MW01012474

THE ENCYCLOPEDIA OF CHICAGO

KOESTER & ZANDER
KOESTER & ZANDER
KOESTER & ZANDER REAL ESTATE
HE CUNARD LINE
GOODFRIEND SHIR
ELSTON AV
FREDRIKSEN ICE CO.
FRANK M. HALLENBECK PHOTO.

THE ENCYCLOPEDIA OF CHICAGO

EDITED BY James R. Grossman
Ann Durkin Keating
Janice L. Reiff

CARTOGRAPHIC EDITOR Michael P. Conzen

THE ENCYCLOPEDIA OF CHICAGO HAS BEEN DEVELOPED BY **THE NEWBERRY LIBRARY** WITH THE COOPERATION OF **THE CHICAGO HISTORICAL SOCIETY.**

THE UNIVERSITY OF CHICAGO PRESS *Chicago and London*

James R. Grossman is vice president for research and education at the Newberry Library and visiting professor of history at the University of Chicago. He is the author of *Land of Hope: Chicago, Black Southerners, and the Great Migration* (1989) and *A Chance to Make Good: African Americans, 1900–1929* (1997), and is coeditor of Historical Studies of Urban America, a University of Chicago Press book series.

Ann Durkin Keating is professor of history at North Central College in Naperville, Illinois. She is the author of *Building Chicago: Suburban Developers and the Creation of a Divided Metropolis* (1988); *Invisible Networks: Exploring the History of Local Utilities and Public Works* (1992); and *Chicagoland* (forthcoming).

Janice L. Reiff is associate professor of history at the University of California, Los Angeles. Author of *Structuring the Past: The Use of Computers in History* (1991), she is also a coeditor of *The Settling of North America: The Atlas of the Great Migrations into North America from the Ice Age to the Present* (1995).

Michael P. Conzen is professor of geography at the University of Chicago. He has authored and edited numerous books, including *The Making of the American Landscape* (1990), *A Scholar's Guide to Geographical Writing on the American and Canadian Past* (1993), and *1848: Turning Point for Chicago, Turning Point for the Region* (1998).

The University of Chicago Press, Chicago 60637
The University of Chicago Press, Ltd., London

Printed in the United States of America

13 12 11 10 09 08 07 06 05 04   1 2 3 4 5

ISBN: 0-226-31015-9

Library of Congress Cataloging-in-Publication Data

The encyclopedia of Chicago / edited by James R. Grossman, Ann Durkin Keating, Janice L. Reiff ; cartographic editor, Michael P. Conzen.
p. cm.
"The encyclopedia of Chicago has been developed by the Newberry Library with the cooperation of the Chicago Historical Society."
Includes bibliographical references and index.
ISBN 0-226-31015-9 (alk. paper)
1. Chicago Region (Ill.)—Encyclopedias. 2. Chicago Region (Ill.)—History—Encyclopedias. I. Grossman, James R. II. Keating, Ann Durkin. III. Reiff, Janice L. IV. Newberry Library. V. Chicago Historical Society.
F548.3.E53 2004
977.3′11′003—dc22

2004003487

Frontispiece: Traffic on Dearborn and Randolph, 1909. Photographer: Unknown. Source: Chicago Historical Society.

∞ The paper used in this publication meets the minimum requirements of the American National Standard for Information Sciences—Permanence of Paper for Printed Library Materials, ANSI Z39.48-1992.

FUNDING

MAJOR FUNDING PROVIDED BY

The National Endowment for the Humanities*

The John D. and Catherine T. MacArthur Foundation

The City of Chicago

The State of Illinois

FOUNDING PATRONS

Bank One

The Boeing Company

BP Foundation

ADDITIONAL FUNDING

Sara Lee Foundation

Otho S. A. Sprague Memorial Institute,
in honor of Charles C. Haffner III

*Any views, findings, conclusions or recommendations expressed in this publication do not necessarily represent those of the National Endowment for the Humanities.

CONTENTS

MAPS

MAPS IN COLOR

STAFF AND CONSULTANTS

MANAGING EDITORS
Douglas Knox (2000–2004)
John H. Long (1998–2000)
Carol Summerfield (1994–1998)

ILLUSTRATION EDITORS
Rosemary Adams
Russell Lewis

CONSULTING EDITORS
Philip V. Bohlman
Louis P. Cain
Susan Manning
Leslie Reagan
Steven A. Riess
Carl Smith
Lynn Y. Weiner

CARTOGRAPHIC DESIGN
Dennis McClendon

STAFF
Wallace Best
David Blanke
Emily Brunner
Kate Caldwell
Catherine Clement
Anastasia Christman
Steven Essig
Sarah Fenton
Erik Gellman
Daniel Greene
Toby Higbie
Allyson Hobbs
Rebekah Holmes
D. Bradford Hunt
Brandon Johnson
Gwen Jordan
Gerald Kendrick
Jonathan J. Keyes
Alexia Koelling
Jennifer Koslow
Ian McGiver
Robert Morrissey
Tracy N. Poe
Steven R. Porter
Marina Post
Christina Reynen
Beth Rillema
Kendra Schiffman
Amanda Seligman
Elizabeth Siarny
Laurel Spindel
Tracy Steffes
Adam H. Stewart
Timothy Straveler
Christopher Thale
Leigh Tomppert
Derek Vaillant
Mark R. Wilson

ACKNOWLEDGMENTS

This encyclopedia represents a collaboration among not only its three editors but also hundreds of individuals across a decade of work. It is impossible to acknowledge our debt to each of these friends and colleagues without consuming vast quantities of precious space in this publication. What follows, therefore, is necessarily abbreviated, an understatement of our dependence on the collective generosity that has made this project possible.

A project of this scope requires considerable resources, and we were fortunate to receive early support from the National Endowment for the Humanities. NEH staff not only guided us through the grant proposal process but subsequently also shared with us their expertise and their contacts. We are aware that much of the work at the NEH is done by staff members who never cross our line of sight, but our most direct contacts were with Jane Aikin, our initial program officer, Joseph Herring, George Farr, and Robert Anderson. Subsequent funding came from the John D. and Catherine T. MacArthur Foundation, the City of Chicago, the State of Illinois, Bank One, the Boeing Company, the BP Foundation, the Sara Lee Foundation, and the Otho S. A. Sprague Memorial Institute. None of this funding would have been available without the assistance of Charles Cullen, Toni Harkness, Cindy Mitchell, Steve Gates, W. G. Jurgensen, Rebecca Riley, Burton Natarus, and Richard M. Daley.

As important as the initial NEH grant were the support and encouragement provided at the outset of the process by civic leaders and scholars willing to lend their names and their time to help this project take shape. Our Advisory Board, which provided ideas, criticism, and links to community resources, included Stanley Balzekas, Lerone Bennett, Jr., Alice Calabrese, Ann S. Coyne, Charles Cullen, Mary Dempsey, William Erbe, James Ford, Richard J. Franke, Douglas Greenberg, Michael Harkins, Neil Harris, Walter Kelly, Louise Año Nuevo Kerr, Richard Newhouse, Leslie Orear, Stephanie Quinn, Rebecca R. Riley, Allen Schwartz, Harold Byron Smith, Susan Stob, Dempsey Travis, Helen Valdez, and Leah Zell Wanger. Editorial Board members met in small groups to work through long lists of potential entries, struggle with us over how the entries might fit together, and recommend authors. Nearly all wrote entries themselves or read entries in their areas of expertise: Michael Anania, James Barrett, Ellin Beltz, Larry Bennett, Henry Binford, Philip Bohlman, Charles Branham, Robert Bruegmann, Louis Cain, Lizabeth Cohen, Kathleen Neils Conzen, Michael Conzen, William Cronon, Irving Cutler, Gerald Danzer, Maria de los Angeles Torres, Pierre deVise, Michael H. Ebner, Lewis Erenberg, Maureen Flanagan, Timothy Gilfoyle, Elliott Gorn, Donald Haider, Hjordis Halvorson, Ronne Hartfield, Arnold Hirsch, Susan Hirsch, Suellen Hoy, Mary Ann Johnson, Theodore Karamanski, Martin E. Marty, Jeffrey Mirel, David Moberg, Patricia Mooney-Melvin, Archibald Motley, Marjorie Murphy, Anthony Orum, Dominic Pacyga, Diane Pinderhughes, Harold Platt, Barbara Posadas, Christopher Reed, Steven Riess, George Roeder, Steven Rosswurm, John Rury, Thomas Schlereth, Ellen Skerrett, Carl Smith, Rayman Solomon, Christopher Thale, Louise Wade, Richard Wang, Lynne Warren, and Lynn Weiner.

These individuals represent a broad cross-section of cultural and educational institutions, but three particular institutions stand out for their support of the project. Without the patient support of the Newberry Library, North Central College, and the University of California, Los Angeles, the editors of this book could not have invested the necessary time and energy. We are grateful to these institutions for facilitating our collaboration and for making our participation possible.

The other institutions that have played essential roles are the libraries and other places that provided research advice and materials: Special Collections and Municipal Reference Collection of the Chicago Public Library's Harold Washington Library Center, Chicago Architecture Foundation, DuPage County Historical Museum, Lake County Discovery Museum, WTTW-TV, and the libraries at the University of Chicago, University of Illinois at Chicago, and Northwestern University. Beyond Chicago we are grateful to the Library of Congress for visual materials. Our authors and research staff also benefited from the assistance of countless librarians, archivists, volunteers, and other individuals at public libraries across metropolitan Chicago, genealogical and historical societies, government agencies, consulates, cemeteries, churches, and a wide variety of civic organizations.

Most of the research took place at the Newberry Library and the Chicago Historical Society. Newberry staff other than those working directly on the encyclopedia but who have played a significant role in this project include John Aubrey, John Brady, Richard Brown, Janice Dillard, Rhonda Frevert, Catherine Gass, Paul Gehl, Krista Geier, Hjordis Halvorson, Fred Hoxie, Robert Karrow, Pat Morris, John Powell, Jack Simpson, Karen Skubish, Karen Smith, Helen Hornbeck Tanner, and Mary Wyly. Project interns have been Sara Berndt, Liz Bird, Sarah Bowen, Theresa Channell, Brian Feltes, Jonathan Heller, Helen Hoguet, Mandi Isaacs, Elliot Lee, Lynn Leverenz, Ron Martin, Ben Mason, Peter Noll, Hai-Dang Phan, and Shannon Thompson.

Collaboration with the Chicago Historical Society began when Ellsworth Brown generously signed on to a partnership without hesitation despite the rather vague nature of the enterprise that we placed on the table. His successors, Douglas Greenberg and Lonnie Bunch, have continued that commitment. We also have valued the assistance of Rosemary Adams, Scott LaFrance, Russell Lewis, Sarah Marcus, Aimee Marshall, Archibald Motley, Jr., and Jordan Walker. This collaboration will take tangible form in a World Wide Web–based encyclopedia located at the Chicago Historical Society.

The Newberry's other main partner has been the University of Chicago Press. Penny Kaiserlian shepherded a proposal that represented mainly a statement of vision and purpose. Linda J. Halvorson picked up the mantle after Penny left the Press and has provided essential expertise and experience in reference publishing. Carol Saller and Russell Harper patiently copyedited the substantial manuscript. Aware that many members of the Press staff have worked behind the scenes to transform hundreds of electronic files into a book, we can specifically acknowledge only those whom we have come to know during the course of developing, editing, producing, and promoting the project: Lain Adkins, Joseph Alderfer, Bruce Barton, Michael Brehm, Perry Cartwright, Siobhan Drummond, Paula Duffy, Ellen Gibson, Sylvia Hecimovich, Erin Hogan, Carol Kasper, Mary Laur, John Muenning, Christopher Rhodes, and Anita Samen. Margie Towery expertly produced the index under a seemingly impossible deadline.

Many other friends and colleagues have helped in various ways over the past decade. Suellen Hoy, Kenneth T. Jackson, and David Van Tassel all played important roles in the project's initiation. Charles Wilson offered his considerable experience and wisdom at an especially useful moment. Mary Dempsey has been a consistent supporter, and Bill Parod and John Swenson provided generous advice on specific aspects in the later stages. Terry, Kate, Sarah, and Olivia Reiff and Helen Hornbeck Tanner graciously shared their homes and their support with the encyclopedia and its long-distance editor. From beginning to end Ann Billingsley and John Keating tolerated the endless meetings and piles of paper, while still remaining willing to share their knowledge of Chicago's civic culture. Betsy and Jack Keating and Ruth and Alice Grossman have simply been patient, waiting for a glimpse of life without an encyclopedia task on the calendar.

Most important, however, have been the staff, who are listed elsewhere in this volume. One of the great joys of a project that is so big and takes so long is the opportunity to work so closely with the energetic young scholars who join its staff. Douglas Knox, who joined the project as a research assistant and finished it off as the managing editor, has been our anchor. The point is simply made: without Doug there would be no encyclopedia.

CONTRIBUTORS

Andrew Abbott
University of Chicago

Carl Abbott
Portland State University

William J. Adelman
University of Illinois at Chicago

Gerald W. Adelmann
Openlands Project / Canal Corridor Association

Jeffrey S. Adler
University of Florida

Tony Adler
Freelance writer

Jane Aikin
Independent scholar

James Akerman
Newberry Library

Peter T. Alter
Chicago Historical Society

Wilbur Applebaum
Illinois Institute of Technology

Joseph L. Arnold
University of Maryland, Baltimore County

Gabriela F. Arredondo
University of California, Santa Cruz

Peter M. Ascoli
Chicago, IL

J. S. Aubrey
Newberry Library

Thomas A. Auger
Atlanta, GA

Jacob Austen
Roctober Magazine

Steven M. Avella
Marquette University

William Ayers
University of Illinois at Chicago

Robin F. Bachin
University of Miami

Julia Sniderman Bachrach
Chicago Park District

Beatriz Badikian-Gartler
Chicago, IL

David A. Badillo
University of Notre Dame

Youngsoo Bae
Seoul National University

Geoffrey Baer
WTTW

Beth Bailey
University of New Mexico

William Leslie Balan-Gaubert
University of Chicago

Francisco E. Balderrama
California State University Los Angeles

Peter C. Baldwin
University of Connecticut

Charles J. Balesi
Highland Park, IL

Stan Barker
National Amusement Park Historical Association

James R. Barrett
University of Illinois at Urbana-Champaign

Dave Bartlett
South Suburban College

Ann Barzel
Chicago, IL

Thomas Bauman
Northwestern University

Eva Becsei
University of Illinois at Chicago

David T. Beito
University of Alabama

Jon Bekken
Albright College

James Belpedio
Becker College

Larry Bennett
DePaul University

David Bensman
Rutgers University

Molly W. Berger
Case Western Reserve University

Ira Berkow
The New York Times

Chad Berry
Maryville College

Wallace Best
University of Virginia

Joseph C. Bigott
Purdue University Calumet

Roger Biles
East Carolina University

Henry C. Binford
Northwestern University

Bradley J. Birzer
Hillsdale College

Timuel Black
Chicago, IL

Cynthia M. Blair
University of Illinois at Chicago

G. Robert Blakey
Notre Dame Law School

David Blanke
Texas A&M University–Corpus Christi

Edith Blumhofer
Wheaton College

Thomas G. Bobula
Windy City Weather Company

John Bodnar
Indiana University

Lisa Krissoff Boehm
Worcester State College

Philip V. Bohlman
University of Chicago

Rachel E. Bohlmann
Newberry Library

Linda J. Borish
Western Michigan University

Leon Botstein
Bard College

Mark J. Bouman
Chicago State University

Devereux Bowly, Jr.
Chicago, IL

Jonathan Boyd
Independent scholar

Robert R. Boyle
Newberry Library

Seth Brady
University of Chicago

Stuart Brandes
University of Wisconsin

Charles Branham
DuSable Museum of African American History

Virginia Lieson Brereton
Tufts University

Winstanley Briggs
Newberry Library

Judith Brodhead
North Central College

David Brodherson
Independent scholar

Charlotte Brooks
University at Albany, SUNY

H. Allen Brooks
University of Toronto

Clayton W. Brown
Kildeer, IL

R. Ben Brown
Independent scholar

Richard H. Brown
Newberry Library

Catherine Bruck
Illinois Institute of Technology

Robert Bruegmann
University of Illinois at Chicago

Jeffrey A. Brune
University of Washington

Emily Brunner
University of Chicago

Roger Bruns
National Archives

Paul A. Buelow
Franklin College

Beth Anne Buggenhagen
University of Rochester

David Buisseret
University of Texas at Arlington

Douglas Bukowski
Berwyn, IL

Wendy Burgess
North Park University

Edward M. Burke
Chicago City Council

Tramayne M. Butler
University of Michigan

Cathleen D. Cahill
University of Chicago

Louis P. Cain
Loyola University Chicago

Louise Cainkar
University of Illinois at Chicago

Alice Calabrese
Chicago/Suburban Library Systems

Lendol Calder
Augustana College

Kate Caldwell
University of Chicago

Dominic Candeloro
City of Chicago Heights, Mayor's Office

Adrian Capehart
University of Illinois at Chicago

Heidi Pawlowski Carey
Chicago Architecture Foundation

E. Wayne Carp
Pacific Lutheran University

Fred Carstensen
University of Connecticut

F. Willis Caruso
John Marshall Law School

Jeanette L. Casey
Northwestern University Library

Dana Caspall
DePaul University

Lisa Cervac
Highwood Historical Society

Jeffrey Charles
California State University, San Marcos

Katherine A. Chavigny
Sweet Briar College

Harvey M. Choldin
University of Illinois at Urbana-Champaign

Richard Christiansen
Chicago, IL

Elin B. Christianson
Hobart Historical Society

J. R. Christianson
Luther College

Lawrence Christmas
Northeastern Illinois Planning Commission

Mark Clague
University of Michigan

Emily Clark
Forest Park, IL

Jean Guarino Clark
Chicago, IL

Charles E. Clifton
Chicago, IL

Kenneth Cmiel
University of Iowa

Peter A. Coclanis
University of North Carolina

Charles Adams Cogan
Carleton College

Andrew Wender Cohen
Syracuse University

Mike Conklin
Chicago Tribune

Steven Conn
Ohio State University

Nathan Daniel Beau Connolly
University of Michigan

Kathleen Neils Conzen
University of Chicago

Michael P. Conzen
University of Chicago

William T. Corcoran
St. Linus Church

Don Coursey
University of Chicago

David Cowan
Chicago, IL

Alicia Cozine
Minneapolis, MN

Tiffany L. Crate
Chicago, IL

Dennis H. Cremin
National Trust for Historic Preservation

Lynne Curry
Eastern Illinois University

Irving Cutler
Chicago State University

Nancy Daffner
Alpharetta, GA

Stephen Daiter
Chicago, IL

Gerald A. Danzer
University of Illinois at Chicago

Sharon S. Darling
St. Charles, IL

KarenMary Davalos
Loyola Marymount University

Kevin Davis
Wheaton, IL

Louis Delgado
Loyola University Chicago

José R. Deustua
Eastern Illinois University

Tracey Deutsch
University of Minnesota

Michael J. Devine
Truman Presidential Library

Pierre deVise
Roosevelt University

Andrew J. Diamond
University of Michigan

Amina J. Dickerson
Kraft Foods

James Diedrick
Albion College

Diane Dillon
Newberry Library

Steven J. Diner
Rutgers University

L. Mara Dodge
Westfield State College

Mel Doering
Valparaiso University

Bernardine Dohrn
Northwestern University

Spencer Downing
University of Central Florida

Margaret D. Doyle
Chesterton, IN

Melvyn Dubofsky
Binghamton University, SUNY

Perry R. Duis
University of Illinois at Chicago

John T. Durkin
Chicago, IL

Jonathan H. Ebel
University of Chicago

Michael H. Ebner
Lake Forest College

R. David Edmunds
University of Texas at Dallas

Robin Einhorn
University of California, Berkeley

Susan K. Eleuterio
Illinois Arts Council

Melvin Patrick Ely
College of William and Mary

Kathleen L. Endres
University of Akron

J. Ronald Engel
Meadville Lombard Theological School

Dena J. Epstein
University of Chicago

William Erbe
University of Illinois at Chicago

Lewis A. Erenberg
Loyola University Chicago

Paul J. Erickson
University of Texas at Austin

Ellen Eslinger
DePaul University

Steven Essig
Newberry Library

Linda J. Evans
Chicago Historical Society

Sara M. Evans
University of Minnesota

David M. Fahey
Miami University

John Mack Faragher
Yale University

David Farber
Temple University

Paula S. Fass
University of California, Berkeley

Donald J. Fehrenbacher
USDA Natural Resources Conservation Service

Sarah Fenton
Northwestern University

Paul-Thomas Ferguson
Black Hawk College

Riva Feshbach
Newberry Library

Cynthia R. Field
Smithsonian Institution

Eve Fine
University of Wisconsin–Madison

Lisa Michelle Fine
Michigan State University

Paul Finkelman
University of Tulsa College of Law

Paul Fischer
Lake Forest College

John Hall Fish
Chicago, IL

Maureen A. Flanagan
Michigan State University

Franklin Forts
University of Georgia, Athens

Scott Fosdick
University of Missouri–Columbia

Jerry L. Foust
Loyola University Chicago

Margaret L. Frank
Naper Settlement

Elizabeth S. Fraterrigo
Loyola University Chicago

Rhonda Huber Frevert
Burlington (Iowa) Public Library

Roger R. Fross
Lord, Bissell & Brook

Peter Frumkin
Harvard University

Jack W. Fuller
Tribune Co.

Stephanie Skestos Gabriele
Independent curator

Robert Galler
St. Cloud State University

Timothy J. Garvey
Illinois Wesleyan University

Paul F. Gehl
Newberry Library

Erik Gellman
Northwestern University

Gerald R. Gems
North Central College

James Gilbert
University of Maryland

Timothy J. Gilfoyle
Loyola University Chicago

Keith R. Gill
Museum of Science and Industry

Paul Gilmore
California State University, Fresno

Connie Goddard
Roosevelt University

Nathan Godfried
University of Maine

Douglas Gomery
Library of American Broadcasting

Mirza L. González
DePaul University

Joanne L. Goodwin
University of Nevada, Las Vegas

Elliott J. Gorn
Brown University

Michael Grace, S.J.
Loyola University Chicago

Daniel A. Graff
University of Notre Dame

H. Roger Grant
Clemson University

Mary Lackritz Gray
Freelance writer

Adam Green
New York University

Paul Green
Roosevelt University

Daniel Greene
University of Chicago

Paul R. Greenland
Rockford, IL

Owen K. Gregory
University of Illinois at Chicago

Gregory Price Grieve
University of North Carolina, Greensboro

Eric C. Grimm
Illinois State Museum

Max Grinnell
University of Wisconsin–Madison

James Grossman
Newberry Library

Ron Grossman
Chicago Tribune

Paul Groth
University of California, Berkeley

Lori Grove
Western Michigan University

Sarah Gualtieri
Loyola University New Orleans

Betsy Gurlacz
Western Springs, IL

Anita Olson Gustafson
Presbyterian College

Raymond J. Haberski, Jr.
Marian College

Tom Hafen
University of Chicago

Clark "Bucky" Halker
Illinois Humanities Council

Robert L. Hall
University of Illinois at Chicago

Rick Halpern
University College London

Katherine Hamilton-Smith
Lake County Discovery Museum

John P. Hankey
University of Chicago

Eleanor Hannah
University of Minnesota Duluth

Ardith K. Hansel
Illinois State Geological Survey

Mark S. Harmon
Downers Grove Museum

Kevin Harrington
Illinois Institute of Technology

Michael W. Harris
Northwestern University

Richard Harris
McMaster University

Ronne Hartfield
Chicago, IL

Aaron Harwig
North Central College

Christiane Harzig
Universität Bremen

Diana Haskell
Newberry Library

Raymond E. Hauser
Waubonsee Community College

Donald A. Hayner
Chicago Sun-Times

Chad Heap
George Washington University

Paul Heltne
Chicago Academy of Sciences

Wanda A. Hendricks
University of South Carolina

Tricia Redeker Hepner
Michigan State University

Tobias Higbie
Newberry Library

Celia Hilliard
Chicago, IL

George W. Hilton
University of California, Los Angeles

Darlene Clark Hine
Northwestern University

Thomas S. Hines
University of California, Los Angeles

Arnold R. Hirsch
University of New Orleans

Susan E. Hirsch
Loyola University Chicago

Allyson Hobbs
University of Chicago

Beatrix Hoffman
Northern Illinois University

Philip T. Hoffman
California Institute of Technology

Lawrence Daniel Hogan
Union County College

Anna Holian
University of Chicago

Jack M. Holl
Kansas State University

Elizabeth Holland
Chicago Public Library

Melvin G. Holli
University of Illinois at Chicago

Rosemarie P. Holz
University of Nebraska–Lincoln

Michael W. Homel
Eastern Michigan University

Charles Howell
Library of American Broadcasting

Suellen Hoy
University of Notre Dame

Daniela S. Hristova
University of Chicago

Alexandra Hrycak
Reed College

John C. Hudson
Northwestern University

D. Bradford Hunt
Roosevelt University

Andrew Hurley
University of Missouri–St. Louis

Asad Husain
Northeastern Illinois University

Cyril Ibe
Chicago, IL

Melissa Isaacson
Chicago Tribune

Thomas J. Jablonsky
Marquette University

Kenneth T. Jackson
Columbia University

Vernon Jarrett
Chicago, IL

Khoshaba P. Jasim
Truman College

Richard Jensen
University of Illinois at Chicago

John B. Jentz
Marquette University

Richard R. John
University of Illinois at Chicago

Brandon Johnson
University of Chicago

Mary Ann Johnson
University of Illinois at Chicago

Robin A. Johnson
Governmental consultant

Arlan R. Juhl
Illinois Office of Water Resources

Richard Junger
Western Michigan University

Penny Kaiserlian
University of Virginia Press

Theodore J. Karamanski
Loyola University Chicago

Ronald Dale Karr
University of Massachusetts Lowell

Robert W. Karrow, Jr.
Newberry Library

Stanley N. Katz
Princeton University

Thomas O. Kay
Wheaton College

Ann Durkin Keating
North Central College

William Howland Kenney
Kent State University

James S. Kessler
Francis W. Parker School

Jonathan J. Keyes
University of Chicago

Ying-cheng (Harry) Kiang
Northeastern Illinois University

Youn-Jin Kim
Dankook University, Seoul

Vitaut Kipel
Belarusian Institute of Arts and Sciences

Judith Russi Kirshner
University of Illinois at Chicago

Eric Klinenberg
New York University

Geoffrey Klingsporn
University of Denver

Ruth Eckdish Knack
American Planning Association

Anne Kelly Knowles
Middlebury College

Douglas Knox
Newberry Library

Anne Meis Knupfer
Purdue University

Rick Kogan
Chicago Tribune

Adrienne W. Kolb
Fermilab Archives

Andrew T. Kopan
DePaul University

Jennifer Koslow
Newberry Library

Bruce Kraig
Roosevelt University

Anthea Kraut
University of California, Riverside

Paul Kruty
University of Illinois at Urbana-Champaign

Patricia K. Kummer
College of DuPage

Sean J. LaBat
University of Illinois at Chicago

Vinay Lal
University of California, Los Angeles

John Lamb
Lewis University

George A. Lane, S.J.
Loyola Press

James B. Lane
Indiana University Northwest

Elisabeth Lasch-Quinn
Syracuse University

Charles Laurier
Osaka, Japan

B. Pierre Lebeau
North Central College

Georg Leidenberger
Universidad Autónoma Metropolitana, Mexico

Nicholas Lemann
Columbia University

Robin Lester
Francis W. Parker School

Bruce Levy
Southern Methodist University

Jerry W. Lewis
Washington School, District 170, Chicago Heights, IL

Liston E. Leyendecker
Colorado State University

Scott Lien
University of Chicago

Kriste Lindenmeyer
University of Maryland, Baltimore County

J. A. Lindstrom
International Alliance of Theatrical and Stage Employees/Studio Mechanics Local 209

Mary Linehan
Spalding University

Lowell W. Livezey
University of Illinois at Chicago

Dick Locher
Chicago Tribune

Carolyn Loeb
Central Michigan University

Gabe Logan
Northern Illinois University

John H. Long
Newberry Library

Mark Howard Long
Loyola University Chicago

Sarah Ann Long
North Suburban Library System

Odd S. Lovoll
St. Olaf College

David Garrard Lowe
Beaux Arts Alliance

Mary Ting Yi Lui
Yale University

J. Anthony Lukas
New York, NY

Joshua M. Lupkin
Museum of the City of New York

Paula R. Lupkin
Washington University in St. Louis

John F. Lyons
Joliet Junior College

Nasutsa M. Mabwa
City of Chicago Department of Planning and Development

David MacLaren
Loyola University Chicago

Bernard Maegi
Normandale Community College

Jess Maghan
University of Illinois at Chicago

Keith Andrew Mann
Cardinal Stritch University

Christopher Manning
Loyola University Chicago

Sarah S. Marcus
Chicago Historical Society

Victor Margolin
University of Illinois at Chicago

Richard D. Mariner
Chicago Academy of Sciences

Jeanne C. Marsh
University of Chicago

Judith A. Martin
University of Minnesota

Ronald Martin
Loyola University Chicago

Martin E. Marty
Public Religion Project

Louis H. Masotti
Northwestern University

Frances Matlock
Chicago, IL

Victoria Kasuba Matranga
International Housewares Association

Glenna Matthews
University of California, Berkeley

Loomis Mayfield
Chicago, IL

Sandy R. Mazzola
Columbia College

John McAllister
Evanston, IL

James P. McCartin
Seton Hall University

Larry A. McClellan
Governors State University

Dennis McClendon
Chicago CartoGraphics

Deirdre N. McCloskey
University of Illinois at Chicago

Aminah Beverly McCloud
DePaul University

Heather McClure
Council of Latino Agencies

James M. McClurken
Michigan State University

Kathleen McCourt
Quinnipiac University

Ian McGiver
University of Chicago

Steph McGrath
DuPage County Historical Museum

Christopher McKenna
Oxford University

Elizabeth McKillen
University of Maine at Orono

Don McLeese
University of Iowa

Eileen M. McMahon
Lewis University

Patrick M. McMullen
Northwestern University

Stephen G. McShane
Indiana University Northwest Library

Ajay K. Mehrotra
Indiana University, Bloomington

Betsy Mendelsohn
University of Virginia

Joel Mendes
CCIM Institute

Ben K. Mensah
Chicago, IL

Dennis A. Meritt, Jr.
DePaul University

Sherry Meyer
Geneva, IL

Lisa Meyerowitz
University of Chicago

Vincent L. Michael
School of the Art Institute

Gregory Michaelidis
University of Maryland, College Park

Christopher Miller
Marquette University

Patrick B. Miller
Northeastern Illinois University

Randall M. Miller
Saint Joseph's University

Ross Miller
University of Connecticut

Laura Milsk
Southern Illinois University Edwardsville

James J. Miner
Illinois State Geological Survey

Newton Minow
Sidley Austin Brown & Wood

Paul J. Miranti, Jr.
Rutgers University

David Moberg
In These Times

Raymond A. Mohl
University of Alabama at Birmingham

Arwen Mohun
University of Delaware

Patricia Mooney-Melvin
Loyola University Chicago

Anne Moore
Chicago, IL

Nancy G. Moore
Independent scholar

R. Jonathan Moore
University of Illinois at Urbana-Champaign

Robert Morrissey
Yale University

Jennifer Mrozowski
Cincinnati Enquirer

Lucy Eldersveld Murphy
Ohio State University–Newark

Timothy F. Murphy
University of Illinois at Chicago

Carl Nash
University of Chicago

Jan Olive Nash
Loyola University Chicago

Patricio Navia
New York University

Timothy B. Neary
Loyola University Chicago

Bruce C. Nelson
History of Education Quarterly

Charles Nilon
University of Missouri–Columbia

Walter Nugent
University of Notre Dame

Paul D. Numrich
Loyola University Chicago

Rafael Nuñez-Cedeño
University of Illinois at Chicago

Symon Ogeto
Columbia College Chicago

José L. Oliva
Chicago Interfaith Committee on Worker Issues

Magne B. Olson
Chicago State University

Liesl M. Orenic
Carnegie Mellon University

David Orr
Cook County Clerk

Anthony Orum
University of Illinois at Chicago

David M. Oshinsky
University of Texas at Austin

Stephen Packard
Audubon–Chicago Region

Dominic A. Pacyga
Columbia College

Amalia Pallares
University of Illinois at Chicago

Susan Palmer
Aurora University

Nicholas C. Pano
Western Illinois University

Joseph John Parot
Northern Illinois University

Elizabeth A. Patterson
Evanston, IL

Myriam Pauillac
Maisons-Alfort, France

Noel B. Pavlovic
U.S. Geological Survey

Kathy Peiss
University of Pennsylvania

Gina M. Pérez
Hunter College, CUNY

Stephen A. Perkins
Center for Neighborhood Technology

Marilyn Elizabeth Perry
Palatine, IL

Cynthia H. Peters
Newberry Library

Amy T. Peterson
American Intercontinental University Online

Paul W. Petraitis
Chicago, IL

Richard Pettengill
Lake Forest College

Craig L. Pfannkuche
Memory Trail Research, Inc.

Paula F. Pfeffer
Loyola University Chicago

Mark E. Pfeifer
University of Toronto

(Margaret) Dorsey Phelps
Independent scholar

Don Pierson
Chicago Tribune

Laurie Pintar
Loyola Marymount University

Harold L. Platt
Loyola University Chicago

Wendy Plotkin
Arizona State University

Tracy N. Poe
DePaul University

Christopher Popa
Chicago Public Library

Stephen R. Porter
University of Chicago

Barbara M. Posadas
Northern Illinois University

Charles Postel
California State University at Sacramento

Jane Preston
Harvard University

Elizabeth E. Prevost
Northwestern University

Margaret Franson Pruter
DuPage County Historical Society

Robert Pruter
Lewis University

Patrick M. Quinn
Northwestern University

Phyllis Rabineau
Chicago Historical Society

Howard N. Rabinowitz
University of New Mexico

Ronald Radano
University of Wisconsin–Madison

Gail Radford
University at Buffalo, SUNY

John Raffensperger
Chicago, IL

Chas. P. Raleigh
Elmhurst, IL

James Ralph
Middlebury College

Christopher R. Reed
Roosevelt University

Jonathan Rees
Colorado State University–Pueblo

Janice L. Reiff
University of California, Los Angeles

Tina Reithmaier
Newberry Library

Christina A. Reynen
Newberry Library

Steven A. Riess
Northeastern Illinois University

Timo Riippa
Immigration History Research Center

Jontyle Theresa Robinson
Independent scholar

Marilyn Robinson
Batavia, IL

Karen M. Rodriguez
USEPA Great Lakes National Program Office

George H. Roeder, Jr.
School of the Art Institute of Chicago

David R. Roediger
University of Illinois at Urbana-Champaign

Craig H. Roell
Georgia Southern University

Patricia Krone Rose
Concordia University

Franklin Rosemont
Charles H. Kerr Publishing Company

Penelope Rosemont
Charles H. Kerr Publishing Company

Howard Rosen
University of Wisconsin–Madison

Steve Rosswurm
Lake Forest College

Carlo Rotella
Boston College

Kate Rousmaniere
Miami University

Eli Rubin
University of Wisconsin–Madison

Robert Ruck
University of Pittsburgh

Susan Sessions Rugh
Brigham Young University

John L. Rury
University of Kansas

John Russick
Chicago Historical Society

David E. Ruth
Pennsylvania State University, Abington

Robert W. Rydell
Montana State University

Paul Saenger
Newberry Library

Karen Sakash
University of Illinois at Chicago

Rich Samuels
WTTW

Glenn Sandiford
University of Illinois at Urbana-Champaign

A. K. Sandoval-Strausz
University of New Mexico

Beryl Satter
Rutgers University–Newark

R. Craig Sautter
Chicago, IL

Bill Savage
Northwestern University

Karen Sawislak
University of California, Berkeley

June Skinner Sawyers
Chicago, IL

Elizabeth D. Schafer
Loachapoka, AL

David L. Schein
Mount Prospect, IL

Leo Schelbert
University of Illinois at Chicago

Thomas J. Schlereth
University of Notre Dame

Steven Schlossman
Carnegie Mellon University

John R. Schmidt
Park Ridge, IL

Raymond Schmidt
Ventura, CA

Susanne Schmitz
Elmhurst College

Daniel Schneider
University of Illinois at Urbana-Champaign

Richard Schneirov
Indiana State University

John D. Schroeder
Joliet Junior College

John Schultz
Columbia College

Quentin J. Schultze
Calvin College

Franz Schulze
Lake Forest College

Thomas F. Schwartz
Illinois Historic Preservation Agency

Richard A. Schwarzlose
Northwestern University

Richard Schwegel
Chicago Public Library

Larry E. Schweikart
University of Dayton

Joseph P. Schwieterman
DePaul University

Barbara Sciacchitano
North Central College

Helen Sclair
Chicago, IL

Steve Scott
Goodman Theatre

Amanda Seligman
University of Wisconsin–Milwaukee

Charles A. Sengstock, Jr.
Northbrook, IL

Alfred Erich Senn
Vytautas Magnus University

Amy Settergren
Northwestern University

Carolyn A. Sheehy
North Central College

Harry L. Sheehy
Chicago, IL

Peggy Tuck Sinko
Newberry Library

Ellen Skerrett
Chicago, IL

Deborah Ann Skok
Hendrix College

Robert A. Slayton
Chapman University

Carl Smith
Northwestern University

Eric R. Smith
University of Illinois at Chicago

Marc Smith
Chicago, IL

Preston H. Smith II
Mt. Holyoke College

Richard Sobel
Harvard University

June Sochen
Northeastern Illinois University

David M. Sokol
University of Illinois at Chicago

David M. Solzman
University of Illinois at Chicago

Timothy B. Spears
Middlebury College

John W. Stamper
University of Notre Dame

David Starkey
Santa Barbara City College

Tracy Steffes
University of Chicago

Alan Harris Stein
Consortium of Oral History Educators

Bruce Stephenson
Adler Planetarium

Robert E. Sterling
Joliet Junior College

Tom Sterling
Hinsdale, IL

Donald F. Stetzer
LaCrosse, WI

Adam H. Stewart
Loyola University Chicago

Clinton E. Stockwell
Chicago Semester

Lisa Stone
School of the Art Institute of Chicago

Randi Storch
SUNY Cortland

David Stradling
University of Cincinnati

Andris Straumanis
University of Wisconsin–Eau Claire

Margaret (Peg) Strobel
University of Illinois at Chicago

Timothy E. Sullivan
Towson University

Mark Swartz
New York, NY

Marlene Sway
Los Angeles, CA

David S. Tanenhaus
University of Nevada at Las Vegas

Helen Hornbeck Tanner
Newberry Library

Christopher James Tassava
Metropolitan State University

Jon C. Teaford
Purdue University

Jane S. Teague
Glen Ellyn, IL

Mark Tebeau
Cleveland State University

Andrea Telli
Chicago Public Library

David T. Thackery
Newberry Library

Christopher Thale
Columbia College

James R. Thompson
Winston & Strawn

Playford V. Thorson
University of North Dakota

Claudette Tolson
Loyola University Chicago

Dempsey J. Travis
Chicago, IL

Barbara Truesdell
Indiana University

Lance Trusty
Purdue University Calumet

Todd J. Tubutis
Field Museum

Martin Tuohy
Tinley Park, IL

Glennette Tilley Turner
Independent scholar

Paul Tyler
Old Town School of Folk Music

Derek Vaillant
University of Michigan

Ronald S. Vasile
Canal Corridor Association

Rudolph J. Vecoli
University of Minnesota

Sudhir Venkatesh
Columbia University

Susan Vieweg
University of Chicago

Larry Viskochil
Chicago, IL

Harold M. Visotsky
Northwestern University

John von Rhein
Chicago Tribune

Louise Carroll Wade
University of Oregon

Stephen Wade
Hyattsville, MD

Michael Paul Wakeford
University of Chicago

Richard A. Wang
University of Illinois at Chicago

George H. Ware
Morton Arboretum

Lynne Warren
Museum of Contemporary Art, Chicago

Jeffrey Webb
Huntington College

Harold S. Wechsler
University of Rochester

N. Sue Weiler
Chicago, IL

Lynn Y. Weiner
Roosevelt University

Wayne M. Wendland
University of Illinois at Urbana-Champaign

Manfred Wenner
Arizona State University

Carroll William Westfall
University of Notre Dame

Shane White
University of Sydney

Andrew Wiese
San Diego State University

Harold R. Wilde
North Central College

Gerould Wilhelm
Elmhurst, IL

J. Kimo Williams
Columbia College Chicago

Marilyn Thornton Williams
Pace University

Michael Willrich
Brandeis University

Mark R. Wilson
University of Chicago

Susan Marie Wirka
University of Wisconsin–Madison

David Wolcott
Miami University

Arnold Jacob Wolf
K.A.M. Isaiah Israel

Daniel P. Wolk
University of Chicago

Roberta Wollons
Indiana University Northwest

Kenneth K. Wong
Vanderbilt University

Nourou Yakoubou
Chicago State University

David M. Young
Chicago Tribune

Henry Yu
University of California, Los Angeles

Katarzyna Zechenter
University College London

Arthur Zilversmit
Lake Forest College

Kathleen Zygmun-McDonald
Evanston, IL

INTRODUCTION

The Newberry Library lies across the street from Bughouse Square. The unofficial but commonly used name of this small park evokes its long association with the unconventional and the marginal: soapbox orators, prostitutes, cultural nonconformists, and, by the 1980s, homeless men on park benches. In the mid-1990s, on the other side of the square block of cement paths, meager grass, and shade trees, a developer demolished the old Salvation Army office building, revived the park's official name, and successfully advertised luxury residences facing "Washington Square Park"—which now sports a decorative wrought-iron fence and attractive fountain. Like his New York City counterpart who created a neighborhood called "Clinton" where once was a space called "Hell's Kitchen," this entrepreneur understood the malleability and power of place names. This might sound benign—a matter of neighborhood improvement and private profit at the expense of tradition, local color, and the sensibilities of neighborhood old-timers—but often there is much at stake in how a space is named. Names are tied up with boundaries, and groups contesting for turf often name overlapping spaces differently to stake their claims.

The Encyclopedia of Chicago is a mapping of Chicago's geographic turf, complemented by a comparable cartography of boundaries that are more conceptual and topical than spatial. Imagine a map that has been broken up into puzzle pieces, each of which is an identifiable unit of some kind: each encyclopedia entry represents a piece of that puzzle. The piece looks the way it does because of the context in which it was created: each entry was generated within a particular rubric (e.g., reform, public order, literature). Like a city space, an entry's use can be shaped by the process by which its boundaries and its name were determined. The editor's power resembles the developer's, and the encyclopedia as a whole—the combination of the pieces—represents an editorial interpretation of urban history.

Metropolitan History

The editors of *The Encyclopedia of Chicago* began with a commitment to a vision of a metropolitan area whose past, present, and future rest on the principle of interdependence. Seemingly disparate strands and isolated pockets of metropolitan life are best understood as part of an integrated whole, and within broad regional, national, and international contexts. Robert Park's oft-quoted metaphor of the city as "a mosaic of little worlds that touch but do not interpenetrate" is more intuitive than accurate. In Chicago, "Little Italy" and "Greektown" not only touched but deeply interpenetrated, most obviously because residents of these districts and other nearby immigrant neighborhoods passed one another on the street, perhaps attending similar events at Hull House, or the same public schools. Less obviously, but equally important, the historical processes that shaped the lives of these residents were anything but separate. The Gold Coast cannot exist without the slum; the suburb is by definition a place with a relationship to the city.

This commitment to an integrative urban history exists in tension with the nature of the publication itself: structurally, an encyclopedia is a fragmented genre. There is no single narrative. An analytical structure that depends on a reader working through the material in a particular order is impossible. But *The Encyclopedia of Chicago* is more than a reference book comprising discrete frames of information about individual topics. It represents a synthesis of a century of scholarship in urban history in general and on Chicago in particular. It is also the result of a process influenced by the simultaneous creation of an electronic encyclopedia, which places a premium on thinking about links, structure, and the malleability of categories.

The encyclopedia's conceptualization started with geographical space because this is a work of urban history. An ambitious goal was set to move beyond the shifting boundaries of the city to create a *metropolitan* history. This means more than a narrative of a fixed space encompassing Chicago and its collar counties. It requires an interpretive emphasis on the historical dynamics of metropolitan dependence and interaction. City and countryside, sometimes placed in opposition as artifice versus nature, are both artifacts of human creativity, and this encyclopedia begins with the assumption that the history of a metropolis includes not only central city and bedroom suburbs, but also the industrial towns, agricultural centers, and vacation spots that dot its broad landscape. The Burnham Plan extended 60 miles beyond the Loop, not because Daniel Burnham and the Commercial Club were metropolitan imperialists (and they may have been), but because it was clear even in 1909 that a Plan of Chicago couldn't stop at the city boundaries. Nor can an encyclopedia that is both a work of urban history and a comprehensive reference. The problem of spatial definition involves relationships among time, space, and culture. Municipal boundaries change over time; the metropolitan area as a cultural and social entity (and even as an idea) invariably encompasses a territory that transcends physical and political boundaries. Moreover, a place with a diverse population acquires over the years equally diverse understandings of its spaces. Such diversity, of course, is one of Chicago's defining characteristics. Therefore a project with aspirations to define the city historically must somehow find a way to use diversity as a founding principle. The challenge lies in recognizing that diversity does not preclude the centrality of the idea of civic culture, or the interpretive goal of using the city as a venue for synthetic narrative and analysis.

This encyclopedia is intended to serve as a comprehensive reference work for members of the general public, for secondary school students as well as scholars of urban history, for lifelong residents of the Chicago area as well as visitors. Beyond the boundaries of the city's neighborhoods and the region's municipalities, Chicago's history has been significant in many ways for American and even world culture. Readers expecting coverage of skyscrapers and blues music, for example, will find a wealth of relevant entries. The range of topics in the encyclopedia includes architecture, music, literature, the arts, politics, reform movements, social services, health, public order, religion, immigration, housing, public works, labor, and leisure. This expansive agenda for a single volume with a stable binding and text that can be read without a magnifying glass has combined with the editors' interpretive perspective and their emphasis on integrative historical scholarship to shape the contours of what we have included in this book.

Balancing Breadth and Detail

The central tension in a work that seeks to combine encyclopedic detail with integrative analysis lies in the principle of "lumping" versus "splitting." To split is to privilege detail, to amass entries that permit users to learn the essential facts of as many historical phenomena as possible. Each institution has its own history, each community its own portrait, each individual her or his own biography. To lump is to allot higher priority to analysis and comparison, to emphasize relationships, to integrate subject matter *within* entries more than through cross-referencing. This project's interpretive emphasis on the integrative nature of urban life is balanced with its goal of providing comprehensive reference: what matters, therefore, is where we lump and where we split.

The most extensive splitting, yielding the largest proportion of the entries, lies in the areas that will draw the initial attention of most users: who we are and where we live. Ethnicity and residence are, more often than not, the mental maps that help Chicagoans situate themselves in the metropolis. To present Chicago's history as it has been experienced and understood by Chicagoans requires comprehensive coverage of these orientations. Hence all 298 incorporated municipalities in Cook, DuPage, McHenry, Lake, Will, and Kane Counties in Illinois, and Lake and Porter Counties in Indiana, have entries, along with six communities beyond these boundaries. To assure complete geographic coverage of the central city, we selected as a starting point the 77 community areas that Chicago city government and social scientists employ as units of analysis. But because the people who live in these spaces often define their communities in different terms (and sometimes with different boundaries), we also commissioned shorter entries on particular neighborhoods. These 33 neighborhoods, identified by the authors of community-area entries as named spaces with cultural and social staying power, overlap geographically with community areas and represent only a selection of places that Chicagoans have defined as neighborhoods. Some readers will not find an entry under the name that they use to define their community (e.g., Edgebrook, Wrigleyville, the Gap), although such a name is likely to be found in the index. All residents of metropolitan Chicago will find at least one entry on the geographical area that they call home. A broader perspective is presented in the entry "Growth of the Metropolis," which emphasizes the mutual dependence and interrelated histories that individual entries on geographic spaces are by their very nature bound to obscure.

A similar dilemma presents itself with regard to ethnic groups. Like neighborhoods, ethnic boundaries are ever-shifting and nearly infinite. A Calabrian arrives in Chicago and gradually becomes an Italian. A Jewish immigrant from Russia is a "Russian" in the census but a Jew in most other contexts. Lakota migrants from South Dakota to Chicago inhabit a community that describes itself as Native American, but they are likely to continue to identify with their Lakota community back home. Some Mexican Americans consider themselves "Latinos"; others identify more with Mexican heritage than with experiences shared by people from Central and South America. An Iraqi American is also an Arab American. The census offers no solution, as it shifts from decade to decade in the options provided for ethnic identification. Facing the challenge of infinite and overlapping categories, we have chosen to rely on current national boundaries to define the scope and naming of entries on ethnic groups. The cost is obvious: an entry called "Germans" ignores the fact that thousands of Germans came to Chicago before there was a Germany. Language is not the defining characteristic, because Austrians have a separate entry. Arab Americans, many of whom identify in just that way, are split into Egyptians, Saudis, Syrians, and so on. Moreover, Chicago's significant early-twentieth-century Syrian community actually was composed of people we now call Lebanese Christians. Finally, some exceptions could not be avoided; else there would be no entries on Jews, African Americans, southern white migrants, Welsh, or Yankees.

This definitional strategy does not, however, resolve the question of whom to include. Who is here and who isn't? Or, more precisely, who has been here and who hasn't? Numbers alone as criteria for inclusion are insufficient and ahistorical: a community of one thousand in 1845 had an impact on local culture very different from a community of a thousand in the 1990s. But therein lies the solution: a community. What makes a community? This seemingly eternal debate invites no easy answer, and the editors had already sidestepped it by using official designations for entries on suburban municipalities and Chicago community areas. To locate ethnic presence, the editors drew on their observation that every community study in the field of urban history has an obligatory section on institution-building. Hence, any given ethnic group has "been here" if they have built an institution—any institution. New Zealanders have a rugby club. Some groups with small numbers have clubs oriented toward political questions back home. Restaurants count only if they are gathering places on some regular basis, such as the Argo Georgian Bakery on Devon Avenue. On this basis encyclopedia staff located 146 ethnic groups in Chicago. Each has an entry.

Religion proved even more difficult. There is no equivalent to current national boundaries. What would be the threshold for a denomination, or a sect? Here we have chosen to lump groups together rather than split them apart. Lumping allows our authors to weave a more complex story of religious development than they could in an endless series of short pieces on an infinite number of religious entities. Readers looking for histories of Methodists, Lutherans, or Assemblies of God should go to the entry on Protestants. The encyclopedia includes entries on Ba'hai, Buddhists, Eastern Orthodox, Hindus, Jews, Mormons, Muslims, Protestants, Roman Catholics, Sikhs, and Zoroastrians. The stories of individual denominations, sects, and congregations have taken a back seat to broader themes in the history of religion in metropolitan Chicago. These themes include a complex and shifting religious geography, and the region's substantial influence on national and international religious thought and trends. But the book also maps the area's vast matrix of religious institutions, which has infused nearly every aspect of local culture. The entry "Religious Institutions," for example, is less about churches, synagogues, or mosques than about the many ways in which Chicago's faith communities have provided services and generated cultural development.

The problem of where to tell a particular story is hardly limited to entries that navigate the difficult waters of identity. Every category of institutional life raised the question of when to weave together many stories into a synthetic narrative and when to present single strands on their own. Museums, colleges and universities, architectural styles, leisure activities, political organizations, corporations: each could yield an almost infinite set of narrow entries, or a very small set of broad essays covering vast territory. Our integrative approach generated a skew toward the larger picture. Extended essays on such issues as politics, art, work, and leisure offer narrative and analytical frameworks that both mention significant institutions and events and establish contexts for narrower topics covered in shorter entries. Sometimes our strategy grew out of practical considerations. For example, it is possible to identify a satisfactory (if not absolutely comprehensive) list of the generally recognized, accredited, postsecondary educational institutions. Hence each four-year college and university is covered in its own entry (with apologies to the one that we have undoubtedly missed), while "Universities and Their Cities" tells a broad story. Schools, on the other hand, are so numerous that individual entries would be impossible. They are treated together in an essay that maps the evolution of Chicago's school systems. Professional sports teams receive individual coverage; they are limited in number and have readily bounded histories. The stories of other athletic landscapes, such as school, sandlot, and collegiate sports, are told through the more generalized mechanism of entries on individual sports. In contrast to health, where the story is told largely through institutional contexts, music divides more logically by genre. Architecture provided still a different set of issues, given Chicago's vast landscape of significant buildings, trends, and innovations. Each of these important aspects of Chicago's architectural history has received attention, but readers looking for the larger architectural picture, and for the many significant particulars that did not receive individual attention, can turn to the four overview essays that periodize Chicago's architectural history ("Architecture"), and a wide-ranging survey entitled "Places of Assembly."

Businesses posed a distinct challenge, given the thousands of enterprises that have generated commerce in metropolitan Chicago. Here again, coverage is both detailed and broadly contextual. Our solution was driven by the urge to be as comprehensive as possible as well as by the encyclopedia's general orientation toward categorical analysis and broader context. Significant sectors of the regional economy (e.g., iron and steel, meatpacking, chemicals, agriculture) are treated in broad narrative entries, with particular attention to the most dominant companies. A **Dictionary of Leading Chicago Businesses**, which appears as an appendix, includes 236 companies chosen because of national importance, particular significance to metropolitan Chicago, number of employees, or a special Chicago angle. Relative brevity and smaller print have permitted inclusion of far more enterprises than could have been accommodated as regular A–Z entries.

Biography posed an even greater dilemma. A list of the iconic figures who stand astride major themes in Chicago's history, augmented by compilations of famous people in various fields, yielded a list too extensive to include in a volume oriented toward metropolitan integration, comparison, and context—unless these were limited to 250 words or less. What could our readers learn in 200 words about Frank Lloyd Wright or Jane Addams that they could not readily find in dozens of reference books with local or national orientations, including the definitive multivolume and recently revised *American National Biography* (1999)? Very little. Meanwhile, some of the greatest lacunae in the standard biographical dictionaries were already being filled by *Women Building Chicago, 1790–1990: A Biographical Dictionary* (2001). The encyclopedia's reference function could be better served by providing information about individuals who often were relatively obscure, but whose significance is marked by the decision of one or more authors to include them in an entry. The result is a **Biographical Dictionary**, which includes all deceased individuals mentioned in this volume in the context of activities relating directly to Chicago. Thomas Jefferson, for example, is mentioned in an entry but is not in this dictionary; by contrast, Martin Luther King, Jr., is included because his name emerges in the context of his civil rights activism in Chicago. This approach required new research, which enabled us to provide basic data for 2,191 individuals, including dates and places of birth and death and a note about each person's significance to Chicago history.

The other main elements of this book, in addition to the standard encyclopedia entries and the dictionary compilations, are blind entries, interpretive essays, sidebars, a chronological survey of Chicago history in the form of a timeline and "year pages," cross-references, maps, illustrations, tables and statistical appendixes, and an index. Like the standard entries, each of these elements contributes to the aim of creating an integrative history, and each has been prepared either by the editors themselves or by scholars participating in the project.

Elements of the Encyclopedia

The Encyclopedia of Chicago consists of three types of **standard entries**: broad essays, mid-level entries, and basic entries. Broad essays offer scaffolding for a large topic—a starting point for readers who want an overview of, for example, dance, public health, or transportation. Most of these have straightforward titles, but some attempt to pull together disparate strands of material in a way that produces less obvious titles, such as "Places of Assembly." Readers will be guided to these articles by **blind entries** appearing where readers might expect to find more narrowly construed but traditional titles like "Stadiums" or "Convention Centers." (A blind entry is alphabetized like a regular entry but, in place of any accompanying text, directs readers to another entry or entries where that topic is discussed comprehensively.) All broad essays are at least 1,000 words, some reaching as high as 4,000. At the other extreme lie the basic entries. These focus on a specific event, institution, or comparable phenomenon (e.g., Haymarket and May Day, La Leche League, Mr. Wizard, Soldier Field). Most of these are relatively brief, often under 200 words. Major institutions, however, such as the Art Institute of Chicago, receive more extensive coverage. In between the broad entries and basic entries lie the mid-level entries. These perform two functions: they fill in gaps left by broad essays that could not cover the entire terrain of a topic, and they provide context and sometimes comparative analysis for topics covered in basic entries. "Universities and Their Cities," for example, surveys the landscape of postsecondary education, offering an overview of individual institutions that have only very brief individual entries. In some cases basic entries were omitted in favor of the larger view possible in mid-level entries. For example, "Amusement Parks" covers the territory in lieu of entries on Riverview, Joyland Park, and Great America. In general the editors have chosen "forests" over "trees" for entries, and readers who do not find specific entries can use the index to locate contextualized discussions of these topics.

Two types of entries serve less conventional encyclopedia functions. Authors of the 21 **interpretive essays** were asked to reflect on recent scholarship rather than provide comprehensive topical or chronological coverage. "Creation of Chicago Sports," for example, highlights particular themes that explain the shift from nineteenth-century sporting culture to the spectator orientation that emerged by the 1920s. Although this essay ends with a landscape that will seem familiar to modern readers, it offers little information about developments since the 1920s; the interpretive edge of the questions it explores was sharpest during the preceding century. Because they are intended to adapt the insights of current scholarship to broad issues in Chicago history, thereby also indirectly introducing readers to this scholarship, these essays include substantial bibliographical essays rather than the standard listing of up to three recommendations for further reading. A notable exception is "Chicago Studied: Social Scientists and Their City," which weaves its bibliography into the article itself as it explains the use and influence of Chicago as an urban laboratory. Because of their interpretive focus and their more free-ranging orientation, many interpretive essays have titles that are less than obvious. Blind entries at the more obvious points guide readers to this scholarship. "Creation of Chicago Sports" is not topically or chronologically comprehensive enough to be called "Sports"; a reader who looks up "Sports" will be directed to this entry instead. Interpretive essays are indicated by a special icon preceding their titles.

Sidebars, also liberated from the obligation of encyclopedic coverage, serve different purposes, offering perspectives either supplementary or complementary to those presented in the entries with which they appear. Voices of participants in major events and a handful of biographies lend a personal perspective to the related entry's narrative. Other sidebars establish a conversation with their related entry, suggesting an alternative perspective or pointing to additional implications. Sidebars are neither cross-referenced nor accompanied by bibliographies because their close association with an entry would in most cases have produced redundant references. To make it into the encyclopedia, each sidebar had to relate to other entries in addition to the one it accompanies.

This linkage requirement pertained to all entries. Any issue so isolated historically that it could not generate a cross-reference to another entry does not meet this encyclopedia's test of historical significance. Influenced in part by the anticipation of subsequent electronic publication which will permit alternative modes of navigation dependent on comprehensive and imaginative cross-referencing, the process of designating **links** was accorded a high priority. These links fall into two categories: cross-references within the text of an entry (presented in SMALL CAPITALS) and "see also" references at the end of each entry. In some cases entries were selected or conceptualized in part by how they would fit into a larger set of linked articles. The editors identified these links as they read entries, with an eye toward gently nudging readers to appreciate historical relationships that are more interpretive than obvious. Most mid-level and basic entries link "upward" to broad essays. As often as possible the editors have linked an entry to at least one interpretive essay.

The links (i.e., cross-references and "see also's") generate pathways through the encyclopedia, suggesting to readers the various ways in which the editors might fit together pieces of the puzzle. The sheer number of these links creates an almost infinite series of pathways, so in the end readers who spend considerable time working their way through the encyclopedia will work the puzzle in a variety of ways, each of which will generate a different map of metropolitan history. In one case, the editors have themselves drawn the map: a **timeline**. Appearing in a special color insert, the timeline charts Chicago's history for the same period covered by the entries: from glaciation to the opening of the twenty-first century. It highlights major events and processes, including those that took place over many years.

The timeline is complemented by a series of **year pages**, which, using a combination of images, documents, maps, and texts, encourage readers to consider how events, people, institutions, and processes came together at particular moments in Chicago's history. The reasons for the choice of some of the years—such as 1871, the year of the Great Chicago Fire—will be immediately apparent. The significance of other selections, such as 1937, the year of the Memorial Day Massacre, might be less intuitive. Each year page, however, provides a window into what it meant to be in Chicago during a year in which the city experienced substantial change.

These chronologically oriented elements of the encyclopedia are skewed toward the last two centuries of Chicago's evolution. As a work of urban history, this encyclopedia is oriented toward aspects of the metropolitan area's development that signify its formation as an urban place. Yet Chicago's history does not begin with its incorporation as a town in 1833. Even where an entry's narrative begins in the 1830s or just before, we have resisted suggesting that the local history of politics, dance, public health, art, or any other aspect of community life "began" at that time. Similarly, the encyclopedia eschews references to people who arrived in the 1830s or 1840s as "pioneers." By the middle of the nineteenth century American Indians had settled, lived, and worked in the area for centuries, some groups staying for generations before moving on to another location. Arriving in what would eventually become Crete, Illinois, in 1836, Willard and Diantha Wood can be identified as that area's first *landowners*; but they were centuries too late to be considered "early settlers."

This concern with the history of population and land use has received special attention in the encyclopedia's **maps**. The maps stem from no mere decorative impulse, but rather seek to communicate vital features of the urban community's embeddedness in physical space and the unique configurations of place that this has produced over time. The cartography falls into three categories: thematic maps and "thumbnails," newly drawn for this publication, and existing (mainly historical) maps. The thumbnail maps accompany entries on locations and enable readers to situate a place within the metropolitan area. Readers of all entries can refer to the "Metropolitan Chicago Reference Map" that follows this Introduction for spatial orientation and an overview of the metropolitan area. The existing maps serve either as illustrations suggesting how space was perceived at a particular time, or as resources that the editors considered sufficient to the encyclopedia's cartographic imperatives and therefore publishable in their original form. In most cases, however, both the reference and interpretive agendas of the project required the creation of new maps, all of which grew out of a careful process of conceptualization, research, visual design, and scholarly review overseen by the cartographic editor. Topics found in map legends and captions are indexed but are not cross-referenced. The cartography in general suggests new ways of looking at space, time, people, institutions, and historical processes in metropolitan Chicago.

Mapping the Future

American Historical Association president Lynn Hunt observed in 2002 that the many recently published encyclopedias "usually represent a summing up of what has been accomplished rather than a forging forward." This book is intended instead to be both a *platform* for moving forward and part of the *process* of moving forward. Like most reference books it rests on a foundation of work generated by many scholars over many years. But it also has required substantial new research. Project staff found scores of immigrant groups that had begun to establish themselves in Chicago and other American cities but had not yet drawn the attention of scholars. These entries demanded not only primary research but also fieldwork; their lack of bibliographical citations signals a scarcity of published sources. Even more striking is the thin historiography on Chicago's suburbs. Most of the entries on suburban municipalities required considerable digging into primary sources and local histories. In addition, many other entries reflect the imbalance in current scholarship between studies of city and suburb, suggesting the vast territory that remains to be explored. Historians have, for instance, written many fine books on the history of policing in American cities, and a literature has also begun to emerge on firefighting. Research on these activities in suburban communities is at best scarce. The same could be said for a wide variety of topics, from art to machine politics to work culture. Innumerable entries, drawing on slivers of existing scholarship and forays into primary sources, invite further scholarly attention, especially within a metropolitan frame. More than just an expansion of attention beyond the city, metropolitan history demands attention to questions of interdependence that not only have influenced the past but also will shape the future. The editors hope that this publication will whet rather than satisfy the curiosity of its readers, thereby stimulating new research, not just on Chicago but other cities as well.

James R. Grossman
Ann Durkin Keating
Janice L. Reiff

Spring 2004

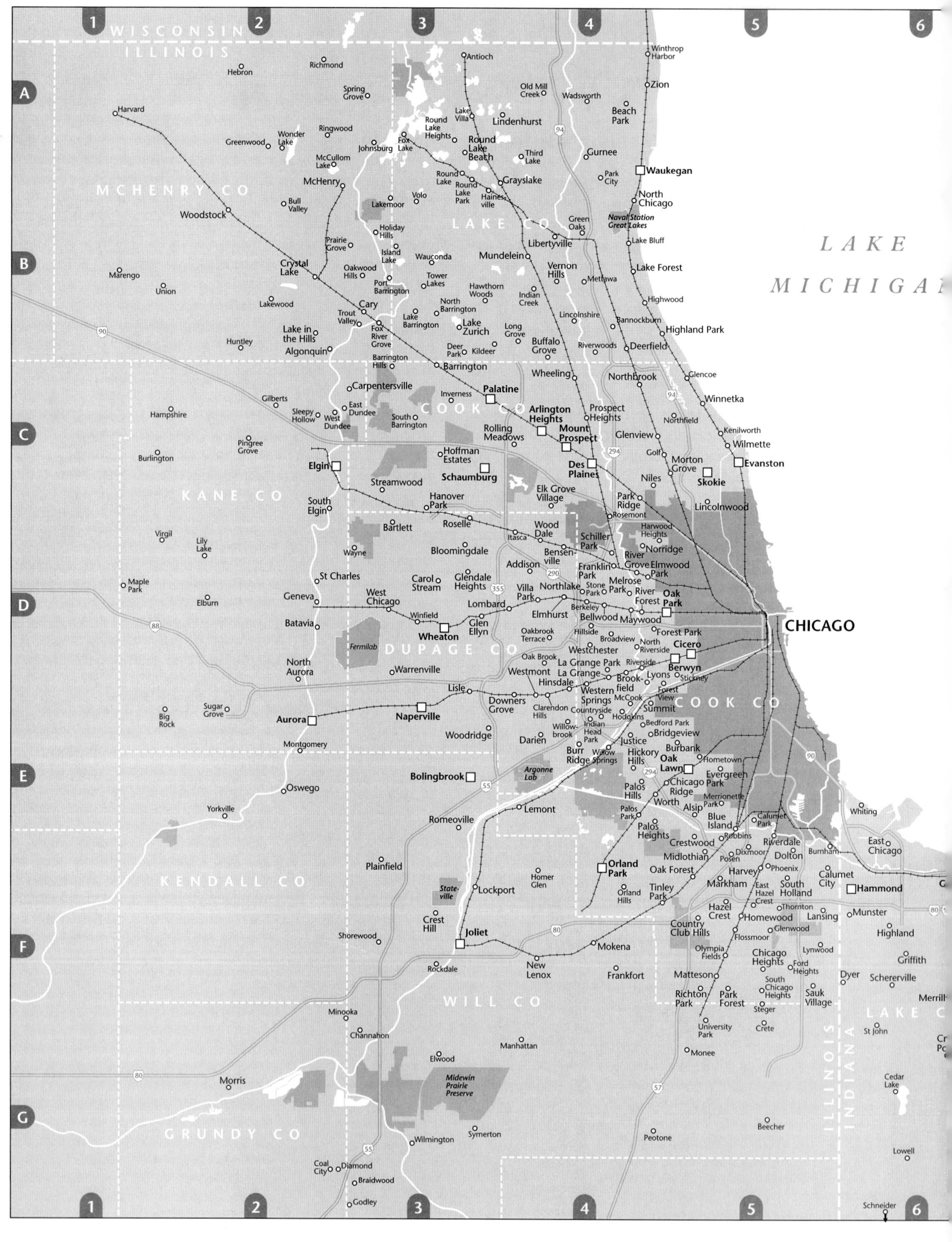

1
2
3
4
5
6
A
B
C
D
E
F
G
WISCONSIN
ILLINOIS
Hebron
Richmond
Antioch
Winthrop Harbor
Zion
Spring Grove
Old Mill Creek
Wadsworth
Harvard
Lake Villa
Lindenhurst
Beach Park
Ringwood
Round Lake Heights
Round Lake Beach
Wonder Lake
Greenwood
Fox Lake
Johnsburg
Third Lake
Gurnee
McCullom Lake
Round Lake
Round Lake Park
Grayslake
Park City
Waukegan
McHenry
MCHENRY CO
Volo
Hainesville
North Chicago
Bull Valley
Lakemoor
Woodstock
Green Oaks
Naval Station Great Lakes
Holiday Hills
LAKE CO
Libertyville
Prairie Grove
Island Lake
Lake Bluff
LAKE
MICHIGAN
Crystal Lake
Wauconda
Mundelein
Vernon Hills
Lake Forest
Marengo
Oakwood Hills
Tower Lakes
Mettawa
Union
Port Barrington
Hawthorn Woods
Indian Creek
Lakewood
Cary
North Barrington
Highwood
Trout Valley
Lake Barrington
Lincolnshire
Bannockburn
Lake in the Hills
Fox River Grove
Lake Zurich
Long Grove
Highland Park
Huntley
Deer Park
Kildeer
Buffalo Grove
Riverwoods
Deerfield
Algonquin
Barrington Hills
Barrington
Glencoe
Wheeling
Northbrook
Carpentersville
Palatine
Inverness
Winnetka
Gilberts
Hampshire
Sleepy Hollow
East Dundee
West Dundee
South Barrington
COOK CO
Arlington Heights
Prospect Heights
Northfield
Rolling Meadows
Mount Prospect
Glenview
Kenilworth
Wilmette
Pingree Grove
Burlington
Hoffman Estates
Golf
Morton Grove
Evanston
Elgin
Schaumburg
Des Plaines
Niles
Skokie
Streamwood
KANE CO
Elk Grove Village
Hanover Park
Park Ridge
Lincolnwood
South Elgin
Rosemont
Bartlett
Roselle
Wood Dale
Harwood Heights
Itasca
Schiller Park
Norridge
Virgil
Lily Lake
Wayne
Bloomingdale
Bensenville
River Grove
Elmwood Park
Addison
Franklin Park
St Charles
Carol Stream
Glendale Heights
Melrose Park
Maple Park
Stone Park
River Forest
Oak Park
Geneva
West Chicago
Villa Park
Northlake
Elburn
Lombard
Berkeley
Winfield
Elmhurst
Bellwood
Maywood
CHICAGO
Batavia
Wheaton
Glen Ellyn
Oakbrook Terrace
Hillside
Broadview
Forest Park
Fermilab
DUPAGE CO
Westchester
North Riverside
Cicero
North Aurora
Oak Brook
La Grange Park
Riverside
Berwyn
Warrenville
Westmont
La Grange
Brookfield
Lyons
Stickney
Hinsdale
Western Springs
Forest View
Lisle
Downers Grove
McCook
COOK CO
Big Rock
Sugar Grove
Clarendon Hills
Countryside
Summit
Aurora
Naperville
Hodgkins
Bedford Park
Willowbrook
Indian Head Park
Bridgeview
Woodridge
Darien
Justice
Montgomery
Burbank
Burr Ridge
Willow Springs
Hickory Hills
Oak Lawn
Hometown
Argonne Lab
Bolingbrook
Evergreen Park
Oswego
Palos Hills
Chicago Ridge
Worth
Merrionette Park
Yorkville
Lemont
Alsip
Whiting
Palos Park
Blue Island
Calumet Park
Romeoville
Palos Heights
Crestwood
Robbins
Riverdale
East Chicago
Midlothian
Posen
Dixmoor
Dolton
Burnham
Plainfield
Orland Park
Oak Forest
Harvey
Phoenix
Calumet City
KENDALL CO
Homer Glen
Markham
East Hazel Crest
South Holland
Hammond
Stateville
Lockport
Orland Hills
Tinley Park
Hazel Crest
Thornton
Lansing
Munster
Crest Hill
Homewood
Country Club Hills
Glenwood
Highland
Shorewood
Joliet
Flossmoor
Mokena
Olympia Fields
Lynwood
Griffith
New Lenox
Chicago Heights
Ford Heights
Rockdale
Frankfort
Matteson
Dyer
Schererville
South Chicago Heights
WILL CO
Richton Park
Park Forest
Sauk Village
Merrill
Steger
Minooka
LAKE C
Crete
St John
Channahon
University Park
Manhattan
ILLINOIS
INDIANA
Monee
Elwood
Morris
Midewin Prairie Preserve
Cedar Lake
GRUNDY CO
Beecher
Symerton
Peotone
Wilmington
Lowell
Coal City
Diamond
Braidwood
Godley
Schneider
90
94
88
290
294
355
55
80
57

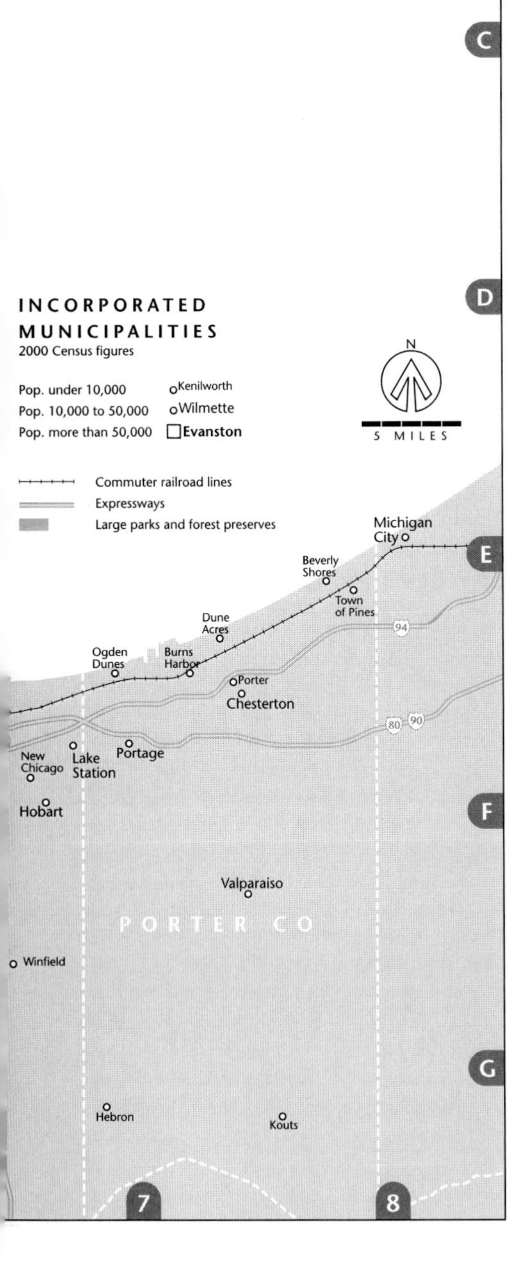

METROPOLITAN CHICAGO REFERENCE MAP

Addison	D-4
Algonquin	C-2
Alsip	E-5
Antioch	A-3
Arlington Heights	C-4
Aurora	E-2
Bannockburn	B-4
Barrington	C-3
Barrington Hills	C-3
Bartlett	D-3
Batavia	D-2
Beach Park	A-4
Bedford Park	E-4
Beecher	G-5
Bellwood	D-4
Bensenville	D-4
Berkeley	D-4
Berwyn	D-5
Beverly Shores	E-8
Big Rock	E-1
Bloomingdale	D-3
Blue Island	E-5
Bolingbrook	E-3
Braidwood	G-3
Bridgeview	E-4
Broadview	D-4
Brookfield	D-4
Buffalo Grove	B-4
Bull Valley	B-2
Burbank	E-5
Burlington	C-1
Burnham	E-5
Burns Harbor	E-7
Burr Ridge	E-4
Calumet City	F-6
Calumet Park	E-5
Carol Stream	D-3
Carpentersville	C-3
Cary	B-3
Cedar Lake	G-6
Channahon	G-3
Chesterton	F-7
Chicago	D-5
Chicago Heights	F-5
Chicago Ridge	E-5
Cicero	D-5
Clarendon Hills	E-4
Coal City	G-2
Country Club Hills	F-5
Countryside	E-4
Crest Hill	F-3
Crestwood	E-5
Crete	F-5
Crown Point	G-6
Crystal Lake	B-2
Darien	E-4
Deer Park	C-3
Deerfield	B-4
Des Plaines	C-4
Diamond	G-3
Dixmoor	E-5
Dolton	E-5
Downers Grove	E-4
Dune Acres	E-7
Dyer	F-6
East Chicago	E-6
East Dundee	C-3
East Hazel Crest	F-5
Elburn	D-2
Elgin	C-2
Elk Grove Village	C-4
Elmhurst	D-4
Elmwood Park	D-4
Elwood	G-3
Evanston	C-5
Evergreen Park	E-5
Flossmoor	F-5
Ford Heights	F-5
Forest Park	D-4
Forest View	D-5
Fox Lake	A-3
Fox River Grove	B-3
Frankfort	F-4
Franklin Park	D-4
Gary	F-6
Geneva	D-2
Gilberts	C-2
Glen Ellyn	D-3
Glencoe	C-5
Glendale Heights	D-3
Glenview	C-4
Glenwood	F-5
Godley	G-3
Golf	C-4
Grayslake	B-4
Green Oaks	B-4
Greenwood	A-2
Griffith	F-6
Gurnee	A-4
Hainesville	B-3
Hammond	F-6
Hampshire	C-1
Hanover Park	C-3
Harvard	A-1
Harvey	F-5
Harwood Heights	D-4
Hawthorn Woods	B-3
Hazel Crest	F-5
Hebron, Ill.	A-2
Hebron, Ind.	G-7
Hickory Hills	E-4
Highland	F-6
Highland Park	B-5
Highwood	B-4
Hillside	D-4
Hinsdale	D-4
Hobart	F-7
Hodgkins	E-4
Hoffman Estates	C-3
Holiday Hills	B-3
Homer Glen	F-4
Hometown	E-5
Homewood	F-5
Huntley	B-2
Indian Creek	B-4
Indian Head Park	E-4
Inverness	C-3
Island Lake	B-3
Itasca	D-4
Johnsburg	A-3
Joliet	F-3
Justice	E-4
Kenilworth	C-5
Kildeer	C-3
Kouts	G-8
La Grange	D-4
La Grange Park	D-4
Lake Barrington	B-3
Lake Bluff	B-4
Lake Forest	B-4
Lake in the Hills	B-2
Lake Station	F-7
Lake Villa	A-3
Lake Zurich	B-3
Lakemoor	B-3
Lakewood	B-2
Lansing	F-5
Lemont	E-4
Libertyville	B-4
Lily Lake	D-2
Lincolnshire	B-4
Lincolnwood	C-5
Lindenhurst	A-4
Lisle	D-3
Lockport	F-3
Lombard	D-3
Long Grove	B-4
Lowell	G-6
Lynwood	F-5
Lyons	D-4
Manhattan	G-4
Maple Park	D-1
Marengo	B-1
Markham	F-5
Matteson	F-5
Maywood	D-4
McCook	E-4
McCullom Lake	A-2
McHenry	B-2
Melrose Park	D-4
Merrillville	F-6
Merrionette Park	E-5
Mettawa	B-4
Michigan City	E-8
Midlothian	E-5
Minooka	F-3
Mokena	F-4
Monee	G-5
Montgomery	E-2
Morris	G-2
Morton Grove	C-5
Mount Prospect	C-4
Mundelein	B-4
Munster	F-6
Naperville	E-3
New Chicago	F-7
New Lenox	F-4
Niles	C-4
Norridge	D-4
North Aurora	D-2
North Barrington	B-3
North Chicago	B-4
North Riverside	D-4
Northbrook	C-4
Northlake	D-4
Northfield	C-5
Oak Brook	D-4
Oak Forest	F-5
Oak Lawn	E-5
Oak Park	D-5
Oakbrook Terrace	D-4
Oakwood Hills	B-3
Ogden Dunes	E-7
Old Mill Creek	A-4
Olympia Fields	F-5
Orland Hills	F-4
Orland Park	F-4
Oswego	E-2
Palatine	C-3
Palos Heights	E-4
Palos Hills	E-4
Palos Park	E-4
Park City	B-4
Park Forest	F-5
Park Ridge	C-4
Peotone	G-4
Phoenix	F-5
Pingree Grove	C-2
Plainfield	F-3
Port Barrington	B-3
Portage	F-7
Porter	E-7
Posen	E-5
Prairie Grove	B-2
Prospect Heights	C-4
Richmond	A-2
Richton Park	F-5
Ringwood	A-2
River Forest	D-4
River Grove	D-4
Riverdale	E-5
Riverside	D-4
Riverwoods	B-4
Robbins	E-5
Rockdale	F-3
Rolling Meadows	C-3
Romeoville	E-3
Roselle	D-3
Rosemont	C-4
Round Lake	A-3
Round Lake Beach	A-3
Round Lake Heights	A-3
Round Lake Park	B-3
Sauk Village	F-5
Schaumburg	C-3
Schererville	F-6
Schiller Park	D-4
Schneider	G-6
Shorewood	F-3
Skokie	C-5
Sleepy Hollow	C-2
South Barrington	C-3
South Chicago Heights	F-5
South Elgin	C-2
South Holland	F-5
Spring Grove	A-3
St. Charles	D-2
St. John	F-6
Steger	F-5
Stickney	D-5
Stone Park	D-4
Streamwood	C-3
Sugar Grove	E-2
Summit	E-4
Symerton	G-3
Third Lake	A-4
Thornton	F-5
Tinley Park	F-4
Tower Lakes	B-3
Town of Pines	E-8
Trout Valley	B-3
Union	B-1
University Park	F-5
Valparaiso	F-7
Vernon Hills	B-4
Villa Park	D-4
Virgil	D-1
Volo	B-3
Wadsworth	A-4
Warrenville	D-3
Wauconda	B-3
Waukegan	A-4
Wayne	D-3
West Chicago	D-3
West Dundee	C-2
Westchester	D-4
Western Springs	E-4
Westmont	D-4
Wheaton	D-3
Wheeling	C-4
Whiting	E-6
Willow Springs	E-4
Willowbrook	E-4
Wilmette	C-5
Wilmington	G-3
Winfield, Ill.	D-3
Winfield, Ind.	G-7
Winnetka	C-5
Winthrop Harbor	A-4
Wonder Lake	A-2
Wood Dale	D-4
Woodridge	E-3
Woodstock	B-2
Worth	E-5
Yorkville	E-2
Zion	A-4

THE ENCYCLOPEDIA OF CHICAGO

A

Abolitionism. Chicago's antislavery community included a variety of activists and sympathizers, including former slaves and evangelical Christians from northeastern states. Among white Chicagoans, opposition to the extension of slavery into new territory was more popular than abolition. To many whites, abolitionist crusades seemed as much a threat to the Republic as slavery itself.

AFRICAN AMERICAN Chicagoans voiced unanimous opposition to slavery but risked reprisal if their actions brought individuals to public notice. Even so, the community, which included many former slaves, took seriously its commitment to UNDERGROUND RAILROAD activity assisting fugitive slaves. John Jones, a prosperous free black tailor, often served as a link between African Americans and white abolitionists. It was to John and Mary Jones's house that John Brown brought his band of militant abolitionists when they came through Chicago in 1859 on their way to Harpers Ferry, Virginia.

Abolitionists first organized in Chicago through churches, beginning around 1839 with prayer meetings led by the minister of the First Presbyterian Church. Members of other churches also participated, on the grounds that slaveholding was a sin. Quinn Chapel African Methodist Episcopal Church also sponsored abolitionist activities, including an organized watch for slave catchers. Institutional support for the abolitionist movement culminated in 1862 when several Chicago churches voted to send a delegation to plead with President Lincoln for an emancipation policy.

Secular abolitionist institutions included the Chicago Anti-Slavery Society and the Chicago Female Anti-Slavery Society. Chicago abolitionists circulated petitions against slavery to be sent to the U.S. Congress. The *Western Citizen,* a Chicago-based NEWSPAPER, served as the official organ of the Illinois Liberty Party and was the primary abolitionist press for Illinois, Indiana, Wisconsin, and Iowa.

Abolitionism enjoyed little success at the ballot box, although one alderman, Ira Miltimore, was elected in 1844, with Liberty Party support. In 1848, the *Western Citizen* endorsed Martin Van Buren, the Free Soil Party's presidential candidate, as the best chance to elect an antislavery man and found itself in step with a majority of Chicago voters. Thereafter, most Chicago abolitionists who voted became a small, radical portion of the free-soil, anti-Nebraska, and REPUBLICAN PARTY coalitions.

Linda J. Evans

Fugitive Slave Law of 1850

Physically distant from the South, and populated mostly by northerners, many with antislavery sentiments, Chicago was a relatively safe haven for fugitive slaves. After the adoption of the 1850 Fugitive Slave Law by the United States Congress, the city's AFRICAN AMERICAN community formed a "Liberty Association" with regular patrols to subvert the legislation by preventing the seizure of blacks in the city by slaveholders and their agents. In October 1850 a slave catcher from Missouri arrived in the city and was informed by leading citizens that his safety was at risk if he stayed. Meanwhile, a slave he had brought with him to help capture the runaway also escaped. On October 21, 1850, the Chicago City Council passed a resolution condemning the new law as "cruel and unjust" and directing the city's police "not to render any assistance for the arrest of fugitive slaves." On October 23 Senator Stephen A. Douglas, in a major speech, condemned the city council resolution. An attempt to rescind the resolution failed and on November 29, 1850, the city council reaffirmed its opposition to the law and its refusal to allow city officials to enforce it. In 1860 John Hossack was convicted in federal district court in Chicago of aiding a fugitive slave who had escaped to Ottawa, Illinois. The jury recommended mercy and Judge Thomas Drummond imposed a fine of only $100 and a sentence of 10 days in jail.

Paul Finkelman

See also: Civil Rights Movements; Fenianism; Politics; Whigs

Further reading: Gliozzo, Charles A. "John Jones: A Study of a Black Chicagoan." *Illinois Historical Journal* 80.3 (Autumn 1987). • Mahoney, Olivia. "Black Abolitionists." *Chicago History* 20.1–2 (Spring–Summer 1991).

Accounting. Chicago's emergence as a major center of professional accountancy began during the 1890s. Initially, Chicago businesses relied on semiprofessional bookkeepers who were usually ill-prepared to develop innovative responses to the bewildering measurement problems associated with new technologies, legal contracts, transactions, management practices, or organizational forms.

A major focus of the early drive to professionalize accounting centered on the founding in 1897 of a state professional association that later became the Illinois Society of Certified Public Accountants. Public accountants provided three distinct services: (1) certification of financial statements; (2) consulting services concerning accounting systems; and (3) tax compliance and planning services after the passage of the federal corporate excise tax (1909) and the federal corporate income tax (1913). The Illinois licensing law (1903) was similar to New York's—both required an examination and practical experience—but the Illinois law provided for reciprocal licensing for practitioners certified in other jurisdictions. Besides encouraging more competitive markets, reciprocity facilitated the building of branch offices and interstate practices.

A unique aspect of Chicago's leading accounting practices was the importance of consulting. The central role of consulting was illustrated by the experience of two early public accounting firms that eventually grew to be giants, Arthur Andersen & Co. and McKinsey & Co. The initial impetus came from a plethora of small- and medium-sized businesses in the Chicago area whose managements were often skilled in either manufacturing or marketing but were not knowledgeable about finance and accounting.

To help clients overcome these weaknesses, Arthur Andersen created a new service in the 1920s known as financial and industrial "investigations." These were specialized studies employing accounting analysis to evaluate markets, organizational structures, plants, or products. Besides assisting business operators, they were also used by bankers in planning mergers or new securities issues. In 1932, this proficiency led to Andersen's selection as the monitor for the financial restoration of Samuel Insull's bankrupt utilities empire. Beginning in the 1960s, Andersen Consulting registered strong, sustained growth because of the advent of new opportunities attributable to the use of electronic data processing. Under the leadership of Leonard Spacek, the firm assisted clients in converting from manual-mechanical to computer-based accounting systems. In 1989, Arthur Andersen & Co. elected to spin off Andersen Consulting, later renamed Accenture, which had grown to become the world's largest consulting practice. The remaining firm, known simply as Andersen, lost its accounting business suddenly in 2002 because of its association with a financial fraud scandal at Enron corporation, one of its clients.

McKinsey & Co. was formed by James O. McKinsey, a CPA and UNIVERSITY OF CHICAGO professor. McKinsey's pioneering *Budgetary Control* (1922) established the intellectual underpinning for a service specialization that supported the formation of his firm three years later and eventually drew it into consultancy. Although budgeting was a practice then thought primarily relevant to the fund accounting procedures of governmental enterprises, McKinsey demonstrated that it also had great utility in business planning and control. The firm avoided the controversy over audit independence that developed in the 1970s, having completely abandoned its accounting practice in 1935. McKinsey & Co. gradually diversified into strategic planning services and became one of the world's largest management consultants.

Chicago also became an important center for accounting education and research. Foremost in this regard was the University of Chicago, which in 1922 was the first U.S. institution to grant a doctoral degree in accounting. Historically, its scholarly agenda was shaped by two initiatives taken in the allied discipline of economics. The first was the long-standing interest of professional economists during the Progressive era in the cost structures of monopolistic and oligopolistic business enterprises. The Interstate Commerce Commission, the Federal Trade Commission, and a host of state regulatory boards sought a better understanding of the economics of high-fixed-cost businesses in order to curb monopoly power or to assure the equity of rate bases. These concerns affected the program in accounting through the emphasis placed on budgeting and cost and managerial accounting. The second initiative began in the 1950s with the rise of positive economics under the leadership of Milton Friedman and others. This aspect had its greatest impact on accounting through the theoretical work of Franco Modigliani and Merton Miller on the functioning of efficient capital markets.

The accounting program at NORTHWESTERN UNIVERSITY, on the other hand, developed more directly in response to the needs of practice. The Northwestern program was founded after the passage of the Illinois CPA law to meet the need of local firms for college-trained accountants. Its closeness to the profession was reflected by the fact that its two earliest chairs, Seymour Walton, of Joplin & Walton, and Arthur Andersen, were both leading practitioners.

Another dimension of accounting education in Chicago involved the activities of proprietary academies and extension institutes. Proprietary schools like the one founded by Seymour Walton after he left Northwestern concentrated on providing rudimentary training in bookkeeping on a part-time basis to the city's large force of CLERICAL workers. It functioned as an adjunct to the local high schools that lacked a commercial arts curriculum. A variant of the proprietary school was the extension institute, which imitated the approach of the city's great retailer, Sears, Roebuck. The LaSalle Extension University supplied accounting education via MAIL ORDER beginning in the 1910s. Eventually, both types of institution were found wanting in preparing candidates for careers in professional accounting, and state licensing authorities mandated the completion of a bachelor's degree as a prerequisite for sitting for the CPA examination.

A fourth development was CPA-firm-sponsored professional education. Initially this took the form of staff training designed to standardize practice procedures among new hires. An early example of such tutelage was the in-house development programs established by Arthur Andersen for his junior accountants in the 1920s. In the 1970s, with the introduction of continuing education requirements by state licensing boards and by the quality-control standards mandated for practices by the American Institute of Certified Public Accountants, firm training also became focused on assuring the continued technical competency of those in the profession. The extent of this training became clear when Arthur Andersen & Co. acquired a former college campus in suburban St. Charles for these purposes.

By the end of the twentieth century, strong connections had been forged to the global economy through the competencies of Chicago's accounting and educational organizations. In these and other ways, professional accounting has been deeply intertwined with the developments that have shaped Chicago.

Paul J. Miranti, Jr.

See also: Business of Chicago; Chicago School of Economics; Management Consulting; Schooling for Work

Further reading: Miranti, Paul J., Jr. *Accountancy Comes of Age: The Development of an American Profession, 1886–1940.* 1990. • Previts, Gary J., and Barbara D. Merino. *A History of Accounting in America: An Historical Interpretation of the Cultural Significance of Accounting.* 1979. • Reckitt, Ernest. *Reminiscences of Early Days of the Accounting Profession in Illinois.* 1953.

ACLU. *See* American Civil Liberties Union

Acting, Ensemble. Ensemble acting in Chicago began in the 1950s with creative collaborations that subsequently evolved into the ensembles that now constitute a major segment of Chicago theater. Like the improvisational movement, the ensemble philosophy in Chicago THEATER first emerged at the UNIVERSITY OF CHICAGO, an institution famous, ironically, for encouraging theory more than practice. University students Paul Sills, Ed Asner, Fritz Weaver, Mike Nichols, and Sheldon Patinkin formed a theater group that eventually grew into the Playwright's Theater Club, a professional repertory theater on Chicago's North Side that performed classics and modern plays. In 1955, the Compass, a group developed by David Shepherd as a theater for "the proletariat," was established with Viola Spolin, the mother of IMPROVISATIONAL THEATER. It was here that Nichols and Elaine May, whom Sills called "the world's fastest humans," first developed the brilliant improvisational sketches that took them to Broadway and launched their distinguished theater and film careers. In the 1960s, Bob Sickinger founded HULL HOUSE Theater, where he created an environment in which young talent could flourish according to a professional standard. These early efforts provided a foundation for the vibrant theater scene that would soon emerge.

In the 1970s and 1980s, resident ensemble companies came to the fore. Stuart Gordon's Organic Theater became known for inventive ensemble-driven pieces like *Warp* and *Bleacher Bums.* In 1974, the GOODMAN THEATRE established Stage 2, a program that supported the collaboration of playwright David Mamet and director Gregory Mosher. Mamet

Second City cast on stage, 1960. Eugene Troobnick, *standing; left to right:* Barbara Harris, Mina Kolb, Andrew Duncan, and Severn Darden. Photographer: Arthur Siegel. Source: Chicago Historical Society.

associates William H. Macy, Joe Mantegna, and Lindsay Crouse often performed in Chicago premieres of both local and national productions of Mamet's plays and, later, in Mamet's films. By 1985, Mosher had established the New Theatre Company, consisting of a resident ensemble of actors, playwrights, and designers that produced new plays in both the Goodman Studio and the Briar Street Theatre. But the company immediately folded when Mosher was tapped to run the Lincoln Center Theater in New York. Robert Falls, who had been artistic director of Wisdom Bridge Theatre, inaugurated in 1986 a new kind of ensemble at the Goodman. Falls quickly assembled a directorial triumvirate consisting of himself, Frank Galati, and Michael Maggio in a partnership modeled on one Falls had observed at the National Theatre in London. Whereas STEPPENWOLF, which featured such actors as John Malkovich, Gary Sinise, Joan Allen, and Laurie Metcalf, was an actor's ensemble in which directing was less crucial to the process than visionary, visceral acting, Falls created a director's ensemble in which the passions of individual directors drove play selection and production concepts. Falls's vision evolved in the 1990s with the addition of such artists as Mary Zimmerman, Henry Godinez, and Regina Taylor to the Goodman artistic roster. Zimmerman, a uniquely gifted director/adaptor of major works of world literature to the stage, did her earliest ensemble work with the Lookinglass Theatre ensemble, which has established its own prominence in the Chicago theater scene. Zimmerman's commitment to ensemble has extended to her casting process: at her auditions she observes multiple actors interacting at once, with special attention to each actor's physical capabilities. Her production of Ovid's *Metamorphoses* went from Chicago's Ivanhoe Theatre to Broadway in 2002, displaying to a larger audience a prime example of Chicago ensemble work.

Andrea Telli
Richard Pettengill

See also: Playwriting; Second City Theatre; Theater Companies

Further reading: Houston, Gary. "A Vital Arrogance." In *Resetting the Stage: Theater Beyond the Loop.* Exhibition catalog. 1990. • Ryan, Sheila. *At the Goodman Theatre: An Exhibition in Celebration of the Sixtieth Anniversary of Chicago's Oldest Producing Theatre, October 12, 1985–January 11, 1986.* 1985. • Sweet, Jeffrey. *Something Wonderful Right Away: An Oral History of the Second City and the Compass Players.* 1978.

Addison, IL, DuPage County, 20 miles W of the Loop. Addison's roots lie in GERMAN and Lutheran tradition. By the 1840s the area was thriving with German newcomers. The town, originally known as Dunklee's Grove, grew to 200 people and had a steam gristmill, a general store, a cobbler's shop and a blacksmith shop. Stagecoaches stopped to change horses along present-day Lake Street.

In the early 1860s a Lutheran teacher training school located in Addison. In 1874, the Evangelical Lutheran Church built an ORPHANAGE to provide the seminary students with teaching experience. The orphan children learned various trades until they were 14 years old, and then were sent to work with area families.

Beginning in 1877 the Orphan Home Association held an Orphan Festival, later the Kinderheim Picnic, which drew large crowds. Music, hymns, games, a BASEBALL game, and tour of the grounds were conducted. Because the festival attracted so many people, the need for a RAILROAD spur line became evident. In 1890 five of Addison's citizens formed the Addison Railroad Company and made an agreement with the Illinois Central Railroad to maintain the line. The train doubled festival attendance from 5,000 to 10,000.

The Lutheran SEMINARY relocated in 1913, and its buildings were occupied by the Chicago City Mission Society, which opened a home for troubled youth referred by the courts. The Addison Manual Training School for Boys and Industrial School for Girls, known as the Kinderheim, opened in 1916. A new, larger facility housing 250 children was built in 1925, adjacent to the Orphan Home. The Kinderheim and the Orphan Home combined in 1940 under the Lutheran Child Welfare Association and operated until 1960. Lutherbrook, a facility for emotionally disturbed children, opened in 1961.

Addison began to grow in area and population when developer Anthony Ross built Normandy Manor on 40 acres he acquired in 1953. In the mid-1950s Green Meadows Estates offered bi-level houses and a shopping center. The Addison population grew from 813 in 1950 to 35,914 by 2000.

In the 1960s the Addison Industrial Commission was formed. While the northwest section of Addison had been developed with single-family housing, in 1983 the village also planned a segregated office research and industrial area. In 1987 the Addison industrial area had 1,000 firms.

Marilyn Elizabeth Perry

See also: DuPage County; Protestants; Religious Geography

Further reading: Eggerding, M. W. "Where Is Addison?" *Greater Chicago Magazine* (1930): 4–7. • Morris, Pearl, and Vivian Krentz. "Addison." In *DuPage Roots,* ed. Richard Thompson, 1985. • Morris, Pearl, and Vivian Krentz. *Addison Village of Friendship: A Centennial Commemorative Book of Addison, Illinois, 1884–1984.* 1984.

Adler Planetarium. The Adler Planetarium & Astronomy Museum was conceived in 1928 on a visit to Europe by Max Adler, a retired executive with Sears, Roebuck & Co. There he saw the newly invented Zeiss planetarium projector, which reproduced the night sky with unparalleled accuracy inside a domed theater. Upon his return, he donated a Zeiss projector to the people of Chicago, with money to build an edifice to house it. The landmark 12-sided building that resulted was designed by Ernst Grunsfeld and opened in 1930 on a small island connected to the shore by a causeway. It was the first modern planetarium in the Western Hemisphere. During the CENTURY OF PROGRESS EXHIBITION (1933–34) a million and a half people visited the planetarium and museum. Its unique position on LAKE MICHIGAN offered then, as it does now, the best view possible of the Chicago skyline.

Even before the planetarium opened its doors, Philip Fox, the Adler's first director, had persuaded Max Adler to purchase the famed Mensing Collection of historic scientific instruments. The two of them recognized that a museum of astronomy would increase the prestige and scientific importance of the new institution. Over the years the Adler's collection of historic instruments has grown, particularly under the curatorship of Marjorie Webster and the late Roderick Webster.

The Adler was operated by the Chicago Park District until 1968, when it incorporated as a nonprofit institution with its own board of directors. Paul Knappenberger arrived as president in 1991, determined to move the Adler to the forefront of public education in astronomy. Today astronomers and historians uphold the scientific standards of exhibits, educational programs, and sky shows. Educators and museum professionals support the public programs and exhibitions and assist the technical staff in producing planetarium shows seen here and around the world.

In 1999 the new glass-enclosed Sky Pavilion opened, wrapped around the Lake Michigan side of the historic 1930 Grunsfeld building. The expanded and completely renovated facilities now house the original Zeiss planetarium theater and the world's first StarRider theater, which offers visitors a computer-simulated virtual ride through the universe. Exhibitions explain current astronomy and its history to visitors in human terms. At the turn of the millennium the Adler Planetarium & Astronomy Museum remained a unique institution, combining planetarium theaters, an astronomy museum, and a historical astronomy collection unequaled in the Americas.

Bruce Stephenson

See also: Leisure; Museums in the Park; Waterfront

Further reading: Knappenberger, Paul, and James Trefil. *A Guide to the Adler Planetarium & Astronomy Museum.* 1999.

Advertising agency Cook, Coburn & Co., in the Kendall Building, corner of Dearborn and Washington, 1874. Artist: Unknown. Source: The Newberry Library.

Advertising. Even though New York City has always been the center of American publishing and BROADCASTING, Chicago became, by the beginning of the twentieth century, the heart and soul of American advertising. Chicago's advertising leadership was forged from the city's unparalleled success in personalized MAIL-ORDER cataloging, nurtured by its pragmatic BUSINESS attitude, and accelerated by the Midwest's democratic culture.

Chicago mail-order pioneers Montgomery Ward and Richard Warren Sears were the first great catalog copywriters. After the Great FIRE OF 1871, Ward began publishing well-illustrated catalogs with product testimonials and personalized copy. By 1883 his catalog advertised a stock of goods worth a half million dollars. Sears and his partner Alvah Curtis Roebuck claimed $53 million annual catalog sales in 1907 based on a circulation of about 5 million catalogs annually. Sears wrote nearly all of the copy himself.

The shift of advertising to the Midwest was stunning. In the 1860s and 1870s, only about 5 percent of the nation's advertising came from west of Philadelphia and New York City. By 1906, 45 percent of all nonlocal advertising in the nation originated west of Buffalo.

One Chicago ad agency—Lord & Thomas—overshadowed all the rest, achieving greater national influence and notoriety than any other agency in the United States. Albert Lasker started at Lord & Thomas in 1898, became general manager in 1904 at a salary of $52,000 per year, and within a decade owned the agency. He traveled the city in a yellow chauffeur-driven Rolls Royce and maintained a suburban estate with a staff of 50. Lasker hired the best copywriters in the business and taught them that advertising was "salesmanship in print"—probably the best-known definition of the advertising business in twentieth-century America.

Lasker sold the public on the idea of orange juice (people previously only ate oranges), built brands such as Goodyear and Van de Kamps, established a "records of results" department that monitored its clients' advertising impact with catalog-response precision, and even used advertising to help defeat Woodrow Wilson's League of Nations. Advertising legend David Ogilvy rightly ranked Lasker as one of the "six giants of modern advertising."

The most legendary American advertising copywriter was Lord & Thomas's Claude C. Hopkins. In his popular autobiography, *My Life in Advertising* (1927), Hopkins captured the populist style of Chicago advertising as literature for the common people. Hopkins is probably the father of consumer advertising for branded goods. He dubbed Schlitz the "beer that made Milwaukee famous," created unparalleled brand equity for Palmolive soap and Pepsodent toothpaste, wrote the "shot from guns" slogan for Quaker Oats, and invented free product sampling through print coupons. Hopkins penned the most influential book ever written about advertising—*Scientific Advertising* (1923).

Lasker sold Lord & Thomas in 1942 to three employees (Messrs. Foote, Cone & Belding). Fairfax Cone led the new company into an unparalleled era of creative broadcast advertising. The agency built some of the most successful broadcast advertising brands of all time, including the "Hallmark Hall of Fame," Clairol's "Does she or doesn't she?" and Dial soap's "Aren't you glad you use Dial?" Cone's client-sponsored broadcast programs helped make superstars out of such performers as Frank Sinatra and Bob Hope. Cone also led the Chicago advertising industry into public PHILANTHROPY, supporting the UNIVERSITY OF CHICAGO, OPERA, and many other endeavors.

The other great modern Chicago ad agency was the Leo Burnett Company. Burnett started the agency in 1935, mortgaging his house in the midst of the GREAT DEPRESSION. In 1989 the agency claimed $3.2 billion annual billings and

This early 1890s trade card for McLaughlin's coffee connected childhood play with future work. Each package of coffee included a picture card, often from a set with a particular theme. Other cards in this set included "The Doctor" and "The Scientist." Artist: Unknown. Source: The Newberry Library.

maintained offices in over 40 countries. Burnett's television campaigns included the Jolly Green Giant, the Pillsbury Dough Boy, Charlie Tuna, Tony the Tiger, and the Marlboro Man. *Advertising Age* ranked Burnett the third most influential person in the history of American advertising.

The *Chicago Tribune* was third nationally among newspapers in total advertising linage from the 1920s into the 1950s, creating and placing ads for thousands of its retail customers. *Advertising Age,* the best advertising trade magazine in the world, was started in the Windy City in 1930. The magazine's critical style set the standard for business JOURNALISM across the country.

By 1980, advertising was among the largest industries in Chicago, with 8,000 employees in over 500 agencies and $6 billion in revenues. Writer and sociologist Hugh Dalziel Duncan called Chicago the nation's home of "commercial magicians and priests of consumption." Chicagoans turned consumption into a "token of an infinitely expanding future of bigger and better things" that people must buy. Chicago businesspeople understood that "the power of style in America is derived from its power to *communicate* to others . . . our power to spend freely and frequently."

Quentin J. Schultze

See also: Global Chicago; Trade Publications

Further reading: Advertising Age. *How It Was in Advertising: 1776–1976.* 1976. • Fox, Stephen. *The Mirror Makers: A History of American Advertising and Its Creators.* 1984. • Goodrum, Charles, and Helen Dalrymple. *Advertising in America: The First 200 Years.* 1990.

Advice Columns. Advice columns have a long history in American journalism, reaching back to the "letters to the lovelorn" that appeared in eighteenth-century MAGAZINES and NEWSPAPERS. Yet perhaps no place rivals Chicago in the history of the newspaper advice column, because it served as the staging ground for the nationally syndicated sister act of Esther and Pauline Friedman, better known as Ann Landers and "Dear Abby," for a significant part of their long and successful careers.

These identical twins, born in Sioux City, Iowa, on July 4, 1918, were christened Esther Pauline and Pauline Esther Friedman. The twins attended Morningside College in Sioux City, where they majored in psychology and JOURNALISM and collaborated on a gossip column in the school newspaper. After dropping out of college to marry in a double ceremony, the two (now Esther Lederer and Pauline Phillips) went in different directions.

"Eppie" Lederer began her career as advice columnist in 1955 when she convinced a *Chicago Sun-Times* editor to give her a chance at the paper's "Ann Landers" column, which had been floundering since the death of the original Ann Landers, a nurse named Ruth Crowley. Lederer's *Sun-Times* column, an immediate success, was distributed nationally through the Sun-Times Syndicate.

Pauline, who lived in northern California, began by helping her sister answer letters and soon decided to pitch an advice column of her own. In January 1956, she began writing for the *San Francisco Chronicle* under the pen name Abigail Van Buren. "Dear Abby" was also a great success, and it was distributed nationally through the McNaught Syndicate from 1956 to 1974. Lured from McNaught to the CHICAGO TRIBUNE–New York Daily News Syndicate in 1974, Phillips reportedly was offered more than 70 percent of gross income from her column, an almost unheard-of deal.

While "Abby" was with the Trib-News Syndicate from only 1974 to 1980, and "Ann" moved through several distributors after the Sun-Times Syndicate, they remained associated with the *Tribune* and the *Sun-Times.* The keen and often public sibling rivalry of the twin sisters seemed to express the historically intense competition between Chicago's major newspapers. Eppie Lederer died in 2002.

Beth Bailey

See also: Television, Talk

Further reading: Weiner, Richard. *Syndicated Columnists.* 1975.

Afghans. Although a few Afghans came to Chicago for university education in the 1930s, they did not have a significant communal presence in the Chicago area until after the Soviet Union invaded Afghanistan in 1979, compelling millions to emigrate. The majority of these emigrants went to Pakistan or Iran; among those who came to the United States, most settled in California, Virginia, or New York. The 2000 census counted 556 Afghan natives in the Chicago metropolitan area, approximately half of them within the city.

Afghans in the Chicago area, most of whom chose Chicago because of friends or family, have neither specific neighborhood nor occupational concentrations. Chicago's two Afghan restaurants, the Helmand Restaurant (1985–1997) and Afghan Cuisine (1999–), have drawn Afghans and other Chicagoans but have not served as primary gathering centers for Afghans. Chicago's Afghans have expressed their communal identity mainly through political action and social gatherings.

During the Soviet occupation of Afghanistan (1979–1989), virtually all of the Afghan organizations in the Chicago area focused on improving the lives of Afghan REFUGEES both in the United States and abroad. Many of these organizations were founded by Afghan immigrants in conjunction with American citizens who had ties to Afghanistan, most often through marriage or Peace Corps service. The Afghan Reconstruction Support Committee, founded in 1983, was instrumental in bringing a handful of *mujahideen* (resistance fighters) to Chicago-area HOSPITALS in 1987 to be treated for injuries before being sent back to Pakistan. The Afghan Women's Task Force, established in 1988 by a group of Afghan and American women in Chicago, supports education for female Afghan refugees living in Pakistan. Community leaders bring Afghans together two times each year—at Nau Roz, the Afghan New Year celebrated on the first day of spring, and for Grandparent's Day in September.

Afghan elders in the Chicago area have been concerned with younger Afghans' lack of interest in maintaining traditional religious practices and language. Some religiously observant Afghans have shared the MUSLIM Community Center, located at Elston and Montrose, with other national groups, including PAKISTANIS and BOSNIANS. But, although many of Chicago's Afghans speak English as well as Dari (Afghan Persian) or Pashto, fewer children were learning these Afghan languages at the close of the twentieth century. Partially in response to this attenuation of tradition, the Afghan Cultural Association of Illinois was founded in 1995 to raise funds in the hope of establishing a cultural center and library for Afghan children.

Daniel Greene

See also: Americanization; Demography

African Americans. Beginning with John Baptiste Point DuSable's trading activities in the 1780s, blacks have had a long history in Chicago. Fugitive slaves and freedmen established the city's first black community

Oscar DePriest

Oscar DePriest was born in Florence, Alabama, to ex-slaves. He arrived in Chicago in 1889. DePriest worked as a painter and decorator, reportedly on occasion passing for white to get a job. He developed his own contracting business and began participating in community affairs. He began his political career as a precinct secretary, but by 1904 was elected to the Cook County Board of Commissioners.

DePriest amassed considerable wealth as a real-estate agent, partly through what later would become known as blockbusting. When the African American population of the Second Ward approached 50 percent in 1915, white leaders of the Republican ward organization backed DePriest for city council. He served one term, becoming the first African American elected to city council in Chicago. He showed interest mainly in civil rights issues and patronage. Indicted for protecting South Side gamblers in 1917, he left his council seat and later won acquittal.

In 1928 he became the first African American congressman elected to the House of Representatives from a northern state and a national symbol for racial pride. He fought for civil rights but took conservative positions on economic issues and lost his seat to a New Deal Democrat in 1934. He served one more term in the city council at the end of the following decade. De Priest devoted the rest of his years to his real-estate business.

Charles Branham

in the 1840s, with the population nearing 1,000 by 1860. John Jones, a tailor, headed most black antislavery and antidiscrimination efforts within the city until his death in 1879. Chicago's white ABOLITIONISTS were also active, but African Americans still suffered from segregation in various public venues, such as SCHOOLS, PUBLIC TRANSPORTATION, HOTELS, and RESTAURANTS. Moreover, black Chicagoans could neither vote nor testify against whites in court.

Finding their newly won liberties circumscribed by the overthrow of Reconstruction, small but growing numbers of black southerners made their way to Chicago, pushing the city's African American population from approximately 4,000 in 1870 to 15,000 in 1890. Increasingly concentrated on the city's SOUTH SIDE, Chicago's black population developed a class structure composed of a large number of DOMESTIC WORKERS and other manual laborers, along with a small but growing contingent of middle- and upper-class business and professional elites.

Formal segregation in Chicago slowly began to break down in the 1870s. The state extended the franchise to African Americans in 1870 and ended legally sanctioned SCHOOL segregation in 1874. A state law against discrimination in public places followed in 1884, but it was rarely enforced and did nothing to address widespread employment discrimination. While not yet confined to the city's nascent ghettos, blacks generally found housing available only within emerging enclaves.

A new cadre of leaders emerged from the business and professional elite to address these issues. In 1878 prominent attorney Ferdinand L. Barnett established Chicago's first black NEWSPAPER, the *Conservator*, which championed racial solidarity and militant protest. Ida B. Wells possessed a history of militant activism long before she moved to Chicago and married Barnett in 1895. Once in Chicago, Wells continued her long-standing antilynching campaign, joined the women's SUFFRAGE, CLUB, and SETTLEMENT HOUSE movements, and played a key role in the conference establishing the NATIONAL ASSOCIATION FOR THE ADVANCEMENT OF COLORED PEOPLE (NAACP) in 1900. Reverdy Ransom, who ministered to the city's black elite at Bethel African Methodist Episcopal (AME) Church, shared Wells's dedication to social causes and, with the help of white activists, established the Institutional Church and Settlement in 1900 to provide a range of SOCIAL SERVICES to the black community.

Steady southern migration raised Chicago's black population to 40,000 by 1910. Recognizing the power that could be derived from this growing community, black leaders began to develop independent black institutions for racial uplift. Between 1890 and 1916 black Chicagoans established PROVIDENT HOSPITAL, the Wabash Avenue YMCA, several black newspapers, including the *Chicago Defender*, and local branches of the NAACP and URBAN LEAGUE. Chicago's black politicians, under the leadership of Ed Wright, Robert R. Jackson, and Oscar DePriest, began to wrest control from white politicians in the predominantly black Second Ward, initiating the development of the nation's most powerful black political organization.

The shift toward a self-help ideology was largely a matter of expedience, though. For during the early years of the twentieth century, Chicago's racial lines hardened. By 1910, 78 percent of black Chicagoans lived in a chain of neighborhoods on the South Side of Chicago. This "BLACK BELT" was an area of aging, dilapidated housing that stretched 30 blocks along State Street and was rarely more than several blocks wide. Moreover, a pattern of education discrimination had reemerged, and blacks were still excluded from the civil service, industrial jobs, and most unions.

WORLD WAR I destabilized this arrangement, as military production requirements overrode racial ideologies that had excluded blacks from industry. With the cessation of Southern and Eastern European immigration and the drafting of young white men into the military, Chicago lost a critical supply of industrial workers at a time of intense need. Industrial jobs previously closed to African Americans suddenly became available. The *Chicago Defender* quickly recognized the significance of this opening and became an important voice encouraging southern blacks to come north to take advantage of Chicago's industrial opportunities.

With at least 50,000 black southerners moving to Chicago between 1916 and 1920, the institutional foundation established before the war provided a base for community development. The old-line AME and Baptist churches experienced considerable growth, exemplified by OLIVET BAPTIST CHURCH, which, with 10,000 members in 1920, was the nation's largest black church. The migrants also added new elements to Chicago's religious culture by establishing Pentecostal and Spiritualist storefront churches that delivered more demonstrative worship services than their more sedate middle- and upper-class counterparts. *Defender* circulation mushroomed, black businesses prospered, and black political candidates won increased representation in the city council.

The bulging pay envelopes and the vibrant community fulfilled migrants' expectations. But with these resources came racial tensions that were not part of migrants' visions of the "Promised Land." Black and white workers tended to regard each other with suspicion, particularly over UNIONIZATION, and with few exceptions (notably in MEATPACKING and garment factories) blacks found themselves generally excluded from the burgeoning labor movement. A general shortage of housing in Chicago made finding a home difficult for all Chicagoans, but the migrants were put into the particularly onerous position of moving into the overcrowded and overpriced Black Belt. Attempts to move into adjoining white neighborhoods sparked violent reactions. These tensions exploded in the summer of 1919, when five days of rioting left 23 black Chicagoans dead and 300 wounded.

Despite the riot and a recession in 1924, blacks' fortunes rose in the 1920s. Between 1925 and 1929, black Chicagoans gained unprecedented access to city jobs, expanded their professional class, and won elective office in local and state government. These years also marked the peak of Chicago JAZZ, which had begun its development well before World War I. In the mid-1920s, at the height of the Jazz Age, blacks and whites walked the STROLL, a bright-light district on South State Street, where nightspots such as the Deluxe Cafe, the Dreamland Cafe, and the Royal Gardens headlined jazz greats like Louis Armstrong, Alberta Hunter, and Joseph "King" Oliver.

The GREAT DEPRESSION undercut many of these gains. By 1939 blacks constituted 40 percent of relief rolls, and half of all black families relied on some government aid for subsistence. Black Chicagoans tried to fight back. In the fall of 1929 the militant *Chicago Whip* foreshadowed later direct-action civil rights activism with its "Spend Your Money Where You Can Work Campaign," which targeted boycotts at chain stores that would serve but not hire blacks. The campaign registered some successes, pushing the number of black employees in stores in the black community to 25 percent and opening up approximately 100 white-collar jobs.

Ironically, the Depression also led to a flowering of Chicago literature and ART. Between 1925 and 1950, Chicago's black literary output rivaled the Harlem Renaissance of the 1920s. Influenced by Robert E. Park and the CHICAGO SCHOOL OF SOCIOLOGY, CHICAGO BLACK RENAISSANCE artists like Richard Wright, Willard Motley, William Attaway, Frank Marshall Davis, and Margaret Walker turned from the Harlem Renaissance's retrospective focus on southern black folk culture to an emphasis on a "literary naturalism" that revealed the nuances of urban ghetto life. St. Clair Drake and Horace R. Cayton exemplified the new intellectual style in their classic *Black Metropolis,* which remains the most detailed portrait of black Chicago in the 1930s and 1940s. Chicago painter Archibald Motley, Jr., offered new impressions of black life, with his exploration of natural and artificial light, in paintings of the South Side's vibrant nightlife. Finally, Gwendolyn Brooks' Pulitzer Prize–winning *Annie Allen* provided a poetic voice to the lives of everyday black Chicagoans with such works as "Beverly Hills, Chicago" and "The Children of the Poor."

Migration from the South slowed during the 1930s but accelerated when WORLD WAR II production created new jobs. In the 1950s, the expanding use of the mechanical cotton picker pushed another wave of black agricultural workers out of the South. Between 1940 and 1960, Chicago's black population grew from 278,000 to 813,000.

What awaited this second GREAT MIGRATION of southern blacks? On the one hand, the South Side of Chicago was the "capital of black America." It was home to the nation's most powerful black politician, Democratic congressman William L. Dawson; the most prominent black man in America, BOXING champion Joe Louis; and the most widely read black newspaper, the *Chicago Defender.* In the late 1930s the CONGRESS OF INDUSTRIAL ORGANIZATIONS finally succeeded in overcoming racial discord in two of Chicago's major industries, steel and meatpacking, enabling some blacks to move further up the ranks to low-level management positions and contributing to a growing black working class able to count on a stable income. The migrants could spend their hard-earned wages in several SHOPPING DISTRICTS with well-provisioned DEPARTMENT STORES, movie theaters, and banks. At night they could go out and hear some of America's best rhythm and blues musicians. The Chicago BLUES scene dated back to the 1930s, but in 1948 Aristocrat records broke new ground and set the tone for rhythm and blues for the next 10 years with the release of Muddy Waters's "I Can't Be Satisfied." Throughout the 1950s Aristocrat, which became the famous CHESS RECORDS label, pumped out a steady supply of R&B hits with some of the nation's most popular artists, including Little Walter, Jimmy Rogers, and Howlin' Wolf.

On the other hand, conditions in Chicago provided these blues artists with much to sing about. Blacks still faced widespread employment discrimination. Stores in the LOOP refused to hire African Americans as clerks. Black bus drivers, POLICE officers, and firefighters were limited to positions serving their own community. CONSTRUCTION trades remained closed. Moreover, the second Great Migration made Chicago's already overcrowded slums even more dilapidated, as more and more people tried to fit into converted "KITCHENETTE" and basement APARTMENTS in which heating and plumbing were poor, if functioning at all. Street crime in African American communities remained a low priority for Chicago's police, and violence, PROSTITUTION, and various other vices soared in black neighborhoods. When Elizabeth Wood, executive director of the CHICAGO HOUSING AUTHORITY (CHA), tried to ease the pressure in the overcrowded ghetto by proposing PUBLIC HOUSING sites in less congested areas elsewhere in the city in 1946, white residents reacted with intense and sustained violence. City politicians forced the CHA to keep the status quo, setting the stage for the development of Chicago's infamous high-rise projects, such as CABRINI-GREEN and the ROBERT TAYLOR HOMES.

In the 1960s, housing and educational issues sparked the Chicago Freedom Movement. Led by Al Raby, the COORDINATING COUNCIL OF COMMUNITY ORGANIZATIONS (CCCO) sponsored a series of school boycotts and a court case to end black school overcrowding, which stemmed from widespread white opposition to SCHOOL DESEGREGATION. Their efforts drew Martin Luther King and the Southern Christian Leadership Conference to Chicago in 1965. In conjunction with the CCCO, King led a series of protests against housing discrimination. The campaign resulted in a stalemate with Mayor Richard J. Daley and made little progress for OPEN HOUSING. Meanwhile, black women, who were rapidly becoming the primary heads of households in the city's steadily deteriorating high-rise projects, built a grassroots movement that resulted in greater tenant involvement in the governance of the city's public housing in the late 1960s.

Black Chicagoans in need of housing found little relief in the suburban housing market. With a few notable exceptions such as AURORA, EVANSTON, OAK PARK, and WAUKEGAN, blacks generally constituted less than 3 percent of the population in Chicago's northern and western suburbs by the end of the twentieth century. They found greater success in moving to southern suburbs, including CHICAGO HEIGHTS, RIVERDALE, and HARVEY, where they migrated in large numbers in the 1950s and 1960s. These communities notably suffered from the decline of local industries in the final third of the twentieth century.

Reeling from the effects of deindustrialization in the 1970s, the Reagan administration's attacks on social welfare programs in the early 1980s, and decades of neglect from the Chicago political machine, black Chicagoans' political activism reignited in Harold Washington's 1983 mayoral campaign. With the support of Latinos and liberal whites, Washington's grassroots campaign defeated the remnants of the Daley machine, making Washington Chicago's first African American mayor. Washington faced intense opposition from a predominantly white city council, whose infamous "Council Wars" blocked most of his initiatives until a 1986 court order forced revisions in the gerrymandering that favored white city council candidates in a city where white voters seldom supported black or Latino candidates. The new city council passed some of Washington's reform agenda, but these initiatives were cut short by his premature death from a heart attack in 1987.

The 1990s saw both continuity and change for black Chicagoans. Racial issues still flared, with several cases of police brutality toward African Americans, controversy over inequitable promotions for African American police officers, and allegations of racial profiling in the affluent suburb of HIGHLAND PARK. Mayor Richard M. Daley attempted to remedy the problems created by the housing projects built by his father in the 1960s with a $1.5 billion plan to remove the city's 51 high-rise projects and replace them with "mixed income" housing. This policy, implemented in the opening years of the twenty-first century, has evoked a mixed reaction from community activists, who have argued that mixed income is but a "euphemism for removal of the poor."

Christopher Manning

See also: Civil Rights Movements; Contested Spaces; Demography; Multicentered Chicago; Politics; Racism, Ethnicity, and White Identity

Further reading: Drake, St. Clair, and Horace R. Cayton. *Black Metropolis: A Study of Negro Life in a Northern City.* 1945; rev. ed. 1993. • Grossman, James R. *Land of Hope: Chicago, Black Southerners and the Great Migration.* 1989. • Spear, Allen H. *Black*

Chicago: The Making of a Negro Ghetto, 1890–1920. 1967.

Agrarian Movements. Although American farmers have maintained an image as independent and self-reliant, they have sustained many interdependent relationships for equipment, horticultural supplies, TRANSPORTATION, marketing, and credit. Nevertheless, it had long been believed in this country that to be successful as a farmer, one had to have only common sense, a strong back, and a little luck with the weather. When this credo failed in the late 1800s, many blamed the middlemen.

As early as 1849, the Chicago-based *Prairie Farmer* began urging northern Illinois farmers to form associations and cooperatives in order to minimize their costs while maximizing their profits. Within 20 years, *Prairie Farmer* editorials blamed the RAILROAD monopolies, grain elevator owners, and the Chicago Board of Trade for the declining fortunes of farmers.

Illinois farmers finally began organizing themselves into county-based cooperatives and associations following the regional 1870 Illinois Producers' Convention in Bloomington. The Order of the Patrons of Husbandry (the Grange) had brief success beginning in 1871, but by the following decade the Farmers' Alliance had become more influential. The Grange and the Alliance, both Illinois branches of national associations, declined following the 1895 legislative act creating the Illinois Farmers' Institute.

The Farmers' Institute comprised individual county-supported organizations, providing its members with innovative farming techniques and the latest practices being developed by the land grant colleges. It merged into the Cooperative Extension Service during the 1940s. County farmer cooperatives continue into the twenty-first century, collectively known as the Farm Service Cooperatives.

One agrarian movement that enjoyed success elsewhere never gained major strength in Illinois: Populism. The depression in the 1890s generated a brief moment of popularity, and a Populist-Labor alliance formed in 1894 for the upcoming elections. While thousands attended mass meetings and torchlight parades in Chicago in support of the alliance, the party received disappointing electoral returns.

Chas. P. Raleigh

See also: Agricultural Journals; Agriculture

Further reading: Scott, Roy V. *The Agrarian Movement in Illinois, 1880–1896.* 1962. • Warner, Donald F. "The Farmers' Alliance and the Farmers' Union." *Agricultural History* 23 (January 1949): 9–19. • Woods, Thomas A. *Knights of the Plow: Oliver H. Kelley and the Origins of the Grange in Republican Ideology.* 1991.

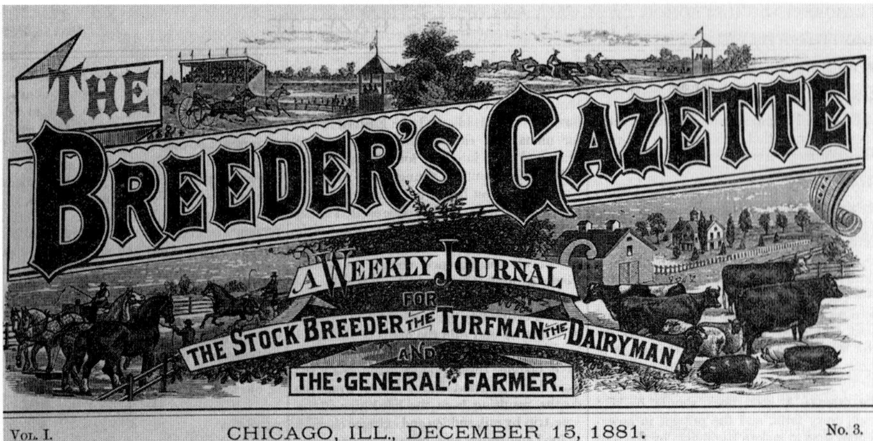

The *Breeder's Gazette* was published in Chicago from 1881 to 1931, when it merged with another publication and moved to central Indiana. Source: Chicago Historical Society.

Agricultural Journals. A rich AGRICULTURAL hinterland, an emerging publishing industry, and a need for specialized information about prairie farming made Chicago a lively center for agricultural journalism. What no one could predict in 1841 when the *Union Agriculturist and Western Prairie Farmer* first appeared was that Chicago would become home to more agricultural journals than any other city in the world.

Founded by the Union Agricultural Society, the monthly *Prairie Farmer,* as it quickly became known, was purchased by John Stephen Wright in 1843. Its publication philosophy, incorporated into its banner "Farmers, write for your paper," made the *Prairie Farmer* the longest continuously published farm journal. Owned briefly (1857–1858) by Chicago printers James and William Medill, then by Henry Emery, who merged it with *Emery's Journal of Agriculture,* this journal continued into the twenty-first century as a publication of the Farm Progress Company of CAROL STREAM.

As the *Prairie Farmer* grew from 500 subscribers in 1841 to more than 12,000 in 1857, when it became a weekly publication, competitors appeared. These included the *Western Enterprise* (1856–1857), *Northwestern Prairie Farmer* (1858–1859; renamed *Farmers' Advocate* in 1859 and merged into *Prairie Farmer* in 1861), the German-language *Der Farmer des Westens* (1856), *Northwestern Agriculturist* (1866), *Rural Messenger* (1868–1872), *Western Farmers' Magazine* (1859–1860), *Chicago Dairy Produce* (1894–1943), *Live Stock Journal* (1900–1915), *American Pigeon Keeper* (1898–1940), *Gardening* (1892–1925), *Farm Life* (1903–1913), *Horse Review* (1889–1932), *Dairy and Creamery* (1898–1904), *Irrigation Age* (1891–1918), *American Fruit Grower* (1883–), and the *Breeders' Gazette* (1881–1964).

Only the last three have enjoyed the success and longevity of the *Prairie Farmer. Irrigation Age* became the *Utah Farmer* when it moved to Salt Lake City in 1917. Both it and *American Fruit Grower* were still publishing at the opening of the twenty-first century. Yet of all these journals, only the *Breeders' Gazette* has rivaled *Prairie Farmer* for contribution to the emergence of the Midwest farmer.

Founded by J. H. Sanders and continued by his son Alvin, the *Breeders' Gazette* was a strong advocate for purebred livestock. Despite the Sanderses' close ties to the UNION STOCK YARD and to the Chicago Fat Stock Show and its successor, the International Livestock Exposition, they were judicious livestock experts who maintained a high degree of integrity in their publication. Much of their success rested on their use of the *Prairie Farmer* model of soliciting information from individual farmers. Copies of their weekly remain one the best sources for the study of livestock development and production between 1880 and 1930.

While Chicago's agricultural journalists have focused on regional content, their most significant contribution has been their role in the establishment of agricultural standards through accurate recording and reporting of the industry.

Chas. P. Raleigh

See also: Meatpacking; Places of Assembly; Trade Publications

Further reading: Bardolph, Richard. *Agricultural Literature and the Early Illinois Farmer.* 1948. • Ogilvie, William Edward. *Pioneer Agricultural Journalists.* 1927; repr. 1973.

Agricultural Machinery Industry. In 1847, Cyrus McCormick decided to consolidate manufacture of his reaper in Chicago. Since developing the first successful reaper in 1831, McCormick had tried selling it through regional licensees who also manufactured the machine. This approach had worked poorly, often producing inferior machines and always producing inferior financial results. McCormick also recognized that the future of American agriculture lay to the West and that Chicago, with the RAILROAD to Galena nearly complete, the ILLINOIS & MICHIGAN CANAL soon to open, and a TELEGRAPH link to the East about to be in place, offered the best location from which to build his BUSINESS.

On August 30, 1847, McCormick, in partnership with Charles M. Gray (later MAYOR of Chicago), bought three lots on the north bank of the CHICAGO RIVER. The two immediately began construction of a factory to build the McCormick reaper. By 1850, with the McCormick factory in full operation, the U.S. census reported 646 people working in the agricultural implement industry in Chicago.

Chicago soon attracted other machinery producers, including George Easterly of Heart Prairie, Wisconsin, who built a Chicago factory to produce his grain header, and John S. Wright, who made a self-rake reaper developed by Jearum Atkins. But the sharp financial panic of October 1857 destroyed or crippled many of McCormick's competitors. In 1860, his factory occupied 110,000 square feet of floor space and, with more than 300 workers, employed nearly a fifth of all wage earners in Chicago's agricultural implement sector.

During the next decade employment in the sector grew quickly—the 1870 Census found nearly 4,000 working in agricultural machinery establishments—but the McCormick Company, though still the largest single employer in the Chicago implement industry, had stagnated. Its products were ill-suited to a shift among many farmers to combined machines that could efficiently harvest both grain and hay, the latter much in demand to feed the livestock in America's burgeoning cities. McCormick harvesters also technically lagged behind specialized self-rakes used for harvesting small grains. As a result, McCormick had shrunk to a regional firm, selling principally in upper Midwest states.

On January 25, 1871, Cyrus McCormick bought 130 acres on the South Branch of the Chicago River, where he hoped to build a new factory. But the Great FIRE OF 1871 put the whole future of the company into question when, on October 9, it destroyed the entire old factory. Within days Nettie Fowler McCormick, the young wife of 62-year-old Cyrus, was on the new site, where she ordered the resumption of full production. Within two years the new McCormick Works replaced the old factory. At the same time the company management, much influenced by Nettie McCormick, refocused on building the business, and the company began to regain ground. By 1880, with McCormick the largest agricultural machinery producer in Chicago, area employment reached nearly 7,000, a fifth of the national total.

A few years earlier, William Deering, a retired merchant from Maine, had come to Plano, Illinois, to superintend another reaper factory his old friend William Gammon had purchased. Deering settled in EVANSTON the following year and, after buying control of the company in 1878, moved it to Chicago in 1880. The William Deering Company soon rivaled the leading McCormick Company, and the Deering factory on the North Branch of the Chicago River employed nearly as many workers as the McCormick plant on the South Branch. A second reaper company was organized to take over the old factory in Plano, but it too relocated to the Chicago area. In 1893, the Plano Company built a new factory in WEST PULLMAN.

In the mid-1880s, as McCormick management tried both to gain closer control over the production processes and to wrestle with the impact of a severe national recession, labor unrest grew rapidly. As a result, the McCormick Works faced several major STRIKES. During one, POLICE used brutal tactics to defend nonunion workers from attacks by strikers as they left the plant on May 3, 1886, leading directly to the protest meeting the next night at HAYMARKET Square, a meeting at which a bomb killed seven policemen. Only a few years later, however, McCormick proudly went through the tumult surrounding the PULLMAN STRIKE with no troubles at all; by then the company paid among the highest factory wages in Chicago and enjoyed high worker loyalty.

In 1902, these three companies—McCormick, Deering, and Plano—together with two others, came together to form the International Harvester Company (Navistar after 1986). The new company controlled more than 80 percent of world production in grain harvesting equipment. International Harvester quickly expanded its Chicago-area facilities. At its peak, in the 1920s and 1930s, the company had six major manufacturing facilities in the Chicago area (plus a steel mill in SOUTH CHICAGO), covering 440 acres, and accounting for a large share of the nearly 23,000 workers in Chicago's agricultural machinery sector in the 1930 census. This accounted for more than half the national total of 41,662.

This was the high-point of the industry in the Chicago area. The GREAT DEPRESSION took a heavy toll, and after World War II both International Harvester and the broader industry undertook all of its expansion outside the Chicago area. As a result, the Chicago-area plants were increasingly outdated and uneconomical. In the 1950s, the McCormick Works was progressively closed down, and the agricultural machinery industry no longer held a significant place in the Chicago-area economy.

Fred Carstensen

See also: Agriculture; Global Chicago; Innovation, Invention, and Chicago Business; Unionization; Work

Further reading: Marsh, Barbara. *A Corporate Tragedy: The Agony of International Harvester Company.* 1985. • Ozanne, Robert W. *A Century of Labor Management Relations at McCormick and International Harvester.* 1967.

Agriculture. Although agriculture was practiced by NATIVE AMERICANS living in the area, it was not until settlers from the eastern United States arrived that Chicago began to emerge as the agricultural leader of the world.

The years between the first schooner-load of grain to leave Chicago in 1839 and the 1865 opening of the UNION STOCK YARD defined Chicago's agricultural heritage. The opening of the ILLINOIS & MICHIGAN CANAL, the construction of RAILROADS, Cyrus McCormick's and Obed Hussey's competitive manufacturing of grain reapers and other implements, the beginning of the Chicago Board of Trade, and the extremely favorable growing seasons of 1849, 1850, and 1851 all combined to strengthen Chicago's importance to the agricultural BUSINESS community.

Likewise, developments after the American CIVIL WAR maintained Chicago's role as the leading agricultural city. Development of the refrigerated railroad boxcar, dredging and expansion of the city's harbor, and the establishment of the corn and livestock belt expanded the agricultural prosperity and reputation of the city.

Chicago's "big shoulders" were broadened with each swing of the farmer's scythe. Grain was and remains at the very center of Chicago's agriculture. Wheat, and later oats, barley, rye, and corn, filled the bellies of livestock and ships alike. Grain culture spread westward from Pennsylvania and Ohio and reached peak production on the prairie lands of Illinois in the 1850s and 1860s. Here, the development of technology for planting and harvesting, combined with the fertile soil and almost perfect CLIMATE, produced bumper crops on an annual basis. By 1860, Illinois was the number one producer of both corn and wheat.

Grain farmers benefited from the ever-expanding TRANSPORTATION system for getting their crop to market. Oxen-pulled carts on crude roads were replaced by horse-drawn wagons on the plank roads of the 1830s. These in turn became obsolete with the opening of the I&M Canal in 1848 and the subsequent railroad construction westward from Chicago in the 1850s. What had been a difficult journey of three or four days to transport a wagon full of grain from the FOX RIVER 35 miles west of Chicago was now a several-hour trip by train to the city.

This mass movement of grain resulted in the commingling of grain at railroad stops and barge tie-ups called elevators. There, a farmer's grain was carefully weighed and graded, with like grades being elevated into large commingled overhead bins. From these bins, gravity provided the impetus and wooden chutes quickly filled the waiting railroad cars and barges. While the elevator created another middleman between the farmer and the purchaser, it facilitated a more reliable delivery system, provided a means to accommodate a larger harvest, minimized the loss of grain to a single seller, and provided for the speculator, who could easily buy or sell the stored grain.

Speculation on the price of grain and other agricultural COMMODITIES has been a critical component in Chicago's agriculture. The Chicago Board of Trade has been the platform allowing access to markets within the United States and throughout the world. Historically, it has provided price stability, setting the minimum price for agricultural commodities and stimulating interest and re-investment in agricultural businesses. While farmers saw speculators as making money off their labor, the Board of Trade facilitated working capital being available for farmers to utilize.

The Chicago Board of Trade provided similar support for the growing beef cattle and hog industry of the mid-1800s. As the railroad link between the eastern markets and the increasing number of Midwestern and trans-Mississippi producers of livestock, the Union Stock Yard became the largest facility of its kind when it opened in 1865. Just as wheat production had moved westward, so had the production of hogs, stripping Cincinnati in the early 1860s of its self-proclaimed status as Porkopolis. Following the arrival of Armour, Swift, and other MEATPACKERS, the Union Stock Yard was easily handling eight to nine million animals each year by the mid-1870s.

This post–Civil War commercial growth brought expansion to the city and its population. Feeding this population and supplying transport materials within the city limits was a large agricultural endeavor unto itself. Following the Great FIRE OF 1871, vegetable and dairy operations moved outside city limits. Vegetable and chicken farms could be found arcing from SOUTH HOLLAND to MAYWOOD. Dairy farms developed in DUPAGE, COOK, and LAKE Counties and in the closer-in areas of WILL and MCHENRY Counties. Creameries and milk-processing facilities were constructed along existing railroad lines, and special milk trains transported this commodity for processing. Hay and oats were cash crops for farmers in the outlying counties, as they were vital for feeding and maintaining the tens of thousands of horses used in Chicago each day. The hay market in Chicago was a huge endeavor, with the Union Stock Yard feeding its livestock 100 tons of hay each day during its peak seasons, in addition to the corn that was fed to select holdings.

After the fire, horses remained the only farm animal permitted to stable within the city limits. They provided necessary cartage between warehouses and businesses, made livery services possible, pulled milk and STREET PEDDLERS' wagons and fire and municipal vehicles, and performed hundreds of other tasks, including functioning as personal transportation. The WASTE from these horses was in excess of 40,000 pounds each day.

Henry Holstein raised hogs, corn, and wheat on his 160-acre farm and operated a windmill to process his neighbors' wheat for shipment to Chicago. From *Combination Atlas Map of DuPage County, Illinois* (1874). Artist: Unknown. Source: The Newberry Library.

In 1872, New Yorker Franklin J. (F. J.) Berry established a small but successful horse market at the corner of Michigan Avenue and Monroe Street. By 1886, Berry was selling 4,000 horses annually. In October of 1888, he moved his operation to the Union Stock Yard and by 1895 was selling 27,000 horses annually. His success was due to his INNOVATIVE sales method: horses brought in by the rail carload were sold individually in a weekly public auction. This method, which allowed Illinois to dominate the national horse market from the late 1880s through the late 1920s, continued into the twenty-first century.

The interest in and specialization of the Chicago livestock market continued well into the twentieth century. Agricultural fairs and specific breed expositions, including the numerous agricultural pavilions of the 1893 WORLD'S COLUMBIAN EXPOSITION, assisted in this promotion. Beginning in 1878, a "fat stock" show was held annually, always in the fall, in order to promote and identify the best examples of purebred species. This evolved into the International Livestock Exposition in 1900 and continued on an annual basis until 1975. J. H. Sanders, founder of the *Breeder's Gazette* in 1881, and son Alvin worked closely with the various large breeders and individual breeders' associations to create this uniquely large, very successful market and exposition.

In the twentieth century, changing technology and the expansion of the Chicago region's population have continued to adversely affect the daily role of agriculture. The Union Stock Yard began declining in the 1950s as better methods of carcass transportation decentralized the meatpacking industry away from the Midwestern transportation centers. Two decades later the Stock Yard itself fell victim to recession and closed. Meanwhile, large GROCERY STORE conglomerates with their own independent supply and distribution systems facilitated the demise of most local fresh-produce growers.

Today, the Stock Yard gate stands as almost a lone sentry against the urban and suburban sprawl that has claimed hundreds of thousands of acres of prime farmland in the collar counties. At the end of the twentieth century, agricultural production continued on a handful of grain and dairy farms that once numbered in the thousands. The recent interest in more wholesome food has sustained a hundred or so seasonal farmers' markets throughout the Chicago region. Specialized products such as free-range chickens, ostrich, llamas, buffalo, and organically grown herbs and vegetables are raised on suburban farmettes. Throughout it all, the South Water Street Market has continued to be the best source of fresh fruits, vegetables, and herbs for Midwestern restaurateurs and independent, up-scale food stores. And the Chicago Board of Trade remains a powerful influence on the world's agricultural markets, despite the fact that most area residents are three to four generations removed from the family farm. Thus, it is these specialized products along with the vastness of the world's grain trade that will define Chicago's agricultural industry for the future.

Chas. P. Raleigh

See also: Agricultural Journals; Agricultural Machinery Industry; County Fairs; Food Processing: Regional and National Market; Prairie Farmer

Further reading: Bogue, Allan G. *From Prairie to Cornbelt: Farming on the Illinois and Iowa Prairies in the 19th Century.* 1963. • Clark, John. *The Grain Trade in the Old Northwest.* 1966. • Cronon, William. *Nature's Metropolis.* 1991.

AIDS (Acquired Immune Deficiency Syndrome). In Chicago, AIDS has affected primarily men who have sex with men, men and women using needle-injected DRUGS, people in heterosexual relations in which one partner is already infected, people receiving tainted transfusions, and the children of infected mothers. In 1999, Chicago ranked sixth in AIDS cases among metropolitan areas in the United States. Since the onset of the disease in the early 1980s, many of the vexing ethical and legal controversies that flared up around the nation bypassed Chicago: questions of quarantine, the placement of schoolchildren with AIDS, the closing of bathhouses as sexual venues, the right of people with AIDS to health care, and so on. Still, the city has had its own controversies, including COOK COUNTY HOSPITAL'S removal of a physician with AIDS from patient contact and citywide controversies related to anti-AIDS education. In the early 1990s, for example, public AIDS posters depicting same-sex couples were defaced by critics who claimed that the posters advocated a homosexual agenda. In response AIDS activists—notably various chapters of the AIDS Coalition to Unleash Power (ACT UP)—staged numerous protests demanding improved AIDS services and education, especially from the city of Chicago itself.

Chicago's NEAR WEST SIDE Medical Center District houses one of the world's largest concentrations of advanced public and private health care facilities, and has been the site of much research on AIDS prevention, drug therapies, and vaccines. Focused on the health care of lesbians and GAY men, the Howard Brown Health Center on the North Side has become the leading private provider of HIV/AIDS services in the Midwest.

Although the number of newly diagnosed cases of AIDS in Chicago has dropped since 1994, certain policy questions remained unsettled at the close of the twentieth century. In the late 1990s, for example, debate continued about the scope of privacy in reporting diagnoses of HIV and AIDS to PUBLIC HEALTH agencies.

The unexpected epidemic gave gay men and lesbians a perspective by which to critique the culture at large through not only political action but the literary arts. Many storefront THEATERS have staged work that documents the impact of the epidemic and charts the gay community's response to it. Despite its toll, AIDS has permanently changed both the political and LITERARY CULTURE of Chicago's large gay and lesbian community.

Timothy F. Murphy

See also: Baths, Public; Epidemics; Gay and Lesbian Rights Movements

Further reading: Adelman, Mara B. *The Fragile Community: Living together with AIDS.* 1997. • Department of Public Health. *An Epidemiologic Profile of HIV/AIDS in Chicago.* 1995. • Murphy, Timothy F. *Ethics in an Epidemic: AIDS, Morality, and Culture.* 1994.

Air Quality. Like most large cities, Chicago has a history of poor air quality. As it industrialized, Chicago relied on the dirty soft COAL of southern Illinois for power and heat. Burned in boiler rooms, locomotives, steel mills, and domestic furnaces, the ubiquitous coal created an equally ubiquitous smoke. Soot soiled everything in the city, ruining furniture, merchandise, and even building facades. Chicago legislated against dense smoke in 1881, but residents and visitors continued to complain about choking clouds and filthy soot. In addition to smoke, the numerous industries surrounding the slaughterhouses produced foul odors and dangerous CHEMICAL emissions, further diminishing air quality. Undoubtedly the poor air increased the severity of several pulmonary diseases, including asthma and pneumonia. Perhaps second only to Pittsburgh in smoke pollution at the opening of the twentieth century, Chicago gained a national reputation for its terrible air, but it also became a leader in regulation. In the early 1900s, a movement to force railroad electrification focused on the Illinois Central's waterfront line and kept the smoke issue in the news. Still, air quality did not significantly improve until coal use began to decline after World War II.

In 1959 the city created the Department of Air Pollution Control. The new department investigated all types of emissions and suggested regulations for several previously ignored sources of pollution, including burning refuse and leaves. Public concern for air quality heightened after a 1962 disaster killed hundreds of London residents, and by 1964 Chicago received more than six thousand citizen air pollution complaints per year. As with the early movement to control smoke, the new activism focused on the potential negative health effects of impure air. Not surprisingly, the LOOP, the CALUMET REGION, and northern LAKE COUNTY, INDIANA, were the most polluted districts in the metropolitan area.

In 1967 the U.S. Public Health Service determined that only New York City's air was more polluted than Chicago's. Impelled by citizen activism and new federal regulations in the 1970s, the city attempted to control the largest polluters, including the massive South Works steel plant. Even as these efforts began to reap benefits, however, the continuing suburbanization and auto dependence of the metropolitan area meant that auto emissions would plague the city for decades to come.

By the 1990s, a decline in heavy industry and effective regulation of auto emissions combined to significantly improve Chicago's air. Chicago no longer ranked among the nation's most heavily polluted cities.

David Stradling

See also: Environmental Politics; Environmental Regulation; Iron and Steel

Further reading: *Air Management.* Chicago: Department of Air Pollution Control, 1962–1968. • Rosen, Christine Meisner. "Businessmen against Pollution in Late Nineteenth Century Chicago." *Business History Review* 69 (Autumn 1995): 351–397. • Stradling, David. *Smokestacks and Progressives: Environmentalists, Engineers, and Air Quality in America, 1883–1953.* 1999.

Airlines. Chicago's geographic location and established position as a major TRANSPORTATION center have made the city attractive to the airline industry from its beginning. The roots of the industry lie in the transport of MAIL for the U.S. Post Office. By the 1920s the Post Office contracted with fledgling airline companies to fly mail throughout the country. Chicago was a pivotal location from the earliest establishment of the Contract Air Mail routes.

Development of the early commercial airline industry grew from a combination of a federal INFRASTRUCTURE of navigation systems and regulations, local boosterism, and private investment. In the 1920s and 1930s communities built airports as a matter of civic pride and attracted private airline companies by promising modern facilities and room for expansion. Chicago's most important airports, O'HARE INTERNATIONAL and MIDWAY AIRPORT, have been operated by city government.

One of the first municipal airports was Chicago Municipal Airport, built in 1927 to replace MAYWOOD Field, the airstrip used for airmail. That year Municipal Airport was a single cinder runway with one square mile of land available for expansion 10 miles southwest of downtown. By 1929, the airport maintained its own post office, stationed a division of the ILLINOIS NATIONAL GUARD, and handled 32 arrivals and departures of passengers, mail, and cargo daily. Municipal Airport cost 10 million dollars to develop. By 1932, it was the busiest airport in the nation and for years claimed the title of World's Busiest Airport. In the early 1930s, it was also the birthplace of the Air Line Pilots Association. In 1949, the Municipal Airport was renamed Midway Airport to commemorate the famous battle in the Pacific. In 1940, the air transportation industry in Chicago employed 822 men and 303 women in both commercial and government jobs; by 1950, the industry employed 3,711 men and 1,431 women.

To compete as an international city, however, Chicago needed an airport with greater growth potential. In 1946, the city purchased over a thousand acres of land northwest of the city. O'Hare opened its 24-million-dollar terminal for commercial passenger traffic in 1955. The airport covered 10 square miles. O'Hare soon dominated Chicago's aviation system with its capacity for handling the new jet airplanes, international flights, and military aircraft through its unique paired tangential runways which allowed for simultaneous takeoffs and landings on six runways. Despite its

United Airlines flight crew at Midway Airport, ca. 1940s. Photographer: Unknown. Source: Chicago Historical Society.

remote location in cornfields 22 miles outside downtown, O'Hare soon usurped Midway's title of World's Busiest Airport. By the early 1960s, O'Hare handled 8 million passengers a year. In 1960, 7,845 men and 3,392 women worked in air transportation in Chicago.

Starting in the 1960s, most scheduled commercial airlines shifted their operations to O'Hare from Midway, causing an economic downturn for the Midway community and a boom for the suburbs surrounding O'Hare. The construction of several expressways accessing the newer airport linked it to both the city and suburbs. Suburbs surrounding the airport, such as ROSEMONT, BENSENVILLE, ADDISON, and ELK GROVE VILLAGE, experienced tremendous growth in population and in light manufacturing and service industries, air freight businesses, and the hospitality industry.

In the late 1990s, approximately 75 commercial, commuter, and cargo airlines served Chicago at Midway and O'Hare. In 1997, approximately 80 million passengers and 1.5 million tons of cargo and mail flew through O'Hare or Midway. In the 1990s, United Airlines and American Airlines provided the majority of commercial scheduled service at O'Hare; Southwest Airlines anchored service at Midway. United Airlines, which grew from the consolidation of several smaller airlines in the late 1920s, is based in the Chicago suburbs. In 2000, United employed approximately 18,000 people in its Chicago operations and approximately 84,000 worldwide.

The pivotal role of the airline industry in Chicago's economy cannot be underestimated. The city's growth as a center of light industry as well as BANKING, consulting, and other white-collar businesses has been linked to air access at O'Hare, Midway, and the city's lakefront airport, Meigs Field. In the early 1990s, Chicago's airports directly employed over 50,000 people, and the industry generated an estimated 340,000 jobs in the metropolitan area through service to visitors and companies that depend on the airports for their existence. PUBLIC TRANSPORTATION by elevated train to O'Hare was finished in 1984 and to Midway in 1993, providing easy access to both airports from downtown and other parts of the city for both travelers and workers. Jobs at the airports are split between Chicago residents and suburbanites, although suburbanites take home the majority of personal income earned at the airports. Despite the economic benefits to suburban Chicago, its relationship with O'Hare has grown tense over issues of noise, growth, and density. In the 1990s, politicians, airlines, and residents began to debate the creation of a third major airport in the far south suburbs, as well as expansion of O'Hare.

Liesl M. Orenic

See also: Business of Chicago; Clearing; Garfield Ridge; Global Chicago; O'Hare; Railroads

Further reading: Harrison, David. "Chicago's Airports: A Legacy of Livelihoods." National Economic Research Associates, Inc., and the City of Chicago. 1993. • Smith, Henry Ladd. *Airways: The History of Commercial Aviation in the United States.* 1942. • Solberg, Carl. *Conquest of the Skies: A History of Commercial Aviation in America.* 1979.

Bessie Coleman: Pioneer Chicago Aviator

Bessie Coleman migrated to Chicago from Texas in 1915. Like many other AFRICAN AMERICANS, Coleman sought better opportunities in northern cities like Chicago. Coleman followed an unusual dream: to become an airplane pilot. Facing prejudice both as a woman and an African American, Coleman was unable to train in the United States. With the encouragement of Robert Abbott, publisher of the *Chicago Defender,* Coleman learned French and gained entrance into the Caudron School of Aviation in France in 1920.

After earning her international pilot's license, she became a barnstormer, with the *Chicago Defender* as her sponsor. Coleman toured the United States. On October 15, 1922, more than 2,000 people came to the Checkerboard Field in MAYWOOD (now Miller Meadow Forest Preserve) for Coleman's first exhibition in Chicago. Coleman died in a plane crash in Florida in 1926.

A group of African American pilots organized the Challenger Air Pilot's Association in 1931, inspired by Bessie Coleman. This association founded an airport at ROBBINS in 1933 to accommodate the needs of African American pilots who faced discrimination at other Chicago airports.

Ann Durkin Keating

Airports, Commuter. Less than a decade before the Wright brothers' groundbreaking flight at Kitty Hawk and more than two decades before the advent of a commercial air TRANSPORTATION system in the United States in 1926, visionaries were writing about commuter air transportation ground facilities. Their ideas would evolve with the development of aircraft ranging on the one hand from the dirigible to the airplane and, on the other, from the Autogiro, the predecessor of the helicopter, to the Airphibian, a convertible automobile/airplane. Many of these commuter airports were planned to be in or near the central business district to accommodate the array of craft carrying passengers, mail, or freight in local hops to and from adjacent suburbs or to and from large outlying airports to coordinate with long-range flights.

The LOOP's Central Post Office, completed in 1932, is an example of such planning. Graham, Anderson, Probst & White designed the post office according to standards proposed in 1927 by Frank E. McMillan, superintendent of the Division of Post-Office Quarters and Engineering. McMillan believed that the 320- by 800-foot roof of the planned two-square-block building, which now bridges the Congress Street spur of the EXPRESSWAY system, would be big enough to facilitate convenient, rooftop airmail. As it turned out, airmail pilots did not use the roof as intended.

To the north of Chicago, Sky Harbor Airport opened in 1929. The facility, which was located approximately five miles west of the suburb of GLENCOE, was also called the North Shore Airport and the Sky Harbor Aviation Country Club. These names reflected the use of the airport as a playground for wealthy Chicagoans as well as a transportation terminal accommodating general and commuter aviation. Architects Alfred P. Allen and Maurice Webster designed the terminal, which combined amenities for entertainment and air travel. Grey Goose Air Lines ferried passengers between this North Shore facility and what became MIDWAY AIRPORT.

For display at the CENTURY OF PROGRESS EXPOSITION of 1933–34, George Fred Keck created an International Style glass-and-steel House of Tomorrow. Keck neatly parked a small biplane in the house's ground-floor hangar to represent the idea of a "flying flivver," a personal commuter vehicle.

In 1948 the city of Chicago opened a commuter airport for wide public use on landfill that had also served as the grounds of the Century of Progress Exposition. Of the array of general aviation and commuter air transportation ground facilities, this airport, which became Meigs Field, emerged as the most important one to serve Chicago over the long run.

In 1920 the city of Chicago began filling extensive parts of LAKE MICHIGAN in order to implement Daniel H. Burnham and Edward H. Bennett's *Plan of Chicago,* published in 1909. One of these fills formed Northerly Island, which eventually became Meigs Field. Despite numerous proposals beginning as early as 1924 to make the island an air transportation facility, the site was employed for other purposes, including the Century of Progress Exposition.

After failing to convince the United Nations to locate on Northerly Island in 1945, the city, with the advice of consulting civil engineer Ralph Burke, returned to the idea of building an air strip here. The field opened in 1948 with the temporary name of Northerly Island Air Strip. The following year the city council renamed the field after Merrill C. Meigs, who was active in local civic affairs and aviation. In 1950 the city added a small wooden terminal and a year later an air traffic control tower. The terminal soon became inadequate, and in 1959 Consoer and Morgan designed a new one, which opened two years later. The exterior of this rectangular building comprised glass, steel, and precast masonry; the taller three-story central block had sheets of glass to allow a vista of the lake and the runway for passengers waiting on the second floor. Mayor Richard M. Daley closed Meigs Field in 2003.

Today, instead of operating from separate fields, commuter aircraft often fly from the main airports in order to facilitate easy transfer between these small craft and the larger airplanes flying longer distances. Moreover, commuter craft carrying even as few as 20 passengers require longer runways than available at general aviation facilities such as the LANSING Municipal Airport to the south of the city or Palwaukee Airport to the north.

David Brodherson

See also: Innovation, Invention, and Chicago Business; Mail Delivery; Maywood; Planning Chicago; Robbins

Further reading: Brodherson, David. "All Airplanes Lead to Chicago." In *Chicago Architecture and Design, 1923–1993: Reconfiguration of a Metropolis,* ed. John Zukowsky, 1993. • Zukowsky, John, ed. *Building for Air Travel: Architecture and Design for Commercial Aviation.* 1996.

Albanians. Prior to gaining its independence in November 1912, Albania was part of the Ottoman Empire. The first wave of Albanian immigration to the United States occurred between 1892 and 1914. Most of the estimated 20,000–30,000 Albanian migrants to the United States during this period were young male Orthodox Christians or MUSLIMS from Southern Albania who had left their homes to improve their economic prospects or avoid service in the Turkish army.

Although the majority of these early Albanian immigrants settled in urban areas of New England, New York, and Pennsylvania, others gravitated to Ohio, Michigan, Indiana, Illinois, and Missouri. Prior to WORLD WAR I, there were small concentrations of Albanians in GARY and WHITING, Indiana, as well as in Chicago, Argo (SUMMIT), and Madison, Illinois. By 1914 approximately 1,000 Albanians resided in greater Chicago and northern Illinois, with an additional 200 to 300 scattered elsewhere in Illinois. Most worked in factories, RESTAURANTS, or the CONSTRUCTION industry.

Chicago's Albanians, like their compatriots elsewhere, were ardent nationalists and in 1908 formed a patriotic organization, *Flamuri i Shqipërisë* (The Albanian Flag), to promote Albanian independence. In 1913, this organization became the Chicago chapter of the newly established (1912) Pan-Albanian Federation of America (VATRA). Other VATRA chapters formed in Argo and Gary and actively supported efforts of the parent organization to safeguard Albania's independence following World War I.

Although some members of the Illinois Albanian community permanently resettled in Albania after the war, others went back to their homeland only to marry, returning to the United States with their wives to raise families. With relatively few Albanian women in Illinois, men, especially Muslims, frequently married outside the group. During the 1920s and 1930s, the state's Albanian population grew slowly but steadily, to about 2,000 on the eve of WORLD WAR II.

St. Nicholas Albanian Orthodox Church (1944) attracted national attention during 1986–87, when some 300,000 persons visited the church to view its "weeping icon" of St. Mary. The focal point for the spiritual and social life of the Greater Chicago Albanian Muslim community is the Albanian American Islamic Center in suburban BERKELEY.

Since the late 1960s several thousand ethnic Albanians from Kosovo, Macedonia, and Montenegro have significantly enlarged Chicago's Albanian community. These newcomers have been especially concerned with promoting the independence of Kosovo and protecting the civil and human rights of Albanians in Macedonia. A small but steady flow of migrants moved from Albania to Illinois in the 1990s, largely for economic opportunity. The majority of the post-1960 arrivals have enjoyed success as owners of restaurants and a variety of small businesses or as construction and factory workers. A small but growing number of Albanian Americans are pursuing careers in the professions. By 2001, there were some 12,000–15,000 residents of Albanian ancestry in Illinois, northwest Indiana, and southern Wisconsin.

Among the most prominent Americans with roots in the Chicago-area Albanian community are Ferid Murad, a 1998 recipient of the Nobel Prize in medicine, and the actor/comedians John and James Belushi.

Nicholas C. Pano

See also: Americanization; Demography; Eastern Orthodox; Multicentered Chicago

Further reading: "Albanians." In *Harvard Encyclopedia of American Ethnic Groups,* ed. Stephan Thernstrom, 1980, 23–28. • Federal Writers Project. *The Albanian Struggle in the Old World and New.* 1939. • Jurgens, Jane. "Albanian Americans." In *The Gale Encyclopedia of Multicultural America,* vol. 1., 1995, 43–54.

Albany Park, Community Area 14, 8 miles northwest of the Loop. Albany Park grew from a sparsely settled farming community to a dynamic urban neighborhood in the course of one generation. In 1868 local entrepreneur Richard Rusk turned an initial 10-acre investment of land into a large farm that included a profitable brickyard along the North Branch of the CHICAGO RIVER and the Rusk Race Track, where late-nineteenth-century Chicagoans often took day excursions to watch HORSE RACING and enjoy the bucolic environs. As Chicago's population exploded in the 1870s and 1880s, the suburban community became increasingly popular. In 1889 Chicago ANNEXED the area along with the rest of JEFFERSON TOWNSHIP.

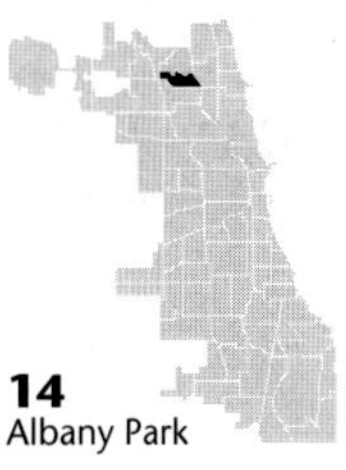

In 1893 a group of investors purchased 640 acres of the nearby McAllister farm for development. The REAL-ESTATE syndicate included four prominent Chicagoans: streetcar magnate DeLancy Louderback, John J. Mitchell of Illinois Trust and Savings Bank, Northwestern Elevated Railroad owner Clarence Buckingham, and transportation mogul Charles T. Yerkes. Louderback, a native of Albany, New York, named the development after his hometown. These investors brought TRANSPORTATION lines to Albany Park that proved essential to the area's early commercial and residential expansion. Electric streetcars ran along Lawrence Avenue between Broadway and Milwaukee Avenue as early as 1896, and the Kedzie Avenue streetcar line extended north to Lawrence Avenue by 1913. Most significant was the extension of the Ravenswood Elevated train to Kimball and Lawrence Avenues by 1907. Beginning in 1904, the Chicago Sanitary District widened and straightened the meandering North Branch of the Chicago River from Belmont to Lawrence Avenues. The river relocation, completed in 1907, defined previously ambiguous property lines and improved sewage disposal in Albany Park.

The completion of the Ravenswood Elevated line set off a building boom clustered around the train terminal at the intersection of Lawrence and Kimball Avenues. Commercial development included small shops, DEPARTMENT STORES, and theaters. Land valued at $52 per front foot in 1909 sold for $2,750 per front foot by 1929. Residential builders constructed BUNGALOWS and two-flats at a furious pace during the 1910s and 1920s. By the 1920s Albany Park was almost completely developed. The 1910 census counted 7,000 inhabitants; by 1920 the number more than tripled to 26,676. In 1930 more than 55,000 people resided in the northwest Chicago neighborhood.

GERMAN and SWEDISH immigrants initially settled the area. After 1912 Albany Park became home to a large number of Russian JEWS leaving the crowded neighborhoods of Chicago's NEAR WEST SIDE. The community remained predominantly Jewish through the 1950s. Between 1910 and 1940 several synagogues and churches, public SCHOOLS, and public parks opened. Albany Park's population reached a high of 56,692 in 1940. After the Second World War, many Jewish families—like the generation before them—moved north, this time to suburban LINCOLNWOOD and SKOKIE.

The suburban exodus led Albany Park into economic and social decline. Population decreased, homes and stores lay vacant, and property values plummeted. In the 1970s, 70 percent of the commercial property along Lawrence Avenue stood vacant. Empty buildings attracted illegal DRUG trade, PROSTITUTION, and GANGS. Relief came in 1978 when city government, the North River Commission, and the Lawrence Avenue Development Corporation cooperated to improve Albany Park's appearance. Albany Park's renewal included streetscape beautification, the Facade Rebate Program, low-interest loans, and other financing packages. Redevelopment efforts led to a decrease in commercial vacancies and an increase in residential property values in the 1980s and 1990s. Albany Park again presented an attractive urban neighborhood for real-estate development and commercial investment.

After the 1970s, Albany Park became a port of entry for immigrants from Asia and Latin America. In 1990 the community area claimed the largest numbers of KOREAN, FILIPINO, and GUATEMALAN immigrants in Chicago. The Korean community played important commercial and civic roles in the revitalization of the area. The number of homes sold increased 125 percent between 1980 and 1989. Albany Park's pattern of population shifts continued in the 1990s, as more prosperous Korean immigrants began moving to northern suburbs. Throughout the twentieth century, Albany Park acted as a gateway community for aspiring middle-class ethnic groups.

Timothy B. Neary

See also: Demography; Infrastructure; Street Railways; Water

Further reading: Ader, Inez C., ed. "Community History of Albany Park." 1944. Manuscript Collection, Sulzer Regional Public Library, Chicago, IL. • Bjorklund, Richard C. "Ravenswood Manor: Indian Prairie to Urban Pride." 1964. Manuscript Collection, Sulzer Regional Public Library, Chicago, IL. • Drury, John. "Old Chicago Neighborhoods: Albany Park." *Landlord's Guide* (August 1950): 6–8.

Alcohol. *See* Drugs and Alcohol; Liquor Distribution

Aldermanic Privilege. Aldermanic privilege refers to the power of Chicago city council members (aldermen) to initiate or block city council or city government actions concerning their own wards. Sometimes written into official council rules, it is often based on unwritten understandings among members or on arrangements with city administrators who find it expedient to routinely comply with aldermanic requests.

Mid-nineteenth-century city councils ordered street improvements and assessments to pay for them only if approved first by the local alderman, but because the alderman was expected to carefully represent local property owners, he enjoyed little independent discretion. By the 1890s, informal understandings among city council members allowed an alderman to "dry up" LIQUOR sales in areas within his ward. As city government acted more vigorously and its regulatory powers grew, "council courtesies" gave members veto power in council votes relative to their wards, notably in cases of ZONING changes and variances. Aldermen regularly intervened in city departments seeking such favors for voters as TREE-cutting, ALLEY cleaning, and permits for driveways and building conversions.

Aldermen, in turn, typically exercised this power only with the approval of their party's WARD committeeman. Those aldermen who were also committeemen acted as "little mayors" of their wards. Reformers objected that aldermanic privilege led to inconsistent application of ordinances, legislative inefficiency, and outright corruption.

Aldermanic privilege reached its zenith in the mid-twentieth century. In 1955, however, Mayor Richard J. Daley centralized zoning variation and driveway permit procedures, denying aldermen veto power and concentrating decision-making in the hands of expert city officials. But changes in the zoning ordinance remain the prerogative of the council, and in the 1980s and '90s members could block city sales or acquisitions of property in their wards. Scandals spurred adoption of an ethics ordinance in 1997, making the exercise of aldermanic privilege more transparent but not eliminating it.

Christopher Thale

See also: Clout; Government, City of Chicago; Machine Politics; Patronage; Political Culture; Real Estate

Further reading: "City Council." Clipping file. Municipal Reference Collection,. Harold Washington Library. • Einhorn, Robin L. *Property Rules: Political Economy in Chicago, 1833–1872.* 1991. • Gable, William R. "The Chicago City Council: A Study of Urban Politics and Legislation." Ph.D. diss., University of Chicago. 1953.

Aldermen. *See* Government, City of Chicago

Algerians. Prior to the 1990s, Chicago's small Algerian population comprised mainly students and professionals in science and medicine. Algeria emerged independent but devastated from its war with France (1954–1962), prompting many of its academic elite to attend French and American universities. Chicago received far fewer students than New York or Washington DC, numbering only about 10 men and women at any given time from the 1960s through most of the 1980s. Community ties remained mostly informal until a constellation of events in Algeria, Europe, and the United States prompted a much larger wave of immigrants in the 1990s.

Tensions between Algeria's secular socialist government and a growing Islamic fundamentalist movement came to a head in 1992, when the government banned the fundamentalists' umbrella organization, the Islamic Salvation Front (FIS). A prominent FIS official, Anwar Haddam, came to Chicago in the mid-1990s to study computer science, having fled the anti-Islamist military coup shortly after he was elected to the Algerian parliament in 1991. Accused of terrorist activities by the Algerian government, Haddam remained in Chicago until December 1996, when he was detained by the Immigration and Naturalization Service. Held for four years in a Virginia prison on secret evidence, without charges, he was released in December 2000.

During the 1990s Algerian worker visas to the European Union declined as U.S. visa slots increased for Algerians and other North Africans. This confluence of events brought Algerians to Chicago seeking employment and refuge from political persecution and turmoil. Settling in a large area on Chicago's near Northwest Side, most of these immigrants arrived less educated and more religious than the small number of Algerians already in Chicago.

Community estimates have placed Chicago's Algerian population at close to 1,000 by the early 2000s. Many men have worked as TAXI drivers, mechanics, and in RESTAURANTS, while most women have either entered DOMESTIC service or have stayed at home. A few have enrolled in local colleges to earn technical degrees.

Several small Algerian SOCIAL SERVICE organizations, most notably the Maghreb

Assembly, emerged in the 1990s to assist these newcomers. Run by several longtime Chicago residents of mostly Algerian and MOROCCAN descent, the Maghreb Assembly has sought to help new immigrants from the Maghreb, the western countries of Islamic North Africa, adjust to secular American life while remaining faithful to the tenets of Sunni Islam. As most Chicago-area immigrants from the Maghreb have not associated closely with MUSLIMS of Middle Eastern descent, Algerians, Moroccans, and a few Tunisians have been encouraged to unite as a common community. Often in conjunction with an area mosque, the organization has taught job skills, English, and the importance of *sirat al-mustaqeem,* the Qur'anic principles of thrift, moderation, and balance. Women have received training in balancing wage work with traditional domestic duties.

Chicago Algerians celebrate the beginning of their revolution against France each November 1, but daily prayers and religious holidays have served to bring Algerians together with other immigrants from the Maghreb countries. Most evenings during the holy month of Ramadan, Algerians join Moroccans and Tunisians at mosques, homes, and restaurants to break the day-long fast. Since 2000 an Algerian-owned café on Lincoln Avenue has donated food for the hundreds of North Africans attending the Ramadan-ending feast of Eid Al-Fitr. During the rest of the year, the café has served as an informal meeting place for North African men before and after work.

Stephen R. Porter

See also: Americanization; Demography; Multicentered Chicago; Refugees

Algonquin, IL, McHenry County, 39 miles NW of the Loop. Algonquin lies in a steep valley where the Fox RIVER cut through the Valparaiso Moraine left by the Wisconsin glacier. The bluffs attracted Paleo-Indian hunters as the glacier melted. A typical Clovis point was found on a hillside just north of the community.

Algonquin was a key point on the heavily traveled trail (now Illinois Highway 62) between Chicago and the Indian settlements at Lake Geneva. Juliette Kinzie used that trail returning home to Portage, Wisconsin, from Chicago in 1830. Her description (*Wau-Bun*) of crossing the river is the first surviving description of the area.

By 1831, several white families had squatted on the prairies beyond Algonquin, but BLACK HAWK WAR fears in 1832 forced them to flee. At war's end, the Gillilan family from western Virginia is said to have been the first to permanently settle there. In 1836, the site known as Cornish's Ferry was renamed Algonquin after Andrew Cornish's sailboat.

Algonquin grew slowly as a trading point for the area's numerous dairy farmers along the Fox River Valley RAILROAD (Chicago & North Western Railway), which entered the community in 1854. Chicagoans riding the line saw a community nestled in the valley reminiscent of a picturesque New England settlement. With attractive scenery, cooling mineral springs, and numerous opportunities for boating and fishing, Algonquin became a natural destination for summer vacationers from Chicago. The turning of the Pingry Hotel into a vacation resort by the Morton family in 1889 foretold the future direction of the community. Algonquin's businessmen incorporated the increasingly busy community in 1890.

While riverine relaxations drew numerous vacationers, other activities like early automobile road and hill-climb races up the northbound highway once used by Juliette Kinzie brought many more. Algonquin's population doubled during summer months through the 1920s as Chicagoans sought to escape the city's summer heat. Dance pavilions and commercial picnic groves crowded dairy cattle pastures. During the GREAT DEPRESSION, many summer cottages became permanent homes as Chicago BUNGALOW buyers faced foreclosure.

Soldiers returning from WORLD WAR II fueled area growth. To many who vacationed in the valley as children, Algonquin seemed a fine place to raise families. They sought to make permanent for their children what had been fleeting summer idylls for themselves. Beginning in 1950 with 1,223 residents, Algonquin experienced a population increase of 60 percent or greater in each of the next three decades. In the 1980s the population more than doubled, reaching 11,663 by 1990, and grew to 23,276 by 2000.

Craig L. Pfannkuche

See also: Metropolitan Growth; Vacation Spots

Further reading: *All About Algonquin.* 1977. • *McHenry County in the Twentieth Century: 1968–1994.* McHenry County Historical Society. 1994. • Nye, Lowell A., ed. *McHenry County, Illinois, 1832–1968.* 1968.

All-American Girls Baseball League. The All-American Girls Baseball League (AAGBL) was founded in 1943 by the owner of the Chicago CUBS, Philip K. Wrigley, to retain BASEBALL'S fans during WORLD WAR II. Originally conceived as a spectacle rather than a sport, the league combined the seemingly dissimilar characteristics of baseball and femininity—including skirts, long hair, and even charm school for the players. Initially a hybrid between baseball and SOFTBALL, the game evolved over the league's 12 seasons into a sport with a smaller ball, longer base paths, and overhand pitching. These changes arose from the fans' interest in the players' skills and management's attempts to differentiate the league from its rival, the National Girls Baseball League, which was closely tied to softball. Drawing recruits from a national network of softball teams, the league peaked in popularity in the late 1940s, with teams in 10 Midwestern cities (such as Racine, Kenosha, South Bend, and Rockford) drawing more than a million fans annually. It began to falter in the 1950s owing to managerial problems, a lack of new talent, and alternative entertainments, especially television.

Cathleen D. Cahill

See also: Creation of Chicago Sports

Further reading: Cahn, Susan M. "No Freaks, No Amazons, No Boyish Bobs." *Chicago History* (Spring 1989): 26–41. • Johnson, Susan E. *When Women Played Hardball.* 1994.

Alleys. Quintessential expressions of nineteenth-century American urbanity, alleys have been part of Chicago's physical fabric since the beginning. Eighteen feet in width, they graced all 58 blocks of the ILLINOIS & MICHIGAN CANAL commissioners' original town plat in 1830, providing rear service access to property facing the 80-foot-wide main streets. But private platting soon produced a few blocks without alleys, mostly in the NEAR NORTH SIDE's early mansion district or in the haphazardly laid-out industrial workingmen's neighborhoods on the NEAR SOUTH SIDE. Remarkably, however, alleys became the overwhelming norm in city platting, as the national land survey imposed its grid framework upon Chicago's expanding street and block pattern. Together, they enabled the city to evolve a "system" of mass-produced services and mass-produced access, one of the civic accomplishments of the century. By 1900, over 98 percent of the city's residential blocks had alleys, and, a century later, the proportion was still well over 90 percent.

Early suburban developments showed a rising ambivalence toward alleys (Olmsted & Vaux's 1869 RIVERSIDE plat contains 31 blocks with and 50 without them). Around WORLD WAR I, "modern" PLANNING theory declared alleys wasteful and undesirable, and the last outer fringes of the city of Chicago, along with the vast majority of suburban territory, were developed thereafter without alleys.

Alleys developed social meanings early on. In middle-class areas, the street represented the respectable front, while the alley saw the servants and suppliers do the dirty work. In working-class areas, alleys provided space for small manufacturing, repair shops, REAR HOUSES, children's play space, and, eventually, garages. Much of Chicago's elevated RAPID TRANSIT SYSTEM came to run along alleys.

Children playing in a South Side alley under the "L," 1941. Photographer: Russell Lee. Source: Library of Congress.

Chicago's alley life, reflecting in many neighborhoods extreme low-rise urban congestion (in contrast to that of New York's tall tenement blocks), spurred intense social criticism by century's end for the health and behavioral "pathologies" it supported, but improvements came slowly. In the core areas, the impact of BUSINESS district expansion, EXPRESSWAYS, PUBLIC HOUSING projects, and large-scale URBAN RENEWAL after WORLD WAR II obliterated thousands of alleys. In the rest of the city and in some RAILROAD suburbs, however, alleys have survived the new millennium largely intact and contribute hugely to the pulse of Chicago's daily life.

Michael P. Conzen

See also: Built Environment of the Chicago Region; Housing Reform; Infrastructure; Northwest Ordinance; Public Health; Streets and Highways

Further reading: Abbott, Edith. *The Tenements of Chicago, 1908–1935.* 1936. • Clay, Grady. *Being a Disquisition upon the Origins, Natural Disposition, and Occurrences in the American Scene of Alleys.* 1978.

Almshouses. Under state law each county has had responsibility for providing a variety of SOCIAL SERVICES to its most destitute residents, and in the nineteenth century each county in the Chicago region established its own almshouse. The Cook County Almshouse (also known variously as the Cook County Poor Farm, Cook County Poorhouse, Cook County Infirmary, Oak Forest Infirmary, Cook County Old-Age Home, and Oak Forest Tuberculosis Hospital) was the only public institution at any jurisdictional level specifically established to provide long-term refuge for the most extremely destitute people in the Chicago area. These were people with chronic physical illnesses or disabilities, mental illness or retardation, elderly people, or single mothers unable to work for a living even during periods when jobs were plentiful. Infamous for its corruption, mismanagement, deplorable living conditions, and maltreatment of inmates, the almshouse was regarded as a refuge of last resort. The number of residents ranged from 75 in 1854 to a peak of about 4,300 in January 1932, but usually the population, of whom approximately 10 percent were children, hovered around 1,000. The insane asylum department housed an additional 500–1,000 persons.

The COOK COUNTY commissioners allocated all almshouse funds and appointed the county agent, who not only determined admission to the almshouse but also distributed any county "outdoor" relief to "deserving" paupers. The commissioners also selected the staffs of the almshouse and the insane asylum. This situation erupted in major scandal nearly once every decade. In 1869, in an effort to make all public and private charitable institutions in Illinois more accountable, the legislature established a State Board of Public Charities. Its five members, private volunteers, were charged with visiting every institution in all 102 counties at least annually. Although they produced valuable biennial written reports and recommendations, they had no authority over the administration of the institutions.

Until the 1940s, almshouse personnel were largely untrained political appointees, but efforts were occasionally made to provide limited differential care. For example, because of concerns that the almshouse was an unfit environment for children, a schoolhouse and teacher were provided on the grounds. Separate cottages were allocated to lying-in patients and individuals with consumption or TUBERCULOSIS. More to prevent pandemonium than to provide special medical care, the county began maintaining an insane asylum in conjunction with the almshouse in 1870. When the almshouse moved from DUNNING to OAK FOREST, the insane asylum stayed behind to be turned over to state management. The Chicago State Hospital at Dunning, established in 1912, still exists.

Although the county almshouse was originally located, from 1835 to 1841, in the center of Chicago on the town square (at Clark and Randolph), all subsequent locations were

DuPage County Almshouse, Winfield, postcard, ca. 1911. Photographer: Unknown. Source: DuPage County Historical Museum.

rural, chosen with the persistent if impractical idea that residents work the land to pay their way. These farms included 160 acres in LAKE TOWNSHIP, 1841–1854; 160 acres five miles from the North Branch of the Chicago River, 1854–1883, expanded to 240 acres with new buildings and a county-constructed railroad station called Dunning, 1883–1910; and, finally, 360 acres in Bremen Township, the Oak Forest Infirmary designed by Holabird & Roche, 1911–1956. The farm ceased operation in 1956 when the institution became licensed as a HOSPITAL, but Oak Forest Hospital of Cook County remained on the site and continues to serve the chronically ill as part of the Cook County Health Care System.

(Margaret) Dorsey Phelps

See also: Housing for the Elderly; Relief and Subsistence Aid; Social Services

Further reading: "The Story of Oak Forest Hospital" and "History of Oak Forest Hospital." Files of the Professional Library, Oak Forest Hospital of Cook County. N.d. • *Biennial Report of the Board of State Commissioners of Public Charities of the State of Illinois.* 1870–1909. • Brown, James. *The History of Public Assistance in Chicago, 1833 to 1893.* 1941.

Alpha Suffrage Club. The passage of the Illinois Presidential and Municipal SUFFRAGE Bill in the summer of 1913 offered AFRICAN AMERICAN women in Chicago the opportunity to merge their social welfare activities with electoral power. This was primarily due to the creation of the first and one of the most important black female suffrage organizations in the state and the city, the Alpha Suffrage Club. Established in January 1913 by black CLUBwoman and antilynching crusader Ida Bell Wells-Barnett and white activist Belle Squire, the club elected officers, held monthly meetings, claimed nearly two hundred members by 1916, issued the newsletter the *Alpha Suffrage Record,* and endorsed candidates. The club is most recognized for its pivotal role in the 1915 election of the first African American alderman in Chicago, Oscar DePriest.

Wanda A. Hendricks

See also: Civil Rights Movements; Feminist Movements; Political Culture; Politics

Further reading: Duster, Alfreda, ed. *Crusade for Justice: The Autobiography of Ida B. Wells.* 1970. • Williams, Katherine E. "The Alpha Suffrage Club." *Half Century Magazine,* September 1916, 12.

Alsip, IL, Cook County, 16 miles SW of Loop. Alsip's population is part of a large suburban fabric that has grown dramatically with the development of SUBDIVISIONS and the convenience of automobiles since the 1950s. Both before and after 1950, Alsip's growth has been tied to that of its neighbors: BLUE ISLAND, OAK LAWN, and WORTH.

The ridge of land known as Blue Island is obvious to visitors to the city of Blue Island or the Chicago neighborhood of BEVERLY immediately to the north. This ridge rises noticeably from approximately 50 to 60 feet above the old lake bed plain to heights of over 650 feet.

West of the ridge another rise of land provided a dry area for settlement with easy access to WATER. To the north and east of this rise was Stony Creek and to the south the Saganashkee Slough. In 1834, the family of Joseph and Hannah Lane settled on the "island" that encompasses much of present-day ALSIP and WORTH. Several generations of Lanes stayed in the immediate area.

Although farming was the dominant occupation on and around "Lane's Island," the presence of good quality clay led Frank Alsip in 1885 to establish the Alsip Brickyard, later run by his son Charles.

By the twentieth century, several CEMETERIES had located in the area. Reluctant to become completely surrounded by cemeteries, the residents voted in 1927 to incorporate. Although the first order of business for the new village was an ordinance to control cemeteries, nonetheless there are five on the borders and three within the village.

Like its neighboring communities, Alsip grew slowly until after WORLD WAR II. Its population stood at 1,228 in 1950, but explosive growth came with building of the Tri-State TOLLWAY in the late 1950s, especially with the opening of the interchange at Cicero Avenue and 127th Street. By 2000, along with extensive commercial growth, Alsip had a population of 19,725 and one of the most congested intersections in the region.

Larry A. McClellan

See also: Cook County

Further reading: "Some History of Lane's Island." *Where the Trails Cross* 16.2 (Winter 1985). • *Alsip: Golden Jubilee, Fiftieth Anniversary.* 1977.

Amalgamated Clothing Workers of America. Chicago played an important role in the formation and growth of the Amalgamated Clothing Workers of America (ACWA), a union of men's clothing workers. In 1910–11, after an unsuccessful STRIKE, these semiskilled immigrants from Eastern and Southern Europe formed a local chartered by the United Garment Workers Union (UGW). Three years later, this local challenged the conservative UGW leadership and its championing of skilled workers, thereby helping to establish the ACWA. A Chicagoan, Sidney Hillman, became president of the new union. The ACWA completely organized Chicago in 1919, soon claiming a membership of 40,000. It secured wage increases and better working conditions and ventured into UNEMPLOYMENT insurance and labor banking. The city became the center of organization campaigns throughout the Midwest, as well as a mainstay of the union nationally.

Beginning in the mid-1920s, however, ACWA membership in Chicago began to shrink. Membership dropped off further during the GREAT DEPRESSION, never recovering except during WORLD WAR II. Chicago continued to provide leadership for the international organization, particularly when Jacob S. Potofsky succeeded Hillman in 1946. The new president extended benefit programs and housing projects to the city and endeavored to reach beyond the stagnating men's CLOTHING industry. In 1976, ACWA members of Chicago, numbering less than three thousand, celebrated the merger of their organization with the Textile Workers Union of America to form the Amalgamated Clothing and Textile Workers Union. In 1995, with the addition of the International Ladies Garment Workers Union, the organization was renamed UNITE (Union of Needletrades, Industrial and Textile Employees).

Youngsoo Bae

See also: Unionization; Work; Work Culture

Further reading: Amalgamated Clothing Workers of America. Research Department. *The Clothing Workers of Chicago, 1910–1922.* 1922. • Bae, Youngsoo. *Labor in Retreat.* 2001. • Fraser, Steve. *Labor Will Rule: Sidney Hillman and the Rise of American Labor.* 1991.

American Civil Liberties Union. Chicagoans have been active in the American Civil Liberties Union (ACLU), on both the local and national levels, since the organization's founding in 1920. Based in New York City, the ACLU evolved from earlier groups that responded to attacks on American pacifists during WORLD WAR I and sought to defend the civil rights of conscientious objectors. The American Union Against Militarism, established in 1916, gave birth to the National Civil Liberties Bureau, which then became the ACLU.

Although initially Chicago did not have a local branch of the ACLU, its residents were among the national organization's most prominent members. Jane Addams stood among the founding members and Clarence Darrow represented the ACLU in its first major case, the Scopes Monkey Trial. In 1929 Chicago members of the ACLU grew alarmed at what they saw as increasing POLICE repression in the city. The group formally incorporated in 1931 as the Chicago Civil Liberties Committee and established a permanent office in downtown Chicago. Although affiliated with the national organization of the ACLU, the Chicago Civil Liberties Committee was an autonomous body. During the 1930s, the group's initial membership of a few dozen grew to about a thousand members.

Many of the cases handled by the committee during its first few years involved defending the rights of AFRICAN AMERICANS, the UNEMPLOYED, and COMMUNIST groups. In addition, the Chicago Civil Liberties Committee investigated charges of police brutality and "third degree" cases of coerced confessions. The CCLC gained a great deal of attention for attacking the local censorship of films and newsreels.

During WORLD WAR II, internal partisan divisions wracked the membership of the Chicago Civil Liberties Committee. Debate surged over the relevance of civil liberties in the Soviet Union, the ACLU's defense of the legal rights of American Fascists, and endorsement of President Roosevelt and his economic policies. In 1945 the national organization of the ACLU accused the CCLC of partisanship and Communist leanings and threatened the committee with expulsion. In response, the CCLC disaffiliated itself from the national organization, but a group of non-Communist members re-formed and reincorporated as the Chicago Division of the American Civil Liberties Union. In 1954, the group changed its name to the Illinois Division of the American Civil Liberties Union in recognition of its expanded activities across the state.

Now known as the ACLU of Illinois, the organization has engaged in hundreds of important CIVIL RIGHTS cases in recent decades. In the mid-1970s, the ACLU of Illinois was widely criticized when it defended the rights of neo-Nazis who sought to hold a public march in SKOKIE, a community with a large Jewish population north of the city, where about 10 percent of the population were German concentration camp survivors. Many local members of the ACLU quit the organization in protest. In the late 1990s, the ACLU of Illinois fought all the way to the U.S. Supreme Court to defeat the city of Chicago's attempts to institute an antiloitering ordinance. The city wanted the ordinance to crack down on GANG activity, but the ACLU saw it as an infringement on the rights of law-abiding citizens.

Ian McGiver

See also: Film Censorship; Free Speech

Further reading: Chicago Civil Liberties Committee. *Pursuit of Freedom: A History of Civil Liberty in Illinois, 1787–1942.* 1942. • Walker, Samuel. *The American Civil Liberties Union: An Annotated Bibliography.* 1992. • Zeigler, Ruth. "The Chicago Civil Liberties Committee, 1929–1938." M.A. thesis, University of Chicago. 1938.

American Giants. During the half century that BASEBALL was segregated by race, black America created its own major leagues. These Negro Leagues showcased black competence and grace at a time when AFRICAN AMERICANS were denied other opportunities. No team better conveyed black baseball's history than the American Giants, who, for four decades, were central to black Chicago, especially as the GREAT MIGRATION swelled its ranks. Chicago, in turn, was the center of black baseball during the 1920s and home to its most important annual event, the East–West all-star game, in the 1930s and '40s.

After the 1910 season, player-manager Andrew "Rube" Foster left the Leland Giants to form the American Giants, who began play in 1911. Perhaps the best black team of the 1920s, the Giants sometimes outplayed and outdrew the WHITE SOX and the CUBS. Relying on speed, defense, and pitching and billed as "The Greatest Aggregation of Colored Baseball Players in the World," the Giants prospered on and off the field. In addition to battling white semi-pro, major league, and Negro League teams, the Giants barnstormed their way across the country and even played in Cuba.

In 1920, Foster founded the first stable black league, the Negro National League (NNL). His Giants won NNL championships in 1920, 1921, 1922, 1926, and 1927. The team later played in the Negro Southern League, the second Negro National League, and then the Negro American League (1937–1952).

For 42 seasons, the American Giants were a source of pride and cohesion to black Chicago. After the 1952 season, in the wake of major league baseball's reintegration, the team disbanded.

Rob Ruck

See also: Leisure; Racism, Ethnicity, and White Identity

Further reading: Clark, Dick, and Larry Lester, eds. *The Negro Leagues Book.* 1994. • Rogosin, Donn. *Invisible Men: Life in Baseball's Negro Leagues.* 1983.

American Plan. During WORLD WAR I, the United States Steel Corporation branded union organizers in its Chicago mills as "German propagandists" and demanded that steelworkers sign a vow against striking called a "Pledge of Patriotism." In the postwar period, other vehemently ANTIUNION employers continued to attack unions as un-American, charging that they subverted individualism and were adversarial and inefficient. In 1921 a convention of Midwestern employers meeting in Chicago formally designated the nonunion or "open shop" the "American Plan."

Implying a linkage between unionism and the Bolshevism of the Red Scare, these American Plan employers pledged that they would neither recognize nor negotiate with union representatives. The most committed refused to purchase materials from unionized vendors or to sell supplies to strikers. A few firms adorned their products with patriotic symbols to indicate that they were made with nonunion labor. After NEW DEAL legislation compelled employers to bargain with unions, the activism of the American Plan subsided.

Stuart Brandes

See also: Americanization; Iron- and Steelworkers; Welfare Capitalism; Work

Further reading: Dunn, Robert W. *The Americanization of Labor.* 1927. • Wakstein, Allen M. "The Origins of the Open-Shop Movement, 1919–1920." *Journal of American History* 51 (1964): 460–475

American Planning Association. Although known by its current name only since 1978, the American PLANNING Association has a far longer history. Its roots go back to the First National Conference on City Planning, held in Washington DC in 1909. By 1917 that informal group had become the American City Planning Institute, later known as the American Institute of Planners.

In 1934, another organization, the American Society of Planning Officials, was formed. Unlike the AIP, whose members were mostly planning consultants, ASPO's seven hundred or so members included citizen planning commissioners, city managers, and other public officials.

In 1938, ASPO, along with 16 other organizations, moved into a building specially constructed for public service associations on the campus of the UNIVERSITY OF CHICAGO in HYDE PARK. The location owed much to the influence of political science professor Charles Merriam, who was on the board of the Spelman Fund, an offshoot of the Rockefeller Foundation, which financed the building at 1313 E. 60th Street. The brainchild of city management expert Louis Brownlow, 1313 housed the Public Administration Clearing House, a nationally known center of municipal research.

In 1978, ASPO and AIP consolidated to form the American Planning Association, blending AIP's more professional and academic perspective with ASPO's broader, national perspective. At the same time, a new group, the American Institute of Certified Planners, was formed to continue AIP's work in certifying planners, providing continuing education, and promulgating a code of ethics. In 1993, the association moved to the LOOP, where it has occupied space in the old People's Gas Building at 122 South Michigan Avenue, designed by Daniel Burnham & Co. in 1911.

Ruth Eckdish Knack

See also: Innovation, Invention and Chicago Business; Merriam Center; Real Estate

Further reading: *Planning* magazine, APA's monthly publication.

American West Indian Association. During the labor shortage of WORLD WAR II, many West Indians were recruited to work in American wartime industry and agriculture under the War Manpower Commission. By the mid-1940s, a substantial number of these newcomers had moved to Chicago, arousing the concern of BARBADIAN, JAMAICAN, and other West Indian professionals already established in the city. In 1944, several of these professionals founded the American West Indian Association (AWIA) with the intention of aiding unemployed and exploited wartime immigrant workers from the islands. By the time the association received its charter in 1950, it had also become the main social and cultural organization for West Indians in Chicago. The AWIA served for more than 30 years as an umbrella organization for Jamaicans, Trinidadians, GUYANESE, Barbadians, BELIZEANS, and other West Indian ethnic groups.

The AWIA held regular meetings at its headquarters in the basement of a member's home at 36th and South Parkway (King Drive). The group organized frequent festivals and fundraisers, as well as social events to celebrate the national holidays of its member ethnic groups. It also hosted dignitaries visiting Chicago from the islands and represented the community to city government and businesses. Beginning in the 1970s, it sponsored scholarships and travel programs for West Indian youth, and coordinated disaster relief during hurricane seasons. In 1970, the first annual West Indian Day was celebrated in Chicago with a flag-raising ceremony at the Civic Center.

By the mid-1970s the AWIA was losing strength. With the recent independence of many West Indian nations, some of the individual ethnic groups under the association's umbrella, particularly Jamaicans, desired their own separate institutions. When a group of Jamaicans in Chicago established the Jamaican American Association in the late sixties, controversy ensued as some in the AWIA felt abandoned. Although many remained committed to the organization, which celebrated its thirtieth anniversary in 1974 with a large party, the association dissolved in the late 1970s, eventually giving way to several separate ethnic organizations.

Many collective activities of the West Indians in Chicago survived the AWIA's demise. Cricket and SOCCER clubs endured. RESTAURANTS like the Hummingbird Supper Club in AUBURN GRESHAM held a weekly West Indian Night through the late 1970s. Pan-Caribbean picnics, like the annual August Carifete on the Midway Plaisance, continued to bring West Indians together socially and culturally through the turn of the millennium.

Robert Morrissey
Frances Matlock

See also: Clubs; Multicentered Chicago; Mutual Benefit Societies

Americanization. Each of Chicago's immigrants has had to come to terms with a new life in a large American city. There have been practical dimensions to this adjustment—learning English and negotiating one's way through the economic and political realities of everyday life. But the process also has involved answering the old question of what it meant to be an American.

Both the timing and content of formal Americanization programs suggest they were often motivated by insecurity on the part of American employers, government officials, and other U.S.-born people. Formal Americanization efforts in Chicago were sparse and rather subdued until 1917–1922. During these years of war, revolution, and labor upsurge, a wide variety of agencies struggled for the hearts and minds of the city's immigrants. The content of Americanization programs promoted by employers and the government, for example, emphasized one's role as a responsible citizen and a loyal, efficient worker.

By 1922 the Chicago Board of Education, which provided most Americanization teachers, had established 31 classes in night schools, 60 in factories, 62 in community centers, and 20 in special "mothers programs." The city's SETTLEMENT HOUSES, YMCAs, churches, and patriotic and fraternal groups cooperated with the board but also sponsored their own programs. The movement reached a crescendo in 1921–22 with a series of large patriotic pageants with thousands of immigrants publicly swearing allegiance, all part of a rather coercive push for "100 percent Americanism." It declined along with immigration between the 1920s and 1960s as a result of immigration restriction, depression, and war.

Many of these classes included instruction not only in English, but also in American history and civics, homemaking, personal hygiene, and vocational training. They were intended to convey not only an understanding

Pageant at Chicago Commons settlement house, 1924. Photographer: Unknown. Source: Chicago Historical Society.

of the language but also a set of appropriately "American" values. Yet this concept of "Americanism" was contested. An understanding of what it meant to be an American could vary enormously between employer and union educational programs, for example. Some immigrants derived their understanding of their new world from involvement with mainstream political parties, others from radical political organizations. The CHICAGO FEDERATION OF LABOR, the city's garment unions, and the WOMEN'S TRADE UNION LEAGUE (WTUL) established their own educational programs with professors and labor activists teaching courses in economics, political economy, history, and literature as well as English. The WTUL organized neighborhood committees to educate immigrant workers, and members of the CHICAGO TEACHERS FEDERATION volunteered to visit immigrant women in their homes. Such programs, which emphasized the rights and responsibilities of workers and the importance of UNIONIZATION and labor solidarity, conveyed values and ideals quite different from those supported by the Chicago Association of Commerce's Americanization Committee.

But whatever the content of these programs, they reached only a fraction of Chicago's immigrants. Even at the movement's height in 1922, no more than 25,000 of the city's more than 300,000 unnaturalized immigrants participated in formal Americanization programs. Thus, most immigrants became acculturated through informal contacts at the workplace, in the SALOON or polling place, through MOVIES or radio, or, in the case of children, in the city's streets, ALLEYS, and PLAYGROUNDS AND SMALL PARKS.

Such contacts might convey not only ideas and values about politics and economics, but also attitudes about race. Much of the violence against AFRICAN AMERICANS in Chicago's 1919 race riot, for example, came at the hands of the more "Americanized" IRISH, while Eastern European immigrants played little part. Yet the prominence of second-generation Slavic people in the post–World War II racial conflicts suggests that newer immigrants had absorbed popular racial prejudices in the intervening generation. These disturbances, considered alongside voting patterns since the 1960s, suggest a movement toward a broader identity on the part of "white ethnics." It seems that becoming American often also involved the construction of a racial identity as "white."

Yet the persistence of distinct ethnic enclaves and organizations from earlier generations, in addition to the more recent influx of Asian, Latin American, African, and other immigrants, all suggest that Americanization in Chicago has been a gradual and uneven process. A visitor to Chicago at the onset of the twenty-first century would be far more likely to be struck by the diversity of the city's popular culture than by any sense of "American" homogeneity.

James R. Barrett

See also: Bilingual Education; Clubs: Fraternal Clubs; Clubs: Patriotic and Veterans' Clubs; Racism, Ethnicity, and White Identity; Schooling for Work

Further reading: *Americanization in Chicago.* The report of a survey made by authority and under direction of the Chicago Community Trust. 1920. • Barrett, James R. "Americanization from the Bottom, Up: Immigration and the Remaking of the American Working Class, 1880–1930." *Journal of American History* 79 (December 1992): 996–1020. • Higham, John. *Strangers in the Land: Patterns of American Nativism, 1860–1925.* 1963.

Amos 'n' Andy. *Amos 'n' Andy,* radio's first hit series, originated on Chicago station WGN as *Sam 'n' Henry* in 1926; it moved to WMAQ under its better-remembered name in 1928. The following year, *Amos 'n' Andy* became a national sensation on the NBC network.

The show's fictional title characters were black southerners transplanted to Chicago (and later, to Harlem). Freeman Gosden and Charles Correll, both white, drew on conventions of "blackface" comedy as they wrote and performed the daily broadcasts. But the pair also tapped into America's curiosity about a fateful, real-life social trend: the great AFRICAN AMERICAN migration to Chicago and other northern cities.

Gosden and Correll endowed even their stereotyped characters with human traits that many listeners found engaging, and they occasionally included sophisticated incidental black characters. *Amos 'n' Andy* drew protests from some African Americans but won the praise of others. The show's move to Hollywood in 1937–38 reflected Chicago's decline as a center of American BROADCASTING.

Melvin Patrick Ely

Freeman Gosden (Amos), *left*, and Charles Correll (Andy), 1930. Photographer: Unknown. Source: Chicago Historical Society.

See also: Great Migration; Leisure; Racism, Ethnicity, and White Identity

Further reading: Barnouw, Erik. *A History of Broadcasting in the United States,* vol. 1, *A Tower in Babel.* 1966. • Ely, Melvin Patrick. *The Adventures of Amos 'n' Andy: A Social History of an American Phenomenon.* 1991. • Wertheim, Arthur Frank. *Radio Comedy.* 1979.

Amusement Parks. Chicago in the 1890s was the birthplace of the amusement park as we know it today. Borrowing the concept of an amusement enclosure from the world's first Midway at the WORLD'S COLUMBIAN EXPOSITION, swimmer/showman Paul Boyton opened Paul Boyton's Water Chute, America's first modern amusement park, at 63rd and Drexel, July 4, 1894. Earlier "amusement parks" centered on natural features such as beaches and picnic groves to attract customers. Captain Boyton's was the first to rely solely on mechanical attractions—specifically, America's first major Shoot-the-Chutes ride. Successful in Chicago, Boyton opened a second park at Coney Island, New York, in 1895, initiating the rise of amusement parks at Coney and throughout America.

Through 1908, Chicago led the nation in its number of amusement parks, including the Chutes, the original Ferris Wheel (at Clark and Wrightwood in Lincoln Park, 1896 to 1903), Sans Souci (WOODLAWN), White City (Woodlawn), Luna Park (NEW CITY), and FOREST PARK. Joyland Park, owned and operated by AFRICAN AMERICANS, was part of the Bronzeville neighborhood during its 1920s heyday. Riverview, at Belmont and Western in NORTH CENTER, was Chicago's largest and longest-running park, surviving from 1904 to 1967. Riverview had the world's first suspended roller coaster (1908) and first parachute ride (1936). Most legendary, however, was the Bobs (1924), perhaps the greatest coaster ever built.

Art Fritz's pony-ride enterprise in suburban MELROSE PARK in 1929 turned into one of the first "kiddielands." By 1944, there were 10 kiddielands in the Chicago area, presaging the explosion of such parks across America in the Baby Boom of the 1950s. Ironically, only Fritz's original survived into the next century.

In the 1960s, as middle-class population shifted to the suburbs, old urban parks like Riverview closed, and California's Disneyland (1955) provided the model for new, outlying "theme parks." Santa's Village, part of the first chain of theme parks, opened in EAST DUNDEE, 1959. Old Chicago, the first indoor shopping mall / theme park (BOLINGBROOK, 1975 to 1980), foreshadowed Canada's West Edmonton Mall and Minnesota's Mall of America. Marriott's Great America (GURNEE, 1976; sold to the Six Flags chain, 1984) brought Chicago into the modern theme park era.

Postcard of Riverview Park, ca. 1909. Photographer: Unknown. Source: Chicago Historical Society.

In 1995, a 148-foot Ferris Wheel—recalling the 1893 original—was erected at the renovated NAVY PIER, a reminder of Chicago's past amusement greatness.

Stan Barker

See also: Entertaining Chicagoans; Leisure; Metropolitan Growth; Shopping Districts and Malls

Further reading: Barker, Stan. "Paradises Lost." *Chicago History* 22.1 (March 1993). • Barker, Stan. *Chicago's Amusement Parks.* Forthcoming.

Anarchists. Anarchists rejected concepts of both private property and organized government in favor of voluntary association and cooperation. Chicago's anarchists were largely skilled, immigrant workers who joined the International Working People's Association (IWPA), which built its organization through local clubs and an anarchist press. By 1886 26 local groups were meeting regularly for lectures and discussions of "the social question." During the 1880s the IWPA published seven NEWSPAPERS in Chicago, in GERMAN, CZECH, NORWEGIAN, and English. Both newspapers and clubs sought to produce a vibrant movement culture that included picnics, parades, festivals, singing societies, and theater groups.

Most anarchists were also trade unionists. In 1884, anarchists established the Central Labor Union (CLU), which came to include some of the city's largest unions. In 1886, the CLU took part in the movement for the EIGHT-HOUR day and tried to organize previously unorganized workers. After the 1886 HAYMARKET Affair, which resulted in eight convictions and the execution of four of the anarchists' most prominent leaders, anarchism could no longer claim to be a mass movement in Chicago and the United States.

Bruce C. Nelson

See also: Socialist Parties; Unionization

Further reading: Avrich, Paul. *The Haymarket Tragedy.* 1984. • David, Henry. *History of the Haymarket Affair.* 1936; rev. ed. 1958. • Nelson, Bruce C. *Beyond the Martyrs: A Social History of Chicago's Anarchists, 1870–1900.* 1988.

Andersonville. Andersonville, located in the southwest corner of the EDGEWATER Community Area, began as a SWEDISH community. In the late 1980s Andersonville became an attractive area of settlement for GAYS AND LESBIANS who sought cheaper homes and apartments north of BOYS TOWN.

Erik Gellman

See also: Neighborhood Succession

Further reading: Pacyga, Dominic A., and Ellen Skerrett. *Chicago, City of Neighborhoods: Histories and Tours.* 1986. • Stuyvesant, Judith Erickson. "Recollections of Andersonville and Swedish Life in Chicago." Collections of the Swedish American Museum, Chicago, IL. 1997.

Angel Guardian Orphanage. Established in 1865 by the five GERMAN ROMAN CATHOLIC parishes of the city to safeguard the German cultural heritage of their dependent CHILDREN, Angel Guardian Orphanage was one of the largest residential child care homes in Chicago. Initially, the Poor Handmaids of Jesus Christ were recruited from Germany to take charge of the facility, located on a 40-acre site at 2001 Devon Avenue. Affected by the wider social welfare debate between institutionalization and home placement, the orphanage changed after 1916 to a "cottage system" in which a small group of children shared a single living quarters and dining facility. In 1973 the Illinois Department of Children and Family Services took a stance in favor of home placement and cut Angel Guardian's subsidies. The orphanage ended its program of child care in 1974 and in 1975 the Misericordia Home for Special Children took over the site, subsequently renamed Misericordia Home North.

Paula F. Pfeffer

See also: Religious Institutions; Social Services

Further reading: Angel Guardian Orphanage Papers. Archives and Records Center, Archdiocese of Chicago, Chicago, IL. • Coughlin, Fr. Roger J., and Cathryn A. Riplinger. *The Story of Charitable Care in the Archdiocese of Chicago, 1844–1997.* 1999.

Angolans. Although numbering fewer than three dozen at the end of the twentieth century, Chicago's Angolans built a united, thriving community, maintaining strong ties to both their homeland and other African immigrants in Chicago. Like the CONGOLESE, with whom they share tribal and linguistic ties, Angolans began coming to the United States in large numbers with the onset of the regional wars of the 1970s. Initially, most REFUGEES fled to France, Belgium, and Portugal, the colonial nations that gave the Republic of Congo and Angola their official languages. European Economic Community restrictions on immigration forced many of them to turn to the United States in the 1980s, to cities such as Philadelphia, St. Louis, Phoenix, and Chicago. In 1992 leaders of these cities' Angolan communities formed the Angolan Community in the USA (ACUSA), whose Chicago branch has actively welcomed and aided new immigrants. It also has hosted yearly celebrations of Angola's Independence Day on November 11.

Because most Angolan immigrants have been single men or small family groups, cut off from the extended family structures common in their homeland, and the community has not clustered in any particular neighborhoods or occupations, formal and informal activities have been important to community life. DANCE festivals, held primarily in Chicago's UPTOWN neighborhood, have featured Kisamba, a popular musical form developed in Angola incorporating African and European influences. These gatherings have provided opportunities to hear news from home, welcome new members, and exchange letters and packages carried by others on frequent trips between the United States and Africa. Despite the political strife that has continued to destabilize Angola, community leaders claim that immigrants' political affiliations and commitments have not precluded peaceful relations among community members in Chicago.

Tracy N. Poe

See also: Demography; Multicentered Chicago

Annexation. At its founding in 1837, the city of Chicago encompassed little more than 10 square miles. It was bounded on the east by LAKE MICHIGAN, on the south by 22nd Street, on the west by Wood Street, on the

Annexations and Additions to the City of Chicago

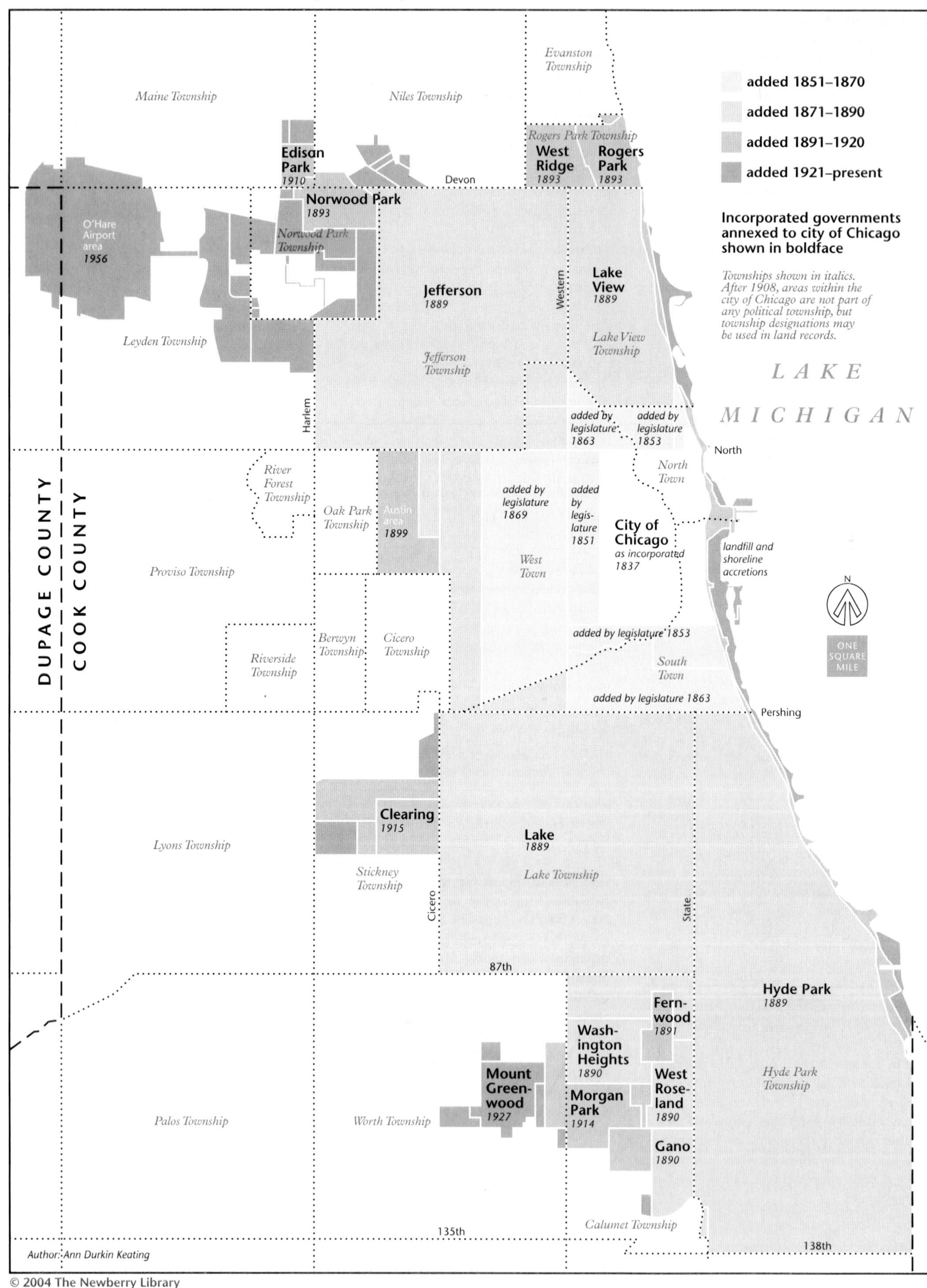

north by North Avenue. East of LaSalle Street, the northern boundary extended to Center Street. These boundaries moved outward via a series of referendums until the city encompassed just over 185 square miles by the end of the century. At first, these annexations were the result of legislative acts, but, beginning in 1889, they were the result of elections. Over the following two decades, Chicago, like many American cities, experienced numerous annexations.

The largest single annexation followed an election on June 29, 1889, when Chicago gained 125 square miles and 225,000 people. It became the (then) largest city in the United States in area and passed Philadelphia to become second in population. That annexation indicates why some suburbs elected to relinquish their autonomy, and others retained theirs.

The rapid growth of urban populations and technology in the late nineteenth century increased public demand for urban services. A larger jurisdiction, the result of annexation, was expected to reduce the cost of providing existing services and provide tax revenues to pay for additional ones. Many suburbs were unable to provide all the services their residents demanded. There were two common problems. First, many suburbs were unable to borrow money for improvements because they were already at their debt limit (typically 5 percent of their assessed valuation). Second, to be cost-effective, the new technologies required populations much larger than most suburbs were likely to have.

Suburban voters favored annexation when they were dissatisfied with the quantity, quality, or cost of public services, particularly sanitary services. One of the reasons LAKE VIEW TOWNSHIP (including RAVENSWOOD) annexed to Chicago in 1889 was to obtain a better sewage system. Prior to 1883, HYDE PARK TOWNSHIP and LAKE TOWNSHIP jointly owned a WATER system. In 1883, Hyde Park installed new waterworks in the densely settled region north of 87th Street; Lake and Hyde Park Townships were annexed to Chicago in 1889. In each of these political jurisdictions, a majority of voters had to vote favorably for annexation to occur. The importance of a water system for effective fire protection played a role in both cases.

An alternative to annexation was the formation of a special governmental body. The Sanitary District Enabling Act of 1889 permitted the creation of a SPECIAL DISTRICT over an area benefited by a common sewage-disposal strategy. Municipalities within such a district would be responsible for collecting sewage, but the Sanitary District would be responsible for disposing of it. The act also required municipalities with direct access to LAKE MICHIGAN to supply water to adjacent municipalities at reasonable cost. The Sanitary District created an alternative to annexation for residents of suburbs adjacent to Chicago. The southern suburb of BLUE ISLAND voted against joining Chicago in 1915, although its neighbor to the north, MORGAN PARK, had joined the year before. Blue Island's assertion of its right to Sanitary District water helped it to preserve its independence. Clearly some suburbs were too small, too poor, too debt-ridden to continue as autonomous municipalities, but others, such as Hyde Park, could have remained independent. In 1889, however, most suburbs looked to Chicago, not to the Sanitary District, as the supplier of sanitary services.

Annexation to Chicago stopped when it reached the established suburban communities where a majority of the residents were supplied with satisfactory public services. In 1892, South Evanston was annexed to EVANSTON after repeated failures to develop its own source of pure water; in 1894, voters rejected the annexation of WILMETTE to Evanston and of Evanston to Chicago. Along with the other North Shore suburbs, Evanston was annexed to the Sanitary District in 1903. In a complicated series of votes, a majority of CICERO voters compelled AUSTIN to join Chicago (1899), OAK PARK detached itself from Cicero (1901), and then Oak Park repeatedly voted down its own annexation to Chicago. It has been argued that temperance considerations contributed to antiannexation votes, but even before the 1889 election the Chicago City Council passed an ordinance permitting the establishment of PROHIBITION districts at the option of local residents.

Suburban annexation activity continued into the twentieth century, but it was relatively minor within Chicago. The village of Niles Center (SKOKIE) increased its size tenfold with a series of annexations between 1924 and 1926. The village of ROSEMONT treated annexation as a tool for creating a city. Incorporated as an area of about 84 acres in 1956, it swiftly began to annex adjacent areas so that it could become a viable municipality. In the last quarter of the twentieth century, NAPERVILLE pursued a vigorous program of annexation to capture increasing tax revenues from its booming neighbors. Annexation today is considered feasible for combined areas in the 50,000 to 100,000 population range.

Louis P. Cain

See also: Flood Control and Drainage; Governing the Metropolis; Government, Suburban; Home Rule; Infrastructure; Metropolitan Growth; Planning Chicago; Water Supply

Further reading: Cain, Louis P. "To Annex or Not? A Tale of Two Towns: Evanston and Hyde Park." *Explorations in Economic History* 20 (1983): 57–72. • Keating, Ann Durkin. *Building Chicago: Suburban Developers and the Creation of a Divided Metropolis*. 1988, esp. chap. 6. • McCarthy, Michael. "The New Metropolis: Chicago, the Annexation Movement,

---

After 1850, Cook County was divided into townships, which administered basic governmental functions. Residents who wanted more than basic services could petition the Illinois legislature for incorporation as a village, town, or city with more extensive powers to provide services and tax local residents. Laid out in 1830, Chicago incorporated as a city in 1837, and by the 1870s all of the townships surrounding the city had also incorporated. Beyond the ring of incorporated townships, parts of townships also sought incorporation by the 1880s. For Chicago, the period of extensive annexations extended from 1851 to 1920. The largest annexation occurred in 1889, when four of five incorporated townships surrounding Chicago (as well as a part of the fifth) were annexed to the city. Most annexations to Chicago during these years came because Chicago offered superior services, from better water connections in the nineteenth century to better high schools in the early twentieth. Later, prior incorporations and suburban resistance to the power and urban complexity of Chicago halted the process.

Skokie's Border with Chicago

Although Chicago's size and population make it the central city of the metropolitan region, it has not been the focus of all annexations. In 1954, for example, Chicago annexed land from the village of SKOKIE, but it was able to do so only because Skokie itself had begun annexing adjacent land three decades earlier, until it bumped up against the edges of seven neighboring municipalities.

Skokie's growth began in 1922, when voters approved a referendum annexing a large swath of unincorporated territory surrounding the original core of Niles Center. A series of smaller annexations in 1925, 1926, 1928, and 1930 brought the village to its maximum size. One of the 1925 annexations made Niles Center adjacent to its closest municipal neighbor to the south, Tessville (LINCOLNWOOD). In 1928 and 1933, Niles Center decreased in size, disannexing two portions of territory to Evanston at the request of the affected voters and property owners.

Skokie lost more land in 1954, when Chicago annexed a quadrilateral bounded by Lunt, Carpenter, Dowagiac, and Central for a hospital that was never built; Skokie, however, retained a block of Ionia south of the annexed land and the strip of Central Avenue required to keep the block contiguous with the rest of Skokie. Ionia connects to Central at an odd angle, accounting for its nickname, the "hockey stick." A subsequent disannexation in 1972 reduced the width of the connecting strip from 100 feet to 1 foot. Finally, in 1974, the village of NILES ceded to Skokie a triangle of land under the westernmost house on the block, in order to clarify responsibility for the street's maintenance.

Amanda Seligman

and Progressive Reform." In Michael H. Ebner and Eugene M. Tobin, eds., *The Age of Urban Reform*, 1977, 43–54.

Anti-Communism. *See* Cold War and Anti-Communism

Antioch, IL, Lake County, 47 miles NW of the Loop. The village of Antioch is located in Antioch Township in the northwest corner of Lake County, Illinois, a region known as the Chain of Lakes. Brothers Darius and Thomas Gage were among the earliest to file land claims and build houses along Sequoit Creek after the winter of 1837. Hiram Buttrick built a sawmill on the creek in 1839. Population reached 300 by 1852.

Some of the early residents were devout followers of the PROTESTANT sect now known as the Disciples of Christ. The name Antioch (a reference to a city in early Christian history) was chosen as the result of an exchange between zealous Disciples and their ridiculing neighbors, who initiated the idea of a biblical name. The settlement was a local center of support for ABOLITIONISM.

Small shops were established in the village, and in 1856 John Elliott built a steam gristmill to accompany the sawmill. The new settlers were mostly of GERMAN, IRISH, and ENGLISH descent.

TOURISM was a spur to Antioch's economy after it became a station on the Wisconsin Central rail line in 1885, between Chicago and Stevens Point, Wisconsin. The recreational possibilities of hunting, fishing, and boating on dozens of small nearby lakes made Antioch a popular vacation spot for Chicagoans. Local farmers transformed their homes into tourist BOARDINGHOUSES, while others built HOTELS and summer cottages. Antioch became the gateway to the Chain of Lakes, including the flowering lotus beds covering hundreds of acres on nearby Grass Lake.

Antioch incorporated as a village in 1892. After a series of fires, the village installed a public WATER system in 1905 and began to build more brick buildings.

Other industries slowly developed alongside tourism. The ice harvesting industry took advantage of the area's lakes and rail service to Chicago. Employers hired hobos from Chicago as seasonal laborers and put them up in BOARDINGHOUSES built near the ice houses.

The Pickard China company moved to Antioch from Chicago in 1937 as it expanded its operation from hand-decorating imported china to full-scale domestic production. Thelen Sand and Gravel has been a prominent local enterprise since 1947.

The village maintained a small-town character with slow growth into the mid-1980s. After 1990 there was more rapid residential development, with developers building hundreds of homes in several new subdivisions. The village population as of the 2000 census was 8,788, with 21,879 in Antioch Township.

Passenger rail service to Antioch, which had ended in 1965, returned in 1996 when Metra opened a new suburban passenger rail line, the North Central, with Antioch as its terminus. Ridership figures turned out to be higher than projected, leading to calls for expanded service.

Douglas Knox

See also: Metropolitan Growth; Sailing and Boating; Vacation Spots

Further reading: *Antioch, Illinois: A Pictorial History, 1892–1992*. Antioch: Lakes Region Historical Society, 1992.

Wisconsin Central trains brought hundreds from Chicago on summer Saturdays to the Chain of Lakes region (ca. 1928). Photographer: Unknown. Source: Lakes Region Historical Society.

Antiunionism. From the late nineteenth century on, Chicago was one of the most heavily unionized American cities, but not for lack of ardent opposition by employers. Their strategies, reflecting both insistence on total managerial control typical of American large-scale BUSINESS and reaction to the radicalism and militancy of Chicago's workers, often made the city as much a global center of antiunionism as it was a "trade union capital of the world." Meatpacker Philip Armour in 1879 captured the managerial ethos: "As long as we are heads of our own houses, we shall employ what men we choose, and when we can't, why, we'll nail up our doors—that's all."

Antiunionism took two basic forms: repression and paternalism. Repressive tactics included firing and blacklisting union sympathizers (Marshall Field & Co. fired workers for being in the company of a union member); recruiting strikebreakers; deploying spies, thugs, and private security forces (including the infamous Chicago-based PINKERTONS); locking out workers to break their union; vilifying unionists as "ANARCHISTS" or "COMMUNISTS"; and exacerbating ethnic conflicts to divide workers. Frequently, owners took advantage of recessions to cut wages, then broke unions by relying on the desperate unemployed to cross picket lines (as the meatpackers did in 1904, destroying a newly created union movement). To present a united front against workers, employers formed associations, such as the RAILROADS' General Managers Association in the 1890s, and to exert business influence over local GOVERNMENT, they formed political groups, such as the Citizens' Association of Chicago in 1874.

Business owners frequently turned to the government to suppress unions and STRIKES through laws against political radicalism, conspiracy, restraint of trade, and even vagrancy; court injunctions against strikes, picketing, and other union activities; POLICE protection of business property and strikebreakers; jailing of labor leaders; and violent—even deadly—attacks on union gatherings, including the police killing of 10 men at a peaceful rally in southeast Chicago near the antiunion Republic Steel plant on MEMORIAL DAY 1937.

In the first decades after the Civil War, businessmen saw Chicago's police as unreliable, that is, occasionally neutral during strikes. In the 1870s and 1880s they formed private armed militias and secured construction of ARMORIES and forts for state militia and federal troops, who were called in to suppress major strikes against the railroads in 1877 and against PULLMAN in 1894. They sought to "professionalize" the police to eliminate working-class sympathies, but the result was a police force whose willingness to support strikebreaking was seldom limited by a concern for civil liberties.

Despite profound business-class influence, local government was not consistently antilabor: a few politicians, including Mayor Carter Harrison and Governor John Peter Altgeld, were largely sympathetic to the labor movement, and twentieth-century machine Democrats relied on union support despite their opposition to union contracts for most public workers. While businesses could count on many elite institutions, including churches and the press, to oppose unions, a few editors, religious leaders, and intellectuals, such as Henry Demarest Lloyd, Jane Addams, and Clarence Darrow, broke ranks to support UNIONIZATION.

While most Chicago businesses openly fought unions, some tried to avoid unionization through paternalism, treating workers more humanely to instill loyalty. George Pullman conceptualized his model factory town south of Chicago to avoid labor unrest, but, like most paternalistic efforts, his idea fell victim to a gap between promise and reality, leading workers to strike in 1894. After WORLD WAR I, when unionizing efforts in steel and MEATPACKING collapsed in the face of internal divisions and employer opposition (reinforced in the steel strike with deadly public and private force), businesses in Chicago joined in the national employer effort to roll back recent union gains with an "open shop" campaign. Many businesses embraced "WELFARE CAPITALISM," which attempted to avoid the irritating aspects of paternalism and, rather than simply avoid unionism, adopted some union principles, but under management control. U.S. Steel, International Harvester, Swift, Armour, and Western Electric were among leading Chicago businesses that provided individualized pay, insurance and promotion incentives (including stock ownership), company-dominated employee representation plans, and family-oriented recreation. Companies, reversing earlier strategies, often broke up close-knit ethnic workgroups as potentially subversive. Some, like Western Electric, initiated surveys and studies to identify sources of worker discontent.

While much of welfare capitalism collapsed with the GREAT DEPRESSION, some programs survived. Sears, Roebuck combined the "soft" and "hard" approaches to union avoidance, using worker surveys as well as the tough tactics of consultant Nathan W. Shefferman, who headed off TEAMSTER organizing through payments to union president Dave Beck. Shefferman pioneered the modern antiunion consulting industry through his techniques of ferreting out union sympathizers and individually pressuring workers to oppose unionization. Shefferman mixed legal and illegal tactics to fight union organizing drives, and his disciples opened influential consulting businesses in Chicago.

Throughout Chicago history a few businessmen, such as banker Lyman Gage in the late nineteenth century, have argued for a détente with the unions. The largely middle-class CIVIC FEDERATION of Chicago, inspired in 1893 by reformer William Stead, promoted social cooperation, including alliances between reformers and labor. The National Civic Federation, founded in Chicago in 1900, became a leading advocate of a labor-capital bargain to recognize unions but assure unhindered production. At times, such as during the two World Wars and from 1945 to the late 1960s, businesses generally were willing to accommodate unions, either because of government pressure or the power of organized labor. But from the 1960s on, many business operations, especially manufacturing branches of large national or multinational corporations, indirectly fought unions by relocating—either to the Sunbelt, where unions were weak, or to foreign countries, often ones with anti-labor regimes. Other large businesses, such as Motorola, tried to avoid unionization by matching union wages and devising human-relations strategies to defuse the buildup of grievances. By the late 1970s and early 1980s, businesses—often relying on specialist antiunion consultants—became more openly aggressive in fighting unionization and breaking unions, as witnessed during the 1985 printing unions' strike at the *Chicago Tribune*. At the close of the twentieth century, unions were losing influence over the city's workforce as emerging industries resisted unionization and new, nonunion firms undercut union dominance in previously well-organized industries such as the HOTEL industry.

David Moberg

See also: American Plan; Haymarket and May Day; If Christ Came to Chicago; Pullman Strike; Railroad Strike of 1877; Sports, Industrial League; Work Culture

Further reading: Barrett, James R. *Work and Community in the Jungle: Chicago's Packinghouse Workers, 1894–1922.* 1987. • Cohen, Lizabeth. *Making a New Deal: Industrial Workers in Chicago, 1919–1939.* 1990. • Schneirov, Richard. *Labor and Urban Politics: Class Conflict and the Origins of Modern Liberalism in Chicago, 1864–97.* 1998.

Antiwar Movements. Many Americans believe in the need for unquestioning patriotism during times of national military crisis. Others have felt it their moral duty to oppose wars that they believed were incompatible with principles of justice, or at odds with their vision of the national interest. From the CIVIL WAR to the Gulf Wars, Chicago has hosted powerful movements opposing national military policies. Particularly important were the roles played by Chicago groups in opposing WORLD WAR I, WORLD WAR II, and the Vietnam War.

When war erupted in Europe in August 1914, President Wilson proclaimed U.S. neutrality and counseled Americans to remain neutral in thought and action. But the president soon pursued policies which his critics charged favored the British. Wilson also began a "preparedness," or rearmament, campaign which many believed was designed to prepare the country for involvement in war. Wilson's sharpest critics in Chicago included IRISH and GERMAN groups, SOCIALISTS, members of the Women's Peace Party, and the leadership of the CHICAGO FEDERATION OF LABOR. Often working together, they staged counterdemonstrations at preparedness parades in the city, opposed the introduction of military training in the SCHOOLS, tried to rally the national labor movement against the war, and vigorously promoted a national campaign to force a referendum on the question of U.S. participation in the war.

Following Wilson's declaration of war against Germany, only the socialists continued to actively oppose the U.S. war effort. But in 1918 the Chicago Federation of Labor created a labor party predicated on anti-militarist and anti-imperialist principles and subsequently spearheaded the drive for a national farmer-labor party committed to these same principles. Although the labor party movement proved short-lived, it provided an intellectual legacy for interwar pacifists who sought to promote the peaceful resolution of conflicts outside the framework of the League of Nations.

Chicago once again became a center of antiwar agitation during World War II, boasting one of the most active "America First" chapters in the country. Profoundly influenced by their experiences during World War I, members of the America First organization believed that American democracy could be preserved only by keeping the nation out of European wars. America First bitterly attacked Roosevelt's policies in support of the allies during 1940–41, arguing that they would provoke a German response which would make American entrance into the war inevitable. Although America First was dominated by conservatives, some left-of-center groups also opposed Roosevelt's policies, charging that he was deceiving the American public on critical foreign policy issues. But as historian Thomas Bailey has noted, "The torpedoes that sank the American battleships in Pearl Harbor also sank America Firstism."

In discrediting isolationism, World War II and the COLD WAR also set the stage for controversial U.S. military interventions in Korea and Vietnam. The antiwar coalition that developed in response to U.S. policy in Vietnam converged on Chicago at the now infamous 1968 Democratic Convention. Protesters held a rally at GRANT PARK to vent their frustrations over the outcome of the convention and

Jane Addams (*right*) and Mary McDowell, 1917. Photographer: Allen, Gordon, Schroeppel and Redlich, Inc. Source: Chicago Historical Society.

were treated savagely by the city's POLICE, with one investigator terming the incident a "police riot." The incident signaled that, as in the World War I era, the DEMOCRATIC PARTY had once again split apart at its seams in response to antiwar agitation.

Elizabeth McKillen

See also: Civil Rights Movements; Congress of Racial Equality (CORE); Feminist Movements

Further reading: Cole, Wayne S. *America First: The Battle against Intervention, 1940–1941.* 1953. • McKillen, Elizabeth. *Chicago Labor and the Quest for a Democratic Diplomacy, 1914–1924.* 1995. • Schneider, James C. *Should America Go to War? The Debate over Foreign Policy in Chicago, 1939–1941.* 1989.

Apartments. From Chicago's earliest experience with multifamily residences until the 1930s, the single-family house remained the norm for a home. Thus, the exterior appearance of flats, apartment buildings, and RESIDENTIAL HOTELS tended to be inspired by whatever was current in the design of the better class of residence.

The first apartments appeared in a "flat craze" serving Chicagoans whom the FIRE OF 1871 had made homeless. Since then, two-, three-, and four-story brick walk-ups with one apartment of four to seven rooms per floor, sometimes ganged at a party wall, have been staples in Chicago. The most graceful grouping, introduced in 1893, gathers four or more sets around a court open to the street to produce a courtyard apartment. Andrew Sandegren and Samuel Crowen designed dozens of the best of these.

Only after 1900 did the number of multifamily buildings under construction exceed the number of single-family residences. Tall apartment buildings first appeared in 1882. Within a decade Clinton J. Warren had shown how elevator apartments could have a distinct visual appearance and functional character distinguishing them from HOTELS. The definitive form of the Chicago luxury apartment, attractive to people who had the means to live in a mansion, arrived in 1900 with Benjamin Marshall's Raymond Apartments at Michigan and Walton (destroyed). In 1911 Marshall built as his own investment the grandest of this group, 1550 North State Parkway. Dozens of others rising the canonic eight to twelve stories proliferated along the northern lakefront, often the design of Marshall, Howard Van Doren Shaw, or Hugh Garden.

After WORLD WAR I, new laws allowed cooperative apartment ventures. Meanwhile, the 1923 ZONING code allowed a generous building envelope along the lakefront. On the GOLD COAST and in HYDE PARK, the affluent middle classes and the wealthy built apartments reaching 23 stories and containing a variety of apartment configurations. Marshall and Shaw designed the best of them while Robert DeGolyer, William Ernest Walker, and McNally and Quinn stand out in the second rank.

Two dramatic designs by Ludwig Mies van der Rohe, the reinforced concrete Promontory Apartments in Hyde Park (1948) and the steel and glass 860–880 North Lake Shore Drive (1951), sanctioned rejecting local and domestic architectural traditions. Since then, Chicago's lakefront high-rise apartments have been part of international modernism and its legacy. The most notable recent development has been the inclusion of apartments into larger complexes like Bertrand Goldberg's Marina City on the Chicago River (1964) and Skidmore, Owings & Merrill's John Hancock Center (1969). And among the commercial buildings and hotels built since 1967 atop the former ILLINOIS CENTRAL RAILROAD railhead east of Michigan Avenue and south of the CHICAGO RIVER are numerous undistinguished apartment buildings.

Carroll William Westfall

See also: Architecture: The First Chicago School; Architecture: The Second Chicago School; Condominiums and Cooperatives; Homelessness and Shelters; Housing Types

Further reading: Baird & Warner, Inc. *A Portfolio of Fine Apartment Homes.* 1928. • Pardridge, A. J., and Harold Bradley. *Directory to Apartments of the Better Class along the North Side of Chicago.* 1917. • Westfall, Carroll William. "Chicago's Better Tall Apartment Buildings: 1871–1923." *Architectura* 21.2 (1991): 177–208.

Aragon Ballroom. The Aragon Ballroom (1106 West Lawrence Avenue) opened its doors in July 1926 and quickly became a center of DANCE-HALL culture in Chicago. Designed by Huszagh & Hill, the interior lavishly recreates a Mediterranean plaza, its arcades surrounding a huge dance floor suspended on a system of springs, cork, and felt.

Located in Uptown, alongside the "L," it drew dancers from across Chicago and the suburbs. In 1927, WGN began live broadcasts from the ballroom, spreading its fame nationwide. Tens of thousands came to the Aragon every week.

After the decline of social dancing in the 1960s, the Aragon survived by hosting rock concerts and other public events. With the recent popularity of salsa and swing, however, the Aragon is again becoming a destination for dancers.

Geoffrey Klingsporn

See also: Entertaining Chicagoans; Ethnic Music; Leisure; Radio Orchestras; Rock Music

Further reading: Banks, Nancy. "The World's Most Beautiful Ballrooms." *Chicago History* 2.4 (1973): 206–215. • Nye, Russel B. "Saturday Night at the Paradise Ballroom: or, Dance Halls in the Twenties." *Journal of Popular Culture* 7.1 (1973): 14–22.

Archdiocese of Chicago. *See* Roman Catholic Archdiocese of Chicago

Archer Heights, Community Area 57, 7 miles SW of the Loop. The urban history of Archer Heights is largely a twentieth-century story. Indians had little use for it except as a part of the passage that connected the Chicago and Des Plaines Rivers. The swamps and prairies of the area interested primarily nineteenth-century land speculators and farmers. After the turn of the century, it became the focus of real-estate developers and manufacturers. Its name reflects both sets of interests. "Archer" refers to Archer Road, which took its name from Illinois & Michigan Canal commissioner and land speculator William B. Archer. For a while the area was known as the Archer Road district. "Heights" stems from the name of an early-twentieth-century subdivision, although it is unclear to what the term referred, since the topography is as flat as any in the region.

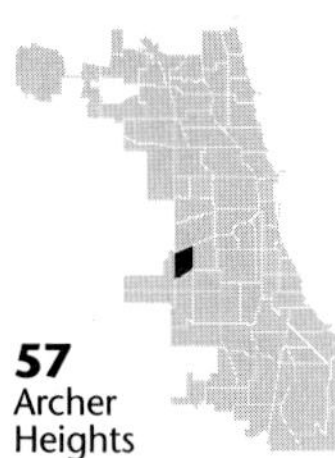

Though most of the land in the area had passed into private hands by the 1850s, until after the turn of the century it either remained undeveloped swamp and soggy prairie, or supported farms and homes of the few settlers. The Illinois & Michigan Canal, which ran where the Stevenson Expressway does now; the Chicago & Alton Railroad, which paralleled the canal; and Archer Road were the first thoroughfares to Chicago, but they had little effect on the area's development in the nineteenth century. Not even the three railroads that encircled it in the 1880s (presently, the Belt, Santa Fe, and Indiana Harbor), or annexation to Chicago in 1889 (from both Lake and Cicero Townships) changed much of the district's character or economic role.

After 1900 speculators developed the southern sections of Archer Heights for residential use, while railroads maintained control of most of the north-side real estate. Archer Avenue offered horsecars in the 1890s and electric streetcars by 1906, which helped attract immigrant laborers. Poles emigrated in the largest numbers, followed by Italians, Lithuanians, Czechs, and Russian Jews. The area saw its largest increase in population between 1920 and 1930. During this decade, modern urban infrastructure and two Catholic parishes, St. Bruno's (1925) and St. Richard's (1928), accommodated the population surge. Though the Great Depression halted most residential construction, the Archer Heights Civic Association (1938), the oldest neighborhood organization on the Southwest Side, looked after the interests of those already living there.

During the 1930s and 1940s industrial and commercial growth overtook residential growth. Industry, initially in the Crawford Industrial District (a project of the Central Manufacturing District) in the 1930s, eventually covered approximately two-thirds of the area, including the Santa Fe Railroad piggyback yard and the Kenwood Manufacturing District. Manufacturing and commercial transport, including Midway Airport, employed many Archer Heights residents. Commercial strips formed along Pulaski Road, Archer Avenue, and 47th Street, the major thoroughfares.

Residential growth picked up again after World War II. Between 1930 and 1950, Archer Heights's population inched along from 8,120 to 8,675. In the following decade it grew to 10,584, and peaked at 11,143 in 1970. By 1980, the population fell to 9,708, and again in 1990 to 9,227, consistent with the decline of Midway as Chicago's main airport. Despite these fluctuations, the community's composition stayed notably consistent. For more than 90 years, its residents have been predominantly white (96 percent in 1990), with a large contingent of foreign-born (27 percent in 1990), and a strong Polish cohort. Only recently has any nonwhite group dented the percentages. In the 1990s, Hispanics, primarily Mexicans, rose to 8 percent of the population. African Americans remain less than 1 percent.

At the close of the twentieth century, approximately 60 percent of the area was devoted to manufacturing and bulk transportation facilities, 30 percent to residences, and 10 percent to commerce. There was no distinct downtown or distinguishing landmarks. The regularity of the modest, well-kept housing combined with the large manufacturing presence established the neighborhood's character. Mostly industrial, mostly blue-collar, and mostly Caucasian, the character of Archer Heights has remained consistent over much of the twentieth century.

Jonathan J. Keyes

See also: Built Environment of the Chicago Region; Transportation

Further reading: Chicago Fact Book Consortium, ed. *Local Community Fact Book: Chicago Metropolitan Area, 1990.* 1995. • Karlen, Harvey M. *Chicago's Crabgrass Communities: The History of the Independent Suburbs and Their Post Offices That Became Part of Chicago.* 1992.

Architecture

OVERVIEW
THE FIRST CHICAGO SCHOOL
THE CITY BEAUTIFUL MOVEMENT
THE PRAIRIE SCHOOL
THE SECOND CHICAGO SCHOOL

OVERVIEW. W. W. Boyington and John Mills Van Osdel were the most prominent architects in Chicago as the city grew from less than 1,000 at its incorporation in 1837 to 325,000 in 1871. Between them, they designed the region's most important buildings, many of which were destroyed in the Fire of 1871. Extant examples of their architecture include Boyington's 1869 Water Tower on North Michigan Avenue and Van Osdel's 1857 McHenry County Courthouse in Woodstock.

However, the distinctive and reknowned story of Chicago architecture seldom begins with Boyington and Van Osdel, because their work is viewed as derivative and utilitarian rather than artistic and groundbreaking. The 1871 fire and Chicago's subsequent meteoric growth drew architects with vision and daring.

The closing decades of the nineteenth century saw the emergence of a group known as the "First Chicago School," famous for Chicago's early skyscrapers. They included architects like John Wellborn Root, Charles Atwood, Dankmar Adler, and Louis Sullivan. Also among them were Daniel Burnham, who was instrumental in the "City Beautiful" movement, which took hold with the 1893 World's Columbian Exposition and influenced architecture and planning for a generation. Other Chicago architects, including Frank Lloyd Wright, Barry Byrne, and George Washington Maher, designed homes, schools, and businesses in what has come to be known as the "Prairie School."

In the mid-twentieth century, a modern style dominated by sheaths of metal and glass, championed by Ludwig Mies van der Rohe, characterized a "Second Chicago School." In the closing decades of the twentieth century a postmodern reaction to the simplicity of the Second Chicago School emerged in the work of architects like Helmut Jahn.

Ann Durkin Keating

See also: School Architecture

Part of a panoramic aerial view, from the Stevens Hotel to the Palmolive Building, 1935. Photographer: Hornby & Freiberg. Source: Chicago Public Library.

THE FIRST CHICAGO SCHOOL. It is no mere accident that in the 1880s Chicago produced a group of architects, now known as the "First Chicago School," whose work would have a profound effect upon architecture.

Within a decade after the FIRE OF 1871, Chicago was a boomtown. By 1890 it had a population of more than a million people and had surpassed Philadelphia to become the second-largest metropolis in the United States. The value of land in the LOOP soared. Quickly, the low buildings constructed just after the fire were seen as an inefficient use of valuable space.

Chicago was ready to experiment with daring solutions. The city that had stood at the center of INNOVATIONS like the PULLMAN sleeping car, the McCormick reaper, and MAIL-ORDER retailing would now be the place where the tall office building would be perfected. One of the keys to this development was the invention of the elevator. Chicago had a special problem, however: it stood upon a swamp.

As early as 1873, Frederick Baumann had proposed that each vertical element of a building should have a separate foundation ending in a broad pad that would distribute its weight over the marshy ground. It was this type of foundation that Burnham & Root used for the Montauk Block (1882) on West Monroe Street. But Baumann's foundation occupied valuable basement space and could support only 10 stories.

Adler & Sullivan developed a far better solution. Dankmar Adler's experience as an engineer with the Union army during the Civil War helped him devise a vast raft of timbers, steel beams, and iron I-beams to float the AUDITORIUM BUILDING (1889). In 1894 Adler & Sullivan developed a type of caisson construction for the Chicago Stock Exchange which quickly became routine for tall buildings across the United States.

The early structures of the First Chicago School, such as the Montauk and the Auditorium, had traditional load-bearing walls of brick and stone, but it was the metal skeleton frame that allowed the architects of the First Chicago School to perfect their signature edifice, the SKYSCRAPER. William Le Baron Jenney constructed the world's first completely IRON-AND-STEEL-framed building in the 1880s. Jenney had in 1853 enrolled in Paris's prestigious École Centrale des Arts et Manufactures. (Among his classmates was Gustave Eiffel.) During the Civil War Jenney had been assigned the task of demolishing buildings and bridges. In the process he had mastered the nuances of metal construction.

In 1868 Jenney established an office in Chicago which became the training ground for a number of leading architects of the First Chicago School, including, among others, Martin Roche, William Holabird, and Louis Sullivan. When, in 1884, the Home Insurance Company asked Jenney to design an office tower, the architect designed an iron skeleton to bear the weight of the structure. After work began, the Carnegie-Phipps Steel Company, realizing the potential of a vast new market, informed Jenney that it could supply him with steel instead of iron beams. Thus the Home Insurance Building at the northeast corner of LaSalle and Adams Streets became a truly seminal structure.

This new construction, while costly, had overwhelming advantages. It was almost fireproof; the thin curtain walls hung from the steel frame allowed for more interior rental space; new floors could be added easily; and since the exterior walls were no longer essential to holding up the building, they could be cut away and replaced by ever larger expanses of glass, an important consideration in the early era of electrical lighting.

While the technical innovations of the First Chicago School had been sensational, what it needed to become a truly notable architectural movement was style. The exterior of the Home Insurance Building, with its gray and green stone columns and its brick upper floors embellished by stone stringcourses and pilasters, was, to say the least, banal. The First Chicago School found its inspiration for style in two totally disparate sources. One was the Louisiana-born architect Henry Hobson Richardson. Although he was trained at the École des Beaux-Arts in Paris, Richardson rejected the *école*'s dictum that the Greek and Roman

Louis Henri Sullivan and the Chicago School

Louis Henri Sullivan, one of America's greatest architects and a key figure in the Chicago School of Architecture, was born in Boston in 1856. His training included a stint at MIT, the École des Beaux-Arts in Paris, and training with Ph.D. architect Frank Furness.

Sullivan worked initially for W. L. B. Jenney soon after he joined his parents in Chicago in 1873. Sullivan's partnership with Dankmar Adler began in 1879, and their first important project was the Central Music Hall in Chicago. The success of the Music Hall and other projects led in 1886 to the commission for the AUDITORIUM BUILDING. While the structure's limestone and granite Romanesque Revival exterior is a stylistic tribute to Sullivan's hero, Henry Hobson Richardson, the flowing foliate decoration of its interior spaces are among the world's earliest examples of art nouveau. At the WORLD'S COLUMBIAN EXPOSITION held in Chicago in 1893, Sullivan's Transportation Building, with its shimmering gold-leafed entrance, boldly dramatized his rejection of the classically inspired Beaux-Arts architecture of the "White City."

The national depression of the 1890s had a devastating effect upon the Adler & Sullivan office and the partnership ended in 1895. This, together with the dominance of the Beaux-Arts architectural style, led to a spiraling downward of Sullivan's career. He would, though, design a small number of superb buildings, including the Schlesinger & Mayer Store in Chicago—now Carson Pirie Scott & Co. He also wrote *The Autobiography of an Idea* before his death in 1924.

David Garrard Lowe

classical style was the ultimate standard of design. Instead, his ideal was the rugged Romanesque of the South of France. In 1870 on Boston's Commonwealth Avenue, Richardson designed the trailblazing Romanesque revival Brattle Square Church, whose tower fired the architectural aspirations of Boston native Louis Sullivan when he was a student at the Massachusetts Institute of Technology. And it was the revelatory presence of Richardson's Marshall Field WHOLESALE Store of 1885, filling the block bounded by Adams, Quincy, Wells, and Franklin Streets, that radically altered the design of Adler & Sullivan's Auditorium Building. Sullivan's original sketches were for an eclectic structure terminating in a high, gabled roof. After the appearance of the Field edifice, Sullivan swept away his original plans and replaced them with a virile, restrained Romanesque revival structure with a single massive tower.

Louis Sullivan was not the only member of the First Chicago School to fall under the spell of Richardsonian Romanesque. It was essential to the designs of Solon S. Beman for the brick and granite Pullman Building of 1883 on Michigan Avenue and the Fine Arts Building of 1885, also on Michigan Avenue. Burnham & Root embraced the Romanesque for the ART INSTITUTE next to the Fine Arts Building and for the Rookery on LaSalle Street, completed in 1888. But it was Sullivan, with his interior of the Auditorium Theater and the entrance to the Chicago Stock Exchange of 1894 on LaSalle Street, who brought Chicago Romanesque to its most complete and impressive development.

The second source of style for the architects of the First Chicago School derived from the very nature of the material they so wholeheartedly adopted: steel. This, curiously, was in contradiction to Richardson's aesthetic principles. He unequivocally rejected the concept of the metal-framed building, championing instead lithic structures with load-bearing walls like his superb Trinity Church, Boston, of 1873. When the architects of the First Chicago School built in stone they generally did so in a Richardsonian Romanesque style. Adler & Sullivan's Walker Warehouse of 1888, which stood on what became Wacker Drive, and the lower floors of Burnham & Root's Masonic Temple Building of 1890 at the corner of State and Randolph Streets are cases in point. But when the Chicago architects moved to metal—iron and steel—they enthusiastically expressed the qualities of the material. This led in two directions. One of the realities of the material was that it lent itself to the sinuous curve, which led Chicago architects, as it did their European contemporaries such as Hector Guimard, to art nouveau. Superb examples include the original design of the light court of the Rookery and the stairways and elevator grills in Adler & Sullivan's Chicago Stock Exchange.

The second aesthetic implication of iron and steel was the right angle, daringly expressed in Holabird and Roche's Tacoma Building of 1889 at the corner of Madison and LaSalle Streets. The 13-story office tower, the first building constructed by using rivets, revealed in its sharp angles the steel structure beneath its curtain walls. This aesthetic was also the controlling factor in the upper floors of Adler & Sullivan's Stock Exchange, where the Romanesque arches of the base were eschewed above for a soaring, simplified elevation whose sole decorative element was the interplay of the planes of the flat wall surface against those of the rhythmic bays. This celebration of the rigid nature of metal is perhaps most brilliantly exemplified by Burnham & Root's Reliance Building (1895) on State Street, completed by Charles B. Atwood after Root's death. There is about the Reliance a marvelous sense of the sharp, almost dangerous, edges of the steel frame lying just beneath its thin, white terra cotta walls. This sensation is enhanced by the

The Rookery Building, 209 South LaSalle, Burnham & Root, late 1880s. Photographer: Unknown. Source: Chicago Historical Society.

fact that two-thirds of the walls are of glass, producing a structure of rare, brittle beauty.

The eclipse of the First Chicago School by an architecture based upon the classical as interpreted by the École des Beaux-Arts was signaled by the WORLD'S COLUMBIAN EXPOSITION held in Chicago in 1893. Louis Sullivan and other architects of the school had expected that the fair, under the architectural direction of Daniel H. Burnham and John Wellborn Root, would be a showcase for Chicago's architecture. But the death of Root in January 1891 ended that hope. Burnham, then the most important architectural voice of the fair, turned for direction to New Yorker Richard Morris Hunt, dean of American architects, who was the first American to graduate from the architectural section of the École des Beaux-Arts. Though Adler & Sullivan designed a spectacularly non-Beaux-Arts Transportation Building for the fair, the style of "The White City" was overwhelmingly Beaux-Arts.

Nonetheless, the First Chicago School was an astonishing and a profoundly important achievement. Its matchless tradition of technical prowess and aesthetic boldness would surface again in Chicago in the 1930s with the arrival of the Bauhaus, and in the following decades in the work of Ludwig Mies van der Rohe and his disciples.

David Garrard Lowe

See also: Built Environment of the Chicago Region; Church Architecture; City as Artifact; Commercial Buildings; Historic Preservation; Public Buildings in the Loop

Further reading: Condit, Carl W. *The Chicago School of Architecture: A History of Commercial and Public Building in the Chicago Area, 1875–1925.* 1964. • Lowe, David Garrard. *The Great Chicago Fire*

in Eyewitness Accounts and Seventy Contemporary Photographs and Illustrations. 1979. • Morrison, Hugh. *Louis Sullivan: Prophet of Modern Architecture.* 1952.

THE CITY BEAUTIFUL MOVEMENT. In Henry Blake Fuller's 1895 novel, *With the Procession*, the artistic young Truesdale Marshall, just returned home from a prolonged grand tour, looked upon his native Chicago as a "hideous monster, a piteous, floundering monster too. It almost called for tears. Nowhere a more tireless activity, yet nowhere a result so pitifully grotesque, gruesome, appalling." Marshall was not alone: many observers of late-nineteenth- and early-twentieth-century America—residents, visitors, and expatriates alike—believed that its cities were ugly. The shapelessness of American cities was due in large measure to the extraordinary speed with which they had developed: between 1860 and 1910, the number of American cities with more than 100,000 residents rose from 8 to 50. By 1910, several cities had passed the one million mark. Such statistics are crucial to understanding the City Beautiful impulse. Despite its preoccupation with aesthetic effect, the movement concerned far more than facade: the quest for beauty paralleled the search for the functional and humane city. Urban PLANNING as the twentieth century would know it developed out of the City Beautiful—both as a phase of it and a reaction to it—and its coalition of planners, of paid experts and unpaid volunteers, of architects, ARTISTS, civic officials, journalists, business people, and interested ordinary citizens.

Daniel Hudson Burnham was indisputably the "Father of the City Beautiful." As director of works of the WORLD'S COLUMBIAN EXPOSITION (1893), he effectively launched the movement that 15 years later would reach its apogee in his epochal *Plan of Chicago* (1909). Burnham's importance as an architect and planner lay chiefly in his ability to direct and stimulate the design efforts of others. His own credo captured the essence of his life and work: "Make no little plans, they have no magic to stir men's blood. . . . Make big plans . . . remembering that a noble, logical diagram once recorded will never die, but long after we are gone will be a living thing asserting itself with ever growing consistency." In his various architectural and planning pursuits, Burnham choreographed large efforts indeed.

Carson Pirie Scott entrance, 1960. Louis Sullivan's design for the massive department store, known as Schlesinger & Mayer for a short time after its opening in 1903, attracted shoppers with elegant ornamentation designed by Sullivan and George Elmslie. Photographer: Hedrich-Blessing. Source: Chicago Historical Society.

Burnham moved with his parents to Chicago in 1854. He became an architect by apprenticing first with William Le Baron Jenney and then in the office of Peter B. Wight, where he met his future partner, John Wellborn Root. Through the 1870s and 1880s, Burnham & Root, and such contemporaries as Adler & Sullivan and Holabird & Roche, helped rebuild the city that had been destroyed in the FIRE OF 1871. In so doing, they developed what would come to be called the Chicago School of SKYSCRAPER architecture. Following Root's premature death in 1891, Burnham turned to a succession of designers, but he never found one who complemented his own talents as completely as Root. With Root's death, Burnham lost both his design gyroscope and his aesthetic self-confidence, and he turned increasingly to the "authority" of historicism. In the 20 years between Root's death and his own, Burnham found his greatest fulfillment as the leader of the City Beautiful movement—an effort to achieve for American cities something approaching a "cultural parity" with Europe's great urban centers.

The central ideological conflict surrounding the City Beautiful pitted invention and INNOVATION against continuity and tradition. The newness and cultural nationalism espoused by Louis Sullivan and Frank Lloyd Wright lay in their quest for a uniquely "American" culture, one with maturity and confidence enough to cease relying so heavily on Old World traditions. Burnham and his allies, by contrast, believed that the sometimes frantic quest for "American-ness"—the obsession with New World originality and horror of all things European—was itself a kind of insecurity, and that maturity would consist in an acknowledgment that America was not culturally isolated from the rest of the world. Burnham and his associates saw the United States as a rightful heir to the traditions of Western culture and chose thus to recall, celebrate, and use those traditions themselves.

Indeed, Europe and its traditions could provide a standard by which critics of America's urban "ugliness" could appeal to the consciousness of a larger constituency. Complementing their "muckraking" contemporaries in JOURNALISM, architects could embarrass

Statue of the Republic and Grand Basin, at the 1893 World's Columbian Exposition. Photographer: Unknown. Source: Chicago Historical Society.

civic leaders into realizing that in civic amenities as in social and political equity, America was somehow woefully behind. City Beautiful advocates could invoke Fuller's heroine: "Keep up with the procession is my motto and lead it if you can."

"Procession" is an apt metaphor for the City Beautiful. However eclectic it became in its borrowings and whatever the style of particular buildings within its plans, the provenance and thrust of City Beautiful planning was classical and Baroque in its emphasis upon processions of buildings and open spaces arranged in groups. For the parallax effect, it depended on the movement of the individual, or the human procession, through space from one specific point to another. Great buildings or monuments were sited so as to become the terminal vistas of long, converging, diagonal axes. The impact on the individual of this arrangement, repetition, and ceremonial procession was, in the Baroque and in the City Beautiful, calculatedly powerful, impressive, and moving.

Burnham launched the City Beautiful movement at the 1893 World's Fair. While the relatively informal lagoon area on the north side of the fairgrounds reflected the picturesque preferences of Frederick Law Olmsted—the designer of New York City's Central Park and a participant in the fair's planning from its earliest sessions—the stately and well-ordered White City formed the seminal image of the City Beautiful approach. Several of the fair's architects had in fact studied at the Parisian École des Beaux-Arts and had garnered their penchant for neoclassicism there. All were imbued with the formal, ordered, and axially oriented imperatives generally associated with Beaux-Arts aesthetics—a point of view that would dominate most City Beautiful design.

The resulting ensemble of neoclassical temples, especially impressive when lighted at night, had much of the "twinkle" and iridescence that Henry James had found in Paris. It was at the World's Fair that Wisconsin historian Frederick Jackson Turner lamented the "end" of the American frontier; but it was there as well that urban reformers drew a suggestive vision of new, *urban* frontiers. The journalist Henry Demarest Lloyd thought the White City revealed to its visitors "possibilities of social beauty, utility, and harmony of which they had not been able even to dream." Henry Adams and William Dean Howells saw it as a suggestive model for the planning of actual cities. The builders of the temporary city had, after all, struggled with the problems posed by actual cities, from the efficacy of streets, sidewalks, WATERFRONTS, and BRIDGES, to the realities of sustenance, TRANSPORTATION, and sewage. But the White City and the movement it embodied continued to have detractors as well. Louis Sullivan saw its influence as a virus that would afflict American architecture for 50 years. Each side of the debate might have taken a different moral from the fact that one of the manual laborers working to create the fantasy was a man by the name of Elias Disney—father of Walt.

For more than a decade following the fair, Chicago lagged behind other cities in the realm of urban planning. Yet during those years Burnham conceived and directed City Beautiful plans for Washington DC (1902), Cleveland (1903), Manila (1904), and San Francisco (1905) from inside his Chicago office. His work also inspired the efforts of other City Beautiful planners, most notably Charles Mulford Robinson and Frederick Law Olmsted, Jr.

The apogee of the City Beautiful came 16 years after the fair in Burnham and Edward Bennett's *Plan of Chicago,* which unified the goals of City Beautiful and City Practical with unprecedented success. Never before had one "city plan" taken into account so much of the surrounding region. The plan encompassed the development of Chicago within a 60-mile radius via a system of radial and concentric boulevards that connected the center to its outlying suburbs and linked the suburbs one with another. One of the plan's most prescient recommendations was for what would become, in Wacker Drive, the modern world's first double-level boulevard for regular and commercial traffic. The CHICAGO RIVER would be straightened and enhanced for more efficient WATER transportation and river-borne commerce. The stations and tracks of competing rail lines would be consolidated into several train stations. A lakefront park system would run 20 miles along Lake Michigan. The elegant, formal downtown would culminate in a refurbished GRANT PARK that would be eastwardly inflected toward a new inner harbor with breakwater causeways stretching far into the lake. At the southern edges of this central park would rise such grandly neoclassical buildings as the SHEDD AQUARIUM and the FIELD MUSEUM OF NATURAL HISTORY, counterpoints to the ART INSTITUTE OF CHICAGO on the park's northern edge. The number and quality of the city's outlying parks would be increased, enhanced, and unified into an integral network.

Parks were central to the City Beautiful impulse and to Burnham's sense of civic harmony. "Fifty years ago," he explained, "before population had become dense in certain parts of the city, people could live without parks, but we of today cannot." Good citizenship, he argued, was "the prime object of good city planning." Civic renewal more generally, Burnham believed, could provide healthy activities to those citizens who could not afford extensive traveling and who thus depended on the city for recreational and cultural enrichment. He worried about the problems that "congestion in city streets begets; at the toll of lives taken by disease when sanitary precautions are neglected." If such needs could be met, Burnham had confidence that "Chicago would be taking a long step toward cementing together the heterogeneous elements of our population, and toward assimilating the million and a half of

Wacker Drive was initially part of Daniel H. Burnham's 1909 *Plan of Chicago*. He envisioned a two-level street to replace the South Water Street Market. This segment, designed by Edward H. Bennett and completed in 1926, is seen here within a decade after construction. Photographer: Unknown. Source: Chicago Historical Society.

people who are here now but who were not here fifteen years ago."

Privately financed in its early stages by the COMMERCIAL CLUB, the BURNHAM PLAN was presented as a gift to the city, which appointed a commission to oversee its development. The Chicago school board agreed to use an elementary version of Burnham's report as an eighth-grade civics textbook. Ministers and rabbis throughout the city delivered sermons on the plan's importance. Brochures, a slide lecture series, a two-reel motion picture, and other advanced promotional devices made their way into people's homes. It was a masterfully orchestrated propaganda campaign. The most important years in the plan's realization were the two decades between its publication in 1909 and the beginning of the GREAT DEPRESSION in 1929. In the teens and twenties, costs exceeded $300 million. For the rest of the century, the Burnham Plan would serve as a base point for the city's changing needs and as proof, perhaps, of Burnham's belief that "a noble, logical diagram once recorded will never die."

Thomas S. Hines

See also: Built Environment of the Chicago Region; Landscape Design

Further reading: Burnham, Daniel H., and Edward H. Bennett. *Plan of Chicago*, ed. Charles Moore. 1909. • Fuller, Henry Blake. *With the Procession*. 1895; 1965. • Hines, Thomas S. *Burnham of Chicago: Architect and Planner*. 1974.

Plan of Chicago: Michigan Avenue northward. From a rendering by Jules Guerin. Source: Chicago Historical Society.

THE PRAIRIE SCHOOL. The Prairie School was a primarily residential architectural movement that began in Chicago yet rapidly spread across the Midwest. Ultimately its influence was felt around the world—most especially in north-central Europe and Australia. Its origins date from the 1890s. Its vitality was largely sapped during the First World War, when homebuilders' attitudes turned conservative and thereafter shunned building concepts that expressed an *idea* rather than traditional architectural forms—ideas such as the relevance of a building to nature and the landscape, the visual expression of natural materials (rather than concealing them behind paint and wallpaper), or the idea of abandoning small, boxy rooms in favor of a more open, integrated interior space.

What, then, nurtured the founding of the Prairie School? First of all, a reservoir of potential clients brought up on the values of the Arts and Crafts movement, those who read the *Craftsman* magazine and the numerous BUNGALOW books and often dabbled in the arts and crafts themselves—whether by making ceramics, doing woodworking, or binding books. By 1916 the *Craftsman* ceased publication for lack of readers, and this date coincides closely with the demise of the Prairie School.

A second factor nourishing the emergence of the Prairie School was the existence of a small group of dedicated individuals obsessed with the idea of creating a new American architecture, an architecture appropriate to the American Midwest and independent of historical styles. The movement attracted more than a score of young men and women, the best known being Louis H. Sullivan and Frank Lloyd Wright.

Louis Sullivan inspired and promoted the movement through the inventive example of his work, his compelling manner of writing and lecturing, and his influence on the many designers who apprenticed in his office. These included Frank Lloyd Wright, George Grant Elmslie, William Purcell, Parker Berry, William E. Drummond, and William L. Steele. Although Sullivan evinced little interest in residential design, his ideas inspired a younger generation. He preached that one must go to school to nature, and this is precisely what the Prairie School architects did.

Among these younger architects, Frank Lloyd Wright was unquestionably the most gifted. Nevertheless, despite his natural talent, it required a full decade—following his six-year apprenticeship with Sullivan—to evolve a fully mature idiom of his own. The Robert W. Roloson rowhouses at 3213–19 S. Calumet, designed in 1894, show the influence of Sullivan on Wright's work. Others, most notably George W. Maher, Hugh M. G. Garden, Robert C. Spencer, Jr., and William E. Drummond, were also creating significant and original work. Yet their designs, with the exception of George Maher's, ultimately proved less viable than the work of Wright.

Maher's work continually enjoyed widespread support from Midwest clients. His genius lay in combining highly personal, original forms that eschewed historicism yet simultaneously embodied the conservative values cherished by his clients; his house designs expressed stability, permanence, and the acquired social status of its inhabitants.

Several of these young architects began sharing loft space in Dwight Perkins's newly built Steinway Hall in the LOOP; this gathering commenced during the winter of 1896–97 and at various times included Perkins, Spencer, and Wright, as well as Myron Hunt, Walter Burley Griffin, Marion Mahony Griffin, and others. The result was a vigorous intellectual and artistic interchange.

But when Wright built a studio next to his OAK PARK home, some among the group, most notably Griffin, were enticed away from Steinway Hall; others just entering the profession also sought apprenticeship at Oak Park—especially after seeing Wright's celebrated exhibition at the Chicago Architectural Club in March 1902. The studio staff at different times included Mahony, Drummond, Griffin, and Barry Byrne. When Griffin left during the winter of 1905–06, Drummond took his place as office manager and chief draftsman, a post later assumed by Robinson. Among the Chicago-area homes designed during these years are the Frederick C. Robie house in HYDE PARK and the Laura Gale, Peter A. Beachy, and Frank W. Thomas houses in Oak Park.

In 1909 Wright closed his Oak Park studio and left for Europe, leaving his remaining employees to enter private practice or join the employ of others—Griffin being the most sought after in this regard. Also in 1909, Elmslie, after spending 20 years in Sullivan's employ, joined Purcell in partnership (George Feick, Jr., was briefly in the firm). The remarkable quality and quantity of their designs attracted commissions for a wide variety of buildings—not just houses but banks, churches, courthouses, stores, and factories. Much of their work was executed in Minnesota.

In 1911 the influential *Western Architect* of Minneapolis switched its editorial policy to favor the Prairie School. For the next five years

Midway Gardens at Cottage Grove Avenue and the Midway, designed by Frank Lloyd Wright, seen here shortly after construction in 1914. Photographer: J. W. Taylor. Source: Chicago Historical Society.

this widely read monthly devoted numerous issues to these architects. These profusely illustrated editions influenced home builders and commercial clients to favor Prairie School and had immediate repercussions on architects in smaller communities across the Midwest and Canada. An illustrative example was Percy Dwight Bentley of La Crosse, Wisconsin, on the banks of the Mississippi. Upon entering private practice, and without the advantage of studying under the movement's notable architects, he immediately began producing designs of the highest quality in the Prairie School mode until after World War I, when his clients began to demand buildings in the Colonial style.

Also in 1911, Walter Burley Griffin, a gifted LANDSCAPE ARCHITECT, entered the international competition for the design of Canberra, the capital city then being planned for the newly independent nation of Australia. Aided by Marion Lucy Mahony's beautiful rendering of his plans, he won this internationally prestigious event in 1912. Canberra stands as Griffin's greatest gift to posterity; despite the distortion of his brilliant scheme by government bureaucrats.

Although Griffin and Mahony, who married in 1911, continued to garner commissions in the United States until after 1915, their energies increasingly focused on Australia, where today they are known as the founders of modern architecture. In 1935, Walter was awarded the contract to design the Lucknow University Library and thereafter removed to India where he received scores of commissions (mostly from Indians rather than the British) before his untimely death in 1937.

Meanwhile Wright had returned from Europe in 1911 and began building Taliesin, his new single-story home near Spring Green, Wisconsin; this was lower and more informal than his earlier prairie houses. As with Griffin, Wright's focus of activity soon shifted west once he procured the commission to design the Imperial Hotel in Tokyo, Japan, which kept him busy until 1922. Repeated trips to Japan by way of Southern California introduced Wright to a new landscape and climate as well as to less conservative clients; this resulted in commissions to design the Barnsdall and various textile-block houses in California during the late teens and early twenties.

Sullivan, between 1906 and 1919, was designing a brilliant series of small-town Midwest banks plus two stately homes and a few low-rise commercial buildings. But he, like the others, had few new commissions after 1919. While Griffin and Wright benefitted from opportunities on the Pacific Rim, these architects who remained in the midwest generally found it necessary to compromise their ideals and design in historical styles. Only Maher's compositions retained a certain, although diminished, public appeal. The intense wave of conservatism that swept the country after the First World War, combined with the demise of the Arts and Crafts movement, signaled a change in taste away from the values of the Prairie School.

H. Allen Brooks

See also: Built Environment of the Chicago Region; Housing Types; Landscape Design

Further reading: Brooks, H. Allen. *Frank Lloyd Wright and the Prairie School.* 1984. • Brooks, H. Allen. *Prairie School Architecture: Studies from the "Western Architect."* 1975. • Brooks, H. Allen. *The Prairie School: Frank Lloyd Wright and His Midwest Contemporaries.* 1996.

THE SECOND CHICAGO SCHOOL. Following the fallow years of WORLD WAR II, residential architecture in Chicago began to reappear as early as the late 1940s, mostly in the form of APARTMENT towers, while the resumption of COMMERCIAL BUILDING waited until roughly a decade later. The two building types, more than any other, represent the functional and stylistic characteristics associated with the Second Chicago School.

The origins of the movement are traceable to two powerfully interactive factors: the advent of modernist architecture as a whole in America and the arrival in Chicago of a single, highly influential figure, Ludwig Mies van der Rohe. One of the major pioneers in the development of modernism in Europe, Mies emigrated from his native Germany in 1937 to assume the headship of the School of Architecture at Chicago's Armour Institute of Technology (later ILLINOIS INSTITUTE OF TECHNOLOGY [IIT]). Several of his important European contemporaries, chiefly Walter Gropius and Marcel Breuer, also took up residence in the United States in the 1930s, where, like him, they sought to advance the cause of modernism by eliminating overt historicist references in building design and concentrating more on neutral forms stripped of ornament and suggestive of a machine technology.

But it was Mies who responded the most creatively to the change of scene, and Chicago proved a locale most nearly ideal in nurturing his ambitions. His first assignment was the reconstitution of virtually the whole of the IIT campus, a commission that did not reach building stage until the last years of World War II but which attracted considerable national attention. In the late 1940s, moreover, Mies had the good fortune to establish a connection with Chicago developer Herbert Greenwald, who appointed him to design a number of high-rise apartment buildings in which he gave further material form to the core principles that occupied him during his American period. Once ensconced in Chicago, he came to regard structure in the abstract as the most important objective of the building art, more than the plan (which was central to his major European work) or the surface treatment of the elevation—hence the emphasis in his American career on the rectilinear frame constructed of familiar industrial building elements that included most notably the wide-flange beam. The standard Miesian building is dependent for its exterior structural materials chiefly on steel (occasionally reinforced concrete) for vertical and horizontal members and glass in broad expanses for fenestration.

By the early 1950s Mies the teacher had begun to produce a generation of students deeply committed to his point of view, while Mies the architect affected just as many independent designers who were impressed by the quality of his built work. These influences made themselves felt most in Chicago, and by the late 1950s, when the city's building as a whole resumed at a brisk pace, the first works suggesting the presence of a Miesian school had been realized. Nonetheless, as the fifties passed into the sixties, the term "Miesian" seemed too personal to accommodate a growing body of Chicago architecture indebted to him but not directly imitative of him, and the notion of a *Chicago* school gained currency. The stylistic features alluded to here fitted much of the work in question, and in some quarters an effort was made to show a kinship with what had come to be regarded as a *first* Chicago school, centering on the metal cage and undecorated (or nearly undecorated) frame of the building. Nevertheless, there are as many differences of expressive intent as similarities between the two groups.

The first large firm to put up the steel and glass high-rise buildings that conform to the main features of the Second School was the Chicago office of Skidmore, Owings & Merrill (SOM). The Inland Steel Building of 1957, the first commercial structure to rise in the LOOP following World War II, was notable for its stainless steel frame, its columns placed outside the curtain wall, and its column-free interior. The two SOM commercial buildings regarded most highly by critics are among the tallest in the city: the John Hancock Center (1969), with its tapering wedge-shaped volume and diagonal exterior bracing, and the 1,454-foot-high Sears Tower (1974), the loftiest building in the United States. Both of these structures are examples of the tubular frame, in which the load is carried not by the traditional cage but mostly by exterior walls conceived as tubes rectangular in plan. (The Sears Tower is composed of nine bundled tubes.) The major architects at SOM

S. R. Crown Hall, College of Architecture, Illinois Institute of Technology, 3630 South State Street, was designed by Ludwig Mies van der Rohe and completed in 1956. Photographer: Unknown. Source: Chicago Historical Society.

Bruce Graham on Modernism

Graham, an architect, designed both the John Hancock Center (1970) and the Sears Tower (1974).

[Y]ou do modern architecture . . . in search of a vocabulary for your country, your city and the architecture you're doing. . . . Most people don't understand architecture. Architecture is the design of space, both interior and exterior. So it's much more closely related to dance than it is to painting or sculpture. Most New York buildings are sculpture. They don't have any sense of space. And it's the idea, of course, in modern architecture . . . to express that space so the *people* understand it rather than imperial palaces and imperial avenues. To look for the character of Chicago, for example. This is what I would call a democratic formed city. The grid . . . means all spaces are equal. That's not true in Paris. Not true in Berlin. It's not true in any of the imperial cities. [A]nd that search for creating as I call a dance is what tells you what's a good architect and what's a bad architect. They don't have the sense of movement of spacing. . . . For example, I'll never forget when the taxi drivers loved the Hancock Building best. And I said that's exactly what I want. I want *them* to understand it; not the people in Wilmette.

Graham, Bruce. Interview with Timothy J. Gilfoyle, Loyola University, on the occasion of the 1999 Making History Awards, Chicago Historical Society.

Looking east on Chestnut Street at the John Hancock Building, 1979. Photographer: Unknown. Source: Chicago Public Library.

who helped significantly to define the character of the Second Chicago School were Myron Goldsmith, Bruce Graham, Fazlur Khan (who was primarily active as an engineer), and Walter Netsch.

C. F. Murphy Associates was responsible for several works of comparable distinction. McCormick Place East (1971), a convention hall notable for its immense trussed roof and recessed glass walls, was designed principally by Gene Summers, a former student of Mies, who based his concept largely on his teacher's 1967 National Gallery in Berlin. Moreover, while credit for the courtroom and office building known as the Richard J. Daley Civic Center belongs as surely to Skidmore, Owings & Merrill and to Loebl, Schlossman & Bennett as to C. F. Murphy Associates, the chief designer was the Murphy firm's Jacques Brownson, another former Mies student. The Daley Center is visually striking for its cladding in Cor-Ten steel, a material identified with the 1960s, but structurally compelling in its huge 87-by-48-foot bays, at the time unprecedented in their dimensions. Most of the buildings erected at O'Hare International Airport were done in the 1960s and 1970s by C. F. Murphy Associates, the majority in deference to Second School principles.

In 1981 the firm changed its name to Murphy/Jahn, acknowledging the role of Helmut Jahn, a German-born architect trained at IIT (though not by Mies), who built the United Airlines Terminal at O'Hare as well as other structures in the Chicago area, although strictly speaking none belong to the Second Chicago School.

Comparably problematical as members of the movement were Bertrand Goldberg and Harry Weese, whose work was more often than not too much their own to be classified with any specific school. Yet it is hard to avoid a reference to Goldberg's Marina City. These twin towers, put up in 1964 and 1967, are composed of concrete, with loads carried by cylindrical cores rather than the usual steel cage-frame, but their outer appearance is declaratively structural. And while Weese was preoccupied more with residential than commercial architecture, no tall building in the city displays a facade more typical of the Chicago frame than his Time-Life Building of 1970.

The seminal role Mies played in the Second Chicago School is apparent in yet another work by his students. In 1968 George Schipporeit and John Heinrich completed Lake Point Tower, an apartment building whose 645-foot height qualified it at the time as the tallest reinforced concrete structure in the world. Once again, a project by the master, an unbuilt 1921 proposal for a glass skyscraper, served as the inspiration for the three sinuously curved lobes that constitute the most striking exterior feature of the building.

Mies himself contributed several works that belong clearly to the Second Chicago School. The most celebrated of these is the pair of apartment towers at 860–880 Lake Shore

Bertram Goldberg's curvilinear design of Marina City (seen here from the east in 1965) stands in sharp contrast to the more general angularity of the modernist style. Photographer: Hedrich-Blessing. Source: Chicago Historical Society.

Drive (1951), which provided the first major realized example of the steel and glass structure that became paradigmatic of the Second School. An even larger enterprise, the Federal Center, erected between 1964 and 1971, consists of a courtroom building, an office building (both curtain-wall structures) and a one-story pavilion occupied by a post office, a threesome that overlooks one of the three great plazas running north and south through Chicago's Loop. The tallest work in Mies's Chicago catalog is the IBM Building of 1971, which takes full advantage of its highly visible site on the north bank of the CHICAGO RIVER.

While the Second Chicago School for the most part came to an end in the mid-1970s, several later structures have exhibited the structural straightforwardness associated with it. Principal among these is the Morton International Building of 1990, designed by Perkins & Will, with Ralph Johnson in supervising capacity. In the 1980s the postmodernist movement began to persuade many observers that the Chicago frame, whose structural neutrality differentiated hardly at all between a courthouse, an apartment tower, an office building, and a convention hall, lacked the symbolic distinctions postmodernism sought to revive. By that time, of course, many of the principals of the large firms had retired, and Mies himself was dead.

Franz Schulze

See also: Built Environment of the Chicago Region; Places of Assembly; Public Buildings in the Loop

Further reading: Schulze, Franz, and Kevin Harrington, eds. *Chicago's Famous Buildings.* 1993.

The 1966 demolition of the old Post Office, with the new Federal Building in the background. Photographer: Gustav D. Frank. Source: Chicago Historical Society.

• Zukowsky, John, ed. *Chicago Architecture and Design, 1923–1993: Reconfiguration of an American Metropolis.* 1993. • Zukowsky, John, ed. *Chicago Architecture, 1872–1922: Birth of a Metropolis.* 1987.

Argentinians. Argentinians have tended to assimilate more quickly into the local population than most other Latin American groups in the United States. Descending mostly from ITALIANS, SPANIARDS, GERMANS, RUSSIANS, POLES, and other Europeans, Argentinian immigrants have generally identified with Euro-American ethnic groups in Chicago. The majority of Argentinians in Chicago are ROMAN CATHOLICS and JEWS.

Immigrants from Argentina have been arriving in Chicago since at least the 1920s, according to the Argentine consulate's offices, which opened in 1927. Most came from Buenos Aires, the capital. Generally, the male head of household arrived first, bringing his family later. Since the 1930s, a steady flow of students has come to Chicago to attend area universities, with many eventually settling permanently in the metropolitan area.

Immigration has tended to follow political events in Argentina. In the 1950s and 1960s, many college students and professionals left the country when the universities were closed down by the government and the economic situation was not favorable. During the political turmoil of the 1970s and 1980s, Argentinians arrived in Chicago as REFUGEES, sponsored by the Lutheran Church and the United Nations.

SOCCER (or *futbol,* as it is known in Argentina) constitutes one of the major recreational activities of Argentinians in Chicago, and the Chicago Pampas soccer club is especially important. Other organizations include the Casa Argentina, a social club with approximately 75 members who gather weekly to play soccer and mingle. The Argentine American Medical Association of the Midwest represents the disproportionately large number of doctors among Argentinian immigrants. Both groups hold special events to commemorate Argentina's national holidays and celebrations with tango music and dancing as well as picnics in the summer.

The popularity of tango music and dancing during the closing years of the twentieth century brought Argentinians into the limelight, evidenced in performances, films, musical revues, and several schools of DANCE, which along with RESTAURANTS, have helped to reverse the earlier invisibility of Chicago's Argentinians.

Beatriz Badikian-Gartler

See also: Demography; Multicentered Chicago

Further reading: Bethell, Leslie, ed. *Argentina since Independence.* 1993. • Foster, David William. *Buenos Aires: Perspectives on the City and Cultural Production.* 1998. • Simpson, John, and Jana Bennett. *The Disappeared and the Mothers of the Plaza: The Story of the Eleven Thousand Argentinians Who Vanished.* 1985.

Argonne National Laboratory, 1956. Photographer: Hubert Henry, Hedrich-Blessing. Source: Chicago Historical Society.

Argo. *See* Summit, IL

Argonne National Laboratory.

Located on 1,700 acres 25 miles southwest of Chicago on Interstate Highway 55, Argonne National Laboratory is one of the U.S. Department of Energy's nine multiprogram scientific laboratories. Established in 1941 as the UNIVERSITY OF CHICAGO's Metallurgical Laboratory (Met Lab), the laboratory was part of the MANHATTAN PROJECT that built America's atomic bomb.

Following WORLD WAR II, the U.S. government continued nuclear research and development at the University of Chicago by establishing Argonne as the first national laboratory on July 1, 1946. Initially, the Atomic Energy Commission designated Argonne as the commission's principal laboratory for nuclear reactor research and development. Other national laboratories shared this mission, however, and in time, Argonne itself became a multiprogram laboratory conducting basic research in physics, high energy physics, and nuclear physics; materials science; applied mathematics and computer science; and biology, medicine, and environmental sciences. From its inception as a national laboratory, Argonne has been operated and managed by the University of Chicago on behalf of the U.S. Atomic Energy Commission (1946–1974) and its successor agencies, the Energy Research and Development Administration (1974–1977), and the U.S. Department of Energy (1977).

From 1946 to 1996, Argonne's staff grew from 1,200 to more than 5,000, while its budget reached $500 million (out of $6.5 billion allocated to the nine national laboratories). Although the largest budget allocations went to the weapons laboratories, for 50 years Argonne's research and development agenda was driven by COLD-WAR priorities to maintain the United States' preeminence in science and technology. In 1994, however, the U.S. government canceled Argonne's Integral Fast Reactor program, leaving the United States without a nuclear reactor research and development program for the first time since 1942.

As a laboratory dedicated to the peaceful applications of science, Argonne has played a leading role in coordinating research and development among government, universities, and private industry. After the collapse of the nuclear reactor program, Argonne turned its attention to a new scientific project. The Advanced Photon Source (APS), dedicated in 1996, produces extremely bright x-ray breams for scientific research. With the ability to illuminate small objects with x-rays 10 billion times brighter than medical x-rays, the APS renewed Argonne's mission in basic and applied science while expanding cooperative research opportunities for materials scientists, chemists, geologists, biologists, engineers, physicians, and physicists from all sectors of the scientific community.

Jack M. Holl

See also: DuPage County; Fermilab; Innovation, Invention, and Chicago Business; Lemont

Further reading: Holl, Jack M. *Argonne National Laboratory, 1946–1996.* 1997.

Arlington Heights, IL, Cook and Lake Counties, 23 miles NW of the Loop. Arlington Heights lies in the southwest corner of Wheeling Township, in an area originally notable for the absence of groves and trees. When the General Land Office began selling land here in 1835, most of the buyers were YANKEES. In 1853 William Dunton, originally from Oswego, New York, persuaded the Illinois & Wisconsin RAILROAD to make a stop here, and laid out a town called Dunton.

By then the area had largely changed its ethnic composition, as many GERMAN farmers from Saxony had arrived during the 1840s. John Klehm might serve as an example; he was at first a potato farmer, supplying the Chicago market, and in 1856 began a nursery for cherry, apple, and pear trees, later moving into spruce, maple, and elm, and then flowers. By the late 1850s the area had become noted for its truck farms, sending dairy products as well as vegetables to Chicago on the railroad.

The little town at the depot slowly grew, acquiring a blacksmith, a cheese factory, a hardware store, and a hotel. It incorporated as Arlington Heights in 1887, when its population numbered about 1,000. Most were farmers, but they were joined by others who worked in

Chicago, for Arlington Heights was an early commuter suburb.

The town developed RELIGIOUS INSTITUTIONS that reflected the origins of its citizens; the first churches were Presbyterian (1856) and Methodist (1858), with a German Lutheran church following in 1860; Catholics had no church here until 1905.

By the turn of the century Arlington Heights had about 1,400 inhabitants, and it continued to grow slowly with a good many farms and greenhouses after WORLD WAR II. By then Arlington Heights was also known for its racetrack, founded in 1927 by the California millionaire H. D. "Curly" Brown upon land formerly consisting of 12 farms. Camp McDonald and two country clubs were founded in the 1930s.

The great population explosion took place in the 1950s and 1960s, when the spread of automobile ownership, together with the expansion of the Chicago-area economy, drove the number of people in Arlington Heights—expanded by a series of ANNEXATIONS—up to 64,884 by 1970. By then virtually all the available land had been taken up, and the formerly isolated depot stop found itself part of a continuous built-up area stretching from Lake Michigan to the Fox River.

David Buisseret

See also: Agriculture; Golf; Horse Racing; Religious Geography; Suburbs and Cities as Dual Metropolis

Further reading: *Chronicle of a Prairie Town: Arlington Heights, Illinois, Its People and Progress.* 1997.

Armenians. The first Armenians came to Chicago during the mid-1800s. Assisted by Protestant missionary teachers and ministers, single men immigrated to obtain an education or to pursue entrepreneurial endeavors in America, as well as to escape the oppression of the Ottoman TURKS. Many planned to return home.

Many of the earliest Armenians in Chicago attained considerable success, most notably the entrepreneurs in the oriental rug trade, which was dominated by Armenians. Some merchants exhibited their rugs at the WORLD'S COLUMBIAN EXPOSITION in 1893. The Armenian Professional Club was founded in 1900, and a scholarship association, the Armenian Educational Society, in 1906.

By the early 1900s, as persecution of Armenians continued in Turkey, Armenians began to realize that their stay in Chicago would be permanent, and the size of the community increased. In 1894 and again in 1909, tens of thousands of Armenians were massacred by Turkish authorities. By 1924 more than 100,000 Armenians had fled to the United States.

Chicago's small established Armenian community offered assistance to the REFUGEES. The Chicago chapter of the Armenian Red Cross helped Armenians locate and assist fleeing family members and orphans. The Armenian Colonial Association had an office in Chicago, which helped newcomers to settle and get jobs, as did the Armenian General Benevolent Union (Chicago chapter founded 1906).

This new generation of Armenian immigrants was initially unable to repeat their predecessors' rapid rise. Many served as laborers in the Pullman shops, the UNION STOCK YARD, or the steel mills of WAUKEGAN, WEST PULLMAN, and downstate Granite City. Since most were still single men or orphans and could not speak English, they lived in BOARDINGHOUSES and ORPHANAGES with other Armenians. These boardinghouses, as well as coffeehouses and communal bathhouses owned by Armenians, became comfortable centers for the new immigrant community, where men could gather on weekends to play backgammon or poker and eat keyma sandwiches.

By 1920, 1,200 Armenians, mostly male, lived in Chicago. With few women in the community, many Armenian men used contacts in other cities and back home to find so-called picture brides whom they married by arrangement. The new families settled in various neighborhoods, sharing houses on the North Side, as well as in EVANSTON, Waukegan, and Indiana Harbor. Between 30 and 60 families settled in West Pullman. Many tried to establish small businesses in West Pullman and elsewhere, especially as Armenian grocers, shoemakers, tailors, and rug merchants and repairers.

PROTESTANT and Armenian Apostolic churches were founded early and became the focal points of the community. The first Parish Council of the Armenian Apostolic Church (an independent branch of the EASTERN ORTHODOX church) was organized in Chicago in 1899 and officially designated as St. Gregory's Parish in 1915. Other early Armenian Apostolic parishes included Holy Savior Church in West Pullman (founded 1924) and St. James in Evanston. Protestant Armenians established their first congregation in 1899 and officially founded the Armenian Congregational Church of Chicago in 1916.

Armenian social and patriotic societies, as well as cultural groups, were formed in the 1920s and 1930s. Patriotic societies included Engerayeen Miyootyoon ("friendship society," WEST PULLMAN), Yeridasartaz Miyootyoon ("youth society," West Pullman), and Chomakhlutzee Patriotic Association (Evanston). In 1922 the AGBU Shant Theatrical Group was formed, and in 1931 the Philo Arts Club became the Armenian National Chorus. Two independent Armenian schools were also established in the 1920s, in West Pullman and Indiana Harbor.

The incorporation of Armenia within the Soviet Union in 1920 factionalized the Chicago community. The Armenian Revolutionary Federation (ARF; or "Tashnag"), was a wing of the ruling party of Armenian independence from 1918 to 1920. The ARF also developed a youth organization called Tzeghagron, which later became the Armenian Youth Federation. The Armenian Henchag Party published its newspaper, *Yeridasart Hayastan,* from its club at Adams and Halsted.The Harachteemagans (Armenian Progressive Party) became active in the 1930s and established a youth group, the Armenian Youth of America. The ARF favored an independent Armenian nation, while the latter two were sympathetic to Soviet rule.

In 1933, this political partisanship and controversy boiled over, producing a major rift in the Apostolic Church. Armenians were one of 30 ethnic groups invited to participate in the 1933 CENTURY OF PROGRESS Exposition, and partisan political disagreements erupted over which flag would fly at the designated "Armenian Day"—the tricolor of independent Armenia, or the red flag of Soviet Armenia. A small "riot" at the fair eventually resulted in a court battle over possession of the Holy Savior Church in West Pullman. ARF supporters won control of Holy Savior, while the other faction seceded and in 1958 founded Saints Joachim and Anne Armenian Apostolic, aligned with the St. James and St. Gregory faction. Armenian All Saints Apostolic Church, aligned with the Holy Savior faction, was founded in 1943. Following the migration of many of its parishioners to the suburbs, All Saints moved in 1980 to a new building in GLENVIEW. Sts. Joachim and Anne Parish moved to PALOS PARK in 1977 and then to PALOS HEIGHTS in 1983. Holy Savior church closed in 1974, donating its estate to All Saints.

The political divide within the Armenian community of Chicago continued into the twenty-first century. Nevertheless, the Armenian community has remained united ethnically, coming together annually for cultural and ethnic events. The most important of these remains the community's recollection every April 24 of the events of 1894 and 1909, which Armenians have defined as genocide at the hands of the Turks.

Robert Morrissey

See also: Demography; Multicentered Chicago

Further reading: Harlan, Sonia. "The Pioneers of the Chicago Armenian Community." Series in *Armenian Mirror-Spectator* (Boston), December 7, 14, 21, 1991. • Kaprielian-Churchill, Isabel. "Armenian Refugee Women: The Picture Brides, 1920–1930." *Journal of American Ethnic History* 12.3 (Spring 1993): 3–29.

Armories. National Guard armories house weapons and military equipment, office space for personnel, drill space for training, and common areas for socializing. The Illinois General Assembly provided no money for armory construction until after 1900; thus all nineteenth-century ILLINOIS NATIONAL GUARD (ING) organizations had to raise funds privately to rent

First Regiment Armory, Michigan and 16th Street, 1891. Photographer: Unknown. Source: Chicago Historical Society.

or construct armory space. In the 1870s near-moribund volunteer militias experienced a nationwide resurgence in popularity. The revived militias, like the First Regiment ING, needed specialized space to store and drill with the increasingly sophisticated military hardware and supplies they required for their training activities, which in turn strained their traditional practice of renting easily modified buildings. Armories also emerged as the locus of militia activities, serving not just as storehouses and drill space, but also as clubhouses and recreational centers for their membership, further changing the requirements for armory design.

Starting in 1890, new specially designed and constructed armories came to mark the urban landscape with distinctive forms. A highly romantic castle style, complete with portcullis gates and turrets, dominated among those rare organizations wealthy enough to build privately. In 1890, the wealthy and socially prestigious First Regiment built their own castle-style armory on South Michigan Avenue. It housed a parade ground, office space for all 12 companies and regimental officers, locker rooms, a gym, a library, several small parlors, and a large weapons storage facility. Chicago's four other National Guard organizations continued to make do with rented facilities of various suitability and cost. Finally in 1907 the state built a modified castle-style armory at 222 East Chicago Avenue to house another Chicago regiment. This armory was demolished to make room for the MUSEUM OF CONTEMPORARY ART in 1993. By the end of 1915, the General Assembly had provided new armories for all infantry regiments in Chicago, completing one for the AFRICAN AMERICAN Eighth ING regiment at 3533 South Giles Avenue in 1915. The only armory with landmark status in Chicago, this facility reopened in 1999 as a public high school. In the 1920s and 1930s, Illinois continued to build or renovate armories for Chicago regiments. As ING companies followed the population out to the suburbs in the 1950s and 1960s, new armories gradually lost much of their distinctive appearance, as they disappeared into suburban light industrial parks and older armories were abandoned or turned to new uses.

Eleanor Hannah

See also: Places of Assembly

Further reading: Fogelson, Robert M. *America's Armories: Architecture, Society, and Public Order.* 1989. • Hannah, Eleanor. "Manhood, Citizenship, and the Formation of the National Guards, Illinois, 1870–1917." Ph.D. diss., University of Chicago. 1997.

Armory Show of 1913. Between March 24 and April 16, 1913, the ART INSTITUTE OF CHICAGO hosted the International Exposition of Modern Art—the famous "Armory Show"—which included 634 works that traced the development of European art from Goya to the Cubists. The show arrived in Chicago fresh from its first, month-long showing in New York. While roughly half the size of the original, it included the addition of an abstract painting by Chicago's own Cubist, Manierre Dawson.

The idea of radical modern ART as displayed at the Armory Show had been introduced to Chicago in 1912 at the W. Scott Thurber gallery in a series of exhibitions of works by Arthur Dove, Jerome Blum, and B. J. O. Nordfeldt. By October 1912 art patron Arthur T. Aldis had persuaded the New York exhibition's organizers, Walt Kuhn and Arthur B. Davies, to include a Chicago venue in their plans. Prior to the show's arrival in Chicago, the *Chicago Tribune* had sent critic Harriet Monroe (whose *Poetry* magazine had begun appearing the previous year) to New York to cover the exhibition, while Chicago lawyer Arthur Jerome Eddy had already purchased postimpressionist works from the show.

Nevertheless, the Armory Show came as a shock to most Chicagoans, provoking a raucous response ranging from moral posturing and parody in the press to honest outrage. The controversy spilled over to so many walks of life that by June 1913 Edward Hale noted in Chicago's *Dial* magazine that the air was "full at present of utterances concerning Futurists, Cubists, Neo-Impressionists, and Post-Impressionism."

The Armory Show changed the progress of art in Chicago. In addition to establishing the importance of avant-garde art in the popular imagination, it prepared the ground for such influential designs as Frank Lloyd Wright's Midway Gardens (1914), which combined modern painting, sculpture, and ARCHITECTURE in a single creation; the founding of the Arts Club in 1916; and the growth of Chicago's many radical exhibition societies of the 1920s.

Paul Kruty

See also: Art Criticism and Scholarship; Literary Cultures; Near North Side

Further reading: Brown, Milton W. *The Story of the Armory Show.* 1963. • Kruty, Paul. "Arthur Jerome Eddy and His Collection: Prelude and Postscript to the Armory Show." *Arts* 61 (February 1987): 40–47. • Prince, Sue Ann. *The Old Guard and the Avant-Garde: Modernism in Chicago, 1910–1940.* 1990.

Armour Square, Community Area 34, 3 miles S of the Loop. The Armour Square Community Area illustrates the difference between a neighborhood and a COMMUNITY AREA. This long thin area (an assemblage of leftovers from adjacent community areas, 21 blocks long, 4–5 blocks wide) is wedged between rail lines, EXPRESSWAYS, and the South Branch of the CHICAGO RIVER. It contains three distinct neighborhoods. AFRICAN AMERICANS dominate the population to the south; the middle section holds recently arrived Hispanics; and along with a few ITALIANS

1

34
Armour
Square

and blacks, CHINATOWN fills the northern section.

Armour Square has been, from the beginning, principally a working-class area. GERMANS and IRISH arrived during the Civil War, and later, SWEDES joined the population. These groups used the area as a way station as they moved southward and climbed upward in social and economic status. Armour Square lay south of the burned area during the Chicago FIRE OF 1871 but was nonetheless greatly affected by the disaster. Laws enacted after the fire required brick or stone construction in the central city. The resulting increase in costs drove many working families out to the edge of the "brick area," and Armour Square received many such families. Armour Square subsequently lost blocks of housing as the tracks of bordering RAILROADS were elevated. These changes cut off the area from neighborhoods to the east and west.

By 1899, Italian immigrants arrived and formed the ROMAN CATHOLIC parish of Santa Maria Incoronata. Commercial operations began to displace housing in the area. Some of the encroaching businesses were extensions of the notorious Levee district just to the east. In 1909, Charles Comiskey built a new baseball park for the Chicago WHITE SOX between 34th and 35th Streets. The old Sox park then became home to the AMERICAN GIANTS of the Negro League. In 1991 the White Sox moved into a still newer stadium just south of the old COMISKEY PARK; the Negro Leagues having long since vanished.

Around 1912, CHINESE living in an enclave at the south edge of the LOOP began a mass movement southward. The Chinese encountered severe racial discrimination, however, and were forced to do business through an intermediary. The H. O. Stone Company acted on behalf of 50 Chinese businessmen to secure 10-year leases on buildings in the new area. Chinatown became a major tourist attraction boasting an impressive entrance gate and many other distinguishing features.

As the city's "BLACK BELT" began to expand during World War I, African Americans moved into Armour Square's southern section, numbering about 4,000 by 1930. This figure remained stable through the GREAT DEPRESSION and World War II until, in 1947, the CHICAGO HOUSING AUTHORITY completed Wentworth Gardens at 37th and Princeton, and the neighborhood reached an all-time high population of over 23,000, with blacks making up nearly half the total. Later, widespread demolition made way for construction of the Dan Ryan and Stevenson Expressways and their interconnecting ramps, which set off a continuing decline in population.

In 1999, Chinese constituted over half the area's population. The Chinese were moving west into BRIDGEPORT and a rejuvenated Chinatown continued as a major tourist attraction with many shops and famed restaurants. An outside investor from Hong Kong developed Appleville apartments, and a consortium of Chinese businessmen and local banks developed Chinatown Square and Jade City apartments. A new Chinatown Park was under construction along the river. Adaptive reuse of old structures, nearby infill housing, and the recently enlarged McCormick Place to the east added energy to the area.

David M. Solzman

See also: Built Environment of the Chicago Region; Fire Limits; South Side

Further reading: "The Chinese in Chicago: The First One Hundred Years." In *Ethnic Chicago: A Multicultural Portrait*, 4th ed., ed. Melvin G. Holli and Peter d'A. Jones, 1995, chap. 13. • The Chicago Fact Book Consortium, ed. *Local Community Fact Book: Chicago Metropolitan Area, Based on the 1970 and 1980 Censuses*. 1984. • Holt, Glen E., and Dominic A. Pacyga. *Chicago: A Historical Guide to the Neighborhoods: The Loop and South Side*. 1979.

Art. From its earliest history, art in Chicago was created in response to the particular nature of the city—first as a rapidly growing gateway to the frontier West, then against the backdrop of industrialization and global commerce. Chicago's earliest ARTISTS were painters and illustrators who created sentimental portraits, landscapes influenced by European examples, and Western subjects for the rapidly growing middle class in the quickly expanding urban center. Many of these artists set up ateliers or were associated with DEPARTMENT STORES, a phenomenon that continued well into the twentieth century, particularly with Marshall Field's, which featured a fine-arts gallery until early in the 1950s. As part of the rebuilding of Chicago after the FIRE OF 1871, great turn-of-the-century industrialists and PHILANTHROPISTS such as Marshall Field, Charles L. Hutchinson, Bertha Honoré Palmer and Potter Palmer, Lambert Tree, Martin A. Ryerson, and others saw the creation of cultural institutions as an obligation of the civic-minded and as a means of social uplift.

The WORLD'S COLUMBIAN EXPOSITION, organized in 1893 largely to celebrate Chicago commerce, featured works by Mary Cassatt and other important painters and sculptors. Created especially for the White City, the only permanent building erected for the fair was a Beaux-Arts palace of fine arts centrally located on Michigan Avenue, which following the exposition became the new home of the ART INSTITUTE OF CHICAGO (founded in 1866 by a group of artists as the Chicago Academy of Design). The FINE ARTS BUILDING, Tree Studios, and many other cultural institutions arose out of the efforts of these patrons and the circle of artists, architects, writers, activists—including Jane Addams, founder of the HULL HOUSE—and other creative people to improve the life of the city. These patrons traveled to Europe and brought back Old Master paintings, including El Greco's *Assumption of the Virgin*, and impressionist and post-impressionist masterpieces—the contemporary art of the day—that eventually formed the Art Institute's collections. Chicago's prestigious social and service clubs, particularly the Union League Club, began collecting art. Institutions such as the RENAISSANCE SOCIETY and the Arts Club were founded in the early years of the twentieth century and, in presenting modern art for its own sake, affirmed that art was an important aspect of civilized urban life.

While Chicago ARCHITECTURE has occupied center stage nationally and internationally, the visual arts have often been a poor stepchild. Local artists, many of them representational painters, sculptors, and printmakers, suffered in comparison to masters imported from Europe and New York, both in the late nineteenth century and as modernism emerged in the early years of the twentieth century. Confronting a reactionary press and with few opportunities to show and often fewer to sell their work, many of Chicago's most ambitious artists adopted a defiant, antimainstream attitude. They championed abstract art in the 1920s when the prevailing style was representational and then promoted figurative styles as abstraction dominated the mainstream in the 1940s and beyond. Several artists, however, did well, including sculptor Lorado Taft, whose casting studios on the SOUTH SIDE later became the art studios for the UNIVERSITY OF CHICAGO. Taft's monumental statues of heroic subjects are now Chicago treasures. Ivan Albright created idiosyncratic portraits and still lifes and later became nationally known when he was chosen to create the dissipated portrait of Dorian Gray in the Hollywood production of Oscar Wilde's *The Picture of Dorian Gray*.

To complicate matters, as a Midwestern city away from the center of the art world, Chicago has seen an almost constant drain of talent. In part this has derived from circumstance; the city has long been a major center for art education, attracting unusually large numbers of young artists who quickly move on after establishing a career. The venerable School of the Art Institute of Chicago dominates a scene that has also included the INSTITUTE OF DESIGN, along with the city's UNIVERSITIES. This sort of besieged mentality influenced aesthetic developments—Chicago's legendary adherence to a figurative, surrealist-tinged tradition—but fed into and perpetuated larger myths about Chicago as "the second city," or, in Carl Sandburg's words, the "City of the Big Shoulders" and "Hog Butcher for the World." These sensibilities, combined with a deep interest in folk and outsider art, gave rise to a distinctive regional feel, especially in post–World War II painting, which included groups of artists dubbed the Monster Roster and the Chicago Imagists.

Chicago art in the 1930s was shaped by the same forces that influenced art elsewhere in the nation, namely the GREAT DEPRESSION and the federally funded Works Progress Administration (WPA). Chicago's brand of social realism differed little from the national norm, influenced as it was by the regional visions of the great muralist Thomas Hart Benton and other social realists. As was typical of the WPA, much art was installed in SCHOOLS, LIBRARIES, post offices, and other public buildings and celebrated the working man and woman, the family, civic life, and the cityscape. Many local artists, including Gertrude Abercrombie, Emil Armin, Eldzier Cortor, Karl Priebe, and Tud Kempf, were employed; the majority of these artists retained a style of social realism, causing their careers to suffer in the 1940s and 1950s.

The growing unrest in Europe in the 1930s brought established European artists to Chicago, although not in the numbers seen in New York. The brilliant achievements of artists and photographers associated with Chicago's world-famous Institute of Design had a direct link to Chicago as a center for commerce. It was business concerns that brought the pioneering Bauhaus (later the Institute of Design) to Chicago in 1937, in large part to upgrade industrial and product design for manufacturing enterprises. Walter Paepcke, president of the Container Corporation of America and founder of the world-renowned Aspen Institute, was a major patron. Although Chicago's postwar captains of industry echoed their predecessors of the turn of the century, there was considerable tension between the ambitions of the Institute of Design's distinguished faculty (e.g., László Moholy-Nagy, Alexander Rodchenko, Serge Chermayeff, and Buckminster Fuller) and the needs of the business community. In the end, financial interests ended the great aesthetic and pedagogical experiment when the institute became affiliated with the ILLINOIS INSTITUTE OF TECHNOLOGY in 1949. Although the heyday of Institute of Design was brief, Moholy-Nagy's philosophy—to train the whole human being as a sensitive, perceptive, problem-solving person rather than merely passing along artistic traditions—electrified students. As these students moved on to teaching positions across the country, this new perspective assumed an enormous impact nationally and internationally. PHOTOGRAPHY continued to flourish at the Institute of Design in the 1950s and 1960s under Aaron Siskind and Harry Callahan, who emphasized experimentation with the camera and with darkroom techniques as well as the development of technical skills.

In the immediate postwar era another federal program, the GI Bill, assumed critical significance. Hundreds of returning soldiers who would not have been able to attend college enrolled in art schools, causing a boom in art education which eventually reached a zenith in the 1990s. Veterans such as Leon Golub, George Cohen, and H. C. Westermann brought a more worldly, mature vision to their artistic output, sowing the seeds for the emergence of a unique Chicago school, the Imagists, in the mid-1960s. Many of these artists were profoundly influenced by a 1951 exhibition by French artist Jean Dubuffet (1901–1985) and by his lecture at the Arts Club, "Anticultural Positions," which stressed the innate creativity of the unschooled individual. Several figures from the prewar scene, however, remained influential and were starting points for later developments. These included Ivan Albright and Gertrude Abercrombie, whose grotesque, detailed figurative style and primitive style, respectively, typify aspects of Chicago art.

Many key patrons, art dealers, and emerging civic and business leaders in the immediate postwar era were University of Chicago alumni who had learned about art and culture directly from artists, many of whom were leaders in the Exhibition Momentum movement. This movement had its genesis when the School of the Art Institute banned student work from its long-standing Annual Exhibitions of Chicago and Vicinity shows in the late 1940s, one of the few places contemporary art was shown in prewar Chicago. Students took matters into their own hands and established a series of highly influential shows, some juried by important New York art world figures, some open to all. Exhibition Momentum artists also set up classes, workshops, and other pedagogical activities for professionals in other fields. These professionals and business leaders, including Joseph Randall Shapiro, Edwin A. Bergman, B. C. Holland, and Richard Gray, exercised major cultural influence in the postwar years.

During the 1930s and into the 1950s, Chicago's AFRICAN AMERICAN communities, mostly on the city's South Side, experienced great growth and artistic achievement. Inspired by the example of the artists of the Harlem Renaissance in New York in the 1920s (many of whom were educated at the School of the Art Institute), Archibald Motley, Jr., who had trained in Europe and achieved success as a painter in New York, worked to set up exhibition and pedagogical opportunities for black artists. The South Side Community Art Center, founded in 1941 and arising out of NEW DEAL social programs, was a seminal institution: artists and writers such as Gwendolyn Brooks, Margaret Burroughs, Elizabeth Catlett, Eldzier Cortor, Gordon Parks, and Richard Wright formed the core of a community working in active exchange with artists centered in nearby HYDE PARK, where housing left over from the Columbian Exposition had formed an artists' colony since the late nineteenth century. In the 1950s, however, artists with interracial friendships found the political climate increasingly hostile, as McCarthyism and the nascent CIVIL RIGHTS MOVEMENT generated heated rhetoric. In 1961, inspired by the activism and people that had brought forth the South Side Community Art Center, Margaret Burroughs founded the DUSABLE MUSEUM, the first Midwest museum celebrating black arts and culture.

In 1966, also on Chicago's South Side, a style exploded on the scene with the first of three exhibitions at the Hyde Park Art Center by a group who called themselves "The Hairy Who." These young painters, including Jim Nutt, Gladys Nilsson, and Karl Wirsum, along with other young artists trained by the School of the Art Institute, quickly became collectively known as the Imagists, a term originally coined by critic Franz Schulze to indicate the preceding generation of Chicago artists, now known as the Monster Roster. The Imagists' figurative style, with its emphasis on distortion, precise

Archibald John Motley, Jr.

Combining a fascination with natural and artificial light, a modernist's sense of color, and a deep respect for the heritage of AFRICAN AMERICANS, Motley's oeuvre provides a compelling record of twentieth-century black urban life. Beginning as a portraitist in the 1910s, Motley subsequently explored his African and southern Creole roots, MEXICAN culture, and life in Chicago's "Bronzeville."

Born in New Orleans, Motley moved north as a child, returning to Louisiana for frequent summer visits. His family settled in Chicago's ENGLEWOOD neighborhood in the 1890s. He graduated from the School of the ART INSTITUTE OF CHICAGO in 1918. These diverse settings informed a consciousness of race evident in group scenes, portraits, and figure studies. *Seated Nude* (c. 1916–18) and *Rita* (c. 1918) are very early works which showed his interest in women, portraiture, and the human form. Motley examined and distinguished ethnic identities and miscegenation through images of women he referred to as mulatresses, octoroons, and quadroons. Sojourns in Paris and Mexico yielded paintings of French-speaking African, West Indian, Euro-American, European, and Mexican women. During the 1930s and '40s, and again toward the end of his career in the 1960s, Motley committed himself to the portrayal of the black experience in genre scenes of Chicago's BLACK BELT.

His work fell into obscurity at midcentury but enjoyed a resurgence in the 1990s, marked by a 1991 retrospective exhibit at the CHICAGO HISTORICAL SOCIETY.

Jontyle Theresa Robinson

craftsmanship, garish colors, puns, and word play, came to define Chicago art both within and outside the city. This "Chicago school" received widespread attention, especially after 1973, when the Imagists were featured in the important international exhibition, the XII São Paulo Bienal.

The emergence of this group coincided with the first museum devoted solely to contemporary art in Chicago, the MUSEUM OF CONTEMPORARY ART, which opened off Michigan Avenue in late 1967 with an ambitious plan for showcasing national and international developments. The Chicago mural movement also emerged in 1967, with the *Wall of Respect,* a paean to black achievements begun under William Walker and the black activist arts organization the Organization of Black American Culture. This mural and the community involvement that it fostered generated over 200 murals by 1975. The civil rights movement, the political activism touched off by the 1968 Democratic Convention, and the emerging pride and social activism of Chicago's rapidly growing Hispanic population all contributed to this now internationally renowned aspect of Chicago art. In the primarily MEXICAN American neighborhood of PILSEN, a mural aesthetic that fused pre-Columbian motifs, popular cultural symbols, and contemporary Latino concerns and issues was pioneered by Mario Castillo, Ray Patlán, and Marcos Raya.

Pablo Picasso's untitled sculpture was placed on Daley Plaza in 1967. While many Chicagoans initially scorned it as unintelligible modern art, it came to be a familiar icon of the city. Photographer: Hedrich-Blessing. Source: Chicago Historical Society.

Continuing the investigation of the ideas of Negritude pioneered by sculptor Marion Perkins, a veteran of the South Side Community Art Center, a group of artists interested in giving visual expression to the goals of the Black Power movement formed AfriCobra in 1968. Led by Institute of Design–trained Jeff Donaldson, AfriCobra's philosophy of self-determination and social responsibility inspired a national and international network of black teachers and artists still active at the end of the century. School of the Art Institute–trained Richard Hunt became one of Chicago's most successful artists, with over 50 public sculptures placed around Chicago.

The formation of the National Endowment for the Arts as part of President Lyndon Johnson's GREAT SOCIETY programs in the late 1960s enabled an explosive growth of arts institutions. Artist-run spaces such as N.A.M.E. Gallery (1973–1997) especially benefited from federal support, and from this gallery a school of conceptually based art emerged in Chicago concomitant to conceptual art's emergence in New York and Los Angeles. Largely overlooked at the time, this form came to dominate in the 1990s and beyond. Also emerging in the 1970s were groups of time-based artists: video, performance, and experimental FILM and music were all explored by collaboratives such as the Editing Center, Chicago Filmmakers, and the Experimental Sound Studios as well as by individuals. Dan Sandin, at the University of Illinois Electronic Visualization Laboratory, undertook some of the first investigations in the nation with the video synthesizer and, as computers developed in the 1980s and 1990s, moved on to virtual reality. The Film Center at the School of the Art Institute (founded 1972, now the Gene Siskel Film Center) was built upon foundations laid by dedicated film buffs that dated back to the 1940s and such organizations as the Documentary Film Group at the University of Chicago and the Magick Lantern Society, both founded in the 1960s. The 1970s also saw both the founding and revitalizing of numerous museums to serve a diversified public, including the Balzekas Museum of LITHUANIAN Culture, the POLISH Museum of America, the Spertus Museum of Judaica, The UKRAINIAN Institute of Modern Art, and the Ukrainian National Museum.

In one of the first such programs in the nation, the Chicago City Council in 1978 unanimously approved a Percent for the Arts ordinance, stipulating that a percentage of the cost of constructing or renovating municipal buildings be set aside for the commission or purchase of art works. Numerous examples of public art soon supplemented the already significant array of public sculpture, many commissioned in the prewar years under the auspices of the Ferguson Fund, an endowment controlled by the trustees of the Art Institute. Chicago's best-known public sculpture, an untitled Picasso in Daley Plaza, however, was a private, much criticized endeavor when it was unveiled in 1967. A 1954 bas-relief by sculptor Milton Horn, *Chicago Rising from the Lake,* carelessly stored and subsequently discovered and reinstalled in 1998 on Chicago's newly developed Riverwalk (the section of the CHICAGO RIVER between the lake and roughly LaSalle Street), became a symbol of the strengths and problems of Chicago's impressive public art collection as major reorganization and consolidation of the program took place in the late 1990s.

In the mid-1980s, along with the rest of the nation, Chicago experienced an art boom. The Chicago International Art Exposition, held annually on NAVY PIER, brought attention to the vital and growing art community. A greatly expanded GALLERY scene emerged, with several distinct districts including the West Loop River North area and Milwaukee Avenue. The Art Institute opened a new wing and began regular presentations of contemporary art for the first time in decades, as it continued to mount blockbuster exhibitions of the impressionist and post-impressionist masters so prominent in its collections. The TERRA MUSEUM opened on Michigan Avenue in 1987. The Chicago Cultural Center, the State of Illinois Gallery (a branch of the downstate Springfield Illinois State Museum), and the numerous ethnic and university galleries presented exhibitions of local artists at unprecedented rates. Chicago's

Mexican American community established the MEXICAN FINE ARTS CENTER MUSEUM in 1982, with a new facility in 1987. The Randolph Street Gallery (1979–1998) began a new era of socially and politically informed shows curated by teams of artists. Chicago has remained a nexus for controversy around works of art, the most infamous involving a School of the Art Institute student who displayed the American flag on the school gallery's floor.

A fire in April 1989 consumed nearly a dozen major galleries and struck a major blow to the River North gallery district. This disaster, combined with rapidly rising rents as the neighborhood became a dining and entertainment center, has continued the historic process of changing artists' neighborhood and gallery districts, in the 1990s relocating respectively to the near northwest WICKER PARK/BUCKTOWN and the near west Fulton Street Market/UNIVERSITY OF ILLINOIS neighborhoods. The completion in 1996 of a new and architecturally controversial building by the Museum of Contemporary Art located just off the major North Michigan Avenue shopping district signaled the maturation of the presence of art as a vital force in Chicago, affirming the ideals of Chicago's founders that art is an essential component in a great city.

Lynne Warren

See also: Art Centers, Alternative; Art, Public; Federal Art Project; Graphic Design; Industrial Art and Design

Further reading: Prince, Sue Ann, ed. *The Old Guard and the Avant-Garde: Modernism in Chicago, 1910–1940.* 1990. • Sparks, Esther. *A Biographical Dictionary of Painters and Sculptors in Illinois, 1808–1945.* 1972. • Warren, Lynne, ed. *Art in Chicago, 1945–1995.* 1996.

Art Centers, Alternative. In the parlance of the contemporary ART world, an "alternative space" indicates a gallery or center that by circumstance or mission exists outside of, or in opposition to, mainstream art institutions, particularly museums and commercial galleries. In Chicago, many of these have taken the form of artists' cooperatives or not-for-profit spaces founded by ARTISTS to further their work in the face of resistance from established institutions. Alternative spaces are largely a post–WORLD WAR II phenomenon, but there were some important precedents, including the Art Building Gallery, founded in 1862 to provide local and foreign artists free exhibition space; the Academy of Design (incorporated in 1869), an art school and membership exhibition gallery which later became the ART INSTITUTE OF CHICAGO; the Neo-Arlimusc group, founded in 1926 by artist Rudolph Weisenborn to further exchanges between all forms of creative practice; and the Artists Union of Chicago (1936–1938), an outgrowth of the John Reed Club, organized to mediate between artists and the NEW DEAL Federal Art Project.

In 1948 the resistance of the curators of the Art Institute's "Annual Exhibition by Artists of Chicago and Vicinity" to the new vision of artists educated at the School of the Art Institute on the GI Bill spawned the important artists' group Exhibition Momentum. This group's series of large exhibitions, organized by members, often juried by high-profile New York artists and curators, and mounted in donated space, continued until 1964 and demonstrated to hundreds of local artists that they were capable of determining their own fate.

The true era of the Alternative Space, however, was the 1970s. Fed by a huge increase in art school graduates in the late 1960s and by grants from the newly established National Endowment for the Arts (NEA), N.A.M.E. Gallery (1973–1997) and feminist co-ops Artemisia Gallery (1973–2003) and ARC Gallery (1973) formed the core of an exciting alternative scene on Hubbard Street west of State. A number of media-specific cooperatives joined the big three: the Center for New Television (later the Editing Center) sponsored new video; Chicago Filmmakers (1973–) showed independent film; Bookspace (1978–1980s) presented artists' books; and Lill Street Gallery (1980–) promoted ceramics.

While founded in reaction to existing institutions, most alternative spaces quickly became a vital part of the Chicago art community, promoting new talent, new media, and styles of art that often moved easily into the embrace of commercial GALLERIES. Member burnout, financial burdens (particularly increased rents due to GENTRIFICATION of a succession of neighborhoods "homesteaded" by the galleries), and pressure from the NEA in the 1980s and early 1990s pushed the evolution of such spaces as N.A.M.E. and Randolph Street Gallery (1979–1998) toward a more conventional board-director structure, with the concomitant perception by the younger generation that these spaces were just another aspect of the established mainstream. Such galleries as WPA (1981–1986) and the Uncomfortable Spaces cooperative of commercial galleries (principally Ten in One, Tough, and Beret International) were founded to further the aims of younger artists amidst the general feeling at the close of the century that the Alternative Space was no longer a viable paradigm for the promotion and exhibition of visual arts in Chicago.

Lynne Warren

See also: Hyde Park Art Center; Museum of Contemporary Art; Renaissance Society

Further reading: Larson, Kay. "Rooms with a Point of View." *Artnews* 76.8 (October 1977): 32–38. • Warren, Lynne, ed. *Alternative Spaces: A History in Chicago.* 1984. • Warren, Lynne, ed. *Art in Chicago, 1945–1995.* 1996.

Art Colonies. There is a long tradition of ARTIST colonies in Chicago and summer outposts some distance from the city. The most famous artist colony, at 57th Street and Stony Island Avenue in HYDE PARK, was located in a pair of one-story frame buildings that had been constructed to house concessions for the WORLD'S COLUMBIAN EXPOSITION of 1893. Among the few buildings not demolished after the fair, the complex soon became a haven for artists, literary figures including Sherwood Anderson, and related businesses such as used bookstores.

The 57th Street Artist Colony had two nearby satellites. Cable Court, located a few blocks northwest, was a narrow, dark street, surrounded by three- and four-story tenement buildings occupied by artists and fellow travelers. Further west, at Kenwood Avenue, a third cluster occupied several buildings but centered on 1328 East 57th Street, where John Dewey had founded the Laboratory School of the UNIVERSITY OF CHICAGO in 1896. In the 1940s the first floor housed the Little Gallery owned by Mary Louise Womer, who with others founded the 57th Street Art Fair in 1948, the first of Chicago's community ART FAIRS. Among the artists displaying their work was Gertrude Abercrombie, with her surreal paintings propped up against her ancient Rolls Royce automobile parked at the curb.

In 1898, Lorado Taft and a small group established the Eagle's Nest artist colony overlooking the Rock River near Oregon, Illinois, 80 miles west of Chicago. The summer facility originally had tents and, later, cottages and studios. The activities at Eagle's Nest included not only visual arts but historical pageants in elaborate costume. Regular visitors included Harriet Monroe.

Ox-Bow, in Saugatuck, Michigan, was founded as a summer artist colony in 1910 under the auspices of the ART INSTITUTE OF CHICAGO Alumni Association; it remains active as an outpost of the School of the Art Institute. Faculty members have included Ed Paschke, architect Thomas Tallmadge, and Alphonso Iannelli. Also located in Michigan, John Wilson's Lakeside Center for the Arts thrived in the 1970s and 1980s with artists such as Richard Hunt and Roger Brown. It had an outpost of the Landfall Press of Chicago, a well-known printmaker.

The Hyde Park artist colonies were among the casualties of URBAN RENEWAL around 1960. In addition, the GENTRIFICATION of Hyde Park pushed artists to the North Side, especially OLD TOWN, which still has its own art fair each year. Artists also clustered elsewhere, including the NEAR NORTH SIDE's Tree Studios, restored and commercialized in 2002, and Italian Court, formerly on Michigan Avenue. In the closing decades of the twentieth century, skyrocketing REAL-ESTATE values in OLD TOWN and LINCOLN PARK drove artists further west to neighborhoods such as WICKER PARK and BUCKTOWN.

Devereux Bowly, Jr.

See also: Art; Art Centers, Alternative; Palos Park; West Town

Art Criticism and Scholarship. The history of ART criticism in Chicago starts with *Art Review* (1870), which closed after the Great FIRE OF 1871. Several periodicals made appearances before the WORLD'S COLUMBIAN EXPOSITION of 1893 created an awareness of the arts. Some, like Mrs. T. V. Morse's *Arts for America* (1892–1900), had a largely female staff and a national circulation. *Fine Arts Journal* was edited by ARTISTS, and it survived from 1899 to 1919; the *Chicago Evening Post* started to offer serious literary and art criticism in 1908. Lorado Taft published his pioneering *History of American Sculpture* in 1903; built on his fame as the pre-eminent local sculptor, it became a classic.

The ARMORY SHOW exhibition (1913) focused criticism on modernism. Harriet Monroe, founder of *Poetry* magazine and art critic for the *Chicago Tribune,* understood the modernists and lambasted conservative critics such as Taft and George Zug, who objected on either aesthetic or moral grounds. The interwar period was dominated by two critics, Eleanor Jewett of the *Chicago Tribune* beginning in 1917, and, starting in 1924, Clarence J. Bulliet, first with *Post's Magazine of the Art World* and then with the *Chicago Daily News* when it subsumed the *Post* in 1932. Jewett, a McCormick family member, supported academic art while condemning all modernism as immoral; Bulliet was widely read and wrote the first of his seven art books, *Apples and Madonnas,* in 1927, in support of modernism. He was influential, as his weekly was the largest such American publication in the late 1920s. There was not much written outside of the NEWSPAPERS and occasional exhibition catalogs. J. Z. Jacobson's *Art of Today: Chicago, 1933* (1932) was the first book devoted to the contemporary art of Chicago. By the time the CENTURY OF PROGRESS exhibition opened in 1933, modernism's legitimacy was secure.

After the WPA experience and WORLD WAR II, the critical agenda turned to defining Chicago art. The critics who supported the "Momentum" artists questioned Chicago's receptivity to new ideas. Using New York jurors underscored the provincial nature of the Chicago art scene, at the same time that national art periodicals began to note the exhibitions here. None of the art critics in the late 1950s and 1960s captured attention like Jewett and Bulliet. NORTHWESTERN UNIVERSITY professor James Breckenridge wrote for the *Herald-American,* and the "Momentum" artist turned art historian Franz Schulze wrote for the *Daily News* and for the *Chicago Sun-Times* when the former folded. Schulze, like his freelance peer Harold Haydon, reflected both a broader base and an appreciation of the work of the younger generation of figural expressionists that became identified as the Chicago School. Schulze's book, *Fantastic Images: Chicago Art Since 1945* (1972), was the first in 40 years to examine the specific contributions of local artists.

A new age of criticism arose in the 1970s, when Chicago's critics served as the local correspondents for such national art periodicals as *Art in America* and *Art News.* The opening of the MUSEUM OF CONTEMPORARY ART provided a contemporary focus that the more comprehensive ART INSTITUTE OF CHICAGO could not, and the growth of the art GALLERIES expanded opportunities to write about art. The *New Art Examiner,* which began in Chicago in 1973, increased national awareness of Chicago's artists in the decades following, while such critics as the *Tribune*'s Alan Artner brought news of European art to his readers. Dennis Adrian of the School of the Art Institute has been especially influential in defining and promoting the Chicago School of local artists.

David M. Sokol

See also: Literary Cultures; Newspapers

Further reading: Prince, Sue Ann. *The Old Guard and the Avant-Garde: Modernism in Chicago, 1910–1940.* 1990. • Schulze, Franz. *Fantastic Images: Chicago Art Since 1945.* 1972.

Art Fairs. Since the 1950s juried ART fairs, organized by community volunteers and nonprofit groups in neighborhoods in and around Chicago, have enabled local ARTISTS to exhibit, market, and sell their artwork directly to the public, free of the gallery system. Informal and family-oriented, these events allow artists to showcase their work to the public with complete control of how their work is installed and represented. Art Chicago and SOFA, the annual art expositions held at NAVY PIER, are two examples of commercial enterprises that invite GALLERIES and art dealers from around the world to market and sell the work of artists that they represent. While these events are often called art fairs, they differ from the neighborhood fairs in that they do not have a direct relationship with local communities or Chicago artists.

Two of the oldest juried art fairs in Chicago are the 57th Street Art Fair and the OLD TOWN Art Fair. In 1948 Mary Louise Womer, a HYDE PARK gallery owner, conceived the idea of the 57th Street Art Fair as an opportunity for local artists to meet one another and to sell their art directly to the community. With local sponsorship, the first fair consisted of 50 artists, many of them students from the School of the ART INSTITUTE and the INSTITUTE OF DESIGN. Since 1950, a volunteer committee has organized and sponsored the fair with a juried panel of professional artists to select the participants. Exhibitors have included Richard Hunt, Leon Golub, Claes Oldenburg, Margaret Burroughs, and Gertrude Abercrombie. In 1950 the first Old Town Art Fair was organized along a couple blocks in LINCOLN PARK West. Because the fair was open to public participation, the art ranged from amateur craft objects to masterfully executed paintings and sculpture. In 1958, a small committee was formed to establish regulations and a jury of established artists was implemented to create a more balanced display of media and to improve the quality of the art. By the end of the twentieth century each of these fairs annually showcased more than 300 artists.

The art fair system has developed into an important Chicago tradition that links both amateur and professional artists to Chicago communities. Based on the models of the 57th Street and Old Town Art Fairs, neighborhood art fairs have been established in BARRINGTON, EVANSTON, HINSDALE, HOMEWOOD, NAPERVILLE, OAKBROOK, Peoria, PARK FOREST, Rockford, SKOKIE, WILMETTE, WOODSTOCK, and other outlying areas.

Stephanie Skestos

See also: Street Life

Further reading: Baugher, Shirley. *Our Old Town: The History of a Neighborhood.* 2001. • Richman, Julie, and Mary Louise Womer. *Chicago's 57th Street Art Fair: The First 50 Years, 1948–1997.* 1997.

Art Galleries. *See* Galleries

Art Institute of Chicago. From modest beginnings as a tiny academy, the Art Institute of Chicago has grown into an internationally renowned institution, comprising a premier collection of ART objects from around the globe, a top-ranked art school and library, and a diverse array of temporary exhibitions and public programs. Throughout its history the institute has served as a barometer of the role of art in Chicago.

The institute traces its origins to the Chicago Academy of Design, established by local artists in rented rooms on Clark Street in 1866. Financed by members' dues and patrons' donations, the academy offered classes and staged regular receptions and exhibitions. In 1870 the organization moved into its own building on Adams Street, adding a lecture series to its program. After the building was destroyed in the FIRE OF 1871, the academy was plagued by financial and managerial problems. In an effort to stabilize the institution, business leaders created a board of trustees in 1878. Within a year they decided to organize a new institution, and resigned to found the Chicago Academy of Fine Arts; its expanded mission included collecting as well as offering education and exhibitions. This new incarnation represented a decisive shift from a school run by ARTISTS to a multifaceted institution superintended by the city's mercantile elite. In 1882 the academy changed its name to the Art Institute of Chicago and elected as president Charles L. Hutchinson, a banker who would lead the institution until his death in 1924. For the trustees, the institute, along with other new educational and arts organizations, served to offset Chicago's materialism and improve its image. They realized that the city's continued economic growth depended on its transformation from a center identified with commerce to a cosmopolitan place filled with cultural offerings. In turn, the institute benefited from the businessmen's managerial skills and financial generosity.

The institute's early history reflected as well as countered Chicago's capitalist ethos: situated symbolically within the city's commercial downtown, it financed its first buildings and acquisitions through business deals and speculation. It also was committed to expansion. During the 1880s the institute outgrew two successive structures at the corner of Michigan Avenue and Van Buren Street, both designed by Chicago architects Burnham & Root. In 1891 the institute and the WORLD'S COLUMBIAN EXPOSITION agreed to share the cost of erecting a new building on the lakefront, which would be used temporarily for the fair's scholarly congresses in 1893. Designed by Boston architects Shepley, Rutan, and Coolidge, the building announced its elevated purpose through its neoclassical design (recalling the humanist ideals of the Renaissance as well as the ARCHITECTURE of many European museums) and the names of famous artists carved into its entablature. The architects' plan was realized in stages as funds became available; over the course of the twentieth century, connecting structures were added to the rear and sides, but none challenged the symbolic prominence of the 1893 building.

The collections likewise mirrored the ambitions and tastes of the institute's leaders and evolving mission. The earliest holdings were instructional objects, most notably a large group of casts of European sculpture. In the 1890s the focus turned, reflecting beliefs that a civic museum should feature masterpieces, a category then meaning original artworks from Europe. The first major acquisition was the Demidoff collection of seventeenth-century Dutch paintings; Hutchinson and fellow trustee Martin Ryerson advanced money for the purchase, and the board subsequently found patrons to donate the pictures to the museum. A series of bequests in the 1920s and 1930s deepened the holdings in Old Master and modern works and established the institute's preeminence in impressionist and post-impressionist painting.

Between 1890 and 1917, the institute was transformed from a separate sphere intended to realize the ideals of its patrons to an institution dedicated to bringing art to a wider public and serving as the hub of the city's artistic life. The institute has continued to pursue this mandate through a program of temporary exhibitions, lectures, concerts, and classes. The museum has also broadened the range of its collections to encompass Asian, African, Amerindian, and American arts and has expanded into new media including PHOTOGRAPHY and architecture.

The institute's character has also been shaped by its art school. While sharing a dedication to art and education, the museum and school have often disagreed about space, funds, and basic priorities. The museum emphasizes the systematic study and preservation of fine art, paying most attention to foreign art from the past. In contrast, the school is more oriented toward the present and the local, embracing experiment, spontaneity, and applied as well as fine arts. Course offerings in drawing, painting, sculpture, and anatomy were supplemented by more practical instruction in architecture, illustration, and wood carving before 1900, and a separate curriculum in industrial design was added in the 1920s. The museum and school diverged further after 1945, when the rise of abstract expressionism made the historical collections seem less relevant to artists, and a series of disagreements over leadership and administration culminated in a faculty strike in 1965. A clearer definition of the school's status and reporting structure resulted. The school has continued to expand in new directions, adding courses in emerging media (such as performance, video, and the Internet) and degree programs including art education, art therapy, arts administration, HISTORIC PRESERVATION, and writing.

The activities of the museum and school have been supported by the Ryerson and Burnham Libraries, one of the premier research facilities for the study of art and architecture in the United States. In addition to books and periodicals, the library houses prints, photographs, architectural drawings, archives, and ephemera.

Diane Dillon

See also: Armory Show of 1913; Industrial Art and Design; Museum of Contemporary Art; Terra Museum of American Art

Further reading: Horowitz, Helen Lefkowitz. *Culture and the City: Cultural Philanthropy in Chicago from the 1880s to 1917.* 1976. • Mancoff, Debra N. "The Art Institute of Chicago: An Introduction." In *Art Institute of Chicago, Treasures from the Art Institute of Chicago,* 2000, 13–17. • Marzio, Peter C. "A Museum and a School: An Uneasy but Creative Union." *Chicago History* 8 (Spring 1979): 20–23, 44–52.

Lorado Taft and Chicago Sculpture

Lorado Taft was a sculptor, author, and educator in Chicago for nearly five decades. After education at the University of Illinois in Urbana (1875–1880) and training in Paris (1880–1885), Taft returned to Chicago where he opened a studio and joined the faculty of the Art Institute in 1886. By 1891 his growing reputation led to an important assignment to design sculpture for William Le Baron Jenney's Horticultural Building (1893) at the WORLD'S COLUMBIAN EXPOSITION. He subsequently completed several more large-scale public projects, including *Blackhawk* (Oregon, Illinois, 1911), *The Columbus Fountain* (Washington DC, 1912), *The Fountain of the Great Lakes* (Chicago, 1913), *The Fountain of Time* (Chicago, 1922), and *Alma Mater* (Urbana, 1929). To help promote his interest in art as civic beautification, Taft became a prolific author as well, contributing numerous articles to newspapers and journals throughout his career. His most significant publication was *The History of American Sculpture* (1903), the first comprehensive survey of his field.

Taft was also an integral part of the Chicago cultural community that included such figures as Henry Blake Fuller, Hamlin Garland, and Ralph Clarkson. Together with these and other writers and artists, he participated in several prominent art clubs and organizations, including the Central Arts Association of America, the Chicago Society of Artists, the Little Room Studio Club, and the Eagle's Nest ARTISTS' COLONY (in nearby Oregon, Illinois). In 1907 he opened the Midway Studios as a traditional atelier, training many more young artists who worked as his student assistants over the following three decades.

Timothy J. Garvey

Art, Public. Chicago is known for its public sculpture, though it also has a rich tradition in murals and other forms of decoration of public spaces. The first forms were the panoramas and cycloramas that were painted and exhibited before being sent on the road, starting in the late 1850s, but the earliest surviving works are two sculptures by Chicagoan Leonard W. Volk, a *Volunteer* FIRE FIGHTERS' *Monument* (1864) and *Our Heroes* (1869), the Rosehill CEMETERY monument to the slain Union forces. The Great FIRE OF 1871 and the economic depression of the 1870s dampened enthusiasm for public art, but a rash of tombs, statutes, and fountains followed in the next decade. Augustus Saint-Gaudens was the most famous of those who worked here, completing both the naturalistic *Abraham Lincoln* and *Bates Fountain* (1887) in LINCOLN PARK. Other sculptors chose to enter the numerous competitions at the time of the WORLD'S COLUMBIAN EXPOSITION, and some moved to the city in anticipation of work for the

Lorado Taft, *The Fountain of the Great Lakes,* in 1929. Photographer: Unknown. Source: Chicago Historical Society.

fair. The exposition was the setting for much temporary public art, including the Mary Cassatt murals installed at the Woman's Pavilion, and it inaugurated an era of mural painting. The South PARK DISTRICT commissioned murals for its fieldhouses around the turn of the century, and many have been refurbished. A major mural cycle was Lawrence C. Earle's *History of Chicago* (1909) for the Chicago National Bank. Frederic Clay Bartlett and William Penhallow Henderson turned to mural painting after the fair and produced notable pieces at Midway Gardens (1914) and the UNIVERSITY OF CHICAGO (1905).

Much public art was produced in the period between the fair and WORLD WAR I: statues of such famous men as Shakespeare, Franklin, Garibaldi, Leif Ericson, Hans Christian Andersen, and Kosciuszko appeared in a 10-year period, as well as monuments to the Confederate dead and the FORT DEARBORN Massacre and several major fountains. The Ferguson Fund, created in 1905 to "memorialize events in American history," bore first fruit with Lorado Taft's Fountain of the Great Lakes. Nearly a score of other notable works ensued, such as Taft's *Fountain of Time* (1922) at the Midway. Whether such abstract works as Henry Moore's *Sundial* (1980), at the ADLER PLANETARIUM, and Richard Hunt's *Slabs of the Sunburnt West* (1975), on the UNIVERSITY OF ILLINOIS AT CHICAGO's campus, fit the spirit of the bequest has inspired considerable disagreement.

In the 1920s, such works as Ivan Mestrovic's *Indians* (1928) and Parisian Marcel Loyau's sculptures for the Buckingham Fountain, the world's largest at the time (1927), captured the city's imagination. The GREAT DEPRESSION and war years limited opportunities for large public works of sculpture, yet *Ceres* (1930), atop the Board of Trade Building, by the expatriate Chicagoan John Storrs, is a striking art deco departure from naturalist modeling.

The FEDERAL ART PROJECT in Illinois was responsible for hundreds of fresco and oil murals in SCHOOLS, HOSPITALS, and post offices, in Chicago and the suburbs. Lane Technical High School alone was graced with abstract figurative work by John Walley, historic narratives by Edgar Britton, and scenes of contemporary life by Mitchell Siporin. Ethel Spears, Mildred Waltrip, and others painted in both Chicago and OAK PARK but lived to see their work destroyed or removed in response to changing taste and values. The revival of mural painting in the 1960s had a more positive effect on the extant work of the 1930s, stimulating an interest in preservation and restoration that continued into the 1990s. In other media, eastern artist Henry Varnum Poor produced ceramic tile murals of Carl Sandburg and Louis Sullivan for the UPTOWN Post Office (1943).

The 1960s were a golden age for public art, with both increased attention to sculpture and a new generation of muralists coming of age. Well-known European sculptors received major commissions: Antoine Pevsner, Henry Moore, and Ruth Duckworth for the University of Chicago, and Pablo Picasso, for his sculpture (1967) at the Daley Plaza. The Picasso, Marc Chagall's mosaic *The Four Seasons* (1974), and Claes Oldenburg's *Bat Column* (1977) were all originally derided but have become as popular as some of the historical pieces. The pivotal piece in the revival of murals for the public was William Walker's *Wall of Respect* (1967), depicting AFRICAN AMERICAN heroes. Soon, African American, Hispanic, and Anglo artists were involved in projects that brought together multiple artists, often with the addition of untrained community-area adults and teenagers, through such organizations as the Chicago Mural Group, the Public Art Workshop, and Latino artists of the Movimiento Artistico Chicano, through the 1970s and beyond. While some of the mural walls have institutional settings, others were painted on the train embankments that run through the neighborhoods. The work ranges from exaggerated naturalism inspired by Diego Rivera and his contemporaries to GRAFFITI-like pieces that reflect the artists' origins as subway "taggers."

David M. Sokol

See also: City as Artifact; War Monuments

Further reading: Bach, Ira J., and Mary Lackritz Gray. *Chicago's Public Sculpture.* 1983. • Chicago Council on Fine Arts. *Guide to Chicago Murals: Yesterday and Today.* 1978. • Riedy, James L. *Chicago Sculpture.* 1981.

Art, Self-Taught. Chicago is notable for engendering exceptional self-taught ARTISTS and for the unusually vigorous acceptance of self-taught ART into the city's art culture. Often referred to as outsider art, self-taught art generally encompasses the work of artists not educated in or oriented to the mainstream art world. Self-taught art differs from folk art, which refers to works of art and craft deriving from ethnic, community, and/or family traditions from both rural and urban environments.

An early instance of the recognition of self-taught art in the city occurred at the Arts Club of Chicago. In 1941 the Arts Club mounted 39 paintings by Horace Pippin, an AFRICAN AMERICAN self-taught artist from Pennsylvania, in an exhibition including works by Dali and Leger. In 1951 Jean Dubuffet delivered an influential lecture, "Anti-Cultural Positions," also at the Arts Club, introducing the European concept of the artist outsider. In the 1960s artists, educators, curators, dealers, and collectors recognized works by area self-taught artists, finding their works consistent, provocative, and highly original. Chicago Imagist artists embraced self-taught art and credited its influence on their work.

Exhibitions since the early 1960s included *Outsider Art in Chicago* at the MUSEUM OF CONTEMPORARY ART in 1979. In 1991, Intuit: The Center for Intuitive and Outsider Art (originally Society for Outsider, Intuitive, and Visionary Art) formed, solidifying Chicago as a national center for the exhibition and interpretation of self-taught art. Chicago-area self-taught artists such as Henry Darger, Joseph Yoakum, Lee Godie, Aldo Piacenza, William Dawson, and Mr. Imagination have achieved international acclaim.

Lisa Stone

See also: Art Centers, Alternative; Art Institute of Chicago

Further reading: Patterson, Tom. *Reclamation and Transformation: Three Self-Taught Chicago Artists.* 1994. • Tuchman, Maurice, and Carol S. Eliel. *Parallel Visions: Modern Artists and Outsider Art.* 1992.

Artists, Education and Culture of.

Early in the twentieth century, Chicago artists and civic leaders believed that the city's accumulating wealth and their own ambitions soon would make it, in novelist Theodore Dreiser's words, "first in art achievement." Chicago did win renown for its art collections and schools for educating artists. This renown seldom extended to Chicago's ART makers, yet by the beginning of the twenty-first century this increasingly diverse group of artists had created a substantial legacy. The city's limitations, as much as its strengths, shaped this legacy. New York always far surpassed Chicago in the number and overall importance of its patrons, GALLERIES, critics, and art publications, as well as artists. Chicago's outside-the-spotlight position could be an asset for artists who wished to develop gradually maturing personal styles, be playfully irreverent toward prevailing practices in the arts, or expand the definition of art. Yet Chicago artists also connected with kindred spirits in their city and with national and international art worlds, participating in ongoing debates such as the persistent one between defenders and critics of tradition.

These connections developed slowly. The external world felt Chicago's influence in POLITICS and industry decades before the city became a presence in the arts, initially as a market for works produced elsewhere. Although by the mid-1850s Chicago had attracted well-known portrait painter G. P. A. Healy and sculptor Leonard W. Volk, well-to-do citizens who sought art usually looked to Europe or the East Coast. This remained true at the time of the 1893 WORLD'S COLUMBIAN EXPOSITION, described by sculptor Augustus Saint-Gaudens as "the greatest meeting of artists since the fifteenth century." Most were only visitors and less then 10 percent of the artworks on display were by Chicago artists, trained mainly in Paris, Munich, Düsseldorf, and Rome. Yet works at the exposition by painters and sculptors such as Alice D. Kellogg and John Donoghue gave promise of things to come.

Although Paris-trained, Donoghue and Kellogg initially had studied at the Chicago Academy of Design. Artists formed the academy in 1866 (incorporated in 1869) to offer art classes and exhibitions. Business leaders supplanted this financially troubled organization by incorporating in 1879 a new Chicago Academy of Fine Arts, renamed the ART INSTITUTE OF CHICAGO in 1882. It included a museum and a school. Subsequently the School of the Art Institute became one of the most influential in the country, as did the museum, for which patrons such as Martin Ryerson and Bertha Honoré Palmer acquired works by Degas, Manet, and many others.

The Art Institute seldom acquired works by Chicago artists, who received some support from a variety of other institutions such as the NEWBERRY LIBRARY, which first purchased and exhibited local work in the 1880s. The following decade a range of creative activities received nourishment at the 57th Street ARTISTS' COLONY, which later attracted writers Floyd Dell and Henry Miller. Also important were the low-rent studios erected in 1894 by Judge Lambert Tree and the FINE ARTS BUILDING, designed to bring together artists, musicians, writers, and craftspeople. Jane Addams added the Butler Art Gallery (1891) two years after opening HULL HOUSE. There in 1897 artists and supporters created the Chicago Society of ARTS AND CRAFTS, which championed decorative arts and a nonhierarchical definition of art, as Addams did by encouraging immigrant crafts. At the Little Room, artists such as painter Ralph Clarkson mingled with Addams and writers Henry Blake Fuller, Hamlin Garland (who credited impressionist painters with teaching him to see anew), and poet Harriet Monroe.

The number of artists available to participate in such interchanges grew. Between 1865 and 1900 the number of Chicagoans listed as "artists" in city directories increased from dozens to several hundred. Many, whose professional and social lives were likely to be quite different from the artists who met in the Little Room, were engaged in such specific commercial tasks as hand painting factory-produced ceramic pieces. Women did this hand painting; men usually received commissions for portraits, designed stained glass, and taught advanced students. The burgeoning PUBLISHING industry also mostly employed men, although women served as book illustrators. By the 1890s fields such as ADVERTISING, crystal cutting, FURNITURE and LEATHER product design, and metalwork, along with the emerging institutional support, made the artist's life more viable in Chicago than in St. Louis or Cincinnati, and comparable to that in Philadelphia or Boston. Chicago augmented New York's preeminence by launching the careers of many fine and commercial artists who then moved there.

Perhaps the most prominent Chicago artist at this time was Lorado Taft, who in addition to making monumental sculptures and teaching at the School of the Art Institute published in 1903 his influential *The History of American Sculpture.* The first work completed with support from the Ferguson Fund, created in 1905 to finance public monuments and sculptures in the city, was his *Fountain of the Great Lakes,* dedicated in 1913. Taft's vision of an uplifting high culture grounded in classical principles of artistic order and harmony received a challenge in that year from the ARMORY SHOW. The show featured works that made unconventional use of color and form and refused to idealize the human form. European artists created most of the controversial works, although one of the few nonrepresentational paintings in the exhibition was by Chicago resident Manierre Dawson. Earlier, the W. Scott Thurber Gallery (designed by Frank Lloyd Wright) and one or two others had exhibited works by local modernists such as Jerome Blum, and a few collectors, notably Arthur Jerome Eddy, purchased modernist work. Most of Chicago's 10 or so commercial galleries, and dozens of art-related associations such as the Friday Club, favored traditional styles.

However, the Armory Show encouraged dissident artists such as Stanislaus Szukalski, who arrived from Poland in 1913. Because the Art Institute's Annual Exhibition of Artists of Chicago and Vicinity slighted modernist work, abstract artist Rudolph Weisenborn and others created a Salon des Refusés and the Chicago No-Jury Society of Artists. They exhibited works in the 1920s at sites such as Marshall Field's. The more traditional Palette and Chisel Club, founded in 1895 by artists who wanted to share the cost of models, offered another venue. The Renaissance Society, traditionalist when founded at the University of Chicago in 1915, began in the late 1920s to challenge prevailing conceptions of art, leading to such exhibitions as *American Primitives* (1931). The Arts Club, promodernist from its founding in 1916, brought Fernand Léger to Chicago in 1930 to show his film *Le Ballet Mécanique*.

As encoded in its name, during its brief existence Neo-Arlimusc (1926–1928) encouraged interactions among artists, littérateurs, musicians, and scientists, as did Margaret Anderson's *A Little Review* a decade before. Contacts with writers Theodore Dreiser and Sherwood Anderson, the latter of whom exhibited paintings in Chicago, helped sustain modernist painter Jerome Blum, whose aspirations met family and public resistance and who found the physical city's predominant grays and browns dispiriting. In later years visual artists met other creative figures, including out-of-town visitors such as Thorton Wilder, Dizzy Gillespie, and Sarah Vaughan, at painter Gertrude Abercrombie's Hyde Park home. Painter and patron Frederick Clay Bartlett's remarkable gift, the Helen Birch Bartlett Memorial Collection (1926), brought to the Art Institute over 20 major works, including Georges Seurat's *Sunday Afternoon on the Island of La Grande Jatte* (1884–86), which influenced many Chicago artists.

Such organizational and cultural opportunities did not satisfy all the needs of Chicago artists. Clarkson in 1921 listed over 70 who had left for better opportunities elsewhere, and following decades brought similar reports. Yet the ties between art and commerce, encouraged by organizations such as the Chicago Association of Arts and Industries, founded in 1922, far surpassed those in any American city other than New York. A 1925 index of advertising artists and illustrators listed 750. Many lost their jobs in the 1930s, yet that decade created additional links among fine and commercial art, industry, and education. Chicago's Century of Progress Exposition of 1933–34 attracted industrial and interior designers to work on its various buildings and displays and brought commissions to many painters and sculptors, some local. With support from the Association of Arts and Industries and then from Container Corporation of America founder Walter Paepcke, émigré László Moholy-Nagy helped establish the New Bauhaus (1937). Moholy-Nagy drew on his experience at the Bauhaus in Germany to teach students how to infuse such utilitarian tasks as product design with a highly developed aesthetic sensibility rooted in cultivation of their sensory and intellectual faculties.

The federal government played the largest new role in sustaining Chicago artists through the Great Depression years. The Federal Art Project and other agencies employed hundreds and left legacies such as the South Side Community Art Center (1941). Project administrators urged painting of scenes of American life, reinforcing local interest in regionalism, but with a stylistic diversity exemplified by the more than 50 artists presented in J. Z. Jacobson's *Art of Today: Chicago, 1933*. The immensely popular exhibitions of earlier and contemporary art at the Art Institute held in conjunction with the Century of Progress Exposition demonstrated public interest in a variety of work including modernist art. Concerned by such trends, the conservative Society for Sanity in Art, established by Josephine Hancock Logan in 1936, called for traditional art as represented in the exemplary collection of the Union League Club.

During World War II, enrollment in Chicago's art schools declined (at the School of the Art Institute it dropped 50 percent between 1938 and 1943) as students entered the military. Those who remained learned to respond to wartime needs, for instance by using less fabric, in short supply thanks to military demand, in their fashion design classes. At war's end the GI Bill helped fill the city's colleges, including its art schools, with former soldiers who brought a new level of maturity and intensity to undergraduate education. Enrollments at the School of the Art Institute and elsewhere surpassed earlier highs. The New Bauhaus in 1944 became the Institute of Design, affiliated from 1949 with the Illinois Institute of Technology (IIT). The Institute of Design made Chicago a national center for study of photography. Its socially oriented and rationally grounded design tradition presented an invigorating contrast to expressive and personal approaches more typical at the School of the Art Institute.

Galleries became more relevant to Chicago artists when in the 1950s Allan Frumkin and Fairweather-Hardin brought contemporary art from New York and Europe and showed local work, encouraging dozens of other galleries to do the same. Serious collectors with local interests appeared, including Jory and Joseph Randall Shapiro, who made their collections accessible to artists and led in founding the Museum of Contemporary Art (1967). Other new venues for seeing and showing included the Terra, Smart, and Block museums. The gift of the Bergman Collection gave the Art Institute a superb surrealist collection. Also important were community venues such as the 57th Street Art Fair, established in 1948 and soon followed by the Old Town Art Fair.

In the 1960s and 1970s, outlying institutions such as the College of DuPage, as well as institutions in or close to the city such as the University of Illinois at Chicago, Roosevelt University, and Columbia College, joined the School of the Art Institute as significant employers of artists, making issues such as a school's part-time faculty benefits important factors. Influential teachers from this period included Kathleen Blackshear, Harry Callahan, Aaron Siskind, George Cohen, Ed Paschke, Ray Yoshida, and Robert Loescher.

Both institutional growth and resistance to it generated artistic energy. In 1947, the Art Institute excluded students from the Chicago and Vicinity show, leading to Exhibition Momentum, which brought renowned artists to jury exhibitions in 1948 and after. Yet distinctions between mainstream and alternatives blurred. Venerable organizations became receptive to a wider range of art, as shown by Katherine Kuh's career. Director of a gallery that showed controversial modernist works in the 1930s, Kuh became the first curator of modern art at the Art Institute the following decade. She later assembled a contemporary collection for First National Bank of Chicago. Ethnographic collections at the Field Museum and the Oriental Institute inspired Leon Golub, Nancy Spero, and others as they challenged both traditional and contemporary practices, leading to the first grouping of Chicago artists to receive national attention, the Monster Roster. Another group to achieve this status was the Hairy Who, first shown in 1966 at the Hyde Park Art Center, founded in 1939 and which under the later leadership of Don Baum and with

South Side Community Art Center

Developed as part of the Federal Art Project, the South Side Community Art Center at 3831 South Michigan Avenue was formally dedicated by Eleanor Roosevelt in 1941. Its purpose was to make art and culture available to minority groups and to provide jobs in the arts for artists and other cultural workers. The center, whose alumni include Charles White, Bernard Goss, George Neal, Eldzier Cortor, Gordon Parks, Archibald Motley, and Margaret Goss Burroughs, continues to offer classes and inspire young artists. Margaret Burroughs, artist, poet, and founder of the DuSable Museum of African American History and Culture, recalls the center's origins.

In my early twenties, I stood on the corner of 39th Street and South Parkway (then Grand Boulevard) with a can collecting a "mile of dimes" to purchase the mansion which housed the center. We reached our goal and were able to purchase the property for $12,000. The local W.P.A. administration sent in workmen who renovated the building into galleries, workshops, studios, and offices.

In May 1941 Mrs. Eleanor Roosevelt came from Washington to cut the ribbon. It was quite an event. 37th Street to 39th Street was crowded with community residents who came to catch a glimpse of our then First Lady.

financial support from Ruth Horowitz championed community arts education and emerging Chicago artists. Critics Franz Schulze and Dennis Adrian helped bring attention to these artists. Writing on Chicago art further benefited from the establishment in 1973 of the *New Art Examiner.*

The black neighborhood mural movement in the early 1960s built on the AFRICAN AMERICAN community's tradition of trading art works for goods and services. Establishment of the DUSABLE MUSEUM (1961) placed into historical context the work of African American artists such as Archibald Motley, Jr., who graduated from the School of the Art Institute in 1918 and whose paintings memorably documented life in Chicago's Bronzeville. The CIVIL RIGHTS MOVEMENT encouraged Motley to deal more explicitly with racial issues by the 1960s. Opposition to American involvement in Vietnam also generated activist art. In November 1968 the Feigen Gallery exhibited works protesting repression of dissenters during the recent Democratic Convention. Vietnam veterans did not have the immediate impact on the Chicago art community that those from WORLD WAR II did, but after its establishment in 1996 the Chicago-based National Vietnam Veterans Art Museum displayed their work.

Social activism sparked creation of the multiracial Chicago Mural Group (1970), the Public Art Workshop (1972), and Movimiento Artistico Chicano (1975). Artists' cooperative galleries proliferated, including N.A.M.E. and several with a feminist emphasis, such as ARC and Artemesia, outgrowths of women artists' group the West End Bag, sparked by Ellen Lanyon. Beginning in the 1960s the National Endowment for the Arts and the Illinois Arts Council provided modest but often crucial support for organizations and individual artists.

Chicago continued to export artists. Perhaps the most widely recognized Chicago painter at midcentury, Ivan Albright, left after the city demolished the building that housed his studio. Claes Oldenburg, Red Grooms, Golub, Spero, Martin Puryear, Ellen Lanyon, and many others departed, often in search of better opportunities to exhibit, sell, and receive recognition for their work. Artists who left frequently expressed affection for Chicago, as did sculptor H. C. Westermann, who valued its commercialism and abundance of industrial materials. Others remained, or returned after stints elsewhere, including Jim Nutt, Gladys Nilsson, Kerry James Marshall, and Paschke. The city provided a receptive environment for self-taught artists such as Mr. Imagination. Artists including Roger Brown, Yoshida, and Karl Wirsum built inspiring collections of unconventional works that they made accessible to others. Novelist Leon Forrest considered visual artists indispensable to the "ideal community" for nurturing his own work, and many Chicago artists thrived on their interactions with local writers, musicians, architects, and performers. The Percent for the Arts Program established in 1978 required 1 percent of the cost of new public buildings be set aside to purchase art for the site. Various gigantic exhibitions such as Art Chicago and Chicago International Art Exposition have given Chicago artists additional exposure and made art from around the world accessible to them.

George H. Roeder, Jr.

See also: Art Criticism and Scholarship; Art, Public; Graphic Design; Literary Cultures

Further reading: Prince, Sue Ann, ed. *The Old Guard and the Avant-Garde: Modernism in Chicago, 1910–1940.* 1990. • Schulze, Franz. *Fantastic Images: Chicago Art Since 1945.* 1972. • Warren, Lynne, ed. *Art in Chicago, 1945–1995.* 1996.

Arts and Crafts Movement. In the 1890s the principles of the British Arts and Crafts movement found a sympathetic audience in Chicago among art workers, educators, and others involved in progressive cultural and social reforms. Convinced that industrial capitalism had caused the degradation of work and the human spirit, the movement advocated a reunification of ART and labor, of ARTIST and artisan. Arts and Crafts societies, guilds, and schools spread "the craftsman ideal" and promoted hand workmanship as a moral regenerative force. HULL HOUSE, a social settlement founded by Jane Addams, became the center of the movement. It sponsored a variety of handicraft activities and shops and served as headquarters for the Chicago Arts and Crafts Society, founded in 1897.

Oscar Lovell Triggs, an English instructor at the University of Chicago, helped found the Industrial Art League of Chicago in 1899. Along with Frank Lowden, Emil Hirsch, Newton Partridge, and E. P. Rosenthal, Triggs was an officer of the league, which disbanded in 1904. Source: Chicago Historical Society.

Less a style than an approach toward the making of objects, the Arts and Crafts philosophy found tangible expression in the revival of traditional crafts, particularly metalwork, ceramics (art pottery, hand-painted china, architectural terra cotta), stained and cut glass (art glass), FURNITURE, books, and weaving.

A number of small shops specializing in Arts and Crafts goods grew up in the Chicago area. Highly skilled metalsmiths hand wrought silver tableware, trophies, and jewelry at the Kalo Shop, the Jarvie Shop, Petterson Studios, and Chicago Art Silver Shop, creating a distinctive Chicago style perpetuated by the Cellini Shop (EVANSTON), Mulholland Brothers (AURORA), the Randahl Shop (PARK RIDGE), and the Tre'O Shop (Evanston).

The Pickard China Company and numerous studios hand painted porcelain. Other small shops crafted leather goods, hand printed books, cut and engraved glass, or made intricate leaded glass windows and light fixtures. Small workshops and large factories turned out straight-lined furniture in the Mission style for thousands of new BUNGALOWS.

The city's leading producers of art pottery were primarily engaged in the manufacture of architectural terra cotta. Frank Lloyd Wright and several architects associated with the Prairie School designed Teco ware, a molded art pottery produced at the American Terra Cotta & Ceramic Company's factory near CRYSTAL LAKE.

By 1914 these handicrafts industries, as well as the Arts and Crafts movement itself, had reached their peak of popularity and were turning into LEISURE activities or personal and social therapy.

Sharon S. Darling

See also: Architecture: The Prairie School; Art; Art Colonies; Fine Arts Building; Settlement Houses

Further reading: Darling, Sharon S. *Chicago Ceramics and Glass.* 1979. • Darling, Sharon S. *Chicago Metalsmiths.* 1977. • Darling, Sharon S. *Teco: Art Pottery of the Prairie School.* 1989.

Arts Funding. Chicago's traditions of arts funding have roots in the BUSINESS community and civic leadership of the mid-nineteenth century. In the 1860s and '70s, early antecedents of cultural institutions grew from arts programs organized by members of elite CLUBS. During the same period, THEATER and music organizations gained strength in ethnic neighborhoods with more grassroots support. The swell of civic support to build the AUDITORIUM Theater in 1886 began a tradition of broad-based backing in addition to bringing together wealthy PHILANTHROPISTS who went on to found other major Chicago cultural institutions. The WORLD'S COLUMBIAN

EXPOSITION in 1893 was pivotal in establishing Chicago as a cosmopolitan, cultural city and brought local, national, and international attention. The virtually concurrent establishment of the CHICAGO SYMPHONY, ART INSTITUTE, and FIELD MUSEUM went hand in hand with the ambitions of the city's aggressive business developers. More specifically community-based arts efforts included programs in music, literature, and visual arts for immigrants at HULL HOUSE, founded in 1889. The establishment of the Chicago COMMUNITY TRUST in 1915 encouraged individual philanthropy, and a Trust survey in the early 1920s showed that culture and education received the largest share.

The mix of corporate, individual, and private foundation grants remained the mainstay of arts funding into the 1960s. During that decade, the establishment of the National Endowment for the Arts and the Illinois Arts Council seeded growth in small and midsize arts organizations. These agencies also encouraged greater community participation and funding of arts programs, commonly awarding matching grants and focusing on community-based and culturally specific organizations. Support for the arts by Chicago city government strengthened in the 1980s and 1990s, spurring corporate and foundation leadership in the funding of arts resources, a development reminiscent of the industrialist backing of the previous century. Chicago became, at the end of the twentieth century, a national model for public-private partnerships in support of the arts.

Jane Preston

See also: Art; Dance; Government, City of Chicago; Theater, Ethnic

Further reading: Horowitz, Helen Lefkowitz. *Culture and the City: Cultural Philanthropy in Chicago from the 1880s to 1917.* 1976. • McCarthy, Kathleen D. *Noblesse Oblige: Charity and Cultural Philanthropy in Chicago, 1849–1929.* 1982. • McCarthy, Kathleen D. *Women's Culture: American Philanthropy and Art, 1830–1930.* 1991.

Ashburn, Community Area 70, 10 miles SW of the Loop. Improvement in greater Ashburn began with the coming of the RAILROADS, just after the area was ANNEXED to Chicago as part of the town of LAKE. The original 1893 subdivision, Clarkdale (named after its developer), was platted near 83rd and Central Park along the new Chicago & Grand Trunk Railway in the hope that the area would flourish after the WORLD'S COLUMBIAN EXPOSITION. By 1894 the early DUTCH, SWEDISH, and IRISH population had built only 30 homes; 11 years later just 18 more residences had been added.

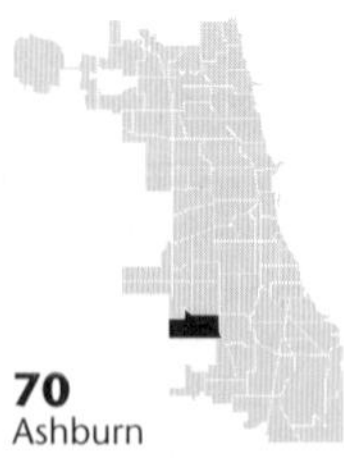

Chicago's first airport, Ashburn Flying Field, opened in 1916, spurring Chicago's drive to be an aviation center. During World War I it became a training camp for the Signal Corps, and Ashburn's population rose to 1,363. Afterward it had U.S. Post Office airmail contracts but, being situated on marshy prairie land, quickly lost them due to the field's remoteness and the prohibitive drainage costs. In 1927 Municipal Airport (now MIDWAY) opened, and further interest in Ashburn diminished. Ashburn Field remained open until 1939; in the 1950s the site became Scottsdale, a suburban-style mall and SUBDIVISION.

By the eve of WORLD WAR II the population had shrunk to 731. The years during and after the war were marked by industrial expansion between Pulaski and Cicero in Ashburn and neighboring WEST LAWN. This included Chrysler's 1943 Dodge plant for the manufacture of bomber engines, Tucker's AUTOMOBILE MANUFACTURING in 1946–7, and Ford's Korean War production. In 1960 the boundary between the two COMMUNITY AREAS was redrawn, creating Ashburn's jagged northern perimeter and uniting the industrial areas within the boundaries of West Lawn.

The automobile and the post–World War II baby boom spurred the community to meteoric growth. For over two decades the prairie surrendered to new housing construction, and population peaked at 47,161 in 1970. The prairie plants on the site were replanted in Marquette Park. The new neighborhoods—Ashburn, Wrightwood, Scottsdale, and Parkview—were predominantly white, until a 1993 subdivision, Marycrest, emerged racially mixed.

In the 1960s Ashburn was the site of significant racial strife over SCHOOL DESEGREGATION. In subsequent decades, SCHOOLS, churches, and neighborhoods integrated with the Greater Ashburn Planning Association (GAPA), working to minimize racial conflict.

Though hardly ostentatious, Ashburn has maintained an extremely high homeownership rate. Many early residents have moved to the southwestern suburbs; Ashburn Baptist Church has a satellite parish in ORLAND PARK. Retirement housing is under development to help families age in place—if the old stay it is hoped the young also will. Racial STEERING is not tolerated: "for sale" signs have been cooperatively banned; lawsuits are filed against realtors who do not comply. In recent years the only signs that have appeared on Ashburn lawns—en masse—read: "We're sold on Ashburn." A 1990 home equity assurance program protects property values.

Economic and aesthetic greening are paramount concerns. Having suffered a significant loss of industry and commerce, GAPA actively courts a diverse range of employers; it was also instrumental in the city's designation of a Tax Increment Financing District along Columbus Avenue. The 2000 census population was 39,584.

Sherry Meyer

See also: Contested Spaces

Further reading: Karlen, Harvey M. *Chicago's Crabgrass Communities: The History of the Independent Suburbs and Their Post Offices That Became Part of Chicago.* 1992. • Kitagawa, Evelyn M., and Karl E. Taeuber, eds. *Local Community Fact Book of Chicago.* 1963. • Young, David, and Neal Callahan. *Fill the Heavens with Commerce: Chicago Aviation, 1855–1926.* 1981.

Associated Negro Press. The Associated Negro Press, a national and international news agency, was established in Chicago in 1919 by Claude Barnett. A graduate of Tuskegee Institute, Barnett was deeply influenced by the self-help/service-to-the-race philosophy of Tuskegee's founder, Booker T. Washington, and served on the governing boards of such organizations as Supreme Liberty Life Insurance, the American Negro Exposition in Chicago of 1940, and Tuskegee.

With correspondents and stringers in all major centers of black population, ANP provided its member papers—the vast majority of black NEWSPAPERS—with a twice-weekly packet of general and feature news that gave AFRICAN AMERICAN newspapers a critical, comprehensive coverage of personalities, events, and institutions relevant to the lives of black Americans.

After 1945, ANP established a significant presence in Africa. By the late 1950s some 75 African papers subscribed to the service's weekly news packets in French as well as English.

Beset by climbing debts and Barnett's failing health, ANP ceased operation in midsummer 1964. His Associated Negro Press provided a vital service to one of black America's most important institutions during an era when African American newspapers realized record circulations, profits, and influence.

Lawrence Daniel Hogan

See also: Chicago Defender; Insurance; Politics and the Press

Further reading: Claude A. Barnett Papers. Chicago Historical Society, Chicago, Illinois. • Hogan, Lawrence. *A Black National News Service: The Associated Negro Press and Claude Barnett.* 1984. • Johnson, James Wesley. "The Associated Negro Press: A Medium of International News and Information." Ph.D. diss., University of Missouri at Columbia. 1976.

Association for the Advancement of Creative Musicians. The Association for the Advancement of Creative Musicians (AACM) represents one of the greatest organizational and aesthetic successes of modern AFRICAN AMERICAN music. Founded by SOUTH SIDE musicians in 1965, it served initially as a grassroots clearinghouse for local performances of a range of JAZZ-based styles. Most commonly practiced was a startlingly original kind of experimental improvised music, which, in its difficulty and close-knit collective interaction, became a modernist marker of the radical collectivist politics many of the organization's members espoused.

This linkage of black-arts political themes and a powerful, new improvised music rapidly drew national attention, particularly through the help of two local institutions: *Down Beat,* the nation's major jazz MAGAZINE, and Delmark, the BLUES record label, which recorded several AACM artists. The AACM distinguished itself by advancing an intricate and abstract "collective" improvisational style that grew out of the informal sessions led by one of its founders, Muhal Richard Abrams. Delmark's releases of AACM recordings (including those led by Abrams, Roscoe Mitchell, Joseph Jarman, and Anthony Braxton) documented this originality, and their appeal motivated these and other AACM artists to travel first to Paris and then New York in order to advance their musical careers.

Although the AACM is best known for this formative moment, it has, since then, continued to enhance the musical life of Chicago and the world. As a training ground, the organization has produced a continual flow of internationally recognized musicians (George Lewis, Henry Threadgill, Chico Freeman) and has become a viable symbol of artistic "self-help," fundamental to the African American tradition.

Ron Radano

See also: Civil Rights Movements; Ethnic Music; Record Publishing

Further reading: Radano, Ronald M. *New Musical Figurations: Anthony Braxton's Cultural Critique.* 1993.

Assyrians. Prior to WORLD WAR I, Assyrians dwelled largely among Kurds, TURKS, Azeris, and Arabs in what is now southeastern Turkey, northern Iraq, and northwestern Iran. Bearers of the ancient Syriac Christian heritage, they speak Modern Syriac ("Modern Assyrian"), a form of Aramaic. Since World War I, they have scattered, yet their nationalistic consciousness has deepened. The tight-knit Chicago community, numbering 15,683 according to the 2000 census (community estimates report several times that many), has long been one of the largest and most active in the Assyrian diaspora.

Exposure to American Presbyterian missionaries in Iran first prompted Assyrians to come to America. Early arrivals, from 1889 on, were young men who had attended missionary schools and came to continue their studies or, later, to seek work. A number of key missionaries in Iran were Chicagoans, including several members of the prominent Shedd family. The young men settled around Clark and Huron, near RELIGIOUS INSTITUTIONS familiar to them. By 1920, the majority were employed as HOTEL and RESTAURANT workers or as janitors.

World War I had calamitous consequences, as approximately one-third of the 310,000 Assyrians remaining in their homeland perished. Assyrians in Chicago saw their numbers swell with REFUGEES: from 1,422 in 1920 to 2,327 in 1924, according to community estimates.

These events hastened organizational development. To save and rebuild the lives of the refugees, Assyrians cooperated with ARMENIANS in the Armenian SYRIAN Relief Committee and established village aid societies and ladies' sewing bees. Several nationalistic social clubs emerged, including the still-existing Assyrian American Association, or *Šôtāputa* (founded 1916).

From the 1910s through the 1930s, Chicago's Assyrian community cultivated a rich social and cultural life, as its members advanced economically and moved northward into such neighborhoods as LINCOLN PARK and LAKE VIEW. Integrating themselves into the life of Chicago through the assertion of their ethnicity, Assyrians established a persisting pattern. During World War I, they assiduously sold Liberty Bonds, and in 1918 they organized the 100-member-strong Assyrian American Illinois Volunteer Training Corps, or *Pôj Surêta* ("Assyrian Battalion"). In 1947, Assyrian veterans established the American Assyrian Amvet Post, which has remained active into the twenty-first century.

Assyrians also organized their own congregations, conducting services in Syriac, within the fold of established denominations. The Carter Presbyterian Church—until the 1970s, the largest Assyrian congregation—was spawned by the FOURTH PRESBYTERIAN CHURCH. Smaller congregations also flourished: Chaldean (Roman) Catholic, Congregational, Pentecostal, Lutheran, and Brethren, in addition to the Assyrians' ancestral Church of the East, which has had strong ecumenical ties with the Episcopal Church.

From the 1920s through the 1950s, the inflow of Assyrians to Chicago seldom exceeded a trickle. Since the 1960s the pace of immigration has quickened, from Syria, Lebanon, and above all Iraq. Assyrians in Iraq tended to work for the British military or foreign contractors. Nationalization of enterprises destabilized their economic position and spurred emigration, which the Iran-Iraq War (1980–1988), the Persian Gulf War (1991), and pervasive government oppression accelerated.

This new migration coincided with the waning of the "old" community. As the mostly IRANIAN Assyrians migrated out of Chicago (especially to California) or assimilated into American society, the mostly IRAQI Assyrians replenished and augmented the existing American Assyrian institutions. Since 1992, they have held an annual Assyrian New Year's Parade on honorary "King Sargon Boulevard" (a stretch of Western Avenue).

Internally diverse, these later immigrants typically have found employment as workers in midsize factories and as store clerks, bank tellers, and mechanics. More and more have become professionals such as doctors, engineers, and accountants, or retailers. By 1990, Assyrians owned as many as four hundred North Side video rental shops. Recently, operating dollar store franchises has become an attraction.

Chicago's Assyrian families have toiled to support or rescue relatives facing dire circumstances in the Middle East. By activating their extensive family support networks, such efforts have kept alive a strong sense of Assyrian identity.

Daniel P. Wolk

See also: Americanization; Demography; Multicentered Chicago

Further reading: Ablahat, Rev. Haidow, et al. *Dedication of the Carter Memorial Assyrian-Persian Chapel, 52–54 West Huron Street, of the Fourth Presbyterian Church of Chicago.* 1914. Ashurbanipal Library, Chicago, IL. • *Holy Catholic Apostolic Church of the East (Assyrian Nestorian) Vs. His Beatitude, Mar Eshai Shimun, Patriarch of the East and of the Assyrians, et al.* 42 C 3763 (1942). Clerk of the Circuit Court of Cook County, Chancery Division. • Stein, Edith M. "Some Near Eastern Immigrant Groups in Chicago." M.A. thesis, University of Chicago. 1922.

Athletic Clubs. *See* Fitness and Athletic Clubs

Auburn Gresham, Community Area 71, 9 miles SW of the Loop.

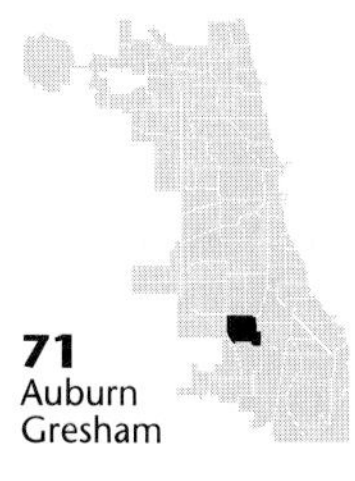

The low, flat, swampy land upon which Auburn Gresham was built was located in the southeast section of the Town of LAKE that was ANNEXED into Chicago in 1889. Early settlers were GERMAN and DUTCH truck farmers. When railroad lines were laid in the mid-nineteenth century, IRISH RAILROAD WORKERS came to the area. The WORLD'S COLUMBIAN EXPOSITION in 1893 attracted prospective homesteaders to the SOUTH SIDE through the extension and improvement of city services to the area, including streetcar lines. Between 1913 and 1918, the city further extended the lines on Halsted to 119th Street and the cars on Racine and Ashland Avenues to 87th Street. The 79th Street line ran from Western Avenue to LAKE MICHIGAN beaches.

Auburn Gresham's accessibility to TRANSPORTATION made the neighborhood an easy sell for developers looking to attract families who were trying to escape older and more congested sections of the city. Many Auburn Gresham residents migrated from the working-class neighborhoods of BRIDGEPORT, Canaryville, and BACK OF THE YARDS as well as from ENGLEWOOD. Twenty-one percent of Auburn Gresham's population were of Irish stock in the 1930s. German Americans, SWEDISH Americans, and some POLISH, ITALIAN, and FRENCH Americans also took up residence in the area. Many stockyard workers commuted to work on the Halsted streetcar. City workers such as POLICE and FIREFIGHTERS, as well as railroad and CONSTRUCTION WORKERS, found the neighborhood convenient. Between 1920 and 1930 the population of Auburn Gresham nearly tripled, from 19,558 to 57,381. Most of the housing built there were BUNGALOWS, two- and three-flats, and apartment buildings.

Approximately 44 percent of Auburn Gresham's population were ROMAN CATHOLICS, concentrated into five large parishes. The other residents worshiped at six Lutheran churches, three Methodist congregations, two Episcopal churches, and small Presbyterian, Baptist, and nonaffiliated congregations. Ethnic groups tended to live near their respective churches. Many Catholics were clustered near St. Leo's and St. Sabina's parishes. There was no overt PROTESTANT-Catholic hostility here as in other Chicago neighborhoods, probably because few residents were nativists of Anglo-Protestant stock.

Auburn Gresham weathered the GREAT DEPRESSION and WORLD WAR II and enjoyed the peaceful and prosperous fifties. By the end of the 1950s, AFRICAN AMERICANS seeking housing beyond the overcrowded and decaying BLACK BELT began to move into neighborhoods adjacent to Auburn Gresham. While this provoked racist anxieties among many residents, in 1959 several churches and civic organizations formed the Organization of Southwest Communities (OSC). Modeled on Saul Alinsky's community organizing tactics, the OSC's goals were to maintain property values and appearances, stop BLOCKBUSTING by real-estate agents, educate residents to dispel racist stereotypes, and prevent violence while allowing peaceful, stable integration.

In its first five years of existence, OSC enjoyed wide and even enthusiastic support from residents who felt protected from property-value declines and racial violence. In the 1960s, however, crime in the Gresham police district rose at a faster rate than in the city as a whole. Crimes ranged from purse snatchings and bicycle thefts to home break-ins. At the same time, Auburn Gresham's population increased dramatically. For the previous 20 years it had remained relatively stable, but between 1960 and 1970 the population grew from 59,484 to 68,854. The swell of cars and noise made the area less appealing, and parking difficulties at night made crime-fearing residents more anxious.

City and national events also played a role in chilling race relations in Auburn Gresham. In 1966 violence greeted the civil rights march of Martin Luther King, Jr., in nearby Marquette Park. King's death in Memphis on April 4, 1968, set off riots in Chicago and across the county. Many white residents in Auburn Gresham came to the conclusion that violence was an inevitable byproduct of racial mixing.

By 1970 Auburn Gresham was 69 percent black, including many middle-class federal employees and CTA workers. Most African Americans initially settled in the eastern portion of the neighborhood. While OSC could not maintain integration, it did make the transition from white to black more peaceful and less destructive to property values and a less embittering experience for many.

Eileen M. McMahon

See also: Civil Rights Movements; Community Organizing; Neighborhood Succession; Racism, Ethnicity, and White Identity

Further reading: McMahon, Eileen M. *What Parish Are You From? A Chicago Irish Community and Race Relations.* 1995. • Pacyga, Dominic A., and Ellen Skerrett. *Chicago, City of Neighborhoods: Histories and Tours.* 1986.

Auditorium Building. The Auditorium is one of Chicago's architectural masterpieces. Built in 1888 on the northwest corner of Congress and Michigan, it combines Dankmar Adler's engineering ingenuity with Louis Sullivan's architectural virtuosity. It was the brainchild of Ferdinand Peck, a Chicago impresario devoted to bringing the city a world-class opera house and theater. A HOTEL and office block were added in 1890 to ensure the theater's economic viability.

Adler and Sullivan received the commission based on Adler's expertise in acoustics and engineering. After preliminary, ornate designs, Peck accepted Sullivan's final scheme, which derived much of its character from H. H. Richardson's recently completed Marshall Field WHOLESALE Store, also in Chicago. Richardson's building was a warehouse that employed strong, solid massing without excessive ornament. The beauty of Sullivan's design (built 1887–1889) comes from his focus on the structure's overall mass and repetition of streamlined patterns to give this large building (63,350 square feet) with many uses a unified look. Sullivan's muted exterior stands in contrast to his elaborate interior designs, based on organic motifs.

The Auditorium demonstrates Adler's technical ability to accommodate a variety of uses, from POLITICAL CONVENTIONS to grand OPERA, under one roof. Innovations in foundation technology allowed the large, heavy building to be constructed on notoriously marshy land, and the latest techniques were employed to give the building uninterrupted spans.

The Auditorium fell into disuse with the completion of Chicago's Civic Opera Building in 1929, and the GREAT DEPRESSION furthered its demise. During WORLD WAR II, portions of the building were used by the United Service Organization (USO). In 1946, ROOSEVELT UNIVERSITY purchased the

Interior of Auditorium Building, designed by Dankmar Adler and Louis Sullivan and constructed in 1889. Photographer: J. W. Taylor. Source: Chicago Historical Society.

structure and began converting the hotel and office spaces into classrooms and school offices. The theater was renovated in 1967, and continues in operation today.

Heidi Pawlowski Carey

See also: Architecture: The First Chicago School; Entertaining Chicagoans; Places of Assembly; Theater Buildings

Further reading: Condit, Carl W. *The Chicago School of Architecture.* 1964. • Jordy, William H. *Progressive and Academic Ideals at the Turn of the Twentieth Century.* Vol. 4, *American Buildings and Their Architects.* 1972.

Audy Home. (Juvenile Temporary Detention Center). In 1899, the women of HULL HOUSE and the men of the Chicago Bar Association succeeded in passing legislation to remove children from adult JAILS and adult poorhouses by establishing the world's first JUVENILE COURT. The separate court was part of a sustained campaign to transform the maltreatment of children by abolishing child labor, establishing compulsory education, creating public PLAYGROUNDS, and strengthening immigrant family life. One dilemma was where to hold children awaiting their first court appearance.

Initially, boys were held in a cottage and stable at 233 Honore Street, while girls were housed at an annex of the Harrison Street POLICE station. Although these arrangements were recognized as an improvement over city jail, escapes, attacks, and underfunding within the first two years led to the establishment of the Detention Home, operated by the Juvenile Court Committee (JCC) in conjunction with the city and county. Children were fed for eleven cents per day, but JCC PHILANTHROPISTS persuaded the Chicago Board of Education to provide a teacher in 1906, and by 1907 a new court building was established with facilities which separated delinquent boys, delinquent girls, and dependent CHILDREN.

Today's Juvenile Temporary Detention Center, located above the 31 courtrooms constituting Juvenile Court, has an official capacity of 489 youngsters awaiting delinquency adjudication or trial in adult criminal court. Popularly still known as the "Audy Home," this facility's overcrowding and economic distress, as well as questions about appropriate programming, punishment, and safety, continue to challenge reformers. The center's Nancy B. Jefferson School, operated by the Chicago Board of Education, teaches 500 detained children each day.

Bernardine Dohrn

See also: Children and the Law; Juvenile Justice Reform; Social Services

Further reading: Knupfer, Anne Meis. "The Chicago Detention Home." In *A Noble Social Experiment? The First Hundred Years of the Cook County Juvenile Court, 1899–1999,* ed. Gwen Hoerr McNamee, 1999. • McNamee, Gwen Hoerr. "The Origin of the Cook County Juvenile Court." In *A Noble Social Experiment?*

Aurora, IL, DuPage and Kane Counties, 35 miles W of the Loop.

The city of Aurora, the economic anchor of the FOX RIVER Valley area, has a population of over 110,000. It began in 1834 (incorporated in 1845), when Joseph and Samuel McCarty came from New York looking for a river site to build a mill. A strategic bend in the Fox River at this location satisfied the McCarty brothers. The river served as a power source for mills and early factories even as periodic floods destroyed businesses, bridges, and dams.

In 1854 a second town incorporated west of the river, and three years later, the separate municipalities united. To ease political tensions between the two, civic offices were located on an island in the river; ward boundaries ended at the river, and the mayor was elected from alternate sides until 1913. While initially the east side was much larger both geographically and in population than the west side, the river now divides the town through its general geographic center.

Following the establishment of textile mills and gristmills, Aurora became a manufacturing center, primarily of heavy-machine building equipment. In 1856 the Chicago, Burlington & Quincy RAILROAD located its railcar construction and repair shops in Aurora to become the town's largest employer until the 1960s. These businesses were located primarily on the east side and provided employment for four generations of European immigrants. Aurora's professional and managerial workers came from YANKEE stock and settled across the river, making the west side more affluent. The combination of these three factors—a highly industrialized town, a sizable river that divided it, and the Burlington's shops—account for much of the dynamics of Aurora's political, economic, and social history.

Aurora's character formed early. Philosophically, the town was inclusive and tolerant, welcoming a variety of European immigrants and openly supporting abolitionist activity prior to the CIVIL WAR. MEXICAN migrants began arriving after 1910.

Socially, the town was progressive in its attitude toward education, religion, welfare, and women, for example, establishing the first free public school district in Illinois in 1851 and a high school for girls in 1855, supporting 20 congregations (including two AFRICAN AMERICAN churches) representing nine denominations in 1887, and establishing a YWCA in 1893 which is still in operation today.

As late as the post–World War II boom, manufacturing companies continued to locate in Aurora to take advantage of the abundant workforce, good TRANSPORTATION, and favorable economy. Few labor problems affected Aurora.

With the closing of many factories in the 1980s, the town's UNEMPLOYMENT rate reached 16 percent. In response, Aurora initiated downtown redevelopment and border ANNEXATIONS, welcoming riverboat casinos, mixed-use business parks, and residential communities to create 20,000 jobs.

In 2000 Aurora's population was 32 percent Hispanic and 11 percent black. The city remains a self-sufficient community, independent of Chicago for its identity, but connected to it through the economic patterns that tie suburbs, edge cities, and central cities together. Aurora is frequently referred to as a Chicago suburb, most often by the nonlocal media or for promotional purposes.

Catherine Bruck

See also: Economic Geography; Kane County; Metropolitan Growth

Further reading: Barclay, Robert. *Aurora, 1837–1987.* 1988. • Derry, Vernon. *The Aurora Story.* 1976. • Palmer, Susan L. "Building Ethnic Communities in a Small City: Romanians & Mexicans in Aurora, Illinois, 1900–1940." Ph.D. diss., Northern Illinois University. 1986.

Aurora University. Aurora University originated in 1893 as Mendota College (Mendota, Illinois), founded by a Midwestern group of Advent Christians. The Advent Christian denomination was one of many outgrowths of the nineteenth-century Millerite Movement. In 1912, the school moved to AURORA, a larger town with a record of impressive economic development that promised the college greater opportunities. Initially Aurora College was a liberal arts school composed mostly of Advent Christians drawn from around the country. That began to change as the effects of the GREAT DEPRESSION and WORLD WAR II created a more diverse student body and began to transform the college into more of a secular, regional liberal arts school with a growing emphasis on professional programs. In 1985, Aurora College became Aurora University. Today the university also has satellite professional programs in Chicago and Wisconsin.

Susan Palmer

See also: Universities and Their Cities

Further reading: Anderson, Charles W. *Building on the Foundation.* 1990. • Anderson, Charles W. *Upon a Rock.* 1987.

Austin, Community Area 25, 7 miles W of the Loop. Austin, on Chicago's western border, evolved from a country village to a dense urban neighborhood between 1870 and 1920. For the next 50 years this was a large community of solidly middle class residents, but since 1970 it has experienced a profound social and economic transformation. Austin had three important early influences: its founder, Henry Austin (also instrumental in OAK PARK's development); transit lines, notably the Chicago & Northwestern RAILROAD and the Lake Street Elevated; and a rivalry with neighboring Oak Park.

Austin was created in 1865, when developer Henry Austin purchased 470 acres for a temperance settlement named "Austinville" (Chicago Avenue to Madison Street, and Laramie to Austin Boulevard). Austin's intentions for the settlement were clear: home ownership, public amenities such as tree-lined parkways, and gracious living—though Austin himself lived in Oak Park. The village had nearly 1,000 residents by 1874, owing largely to steadily improving suburban railroad service. With over 4,000 residents by the 1890s, Austin was the largest settlement in Cicero township. In 1899, Austin was voted out of the township and into Chicago by residents of other parts of the township. Austin's residents sought to maintain an independent identity after ANNEXATION. An ambitious illustration was the 1929 construction of Austin Town Hall, modeled on Philadelphia's Independence Hall.

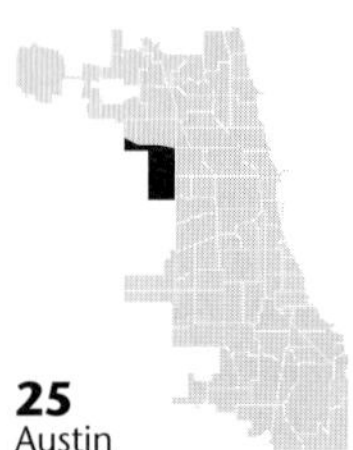
25
Austin

By 1920 Austin was one of Chicago's best-served commuter areas, with STREET RAILWAYS to downtown Chicago every half mile, the busiest being the Madison Street "Green Hornet." The area was also served by the Lake Street "L" RAPID TRANSIT. Commerce in Austin followed transit lines, with significant business development along Madison Street, Chicago Avenue, and Lake Street. Despite its commercial range and volume, Austin lacked the intense retail centrality of West Garfield Park (on Madison, from Pulaski to Cicero) or of Oak Park (at Lake and Harlem). In 1950 Austin was a predominantly residential community, with major industrial corridors to the east, north, and south.

Austin early attracted upwardly mobile GERMANS and Scandinavians, followed by IRISH and ITALIAN families. These groups built the community's mid-twentieth-century landmarks: a half-dozen sizable ROMAN CATHOLIC parishes, which annually educated thousands of children and provided the social base for much of the community. By the 1930s GREEK migrants had arrived in south Austin, building their own landmark, the Byzantine-style Assumption church. Austin had 130,000 residents by 1930.

Dense housing development almost completely supplanted the village landscape of large frame homes in the early twentieth century: north Austin sprouted brick two-flats, small frame houses, and the ubiquitous brick story-and-a-half bungalow; in south Austin, rowhouses, sizable corner apartment blocks, and a multitude of brick three-flats and courtyard apartment buildings flourished. Despite the massive scale change, the nineteenth-century village residential core is still visible in the Midway Park area north of Central and Lake, a designated National Register historic district (1985). This neighborhood boasts stately neoclassical and Queen Anne–style homes, many designed by architect Frederick Schock, as well as several structures by Frank Lloyd Wright and his students.

Austin's crown jewel was Columbus Park (1920). Designed in a prairie mode by renowned LANDSCAPE ARCHITECT Jens Jensen, the park featured a lagoon, a GOLF course, athletic fields and a SWIMMING pool, as well as winding paths and an imposing refectory overlooking the lagoon. Assaulted by EXPRESSWAY construction in the 1960s, the park was extensively restored in 1992.

Austin's DEMOGRAPHIC profile shifted dramatically beginning in the late 1960s. By 1980 Austin's population was predominantly AFRICAN AMERICAN, more than 96 percent in south Austin. Like other west-side communities, Austin experienced housing disinvestment, vacancy, and demolition, as well as loss of jobs and of commerce as its white population moved to the suburbs and to Chicago's Northwest Side. Neighborhood groups like the Organization for a Better Austin have worked to stabilize the community, as have nonprofit housing developers aided by SOUTH SHORE Bank.

Judith A. Martin

See also: Historic Preservation; Housing Types; Neighborhood Succession; Suburbs and Cities as Dual Metropolis; Transportation

Further reading: Martin, Judith A. "The Influence of Values on an Urban Community: The Austin Area of Chicago, 1890–1920." M.A. thesis, University of Minnesota. 1973. • Pacyga, Dominic A., and Ellen Skerrett. *Chicago, City of Neighborhoods: Histories and Tours.* 1986. • Sinkevitch, Alice, ed. *AIA Guide to Chicago.* 1993.

Austin High Gang. Chicago-style JAZZ began on the far West Side when six student musicians from AUSTIN High School got together at a local ice cream parlor to listen to their favorite hot music—jazz. After they discovered the 1922 recordings of the New Orleans Rhythm Kings (NORK), they made a collective decision to pursue jazz careers. The musicians were Bud Freeman (saxophone), Jim Lanigan (string bass/tuba), Dick McPartland (banjo/guitar), Jimmy McPartland (cornet), Dave North (piano), and Frank Teschemacher (clarinet). They were joined by drummer Dave Tough from nearby OAK PARK.

By 1923 they were going to the black SOUTH SIDE to hear King Oliver's Creole Jazz Band, which became the most important influence on their music. Although they did not record as a group, McPartland, Freeman, Teschemacher, and Lanigan are on the 1927 recordings of the McKenzie and Condon's Chicagoans in which the Chicago style is documented.

Richard A. Wang

See also: Entertaining Chicagoans

Further reading: Kenney, William Howland. *Chicago Jazz: A Cultural History, 1904–1930.* 1993. • Smith, Charles Edward. "The Austin High Gang." In *Jazzmen,* ed. Charles Edward Smith and Frederic Ramsey, Jr., 1939. • Steiner, John. "Chicago." In *Jazz: New Perspectives on the History of Jazz,* ed. Nat Hentoff and Albert McCarthy, 1959.

Australians. Like Australians in other major U.S. cities, most of Chicago's Australians have assimilated easily owing to their small numbers, their knowledge of English upon arrival, and the fact that their migration constitutes a transfer from one advanced industrialized country to another. Unlike many other ethnic groups, Australians living in Chicago have maintained neither an active organizational presence, nor significant neighborhood or occupational concentration.

Chicago's small Australian population increased soon after WORLD WAR II, with the arrival of war brides, Australian women who married American servicemen stationed in the Pacific theater. Since the end of World War II, most Australians who have moved to the Chicago area have been drawn by employment opportunities. In 1998, the Australian-American Chamber of Commerce estimated that a few thousand Australians were living in the Chicago area.

The Australian federal government maintained a general consulate office in Chicago from 1971 to 1993 and an Australian-American Chamber of Commerce from 1987 to 1998, each of which closed as a result of cutbacks following an economic depression in Australia during the mid-1990s. The Australian Trade Commission has maintained representation in Chicago, despite the closing of all other Australian governmental offices in the area.

Following the closing of the Chamber of Commerce, the Down Under Club, a not-for-profit social organization founded in 1986, became the only organized body attempting to bring together Australians in the Chicago area. The Down Under Club, which has never recorded more than a hundred members, sponsors social functions for Anzac (Australian and NEW ZEALANDER Army Corps) Day in April, and celebrates the running of the Melbourne Cup HORSE RACE on the first Tuesday of each November.

Daniel Greene

See also: Multicentered Chicago

Austrians. With nearly 40,000 residents of Austrian ancestry at the end of the twentieth century, Chicago is, at least symbolically, the most Austrian city outside of Austria itself. Austrian ethnicity and national affiliation, however, must be interpreted from four distinct historical paths, both European and American. First, Austrian identity in Chicago historically derives from the multicultural mosaic of the Austro-Hungarian Empire, whose populations spoke various Slavic, Hungarian, Romanian, Italian, and Yiddish languages, as well as GERMAN, especially in German-speaking "speech islands." Second, European Austrian identity alternately accepted and rejected a larger Germanic culture, dependent on the military and cultural hegemony of Germany; a similarly ambivalent relation with German American culture has persisted in Chicago. Third, Austrian identity may be constructed as a secondary affiliation, behind primary cultural connections to a province or city, such as Styria, Vienna, or the Danube Swabian region of southwestern Romania and northern SERBIA. Fourth, Austrian identity in Chicago may result from postethnic decision-making, in which immigrants from one region or dialect region may participate in the activities of another or join organizations that espouse a unified Austrian national culture, which in turn welcomes non-Austrians as different as HUNGARIANS or SLOVAKS from the former empire or war brides returning after World War II.

Neither the magnitude of Austrian emigration nor the evolution of distinctive forms of Austrian American identity can be readily documented. During the nineteenth century, the Austro-Hungarian Empire did not keep emigration statistics. Statistics used to track immigration to the United States, moreover, inevitably illustrate different patterns of Austrianness. In the 1970 census only 71 percent of Austrians in Chicago reported German as their mother tongue; the figure was considerably lower among older Austrian immigrants. Census statistics from Americans of Hungarian, ROMANIAN, CZECH, and JEWISH descent often report German as the mother tongue, thus suggesting strong affiliation with Austria as a cultural, if not national, homeland. Emigration and immigration data, nonetheless, do illustrate one persistent phenomenon, namely, that Austrian identity in Europe and in North America—and especially in Chicago—depended from the beginning on the interaction of minority and ethnic groups and shifting processes of multiculturalism.

Beginning in 1890, Chicago became the most important destination of Burgenlanders (from Burgenland, a region in eastern Austria) immigrating to North America. Economic necessity was the primary motivating factor, for though Burgenland was rural, many Burgenlanders did not own land, obligated instead to do handwork or weekly labor in Vienna. The Burgenland immigration to Chicago took place during three periods: (1) from about 1890 to 1914; (2) from the collapse of the Austro-Hungarian Empire at the end of WORLD WAR I (1918) until the rise of National Socialism in the 1930s; (3) post–WORLD WAR II. Immigration between the world wars was not only the most extensive, it also played the most critical role in shaping Burgenland-Chicago identities. During this period most Burgenlanders worked in the stockyards, for RAILROADS, or in related industries, such as in foundries and CONSTRUCTION. The first immigrants were often single men, hoping to earn enough money to return to Austria, and many were able to return (as many as 35 percent). A "Little Burgenland" took shape, roughly stretching along the railroad lines paralleling what is today the corridor of the Stevenson Expressway.

Austrian culture in Chicago has included both concentration in neighborhoods like Little Burgenland and dispersion, for which a single Austrian identity may be less crucial than affiliation to other ethnic or cultural groups and institutions. Whereas Little Burgenland depended on access to employment, the much reduced neighborhoods at the end of the twentieth century depended on previous structures for maintaining cultural and social relations. Taverns and churches survived in some neighborhoods, providing not only opportunities for Austrians to gather together but facilities for ethnic CLUBS and venues for visiting musical groups.

Dispersion of Austrians in Chicago, beginning in the 1950s and extensive by the 1990s, has altered many forms of ethnic affiliation from the immigrant generations but has also supplanted these with other ways of maintaining Austrian ethnicity and culture. There are still recognizable areas in which Austrians, especially Burgenlanders, have resettled in significant numbers, especially on the North Side of the city, near the junction of the Kennedy and Edens Expressways, and in the southwestern suburbs. In order to draw a critical mass, Austrian cultural activities often take place in symbolic communities. The LINCOLN SQUARE neighborhood, notable for its German American cultural activities, was never the home to Austrians in Chicago, but a symbolic form of Austrianness is undergirded by local shops (e.g., Delicatessen Meyer) and the choice of Austrian CHORAL societies to rehearse and perform in the DANK-Haus on Western Avenue. Many Austrians in Chicago, moreover, maintain extensive contacts with Austria. Touring Austrian musicians will usually include Chicago on their itinerary. Young Austrians in Chicago, such as the winner of the annual "Miss Burgenland" contest, are awarded opportunities to visit Austria as symbolic ambassadors of Austrian culture in Chicago.

The presence and transformation of Austrian culture in Chicago has depended on an institutional life woven into a variety of cultural institutions, which assume three forms. First, there are cultural organizations that retain fairly extensive connections with Austria. The most significant German-language press for Austrians, for example, is the newsletter of the *Burgenländische Gemeinschaft* (Burgenland Society), which extensively reports news and cultural events in both Chicago and Burgenland. Second, there are cultural organizations that interact with other Central and East Central European ethnic communities, especially the Bavarians and the Czechs and other former Habsburg ethnic communities, thereby reformulating and resituating European patterns of multiculturalism to the United States. Third, and especially at the end of the twentieth century, many Austrian cultural organizations consolidate a North American web of institutions that sponsor Austrian culture, especially the arts. The monthly *Austrian-American* newsletter, for example, is published in Chicago, and much of its news comes from Chicago, but it consciously represents a much larger ethnic identity.

Austria itself, therefore, assumes new symbolic forms in the activities of these American cultural organizations—activities that emerge from a mosaic of historical, regional, and transnational identities. Austrian culture and identity in Chicago are the products of a small community that relies on a historically conscious institutional culture and the active use of expressive culture to create a malleable identity. Austrians in Chicago therefore maintain a creative culture, one that has responded historically to the complex conditions of Austrian identity, both in Austria and, especially during the twentieth century, in Chicago.

Philip V. Bohlman

See also: Americanization; Demography; Multicentered Chicago

Further reading: Chmelar, Johan. "The Austrian Emigration, 1900–1914." *Perspectives in American History* 7 (1973): 275–378. • Dujmovits, Walter. *Die Amerikawanderung der Burgenländer.* 1975; 2nd ed. 1992. • Goldner, Franz. *Austrian Emigration: 1936–1945.* Trans. Edith Simons. 1979.

Automobile Manufacturing. Although two early automobiles were exhibited at the WORLD'S COLUMBIAN EXPOSITION of 1893—the prototype Morrison electric and a gasoline-powered car from Germany—horseless carriages didn't receive much notoriety until the *Chicago Times-Herald* offered $5,000 in prizes to the winner of a round-trip race between Chicago and EVANSTON two years later. The race attracted considerable attention because two cars were able to finish despite the fact that a storm had deposited a foot of snow on the Chicago area two days earlier.

What was possibly the nation's first auto show was held in conjunction with the race. A modest 12 automobiles were exhibited in a donated Studebaker Company wagon and buggy showroom on South Wabash Avenue. Annual auto shows at which builders exhibited production and futuristic vehicles did not begin in Chicago until after 1900. Except during major wars they continued through the end of the century. Road races and "reliability runs" intended to demonstrate the durability of motor cars were also popular in the early twentieth century.

The 1895 race in a way marks the beginning of Chicago's auto manufacturing industry; at least six local tinkerers tried to build vehicles for the race but were unable to complete them in time. In the final five years of the nineteenth century at least 22 local companies were formed to build and sell horseless carriages, and at least 12 got their vehicles into production.

Although Chicago never quite rivaled Detroit as the nation's auto capital, during the first decade of the twentieth century no less than 28 companies produced 68 models of cars in the Windy City and its environs. Chicago's industrial base, which included a profusion of machine shops able to turn out automotive components, established the city as a center of manufacture of AUTOMOBILE PARTS through the twentieth century. The fact that the city was a RAILROAD center enabled customers to travel to Chicago from all over the Midwest to buy cars built locally as well as in Detroit. In the decades before rural roads were paved to permit intercity travel by auto, out-of-town customers would buy cars along Auto Row south of the LOOP and ship them home by train.

Many early manufacturers also built light delivery trucks, which for a time provided more of an impetus for the conversion from horsepower to motor vehicles than did autos because they were less expensive to operate than horse-drawn drays. Trucks also enabled Chicago to reduce pollution from dung and urine deposited by horses on the streets and to avoid epizootic diseases which decimated urban horse populations in the late nineteenth century. Several auto manufacturers, such as INTERNATIONAL HARVESTER COMPANY and Diamond T Motor Car Company, successfully converted to heavy truck production. International Harvester, which became Navistar Corporation in 1986, was one of the nation's largest builders of large trucks and school buses.

A motorized farm buggy known generically as the "highwheeler" because of its wagon-style wheels was developed in Chicago, which became the center of manufacture of that type of car between about 1903 and 1912, when the Model T Ford drove it from the market. Holsman Automobile Company, International Harvester, Staver Carriage Company, and SEARS, ROEBUCK & Co. combined built nearly 18,000 highwheelers in Chicago. Sears sold them through its catalog.

Woods Motor Vehicle Company manufactured more than 13,500 electric and dual-powered cars between 1896 and 1918, when it went out of business. Other well-known Chicago auto manufacturers included Checker Motors Corporation, a taxicab builder which moved to Kalamazoo, Michigan; Yellow Cab Manufacturing Company, one of auto-leasing company founder John Hertz's ventures; and Thomas B. Jeffery & Co., a BICYCLE maker who developed the Rambler auto and moved his manufacturing operations to north suburban Kenosha, Wisconsin. The Rambler was the most popular auto developed in Chicago. More than 4.2 million were sold between 1902 and their discontinuance in 1969 by the successor American Motors Corporation. As the twentieth century ended, the Rambler factory in Kenosha was used to build engines for Chrysler Corporation autos.

The auto manufacturing industry in the Windy City began to decline by WORLD WAR I as Detroit-made cars became dominant, although the Chicago area remained an important center for auto parts and steel used to make cars. At the end of the twentieth century, Ford Motor Company maintained an assembly plant in HEGEWISCH, and Chrysler Corporation maintained one in in Belvidere, but the last Chicago manufacturer of consequence was Elgin Motor Car Company, which built 16,784 conventional cars in suburban Argo (SUMMIT) between 1916 and its bankruptcy in 1924. In 1946, Preston Tucker organized his company and planned to build the "Torpedo" in a factory in the WEST LAWN Community Area. Detroit was so dominant that he had no chance of success. The company was bankrupted in 1949 after producing only 51 vehicles.

David M. Young

See also: Business of Chicago; Economic Geography; Innovation, Invention, and Chicago Business; Iron and Steel; Near South Side

Further reading: Flink, James J. *America Adopts the Automobile.* 1970. • Young, David M. *Chicago Transit.* 1998.

Automobile Parts. The manufacture of automobile parts was never one of Chicago's largest industries. Nevertheless, the history of the auto parts industry cannot be written without Chicago-based companies. The production and distribution of car and truck parts employed thousands of area residents engaged in delivering many of the approximately 15,000 parts used in a modern automobile.

In 1900, when the nascent automobile industry was still closely related to the BICYCLE industry, Chicago companies such as the Western Wheel Works and Smith Steel Stamping were among the earliest makers of parts for gasoline-powered vehicles. As the auto industry grew at an explosive rate, new parts makers sprung up in and around the city. During the 1920s, as many as six hundred companies in the Chicago area made auto parts and accessories. Most were quite small, and many went out of business or were bought out by larger firms. Still, metropolitan Chicago boasted dozens of small-scale manufacturers and distributors of auto parts through the end of the twentieth century.

Several Chicago companies, including Stewart-Warner, Maremont, and Borg-Warner, became leaders in various sectors of the industry. Stewart-Warner, a maker of speedometers and other gauges, was descended from the Stewart Company, a Chicago company founded in 1905, and the Warner Instrument Company, which originated a year earlier in South Beloit, Wisconsin. By the 1970s, Stewart-Warner employed about 5,000 people in the Chicago area. Another local industry leader descended from Maremont, Wolfson & Cohen, Inc., established in Chicago in 1903. In 1933 this maker of truck yokes and springs became Maremont Automobile Products, Inc., and manufactured shock absorbers, mufflers, and other parts. The largest and best known of all the Chicago-based auto parts companies during the twentieth century was Borg-Warner Corporation, created from several Midwestern auto parts makers in 1928. Borg-Warner saw its annual sales rise from about $54 million in 1929 to over $600 million by 1957. During the 1950s, it supplied many of the new automatic transmissions installed in the vehicles assembled by Detroit giants such as Ford. By the end of the twentieth century, the company (still headquartered on Chicago's Michigan Avenue) sold nearly $2.5 billion worth of auto parts annually and employed a global workforce of over 13,000 people.

By the late twentieth century, intense global competition in the auto parts industry made it difficult for local manufacturing firms to prosper. Borg-Warner, despite its continued growth, no longer manufactured as many parts at local plants. Some companies were forced to retrench. OAK BROOK's Champion Parts, Inc., once the leading independent American rebuilder of parts such as carburetors and alternators, was having trouble remaining profitable in the 1990s. Navistar International, the descendant of International Harvester that sold truck engines and parts as well as finished vehicles, trimmed domestic operations and opened overseas factories to reverse large losses and return itself to profitability. Warshawsky & Co., an auto parts catalog company based on the SOUTH SIDE, laid off about five hundred workers when it closed a large warehouse in 1996. Other local parts makers, including Maremont and BROADVIEW's Robert Bosch Corporation, became subsidiaries of foreign companies. At the end of the century, Chicago-area companies continued to participate in what had become a highly competitive GLOBAL industry.

Mark R. Wilson

See also: Agricultural Machinery Industry; Automobile Manufacturing; Business of Chicago

Further reading: Achilles, Rolf. *Made in Illinois: A Story of Illinois Manufacturing.* 1993. • Oursler, Will. *From Ox Carts to Jets: Roy Ingersoll and the Borg-Warner Story.* 1959. • Yost, Robert Jeffrey. "Components of the Past and Vehicles of Change: Parts Manufacturers and Supplier Relations in the U.S. Automobile Industry." Ph.D. diss., Case Western Reserve University. 1998.

Automobile Racing. *See* Motor Sports

Automobiles. *See* Motoring

Avalon Park, Community Area 45, 10 miles SE of the Loop. The area now known as Avalon Park was so swampy during most of the nineteenth century that the few houses located there had to be perched on stilts to avoid flooding and infestation. The main natural features were Mud Lake and Stony Island. For a time, Avalon Park's isolation made it a site for WASTE DISPOSAL. The borders of the community are South Chicago Avenue and the Chicago SKYWAY to the northeast, 87th Street on the southern edge, and the ILLINOIS CENTRAL RAILROAD to the west. A 30-acre park by the same name is situated on the southwestern corner of Avalon Park.

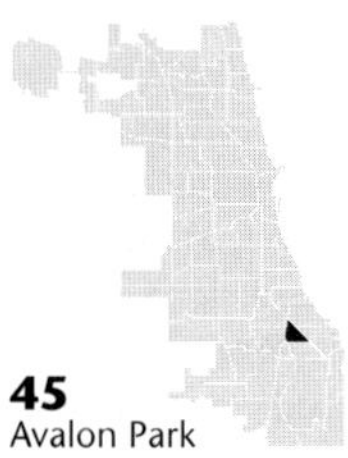
45
Avalon Park

Although swampy conditions discouraged early attempts at permanent settlement, RAILROAD WORKERS of GERMAN and IRISH descent began to reside in the northern section of the community by the late 1880s. In addition to railroad workers, skilled mechanics, many of them Germans employed in nearby PULLMAN or BURNSIDE, also made Avalon Park their home. ANNEXATION to Chicago in 1889, the World's Columbian Exposition of 1893, and the installation of drainage in 1900 stimulated residential growth.

Like many communities, Avalon Park's history has been characterized by successive waves of home building and population growth, although its population began to decline after 1970. The most active period of single-family home building occurred between 1900 (just after drainage) and 1910. In 1910 the name of the community, which had unofficially been "Pennytown," was officially changed to Avalon Park. A second housing boom occurred in the 1920s, and a third after World War II, when single-family brick BUNGALOWS and a few apartments were constructed. The postwar boom coincided with a rise in jobs in nearby steel mills and industrial plants.

By 1930 more than 10,000 people resided in Avalon Park, up from 2,911 a decade before. The community has been primarily residential, served by a shopping district at 79th Street and Stony Island, as well as several schools and churches. Owner-occupancy rates have consistently been over 70 percent in recent decades.

Transitions have happened in Avalon Park along both class and racial lines. By 1930, 19 percent of the community's residents were of SWEDISH origin, having joined the earlier, predominantly German and Irish residents. Most were railroad, steel mill, and factory workers. The AFRICAN AMERICANS who began to move into Avalon Park during the 1960s, however, like their neighbors in adjoining CHATHAM, were for the most part middle-class doctors, lawyers, businessmen, and other professionals. In 1970 Avalon Park reached a population high of 14,412, of whom 83 percent were African American. By 1980 Avalon Park's African American residents made up 96 percent of the population of 13,792.

Avalon Park's population dropped significantly by the end of the century, falling to 11,147, just below the level of 1950. In the late 1990s, to counter this trend, REAL-ESTATE developers planned several multiunit housing developments along 83rd Street.

Wallace Best

See also: Neighborhood Succession; South Side

Further reading: "South Side Camelot." *Chicago Tribune,* April 17, 1992. • "South Side Living." *Chicago Tribune,* January 31, 1998. • Chicago Fact Book Consortium, ed. *Local Community Fact Book: Chicago Metropolitan Area, 1990.* 1995.

Avondale, Community Area 21, 6 miles NW of the Loop. The Avondale Community Area lies west of the North Branch of the CHICAGO RIVER between Addison on the north and Diversey on the south. It stretches westward to the tracks of the Soo Line RAILROAD (originally the Chicago, Milwaukee, St. Paul Pacific). At the beginning of the nineteenth century, the area was prairie along the route of a meandering Indian trail. After 1848, the trail was straightened and planked as Milwaukee Avenue. Avondale developed along this road, as well as along the railroad lines that subsequently paralleled it west of the Chicago River.

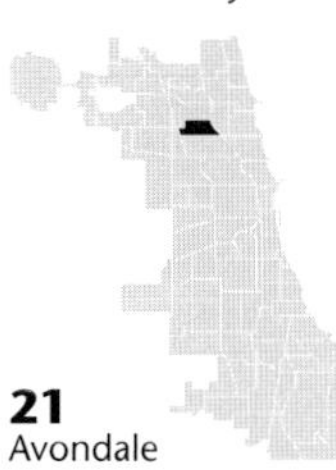
21
Avondale

The Milwaukee road's planks, however, broke under heavy loads or warped in the sun. Further, the road was interrupted by tollgates, which added the insult of expense to the very uncertain and uncomfortable ride along the planks. In 1889, some citizens of Avondale dressed as Indians rioted and burned down the tollgate, killed its owner, and stripped the planks from the stringers for firewood.

More farms appeared after the Chicago, Milwaukee, St. Paul & Pacific tracks were extended to Milwaukee in 1870, and in 1873, a post office was built at the corner of Belmont and Troy where the Chicago & North Western Railway made a stop. In the 1880s, a small group of about 20 AFRICAN AMERICAN families settled east of Milwaukee Avenue and built the first church in Avondale, the Allen Church.

Rapid growth began in 1889 when the area was ANNEXED to the city of Chicago. Soon, the city hard-surfaced the road. Further TRANSPORTATION improvements including the electrification and extension of the STREET RAILWAY lines on Milwaukee and Elston Avenues and the construction of the Logan Square branch of the Elevated line led to prodigious development between 1890 and 1920. The railroads and a horsecar line on Milwaukee Avenue provided relatively rapid transportation to jobs in the city.

By 1920, the population exceeded 38,000. More than one-quarter of these residents were foreign-born, mostly GERMANS along with some SWEDES and AUSTRIANS. By 1930 POLES constituted 33 percent of the population of 48,000. As new waves of Poles entered the community from the tenements west of the city center, German, Scandinavian and even some of the earlier Polish residents began to move further northwest. Poles remained the dominant ethnic group in 1980, but by 1990 Hispanics accounted for 37 percent of the total population.

Avondale developed as a working-class community, since the rail lines and the river served to attract industry. Numerous clay pits and brick factories were concentrated near Belmont Avenue in an area that came to be known as Bricktown. This brick was much in demand after the FIRE OF 1871 demonstrated the necessity of using brick for city construction to avert further conflagrations. After 1920, Grebe's Boatyard occupied the west bank of the Chicago River north of Belmont. Grebe's created luxury powered yachts for wealthy patrons, but the yard also produced minesweepers and numerous other small naval vessels during WORLD WAR II. Across the river rose Riverview AMUSEMENT PARK with its storied roller coaster, "The Bobs." Riverview Park is gone now and so is the boatyard. Today, along the river, luxury townhouses, condominiums, and shopping malls are replacing the old industrial belt, causing the loss of many of the industrial jobs that have for so long supported this old working-class neighborhood.

David M. Solzman

See also: Economic Geography; Rapid Transit System; Shipbuilding; Toll Roads

Further reading: The Chicago Fact Book Consortium, ed. *Local Community Fact Book: Chicago Metropolitan Area, Based on the 1970 and 1980 Censuses.* 1984. • Schnedler, Jack. *Chicago.* 1996. • Solzman, David M. *The Chicago River: An Illustrated History and Guide to the River and Its Waterways.* 1998.

B

Back of the Yards. Situated in a heavily industrialized location, populated by successive generations of immigrant people, and animated by some of the most dramatic social conflicts of modern times, Back of the Yards focused the attention of novelists, activists, and social scientists alike for most of the twentieth century. Located in the community area of New City, the neighborhood extends from 39th to 55th Streets between Halsted and the railroad tracks along Leavitt Street, just south and west of the former Union Stock Yard and adjacent packing plants, a giant sprawl that was until the 1950s the largest livestock yards and meatpacking center in the country.

The concentration of railroads in the mid-nineteenth century, the establishment of the Union Stock Yard in 1865, and the perfection of the refrigerated boxcar by 1880 led to a giant expansion of meatpacking in the neighborhood. Part of the town of Lake until annexation by Chicago in 1889, Back of the Yards was settled by skilled Irish and German butchers, joined in the 1870s and 1880s by Czechs. Here in 1889, developer Samuel Gross built one of his earliest subdivisions of cheap workingmen's cottages. By the turn of the century the area was transformed into a series of Slavic enclaves dominated by Poles, Lithuanians, Slovaks, and Czechs, with most communities organized around ethnic parishes serving as social and cultural as well as spiritual focal points for residents' lives. Small numbers of Mexican immigrants entered Back of the Yards and neighboring Bridgeport as early as World War I and the 1920s, but the community retained its Slavic character until the 1970s, when it gradually became a largely Chicano community with a minority of African Americans.

Immortalized for its pollution, squalor, and poverty in Upton Sinclair's *The Jungle* (1906), government reports, and University of Chicago sociology studies, Back of the Yards was, in fact, characterized by particularly vibrant and cohesive working-class communities over time. The sprawling stockyards and adjacent plants with their unique combination of pollution, erratic work schedules, occupational diseases, and low wages exacted a heavy toll on the community in the years up to the Great Depression, but workers and their families organized a series of struggles in and outside the plants to improve and protect their communities.

In the Depression and World War II years residents created two key social movements: the Packinghouse Workers Organizing Committee (later the United Packinghouse Workers of America, or UPWA-CIO) and Back of the Yards Neighborhood Council (BYNC). The UPWA-CIO, a particularly effective industrial union movement, became a progressive mainstay of the labor movement. The BYNC, a coalition of dozens of neighborhood and parish groups, became Saul Alinsky's model for community organizing throughout the country. While the UPWA-CIO raised wages, stabilized employment, and fought for civil rights in the plants, the BYNC galvanized a broader

Aerial view of the Union Stock Yard, 1936, looking toward the southeast. Photographer: Unknown. Source: Chicago Historical Society.

community identity among the diverse ethnic groups and addressed an array of community problems.

With the end of Chicago's meatpacking industry by the 1960s, Back of the Yards once again faced serious problems of economic decline and physical deterioration. At the end of the twentieth century, as the city worked to develop a new manufacturing district on the site of the old Union Stock Yard, the newer residents resumed the old struggle to maintain a strong community.

James R. Barrett

See also: Economic Geography; Environmental Politics; Lake Township; Packinghouse Unions; South Side

Further reading: Barrett, James R. *Work and Community in the Jungle: Chicago's Packinghouse Workers, 1894–1922.* 1987. • Jablonsky, Thomas J. *Pride in the Jungle: Community and Everyday Life in Back of the Yards Chicago.* 1993. • Slayton, Robert A. *Back of the Yards: The Making of a Local Democracy.* 1986.

Back of the Yards Neighborhood Council. The Back of the Yards Neighborhood Council (BYNC) is one of the oldest community organizations in America still functioning. Founded in New City on the Near South Side in 1939 by Saul Alinsky and Joseph Meegan, the council was dedicated to their motto, "We the people will work out our own destiny."

The BYNC set the pattern for what is known as the Alinsky school of organizing. An outside organizer would work with local leaders to create a democratic organization where people could express their needs and fears, and gain improvements in their conditions via direct action. Membership in the council was based on organizations, rather than individuals, thus using the neighborhood's existing social institutions.

The initial efforts of the council centered around basic organization and economic justice. Overcoming nationalistic hatreds in this ethnically diverse community, they managed to join the ROMAN CATHOLIC Church and radical labor unions in common cause.

In the 1950s the council turned to neighborhood conservation. They pressured local banks to release funds for mortgages and building upgrades; in the first year alone there were 560 home-improvement loans in this local area. Between 1953 and 1963, the council fostered the rehabilitation of 90 percent of the community's HOUSING stock.

In 1981, Meegan resigned as executive secretary after 42 years of leadership, and was succeeded by Patrick Salmon. Since then, the council has concentrated on economic development and employment, assisting, for example, in the opening of Damen Yards Plaza, and helping to direct jobs toward local residents, who were increasingly MEXICAN and AFRICAN AMERICAN.

Robert Slayton

See also: Community Organizing; Meatpacking; Neighborhood Associations; New City; Packinghouse Unions

Further reading: Horwitt, Sanford. *Let Them Call Me Rebel.* 1989. • Jablonsky, Thomas J. *Pride in the Jungle: Community and Everyday Life in Back of the Yards Chicago.* 1993. • Slayton, Robert. *Back of the Yards.* 1986.

Bahā'ī. The Chicago Bahā'ī community began in the 1890s as a small group of American converts and IRANIAN immigrants. There were perhaps two to three hundred Bahā'īs in Chicago before 1910. After 1903 the project of building a major temple in Chicago served as the focal point for organizing and evangelizing throughout the United States and internationally. Abdul Baha, the son of the religion's founder, Bahā'u'llāh, dedicated the WILMETTE temple site in 1912 on a visit to the United States, during which he spoke against racial discrimination at HULL HOUSE and before the fourth annual convention of the NATIONAL ASSOCIATION FOR THE ADVANCEMENT OF COLORED PEOPLE. Dedicated in 1953, the Bahā'ī Temple remains a renowned architectural landmark and the headquarters of the Bahā'ī faith in the United States.

Douglas Knox

See also: Church Architecture

Further reading: Whitmore, Bruce W. *The Dawning Place: The Building of a Temple, the Forging of the North American Baha'i Community.* 1984.

Bahā'ī Temple, Wilmette, 1971. Photographer: Calvin Hutchinson. Source: Chicago Historical Society.

Ballet. Although European ballet dancers visited Chicago as early as 1838, a local company was not formed until 1922. Considered one of the earliest American ballet companies, the Pavley-Oukrainsky Ballet was associated with the Chicago Grand Opera and toured for the next dozen years led by Serge Oukrainsky and Andreas Pavley. Adolph Bolm, succeeding the two as director of the CHICAGO OPERA BALLET, was ballet master of Chicago Allied Arts, a showcase for modern ballet, music, and stage design, from 1924 to 1927. Allied Arts dancer Ruth Page established several performance companies based in Chicago, gave solo concerts, was ballet mistress for LYRIC OPERA of Chicago from 1954 to 1970, and choreographed several classic works, including the annual *Nutcracker*, presented by Tribune Charities from 1965 to 1997.

Ruth Page's Chicago Ballet Company performing a scene from *Camille* for a Saturday-afternoon dance program on WBBM-TV, 1966. Photographer: Unknown. Source: The Newberry Library.

Leading schools of ballet included the Edna McRae School (1925–1964) and the Stone-Camryn School of Ballet (1941–1981), the latter particularly successful placing its graduates in professional companies. Founders Bentley Stone and Walter Camryn both danced with the Chicago Civic Opera Ballet and both were directors of the Federal Dance Theatre Project. With Page, Stone cofounded the Page-Stone Ballet, which toured widely and became the first American ballet company to visit South America.

At the opening of the twenty-first century, Chicago's companies included Ballet Chicago, growing out of the dissolution of Maria Tallchief's CHICAGO CITY BALLET (1980–1987); Ballet Theater of Chicago (founded 1996); and JOFFREY BALLET OF CHICAGO. The Joffrey, formerly a New York–based touring company founded as the Robert Joffrey Theatre Ballet in 1956 by Robert Joffrey and Gerald Arpino, moved its base of operation to Chicago in 1995. Although Chicago has nurtured scores of nationally recognized dancers, classic ballet struggles for corporate support and popular recognition.

Diana Haskell

See also: Dance; Dance Companies; Dance Training

Further reading: Dance Collection. Newberry Library, Chicago, IL.

Balloon Frame Construction. A popular myth suggests that a Chicago carpenter, George W. Snow, invented the balloon frame in 1832 and revolutionized CONSTRUCTION practice. Chicago architect John M. Van Osdel erroneously attributed the invention to Snow in 1883, and subsequent histories accepted the story. But they did so without examining physical evidence. The oldest buildings that remain in metropolitan Chicago suggest that the balloon frame was not a revolutionary idea; nor was it invented by Snow or any other Chicagoan.

During the colonial period, carpenters simplified the timber frame to allow for rapid construction with standardized materials. The Beaubien Tavern on the plank road between Chicago and NAPERVILLE, in what is now LISLE, reflected these changes. The frame employed smaller, standardized timbers. All mortises and tenons were very simple. The roof was a system of small common rafters held in place by nails. Joinery did not attach it intimately to the frame. Heated by stoves, the building had no need for a large, central fireplace.

A minimal difference existed between the tavern's box frame and early balloon frames. Timber girts supported the tavern's second-story floor joists. They were tenoned, pinned, and braced to mortised corner posts. The balloon frame eliminated these elements by nailing a one-by-four-inch board, called a ledger or ribband, into vertical studs that ran continuously to the height of the building. The studs were notched to accommodate the ledger. The second-floor joists were also notched and then hooked onto the ledger. The joists were then nailed to the studs.

The idea was not original. Carpenters in seventeenth-century Virginia employed a similar method when confronted with pressures to build rapidly. But no matter the type of frame, carpenters could not reduce substantially the handwork necessary for building a house until the 1880s. Then, Chicago carpenters replaced mortised-and-tenoned timber sills with box sills that used only dimensional lumber joined by nails. By this time, factories produced most windows, doors, and trim, as well as kiln-dried dimensional lumber with tighter tolerances. Carpenters on the site merely fit and installed these products.

The balloon frame evolved slowly over the course of the nineteenth century. It resulted from modest shifts in the practice of many carpenters over time. Most likely, Chicago gained a reputation for the invention owing to factories like the Lyman Bridges Company that produced ready-made houses with balloon frames that were sold to various Western cities attempting to meet the needs of rapidly expanding populations.

Joseph C. Bigott

See also: Architecture; Building Trades and Workers; Built Environment of the Chicago Region; Housing Types; Housing, Mail-order; Innovation, Invention, and Chicago Business

Further reading: Field, Walker. "A Reexamination into the Invention of the Balloon Frame." *Journal of the American Society of Architectural Historians* 2 (October 1942). • Sprague, Paul E. "Chicago Balloon Frame: The Evolution during the Nineteenth Century of George W. Snow's System for Erecting Light Frame Buildings from Dimension Lumber and Machine-made Nails." In *The Technology of Historic American Buildings: Studies of the Materials, Craft Processes, and the Mechanization of Building Construction,* ed. H. Ward Jandl, 1983. • Van Osdel, John M. "History of Chicago Architecture." *Inland Architect* (April 1883).

Bands, Early and Golden Age. Drawing on a tradition that began before the founding of the Republic, military and brass bands became an inextricable and significant element of the cultural milieu of Chicago, from its earliest days into the twentieth century. Though first associated almost exclusively with civic and military occasions, bands became ubiquitous in the city's daily life, some even achieving worldwide reputations during the so-called Golden Age of Bands, roughly between 1880 and 1920.

In 1840, the first Chicago band, 16 pieces strong and led by Nicholas Burdell, was organized to "discourse sweet music" at public and civic events. It was supported by private subscriptions, but its silver instruments were to remain city property. In the next few years, other miscellaneous bands appeared. Like Burdell's ensemble, they were typically amateur and temporary.

It was during the 1850s that Chicago bands, organized principally to accompany militia units, became a more permanent fixture of the city's landscape. The Garden City Guards established the Garden City Band in 1853 to perform for drills and parades. Similarly, the Light Guard Band in 1854 and the National Guard Band in 1855 performed for their respective units. By 1860, Chicago had five resident militia bands. Like their predecessors, they relied on private contributions, often solicited at special promenade concerts. The band musicians were predominantly of GERMAN descent, and, borrowing from the German *Verein* tradition, they operated the bands as cooperatives.

After the CIVIL WAR, a few street bands, such as the ones led by Billy Nevans and Silas Dean, added to the number of local groups. With midcentury refinements to brass and wind instruments, the military/brass band became more versatile in sound and function. The most accomplished in the city, formed in 1866, was the Great Western Light Guard Band, which, with as many as 100 players at times, was capable of hosting concerts of popular and even, when some members doubled on string instruments, symphonic music.

In the wake of the Great FIRE OF 1871 and a devastating depression, musical performance and band organization suffered. Toward the end of the 1870s, cooperative ensembles disappeared, and gradually successful business bands began to emerge, such as those led by Johnny Hand, Adolph Liesegang, Johnny Meinken, and the Frieburg brothers. The larger bands nonetheless could not exist without a subsidy. Some, such as AUSTIN'S First Regiment Band, continued to seek affiliation with a militia. Others, like the Lyon & Healy Music Store Band and the Pullman Band, had commercial sponsors.

Still, as the nation entered the Golden Age of Bands in 1880, Chicago bands were not numerous. Within the next 10 years, however, the city witnessed a virtual explosion in band music. Outdoor concerts were a summer staple at city parks, while military-uniformed bands performed throughout the year at theaters, SALOONS, museums, ballparks, and dances. By 1890, there were over 80 resident professional bands and countless ETHNIC and amateur ensembles. Finally, under the impetus of the WORLD'S COLUMBIAN EXPOSITION in 1893, Chicago came to possess its own renowned touring wind concert bands. Most notable were Phinney's United States Band, A. F. Weldon's Second Regiment Band, and the legendary Thomas P. Brooke's Chicago Naval Marine Band, which rivaled the nation's best before its demise in 1906.

Although the number of bands continued to increase, after 1910 Chicago produced only

Beck's American Band, Englewood (no date). Photographer: Unknown. Source: Chicago Historical Society.

one more concert band, Bohumir Kryl's Chicago Band. By 1920, the Golden Age of Bands was over, giving way to modern influences in the culture. Yet the early bands of Chicago had left an indelible mark on its music, the legacy of which can still be heard in school presentations, public parades, and even in some JAZZ and ROCK bands.

Sandy R. Mazzola

See also: Music Publishing; Musical Instrument Manufacturing; Outdoor Concerts; Street Life

Further reading: Hazen, Margaret H., and Robert M. Hazen. *The Music Men.* 1987. • Mazzola, Sandy R. "Bands and Orchestras at the World's Columbian Exposition." *American Music* 4/4 (Winter 1986). • Mazzola, Sandy R. "Chicago Concert Bands at the Turn of the Century." *Journal of Band Research* 29/1 (Fall 1993).

Bangladeshis. Like other South Asian immigrants, the majority of Bangladeshis did not arrive in Chicago until after 1965 when the newly amended Immigration and Nationality Act liberalized the regulations on South Asian immigration to the United States. In fact, because Bangladesh did not gain national independence until 1971, many of the early immigrants arriving from the region were East Pakistan nationals. The first wave of immigrants, those arriving in the late 1960s and early 1970s, were generally graduate students and young professionals who tended to settle in and around major urban areas and initial ports of entry such as New York and Los Angeles. But because of its educational and economic opportunities Chicago has also developed a relatively large and vibrant Bangladeshi community. The 2000 federal census officially reported 712 Bangladeshis living in the Chicago metropolitan area. Local community leaders estimate, however, that nearly four thousand Bangladeshis lived in the greater Chicago region at the close of the twentieth century, many of them Bengali-speaking MUSLIMS.

Though small in number and scattered across the metropolitan area, the Bangladeshi community in Chicago is a socially and culturally active ethnic group. The Bangladesh Association of Chicagoland has been the community's official organization since 1980. In addition to disseminating information regarding health care, literacy, and immigration and citizenship, the association also provides assistance with employment and other issues related to assimilation into American society.

Every March 26, Chicago's Bangladeshi community celebrates the national independence of Bangladesh with a citywide, day-long cultural festival. Since 1994 the day has been recognized by the state of Illinois and the city of Chicago as Bangladesh Day. The ceremonies usually begin with an assembly near Devon Avenue—the symbolic and commercial hub of Chicago's South Asian communities. After opening remarks by community leaders and local politicians, the celebration proceeds with a parade along the portion of Devon Avenue (West Devon Avenue between North Ravenswood Avenue and North Damen Avenue) that has been officially designated "Sheikh Mujib Way," in honor of the founder of Bangladesh. The day of festivities concludes with a dinner and cultural show. Bangladeshi culture is also on display on Chicago's local television channels, where every Saturday Bangladeshi DANCE recitals, POETRY readings, and plays are broadcast.

Chicago's skyline has also had a Bangladeshi influence. Fazlur R. Khan, a structural engineer and founding president of the Bangladesh Association of Chicagoland, played an instrumental role in designing the Sears Tower and the John Hancock Center. The portion of Franklin Street adjacent to the Sears Tower has received the honorary designation "Fazlur Khan Way."

Ajay K. Mehrotra

See also: Demography; Indians; Multicentered Chicago; Pakistanis

Banking, Commercial. Chicago's economic growth reached the point that it needed banking institutions just at the time that a fierce debate over banks and paper money engulfed the nation. Although the Bank of Illinois already was operating in 1817, chartered banking was not authorized until the following year, by the 1818 Illinois Constitution. The state bank closed 10 years later, when its notes plummeted in value. The bank's notes failed to maintain their value for a number of reasons: the bank failed to maintain sufficient gold and silver; there was a fire that destroyed the bank, followed by a robbery of the temporary quarters; and changes in state law made it difficult to collect debts. Banks received their charters from the state legislature, and this process made the chartering of banks a highly political process. Under the charter provisions of virtually all states, banks were permitted to issue notes based on gold or silver coin called *specie*. When a bank could not redeem its notes in specie, it had to close, a problem many Illinois banks faced after the panic of 1837, at which time the Second State Bank, created in 1835 with a branch in Chicago, also failed. Most Chicago banks failed during, or shortly after, that panic.

These circumstances generated a hostility to banks throughout the Old Northwest and might have doomed Chicago to slow growth, starved for credit, had it not been for the appearance of "private" (i.e., unchartered) banks. One of the first of those was created by Gurdon Hubbard, under the title Hubbard and Balestier, in the 1830s. More important was the bank of George Smith, a Scottish land speculator and investor, who played a crucial role in the city's early financial history. Smith created the Scottish Illinois Land Investment Company in 1837 by investing in Chicago properties, and, in the process of handling the REAL-ESTATE business, the company started to discount bank notes from other cities and states. Although the company split in 1839, with Smith moving to Wisconsin, his banking activities shaped Chicago.

Smith re-entered banking in Chicago later that year, first by creating the Wisconsin Marine and Fire INSURANCE Company and second by founding George Smith and Company in Chicago. The latter was not a chartered bank, and therefore could not issue notes, but it could circulate certificates from the Wisconsin business. Smith called his certificates "checks," and by 1842, "George Smith's money," redeemable in specie, was in sharp demand throughout the Chicago region. Within two years, all Illinois banks other than Smith's had disappeared. By 1854, George Smith's banks supplied nearly 75 percent of Chicago's currency.

The Illinois legislature passed a "free banking" law in 1851 in which a bank no longer had to obtain a charter from the legislature but could secure a general incorporation charter from the secretary of state. The first Chicago bank under the new constitution, the Marine Bank, appeared that same year and developed close ties with William Ogden and other influential Chicago leaders in RAILROADS, industry, and real estate. The appearance of the Marine Bank was followed shortly by the Merchants and Mechanics Bank, then, rapidly, eight more institutions. As a result of the new law, Illinois banking capital nearly quadrupled in the mid-1850s.

Although Chicago witnessed 204 business failures during the recession following the panic of 1857, less than 10 percent of Illinois' banks failed and the politicians praised the banking system for its performance. However, in 1858, Chicago bankers started to refuse the

Illinois & Michigan Canal scrip issued by the State Bank of Illinois. Source: Chicago Historical Society.

notes of "country banks," many of which were backed by bonds from the South. The discounting of non-Chicago notes and the continued collapse of the country bank notes' value led to calls for the abolition of all banks in the state. Instead, the problems were addressed with reforms in the free banking laws.

With the passage of the National Bank Act (1863), Chicago added five new nationally chartered institutions, all developed out of existing private banking houses. Illinois encouraged large "unit" banks as epitomized by the Central Trust Company of Illinois, which opened in Chicago in 1902 as a "big bank for small people." Its president, former U.S. comptroller Charles Dawes, opposed branch bank legislation at the state and national levels. The national banks were created first and foremost to finance the CIVIL WAR, and thus gained important advantages over state banks in securities acquisition and sales. In 1891, for example, Chicago's FIRST NATIONAL BANK took $1.2 million in the city's bond issue—the entire amount. When the bank's bond department could not handle mortgage or real-estate loans, the bank organized a "security affiliate," First Trust and Savings Bank, to deal specifically in securities. This represented a revolution in securities financing and was quickly copied by New York institutions, which referred to it as "the Chicago Plan." Later, during the GREAT DEPRESSION, critics of the banking system pointed to the interlocking of banks with securities affiliates as a cause of the weakness that led to the banking collapse in the 1930s. In fact, this system strengthened the banks by giving them more flexibility in their portfolios. Since only the state bank was allowed to have branches, its failure effectively ended branching in Illinois.

Chicago bankers also led the way in creating a system of preventing panics through the Chicago Clearing House. James B. Forgan of First National Bank initiated the new clearing system in 1905 and ran it effectively. Clearinghouses allowed the city's banks to settle all their outstanding obligations with each other at the end of each business day. This enhanced information transmission among the banks and reduced the risk of panics. After the panic of 1907, however, many concluded that only a national "lender of last resort" could prevent future panics, leading to a reform movement. Forgan served on the Currency Commission of the American Bankers Association and helped shape the reform legislation that became the Federal Reserve Act of 1913. Forgan, meanwhile, had found a way around the branch bank restrictions by establishing new, but clearly related, unit banks in areas outlying Chicago, thus forming an early "chain" bank—the second most efficient form of banking next to branching. Chain banks, unlike branch banks, might have the same owners, but they could not commingle assets or liabilities: each, essentially, had to stand on its own. This was a weaker structure than branching, because branch banks could shift assets around to "trouble spots."

After the creation of the "Fed," Chicago was designated a headquarters city of a Federal Reserve District Bank, and the city's national banks soon opted to have Chicago designated a central reserve city in the new system, under which all national banks had to carry a 25 percent reserve. That attracted the balances of banks designated as country banks to Chicago, which, by 1914, had $205 million in interbank balances, or nearly six times more than

Crowd gathered outside the Milwaukee Avenue Bank at 739–47 (formerly 409–15) Milwaukee Avenue during its August 1906 failure. Photographer: Unknown. Source: Chicago Historical Society.

in 1887. George Reynolds' Continental and Commercial National Bank of Chicago was the leader in handling correspondent business. Banks already had started to specialize in either commercial operations, which financed agriculture, trade, and businesses, or large-scale capital investment, often through a syndicate of many institutions, to build railroads or other capital-intensive enterprises.

After 1900, Chicago emerged as a major source of investment funds. By this time, a difference had emerged between "investment banks" (such as J. P. Morgan), which dealt extensively with providing start-up capital for large, new enterprises, and commercial banks, which provided loans for BUSINESS operations on a more short-term basis. From 1900 to 1928, Chicago's banks, most of which were commercial banks, underwent a period of rapid expansion, with aggregate net worth growing nearly sixfold. During that same period, the nation's percentage of total banks made up of national banks shrank from 60 percent to 36 percent, indicating the strong advantages offered by state charters, including lower capitalization requirements. Like bankers in other major cities, Chicago's financial leaders had no reason to see a threat in the near future: in the 1920s alone, Chicago banks marketed $2.5 million in public utilities, and at the end of the decade Chicago stood behind only New York and London as a great money center.

But the correspondent system that had generated much of that growth rebounded negatively to the city's banks when the agricultural downturn of the 1920s caused the collapse of many unit banks in farm states. Their balance withdrawals started to weaken Chicago's major institutions. After the Great Crash of 1929, a national banking panic materialized. Research suggests that the complaints about banks' "speculation" causing the crash were exactly wrong: banks with securities affiliates, such as First National, were less likely to fail than banks *not* involved in the market. There were exceptions, of course: the collapse of Samuel Insull's Midwest utilities empire helped weaken the Continental Illinois Bank. From 1929 to 1930, more than 30 Chicago banks went out of business. In addition, more than 100 banks sought to strengthen themselves through mergers. In 1931, the collapse of Insull-related securities spread through the banking community, with runs forcing 25 banks to close in a matter of days. Research has suggested that most of the failures between 1930 and 1933 resulted more from weakening portfolios related to government securities they held than to declining real-estate prices that might indicate poor management of mortgage lending.

By 1933, President Franklin Roosevelt concluded that only a national "bank holiday" would restore the system. Soon thereafter Congress changed most of the banking laws. Banks could not have securities affiliates under the Glass-Steagall Act. The Federal Deposit Insurance Corporation (FDIC) was formed, although subsequent research has shown conclusively that the state deposit insurance schemes of the 1920s contributed to the banking problems in the agricultural states. The

Insull securities empire also had held large amounts of tax-anticipation warrants, suggesting that the deteriorating condition of the municipalities themselves contributed to the weakness of the financial structure.

Chicago banks stabilized, but only after huge losses: Continental Illinois National Bank wrote off $110 million in a two-year period. Full recovery did not occur until after WORLD WAR II. Between 1959 and 1968, 56 new banks were established in Cook County, with Chicago having 240 offices in 1960 and 295 by 1968. Deposit concentrations held by Chicago's banks as a share of all Illinois banks rose during that period from 43.9 percent to 45.1 percent. Gross loans doubled, and total assets increased by more than 70 percent.

The integrated financial market of the United States allowed Chicago banks to invest in Arizona real estate, lumbering in Maine, and businesses throughout the United States. One of the most important new sources of demand for loans was in oil and gas drilling and exploration. Ironically, oil and gas investments contributed to the downfall of what many insiders called Chicago's best-managed bank, Continental Illinois. In the late 1970s and early 1980s, a small Oklahoma City bank, Penn Square Bank, had begun offering "participations" in oil and gas loans that it originated. By 1982, Continental Illinois held $1.1 billion of Penn Square's "participations," which constituted 17 percent of Continental's energy loans. In mid-1982, however, the oil and gas loans went sour, and in May a run struck the bank. Continental Illinois threatened to collapse and had to be bailed out by loans from the federal government in 1989 because the bank had correspondent accounts from more than 175 banks, each of whom had at least half their capital in the struggling institution.

While Continental Illinois recovered temporarily, the importance of the integrated and international market was apparent: Chicago banks would no longer stand isolated as the "kings" of Midwest banking. Without branching, it was only a matter of time before Chicago's largest banks became relatively small and therefore takeover targets. During the merger waves of the 1980s and 1990s, Continental's many business interests were split; its commercial banking business became part of First National. The National Bank of Detroit (NBD) merged with First National to form First Chicago NBD, and the resulting firm then joined Banc One, a Columbus, Ohio, firm that moved its headquarters to Chicago. The HARRIS TRUST was acquired by the Bank of Montreal, while the LaSalle Bank was purchased by ABN-AMRO, a Dutch firm. This left the Northern Trust as the only one of Chicago's major banks that retained Chicago ownership, and it has increased rapidly the number of its branches. These acquisitions effectively marked the end of Chicago's regional advantage as a financial center, due in large part to Illinois' limitations on branch banking. The rise of the Internet and electronic banking might have given Chicago's banks some advantages that the law denied them. For example, with electronic/Internet banking, branches became less important, and Chicago banks could have engaged in "interstate banking" without having physical branches. However, electronic banking remained in its infancy and did not mature fast enough to keep the large Chicago banks independent of outside interests.

Larry E. Schweikart

See also: Consumer Credit; Insurance; Management Consulting; Savings and Loans

Further reading: Klebaner, Benjamin J. *Commercial Banking in the United States: A History.* 1974. • James, F. Cyril. *The Growth of Chicago Banks.* 2 vols. 1938. • Smith, Alice E. *George Smith's Money: A Scottish Investor in America.* 1966.

Bannockburn, IL, Lake County, 25 miles NW of the Loop. The village of Bannockburn is a somewhat inconspicuous upper-middle-class suburb that has catered to its mostly residential population through ZONING and service provisions. Established in 1924 by developer William Aitken, the settlement was intended to be an exclusive community for members of his bridge group and country club. The original charter called for homes to be built on no less than one-acre plots; the community has since expanded requirements to two acres.

Bannockburn is, in part, a product of TRANSPORTATION systems of the middle and second half of the twentieth century. Located along the Tri-State Tollway, the village has served as a convenient location for those who COMMUTE by automobile. With narrow, winding local roads, residents have created a refuge from surrounding development and a model community built upon a "garden suburb" philosophy.

Easy access to highways and EXPRESSWAYS also has provided the village with its most sustained challenge. Due to increased development west along Lake-Cook Road and north on the tollway, traffic has become a major problem for residents. Beginning in the late 1980s, local politicians began lobbying the Illinois State Toll Highway Authority for a sound barrier to protect residents from noise. The issue was been consistently prevalent and polarizing in local politics throughout the 1990s.

Bannockburn was almost entirely residential until 1968, when the community split over the development of an industrial park. A proposal was eventually approved, and since then several new corporate parks on the northern edge of the village supplement the tax base, with little impact on the residential community. In 1984, the suburb zoned its first commercial area along Route 22, one of the town's few major thoroughfares.

Responding to residents' desire for low taxes, Bannockburn has traditionally provided few municipal services. It was not until the late 1970s that the village fielded a full-time police department, and until 1992 the village had no city hall. The village has continued to rely on agreements with neighboring DEERFIELD for many public services, such as a library, park district, and fire protection. The only public school—Bannockburn Elementary School—served as the administrative headquarters for most of the twentieth century.

Perhaps because of its reclusive nature oriented toward its residents' comfort and privacy, the village has been home to more than its share of sports celebrities. Former Bears coach Mike Ditka and former Bulls coach Phil Jackson both owned homes there, along with Cubs legendary third baseman Ron Santo. In line with this tradition, the town was home to baseball great Kirby Puckett when he played for the team at Trinity College (now part of TRINITY INTERNATIONAL UNIVERSITY).

Despite Bannockburn's growth during the second half of the twentieth century, it has remained smaller than most Chicago suburbs. In 2000, the population was only 1,429, of whom 88 percent were white. Asian Americans accounted for the largest segment of the small minority population.

Adam H. Stewart

See also: Government, Suburban; Suburbs and Cities as Dual Metropolis; Toll Roads

Barat College. Founded in Chicago in 1858 as a school for ROMAN CATHOLIC women, Barat College remains a committed heir to the nineteenth-century teaching tradition of its French namesake, St. Madeleine Barat. After relocating to LAKE FOREST in 1904, Barat expanded its mission, obtaining a charter as a four-year college in 1918. Although still explicitly Catholic, Barat came under the supervision of an autonomous Board of Trustees in the late 1960s and received no direct financial support from the Catholic Church.

Barat began admitting men in 1982, and its student body grew to 850 by the year 2000. In early 2001, Barat became a part of DEPAUL, the nation's largest Catholic university, to ensure its own survival and extend DePaul's reach to include Barat's 30-acre wooded campus along the North Shore.

Sarah Fenton

See also: Loyola University; Saint Xavier University; Universities and Their Cities

Barbadians. Small numbers of Barbadian professionals, students, and entrepreneurs moved to the Chicago area in the 1910s and

1920s. Substantial numbers of Barbadians, however, did not arrive in Chicago until WORLD WAR II, when many were recruited, along with other West Indians, to work in war industries under the War Manpower Commission. With a troubled economic situation on the island of Barbados, opportunities in Chicago attracted emigrants, the majority of whom were laborers. Before long, a small community of Barbadians—or "Bajans"—was scattered across the SOUTH SIDE, with a small colony concentrated around 39th and Vincennes.

Some Barbadians joined Episcopalian parishes like St. Edmunds (61st and Michigan). St. Augustine's African Orthodox Cathedral (5831 S. Indiana) also attracted a large number of Barbadians, and became a focal point for the community.

The Barbadian immigrant generation maintained a separate and distinct identity apart from Chicago's AFRICAN AMERICANS. Working-class Barbadians encountered considerable prejudice when they arrived, suffering insults and attracting harassment on account of their island identity and British-influenced culture.

In 1944, pioneering Barbadian professionals collaborated with other West Indians in Chicago to found the AMERICAN WEST INDIAN ASSOCIATION (AWIA), which included JAMAICANS, GUYANESE, Trinidadians, and others. In addition to aiding workers, the AWIA sponsored festivals and celebrations like Guy Fawkes Day. In 1955 and 1969, it hosted prime ministers of Barbados visiting Chicago. Barbadians also participated in the Pan-American Association, which united Caribbean ethnic groups with other Latin American groups beginning in the 1940s. The community's first major celebration was occasioned by Barbadian independence in 1966.

Sporting associations have always been a focal point for the Barbadian community. Since the 1950s, Barbadians have joined other West Indians in summer cricket leagues at WASHINGTON PARK and elsewhere. Teams have included the West Indian Cricket Club, Windy City Cricket Club, Sunlight Cricket Club, and Lucas Cricket Club.

After the AWIA dissolved in the 1970s, Chicago's approximately 500 Barbadians were left without strong organization. Community leaders recall that at least two Barbadian community associations were founded between the dissolution of the AWIA and the early 1990s, but neither endured. An annual Barbados Day picnic was celebrated for some time by the community, but it also ended. In 1994, however, the Barbados Caribbean American Association was founded as a local chapter of the National Association of Barbadian Organizations to carry on the cultural mission formerly pursued by the AWIA. In addition to dances and Independence Day celebrations (each November 30), the organization was dedicated to fundraising and charity projects for schools in Barbados. At the end of the 1990s, Barbadians also continued to participate in the cricket associations and in the annual Carifete on the Midway Plaisance. Community leaders estimated the size of the community at approximately 1,000 at the close of the twentieth century.

Robert Morrissey

See also: Demography; Multicentered Chicago

Barrington, IL, Cook and Lake Counties, 32 miles NW of the Loop. While the oak grove and prairie land that lay between Chicago and the Fox RIVER in the 1830s were both attractive and fertile, fear of Indian attack during the 1832 BLACK HAWK WAR and the lack of milling facilities kept Eastern farmers from entering the area. After the war, mills were erected along the Fox River at Dundee and ALGONQUIN, and land-hungry Yankees flowed in.

William Butler Ogden became interested in connecting the developing northwest to Chicago's growing port facilities. He gained control of the Chicago, St. Paul & Fond du Lac RAILROAD (later the Chicago & North Western Railway) in 1854 and pushed its tracks to the northwest corner of COOK COUNTY, where a station named Deer Grove was built.

Although it meant improved profits, many area farmers feared the railroad would bring too many SALOONS and IRISH Catholics to the area. In response to the opposition, Robert Campbell, a civil engineer working for the Fond du Lac line, purchased a farm two miles northwest of Deer Grove and platted a community there in 1854. At Campbell's request, the railroad moved the station building to his new community, which he called Barrington after Barrington, Massachusetts, the original home of a number of area farmers.

The prosperity of the CIVIL WAR era increased Barrington's population to 300 in 1863. Because leaders believed the growing community needed tax-supported improvements, an election to incorporate Barrington was held on February 16, 1865. Homer Willmarth became the first village president. The village prospered as many Chicago grain merchants whose homes were destroyed in the FIRE OF 1871 decided to construct opulent Queen Anne–style residences along Barrington's tree-shaded streets.

Although the Elgin, Joliet & Eastern Railway was built through Barrington in 1889, the village continued to serve AGRICULTURALLY based trading interests into the twentieth century. Dairy farming was the major activity on the meadows and woodlots surrounding the community. Fueled by post–WORLD WAR I prosperity, however, a number of Chicago business leaders built their residences on large woodland tracts around the village, bringing an end to dairying.

The large estate acreage that tended to remain in family hands decade after decade protected Barrington from the densely packed residential developments that came to neighboring communities in the 1950s and 1960s. Barrington's population grew from 3,213 in 1930 to only 5,435 in 1960. But with the construction of the Northwest TOLLWAY five miles to the south in the early 1960s, development did come to Barrington's south side. Population reached 10,168 in 2000.

Proud of its reputation as an estate community, Barrington's leaders continue their opposition to dense population developments replacing estate acreage as it comes up for sale. A proposal to turn the Elgin, Joliet & Eastern Railway into a suburb-to-suburb commuter line with Barrington as a major stop met strong disapproval based on the fear that, as happened with the towns along the Northwest Tollway, such a transportation development would clog the city with traffic and noise.

Craig L. Pfannkuche

See also: Local Option; Metropolitan Growth; Prohibition and Temperance; Suburbs and Cities as Dual Metropolis

Further reading: Lines, Arnett C. *A History of Barrington, Illinois.* 1977. • Messenger, Janet. "Country Living." *Northshore Magazine,* December 1997, 73–94. • Sharp, Cynthia Baker. *Tales of Old Barrington.* 1976.

Barrington Hills, IL, Cook County, 34 miles NW of the Loop. Fanning out over the four counties of LAKE, COOK, KANE, and MCHENRY, the village of Barrington Hills, at 28.6 square miles, is geographically among the largest in Illinois. Property owners enjoy expansive vistas on minimum five-acre sites where both farming and horse raising are allowed.

The rich farmland and abundant water supplies attracted settlers Jesse Miller and William Van Orsdal in 1834. In the early 1840s other farm families arrived, many of whom were GERMAN, ENGLISH, and IRISH immigrants, and formed a town near present-day Sutton Road and Route 68. Initially called Miller's Grove, the community was later named Barrington Center. Farmers brought their crops to nearby markets on the FOX RIVER in EAST DUNDEE. Dairy farmers supported a cheese factory in the late nineteenth century.

Barrington Center Church (used by a KOREAN Wesleyan church in the beginning of the twenty-first century) was built in 1853 and used as an army recruiting station during the CIVIL WAR. Industry came to the area for a short period in the 1890s, when American Malleable Iron Company built a plant on the northern fringe of Barrington Hills along Highway 14. The company hired hundreds of HUNGARIAN workers and constructed a residential community for their workers which they called Chicago Highlands. The foundry closed in 1903 and the workers deserted their homes.

At the turn of the century, executives working in Chicago sought the quiet and openness that Barrington Hills offered. Many of the rolling farms subdivided into large estates where owners turned from agriculture to horse breeding and riding. By the 1920s residents began marking bridle paths. The Fox River Valley Hunt Club, founded in the late 1930s, aided in continuing the system of trails which traversed both private properties and forest preserve land. By the late 1980s over 70 miles of paths could be found.

The Barrington Horse Show began in 1945. It was held on various estates until 1965, when the 15-acre Barrington Countryside Riding Center became its permanent home. The village is home to Hill 'N Dale Farms, belonging to Richard Duchossois, owner of the Arlington Racetrack, and Bill McGinley's Horizons Farms, which exalt the equestrian flavor of the community. The community's identification with horses can be seen in names like Broncos and Colts for school teams, stores catering to saddlery and riding outfits, and subdivisions with names such as Saddlewood and Steeplechase and roads such as Bridlewood Trail and Surrey Court.

A desire to retain the rustic landscape led to village incorporation in 1957. In 1962 Barrington Hills annexed the neighboring town of Middlebury (incorporated in 1953). The Barrington Area Council of Governments (BACOG) formed in 1970 to preserve the resources of the seven villages that constitute the Barrington area.

Barrington Hills has 6,000 acres of FOREST PRESERVE, constituting 42 percent of the village landscape. The largest is Spring Creek Nature Preserve, which measures 4,000 acres of prairie, stream, slough, and woods. Into the 1990s farmers still retained about 3,000 acres of land. Residential properties of over one acre covered 30 percent. Devoid of a downtown center, the village has a small shopping strip along Route 14. With a population of 3,915 in 2000, Barrington Hills has kept its rural flavor as industrial and commercial development has sprung up around its borders.

Marilyn Elizabeth Perry

See also: Horse Racing; Suburbs and Cities as Dual Metropolis

Further reading: League of Women Voters of the Barrington Area, Illinois. *In and Around Barrington.* 1990. • Lines, Arnett C. *A History of Barrington, Illinois.* 1977. • Messenger, Janet. "Country Living." *North Shore* (December 1997): 73–94.

Bartlett, IL, Cook, DuPage, and Kane Counties, 30 miles W of the Loop. The town of Bartlett began in a woodland and still retains much of its picturesque and historical beauty. Victorian houses and farmhouses stand alongside ranches, BUNGALOWS, and Sears MAIL-ORDER HOUSES.

In 1844, Luther Bartlett purchased a 320-acre farm in Wayne Township along with his brother Lyman. Although Lyman eventually left the community, Luther became a farmer and sheep breeder, remaining in Bartlett until his death in 1882.

Bartlett built the Bartlett Manufacturing Company, which produced patent neck yokes. Although this created job opportunities for many of the villagers, the company failed in 1878 during an economic depression. In 1873 Bartlett laid an economic cornerstone for the village: subdividing 40 acres of property, he donated half of the land to the Chicago & Pacific RAILROAD (which was succeeded in 1880 by the Chicago, Milwaukee & St. Paul Railroad) for a train station and switching yard. Because of his donations the town was named for him.

The Bartlett station attracted butter- and cheese-making operations, which then drew a cooper shop to the area. In 1880 the shop employed over 25 employees, who put together 140,000 cheese boxes and 39,000 butter tubs. Bartlett was incorporated in 1891. At the turn of the century nearly three-fourths of the residents were GERMAN-born or were of German heritage.

In 1915 attorney Charles Erbstein purchased a 210-acre estate along present-day Lake Street (Route 20), naming the estate Villa Olivia after his daughter. From this location Erbstein broadcast a radio program beginning in 1922. The station moved to larger quarters the following year and the broadcast went national. The CHICAGO TRIBUNE later purchased the station.

Two private nine-hole GOLF courses were built on the Villa Olivia property in 1924 and 1926, and upon Erbstein's death his widow turned the property into a country club. She managed the property until it was sold in 1953. In 1975 a ski hill was added and a restaurant with banquet rooms.

Bartlett had just 716 residents in 1950, and resisted residential growth until the mid-1970s when the Boise Cascade company planned to develop 540 acres south of the village. Although the plan was finally approved, Boise Cascade backed out in the face of residents' opposition and subsequently sold to other developers. By decade's end approximately 3,500 residences had gone up, including townhouses, CONDOMINIUMS, and single-family houses.

The 1980s and 1990s brought new population growth and ANNEXATIONS. Bartlett's population soared from 19,373 in 1990 to 36,706 in 2000.

Marilyn Elizabeth Perry

See also: Agriculture; DuPage County; Suburbs and Cities as Dual Metropolis

Further reading: Alft, E. C. *Hanover Township: Rural Past to Urban Present.* 1980. • *Centennial Celebration—1991: Bartlett, Illinois.*

Baseball. The history of baseball in Chicago is usually associated with the two major league teams that call the city home—the CUBS and the WHITE SOX. But Chicago's baseball history actually encompasses many different levels of the diamond sport.

The earliest recorded game in the Chicago area was played in August 1851 between amateur teams from JOLIET and LOCKPORT. The Union Baseball Club was organized in Chicago in 1856; city newspapers first reported on its August 1858 game against the Excelsiors. Baseball experienced a rapid growth in popularity in Chicago after the CIVIL WAR. By 1867 there were 45 amateur teams competing in the city. By 1870 the NEWSPAPERS of Chicago were reporting the results of games played between amateur teams, company teams, and youth teams.

Encouraged by the growing attendance at games between the top-flight amateur teams, the city's eight strongest clubs decided to join together in organizing the Chicago City League in 1887. With the players sharing in the proceeds from the gate receipts collected at the enclosed ballparks, these teams moved into the ranks of semiprofessional baseball. The Chicago City League reached its nineteenth-century peak in popularity in 1890, but the circuit was disbanded after the 1895 season when the better teams opted to play the financially more attractive schedules of an independent.

Semiprofessional baseball in Chicago and surrounding suburban areas continued to grow from 1900 to 1910, both in overall quality of play and fan attendance at the city's dozen enclosed ballparks. During this period Chicago's legendary semipro teams—the Logan Squares, the Gunthers, and the West Ends—were all organized. Similar expansion also continued in the ranks of Chicago amateur baseball and in the industrial leagues. In the days before SOFTBALL became a popular recreational sport, amateur baseball fulfilled that role in Chicago. The city's newspapers carried reports of games in a wide range of leagues sponsored by organizations such as churches, corporations, fraternal orders, banks, HARDWARE dealers, and jewelers.

The Chicago City League returned to operation in 1909 with six teams, at least three of

"Playground Ball" at Marshal Swenie Playground, Polk Street east of Halsted, 1907. This was one of many illustrations of small parks published in the Special Park Commission's *Annual Report* for that year. Photographer: Unknown. Source: Chicago Public Library.

which were described as "professional" clubs, including the AFRICAN AMERICAN Leland Giants, one of many teams to emerge as a result of baseball's racial segregation. Chicago claimed a unique place in baseball history on the night of August 27, 1910, as the LOGAN SQUARES and ROGERS PARK played the sport's first successful night game under artificial lights at COMISKEY PARK.

After 1911, the overall quality of Chicago's semipro teams began to decline. The top clubs returned to playing as independents and the City League was no longer the major attraction it had once been. During WORLD WAR I, the Chicago area was home to the team fielded by the GREAT LAKES NAVAL STATION. Featuring seven former major league players in its lineup, Great Lakes won the 1918 Navy Championships. In the 1920s, Chicago baseball fans increasingly turned their attention to the CUBS, WHITE SOX, and the AMERICAN GIANTS of the National Negro League. The number of semiprofessional teams in the city declined substantially, and through the next two decades Chicago's remaining clubs played in a circuit commonly called the "Midwest League." Since the 1950s, semipro baseball in the Chicago area has been primarily made up of teams playing as independents.

In 1871, NORTHWESTERN UNIVERSITY played its first baseball game against non-Northwestern competition. The UNIVERSITY OF CHICAGO won or shared four Big Ten Conference championships before it left the league in 1947. The Maroon baseball teams also took several exhibition tours to Japan, the first in 1910.

The first interscholastic baseball game in Chicago was played in October 1868 between two private prep schools, Chicago Academy and Beleke Academy. In 1890 seven public high SCHOOLS organized the Cook County League amidst the rapidly spreading popularity of baseball among the city's secondary schools. The Chicago Public League came into existence in 1914; Crane High School won the league's first baseball championship.

From 1920 to 1926, the Chicago Public League high-school champion played the New York City champion in a series of intercity championship games, winning three of seven games. The Illinois High School Association held its first annual state baseball tournament in 1940. CICERO Morton in 1943 and Chicago Lane Tech in 1945 were the first Chicago-area schools to win the state championship. The American Legion sponsored youth baseball leagues beginning in the 1920s. Following WORLD WAR II, Little League baseball spread throughout Chicago and its suburbs, bringing

Andrew "Rube" Foster: A Baseball Legend

Rube Foster left school after the eighth grade to become a ballplayer but was limited to all-black teams, because the major and minor leagues were segregated after 1898. After an outstanding career, Foster moved to Chicago and became the Leland Giants' playing manager in 1907. Three years later, his squad capped repeated semipro championships against local white leagues with a closely fought but unsuccessful series against the Chicago CUBS.

In 1910 Foster gained control of the Leland Giants, in partnership with white saloonkeeper John Schorling. After an extraordinary 123–6 record in 1910, the team was renamed the American Giants. An outstanding recruiter and negotiator, Foster always secured for his teams at least half of all nonleague game proceeds; his players earned more than black postal workers or schoolteachers.

On February 13, 1920, Foster piloted the formation of the Negro National League (NNL), in part to promote economic development in black communities. As president and treasurer of the eight-team circuit, Foster ran it benevolently, wiring money to keep struggling traveling teams afloat, and trading his own star players to keep the league competitive.

In 1926 Foster suffered a nervous breakdown and was committed to an insane asylum. His beloved league collapsed in 1930, partly due to the GREAT DEPRESSION, but mainly from the loss of its leader. In 1981 he was elected to the Baseball Hall of Fame.

Steven A. Riess

Rube Foster of the Leland Giants baseball team, 1909. Photographer: Unknown. Source: Chicago Historical Society.

thousands of boys—and eventually girls—onto the baseball diamond.

By the final years of the twentieth century, minor league baseball had also come to Chicago. Going into the 2002 season, the metropolitan area was home to the COOK COUNTY Cheetahs (playing in CRESTWOOD), the KANE COUNTY Cougars (in GENEVA), the SCHAUMBURG Flyers, and the GARY Railcats.

Raymond Schmidt

See also: Creation of Chicago Sports; Leisure; Sports, High-School; Sports, Industrial League

Further reading: Federal Writers' Project (Illinois). *Baseball in Old Chicago.* 1939. • Pruter, Robert. "Youth Baseball in Chicago, 1868–1890: Not Always Sandlot Ball." *Journal of Sport History* 26.1 (Spring 1999): 1–28. • Schmidt, Raymond P. "The Golden Age of Chicago Baseball: Neighborhood Parks and the Semi-Pros, 1890–1910." Unpublished manuscript article.

Baseball, Indoor. Indoor baseball was invented by George Hancock in 1887 at the Farragut Boat Club on Chicago's SOUTH SIDE. The basic equipment was a mushy soft 17-inch ball and a stick-like bat. No gloves were worn and bases were only 27 feet apart. The game spread like wildfire across the Chicago area, and by the winter of 1891–92 there were more than a hundred teams organized in flourishing amateur leagues. Colleges and high schools, girls and boys, embraced the sport. Around 1907, players began taking the game outdoors, calling it "playground ball" and later "SOFTBALL." The indoor version went into steep decline in the 1910s, most assuredly because of the rapid growth of BASKETBALL, a game far better designed for indoor play. By the early 1920s, indoor baseball was a dead sport, but it left as its progeny the playground game most peculiar to Chicago, 16-inch slow-pitch softball.

Robert Pruter

See also: Creation of Chicago Sports; Leisure; Softball, 16-Inch; Sports, High-School

Further reading: Cole, Terrence. "'A Purely American Game': Indoor Baseball and the Origins of Softball." *International Journal of the History of the Sport* 7.2 (September 1990): 287–296. • Dickson, Paul. *The Worth Book of Softball: A Celebration of America's True National Pastime.* 1994. • Gems, Gerald R. *Windy City Wars: Labor, Leisure, and Sport in the Making of Chicago.* 1997.

Basketball. Basketball was invented in December 1891 by James Naismith at the YMCA's School for Christian Workers (now Springfield College) in Springfield, Massachusetts. Within months, the game spread across the country through a network of YMCAs. By February of 1893, teams at Chicago-area Ys had formed into a league.

Collegiate basketball also came to Chicago from Springfield College in the person of Amos Alonzo Stagg, the UNIVERSITY OF CHICAGO's new faculty coach, who had played on the Springfield teachers' team in the first public basketball contest. Intramural basketball games began at the university in 1893, but only one outside game was played, against the university's affiliate school, MORGAN PARK Academy. Early in 1894, Stagg formed the university's first varsity squad to compete in the YMCA league. In 1896, Chicago played in the world's first intercollegiate five-man squad competition, against the University of Iowa on January 18 in Iowa City.

High-school basketball in Illinois flourished first as a girls' sport. In the fall of 1895, AUSTIN High girls started a team and played against college squads. On December 18, 1896, they met OAK PARK in the first interscholastic high-school basketball contest in Illinois. Unlike elsewhere in the country, local teams did not play under modified rules for girls. This equality led to their undoing; under pressure from educators, girls in Illinois were forced out of basketball competition by 1910.

In 1899, ENGLEWOOD High formed the first permanent high-school boys' team and met ELGIN High the following year for the first interscholastic high-school boys' contest held in Illinois. The boys' game grew rapidly and 1908 saw the inauguration of the first boys' state tournament, held at Oak Park High School. In its first decades, the tourney was dominated by downstate schools.

During the first decade of the century, basketball swept throughout Chicago like a

Roger Ebert on *Hoop Dreams*

A film like "Hoop Dreams" is what the movies are for. It takes us, shakes us, and makes us think in new ways about the world around us. It gives us the impression of having touched life itself.

"Hoop Dreams" is, on one level, a documentary about two African-American kids named William Gates and Arthur Agee, from Chicago's inner city, who are gifted basketball players and dream of someday starring in the NBA. On another level, it is about much larger subjects: about ambition, competition, race and class in our society. About our value structures. And about the daily lives of people like the Agee and Gates families, who are usually invisible in the mass media, but have a determination and resiliency that is a cause for hope. . . .

One image from the film: Gates, who lives in the Cabrini Green project, and Agee, who lives on Chicago's South Side, get up before dawn on cold winter days to begin their daily 90-minute commute to Westchester [where they attend St. Joseph High School on basketball scholarships]. The streetlights reflect off the hard winter ice, and we realize what a long road—what plain hard work—is involved in trying to get to the top of the professional sports pyramid. . . .

We know all about the dream. We watch Michael Jordan and Isiah Thomas and the others on television, and we understand why any kid with talent would hope to be out on the same courts someday. But "Hoop Dreams" is not simply about basketball. It is about the texture and reality of daily existence in a big American city.

Ebert, Roger. "Hoop Dreams." *Chicago Sun-Times*, October 21, 1994.

whirlwind, as church, CLUB, SETTLEMENT HOUSE, and other amateur leagues for men and women were formed around the sport. That enthusiasm was also fueled by the national success of the University of Chicago teams. Under Coach Joseph E. Raycroft and with players like hall of famers John Schommer and Pat Page, the team compiled a 78–12 record from 1900 to 1909.

The biggest local basketball event in the 1920s was the National Interscholastic Basketball Tournament, held every March at the University of Chicago. At the invitation of Coach Stagg, champion high-school teams from across the country would converge on the city. Chicago NEWSPAPERS devoted the biggest coverage of the winter season to this extravaganza. Metropolitan Chicago's only winner in the tournament was CICERO's Morton High School in 1927.

Coach Lennie Sachs built LOYOLA UNIVERSITY into a national power in the late 1920s, and competed with DEPAUL for fans during the 1930s. Chicago fans during the 1940s were primarily enamored with the college game. DePaul won national recognition under Coach Ray Meyer, winning the prestigious National Invitation Tournament (NIT) in 1945 behind future hall of famer George Mikan. Regular doubleheaders of college games filled the CHICAGO STADIUM.

The professional game grew slowly and with difficulty in Chicago. Chicago BEARS owner George Halas sponsored the Chicago Bruins in the short-lived American Basketball League (1925–1931). The most successful local professional team was the Harlem Globetrotters, founded in 1926 by Abe Saperstein. In 1940, this barnstorming AFRICAN AMERICAN team captured the title at the *Chicago Herald-American*'s World Professional Basketball Tournament and established their national popularity.

George Halas revived his Chicago Bruins in 1939 to play in the Midwest professional loop, the National Basketball League (NBL), but disbanded them again in 1942. In 1947, the American Gears, founded in 1944, won the NBL tournament with superstar George Mikan. The team collapsed the following year when its owner, Maurice White, tried to form a rival league. The Chicago Stags made its debut in 1946 as a member of the Basketball Association of America (BAA), but the franchise dissolved in 1950, one year after the NBL merged with the BAA to form the National Basketball Association (NBA).

The emergence of African American players was signaled by the success of two all-black Chicago high-school teams, DuSable, which took second in the state championship series in 1954, and Marshall, which took state titles in 1958 and 1960. These successes on the high-school level were followed by Loyola University's surprising 1963 National Collegiate Athletic Association (NCAA) championship, with four African Americans on Coach George Ireland's starting team.

Chicago struggled for a professional franchise in the 1960s. The Chicago Packers searched for wins and audiences in 1961–62, took a new name, the Zephyrs, in 1963, then left for Baltimore. In 1966, the NBA awarded the city another franchise, for the BULLS, Chicago's first pro basketball team that succeeded both at the box office and on the floor. It contended for the NBA championship in the 1970s and filled Chicago Stadium despite the growing appeal of the college game in the city. DePaul University, still under the aegis of Coach Ray Meyer, again emerged as a national power in the 1970s and regularly contended for the NCAA title.

The 1970s saw a return of women's basketball in Chicago area colleges and high schools, reflecting a trend nationally. The first state tournament for high-school girls was inaugurated in 1977, and schools such as Maine West in DES PLAINES and Chicago's Marshall captured state titles and did much to extend the popularity of the game. The city also fielded the Chicago Hustle in the short-lived Women's Professional Basketball League from 1978 to 1981.

Despite the ongoing success of boys' high-school programs, especially at schools like MAYWOOD'S Proviso East and Chicago's Martin Luther King, which won four and three state championships respectively, the focus of Chicago basketball fans in the 1990s was primarily on the Chicago BULLS. The best professional team of the decade, the Bulls won six NBA titles behind the consensus greatest player in the history of the game, Michael Jordan.

Robert Pruter

See also: Creation of Chicago Sports; Sports, High-School

Further reading: Hill, Bob, and Randall Baron. *The Amazing Basketball Book: The First 100 Years.* 1987. • Johnson, Scott. "The Origins of High School Basketball in Chicago." Unpublished manuscript. 1991. • Lindberg, Richard, with Biart Williams. *Armchair Companion to Chicago Sports.* 1997.

Batavia, IL, Kane County, 34 miles W of the Loop. On their way west in the mid-1830s, settlers found by the FOX RIVER a valley rich in farmland, quarry stone, timber, and waterpower. Known initially as "Head of Big Woods," the area was renamed Batavia by Judge Isaac Wilson after his hometown in New York.

In 1854, the Newton Wagon Company was the first large factory to take advantage of the area's natural resources. Three major windmill factories joined the wagon company and were so productive that by 1890, Batavia was recognized as the leading windmill manufacturing city in the world, generating a nickname, "The Windmill City."

Following the Great Chicago FIRE OF 1871, quarries in Batavia shipped Niagara limestone to help with the city's rebuilding. Many SWEDISH immigrants who lost their jobs because of the fire came out of the city to work the quarries, joining the ENGLISH, IRISH, and GERMANS already there. Three RAILROADS served Batavia's citizens and industries.

In the last quarter of the nineteenth century, the VanNortwick Paper Company produced most of the newsprint used by the *Chicago Tribune*, and the Western Paper Bag Company made two to three million paper bags daily until the adjacent woods were depleted.

In 1867, Richard J. Patterson established a sanitarium for women in a former high-school building. Mary Todd Lincoln, widow of the assassinated president, stayed at the sanitarium in the summer of 1875.

By the census of 2000, Batavia's population had reached 23,866. The city's many styles of architecture range from the 1850s farmhouse to the 1990s townhouse. Yet the city is bounded by institutions that have limited its sprawl. The Fabyan FOREST PRESERVE is located directly north of Batavia. In 1912, the Loyal Order of the Moose, a fraternal organization founded in 1888, chose a 1,200-acre estate south of Batavia as the site for its international offices and established Mooseheart, a boarding school serving thousands of boys and girls of deceased lodge members. Congress approved a site east of Batavia for the FERMI National Accelerator Laboratory in 1966. Groundbreaking took place in 1968, and the facility was dedicated May 15, 1974.

Inhabitants of the city are proud of the completion in 1998 of a downtown riverwalk built entirely with volunteer help and funding.

Marilyn Robinson

See also: Clubs, Fraternal Clubs; Economic Geography; Housing Types

Further reading: Mair, Thomas A. *Batavia Revisited.* 1990. • Robinson, Marilyn, and Jeffery D. Schielke. *John Gustafson's Historic Batavia.* 1998. • Robinson, Marilyn. *Batavia Places and the People Who Called Them Home.* 1996.

Baths, Public. By the late 1800s personal cleanliness had become a cultural norm for Americans, necessary for social acceptance, symbolic of good character, and essential for the protection of PUBLIC HEALTH from infectious diseases. The urban poor and working class, without bathing facilities in their homes, were not able to conform to this standard of cleanliness. During the Progressive era, reformers urged city governments to build public baths for the poor, and Chicago's GOVERNMENT responded by building 21 small and utilitarian public bathhouses in poor and immigrant neighborhoods between 1894 and 1918.

A women's reform organization in Chicago, the Municipal Order League (later renamed the Free Bath and Sanitary League), led the campaign for public baths. Three women physicians, Gertrude Gail Wellington, Sarah Hackett Stevenson, and Julia R. Lowe, headed the crusade. Beginning in 1892, Wellington led in the effort, utilizing the network of women reformers in Chicago centering in the SETTLEMENT HOUSES, especially Jane Addams's HULL HOUSE, as well as the Chicago Woman's Club and the Fortnightly Club. These women gained support for the cause of public baths from the press and the city government under Mayor Hempstead Washburne and city council finance committee chairman Martin Madden. Chicago's first public, bath located at 192 Mather Street, near Hull House on the NEAR WEST SIDE, opened in 1894. It was named after assassinated mayor Carter H. Harrison and

This 1950 photo by Mildred Mead shows the still-operating William Mavor bath, constructed in 1900 and named after a Chicago alderman. The third municipal bath opened by the city of Chicago, it was located at 4645 Gross (later McDowell) Avenue. Photographer: Mildred Mead. Source: Chicago Historical Society.

cost $20,649. Thereafter, Chicago public baths were generally named after prominent local citizens.

Although some American cities built elaborate, monumental, and expensive public baths, Chicago conformed to the bath reformers' ideal that public bathhouses should be modest, unpretentious, strictly functional, free, and located in poor and immigrant neighborhoods readily accessible to bathers. Chicago's bathhouses generally contained between 20 and 40 showers, with attached dressing rooms, and a waiting room. There were no separate sections for men and women; two days a week were reserved for women, girls, and small children with their mothers. Bath patrons did not control water or temperature, which were regulated by an attendant who turned on the shower for 7 to 8 of the 20 minutes allowed for a bath.

In spite of this functional emphasis, bath patrons utilized the public baths more to cool off in the summer than to bathe in the winter months. Additionally, utilization of the public baths began to decline even as the city opened new baths. Peak attendance was reached in 1910, when a total of 1,070,565 baths were taken in the 15 bathhouses in operation; by 1918, when 21 bathhouses were open, utilization had declined to 709,452 baths. The opening of bathing beaches and SWIMMING pools in the early 1900s, as well as HOUSING REFORM laws which required private toilets in APARTMENTS (many landlords added bathtubs as well), contributed to the decline in public bath usage.

After WORLD WAR II, Chicago began to close down its public bathhouses. By the 1970s only one bathhouse remained open, to serve Skid Row residents, and that too closed in 1979.

Marilyn Thornton Williams

See also: Leisure

Further reading: Glassberg, David. "The Design of Reform: The Public Bath Movement in America." *American Studies* 20 (Fall 1979): 5–21. • Hanger, G. W. W. "Public Baths in the United States." In *Bulletin of the Bureau of Labor,* no. 54 (1904): 1245–1367. • Williams, Marilyn Thornton. *Washing "The Great Unwashed": Public Baths in Urban America, 1840–1920.* 1991.

Batswana. While a few individuals may have settled in Chicago earlier, the majority of Batswana came to Chicago in the 1990s on educational scholarships. The Botswana government has sponsored hundreds of students and professionals every year to obtain advanced degrees around the world, particularly in the United Kingdom, the United States, and Australia. The vast majority of Batswana students have returned home immediately after completing their educations, although a small number have remained to work for a few years. Community estimates suggested approximately 20 Batswana in Chicago in 2002, nearly all of them students specializing in a range of studies.

Batswana in Chicago meet for SOCCER, informal parties, and holidays and sometimes travel to larger Batswana communities in Michigan, New York, California, Washington DC, or Atlanta for large events like Batswana Independence Day (September 30). Chicago Batswana also remain connected to a larger community through Bosuinusa, an organization of Botswana students in the United States that organizes events and conferences and also maintains an active Internet newsgroup with more than a hundred participants.

Tracy Steffes

See also: Demography; Multicentered Chicago

Beach Park, IL, Lake County, 39 miles N of the Loop. This semirural community encompassing 7.5 square miles lies between the larger LAKE COUNTY towns of ZION and WAUKEGAN. Fearing forcible ANNEXATION to either Zion or Waukegan and the impact of the growth and development in those towns, Beach Park residents voted for incorporation in 1988. Although Waukegan attempted to block it, the referendum passed by a large margin.

Beach Park was completely rural until the 1930s, when people from Chicago and Milwaukee constructed campgrounds and mobile-home parks in the area. Though containing neither a "beach" nor a "park," the community was ideal for vacations as well as permanent residency, because of its proximity to the Illinois Beach State Park, located directly east. As intended by area residents and village officials, Beach Park began as a community unencumbered by tract housing, factories, or commercial development. By the time of its incorporation as a village, the community was still characterized by varied HOUSING TYPES, including a large number of single-family and MOBILE HOMES, and was free of industrial or commercial development.

Though the rate of population growth in Beach Park fell far short of its two neighbors, the number of residents rose steadily from 8,468 in 1980 to 9,513 in 1990 and 10,072 by 2000. These residents were predominately white and middle class.

At the time of incorporation, Beach Park residents, hoping to maintain the semirural character of the village, resolved that there would be no property taxes levied and therefore no funds available for roads, streets with curbs, streetlights, or police. The "home rule" style of government that residents and village officials adopted not only guaranteed independence from Zion and Waukegan, but that the character of the community would always differ from these neighboring Lake County towns.

Wallace Best

See also: Governing the Metropolis; Vacation Spots

Further reading: "Beach Park's Founding Fathers Fight for Control." *Chicago Tribune,* March 11, 1993. • "Primary May Put a New Town on the Map." *Chicago Tribune,* March 14, 1988.

Team owner and head coach George Halas with members of the 1935 Chicago Bears. Photographer: Unknown. Source: Chicago Historical Society.

Bears. The Chicago Bears professional FOOTBALL team began in 1920 as the Decatur Staleys, an industrial team sponsored by the A. E. Staley Company, a starch manufacturer. Organized and coached by Chicago native and former University of Illinois player George S. Halas, the Staleys recruited employees and former college players and helped establish the American Professional Football Association, which became the National Football League in 1922.

Franchises cost $100 and the average payout for each player in 1920 was $125 per game. In 1921, after a business recession cut starch profits, A. E. Staley suggested to Halas that the future of professional sports would lie in big cities and paid Halas $5,000 to take the team to Chicago and keep the nickname Staleys for one season. The Racine Cardinals and Chicago Tigers already were playing professional football in Chicago. Halas received permission from Cardinals owner Chris O'Brien to share territorial rights. Halas made Ed "Dutch" Sternaman a partner and cocoach.

The Staleys played in Cub Park, the baseball stadium later renamed WRIGLEY FIELD. Halas and Sternaman renamed their team the Bears because, they said, football players are bigger than baseball players.

Halas was a player as well as coach during the 1920s and was responsible for assembling a team that compiled only one losing record in its first 25 years. During that period, the Bears won the league championship six times and became known as the "Monsters of the Midway."

In the fall of 1925, Halas signed University of Illinois star senior Harold "Red" Grange when the college football season ended. Grange's manager, C. C. Pyle, operator of a movie theater in Champaign, arranged a barnstorming tour that brought national recognition to the Bears and the league. On Thanksgiving Day, 1925, Grange and the Bears played the Chicago Cardinals to a scoreless tie in Wrigley Field before the biggest crowd the league had drawn, 36,000. The team played eight games in 12 days in St. Louis, Philadelphia, New York City, Washington, Boston, Pittsburgh, Detroit, and Chicago. A crowd of 73,000 watched the game against the Giants in New York. The team played nine more games in the South and West, including a game that drew 75,000 to the Los Angeles Coliseum.

After the team's first losing season, in 1929, Halas hired former University of Illinois assistant Ralph Jones to coach. Jones refined the T formation, and the Bears won the league's first postseason game to decide the championship, in 1932, by defeating the Portsmouth Spartans 9–0. Because of inclement weather, the game was played indoors in CHICAGO STADIUM on an 80-yard field.

The Bears lost $18,000 in 1932. Halas borrowed money to buy out Sternaman for $38,000 and reinstated himself as coach in 1933. The Bears won the league championship in 1934. In 1936, the Bears made tackle Joe Stydahar their first choice in the league's first player draft. In 1939, they drafted Columbia quarterback Sid Luckman. The following year, they defeated the Washington Redskins 73–0 for the championship in the most lopsided game in NFL history. With the help of former UNIVERSITY OF CHICAGO and Stanford coach Clark Shaughnessy, Halas's offense perfected the T formation with "man in motion." The game against Washington was the first championship carried on network radio, BROADCAST to 120 stations. It further popularized the NFL and helped revolutionize offensive football in colleges and the pros.

With future Hall of Fame players Luckman, Stydahar, Bronko Nagurski, Danny Fortmann, George McAfee, George Musso, and Clyde "Bulldog" Turner, the Bears of the early 1940s dominated the NFL, winning titles in 1940, 1941, 1943, and 1946, and losing the 1942 championship after compiling an undefeated regular season. Halas joined the Navy in 1942, and several players also left for service in WORLD WAR II. Heartley "Hunk" Anderson and Luke Johnsos were co-coaches until Halas returned in 1946.

Halas made Paddy Driscoll coach in 1956–57 before returning himself until 1968, when he retired at age 73 after winning a league record 324 games, including his last championship, in 1963. Halas died in 1983, leaving the team to his daughter, Virginia Halas McCaskey. The Bears won the 1985 Super Bowl championship with former player Mike Ditka as coach. In 1997, the Bears became the first team in the NFL to reach 600 victories.

Don Pierson

See also: Leisure; Soldier Field; Sports, Industrial League

Further reading: Halas, George, Gwen Morgan, and Arthur Veysey. *Halas by Halas.* 1979. • Rollow, Cooper. *Bears 1977 Football Book.* 1977. • Whittingham, Richard. *The Bears: A 75-year Celebration.* 1994.

Beat Generation. Chicagoans played key roles in the emergence of the Beat Generation. The editors of the UNIVERSITY OF CHICAGO's student-run literary MAGAZINE, *Chicago Review,* planned in their Winter 1959 issue to continue their publication of excerpts from *Naked Lunch,* by William S. Burroughs, and "Old Angel Midnight," by Jack Kerouac. *Chicago Daily News* columnist Jack Mabley decried what he considered the publication of obscenity, and the university's administration suppressed the magazine. The editors, including Irving Rosenthal and Paul Carroll, went independent, raising money with a series of celebrated public readings featuring Beat writers Allen Ginsberg, Peter Orlovsky, and Gregory Corso. The first issue of *Big Table* (named for a note Kerouac wrote to himself about his workspace: "Get a bigger table.") ran into trouble with postal authorities, who, amidst allegations of obscenity, refused to ship copies. Judge Julius J. Hoffman, better known for the CHICAGO CONSPIRACY TRIAL, found *Big Table* 1 not obscene, and some important works achieved their first American publication here.

Bill Savage

See also: Free Speech; Literary Cultures

Further reading: Brennan, Gerald. "Big Table." *Chicago History* 17.1 and 2 (Spring and Summer 1988): 4–23. • Morgan, Ted. *Literary Outlaw: The Life and Times of William S. Burroughs.* 1988. • Nicosia, Gerald. *Memory Babe: A Critical Biography of Jack Kerouac.* 1983.

Bedford Park, IL, Cook County, 12 miles SW of the Loop. The village of Bedford Park has its roots in the planned industrial development known as the Clearing Industrial District. In 1888 railroad entrepreneur Alpheus B. STICKNEY bought land here in order to create a huge RAILROAD switching yard. In 1898 Henry H. Porter incorporated the Chicago Transfer and Clearing Company (CT&C), which soon after purchased Stickney's operation.

In 1905 the Chicago & Joliet Electric Railway was extended to the region, along Archer Avenue, making it possible for workers from Chicago to COMMUTE to jobs in the area. In 1906 the Corn Products Refining Company, run by Edward T. Bedford, purchased a hundred acres from the CT&C, and by 1915 "Ma Corn," as the corn milling plant came to be known, provided employment for hundreds of workers. In 1919 Corn Products purchased land for a management housing complex. This two-block area served as the beginning of Bedford Park's residential district. In 1940 the Town of Bedford Park incorporated.

Bedford Park has remained mostly industrial, with thousands of workers pouring into the village each day. The sheltered residential area, just off Archer Avenue, spans four blocks, comprising some two hundred homes. There are no restaurants, grocery stores, gas stations, or churches in this area. Owing to its industrial tax base, the village offers low taxes and high-quality services, including an outstanding library.

Ronald S. Vasile

See also: Built Environment of the Chicago Region; Economic Geography; Interurbans

Further reading: Frisbie, Richard, ed. *High Point on the Prairie: The Bedford Park Clearing Industrial Association at Seventy-five Years; The Village of Bedford Park at Fifty Years.* 1992. • Hill, Robert Milton. *A Little Known Story of the Land Called Clearing.* 1983. • Swanson, Elmay. *Out of My Mind: An Informal History of Bedford Park.* 1990.

Beecher, IL, Will County, 37 miles S of the Loop. Timothy L. Miller successfully raised then-rare longhorn Hereford cattle here by the 1870s. An influx of GERMAN settlers was followed by incorporation in 1883 and the arrival of the Chicago and Eastern Illinois RAILROAD in 1905. Beecher changed very slowly in subsequent decades. The Shady Lawn GOLF Course inhabits the former Miller estate, and a café occupies the 1850 Old Stage Tavern building. Over 53 percent of its residents claim German heritage, and five of its seven churches represent the Lutheran denomination.

Erik Gellman

See also: Agriculture; Will County

Belarusians. Belarusian immigrants began to settle in Chicago around the end of the nineteenth century. Labeled "RUSSIANS" if they were of EASTERN ORTHODOX faith, or "POLES" if they happened to be ROMAN CATHOLICS, Belarusians were not mentioned by name in any statistical reference sources. According to the program published in celebration of Whiterussian Day in 1930, drawing on records of the Belarusian Committee in Prague, there were by then approximately 25,000 Belarusians living in Chicago.

The Republic of Belarus is located in roughly the center of Europe. Between the fourteenth and eighteenth centuries, what is now known as Belarus became an integral part of the Grand Duchy of Lithuania; the native population was then known as Licviny (roughly translated: "LITHUANIANS"). The Russian Empire occupied the multinational state called Lithuania in 1795 and began an aggressive policy of russification. Consequently, when ethnic Belarusian peasants arrived on America's shores, they usually accepted whatever classification was assigned them. Most were labeled Russians since, from a political standpoint, they had emigrated from the Russian Empire. From 1919 to 1991, the independent Republic of Belarus was known as the Byelorussian Soviet Socialist Republic.

Beginning in the early 1900s, however, political self-awareness gradually took hold both in the homeland and among Belarusians abroad. The first Belarusian organization in Chicago—the White Russian National Committee—was established in 1920. At a convention called by the committee in 1923, the White Ruthenian National Association was established, opening its offices on the NEAR WEST SIDE. The association launched an ambitious range of programs, including the celebration of Belarusian Independence Day (March 25), the opening of a Sunday School, publication of a newspaper (*Belaruskaja Trybuna,* 1928–1932), and sponsorship of a weekly radio hour conducted in Belarusian.

During the 1920s, several other Belarusian organizations were formed in Chicago, among them the White Ruthenian Aid Committee, whose goal was to provide assistance to Belarusian schools in the homeland; the White Russian-American Club; and the White Russian People's Society of the City of Chicago. During the early 1930s, the group's most active organization was the White Russian-American Citizens Association. A decade later, in October 1941, the state of Illinois granted a charter to the White Russian American National Council, which has remained active ever since.

The arrival of 5,000–10,000 Belarusian immigrants to Chicago in the late 1940s and early 1950s prompted the formation of additional organizations. One of these, the Organization of Belarusian-American Youth in the State of Illinois, initiated and continues to sponsor a radio hour in Belarusian. Since its establishment in 1973, however, Belarusian-oriented activities have been organized most aggressively by the Belarusian Coordinating Committee, which oversees such activities as participation in MUSEUM OF SCIENCE AND INDUSTRY Christmas Programs and coordinates a variety of ethnic community parades.

Chicago's orthodox congregation, St. George Belarusian Orthodox Parish, in WEST TOWN, under the jurisdiction of the Ecumenical Patriarchate, has developed many cultural and youth programs. Christ the Redeemer in LOGAN SQUARE offers academic and religious programs to Roman Catholic Belarusians. Both congregations have provided assistance to the Belarusian victims of the 1986 Chernobyl nuclear reactor catastrophe.

Vitaut Kipel

See also: Demography; Eastern Orthodox; Multicentered Chicago

Further reading: Kipel, Vitaut. *Belarusans in the United States*. 1999.

Belgians. James Oliver Van de Velde, consecrated the second bishop of the ROMAN CATHOLIC ARCHDIOCESE OF CHICAGO in 1849, was among the first Belgians to arrive in Chicago. The Henrotin family (Joseph and Ferdinand) arrived around the same time and remained prominent in the city as physicians, financiers, and consuls for several generations.

A small cadre of Belgian businessmen established an early presence in Chicago, opening a consulate office in 1854 that remains the oldest in the city. Consul Adolphe Poncelet's 1855 report to the Belgian government identified 83 Belgians in Chicago with 24 different professions. Substantial settlement in Chicago awaited the 1880s, when population growth and epidemics at home caused many Belgian workers to emigrate to the United States. Many settled farms in Wisconsin, Michigan, and Minnesota, but substantial numbers of Belgian immigrants soon looked toward employment opportunities in industrial centers like Chicago. Initially seasonal laborers supplementing farm income during the winter, they gradually settled permanently in the city.

Belgian immigrants to Chicago at the turn of the century came largely from East Flanders. They settled primarily in LOGAN SQUARE, where St. John Berchmans Church was organized in 1903–4 by the archdiocese as a national parish for Belgian ROMAN CATHOLICS. The largely Flemish Belgian population increased through the 1910s and 1920s as men came to find work and were later joined by their families. By 1920, following the two most significant decades of Belgian immigration to the United States, Chicago was home to 3,079 Belgians. Immigration from Belgium diminished significantly after 1920 and reached a low point during the 1930s.

Around the turn of the century, Belgians began to find work in plumbing, building maintenance, and especially janitorial work. A large percentage of Belgians joined the Flat Janitors Union (Local 1), and Belgians eventually occupied a significant portion of the janitorial positions in LAKE VIEW and downtown buildings. In 1914, they organized the Belgian American Janitors Club, which served as a mutual aid and social organization for its members.

A stretch of Fullerton Avenue near Western Avenue burgeoned as the focal point for the Chicago Belgian colony's clubs, taverns, and businesses. In 1909, the first Belgian cultural organization, Kunst-En Broederliefde, established its headquarters at 2532 West Fullerton. In 1915, the Belgian American Janitors Club was reorganized as the Belgian American Club of Chicago and soon was planning dances and cultural events using the clubhouse built in 1921 by the All Belgians Are Equal Club. By the 1930s, at least seven Belgian taverns and several Belgian bakeries and delis stretched along Fullerton. While Logan Square was clearly the heart of the community, there were also Belgians living on the SOUTH SIDE, where De Jonghe Restaurant was the local meeting place. This Belgian restaurant would later move to East Monroe and become a famous eatery serving the house specialty "Shrimp De Jonghe."

Soon after the founding of the Janitors Club, Belgian women began organizing their own CLUBS. The Belgian American Ladies Society (1915), a social organization, and the Queen Elizabeth Club (1915), a civic and charitable organization, together had membership of nearly 200.

In 1960 the Chicagoans organized a chapter of the United Belgian American Society of the Midwest. This umbrella organization helped to unite Chicago's Flemish-speaking Belgians, in addition to connecting Belgians across the Midwest through annual conventions beginning in 1963. The United Belgian American Society continued to hold dances, BOWLING tournaments, bingo games, and the annual Belgian Night beauty pageant, which ran from 1962 to 1975 and attracted crowds of over 750.

The sixties also saw the founding of the Center for Belgian Culture, an effort to preserve Belgian heritage in the midst of the dissolution of the Belgian neighborhood in Logan Square as older Belgians moved to the suburbs and out of state. St. John Berchmans transformed along with the Logan Square neighborhood into a predominantly Hispanic and POLISH congregation, and the Belgians on the South Side gradually moved out of the neighborhood.

In 1970, an economic downturn and tax increases prompted another wave of immigration from Belgium. This new influx differed from earlier patterns because it included a significant number of Walloons, or FRENCH–speaking Belgians. By 1980, there were perhaps 75 families from Wallonia in Chicago. The 2000 census enumerated 7,303 persons with Belgian first ancestry in Cook and collar counties.

Robert Morrissey
Christina A. Reynen

See also: Americanization; Demography; Multicentered Chicago

Further reading: Griffin, Rev. Joseph A. *The Contribution of Belgium to the Catholic Church in America*. 1932. • Poncelet, Adolphe. "Rapport au Ministre des Affaires Étrangères de Belgique, daté de Chicago, le 22 septembre 1855." *Le Moniteur Belge*, January 16, 1856. • de Smet, Antoine. *Voyageurs belges aux États-Unis du XVIIe siècle à 1900*. 1959.

Belizeans. Substantial numbers of Belizeans first migrated to Chicago during the 1940s and 1950s. Many were hired as DOMESTIC WORKERS in the affluent suburbs of the North Shore; others had been recruited to Florida citrus farms in the first half of the century and joined the "GREAT MIGRATION" of black SOUTHERNERS to Chicago which continued through the 1960s. Still others worked in the Farm Work Program and the War Manpower Commission during WORLD WAR II and eventually made their way to Chicago after the war. When Hurricane Hattie struck Belize in October of 1961, devastating the country and leaving thousands homeless, another substantial wave of immigrants arrived in Chicago. In 1999, community leaders estimated 35,000 Belizeans living in Chicago, although the 2000 census counted only 4,242 in the metropolitan area.

Like most other immigrants, Belizeans established a pattern of "chain migration" as individuals, once established in Chicago, attracted and then assisted family members, relatives, and friends. Because so many were employed in domestic service in EVANSTON, KENILWORTH, and GLENCOE, a large concentration of Belizeans settled in neighborhoods on the North Side (along Howard Street in ROGERS PARK) and in Evanston. Hispanic Belizeans from the North and West of Belize established communities in WAUKEGAN and ZION. A small community of indigenous Caribbean *Garifuna* from Belize settled on the far SOUTH SIDE of the city.

In addition to domestic service, many Belizeans have done CONSTRUCTION and carpentry. Others have advanced into professions as nurses, bankers, and doctors. Many have opened small businesses and RESTAURANTS, especially on the North Side.

The Belizean Cricket Association of Chicago, formed sometime in the 1950s, was probably the first Belizean community organization in Chicago. Belizeans also participated in the AMERICAN WEST INDIAN ASSOCIATION, founded in 1944 as a social and cultural organization and as an advocate for exploited wartime immigrants. In 1971, Chicago Belizeans organized the Belizean Social Club, which served as an aid society and sponsored dances, benefits, field trips, and cotillions throughout the 1970s and 1980s. In 1980, the club organized the first annual Belizean Day in WASHINGTON PARK. The annual festival, which attracted two thousand participants in 1999, features traditional Belizean music and dancing as well as ethnic foods such as rice and beans, conch fritters, and potato pound. In 1998, Mayor Richard M. Daley declared the first Sunday in August to be Chicago Belizean Day.

In addition to the Belizean Social Club, the Hemenway Methodist Church on Chicago Avenue in Evanston became a social as well as spiritual center for the Belizean community.

Chicago's Belizeans have maintained strong ties with their homeland through several other organizations founded in the 1970s and 1980s. The Belizean American Association, dedicated to disaster relief, educational aid, and other charities in Belize, was founded in 1971 and reorganized as the Belize Association of Illinois in the early 1990s. In 1985 the Belizean NURSING Association was established to aid hospitals in Belize. The Chicago Belizean Sporting Association, formed to support athletics in Belize, was founded in the late 1980s. Belizean activity in sporting organizations has also included Evanston Cricket Club, the West Indian Cricket Association, and several Washington Park–based teams. Belizeans also participated in the 1970 founding of the West Indian Jets SOCCER team, which was still active at the turn of the millennium.

The Belize Cultural Association was founded in 1987 with a mission to preserve the ethnic heritage of Belize—Creole language, ethnic dances, and performing arts—among the young Belizeans living in Chicago. The Belize Cultural Association has sponsored choirs, dance troupes, and the annual Miss Belize U.S.A. pageant.

Robert Morrissey

See also: Americanization; Demography; Multicentered Chicago

Bellwood, IL, Cook County, 13 miles W of the Loop. The suburb of Bellwood is bounded by the Eisenhower EXPRESSWAY to the south, the Proviso yards of the Union Pacific RAILROAD to the north, and the suburbs of MAYWOOD to the east and HILLSIDE and BERKELEY to the west. With rail and highway TRANSPORTATION readily available, Bellwood developed a strong manufacturing base, yet remains essentially a residential community of single-family houses.

Consisting primarily of level prairie, the area was mainly farmland until the early 1890s when the first two SUBDIVISIONS were established. The first subdivision attracted a handful of businesses, including several taverns. Tavern owners were the first to push for incorporation, in response to dry Maywood's attempt to annex the subdivision. The village of Bellwood was incorporated on May 21, 1900, taking the name of a second early subdivision, Bellewood.

Bellwood's population grew steadily between 1900 and 1930. The 1910 population of 943 doubled by 1920 as more people, many of GERMAN and RUSSIAN descent, moved to the village. The 1926 ANNEXATION of land west of Mannheim Road, plus continued migration, accounts for the jump to 4,991 residents in 1930.

After WORLD WAR II, large industries, several of which became major employers in the near western suburbs, located in the eastern part of the village along the Indiana Harbor Belt tracks. Rail passenger service, available via the Chicago, Aurora & Elgin Railway (INTERURBAN) and the Chicago & North Western Railway, encouraged residential development in other parts of Bellwood. The completion of the Eisenhower EXPRESSWAY in the 1950s made Bellwood's location even more attractive for prospective commuters, even as it contributed to the demise of the Chicago, Aurora & Elgin in 1957. The population jumped to 8,746 in 1950, then more than doubled to 20,729 in 1960, and included people of Italian, Serbian, and Polish descent. Construction slowed considerably as little vacant land remained, and the population peaked in 1970 with 22,096 residents.

The 1970s brought racial change to the community—and involvement in a U.S. Supreme Court case. In 1975 the village of Bellwood filed a lawsuit accusing a local REAL-ESTATE firm of racial STEERING. Four years later a landmark ruling by the Supreme Court granted municipalities the legal right to use testers and to sue when discrimination occurred. Bellwood's black population grew from 1.1 percent in 1970 to 35 percent in 1980 and to 70 percent in 1990.

Today, several of Bellwood's large manufacturers remain, but the loss of other large industries has caused a decline in employment and in tax dollars. However, a number of smaller industries and commercial enterprises brought some new construction to the village. Like the trees planted in village parkways, Bellwood, with its many brick BUNGALOWS, ranches, and Georgians, has matured, but in many respects it remains the largely residential suburb that it has been for the last 50 years.

Patricia Krone Rose

See also: Economic Geography; Open Housing; Prohibition and Temperance

Further reading: Kerch, Steve. "Village Has an Appetite for the Variety of Life." *Chicago Tribune,* July 6, 1991. • Zygowicz, Kathryn. *Bellwood 1900–1975: The Heart of Proviso Township.* 1975.

Belmont Cragin, Community Area 19, 8 miles NW of the Loop. Belmont Cragin is a community built on commerce and industry. The first business was a SALOON opened by George Merrill sometime after 1835, when he settled with his family at the intersection of Armitage and Grand Avenues. Operating the saloon out of his home, Merrill catered to truck farmers carrying produce over the plank road to the city. The corner, named Whiskey Point, prompted many colorful and romanticized legends but attracted few permanent residents.

In 1862 Michael Moran established a hotel at Whiskey Point, but the area remained rural until 20 years later, when Cragin Brothers & Company moved their tin plate and sheet iron processing plant near Whiskey Point. The plant and warehouses covered 11 acres, and the Chicago, Milwaukee & St. Paul RAILROAD built a station at Leclaire Avenue to accommodate all the employees. Cragin also purchased a rivet company and moved machinery and workers from Connecticut to the location. Job opportunities and rail service brought settlers and a new-housing boom to the town, now named Cragin. Within the first two years the population rose to 200, and the community boasted a general store, two schoolhouses, and a Congregational church.

Railroads drew more factories and workers to the area, which was annexed into Chicago as part of JEFFERSON TOWNSHIP in 1889. The Belt Railway Company extended its service in 1883, and plants developed in the new neighborhoods of Hanson Park and Galewood. In the same year the Washburn and Moen Manufacturing Company launched a branch for its wire products, and the Western Brick and Tile Company found Galewood's superior clay SOIL conducive to business. By 1891 Westinghouse, Church, Kerr & Company Iron Works, the Pitts Agricultural Works Warehouse, and the Rice and Bullen Malting Company brought more people into Cragin.

In 1922 W. F. Hall PRINTING Company erected a plant on 17 acres adjacent to the Northwestern railroad line, which further spurred manufacturing development. SWEDISH, GERMAN, and IRISH workers were among the earliest to move near these factories. By 1920 jobs drew POLES and ITALIANS as well, and the population of the area more than quadrupled in the next decade. By 1930 the population escalated to 60,221, one-third foreign-born. Slower growth ensued. In the 1930s the community area became known as Belmont Cragin. Builders inundated the area to fill the housing needs of area workers. Bungalows, Cape Cods, and two-flats offered a range of HOUSING TYPE choices. Especially popular was the subdivided residential neighborhood on the eastern border named Belmont Park.

SHOPPING DISTRICTS added to the commercial atmosphere. In the 1940s Belmont-Central was constructed with a dozen stores, a parking lot, and a children's playground. During the postwar years the CHICAGO TRANSIT AUTHORITY extended its Belmont Street bus service beyond Central, transporting new patrons into the district. A 1981 addition of a nearby PARKING garage continued to contribute to business prosperity. In March 1976 the opening of the Brickyard Shopping Mall on the former site of the Carey Brickyard property at Narragansett and Diversey added new vitality to the community, drawing city shoppers away from suburban malls.

Belmont Cragin's overall population grew by more than 6 percent in the 1980s and 37 percent in the 1990s. The Hispanic population grew from 3,072 in 1980 to 16,846 in 1990. By the 2000 census the area was 65 percent Hispanic. POLISH immigrants and businesses also came to the area during these years. A number of young middle-class professionals joined blue-collar laborers in the area. Residents formed an active coalition called the Northwest Neighborhood Federation to address increases in crime, GANGS, and school overpopulation.

By 1995, Hall Printing and other plants had closed their doors. The area experienced a drop in manufacturing employment and a decline in retail activity during the 1980s. Concerns over UNEMPLOYMENT and an increasing poverty level have led residents to organize a home reinvestment campaign and to study ways of reviving the commercial climate in the area.

Marilyn Elizabeth Perry

See also: Annexation; Economic Geography; Iron and Steel; Metropolitan Growth

Further reading: Clipping file. Chicago Public Library, Portage-Cragin branch. • Karlen, Harvey M. *Chicago's Crabgrass Communities: The History of the Independent Suburbs and Their Post Offices That Became Part of Chicago.* 1992. • Krob, Gregory James. "The Economic Impact of a Regional Shopping Center on the Central City: A Study of the Brickyard Shopping Center, Chicago, Illinois." M.A. thesis, University of Illinois at Chicago. 1982.

Benedictine University. In 1885, two assemblies of Benedictine monks—one from Pennsylvania, the other from Ohio—journeyed west and joined forces to serve the CZECH and SLOVAK immigrants who had begun settling in Chicago at midcentury. They named their new parish St. Procopius Abbey in honor of the first canonized Czechoslovakian saint. In 1887, St. Procopius College became the first Czech school of higher learning in the United States. After moving to LISLE—onto farmland purchased by the monks 30 miles west of Chicago—in 1901, the school began to extend its reach beyond the Czech community. It became coeducational in 1968 and, after adding several graduate programs, was renamed Benedictine University in 1996.

Sarah Fenton

See also: Roman Catholics; Universities and their cities

Beninese. Prior to the 1990s most Beninese preferred to migrate to France and Belgium because of the shared language, lower costs, and availability of visas. Educational and economic opportunities began to draw Beninese to New York in the 1980s, and, like other West African groups, they carved out a niche in African clothing and hairbraiding. As the community grew in size in the 1990s, Beninese began to move to Chicago and other major cities in search of economic opportunities, encouraging friends and family to follow. In Chicago, many Beninese women established African hairbraiding businesses catering to the city's large AFRICAN AMERICAN community, while men entered occupations including TAXI cab driving, HOTEL management, and trading. Building off ties to and the success of the earlier group, a new wave of younger and more educated migrants from Benin and Europe came to Chicago in the late 1990s for graduate education and professional opportunities. Community members in 2001 estimated 150 to 200 Beninese in Chicago, and the number was rapidly growing.

Beninese have begun to organize as a community in Chicago and nationwide. The Association of Beninese Nationals in the U.S.A. (ARBEUA) was founded in 1984 in Washington DC as a social, cultural, and mutual aid organization to unite all Beninese in the United States. The organization maintains a national General Assembly and Executive Board which holds meetings and organizes cultural activities in Washington DC. In 1999, Beninese in Chicago established a Chicago chapter of the organization, which primarily organizes social and cultural events like monthly parties, summer picnics, and an annual Independence Day celebration on August 1. The organization also financially assists members in need.

In addition to involvement in ARBEUA, Beninese in Chicago come together through personal ties and professional activities. Since most Beninese have been drawn to Chicago through a network of family and friends, the Beninese community is particularly tight-knit. It is also closely tied to other West African communities, including the MALIAN, IVORIAN, SENEGALESE, and TOGOLESE communities with whom it shares many cultural similarities and kinship ties. Many Beninese are involved in *tontine* groups, small money-gathering cooperatives based on trust and oral agreement. Each member of a tontine contributes a set amount of money at regular intervals and then takes a turn drawing the full amount. Through the discipline of the tontine, members can collect at one time what it might take them a considerable amount of time to save on their own. Beninese are also active professionally and formed the African Hairbraiding Association of Illinois in 2001 to lobby the state for a new form of licensing. Under the Illinois Cosmetology Act, hairbraiders are required to obtain a general cosmetology license which requires training in areas unrelated to hairbraiding.

Tracy Steffes

See also: Demography; Multicentered Chicago

Bensenville, IL, DuPage County, 17 miles W of the Loop. The village of Bensenville occupies the northeastern corner of DUPAGE COUNTY near O'HARE AIRPORT. Bensenville has evolved from rural farming community to railroad town to mature airport suburb, reflecting the changes of the Chicago area.

As in other DuPage communities, the POTAWATOMI tribe represented the largest Indian presence, before their removal after 1833. New Englanders Hezekiah Dunklee and Mason Smith established claims near SALT CREEK soon after the Indian removal in a wooded grove west of present-day Bensenville in ADDISON Township. Political strife in Europe contributed to building the area's population, as many GERMAN immigrants settled in the area.

These farmers raised wheat and dairy products. A stage road connecting Chicago, Elgin, and Galena and a plank road that paralleled Irving Park Road promoted travel, trade, and settlement in the region. The opening of the Galena & Chicago Union RAILROAD in 1849 to the south also contributed to growth and provided a glimpse into the role of TRANSPORTATION in the community's future.

In the early 1870s, Dietrich Struckmann, T. R. Dobbins, and Roselle Hough purchased and subdivided the land that would become Bensenville. The Chicago, Milwaukee, & St. Paul Railroad began service between Chicago and Elgin with a stop in the area. Discussion of incorporation soon began, and on May 10, 1884, the measure passed handily.

During the next 30 years, Bensenville began to resemble a suburb. The first school opened in 1886, and storm sewers were constructed a year later. Other amenities, such as TELEPHONE service, concrete sidewalks, and electricity, followed in the early 1900s. Most significant, the Chicago, Milwaukee, & St. Paul constructed a roundhouse and freight yard in Bensenville in 1916. The yard provided many jobs and attracted new residents, including many MEXICANS. Bensenville soldiered quietly forward through the twenties and thirties, reaching a population of 1,869 by 1940.

In 1940 the federal government announced plans to construct an aircraft plant to manufacture cargo planes just outside Bensenville in Cook County. The plant operated from 1943 to 1945. Chicago purchased the complex in 1946 to develop a large airport. The proposed airport required additional land in unincorporated DuPage County, which Chicago planned to acquire. Nearby Bensenville challenged Chicago's right to annex this land in court, but lost. Many unincorporated Bensenville structures were moved or demolished to accommodate portions of O'Hare Airport, which began domestic commercial service in 1955.

Bensenville's population grew dramatically after World War II, doubling by 1950 and nearly tripling by 1960. O'Hare provided the catalyst for increased industrial development between the airport and residential areas, but the airport also created substantial noise pollution. Bensenville joined 16 other area suburbs in 1969 in forming the O'Hare Area Noise Abatement Council to address this issue.

Like its eastern DuPage neighbors, Bensenville has nearly reached its limits in land development. The village still attracts residents from many ethnic backgrounds, including INDIANS, East Asians, and Eastern Europeans, and grew slightly, to a population of 20,703, in 2000.

Aaron Harwig

See also: Demography; Metropolitan Growth; Railroads; Transportation

Further reading: Jones, Martha Kirker. *Bensenville.* 1976. • *Knowing Our History, Learning Our Culture.* Videotape. Bensenville Community Library, 1993. 42 min. • Ritzert, Kenneth. "Bensenville." In *DuPage Roots,* ed. Richard Thompson, 1985.

Berkeley, IL, Cook County, 14 miles W of the Loop. Berkeley is located on COOK COUNTY'S western border. With Interstates 290 and 294 forming its western and part of its southern boundary, and the Union Pacific RAILROAD (formerly the Chicago & North Western) and the large Proviso classification yard to the north, Berkeley has ready access to the metropolitan region. Yet the TRANSPORTATION corridors that make Berkeley accessible to distant places also serve to separate the village from its nearest neighbors, creating a small-town atmosphere.

Beginning in 1835 the area that was to become Berkeley was home to farmers, most of GERMAN and DUTCH ancestry. Settling on farms that ranged from 40 to 160 acres, the Dutch tended to be truck farmers, while the Germans did general farming. This small group of farm families established a one-room school called Sunnyside in 1848. Now housed in a larger and newer building, Sunnyside Elementary School still operates today. A short distance west on St. Charles Road (which was completed in 1836), farmland was donated for what is now known as Old Settler's CEMETERY.

The 1902 completion of the Chicago, Aurora & Elgin Railroad (INTERURBAN) gave the area its first passenger rail service at a stop called Berkeley. SUBDIVISION in 1908 and again in 1914–1915 brought residential construction and new residents, many of whom were ENGLISH, to the area. At the initiative of these newcomers, the village of Berkeley incorporated in 1924.

The population growth of the early 1900s paled by comparison to the population boom Berkeley experienced after WORLD WAR II when the village population tripled from 1,882 in 1950 to 5,792 in 1960. At the same time, Berkeley lost a number of houses when the construction of the Interstate 290 extension in the late 1950s cut a north-south swath through the western section of the village. With traffic diverted to the new EXPRESSWAY system, the Chicago, Aurora & Elgin terminated its passenger service in 1957, but its route is still marked through the village by the Prairie Path for BICYCLING.

Berkeley's land purchase from the railroad in the 1960s extended its northern boundary, allowing for the addition of a small industrial park. In 2000, the facility's 12 light industries included electrical contractors, PRINTING companies, warehouses, wholesalers, and the World Dryer Corporation, one of the world's largest manufacturers of hand dryers.

Berkeley has remained predominantly a residential community, however. Many of the people who bought homes in the 1950s stayed in the village through the 1990s. At the opening of the twenty-first century the village expected significant residential turnover as these long-term homeowners sold their properties.

Patricia Krone Rose

See also: Built Environment of the Chicago Region; Economic Geography; Land Use

Further reading: Johnson, Rosemarie. *From Oats to Roses: The History of Berkeley.* 1974. • Young, Linda. "A Quiet Place with Come-Back Spirit." *Chicago Tribune,* September 18, 1993.

Berwyn, IL, Cook County, 9 miles W of the Loop. In June 1856, Thomas Baldwin bought 347 acres in the southern section of modern-day Berwyn from the ILLINOIS & MICHIGAN CANAL Company, hoping to create an affluent community called LaVergne. Baldwin's property became part of CICERO Township in 1857. With the canal a mile to the south, LaVergne was initially accessible only via the Ogden Avenue plank road. The Chicago, Burlington & Quincy RAILROAD ran through the area by 1864, but did not stop in LaVergne until a decade later.

By 1880, a REAL-ESTATE syndicate that included Marshall Field had acquired Baldwin's land and platted a new LaVergne subdivision. Large numbers of SWEDISH immigrants settled north of the railroad tracks on a section of Baldwin's former property soon known as Upsala. The Mutual Life Insurance Company acquired the northernmost portion of the canal company land, surveying and subdividing it in 1887. More than a mile removed from LaVergne and Upsala, the area developed quite independently.

In 1890, the Field syndicate sold 106 acres to investors Charles E. Piper and Wilbur J. Andrews. The developers subdivided the land, constructing STREETS, sidewalks, and sewers, and named the new subdivision Berwyn, after a Philadelphia suburb listed on a Pennsylvania Railroad timetable. Middle-class Chicagoans were quickly drawn to the desirable new community, with its many amenities. In 1891 Piper and Andrews acquired additional land, nearly doubling the town's size.

By 1900 Chicago was hungrily annexing surrounding communities. To prevent its ANNEXATION, Berwyn voted in 1901 to separate from Cicero Township and become an independent village. Only seven years later Berwyn incorporated as a city. The community began to draw large numbers of Czechoslovakian families, along with GERMANS, POLES, and ITALIANS. Population more than doubled between 1910 and 1920, with new building concentrated in south Berwyn. Because the city prohibited heavy industry within its borders, the community remained largely residential. Many Berwyn residents worked at the nearby Hawthorne Works of the Western Electric Company. Thus Berwyn suffered a great loss when in July 1915 the excursion boat EASTLAND, chartered for a company outing to MICHIGAN CITY, Indiana, capsized in the CHICAGO RIVER, drowning 812.

Berwyn experienced phenomenal growth during the 1920s, gaining a reputation as Chicago's fastest-growing suburb. The city's stringent BUILDING CODES resulted in block upon block of well-built, two-story brick BUNGALOWS. To serve its expanding population, Berwyn established an independent park district and created Illinois' first municipal health district. The street improvements that sparked the boom also helped unify north and south.

Berwyn's growth slowed substantially during the GREAT DEPRESSION, but the community experienced a second building boom after WORLD WAR II, pushing its population to 54,226 in 1960. Population began to fall thereafter, as longtime residents aged and their offspring moved away. By 1990 some of these children were returning to Berwyn to raise their own families. Often more affluent than their parents, they demanded new services and drove up real-estate prices, leaving old-timers "house poor." And while Berwyn's CZECH heritage retained its importance, increasing ethnic diversity further tested the city. Despite these challenges, however, Berwyn remains a solidly middle-class bedroom community.

Elizabeth A. Patterson

See also: Annexation; Metropolitan Growth; Oak Park, IL; Taylorism; Telephony

Further reading: *Berwyn Views.* Miscellaneous pamphlets on Berwyn. Undated. Chicago Historical Society, Chicago, IL. • Chicago Fact Book Consortium, ed. *Local Community Fact Book: Chicago Metropolitan Area, 1990.* 1995. • *Twenty-five Years of Progress with Berwyn, Cicero, and Stickney, November 1951: The Life Newspapers' Silver Anniversary Edition.* 1951.

Beverly, Community Area 72, 12 miles S of the Loop. Known for its spacious homes, TREE-lined streets, and racially integrated population, Beverly has retained its reputation as one of Chicago's most stable middle-class residential districts. Originally part of the village of WASHINGTON HEIGHTS (1874), this area was ANNEXED to Chicago by 1890 but remained sparsely settled for decades. Residents often identify their community as "Beverly Hills," a reference to the glacial ridge just west of Longwood Drive, the highest point in Chicago. Whether the community was named after Beverly, Massachusetts, or Beverly Hills, California, remains subject to debate, but in the 1890s, the Rock Island Railroad designated its 91st Street station "Beverly Hills" and by WORLD WAR I, the telephone company had established a Beverly exchange.

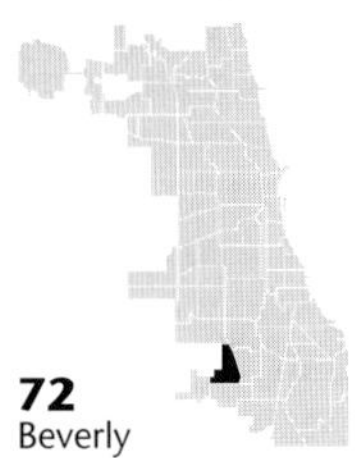

In 1886, real-estate developer Robert Givins constructed a limestone castle at 103rd and Longwood Drive in the Tracy SUBDIVISION of Washington Heights, but the surrounding neighborhood did not achieve residential maturity for decades. The situation was the same north of 95th Street, where CIVIL WAR general Edward Young and W. M. R. French, the first director of the ART INSTITUTE, had built homes along Pleasant Avenue in the 1890s. Vast sections of Beverly, especially the area south of 99th Street and west of Western, remained prairie until the 1940s and 1950s.

From its earliest days, this community symbolized upward social mobility, first for white Anglo Saxon PROTESTANTS, and later for IRISH ROMAN CATHOLICS and AFRICAN AMERICANS. Like MORGAN PARK to the south, Beverly has always been a dry area, prohibiting SALOONS and the sale of liquor in the area east of Western Avenue. The community's suburban setting was further enhanced by Ridge Park with its imposing fieldhouse (1912) designed by local architect John Todd Hetherington and by its close proximity to Beverly and Ridge Country Clubs and the Dan Ryan FOREST PRESERVE. Its housing stock remained predominantly single-family with only a few APARTMENT buildings clustered along the Rock Island Railroad tracks that link Beverly to downtown Chicago. Although the 95th Street commercial district included a variety of shops and restaurants, it never rivaled ROSELAND's Michigan Avenue or 63rd and Halsted. Indeed, the Beverly Theater was built outside the community's boundaries at 95th and Ashland Avenue in the mid-1930s and residents did not have their own branch of the CHICAGO PUBLIC LIBRARY until 1981.

Beverly's churches and public SCHOOLS reflected the community's growth from east to west. Bethany Union (1872) and Trinity Methodist (1896), originally located on Prospect Avenue, built architecturally significant houses of worship in the 1920s closer to Longwood Drive.

In the 1920s, Beverly's ethnic composition expanded to include Irish Catholics and GERMAN Lutherans who established St. Barnabas church and school (1924) and St. John Divine Lutheran (1929). However, anti-Catholic sentiment ran so high that residents had property at 100th and Longwood Drive condemned for a public park to prevent its use by the Catholic congregation. But St. Barnabas parish persisted and in 1936, a second Catholic parish, Christ the King, was organized in north Beverly. By the time St. John Fisher was formed in 1948 in the newest section of the community, Catholics had become the largest denomination in Beverly.

Beyond the post–WORLD WAR II baby boom, Beverly's increase in population between 1940 and 1960, from 15,910 to 24,814, was due in large measure to racial change in such neighborhoods as ENGLEWOOD, Normal Park, and SOUTH SHORE. The community's churches experienced new growth and many embarked on ambitious building campaigns. Beverly's Unitarians, who had purchased the landmark castle in 1942, for example, welcomed families from the People's Liberal Church of Englewood. In 1949, members of Bethlehem SWEDISH Lutheran Church at 58th and Wells Street financed a new complex at 94th and Claremont Avenue. Among the new houses of worship constructed in the community were St. Paul Union (1944), Society of Friends (1948), Ridge Lutheran (1948), Beverly Covenant (1952), Christ the King (1953), St. John the Divine (1953), the Episcopal Church of the Holy Nativity (1954), Salem Baptist (1955), St. John Fisher (1956), and St. Barnabas (1969). From the late 1950s until 1974, the community also included Beth Torah Synagogue.

In 1971, the Beverly Area Planning Association (1947) was reorganized to respond to residents' concerns about "BLOCKBUSTING" by REAL ESTATE brokers interested in profiting from rapid racial change. BAPA's annual home tours brought thousands of visitors to the community, and the group promoted Beverly's and Morgan Park's inclusion on the National Register of Historic Places in 1975. In 1981, the city of Chicago granted landmark status to the Prairie-style BUNGALOWS designed between 1909 and 1914 by Walter Burley Griffin on the 1700 block of West 104th Place, as well as 12 blocks on Longwood Drive and three blocks along Seeley Avenue between 98th and 110th Streets. The Ridge Historical Society (1971) maintains a library and museum to aid residents and researchers in documenting the community's past.

Like Chicago's HYDE PARK and ROGERS PARK, Beverly is a racially integrated neighborhood but the community has no large institutional anchor comparable to the UNIVERSITY OF CHICAGO or LOYOLA UNIVERSITY. In 1995, Beverly became one of the city's neighborhoods to adopt cul-de-sacs. The 11 concrete cul-de-sacs and diverters in the area north of 95th Street restricted automobile access to north Beverly to three points of entry: 91st and Western; 95th and Leavitt; and 95th and Damen. Critics charged that the traffic plan was racially motivated, but Alderman Virginia Rugai cited security concerns expressed by both black and white residents.

Ellen Skerrett

See also: Historic Preservation; Prohibition and Temperance; Religious Geography; South Side

Further reading: Commission on Chicago Landmarks and the Chicago Department of Planning and Development. *Chicago Historic Resources Survey.* 1997. • Pacyga, Dominic A., and Ellen Skerrett. *Chicago, City of Neighborhoods: Histories and Tours.* 1986.

Beverly Shores, IN, Porter County, 36 miles E of the Loop. The resort community of Beverly Shores, Indiana, lies among the sand dunes of Lake Michigan's southern shore, surrounded by INDIANA DUNES National Lakeshore. The history of Beverly Shores is linked to that of the electric INTERURBAN rail line initially known as the Chicago, Lake Shore & South Bend, which began to provide through-service from South Bend to Chicago shortly after 1900. Chicago utilities magnate Samuel Insull reorganized the railroad as the Chicago, South Shore & South Bend in 1925, investing millions in upgrades and ADVERTISING to encourage commuters and vacationers to ride the line. Among the improvements was a series of tile-roofed, Spanish revival depots, one of which appeared in the nascent community of Beverly Shores.

Beverly Shores was the brainchild of the Frederick H. Bartlett Company, Chicago's largest REAL-ESTATE developer of the era. Encouraged by Insull's investments and the opening of the Dunes Highway several years before, the Bartlett Company purchased 3,600 acres of duneland west of MICHIGAN CITY in 1927. The company envisioned Beverly Shores, named for Frederick Bartlett's daughter, as only one portion of a much larger development rivaling Atlantic City. The crash of 1929 led the Bartlett Company to scale back its grand plans, but Beverly Shores nevertheless began to take shape shortly thereafter.

To lure buyers, Robert Bartlett, who purchased the venture from his father's company in 1933, built roads, a school, a championship GOLF course, a botanical garden, a riding academy, and a Florentine revival hotel. He relocated six model houses and a recreated colonial village from the CENTURY OF PROGRESS World's Fair to Beverly Shores. He enticed a group of players from the GOODMAN THEATRE of Chicago to present weekend performances at the Beverly Shores playhouse. His salesmen fanned out across Chicago's neighborhoods, recruiting potential buyers and transporting them to Indiana on special South Shore trains. Bartlett's promotional efforts met with success, and both VACATION homes and year-round residences appeared amidst the dunes during the thirties and forties.

When Robert Bartlett withdrew from Beverly Shores in 1947, the community was forced to incorporate in order to provide services for its residents. By this time, activists in Indiana and Chicago, fearing further industrial intrusions into the dunes LANDSCAPE, had begun to lobby for creation of a national lakeshore park. Through the efforts of the Save the Dunes Council (founded in 1952), among others, Congress established the 8,330-acre Indiana Dunes National Lakeshore in 1966. In 1976, the park's boundaries were expanded to include part of Beverly Shores, leaving the remainder of the village an island surrounded by parkland.

Beverly Shores still struggles with its island status; a smaller tax base makes providing services a challenge. But the village increasingly looks to its past to strengthen its future. Just outside the village proper, the National Park Service has plans to rehabilitate the five remaining Century of Progress houses. More important for village residents, the shuttered South Shore depot has been renovated, and the remainder of the landmark station serves as a museum of Beverly Shores' unusual history.

Elizabeth A. Patterson

See also: Conservation and Preservation; Dune System; Environmental Politics; Leisure; Metropolitan Growth

Further reading: Cohen, Ronald D., and Stephen G. McShane, eds. *Moonlight in Duneland: The Illustrated Story of the Chicago South Shore and South Bend Railroad.* 1998. • Engel, J. Ronald. *Sacred Sands: The Struggle for Community in the Indiana Dunes.* 1983. • Miscellaneous Newspaper Clippings and Pamphlets on the Chicago, South Shore & South Bend Railroad; House of Tomorrow; Indiana Dunes; Save the Dunes Council. Chicago Historical Society, Chicago, IL.

Bicycling. Chicago's bicycling boom reached its peak at the end of the nineteenth century. The first bicycles, known as velocipedes but nicknamed "boneshakers," appeared in Chicago in the late 1860s. Heavy metal tires made pedaling these 150-pound bicycles arduous work. The introduction of the "high-wheeler" in the late 1870s made cycling easier yet required riders to climb atop a 54-inch front wheel. Those who were neither athletes nor acrobats chose to watch cyclists rather than ride. Chicagoans gathered at the Chicago Coliseum to watch six-day endurance races held on indoor tracks, and spectators lined the streets from Michigan Avenue's Leland Hotel to PULLMAN to watch the annual Pullman bicycle race.

The high cost of a high-wheeler limited bicycle ownership to the upper class. Wealthy cyclists willing to spend $200 to $400 for a bicycle donned elegant riding uniforms and joined wheelman's clubs. By the late 1890s, 54 clubs boasted more than 10,000 members. Some clubs constructed ornate buildings equipped with gymnasiums to enable members to exercise during the winter. Wheelmen used their political clout to lobby for bicycle-friendly legislation, including a state highway system, protection on desolate roads, and smoother street surfaces. Carter H. Harrison II capitalized on cyclists' political proclivities during the mayoral election of 1897. A campaign poster featured a cycling Harrison identified as "Not the Champion Cyclist; But the Cyclists' Champion." Harrison attributed his victory to strong support from cyclists, and he rewarded his constituents with a bicycle path along Sheridan Road from EDGEWATER to EVANSTON.

Middle-class buyers took advantage of improvements in bicycle technology and installment plans to purchase bicycles during the 1890s. Mass production lowered prices to $40–$120, and, by 1898, less expensive models cost only $20.

The "safety" bicycle, a lighter model with smaller tires, introduced more women to the sport. Many Chicago women relished the opportunity to wear voguish bloomers and divided skirts and to accompany a male companion on a ride. A May 1897 *Chicago Post* article observed, "The fashionable girl no longer lolls about in tea gowns and darkened rooms, but stands beside you in short skirts, a sailor hat, low shoes and leggings, ready for a spin on the wheel." While the women's clothing industry enjoyed a cycling-induced boon, not all bystanders greeted women's cycling with enthusiasm. Critics questioned the propriety of the new women's clothing and objected to unsupervised encounters between men and women.

By the late 1890s, Chicago was the "bicycle-building capital of America." According to the 1898 Chicago Bicycle Directory, approximately two-thirds of the country's bicycles and accessories were manufactured within 150 miles of the city. In 1895, GERMAN immigrant Ignaz Schwinn and meatpacker Adolph Arnold formed Arnold, Schwinn & Co. The company withstood many of the industry's booms and busts and, when adults' attention shifted to the automobile, Schwinn expanded the bicycle market for children. Lower prices and heartier "balloon" tires increased the popularity of children's models such as the Varsity, the Sting-Ray, and the Phantom.

Keeping with the tradition begun by Carter H. Harrison II, Mayor Richard J. Daley played a critical role in developing Chicago's bikeway system. During the 1950s, the city had a limited number of bike paths. By the early 1970s, Daley's administration announced the completion of an elaborate network that included an expanded lakefront path and on-street bicycle lanes. In May 1971, Daley unveiled a 34-mile bicycle route, and, in August 1972, he inaugurated rush-hour bicycle lanes on Clark and Dearborn Streets. During the 1970s, soaring gas prices and heightened concern about energy and air pollution bolstered public support for Daley's bicycling programs.

During the 1990s, Mayor Richard M. Daley, an avid cyclist, furthered Chicago's reputation as a bicycle-friendly city. In 1991, Daley created the Mayor's Bicycle Advisory Council to encourage bicycling. In the following decade over one hundred miles of bikeways have been constructed or improved and almost eight thousand bicycle racks have been installed. Bike Chicago, a month-long celebration begun in May 1991, has included events such as Bike to Work, Mayor Daley's Lakefront Bike Ride, and Bike the Drive, which was added in June 2002. Bicycle advocacy groups including the Chicagoland Bicycle Federation and Chicago Critical Mass have promoted the bicycle as a viable means of TRANSPORTATION. Since September 1997, Chicago Critical Mass has sponsored monthly rides from Daley Plaza to busy intersections and expressways in order to challenge "car culture" and to assert bicyclists' right to the roads. In November 2001, *Bicycling* magazine honored Chicago as the "Best Cycling City in the United States" of cities with more than one million residents.

Allyson Hobbs

See also: Commuting; Consumer Credit; Leisure; Mayors

Further reading: "Bicycles, Routes, Chicago." Clipping file. Municipal Reference Collection, Chicago Public Library. • "Sports, Cycling." Clipping file. Chicago Historical Society. • Bushnell, George D. "When Chicago Was Wheel Crazy." *Chicago History* 4.3 (Fall 1975): 167–175.

Bilingual Education. Changes in the prevailing political climate coupled with immigration patterns have historically led to the expansion or diminishment of bilingual education in Chicago's SCHOOLS. Instruction in GERMAN was common during the nineteenth century, sometimes to the exclusion of English. The earliest German schools had a religious focus, with ministers providing instruction. By the late nineteenth century, POLISH and Slavic immigrant groups were also incorporating their native language into their children's schooling. Bilingual teachers were readily available within their religious and social communities.

Between 1890 and 1914 waves of ITALIAN, GREEK, Polish, and JEWISH immigrants settled in Chicago, prompting increased xenophobia and AMERICANIZATION campaigns. Schools became the central institution for socializing immigrants into the "American" way of life, which included the English language. The Edwards Law of 1889 required that all parochial and public schools in Illinois teach in English. Germans were outraged. The law was repealed in 1893, but it allowed English-only instruction to gain momentum. Many families encouraged their children to give up their native languages. Bilingual education ceased entirely amid strong anti-German sentiments after the U.S. entry into WORLD WAR I. By 1923 another English-only law was in force, and immigrant schoolchildren were immersed in a language they could not always comprehend.

Bilingual education remained dormant for the next five decades, until the socially conscious 1960s gave rise to numerous programs for "disadvantaged" children. Riding on the tails of the GREAT SOCIETY programs was the 1968 Bilingual Education Act, originally designed to improve the condition of poverty-stricken Hispanic children. Its federally funded grants initiated the first modern bilingual programs in Chicago. Between 1968 and 1973 bilingual education took root in Chicago, fueled by a state mandate in 1973 (with funding provided) that required instruction in a child's native language when 20 or more students at a single school spoke the same language.

Bilingual education was implemented before an adequate infrastructure of materials, teacher training programs, and expertise existed. Program developers struggled with what bilingual education meant and who it was intended to benefit. Should the native language be maintained? Should English-speaking children be involved? How is English proficiency determined? When should a student's participation in bilingual education cease? As bilingual education expanded in the 1970s and 1980s, experimentation continued with the exploration of different approaches to and components of bilingual education, encompassing student assessment, teacher training, parent involvement, materials development, and program evaluation. Various program designs emerged depending on the number of students and language groups served, the availability of native-language resources, and the goals of the communities.

The first bilingual teachers were trained on the job, primarily by their own experience and via networking opportunities and local conferences. In 1975 the National Association of Bilingual Education held its fourth annual conference in Chicago, bringing recognition to the pioneering efforts of Chicago educators and providing a forum for bilingual practitioners. In 1976 the state added a language test as a requirement for teacher certification. In 1985 further demands were made on bilingual teachers when the state identified five areas of knowledge—assessment, methods and materials, theoretical foundations, cross-cultural studies, and second-language acquisition—that all bilingual teachers needed in order to obtain approval to teach in a bilingual program. Along with federal funding, these requirements provided an incentive to Chicago colleges and universities to begin or expand bilingual teacher training programs. Still, a shortage of bilingual teachers continued to plague the field into the twenty-first century.

The first bilingual education program in Chicago was opened for Spanish-speaking students in 1968 at Lafayette School. By 1973 more than 12,000 preschool through high-school children were enrolled in 64 bilingual programs serving Spanish, Arabic, Cantonese, Greek, and Italian-speaking students. In 1980 bilingual programs were operating in 183 schools serving 28,337 students in 19 languages. The top five language groups included Spanish, Polish, KOREAN, VIETNAMESE, and ASSYRIAN. In 1990, 44,955 students were identified as needing bilingual education.

By the end of the twentieth century, shifting demographics had placed more than 68,000 students in bilingual programs. The top languages included Spanish, Polish, Urdu, Cantonese, and Arabic. Bilingual teacher shortages led to temporary provisional certification for bilingual persons with baccalaureate degrees in other fields. Increasing numbers of "dual language" programs, including those in which English-proficient students studied a second language, were initiated. But the press for English was at its greatest since WORLD WAR I, creating new program dilemmas and policies which limited students' participation in bilingual education to three years. Instead of widespread xenophobia, which had characterized the resistance to native-language instruction in the early part of the century, an emphasis on increased educational accountability and high-stakes English testing policies resulted in less instruction provided in the native language.

Karen Sakash

See also: Catholic School System; Demography; Progressive Education

Further reading: *Celebrating Linguistic and Cultural Diversity: 25 Years of Bilingual Education in Chicago Public Schools.* Board of Trustees, Chicago Public Schools, Department of Language and Cultural Education. 1995. • *Implementation Handbook for Bilingual Education Programs in the Elementary Schools.* 1988 and 1991. • *Public School Bilingual Census Summary by Language Group.* City of Chicago School District 299, Illinois State Board of Education. Annual.

Billy Graham Center. The Billy Graham Center opened on the campus of WHEATON COLLEGE in September 1980. Funded by the Billy Graham Evangelistic Association, the 200,000-square-foot facility was a gift to Wheaton College in honor of Billy and Ruth Graham, members of the Wheaton College class of 1943. The center houses a museum that features an introduction to the history of evangelism in America and detailed representations of the life and labors of Billy Graham. The center library is dedicated primarily to evangelism and missions, and its archives feature the papers of nondenominational evangelical agencies. The Billy Graham Center houses the Wheaton College Graduate School as well as several departments of the college. Its administration oversees institutes dedicated to prison ministries, MUSLIM studies, and evangelism. The center is a hub for conferences and, though part of Wheaton College, also serves the church at large as a site for instruction and inspiration for "furthering the global cause of Christ."

Edith Blumhofer

See also: Missionary Training Schools; Moody Bible Institute; Protestants; Religion, Chicago's Influence on

Further reading: Malik, Charles. *The Two Tasks.* Pamphlet. 2000. Billy Graham Center, Wheaton, IL. • Shuster, Robert D., et al., comps. *Researching Modern Evangelicalism: A Guide to the Holdings of the Billy Graham Center.* 1990.

Birthing Practices. Throughout the nineteenth and early twentieth centuries in Chicago, childbirth customarily occurred at home rather than in a HOSPITAL. Although obstetrics had been offered as a medical specialty at Rush Medical College since before the Civil War, physicians usually attended birthing women in their own homes. Because infectious diseases spread easily throughout hospital wards, those institutions were considered dangerous places for both mother and child.

Women received few prenatal medical services before the twentieth century, and only four prenatal CLINICS operated in the city prior to 1900. These were located at the MARY H. THOMPSON HOSPITAL, the Chicago Lying-In Hospital, the Central Free Dispensary, and the Chicago Polyclinic. To prepare themselves for the birth of a child, expectant mothers gleaned information from a variety of sources, including experienced friends and family members, midwives, physicians, PUBLIC HEALTH nurses, and the pages of advice manuals.

The custom of using midwives to assist in childbirth remained popular, especially among Chicago's European immigrant communities. Until WORLD WAR II, midwives attended approximately 45 percent of all deliveries in the city; nearly 75 percent of all midwives registered in the state of Illinois practiced in Chicago. A 1908 study found that ITALIAN, Slavic, and GERMAN immigrant families were most likely to use their services, while midwives attended approximately one-third of births to native-born women. Locally known and respected HEALTH CARE practitioners, midwives had the advantage of knowing the mother's own language, customs, and beliefs. They

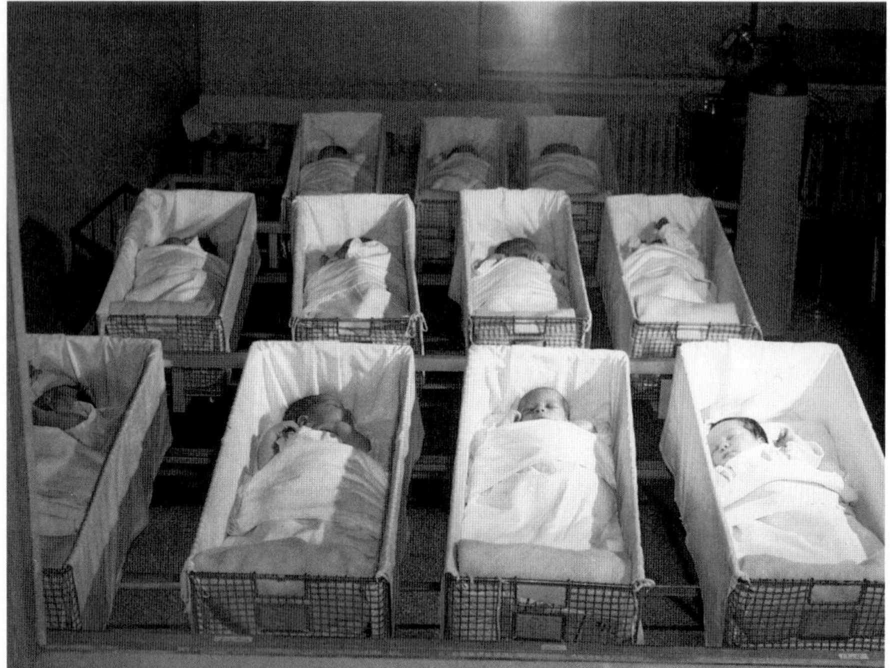

Newborn babies, Provident Hospital, 1942. Photographer: Jack Delano. Source: Library of Congress.

usually charged less to attend a delivery than physicians did, and midwives' services included caring for the mother for several days following the birth. In addition, many cultures proscribed men's presence in the birthing room, believing it to be an appropriate place for females only. It was not uncommon for women to use the services of more than one practitioner during childbirth. For example, a midwife or public health nurse might be called to attend an apparently normal delivery but a physician summoned if complications arose.

Childbirth remained extremely hazardous during the first half of the twentieth century. "Childbed fever," a common term for puerperal sepsis, or the onset of infection following childbirth, was a well-known danger of the postpartum period. The Chicago Board of Health identified such infections as the second leading cause of death for adult women in the city, following TUBERCULOSIS. The lack of prenatal medical services available to women meant that serious medical conditions such as ectopic pregnancy (implantation of the fertilized egg in the fallopian tube rather than the uterus) and eclampsia (a drastic increase in blood pressure) went undetected until they became life-threatening.

At the turn of the nineteenth century, concerns for the well-being of the mothers and babies of Chicago prompted a vigorous movement for more hygienic maternal and infant health practices. In the 1930s, Joseph B. De Lee, director of the Chicago Lying-In Hospital, spearheaded a major campaign to improve sanitary conditions in hospital maternity wards throughout the city. The widespread use of antibiotic drugs after World War II helped control the incidence of infection following childbirth, and this, along with increased use of anesthesia and pain relief during delivery, rendered hospitals more attractive to birthing women.

Lynne Curry

See also: Family Planning; La Leche League; Nursing and Nursing Education

Further reading: Bonner, Thomas Neville. *Medicine in Chicago, 1850–1950.* 1991. • Curry, Lynne. *Modern Mothers in the Heartland: Gender, Health, and Progress in Illinois, 1900–1930.* 1999. • Leavitt, Judith Walzer. *Brought to Bed: Childbearing in America.* 1986.

Black Belt. From the turn of the twentieth century until after World War II, the term "Black Belt" was commonly used to identify the predominately AFRICAN AMERICAN community on Chicago's SOUTH SIDE. Originally a narrow corridor extending from 22nd to 31st Streets along State Street, Chicago's South Side African American community expanded over the century until it stretched from 39th to 95th streets, the Dan Ryan Expressway to LAKE MICHIGAN.

Wallace Best

See also: Contested Spaces; Neighborhood Succession; Polonia; Redlining; Restrictive Covenants; Urban Renewal

Further reading: Chicago Commission on Race Relations. *The Negro in Chicago: A Study of Race Relations and a Race Riot.* 1922. • Drake, St. Clair, and Horace R. Cayton. *Black Metropolis: A Study of Negro Life in a Northern City.* Rev. ed. 1993. • Philpott, Thomas Lee. *The Slum and the Ghetto: Neighborhood Deterioration and Middle-Class Reform, Chicago, 1880–1930.* 1978.

Black Hawk War. The Black Hawk War (April–July 1832) quelled the last Indian resistance to white settlement in the region around Chicago. The famous SAUK leader, Black Hawk, and his thousand followers had been expelled from Illinois in 1831, but returned from Iowa carrying seeds for planting. Hostilities commenced after inexperienced militia attacked an Indian delegation approaching with a white flag. Thereafter, Black Hawk and Indian supporters joined in warfare that provoked the mobilization of about seven thousand American soldiers, bringing the first regular army troops—and the first cholera EPIDEMIC—into the Upper GREAT LAKES. Most of Black Hawk's band was killed trying to flee west. Black Hawk with his son and the Winnebago Prophet, surrendered at Prairie du Chien, Wisconsin, and were imprisoned until the summer of 1833. In that year, POTAWATOMI ceded the last of their lands in northeastern Illinois, promoting the first development of the Chicago area.

Helen Hornbeck Tanner

See also: Chicago in the Middle Ground; Fort Dearborn

Further reading: Black Hawk (Ma-ka-tai-me-she-kia-kiak). *Black Hawk: An Autobiography.* Ed. Donald D. Jackson. 1955. • Lurie, Nancy O. "In Search of Chaetan: New Findings on Black Hawk's Surrender." *Wisconsin Magazine of History* 71.3 (Spring 1988): 163–183. • Tanner, Helen Hornbeck, ed. *Atlas of Great Lakes Indian History.* 1987, 151–154.

Black Panther Party. The Black Panther Party of Chicago emerged on the city's West Side in the autumn of 1968. As one of 45 Black Panther chapters around the country, the "Illinois Chapter" gained over 300 new members within four months of its founding because many young black Chicagoans identified with the Panthers' militant denunciations of RACISM, capitalism, and POLICE brutality.

By the middle of 1969, the Chicago Panthers' neighborhood roots and class-based critiques of American political economy helped them form a radical partnership with Latino and white Chicagoans called the "Rainbow Coalition." This coalition targeted Chicago's structural inequalities by placing programs like free breakfast and free legal consultation at the service of the city's disadvantaged populations.

The militant image and rhetoric that attracted so many radical Chicagoans to the Panthers' ranks, however, hindered the effectiveness of the party's programs. It alienated more conservative and influential sectors of the AFRICAN AMERICAN community and left the group open to negative publicity in the mainstream press. Moreover, the Panthers' programs presented a political threat to Mayor Richard J. Daley, who perceived the party's service projects as an attempt to preempt the authority of city hall.

The party's militant image also prompted federal and local authorities to raid Panther property on three separate occasions in 1969, ostensibly to look for fugitives and illegal weapons. The final raid, on the morning of December 4, crippled the organization and claimed the lives of Illinois chapter deputy chairman Fred Hampton and Panther Mark Clark. Without effective leadership and a broad base of community support, the Chicago Black Panther Party could not weather the internal differences that eventually sapped the group's remaining resources in 1973.

Nathan Daniel Beau Connolly

See also: Chicago Conspiracy Trial; Civil Rights Movements; Community Organizing; Congress of Racial Equality (CORE); Haymarket and May Day; Social Services

Further reading: Hampton, Henry, Steve Fayer, and Sarah Flynn, eds. *Voices of Freedom: An Oral History of the Civil Rights Movement from the 1950s through the 1980s.* 1990. • Joravsky, Ben, and Eduardo Camacho. *Race and Politics in Chicago.* 1987. • Rice, Jon. "Black Radicalism on Chicago's West Side: A History of the Illinois Black Panther Party." Ph.D. diss., Northern Illinois University. 1998.

Black Sox Scandal. On October 1, 1919, the Chicago WHITE SOX, whom many observers believed to be one of the best BASEBALL teams ever, lost the opening game of the World Series to the Cincinnati Reds, nine to one. This shocking defeat was an omen, for the White Sox lost the series five games to three. A year later, fans found out why. Several team members testified in a Chicago courtroom that they had intentionally thrown the World Series through an arrangement with a nationwide GAMBLING syndicate. Eight White Sox players, including star pitcher Eddie Cicotte and renowned outfielder "Shoeless" Joe Jackson, were charged with conspiracy to defraud the public, conspiracy to commit a confidence game, and conspiracy to injure the business of team owner Charles A. Comiskey. The trial lasted 14 days, and on August 2, 1921, the jury found the players not guilty, clearing them of all charges. Despite their acquittal, newly appointed baseball commissioner Kenesaw Mountain Landis expelled all eight players from major league baseball in an attempt to assure the American public of the purity of the game. The story of the betrayal and expulsion of the "Black Sox," and the sense of injustice it provoked, has maintained a powerful hold on American popular culture, and has been memorialized in literature and film.

Robin F. Bachin

See also: Crime and Chicago's Image; Leisure

Further reading: Asinof, Eliot. *Eight Men Out: The Black Sox and the 1919 World Series.* 1963. • Burk, Robert F. *Never Just a Game: Players, Owners, and American Baseball to 1920.* 1994. • Riess, Steven A. *Touching Base: Professional Baseball and American Culture in the Progressive Era.* 1980.

Blackhawks. Professional ICE HOCKEY came to Chicago in 1926 when Major Frederick McLaughlin, a local coffee millionaire, purchased the Western Canadian Hockey League's Portland (Oregon) Rosebuds and moved the team to Chicago, renaming them the Blackhawks after his former army division. The Blackhawks played at Chicago Coliseum, 16th and Wabash, before moving into CHICAGO STADIUM in 1929.

The Blackhawks won Stanley Cups in 1934 and 1938. Because McLaughlin was obsessed with the idea of an all-American team, many of the Blackhawks' players during the 1930s were Americans from Minnesota, which outraged some Canadians. Bill Stewart, who coached the team to the 1938 Stanley Cup, was the first American-born manager to accomplish the feat.

Despite the presence of many talented players, the 1940s and 1950s were dismal years for the Blackhawks, who finished in last place nearly every season and made the playoffs only once. As part of a rebuilding effort, team ownership brought General Manager Tommy Ivan to Chicago from the Detroit Red Wings in the 1950s. Ivan developed a productive system of farm teams that supplied the Blackhawks with fresh, new talent.

The Blackhawks developed into a formidable force during the 1960s, winning the Stanley Cup in 1961, finishing first in 1967, and reaching the Stanley Cup finals in 1961–62 and 1964–65. Forwards Bobby Hull and Stan Mikita, as well as goaltender Glenn Hall, were among the NHL's best players.

Led by longtime coach Billy Reay, the Blackhawks enjoyed first-place finishes in 1969–70 and 1970–71 and made it to the Stanley Cup finals in 1970–71 and 1972–73. After a gradual rebuilding process during the 1980s, the team enjoyed a resurgence during the 1990s, reaching the Stanley Cup finals in 1991–92 and finishing first in the NHL in 1992–93. It also was during the 1990s that the Blackhawks moved into the UNITED CENTER.

Paul R. Greenland

See also: Entertaining Chicagoans; Leisure; Skating, Ice

Further reading: Greenland, Paul. *Hockey Chicago Style: The History of the Chicago Blackhawks.* 1995. • Pfeiffer, Gerald L. *The Chicago Blackhawks : A Sixty Year History, 1926–1986.* 1987. • Vass, George. *The Chicago Black Hawks Story.* 1970.

Blind Trusts. A blind trust is a legal mechanism that allows property owners to conceal their identities. Public records bear only the name of a front person, who does not actually control the property. Blind trusts permit owners to buy and sell property without public scrutiny. They make it difficult for casually interested parties to make purchase offers on buildings and for tenants to know to whom to take their complaints. Although no Illinois statute deliberately established the legality of the blind trust, state courts have recognized its validity.

During the 1960s, the blind trust became a target of AFRICAN AMERICAN housing activists. A favorite tactic was to picket outside the homes and offices of people who owned poorly maintained apartment buildings and houses purchased "on contract." The Contract Buyers' League (CBL) worked to help African Americans renegotiate the payment terms of the contracts on their homes. The use of blind trusts hindered efforts both to shame property owners and to negotiate with them. In 1969, the CBL pressured the Illinois legislature into requiring the identification of owners of residential property bought on contract.

Amanda Seligman

See also: Housing Reform; Open Housing; Real Estate; Redlining

Further reading: "Comment: Some Aspects of Illinois Land Trusts." *De Paul Law Review* (Autumn-Winter 1958): 385–393. • Conrad, Mary. "Trusts—Illinois Land Trusts—A Beneficial Interest Is a 'General Intangible' under U.C.C. Article 9." *De Paul Law Review* 18 (1969): 875–885.

Block 37. The story of Block 37 is the history of the American downtown in microcosm. At the center of Chicago, this typical urban block missed no trend, from the first office buildings in the 1870s to the early SKYSCRAPERS of the 1890s and the supermarkets of the 1930s. Even through long decades of decline, from the perceived street anarchy of the 1960s to the massive URBAN RENEWAL of the 1980s that finally demolished the block, Block 37 has mirrored the enthusiasms and fears of the city. The MOVIE PALACES, seedy political hangouts, fine billiard parlor, novelty store, and gourmet food hall made it a primary destination for those seeking the LOOP's pleasures. Also a place of WORK where small NEWSPAPERS were published, violins repaired, hair cut, and fortunes read, this one city block, in its prime, attracted thousands of people an hour. On a typical day it housed the population of a small town, only to be completely empty at night. All the city's variety was packed into 16 buildings of various size and condition. Its landlords, high and low, were among Chicago's first families and fabled entrepreneurs. A scene for brilliant acts of charity and extraordinary moments of predation, Block 37 was a prime arena for the urban arts, from fly-by-night retailing and three-card monte to international REAL-ESTATE deals involving hundreds of millions of dollars. To understand the rise and fall of this one block in some of its daunting detail is to appreciate Chicago's unique attraction to city lovers and haters alike. To know Block 37 is to know Chicago.

Favored by its unique geography, the land that was to become Block 37 already had a rich history before the first Europeans canoed into the swampy prairie on LAKE MICHIGAN. At least 100 years before Chicago was surveyed, scribed, and squared, the POTAWATOMIS pursued an active commercial life on the site. With its proximity to the lake and to the main branch of the CHICAGO RIVER, the block was important too after FORT DEARBORN was established and the area became a key area of settlement of the Northwest Territories.

The block was platted in James R. Thompson's 1830 survey and numbered as one of the city's original 58 blocks. Its strategic location between State and Dearborn Streets to the east and west and Randolph and Washington to the north and south assured that the block's original eight lots, equally cut from only 120,000 square feet of ground, would become fully deployed in the city's remarkable political, commercial, and industrial development.

After Chicago's incorporation as a town in 1833, Block 37, situated only several hundred yards from the COOK COUNTY courthouse and across the street from the city's largest bank, boomed along with the city. When the Great FIRE of October 8, 1871, razed the entire downtown, the block had already been densely developed for decades. Rebuilt immediately after the fire at over four times its original square footage and increasingly added to over the next century, Block 37 shared the fortunes of other American downtowns from New York to San Francisco. Resiliently prosperous and endlessly inventive in the sort of commerce it could support, the block survived not only the fire, but a worldwide Depression and a host of cunning MAYORS and dealmakers, until it finally fell prey in 1989 to the final "improvement" that flattened, in the name of urban renewal, every one of its buildings—including, without distinction, its architectural treasures and notorious firetraps.

Block 37 was, in the end, a victim of the very trends that it had so efficiently exploited in the past. After the WORLD WAR II, as Chicago's population began its permanent migration away from the core and out to the suburbs, the block started to suffer from the neglect that would eventually make it a candidate for URBAN RENEWAL. Beginning in the early 1960s, the historic LOOP was bypassed for the redevelopment of North Michigan Avenue. The old downtown was perceived and relentlessly advertised as hopelessly decayed and dangerous. The once superior location of Block 37 at the matrix of the city's political, commercial, and social life now doomed it. By the 1970s, State Street had lost its preeminence as a SHOPPING center to the DEPARTMENT STORES on Michigan Avenue and to the large regional malls multiplying out in the suburbs. The entertainment "rialto" along Randolph—Chicago's equivalent to Times Square—had closed down its live shows and was subsisting on pornography and action films, while on Washington Street, the gourmet shop Stop and Shop, a city institution, went out of business. Offices for lawyers, political activists, and skilled artisans on the block's Dearborn Street side went unrented as the center of Chicago shifted to the grand new towers of the West Loop. None of the billions of dollars flooding the city during the SKYSCRAPER boom of the 1980s reached Block 37 in time.

Ironically, the block's very dereliction became its last chance. Speculators and city hall insiders had written down the land values of the entire North Loop to the point in 1979 when the Chicago PLAN Commission declared 26.74 acres, seven full or partial blocks including Block 37, "blighted." This designation qualified the area for a "taking." Once valuable commercial property was seized from its lawful owners, condemned, and written down as worthless. After speculators had delayed the taking almost a decade and bid up land costs, the city paid nearly $250 million for the entire North Loop, including nearly $40 million for Block 37 alone. In 1983 a local development group, JMB, won the rights to develop the entire block. A series of delays, beginning with a challenge from HISTORIC PRESERVATIONISTS and prolonged by costly legal battles, put off the block's demolition until 1989, when the city completely leveled the land and traded the title to the developers for $12.5 million, less than a third of what it had paid. Plans to build two towers and a large retail mall fell prey to the national real-estate crash of 1990. For almost a decade, the block was put to temporary use as a winter SKATING rink and a summer student ART gallery. At the opening of the twenty-first century, this once diverse and active place still lies empty, an unwanted orphan of progress. The history of Block 37 will continue to mirror the rise and fall of Chicago's downtown. Its long and various history is an intimate calibration of the history of a great American city.

Ross Miller

See also: Business of Chicago; Economic Geography; Political Culture

Further reading: Miller, Ross. *Here's the Deal: The Buying and Selling of a Great American City.* 1996.

Blockbusting. "Blockbusting" refers to the efforts of REAL-ESTATE agents and real-estate speculators to trigger the turnover of white-owned property and homes to AFRICAN AMERICANS. Often characterized as "panic peddling," such practices frequently accompanied the expansion of black areas of residence and the entry of African Americans into neighborhoods previously denied to them. In evidence as early as 1900, blockbusting techniques included the repeated—often incessant—urging of white homeowners in areas adjacent to or near black communities to sell before it became "too late" and their property values diminished. Agents frequently hired African American subagents and other individuals to walk or drive through changing areas soliciting business and otherwise behaving in such a manner as to provoke and exaggerate white fears. Purchasing homes cheaply from nervous white occupants, the panic peddler sold dearly to African Americans who faced painfully limited choices and inflated prices in a discriminatory housing market. Often providing financing and stringent terms to a captive audience, the blockbuster could realize substantial profits.

Blockbusting depended upon a high degree of residential segregation and provided the means for transferring white property into black hands at a time when mainstream real-estate and financial institutions refused to sell to blacks or facilitate their movement into all-white neighborhoods. Even as late as 1951, major newspapers continued to run separate ads for "colored" housing, thus fostering, as well as reflecting, the conditions that gave rise to such market manipulation. Especially evident in the wake of black population increases associated with the first and second GREAT MIGRATIONS, the movement into newer, outlying neighborhoods was fueled by increased demand for housing on the part of blacks, the growing ability of a rising middle class to pay for it, and the desire for a better life and escape from the more impoverished sections of the urban core. Working virtually, if not covertly, in tandem, "respectable" real-estate agents flocked to do business in transitional areas once they had been broken by the maverick blockbusters. The net result was a gold-rush effect that destabilized residential communities as it maximized racial tensions and fears.

Attempts to combat blockbusting and stabilize white ethnic neighborhoods culminated in the 1971 passage of a series of ordinances that prohibited the placement of "For Sale" and related signs on residential property. The Illinois Supreme Court ultimately ruled such measures unconstitutional. Subsequent efforts to thwart panic peddling included the promotion of home-equity insurance plans. Pioneered by OAK PARK in 1978 in the effort to manage suburban integration, such proposals were picked up by neighborhood groups on the Southwest and Northwest Sides in an attempt to maintain the racial status quo. A coalition of such groups known as Save Our Neighborhoods/Save Our City (SON/SOC) emerged after Harold Washington's 1983 election to push various home-equity insurance measures, including a referendum. A source of tension and racial polarization, the referendum passed in November 1988—under new state law and over city opposition—allowing the establishment of home-equity districts in selected precincts.

Arnold R. Hirsch

See also: Community Organizing; Contested Spaces; Open Housing; Redlining; South Side; Steering

Further reading: Bennett, Larry. *Fragments of Cities: The New American Downtowns and Neighborhoods.* 1990. • Helper, Rose. *Racial Policies and Practices of Real Estate Brokers.* 1969. • Hirsch, Arnold R. *Making the Second Ghetto: Race and Housing in Chicago, 1940–1960.* 1983.

Bloomingdale, IL, DuPage County, 24 miles W of the Loop. After the BLACK HAWK WAR, easterners teemed into what would become the Chicago metropolitan area in search of farmland. Brothers Lyman, Harvey, and Silas Meacham all staked squatter claims near a grove that later bore their name.

While initially there was little to distinguish Meacham's Grove from other acreage in northeastern Illinois, Frink and Walker's stage line soon ran through the settlement on its route between Chicago and Rockford. By the end of the 1830s several hundred wagons and travelers moved through the area. GERMAN immigrants diversified the population and in 1845 Bloomingdale became one of the first villages to be platted in the northern part of DuPage County. The town served as a trading center, a stage stop, and a location for the first churches—initially Baptist and Methodist, and subsequently Lutheran.

Envisioning increased development potential with a RAILROAD connection, two of the area's largest landholders, B. F. Meacham and Roselle M. Hough, each donated large tracts of land to the Chicago & Pacific Railroad (Chicago, Milwaukee & St. Paul) in 1873 in exchange for a stop near their landholdings. The platted community of Bloomingdale was south of the railroad stop, while a new village named ROSELLE was platted to the north. Both villages fostered industrial settlement during the 1870s.

The village of Bloomingdale was officially incorporated in 1889, and included the platted towns of Roselle and Bloomingdale. Both areas shared such items as library books and a fire engine. In 1922, however, the two villages separated and reincorporated individually.

Development remained slow in Bloomingdale until the 1950s. The 1960s saw the creation of a full-time police department and a new post office. In 1965 the Baptist church, purchased in 1892 by the township, was sold to the Bloomingdale Park District for a dollar and converted into the Bloomingdale Park District Museum.

During the 1970s the population grew as the TOLL ROAD system spurred growth across DUPAGE COUNTY. Three shopping centers were constructed, including Old Town Square, Stratford Square, and Old Town shopping center, which is the site of the original town and is a turn-of-the-century shopping and professional area, complete with replicas and renovations of historic buildings.

Jane S. Teague

See also: Metropolitan Growth; Shopping Districts; Suburban Government

Further reading: Sanborn, Dorothy. *History of Roselle, Illinois.* 1968. • Thompson, Richard A., ed. *DuPage Roots.* 1985.

Blue Island, IL, Cook County, 16 miles S of the Loop. Blue Island stands on the southern end of an ancient GLACIAL ridge five miles long, extending northward along Western Avenue and Vincennes Road from 131st Street to 87th Street. The ridge stood as an island in glacial Lake Chicago, the predecessor of LAKE MICHIGAN. Bands of OTTAWAS, OJIBWAS, and POTAWATOMI lived along the Little Calumet River and Stony Creek until 1835.

To a springtime traveler on the Vincennes Trail, the glacial bluff that rose out of the prairie south of Chicago took on a bluish hue from haze or blue wildflowers. In 1836 the first inn opened along the Vincennes Trail at Blue Island. Excavation of a Calumet–Blue Island feeder canal in the 1840s diverted water from the Little Calumet River to the ILLINOIS & MICHIGAN CANAL near Lemont. Transplanted YANKEES established the village as an AGRICULTURAL market center. GERMAN agricultural laborers began arriving in the 1850s, and by the 1890s they had usurped political and economic power from the Yankees.

Small-scale factories, brickyards, BREWERIES, and cigar shops arose after 1880. Between 1886 and 1889 workers affiliated with KNIGHTS OF LABOR Local Assembly 6581, and in 1893, organized Local 3 of what became the United Brick and Clay Workers Union.

RAILROADS bolstered employment until the 1950s. The Chicago, Rock Island & Pacific Railroad arrived in 1852; its 1868 brick depot at Vermont Street remains in use today. Between 1888 and 1893 several belt railroads crossed the southern and western parts of town, while the Rock Island line constructed an expansive freight yard, shops, and roundhouse. Engineers and craftsmen lived in the respectable center of town; laborers lived across the tracks on the east side. During the 1894 PULLMAN STRIKE, American Railway Union President Eugene V. Debs exhorted RAILROAD WORKERS to stop Rock Island traffic. Two Rock Island trainmen blocked the line on June 30 by derailing a slow-moving train just south of the Vermont Street station. Although local railroaders remained disciplined, riotous brickmakers toppled cars and jeered strikebreakers, prompting a federal injunction and suppression of the STRIKE nationwide. Early the morning of July 4, 1894, the Fifteenth U.S. Infantry arrived in Blue Island and imposed martial law. While protests and violence raged elsewhere after July 4, Blue Island quickly succumbed under the occupying army.

In 1901 Blue Island incorporated as a city to avoid ANNEXATION by Chicago. In 1915 residents rejected annexation while nearby MORGAN PARK joined Chicago. ITALIANS, POLES, and SLOVAKS settled in Blue Island between 1900 and 1920, but AFRICAN AMERICANS who were excluded from the town incorporated ROBBINS in 1917. Population plateaued at 16,000 to 21,000 between 1930 and 1990. Despite chain stores and Western Avenue's designation as the Dixie Highway in the 1920s, the central business district declined. Political and fiscal conservatism blocked annexation of the future ALSIP industrial district. Landlocked industries left the city. During the 1990s, however, the city appeared to revive slowly. Old industries such as Modern Drop Forge and Clark Oil Refineries thrived, while antique stores, theaters, and MEXICAN restaurants lined Western Avenue.

Martin Tuohy

See also: Calumet River System; Contested Spaces; Economic Geography; Water

Further reading: Jebsen, Harry, Jr. "Blue Island, Illinois: The History of a Working Class Suburb." Ph.D. diss., University of Cincinnati. 1971. • Jebsen, Harry, Jr. "Preserving Suburban Identity in an Expanding Metropolis: The Case of Blue Island, Illinois." *Old Northwest* 7.2 (Summer 1981): 127–145. • Volp, John H. *The First Hundred Years, 1835–1935: Historical Review of Blue Island, Illinois.* 1938.

Blues. As legendary guitarist Robert Johnson put it, Chicago has been a "sweet home" for the blues. The most recognizable cultural signature this city has produced, Chicago blues has diverse and contradictory roots: AFRICAN AMERICAN migration from the South and the growth of the modern music industry; regional folk genius and ethnic entrepreneurial savvy. This rich sense of origin and history makes blues music such a celebrated civic resource, one that still shapes cultural and social practice throughout the Windy City.

The earliest geographic origins of the blues are uncertain, given the multiple versions appearing across the African American South near the turn of the century. In Chicago, the emergence of blues culture in the 1920s coincided with increased musical performance and recording nationwide and paralleled the dramatic growth of black urban enclaves during the GREAT MIGRATION. Alberta Hunter, Cow Cow (Charles) Davenport, and Blind Lemon Jefferson were among the first blues artists to record locally, under the supervision of J. Mayo "Ink" Williams of Paramount Records. Williams gathered other musicians of note, including Tampa Red (Hudson Whittaker), Big Bill (William) Broonzy, and Georgia Tom, who

Willie Dixon and the Blues

Willie Dixon—blues artist, songwriter, and studio producer—was born in Vicksburg, Mississippi, in 1915. During a Depression youth spent alternately as a laborer, prison inmate, and train hobo, Dixon first displayed the talent that later established his fame, writing songs for diverse Vicksburg musicians. His first motivation for coming to Chicago in 1936 was BOXING: Dixon won a Golden Gloves title and sparred with world champion Joe Louis, before shoddy management ended his prizefighting career. Dixon retooled himself as a musician, playing bass through the 1940s with several groups and becoming involved with the emerging blues recording industry in Chicago. Dixon's best work came during his years at CHESS RECORDS (1951–1956; 1959–1971). Rising from accompanist to studio manager, Dixon worked with countless artists, including Muddy Waters, Howlin' Wolf, Chuck Berry, and Koko Taylor. During an intermediate stint with Cobra Records (1956–1959), Dixon worked with many in the "second generation" of blues talent—Buddy Guy, Otis Rush, Magic Sam—cementing his reputation as preeminent impresario within the postwar blues scene. In spite of Chess's collapse in 1971 and the decline of the blues' commercial appeal, Dixon maintained an active professional life, continuing his festival work and organizing the Chicago Blues All-Stars touring group. In 1982, he started the Blues Heaven Foundation, a group promoting awareness about blues among urban youth and helping musicians regain royalty rights, a struggle Dixon waged until his death in 1992.

Adam Green

Blues musicians on Maxwell Street, ca. 1950–51. Photographer: Jerome Joseph. Source: Chicago Historical Society.

later modernized GOSPEL music as composer Thomas Dorsey. Although Hunter, Broonzy, and others performed across the SOUTH SIDE, and despite an abundant audience of migrants, there was not yet the extensive network of blues clubs that emerged in later years.

Like the rest of the economy, music production suffered during the GREAT DEPRESSION. Between 1926 and 1932, annual sales of phonograph records in the United States plummeted from $126 to $6 million; sales for black performers decreased from $5 million to only $60,000. The decline slowed the migration of blues artists, whose motivation for coming to Chicago, like other black southerners, included economic opportunity. Still, the city continued to serve as incubator of blues music, as musicians awaited the resurgence of the record industry. Tampa Red and Bill Broonzy were joined by such talents as Memphis Minnie (Douglas), Lil Green, Memphis Slim (Peter Chatman), and Sonny Boy (John Lee) Williamson. With the wartime emergence of local labels such as Bluebird, Chicago became the national center for blues recording—hits like Lil Green's "Romance in the Dark" (1940), Minnie's "Me and My Chauffeur Blues" (1941), and Williamson's "Elevator Woman" (1945) exemplified post-Depression popular music for blacks, North and South. As the community of artists and entrepreneurs grew, blues culture revised the geography of black Chicago. Legendary clubs such as Silvio's, Gatewood's Tavern, the Flame Club, and the 708 opened along Indiana Avenue on the South Side and Lake Street on the West Side, serving as community centers for migrants arriving in ever greater numbers during the 1940s. Blues music also moved beyond studio and stage. The outdoor market on MAXWELL STREET became a regular weekend venue, and newly arrived musicians found work playing "rent parties" across the South and West Sides.

During the 1950s, Chicago blues flourished, developing the signatures—use of rhythm sections and amplification; reliance on guitar and harmonica leads; and routine reference to Mississippi Delta styles of playing and singing—that identify it today. Consolidation of blues recording continued, with new labels CHESS, Vee-Jay, and Cobra all signing and producing large numbers of artists. Of these, the most prominent was Chess, whose first generation of artists—Muddy Waters (McKinley Morganfield), Little Walter (Jacobs), Willie Dixon, Howlin' Wolf (Chester Burnett)—were exemplars of Chicago blues style. The distinctive sound of these artists restructured popular music, providing fundamental elements for subsequent genres like soul and rock and roll. Indeed, the work of Waters on songs like "Rollin' Stone" (1950) and "Hootchie Cootchie Man" (1954) had international influence, subsequently inspiring the Beatles, the Rolling Stones, and other British bands. Dixon was also a figure of special note—in addition to playing bass and writing for artists ranging from Waters to Chuck Berry and Bo Diddley, he supervised most of the studio sessions at Chess beginning in the mid-1950s.

A key catalyst to the blues' postwar popularization were "black-appeal" DISC JOCKEYS, such as Al Benson and Big Bill Hill, who ensured that records released by Chess, Vee-Jay, and other labels received public exposure. By the late 1950s and early 1960s a new generation of West Side artists, including Otis Rush, Magic Sam (Maghett), and Buddy (George)

Blues Clubs in Chicago

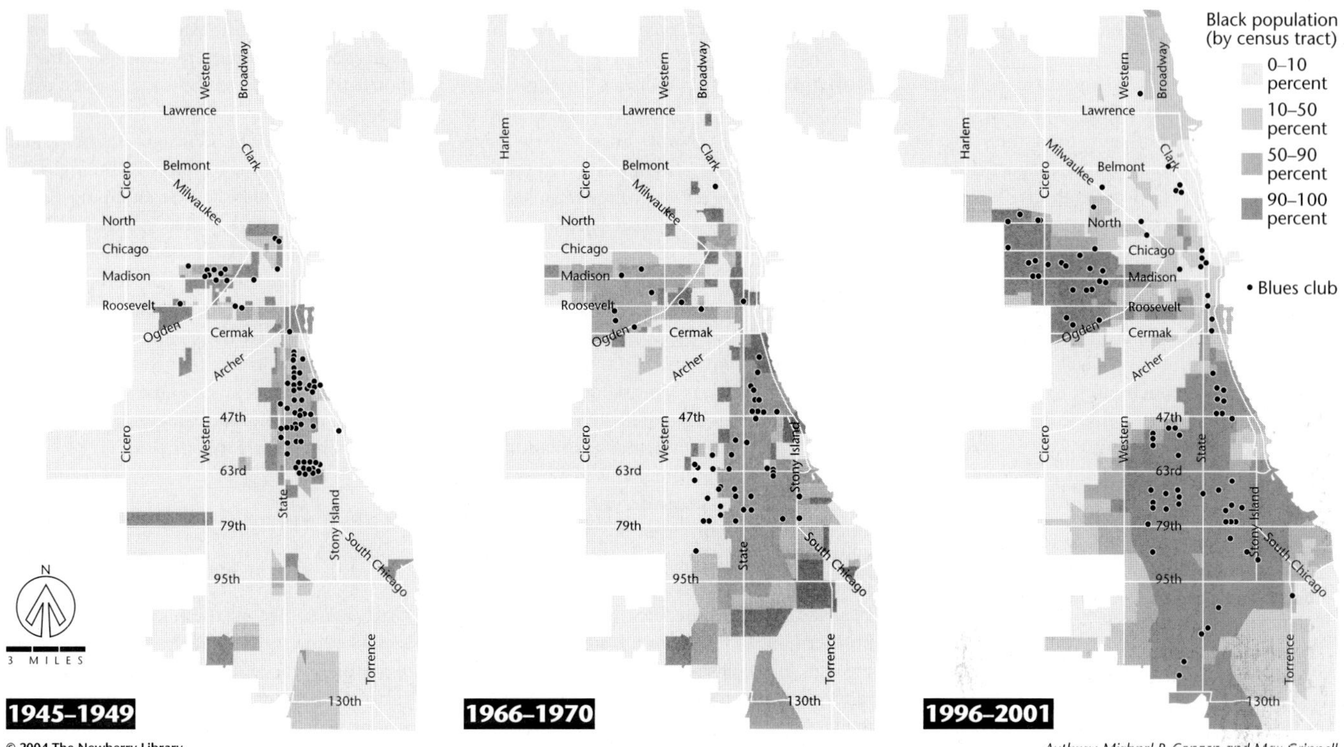

Authors: Michael P. Conzen and Max Grinnell

Though one could hear the blues in 1920s Chicago, the club scene was not well developed until the 1940s. Blues musicians performed regularly at bars and other entertainment venues in African American communities on both the South and West Sides in the '40s, but rarely outside these areas. Blues clubs spread out as the city's black population grew and the genre's popularity rose, but most remained in or close to African American neighborhoods. By the 1990s, the blues had become widely fashionable, and while the historic pattern largely held, some clubs, especially those downtown and on the North Side, catered to largely non–African American audiences.

Guy, carried the work of Waters, Dixon, and other Chess artists even further. Chicago blues soon attracted substantially broader audiences. In 1959, Dixon and Memphis Slim toured England and the Middle East: they would return to Europe in 1962 with a full roster of artists to perform in the first of many annual American Folk Blues Festivals.

The history of Chicago blues since the 1960s has been a contradictory one, combining periods of recession and renewal. By the end of the 1960s, blues had infrastructural as well as aesthetic presence. WVON, the all-day radio station opened by Chess owners Leonard and Phil Chess in 1963, maintained a healthy blues playlist, augmenting programming from other local stations. Blues NIGHTCLUBS continued to shape black neighborhoods on the South and West Sides; Roosevelt Road, Madison Street, and 43rd Street became blues thoroughfares. With the failure of Cobra Records in 1959 and Vee-Jay in 1966, Chess stood as the only remaining major label and, under the supervision of Willie Dixon, consolidated the remaining talent. Old rivals such as Buddy Guy and Otis Rush were signed, along with newcomers Etta James, Little Milton (Campbell), and Koko Taylor. Yet blues music found itself at a disadvantage commercially next to soul, gospel, and other new genres of black popular music. Chess went out of business in 1975, by which time most older clubs were closing down.

While Chicago blues did not recapture its centrality to the civic life of the African American community, a renaissance has been building since the late 1960s, when blues found a new audience drawn from followers of ROCK MUSIC searching out roots artists. Such local labels as Delmark, which recorded Junior Wells (Amos Blakemore) and Magic Sam (Sam Maghett), and Alligator, which recorded Koko Taylor and Lonnie Brooks (Lee Baker, Jr.), built a new national audience for Chicago blues. Old-line clubs (notably the Checkerboard) on the South and West Sides have been joined by new venues on the South, West, and North Sides (notably Kingston Mines) serving the tourist industry and predominantly white fans of blues. In 1984 Chicago inaugurated an annual blues festival. Continued participation in Chicago blues culture underscores that, as in earlier times, the music serves as "living history," shaping both memories of and hopes for urban social life.

Adam Green

See also: Entertaining Chicagoans; Ethnic Music; Multicentered Chicago; Music Publishing; Outdoor Concerts; Record Publishing; Rhythm and Blues

Further reading: Keil, Charles. *Urban Blues.* 1966, 1991. • Palmer, Robert. *Deep Blues.* 1981.

Board of Trade. *See* Commodities Markets

Boardinghouses. Residential boarding arrangements in the Chicago metropolitan area are at least as old as the taverns of the FORT DEARBORN trading settlement. During Chicago's early boom years, when housing facilities lagged behind population growth, many visitors and newcomers found lodging and meals in the households of private citizens.

By the 1880s, boarding was an established way of life. Private boardinghouses typically consisted of a married couple (with or without children) who kept several boarders, generally single, unrelated individuals. While married couples occasionally boarded, families with children rarely lived in boardinghouses.

Women usually took primary responsibility for boarders. For many women, keeping boarders and lodgers was a readily available way to earn money that permitted a flexible schedule and was compatible with caring for children. A married woman's income from boarding was often more reliable than her husband's income, and could well be the primary income for the household. Keeping boarders was also a source of income for some widows and mature single women.

For many landlords and boarders, the household intimacy of boarding was part of its appeal. Boarders not only took their meals within the household, but often participated in family activities. Boardinghouse residents met daily in the shared spaces of the dining room and the parlor. Late-nineteenth-century reformers approved of the family environment of boardinghouses, which they felt acted as a welcome social restraint on boarders.

Native-born white and black Americans often lived in boardinghouses when they were single and new to the city. After the 1880s, more and more single young women and men were employed in clerical jobs in the new SKYSCRAPERS, and many of them lived in boardinghouses.

Boarding was more prevalent among immigrants than among the native-born in early twentieth-century Chicago and other large cities. Boarding provided a cultural haven for homesick new immigrants who sought out households where they could speak their native tongues. Housing arrangements were often made through informal networks rather than public advertising.

Larger and more commercial boardinghouses existed in outlying industrial areas, such as near suburban railroad shops. In some of the more crowded arrangements, workers shared bedding and slept in shifts in a "hot bed." In some working-class boardinghouses, each boarder's food was purchased and cooked separately. In other situations residents themselves took turns cooking.

Well before 1900, other arrangements began to supplant boarding. Many tenants preferred to lodge without common meals or to live in larger, more anonymous rooming houses, where a "light housekeeping room" included a gas fixture for cooking on a single burner. In a rooming house residents could keep their own hours, enjoy greater privacy, and perhaps entertain guests more easily.

Landlords, too, could prefer lodgers to boarders for many of the same reasons. Boardinghouse families began to prefer their privacy to the affective ties of an extensive surrogate family. The decline of boarding could be seen as parallel to the transformation of the semipublic "parlor" into the twentieth-century private "living room" in which boarders would seem to be strangers.

Douglas Knox

See also: Apartments; Demography; Housekeeping; Kitchenettes; Residential Hotels

Further reading: Abbott, Edith. *The Tenements of Chicago, 1908–1935.* 1936. • Meyerowitz, Joanne. *Women Adrift: Independent Wage Earners in Chicago, 1880–1930.* 1988. • Monroe, Day. *Chicago Families: A Study of Unpublished Census Data.* 1932.

Boating. *See* Sailing and Boating

Bohemians. *See* Czechs and Bohemians

Bolingbrook, IL, Will and DuPage Counties, 26 miles SW of the Loop. Few communities demonstrate the interstate highway system's profound influence on suburban development as well as Bolingbrook. The opening of Interstate 55 in the early 1960s made the farm fields of northern WILL COUNTY more accessible to Chicago, attracting developers and residents. Incorporated in 1965, Bolingbrook grew from thinly settled farmland to the second-largest community in Will County (behind JOLIET) in less than 10 years.

The POTAWATOMI lived in this area from the late 1700s. In 1816, the Indians ceded a 10-mile-wide area on both sides of the DES PLAINES RIVER to the U.S. government. The northern line of the "Indian Boundary" passed through Bolingbrook. The area's first white residents settled west of Bolingbrook where the DUPAGE RIVER splits into its east and west branches.

Captain John Barber of Vermont came to Bolingbrook in 1832. Barber and his family claimed 211 acres near the intersection of two Indian trails (today's Route 53 and Boughton Road), where they operated a dairy farm. Barber named the area Barber's Corners, a designation that lasted until Bolingbrook's incorporation. Other settlers, many from Vermont, made their homes in Barber's Corners and established sawmills and gristmills, a tavern, a post office, and a cheese factory.

AGRICULTURAL ways of life continued into the first half of the twentieth century. While other communities developed in proximity to railroads or the Illinois & Michigan Canal, the Bolingbrook area continued to rely on roads for TRANSPORTATION. Fittingly, roads would propel the region's transformation after World War II.

President Dwight Eisenhower helped determine Bolingbrook's future when he signed the Interstate Highway Act into law in 1956. The legislation prompted the decision to replace U.S. Route 66, which ran just south of Bolingbrook, with a limited-access superhighway. The EXPRESSWAY, designated Interstate 55, would be constructed closer to the Bolingbrook area, promoting faster travel to and from Chicago.

Dover Construction Company developed Westbury, Bolingbrook's first subdivision, west of Route 53 and north of I-55 on Briarcliff Road. Colonial Village, an even larger development east of 53, followed. An attempt to incorporate the two subdivisions in 1963 failed by more than a three-to-one margin. In 1965 proponents for incorporation mounted a stronger effort, which succeeded. Bolingbrook's affordable housing, combined with its newfound proximity to Chicago, attracted thousands of residents. By 1972, 15,000 called Bolingbrook home.

In 1975, the Old Chicago entertainment complex opened for business in Bolingbrook. Touted as "the world's first shopping center/amusement ride park," Old Chicago combined vaudevillian themes with county fair–type rides and two hundred stores. The complex never lived up to expectations and closed in 1980.

Bolingbrook participated in the area's massive growth in the 1980s and 1990s. New subdivisions have pushed the population to over 50,000, while large areas of open land remain available for development.

Aaron Harwig

See also: Amusement Parks; Land Use; Metropolitan Growth

Bolivians. Among the smallest of Chicago's Latino ethnic groups, Bolivians are also less residentially concentrated. They live in various parts of the city, mixed among other Latino groups or in areas with other ethnic and national groups. They also are economically and ethnically diverse. Affluent Bolivian professionals, mainly physicians, live in suburban communities; laborers and undocumented immigrants live largely in poor districts in the inner city. Chicago's Bolivians reflect patterns in the mother country, where a large majority trace their origins and culture to the Aymara, an Indian society conquered by the Incas in the fifteenth century, before the Spaniards arrived in the Andes. Others are Quechua, and just a small minority could be considered of Spanish descent.

The arrival of Bolivians in Chicago and in the Midwest in general is linked to expropriations and revolutionary changes after 1952, when a populist party, the Revolutionary Nationalist Movement (MNR), took control of the government. Land reform and the nationalization of mining companies stimulated one of the first waves of Bolivian emigration to the United States, particularly of people with economic and educational means. From 1964 to the late 1970s Bolivia experienced several military regimes, some very repressive, producing another wave of less affluent immigrants escaping political persecution. Finally, in the 1980s and particularly during the MNR administration of Víctor Paz Estenssoro, another wave of immigrants came to the United States for economic reasons. Bolivia experienced at that time high inflation rates and high unemployment, tempting many Bolivians to look abroad.

Chicago's small Bolivian presence was magnified in 1994 when SOCCER's World Cup competition took place in the United States, with some of the games played in Chicago's Soldier Field. The Bolivian national team's participation produced a national jubilee, and Bolivians from Chicago, elsewhere in the United States, and back home congregated to celebrate their national team, waving flags and singing Bolivian songs, including the national anthem.

Bolivians in Chicago try to recreate their culture and traditions in spite of their isolation and dispersion. Latino festivals include Bolivian food stalls and music groups playing particularly Andean tunes, including *waynos, taki raris,* and *sikuris.*

José R. Deustua

See also: Demography; Multicentered Chicago

Book Arts. The arts of calligraphy, illumination and engrossing, hand press work, fine and decorative binding, type design, and graphic design depend for their cultivation on the existence of an audience of bibliophiles. In Chicago, starting in the decades just before and after the Fire of 1871, this audience was drawn largely from the city's thriving commercial printing and publishing industries and from its intermittently flourishing literary circles.

Chicago in the 1860s had many small bookshops and commercial printing establishments. The bookstores served general readers of all sorts and also catered to a few upper-end buyers among the city's elites who were amassing considerable libraries. The most ambitious of these collectors bought more on the book markets in eastern U.S., English, and European cities, but their tastes and interests affected the Chicago book market too. Notable libraries of English and continental history and literature and fine printing were amassed by John A. Spoor, John Wrenn, Horace Hawes Martin, Emma Hodge, and Nicholas Senn. Several such collectors, most notably James Ellsworth and printer Robert Fergus, were important innovators in the taste for collecting Americana. Inevitably, they were also avid collectors of materials on Illinois and the Midwest. The destruction of book stocks and private libraries in the fire created an instant market for local-history rarities; Fergus responded by founding the Fergus Historical Records, consisting of reprints of early narratives. An equally influential collector in a completely different field was Coella Lindsay Ricketts, a lettering artist, who began in the 1880s to amass the largest collection of calligraphic books and manuscripts in the Midwest.

Meanwhile, the commercial printing industry was also contributing to the growth of the bibliophile public. Many of the early printing houses were associated with newspapers, but there were also shops that concentrated on advertising job work, railroad tickets and timetables, and theater printing. Several small to midsize binderies also served the city. The fire swept away many of these businesses and led to consolidation, so that the trade and manufacture of books was much more concentrated from the mid-1870s onward. By the mid-1880s, A. C. McClurg was by far the city's largest bookstore and an active publisher as well; meanwhile, Alfred J. Cox & Co. dominated the field of trade binding. Printing remained somewhat more decentralized, perhaps because the immense growth of advertising, trade magazine and directory publishing, and railroads in the decades after the fire created so great a demand for job printing that small and midsize concerns like M. A. Donohue and the Franklin Press could thrive alongside emerging large firms like R. R. Donnelley & Sons and Rand McNally.

Before the fire, Chicago had no type foundries or manufacturers of printing presses or related machinery. The booming printing business of the 1870s and 1880s changed all that; by 1900, Goss and Miehle presses, Dexter paper folders and cutters, and many other Chicago brands were known around the world, while Barnhart Brothers and Spindler supplied type to a large part of the Midwest. These concerns employed large numbers of craftspeople and managers who were interested in the book arts more generally, and who created familiarity with and demand for beautiful printed objects.

The Arts and Crafts movement that originated in England in the 1880s found fertile ground among this printing industry constituency. The Chicago Literary Club (founded 1874) and the Caxton Club (founded 1895) were groups of bibliophiles who responded immediately to the new aesthetics. Key individuals in bringing the new sensibility to the Chicago book world were Herbert Stuart Stone, son of the pioneer journalist Melville Stone, Ingalls Kimball, and William Irving Way. The two firms of Stone & Kimball and Way & Williams were synonymous in 1890s Chicago with the production of finely printed works of literature, often illustrated by Chicago artists; but neither company ever found a stable market and both folded within a few years. Stone & Kimball's *Chap-Book* published Chicago and international writers and illustrators from 1894 to 1898. Among the artists who worked for the two high-end publishers and went on to long and successful careers were Frederic Goudy, Will Ransom, Frank Holme, and J. C. Leyendecker. The work of some of these same Chicago artists was much more widely distributed by A. C. McClurg, which never claimed high-end production values but which nonetheless aped the look made fashionable by more expensive books.

The twentieth century saw a continuation of the fruitful pattern of exchange between purely commercial printing and high-end book arts. Fine printers proliferated, many just hobbyists but others with excellent design and production standards that influenced the best printing by more commercial presses. Chief among these was Ralph Fletcher Seymour, proprietor of the Alderbrink Press, which maintained the flavor and standards of Arts and Crafts printing up to the 1950s. The Chicago commercial art tradition in this period was represented by Oswald Cooper, the city's most original lettering artist and type designer. Recognizing the employment opportunities provided by the printing trades, Hull House offered basic courses in bookbinding taught by Ellen Gates Starr and Florence Kelley.

Large 8vo, printed in black and red. 231 copies, 200 for sale at $3.00 ❦In press.
A DISSERTATION ON ROAST PIG. By Charles Lamb, with a critical introduction by C. L. Hooper of the Northwest Division High School, Chicago. 16mo, 225 copies on Japan vellum, bound in parchment. 200 for sale. Price to be announced later. ❦In preparation.
The TRAVELLER & The DESERTED VILLAGE Two poems by Oliver Goldsmith. Price and further particulars to be given later. ❦In preparation.

(2)

Park Ridge, July 28, 1903.

Prospectus for the short-lived Village Press, 1903. The proprietors of one of several fine-press ventures of the period here express in words and ornament the philosophy of the Arts and Crafts movement. Artist: Frederic W. Goudy and Will H. Ransom. Source: The Newberry Library.

In the 1920s, big Chicago printing firms hired designers from outside the city who fostered yet another aesthetic current, that of modernism. William A. Kittredge at R. R. Donnelley & Sons and Douglas C. McMurtrie at Cuneo Press and later Ludlow Typograph Company were the most important of these new arrivals. Together with Ernst F. Detterer, teacher at Chicago Normal School and later the School of the Art Institute, they schooled and patronized a new generation of lettering and type artists, most notably type designer R. H. Middleton and calligrapher James Hayes.

Chicago's native modernist movement received exciting new stimulus in 1938 when a group of exiled designers from the German Bauhaus arrived here and began training students at the Institute of Design, then and now informally called the New Bauhaus. The arrival of László Moholy-Nagy, Herbert Bayer, and György Kepes was promoted by Walter Paepcke of the Container Corporation of America, who, a few years later, also helped

Albert Kner settle in as designer at Container Corporation.

Since the end of World War II, Chicago book arts have remained deeply indebted to Bauhaus ideals. Even such traditional arts as calligraphy and binding responded to Bauhaus modernism, and it was the functionalism of that movement, combined with the horrors of destruction witnessed during the war, that led to the first experiments in conservation binding and the first laboratories for restoration in the city. R. R. Donnelley & Sons was a leader in this field, devoting more and more of the energies of their fine bindery, founded in the 1920s, to conservation work; and in 1964 the NEWBERRY LIBRARY became the first American library to appoint a full-time conservator, Paul Banks. This same combination of functionalism and modernism informed the career of Elizabeth Kner, sister of Albert, who emigrated to Chicago in 1950 and trained or influenced a whole generation of fine and conservation binders in the city.

Exhibits of book arts have long kept the general public aware of this vital part of Chicago's heritage. In the early years these were sponsored by the CHICAGO PUBLIC LIBRARY and some of the city's private clubs. From the 1890s, the Caxton Club, the ART INSTITUTE, and the Newberry Library regularly showed book artists. The 1927 founding of the Society of Typographic Arts created another regular and highly influential venue, and in the same decade R. R. Donnelley & Sons opened an elegant gallery inside their corporate headquarters building on 26th Street. Since World War II, the Chicago Book Clinic, publisher Scott Foresman, and Kroch's & Brentano's Bookstore have sponsored shows. In 1969, the UNIVERSITY OF CHICAGO opened a book exhibit gallery in the new Joseph Regenstein Library. In recent years these established institutions have been joined by small nonprofit ventures such as the Chicago Calligraphy Collective, Paper Source, Artist's Book Works, and COLUMBIA COLLEGE's Chicago Center for Book and Paper Arts, founded in 1995.

Paul F. Gehl

See also: Literary Cultures; Presses, University; Printer's Row

Book Publishing. *See* Publishing, Book

Bootlegging. Despite national PROHIBITION, many Chicagoans sought alcoholic beverages during the 1920s. To meet this demand, large organizations BREWED beer and imported and distributed LIQUOR; thousands of families manufactured bootleg, providing access to the decade's prosperity; and neighborhood "soft drink parlors" sold these illegal products. Bootlegging thus undermined the Prohibitionists' great social experiment. Official efforts to stop bootlegging were halfhearted, though supply restrictions meant bootleg booze was often of inferior quality. Competition over bootlegging markets turned so violent that GANGS, alcohol, and crime became a permanent part of Chicago's reputation.

Christopher Thale

See also: Crime and Chicago's Image; Local Option; St. Valentine's Day Massacre

Further reading: Allsop, Kenneth. *The Bootleggers and Their Era.* 1961. • Blocker, Jack S. *American Temperance Movements: Cycles of Reform.* 1989. • Haller, Mark H. "Bootlegging: The Business and Politics of Violence." In *Violence in America,* vol. 1, *The History of Crime,* ed. Ted Robert Gurr. 1989.

Bosnians. Bosnians first migrated to Chicago in the late nineteenth century with other South Slavic immigrants, including SERBIANS, CROATIANS, SLOVENES, and BULGARIANS. Early migrants from Bosnia-Herzegovina were generally young, unskilled male laborers who came in search of economic opportunities. Many found jobs in the CONSTRUCTION and mining industries, building roads, downtown buildings, and TUNNELS for the CHICAGO TRANSIT AUTHORITY (CTA). Bosnian Serbs and Croats migrated toward growing Serbian and Croatian communities on the SOUTH SIDE of the city. While these Bosnian Christians identified with nationals from Croatia and Serbia, Bosnian MUSLIMS identified themselves exclusively as Bosnians.

Bosnian Muslims were early leaders in the establishment of Chicago's Muslim community. In 1906, they established Dzemijetul Hajrije (The Benevolent Society) of Illinois to preserve the community's religious and national traditions as well as to provide mutual assistance for funerals and illness. The organization established chapters in GARY, Indiana, in 1913 and Butte, Montana, in 1916 and is the oldest existing Muslim organization in the United States. The Bosnian Muslim community received a new influx of migrants after WORLD WAR II who were displaced by the war and Communist takeover. This new wave of REFUGEES included many well-educated professionals, some of whom were forced to take lower-skilled jobs as TAXI cab drivers, factory workers, chauffeurs, and janitors. As the population increased in the early 1950s, the community invited Sheik Kamil Avdich, a prominent Muslim scholar, to become the first permanent imam (religious minister). Under Imam Kamil's leadership, the Muslim Religious and Cultural Home was established to raise funds for a mosque, which opened on Halsted Street in 1957. In 1968, the organization's name was changed to the Bosnian American Cultural Association, and in the early 1970s it purchased land in NORTHBROOK to build a larger mosque and cultural center. The Islamic Cultural Center of Greater Chicago has remained an important center for Muslim religious activity, serving Bosnian and non-Bosnian Muslims in metropolitan Chicago.

The war in Bosnia-Herzegovina from 1992 to 1995 brought the largest influx of Bosnian refugees to Chicago. Chicago became the most popular United States destination for Bosnian refugees, and, according to community estimates in 2002, an estimated 40,000 Bosnians settled in the city. Comprising Bosnian Muslims, ROMAN CATHOLICS, EASTERN ORTHODOX, JEWS, and "other" (of mixed background), the new Bosnian community has settled in the northern part of the city, between Lawrence and Howard, from Clark to the lake. Victims of ethnic cleansing efforts, many of the refugees suffered from post-traumatic stress disorder as a result of gruesome experiences in concentration camps and the death of family and friends. The Illinois Department of Human Services founded the Bosnian Refugee Center in 1994 with the help of public and private agencies to assist the newcomers, and in 1997 it became the nonprofit Bosnian & Herzegovinian American Community Center. Staffed by Bosnian refugees from all backgrounds, the center serves all refugees by providing community services that include educational and family programs, counseling, and cultural activities.

Asad Husain

See also: Americanization; Demography; Rogers Park; Yugoslavians

Further reading: Miller, Olivia. "Bosnian Americans." In *Gale Encyclopedia of Multicultural America,* 2000.

Boss Politics. *See* Patronage

Bowling. Until the mid-twentieth century, Chicago was one of the foremost bowling hotbeds in the United States. As early as 1851 the city of Chicago had licensed five bowling alleys, and for the balance of the nineteenth century the popularity of the game and the number of bowling centers grew rapidly, centered primarily among GERMANS living on the North Side. By 1900 Chicago NEWSPAPERS were regularly reporting results from organized bowling leagues around the city, and by 1910 the city boasted 230 bowling alleys.

In January 1901 Chicago received endorsement as one of the nation's leading bowling centers when the American Bowling Congress (ABC) conducted its inaugural national men's tournament on the lanes in the Welsbach Building on Wabash Avenue in the LOOP. Chicago subsequently hosted five other ABC tournaments. That same weekend the Chicago Women's Bowling Association sponsored a tournament which it billed as the first United States women's championships. While this tourney was short-lived, Chicago would play host to Women's International Bowling Congress tournaments in 1920 and 1935.

The American Bowling Tournament, at the Coliseum, 1929. Photographer: Unknown. Source: Chicago Historical Society.

In 1911 the top men bowlers of Chicago organized the now-legendary Randolph League, a prestigious circuit that operated until 1946. Another circuit for the city's top-flight men bowlers, organized in the early years of the twentieth century, was the Classic League, the spirit of which continues in the city's various major leagues.

In 1921 Louis Petersen opened Archer-35th Recreation, a bowling alley on the second floor of a building at 2055 W. 35th Street on the SOUTH SIDE. That same year he launched an open singles tournament that became known as the Petersen Classic, which annually drew thousands of bowlers from around the country. When the old bowling alley closed in 1993, the Petersen Classic was moved to a suburban location.

In 1927 the *Chicago Herald-Examiner* inaugurated the Weekly High Game Bowling Contest, a tournament for men and women league bowlers. The event soon became an annual women's team handicap tournament, known as the *Herald-American* Women's Bowling Classic from the 1950s until its demise in the mid-1960s. In 1961 the *Chicago Sun-Times* joined with the Bowling Proprietors' Association to cosponsor an annual handicap tournament for individual men and women bowlers, called Beat the Champions, which remained in operation at the end of the century.

Another major Chicago bowling event, the All-Star Tournament, began in 1941 under the cosponsorship of the Bowling Proprietors of America and *Chicago Tribune* Charities. This grueling marathon tournament, usually held at the Chicago Coliseum, determined the national individual match game championship. A women's division was added in 1949, before the annual competition was moved out of Chicago in 1957.

Television provided a major stimulus to the sport's increasing popularity in the 1950s. In 1952, WMAQ-TV launched *Championship Bowling,* a weekly one-hour show featuring taped matches between professional bowlers. For many years the shows were filmed at the Faetz-Niesen Lanes and were announced by sportscaster "Whispering" Joe Wilson. In the mid-1950s, WBKB-TV carried *Universal Bowling Clinic,* a weekly half-hour program featuring bowling news and lessons and cohosted by Sam Weinstein and hall-of-fame bowler Paul Krumske. Long after local bowling shows had disappeared from Chicago television, Weinstein, known as the Tenpin Tattler, carried on with a weekly radio program about bowling until the 1990s.

Raymond Schmidt

See also: Bridgeport; Leisure

Further reading: American Bowling Congress. *First Fifty Years, 1895–1945.* 1945. • Jones, Thomas C., ed. *The Halls of Fame: Featuring Specialized Museums of Sports, Agronomy, Entertainment, and the Humanities.* 1977. • Riess, Steven A. *City Games: The Evolution of American Urban Society and the Rise of Sports.* 1989.

Boxing. Throughout much of the nineteenth century, boxing was part of Chicago's bachelor subculture where bouts for small bets were held in the back rooms of SALOONS. The first notable professional prizefight in the city was held in 1885, between bare-knuckle champion John L. Sullivan and Jack Burke at the Driving Park Racetrack.

Boxing flourished in the late 1890s at Tattersall's at 16th and Dearborn. A match there between famed champion Bob Fitzsimmons and Englishman Jim Thorne was the first prizefight in the city to attract an upper-class clientele. Following a rigged boxing match between Terry McGovern and Joe Gans in December of 1900, prizefighting was banned in the city early in 1901, a ban upheld for more than a quarter century. Amateur matches continued to be held in the city, however, by such organizations as the Chicago Athletic Association (CAA).

Following agitation to end the ban, notably by the *Chicago Tribune,* boxing was legalized

Golden Gloves Finals program, Chicago Stadium, March 10, 1944. Creator: Chicago Tribune Charities, Inc. Source: Chicago Historical Society.

in 1926, upon which the Illinois Boxing Commission was organized. In 1927, in the largest live boxing gate in history, 128,000 fans at SOLDIER FIELD watched Gene Tunney defeat Jack Dempsey in the famous "long-count" fight. The CHICAGO STADIUM, opened in 1929, became an important boxing venue, hosting many major championship bouts.

In 1928, the *Chicago Tribune* inaugurated the Golden Gloves amateur competition. The sport thrived, with boxers being trained and promoted by such private gyms as Coulon's (1154 East 63rd Street), founded in 1925 by one-time bantamweight champion Johnny Coulon. The ROMAN CATHOLIC ARCHDIOCESE OF CHICAGO was important in the sport's promotion, becoming the biggest sponsor of youth boxing through the CATHOLIC YOUTH ORGANIZATION, the Knights of Columbus, and the Catholic High School League. The Chicago PARK DISTRICT also nurtured and promoted boxing in the city.

The Marigold Gardens on the North Side emerged in the 1930s as the most significant venue for local professional bouts. Lightweight Barney Ross became a hero in the West Side JEWISH community in the 1930s. In the 1940s, middleweight Tony Zane, from Gary, also captured the city's fancy.

In 1949, boxing promoter James Norris and Chicago Stadium owner Arthur Wirtz formed the International Boxing Club, which controlled pro boxing competition before being broken up by the federal government as a monopoly in 1957. During that time the Chicago Stadium played host to many of the biggest fights in the country, featuring such boxers as Sugar Ray Robinson, Rocky Marciano, and Floyd Patterson. In 1961, Wirtz ended boxing matches at the Stadium, and thereafter Chicago declined as a boxing town.

Since the early 1960s, boxing in the city has been basically a club sport, with fight cards featuring local boxers holding matches in hotels, many promoted by former heavyweight champion Ernie Terrell (a product of the West Side). The premier private gym in the city since the late 1970s has been the Windy City Boxing Club, producing such fighters as Andrew Golota and Angel Manfredy. In 1994, the Golden Gloves opened the tournament to women.

Robert Pruter

See also: Creation of Chicago Sports

Boy Scouts. *See* Scouting

Boys Town. The boundaries of the neighborhood known as Boys Town stretch from about 3100 to 3800 North Halsted. The unofficial designation of Boys Town as an area within LAKE VIEW dates back to 1970, when residents marched here in the first annual Gay Pride Parade.

The city of Chicago proposed a $3.2 million facelift for the area in 1997. These improvements included a plan to commemorate Boys Town's GAY AND LESBIAN residents that would mirror similar efforts on behalf of residents in Chicago's ethnic-identified neighborhoods. The city erected eleven pairs of 23-foot-high art-deco-style pillars with rainbow rings in 1998.

Erik Gellman

See also: Gay and Lesbian Rights Movements

Further reading: Engelbrecht, P. J. "Proud Pylons Rise over Boys Town." *Outlines,* October 7, 1998. • Reed, Christopher G. "There's No Place Like Home: Making Chicago's 'Boys Town.'" In *(A) Way Stations: The Architectural Space of Migration,* ed. Paul duBellet Kariouk and Mabel Wilson. 2002. • Wockner, Rex. "America's First Official Gay Neighborhood Debuts." *Stonewall Journal* (January 1999).

Bozo's Circus. Chicago-based *Bozo's Circus,* featuring the antics of a clown with startling red hair, was the nation's longest-running children's television program. The Bozo character originated in Los Angeles in 1946, when Alan Livingston created the clown for a series of Capitol Records children's albums. KTTV-TV aired the first televised Bozo program there in 1949. Larry Harmon, one of the first Bozos, purchased the rights to franchise the clown nationwide in 1956. Chicago's *Bozo's Circus* premiered on WGN-TV in 1961 with Bob Bell as the clown, broadcasting every weekday at noon. Its circus acts, comedy skits, cartoons, and audience games, overseen by the beaming Ringmaster Ned (Ned Locke), were a hit with local children. During the 1960s and '70s, the wait to appear in the studio audience stretched to several years.

WGN's *Bozo* began airing nationally in 1978. Bob Bell retired in 1984 and was replaced by Joey D'Auria. A dwindling audience finally led WGN to cancel the program in 2001.

Beatrix Hoffman

See also: Broadcasting; Entertaining Chicagoans

Further reading: "Bozo" subject file. Museum of Broadcast Communications Archives, Chicago, IL. • *Bozo 25th Anniversary Special.* Video, MBC Archives. WGN, 1986. • Hyatt, Wesley. "Bozo the Clown." In *The Encyclopedia of Daytime Television,* 1997, 67–68.

Braidwood, IL, Will County, 52 miles SW of the Loop. Incorporated only nine years after William Henneberry discovered COAL here in 1864, Braidwood soon became a major coal supplier to Chicago. IRISH, WELSH, SCOTTISH, and CZECH miners, including future MAYOR Anton Cermak were among those who found WORK in the mines, which were the site of STRIKES in 1868, 1874, and 1877. Two nuclear power plants were built near Braidwood in the 1980s.

Brandon Johnson

See also: Coal City; Environmental Politics

Further reading: Gutman, Herbert. "Labor in the Land of Lincoln." In *Power and Culture: Essays on the American Working Class.* 1992. • *The History of Will County, Illinois.* 1878.

Brazilians. Chicago's early Brazilians included a small diaspora of Southern and Eastern Europeans who, after fleeing the devastation of post–WORLD WAR II Europe for Brazil, eventually circumvented restrictive American immigration laws to settle in Chicago. From the late 1940s through the 1950s this group, including a handful of PORTUGUESE JEWS, gravitated toward Chicago communities representing their birthplace cultures and generally eschewed a strong Brazilian identity. Since the small population of other Brazilians in postwar Chicago was largely transient, no recognizable Brazilian community developed until the early 1970s.

Beginning in the mid-1960s a small but growing stream of Brazilians sought better living standards by migrating to Chicago. While most single men returned to Brazil within several years, families tended to settle in Chicago for longer periods, establishing Chicago's first Brazilian community. The men often worked in manufacturing or as mechanics, while many women either joined their husbands at the factories or labored in DOMESTIC WORK.

While Chicago Brazilians have never concentrated in a single neighborhood, a SOCCER group begun in 1970 helped forge an otherwise disparate group of people into an active community. Organized by a handful of young men, the Flyers Soccer Club quickly grew from a sports team into a multifaceted organization, also referred to as the Luso-Brazilian Club. From 1970 to 1985 the club's LAKE VIEW–area headquarters doubled as the organizational center of the community, sometimes hosting celebrations and dances for several hundred area Brazilians and a handful of Portuguese. The club limited itself to playing soccer beginning in 1985, as many of its members had left Chicago for other American cities with either warmer climates, like Miami and Los Angeles, or larger Brazilian and Portuguese communities, like New York City, Newark, and Boston.

Ironically, the Flyers Club downsized as a new, larger wave of Brazilians began settling in Chicago. From the mid-1980s through the 1990s Brazilian immigration to the United States skyrocketed, spurred by economic crises at home. But while cities like New York could boast tens of thousands of Brazilians by the late 1990s, Chicago Brazilians numbered no more than several thousand at the new millennium. This new group differed from both larger American Brazilian communities and earlier Chicago Brazilians in its greater education and affluence. Some of these professionals were transferred to Chicago by their Brazilian employers, while others came to fill shortages in NURSING and software engineering.

While no single organization represented Chicago Brazilians in the 1990s as the Flyers did in the 1970s and 1980s, several entities have served to keep the community connected and active. A few area churches—ROMAN CATHOLIC, Baptist, and Seventh-Day Adventist—regularly hold services in Portuguese for their Brazilian parishioners. A Brazilian-owned GROCERY near Armitage and Western Avenues became an informal meeting place and communication center of sorts for Brazilians in 2000. Some Latin-themed RESTAURANTS and clubs began featuring Brazilian dishes and drinks, as well as live music played by the popular Chicago Samba. With musicians based out of both Chicago and St. Louis, Chicago Samba had developed into the community's roving linchpin by the mid-1990s. Not only has the band brought hundreds of area Brazilians together on a regular basis, but it has regularly apprised people of upcoming community events through its extensive fan mailing list. One such event was a festive gathering of approximately 750 Brazilians who, from the basement of an area church, watched the Brazilian soccer team win the 2002 World Cup finals.

Stephen R. Porter

See also: Demography; Ethnic Music; Multicentered Chicago

Breakfast Club. The longest running network series in radio history, the *Breakfast Club* was emblematic of the freewheeling style of the golden age of Chicago BROADCASTING. Almost two years after its 1933 debut, host Don McNeill decided that scripts interfered with the informal atmosphere he wanted. NBC's executives reluctantly agreed to an ad-libbing experiment that continued on the air, five mornings a week, until the show's final broadcast, on December 27, 1968.

The hour-long broadcast was divided into 15-minute segments, each beginning with a call to breakfast. During "Memory Time," McNeill might read a poem or brief essay. Halfway through the show, he would invite listeners to "March Around the Breakfast Table." There was a daily moment of silent prayer.

The show published its own yearbook, which some years sold over 130,000 copies. It received 6,000–10,000 letters a month. In 1944, sponsor SWIFT & CO. offered free membership cards in a *Breakfast Club* fan club. One million fans, including Supreme Court Justice William O. Douglas, joined. Within a few weeks, the sponsor closed the club: the gimmick had cost the company $50,000.

The show's success stemmed from McNeil's ability to project a folksy personality. The broadcast began with a singing welcome: "Good morning Breakfast Clubbers, good morning to ya, we woke up bright and early just to howdy-do ya." A POW in a German prison camp was said to cheer fellow American internees by singing the *Breakfast Club* theme song.

McNeill surrounded himself with complementary talent: the show's longtime clown and resident heckler Sam Cowling, crooner Johnny Desmond, and Marion and Jim Jordan, creators of FIBBER MCGEE AND MOLLY. Before joining KUKLA, FRAN AND OLLIE, Fran Allison was the show's busybody Aunt Fanny.

The show originated at the MERCHANDISE MART and later broadcast before live audiences at the Opera House, the Morrison Hotel, the Sherman House, and the Allerton Hotel. In 1946, 17,000 fans filled Madison Square Garden for a New York broadcast. Years later, McNeill ended his last broadcast by joining with listeners in silent prayer. After a few seconds, he said: "Amen. And if you want peace where you are, don't ever forget Don McNeill and the gang saying so long and be good to your neighbor."

Ron Grossman

See also: Entertaining Chicagoans

Further reading: Doolittle, John. *Don McNeill and his Breakfast Club.* 2001.

Breweries. During the nineteenth century, beer making was transformed from a small-scale, seasonal activity for local consumers into a highly mechanized big BUSINESS. Outside of New York City, Chicago became the nation's largest center of the malt LIQUOR industry. In addition to its looming economic importance, brewing had several other major impacts on the city in the areas of science, technology, ARCHITECTURE, POLITICS, and culture.

In 1833, GERMAN immigrants established the first brewery in Chicago. Soon renamed the Lill and Diversey Brewery, it made ENGLISH-style ales and porters. In 1847, however, John A. Huck opened the first German-style or lager beer plant and an adjacent beer garden on the NEAR NORTH SIDE. The city's swelling numbers of IRISH as well as GERMANS preferred this lighter, more carbonated cold drink, relegating traditional brews to a small specialty market. The brewery's insatiable demand for ice in making and storing its highly perishable food product was largely responsible for creating the ice business in Chicago. In a similar way, its needs for strong animals to pull wagons laden with heavy barrels of beer to SALOONS and RESTAURANTS across the city on a weekly basis helped establish breeding farms for the biggest type of "city" horses.

From 1860 to 1890, brewing underwent a profound scientific and technological revolution. Louis Pasteur's work on beer yeast identified germs and other microorganisms as the main reason why such a large proportion of the beer went bad. The virtually complete domination of the industry in Chicago by German immigrants and their offspring meant that the city became a leading center of "scientific brewing," boasting a special school, the Siebel Institute of Technology. Successful businessmen such as Conrad Seipp, Peter Schoenhofen, Michael Brand, and Charles Wacker, giants in the brewing community, underwrote the inventions that helped bring refrigeration machines to a point of commercial practicality. They also replaced the traditional brewmeister with university-trained chemists. The malting business grew in tandem, branching off to form an important industry in its own right. Applying more and more energy in the form of heat, power, and cooling, beer making became one of the country's most highly automated and mechanized industries, complete with assembly lines in the bottling plant. By 1900, Chicago's 60 breweries were making over 100 million gallons a year.

At the same time, however, the half-century campaign for temperance was becoming a highly charged political issue, full of ethnocultural, gender, and class meaning. Concerns about new waves of European immigrants, women's changing roles, and working-class militancy fueled the attack on the neighborhood saloon as the city's greatest social evil. With the coming of WORLD WAR I, the forces of reform won passage of the Eighteenth Amendment, marking the end of Chicago's role as a vibrant center of INNOVATION. After the repeal of PROHIBITION in 1933, the city's brewing industry did not recover in the face of competition from national brand names selling beer in cans. One by one, the city's breweries closed their doors.

Industrial beer making in Chicago languished until the 1980s. Attempts to reopen some of the old large-scale breweries ultimately failed, but microbreweries (small-scale brewing companies) and brewpubs (restaurants with attached breweries) kept the city's beer-making tradition alive.

Harold L. Platt

See also: Entertaining Chicagoans; Schooling for Work

Further reading: Angle, Paul M. "Michael Diversey and Beer in Chicago." *Chicago History* 8 (Spring 1969): 321–326. • Duis, Perry. *The Saloon: Public Drinking in Chicago and Boston.* 1983. • *One Hundred Years of Brewing: A Supplement to the Western Brewer.* 1903.

Brickmaking. *See* Quarrying, Stonecutting, and Brickmaking

Bridgeport, Community Area 60, 3 miles SW of the Loop. Before the FORT DEARBORN Massacre, Charles Lee owned a farm along the South Branch of the CHICAGO RIVER. In April 1812 Indians raided Lee's farm and killed two whites at a place known as Hardscrabble, all on the current site of Bridgeport.

The beginning of the construction of the ILLINOIS & MICHIGAN CANAL in 1836 gave birth to Bridgeport. Canal commissioners probably named the new town, which included the northern terminus of the canal, to distinguish it from an earlier privately planned settlement, Canalport. First IRISH canal workers, and then GERMANS and NORWEGIANS arrived to WORK under Chief Engineer William Gooding. Many lived along Archer Avenue, named after William Beatty Archer, who supervised construction of the canal. The canal opened in 1848 and guaranteed Bridgeport's position as an industrial center. LUMBER yards, manufacturing plants, and packinghouses opened along both the river and canal. Drovers bringing livestock to Bridgeport packers often crowded Archer Road, a thriving commercial strip.

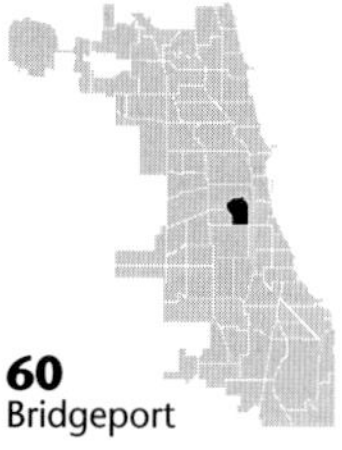

Most packers relocated to the UNION STOCK YARD after 1865 but the MEATPACKING industry remained a major employer of Bridgeport residents. Also in 1865 the Union Rolling Mill began operation. Other manufacturers arrived, and in 1905, the CENTRAL MANUFACTURING DISTRICT opened in the western section of Bridgeport.

In 1850 enough Irish lived along Archer Avenue to organize St. Bridget's, the first of four Irish ROMAN CATHOLIC parishes. The district soon attracted other immigrant groups. Germans settled in the neighborhood originally called Dashiel north of 31st Street and east of Halsted Street. The First Lutheran Church of the Trinity (1863), Holy Cross Lutheran Church (1886), St. Anthony Catholic Church (1873), and Immaculate Conception Catholic Church (1883) were all originally German congregations. CZECH Catholics organized St. John Nepomucene Parish in 1871. POLES and LITHUANIANS settled along Morgan Street. The Poles established St. Mary of Perpetual Help Parish (1886) and St. Barbara's (1910), while the Lithuanians opened St. George Church in 1892. Frame and brick cottages and two-flats with small backyards made up the majority of the housing stock. Small stores, SALOONS, fraternal halls, and SCHOOLS soon joined the churches lining the streets. After 1880, as streetcars made their way up and down Halsted and 35th Streets, the intersection of those two thoroughfares developed into a small but important shopping strip, eventually replacing Archer Avenue as the neighborhood's commercial district.

Bridgeport residents, while primarily working in local industries, often looked beyond the factories. After the CIVIL WAR the Irish in particular saw the expanding role of the municipal GOVERNMENT as an opportunity for upward mobility. Bridgeport's politicians actively pursued PATRONAGE jobs as options for their constituencies. When the Democratic MACHINE came to power in 1931 under MAYOR Anton Cermak, Bridgeport politicians provided an important part of the coalition. After Cermak's death two Bridgeport natives, Patrick A. Nash and Edward J. Kelly, dominated city government. In 1955 Richard J. Daley, who hailed from the Bridgeport neighborhood of Hamburg, took office. As mayor and chairman of the Cook County DEMOCRATIC PARTY, Daley controlled one of the most powerful machines in urban America until his death in 1976. Bridgeport's disproportionate share of patronage provided a stable economic base for the neighborhood. In 1989 his son, Richard M. Daley, became the fifth mayor of Chicago born in Bridgeport.

Bridgeport once stood as a bastion of white ethnic communities. Racial and ethnic strife has always been part of its history. An almost legendary clash between the Germans and the Irish occurred in 1856. During the CIVIL WAR pro-Confederate rallies were held in the neighborhood. In the twentieth century Polish and Lithuanian GANGS often clashed along Morgan Street. While in the 1990s AFRICAN AMERICANS made up less than 1 percent of the community area's population, the number of

MEXICAN and CHINESE residents has grown. Meanwhile the traditional white ethnic population has grown older and smaller. Bridgeport is adjacent to the booming Chinese community in ARMOUR SQUARE, and lies just to the south of PILSEN, home to the city's largest Mexican community. In addition, while Bridgeport remains a largely working-class community, its location to the south of the city's expanding LOOP puts it in the direct line for future investment and development. Already new housing in the form of expensive townhouses and single-family houses has appeared in the district. In turn older housing has been restored and modernized.

Dominic A. Pacyga

See also: New City; Transportation; Water

Further reading: Holt, Glen, and Dominic A. Pacyga. *Chicago: A Historical Guide to the Neighborhoods: The Loop and South Side.* 1979. • Pacyga, Dominic A., and Ellen Skerrett. *Chicago, City of Neighborhoods: Histories and Tours.* 1986. • Pierce, Bessie Louise. *A History of Chicago.* 3 vols. 1937–1957.

Looking east along the Chicago River at the LaSalle Street Bridge prior to completion, 1928. Photographer: Unknown. Source: Chicago Historical Society.

Bridges. Nineteenth-century Chicago's geography presented unusual requirements. A narrow river, with low banks, ran through the heart of the city, requiring frequent crossings. Yet the navigable river was one of the world's great ports, and the low bridges had to accommodate frequent passage of masted ships.

Ferries provided an initial solution, but by 1833 a log bridge allowed an uneasy passage to the West Side. The first drawbridge was constructed in 1834, but its approaches impeded navigation and it was torn down in 1839. Although South Siders had hoped to keep trade on their side of the river, a new floating bridge was built in 1840, and three more soon followed. All were swept away in an 1849 spring flood, but replacements soon followed, and the first municipally funded bridge opened in 1857. By 1871, the city had 27 movable bridges.

Most of these were swing bridges, which turned on a center pier to swing out of the way of ships. The narrow channel saw frequent collisions between sailing ships and bridges, spurring the search for other solutions.

Frequent bridge openings vexed the city, making the North and West Sides less desirable. Tunnels built at Washington Street (1869) and LaSalle Street (1871) proved extremely useful for cable cars, which could not cross an openable bridge, and a third was built near Van Buren Street (1894).

A new type of bridge, the Scherzer rolling lift bridge, was designed in 1894 for the Metropolitan West Side Elevated Railroad and nearby Van Buren Street crossings. This type of bridge rolled back like a rocking chair to open, its trusses having curved ends with overhead counterweights on shore. Chicago still has a few Scherzer-type bridges, notably the Cermak Road bridge and the now-inoperable "Eight-Track" RAILROAD bridges near Western Avenue. Newer examples can be found in JOLIET.

The bridge most identified with Chicago, the trunnion bascule, was developed in 1900, and the first one built, opened in 1902, remains at Cortland Street. The bridge's leaves are suspended on axles (trunnions), with the counterweights in a riverbank pit. The new design proved efficient to operate and allowed trusses to be set at banister height and eventually moved underneath the road deck altogether. After 1910, involvement of the Chicago Plan Commission and architect Edward Bennett improved such architectural elements as bridge houses.

At the beginning of the twenty-first century, the city had 37 operable street drawbridges, including 5 over the CALUMET RIVER, opened nearly 30,000 times a year. Only a few were attended full-time; bridge tenders drove from bridge house to bridge house to open the others. The U.S. Coast Guard has accepted lower vertical clearances for the North and South Branches outside downtown, and bridges there no longer move or were built as fixed spans. At the outbreak of WORLD WAR II, the new Western Avenue bridge was temporarily converted to a lift bridge, and machinery was installed in other spans on the SANITARY AND SHIP CANAL to allow warships to reach the Gulf of Mexico.

A few drawbridges of other types are still found in Chicago. Inoperable swing bridges survive on two railroads over the Sanitary and Ship Canal, as does a cantilevered "retractable" bridge over a slip near 3101 West 31st Street. Vertical lift bridges, with towers at each end to raise a center span, are found on three Calumet River railroad crossings, on Torrence Avenue, and at Amtrak's Union Station approach near 18th and Canal.

Dennis McClendon

See also: Chicago River; Innovation, Invention and Chicago Business; Planning Chicago; Streets and Highways; Transportation; Water

Further reading: Becker, Donald N. "Development of the Chicago Type Bascule Bridge." *American Society of Civil Engineers Papers,* February 1943. • Becker, Donald N. "Early Movable Bridges of Chicago." *Civil Engineering* (September 1943). • City of Chicago, Department of Public Works. *Chicago Bridges.* 1984.

Bridgeview, IL, Cook County, 13 miles SW of the Loop. NATIVE AMERICAN artifacts have been found in Bridgeview near Archer Avenue, evidence of a long human occupation. Archer runs through the northwestern edge of the town, and one of the earliest homes in what is now Bridgeview was built near this old Indian trail in the 1830s. By the 1870s GERMAN farmers had moved to the area, growing corn for livestock as well as hay, wheat, and potatoes. By the 1880s former Chicago MAYOR "Long John" Wentworth owned land in the area.

The settlement remained a sleepy farming community until the 1920s, when in spite of an influx of ITALIAN farmers, farming began to decline. By 1924 REAL-ESTATE developers began to build homes between 71st and 75th Streets, in the Frederick H. Bartlett SUBDIVISION. Many residents worked at the huge Corn Products International plant in neighboring BEDFORD PARK. The Harlem AIRPORT at 87th Street and Harlem Avenue operated from the 1920s until the 1950s. The effects of the GREAT DEPRESSION slowed development, but in 1936–37 the Bartlett Real Estate Company resumed building houses. Local residents chose the name Bridgeview by one vote over Oketo, the latter a street name in the village today. "Bridgeview" was chosen for the view of the area from the Harlem Avenue BRIDGE. The Bridgeview Community Club, founded in 1938, became the center of local activities.

In 1947 voters decided to incorporate as a village of approximately 500 residents. After incorporation the village began installing streetlights and replacing failing wells with WATER from Lake Michigan. Ten years after incorporation population had surged to roughly 3,600, and by 1960 it had more than doubled, to 7,334.

Once Lake Michigan water became available, more industries moved to Bridgeview. The Indiana Harbor Belt Railroad played a key role in development of the area, as did the town's close proximity to MIDWAY AIRPORT and Interstates 294 and 55. For a time Bridgeview was known for its large truck terminals, and truck traffic has remained heavy: in 1998 the town had the dubious distinction of being named by the Environmental Protection Agency as the major source for cancer-causing pollutants in Cook County.

Over the 1960 and 1970s, Bridgeview acquired a fire department, a municipal center, a park system, and a library. In the early 1980s longtime Bridgeview mayor John Oremus pitched the bold idea of a dozen or more southwest suburbs uniting into a single city, but many opposed it. Oremus dominated politics for decades until 1999, when he chose not to run for reelection.

The town's motto, "A Well Balanced Community," is indicative of a diversified economy, split between industry, retail, and service-oriented businesses. The village receives over $13 million in tax revenues a year. The 2000 population was 15,335, only slightly larger than it had been 20 years earlier. Ethnic groups represented in large numbers include POLES, Germans, and IRISH. Arab Americans are a growing presence, making up 7 percent of the population. In 1981 an Islamic social club was established, and by 1984 it had became a mosque. Two Islamic schools educate hundreds of students.

Ronald S. Vasile

See also: Expressways; Industrial Pollution; Muslims; Religious Geography; Suburban Government; Transportation

Further reading: Krbecek, Norene. "Unpublished History of Indian Springs School District #109." Bridgeview Public Library, Bridgeview, IL. • Peksa, Rich. *A History of Bridgeview, Illinois.* 1972.

Brighton Park, Community Area 58, 6 miles SW of the Loop. Brighton Park takes its name from the Brighton livestock market in England and is bounded roughly by the Stevenson EXPRESSWAY and 48th, Western, and Kimball Streets. Construction of the ILLINOIS & MICHIGAN CANAL and Archer Avenue drew early settlers. Henry Seymour subdivided land north of Pershing Road in 1835. By 1851, there was a small settlement named Brighton Park near the Blue Island Avenue Plank Road (now Western Avenue). In 1855 Mayor Long John Wentworth opened the Brighton Race Track.

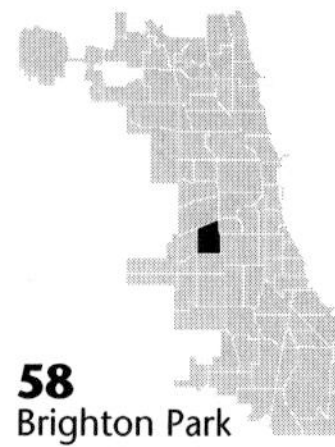

In the late 1850s Brighton became a livestock trading center. A stockyard was built in 1857 at the corner of Archer and Western, and in 1861 a state fair was organized by the U.S. Agricultural Society. The completion of the UNION STOCK YARD in 1865 forced the closing of Brighton's yards. Instead, Brighton Park attracted other industries, including the Northwestern Horse Nail Company, a cotton mill, a silver smelting and refining company, and the Laflin and Rand Company, a firm that manufactured explosives. On August 29, 1886, lightning struck one of Laflin and Rand's warehouses, leaving a 20-foot crater and damaging property for miles around. After heated meetings, the citizens ordered all powder mills to leave the area. The mills relocated to BLUE ISLAND, Illinois.

The Chicago & Alton RAILROAD established a roundhouse in the community, and industrial employment attracted GERMAN and IRISH workers. In 1887 the Santa Fe Railroad moved in, building its Corwith Yards, then the busiest in the nation.

In 1889 Brighton Park was ANNEXED to the city of Chicago as part of LAKE TOWNSHIP. By the 1880s and 1890s INFRASTRUCTURE and transportation improvements drew even more diverse populations. FRENCH and Eastern European JEWS settled in the community, followed by POLES, LITHUANIANS, and ITALIANS.

Much of the ethnic character of the community was carried by the churches. The first churches in the community were PROTESTANT, serving the YANKEES who owned and managed the early firms. The Brighton Park Baptist Church dates from 1848, and the McKinley Park Methodist Church first met in 1872. In 1878 Irish ROMAN CATHOLICS established St. Agnes Church. By 1892 French Catholics had established St. Jean Baptiste church at 33rd and Wood Streets. Later, Italians, Poles, and Lithuanians found jobs and homes in Brighton Park. They developed their own churches, including Five Holy Martyrs in 1908 (Polish); Immaculate Conception in 1914 (Lithuanian); St. Pancratius in 1924 (Polish); and St. John's Polish National Parish, also in 1924.

Industrial parks such as the CENTRAL MANUFACTURING DISTRICT opened in 1905, and the Kenwood Manufacturing District opened on the southern border around 1915. The Crane Manufacturing Company opened a plant in 1915, providing more jobs. By 1930, Brighton Park reached residential maturity, peaking at 46,552 people, 37 percent of Polish descent. Deindustrialization, exemplified by the closing of Crane's in 1977, weakened the area's economy, and population declined by one-third between 1930 and 1980.

Although the community remains largely residential, there is a growing commercial section. The community maintains monuments to European connections, including the Balzekas Museum of Lithuanian Culture and the Polish Highlander Alliance. By 2000 the population had grown to 44,912, 69 percent of MEXICAN origin.

Clinton E. Stockwell

See also: Economic Geography; Horse Racing; Meatpacking; South Side

Further reading: Chicago Fact Book Consortium, ed. *Local Community Fact Book: Chicago Metropolitan Area, 1990.* 1995. • Hamzik, Joseph. "Brighton Park History." Binders, 1952–1976. Brighton Park Public Library. • Hamzik, Joseph. "Gleanings of Archer Road." December 1961. Brighton Park Public Library.

Broadcasting. Chicago emerged as a broadcasting center because its first radio stations, thanks to geography, were heard from the eastern seaboard to the Rockies and beyond. Its broadcasting flourished when Chicago became a central switching point for transcontinental network lines, allowing the city's production facilities to re-feed programming to the various time zones with relative economy in the days before audio and videotape. It survived because three generations of broadcasters, both on-air and behind the scenes, were consistently able to retool the broadcast media and sell them to an evolving market.

Chicago's age of broadcasting began the evening of November 11, 1921, when KYW (licensed to Westinghouse Electric and Manufacturing Company and operated jointly with Commonwealth Edison) began regular scheduled programming. For the next two months, KYW aired live performances of the Chicago Grand OPERA Company—and nothing else. Managers of a later era might cringe at the thought of an "opera-only" station. But in

Judith Waller and Chicago Radio

Judith Waller—Chicago's "First Lady of Radio"—believed that broadcasting's potential as an educational medium was unlimited. She developed network programs that ranged from radio's *University of Chicago Roundtable* to television's *Ding Dong School.* Her *Radio, the Fifth Estate,* published in 1946, is the most thorough treatment of the broadcast practices of radio's golden age.

Chicago's *Daily News* hired Waller in April 1922 to put its newly licensed radio station on the air. Under her leadership, WMAQ evolved from a two-person operation into one of the nation's leading stations. WMAQ was the home of *Amos 'n' Andy* and the first station to broadcast a complete home season of a professional BASEBALL team (thanks to Waller's negotiations with the Chicago CUBS).

When NBC purchased WMAQ in November 1931, Waller became the director of public affairs programming for the network's Central Division, a position she held until her 1957 retirement.

Rich Samuels

1921, only a year after Westinghouse's pioneer KDKA went on the air in Pittsburgh, the content of programs was secondary to the novelty of the medium. Westinghouse claimed there were 200 radio receivers in Chicago when the 1921 opera season began, 25,000 when it ended. KYW's live opera broadcasts were a major factor in the spread of America's "radio craze" and the creation of a local radio boom.

By the spring of 1923, 20 Chicago radio stations cluttered the largely unregulated dial. Many (including WBU, licensed to the city of Chicago, and WHT, separately licensed to Mayor William Hale Thompson) did not last the decade. Most that made the cut were owned by established BUSINESSES with pockets deep enough to absorb the losses until radio could pay its own way. WMAQ survived thanks to the backing of the *Chicago Daily News* (as well as the skills of general manager Judith Waller); WBBM thanks to a collaboration between the brothers H. Leslie and Ralph Atlass and the Stewart Warner Corporation; WGN thanks to its ownership by the *Chicago Tribune;* and WLS thanks to Sears, Roebuck (and, after 1928, Prairie Farmer Publishing) and its rural-oriented programming. KYW, meanwhile, forged an alliance with the Hearst papers that lasted until its license was transferred to Philadelphia in 1934. Two stations survived thanks to their institutional affiliations: WCFL (licensed to the CHICAGO FEDERATION OF LABOR) and WMBI (licensed to the MOODY BIBLE INSTITUTE). Lower-powered WCRW, WEDC, and WSBC thrived because of their foreign-language programming.

The extension of AT&T's network lines to the West Coast in November 1928 turned Chicago into a national radio production center. Both NBC and CBS were committed to an 18-hour broadcast day. The time couldn't be filled without Chicago's participation.

Locally produced prime-time shows like Freeman Gosden and Charles Correll's AMOS 'N' ANDY and Marion and Jim Jordan's FIBBER MCGEE AND MOLLY were among the nation's most popular. But Chicago's network output was most substantial during the daytime, beginning with Don McNeill's BREAKFAST CLUB (1933–1968), and continuing with hours of SOAP OPERAS, a genre pioneered in Chicago. For many, the highlight of the broadcast day was *Vic and Sade* (1934–1946). Writer Paul Rhymer's low-key comedy with a distinct Midwestern flair provided 15 minutes of welcome relief from the drama of the soaps.

Chicago rapidly lost its status as a network radio production center following the end of WORLD WAR II. But the completion of the coaxial cable linking the East Coast and Midwest in January 1949 turned it into the origination point of some of early television's most memorable programs. WBKB (licensed in 1939 to the Balaban and Katz theater chain) had already trained the medium's first generation of technicians and producers. Network radio's departure had left a substantial pool of underutilized talent. Critics called the programming that resulted the "CHICAGO SCHOOL OF TELEVISION." Technically innovative on the one hand, simple and straightforward on the other, the "Chicago School" was above all characterized by the belief of its proponents that television was a unique medium unto itself.

Program cover for the 13th anniversary of the Slavic Song and Dance Festival, 1946. The festival's director, George Marchan, was host of the *Jugoslav Radio Hour* on WGES. Source: Chicago Historical Society.

By the mid-1950s, most of Chicago's major network television talents had been lured to the East or West Coasts. Emerging videotape technology meant that Chicago's studios were no longer necessary for live network broadcasts. At WGN-TV in particular, children remained a key target of local programming. A generation of Chicago's youth grew up watching *Garfield Goose and Friend,* while at least two generations watched (and hoped they could acquire tickets for) BOZO'S CIRCUS. But increasingly Chicago's commercial stations directed their resources toward local news coverage. The quality of local television news in Chicago generally remained high, thanks to the city's strong NEWSPAPER tradition and seasoned radio journalists like Clifton Utley and Len O'Connor who brought their skills to the video medium. Meanwhile, WTTW (licensed in 1955) evolved into the nation's most-watched public television station.

Chicago's radio stations searched for new identities in the post-network era. In 1960, WLS abandoned its rural audience and adopted a fast-paced top-40 format. WCFL followed suit a few years later. WMAQ shifted from middle-of-the-road to country and western. WBBM experimented with an all-talk format, then shifted to all news. Phil and Leonard Chess, owners of CHESS RECORDS, purchased suburban Cicero's WHFC and changed its call letters to WVON. For the first time, Chicago had a station that targeted AFRICAN AMERICANS around the clock (Chicago's pioneer black radio personalities—Jack L. Cooper, Al Benson, and Sam Evans—had settled for small slices of time on primarily foreign-language stations). WGN was the lone holdout as a "full-service" station.

In the 1970s music, for the most part, moved to the FM band. Three decades after Zenith Radio's Eugene McDonald put experimental station W51C on the air, FM had become profitable. Popular music dominated the dial. But Chicago's audience still supported two fine-arts stations, WFMT and WNIB. Paul Harvey remained Chicago's lone network radio personality. His daily news and commentary broadcasts were almost as long-lived as the ABC network that carried them.

But long after satellite dishes supplanted the network lines that once made Chicago a broadcasting hub, tens of millions of Americans continued to watch Chicago-made programs, thanks to the growing popularity of syndicated daytime TELEVISION TALK shows. Phil

Foreign-Language Broadcasting in the Chicago Area, 1956–1995

✧ less than one hour ○ 1 to 10 hours ◎ 10 to 20 hours □ 20 to 200 hours ★ more than 200 hours

	1956	1957	1958	1959	1960	1961	1963	1964	1965	1966	1967	1968	1969	1970	1971	1972	1973	1974	1975	1976	1977	1978	1979	1980	1981	1982	1983	1984	1985	1986	1987	1988	1989	1990	1991	1992	1993	1994	1995
Arabic																					✧												✧	○	○	○	○	○	○
Armenian										✧																					✧	✧		✧	✧	✧	✧	✧	
Bohemian	○	○	◎		○	○		○	○	○		○	○	○	○																								
Croatian	○	○	○	○	✧	✧		✧	✧	✧																						○	○	○	○	○	○	○	○
Czech		◎				○		○	○																							○	○	○	○	○	○	○	○
Finnish										✧									✧	✧																			
French					✧	✧				○			○	✧	○		○	○	○	○	○		○	○	○	○	○	○	○	○									
Gaelic				○			○																																
German	○	○	◎	◎	◎	◎	□	○	◎	□	□	◎	□	□	□	○	○	○	○	◎	□	□	□	□	□	□	□	◎	□	□	□	◎	□	○	○	○	□	□	◎
Greek	○	○	○	○		✧	○	○	○	○	○	✧	○	○	○	○	○	✧	✧	○	◎	□	◎	◎		○	◎	□			□	□	□	□	○	□	□	◎	□
Hebrew																																	✧	✧	✧	✧	✧	✧	✧
Hindi																															○	○	○	○	○	○	○	○	○
Hungarian	○	○	○	○	○	○	✧	○		○																													
Irish	○							○		○										○											○	○	◎	◎	○	◎	○	◎	◎
Italian	□	□	□	□	□	□	◎	□	□	□	◎	□	□	□	□	○	○	□	◎	□	□		□	□	□	□	□	□	□	□	□	□	□	□	□	□	◎	□	□
Japanese																						✧	✧	✧	✧	✧	✧												
Jewish								✧	✧	✧	○																				○	○	○	✧					
Korean																															□	○	○				◎	◎	
Latin													✧		✧																								
Latvian	✧		✧	✧																																			
Lithuanian	○	○	◎	○	○	◎	○	◎	◎	◎																					○	○	◎	◎	◎	◎	◎	◎	◎
Macedonian		✧																																					
Native American																						✧		○	✧														✧
Polish	□	□	□	□	◎	□	□	□	□	□	□	□	□	□	□	○	○	□	○	□	□	□	□	□	□	□	□	□	□	□	□	□	□	□	□	□	□	□	□
Portuguese																						○							✧										
Rumanian	✧	✧	○	○			✧							✧																									
Russian						✧								✧	✧			✧	○	○	✧										○	○	○	○	✧	✧	○	○	○
Scandinavian	✧		✧		○	○																																	
Scottish										✧																								✧	✧	✧			
Serbian	○	✧	○	○		○	○	○	○	□	✧	✧		✧																	○	○	○	○	○	○	○	◎	◎
Slovak	○	○	○	○	✧	✧	✧	○	○											✧																			
Slovenian		✧								○								✧	○													✧		✧	✧	✧	✧	✧	✧
Spanish	□	□	□	□	□	□	□	□	□	□	□	□	□	□	□	□	□	□	□	□	★	★	★	□	★	★	★	★	★	★	★	★	★	★	★	□	★	★	★
Swedish	○	✧																																					
Ukrainian	○	○	○	○						✧		✧	✧	✧	○	✧		✧	✧	○	○	○	○								○		◎	◎	◎	◎	◎	○	○
Yiddish	○	○	○	✧																																			
Yugoslav	○	○	○	○		○	○	○	✧				○	✧	✧		✧	✧	○	✧	✧																		

Source: Broadcast Yearbook

Donahue pioneered the genre. Oprah Winfrey perfected it. Jenny Jones and Jerry Springer threw it (sometimes literally) into the arena of controversy. And Chicago remained a national broadcast production center.

Rich Samuels

See also: Entertaining Chicagoans; Ethnic Music; Journalism; Public Broadcasting

Further reading: *Broadcasting Magazine.* Various issues. • Gonciar, Elizabeth. *The Adventures of Broadcasting in Chicago.* Mimeographed pamphlet. 1942. Illinois Writers Project. • *Variety.* Various issues.

Broadview, IL, Cook County, 12 miles W of the Loop. The village of Broadview incorporated in 1914 in response to MAYWOOD's offer to ANNEX this land along its southern boundary. The approximately 200 residents who voted for incorporation included farmers scattered throughout the village and approximately 20 homeowners in the northern section. They established boundaries that were nearly identical to the present perimeter, except that the village included the land to the east and west of 1st Avenue between Roosevelt Road and Cermak Avenue. Initially a two-mile auto racetrack was built on the property along 1st Avenue, and in 1919 an airfield was constructed nearby. Known as Checkerboard Air Mail Field, the AIRPORT operated as Chicago's airmail center until 1923. Eventually this land became part of the FOREST PRESERVE District of COOK COUNTY. To the west of 1st Avenue the U.S. government planned construction of Edward J. Hines HOSPITAL. The eastern portion of this tract was turned over to the Post Office Department and used as an airmail field from 1922 to 1927, eventually becoming part of the village of Maywood and home to LOYOLA UNIVERSITY Medical Center.

Most of Broadview's initial residential development took place north of Roosevelt Road, but beginning around 1940, construction began south of that line as large numbers of Cape Cods, Georgians, BUNGALOWS, and raised ranches were built. Village population peaked in 1970 with over 9,600 residents. The housing has changed little in appearance, but a significant amount of residential turnover has occurred in the last 30 years as AFRICAN AMERICANS, who made up less than 6 percent of Broadview's population in 1970, accounted for 30 percent in 1980 and 74 percent in 2000.

The post–World War II years brought not only massive residential construction, but also a village-wide commitment to set aside nearly half of Broadview's land for industry. Land along 25th Avenue and the Indiana Harbor Belt RAILROAD near Broadview's western boundary and land along the ILLINOIS CENTRAL RAILROAD was designated as industrial. A wide variety of industries located here, including International Harvester on the largest industrial tract in the village. As some of the long-standing employers moved out, other manufacturers and new commercial development moved in.

Until recently, Roosevelt Road was the only commercial district. The 1994 addition of Broadview Village Square Mall (on the former International Harvester property) brought an additional revenue base and reinforced Broadview's motto: "A Balanced Community—Residential, Commercial, Industrial."

Patricia Krone Rose

See also: Economic Geography; Land Use; Transportation

Further reading: *Broadview Golden Jubilee, 1914 to 1964*. Pamphlet. Broadview Public Library, Broadway, IL. • Presecky, William. "This Town Built Around Jobs." *Chicago Tribune*, October 9, 1993.

Bronzeville. *See* Grand Boulevard

Brookfield, IL, Cook County, 13 miles SW of the Loop. Brookfield, a middle-class bedroom community, is a near-western suburb of Chicago. There is little industry or major business in the village, although the BROOKFIELD ZOO draws substantial numbers of visitors. Major settlement of the area began in 1889 when the Chicago REAL-ESTATE developer S. E. Gross opened his SUBDIVISION of Grossdale. The area became popular as a suburban home site due to its easy proximity to downtown Chicago via the Chicago, Burlington & Quincy Railroad (now METRA). The first building Gross erected in the new subdivision was a train station. (In 1981, the station was moved across the tracks and now houses the Brookfield Historical Society. It is on the National Register of Historic Places.) Gross later added the subdivisions of Hollywood (1893) and West Grossdale (1895), each with its own train station. Residents voted to incorporate as the village of Grossdale in 1893.

In the early years the community was heavily influenced by Gross. He named numerous streets in the subdivisions after family members, and in 1895, against the wishes of area residents, changed the name of his Hollywood subdivision to East Grossdale. In 1901, the community's ambivalence about his strong presence generated an unsuccessful attempt to change the village's name to Montauk. Sentiment for a name change persisted and became the platform of the victorious Independent Party in the 1905 election. A contest to choose a new name yielded "Brookfield" in respect for SALT CREEK, which runs through the area. During this period the name of the East Grossdale subdivision reverted back to Hollywood and the West Grossdale subdivision was renamed Congress Park.

The housing stock in the village ranges from Victorian homes built by Gross in the late nineteenth century to BUNGALOWS of the 1920s and more modern homes built during the post–World War II building boom. The village board system of government continued in Brookfield until a 1947 ordinance called for a village manager, a structure permanently adopted in 1951. In 1952 Brookfield received an All-American City award from the National Municipal League and *LOOK* magazine, in recognition of "intelligent, purposeful, citizen action." The village's main claim to fame, however, is the Chicago Zoological Park, commonly known as Brookfield Zoo. The zoo is located on land given to the FOREST PRESERVE District by Edith Rockefeller McCormick in 1919. The village's population reached a high of over 20,000 in the 1960s, declining slightly to 19,085 in 2000.

Emily Clark

See also: Government, Suburban; Housing Types; Planning Chicago; Real Estate

Further reading: *Brookfield, Illinois: A History*. 1994.

Brookfield Zoo (Chicago Zoological Park). By June 30, 1934, when the Brookfield Zoo officially opened, local residents had been working to build it for almost 15 years. In 1919, Edith Rockefeller McCormick gave 83 acres of land to the Cook County FOREST PRESERVE District for a large modern zoo, and the district responded by adding another 98 acres. In 1920, a group of prominent Chicagoans joined to make the zoo a reality and, in 1921, incorporated the Chicago Zoological Society. The following year, building began and George Frederick Morse, Jr., was hired as the society's first manager. Not until 1926, after county residents approved a zoo tax, did serious construction begin, only to falter in the GREAT DEPRESSION. But by late in 1931 momentum had returned to building what would become America's first zoo with barless exhibits. Visitors from all over the Midwest came to visit the zoo and its most famous residents: Ziggy, a popular male elephant, and Su-Lin, the first giant panda in an American zoo and the first of three pandas at Brookfield.

Its development interrupted by WORLD WAR II, the zoo expanded in size and commitments in the decades following. A Veterinary Hospital (1952), a Children's Zoo (1953), and the famous central fountain (1954) were built. Zoo leadership took advantage of new media opportunities, including television, and formalized education programs. The first curator of research, George B. Rabb, was hired in 1956. Despite these innovations, the zoo struggled with deficits and a declining physical plant through much of the 1960s. Then, helped by a large bond issue from the Forest Preserve District, close attention to zoo governance and visitor services, and Rabb's appointment as director in 1976, the zoo began to recreate itself as one of the nation's best, especially in its institutional commitment to international conservation and environmental awareness.

Tropic World was born, one of the world's largest themed great ape enclosures. Olga the walrus became a household name as hundreds of Chicago-area residents came to see her antics. The focus of the zoo turned dramatically toward people: visitors and those who would ensure its viability in the future. The Seven Seas Panorama was built and improvements were made to the Aquatic Bird House. Conservation biology became an important focus of the institution, as Rabb became chair of the

Federal Art Project poster 1937. Artist: Carken. Source: Library of Congress.

Species Survival Commission for the International Union for the Conservation of Nature. Facility and staff changes helped to reinforce Brookfield's leadership position in this important arena.

More recent exhibits promote conservation education. Visitors are encouraged to observe and enjoy the animals in realistic natural settings. Brookfield has continually pioneered new zoo experiences that point the way for other institutions.

The zoo is still owned by the Cook County Forest Preserve District and managed by the Chicago Zoological Society. With an animal collection numbering about 450 species and 3,100 specimens, attendance in 1998 was 2,200,000.

Dennis A. Meritt, Jr.

See also: Lincoln Park Zoological Gardens; Park Districts; Taxation and Finance

Further reading: Ross, Andrea Friederici. *Let the Lions Roar.* 1997.

Brotherhood of Sleeping Car Porters. The International Brotherhood of Sleeping Car Porters and Maids was the first African American labor union chartered by the American Federation of Labor (AFL). Pullman porters, dissatisfied with their treatment by the Chicago-based Pullman Company, sought the assistance of A. Philip Randolph and others in organizing their own union, founded in New York in 1925. The new union assigned Milton P. Webster to direct its organizing in Chicago, home to the largest number of Pullman's 15,000 porters.

For African Americans, porter and maid jobs, when supplemented with tips, paid better than many other opportunities open to them, yet less than those jobs on Pullman cars denied to them by their race. Porter and maid jobs also retained African Americans in servile relations to white passengers. Moreover, segregation persisted even in the North, where blacks were limited in where they could spend their stopovers while on the job.

In addition to the often overlooked maids who organized for the union, the wives of porters also assumed an important role in the decade-long struggle for union recognition. Their auxiliary functions and support were significant contributions to the union's efforts. More than half of Chicago's "Inside Committee" were women.

As a black organization, not just a union, the Brotherhood was an important early component of the Civil Rights movement. Porters distributed the Chicago Defender after that black newspaper was banned from mail distribution in many southern states. The Pullman Company's recognition of the union in 1937 and the expansion of Brotherhood membership and activities slowly fractured segregation within the AFL.

In 1978, the decline of the railroad industry led the Brotherhood of Sleeping Car Porters to merge with the much larger Brotherhood of Railway, Airline, Steamship Clerks, Freight Handlers, Express, and Station Employees.

Eric R. Smith

See also: Racism, Ethnicity, and White Identity; Railroad Workers; Unionization; Work Culture

Further reading: Chateauvert, Melinda. *Marching Together: Women of the Brotherhood of Sleeping Car Porters.* 1998. • Harris, William H. *Keeping the Faith: A. Philip Randolph, Milton P. Webster, and the Brotherhood of Sleeping Car Porters, 1925–37.* 1977. • Wagner, Paul, and Jack Santino, prods. *Miles of Smiles, Years of Struggle.* Documentary film. 1983.

Bucktown, Part of the West Town and Logan Square Community Areas. Roughly bounded by North, Ashland, Western, and Fullerton Avenues, Bucktown supposedly takes its name from the goats that roamed its streets at the turn of the twentieth century. Originally a primarily Polish working-class area of small homes, saloons, and churches, it has experienced significant gentrification in recent years.

Steven Essig

See also: Multicentered Chicago

Further reading: Fremon, David. *Chicago Politics Ward by Ward.* 1988.

Bud Billiken Day Parade. In 1923 Chicago Defender founder Robert S. Abbott and his managing editor, Lucius Harper, formed the Bud Billiken Club. Abbott had long expressed a concern for Chicago's African American youth, and the success of the *Defender*'s "young people's page" convinced him that a club would also be popular. Harper apparently chose the name "Bud" because it was his own nickname, and "Billiken" because of its association with of an ancient Chinese mythical character believed to be the guardian angel of all children. By 1929 the Bud Billiken Club, with its membership cards and identification buttons, was so popular among Chicago's black youth that Abbott decided to initiate an annual parade to celebrate it. He led the first parade in his Rolls Royce, and Frank Gosden and Charles Correll of Amos 'n' Andy fame were the first guests of honor.

Since the 1940s the Bud Billiken Day Parade has been sponsored by the Chicago Defender Charities, and has become known as the oldest African American parade in the country. Participants in the parade, which proceeds south on Dr. Martin Luther King Jr. Drive from 39th to 51st streets culminating with a picnic in Washington Park, have included presidents Truman, Kennedy, and Johnson; Nat King Cole; Michael Jordan; and Muhammad Ali. Toward the late 1990s spectator estimates of the Bud Billiken Day parade, held on the second Saturday of August, ran into the millions, and the event was routinely considered one of the largest of its kind in the United States.

Wallace Best

See also: Clubs: Youth Clubs; South Side; Street life

Further reading: "Who Was Bud Billiken?" *Chicago Sun-Times,* August 13, 1977. • Calloway, Earl. "A History of Bud Billiken Day." *Chicago Defender,* August 8, 1998.

Buddhists. Buddhism had a minimal presence in Chicago prior to World War II. Of traditionally Buddhist populations, only the Chinese and Japanese had any appreciable local settlement by 1940, but neither group had yet established an institutional Buddhist expression.

Representatives of some Asian Buddhist traditions attended the World's Parliament of Religions held in conjunction with the World's Columbian Exposition of 1893. Afterwards, at a ceremony conducted by Anagarika Dharmapala of Ceylon, Jewish businessman C. T. Strauss became the first formal convert to Buddhism on American soil. A branch of Dharmapala's Maha Bodhi Society opened subsequently in Chicago, attracting a mostly professional clientele of converts and spiritual seekers. Two enterprises based in the region kept Buddhism in the American public eye in the early decades of the twentieth century: the Theosophical Society, which established its permanent headquarters in west suburban Wheaton in 1926, and Open Court Publishing Company, founded in 1887 in downstate LaSalle.

Significant Buddhist presence in the Midwest dates from the arrival of several thousand former Japanese American internees beginning in June 1942. Two Japanese Buddhist temples emerged on Chicago's South Side soon thereafter: Midwest Buddhist Temple (1944), a member of the Jodo Shinshu Buddhist Churches of America, and Buddhist Temple of Chicago (1944), a nonsectarian temple founded by Gyomay Kubose. Both temples subsequently relocated to the North Side, and in 1971 Midwest Buddhist Temple erected the region's only newly constructed immigrant Buddhist temple, with an exterior Old World architecture, in Lincoln Park. Three more Japanese temples opened in the 1950s and 1960s, while several other Asian American groups (BURMESE, Chinese, Kampuchean, KOREAN, LAO, THAI, VIETNAMESE) have established temples since 1970. The number of these temples in the region doubled (from 8 to 16) in the 1980s, and more than doubled again by the end of the 1990s. Over half can be found on Chicago's North Side, several in the UPTOWN area. Outside the city, notable older temples include the Thai Buddhist Temple (Wat Dhammaram, 1976) in unincorporated southwest Cook County, which opened a striking multipurpose facility in the early 1990s, and Wat Phothikaram (1982) in Rockford, the Lao temple featured in the video documentary *Blue Collar and Buddha*.

Two Japanese clergy stimulated local American-convert participation in Buddhism in the postwar period. Kubose's Buddhist Temple of Chicago drew as many as 30 converts to its services in the late 1940s and early 1950s. In 1955 Kubose created the American Buddhist Association to facilitate outreach beyond the Japanese community. Soyu Matsuoka Roshi, abbot of the Zen Buddhist Temple of Chicago (1949), began to attract both white and AFRICAN AMERICAN practitioners in the early 1960s. As a result of sustained indigenous interest since the 1960s, the region today contains about 30 Buddhist centers that serve a predominantly non-Asian constituency, plus a few Asian American temples that accommodate non-Asian converts. Zen traditions account for about half of the non-Asian centers, TIBETAN traditions about one-fourth. The Nichiren Shoshu Temple for the Midwestern states opened in west suburban West Chicago in 1981, and a new Soka Gakkai International center opened in 1995 in the NEAR SOUTH SIDE, both groups claiming a significant number of African American members. Formal inter-Buddhist cooperation among several Asian and non-Asian groups occurs through the Buddhist Council of the Midwest (1987), especially in its annual International Visakha celebration. The council cosponsored the centennial commemoration of the World's Parliament of Religions in 1993.

Greater Chicago's Buddhist population at the close of the twentieth century comprised a variety of ethnic and sectarian identities. The immigrant groups, most into only their second generation, faced a complex AMERICANIZATION process which included the task of separating Old World, culture-specific aspects from more universal elements of Buddhism shared cross-culturally among them. The convert groups, somewhat insulated by sectarian distinctions, nevertheless have brought a common, American cultural perspective to their Buddhist practices. At the dawn of the new century it remained unclear whether a uniquely "American" brand of Buddhism would emerge in urban centers like Chicago, or whether Buddhism in America would remain pluralist.

Paul D. Numrich

See also: Demography; Religious Institutions

Further reading: *Buddhist Churches of America*, vol. 1, *75 Year History, 1899–1974*. 1974. • Kubose, Gyomay M. *American Buddhism: A New Direction*. 1976. • Numrich, Paul David. *Old Wisdom in the New World: Americanization in Two Immigrant Theravada Buddhist Temples*. 1996.

Buffalo Grove, IL, Cook and Lake Counties, 26 miles NW of the Loop.

New Englanders established the first farms in the area, followed in the 1840s by Melchior Raupp and other GERMANS. Farmers carried their harvest in wagons along 34 miles of dirt roads to Chicago. Mainly ROMAN CATHOLICS, these German settlers raised $300 and donated seven acres of land to build St. Mary's Church in 1852. Although a few years later arsonists destroyed the church, it was rebuilt in 1899 at Buffalo Grove Road and Lake-Cook County Road. Additions enlarged the structure in the 1980s.

Around the turn of the century dairy farming was extensive, prompting J. B. Weidner to build a cheese factory. When the price of milk rose, the cheese factory closed. In 1899 Little Mike's Place located across from St. Mary's Church and had a bar, dining room, dance hall, sleeping rooms, and a place for horses. A century later the establishment remained in operation with its original bar intact as Lou Malnati's Pizzeria.

In the 1930s Dundee Road became the first state concrete road in northern Illinois, improving automobile access. Development began in earnest in 1957 when builder Al Frank purchased one hundred acres of farmland and began building ranch-style houses, generally without basements.

Following incorporation in 1958 the village grew from 164 to 1,492 residents within two years. Other developers, including William Levitt, who built Long Island's Levittown, entered the market. Population escalated with large SUBDIVISIONS such as Strathmore and the Woodlands at Fiore. In the 1970s Jewish families flocked to the area, and by the early 1990s there were six synagogues in Buffalo Grove. At the end of the twentieth century JEWS constituted approximately 30 percent of the village's population.

Growth has not been limited to residential SUBDIVISIONS. Buffalo Grove Commerce Center was developed in 1981 with 50 acres of light industrial park at Lake-Cook Road and the Soo Line Railroad tracks. In the mid-1980s Corporate Grove industrial park was erected to the east and Buffalo Grove Business Park was constructed to the west. Expansion continued into the 1990s to the north with Arbor Creek Business Centre at Aptakisic Road and Barclay Boulevard, and Covington Corporate Center on Busch Road.

By the end of the twentieth century the village had grown from 67 acres at incorporation to approximately 5,000. Population in 2000 stood at 42,909.

Marilyn Elizabeth Perry

See also: Expressways; Land Use; Suburbs and Cities as Dual Metropolis

Further reading: Clipping file. Indian Trails Public Library, Wheeling, IL. • Polzin, Michael. "Charging Ahead." *North Shore Magazine*, July 1991, 38–41, 93–102. • Stritch, Samuel Alphonsus Cardinal. *Solemn Blessing and Dedication of St. Mary's School, Buffalo Grove, Illinois*. 1947. Booklet, Indian Trails Public Library, Wheeling, IL.

Bughouse Square. Bughouse Square (from "bughouse," slang for mental health facility) is the popular name of Chicago's Washington Square Park, where orators ("soapboxers") held forth on warm-weather evenings from the 1910s through the mid-1960s. Located across Walton Street from the NEWBERRY LIBRARY, Bughouse Square was the most celebrated outdoor FREE-SPEECH center in the nation and a popular Chicago tourist attraction.

In its heyday during the 1920s and 1930s, poets, religionists, and cranks addressed the crowds, but the mainstays were soapboxers from the revolutionary left, especially from the INDUSTRIAL WORKERS OF THE WORLD (IWW), Proletarian Party, Revolutionary Workers' League, and more ephemeral groups. Many speakers became legendary, including ANARCHIST Lucy Parsons, "clap doctor" Ben Reitman, labor-wars veteran John Loughman, SOCIALIST Frank Midney, feminist-Marxist Martha Biegler, Frederick Wilkesbarr ("The Sirfessor"), Herbert Shaw (the "Cosmic Kid"), the Sheridan twins (Jack and Jimmy), and one-armed "Cholly" Wendorf.

A Bughouse Square Committee, headquartered at Newberry Library, has continued to organize free-speech gatherings there each July in conjunction with the library's annual book sale.

Franklin Rosemont

See also: Haymarket and May Day; Hoboes; Lectures and Public Speaking; Near North Side; Park Districts; Playgrounds and Small Parks

Further reading: Beck, Frank O. *Hobohemia*. 1956. • Rosemont, Franklin, ed. *From Bughouse Square to the Beat Generation: Selected Ravings of Slim Brundage, Founder and Janitor of the College of Complexes*. 1997.

Building Codes and Standards. From the city's inception in 1837, Chicago's Health Department regulated the BUILT ENVIRONMENT to reduce threats from fire and disease.

Within a generation, the regulations addressed numerous issues concerning the CONSTRUCTION, alteration, and maintenance of residential, industrial, and commercial structures. In 1875, the city codified these regulations and created a Department of Buildings to administer the code.

The code never satisfied reformers. In the 1890s, HULL HOUSE residents investigated their neighborhood to reveal the extent of sanitation problems among the poor. Despite a revision of the code, problems remained, due to severe overcrowding. So in 1900, the City Homes Association commissioned a much larger survey directed by Robert Hunter. Hunter canvassed immigrant neighborhoods and presented a sophisticated statistical analysis. Social scientists Edith Abbott and Sophonisba Breckinridge expanded this work in their attempt to establish a scientific basis for the study of poverty. Their efforts led to TENEMENT codes setting minimum requirements for light, air, ventilation, and plumbing.

Understaffed and often corrupt, the Department of Buildings could not enforce even minimal requirements. Consequently, older structures were seldom brought up to code, especially in areas where properties were purchased on speculation that the business district would expand. However, the code affected new buildings by requiring fireproof construction for tenements of greater than three stories. The cost of meeting this requirement effectively set a limit upon the height of tenements in Chicago.

After 1920, major advances occurred in the scientific and engineering basis for establishing building codes. Under Herbert Hoover, the Department of Commerce created national standards encouraging greater uniformity in the codes of the nation's largest cities. Chicago also accepted the recommendations from organizations such as the American Society for Testing and Materials, the National Association of REAL ESTATE Boards, the National Fire Protection Association, and the American PUBLIC HEALTH Association.

By 1950, Chicago's code was woefully out of date. Its restrictive language did not allow builders to use plywood or drywall, products commonly allowed by suburban codes. PATRONAGE, politics, and petty corruption thwarted efficient administration.

Conditions improved with an increase in the number of career bureaucrats who improved enforcement with the help of an extensive survey of housing conditions throughout the city. The plan for URBAN RENEWAL targeted areas for demolition and redevelopment while concentrating energies on areas likely to deteriorate unless monitored. However, politics still determined the level of enforcement.

By 1970, the city devised an institutional method for continually updating the code by placing policy decisions in the hands of bureaucrats, architects, developers, trade unions, and builders. In 1983, this system accommodated the rehabilitation movement by relaxing the code, facilitating GENTRIFICATION in old neighborhoods as older homes could be restored to the new regulation. Interest groups also lobbied successfully for code regulations that made Chicago more accessible to the disabled.

Building inspection at 2358 South Indiana, 1953. Photographer: Unknown. Source: Chicago Historical Society.

Enforcement of the building code, at a minimal level, protected health and safety by ordering the repair or demolition of substandard structures. In declining areas, however, the cost of rehabilitation has led to abandoned buildings. Most troublesome, a cumbersome court system with protracted legal proceedings has never provided an efficient means for obtaining compliance from code violators.

Joseph C. Bigott

See also: Environmental Regulation; Housing Types; Planning Chicago

Further reading: Abbott, Edith, and Sophonisba P. Breckinridge, et al. *The Tenements of Chicago, 1908–1935.* 1936. • Chicago Association of Commerce. *Building Regulation in Chicago: An Analysis and Recommendations.* 1945. • Jones, Bryan D. *Governing Buildings and Building Government: A New Perspective on the Old Party.* 1986.

Building Trades and Workers.

The modern CONSTRUCTION industry and organizations of journeymen and contractors originated in the commercial, industrial, and urban transformations of the early nineteenth century. As large-scale merchant builders took over from the master artisans in the various special crafts required to erect a building, they relegated many to the position of labor subcontractors. These changes were well underway by midcentury, when Chicago experienced its greatest growth. With the advent of factory-made materials, many workers, especially those in the carpentry trade—the largest of the construction crafts—became little more than installers of prefabricated products, often paid by the piece. Under the "piecework" system speculators bypassed masters and their broadly trained journeymen, allowing easily trained, lower paid "greenhorns" who were often recent immigrants to threaten the integrity of the crafts.

By the 1870s unions of skilled building tradesmen had taken root in almost all city crafts. Though they were at first little more than makeshift bodies relying on the enthusiasm of the moment, these early unions embodied a basic labor demand: that all journeymen receive a standard minimum wage. Payment of a standard wage would remove contractors' incentive to employ lower paid pieceworkers and cement class solidarity among journeymen.

No building trades unions won stable contracts until the great EIGHT-HOUR DAY movement surrounding the HAYMARKET Tragedy of 1886. By that time many unions employed paid walking delegates (now called business agents), required initiation fees and dues, and offered burial, sick, and other benefits.

In 1887, after the bricklayers and carpenters had won the eight-hour day, the contractors formed strong employers' associations and mounted an "open shop" counterattack to destroy the power of the walking delegates to enforce union standards at the widely scattered building sites. After a short but bitter battle, Judge Murray F. Tuley arbitrated a precedent-setting trade agreement in which the bricklayers and mason contractors agreed to regularized collective bargaining for the first time. By 1890 the bricklayers and other trades had joined together in the first viable building trades council. Under its leadership journeymen from all organized trades could STRIKE a building under construction in unison—the "sympathy strike"—leaving the contractor without a workforce. They were often aided by a hands-off approach from Chicago POLICE.

In 1890–91, during construction of the WORLD'S COLUMBIAN EXPOSITION, carpenters, painters, plumbers, steam fitters, iron workers, and others in the building trades used their favorable bargaining position and newfound strike methods to win agreements similar to those of the bricklayers.

During the 1890s the contractors' associations fell into disarray. Under the two-fisted leadership of Martin "Skinny" Madden, the unions parlayed their ability to mount sympathy strikes into union control over the industry. The depression from 1893 to 1897, however, forced the unions to accept agreements to WORK only for association contractors, thus artificially strengthening their employers. Soon, the agreements were expanded into three-cornered arrangements in which unions and the associations of contractors and material manufacturers gained monopolies within their respective markets.

In 1900–01, the contractors locked out the unions, claiming that these exclusive agreements raised material prices to exorbitant levels and that sympathy strikes created intolerable unpredictability in the market for contractors. Under intense pressure from Chicago business, DEMOCRATIC mayor Carter Harrison II used the police to protect strikebreakers, and the Great Lockout of 1900–01 ended in union defeat. Though most labor gains from the late nineteenth century remained, the exclusive agreements were abolished and the unions accepted "the eight cardinal principles" in which they acknowledged the supremacy of the contractors in the industry.

The first 11 years of the twentieth century were years of peace in the construction industry and accomplishments such as the establishment of jointly run apprenticeship programs. But, gradually, the rise of new construction methods led to union rivalry over control of the new work. By 1913, fully 75 percent of all work stoppages resulted from jurisdictional disputes between unions. In 1915, general contractors led by the Builders' Association were able to initiate a lockout and force the unions to accept a "uniform form of agreement" as the basis of all labor agreements and a Joint Conference Board, which still functions to resolve disputes.

The last great episode of industrial conflict in the Chicago construction industry occurred in the early 1920s. The city's largest employers and builders combined to impose the open shop on contractors and unions alike. Using many unions' unwillingness to abide by Judge Kenesaw Mountain Landis's 1921 arbitration award, outside employers established a Citizens Committee which labeled as "outlaw" unions that rejected the award and bound contractors not to bargain with them.

No struggle in the history of the construction industry in the city was fought with more bitterness and violence. The carpenters and painters split from the building trades council and led successful opposition to the Landis Award. A major reason for their victory was the massive 1920s building boom in which speculative builders operating in the outlying residential areas employed the journeymen outlawed by the Citizens Committee. A troubling byproduct of the conflict was the use by many building trades unions of professional thugs to intimidate nonunion workers and contractors through bombings and beatings. By the late 1920s, Al Capone and his gangsters had turned the tables on union members by taking control of many of the smaller building trades unions.

By the end of the decade, most contractors returned to union recognition. An extended era of cooperation and nonadversarial bargaining relations began, which was reinforced by two developments. The first was the pro-collective-bargaining legislation of the NEW DEAL in the 1930s and 1940s. Second, after WORLD WAR II, a 30-year building boom, whose yearly average of residential units built approached that of the 1920s, permitted contractors to pass union wages onto the public. In the early 1980s, the construction industry was hit with a major recession, followed by substantial expansion from the late 1980s to the end of the century.

Most worrisome to labor has been the decline, beginning in the 1970s, of general contractors employing all the basic trades (carpenters, painters, iron workers, laborers, cement masons, bricklayers) to build a building. General contractors have been replaced by project managers whose entire business is brokering bids to subcontractors. As a result, there is more specialization in the basic trades, more cutthroat bidding, a resurgence of piecework, and more white-collar middlemen in the industry. Though union contractors still control a majority of residential, industrial, and commercial work in the metropolitan area, the short duration of most contracts makes it difficult for business agents to police collective-bargaining agreements and has allowed small immigrant-owned nonunion firms a niche in the basic trades.

Since the 1970s, the building trades have opened their doors, reluctantly at first, to African American, Latino, and even a trickle of women workers. By the 1980s, apprenticeship programs had been integrated and many unions had outreach programs. The carpenters district council claimed at the end of the century that approximately 20 to 25 percent of its membership is black or Latino. Union leadership, however, remained largely white and male.

Richard Schneirov

See also: Building Codes and Standards; Built Environment of the Chicago Region; Chicago Crime Commission; Mafia; Quarrying, Stonecutting, and Brickmaking; Unionization; Work Culture

Further reading: Hoyt, Homer. *One Hundred Years of Land Values in Chicago.* 1929. • Montgomery, Royal E. *Industrial Relations in the Chicago Building Trades.* 1927. • Schneirov, Richard, and Thomas J. Suhrbur. *Union Brotherhood, Union Town: The History of the Carpenters' Union of Chicago, 1863–1987.* 1988.

Built Environment of the Chicago Region. ARCHITECTURE has always loomed large in accounts of Chicago. Famous architects like William Le Baron Jenney, Daniel Burnham, Louis Sullivan, Frank Lloyd Wright, Mies van der Rohe, and Skidmore, Owings & Merrill are firmly embedded in local history and lore, as are buildings celebrated in architectural history like the Monadnock, Rookery, AUDITORIUM BUILDING, Robie House, and Sears Tower. The particular kind of fascination with architecture seen in Chicago suggests certain characteristic attitudes. Whereas in older European and American cities the major monuments are often palaces, governmental buildings, and great cathedrals, Chicago's monuments have more often than not been business buildings, houses, SCHOOLS and churches. In its concentration on these landmarks of daily use, the city seems to celebrate its democratic, mercantile, and middle-class character. The creation of a comfortable built environment for a very large portion of the population, more than any individual buildings, no matter how successful, stands as the Chicago area's crowning architectural achievement.

From the Founding to the Fire

For the great city of Chicago to rise from its marshy site a number of important infrastructure works were necessary. In the years before the Great Fire the most important were the construction of the ILLINOIS & MICHIGAN CANAL between 1836 and 1848, the WATER system designed by engineer Ellis Chesbrough in the 1860s, and the city's great RAILROAD system. Despite these impressive works, however, the city itself during most of the mid-nineteenth century would have looked to most observers little different from many other young and fast-growing Midwestern cities. Small, mostly wood, buildings straggled alongside unpaved roads that were alternately dusty and muddy. Even the most conspicuous structures in the city were relatively small and unimpressive by the standards of larger Midwestern cities like St. Louis, not to mention those of Eastern cities and the European capitals. It was not until the last years before the fire that great commercial emporia like Marshall Field and hotels like the Palmer House rising on State Street gave Chicago buildings to rival those in more established places.

From a small gridiron plat around the meeting of the south and north forks of the CHICAGO RIVER, the city bounded outward by annexing adjacent development, virtually all of it laid out in conformity with the original plat and the regular mile-square grid pattern of the American land survey specified by Congress in 1785. The relatively low density of Chicago's residential neighborhoods and the high percentage of single-family detached homes rather than the tightly packed tenements and row houses of cities in the eastern United States and Europe was in part the result of a new construction technique, the BALLOON FRAME. Although this technique, in which the use of LUMBER in standardized sizes and machine-cut nails made possible rapid and inexpensive construction, has sometimes been claimed as a Chicago invention, this claim is dubious. Not only do the origins of the balloon frame appear to go back well before the founding of Chicago, but it was also only one step in a long process of substituting prefabrication for handwork. Whatever its origin, the balloon frame undoubtedly helped make possible, during the middle decades of the nineteenth century, a CONSTRUCTION boom in Chicago unmatched by any city up to that date. By the time of the Great Fire a large part of the population, including many factory workers, could afford what was then the extraordinary luxury of a single-family detached home, often a small one-story or story-and-a-half frame or brick house known as a workman's cottage. Entire neighborhoods of these cottages were erected on all sides of the central business district. Many can still be seen today in close-in neighborhoods like BRIDGEPORT on the SOUTH SIDE or OLD TOWN on the North Side.

Another reason the city could grow so quickly and at densities so much lower than older cities was that Chicago grew up with PUBLIC TRANSPORTATION. During the years before the fire, the horse-drawn STREET RAILWAY and the cable car allowed a vast expansion of the settled area. The advent of the steam railroad permitted suburban settlements well beyond the continuously developed urban fabric. Many of these railroad suburbs were upper-middle-class enclaves. RIVERSIDE, designed by Frederick Law Olmsted and Calvert Vaux with large lots, carefully planned curving streets, and generous public open spaces, was the most famous early American suburb in the picturesque mode. Other outlying communities, like BLUE ISLAND, were industrial, accommodating factories and working-class housing. By the time of the Great Fire, suburbs radiated outward from the central city along the railroad lines like beads on a necklace.

From the Fire to the First World War

The Great FIRE OF 1871 wiped out much of the central area of Chicago. Because much of the INFRASTRUCTURE and industrial capacity of the city had already decentralized, this disaster did not destroy the city's production capacity. Moreover, with the aid of insurance money and investment funds drawn primarily from Eastern cities, the city rebuilt rapidly. Despite new laws enacted to guard against the worst fire hazards, the immediate post-fire rebuilding tended to reproduce the pre-fire configurations.

In the years between the Great Fire and the First World War, Chicago became a great industrial power and had its period of greatest sustained growth. It captured the imagination of individuals around the world as the "shock city" of its day, the place where people came to see the emerging metropolis of the future. This growth was made possible in part by a vast expansion in basic infrastructure. Perhaps the most striking improvement was a massive program to remove the health hazards caused by dumping untreated sewage into the lake, which was where Chicago got its fresh WATER SUPPLY. The solution, finally completed at the turn of the century after monumental engineering work directed by the newly formed Sanitary District of Chicago, was to reverse the flow of the CHICAGO and CALUMET RIVERS. Another major public undertaking was the creation, by the federal government, of a major port at Lake Calumet by dredging that started at the end of the 1860s. Finally, there was the extension of the TRANSPORTATION system and the appearance of the electric streetcar and then, starting in the early 1890s, the elevated RAPID TRANSIT train.

The most striking physical manifestation of the city's modernity was seen in the LOOP, the central business district named originally for a circuit of cable car lines that encircled it and reinforced, after 1897, by the Loop elevated. Here, starting in the 1880s, a group of buildings burst through the four- to five-story plateau that had marked the upper limit of practical commercial construction until that time. Promptly dubbed SKYSCRAPERS, these new buildings had become practical with the advent of the passenger elevator, new methods of foundations and fireproofing, and other technological advances. Skyscrapers had actually appeared in New York in the 1870s, a decade earlier than in Chicago, but because Chicago's business district was smaller and the pace of construction greater in the 1880s, it was along broad, regular streets like Dearborn and LaSalle in Chicago's Loop where these buildings found their most striking and characteristic expression as a cliff of large, rectangular structures with relatively little ornament but enormous plate glass windows. Although they were a source of civic pride, their enormous scale and fears about their safety also inspired intense hostility. This novel cityscape attracted worldwide attention and comment.

These office buildings, lofts, and retail buildings were the work of a large number of urban professionals, including developers like the Brooks brothers of Boston, agents like Owen Aldis, architects like William Le Baron Jenney, Burnham & Root, Holabird & Roche, and Adler & Sullivan, engineers like Charles Strobel, William Sooy Smith, and Corydon T. Purdy, and contractors like George A. Fuller, who developed the first large-scale general contracting firm in the country. All of these men played major roles in the creation of the first buildings with complete metal skeletons and relatively thin exterior claddings, a system that finally came of age about 1890.

As land prices rose in the business district, activities that required large amounts of inexpensive space tended to move further afield. This led to the creation, among other industrial areas, of the Chicago UNION STOCK YARD starting in the 1860s, the company town of PULLMAN in the 1880s, and the Central Manufacturing District, perhaps the country's first planned industrial district, at the turn of the century.

Explosive growth also brought congestion, noise, and pollution. This led, in turn, to a constant outward movement of families searching for greener, less congested living environments. In this process of dispersal the city's residential areas came to be marked by an increasing segregation and contrast between rich and poor neighborhoods, ranging from the slums and tenement areas close to the Loop to the mansions of the GOLD COAST, relocated in the late nineteenth century from just south of the business district to north of the Loop. Both poor and affluent areas were relatively small in area, though, compared to the large working- and middle-class SUBDIVISIONS that pushed outward in all directions. During these years residential developers, led by Samuel E. Gross, perhaps the country's largest, transformed the housing industry by building large numbers of units and entire subdivisions at a time. Single-family houses were interspersed with the city's characteristic two-flat and three-flat APARTMENT buildings as well as, in affluent areas, the newly fashionable "French flats," or apartment buildings for the affluent.

Complementing the new residences were the neighborhood SCHOOLS, churches, and other community buildings as well as miles of retail frontage along arterial streets, particularly the major diagonal roads and the large streets that ran along the mile-square grid lines. Also complementing the residential subdivisions was a major system of parks and boulevards, projected in the late 1860s but not finished for several decades, that encircled the built-up portion of the city from JACKSON PARK in the south to LINCOLN PARK in the north. This system was in part a sanitary effort, offering what citizens of the time thought of as reservoirs of light and air in a congested and polluted city and in part a means to enhance the REAL-ESTATE value of adjacent property.

The same diversity marked the railroad suburbs beyond the city limits. At the upper end of the scale were elegant places like EVANSTON and KENILWORTH on the North Shore. The most affordable included some of the suburbs to the south like DOLTON or EAST CHICAGO in Indiana. In the middle range, on all sides of the city, were the vast majority of suburban communities. Beyond the suburbs, booming satellite industrial cities like JOLIET, AURORA, WAUKEGAN, and GARY, Indiana, each had a business center and outlying districts as well as a range of economic activities, income levels, and building types similar to those of Chicago itself but on a reduced scale.

This period also saw the first efforts at systematic city planning. The White City, the

World's Columbian Exposition of 1893, with its coordinated planning and clean white architecture, marked a strong contrast with the often chaotic gray city to the north. It became a model for subsequent planning efforts and a major inspiration for the famous 1909 *Plan of Chicago* by Daniel Burnham and Edward Bennett and many subsequent plans across the Chicago area and the nation. Although most of the ideas espoused in the plan had been formulated by others in the years prior to its publication, and although only a few of its provisions were actually executed, this plan quickly became the country's most famous urban planning document and has exerted a hold on the imagination of Chicagoans ever since.

Between the Wars

Between the world wars, particularly during the boom years of the 1920s, a continued increase in density of land use in and around the Loop was accompanied by a continued outward push of residential development at ever lower densities at the perimeter. This pattern was possible because increased affluence had led to greater personal mobility, particularly after a dramatic increase in the 1920s in car ownership and the construction of new and better roads. By the onset of World War II an entire expressway system for the metropolitan area had been planned, and a stretch of Lake Shore Drive with limited access and cloverleafs, one of the earliest such installations in the country, had already been constructed. Another key piece of infrastructure of these years was Municipal (later Midway) airport, which opened in 1927 and soon became the nation's busiest.

Within the Loop a new generation of sleek new high buildings, often with towers made possible by the provisions of the 1923 zoning ordinance, dominated the skyline. The completion of a bridge over the Chicago River at the north end of Michigan Avenue and its continuation as a great commercial boulevard made possible a new retail district north of the river that would eventually eclipse State Street as Chicago's most important center for upscale shopping.

The increasing affluence of the 1920s also allowed for a vast expansion in residential development. Within the city and inner suburbs a large number of solid but modest structures known as "Chicago bungalows," really an updated version of the worker's cottage, created a broad band on all sides of the city center and extending outward to suburbs like Berwyn, which had a particularly spectacular collection of these houses. Another important development was the growth of apartment districts in places like Uptown, Rogers Park, Hyde Park, and South Shore, where railroad and rapid transit lines provided easy acess to downtown. With the rapid development of new residential districts and the increasing use of the automobile came the growth of regional shopping and business centers, the most notable located at the elevated stations at Englewood on the South Side and Uptown on the North Side. These became miniature versions of downtown with their own department stores, specialty shops, movie theaters, and other urban services. Development further out grew even more quickly, with new subdivisions around existing railroad suburbs and entirely new communities in areas opened up by the automobile. As in previous eras, these suburbs ranged from elegant upper-income places to working-class suburbs and industrial satellites.

Home Building and Sanborn Insurance Atlases

A house's exterior can tell a lot about its builder. A large, distinctive house of brick or stone was probably designed by an architect and built to order. A modest, single-story, and equally unusual frame house might have been built by the owner, especially if it differs from its neighbors in style, materials, and street setback. An imperfection is a giveaway. In contrast, uniformity of any kind indicates the activity of a professional who built "on spec." Even when speculative builders tried to create diversity, as Samuel Gross did on Alta Vista Terrace in Chicago's Lake View Community Area, they left their mark. Many Chicago areas were developed with a singular vision. Riverside was the province of the custom builder and Stone Park of the owner-builder. Whole districts were speculatively built during the building booms of the 1880s, the 1920s, and after World War II.

Where redevelopment, renovation, and infill have left their mark an excellent source of information about original development is the Sanborn fire insurance atlas. Prepared and revised irregularly for fire insurance purposes for thousands of cities across the United States, the Sanborn maps show structures that were attached to the land. For each dwelling they show construction material, number of stories, external dimensions, and location on the lot.

A Sanborn streetscape reveals at a glance the presence of different types of builders. A good, because unexceptional, example is the pair of blocks on North Newcastle between Diversey and Wellington Avenues. In 1951 the Sanborn shows that on the west side, south of George, were nine dwellings. No two were identical; most were of frame construction; three sat at the back of the lot; and one that occupied a double lot (number 2842) had an unusual footprint. Here is the sign of the owner-builder. One block over were rows of brick veneer bungalows of almost identical design and size. They were surely the product of speculative builders.

Comparing Sanborns for successive years offers insights into the development process. The evolution of the block bounded by Newcastle, New England, Diversey, and George reveals the extended process that was typical of owner-development. Nine dwellings existed here in 1919, but by 1951 there were still vacant lots. In the interim two dwellings on North New England (numbers 2843 and 2853) had been replaced, while others, including two on North Newcastle (numbers 2832 and 2842) were extended. Improvement and replacement were common as owner-builders saved and prospered. In contrast, blocks of speculative construction were completed in a single building season.

Richard Harris

The Postwar Decades

After the Second World War most of the building patterns already established in the 1920s resumed but on a larger scale. The long boom of the postwar decades included tremendous investment in infrastructure, particularly for automobile and air travel. Construction of the region's expressway system, projected in the 1930s, started in earnest after the war with local funding but was greatly accelerated by the federal funds available through the Interstate Highway Act of 1956. At the same time, the area's public transportation system, temporarily buoyed by ridership increases during World War II, continued a long decline. The Chicago Transit Authority, created in 1947 to take over private transit operations, first required a subsidy in 1970 and has, since then, seen round after round of subsidy hikes and ridership declines. Along with a rise in automobile travel came an enormous increase in air travel, particularly with the development of the commercial airline and the creation of a new airport, O'Hare Field, which soon took over from Midway the title of the nation's busiest.

Despite the apparent vigor of the region, there was considerable concern about the future. Chicago's industrial plant had not been updated sufficiently during the long years of the Great Depression and war to keep pace with developments in the Sun Belt and elsewhere. Much of the central business district was old and congested. Beyond the Loop were square miles of industrial and residential land that were considered obsolete and blighted. Civic and government leaders hoped to counter these problems with new planning techniques and an aggressive program of urban renewal.

In the Loop itself, after a relatively short postwar lull, a building boom in the late 1950s through the 1960s that rivaled those of the 1880s and 1920s was initiated largely by private real-estate interests. The new structures included some of the largest and tallest office buildings in the world, notably Sears Tower and the John Hancock Building, both by Skidmore, Owings & Merrill, Chicago's most successful postwar corporate architecture firm. Other major undertakings in the central business district included a large planned development at Illinois Center, an enormous convention center complex at McCormick Place along the lakefront to the south of the Loop, and, to the north along Michigan Avenue, the creation of elaborate mixed-use complexes, starting with Water Tower Place in the early 1970s.

The prognosis for residential areas around the Loop, however, was less bright. Here postwar planners saw mostly older houses, decay, and blight. They initiated aggressive urban renewal programs that resulted in the demolition and rebuilding of large areas, including, for example, most of the NEAR SOUTH SIDE. In the place of the demolished structures rose new houses and apartment buildings such as Prairie Shores and Lake Meadows, institutional structures like a new MICHAEL REESE HOSPITAL, and a new campus for the ILLINOIS INSTITUTE OF TECHNOLOGY. In some cases, like the townhouses in Hyde Park on the South Side and the apartments of SANDBURG VILLAGE on the North Side, the planners' intentions of stabilizing neighborhoods and retaining middle-income residents in the city were at least partially realized. On the other hand, the creation of massive PUBLIC HOUSING projects, particularly the high-rise apartment buildings of the ROBERT TAYLOR HOMES on the South Side and the CABRINI-GREEN complex on the North Side, proved to be highly problematic.

Many of the most successful developments seemed to have had nothing to do with planning. Many older, apparently decaying neighborhoods near the center that were spared demolition from urban renewal bounced back as middle- and upper-middle-class communities through a process of private restoration and GENTRIFICATION. This change coincided, however, with a continuous loss of jobs and income in many neighborhoods further out. Large parts of the South and West Sides, particularly, were hard hit as high-paying industrial jobs disappeared, and racial and ethnic change created instability.

While city population declined after World War II, suburban development boomed. At one end of the spectrum were places like BARRINGTON HILLS to the northwest and OAK BROOK to the west. Here substantial houses occupied lots that often exceeded an acre in size. At the other end of the scale was PARK FOREST, a planned community developed immediately after the war in the far south suburbs that contained a mix of small ranch houses (the postwar equivalent to the interwar bungalows) and garden apartments as well as a shopping center and a wide variety of community structures. This attempt to completely master plan a community, while widely hailed and intensively studied, never became typical. Instead most development proceeded as it had in the past, with a patchwork of residential subdivisions and industrial and retail development all done by private interests and schools, parks, and public buildings put in place by local governments. The vast majority of suburban development was based on subdivisions of middle-class ranch houses and split-levels with four to eight houses per acre, for example, in MORTON GROVE and NILES to the north or FRANKLIN PARK and MELROSE PARK to the west.

With the residential growth came major new business developments. Industrial concerns continued their push out from the center to the periphery, occupying newly created complexes for themselves or quarters in planned industrial parks. Located just west of O'Hare Airport, for example, the Centex Industrial Park was the largest of its kind in the country. Along with the industrial parks came office parks and SHOPPING DISTRICTS, such as a trio of pioneering open-air centers in the 1950s, including River Oaks in the south suburbs, OAK BROOK in the west suburbs, and Old Orchard in the north suburbs.

Since the 1970s

In recent decades renewal at the core has proceeded at the same time as continued outward growth. Despite all of the fears, particularly during the dark years of industrial decline and civil unrest in the late 1960s and early 1970s, Chicago's central area did not collapse. An increase in the number of jobs in the Loop devoted to high-level corporate, financial, and legal business as well as a growing economy based on TOURISM and culture led to a massive office building boom starting in the 1980s. The central area also saw an increasing residential population, with the conversion of loft and office buildings like those in the PRINTER'S ROW area just south of the Loop, the construction of large new apartment buildings such as Presidential Towers just west of the Loop, and the development of entire new residential neighborhoods like the one at DEARBORN PARK just south of the Loop. Meanwhile, gentrification spread from a small nucleus in Old Town on the Near North Side to include very substantial areas of the North and Northwest Sides. By 2000, new building and rehabilitation were evident even in some of the most depressed areas of the West and South Sides, giving reason for some optimism despite continuing high rates of poverty and crime in many neighborhoods in the city and growing problems in some of the inner-ring suburbs and elsewhere in the area.

Despite the stabilization and revitalization of the core, the majority of growth in the metropolitan area has continued to take place at the periphery. In some key areas important new infrastructure has been constructed. Some of the area's most difficult problems of flooding and wastewater treatment were addressed by new wastewater treatment facilities and the massive Tunnel and Reservoir Project (TARP, more commonly known as the DEEP TUNNEL), which stores water after heavy rains until wastewater treatment plants have the capacity to treat it. The transportation infrastructure, on the other hand, has not kept up with demand. Although automobile ownership and use has continued to increase, relatively few new highways have been built, and public transit has not managed to maintain, let alone increase, its share of trips areawide. The result has been increasing congestion. Much the same problem plagues the city's airports. Even with massive rebuildings at O'Hare and Midway, the region's air traffic system has become increasingly inadequate, threatening the region's economic vitality and quality of life.

Despite well-meaning regional plans, most of the development in the area has been due to private initiative more than public planning, which is largely local and often quite piecemeal. By 2000, new suburban residential developments had pushed to the east along

Philip Klutznick: Shopping as a Real-Estate Deal

Philip M. Klutznick's work as a real-estate developer in the second half of the twentieth century had a profound effect on the Chicago region. He was instrumental in the development of PARK FOREST as a community planned around a shopping center in the late 1940s. His subsequent involvement in the creation of OAK BROOK and Old Orchard Shopping Centers related to his understanding of the important role that shopping centers could play in suburban life.

Old Orchard, designed as an outdoor, unenclosed shopping mall with a good mix of high-quality competitive merchants, was meant to attract a year-round patronage of people who would enjoy walking around the mall as part of their experience of shopping.

Klutznick brought this perspective into Chicago in 1973, when Marshall Field's asked him to help develop a new store on the Near North Side:

> Several sites considered for the Marshall Field store proved too costly or were unavailable. But one location near the north end of Michigan Avenue seemed to have real possibilities. It was owned by the liquor firm of Joseph Seagram and Company, whose principal stockholder was the Sam Bronfman family. Sam was an old friend whom I used to see in New York when I was working at the United Nations.

Klutznick arranged the sale of the Seagram property for $10 million, as well as additional property from the John Hancock Life Insurance Company. On the site, Klutznick supervised development of Water Tower Place.

Klutznick, Philip M., and Sidney Hyman. *Angles of Vision: A Memoir of My Lives.* 1991, 190, 310–311.

LAKE MICHIGAN toward the Michigan border, to the south toward Kankakee, to the west well past the FOX RIVER, and to the north deep into southern Wisconsin. House sizes at all economic levels have increased, although lot sizes have declined and increasingly large numbers of rental apartments and row houses have started to appear in the suburbs.

Along with the residential developments have come new shopping centers, strip malls, discount centers, and other retail establishments. Office, business, and industrial parks, like the Meridian Business Park in AURORA, have grown in size and sophistication. The most spectacular phenomenon of the last several decades has been the rise of large outlying business centers. The most important is located at SCHAUMBURG, surrounding the Woodfield Mall, an enclosed shopping center that was the largest in the country at the time of its completion in 1971. Around the mall has grown a large collection of office, retail, and HOTEL buildings that at the opening of the twenty-first century constituted the largest business district in Illinois outside of Chicago's Loop. Together with other business centers like the master-planned center at Oak Brook and the largely unplanned centers near O'Hare airport and ROSEMONT, these business districts have helped create what is effectively a multinucleated structure for the metropolitan area.

One of the most remarkable aspects of this outward expansion since the 1920s has been the relatively slow growth in population but large increase in occupied land. For an increasing number of critics this constitutes "sprawl," an undesirable, uncoordinated, and wasteful development pattern. The decline in density has actually slowed since World War II, however, and ENVIRONMENTAL problems, while significant and troubling, are perhaps less worrisome, at least at the local level, than they were in the past. It is perhaps more useful to consider recent developments, like the history of Chicago's development from the beginning, as an apparently hasty, unplanned, and chaotic process that, nevertheless, has actually been marked by a great deal of internal order and can be seen as the logical result of a vast increase in wealth, mobility, and choice by a very large number of Chicagoans.

Robert Bruegmann

See also: Commercial Buildings; Church Architecture; Economic Geography; Housing Types; Land Use; Landscape Design; Metropolitan Growth; Places of Assembly; Planning Chicago; Suburbs and Cities as Dual Metropolis

Further reading: A basic source for the development of the built environment for the Chicago area remains Harold M. Mayer and Richard C. Wade, *Chicago: Growth of a Metropolis* (1969), a durable classic still unsurpassed as a treatment of the built environment of a large American city. During the decades between the 1950s and 1970s, Carl Condit created a large corpus of work on the architecture and infrastructure of the city that remains a valuable resource. His most important books include *The Chicago School of Architecture* (1964); *Chicago, 1910–29: Building, Planning, and Urban Technology* (1973); and *Chicago, 1930–70: Building, Planning, and Urban Technology* (1974).

These large compendia are complemented by important works on more specific topics, such as Frank A. Randall, *History of the Development of Building Construction in Chicago* (1949; second edition 1999), which remains the best source for information about buildings in the Central Business District, and Chicago Department of Public Works, *Chicago Public Works: A History* (1973), which provides a good overview of public infrastructure development.

Since the 1970s a number of books have appeared that look into other parts of the story of building the Chicago region from new perspectives. Among these are Ann Durkin Keating, *Building Chicago: Suburban Developers and the Creation of a Divided Metropolis* (1988), which gives an excellent account of the relationship between city building, metropolitan services, and governmental structure; Daniel Bluestone, *Constructing Chicago* (1991), which has excellent chapters on aspects of Chicago development that had been somewhat neglected earlier, notably the park system, public buildings, and religious, civic, and cultural facilities, as well as an excellent treatment of the history of the skyscraper; and Miles Berger, *They Built Chicago: Entrepreneurs Who Shaped a Great City's Architecture* (1992), a very good account of the financial underpinnings of Chicago's famous buildings. In *The Architects and the City: Holabird & Roche of Chicago, 1880–1918* (1997), Robert Bruegmann discusses a wide variety of building types in the urban fabric as seen through the lens of the work of a single large firm. Finally, a two-volume set of catalogs created for exhibitions held at the Art Institute of Chicago and edited by John Zukowsky, *Chicago Architecture, 1872–1922: Birth of a Metropolis* (1987) and *Chicago Architecture and Design, 1923–1993: Reconfiguration of an American Metropolis* (1993), provide multiple perspectives on a wide variety of subjects connected with the built environment of the city.

Bulgarians. When, in 1893, the famous Bulgarian writer Aleko Konstantinov recounted his journey to the WORLD'S COLUMBIAN EXPOSITION, he could not have known that his remarkable book *Do Chikago i nazad* (To Chicago and Back) would become instrumental in the immigration and the choice of final destination of generations of Bulgarians. By the year 2000 the Chicago area was among the largest Bulgarian settlements in the United States. The census counted 5,683 people of Bulgarian ancestry in metropolitan Chicago, and unofficial community estimates ranged from 20,000 to 30,000.

The first Bulgarians who began to arrive in Chicago, as early as 1870s, were students sent by American Protestant missionaries for further study in the United States. Most returned, but those who remained formed the basis of an ethnic presence.

There were two major waves of Bulgarian immigration to the United States. In the beginning of the twentieth century, unemployment and overpopulation stimulated emigration. Approximately 50,000 predominantly single men from Bulgaria proper ("the kingdom") and from its lost territory of Macedonia moved to the United States in the first years of the twentieth century. Most were peasants or unskilled laborers who worked in mines, steel mills, or railroad construction.

The second wave began with the fall of state socialism in Eastern Europe. After 1989, thousands of young, well-educated Bulgarians arrived in Chicago, not with the intention of earning some money and returning back home as many of their predecessors had, but intent on building a new life in America. Between those two waves, because of the U.S. restriction on immigration in the period from 1924 to 1965 and changes in Bulgarian emigration regulations, only small numbers of job-seeking youths and opponents to the Communist regime emigrated.

Bulgarians initially formed a distinct community centered on Adams Street, just east of Halsted. The first two Bulgarian bookstores in the United States opened there, as well as a growing number of bakeries, taverns, and travel and employment agencies. Later, numerous Bulgarian families that had traveled to America through Germany settled among GERMANS in LINCOLN SQUARE or in ALBANY PARK before moving to the northern suburbs.

In 1902, the first Bulgarian newspaper, *Struggle*, appeared in Chicago, followed by *Bulgarian News* a year later. Around 1905, the first Bulgarian Protestant Group was organized. An evangelical mission *Zhivot* (Life), a neighborhood cultural club, and a few fraternal and MUTUAL BENEFIT SOCIETIES were started in 1911. The two Bulgarian EASTERN ORTHODOX churches, St. Sophia, established in 1938, and St. John of Rila, founded in 1996, have been not only religious places but also social centers devoted to maintaining ethnic awareness, language, and traditions through Sunday schools and social gatherings. The numerous political organizations that Bulgarians have joined or established, such as the Macedonian Political Organization (founded 1922), the Bulgarian Socialist Labor Federation (1910–1917), the American Slav Congress (1930s), the right-wing Bulgarian National Committee—Free and Independent Bulgaria (founded 1949), and the Bulgarian National Front (founded 1958), have also aimed at preserving ethnic pride. Chicagoans of Bulgarian descent more recently contributed to metropolitan culture with the festivities on the occasion of the donation of the bust of Aleko Konstantinov to the UNIVERSITY OF CHICAGO in November 1996.

Daniela S. Hristova

See also: Americanization; Demography; Multicentered Chicago

Further reading: *25th Anniversary Jubilee Almanac of "Naroden Glas," the Oldest Bulgarian National Newspaper in America* [in Bulgarian]. 1933. • Abbott, Grace. "The Bulgarians of Chicago." *Charities and the Commons* 21 (January 1909): 653–660. • Altankov, Nikolay. *The Bulgarian-Americans.* 1979.

Bull Valley, IL, McHenry County, 52 miles NW of the Loop. Local residents voted to incorporate in 1977 to protect their estate-style development, tucked into hilly, wooded terrain. Containing historic 1850s buildings such as the noted Terwilliger and Stickney houses, the carefully developing community still prizes its rural atmosphere. The population in 2000 was 726.

Craig L. Pfannkuche

See also: McHenry County

Further reading: *McHenry County in the Twentieth Century, 1968–1994.* McHenry County Historical Society. 1994.

Bulls. It would seem the Chicago Bulls have been around forever. Six NBA championships create a sense of history, especially when they occur within eight years. Yet the franchise wasn't born until 1966, as an expansion team with Johnny "Red" Kerr as coach, and not until the 1990s did the Bulls become one of the most successful dynasties in all of sports.

The Bulls enjoyed a mini-boom with the playoff teams of the early seventies featuring coach Dick Motta and such stars as Jerry Sloan, Bob Love, and Chet Walker. In the late eighties, when new owner Jerry Reinsdorf and general manager Jerry Krause drafted Scottie Pippen and Horace Grant and traded for veteran center Bill Cartwright to join veteran guard John Paxson and their superstar, Michael Jordan, the Bulls dynasty began to take shape under coach Doug Collins.

The 1989 hiring of Phil Jackson as head coach provided the final puzzle piece for the hungry team that prided itself on a disciplined offense and a fierce pressing defense. The Bulls knocked off division nemesis Detroit in a four-game sweep in the 1991 Eastern Conference Finals, then dismantled the Lakers in the NBA Finals. The Bulls put together their first "three-peat" by sprinting through the Eastern Conference then running over Portland in the '92 Finals and Phoenix in '93.

The shocking "retirement" of Jordan beginning October 6, 1993, coincided with the team's two-year absence from the NBA Finals. But Jordan's dramatic comeback in the spring of '95 and return to greatness reinstated the Bulls at the very top of the pack. The addition of such players as Ron Harper, Dennis Rodman, Toni Kukoc, and Steve Kerr helped the Bulls capture three more NBA titles, against Seattle in '96, then Utah in '97 and '98, for a second "three-peat" and six championships in all. For Jordan, it was also a crowning moment with his sixth Finals MVP award to go along with five regular-season MVPs and 10 scoring titles in his 13-year career.

With the 1998 departure of Jackson, Jordan, and others from the championship squad, the team started to rebuild. Meanwhile, the statue of Michael Jordan at the UNITED CENTER reminds Bulls fans of the team's past and sets high expectations for the future.

Melissa Isaacson

See also: Basketball; Creation of Chicago Sports

Further reading: Isaacson, Melissa. *Transition Game: An Inside Look at Life with the Chicago Bulls.* 1994. • Sachare, Alex. *The Chicago Bulls Encyclopedia.* 1999.

Bungalow Belt. Powerfully combining ARCHITECTURE, housing distribution, race, and POLITICS, "bungalow belt" is a quintessential Chicago term, referring generally to the bungalow-style single-family houses built in the 1910s and 1920s in a collar just inside the limits of the city of Chicago. A variety of racial and ethnic groups have owned these homes, from AFRICAN AMERICAN families on the far SOUTH SIDE to Orthodox JEWISH families on the far North Side. Despite this diversity, this term generally connotes the primarily white residents of the far Northwest and Southwest Sides who became the main support of Richard J. Daley and his DEMOCRATIC machine after 1968.

Ann Durkin Keating

See also: Built Environment of the Chicago Region; Housing Types; Political Culture

Further reading: Bigott, Joseph C. *From Cottage to Bungalow: Houses and the Working Class in Metropolitan Chicago, 1869–1929.* 2001. • Biles, Roger. *Richard J. Daley: Politics, Race, and the Governing of Chicago.* 1995. • Grimshaw, William. *Bitter Fruit: Black Politics and the Chicago Machine, 1931–1991.* 1992.

Bungalows. The word "bungalow" derives from the British colonial experience in India. After 1900, architects, builders, and developers adopted the term to describe modern houses built throughout the United States. In Chicago, a few architects had begun to design and build expensive, Craftsman-style, California-influenced bungalows in affluent locations of the city by 1910. When the housing market boomed in the twenties, developers throughout the metropolitan region marketed lower-priced "bungalows" to an expanding range of middle-class families. These structures all had modern plumbing, electricity, and central heating.

Within the city limits, a common form of bungalow was a rectangular brick structure with a modestly pitched, hip-raftered roof and a small distinctive front porch. It fit on narrow city lots and followed the floor plan of earlier one-story working-class houses. However, builders constructed a great variety of structures even in the city's classic "BUNGALOW BELT." Variety was still more common in the suburbs, especially those with larger lots that allowed builders greater freedom. Suburban bungalows were often one-and-one-half-story frame structures with steeply pitched roofs. These houses had bedrooms on the second floor, separated from the kitchen, parlor, and dining room.

By 1930, one-fourth of all residential structures in metropolitan Chicago were less than 10 years old, many of them bungalows, ranging in cost from about $2,500 to $10,000. A form of bungalow continued to be built in working-class areas of the SOUTH SIDE in the 1960s. However, the bungalow lost popularity among house buyers after WORLD WAR II, as ranches and split-levels became the dominant house forms in new areas. Recently, "historic" bungalows have resurged as popular housing in GENTRIFYING areas of the city. Promoters have praised the aesthetic virtues of an older style, most notably its woodwork and "craftsmanship." However, location and affluence apparently matter more than aesthetic values. In poor areas of the city, the same types of bungalow serve as affordable but out-of-date housing.

Joseph C. Bigott

See also: Built Environment of the Chicago Region; Housing Types; Metropolitan Growth

Further reading: Bigott, Joseph C. "Modest Bungalow Makes Metropolitan History." *Historic Illinois* 24.3 (October 2001): 3–6. • Bigott, Joseph C. *From Cottage to Bungalow: Houses and the Working Class in Metropolitan Chicago, 1869–1929.* 2001. • Pacyga, Dominic A., and Charles Shanabruch, eds. *The Chicago Bungalow.* 2001.

Burbank, IL, Cook County, 12 miles SW of the Loop. Burbank is one of the younger communities in COOK COUNTY. Incorporated in 1970, it is bordered by Chicago on the east, OAK LAWN on the south, BRIDGEVIEW on the west, and BEDFORD PARK on the north. The early history of Burbank features a series of false starts and frustrated plans.

The Burbank area contained scattered farms when in 1850 it became the southeastern portion of Lyons Township. One of the earliest roads to run through the area was the diagonal State Road that connected Ridgeland/Narragansett Avenues to Cicero Avenue. By 1871, State Road attracted the attention of a Pittsburgh investor who laid out a subdivision along this route that apparently never materialized. Instead GERMAN and DUTCH truck farmers settled in the area.

Railroad executive A. B. Stickney planned a massive freight RAILROAD transfer center that included the northern part of Burbank, but the 1893 depression curtailed his plans. In 1901, this area became the southern end of the newly formed Stickney Township, an 18-square mile tract split from the eastern side of Lyons Township.

The subdivision boom of the 1920s spread to this area as REAL-ESTATE developers bought up farmland and platted SUBDIVISIONS. But the ongoing drainage problems, poor roads, and inadequate WATER and sewer systems, as well as the GREAT DEPRESSION, dampened the enthusiasm of many would-be buyers.

The creation of the South Stickney Sanitary District in 1952 changed the course of Burbank's history. By 1959 the area known as South Stickney or Burbank Manor had a water and sewer system for the first time, and the flooding problems diminished. Roads were improved and streetlights installed. The area's population tripled during this decade, reaching an estimated 20,720 in 1960.

Burbank was the last part of Stickney Township to incorporate. In 1970, to avoid ANNEXATION by Chicago, residents formed the city of Burbank. The name was taken from the local Luther Burbank Elementary School, named after the famous horticulturist. Six years later, in 1976, the city's population peaked at 29,448. By 1979, nearly all of the city's land was subdivided. Burbank's population declined to 27,902 in 2000.

More than half of the city's revenue comes from retail sales taxes. Stores are concentrated along Harlem and Cicero Avenues, the city's main north-south thoroughfares, with some retail businesses also on 79th and 87th Streets. There is almost no manufacturing in Burbank.

The city covers approximately four square miles, only slightly larger than it was in 1970. A mayor, treasurer, city clerk, and seven aldermen run the government. Burbank's mostly white, middle-class residents drive to their places of business; almost half WORK in Chicago. Although there is no train service in Burbank, buses link residents to the CHICAGO TRANSIT AUTHORITY.

Betsy Gurlacz

See also: Commuting; Flood Control and Drainage; Government, Suburban

Further reading: Hill, Robert Milton. *A Little Known Story of the Land Called Clearing.* 1983. • *Our Township Government: Stickney's History from Indians to Skyscrapers.* 1942. • *Pioneers of Progress: The History of Stickney Township.* 1969.

Burlington, IL, Kane County, 48 miles W of the Loop. In 1851, Andrew Pingree platted Burlington, which had three cheese factories by 1878 and incorporated as a village in 1906. The last dairy plant closed in the 1970s. Burlington has been home to small plastics companies in recent decades and had a population of 452 in 2000.

Erik Gellman

See also: Kane County

Burmese. Burmese immigrants began coming to Chicago in large numbers in the early 1960s. A nation encompassing three major ethnic groups—INDIANS, CHINESE, and ethnic Burmese—Burma (Myanmar) was overrun by an anti-Communist military dictatorship in 1962. Nationalizing businesses and industry, the military regime prompted thousands of Indians and Chinese to flee to Nepal and Taiwan, from which some eventually emigrated to American cities. In 1964, the military targeted members of the opposing Burmese Socialist Program Party, prompting its members as well as political moderates to flee the country. Human rights violations and political repression continued through 1988, when a major student uprising in favor of democracy was crushed in Rangoon, sending thousands more into exile on the Burma/Thailand border.

By 1967, Chicago had become a destination for Burmese of all ethnicities able to obtain passports through bribery and political connections. Well-educated Burmese immigrants found relatively easy entry to the United States during the Vietnam War era and established a chain migration pattern to the city. In 1991–92, following the student rebellion, several hundred Burmese exiles living in camps in Thailand were granted entry to the United States as REFUGEES. Many received assistance from voluntary agencies and sponsors in Fort Wayne, Indiana, from which some later moved to Chicago.

By the late 1960s, Chicago had a sizeable community of Burmese immigrants, who in 1970 founded two organizations to provide aid and a cultural center for the newcomers. The Burmese-Chinese Association was established in CHINATOWN, where many of the ethnic Chinese from Burma settled. The Burmese-American Association of Chicago served members of the ethnic Burmese community, many of whom lived on the North Side, though not concentrated in any particular neighborhood. These associations provided the center of the Burmese community through the 1970s. By 1980, there were perhaps 500 Burmese families living in Chicago.

Most Burmese and Chinese Burmese practice Theravada Buddhism. In 1984 the Burmese BUDDHIST Association was formed. In 1987, the association purchased a building in Elmhurst which became its headquarters. The Buddhist Association grew throughout the late 1980s and early 1990s, maintaining cultural activities and religious holidays like the "Waso" and "Kathina" robe offerings, and the annual "Thingyan" celebration in April, in which the community pays its respects to elders. The Burmese Buddhist Association also continued to sponsor community picnics and social affairs.

In the wake of the defeated 1988 student uprising, some members of Chicago's Burmese community united in a strong political movement. The Burmese Community Development Association was organized in 1989 to send moral support to freedom fighters in the homeland, as well as to apply diplomatic pressure to the U.S. government and promote military intervention. At a conference in Chicago in 1990, the Development Association united with 10 other Burmese Associations from around the world to create the Burma Democratic Council International, which protested the military government in Burma/Myanmar and supported the resistance.

Community leaders estimated approximately 2,000 Burmese of all three ethnicities in Chicago at the close of the twentieth century. Many were working in service industries or in professions and generally considered themselves middle class. Because many hope to return to Burma in the future, close ties remain between the immigrants and the homeland. In 1991, Burmese doctors assembled to form the Midwest Burmese Medical Association. Members collected medical equipment and raised funds to donate to hospitals in Burma, and they traveled to Burma to instruct health care workers there.

Robert Morrissey

See also: Cambodians; Demography; Multicentered Chicago

Further reading: Oo, Aung Saw. *Burma's Student Movement: A Concise History.* 3rd ed. 1993.

Burnham, IL, Cook County, 18 miles S of the Loop. In 1883 a group of investors including George Pullman hired Telford Burnham to develop a commercial and residential plan for the point where the branches of the CALUMET RIVER meet before flowing north to Lake Calumet and Lake Michigan. The investors were aware of the growing steel industries across the CALUMET REGION. The Hammond Lumber Company had just built 500 feet of dock for shipping.

While investors hoped for commercial development in Burnham as well, TRANSPORTATION and housing needs were being spurred by the growing steel industries. The strong demand for workers' housing led to residential growth in Burnham, HEGEWISCH, and West Hammond (CALUMET CITY). These growing areas were closely connected to HAMMOND.

In 1907 residents voted to incorporate as the village of Burnham. The village's boundaries were (and are) Hammond on the east, Chicago on the north, and Calumet City to the south and west.

For 40 years, from 1908 to 1948, the history of Burnham was tied to the activities of its mayor, John Patton. When first elected, "Johnny" Patton was the youngest mayor in Illinois. Over the years, he developed the

CLOUT to bring Chicago WATER and sewer services into Burnham along with "pleasure-loving people." Only 40 minutes from the Loop, by car or the South Shore INTERURBAN line, the village was a lively place and Johnny was called the "livest wire of them all." One account from 1920 refers to it as the "cabaret town" of Cook County and adds that of all the small towns in the country, Burnham is "perhaps the one most often visited by amusement seeking visitors."

Even into the 1950s, Burnham was home to 11 taverns in its small central core. The oldest neighborhood, mostly housing for workers in regional industries, connects with the old center of town. In this area, several small factories and an industrial zone follow the river which cuts through Burnham. Rail lines still crisscross through the community, and on the west side is newer, postwar housing.

Burnham had 328 residents in 1910, 865 in 1940. Most of the housing on the west side was built after World War II, and this growth is reflected in the population increase from 1,331 in 1950 to 4,030 in 1980.

Early in its development, the village of Burnham created a public GOLF course on its eastern edge as an added attraction for its amusement seekers. This continues today as Burnham Woods, a public course owned and operated by the FOREST PRESERVE District of Cook County.

Although the big plans for docks and shipping never came to pass, Burnham continues as a predominantly residential village in the fabric of suburban communities tied together just south of Chicago.

Larry A. McClellan

See also: Governing the Metropolis; Underground Economy; Vice Districts

Further reading: "The Story of Burnham." *Hammond Times,* November 28, 1955. • Beaudette-Neil, E. Palma. *Thornton Township, Cook County, Illinois.* 1921, 75, 77. • McClellan, Larry A. "Burnham's Growth Shaped by Steel and the Calumet." *Star,* August 30, 1998.

The Plan of Chicago Downtown: What Was Accomplished

Congress Parkway
Envisioned in the *Plan* as a great boulevard to the west and the central spine of the city. When opened as an expressway in 1956, it included a transit line but had lost most of its "parkway" amenities.

Arterial street widening
Many miles of arterial streets were widened in the 1920s, with increased urgency due to burgeoning auto use.

Civic Center
Never attempted. A new City-County Building was under construction downtown even as *The Plan of Chicago* was being written.

Chicago River straightening
Accomplished as planned, 1927–29, but additional through streets were never opened, blocked by railroad facilities.

Roosevelt Road
Widened in 1926 as part of the *Plan*'s Inner Circuit" of roadways to route traffic around the central business district. Not extended across railroad tracks into Grant Park until 1997.

Grant Park
Cultural center of museums and libraries planned by Burnham was blocked by Montgomery Ward decisions limiting buildings in Grant Park; compromise site was found for Field Museum south of Roosevelt Road. Landfill and formal landscaping was guided by Bennett during the 1920s.

Northerly Island
Landfill for "Island No. 1" was constructed by South Park Commission in late 1920s. Intended as a combination of port and recreational facilities, the island (now a peninsula) was considered for an airport as early as 1924. Used for Century of Progress Exposition, 1933–34; and as Meigs Field airport, 1948–2003.

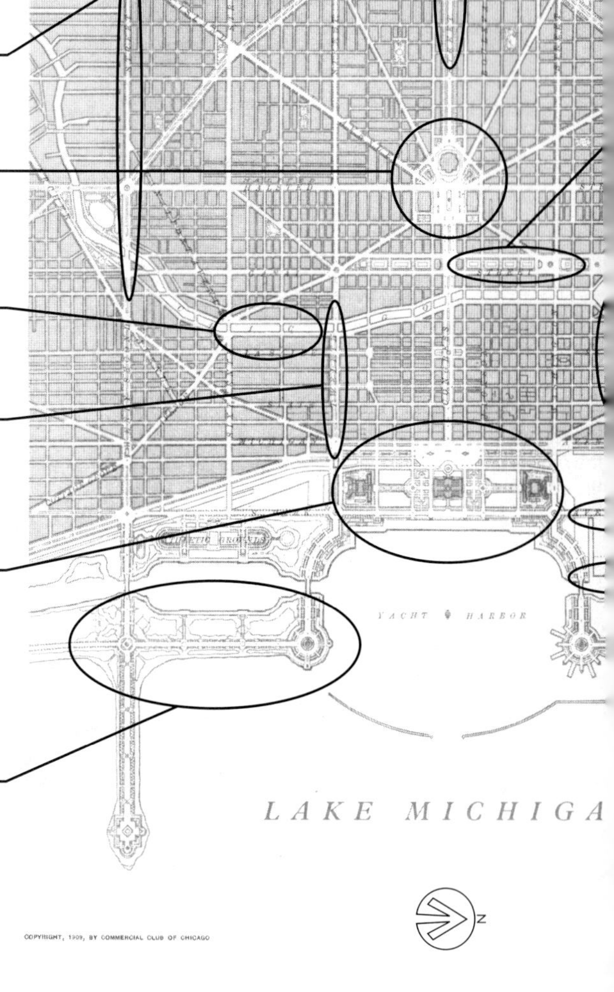

Burnham Plan. The visionary *Plan of Chicago* (1909) creates pictures of a City Beautiful, calls upon civic character to realize the goal, and characterizes Chicagoans as a people who can and will act in the best public interest to realize the vision. Such a combination of idealism and imagination distinguishes this work of Daniel Hudson Burnham and Edward H. Bennett, and the civic-minded citizens of the COMMERCIAL CLUB OF CHICAGO and the former Merchants Club who commissioned the work.

The plan consisted of a system of parks and broad avenues that transcended the street grid in a pattern reminiscent of the French Baroque tradition favored for nineteenth-century Paris. The physical integration of systems of TRANSPORTATION and systems of recreation was the organizing principle for the buildings, streets, and parks. In the following decades, as a result of a flexible and well-publicized planning process, the *Plan of Chicago* inspired the creation of a permanent greenbelt around the metropolitan area, the development of the lakefront parks with cultural enhancements such as the FIELD MUSEUM of Natural History, and the establishment of new transportation elements, from road to river to rail.

As a collaborative product, the work is unusually seamless. Nevertheless, it is clear that Edward Bennett, trained in the symmetrical sequential planning of space at the École Nationale Supérieure des Beaux-Arts, brought to the work formal training in large-scale design. He directed the planning and the preparation of the drawings. Daniel Burnham, self-taught and public-spirited, brought his experience and salesmanship from previous planning projects to the analysis and problem-solving aspects, both functional and popular. The *Plan of Chicago* represented a synthesis of lessons learned from the careers of both men, who together or individually developed plans for WORLD'S COLUMBIAN EXPOSITION and projects in Cleveland, the District of Columbia, San Francisco, and Manila.

The *Plan of Chicago*'s magnificent illustrations, maps, and plans created an enduring image. Generation's of schoolchildren throughout the city studied the plan in a manual prepared in 1911 by Walter D. Moody. Although planning in ensuing decades moved away from the design principles of the *Plan of Chicago,* the plan itself and its authors remain a familiar presence in Chicago urban thinking.

Cynthia R. Field

See also: Architecture: The City Beautiful; Magnificent Mile; Planning Chicago; Planning, City and Regional; Waterfront

Consolidated railroad stations

A new Union Station and adjacent street improvements were planned and built 1916–25 in line with the new North Western Station, but further consolidation of the six downtown railroad stations was never accomplished. The new Main Post Office was built south of Van Buren rather than between Madison and Adams.

New diagonal avenues

Ogden Avenue was the only one ever attempted, extended in the early 1930s across two costly bridges and through the densely built Old Town area. The entire route from Chicago Avenue to Lincoln Park had been vacated and removed by 1993.

Two-level riverfront drives

Wacker Drive displaced the city's produce market in 1926. An extension along the east bank of the South Branch opened in conjunction with the Eisenhower Expressway in the late 1950s. Similar drives along the facing riverbanks were never attempted, though space was left in 1928 in front of the Merchandise Mart.

Michigan Avenue bridge

Double-level boulevard bridge opened in 1920, extending the business district across the river and beginning the transformation of North Pine Street into a world-renowned retailing avenue.

Link bridge

Lake Shore Drive bridge opened 1937 east of location anticipated in the *Plan* for the extension of South Park Avenue.

Municipal piers

"Municipal Pier No. 2" (now Navy Pier) was completed in 1916, but at the foot of Grand Avenue rather than Chicago Avenue. As suggested in the *Plan*, recreational amenities such as a ballroom were integrated with shipping facilities.

Dennis McClendon

Further reading: Condit, Carl W. *Chicago, 1910–29: Building, Planning, and Urban Technology* (1973); and *Chicago, 1930–70: Building, Planning, and Urban Technology* (1974).

Burns Harbor, IN, Porter County, 32 miles SE of the Loop.

In 1962, Bethlehem Steel announced it would build its largest steel plant to date at Burns Harbor. In 2001, it ranked as one of the most efficient steel plants in the United States. Fewer than 1,000 residents lived in Burns Harbor at the end of the century.

Erik Gellman

See also: Iron and Steel

Burnside, Community Area 47, 11 miles S of the Loop. Burnside, the smallest of Chicago's community areas, is bounded entirely by RAILROADS—a distinctive and difficult-to-access triangle marked by the ILLINOIS CENTRAL RAILROAD on the west, the Rock Island on the south, and the New York Central on the east. Interestingly, it occupies a different physical place from what earlier Chicagoans knew as Burnside, an area that lies almost entirely in the community areas of ROSELAND and CHATHAM. Only with the mapping of UNIVERSITY OF CHICAGO sociologists did the area once known as Stony Island and subsequently the Burnside Triangle become Burnside.

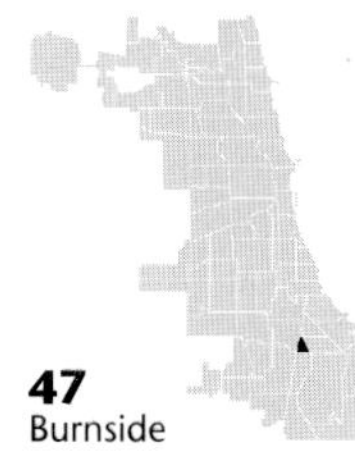

Situated on the low, swampy land surrounding Lake Calumet, the Triangle originally seemed more appropriate for industrial rather than residential development. When the Illinois Central established its Burnside station, named after former company official and Civil War general Ambrose Burnside, in 1862, what little development occurred took place west of the tracks. Not until the 1890s, when the Illinois Central Railroad (IC) began building a roundhouse and repair shops south of 95th Street on what is now the site of CHICAGO STATE UNIVERSITY, did developer W. V. Jacobs purchase and subdivide land in the Triangle. Settlement there proceeded slowly compared to the rest of Burnside. By 1911, when the entire area was embroiled in a STRIKE against the IC, the Triangle had become home to a small population of the newest immigrants—HUNGARIANS, ITALIANS, UKRAINIANS, and POLES most prominently—who occupied the least skilled jobs in the IC Burnside shops, the New York Central Stony Island shops, the Calumet & South Chicago street railway shops, the PULLMAN Car Works, Burnside Steel, and other factories nearby.

With their 400 homes and BOARDINGHOUSES spread sparsely over the 30 blocks of Burnside, residents had to build many of their own institutions because city institutions, with the exception of Perry Public School, were located primarily west of the IC tracks. Two churches were among the most important: the Hungarians' Our Lady of Hungary ROMAN CATHOLIC Church and the Ukrainians' Sts. Peter and Paul Church. These, along with the Burnside Settlement and the SCHOOL, offered citizenship classes, educational programs, and a variety of other opportunities and services. SALOONS, some with meeting halls, provided another venue where residents who lived in adjoining wooden homes and boardinghouses could meet.

Its well-defined physical boundaries (enhanced when the railroads were raised in the 1920s), small size, and residents' ethnic ties and common work experiences made Burnside a well-defined community socially in the years between the World Wars. They also meant Burnside attracted little outside attention. Even in the political arena, where it moved between the Ninth and Tenth Wards, it garnered little CLOUT and few rewards.

Only after World War II did the vacant residential land in Burnside attract the attention of developers and potential new residents. New single-family homes began to appear, especially in the most northerly, undeveloped areas. Homes for the middle class, they gradually changed the nature of Burnside, first by class and then, beginning in the 1960s, by race, as middle-class AFRICAN AMERICANS built their own homes or occupied those of European-heritage residents who left the neighborhood. In the mid-1970s, Burnside, like other SOUTH SIDE neighborhoods, suffered from the scandals associated with Federal Housing Authority loans that led to a high number of foreclosures.

By the end of the twentieth century, Burnside had again become a comfortable residential community, still well defined by the railroads that created it and still underserved by the city outside its boundaries.

Janice L. Reiff

See also: Americanization; Chicago Studied; Economic Geography; Multicentered Chicago; Railroad Workers

Further reading: City of Chicago, Department of Planning and Development. *Demographic and Housing Characteristics of Chicago and Burnside: Community Area #47 Profile*. 1994. • Davis, Berenice Davida. "Housing Conditions in the District of Burnside." M.A. thesis, University of Chicago. 1924.

Burr Ridge, IL, DuPage County, 17 miles SW of the Loop. Burr Ridge's gently rolling hills were carved by glaciers at the end of the last ice age, and most of the village lies on the Valparaiso Moraine. Flagg Creek, a tributary of the DES PLAINES RIVER, runs through town.

Joseph Vial erected a log cabin near Wolf and Plainfield Roads in 1834. Vial also ran a HOTEL on the stagecoach line, and the Vial family was actively involved in Lyons Township politics and the creation of the Lyonsville Congregational church. The first DEMOCRATIC Convention in Cook County was held here in 1835. After 1848, farmers shipped their goods to Chicago along the ILLINOIS & MICHIGAN CANAL. A small settlement of GERMAN farmers also inhabited Flagg Creek by the 1880s.

In 1917 the International Harvester Company purchased 414 acres for an experimental farm, where it tested the world's first all-purpose tractor, the Farmall. Also in 1917, the COOK COUNTY Prison Farm (also known as the Bridewell Farm) began operation in what is now Burr Ridge.

In 1947 developer Robert Bartlett, whose company also developed Beverly Shores and COUNTRYSIDE, established the Hinsdale Countryside Estates out of a former pig farm. In 1956 these residents decided to incorporate as the village of Harvester, in honor of International Harvester.

In the 1940s Denver Busby bought 190 acres that became known as the Burr Ridge dairy farm. He later launched the Burr Ridge Estates, with five-acre home sites. In 1961 the International Harvester Company and the Burr Ridges Estates merged with Harvester, changing the community's name to Burr Ridge. The town name is derived from a group of bur oaks (scientists spell it with one r) on a ridge. By 1963 the population had more than doubled, to 790, and by 1975 it had soared to over 2,200.

In 1969 Chicago Mayor Richard J. Daley floated a proposal to build low-income SUBSIDIZED HOUSING on the prison farm property, but REPUBLICAN-dominated DUPAGE COUNTY squashed the idea. The prison farm site became the Ambriance SUBDIVISION, a gated community of multimillion-dollar homes. Other farms gave way to the Carriage Way subdivision, and in 1971 additional farmland became the Braemoor neighborhood. An area known as Valley View, once owned by a Chicago industrialist and later by the Chicago chapter of the Boy SCOUTS of America, was developed in the early 1970s as the Burr Ridge Club. The village also has five corporate parks. As with other towns in the industrial corridor southwest of Chicago, close proximity to Interstates 294 and 55 spurred development in Burr Ridge.

By 1990 the population had risen to 7,669, a 100 percent increase over 1980. Into the 1990s Burr Ridge continued to aggressively annex surrounding land, growing to include seven square miles. The 1998 median home value weighed in at $470,000. An $8 million project at the turn of the century upgraded WATER mains, with water coming via BEDFORD PARK. The Robert Vial home, relocated to Pleasant Dale Park, now houses the Flagg Creek Historical Society.

Ronald S. Vasile

See also: Agricultural Machinery Industry; Glaciation; Innovation, Invention, and Chicago Business

Further reading: "Farmers Till the Rich Soil." *Doings*. September 3, 1981. • "Village of Burr Ridge: A Very Special Place." 1998 Calendar and Annual Report. • McCullough, Purdie. "A Very Special Place." Burr Ridge Bicentennial Committee, 1976.

Bus equipped for wheelchairs, State Street and Randolph, 1992. Photographer: Janet Schleeter. Source: Chicago Historical Society.

Bus System. Although PUBLIC TRANSPORTATION systems in the Chicago area at the opening of the twenty-first century operated a system of nearly 2,900 buses providing 326 million rides annually, an estimated 14,000 buses in the region were privately owned and operated in charter service and for schools, corporations, churches, and airports. The largest single system, with 1,882 buses, was operated by the CHICAGO TRANSIT AUTHORITY. PACE was operating more than 600 buses in the suburbs.

The use of transit buses varies from fixed routes (where stops are marked by signs and buses operate on schedules) to dial-a-ride service (in which the patrons, usually elderly or handicapped persons, must telephone in advance for pickup).

The standard transit bus in the United States, which has an entry door in front next to the driver, an exit door in the rear, and the engine under the floor, was developed in 1927 by Twin Coach Company for Chicago Surface Lines (CSL) as a cheaper alternative to extending streetcar lines. That design has grown into a vehicle 102 inches wide and 40 feet long seating 40 passengers. Transit buses were an offshoot of heavy-duty trucks developed during World War I, whereas small motor buses were developed from automobiles in the 1890s.

The prototype transit bus resulted from a battle between CSL (a STREET RAILWAY) and Chicago Motor Coach Company to provide service in outlying areas of Chicago. The bus company was controlled by John D. Hertz, who founded Yellow Cab Company and the rental car company bearing his name. Although the street railway was successful in its court bid to protect routes on which it held franchises but had not yet extended streetcar lines, CSL was forced to buy buses to provide the service.

Chicago transit systems have also experimented with larger vehicles. Chicago Motor Coach Company in 1933 bought a series of 72-passenger, double-decked buses called "Queen Marys" because of their size. Their use was limited, however, because they were too tall to clear many railroad viaducts.

When it was absorbed by the CTA in 1947 the CSL street railway had 411 buses. Chicago Motor Coach had 595 buses when it was bought by the CTA in 1952. The transit agency replaced its streetcar fleet with buses in the 1950s to reduce costs. Buses are operated with one employee, a driver; whereas streetcars required two, a motorman and a conductor.

Buses have not proved to be as influential in shaping development in Chicago as were the street railways because they have generally followed street railway routes. Surface-system ridership in Chicago, which includes both buses and streetcars but not RAPID TRANSIT, declined from 641 million passenger trips annually in 1952 to 287.6 million in 1997.

David M. Young

See also: Built Environment of the Chicago Region; Commuting; Land Use; Transportation

Further reading: Krambles, George, and Arthur H. Peterson. *CTA at Forty-five: A History of the First Forty-five Years of the Chicago Transit Authority*. 1993. • Mroz, Albert. *The Illustrated Encyclopedia of American Trucks and Commercial Vehicles*. 1996. • Young, David M. *Chicago Transit: An Illustrated History*. 1998.

Business of Chicago. Business and Chicago have been inextricably bound since the city's beginnings in the early nineteenth century. Although there is no truth to the story that *Chicago* is POTAWATOMI for "let's make a deal," economic and business concerns have not merely shaped but determined Chicago's destiny for almost two hundred years. After an initial period of settlement and environmental/economic accommodation, the city entered into a remarkable phase of economic expansion between about 1850 and 1930. Chicago's economic performance since that time has been less impressive, but the city, having adjusted to a series of economic shocks and dislocations in the 1970s and 1980s, remains the most important economic and business center in the interior of the United States. Indeed, with its increasingly diversified economy, metropolitan Chicago appears well poised to continue as the economic powerhouse, if not the growth engine, for the greater Midwest.

European penetration of the GREAT LAKES region began relatively early during the socalled Age of Discovery. By the late seventeenth century, numerous FRENCHMEN—most notably Louis Jolliet and Jacques Marquette—had explored the area along the southwestern shore of LAKE MICHIGAN. Throughout the eighteenth century, the area's marshy grounds were traversed by various trappers, traders, "projectors," and "adventurers" from Europe and elsewhere in the Americas. The intensity of European and African commercial penetration increased markedly in the early nineteenth century, illustrated in stylized form by the establishment, destruction, and reestablishment of the FORT DEARBORN site on what is now Michigan Avenue in the period between 1803 and 1816.

Until recently few scholars viewed Chicago's early development in a fully commercial framework, arguing instead that slow, desultory, rather aimless economic encounters among traders, frontier farmers, Indians, and government contractors of one type or another characterized the area's economy until the 1830s. The same scholars then argue that during the 1830s Chicago experienced a wild period of boom and bust, based on furious but ultimately unsustainable land speculation, before establishing a firm foundation as a trading center in the 1840s.

Today most students of the economic development of the southern Great Lakes region, including Chicago and environs, embed the area from the start in the context of an expanding capitalist market in the Western world. The FUR TRADE, military installations, public investment in INFRASTRUCTURE, private REAL-ESTATE speculation, and the marketing of farm products, however prosaic and seemingly petty, are all viewed as expressions of the region's gradual, piecemeal and incremental, but ultimately inexorable incorporation into capitalist financial and product markets of extraregional, indeed, national and even international scope. When viewed in this way, Chicago's development after 1830 seems less sudden and abrupt and less implausible. This is not to suggest that Chicago qua Chicago was foreordained or inevitable, merely that, given American capitalism's nineteenth-century trajectory, the development of an urban center such as Chicago somewhere in the southern Great Lakes region of the Midwest is readily understandable.

By the early nineteenth century an expanding capitalism was transforming the area economically from a site of irregular or intermittent cross-cultural trade in resources and "preciosities" to a site of regular, routinized production and exchange of agricultural commodities and manufactured goods conducted and organized under Euro-American auspices. Such expansion manifested itself in a variety of ways: in state formation and in the build-up in the administrative capacity of the U.S. government in the region; in the capitalist state's increased police powers and its move to monopolize organized violence; and in rising public and private investment in TRANSPORTATION infrastructure. The completion of the Erie Canal in 1825 was particularly important in this last regard, for by linking the Great Lakes with Buffalo, Albany, and by extension with New York City and the Atlantic world, the canal at once signaled and helped to bring about a shift in the locus of economic power in the Old Northwest from the Ohio Valley to the southern shoreline of the Great Lakes, from Cincinnati and Louisville to Cleveland and, increasingly, to Chicago. The Erie Canal did not do this all at once, of course, but with its completion and early success, visionary entrepreneurs began to sense and more importantly to invest in the future of cities on the Lakes' southern shores. These investors were as prescient as they were vigorous, but in retrospect it is clear that the Great Lakes region generally and the Chicago site specifically were good bets in the first half of the nineteenth century.

One might begin with resources, not merely because they were bounteous in the Midwest—although they certainly were—but because the particular constellation of resources available in the Great Lakes region was remarkably appropriate for rapid economic development in the nineteenth century. There was the SOIL, for example, soil of great natural fertility, and WATER, water in almost unimaginable and seemingly inexhaustible quantities. And there were prairies, pancake flat and most fortuitous in the coming age of the RAILROAD, as well as vast deposits of iron ore and COAL, which proved propitious indeed as America turned to steam and steel.

A formidable stock of social and cultural resources complemented these natural resources. Settlement was dominated by farmers and artisans who, whether of YANKEE or GERMAN origins, were accustomed to disciplined labor, rational calculation, and patient accumulation. Equally determined migrants from other lands followed and, despite vast differences in cultures and traditions, either bought into, or at least behaved in a manner consistent with, the economic and social expectations and ethos of their Euro-American neighbors. Such resources, conjoined with the relatively liberal and egalitarian developmental policies associated with the Midwestern states, help to explain both the rural and urban opportunities available in the southern Great Lakes region and, ipso facto, the region's inflows of labor and capital. Indeed, the area was nothing if not ready for what the novelist Richard Powers has aptly referred to as the "tireless nineteenth century."

If the best opportunities early in the century were still in the procurement of raw materials, cross-cultural trade, government contracting, and land speculation and development, commercial AGRICULTURE soon entered fully into the mix. Along with commercial agriculture—small grains and cattle plus corn and hogs, most notably—came increased trade and the beginnings of what might be called Chicago's agro-industrial complex. Because production, exchange, and consumption were closely, even organically linked in the Midwest (unlike the case in the American South among other places), town and country, or, more accurately, field, forest, and factory, fostered and supported one another in a mutually ramifying, virtuous economic cycle. Well before 1850, indeed, even before the much-ballyhooed completion in 1848 of the ILLINOIS & MICHIGAN CANAL connecting Chicago to the Mississippi River system via the Illinois and CHICAGO RIVERS, the city on the southwestern shore of Lake Michigan was emerging as one of the more important urban nodes in the Midwest's regional economy. Chicago's population grew accordingly, from about 200 inhabitants in 1833 to almost 5,000 in 1840 and nearly 30,000 in 1850.

Yet resources, impersonal market forces, and capitalism's "systemics" cannot fully explain Chicago's development. Despite the city's many locational advantages, an equal number of disadvantages—poor drainage, endemic disease, a late start—had to be overcome if the city was to outcompete other commercial centers to become the jewel in the Midwestern urban crown. Here, many scholars point to yet another advantage Chicago enjoyed over its rivals: an advantage in human capital, specifically in entrepreneurship.

Whatever attribute or complement of attributes one chooses to emphasize in defining entrepreneurship—risk receptivity, vision, creative INNOVATION, deal-making, enlightened management, and the like—Chicagoans have never seemed lacking. Although some economists assume that economic behavior is entirely positional, and that sociocultural qualities such as entrepreneurship are randomly distributed among human beings, Chicago's early history suggests otherwise. In this regard, it is most instructive to plot Chicago's historical trajectory against the trajectories of some of its early urban rivals, places with more or less similar structures of opportunity, places such as Kenosha, Racine, and even Milwaukee and St. Louis. The historical differences among these places cannot be attributed solely to structural factors, locational differences, first-mover advantages, timing, or luck. A residual remains, some part of which arguably is explicable by invoking entrepreneurship.

In any case, in the 1830s and 1840s, risk-receptive, visionary, creative, deal-making businessmen and women were busy making Chicago work. Not only was the city establishing a hinterland, it was beginning to develop entrepôt and manufacturing functions—trading, milling, butchering, tanning, BREWING, distilling, sawing, planing, and, most portentously, fabricating products for local, regional, and, in some cases, extraregional markets. In so doing, Chicago and Chicagoans—aided by governmental policies supporting development and a legal system promoting the "release of entrepreneurial energy"—were setting the stage for the amazing period of economic expansion about to unfold.

Chicago's economic dynamism between the 1850s and the 1920s is the stuff of legend. Seldom before in world history had an urban center grown so rapidly, been transformed so dramatically, or captured and conveyed the regnant spirit of the age so thoroughly. Chicago had developed big shoulders indeed by the 1920s, and this development was due more than anything else to sweaty WORK and heavy lifting. In the age of industrial capital, Chicago had become America's industrial capital, there to remain for most of the twentieth century.

The city's will to power—one of Chicago's official mottoes, revealingly, is "I will"—can be said to have begun, metaphorically at least, in 1847. In that year, a Virginia native named Cyrus Hall McCormick migrated from Cincinnati to Chicago and brought with him a business enterprise, the McCormick Harvesting Machine Company, which captured and embodied the epoch of Chicago's industrialization. Not only was the factory McCormick established in 1848—the McCormick Reaper Works, located between North Water Street and the Chicago River, just east of what is now Michigan Avenue—large and centralized, but its metal-fabricating technologies and the agro-industrial tenor and cast of the products produced were avatars of the city's subsequent manufacturing orientation. McCormick later marketed its products not just in the Midwest or even the United States, but all over the world.

Between 1850 and the 1920s Chicago was transformed—or more accurately and actively, it *transformed itself*—from an earnest little regional trading node in the interior of the United States into the nation's second largest city. Served only by the Galena and Chicago Union in 1850, the city was the greatest railroad center in the world by 1856. In possession of but rudimentary manufacturing facilities at midcentury, Chicago formed the core of one of the most heavily industrialized regions on earth before 1900. A nice little trade, distribution, and supply center for Great Lakes' farmers in 1850, Chicago had extended its hinterland into the Rockies within a few decades and developed into a world emporium before the turn of the century. How and why?

As the American economy grew, the northeastern quadrant of the United States—the area east of the Mississippi River and north of the Ohio River—came to constitute the nation's manufacturing core. As transportation and communications improvements linked the West more closely with other regions, Chicago, well positioned to take advantage of such developments, began to assume more and more economic functions, of greater and greater sophistication and complexity. The city's growth and dynamism began to seem irresistible, inexorable, inevitable: the juggernaut of the southern Great Lakes, indeed, of the United States. Wherever one looks—transport, trade, finance, manufacturing, services—one finds Chicago on the move. The city's primacy in the U.S. transportation system grew, for example, with the simultaneous, mutually reinforcing development of the West and the American railroad network. As a "gateway" to the West, moreover, Chicago benefited coming and going, serving as both a staging point (commercially and financially in particular) for migrants west and a collection and processing point, later on, for the fruit—or, more accurately, the grain and meat—of their labor. At the same time, Chicago's economic relationships with its immediate hinterland in the Great Lakes region intensified as well, with the city's mercantile community not merely facilitating but, in many cases, making possible increased production and consumption in the region.

As the city's population grew, internal multiplier effects came into play: more people meant more CONSTRUCTION, provisions, services, entertainment, etc., which, in turn, led to more jobs and more people, and perforce to iteration after iteration of the same process. Chicago's population grew from just under 30,000 in 1850 to about 300,000 by 1870 then to almost 1.1 million by 1890. By 1910 the city's population had doubled again to almost 2.2 million, and Chicago's population grew by another 55 percent or so over the next two decades, approaching 3.4 million by 1930. Some of this growth came from ANNEXATION, but most was "real," the result of natural increase (an excess of births over deaths among the resident population), rural migration (from the Midwest and, increasingly, from the South), and from foreign immigration (particularly from Southern and Eastern Europe).

For all its railroads, western connections, trade and commerce, and internal multipliers, Chicago between 1850 and 1930 evokes images of manufacturing, the heavier the better. However important the ILLINOIS CENTRAL, Sears, Roebuck & Co., or the Board of Trade—and they were important indeed—in the mind's eye Chicago, during this period, butchered hogs, made tools, and stacked wheat. With apologies to Carl Sandburg, Chicago meant IRON AND STEEL too, and FURNITURE, clothes, and tobacco, as well as a thousand and one other manufactures. In 1890, Chicago was the leading center of slaughtering and MEATPACKING, LUMBER production, and furniture manufacturing in the United States. By that time the city was also the nation's leading manufacturer of foundry and machine-shop products, the second leading manufacturer of CLOTHING and apparel, the third largest manufacturer of tobacco products, and a leading producer of iron and steel, industries that would grow dramatically in the years to come.

By 1930 Chicago, had become even more of a manufacturing town. Moreover, many of the early processing activities—sawing and planing lumber, milling, and meatpacking—lost ground in relative terms to higher-order industries based on metal fabrication, particularly the fabrication of iron and steel. In 1930 the "Chicago Industrial Area"—comprising a five-county area in northeastern Illinois and adjacent LAKE COUNTY in northwestern Indiana—was the second largest manufacturing area in the U.S., behind only the "New York City Industrial Area," which had over twice as many people. In per capita terms, Chicago's value of manufacturing product and value-added by manufacturing exceeded New York's in 1930, as did the manufacturing proportion of the labor force. In qualitative terms, too, vast differences distinguished the two areas: Chicago was America's center of heavy industry, New York, the center of light industry. Chicago, in the eyes of Chicagoans and non-Chicagoans alike, typified large-scale, centralized, capital-intensive, heavy industry.

This view of Chicago is not so much wrong as incomplete, both in terms of the city's manufacturing sector specifically and of its economy as a whole. Although the electrical machinery industry, iron and steel production, and machine-shop and foundry production constituted the three largest components of Chicago's manufacturing economy in 1930, employment in other, less "brawny" manufacturing sectors was extremely significant as well. There were, for example, over 30,000 Chicagoans employed in the clothing industry in 1929, over 25,000 employed in PRINTING and PUBLISHING, and another 18,000 employed in the furniture industry. If many Chicago workers labored in huge integrated mills—the average number of wage earners

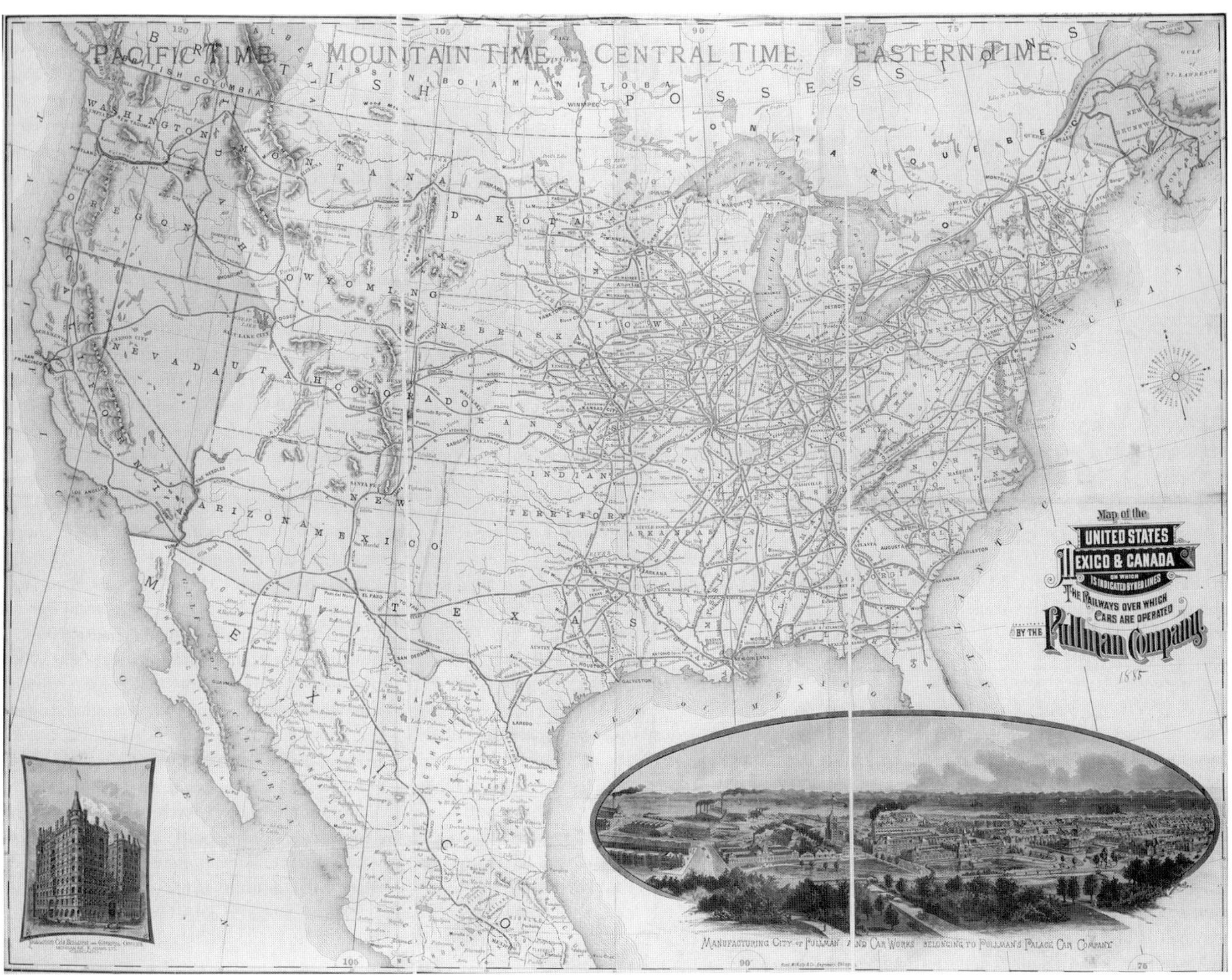

The Pullman Company advertised all of its ventures widely. This map shows the reach of the company's North American rail service, with an inset depicting the town of Pullman, still under construction in 1885. Artist: Unknown. Source: Chicago Historical Society.

in Chicago's 36 iron- and steelmaking facilities in 1929 was 1,261—many other Chicagoans toiled in much smaller manufacturing establishments. One of the great canards about American industrialization is that by the late nineteenth century all of the manufacturing action was occurring in big, vertically or horizontally integrated units controlled by large corporations. In reality, much of America's manufacturing output continued to come out of small- and medium-sized family-owned firms, producing small "batches" of specialized goods. In Chicago, such firms could be found everywhere but seemed to locate most commonly on the West and North Sides, with big mills dominating production on the South and Southeast Sides of the city.

As Chicago's manufacturing sector evolved, as its output became at once more varied and more sophisticated, the markets for manufactured goods produced in the city changed as well. With the relative shift away from processing activities and toward fabricating industries, the city was able increasingly to pursue import substitution policies and to export fabricated goods (rather than just raw materials, agricultural commodities, and processed manufactures) out of the region. By the 1920s, electrical machinery, iron and steel products, machine tools, and fabricated metals from Chicago were being sold not merely throughout the United States, but all over the world.

Chicago's formidable industrial prowess provides a ready explanation of the city's economic dynamism between the 1850s and 1930. But the city's expansion and growth *during* this period, *before* this period, and *after* this period owed much to trade and finance, to transportation-related activities, and to a variety of service activities. Chicago became the Midwest's great WHOLESALE and RETAIL emporium during this period and retained many of its marketing functions for areas further to the west. Its bankers and financiers provided credit and financial services for much of the region, and the city's commodities exchanges, however controversial, helped bring greater order and stability to American agriculture. Chicago remained the leading railroad center in the country, and, as the U.S. automotive-industrial complex became increasingly centralized in the Great Lakes region, Chicago came to play a leading role in the AUTOMOBILE and trucking industries too. Finally, as the city's population grew wealthier and more sophisticated, Chicago began to invest more in human capital—in education and in health care, most notably—and to spend more on sports, entertainment, and the arts, that is to say, on cultural capital. As a result, service-related activities—the food, beverage, and lodging industries, for example—grew as well. All in all, Chicago, circa 1930, was at its apogee. Would this mighty city's amazing growth ever end?

This question is more difficult to answer than appears at first glance. On the one hand, the city has clearly experienced some periods of tough economic sledding over the

The Illinois Tunnel Company's new storage warehouse, ca. 1910, Taylor Street at the Chicago River. Photographer: Unknown. Source: Chicago Historical Society.

past 70 years. Like most other cities in the industrial Midwest, Chicago suffered terribly during the GREAT DEPRESSION, as the demand for Chicago-made capital goods and consumer durables plummeted. Similarly, both the city and the entire metropolitan region have been hurt by the decline of jobs in heavy industry over the past 30 years—the region lost a staggering 188,000 jobs in this sector during the 1980s alone. On the other hand, Chicago's economy grew robustly during the Second World War, for most of the period between 1945 and the early to mid-1960s, and during the 1990s. Chicago's economic performance, once amazing, has been solid since its apogee. To appropriate and adapt a conceptualization initially developed by historian John Higham, the period can be seen as one in which the city moved in economic terms from "boundlessness" to "consolidation."

DEMOGRAPHIC as well as economic data support the theme of "consolidation." Although the growth rate of the *city* of Chicago has been negligible (and, at times, negative) over the past 70 years, the Chicago metropolitan area has grown at a robust rate over much of the period. According to the 2000 census, greater Chicago constituted the third largest metropolitan area in the U.S., behind only Los Angeles–Riverside–Orange County and the New York City–Northern New Jersey–Long Island metropolitan conurbation. As such, "Chicago," with more than 8 million inhabitants, is still by far the largest urban center in the "fly-over district" of inland America.

Metropolitan Chicago's economy has experienced relatively robust growth for much of the period too, despite severe problems related to industrial readjustment and restructuring during the 1970s and 1980s. Indeed, the Chicago *area*'s economy as a whole continues to perform well, and, in some ways, Chicago's more diversified and balanced economy at the turn of the twenty-first century is healthier and more stable than ever before. Even the situation in manufacturing is more complicated than often assumed. Manufacturing has declined in relative terms in the Chicago area, particularly the manufacturing proportion of the area's labor force, but total manufacturing output has continued to grow, and the Chicago Standard Metropolitan Statistical Area ranks third behind New York and Los Angeles in most measures of industrial might. Chicago remains, according to almost every index, one of the most important industrial areas in the U.S. and in the world. Given Chicago's continuing importance as a center of trade, finance, and transport—air as well as rail and highway—how does one evaluate and interpret the modern economic experience of (metropolitan) Chicago?

One important consideration in attempting to answer this question is the relationship of Chicago to the Midwest. Unlike the situation during the period of Chicago's great ascent, the Midwest since the 1930s has been in a period of relative decline. The income elasticity of food, generally speaking, is low, which, not surprisingly, hurt the AGRICULTURAL Midwest; and with the expansion of capitalist markets in the U.S. and national economic integration, relatively underdeveloped or undeveloped American regions—in the South and West in particular—began to develop rapidly. To some extent, their development came at the expense of older regions, including the Midwest. In an efficient capitalist economy such as that in the modern U.S., standard economic

Ore shipments to steel mills near 101st Street and the Calumet River, 1951. Photographer: C. J. Horecky. Source: Chicago Historical Society.

theory predicts that costs of production will converge with growth rates over time. Areas with very high growth rates, such as the Midwest in the late nineteenth and early twentieth centuries, would not be expected to sustain those rates as other areas developed, but to slow down and decline in relative terms over time. This is more or less what has occurred in the southern Great Lakes region, including metropolitan Chicago, since the 1930s.

Indeed, when one compares Chicago's structure of economic opportunity in the post-1930 period with the opportunities afforded the city in the period between the 1850 and 1930, one is struck by how much more constrained and limited Chicago's possibilities and options have been over the past 70 years than during the period of the city's ascent. Chicago's rise was in large part an expression, if not the embodiment, of the Midwest and its manifold resources: flat, fertile prairies during the great age of agricultural and railroad expansion; coal and iron ore during the age of steel; food, fibers, and raw materials during a period of rapid population increase, urbanization, industrialization, and economic growth in the U.S. To be sure, since the 1930s the U.S. economy has continued to develop, but hardly in the same way. The Midwest's comparative advantages have proved less compelling, and Chicago and Chicagoans have had to live with this painful, unvarnished truth. One can argue that metropolitan Chicago has fared pretty well under the circumstances, and that both the city and its inhabitants deserve high marks for devising and implementing sound development strategies and displaying considerable entrepreneurship.

Chicago has maintained a strong, increasingly high-tech industrial profile, for example, and has remained a center for wholesale and retail trade, distribution, and industrial and commercial exhibitions. The city has a huge presence in publishing, and it is one of the leading centers of finance, banking, and INSURANCE in the United States. Chicago, moreover, is still the major transportation node for the nation's interior: O'HARE International remains one of the busiest airports in the world; the city handles more railroad freight than any other U.S. city; Chicago has excellent highway connections and massive trucking and intermodal transport capacity; and it is a major inland port. With the opening of the ST. LAWRENCE SEAWAY in 1959, Chicago became a world rather than lake port.

Chicago has survived depression and war, the postwar boom, the retrenchment and restructuring of the 1970s and '80s, and the go-go 1990s with a good deal of its pride and prosperity intact. Although it will likely never again experience a period resembling 1850–1930, and although the city faces countless economic challenges—poverty, inequality, declining infrastructure, and insufficient investment in human capital, for starters—Chicago in many ways and for many people remains even today the "I will" city "that works." Whether it will remain so in the future as capitalist market integration intensifies in our increasingly "borderless" economic world is the challenge facing Chicagoans in the generations to come.

Peter A. Coclanis

Patrick Ryan (Aon Corporation) on the New Economy

Well, I think that what has caused the change, probably is the sophistication of business, the globalization of business. Risks have become much more complex with high technology. If something blows up or burns, you know, drops through the ground from an earthquake, you've got huge investments in technology and business is interrupted, and it can have a ripple effect around the world. So the risks are just much greater. Secondly, through various forms of deregulation, the business has become much more competitive. It was, in many ways, very tightly regulated to a point that in many states everybody had to charge the same price, the same form. You couldn't differentiate your product; everybody paid the same. So it was really like a utility. Through deregulation, market forces took over and made the business much more competitive, drove prices down, which, you know, demanded efficiencies.

Ryan, Patrick. Interview with Timothy J. Gilfoyle, Loyola University, on the occasion of the 1998 Making History Awards, Chicago Historical Society.

Gilfoyle, Timothy J. "Wisconsin's Finest: Interviews with William Cronon, Abner Mivka, and Patrick Ryan." *Chicago History* (Summer 1999): 54–72.

See also: Chicago in the Middle Ground; Commercial Banking; Commodities Markets; Dictionary of Leading Chicago Businesses, 1820–2000 (p. 909); Economic Geography; Food Processing: Regional and National Market; Innovation, Invention, and Chicago Business; Global Chicago; Metropolitan Growth

Further reading: The best overview of urban development in the Midwest is Jon C. Teaford's *Cities of the Heartland: The Rise and Fall of the Industrial Midwest* (1993). Chicago's early economic history is vividly described by William Cronon in *Nature's Metropolis: Chicago and the Great West* (1991), which should be read in concert with Peter A. Coclanis, "Urbs in Horto," *Reviews in American History* 20 (March 1992): 14–20. For insightful analyses of the systemics of Chicago's economic development, see, for example, David R. Meyer, "Emergence of the Manufacturing Belt: An Interpretation." *Journal of Historical Geography* 9 (April 1983): 145–174; Meyer, "Midwestern Industrialization and the American Manufacturing Belt in the Nineteenth Century," *Journal of Economic History* 49 (December 1989): 921–937; William N. Parker, "The Industrial Civilization of the Midwest," in Parker, *Europe, America, and the Wider World: Essays on the Economic History of Western Capitalism,* vol. 2 of 2 (1991), 215–257; Brian Page and Richard Walker, "From Settlement to Fordism: The Agro-Industrial Revolution in the American Midwest," *Economic Geography* 67 (October 1991): 281–315.

Cable Cars. *See* Street Railways

Cabrini-Green, neighborhood in the Near North Community Area. Formerly "Swede Town" and then "Little Hell," the site of the Cabrini-Green public housing complex was notorious in the early twentieth century for its inhabitants' poverty and dilapidated buildings. During World War II, the CHICAGO HOUSING AUTHORITY razed Little Hell and built a low-rise apartment project for war workers, naming it the Frances Cabrini Homes after the first American canonized by the Catholic Church. CHA further transformed the area with the high-rise Cabrini Extension (1958) and William Green Homes (1962). The original population of Cabrini-Green reflected the area's prior ethnic mix; poor ITALIANS, IRISH, PUERTO RICANS, and AFRICAN AMERICANS lived among the war workers and veterans. Racial segregation overtook Cabrini-Green by the early 1960s.

The large new APARTMENTS and large swaths of recreation space failed to mend the area's poverty. The difficulty blacks had finding better, affordable housing gave Cabrini-Green a permanent population. CHA failed to budget money to repair buildings and maintain landscaping as they deteriorated. Cabrini-Green's reputation for crime and gangs rivaled Little Hell's. The murders of two white police officers in 1970 and of seven-year-old resident Dantrell Davis in 1992 drew national attention.

Increasing real-estate values in the late twentieth century led housing officials to propose replacement of the complex with mixed-income housing. Residents argued however that such a move would displace them permanently, completing the slum removal effort begun with the building of Cabrini Homes half a century earlier.

Amanda Seligman

See also: Contested Spaces; Crime and Chicago's Image; Gentrification; Housing Reform; Near North Side; Neighborhood Succession; Subsidized Housing; Tenements

Further reading: Bowly, Devereux, Jr. *The Poorhouse: Subsidized Housing in Chicago, 1895–1976.* 1978. • Marciniak, Ed. *Reclaiming the Inner City: Chicago's Near North Revitalization Confronts Cabrini-Green.* 1986.

Frances Cabrini Homes, Near North Side, ca. 1942. Photographer: Unknown. Source: University of Illinois at Chicago.

Calumet City, IL, Cook County, 19 miles S of the Loop. Calumet City is located across the southeast boundary of the city of Chicago at the state line between 143rd Street and 163rd Street, east of the Bishop Ford Freeway. It is north of LANSING and southeast of DOLTON. Originally known as West Hammond, Calumet City shares State Line Road with HAMMOND.

Founded in 1893 when the population consisted mainly of GERMAN Lutheran farmers, the early community depended heavily on the factories and commerce of Hammond. The 1900 population of 2,935 grew to 7,492 by 1920. By that time, POLES outnumbered Germans, with residents of IRISH ancestry in third place. Poles were so politically powerful in the community that a Polish American was elected village president in 1900 and in 1902 one municipal party was able to field a slate made up completely of candidates with Polish names.

When Indiana went dry in 1916, West Hammond became an attractive watering hole for the drinkers of northwest Indiana. Bootleggers like Al Capone built on this base when national PROHIBITION came into play, and the town of West Hammond, just 30 minutes from downtown Chicago, gained a reputation as a "Sin City," where GAMBLING, PROSTITUTION, and illegal booze joints created a pre–Las Vegas strip on State Street. Hardworking residents were so dismayed by the town's bad reputation that they voted in 1923 to change the name to Calumet City. Despite the city's notoriety, the population grew from 7,500 to 12,300 during the 1920s, reaching 25,000 in 1960, 32,956 in 1970, and 39,697 in 1980. Since the 1920s various mayors and citizen groups battled to shut down the State Street bars with varying success, until Mayor Jerry Genova's efforts in the 1990s seemed to bring that chapter of the city's history to an end.

In 1966 investors spent $35 million and built the 80-store River Oaks Shopping Center. The center's excellent location on U.S. Route 6, a few miles from the Bishop Ford Freeway, brought customers from Chicago's SOUTH SIDE, and a renovation in the early 1990s (completely enclosing the previously open-air mall) maintained its drawing power.

In 2000 Calumet City's population was 39,071, with 54 percent AFRICAN AMERICAN and 11 percent Hispanic. Thirteen percent of Calumet City residents reported Polish ancestry, with smaller percentages of German, Irish, and Italian ancestry.

Dominic Candeloro

See also: Economic Geography; Expressways; Lake County, IN; Shopping Districts and Malls; Underground Economy

Further reading: McGahen, Adeline. "Calumet City Centennial Celebration." Calumet City Public Library. 1993.

Calumet Heights, Community Area 48, 11 miles SE of the Loop. Calumet Heights lies on Chicago's Southeast Side, bounded by 87th Street on the north, South Chicago Avenue on the east, and railroad lines on the west and south (along 95th Street). The community takes its name from the nearby CALUMET RIVER and from the ridge of Niagara limestone that runs through the area.

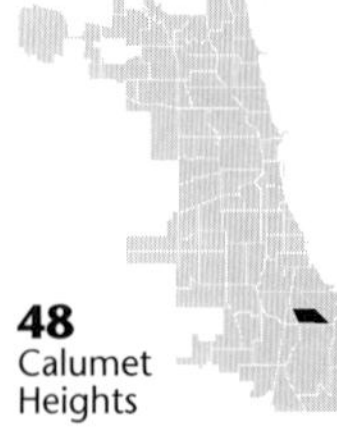

The swampy Calumet Heights region remained largely unoccupied throughout much of the nineteenth century. Though travelers passed through, few settled. In the 1870s, the Calumet and Chicago Canal and Dock Company acquired property in what was by then part of the incorporated Township of Hyde Park, holding it for future use. In 1881, the New York, Chicago & St. Louis RAILROAD built rail yards at the area's western border, and a small settlement began to develop nearby. A new QUARRY near 92nd Street prompted further settlement. REAL-ESTATE developer Samuel E. Gross purchased a portion of the Calumet and Chicago Company's land in 1887, creating the new Calumet Heights SUBDIVISION. Though Chicago annexed the entire HYDE PARK TOWNSHIP just two years later, and the adjacent Stony Island and South Chicago Heights subdivisions followed in 1890 and 1891, residential growth remained slow for several decades.

By 1920, Calumet Heights had 3,248 residents, many of them, especially in the eastern section, foreign-born. During the following decade, the community experienced a surge in residential building, and population more than doubled, to 7,343 by 1930. The large foreign-born population included many POLES, ITALIANS, IRISH, and YUGOSLAVIANS. The new housing included many single-family homes, though an area of apartments also developed west of Stony Island Avenue, between 87th and 91st Streets. Building slowed dramatically during the GREAT DEPRESSION, however, and much of Calumet Heights remained vacant.

The postwar years saw renewed growth. The 92nd Street quarry was filled in and a group of small homes constructed there. A shopping area developed around Stony Island Avenue and 87th Street. The community's population grew to 9,349 in 1950, and surged to 19,352 in 1960.

Between 1960 and 1980 the Calumet Heights community experienced a sea change in its population. A few AFRICAN AMERICANS began to move in during the early 1960s. By 1970, they made up 45 percent of the population; by 1980, more than 86 percent. Louis Rosen, whose family remained in Calumet Heights well beyond most of their white neighbors, documented this change in *The South Side: The Racial Transformation of an American Neighborhood* (1998).

Throughout the last decades of the twentieth century, Calumet Heights remained solidly middle class, with many professionals and other white-collar workers being drawn to its well-kept homes. In 1990, nearly three-quarters of the homes were single-family, and of these, four of five were owner-occupied.

Calumet Heights comprises two distinct residential areas. The Stony Island Heights neighborhood occupies the eastern two-thirds of the community. More affluent still is the Pill Hill neighborhood, said to be named for the large number of doctors from nearby South Chicago

Hospital who own spacious homes perched upon the Stony Island ridge.

Elizabeth A. Patterson

See also: Neighborhood Succession; South Side

Further reading: Chicago Fact Book Consortium, ed. *Local Community Fact Book: Chicago Metropolitan Area, 1990.* 1995. • Kouri, Charles. "Upwardly Mobile: Calumet Heights a 'High-End' Community." *Chicago Tribune,* November 22, 1991. • Richardson, Cheryl Jenkins. "Communities: At Home in Calumet Heights." *Chicago Tribune,* November 23, 1998.

Calumet Park, IL, Cook County, 15 miles S of the Loop. Calumet Park began as an appendage of BLUE ISLAND. Originally calling their town Caswell, two to three hundred ethnically mixed residents incorporated as DeYoung in 1912. Soon POLISH immigrants gained control of the village, changing its name first to Burr Oak and then to Calumet Park in 1925.

During Prohibition, Calumet Park served as a bootlegging and GAMBLING town for Al Capone, providing a haven for minor CRIME, which provided revenue for the village. The population reached 1,593 in 1940.

After World War II, Interstate 57 cut through Calumet Park, dividing the community in two. But direct access to the LOOP encouraged a population boom as builders filled the village with small brick houses. As the population expanded, the community became close-knit, with relatives frequently living nearby. By 1970 the population reached 10,069, with 60 businesses, most located along the commercial strips of 127th Street and Ashland Avenue. Even so, Calumet Park depended upon larger neighbors like Blue Island for jobs and significant purchases.

Like many southern suburbs, Calumet Park experienced dramatic changes within the lifetime of its post–World War II settlers. In 1949, St. Donatus, a parish on the Blue Island border, established a ROMAN CATHOLIC mission in Calumet Park to serve a population of predominantly IRISH and Polish Catholics. Twenty-five years later, the mission evolved into Seven Holy Founders Church, the village's dominant religious institution. The parish and the Calumet Park Recreation Association united the community, which built a public SWIMMING pool and a small library in 1964. By 1980, one-fourth of the population was over 65.

As late as 1975, only 12 AFRICAN AMERICAN families lived in the village. But within 10 years, blacks became the dominant population, accounting for 72 percent by 1992. The transition from white to black suburb produced conflict. In the summer of 1992, within weeks of each other, two black prisoners died in the village jail, allegedly by suicide. The incidents attracted the attention of Chicago Alderman Robert Shaw, whose protests against the all-white POLICE force provided headlines for Chicago papers. Fearful of GANGS, the village created ordinances establishing curfews for children and prohibitions against gatherings of three or more people. Enforcement increased racial tensions, leading to the election of Buster Porch in 1996 as the first African American mayor of Calumet Park.

Joseph C. Bigott

See also: Expressways; Neighborhood Succession

Further reading: "Cal Park—It's the Village That Works." *Chicago Sun-Times,* January 11–12, 1980. • "Cal Park: A Town Torn with Tension." *Chicago Sun-Times,* July 6, 1992. • Calumet Park Community Improvement Association. *Calumet Park: The Place to Be . . . It's a Great Community.* 1975.

Calumet Region. Although the Calumet region has no fixed boundaries, most Chicagoans understand it to be the part of the metropolitan area surrounding Lake Calumet and the CALUMET RIVER SYSTEM. By the 1880s, the heavy industry beginning to dominate the region also helped to define it. The relationship between the two definitions was apparent in a 1957 Chicago report that described the region as lying south of 79th Street, stretching from JOLIET to GARY, Indiana. That region supplied 95 percent of the metropolitan area's jobs in primary metal industries, 72 percent in petroleum and coal products, 30 percent in CHEMICALS, stone, clay, and glass products, and 21 percent in transportation equipment.

Janice L. Reiff

See also: Economic Geography; Iron and Steel; South Side

Further reading: "The Calumet Area—Here's How City Defines It." *South End Reporter,* April 21, 1957.

Calumet River System. The Calumet river system is a network of waterways, some human-made and others transformed by two centuries of human straightening, widening, dredging, channelizing, and damming, as well as by INDUSTRIAL POLLUTION and landfilling of nearby marshes.

Thousands of years ago the Konomick River flowed west from LaPorte County, Indiana, to near RIVERDALE, where it emptied into LAKE MICHIGAN, which was then much larger. Centuries of wave action and drifting sand filled in the southern end of the lake, and by the late eighteenth century, the Konomick made a hairpin turn in the vicinity of Riverdale then flowed back east to the Miller area of GARY, where it emptied into Lake Michigan. Between 1809 and 1820, a channel was cut from the northern section of this river through the marshes to SOUTH CHICAGO. Now the southern part of the Konomick—or the Little Calumet—flowed around the hairpin turn and into this new channel and emptied into the lake at South Chicago. Another channel linked it to Lake Calumet as well. The northern portion, or Grand Calumet, was deprived of the waters of the Little Calumet, and it flowed so sluggishly that by 1872 sand bars completely covered its outlet, and its flow was reversed.

In 1823 a government engineer proposed placing the terminus of a canal between Lake Michigan and the Illinois River at South Chicago, but this plan for the ILLINOIS & MICHIGAN CANAL was turned down in favor of a CHICAGO RIVER terminus. The Calumet watershed remained flat and marshy and its

The Calumet Region

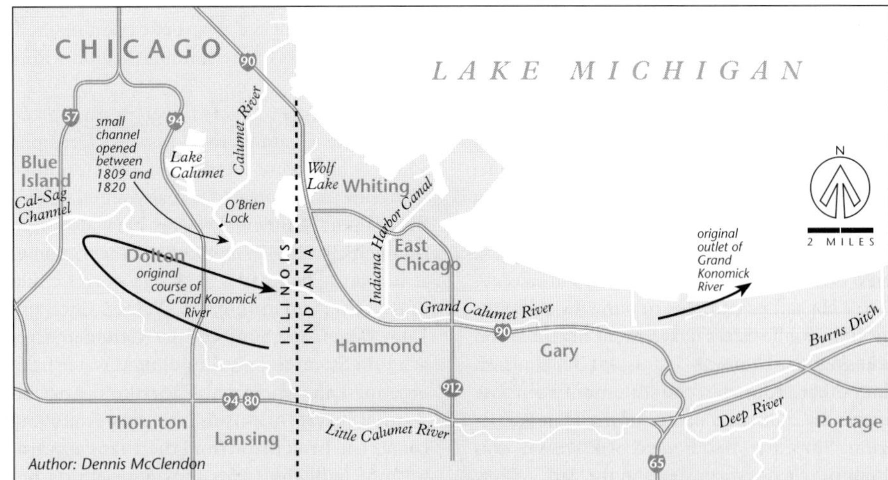

Politicians who established the Illinois-Indiana boundary showed no regard for the beach-ridge controlled geography of the Grand Calumet and Little Calumet Rivers, nor have later engineers and businessmen intent on industrializing their watershed. The natural courses of drainage have been thoroughly redesigned for urban and industrial convenience.

Illinois Steel Works and harbor entrance, Calumet River, South Chicago, between 1890 and 1901. Photographer: Detroit Publishing Company. Source: Library of Congress.

waterways unnavigable. Only when downtown Chicago began to fill up and expanding heavy industry found itself short on space did developers and industrialists turn to the Calumet area, where they could still enjoy proximity to Chicago's Transportation, markets, labor force, and Business services.

Industrial development became possible in 1869, when Congress appropriated money for a harbor at South Chicago. In the 1890s, the Calumet River was straightened and dredged. Industry began moving into the area in the 1870s, and by the early twentieth century the Pullman Company, the South Works of U.S. Steel, and other industries had been established in southeast Chicago and Hammond. To accommodate industry, the channel of the Grand Calumet was moved and straightened. The Indiana Harbor Canal connecting the Grand Calumet with Lake Michigan at East Chicago was completed in 1906, and industries moved to its banks. Burns Ditch, completed in 1926, connected the Little Calumet with Lake Michigan in Porter County, draining thousands of acres of marsh and facilitating development. Parts of the Grand Calumet and Little Calumet drained into the lake at these new outlets, depending on rainfall and lake levels. This harbor complex became the most important on the Great Lakes. With steel mills, oil Refineries, chemical plants, packinghouses, and other industries, the Calumet system became the industrial center of the Chicago region. Since the model town of Pullman was built near its western shore in the early 1880s, Lake Calumet has been drastically altered. Vast areas of it have been filled in with refuse and converted to use as parkland and docks, while extensive dredging has deepened other parts to accommodate shipping.

Industries dumped wastes into Calumet waterways, and sewers deposited human wastes in increasing amounts as industry and population grew. The currents flowing into the lake were inadequate to get rid of sewage and industrial wastes, and frequent dredging was necessary to keep channels open. In 1922, the Metropolitan Sewage District dug the Calumet-Sag Channel from the Little Calumet River to the Sanitary and Ship Canal (which paralleled the old Illinois & Michigan Canal). This altered the flow of the rivers and diverted wastes to the Illinois River and away from Lake Michigan. But river direction remained subject to flooding and to Water levels in Lake Michigan, and, with Calumet-area wastes periodically entering Lake Michigan, Chicago's drinking water had a distinctive phenol taste. In 1922, the sewage district's first sewage treatment plant opened, serving that part of the Calumet region within Illinois.

Still, pollution remained a very serious problem in the Calumet river system. Dredging spoils, which were often toxic, were dumped alongside its waterways for many years, and industrial and municipal wastes have also been dumped nearby. In the 1960s, the Calumet River was so polluted that sludge worms could not survive, and in 1965 the O'Brien Lock and Dam began operating on the Calumet River at 130th Street to prevent polluted water from entering Lake Michigan. Efforts to restrict industrial Waste Disposal into area rivers and canals had been made from the 1920s onward, but not until the 1970s did these efforts begin to be effective in cleaning up waterways. As of 2000 a number of river bottom locations remained so heavily polluted as to be active federal Superfund sites.

Christopher Thale

See also: Economic Geography; Flood Control and Drainage; Iron and Steel; Transportation; Waste, Hazardous; Water Supply

Further reading: Colten, Craig E. *Industrial Wastes in the Calumet Area, 1869–1970: An Historical Geography.* 1985. • Kay, Robert T., et al. *Characterization of Fill Deposits in the Calumet Region of Northwestern Indiana and Northeastern Illinois.* 1997. • Moore, Powell A. *The Calumet Region: Indiana's Last Frontier.* 1959.

Cambodians. Although a small number of Cambodians, many of them affiliated with the U.S. military, immigrated to Chicago prior to 1975, most of the Cambodians in Chicago came as Refugees in the years following 1975, when the brutal Khmer Rouge regime seized control of Cambodia, killing millions. With the overthrow of the Khmer Rouge by Vietnamese forces in 1979, refugees escaped on foot to camps in Thailand, where international voluntary agencies assisted their emigration. From 1979 to 1985, groups like Catholic Charities, Lutheran Child and Family Services, Jewish Family and Community Service (a local affiliate of Hebrew Immigration Association), Travellers and Immigrants Aid, and Third World Services, along with many family sponsors, helped thousands of Cambodians settle in Chicago.

The 2000 census counted 3,364 Cambodians in the metropolitan area, though community estimates ran to several times that number. Many settled in the economically disadvantaged area of Uptown, which presented its own inner-city obstacles to survival for the refugees. As years passed, others settled in Albany Park, making it and Uptown the two major Cambodian neighborhoods in the city.

The Cambodian Association of Illinois (CAI) was founded in 1976 by a group of Cambodian volunteers in cooperation with the Chicago Office of Refugee Resettlement to assist the war-torn Cambodian refugees, many of whom came alone and almost all of whom had lost family members during the Khmer Rouge regime. Since many were suffering from post-traumatic stress disorder and had limited education (most educated Cambodians had been killed by the Khmer Rouge), CAI fostered educational, health, aid, and cultural programs to help the refugee community with its ongoing battle for survival. In 1980, CAI was formally incorporated and established its first community headquarters at 1105 W. Lawrence.

Other centers of the Cambodian community were established during the 1980s as refugees continued to arrive. In 1986 and 1989, respectively, the Cambodian Buddhist Association (1228 W. Argyle) and the Kampuchean Buddhist Society (4716 N. Winthrop) were founded as spiritual centers for Chicago's Cambodian community. In 1979, Uptown Baptist Church began to hold services in the Khmer language.

With limited education, most Cambodian refugees sought jobs in factories, crafts, and blue-collar service jobs. English as a Second Language and other educational programs provided at CAI helped Cambodians to adjust to American life, but poverty remained a major problem, with 49 percent of Cambodians in Chicago living beneath the poverty line at the end of the 1990s.

Although relations between Cambodians and other Southeast Asian groups such as LAOTIANS and Vietnamese became increasingly friendly in the United States, the Cambodian community has remained a largely separate group in Chicago. In 1999, CAI moved its headquarters to an expanded facility, located at 2831 W. Lawrence, which continued to serve as the focal point for the Cambodian community. Continuing its aid programs for the immigrants (who in 1999 still constituted 80 percent of the community), the CAI also sponsored youth programs such as the Cambodian Traditional Dance Troupe, the Khmer Future Leaders Project, and Cambodian Youth Council. These aimed to preserve the Cambodian culture among the first generation of Cambodians born in America.

Robert Morrissey

See also: Americanization; Demography; Multicentered Chicago; Religious Geography

Further reading: "Cambodians Have a Home, a Place to Honor Memories." *Chicago Tribune,* May 14, 1999. • Khim, Borita. "Cambodians." In *The Ethnic Handbook: A Guide to the Cultures and Traditions of Chicago's Diverse Communities,* ed. Cynthia Linton. 1996.

Cameroonians. The first Cameroonians in Chicago came as students in the early 1960s. More permanent immigrants began arriving in the 1990s during political unrest in Cameroon occasioned by the birth of a multiparty system. Many fled to escape imprisonment, torture, and political repression within the strife-ridden country. Approximately 300 to 400 Cameroonians arrived annually in Chicago from 1994 to 2000. Community leaders estimated that roughly 1,500 Cameroonians lived in Chicago at the turn of the millennium, with another 500 or so living in the suburbs.

Because visas were granted most readily to those with advanced education, and because so many professionals were openly critical of the government and therefore particularly vulnerable to political repression, many Cameroonian emigrants were professionals. Community leaders identify medicine, engineering, NURSING, pharmacy, and computer programming as significant areas of employment. A smaller working-class segment of the population has found work in blue-collar service jobs. Although Cameroonians settled in various neighborhoods throughout the city, a significant percentage of them made their homes in the ROGERS PARK area.

Political activism has provided the focus for several Cameroonian community groups in Chicago. In 1991, Cameroonians formed an overseas wing of the Social Democratic Front, an opposition party, in order to support the cause of political pluralism. This U.S. SDF party later grew into a national movement with affiliates in several other American cities. The group raised funds to support the movement in Cameroon, and also pressured the U.S. Senate and the United Nations to stop the sale of arms to the Cameroon government. Soon after, another group of mostly French-speaking Cameroonians in Chicago formed a wing of the Cameroonian People's Democratic Movement, waging its own campaign of political activism in support of the government.

In 1998, Cameroonian leaders founded the first nonpolitical Cameroonian community group in Chicago. The Association of Cameroonians in Illinois aimed to unite Cameroonians of all political persuasions, providing assistance to immigrants and mutual aid to members of the community, and acting as a collective body to represent Cameroonians to the city government. The community also commemorated annual celebrations, including Cameroonian Independence Day, which falls on May 20.

Robert Morrissey

See also: Burmese; Demography; Multicentered Chicago; Refugees

Camp Douglas, prisoner-of-war detention center. Founded in the fall of 1861 as a training camp and staging center for Union forces, Camp DOUGLAS was named after Stephen A. Douglas, whose property south of the city provided its site. In 1862 the camp was hastily adapted to serve as a prison for rebel soldiers captured by Ulysses S. Grant at Fort Donelson. Due to occasional prisoner exchanges during the first two years of the CIVIL WAR, the number of prisoners in the camp fluctuated, although for a time it was the largest military prison in the North. By the end of the war a total of 26,060 men had been incarcerated there.

Escapes were frequent from the camp, but only the abortive November 1864 "Chicago Conspiracy" roused broad concern. Federal informants foiled an ill-conceived attempt by local ANTIWAR activists and die-hard prisoners to disrupt the 1864 election with a mass prison break.

Like all Civil War prisons, Camp Douglas had a high mortality rate: one prisoner in seven died in Chicago. Poor sanitation, hastily constructed buildings, and harsh weather conditions were to blame. In June 1862 a U.S. Sanitary Commission agent decried the camp's "foul sinks," "unventilated and crowded barracks," and "soil reeking with miasmatic accretions" as "enough to drive a sanitarian to despair." By the end of the war more than 4,000 rebels had died in the camp.

Theodore J. Karamanski

See also: Copperheads; Jails and Prisons; South Side

Further reading: Karamanski, Theodore J. *Rally 'Round the Flag: Chicago and the Civil War.* 1993. • Levy, George. *To Die in Chicago: Confederate Prisoners at Camp Douglas, 1862–1865.* 1994.

Canadians. In addition to the FRENCH Canadian population, Chicago has long been home to significant numbers of English-speaking Canadians. For many Anglo-Canadians, migration to the United States was an extension of internal migration patterns by which ambitious young people sought economic opportunities in towns and cities. For much of the nineteenth century, travel between Canada and the United States was not a noticeably different experience from travel within either country. Immigrants were not screened at the U.S. border until the 1890s, and Canadians moving to the U.S. did not need visas until 1924. Canadians were exempt from the quota system imposed on overseas immigrants in 1924, but in the 1930s the GREAT DEPRESSION closed off the economic opportunities that had attracted Canadians to the United States.

Movement between Canada and Chicago became easier in 1854 with the opening of the Great Western RAILROAD, which connected Ontario to Chicago. Many Canadians passed through Chicago on their way to other destinations, but significant numbers settled in the Chicago metropolitan area. After 1866, more residents of the Canadian province of Ontario moved to the United States because population growth and changes in AGRICULTURE limited economic opportunities in rural Ontario. According to the 1880 census, Chicago was home to nearly 14,000 people born in Canada, making Canadians the third largest immigrant group in the city after the GERMANS and IRISH. By 1900, more than 34,000 Canadian immigrants and almost 55,000 children of Canadian immigrants lived in the city of Chicago. Most Anglo-Canadian immigrants to Chicago came from Ontario and from the prairie provinces of Alberta, Manitoba, and Saskatchewan.

Chicago's Anglophone Canadian population has left few traces that historians can discern. English-speaking Canadians did not face linguistic or social barriers preventing them from participating in English-speaking Chicago society and had little incentive to form separate ethnic schools or churches or to congregate in ethnic neighborhoods. Canadians divided among a number of religious denominations and joined general English-language churches rather than starting their own Canadian congregations. Furthermore, some of Chicago's Canadians were born in Europe or were the children of European immigrants, and these might have identified as much with their European ethnicity as with Canada.

Although Chicago's English-speaking Canadians did not create many institutions to foster a sense of Canadian ethnicity, there is evidence that they did identify with their home country and with the British Empire. From the 1880s to the 1900s, a weekly newspaper, the *Canadian American,* was published in Chicago. Around the same time, the *Western British American* encouraged a sense of British imperial identity by reporting on events in British dominions and carrying news of Chicago's Canadian, English, Irish Protestant, Scottish, and Australian communities. Both newspapers refer to Canadian clubs in Chicago.

Chicago continues to be home to many English-speaking Canadians and to a smaller number of Francophone Canadians. In 2000, approximately 16,000 people who were born in Canada lived in the Chicago metropolitan area. Most have come to Chicago to pursue professional opportunities or because they have married Americans who wish to remain in the country. Although many Canadians in Chicago feel a sense of kinship or "cousinhood" with Americans, many stress the differences between Canadian and American culture and maintain a sense of distinctive Canadian identity. Nationwide, Canadian immigrants are the national group whose members are least likely to become naturalized American citizens, even after many years of residence in the United States.

Several institutions in Chicago continue to foster Canadian identity. The Canadian Club of Chicago, founded in 1942, promotes commerce between the United States and Canada and provides opportunities for Canadians in Chicago to socialize with each other. Members include Canadians, former Canadians, and Americans with an interest in Canada. The club provides lectures on business topics as well as social events such as outings to ice hockey games. The Canadian Women's Club sponsors social and philanthropic activities.

Emily Brunner

See also: Americanization; Demography; New Zealanders

Canals. *See* Illinois and Michigan Canal; Sanitary and Ship Canal

Canaryville. "Canaryville" enjoyed a reputation as one of the toughest neighborhoods in the city from the late nineteenth through much of the twentieth century. A largely Irish community on the South Side adjacent to Bridgeport in the New City community area, it stretches from Fortieth to Forty-Seventh Street between Wentworth Avenue and Halsted, with the "Black Belt" to the east and the late Union Stock Yard to the west. Given its close proximity to the stockyards, the area's physical environment and economic life were shaped by livestock and meatpacking from the 1860s until the industry's decline in the postwar era. Canaryville's name may originally have derived from the legions of sparrows who populated the area at the end of the nineteenth century, feeding off stockyard refuse and grain from railroad cars, but the term was also applied to the neighborhood's rambunctious youth, its "wild canaries." Gangs helped establish the neighborhood's truculent reputation and were active in attacks on African Americans during the 1919 Race Riot. Boasting a strong Democratic Party machine throughout the twentieth century, Canaryville also embraced a rich Roman Catholic cultural life centered on St. Gabriel's Parish. With the closing of the stockyards and the International Amphitheatre, population in the area began declining in the 1960s. Still populated largely by Irish, Canaryville now includes a sizeable Mexican community.

James R. Barrett

See also: Back of the Yards

Further reading: Davis, Myron. "Canaryville." University of Chicago Research Paper, doc. 1a, in "Documents: History of Bridgeport." 1927. Chicago Historical Society. • Pacyga, Dominic A., and Ellen Skerrett. *Chicago, City of Neighborhoods: Histories and Tours.* 1986. • Wade, Louise Carroll. *Chicago's Pride: The Stockyards, Packingtown, and the Environs in the Nineteenth Century.* 1987.

Capital Punishment. Illinois has had a death penalty since the Northwest Ordinance of 1787, which provided for death in cases of treason, murder, arson, horse stealing, and rape.

In Chicago, a bitter legacy of justice is found in the 171 executions that took place between 1840 and 1962, three of which were public. In 1859, state legislation moved all hangings to inside the jail in the county where the condemned was sentenced. From then until 1928, 101 individuals were hanged in Cook County at the county jail. In 1928, both the method and location of execution in Illinois were changed—from hanging to electrocution, and from county jails to the state penitentiaries at Joliet and Menard—with one exception: counties having populations over one million were to retain jurisdiction over their executions, thereby making the Cook County Jail the only local facility in the state eligible to maintain its own electric chair. From 1928 until the execution of James Dukes in 1962, 67 men were electrocuted in Cook County.

The attack on capital punishment in the United States intensified after the end of World War II and culminated on June 29, 1972, in the U.S. Supreme Court decision in the landmark case of *Furman v. Georgia.* The Court ruled that the death penalty as applied in the various states was arbitrary and capricious, constituting "cruel and unusual punishment" in violation of the Eighth Amendment. But as states began to enact new death-penalty laws designed to conform to the standards required by the *Furman* decision, the number of death-row prisoners again began to rise.

As the twentieth century drew to a close, the wisdom and morality of the death penalty remained a controversial issue in Chicago's legal and civic community. Execution by lethal injection was instituted in 1990 at Stateville Prison in Joliet. In September 1998, the state of Illinois transferred the capital punishment lethal-injection execution chamber to the new "supermaximum security" prison at Tamms, Illinois.

Jess Maghan

See also: Court System; Homicide

Further reading: Sturman, John David. "An Abolitionist Perspective on the History of the Death Penalty in Illinois with Commentary." M.A. thesis, University of Illinois at Chicago. 1995.

Cardinals. One of the least successful franchises in professional football history, the Chicago Cardinals originated on the city's South Side in the late nineteenth century as the Morgan Athletic Club. In 1920 the team was a founding member of the league that became known as the National Football League two years later, and it won the NFL championship in 1925. Lean years followed; the Cardinals played consistently losing football over the next two decades at Comiskey Park in the shadow of the more popular and successful Bears.

The team enjoyed short-lived success in the early postwar years, winning a second NFL championship in 1947 under coach James Conzelman, with the "Dream Backfield" of Paul Christman, Pat Harder, Elmer Angsman, and Charley Trippi exploding for long touchdowns in a 28–21 win over the Philadelphia Eagles. The Eagles reciprocated in 1948, defeating the Cardinals 7–0 during a blinding snowstorm. In 1959, the Bidwell family, owners of the team, briefly grabbed national attention by trading star running back Ollie Matson to the Los Angeles Rams for eight players and a draft pick. In 1960 the franchise deserted Chicago for St. Louis.

David M. Oshinsky

See also: Leisure

Further reading: Baxter, Russell, and John Hassan, eds. *The Ultimate Pro Football Guide.* 1998. • Treat, Roger. *The Official National Football League Football Encyclopedia.* 1959.

Carol Stream, IL, DuPage County, 26 miles W of the Loop. A veteran of the War of 1812, Anning S. Ransom, came to farm this area around 1840. He was followed in 1844 by Vermonter Daniel Kelley, who purchased 1,400 acres and settled at "Tall Trees"

with his wife to raise Spanish Merino sheep. The Kelleys and their 11 children all became actively involved in WHEATON'S political and business life. Daniel Kelley donated land for the Chicago & Great Western Railway, and the area around the RAILROAD stop became known as Gretna after 1887. GERMAN farm families, largely ROMAN CATHOLICS from Southern Germany, immigrated and established St. Stephen's Catholic Church in 1852. St. Stephen's served the area for 20 years and became the mission church for six additional DUPAGE COUNTY parishes.

AGRICULTURE dominated Gretna's economy until the 1950s, and Gretna's Harbecke-Landmeier farm so typified successful farm life that it became the site for the 1953–1955 television show *Out on the Farm.* In the mid-1950s Wheaton resident Jay Stream was among a group who selected the farmlands of Gretna for a community development whose industrial base would significantly defray the costs of its public services. Stream built housing tracts and the first shopping center and supermarket in DuPage County for its residents. The area was renamed after Jay Stream's daughter Carol.

By November 1958 hundreds of residents had moved into Carol Stream. The village incorporated in 1959 and passed a 5 percent utility tax with no village property taxes levied (except for library purposes and sewer and water bond issues). This arrangement remained in effect through the 1990s.

In the early 1960s office and industrial parks (particularly warehousing) were developed, which are served by the ILLINOIS CENTRAL RAILROAD. Tyndale House Publishing Company moved to Carol Stream in 1980. The village grew from 15,472 residents in 1980 to 40,438 in 2000.

Jane S. Teague

See also: Metropolitan Growth; Suburbs and Cities as Dual Metropolis

Further reading: Thompson, Richard A., ed. *DuPage Roots.* 1985.

Carpentersville, IL, Kane County, 37 miles NW of the Loop. Carpentersville had its origins in 1837 when the rising FOX RIVER prevented Charles and Daniel Carpenter from traveling west. They decided to stay and began a settlement that they named Carpenter's Grove. In 1851 Charles's son, Angelo, platted the land and renamed the town Carpentersville, which was incorporated in 1887. He acquired a dam and then a mill, which he converted into a yarn and flannel factory. Progress of the new industry was evident along the riverbank, where fabrics doused in colorful dyes were hung to dry.

In 1864 Carpenter established an IRON foundry and blacksmith shop called the Illinois Iron & Bolt Company. The company later acquired the Star Manufacturing Company, which produced AGRICULTURAL MACHINERY. During the 1870s and 1880s GERMAN, SWEDISH, and POLISH immigrants came to work in the factories. Carpenter housed the workers, built a church, and held cultural events. Although he moved to ELGIN in 1875, Carpenter continued his business interests in Carpentersville. He persuaded the Chicago & North Western RAILROAD to extend its tracks from EAST DUNDEE to the area and built an iron bridge with his own funds to accommodate the rail line. By 1912 Carpenter's two companies employed 2,000 people. Star Manufacturing remained in Carpentersville until 1977.

The community remained small until the mid-1950s, when gentleman farmer Leonard W. Besinger began a community named Meadowdale north of Carpentersville. By 1956 Besinger had accumulated more than 2,600 acres. Other area residents thwarted his attempts to incorporate Meadowdale as an independent town. So Besinger had Carpentersville ANNEX the property.

In its first two years, more than 700 houses were sold in Meadowdale. The prefabricated homes were economically priced, and had no basements. A carport served as a garage. Lots were small and living space averaged 960 square feet. Prospective buyers toured model homes and sometimes waited three to four hours for a salesperson, but by 1982 the complex consisted of 6,000 houses and approximately 1,000 APARTMENT units.

Meadowdale Shopping Center was built in 1957 as an early regional mall, featuring a restaurant overlooking a SKATING area. When the Northwest TOLLWAY opened in 1958, it offered COMMUTERS easier access to the community. That same year, Besinger built Meadowdale Raceway (later Illinois International Speedway), which attracted as many as 200,000 spectators at a time. The track was plagued with problems, however and closed in 1970.

In 1992 the village annexed 1,100 acres of farmland to the west. In an attempt to bring a new image to the area, housing developments advertised their location as "West Carpentersville." The village's population remained around 23,000 from 1970 to 1990 but grew to 30,586 in 2000.

Marilyn Elizabeth Perry

See also: Government, Suburban; Kane County; Metropolitan Growth; Shopping Districts and Malls

Further reading: "Provisional League of Women Voters." *Fox Valley Four* 1971. • Bullinger, Carolyn J., ed. *Dundee Township, 1835–1985.* 1985.

Cartography. *See* Mapmaking and Map Publishing; Mapping Chicago

Cary, IL, McHenry County, 39 miles NW of the Loop. In 1853 the Illinois & Wisconsin RAILROAD began grading a line from Chicago to Janesville, Wisconsin. The following year track layers threw a trestle across the FOX RIVER before economic problems stalled construction. Reorganized as the Chicago, St. Paul & Fond du Lac, the railroad resumed construction through CRYSTAL LAKE to Janesville in 1855. During that pause, engineers found that the valley's west bluff was composed of gravel left behind by the Wisconsin glacier. Pits quickly opened and trains were loaded with gravel to level the railroad right-of-way and fill in the long trestles leading to the Fox River bridge.

Noting the activity, local farmer William Cary platted a town site in 1856 one mile northwest of the Fox River beyond the pits. The railroad quickly accepted the site as "Cary Station" and a post office was established. When street improvements became necessary, residents incorporated their community as Cary in 1893 with L. E. Mentch as president.

Besides accommodating area farmers, Cary served the workers who operated the pits for the railroad, which had become the Chicago & North Western Railway in 1859. In the late 1890s, the double tracking of the North Western's main lines and the elevating of its tracks in Chicago increased demand on the ever expanding pits.

Away from the pits, rolling grasslands provided superb pasturage for dairy cattle. From the 1880s, early morning trains daily hauled thousands of cans of fresh milk into Chicago for sale to families. By 1903, Borden Dairy opened a large bottling plant in Cary. Shortly after, the Oatman Milk Company opened its doors.

Chicagoans quickly discovered that the source of their milk and cream was the Fox River Valley, which also provided a marvelous setting for resort VACATIONS. Boardinghouses and hotels that sprang up at Cary to lodge rail and pit workers soon bulged with additional tenants taking advantage of the pure air and clean, fish-filled waters. Family-run resorts lined the west bank of the river around Cary.

One resorter was John Hertz, who had made a fortune expanding the Parmelee Transfer Service into Chicago's Yellow Cab Company. Deeply involved in horse breeding, Hertz purchased 940 acres that became home to two Kentucky Derby winners. In 1943, Hertz sold the land to the Chicago-based Curtiss Candy Company, which experimented in cattle breeding. The Curtiss Company sold the land to a housing developer in the 1950s.

The population of Cary grew steadily from 943 in 1950 to 6,640 in 1980 and continued to grow, reaching 15,531 in 2000.

With the ever increasing demand for gravel for CONSTRUCTION causing uninterrupted expansion of Cary's gravel pits toward the same areas where housing is expanding, serious tensions have grown between those historic forces. It remains to be seen how the conflict will be resolved as the clash over what little open land remains in Cary continues.

Craig L. Pfannkuche

See also: Food Processing: Local Market; Leisure; Quarrying, Stonecutting, and Brickmaking

Further reading: *Cary Me Back.* 1993. • *McHenry County in the Twentieth Century, 1968–1994.* McHenry County Historical Society. 1994. • Nye, Lowell A., ed. *McHenry County, Illinois, 1832–1968.* 1968.

Catholic Charities. Incorporated in January 1918, Catholic Charities became the central agency coordinating fundraising efforts in the ROMAN CATHOLIC ARCHDIOCESE OF CHICAGO for relief work among the poor. It has grown into one of the largest not-for-profit SOCIAL SERVICE agencies in the United States, annually serving nearly 500,000 "Cook and Lake County residents of all religious, national, social, racial, and economic backgrounds."

Since the 1840s, Chicago's ROMAN CATHOLICS had sustained a multitude of charitable organizations—ORPHANAGES, HOSPITALS, industrial schools, homes for unwed mothers, day nurseries, and homes for the blind and the aged. But the demand outstripped the resources of ethnic parishes and religious orders. Archbishop George W. Mundelein articulated the advantages of the new system: not only would Catholic Charities be more efficient, it would "eliminate the need for our Sisters begging and . . . let them return to the more necessary work of caring for the sick and looking after the deserted, the dependent, the delinquent."

Catholic Charities expanded its services in the 1920s to include adoption. During the GREAT DEPRESSION of the 1930s, 4,300 volunteers from the parish-based ST. VINCENT DE PAUL SOCIETY (1857) aided families in obtaining financial assistance through the Chicago Relief Administration. Maternal and child care continued to be a priority after World War II, and in the 1960s, Catholic Charities began to administer federal funds from the "War on Poverty." By the end of the twentieth century, Catholic Charities was the largest private charitable agency in the Midwest. In addition to providing food, clothing, and other assistance to abused and neglected children, pregnant women, and victims of domestic violence and substance abuse, the agency has utilized former parochial schools and CONVENTS as shelters for homeless women and families and built new residences for senior citizens.

Ellen Skerrett

See also: Great Society; Housing for the Elderly; Relief and Subsistence Aid; Religious Institutions; United Charities

Further reading: Coughlin, Roger J., and Cathryn A. Riplinger. *The Story of Charitable Care in the Archdiocese of Chicago, 1844–1997.* 1999. • *The Housing Crisis in Our Neighborhoods.* 8-page pamphlet distributed by the Catholic Charities of Chicago, October 1999. • Mundelein, George W. *Two Crowded Years.* 1918.

Catholic School System. Catholic education in Chicago began simply enough on June 3, 1844, with a boys' school at the rear of St. Mary's Church at Madison Street and Wabash Avenue. Newly appointed bishop William J. Quarter embarked on an ambitious program to provide ROMAN CATHOLIC immigrants with an entire system from grammar grades through college. St. Mary of the Lake University, the first institution of higher learning in Chicago, was dedicated on July 4, 1846. Wracked by conflict after Quarter's death in 1848, the university and its SEMINARY department survived only until 1866. Much more successful were the parish-based grammar SCHOOLS and CONVENT academies that came to be a distinguishing feature of the urban landscape.

Parochial schools not only eventually met the needs of diverse ethnic and racial groups—IRISH, GERMANS, POLES, CZECHS AND BOHEMIANS, FRENCH, SLOVAKS, LITHUANIANS, AFRICAN AMERICANS, ITALIANS, and MEXICANS—but they were primarily the creation of Catholic nuns, often immigrants themselves, who lived in neighborhood convents close to the families they served. Virtually all of the city's 24 PARISHES supported parochial schools by the time of the Great FIRE OF 1871, a trend that continued for nearly a century.

Built with voluntary contributions, Catholic schools sought to preserve culture and transmit faith while educating the children of immigrants for American citizenship. Nativists decried the existence of a separate Catholic school system and defeated efforts by Catholics to obtain a share of the state's educational fund in the 1850s and 1860s. The multiethnic character of Chicago's parochial schools was brought into sharp relief during the controversy over the Edwards Law (1889), a compulsory education measure that required instruction solely in English and gave local school boards the authority to regulate private schools. Catholics collaborated with German Lutherans to force the repeal of the Edwards Law, with 30,000–50,000 Catholic protesters taking the streets on October 30, 1890, in a torchlight procession.

Catholic elementary school enrollment in Chicago tripled between 1900 and 1930, from 49,638 to 145,116. Despite the decrease in family size during the GREAT DEPRESSION, by 1942 Catholics still supported 264 grammar schools in the city as well as a network of 59 secondary schools. Of these high schools, 28 were for girls, 14 were for boys, and 17 were coed. While women's colleges such as SAINT XAVIER (1912), BARAT (1918), Rosary (1922), and Mundelein (1930) continued to struggle for survival, older institutions such as LOYOLA (1870) and DEPAUL (1898) soon benefited from returning veterans, whose post–WORLD WAR II education was funded by the GI Bill.

Although enrollment in Chicago's Catholic schools peaked during the "baby boom" of the 1950s, parochial schools in older industrial neighborhoods and on the city's South and West Sides began to experience the effects of dramatic ethnic and racial change. However, in welcoming "every Catholic child of the Negro race, whether his parents be Catholic or not," parochial schools continued to be, in the words of the *Chicago Defender,* "a blessing especially to poor black families." Archbishop John P. Cody's decision to restrict the construction of elementary schools in the suburbs of

Robert Galvin on Catholic Schools and Virtual Perfection

Robert Galvin was the chairman of the board of Motorola.

I went to St. Jerome's on Lunt Avenue in Rogers Park. I got a superb education there. I remember elements of that, and at that time, it was staffed entirely by the Sisters of Mercy . . . On a given occasion, whatever the grade was—4th, 5th or 6th, and I think the nun's name was Sister Mary Norberdette—the assignment was announced that on Friday there would be a test on fractions to decimals, decimals to fractions. . . . And she said there was only one grade acceptable, and that was 100 percent. . . . here was a nun that was generating a standard, a level of expectation of perfection . . . that era starting in the 70s where people began to question the American quality of goods and services and weren't others, like the Japanese, doing better. And eventually I put two and two together, and I in effect said to certain "in" audiences, isn't it interesting that I was given the introduction to the right standard in 4th, 5th or 6th grade when this nun said, "There's only one acceptable answer—100 percent."

Galvin interview with Timothy J. Gilfoyle, Loyola University, on the occasion of the 1995 Chicago Historical Society Making History Awards.

Gilfoyle, Timothy J. "Quarks, Neutrinos, and Virtual Perfection: Interviews with Robert W. Galvin and Leon M. Lederman." *Chicago History* (Summer 1996): 56–62.

Cook and Lake Counties marked the end of the school-centered model of Catholic parish life. Since 1966, the Archdiocese of Chicago has closed more than half its urban schools. Chicago's 139 Catholic elementary schools and 25 high schools enrolled 61,769 students in 2002.

Ellen Skerrett

See also: Americanization; Bilingual Education; Roman Catholic Archdiocese of Chicago; Schools and Education

Further reading: *Golden Jubilee of the New World, 1892–1942.* 1943. • Koenig, Rev. Msgr. Harry C., ed. *A History of the Parishes of the Diocese of Chicago.* 2 vols. 1980. • Sanders, James W. *The Education of an Urban Minority: Catholics in Chicago, 1833–1965.* 1977.

Catholic Worker Movement. During its heyday in the late 1930s and early 1940s, the Chicago Catholic Worker was the most significant offshoot of Dorothy Day's group in New York City. It ran houses of hospitality (St. Joseph's, the longest lasting and most important, opened in 1938) where members lived and practiced works of mercy. Its rejection of pacifism and revolutionary rhetoric, close connection with the Church hierarchy, and immersion in the Congress of Industrial Organizations in Chicago distinguished it from its parent organization. The Chicago Catholic Worker, especially its newspaper published from 1938 to 1941, launched the careers of many prominent Roman Catholic journalists and lay activists, including John Cogley, Edward Marciniak, and James O'Gara.

Steve Rosswurm

See also: Religious Institutions; Settlements, Religious

Further reading: Piehl, Mel. *Breaking Bread: The Catholic Worker and the Origin of Catholic Radicalism in America.* 1982. • Sicius, Francis J. *The Word Made Flesh: The Chicago Catholic Worker and the Emergence of Lay Activism in the Church.* 1990.

Catholic Youth Organization. Officially founded in 1930, the Catholic Youth Organization (CYO) built upon previously initiated Holy Name Societies in parishes throughout the Chicago Archdiocese. Centralized in a downtown office and led by the legendary and controversial Bishop Bernard J. Sheil, the CYO sought to combat delinquency, Americanize ethnic Catholics, and bridge social divisions during the Great Depression. Whereas previous Americanization efforts of Cardinal George Mundelein had met with meager success, the CYO fostered widespread Catholic unity even as it furthered the Church's inclusion in the mainstream culture. The CYO offered a wide-ranging system of social services, community centers, and vacation schools; but its greatest publicity resulted from an extensive and comprehensive sports program that claimed the world's largest basketball league (430 teams) and an international boxing team. Such CYO ventures included American Indians, African Americans, Asians, and Jews, which catapulted Bishop Sheil to national prominence as a social activist and labor leader.

Gerald R. Gems

See also: Clubs: Youth Clubs; Creation of Chicago Sports; Leisure; Roman Catholic Archdiocese of Chicago; Roman Catholics

Further reading: Gems, Gerald R. "Sport, Religion, and Americanization: Bishop Sheil and the Catholic Youth Organization." *International Journal of the History of Sport* 10:2 (August 1993): 233–241. • Carroll, Mary Elizabeth "Bishop Sheil: Prophet without Honor." *Harper's Magazine* 211.1266 (1955): 45–51. • Treat, Roger L. *Bishop Sheil and the CYO.* 1951.

Catholics. *See* Eastern Orthodox; Roman Catholics

Cedar Lake, IN, Lake County, 37 miles S of the Loop. Attractive to settlers in the 1830s for its excellent farming and grazing land, the town lies on the northwest corner of Cedar Lake. Recreation opportunities, including boating, fishing, sailing, and golf, have drawn visitors and residents. Most residents either fill recreation-related jobs or commute to nearby manufacturing opportunities.

Erik Gellman

See also: Leisure; Vacation Spots

Cemeteries. In Chicago, the living and the dead have always sought the same space, high and dry land with good transportation. In the city's earliest years, both populations shared settlements at Fort Dearborn and along the rivers. Regular burying grounds near Lake Michigan, at the edges of town, one at Chicago Avenue and the other at Twelfth Street, established in 1835, were short-lived. The dead were standing in the way of the living.

In 1843, a cemetery complex began on the Green Bay beach ridge at North Avenue and slowly extended north with the 60-acre "City Cemetery" and south with the smaller "Catholic Cemetery." A Jewish Burial Society bought six-sevenths of an acre in City Cemetery in 1846. Four years later, the city added 12 acres to its cemetery by purchasing the adjacent estate of Jacob Milleman, a victim of cholera.

Citing the proximity of the burial grounds to the city's water supply as hazardous to public health, Chicago's sanitary superintendent, physician John Rauch, requested the abandonment of the city cemetery as early as 1858. Burials, however, continued until 1866, when Chicago lost a lawsuit filed by the Milleman heirs, who claimed $75,000 was owed to them as a result of the mistake-ridden sale of 1850. The city chose to move the bodies to private cemeteries located outside of the city limits and return the land to the heirs.

The Great Removal began. City Cemetery bodies were wagoned to Graceland, Oakwoods, Rosehill, and Wunder's cemeteries. The Roman Catholic choices were Calvary in Evanston and St. Boniface in Chicago. Jews had moved their burial ground to Belmont and Clark in 1856.

Chicago city government attempted to prohibit any new burials within the city throughout the late nineteenth century. Yet, as the city annexed additional land, it found itself contending with existing cemeteries inside its limits. Graceland, for instance, was situated two miles north of the city until the great annexation of 1889. The state of Illinois protected these private cemeteries from city bans on burials. Still, Chicago was able to exercise some control over their extension by passing an ordinance in 1931 that made it unlawful for cemeteries to expand

Waldheim Cemetery

Waldheim Cemetery, now known as Forest Home, is located approximately 10 miles west of downtown Chicago on both sides of the Des Plaines River.

The area was once a burial ground for Potawatomi Indians. In the 1830s, Leon Bourassa, a French trapper, purchased land from the government. Prussian Ferdinand Haase bought it and developed it as a farm, Haase Park picnic grove, and as a site for gravel mining.

In 1873, Haase established German Waldheim Cemetery on his land. The only German nondenominational cemetery in the Chicago area, Waldheim did not discriminate based on race or political affiliation. In 1876, Haase established a second nonsectarian cemetery, Forest Home (English for *Waldheim*), for English-speaking citizens. The two cemeteries were merged in 1968 as Forest Home.

No cemetery better represents a cross section of society, with labor leaders, society leaders, gypsies, American Indians, African Americans, and rich and poor lying side by side for eternity. Near the Haymarket Martyrs Monument, designated a National Historic Landmark in 1997, is "Dissenters Row" and the graves of over 60 labor activists, including Emma Goldman, Elizabeth Gurley Flynn, and Ben Reitman.

Others buried here are the parents of Ernest Hemingway, the Austin Family, dancer Doris Humphrey, several Prairie School architects, evangelist Billy Sunday, members of the Cigar Makers International Union #14, and Adolph Strasser, who cofounded the AFL with Samuel Gompers.

William J. Adelman

or change their boundaries without a special permit.

Regardless of the wranglings over legalities, transportation had already affected interment practices. No longer were burial grounds only a walk away. Suburbs like FOREST PARK and NILES became available with their "cities of the dead." The first motor-driven hearse appeared in 1900. As roads improved and distance was no longer a primary locational factor, ethnic and religious groups established new cemeteries. These early necropoli were segregated, exclusive, and excluding. Later immigrants have found space in extant cemeteries, only nominally integrating them. Segregation continues for the dead as well as the living.

All burial space is endangered. The dead continue to stand in the way of the living.

Helen Sclair

See also: Epidemics; Funeral Service Industry; Religious Institutions

Further reading: Pattison, William D. "The Cemeteries of Chicago: A Phase of Land Utilization." *Annals of the Association of American Geographers* 45.3 (September 1955). • Sclair, Helen. "Chicago's Ethnic Cemeteries." In *Ethnic Chicago,* ed. Melvin G. Holli and Peter d'A. Jones, 1995. • Simon, Andreas. *Chicago: The Garden City.* 1893.

Center for Neighborhood Technology. The Center for Neighborhood Technology is a nonprofit organization that promotes just and sustainable communities. Its work includes policy research and coalition building.

Founded in 1978, the center has anchored coalitions around energy policy, housing conservation, tax scavenger sale reform, the proposed 1992 World's Fair, the proposed Lake Calumet Airport, and the Commonwealth Edison franchise renewal. For 20 years, it published *The Neighborhood Works,* covering the community organizing and environmental beat.

In partnership with community groups, the center has made 12,000 housing units and 170 nonprofit-owned buildings energy efficient and helped small metal finishers comply with environmental regulations. The center also works on nontoxic alternatives to dry cleaning.

Since 1990, the center has focused on turning the "hidden assets" of urban areas into economic opportunities. Its regional TRANSPORTATION coalition promotes smart growth strategies. Its Location Efficient Mortgage and Connections for Community Ownership programs offer market incentives for sustainable development.

Stephen A. Perkins

See also: Environmentalism; Housing Reform; Neighborhood Associations; Planning Chicago

Central Manufacturing District. The Central Manufacturing District (CMD) was a 265-acre industrial park created in 1905 by Frederick Henry Prince, an East Coast investor. Bounded roughly by 35th Street to the north, Morgan Street to the east, Pershing Road to the south, and Ashland Avenue to the west, the CMD was the first planned manufacturing district in the United States. Prince acquired the Chicago Junction RAILROAD at the turn of the century as a switching line that transported goods from the Chicago UNION STOCK YARD to major trunk railroad lines. Recognizing the potential, Prince developed the CMD as a way to enhance and expand business operations.

By 1915, some two hundred firms were using the CMD, many renting space with the option to buy, providing a work location for 40,000 people when combined with the Union Stock Yard. The CMD functioned as private banker, BUSINESS incubator, and maintenance operator, including landscaping and upkeep of the grounds.

In 1915, Prince began a second 90-acre industrial park on the south side of Pershing Road. Highly successful, the CMD has developed industrial parks across the metropolitan area including those in ITASCA, ST. CHARLES, PHOENIX, and AURORA. In 1983, the Meridian Business Campus in Aurora was designed to provide connections between office, research, and production facilities. Newer parks have also been adapted for intermodal transit for trucking and storage. The CMD spawned copycat developments such as the CLEARING Industrial Park in 1909 and the CENTEX Industrial Park in ELK GROVE in 1956.

Clinton E. Stockwell

See also: Bedford Park, IL; Economic Geography; McKinley Park; Meatpacking

Further reading: Cutler, Irving. *Chicago: Metropolis of the Mid-Continent.* 1982. • Mayer, Harold M., and Richard C. Wade. *Chicago: Growth of a Metropolis.* 1969. • Pacyga, Dominic A., and Ellen Skerrett. *Chicago, City of Neighborhoods: Histories and Tours.* 1986.

Century of Progress Exposition. (May 27, 1933–November 12, 1933; May 26, 1934–October 31, 1934)

Originally intended to commemorate Chicago's past, the Century of Progress Exposition came to symbolize hope for Chicago's and America's future in the midst of the GREAT DEPRESSION.

This was the second world's fair that Chicago had hosted, and by the time it closed, it had been visited by nearly 40 million fairgoers. As was the case with the 1893 WORLD'S COLUMBIAN EXPOSITION, the Century of Progress Exposition was conceived in an atmosphere of economic, political, and social crisis, shaped this time by the economic recession that followed America's victory in WORLD WAR I, the ensuing Red Scare, Chicago's 1919 RACE RIOTS, and Chicago's notorious gangster violence. These threats to social order led Chicago's political and cultural authorities to organize the 1921 Pageant of Progress along the Municipal Pier (NAVY PIER). The festival's success in attracting over a million visitors during its two-week run inspired a diverse group of Chicago's business and civic authorities to propose another world's fair that would build confidence in the fundamental soundness of the American economy and political system. A decade later, the fair they initiated assumed national importance during the Great Depression, the nation's worst crisis since the CIVIL WAR.

In the course of trying to win support from the city for their plans for a fair that would ultimately be built on Northerly Island (a narrow strip of reclaimed land just southeast of the LOOP that had been developed as part of the BURNHAM PLAN), exposition promoters pointed to the resurgent world's fair movement across the Atlantic. In 1922, the French government sponsored a colonial exposition in Marseilles. The British followed suit in 1924–25 with the British Empire Exhibition on the outskirts of London. Then Paris hosted the 1925 Exposition Internationale des Arts Decoratifs et Industriels Modernes.

Together with a world's fair closer to home, the 1926 Philadelphia Sesqui-Centennial International Exposition, these expositions sparked Chicago's political and business leaders to action. In 1927, they selected oil tycoon Rufus C. Dawes to serve as chairman of the exposition board. He invited his brother, Charles G. Dawes, a former U.S. senator and vice president of the United States, to serve as chairman of the exposition's finance committee and selected military engineer and future president of NBC Lenox R. Lohr to direct the fair's operations. In the wake of the 1929 stock market crash, the Dawes brothers' wealth and prestige, together with Lohr's managerial prowess, proved vital for the exposition's success. The Dawes brothers persuaded a notable array of local BUSINESS figures, including Julius Rosenwald, head of Sears, Roebuck & Co., to secure $12 million in gold notes required to underwrite the initial costs of a fair that would ultimately cost more than $100 million. With that guarantee in tow, the Dawes brothers prevailed upon Congress to authorize construction of a U.S. government building and to issue invitations to foreign governments to participate in the fair.

In addition to lending and securing financial and political support for the Century of Progress Exposition, Rufus Dawes played a pivotal role in giving the fair its thematic direction. In 1928, at the suggestion of several Chicago physicians and scientists, who saw in the fair an opportunity to cement alliances between the business and scientific communities and to rebuild public trust in science after the devastation wreaked by chemical weapons in the First World War, Dawes agreed to turn the fair into an "exposition of science and industrial development." To give form and substance to this idea, Dawes asked the National Research Council to lend assistance. In exchange for their help in formulating a philosophy of science for the fair, he agreed to scientists' requests for a separate Hall of Science that would give the fair its unofficial motto: "Science Finds, Industry Applies, Man Conforms."

Lohr was asked to bring this vision to fruition. Under his close supervision, the architectural design of the fair was entrusted to a commission consisting of Edward H. Bennett, Arthur Brown, Jr., Daniel Burnham, Jr., Hubert Burnham, Harvey Wiley Corbett, Paul Philippe Cret, John A. Holabird, Raymond Hood, and Ralph T. Walker. Unlike earlier fairs, which gave architects responsibility for individual buildings, Century of Progress Exposition authorities, with some exceptions, agreed to give architects responsibilities for buildings in particular areas of the fair. Bennett, for instance, had responsibility for the area north of the fair's central lagoon, while Hubert Burnham received charge over an area south of the 23rd Street entrance. Joining these architects in planning the fair were prominent theater designer Joseph Urban and exhibit designers (and soon-to-be prominent Chicago architects in their own right) Louis Skidmore and Nathaniel Owings. Together, architects and designers developed a modernistic vision for the fair that, with its emphasis on streamlined surfaces and bright colors, differed markedly from the monochromatic, Beaux-Arts design of the 1893 fair. What the 1933–34 fair had in common with its predecessor was criticism from a famous architect. Just as Louis Sullivan condemned the ARCHITECTURE of the 1893 fair, so Frank Lloyd Wright, who had been denied a role in designing the 1933–34 fair, blasted its architecture as a "sham."

When the Century of Progress Exposition opened, numerous buildings and exhibits drove home the message that cooperation between science, business, and government could pave the way to a better future. With the Hall of Science serving as the cornerstone, nearly two dozen corporations, contrasted with only nine at the 1893 fair, erected their own pavilions and developed displays that insisted that Americans needed to spend money and modernize everything from their houses to their cars. Several model homes, including George Keck's House of Tomorrow, featured synthetic building materials and forecast a future where dishwashers and air conditioning would be commonplace household items.

President Franklin D. Roosevelt was so taken with the power of the fair to stimulate spending on consumer durable goods, and thereby complement the federal government's efforts to jump-start the economy, that he urged Dawes to reopen the fair in 1934, which the exposition corporation agreed to do. Roosevelt was not alone in his enthusiasm. Henry Ford, who had insisted that his company not participate in the 1933 fair, switched gears after seeing the publicity that rival General Motors had generated for its products through its working model of a G.M. assembly line. By all accounts, the Ford Building, with its gigantic globe highlighting Ford's operations around the world, was the most popular corporate attraction at the 1934 fair.

The drive to promote consumer spending was also apparent in the multitude of entertainments offered by the fair. In addition to its Skyride, with rocket cars carrying visitors 219 feet above the fairgrounds, the exposition boasted an Enchanted Isle for children, an Odditorium with variations on old-time "freak shows," and various ethnic and ethnological villages. The hit of the Midway, and in many respects of the fair itself, proved to be a striptease show featuring Sally Rand's fan dance in the Streets of Paris concession. Rand, a local dancer and aspiring movie actress, had a talent for self-promotion and parody. She originally intended her show as a spoof on Chicago's high-society matrons who insisted on overdressing at a time when many Americans barely had money to clothe themselves. By taking it off, she was putting them on. In the process, she made the Streets of Paris one of the most profitable concessions at the fair.

The fair suggested that America, despite the Depression, was well on the way toward becoming a consumer paradise. Whether it would be paradise predicated on mutual respect and equal opportunity was an open question. With the exception of Jean Baptiste Point DuSable, the AFRICAN AMERICAN who established Chicago's roots and whose cabin was reproduced at the fair, very few exhibits noted African American contributions to Chicago's development. To the contrary, several concessions, notably the Darkest Africa show, openly ridiculed African Americans. Furthermore,

The cables attached to the 12 towers of the Travel and Transport Building, designed for the Century of Progress Exhibition by Edward H. Bennett, John Holabird, and Hubert Burnham, held a suspended dome that allowed for clear, unobstructed, and relatively inexpensive exhibit space inside the building. Photographer: Unknown. Source: Chicago Historical Society.

The Century of Progress Exhibition offered businesses a chance to advertise and display their products. That was also true for companies that provided services to the fair, like Chicago-based Greyhound, which moved some 20 million attendees around the 428-acre site in special buses like the one above. Photographer: Kaufmann & Fabry. Source: Chicago Historical Society.

despite early promises from exposition directors, African Americans were discriminated against in exposition employment practices and were refused service in several restaurants on the fairgrounds. Some African Americans boycotted the fair; others, aware that the fair was attempting to chart a roadmap to the future, determined to use the exposition to change the direction America was heading. With the help of the NATIONAL ASSOCIATION FOR THE ADVANCEMENT OF COLORED PEOPLE, a handful of African American state legislators held up legislation authorizing a continuation of the fair into 1934 until exposition management agreed to wording in the legislation that forbade racial discrimination on the fairgrounds. No small accomplishment in an era when segregation was commonplace and RACISM its ideological underpinning, the NAACP's success in transforming the Century of Progress Exposition into a laboratory for advancing the cause of CIVIL RIGHTS helped energize a new generation of Chicago's civil rights activists.

Unlike African Americans, who had some success in shaping practices at the Century of Progress Exposition, women were largely ignored by the fair's corporate leadership. In 1893, federal legislation had mandated the inclusion of women's exhibits in the World's Columbian Exposition. In 1933, no such congressional mandate existed, and the result was that women found little representation in the Century of Progress Exposition apart from midway shows where they were represented as commodities. In 1933–34, there was no Woman's Building, and exhibits depicting the contributions of women to America's national progress were few and far between. If the fair was any indication, progress in the area of women's rights would not automatically follow from the growing power of corporations in American life.

The Century of Progress Exposition was not without its flaws and critics. But critics found little sympathy among those who, in the midst of the Great Depression, found employment, entertainment, and education at the fair. Perhaps the best measure of its success lay in expositions that followed in its wake. By the close of the decade, civic authorities in Dallas, San Diego, Cleveland, San Francisco, and New York had held major fairs that helped shore up national faith in the "world of tomorrow"—the theme of the 1939 New York World's Fair. While the Century of Progress Exposition left no permanent buildings, its profits enriched several Chicago museums, including the MUSEUM OF SCIENCE AND INDUSTRY, which also received some of the exposition's exhibition materials for its permanent collections. Exposition land was later occupied by Meigs Field and McCormick Place. Perhaps the exposition's most lasting bequest was to remind Chicagoans and Americans alike of the distance they had traveled and of the distance they had yet to journey in defining the meaning of progress.

Robert W. Rydell

See also: Entertaining Chicagoans; Innovation, Invention, and Chicago Business; Landscape Design; Leisure; Navy Pier; Waterfront

Further reading: Findling, John E. *Chicago's Great World's Fair.* 1994. • Rydell, Robert W. *World of Fairs: The Century of Progress Expositions.* 1993.

CHA. *See* Chicago Housing Authority

Chambers of Commerce. For most of the twentieth century, the city of Chicago had no organization named the Chamber of Commerce, but it did have an Association of Commerce and Industry, formed in 1904. Not until 1992 did it take the name Chicagoland Chamber of Commerce. Overshadowed by the world-famous Board of Trade and by the socially prominent COMMERCIAL CLUB, the Association of Commerce and Industry played a key role in boosting Chicago and its business concerns. From its initial founding under the leadership of John Shedd of Marshall Field & Co., the association has gathered representatives of local businesses who meet regularly and work to strengthen the economic interests of Chicago. The association has extended the geographical reach of Chicago commercial interests, sending members to towns across the country recruiting business, distributing reams of booster literature, and helping to attract conventions. Its research bureau has provided market information to its members and statistics useful in lobbying local, state, and national governments, and members have fervently supported city improvement efforts promising growth and development.

The association has also helped organize groups of businessmen similar to its own, playing a key role in founding the Illinois Chamber of Commerce. The association's sixth president, Harry Wheeler, became the first president of the U.S. Chamber of Commerce in 1912. Throughout its existence, the association has remained remarkably consistent in promoting what it calls "the great Central Market," though its recent emphasis on GLOBAL trade and on regional economic planning reflect how that market has changed.

Businessmen within the city and in suburban communities surrounding Chicago also formed their own chambers, most of them in the 1920s, sometimes renaming existing businessmen's associations as chambers of commerce or associations of commerce and industry. These local chambers' sponsorship of events such as GOLF tournaments, pet parades, and holiday festivals encourage civic involvement and establish local identity within a sprawling metropolis, while promoting the commercial interests of their retail areas.

The Chicago area is also home to regional chambers of commerce, such as the Chicago Southland Chamber of Commerce, and chambers representing particular groups within the city, such as the Cosmopolitan Chamber of Commerce, the Chicago Area GAY AND LESBIAN Chamber of Commerce, and the POLISH-American Chamber of Commerce. Other local organizations, such as the FRENCH-American Chamber of Commerce of Chicago and the America-Israel Chamber of Commerce Chicago facilitate economic exchange between Chicago and other countries. Together, these chambers of commerce link Chicago's regional markets in a vital network with not just one but many centers.

Jeffrey Charles

See also: Governing the Metropolis; Metropolitan Growth; Retail Geography; Tourism and Conventions

Further reading: *Chicago Faces and Places.* Chicago Association of Commerce and Industry. 1979. • Miller, Louisa Drucilla. "The Chicago Association of Commerce: Its History and Policies." Ph.D. diss., University of Chicago. 1941.

Channahon, IL, Will County, 43 miles SW of the Loop. Channahon, reportedly named from a POTAWATOMI word meaning "meeting of waters," rests at the confluence of the DES PLAINES, Kankakee, and DUPAGE Rivers. The town grew in the 1840s with the construction of the ILLINOIS & MICHIGAN CANAL, but its growth slowed as RAILROADS replaced waterway connections. More recently, oil and CHEMICAL corporations, interstate highways (55 and 80), and affordable new housing have attracted new residents.

Erik Gellman

See also: Transportation; Water

Charity Organization Societies. Charity Organization Societies (COS) began in the eastern United States during the 1870s to improve the organization of SOCIAL SERVICES. A vast number of independent groups had formed to ameliorate the problems of poverty caused by rapid industrialization, but they operated autonomously with no coordinated plan. COS founders wanted to reform charity by adding a paid agent's investigation of the case's "worthiness" before distributing aid. Furthermore, they believed that unregulated and unsupervised relief caused rather than cured poverty, so a volunteer "friendly visitor" offered advice and oversaw the family's progress. COS views dominated charity philosophy until the 1930s and influenced the face of social welfare as it evolved during the Progressive era.

Chicago charities adopted these principles later than eastern cities, in the 1890s. The first local charity organization society formed in 1883, but three years later it folded into the older and larger CHICAGO RELIEF AND AID SOCIETY (founded 1857) with little effect upon charity methods. COS proponents tried again to implement the principles of organization in 1893 when Chicago, already suffering from the national economic depression, experienced severe unemployment with the close of the WORLD'S COLUMBIAN EXPOSITION. A new agency, the Central Relief Association (later the Bureau of Organized Charities), formed to coordinate benefits between agencies and implement investigation methods. It also attempted to make services available without regard to nationality or religion. In 1909, the UNITED CHARITIES of Chicago incorporated both the Bureau of Charities and the Relief and Aid Society.

By the 1920s, ideas about social INSURANCE and publicly funded entitlements began to replace COS concerns about public aid, resulting in a partnership between public and private agencies in the delivery of social services. Furthermore, social research and professional training had developed extensively during the intervening years and most SOCIAL SERVICE EDUCATION moved to universities, such as the School of Social Service Administration at the UNIVERSITY OF CHICAGO.

Joanne L. Goodwin

See also: Great Society; New Deal; Philanthropy; Relief and Subsistence Aid; Religious Institutions; Subsidized Housing

Further reading: McCarthy, Kathleen D. *Noblesse Oblige: Charity and Cultural Philanthropy in Chicago, 1849–1929.* 1982. • Watson, Frank Dekker. *The Charity Organization Movement in the United States: A Study in American Philanthropy.* 1922.

Charles H. Kerr & Co. Charles H. Kerr & Co., the SOCIALIST publishing house, was founded in 1886 by Charles Hope Kerr (1860–1944), son of ABOLITIONIST parents. Initially Unitarian oriented, the Kerr Company quickly embraced social reform and in 1899 adopted a Marxist outlook. It remained the largest purveyor of revolutionary socialist literature in the English-speaking world until the late 1920s.

Close to the Socialist Party and the INDUSTRIAL WORKERS OF THE WORLD, Kerr brought out many Marxist classics, including the first complete English edition of *Capital* (1906–1909), as well as works by anarchist Peter Kropotkin, feminist Matilda Joslyn Gage, Irish revolutionist James Connolly, animal rights crusader J. Howard Moore, such noted U.S. socialists as Eugene V. Debs, "Mother" Jones, Upton Sinclair, Jack London, Gustavus Myers, Carl Sandburg, William D. Haywood, Mary E. Marcy—whose *Shop Talks on Economics* (1911) sold over two million copies—and, more recently, Staughton Lynd, C. L. R. James, and Carlos Cortez.

Because of its opposition to WORLD WAR I, Kerr & Co. was denied access to the mail under the Espionage Act, but somehow the firm survived. As a nonprofit cooperative, it has continued to publish classics of the international Left, and new works of critical theory, labor history, and radical humor.

Penelope Rosemont

See also: Anarchists; Feminist Movements; Publishing, Book; Red Squad

Further reading: Roediger, David, and Franklin Rosemont. "Charles H. Kerr Publishing Company: A Century on the Left." *Workers' Democracy* 21 (Fall 1986). • *The Charles H. Kerr Company Archives, 1885–1985: A Century of Socialist and Labor Publishing.* 1986. A guide to the Kerr Company Archives. The Newberry Library, Chicago, IL. • Ruff, Allan. *"We Called Each Other Comrade": Charles H. Kerr and Company, Radical Publishers.* 1997.

Charters, Municipal. Through municipal charters, state governments grant powers of local government to cities. Such a legal conveyance of power is necessary because the U.S. Constitution specifies only two levels of government, national and state, and all municipalities are considered legal creatures of their states. Typically, municipal charters specify the municipality's type of governing structure, its political offices, its financial powers including TAXATION, and the limits of its HOME RULE powers. States invariably reserve to themselves certain powers over a city. This arrangement has caused power struggles between cities and states, especially when the growth of cities like Chicago far outstripped that of any other municipalities in their states in the late nineteenth and early twentieth centuries.

Chicago's earliest charters reflected its small population, restricted geographic area, and limited governing needs. These first town charters were conferred in 1833 and 1835, when only a few hundred settlers clustered on a small site along LAKE MICHIGAN. Under its town charters, Chicago was governed by an elected Board of Trustees which wielded little political or financial power. In 1837 Chicago received its first city charter, which divided the city into six WARDS, allowed for a MAYOR elected to a one-year term, and legally incorporated Chicago as a municipality. The city grew so rapidly thereafter that new charter legislation was constantly needed. In 1847 charter legislation increased the wards to nine and designated annual elections for a city attorney, treasurer, tax collector, and surveyor. Still another charter was granted in 1851, followed by more charter legislation in 1853, 1857, and 1861. These acts extended Chicago's city limits, strengthened the mayor's powers of appointment over all municipal offices that were not elected, and consolidated a variety of small governing boards into a Board of Public Works. In 1863 Chicago sought and received yet another new charter, which divided the city into 16 wards and extended the one-year terms of elected municipal officials to two years.

Outside of Chicago in COOK COUNTY, the TOWNSHIPS of CICERO, LAKE VIEW, JEFFERSON, and HYDE PARK had also received special municipal charters from the state legislature by 1870. In addition, BARRINGTON, PALATINE, WINNETKA, and GLENCOE had received special municipal charters. DES PLAINES and EVANSTON incorporated under the state's general town incorporation act.

In 1870, Illinois wrote a new constitution, which halted the practice of granting individual charters to cities. For the next 100 years, Chicago and all municipalities in Illinois were subject to the Cities and Villages Act, a general incorporation act that enumerated the governing powers given to all cities and villages in the state, forbade special legislation to meet specific urban circumstances, and reserved significant powers to the state legislature. Dozens of suburban communities used this legislation to organize incorporated suburban governments. Chicagoans, however, fought the act, arguing that the city's sizeable population, growing industrial base, and expanding geographic area differed sufficiently from the rest of the municipalities of the state to warrant special charter legislation. They also charged that the act reflected the legislature's desire to restrict the city's power within the state, a credible accusation considering the constitutional convention's initial attempt to permanently restrict the number of legislative representatives from Chicago.

Decades of hostility between Chicago and the state legislature over Chicago's political and fiscal powers ensued. In 1902 a group of Chicagoans, led by the CIVIC FEDERATION, began a movement to secure a new municipal charter for the city. Seventy-four men from business, civic, and social organizations met and wrote an enabling amendment to the state constitution that would allow the legislature to write a new charter specifically for Chicago. Chicago voters ratified the amendment, subsequently sometimes referred to as Chicago's "little charter," in 1904, and in 1906–7, 74 men, appointed by various political bodies and politicians, assembled as a charter convention to draft a new municipal charter. This convention produced a document that proposed to alter the city's governing structure by consolidating the existing separate governing bodies of the PARK DISTRICTS, board of education, and library board into the municipal government, increase the city's financial and taxing powers, and provide a significant grant of home rule power to Chicago.

The state legislature significantly altered this draft charter and returned it to Chicago voters for their approval. Chicago businessmen, their organizations, and the REPUBLICAN PARTY strongly backed ratification of the charter; other Chicagoans disagreed. Middleclass progressive reformers such as Raymond Robins, Margaret Dreier Robins, Louis Post, and Jane Addams, as well as the CHICAGO FEDERATION OF LABOR and the CHICAGO TEACHERS FEDERATION, rejected the charter, claiming it neither gave Chicago home rule nor sufficiently reformed its government. Ethnic groups in United Societies for Local Government opposed the charter because it failed to free the city from the state's alcohol restriction laws. Women organized across class and ethnicity to urge male voters to reject the charter because it did not provide municipal SUFFRAGE for women. The DEMOCRATIC PARTY and its working-class, ethnic constituency charged that the legislature had rearranged the city's ward configuration to favor the city's middle- and upper-class neighborhoods. Charter opponents especially objected to accepting a charter they believed reflected the legislature's hostility toward Chicago. Not only had the legislature changed the original document in unpalatable ways, several legislators had attempted to trade the charter's approval for the city's agreement to accept permanent restriction on the number of legislators to be elected from Cook County. In September 1907, Chicagoans overwhelmingly rejected this proposed charter, believing that the city should seek better charter legislation.

In 1909 and 1914–15, Chicagoans again sought new charter legislation, but these efforts also failed. Subsequently, women's organizations, the Chicago Federation of Labor, and male civic reform organizations looked for charter relief in a new state constitution. These groups were disillusioned once again when the hostility between Chicago and the state influenced both the delegate selection to a 1920 constitutional convention and the document that emerged. In 1922, Chicago and Cook County voters defeated a proposed state constitution that, although promising Chicago more self-government, would have permanently restricted Cook County's representation in the state legislature. The constitution failed throughout the state, but the margin of rejection outside of Cook County was 2 to 1, compared to 20 to 1 among Cook's voters.

Across the next three decades, Chicago continued to express its dissatisfaction and even considered seceding from the state. Chicago continued to propose new charter legislation to the General Assembly, and in the 1950s, a new generation of specialists in municipal governance revived cries for charter relief. They pointed to Chicago's situation as the only city of its size in the state and therefore forced to function under general incorporation statutes while at the same time existing state legislation prevented Chicago from making changes to its governing structure that were allowed to all other cities in the state.

Chicago gained new home rule powers only with passage of a new state constitution in 1970. This constitution gives municipalities with a population over 25,000 broader home rule powers, although Chicago (as the only municipality with a population of more than 500,000) is still subject to special restrictions and remains one of the very few special charter municipalities in the state, meaning that it retains the municipal governing structure established by a charter issued prior to 1870. In Cook County, Cicero, Glencoe, and Winnetka are also special charter municipalities.

Maureen A. Flanagan

See also: Annexation; Governing the Metropolis; Government, City of Chicago; Politics; State Politics

Further reading: Einhorn, Robin L. *Property Rules: Political Economy in Chicago, 1833–1872.* 1991. • Flanagan, Maureen A. *Charter Reform in Chicago.* 1987. • Merriam, Robert E., and Norman Elken. *The Charters of Chicago: A Summary.* 1952.

Chatham, Community Area 44, 10 miles S of the Loop. Since the mid-1950s, Chatham has been a stronghold of Chicago's AFRICAN AMERICAN middle class. Defined by a jagged boundary lying within 79th and 95th Streets, the ILLINOIS CENTRAL RAILROAD and the Dan Ryan EXPRESSWAY, Chatham contains one of the most solidly middle-class African American populations in the city, and is home to several of the most successful black businesses in the country.

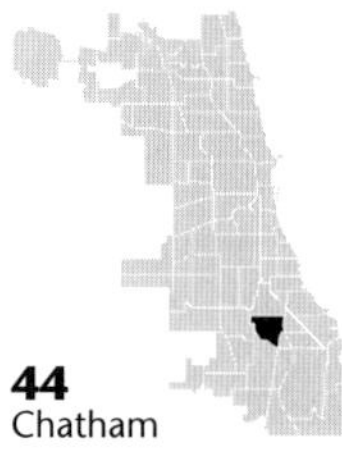

More suitable for duck hunting than for human habitation, the swampy area was known as "Mud Lake" to hunters and as "Hogs Swamp" to the farmers who began to settle the western region of Chatham during the 1860s. The first buildings in the area were corncribs assembled by the Illinois Central in 1860 along the tracks between 75th and 95th Streets. Industrial development began to the north after 1876 when Paul Cornell, founder of Hyde Park, established the Cornell Watch Factory at 76th and the Illinois Central tracks. By 1900, steel mills that had been built along the lakefront and the CALUMET RIVER provided work for European immigrants settling in Chatham.

Population growth and residential expansion in Chatham began in earnest in the 1880s with the subdivision of three small areas that constituted the community. The first permanent residents in the eastern portion of Chatham were ITALIAN stonemasons, who in the mid-1880s built frame houses in what is now AVALON PARK. When Chatham was annexed to Chicago as part of HYDE PARK TOWNSHIP in 1889, HUNGARIAN and IRISH railroad workers inhabited the Dauphin Park subdivision, also in the eastern portion of what is now Chatham. With the 1914 subdivision of central Chatham as Chatham Fields, strict ZONING codes and property standards became a characteristic feature of the entire community.

The 1920s brought dramatic increases in both property values and the population of Chatham. As new residents of mostly SWEDISH, Irish, and Hungarian American origin took occupancy in numerous BUNGALOWS, the population swelled from 9,774 to 36,228 by the end of the decade, and the community evolved from working class to middle class. Another boom started in Chatham toward the end of the GREAT DEPRESSION with the development of the Chatham Park housing complex in 1941, which stimulated the growth of Cottage Grove Avenue as a SHOPPING DISTRICT. By 1959, the mostly JEWISH occupants of Chatham Park converted the complex into what was claimed to be the first cooperative rental property in Illinois.

As in many other neighborhoods in Chicago, racial transition occurred in Chatham quite rapidly. In 1950 the African American residency of Chatham was less than 1 percent. By 1960 it had jumped to 63.7 percent. Unlike many other neighborhoods, however, Chatham's experienced a relatively uncontested racial transition. While the West Chatham Improvement Association attempted to keep the area reserved for whites, other community leaders wanted to avoid the violence that occurred just to the north in GREATER GRAND CROSSING. Several area churches, for example, welcomed blacks into their congregations, and the Chatham–Avalon Park Community Council began in 1955 to include African American residents in their organization. Owing partly to the scare tactics of some REAL-ESTATE agents, however, whites left Chatham in large numbers in the 1950s and 1960s. The 1990 census reported 99 percent of Chatham's residents as African American.

Chatham has the distinction of being perhaps the only neighborhood in Chicago that developed from a European American middle-class community into one composed of middle-class African Americans. Middle-class African Americans were, in fact, drawn to the area precisely because of its strict property standards, high levels of community organization, and good SCHOOLS. When the racial changeover was completed, African American Chathamites worked diligently to maintain the middle-class character of their community.

Some of the most successful black businesses have been located in Chatham, including the Johnson Products Company (Ultra Sheen Hair Products), the Independence Bank of Chicago, Seaway National Bank of Chicago, and a branch of the Illinois Service Federal Savings and Loan Association. Independence Bank of Chicago was one of the nation's largest black-owned banks until 1995, when it was acquired by another corporation.

Toward the end of the 1990s Chatham seemed on the brink of another transition as reports of crime, property neglect, and economic instability were in the rise. More important, the declining population—down from a 1970 high of 47,287 to 37,275 in 2000—was aging. Community leaders and residents, however, devoted their energies to a number of revitalization projects designed to assure that Chatham would remain, in the words of real-estate developer Dempsey Travis, "the jewel of the Southeast Side of Chicago."

Wallace Best

See also: Condominiums and Cooperatives; Cosmetics and Hair Care Products; Economic Geography; Neighborhood Succession

Further reading: Gregory, Mae. "Chatham 1865–1987: A Community of Excellence." Harold Washington Library, Special Collections. • Mayer, Harold M., and Richard C. Wade. *Chicago: Growth of a Metropolis.* 1969. • Neufeld, Steve, and Annie Ruth Leslie. "Chatham." In *Local Community Fact Book: Chicago Metropolitan Area, 1990*, ed. Chicago Fact Book Consortium. 1995.

Chemicals. Although the chemical industry has never represented one of the leading economic sectors in Chicago, the metropolitan region has been home to several significant chemical-making enterprises. A center for the production of soap and other basic chemical goods since its early years, the Chicago region became an important producer of industrial chemicals during first half of the twentieth century. By the end of that century, several of the world's leading chemical-producing corporations were headquartered in the city.

During the first part of the city's history, the production of chemicals was not a particularly important part of the local economy. The city was home to a few chemical-making companies of some significance during this period. The factory of J. V. Z. Blaney, which employed about 15 Chicagoans during the 1850s to manufacture various chemicals, was reportedly one of the leading producers of chemicals in the western part of the United States. Two decades later, during the 1870s, the Chicago Union Lime Works employed about 200 local residents at its large factory. With the capacity to produce lime (calcium oxide) at the rate of 1,300 barrels a day, this establishment was a major supplier to the makers of lime-using products such as cement and bleach. By the 1880s, another basic chemical, sulfuric acid, was being produced down the ILLINOIS & MICHIGAN CANAL, at the zinc works of Matthiessen & Hegeler in La Salle.

During the first half of the twentieth century, the local chemical industry grew rapidly. Several Chicago firms became leading suppliers of water treatment products. The Dearborn Chemical Company, established in 1888 by chemist William H. Edgar, specialized in making water treatments that would reduce the formation of mineral deposits in boilers and other industrial equipment. The Chicago Chemical Company, founded in 1920 by H. A. Kern and Frederick Salathe (a chemist for the Standard Oil Company of Indiana), made water treatment products such as sodium aluminate. In 1927, this company merged with a competitor to form the National Aluminate Corporation (later Nalco), which soon grew to encompass subsidiaries in Texas and New York. By the late 1940s, Nalco was producing 181 different chemicals, many of them for water treatment; by the late 1970s, it employed about 1,700 men and women in the Chicago area. At the end of the twentieth century, Nalco—still headquartered in the area—stood as one of the leading firms in the chemical industry. Another local company, W. R. Grace & Co., founded in 1887 and based in LAKE ZURICH, was also a leading dealer in water treatment products.

Among the several large industrial chemical factories established in the area during the early twentieth century, only some were owned by local interests. One of the home-grown operations was the Victor Chemical Works, which was started by the GERMAN-born August Kochs in 1902. Kochs, who for several years had been experimenting with the manufacture of baking powder, directed the production of monocalcium phosphate at the Victor plant in CHICAGO HEIGHTS. By the 1910s, Victor was making ammonium phosphate and sulfuric acid. By the 1960s, the company (then controlled by the Stauffer Chemical Company) employed more than 1,000 Chicagoans.

Many of the chemical factories that sprung up in the metropolitan area during the early twentieth century were controlled by large corporations based outside the region. One of the largest of these establishments was the EAST CHICAGO plant of the Grasselli Chemical Company, which made acetic acid and other industrial chemicals. The Grasselli works (which was eventually taken over by DuPont) employed about 500 men by 1910 and more than 1,000 by the middle of the GREAT DEPRESSION. Other nonlocal firms with chemical factories in the Chicago region during this period included Union Carbide & Carbon Corporation, which owned plants that made industrial gases; Sherwin-Williams, which had dye-making operations in addition to its paint works; and the Interchemical Corporation, another maker of paints and inks.

Some of the most important parts of Chicago's chemical industry have been located not in firms that specialized in the production of chemicals but rather in divisions or subsidiaries of large companies better known for other products. Leading MEATPACKING firms such as Armour and Swift, for example, used waste from their slaughterhouses to manufacture soap, glue, and fertilizer. In the twentieth century, the Quaker Oats Company used byproducts from its FOOD PROCESSING plants to manufacture furfural and other chemicals. And Standard Oil of Indiana (later known as Amoco and then BP) created a chemicals division to complement its petroleum business.

By the end of the twentieth century, the industrial production of chemicals in the Chicago area had declined, but Chicago was home to several major chemical-making corporations. Morton, an important Chicago company since a Nebraskan named Joy Morton began to expand the salt marketing firm he took over in the 1880s, became a producer of chemicals during the twentieth century. By the 1950s, Morton—which continued to be based in Chicago but had operations around the world—was making photographic chemicals, adhesives, dyes, and a variety of other goods. At the end of the twentieth century, Morton stood as one of the world's leading makers of specialty chemicals and chemical preparations. Among the other leading chemical-making corporations with headquarters in the Chicago area at this time were IMC Global, a leading producer of phosphate fertilizers; CF Industries, a maker of nitrogenous fertilizers; the FMC Corporation, a leading supplier of soda ash (sodium carbonate) and insecticides; and CBI Industries (a descendant of the Chicago Bridge & Iron Company), which produced carbon dioxide and other industrial gases.

Mark R. Wilson

See also: Business of Chicago; Economic Geography; Medical Manufacturing and Pharmaceuticals; Refining

Further reading: Haynes, Williams. *American Chemical Industry.* 6 vols. 1945–1954.

Chess Records. Founded in 1950, Chess Records captured a vibrant new style of American music with roots in the American South that influenced and inspired ROCK and roll pioneers from Chuck Berry to the Rolling Stones. It has become synonymous with American RHYTHM AND BLUES.

Leonard and Phil Chess, immigrants from Poland, began recording acts performing at their Club Macambo at 3905 Cottage Grove after World War II. In 1947 the brothers formed the Aristocrat Record Corporation, which reorganized in 1950 when they left the nightclub business to concentrate on making records as the Chess Recording Company. They added a subsidiary BLUES label, Checker, in 1952.

Located in the heart of Bronzeville at 4750 Cottage Grove, the Chess Company was well established by 1954, featuring blues and R&B hits by Muddy Waters, Howlin' Wolf, Little Walter, Sonny Boy Williamson, Gene Ammons, and Willie Mabon.

In 1956 the Chess brothers diversified into JAZZ recording under the Argo label, retaining a crack production team of arranger/composer Willie Dixon and Malcolm Chisholm, a recording engineer with Universal Studios. As rhythm and blues begot rock and roll, Chess was there with hits by Chuck Berry, Bo Diddley, and the Flamingos.

By 1957 the company had consolidated operations in a move to a two-story office complex at 2120 Michigan Avenue. Over the next 10 years, "2120" produced hits for Little Milton, Etta James, the Dells, Koko Taylor, the Rolling Stones, and the Yardbirds. Today it is a Chicago Landmark and home to Willie Dixon's Blues Heaven Foundation.

Leonard Chess's son, Marshall, took command in 1969 as president of the company, which was sold to GRT later that year. MCA continues to issue the classic and influential recordings of Chess Records.

Paul W. Petraitis

See also: Record Publishing

Further reading: Oliver, Paul, ed. *The Blackwell Guide to Recorded Blues.* 1989. • Ruppli, Michel, comp. *The Chess Labels: A Discography,* vol. 1 of 2. 1983. • Wilcock, Donald E., with Buddy Guy. *Damn Right I've Got the Blues: Buddy Guy and the Blues Roots of Rock-and-Roll.* 1993.

Chesterton, IN, Porter County, 36 miles SE of the Loop. When Indiana became a state in 1816, the northern portion, which bordered on LAKE MICHIGAN, was a densely forested area inhabited largely by POTAWATOMI. The first non-Indian settler in what is now the town of Chesterton was Jesse Morgan, who built a cabin on the Detroit–Fort Dearborn Post Road. His house became a stopping place for the stagecoach, and a post office from 1833 to 1853.

In the early 1830s William Thomas bought a large tract of land originally owned by a Potawatomi Indian woman, Mau-Me-Nass. A settlement known as Coffee Creek grew up around his cabin, sawmill, and general store. In 1852 the town was platted with the name of Calumet. The Michigan Southern RAILROAD ran through the town toward Chicago on land donated by William Thomas II. In succeeding years other railroads crossed the area, and Calumet became a busy railroad center.

Railroad construction drew IRISH workers in the 1850s, followed in the sixties and seventies by SWEDES and GERMANS. Many of the Swedish settlers stayed to own homes, farms, and businesses.

In 1869 Calumet was incorporated as the Town of Chesterton, the name apparently derived from that of Westchester Township, in which it was located. The incorporation failed in 1878, owing to an inadequate tax base. Reincorporation occurred in 1899; this time planners were careful to take in sufficient territory to raise the necessary taxes. ANNEXATION brought in additional land in later years.

By 1880 Chesterton was a well-established town with several small factories. The Hillstrom Organ Factory relocated from Chicago in 1880 and became the town's main industry. A growing preference for pianos over organs resulted in the sale of the factory to private investors by the Hillstrom estate in 1898, and the eventual closure of the factory in 1920. Other small industries included a china factory and a glass factory. The *Chesterton Tribune* has been published continuously since 1884. The Chesterton State Bank was founded in 1890 by George Morgan (son of Jesse Morgan) and Joseph C. Gardner. In the early 1900s electricity and TELEPHONES became available, along with INTERURBAN transportation to nearby towns. The Chicago, South Shore & South Bend INTERURBAN still serves the area.

Since WORLD WAR II growth has been rapid in Chesterton. The opening of BURNS HARBOR and the establishment of Bethlehem Steel's Burns Harbor Division in the early 1960s increased the economic health of Westchester Township. Through the efforts of Sen. Paul Douglas of Illinois, and other interested groups, the INDIANA DUNES National Lakeshore was established in 1966. This park, together with the Indiana Dunes State Park, which opened to the public in 1926, preserves the remaining dunes of the south shore of Lake Michigan for recreational use.

With a population of 10,488 in 2000, Chesterton is the largest town in Westchester Township. Since 1980, business development has occurred largely at the junction of Indian Boundary Road and State Highway 49. Sand Creek Country Club and the Sand Creek residential development, the largest of many new SUBDIVISIONS, are nearby, located in the area originally settled by Jesse Morgan.

Margaret D. Doyle

See also: Conservation and Preservation; Economic Geography; Governing the Metropolis

Further reading: *History of Porter County.* 1912. • Local History Archives. Westchester Public Library, Chesterton, IN. • Moore, Powell A. *The Calumet Region: Indiana's Last Frontier.* 1959.

Chicago. The name "Chicago" derives from a word in the language spoken by the MIAMI and ILLINOIS peoples meaning "striped skunk," a word they also applied to the wild leek (known to later botanists as *Allium tricoccum*). This became the Indian name for the CHICAGO RIVER, in recognition of the presence of wild leeks in the watershed. When early FRENCH explorers began adopting the word, with a variety of spellings, in the late seventeenth century, it came to refer to the site at the mouth of the Chicago River.

Ann Durkin Keating

See also: Chicago in the Middle Ground; Flags and Symbols; "Windy City"

Further reading: Swenson, John F. "Chicagoua/Chicago: The Origin, Meaning, and Etymology of a Place Name." *Illinois Historical Journal* 84.4 (Winter 1991): 235–248.

Chicago (Chicago Transit Authority). Long-lived ROCK band featuring sax, trombone, and trumpet, and an extremely successful melodic ballad style. Formed in Chicago in 1967 as the "Big Thing," the band's first producer, James Guercio, suggested the name "CHICAGO TRANSIT AUTHORITY," later shortened to "Chicago" after the CTA threatened to sue. Relocating to Los Angeles in 1968, the band signed to Columbia, releasing its first album in 1969. It went gold, the first of 18 albums to reach gold or platinum status. "Chicago" will be remembered both for their pioneering jazz-rock of "25 or 6 to 4" and ballads "Hard to Say I'm Sorry" and "You're the Inspiration." Their 1995 album "Night & Day" was an interpretation of the big bands of the 1930s and '40s.

Original members: Peter Cetera, Terry Kath, Robert Lamm, Lee Loughnane, James Pankow, Walter Parazaider, Danny Seraphine.

Jeanette L. Casey

See also: Chicago Sound; Jazz

Further reading: MacDonald, Meg. "Chicago." In *Contemporary Musicians,* vol. 3. 1990, 32–34. • Stambler, Irwin. *Encyclopedia of Pop, Rock and Soul.* 1989, 117–120.

Chicago Academy of Sciences. Founded in 1857 and chartered in 1865, the Chicago Academy of Sciences was guided in its early years by Robert Kennicott and William Stimpson, close collaborators of an early leader of the Smithsonian Institution. The academy, with one of the best natural history collections in America, built a museum at Wabash and Van Buren, but its exhibits, collections, and library were destroyed in the FIRE OF 1871. The academy rebuilt and lost its building during the economic turmoil of the 1880s.

After renting space for several years, the academy built the Matthew Laflin Memorial Building, opening in LINCOLN PARK in 1894. This relationship with the PARK DISTRICT formed the model of capital and operating support for museums which has been the foundation for Chicago's unique MUSEUMS IN THE PARKS arrangement. The academy pioneered ecological dioramas, loan boxes for schools, a forerunner of the modern planetarium called the Atwood Celestial Sphere, and the use of still and motion PHOTOGRAPHY in the documentation of natural history. However, by the mid-1930s, these leadership positions had been overtaken by larger or specialty organizations. The academy languished as a museum but flourished as a research institute during the 1940s and 1950s. In 1958 William J. Beecher began a process of renovation of building, exhibits, and programs. Fueled in part by post-Sputnik funding, the academy became known as a site for teacher training and as a home for the growing ENVIRONMENTAL movement.

By the 1990s the academy was serving over a quarter of Chicago public SCHOOLS with teacher training and educational outreach programs. In 1991 the academy founded the International Center for the Advancement of Scientific Literacy, which conducts the biannual assessment of adult scientific literacy for the National Science Foundation. The academy was also home to the Chicago Peregrine Release and Restoration Project, natural history collections and archives extending back to the 1840s, and the Nature, Polis, and Ethics Project.

In 1999 the academy opened its new home on Lincoln Park's North Pond, the Peggy Notebaert Nature Museum. Surrounded by gardens containing representatives of five major regional ecosystems, the museum maintains a diverse exhibits program ranging from the ecological history and future of the region to butterflies and the human home as an ecological entity.

Paul Heltne

See also: Field Museum; Landscape; Plant Communities

Chicago Area Project. The Chicago Area Project (CAP), a pioneering delinquency prevention program, was incorporated in 1934 by Clifford R. Shaw, with support from prominent sociologists at the UNIVERSITY OF CHICAGO and the Illinois Institute for Juvenile Research. Shaw believed that juvenile delinquency was a natural product of deteriorating neighborhoods in the modern industrial city. Suspicious of psychological explanations of delinquency and of programs aimed solely at reforming individual delinquents, he created CAP as a new form of grassroots community organization. Its goal was to prevent delinquency by eliciting local residents' active participation in community self-renewal.

CAP sponsored COMMUNITY ORGANIZING committees composed of residents of high-delinquency neighborhoods. Shaw worked as much as possible through existing institutions, such as the Catholic church in the predominantly POLISH neighborhood of Russell Square.

CAP's initial programs took three main forms. First, it organized recreation; the Russell Square Community Committee (RSCC), for example, sponsored a boys' club and athletic leagues. Second, it sought to improve neighborhood conditions; the RSCC cleaned up local parks and established a summer camp operated by community residents. Third, it intervened directly with delinquents; workers provided informal guidance ("curbstone counseling") to youth GANG members. Street workers also mediated with police and school officials when neighborhood youths were arrested or experienced difficulty in school. In addition, they supervised convicted offenders from the neighborhood when they were placed on parole.

CAP grew from 3 community committees in the 1930s to as many as 80 in the late 1960s. In many neighborhoods, the European ethnic groups whom CAP originally served were succeeded by Hispanics and African Americans. CAP has nonetheless remained an influential mechanism for community organizing.

David Wolcott
Steven Schlossman

See also: Back of the Yards Neighborhood Council; Children and the Law; Juvenile Justice Reform; New City; Playgrounds and Small Parks

Further reading: Bennett, James. *Oral History and Delinquency: The Rhetoric of Criminology.* 1981. • Kobrin, Solomon. "The Chicago Area Project—A 25-Year Assessment." *Annals of the American Academy of Political and Social Sciences* 322 (March 1959): 19–29. • Schlossman, Steven L., and Michael Sedlak. "The Chicago Area Project Revisited." *Crime and Delinquency,* 26 (July 1983): 398–462.

Chicago Bears. *See* Bears

Chicago Blackhawks. *See* Blackhawks

Chicago Black Renaissance. Although the Harlem Renaissance of the 1920s has gained greater prominence, the black aesthetic movement in mid-twentieth-century Chicago also produced an influential flowering in the arts. The "GREAT MIGRATION" brought tens of thousands of southern AFRICAN AMERICANS to the city, where they contributed to the development of an urban culture reflected in the visual and performing arts, literature, and music. Chicago became a pioneering center for recording and performing music. The *Chicago Defender* promoted black fine arts and publicized the works of ARTISTS and the institutions that supported and nurtured their creativity. The SOUTH SIDE Community Art Center and

Chicago Area Project workshop for neighborhood leaders, 1964. Fifty students, mostly adult volunteers, received certificates for taking a 12-session course held in the DePaul University downtown center and sponsored by the Division of Community Services of the Illinois Youth Commission, the Chicago Federation of Community Committees, and the Department of Sociology of DePaul University. Photographer: Unknown. Source: Chicago Historical Society.

the NEW DEAL's Works Progress Administration nourished artistic creativity and organized art workshops for black citizens.

Literature

The spirit of the city, conflict between the races, questions of identity, and the quest for meaning and dignity anchor the novels, poems, and short stories of Langston Hughes, Richard Wright, Arna Bontemps, Margaret Walker, and Gwendolyn Brooks. In 1936, Wright founded the South Side Writers Group, whose membership included Bontemps and Walker, in order to provide inspiration and encouragement to budding writers and space to experiment with new themes and subjects. The publication in 1940 of *Native Son* catapulted Wright into national prominence. Its evocative exploration of slum and ghetto, class and race, complements its social-science counterpart, the classic *Black Metropolis* of St. Clair Drake and Horace R. Cayton.

In 1941 Gwendolyn Brooks attended a class on modern POETRY that Inez Cunningham Stark conducted at the South Side Community Art Center. Her award a few years later at the Midwestern Writer's Conference led to the publication of her first book of poetry, *A Street in Bronzeville*. Her next book, *Annie Allen*, won the Pulitzer Prize in 1950, and in 1968 Brooks was named Poet Laureate of Illinois. In 1969, with the publication of *Riot*, Brooks began a long association with Haki Madhubuti's Third World Press.

Visual Art

Four early black visual artists, all of whom received training at the School of the Art Institute of Chicago, captured the dynamic spirit of black Chicago: William Edouard Scott, Charles White, Archibald John Motley, Jr., and Eldzier Cortor. Scott painted impressionist landscapes, portraits, and murals, including the murals depicting black achievement on the walls of the Tanner Art Gallery in the Chicago Coliseum when it was the site of the American Negro Exposition in 1940. White worked with the mural division of the Illinois FEDERAL ART PROJECT and became a prominent graphic artist. Motley's early works provoked controversy with his depictions of JAZZ culture and celebration of black sensuality. His paintings, joyous celebrations of the vitality of urban black life, provide vivid images of black social activities in the 1920s and 1930s. Cortor was among the first African American artists to take the beauty of black women as his major theme. In 1946, *Life Magazine* published one of his full-length seminude female figures.

Music

The Chicago Black Renaissance witnessed the emergence of JAZZ, the evolution of GOSPEL music, and the rise of urban BLUES. In 1922 King Oliver invited trumpeter Louis Armstrong to join his Creole Jazz Band in Chicago. Armstrong quickly eclipsed Oliver, demonstrating an impressive skill as an improvising soloist. He remained mostly in Chicago for the next three decades, where his recordings and radio BROADCASTS defined and dominated Chicago jazz.

Thomas Dorsey, known as the "Father of Gospel Music," wrote over four hundred songs that revitalized black religious music. A distinctly urban music, gospel featured pianos, tambourines, drums, cymbals, and steel tambourines. Contralto Mahalia Jackson was most responsible for the acceptance and widespread popularity of gospel music. She arrived in Chicago in 1927 and by 1945 was selling millions of records featuring Dorsey's compositions, including "Take My Hand, Precious Lord."

Dance

DANCE HALLS and social clubs became important venues for black Chicagoans who sought release and pleasure after working in stockyards, factories, and STEEL mills. At the other end of the spectrum, Katherine Dunham organized *Ballets Negres* and in 1931 presented one of her compositions, "Negro Rhapsody," at the Beaux Arts Ball in Chicago. In 1945, she founded the Katherine Dunham School of Arts and Research. Dunham's race consciousness and appreciation of black aesthetics emerged in her choreography and her ethnographic studies of West Indian dance.

Darlene Clark Hine

See also: Art; Art Centers, Alternative; Entertaining Chicagoans; Fiction; Literary Cultures; Sacred Music

Further reading: Bone, Robert. "Richard Wright and the Chicago Renaissance." *Callaloo* (Summer 1986): 446–468. • Floyd, Samuel. *The Power of Black Music: Interpreting Its History from Africa to the United States.* 1995. • Reed, Christopher. *The Chicago NAACP and the Rise of Black Professional Leadership, 1910–1966.* 1997.

Chicago Botanic Garden. Spanning a 385-acre site of once-swampy marshland in suburban GLENCOE, the Chicago Botanic Garden is the culmination of nearly a century's work by the Chicago Horticultural Society. Formed in 1890 to help keep the city true to its motto "Urbs in Horto" (Garden City), the society lost much of its momentum in the early twentieth century, letting its charter lapse during the GREAT DEPRESSION. The WORLD WAR II "victory gardens" campaign helped revive the organization and renew interest in a large public garden.

The Garden (comprising more than 20 individual gardens) is a joint project. The Cook County FOREST PRESERVE turned the land over to the Horticultural Society in 1965, creating a major public-private partnership. Planting began in 1972, and the Garden opened to the public later that year. Its choice of exhibits makes the Chicago Botanic Garden an archetypal Chicago institution: while preserving a peculiarly Midwestern flavor, it has also featured plant life from environs as far and diverse as Russia and Japan. Though located in the suburbs, the Garden is accessible by METRA; it served nearly 900,000 visitors in 1998.

Sarah Fenton

See also: Conservatories; Gardening; Landscape Design; Morton Arboretum; Plant Communities

Chicago Bulls. *See* Bulls

Chicago Chinese News. *Chicago Chinese News* began publishing in 1991 under the name *Chicago Chinese Times.* In 1998, the daily NEWSPAPER was renamed and changed to a weekly publication. A subsidiary of Houston-based Southern CHINESE Newspaper Group (SCNG), *CCN* at the turn of the century maintained the highest circulation of the area's CHINESE-language newspapers at 10,000. SCNG also was publishing newspapers in eight other U.S. cities, and its Taipei office was covering news from Taiwan, Hong Kong, and the People's Republic of China. The Chicago CHINATOWN office had four reporters covering local news.

With its international organization, *CCN* stands in sharp contrast to Chicago's earlier Chinese newspapers, the first of which, the semimonthly *Chinese American,* began publication in 1893. Since then, several political and community organizations have published their own newspapers, though they were often poorly funded and appeared infrequently and briefly. With the growth of Chinese communities after the passage of the 1965 Immigration Act, however, *Chicago Chinese News* serves as an excellent example of Chinese newspapers in metropolitan America.

Mary Ting Yi Lui

See also: Associated Negro Press; Journalism; Politics and the Press; Press: Neighborhood Press

Further reading: Lai, Him Mark, and Karl Lo. *Chinese Newspapers Published in North America, 1854–1975.* 1977, 5; 24–32. • Moy, Susan Lee. "The Chinese in Chicago: The First One Hundred Years, 1870–1970." M.A. thesis, University of Wisconsin–Madison. 1978, 106–107. • Moy, Susan Lee. "The Chinese in Chicago: The First One Hundred Years." In *Ethnic Chicago: A Multicultural Portrait,* ed. Melvin G. Holli and Peter d'A. Jones, 1995, 378–408.

Chicago City Ballet. Maria Tallchief, former prima ballerina of the New York City Ballet, founded the Chicago City Ballet in 1974 in order to provide the city with a company of national prominence. At first, the company served the LYRIC OPERA, but in January 1980 it became an independent organization, funded generously by Henry Paschen, Tallchief's husband. In 1982, Tallchief brought in Paul Mejia as co–artistic director. Mejia BALLETS were added to a repertoire of Balanchine works. By the spring of 1987 the company's finances were in crisis. Mejia's contract was not renewed, and the board of directors hired a single artistic director, Daniel Duell. In September, the company performed at the Chicago Theatre under the direction of Duell, who bravely came on stage and played the flute for soloist Sherry Moray in his ballet "Ave Maria." Paschen withdrew his support in October, and the Chicago City Ballet was forced to disband.

Nancy G. Moore

See also: Dance; Dance Companies

Further reading: Smith, Sid. "It May Be Curtains for City Ballet." *Chicago Tribune,* November 11, 1987.

Chicago Commons. Chicago Commons was established in the fall of 1894 and modeled on HULL HOUSE. Founder Graham Taylor had come to Chicago Theological SEMINARY to teach applied Christianity and wanted to live in an immigrant, working-class area. With his wife and four children, he moved to an IRISH, GERMAN, and Scandinavian neighborhood in the northwest part of the city. As other residents joined them, this SETTLEMENT HOUSE started a KINDERGARTEN, CLUBS and classes, and a civic forum for the discussion of current events. In 1901, it constructed a five-story building on Grand Avenue with a gymnasium, auditorium, activities rooms, and living quarters for two dozen residents.

Lea Demarest Taylor succeeded her father as director in 1922 and remained in that post until 1954. She adjusted the settlement program to meet the needs of Spanish-speaking neighbors in the 1930s and AFRICAN AMERICANS in the 1940s and 1950s. Chicago Commons took the lead among Chicago settlements in fighting for adequate relief stipends and job programs during the GREAT DEPRESSION and in promoting racial integration in its neighborhood. But in 1947 the city of Chicago announced plans to build a freeway through that neighborhood, and the settlement merged with Emerson House to become Chicago Commons Association in 1948. The Grand Avenue building was sold and the proceeds used to establish other community centers which sponsored activities but no longer housed residents. The Chicago Commons Association was administering six such centers and three summer camps at the time of Lea Taylor's death in 1975. Since then, Chicago Commons has continued to provide a variety of SOCIAL SERVICES in neighborhoods with few resources.

Louise Carroll Wade

See also: Religious Institutions; Social Gospel in Chicago

Further reading: Taylor, Graham. *Chicago Commons through Forty Years.* 1936. • Trolander, Judith Ann. *Professionalism and Social Change: From the Settlement House Movement to Neighborhood Centers, 1886 to the Present.* 1987. • Wade, Louise Carroll. *Graham Taylor, Pioneer for Social Justice, 1851–1938.* 1964.

Chicago Community Trust. The Chicago Community Trust has played a central role in encouraging and managing PHILANTHROPY in metropolitan Chicago since its founding in 1915. Banker Albert W. Harris established the second community foundation in the United States with an initial endowment of $600,000 to create permanent funds for grants to address civic affairs, education, culture, health, and SOCIAL SERVICES in subsequent generations. The trust had only four executive directors in its first 85 years, each establishing priorities responsive to changing community and financial resources. From its founding, a volunteer governing board appointed by outside civic leaders has overseen operations.

In 1919, the trust undertook its first community assessment, establishing an ongoing practice of identifying and responding to current needs in Chicago. Endowment funds grew in the 1920s with new donor participation and services to individuals and families to channel funds to agencies serving their philanthropic interests. Even with emphasis on relief funds in the 1930s, the trust's endowment grew to almost $5 million by 1939, a figure that almost doubled in the in the early 1940s. By the early 1960s the trust's assets exceeded $50 million.

In the 1970s, the trust published its first formal guidelines and program areas for grant seekers, continuing to survey the community to determine priorities. In 1977, permanent endowment funds surpassed $100 million, and growth accelerated in the next two decades, reaching over $1 billion in 2000, placing the Chicago Community Trust as the fourth largest among 550 U.S. community foundations.

Jane Preston

See also: Arts Funding; MacArthur Foundation

Further reading: Loomis, Frank Denman. *The Chicago Community Trust: A History of Its Development, 1915–1962.* 1962 • McCarthy, Kathleen D. *Noblesse Oblige: Charity and Cultural Philanthropy in Chicago, 1849–1929.* 1982

Chicago Conspiracy Trial. In September 1969, under a new federal antiriot statute, David Dellinger, Rennie Davis, Tom Hayden, Abbie Hoffman, Jerry Rubin, John Froines, Lee Weiner, and Bobby Seale went on trial in the Federal Building at Jackson and Dearborn, charged with crossing state lines with the intent to incite ANTIWAR riots and disrupt the 1968 DEMOCRATIC National Convention in Chicago. Judge Julius Hoffman ruled that "the substance of the crime was a state of mind." The six-month spectacle included outspoken protests, the binding and gagging of defendant Bobby Seale, and federal marshals struggling with defendants and spectators.

The jury dismissed the conspiracy charges, but found five defendants guilty of "intent." The Seventh Circuit Court of Appeals remanded the five for separate retrials, ruling that the evidence could as easily lead a jury to acquit as to convict. The government never retried the five.

John Schultz

See also: Court System; Free Speech; Political Conventions; Politics; Red Squad

Further reading: Schultz, John. *The Chicago Conspiracy Trial.* 1993.

Chicago Crime Commission. The Chicago Crime Commission is a nonpartisan, anticrime organization founded by businessmen in 1919 after a notorious payroll robbery. In the 1920s, under its active operating director, Henry Barrett Chamberlin, an attorney and former newspaper editor, the commission gained a prominent publicity and advocacy role and became the nation's leading citizen crime commission at a time of intense concern about organized crime and ineffective law enforcement. The new commission focused on crimes against property, which it saw as the work of a highly sophisticated BUSINESS: "Modern crime, like modern business, is tending towards centralization, organization and commercialization. Ours is a business nation. Our criminals apply business methods."

The commission advocated a more efficient, rigorous criminal justice system that would deter with certain, harsh punishment. As public watchdog, it monitored POLICE, COURTS, and corrections institutions for lenience, laxity, and corruption. It decried political interference. In the late 1920s, the commission campaigned unsuccessfully against the widespread practice of plea bargaining, which it portrayed—many said unfairly—as the product of judicial inefficiency and corruption.

The commission's efforts to arouse citizens' indignation produced its most successful publicity maneuver, the 1930 release of a "public enemies" list, headed by Al Capone. Drawing on the work of its "Secret Six" investigative unit, the commission was among the organizations that called for the ultimately successful tax-evasion prosecution of Capone in 1931.

In later years, the commission worked actively to combat organized crime. In 1951, longtime executive director Virgil Peterson was a prominent witness in the sensational televised hearings conducted by Estes Kefauver's Senate Organized Crime Committee. Local syndicates, Peterson warned, had evolved into a dangerously sophisticated national mob.

The commission's visibility has faded in recent decades, but it has remained active—monitoring courts and police, campaigning against legalized GAMBLING, and pushing for punitive responses to problems associated with street GANGS (designated "Public Enemy No. 1" in 1995) and illegal drugs.

David E. Ruth

See also: Crime and Chicago's Image; Mafia; Underground Economy

Further reading: Files of the Chicago Crime Commission, including its annual reports and periodic *Bulletin* (later titled *Criminal Justice*). • Hoffman, Dennis E. *Scarface Al and the Crime Crusaders: Chicago's Private War against Capone.* 1993. • Peterson, Virgil W. *Crime Commissions in the United States.* 1945.

Chicago Cubs. *See* Cubs

Chicago Defender. Robert Sengstacke Abbott produced the first issue of the *Chicago Defender* on May 6, 1905. What began as a four-page handbill quickly became the most important black metropolitan NEWSPAPER in America. Flaming headlines and indignant editorials chronicled the plight of AFRICAN AMERICANS in sensational detail. Its commitment to safeguarding civil liberties opened a new space for blacks to air their views and to voice their discontent. Abbott's conviction that "American Race Prejudice must be destroyed" led the *Defender* to fight against racial, economic, and social discrimination, baldly reporting on lynching, rape, mob violence, and black disfranchisement. It championed fair housing and equal employment and was a chief proponent of the "spend your money where you can work" campaign.

The *Defender* remains most significant for the active part it played in the GREAT MIGRATION. Most southern migrants got their first glimpse of life in Chicago in the pages of the *Defender*, glimpses that made the city a striking symbol of the migration even for those moving elsewhere. Setting departure dates and showing pictures of the best schools, parks, and houses in Chicago next to pictures of the worst conditions in the South, the *Defender* stirred migration fever across much of the South. Southern cities banned the newspaper and exacted serious penalties on anyone found distributing or reading it.

The "World's Greatest Weekly" also constituted a revolutionary departure for black newspapers and set new standards for African American JOURNALISM. The *Defender* devoted columns to editorials, society news, culture, and local POLITICS, printing what many black

Southern Distribution of the *Chicago Defender*

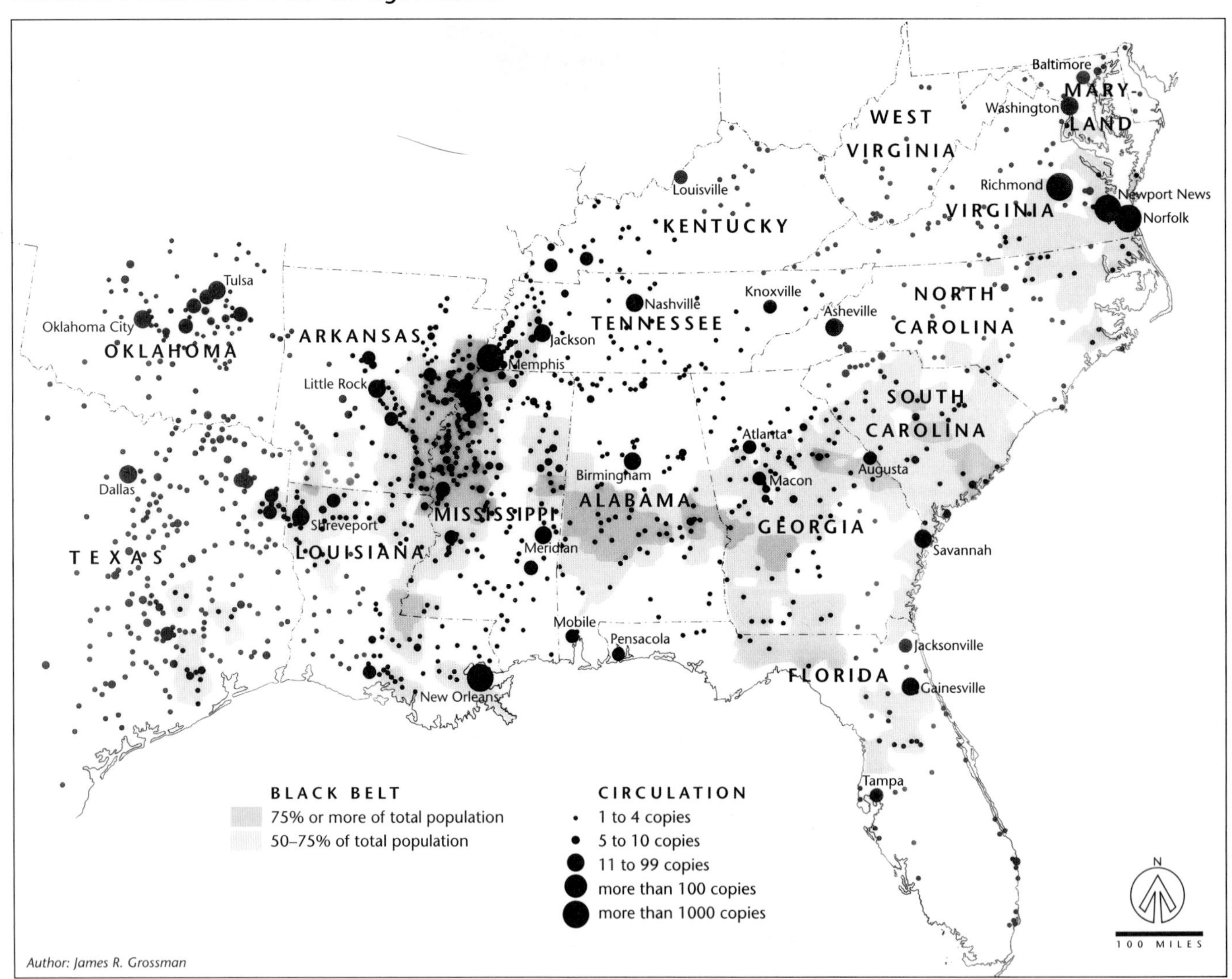

The *Chicago Defender* shipping list, which ran to 64 galley-sized pages, was obtained by Military Intelligence "in strict confidence" from the *Defender*'s distributor during the post–World War I federal investigations of radicals. The *Defender*'s circulation of approximately 50,000 in 1916 was an important factor in the "Great Migration" of black Southerners to northern cities. "I bought a Chicago Defender and after reading it and seeing the golden opportunity I have decided to leave this place at once," wrote a Tennessee railroad worker in 1917. By 1919 the *Defender*'s advocacy of migration had won new subscribers, especially in the South, which contributed three-fourths of its approximately 130,000 circulation that year.

southerners were afraid to whisper among themselves. For its part in encouraging the Great Migration, voicing the discontent of blacks, and revolutionizing black journalism, the *Defender* stands as one of the most powerful organs of social action in America.

Wallace Best

See also: Associated Negro Press; Bud Billiken Day Parade; Dziennik Związkowy; South Side

Further reading: Green, Adam Paul. "Selling the Race: Cultural Production and Notions of Community in Black Chicago, 1940–1955." Ph.D. diss., Yale University, 1998. • Grossman, James R. *Land of Hope: Chicago, Black Southerners, and the Great Migration.* 1989. • Ottley, Roi. *The Lonely Warrior: The Life and Times of Robert S. Abbott.* 1955.

Chicago Federation of Labor. Founded in 1896, the Chicago Federation of Labor (CFL) quickly emerged as the nation's most powerful central labor council. Owing to its ability to forge unified militancy from a politically diverse membership, the CFL proved an enduring working-class organization in Chicago, achieving its greatest prominence in the first half of the twentieth century.

Led by IRISH immigrant John Fitzpatrick, the CFL built upon its base of craft unions to foster the organization of teachers, service workers, and factory operatives. By 1910, the CFL's membership of 245,000 represented one-half of the city's workforce, including 35,000 women.

Employing radicals such as COMMUNIST William Foster, the CFL pioneered in industrial organization techniques during the late 1910s. Through its influential NEWSPAPER and radio station, the CFL also spurred the political and cultural integration of Chicago's diverse workforce in the 1920s. The interunion cooperation achieved by the CFL in the packinghouses and steel mills, though ultimately unsuccessful, served as a model for future union efforts of the late 1930s. After the AF of L and the CIO merged in the mid-1950s, the Cook County Industrial Union Council, the SOUTH CHICAGO Trades and Labor Assembly, and the Calumet Joint Labor Council joined the CFL. At the beginning of the twenty-first century, the CFL still commanded a membership of over 500,000.

Daniel A. Graff

See also: Congress of Industrial Organizations; Iron- and Steelworkers; Packinghouse Unions; Unionization; WCFL; Work; Work Culture

Further reading: Barrett, James R. *Work and Community in the Jungle: Chicago's Packinghouse Workers, 1984–1922.* 1987. • Cohen, Lizabeth. *Making a New Deal: Industrial Workers in Chicago, 1919–1939.* 1990. • Newell, Barbara Warne. *Chicago and the Labor Movement: Metropolitan Unionism in the 1930s.* 1961.

Chicago Federation of Musicians. The first permanent trade union among Chicago musicians, the Chicago Federation of Musicians (CFM) drew upon a well-established tradition of local musicians' protective organizations.

The origins of CFM can be traced to the Chicago Musicians' Protective Union (CMPU), founded in June 1864 by GERMAN American band musicians as a member of the city's General Trades Assembly. CMPU practically dictated working policies for local musicians, especially in the city's theaters and museums. Only a serious depression forced its demise in 1877.

In 1880, a resurrected CMPU emerged as the Chicago Musical Society (CMS), which conspicuously avoided affiliation with other labor organizations, although it did help to establish a National League of Musicians in 1886. Meanwhile, a few competing local musicians' unions sprouted, including a KNIGHTS OF LABOR affiliate.

When conductor Theodore Thomas defeated a CMS attempt to limit membership in the new Chicago Orchestra to local musicians, CMS in 1891 joined the American Federation of Labor. In 1896 it was a founding member of the American Federation of Musicians (AFM). A series of bitter jurisdictional disputes ensued, ultimately leading in 1901 to the Chicago Federation of Musicians, Local 10, AFM, an amalgamation of dissident CMS members and other musicians' unions. Excluded AFRICAN AMERICAN members established segregated Chicago Local 208.

Under its longtime president James Caesar Petrillo, CFM created a virtual closed shop after 1922. In 1966, Local 10 and Local 208 finally merged. Despite succeeding setbacks, Local 10-208 was still the third largest representative body of musicians in America through the 1990s.

Sandy R. Mazzola

See also: Chicago Federation of Labor; Chicago Symphony Orchestra; Unionization; Work; Work Culture

Further reading: Leiter, Robert D. *The Musicians and Petrillo.* 1953. • Mazzola, Sandy R. "Orchestras of Chicago: A Musical and Economic History." In *Transactions of the Illinois State Historical Society,* ed. Mary Ellen McElligott and Patrick H. O'Neal, 1988.

Chicago Hebrew Institute. Organized in 1903 on the NEAR WEST SIDE of Chicago to promote the moral, physical, religious, and civic welfare of JEWISH immigrants and residents, the Chicago Hebrew Institute served as a key institution in the AMERICANIZATION of Eastern European immigrants. In addition to classes in citizenship, English, commerce, domestic science, Jewish culture, literature, art, physical culture, drama, and music, it offered Jewish people a diverse range of experiences in Jewish American life, through programs in adult education, along with a library, a Jewish museum, and a summer camp for girls.

Philip L. Seman, director from 1913 to 1945, described the institute as "frankly Jewish and staunchly American." The institute changed its name to the Jewish People's Institute in 1922 and operated from a new building in NORTH LAWNDALE after 1926. A forerunner of today's JEWISH COMMUNITY CENTERS, the Jewish People's Institute served as a major community center for Chicago Jewry and gained national recognition with its successful programs in education and religion, along with vocational and recreational activities.

Linda J. Borish

See also: Settlement Houses; Social Services

Further reading: Cutler, Irving. *The Jews of Chicago: From Shtetl to Suburb.* 1996. • Meites, Hyman L. *History of the Jews of Chicago.* 1927. • Seman, Philip L. "Democracy in Action." *Chicago Jewish Forum* (1943): 49–54.

Chicago Heights, IL, Cook County, 26 miles S of the Loop. Chicago Heights is located six miles from the Indiana border at the crossroads of Lincoln Highway (Route 30) and Dixie Highway (Hubbard's Trail). Absalom Wells built a cabin on the ridge above Thorn Creek in the 1830s and was the first farmer in the area that was called Thorn Grove by the 1840s. The First Presbyterian Church established a place of worship and a cemetery for the rural community.

In the early 1890s a group of Chicago developers led by Charles Wacker determined to establish "Chicago Heights" as an outer-ring industrial suburb. They successfully recruited large-scale heavy industries such as Inland Steel, and built the impressive Hotel Victoria (designed by Louis Sullivan). Community growth and development progressed rapidly. Chicago Heights boasted a population of 19,653 in 1920. ITALIAN, POLISH, SLOVAK, LITHUANIAN, IRISH, and AFRICAN AMERICAN workers poured into the East Side and Hill neighborhoods to be close to the heavy industries. The downtown area served as the retail, BANKING, TRANSPORTATION, and entertainment center for nearby communities and rural settlements in a 15-mile radius. Local pride (and commerce) swelled when city fathers persuaded the Lincoln Highway Association (in 1916) to route the first transcontinental highway through the city, making it "the Crossroads of the Nation." The city gained some notoriety as a stomping ground for top bootleggers during the PROHIBITION era and, because of its industrial base, was hit hard by the GREAT DEPRESSION in the 1930s. Chicago Heights factories worked around the clock in the 1940s to produce steel, CHEMICAL, and war materials of every sort. WORLD WAR II set the stage for a golden era that saw residential expansion to the north and west, prosperity for downtown retailers, and (in the mid-1950s) the coming of a new Ford stamping plant that provided employment for thousands. In the 1950s Bloom Township High School also gained a high level of recognition in sports and academics.

Changing retail patterns including competition from the PARK FOREST Plaza brought big challenges to the commercial center in the 1970s. Heavy manufacturing employment became less reliable as well.

The diverse population of Chicago Heights peaked at 40,900 in 1970 and declined to 32,776 in 2000, with the percentage of African American and Hispanic minorities on the rise. The prosperity of the late 1990s brought stabilization of the industrial base, a movement for renewal of the old East Side and Hill neighborhoods, a preservation movement, and continued challenges in the commercial sector.

Dominic Candeloro

See also: Economic Geography; Iron and Steel; Iron- and Steelworkers; Land Use; Shopping Districts and Malls

Further reading: Beeson, F. S. *History of Chicago Heights, Illinois, 1833–1938.* 1938. • Candeloro, Dominic, and Barbara Paul. *Images of America: Chicago Heights.* 1998. • Candeloro, Dominic. "Suburban Italians: Chicago Heights 1890–1975." In *Ethnic Chicago,* ed. Melvin Holli and Peter d'A. Jones, 1981.

Chicago Historical Society. The Chicago Historical Society, organized by BUSINESS leaders in 1856 to foster an appreciation for local and national history, is Chicago's oldest cultural institution. The Great FIRE OF 1871 destroyed the society's 1868 building at the northwest corner of Dearborn and Ontario Streets, and most of its collection. Operating from temporary quarters on the same site, the society rebuilt its collections. In 1896, a new permanent facility designed by Henry Ives Cobb replaced the temporary structure.

The 1920 acquisition of thousands of manuscripts and artifacts from the estate of Charles F. Gunther helped the historical society become a nationally known collection of decorative and industrial arts, paintings and sculpture, and costumes. The Gunther Collection's unusually rich materials in seventeenth-century, eighteenth-century, and CIVIL WAR history (including Abraham Lincoln's deathbed) also enhanced both the American history and the Chicago history collections.

In 1932, the society moved to a new red brick Georgian-style facility at the corner of Clark Street and North Avenue in LINCOLN PARK designed by Graham, Anderson, Probst & White. There, under the guidance of director Paul Angle (1945–1964), the historical society first turned to interpreting the city's history. Director Harold K. Skramstad, Jr. (1974–1981), drew upon the scholarship of urban historians to shape the innovative Chicago History Galleries, opened in 1979.

Encouraged by the Chicago Park District's 1981 decision to issue matching bonds for capital improvements to museums on its land and the new leadership of Ellsworth H. Brown, (1981–1993), the historical society initiated self-studies of its facility requirements, collecting scope, and audience. Capital expansion and renovation of the main facility began in 1986, resulting in a new wing and an underground storage facility, interior remodeling, and a new facade designed by the architectural firm Holabird & Root.

During the presidency of Douglas Greenberg (1993–2000), the society committed itself to documenting and interpreting Chicago's diverse populations. New initiatives—studying the history of the city's neighborhoods, establishing an Internet presence, developing facilities for oral and video history, enhancing its research center—distinguished it among its peer institutions. A 1998 mission statement reflected a new commitment to history education and the civic role of museums and libraries in American cities.

Under the leadership of Lonnie G. Bunch, who became president in 2001, the historical society has enhanced its role in history education while emphasizing its function as a history museum rooted in its transformed Chicago history galleries.

Michael H. Ebner

See also: City as Artifact: The Above-Ground Archaeology of an Urban History; Lincoln Park; Museums in the Park; Near North Side

Further reading: Angle, Paul M. *The Chicago Historical Society, 1856–1956: An Unconventional Chronicle.* 1956. • Silvestro, Clement. "The Candyman's Mixed Bag." *Chicago History* 2.2 (Spring 1972): 86–99. • York, Byron. "The Pursuit of Culture: Founding the Chicago Historical Society." *Chicago History* 10.3 (Fall 1981): 141–150.

Chicago Housing Authority. The initial goal of PUBLIC HOUSING was to provide decent housing for poor and low-income households. There have been two categories of public housing in Chicago: for families and for the elderly.

Founded in 1937, the Chicago Housing Authority (CHA), has been responsible for all public housing in the city of Chicago. It is a municipal not-for-profit corporation, governed by commissioners who are appointed by the mayor. Social reformer Elizabeth Wood was CHA's first executive secretary, serving with distinction until 1954.

The first public housing projects were made possible by the Public Works Administration and then the federal Housing Act of 1937. Prior to WORLD WAR II there were four projects, all composed of low-rise (two-to-four-story) buildings. Three projects were opened in 1938: Jane Addams Houses on the NEAR WEST SIDE, comprising 32 buildings for 1,027 families; Julia C. Lathrop Homes on the North Side for

Poster for the dedication ceremony for Ida B. Wells Homes, 1940. Designer: Unknown. Source: Library of Congress.

925 families; and Trumbull Park Homes on the far SOUTH SIDE for 426 families. Unlike these three, which were built for whites (although 2.5 percent of the units in the Jane Addams Houses were initially assigned to AFRICAN AMERICAN families), a fourth project, Ida B. Wells Homes, in the ghetto, was for blacks. Far larger than the other projects, it housed 1,662 families.

The racial segregation embodied in these developments was in compliance with federal policy (the "Neighborhood Composition Rule"), which required that the tenants of a housing development be of the same race as the people of the area in which it was located. Managers were selective in choosing among the thousands of families who applied for apartments. There had to be one employed breadwinner and the tenants had to behave according to prescribed rules.

During World War II, CHA was redirected to create housing for the workers in war industries. Two large projects had some units for black families, but, in addition, one very large project, Altgeld Gardens, built in RIVERDALE at the edge of the city with 1,500 units, was designed exclusively for black war workers. After the war, CHA provided several thousand units of temporary housing for veterans, in such forms as temporary plywood houses and Quonset huts. Abandoning the Neighborhood Composition Rule, CHA introduced a short-lived policy of racial integration, which precipitated a series of violent white-black confrontations.

Chicago Housing Authority Family Projects, 1985

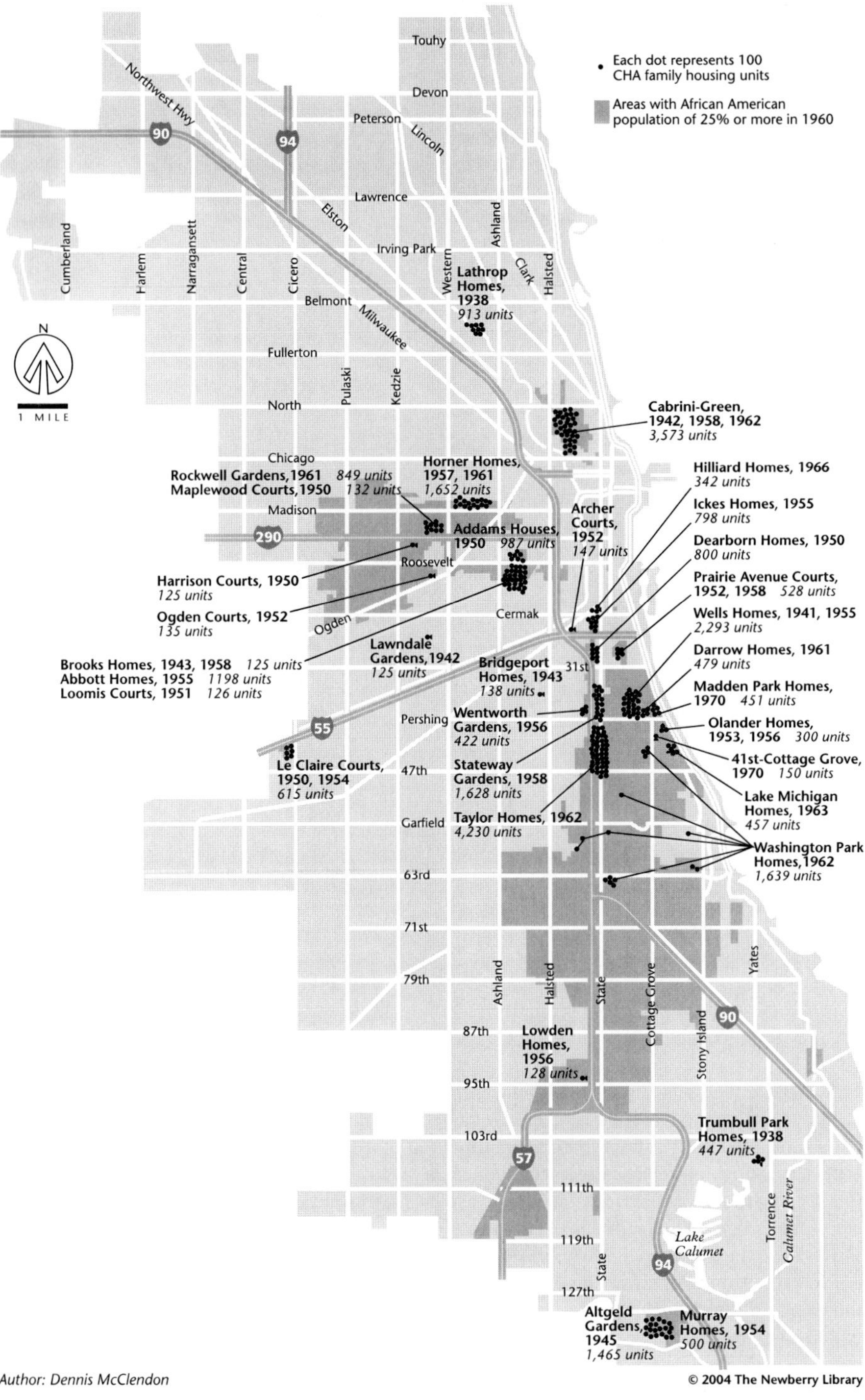

Author: Dennis McClendon

The Chicago Housing Authority (CHA) was established in 1937 to provide housing for poor and low-income city residents. From 1937 to 1968, the CHA built numerous apartment complexes, initially low-rise, and operated by managers empowered to exclude potential tenants whom they thought might be troublesome. A few were racially diverse. At first, projects were placed in both white and black areas, but white aldermen later blocked their construction in white areas. After 1955 most public housing was built in tower projects on superblocks placed in or on the margins of black neighborhoods in spaces opened up through urban renewal programs. Under pressure to relocate residents displaced by freeway construction and urban renewal, the CHA abandoned tenant selection, and long-term maintenance of the no-frills structures became highly problematic, especially given the unusually high proportion of children in the buildings and inadequate maintenance by the agency. After charges that the city perpetuated racial segregation through its public housing policy of building only in black areas, and the withdrawal of significant federal funding for new construction, the existing pattern was frozen in space. As high-rise public housing has been declared a broad failure, policy since 1996 has led to the demolition of several prominent projects, including many units of the Robert Taylor Homes, Stateway Gardens, and Cabrini-Green complexes.

When Congress passed the Housing Act of 1949, which provided substantial funding for public housing, CHA was ready with a map of proposed sites for projects to be built on open land throughout the city, but the city council rejected this map altogether. White aldermen rejected plans for public housing in their wards. CHA's policy thereafter was to build family housing only in black residential areas or adjacent to existing projects. This rejection explains the concentration of public housing in the city center on the South and West Sides.

Most of the high-rise projects of the 1950s and 1960s took one basic form. They were larger than the earlier developments, ranging from 150 to 4,415 APARTMENTS (averaging about 1,027). Most were built in superblocks: streets that had previously traversed the redeveloped areas were ripped up, replaced by what were supposed to be grassy areas. The structures were high-rise apartment buildings with elevators, many reaching 15 to 19 stories. In style, they were modern but plain, following a "no-frills" principle. Designers of postwar projects included Bertrand Goldberg; Holabird, Root & Burgee; Keck & Keck; Shaw, Metz & Associates; and Skidmore, Owings & Merrill. Three high-rise projects were opened in 1955. Grace Abbott Homes was the largest, with 1,200 apartments in 40 buildings covering what had been 10 city blocks.

Several projects like CABRINI-GREEN on the NEAR NORTH SIDE grew by accretion. It began with Frances Cabrini Homes, a low-rise development of 586 units, opened in 1942. Cabrini Extension was built in 1958; it had 1,925 units in 15 buildings. Then in 1962 William Green Homes was built on another adjacent site with 1,096. Altogether, Cabrini-Green had 3,607 units.

A series of large projects formed "the State Street Corridor," a narrow zone of public housing, more than four miles long. The corridor included STATEWAY GARDENS (1958), which comprised eight buildings; and ROBERT TAYLOR HOMES (1962), the largest public housing project in the United States. When it opened, Robert Taylor Homes had 4,415 units in 28 identical 16-story buildings.

After 1950, public housing began rapidly to deteriorate. Some buildings had serious design flaws. All buildings were subject to hard use and were badly maintained, which accelerated their deterioration. CHA managers stopped screening applicants and the socioeconomic mix of tenants changed, as the CHA was directed to accommodate all families who had been displaced by URBAN RENEWAL, EXPRESSWAY construction, and other forms of slum clearance.

By the late 1950s, it was apparent that there were serious physical problems in the high-rise projects. Nonetheless, CHA continued to build high-rise projects in black districts until 1968, when the federal government stopped funding high-rise buildings for family housing. All told, CHA built 168 high-rise buildings with approximately 19,700 apartments for families.

In 1966 a group of tenants sued the CHA, alleging that the agency was perpetuating racial segregation by siting projects in the ghetto. In GAUTREAUX *v. Chicago Housing Authority,* a federal judge enjoined CHA from building additional family housing in black residential areas. He ordered the agency to build scattered-site housing elsewhere in the city. Thereafter the authority built no more than a handful of scattered-site dwellings.

Following the *Gautreaux* decision, almost all of the housing built by CHA was for elderly tenants, housing that could be built in white sections of the city. CHA erected its first project for the elderly in 1959, and between 1961 and 1976 the CHA built 46 developments, totaling 9,607 units.

Family high-rise projects continued to exhibit social problems and the buildings continued to deteriorate. In 1996, the federal department of Housing and Urban Development (HUD) took control of the CHA, on the grounds of mismanagement and poor performance. At about the same time, HUD introduced a radical change of policy, advocating demolition of failed high-rise buildings. Chicago demolished several high-rise buildings in 1996 and 1997, planning to redevelop those areas with a mix of public housing and housing for middle-income households. The CHA regained control from the federal government, as it undertook continued demolition and redevelopment.

Harvey M. Choldin

See also: Built Environment of the Chicago Region; Housing for the Elderly; New Deal; Planning Chicago; Public Works, Federal Funding for; Racism, Ethnicity, and White Identity; South Side; Subsidized Housing

Further reading: Devereux, Bowly, Jr. *The Poorhouse: Subsidized Housing in Chicago, 1895–1976.* 1978. • Hirsch, Arnold R. *Making the Second Ghetto: Race and Housing in Chicago, 1940–1960.* 1983. • Meyerson, Martin, and Edward C. Banfield. *Politics, Planning, and the Public Interest: The Case of Public Housing in Chicago.* 1955.

Chicago Industrial School for Girls. *See* House of the Good Shepherd/Chicago Industrial School for Girls

Ancient Indian Earthworks in the Chicago Region

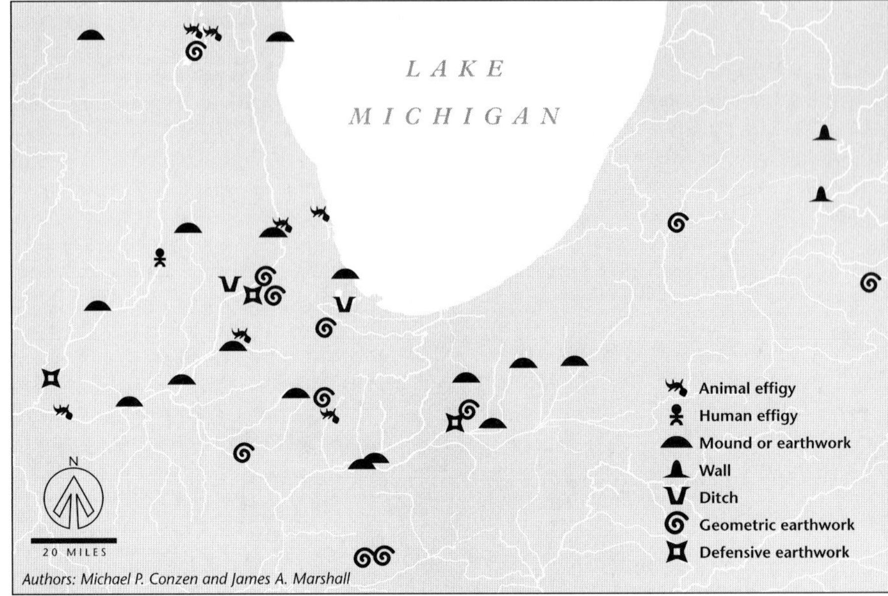

Patient research in field and archive has documented the existence of a remarkably extensive and diverse distribution of Indian earthworks in the Chicago region dating from ancient times. Many sites are difficult to associate with any particular people or time period. Similarly, their individual functions remain largely obscure, and some no longer survive, such as the mound that was once near the 79th Street beach on Chicago's South Side.

Chicago in the Middle Ground. Archaeological evidence and NATIVE AMERICAN oral tradition indicate that Chicago was a crossroads of trade during the late pre-Columbian period. Artifacts suggest many people passed through the region carrying trade goods from Mississippian settlements to the south, or copper from Lake Superior, but these travelers probably were itinerant traders or small groups of hunters harvesting the rich fauna of the region. By the mid-seventeenth century the MIAMIS had established some villages along the Chicago and DES PLAINES Rivers, but during the 1650s they abandoned the region, moving first west of the Mississippi and then to Wisconsin. During the 1670s FRENCH travelers encountered winter camps of ILLINOIS hunting in the region. The Miamis reoccupied the region in the 1690s, forming two villages on the CHICAGO RIVER, one of 2,500 inhabitants near the river's mouth and another about three miles upstream. Other Miami villages were located on the CALUMET RIVER near the modern Indiana border, and at the junction of the Des Plaines and Kankakee rivers.

The Miamis abandoned their Chicago villages during the first decade of the eighteenth century, moving to the Maumee and Wabash Valleys in Indiana, while the Illinois ceased to hunt in the region and relocated down the Illinois Valley toward the Mississippi. Meanwhile, POTAWATOMIS, SACS, and OTTAWAS from Michigan and Wisconsin began to hunt in the Chicago region, but no permanent villages were established because of warfare between the French and the Foxes, which embroiled much of northern Illinois and southern Wisconsin until the late 1730s. During the 1740s however, the Potawatomis constructed a permanent village on the Chicago River, and within a decade they had been joined by Ottawas and Chippewas. These three tribes established mixed settlements along the Des Plaines and Kankakee rivers, eventually forcing the Illinois from the Lake Peoria region, which the Potawatomis occupied prior to the American Revolution.

The intermittent NATIVE AMERICAN communities at Chicago maintained close ties with the French. Jesuit priests, traders, and French officials visited the region during the last quarter of the seventeenth century, and as Native Americans returned to the region, their relationship with the French intensified. In 1673 Father Jacques Marquette and trader Louis Jolliet passed over the Chicago PORTAGE from the Des Plaines River, and the following year Marquette and two companions spent the winter at a bivouac on the Chicago River, where they obtained food from hunting camps of Illinois Indians and from two French traders who recently had entered the region. Father Claude Allouez crossed over the portage in 1676–77, and one year later he was followed by Robert Cavelier de La Salle, who passed along the lakeshore en route from Green Bay to the St. Joseph River. During the following two

Chicago's Place in the Water Routes of the Indian World, 1600–1830

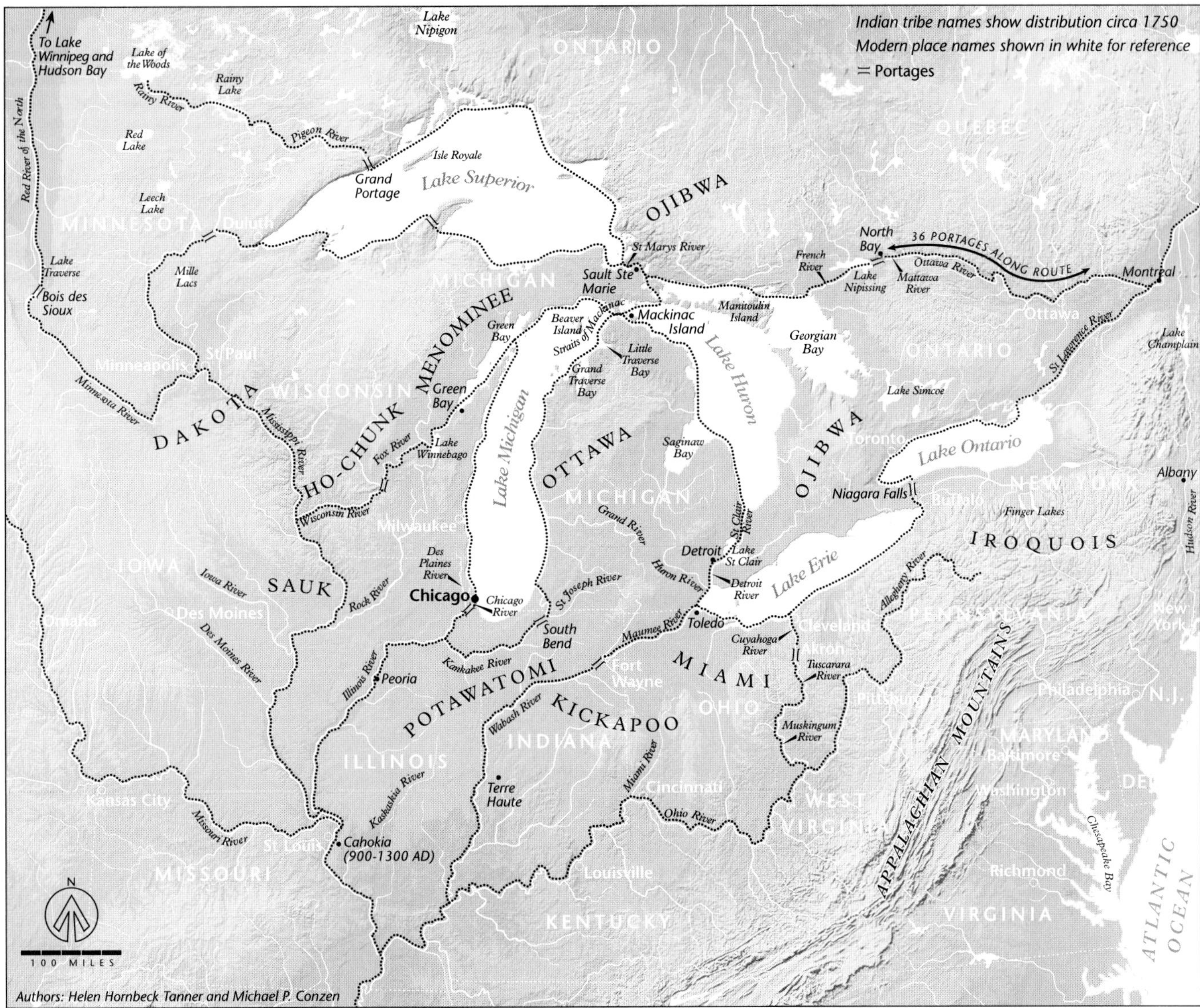

For centuries the Chicago area represented for Native Americans just one of a number of key portages for long- distance canoe travel between the Great Lakes and the river network of the Mississippi Basin. These routes were vital for seasonal migrations and periodic trade between populations bordering the Great Lakes and the middle Mississippi Valley. These corridors of interregional movement proved essential to the successful development of the fur trade following contact with Europeans, a trade that flourished in the Chicago area until the opening decades of the nineteenth century.

decades a series of French traders, priests, and officials used the portage, occasionally caching trade goods near the river's mouth, but with the possible exception of French traders who resided among the Miamis, no official French residence was established until 1696, when Father Pierre Pinet established the MISSION OF THE GUARDIAN ANGEL. The mission remained near the mouth of the Chicago River for only one year but was reestablished in 1698, before being permanently abandoned in 1700, when Pinet left the region to minister among the Illinois at Cahokia.

After 1700 the French maintained no official presence at Chicago, and their influence in the region temporarily declined. For a quarter century between 1710 and 1735, French hegemony in Illinois and Wisconsin was challenged by the MESQUAKIE or Fox Indians, a tribe from Wisconsin who resented French attempts to trade firearms to the Sioux. Warfare between the Foxes and the French and their allies spread across the region, and the Foxes so disrupted the French FUR TRADE that travelers between the GREAT LAKES and French settlements in southern Illinois avoided the Chicago portage in favor of the more circuitous Wabash route. Consequently, French traders and their Native American allies withdrew from the Chicago region while the Foxes established a village on Lake Pistakee, in modern Lake County. In 1733, after a series of French military victories, the Foxes finally withdrew to Wisconsin and French traders again traversed and traded at the Chicago portage.

After 1740 French influence in the region again increased. French traders, both licensed and unlicensed, permeated the western Great Lakes, and many married Native American women who produced families of MÉTIS, or mixed-blood, children. This intermarriage of French and Native Americans produced a society and culture that would dominate Chicago and much of the Great Lakes region through the first decades of the nineteenth century. Described by historian Richard White as "the middle ground," the emergent society incorporated both Native American and French

Indian Settlement Pattern in the Chicago Region, circa 1830

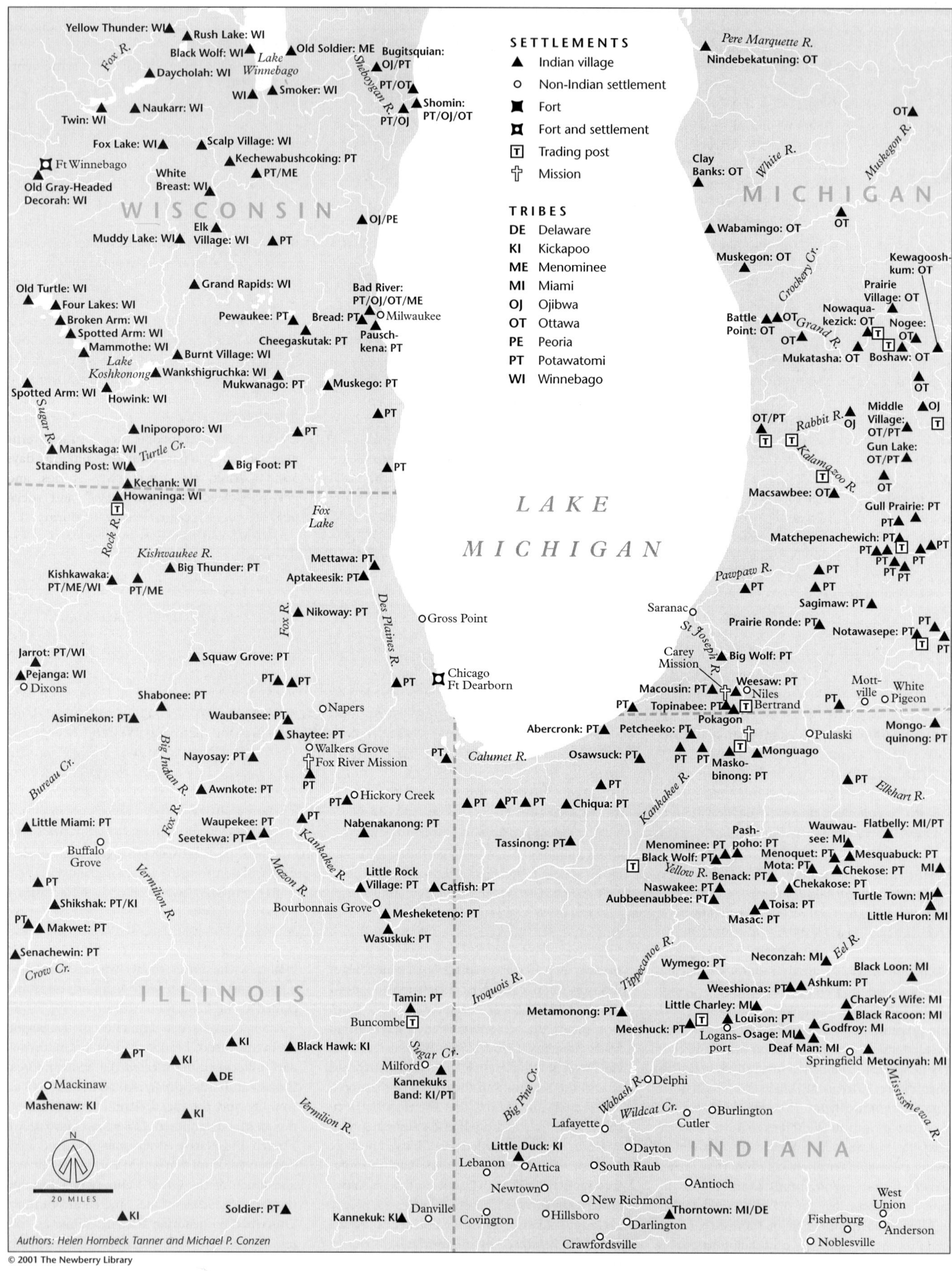

cultural patterns but reshaped them into an indigenous blend.

The middle ground's biological and cultural fusion produced advantages to all concerned. By marrying into leading Native American families, French traders gained access to and support from widespread kinship networks that functioned throughout the Great Lakes and the Illinois country. Married to women from prominent Native American families, the traders were welcomed into tribal hunting camps scattered throughout the region, and their kinship ties also facilitated the exchange of commodities. In turn, Native American people gained access to merchants who supplied them with trade goods and other products increasingly critical to their way of life. In addition, those merchants were bound through familial obligations to provide trade goods to all members of the kinship network. In the Chicago region the marriages of traders such as Antoine Ouilmette, Jean Baptiste Point DuSable, and Jean Baptiste Beaubien to Native American women provide good examples of these unions.

These Native American women contributed markedly to their family's success. Since their husbands often were absent on trading expeditions, the women sometimes supervised and maintained their husbands' trading posts. Marie Madeline Réaume L'Archeveque Chevalier, an Illinois woman living in southwestern Michigan, and Madelaine LaFromboise, an Ottawa woman, operated their own trading companies after becoming widows. Although relatively little corn or other grain was grown at Chicago, Native American women in adjoining areas, particularly the St. Joseph Valley in Michigan, produced surplus foodstuffs which were transported throughout the Lake Michigan region, providing food for the traders, voyageurs, and engagees involved in the fur trade.

The marriages produced significant numbers of Métis children, who served as ambassadors of the middle ground, often negotiating political, economic, or social differences among tribal peoples, Europeans, and, later, Americans. The Langlade family, Métis-Ottawa residents of the Mackinac region, exercised considerable influence in the Chicago region during the French period, while Billy Caldwell, Alexander Robinson, and Madore Beaubien provided leadership for the Potawatomis at Chicago while also serving the interests of the American government. Their ethnic identities were mutable: sometimes they acted in consort with and were identified as part of the Native American community, at other times they identified as Europeans or Americans.

In the late eighteenth century the small Native American and métis community that had settled at Chicago retained close ties to the French community in southern Illinois as well as to communities in Mackinac and Detroit. Among the most prominent was Jean Baptiste Point DuSable, an Afro-French fur trader whose partners traded along the Illinois River from Peoria to Cahokia. DuSable himself was trading during the 1770s near present-day Michigan City, where he was arrested briefly in 1779 by British officials who suspected him of rebel sympathies. By the late 1780s he began developing a farm near the mouth of the Chicago River, where he also did some trading. He erected a spacious five-room "mansion" with a long covered porch modeled after French creole homes in the American Bottom. DuSable prospered during the 1790s, entertained travelers who passed over the portage, and was highly respected by both Native American and métis inhabitants. In 1800, however, he sold his holdings at Chicago and moved to Spanish Upper Louisiana near present-day St. Charles, Missouri.

Most houses at Chicago were less imposing than the DuSable residence. Houses were constructed of logs, but generally following the old French-Canadian fashion, with rough-hewn logs set vertically in a trench rather than placed horizontally. The logs were chinked with grass and mud, then covered with either bark or lumber. The structures featured high-pitched, thatched or shingled roofs, with a fireplace and rude chimney in the center rather than at one end of the dwelling.

In 1803, the United States built Fort Dearborn on the south side of the Chicago River. By 1810 settlement at Chicago clustered at several places. North of the river's mouth were the Kinzie family, whose patriarch John Kinzie occupied DuSable's old mansion. Further north, at Grosse Pointe (Wilmette), Antoine Ouilmette and his relatives maintained a trading post where the road to Milwaukee left the Chicago community. On the south side of the river, near Fort Dearborn, Jean Baptiste Beaubien and his family maintained a trading establishment and occupied a series of log houses. Further south was Hardscrabble, (modern Bridgeport), where the southern branch of the river emerged from Mud Lake. Here lived Alexander Robinson and members of the Bourassa, LaFramboise, and Chevalier families. Finally, to the west, along the Des Plaines in modern Riverside, several villages of Potawatomis had erected their cabins and wigwams.

These physically separated settlements shared a focal point of social activity at Wolf Point, where the two forks of the Chicago joined before flowing east into Lake Michigan. Here people met to drink considerable quantities of French brandy, British rum, and American bourbon and to wager furs, trade goods, and other valuables on card games, shooting matches, and horse races. Here also outdoor dances were held on warm summer nights, and while fiddles, flutes, and mouth organs played Creole or frontier melodies, Métis women danced with their husbands or with eligible bachelors from among the ranks of traders and voyageurs. Wolf Point also was the scene of considerable Potawatomi festivity, and tribespeople from the separate camps assembled to celebrate seasonal ceremonies and to dance to traditional songs and drumbeats. During the winter, people met at rude taverns near the point to pass away the cold gray days and to drink, play cards, swap stories, and gossip. Indeed, the "frolicking" and social activities of Chicago's residents during this period seemed to transcend economics and ethnicity.

John Kinzie is a good example of someone who negotiated this social and economic world. Born in Quebec in 1763, Kinzie moved to Detroit as a boy after his widowed mother married Thomas Forsyth, a Scots-Irish merchant at Grosse Point, Michigan. There Kinzie was raised amidst Creole and Métis contemporaries, and as a young man he married Margaret Mackenzie, born in Virginia but captured as a young child and reared by the Shawnees. After the revolution Margaret returned to Virginia with their three children and Kinzie married a second time, to Elizabeth McPhillip, a Detroit widow, but also a former Indian captive with important ties to the tribes. Kinzie, who first traded in the Sandusky region, continued to trade in Michigan, but after 1803 he relocated to Chicago, where he traded with the surrounding Native American communities. He built a new trading post on the south side of the river, near the newly established Fort Dearborn, and eventually supplied the garrison with both luxuries and necessities. He also forced Métis Jean Lalime to relinquish DuSable's large house, which he then occupied with his family. When Lalime protested the loss of his property, Kinzie first quarreled with the man then killed him.

Kinzie's ascension at Chicago continued the pattern of white traders married to Native American (or captive) women, and as Kinzie's trading establishment grew, he employed large numbers of Métis, even some, including Billy Caldwell and Alexander Robinson from Michigan. Moreover, he also cemented his ties with Métis traders at Milwaukee, apprenticing their

As Euro-Americans penetrated the Chicago region in the 1820s, they encountered a widespread network of Indian villages occupied by people of many distinct tribes, some places containing families of more than one group. This comparatively dense pattern of settlements favored sites along the margins of rivers and lake shores, wherever fish, game, and plant resources were abundant. By 1830, American intrusion was evident in the villages and small towns along the Wabash Valley of Indiana, and in the thin scatter of trading posts, forts, villages, and Christian missions across other parts of the area.

part-Potawatomi children as servants or employees in his household. Yet by 1800 the Indian trade at Chicago was no longer financed by or dependent upon traders at Peoria or southern Illinois. Its new ties were to Mackinac and Detroit, and trading houses at those locations supplied the Chicago community with most of its goods and finances. Moreover, the Great Sac Trail, an overland route between the upper Mississippi Valley and British Indian Department offices in Ontario, passed just south of Chicago, providing additional ties between Kinzie and other traders with merchants at Detroit or in Canada.

The War of 1812 marked the death knell for the middle ground at Chicago. In August 1812 the first Fort Dearborn (built in 1803) was evacuated by the garrison, and as the troops and a party of civilians traversed the lakeshore en route toward Fort Wayne they were attacked and defeated by pro-British Potawatomis. Kinzie and his associates lost their property, and when they returned to Chicago following the war, the pace of change overwhelmed them. The fort was rebuilt and regarrisoned in 1816, but the middle ground was falling apart. The fur trade in the Chicago region declined rapidly, and the American Fur Company gained control of the remaining traffic. Kinzie, Beaubien, and other Métis traders were employed by the company, but they were given secondary roles. New groups of Americans, YANKEES (New Englanders from the east), moved into the region and the old way of life disintegrated.

Some of the Métis, including Mark Beaubien, opened inns or taverns to serve the newcomers, but they became alienated from the more aggressive, highly organized, and systematic Yankees. Moreover, within two decades both the Native Americans and the Métis found that they no longer had a place at the Chicago portage. The onrushing American population demanded access to Native American lands in the region, and the government signed a series of TREATIES with the Potawatomis and other tribes which transferred their lands to the United States and provided for the removal of Native Americans across the Mississippi. Ironically, the large Métis population which inhabited the portage now found that their separate identity as Métis was no longer accepted by the newcomers. The Yankees lumped all people of Native American descent together as "Indians, pure or half-breeds," and demanded that the Métis traders and their families join with the Potawatomis and remove to the west. Those few Métis families who remained at Chicago did so only by de-emphasizing their Native American heritage, identifying with the new ruling class, and adopting the Yankees' cultural values.

In making these changes, they entered a new and different world. Economic activities within the middle ground had been focused upon the fur trade, and individuals, families, and extended kinship groups all had endeavored to produce enough commodities to maintain a comfortable existence. But their efforts had been much more communal, and ties to family and clan had taken precedence over the accumulation of wealth by individuals. Hospitality and generosity had been highly valued, and people enjoyed the present; they did not regularly postpone the pleasures of the day for anticipated benefits to be obtained in the distant future. In addition, one's identity was to family and clan, which in turn transcended "race" as it was defined by the Yankees. One might be a Beaubien or a Kinzie, with family ties to Ottawa, Potawatomi, Creole, or Scots-Irish families, but one envisioned one's identity within that multifaceted framework, rather than in terms of a mutually exclusive racial category.

The new society cherished different values. Its members believed that future happiness could be assured only by limiting one's enjoyment of the present, and that wealth should be amassed and hoarded by individuals, rather then shared with a large network of family members and kin. Thrift and saving was valued over generosity, and men were honored for the treasures they accumulated rather than for their hospitality to relatives and friends. Moreover, as the decades passed, ethnic delineations were sharpened. Métis, regardless of their family ties or former acceptance by the old community, were barred from joining a new socioeconomic elite. Race became an exclusionary device, leaving little place for people of mixed heritage. The middle ground was ending. Chicago had entered a new age.

R. David Edmunds

A Folklore of the Middle Ground

In 1951, Nelson Algren published his complex essay exploring the psyche of Chicago. He began with a common romanticized folklore of the middle ground:

To the east were the moving waters as far as the eye could follow. To the west a sea of grass as far as wind might reach.

Waters restlessly, with every motion, slipping out of used colors for new. So that each fresh wind off the lake washed the prairie grasses with used sea-colors: the prairie moved in the light like a secondhand sea....

The portage's single hotel was a barracks, its streets were pig-wallows, and all the long summer night the Pottawattomies mourned beside that river: down in the barracks the horse-dealers and horse-stealers were making a night of it again. Whiskey-and-vermilion hustlers, painting the night vermilion.

In the Indian grass the Indians listened: they too had lived by night.

And heard, in the uproar in the hotel, the first sounds of a city that was to live by night after the wilderness had passed. A city that was to roll boulevards down out of pig-wallows and roll its dark river uphill.

That was to forge, out of steel and blood-red neon, its own peculiar wilderness.

Yankee and *voyageur,* the Irish and the Dutch, Indian traders and Indian agents, half-breed and quarter-breed and no breed at all, in the final counting they were all of a single breed. They all had hustler's blood. And kept the old Sauganash in a hustler's uproar.

They hustled the land, they hustled the Indian, they hustled by night and they hustled by day. They hustled guns and furs and peltries, grog and the blood-red whiskey-dye; they hustled with dice or a deck or a derringer.

Algren, Nelson. *Chicago: City on the Make.* 1951.

See also: Black Hawk War; Multicentered Chicago; Native American Religion

Further reading: Beaubien, Frank G. "The Beaubiens of Chicago." *Illinois Catholic Historical Review* 2 (July 1919 and January 1920): 96–105, 348–364. This two-part essay contains considerable information regarding the Beaubien family and their associates at Chicago.

Chicago Area Archaeology. Bulletin no. 3 of the Illinois Archaeological Survey. 1961. This bulletin contains a series of essays that focus upon the archaeology of the Chicago region.

Chicago Historical Society. Holdings include several collections of papers and documents that provide considerable information about Chicago during the last decades of the eighteenth and first decades of the nineteenth centuries. Among the most important collections are the papers of the following: American Fur Company, Beaubien Family, Madore Beaubien, Billy Caldwell, Gurdon S. Hubbard, John Kinzie, Juliette Kinzie, John Harris Kinzie, and Alexander Wolcott.

Clifton, James A. "Merchant, Soldier, Broker, Chief: A Corrected Obituary of Captain Billy Caldwell." *Journal of the Illinois State Historical Society* (August 1978): 185–210. This essay traces the career and adaptability of this Métis leader and argues that ethnic identity at Chicago was mutable.

Edmunds, R. David. *The Potawatomis: Keepers of the Fire.* 1978. This volume offers a good survey of the Potawatomis at Chicago from their first contact with the French through their removal from Illinois.

Edmunds, R. David, and Joseph L. Peyser. *The Fox Wars: The Mesquakie Challenge to New France.* 1993. This history of the conflict between the French and the Mesquakies illustrates that the warfare was very disruptive to French occupation of the Chicago region and also indicates that not all Native Americans were integrated into the "Middle Ground" or French alliance.

Kinzie, Juliette. *Wau-Bun: The "Early Day" in the North-West.* 1932. Although some information in this small volume seems questionable, it contains reminiscences of Chicago during the first three decades of the nineteenth century and offers valuable information regarding the Fort Dearborn attack.

National Archives. The National Archives of the United States hold a plethora of records that focus upon Chicago during the first three decades of the nineteenth century. Particularly important are Records of the Bureau of Indian Affairs (RG 75), Letters Received by the Office of Indian Affairs (M234), Chicago Agency, 1824–1827; Records of the Secretary of War Relating to Indian Affairs, Letters Received (M271), 1800–1823, and Letters Sent (M15), 1800–1824; and Records of the Superintendent of Indian Trade, Letters Received (T58), 1806–1824, and Letters Sent (M16), 1807–1823. In addition, the Records of the Office of the Secretary of War (RG 107) also contain information on Chicago during this period. See Letters Received by the Secretary, Main Series (M221), 1801–1835, Letters Received by the Secretary, Unregistered Series (M222), 1805–1836, and Letters Sent by the Secretary Relating to Military Affairs (M6), 1800–1816.

Peterson, Jacqueline. "Goodbye, Madore Beaubien: The Americanization of Early Chicago." *Chicago History,* n.s., 9 (Summer 1980): 98–111. This essay examines Métis and Creole society at Chicago and traces its demise after the War of 1812. It contains excellent information on the Beaubien and Kinzie families.

Peterson, Jacqueline. "Wild Chicago: The Formation and Destruction of a Multiracial Community on the Midwestern Frontier, 1816–1837," in *The Ethnic Frontier: Essays in the History of Group Survival in Chicago and the Midwest,* ed. Melvin G. Holli and Peter d'A. Jones, 1977, 26–71. This essay offers an excellent analysis of life at Chicago during the first three decades of the nineteenth century.

Quaife, Milo Milton. *Chicago and the Old Northwest, 1673–1835.* 1913. Although written in the early twentieth century, this volume remains the most detailed account of events at Chicago during these years—an excellent reference source for individuals, events, places, and other factual information.

Sleeper-Smith, Susan. *Indian Women and French Men: Rethinking Cultural Encounter in the Western Great Lakes,* 2001. This volume provides excellent insights into the critical roles played by Native American and Métis women in the Lake Michigan–Illinois region during the eighteenth and early nineteenth centuries.

State Historical Society of Wisconsin. The Draper Manuscripts, contained within the society's holdings, contain significant materials that focus upon the Chicago region during the period of the American Revolution and the War of 1812. Particularly important are Draper's Notes and the Thomas Forsyth Papers.

Tanner, Helen Hornbeck, ed. *Atlas of Great Lakes Indian History.* 1987. This indispensable reference work, with its excellent maps and texts, is critical for any study of Native American occupancy of the Chicago region.

White, Richard. *The Middle Ground: Indians, Empires, and Republics in the Great Lakes Region, 1650–1815.* 1991. This volume contains an excellent description of the multiethnic society and culture that emerged in the Great Lakes region during these years. Although it does not focus specifically upon the Chicago region, it provides a very valuable analytical framework through which the Creole and Métis societies at Chicago may be studied.

Chicago Jazz Ensemble. In 1965, William Russo organized the Chicago Jazz Ensemble, performing to critical acclaim for three years before disbanding. By offering a variety of historical JAZZ, the ensemble preceded similar "repertory" bands by a quartercentury.

Under auspices of COLUMBIA COLLEGE CHICAGO, Russo successfully revived the group in 1991, presenting classic works from Jelly Roll Morton (1926) to Miles Davis (1959) with period phrasing and articulation. New compositions, such as Russo's "Chicago Suite No. 1," included on the ensemble's CD debut, *The Chicago Jazz Ensemble: Conducted by William Russo* (Chase Music Group, 1997), expanded their repertoire. A second CD, *Kenton a la Russo* (Hallway Records, 2000), presented arrangements Russo had done for Stan Kenton in the 1950s, as well as newer originals, including *Road Runner* (1998).

As the historicist ensemble, made up largely of professionals, continued to move toward a full-time status, it regularly appeared at clubs, concerts, and festivals.

Christopher Popa

See also: Entertaining Chicagoans; Ethnic Music

Further reading: Chicago Jazz Ensemble. *The Chicago Jazz Ensemble: Conducted by William Russo.* Compact disc. Chase Music Group, CMD 8052. 1997. • Helland, Dave. "Repertory Big Bands: Jazz's Future-Past." *Down Beat* 64.1 (1997): 34–37. • Reich, Howard. "Riding a Rave: Chicago Jazz Ensemble Reaps Praise at Home and Abroad." *Chicago Tribune,* September 28, 1997, sec. 7, p. 11.

Chicago Lawn, Community Area 66, Cook, 8 miles SW of the Loop. The locals call Chicago Lawn "MARQUETTE PARK" because the 300 acres of parkland by that name dominates the southern portion of the neighborhood. It remained mostly farmland with some scattered settlements until the 1920s, when developers lured managers and skilled stockyard workers to this BUNGALOW belt community. Between 1920 and 1930 the population increased from 14,000 to 47,000. Ethnic groups starting with the GERMANS and IRISH began the exodus from BACK OF THE YARDS and ENGLEWOOD. POLES, Bohemians, and LITHUANIANS followed them. Most residents belonged to various Protestant denominations, but Chicago Lawn also was home to many ROMAN CATHOLIC churches and schools as well as a Carpatho-Russian Orthodox church. It was a thriving urban neighborhood as the Depression hit the nation. This economic catastrophe did not entirely stop its growth. By 1940 its population reached 49,291.

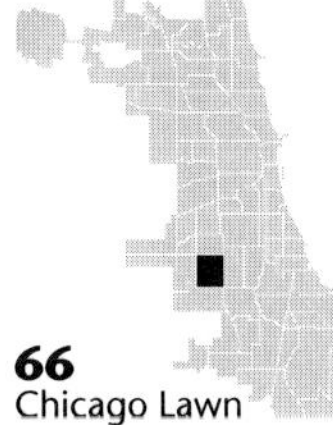

Chicago Lawn's residents formed tightly knit communities around their respective churches and schools. The Lithuanians, however, maintained an especially notable presence, establishing a network of institutions that earned their community the label of Lithuanian Gold Coast. They formed some of the richest SAVINGS AND LOANS in the city. The Lithuanian Sisters of St. Casimir founded Holy Cross Hospital in 1928 and Maria High School in 1952. The Lithuanian Youth Center in GAGE PARK was also a vital component to maintaining an exclusive Lithuanian identity.

Chicago's changing racial DEMOGRAPHICS had a profound impact on Chicago Lawn. By 1960 its population swelled to over 51,000 as whites fled Englewood and WEST ENGLEWOOD. In the mid-1960s Chicago Lawn became a target for CIVIL RIGHTS groups' OPEN HOUSING marches. In 1966 a march led by Martin Luther King, Jr., into Marquette Park met a violent reaction. King himself was hit by a rock. Violence also erupted in the neighborhood when Gage Park High School attempted integration. To add to the neighborhood's notoriety, the American Nazi Party opened a headquarters here aiming to further fan the flames of racial tension. However, the Nazis did not find the sympathetic support they expected. Many East European immigrants had their own horror stories about the Nazis. The primary resistance to integration came from fear of declining property values by people who put their life savings into their homes and disruption of ethnic bonds, especially for the Lithuanians. From their point of view, Chicago had no model of workable integrated neighborhoods, and Chicago Lawn would disintegrate from racial change.

By 1990 AFRICAN AMERICANS composed 27 percent of the population. Hispanic groups accounted for 28 percent. Arabs have also taken up residence. Some Irish, Poles, and Lithuanians still remain. However, most have moved further south and west. Many Lithuanians have reestablished a community in LEMONT. A number of groups have worked to keep the area economically vital, and a tenuous peace exists in this ethnically and racially diverse neighborhood.

Eileen M. McMahon

See also: Contested Spaces; Neighborhood Succession; Racism, Ethnicity, and White Identity; School Desegregation

Chicago Literary Renaissance. Between the Great FIRE OF 1871 and the mid-twentieth century, there were at least three surges of Chicago writing that helped shape the development of American literature. The first wave, cresting at the turn of the century, featured the path-marking Midland realism of Hamlin Garland, Robert Herrick, Henry Blake Fuller, and Theodore Dreiser and the popular humor of George Ade, Eugene Field, and Finley Peter Dunne. The third wave, cresting in the 1940s, produced the neighborhood novels of James T. Farrell, Richard Wright, and Nelson Algren, the work of the South Side Writers Group, and the budding careers of Gwendolyn Brooks and Saul Bellow.

But the term "Chicago Renaissance," as it is usually used, applies more precisely to the second wave of Chicago writing. It describes a gathering of writers, a flowering of institutions that supported and guided them, and the outpouring of writing they produced between about 1910 and the mid-1920s. Major figures include novelists Dreiser (whose career extended well into this period), Sherwood Anderson, and Floyd Dell; poets Carl Sandburg, Harriet Monroe, Edgar Lee Masters, and Vachel Lindsay; reporters Ben Hecht and Ring Lardner; and editors and critics Monroe, Dell, Margaret Anderson, and Henry Justin Smith. In this period, Chicago's NEWSPAPERS often served as incubators for LITERARY CAREERS. Little magazines like Monroe's *Poetry,* Margaret Anderson's *Little Review,* Dell's *Friday Literary Review,* the *Dial,* and the *Chap-Book,* orchestrated an encounter between American and European innovators. These magazines introduced not only Chicago writers but also Pound, Yeats, Joyce, and Lawrence to the American literary scene. While Jane Addams and HULL HOUSE provided a guiding force for social reformers, the Hull House Theater joined the Little THEATRE and Players' Workshop in offering venues for experimental drama. The UNIVERSITY OF CHICAGO nurtured both literary and social scientific exploration of urban life. Writers' groups, especially the Little Room group and the reporters' roundtable at Schlogl's restaurant, encouraged networks of influence and inspiration. Looser alliances of female artists and editors—among them Monroe, Addams, Margaret Anderson, Edith Wyatt, Susan Glaspell, Clara Laughlin, and Margery Currey—struggled to extend and break through the conventional limits on women's participation in artistic, civic, and domestic life.

At one time or another several books of the Chicago Renaissance have been regarded by critics as representative masterpieces: Masters's *Spoon River Anthology* and Sherwood Anderson's *Winesburg, Ohio,* two cosmopolitan looks back at the small-town world left behind; Sandburg's much-quoted *Chicago Poems;* Dreiser's entrepreneurial epic *The Titan;* and visiting muckraker Upton Sinclair's portrait of stockyard brutality in *The Jungle.* Dreiser's earlier novel *Sister Carrie,* tracing the career of a small-town Midwestern woman in the big city, looms with increasing authority over the whole of Chicago writing since 1900. Uncelebrated when it was published, *Sister Carrie* has in recent decades been elevated to most short lists of American and urban masterworks.

The Chicago Renaissance "brought the world to Chicago and Chicago to the world," as literary critic Carla Cappetti puts it. If American and international observers had already accepted Chicago's furious growth, industrial productivity, and bruising social dynamics as important social facts, it was only in the 1910s that prominent intellectuals began to respond to the *writing* that Chicago produced as culturally significant. H. L. Mencken led the way, identifying Chicago and its hinterland as "the Literary Capital of the United States." Mencken argued that "Chicago habits of mind" produced an original, genuinely national literature that made art from the principal stories and idioms of American life: the westering of the wellsprings of American culture, the rise of the metropolis and the concomitant crisis in the small towns from which so many Chicago writers of the period came, the clash and combination of a democratic culture's heterogeneous voices. Subsequent generations of critics would continue to seek the significance of Chicago writing in its emphasis on working people and the hard facts of city life.

European and expatriate high modernism eclipsed Chicago realism by the late 1920s, when an exodus of novelists, poets, editors, critics, and reporters from Chicago to points east marked the waning of Chicago literature's second wave. Still to come, though, was the third wave in the 1930s and 1940s. That being the case, we might more profitably regard the period between the Great Fire and the mid-twentieth century as a single renaissance in which Chicago's writers, engaging with landscape and humanity in compelling motion around them, did much to give form and meaning to our imaginative encounter with modern urbanism.

Carlo Rotella

See also: Fiction; Chicago Black Renaissance; Poetry

Further reading: Duncan, Hugh Dalziel. *The Rise of Chicago as a Literary Center from 1885 to 1920: A Sociological Essay in American Culture.* 1964. • Kramer, Dale. *Chicago Renaissance: The Literary Life in the Midwest, 1900–1930.* 1966. • Smith, Carl S. *Chicago and the American Literary Imagination, 1880–1920.* 1984.

Edward Eggleston and Literary Realism

In the 1870s, Edward Eggleston achieved wide national fame for his novels of rustic life in the antebellum Midwest: *The Hoosier Schoolmaster, The End of the World, The Mystery of Metropolisville, The Circuit Rider,* and *Roxy.* Although written after Eggleston left the Midwest to pursue an editorial career in New York, these novels reflect the techniques of American literary realism.

Lured in 1866 to Chicago by Alfred Sewell, publisher of *The Little Corporal,* the first magazine in America written solely for children, Eggleston quickly assumed a number of important positions within the Chicago JOURNALISM community. During a period as the author of the *Chicago Evening Journal*'s "Our Saturday Feuilleton," Eggleston assumed the narrative guise of a *flâneur,* or urban wanderer, who strolled the streets in search of novelty and adventure. Experimenting with both literary realism and the tone of lighthearted earnestness, Eggleston conveyed to his urban readers a sense of the city as site of paradox. In particular he both praised and criticized many of the institutions responsible for the rise of modern mass society. An urban journalist himself, he disdained the urban media's ability to beguile the population with gossip, or what he called "sensations"; he fretted about the streetcar's tendency to mingle populations and increase anonymity, thus creating at once "sublime democratic possibilities" and the "absolute negation" of social identity; and he saw the DEPARTMENT STORE as a "popular educator," capable of maintaining public standards of order and decorum, yet generating, at the same time, new, potentially dangerous forms of social desire at the dawn of consumer society.

In 1870, Eggleston left Chicago for New York. Although the city itself never again served as the subject of Eggleston's writing, when Hamlin Garland called him "the father of us all," he acknowledged Edward Eggleston's place as a precursor of the Chicago literary renaissance, the movement that made Chicago and the Midwest the focal point of American writing.

Bruce Levy

Chicago Marathon. Inaugurated in September 1977, the Chicago Marathon grew from modest beginnings into an athletic event of international stature. The first running of the race drew 5,000 competitors, though it was covered only locally and drew regionally for participants. The 2001 race attracted participants from 74 countries, with 28,830 finishers. Live television coverage and $300,000 in prizes have added to the race's reputation. So has expansive corporate sponsorship from LaSalle Bank.

Beginning and finishing in GRANT PARK, the fast, flat course traverses many city neighborhoods and has drawn elite runners from around the world. In 1999 Khalid Khannouchi set a world record for men, and in 2001 Catherine Ndereba set a world record for women.

Patrick B. Miller

See also: Creation of Chicago Sports; Leisure

Chicago Opera Ballet. While a series of companies appeared in conjunction with Chicago OPERA in the first half of the twentieth century, the Ruth Page Chicago Opera Ballet (commonly referred to as the Chicago Opera BALLET) was founded in 1955 out of an alliance between Ruth Page and the Chicago Lyric Opera. A significant figure on Chicago's ballet scene since the 1930s, Page established this company to tour independently when not performing with the LYRIC OPERA during its regular seasons. In particular, the company became renowned for its repertory of "opera-into-ballets," a genre that Page herself innovated by translating the plots and musical scores from well-known operas into balletic terms. Featuring a number of famous artists as principal dancers, including Kenneth Johnson,

Alicia Markova, Marjorie Tallchief, and Maria Tallchief, the company continued until 1969, although it was known after 1966 as Ruth Page's International Ballet. At the end of the twentieth century, no permanent affiliation existed between Chicago opera and a local ballet company.

Anthea Kraut

See also: Dance; Dance Companies

Further reading: Ann Barzel Dance Collection. The Newberry Library, Chicago, IL.

Chicago Political Equality League. The Chicago Woman's Club founded the Chicago Political Equality League in 1894. Prominent clubwomen Ellen Henrotin and Mary Wilmarth, suffragist Catharine Waugh McCulloch, and Unitarian minister Celia Parker Woolley organized this group to work for women's full political equality. The league began with an elite membership of approximately 100, drawn heavily from the Chicago Woman's Club. The membership expanded to 1,400 in 1913–14. Over time its members included a broad range of Chicago women, including SETTLEMENT HOUSE founder Jane Addams, African American activist Ida B. Wells-Barnett, teachers' union leader Margaret Haley, and public schools' superintendent Ella Flagg Young.

The league circulated SUFFRAGE literature and petitions on the ward and precinct levels in the city and lobbied the state legislature to grant women the right to vote. In 1912, it formed alliances with the Chicago WOMEN'S TRADE UNION LEAGUE and middle-class and settlement-house women's CLUBS to put a municipal suffrage advisory ballot before Chicago male voters. This referendum failed, but the state legislature granted Illinois women partial suffrage the following year. The league then campaigned for women's voter registration and for women poll judges in Chicago, marched in national suffrage parades, and worked with the national suffrage movement for full suffrage. It also held study classes and public meetings that debated every aspect of women's political, legal, and economic status. Its members worked for municipal housing reform and social welfare for children. They joined picket lines in support of striking women workers. The league disbanded in 1920 after the national suffrage amendment was ratified.

Maureen A. Flanagan

See also: Feminist Movements; Good Government Movements; Politics

Further reading: Buechler, Steven M. *The Transformation of the Woman Suffrage Movement: The Case of Illinois, 1850–1920*. 1986. • Chicago Political Equality League. *Annual and Yearbook*. 1895–96 to 1920. Chicago Historical Society. • Frank, Henrietta Greenebaum, and Amalie Hofer Jerome. *Annals of the Chicago Woman's Club for the First Forty Years of Its Organization, 1876–1916*. 1916.

Chicago Public Library. According to legend, the Chicago Public Library began with the donation of books by British citizens after the FIRE OF 1871. In fact, efforts had been underway before that to augment private libraries with a public institution. These efforts reached fruition in 1872, when the city organized a board under the Illinois Library Act. The board's mandate was to provide service to the "common man." The first librarian, William Poole, concentrated on building up the library's collections and on public access via delivery stations throughout the city. By 1909, two-thirds of the circulation took place through deposit stations.

In the 1890s the library's priorities shifted from service to uplift. This corresponded with Chicago's larger cultural renaissance, which included the creation of the NEWBERRY and CRERAR research libraries. The three libraries agreed to divide the areas of study among them—the humanities to the Newberry, the sciences to Crerar, and popular collections to the public library. In 1897, the new main branch opened in an opulent structure in the LOOP. The ARCHITECTURE as well as the books were meant to influence and uplift patrons. At the same time, politicians drastically cut the budget for acquisitions and neighborhood services.

The ideals of progressive reformers soon returned the library to its mission of service, exemplified in librarian Henry Legler's 1916 proposal, "A Library Plan for the Whole City." The plan, which called for an extensive network of neighborhood libraries and regional districts, was carried out by Legler's assistant, Carl Roden. During Roden's tenure as librarian (1918–1950), the branch library system grew by 50 percent and circulation reached stunning heights, though expenditures and book purchases were low in the wake of the GREAT DEPRESSION. During the three decades after 1950 the public library remained limited by its financial resources.

By 1969, 59 branch libraries were in operation, but they were overburdened. What caught the public's attention and dominated it for the next two decades, however, were the needed renovations to the library's central building. In 1977, the refurbished building reopened as Chicago's Cultural Center, also housing the library's new special collections unit. The rest of the collections, however, remained without a central building until 1991. In the meantime, the library's board debated plans for the new site while the budget, staff, and hours were cut and circulation dropped. Following strong support from Mayor Harold Washington, the new central library was built on the corner of Congress Parkway and State Street and was named in his honor. Its completion signaled a renewed emphasis on public service.

Mayor Richard M. Daley made branch libraries a priority and supported a special bond measure to rebuild them. In 1995, under the leadership of Library Commissioner Mary Dempsey, the library revised its mission statement and developed a Five-Year Strategy for growth that brought renewed vigor to the system. Between 1989 and 2002, it has built or renovated 41 libraries and begun construction on numerous others. Another 14 new neighborhood projects were scheduled for completion by 2004. A commitment to outreach, manifested in public programs, exhibits, and special events, has dramatically increased use of the library.

Cathleen D. Cahill

See also: Governing the Metropolis; Libraries: Suburban Libraries

Further reading: *The Chicago Public Library: Celebrating 125 Years, 1873–1998*. 1997. • Harris, Neil. "By the Book" and "By the Book II." *Chicago Times Magazine* 1.2:62 (Jan–Feb 1988) and 1.3:66 (Nov–Dec 1987). • Horowitz, Helen Lefkowitz. *Culture and the City: Cultural Philanthropy in Chicago from the 1880s to 1917*. 1976.

Chicago Relief and Aid Society. The Chicago Relief and Aid Society, founded in 1851, sought to exercise a "scientific" and "disinterested" model of urban alms giving. Elite male Chicagoans modeled the institution on New York's Association for Improving the Condition of the Poor—a pioneering alternative to what was viewed as the overly sentimental practices of early forms of benevolence, which encouraged sympathetic identification between the charity worker and the client. Practitioners of "scientific charity" believed in the rigorous investigation of all applicants by experts; only the "worthy poor"—those brought to a state of want through no fault of their own—should be granted temporary aid meant to restore them to self-sufficiency. Excessively generous support, it was believed, would instill habits of dependency.

The Relief and Aid Society was one of dozens of sources for charity in Chicago in the mid-nineteenth century; others were run by COOK COUNTY, religious groups, ethnic associations, trade unions, and women's committees. The society functioned on a relatively small scale until the Great FIRE OF 1871, when MAYOR R. B. Mason, at the request of a delegation of prominent businessmen, designated this organization as the "official" agent for the distribution of millions of dollars of "fire relief."

Many acclaimed the society's fire relief as a triumph of organization and system, while others bitterly complained that the suffering of many Chicagoans, particularly immigrant workers, too often was seen as beyond the pale of the society's mission. The Relief and Aid Society closed the books on their fire relief effort with $600,000 of the funds donated to the city left unspent, having come to the conclusion that all "honest need" born of the fire had been addressed. This surplus provided an operating budget that allowed the organization to build a new headquarters and suspend all new fundraising until the mid-1880s. In 1909, the society was absorbed into the UNITED CHARITIES of Chicago.

Karen Sawislak

See also: Almshouses; Relief and Subsistence Aid; Social Services

Further reading: Katz, Michael B. *In the Shadow of the Poorhouse.* 1986. • McCarthy, Kathleen D. *Noblesse Oblige: Charity and Cultural Philanthropy in Chicago, 1849–1929.* 1982. • Sawislak, Karen. *Smoldering City: Chicagoans and the Great Fire, 1871–1874.* 1995.

Chicago Ridge, IL, Cook County, 15 miles SW of the Loop. Chicago Ridge's irregular shape is bounded by OAK LAWN on the north and east, BRIDGEVIEW on the west, and WORTH on the south. Its early geographic and historical context parallels that of Worth.

The path of Stony Creek arcs through the village. It is not only an old creek but also the remnants of a feeder canal for the ILLINOIS & MICHIGAN CANAL that reached from the Little Calumet River westward through the Saganashkee Slough. Although the work on the feeder canal brought some settlers in the 1840s, GERMAN and DUTCH farmers arrived after the 1850s.

Settlement increased with the coming of the Wabash, St. Louis & Pacific RAILROAD in 1882. Later, the Wabash would be crossed in the middle of Chicago Ridge by the Chicago & Calumet Terminal Railway, which also established rail yards in the village.

In 1898, the Paul E. Berger Company, manufacturers of cash registers and slot machines, located adjacent to the railroad. The Berger Company built housing for its employees, and a settlement emerged around the factory, with a tavern, rooming house, and grocery store. The first post office opened in 1900 in the Berger factory, and in 1902 the Wabash Railroad established a train station.

Both Chicago Ridge and Worth benefited from the activity and economic influences of a racetrack operating on 111th Street. Local residents proudly recall that a member of one of the founding families of the Chicago Ridge area, Fred Herbert, won the Kentucky Derby in 1910. The racetrack was torn down in 1911 and is now the site of Holy Sepulchre CEMETERY.

After Oak Lawn incorporated in 1909, Chicago Ridge and Worth both considered the move. An incorporated government could replace wooden sidewalks, deal with the stagnant waters in the swampy areas, initiate local municipal services and provide locally elected and accountable officials. Both Chicago Ridge and Worth incorporated in 1914. Chicago Ridge grew from 176 in 1920 to 888 in 1950. With the great demand for housing and the expansion of road networks to include EXPRESSWAYS, Chicago Ridge was poised for growth. Along with a strong new industrial and commercial base, the population increased dramatically, to 5,748 in 1960 and 14,127 in 2000.

Larry A. McClellan

See also: Economic Geography; Government, Suburban; Horse Racing

Further reading: "Village of Patriotism, Chicago Ridge, 1914–1974." Diamond Jubilee Souvenir Edition. *Worth-Palos Reporter,* July 4, 1974. • Pote, Anne. *A World of Thanks; In the "Olden" Days: An Outline History of Chicago Ridge, Illinois.* 1976.

Chicago River. To many Chicago residents, the Chicago River is a body of WATER dyed green on St. Patrick's Day, or a river that flows backwards from its original mouth at LAKE MICHIGAN, or the cause of a 1992 FLOOD in the LOOP. The river is also a part of a system that includes the North Branch, South Branch, and Main Stem of the Chicago River, as well as 52 miles of constructed waterways: the North Shore Channel, the SANITARY AND SHIP CANAL, and the Calumet Sag Channel. The river system has played a central role in the history of Chicago and is an example of the link between nature, natural resources, and urban development.

Before Euro-American settlement and the development of Chicago and its suburbs, the North Branch of the Chicago River was fed by three small streams with headwaters near present-day DEERFIELD, GLENCOE, and WINNETKA. The tributary flowed through upland oak savannas and maple forest and through a wet prairie formed in the till plain of ancient Lake Chicago. From its headwaters near Racine and Pershing, the South Branch flowed through the same wet prairie and joined the North Branch at Wolf Point, near the future site of the Merchandise Mart. The main stem of the river flowed east through wetlands and marshes into Lake Michigan. This mixture of wetlands, marshes, and forest supported a large number of wildlife species and made the area an important factor in the FUR TRADE, first by the POTAWATOMI, then by settlers of African and European descent.

The river was crucial in Chicago's development as a major center of the LUMBER and MEATPACKING industries during the nineteenth century. Access through the ILLINOIS & MICHIGAN CANAL to the DES PLAINES RIVER and the Mississippi River system provided opportunities for trade and shipping throughout the Midwest. A series of wholesale lumber docks was developed along the river near its connection to the canal at BRIDGEPORT. Meatpacking plants and the stockyards used the river as a drainage system with two sewers, one of them infamously known as "Bubbly Creek" emptying directly into the South Branch. Water from the South Branch upstream of the stockyards was used as a source of fresh water for cattle troughs.

By the 1870s the dumping of waste from industrial and commercial development led to visible signs of pollution and increased concern about threats the river posed to PUBLIC HEALTH. Between 1889 and 1910 the Metropolitan Sanitary District of Greater Chicago completed two major engineering projects to direct the flow of the river into the Des Plaines River and divert wastes away from Lake Michigan. The 28-mile Sanitary and Ship Canal was constructed between 1889 and 1900. Locks located near Lake Michigan and at LOCKPORT diverted the flow of the North Branch, South Branch, and Main Stem into the canal and to the Des Plaines River. The completion of the 8-mile North Shore Channel in 1910 diverted wastes from the northern suburbs from Lake Michigan into the North Branch.

Two additional projects were completed in the 1920s that helped form the Chicago River System. In 1922 the 16-mile Cal-Sag Channel was constructed between BLUE ISLAND and Sag Bridge to link the Little Calumet River to the Sanitary and Ship Canal. In 1928 the final major engineering project on the river system straightened the channel of the South Branch between 18th and Polk by digging a new channel 850 feet west of Clark Street and filling the old river channel. This project improved rail access to the Loop and was part of the 1909 BURNHAM PLAN.

With the decline in industrial and commercial activities associated with the river system, increased attention has been paid to its ecological and aesthetic values. Toward the end of the twentieth century, the "DEEP TUNNEL" project of the Metropolitan Water Reclamation District was designed to divert all stormwater runoff from the Chicago River System. In 1992 the Chicago Rivers Demonstration Project was initiated to assess the ecological condition of the river system, make recommendations for restoration programs, and identify opportunities for increased public use of the river and the lands associated with it. The study identified more than 30 vegetation classes associated with lands bordering the rivers that provide habitat for wildlife species and opportunities for recreation for Chicago-area residents.

Charles Nilon

See also: Bridges; Riverine Systems; Waste Disposal; Waterfront

Further reading: Hill, Libby. *The Chicago River: A Natural and Unnatural History.* 2000. • Gobster, Paul, and Lynne Westphal. *People and the River.* 1996. • Solzman, David. *The Chicago River: An Illustrated History and Guide to the River and Its Waterways.* 1998.

Chicago School of Architecture.
See Architecture

Chicago School of Economics. The free-market, antisocialist approach of the UNIVERSITY OF CHICAGO Department of Economics, typified by Milton Friedman, came to be known as the Chicago School of Economics. Like other Chicago schools it developed from the university's isolation and talk, and its unconventional hiring. Leading figures were Frank Knight in the 1930s and 1940s, and Gary Becker and Robert Lucas in the 1980s and 1990s. The most creative and fact-oriented period came from the chairmanship of Theodore Schultz (1946–1961), eventually resulting in eight Nobel Prizes between 1976 and 1995, many more than at any other university (Friedman, Becker, Lucas, Schultz, Ronald Coase, Robert Fogel, George Stigler, and Merton Miller). The school became by the 1990s the mainstream of economics worldwide.

Deirdre N. McCloskey

See also: Chicago School of Sociology; Chicago Studied: Social Scientists and Their City; Universities and their Cities

Chicago School of Sociology. When the UNIVERSITY OF CHICAGO was founded in 1892, it established the nation's first department of sociology. The study of sociology was still a relatively undeveloped field, but by the 1920s the department had become nationally famous and graduates of its Ph.D. program dominated newly formed sociology programs across the country. During its early history, Chicago sociology was connected with progressive reform programs, including Jane Addams's HULL HOUSE project. The department pioneered research on urban studies, poverty, the family, the workplace, immigrants, and ethnic and race relations, and developed important research methods using mapping and survey techniques.

Henry Yu

See also: Chicago Studied: Social Scientists and Their City; Settlement Houses; Universities and Their Cities

Further reading: Bulmer, Martin. *The Chicago School of Sociology: Institutionalization, Diversity, and the Rise of Sociological Research.* 1984. • Kurtz, Lester R. *Evaluating Chicago Sociology: A Guide to the Literature, with an Annotated Bibliography.* 1984. • Lal, Barbara Ballis. *The Romance of Culture in an Urban Civilization: Robert E. Park on Race and Ethnic Relations in Cities.* 1990.

Chicago School of Television. Five network programs produced in NBC's Chicago studios between 1949 and 1955—KUKLA, FRAN AND OLLIE, *Garroway at Large, Studs' Place, Hawkins Falls,* and DING DONG SCHOOL—composed the canon of what New York critics almost immediately began calling the "Chicago School" of television.

The guiding axiom of the Chicago School performers and production staff was that television was neither theater nor film, but a unique, new medium. The corollary followed that television performances should not be directed at a studio audience, but at the viewers at home who watched singly or in small groups.

Informality and spontaneity were the hallmarks of the Chicago School programs, largely because they were seldom scripted. Burr Tillstrom (creator of the Kuklapolitans) and Fran Allison worked from a simple rundown. Likewise Garroway, even though his variety show included elaborate production numbers. A two-page plot summary guided Studs Terkel and his colleagues. They improvised the rest.

Technical necessity, rather than the desire to propagate an esthetic, created the Chicago School. When coaxial cable linked the East Coast and Midwest in January 1949, New York lacked the production facilities to fill an evening schedule. Chicago's task was to fill the gap—at low cost.

The success of the Chicago School, coupled with technological advances, assured its demise. Many of its principal exponents were summoned to New York for more important tasks. The extension of coaxial cable to the West Coast in 1951 left Chicago's facilities superfluous and, by the mid-1950s, generally deprived of network productions.

Rich Samuels

See also: Broadcasting; Entertaining Chicagoans; Improvisational Theater; Public Broadcasting; WBBM; WGN; WLS; WMAQ

Further reading: Mills, Ted. "Television's 'Chicago School' Carries On—Far From Chicago." *Variety,* January 5, 1955. • Sternberg, Joel. "A Descriptive History and Cultural Analysis of the Chicago School of Television." Ph.D. diss., Northwestern University. 1973. • Terkel, Studs. "Studs Terkel's Chi TV Lament: 'East Coast Gets Curiouser and Curiouser.'" *Variety,* November 30, 1954.

Chicago Sound. The "Chicago Sound" or "Style" has meaning only in the context of a particular musical genre. It does not refer to any specific immutable quality that is idiosyncratic to music made in Chicago. Yet while many important musicians, ensembles, and musical movements—in popular music, art music, and ETHNIC MUSIC—have roots in the city's fertile cultural landscape, in three genres—JAZZ, BLUES, and art music—the intersection of imported musical tradition with the energy and vitality of the surrounding urban culture has been so dynamic as to create a sound or style that is recognized as distinctive to Chicago. The markers of what constitutes "Chicago Style" in one genre, however, are unrelated to those of another.

The GREAT MIGRATION of AFRICAN AMERICANS to Chicago in the first half of the twentieth century produced, in jazz and, later, the blues, two of the city's most enduring contributions to popular music. In the 1910s and 1920s southern African American folk music traditions (especially those of New Orleans) were grafted onto the SOUTH SIDE's vibrant cabaret and DANCE HALL scene, producing a faster and flashier "hot" version of New Orleans's collective-improvisation small-group jazz. Louis Armstrong, Jelly Roll Morton, Joseph "King" Oliver, Earl Hines, and Lil Hardin Armstrong were among the influential African American musicians who worked on the South Side in the 1920s. White musicians from the Chicago area such as Jimmy McPartland, Bud Freeman, Mezz Mezzrow, Mugsy Spanier, and Dave Tough—plus others from the Midwest, including Bix Beiderbecke, Hoagy Carmichael, and Eddie Condon—wholeheartedly embraced this exuberant new sound and made their own contributions to it. In this hothouse environment of innovation and loosened social inhibitions that characterized PROHIBITION-era Chicago, jazz, aided by the nascent recording industry, quickly grew from a regional and racial phenomenon into the music that would define an era. The more jagged syncopations and collective improvisations of early jazz were superseded by smoother, more supple swing rhythms, and individual, more virtuosic improvisations. In addition, as the lines between small-group jazz bands, which often performed from memory, and large dance orchestras became less distinct, written arrangements became more common. These trends were the precursors of the Swing Era, when jazz enjoyed its greatest popularity. Benny Goodman and Gene Krupa, important Swing Era musicians and bandleaders, grew up and learned to play jazz in 1920s Chicago.

In their first major encounter with Chicago culture, southern music traditions got dressed up (literally in the case of the musicians), becoming more refined and sophisticated. In the late 1940s, however, Delta blues musicians who brought their old-time rural blues with them to Chicago did not smooth off the rough edges. The expressive possibilities of the distortion and volume provided by electrical amplification had already begun to be exploited in the Delta in the 1940s, and this new sound became a hallmark of Chicago blues. The old-style rolling Delta blues accompaniment of a fingerpicked acoustic guitar was left behind for a new sound—hard-edged, searing, and raw—of electric guitar and harmonica lead driven by a rhythm section of piano, rhythm guitar, bass, and drums. Delta musicians who migrated to Chicago—such as Muddy Waters, Elmore James, Howlin' Wolf, John Lee Hooker, Little Walter, and John Lee "Sonny Boy" Williamson—along with Chicagoans Willie Dixon and the record producers and promoters Leonard and Phil Chess of CHESS RECORDS, were instrumental in creating a unique sound that still retains its identity. This sound was a significant influence on RHYTHM AND BLUES and American and British ROCK and roll of the 1960s and 1970s.

In another realm altogether, the Chicago Sound refers to a distinctive style of orchestral brass playing that developed in the brass section of the CHICAGO SYMPHONY ORCHESTRA in the 1950s under the baton of Fritz Reiner. Led by principal trumpet Adolph Herseth and anchored by tubist Arnold Jacobs, the section's sound—characterized by its rhythmic drive and precision, as well as the clarity, consistency, and fullness of its tonal color throughout the entire section and in all dynamic ranges—had an identity distinct from other orchestral brass sections. Through its recordings, radio BROADCASTS, and performances, especially several international tours during Georg Solti's tenure as music director, this unmistakable sound and high standard of performance helped define the Chicago Symphony Orchestra as a world-class institution. It also made Chicago an international center for the study of brass instrument performance.

As the various Chicago Sounds continued to evolve and as other styles and traditions absorbed and adapted certain aspects of them, their distinctiveness diminished. Nevertheless, two of these Chicago Sounds—the Chicago Symphony Orchestra brass section at Symphony Center and the blues in Chicago NIGHTCLUBS—can still be heard today. In jazz, however, the Chicago Sound has long since metamorphosed into a larger performance tradition and exists now only on recordings.

John McAllister

See also: Austin High Gang; Classical Music; Music Clubs; Polka; Record Publishing

Further reading: Herzhaft, Gerard. *Encyclopedia of the Blues.* Trans. Brigitte Debord. 1992. • Kenney, William Howland. *Chicago Jazz: A Cultural History, 1904–1930.* 1993. • Palmer, Robert. *Deep Blues.* 1982.

Chicago Stadium. The Chicago Stadium was the city's premier all-purpose indoor arena for 65 years. Built for $7 million by West Side promoter Paddy Harmon, it opened with a BOXING match on March 28, 1929. After that came midget car races, rodeos, POLITICAL CONVENTIONS, rock concerts, water shows, six-day BICYCLE races, circuses, SOCCER games, and church services.

Situated close to the LOOP at 1800 W. Madison, the Stadium, as it was known, was built to offer affordable seats with unobstructed views. Constructed with steel trusses that spanned 266 feet without supports, it was one of the biggest arenas of its kind, drawing crowds up to 20,000.

Here Chicagoans saw championship hockey, BASKETBALL, and even FOOTBALL—the BEARS were forced inside by snow and cold in 1932. Franklin D. Roosevelt was nominated on the Stadium floor, Bobby Hull skated across it, and Michael Jordan flew off it.

Outside, fans would crowd by the Stadium's fabled Gate 3 1/2 to see sports stars and performers like Frank Sinatra, Elvis Presley, and ice-skating superstar Sonja Henie. Inside, they'd get an earful. With the acoustics of a shower stall, it was renowned for its crowd noise and booming pipe organ.

Owner William Wirtz leveled the aging Stadium in 1995 in favor of the UNITED CENTER, a sleek, modern arena built next door.

Donald A. Hayner

See also: Entertaining Chicagoans; Ice Hockey; Leisure; Near West Side; Places of Assembly

Further reading: *Chicago Daily News.* Various issues. • *Chicago Sun-Times.* Various issues. • Hayner, Don, and Tom McNamee. *The Stadium, 1929–1994: The Official Commemorative History of the Chicago Stadium.* 1993.

Chicago State University. Begun as an experimental teacher training school by the Cook County Board of Commissioners in 1867, the COOK COUNTY Normal School registered 13 students in temporary quarters in BLUE ISLAND. In 1869 it moved to ENGLEWOOD, where it stayed until 1972. When, in 1897, the county board decided it could no longer finance the school, the Chicago Board of Education took over what was renamed the Chicago Normal School. It remained a city institution, undergoing several name changes, until it came under state control in 1965, gaining the name Chicago State University in 1971. The 161-acre modern campus at 95th and King Drive was occupied in 1972 and includes dormitories.

Teacher education has remained a major focus, and expanding enrollments in recent years have enlarged the Colleges of Arts and Sciences, Business and Administration, and Health Sciences. The university grants bachelor's and master's degrees, offers a variety of nontraditional and innovative programs, and currently enrolls more than 9,000 students, mostly from the city of Chicago. AFRICAN AMERICANS have become the largest contingent of the student body. Service to first-generation college students, working adults, and minorities has remained a high priority.

Magne B. Olson

See also: Northeastern Illinois University; Progressive Education; Schools and Education; Universities and Their Cities

Further reading: Kearney, Edmund W., and Maynard E. Moore. *A History: Chicago State University, 1867–1979.* 1979.

Chicago Studied: Social Scientists and Their City. More than any other city in America, if not the world, Chicago has been the studied city. Studies of Chicago have shaped discipline after discipline and, indeed, beyond the world of academia, have played central roles in American urban policy. To some extent this reflects accidents of geography and history. More than most cities, Chicago developed as and remains a cohesive unit. Unlike New York, it is not an assemblage of adjacent cities separated by rivers and harbors. Unlike Los Angeles, it is not a network of transportation arteries in which local agglomerations grow.

The crucial accidents do not concern Chicago alone. The great growth years of the city after the FIRE OF 1871 were also those of the American university and the academic disciplines that dominate it. The UNIVERSITY OF CHICAGO grew precociously, a vast endowment from John D. Rockefeller establishing what would be Chicago's dominant scholarly institution through most of the twentieth century. With the nation's fastest-growing major city at their doorstep, University of Chicago social scientists concerned to build their fields turned at once to the city as laboratory. What they made of the opportunity is evident in the "Chicago Schools" of political science and sociology. To be sure, one of the great CHICAGO SCHOOLS—ECONOMICS—did not study the city but merely grew there. But the others built themselves on studies of the raw and growing city around them.

Across the various social sciences concerned with modern societies—sociology, political science, geography, history, and public policy—Chicago has been an enduring fascination. And those studies of Chicago evince a number of basic themes. The first is that of the tabula rasa. Chicago has often been envisioned as growing in a vacant space, whether that space be geographical, social, or even symbolic. Second, studies of Chicago have focused on the physical and infrastructural layout of the city created in that space. While one might imagine that the flat prairie landscape would turn attention to purely social structure, students of Chicago turned to the man-made aspects of physical geography: to rail lines and canals, to major arteries and their effects, to park systems. Their studies of social structure were overwhelmingly geographic, emphasizing the "mosaic of little worlds" formed by the physical juxtapositions of social groups.

Third, Chicago scholars have been overwhelmingly concerned with the dynamics of city life, with culture contact, change, and assimilation. For them, no city is static. Indeed, the story of the city is the dynamic filling of the tabula rasa and of the conflicts that ensue. Fourth, Chicago is seen as a paradigm. This emerges most clearly in Ernest W. Burgess's famous map of the concentric zones of city development, probably the most famous single visual document in the history of sociology. Burgess intended that map as a universal description of city development. But when asked at one talk what the diagonal blue line down the right center of the picture was, he said without a second thought, "Oh, that's the lake." That is how paradigmatic most Chicagoans thought their city to be.

Finally, Chicago scholars always saw the city as enmeshed in various larger structures.

Chicago's debt to its position in TRANSPORTATION networks was always clear, but scholars have looked beyond that to study Chicago's relation to larger economies and DEMOGRAPHIES.

These themes help organize a discussion of studies of Chicago. While it is tempting to chronicle the image of Chicago discipline by discipline, a thematic organization is preferable not only because of its conceptual clarity, but also because the disciplines in fact dramatically affected one another. Studies of Chicago were dominated by the University of Chicago until well into the postwar period, and the university's organization of the social sciences into a single division meant that disciplinary boundaries counted for little.

We begin, then, with the theme of the tabula rasa. Much of the work on Chicago has emphasized the notion of a clean slate, a bare setting into which reality pours like so much flooding water. In the first instance, this vacancy was physical. The physical land that would become Chicago seemed nearly a featureless LANDSCAPE, relieved by a small river, extensive swamps, and an almost imperceptible ridge dividing the Atlantic and Gulf watersheds. Many authors would see this landscape as a slate on which nearly anything could be inscribed by human ingenuity and effort. Roads and RAILROADS could be placed at will. Even the river would be reversed. Only the lake was an immovable fact, and even that would be remodeled in the building of Lake Shore Drive, GRANT PARK, and the Northerly Island.

The vacancy was in the second instance symbolic. Chicago for many writers was an act of imagination. William Cronon's magisterial history attributed Chicago's greatness, ultimately, to the vast dreams that envisioned and built an entrepôt city. Not for nothing did Chicago invent the concretization of the future in the present via the mechanism of futures markets. Unlike other cities with their long and complex histories, Chicago had a clean slate, symbolized by the great fire and subsequent redevelopment; it could become what it dreamed and willed.

The vacancy was in the third instance social. Writers from the HULL HOUSE surveyors forward to William I. Thomas and Florian Znaniecki and beyond stressed the sudden freedom of immigrants released from the controls and fixities of Europe to the unrestrained competition of the new city. For Thomas the very groups themselves had to reinscribe and reconstruct themselves. Studying the situation a generation later, Burgess, and still later Everett C. Hughes, saw the ethnic groups fully enacted but constantly rewriting the city's social landscape through the endless processes of ethnic succession.

The tabula rasa view did not emerge in the first generation of studies of Chicago. That first generation was very much bound up with reform POLITICS. For reform politics, the city was not something seen in the abstract, de novo, but rather something seen very much for what it was, at any given moment, with all its historical warts. Progressives like Jane Addams and Albion W. Small and even the subsequent generation of Charles E. Merriam and W. I. Thomas were thoroughly enmeshed in such an immediate view of the city. It was only in the next generation—the generation taught by Robert E. Park—that newly scientizing sociology and political science began to ask the abstract questions that not only conceived of scientific knowledge of the city de novo but in the process conceived of the city itself as the outcome of an abstract, theoretically conceived developmental process in a largely characterless setting. This new view reflected not only the scientizing impulse but also the youth of the new scholars and their relative detachment—at least by comparison with Addams, Small, Thomas, and Merriam—from the realities of Chicago's political life.

A second basic theme followed from this first theme of tabula rasa. The relative absence of environmental determination of city development meant a correspondingly increasing importance for man-made landscape features and for the mutually determining quality of internal social groupings. In the first place, this meant a focus on the extraordinary importance of roads, RAILROADS, streetcar lines, canals, and other means of transport, not only for their direct impact in determining development, but also in their creation of "ecological" barriers that determined the ebb and flow of community life. Geographers like Harold M. Mayer and Richard C. Wade emphasized the centrality of such structures within the city; Cronon and many others emphasized the importance of the regional transportation structure environing the city.

Ecological barriers interacted with social life itself to produce "natural areas," a concept that was foundational to Chicago sociology with its vision of a city of neighborhoods. An enduring debate has concerned whether Park, Burgess, and their students saw natural areas that were already present or defined them into existence with their intensive study. But the fact remains that a generation of research on natural areas from 1920 to 1940 construed the city at a level of geographic detail completely unmatched elsewhere and, in the process, gave Chicago's internal "COMMUNITY AREAS" the names that still label them 75 years later. Neighborhoods and natural areas were the units of what latter-day Chicagoan Gerald D. Suttles would call the man-made city. This focus on natural areas has endured into the present. Only in the last two decades have a handful of writers in the new social and labor history begun to think of the "units" of Chicago as being trade unions, gender subgroups, or even social classes.

In some incarnations, the natural areas view seemed quite static. But later ecologists like Hughes and Wirth would emphasize the dynamism implicit in much of the earlier writing. The early Chicago School focused on description. But one important aspect of description conduced strongly to the dynamic emphasis. The legacy of the reform tradition to the descriptive scientism of the Chicago School in the 1920s was an intense focus on what W. I. Thomas had called social disorganization. The new sociologists and political scientists studied this phenomenon in comprehensive geographical detail, following the natural areas paradigm. Hence came the dozens of studies of DANCE HALLS, brothels, insanity, divorce, nonvoting, suicide, and other forms of socially problematic behavior of interest to the reformers. The greatest of these bodies of social disorganization studies was the ecological analysis of crime and delinquency, dominated by Clifford R. Shaw, Henry D. McKay, and other sociologists at the Institute for Juvenile Research.

Studies of Chicago by sociologists, geographers, and political scientists reached their mystical apogee in the 1920s with Burgess's celebrated zone map of the city, published in 1925. Burgess's map was equally indebted to the static descriptive tradition of the ecologists, on the one hand, and the extraordinary focus of Chicago studies on change and process, on the other. Location in space was no more important than location in time.

Three broad subthemes characterized this dynamic mode of Chicago studies. The first was the subtheme of culture contact and conflict. First celebrated in Thomas and Znaniecki's monumental study of the POLISH peasant, published in 1918, the culture contact theme stretched through the decades down to Suttles, Albert Hunter, William Kornblum, Ruth Horowitz, and others. These scholars all saw ethnic groups in contact and contention. They saw community succession. They saw institutional transformation. For all of them, ethnic groups defined themselves in this process of ecological succession and change, acquiring in that process particular qualities—by virtue of particular ethnic contrasts—that would later come to be seen as generic to those ethnic groups beyond the immediate Chicago context. A conspicuously important subset of this work concerned AFRICAN AMERICANS; works including E. Franklin Frazier's studies of the black family and Horace R. Cayton and St. Clair Drake's monumental community study would shape white America's perception of black communities for decades.

A second subtheme concerned the changes such succession implied in community institutions. In the 1930s, Samuel C. Kincheloe studied church succession, and Everett Hughes studied the REAL-ESTATE board. In the 1950s, Morris Janowitz published his study of the community press. Later students were to study HOSPITALS, JAILS, and cultural institutions. Again and again, the theme was underscored.

Community institutions were both stakes and actors in the continuous ebb and flow of ethnic groups.

Finally, a third strand of dynamic studies concerned city POLITICS. Here, the defining figure was Charles Merriam, whose decades of central involvement in Chicago reform politics in the first half of the twentieth century gave him and his students an access to political knowledge unmatched elsewhere. Merriam remained committed to reform, and his work on Chicago never left the reform agenda. But his student and collaborator Harold F. Gosnell played the scientizing role that Park had played in sociology, turning studies of political Chicago in a more abstract direction, away from the practical questions of reform success and failure to the more general questions of voting and other forms of participation. Gosnell's work in the 1920s and 1930s on MACHINE POLITICS and African American politicians was to shape for decades the perception of city politics in the United States. His painstakingly scientific descriptions remain readable and relevant today.

The dynamic strand of studies of Chicago is completed by another genre that, while not always academic in tone, has played a central role in defining the city's image of itself—or at least its POLITICAL CULTURE. This is what we might call the "gritty politics" genre, books that revel in the rough-and-tumble, occasionally corrupt, always exciting details of life in a big-city machine. Milton L. Rakove, William J. Grimshaw, and others have written recent works in this tradition, which looks back directly to Merriam with his active commitment to particular views of city life. (Newspaper columnist Mike Royko's *Boss* is probably the most famous book in this genre.) Here too the focus is on the dynamics of urban life and politics, but the aim is less systematic and certainly less abstract and generalizing. One has only to contrast Grimshaw's engaged view of urban politics with the detachment of James Q. Wilson (Gosnell's successor as an analyst of black politicians) to see the difference.

This tension between particularizing and generalizing views of Chicago brings us to another major theme in Chicago studies, that of Chicago as paradigm. There are some central works about Chicago that view it primarily as a unique, individual location. By far the most important is Bessie L. Pierce's history of Chicago, published in three volumes from 1937 to 1957. The book was solicited and supported by the leaders of the Chicago Schools of Sociology and Political Science; Pierce was invited to Chicago specifically to write it, by a University of Chicago committee including Park and Merriam. Yet where the CHICAGO SCHOOL OF SOCIOLOGY ultimately developed what had pretensions to being a general description of urban development and process, Pierce's extraordinary mastery of detail produced a work that insists upon Chicago's uniqueness. So to some extent did Cronon's attempt to see the city in its full regional context, although the book does consistently invoke general theoretical arguments.

Bessie Louise Pierce and Chicago History

Bessie Louise Pierce (1888–1974) devoted 44 of her 86 years to writing a history of Chicago. A native of rural Michigan, she taught in Iowa schools, earned degrees at the University of Iowa, and then taught there. In the late 1920s the University of Chicago decided to examine the city from the standpoints of all the major social-science disciplines, including history. Pierce was recruited to the Midway in 1929 to write the historical volume. She produced one in 1937, but it went only to 1848. A second, up to the 1871 fire, came in 1940; a third took until 1957. Assisted by as many as a dozen graduate students, Pierce brought the story to the 1893 World's Columbian Exposition. She continued working on a fourth volume, to go through 1915, until she died.

The three published volumes received much praise (including the city's Distinguished Service Award in 1959) and lasting respect. They are both reference works and good reads, anecdotal and picturesque, seldom analytical.

Pierce also published *Public Opinion and the Teaching of History* (1926), *Civic Attitudes in American School Textbooks* (1930), and *Citizens' Organizations and the Civic Training of Youth* (1933), which drew on her early schoolteaching and reflected her Yankee-Progressive outlook. In 1933, coincident with the Century of Progress celebration, she brought out *As Others See Chicago*, compiling the views of visitors to the city from its early days. She retired in 1953, returned to Iowa City in 1973, and died there on October 3, 1974.

Walter Nugent

But the majority of work on Chicago has seen the city as emblematic, the quintessential modern, or American, city. Ideas developed for analyzing Chicago were seen as generally applicable; indeed, they were often applied in dissertations at other universities describing other cities. Roderick D. McKenzie and Amos H. Hawley went on to develop full-scale theories of human ecology with completely general pretensions. Robert Park's fascination with "natural history," a concept which for him was best instantiated by the race relations cycle, led him to see it everywhere: in GANGS, in STRIKES, in revolutions. Natural areas, ecological succession, natural history, assimilation and accommodation, social disorganization, ecological analysis: all these concepts and many more were developed in the analysis of Chicago and passed on into the general heritage. The theoretical and descriptive apparatus built up to study Chicago became the stock and trade of all of urban sociology and, indirectly, of such other fields as the sociology of occupations, which was recast by Everett Hughes and his followers into an ecological model suspiciously like the one Burgess had evolved for Chicago.

Beyond this scientifically paradigmatic quality, Chicago as envisioned by its students had a symbolically paradigmatic quality. It was the ultimate American city, complex and multiethnic, yet coherent in ways New York could not be. The northeastern cities were in fact more ethnically heterogeneous than was Chicago, but through virtuosic description Chicago became the paradigmatic example of a socially complex yet somehow unified city. It may be that analysts of Chicago turned to ethnicity for arbitrary reasons: because of their own backgrounds or because of the ethnic political machine's long survival. Yet it is striking that studies of Chicago seem to have been so dominated by the concept of ethnic groups. There is surprisingly little about class. There is only a tiny handful of class-based studies of labor in Chicago despite the celebrated events of PULLMAN and HAYMARKET. Nor is there much work on Chicago's upper class by comparison with the well-studied elites of New York, Boston, and Philadelphia.

Yet Chicago has served as an archetype of reform politics, and Chicago's history as a prime example of the successes and failures of reform. Merriam's long obsession with clean government provides an important strand of this tradition, as does Gosnell's pursuit of the problems of voting, and the gritty politics tradition with its delight in exposés. There has been no single school of policy studies based on Chicago, but studies of the city have produced a number of works with enormous national influence. From *Hull House Maps and Papers* (1895) and Upton Sinclair's THE JUNGLE (1906) forward, books on Chicago have shaped national consciousness. Homer Hoyt's massive ecological study of land values, first published in 1933, would prove the unwitting foundation of REDLINING in federal loan policies, turning ecological succession into a self-fulfilling prophecy. William H. Whyte's *The Organization Man*—based on study of the far south suburb of PARK FOREST—would shape conventional wisdom on the consciousness of the 1950s. James Q. Wilson's influential work—both on black politicians and later on city government in general—would owe more to Chicago than any other city. William Julius Wilson's *The Truly Disadvantaged* would play a similar role in a later generation.

The image of Chicago in public policy has thus been less a consistent picture built up by a long tradition than a series of extraordinary portraits generated by committed analysts. In this sense, the political image of Chicago has stayed in the engaged tradition of Merriam, rather than drifting in the scientific direction begun by Gosnell. As for the other themes of Chicago studies, they continue as consistent traditions into the present. The notion of a physical landscape remade by human effort, the concepts of location in human and social space and in human and social time—these are still the touchstones of important schools of sociology, political science, and geography.

At the end of the twentieth century, Chicago loomed behind the imagination of the social sciences as New York had done at the end of the nineteenth century. Within the social scientific imagination, New York had been a way station in the odyssey of the European immigrant, a place physically separated from, but still socially encumbered by, European traditions of social identity and place. Against the image of New York, social scientific studies of the city made Chicago the *American* city, the urban outcome of the economic jostling of liberated, self-determined individuals upon the unbounded western prairie. As the American westward odyssey reached the Pacific Ocean, that barrier provided a new metaphor for contact with a world now understood as global and, ironically, reaching to the east. The "Pacific Rim" came to be imagined as a point of foreign penetration into America as much as a gateway for expansion of the American psyche outward. Near the southernmost point of U.S. expansion, a new paradigm was proclaimed within cities named and previously colonized by Spaniards. Through continually redefining lenses, the American city emerged within the social scientific imagination as postmodern Los Angeles. As the congealed instantiation of disintegrated, "polynucleated" urban form, the metaphor of Los Angeles was a rejection of Chicago's rational inscription of place upon prairie. Emphasizing empirical links to world systems and theoretical links to European social thought, "new urbanists" like Mark Gottdiener claimed to vanquish the Chicago model of an "ecological" order growing in concentric pattern from the downtown business district.

The scholarly energy given by postmodern urban social theorists to severing the intellectual tentacles of Chicago studies suggests that this grip is not so easily dislodged. Several of the classic works on Chicago—notably the books of Thomas and Znaniecki, Cayton and Drake, and Hoyt—emphasized the relation of events in Chicago to events in the social and economic structure beyond it, and it is a tradition continued in the present by writers like Cronon and W. J. Wilson. It may be that the globalization theorists will soon bring us back to Thomas and Znaniecki's analysis of migration.

Andrew Abbott
Jolyon Wurr

See also: Built Environment of the Chicago Region; City as Artifact; Land Use; Multicentered Chicago; Neighborhood Succession; Universities and Their Cities

Further reading: Addams, Jane. *Twenty Years at Hull-House.* 1910. • Anderson, Nels, and Council of Social Agencies of Chicago. *The Hobo: The Sociology of the Homeless Man.* 1923. • Banfield, Edward C., and James Q. Wilson. *City Politics.* 1963. • Cressey, Paul Goalby. *The Taxi-Dance Hall: A Sociological Study in Commercialized Recreation and City Life.* 1932. • Cronon, William. *Nature's Metropolis: Chicago and the Great West.* 1991. • Drake, St. Clair, and Horace Cayton. *Black Metropolis: A Study of Negro Life in a Northern City.* 1945. • Frazier, Edward Franklin. *The Free Negro Family: A Study of Family Origins before the Civil War.* 1932. • Frazier, Edward Franklin. *The Negro Family in Chicago.* 1932. • Gosnell, Harold Foote. *Getting Out the Vote: An Experiment in the Stimulation of Voting.* 1927. • Gosnell, Harold Foote. *Negro Politicians: The Rise of Negro Politics in Chicago.* 1935. • Gosnell, Harold Foote. *Machine Politics: Chicago Model.* 1937. • Grimshaw, William J. *Bitter Fruit: Black Politics and the Chicago Machine, 1931–1991.* 1992. • Hawley, Amos Henry. *Human Ecology: A Theory of Community Structure.* 1950. • Hoyt, Homer. *One Hundred Years of Land Values in Chicago.* 1970. • Hughes, Everett Cherrington. *The Chicago Real Estate Board: The Growth of an Institution.* 1979. • Hughes, Everett Cherrington, and Helen MacGill Hughes. *Where Peoples Meet: Racial and Ethnic Frontiers.* 1952. • Janowitz, Morris. *The Community Press in an Urban Setting.* 1952. • Kincheloe, Samuel C. *The American City and Its Church.* 1938. • Mayer, Harold M., and Richard C. Wade. *Chicago: Growth of a Metropolis.* 1969. • Merriam, Charles Edward. *A History of American Political Theories.* 1903. • Merriam, Charles Edward. *Primary Elections: A Study of the History and Tendencies of Primary Election Legislation.* 1908. • Merriam, Charles Edward. *Chicago: A More Intimate View of Urban Politics.* 1929. • Park, Robert Ezra, and Ernest Watson Burgess. *Introduction to the Science of Sociology.* 1921. • Park, Robert Ezra, Ernest Watson Burgess, Roderick Duncan McKenzie, and Louis Wirth. *The City.* 1925. • Pierce, Bessie Louise. *A History of Chicago: The Beginning of a City, 1673–1848.* 1937. • Pierce, Bessie Louise. *A History of Chicago: From Town to City, 1848–1871.* 1940. • Pierce, Bessie Louise. *A History of Chicago: The Rise of a Modern City, 1871–1893.* 1957. • Rakove, Milton L. *Don't Make No Waves—Don't Back No Losers: An Insider's Analysis of the Daley Machine.* 1975. • Residents of Hull-House. *Hull-House Maps and Papers: A Presentation of Nationalities and Wages in a Congested District of Chicago, Together with Comments and Essays on Problems Growing Out of the Social Conditions.* 1895. • Royko, Mike. *Boss: Richard J. Daley of Chicago.* 1971. • Shaw, Clifford Robe, and Ernest Watson Burgess. *The Jack-Roller: A Delinquent Boy's Own Story.* 1930. • Shaw, Clifford Robe, Frederick McClure Zorbaugh, Henry Donald McKay, and Leonard S. Cottrell. *Delinquency Areas: A Study of the Geographic Distribution of School Truants, Juvenile Delinquents, and Adult Offenders in Chicago.* 1929. • Sinclair, Upton. *The Jungle.* 1920. • Suttles, Gerald D. *The Social Order of the Slum: Ethnicity and Territory in the Inner City.* 1968. • Suttles, Gerald D. *The Social Construction of Communities.* 1972. • Suttles, Gerald D. *The Man-Made City: The Land-Use Confidence Game in Chicago.* 1990. • Thomas, William Isaac, and Florian Znaniecki. *The Polish Peasant in Europe and America: Monograph of an Immigrant Group.* 1918. • Thrasher, Frederic Milton. *The Gang: A Study of 1,313 Gangs in Chicago.* 1926. • Whyte, William Hollingsworth. *The Organization Man.* 1956. • Wilson, James Q. *Negro Politics: The Search for Leadership.* 1960. • Wilson, William J. *The Truly Disadvantaged: The Inner City, the Underclass, and Public Policy.* 1987. • Wirth, Louis. *The Ghetto.* 1928. • Wirth, Louis. "Urbanism as a Way of Life: The City and Contemporary Civilization." *American Journal of Sociology* 44 (1938):1–24. • Zorbaugh, Harvey Warren. *Gold Coast and Slum: A Sociological Study of Chicago's Near North Side.* 1929.

Chicago Sun-Times. Although the *Chicago Sun-Times* was launched in February 1948 through the merger of the morning *Chicago Sun* and the evening *Times,* it is in a sense the city's oldest daily—continuing the *Chicago Evening Journal,* published from 1844 until 1929, when it was re-launched as the *Daily Illustrated Times.*

In contrast to the stodgy *Journal,* the *Daily Times* was a sprightly, progressive paper. The *Times* used tabloid format and style to appeal to a mass audience with hard-hitting reporting, lots of photographs, and a heavy dose of carefully chosen features. It was bought in 1947 by DEPARTMENT STORE heir Marshall Field III, who was looking for PRINTING presses for his *Chicago Sun,* founded in December 1941 to challenge the *Tribune*'s monopoly in the morning field.

Field's heirs lacked his liberal politics and his commitment to newspapering, and the *Sun-Times* gradually moved to the right, endorsing Richard Nixon for president in 1968.

In 1984 the Field family sold the *Sun-Times* to Rupert Murdoch's News Corporation, prompting popular columnist Mike Royko to flee to the *Tribune.* Murdoch sold the paper two years later to its managers and an investment partnership, who in 1994 sold the *Sun-Times* and its chain of community papers to Conrad Black's American Publishing Company.

Jon Bekken

See also: Journalism; Newspapers

Further reading: Becker, Stephen. *Marshall Field III.* 1964. • Meyers, Walter C. "Chicago's Mister Finnegan: A Gentle Man of the Press." Ph.D. diss., Northwestern University. 1959. • Weston, Mary Ann. "The *Daily Illustrated Times:* Chicago's Tabloid Newspaper." *Journalism History* 16 (3/4) (Autumn–Winter 1989): 76–86.

Chicago Symphony Orchestra. C. Norman Fay could never have known how successful his efforts would become when he marshaled the support of 50 like-minded Chicago businessmen to entice conductor Theodore Thomas from New York with promises of a permanent, full-time orchestra, a 28-week season, competitive wages for his musicians, and complete artistic freedom unfettered by box-office receipts or administrative burdens. When the Chicago Orchestra presented its first concert in the AUDITORIUM Theater on October 16, 1891, Thomas created a recipe for success that has served the ensemble through its history: audience education and community service based upon uncompromising artistic excellence.

Thomas died January 4, 1905, just weeks after dedicating the new Orchestra Hall that 8,000 contributors had built at his request. Another GERMAN-born maestro, Frederick Stock, succeeded Thomas and continued an illustrious conducting tradition which would later include Désiré Defauw, Artur Rodzinski, Rafael Kubelik, Fritz Reiner, Jean Martinon, Sir Georg Solti, and Daniel Barenboim. In 1919, Stock established the orchestra's first children's concerts and created the Civic Music Student Orchestra (now the Civic Orchestra of Chicago), a unique training ensemble intended to develop native talent that is still operating today. Another function of the orchestra was to help overcome the city's rough-hewn image and place Chicago onto the world's cultural stage. After over 900 recordings (1916–), 56 of which have won Grammy Awards (1960–), regular radio broadcasts, television appearances, numerous domestic and overseas tours, the "CHICAGO SOUND," with rich brass sonorities complemented by virtuosic wind and string playing, has indeed elicited worldwide admiration.

Mark Clague

See also: Chicago Federation of Musicians; Classical Music; Entertaining Chicagoans; Radio Orchestras

Further reading: Otis, Philo Adams. *The Chicago Symphony Orchestra: Its Organization, Growth and Development, 1891–1924.* 1924. • Schabas, Ezra. *Theodore Thomas: America's Conductor and Builder of Orchestras, 1835–1905.* 1989. • Thomas, Rose Fay. *Memoirs of Theodore Thomas.* 1911.

Chicago Teachers Federation.

The Chicago Teachers Federation, founded in 1897 and powerful through the 1930s, was organized by and for women elementary school teachers. At its height in the early 1900s, over half of all Chicago elementary school teachers were members of the federation.

The federation fought for teachers' rights and improved working conditions, but it also played a prominent role in Chicago progressive reform. Former elementary teacher Margaret Haley, the federation's paid business representative, spearheaded a legal challenge of corporate tax exemptions and drew Chicago's teachers into municipal reform and woman SUFFRAGE campaigns. To bolster its authority, the federation made unprecedented alliances with organized labor, affiliating with the CHICAGO FEDERATION OF LABOR in 1902. In 1916, the Chicago Teachers Federation became Local 1 of the newly formed American Federation of Teachers. In 1917, however, the federation was forced to withdraw from both organizations under the Loeb rule, which prohibited Chicago teachers from membership in any organization affiliated with trade unions.

Between 1897 and the 1920s, the federation was known to teachers throughout the nation as the only organized advocate for women elementary teachers, and it developed great political clout in Chicago and in the larger educational community. Haley's leadership was eventually challenged by competing teacher organizations, which amalgamated in 1937 into the Chicago Teachers Union.

Kate Rousmaniere

See also: Feminist Movements; Good Government Movements; Schools and Education; Unionization; Work Culture

Further reading: Chicago Teachers Federation. Papers. Chicago Historical Society. • Hogan, David. *Class and Reform: School and Society in Chicago, 1880–1930.* 1985. • Murphy, Marjorie. *Blackboard Unions: The AFT and NEA, 1900–1980.* 1990.

Mary Abbe presides at overflow meeting of the Chicago Teachers Federation, 1920s. Photographer: Unknown. Source: Chicago Public Library.

Chicago Title and Trust.

The Chicago Title and Trust Company was born of disaster and grew from unrivaled opportunity. The Great FIRE of October 8, 1871, that destroyed a substantial portion of the city of Chicago might have also prevented its orderly and timely rebuilding had it not been for the "abstract men" who had prepared meticulous indices and abstracts of all land transactions in COOK COUNTY since 1847. Official property records prepared and stored in the courthouse were turned to dust in the flames. Fortunately for the city, three abstract firms, using a system of indexing and summarizing land trading pioneered by Edward A. Rucker, independently salvaged their records. With a minimum of legal challenge and political wrangling, clear title to property was maintained after the fire. The state of Illinois gave the abstracted land titles the status of law in all courts by passing the Burnt Records Act of 1872. Chase Brothers & Co., Jones & Sellars, and Shortall & Hoard consolidated their records and earned for their efforts a legal monopoly on all land dealings in Cook County. The Illinois General Trust Company Act of 1887 allowed the company (renamed Chicago Title and Trust in 1891) to act as executor, administrator, guardian, and trustee for corporations and individuals. With its archive of land tracts and roster of "BLIND TRUSTS," CT&T remained the only legal title company operating in Cook County until the 1960s, when the franchise was first opened to out-of-state companies. With their unique inside view of city land dealing, the officers of Chicago Title often found themselves at the critical boundary between POLITICS and BUSINESS. Under the leadership of men like Holman Pettibone, the company had a discreet and nearly invisible role in the PLANNING and development of modern Chicago.

Ross Miller

See also: Real Estate; Urban Renewal

Further reading: Miller, Ross. *American Apocalypse: The Great Fire and the Myth of Chicago.* 1990. • Miller, Ross. *Here's the Deal: The Buying and Selling of a Great American City.* 1996.

Chicago to Mackinac Race.

The Chicago Yacht Club's annual Chicago to Mackinac Race is the world's oldest and longest freshwater sailboat race. Each July, nearly three hundred boats make the 333-mile trip to Mackinac Island in two to three days. Sailors, some of whom have competed in over 25 "Macs" and are called "Island Goats," consider the race an outstanding test of boats and crews because of LAKE MICHIGAN's unobstructed waters and highly changeable weather conditions. Despite those conditions, there has never been a fatality and only one boat has been lost.

The sloop *Vanenna* won the first race in 1898 against four boats. In 1911, *Vencedor* ran aground and broke up in hurricane-force winds. That same year, *Amorita* finished first

Sailboats going through the gap in the breakwater at Van Buren Street prior to the beginning of the Chicago to Mackinac Race, 1905. Photographer: Unknown. Source: Chicago Historical Society.

with a time of 31 hours, 14 minutes, 30 seconds—a record that stood until 1987, when *Pied Piper* finished in 25 hours, 50 minutes, 44 seconds. Because of handicap rules, neither boat actually won its record-setting race. In 1998, Steve Fossett's catamaran *Stars and Stripes*, sailing in a special "open" division that allows multihull boats, set an all-time record of 18 hours, 50 minutes, 32 seconds.

Geoffrey Baer

See also: Creation of Chicago Sports; Great Lakes System; Leisure; Sailing and Boating; Waterfront

Further reading: Tank, Deane, Sr., ed. *Tales of the Mackinac Race, 1898–1998.* 1998.

Chicago Transit Authority. In 1997, the Chicago Transit Authority (CTA) was the second-largest transit system in the United States, with approximately 1,900 buses and 1,150 RAPID TRANSIT cars carrying almost 419 million passenger trips a year (1997).

The CTA was created in 1945. Chicago's elevated and street railway companies were owned by corporations that had become hopelessly mired in bankruptcy during the GREAT DEPRESSION because of overregulation by the city, corruption, and poor financial practices. The emergence of the automobile as a competitor made their successful reorganization unlikely despite high ridership during World War II. The state legislature empowered the new CTA to pay over $12 million for the city's elevated railway system and $75 million for its street railways. The money bought 3,560 streetcars, 152 electric buses, 259 motor buses, and 1,623 rapid transit cars.

The CTA eventually replaced all its streetcars with buses and abandoned six of its elevated lines. By 1963, it had begun a program of expansion that led to new lines to north suburban SKOKIE, O'HARE INTERNATIONAL AIRPORT on the Northwest Side, and MIDWAY AIRPORT on the Southwest Side, and in the median strip of the Dan Ryan EXPRESSWAY.

The law creating the CTA did not make any provision for subsidies. Deficits resulting from increased service, declining ridership, and inflation that drove up costs resulted in creation of the REGIONAL TRANSPORTATION AUTHORITY in 1974 to levy taxes to subsidize mass transit. At the end of the twentieth century, the agency was receiving about half its operating revenues from fares and the balance from federal, state, and regional subsidies.

David M. Young

See also: Bus System; Commuting; Public Transportation

Further reading: Cudahy, Brian J. *Destination Loop: The Story of Rapid Transit Railroads in and around Chicago.* 1982. • Krambles, George, and Arthur H. Peterson. *CTA at Forty-five: A History of the First Forty-five Years of the Chicago Transit Authority.* 1993. • Young, David M. *Chicago Transit: An Illustrated History.* 1998.

Chicago Tribune. For most of the city's history, the *Chicago Tribune* has been Chicago's leading NEWSPAPER in terms of both local circulation and national influence. Led by a series of ambitious editors and publishers, the *Tribune* was one of a small handful of major American daily papers published continuously from the mid-1800s into the twenty-first century. By the late twentieth century, when it was owned by a corporation that took the name of the paper, the *Tribune* stood as the flagship of a national media empire.

Founded in 1847, the *Chicago Daily Tribune* was transformed by the arrival in 1855 of editor and co-owner Joseph Medill, who turned the paper into one of the leading voices of the new REPUBLICAN PARTY. Daily circulation grew from about 1,400 copies in 1855 to as high as 40,000 during the CIVIL WAR, when the paper was a strong supporter of President Lincoln and emancipation.

After an eight-year period in which the paper was dominated by liberal maverick editor Horace White, Medill regained control in 1874. Driven in part by competition from the *Chicago Daily News* and other papers, the *Tribune* gradually introduced more illustrations and reduced its price from five cents per copy to a penny. In 1901, two years after Medill's death, it installed its first color press.

In the following decade, the *Tribune* was led by Medill's son-in-law Robert Patterson and editor James Keeley. Presenting itself as a champion of reform, the paper set its sights on political corruption. The targets of its investigations and editorials included not only Democrats but also Republican MACHINE politicians such as U.S. Senator William Lorimer, whom the *Tribune* forced out of Congress.

Between the 1910s and the 1950s, the *Tribune* prospered under the leadership of Medill's grandson Robert R. McCormick. Calling his operation the "World's Greatest Newspaper," McCormick succeeded in raising daily circulation from 230,000 in 1912 to 650,000 by 1925, when the *Tribune* stood as the city's most widely read paper. In 1925, when it moved into the Tribune Tower on North Michigan Avenue, the paper employed about two thousand men and women. During the 1930s and 1940s, McCormick used the *Tribune*'s editorial pages to attack the NEW DEAL and promote isolationism and anti-Communism.

After McCormick died in 1955, the *Tribune* moved toward a more moderate (if still Republican) editorial stance, as it increasingly became the product less of individual personalities than of a large BUSINESS corporation. Meanwhile, the *Tribune*'s younger media cousins were growing faster than the newspaper itself. This development had begun under McCormick, who oversaw the founding of WGN (after "World's Greatest Newspaper") radio in 1924 and WGN television in 1948. By the end of the twentieth century, when the newspaper's parent company (the Tribune Company) was a national media giant that employed close to six thousand Chicago-area residents, the future of traditional print dailies was uncertain. Nevertheless, the *Tribune,* now available in electronic form, continued to be Chicago's leading newspaper.

Mark R. Wilson

See also: Cold War and Anti-Communism; Journalism; Machine Politics; Politics and the Press

Further reading: Kinsley, Philip. *The Chicago Tribune: Its First Hundred Years.* 3 vols. 1943–1946. • Mott, Frank Luther. *American Journalism: A History, 1690–1960.* 3rd ed. 1962. • Wendt, Lloyd. *Chicago Tribune: The Rise of a Great American Newspaper.* 1979.

Chicago White Sox. *See* White Sox

Chicago Women's Liberation Union. The Chicago Women's Liberation Union (CWLU, 1969–1977) was founded by women from the CIVIL RIGHTS MOVEMENT and Students for a Democratic Society. Its pamphlet, *Socialist Feminism: A Strategy for the Women's Movement* (1972), circulated widely and is apparently the first use of "socialist feminism," a term that identified feminists who used Marxist and SOCIALIST ideas while criticizing them for inattention to gender.

The union's programs raised consciousness, challenged power structures through direct action, and provided services for women. Committed to democratic and decentralized structures, union members chose to develop accountable leaders, rather than dismiss altogether the notion of leadership.

Individual chapters were linked through a steering committee, outreach newspapers (*Womankind, Blazing Star,* and *Secret Storm*), and an internal newsletter. "JANE" (or "the Service") provided first referrals and then clandestine abortions. Later, the Abortion Counseling Service and the Health Evaluation and Referral Service (HERS) advocated quality health care.

The CWLU influenced the development of women's studies programs locally, ran a Liberation School, organized high-school girls, and offered courses at Dwight Correctional Institution. Its rock band recorded *Mountain Moving Day* in 1972. The Graphics Collective marketed silk-screen posters nationally. The CWLU organized sports teams and challenged sexism in the Chicago PARK DISTRICT.

With the Chicago chapter of the National Organization for Women, the CWLU successfully sued Chicago for sex discrimination on behalf of city "janitresses." Blazing Star, the lesbian chapter, worked for a lesbian and gay rights ordinance. Action Coalition for Decent Childcare (ACDC) won changes in licensing codes for day care providers, and the Legal Clinic offered advice on tenant issues and divorce.

Although most members were European American, the CWLU supported the Black Panthers, worked with the PUERTO RICAN Socialist Party, and organized against racial discrimination in gay and lesbian bars.

Margaret Strobel

See also: Feminist Movements; Gay and Lesbian Rights Movements

Further reading: DuPlessis, Rachel Blau, and Ann Snitow, eds. *Feminist Memoir Project: Voices from Women's Liberation.* 1998. • Strobel, Margaret. "Consciousness and Action: Historical Agency in the Chicago Women's Liberation Union." In *Provoking Agents: Theorizing Gender and Agency,* ed. Judith Kegan Gardiner, 1995, 52–68.

Chicago Youth Symphony Orchestra. Inspired by their children's summer at Interlochen's National Music Camp, a group of parents formed the Youth Orchestra of Greater Chicago in 1946 with the founding principle of providing a superior music experience to talented high-school musicians. In the decades following the first concert, conducted by Harold Finch on November 14, 1947, the organization grew to consist of a 120-piece symphony orchestra (CYSO) drawn from around 50 area high schools, the Chicago Youth Concert Orchestra, a training ensemble, and the elite Encore Chamber Orchestra. Conductors have included Désiré Defauw (1954–1958), Michael Morgan (1989–1993), and Rossen Milanov (1998–), and many alumni play in professional ensembles nationwide and throughout the world. Tours to Europe and Japan, radio broadcasts, recordings, and awards, including Orchestra of the Year (1993) by the Illinois Council of Orchestras and an ASCAP for adventurous programming (1994 and 1995), have elevated the CYSO's status to among the finest youth training ensembles in the country.

Richard Schwegel

See also: Classical Music; Schooling for Work

Further reading: Chicago Youth Symphony Orchestra. *Golden Anniversary Commemorative Book, 1946–1966.* 1996.

Chicagoland. Col. Robert R. McCormick, editor and publisher of the *Chicago Tribune* for most of the first half of the twentieth century, usually gets credit for putting "Chicagoland" into common parlance. In McCormick's time, it referred to the city and its grain, timber, and livestock hinterlands covering parts of five states (Illinois, Indiana, Wisconsin, Michigan, and Iowa), all of which were served by rail delivery of the colonel's newspaper. Later in the century it came to mean a smaller, denser area of city and suburbs in three states stretching from northern Indiana to southern Wisconsin.

Jack W. Fuller

See also: Agriculture; Suburbs and Cities as Dual Metropolis

Further reading: "The Colonel's Century." *Time,* June 9, 1947, 60. • Cronon, William. *Nature's Metropolis.* 1991.

Children and the Law. Chicago was to Progressive-era children's rights advocates what Boston was to antebellum ABOLITIONISTS. While neither effort originated in either city, both served as incubators for movement leadership. Influential individuals from Chicago helped to redefine childhood and encouraged the passage of new laws regulating CHILDREN'S HEALTH, labor, education, and dependency.

Chicago's meteoric growth from frontier settlement to modern city paralleled a growing awareness of the transformed function of childhood and family life in a more urban and industrialized America. In *Some Ethical Gains through Legislation* (1905), Florence Kelley asserted "a right to childhood" that was being threatened by such change. Kelley and other child welfare advocates were primarily linked through Jane Addams's and Ellen Gates Starr's HULL HOUSE (1889), located on Chicago's Halsted Street.

Chicago's influence in the growing national child welfare movement is clear. On March 31, 1905, Chicagoans Jane Addams and Mary McDowell joined Lillian D. Wald, founder of New York's Henry Street Settlement, and Edward T. Devine, editor of the journal *Charities,* for a meeting at the White House with President Theodore Roosevelt. The group urged Roosevelt to establish a federal bureau to investigate and report on the nation's youngest citizens. It took seven more years of lobbying, but President William Howard Taft signed the U.S. Children's Bureau into law on April 9, 1912, and named as the agency's first chief another Hull House resident, Julia C. Lathrop. With this appointment, Lathrop became the first woman to head a federal agency. Many of her staff were trained at the Chicago School of Civics and PHILANTHROPY, thereby creating a legacy linking Chicago and national child welfare reform.

Although the U.S. Children's Bureau had no legal authority, it acted as the major lobby for children at the national, state, and local levels. Lathrop quickly implemented tactics that she learned while in Chicago. Infants and young children were dying at alarming rates. Hull House workers had conducted surveys in an effort to identify the reasons why so many children died of what seemed to be preventable causes. Beginning in 1915, Lathrop instituted a plan encouraging states to require birth registration programs. The issuing of birth certificates led to greater use of physicians and visiting nurses at births, rather than uncertified midwives. The effort also furthered the establishment of clean milk distribution centers and child health CLINICS for the poor. By 1920 the Children's Bureau had a staff of 196, nearly half of which (86) were stationed in Chicago.

The U.S. Children's Bureau's biggest success was passage of the 1921 Sheppard-Towner Maternity and Infancy Act, which provided federal funds matched by states for programs designed to reduce the nation's high infant mortality rate. Limited to education and diagnosis, Sheppard-Towner funds could not be used for direct medical care. Still, beginning in March 1922, Sheppard-Towner funds paid the salaries of visiting nurses and provided funds to implement educational programs and free diagnostic clinics for young children and pregnant women. But opponents, initially led by the Illinois Medical Association, labeled Sheppard-Towner socialized medicine, and Congress allowed funding for the program to expire in 1929. Ironically, since the idea came from Illinois' Julia Lathrop, Illinois was one of the three states—Connecticut and Massachusetts were the others—that refused to pass matching funding for Sheppard-Towner. Nonetheless, in Illinois, the focusing of public attention on children's health helped increase public spending and reduce the state's infant mortality rate by 50 percent between 1920 and 1930.

Child labor was another controversial legal reform connected to birth registration. American children had always labored. But by the mid-nineteenth century some reformers argued that working in the nation's mines, streets, and factories harmed children's health and produced unproductive adults. Massachusetts and Connecticut passed the nation's first child labor regulations in 1842, limiting the workday to 10 hours for children under 12 and 14 years of age, respectively. Illinois followed, making it illegal by 1900 for children under 14 to work for wages. Over the next two decades the successful implementation of a birth certificate program and a growing labor movement in Illinois and Chicago focused enforcement on child labor regulations. When Congress passed the nation's first federal child labor law in 1916 (the Keating-Owen Act), another Chicago Hull House resident, Grace Abbott, came to Washington to enforce the legislation. But Abbott returned to Chicago when the U.S. Supreme Court declared the law unconstitutional in 1918 (*Hammer v. Dagenhart,* 247 U.S. 251). Abbott returned to Washington in 1921 as the second U.S. Children's Bureau chief, a position she held until July 1, 1934.

Child labor regulation and compulsory school attendance laws also went hand in hand. The first public SCHOOLS opened in Chicago in the 1830s. After the Civil War, a parallel system of largely Catholic parochial schools arose to accommodate the desires of many immigrant parents. By the 1880s Illinois passed compulsory school attendance laws for children up to age 14. Birth certificates enabled enforcement, and Chicago's schools became a symbol of opportunity for immigrant families and southern AFRICAN AMERICANS migrating north. Problems of racial discrimination endured, and white flight to the suburbs has hampered the effectiveness of court-ordered SCHOOL DESEGREGATION since the end of World War II. But compulsory school attendance requirements have remained an important factor, with the Chicago Public Schools in the late 1990s instituting required summer attendance for children with egregiously subpar test scores.

Chicago and Illinois were also pioneers in the area of child dependency legislation. In 1911 Illinois and Missouri became the first states to enact MOTHERS' PENSION laws. Advocates argued that children deprived of a male breadwinner should not also be deprived of a "normal home life." Mothers' pensions offered cash payments so that children could remain in their own homes in the case of a father's death, desertion, or imprisonment. Lathrop and Abbott promoted the idea at the national level. By 1921, 40 states had programs similar to Illinois', and by 1931 only Georgia and South Carolina had no mothers' pension programs. In 1935, state mothers' pensions were replaced by the Social Security Act's Aid to Dependent Children program (later, Aid to Families with Dependent Children). Grace Abbott helped write this seminal legislation.

Children from families who became totally dependent upon the state for their care were also a part of Chicago's early efforts. After a 30-year campaign, in 1899 Chicago reformers established the nation's first state-sanctioned JUVENILE COURT. Reformers argued that children who appeared before the courts were "handicapped by immaturity of body and mind [and] by a lack of effective parental control." Some were dependent due to the death of parents, others because of physical or mental disabilities, illegitimacy, or socially unacceptable behavior. Like the mothers' pension movement, juvenile courts quickly spread throughout the United States. But the application of juvenile court laws was inconsistent. Even in Chicago, juvenile court authority has led to a complex bureaucracy. Reform schools, institutions, and foster care became the primary course of "treatment," and efforts focused on individual children rather than the entire family as originally envisioned.

The very definition of childhood has been at the heart of legal reforms for children. Fourteen was generally accepted as the limit of childhood during the nineteenth century. By 1925 Illinois child welfare advocates had successfully extended the definition to 16 for juvenile court jurisdiction, many child labor laws, and minimum age at marriage laws. From 1925 through the 1970s, the legal age of childhood was generally raised to 18. But since 1980 there has been a growing ambivalence about children's legal dependency. Debates over appropriate punishment for juvenile violent offenders and the 1996 Welfare Reform Act's five-year limitations show that the redefinition of the legal status of children continues.

Kriste Lindenmeyer

See also: Birthing Practices; Catholic School System; Children, Dependent; Juvenile Justice Reform; Kindergarten Movement

Further reading: Chambers, Clarke A. *Seedtime of Reform: American Social Service and Social Action, 1918–1933.* 1963. • Costin, Lela B. *Two Sisters for Social Justice: A Biography of Grace and Edith Abbott.* 1983. • Gitten, Joan. *Poor Relations: The Children of the State in Illinois, 1818–1990.* 1994.

Children, Dependent. The chaotic and stunning growth of the city was the first source of Chicago's dependent children problems. By the 1850s, disease, desertion, and poverty—the three nineteenth-century sources of dependent children—were already apparent. The first ORPHANAGES appeared in the city in response to the cholera EPIDEMIC of 1849. Parents on their way west were known to abandon their children on the streets of Chicago. The 1851 city charter noted children "destitute of proper parental care, wandering about the streets, committing mischief." Two years later, a COOK COUNTY Grand Jury complained that the women and children's section of the county poorhouse was "so crowded as to be very offensive."

City leaders responded by building institutions for dependent children. These privately owned institutions, usually organized along religious lines, aimed at keeping poor children from mixing either with adults in the county poorhouse or with delinquent children in reformatories or JAILS. The Chicago Home for the Friendless and Chicago Foundling HOSPITAL were created in the 1850s for abandoned infants. Orphanages like ANGEL GUARDIAN ORPHANAGE, the Protestant Chicago Orphan Asylum, and the Marks Nathan Jewish Orphan Asylum were built either in or around downtown. They housed children under 12 years of age. Industrial schools were founded for children between 11 and 16. A cross between orphanages and training schools, industrial schools tried to teach adolescents some sort of marketable skill.

Still, the system was overwhelmed. As ROMAN CATHOLICS, JEWS, and EASTERN ORTHODOX migrated to the city between the 1880s and WORLD WAR I, the number of dependent children grew geometrically. There was never enough room in the children's institutions for those needing help. Poor children continued to live on the streets, stay with their mothers in the county poorhouse, or wind up in jail or the Chicago Reform School simply because there were not enough separate resources in institutions for dependent children.

While most of the poor were grateful for the children's institutions, some kept their distance. Until World War I, some poor children without parents banded together on the streets, making money by everything from selling NEWSPAPERS to PROSTITUTING themselves. Similarly, mothers in the Cook County poorhouse clung to their children, resisting the efforts of welfare reformers to put them in orphanages.

Beginning in the 1890s, reformers like Jane Addams of HULL HOUSE, Louise de Koven Bowen of the JUVENILE PROTECTION ASSOCIATION, and Professor Charles Henderson of the UNIVERSITY OF CHICAGO began attacking the nineteenth-century institutional system. In general, they wanted dependent children to remain at home, with foster care the next best option. In 1899, the Cook County JUVENILE

Court, the first in the nation, opened with a mission to remove children from the adult criminal justice system. In 1911, Illinois passed the first law in the nation giving widowed mothers some financial aid, to help keep children with their mothers and out of orphanages.

Despite the reforms, between 1890 and 1920, new orphanages and industrial schools continued to open. And the existing children's institutions grew larger. Only later—between the two world wars—was progressive reform institutionalized in Chicago, with a significant increase in foster care, led by Protestant and Jewish social workers. Institutions themselves began trying to simulate a family environment. Between 1910 and 1930, most orphanages moved away from the center of the city to either suburban or rural surroundings. Several Catholic institutions moved to the northwest corner of the city and subsequently to the country. The Illinois Industrial School for Boys relocated from the Near West Side to Glenwood; the Illinois Industrial School for Girls moved to Park Ridge.

On the eve of World War II, thousands of Chicago children still lived in institutions, as many as lived in foster homes. The child welfare system had grown to accommodate the immigrants of 1880–1917 but it had not moved children out of institutions.

One new group of dependent children was not accommodated by the system's expansion. In the years after 1916, African American dependent children first appeared in large numbers in Chicago. Protestant institutions simply refused to take them. Catholic orphanages took a few, but their priority was to children of their own faith, and African Americans were overwhelmingly Protestant. The two small existing homes for African American children, the Amanda Smith Home for girls and the Louise Manual Training School for Colored Boys, closed in 1919 and 1920. Efforts to build a black foster care system in the 1920s and 1930s did not come to much. Hence, the African American community, where poverty rates were highest, had almost no social service support. It should not be surprising that by the 1940s African American children were disproportionately in correctional institutions like the St. Charles Reformatory or the Geneva School for Girls. There was simply no place else for poor parentless African American children to go.

Since World War II, there have been four important changes for dependent children in Chicago. First, the civil rights movement brought African Americans into the child welfare system between 1955 and 1970. Second, the nineteenth-century orphanages closed and home foster care became the norm for children who had to live away from their biological parents. The orphanages were shut down in two stages, the first between 1945 and 1955 and the second in the mid-1970s. Third, the state took over the management of the child welfare system. The Illinois Department of Children and Family Services (DCFS) was created in 1964. Five years later, the historic "children's division transfer" occurred, and, for the first time, practically every dependent child in Chicago became the responsibility of a public authority. Finally, during the 1980s and 1990s, new and brutal forms of adult drug dependency brought another group of dependent children into the orbit of the child welfare system. Adult use of crack cocaine created a growing pool of children needing homes in which to live, despite the generally strong economy.

Kenneth Cmiel

See also: Children and the Law; Drugs and Alcohol; Religious Institutions; Schooling for Work

Further reading: Cmiel, Kenneth. *A Home of Another Kind: One Chicago Orphanage and the Tangle of Child Welfare*. 1995. • Harwood, Naomi. "The History and Care of Dependent Children in Cook County until 1899." Field Study, School of Social Service Administration, University of Chicago. 1941. • McCausland, Clare. *Children of Circumstance: A History of the First 125 Years of the Chicago Child Care Society*. 1976.

Children's Health. In the mid-nineteenth century, children paid the highest price for poor health conditions in Chicago. In many years children under five represented more than half of all deaths that occurred in the city. Infant mortality rates (the number of deaths of children under two years of age for every 1,000 live births) also remained high throughout this period. Respiratory and diarrheal diseases accounted for the majority of these untimely deaths.

As the links between germs and illness became more widely understood, children's

THE RIGHT WAY TO KEEP BABY'S MILK

Infant Welfare Society poster, ca. 1910s. Milk, considered a fundamental part of a healthy child's diet, could also be a killer. When left at room temperature, it offered germs a very agreeable environment. Armed with new knowledge about the transmission of the disease at the turn of the twentieth century, reformers set out to educate consumers on the virtues of keeping milk cool and protected. Source: Chicago Historical Society.

health reformers stressed disease prevention through appropriate hygiene as the most effective means of reducing high rates of infant and childhood mortality. Sanitary engineering improved overall health conditions in the city, and by the early twentieth century several important public health measures had been put in place. In 1908 Chicago became the first city in the world to require the pasteurization of its milk supply, and the chemical treatment of the city's water supply began in 1913. Widespread reductions in childhood disease and death could not be fully realized, however, until significant numbers of families adopted appropriate daily hygiene practices within their own households, measures such

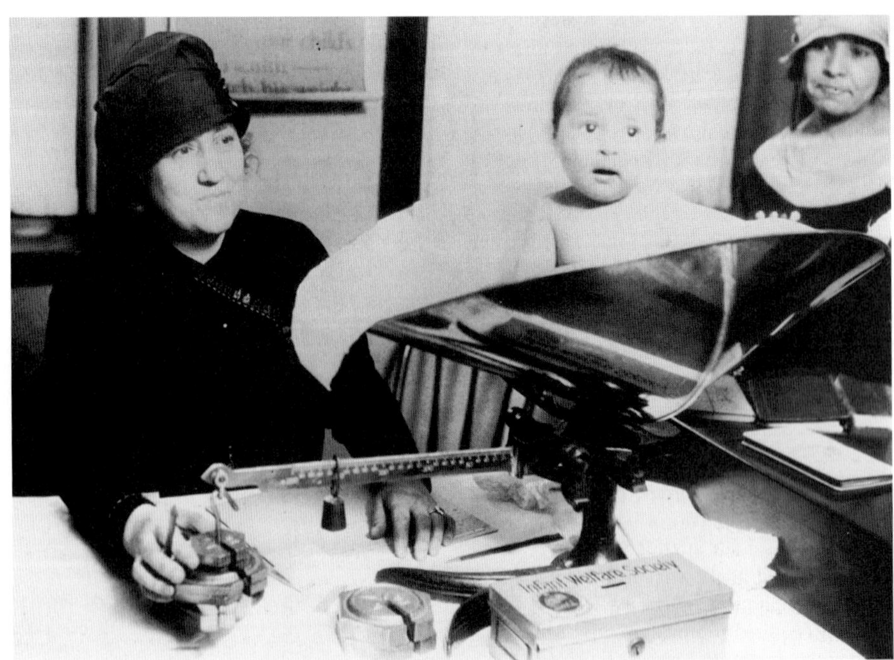

Weighing a baby at Hull House clinic, 1930s. Photographer: Wallace Kirkland. Source: University of Illinois at Chicago.

as frequent hand washing and the sterilization of baby bottles.

Public and private agencies, including the Visiting Nurse Association (founded in 1889), the Elizabeth McCormick Memorial Fund (1908), and the Infant Welfare Society of Chicago (1911), worked to popularize the germ theory among the city's inhabitants. Activities included the publication of child care literature, demonstrations of infant hygiene practices, and the distribution of pasteurized milk in sterilized bottles at low cost to needy families. Reformers also campaigned against the use of patent medicines, as such nostrums often contained narcotics dangerous to children. Immunizations became another important means of preventing illness. In 1917, for example, city school children began to receive immunizations against diphtheria.

In the 1880s, pediatrics became part of the medical school curriculum in Chicago. As medical practitioners began to regard the health care needs of children as being different from those of adults, the city's HOSPITALS set aside special wards for the treatment of children. A hospital designated especially for sick children, Children's Memorial, was founded in 1882. Unfortunately, many of these institutions proved quite hazardous in their early years owing to unsanitary conditions. Their poor reputation among the public prompted reformers to look for more innovative venues for the treatment of children. Neighborhood well-baby CLINICS, visiting NURSE services, and outdoor "baby tents" served as alternative centers for children's health care in the early decades of the twentieth century. Reformers also promoted "better baby contests," in which youngsters were weighed, measured, and examined by medical personnel as a way to disseminate information to parents as well as to stimulate community interest in children's health. Beginning in the 1930s, increased attention began to be paid by the Chicago health care community to prenatal health care, thus helping to improve the life chances of infants under 30 days old.

Lynne Curry

See also: Birthing Practices; Children, Dependent; Epidemics; Horse Keeping; Tuberculosis

Further reading: Bonner, Thomas Neville. *Medicine in Chicago, 1850–1950*. 1991. • Curry, Lynne. *Modern Mothers in the Heartland: Gender, Health, and Progress in Illinois, 1900–1930*. 1999. • Meckel, Richard A. *Save the Babies: American Public Health Reform and the Prevention of Infant Mortality, 1850–1929*. 1990.

Children's Museums. Chicago is home to a number of museums designed especially for young people, including the Chicago Children's Museum (CCM), located on NAVY PIER, and the Kohl Children's Museum in suburban WILMETTE.

Kohl was founded in 1985 by former elementary school teacher Dolores Kohl to serve as a resource center for teachers as well as a place for parents to take part in educating their children outside the confines of a traditional school setting. The museum has grown, from serving 47,000 visitors in its first year to 200,000 by the turn of the century.

The CCM was founded in 1982 by the JUNIOR LEAGUE of Chicago in response to cuts in the arts education budget of the city's public SCHOOLS. Expressways—as the CCM was then called—had its humble beginnings in two hallways of the CHICAGO PUBLIC LIBRARY. It moved to LINCOLN PARK in 1986 and to North Pier in 1989, before changing its name and opening at Navy Pier in 1995. With each move, the CCM occupied more space and served a larger audience: its home at Navy Pier was two and a half times the size of its North Pier location and served nearly 600,000 visitors in its opening year alone, more than any other children's museum in the U.S., save the one in Indianapolis.

Though Kohl and the CCM are miles apart and share no formal affiliation, they do share a guiding commitment to participatory, "hands-on" learning reminiscent of celebrated Chicago educator John Dewey. They also share an interest in helping children cope with issues specific to city living: in the late 1990s, the CCM housed a "Prejudice Bus," which dealt with different kinds of discrimination, and "All About Garbage," a lesson on city refuse and recycling, while Kohl's "All Aboard" took children on a mock CHICAGO TRANSIT AUTHORITY train ride through the streets of Chicago.

Other children's museums include the Dupage Children's Museum (1987) in NAPERVILLE, the Bronzeville Children's Museum (1993) in EVERGREEN PARK, and Health World (1995) in BARRINGTON. In 2003 OAK PARK'S Wonder Works (1991) reopened after having been closed for several years.

Sarah Fenton

See also: Leisure; Museum of Science and Industry; Progressive Education

Chileans. Chileans have resided in Chicago since the late nineteenth century, but the first formal organization, the Club Chileno, dates back only to the 1950s. During the 1960s and 1970s, more than two hundred Chilean economists attended the UNIVERSITY OF CHICAGO with the sponsorship of the Ford Foundation. They had a limited influence among the HYDE PARK academic community but not in the city, as a majority of them returned to Chile. Nonetheless, their political and economic influence in the 1970s and 1980s made the University of Chicago a household name in their native country.

A more permanent settlement of Chileans resulted from the 1973 military coup in Chile. Thousands of Chileans were sent into exile, a few hundred of whom moved to Chicago under the auspices of church organizations and an ad-hoc Committee to Save Lives in Chile. These exiled families, unlike Chilean exiles elsewhere, did not form residential communities. They were, however, politically active and soon organized Casa Chile and other cultural and political groups aimed at helping exiles and denouncing human right abuses. Most exiles intended to return to Chile when the political situation changed, and many did after the restoration of democracy in 1990. Many of their children, however, attended college, married, and permanently settled in the area. Members of this group have made an impact on local cultural and political life, through such organizations as the Pablo Neruda Cultural Center and the Rodrigo Rojas–Chilean Alliance of University Students at the UNIVERSITY OF ILLINOIS AT CHICAGO. With the return of democracy to Chile, many of these organizations disbanded, but their members joined other existing human rights and political organizations where they continue to be active.

A third wave of Chileans, mostly students and relatives of local residents, completes the Chilean presence in the area. Several doctors and university professors of Chilean origin now live and teach at institutions of higher education in the city, primarily in medical schools. Young entrepreneurs as well as corporate executives also have settled in the area. The Chilean community in the 1990s also attracted Spanish-language poets and supported a musical folkloric group, Los Sudacas. A local amateur SOCCER team, Arauco, has won several championships.

Official Chilean presence has existed through a consulate. Protests to denounce human right abuses were common during the 1970s and 1980s in front of the consulate, which was eventually closed in the late 1980s. With the return of democracy to Chile, Fernando Ayala was sent to Chicago as consul general in 1993. Consul Ayala's leadership converted the consulate into a center for Chilean cultural and social activities, including an official Chilean Independence reception every September 18, with attendance reaching as high as 1,500. The consulate also has developed partnerships with local organizations to sponsor other cultural and social events. According to the Chilean Consulate, 2,500 Chileans resided in the Chicago metropolitan area by the late 1990s.

Patricio Navia

See also: Chicago School of Economics; Demography; Ethnic Music; Multicentered Chicago; Medical Education; Universities and their Cities

Further reading: "Beyond Potluck Gourmet Clubs Grow, as Home Cooks Get More Sophisticated." *Chicago Tribune,* November 9, 1997. • *Abra Palabra* (literary magazine). 1995–1998.

Chinatown. In 1890, 25 percent of the city's 600 CHINESE lived along Clark between Van Buren and Harrison Streets, in an area called

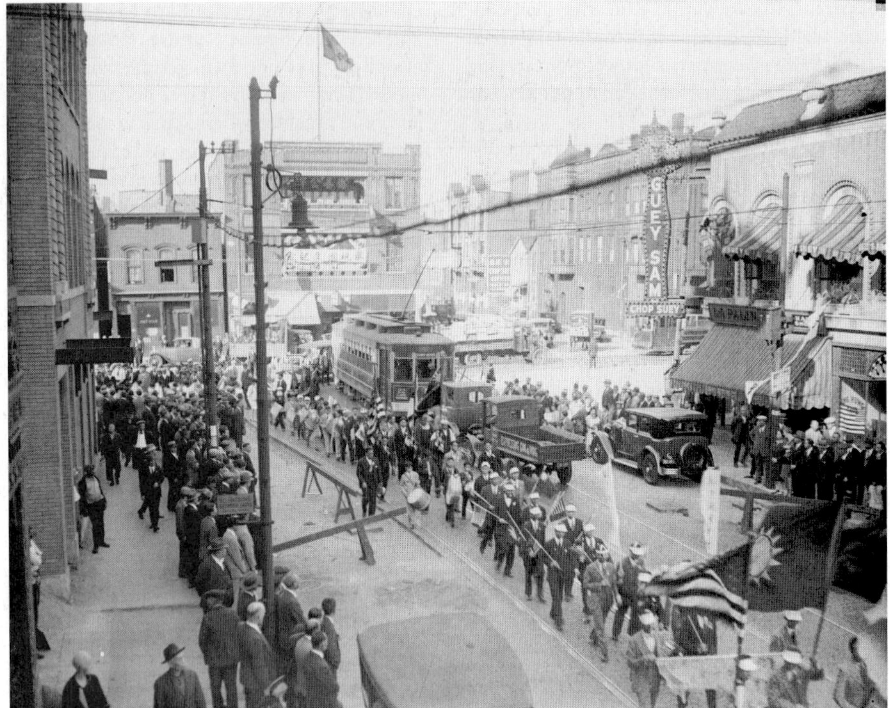

Parade in Chinatown, 1928. Photographer: Unknown. Source: Chicago Historical Society.

the Loop's Chinatown. After 1910 Chinese from the Loop moved to a new area near Cermak Road and Wentworth Avenue, mainly for cheaper rent. Chinatown expanded before 1980 into Armour Square and by 1990 into Bridgeport. In 2000 Chicago had 32,187 Chinese residents, 33 percent of whom lived in Chinatown and adjacent areas.

Chinese have also concentrated in the so-called New Chinatown area, centered along Argyle Street between Sheridan Road and Broadway in Uptown. There were more Vietnamese than Chinese there in 2000, with smaller numbers of and Koreans as well.

For decades, Chinatown has been a unique tourist attraction in Chicago. A colorful gate decorated with a Chinese inscription declaring "The world is for all" stands at the intersection of Cermak Road and Wentworth Avenue. Nearby is a landmark of Chinese architecture, the former Chinese Merchants Association Building. Adorned with red and green pagodas, flowers, and lion sculptures, the building houses a library, meeting rooms, and a shrine. The Chinatown Square mall located near Archer and Wentworth Avenues has a pagoda structure and 12 statues representing the animals of the Chinese zodiac. Tourists shop for oriental gifts or groceries or enjoy Chinese food; along Wentworth Avenue between 22nd and 24th Streets there are at least 30 Chinese restaurants. Printers and bakeries are found in the commercial areas along Wentworth Avenue and Cermak Road.

Chinatown is fragmented by many transportation lines. The New York Central Railroad and the Dan Ryan Expressway parallel its east boundary closely. The Santa Fe Railroad parallels the South Branch of the Chicago River, which forms its northwest boundary. The Pennsylvania Railroad cuts Chinatown from north to south along Canal Street. The Stevenson Expressway cuts Chinatown from east to west along 26th Street.

Chinatown is overcrowded. The residential areas have mostly two-story structures, both old and new. High-rises include the Archer Court and Chinatown Elderly apartments for low-income seniors. In response to a critical shortage of open space, the city of Chicago is building a 12-acre park along the east bank of the South Branch of the Chicago River from 16th to 21st Streets. The park has an indoor swimming pool, playing fields, a Chinese teahouse pavilion, and rose garden.

Ying-cheng (Harry) Kiang

See also: City as Artifact; Demography; Food Processing: Regional and National Market; South Side

Further reading: Kiang, Harry. *Chicago's Chinatown.* 1992.

Chinese. The first Chinese immigrants to Chicago arrived in the early 1870s from the West Coast of the United States. Lured by the gold rush and job opportunities abroad in the face of economic crisis in southern China, male Cantonese laborers began migrating to California in the early 1850s. Intending only temporary stays, they were willing to work long hours at menial and even dangerous jobs in agriculture, mining, small industries, and railroads in order to support families back home. With the completion of the transcontinental railroad, which had employed thousands of Chinese laborers, and growing legal discrimination and harassment in California, many Chinese migrated eastward in the 1870s to major cities like Chicago, New York, and Boston. Chinese settlers in Chicago attracted other migrants from the West Coast, and the population grew steadily, from 172 in 1880 to 1,179 in 1900 and 2,353 in 1920.

The growth of Chicago's Chinese community was limited by U.S. immigration policies and by anti-Chinese sentiment. Congress passed the first Chinese Exclusion Law in 1882, which barred Chinese immigration to the United States and prohibited Chinese from attaining American citizenship. Exclusion, which lasted until World War II, not only placed severe restrictions on the growth of the Chicago community and convinced many people to return to China, it profoundly influenced demography and family life by imposing a significant gender imbalance. In 1910 there were 65 Chinese women and 1,713 men in Chicago, and by 1926 women still constituted less than 6 percent of the population. The severe shortage of women made normal family life impossible for many Chinese, delaying the growth of a second generation of Chinese Americans and contributing to the sense among Americans that Chinese were "alien." While anti-Chinese sentiment was not as strong in Chicago as on the West Coast, it nevertheless significantly shaped where Chinese lived and worked. Many Chinese, faced with limited occupational opportunities, opened laundries, which were considered difficult and undesirable to own and run. Some carved out a niche in the restaurant business. Concerned about being targets of hostility, most Chinese in Chicago chose to disperse themselves across the city rather than live in Chinatown like Chinese in most other American cities.

Despite the obstacles, Chinese in Chicago built a vibrant community center in Chinatown and established a variety of organizations for mutual support. The first Chinatown was established in the 1880s near Clark and Van Buren, and, though it was not a major residential enclave, it was home to several Chinese family associations, Tong organizations, groceries, and a Chinese Baptist Mission. Rising rents and internal factionalism led Chinese leaders to expand to a second Chinatown, located near Wentworth and 22nd Street (Cermak Road), around 1910, and in the next several decades the community continued to expand its boundaries and attract businesses and residents. In 1906 the Chicago affiliate of the national Chinese Consolidated Benevolent Association was founded, and it quickly became the largest organizational force in Chicago's Chinese community. This quasi government provided social services, arbitrated disputes, certified documents, maintained order in the

Chinese citizens registering for the draft, 1917. Photographer: *Chicago Daily News*. Source: Chicago Historical Society.

community, and guarded treaty rights. In addition to the Chinese Association, family societies were important sources of mutual support, providing aid and protection to members, preserving cultural heritage, and enforcing family codes. Many Chinese organized politically in the powerful labor organization known as the Mon Sang Association and in the local branch of the Chinese Nationalist League after Sun Yat-sen's 1910 visit to Chicago.

Changes in U.S. immigration policy during and after World War II led to the end of Chinese exclusion and opened the door to new and diverse waves of Chinese immigration in the second half of the twentieth century. In 1943, Chinese exclusion laws were repealed and small quotas established for Chinese immigration, allowing many families to reunite and for the first time admitting significant numbers of Chinese women to the United States. The establishment of the People's Republic of China in 1949 caused a large influx of Chinese immigrants in the 1950s, primarily Mandarin-speaking professionals who were displaced by the revolution and entered the United States under more lenient REFUGEE policies. Socially and culturally different from earlier Cantonese migrants, the new Mandarin Chinese tended not to settle in Chinatown but instead dispersed across the city and suburbs. Chinese from Hong Kong and Taiwan migrated to Chicago throughout the 1950s and 1960s, and ethnic Chinese from Southeast Asia came after the fall of Saigon. The Chinese community doubled from 3,000 to 6,000 in the 1950s and doubled again, to 12,000, by 1970.

In the mid-1970s, in an era of significantly raised annual quotas under the 1965 Immigration Act, another major surge of immigration from mainland China occurred when China and the United States renewed relations. The Chinese community has continued to rapidly expand through steady migration, the 1990 census showing the city of Chicago's Chinese population to be over 23,000 and the 2000 census counting almost 34,000, with nearly 74,000 in the metropolitan area.

The rapid influx of Chinese in the past several decades and the increasingly diverse nature of Chinese immigration has caused changes in Chicago's Chinese community. With the constant influx of migrants, Chinatown has swelled in size. In the 1970s, entrepreneurs established a New Chinatown on Argyle Street in UPTOWN, which has alleviated some of the population pressure in the large SOUTH SIDE Chinatown and attracted many Southeast Asians, including VIETNAMESE, LAOTIAN, and CAMBODIAN refugees. In addition, the rapid growth of the Chinese community and renewed gender balance has rendered traditional family associations less necessary and new types of social service agencies more attractive. During the 1980s and 1990s, Chinese social service organizations proliferated to provide counseling, training, education, and other services. In addition, a range of new Chinese professional, business, cultural, and social organizations have grown with the expanding community, and Chinese media have developed to serve the community. Major Chinese holidays and festivals like Chinese New Year and Moon Festival draw together not only different Chinese, they also bring together other Asian communities with Chinese heritage, including MALAYSIANS, SINGAPOREANS, and other Southeast Asians.

Tracy Steffes

See also: Americanization; Armour Square; Multicentered Chicago; Street Life

Further reading: Fan, Ting C. "Chinese Residents in Chicago." Ph.D. diss., University of Chicago. 1926. • Moy, Susan. "The Chinese in Chicago: The First One Hundred Years." In *Ethnic Chicago: A Multicultural Portrait*, ed. Melvin G. Holli and Peter d'A. Jones, 1997. • Tong, Benson. *The Chinese Americans*. 2000.

Chippewas. *See* Ojibwa

Choral Music. Understanding choral music in Chicago's cultural life requires a nineteenth-century perspective on music in participation. An 1848 convention of Chicago's religious denominations proclaimed "(1) that music is . . . one of the most powerful . . . means used for the elevation, spiritually, of mankind; (2) that instruction in vocal music should begin in public and private schools . . . ; (3) that . . . vocal music is conducive to health and all who have at heart the physical as well as spiritual welfare of mankind will advocate its study." Rather than emphasizing stars, virtuosity, publicity, and the national stage, Chicago's choral music tradition perpetuates community ideals of participation, education, uplift, civic pride, and the local stage.

European immigrants brought choral singing to Chicago, especially its churches. Chicago's first regular quartette choir was organized in 1936 at St. James's Church, and Chicago's first choral society, the Chicago Sacred Music Society (formed 1842), grew out of religious practice. The city's diverse churches have encouraged congregational singing, and many have supported large volunteer or semiprofessional choirs with paid soloists. Groups such as the Lutheran Choir of Chicago (1947–) perpetuate this tradition.

Secular singing societies, including the Choral Union (1846–1848) and Mozart Society (founded 1849), were prominent among the few organizations performing CLASSICAL MUSIC regularly in Chicago until the 1890s. Choirs also thrived within immigrant communities, especially the GERMAN, Scandinavian, and Bohemian *Männerchöre* (men's choruses). Numbering over 60 in 1885, Chicago's men's choruses provided a vital social network and preserved ethnic identity. The Männergesangverein (1852) was among Chicago's earliest ethnic choral societies, while the Germania Männerchor (founded 1865) and the Concordia (which split from Germania in 1866) competed to increasing artistic praise. In 1868, Chicago hosted the 16th annual *Sängerfest* (singers' festival), attracting an international collection of a thousand voices.

Chicago's nonethnic choruses, often modeled on singing societies from New York or Boston, recruited talent from and soon marginalized the ethnic choirs. George Upton, in his *Musical Memories* (1908), places the city's "best voices" in the Chicago Musical Union (1857–1865). The Union premiered George Root's *Haymakers* and performed Chicagoland staples—Haydn's *Creation* and Rossini's *Stabat Mater.* Competition between societies was intense. The Musical Union disbanded because its best members joined the Mendelssohn Society (1858–1865). The Oratorio Society (1869–1873), led by Hans Balatka, was, like nearly all of the city's cultural organizations, decimated by the 1871 fire. Members of Boston's Handel and Haydn Society donated replacement musical scores, but, after a single 1872 performance of Handel's *Messiah,* the Oratorio Society's library again fell victim to fire.

Chicago's leading post-fire choral societies were established in 1872: the 200-member mixed chorus of the Beethoven Society and the 33-member men's chorus of the Apollo Musical Club (now Apollo Chorus of Chicago and still among the largest American volunteer choirs). Like the Beethoven Society, the Apollo Club initially performed semiprivate concerts for 1,500 contributing "Associate Members." Director William Tomlins (active 1875–1898), whose emotive style expanded Apollo membership to over 500 singers, programmed "Workingmen's" outreach concerts, initiated Chicago's annual *Messiah* tradition, and helped provide choral instruction to Chicago's public schools. In 1876, the club admitted a women's auxiliary chorus and began performing as a mixed ensemble. Women became full members in 1885. At the World's Columbian Exposition, the Apollo joined a 5,700-voice chorus for the fair's dedication.

Choirs such as those of the Hull House music school (founded 1893) provided a conduit for social assimilation—an ideal of turn-of-the-century immigration policy. Founded in 1913, the Civic Music Association linked many ethnic, corporate, and neighborhood choirs, ranging from the Volkslieder Verein and the Peoples Gas Choral Society to the Civic Music Club of Sherman Park and many local young women's and children's choruses. The Civic Music Association held community sings (beginning 1916) at which 1,500–5,000 people sang patriotic and popular songs to enhance the Americanization process. A *Chicago Herald* review described a young woman singing Stephen Foster's "Old Folks at Home":

> [She] trembled with the earnest fervor of her song. . . . She may have been Hungarian, or Lithuanian or perhaps Italian, but in her own heart she knew she was American. . . . Those . . . who do not believe the races can fuse and mass in the unity of a common ideal—let them go down to the pier. . . . They will join in the singing.

In 1896, the Chicago Symphony Orchestra founded a small professional chorus, although it disbanded after two years because of recruiting and financial troubles. Margaret Hillis established a new Chicago Symphony Chorus in 1957 (directed by Duain Wolfe since 1994) to perform, record, and tour with its namesake. Similarly, the Chicago Park District organized the Grant Park Symphony Chorus (1962–). With other professional choirs, including Music of the Baroque (ca. 1972–), Oriana Singers (1979–), His Majestie's Clerkes (1982; now Bella Voce, directed by Anne Heider), and Chicago a Capella (1993–; directed by Jonathan Miller), Chicago enjoys a full gamut of historical and contemporary styles.

Chicago's black community presented oratorios and concert operas among other works in the Choral Study Club (founded 1900), Umbrian Glee Club (1895–), and Federal Glee Club (founded 1910, by the city's black postal workers). James Mundy and J. Wesley Jones staged "Battles of the Choirs" (1930s). The four-part, mixed-choral tradition in gospel began when Thomas Dorsey, Theodore Frye, and Magnolia Lewis Butts formed a choir at Chicago's Ebenezer Baptist Church (1931), while Dorsey, Frye, and Sallie Martin organized the National Convention of Gospel Choirs and Choruses (1932–). Kenneth Morris, director at First Church of Deliverance, revolutionized gospel by introducing the Hammond organ (1939). Along with Morris's

Apollo Chorus, 1924. Photographer: Gino-Fish. Source: Chicago Historical Society.

choir, the Roberta Martin Singers, the Soul Children, and the Thompson Community Singers (1948–) form the core of Chicago's contemporary gospel choral style. Organist Maceo Woods added the Christian Tabernacle Concert Choir in 1960.

Each of Chicago's universities maintains several choral groups, sometimes incorporating both students and community members. The UNIVERSITY OF CHICAGO sponsors a University Chorus, a Motet Choir, and the semiprofessional Rockefeller Chapel Choir. DEPAUL and NORTHWESTERN universities offer all-student choirs in their professional schools of music.

As public school music budgets have evaporated, the Chicago Children's Choir has grown to involve 2,700 (in 1997) elementary to high-school students in a comprehensive tuition-free music education program, including 32 elementary schools, 6 neighborhood choirs, and the premier Concert Choir. Reverend Christopher Moore founded the multiracial, multicultural program at Hyde Park's First Unitarian Church in 1956, hoping that "young people from diverse backgrounds could better understand each other and themselves by learning to make beautiful music together."

The Halevi Choral Society (1926–, founded by Harry Coopersmith and Hyman Reznick; directed by Judith Karzen since 1984) preserves the multifaceted JEWISH choral music tradition, while the William Ferris Chorale (1972–, directed by William Ferris until his death in 2000) presents "composer festivals" to support contemporary choral music. In 1982 over 25 nationalities were represented by Chicago's ethnic choirs, including the Lira Singers (POLISH) and the Österreichischer Gemischter Chor (AUSTRIAN). *Männerchöre, Damenchöre* (women's choruses), and *Kinderchöre* (children's choruses)—including the Rheinischer Gesangverein, Damenchor Lorelei, Steirer Damenchor, and the Deutsch-Amerikanischer Kinderchor—continue to thrive. Chicago's volunteer men's choruses, the Windy City GAY Chorus (1979–), the New Tradition Men's Chorus (1981–, directed by Jay Giallombardo), and the Chicago Gay Men's Chorus (1983–), have also experienced an artistic renaissance. The two gay choirs began as social organizations but immediately became symbols of gay pride and instruments of social outreach. These and choirs such as the CHICAGO DEFENDER's 1930 Massed Chorus or the CHICAGO HOUSING AUTHORITY's choral projects of the 1990s demonstrate continuing links between choral singing, artistic growth, social networks, and community activism.

Mark Clague

See also: Ethnic Music

Further reading: "Chicago." In *The New Grove Dictionary of American Music,* vol. 2., ed. H. Wiley Hitchcock and Stanley Sadie, 1986. • Boyer, Horace Clarence. *How Sweet the Sound: The Golden Age of Gospel.* 1995. • Bryan, Mary Lynn McCree, and Allen F. Davis, eds. *100 Years at Hull-House.* 1990.

Church Architecture. From the earliest days of human history, people have designated sacred places, a construction of stones, an ark, an oracle, a shrine, a grotto, a temple to God, a mosque, a synagogue, and, in the Christian era, basilicas, churches, and cathedrals. There were more than two thousand churches in Chicago at the opening of the twenty-first century, and motorists traveling on Chicago EXPRESSWAYS could see a skyline of steeples, perched atop buildings designed expressly for the purpose of Christian worship.

Chicago's earliest Christian house of worship was probably a log cabin, built opposite Wolf Point near the CHICAGO RIVER in 1831 by Methodists. The direct descendants of that congregation moved to the corner of Clark and Washington Streets in 1838, and a building completed in 1923 now houses the Chicago Temple First United Methodist Church, as well as 18 floors of commercial office space, under its Gothic spire.

A ROMAN CATHOLIC church showcased BALLOON FRAME architecture—a simple, inexpensive, and efficient wooden building technique—in 1833, when Augustine Deodat Taylor designed and built St. Mary's Church on Lake Street just west of State. The balloon frame would subsequently become a major feature of Chicago's residential architectural landscape.

Chicago's early Christian ARCHITECTURE was predominantly PROTESTANT, and the prevailing architectural style was Gothic, with its tall vertical lines and pointed arches. St. James Episcopal Cathedral (1856 and 1875), at Wabash and Huron, the First Baptist Congregational Church (1869), at Ashland and Warren Boulevard, the Second Presbyterian Church (1872), on South Michigan Avenue, Trinity Episcopal Church (1873), at 26th and Michigan, and Holy Name Cathedral (1874–75), at State and Superior, are all examples of a Gothic style with Victorian American variations.

Many nineteenth-century churches were built of limestone. QUARRIED in the nearby JOLIET area, limestone had the distinction of turning a soft grayed yellow when its iron content oxidized. IRISH immigrants built one of Northeastern Illinois' first churches out of limestone in 1833 while working on the ILLINOIS & MICHIGAN CANAL in LEMONT; the present St. James of the Sag was built in the same spot on Archer Avenue two decades later. OLIVET BAPTIST CHURCH (1875–76; originally First Baptist), at 31st and King Drive, St. James Church (1875–80), at 29th and Wabash Avenue, the Church of the Ascension (1882–87), on LaSalle Drive at Elm, and First Immanuel Lutheran Church (1888), at 1124 South Ashland Avenue, as well as the city's famed Water Tower (1869), were made in whole or in part of Joliet limestone. AFRICAN AMERICANS built Quinn Chapel AME Church (1891–94) at 24th and Wabash Avenue. Quinn's limestone facade houses the oldest African American congregation in the city.

In the nineteenth-century, in the wake of political upheavals in Europe and Ireland's Great Famine in the 1840s, large numbers of Irish, GERMAN, and POLISH Catholic immigrants came to Chicago, settled new neighborhoods, and built large, beautifully decorated churches. Houses of prayer and expressions of faith, these churches were also statements of religious identity and ethnic pride, distinguishing the emerging ROMAN CATHOLIC minority from the prevailing Protestant majority in late-nineteenth-century Chicago.

Under the leadership of Rev. Arnold Damen, S.J., Irish Catholics built the monumental Holy Family Church (1857–60) on Twelfth Street with a 236-foot tower, the tallest structure in the city until the Monadnock Building went up in 1889. German Catholic immigrants built St. Joseph's Church (1872) on Orleans Street, as well as St. Michael's (1866 and 1873) at Cleveland and Eugenie, which would become the defining structure of the OLD TOWN neighborhood. Polish Catholic immigrants built St. Stanislaus Kostka (1877) on Noble Street and subsequently many other magnificent churches in a variety of architectural styles that continue to define Polish neighborhoods all over Chicago.

Catholic immigrant congregations used all the classical architectural styles of Europe—Byzantine, Romanesque, Roman basilica, French Gothic, English Gothic, and Renaissance. Some Catholic churches even used American Colonial and Congregational styles—including St. Mary's Cathedral (1843), a brick church at Madison and Wabash that was destroyed in the FIRE OF 1871; St. Bartholomew (1937), on Lavergne at Addison; and most notably the chapel of St. Mary of the Lake Seminary (1925), in MUNDELEIN.

The evangelical Moody Church, founded by Dwight L. Moody in 1864 (as the Illinois Street Church), stood at the corner of Chicago and LaSalle from 1873 to 1915, when it moved to North Avenue and Clark Street to a building completed in 1925. The Moody Church's large auditorium has hosted world missions conferences and evangelistic crusades.

Among the most prolific Chicago church architects from the 1890s to the GREAT DEPRESSION was Henry Schlacks, who was known to tour the cathedrals of Europe during the summer, sketch their details, and then incorporate their elements into his designs of Chicago churches. Thus St. Paul's (1897), at 22nd Place and Hoyne, is modeled after the Cathedral of St. Cortin in Normandy. St. Adalbert (1912–14), on West 17th Street, and St. Mary of the Lake (1913–17), on North Sheridan Road, are

Chicago Rapid Transit Company poster by Rocco D. Navigato, depicting the Chicago Temple, 77 West Washington, 1920s. Artist: Rocco D. Navigato. Source: Chicago Historical Society.

Holy Name Cathedral, 1979. Photographer: Unknown. Source: Chicago Historical Society.

St. Mary's Catholic Church, built in 1833. Photographer: Unknown. Source: Chicago Historical Society.

Second Presbyterian Church, pre-1871. Photographer: Unknown. Source: Chicago Public Library.

grand Roman basilica–style churches modeled after St. Paul's Outside the Walls in Rome. St. Ignatius Church (1916–17) in ROGERS PARK is a splendid Renaissance church.

Several Chicago architects known best for their secular designs built houses of worship as well. Louis Sullivan designed the Holy Trinity Orthodox Cathedral (1903), on North Leavitt Street—a genuine touch of Holy Russia in Chicago. Sullivan and his partner Dankmar Adler were also known for their synagogues, including KAM Temple (1890–91), at 33rd and Indiana Avenue, which since 1922 has served as the Pilgrim Baptist Church. John Wellborn Root (of Burnham & Root) designed St. Gabriel Catholic Church (1887–1888), near the stockyards at 45th and Lowe, for Irish Catholic immigrants, and the Lake View Presbyterian Church (1887–88), at Addison and Broadway.

Howard Van Doren Shaw, a Chicago architect who received the American Institute of Architects gold medal, designed several churches, including the Fourth Presbyterian Church (1912–14), at Delaware and Michigan, and the Second Presbyterian Church (1872–74), at 16th and Michigan. In both of these edifices, Shaw worked with existing conditions; in the case of the Second Presbyterian, he was responsible for rebuilding the original church after its devastating fire in 1901. The original structure by the famous Eastern architect James Renwick was remodeled to include interior decorations by Frederic C. Bartlett and art glass windows by Louis Comfort Tiffany, John LaFarge, Louis Millet, Sir Edward Burne-Jones, and William Morris. Fourth Presbyterian was designed in association with the Eastern architect Ralph Adams Cram in 1912. Besides Shaw's contributions to the design of the church, he was responsible for the beautiful court, fountain, and manse.

Ludwig Mies van der Rohe designed St. Savior Episcopal Chapel (1952), at ILLINOIS INSTITUTE OF TECHNOLOGY, in his characteristically simple, linear style. St. Savior is the only building Mies designed and built for a religious purpose. Its simple English bond brick walls, its travertine altar built out of a solid block of stone, and its stainless steel cross speak to the essence of theological rationality.

St. Stanislaus Kostka Church, 1300 North Noble, 1910s. Photographer: Percy H. Sloan. Source: The Newberry Library.

Interior of St. Stanislaus Kostka, 1942. Photographer: Unknown. Source: Chicago Historical Society.

St. Ignatius Church, Greenwood and Loyola Avenues, 1910s. Photographer: Percy H. Sloan. Source: The Newberry Library.

Frank Lloyd Wright deliberately designed Unity Temple (1906–9) in nearby OAK PARK without any traditional Christian symbolism. Wright's former employees Guenzel and Drummond also designed several churches of note, among them the First Congregational Church of Austin (1908) at 5700 West Waller. St. Thomas the Apostle Catholic Church (1922–24), at 5472 South Kimbark, was designed by Francis Barry Byrne, who went on to become a noted designer of Catholic churches, including the cathedral of Cork in Ireland.

Many of Chicago's splendid Byzantine-style churches are distinguished by their large central domes and their icon screens. St. Nicholas Ukrainian Catholic Cathedral (1913–15), on Oakley Boulevard at Rice Street, was designed by Worthmann and Steinbach; St. Clement Church (1917–18), at 642 West Deming Place, by George D. Barnett; KAM Isaiah Israel

Holy Trinity Russian Orthodox Church, 1121 North Leavitt Street, 1958. Photographer: Unknown. Source: Chicago Historical Society.

Pilgrim Baptist Church, Easter Sunday, 1941. Photographer: Russell Lee. Source: Library of Congress.

Interior of Unity Temple, Oak Park, 1965. Photographer: Hubert Henry, Hedrich-Blessing. Source: Chicago Historical Society.

Unity Temple, Oak Park, 1913. Photographer: Percy Sloan. Source: The Newberry Library.

Temple (1923–24), on Greenwood at Hyde Park Boulevard, by Alfred Alschuler; SS. Volodymyr and Olha Church (1973–75), at 735 North Oakley Boulevard, by Jaroslaw Korsunsky; and the ultramodern St. Joseph's Ukrainian Church (1975–77), at 5000 North Cumberland Avenue, by Zenon Mazurkevich. St. Simeon Mirotovici (1968–69) on East 114th Street is an exact replica of a fifteenth-century Serbian monastery church.

Three fine Chicago churches were designed in the Richardsonian Romanesque style reminiscent of Henry Hobson Richardson's Trinity Church in Boston. They are the Church of the Epiphany (1885), at Ashland and Adams Street, designed by Burling & Whitehouse; St. Gabriel Church (1887–88), at 45th and Lowe, by Burnham & Root; and the Metropolitan Community Church (1889), at 41st and King Drive, by Solon S. Beman.

Gothic-style churches abound in Chicago: French Gothic, English Gothic, and Victorian Gothic. Among the finest are St. Alphonsus (1889–97), at Southport and Wellington, designed by Schrader & Conradi of St. Louis; St. Paul's, by Henry Schlacks: St. James Chapel (1917–20), at Rush and Pearson Streets, by Gustav Steinbach of New York and Zachary Davis of Chicago; and Queen of All Saints Basilica (1956–60), at 6280 North Sauganash Avenue, designed by Meyer & Cook.

Chicago's English Gothic masterpieces include Shaw's Fourth Presbyterian; Our Lady of Mt. Carmel (1913–14), at 690 West Belmont, designed by Chicago architects Egan & Prindeville; Bond Chapel (1925–26), at the University of Chicago, by Coolidge & Hodgdon; St. Thomas Aquinas, now St. Martin de Porres (1923–25), at 5112 West Washington Boulevard, by Karl Vitzthum; St. Chrysostom (1925–26), at 1424 North Dearborn, by Chester H. Wallace; St. Sabina (1925–33), at 78th and Throop, by Joe McCarthy; St. Viator (1927–29), at 4170 West Addison Street, by Charles L. Wallace; St. Gertrude (1930–31), on Glenwood at Granville in Rogers Park, by James Burns; and the First Unitarian Church of Chicago (1929–31), at 57th and Woodlawn, by Denison B. Hull.

Among the finest Renaissance-style designs are Our Lady of Sorrows Basilica (1890–1902), at 3101 West Jackson Boulevard, designed by Engelbert, Pope & Brinkman; St. John Cantius Church (1893–98), at 825 North Carpenter Street, and St. Hedwig Church, at 2226 North Hoyne (1899–1901), both designed by Adolphus Druiding; Corpus Christi Church (1914–16), at 49th and King Drive, by Joe McCarthy; St. Mary of the Angels (1914–20), at 1850 North Hermitage, by Worthmann & Steinbach; Annunciation Cathedral (1910), at 1017 North LaSalle Drive, by N. Dokas; and St. Josaphat Church (1900–02), at 2311 North Southport, by William J. Brinkman.

Twentieth-century churches departed somewhat from their nineteenth-century antecedents. Several churches designed by Edward

Icon of Annunciation, St. Nicholas Ukrainian Church, 2238 West Rice Street. Photographer: Unknown. Source: Chicago Historical Society.

Rockefeller Chapel, University of Chicago (no date). Photographer: Jun Fujita. Source: Chicago Historical Society.

Madonna della Strada Chapel, Loyola University, 1951. Photographer: J. Sherwin Murphy. Source: Chicago Historical Society.

Interior of Seventeenth Church of Christ, Scientist, 55 East Wacker Drive, 1968. Photographer: James Hedrich. Source: Chicago Historical Society.

D. Dart—in clean, brick-and-glass style—are in this category: First St. Paul's Lutheran Church (1969–70), at 1301 North LaSalle, and St. Procopius Abbey Church (1968–70), at BENEDICTINE UNIVERSITY in LISLE, are both Dart designs. The Seventeenth Church of Christ, Scientist (1968), at 55 East Wacker Drive, designed by Harry Weese, has clean, modern lines as well. Madonna della Strada Chapel (1938–39), on LOYOLA UNIVERSITY's Lake Shore Campus, designed by Andrew

Rebori, is another example of modern religious architecture.

Many architects, many Christian traditions, and a spectrum of architectural styles; sacred places built by people as houses of worship. Some grand soaring edifices, some simple rooms, but all places where people deliberately come together to pray, to build community, to support one another, to find peace and strength for the challenges of their daily lives and to find inspiration to serve their brothers and sisters in the city.

George A. Lane, S.J.

See also: Baha'i; Buddhists; Eastern Orthodox; Hindus; Judaism; Muslims

Further reading: Lane, George A. *Chicago Churches and Synagogues: An Architectural Pilgrimage.* 1981.

Cicero, IL, Cook County, 7 miles W of the Loop. The town of Cicero, bordered on the north and east by Chicago, is the suburb nearest to downtown. Named for a town in New York State, Cicero has the only town form of government in Cook County, and is governed by a board of trustees. Present-day Cicero, 5.5 square miles, is less than one-sixth of its original 36 square-mile area.

Ogden Avenue, a former Indian trail, was one of the early thoroughfares through Cicero. The first homesteaders in the town settled on the highest and driest part of Cicero (now OAK PARK). Other families settled along Ogden Avenue, Lake Street, and Cermak Road (22nd Street). When the Galena & Chicago Union RAILROAD was built westward from Chicago in 1848, Cicero became the first western suburb connected to the city by rail.

In 1857 inhabitants formed the township of Cicero in order to levy taxes for roads and drainage ditches. In 1869 Cicero was incorporated as a town, and that same year, Chicago ANNEXED 11 square miles along Cicero's eastern edge. The town's population of 3,000 dropped 50 percent as a result.

Cicero's location on several rail lines influenced the Chicago & North Western Railway and the Chicago & Alton Railroad companies to establish manufacturing and repair shops there. Small communities began to develop around these and other industries, such as the Brighton Silver Smelting & Refining Company and the Brighton Cotton Mill.

During the 1880s new residents were drawn to the industries in the northern part of the town along the Galena & Chicago Union Railroad. As these communities expanded they began to meld. Some of these areas later separated from Cicero; others, such as Clyde and Hawthorne, remained as names of railroad stops.

In 1889 Chicago again annexed territory along Cicero's eastern border, and by 1897, STREET RAILWAYS ran from the city into Cicero. In 1899, Chicago annexed its last portion of Cicero, including the AUSTIN area. Cicero ceded the Hawthorne Race Track to STICKNEY in 1900, and in 1901, Oak Park and BERWYN separated from Cicero.

Western Electric established a TELEPHONE equipment manufacturing plant in Cicero in 1904 employing more than 20,000 people, a number that dwarfed the population of Cicero, which was only 14,557 in 1910. Cicero's population more than quadrupled over the next 20 years, with the majority of newcomers Eastern European immigrants. Yet there was still enough open land for Cicero Field, one of Chicago's earliest airfields.

Cicero's position at the edge of Chicago attracted criminal elements wishing to evade Chicago's law enforcement agencies. In the mid to late 1920s, the gangster Al Capone established his headquarters in Cicero. At the end of the century government officials were convicted on charges of corruption that recalled the town's earlier reputation.

Racial tensions surfaced in Cicero throughout the 1950s and 1960s when residents resisted AFRICAN AMERICANS moving into their community. At the end of the twentieth century, although Cicero had virtually no black residents, people of Hispanic or Asian ancestry contributed to its mixture of ethnic cultures. Ethnic tensions surfaced in town politics as an entrenched Republican organization reluctantly shared power with an emerging Hispanic majority.

Betsy Gurlacz

See also: Civil Rights Movements; Crime and Chicago's Image; Economic Geography; Racism, Ethnicity, and White Identity

Further reading: Anderson, Alan B., and George W. Pickering. *Confronting the Color Line: The Broken Promise of the Civil Rights Movement in Chicago.* 1986. • Clark, Eugene. "History of Cicero by a Ciceronian." Cicero Library Reference Desk, Cicero, IL. • Spelman, Walter Bishop. *The Town of Cicero: History, Advantages, and Government.* 1923.

City Beautiful Movement. *See* Architecture: The City Beautiful Movement

City Club of Chicago. Founded in 1903, the City Club of Chicago was established as a nonpartisan, nonprofit organization to investigate and improve urban conditions and affairs in Chicago. Like most Progressive-era urban reform organizations, the City Club took its civic improvement mandate seriously, serving as a forum to discuss and study issues of particular concern to Chicagoans. The club conducted much of its active work through numerous "civic committees," which together functioned as its main investigative and educational arm. The civic committees addressed a broad spectrum of relevant topics, including municipal revenues; tax reform; PUBLIC HEALTH, education, and welfare; local TRANSPORTATION; city PLANNING; housing conditions; public ART; parks and public PLAYGROUNDS; GAS, electricity, and WATER SUPPLY; harbors, wharves, and BRIDGES; fire protection and POLICE service; civil service and ballot reform; labor conditions; and immigration policy.

The City Club, starting with 175 dues-paying members, grew to nearly 1,000 active members in the early 1950s. Club membership began to decline, however, with the advent of Mayor Richard J. Daley's administration, as the DEMOCRATIC PARTY increasingly controlled the city's reform environment. When Mayor Daley died in 1976, the club had as few as 60 members. In the late 1970s and early 1980s, membership began to grow again, as new leadership, largely directed by Larry Horist and Tom Roeser, infused the seemingly dormant civic organization with renewed interest, activity, and fundraising efforts.

Attracting leading citizens of Chicago's business and professional community, the City Club counted lawyers, physicians, bankers, college professors, religious leaders, social workers, city planners, engineers, and newspaper editors among its ranks. For much of its early history, at least until the 1940s, membership was exclusive; admission required the support of at least two other club colleagues. Members kept abreast of important issues and events through the club's publication, the *City Club Bulletin;* at times billed as a "journal of active citizenship," the newsletter had an erratic run lasting from 1907 through the late 1980s.

Susan Marie Wirka

See also: Commercial Club of Chicago; Good Government Movements; Political Culture; Woman's City Club

Further reading: *City Club Bulletin.* Chicago Historical Society. • City Club of Chicago. Research collection. Chicago Historical Society.

City Council. *See* Government, City of Chicago

City Homes Association. The City Homes Association was a HOUSING REFORM organization created by middle- and upper-class white reformers (including Jane Addams) in 1900 for improving lodging houses and tenements as well as establishing small parks and playgrounds in Chicago. Emerging from the earlier Improved Housing Association, it created committees on PLAYGROUNDS AND SMALL PARKS, the enforcement and amendment of existing laws and ordinances, TENEMENTS, lodging houses, publication, and an investigating committee. The investigating committee was responsible for its most famous product: the publication of

Tenement Conditions in Chicago in 1901. This study examined tenement and neighborhood conditions in three areas—the NEAR WEST SIDE, the near Northwest Side (near Division and Ashland Streets in WEST TOWN), and the Bohemian district southwest of Blue Hill Avenue (LOWER WEST SIDE). Authored by Robert Hunter, who wrote the 1904 classic study *Poverty* in New York, the study deplored conditions in Chicago's dense and dilapidated one- to four-story tenements and the neighborhoods in which they were located. It discovered a proliferation of privy vaults and overflowing garbage and manure boxes that threatened the quality of life and health of the neighborhoods' largely immigrant populations. The findings led to the enactment of Chicago's 1902 Tenement House Ordinance, covering all housing of two or more apartments.

The association also assisted in the establishment of the Municipal Lodging House (1902–1917) and in the hiring of Charles Ball, a highly qualified sanitary engineer, as sanitary bureau chief in 1907. Most active from 1900 to 1910, the organization no longer existed after 1914.

Wendy Plotkin

See also: Boardinghouses; Infrastructure; Public Health; Settlement Houses; Water

Further reading: Abbott, Edith. *The Tenements of Chicago, 1908–1935*. 1936. • Hunter, Robert. "Housing Reform in Chicago." *Proceedings of the National Conference of Charities and Correction*, 29th sess., Detroit, May 28–June 3 (1902): 343–351. • Philpott, Thomas Lee. *The Slum and the Ghetto: Neighborhood Deterioration and Middle-class Reform, Chicago, 1880–1930*. 1978.

City News Bureau. In 1890 *Chicago Daily News* publisher Victor Lawson, having persuaded local NEWSPAPER competitors that cooperative gathering of POLICE and other routine news would reduce the cost of rapidly growing reporting staffs and would train reporters for their newsrooms, organized the City Press Association of Chicago, supported in the beginning by 8 publishers of 10 Chicago dailies.

Renamed City News Bureau in 1910, the agency was fulfilling the same reporting and training missions when Chicago's *Sun-Times* and *Tribune* shut it down on February 26, 1999, because of costs.

After 1893, City News delivered copy to newspapers via underground pneumatic tubes, replaced by Teletype in 1961. A no-nonsense boot camp for beginners, City News turned out hundreds of alums, notably JOURNALISTS Mike Royko, Seymour Hersh, Clayton Kirkpatrick, Carole Simpson, Herman Kogan, Jack Mabley, Anne Keegan, novelist Kurt Vonnegut, actor Melvyn Douglas, sculptor Claes Oldenburg, and author Charles MacArthur, co-author of the play *The Front Page*, which captured the rambunctious City News style.

Richard A. Schwarzlose

See also: Associated Negro Press; Chicago Tribune; Literary Cultures

Further reading: Dornfeld, Arnold A. *"Hello, Sweetheart, Get Me Rewrite!": The Story of the City News Bureau of Chicago*. 1988. (Published in 1983 as *Behind the Front Page*.) • Howlett, Debbie. "Legendary News Bureau to Close / City News in Chicago Was Training Ground for Renowned Writers." *USA Today*, February 26, 1999.

Civic Federation. Founded amidst the 1893 economic depression, the Civic Federation of Chicago began as a relief organization but soon addressed a great variety of the city's social and political problems, including political corruption, union-employer disputes, and inefficient public administration. It soon underwent a transition from a broadly oriented reform organization to an agency specializing in TAXATION.

Led by banker Lyman Gage and journalist Ralph Easley, the Civic Federation became a quintessential Progressive-era reform organization. In 1900, Easley formed the widely acclaimed National Civic Federation, which despite its name functioned independently of the Chicago organization. Departing from the elitist strategies of previous civic groups, the Civic Federation of Chicago sought to gain broad popular support for its nonpartisan reform proposals. During its early years, membership crossed class boundaries and included trade unionists from the CHICAGO FEDERATION OF LABOR and social reformers like Jane Addams. The Civic Federation engaged in such innovative strategies as petition campaigns, protests at City Hall, and newspaper publicity. Yet it opposed measures that called for greater direct democracy, such as the initiative and referendum, and instead promoted centralization of government as well as rule by professionally trained experts. Municipal problems, increasingly complex in nature, were to be removed from politics altogether and subjected to rational, fact-based solutions, for which the federation's numerous published investigations would form the basis.

The unions left the Civic Federation soon after the turn of the century, and by 1917 it focused on taxation and efficiency in public administration, leaving other tasks to separate organizations that had grown out of its earlier activities such as the Chicago Bureau of Charities and the Municipal Voters League. As governmental functions widened during the early twentieth century, the federation sought to augment public revenues by streamlining municipal administration, thereby avoiding higher taxes. Since the 1920s, by means of policy statements and research assistance to legislators, it has fought to minimize public spending, serving as a watchdog on government finance and administrative efficiency.

In 1929, as the Civic Federation operated increasingly on the state level, it omitted "Chicago" from its name. Three years later, it merged with the Chicago Bureau of Public Efficiency, founded in 1910. Temporarily known as the Civic Federation and Bureau of Public Efficiency, it dropped the latter part of that name in 1941. It is considered the oldest taxpayers' research organization in the country.

Georg Leidenberger

See also: City Club of Chicago; Commercial Club of Chicago; Good Government Movements; Governing the Metropolis

Further reading: Hogan, David John. *Class and Reform: School and Society in Chicago, 1880–1930*. 1985. • Levine, Daniel. *Varieties of Reform Thought*. 1964. • Weinstein, James. *The Corporate Ideal in the Liberal State, 1900–1918*. 1968.

Civil Rights Movements. Agitation for civil rights has been a regular feature of the Chicago scene, and AFRICAN AMERICANS have been the leading—though not the only—insurgents in this fight. It is difficult, however, to speak of a civil rights movement in Chicago before WORLD WAR II.

Unlike white immigrants, African Americans had to battle for legal recognition of their citizenship rights. Before the CIVIL WAR Illinois was a free state, but its laws prohibited the immigration of African Americans and voting by blacks. And even though Chicago was a center of antislavery activity, city schools and places of public accommodation were racially segregated.

Black Chicagoans resented these restrictions. In 1870 they gained the right to vote, in 1874 they hailed a state law forbidding segregated education, and a decade later they successfully urged the state legislature to endorse a sweeping civil rights measure which provided "that all persons . . . shall be entitled to the full and equal enjoyment of . . . inns, restaurants, eating houses, barber shops, theatres, and public conveyances on land and water and all other public accommodations." After a legal challenge in 1896, the Illinois legislature more directly stated the scope of the Illinois Civil Rights Act of 1885.

City practices did not match the color-blind rhetoric, however. Beyond the BLACK BELT, black Chicagoans faced discriminatory treatment. Restaurants and hotels regularly turned away black patrons. Theaters often seated African Americans only in the balcony. And despite the 1885 civil rights law, it was difficult to obtain a conviction for discriminatory practices.

By the early twentieth century, race relations in Chicago had become more tense than they had been in over a generation. Out of this climate, which was part of a nationwide trend, emerged the Chicago branch of the NATIONAL ASSOCIATION FOR THE ADVANCEMENT OF COLORED PEOPLE. Founded in 1910 by black and

Martin Luther King, Jr., in Chicago

During the first decade of his public career, Martin Luther King often visited Chicago to build support for the black freedom struggle. But in the summer of 1965, the nature of King's connection to Chicago changed. Responding to requests from local civil rights forces, King and the Southern Christian Leadership Conference (SCLC) joined the fight against school superintendent Benjamin Willis and Chicago's segregated public schools. By the fall, SCLC had allied with the Coordinating Council of Community Organizations to launch a campaign to end slums in the city, which would become known as the Chicago Freedom Movement.

King relied on his lieutenant James Bevel to energize the first phases of the campaign, but in January 1966 he captured national headlines when he moved his family into a dingy apartment in the West Side ghetto. It was not until June that King and his advisors, under pressure to produce results, settled on a focus for the Chicago movement. King himself participated in two dramatic marches into all-white neighborhoods during a two-month open-housing campaign during the summer of 1966. These fair-housing protests brought real estate, political, business, and religious leaders to the conference table for "summit" negotiations.

In late August, King and Mayor Richard J. Daley announced that an agreement had been reached: the marches would stop, while city leaders promised to promote fair housing. King hoped that the "summit" accord would be an important step toward making Chicago an open city, but black militants denounced the settlement and the Daley administration never fulfilled its promises.

James Ralph

Protestors demonstrate against racial discrimination at the White City Roller Rink (63rd and South Parkway, later King Drive) in 1949. The Congress of Racial Equality (CORE), established in 1942, staged protests and sit-ins like this one throughout the 1940s and 1950s to break down racial barriers in housing, public accommodations, and recreational activities. Photographer: Kaufmann & Fabry. Source: Chicago Historical Society.

white racial progressives, the Chicago NAACP championed a vision of a just society, even if other groups eclipsed its efforts during the 1910s.

Black activism reached a new peak with the coming of the Great Depression. A black newspaper, the *Chicago Whip*, led a "Don't Spend Your Money Where You Can't Work" campaign. The Communist Party spurred agitation over employment rights and access to public accommodations. And local residents protested segregated schools.

It was a new organization, however, that specialized in nonviolent direct action. Founded in 1942 in Chicago by James Farmer and other followers of Gandhian tactics, the Congress of Racial Equality staged sit-ins and other protests against discriminatory Chicago restaurants and recreational centers. In the late 1940s activists of the United Packinghouse Workers union also targeted segregated eateries. By the early 1960s, most public accommodations in the city were open to African Americans.

The broad range of insurgency in the 1930s and 1940s was impressive, but it represented less a cohesive movement than a series of distinct efforts to secure more opportunities for African Americans. In the early 1960s, however, unequal educational opportunities and the imperial style of school superintendent Benjamin Willis spurred black parents, especially on the far South Side, to protest public school policies. The emergence of local, grassroots movements laid the foundation for the great school boycotts of October 1963 and February 1964 in which 400,000 students missed school.

A new organization, the Coordinating Council of Community Organizations (CCCO), founded by the Chicago Urban League, the Chicago NAACP, and a number of other groups, sought to harness the emerging protest energies. By 1965, CCCO comprised 40 affiliates, including largely white groups like the Catholic Interracial Council and more militant black groups like Chicago CORE. During the summer of 1965, CCCO staged almost daily marches against Willis and segregationist school policies. Never before had Chicago experienced such a dramatic and sustained demand for racial justice.

CCCO's activism did not yield substantive results. In September 1965, it joined forces with Martin Luther King's Southern Christian Leadership Conference to launch the Chicago Freedom Movement, which sought to end slums and extend equal opportunities to all Chicagoans. The high point of the Chicago Freedom Movement was a two-month campaign in the summer of 1966 to end housing discrimination in metropolitan Chicago.

By mid-1967, however, the Chicago Freedom Movement was over, and CCCO was disintegrating. The Black Power impulse—which questioned interracial activism and nonviolent direct action—pulsated through black Chicago. As the rise of the Black Panther Party and the urban uprisings of 1966 and 1968 attested, a new protest universe had emerged. Only the regular mass meetings of Jesse Jackson's Operation Breadbasket, which later became Operation PUSH, and the deep commitment among African Americans to Harold Washington's mayoral campaigns in the 1980s carried on the movement qualities of the first half of the 1960s.

James Ralph

See also: Abolitionism; Contested Spaces; Feminist Movements; Gay and Lesbian Rights Movements; Political Culture; Suffrage; Willis Wagons

Further reading: Anderson, Alan B., and George W. Pickering. *Confronting the Color Line: The Broken Promise of the Civil Rights Movement in Chicago.* 1986. • Ralph, James R., Jr. *Northern Protest: Martin Luther King, Jr., Chicago, and the Civil Rights Movement.* 1993. • Reed, Christopher Robert. *The Chicago NAACP and the Rise of Black Professional Leadership, 1910–1966.* 1997.

Civil War. (1861–1865). The Civil War was a crucial event in the development of nineteenth-century Chicago. The war came at a time when the city's commercial economy and TRANSPORTATION links had matured to the point of providing the foundation for substantial industrialization.

The opening of the UNION STOCK YARD on Christmas Day, 1865, is symbolic of the Civil War's impact on Chicago. The war directed the flow of vital food commodities away from Chicago's most persistent urban rivals, which were too close to the front lines during the first two years of the war and were hurt by stoppages of trade on the Mississippi and Ohio Rivers. Because the war cost St. Louis its status as the major grain distribution center and Cincinnati lost its distinction as the pork-packing capital, Chicago emerged as the logical center for the MEATPACKING, wheat distribution, and related industries. Heavy industry took root in Chicago during the war to provide Union forces with the rolling stock and rails needed to transport troops and supplies. The first steel rails made in America came off the North Chicago Rolling Mill in 1865. Although Chicago wasn't one of the North's main procurement centers, Chicago-area firms sold millions of dollars' worth of horses, hardtack, preserved meats, tents, saddles and harnesses, and other supplies to the state of Illinois and the U.S. Army for the troops.

The Civil War also helped spur industrialization by bringing stable banking to Chicago for the first time. The First National Bank of Chicago was founded in July 1863, and by war's end the city boasted 13 national banks, more than any other city in America. The $30 million in deposits at those banks was the capital foundation necessary for industrial expansion. By 1870 the number of factories in Chicago had tripled since the outbreak of the war, and the city's population had nearly tripled as well.

The Civil War divided Chicago, not as dramatically as it did the Union but in nonetheless important ways. Racial tensions ran high. In 1862 the city suffered its first RACE RIOT when white TEAMSTERS tried to prevent AFRICAN AMERICANS from using the omnibus system. The Chicago City Council voted to segregate the public SCHOOLS. The *Chicago Times*, a DEMOCRATIC PARTY organ, was the nation's loudest and most persistent critic of Lincoln and emancipation. In June 1863, the Union Army closed the *Times* at bayonet point. Only when mobs of Democratic supporters threatened to destroy the Republican *Chicago Tribune* did Lincoln order the suppression to cease. Suspicions ran so high that Republicans in 1864 accused a small group of disgruntled Democrats of conspiring with Confederate secret agents to disrupt voting in the presidential election by liberating the prisoners of war at CAMP DOUGLAS. The alleged conspirators were arrested on the eve of the balloting.

Mary Livermore and the U.S. Sanitary Commission

Mary Livermore (1820–1905) was a Christian philanthropist, abolitionist, and suffragist in nineteenth-century Chicago. As a reporter for the *Northwestern Christian Advocate,* she was the only female correspondent to cover the 1860 Republican National Convention's nomination of Abraham Lincoln. During the Civil War she played a vital role on the home front, serving as codirector of the Northwestern Branch of the U.S. Sanitary Commission from 1862 to 1865. That experience brought her into association with the most politically conscious women in Illinois and raised her awareness of the legal obstacles that prevented women's public service. In 1869, Livermore founded the Illinois Woman Suffrage Association and served as its first president.

In 1888 Livermore published *My Story of the War,* where she explained her involvement with the Sanitary Commission during the Civil War:

> Organizations of women for the relief of sick and wounded soldiers, and for the care of soldiers' families, were formed with great spontaneity at the very beginning of the war.... When the local aid society of which I was president, merged its existence in that of the Sanitary Commission, I also became identified with it.... Here, day after day, the drayman left boxes of supplies sent from aid societies in Iowa, Minnesota, Wisconsin, Michigan, Illinois and Indiana. Every box contained an assortment of articles, a list of which was tacked on the inside of the lid.... beautifully made shirts, drawers, towels, socks, and handkerchiefs, with "comfort-bags" containing combs, pins, needles, court-plaster, and black sewing-cotton, and with a quantity of carefully dried berries and peaches.

Theodore J. Karamanski

Camp Douglas, located on the city's SOUTH SIDE, was one of the largest POW camps in the North. At times more than 10,000 rebel soldiers were held behind its stockade, 4,457 of whom perished. The majority of the deaths were due to poor sanitary and medical facilities at the camp.

While Confederate soldiers suffered in appalling conditions on the SOUTH SIDE, Chicago women played an important role improving the lot of Union soldiers at the front. The Sisters of Mercy nursed wounded men in numerous makeshift HOSPITALS. Mary Livermore and Jane Hoge rallied the women of the Midwest through the operation of two gigantic fairs in 1863 and 1865. At the hastily assembled but elaborately decorated Northwest Sanitary Fairs, donated items were sold to fund medical supplies and treats for the troops. The 1863 Chicago fair was imitated throughout the North. The public affairs experience won by Chicago women during the war helped to fuel the embryonic women's rights movement in postwar Illinois.

Although the war was controversial in Chicago, support for the Union ran strong. Cook County sent 22,436 men to fight, approximately two-thirds of them from Chicago. Surrounding counties together sent 13,516 men, more than half of them from Kane and Will counties. The draft was little used in Chicago because of enthusiastic enlistment rallies and generous bounties. Chicago MUSIC PUBLISHER George Frederick Root produced many of the most popular Union war songs for use at city rallies, including "Battle-Cry of Freedom" and "Tramp, Tramp, Tramp."

Nearly four thousand Chicagoans died in the Civil War. Respect for their memory and pride in their accomplishment is preserved today in the numerous war heroes, frozen in bronze, standing over GRANT PARK, LINCOLN PARK, and the city's historic CEMETERIES.

Theodore J. Karamanski

See also: Abolitionism; Copperheads; Feminist Movements; Food Processing: Regional and National Market; Iron and Steel; Republican Party; Sanitary Commission; Underground Railroad

Further reading: Karamanski, Theodore J. *Rally 'Round the Flag: Chicago and the Civil War.* 1993.

Clarendon Hills, IL, DuPage County, 18 miles W of the Loop. Clarendon Hills, a commuter village along the Chicago, Burlington & Quincy RAILROAD, roughly encompasses the area between Ogden Avenue, Kingery Highway, Richmond Avenue, and 55th Street. The village consists of elevated prairie land with small rolling hills to the north and large hills to the south, many rising to as much as 70 feet above Lake Michigan.

When the Chicago, Burlington & Quincy Railroad began service here in 1864, farmers initially used it as a milk stop. But the scenic terrain soon attracted speculators, headed up by James M. Walker, then president of the railroad, who hoped to develop a COMMUTER suburb. The area was platted in 1873 with a design inspired by the principles of landscape architect Frederick Law Olmsted, as seen locally at RIVERSIDE. Accordingly, numbered lots of various shapes and sizes were placed along winding streets which followed the natural contours of the land. The area was named Clarendon Hills after a Boston suburb. Despite the hills, winding plat, and influential backers, Clarendon Hills languished.

North of the railroad tracks, Henry C. Middaugh had acquired 270 acres in 1869. Instead of immediately subdividing his property, he farmed the land and hoped to attract other wealthy investors to do the same. He tile-drained his land, planted trees, and in 1893 built an elegant 20-room mansion. The Middaugh Mansion, which entered the National Register of Historic Places in 1978, was meticulously constructed. Bronze screws were used instead of nails, and Middaugh supposedly used a billiard ball to test the floors for levelness. Despite local preservation efforts, the mansion was razed in June 2002.

In the 1920s residential development began in earnest. Residents incorporated as a village in 1923. The one-room schoolhouse was replaced by a two-room brick building. The first police officer was appointed in 1924, and a business district developed to serve the growing population, which included many commuters. Additional subdivisions were made north of the railroad station.

A real boom in Clarendon Hills followed World War II. Population increased from 933 in 1930 to 5,885 by 1960. Ranches, Cape Cods, and split-levels were built on the odd-shaped lots platted almost a century before. New residents organized Episcopal, Roman Catholic, and Lutheran congregations. The Lions Club, formed in 1950, built the community's first public swimming pool. The population of Clarendon Hills in 2000 was 7,610.

Tom Sterling

See also: DuPage County; Historic Preservation; Planning Chicago

Further reading: Knoblauch, Marion. *DuPage County Guide*. 1948. • Shockey, Celia Perry. "Clarendon Hills." In *DuPage Roots*, ed. Richard Thompson, 1985, 133–137.

Classical Music. Classical music has served Chicagoans in a broad variety of ways. Some have used it as a means of artistic expression, others as a way of making a living. Classical music can be a path to personal enrichment and accomplishment or a marker of social status. It can be a focus of research and historical study or a means of entertainment and source of personal pleasure. For the city as a whole, classical music has served as a signal of Chicago's cultural sophistication and economic strength. Cultural events and institutions were one means of placing Chicago's civic vitality above that of rival cities and proclaiming its coming of age to the nation and the world. In a city of superlatives, Chicago's musical culture could likewise excel. To combat pejorative labels such as "Porkopolis" or "Second City," civic boosters strove to make Chicago a "First City" of the arts.

Classical music was heard in Chicago at least from the time of its incorporation and city charter in the 1830s. Early settlers such as Mark Beaubien (fiddle), John Kinzie (violin), and Jean-Baptiste Beaubien (piano) owned instruments and played for dances at the Sauganash Tavern. A Miss Wythe opened the first school of music in July 1834; Samuel Lewis opened a second the following year, and a shipment of pianos arrived in 1835. Short-lived amateur performing groups began with the Old Settlers' Harmonic Society (1835–36, also called the Chicago Harmonic Society) and soon included the Chicago Sacred Musical Society (1842), the Chicago Choral Union (1846–48), and the Mozart Society (1849). In 1847, Frank Lumbard was appointed vocal teacher in the public schools, a move that placed music education at the core of the civic enterprise.

As Chicago expanded, its growing audiences could attract touring artists. Musicians visited intermittently, offering recitals that mixed classical and popular music with virtuoso feats. In 1848 the pianist Richard Hoffman arrived. Soprano prodigy Adelina Patti performed with violinist Ole Bull in 1853, '54, and '57, and with her family troupe in 1860. Pianist Louis Moreau Gottschalk visited several times in the 1860s. The Germania Orchestra visited in 1853, giving the city its first complete symphony (Beethoven's Second), while Theodore Thomas's orchestra began giving almost annual concerts in 1869. The city's first music venues included Rice's Theatre (opened 1847), Tremont Music Hall (opened 1850), McVicker's Theatre (1857–71, reopened 1872), and Central Music Hall (1879–1900). When Crosby's Opera House was dedicated in 1865, Chicago boasted a first-class hall. Its 3,000 seats further helped to attract touring musicians with promises of large receipts. Yet in a fickle cultural marketplace, theater owners hedged their investments by combining stages with retail, office, or hotel space to enhance profits.

Before the 1890s Chicago's most regular concerts were provided by amateur music societies, especially choral groups. European immigrants formed choruses, such as the Männergesangverein (1852), that paved the way for the Musical Union (1858–66), the Oratorio Society (1868–71), the Apollo Club (1872–, later renamed the Apollo Chorus), and the Beethoven Society (1873). Julius Dyhrenfurth and later Hans Balatka conducted the city's first orchestra, the Philharmonic Society (1850–68). Former Germania Orchestra trumpeter Henry Ahner founded a second ensemble in 1856 that performed for only two years. Thomas's Summer Night Concerts in the Exposition Building (1877–91) helped build an audience for symphonic repertory with programming attractions such as "Ballroom Night," "Symphony Night," "Une nuit française," and "Request Nights."

Beginning with the Chicago Jubilee of 1873, for which bandleader Patrick Gilmore combined spectacular music with huge choral and orchestral forces to celebrate the city's rebuilding from the Fire of 1871, musical festivals drew huge, broad-based middle- and upper-class audiences to choral, operatic, and symphonic performances. Usually running for just a few weeks, these festivals captivated social life and garnered extraordinary publicity to further enhance the prestige of the burgeoning metropolis. The 1881 Sängerfest, the May Festivals of 1882 and '84, the opera craze of 1883, and the 1885 Chicago Grand Opera Festival justified the construction of the 4,200-seat Auditorium Theater (1889), a cultural ecosystem combining theater and 500-seat recital hall with revenue-producing hotel, retail, and office spaces (including a school of music), plus ample social facilities (restaurants, meeting spaces, ballroom, and an observation deck). Adelina Patti, the Apollo Chorus, and organist Clarence Eddy dedicated the theater on December 9. A utopian endeavor, the Auditorium addressed social tensions by drawing patrons from across Chicago society to "lessen the gulf between classes" while committing the elite to philanthropy.

The foundations laid by Chicago's amateur music societies, touring musicians, and civic festivals enabled the creation of the city's first permanent professional ensemble. In 1890, C. Norman Fay and the Orchestral Association gave Thomas unprecedented artistic control to establish the Chicago Orchestra (now Chicago Symphony Orchestra [CSO]). Its opening concert in the Auditorium on October 16, 1891, included Wagner's *Faust Overture*, Beethoven's Fifth Symphony, Tchaikovsky's Piano Concerto no. 1, and Dvořák's *Husitská Overture*. Although the orchestra struggled to attract a subscription audience and ran financial deficits, the construction of the 2,566-seat Orchestra Hall (1904–) solved its space problems and affirmed the city's commitment to the ensemble. Shaped by conductors including Frederick Stock (1905–42), Fritz Reiner (1952–63), and Sir Georg Solti (1969–91), the CSO has become the nucleus of Chicago's musical culture while attaining international prominence with tours and award-winning recordings. Cut off from imported talent by World War I, Stock founded the Chicago Civic Music Student Orchestra (1919–, later renamed the Civic Orchestra of Chicago) as a training ensemble for American musicians. The Chicago Symphony Chorus formed in 1957 under the direction of Margaret Hillis. In 1997, a renovated Orchestra Hall reopened as Symphony Center, with additional rehearsal space, a restaurant, and an interactive education center.

Although opera had been heard in Chicago since 1850, performances were often far between, as the city did not support its own resident company. Nevertheless, by 1875 more than 60 operas, many recent works, had been performed for enthusiastic audiences. The 1885 opera festival reportedly attracted over 100,000 attendees. In some neighborhoods, ethnic audiences supported small-scale, local operatic performances. In 1910, the Chicago

Chicago Symphony Orchestra and Theodore Thomas, Auditorium Theater, 1897. Photographer: Unknown. Source: Chicago Historical Society.

Grand Opera Company, formed from the remnants of Oscar Hammerstein's bankrupt New York–based troupe featuring soprano Mary Garden, opened with Verdi's *Aïda*. With star power, strong financial backing from Harold and Edith McCormick, and innovative artistic direction from Cleofante Campanini, Chicago opera rose to immediate national prominence. Running continual deficits for star singers and lavish productions, the company went bankrupt only to be reorganized under a series of monikers.

Electricity magnate Samuel Insull brought financial discipline to the opera administration and built the Civic Opera House (1929–) to escape the inevitable default of the Auditorium's construction bonds. Rosa Raisa as Aïda and Charles Marshall as Radames dedicated the new hall on November 4. The building's 45 stories included over 700,000 square feet of rentable space that was to support the company. Unfortunately, Black Tuesday, signaling the beginning of the GREAT DEPRESSION, occurred just a week before the dedication, putting the company's financial plans in jeopardy. After years of Chicago opera's decline, Carol Fox organized the Lyric Theatre (1954–, later renamed LYRIC OPERA of Chicago) and presented the American debut of Maria Callas (1954). Known as "La Scala West" because of its predominantly Italian repertory, the company continued to grow under Fox's successor Ardis Krainik; her introduction in 1985 of supertitles offering translation of the libretto during performance attracted thousands of new subscribers. In 1974, Alan Stone founded Chicago Opera Theatre, presenting three annual productions in English.

These developments accompanied a gradual shift in patronage from music as an independent business striving to return profit for independent IMPRESARIOS to the civic musical institutions supported by an association of PHILANTHROPISTS for the benefit of the community. Yet festivals did not end with the shift to resident companies. RAVINIA Park, built in 1904 in HIGHLAND PARK as an upscale amusement, became the site of music, dance, and theater events. Orchestral concerts and operatic excerpts were offered during Ravinia's first decade. In 1915, whole evenings of opera were offered, and from 1919 to 1931 star singers appeared. Reinstated after the Depression, the Ravinia series has featured the CSO since 1936. Music directors have included Seiji Ozawa (starting in 1964), James Levine (starting in 1971), and Christoph Eschenbach (starting in 1994). Performances are held in the 3,200-seat, open-air Ravinia Pavilion with picnic seating for 15,000 on the surrounding lawn; more than 500,000 listeners attended in 2002. In 1934 a municipal summer orchestra was organized by musicians' union chief James C. Petrillo, putting players back to work in a WPA bandshell at the lakefront's GRANT PARK. The shell was rebuilt in 1978 and named in honor of Petrillo. The annual summer series now includes a resident Grant Park Symphony and Chorus.

In America, no less in Chicago, teaching is the mainstay of many musicians. Individual instruction provides essential income but also supports music's role as a vehicle of personal transformation. A healthy base of amateur musicians also provides a core audience to support live performance. Chicago's music schools nurtured amateur and aspiring professionals and offered an active recital calendar. Florenz Ziegfeld, Sr., founded the Chicago Academy of Music (later renamed the Chicago Musical College) in 1867 and imported European musical talent as faculty and for a public performance series. Other educational institutions have included the Chicago Conservatory of Music and Dramatic Art (1884–ca. 1905), the American Conservatory of Music (1886–), and the Sherwood Music School (1897–). Chicago universities such as NORTHWESTERN (which initiated music instruction 1873 and a school of music in 1895), DEPAUL (whose school of music dates to 1912), and ROOSEVELT (which merged with Chicago Musical College in 1954), have maintained nationally recognized schools of music, drawing from the city's elite performance groups for faculty. The UNIVERSITY OF CHICAGO's Music Department (1933–) has focused exclusively on composition, music theory, ethnomusicology, and history.

Founded in 1913, the Civic Music Association encouraged music instruction, concert attendance, and community singing. As public school music has suffered from budget woes, other organizations have provided important early training to a diverse student population. The Chicago Youth Symphony (1946–) has united top high-school players from throughout the region. The Chicago Children's Choir (1956–) has supported choirs in public elementary schools, neighborhood choirs, and a 125-voice concert choir. The Merit Music Program has offered a comprehensive program of performance and instruction that has reached 30,000 students since 1979. Merit, with its motto "Making Music . . . Building Lives," has perpetuated the city's ideal of cultural democracy. Projects such as Urban Gateways and the Kraft Family Concerts have brought music to the schools and underserved communities.

Attracted to the city by church or teaching jobs, prominent composers active in Chicago

James C. Petrillo: The Man Behind the Petrillo Band Shell

Born in Chicago, James C. Petrillo became active in the CHICAGO FEDERATION OF MUSICIANS, Local 10 of the AFM. He served as president of the local from 1922 to 1962. His union adjusted to lost opportunities in VAUDEVILLE and movie theaters but made gains in radio and recordings. National president of the AFM from 1940 to 1958, he organized a recording STRIKE during World War II to protest free airplay of recorded pieces. In 1935, Petrillo's free concert series in Chicago's GRANT PARK began, and the park's band shell bore his name.

Dennis H. Cremin

included organist Dudley Buck (1839–1909) and Frederick Grant Gleason (1848–1903). Twentieth-century composers associated with the city included Felix Borowski (1872–1956), who taught in Chicago from 1897 until his death; Chicago native and society businessman John Alden Carpenter (1876–1951), who enjoyed critical success writing BALLETS like *Krazy Kat* (1921) and *Skyscrapers* (1926) as well as piano works and art songs; modernist Ruth Crawford, who studied at Chicago's American Conservatory (1921–29); and African American composer Florence B. Price, who moved to the city in 1926 and had her Symphony in E Minor performed by the CSO in 1933 at the CENTURY OF PROGRESS EXPOSITION. Leo Sowerby taught at the American Conservatory, while Ralph Shapey, Easley Blackwood, Shulamit Ran, and John Eaton have held faculty positions at the University of Chicago. M. William Karlins and Alan Stout have been the linchpins of Northwestern's composition department.

Women's Symphony Orchestra of Chicago, 1952. Photographer: Unknown. Source: Chicago Historical Society.

Chicago has a history of supporting new music in its programming and commissions. Philanthropist Paul Fromm established the Fromm Music Foundation in 1952 to support composers and performance. Shapey founded the Contemporary Chamber Players in 1964, while the CSO has employed three composers-in-residence: John Corigliano (1987–90), Ran (1990–97), and Augusta Reed Thomas (1997–). Ran, who won the Pulitzer Prize in 1991, has also served as composer for the Lyric Opera. In addition to commissioning *Amistad* (1997–98) from Anthony Davis, Lyric Opera has established a long-running collaboration with composer William Bolcom, resulting in *McTeague* (1992–93), *A View from the Bridge* (1999–2000), *The Wedding* (2004–5), and a commission for the 2009–10 season.

Chicago's major ensembles and educational institutions provide a base of instrumentalists for a variety of smaller ensembles and chamber groups. Early music ensembles include Music of the Baroque (1972–) and the NEWBERRY Consort (1986–), as well as the chorus His Majestie's Clerkes (1982–, later named Bella Voce). Chamber ensembles include the Vermeer Quartet (1969–), the Ying Quartet (1992–), Chicago Pro Musica (1979–), the Chicago Chamber Musicians (1986–), and the Rembrandt Chamber Players (1990–).

Classical music's association with education and elite status, the very aspects used to elevate a cultured Chicago within the national imagination, could also lend respect to groups burdened by discrimination. Even before the Second World War, the Women's Symphony Orchestra of Chicago (formed in 1925 by Ebba Sundstrom) gave musicians like Helen Kotas opportunities that would help her become principal French horn of the CSO and, later, the Lyric Opera orchestra. Parallel to Harlem, Chicago supported its own black artistic renaissance. The Umbrian Glee Club (1895–) would give performances in Orchestra Hall, while Pedro Tinsley founded a Choral Study Club in 1900 that performed European choral works. Two years later, Chicago Local 208 incorporated within the American Federation of Musicians, the first black musicians' union to do so. Chicagoans N. Clark Smith and J. Berni Barbour established the first black music publishing company in 1903. Smith also formed an orchestra (1902–5) and composed a *Negro Folk Suite* (1924). William Hackney produced annual "all-colored" composers concerts in Orchestra Hall (1914–16), and in 1919 Nora Holt founded the NATIONAL ASSOCIATION OF NEGRO MUSICIANS, which held its first convention in Chicago. The 1920s saw the formation of the South Side Opera Company, while the 1940s produced the Chicago Negro Opera Guild. The Chicago Sinfonietta (1987–), conducted by Paul Freeman, continues to represent the city's social mix on the concert stage in fulfilling its mission to achieve "excellence through diversity."

Chicago is also home to rich collections of primary research materials for music. The Newberry Library holds rare sources for Renaissance and American music, and, along with the CHICAGO HISTORICAL SOCIETY and CHICAGO PUBLIC LIBRARY, preserves personal papers of many Chicago musicians. The public library also houses the Chicago BLUES Archive, while a large collection of musical instruments dating back to the 1893 WORLD'S COLUMBIAN EXPOSITION can be found at the FIELD MUSEUM. Northwestern's music library includes collections relating to Henry Cowell and John Cage as well as part of the Moldenhauer Archive of twentieth-century manuscripts. The University of Chicago's music library houses the Chicago JAZZ Archive, while COLUMBIA COLLEGE supports the unique holdings of the Center for Black Music Research (1983–).

Chicago entrepreneurs invested heavily in the music industry, and the city's manufacturing and transportation resources made it a center of MUSICAL INSTRUMENT MANUFACTURING, MUSIC PUBLISHING, and recording. Founded as a distributor in 1857, the W. W. Kimball Company began organ manufacture in 1881 and built pianos from 1885. Best known for harps, Lyon & Healy began as a retail shop in 1864 and turned to instrument building in 1885. Organ builders have included Story & Clark, Wilcox & White, and Estey. Percussion manufacturers have included J. C. Deagan & Co. as well as Ludwig, active in Chicago from 1909 to 1930. Piano makers have included Julius Bauer & Co. and the J. P. Seeburg Piano Company, which built a coin-operated player piano—a predecessor to the jukebox. Chicago publishers have included Root & Cady, Clayton F. Summy, and Carl Fischer. In 1964 the University of Chicago Press began offering critical editions of Renaissance Music, later adding series devoted to Rossini and Verdi. As early as 1889, Chicago had become the third largest music industry center in the United States by grossing over $7 million in music products.

The development of classical music in Chicago has followed the growth of the city, including its rapid rise in the second half of the nineteenth century as a major metropolitan center and its twentieth-century maturity and international presence. By appealing to the city's educational, commercial, artistic, and competitive needs, classical music has secured a place in Chicago's multifaceted cultural life.

Mark Clague
J. Kimo Williams

See also: Chicago Sound; Entertaining Chicagoans; Ethnic Music; Music Clubs; Outdoor Concerts; Theater Buildings

Further reading: Schabas, Ezra. *Theodore Thomas: America's Conductor and Builder of Orchestras, 1835–1905.* 1989. • Upton, George Putnam. *Musical Memories.* 1908.

Clearing, Community Area 64, 10 miles SW of the Loop. Chicago ANNEXED much of the area known as Clearing in 1915, with other segments added in 1917 and 1923. It is bounded by 65th Street to the south, 59th Street to the north, Harlem to the west, and Cicero to the east and includes about half of Midway Airport.

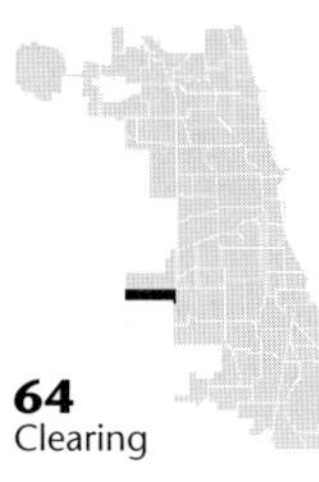

DUTCH and GERMAN farmers lived in the area by the mid-nineteenth century. The area's most extensive landholder was Long John Wentworth, a U.S. Senator and MAYOR of Chicago. Wentworth built a house in 1868 at the corner of what is now 55th and Harlem. The 4,700 acres owned by Wentworth included land in what eventually became Clearing, GARFIELD RIDGE, and SUMMIT. Clearing received its name from a proposed railway-switching yard. A. B. STICKNEY, president of the Chicago Great Western RAILROAD, laid out a plan in 1888 for a one-mile circle, called Stickney's Circle. This circle would allow workers to unload and load goods, avoiding the rail congestion closer downtown. This scheme failed, so the enterprising Stickney tried to cut a deal in 1891 with the upstart Chicago National Stockyards to rival the UNION STOCK YARD. This effort also failed, in part because of a national economic depression from 1893 to 1897. "Stickney's Circle" became "Stickney's Folly."

In 1909, George Hill established a hardware store, one of the first businesses in Clearing. Three years later, residents voted to incorporate as a village. By 1915, the Chicago Transfer and Clearing Company connected the freight car switching hub with 18 industries, and Clearing was annexed to the city.

From those 18 industries in 1915, the Clearing Industrial District grew to more than 90 by 1928. Land in Clearing and Garfield Ridge owned by the Chicago Public SCHOOLS was leased to the city in 1926 for the purpose of building an airport on the Southwest Side. In 1927, Mayor William Hale Thompson dedicated the Chicago Municipal Airport. In 1928 there were 4 runways, expanding to 16 by 1941. By 1949 the airport was renamed MIDWAY AIRPORT to honor victories at Midway Island during World War II.

Clearing entered a postwar residential and economic boom, and its population grew from 6,068 in 1940 to a peak of 24,911 in 1970. By 1970, some 300 firms had located in what is now known as the Bedford-Clearing Industrial District. During the economic recession from 1974 to 1984, over half of those companies left Clearing for other locations, reducing the number of firms to 175 and reducing the number of workers from 50,000 to just over 19,000. Since 1985, with the resurgence of Midway Airport, some stability has returned.

Clinton E. Stockwell

See also: Economic Geography; Railroads

Further reading: Chicago Fact Book Consortium, ed. *Local Community Fact Book: Chicago Metropolitan Area, 1990.* 1995. • Hill, Robert Milton. *A Little Known Story of the Land Called Clearing.* 1983. • Swanson, Stevenson. *Chicago Days: 150 Defining Moments in the Life of a Great City.* 1997.

Clerical Workers.
Chicago's explosive growth and economic development during the late nineteenth century multiplied the demand for office workers. Clerks of many sorts, bookkeepers, typists, stenographers, and receptionists found positions in expanding bureaucracies in the service and business sectors. Many of these new workers were women. The male clerk, the young, aspiring company man who was a common feature of small nineteenth-century offices, was gradually replaced by the young female, who was expected, or allowed, to remain at her job only until she got married.

This transition derived from a combination of Chicago's characteristics. As a terminus for immigrants and migrants, Chicago attracted young women looking for work. For women who had the right qualifications, which at that time meant literate, young, and white, positions in office WORK did seem appealing given the limited opportunities available. The newly invented typewriter was paired with stenography to create the stenographer-typist just as a large number of Chicago's private business colleges began teaching these skills. Chicago was home to the nation's first SKYSCRAPERS, urban workspaces that women believed were modern, safe, and clean. Despite the concerns of female reformers like Jane Addams, who warned of the dangers faced by solitary working girls, many philanthropic and benevolent organizations like the YWCA, the Eleanor Association, and WOMAN'S CITY CLUB created service institutions, residential clubs, and rest areas in the LOOP to accommodate the needs of this new feature of the downtown business district: the working girl. By the 1920s, courses in all the skills necessary for the office became regular and popular in a variety of curricula offered by the Chicago Board of Education in the city's public school system.

In this era of transition, Chicago's female clerical workers experienced a wide range of working conditions. Public stenographers had their own offices in large office blocks or hotels and contracted for work from the various office suites. A stenographer-typist might work for a single boss much like a private secretary today, or she might work in a large office with many other stenographer-typists in a more factory-like setting. A clerk or bookkeeper could also find herself in a wide range of possible jobs depending on size and type of firm or the type of office machinery she could operate. Even though women could expect only very limited job mobility, young white women flocked to these positions, especially stenography-typing, since it offered the best wages, hours, and working conditions for women without professional training.

Chicago witnessed some of the earliest efforts to organize clerical workers. Organizing Chicago's stenographer-typists was on the agenda of Chicago's branch of the WOMEN'S TRADE UNION LEAGUE from the start. In 1905, the Stenographers' and Typewriters' Union #11691 appeared in a directory of unions affiliated with the CHICAGO FEDERATION OF LABOR. Until 1912, when the union ceased to exist, it provided a wide range of services to its several hundred members.

By 1920, the majority of Chicago's clerical workers were U.S.-born white females of foreign or mixed parentage and under the age of 24. Companies employing these clerical workers were challenged to create separate occupational hierarchies and in some cases even separate workspaces for men and women. Some Chicago companies, particularly RAILROADS, attempted to bar women from employment because employers did not want to have to promote women within their ranks. The new larger office staff prompted many companies to adapt scientific management techniques originally designed for factories. Nevertheless, for immigrant daughters, clerical work might have been seen as a way to escape the danger and degradation of the factory and the slum or ghetto. They saw clerical work, as well as other white-collar occupations such as clerking in DEPARTMENT STORES and teaching, as a way to "AMERICANIZE" themselves.

Since 1920, the clerical labor force has become more DEMOGRAPHICALLY diverse, even though individual firms or industries, until quite recently, have discriminated on the basis of age, marital status, race, and ethnicity. Because of the CIVIL RIGHTS MOVEMENTS and legislation of the 1950s and 1960s, minority women made some inroads into a wider variety of office positions. As a result, women of all backgrounds have used clerical jobs

Women taking civil service exam for government employment as stenographers, 1909. Photographer: Unknown. Source: Chicago Historical Society.

for self-support and to provide vital income for their families. Recently, computer technology has accelerated the trend toward factory-like office work. Early efforts at UNIONIZING clerical workers in the 1930s were revived in the 1960s and 1970s, as the concentration of large numbers of women in typing pools or word-processing centers along with the recent women's movement created favorable conditions for this activity.

Lisa Michelle Fine

See also: Economic Geography; Schooling for Work; Work Culture

Further reading: Cavan, Ruth Shonle. *Business Girls: A Study of Their Interests and Problems.* 1929. • Fine, Lisa M. *The Souls of the Skyscraper: Female Clerical Workers in Chicago.* 1990. • Meyerowitz, Joanne J. *Women Adrift: Independent Wage Earners in Chicago.* 1988.

Climate. Chicago's climate is attributable to its location, roughly halfway between the equator and the North Pole and in the interior of a large continent. These conditions produce relatively large annual and day-to-day swings in temperature. Precipitation is greater during the warm half of the year. The proximity of LAKE MICHIGAN to the city produces a lake effect—cooler breezes off the lake during warm-season days and cold-season nights (providing the lake is not frozen), and warmer breezes during cold-season days (again, providing the lake is not frozen) and warm-season nights. Most apparent along the lakeshore, this lake effect can also be noted several miles inland. Northeast winds in winter can produce heavy, lake-effect snowfalls.

Chicago's weather records begin in the 1830s, first taken by medical staff at FORT DEARBORN, then continuing with those of the U.S. Army Signal Corps and the U.S. Weather Bureau, now the National Weather Service. Originally located in the downtown area, observing sites moved to MIDWAY AIRPORT in 1928 and O'HARE AIRPORT in 1958. Temperatures at the airports, being further from the urban center, are systematically cooler by a few degrees.

Chicago's summers are dominated by warm, humid air originating over the Gulf of Mexico, with occasional incursions of air from the Pacific Ocean, resulting in daily high temperatures generally in the low 80s with lows about 20 degrees Fahrenheit lower. The relatively high humidity occasionally yields unbearably high temperature-humidity indexes, as the death toll during the summer of 1995 attests. Days dominated by Pacific air, on the other hand, bring respite, with highs generally in the 60s and 70s. Summer is the wettest season of the year, with rainfall generally three to four inches per month, though there is great variability, as the drought of 1988 and the floods of 1993 demonstrate. Summer rainfall is almost totally showery and associated with thunderstorms. Hail and a few TORNADOES have occurred rarely and have affected only a few square miles.

Winter days are generally dominated by air from the Pacific, with several incursions each year of air from Arctic Canada. January temperatures generally peak in the low 30s, although Arctic air limits highs to the single digits and occasionally below zero. High wind chills in winter are due to high winds attributable to the relatively flat surrounding prairie and lake and the canyon effect of the tall buildings in and near the LOOP. Winter months generally experience one and a half to two inches of precipitation, a combination of rain and snow. Most winters, Chicago experiences two to three storms with at least six inches snowfall each, sometimes accompanied by strong winds. Heavy snowfalls during winters of the mid- and late 1970s severely tested Chicago, as did the snowfall of January 26–27, 1967, when more than 20 inches fell, accompanied by winds gusting between 50 and 70 miles per hour. Fifty-six people died, untold numbers were injured, and total losses were estimated at $1.74 million. Snow was hauled to rural areas and the lake for disposal.

The average annual temperature for Chicago, based on data from 1961 to 1990, is 49.0 degrees Fahrenheit but has varied from 42.5 (Loop, 1864) to 54.3 (University of Chicago, 1987). Average annual precipitation (1961–1990) is 35.82 inches but has varied from 21.19 inches (University of Chicago, 1956) to 49.35

Chicago's Weather Extremes

Temperature	Highest recorded temperature	105°F	July 24, 1934
	Lowest recorded temperature	−27°F	January 20, 1985
	Most number of days in a year with temperatures at 90°F	47	1988
	Most number of consecutive days in a year with temperatures below 32°F	43	1976–77
Precipitation	Most recorded precipitation in a 24-hour period	6.24 inches	August 12–13, 1987
	Most recorded precipitation in a month	17.1 inches	August 1987
Snowfall	Most recorded accumulated snowfall in a 24-hour period	23 inches	January 26–27, 1967
	Most recorded accumulated snowfall in a season	89.7 inches	Winter, 1978–79

Source: WGN Weather data compiled from National Weather Service records, with data from 1872 to 2000.

inches (O'Hare, 1983). Annual average winter snowfall is 38.7 inches (1961–1990), varying from 9.8 inches (Loop, 1920–21) to 83.7 inches (O'Hare, 1978–79).

The trend of average annual temperatures in Chicago indicates warming of two to three degrees from the mid- to late 1800s to the first half of the twentieth century, with cooling of one to two degrees thereafter. The cooling after about 1960, however, may be due to the fact that data after 1958 were taken at O'Hare, as opposed to Midway and the Loop. The trends (though not necessarily the magnitudes) in Chicago temperature are similar to the average of the United States but not other areas in the world.

Average annual precipitation at Chicago, like most other Upper Midwestern sites, exhibits great year-to-year variability. In spite of the variability, the trends suggest a decline of perhaps five inches from the second half of the nineteenth century to the first half of the twentieth, with a rather substantial increase beginning about 1960 and continuing thereafter.

Wayne M. Wendland

See also: Air Quality; Seiches; Snow Removal

Further reading: Bryan, A. A., H. Hoffman, W. M. Wendland, and P. Daily. *Local Climatological Data Summary, Chicago Ill., 1830–1993.* Misc. Pub. 98–16. Illinois State Water Survey. 1994. • Cox, H. J., and J. H. Armington. *The Weather and Climate of Chicago.* 1914.

Waiting room at the Municipal Tuberculosis Sanitarium, 1941. Photographer: Edwin Rosskam. Source: Library of Congress.

Clinics and Dispensaries. In nineteenth-century American cities, those who were sick but could not afford private medical attention often found aid at a dispensary, a walk-in clinic dealing mostly with nonacute illnesses. Following a British model, PHILANTHROPISTS, physicians, and civic leaders began building dispensaries in East Coast American cities shortly after the Revolution. This idea migrated westward with doctors until nearly every city had at least one dispensary. In Chicago in the early 1840s, the sick poor could visit the "City Dispensary" at the recently opened Rush Medical College. Like the many other proprietary medical schools in the United States before the CIVIL WAR, Rush College needed to attract fee-paying students, and the ability to offer students clinical training in a dispensary at a time when no permanent general HOSPITALS existed in the city was a great advantage. Thus, for one hour in the mornings, while student doctors observed, Rush professors treated the indigent poor. Later medical schools in Chicago also established dispensaries.

Chicago's growing population of poorly paid and ill-housed workers provided a large and needy clientele for free medical care. A visit to a dispensary, however, was unlikely to mean a thorough examination. Typically, a patient had a long wait on a hard bench in a crowded room, followed by a brief interview with a physician who wrote a number on a slip of paper. This paper could be exchanged for a medication at the attached pharmacy. Despite the cursory nature of their services, dispensaries proliferated. Before the Great FIRE OF 1871, Chicago had nine; by the 1890s dozens operated across the city. Several of Chicago's social SETTLEMENTS, such as HULL HOUSE and CHICAGO COMMONS, briefly ran their own dispensaries. The JEWISH Aid Society founded the West Side Free Dispensary near MAXWELL STREET. Other religious groups, including the SALVATION ARMY and the Bohemian, Dunkard, and Bethesda missions, sponsored dispensaries as well. The Chicago Lying-In Hospital began as a dispensary. Companies such as the Chicago & Northwestern Railroad established their own facilities for employees. Large dispensaries like the Central Free and the West Side Free ran daily and weekly clinics specializing in various ailments.

During the early years of the twentieth century, Chicago's Health Department used existing dispensaries to disseminate information about venereal, mental, and childhood diseases and maternal welfare. The department set up seven TUBERCULOSIS dispensaries of its own in 1907 and a Municipal Venereal Disease Clinic in 1910. Beginning in 1915, it established dental clinics in Chicago public SCHOOLS.

As modern general hospitals established outpatient departments with well-equipped laboratories and greater therapeutic resources, the older, freestanding dispensaries gradually disappeared, but the idea of free or low-cost clinics survived in underserved urban areas. In the era of the GREAT SOCIETY of the 1960s, community leaders saw neighborhood health centers under local control as an answer to uneven distribution of health care. The Mile Square Health Center and the East Lawndale Health Center opened in the late 1960s. In 1970, the city's Board of Health maintained dispensary-like institutions: 35 infant welfare stations, 18 prenatal clinics, and 6 FAMILY PLANNING clinics.

Paul A. Buelow

See also: Birthing Practices; Drug Retailing; Medical Education; Public Health

Further reading: Bonner, Thomas N. *Medicine in Chicago, 1850–1950: A Chapter in the Social and Scientific Development of a City.* 2nd ed. 1991. • Buelow, Paul A. *The Dispensary Comes to Chicago: Health Care and the Poor Before 1920.* Ph.D. diss., University of Illinois at Chicago. 1997. • Rosenberg, Charles E. "Social Class and Medical Care in 19th-Century America: The Rise and Fall of the Dispensary." *Journal of the History of Medicine and the Allied Sciences* 29 (1974): 32–54.

Clothing and Garment Manufacturing. Clothing, traditionally made at home or by custom tailors, began to be commercially produced in the early nineteenth century. In Chicago this industry developed rapidly after the Great FIRE OF 1871 and remained one of the most dynamic sectors until the GREAT DEPRESSION.

Starting from the 1860s, the city's men's clothing merchants employed tailors and had ready-to-wear clothes made at their shop. The industry expanded in the next decade, as merchant-manufacturers like Harry Hart and Bernard Kuppenheimer produced suits as well as work clothes and marketed them in the Midwestern and Southern states. Those years also saw women's clothing production added to the industry, when manufacturers like Joseph

Women's Garment Factories in Chicago in 1925

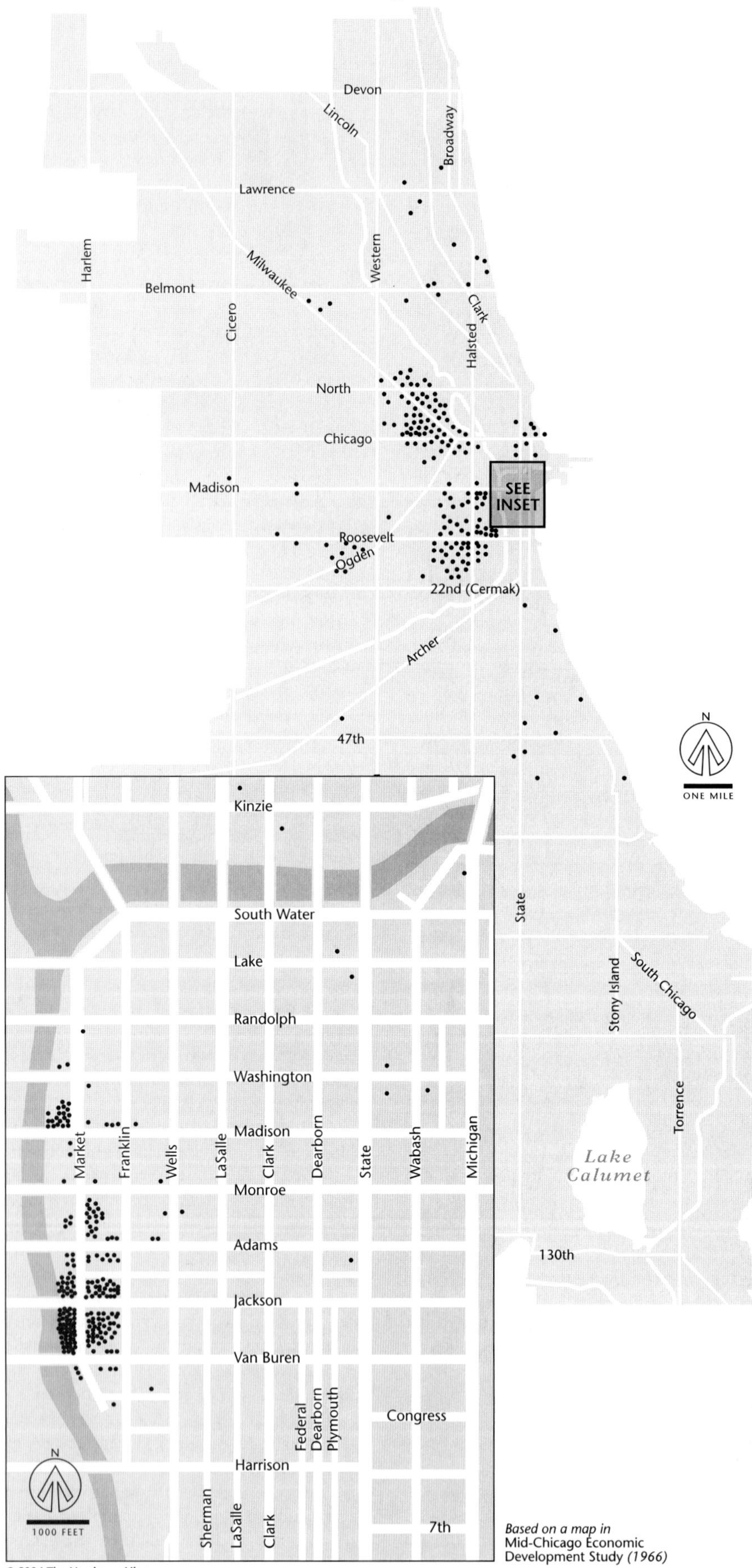

Chicago once had a thriving women's garment manufacturing industry. In 1925, during its heyday, it was located principally in three concentrations. The main garment district was on South Market Street (the site of later South Wacker Drive) between Monroe and Van Buren Streets. Secondary concentrations were found on the Near West Side, both southwest of downtown and around Milwaukee Avenue between Chicago and North Avenues. The industry declined with foreign competition and outsourcing of production.

Beifeld began producing ready-made cloaks. Chicago was increasingly involved in nationwide competition, which led to the sweating system in the 1880s. Manufacturers sent out WORK to be done by contractors and subcontractors, who often opened tiny shops in poor districts, the NEAR WEST SIDE in particular, and hired immigrants for long hours at low wages. In the early 1890s, urban reformers engaged in an anti-sweatshop campaign in Chicago and across the country.

By that time, however, Chicago was already turning to the factory system. Trying to secure an edge against their New York and Philadelphia competitors, manufacturers began producing better grades of garment with fine material and workmanship. They established large factories, where each worker took up only one segment of the whole production process and dexterously performed it. They also endeavored to improve the public image of ready-made garments through national ADVERTISING. The pioneer in this arena was Joseph Schaffner of HART, SCHAFFNER & MARX, a Chicago firm that was to grow into a giant, employing 8,000 workers and leading the U.S. clothing industry in the early twentieth century. These efforts, aimed at the emerging urban middle classes, led to industrial expansion. By the end of the century, Chicago became the second largest production center for men's clothing, with its output roughly amounting to 15 percent of the national total. New York as the center of fashion dominated women's clothing, attracting numerous small shops and producing four-fifths of the national output. With only 4 percent of the women's market, Chicago concentrated on cloaks and suits and attempted to establish only a relatively few small factories.

Although the factory system never entirely replaced sweating, it led to modern labor relations. Ethnic diversity particularly characterized Chicago's workforce, which included a significant number of SWEDES, CZECHS, POLES, and LITHUANIANS, in addition to JEWS and ITALIANS. The workforce remained further fragmented by gender and skill. Women constituted the majority on the shop floor but had little access to high-paying jobs. Cutters, mostly of GERMAN or IRISH descent, despised tailors. Yet factories, mainly located close to immigrant settlements in the Northwest, Near West,

Margaret Dreier Robbins with garment strikers, 1915. Photographer: Unknown. Source: Chicago Historical Society.

Men in front of a union tailor shop, 1354 West Taylor Street (no date). Photographer: Unknown. Source: University of Illinois at Chicago.

Women in the Garment Industries

After the Civil War, the garment industry grew in downtown Chicago. Immigrant women often took this low-paying, sometimes dangerous WORK. In 1882, the German-language *Chicagoer Arbeiter-Zeitung* published a piece called "The Fate of Women Workers," in which a young German woman described work in a garment factory:

> In the factories they constantly make deductions on the flimsiest pretexts. For example, there's a company on Wabash Avenue. They employ "80 hands for overalls," trousers made from stiff material. The machines are steam powered and most of them are old and on their last legs. Often when you have to double-stitch, the needle breaks off. One of these costs 50 cents, and the girls have to pay for it themselves whether it was their fault or not. . . .
>
> The worst is that the factories usually don't have light, and slowly but surely the women ruin their eyesight. It's as bad in the evening as it is during the day. The gasometer is turned down to half pressure, and the flame is barely as big as a match. . . . An *overall* seamstress makes $4 to $5 if she's good. . . . Most live with their parents. But a lot of them have to "board" . . . and the cheapest is $3 a week—if, that is, you share a room with another girl.

Keil, Hartmut, and John B. Jentz, eds. *German Workers in Chicago: A Documentary History of Working-Class Culture from 1850 to World War I.* 1988, 80–81.

or Southwest districts in addition to the LOOP, helped workers cultivate close social networks and resort to collective action. In men's clothing, a general STRIKE involving over 40,000 workers and lasting for 14 weeks in 1910–11 prompted the formation of a local union of immigrant workers. This organization, chartered by the United Garment Workers, helped launch the AMALGAMATED CLOTHING WORKERS OF AMERICA (ACWA) in 1914. Under the leadership of Sidney Hillman, the ACWA completely organized Chicago in 1919 and claimed a membership of 41,000 in the following year. The International Ladies' Garment Workers' Union (ILGWU) helped the small and unstable local women's clothing unions of the city to form a joint board in 1914. The joint board conducted unionization campaigns and soon secured a citywide agreement with employers. By 1920, the ILGWU claimed a membership of 6,000, two-thirds of Chicago's women's clothing workforce.

The mid-1920s turned out to be a high point. With a larger share of the national market than before and with labor relations stabilized through collective bargaining, Chicago's clothing industry was faced with new challenges.

Men looked for lower-priced garments, spending more money on automobiles, radios, and other modern conveniences; women preferred the dress and waist to the coat and skirt, often wearing the suit. Manufacturers were less interested in technological INNOVATIONS than in concessions to be made by the unions. When the ILGWU lost a major strike in 1924, the ACWA retreated without completely giving up high wage rates. Consequently, large men's clothing firms tried to maintain sales by integrating retail outlets, but small ones began to leave for nonunion towns in the Midwestern countryside.

By the late 1920s, overview Chicago's clothing industry was already on the decline, a tendency greatly accelerated by the GREAT DEPRESSION. The NEW DEAL revived women's clothing; government contracts for military uniforms boosted men's; and postwar prosperity temporarily benefited both. Soon, however, manufacturers began to leave Chicago, many settling in the South, where labor expenses were lower. Lower production costs fit American preferences for spending less on clothing than on homes, home appliances, and automobiles, and for informal wear that accommodated increasing LEISURE time and the suburban lifestyle. Lower costs also made it easier to compete with imports, particularly those made in low-wage countries in Northeast Asia, which were taking an expanding share of the American market. By the mid-1970s, Chicago had only 7,000 workers engaged in the clothing industry. The few manufacturers still remaining in the city have attempted to integrate the making of men's and women's clothing and to experiment with new technologies like laser cutting or programmed sewing.

Youngsoo Bae

See also: Antiunionism; Business of Chicago; Economic Geography; Housekeeping; Work Culture

Further reading: Amalgamated Clothing Workers of America. Research Department. *The Clothing Workers of Chicago, 1910–1922.* 1922. • Carsel, Wilfred. *A History of the Chicago Ladies' Garment Workers' Union.* 1940. • Cobrin, Harry A. *The Men's Clothing Industry: Colonial through Modern Times.* 1970.

Clout. In the mid-twentieth century, Chicago writers coined the term "clout" to mean political power and influence. This political usage probably was taken from the baseball expression "What a clout!" which described a powerful hit.

In Harold Gosnell's *Machine Politics* (1937), a Chicago precinct captain claimed that no one could "get anywhere" in POLITICS "without clout from behind." In 1958, Irv Kupcinet wrote that defendants in Chicago trials are "found innocent on the age-old legal premise of reasonable doubt—not . . . reasonable clout." Clout's association with Chicago politics was solidified by Len O'Connor's *Clout: Mayor Daley and His City* (1975).

Royko: What Clout Is . . .

In a column entitled "What Clout Is and Isn't," which appeared in the *Daily News* on June 7, 1973, Mike Royko tackled a definition of clout:

[W]hat clout is in Chicago is political influence, as exercised through patronage, fixing, money, favors, and other traditional City Hall methods.

The easiest way to explain clout is through examples of the way it might be used in conversation.

"Nah, I don't need a building permit—I got clout in City Hall."

"Hey, Charlie, I see you made foreman. Who's clouting for you?"

"Lady, just tell your kid not to spit on the floor during trial and he'll get probation. I talked to my clout and he talked to the judge."

"My tax bill this year is $1.50. Not bad for a three-flat, huh? I got clout in the assessor's office."

"Ever since my clout died, they've been making me work a full eight hours. I've never worked an eight-hour week before."

"My clout sent a letter to the mayor recommending me for a judgeship. Maybe I'll enroll in law school."

Get the idea? Clout is used to circumvent the law, not to enforce it. It is used to bend rules, not follow them.

Royko, Mike. *Sez Who? Sez Me.* 1982, 101.

By the 1970s, the query "Who's your clout?"—questioning one's ability to reach and persuade those in power—had found wide national usage beyond its Chicago origins.

Daniel Greene

See also: Government, City of Chicago; Machine Politics; Patronage; Political Culture; Shakman Decrees

Further reading: "Kup's Column." *Chicago Sun-Times,* December 14, 1958. • Safire, William. *Safire's Political Dictionary.* 1978.

Clubs

OVERVIEW
FRATERNAL CLUBS
LITERARY CLUBS
PATRIOTIC AND VETERANS' CLUBS
WOMEN'S CLUBS
YOUTH CLUBS

OVERVIEW. Put three people together, the German adage holds, and they will form a club. The same can be said about Chicagoans. Starting with the city's earliest residents, Chicagoans have joined clubs and organizations of all kinds and sizes that claimed all kinds of purposes. Ethnic clubs provided safe havens for newcomers and provided services and skills they needed to cope with life in Chicago and the United States. As immigration slowed, the same clubs helped preserve cultural traditions from "home." Religious denominations created organizations to serve the needs of men, women, and children and to provide services to congregations. Improvement associations brought neighbors together to solve community problems, welcome new residents, and—sometimes—keep others from moving in. From the purely social Jolly Bachelors to the firmly political ALPHA SUFFRAGE CLUB to the clubs that, like Ragen's Colts, defy easy categorization, Chicagoans have created a rich network of institutions that have both reflected and shaped every aspect of life in the metropolitan region.

Janice L. Reiff

See also: Fitness and Athletic Clubs; Mutual Benefit Societies; Neighborhood Associations; Religious Institutions

FRATERNAL CLUBS. Ritual and regalia distinguish fraternal societies from other social clubs and service organizations. Local lodges were affiliated with a national fraternal organization. The Freemasons were the oldest and most prestigious fraternal society, and other fraternal organizations imitated its ceremonies. In the 1890s there were hundreds of fraternal orders, thousands if one counts splinter groups, brief-lived organizations, and local societies.

At fraternalism's peak of popularity in the late nineteenth century, most middle-class and many working-class men belonged at least briefly to a lodge. Millions of lodge brothers paraded in colorful fraternal dress, honored their officers with extravagant and even ridiculous titles, and found a sense of community at the lodge hall. Many fraternal societies provided their members with life insurance and sometimes with sickness insurance. The best-known fraternal societies accepted only white men and often only PROTESTANTS as members, although many had auxiliaries for women. There also were auxiliaries for youth, sometimes with quasi-military drill teams. Other fraternal societies sprang up for the excluded to meet their need for sociability and a sense of personal and collective importance. Immigrants and blacks, ROMAN CATHOLICS and JEWS had their own societies. GERMAN, Scandinavian, and East European lodges for many years operated in their own languages. There were other specialized orders, notably the temperance fraternal societies that provided mutual support in the battle for individual sobriety and prohibition.

The publication in 1893 of the Chicago Directory of Lodges and Benevolent Societies highlighted the popularity of fraternal societies in Chicago during the late nineteenth century. It listed various kinds of Masons, the Independent Order of Odd Fellows, the Ancient

Order of United Workmen, the Deutscher Order Harugari, the Ancient United Order of Druids, the Knights of Pythias, the Independent Order of Free Sons of Israel, the Order of the Red Cross, the Independent Order of Sons of Hermann (a society for German immigrants), the Independent Order of Red Men, the Kesher Shel Barzel (a Jewish society), the Independent Order of Foresters, the rival Ancient Order of Foresters, the Benevolent and Protective Order of Elks, the Royal Arcanum, and others, but omitted more fraternal societies than it included. For instance, it failed to mention AFRICAN AMERICAN organizations such as the United Brothers of Friendship and Sisters of the Mysterious Ten and temperance societies like the Good Templars.

The best-known fraternal organizations in the United States have been the Masons, the Odd Fellows, and, most recently, the Elks. Chicago's first Masonic lodge was chartered in 1843. Numerous and mostly middle class, the Masons constructed the Chicago Masons Temple in 1892, which at 22 stories was then the world's tallest building. The Odd Fellows chartered their first Chicago lodge in 1844. By 1923 this order counted 89 Chicago lodges with nearly 28,000 members. Adapting to a changing population, the Odd Fellows chartered a Spanish-speaking lodge in 1971. The first Elks lodge in Chicago was chartered in 1876 and was especially popular among actors. Unlike most fraternal societies that declined in membership in the early 1900s, the Elks added members until well after World War II. The Elks reached their greatest Chicago membership, 4,300 in four lodges, in 1958. By the end of the twentieth century their Chicago-area lodges were all located in the suburbs, outside the city limits.

Many of the black fraternal organizations active in Chicago were the segregated and unacknowledged counterparts of white societies such as the Masons, the Odd Fellows, and the Elks, but newcomers from the southern states brought with them new societies such as the True Reformers. Lodge membership played an important role in community politics. By the eve of WORLD WAR II, the Chicago membership of black fraternal orders had fallen to about 10,000, mostly middle class and few of them active in their organizations.

Even in their heyday fraternal societies had enemies. Evangelical ministers and women dominated the anti-secret-society National Christian Association, organized in Illinois in the late 1860s. Its leader was the founder and first president of WHEATON COLLEGE, which as a result became an anti-secret-society stronghold. To expose the fraternal societies, the National Christian Association's publisher, Ezra A. Cook of Chicago, printed many secret society rituals. The Roman Catholic Church also condemned membership in secret societies, so Catholic fraternal societies such as the Knights of Columbus emphasized that their ritual was not secret.

In the twenty-first century, ritual and regalia have lost their appeal. To most people, they appear absurd. The lodge members who remain are often elderly. Other than the Masons, the Odd Fellows, and the Elks, few fraternal societies survive except as mutual insurance organizations whose members seldom meet.

David M. Fahey

See also: Clubs: Youth Clubs; Danes; Leisure; Mutual Benefit Societies; Norwegians; Swedes

Further reading: Dumenil, Lynn. *Freemasonry and American Culture, 1880–1930*. 1984. • Ferguson, Charles W. *Fifty Million Brothers*. 1937. Reprinted 1979. • Schmidt, Alvin J. *Fraternal Organizations*. 1980.

LITERARY CLUBS. Literary clubs exemplified Chicago's progress from an emerging city focused on the marketplace toward one in which some of its citizens had the LEISURE to promote and patronize the arts. These clubs often incorporated both literary study and social concern. Early clubs held literary debates, hosted lectures, and established libraries and included the Chicago Polemical Society (founded 1833), Chicago Lyceum (1834), and the Young Men's Association (1841). By the early 1870s the women of the Fortnightly Club met to engage in both social intercourse and intellectual development. In 1874 the all-male Chicago Literary Club began meeting to share their love of literature. The club published selected papers of members on topics including POLITICS, the labor movement, and CIVIL WAR reminiscences. The Fortnightly Club and the now coed Chicago Literary Club, the city's longest-lived literary clubs, have continued to meet weekly into the twenty-first century.

Chicago's educated middle-class AFRICAN AMERICANS instituted literary clubs of their own and participated in mixed-race clubs such as the Frederick Douglass Center's Woman's Club. Since the 1960s the formal, organized literary clubs (in Chicago as elsewhere) have had to compete with proliferating informal reading groups which may center on a local library branch, a bookstore, or just a hospital living room. In 2000 the CHICAGO PUBLIC LIBRARY started a program to promote broader and more unified group reading under the banner of "One Book, One City," which recommends a single book to be read and discussed all over town.

Rhonda Huber Frevert

See also: Lectures and Public Speaking; Libraries: Suburban Libraries; Literary Cultures

Further reading: Andrews, Clarence A. *Chicago in Story: A Literary History*. 1982. • Chicago Literary Club. *The Chicago Literary Club: The First Hundred Years, 1874–1974*. 1974. • Knupfer, Anne Meis. *Toward a Tenderer Humanity and a Nobler Womanhood: African American Women's Clubs in Turn-of-the-Century Chicago*. 1996.

PATRIOTIC AND VETERANS' CLUBS. The first veterans' organization to have substantial membership and influence in Chicago and around the country was the Grand Army of the Republic, an organization for CIVIL WAR Union veterans. The official founder of the GAR, Dr. Benjamin Franklin Stephenson of

Grand Army of the Republic drum corps members stand on a train platform, 1906. Photographer: Unknown. Source: Chicago Historical Society.

Like many other American Legion posts, Roseland Post 49 was involved in a wide array of civic activities. Here they lead the 50th anniversary parade of the Roseland Moose. Photographer: Unknown. Source: Chicago Historical Society.

Springfield, Illinois, installed the first GAR post in Decatur, Illinois, in 1866. Historians also credit the impetus for the organization's founding to Illinois governor Richard J. Oglesby, who hoped that a veterans' organization would support his U.S. Senate bid against Lyman Trumbull. The GAR in Chicago, as in the rest of the country, lobbied for veterans' pensions, provided aid to disabled veterans, raised money for veterans' widows and children, and petitioned for the national recognition of Memorial Day. They responded to disasters such as the Chicago Fire by organizing relief campaigns. Chicago-area GAR posts also became a fixture of parades in the city and marched at "German Day" at the WORLD'S COLUMBIAN EXPOSITION on June 15, 1893.

The late 1800s saw the rise of a self-conscious patriotism in the United States. The influx of immigrants, especially into urban areas like Chicago, and the nation's growing international power prompted a search to delineate the roots and rituals of an American identity. Clubs such as the Veterans of Foreign Wars (founded 1899) and the American Legion (founded 1919) gained membership and influence, especially as GAR veterans passed away. These organizations have continued the work of the GAR. They also champion their interpretation of patriotism through activities such as promoting public display of the flag and evaluating history books for their depictions of the wars of the United States.

During the late 1800s, genealogically based patriotic clubs became popular, the two best known being the Sons of the American Revolution (founded 1889) and the Daughters of the American Revolution (founded 1890). Both organized Chicago chapters very early in their development. These clubs have provided a venue for sociability, the assertion of status, and participation in activities the organization identifies as promoting patriotism. Like the veterans' organizations, the work of these patriotic clubs is largely at the grassroots level: sponsoring history essay contests in the schools, preserving historic sites and records, supporting patriotic holidays and rituals, providing citizenship training for immigrants, and—more controversially—taking stands as an organization against "un-American" activities or views contrary to the organization's own definitions of patriotic activities and beliefs.

Barbara Truesdell

See also: Americanization; Fire of 1871; Mutual Benefit Societies; World War I; World War II

Further reading: Davies, Wallace Evan. *Patriotism on Parade: The Story of Veterans' and Hereditary Organizations in America, 1783–1900.* 1955. • Gibbs, Margaret. *The DAR.* 1969. • McConnell, Stuart. *Glorious Contentment: The Grand Army of the Republic, 1865–1900.* 1992.

WOMEN'S CLUBS. At its height between 1890 and 1920, the women's club movement extended its concerns of child and family welfare to social motherhood, as many women's clubs promoted civic betterment, in addition to traditional PHILANTHROPIC work. Clubwomen conjoined maternalist practices to more political agendas, including women's SUFFRAGE and legislation for children and working mothers. Generally stratified by class, ethnicity, and race, Chicago's women's clubs engaged in a wide variety of activities, depending upon institutions, traditions, and resources within their own communities.

The Chicago Woman's Club, of those clubs dominated by well-to-do white women born in the United States, stood out as among the most active. Formed in 1876, the club originally focused on self and social improvement; members studied classical literature and ART, while also establishing KINDERGARTENS and homes for fallen women. By the late 1880s, their efforts turned to state-building reform, most notably the improvement of state facilities for dependent children, orphans, and female prisoners, as well as legislation for compulsory education and against child labor. The Chicago Woman's Club's members—particularly Julia Lathrop, Jane Addams, and Lucy Flower—were so influential that they largely ushered in the Illinois Juvenile Court Law of 1899, which created the first JUVENILE court in the United States.

The Chicago Woman's Club also worked in conjunction with other elite white women's clubs through the League of Cook County Clubs. League delegates returned to their respective clubs to organize them around key pieces of legislation, such as the truant school bill. The HULL HOUSE Woman's Club and other SETTLEMENT clubs, as well as other city and suburban women's clubs, also raised funds for PLAYGROUNDS and vacation schools. This alliance of women's clubs established citywide improvement associations aimed at street sanitation, garbage removal, and school conditions. Women's club strategies and motives were noticeably different from those of the men's clubs. For example, the Woman's City Club circumscribed its interest in vocational education around child welfare, whereas its male counterpart, the City Club, was motivated more by BUSINESS interests.

AFRICAN AMERICAN women's clubs, too, conjoined traditional concerns of child and family welfare to political activism. However, unlike their white counterparts, they faced a variety of obstacles: RACISM, insufficient financial resources, and lack of cooperation from mainstream organizations. Consequently, they created and sustained multiple community organizations, including day nurseries, kindergartens, settlements, and homes for working girls, dependent children, and the aged and infirm. Through letter-writing campaigns to legislators, they also protested discrimination in schools and employment. Their strategies of educating voters on political platforms, of canvassing door-to-door, and forming voting blocs were most successful in the 1915 victory of Chicago's first African American alderman, Oscar dePriest.

Immigrant women, too, formed their own clubs, many of which were parish organizations and dramatic, literary, and singing church circles. They also sought to assist those in need, most notably newcomers, destitute women, neglected children, and the aged. Like other ethnic clubs, they were concerned with

Members of the West Side Women's Federated Club, 1950s. Photographer: Unknown. Source: Chicago Public Library.

preserving cultural traditions. For example, the POLISH Women's Alliance, formed in 1898, organized a reading room for women, as well as schools to teach their language, history, and culture. Although deeply concerned with political issues, such as suffrage and women's advancement, they did not align themselves with other Chicago women's clubs because of language differences as well as a strong sense of Polish nationalism.

Settlements also formed mothers' and women's clubs, primarily to Americanize immigrant women. Most offered instruction in cooking, sewing, childcare, and HOUSEKEEPING, as well as sponsored social hours. Immigrant women's responses to middle-class settlement workers' club programs varied. In many cases, they resisted activities which were demeaning to their cultural traditions but adopted programs of benefit to their children's health.

Anne Meis Knupfer

See also: Alpha Suffrage Club; Children and the Law; League of Women Voters; Leisure; Playground Movement; Politics; Waste Disposal

Further reading: Flanagan, Maureen A. "Gender and Urban Political Reform: The City Club and the Woman's City Club of Chicago in the Progressive Era."*American Historical Review* 95 (October 1990): 1032–1050. • Knupfer, Anne Meis. *Toward a Tenderer Humanity and a Nobler Womanhood: African American Women's Clubs in Turn-of-the-Century Chicago.* 1996. • Wycoff, Catherine E. "Identity, Culture, and Community: Immigrant Youth and Settlement Workers in Chicago, 1919–1939." Ph.D. diss., University of Illinois at Urbana-Champaign. 1999.

YOUTH CLUBS. Youth clubs and sports have been a part of Chicago's social world from its earliest days. Many were spontaneously generated by young women and men who were interested in particular sports and the possibilities of participation. Others have emerged from the efforts of educational, reform, ethnic, neighborhood, and political organizations interested in shaping children's and young adults' current lives and their social roles in the future.

The YOUNG MEN'S CHRISTIAN ASSOCIATION, established in Chicago in 1858, first attempted to organize youth and young men in order to promote temperance and wholesome lifestyles. It met with limited success until it began incorporating sports and games into its programs in the 1870s. Fueled by the widespread interest in BASEBALL during the CIVIL WAR, young men, boys, and employers began organizing competitive teams and leagues.

By the 1880s, high-school students had organized their own baseball, TENNIS, and FOOTBALL teams. They formed the student-run Cook County Athletic League in 1885. The growing interest in tennis resulted in the organization of clubs with their own facilities in several middle-class neighborhoods during the decade. By the 1890s a BICYCLING fad fostered hundreds of clubs, some organized by particular ethnic groups. Cycling held a particular appeal for young women, who found in it a means to challenge Victorian norms, as they adopted pants or bloomers and eschewed chaperones during social excursions.

Such neighborhood associations produced economic as well as social opportunities. Neighborhood sports teams publicly challenged others in the NEWSPAPERS. The most successful, like the ROSELAND Eclipse baseball team, attracted the best players and constructed their own stadiums, thereby achieving semipro status. Like the commercialized model of the professional teams, the semipros enjoyed paying spectators and loyal fans. Such loyalty often promoted rivalries and GAMBLING among neighborhood, ethnic, and religious factions.

Girls formed a high-school BASKETBALL league in 1900. Meanwhile, boys' teams engendered intense rivalries and consequent abuses, such as the use of ineligible players. Faculty members moved to gain greater control over students' extracurricular activities by the turn of the century. By 1913, school authorities and private sponsors reorganized the Cook County Athletic League as the Chicago Public Schools Athletic League under adult regulations. The ongoing rivalry between the Public League and its counterpart the Catholic League fostered the Prep Bowl, an annual city championship football game that drew more than 120,000 to SOLDIER FIELD in 1937. The CATHOLIC YOUTH ORGANIZATION incorporated sports activities in a comprehensive program under its religious banner that covered PARISHES in Chicago and all COLLAR COUNTIES.

Politicians, too, noticed the widespread interest in sport and the growth of athletic clubs and adopted them for their own purposes. Frank Ragen, for example, adopted the stockyard district's Morgan Athletic Club, trading their support for his political aspirations with financial and political support for their social and athletic activities. With more than two thousand members, they helped him rise to Cook County commissioner and became infamous with their belligerent role in Chicago's 1919 RACE RIOT. Similar clubs proliferated in other neighborhoods and among different ethnic groups, often to protect their immigrant and working-class neighborhoods from perceived transgressors. The social-athletic clubs of the BRIDGEPORT area produced several Chicago MAYORS, including Richard J. Daley. By the 1920s, more than 1,300 of these clubs operated in the city alone.

Progressive reformers tried to channel youth club activities into organized and supervised programs in the SETTLEMENT HOUSES and PARK DISTRICTS with limited success. Sports proved attractive to immigrants and working-class youth, and PLAYGROUND directors offered numerous tournaments and city championships, as well as physical FITNESS tests, for both boys and girls. Corporate interests hoping to inculcate competition, cooperation, and discipline as work values readily sponsored such activities. Thousands participated in the sports, crafts, and dances offered by civic authorities aimed at assimilation. Settlements, such as HULL HOUSE and the Chicago HEBREW INSTITUTE, had particular success in their efforts to AMERICANIZE immigrant youth. The YMCA and churches sponsored clubs and

Ethnic organizations often sponsored a wide range of clubs and activities for children and young adults. In this portrait, ca. 1915, the Chicago Hebrew Institute celebrated its sports programs and young athletes. Photographer: Taylor & Lytle. Source: Chicago Historical Society.

athletic teams for the growing AFRICAN AMERICAN community on the South Side after World War I, and the Catholic Youth Organization addressed similar concerns among its constituents by the 1930s.

Many youth clubs spurned such direction, however, and opted for autonomy. By the 1930s smaller groups, known as basement clubs, operated from such neighborhood locations. Sandlot athletic teams known as prairie leaguers competed on the diminishing open spaces or the city's vacant lots. Some others, particularly those with political protection, managed to take over the neighborhood parks and playgrounds and use them as headquarters for their sport, social, and gambling activities.

Other clubs fostered ethnic pride and adherence to European cultures. GERMAN Turner societies, CZECH Sokols, and POLISH falcon clubs were all established in Chicago during the nineteenth century to maintain the language and customs of their homeland. By the 1920s, however, the interest of youths in sports forced many to adopt English and sponsor teams in American sports as well as gymnastics and SOCCER in order to attract and retain members.

By the mid-twentieth century, ethnic youth had largely assimilated into the American mainstream. Few ethnic clubs remained, although new ones appeared by the latter twentieth century along with a resurgent interest in soccer. Boys' clubs, YMCAs, and church groups still try to attract city youth; but GANGS have foregone sporting ventures in favor of more lucrative activities. The few remaining ethnic clubs and many sports clubs have moved to the suburbs, where they maintain headquarters and promote rapidly growing youth sports organizations.

Gerald R. Gems

See also: Creation of Chicago Sports; Political Culture; Prohibition and Temperance; Sports, Industrial League; Turnvereins

Further reading: Gems, Gerald R. *Windy City Wars: Labor, Leisure, and Sport in the Making of Chicago.* 1997. • Halsey, Elizabeth. *The Development of Public Recreation in Metropolitan Chicago.* 1940. • Thrasher, Frederic M. *The Gang.* 1927.

Coal City, IL, Grundy County, 53 miles SW of the Loop. Coal City, incorporated in 1881, is situated among the vast COAL reserves that lie just south of Chicago. Peter Lansett, a CANADIAN, has been credited with the 1820 discovery of coal in the area. It was only later in the nineteenth century, however, that the mines around the village made Coal City a major contributor of coal to Chicago. By the twentieth century, the manufacturing of wallpaper, CHEMICALS, concrete, and CLOTHING began to complement the village's mining industry.

On February 16, 1883, one of Illinois' worst mine disasters stunned the citizens of Coal City and nearby BRAIDWOOD. That morning, a worker at the DIAMOND mine (which lies a short distance from the Coal City limits) noticed an unusual amount of water flowing to the bottom of the mine shaft. The alert miner raised the alarm, but within minutes the mine was flooded, trapping and killing at least 69 men. Defects in the mine's construction made it impossible for the trapped miners to move to the surface using the mine's escapement shaft.

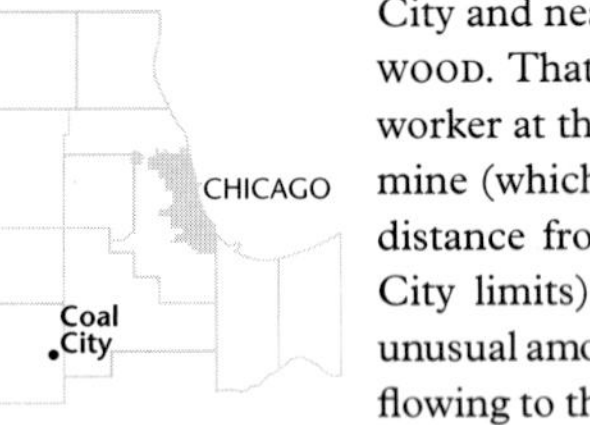

The Diamond mine disaster moved state legislators to overhaul an 1871 law that allowed

individual counties to appoint their own mine inspectors. Realizing that counties often did not take the examination of mines seriously, the Illinois General Assembly passed legislation in 1883 that eventually led to the appointment of five state inspectors of mines.

Coal City's importance as a coal mining center has declined over the twentieth century. By 1969, only one strip mine north of the village was still in operation. Construction of Interstate 55 and at least two Commonwealth Edison nuclear power plants nearby has encouraged growth in postwar Coal City. The village had a population of 4,797 in 2000. Much of the landscape around Coal City's mines has been reforested and serves as an outdoor recreation area.

Brandon Johnson

See also: Economic Geography; Expressways; Land Use; Occupational Safety and Health

Further reading: *A Compilation of the Reports of the Mining Industry of Illinois from the Earliest Records to the Close of the Year 1930.* 1931.

Coal Mining. Like farming, mining is one Illinois economic activity carried out to a much greater extent outside the Chicago metropolitan area than inside it. Only the northeastern fringes of the state's vast deposits of bituminous coal were located near Chicago. But these WILL COUNTY deposits were the object of considerable mining activity for nearly a century.

Mining activity was centered at a town named for James BRAIDWOOD, a SCOTTISH emigrant who sunk the first shaft for the Chicago & Wilmington Coal Company (C&W). Located about 60 miles from downtown Chicago, not far from the tracks of the Chicago, Alton & St. Louis RAILROAD, these mines were well-suited to supply a portion of the big city's growing demand for fuel. Five years after mining began in 1865, workers at the Braidwood mines produced a one-year output of roughly 230,000 tons of coal, most of which was consumed in Chicago. By this time, the town was dominated by Chicago-based C&W, which employed nearly a thousand men to take coal out of the shallow deposits. Many of these early miners were veterans of the industry who emigrated from Scotland and England during the 1860s.

Through the 1880s, when coal production at the Braidwood mines was at its height, conflict between C&W and its employees was severe enough to attract national attention. From the earliest years of coal mining in northern Illinois, Scottish emigrants such as John James and Daniel McLaughlin built associations among the miners. By the 1870s, many of these workers were members of a group called the Miners' Benevolent and Protective Association of the Northwest. A brief STRIKE in 1868 was followed by a more severe conflict in 1874, during a nationwide economic downturn when about a quarter of the Braidwood miners were out of work. C&W responded by hiring replacement workers and a private security force from the PINKERTON National Detective Agency of Chicago. But the miners managed to attract a great deal of support from Braidwood residents and the general public, and the conflict ended when the workers agreed to accept a wage cut that was smaller than the one originally proposed. During a similar strike in 1877, the replacement workers and Pinkertons were backed by Illinois troops called out by Governor Cullom, and the miners lost. They lost again in similar disputes in 1889 and 1894.

Coal production in Will County began to decline after the 1880s, as miners exhausted the most easily reached portions of the shallow local deposits. Output appears to have peaked around 1882, when two thousand miners raised 650,000 tons from the Braidwood shafts. Mining activity declined steadily over the next few years. The local industry was hit by a deadly disaster in February 1883, when rain and melted snow flooded a DIAMOND Coal Company mine. The sudden rush of water killed 61 men and boys. Over the next few years, the local mines became less productive and accounted for a smaller and smaller piece of Illinois' large coal industry. By 1892, Will County mines produced only 114,000 tons, less than a fifth of what they had a decade before and under 1 percent of the state's total output in that year. Increasingly, Bohemians, ITALIANS, and other Europeans came to work the mines.

Coal mining in the Braidwood during the twentieth century never approached the peaks it had reached in the 1870s and 1880s, but there was a small revival starting in the 1920s made possible by strip-mining. In the late 1920s, the Northern Illinois Coal Company (NIC) began to employ power shovels and earth-moving equipment to unearth coal by displacing huge volumes of soil and rock. Over the next 25 years, Will County strip-mining operations produced nearly 30 million tons of coal, making it one of the leading strip-mining areas in Illinois. In 1940, NIC employed over four hundred men, and another company, the WILMINGTON Coal Mining Corporation had a smaller strip-mining operation in Braidwood. Like the traditional mines that had been so important to the area in the nineteenth century, however, these strip mines were active for only a generation. By the 1960s, the last coal mining operations in the Chicago region were closed.

Mark R. Wilson

See also: Air Quality; Antiunionism; Czechs and Bohemians; Gas and Electricity; Illinois National Guard; Iron and Steel; Occupational Safety and Health; Quarrying, Stonecutting, and Brickmaking; Unionization

Further reading: Gutman, Herbert G. "The Braidwood Lockout of 1874." *Journal of the Illinois State Historical Society* 53.1 (1960): 5–28. • Illinois Department of Mines and Minerals. *A Compilation of the Reports of the Mining Industry of Illinois from the Earliest Records to the Close of the Year 1930.* 1931. • U.S. Department of the Interior, Census Office. *Report on the Mining Industries of the United States.* 1886.

Coffeehouses. Throughout the first half of the twentieth century, coffeehouses played a major role in developing and sustaining Chicago's many ethnic neighborhoods. The café had traditionally played a major role in European community life, serving as a community center, library, and meeting place for influential politicians, journalists, intellectuals, and businessmen. European immigrants brought this tradition with them to Chicago in the early twentieth century. Each of Chicago's ethnic communities at some time defined themselves by the food, music, and activities sponsored at the neighborhood coffeehouse.

The Knickerbocker Coffee Shop at 163 East Walton was a center of the GERMAN community. Opened in 1918, Glaser's Café at 3551 West 26th Street was a crossroads of the CZECHOSLOVAKIAN community. In addition to coffee, a visitor to Glaser's could find Bohemian cuisine, musicians, newspapermen, and politicians, including future mayor Anton Cermak. Amato's Café at 914 S. Halsted Street was a prime meeting spot in LITTLE ITALY. Open all night, Amato's was especially popular with OPERA singers and ITALIAN American politicians. The Idraft SWEDISH Cooperative Café at 3204 Wilton Avenue was a SWEDISH Community Center and an informal library, public bakery, LECTURE hall, and card room for Chicago's Swedish families. The influx of AFRICAN AMERICANS from the South brought a developing JAZZ culture to Chicago from New Orleans that first surfaced in SOUTH SIDE cafés. The jazz scene began among a row of cafés on State Street between 31st and 35th Streets known as "the STROLL." The Royal Gardens Café (renamed Lincoln Gardens in 1920) at 31st and Cottage Grove first showcased for white audiences New Orleans legends including King Oliver and Jelly Roll Morton. The Pekin Inn at 27th and State was a favorite among the gangsters of the roaring twenties.

A Chicago coffee shop, 1941. Photographer: John Vachon. Source: Library of Congress.

The European tradition of conducting politics in the coffeehouse blended with Chicago's jazz culture to produce a new tradition: the beatnik coffeehouse. Medici in HYDE PARK was founded in 1958, providing important meeting places for law students, CIVIL RIGHTS workers, and JOURNALISTS. Also founded in 1958, No Exit in ROGERS PARK provided a forum for FOLK MUSICIANS and beat POETS.

Since the late 1980s, chain coffee stores such as Starbucks as well as "cybercafés" such as the Interactive Bean have become central to the Chicago region's coffee-drinking habits.

Eli Rubin

See also: Dance Halls; Leisure; Places of Assembly; Restaurants

Further reading: "From the Editor." *Chicago History* (Spring 1996): 3. • "This Coffee Has Been Percolating for Centuries." *Chicago Tribune,* April 26, 1996. • Drury, John. *Dining in Chicago.* 1931.

Cold War and Anti-Communism. From the late 1940s through the 1950s, as the governments of the United States and the Soviet Union confronted each other in a Cold War, anti-Communism dominated American domestic politics. In Chicago, as elsewhere, conservative politicians and pressure groups as well as city NEWSPAPERS sought to expose Communist subversion and discredit liberal causes.

The tone of postwar anti-Communist activity in Chicago was set by the Illinois legislature. In August 1947 the legislature created the Seditious Activities Investigation Commission, otherwise known as the Broyles Commission, after its chairman, REPUBLICAN senator Paul Broyles, to probe Communist influence in the state. The commission identified the education system as the most vulnerable to Communist penetration. In 1949 the commission held hearings to investigate the political activities of professors at the UNIVERSITY OF CHICAGO, but, with the faculty publicly defended by university chancellor Robert Hutchins, the hearings accomplished little.

Taking their cue from the Broyles Commission, Chicago anti-Communists singled out the public SCHOOLS for attack. Throughout the 1950s the *Chicago Tribune* condemned Communist teaching and campaigned, often successfully, for the removal of liberal texts from the schools. In October 1950, Chicago Board of Education president William B. Traynor established a committee to study ways to promote patriotism and combat Communism in the schools. In 1955, the school Board of Examiners asked candidates for teaching jobs to declare their membership in "subversive" organizations and denied certification to some individuals on political grounds.

Anti-Communists also sought the introduction of loyalty oaths for public sector workers. In the early 1950s, Paul Broyles, backed by the American Legion, sponsored a series of bills which sought to outlaw the COMMUNIST PARTY and to require loyalty oaths for public sector workers. DEMOCRATIC governor Adlai Stevenson vetoed the bills, but in July 1955 the new Republican governor William Stratton signed a bill which forced public workers to take a loyalty oath. Three Chicago public school teachers refused to sign the pledge. The AMERICAN CIVIL LIBERTIES UNION filed a suit in the name of one, Shirley Lens, claiming the oath was unconstitutional, but in 1956 the Illinois Supreme Court upheld a circuit court decision to dismiss the suit.

Throughout the 1950s many individuals and organizations in Chicago suffered from accusations of Communist sympathies. Investigated by the House Un-American Activities Committee, many left-leaning unions such as the United Public Workers; United Electrical, Radio and Machine Workers; and the United Packinghouse Workers of America found it difficult to prosper in the city. The Chicago POLICE Department's "RED SQUAD" prepared thousands of files on allegedly subversive organizations and individuals and hampered their activities. With its members blacklisted by the late 1950s, the Chicago Communist Party, never larger than a couple of thousand, had dwindled to a dedicated few. After it was apparent that Communism posed little threat to American society, anti-Communism subsided. However, the Red Squad continued activities until 1975, the loyalty oath stayed on the statute books until 1983, and the Cold War dragged on until the fall of the Soviet Union in 1991.

John F. Lyons

See also: Chicago Conspiracy Trial; Free Speech

Further reading: Harsha, E. Houston. "Illinois, the Broyles Commission." In *The States and Subversion,* ed. Walter Gellhorn, 1952, 54–139. • Selcraig, James Truett. *The Red Scare in the Midwest, 1945–1955: A State and Local Study.* 1982.

Collar Counties. "Collar counties" is a term applied to the five counties that surround the centrally located Cook County in the Chicago metropolitan area: DuPage County, Kane County, Lake County, McHenry County, and Will County. There is no documentation of the origin of the term, but it probably came into use in the 1960s or 1970s. It is widely used in urban planning and public policy circles and in the media. As metropolitan growth begins to extend into counties outside the ring established by collar counties, the term may begin to lose some of its meaning and utility as a descriptor of the metropolitan region.

Richard D. Mariner

See also: Metropolitan Growth; Suburbs and Cities as Dual Metropolis

College All-Star Football Game. Initiated in 1934 by Arch Ward of the *Chicago Tribune,* the College All-Star Game FOOTBALL series was played annually in Chicago through 1976. Soon achieving status as the official opening of each football season, the game placed Chicago in the national sporting limelight each year as hundreds of NEWSPAPER writers from around the country attended.

Matching a team of graduated All-American players from the previous season against the defending National Football League professional champion, the games were all played at SOLDIER FIELD—except for two games held at NORTHWESTERN. During its lifetime the series raised approximately $4 million for various Chicago-area charities.

Raymond Schmidt

See also: Creation of Chicago Sports; Leisure; Philanthropy

Further reading: Littlewood, Thomas B. *Arch: A Promoter, Not a Poet.* 1990. • Schmidt, Raymond. *Football's Stars of Summer: A History of the College All-Star Football Game Series of 1934–1976.* 2001.

Colleges, Junior and Community. The public junior college movement was born in the Chicago area due to the leadership of William Rainey Harper and J. Stanley Brown. Harper, the first president of the UNIVERSITY OF CHICAGO, distinguished between the general education of the first two years of college life and the specialized focus of the last two years. This distinction generated the term "junior college."

Harper believed that junior college–level work could also be done at "cooperating" high schools in a fifth and sixth year. By 1899, Brown, superintendent of the Joliet Schools, had developed a six-year school at JOLIET Township High School. Thus evolved Joliet Junior College in 1901, the nation's oldest continuous public community college. With Harper's successors at Chicago uninterested in the junior colleges, their guidance passed to the University of Illinois.

Although born in Illinois, the junior college movement took root and flourished in California, while in Illinois lack of leadership, an excessively localized school system, and fiscal conservatism slowed the development of a public junior college system. Chicago founded its system in 1911, with Crane Technical High School (later Crane Junior College), which by 1931 had become the nation's largest junior college. In 1924 Morton Junior College was established in CICERO and LaSalle-Peru-Oglesby Junior College (now Illinois Valley Community College) in LaSalle. Thornton Junior College in HARVEY (1927, now South Suburban College) followed, along with Lyons Township Junior College (1929, annexed to College of DuPage in 1967). As extensions of high schools these colleges operated under questionable legal authority. Legislation legitimated Chicago's Crane in 1931, and the suburban colleges six years later. Junior colleges outside of Chicago were all based on township or community districts, and until 1940 all were located in northern Illinois.

Crane Junior College closed in 1933, a victim of the GREAT DEPRESSION. In 1934 the federal government provided Chicago with free junior college courses under the Civil Works Educational Service. That year, Chicago reopened its junior college with three branches enrolling nearly 3,800 students. Proviso Township started a junior college at MAYWOOD in 1935 which closed after a year. Maine Township Junior College opened at DES PLAINES in 1939, but closed in 1942.

The public junior college had developed as the first two years of a traditional liberal arts college, funded as part of the common schools. After WORLD WAR II the name "community college" began to replace "junior college" and vocational, technical, and adult education were added to its function. Returning veterans, funded by the GI Bill, increased the demand for college education. EVANSTON Community College opened in 1946 and closed in 1952. ELGIN opened as an extension of the University of Illinois in 1946 and became Elgin Community College in 1949. In 1957 Bloom Community College (now Prairie State College) opened in CHICAGO HEIGHTS.

In 1955 the General Assembly initiated state support for community colleges, which was increased in 1957 and 1959. Legislators added a bill in 1959 encouraging the building of independent colleges with separate boards and taxing authorities. Thus, Triton Community College in RIVER GROVE was organized in 1964, and William Rainey Harper College at PALATINE, in 1965.

The greatest stimulus for the development of public community colleges was the Illinois Junior College Act of 1965, which included community colleges within higher education, rather than as part of the common schools. It provided financial encouragement for the establishment of new community colleges and the separation of the older colleges from high schools. Metropolitan Chicago responded by establishing Waubonsee Community College at SUGAR GROVE (1966), Kankakee Community College (1966), College of DuPage at GLEN ELLYN (1967), Moraine Valley Community College at PALOS HILLS (1967), McHenry County College (1967), College of Lake County at GRAYSLAKE (1967), and Oakton Community College (1969). Community colleges grew rapidly in the following decades. The Chicago City College evolved into a multicampus operation with a TV College. The College of DuPage became the largest single institution of higher education in the state.

Along with growth came conflict. The Cook County College Teachers Union, American Federation of Teachers, Local 1600, founded in 1965, went on to organize most of the Chicago-area community colleges. Since then, Chicago faculty have conducted STRIKES at various campuses.

Dave Bartlett

See also: Schooling for Work; Special Districts

Further reading: Hardin, Thomas L. "A History of the Community Junior College in Illinois: 1901–1972." Ph.D. diss., University of Illinois. 1975. • Meisterheim, Matthew. "A History of the Public Junior College in Illinois, 1900–1965." Ed.D. diss., Northern Illinois University. 1973. • Smith, Gerald W. *Illinois Junior-Community College Development: 1946–1980.* 1980.

Colombians. By the late 1990s Colombian immigrants constituted Chicago's largest group of South Americans and had established an active community in the city. Colombians began arriving in Chicago around 1950; in 1970 the U.S. census counted approximately 3,500 Colombians in Chicago; by 2000, approximately 11,000. Pointing to the Census Bureau's regular undercounting of Latin American immigrants, however, community leaders and consular officials contend that the correct number might be several times larger.

Chicago's early Colombian colony was drawn from the professional classes of the nation's Caribbean coast, many of whom emigrated in the 1950s during a period of extremely bitter civil warfare known as La Violencia (1948 to 1957). The influx into Chicago of skilled *costeños,* or coastal Colombians, increased in the 1960s and 1970s, when a slowing national economy, combined with the inability of the coastal region to generate jobs for the graduates of its growing university system, persuaded many *costeños* to follow friends and family to Chicago. In the 1980s and 1990s, Colombia's continued urbanization and falling transportation costs fostered far greater regional and class diversity among emigrants. As a result, Chicago Colombians' traditional concentration in professional and technical work broadened to include increasing numbers of blue-collar and unskilled workers in the city's light industrial and service sectors.

Chicago's Colombians have been atypical of the city's immigrants and of Colombian Americans elsewhere in their pattern of settlement. Rather than form neighborhood enclaves, they have tended toward a dispersed residential pattern. While they initially settled in apartments on the North Side, where many of the city's PUERTO RICANS also lived, as soon as their earnings allowed, most Colombians moved to private homes in such northern suburbs as SKOKIE, EVANSTON, and ARLINGTON HEIGHTS. More recent arrivals have followed a similar residential path, albeit with a slightly greater proportion inside the city. Colombian businesses have also been quite dispersed, though a small concentration has formed along Lincoln Avenue. For many years Colombian immigrants socialized almost exclusively among themselves and with CUBANS. In recent years, however, there has been a noticeable shift toward sociability and intermarriage within a Chicago Latino community less segmented by nationality.

Numerous social and professional associations, rather than residential concentration, have provided the basis for Colombian community in Chicago. Within a few years of arrival, immigrants established the Club de El Dorado and Club Colombia, which organized monthly dinners and other social events. CartaMed (Cartagena Medical Alumni Association) originated in the 1960s as a society of physicians trained at the University of Cartagena. It was soon expanded to include other professional occupations, and eventually came to function as a MUTUAL-BENEFIT and community fund-raising organization which also provided aid to Colombian newcomers to Chicago. The Colombian consulate has also served as the nucleus of a community in which many people have maintained Colombian citizenship and closely followed political affairs in the homeland. Among the most enduring of many Chicago Colombian organizations is Colombianos Unidos Para Una Labor Activa, whose July 20 celebration of Colombian independence drew many thousands of participants each year in the late 1990s.

A. K. Sandoval-Strausz

See also: Demography; Multicentered Chicago

Further reading: Baldassini, José G. "Acculturation Process of Colombian Immigrants into the American Culture in Bergen County, N.J." Ph.D. diss., Rutgers University. 1980. • Cruz, Ines, and Castaño, Juanita. "Colombian Migration to the United States." In *The Dynamics of Migration: International Migration.* 1976. • Walton, Priscilla Ann. *Having It Both Ways: The Migration Experience of Colombian Professionals and Their Families in Chicago.* 1974.

Columbia College. Established in 1890 by Mary Blood and Ida M. Riley as a women's speech college, Columbia began training radio broadcasters, writers, and technicians in the 1930s and later expanded into television.

By the 1960s Columbia was well known but small and financially precarious. In 1963 Mirron "Mike" Alexandroff became president, envisioning Columbia as a school of arts and communications in a liberal arts context. Reaffirming its earlier emphasis on hands-on education by people working in the arts, Columbia adopted an experimental, antibureaucratic approach to learning. The college embraced open enrollment, holding classes throughout Chicago to connect learning with the city's communities. A sense of excitement pervaded the college, which grew to include an innovative and award-winning FICTION-writing program and a highly regarded FILM- and video-making program.

Accredited in 1974, Columbia established a graduate division in 1981. Institutional growth diminished some of the earlier sense of excitement, as the college grew to over 9,000 students by the end of the century. In 1998, Columbia's part-time instructors, who taught over two-thirds of its classes, voted for union representation.

The college moved to 600 South Michigan Avenue in 1976 and by 2001 included 13 buildings in the South Loop. Tuition in 2001 remained among the lowest for Illinois private colleges.

Christopher Thale

See also: Broadcasting; Unionization; Universities and Their Cities

Further reading: Kundrat, Theodore V. "Columbia College in Retrospect." A series in Columbia College Alumni News, 1986–1987. • Silverstein, Louis, ed. *An Oral History of Columbia College*. 3 vols. 2000.

Columbian Exposition. *See* World's Columbian Exposition

Comiskey Park. Comiskey Park (renamed U.S. Cellular Field in 2003) is home to American League Baseball's Chicago White Sox. The original Comiskey Park, built in 1910 at 35th Street and Shields Avenue, was dubbed the "baseball palace of the world" for its modern steel and concrete construction. When it was torn down after the 1990 season to make room for a new stadium across 35th Street, Comiskey Park was the oldest professional baseball park in operation.

In 1908, Charles A. Comiskey, first owner of the White Sox, purchased 15 acres between 34th and 35th and Wentworth and Shields in an area housing working-class ethnic whites. Architect Zachary Taylor Davis, a graduate of nearby Armour Institute (Illinois Institute of Technology), integrated Comiskey Park into its surroundings by creating a stadium with sloping Romanesque archways and red pressed brick reflective of the neighborhood ethnic churches. Inside, the dimensions were 362 feet down the right and left field lines and 440 feet to deep center field—a pitchers' park, as Comiskey wanted.

On July 1, 1910, the White Sox played their first game in the fireproof park, made entirely of steel and concrete, which seated 32,000, including 7,000 in twenty-five-cent bleachers. A trolley from downtown brought businessmen to late-afternoon games after work. Fans from nearby South Side communities attended on Sundays. Night baseball, initiated August 14, 1939, allowed working-class fans even greater access. Growing numbers of African Americans attended Comiskey as well. From 1933 to 1950, Comiskey Park hosted the Negro League East-West All-Star Game. On July 5, 1947, Larry Doby of the Cleveland Indians became the first African American to play in the American League, debuting during a doubleheader at Comiskey.

Comiskey Park also hosted other events. On July 6, 1933, Comiskey hosted the first Major League All-Star game. On June 22, 1937, Joe Louis defeated James Braddock at Comiskey to become heavyweight boxing champion of the world. The Chicago Cardinals of the National Football League played there from 1922 to 1925 and from 1929 to 1959. Comiskey also hosted church festivals, musical extravaganzas, picnics, and auto polo events.

In 1926–27, Comiskey added grandstands at field level and second base to bring the seating capacity to 52,000. Owner Bill Veeck, Jr. (1959–1961; 1975–1981), added an exploding scoreboard in 1960 which featured pinwheels and fireworks after Sox home runs. He also installed group picnic areas at center field and showers in the bleachers.

When Jerry Reinsdorf and Eddie Einhorn bought the team in 1981, they began pushing for a new Comiskey Park. After threats to move the team to suburban Addison, the owners and Mayor Harold Washington successfully lobbied the state legislature for permission to build a new stadium in Chicago. The problem of displacing residents and politics stalled construction until 1989, when ground was finally broken for the new Comiskey, built with a seating capacity of 44,702 and without the obstructed-view seats of the old park. On September 30, 1990, the White Sox played their last game at old Comiskey. They played their first game at the new Comiskey Park on April 18, 1991.

Robin F. Bachin

See also: Armour Square; Creation of Chicago Sports; Cubs; Leisure; Places of Assembly; Wrigley Field

Further reading: Benson, Michael. *Ballparks of North America: A Comprehensive Historical Reference to Baseball Grounds, Yards, and Stadiums, 1845 to Present*. 1989. • Bukowski, Douglas. *Baseball Palace of the World: The Last Year of Comiskey Park*. 1992. • Riess, Steven A. *Touching Base: Professional Baseball and American Culture in the Progressive Era*. 1980.

Comiskey Park, 1910. Photographer: Barnes-Crosby. Source: Chicago Historical Society.

Commercial Buildings. Chicago was founded for and by commerce. Perhaps its first building, Jean Baptiste Point DuSable's trading post at the mouth of the Chicago River, was a commercial structure. When the city shed its frontier identity in the 1830s, all of its buildings were rough-and-ready frame structures offering only roofs, walls, windows, and enough space on the facade for a sign.

Chicago's first commercial district was Lake Street, near its bustling commercial riverfront. First floors held retail and wholesale outlets, while upper floors were used for inventory, or even public assembly. The organization of the first Jewish minyan in Chicago in 1845 took place above a store at Lake and Wells Streets. Similarly, early Episcopal services in the 1830s were often held in John Kinzie's Tippecanoe Hall at State and Kinzie Streets. By the 1850s commercial buildings lined Lake Street from Wabash to Wells, many in the popular Italianate style with flat-topped rooflines ornamented with overhanging cornices supported by brackets. The city's first architect, John Mills Van Osdel, designed a cast-iron facade—well suited to the more elaborate versions of the Italianate style—for a Lake Street edifice in 1856.

By 1870 the demand for commercial space exceeded the boundaries of a single downtown street. Potter Palmer bought property on State Street, and with the help of the Field & Leiter store and his own luxury HOTEL, shifted commercial interests away from Lake Street. The Page Brothers Building (1872) exemplifies the shift with its cast-iron facade on Lake Street supplemented by a brick facade added on State Street. The Great Fire of 1871 stimulated commercial architecture, clearing the downtown of homes and stables. The entire LOOP was rebuilt with four-to-five story Italianate buildings that had retail stores below and offices above. State Street hosted ever larger DEPARTMENT STORES, from the six-story, quarter-block Field & Leiter store of 1873 to William Le Baron Jenney's eight-story, half-block Second Leiter Building of 1891. The even more significant WHOLESALE business of these merchants led to the creation of the epochal Marshall Field Wholesale Store, design by H. H. Richardson in 1885 at Adams and Franklin Streets. By 1914 Marshall Field & Co.'s store by D. H. Burnham & Co. filled a full block, joined by block-long retail behemoths like Carson Pirie Scott & Co. (Louis Sullivan, 1899, 1906), the Fair Store (Jenney, 1891), and A. M. Rothschild & Co. (Holabird & Roche, 1912).

Offices climbed the streets to the west, with Burnham & Root's Montauk Block of 1881–82 rising to an unprecedented eight stories, to be dwarfed by Jenney's pioneering skeleton-frame Home Insurance Building in 1884–85. The Chicago School architects who transformed Jenney's apogee into artistry helped invent mixed-use buildings, from the hotel-office-theater complex of the great AUDITORIUM BUILDING (1889, Adler & Sullivan) and the office-theater Schiller Building (1891, Adler & Sullivan) to the many music stores and factories with recital halls that lined Wabash Avenue, and the bank-office combinations of LaSalle Street. The skeletal frame allowed for larger shop windows, and the modern glass-front store was born.

On LaSalle Street, home to exchanges like the venerable Chicago Board of Trade, captains of finance lavished decorations on opulent banking lobbies, notably Continental Bank's famed second-story classical space with massive murals by BURNHAM PLAN illustrator Jules Guerin, completed in 1924. The orange stone facade of the Northern Trust Company Building (1905, Frost & Granger) evokes the scale of the street before it became a canyon of towers in the 1920s.

Mingling with downtown palaces, banks, and hotels were cheap amusements housed in cheap buildings with massive marquees blotting out any architecture that might exist below. Over time they grew into nickelodeons showing one-reel films supplemented by stage acts, and eventually, in the 1910s and 1920s, into lavish vaudeville MOVIE PALACES, where the entertainment began on the building facade and continued into auditoriums that evoked ancient Rome, imperial France, Mongol China, Persia, Byzantium, Renaissance Florence, and medieval Spain—sometimes all at the same time. Downtown landmarks like the Chicago Theatre (1921, Rapp & Rapp), McVicker's, the Oriental, the State-Lake, the Woods, and the United Artists were matched by neighborhood wonders like the Marbro, the Tivoli, the Uptown, the Central Park, the Avalon, and the Regal.

The spread of movie palaces in the automobile age presaged the spread of commercial buildings from the Loop to the neighborhoods and suburbs. By 1930, Marshall Field & Co. had created smaller versions of its downtown store in EVANSTON and OAK PARK, while neighborhood retailers like Goldblatt's and Wieboldt's were moving downtown. Chicago developed regional SHOPPING DISTRICTS at 47th and Ashland, 63rd and Halsted, Irving Park and Pulaski, and many other locations. Certain areas catered to specialized industries, such as "Automobile Row" on South Michigan Avenue, or the MAXWELL STREET Market, an open-air European-style market that resisted every effort at modernization until its destruction in the 1990s.

In 1916 the Chicago area gave birth to one of the first auto-oriented shopping centers in the nation with the construction of Howard Van Doren Shaw's Market Square in LAKE FOREST, and the region later helped pioneer the modern postwar shopping center when PARK FOREST Plaza opened in 1949. Ten major shopping centers, surrounded by PARKING, were built between 1952 and 1969, followed by another 13 in the 1970s. The spread of regional shopping malls and the construction of interstate EXPRESSWAYS led to the decline of downtown retail, although North Michigan Avenue blossomed in the 1990s as a luxury and tourist destination with its postmodern high-rise malls and specialty shops.

Vincent L. Michael

See also: Architecture; Built Environment of the Chicago Region; Economic Geography; Magnificent Mile; Retail Geography

Further reading: Harris, Neil. "Shopping—Chicago Style." In *Chicago Architecture 1872–1922.* ed. John Zukowsky, 1987. • Schulze, Franz, and Harrington, Kevin. *Chicago's Famous Buildings,* 4th ed. 1993. • Sinkevitch, Alice, ed. *AIA Guide to Chicago.* 1993.

Commercial Club of Chicago. The Commercial Club of Chicago began when two predecessor clubs, the Commercial Club, organized in 1877, and the Merchants Club, organized in 1896, were united in 1907. An elite group of successful Chicago businessmen, the Commercial Club promoted the economic development of the city. The club's most active members—men like George Pullman, Marshall Field, Cyrus McCormick, George Armour, and Frederic Delano—were the same men who forged Chicago into a leading industrial and commercial center.

The Commercial Club patterned itself after traditional civic improvement clubs, holding regular meetings to discuss pertinent reform issues of the day. During the height of the Progressive era, the club took a particular interest in developing vocational training programs for youngsters entering the wage labor force. Toward that end it founded the Chicago Manual Training School and supported similar "practical education" projects, including the Illinois Training School Farm at Glenwood and the St. Charles School for Boys. The club also sponsored and translated studies of vocational education in Europe for an American audience.

The Commercial Club's most striking achievement was its support and publication of Daniel Burnham's *Plan of Chicago* (1909). BURNHAM'S PLAN was a masterpiece of city PLANNING, providing a blueprint for the future growth and development of the entire Chicago region. A longtime member of the club, Burnham was uniquely positioned to link the commercial prosperity of the city with emerging City Beautiful principles to make Chicago both a profitable and pleasurable place to live.

Beyond Burnham's plan, the Commercial Club addressed many other progressive reform issues during the 1920s and 1930s. Under the rubric of "civic beauty and social unity," club members supported street cleaning and paving projects, smoke abatement and sanitation schemes, and the development of city parks and PLAYGROUNDS. They also kept abreast of key social reform movements by regularly studying issues like juvenile delinquency, race relations, and old-age pensions. Throughout its history, the club remained actively interested in the lives of its membership, following closely some members' military service and sponsoring numerous trade-related trips to observe economic development in Cuba, Puerto Rico, and Panama. In the late 1990s, the club again sought to foster the development of an ambitious program of regional planning with the publication of its report *Chicago Metropolis 2020: Preparing Metropolitan Chicago for the 21st Century.*

Susan Marie Wirka

See also: Architecture: The City Beautiful; City Club of Chicago; Good Government Movements; Schooling for Work

Further reading: Burnham, Daniel H., and Edward H. Bennett. *Plan of Chicago.* 1909; repr. 1970. • Commercial Club of Chicago. Research collection. Chicago Historical Society. • Glessner, John J. *The Commercial Club of Chicago: Its Beginning and Something of Its Work.* 1910.

Commodities Markets. Chicago's ascendant commodity markets were the result of the city's strategic position within the nation's TRANSPORTATION network and its close

Interior, Chicago Board of Trade, ca. 1900. Photographer: Unknown. Source: Chicago Historical Society.

proximity to some of the most productive farmland in the world. The unprecedented production of corn, wheat, and hogs within Chicago's immediate environs plus the cattle and LUMBER shipped in from the upper Midwest and Canada filled the city's enormous mechanical grain elevators and vast stockyards. The immense volume of AGRICULTURAL produce forced the city's commercial community to use their ingenuity (and state law) to temporarily store then ship these goods to domestic and international markets.

The completion of the ILLINOIS & MICHIGAN CANAL in the fall of 1847 and its opening in the spring of 1848 inspired the formation of the Chicago Board of Trade, the city's first voluntary association of businessmen. The Board of Trade reorganized in 1850 to conform to a law governing boards of trade passed by the Illinois General Assembly in 1849.

The city's merchants adopted their procedures to handle grain in bulk, not in bags, as traditionally had been the case. The first small shipment of grain in bulk had occurred in 1839. Chicago's grain traders gained national recognition as a reliable and competitively priced source of grain during the 1850s.

The Board of Trade enhanced its role in the grain trade by implementing regulations for grading grain. The state legislature recognized its regulations by granting it a special charter in 1859. The special charter gave the board the power to impose rules and regulations for handling of grain and to arbitrate disputes between commodity merchants.

During the CIVIL WAR the Union quartermaster procured supplies with contracts that postponed delivery of commodities until they were needed and payment was secured. These contracts created a market in "seller's" or "buyer's" options for the future delivery of commodities. Delivery before a date was "optional" because of the risks of transporting commodities to Chicago. Speculative purchases and sales of commodities were also inspired by these options. Regulations governing them were published by the Board of Trade in October 1865. These crude seller's or buyer's options evolved into "futures" contracts by the end of the 1870s.

Merchants bought and sold grain for cash, storage, or for future delivery. Elevator operators stored grain until it could be shipped after navigation opened on the GREAT LAKES or by RAILROAD. Commission merchants received a fee for satisfying the demands of buyers and sellers of grain or provisions. Speculators bought and sold commodities when it was profitable.

The Illinois Constitution of 1870 placed railroads and elevators under the control of a Railroad and Warehouse Commission. The commission had the power to regulate rail and storage rates and to inspect public grain elevators. Ira Munn, an elevator operator in Chicago and a former president of the Board of Trade, challenged the legality of the commission in *Munn v. Illinois.* The case was appealed to the U.S. Supreme Court in 1876. In the

Updating the chalkboard at Board of Trade, 1948. Photographer: Gordon Coster. Source: Chicago Historical Society.

spring of 1877, the Supreme Court affirmed the commission's power as being in "the public interest."

The Board of Trade sued to prevent the unauthorized use of its quotations in *Board of Trade v. Christie Grain and Stock Company* (1905). Justice Oliver Wendell Holmes, Jr., wrote the brief for the majority affirming the board's ownership of its quotations and speculation as a means that an economy adjusts to changing conditions. By legitimating speculation, "hedging," or shifting risk to speculators by merchants, was recognized.

Chicago's grain market became the world's preeminent commodity market by the end of the nineteenth century. Although the Board of Trade was the predominant market in membership and in trading volume, Chicago was also the location of smaller but influential markets. The Chicago Open Board of Trade was organized in 1880 and has survived as the MidAmerica Commodity Exchange and is a subsidiary of the Chicago Board of Trade. A butter and egg exchange that traces its roots to the post–Civil War era was reorganized in 1919 as the Chicago Mercantile Exchange. The remnants of a local produce market are still visible at the intersection of Halsted and Randolph Streets.

During World War I, representatives of Chicago's commodity markets staffed the government agencies created to procure, handle, and distribute the nation's food supplies. The federal government established grades for wheat, corn, and oats while in control of the grain trade. The futures market was closed from September 1917 until May 1920.

After the armistice in November 1918, foreign governments were given access to the nation's grain supplies. Their activities disrupted the grain market and resulted in the federal regulation of commodity markets with the passage of the Grain Futures Act of 1922. The Federal Warehousing Act of 1931 extended federal oversight to grain elevators.

The viability of Chicago's commodity markets was challenged during the 1920s by the depression in farm prices, subsidized grain exports by foreign governments, and by competition for investors' capital from securities markets. The nation's farmers coped with the relentless decline in prices by seeking help from the federal government. The decade ended with the passage of the Agricultural Marketing Act of 1929, which created the Federal Farm Board and made the federal government a competitor in the private grain market.

Chicago's commodity markets entered the 1930s in a weakened condition. The Federal Farm Board began to intervene in the grain market and the markets for commodities began to shift to the south and west. The amount of grain received in the city declined in 1934 to a level unprecedented since the 1870s. Congressional suspicion that grain markets were responsible for the decade's low grain prices inspired a revision and enhancement of commodity market regulation, the Commodity Exchange Act of 1936.

The imposition of price controls and the appropriation of commodities by the federal government after the United States' entry into World War II in December 1941 postponed futures trading until the end of the war. But the federal government still retained a substantial and a continuing interest in the agricultural economy with the commencement of the Cold War.

As federal control over commodity prices and production began to recede in the 1960s, Chicago's exchanges began to diversify their trading out of agricultural commodity futures. The Board of Trade initiated trading in silver futures in 1969, and along with the Mercantile Exchange commenced trading in gold futures in 1974. The board opened the Chicago Board Options Exchange in 1973. A futures contract in government-insured mortgages began to trade on the board in 1975. The Mercantile Exchange began its futures market in financial instruments with contracts for foreign exchange in 1972, for Treasury bills in 1976, and for Standard & Poor's stock index futures in 1982. The Board of Trade's most successful contract, federal government bond futures, began trading in 1977. Innovations in Chicago and other commodity markets in futures contracts for financial instruments, metals, and other commodities led Congress to replace the obsolete Commodity Exchange Act of 1936 with the Commodity Futures Trading Act of 1974.

Chicago's commodity markets recast themselves as futures exchanges for financial instruments and other commodities by the end of the twentieth century. Their position in world markets might not be as dominant as it was at the end of the nineteenth century. At the beginning of the twenty-first, they must successfully challenge the competition to their floor-based, open-outcry trading system from foreign exchanges and from electronic trading.

Owen K. Gregory

See also: Business of Chicago; Economic Geography; Food Processing: Regional and National Market

Further reading: Andreas, Alfred Theodore. *History of Chicago.* 3 vols. 1884. Reprint, 1975. • Chicago Board of Trade. *Annual Report.* Various years, 1859–1940. • Taylor, Charles H., ed. *History of the Board of Trade of the City of Chicago.* 3 vols. 1917.

Communist Party. The American Communist Party was born in Chicago in 1919 and headquartered there until 1927, when its headquarters and newspaper, the *Daily Worker,* moved to New York. During the 1920s, Chicago's party members dealt with factionalism, reorganization, and police persecution. Before 1925, membership hovered around 2,400, organized into 36 neighborhood and union groups in the needle, metal, and building trades; printing; railroads; and food industries. Through party-organized workers' schools, foreign-language federations, fraternal organizations, and literary, youth, and theater groups, party influence extended beyond its membership. The party also fought racial discrimination in factories, and in October 1925 organized the American Negro Labor Congress to bring AFRICAN AMERICANS into the labor movement.

In the 1930s, the Communist Party in Chicago reached its largest audience through organizing the unemployed and protesting evictions and cuts in relief. BLACK BELT organizers recruited protesters at WASHINGTON PARK, while Communists in BACK OF THE YARDS built alliances with community activists like ROMAN CATHOLIC bishop Bernard Sheil and Saul Alinsky. When police killed two black workers protesting an eviction in 1931, Communists led an interracial funeral procession estimated at 60,000 by the party and 15,000 by the *Chicago Daily News.*

Chicago's party members also succeeded in organizing industrial unions in MEATPACKING and metals despite periodic police harassment. During the Popular Front of the late 1930s, Communism's popularity increased among ARTISTS, writers, and intellectuals. By the end of the decade, the party claimed approximately 3,000 members, exercised influence in cultural organizations, and published its own newspaper, the *MidWest Daily Record.*

The Nazi-Soviet pact of 1939 suspended antifascist alliances. After the war, the Taft-Hartley Act required unions to purge Communist leaders. In 1956 numbers and influence decreased further as Khrushchev denounced Stalin and the Soviet Union suppressed the Hungarian Revolution. After the 1989 disintegration of the Soviet Union, prominent party members split off and formed the Committees of Correspondence, which had its founding meeting in 1994 in Chicago. A small Chicago Communist Party remained at the close of the twentieth century.

Randi Storch

See also: Socialist Parties; Unionization

Further reading: Isserman, Maurice. *Which Side Were You On? The American Communist Party during the Second World War.* 1982. • Klehr, Harvey. *The Heyday of American Communism: The Depression Decade.* 1984. • Laswell, Harold Dwight, and Dorothy Blumenstock. *World Revolutionary Propaganda: A Chicago Study.* 1939.

Chicago's Community Areas

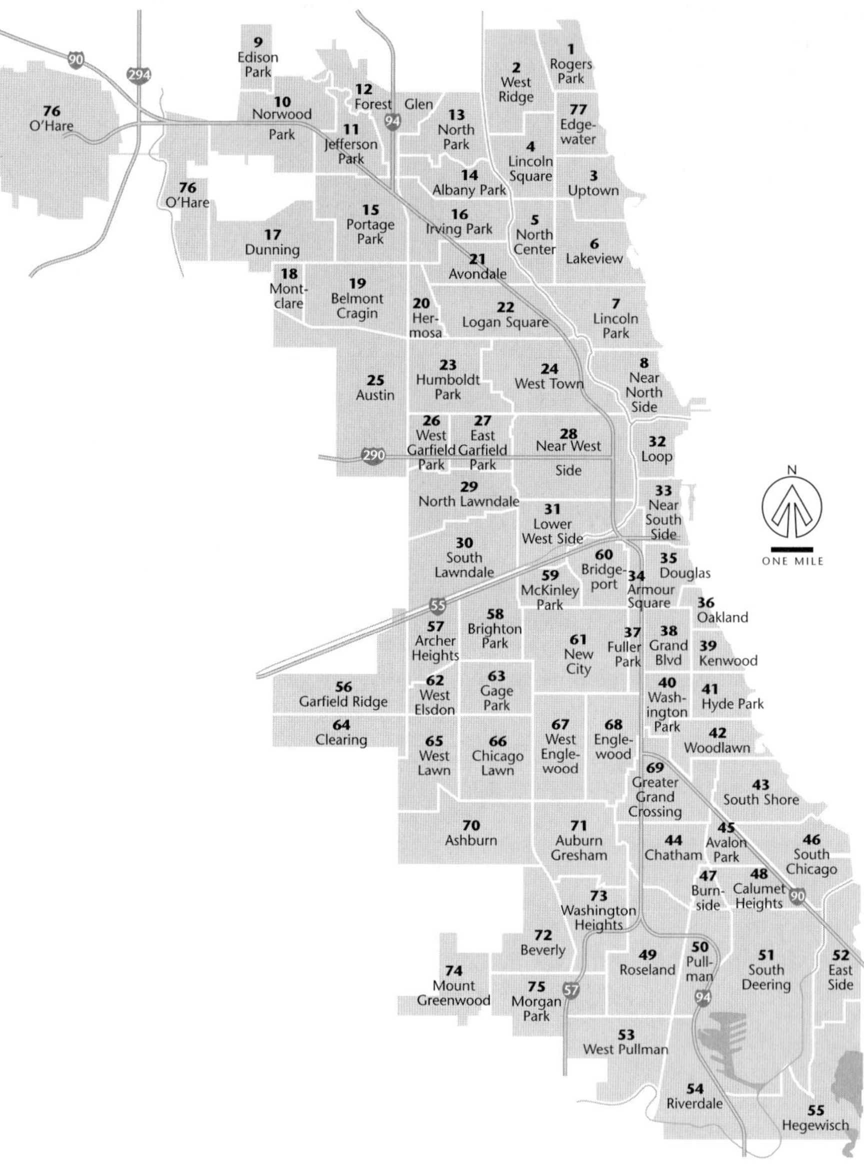

Established in the 1920s by University of Chicago sociologists conducting urban research, these zones represented moderately coherent social character across urban space at this generalized geographical scale. These so-called community areas have been widely used ever since as a convenient means of summarizing social and physical features of spatial units smaller than the city as a whole and have provided stable boundaries for the compilation of census data. From the beginning, however, they have only unevenly reflected the actual experience of community within each area, and over time many of them have become even less indicative of the perceptions of their residents, whose characteristics have shifted considerably because of migration. As ossified zones, they capture neither individual community identity nor the territorial reality of social groups. Their stable boundaries remain useful, however, as subdivisions of city space that facilitate the study of community change.

Community Areas. In the nineteenth century, the United States Bureau of the Census used the WARD SYSTEM to break down data within cities. This approach was unsuited for comparisons across time, because ward boundaries changed with each census cycle. The Federated Churches of New York pioneered the concept of the census tract in 1902; Chicago first used census tracts in 1910.

Members of the UNIVERSITY OF CHICAGO'S Local Community Research Committee wanted the information gathered by the Census Bureau to reflect real, not arbitrary, divisions within the city. Sociologist Robert Park argued that physical barriers such as rivers, parks, and railroads created "natural areas" within cities. These natural areas had distinctive histories and consistent rates of various social ills, regardless of who lived there. Chicago's Department of PUBLIC HEALTH also had an interest in reporting local variations in birth and death rates. The two institutions collaborated to produce a map with 75 community areas, into which 935 census tracts were distributed. The University of Chicago Press published editions of the 1920, 1930, and special 1934 census with information presented for each community area. The *Local Community Fact Book* series continued this tradition after each census except 1970.

With two exceptions, there have been only minor changes in the community area map. Because the original map was designed after the great wave of ANNEXATIONS at the end of the nineteenth century, O'HARE (CA 76) was the only addition to the city that needed a separate designation. In 1980, EDGEWATER wrested a symbolic secession from Uptown, and was recognized as a distinct entity (CA 77).

Despite the uses scholars and planners have found for the concept of community areas, they do not necessarily represent how Chicagoans think about their city. Scholars have challenged the validity of the idea of "natural areas" since its inception. Prominent neighborhoods such as PILSEN and BACK OF THE YARDS are subsumed into the less familiar LOWER WEST SIDE and NEW CITY. Many ROMAN CATHOLICS are as comfortable with the names of parishes as of community areas. And the virtue of the community areas, their stability, means that they cannot accommodate transformations in the geography of Chicago, such as the mid-twentieth-century EXPRESSWAYS that cut through once-coherent neighborhoods.

Amanda Seligman

See also: Armour Square; Chicago School of Sociology; Chicago Studied: Social Scientists and Their City; Metropolitan Growth; Multicentered Chicago; South Side

Further reading: Burgess, Ernest W., and Charles Newcomb, eds. *Census Data of the City of Chicago, 1920.* 1931. • Hunter, Albert. *Symbolic Communities: The Persistence and Change of Chicago's Local Communities.* 1974. • Smith, T. V., and Leonard D. White, eds. *Chicago: An Experiment in Social Science Research.* 1929.

Community Colleges.

See Colleges, Junior and Community

Community Organizing.

In late winter 1939, as Saul Alinsky and Joe Meegan crisscrossed the southwest-side Packingtown area, canvassing local priests and urging their parishioners to attend the inaugural meeting of the BACK OF THE YARDS NEIGHBORHOOD COUNCIL (BYNC), they were inventing the modern community organization. Alinsky had come to Packingtown representing the Chicago Area Project, a program sponsored by the Illinois Institute for Juvenile Research to combat juvenile delinquency through neighborhood improvement efforts. Meegan was a local park director. The organization they built, the BYNC, became the prototype of community organizations across the country. Structurally, the BYNC was a neighborhood congress, representing the various church parishes and other communal organizations in Packingtown. The BYNC's agenda was expansive: to attract resources to its neighborhood, thereby promoting social and economic uplift. Most tellingly, the BYNC was confrontational, using conflict with the packinghouse owners and city government as the lightning rod to draw resident commitment. Alinsky made a career of organizing, later developing campaigns in St. Paul, Minnesota, southern California, New York City, and upstate New York. His organizing team, the Industrial Areas Foundation, initiated other important organizing efforts in Chicago, notably the Organization for the Southwest Community in the late 1950s, and a few years later, the WOODLAWN ORGANIZATION.

In his latter years Alinsky assumed the role of elder statesman of organizing, sparking a new generation of organizers, who in some cases substantially reworked his tactical program. Chicago has remained a center of community organizing. During the 1970s, one of the nation's most important training centers for organizers, the Midwest Academy, was founded in Chicago. In the early years of that decade, an ambitious organizing effort known as the Citizens Action Program (CAP—originally the Campaign Against Pollution) forged a new model of Alinsky-style organizing. CAP sought to mobilize a citywide constituency by focusing on an array of public policy issues—including air pollution, expressway plans, and mortgage lending practices—and financed its operations through member dues. Though CAP collapsed in the mid-1970s, its agenda-setting, coalition-building, and fund-raising strategies were adopted by many subsequent organizing campaigns.

Since the 1970s Chicago has been the site of numerous organizing campaigns. Often groups have responded to neighborhood demographic or economic changes. Many contemporary organizing efforts have substituted a community development emphasis for Alinsky's more directly confrontational tactics, thus seeking to upgrade neighborhood conditions through indigenous efforts or by working with government or other institutions outside the neighborhood.

Larry Bennett

See also: Environmentalism; Meatpacking; Neighborhood Associations; New City; Packinghouse Unions; Politics

Further reading: Alinsky, Saul D. *Reveille for Radicals.* 1946. • Bennett, Larry. *Neighborhood Politics: Chicago and Sheffield.* 1997. • Horwitt, Sanford D. *Let Them Call Me Rebel: Saul Alinsky—His Life and Legacy.* 1992.

Race and Community Organizations in Austin

White Austinites responded to African American neighbors in the 1960s by forming community organizations whose policies varied between tepidly welcoming and unabashedly hostile.

The Austin Tenants and Owners Association (1965–1966), founded by block-club organizer Marcella Kane, lobbied property owners, banks, and real-estate dealers about housing concerns. ATOA tried to preserve Austin's character by making sure that buildings were well maintained and housing contracts were racially fair. The group of clergy that sponsored the Austin Community Organization (1964–1966) intended to provide a platform for local residents. ACO's efforts attracted animosity from whites hostile to its "integrationist" sentiments without winning much African American support. In 1966, Catholic priests withdrew their money from ACO and hired Saul Alinsky's student Tom Gaudette to form the Organization for a Better Austin. OBA's controversial tactics of community protection unapologetically played on white racism. Among OBA's leaders were the future anti-redlining activist Gale Cincotta and a police spy.

ACO and OBA consistently faced organized opposition. The United Property Group (1959–1965) was explicitly dedicated to keeping African Americans out of homes and schools in West Garfield Park and Austin. The Town Hall Assembly (1967) replaced the defunct UPG and concentrated on maintaining school boundary lines that segregated students by race. THA, which appeared moderate in comparison to the overtly racist UPG and the flamboyant OBA, won support from white business owners and residents in North Austin.

Amanda Seligman

Community Service Organizations.

Residents of metropolitan Chicago have a long and distinguished tradition of community service, and a multitude of organizations have expressed Chicagoans' civic and charitable impulses. By the 1850s, associations dedicated to service appeared among residents inspired by religious interests (such as the YOUNG MEN'S CHRISTIAN ASSOCIATION or the St. Vincent de Paul Society) or by ethnic solidarity (MUTUAL BENEFIT SOCIETIES like the Hibernian Benefit Society or the Dania Club.) Others, such as the Ladies Benevolent Association (1843) and the male-dominated Chicago Relief Society (1850) gathered the upper classes to serve the poor.

The late nineteenth century saw more generalized service efforts, as a combination of changes—including the explosive growth of the city and the diversity of mass immigration—generated new concern for the community welfare, while the increasing prosperity of Chicago's middle and upper classes, and the emerging presence of women in public life, supplied new organizational energies. Crucial to the expansion of community service among Chicago's upper and middle classes were the Chicago's Woman's Club (1876) and an increasing number of AFRICAN AMERICAN women's clubs that joined together in the 1890s to create the Chicago Federation of Colored Women's Clubs. The efforts of these women in city neighborhoods and communities throughout the metropolitan region not only created a number of welfare, youth-oriented, and cultural institutions, they also articulated a new vision of responsibility to the community. New religious organizations, such as the Church of Christ's Community Renewal Society (1882), though still denominationally based, dedicated themselves to more broadly defined community service. By the early twentieth century, ethnically based clubs such as the Bohemian Charitable Association (1910) had moved beyond mutual benefit to community service. Businessmen's clubs, such as the Standard Club (1869), a prominent JEWISH organization, adopted this nonsectarian gospel of service. New businessmen's organizations explicitly dedicated to service, such as Rotary (founded in Chicago in 1905), were formed. The agencies that would become spear heads of Progressive reform in Chicago—HULL HOUSE, CHICAGO COMMONS, the Chicago School of Civics and PHILANTHROPY, and the NORTHWESTERN UNIVERSITY Settlement—drew upon and helped organize this service orientation.

By the 1920s community service was thoroughly bureaucratized and becoming increasingly professionalized, as overarching organizations such as the Chicago COMMUNITY TRUST, the Chicago Bureau of Charities, the Association of Catholic Charities, and the Jewish Charities of Chicago helped administer and fund a variety of civic and charitable organizations. The impact of this centralized organizing was twofold. On the one hand, the professionalization of these agencies left less room for voluntarism, dampening the eager energy that had launched new service activities in the Progressive era. On the other hand, the ethnic and religious boundaries that had previously channeled civic organizing became less sharply defined. During the GREAT DEPRESSION, which nearly overwhelmed the capacity of older charitable societies, a new type of community organization appeared—a multiethnic and at times multiracial organization working to preserve the vitality of individual Chicago neighborhoods. The pioneers of this type of community service were the Chicago Area Project, founded by UNIVERSITY OF CHICAGO sociologist Clifford Shaw in 1934, and the BACK OF THE YARDS NEIGHBORHOOD COUNCIL, organized in 1939 by Saul Alinsky. After WORLD WAR II, neighborhood groups such as the HYDE PARK–KENWOOD Community Conference, the WOODLAWN ORGANIZATION, the NORTHWEST COMMUNITY ORGANIZATION, and the UNITED NEIGHBORHOOD ORGANIZATION attempted to fight the deterioration of their neighborhoods and halt unwanted "slum clearance" projects. These groups remain active today, helped by funding from foundations and the Chicago Association of Neighborhood Development Organizations (1979). The success of these community groups in serving their local areas has ensured Chicago remains a city of thriving neighborhoods.

Chicago's suburban satellites early established their own women's CLUBS, businessmen's clubs, and community welfare organizations, particularly in the prosperous North Shore area. Yet because most suburbs experienced their dynamic growth after 1920, when the systematizing of the service impulse was complete, many suburban residents who wished to serve their community joined local chapters of national organizations rather than creating their own clubs. This was particularly the case after World War II, when men flocked to BUSINESS clubs such as ROTARY, Kiwanis, Lions, and the Jaycees, and civically minded women joined the JUNIOR LEAGUE, the LEAGUE OF WOMEN VOTERS, or clubs affiliated with the General Federation of Women's Clubs. The multiplicity of these organizations left suburban residents open to charges of conformity and "joinerism," but these organizations guaranteed that every suburban center, no matter how new, could tap a reservoir of community activism.

Today, in both Chicago and its suburbs, residential privatism has seemingly intensified, and many express fears of an attenuated community spirit. Yet even as the metropolis continues to sprawl outward, diffusing charitable energy and resources, Chicago's myriad service organizations remain bulwarks of civic responsibility.

Jeffrey Charles

See also: Clubs: Patriotic and Veterans' Clubs; Clubs: Women's Clubs; Coordinating Council of Community Organizations; Press: Neighborhood Press; Relief and Aid Society, Chicago; Settlement Houses

Further reading: Cohen, Lizabeth. *Making a New Deal: Industrial Workers in Chicago, 1919–1939.* 1990. • Henig, Jeffrey R. *Neighborhood Mobilization: Redevelopment and Response.* 1982. • McCarthy, Kathleen. *Noblesse Oblige: Charity and Cultural Philanthropy in Chicago, 1849–1929.* 1982.

Commuting. The emergence of commuting in Chicago and its ever-growing importance in the daily urban experience is a concomitant of the region's long-term population growth, the spatial expansion of the urban BUILT ENVIRONMENT, and the increasing separation of home and WORK for most residents over time. The history of commuting is one of changing LAND-USE patterns, lengthening distances and changing geometry of travel, evolving modes of TRANSPORTATION, shifts in the social composition of commuters, and the rise of a metropolitan commuter culture. As Chicago became metropolitan, commuting involved more and more people, a more complex geography of movement, and a sequence of technological innovations adding variety to the transportation system. The interconnected elements can be viewed from the perspective of five broad eras of commutation.

From its beginning in 1830 until the mid-1850s most of the city was walkable, contained within a radius of about two miles from the center. Many residents worked in or close to home, and only the well-to-do could afford to cluster in a few prestigious districts removed from the central area. In the GROCERY trade, for example, retail grocers of necessity lived above their stores, scattered throughout the town's neighborhoods, whereas most WHOLESALE grocers made a fine enough living to reside a carriage ride away on a street with social cachet. Chicago's bankers at that time, except for a very few who rented central HOTEL rooms, all lived in quiet districts away from the noise and hubbub of downtown, giving sociogeographical definition to the phrase "bankers' hours."

In 1856, Paul Cornell initiated the railroad suburb in greater Chicago, when he persuaded the ILLINOIS CENTRAL RAILROAD to operate local passenger service to HYDE PARK, six miles south of the city center. Within the city proper, horse omnibus lines began in 1850 and steadily multiplied their routes as the built-up area expanded, to be superseded by the STREET RAILWAY in 1859. Three years later, 3,512,272 passengers were being carried annually by horsecar through the city. More dramatic, however, was the emerging commuter train service, offered on RAILROADS which by the 1880s fanned out in 15 different directions, creating a large metropolitan pattern resembling the spokes of a giant wheel. Such suburban commutation stimulated the development of strings of railroad suburbs out to a distance of 30–40 miles and enabled an enlarged class of business managers and well-paid professionals to live in semirural settings far from their city offices, a pattern deeply etched on the region by 1934 and still operating today.

A third phase in commuter history may be said to have arrived with the mechanization of street railways in the 1880s and the appearance of RAPID TRANSIT service the following decade. As railroad commuting produced a roughly star-shaped outline to the metropolitan built-up area as a whole, steam-driven cable car and later electric streetcar service along most major Chicago streets made possible a new level of access from the city's burgeoning neighborhoods. Commuters could now reach downtown as well as factory sites along developing river and rail corridors within the core areas of the urban mass. This trend greatly increased the daily flows of workers to and from the central business district, but it also promoted crosstown commuting to noncentral jobs and local SHOPPING DISTRICTS. The addition of elevated rapid

Chicago: Commuting in the Walking City in 1854

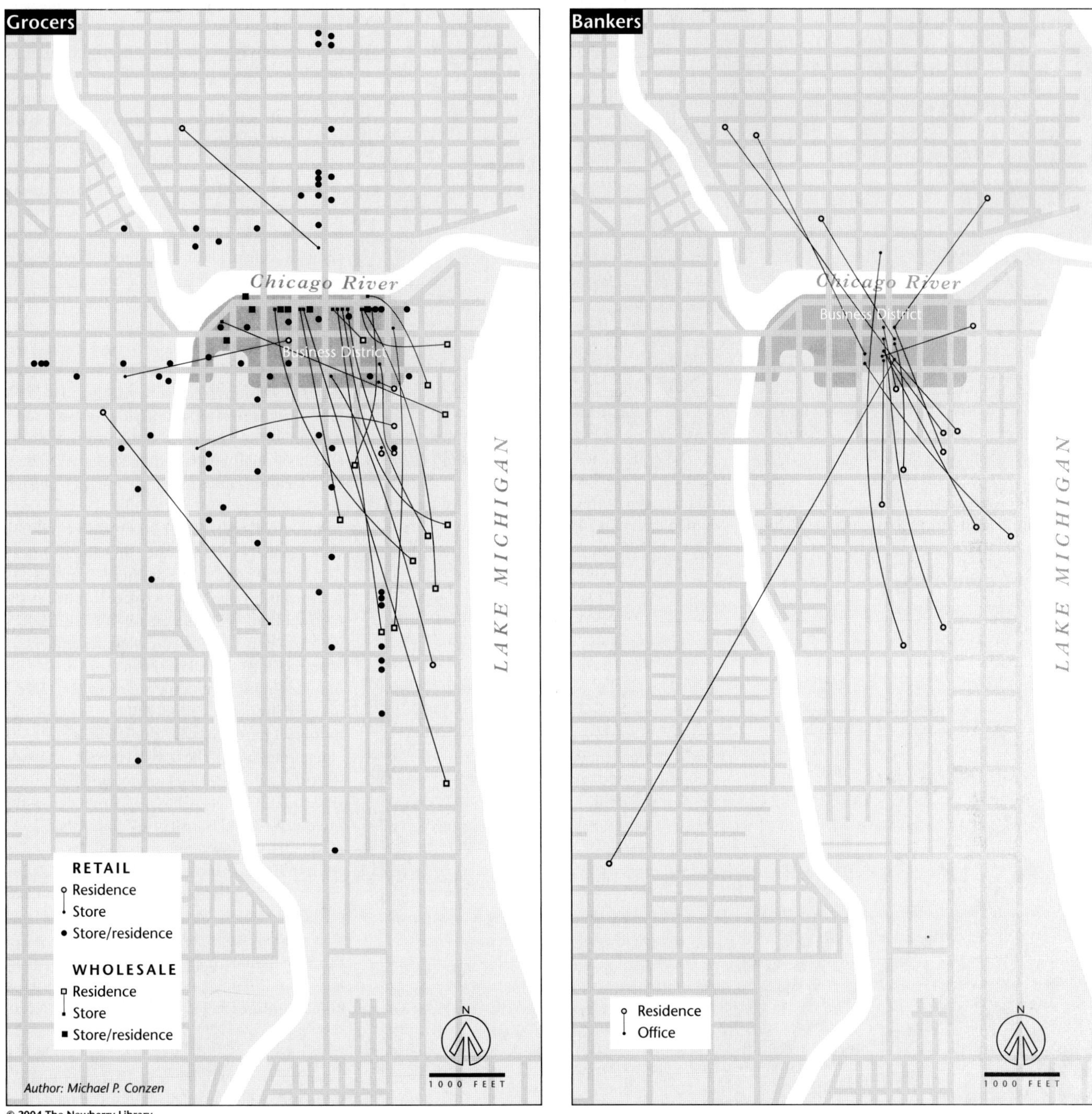

Chicago in 1854 was still a walking city for most of its residents. The town's small spatial extent and the wide scatter of job sites ensured that the streets daily teemed with pedestrians going back and forth about their business. For many, work and residence were at the same address: retail grocers, for example, generally lived above their stores, to be close to their neighborhood customers. Wholesale grocers, whose warehouses lined South Water Street in the heart of the business district, accumulated enough wealth to live away from the bustle in the elegant section running south behind Michigan Avenue. Not one lived north of the river, perhaps to avoid dependence on risky bridge access to their premises. Bankers likewise lived removed from downtown, some perhaps a carriage ride away, but most less than a 20-minute walk from the office.

transit service between 1892 and 1915, tied together in the famous "LOOP" circuit around the downtown created in 1911, served to further concentrate centripetal movement from outskirts to center. INTERURBAN railroads extended the geographical reach of low-cost commuting from satellite cities in the metropolitan region.

With the rapid spread of automobile ownership by the 1920s, commuting became somewhat more spatially and socially diffuse, but the focus on downtown was still overwhelming, forcing major changes in downtown land use to accommodate cars in PARKING lots and new parking structures. Between the 1920s and 1950s, the "rush hour" became a fixture of Chicago urban life, as cars—parked and moving—jostled with streetcars and, after

Commuters waiting for southbound trains, 1941. Photographer: John Vachon. Source: Library of Congress.

Railroad Commuting to Chicago in 1934

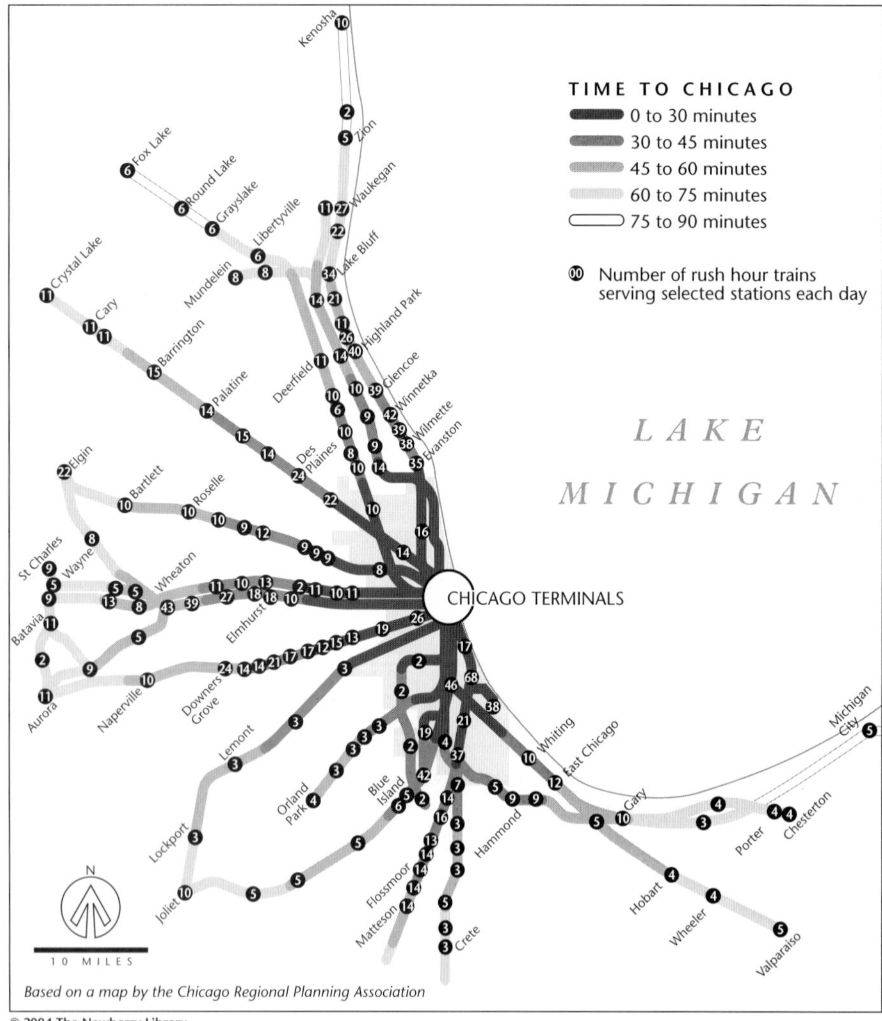

1927, buses for street space created in the horse and carriage era. By 1940, Chicago's Loop received 603,000 daily commuters, of whom over 113,000 came in from the suburbs. Significantly, one-quarter of all commuters drove in by car, one-quarter took the streetcar, one-quarter the elevated trains, one-eighth the commuter trains, and the rest came by BUS or other means.

Continued METROPOLITAN GROWTH and densification of the inner built-up area generated traffic volumes and congestion sufficient to spur the construction of limited-access superhighways. These consisted of urban parkways, beginning with Lake Shore Drive in 1933, and EXPRESSWAYS, starting with the Congress (now Eisenhower) Expressway in 1955–1960. The new superhighways, when linked to their suburban extensions (themselves designed to serve long-distance travel), did widen the regional catchment area for commuters to the city of Chicago. But they also fed a new pattern of "reverse" commuting from the central city to the suburbs. Already in 1960, while about 330,000 suburbanites worked in Chicago, over 100,000 Chicagoans worked in the suburbs. In recent decades the automobile has become the essential means for commuters to get to work in the metropolitan area, as with all other American metropolitan regions. Equally striking, however, has been the survival of a historical legacy of mixed transportation options, at least in the inner metropolitan zone. Many districts there harbor commuters who prefer walking, bicycling, or taking public transit to work, a pattern well illustrated in 1980 and not much changed since then. Chicago has even pioneered the building of rapid transit lines along expressway median strips to extend such choice.

Metropolitan decentralization of population and jobs during the second half of the twentieth century changed regional commuting from a centripetal to a largely diffuse pattern. At the same time, it pushed the working class and many of the poor into the ranks of regional commuters for the first time. The recent

---

If streetcars moved commuters within the core of the industrial-era city, railroads served that function further out and pioneered a white-collar commuter business. Beginning with daily trains from Hyde Park in 1856, Chicago's railroads developed a complex octopus-like network of commuter service which by 1934 reached such distant places as Michigan City (Indiana), Kenosha (Wisconsin), and Fox Valley towns from Elgin to Aurora. Most daily commuters, however, originated from suburbs within a one-hour ride of Chicago's Loop, as reflected in the number of daily trains on each line. Strikingly, the managerial and office-worker ebb and flow by this date already favored the white-collar bedroom communities of the North Shore and western suburbs over the southern suburbs, most of which were more industrial in character.

Commuting to Chicago in 1970

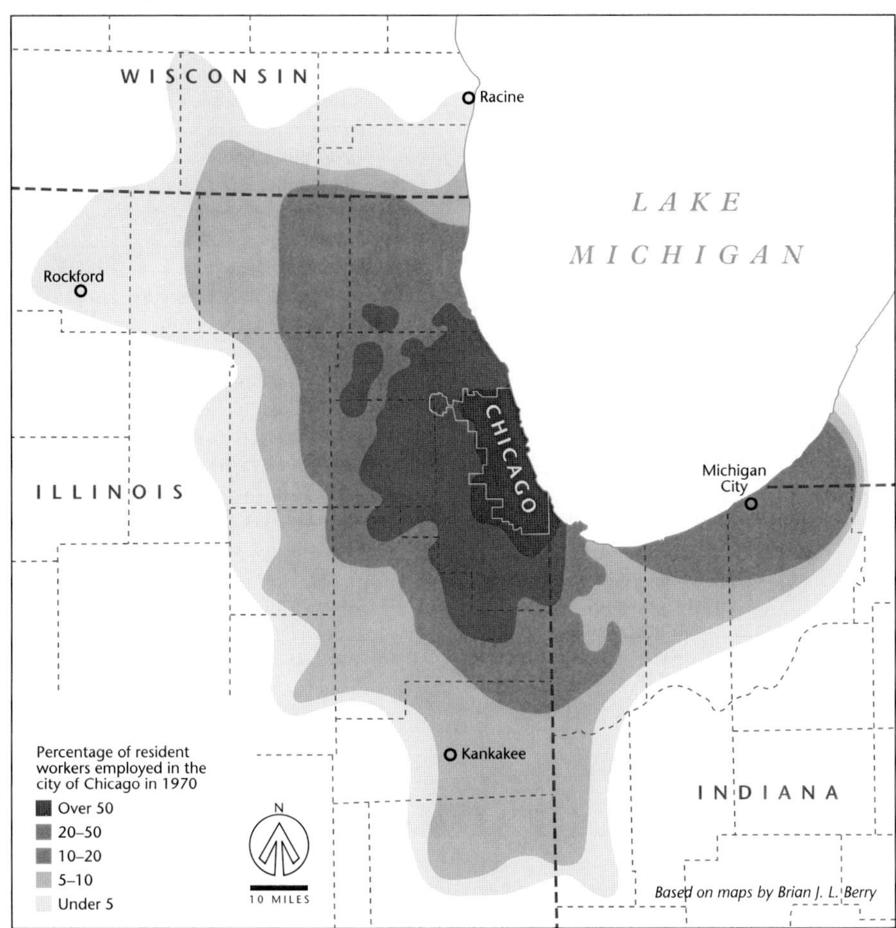

Automobiles have been used to commute to central Chicago since the early twentieth century, but driving to work did not become a truly mass phenomenon across the metropolitan area until the advent of the superhighway. By 1970, commuting by car had etched a pattern of vast proportions, drawing to Chicago over half of the resident workers of communities that spanned five counties in a daily centripetal vortex. However, as jobs began to decentralize within the metropolitan area following World War II and moved outwards even faster during the 1960s, commuting flows became more complex, and "reverse" commuting from the city of Chicago to suburban job sites assumed significance. Nevertheless, the drawing power of Chicago's Loop remained undiminished. More than 1 in 10 workers in large parts of the collar counties in 1970 commuted, by various means of transport, to the city's central business district.

Reverse Commuting from Chicago in 1970

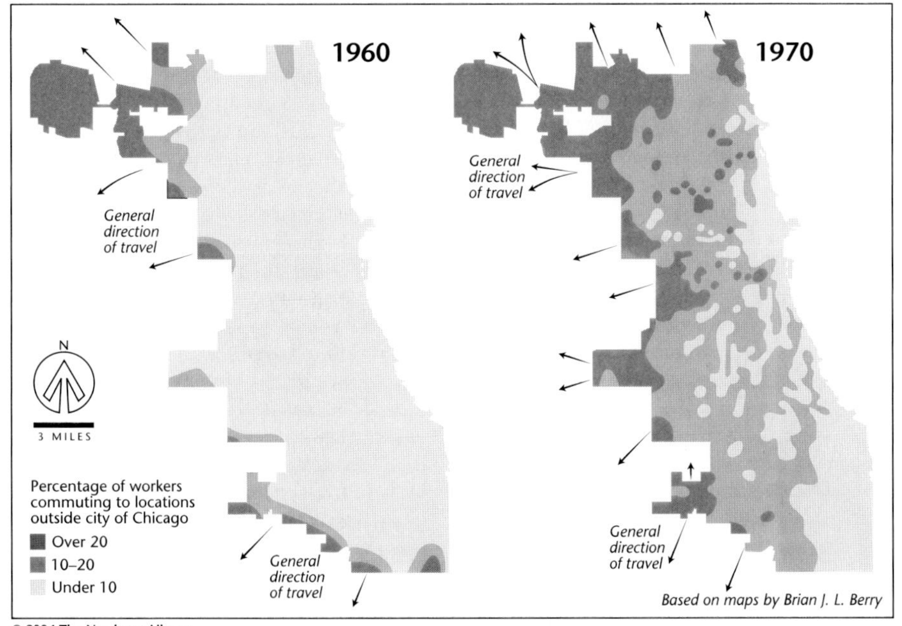

Downtown Commuting

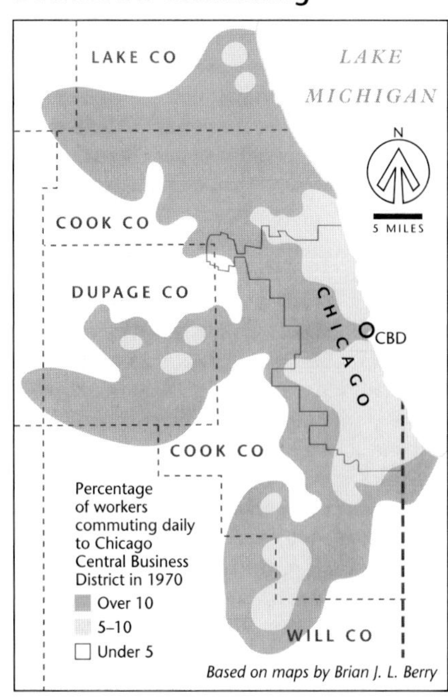

repopulating of the city center with its globalizing management functions has revivified the multimodal transportation environment of the core. As the new millennium dawned, "edge cities" in metropolitan Chicago were showing increasing interest in rapid transit links with O' HARE INTERNATIONAL AIRPORT and the city of Chicago.

Michael P. Conzen

See also: Economic Geography; Multicentered Chicago; Parking; Public Transportation; Streets and Highways; Suburbs and Cities as Dual Metropolis; Toll Roads

Further reading: Berry, Brian J. L. *Case Studies of Commuting Fields and Metropolitan Definition.* 1966. • Breese, Gerald W. *The Daytime Population of the Central Business District of Chicago, With Particular Reference to the Factor of Transportation.* 1949. • Cudahy, Brian J. *Destination Loop: The Story of Rapid Transit Railroading in and around Chicago.* 1982.

Company Housing. While most companies have preferred to leave the housing of their workers in the hands of REAL-ESTATE speculators, a few have directly intervened to provide housing. In Chicago, company housing dates from the great industrial expansion of the late nineteenth century.

The most ambitious and controversial project of company housing was conceived by railroad car magnate George M. Pullman, who in 1880 founded the town of PULLMAN on Chicago's southern suburban fringe. As part

The Journey to Work in Chicago in 1980

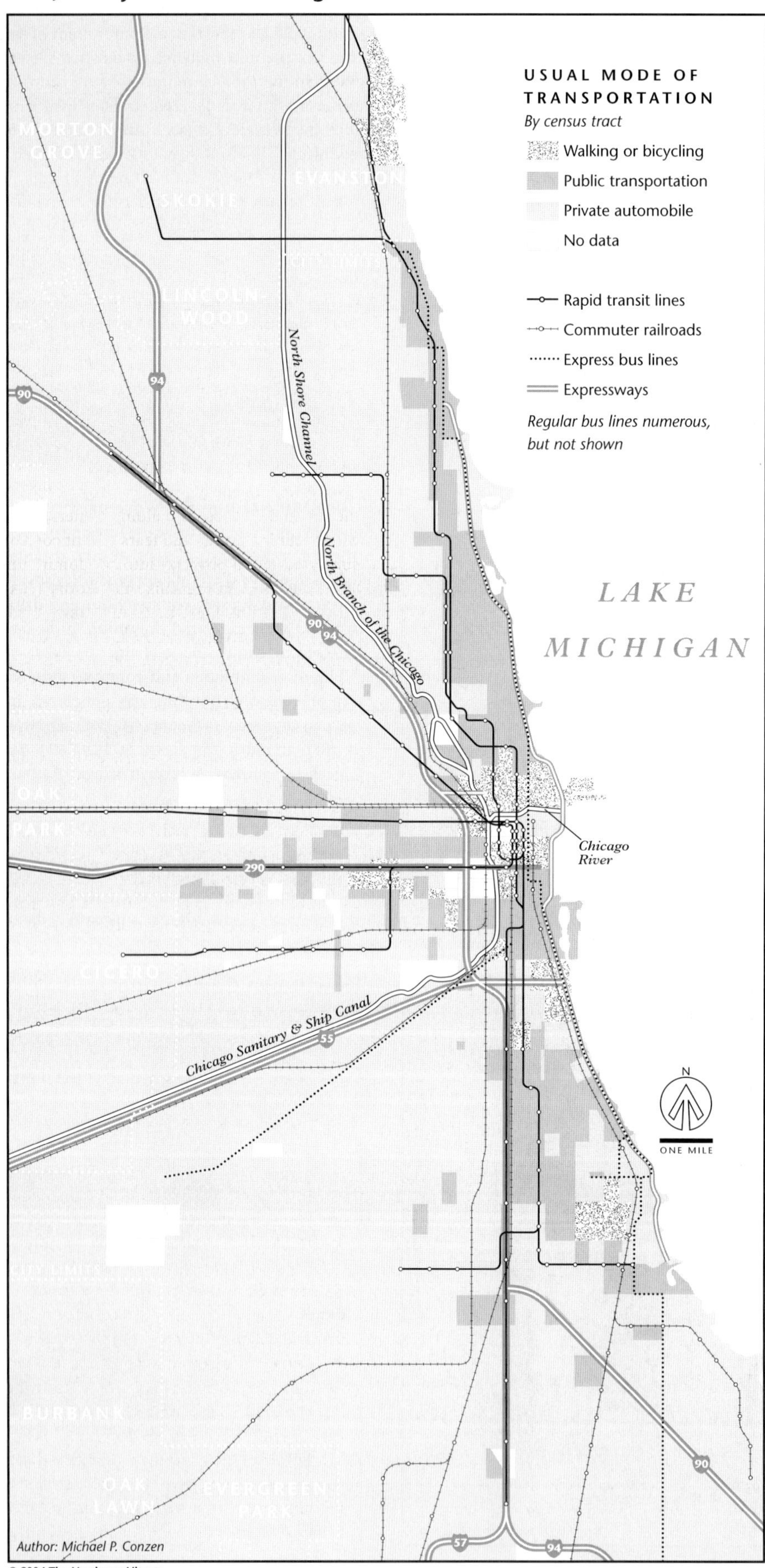

Chicagoans built an impressive system of public transport during the twentieth century, providing the city's commuters with several alternatives to the automobile. However, the rapid transit network has always strongly favored the Loop, so as jobs decentralized across the metropolis this centripetal system could no longer conveniently serve commuters going elsewhere. Therefore, by 1980 the choice of means to reach work for residents in the central city was becoming highly fragmented. Extensive zones existed on the city's North, South, and West Sides in which more people took public transport to work than other means. This correlates with the geography of the public transport system. In particular areas, such as around the downtown business core, hospitals, and universities, more people walked or bicycled to work than took other means. Elsewhere, the automobile prevailed as the means of getting to work, even in districts with good bus service and access to rapid transit.

of Pullman's paternalistic social vision, his housing was designed to foster in workers the virtues of industriousness, temperance, thrift, and cleanliness. All dwellings, from the bachelor APARTMENTS to the free-standing houses, featured running water, GAS, and garbage disposal. The Pullman companies maintained total control over housing: they owned the land and buildings, set the rents, screened (and evicted) tenants. In the Strike of 1894, workers protested against Pullman's refusal to lower rents during a depression.

Other industrialists opted for less intervention, building housing that they then sold to workers. Shortly before his death in 1884, Cyrus Hall McCormick instituted a program of welfare assistance that included the construction of "model cottages" to be sold at cost to his employees at the McCormick Reaper Works. U.S. Steel Corporation, negatively influenced by Pullman's example, pursued an even more hands-off approach in developing the town of GARY, INDIANA, in the 1900s. Through the Gary Land Company, it sold lots and built houses for employees of the steel-working industries south of Chicago.

Anna Holian

See also: Housing Reform; Roselle, IL; Welfare Capitalism; West Dundee, IL

Further reading: Buder, Stanley. *Pullman: An Experiment in Industrial Order and Community Planning, 1880–1930.* 1967. • Crawford, Margaret. *Building the Workingman's Paradise: The Design of American Company Towns.* 1995. • Ely, Richard T. "Pullman: A Social Study." *Harper's New Monthly Magazine* 70 (December 1884–May 1885).

Concerts, Outdoor. *See* Outdoor Concerts

Concordia University. In April 1847, a group of GERMAN Americans from around the Midwest assembled in Chicago and formed the Lutheran Church Missouri Synod. Over the next century, the Missouri Synod grew to become the second largest Lutheran body in the United States, and in 1992 it formed the Concordia University System to oversee the 2 SEMINARIES and 10 colleges affiliated with its teachings. Concordia University is one such school. Established in 1864 in ADDISON, Illinois, the school initially focused on training educators. In 1913, Concordia relocated its growing student body of both undergraduate and graduate students to a 40-acre campus in RIVER FOREST, a tree-lined suburb 10 miles west of Chicago.

Sarah Fenton

See also: Protestants; Universities and Their Cities

Condominiums and Cooperatives. Built amidst housing shortages and rising costs after WORLD WAR I, the first cooperatives in Chicago offered middle-income and well-to-do city dwellers a form of home ownership in the city. Rather than own their unit, members in a cooperative have a share in a corporation that owns the building. Members are entitled to occupy one unit and are responsible for a share of the corporation's cost of operation, which often includes mortgage payment, taxes, utilities, and maintenance fees. The GREAT DEPRESSION bankrupted over 75 percent of the cooperatives in Chicago, but housing shortages after WORLD WAR II combined with favorable new federal policies, including FHA insurance of blanket mortgages on cooperatives and new types of subsidies, encouraged a new wave of cooperative building in Chicago. A variety of cooperatives can be found today in many parts of the city, including luxury co-ops on the GOLD COAST, middle-income co-ops in HYDE PARK, senior co-ops on the North Side, and limited-equity co-ops (subsidized, price-controlled) on the SOUTH SIDE.

American Furniture Mart, Lake Shore Drive at Erie Street, 1938. With the decline of the city's wholesale furniture trade, the building was converted to residential condominiums and offices in 1979. Photographer: Unknown. Source: Chicago Historical Society.

While cooperatives remain a viable housing option in the city, they have been outpaced in recent decades by a newer housing form introduced from Puerto Rico. Condominiums first appeared in Chicago after the 1963 Illinois Condominium Property Act authorized their construction. Condominium ownership is a different legal form; rather than own stock in a company like cooperatives, owners have exclusive ownership of the space in their unit as well as common ownership of common areas and facilities. Condo owners have individual mortgages rather than a share in a blanket mortgage. Generally less expensive than single-family homes, condominiums thus became an attractive housing option for many, and within a decade new condominiums were built along the northern lakefront in the city and in many northern and western suburbs. Condominium construction took off rapidly in the city in the 1970s, as building owners, faced with declining profits and fears of rent control, converted rental property into condominiums at a rapid pace in areas like the LOOP, NEAR NORTH, LINCOLN PARK, LAKE VIEW, Hyde Park, and EDGEWATER. In the Loop, for example, condominiums were nonexistent in 1970 but accounted for nearly half of its housing in 1980. Condominium construction and conversion remained steady in the 1980s and 1990s in Chicago but increased in many Chicago suburbs, particularly in DUPAGE COUNTY.

Like neighborhood associations and GATED COMMUNITIES, cooperatives and condominiums raise questions about private governance. Condominiums and cooperatives are governed by elected boards that can set criteria for the appearance of units or exclude undesirable members.

Tracy Steffes

See also: Apartments; Housing Types; Real Estate

Further reading: Clurman, David, and Edna Hebard. *Condominiums and Cooperatives.* 1970. • McKenzie, Evan. *Privatopia: Homeowner Associations and the Rise of Residential Private Government.* 1994. • Shales & Co. *Condominium Conversions in Chicago: Facts and Issues.* 1979

Congolese. Congolese migration to Chicago has been shaped by the political situation in the Democratic Republic of Congo (formerly Zaire). The 32-year dictatorial reign of Mobuto Sese Seko ended in 1997 but left behind a legacy of violence, corruption, and economic collapse which continues to plague the country. While a few Congolese might have arrived in Chicago following Congolese independence in 1960, the first major wave of Congolese migrants were students in the 1980s. Most students anticipated a temporary stay for educational purposes, but the deteriorating political and economic situation at home led many of them to remain in the United

States. The escalation of conflict in the 1990s created a wave of political REFUGEES which has swelled the size of the Congolese community in Chicago from around 50 to several hundred, according to community estimates in 2001. Among the recent refugees are a distinct group of Tutsi-Congolese, ethnic Tutsis from Rwanda who settled in the Congo and became citizens a generation or more ago but faced ethnic and political backlash.

Recent political refugees have had a more difficult adjustment to life in Chicago than earlier students and professionals. Recent immigrants tend to have less experience with English than earlier migrants. In addition, professional expertise and education acquired in the Congo are often not recognized by United States employers, and consequently many educated Congolese have had to take unskilled and low-paying jobs like dishwashing and TAXI CAB DRIVING. Although some families were able to migrate together, many refugees had to flee their homes and leave their families behind.

Although Congolese in Chicago have come from a range of ethnic and religious backgrounds, they have attempted to overcome divisions and organize into a single Congolese community. Earlier Congolese settlers have become active not only in providing assistance but in creating and nurturing a Congolese cultural identity. Congolese leaders formed the Congolese Association in the early 1990s as an informal social and mutual aid organization. It created a constitution and formal structure in 1994 and sponsored social events and gatherings until the late 1990s, when it struggled with institutional difficulties and became inactive. In 2001, Congolese leaders formed the New Community Church of Chicago in EVANSTON to build a strong, spiritual community of Congolese from different religious backgrounds. The church sponsors a variety of activities and assists members, creating a surrogate family for some. In addition, Congolese gather annually for major holidays like New Year's Day and Independence Day (June 30), celebrating with traditional Congolese food, music, and dancing.

Tracy Steffes

See also: Demography; Multicentered Chicago

Congress of Industrial Organizations. Union presidents, including John L. Lewis of the United Mine Workers, founded the Committee for Industrial Organization in November 1935. Fed up with the refusal of the American Federation of Labor (AFL) to organize unskilled and semiskilled factory workers, Lewis and his allies provided the money and organizational framework for their mobilization and UNIONIZATION. The committee formalized its break with the AFL when it held its first convention in 1938, renaming itself the Congress of Industrial Organizations (CIO). In 1955, the CIO merged with the AFL to form the AFL-CIO.

It took many battles—on the picket lines and shop floor, in the courts and the neighborhoods—to build the CIO. Organizers faced employers who were both sophisticated and stubborn, with long histories of ANTIUNION campaigns that often turned to violence. Other things, though, were conducive to organizing: Depression UNEMPLOYMENT, which undermined employees' loyalty to their companies; a firmly prolabor ROMAN CATHOLIC Church; a working-class that had maintained its own institutions and a sense of itself; and the presence of many radicals, often COMMUNISTS, who had spent years organizing in the trenches. Among the key events from the 1935 to 1942 period that marked the initial phase of organizing and institutionalizing the CIO were the MEMORIAL DAY MASSACRE, when Chicago POLICE officers attacked striking Republic Steel workers on May 30, 1937; the PACKINGHOUSE WORKERS' mass rally at the Coliseum on July 16, 1939, when Bishop Bernard Sheil and John L. Lewis voiced their approval of industrial unionism; and, in early 1941, the Farm Equipment Workers' successful strike against International Harvester.

Steelworkers, who accounted for 100,000 to 125,000 of Chicago-area CIO members, on average, throughout much of its history, were at its core. Packinghouse workers—averaging about 40,000 members—and farm equipment workers—about 25,000—came next. Other CIO members have included auto workers, clothing workers, retail and wholesale workers, and electrical workers.

Joseph Germano, director of the Steelworkers District 31 from 1940 until his retirement in 1973, led the CIO's liberal, anti-Communist wing. A virtual dictator of his district, the largest in the Steelworkers, Germano was virulently antiradical, but also pro-CIVIL RIGHTS and, when necessary, a militant trade unionist. Herbert March, of the United Packinghouse Workers, Grant Oakes, of the Farm Equipment Workers, and Hilliard Ellis, of the United Automobile Workers, led the "Communist" wing. Matters came to a head at the 1947 Illinois CIO convention, which featured repeated thuggish attacks on "Communists," when the Steelworker-dominated meeting purged itself of the left. In the following years, the Steelworkers played the leading role in the CIO's partnership with the Democratic Party.

In the hindsight afforded by years of deindustrialization and antiunion attacks, the CIO's successes (increased on-the-job dignity, advancements in civil rights, higher wages, and improved benefits), impressive enough at the time, seem virtually incredible.

Steve Rosswurm

See also: Great Depression; Iron and Steel workers; Work; Work Culture

Further reading: Cohen, Lizabeth. *Making a New Deal: Industrial Workers in Chicago, 1919–1939.* 1990. • Halpern, Rick. *Down on the Killing Floor: Black and White Workers in Chicago's Packinghouses, 1904–1954.* 1997. • Newell, Barbara Warne. *Chicago and the Labor Movement: Metropolitan Unionism in the 1930s.* 1961.

Congress of Racial Equality (CORE). Black and white activists from the Christian pacifist movement, including James Farmer and George Houser, created the Chicago Committee of Racial Equality, the first chapter

James Farmer: A Chicago Lunch Counter Sit-In

James Farmer came to Chicago in 1941 to work as the race-relations secretary with the Fellowship of Reconciliation, a pacifist organization. Farmer, a recent graduate of Howard University, convened an interracial group, mostly University of Chicago graduate students, to study Gandhi and his pacifist model for social change. This group evolved into the Committee of Racial Equality (CORE), which became an important force in the civil rights movement.

CORE set about fighting segregation in Chicago through direct-action techniques. Its first success was at a restaurant called the Jack Spratt Coffeehouse on 47th Street in Kenwood. The restaurant refused to serve African Americans. Farmer explained CORE's direct action:

> We went in with a group of about twenty—this was a small place that seats thirty or thirty-five comfortably at the counter and in the booths—and occupied just about all of the available seats and waited for service. The woman was in charge again [the manager they had encountered on a previous visit]. She ordered the waitress to serve two whites who were seated at the counter, and she served them. Then she told the blacks, 'I'm sorry, we can't serve you, you'll have to leave.' And they, of course, declined to leave and continued to sit there. By this time the other customers who were in there were aware of what was going on and were watching, and most of these were university people, University of Chicago, who were more or less sympathetic with us. And they stopped eating and the two people at the counter she had served and those whites in the booth she had served were not eating. There was no turnover. People were coming in and standing around for a few minutes and walking out. There were no seats available.

Ultimately, CORE succeeded in desegregating this restaurant and fought for equal treatment in other public venues. CORE's techniques would later play a significant role in attacking racial segregation in the Deep South.

Raines, Howell. *My Soul Is Rested.* 1977, 31.

of CORE, in 1942. The interracial group advocated nonviolent direct action to address racial discrimination. Not a mass membership organization, CORE depended on a small group of disciplined activists to conduct their campaigns to desegregate public accommodations, workplaces, and housing. Pioneering the use of sit-ins and other civil disobedience for CIVIL RIGHTS causes, the Chicago chapter reached a high point when the organization desegregated White City Roller Rink in 1946. After a failed employment campaign at a DEPARTMENT store the following year, the chapter became inactive during the 1950s until its disaffiliation.

A reorganized Chicago chapter benefited from CORE's nationally prominent Freedom Rides through the South in 1961. Its efforts to desegregate Chicago public SCHOOLS brought attention to enduring racial segregation in the North. The movement crested in 1963, when activists moved beyond picketing and petitioning and sat in at the Board of Education to protest the construction of mobile classrooms for overcrowded black schools. Their direct-action protest attracted more working-class blacks, leading the chapter to de-emphasize its Gandhian roots in nonviolence and interracialism. Chairman Robert Lucas, critical of the failure of the Martin Luther King–led OPEN HOUSING campaign to extract concrete concessions from Mayor Richard J. Daley, led a march in CICERO in 1966. The organization was in decline even before the ill-fated march and remained a paper organization through the rest of the 1960s. The Chicago chapter's efforts to address de facto segregation in schools, housing, and employment anticipated and typified the CIVIL RIGHTS MOVEMENT's difficulty in significantly altering entrenched patterns of racial subordination.

Preston H. Smith II

See also: Black Panther Party; Coordinating Council of Community Organizations; National Association for the Advancement of Colored People (NAACP); School Desegregation; Willis Wagons

Further reading: Anderson, Alan B., and George W. Pickering. *Confronting the Color Line: The Broken Promise of the Civil Rights Movement in Chicago.* 1986. • Meier, August, and Elliot Rudwick. *CORE: A Study in the Civil Rights Movement, 1942–1968.* 1973. • Ralph, James R., Jr. *Northern Protest: Martin Luther King, Jr., Chicago, and the Civil Rights Movement.* 1993.

Conservation Areas. In the late 1940s and early 1950s, conservation areas were primarily residential districts whose physical condition urban planners judged to be between "near-blighted" and "stable." The 1943 *Master Plan of Residential Land Use of Chicago* found that 56 square miles of Chicago constituted conservation areas. After the Urban Community Conservation Act of 1953 became Illinois law, Chicago established the Community Conservation Board, empowered to recognize tracts of 40 acres or more as conservation areas. Officially designated conservation areas, including Hyde Park and Uptown, were eligible to receive improvement funds and city planning services. Although conservation was theoretically distinct from urban renewal, in practice the two often blurred.

Amanda Seligman

See also: Planning Chicago

Further reading: Chicago Plan Commission. *Master Plan of Residential Land Use of Chicago.* 1943. • *Conservation: A Report to the Conservation Committee of the Metropolitan Housing and Planning Council by Its Conservation Study Staff.* 1953. • Hirsch, Arnold R. *Making the Second Ghetto: Race and Housing in Chicago, 1940–1960.* 1983.

Conservatories. Concerned with the ill effects of industrialization, many nineteenth-century city dwellers became fascinated with horticulture. This, along with advances in building technology, led to the development of conservatories in Europe early in the century. The first conservatories in the United States were introduced in the eastern states in the late 1860s. In Chicago, soon after the city's three park commissions were organized in 1869, there was great interest in creating such "tropical paradises" as well as fanciful gardens.

The LINCOLN PARK Commission established a greenhouse in 1877 and planted an adjacent formal garden in 1880. The greenhouse was replaced with a much more substantial and exotic conservatory, designed by Joseph Lyman Silsbee and M. E. Bell. As the new conservatory was being constructed in stages between 1890 and 1895, an informal perennial garden, called Grandmother's Garden, was planted to its west.

The West and South Park Commissions also built conservatories, bringing the total to five within Chicago's public parks by the late 1890s. The West Park System replaced utilitarian greenhouses in HUMBOLDT, Douglas, and GARFIELD PARKS with three small conservatories between 1886 and 1888. One was designed by architect William Le Baron Jenney, and the other two were by the firm of Fromann and Jebsen. In WASHINGTON PARK, the South Park Commission replaced earlier greenhouse facilities with an impressive conservatory perched above ornate sunken gardens in 1897. The building was demolished in the 1930s.

Owing to political corruption within the West Park System, by the early 1900s the three glass houses in Humboldt, Douglas, and Garfield Parks were poorly maintained. In 1905, Jens Jensen was appointed as superintendent and chief LANDSCAPE architect by a reform-minded board. He demolished all three conservatories to construct one centralized facility in Garfield Park, intended as the world's largest conservatory. Jensen, who is considered dean of the Prairie style in landscape architecture, developed a revolutionary design for the Garfield Park Conservatory. In contrast to most conservatories, which looked like palaces or chateaus, Jensen wanted the structure's form to emulate the "great haystacks" of the Midwest. His unique approach for the interior, considered "landscape GARDENING under glass," featured compositions with open vistas surrounded by artfully arranged plantings.

Jensen's design improvements during the West Park Commission's era of reform included

Interior view, Lincoln Park Conservatory, 1906. Photographer: Unknown. Source: Chicago Historical Society.

Washington Park Conservatory, 56th and Cottage Grove, designed by D. H. Burnham & Co., built in 1897. Photographer: J. W. Nolan. Source: Chicago Historical Society.

outdoor gardens in Humboldt, Douglas, and Garfield Parks. These elaborately planted gardens combined Midwestern wildflowers with non-native annuals. To provide shady seating areas, Jensen used open shelters called pergolas in Humboldt and Garfield Parks and a larger Prairie-style building known as Flower Hall in Douglas Park. There are water features in all three gardens.

Chicago's suburbs include several other examples of historic gardens and one other conservatory. Among these are Jens Jensen's Shakespeare Garden (1915) and the Merrick Rose Garden, both located in EVANSTON. Gardener's Memorial in HIGHLAND PARK was created to commemorate three local naturalists, including Jens Jensen. In OAK PARK, a 1914 community effort had residents bringing back plants from foreign places. This culminated in the construction of the Oak Park Conservatory in 1929.

Julia Sniderman Bachrach

See also: Architecture: The Prairie School; Chicago Botanic Gardens; Landscape Design; Leisure; Morton Arboretum; Park Districts; Plant Communities

Further reading: *Annual Reports of the Chicago Park District.* Various years, 1935–1960. • *Prairie in the City: Naturalism in Chicago's Parks, 1870–1940.* Chicago Historical Society, in cooperation with the Morton Arboretum and the Chicago Park District. 1991.

Construction. One of the most remarkable aspects of the history of the Chicago region has been the rapid development of the BUILT ENVIRONMENT. In the early 1800s, the local LANDSCAPE was not dominated by human settlements. Only a few decades later, Chicago stood as a thoroughly constructed place, in which buildings, roads, and other human creations filled the landscape. This tremendous growth rested upon the efforts of thousands of people—including carpenters, masons, contractors, developers, and regulators—who worked in the field of construction. Few of the city's industries have employed more people, and few have been so volatile or so closely connected to the activities of government. Virtually every piece of Chicago's modern landscape stands as a testament to decades of developments in the city's construction industry.

The extraordinary growth of Chicago's built environment has proceeded at an uneven pace. Among the city's building boom periods, during which structures were erected at a rapid pace and construction workers were in high demand, have been the mid-1850s, 1864–1873, the 1880s, the 1901–1916 period, the 1920s, the 1950s, the 1980s, and the late 1990s. The overall rate of expansion was greatest between the 1830s and the 1920s, when Chicago grew from a tiny settlement into one of the world's largest cities. In 1840, there were fewer than one thousand structures in the Chicago area. This figure passed 10,000 around 1854 and 100,000 during the 1880s. By the end of the 1920s, the city contained roughly 400,000 buildings, most of them one- or two-family dwellings.

Chicago has long been associated with the development and construction of inexpensive residential buildings. In the early 1830s, Chicago carpenter Augustine D. Taylor became one of the pioneers of BALLOON FRAME CONSTRUCTION, which cheapened housing costs by avoiding the use of heavy posts and beams. During the latter part of the nineteenth century, Chicago developers such as Samuel E. Gross erected thousands of houses around the city and suburbs and offered prospective buyers innovative finance plans that allowed them to pay in periodic installments. Similar arrangements lay behind the city's BUNGALOW boom of the 1920s, when as many as 100,000 one-story cottages went up in Cook County alone. Many of these bungalows were financed by local building and loan associations, often tied to particular ethnic groups. By this time, most new houses were made of brick and featured central heating, electricity, and indoor plumbing.

In commercial construction, Chicago became a world leader in building technologies and business organization. Starting in the 1880s, Chicago architects, engineers, and builders created structures with deep foundations and steel skeletons that allowed them to reach extraordinary heights. The construction of the world's first SKYSCRAPERS relied on the designs of leading Chicago architects such as William L. Jenney, Burnham & Root, and Holabird & Roche. Equally important was the role of a new kind of construction contractor. The building of the first skyscrapers went hand in hand with the rise of large general contracting firms that coordinated the activities of the dozens of building specialists and hundreds of workers involved in the creation of these huge structures. The pioneering general contracting firm was led by George A. Fuller, who came to Chicago in 1883. The rise of general contracting firms such as Fuller's, which responded to the complex problems associated with the building of large structures, was part of the ongoing industrialization of construction.

The late-nineteenth-century revolution in construction methods, which affected the small dwellings of Chicago families as well as the city's huge skyscrapers, was partly a matter of technological INNOVATIONS and the rise of a manufacturing sector that provided cheap, mass-produced building supplies. New construction materials, such as structural steel and reinforced concrete, were used in the early skyscrapers. In Chicago, which featured wet and unstable soils, the big buildings also depended upon innovations in foundation digging. Starting in the 1880s, Chicago engineers and construction workers used compressed air to create deep caissons that allowed them to anchor the tall buildings in bedrock. Other key building technologies introduced during this period were not as spectacular but were no less important. By the middle of the nineteenth century, a few buildings were starting to be outfitted with modern conveniences such as running WATER, GAS, steam heating, and even indoor toilets. During the 1880s and 1890s, these conveniences were installed in larger numbers of new homes and buildings and became available to more of Chicago's residents. The considerable rise in the quality of the city's housing stock during this period was possible because manufacturers were producing large quantities of cheap building supplies

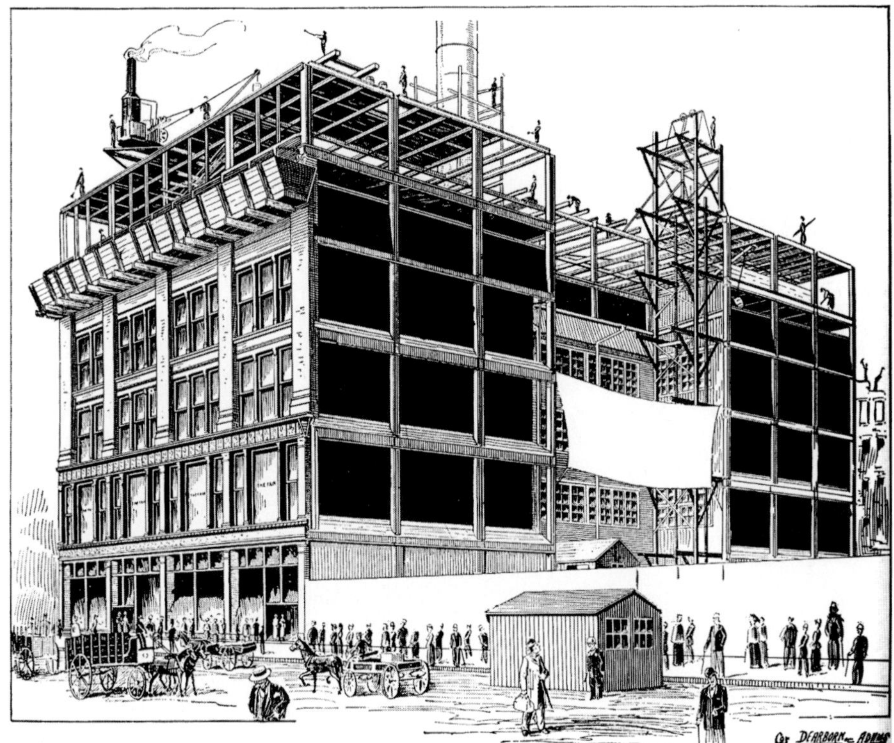

Illustration accompanying William Le Baron Jenney, "Chicago Construction of High Buildings on a Compressible Soil," *Inland Architect and News Record,* November 1891, showing construction of "The Fair" department store in downtown Chicago. Source: The Newberry Library.

such as plumbing fixtures, shingles, and premade doors and windows. Among the leaders in the late-nineteenth-century American building supply industry were Chicago companies like the plumbing and heating equipment companies of Richard T. Crane and Ludwig Wolff. By 1900, when elevators and electric lights were present in Chicago structures, many of the technologies and conveniences that late-twentieth-century residents would expect from buildings were already in place.

Throughout Chicago's history, the construction industry has seen considerable conflict between workers and employers. Construction workers have tended to be highly UNIONIZED and successful in retaining craft traditions. By the 1890s, the Chicago BUILDING TRADES Council included about 30,000 workers in 31 separate trade unions. This association was soon countered by Chicago's contractors, who in 1899 created the Building Contractors' Council. Between 1899 and 1901, the contractors won several disputes with their employees over the control of the workplace. The most severe labor disputes in the history of the Chicago construction industry occurred in the early 1920s. In 1921, when the local construction industry was still in a severe slump and UNEMPLOYMENT was high, workers refused to accept wage cuts of about 25 percent and employers locked them out. Even after official arbitrator Judge Kenesaw Mountain Landis endorsed proposed wage cuts, workers refused to accept them, provoking Chicago BUSINESS leaders to form a "Citizen's Committee" to uphold the Landis award. In the end, and after two deaths, a new construction boom helped the workers to defeat the wage cut. By 1926, most leading contractors agreed to pay rates higher than the Landis ruling and to hire union workers for most tasks. The unions remained strong in the years that followed.

The construction industry in the Chicago area has long been subject to governmental regulations about materials, safety, and LAND USE. As early as 1833, the city enacted municipal rules for construction, many of which were designed to prevent fires. By the 1850s, wooden structures were banned from the central business district. After the terrible FIRE OF 1871, building codes became a major political issue. The next mayoral election was won by Joseph Medill, who ran on a "fireproof" ticket that fought for the extension of the brick-only district. A BUILDING CODE was enacted by Chicago in 1881, and the city's Board of Health soon set new standards for light, ventilation, and plumbing. By the time the city's building code underwent a major revision in 1910, the rules governing local construction covered the numbers of doors and sizes of vents, as well as fireproofing and fire escapes. In the 1910s, local ordinances began to govern not only construction practices but the kind of buildings that could be erected in certain areas. As early as the 1880s, REAL-ESTATE developers and local communities had begun to attach restrictions to real-estate transactions in an attempt to control land use in certain areas. By the 1910s, these restrictions were increasingly upheld by the courts; meanwhile, local governments began to create their own land-use regulations. In 1919, the Illinois General Assembly passed a ZONING law modeled on similar legislation created three years earlier in New York. The new law allowed Chicago and other localities to create geographical zones that carried restrictions on building height, area, and land use.

Government agencies were also the industry's leading customers. By 1890, Chicago had spent about $11 million on sewers. During the 1830s and 1840s, Illinois spent millions of dollars to complete the ILLINOIS & MICHIGAN CANAL, over $3 million more was paid to contractors during the late 1860s in order to deepen it. The 1890s saw the creation of another major waterway, the Chicago SANITARY AND SHIP CANAL, a $60 million building project that employed as many as 8,500 men at once. From the city's early years, many of Chicago's construction contractors depended on government orders for a large fraction of their business. Government expenditures on building projects became even more important to the industry during the twentieth century. By the 1970s, between one-quarter and one-half of the value of all new construction in the Chicago region—which totaled roughly $2 billion a year—was paid for by public agencies in any given year. The construction of large numbers of PUBLIC HOUSING units, which responded in part to the decline in construction during the GREAT DEPRESSION, peaked between the 1940s and the 1960s. By the 1970s, the CHICAGO HOUSING AUTHORITY (CHA) owned buildings that had cost over $560 million and were home to about 140,000 tenants. Even more government spending was devoted to the construction and maintenance of roads for automobiles. Chicago's EXPRESSWAY system, much of which was built during the 1950s, cost roughly $1.1 billion to create. By the end of the twentieth century, federal, state, and local governments were paying several hundred million dollars a year for the construction and maintenance of roads in the Chicago region.

Given that the construction industry has always involved large transactions between government agencies and contractors, it is hardly surprising that it has often been surrounded by rumors and allegations—some of them well-founded—about corruption and other illegitimate activity. During the 1880s, the *Chicago Tribune* ran a series of articles exposing corruption in the awarding of construction contracts by the COOK COUNTY commissioners. In 1922, when the Illinois legislature completed an extensive investigation of Chicago's construction industry, it concluded that bribery, graft, and extortion were widespread. Contractors and union officials, as well as government officers, were frequently accused of illegal activity. William Lorimer, a leading Republican politician in Chicago at turn of the twentieth century, was one of several local politicians of his generation who profited from public contracts to construction companies they owned. Ed Kelly, one of the city's leading Democrats, was involved in many questionable transactions when he served as chief engineer of the city's Sanitary District during the 1920s. After an investigation that ended in 1928, Kelly was charged with defrauding the Sanitary District by awarding inflated construction contracts—including some that went to close acquaintances—for sewage plants, roads, and Soldier Field. (These accusations did not prevent Kelly from being chosen mayor in 1933.) During the latter part of the twentieth century, charges of cronyism and lack of competition in the awarding of government contracts still abounded.

As the twenty-first century began, the construction industry in the Chicago area was still mostly recognizable as the descendant of what it had been during the 1920s. Building techniques and tools were more sophisticated, but changes after 1920 were less radical than those that had transformed the industry between the Civil War and the Jazz Age. The geography of construction changed with the expansion of the suburbs and then, in the 1990s, the residential redevelopment of the city. But the organization of work in the building trades was relatively resistant to change. Compared to many sectors of the economy, the construction industry featured relatively small firms and a workforce that remained highly unionized and at least somewhat connected to craft traditions. The region's largest firms, such as Pepper Construction and the Walsh Group, recorded as much as several hundreds of millions of dollars in annual revenues by the end of the 1990s, but they were considerably smaller than the multinational corporations that dominated many other industries.

The pattern of relatively slow long-term change in the modern construction industry applied even to one of its most important developments during the second half of the twentieth century—the participation of women and minority ethnic groups as both workers and contractors. During the 1960s and 1970s, federal affirmative-action programs gave a small boost to the numbers of African Americans and other minorities in the skilled construction trades. Government contracting rules began requiring that a share of public business go to firms owned by women or members of certain ethnic minorities. As the twentieth century came to a close, however, men of European descent still dominated the local industry, and established contractors had begun to challenge affirmative-action measures.

Mark R. Wilson

Loan store, northwest corner of Dearborn and Washington, 1962. City Hall is visible in the background. Photographer: Unknown. Source: Chicago Historical Society.

See also: Architecture; Housing Types; Occupational Safety and Health; Public Works, Federal Funding for; Savings and Loans; Strikes

Further reading: Bonshek, Jane. "The Skyscraper: A Catalyst of Change in the Chicago Construction Industries, 1882–1892." *Construction History* 4 (1988): 53–74. • Prosser, Daniel J. "Chicago and the Bungalow Boom of the 1920s." *Chicago History* 10.2 (1981): 86–95. • Radford, Gail. "New Building and Investment Patterns in 1920s Chicago." *Social Science History* 16.1 (1992): 1–21.

Consulting. *See* Management Consulting

Consumer Credit. From 1910 to 1940, household finance was transformed by a revolution in consumer credit. A credit system that had been disorganized, disreputable, and poorly capitalized was replaced by a new corporate system that was regulated by the state, widely promoted, and in such demand that living on credit became part of the American way of life. Chicagoans played an important role in this transformation.

Credit for consumption is as old as the city itself. Wages for late-nineteenth-century workers were so low that the slightest upsets—from illness, injury, layoffs, or firings—left households in need of borrowed money. Before the credit revolution, borrowers obtained credit from a market that was highly stratified on the basis of social class.

Pawnbrokers served the needs of the poorest. In 1897, 68 pawnbrokers operated shops on State, Clark, and Halsted Streets. Small loan lenders lent money to wage-earners on security of chattel mortgages or wage assignments. The first professional small loan lenders in the country appeared in Chicago in 1870. By 1916, the city led all others in loan offices, with 139 offices lending to one out of five families. Operating illegally under the state's restrictive usury laws, most lenders were honest, but the few who were not gave the entire industry a reputation for remorseless extortion. A third source of credit was the city's retailers. Street peddlers and "borax" stores sold cheap goods on installments to low- and moderate-income customers, while thousands of neighborhood shopkeepers sold "on tic." At Marshall Field's, well-to-do customers were allowed charge accounts.

By 1906, Chicago's leading installment seller was the Spiegel House Furnishing Company. Spiegel boasted, "We Trust the People—Everywhere," and their mail order department spread the gospel of small, easy payments from coast to coast. Spiegel's example prodded Sears and other retailers to follow suit. The result was a credit revolution marked by "the installment plan."

Another leader in the credit revolution was the Household Finance Corporation. Founder Frank Mackey opened a loan office on Madison Street in 1885. In 1894 he moved his headquarters from St. Paul, Minnesota, to Chicago. In 1905, Household became the first

Monthly payments made it possible for consumers to buy expensive items like this chair advertised by Spiegel's in a 1905 issue of the *Woman's Magazine*. Artist: Unknown. Source: Chicago Historical Society.

The color line has reached the north.

Cartoon by John T. McCutcheon, *Chicago Tribune*, July 28, 1919. Artist: John T. McCutcheon. Source: Chicago Tribune.

cash lender to offer monthly installment terms. Household also pioneered in the fight for a Universal Small Loan Law, a reform of the usury laws that ended the era of the "loan shark" and began the era of the personal finance company. Growth in the 1920s made Household the largest personal finance company in the nation. Other consumer finance companies, including Universal CIT Credit Corporation and General Finance Corporation, joined Household in making Chicago their home.

After 1930, consumer credit became more available from credit unions, commercial banks, and issuers of credit cards. Buying "on tic" and pawnbroking declined. But in the 1970s the share of the population operating outside the mainstream financial system grew markedly. In the 1980s and 1990s pawnbrokers returned in numbers and Chicago led the way in another credit innovation: high-interest "payday" loans from check-cashing outlets, of which there were more than 560 in 1985.

Throughout the city's history, consumer credit has enabled Chicagoans both to survive financial emergencies and to improve their standard of living.

Lendol Calder

See also: Banking, Commercial; Department Stores; Savings and Loans; Underground Economy

Further reading: Calder, Lendol. *Financing the American Dream: A Cultural History of Consumer Credit.* 1999. • Caskey, John P. *Fringe Banking: Check-Cashing Outlets, Pawnshops, and the Poor.* 1994. • Kogan, Herman. *Lending Is Our Business: The Story of Household Finance Corporation.* 1965.

Contested Spaces. Sunday, July 27, 1919, dawned hot in Chicago. As the day wore on, city dwellers crowded onto the beaches lining LAKE MICHIGAN seeking relief from the heat. Late that afternoon, 17-year-old Eugene Williams dove off a raft that had wandered toward the 29th Street beach. The AFRICAN AMERICAN teenager was unaware of a confrontation earlier that day when black Chicagoans had walked onto a space conventionally limited to whites. Spotting him in the water, a group of bathers began throwing stones at Williams, who struggled, disappeared, and drowned. As news of his death spread, further violence erupted on the beach and extended out from it. Four days of rioting followed, engulfing large sections of the city. When the violence subsided, 38 persons were dead, 537 were injured, and over 1,000 were left homeless.

Sometime late on the night of Williams's death, *Chicago Tribune* cartoonist John T. McCutcheon sketched a drawing depicting two groups of Lake Michigan bathers, one white and the other black, facing off across a rope. The cartoon represented widespread assumptions that divided the city of Chicago spatially into areas understood to be black or white, though not marked off as in the Jim Crow South. The beach near where Williams drowned was not officially maintained by the city. It was, nonetheless, widely used and hotly contested. Informal segregation reflected the changing racial boundaries of the neighborhoods nearby. Between the "white" beach and a "black" beach immediately to the north lay an invisible line in the sand and water, a line that Williams crossed and that McCutcheon gave physical form in his powerful cartoon. In the aftermath of the riots, the Chicago City Council considered codifying that line through a proposed ordinance that read, in part,

> Resolved that a commission composed of members of both races be formed for the purpose of investigating the causes of the recent riots and to ascertain if it is possible to equitably fix a zone or zones which shall be created for the purpose of limiting within its borders the residences to only colored or white persons.

The ordinance failed to pass, but much of white Chicago hardened its commitment to racial separation in certain aspects of daily life, especially as the city's black population swelled with continued migration from the South. Continuing demands by black Chicagoans for equality ensured that the city's racial boundaries would remain sites of negotiation and conflict.

Contests over space in the Chicago region both predated and long outlived Eugene Williams's fateful swim. In 1812, struggles between peoples—the United States, Great Britain, and various Indian nations—who viewed the western Great Lakes in starkly different ways led to the abandonment of a fort on the banks of the Chicago River and the loss of life on the site that has since become the PRAIRIE AVENUE Historic District. That contest, familiarly known as the FORT DEARBORN Massacre, became the city's foundational event, symbolized by one of the four stars on the city's FLAG. Throughout Chicago's history, spatial contestation encompassed a wide variety of issues, from race relations to divergent views on LAND USE. Chicagoans, like residents of other cities, have divided over all aspects of urban space, from how it is planned to how it is experienced in everyday life, to the less tangible question of how it is perceived.

Twenty-five years before Williams died, Pullman workers provided a vivid example of how conflict could grow out of vastly different understandings of a space. From its inception in 1880, the planned community of PULLMAN was carefully advertised and widely accepted as one solution for various ills that made many of Chicago's working-class neighborhoods unpleasant and even dangerous areas in which to live. With its attractive brick buildings and numerous amenities, Pullman seemed an ideal home for workers and their families. To many who lived there, however, Pullman was less a well-designed ideal than a paternalistic nightmare. As one worker explained:

> We are born in a Pullman house, cradled in a Pullman crib, paid from a Pullman store, taught in a Pullman school, confirmed in a Pullman church, exploited in a Pullman shop, and when we die we'll be buried in a Pullman grave and go to a Pullman hell. (*Chicago Evening Journal,* February 16, 1918)

These divergent understandings of Pullman not only helped to launch the STRIKE in May of 1894; they also served as critical elements in the progress of the strike and the subsequent fate of the town.

To those who perceived the town to be what the Pullman Company claimed it to be, the workers' demands seemed inappropriate at best and ungrateful at worst. Strikers, on the other hand, sought support by demonstrating their vision of Pullman's space to visiting delegates from the American Railway Union and anyone else willing to listen, including state officials, who eventually forced the Pullman Company to sell the town.

These two perspectives on Pullman demonstrate how different the same space can look to various observers, and the implications of such differences. But Pullman, like other working-class neighborhoods tied to nearby employment, also provides a stark contrast to a very different kind of community—bedroom suburbs like PARK FOREST, where William Hollingsworth Whyte profiled the world of the classic "Organization Man" in the 1950s. For residents of Pullman, work, home, and even LEISURE were located in a relatively small geographic area that included the model town and parts of nearby communities. Men and women spent their days in different workspaces but shared a comparable social geography. For many male residents of Park Forest, everyday space included their working lives in downtown Chicago and the commuter trains that brought them there; for many of their wives, everyday space was more likely to be in Park Forest itself.

Though few have been as violent as that of 1919, contests over space have been a consistent part of Chicago's history. Some have been ongoing, created by legal requirements, social differences, environmental factors, or the REAL-ESTATE market, with its pressure for ever more space and rising values. Others have been shorter lived, the product of a particular issue or climate. Some have been largely symbolic, with practical effects reaching far beyond the metropolitan region. Many took a long time to come to the public's attention, sometimes quietly, sometimes dramatically. This essay provides one way of thinking about metropolitan space by contemplating a set of spatial contests across a variety of arenas—political, economic, social, and environmental. To a much greater degree than physical places, spaces are not static: space changes as planned uses, actual uses, and the meanings associated with those uses compete and evolve.

Governmental entities at all levels are instrumental in both defining and PLANNING space. Even after early contests about how states and counties would organize the place that became metropolitan Chicago were resolved, various governmental entities continued to divide the physical space into sometimes competing entities. A property tax bill readily indicates the number of overlapping agencies (PARK DISTRICTS, SCHOOL districts, SPECIAL DISTRICTS, sanitation districts, etc.) that have evolved to govern metropolitan space. During the early years of the GREAT DEPRESSION, the taxes demanded by those different entities led to a short-lived TAX STRIKE that spread from the metropolitan region across the state and left the city of Chicago in even more desperate financial straits. ZONING is perhaps the classic twentieth-century example of governmental definition of urban space. The use of eminent domain to redefine the uses of particular spaces for greater community needs like EXPRESSWAYS and public institutions is another.

Congressional districts and city wards are two sets of political spaces that change according to law and custom. Congressional districts are redrawn every 10 years as population changes and states gain or lose seats in the U.S. House of Representatives. During most of the nineteenth century and the first years of the twentieth, Illinois gained population and seats, necessitating the regular redrawing of congressional district lines after each census. Beginning with the redistricting following the 1870 census, Illinois turned to a policy of determining congressional districts by measuring spaces rather than people, which at the time was legal since population mattered only in terms of how many representatives a state deserved. Chicago was growing rapidly—its population accounting for almost a third of the total Illinois population—and downstate legislators feared the city's potential influence in STATE POLITICS. One way to thwart that power was to draw congressional boundaries that created districts of roughly equal space, even if very unequal population. For nearly a century, that strategy—supported by a similar strategy in state legislature districts—ensured that Chicago's political influence would not grow concomitant with its population.

Even as the state emphasized territory, city leaders fastened on a different formula for the organization of wards and representation in the city council. As class and ethnic pockets grew and shaped affiliations to political issues and parties, ward lines began to follow the perceived socioeconomic boundaries of the city's neighborhoods. As wards grew geographically smaller and were represented by one council member rather than two and as patterns of residential clustering and segregation sharpened, individual wards came to be seen as the domain of particular groups and parties. In the first half of the twentieth century, wards provided ethnic and racial groups with access to political power and added to the importance of neighborhoods in the fight for resources.

In 1962, the U.S. Supreme Court ruled in *Baker v. Carr* that districting schemes allowing huge discrepancies in population were unconstitutional. New contests over redistricting erupted as different political players tried to maximize their "CLOUT" through the old practice of gerrymandering—drawing political boundaries to enhance the voting strength of one group at the expense of others. Reapportionment has since become hotly contested, as political parties have sought to juggle legislative boundaries to improve their electoral chances, interest groups have worked to secure or preserve an electoral voice, and incumbents have placed a priority on retaining their seats.

If politicians have shaped and reshaped space to determine the distribution of power, others in government have used the power to define space to shape perceptions and realities of how people inhabit those spaces—and how much those inhabitances are worth. Between 1935 and 1940, the Home Owners' Loan Corporation, a federal agency established in 1933, launched a massive survey to determine current and future values of real estate to help lenders decide which neighborhoods would be good lending targets. Surveyors visited neighborhoods, consulted local institutions, and filed reports that assigned ratings of "A," "B," "C," or "D" to each community surveyed. An "A" or "B" rating encouraged lenders. A "C" discouraged them, and a "D" meant that residential lending virtually disappeared from these "REDLINED" communities.

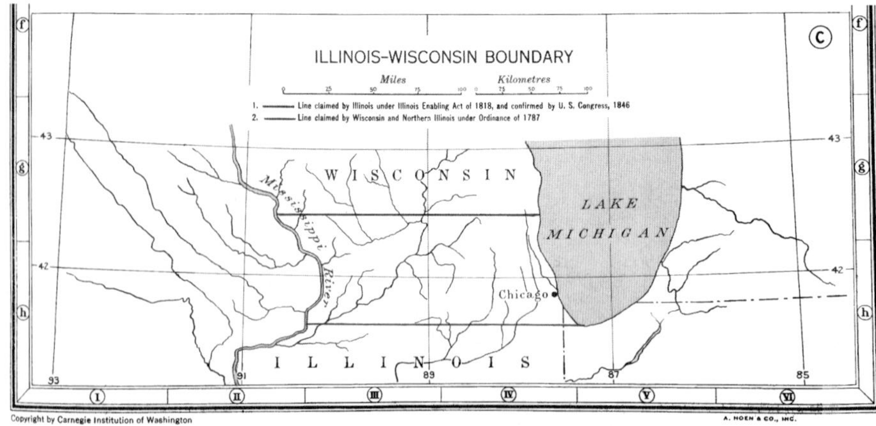

The changing Illinois-Wisconsin boundary line. Cartographer: Charles O. Paullin. Source: The Newberry Library.

Racial Restrictive Covenants on Chicago's South Side in 1947

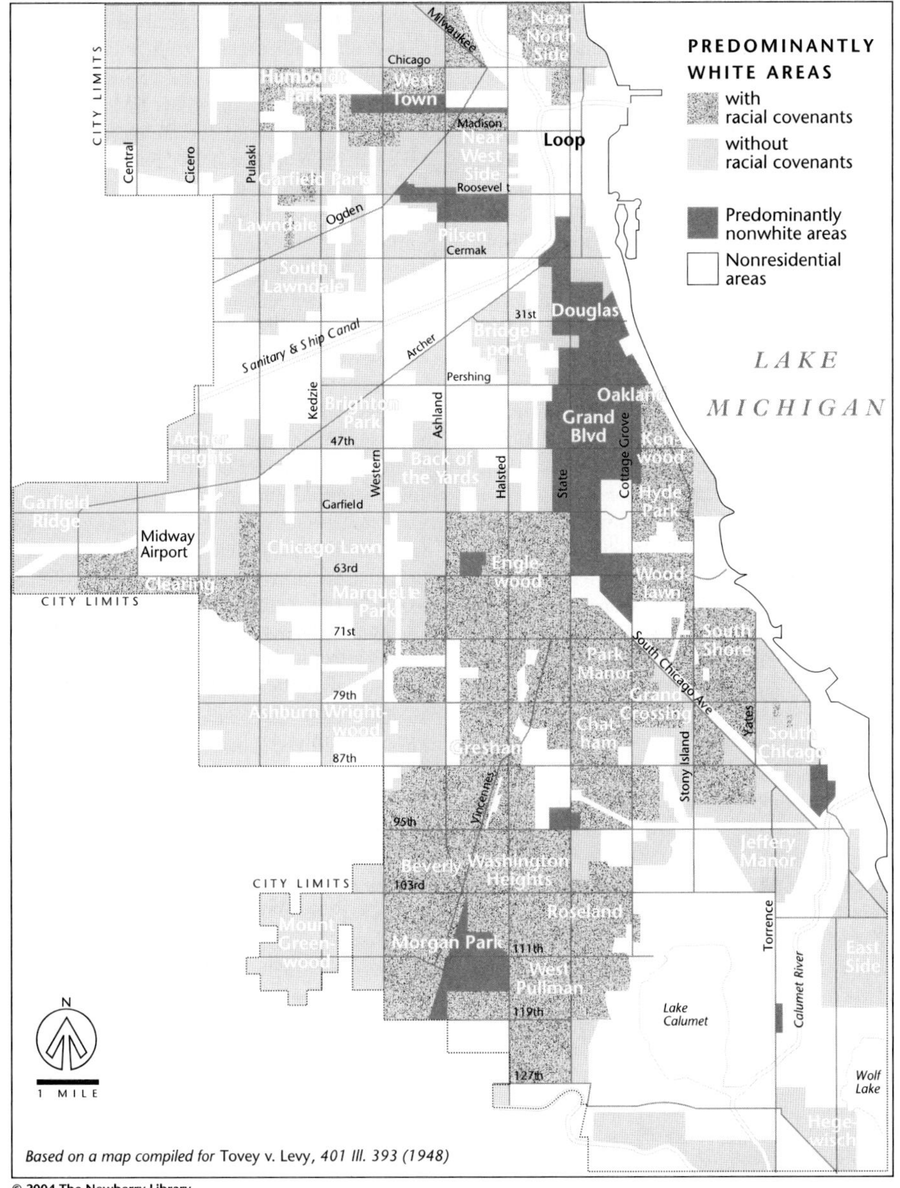

Based on a map compiled for Tovey v. Levy, *401 Ill. 393 (1948)*

From 1916 until 1948, racially restrictive covenants were used to keep Chicago's neighborhoods white. In language suggested by the Chicago Real Estate Board, legally binding covenants attached to parcels of land varying in size from city block to large subdivision prohibited African Americans from using, occupying, buying, leasing, or receiving property in those areas. This map stems from one used in a lawsuit (*Tovey v. Levy*, 1948) that was brought to enforce covenants. It shows that in 1947 covenants covered large parts of the city and, in combination with zones of nonresidential use, almost wholly surrounded the African American residential districts of the period, cutting off corridors of extension. Many of the neighborhoods encumbered with racially restrictive covenants were subsequently settled by African Americans once the covenants had been declared unconstitutional.

Although not applied uniformly across the country, these categories were applied in Chicago and elsewhere in ways that reinforced existing prejudices and practices. Older neighborhoods, built before central heating and modern plumbing, were flagged as poor targets for the new long-term mortgages and for home improvement loans to be guaranteed by the federal government. So, too, were neighborhoods experiencing ethnic or racial change. "Mixed" neighborhoods received similarly low marks, as did neighborhoods where older industries had closed or moved to new suburban locations. Newer neighborhoods and more homogenous and well-to-do neighborhoods received high marks for secure lending. By 1939, most residential space in the Chicago metropolitan area had been surveyed and rated, and the ratings helped to shape a new residential geography once World War II ended. Mortgage money flowed into new developments in the suburbs and, to a more limited extent, into the city's "A" and sometimes "B" communities. At the same time, "C" communities were flagged as risky bets, neighborhoods that might be improved but might also fall into the category of "blight." The "D" communities were dismissed as already blighted. Such classifications shaped the perceptions of, experiences in, and planning for those spaces for decades. They helped to stimulate the postwar boom in the suburbs and the outlying areas of the city, where financing for housing development and purchase became more readily available than in the older sections of the central city. They helped shape the contours of URBAN RENEWAL as well, encouraging white Chicagoans in the belief that the presence of African Americans lowered property values and providing tacit support for agencies to limit residential lending in mixed and African American neighborhoods.

By the 1960s, Chicago had become a symbol of the problems associated with spatial segregation and the efforts to dismantle it. Perhaps no effort highlighted that symbolism more substantially than the Chicago Freedom Movement in 1966. Local CIVIL RIGHTS leaders invited Martin Luther King, Jr., to fight for OPEN HOUSING in Chicago and to help dismantle the formal and informal practices that had made the city the most racially segregated in the nation: 9 of 10 white Chicagoans or 9 of 10 black Chicagoans would have had to move within the city for Chicago to achieve some kind of neighborhood racial parity. From NORTH LAWNDALE (where King took an apartment) to Soldier Field and City Hall (where protesters demanded open housing), city spaces became sites of contests over space. The most infamous of these was surely the one at the border of MARQUETTE PARK, where hostile whites screaming racial epithets at marchers protesting the practices of real-estate agents helped mold a new image of working-class ethnic whites. No image was stronger than that of King bleeding from the forehead after being struck by a brick thrown by a white demonstrator.

A different kind contest over space, relating more to its use in the past, has taken place in metropolitan Chicago's industrial districts. From the unwelcome stench of Chicago's sewage in downstream cities like LOCKPORT after the CHICAGO RIVER changed direction, to the polluted air that contributed to the respiratory problems of all who lived downwind from a steel mill or a CHEMICAL plant, concerns over the environment have produced their own contests over space. For generations, many of the region's industries created toxic WASTE and pollutants along with their products and the jobs necessary to create them. The pages of Upton Sinclair's THE JUNGLE are filled with vivid descriptions of such

Trumbull Park Homes Race Riots, 1953–1954

South Deering erupted in violence in 1953 over the issue of racial integration at the neighborhood's lone public housing project, Trumbull Park Homes, located at 105th Street and Yates Avenue. Since 1937, the Chicago Housing Authority (CHA) had maintained an unstated policy to house only whites at projects that, like Trumbull Park, were located in entirely white neighborhoods. However, the project was "accidentally" integrated on July 30, 1953, because the CHA assumed that Betty Howard, an exceptionally fair-skinned African American, was white. Beginning on August 5 and continuing nightly for weeks thereafter, crowds of whites directed fireworks, rocks, and racial epithets toward Betty and Donald Howard's apartment. Police responded with a show of force but few arrests. South Deering leaders openly pressured Chicago politicians and the CHA to remove the Howards, while progressive forces argued for further integration. In October, after lengthy debate, the CHA's commissioners reluctantly agreed to move in 10 additional black families, triggering a new round of white violence directed at blacks. A massive police presence prevented full-scale rioting, but chronic racial tension and sporadic violence continued through the 1950s. Not until 1963 could African Americans openly use a neighboring public park without police protection. The conflict claimed the career of the CHA's progressive executive director, Elizabeth Wood, who had pushed the CHA's commissioners to further integrate the project. White violence had succeeded in blocking any further racial integration beyond the token black population in the project.

D. Bradford Hunt

pollution in and around the stockyards, from the canning room floors to the banks of the infamous "Bubbly Creek." Over time, pollutants built up, devastating the land in and around the plants, tainting nearby water sources, and filling the air with particulate matter. Moreover, assumptions about the degraded nature of those spaces combined with zoning regulations to encourage the nearby placement of other environmental threats such as landfills. For much of the last half of the nineteenth century and first half of the twentieth, pollution was taken for granted as a fact of industrialization and a characteristic of working-class life on the job and at homes near the plants. A community newspaper described the drive down the Calumet Expressway in 1964, from 103rd to the city limits, as "a path only for the strong of stomach."

Even as such areas emerged, migration and business patterns meant that the neighborhoods surrounding those areas changed as well. As industrial wages improved with unionization, many workers at the plants moved away from the worst of the pollution, leaving their former homes available for families that, because of discriminatory practices or limited incomes, had fewer housing choices. As industries started to close, communities from Waukegan to Michigan City were left economically devastated as well. In response, activists, union leaders, and politicians helped launch local and national programs for environmental justice. Plans for transforming "brownfields," the Environmental Preservation Agency's designation for the most polluted of these spaces, involved both removing the most toxic pollutants and bringing in new uses that might help sustain the neighborhoods around them.

As the image of the active smokestack has shifted over the years from implying a productive space providing lucrative employment to conjuring an arena clouded by industrial pollution, Chicagoans have become accustomed to contested spaces generating equally fierce debates about what is above their homes. When, in 1947, Chicago planners decided Municipal Airport (Midway) could not adequately meet the future demands of air traffic (and local residents had begun to protest the noise), the city began developing O'Hare International Airport and, in 1956, annexed it to the city. In the intervening five decades, developers and urban growth have transformed the former farmland to the city's northwest, little disturbed by the air traffic, into expensive residential suburbs greatly bothered by ceaseless jet noise. The political climate has also changed as suburbs developed new clout and noise has become an issue for government regulation. NIMBY (Not In My Back Yard) politics in the neighborhoods around O'Hare have become powerful enough to contest the will of the city of Chicago. As a result, further O'Hare expansion has been caught up in complicated negotiations between Chicago, O'Hare's nearby suburbs, and more distant locations like Peotone and Springfield, Illinois, Gary and Indianapolis, Indiana, and even Washington DC.

What constitutes the "success" of a given space can thus mean something different to its residents, planners, and developers. This is clearest in the case of urban gentrification, but it can also be witnessed in rural areas. In Kane and McHenry Counties, efforts are underway to preserve farms and farmlands from what seems to be the unrelenting spread of residential, commercial, and industrial development. Interested in maintaining a way of life and a historical identity, as well as managing the inevitable demands of growing populations, residents of those counties have come together to limit development. Standing in sharp opposition to this movement are developers and farm owners who know that homes and businesses make their acreage far more valuable than do soybeans or corn.

Although this contest on the outer edges of the metropolitan area may seem very different from other struggles over space, it is part of an ongoing contest that began with the settlement of Chicago itself. The contest between rural and urban space is as important a part of the city's experience as the struggles over race and ethnicity, which themselves often involve contested city spaces and boundaries. All of these struggles involved planned spaces, perceptions about kinds of spaces, and historical uses of space, and have much to do with how people use their space.

Janice L. Reiff

See also: Economic Geography; Environmental Politics; Government, City of Chicago; Multicentered Chicago; Planning Chicago; Race Riots; Work Culture

Further reading: The literature of urban space is voluminous, as are the studies that document Chicago's ongoing contests over space. The most important

Richard Brummel harvesting soybeans on one of the last farms in the Naperville area, October 2000. Photographer: Mario Petitti. Source: Chicago Tribune.

Painting by Richard Estes, *Michigan Avenue with View of the Art Institute,* 1984. Source: The Art Institute of Chicago.

The City as Artifact: The Above-Ground Archaeology of an Urban History

God made the country," wrote William Cowper, "and man made the town." Modern cities, Chicago among them, are humankind's largest collections of ART, ARCHITECTURE, and artifice. The Chicago cityscape can be thought of as a huge Rosetta stone, as a historical landscape that is, at once, a panorama and a palimpsest. Metropolitan Chicago, encompassing eight counties and more than five thousand square miles, is an even larger three-dimensional history text to explore.

Chicago's artifact assemblages exist in two main forms: (1) as artifacts that can be found in situ (still in place), like Leonard Volk's *Stephen A. Douglas Memorial* (1881), with "The Little Giant" standing atop a 46-foot marble column overlooking the Illinois Central Railroad right-of-way that he successfully lobbied Congress for in 1853; and (2) as extant artifacts in museums, historical societies, libraries, and other cultural institutions, like the Richard Estes painting *Michigan Avenue with a View of the Art Institute.*

In the first instance, metropolitan Chicago can be understood as a massive, outdoor museum without walls, a historical landscape accessible to residents and visitors any time, day, or season. Repositories that collect and curate a city's cultural memory, on the other hand, display their material culture (an archaeological term used here as largely synonymous with artifacts) in a more restricted and manipulated context. Together, the city and its repositories provide historical information and insight for understanding Chicago as a collective (and collected) artifact of past and present urban life. Together, they are the result of innumerable individual and communal decisions made by surveyors, land speculators, homeowners, INSURANCE companies, REAL-ESTATE developers, ARTISTS, ZONING boards, investors, architects, city councils, URBAN RENEWAL ("removal" to some) experts, individual and corporate businesses, engineers, demolition contractors, architectural firms, and city planners.

To explore metropolitan Chicago history outdoors, one might employ a technique that anthropologist John Cotter and I have called "above-ground archaeology." This way of looking at urban artifacts is indebted to traditional (below ground) archaeology practice but without the laborious digging, applying basic archaeological techniques to the study of contemporary landscapes. Among the most useful methods are (a) *stratification,* the identification of the layering of different cultural remains in a specific geographical site; (b) *typology,* the classification of artifacts by form or type categories; (c) *iconography,* the study of the meanings of symbols and symbolic systems; (d) *serration,* a method of dating artifacts by arranging and comparing them as to design, material, workmanship, or style; and (e) *diffusion,* the tracing of cultural patterns, particularly when embodied in artifacts such as dwellings or workplaces, as to their geographical origin and subsequent spatial distribution.

In the past decade, archaeologists themselves have endorsed such an approach in studying the American landscape. "Archaeological methods can profitably be applied to any phase or aspect of history," argues Grahame Clark. "A coherent and unified body of subject matter entirely appropriate to the archaeologist," writes James Deetz, "is the study of all the material aspects of culture in their behavioral context, regardless of provenance." Applying the archaeological methodology that Clark suggests to the range of material data Deetz wishes to survey, contemporary archaeologists have shown how important information and insight about human behavior, past and present, can be extracted from urban material culture data without necessarily having to physically excavate it. Historical and cultural geographers concur with this assumption. The student of the cultural landscape is a kind of contemporary archaeologist, with somewhat different materials, similar methods, and nearly identical motives. In addition to its obvious debts to archaeology as traditionally conceived, above-ground archaeology borrows much of its theory and practice from related fields such as art history, cultural geography, architectural history, toponymy, history of city and town PLANNING, urban folkways research, and the history of technology.

Photograph by Jay Wolke, *The Running Horse—Dan Ryan Expressway,* 1985.

Geologic/Geographic Influences

Chicago, like several of its nineteenth-century economic rivals (e.g., Cincinnati, St. Louis), is in part the *way* it is because of *where* it is. The glacial waters of what geologists (and some pre-1800 MAPMAKERS) call Lake Chicago (now LAKE MICHIGAN) found their way through the drainage divide via two valleys, or sags, en route westward to the Mississippi, recognizable today as the Calumet Sag Channel and the Chicago SANITARY AND SHIP CANAL.

As the ice sheet retreated irregularly, it occasionally paused long enough to permit shore currents to create spits, bars, islands (surviving in place names such as Stony Island and Blue Island), and beaches, as well as a spoke-like pattern of drainage beds radiating out from the mouth of the CHICAGO RIVER. In later times, these sandy strips were the only well-drained ground in the spring, and the indigenous peoples used them for overland travel when the surrounding area was waterlogged. In the city plan, some of the major streets that deviate from James Thompson's original grid plan—such as North Clark Street, the appropriately named Ridge Avenue, and Milwaukee and Vincennes Avenues—are fossils of these glacial formations and Indian pathways.

The above-ground archaeologist finds other spatial history both on current Chicago road maps and when driving its highways. Along the South Branch of the Chicago River (e.g., from Cermak Road to 95th Street), the city's past TRANSPORTATION types remain visible in a horizontal stratigraphy. Within a mile of each other, on either side of Interstate 55, lie an old glacial streambed (ca. 13,500 BP); an Illini Indian foot trail (ca. AD 1400–1600); the PORTAGE route of the French *coureurs de bois* (ca. 1793); a nineteenth-century drover trail and plank road that became Archer Avenue (ca. 1836 and later immortalized by Finley Peter Dunne as the tavern site of "Mr. Dooley"); the path of the ILLINOIS & MICHIGAN CANAL (ca. 1848); and the road bed of the Chicago & Alton Railroad (ca. 1860). All surround the most recent transportation corridor, I-55, which, as a part of the National System of Interstate and Defense Highways, owes part of its origin to the COLD WAR, being a planned evacuation route in time of nuclear holocaust. Chicago photographer Jay Wolke has captured part of the material culture of this corridor in his contemporary image of *The Running Horse—Dan Ryan Expressway* .

Landscape Vegetation

In a city whose very name derives from an Indian reference to wild garlic (stinking onion) and whose Latin motto (*Urbs in Horto*) promotes "a city in a garden," the above-ground archaeology student should expect evidence of how past plantings continue in the present urban environment. The city's parks, botanical gardens, estates, CONSERVATORIES, CEMETERIES, FOREST PRESERVES, and arboretums, despite their seeming naturalness, betray human hands on the land. Some of their LANDSCAPE authors are nationally famous: Frederick Law Olmsted (JACKSON and WASHINGTON PARKS, 1872; the suburban plan for RIVERSIDE, Illinois, 1869); Ossian Cole Simonds (GRACELAND CEMETERY, 1878); and Jens Jensen (GARFIELD, HUMBOLDT, and Douglas Parks, 1906–1910). The placement, size, design, and vegetation in their artful yet changing collections of plants demonstrate a perennial issue in human history: the relationships between nature and culture.

Chicago's parks illustrate a miniature history of this relationship and also reveal the interconnections between plants and POLITICS. Compare, for instance, the pleasure garden

Mural by Richard Haas, *Homage to the Chicago School,* 1980. 1211 North LaSalle Street. Photographer: Thomas Schlereth.

park (e.g., Jackson Park) of the 1850–1900 era; the Progressive reform park (e.g., Pulaski Park), first appearing about 1900 to 1920; followed by the recreational facility park (e.g., Seward Park), first developed in the 1930s.

In addition to these formal, public landscapes, one also finds vernacular "natural" material culture throughout the Chicago region. For instance, well into the twentieth century, Indian trail trees, like the one at 630 Lincoln Street in WILMETTE, survived in northern Illinois. POTAWATOMI Indians bent or buried young tree sprouts or saplings to indicate the direction of their travel routes east and west, to designate sources of fresh water, and to mark the path to the Chicago Portage.

In a highly urbanized area such as metropolitan Chicago, many examples of the city's early plants survive only in the area's place nomenclature. Consequently, the alert aboveground archaeologist must be a recorder and interpreter of such data. Often such names are small time capsules containing linguistic, historic, geographic, and folkloristic information about local history.

For instance, those who fly into O'HARE AIRPORT in Chicago have baggage tags labeled "ORD." That abbreviation recalls not the name of the person (World War II flyer Edward O'Hare) for whom the airport is named, but its former land use as a productive fruit-growing region known as Orchard Place. Samuel J. Walker, a Kentuckian who moved to Chicago and subsequently bought up much of the land around Reuben Street from Madison to 12th Street, decided to rename the street Ashland to honor his native state's political hero, Henry Clay, whose Kentucky home was known as Ashland. Warner left still another marking on the land when he planted both sides of his residential avenue with rows of white ash.

Street and Road Names (Histories)

Streets—be they boulevards or parkways, ALLEYS or avenues—are a city's conduits of people and products. Chicago's commercial/retail/tourist "Main Street" has shifted over the city's history from Lake to State to Michigan. Residential avenues of affluence have also migrated: from South Michigan Avenue to PRAIRIE AVENUE to North Lake Shore Drive to suburban lanes.

Street names often commemorate the presence of earlier peoples in a region (Chippewa, ILLINOIS, Potawatomi); the first people on a city block (Kinzie, Huey, Farrell); the first people on the block who developed adjoining blocks (Diversey, Belden, Palmer). As might be expected, in Chicago's toponymy we find numerous city fathers (Ogden, Damen, Elston); heroes (Lincoln, Altgeld, Cermak); and builders (Jensen, Burnham, Mies van der Rohe).

To the street historian every building is a historic site. Additions to a structure often reveal parts of its history; for example, in 1974, the Chicago firm of Skidmore, Owings & Merrill completed the Sears Tower, then the tallest example of mega-architecture in the world. A decade later, they felt the need to renovate the building's ground floor and add an atrium whose form recalls Joseph Paxton's Crystal Palace design for the first world's fair in London in 1851. Why? Building users complained it took herculean efforts to enter or exit the structure from perennially windswept Wacker Drive. Buildings half finished also tell aboveground archaeology tales. For almost a century, anyone walking along Dearborn or Clark could look up at Henry Ives Cobb's NEWBERRY LIBRARY and, on its side elevations, see a half-complete Romanesque arch—an unintended historical marker to the city's financial crisis of 1893. Also on the city's NEAR NORTH SIDE, one encounters an artifact assemblage by one artist dedicated to another. On the four sides of a 1929 APARTMENT hotel converted into a 1981 apartment building, urban muralist Richard Haas executed a trompe l'oeil, his *Homage to the Chicago School* (1980). The 16-story artwork is primarily a visual paean to Louis Sullivan; it includes an illustration of the architect's terracotta-ornamented window from the Merchants National Bank in Grinnell, Iowa, rising above the famous Golden Entrance to his 1893 WORLD'S COLUMBIAN EXPOSITION Transportation Building. Between these two facades, Haas added a playful "reflection" of the Chicago Board of Trade Building (1930), two miles south.

Mural art, almost always public and frequently political, provides a range of historical evidence for the city observer. Chicago abounds in striking examples. For instance, neighborhood ethnicity is portrayed in William Walker's *History of the Packinghouse Worker* (1974) on the Charles A. Hayes Family Investment Center; *I Welcome Myself to a New Place* (1988), by Olivia Gude, Marcus Jefferson, and

Mural by William Walker, *History of the Packinghouse Worker,* 1974. 4859 South Wabash. Photographer: Catherine Gass.

I Welcome Myself to a New Place: Roseland Pullman Mural, by Olivia Gude, Jon Pounds, and Marcus Jefferson of Chicago Public Art Group, 1988. 113th Street at Cottage Grove Avenue. Photographer: Catherine Gass.

Mural by Marcos Raya et al., *Casa Aztlan,* 1977. 1831 South Racine Avenue. Photographer: Thomas Schlereth.

Jon Pounds, is a history book on an underpass wall in Pullman; Marcos Raya and others depict Latino history on the front entrance of Casa Aztlan, a local community center at 1831 S. Racine in Chicago's Pilsen district, formally a Czech neighborhood now inhabited by Spanish-speaking Americans. On the Northwest Side, the Humboldt Park murals relate the past of a German community that is also commemorated in city streets elsewhere named Goethe, Schiller, and, of course, Humboldt Boulevard and Humboldt Drive.

The above-ground archaeologist walking the city's streets should watch for what I call "time collages" and what below-ground archaeologists call a "tell." Often one will find, lined up along a single streetscape or clustered about a civic space, a series of artifacts from different eras of a community's history. An above-ground researcher can discover architectural styles (in Oak Park, for example) layered horizontally just as the below-ground archaeologist searches in a vertical stratigraphy. Such time collages also reveal changes in land use, economic and social status, and aesthetic and design tastes, as well as shifts in population densities.

In Chicago, typical time collages lend themselves to a variety of personal explorations. One can walk up or down Dearborn Street (from Congress to Wacker or the reverse), carefully looking left and right to see a century of modern office/skyscraper designs. Another approach is to follow the Chicago River's course, remembering two things: first, a definition of material culture is "all artifacts are a manipulation of nature," and originally the Chicago River emptied into Lake Michigan, but human engineering reversed its natural course in the second half of the nineteenth century; second, Chicago boasts more moveable bridges than any city in the world—46 of varying types and sizes. One might also position oneself at the corner of Chicago and Michigan Avenues and, turning in a circle, note the diverse land uses of the Chicago Tower and Pumping Station (1866, 1869), the Fourth Presbyterian Church (1914), the John Hancock Center (1969), the Palmolive Building/Playboy Building (1929), and Water Tower Place (1976).

Urban Shards

To the archaeologist who "does the dirt" for his or her data, a shard is a fragment of material culture. Above-ground archaeology shards include what art historian George Kubler calls "prime objects" and archaeologist Robert Ascher labels as "superartifacts"—that is, famous material culture icons of the Chicago built environment. Among these shards are the city's central transit track, created in the 1880s and popularly known as "the Loop"; the Jane Addams Hull House (1889); the Frank Lloyd Wright Robie House (1906–9); and the nation's first MacDonald's fast-food restaurant (1955) in Des Plaines.

Above-ground archaeologists also use the term "shard" in its traditional meaning: an incomplete piece, part, or physical remain surviving from the past. In an urban complex such as Chicago—once described by Carl Sandburg as continuously being "built up" and simultaneously "torn down"—the city's physical past is most often piecemeal. A lonely 1879 Union Stock Yard Gate at 850 West Exchange stands bereft of its nineteenth-century context. Twin equine heads on a Pullman gasoline station (11201 S. Cottage Grove Avenue) recall the building's original use (ca. 1881) as a livery stable. The Board of Trade Building (141 W. Jackson Boulevard) provides a hybrid view of the architectural, sculptural, and interior design preferences of the art deco 1930s in comparison with the postmodern ambitions of the 1980s. The remodeling (1980) of the Mergenthaler Linotype Building (531 S. Plymouth Court) includes a modern colorful facade plus a playful incorporation of a facade section ofTom's Grill and Sandwiches, a former adjacent eatery, as a sculptural *objet trouvé.* Even the Chicago Historical Society has had its migrations and additions—from being headquartered in an 1892 Romanesque building (still extant at 632 N. Dearborn and currently a nightclub) to a 1932 Colonial Revival structure (North Avenue and Clark Street) to which a modern International Style addition was affixed in 1988.

Detail of *Fragments of Chicago's Past.* Permanent installation in the architecture gallery of the Art Institute of Chicago. Photographer: Robert Lifson. Source: The Art Institute of Chicago.

The above-ground archaeologist can ascend a skyscraper and decipher one of the country's most intriguing urban spaces. Painting by Roger Brown, *Land of Lincoln,* 1978. Source: School of the Art Institute of Chicago.

Urban shards can also result from deliberate attempts to embellish artifacts. In addition to its homage to medieval Gothicism (particularly the Rouen Cathedral in France), Chicago's Tribune Tower (designed by Howells & Hood, 1925) features a stone screen depicting characters (a howling dog and Robin Hood figure) that serve as visual references to the architect's surnames. As Chicago's retort to New York's Woolworth Building (1913), the tower also features, on its lower elevations, an extravaganza of assorted building pieces from well-known structures throughout the world, including a fragment of the Great Wall of China.

A shard assemblage of a different time and place is the massive sculpture (now demolished) executed by Nancy Rubins for Berwyn in 1980. An *objet trouvé* artist, Rubins scoured the streets of Berwyn for artifacts that its residents had discarded. As below-ground archaeologists have often dug trash dumps and even privies in search of important cultural information, Rubins searched amongst and then structured Berwyn's communal remains into a 30-foot sculpture she called "Big Bil-Bored." Big Bil's demise in 1998 illustrates three maxims every above-ground archaeologist must continually remember: first, most material culture, despite its physicality and seeming temporal tenacity, is ephemeral; second, humans destroy more artifacts than they save; third, with the exception of structures whose interior spaces are accessible, much of the above-ground archaeology of the city deals with public rather than private history.

Chicago's often tardy historic preservation movement has yielded other urban shards. Many of Louis Sullivan's buildings have been demolished, but fragments of his work enjoy a second life; for instance, the main entrance to his Stock Exchange Building (which Alice Sinkevitch calls the "wailing wall of the city's preservation corps") has been relocated to the grounds of the Art Institute at Monroe Street and Columbus Drive. The Art Institute also salvaged Sullivan's exquisitely stenciled Trading Room and reconstructed it as, perhaps, one of the first commercial period rooms in the United States. New York's Metropolitan Museum of Art took home an interior Sullivan copper staircase to display in its American Wing.

The ultimate Chicago tribute, at least to date, to the architectural shard, is Pauline Saliga's museum exhibition and published checklist, *Fragments of Chicago's Past: The Collection of Architectural Fragments at the Art Institute of Chicago.* Innumerable building parts from Chicago, once in situ, are now in museum. Among the more intriguing relics now ensconced in the Art Institute are an engaged capital from the 1887–88 Church of the Covenant; a playful fish ornament from the base of the 1907–8 Oliver Building; and the study model for the head of a sprite for the 1913–14 Midway Gardens.

Sculpture by Nancy Rubins, *Big Bil-Bored,* 1980. Cermak Road and Harlem Avenue, Berwyn. Photographer: Thomas Schlereth.

Historical Markers

The fragments in the Art Institute's collections have become artifacts with two meanings. Their first significance is the context for which they were originally made. Their second meaning is their selection (and periodic display) as artifacts enshrined in a museum.

Historical markers and monuments erected outside a community's museums, historical societies, and other cultural institutions also have a double existence. First, they provide the above-ground archaeologist with three types of visual/verbal information: (a) about a vanished historic site (e.g., the brass markers embedded in the pedestrian sidewalks on the southwest side of the Michigan Avenue Bridge, which outline the perimeters of FORT DEARBORN between 1803 and 1816; (b) about an event (e.g., the plaque on the Jackson Boulevard corner of the Continental Illinois National Bank Building, which notes that in 1883 an association of railroad executives met in Chicago and voted to adopt Standard Railway Time for the entire country); or (c) about an individual (e.g., the sculptures of Abraham Lincoln by Augustus Saint-Gaudens: the "seated" Lincoln in Grant Park [1908] and the "standing" Lincoln in Lincoln Park [1887]).

Like these examples, most historic markers are deliberately celebratory. The four stars on Chicago's FLAG, for example, mark four events in the city's material culture history: its founding, the fire, and two world's fairs. The Marquette Building (1893–95) interior honors the 1674–75 expedition of Jacques Marquette in an ensemble of sculpture, mosaic, and bronze. In the Second Franklin Building (720 S. Dearborn Street), one finds Oskar Gross's colorful mosaic murals depicting the history of printing.

A few of Chicago's historical monuments, however, have been artifacts of controversy and contest. Consider the tempestuous history of the historic site known (depending on one's politics) as the HAYMARKET Square Riot, Massacre, Bombing, Affair, or Anarchy. The only nearby tangible reminder of the 1886 disturbance is the sculpture now at the Timothy J. O'Connor Police Training Academy (1300 W. Jackson Boulevard). A POLICE officer, his arm upraised, restrains an invisible mob, commanding peace, "In the name of the people of Illinois." There has been, however, little peace surrounding this icon of order. Its plaques at the base were stolen in 1903. Later, a streetcar motorman rammed into the statue, claiming he hated to look at it. Moved to Union Park in 1928, the sculpture remained unmolested until the civil turbulence of the 1960s, when it was defaced with black paint and twice bombed. At one time, the sculpture was placed under 24-hour guard and moved to Central Police Headquarters, from which it was transferred to its present site in 1976.

A region's cemeteries contain historic monuments to personal histories. The above-ground archeologist looks at them as documents of cultural geography, public sculpture, and historical markers. To be sure, the rich and famous are frequently most prominent, often trying to best each other with gigantic mausoleums in death as they did with their ostentatious mansions in life. In Chicago's many cemeteries, two stand out: the Couch Mausoleum in LINCOLN PARK and the Ludwig Mies van der Rohe grave in Graceland Cemetery. In the latter site, Chicago's most famous architectural modernist lies under a single rectangular black granite slab parallel with the earth—a horizontal curtain-wall SKYSCRAPER in miniature.

Few know who the Couches were or why they are still interred in a city park. Ira Couch built Tremont House, an early Chicago HOTEL. The further explanation as to why the mausoleum has survived since Ira's death in 1857 is important to thinking of the city as artifact, a space crafted by both private and public decisions. The family tomb is where it is for three reasons: (1) present-day Lincoln Park was once a municipal burying ground (from which the Couch Mausoleum is the only extant above-ground tomb); (2) when park officials demanded the Couches remove their deceased kin to make way for the park, they refused; and (3) when the issue came before the Illinois Supreme Court, the justices ruled to let the Couches rest in peace.

Controversial sculpture honoring the police presence during the Haymarket riots. John Gelert, *Haymarket Riot Monument,* 1889. Photographer: A. Witteman. Source: Chicago Historical Society.

Glorifying the workers' cause, another Haymarket monument stands in Forest Home Cemetery in Forest Park. Sculpture by Albert Weinert, *Haymarket Martyrs' Monument,* 1893. Source: Chicago Historical Society.

To consider the city as a laboratory recalls Chicagoan John Dewey's advocacy of the laboratory school—an artifact still extant on the University of Chicago's campus. To this author, it also prompts remembering Dewey's insistence that "all history is local history." So believes the above-ground archaeologist. As with the below-ground archaeologist, the researcher who works primarily above ground does not solve every historical riddle in the field. Indeed, above-ground archaeology cannot be done without the data we normally find in local and city libraries, archives, and municipal record offices. The extant cityscape, however, always beckons. The past is visual as well as verbal. It survives in space as well as in time. "Reading the landscape is a humane art," geographer D. W. Meinig reminds us, "unrestricted to any profession, unbounded by any field, unlimited in its challenges and its pleasures."

Thomas J. Schlereth

See also: Art, Public; Built Environment of the Chicago Region; Chicago Studied; Historical Preservation; Mapping Chicago

Further reading: British landscape historians and historical archaeologists pioneered the idea of above-ground archaeology even though they did not use this particular terminology. Examples of their work include Maurice Beresford, *History on the Ground: Six Studies in Maps and Landscapes* (rev. ed. 1971); Michael Aston and Trevor Rowley, *Landscape Archaeology: An Introduction to Field Work Techniques on Post-Roman Landscapes* (1974); Penelope Lively, *The Presence of the Past: An Introduction to Landscape History* (1976); and W. G. Hoskins, *The Making of the English Landscape* (1955, 1963).

Perhaps the most useful introductions to the principles, practices, and problems of applying modern archaeological research to social history are Grahame Clark's *Archaeology and Society* (1964) and James Deetz's *Invitation to Archaeology* (1967).

American above-ground theory and practice can be found in John L. Cotter, "Above-Ground Archaeology," *American Quarterly* 26.3 (August 1974): 266 280; Thomas J. Schlereth, "Above-Ground Archaeology: Discovering a Community's History through Local Artifacts," in *Artifacts and the American Past* (1980, 1996): 183–203; and Peirce F. Lewis, "Axioms for Reading the Landscape: Some Guides to the American Scene," in *Material Culture Studies in America,* comp. and ed. Thomas J. Schlereth (1982): 174–182. In order to view the natural history of the Midwest landscape and cityscape as cultural history, consult William Thishler, *Midwest Landscape Architecture* (2001); Robert E. Grese, *Jens Jensen: Maker of Natural Parks and Gardens* (1992); Floyd Swink and Gerould Wilhelm, *Plants of the Chicago Region* (1994); and Glen Cranz, "Changing Roles of Urban Parks: From Pleasure Garden to Open Space," *Landscape* 22.3 (Summer 1978): 9–18. *Reading the Landscape of America* (1957, 1975), by the late May T. Watts, a naturalist at the Morton Arboretum, is a classic, as are two works in place name history by George Stewart: *Names on the Land: A Historical Account of Place-Naming in the United States* (1958) and *American Place Names: A Concise and Selective Dictionary for the Continental United States of America* (1970).

To understand the historical significance of American streets and roads, see Grady Clay, *Close-Up: How to Read the American City* (1973); Anthony Vidler, "The Scenes of the Street: Transformations in Ideal and Reality, 1750–1871," in *On Streets* (1978): 29–112; Bernard Rudofsky, *Streets for People: A Primer for Americans* (1969); and Thomas J. Schlereth, *Reading the Road* (1996).

For interpreting prime objects, see George Kubler, *The Shapes of Time: Remarks on the History of Things* (1962). On "superartifacts," see Robert Ascher, "Tin*Can Archaeology." in Thomas J. Schlereth, *Material Culture Studies in America* (1982): 325–340. On architectural fragments, see Pauline Saliga, *Fragments of Chicago's Past: The Collection of Architectural Fragments at the Art Institute of Chicago* (1990).

books on urban space for this essay were Henri Lefebvre, *The Production of Space* (1974; English translation by Donald Nicholson-Smith, 1991); Kevin Lynch, *The Image of the City* (1980); and the many works of David Harvey, most especially *Social Justice and the City* (1973). These approaches toward urban space must, however, be considered in light of the rich scholarship on urban space by the scholars of the Chicago School who helped to introduce space as an important issue for understanding Chicago and all cities. Among these are Louis Wirth, "Urbanism as a Way of Life," *American Journal of Sociology* 44.1 (1938): 1–24; Ernest W. Burgess, "The Growth of the City: An Introduction to a Research Project," in Robert E. Park and Ernest W. Burgess, eds., *The City* (1926); and more recent scholarship such as Albert Hunter, *Symbolic Communities: The Persistence and Change of Chicago's Local Communities* (1974); Gerald D. Suttles, *The Social Construction of Communities* (1972); and the many works of Brian J. L. Berry.

To learn more about particular topics in the essay, see Allen H. Spear, *Black Chicago: The Making of a Negro Ghetto, 1890–1920* (1967); William M. Tuttle, *Race Riot: Chicago in the Red Summer of 1919* (1972); Chicago Commission on Race Relations, *The Negro in Chicago: A Study of Race Relations and a Race Riot in 1919* (1922); Janice L. Reiff, "Rethinking Pullman: Urban Space and Working Class Activism," *Social Science History* 24.1 (2000): 7–32; William H. Whyte, *The Organization Man* (1956); Edward C. Banfield, *Political Influence* (1961); Ross Miller, *Here's the Deal: The Buying and Selling of a Great American City* (1996); Anna J. Merritt, ed., *Redistricting: An Exercise in Prophecy* (1982); Gail Radford, *Modern Housing for America: Policy Struggles in the New Deal Era* (1996); Kenneth T. Jackson, *Crabgrass Frontier: The Suburbanization of the United States* (1985); Donald Alexander Downs, *Nazis in Skokie: Freedom, Community, and the First Amendment* (1985); James Ralph, *Northern Protest: Martin Luther King, Jr., Chicago, and the Civil Rights Movement* (1993); David J. Garrow, ed., *Chicago 1966* (1989); Felix M. Padilla, *Puerto Rican Chicago* (1987); Andrew Hurley, *Environmental Inequalities: Class, Race, and Industrial Pollution in Gary, Indiana, 1945–1980* (1995); David N. Pellow, *Garbage Wars: The Struggle for Environmental Justice in Chicago* (2002); Arnold R. Hirsch, *Making the Second Ghetto: Race and Housing in Chicago, 1940–1960* (1985); and the *Journal of Urban History* 29.3 (2003), a special issue devoted to Hirsch's book.

Convention Centers. *See* Places of Assembly; Tourism and Conventions

Convents. "Convents" generally refer to houses where ROMAN CATHOLIC women live under religious vows. They became common in Chicago and other industrial cities early in the nineteenth century. The first ones, like that established on Chicago's Wabash Avenue by Mother Agatha O'Brien and four other Sisters of Mercy in 1846, resembled the SETTLEMENT HOUSES of the 1890s. But before Jane Addams and Ellen Gates Starr were born, the Mercys and several other communities had begun building a network of services for the urban poor that included elementary and Sunday schools, ORPHANAGES and HOSPITALS, employment bureaus and industrial schools, as well as the city's first Magdalen Asylum. Some of these mid-nineteenth-century institutions, such as Mercy Hospital and the HOUSE OF THE GOOD SHEPHERD, still exist. Thus, when HULL HOUSE opened in 1889, most Chicagoans would not have considered it extraordinary to see a group of women living among immigrants and working selflessly on their behalf. By 1889, Chicago had over 60 convents.

Unlike most "settlers," Catholic sisters before the 1920s were not usually middle-class. Many came from immigrant families and were IRISH, like the Catholic clergy and laity of that time. But by the 1920s, when Chicago's convents numbered over 200 women from other ethnic groups—particularly GERMAN, POLISH, ITALIAN, LITHUANIAN, and SLOVAK—entered religious communities of the Irish or those of "their own." In 1911, the Sisters of St. Casimir, a Lithuanian congregation, established their motherhouse in Chicago and immediately opened an academy there. By 1921, they were teaching in nine Lithuanian parish schools. Large numbers of Polish and German nuns did similar work. Some also nursed in hospitals and homes. In unusual fashion, the Poor Handmaids of Jesus Christ, a German order of NURSING and teaching sisters, staffed the Municipal Isolation Hospital (for smallpox patients) for over 60 years. Mother Katharine Drexel's Sisters of the Blessed Sacrament (for NATIVE AMERICANS and AFRICAN AMERICANS), who came to the SOUTH SIDE in 1912, remain active at St. Elizabeth's at 41st and Michigan.

In city and suburban neighborhoods, most convents were visible to passersby since they were often adjacent to Catholic churches and schools. Yet a good many could not be seen, situated as they were within large medical, charitable, and educational institutions operated by religious communities and scattered across Chicago. The Sisters of the Good Shepherd, for example, lived and worked quietly inside the imposing four-story House of the Good Shepherd at Grace and Racine on Chicago's North Side; while the Ladies of Loretto made their home on the third floor of an impressive brick academy in WOODLAWN on the South Side. Other nuns resided within hospitals, orphanages, and UNIVERSITIES where they fulfilled their missions. By 1945, over nine thousand Catholic sisters lived in convents in the ROMAN CATHOLIC ARCHDIOCESE OF CHICAGO.

Organized religious life among women of like mind resulted in efficacious service. During the nineteenth century, PROTESTANT women such as educator Catherine Beecher and reformer Mary Livermore viewed Catholic sisterhoods as an effective force for good—one they encouraged Protestants to emulate. The opportunity to lead useful lives, to do good, to act in ways that would not have been permitted for women of the Victorian era, and to accomplish something important in life fueled the idealism and aspirations of generations of young women into the 1950s and early 1960s. As a result, they chose what they and their families often considered "the better part," over motherhood or spinsterhood.

During the prosperous years following WORLD WAR II, Americans began to experience profound social and cultural change—Catholic women (both inside and outside convents) included. They benefited from opportunities for advanced education that, along with the CIVIL RIGHTS and women's movements and the sweeping reforms of the Second Vatican Council, transformed religious life. Many nuns left their convents for married life or professional careers; those who stayed not only altered their dress but also committed themselves to new forms of Christian service. However, the reduction to fewer than five thousand sisters in the Chicago Archdiocese by 1990, many of them retired, and the adoption of new ministries resulted in the closing of dozens of institutions and convents. Those that remain open frequently assist the inner-city poor, battered women, and neglected or handicapped children as well as continue the traditional roles of teaching and nursing.

Suellen Hoy

See also: Catholic School System; Feminist Movements; Parish Life; Public Health; Religious Institutions

Further reading: Hoy, Suellen. "Caring for Chicago's Women and Girls: The Sisters of the Good Shepherd, 1859–1911." *Journal of Urban History* 23 (March 1997): 260–294. • Hoy, Suellen. "Walking Nuns: Chicago's Irish Sisters of Mercy." In *At the Crossroads: Old St. Patrick's and the Chicago Irish,* ed. Ellen Skerrett, 1997, 39–51. • Thompson, Margaret Susan. "Women, Feminism, and the New Religious History: Catholic Sisters as a Case Study." In *Belief & Behavior: Essays in the New Religious History,* ed. Philip R. Vandermeer and Robert P. Swierenga, 1991, 136–163.

Cook County. When Cook County was organized in 1831 with approximately 100 residents in 2,464 square miles, it encompassed much of what is today LAKE, DUPAGE, WILL, MCHENRY, and Cook counties. Because of population growth in northeastern Illinois in the 1830s, Cook County lost over half its territory, but continued to increase in population. By 1839, it comprised 954 square miles and followed its current irregular boundaries. It had expanded to a population of over four thousand.

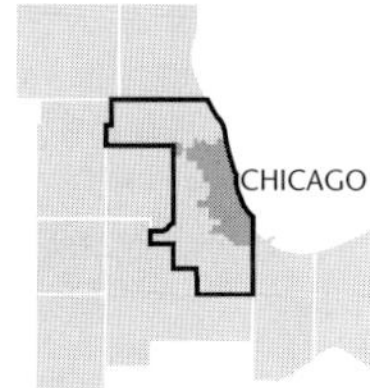

Although Daniel Pope Cook is the namesake of the county, there is no evidence that he ever visited the area. Cook served as the first Illinois attorney general and the second U.S. congressman from Illinois.

The first Cook County Board met in 1831 with three members: two from Chicago and one from NAPERVILLE (DuPage did not become a separate county until 1839). As the basic unit of local government, the board was charged with a host of responsibilities and met initially for two days at FORT DEARBORN. The board set the county seat at Chicago, requested 10 acres of land from the state for public buildings, and appointed a county clerk. Soon after, the board established a REAL-ESTATE tax, built an ALMSHOUSE, supervised licensing of taverns and a ferry across the CHICAGO RIVER, and began construction on two highways: one west to DuPage (Ogden Avenue); and another southwest (Archer Avenue). The county had direct responsibility for the poor, the sick, and prisoners, as well as for roads, courts, elections, and TAXATION. These basic functions remain central to Cook County government today.

During the 1830s and 1840s, farmers purchased most of the available land in the county and began raising crops and livestock. Without RAILROADS, some farmers hauled their harvest to Chicago, but others went to closer, smaller settlements. By 1840, WHEELING, Gross Point (now WILMETTE), LYONS, SUMMIT, BRIGHTON, WILLOW SPRINGS, Calumet, BLUE ISLAND, and THORNTON were thriving settlements. Most were AGRICULTURAL centers, serving the farmers in their vicinity with small stores, churches, and schools.

In 1848, the Illinois legislature voted to allow counties to adopt township governments. Cook County subdivided initially into 27 TOWNSHIPS, which took on some of the county responsibilities: collecting taxes, running SCHOOLS, supervising elections, and maintaining local roads. Township supervisors served as county board members.

Between 1860 and 1890, the area of contiguous urban settlement grew substantially. By 1870, the Cook County Board was an unwieldy group of more than 50 town supervisors. Although over 85 percent of the population of the county resided within the city of Chicago, fewer than half of the board representatives were from the city. To remedy this problem, the state changed the organization of the board. The new 15-member board had 10 representatives elected from Chicago. After the 1889 ANNEXATION, which shifted more than 225,000 county residents to within the city and expanded the city's physical size from 43 to 169 square miles, over 90 percent of the county's population lived within the city.

The railroad (and increasingly STREET RAILWAYS) allowed Chicagoans to live and work in noncontiguous suburban areas. While farming in Cook County did not disappear, outlying growth by 1900 was decidedly suburban. The initial development and extension of the Elevated fostered the rise of population centers at OAK PARK, EVANSTON, UPTOWN, and HYDE PARK.

Many of the farms on Chicago's Far Northwest and Southwest Sides disappeared in the face of the speculative building boom of the 1920s. Industrial and residential developers began to work on suburban farmland convenient to bus, truck, and automobile traffic. By 1940, the proportion of the county's population living within Chicago had dropped to 83 percent.

After 1945, with the availability of FHA and VA insured loans, new EXPRESSWAYS, and the move of many businesses to suburban locations, suburban population in the county burgeoned. SKOKIE and OAK LAWN were among the most quickly growing suburbs during the 1950s and 1960s, with thousands of single-family houses built in each. The 1970s and 1980s saw the development of most of the remaining farmland in the county. By then, contiguous urban growth had engulfed both the remaining farms and the suburban residential and industrial areas that had once been distinct from the city center. No further annexation by the city took place, however, and by 1990 the city comprised only 55 percent of the county's population.

Ann Durkin Keating

See also: Cook County Hospital; Court System; Forest Preserves; Governing the Metropolis; Government, City of Chicago; Government, Suburban; Jails and Prisons; Public Health; Suburbs and Cities as Dual Metropolis

Further reading: Andreas, A. T. *History of Cook County.* 1884. • Johnson, Charles B. *Growth of Cook County,* vol. 1. 1960. • Keating, Ann Durkin. *Building Chicago: Suburban Developers and the Creation of a Divided Metropolis.* 1988.

Cook County Hospital. Northwest Territory law and the Illinois General Assembly assigned the care of paupers to the counties. From 1832 until 1866, COOK COUNTY fulfilled this obligation by providing a minimum of food and medicine for patients in temporary HOSPITALS or private homes. Physicians and students from Rush Medical School provided free medical care.

A permanent hospital was built by the city of Chicago in 1857 at the urging of Brockholtz McVicar, who had been the commissioner of health during the cholera EPIDEMICS of 1849 and 1854. Rush Medical School used the building at 18th and Arnold Streets as a teaching hospital until the CIVIL WAR, when it became an army hospital. After the war, the city traded it to Cook County for 160 acres of property which had been used as a reform school. The "Old County Hospital" opened in 1866 in the same building, a three-story brick and limestone structure with "all the modern conveniences," including a knife, saw, and chisel for autopsies.

From its beginning, the Cook County Hospital was a center for MEDICAL EDUCATION. The first internship in the country was started there in 1866. Neither the interns, chosen by competitive examination, nor the attending physicians were paid, but they gained wide experience with every sort of disease.

Corrupt political appointees controlled hospital purchasing and personnel. The physical plant deteriorated and the building became infested with rats and roaches. As city population increased in the 1870s, the hospital became more crowded. Despite public indifference, physicians prevailed upon the county in 1876

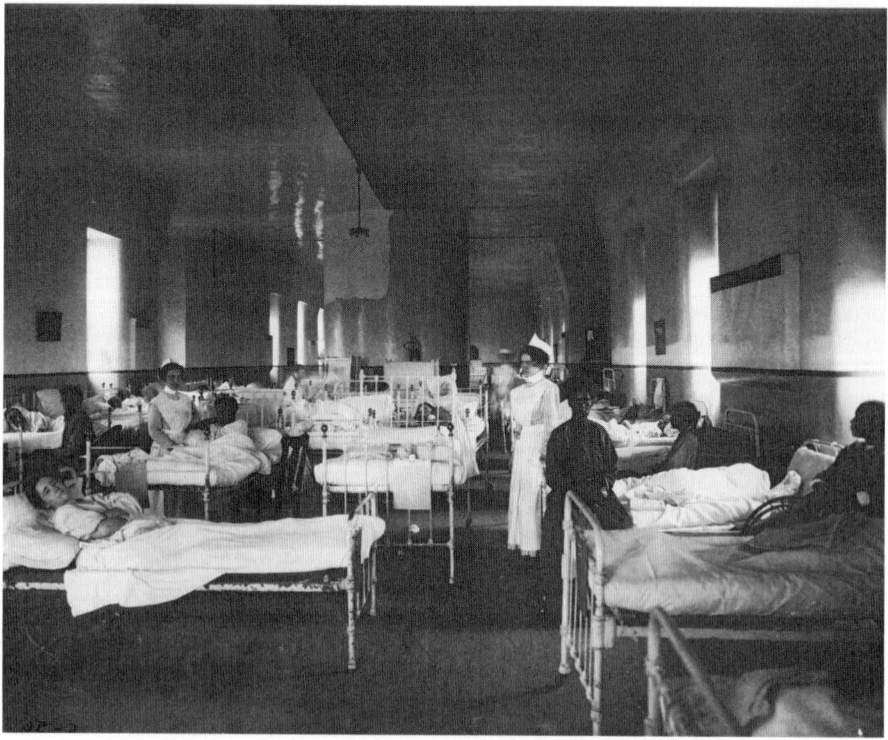

Old Cook County Hospital, ca. 1900. Photographer: Unknown. Source: Chicago Historical Society.

to build a new 300-bed facility between Harrison, Polk, Lincoln, and Wood Streets. Political corruption worsened, and, after almost the entire medical staff resigned, the politicians appointed poorly qualified physicians. In 1886 newspaper articles described the PATRONAGE-ridden hospital as a "roadhouse" for politicians.

A new era of scientific medicine commenced in 1877 with the arrival of Christian Fenger, a Danish surgeon trained in the best European clinics. Fenger paid $1,000 for his hospital position and quickly established himself as an outstanding surgeon, scientist, and teacher. The interns trained by Fenger became leaders in American medicine and remained on the hospital staff as attending physicians and teachers.

During the early 1900s, political corruption declined, and new civil service laws required that attending physicians pass an examination for staff appointment. As a result, the best surgeons and physicians in Chicago volunteered their services to care for the sick poor and to teach interns. A huge new hospital was completed in 1916, anchoring a complex that eventually grew to 3,000 beds. The original building has been periodically remodeled and remained in use until 2002, when the new John H. Stroger, Jr., Hospital of Cook County opened.

From the 1920s until immediately after WORLD WAR II, the Cook County Hospital, despite continued political problems and a seriously deteriorating physical plant, was regarded as one of the world's great teaching hospitals. Interns, residents, and graduate physicians came for experience and to see outstanding medical and surgical work. Scientific INNOVATIONS included the world's first blood bank and the surgical fixation of fractures.

A desperate shortage of NURSES, poor intern pay, and a lack of modern facilities plagued the hospital following World War II. During the 1960s, voluntary attending physicians were largely replaced by full-time, paid doctors. Young and socially conscious, many of these physicians rebelled against the "old guard" who had run the hospital for years. In 1969, in an attempt to reduce political influence, the state legislature assigned the responsibility for running the hospital to a citizens' commission. Amidst great turmoil, the Cook County Board of Commissioners retained control of the budget, and in 1975 cutbacks provoked a strike among interns and residents, closing the hospital. The County Board of Commissioners retook complete control in 1979.

Cook County Hospital has always been open to all patients, generally poor or destitute, and often alcoholic. European immigrants filled the wards until the years following World War I. During the 1910s and 1920s, Chicago's rapidly increasing AFRICAN AMERICAN population turned to Cook County and PROVIDENT HOSPITAL in the face of widespread exclusion. The hospital population became almost entirely black until the recent wave of Hispanic and Asian immigrants arrived in the city.

The advent of federal programs such as Medicare resulted in more poor patients being treated at private hospitals. These programs as well as the trend to outpatient care has reduced the number of patients at Cook County Hospital.

John Raffensperger

See also: Clinics and Dispensaries; Public Health

Further reading: Raffensperger, John G., and Louis G. Boshes, eds. *The Old Lady on Harrison Street: Cook County Hospital, 1833–1995.* International Healthcare Ethics, vol. 3. 1997.

Cook County Morgue. Since at least 1842, for which the earliest records exist, the morgue has served as the site of official inquiry into every questionable death in COOK COUNTY. Housed in the City Hospital until 1876 and in COOK COUNTY HOSPITAL afterwards, the "deadhouse" was administered first by an appointed "curator" and then, after 1864, an elected coroner. Between 1872 and 1911, the coroner investigated more than 75,000 deaths. Coroners oversaw the inquest process, but staff pathologists actually performed the autopsies, using them to determine the cause of each decedent's demise, train Cook County medical students, and generate valuable medical knowledge. (By 1900, the work of Christian Fenger and his protégés had established Chicago as a world center of pathology research.) In determining the manner of death, inquest juries considered pathologist's conclusions as well as the findings of POLICE, the county state's attorney, and coroner's office investigators. During these deliberations, held in the morgue itself, coroners could exclude certain evidence, shaping juries' verdicts and advancing or retarding criminal investigations into particular deaths.

The coroner's office was rife with PATRONAGE from the start; the first coroner resigned in 1865 to protest interference with his work. Later coroners and their loyal, practically permanent inquest jurors rubber-stamped the findings of police and prosecutors. Though pathologists' attempts at reform withered, several incidents in the late 1960s led county voters to abolish the elected coroner in favor of a credentialed medical examiner. After his hiring in 1976, the first medical examiner stated as his goal "to get the facts and truth in an entirely neutral professional approach." Since then, medical examiners and their pathologists and roving investigators have inquired into every questionable death in the county and recommended that county law enforcement officials either pursue or drop criminal investigations. By the end of the twentieth century, the medical examiner's office was investigating about five thousand deaths every year at its West Side facility. In 1995, the chief medical examiner, Dr. Edmund R. Donoghue, achieved a degree of prominence by calling attention to the deadly effects of that summer's heat wave.

Christopher James Tassava

See also: Court System; Homicide; Public Health

Further reading: Bonner, Thomas N. *Medicine in Chicago, 1850–1950: A Chapter in the Social and Scientific Development of a City.* 1957. • Fahey, Richard P., and Deborah J. Palmer. *An Inquest on the Cook County Coroner.* 1971.

Coordinating Council of Community Organizations. The precise origins of the Coordinating Council of Community Organizations (CCCO) are murky, but it emerged against the backdrop of mounting dissatisfaction with the policies of Chicago school superintendent Benjamin Willis in the early 1960s. Black parents staged sit-ins against overcrowded SCHOOLS and pursued legal action against school segregation. CCCO harnessed this unrest to organize two massive school boycotts in October 1963 and February 1964.

In 1964 Al Raby, a black schoolteacher, was elected convener of CCCO. Raby presided over a broad—and often quarrelsome—coalition of groups including the more militant Chicago CONGRESS OF RACIAL EQUALITY (CORE) and Chicago Area Friends of SNCC and the more moderate Chicago Catholic Interracial Council and the Chicago URBAN LEAGUE. In the summer of 1965 Raby led CCCO marches on city hall to force Mayor Richard J. Daley to remove Willis and to endorse school integration. CCCO also turned to Martin Luther King, Jr., and the Southern Christian Leadership Conference (SCLC) for assistance, and by September 1965 SCLC had committed itself to working with CCCO in a joint venture to bring racial justice to the city.

The SCLC-CCCO alliance was strained, even as it led a two-month campaign against housing discrimination in the summer of 1966. The dramatic protests brought real-estate agents and city leaders to the bargaining table, and a "summit" agreement on promoting fair and OPEN HOUSING was reached. The promise of the accord, however, was never realized—though it did give birth to the Leadership Council for Metropolitan Open Communities. Disillusionment over the lack of progress and growing doubts about interracialism widened the rifts within CCCO. In late 1967, Raby resigned as convener and CCCO quickly disintegrated.

James Ralph

See also: Civil Rights Movements; Contested Spaces; School Desegregation; Willis Wagons

Further reading: Anderson, Alan B., and George W. Pickering. *Confronting the Color Line: The Broken Promise of the Civil Rights Movement in Chicago.* 1986. • Ralph, James R., Jr. *Northern Protest: Martin*

Luther King, Jr., Chicago, and the Civil Rights Movement. 1993.

Copperheads. "Copperheads" were northerners who opposed the United States Army's defense of the Union during the Civil War, though Republicans also used the term to describe northern Democrats in general, in order to charge the Democrats with disloyalty. In Chicago, there were many Democrats, but few openly disloyal Copperheads. In 1861, the city's leading Democrat, Stephen Douglas, called on his party to support the Lincoln administration, and most Democrats rallied to the Union war effort with enthusiasm. By 1863, however, discontent with several of the administration's war measures–taxes, banking policies, conscription, infringements on civil liberties, and especially the Emancipation Proclamation–caused an upsurge of antiwar feeling. Wilbur Storey's *Chicago Times* was nationally famous for its strident antiwar stance, extreme racism, and suppression by military authorities, though it seems never to have represented a large local constituency. A few local residents participated in an abortive conspiracy to mobilize the Confederate prisoners of war held at Camp Douglas as the nucleus of an insurrection aimed at establishing a pro-South "western confederacy," but this effort went nowhere. Luckily for Chicago, conscription occurred peacefully, with no outbreaks resembling the bloody New York City draft riots of July 1863, which might have strengthened a popular Copperhead following.

Among local politicians, most active Copperheads were southern migrants to the city like former mayors Buckner Morris and Levi Boone. Most Democrats, however, including the wartime mayor Francis C. Sherman, sustained the difficult position of maintaining their identity as a loyal opposition, separate from the Republicans, throughout the war.

Robin Einhorn

See also: Politics

CORE. *See* Congress of Racial Equality (CORE)

Cosmetics and Hair Care Products. Chicago residents participated in the rise of the cosmetics industry during the twentieth century not only as consumers but also as producers and distributors. As they spent more time and money on personal grooming and so-called beauty products, the area's women—and men, to a lesser extent—participated in a development that was going on throughout much of the United States and the industrialized world. Chicago played a more distinctive role in the development of the cosmetics and hair care industries through the leadership of several of the area's business firms in this economic sector. At the same time, Chicago entrepreneurs built one of the most important of the industry's subsectors: hair care products and cosmetics designed for consumers of African descent.

Two leading cosmetics and hair care products makers, Helene Curtis and Alberto-Culver, grew into big businesses while they were headquartered in Chicago. In 1927, Gerald Gidwitz and Louis Stein started a cosmetics manufacturing company in Chicago. During the years following World War II, Stein named the company Helene Curtis, combining the names of his wife and son, and the company expanded with the success of products such as "Suave," one of the first modern shampoos. By the 1950s, Helene Curtis was also selling hairspray and deodorant and it had branches around the world. Meanwhile, a competitor arrived from California. In 1955, Leonard and Bernice Lavin moved the Alberto-Culver Company from Los Angeles (where it had started as a supplier of hair care products to the film industry) to Chicago; by 1960, the company was moving into a new headquarters and manufacturing facility in nearby Melrose Park. Like Helene Curtis, Alberto-Culver prospered by selling branded lines of products such as shampoo and deodorant—items that, although they were virtually unknown before the twentieth century, many consumers now regarded as indispensable.

The development, manufacture, and marketing of cosmetics and hair care products for African Americans was led by Chicago firms for much of the twentieth century. During the 1910s and 1920s, the Kashmir Chemical Company of Claude A. Barnett, a graduate of the Tuskegee Institute, manufactured specialty hair care products. In 1935, S. B. Fuller established the Fuller Products Company, a cosmetics company, on the city's South Side. Fuller, the first African American member of the National Association of Manufacturers, led the company through an expansion that peaked in the 1950s. By that time, an army of 5,000 salesmen sold nearly $20 million a year worth of various Fuller Products cosmetics—to European Americans as well as African Americans. One of Fuller's employees, George Johnson, left the company in 1954 to start his own business. Along with Chicago barber Orville Nelson, Johnson created the company that would soon become the most important of all manufacturers of African American hair care products: the Johnson Products Company. The company's "Ultra Wave" hair straightener proved popular, as did its "Ultra Sheen" and "Afro Sheen" lines, and by the end of the 1960s annual sales were over $10 million. During the 1970s, as sales expanded even further, Johnson Products ranked as the largest African American–owned manufacturing company in the nation. Johnson Products was not the only Chicago company engaged in the manufacture of beauty products for African American consumers. The Johnson Publishing Company, creator of *Ebony* magazine, entered the cosmetics business in the 1970s. And Johnson Products' leadership in the hair care sector was challenged by Chicago's own Soft Sheen Products Inc., a company established in the 1960s by Edward Gardner that found success with brands such as "Care-Free Curl."

Chicago's status as a center of the hair care and cosmetics industry declined during the last years of the twentieth century. Johnson Products encountered declining profits and market share by the mid-1970s, when large cosmetics companies such as Revlon and Avon began to target African American consumers. In 1993, the company left local hands when it was sold to the Ivax Corporation, a large company based in Miami. Soft Sheen, which had about 400 employees in the Chicago area and $100 million in annual sales by the mid-1990s, was sold in 1998 to French company L'Oreal. Helene Curtis, which had grown into a billion-dollar company by the early 1990s, experienced declining growth after the 1980s and was bought in 1996 by Unilever, the huge British-Dutch corporation. Of the several Chicago companies that had been so prominent in the industry since the 1950s, only Alberto-Culver—with about $2 billion in annual sales and 16,000 employees worldwide—was still based in Chicago at the end of the century.

Mark R. Wilson

See also: Economic Geography; Innovation, Invention, and Chicago Business; Retail Geography

Further reading: *Crain's Chicago Business.* Various issues. • Robinson, Greg. "Johnson Products." *Encyclopedia of African-American Culture and History,* vol. 3. 1972. • Silverman, Robert Mark. "The Effects of Racism and Racial Discrimination on Minority Business Development: The Case of Black Manufacturers in Chicago's Ethnic Beauty Aids Industry." *Journal of Social History* 31.3 (1998): 571–597.

Costa Ricans. Unlike many other Latin American groups, Costa Ricans have never had to flee their country on account of political oppression or economic crisis. Instead, they have come to the United States largely for opportunities in education and business, and have tended to arrive through legal immigration channels.

Costa Ricans have been coming to the Chicago area since the late 1930s. Some came to start businesses or to find better jobs in factories and restaurants, although many came to attend local universities. In the late 1940s and 1950s, Benedictine Friars in a Costa Rican high school encouraged a considerable number to attend Illinois Benedictine University. Others matriculated at the University of Illinois at Chicago, Northwestern, and other area schools. After graduating, many entered the professions as doctors and engineers.

Small businesses undertaken by Costa Ricans in Chicago have included RESTAURANTS, clothing stores, and auto repair shops. One restaurant, Irazu, has become an informal meeting space for the community.

A handful of Costa Rican families settled in UPTOWN and ROGERS PARK in the 1950s. Later, another concentration of Costa Ricans formed on the North Side near Milwaukee and Fullerton. Others have spread out across the North Side and into the suburbs.

Several ROMAN CATHOLIC Churches have served as spiritual centers for Costa Ricans in Chicago, including St. Ita's Church (5500 N. Broadway) and St. Benedict's (2215 W. Irving Park). Each year on August 2, the Costa Rican Catholic community has honored its patron saint, Our Lady of Angels, with a mass at Our Lady of Lourdes (4640 N. Ashland).

Costa Rican immigrants participated in the Pan American Council of Chicago, a friendship and cultural organization of Caribbean and Central American ethnic groups formed in 1939. In 1986, Costa Ricans established the Chicago Costa Rican Cultural Association as a chapter of the Central American Civic Society of Chicago. This group organized cultural celebrations and programs, including the annual Independence Day Parade (September 15), throughout the 1980s. The September affair included a beauty pageant and party for all the Central American groups in Chicago. The Costa Rican Cultural Association also organized periodic picnics and parties featuring Costa Rican music and *folklórico.* Costa Rican Mothers Day (August 15) has been commemorated each year with a picnic, drawing hundreds of Costa Ricans together. In the early 1990s, *Asociación de Damas Costarricenses* was founded as a benevolent organization to aid needy children and elderly persons at home in Costa Rica.

In the 1970s and 1980s, the Chicago Costa Rican community organized two SOCCER teams, *Saprisa* and *Alajuela,* which competed against other Latin American teams in LINCOLN PARK every summer. Although the teams dissolved in the 1990s, soccer has remained a major pastime for many Costa Ricans in Chicago.

Because few Costa Ricans immigrate to the United States illegally, census figures are relatively reliable. The 1990 U.S. census found 1,845 Costa Ricans in Chicago and GARY, Indiana. Community leaders estimated between 1,500 and 2,000 in Chicago at the turn of the millennium; the 2000 census counted 1,119 in the metropolitan area.

Robert Morrissey

See also: Demography; Guatemalans; Multicentered Chicago; Nicaraguans

Council on Fine Arts. Authorized by a 1975 ordinance to encourage public support for and understanding of the arts, the 15-member, mayor-appointed Chicago Council on Fine Arts (CCFA) began work in December 1976, led by Executive Director (and noted cultural activist) Heather Morgan. Under Morgan and her successors, the CCFA initiated a host of innovative projects: a "culture bus" to major arts centers; free performances in the Daley Civic Center and other venues; guidebooks and calendars for potential arts patrons; artists-in-residence in previously underserved communities; and CityArts, providing funding and assistance for emerging arts groups. In 1984, the council (renamed the Chicago Office of Fine Arts) was combined with the Mayor's Office of Special Events and the Office of FILM and Entertainment Industries to constitute the Department of Cultural Affairs.

Steve Scott

See also: Arts Funding; Government, City of Chicago; Museums in the Park

Further reading: Kilian, Michael, Connie Fletcher, and F. Richard Ciccone. *Who Runs Chicago?* 1979. • Tigerman, Thomas Hart, ed. *Growing Up with Art: Educator's Guide to Chicago's Cultural Resources.* 1982.

Council Wars. *See* Political Culture

Country Club Hills, IL, Cook County, 23 miles S of the Loop. Residential use covers most of the four square miles of the village, which is a classic example of an automobile suburb initiated in the 1950s. It is adjacent to the interchange of Interstates 80 and 57 and several miles from METRA rail stations.

Although the area was farmed in the nineteenth century, the current community emerged from the large SUBDIVISION activity of Joseph E. Merrion, a major Chicago-area housing developer. In 1955, he sought to build a large housing tract for middle-income home buyers. Perhaps influenced by the success of PARK FOREST to the south, Merrion created an environment with fairly large lots, curving streets, and ranch-style houses. East of Cicero Avenue, both north and south of 183rd Street, Merrion's original plan remains visible. Later development, by Merrion and others, took on more conventional subdivision forms. In 1957 and 1958, *American Home* magazine awarded recognition to Merrion for offering among the best home buys in the Midwest. Earlier, Merrion had built more conventional subdivisions that were core to other villages like HOMETOWN and MERRIONETTE PARK.

He named his new effort Country Club Hills, seeking to evoke that atmosphere and highlight a variety of nearby GOLF courses and country clubs. However, his Country Club Hills did not have a country club, although a driving range was eventually built in a community park.

Response was enthusiastic, and by the end of 1956 over one hundred homes had been built. With continuing growth, the Country Club Hills Home Owners' Association was formed in early 1958 to seek basic services. The association worked with local SCHOOL DISTRICTS, townships, and the developer to improve community conditions and moved rapidly to consider incorporation. With over four hundred homes in place, a special election established the city of Country Club Hills in July of 1958.

Along with several areas of commercial development, the city continued steady population growth, reaching 6,920 in 1970, 14,676 in 1980, and 16,169 in 2000. Country Club Hills is one of a cluster of predominantly middle-class suburbs south of Chicago that has experienced significant racial change. In 1990, 57 percent of the city's population was African American by 2000, the percentage had grown to 83 percent.

The community has benefited from the work of an activist city government and has paid attention to its historic roots. Merrion's development was close to the site of the old Cooper's Grove settlement dating to the 1840s, with the historic St. John Evangelical Lutheran Church organized in 1849. One of the earliest congregations south of Chicago, it started with two wooden structures, built in 1851 and replaced in 1857. The current church was completed in 1874 using Joliet limestone and stands today as one of the most historic buildings in the south region.

The community library district was established in 1960 and, in 1975, joined with residents in HAZEL CREST to form the Grande Prairie Library District.

Larry A. McClellan

See also: Built Environment of the Chicago Region; Expressways

Further reading: Country Club Hills Public Library District. *From Cooper's Grove to Country Club Hills.* 1976. • Kukec, Anna Marie. "Country Club Hills, Profile." *Chicago Tribune,* January 19, 1998. • Nordbrock, Richard R. *The Story of St. John's Evangelical Lutheran Church, Missouri Synod, Organized July 5, 1849.* 1990.

Countryside, IL, Cook County, 15 miles SW of the Loop. Most of what is now the city of Countryside once stood as fertile farmland. One of the earliest landowners, Joseph Vial, arrived in 1833. The area remained sparsely settled for much of the nineteenth century. A few self-sufficient farmers established a schoolhouse, and some worshipped at the Lyonsville Congregational Church. Around 1917 the Marx Brothers comedy team bought a chicken farm near Joliet and LaGrange Roads. Groucho Marx later claimed that the brothers spent

too much time at WRIGLEY FIELD watching the Chicago CUBS to make the farm economically viable.

In 1929 a large tract of land known as Sherman Gardens was subdivided and a few lots were sold. However, it was not until after World War II, with the postwar housing boom, that significant growth came to this area, known to many residents as South LA GRANGE. The first concentrated development took place in 1947 with the construction of the LaGrange Terrace subdivision. The Don L. Dise SUBDIVISION followed in 1954, and later Edgewood Park opened in two phases. Homeowner associations were formed in 1949 and 1960 to address sewage disposal and procurement of an adequate WATER SUPPLY in the face of failing wells. The Countryside Sanitary District was created in 1959. The activities of the homeowners groups paved the way for the incorporation of Countryside in 1960.

In 1962, 80 acres of undeveloped land were turned into the Dansher Industrial Park. McCook supplied water from LAKE MICHIGAN to Countryside in 1964. A new city hall opened in 1967, and by 1970 the population stood at 2,864. After annexing an area south of Joliet Road in 1971, the city moved to provide water for that area. The Pleasantview Fire Protection District serves Countryside and adjacent towns.

Countryside's thriving business community, including automobile dealerships along LaGrange Road and shopping plazas along LaGrange and Joliet Roads, generated enough commercial sales taxes in the twentieth century to allow the city to levy neither real-estate nor corporate taxes. The 2000 population stood at 5,991. A portion of old Route 66 runs through Countryside, and Interstates 294 and 55 pass through the southern edge of the city. Three different elementary school districts serve Countryside, with high schoolers attending Lyons Township High School District. Two Cook County FOREST PRESERVES provide recreational opportunities, and the Countryside Recreation Department maintains seven recreation areas.

Ronald S. Vasile

See also: Metropolitan Growth; Streets and Highways

Further reading: Chandler, Charlotte. *Hello, I Must Be Going: Groucho and His Friends.* 1992, 152–153. • City of Countryside. *Countryside: Illinois Community Guide.* 1998. • Sun Newspapers. *1990 Countryside Anniversary Book.* 1990.

County Fairs. The American county fair developed in the early nineteenth century when AGRICULTURAL reformers in the northeastern United States organized local exhibitions to promote modern farming. Typical events included livestock judging, exhibits of new agricultural implements and techniques, and plowing contests.

Left to right: Ida Honore Grant, Grace Brown Palmer, and Bertha Honore Palmer, at Lake County Fair, Lake Forest, July 1916. Photographer: Unknown. Source: Chicago Historical Society.

The Union Agricultural Society (1839), which published the *Prairie Farmer* from Chicago, drew members from counties throughout Northeastern Illinois and held its first annual fair in NAPERVILLE in 1841. Numerous county agricultural societies were organized a decade later, including Porter and LAKE Counties, Indiana (both 1851), and LAKE (1851), MCHENRY (1852), and DUPAGE (1853) Counties in Illinois. Each of these societies soon began holding annual fairs and acquiring land for permanent fairgrounds.

The Chicago Mechanics Institute (1837) held annual fairs highlighting mechanical inventions beginning in 1845. In 1855 it organized a state agricultural and mechanical fair, which drew tens of thousands of visitors to a 50-acre plot of prairie near BRIDGEPORT.

Entertainment became important as fairs competed with national expositions during what is considered the golden age of agricultural fairs between 1870 and 1910. Chicago's fair board, incorporated in the 1870s, sought a permanent location in its northwest farm communities to provide a one-half-mile oval track for harness racing and speed trials. HORSE RACING was so popular that by 1900, 80 of the 102 Illinois county fairs featured trotting and pacing competitions. BICYCLE races, balloon ascensions, and eventually automobile races and airplane demonstrations were common features, while plowing matches and evening lectures were replaced with pyrotechnic displays.

Early in the decade of the 1900s, the Illinois Farmers' Institute began encouraging boys and girls to exhibit fair entries. The Institute began sponsoring regional and county chapters of a new national youth movement called 4-H, whose 4-leaf clover insignia with embossed H's signified the emphasis on Head, Heart, Hands, and Health. Perhaps the 4-H movement, which provided an important revitalization of livestock and domestic arts competition, was a reaction to the growing bawdiness of fairs. 4-H chapters continued to flourish in Cook and suburban counties into the twenty-first century, encouraging teenagers in local, county, state, and national competitions.

The 1916 Cook County Fair found a final home in PALATINE Township. Charles E. Dean, Sr., a well-respected trainer of harness racers, had constructed a racetrack on his 120-acre farm. Dean's Fairgrounds Park provided the ideal location for annual harness events in conjunction with the six-day Labor Day weekend fair. Fair-sponsored horse racing continued on Dean's property through 1928.

Urbanization and financial difficulties ended the Cook County Fair. Although the 1924 fair set attendance records by blending urban and rural interest, the costs of permanent grounds and world-class entertainment were debilitating. Numerous attempts to reinstate the Cook County Fair failed, including an 11-day event in 1948 at SOLDIER FIELD. County fairs have survived in surrounding counties, however, despite the diminishing presence of agriculture.

Marcia Lautanen-Raleigh
Charles P. Raleigh

See also: Agricultural Machinery Industry; Clubs: Youth Clubs; Leisure

Further reading: Illinois Department of Agriculture. *Transactions.* 1875, 1899, 1919, and 1930. • Ross, Earle D. "The Evolution of the Agricultural Fair in the Northwest." *Iowa Journal of History and Politics* 24 (1926): 445–480. • Schmidt, Louis Bernard. "Some Significant Aspects of the Agrarian Revolution in the United States." *Iowa Journal of History and Politics* 18 (1920): 371–395.

Court System. From the establishment of its first court of record in 1831, Chicago has developed an innovative and influential court system. Chicagoans created the first JUVENILE COURT to deal with the unique problems of young offenders, as well as a widely copied municipal court system. The COOK COUNTY court system, established in 1964, is now the largest unified system in the world. The federal court judges who sit in Chicago have made and continue to make major contributions to American jurisprudence.

Though Chicago was within the jurisdiction of territorial courts, and later that of circuit courts established under the Illinois Constitution of 1818, no court was held in the area until the 1820s, when John Kinzie was appointed the first justice of the peace for Chicago. Once Cook County was established in 1831, Chicago, as its county seat, was visited periodically by circuit judges who went from county to county hearing both civil and criminal cases. As other counties were organized, they too began holding circuit court terms several times

Cook County Circuit Court, 1910, with Judge George Kersten presiding; the jury is in the background. Circuit Court had many branches, each with its own judge, and it was only one of several types of courts with overlapping jurisdictions. These courts were unified in 1964. Photographer: Unknown. Source: Chicago Historical Society.

per year. Justices of the peace provided more accessible and immediate grassroots justice in hundreds of locations throughout the region. Chicago established other courts to deal efficiently with ordinance violations and minor crimes, and to handle the enormous volume of business in what was becoming the Midwest's business and financial center. A federal district court was established in Chicago in 1848.

The court system elaborated in the Illinois Constitution of 1870 made little provision for specialized courts, and at its base were justice courts often staffed by nonprofessionals. While this structure seemed to meet the needs of homogeneous agricultural counties, it was inadequate for Chicago's large and diverse population and problems. The city, home to a well-organized bar and many social and governmental reformers, met the task of developing new approaches.

Juvenile crime was one pressing problem of the late nineteenth century, especially in poor immigrant city neighborhoods, where reformers worried about lax supervision of children. When children ran afoul of the law, the only legal remedy was to try them as adults and incarcerate them with older offenders. Reform-minded Chicagoans began campaigning for an alternative. At the forefront of the movement were Lucy Flower of the Chicago Woman's Club, Julia Lathrop of HULL HOUSE, Timothy D. Hurley of the Catholic Visitation and Aid Society, and members of the Chicago Bar Association. This alliance convinced the state legislature to establish the Cook County Juvenile Court effective July 1, 1899.

This law allowed juvenile court judges to avoid treating children as criminals to be incarcerated. Instead, the court could find that children were delinquent, dependent, or neglected. This finding allowed the court a variety of alternatives, including probation at home or in a foster home, or placement in a training school or reformatory. The court was not allowed to incarcerate a child with adult offenders. This formula, the specialized court and the delinquent, dependent, and neglected statuses, became widely copied in cities around the United States.

The 1870 constitution also established for Cook County a variety of courts with overlapping jurisdictions and little coordination, including a circuit court, superior court, and criminal court. In addition, every city could establish a city court that had concurrent jurisdiction with the circuit court. Moreover, certain courts of specialized jurisdiction were authorized and called county courts. To exacerbate the confusion, every one of the towns (or precincts) into which Illinois was divided—including eight towns partly or wholly within Chicago—had a justice of the peace court, and some communities had police magistrates' courts as well. Justice of the peace courts could hear matters up to $200, then a substantial sum, and their geographic jurisdiction extended throughout the entire county. Justices collected fees, filed papers, issued judgment, and so on. By 1904, Cook County had 52 of these justice of the peace courts. One notable abuse of this system was that it allowed creditors to file collection cases against city-dwelling debtors in front of sympathetic justices of the peace in remote areas of the county. The debtor-defendants seldom could appear to defend their cases, and some justices engaged in outright collusion with creditors, garnering fees but effectively denying meaningful process to working-class or poor defendants.

The first successful attempt to deal with these problems came in 1904, when reformers amended the state constitution to allow Cook County to establish a court system that differed from those in the other counties. The state legislature passed a law establishing the Municipal Court of Chicago in 1905, replacing the city's justice of the peace courts with municipal courts, and removing the city from the jurisdiction of the remaining suburban justice of the peace courts in Cook County. By the 1930s the municipal court had dozens of branches, with a variety of specialties, such as garnishments, rent, domestic relations, and traffic. This provided a cure for some of the problems of the Chicago judicial system. By 1927, 39 cities had adopted a similar municipal court system. However, it did not eliminate political corruption in the courts. Moreover, the judges in the circuit, superior, and criminal courts retained their independence, and the older system, including justice courts, remained in the suburbs and COLLAR COUNTIES. So the calls for reform continued.

An effective solution to the inefficiency and, to an extent, the corruption of the judicial system emerged in 1964. A constitutional amendment consolidated all the disparate trial courts in the state into 19 unified circuit courts. By then, Cook and DUPAGE Counties had their own circuit courts, MCHENRY and LAKE Counties together had formed the Nineteenth Circuit Court, while other collar counties were part of larger circuits. Within each circuit court, three levels of judges—circuit judges, associate judges, and magistrates—handled all judicial matters. The chief judge was given power over all the other judges to establish uniform rules of operation and procedure, and many courts and judges specialized in particular types of cases, especially in Cook County. The crazy quilt of overlapping jurisdictions and independent judges was finally ended. The 1970 constitution made some minor adjustments to the system. For instance, appointed magistrates became appointed associate justices. In 1989, the legislature established judicial subcircuits to increase the diversity of the judiciary.

At the opening of the twenty-first century, the Circuit Court of Cook County was the largest unified court system in the world, with 400 judges assigned to 14 specialized divisions of geographic districts. The specialized divisions, such as probate and the juvenile division, which has continued the work of the 1899 juvenile court, allow the judges to develop expertise in various areas of the LAW. The geographical divisions provide forums for local law enforcement to deal with local problems. Meanwhile, the power of the chief judge to control the entire structure allows the court to address the changing needs of Cook County.

In addition to city and county courts, Chicago is also a center of the national judiciary. Of particular importance, the influential U.S. Circuit Court of Appeals for the Seventh Circuit sits in Chicago. During the twentieth century, two members of that court were elevated to the United States Supreme Court, Sherman Minton, who served on the Supreme Court from 1949 to 1956, and John Paul Stevens, who was appointed in 1975. In 1999, Ann C. Williams became the first AFRICAN AMERICAN to sit on the Seventh Circuit. This court has close ties to the UNIVERSITY OF CHICAGO Law School. As of 2001, at least two of the sitting judges, Richard Posner and Frank Easterbrook, continued to hold positions on the University of Chicago Law School while sitting on the bench. The Seventh Circuit has become known for advocating the use of economic analysis in deciding federal cases.

R. Ben Brown

See also: American Civil Liberties Union; Children and the Law; Jails and Prisons; Legal Aid; Police

Further reading: Getts, Victoria. *The Juvenile Court and the Progressives.* 2000. • Lepawsky, Albert. *The Judicial System of Metropolitan Chicago.* 1932. • Solomon, Rayman L. *History of the Seventh Circuit, 1891–1941.* 1981.

Cradle Society, The. Founded in 1923 by Florence Walwrath, the Cradle Society was among the first private adoption agencies to place infants with families. Before World War II, the Cradle's national reputation rested in part on its pioneering scientific methods in health care, which drastically reduced infant mortality. It also was praised and criticized for placing babies with Hollywood celebrities and out-of-state childless couples.

In the 1940s, the Cradle began to incorporate professional social work practices and evolved into a comprehensive adoption agency. In the 1990s the agency once again reevaluated its policies, incorporating "open adoptions" (in which birth families remain in contact with adopted children) into its program.

E. Wayne Carp

See also: Demography

Further reading: Carp, E. Wayne. *Family Matters: Secrecy and Disclosure in the History of Adoption.* 1998. • Clark, Neil M. "Filling Empty Arms." *American Magazine* 110 (September 1930): 24–25, 82–86. • Pfeffer, Paula, "Homeless Children, Childless Homes." *Chicago History: The Magazine of the Chicago Historical Society* 61 (Spring 1987): 51–65.

Creation of Chicago Sports. Sport lies at the heart of one of Chicago's founding legends. When the city was a frontier boomtown, as the story goes, local authorities staged a dogfight, knowing that such an event would attract the town's most notorious characters. As soon as the battle began, POLICE moved in, arrested every thief and desperado, and showed them to the city borders. Thus was Chicago cleansed.

Ring Lardner and Chicago Sports Reporting

Ring Lardner, a major figure in the tradition of American vernacular literature, perfected his craft and rose to fame while working as a sportswriter on a series of Chicago NEWSPAPERS. Lardner came to Chicago in the fall of 1907 and began a 12-year Chicago sportswriting career that took him to the *Inter-Ocean Examiner* and the *Tribune*. In 1913, when he was 28, Lardner took over the widely read *Tribune* column "In the Wake of the News," which freed him from the pressure of regular BASEBALL reporting and allowed him to develop the distinctive literary gifts on which his fame rests. Combining an ironic perspective, verbal economy, and a gift for dialect, Lardner built a large and loyal audience for his "Wake" columns—including such budding young writers as OAK PARK resident Ernest Hemingway, whose parodies of Lardner in his high-school newspaper suggest an important stylistic indebtedness.

Many of Lardner's "Wake" columns feature characters and dialogues that anticipate his first national success, "A Busher's Letters Home," published serially in the *Saturday Evening Post*. These letters, written by an imaginary WHITE SOX rookie named Jack Keefe to his friend in Indiana, reveal Lardner's unerring ear for American vernacular.

James Diedrick

While the story is probably apocryphal, it contains a germ of truth. Early Chicago had only the most primitive sports. Until about 1850, men outnumbered women, and a bachelor subculture encouraged drinking and GAMBLING, as well as activities like billiards and HORSE RACES. As Chicago began its rapid growth in the years just before and after the CIVIL WAR, new recreations emerged. BOXING, BASEBALL, and cricket, all in vogue in the east, especially in New York City, made their appearance here. During the final decades of the nineteenth century and the opening years of the twentieth, a new sporting culture emerged, one no longer on the fringes but in the mainstream of American life.

Prizefighting offers a good example of the older ways. Bare-knuckle boxing remained an outlaw sport throughout America for most of the nineteenth century, and occasional furtive bouts held in or near Chicago—fighters and fans often crossed over into Indiana to elude constables—were sporadic, spontaneous, crude affairs, patronized mostly by men of working-class or lower status. Prizefights hardly suited earnest Victorians—more precisely, those social, economic, and religious elites rising to power in the city, as well as the growing middle class aspiring to respectability. Boxing remained illegal until fights with gloves under the Marquis of Queensbury rules were established toward the end of the century.

Saloon-centered sports like boxing, billiards, dogfighting, and bear baiting were viewed as disruptive by businessmen, the clergy, and other middle-class Chicagoans. Such activities tempted men away from their jobs and toward gambling and drinking, swearing and Sabbath-breaking. More, the raw physicality of these sports offered a world at odds with the quiet virtues of home and family. Sports' rise to respectability—not only in Chicago, but throughout America—came when new athletic games displaced the ancient blood sports—or, more precisely, banished them to the fringes of lower-class and ethnic neighborhoods. Reformed sports were justified by a new ideology that merged athleticism with morality. Clean sports, reformers argued in the late nineteenth century, taught lessons in teamwork and self-sacrifice, in steady habits, leadership, and self-discipline. The YOUNG MEN'S CHRISTIAN ASSOCIATION, first founded in England, came to Chicago just before the Civil War, and by the 1870s, leaders like evangelist Dwight Moody and businessmen such as Cyrus McCormick, George Pullman, and Philip Armour helped the YMCA use athletics to spread the gospel of hard WORK and sobriety.

Baseball was the first major team sport that was part of the new ethos. It emerged in New York City in the mid-nineteenth century, and by the Civil War, amateur teams ranged along the Atlantic coast. The sport attracted many substantial middle-class citizens, and advocates emphasized how it taught manly fortitude. The Chicago Base Ball Club, founded in 1858, was followed by three more "nines" before the Civil War. Then the game's popularity exploded. Nearly 50 amateur clubs played here by 1867. Soon the Board of Trade fielded teams, and local magnates like Marshall Field and Potter Palmer sponsored clubs. Rivalries with Milwaukee and St. Louis quickly emerged, and, by 1870, a Chicago merchant put up $15,000 and founded the White Stockings, the city's first professional team, eventually renamed the Chicago CUBS. (America's first professional team was the 1869 Cincinnati Red Stockings.) Operated by William Hulbert, the White Stockings lured such stars as Albert Spalding away from the Boston Red Stockings and Cap Anson from the Philadelphia Athletics. The team quickly joined with other avowedly professional teams to form the National League of Professional Base Ball Clubs.

With migrants from the hinterlands and European immigrants pouring in, the city doubled in population every decade to 1890 and continued to add half a million new residents each decade until the GREAT DEPRESSION. Sports in particular and LEISURE in general consumed more and more of people's time and energy. Chicago's cultural elites often viewed newcomers as a disorderly rabble in need of discipline. For their part, the working classes labored hard under the new manufacturing regime, and they sought to fill their precious free time with exuberant pleasures. The very word "sport" measured the change. In 1850, a sport (or sporting man) was one who frequented the track, hung out in brothels and bars, spoke knowingly of the great pugilists, made money by his wits, and lived to gamble. By 1900, however, the more common usage of sport—the one we still use today—implied healthful athletic competition between teams or individuals.

The new sporting ideal did not, however, bring unity to Chicago's disparate classes, races, or ethnic groups. Many among the wealthy played in splendid isolation, competing against each other at exclusive yacht CLUBS, GOLF courses, athletic clubs, and COLLEGES, a whole host of institutions designed to mark the boundaries of caste and class. Even well-off JEWS, Catholics, and AFRICAN AMERICANS were excluded from these elite sporting venues.

But the class boundaries of the sports world were never wholly impermeable. The competitive nature of sport and the desire to win meant that even elite sports organizations—a rowing club, for example—might obtain "ringers," athletes retained for their ability, not their membership in an elite group. Moreover, sports, like the American social structure itself, contained some flexibility. For example, a few small entrepreneurs grew wealthy by manufacturing sporting merchandise, men like former ballplayer Albert Spalding and SWISS immigrant John Brunswick. In addition, middle-class communities formed their own versions of elite sporting organizations, including country clubs with golf courses and TENNIS courts and, by 1890, hundreds of BICYCLING clubs. Various immigrant groups re-created some of their old games from home, such as the German *Turnverein,* where gymnastics was part of a larger cultural agenda, including an ideological commitment to socialism. Even baseball could at once unite citizens in a shared culture—the game was, after all, the national pastime—while still marking group boundaries, as labor unions and country clubs sponsored their own amateur nines.

More new sports entered the scene shortly before the turn of the century, most notably BASKETBALL and college FOOTBALL. James Naismith invented basketball at the Springfield, Massachusetts, YMCA in 1891, and it spread rapidly. Within two years, the game was played at the UNIVERSITY OF CHICAGO and in urban YMCAs. HULL HOUSE quickly incorporated the game into its youth programs, Chicago high schools formed leagues for boys and girls and launched the first statewide tournament in 1908, and neighborhoods too created teams and built PLAYGROUNDS. Within a scant few years, basketball had grown into one of Chicago's most popular sports, especially among working-class males.

Football's early beginnings were much more elite. Informal versions of the game that we know as SOCCER were played in early-modern England and in the American colonies, though teams consisted of anyone who wanted to participate, playing fields were pastures or other open spaces, balls were inflated animal bladders, and goals local landmarks. Chicago had its own League of Association Football (soccer) beginning in 1883, which began with five neighborhood teams, and the sport continued to grow in popularity. Shortly after the Civil War, however, a new American version of the game developed at elite eastern colleges, the forerunner of the run-pass-and-kick football we know today. By the 1880s, Ivy League college games attracted thousands of fans (many of them unaffiliated with any college) and garnered ever-increasing space in the newspapers.

Chicago followed the national trend: high-school students were organized into the Cook County Football League, NORTHWESTERN UNIVERSITY began intercollegiate play in 1882, and, shortly after its founding, the University of Chicago competed against other Midwestern powerhouses such as Michigan and Wisconsin. Chicago President William Rainey Harper recognized the value of athletics for publicity, and in Amos Alonzo Stagg he found a football coach who could build a nationally competitive program; indeed, during the first decade of the twentieth century, Chicago was America's predominant football power. Building on the Maroon's success, football spread throughout the city, with countless club, school, and PARK DISTRICT teams. The city's first professional team, the Chicago CARDINALS, did not arrive until 1920 (the year the National Football League was founded), but the college game continued to attract greater crowds and press coverage throughout the 1920s. Indeed, amateur football laid the groundwork for the professional game, which originated in the GREAT LAKES region after WORLD WAR I.

By the Progressive era, a sporting trend had taken hold of America that differed markedly from anything before. The old blood sports still lingered, but the new direction was clear. Modern sports had carefully formulated rules, regulatory bodies (such as the National Collegiate Athletic Association, founded in 1906), increasingly sophisticated record keeping, and uniform rules of entry (for white males, that is, since blacks and women were routinely excluded). Sports were now highly commercialized activities—repeatable spectacles played before paying audiences. Equally important, a new sports ethos was ascendant, one that argued for the moral value of wholesome physical activity. Chicago journalists disseminated both this new ethos and daily information about the games themselves. The city's newspapers were among the nation's first to develop entire pages and even sections for sports, and local writers cultivated a unique narrative style. Moreover, by the early twentieth century, sports had influential new patrons: big businesses that founded industrial leagues; private organizations like the YMCA that sought clean, alcohol-free activities; and government-sponsored SCHOOLS, parks, and playgrounds, all looking for wholesome alternatives to street culture. Perhaps most important in spreading the gospel of Chicago sports, local teams competed quite successfully in these years, especially the Cubs during the first decade of the century, the Chicago WHITE SOX during the World War I era, and Stagg's University of Chicago football teams.

Divisions of class and ethnicity did not disappear from sports; the wealthy still retreated to exclusive country clubs, and immigrants like the Bohemians and the POLES continued to build community through their own Old World athletic associations, the Bohemians' Sokols and the Polish Falcons. But sport, along with other leisure activities of the rising consumer culture, increasingly created bonds among diverse Americans. To be a Cubs or a White Sox fan was to be a true Chicagoan, and therefore a true American. Fandom was a bond that united a city of strangers. The children of immigrants, especially, found that knowledge of batting averages and boxing champions could be part of the process of AMERICANIZATION, of fitting in and belonging. This second generation did not so much lose its ethnic identity as take on a dual identity. One could be Polish *and* American, ITALIAN *and* American, Jewish *and* American.

One of the most remarkable things about sports by the early twentieth century was the sheer amount of it; Chicago was awash in sports. Partly this was because the boundaries that later emerged between professional and amateur games were much more fluid. Baseball, for example, was the most popular sport of the era, with semiprofessional teams proliferating all over the city. Companies such as Sears, Roebuck and Illinois Steel sponsored clubs to retain worker loyalty. Other teams represented neighborhoods, such as the LOGAN SQUARES, and still others, such as Cap Anson's Colts, were promoted by individuals. These latter two were members of the Chicago League, and their games against each other were well attended and received extensive newspaper coverage. Working-class men supplemented their wages by playing semipro games and betting on their own teams. Excluded from such white neighborhood and industrial leagues, African Americans organized their own teams during these years. Mostly they played black clubs from other cities, but plenty of games pitted white against black teams. Indeed, even professional organizations—the White Sox and

Soccer team, George M. Pullman Free School of Manual Training, 1922. Photographer: Unknown. Source: Chicago Historical Society.

Cubs, for example—played against semipro teams, including African American ones. Latinos too, especially in GARY and HAMMOND, formed their own teams and leagues.

Athletics also had become a marker of masculinity, a male realm, a place where men displayed physical prowess and fortitude.

Boxer Bob Fitzsimmons (card), 1894. Photographer: Unknown. Source: Chicago Historical Society.

Increasingly, sport became a lingua franca; at the office, during lunch break in the factory, over a beer after work, men came together to talk of sports. Moreover, team games modeled a masculine ideal, one much like the business world—cooperative within the organization, competitive without.

Nevertheless, substantial numbers of women played in the early years of the twentieth century. Some schools offered athletic programs for girls, and industrial leagues for working-class women opened up opportunities too. Tennis and basketball were sports of choice for high-school and college girls. And among working-class women, the Western Electric Company, for example, had 28,000 members in its recreation program by the mid-1920s, including an 8-team women's baseball league and 26 women's BOWLING teams. SWIMMING and volleyball also were remarkably popular with women, especially in programs offered by the Chicago Park District. Numbers suggest the growing popularity of sports among Chicago women: shortly before World War I, 1,400 women entered a track meet hosted by the Park District and the Chicago *American* newspaper; during the same period, a citywide SOFTBALL tournament attracted 900 women's teams, and a local woman's basketball championship drew 1,200 teams. While the old Victorian notion that physical strenuosity and competition harmed women still persisted in some quarters, thousands of female Chicagoans nonetheless took every opportunity to play sports through neighborhood, park, and industrial leagues.

The post–World War I era marked a watershed in Chicago sports history. Consider four seminal events. In 1919, several members of the Chicago White Sox conspired with gamblers to deliberately lose the World Series to the Cincinnati Reds. The "Black Sox" scandal besmirched baseball's hard-won image as an honest sport, and many predicted the game's ruin. But team owner Charles Comiskey and his attorneys managed to salvage the situation. Eight indicted White Sox players were cleared in court, then banned from the game by baseball's new commissioner, Kenesaw Mountain Landis. Landis's decree was draconian and unjust, but it sent a message that the national pastime had been cleaned up. With a strong commissioner's office regulating the game, baseball owners went on to build new stadiums and fill them with unprecedented numbers of fans. Instead of declining, baseball entered a new golden age, and the rise of the game's greatest star, Babe Ruth, was emblematic of this triumph.

Prizefighting too staged its greatest triumphs during these years, and shook off its old outlaw stigma. The ring had an initial burst of respectability at the turn of the century when the new Marquis of Queensbury rules seemed to sweep away the corruptions of the old bare-knuckle era. But when Jack Johnson—proud, defiant, and black—became heavyweight champion in 1908, the rising RACISM of the era elicited a search for a "great white hope" who could defeat him. Not until Johnson lost his title in 1915 to Jess Willard could the champion once again embody white manhood. The 1920s brought the ring's apotheosis, and the high point of the decade came in 1927, when over 100,000 people attended the Dempsey-Tunney championship fight in Chicago's new SOLDIER FIELD, a stadium dedicated to the American servicemen who had fought overseas in the Great War. Tunney's victory (he was known as the "Fighting Marine") in this shrine to patriotism signaled the growing ties between sport and nationalism. Indeed, the 1920s were an era when the localism of neighborhood and ethnicity lost some of its allure to a citywide and nationwide mass culture. As the old immigrants aged, a new generation that knew only American ways emerged, a group in which commercialized mass leisure found its most fertile ground.

Yet if sport in the 1920s knit together many Chicagoans from across the city as fans, the divisions of race grew deeper. The horrific 1919 Chicago RACE RIOT, after all, began on a segregated beach on the SOUTH SIDE with the stoning of an African American teenager who inadvertently crossed an invisible barrier separating black from white swimmers. Athletics developed their own version of America's deepening segregation. Jim Crow discrimination in sport flowered in 1887, when legendary Chicago White Stockings star Cap

Anson refused to let his team play against a top African American pitcher, achieving a policy of discrimination that soon spread throughout the league. In the coming years, several black teams came and went, but the most successful institutional response was the Negro National League, founded in 1920 by player-manager-owner Rube Foster, who brought together entrepreneurs from several Midwestern cities in Chicago. The Negro League served its purpose, prospering until baseball was reintegrated in 1947, when Jackie Robinson joined the Brooklyn Dodgers. The Negro League produced a generation of great athletes, and the teams themselves grew into important businesses in African American communities. Moreover, black baseball developed a distinctive style based less on power than on aggressive base-running. Chicago remained the capital of black baseball in America in that era, hosting the annual East–West all-star game, which filled the South Side's Sox Park every year.

A fourth development of the 1920s was the rise of the National Football League. The father of professional football, George Halas, was the son of Bohemian immigrants. Raised in Chicago's PILSEN neighborhood, he first developed a love of sport at his neighborhood Sokol. In school, however, he played American games. He found his way into industrial-league football and then played for the University of Illinois. The Staley Starch Company of Decatur offered him a job setting up industrial-league teams to improve employee morale. Semiprofessional football was strongest in midsize Great Lakes cities like Canton, Ohio, and Green Bay, Wisconsin. When Halas contacted the owner of the Canton team to arrange a game in 1920, he was invited to the first meeting of the American Professional Football Association. Representatives of eight teams met in an auto showroom in Canton, worked out a schedule for the next season, and agreed not to tamper with either college athletes or each other's players. Each owner was asked to put up $100, though Halas later remarked that he doubted there was that much money in the whole room. Nonetheless, Halas rapidly emerged as the leader of the new league, and he left Decatur to start a team in Chicago. The new circuit almost immediately outgrew its parochial origins, taking on the name the National Football League, and the Chicago BEARS became one of the flagship teams.

By the 1920s, sports had taken on the forms we recognize today. The games themselves, their leagues, regulatory agencies, urban stadiums, and media coverage—even electronic journalism began in the 1920s with radio BROADCASTS—all were in place. The Great Depression and WORLD WAR II certainly curtailed the growth of sport, but in the second half of the twentieth century, athletic culture once again exploded. Since the 1920s, sports have gotten much bigger: greater revenues, higher salaries, more consumer goods, larger audiences, fuller coverage over television and cable networks, new leagues, and so forth. By the last decades of the twentieth century, professional football and even basketball vied with baseball as our predominant game. Still, the games themselves and the institutional structures of modern sports had been in place since early in the century.

Sports have also become much more international in scope. Baseball recruits star players from Asia and Latin America, many Europeans and Africans consider basketball their favorite sport, and American children idolize the great soccer players from around the world. From the 1920s on, Al Capone was Chicago's most internationally recognizable citizen, until he was replaced first by Muhammad Ali in the 1960s, then by Michael Jordan in the 1990s. As sports have become less parochial, old prejudices have subsided too. African Americans, Latinos, and women—especially since the passage of Title IX of the Education Acts opened up school sports—are more visible and more accepted as sports heroes than ever before. Although team ownership and management remain mostly the province of white males, that too is slowly changing. Perhaps the greatest change has been the sheer amount of sports marketing around the world and the pervasiveness of athletic imagery for selling goods.

If a Chicago sports fan from the 1920s were magically transported to the 1990s to witness the city's greatest sports triumph, the Chicago BULLS' sixth championship of the decade, that fan would have been surprised by the sheer magnitude of the spectacle, and stunned that the team's leader, a black man, had become the most famous human being in the world. But our fictitious fan would have been familiar with the commercialism, the emotional outpouring, and the civic pride of that event, for since the early twentieth century, sports have been central to Chicago life and identity. Our teams and recreations remain fundamental to our urban self-definition.

Elliott J. Gorn

See also: Entertaining Chicagoans; Fitness and Athletic Clubs; Sports, High-School; Sports, Industrial League Street Life; Work Culture

Further reading: For general works on sports history, see Elliott J. Gorn and Warren Goldstein, *A Brief History of American Sports* (1993); Benjamin Rader, *American Sports: From the Age of Folk Games to the Age of Spectators* (1983); and Allen Guttmann, *From Ritual to Record: The Nature of Modern Sports* (1978). Steven Riess has written two innovative works on sport and urban life—*Touching Base: Professional Baseball and American Culture in the Progressive Era* (1980), and *City Games: The Evolution of American Urban Society and the Rise of Sports* (1989). Several fine works have concentrated on particular American cities, for example Melvin Adelman, *A Sporting Time: New York City and the Rise of Modern Athletics* (1986); Roy Rosenzweig, *Eight Hours for What We Will: Workers and Leisure in an Industrial City* (1983); Rob Ruck, *Sandlot Seasons: Sport in Black Pittsburgh* (1987); and Stephen Hardy, *How Boston Played: Sport, Recreation, and Community* (1982). The indispensable work on sport in Chicago is Gerry Gems, *Windy City Wars: Labor, Leisure, and Sport in the Making of Chicago* (1997).

Histories of particular sports are especially useful. For baseball, see Warren Goldstein, *Playing for Keeps: A History of Early Baseball* (1989); Peter Levine, *A. G. Spalding and the Rise of Baseball* (1985); Harold Seymour, *Baseball: The Early Years* (1960), and *Baseball: The People's Game* (1990); and David Q. Voight, *American Baseball: From Gentleman's Sport to the Commissioner System* (1966). For boxing, see Elliott J. Gorn, *The Manly Art: Bare-Knuckle Prize Fighting in America* (1986); Jeffrey Sammons, *Beyond the Ring: The Role of Boxing in Modern Society* (1988); and Randy Roberts, *Jack Dempsey, The Manassa Mauler* (1979). Michael Oriard, *Reading Football: How the Popular Press Created an American Spectacle* (1993), and *King Football: Sport and Spectacle in the Golden Age of Radio and Newsreels, Movies and Magazines, the Weekly and Daily Press* (2001), are outstanding histories of the game; and for the founding of the National Football League, see Marc S. Maltby, *The Origins and Early Development of Professional Football* (1997).

There are surprisingly few good works on sports in Chicago. In addition to Gems, see Robin Lester, *Stagg's University: The Rise, Decline, and Fall of Big-Time Football at Chicago* (1995); Lizabeth Cohen, *Making a New Deal: Workers in Industrial Chicago* (1990); James T. Farrell, *My Baseball Diary* (1957); and Ray Schmidt, "The Golden Age of Chicago Baseball," *Chicago History* (Winter 2000): 39–59.

Credit. *See* Consumer Credit

Crerar Library, John. The John Crerar Library, a public research library for the natural and social sciences, opened April 1, 1897.

John Crerar came to Chicago from his native New York City in 1862 to establish A RAILROAD SUPPLY firm. His will gave the city a portion of his estate (estimated at approximately $2.6 million) as an endowment for a free public library, selected "to create and sustain a healthy moral and Christian sentiment." To comply with Crerar's wishes and to complement area LIBRARIES, the directors decided to limit the collections to the sciences, adding medicine to the library's scope in 1906.

The Crerar's technology resources attracted a large clientele from Chicago-area business and industry. Its equally outstanding collections of historical and rare materials drew scholars from many countries. To assist the post–WORLD WAR II expansion in scientific research, the directors established an innovative fee-based research service for industry and government. In 1951 they decided to limit the collection to current science, technology, and medicine.

The Crerar Library opened in the Marshall Field building, moving in 1921 to its own home at the northwest corner of Randolph Street and Michigan Avenue. The building became overcrowded in the 1950s, and because endowment income no longer covered operations, the directors contracted with the ILLINOIS INSTITUTE OF TECHNOLOGY to provide library services. The library moved to the IIT campus in 1962. By the mid-1970s, however, the facility had become inadequate and in 1980 Crerar and IIT agreed to terminate the contract within four years. The directors consolidated the collection with the UNIVERSITY OF CHICAGO'S science collection in a new building opened in 1984. The merger, among the largest in American library history, resulted in a collection of 900,000 volumes. The John Crerar Library, now in HYDE PARK, retains its name and its status as a free public library.

Jane Aikin

See also: Chicago Public Library; Innovation, Invention, and Chicago Business; Newberry Library

Further reading: Bay, J. Christian. *The John Crerar Library, 1895–1944: An Historical Report Prepared under the Authority of the Board of Directors by the Librarian.* 1945. • Carnahan, Paul A. *A Guide to the Historical Records of the John Crerar Library, 1828–1984.* Edited by Richard L. Popp. 1991. • John Crerar Foundation. *The John Crerar Library.* 1984.

Crest Hill, IL, Will County, 33 miles SW of the Loop. Crest Hill incorporated in 1960 to avoid ANNEXATION to JOLIET. The city annexed the land encompassing the Stateville Correctional Center in 1987, which subsequently accounted for the majority of Crest Hill's taxes. The 2000 population was 13,329, including 2,571 prisoners.

Erik Gellman

See also: Jails and Prisons; Will County

Crestwood, IL, Cook County, 17 miles S of the Loop. Crestwood shares an early history with the adjoining communities of ALSIP, WORTH, PALOS HEIGHTS, and ROBBINS. All were part of the marshlands surrounding the Saganashkee Swamp which were drained for farming and which provided the route for the Calumet-Sag Channel built from 1911 to 1922. From the middle of the nineteenth century, the area included scattered farms and the beginnings of small market towns as RAILROAD stops were established. In the early twentieth century, pressures for residential development grew in the Crestwood area with the establishment of large FOREST PRESERVES to the west and the Midlothian Country Club to the south.

In 1927, residents around the country club incorporated as the village of MIDLOTHIAN. Following that lead, with a population of around 400, the residents from the area north of Midlothian to the Cal-Sag Channel incorporated as the village of Crestwood in 1928. As housing continued to develop, Kostner and Cicero began to develop as commercial streets for the village. In the 1920s, the Midlothian Turnpike, once a Native American trail, was improved and motorists used it as their route from BLUE ISLAND to the Midlothian Country Club. Through the 1920s and 1930s, few residents had cars, and many walked to Midlothian or to Blue Island to use trolley and train lines to commute to WORK in the city.

Typical of other suburban towns, Crestwood saw the growth of a rich variety of local organizations, many following the lead of the Crestwood Boosters Club formed in 1947. These included scouting, Little League, and other recreational and women's groups.

Crestwood experienced significant residential growth in the 1960s and 1970s. Its population grew from 1,213 in 1960 to 10,852 in 1980, with little change in the two decades after that.

Both in its early years and throughout its growth, the population of Crestwood has been predominately of GERMAN background, with other families of POLISH, ITALIAN, SLOVAK, and ENGLISH extractions. The minority population was under 10 percent in 2000.

A substantial transformation in the village revolved around the Howell Airport located at Cicero Avenue and State Route 83. For many years, Howell had served as one of the busiest general aviation AIRPORTS in the region. However, it was replaced by a large shopping complex known as RiverCrest Centre that opened in 1990. This commercial area, along with related business areas along Cicero Avenue, gave Crestwood an extremely strong local tax base.

Larry A. McClellan

See also: Golf; Metropolitan Growth; Water

Further reading: *Great Today, Greater Tomorrow: Village of Crestwood.* 1976[?].

Crete, IL, Will County, 30 miles S of the Loop. Located just south of Cook County, Crete grew alongside the wagon road known as Vincennes or Hubbard's Trail, later the route of the Dixie Highway and Illinois Route 1.

Among the first landowners were the family of Willard and Diantha Wood, who arrived in 1836. By the mid-1840s a small market center had developed in the community known as Wood's Corners. In 1843, Wood served as the first postmaster and selected the name Crete from the New Testament writings of St. Paul. Wood platted the village in 1849, served in elected positions, donated land for churches, and built a frequently used hotel. Immigrant GERMANS arrived in the 1840s and 1850s. Into the twentieth century, German could be heard as often as English in Crete.

Due mainly to families associated with the Congregational Church, Crete was a key stopping point on the UNDERGROUND RAILROAD, and strong ABOLITIONIST sentiment led to a large enlistment for the CIVIL WAR.

Initial businesses related to farming, with a woodworking plant established in 1869. Also in 1869, the Chicago, Danville & Vincennes RAILROAD came through Crete, connecting to markets in Chicago.

With a rail line and established businesses, Crete grew as the commercial center for eastern WILL COUNTY, incorporating in 1880. In 1893, a local entrepreneur built the Hattendorf Hotel for visitors to the WORLD'S COLUMBIAN EXPOSITION in Chicago. However, Crete was too far south to benefit from the fair visitors. In 1906 the Chicago and Southern Traction Company, an INTERURBAN line between Chicago and Kankakee, tied Crete more closely to the Chicago region. In 1926, Chicago and Kentucky businessmen built Lincoln Fields, later renamed Balmoral Park racetrack, on 1,000 acres south of Crete. Also in 1926, Chicago interests purchased land east of the village and created Lincolnshire, planning four GOLF courses and upscale commuter-oriented housing.

Throughout the twentieth century, Crete has added large residential areas while at the same time seeking to preserve its historic central core. The population grew from 760 in 1900 to 2,298 in 1950 and 7,346 in 2000.

Larry A. McClellan

See also: Agriculture; Horse Racing; Streets and Highways

Further reading: Crete Area Historical Society. *A Pictorial History of Crete.* 1986. • Lazaros, Ettarose, and Phyllis Monks. *Crete, 1836–1980.* Edited by Audrey DeMuth. 1980.

Crime and Chicago's Image. Chicago's criminal reputation long preceded Al Capone and the beer wars. Born in the same years as the sensationalist penny press and Americans' new fears of a masterless working class, the city seemed even to its earliest observers a hotbed of crime and immorality. Stories of murder, rape, theft, arson, and other mayhem filled the frontier town's many NEWSPAPERS. In its 1840 complaint that "the business of stealing horseflesh," has been "reduced to a regular system," the *Tribune* echoed the perception of countless Chicagoans. The same year, the city's first hanging—with 2,500 reportedly in attendance—confirmed the view.

By the end of the 1840s, observers both within the city and beyond regularly noted the existence of an identifiable criminal underworld. In the words of the *Democrat,* it was "getting to be a notorious fact that robbers, pickpockets, thimble riggers [literally, those who played the three-shell game, but more broadly any who used sly tricks to cheat], &c., &c., are perfectly at home in our city."

Al Capone

Born in Brooklyn to Neapolitan immigrants, Alphonse Capone quit school at 14. Young Capone joined a street GANG, earned a local reputation for violence, and received his later famous scar, probably in a bar fight. He came to Chicago, probably in 1919, to work with John Torrio, an associate from his old Brooklyn gang who now served as lieutenant for SOUTH SIDE vice kingpin Jim Colosimo. After Colosimo's murder in 1920, Torrio took over, expanding operations in GAMBLING and PROSTITUTION. He entered the lucrative new field of bootlegging, operating BREWERIES, distilleries, and a ruthless LIQUOR DISTRIBUTION system. First operating the outfit's Four Deuces vice joint, Capone soon became Torrio's chief assistant. When Torrio fled Chicago in 1925 after a nearly fatal attack from rivals, Capone became the leading partner in the expanding organization.

The organization consolidated its control of the Chicago-area underworld in the "beer wars" of 1924 to 1930. The hundreds of casualties included Dion O'Banion, hijacker and leader of a North Side gang, his successor Hymie Weiss, and the seven victims of the infamous ST. VALENTINE'S DAY MASSACRE of 1929. The killings of Assistant State's Attorney William McSwiggin (1926) and *Chicago Tribune* reporter Jake Lingle (1930), both posthumously regarded as corrupt, illuminated the long reach of underworld influence.

Capone fascinated Americans preoccupied with crime and the social turmoil it symbolized. Popular accounts simultaneously celebrated and condemned a *public* enemy found to bear an uncanny resemblance to ordinary, noncriminal Americans. In his multiple roles as businessman, patriarch, spender, and playboy, Capone illuminated the lives of millions of urban Americans.

Capone was convicted in 1929 of carrying a concealed handgun and spent 10 months in a Philadelphia jail. A Treasury Department investigation led to his 1931 conviction for failure to report income and pay taxes; he was imprisoned, for a time in the newly opened Alcatraz, until 1939. His mind ravaged by syphilis, Capone spent his last years in his Miami estate.

David E. Ruth

The visibility of vice enhanced the city's criminal reputation. At midcentury, Chicago reportedly had more GAMBLING establishments than the larger city of Philadelphia and more per capita than New York. Vice first concentrated in an area along the CHICAGO RIVER known as "the Patches," places, as the *Tribune* put it, of "the most beastly sensuality and darkest crimes."

So wicked was the city's reputation that many saw the FIRE OF 1871 as divine retribution against a modern-day Sodom and Gomorrah. Lawlessness after the conflagration gave no cause for optimism. "The city," one newspaper reported, "is infested with a horde of thieves, burglars and cut-throats, bent on plunder, and who will not hesitate to burn, pillage and even murder."

Fire did not bring redemption, and Chicago's reputation darkened in the late 1800s. Violent labor disputes—especially the HAYMARKET crisis—added to the image of lawlessness. By the 1890s the notorious Levee VICE DISTRICT attracted criticism—and visitors—from around the world. Chicago "makes a more amazingly open display of evil than any other city known to me," a visitor from London exclaimed. "Other places hide their blackness out of sight; Chicago treasures it in the heart of the business quarter and gives it a veneer."

The WORLD'S COLUMBIAN EXPOSITION of 1893 focused attention on the city's sins as well as its achievements. William T. Stead's *If Christ Came to Chicago* (1894), which used the city to symbolize modern corruption, and detective Clifton Wooldridge's *Hands Up!* (1901), a popular account that detailed the many arrests he made at the exposition, added to the city's sordid reputation. So too did the sensational story of Herman Mudgett, the confessed killer of 27, many of whom were exposition visitors boarding at his SOUTH SIDE Gothic "castle"—a horror house, readers across the country learned, with secret passages, torture chamber, and crematorium.

The efforts of Progressive-era muckrakers and reformers ironically added new layers to the city's criminal reputation. "Chicago, in the mind of the country," George Kibbe Turner wrote in *McClure's* (1907), "stands notorious for violent crime." His tracing of that crime to widespread official corruption indicted much of the city. Assistant Attorney General Clifford G. Roe's media-savvy campaign against "white slavery" and the widely publicized VICE COMMISSION report, *The Social Evil in Chicago* (1911), put the city at the center of a nationwide PROSTITUTION scandal. The tradition

Robert Harland's *The Vice Bondage of a Great City* (1912) typified early twentieth-century portrayals of Chicago as riddled with vice. The book's refrain, "Chicago is the Wickedest City in the World," punctuates references to the specific temptations that await the innocent visitor. Artist: unknown. Source: Chicago Historical Society.

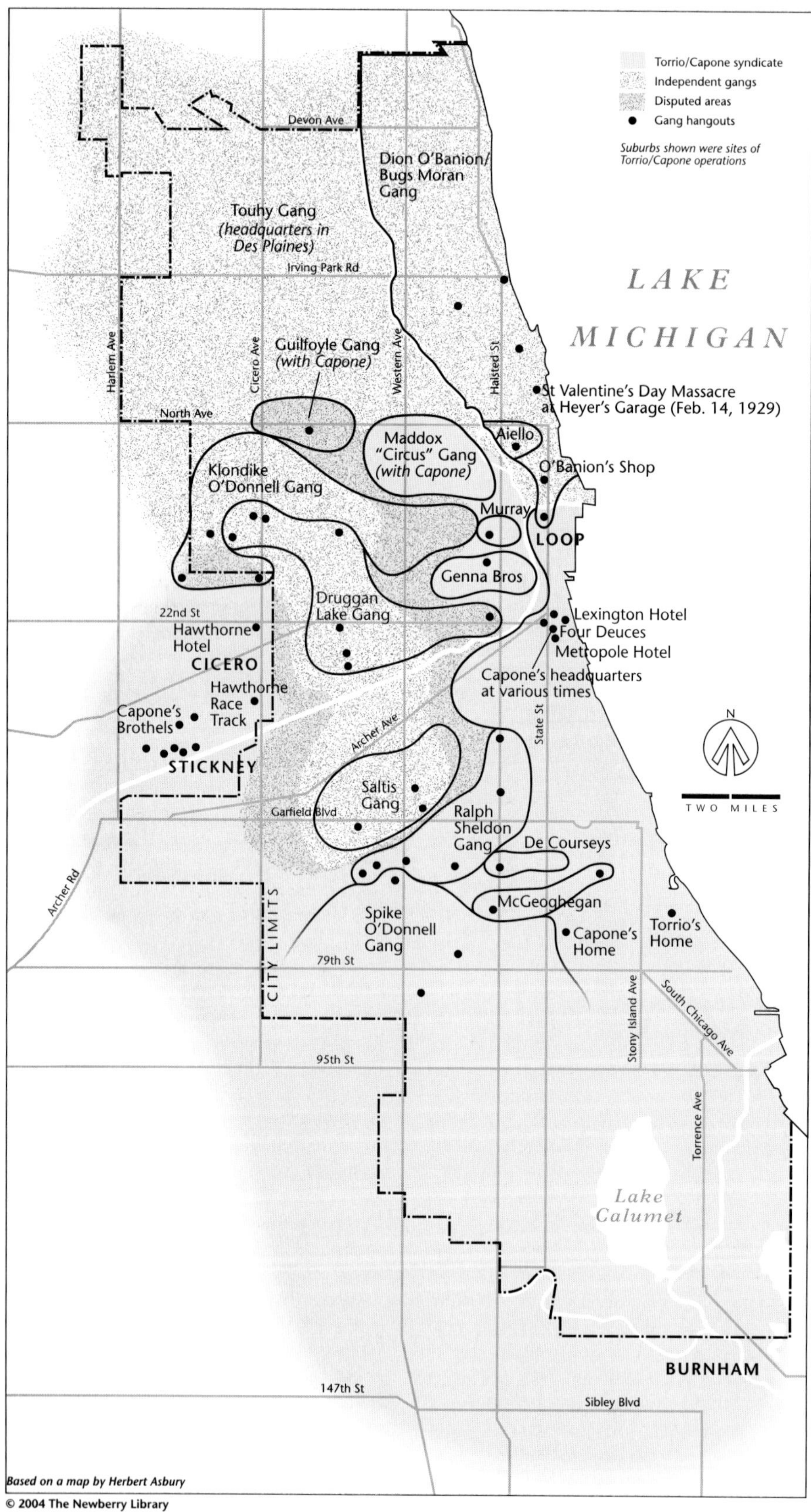

Organized Crime in 1920s Chicago

The long-standing reformist theme of shadowy conspirators seeking "control" of the city and suburbs captured public attention in Chicago and beyond when bootlegging and vice entrepreneurs John Torrio and Al Capone rose to prominence amidst shocking violence. This map is redrawn from an impressionistic map in Herbert Asbury's popular *Gem of the Prairie* (1940), itself based on earlier depictions of organized crime during the bootlegging era. Ignoring many illegal businesses—from neighborhood "soft drink parlors" to international liquor marketing networks—as well as public demand for booze, this focuses on the violent competition among gangs to dominate illegal markets in urban space. The fuzzy and ever-shifting "turf" of major gangs around 1925 is captured on this map at one moment in time, which subtly suggests that no area—perhaps no Chicagoan—was outside the control of some gang.

of investigation and exposure continued in the 1920s and 1930s, especially in research conducted by members of the influential CHICAGO SCHOOL OF SOCIOLOGY that helped make the city's criminal subculture the most intensively studied in the world.

The killing of vice leader Jim Colosimo in 1920, the first year of national Prohibition, signaled a new phase in Chicago violence. The bloody beer wars of 1924–1930 made Al Capone famous and the city synonymous with the new phenomenon of gangsterism. Chicago's notoriety grew in a series of violent episodes: the 1924 shooting of GANG leader Dion O'Banion in his North Side flower shop, the 1926 machine-gunning of Hymie Weiss on the steps of Holy Name Cathedral, the 1929 ST. VALENTINE'S DAY MASSACRE of seven men in a Clark Street garage. Widely reported in the national and international press, these incidents were the subject of popular contemporary books and plays. Even more important, *Underworld* (1927), *Public Enemy* (1931), *Scarface* (1932), and scores of lesser films broadcast to eager audiences dramatic tales of Chicago criminality. As one journalist put it in 1930, "In all the seven seas and the lands bordering thereon there is probably no name which more quickly calls up thoughts of crime, violence and wickedness than does that of Chicago."

Yet even during the twenties and thirties, Chicago's levels of violence and vice were never especially high. Instead the city's reputation was a matter of myth and symbol. For Chicago—in its booming growth, unrestrained energy, and sometimes explosive conflicts—symbolized for many the promises and perils of America's urban future. In its "excessiveness," one writer on crime explained, Chicago "is like other American cities—only more so." The myths of Chicago crime were compelling because they spoke to larger concerns—about morality, economic competition, ethnicity, sexuality, the pursuit of pleasure, and its dangers.

Capone and his peers have continued to loom extraordinarily large in popular perceptions of Chicago. Reinforcing those perceptions has been a steady stream of books, television series, and films as varied as *The Roaring*

Twenties (1939), *Al Capone* (1959), *Some Like It Hot* (1959), and *The Untouchables* (1987). Though resented by some Chicagoans, the city's criminal reputation has taken on new meanings in the form of nostalgia, compelling as an odd source of civic pride and, perhaps, as a reminder of a time when urban disorder seemed more contained, rational, and controllable than it does today.

David E. Ruth

See also: Black Sox Scandal; Chicago Crime Commission; Chicago Studied: Social Scientists and Their City; Homicide; Lexington Hotel; Mafia; Police; Prohibition and Temperance

Further reading: Asbury, Herbert. *Gem of the Prairie: An Informal History of the Chicago Underworld.* 1940. • Ruth, David E. *Inventing the Public Enemy: The Gangster in American Culture, 1918–1934.* 1996.

Croatians. A Croatian-language encyclopedia published in Yugoslavia in 1942 included a three-page entry on Chicago, illustrated by a photograph of the lakefront and a map of local Croatian settlement. Because Chicago was a magnet for both peasants and political activists emigrating from Croatia, the historian of Croatian immigrants in the United States called Chicago the "Second Croatian Capital." Croatian immigration is difficult to measure because Croatia's lack of political autonomy prompted U.S. immigration and census officials to lump them with SLOVENES or YUGOSLAVIANS. That lack of national independence, however, nourished American Croatians' ethnic ties and kept their attention on the political reconfiguration of Southern Europe. The nearly continuous flow of migrants from the Balkans to Chicago made the city a place where both Europeans and Americans could renew Croatian politics and culture.

Although Croatians had traveled to southern and western North America since the sixteenth century, only in the middle of the nineteenth century did they reach the Midwest. A few itinerant Croatian peddlers of religious jewelry conducted businesses from Chicago. The collapse of farming and the blight of phylloxera on Dalmatian vineyards brought a few hundred thousand Croatians to the industrial Northeast, beginning in the 1880s. The majority stopped in the Allegheny Valley to work in the burgeoning mining and steel industries. Some passed through Chicago on their way to jobs in heavy industry and coal mines in the West. But many headed directly for Chicago, where Croatian saloonkeepers, who doubled as labor and steamship agents, reported that work was available.

Former farmers found jobs in the stockyards, at factories such as International Harvester and Crane Brothers Manufacturing Company, in the BUILDING TRADES, and on the surface rails. Some left the city in the summers for CONSTRUCTION work. In nearby WHITING, Indiana, Croatians worked in oil refineries. Most migrants were single men who paid to live in BOARDINGHOUSES run by Croatian wives who did laundry and prepared meals. Women worked in packinghouses or other factories, or set up small shops.

The small colony living south of the LOOP in the early twentieth century grew into several distinct settlements, each with its own ROMAN CATHOLIC church and priest from Croatia. Migrants from the Dalmatian region settled near Wentworth Avenue in ARMOUR SQUARE and opened St. Jerome's in 1912. Another group concentrated in PILSEN and worshiped at Holy Trinity Croatian Catholic Church after 1914. Financially successful Croatians gathered in ENGLEWOOD. A third group of migrants settled in the far southeastern part of the city. Initially they worshiped with Slovenes at St. George's at 95th and Ewing, but in 1914 they dedicated Sacred Heart Church. Between 15,000 and 50,000 Croatians settled in Chicago before World War I slowed European emigration.

Even as the establishment of Croatian PARISHES solidified immigrants' attachments to particular neighborhoods, political organizations made Chicago the center of American debate over Croatia's proper role within the Austro-Hungarian Empire, and, after World War I, within the Kingdom of SERBS, Croats, and Slovenes (Yugoslavia after 1929). Between 1892 and 1943, 44 Croatian NEWSPAPERS and MAGAZINES were published in the Chicago area. Some reflected the active SOCIALIST contingent; others debated the future of the Balkans. The most important of these was *Hrvatska Zastava (Croatian Flag)*, which began publication in 1901; in 1912, it became the organ of the Croatian Alliance, advocating a federal South Slavic state ruled by all three nationalities. Chicago also hosted several national conferences that debated Croatian governance. A constant flow of Croatians back and forth between Europe and America ensured continued attention to the state of politics in Europe, until American immigration restrictions established in the 1920s limited the number of "Yugoslav" migrants to the United States.

Chicago's Croatians became less active in European affairs during the 1920s and 1930s, but maintained cultural coherence through a variety of festivals, CLUBS, and fraternal associations. Churches and picnic groves, especially the Yugoslav Benevolent and Pleasure Club and the Sacred Heart Church, hosted picnics and festivals in the summertime. Croatian Americans joined lodges of the Croatian Catholic Union, headquartered in GARY, Indiana. In 1935, Ivan Majdak of BERWYN founded the Croatian-American Radio Club, which broadcast a weekly radio program on WGES. The Croatian Woman's Society supported charitable causes: during World War II they sent packages to soldiers in Europe, and during the 1990s they collected funds to help victims of the war in Bosnia. Similarly, the singing society *Zora* ("Dawn," one of the first Croatian choral societies in the United States), ethnic SOCCER teams, *Kolo* or circle dances, and *tamburitza* music reminded Chicago's Croatians of Europe.

After WORLD WAR II, another wave of Croatian migrants sought out Chicago. Attracted by Chicago's reputation in Croatia, political refugees and intellectuals fleeing Marshal Tito's rule in Communist Yugoslavia reinvigorated the ties of a community that had begun to marry outside its ethnic bounds and disperse across the city and suburbs. The Pilsen colony scattered as MEXICANS moved there, but Holy Trinity's school continued to be staffed by Croatian clergy, even after the mid-1960s when most of the graduates had Hispanic surnames. Chicago's growing community of Croatian MUSLIMS established their own mosque in 1957. The founding of the Croatian Folklore Group of Chicago created another opportunity for sustaining ethnic traditions. Many of the political migrants settled in ROGERS PARK and worshiped at the Angel Guardian Croatian Catholic Church. The 1960s also brought economic REFUGEES from Yugoslavia.

Chicago's awareness of local Croatian nationalism and culture reawoke during the 1970s. Edward Vrdolyak, the son of Croatian saloonkeepers from the Southeast Side, was elected Tenth Ward alderman in 1971. Michael A. Bilandic, who had gone to Croatian-language school at St. Jerome's, became MAYOR after the death of Richard J. Daley in 1976 and was elected in his own right for another term. Beyond the sudden popularity of Croatian greetings in city hall, Bilandic's ancestry was highlighted by his appearance at negotiations with Croatian nationalists who held six hostages at Chicago's West German consulate in August 1978. Several national conferences on Croatia's future and celebrations of Croatian Independence Day were staged at the LaSalle Hotel.

In the 1990s Croatia and Chicago continued to feel one another's influence. One of the most active lodges of the Croatian Catholic Union reported from WAUKEGAN, and Chicagoan Myrna T. Jurcev served as the CCU's national secretary-treasurer. A large sign on 53rd Street in HYDE PARK reminded passers-by that "Croatia is dying to be free." Although the original concentrations of Croatians in Chicago have dispersed, the city's role as a political and cultural center kept Croatian ethnicity intact and distinct from that of other Balkan emigrants.

Amanda Seligman

See also: Bosnians; Demography; Ethnic Music; Iron and Steel; Multicentered Chicago

Further reading: Prpic, George J. *The Croatian Immigrants in America.* 1971. • Zivich, Edward A. *From Zadruga to Oil Refinery: Croatian Immigrants and*

Croatian Americans in Whiting, Indiana, 1890–1990. 1990.

Crown Point, IN, Lake County, 35 miles SE of the Loop. Originally named Lake Court House, Crown Point was settled in 1834, and has served as the county seat of LAKE COUNTY, INDIANA, since 1840. The name was changed to Crown Point in 1845. Between 1915 and 1940, Crown Point was a popular elopement destination for Chicago-area couples because there was no waiting period to obtain a marriage license. The 2000 population was 19,806.

Peggy Tuck Sinko

See also: Leisure

Further reading: Moore, Powell A. *The Calumet Region: Indiana's Last Frontier.* 1959.

Crystal Lake, IL, McHenry County, 43 miles NW of the Loop. In her memoir *Wau-Bun,* Juliette Kinzie described seeing in 1830 "a beautiful sheet of water, now known as Crystal Lake." Ziba Beardsley's 1835 description of the lake as "clear as crystal" named both lake and community. Beman Crandall and Christopher Walkup platted the east shore village in 1840.

In 1855, residents believed that the Illinois & Wisconsin RAILROAD would follow the Big Foot Trail through the hamlet without any local investment. However, without any Crystal Lake investors, the railroad chose a route over a mile to the north. Building northward from ALGONQUIN, the Fox RIVER Valley RAILROAD skirted the village to the east. After the rival track gangs attacked each other at the crossing point, peace came when the Wisconsin line bridged the Fox River's rails.

The consolidated line known as the Chicago & North Western erected a station near the junction and laid a spur to Crystal Lake. Two villages developed: Nunda at the junction and Crystal Lake. Each village incorporated independently in 1874, but in 1908, Nunda became North Crystal Lake and in 1914 the two communities merged to form the city of Crystal Lake, with most commercial activity shifting to the station area.

In 1863 at the end of the Crystal Lake rail spur, Charles Dole of Chicago's Armour and Dole established an expansive estate including the lake bottom. Dole had ice cut from the lake, which he shipped to Chicago even during summer months; well-insulated ice houses lined the shore. Popular in Chicago as Knickerbocker Ice, its quality attracted many vacationers to the lake. Resorts and boardinghouses rose around the north shore while the Dole family hosted picnics and public outings along their beachfront. In 1912 citizens took legal action to ensure public access to the lake, and in 1921 a Crystal Lake Park District was established. Unfortunately, lake bottom ownership was not clearly resolved.

Crystal Lake's reputation as a resort lasted throughout the 1920s, and wealthy vacationers built homes in the woods along the lake's south shore. Facing unwanted expansion from the city of Crystal Lake, south shore residents incorporated as Lakewood in 1933.

The area's population remained stable from the 1930s through the 1950s. When the Ladd family's large Coventry SUBDIVISION quickly sold out to pilots based at Chicago's expanding O'HARE AIRPORT in the early 1960s, Crystal Lake became the center of a land rush. From the Ladd success to 1980, the city's population doubled, reaching 18,590, and the commercial activity of the retail center moved away from the railroad. By 2000 the population had grown to 38,000. As the lake grew increasingly crowded, the city of Crystal Lake, the Crystal Lake Park District, the village of Lakewood, and a lakeshore property owners group continued to contest lake ownership and control. To alleviate the problem, the city of Crystal Lake devised a plan to create a lake from a large gravel pit on the southeast side of the city for recreational use.

Craig L. Pfannkuche

See also: Government, Suburban; Leisure; Meatpacking; Vacation Spots

Further reading: Heisler, James, Susan Riegler, and Roberta Smith, eds. *Crystal Lake, Illinois: A Pictorial History.* 1986. • *McHenry County in the Twentieth Century, 1968–1994.* McHenry County Historical Society. 1994. • Nye, Lowell A., ed. *McHenry County, Illinois, 1832–1968.* 1968.

CTA. *See* Chicago Transit Authority

Cubans. Cubans began migrating to Chicago during the 1950s. A few were attracted by economic opportunities, but most were political dissidents fleeing Fulgencio Batista's repressive regime. Although some returned to the island with the triumph of the Cuban revolution in 1959, the majority stayed, leaving approximately 2,500 Cubans in Chicago in 1960.

Opposition to the Castro government set in motion consecutive emigration waves, bringing 20,000 Cubans to the Chicago area between 1960 and 1973 and smaller numbers thereafter. White professionals, mainly doctors, dentists, lawyers, engineers, accountants, and teachers, constituted the majority of the first group of political refugees (1960–62). The "freedom flights," which permitted Cubans to reunite with their families in the United States, propelled the second wave, of approximately 20,000 Cuban exiles, between 1966 and 1973. Stricter immigration policies subsequently limited the flow largely to Cubans coming from third countries, especially Spain and Mexico. The third wave, known as the Mariel boatlift, arrived in 1980. This group comprised mainly single men in their twenties, mostly colored and poor, with no relatives in Chicago. The fourth and most recent wave included *balseros* (boat people) of similar social status who had been picked up by U.S. Coast Guard ships, beginning in 1990. By the end of 1996 about 2,000 *balseros* had settled in the Chicago area, many relocated to the city by CATHOLIC CHARITIES.

In contrast with the Cuban exiles of the 1960s and the 1970s who left the island for political reasons, the last two waves left mostly for economic reasons. Cubans who have come to Chicago since 1980 have been younger and less educated. Later immigrants, arriving after the 1994 U.S. laws changed Cuban REFUGEE status from political to economic, have received fewer economic and health benefits from the U.S. government.

According to Latino Institute data (1995), most Chicago-area Cubans live in COOK COUNTY (14,437), with others scattered across DUPAGE (1,286), KANE (264), LAKE (539), MCHENRY (99), and WILL (185) Counties. Approximately 7,000 Cubans have migrated to the suburbs, constituting the highest percentage of any Hispanic group. They live in MAYWOOD, MELROSE PARK, MORTON GROVE, NORTHBROOK, OAK PARK, PARK RIDGE, STONE PARK, and SKOKIE. Unlike other Hispanics, who are more likely to live in *barrios,* Cubans who have remained in the city have dispersed to such North and Northwest Side neighborhoods as LOGAN SQUARE, EDGEWATER, ALBANY PARK, and IRVING PARK. In 1979, 45 percent of Cuban Americans in Cook County owned their homes, compared with only 35.8 percent of other Hispanic groups.

Although most Cubans are ROMAN CATHOLIC, there are some PROTESTANTS, mainly Baptists, Methodists, Pentecostals, and Jehovah's Witnesses. Catholic Cubans in Chicago celebrate the feast of Our Lady of Charity, the patroness of the island, on September 8, with masses at Saint Ita in Chicago, Saint Lambert in SKOKIE, and Sacred Heart in MELROSE PARK. The main celebrant, flown from Miami or New York, is usually a Cuban priest known for his patriotic zeal. Many Cubans practice *Santería,* a syncretic manifestation of Catholicism and African religion. All *Santeros* (Santería priests) celebrate the feast of Our Lady of Charity (Ochún) on Sept. 8, St. Barbara (Changó) on December 4, and St. Lazarus (Babalú) on December 17.

More likely than other Hispanic minorities to be business owners, Chicago's Cubans have moved into food markets, jewelry and retail clothing stores, REAL-ESTATE and INSURANCE brokerages, investment, marketing, and CONSTRUCTION companies. Cuban women have high rates of participation in the labor force, often in male-oriented careers such as medicine, DENTISTRY, and LAW. Education is even more prevalent, including high school, college, and university faculty.

The Cuban American CHAMBER OF COMMERCE, founded in 1969, counts 184 active members and manages a powerful credit union. Every year it confers the prestigious "Mercurio" award to a distinguished Cuban in an artistic, professional, or political field. In addition to offering various services to Cuban and other Latino communities, it traditionally sponsors or cosponsors patriotic festivities such as January 28, the birth date of José Martí, national hero and martyr of the Cuban War of Independence (1895–1898).

Politics on the island and U.S. foreign policy continue to form an essential component of Cuban American identity and POLITICAL CULTURE. Chicago has harbored various Cuban political organizations, mostly with headquarters in Miami. Important groups that have struggled against Castro's government and for political change in Cuba over the years are Abdala, CID (Independent and Democratic Cuba), FOCI (Federation of Cuban Organizations of Illinois), JPC (Cuban Patriotic Council), and CANF (Cuban American National Foundation). Although most community members do not perceive serious internal conflicts, divisions persist over relations with the Castro regime. Anti-Communists criticize Cubans who advocate lifting the U.S. trade embargo or inviting artists from the island to perform in the United States. The most fervent opponents of Castro even condemn visits to the island and sending money to relatives back home. A stronger consensus persists, however, in the hope for a democratic change in Cuba.

Mirza L. González

See also: Americanization; Cold War and Anticommunism; Demography; Multicentered Chicago; Puerto Ricans

Further reading: González-Pando, Miguel. *The Cuban Americans.* 1998. • Masud-Piloto, Felix. *From Welcomed Exiles to Illegal Immigrants: Cuban Migration to the U.S. (1959–1995).* 1996. • Pérez-Firmat, Gustavo. *Life on the Hyphen: The Cuban-American Way.* 1994.

Cubs. The Cubs are the only original National League (NL) franchise to play every season in its original city. The team, first known as the White Stockings, was organized in 1870 to advertise the city. The squad joined the new National Association in 1871 but missed two years following the Great FIRE OF 1871. In 1876 team president William Hulbert organized the NL with other team owners. Pitcher-manager Albert G. Spalding, who led the White Stockings to their first NL pennant, became the team's president and chief stockholder in 1882. Under player-manager Adrian "Cap" Anson (1879–1897), the team dominated the NL in the early 1880s with five pennants (1880–1882, 1885–1886). The club played at five ballparks before moving into the $30,000 West Side Park (Polk and Walcott) in 1893.

Following Anson's dismissal, the team was known as the Orphans, and briefly in 1902, Selee's Colts, after new manager Frank Selee. In 1905, Spalding sold the team, then referred to as the Nationals or Cubs, to the team's press agent, Charles W. Murphy, for $105,000. The following year, under manager Frank Chance (1905–1912), the Cubs went 116–36, the best record in major league history, but lost the World Series to the Chicago White Sox. Officially adopting the Cubs moniker in 1907, the team, led by a great pitching staff including Mordecai "Three-Finger" Brown, won three straight pennants (1906–1908), two world championships over the Detroit Tigers, and another pennant in 1910. In 1916, the club was sold for $500,000 to a syndicate led by Charles Weeghman, who in 1914 had built the ballpark at the corner of Clark and Addison Streets that in 1926 was named Wrigley Field. In the war-shortened 1918 season the Cubs won the pennant but lost the World Series to the Boston Red Sox, led by pitcher Babe Ruth. Two years later, William Wrigley became the team's majority owner.

In 1929, manager Joe McCarthy's future Hall of Famers Rogers Hornsby, Hack Wilson, Gabby Hartnett, Riggs Stephenson, and Kiki Cuyler led the Cubs to a pennant, but they lost the World Series to the Philadelphia Athletics. One year later, Wilson hit 56 homers and drove in a record 191 runs, a major league mark that many pundits consider unlikely to be surpassed. Philip K. Wrigley became team owner in 1932, and manager Charlie Grimm piloted the squad to the NL championship. They lost the World Series to the New York Yankees in four games highlighted by Babe Ruth's alleged called shot into the center field bleachers in game three. The Cubs won another pennant in 1935 but lost the World Series to the Detroit Tigers. In 1938, catcher-manager Gabby Hartnett's legendary "Homer in the Gloamin'" helped the Cubs capture the pennant, only to be swept again by the Yankees in the World Series. The Cubs won their last pennant in 1945, losing the World Series in seven games to the Tigers.

For years thereafter, loyal fans, encouraged by the Wrigleys' fan-friendly environment that included free television coverage beginning in 1948, suffered through poor seasons. The team was integrated in late 1953 with Gene Baker and fan favorite Ernie Banks, who hit a career 512 home runs. The innovative "college of coaches," which introduced a variation on collective management between 1961 and 1965, was more provocative than it was successful. In 1969 manager Leo Durocher's squad with Ron Santo, Billy Williams, and Ferguson Jenkins led the pennant race for most of the season, only to be overtaken by the New York Mets.

In 1981 the Wrigleys sold the team to the Tribune Company for $20.5 million. Attending Cubs games became enormously popular with upscale Chicagoans as well as tourists, abetted by competitive teams, an appealing ballpark, and popular announcer Harry Caray on superstation WGN from 1982 to 1998.

In 1984 the Cubs went 96–65 and, led by manager Jim Frey, MVP Ryne Sandberg, and Cy Young pitcher Rick Sutcliffe, won the NL Eastern Division championship but lost the playoffs to the San Diego Padres. Sandberg and Sutcliffe, together with Andre Dawson, led the Cubs to the 1989 NL Eastern Division championship, but manager Don Zimmer's club fell to the San Francisco Giants in the playoffs. In 1998 Sammy Sosa hit 66 home runs, and, in 1999, a record-setting year for Cubs attendance, he led the club to the playoffs, where they were swept by the Braves.

The Cubs finally won a postseason series in 2003, against the Braves. But the pennant eluded them once again, as they lost a seven-game league championship series to the Florida Marlins.

Steven A. Riess

See also: Creation of Chicago Sports; Leisure; Tinkers to Evers to Chance; Wrigley Field

Further reading: Gentile, Derek. *The Complete Chicago Cubs.* 2002. • Holtzman, Jerome, and George Vass. *Chicago Cubs Encyclopedia.* 1997. • Riess, Steven A. *Touching Base: Professional Baseball and American Culture in the Progressive Era.* 1999.

Cypriots. Although GREEK Cypriots have a distinct history and identity, they are closely aligned with the city's Greek population. Greek Cypriots attend Greek Orthodox churches, and the most important holiday is Greek Independence Day on March 25, rather than Cypriot Independence Day on October 1. The main community organization, the Cypriot Brotherhood, is analogous to societies for the descendants of people who came from various parts of Greece.

Greek Cypriots began arriving in Chicago during the first third of the twentieth century, but numbers were small until the 1960s and '70s. Most early immigrants came seeking economic and professional opportunities. The last large wave of Cypriot immigration took place between 1974 and 1976, when a Greek-sponsored coup and TURKISH invasion of the island forced many Cypriots to leave their homes. Most Cypriots emigrated to England or Australia rather than the United States, and London is home to the biggest Cypriot community outside of Cyprus. Most Chicago Cypriots have relatives in London, and some lived there before moving to the United States.

At the opening of the twenty-first century, approximately 1,500–2,000 Greek Cypriots lived in metropolitan Chicago, with no concentration in a single neighborhood. Many Cypriots are professionals or own small businesses, particularly RESTAURANTS and CONSTRUCTION firms. They are represented by the Cypriot Brotherhood, which aims to preserve Cypriot customs and foster a sense of community. The Cypriot Brotherhood is open to any man or woman whose family is from Cyprus, although in practice all members are Greek Cypriots.

Chicago's Turkish Cypriots are more difficult to document than their Greek counterparts. Given the low rate of emigration among Turkish Cypriots, it seems likely that there are few Turkish Cypriots in the Chicago area and that they would participate in Turkish organizations rather than separate Cypriot institutions.

Emily Brunner

See also: Demography; Eastern Orthodox

Czechs and Bohemians. Czech immigration to Chicago began in the 1850s, after the RAILROADS had linked the city to the East Coast. In the following two decades the cost and duration of emigration from Europe decreased markedly, as the transatlantic journey dropped from an average of 44 days in 1850 to an average of 9.7 days in 1875. Czech emigration swelled as faster railroads to port cities like Hamburg facilitated that leg of the journey as well. Chicago's Czech-born population reached its peak in the 1870s, and the Czech immigrant community remained important in the city long after immigration restrictions were imposed in the 1920s.

Chicago's Czech community followed a common pattern of migration from inner-city working-class neighborhoods to middle-class areas further out and on to the suburbs. This gradual movement followed the economic progress of many Czech immigrants and the influx of other ethnic groups. In the 1850s and 1860s many Czech immigrants settled on the NEAR WEST SIDE. The neighborhood, known as "Prague," centered on the ROMAN CATHOLIC parish of St. Wenceslaus at DeKoven and Desplaines Streets and was largely spared by the Chicago FIRE OF 1871. Movement south and west in the 1870s and 1880s generated a second working-class Czech community, dubbed "PILSEN," which included the Czech congregation of St. Procopius, founded in 1875. By the 1890s, Czechs were colonizing middle-class neighborhoods like SOUTH LAWNDALE (popularly known as "Czech California"), where they established several churches, SCHOOLS, and Sokol halls. As the Czechs continued to move south and west, other immigrant groups moved into the neighborhoods they left, with immigrants from POLAND, CROATIA, SLOVENIA, LITHUANIA, and other Slavic areas settling in Pilsen around the turn of the century. By the 1930s many Czechs were moving into such suburbs as CICERO, BERWYN, and RIVERSIDE.

Religious or philosophical differences divided Chicago Czechs and their institutions. Although most Czechs in the Austro-Hungarian Empire were content to subscribe to the state religion on official documents, with the result that the overwhelming majority identified themselves as Catholics, many emigrants espoused FREE THOUGHT (rationalist) and SOCIALIST views in the United States. The immigrant institutions founded as the Czechs became established, including MUTUAL BENEFIT SOCIETIES, fraternal organizations, SAVINGS AND LOAN associations, and gymnastic societies (Sokols), were frequently identified with one group or another within the community. Schools were attached either to Catholic PARISHES or to freethinkers' societies. Burial was equally segregated: the Czech National Cemetery, a CEMETERY for freethinkers, was founded in 1877 and remains in existence today. The immigrant press was also divided. By the 1920s there were four main Czech-language NEWSPAPERS in Chicago: the *Narod* (Nation, founded 1894) served the Catholic community, *Svornost* (Concord, founded 1875) served the freethinkers, *Spravedlnost* (Justice, founded 1900) served the socialists, and the *Denní Hlasatel* (Daily Herald, founded 1891) was a "neutral" paper for the larger Midwestern Czech community.

By the turn of the century, Chicago was the third-largest Czech city in the world, after Prague and Vienna. In addition to their local concentration, Chicago Czechs lived at the center of a network of Midwestern Czech communities, including significant populations in Ohio, Iowa, Wisconsin, Nebraska, Minnesota, and Missouri.

Chicago's Czech immigrants possessed few marketable skills, and in the 1880s, working at unsteady jobs, notably as LUMBER shovers in the "lumber district" adjoining Pilsen, they earned less than nearly all other major ethnic group in the city. Eschewing traditional craft unions, they readily employed the mass STRIKE to better their economic situation, drawing on their dense associational network. Whole neighborhoods joined to keep out strikebreakers, playing a prominent part in street fighting with POLICE and militia in the Great RAILROAD STRIKE OF 1877 and other labor conflicts. The event that precipitated the HAYMARKET tragedy was a violent clash between heavily Bohemian lumber shovers and the police. Led by socialist-leaning freethinkers, Bohemians turned readily to the Socialist Labor Party at the end of the nineteenth century. By the 1910s and 1920s, however, Czechs earned more and worked at a wider range of occupations, including as operatives at Western Electric. Their energies were devoted more to ethnic and neighborhood organizations than to radical or unionist activity.

Early Czech immigrants largely voted for the REPUBLICAN PARTY because of their opposition to slavery. However, Chicago Czechs changed their allegiance in local POLITICS after the DEMOCRATIC PARTY nominated a Czech for alderman in 1883. Czech support for the Democrats continued well into the twentieth century, peaking with the election of Anton Cermak, a Czech immigrant, as the Democratic mayor of Chicago in 1931.

Anton J. Cermak was born in Bohemia and emigrated to the United States as a boy. He grew up in Chicago and lived in the heart of the immigrant community, in Lawndale, from 1892 until his death in 1933. He sold REAL ESTATE in the neighborhood and had close ties to Czech banks. After election to the state legislature before WORLD WAR I, the virulently anti-Prohibition Cermak became secretary of the United Societies for Local Self-Government, a coalition of GERMANS, Czechs, other immigrant communities, and BREWING and distilling interests. When Mayor Bill Thompson began enforcing the SUNDAY CLOSING laws in October 1915, Cermak led the opposition. The defeat of Germany in World War I, PROHIBITION, and the imposition of severe immigration controls changed politics in Chicago. Fewer new Czech arrivals led to a decline in the use of the Czech language, but the Czech political voice remained solidly Democratic.

During World War I, Chicago's Czechs had vigorously promoted American entrance into the war against Germany and Austria as part of the drive for Czech independence. After WORLD WAR II, Chicago again became a center for Czech political activity. Of the 91,711 foreign-born United States residents claiming Czech as their mother tongue in the 1960 census, 18,891 lived in Chicago, where this new wave of political immigrants established their base of operations. *Svobodné Ceskoslovensko* (Free Czechoslovakia) began publishing in Berwyn in 1939, and the Alliance of Czechoslovak Exiles in Chicago with its *Zpravodaj* (Reporter) was founded in 1959. The Czechoslovak National Council, which had been founded during World War I to coordinate aid to Czechoslovakia, began publishing a *Vestnik* (Bulletin) after World War II and actively lobbied for Czechoslovak causes in Washington during the COLD WAR.

Alicia Cozine

See also: Americanization; Demography; Multicentered Chicago

Further reading: Gotfried, Alex. *Boss Cermak of Chicago: A Study in Political Leadership,* 1962. • Schneirov, Richard. "Free Thought and Socialism in the Czech Community in Chicago, 1875–1887." In *Struggle a Hard Battle: Essays on Working-Class Immigrants,* ed. Dirk Hoerder, 1986, 121–142.

D

Daily Herald. The ARLINGTON HEIGHTS–based *Daily Herald* started in 1872 as the *Cook County Herald,* a weekly devoted to agricultural news and the BUSINESS needs of northwestern county residents. In 1889, Hosea C. Paddock bought the NEWSPAPER for $175, printing half in GERMAN for immigrant farmers.

Stuart R. and Charles Paddock, Sr., Hosea's sons, took control in 1920, renaming it the *Arlington Heights Herald* in 1926. It prospered with the suburban settlements growing along the Chicago & North Western's northwest line. By the end of WORLD WAR II, its circulation surpassed 10,000, as the *Herald* championed the development of Chicago's northwestern suburbs.

As population followed the four-lane highways from the city, the *Herald* became a triweekly in 1967. A third generation of Paddocks asserted control in 1968, adding national and international news and making the paper a daily in 1969. The *Daily Herald,* as it was renamed in 1977, remains the flagship of family-owned Paddock Publications, Inc.

The *Daily Herald* expanded into LAKE and DUPAGE COUNTIES in the 1980s and KANE and MCHENRY COUNTIES during the 1990s. As its circulation climbed to 130,000, the publishers added news about Chicago, arts, and entertainment and initiated an unsuccessful antitrust lawsuit against the two Chicago dailies. It continues to be an important newspaper presence in the lucrative northwest suburban market.

Richard Junger

See also: Agricultural Journals; Journalism; Press: Neighborhood Press; Suburbs and Cities as Dual Metropolis

Further reading: Allen, Jim. "Newspaper Picks Up Speed to Keep Pace with Suburbs." *Daily Herald,* May 9, 1998. • Kennedy, Kristy. "From $175 to Driving Force in the Community." *Daily Herald,* October 12, 1997.

Daily Southtown. Known for much of its existence as the *Southtown Economist,* the *Daily Southtown* was founded as the weekly *Englewood Economist* in 1906. The early *Economist* was marketed toward residents who wanted to save money by shopping in their own white, native-born, working-class neighborhood. The paper targeted BEVERLY and surrounding neighborhoods in 1920, renaming itself the *Southtown Economist.* It became a twice-weekly in 1940 but remained a community NEWSPAPER into the 1960s, when it purchased first the BLUE ISLAND *Sun-Standard* and then the Pointer newspaper chain that included various community newspapers. The demise of the afternoon *Chicago Daily News* spurred the *Economist* to become a six-afternoons-per-week daily in 1978, covering south and southwestern Chicago and adjoining suburbs.

St. Louis-based Pulitzer Publications Company, hoping to enter the lucrative Chicago market, purchased it from owner Bruce Sagan in 1986. Pulitzer's effort failed, and the renamed *Daily Southtown* was sold to Toronto-based Hollinger International, the parent company of the *Sun-Times* and the suburban Star Publications and Pioneer Press chains, for $31.9 million in 1994. The combination gave Hollinger a city and suburban penetration that it lacked in the *Sun-Times*'s competition with the *Tribune.*

The *Daily Southtown* achieved its greatest circulation during the early and mid-1990s at nearly 60,000 copies, making it the fifth-largest circulating daily in the Chicago metropolitan area. It moved to a new editorial plant in TINLEY PARK in 1996 and launched a Web site in 1997.

Richard Junger

See also: Englewood; Press: Neighborhood Press; Press: Suburban Press; Retail Geography

Further reading: Sullivan, Gerald E., ed. *The Story of Englewood, 1835–1923.* 1924.

Dance. Technical versatility and theatrical flair have always been a hallmark of Chicago's great dancers and DANCE COMPANIES, represented at the end of the twentieth century in the work of HUBBARD STREET DANCE CHICAGO and the JOFFREY BALLET. Nacho Duato's *Rassemblement* (1990), in the Hubbard Street repertory, required competence in Graham technique, while the Joffrey's *Frankie and Johnny,* originally choreographed by Ruth Page and Bentley Stone in 1938, proposed the disintegration of technique as a choreographic analogue to social disorder. BALLET training alone has never pleased a Chicago audience so much as ballet combined with movement traditions that blur the distinction between stage dancing and the participatory dance of school gymnasiums, DANCE HALLS, cabarets, and impromptu neighborhood gatherings. Concerts of IRISH step dancing by world-class competitive performers such as the Trinity Irish Dancers were very popular throughout the 1990s. At the beginning of the twentieth century, Chicagoans took an interest in a new system of physical training imported from Hellerau, Germany, called Dalcroze eurhythmics. Initially conceived by SWISS composer Emile Jaques-Dalcroze as a classroom exercise for music students, eurhythmics was offered in 1913 at the Hinman School of Gymnastic and Folk Dancing in HYDE PARK along with classes in clogging and ballet. Typical of Chicago's eclectic

Ruth Page: A Chicago Dance Institution

Dancer, choreographer, and ballet director, Ruth Page (1899–1991) was a pioneer in creating works on American themes. To the classical ballet vocabulary she added movements from sports, popular dance, and everyday gestures.

Born in Indianapolis, Ruth Page studied with Adolph Bolm in New York, and after a tour with the company of Anna Pavlova's ballet company she joined Bolm's Ballet Intime. In 1919 she came to Chicago to dance the leading role in *Birthday of the Infanta,* choreographed by Bolm to a score by Chicagoan John Alden Carpenter. After dancing in a Broadway musical, she returned to Chicago in 1924 as principal dancer with Bolm's Allied Arts Ballet. From 1926 to 1931 she was principal dancer and choreographer for the RAVINIA Opera Company. While dancing and directing the ballet ensemble for the Chicago Opera Company (from 1934 to 1945, with several off-seasons), Page codirected with Bentley Stone the Dance Project of the Works Progress Administration's Federal Theatre (1938 and 1939). From 1954 to 1969 she directed the ballet for Chicago LYRIC OPERA and toured America in the company known as Ruth Page's Opera Ballet, choreographing full-scale ballets on opera subjects. In 1965 Page choreographed a large-scale production of *The Nutcracker,* which was presented annually through 1997 by the Chicago Tribune Charities in the Arie Crown Theatre. On retiring from active choreography, Page created the Ruth Page Foundation, which established a dance center.

Ann Barzel

Ruth Page at her 87th birthday, 1986. Photographer: Sheila Malkind. Source: The Newberry Library.

dance history is that the first theatrical display of Dalcroze eurhythmics was provided by the popular Pavley-Oukrainsky Ballet in association with the Chicago Grand Opera.

Andreas Pavley and Serge Oukrainsky gave Chicagoans a remarkable introduction to the dances of the pre–World War I European avant-garde. During the 1916–17 Chicago OPERA season, when the two men were principal dancers, they organized a Chicago school which in time would support America's first major touring ballet company—the Pavley-Oukrainsky Ballet. From 1919–1931, they also directed an influential summer dance camp on a 22-acre bluff overlooking LAKE MICHIGAN in South Haven, Michigan. At one point, the mailing list for this camp contained 8,000 names. Photographs reveal barefoot dancers posed in the branches of trees and along the lakeshore in attitudes reminiscent of Swiss attempts to imbue dancing with the rhythms and visual patterns of nature. Prospective students were expected to be thoroughly familiar with classical ballet technique, as well as pantomime, and to know the difference between "Oriental" and "Grecian" gesture. Many of Chicago's earliest professional dancers studied in the eclectic Pavley-Oukrainsky schools, including Edna McRae, Doris Humphrey, Anna Ludmila, Berenice Holmes, Bentley Stone, Harriet Lundgren, Mark Turbyfill, Edward Caton, and Iva Kitchell. Portia Mansfield, who taught dance from Hyde Park to KENILWORTH in order to subsidize the newly formed Perry-Mansfield School of Theatre and Dance in Colorado, credited Pavley and Oukrainsky with liberating ballet from the exacting technique of the French and Italian schools. In retrospect, she found that what she had learned from them in Chicago came very close to MODERN DANCE.

Andreas Pavley, Anna Ludmila, and Serge Oukrainsky, circa 1920. Photographer: Unknown. Source: The Newberry Library.

Chicago's first European-trained modern dancers, Diana Huebert and Grace Cornell Graff, never became the devoted acolytes of their teachers (Raymond Duncan, Rudolph von Laban, and Mary Wigman), as was common in New York, where modern dancers were discouraged from associating with the ballet world. In the late 1920s, when Graff made her debut with the innovative Adolph Bolm company, the Chicago dance community was not divided over the legitimacy of ballet versus modern dance but rather over the question of ballet's ethnicity. Supporters of Bolm, who had been a soloist with the Maryinsky Theatre Ballet in St. Petersburg, Russia, complained that Pavley and Oukrainsky were not "RUSSIAN" enough, while Laurent Novikoff, who joined the opera in 1929, was "only from Moscow." When the young Katherine Dunham moved to Hyde Park in 1927, the big problem for her was breaking the color barrier in downtown ballet studios, not her interest in combining the study of ballet technique with Indonesian, West Indian, and AFRICAN AMERICAN dance practices. The unusual success in the 1930s of the Chicago Dance Unit of the Works Progress Administration's Federal Theatre Project may be traced to this earlier history in which ballet and modern dance in all its variety coexisted on the same stage.

From the Pavley-Oukrainsky era, through the GREAT DEPRESSION years, and until World War II, Chicago supported a spectacular array of dance traditions not seen in the city again until the early 1970s. In just the first weeks of January 1931, Angna Enters was at the Studebaker Theatre, followed by La Argentina, Mary Wigman, and the Denishawn Dancers in separate recitals at Orchestra Hall. In association with the 1933 CENTURY OF PROGRESS World's Fair, Chicagoans saw the infamous fan dance of Sally Rand, a pageant of dance history starring Anna Ludmila, Edward Caton, and Walter Camryn, plus Ruth Page's West Indian ballet, *La Guiablesse,* with its nearly all-black cast of SOUTH SIDE dancers, including Katherine Dunham and Talley Beatty. Among local dance events sponsored by the Federal Theatre Project, the summer 1938 premiere of *Frankie and Johnny* by the Page-Stone Ballet was the most successful. On the same program was a modern dance with political import, *Behind This Mask,* choreographed by Grace and Kurt Graff, who had opened the Little Concert House and Studio of Dance in Hyde Park in 1935. During the war years of the 1940s, when dancers had to find support from sources other than the WPA and the opera, the UNIVERSITY OF CHICAGO in Hyde Park, the GOODMAN THEATRE, and the downtown campus of NORTHWESTERN UNIVERSITY provided the space for solo and collaborative performance.

The dancers who shaped the Chicago dance scene in the postwar years—from Gus Giordano, who opened his EVANSTON jazz studio in 1952, to Shirley Mordine, who founded the Dance Center of COLUMBIA COLLEGE in 1969—began their work in a relatively undeveloped cultural environment for dance production in comparison to the vibrant days of Pavley and Oukrainsky, Adolph Bolm, and the Page-Stone Ballet. WORLD WAR II had drained the dance community of much of its vitality, including public recognition of the city's history as a major American dance center. For the gifted soloist Sybil Shearer, who had never felt entirely free to dance as she pleased in fractious Manhattan, Chicago's amnesia about its defining role in dance history was a compelling reason to move here in 1943. For the young Darlene Blackburn, who became one of the city's most influential teachers of African dance, this loss of identity meant going to the public library to find out about Katherine Dunham. Maggie Kast, who cofounded the

Auditions at the Ruth Page School of Dance for an annual production of the *Nutcracker* ballet, 1988. Photographer: Sheila Malkind. Source: The Newberry Library.

Chicago Contemporary Dance Theatre with Neville Black in 1963, was at first one of the very few members of the dance community familiar with the technical innovations of Martha Graham and Merce Cunningham. For Nana Shineflug, originally an Edna McRae student, the Harper Theatre Dance Festival (1965–1975) in Hyde Park provided the first extended opportunity to see the nation's leading modern dancers.

By the early 1970s, dance of all kinds once again filled Chicago's theatres and art GALLERIES, spilling out onto State Street and the Civic Plaza. In addition to wildly popular visits from the Joffrey Ballet, which would relocate to Chicago in 1995, and the Alvin Ailey American Dance Theater, local artists began to draw attention at MOMING DANCE AND ARTS CENTER. The Chicago Repertory Dance Ensemble provided serious competition for the Hubbard Street Dance Company from 1981 to 1992. As the twentieth century drew to a close, plans had been approved for Music and Dance Theater Chicago, a 1,500-seat, state-of-the-art auditorium to be shared by 12 local dance companies and situated downtown in the new Millennium Park.

Nancy G. Moore

See also: Dance Training; Entertaining Chicagoans; Folk and Traditional Dance; Tap Dance

Further reading: Ann Barzel Research Collection. Chicago Dance Collection, Newberry Library, Chicago, IL. • Chicago Dance, Vertical Files. Visual and Performing Arts Division, Harold Washington Library, Chicago, IL. • Vivian G. Harsh Research Collection of Afro-American History and Literature. Carter G. Woodson Regional Library, Chicago, IL.

Dance Companies. From Akasha to XSIGHT!, Chicago has a rich DANCE history, comprising a variety of different types and sizes of dance companies. The 1900 edition of the *Chicago Business Directory* listed 35 "Dancing Academies" but no "Dance Companies." A 1985 survey by the MACARTHUR FOUNDATION found Chicago had approximately 40 dance companies. At the opening of the twenty-first century, Chicago's dance companies combined dance forms and ethnic dances to reflect the energy of the city's diverse population.

Dance companies require two ingredients: well-trained dancers and venues that support dance. Chicago has supplied both ingredients. Since 1900 Chicago's "dance academies" have showcased an outstanding lineage of dance teachers, from Merriel Abbott, Mary Wood Hinman, and Edna McRae at the beginning of the century to Lou Conte, Daniel Duell, Gus Giordano, Larry Long, Shirley Mordine, Harriet Ross, and Nana Shineflug nearly one hundred years later.

In the early years the OPERA provided a source of employment for dancers and a place to develop and expand their craft. Starting in 1910 with the Chicago Grand Opera Company's first BALLET master Luigi Albertieri (protégé of Enrico Cecchetti, Anna Pavlova's instructor), the opera became a base from which successful Chicago resident dance companies emerged. In 1922 two émigré dancers, Andreas Pavley and Serge Oukrainsky, among the opera's most illustrious early ballet masters, created Chicago's first independent ballet company, the Pavley-Oukrainsky Ballet, which toured nationally and internationally until Pavley died in 1931.

Dance companies thrive in atmospheres that foster creative exchanges among artists in a variety of fields. The Chicago Grand Opera offered a fertile environment for collaborative efforts between ARTISTS, musicians, and dancers. In 1919, Adolph Bolm was invited by the opera to stage an original ballet. Based on a story by Oscar Wilde, Bolm's *The Birthday of the Infanta* had music by Chicago composer

John Alden Carpenter and decor by the American designer Robert Edmond Jones. Midwest dancer Ruth Page starred as the infanta. When Pavley and Oukrainsky left the opera in 1922 to form their company, Bolm became the opera's ballet master. Subsequently he helped establish Chicago's Allied Arts, considered the first ballet theater in the United States, which he directed from 1924 to 1927. Allied Arts ceased for lack of funds, but the Adolph Bolm Ballet continued.

VAUDEVILLE, motion picture, and stage THEATERS also provided opportunities for Chicago dancers in the 1920s. At the GOODMAN THEATER, modern dancer Diana Huebert and poet Mark Turbyfill (who had danced with Bolm) performed an avant-garde piece that combined words and movement.

The spirit of experimentation continued in the 1930s and included a pioneering attempt by Turbyfill and his former student Katherine Dunham (a student of anthropology at the UNIVERSITY OF CHICAGO) to organize an AFRICAN AMERICAN ballet company in Chicago. Although short-lived, the company anticipated the development of black concert dance over subsequent decades. In 1933 Ruth Page choreographed *La Guiablesse,* based on a Martinique legend about an evil spirit, which featured Page along with Dunham, Talley Beatty, and an all-black supporting cast. Dunham was appointed director of ballet in 1938 for the Federal Theatre in Chicago, a part of the Works Progress Administration (WPA) which centered all dance activity in one company. In 1938 Dunham choreographed *L'Ag'Ya,* based on her ethnographic research in Martinique, for the WPA. The WPA dance project and the Chicago Civic Opera (which closed in the GREAT DEPRESSION but reopened in 1934 with Ruth Page as ballet mistress) were unique not only in the jobs they offered to dancers but also in the high degree to which dance forms—ballet, modern, jazz—were intermingled. Such experimentation lent Chicago dance a distinctive vitality in the years between the two world wars.

Chicago's stature in the international dance community increased after World War II. So did the number of ethnic dance companies, whose broad range included Muntu Dance Theatre of Chicago, Ensemble Espagnol, Natyakalalayam Dance Company, Teresa y Los Preferidos, and Trinity Irish Dance Company. Companies as distinct as Gus Giordano JAZZ DANCE Chicago, HUBBARD STREET DANCE CHICAGO, and the JOFFREY BALLET of Chicago added the city's name to their company's logo and in their international tours boasted of their Chicago connection.

The opera remained a source of jobs for dancers and a springboard for ballet companies such as Page-Stone Ballet (Ruth Page and Bentley Stone), Ruth Page's Chicago Ballet Company, and Maria Tallchief's CHICAGO CITY BALLET. As Chicago continued to grow in the postwar period as a cultural and commercial center, the city also offered dancers opportunities to work in trade and industrial shows, commercials, and hotel and nightclub revues. Dance companies such as the Chicago Moving Company and Mordine and Company initiated outreach programs, utilizing federal, state, or private support to bring dance to Chicago residents, often in SCHOOLS and community centers.

The strength and stability of a dance company's internal organization and management are crucial to its ability to raise money and sustain itself. In the late twentieth century, with the proliferation of Chicago dance companies, these criteria have assumed even greater importance. The Chicago Ballet Company (disbanded in 1978) and Chicago City Ballet (disbanded in 1987) foundered, owing in part to financial problems and divisions between the board of directors and the company's artistic director. Other dance companies, such as Hubbard Street Dance Chicago, have a strong history of cooperation between the artistic director, general manager, and board of directors and have maintained firm financial footing.

Carolyn A. Sheehy

See also: Arts Funding; Dance Training; Folk and Traditional Dance; MoMing Dance and Arts Center; Tap Dance; Theater Companies

Further reading: Anderson, Jack. "Chicago Was Once America's Ballet Capital." *New York Times,* April 1, 1984. • Barzel, Ann. "Dance in Chicago—An Early History." *American Dance* 2.1 (1986): 27–31. • Martin, John Joseph. *Ruth Page: An Intimate Biography.* 1977.

Dance Halls. Dance halls have played central roles in Chicago's civic life. In the 1820s and 1830s, Mark Beaubien's Sauganash Tavern built community with drink and dance as Beaubien fiddled for POTAWATOMIS, Creoles, SOUTHERNERS, and YANKEES who danced in an informal atmosphere of male democracy that transcended class and race. With incorporation, settlement, and social stratification, the DANCE hall, symbolic of urban wildness, threatened Victorian values of work, order, and restraint. The upper and middle classes danced in the privacy of their homes to safeguard young women. Lower- and working-class dances were also largely private until the 1890s. Ethnic MUTUAL BENEFIT SOCIETIES and social CLUBS rented space in SALOONS, occasionally selling tickets. The most notorious dance halls crowded the VICE DISTRICT in an atmosphere of male anarchy. Freiberg's Dance Hall on 22nd Street between Wabash Avenue and State Street was typical. It had a long bar, a hall with small tables, an orchestra in the balcony, and female performers and PROSTITUTES who pushed liquor and sex. Freiberg's ran almost continuously from 1901 to 1914, when women reformers forced its closure.

Dance halls were a familiar part of many communities. In this photo from 1911, Freiberg's Dance Hall, at 20 East 22nd Street, provided a place for residents of its Near South Side neighborhood and visitors arriving on the "L" to dance. Photographer: Unknown. Source: Chicago Historical Society.

Because of close links with vice, dance halls only slowly gained public acceptance. By 1900 saloonkeepers opened annexes for dancing to meet the needs of the growing working classes who sought release from factory routine. Through World War I, reformers tried to stop alcohol consumption, regulate the types of dances (especially the new ragtime "close-holds"), and open municipal halls as alternatives for the young women who named dancing their favorite recreation. Attempts at regulation alerted entrepreneurs to the dance hall's commercial potential. In 1922 the Karzas brothers opened the Trianon at 63rd Street and Cottage Grove Avenue with a major society gala, a "no JAZZ" policy, and floor spotters to police the crowd. Like its North Side sister the ARAGON (1926–), the Trianon attracted white lower-middle- and working-class youth. Free of ties to lower-class vice, the Karzas used design and decoration to evoke refinement and luxury for ordinary people while uplifting "dangerous" sexuality to the level of romance.

The quest for decorum also led to the rigid racial segregation in the new dance-hall public culture. The Trianon, White City Ballroom and Casino, and the Coconut Grove Ballroom had a whites-only policy. Thus, dance halls emerged for the AFRICAN AMERICANS streaming to the SOUTH SIDE. Lincoln Gardens, Dreamland Ballroom, and many others dotted "the STROLL" at Thirty-Fifth and State; later in the 1920s the Savoy Ballroom opened on

Forty-Seventh. Home to the jazz that accompanied newcomers from New Orleans during the GREAT MIGRATION, the dance halls also helped southern blacks adjust to urban, albeit segregated, patterns of entertainment.

Dance halls flourished through World War II, but postwar domesticity, white flight, suburbanization, and television aided their decline. Whites desired to escape the growing black communities and their demands to be allowed into formerly all-white halls. Many halls closed rather than integrate.

In an age of privacy, the era of the grand urban dance halls has ended.

Lewis A. Erenberg

See also: Entertaining Chicagoans; Leisure; Prohibition and Temperance; Stroll, The

Further reading: Erenberg, Lewis A. *Swingin' the Dream: Big Band Jazz and the Rebirth of American Culture.* 1999.

Dance Training. In Chicago, DANCE classes were multicultural and technically diverse long before such training was the norm for professional dancers. Mary Wood Hinman, an innovative Chicago educator who thought that the study of dance should include familiarity with its history, taught ballroom, folk and interpretive dance, pantomime, and BALLET in the years before WORLD WAR I. One of her students was Doris Humphrey, who opened a dance studio in OAK PARK before leaving town in 1917 for an illustrious career as a MODERN dancer. The Chicago Association of Dancing Masters, founded in 1912 by a German ballroom dancer named Frederick Kehl, provided a forum for the study of all the latest social dances, as well as "stage dancing." By 1924, the association was offering classes in Bar Technique and Port de Bras, Oriental, Castanet, Eccentric, Scotch and Irish FOLK DANCE, and Grecian Ballet.

From its earliest manifestation in 1910, the Chicago Opera employed a series of distinguished ballet directors, including Andreas Pavley and Serge Oukrainsky, with whom Doris Humphrey also studied. Pavley had learned Dalcroze eurhythmics in Geneva and specialized in a languorous "plastique," while Oukrainsky had worked alongside Ida Rubinstein and Natalia Trouhanova as a protégé of the ballet master of the Paris Opéra, Ivan Clustine. Humphrey, as well as dancers like Edna McRae—who would go on to become Chicago's most influential dance teacher—were thus exposed to international folk dance traditions and the European avant-garde well before "MODERN DANCE" was taught in America as a revolutionary alternative to ballet.

By the end of the twentieth century, dance training in Chicago was provided by over 70 private schools of dance, notable academic programs at NORTHWESTERN UNIVERSITY, COLUMBIA COLLEGE, and Northern Illinois University, and by the Chicago National Association of Dance Masters, then in its ninth decade—but no longer at the OPERA. Prominent studios for the study of ballet included Daniel Duell's Ballet Chicago and the Ruth Page Foundation School of Dance. The Lou Conte Dance Studio, opened in 1974, expanded dramatically to offer nearly 60 classes a week in ballet, JAZZ, TAP, modern dance, hip-hop and tai chi. Beginning in 1988, the dances of Doris Humphrey were taught once again in Oak Park by the artists of the modern dance company Momenta.

Nancy G. Moore

See also: Dance Companies; Theater Training

Further reading: Ann Barzel Research Collection. Chicago Dance Collection, Newberry Library, Chicago, IL. • Barzel, Ann. "Chicago's 'Two Russians': Andreas Pavley and Serge Oukrainsky." *Dance Magazine* (June 1979): 63–94. • Barzel, Ann. "European Dance Teachers in the United States." *Dance Index* 3:4–6 (1944): 56–100.

Bob Fosse: His Chicago Beginnings

Born and raised on the North Side, Bob (Robert Louis) Fosse graduated from Ravenswood Grade School and Amundsen High School. Fosse (pronounced FAW-see) developed his distinctive dancing style as half of a teenage duo, the Riff Brothers, performing in amateur shows, lodge halls, vaudeville houses and strip joints around the city before moving to New York after World War II to become a Broadway show dancer. He rose from lead dancer (*Call Me Mister,* 1946) to choreographer (*The Pajama Game,* 1954) to director-choreographer for stage (*Redhead,* 1959) and screen (*Sweet Charity,* 1969). In 1973, he won the director's triple crown of Academy Award (*Cabaret*), Tony Award (*Pippin*), and Emmy Award (*Liza with a Z*).

Richard Christiansen

Danes. Danes began to emigrate in significant numbers after Denmark suffered defeat by Bismarck's Prussia in 1864. Some fled from the conquered duchy of Schleswig to escape Prussian rule. Many Danish immigrants had urban backgrounds, with one out of five coming from the capital city of Copenhagen. In America they gravitated toward cities. During the 1870s, cheap grain from Russia and the American heartland flooded European markets, depressing local agriculture. This led Danes from rural areas to join the emigrants heading for America. Over 300,000 Danes emigrated in the years 1840–1914, with peak years 1881–1883 and 1903–1905.

Danish immigrants tended to be young, skilled, and well educated. Many single men came, and some families, but young women often stayed home, creating a gender imbalance among the immigrants. The flow of Danish migration was toward the Midwest.

The written Danish language was the same as NORWEGIAN, and SWEDES could understand it as well, so Danes often lived in mixed Scandinavian communities and intermarried with Norwegians and Swedes. The earliest Danish community in Chicago was around Randolph and LaSalle Streets in the 1860s. Around 1870, some Danes established a SOUTH SIDE enclave around 37th and State Streets that persisted until the 1920s, but the main axis of Danish and Norwegian settlement crossed the Chicago River and moved northwest along Milwaukee Avenue during the 1870s. By 1880, two-thirds of the city's 6,000 Danes lived in Milwaukee Avenue neighborhoods. A new, heavily Norwegian and Danish neighborhood also began to take shape east of HUMBOLDT PARK. By 1910, there were 18,500 first- and second-generation Danes in the city. Scandinavians had abandoned Milwaukee Avenue to ITALIAN and East European immigrants, and North Avenue was the new Danish-Norwegian commercial center. Humboldt Park remained a major Scandinavian community for a couple of decades, but Danes began to disperse around 1920 to western and northern suburbs.

Most commonly, Danish men joined other Scandinavians to work in the BUILDING TRADES as carpenters, masons, painters, FURNITURE makers, and contractors. Many also became small-scale entrepreneurs of GROCERY, tobacco, and clothing stores, ethnic HOTELS, taverns, and cafes. Some Danish families specialized in market gardening and dairying on the fringes of the city. Danish women generally found work in DOMESTIC WORK or shop clerks.

Early immigrant luminaries met at the "Round Table" in Wilken's Cellar at Randolph and LaSalle, where the Danish consul, Emil Dreier (1832–1892), generally presided. In 1862, Danish immigrants established Dania as a social CLUB to hold masquerade balls, and the organization grew to sponsor a library, English night school, mutual aid fund, and missing-persons bureau. Trinity Lutheran Church was founded in 1872, followed by several other Lutheran and Baptist churches. A Danish veterans' society was founded in 1876, the Danish Brotherhood in 1883, and various choral groups from 1886. Many Danish ethnic organizations emerged toward the turn of the century, including societies for gymnastics, cycling, FOOTBALL, hunting, fishing, sharpshooting, and theater. Chicago had a daily Danish-Norwegian NEWSPAPER, *Skandinaven,* for over 50 years and from five to seven weeklies for several decades.

Danish Chicago included an active elite of ARTISTS, journalists, clergymen, and professionals. The sculptors Carl Rohl-Smith and Johannes Gelert contributed monuments to the city. Jens Jensen, the leading landscape designer of the Prairie School, designed

Chicago's west parks and boulevards, besides promoting FOREST PRESERVES and state parks. Christian Fenger, an internationally renowned surgeon, taught at NORTHWESTERN UNIVERSITY and Rush Medical College. Max Henius, a chemist, founded the American Academy of Brewing and made Chicago an international center of the BREWING industry.

J. R. Christianson

See also: Demography; Multicentered Chicago; Mutual Benefit Societies

Further reading: Friedman, Philip S. "The Danish Community of Chicago." *The Bridge: Journal of the Danish American Heritage Society* 8.1 (1985): 5–95. • Lovoll, Odd S. "A Scandinavian Melting Pot in Chicago." In *Swedish-American Life in Chicago: Cultural and Urban Aspects of an Immigrant People, 1850–1930,* ed. Philip J. Anderson and Dag Blanck, 1992, 60–67. • Nielsen, George R. *The Danish Americans.* 1981.

Darien, IL, DuPage County, 20 miles SW of the Loop. The city of Darien lies in southeastern DUPAGE COUNTY, north of the DES PLAINES RIVER. The youngest municipality in the county at the opening of the twenty-first century, Darien exemplifies the massive suburban development that occurred outside Chicago after World War II. Darien is often associated with the nearby ARGONNE NATIONAL LABORATORY.

The first permanent settlement in the area, known as Cass, grew up along a stagecoach route between Chicago and Ottawa (paralleled by Interstate 55 today). An inn operated by Thomas Andrus served the community as well as travelers. Cass was initially a thriving town assisted by trade along the nearby ILLINOIS & MICHIGAN CANAL, which opened in 1848.

In the 1850s, a group of GERMAN Lutherans moved into the area north of Cass (near Cass Avenue, Plainfield Road, and 75th Street) and began to develop their own community, which became known as Lace. Ethnic, language, and religious differences limited communication and cooperation between Cass and Lace. Nearby LEMONT overshadowed Cass, while Lace grew and by the 1890s featured a Lutheran church, a town hall, a post office, and a schoolhouse.

Farming provided the largest source of employment and commerce in the Darien area from the late nineteenth century until World War II. The region's distance from the Burlington Northern RAILROAD, which ran north through Downers Grove, along with the cessation of trade on the Illinois & Michigan Canal, limited the residents' occupational choices.

The Darien area underwent radical changes after WORLD WAR II. In 1946, the federal government announced plans to acquire land to construct Argonne National Laboratory. The nuclear research facility opened a year later. Widespread usage of the automobile, combined with the expansion and improvement of the road system, helped lay the groundwork for suburban housing development. Area farmers began selling land to developers.

Developers created four major residential SUBDIVISIONS: Marion Hills, Brookhaven, Clairfield, and Hinsbrook. Throughout the 1960s, the four subdivisions struggled with the issue of incorporation. While some residents enjoyed the lower taxes which unincorporated living allowed, others disliked depending on DuPage County for police protection and road maintenance. Some subdivisions considered incorporation into nearby WESTMONT and WILLOWBROOK.

In 1968, while riding together in a Fourth of July parade, the presidents of the four homeowners associations began to discuss seriously incorporation as their own municipality. In December 1969, an incorporation referendum passed by a scant 42 votes, out of 2,000 cast. Sam Kelly, the first mayor of the new city, suggested the name "Darien," inspired and impressed by a community in Connecticut by the same name. By 2000 Darien had grown to 22,860 residents.

Aaron Harwig

See also: Agriculture; Expressways; Metropolitan Growth

Further reading: Elbe, Anita. "Darien." *DuPage Roots,* ed. Richard Thompson, 1985.

Dearborn Park. The Dearborn Street Station served as a major national rail terminus in the NEAR SOUTH SIDE community area. Downtown business leaders convinced George Halas in 1977 to bestow 51 acres of railroad yards for redevelopment as Dearborn Park. The resulting APARTMENTS and townhouses along tree-lined walkways were hailed as models of URBAN RENEWAL.

Erik Gellman

See also: South Side

Further reading: Wille, Lois. *At Home in the Loop: How Clout and Community Built Chicago's Dearborn Park.* 1997.

Deep Tunnel. The $4 billion Tunnel and Reservoir Plan (TARP), better known as "The Deep Tunnel," is the Metropolitan Water Reclamation District of Greater Chicago's answer to water pollution and sewer backup problems in 52 municipalities in COOK COUNTY. Begun in 1975, and at one time the nation's largest municipal WATER pollution control project, it involves the construction of 109 miles (174 kilometers) of tunnels 9 to 33 feet (3 to 10 meters) in diameter excavated in dolomitic limestone bedrock as much as 350 feet (107 meters) below the surface. These tunnels will collect combined sanitary and storm sewer flows and convey them to surface reservoirs, such as QUARRIES, for storage until the area's water reclamation plants can treat and safely discharge the effluent.

The first phase of construction, 85 percent complete in 1999, is designed to minimize water pollution by reducing the discharge of untreated sewage into the area's streams and LAKE MICHIGAN, the source of the region's drinking water. Phase 2, begun in 1990, will reduce sewer backup into homes and businesses if adequate flood storage capacity can be constructed or acquired. The entire project is expected to be completed after 2015.

Because of the region's aging INFRASTRUCTURE and high runoff characteristics, frequent large storms can cause commingling of sanitary and storm sewer flows that exceed the system's ability to handle the load. The Deep Tunnel is designed to reduce and nearly eliminate the release of untreated water to streams, Lake Michigan, and people's basements.

David L. Schein

See also: Environmental Politics; Environmental Regulation; Flood Control and Drainage; Industrial Pollution; Tunnels; Water Supply

Further reading: American Society of Civil Engineers. "The Tunnel That Cleaned Up Chicago." *Civil Engineering,* July 1986.

Deer Park, IL, Lake County, 31 miles NW of the Loop. POTAWATOMI Indian trails marked the way for Deer Park's early settlers. George Ela settled in the area in 1835, claiming 281 acres of land in a grove that later became Deer Grove FOREST PRESERVE.

YANKEE farmers followed, and in 1854 the Illinois & Wisconsin RAILROAD (Chicago & North Western Railway) laid track from Chicago. When the railroad sought to buy land surrounding the station in hopes of building a village, its attempts were blocked by the landowners, Ezekiel Cady and Barney Elfrink, who did not want the serenity of the area disturbed. In response, the railroad moved the depot two miles west to BARRINGTON. Subsequently the general store was carted by oxen to the new location.

The community remained quiet and rural, a feature attracting gentlemen farmers to the area in the early 1900s. Residents continued to enjoy the country atmosphere. In 1957 when a developer sought to put more than four houses on an acre, the community banded together to

Chicago's Deep Tunnel System in 2003

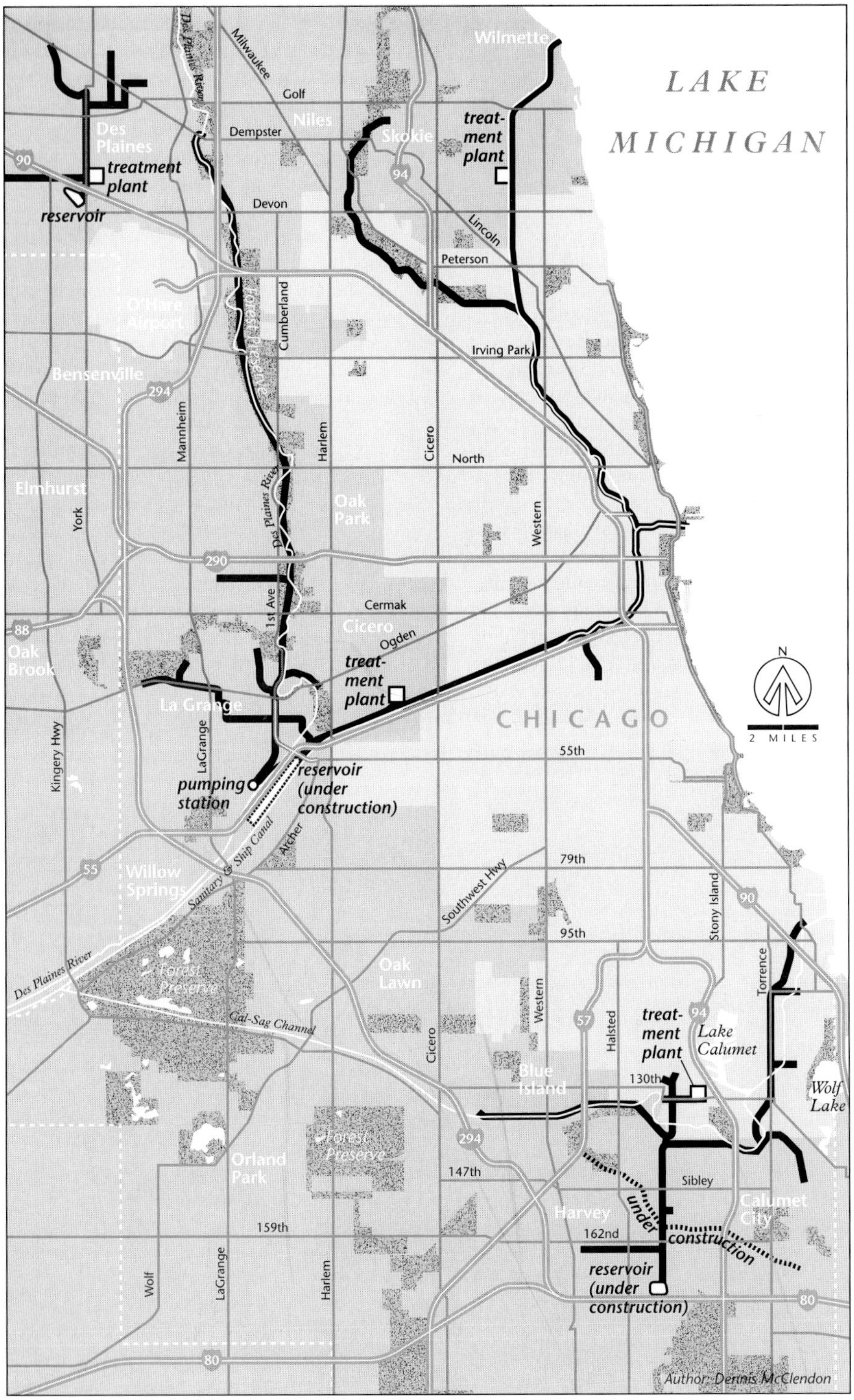

The Deep Tunnel System was created to ameliorate the sewer and pollution problems of storm runoff events. Most of it has been built under existing waterways where storm sewers and other runoff sources already converge, resulting in a discontinuous network as a whole. Such waterway locations, publicly owned, also simplified construction. The system is designed to collect excess stormwater into reservoirs for later treatment and gradual release.

incorporate as a village and passed an ordinance restricting residences to one house per acre. The first SUBDIVISION, Oak Ridge, won approval in 1959 when the village annexed 40 acres of land to the east of Ela Road. The village had 476 residents in 1960. Most businesses located near Deer Park's southeastern boundary of Rand and Lake-Cook Roads.

Deer Park remained a sleepy community until late in the 1970s, when larger houses were built. The population grew from 1,368 in 1980 to 3,902 in 2000. Although community residents fought to maintain a country atmosphere, protesting various projects that the village trustees saw as good for the tax base, in the early 1990s residents unsuccessfully opposed the building of the Brunswick Deer Park Lanes BOWLING alley.

In the late 1990s, Deer Park Town Center was approved by village trustees over the objections of residents. The 500,000-square-foot center was to be erected on 86 acres at U.S. Highway 12 and Long Grove Road. The center would include shopping, restaurants, and a cinema. Other mixed-use projects were planned for the area.

Marilyn Elizabeth Perry

See also: Lake County, IL; Land Use; Suburbs and Cities as Dual Metropolis

Further reading: The League of Women Voters of the Barrington Area, Illinois. *In and Around Barrington.* 1990. • Lines, Arnett C. *A History of Barrington, Illinois.* 1977. • Loomis, Spencer. *A Pictorial History of Ela Township.* 1994.

Deerfield, IL, Lake County, 22 miles NW of the Loop. Deerfield lies in the prairie of northern Illinois, surrounded by farmlands and forests. The POTAWATOMI once inhabited the area and used the nearby DES PLAINES, FOX, and CHICAGO RIVERS as a means of transportation.

Jacob Cadwell settled in 1835, and the area became known as Cadwell's Corner. Farmers were attracted by the availability of land and fertile soil, and by the close proximity of rivers. The waterways allowed residents to ship their goods such as timber, venison, and wheat to the markets in Chicago as well as to bring supplies to the area.

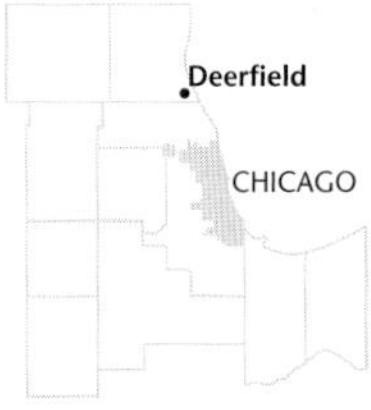

In 1840, the village was renamed Le Clair. Although many of the original settlers were of IRISH descent and wanted to change the name to Erin in honor of their homeland, in 1849 a settler named John Millen encouraged people to change the name to Deerfield, after Millen's hometown in Massachusetts, and because of the area's heavy deer population. The opening of the Milwaukee RAILROAD in 1872 attracted new residents who COMMUTED to work in the city. The village was incorporated in 1903, but in 1910 Deerfield was still a small town with a population of only 476.

The completion of the Edens EXPRESSWAY in 1959 enticed Chicagoans to Deerfield just as the proximity of rivers had attracted settlers to the area a century before. The population of

Deerfield increased from 7,009 people in 1957 to 11,786 people in 1960. By 2000, the number of people living in the village stood at 18,420, of whom 96 percent were white. The median household income was $107,194.

The village faced a setback in 1991 when the main industry in the area, Sara Lee, moved after 27 years of operation in Deerfield. The area's economy continued to thrive, however, because of Deerfield-based Baxter International, as well as the growth of the REAL-ESTATE and service industries.

Thomas A. Auger

See also: Economic Geography; Suburbs and Cities as Dual Metropolis

Further reading: Deerfield, Bannockburn, Riverwoods Chamber of Commerce. "A Look at . . . Deerfield, Bannockburn, Riverwoods." 1990. • Reichelt, Marie Ward. *History of Deerfield, Illinois.* 1928.

Defender. *See* Chicago Defender

Democratic Party. The modern Democratic Party in Chicago emerged in the generation that followed the FIRE OF 1871. Carter H. Harrison I (1879–1887, 1893) and his son, Carter H. Harrison II (1897–1905, 1911–1915), were each elected MAYOR five times as Democrats, winning 10 of 17 contests between 1879 and 1911. Native white American PROTESTANTS, but less moralistic than many of their REPUBLICAN counterparts, the Harrisons also drew on personal charisma to form alliances with varied immigrant groups. Among the shrewdest of the city's early professional politicians, these pioneers in the development of interethnic coalitions failed nonetheless to create a dominant organization.

Factionalism rooted in personality-based POLITICS remained the hallmark of the Democratic Party well into the twentieth century. Politicians clamored around the Harrison crowd, while "reform-minded" Democrats surrounded Edward F. Dunne, even as a third group—led by Roger C. Sullivan—made the greatest inroads in organizing the IRISH. Solidifying an ethnic base within the Democratic Party allowed Sullivan to mold the nucleus of an organization.

Sullivan died in 1920 and was replaced at the head of the Irish faction by George Brennan. Perhaps equally important to Democratic politics in this era was three-time Republican mayor William Hale (Big Bill) Thompson (1915–1923, 1927–1931). Effectively exploiting a rapidly expanding base of AFRICAN AMERICAN voters, Thompson appealed to racial identity in addition to GERMAN ethnic nationalism in a series of tumultuous electoral efforts. Democrats countered with appeals to ethnic pluralism. By running racially polarizing campaigns in the 1920s, the Brennan Democrats contributed to the evolution of "whiteness" as a political identity among European immigrants and their children. Anton Cermak, a foreign-born CZECH and a West Side Democrat, recruited those deeply opposed to PROHIBITION and others, such as JEWS, similarly stung by nativism. With "personal liberty" as a slogan, Cermak assumed powerful positions as president of the COOK COUNTY Board of Commissioners in 1922 and chairman of the party organization following George Brennan's death in 1928. His ticket balancing produced a broadly based Democratic coalition, including an Irish component.

Elected mayor in 1931, Cermak passed the party chairmanship to Pat Nash, who exemplified a more professional, and less narrowly ethnic, wing of the Irish contingent. Following Cermak's assassination, Nash selected Edward J. Kelly to serve as mayor. Kelly (1933–1947) expanded the party's base and resources by bringing African Americans into the

Democratic National Convention, Chicago Stadium, June 27, 1932. The convention nominated Franklin Roosevelt for president. The banner honoring Chicago's Democratic mayor, Anton Cermak, was left over from his mayoral campaign a year earlier. In 1933 Cermak was killed in Florida by an assassin aiming for Roosevelt, and thousands of people again filled the Chicago Stadium for Cermak's funeral. Photographer: Unknown. Source: Chicago Public Library.

Democratic fold, tapping the NEW DEAL's federal largesse, and running a "wide-open" town congenial to organized crime. After World War II, the racial tensions generated by white reactions to a rapidly expanding black community, and the corruption associated with his administration, led the organization to dump Kelly as its standard-bearer.

Jacob Arvey, who followed Pat Nash as party chair, orchestrated a dalliance with respectability that witnessed the nomination of such "blue-ribbon" candidates as Martin H. Kennelly for mayor in 1947, and Paul Douglas and Adlai Stevenson II for U.S. senator and governor, respectively, in 1948. Two-term mayor Kennelly, a caretaker possessing neither the will nor the skill to dominate, cultivated a "clean" image which gave organization Democrats time to reorganize while he alienated African Americans and party regulars. By 1955, Richard J. Daley had seized the party chair and, with the support of William Levi Dawson's SOUTH SIDE black "sub-machine," executed a coup that placed him in the mayor's office.

Daley's 21-year administration (1955–1976) represented the apotheosis of the "machine" or Cook County Democratic Organization. He professionalized the city bureaucracy, centralized power by refusing to surrender the party chair, and, by the end of his reign, shifted the organization's base to the white urban fringe from the growing black core. By the 1970s, electoral results indicated the party's shaky grip on a racially polarized electorate even as hostile Republican prosecutors thinned the ranks of scandal-ridden party leaders. Daley's death in 1976 subsequently precipitated a revival of Democratic infighting in which bureaucrats fought ward leaders and ward barons battled among themselves. Jane Byrne's stunning victory over Daley successor Michael Bilandic following the "blizzard of '79" marked the beginning of the end.

The court-sponsored "SHAKMAN DECREES" compounded the party's problems at the same time by undermining the traditional PATRONAGE system. Resurgent factionalism and the rise of new forces beyond the organization's control became apparent with Harold Washington's victory over Jane Byrne and Richard M. Daley in a three-cornered primary in 1983. With the white vote split, Washington combined support from a highly motivated African American community with Latinos and "anti-machine" reformers to become not only the party's nominee but, ultimately, the city's first black mayor. The age of the Democratic "machine" apparently had passed.

Washington's administration seemed to confirm the obituary. The new mayor refused to surrender city council control to the party's white leadership. Confronting implacable opposition from large numbers of white Democrats, Washington relied less on party POLITICS than on personal popularity, racial loyalties, liberal public policy, and fiscal responsibility to maintain his coalition. His death in 1987, however, derailed the construction of a local Democratic Party built upon a new coalition of black, Latino, and liberal white voters. By the 1990s, Richard M. Daley had built a new model of city hall power, but it remained unclear at the turn of the century whether the foundation was the party or the mayor's shrewd and effective personal leadership.

Arnold R. Hirsch

See also: Copperheads; Kelly-Nash Machine; Machine Politics; Political Culture; Racism, Ethnicity, and White Identity

Further reading: Biles, Roger. *Richard J. Daley: Politics, Race, and the Governing of Chicago.* 1995. • Gottfried, Alex. *Boss Cermak of Chicago: A Study of Political Leadership.* 1962. • Grimshaw, William J. *Bitter Fruit: Black Politics and the Chicago Machine.* 1992.

Demography.

Chicago as a Modern World City

The modern rise of population in world history began around 1750, and Chicago became an exemplary part of it roughly a century later. Abundant sources of food, and the means of transporting them, were crucial for that rise, and Chicago became a focal point of both. Although people have seldom praised Chicago's CLIMATE, the city was blessed in its formative years with freedom from both drought and floods, along with the right amount of sunshine and rainfall to nourish corn, wheat, and livestock. While no one could call the flat prairies stretching westward from LAKE MICHIGAN dramatic, they placed no topographical obstacles to Chicago's future as a rail and shipping center. In its first 50 to 75 years, Chicago was almost perfectly placed between America's industrializing Northeast and its farm-frontier West; it was also almost perfectly timed to take maximum advantage of RAILROADS and steamships, which were the advanced TRANSPORTATION technology of the era. As a consequence, Chicago soared from empty prairie and mud flats to world metropolis in a breathtakingly short sequence.

In 1820, when New York became the first American city with 100,000 people, Chicago hardly existed. But in 1860, when nine cities reached that size, Chicago was one of them; and in 1890, it became the third in the United States to reach 1,000,000, after New York and Philadelphia. By 1890, having burst from the ashes of 1871 to achieve metropolitan rank, it was earning the ambivalent reputation that all great cities had at that time—awesome in its bulk and wealth, yet condemned for its fleshpots, diseases, and poverty. It did not fit into a still-rural America: it was frighteningly large, and its hundreds of thousands of foreign-born residents aroused nativist as well as antiurban suspicions. And it kept on growing.

Among world cities, Chicago's explosive growth prior to 1915 was almost unique. From about 4,000 when it was first chartered as a city in 1837, Chicago leapt to 109,000 in 1860. It was the youngest city in the United States with more than 100,000, and one of only three in the Midwest, together with St. Louis and Cincinnati. The FIRE OF 1871 razed much of Chicago, and the national depression from 1873 to 1878 should have finished it off. But in 1880 the census recorded 503,000 inhabitants—whereupon it doubled to over a million in 1890 (passing Philadelphia to become the "second city") and doubled again, to 2.2 million, by 1910. Numbers kept climbing, though never again that fast. Chicago's population peaked at 3,621,092 in the census of 1950 and has slipped since then; in 2000 it was 2,896,016. But that was just the core city; together with the suburbs, the metropolitan area from Kenosha southward around Lake Michigan beyond GARY was home to 9,157,540 people in 2000.

To start small and multiply several times in a few decades was not rare in the nineteenth century: Detroit expanded 13 times over, from 9,000 to 116,000, between 1840 and 1880; and St. Louis, 22 times over, from 16,000 to 351,000. But Chicago, going from 4,000 to 503,000 in the same 40 years, multiplied 126 times over. Then, despite its size, it doubled and redoubled. Increasing from half a million to a million, as Chicago did in the single decade of the 1880s, was truly rare, matched only by Los Angeles in the 1920s. Not even New York ever managed that. By 1900, Chicago was yet to observe its 70th birthday, but only one city in the Americas (New York) and four in Europe (London, Paris, Berlin, and Vienna), all much older, were more populous. Soon after, the growth curve flattened out, but at the close of the twentieth century, Chicago—the city itself, COOK COUNTY, and the Consolidated Metropolitan Area—was still third largest in the United States. Elsewhere in the hemisphere, however, São Paolo and Mexico City had become five or six million larger, Rio de Janeiro and Buenos Aires were slightly bigger, and Toronto was within hailing distance.

Birthing and Dying in Chicago's History

Growth (or decline) of populations can come from only two sources: the net balance of births and deaths, and whether more people migrate to a place than leave it. Chicago's "natural" demography—its births and deaths—account for part of its exceptional growth. Migration boosted it tremendously in the age of railroads and heavy industry; outbound migration to southern California and elsewhere in the Sunbelt slowed it after 1920; and its ability to keep pace with technology and to continue to provide opportunity have stabilized, preserved, and reinvigorated it.

Migrants to Chicago

Thea Kronborg was a rather incurious migrant to Chicago in Willa Cather's *The Song of the Lark* (1915):

> During this first winter Thea got no city consciousness. Chicago was simply a wilderness through which one had to find one's way. She felt no interest in the general briskness and zest of the crowds. The crash and scramble of that big, rich, appetent Western city she did not take in at all, except to notice that the noise of the drays and street-cars tired her. The brilliant window displays, the splendid furs and stuffs, she scarcely noticed.

In contrast, the heroine of Theodore Dreiser's *Sister Carrie* (1900) is interested in Chicago from the moment she debarks a train from Wisconsin:

> The entire metropolitan center possessed a high and mighty air calculated to overawe and abash the common applicant, and to make the gulf between poverty and success seem both wide and deep.
>
> Into this important commercial region the timid Carrie now wended her way. She walked east along Van Buren Street through a region of lessening importance until it deteriorated into a mass of shanties and coalyards and finally verged upon the river. She walked bravely forward, led by an honest desire to find employment and delayed at every step by the interest of the unfolding scene, and a sense of helplessness amid so much evidence of power and force which she did not understand. These vast buildings, what were they? These strange energies and huge interests—for what purposes were they there?

Chicago's patterns of fertility and mortality, as in the rest of the United States and Europe, fluctuated vigorously and perilously throughout its first hundred years. Frontier Chicago almost certainly had a high birth rate. The national rate in the mid-nineteenth century hovered around 50 (live births per thousand people per year), well above the height of the baby boom in the mid-1950s (around 25) and about triple what it is today (14 to 15). For this reason alone, immigration aside, Chicago and the rest of the United States grew enormously fast. But Chicago's nineteenth-century fertility rates will never be known precisely, because most vital records burned in the Great FIRE OF 1871. Irregular reporting practices leave the post-fire data inadequate, even for births; the Board of Health complained in 1873 that "the midwives, and Chicago boasts of a large number, many of whom are very ignorant but still do a large practice among the poorer classes of people, do not send reports of births as they should." This uncertainty continued until 1925, when the Chicago SCHOOLS began requiring incoming pupils to produce a birth record in order to establish their age. By 1898, when about two-thirds of the city's births were probably being reported, the birth rate was about 28, a little below the national rate of 32 but close to normal for large cities. By 1921, when virtually all births were reported, Chicago's rate was 20.5, the nation's, 28.1. After that, Chicago's fertility continued to parallel the nation's: low in the depressed 1930s, up to 26 or more in the final years of the baby boom, down to 19 by the baby bust of the early 1970s, slipping further by 2000.

Deaths and their causes can be tracked much more accurately. Contagious diseases claimed most people until well into the twentieth century. The people and their health officials kept believing that contagion could be controlled, though they were often at a loss as to how. EPIDEMICS struck frequently and viciously. Chicago had a Board of Health as early as the 1830s, but until the germ theory, pasteurization, vaccines, and dependable systems of sewerage and pure WATER came about—all roughly between 1890 and 1910—the citizenry were virtually defenseless against contagion and, often, sudden death. If a killer was a virus, as with the influenza pandemic of 1918—the worst single demographic disaster in human history—nothing could stop it until it ran out of new victims. In one unusual case, an outbreak of typhoid fever among ITALIAN immigrants on the near Northwest Side in 1928 turned out to result from their practice of scooping minnows from the CHICAGO RIVER and eating them raw with olive oil and spices, as they customarily did with sardines on the coast of Italy. This mini-epidemic was quickly stopped. By the closing decades of the twentieth century, Chicago (like the rest of the industrialized world) had rid itself of most contagious diseases, and when its people died, the causes were usually chronic diseases connected with aging (and, to some extent, accidents, HOMICIDES, and a few bafflers like AIDS and antibiotic-resistant TUBERCULOSIS).

Progress in PUBLIC HEALTH, measured by falling death rates and control of contagion, characterized Chicago's demographic history in the early twentieth century. Tuberculosis mortality dropped by half between 1893 and 1920 and continued to drop. A society is often regarded as having become truly modern when fewer of its people die of contagion than from chronic causes such as heart disease, cancer, and kidney failure, and by the 1920s Chicago turned that crucial corner. Pasteurization, vaccinations, and school-taught hygiene brought results. But fatal accidents—at work, in the home, and in motor vehicles—increased, and occasional disasters such as the Iroquois Theater fire of 1903 and the sinking of the cruise boat EASTLAND in the Chicago River in 1915 each killed enough people to bump up the death rate for those years.

The PROHIBITION era smeared Chicago with a reputation for homicides, although suicides always outnumbered them. The Board of Health took pains to report that homicides in 1929, including gunshot deaths, occurred much less often than in Atlanta, Birmingham, or New Orleans (though it had to admit that New York and Los Angeles were less homicidal), and therefore the city did not deserve its gangster reputation. But the stereotype persisted, reinforced by killings like the ST. VALENTINE'S DAY "MASSACRE" in 1929 and the shooting of John Dillinger in 1934. Contagions killed more people than murders or suicides did, afflicting immigrants and AFRICAN AMERICANS more than native whites. Despite its Capone-era dangerous reputation, Chicago became safer for everyone by the 1930s.

By then its growth rate, though still considerable, had slowed substantially since the 1880s. Chicago kept attracting newcomers: in the late 1920s, net migration accounted for about 44,000 additions each year, while natural increase (births over deaths) averaged only about 22,000. Chicago no longer topped the national growth list, however; in the 1920s, that honor had fled, along with many Midwesterners, to Los Angeles. After WORLD WAR II, Chicago's efforts at public health and demographic safety differed little from those in other large American cities. All fought polio outbreaks, defeated tuberculosis with antibiotics, and tried to stop the rise of sexually transmitted diseases. These were the new contagions in Chicago too; about 40,000 cases of gonorrhea appeared each year in the late 1960s and early 1970s, and an AIDS Task Force created in 1982 watched almost helplessly as hundreds died each year, approximately 1,000 in 1993. By the 1980s and 1990s, Chicago's birth, death, and health picture was not remarkable within the North American context. Compared to some other world areas, however, it was much safer, and that was one of the reasons why it continued to attract immigrants.

A City of Migrants and Ethnics

Chicago has long been known as an ethnic city. Throughout its history it has, to be sure, attracted native-born Americans. In its early decades (the 1840s to 1870s), business and professional people arrived from New England and elsewhere in the Northeast and constituted most of the early civic elite; few came from the South (though Cyrus McCormick and Mayors Carter Harrison senior and junior came from Virginia families), and the city never had the southern "feel" of St. Louis or Cincinnati. When Midwestern boys and girls started leaving parental farms for city opportunities, a rural-to-urban migration lasting from the 1880s until at least the 1940s, Chicago always attracted a hefty share. And from the 1910s to the late 1960s, African Americans migrated from the South to Chicago by the hundreds

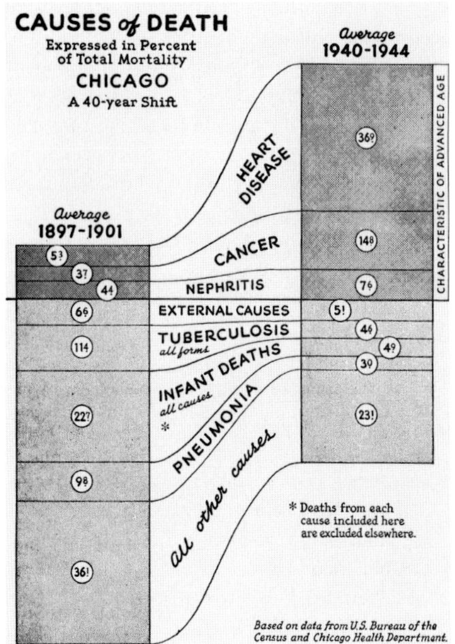

Advancements in medical knowledge and changes in public health practice in the early twentieth century led to a significant shift in the leading causes of mortality in Chicago. Increasingly, Chicagoans died from complications associated with chronic illness rather than from contagious disease. Creator: U.S. Public Health Service. Source: The Newberry Library.

of thousands. Migration of native-born Americans has always enriched Chicago.

Immigration from abroad, however, has been the city's hallmark characteristic in the public mind. When the U.S. Post Office issued a stamp in 1943 to commemorate Poland's occupation, it did so in Chicago, the heart of Polish America. Chicago's Jewish community, at first German and later Eastern European, has been larger than any in the United States except that of New York, Philadelphia, and Los Angeles through most of the twentieth century. One on top of another, European peoples tumbled in, starting with IRISH in the 1840s, quickly followed by GERMANS, British, and Scandinavians; then, overlapping with them, CZECHS, LITHUANIANS, SERBS, CROATS, GREEKS, and CHINESE; and recently, Mexicans, Caribbeans, and a broad-sourced array of Central Americans and Asians, along with a new (and smaller) wave of Eastern Europeans.

When the flood of Irish, Germans, and others inaugurated the third stage of American immigration history in the 1840s and 1850s, Chicago was ready. This stage lasted until Congress closed the door in the 1920s. Thus Chicago's period of most rapid growth coincided almost exactly with Europe's mass migration to the Americas. Railroads in and out of the city, and STREET RAILWAYS within it, promoted mobility. Chicago's industries always seemed to demand workers, and from 1890 to 1920, half of the 400,000 (by 1919) wage earners were occupied in IRON AND STEEL, MEATPACKING, the CLOTHING AND GARMENT INDUSTRY, PRINTING and PUBLISHING, railroading, or electrical machinery. The city was already half foreign-born in 1860, and by 1890, 79 percent of Chicagoans were born abroad (most of them in Europe) or were children of immigrants. By 1920, a traveler going south on Halsted Street from its beginning on the North Side met, one after another, SWEDES, Germans, Poles, ITALIANS, Greeks, Russian and Polish JEWS, Czechs, Lithuanians, and Irish—and very soon, blacks. And by the late 1990s, maintaining Chicago's history of ethnic mixes, to travel west on a main North Side boulevard like Lawrence Avenue meant encountering yuppie Anglo-Americans, African Americans, Latinos, KOREANS, VIETNAMESE, and others, before reaching largely Anglo-white suburbia.

During the period from 1924 to 1965, when U.S. immigration was cut off except for certain war REFUGEES and others, Chicago's ethnics consolidated, increased, and multiplied, and gave their character to city neighborhoods.

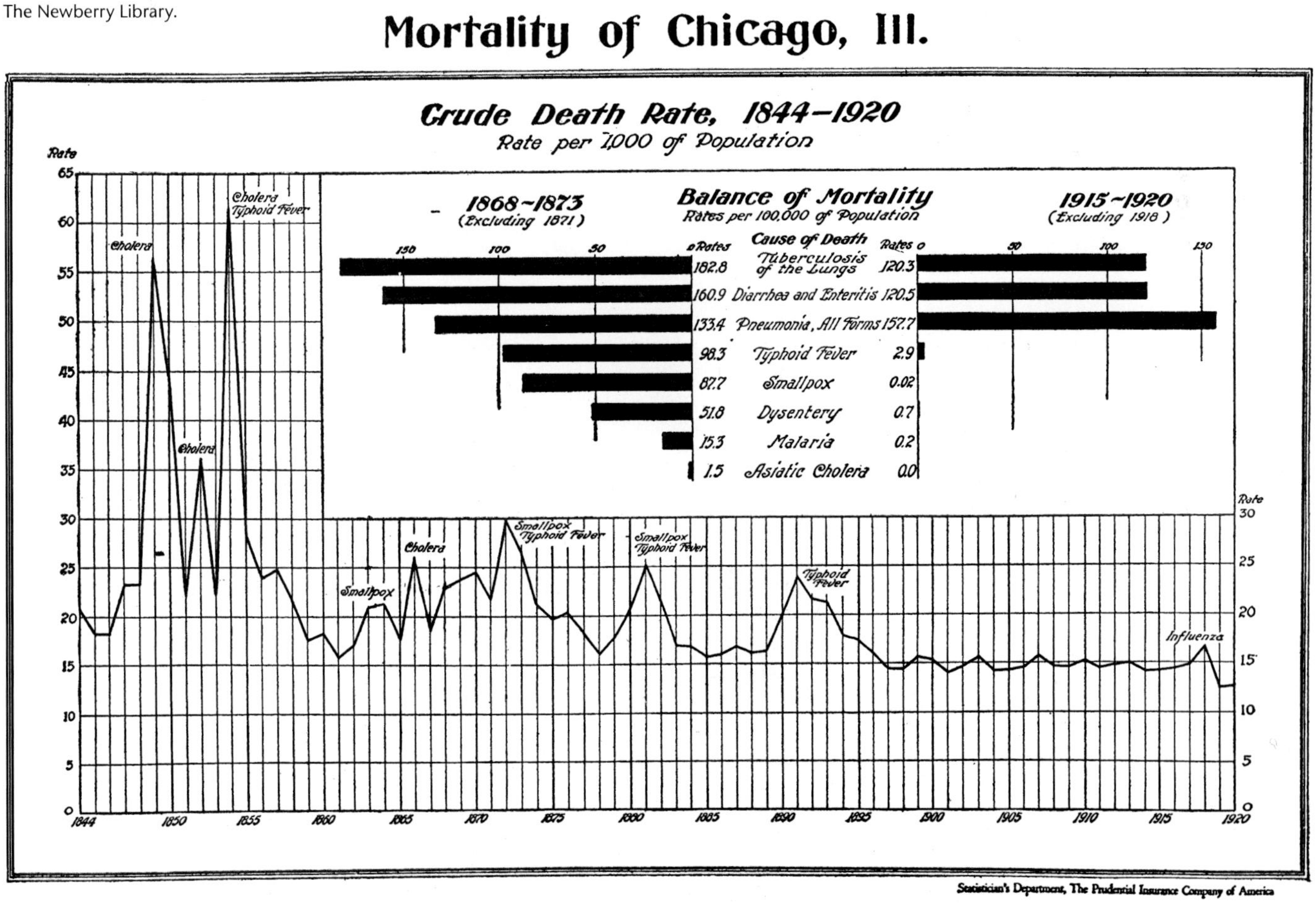

Mortality of Chicago, Ill.

Crude Death Rate, 1844–1920

Rate per 1,000 of Population

Balance of Mortality — Rates per 100,000 of Population

Cause of Death	1868–1873 (Excluding 1871) Rates	1915–1920 (Excluding 1918) Rates
Tuberculosis of the Lungs	182.8	120.3
Diarrhea and Enteritis	160.9	120.5
Pneumonia, All Forms	133.4	157.7
Typhoid Fever	98.3	2.9
Smallpox	67.7	0.02
Dysentery	51.8	0.7
Malaria	15.3	0.2
Asiatic Cholera	1.5	0.0

Statistician's Department, The Prudential Insurance Company of America

New understandings of disease in the early twentieth century led Chicago health officials to implement more effective preventive measures which, in turn, helped to dramatically decrease the mortality rate for many nineteenth-century killers. Creator: Prudential Insurance Co. Source: The Newberry Library.

Changing Origins of Metropolitan Chicago's Foreign-Born Population

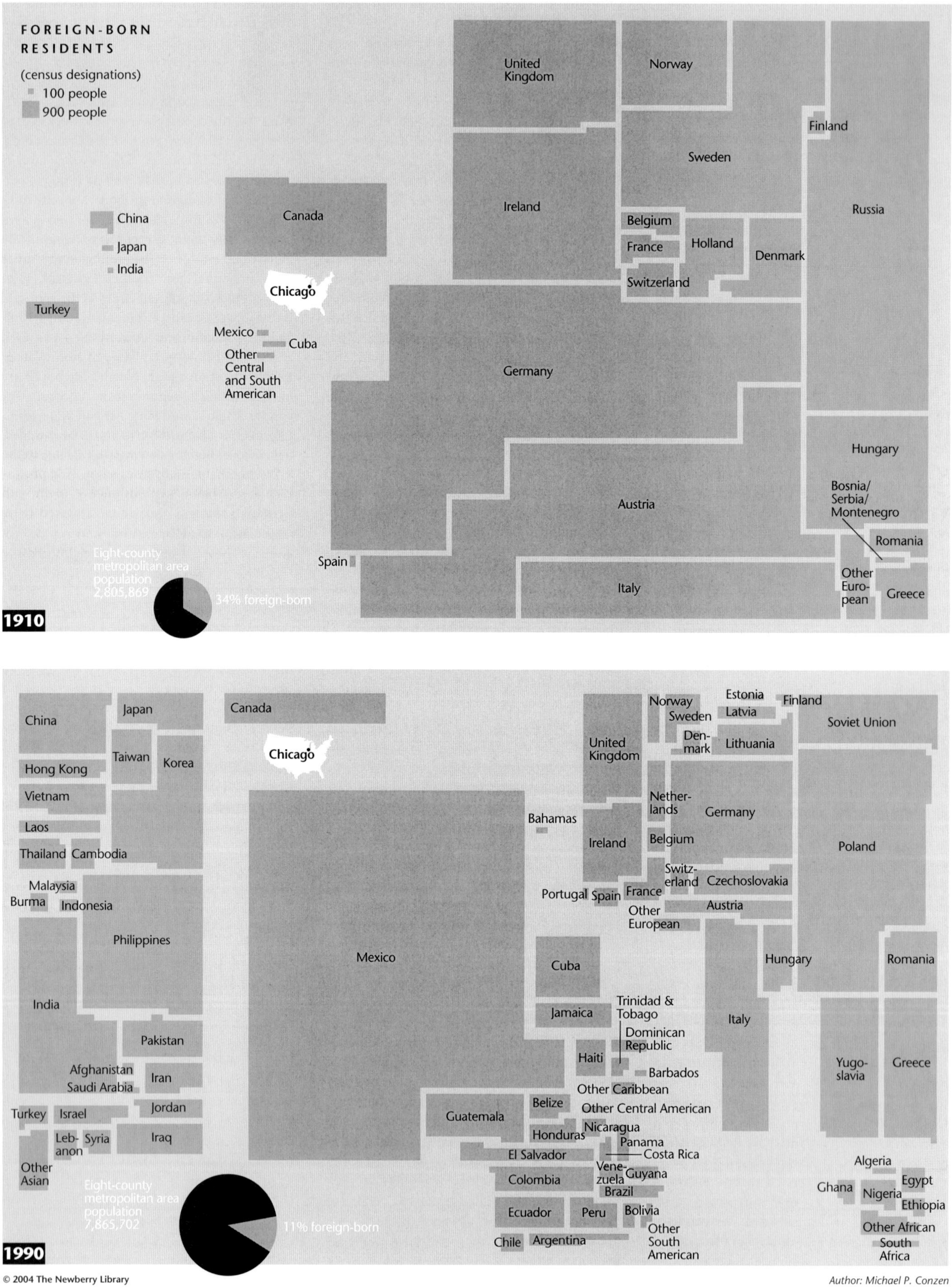

Author: *Michael P. Conzen*

This map shows the dramatic shifts in world migration patterns to metropolitan Chicago that have widened the region's diversity of foreign-born residents. In 1910 the area was already a multicultural region, with more than 900,000 residents born in foreign countries. They came overwhelmingly from Europe, with Germans the largest single group. The region was also home to almost 38,000 Canadian-born residents. Only a handful of Chicagoans came from Asia or Latin America. By 1990, metropolitan Chicago drew from around the globe. The region had more residents born in Latin America than Europe, almost as many from Asia, and thousands from Africa and the Caribbean. Mexicans now formed the largest single group. This cartogram is based on census data and reflects official nation-state designations. For example, Poland was not an independent country in 1910. Similarly, in 1990 the Soviet Union still existed, though some of its constituent parts (such as Lithuania) had already broken off. As a result, country data in some cases may not be comparable.

Many JAPANESE Americans who had been imprisoned in "relocation camps" during World War II opted to settle in Chicago after they were released rather than return to their homes on the West Coast; from only 400 before 1941, the area's Japanese Americans swelled to 20,000 just after 1945. European refugees—the "displaced persons" from Eastern and Central Europe—sought and found help from relatives and friends already living in Chicago who would help them get a fresh start. (Chain migration never stopped; Poles and Irish still arrived in the 1990s.)

By far the most visible, numerous, and culturally significant migrants in this period, however, were African Americans. In the 1960s, Illinois (the Chicago metropolitan area mostly) had a net overall in-migration of about 20,000, not a large number compared to nearly a million to Florida and two million to California. But the net Illinois figure disguised a white outflow nearly as large as a black inflow. The result was a continued rise in the black share of Chicago's population. The area's African American population, only 2 percent of the total in 1910, rose to 7 percent by 1930. The Depression-ridden 1930s brought it up only slightly, to 8 percent, but the "Second GREAT MIGRATION" that began in World War II increased it to 14 percent in 1950, 23 percent in 1960, and 38 percent by 1975. By then, the rush out of Mississippi, Arkansas, and Alabama (the three states contributing blacks most heavily to Chicago) had ceased, as the Deep South became more tolerable and Chicago's ghettoes on the South and West Sides less so.

As black migrants arrived from the distant South, white migrants most often came from nearby (Illinois, Michigan, and Wisconsin)—and hence the cultural differences sharpened rather than dulled. Within the city and its suburbs, segregation of living space never stopped. As whites left in droves for suburbs to the north, west, and south, few blacks or Latinos could follow, except to certain factory towns like Gary or JOLIET. In Chicago's history, the flows from one neighborhood to another, or one municipality to another, have never been smooth. Conflict, erupting at times into a RACE RIOT (1919) or street battles (the late 1960s), has never rested far below the surface.

Since 1965, migration to the United States has been heavy from Latin America and Asia, and Chicago has attracted many of these newcomers. Because of geographical distance, however, Chicago's magnetic force has not matched southern California and other parts of the West and Sunbelt; and it has not drawn proportionately as many immigrants as it did before 1924. By 1975, Mexicans prevailed in once-Czech PILSEN, in SOUTH LAWNDALE, in BACK OF THE YARDS, and in SOUTH CHICAGO. PUERTO RICANS did business along Division Street and into the near Northwest Side; CUBANS, in UPTOWN and northward to ROGERS PARK. FILIPINOS and Vietnamese, with other Asians, settled along North Broadway. As the sources and sizes of migrations changed, Chicago continued into the twenty-first century as a major entrepôt.

The odd thing about Chicago is that it has kept growing—not at the phenomenal rate of the 1880s, to be sure, but enough to maintain its third-city rank—and in all of its parts. The central city attracts Latinos and Asians as it used to attract Europeans and African Americans. The suburbs keep spreading; edge cities emerge; even the older satellites like WAUKEGAN, ELGIN, AURORA, and Joliet revivify. Chicago, the premier case of American urban growth and diversity from the 1840s to the 1920s, ceded growth-rate leadership to Los Angeles and a few other Sunbelt cities in the late twentieth century; but it remained the demographic center of the Midwest.

Walter Nugent

See also: Business of Chicago; Chicago Metropolitan Population (table, p. 1005); Chicago's Residential Patterns According to Census Racial Categories in 2000 (color map, p. C8); Economic Geography; Metropolitan Growth; Multicentered Chicago

Further reading: Statistics on the size of American and world cities at different times are most easily found in the *Historical Statistics of the United States, Colonial Times to 1970* (1975), published by the United States Census Bureau, and in two of B. R. Mitchell's compilations, *European Historical Statistics, 1750–1970* (1975), and *International Historical Statistics: The Americas and Australasia* (1983). The volumes on population of the successive United States censuses also provide relevant information, such as the proportion of native-born and foreign-born in cities. For information on Chicago's birth rates, rates and causes of death, epidemics, and public health measures, the intermittent *Report* of the Chicago Board of Health is extremely helpful, especially those issued prior to the 1930s; more recent reports are much briefer and oriented more toward public relations than toward social science.

For recent information on Chicago's population, more useful are the volume issued by the city's Department of Planning and Development in 1994, *Demographic Characteristics of Chicago's Population: Community Area Profiles,* and the *Local Community Fact Book: Chicago Metropolitan Area, 1990,* published by the Department of Sociology of the University of Illinois at Chicago in 1995.

Older informative works include Helen R. Jeter, *Trends of Population in the Region of Chicago* (1927), I. N. Fisher, *The Impact of Migration on the Chicago Metropolitan Population* (1973), and Irving Cutler, *Chicago: Metropolis of the Mid-Continent* (1976).

Useful secondary works include Melvin G. Holli and Peter d'A. Jones, *Ethnic Chicago: A Multicultural Portrait* (4th ed., 1995); Suellen Hoy, *Chasing Dirt: The American Pursuit of Cleanliness* (1995); Walter Nugent, *Crossings: The Great Transatlantic Migrations, 1870–1914* (1992); Dominic A. Pacyga and Ellen Skerrett, *Chicago: City of Neighborhoods, Histories and Tours* (1986); and Robert Isham Randolph, "The History of Sanitation in Chicago," *Journal of the Western Society of Engineers* (October 1939).

Dentistry. Chicago has played a leading role, both nationally and internationally, in the development of dentistry as a scientific profession. Individual accomplishments begin with Greene Vardiman Black, often referred to as the father of modern dentistry. At the turn of the nineteenth century, he developed dental materials, techniques, and instruments still in use today, established the scientific basis for research in dentistry, instituted rigorous standards for dental education as a founder and dean of NORTHWESTERN UNIVERSITY Dental School, and took a significant leadership role in organized dentistry.

Pioneers also included Black's contemporary Truman W. Brophy, a renowned oral surgeon who developed innovative techniques for correcting cleft palate and harelip, and a founder of the College of Dental Surgery in 1883 (later affiliated with LOYOLA UNIVERSITY); Charles Nelson Johnson, early twentieth-century dental educator, prominent leader in organized dentistry, and distinguished editor of professional dental journals; and Walter Webb Allport, late-nineteenth- and early-twentieth-century clinician, educator, researcher, noted publisher of patient educational materials, and organizer of the World's Columbian Dental Congress.

Since 1918, Chicago has been home to the American Dental Association. National associations for dentistry's principal specialty areas are also headquartered here. The ADA's local affiliate—the Chicago Dental Society—has played a unique role in organized dentistry, far transcending its geographic boundaries. Its annual Midwinter Meeting in February—a tradition that dates back to 1865—is the second largest such gathering in the country, hosting over 32,000 dental professionals from all over the world.

For most of the twentieth century, Chicago has had three dental schools: Northwestern

University Dental School, Loyola University School of Dentistry, and UNIVERSITY OF ILLINOIS AT CHICAGO College of Dentistry. In the latter part of the century, however, in the face of a perceived oversupply of dentists, the high costs of dental education, and in some cases the redefining of a parent university's long-term goals, a number of private dental schools throughout the country closed their doors, including Northwestern's and Loyola's. The College of Dentistry at the University of Illinois, like most of the country's state-sponsored dental schools, has kept its doors open, reflecting the state's responsibility to its citizens to provide a supply of qualified dentists, even though the cost of doing so invariably exceeds revenues generated from student tuitions and patient fees.

Harry L. Sheehy

See also: Medical Education

Further reading: Black, G. V. "Limitations of Dental Education." *Illinois Dental Journal* 55.6 (September–October 1986): 508–511. • McCluggage, Robert W. *A History of the American Dental Association.* 1959. • Orland, Frank J. "Distinguished Dentists of Early Chicago." *Bulletin of the History of Dentistry* 24.1 (April 1976): 1–15.

This 1903 cartoon by John T. McCutcheon captured the excitement of shopping at Marshall Field's on the special Children's Day and for shoppers coming downtown on other days as well. Artist: John T. McCutcheon. Source: The Newberry Library.

Department Stores. In the last two decades of the nineteenth century, Chicago established itself as a leader in the development of the department store, a central feature and symbol of the nation's emerging consumer culture. The most important figure in the rise of this local industry was Marshall Field, and his establishment has received credit for being one of the three that most influenced the nationwide development of the department store (the other two were in New York and Philadelphia). In the mid-1850s the young Field moved to Chicago and worked his way through various retail establishments. Field's early partnerships with Potter Palmer and Levi Leiter were significant precursors to the establishment of MARSHALL FIELD & COMPANY in 1881. Along with Marshall Field's, other establishments in the late nineteenth and early twentieth centuries also thrived in the Loop shopping district, including CARSON PIRIE SCOTT & COMPANY, MANDEL BROTHERS, the FAIR, and SCHLESINGER & MAYER.

The development of the department store posed a serious threat to smaller retailers. Many small merchants tried to rally the public against the new behemoths, but they failed to gain much support. Rather than rally to the side of traditional merchants, Chicago shoppers embraced the new form of retail. The opening of the new Marshall Field's State Street store in 1902, only a few years after anti–department store protests, signaled that this newer type of institution had won the admiration of consumers. The opening was a sensational event, and the store decided not to start selling items on its first day of BUSINESS so that more of the eager public would be able to pass through.

The new Marshall Field's store was more than a place for people to spend their money; the 12-story building became a public landmark and spectacle. The store's magnificent architecture alone was enough to inspire visitors' awe. The highlight of the Marshall Field store was the Tiffany Dome (1907), a glass mosaic covering six thousand square feet, six floors high. Other stores, most notably Schlesinger & Mayer, also offered opulent buildings to house their goods. The Schlesinger & Mayer store, which Carson Pirie Scott later bought, was the last large COMMERCIAL BUILDING designed by Louis Sullivan, and many of his admirers regard it as the culminating work in his career.

Service was yet another part of the department store allure. More than any other establishment, Marshall Field's gained a reputation for pampering its customers. Field's sent all its elevator operators to charm school, was the first to offer a personal shopping service, and even maintained an information desk with personnel who spoke several languages and answered any question about the store or about the city in general.

In addition to affecting consumer habits, department stores had a significant impact on the city's labor force. In 1904 Marshall Field's alone employed between 8,000 and 10,000 people, but the stores' effect on labor was more than quantitative. Traditional retail stores needed employees who could be responsible for a variety of tasks, but department stores hired many more workers, which enabled them to specialize. As a result, many of the jobs in department store WORK required fewer skills, and the greater size of the stores meant that top executives could earn much greater salaries. Probably the most significant impact that the department store had on labor was that it brought women into the retail workforce. Traditional retail stores had believed that their work was too demanding for women, but department store managers reasoned that many of the specialized positions in their stores, especially in sales and CLERICAL WORK, did not require manly characteristics and could be filled by a lower-paid female workforce.

With few other options available to them, many women coveted work in department stores, even though the industry paid them extremely low wages. As women came to dominate many of the sales and clerical positions, the department stores received increasing criticism for the way they treated these employees. In 1913, executives from Marshall Field and Carson Pirie Scott found themselves involved in state legislative hearings on a proposed minimum wage. The stores' labor practices gained even more notoriety as the executives testified that they could double the pay of their female employees and still make a profit, yet they still refused to pay women a living wage.

In the 1920s Chicago's department stores expanded their reach and opened small branches elsewhere in the city and in the outlying metropolitan area, joining other local department stores like Wieboldt's and Goldblatt's. However, it was not until after WORLD WAR II that suburban shopping centers, with full-size department stores, developed fully. In the

1950s Field's was part of the group that developed one of the metro region's first suburban shopping centers, Old Orchard (SKOKIE).

Along with continuing decentralization, the influx of stores based in other parts of the country has become the most noticeable recent development in Chicago's department store industry. Many of these new stores that have opened in Chicago have come from New York, such as Bloomingdale's and Saks Fifth Avenue, as well as from other parts of the country, such as Neiman-Marcus of Dallas and Nordstrom of Seattle. After a century of development, department stores seem to have lost none of their popularity, but today Chicago has far fewer locally owned department stores than it did in the late nineteenth and early twentieth centuries.

Jeffrey A. Brune

See also: Architecture: The First Chicago School; Retail Geography; Retail Workers; Shopping Districts and Malls; Work Culture

Further reading: Benson, Susan Porter. *Counter Cultures: Saleswomen, Managers, and Customers in American Department Stores, 1890–1940.* 1986. • Siry, Joseph. *Carson Pirie Scott: Louis Sullivan and the Chicago Department Store.* 1988. • Wendt, Lloyd, and Herman Kogan. *Give the Lady What She Wants! The Story of Marshall Field & Company.* 1952.

DePaul University. A metropolitan institution with campuses in the heart of Chicago and its outlying suburbs, DePaul is also (since 1998) the largest ROMAN CATHOLIC university in the United States. In 1875 its founding Vincentian fathers traveled to Chicago from LaSalle, Illinois, and established a church at 1010 West Webster Avenue on the city's North Side. There, in a building shared with a Catholic high school, they opened St. Vincent's College in 1898. The first intercollegiate FOOTBALL and BASEBALL teams formed two years later. In 1907, the school was rechristened DePaul University, a name taken from the seventeenth-century father of the Vincentian order, St. Vincent DePaul. Nearly two hundred students enrolled that year. In 1911, DePaul became one of the first Catholic colleges in the United States to admit women, and Sisters Mary Leahy and Mary Teresita earned bachelor's degrees there the next year.

DePaul contributed personnel and facilities to both World Wars: the college theater was transformed into army barracks in 1918, and 280 students were inducted later that year. In the early 1940s, the school provided free instruction to men and women seeking war industry jobs, as well as V-1 training for young men looking to become navy officers.

After WORLD WAR II, enrollment jumped (to 11,500 in 1948), and the school established a master's program in business administration. This marked the start of a transformation in the school's academic culture. In 1964, the Reverend John R. Cortelyou, a natural scientist and the first nontheologian to act as school president, DePaul became the first American Catholic school to alter its curriculum by adding courses in existentialism and phenomenology to the philosophy program. By 1967, the departments of philosophy, psychology, and biology all had accredited doctoral programs.

That same year a core curriculum was established for all undergraduates, now students of the reorganized DePaul College. After expanding its academic offerings, the school sought to diversify its student body. In 1982 DePaul joined forces with LOYOLA and Mundelein Universities to form the Hispanic Alliance, a program designed to improve opportunities in education for the city's growing Latino population. Three years later the three schools formed the Hispanic Women's Project. When enrollment reached 14,699 students in 1988, DePaul needed a new library. Planning began the following year, and, in 1992, Archbishop Joseph Cardinal Bernardin dedicated the LINCOLN PARK Campus Library, a $25 million building and the first freestanding library in the school's history.

Sarah Fenton

See also: Barat College; Catholic School System; Religious Institutions; Universities and Their Cities

Depression. *See* Great Depression

Desegregation. *See* School Desegregation

Design. *See* Graphic Design; Industrial Art and Design

Des Plaines, IL, Cook County, 17 miles NW of the Loop. Des Plaines is a suburban TRANSPORTATION hub. Trains, buses, and highways provide a network bringing commuters and visitors from Chicago to Des Plaines and beyond. The DES PLAINES RIVER provided the earliest means of transportation. The river was variously known as Le Plein, Aux Plaines, and Oplain until GERMANS settled in the village and called it Des Plaines. In 1869 the town became Des Plaines by act of the state legislature.

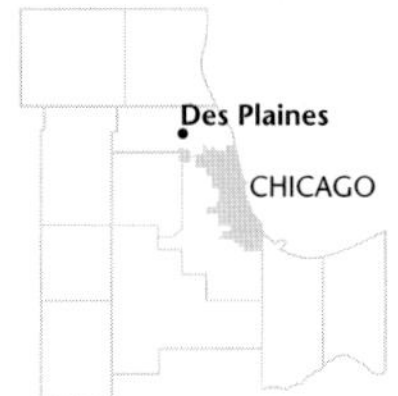

In 1835 Socrates Rand settled on the river's west bank; in 1837 he opened his home for Episcopal services and in 1838 operated the first school in the cheese room of his cabin. An important community member, Rand helped to build the RAILROAD by providing timber for a sawmill, and became the first township chairman. In 1857 the first SUBDIVISION was named for him.

The Illinois & Wisconsin Railroad (later known as the Chicago & North Western Railway) came through Des Plaines in 1854 with a depot located near the river. Train service and the extension of the North West Plank Road brought industry and laborers. In 1873 the settlement was incorporated as a village. The 1880 census figured population at 818.

Flooding posed a constant threat. Although 10 BRIDGES crossed the river in Des Plaines, their wood construction made them temporary, since spring floods could wash them away. The Great Flood of 1881 hindered travel for many weeks. Although the addition of brick culverts somewhat secured the bridges, heavy flooding continued to wear away at them. The first steel bridge crossed the river in 1900.

In the summer months the idyllic river setting enticed Chicagoans to board trains for Des Plaines to picnic or camp. As many as 8,000 people came in a day, disrupting the quiet community and annoying townspeople whose flower gardens were trampled by visitors. The Des Plaines Methodist Camp Ground, established in 1860, drew Methodists from across the region. Northwestern Park's pavilion provided another attraction when it opened for dancing in the early 1900s. In 1918 Cook County's FOREST PRESERVE District created favorable water levels for boating, swimming, and fishing by constructing a dam two miles north of Des Plaines.

Growth accelerated in the 1920s and the population more than doubled to 8,798 in 1930. A city form of government was adopted in 1925 and the village of Riverview was annexed. Orchard Place was added in 1949, with adjacent land becoming part of O'HARE INTERNATIONAL AIRPORT. Des Plaines grew to eight square miles, as a center for both suburban residential growth and light industry.

In 1955 Des Plaines became home to the McDonald's Corporation's first restaurant. The community welcomed Oakton Community College in 1969. Population reached 57,239 in 1970 and declined to about 53,000 in the following two decades. By 2000 the population had grown to 58,720, with 17 percent Hispanic, 8 percent Asian, and 1 percent African American.

Connections for workers continue to make Des Plaines an attractive community for commuters. Next-door to O'Hare Airport, townspeople have access to numerous daily trains, extensive bus lines, major roads such as Rand Road and Northwest Highway, and TOLLROADS and EXPRESSWAYS.

Marilyn Elizabeth Perry

See also: Entertaining Chicagoans; Flood Control and Drainage; Religious Geography; Streets and Highways

Further reading: Henkes, Mark. *Des Plaines: A History.* 1975. • Johnson, Donald S. *Des Plaines, Born of the Tallgrass Prairie: A Pictorial History.* 1984. • Smith, Hermon Dunlap. *The Des Plaines River, 1673–1940: A Brief Consideration of Its Names and History.* 1940.

Des Plaines River. The Des Plaines is not only the longest stream within the Chicago region, it is also of great historic importance. This river combines its flow with that of the Kankakee southwest of JOLIET to create the Illinois River, a significant tributary of the Mississippi. In 1673, when Marquette and Joliet made their historic voyage of discovery, Indians showed them a preferred route from the Mississippi Valley to the Great Lakes. This route lay up the Illinois River and continued along the Des Plaines to the Chicago PORTAGE. So the Des Plaines, long traveled by native peoples, became the principal water route westward from LAKE MICHIGAN toward the Mississippi.

The Des Plaines rises in wetlands near Union Grove, Wisconsin, and flows 150 miles (105 miles in Illinois) southwest to its confluence with the Kankakee. A major tributary, SALT CREEK, joins the Des Plaines near LYONS. Just to the south of this confluence, the Des Plaines passes through a continental divide between the GREAT LAKES and Mississippi River systems. In this area, during periods of wet weather, the Des Plaines sometimes poured part of its flow eastward into Mud Lake toward the Chicago River rather than in the usual westward direction toward the Mississippi. This wetland between the Des Plaines and the Chicago River was long known as the Chicago Portage.

Southwest of the old portage, the Des Plaines now follows an altered channel north of its original path. This channel was shifted slightly to the north to make room for the construction of the Chicago SANITARY AND SHIP CANAL, which reversed the flow of the CHICAGO RIVER. Today, if one stands near the Santa Fe Railroad bridge near Stony Ford, it is possible to view the original 8,000-year-old river channel to the north and the altered 100-year-old channel to the south. At LOCKPORT, south of the confluence between the Sanitary Canal and the Des Plaines, the river resumes its original course. The DUPAGE RIVER, largest tributary of the Des Plaines, joins the Des Plaines just above its confluence with the Kankakee.

Today the Des Plaines is very much changed from its original character. Massive urban development pervades the stream's drainage area, and flooding is a continuing problem. Filled-in wetlands and pavement result in rapid runoff from rainstorms. Now the stream rises more rapidly after storms than in the past, when adjacent wetland areas absorbed rain and slowed its movement into the river. These conditions also tend to make the river somewhat deeper than in the past. When the route for the ILLINOIS & MICHIGAN CANAL was surveyed in the early 1800s, it was necessary to create a 100-mile canal from the Chicago River southwestward to the Illinois River near La Salle to find water of sufficient depth for year-round navigation. Although degraded by urban development, the Des Plaines is on the rebound. Today, canoe races and leisurely water trips follow the Des Plaines Water Trail with its numerous boat launches and nature preserves.

David M. Solzman

See also: Landscape; Riverine Systems

Further reading: Northeastern Illinois Planning Commission, Openlands Project, Illinois Paddling Council, eds. *Northeastern Illinois Regional Water Trails: Map and Plan Summary.* 1999. • Solzman, David M. *The Chicago River: An Illustrated History and Guide to the River and Its Waterways.* 1998.

DeVry Institutes. A leader in the field of for-profit higher education, DeVry has been important not only as a Chicago-area school, but also as a business enterprise operating at the national level. DeVry Institutes was founded in 1931 by Herman DeVry as an ELECTRONICS repair school, with campuses in Chicago and Toronto. Its main Chicago campus was built on North Campbell Ave., west of the city's LAKE VIEW neighborhood, on the site of the old Riverview Park. Between 1967 and 1987, DeVry Institutes was owned by Bell & Howell, the large Chicago-based camera and imaging equipment company. In 1987, when the school was struggling, Bell & Howell sold it to Dennis Keller and Ronald Taylor, founders of another Chicago-based, for-profit higher education chain, the Keller Graduate School of Management. This merger produced DeVry, Inc., with its corporate headquarters in suburban OAKBROOK TERRACE. By the beginning of the twenty-first century, when it opened its first campus in New York City, DeVry was one of the world's leading for-profit educational enterprises, with about 50,000 students at 23 campuses across the country.

Mark R. Wilson

See also: Schooling for Work

Further reading: Martin, Rachel. "DeVry Incorporated." *International Directory of Company Histories* 29 (2000): 159–161.

Dial Magazine. The *Dial,* a journal of literary critics, was founded by Francis Fisher Browne in 1880. A native of Vermont, Browne edited the *Lakeside Monthly* from 1869 to 1874 and was literary editor of the *Alliance,* 1878–79. He envisioned his new literary journal in the genteel tradition of its predecessor *Dial* (Boston, 1840–1844), with book reviews, articles about current trends in the sciences and humanities, and long lists of current book titles. Although published in a city reputedly indifferent to literary pursuits, the *Dial* attained national prominence, absorbing the *Chap-Book* in 1898. Known for its unswerving standard in design and content, the *Dial* changed character after its sale by the Browne family in 1916 and subsequent removal to New York in 1918, where it ceased publication in 1929.

Diana Haskell

See also: Chicago Literary Renaissance; Literary Cultures

Further reading: F. F. Browne Papers. The Newberry Library, Chicago, IL. • Joost, Nicholas. *The Dial, 1912–1920: Years of Transition.* 1967. • Mosher, Frederic John. "Chicago's 'Saving Remnant': Francis Fisher Browne, William Morton Payne, and the *Dial* (1880–1892)." Ph.D. diss., University of Illinois. 1950.

Diamond, IL, Grundy County, 52 miles SW of the Loop. Named after the coal synonym "black diamond," the area attracted miners by the early 1870s. In 1883 tragedy struck when a mine shaft flooded, killing 74 men. Incorporated in 1895, the village nearly disappeared after coal mining ended in the early 1900s. The town reincorporated in 1949 and had a population of 1,393 at the end of the century.

Erik Gellman

See also: Economic Geography; Quarrying, Stonecutting, and Brickmaking

Dick Tracy. Dick Tracy was born in the gang warfare of Prohibition. With machine-gun fire and POLICE chases reverberating in its ears, the edgy public clamored for protection and news. As NEWSPAPERS responded, a unique feature came to life. Artist Chester Gould presented his new comic strip, "Plainclothes Tracy," to enthusiastic *Chicago Tribune* editor Joseph Patterson. Renamed "Dick Tracy," the square-faced, no-nonsense crime fighter was off and running on October 4, 1931.

Gould's "Tracy" found himself chasing Capone, Dillinger, and Pretty Boy Floyd as thinly disguised characters named Pruneface, Flattop, and Putty Puss. The strip introduced dazzling car chases, fierce gun battles, and death-defying scenarios to the comics.

Dick Tracy continued into the twenty-first century with Pulitzer Prize–winning cartoonist Dick Locher and columnist Michael Kilian. Tracy still pursues outlandish characters, revealing that chisel-jawed icon protruding into the many faces of modern crime.

Dick Locher

See also: Crime and Chicago's Image; Gangs; Prohibition and Temperance

Further reading: *Dick Tracy's Fiendish Foes: A 60th Anniversary Celebration.* 1991.

Dime Novels. The dime novel was the dominant popular fiction form in late-nineteenth-century America. The New York firm Beadle and Adams published the first dime novels in June 1860, and they were rapidly imitated.

Millions were eventually published, providing American readers from the CIVIL WAR to WORLD WAR I with accessible, inexpensive reading while shaping attitudes about cities, crime, and especially the American West. Early dime novels were small (four by seven inches) and typically about a hundred pages long, with illustrated covers of colored paper. The genre represented a revolution in merchandising and distribution rather than content; many early dime novel adventure stories had previously appeared in story papers or MAGAZINES. In the early 1900s, challenged by new forms of cheap reading and other popular entertainment, and by increases in postal rates, dime novels gradually died out.

Simultaneous with its period of explosive growth, Chicago began to appear in dime novels starting in the 1870s, when stories focusing on detective heroes and urban crime became popular. As these new types of stories appeared, the price for some series fell (many sold for a nickel) and the format changed, with many novels being printed on larger paper. The new interest in city tales, combined with the continuing appeal of Westerns, made Chicago a popular setting for stories shifting between the East and West, as in *Deadwood Dick, Jr.'s Chase across the Continent; or, A Race for a Ruthless Rogue* (1889) and *Belle Boyd, The Girl Detective: A Story of Chicago and the West* (1891). The city's affluence, and the crime that accompanied it, made Chicago an appealing setting for detective stories such as *Lion Heart Lee, the Lakeside Detective; or, Saved by the Skin of His Teeth* (1891). Real events often appeared in dime novels, as in *The Red Flag; or, The Anarchists of Chicago,* which revolves around the HAYMARKET and McCormick Reaper Works riots of 1886. No Chicago event proved more fertile for dime novel authors than the WORLD'S COLUMBIAN EXPOSITION of 1893. Stories of pickpockets and con men taking advantage of the crowds that converged upon Chicago were widespread, inspiring novels like *The Infanta Eulalia's Jewels; or, Old Cap Collier among the Crooks at the World's Fair* (1893) and *Jocko, the Talking Monkey; or, The World's Fair Globe Trotters* (1892). Such novels, along with the fair itself, helped promote the image of Chicago as a new international metropolis.

Paul J. Erickson

See also: Chicago Literary Renaissance; Crime and Chicago's Image; Fiction; Literary Images of Chicago

Further reading: Brooks, Edwin. "Chicago Dime Novels." *Reckless Ralph's Dime Novel Round-Up,* 9.108 (August 1941): 3. • Denning, Michael. *Mechanic Accents: Dime Novels and Working-Class Culture in America.* 1987. • Johannsen, Albert. *The House of Beadle and Adams and Its Dime and Nickel Novels.* 2 vols. 1950.

Ding Dong School. Billed as "The NURSERY SCHOOL of the Air," *Ding Dong School* was the brainchild of Judith Waller, an NBC executive. She engaged Frances Horwich, professor of education at Chicago's Roosevelt College, to develop an on-screen child-participation format that would appeal to preschoolers and their parents.

Chicago broadcasts began on WNBQ-TV in October 1952 and nationally a month later. The show received a Peabody Award in 1953 for children's programming and three Emmy nominations as best Children's Program from 1953 to 1955, when production moved to New York. From 1957 to 1959, Horwich, who owned the rights to the program, originated the final 130 episodes, carried locally on WGN, from Los Angeles. *Ding Dong School* remained in syndication until 1965.

"Miss Frances" gave daily instruction in various activities for children and ended each program with a brief lecture on parenting. Although influential for later children's programs, *Ding Dong School* eventually closed, due to competition from children's cartoons.

James R. Belpedio

See also: Bozo's Circus; Broadcasting; Kukla, Fran and Ollie; Roosevelt University

Further reading: Brown, Les. *Les Brown's Encyclopedia of Television.* 1982 • McNeil, Alex. *Total Television: A Comprehensive Guide to Programming from 1948 to 1980.* 1980 • Wilk, Max. *The Golden Age of Television.* 1976.

Disc Jockeys. The disc jockey became important in Chicago radio during the 1930s, well before the term "disc jockey" was coined in the 1940s. The city's first disc jockey was Halloween Martin, whose show, *Musical Clock,* was a morning staple on various stations from 1929 to 1946. In black-appeal radio, the disc jockey role was pioneered both locally and nationally by Jack L. Cooper, who began playing records on WSBC in 1931. Former SWIMMING great Norman Ross, Sr., built a tremendous following for his light classics program, *400 Hour,* on WMAQ from 1935 until his death in 1953.

One of postwar Chicago's most notable disc jockeys was Dave Garroway, whose familiar manner and wry humor drew many fans to his *1160 Club* JAZZ show on WMAQ. Al Benson succeeded the urbane Cooper in popularity after joining WGES in 1945. Calling himself "the Old Swingmaster," Benson appealed to newly arrived Southern migrants with down-home gutbucket BLUES and R&B.

The preeminent disc jockey of the 1950s, Howard Miller, began BROADCASTING on WIND in 1948. By 1957 he commanded the country's largest local audience and was described by *Time* as "the nation's biggest single influence on record sales." Miller's principal rival was the more rambunctious Art Hellyer, who broadcast his *Morning Madcap* show on WCFL.

During the 1950s, Herb "Kool Gent" Kent used his everyday conversational style to surpass Al Benson in popularity. His success led CHESS RECORDS' Leonard Chess to create WVON in 1963 as the first 24-hour station for the city's African American community. Don Cornelius, an up-and-coming star at WVON, later developed the dance show *Soul Train.*

WLS introduced Chicago in 1960 to Dick Biondi, one of America's most famous ROCK 'n' roll disc jockeys, whose frantic screaming style epitomized the era. Another notable WLS deejay was Larry Lujack, whose low-key sarcastic delivery attracted an immense following in the 1970s.

Symbolizing the end of the golden age of the disc jockey was the audience battle between Howard Miller at WIND and Wally Phillips at WGN. Phillips would emerge as the city's most popular deejay with his morning show (1965–1986). The two radio hosts gradually stopped playing records, helped move AM radio from a music-based format to a talk-based format, and transformed themselves from disc jockeys to talk show hosts, helping to usher in the era of "talk radio." While disc jockeys continued to flourish in Chicago radio where recorded music was the format, they no longer were the most popular radio personalities.

Robert Pruter

See also: Breakfast Clubs; Classical Music; Entertaining Chicagoans; Ethnic Music; Radio Orchestras

Further reading: Ghrist, John Russell. *Valley Voices: A History of Radio Broadcasting in Northern Illinois and Northwest Indiana from 1910 to 1992.* 1992. • Lieberman, Philip A. *Radio's Morning Show Personalities: Early Hour Broadcasters and Deejays from the 1920s to the 1990s.* 1996. • Salowitz, Stew. *Chicago's Personality Radio: The WLS Disc Jockeys of the Early 1960s.* 1993.

Dixmoor, IL, Cook County, 17 miles S of the Loop. Dixmoor has the unusual distinction of having thousands of people daily drive right over it: Interstate 57 passes over the village's streets. Despite this intrusion, Dixmoor still exhibits important traces of the history of the region. Its eastern boundary parallels the Little Calumet River and the old BLUE ISLAND–THORNTON Road. This is the path of the original Vincennes Trace that in the 1820s and 1830s reached from the small settlement of Chicago down to Vincennes in Indiana.

Western Avenue constitutes the western edge of the village. Since 1915 this part of Western Avenue has been Dixie Highway, a designation which came as national roadways were being established and entrepreneurs sought to link points in the north, including Chicago, with passable roads going through to Florida. The tracks of the Grand Trunk Western RAILROAD cut through the center of Dixmoor. From 1907 to 1926, an INTERURBAN from Chicago to Kankakee, the Chicago and Southern Traction Company, ran alongside the Grand Trunk line through the village.

Because of its proximity to industrial jobs in BLUE ISLAND and HARVEY, the area's original development was residential. To counter attempts of both Blue Island and Harvey to annex the area, residents voted for incorporation in 1922. As the owner of more than 70 lots, Charles Special played a key role in the ANNEXATION process and served as the first president of the village. It was in his honor that the village, for a while, was named Specialville. In 1929 residents petitioned the secretary of state to change the name of the village to Dixmoor, possibly to recognize proximity to Dixie Highway.

After incorporation, the village provided municipal services including electric streetlights, sewers, and Lake Michigan WATER. From the time of incorporation, much of the employment base for Dixmoor was tied to the metal-fabricating industries in Harvey. The large Wyman-Gordon plant was situated partially in both communities. The loss of these manufacturing facilities in the Harvey area from the 1960s through the 1980s adversely affected both employment and municipal revenues for Dixmoor and its surrounding towns.

Integration in Dixmoor began in the 1960s. By 1990, 58 percent of the population was AFRICAN AMERICAN, a ratio that remained the same in 2000. While racial integration was largely peaceful, during the summer of racial unrest across the country in 1964, Dixmoor gained unusual notice due to a brief (one-day) confrontation and riot. The "Gin Bottle Riot" involved over 1,000 persons and local and state police. In the closing years of the twentieth century, new housing starts brought growth in Dixmoor. Because the community is landlocked, this new growth came as redevelopment of existing property.

Larry A. McClellan

See also: Civil Rights Movements; Contested Spaces; Neighborhood Succession; Streets and Highways

Further reading: McClellan, Larry A. "Dixmoor on the Dixie Highway." *Star,* October 26, 1997, South Suburban edition. • Wolf, Wayne L. *The Gin Bottle Riot of 1964: Harvey and Dixmoor in Flames.* 1977. • Zimmerman, Jacob F. *History of the Incorporated Municipalities of Thornton Township.* 1938.

Dolton, IL, Cook County, 18 miles S of the Loop. Dolton and RIVERDALE were practically one community until each incorporated as a village in 1892. Dolton includes areas known as Berger, Greenwood, Marydale Manor, and Yard Center.

The Dolton area is drained by the Little Calumet River, which forms part of Dolton's southern border as it flows west toward BLUE ISLAND, where it originally turned east and touched Dolton's northeast corner. Significant evidence of human habitation in the area of Dolton was found at the Anker Site on the north shore of the Little Calumet on the south edge of Dolton, which dates to about AD 1400 to 1500. Although the tribe could not be identified, the MIAMI and ILLINOIS were known to have lived in the area during that period.

George Dolton settled where the old Indian trail (Lincoln Avenue) crossed the Little Calumet River in 1835 and operated a ferry with J. C. Matthews, who arrived in 1836. Dolton and Vincent Matthews operated the ferry until 1842, when a toll bridge was built that operated until 1856. This activity took place along Indiana Avenue in what is now the village of Riverdale and the Riverdale community of Chicago and was known as "Riverdale Crossing."

Dolton's sons settled here, and it is for them that the town is named. A period of GERMAN immigration intensified in the late 1840s. The earliest industries were a distilling company and a lumber company located on the CALUMET RIVER. The coming of the RAILROADS stimulated Dolton's growth. The 1850s began a period of rail expansion that has characterized Dolton's physical setting and brought in IRISH Catholics who worked in constructing the railroads. From 1866 to 1910 the village was known as Dolton Station. Hay and grain were the earliest agricultural products. By the 1890s Dolton was a center for producing agricultural products for Chicago, such as potatoes, asparagus, cabbage, onions, sugar beets, eggplants, and lima beans. This early agricultural activity lead to the area's packing and canning industries.

In 1885 Dolton's clay deposits began to be exploited and eventually supplied three brick companies. In 1911 the brick workers conducted a successful one-month strike over an attempt to reduce wages. The mixture of railroads and the Little Calumet River proved to be a good site for industry. Dolton grew as a center for truck farming and manufacturing. It has produced bakery equipment, brass castings, shipping containers, cement, FURNITURE, agricultural equipment, steel tanks, and CHEMICALS. This diverse activity attracted an ethnically varied workforce. In the 1960s the Calumet EXPRESSWAY (now the Bishop Ford Freeway) improved automobile and truck access to Chicago by two interchanges serving Dolton. In recent years large numbers of AFRICAN AMERICANS have moved to Dolton. The 2000 census reported a population of 25,614 with 14 percent white, 82 percent black, and 3 percent Hispanic.

Dave Bartlett

See also: Agriculture; Quarrying, Stonecutting, and Brickmaking

Further reading: Bluhm, Elaine A., and Allen Liss. "The Anker Site." In *Chicago Area Archaeology,* 2nd ed., ed. Elaine Bluhm, 1983, 89–137. • Cook, Marlene. *Dolton Tattler: Fact, Fiction, and Folklore, 1892–1992.* 1992. • Dolton–South Holland Junior Woman's Club. *Dolton, 1892–1976.* 1976.

Domestic Work and Workers. The explosive economic growth of the latter half of the nineteenth century transformed Chicago into the nation's leading interior metropolis. Men and women of the burgeoning urban middle class sought to display their prosperity through the hiring of domestic servants to perform daily cooking, cleaning, and childcare chores. By 1870, one in five Chicago households employed domestic workers, who accounted for 60 percent of the city's wage-earning women. Over the next half century, domestic service represented the leading occupation of women in Chicago and the nation.

Domestic servants usually lived with the employing family, performing a multitude of household tasks (such as LAUNDRY, ironing, cooking, cleaning, and serving) in exchange for a modest wage plus room and board. Domestic workers were usually young, single women from working-class families whose terms of service lasted until marriage. While comparable or superior in pay to other jobs open to poor, uneducated females, domestic work attracted few native-born women because of the long hours, low status, lack of freedom, and close supervision. Consequently, domestic servants often came from the ranks of the most desperate members of the community, either those too poor to pay for housing or those excluded from other vocations. In late nineteenth-century Chicago, domestic WORK was increasingly performed by IRISH, GERMAN, Scandinavian, and POLISH women.

By the turn of the twentieth century, domestic work had changed little in either substance or status. When a Chicago newswoman went undercover as a live-in servant in 1901, she reported toiling 15 hours daily and performing every household chore except laundry, which was sent out. She made $2.75 per week plus room and board. While her wage was a dollar and a half less than the average, similar conditions compelled some domestic workers to form the Working Women's Association of America (WWAA) in the same year. Aided by reformers such as Jane Addams, the group pushed employers to raise wages, lower hours, allow home visitors, and agree to an established grievance procedure. But the personalized, decentralized nature of domestic work made organizing difficult, and the WWAA disbanded after enrolling only 300 of the city's 35,000 domestic servants. Later efforts at UNIONIZING domestic workers also proved unsuccessful.

In the wake of WORLD WAR I, changes in the national economy and labor market precipitated a transformation in the structure of domestic work and those who performed it. New opportunities for white women in the expanding clerical and sales sectors, restrictions on European immigration, and the GREAT MIGRATION of AFRICAN AMERICANS to urban cities in the North significantly altered the labor market for domestic work. Already in 1900, African American women, only 4 percent of the wage-earning female population in the city, represented 30 percent of domestic workers, and their numbers grew over the next 40 years.

Racially excluded from most occupations, black women soon dominated the domestic service sector in Chicago. Despite limited options, black domestic workers still experienced an improvement in wages compared to similar positions in the South, where it took three weeks to earn the same amount as in one week in Chicago in the 1910s. In contrast to earlier domestic servants, black women were often married with children and hence preferred day work to a living-in situation. By 1920, more domestic workers were living at home than boarding with their employer. By reducing the hours that domestic workers were available for personal service, day work fostered the introduction of electric labor-saving appliances into middle-class homes, further transforming the nature of household work.

While a step up economically from the South, Chicago nonetheless presented newly arrived African American domestic workers with difficult conditions. As late as the 1930s, domestic servants complained of employers offering day work to the lowest bidder at the notorious "slave pens" at the corner of Halsted and Twelfth Streets. While single white women often utilized domestic work as a temporary stop on a track of upward mobility, most African American women were forced to make careers as domestic day workers or laundresses.

In the post–WORLD WAR II period, domestic work receded from prominence as a privilege in middle-class families and an occupational option for working-class women. Commercial facilities outside the home increasingly performed much of the household labor, as in the case of child care centers, nursing homes, and fast-food RESTAURANTS. Even the enduring practice of day work was contracted out to cleaning agencies, who might send a worker once or twice a week to a specific home. Still, while the structure of domestic work had changed, the low pay and status associated with it remained the same. In her 1999 investigations, journalist Barbara Ehrenreich found that corporate cleaning companies paid between $5 to $6 per hour on average. And in Chicago, as elsewhere in the United States, cleaning, cooking, and child care for pay continued to be performed by poor, immigrant, and nonwhite women.

Daniel A. Graff

See also: Foodways; Housekeeping; Housing for the Elderly; Nursery Schools; Work Culture

Further reading: Dudden, Faye E. *Serving Women: Household Service in Nineteenth-Century America.* 1983. • Katzman, David M. *Seven Days a Week: Women and Domestic Service in Industrializing America.* 1978; 1981. • Meyerowitz, Joanne J. *Women Adrift: Independent Wage Earners in Chicago, 1880–1930.* 1988.

Dominican University. The original charter for what would one day become Dominican University was granted by the state of Wisconsin to Santa Clara Academy, which opened as a ROMAN CATHOLIC school for girls in 1848. The Dominican sisters began teaching college-level courses there in 1901, and, less than two decades later, undergraduate enrollment had climbed to 70 students. The college needed a larger campus. In 1918, at the invitation of Archbishop George Mundelein, the renamed Rosary College settled in RIVER FOREST, an affluent suburb eight miles west of Chicago. Though no longer a frontier school, Rosary retained its pioneering spirit, providing free evening courses during the GREAT DEPRESSION and admitting its first AFRICAN AMERICAN student in 1938. Political activism defined campus life in later decades as well: students marched to show their solidarity with the Selma, Alabama, CIVIL RIGHTS marches in 1965 and their opposition to the Vietnam War in the early 1970s. Students also sought changes on-campus, requesting that academic requirements be reevaluated, seminars provided, and men admitted. The Academic Council acquiesced to student demands in 1971, opening a new dormitory housing 50 male students later that year. The number of accredited graduate-level courses increased over the next several decades, and in 1997 the school chose to acknowledge its graduate programs and honor its founding order by once again changing its name, to Dominican University. By 2000, the school's 70-year-old program in library science was the only such program in metropolitan Chicago and one of two in the state.

Sarah Fenton

See also: Barat College; Universities and Their Cities

Dominicans. Although immigration from the Dominican Republic to the United States dates back at least to 1940, a growing influx began in the decade after the 1961 assassination of dictator Rafael Leónidas Trujillo Molina. Having experienced a failed armed insurrection in 1965, a subsequent U.S.-led invasion, and further social-political instability in a depressed economy, Dominicans from all social, religious, and economic backgrounds first began to resettle in great numbers in New York City in the 1970s.

Dominican families have resided in Chicago since 1966. These immigrants were mostly devout ROMAN CATHOLICS from the urban middle class. As New York's industrial production began to decline after 1970, rising UNEMPLOYMENT affected thousands of Dominicans. The hope of finding better job opportunities in metropolitan Chicago's bustling economy attracted unskilled workers, self-employed men and women, mostly male technicians, professionals, PROTESTANT ministers, and a handful of artists. Most found jobs in the MEATPACKING, garment, and ELECTRONICS industries as well as in the service sectors. Notwithstanding their uncertain command of English, they felt accepted in a city that was already home to thousands of Latinos from Mexico, Cuba, and Puerto Rico. With the latter two groups Dominicans have not only a historical affinity, sharing heroes of nineteenth-century Caribbean liberation struggles, but also a common mixed ethnic ancestry going back even further, in which the Afro-Hispanic element stands out. Many Dominicans chose to settle among CUBANS and PUERTO RICANS and blended easily with them in the HUMBOLDT PARK neighborhood and in other areas on Chicago's Northwest Side. Others, mostly professionals, spread to surrounding suburbs, such as BURR RIDGE, DOWNERS GROVE, and NILES.

Although the 2000 U.S. Census counted only 1,651 permanent residents and second-generation Dominicans living in Chicago, consular registers suggest the presence of some 7,500 Dominicans. During the 1990s a small but influential group of university graduates and community activists revived earlier attempts to unite Dominicans around cultural, social, and educational themes. Casa Dominicana, founded in 1991, has sought to instill a sense of Dominican pride in culture, national heritage, and ethnic identity. In 1997 the Chicago City Council commemorated the memory of the Dominican physician Ramón García Camilo for his humanitarian services to Humboldt Park residents. Another organization of professionals emerged under the rubric of Dominican American Midwest Association, whose mission is to address the needs of Dominican Americans in the Midwest on issues concerning education, economics, technology, and culture. It also seeks to monitor and act upon local and national policy issues that affect Dominican Americans.

During the 1990s other initiatives brought historical and cultural presentations ranging from Dominican folklore to merengue music performers to Chicago's museums, SCHOOLS, parks, and libraries. The Dominican-owned gallery Mi Galería introduced Dominican artists and sculptors to Chicago.

Dominicans have found a variety of BUSINESS opportunities in Chicago, including money-transfer agencies, cosmetics stores, beauty salons, car repair shops, household appliance service, nightclubs, RESTAURANTS, and CONSTRUCTION. The thousands of dollars sent annually to relatives and friends back home help sustain the Dominican Republic's political and economical stability.

Rafael Nuñez-Cedeño

See also: Demography; Mexicans; Multicentered Chicago

Further reading: Foner, Nancy. *New Immigrants in New York.* 1987. • Grasmuck, Sherri, and Patricia R. Pessar. *Between Two Islands.* 1991. • Torres-Saillant, Silvio, and Ramona Hernández. *The Dominican Americans.* 1998.

Douglas, Community Area 35, 3 miles S of the Loop. In 1852 Stephen A. Douglas, lawyer, politician, and land speculator, purchased 70 acres of land located along the lake between 33rd and 35th Streets. Douglas built a house at 34 E. 35th Street and donated land to the Baptists who opened the first UNIVERSITY OF CHICAGO in 1860.

At the beginning of the CIVIL WAR (1861), the Union army set up CAMP DOUGLAS between 31st and 33rd Streets, first as a training facility for the Illinois regiment and subsequently as a prisoner of war camp for Confederate soldiers. Forty-four hundred Confederate soldiers died because of poor conditions at Camp Douglas.

Access to both a commuter stop of the ILLINOIS CENTRAL RAILROAD and a growing number of streetcar lines drew a wide range of Chicagoans. After the war, wealthy citizens like Joy Morton, founder of the Morton Salt Company, lived in Groveland Park and Woodland Park, while upper-middle-class families purchased homes along Dearborn, State, Wabash, Indiana, and Michigan Avenues.

The area attracted many of the city's leading JEWISH families, who in 1881 built a HOSPITAL with $200,000 from the estate of MICHAEL REESE. Less than a decade later, the Jewish community completed the Kehilath Anshe Mayriv Synagogue (1890) at 33rd and Indiana. Designed by Dankmar Adler and Louis Sullivan, it has housed the Pilgrim Baptist Church since 1922.

Working-class families employed in the nearby MEATPACKING industry, railroad shops, and BREWERIES constructed small BALLOON FRAME houses and a few brick cottages along Federal Street. IRISH workers built and worshiped at St. James Church (1880) at 29th and Wabash. In 1869, the Sisters of Mercy relocated their MERCY HOSPITAL to 26th and Calumet. In 1889, the Irish helped to establish De La Salle Institute, a Catholic academy for young men. MAYORS Martin Kennelly, Richard J. Daley, Michael Bilandic, and Richard M. Daley graduated from this school.

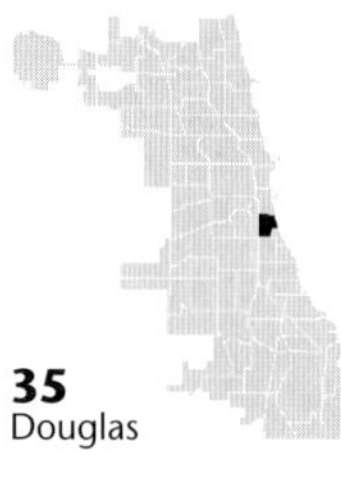

35
Douglas

AFRICAN AMERICANS made their way along the boulevards from the LOOP to Douglas. By the 1890s, the boundaries of the SOUTH SIDE black community expanded southward along a narrow strip known as the "BLACK BELT." Black institutions began to play a prominent role in the community. OLIVET BAPTIST CHURCH, with the city's largest African American congregation, moved from the Loop to 27th and Dearborn in 1893, later purchasing the First Baptist Church at 31st and South Parkway (now King Drive). As an outgrowth of the economic strength of the area, businessman Jesse Binga opened Chicago's first black-owned bank in 1908.

During the 1920s through the 1940s, Douglas, along with the community to the south, GRAND BOULEVARD, became the center of black business and cultural life. Popularly known as the Black Metropolis or Bronzeville, the area exhibited an amazing diversification of professional and commercial interests. By day black people transacted business in companies housed in the Jordan, Overton Hygienic, and *Chicago Bee* Buildings, and at night they went to clubs where they heard musicians like King Oliver, Louis Armstrong, and Jelly Roll Morton.

After the stock market crash of 1929, most of the black-owned banks and INSURANCE companies went out of business. The city's segregated REAL-ESTATE market limited black housing opportunities. Many middle-class houses were converted into APARTMENTS, falling into disrepair.

In 1941, the CHICAGO HOUSING AUTHORITY (CHA) built the Ida B. Wells housing project at 37th and Vincennes. In 1950, the Dearborn Homes at 27th and State were opened. Although this new housing and the single-family dwellings were not enough to provide adequate living space for the 30,000 black newcomers who arrived in the area during World War II, RESTRICTIVE COVENANTS, violence, and intimidation by whites limited options for black people interested in moving out of the community.

In 1952, the CHA completed Prairie Avenue Courts and in 1961 they built the Clarence Darrow Homes. In between, they constructed STATEWAY GARDENS at 35th and State, along with the ROBERT TAYLOR HOMES to the south, replacing all that remained of the worker cottages and tenements along Federal Street.

At the same time public housing was being constructed along Douglas's western border, private developments for middle- and upper-income groups were erected along the eastern border. Michael Reese Hospital and the ILLINOIS INSTITUTE OF TECHNOLOGY (created by the merger of Armour and Lewis Institutes) played pivotal roles in these initiatives. The Lake Meadows apartment complex (31st to 35th Streets east of King Drive); Prairie Shores development (adjacent to Michael Reese); and South Commons (Michigan Avenue south of 26th Street) were completed by the mid-1960s.

Since the late 1980s, there has been a concerted effort to bring the old Black Metropolis back to life. The Mid-South Planning and Development Commission and a number of local community organizations have been in the forefront of this renaissance. The majority of the rebirth has taken place in the area located between the two high-rise developments called "The Gap" (31st to 35th Streets and King Drive to Michigan Avenue) a national historic landmark district.

Adrian Capehart

See also: Historic Preservation; Jazz; Subsidized Housing; Urban Renewal

Further reading: Drake, St. Clair, and Horace R. Cayton. *Black Metropolis: A Study of Negro Life in a Northern City.* Rev. ed. 1993. • Pacyga, Dominic A.,

Stephen A. Douglas

A Quincy lawyer, Douglas was involved in the organization of the DEMOCRATIC PARTY in Illinois in the 1830s, working closely with John Wentworth. As a state legislator, he supported funding of the ILLINOIS & MICHIGAN CANAL. He received strong support from Chicago voters when he entered Congress in the mid-1840s. After his marriage and election to the U.S. Senate in 1847, Douglas moved to Chicago.

Douglas quickly joined the ranks of land speculators in Chicago, making substantial investments on the South Side, including 160 acres near 31st Street and Cottage Grove Avenue, which became the nucleus of the Douglas neighborhood; 2,964 acres in the Calumet region; and 4,610 acres from the ILLINOIS CENTRAL RAILROAD.

Senator Douglas was instrumental in designating Chicago the northern terminus of the Illinois Central Railroad and worked for a transcontinental route. The Illinois Central went through a part of his South Side properties. In 1856, Douglas, seeking to promote the value of his extensive real-estate holdings, donated several acres of land for a college to local Baptists near 31st Street.

Douglas's electoral support in Chicago remained strong until 1858. While he was reelected in the famous 1858 Senate campaign against Abraham Lincoln, he did not carry Chicago. Two years later, 8,094 Chicagoans voted for Douglas for president, while 10,697 cast their ballots for the ultimate winner, Abraham Lincoln.

Ann Durkin Keating

and Ellen Skerrett. *Chicago, City of Neighborhoods: Histories and Tours.* 1986. • Spear, Allan. *Black Chicago: The Making of a Negro Ghetto, 1890–1920.* 1967.

Downers Grove, IL, DuPage County, 21 miles W of the Loop. The village of Downers Grove takes its name from the community's first landowner, Pierce Downer, who came from New York State in 1832 to join his son Stephen, a stonemason who was working on the first Chicago lighthouse. Downer staked his claim to 160 acres of a prime grove surrounded by prairie, turning it into a successful dairy farm. The Downers were followed by others like Walter Blanchard, Israel Blodgett, Henry Carpenter, Henry Lyman, Henry Puffer, and Dexter Stanley, who created a community around their grove.

The year before the Chicago, Burlington & Quincy RAILROAD came through town in 1864, Samuel Curtiss established the first SUBDIVISION in what would become the southeastern side of the central business district. In 1873 local leaders incorporated as the village of Downers Grove.

Growth continued near the village's three railroad stations at Main Street, Belmont, and East Grove. In 1890 E. H. Prince platted an attractive subdivision north and west of the Main Street station. In 1892, just north of the Belmont station, Chicago businessmen, including Marshall Field, founded the first nine-hole GOLF course west of the Appalachian Mountains. North of the East Grove station, POLISH families from Gostyn, Poland, purchased lots, creating the largest ethnic neighborhood in town. In 1891, they founded St. Mary's of Gostyn, the village's oldest ROMAN CATHOLIC church.

Owing to its close proximity to Chicago and its large rail siding, the village became a major site for mail-order HOUSING sold by Sears, Roebuck & Co. between 1908 and 1940. With up to two hundred possible Sears houses identified, Downers Grove has one of the largest concentrations of existing Sears houses in the world.

The Tivoli Theatre was built in 1928. It was the second theater in the nation constructed specifically for sound motion pictures.

With the advent of the EXPRESSWAY system in the post–World War II era, the automobile accelerated Downers Grove's expansion, just as the railroad had done almost a century earlier. The village annexed adjoining unincorporated land and the East-West TOLLROAD provided easy access. By 2000, the village of Downers Grove consisted of 13 square miles, with 48,724 residents. Its diverse economy included corporate headquarters, light industry, service, and retail businesses.

Downers Grove has often had an impact on the state, the nation, and the world through the actions of famous residents. Arthur C. Ducat served as an inspector general of the Union army during the Civil War, and later established the 800-acre Lindenwald Estate on the west side of town. James Henry Breasted became an internationally renowned Egyptologist at the Oriental Institute. Lottie Holman O'Neill was the first woman elected to the state legislature, and served there 40 years (1923–1963). Art Chester made newspaper headlines in the 1930s and 1940s as an air race champion and aircraft designer. Another resident was gold medalist Cammi Granato, who captained the U.S. women's hockey team at the 1998 and 2002 Winter Olympics.

Mark S. Harmon

See also: DuPage County; Metropolitan Growth; Transportation

Further reading: Dunham, Montrew, and Pauline Wandschneider. *Downers Grove, 1832 to 1982.* 1982. • Herrick, Bartle R. *What You Didn't Know about Downers Grove and Didn't Know Who to Ask.* 1982.

Drainage. *See* Flood Control and Drainage

Drug Retailing. Though one might have been able to find a patron of John Kinzie's retail establishment or of Mark Beaubien's hotel in frontier Chicago who would have touted the "medicinal benefits" of the cheap LIQUOR both men dispensed over the counter, the business of drug retailing in early Chicago consisted primarily of odd elixirs, suspect folk remedies, and medicine show potions.

The NEWSPAPERS of the 1830s were filled with advertisements for "cures" such as Dr. William B. Egan's Sarsaparilla Panacea, "the most perfect restorative ever yet discovered for debilitated constitutions and diseases of the skin and bones." Small drugstores such as the one operated by Dr. Edmund S. Kimberly began to dot the frontier town and were in fierce competition with, of all places, bookstores, many of which held exclusive franchises to sell certain remedies.

The CIVIL WAR created a great new demand for DRUGS and furthered the growth of the drug retailing industry. Drugstores (often called apothecaries) began to operate in most city neighborhoods.

In the years following the Great FIRE OF 1871, the drug retailing BUSINESS boomed because of two forces, industry and science. The Industrial Revolution, with its development of manufacturing methods that could be used to mass-produce drugs, coincided with such scientific developments as phytochemistry and synthetic chemistry, resulting in new derivatives of old drugs and new chemical entities.

Though European firms dominated the drug manufacturing industry and would until the 1920s, a late-1880s catalog for the Chicago-based G. D. SEARLE listed 400 fluid extracts, 150 elixirs, 100 syrups, 75 powdered extracts, and 25 tinctures and other drug forms.

Many of those were on display at the opening of the first Walgreen's drugstore at 4134 South Cottage Grove Avenue in 1901, an operation similar to most turn-of-the-century drugstores. Haphazardly arranged in the front windows were clusters of products like the "only genuine old-fashioned" Castile soap, Peerless tooth powder, vegetable tonics, perfumes, and tins and small jars of pills and tablets for ailments ranging from dyspepsia to bronchitis. Along the aisles were cabinets and shelving with medicinal and nonmedicinal products (the latter called "sundries"). At the store's far end, from floor to ceiling, was a wooden grillwork partition behind which medicines were compounded out of the sight of customers. Back there were the tools of the trade: a mortar and pestle, a set of scales, a jar of leeches, a bottle capper, and rows of bottled drugs bearing Latin labels, plus small unfilled bottles and tiers of little drawers that contained various ingredients used in filling prescriptions. It was a dark and uninviting place, though one that played a central role in every neighborhood, as the corner druggist often referred to as "Doc" became the primary source of medical care, diagnosing illnesses and concocting remedies.

That role would diminish during the century, due largely to government regulations, primarily through the Pure Food and Drug Act, passed in 1906. In the early twentieth century there was much agitation and press clamor against nostrums that included tonics with alcohol, syrups that contained cocaine and morphine, ointments to enlarge or reduce bosoms, and lavishly advertised "cures" for cancer, alcoholism, impotence, rupture, and other ailments.

The pharmacist, with increasingly less time devoted to compounding drugs, supplemented his income by adding various elements to the drugstore. One of the most important and romanticized was the soda fountain, where the pharmacist dispensed ice cream sodas and sundaes. They also began offering on their shelves a variety of other products not conveniently handled at any other stores: school supplies, personal grooming aids, baby food.

In the 1920s, 80 percent of the prescriptions dispensed in Chicago pharmacies required a knowledge of compounding. But by the 1940s, only 26 percent did. Further reducing the time pharmacists spent making drugs was the 1951 passage of the Durham-Humphrey Amendment to the Federal Food, Drug and Cosmetic Act, which precluded dispensing a wide class of medications without a physician's prescription.

From that point, drugstores began to assume the look of small supermarkets, with pharmacies tucked into the back. Chains such as Osco and Walgreen's grew as the number of independent drugstores decreased. Large supermarkets and retailers began including pharmacies within their stores. Since most drugs are supplied by manufacturing firms, the druggist today double-checks physicians' orders and watches for contradictions to a prescription. He or she must also keep track of new developments in drugs and drug manufacturing, have a knowledge of shelf life and other storage issues, and be able to judge the reliability and reputations of the manufacturers.

Though buying drugs through the Internet might eventually prove a serious threat to the conventional (and increasingly computerized) pharmacy business in Chicago, it is still possible to find, tucked into the city's corners, practitioners of herbal or alternative medicine, whose stores charmingly resemble drugstores of the past.

Rick Kogan

See also: Grocery Stores and Supermarkets; Mail Order; Medical Manufacturing and Pharmaceuticals; Public Health; Retail Geography

Further reading: Bonner, Thomas Neville. *Medicine in Chicago, 1850–1950.* 1957. • Kogan, Herman, and Rick Kogan. *Pharmacist to the Nation: A History of Walgreen Co., America's Leading Drug Store Chain.* 1989.

Drugs and Alcohol. Chicagoans, like other Americans, have long favored alcohol when they wished to experience intoxication. Whiskey—easy to transport, cheap, and nonperishable—remained Chicago's most popular alcoholic drink in the nineteenth century. Ale was also widely available, not only in general merchandise and GROCERY STORES, but also in SALOONS and the early DEPARTMENT STORES. GERMAN immigrants introduced lager beer to the city in the 1850s. By the 1880s, mass production distillers made lager beer an inexpensive and popular drink for working-class men and women. In the congested neighborhoods of the city, children and younger workers ran the "growler" to local saloons for beer to consume in workshops and tenement households. At the other end of the social scale, the lavish dinner parties of Chicago's cultural elite featured a different wine for each of many courses. Etiquette books, instructing aspiring readers in the finer points of serving wine, cordials, and after-dinner drinks, suggest patterns of acceptable domestic drinking among more affluent Chicagoans.

Chicago was a wide-open town when it came to drinking, but opium smoking, introduced into the city in the 1870s by CHINESE immigrants, drew an uncharacteristically punitive response. Statutes targeting opium dens, passed in the 1880s, resulted in hundreds of arrests per year in areas such as the Levee, the VICE DISTRICT clustered around State Street south of the LOOP.

Far more prevalent was the medical use of opiates and other drugs in late-nineteenth-century Chicago. Doctors, having limited therapeutic alternatives, eagerly prescribed laudanum and other opiated medications, producing a high rate of addiction among their middle-class patients. Proprietary or patent medicines, which could be obtained without prescription, often contained alcohol, opiates, and cocaine. Few laws limited access to these drugs, which could be obtained for medical or recreational purposes alike until Progressive-era laws regulated their sale.

By the turn of the twentieth century, doctors were prescribing far fewer addicting drugs, while labeling laws made it possible to avoid proprietary medicines containing such substances. As the incidence of middle-class use declined, reformers in cities across America turned their attention to the legal but nonmedical use of drugs by the immigrant poor. In 1904, HULL HOUSE settlement workers, alerted to the use of cocaine by adolescent boys living in the surrounding NEAR WEST SIDE, organized to pass and enforce laws controlling druggists' dispensing of narcotics and cocaine. Their success in shutting off this quasi-legal supply of drugs drove recreational drug users to the vice districts—the Levee, along North Clark Street, and west of Hull House—where an UNDERGROUND trade developed to serve them. After public outrage caused the Levee to be shut down in 1912, the illicit drug trade migrated to the BLACK BELT, which by the 1920s hosted a booming commercial LEISURE district centered in the vicinity of 35th and State Streets.

Increasingly aggressive regulation of narcotics and cocaine in the 1910s and 1920s caused habitual users to turn to more potent and efficient forms of their preferred drugs. Opium smokers switched to oral and then injectable opiates, usually morphine, while cocaine users moved from sniffing to injecting the drug, often in combination with morphine. PROHIBITION also accelerated changes in patterns of euphoric-substance use. Enforcement of the Volstead Act diminished the prominence of all-male saloons and unintentionally encouraged the development of more expensive speakeasies patronized by men and women. After repeal, heterosocial drinking patterns persisted. Marijuana smoking, introduced into the city in the 1920s by MEXICAN immigrants seeking work in the steel mills, became popular among youths seeking a cheap alternative to alcohol during Prohibition. White visitors "slumming" in the Black Belt entertainment district could also visit "teapads" or "reefer dens."

Given the concentration of the illicit drug trade in the Black Belt, AFRICAN AMERICANS appeared relatively infrequently in narcotics arrest statistics. By the early 1930s, the average Chicago narcotics addict was a poor, native-born, white adult male over the age of 30 who injected morphine under the skin. Only a few used heroin or cocaine. By 1952, however, most addicts in Chicago injected heroin rather than morphine, and one-third were under the age of 21. A large proportion were the sons of recent migrants to the city and lived in the poorest neighborhoods in the city. Narcotics use among black Chicagoans did not become a public concern until the late 1960s.

Katherine A. Chavigny

See also: Lager Beer Riot; Public Health; Sunday Closings

Further reading: Dai, Bingham. *Opium Addiction in Chicago.* 1937; 1970. • Duis, Perry. *The Saloon: Public Drinking in Chicago and Boston, 1880–1920.* 1983. • Spillane, Joseph. "The Making of an Underground Market: Drug Selling in Chicago, 1900–1940." *Journal of Social History* 32.1 (1998): 27–39.

Dune Acres, IN, Porter County, 32 miles SE of the Loop. Dune Acres, platted in 1923, was envisioned as an exclusive, year-round shore-line community akin to those found along Illinois' north shore. By the 1930s it had quickly become a recreational community of summer homes, many owned by Chicagoans, with few permanent residents. It is now surrounded by the INDIANA DUNES National Lakeshore.

Peggy Tuck Sinko

See also: Lake County, IN; Metropolitan Growth; Vacation Spots

Further reading: Engel, J. Ronald. *Sacred Sands: The Struggle for Community in the Indiana Dunes.* 1983. • Moore, Powell A. *The Calumet Region, Indiana's Last Frontier.* 1977.

Dune System. Although many Chicagoans think of dunes as north or southeast of the city, Chicago itself was built upon dunes. The sand dunes formed after the retreat of the Wisconsin glacier, when sand was abundant and various stages of Lake Chicago, the ancestral LAKE MICHIGAN, were created. Successively lower lake levels formed the Glenwood (14,500–12,200 years before present [YBP]), Calumet (11,800–10,200 YBP), Toleston (<6,300 YBP), and younger dunes. Dunes formed when lake levels were low and eroded when lake levels were high. Dunes at Illinois Beach State Park and SOUTH CHICAGO/GARY are less than 5,000 years old, low in height, and often form linear alternating dunes and wetland depressions called swales. These are low because shoreward movement of sand can occur only when winds are out of the northeast in a region where the prevailing winds are westerly. In contrast, the dunes to the east in Indiana progressively increase in elevation, to

Dunes on South Chicago beach, ca. 1898. Photographer: Unknown. Source: Chicago Historical Society.

212 feet above the lake, as the shoreline curves around to face the prevailing northwest winds. Winter storm winds can pile much sand inland.

Dunes in the Chicago region played an important role in the history of ecology. In the late 1890s, Henry Chandler Cowles discovered the interaction between the geological processes and vegetation development that produced dunes. He studied the process of dune succession whereby a series of different PLANT COMMUNITIES developed over time as dunes built up and became stabilized. For instance, foredunes, the first low dunes to develop above the beach, are often stabilized and increase in height as beach grass (*Ammophila breviligulata*) or cottonwood (*Populus deltoides*) colonizes the sand. The ability of beach grass shoots to grow upward and rhizomes to grow sideways in lines allows the capture of sand and the increase in dune elevation. Likewise, cottonwood can grow upward as it is buried because new roots can sprout from its buried trunk. After the foredune stabilizes, these pioneer plants increase the richness of the soil by depositing and trapping litter. In the early 1950s, Jerry Olson demonstrated that most of the soil development occurs in the first 2,000 years of the dune. Soil enrichment and disturbances then promote the invasion of little bluestem grass (*Schizachyrium scoparius*) and plants such as old field goldenrod, puccoon, sand cherry, and milkweed. Later, jack pines and oaks invade, creating wooded communities. Through the process of succession, much of the older and higher dunes are covered with prairie, oak savanna, woodland, or forest. Dune formation today is limited to where there is abundant sand supply that has not been interrupted by docks, harbors, or fill that blocks the sand movement along the lake and where human disturbance does not hinder the growth of vegetation.

Beaches were important travel routes for Native Americans and early Euro-American settlers, because of the ease of travel, although mosquitoes and sudden storms could make travel uncomfortable or dangerous. Native Americans used dune plants for various purposes including puccoon roots (*Lithospermum caroliniense*) to produce red dye. After settlement, the dunes were an important source of raw materials. In the 1850s white pines were cut from the Indiana Dunes to build the growing metropolis. Later the dunes were a source of sand for fill and construction to expand Chicago and locations for home and industrial development.

Many Chicagoans, including Cowles, Jens Jensen, Stephen Mather, and members of the Prairie Club, found recreation and spiritual renewal in the dunes. On June 3, 1917, the Historical Pageant and Masque of the Sand Dunes of Indiana took place at the present INDIANA DUNES State Park. This drama celebrated and symbolized the spiritually enriching beauty and timelessness of the dunes. Through their efforts a movement was born to protect and preserve the dunes. Perhaps saddest was the destruction in 1963 of Dunes Park, where Cowles did much of his research, to construct a modern steel manufacturing complex. Ironically, this made it possible for Senator Paul Douglas, who lamented the loss, to succeed in passing a bill in Congress in 1966 to establish the Indiana Dunes National Lakeshore.

Noel B. Pavlovic

See also: Ecosystem Evolution; Glaciation; Lumber; Topography

Further reading: Chrzastowski, M. J., and T. A. Thompson. "Late Wisconsinan and Holocene Coastal Evolution of the Southern Shore of Lake Michigan." In *Quaternary Coasts of the United States: Marine and Lacustrine Systems,* ed. Charles H. Fletcher III and John F. Wehmiller, 1992, 397–413. • Cowles, H. C. "The Ecological Relations of the Vegetation on the Sand Dunes of Lake Michigan." *Botanical Gazette* (1899): 27, 95–117, 167–202, 281–308, 361–388. • Fraser, G. S., C. E. Larsen, and N. C. Hester. "Climatic Control of Lake Levels in the Lake Michigan and Lake Huron Basins." In *Late Quaternary History of the Lake Michigan Basin,* ed. Allan F. Schneider and Gordon S. Fraser, 1990, 75–89.

Dunning, Community Area 17, 10 miles NW of the Loop. In 1851 this remote prairie location seemed ideal for COOK COUNTY'S plans to erect a poor farm and asylum for the insane. The county purchased from Peter Ludby 160 acres hemmed in by Irving Park Road and Narragansett, Montrose, and Oak Park Avenues. Both facilities were housed in a three-story building situated atop a ridge.

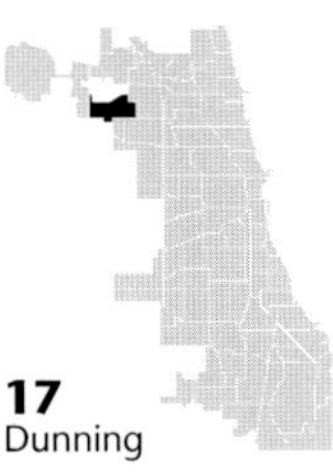

Residents of the poor farm lived with their families growing vegetables, washing their clothes, and attending school on the premises. After 1863 the institution also admitted TUBERCULOSIS patients. The county built a separate building for the insane asylum in 1870. The construction of two more buildings in the 1880s added enough space to accommodate the more than 1,000 patients.

Following the CIVIL WAR, Andrew Dunning purchased 120 acres just south of the county property to start a nursery and lay the groundwork for a village. He set aside 40 acres for the settlement, but proximity to the insane hospital kept settlers away.

Initially TRANSPORTATION links were poor. Although trains brought employees and COMMUTERS from the city, visitors had to walk two and a half miles from the depot to the county farm. After a single three-mile track was extended to the facilities in 1882, the Chicago, Milwaukee & St. Paul "crazy train" brought patients, supplies, and medicines. The county built a station, naming it for Dunning.

In the 1880s and 1890s Dunning's rolling landscape remained sparsely settled. The Scandinavian Lutheran CEMETERY Association bought 65 acres south of Dunning's property in 1886 which became Mount Olive Cemetery. JEWISH families purchased 40 acres between the Scandinavian cemetery and Addison for burials.

Around the turn of the century Henry Kolze inherited a tavern and wooded acreage at Narragansett and Irving Park which he turned into a picnic grove. The idyllic scenery enticed visitors, as did the tavern. With the advent of the Irving Park Boulevard STREET RAILWAY, clubs, churches, and companies held picnics in the grove.

The infirmary, poorhouse, and asylum eventually became overcrowded. Minimal heat in winter, no hot water, and poor ventilation

A picnic grove called the Elm Tree Grove, on West Irving Park Boulevard, 1908. Photographer: Curt Teich & Co. Source: Curt Teich Archives, Lake County Discovery Museum.

contributed to the deaths of many patients and inmates. In 1886 an official investigation found misconduct, gambling, patient abuse, and "influence" in the hiring of medical personnel. After 1910 the poor farm was moved to OAK FOREST, and two years later the state bought the mental hospital and property for one dollar. Although it was called the Chicago State Hospital, many continued to refer to the institution simply as Dunning.

Outside the state facility, the population had grown to only 1,305 by 1909. In 1916 the first housing boom occurred when Schorsch Brothers Real Estate bought a tract west of Austin and south of Irving Park. They called the area West PORTAGE PARK to remove the stigma of association with Dunning.

Following WORLD WAR I the population rose to 4,019, with residents primarily of SWEDISH, GERMAN, and POLISH descent. In 1934 Wright Junior COLLEGE was built in the eastern portion. At its peak in 1970 population reached 43,856 but fell to 36,957 by 1990. The State Hospital property stood in shambles and in the 1970s nearly half the buildings were razed. In that year, the Chicago-Read MENTAL HEALTH Center was established, incorporating the old hospitals.

Dunning moved toward a revival of institutional, commercial, and residential growth in the 1980s and 1990s. The neighborhoods of Schorsch Village, Belmont Heights, Belmont Terrace, and Irving Woods became more desirable. On Narragansett, north of Irving Park, Ridgemoor Estates boasted luxury homes near a GOLF club. New modern facilities were present at Chicago-Read Mental Health Center. Wright Junior College expanded with futuristic-style buildings and a learning resource center at Narragansett and Montrose. By 2000 the population had grown again, to 42,164.

Marilyn Elizabeth Perry

See also: Almshouses; Social Services

Further reading: Johnson, Charles B. *Growth of Cook County,* vol. 1. 1960. • Ryan, David Joseph. "The Development of Portage Park from the Earliest Period to the 1920s." Senior History Seminar, Northwestern University. May 24, 1974. • State Commissioners of Public Charities. *Special Report of an Investigation of the Management of the Cook County Hospital for the Insane.* 1886.

DuPage County. Taking its name from the DUPAGE RIVER, DuPage was established as a separate county from part of COOK COUNTY in 1839, with NAPERVILLE as the county seat. In 1850, DuPage County was organized into nine TOWNSHIPS, through the efforts of state legislator Warren Wheaton (1849–1851). An 1857 attempt to relocate the county seat to WHEATON because of its more central location was defeated, but 10 years later the referendum succeeded in a close election. Naperville resisted turning over the county records, which resulted in a midnight raid by a contingent of CIVIL WAR veterans from Wheaton and Danby (now GLEN ELLYN).

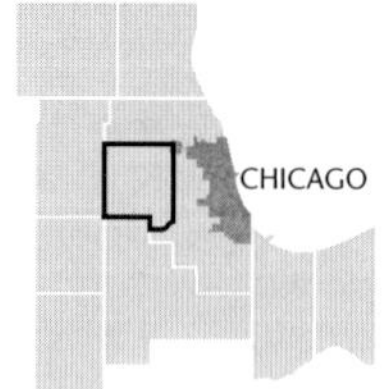

Throughout its history, DuPage County's growth and development have been linked to Chicago and to TRANSPORTATION routes in northern Illinois. When American settlers began arriving in the 1830s, the area that would become DuPage County was already crisscrossed by Indian trails. By 1800 the POTAWATOMI Indians had established four major villages along local rivers. In the 1830s stage routes radiating out of Chicago were established, with way stations in the area of the DuPage River. The first Euro-American settlers in the area were Bailey and Clarissa Hobson and their five children, who came from Orange County, Indiana, by 1832. Hobson built a gristmill on the West Branch of the DuPage River, near present-day Hobson Road, in Naperville. After the 1833 Treaty of Chicago forced the Indians to move west of the Mississippi River, white settlement accelerated. During the 1830s and 1840s, newcomers first claimed land along the branches of the DuPage River and then filled in across the prairies.

As Chicago became a central commercial point for the resources of a wide region, vital transportation routes passed through the area in transit to and from Chicago. In 1836 construction began on the ILLINOIS & MICHIGAN CANAL, which in 1848 linked LAKE MICHIGAN to the Illinois River. Many IRISH immigrants came to work on the I&M Canal and later settled in DuPage County. In the 1840s and '50s plank roads were built, established as private toll roads. The most significant development in transportation was the construction of RAILROADS, beginning in 1848 with the Galena & Chicago Union Railroad. Six railroads and an INTERURBAN line would enter DuPage by the early 1900s. Irish, ENGLISH, GERMANS, ITALIANS, MEXICANS, and AFRICAN AMERICANS came to work on these rail lines and stayed to live in DuPage County.

Chicago grew to be the Midwest's great rail center, with links to the east and west helping to create regional and national markets. DuPage County, by its opportune location, continued both to contribute to this development and to benefit from it. These railroads were most concerned with freight traffic. AGRICULTURAL products and other raw materials from a national market flowed into Chicago, and manufactured goods flowed out. DuPage County contributed grain, produce, livestock, dairy, and other products, which helped to sustain Chicago's population and industry and brought wealth and prosperity to DuPage. NEWSPAPERS and mail now arrived by rail, and TELEGRAPH lines followed the tracks, making the spread of news seem almost instantaneous. Railroad lines with stops in the county offered passenger service, and residents could easily go to Chicago to shop, socialize, or enjoy cultural activities. COMMUTER train service was added between the 1880s and 1910s. Then, as now, the benefits of country or suburban life, with proximity to Chicago, made living in DuPage County attractive. But the county remained primarily agricultural until the decade after WORLD WAR II.

In the 1940s and '50s transportation once again changed the face of DuPage County and led to new developments, resulting in tremendous growth. In 1946 Chicago acquired land

Route 83 looking south across the East-West Tollway (I-88), 1974. Photographer: Unknown. Source: DuPage County Historical Museum.

for O'HARE AIRPORT, including a portion of northeast DuPage. O'Hare opened in 1955 and by 1962 had become the main airport for the Chicago area. In 1958 the era of EXPRESSWAYS and interstates arrived with the completion of the East-West TOLLWAY (now I-88) and the portion of the Tri-State (I-294) that borders DuPage County on the east.

This improved transportation network helped to attract scientific and business developments. In 1947 the Atomic Energy Commission acquired a tract of 3,667 acres in DuPage County as a site for ARGONNE NATIONAL LABORATORY. FERMI National Accelerator Laboratory, the world's most powerful particle accelerator, was established on 6,800 acres (80 percent in DuPage County) and began operating in 1973. In 1958 OAK BROOK, a planned community divided into residential, commercial, industrial, and recreational zones, was incorporated. Chosen for its strategic location near the intersections of I-88, I-294, and Route 83 (the main north-south road at the time) and proximity to O'Hare Airport, Oak Brook contributed to the perception of and growth of DuPage County as a center for business. By the 1980s DuPage touted its Research and Development Corridor along the East-West Tollway as a research and commercial center.

By 2000 more people were COMMUTING into DuPage County for work (256,617) than were commuting out (191,439). The number of DuPage residents who stayed within the county for their work (277,934) had increased, a trend that has continued since 1970.

By 1995, only 5 percent of DuPage's land was identified for agricultural use. By 2000 the county's population had surpassed 900,000. Naperville, now DuPage County's most populous community, has developed into an "edge city."

Steph McGrath

See also: Agriculture; Metropolitan Growth

DuPage River. The 84-mile DuPage River drains most of DUPAGE and western WILL counties, one of the most rapidly developing areas in the Chicago region. This sprawling development tends to degrade the stream and its watershed. Nonetheless, the DuPage River, largest tributary of the DES PLAINES, remains quite a beautiful stream.

The DuPage has two branches. The shallow eastern branch flows through the MORTON ARBORETUM and has not been developed for canoeing. The west branch is an active water trail and passes through FOREST PRESERVES and wooded areas. There are five dams on the west branch, and the stone cascade of WARRENVILLE Dam creates a natural-looking waterfall. The west branch winds through NAPERVILLE, where an attractive riverwalk borders the stream. A dam near CHANNAHON creates a slack water pool where the ILLINOIS & MICHIGAN CANAL crosses the DuPage. The last mile above the confluence with the Des Plaines is a haven for bass fishing.

David M. Solzman

See also: Landscape; Riverine Systems

Further reading: Northeastern Illinois Planning Commission, Openlands Project, Illinois Paddling Council, eds. *Northeastern Illinois Regional Water Trails: Map and Plan Summary.* 1999.

DuSable Museum. The DuSable Museum of African American History is devoted to the history, ART, and culture of the African diaspora. A pioneer among a group of black cultural museums that emerged during the CIVIL RIGHTS MOVEMENT of the mid-twentieth century, it began as the Ebony Museum, and then the Museum of Negro History and Art. The museum's first site was in the home of its founders, artist/educator Margaret Goss Burroughs and her husband Charles Burroughs, whose historic SOUTH SIDE mansion had once been a boardinghouse for AFRICAN AMERICAN railroad workers. During the early 1960s the fledgling museum and the South Side Community Art Center across Michigan Avenue created a small black cultural corridor.

Upon moving to its current home, a former Chicago PARK DISTRICT facility in WASHINGTON PARK, in 1973, the museum was renamed in honor of Chicago's first permanent nonnative settler, Jean Baptiste Point DuSable, an Afro-French trader. An interracial group of educators and activists that included Eugene Pieter Feldman, Gerard Lew, Marian Hadly, Ralph Turner, James O'Kennard, and Wilbur Jones played a central role in the museum's early development. The DuSable quickly became a resource for teaching African American history and culture and a focal point in Chicago for black social activism, particularly because of limited cultural resources then available to Chicago's large black population. Through the years, the museum has served as nerve center for political fundraisers, community festivals, and social and civic events serving the black community. The museum and its founder, Margaret Burroughs, rose to national prominence, and its model has been replicated in other cities around the country, including Boston, Los Angeles, and Philadelphia.

DuSable's holdings have developed largely from private gifts. These include slave-era relics, nineteenth- and twentieth-century artifacts, archival materials such as the diaries of sea explorer Captain Harry Dean, and letters, photographs, and memorabilia of scholar W. E. B. Du Bois, sociologist St. Clair Drake, and poet Langston Hughes. The significant African American art collection includes work by Charles White, Archibald Motley, Jr., Charles Sebree, and Marion Perkins (all of whom studied at the South Side Community Art Center), and numerous works from the WPA period and the 1960s Black Arts Movement. In addition to traditional African art and numerous prints and drawings, the museum owns works by noted artists Henry O. Tanner, Richmond Barthé, and Romare Bearden.

It also has an extensive collection of books and records on African and African American history and culture.

The museum, which receives partial support through the publicly funded PARK DISTRICT tax levy, added the Harold Washington Wing, with additional galleries and a theater, in 1993. It has continued to mount exhibitions, host lectures, festivals, performing arts, and film programs, and provide educational services for students and teachers.

Amina J. Dickerson

See also: Chicago Historical Society; City as Artifact; Mexican Fine Arts Center Museum; Museums in the Park; Nommo

Further reading: Feldman, Eugene Pieter Romayn. *The Birth and the Building of the DuSable Museum.* 1981. • Walker, Lillian O. "A History of the DuSable Museum of African American History and Art." M.A. thesis, Governors State University. 1977. • Williams, Carline Evone Strong. "Margaret Taylor Goss Burroughs: Educator, Artist, Author, Founder, and Civic Leader." Ph.D. diss., Loyola University of Chicago. 1994.

Pageant at Chicago Commons settlement house, 1924. Photographer: Unknown. Source: Chicago Historical Society.

Dutch. The Dutch stand among the first European ethnic groups to settle in the Chicago area. Through the years they left the Netherlands in search of opportunities that were disappearing or unavailable to them at home. Initial Dutch immigration to Chicago, beginning as early as 1839 as part of a wider influx to the Midwest, combined desires to pursue AGRICULTURE, to recreate traditional social structures, and to maintain religious beliefs. Later, urban jobs provided the main attraction for Dutch emigrants.

In the mid-nineteenth century, the middle-to-lower-class PROTESTANT, rural, Dutch immigrants who moved to and around Chicago established three distinct communities that recreated the cultural, social, and geographical patterns of the Netherlands. The first two were agricultural enclaves: in 1846, near Lake CALUMET, Zuid (South) Hollanders founded Lage (Low) Prairie, later known as SOUTH HOLLAND; and in 1849, a few miles to the north, Noord Hollanders settled Hooge (High) Prairie, later known as ROSELAND. The third settlement, just west of the city center, became known as the Groningsche Hoek (Groningen Quarter) as immigrants from the Groningen Province increasingly settled there.

These communities reflected both the provinciality and the diversity of the homeland while expressing the strong Dutch attachment to place of origin, along with their desire to retain the familiar in their lives. Designed as separate and segregated enclaves, they could not stay isolated for long.

As Chicago grew, Dutch solidarity came under pressure. By the 1880s and 1890s, the crush of immigration from other parts of Europe threatened the NEAR WEST SIDE community. Many Groningen Quarter residents sold their holdings and fled to less congested areas. Some reestablished a community a little further to the west in the Douglas Park–NORTH LAWNDALE area, while others moved to the newly established Dutch community in ENGLEWOOD. Still others left for the suburbs of BELLWOOD, MAYWOOD, and SUMMIT to pursue truck farming. At the same time, industrialization took its toll on Dutch autonomy, especially in the Roseland settlement. Industries such as the Pullman Palace Car Company, International Harvester, and the ILLINOIS CENTRAL RAILROAD competed for open land and attracted thousands of Southern European immigrants to the area. Like the West Siders, many Roselanders sold and moved to areas that still afforded a rural setting, particularly South Holland and nearby Indiana. Others decided to remain, accepting and adapting to the new order and flavor of urban life.

Between WORLD WAR I and WORLD WAR II, competition for living space from newly arrived ethnic groups once again prompted a move for the West Side Dutch, this time to the suburbs of CICERO, BERWYN, and OAK PARK. Following World War II, they ventured into the far western suburbs, while many members of the Roseland and Englewood communities joined in the flight from the city by migrating to nearby south and southwestern suburbs.

Despite these migrations, Chicago's Dutch preserved their ethnic identity and promoted cohesiveness through religion, marriage, social CLUBS, and geographic proximity. Religious beliefs proved the strongest bond. Churches and Christian schools formed the institutional focus and remain hallmarks of the Dutch presence. Most early Dutch immigrants belonged to either the Reformed Church or its rival offshoot, the Christian Reformed Church, though later in the century ROMAN CATHOLIC and SOCIALIST Dutch immigrants would challenge the hegemony of these institutions.

Chicago's Dutch earned their livings in numerous ways. Most early immigrants were farmers, first in self-sufficient operations, then as truck farmers supplying the city with fresh produce. General farming gave way to specialized pursuits such as onion and melon raising. Agriculture, however, grew increasingly less important as the city and its industries expanded. Factory work proved attractive to late-nineteenth-century immigrants, who found employment in the PULLMAN works, as well as the RAILROADS, steel plants, and other industries that moved to the Roseland area. Capitalizing on the explosive growth of Chicago, the Dutch also branched out into service industries. South Siders entered the BUILDING TRADES as independent entrepreneurs, while West Siders' familiarity with handling animals led to jobs as TEAMSTERS and refuse haulers. The West Side Dutch dominated the city's commercial refuse business, later expanding into the suburbs. Others sustained local economies, operating small retail shops and providing services for the Dutch communities.

The Dutch reached their high point as a percentage of the population in the earliest stages of their migration. Initially arriving as families, the small nuclei of settlers expanded slowly, and their growth rate fell well behind that of the other immigrant groups, though by 1920, Roseland's Dutch population had increased to approximately 8,750, making it the largest Dutch enclave in the city. Nevertheless, the Dutch accounted for less than 1 percent of Chicago's total population by this time. Twentieth-century immigration from Holland to Chicago has been limited, though the Chicago community remained active into the 1920s, scouting out prospective sites for Dutch settlement in as faraway places as South Dakota and Texas.

Despite slow population growth, dispersion, and apparent assimilation, the Dutch presence in Chicago remains resilient. Pockets of Dutch ancestry still inhabit their traditional spaces, marking their presence with place-names, dedicated CEMETERY sections, churches, and Dutch-supported retirement homes and schools. A fitting symbol of the continuing Dutch influence is TRINITY CHRISTIAN COLLEGE in suburban PALOS HEIGHTS. Established in 1959 by members from the Reformed Church community, this nondenominational institution presently houses the Dutch Heritage Center, a library and research facility for Dutch history in the Chicago area. This institution reflects the active Dutch ethnic consciousness that takes pride in its long association with metropolitan Chicago.

Jonathan J. Keyes

See also: Demography; Iron and Steel; Multicentered Chicago; Protestants; Religious Institutions; Waste Disposal

Further reading: Rowlands, Marie K. *Down an Indian Trail in 1849: The Story of Roseland.* 1987. • Swierenga, Robert P. "Dutch." In *The Harvard Encyclopedia of American Ethnic Groups.* 1980. • Vandenbosch, Amry. *The Dutch Communities of Chicago.* 1927.

Dyer, IN, Lake County, 27 miles S of the Loop. Dyer's beginnings can be traced back as early as 1838, when the State Line House was built facing Old Sauk Trail. In 1857, Philadelphia book publisher Aaron Hart purchased several thousand acres of government land in northwestern LAKE COUNTY at $1.25 per acre—possibly as much as 17,000 acres—in what now comprises GRIFFITH, Dyer, SCHERERVILLE, and HIGHLAND. Hart married Martha Dyer, who is the town's namesake. That year, the Michigan Central RAILROAD established a station at Dyer and built a grain elevator nearby, attracting farmers from as far as 30 miles away.

Within 10 years, a HARDWARE store, a furniture store, a door and blind factory, a distilling plant, and other stores were located near the railroad station. The Louisville & New Albany Railroad ran through the town in 1882, giving Dyer its second railroad and attracting more businesses, including a pickle and sauerkraut factory, a flour mill, a harness shop, a tin shop, and the First National Bank. In the early 1900s, the town had schools, churches, seven SALOONS, two GROCERY STORES, and the county's first Ford automobile agency, Fitch Brothers. The population reached 545 by 1910.

The citizens of Dyer voted to incorporate the town in 1910. In 1915, the Municipal WATER Utility was established to service the main part of the town, and the establishment of the FIRE department soon followed. In 1942, Mount Mercy Sanitarium was founded.

As veterans and their families moved to Dyer after WORLD WAR II, the population climbed. Growth continued and a special census in 1968 showed 4,496 people in Dyer. A small SHOPPING DISTRICT debuted in 1969, followed by the construction of a major APARTMENT complex in 1970. The Dyer Park and Recreation Board, established in 1971, dedicated the Northgate Park in 1974. By 1990, the population had reached 10,923. Three years later, some downtown businesses had to relocate to accommodate a $9 million U.S. 30 reconstruction project. New housing increased after problems with the town's wastewater treatment plant were solved. The 2000 population grew to 13,895. Many of the new residents came from Illinois seeking a quiet suburban community near Chicago. The sanitarium founded in the 1940s, now called St. Margaret Mercy Healthcare Centers, is Dyer's largest employer.

Jennifer Mrozowski

See also: Metropolitan Growth; Transportation

Further reading: Moore, Powell A. *The Calumet Region.* 1959. • *Town of Dyer Bicentennial Book.* 1976.

Dziennik Związkowy. The Polish National Alliance established the *Dziennik Związkowy* (Alliance Daily) in 1908 with Francis Jablonski as its editor. Eventually Chicago's largest POLISH-language NEWSPAPER, it brought its readers local news as well as extensive coverage of issues relating to Poland, including American policies. During WORLD WAR I, the paper supported President Woodrow Wilson's policy of national self-determination for Poland. It promoted the Polish National Fund (Fundusz Narodowy Polski), which raised several million dollars for Polish war relief efforts. Under the editorship of Karol Piatkiewicz (1931–1967), the paper also worked tirelessly for Polish war relief in WORLD WAR II.

Dziennik Związkowy broke with President Franklin Roosevelt in its fierce opposition to the 1945 Yalta Pact. It maintained its militant Cold War stance until the mid-1960s, when its emphasis shifted to strengthening America's and Chicago's Polish communities. Between 1978 and 1990, under the editorial leadership of Jan Krawiec (1968–1985), Anna Rychlinska (1985–1989), and Wojciech Bialaszewicz (1989–), the paper devoted extensive coverage to Pope John Paul II, formerly archbishop of Krakow, and to the activities of Solidarity. By the end of the twentieth century, *Dziennik Związkowy* still reached 25,000 subscribers in the greater Chicago area.

Joseph John Parot

See also: Cold War and Anti-Communism; Press: Neighborhood Press

Further reading: Parot, Joseph John. *Polish Catholics in Chicago, 1850–1920: A Religious History.* 1981. • Pienkos, Donald E. *PNA: A Centennial History of the Polish National Alliance of the United States of North America.* 1984. • *Polish American Studies.* Vols. 1–58. 1942–2001.

E

East Chicago, IN, Lake County, 19 miles SE of the Loop. East Chicago became a leading industrial center by capitalizing on the resources of its metropolitan namesake and its proximity to LAKE MICHIGAN and the CALUMET RIVER. Mills and factory jobs drew tens of thousands of migrants to the region in the 1910s and 1920s. The town grew to the fringes of WHITING, HAMMOND, and GARY, eventually covering more than 12 square miles.

The POTAWATOMI hunted East Chicago's white pine and oak forests and fished its grassy riverways. In 1854, George W. Clark, a farsighted civil engineer connected with RAILROADS, began accumulating land along Lake Michigan. In 1881 a British investment firm bought a parcel of Clark's land, and platting of the SUBDIVISION of East Chicago began in 1888. That same year, the Chicago & Calumet Terminal Beltline (later the Baltimore & Ohio Railroad) linked the settlement to Chicago's trunk rail system. East Chicago incorporated as a town in 1889, and reincorporated as a city in 1893.

After 1901 two events transformed the city's fortunes. First, Inland Steel built a plant at Indiana Harbor, heralding the dawn of East Chicago as an industrial center. Second, in 1903 the East Chicago Company (ECC) took direct control of residential and municipal planning.

The ECC represented Chicago powerbrokers, including Potter Palmer, Jr., and Stanley McCormick. They recognized the need for a new industrial zone outside Chicago and invested heavily in municipal services, oversaw neighborhood planning, and dredged the Indiana Harbor Ship Canal. By 1907, East Chicago boasted a navigable waterway link to Lake Michigan and to the Grand Calumet River.

Enormous freighters, thousands of railcars, and massive pipelines eventually supplied coal, iron ore, limestone, oil, and other materials from around the nation for processing. Steel mills, petroleum REFINERIES, construction, manufacturing, and CHEMICAL factories operated at Indiana Harbor and along its inner canal system.

With immigrants from Eastern and Southern Europe flocking to its factory jobs, the population of East Chicago soared 460 percent between 1900 and 1910, from 3,411 to 19,098. Over 50 percent of the population were not native born. During WORLD WAR I, AFRICAN AMERICANS from the South, and MEXICANS from the Southwest and Mexico, joined the industrial labor force, lifting the population to 54,784 by 1930.

A rivalry developed between Indiana Harbor, the "East Side" home of Inland Steel and most working-class families, and East Chicago's "West Side," the residential enclave of the native-born business community. Locals spoke of the "Twin City" to describe spatial, residential, and class divisions at the heart of the town's identity.

In the 1920s, East Chicago carried a reputation as a freewheeling boomtown with a vibrant VICE DISTRICT and underground network of "blind tigers" serving bootleg liquor. In 1930, federal investigators indicted East Chicago mayor Raleigh Hale and police chief James W. Regan for conspiring to violate PROHIBITION, forcing both men to resign.

Religious practices fostered early community development through ethnic SOCIAL SERVICES and the building of St. Catherine HOSPITAL. By WORLD WAR II, 59 congregations reflecting the ethnic and cultural diversity of the population worshiped in East Chicago: 33 PROTESTANT, 16 ROMAN CATHOLIC, 8 Greek Orthodox, and 2 JEWISH.

After 1930, city growth slowed with only nominal increases, reaching a peak population of 57,669 in 1960. As East Chicago lost its job base in subsequent decades, population declined, to 32,414 in 2000.

Derek Vaillant

See also: Eastern Orthodox; Economic Geography; Environmental Politics; Greeks; Iron and Steel; Italians; Poles; Transportation

Further reading: *Calumet Region Historical Guide.* 1939.

East Dundee, IL, Kane County, 35 miles NW of the Loop. The land east of the FOX RIVER in what is now East Dundee was platted in 1837 for Thomas Deweese, who had laid claim to a large part of the area. Newcomers who settled there were unaware of Deweese's claims and either were forced to pay or were moved out by men hired by Deweese. In 1837 Deweese built a gristmill, and soon after was responsible for the installation of the first BRIDGE. In the 1850s, a large group of Lutheran GERMANS moved into the area. They erected a church and practiced their own traditions, which separated them from their largely SCOTTISH western neighbors.

Using clay from the riverbank, a brickyard started business in 1852. D. H. Haeger became part owner in 1871, the same year the village was incorporated; within a year he was sole owner and had extended the business to include tile. After the FIRE OF 1871, bricks were shipped into the city to help rebuild. By the 1920s the brickyard's production included teaware, luncheonware, and Royal Hickman crystal and glassware.

At the CENTURY OF PROGRESS Exposition in 1934 in Chicago, Haeger Potteries' exhibit included a complete working plant where souvenir pottery was made on the spot. The company, which passed to Haeger's great-grandchildren, employed 200 workers in 1985, most of whom were women. In the 1990s Haeger had a national sales base, attracting many shoppers to its factory, especially during its summertime tent sale.

A historic district along the Fox River and stores on Main Street constitute the commercial part of East Dundee. On Route 25 Santa's Village AMUSEMENT PARK provides rides and games for children.

Development of East Dundee has been slowed by a lack of land. The river is a barrier to the west, and HOFFMAN ESTATES, to the east. Referendums in 1956 and 1962 failed to unite East Dundee and West Dundee, which has prevented East Dundee from reaping any benefit from Spring Hill Mall to the west. Although the village has had limited land expansion, East Dundee's industry and commerce have grown, including the annexation of Rockroad Industrial Park in 1984–85 and the addition of the Spring Hill Ford auto dealership and a shopping center around 1990.

In 2000 population stood at 2,955, with 94 percent white and nearly 4 percent Hispanic. METRA rail service is located south of East Dundee in ELGIN.

Marilyn Elizabeth Perry

See also: Protestants; Quarrying, Stonecutting, and Brickmaking

Further reading: Bullinger, Carolyn J., ed. *Dundee Township, 1835–1985.* 1985. • Provisional League of Women Voters. *Fox Valley Four.* 1971.

East Garfield Park, Community Area 27, 4 miles W of the Loop. East Garfield Park was annexed to Chicago in 1869, but a quarter century elapsed before it was thickly populated. Its western section consisted of Central (GARFIELD) Park, one of three large West Side parks. The designation of the park in 1869 prompted a flurry of REAL-ESTATE dealing, but after subdividing the property south and east of the park for sale, developers provided neither buildings nor infrastructure. Intense trading lasted until the FIRE OF 1871, after which speculators looked outside the city, beyond the reach of the fire limits. Like the residential land, Central Park remained barren, as the corrupt West Park Board ignored William Le Baron Jenney's original designs. Not until 1905, under Jens Jensen's supervision, was the landscaping of Garfield Park undertaken. A few churches (Our Lady of Sorrows, Warren Avenue Congregational) and schools (Marshall) served the small population.

Unreliable TRANSPORTATION service further diminished the West Side's appeal to potential residents. Instead, the railroads that described East Garfield Park's northern, eastern, and southern boundaries attracted manufacturers expanding westward from the NEAR WEST SIDE at the turn of the century. The most notable of such industrial developments was the four-block-long Sears plant along the border with NORTH LAWNDALE. Commercial development likewise followed the tracks of the new Lake Street Elevated after 1893. Two-flats and small APARTMENT buildings were erected to house the population working in local industry. East Garfield Park's early residents were mostly IRISH and GERMAN. Later ITALIANS and Russian JEWS joined them. By 1914, modest homes, commercial buildings, and industry intermixed in East Garfield Park.

A brief postwar prosperity visited the area. The success of the Madison-Crawford SHOPPING DISTRICT in WEST GARFIELD PARK spilled eastward along Madison street. A high-class residential hotel, the Graemere, opened just east of Garfield Park. Flower Technical High School, a vocational school for Chicago's girls, moved from the SOUTH SIDE to 3545 Fulton in 1927. But during the GREAT DEPRESSION and WORLD WAR II, many homes were converted into smaller units, crammed with boarders, and allowed to deteriorate. By 1947, the area was so needy that the Daughters of Charity opened Marillac House at 2822 West Jackson to serve the local poor.

Although Marillac House's original clients were whites, East Garfield Park's racial composition soon began to change. The building of the Congress (Eisenhower) EXPRESSWAY during the 1950s displaced residents from a southern stretch of the neighborhood. AFRICAN AMERICANS, crowded out of the South and Near West Sides, bought and rented homes in East Garfield Park. Finally, a cluster of CHICAGO HOUSING AUTHORITY (CHA) projects—Harrison Courts, Maplewood Courts, and Rockwell Gardens—delineated the western edge of family PUBLIC HOUSING in Chicago and the eastern edge of East Garfield Park by 1960.

Physical conditions deteriorated: absentee landlords ignored tenants' requests for repairs, and vacant lots became increasingly common. At the same time, many institutions welcomed black participation. Warren Avenue Church and Central Presbyterian Church invited interracial membership. The Midwest Community Council sponsored block clubs and promoted URBAN RENEWAL. Marillac House created Neighbors at Work to teach organizing skills. The Institute of Cultural Affairs founded the Fifth City Human Development Project in 1963 to develop local leadership.

In 1966 Martin Luther King's northern CIVIL RIGHTS drive built antislum organizations in several neighborhoods. The East Garfield Park Union to End Slums led rent strikes and pickets against neglectful landlords. Participants also organized the East Garfield Park Cooperative to obtain groceries and housing. A coalition of residents and clergy successfully fended off the CHA's attempt to build more high-rise public housing, arguing that the area already had its share. This promising spurt of activism was undermined by rioting along Madison Street in 1968. Businesses left when they lost their insurance, and federal open-occupancy legislation enabled the dispersal of black residents who wished to leave. Burned buildings were not replaced, as both people and money flowed out of the area.

East Garfield Park lost more than two-thirds of its population to out-migration, from a high of 70,091 in 1950 to 20,881 in 2000. In the 1970s and 1980s, as endemic poverty and UNEMPLOYMENT overtook the area, a DRUG economy and associated criminal activity such as PROSTITUTION filled the economic void. Sporadic reinvestment included the expansion of Bethany Hospital, the building of Ike Sims Village for senior citizens, and the arrival of St. Stephen AME Church.

Amanda Seligman

See also: Contested Spaces; Housing Types; Landscape Design; Neighborhood Succession; Rapid Transit System

Further reading: Bennett, Larry. *Fragments of Cities: The New American Downtowns and Neighborhoods.* 1990. • East Garfield Park Community Collection. Department of Special Collections, Harold Washington Library, Chicago, IL. • *Local Community Fact Book* series.

East Hazel Crest, IL, Cook County, 21 miles S of the Loop. As south and southwest COOK COUNTY has exploded in growth in the past 30 years, East Hazel Crest has maintained its status as the smallest of the southern suburbs. Although it has several small industrial and commercial zones, East Hazel Crest is predominantly residential, with over 90 percent of its housing in single-family units.

The whole village is roughly four hundred acres in an area several blocks wide south of and paralleling Interstate 80. The Calumet stop on the METRA commuter line could be called the East Hazel Crest stop. Mostly east of the ILLINOIS CENTRAL RAILROAD, the village annexed an area west of the IC that includes a small commercial section and the subdivision of Bremerton Woods, which is generally thought of as part of HAZEL CREST.

East Hazel Crest was a part of Hazel Crest (east of the railroad line) when it was incorporated in 1911. When the IC raised its commuter and mainline tracks above grade level, residents felt even more isolated from most of Hazel Crest. In an effort to maintain their quiet, almost rural community, the residents voted for incorporation as their own village in 1918.

For many years, Washington Park racetrack stood south of East Hazel Crest. It was one of the most famous tracks in the metropolitan area and attracted huge crowds. In the 1940s, the owners sought ANNEXATION to the village if it would change its name to Washington Park. However, the small, tight-knit community was not interested.

Since its inception, the majority of the residents have worked in nearby industrial areas and the MARKHAM rail yards. The community has become racially diverse over the past 20 years. In 1990, 31 percent of its population was minority, rising to 48 percent in 2000.

Larry A. McClellan

See also: Government, Suburban; Horse Racing

Further reading: *Illinois Guide and Gazetteer.* 1969. • Rocke, Verva Coleman, ed.; Lucile Ross and Ileane Breslin, co-eds. *Living in Hazel Crest, 1890–1990.* 1990.

East Side, Community Area 52, 13 miles SE of the Loop. The modern history of the East Side was shaped by the entrance of heavy industry into the CALUMET area in the 1870s. Prior to this time, Native Americans had lived off the land, hunting and fishing for their food. Located just south of SOUTH CHICAGO and east of SOUTH DEERING, the region's natural port and its proximity to RAILROADS influenced many firms to locate in the area. Industry flourished, and by the 1920s the East Side, until then known by the names Taylorville, Goosetown, and Colehour, was significant for IRON AND STEEL production.

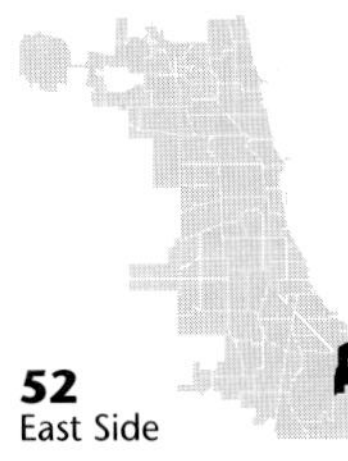

Consequently, settlement exploded. GERMANS and SWEDES established themselves in the late 1800s. The first religious congregation, the Colehour German Lutheran Church, opened in 1874, and a succession of congregations soon followed. CROATIAN, SLOVENE, and SERBIAN immigrants began to arrive in the 1880s, sparking the first signs of nationalist divisions. Germans and Swedes promoted their "American-ness" before their new neighbors. This symbolized a divisive trend that was to continue into the next century.

New settlers were quick to organize their own congregations. Croatians, specifically, formed the Sacred Heart parish at 96th and Escanaba. ITALIANS entered the area in 1914; together with the Slavs, they inhabited the older neighborhoods near the river. Shortly thereafter, Calumet Park was constructed; it influenced the eastward migration of the community. Today it is considered a great resource of the East Side, home to local athletics, a WATERFRONT, and other public entertainment.

The East Side's geography, bordered by water on three sides and shielded by miles of mills, is perhaps symbolic of its voluntary social isolation. The East Side has long been considered a suburb of South Chicago, and its residents have a profound sense of social cohesiveness; family and friendship ties tend to remain stable for many years. Ethnic cohesion has not always been so stable. As new immigrants entered the area after 1900, they often met with antagonism from the older inhabitants. Following WORLD WAR I, ethnic differences began to subside as immigration slowed and a process of AMERICANIZATION influenced the population. The attempted entry of AFRICAN AMERICANS into the area, however, produced particularly bitter and often violent resistance from East Siders. RACE RIOTS exploded at Calumet Park and in the nearby area of Trumbull Park in South Deering following attempts by African American families to move in after World War II. Between 1980 and 2000 the Hispanic population grew from 13 to 68 percent, and the area remained a predominantly working-class enclave.

Industrial conflict arising from the hegemony of local steel has plagued the area since the 1930s. Republic Steel had built a specialty plant, and was one of the area's chief employers. The Steel Workers Organizing Committee (SWOC) launched a campaign to organize the Republic steelworkers in 1937. Greatly supported by local IRON AND STEEL WORKERS, SWOC organized a MEMORIAL DAY march on the plant. As 1,000 people approached the mill gates, Chicago police ordered their retreat. The crowd capitulated, yet police began shooting at the strikers, killing 10 and maiming many more. The massacre sidetracked the drive for UNIONIZATION; Republic Steel was eventually organized in 1941. SWOC was transformed into the United Steelworkers of America in 1942.

The decline of the Chicago steel industry had profound effects on the East Side community. Calumet-area steel producers suffered greatly from depressed economic conditions and international competition. Republic Steel dismissed half its employees in the 1980s. In 1984, the company merged with Jones and Laughlin to form LTV Steel, becoming the country's second largest steel producer, but in 1986 LTV declared bankruptcy, closing operations in Chicago. Layoffs reverberated throughout the East Side, decimating the local economy. The population dropped by several thousand between 1970 and 1980. In 1982, the area became an official "enterprise zone," part of the city's effort to revitalize the local economy. These efforts have not proved very successful. Two decades later, the East Side remained an embattled and struggling community, attempting to recreate its sense of cohesion. In 2000 the Ford Motor Company announced plans to expand onto the site of the former Republic Steel.

David Bensman

See also: Economic Geography; Racism, Ethnicity, and White Identity; Work; Work Culture

Further reading: Bensman, David, and Roberta Lynch. *Rusted Dreams: Hard Times in a Steel Community.* 1988. • Kornblum, William. *Blue Collar Community.* 1974. • Taub, Richard P., et al. *Paths of Neighborhood Change: Race and Crime in Urban America.* 1984.

Eastern Orthodox. The term "Eastern Orthodox" usually refers to those Orthodox Christians who claim Hellenic, Slavic, or Arabic cultural traditions and adhere to the liturgies and customs of the ancient Byzantine church. Eastern Orthodox parishes generally have relied on ethnic identity as a significant organizing principle. Ecclesiastical organizations in the United States exist for ALBANIANS, BULGARIANS, BELARUSIANS, Carpatho-Rusyns, GREEKS, MACEDONIANS, ROMANIANS, RUSSIANS, SERBIANS, SYRIANS, and UKRAINIANS. The majority of Chicago's Eastern Orthodox congregations belong to either the Greek Orthodox Archdiocese of North and South America or the Orthodox Church in America (formerly the Russian Orthodox Greek Catholic Metropolia in North America) or enjoy autocephalous or autonomous status granted by the Ecumenical Patriarch of Constantinople. Some local groups still recognize the authority of church authorities in their countries of origin.

Groups of Greeks, Russians, and Serbs were the first Eastern Orthodox believers to establish permanent Eastern Orthodox churches in Chicago. The Russian population of the city established St. Vladimir's Russian Orthodox parish in 1892 and in 1903 built Holy Trinity Cathedral. The construction of the cathedral, designed by renowned architect Louis Sullivan, was facilitated by a $4,000 donation from Czar Nicholas II of Russia. Belarusians and Ukrainians, traditionally identified as "Russians" by American immigration officials in the early twentieth century, often joined Russian Orthodox parishes. Many Ukrainians, however, were Eastern Rite or Uniate Catholics (Eastern Christians who adhere to the Eastern liturgical tradition but acknowledge the spiritual primacy of the Roman Catholic pope) and soon began to establish their own Ukrainian Catholic parishes, beginning with St. Nicholas parish in 1905.

The city's earliest Greek and Serbian settlers were also quick to found their own ethnic parishes. Chicago's first Greek Orthodox parish, organized in 1892, met in rented quarters until it was able to build Annunciation Greek Orthodox Cathedral in 1910. Greek Orthodox adherents also established the parish of St. Constantine in 1909 on the city's SOUTH SIDE. St. Constantine's became one of the largest congregations in the Greek Orthodox Archdiocese of North and South America. Serbian immigrants living in WICKER PARK first worshipped at Holy Resurrection Church, built in 1905, until the parish moved to its current far Northwest Side location in the 1960s. By the 1970s, the number of Greek Orthodox parishes in the Chicago area had jumped to 28. The increase in Serbian parishes was slightly more modest—19 parishes were still in operation by the 1970s.

Later immigrant groups to Chicago also established their share of Eastern Orthodox churches. Albanians, Bulgarians, Romanians, Carpatho-Rusyns, and Macedonians all founded churches in Chicago. By the 1970s, there were 88 Eastern Orthodox parishes of various ethnic classifications in the city and its environs.

Eastern Orthodoxy's adaptation to modern American culture has not always been smooth. Devotees have left inner-city parishes for the suburbs and parishes have modified liturgical traditions to attract younger followers. Perhaps the most challenging development, however, has been the tendency among some Eastern Orthodox groups to separate from traditional ecclesiastical organizations. Parishes that have traditionally catered to adherents of Eastern European origin, such as Holy Nativity Romanian Orthodox Church on Chicago's far North Side, broke with church authorities in Communist-dominated homelands in the 1960s.

Brandon Johnson

See also: Religious Geography; Religious Institutions; Roman Catholic Archdiocese of Chicago

Further reading: Bezkorovainy, Anatoly, ed. *A History of Holy Trinity Russian Orthodox Cathedral of Chicago, 1892–1992.* 1992. • Bird, Thomas E. "Eastern Orthodox." In *Harvard Encyclopedia of American Ethnic Groups,* ed. Stephan Thernstrom, 1980. • The James Landing Papers. Special Collections, University Library, University of Illinois at Chicago.

Eastland. The steamer *Eastland,* immediately after loading an excursion of Western Electric employees for MICHIGAN CITY, Indiana, capsized into the CHICAGO RIVER on July 24, 1915, killing a reported 844 people—the worst disaster in loss of life in the city's history. The ship as built in 1903 was stable but did not meet specifications in speed and draft. Modifications in 1904 to correct those problems created a chronic problem of top-heaviness. The *Eastland* nearly capsized on July 17, 1904.

The *Titanic* disaster had produced a worldwide movement to increase the boat and raft capacity of ships relative to licensed passenger capacity. Owners who bought the *Eastland* in 1914 after the ship's service on Lake Erie did not inquire into its history. On July 2, 1915, they modified it with additional lifeboats and life rafts on its top deck. The ship capsized on the first occasion when it was loaded to its new licensed capacity.

George W. Hilton

See also: Lake Michigan; Sailing and Boating

Further reading: Hilton, George W. *Eastland: Legacy of the Titanic.* 1995.

Economic Geography. American cities grow or decline because of their roles in the national economy. The village of Chicago became the country's second largest city in 1889 because it captured many of the fastest-growing sectors of that economy. Businessmen and politicians enhanced Chicago's geographical position at the eastern edge of the nation's agricultural heartland, making it the center of multiple TRANSPORTATION networks. These supported wholesale trade and manufacturing which spurred the city's growth. Industry determined the physical development of the city itself, preempting space for zones of commerce and manufacturing and channeling the expansion of residential neighborhoods. During the twentieth century, new economic trends undermined Chicago's position; decentralization favored suburbs over cities, and the rise of the South and West created new centers of competition for the most dynamic sectors of the economy.

Chicago developed because its site was convenient for commerce. For hundreds of years, American Indians gathered each summer to trade where the CHICAGO RIVER enters LAKE MICHIGAN. In 1673 the French explorer Louis Jolliet recognized Chicago's potential for wider trade: it sits on a low divide between the drainage areas of the GREAT LAKES and the Mississippi River, and only one large portage breaks an all-water route between Lake Michigan and the Gulf of Mexico via the Chicago, DES PLAINES, Illinois, and Mississippi Rivers. During the rainy season, the "Chicago PORTAGE" between the Chicago and Des Plaines Rivers could be traversed by canoe. Jolliet suggested cutting a canal across this

This 1860s bird's-eye view of Union Stock Yard suggests the impact of industries on the residential geography of the city. Built on the unsettled prairie, the stockyards attracted hundreds of thousands of workers, whose homes transformed the empty land into residential neighborhoods that, in 1889, were annexed to the city of Chicago. Artist: James Washington Sheahan. Source: The Newberry Library.

portage to link the Gulf and French Canada, but French officials ignored him.

Chicago's first permanent resident, Jean Baptiste Point DuSable, settled near the mouth of the Chicago River in the late 1780s to take advantage of this geography to trade with the Indians. In 1795 the new United States government also recognized the site's potential and acquired a piece of land, six miles square around the mouth of the river, by Treaty with the Indians. Fort Dearborn, erected in 1803, secured the site for Americans. Trading eastern manufactured goods for furs established a base for Chicago's economy, consistent with DuSable's more limited enterprise. After 1819 the American Fur Company, headed by John Jacob Astor in New York, monopolized the fur trade of Chicago and the Great Lakes region. From this point, Chicago's economy was tied to national and international markets and financing. By the late 1820s, overhunting depopulated the game of Illinois, and the American Fur Company left Chicago for points farther west. Rather than wither, however, the village of fewer than a hundred residents began its rapid expansion as others saw new opportunities in the site.

Grain elevators and cargo ships on the Chicago River, before 1871. Photographer: J. Carbutt. Source: Chicago Historical Society.

National business and political leaders created the conditions for the rise of Chicago in order to develop the country's western territories. When New York's Erie Canal connected the Great Lakes to the Atlantic Ocean in 1825, they searched for a port at the western end of the lakes to serve the potential trade with new settlers. Eastern businessmen and Illinois politicians revived Jolliet's vision to connect the lakes to the Mississippi through Chicago, and, in 1829, state legislators began planning the Illinois & Michigan Canal.

For easterners to settle northern Illinois, however, the Indians had to be dispossessed. In 1833 the federal government pressured the united Potawatomi, Chippewa, and Ottawa nations to cede all their lands east of the Mississippi River, opening the path for easterners to seek their fortunes in northern Illinois.

Chicago had no natural harbor, but the sandbar at the mouth of the Chicago River created a sheltered spot for boats. The river became a federal harbor in 1834, when government aid for cutting a channel across the bar, constructing piers, and dredging made the river into the port of Chicago. The state authorized construction of a canal in 1836, and bonds sold well to eastern capitalists. From the mid-1830s, Chicago developed as a transfer point—shipping Midwestern agricultural products to New York and eastern manufactured goods to farmers on the plains.

While many people came to Chicago to engage in this trade, others came because they believed a city would develop around the port. Real-estate speculation fueled town development in nineteenth-century America and was an important avenue to wealth. Speculation in Chicago real estate boomed in 1835 in anticipation of the construction of the canal. Several thousand people, including many New Yorkers, migrated to the city. William B. Ogden, Chicago's first mayor, came to oversee a relative's real-estate investments and bolstered their value by developing transportation facilities. He promoted the first swing BRIDGE to span the Chicago River and link the North and South Sides of the city. In 1836 he helped found Chicago's first RAILROAD, the Galena & Chicago Union, to connect the port to the lead mining center on the Mississippi.

Although most Chicagoans were involved in trade or real-estate speculation, some established factories to process the farm produce and natural resources that were shipped to the city. In 1829, Archibald Clybourne began MEATPACKING, and a LUMBER mill settled near his factory on the North Branch of the Chicago River. The city's first manufacturing district developed there, with the river providing transportation and WASTE DISPOSAL.

The national economic depression of 1837 halted work on the canal and the railroad. Trade atrophied, and Chicago land values plummeted. In 1840, Chicago was a small city of more than four thousand people, with the outline of the transportation network that would make it the center of wholesale trade in the west. Once the national economy revived in the mid-1840s, Chicago's potential came to fruition.

1848 was a key year for the city—the canal was completed, the first railroad opened, the TELEGRAPH reached town, and the Chicago Board of Trade was founded. The canal facilitated trade in bulky goods, not only farm produce but also coal from southern Illinois to fuel the city's homes and industries. Initial plans called for a deep-cut canal to allow boats to pass directly from the lake to the river system, but lack of funds led supporters to settle for a narrow, shallow one. This reinforced Chicago's position as a transfer point where goods were switched from lake boats to barges. Traffic on the canal peaked in 1882. In the long run, Chicago's development as a rail hub was more important for its dominance in WHOLESALING.

Private companies built RAILROADS radiating out from Chicago in all directions to tap the farms of the Midwest. By 1856, 10 trunk railroads ended in Chicago, making the city a breakpoint for railroad traffic as well as waterborne trade. Tracks paralleled the river and canal to facilitate transfers of goods between railroad cars, canal barges, and lake ships. The wholesale traders set up along the river on South Water Street to direct this commerce. By 1854, Chicago claimed title as the greatest primary grain port in the world, and the grain elevators lining the river dominated the skyline. The grain trade grew rapidly as a national speculative futures market developed. The telegraph made such a market technologically feasible, but the Chicago Board of Trade made it a reality. It created standards and measures such as grades of wheat along with an elevator inspection system, giving eastern capitalists enough confidence to invest in grain sight unseen. The lumber trade also boomed, as lumber from the Midwestern woods was shipped by boat across the lake to be milled in the city. A huge lumber district, with sawmills and extensive storage yards, developed on the Chicago River's South Branch. After milling, the lumber was shipped by rail mostly to the west to build farmhouses, barns, and fences.

Chicago merchants combined wholesale and retail operations; they sent dry goods to small stores throughout the Midwest and kept stores in the city center for travelers and residents alike. The large retailers congregated on Lake Street, and Chicago's DEPARTMENT STORES developed as these establishments enlarged and diversified. The downtown rose around the wholesalers and retailers with HOTELS, RESTAURANTS, SALOONS, and less reputable businesses to service traveling men and conventioneers.

Although the wholesale trade was the most important element in Chicago's economy until the 1870s, industries for processing agricultural and raw materials also developed. Pork—salted, pickled, and otherwise preserved—was the primary product manufactured for easterners. At the same time, Chicago businessmen saw the potential of producing goods for farmers in Chicago rather than acting as middlemen for eastern manufacturers. In 1847 Cyrus H. McCormick opened his reaper works and initiated one of the city's most important industries—AGRICULTURAL MACHINERY.

The CIVIL WAR extended the advantages conferred by geography and human initiative. St. Louis, an older and larger city, was Chicago's rival for the western trade. Chicago's railroad network was making the city more attractive to shippers, but Union forces delivered the decisive blow to St. Louis when they closed the Mississippi River during the war. Trade that shifted to Chicago did not return to St. Louis after the war.

Contracts for supplies for the Union forces also stimulated Chicago enterprise, especially among the meatpackers. The packing plants, scattered around the city, had always been a nuisance because they created pollution. Now huge numbers of animals driven through the streets caused total congestion. Chicagoans wanted the plants moved, and the packers needed more space for pens and better access to railroads to minimize production delays. Chicago's first planned manufacturing district—the UNION STOCK YARD—opened in 1865 to solve these problems. The packers and the railroads chose a site just outside the city limits at 39th Street and Halsted Street. With access to the canal and major railroads, it was the prototype of future industrial developments that would move to the edge of the city in search of space and better transportation.

By the end of the Civil War, Chicago was poised to build on its dominance of Midwestern trade and its manufacturing base. Growth came quickly, as the completion of the transcontinental railroad enabled the vast expansion of Chicago's potential market. Federal subsidies underwrote this rapid development, in the form of land grants to railroads laying new track. Once again the joint efforts of politicians and businessmen secured Chicago's future. As the eastern terminus of important western railroads and the western terminus of eastern railroads, Chicago remained the central transfer point for people and freight. In the next decades, railroad building devoured more of Chicago's physical space, and rights-of-way guided the siting of industry and residences.

The Great FIRE OF 1871 decimated the center of the city, but it did not slow development. It spared most of the outlying areas, including the manufacturing district, the lumber district, the Union Stock Yard, the grain elevators, and the railroad freight terminals. This INFRASTRUCTURE supported the rapid rebuilding of the central business district and residential neighborhoods because it gave eastern investors who financed reconstruction confidence that the city would recover and investors would profit.

From 1870 to 1920 Chicago was "the metropolis of the west," the hub of transcontinental trade and the most dynamic center of manufacturing for the new national market. In the 1870s Gustavus Swift financed the development of the railroad refrigerator car, enabling meat butchered in Chicago to be shipped fresh to the East. He established sales offices and refrigerated warehouses in eastern cities and launched a national advertising campaign to overcome consumer fears about meat that was not butchered locally. Other newcomers to the city, like Philip D. Armour, followed his lead, until Chicago's "Big Five" packing companies controlled the nation's meatpacking industry. By 1900 these companies were expanding internationally, both exporting Chicago products and opening subsidiary plants abroad.

As production at the stockyards increased, the residential neighborhoods around the factories grew polluted and congested. The slums of Packingtown were peopled by poor workers, primarily immigrants from Central and Eastern Europe who struggled to support their families and sustain their cultural traditions. Large working-class neighborhoods characterized by INDUSTRIAL POLLUTION, congestion, poverty, and cultural diversity developed wherever industry located.

By 1890 Chicago had a population of more than one million people and had surpassed Philadelphia to become the second-largest city in the nation and the second-largest manufacturing center. The diversity as well as the size of its industries spurred this development. Manufacturing based on the trade in agricultural commodities, like BREWING and baking, flourished. The FURNITURE industry developed from the lumber trade; it prospered even after

Midwest Stock Exchange, 1940. Photographer: Kaufmann & Fabry. Source: Chicago Historical Society.

the woods of the northern Midwest had been decimated and the lumber trade declined in 1880s. Established industries like agricultural machinery also expanded as other manufacturers followed McCormick to Chicago. The creation of International Harvester from these companies in 1902 capped Chicago's leading position in this industry.

New industries such as IRON AND STEEL production also pushed Chicago ahead of other cities. The North Chicago Rolling Mill produced the city's first steel rails in 1865 but soon relocated to SOUTH CHICAGO. This move signaled not only its need for more space but also a new factor in the city's economic geography. The transcontinental railroads skirted the bottom of Lake Michigan, and production costs were minimized for manufacturers who obtained access to both lake boats and railroads by locating there. The new steel plant, which later became the United States Steel South Works, anchored the north end of the vast iron-and-steel-producing district that developed along the lake from South Chicago to GARY, INDIANA. Like the stockyards, it attracted workers, especially immigrants from Eastern and Southern Europe, and created new neighborhoods on the fringes of the city.

Industries that used iron and steel, including those that manufactured machinery, machine tools, and railroad cars and equipment, also developed, most frequently near the steelmaking district. George Pullman, who manufactured railcars, saw the potential of the area around Lake Calumet; major railroads ran nearby and the lake provided an inland harbor accessible to Lake Michigan by the CALUMET RIVER. He built the town of PULLMAN on the western edge of the lake in 1881 to house his workers and a new factory. Unlike most of Chicago's manufacturing districts, Pullman's model town was neither polluted nor congested. It became a tourist attraction—a vision of what people wished the city would be. No other manufacturers followed Pullman's lead in building decent neighborhoods, although others followed him to the CALUMET REGION. In 1889 and 1893 Chicago annexed all these suburban districts as well as extensive territory to the north, more than trebling its area.

Although the combination of space and transportation drew some industries to the edges of the city, many still found the resources of the old central city more useful. Garment manufacturing was one of Chicago's most important industries, and Chicago led the nation in the production of men's CLOTHING thanks to firms such as Hart, Schaffner, & Marx. Garment makers settled in lofts west of the downtown near Chicago's poorest neighborhoods, because the cheap labor of women and children was their most important requirement.

Perhaps the most important resource of the central city was the concentration of modes of communication. Chicago's PRINTING and publishing industry, second only to New York's, developed with companies such as R. R. Donnelley & Sons, which located near the downtown because of the demand for business

Chicago's Evolving Economic Geography

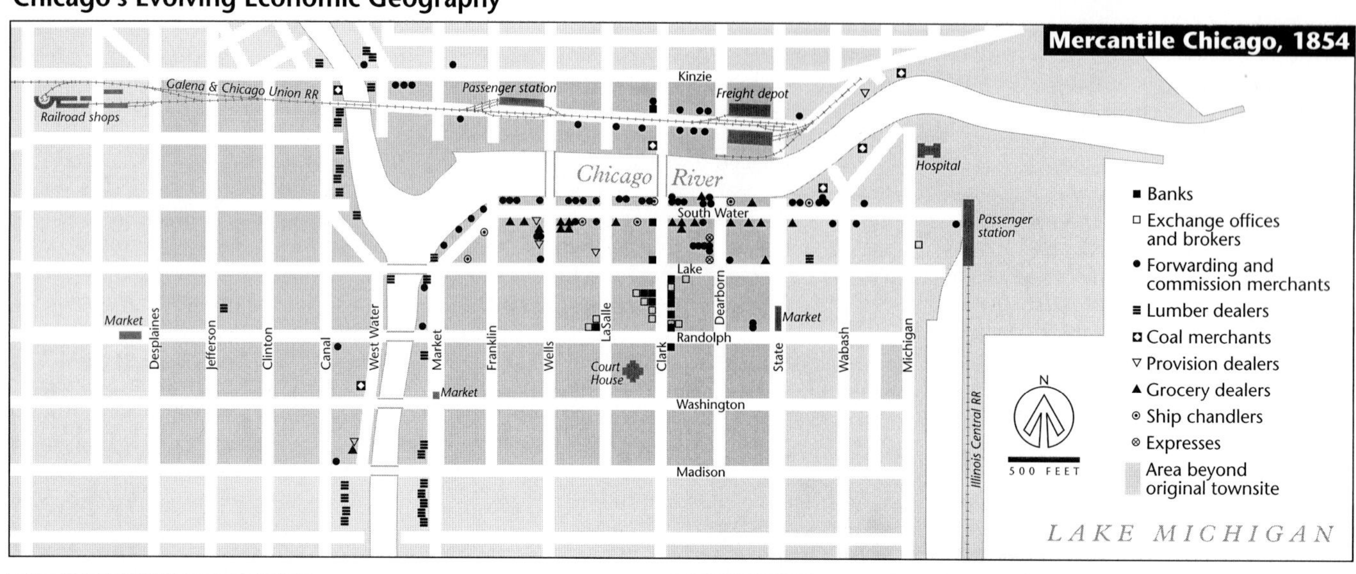

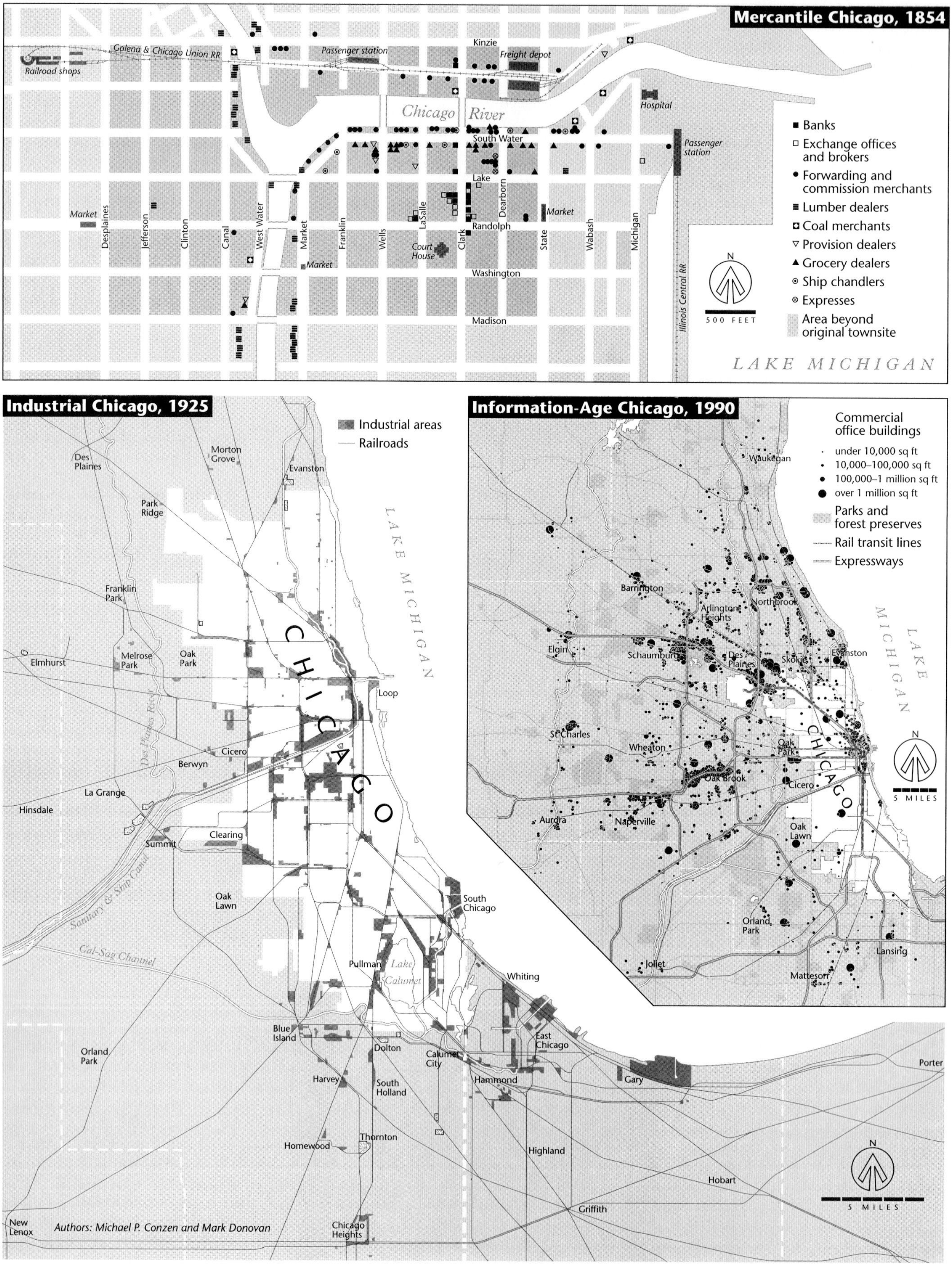

Mercantile Chicago, 1854
Galena & Chicago Union RR
Railroad shops
Passenger station
Kinzie
Freight depot
Chicago River
Hospital
South Water
Passenger station
Lake
Market
Desplaines
Jefferson
Clinton
Canal
West Water
Market
Franklin
Wells
LaSalle
Clark
Dearborn
State
Wabash
Michigan
Market
Randolph
Court House
Market
Washington
Madison
Illinois Central RR
N
500 FEET
LAKE MICHIGAN
Banks
Exchange offices and brokers
Forwarding and commission merchants
Lumber dealers
Coal merchants
Provision dealers
Grocery dealers
Ship chandlers
Expresses
Area beyond original townsite
Industrial Chicago, 1925
Industrial areas
Railroads
Des Plaines
Morton Grove
Evanston
Park Ridge
LAKE MICHIGAN
Franklin Park
CHICAGO
Elmhurst
Melrose Park
Oak Park
Loop
Des Plaines River
Cicero
Berwyn
La Grange
Hinsdale
Clearing
Summit
Sanitary & Ship Canal
Oak Lawn
South Chicago
Cal-Sag Channel
Pullman
Lake Calumet
Whiting
Blue Island
East Chicago
Orland Park
Dolton
Calumet City
Harvey
South Holland
Hammond
Gary
Porter
Thornton
Homewood
Highland
Hobart
N
5 MILES
Griffith
New Lenox
Authors: Michael P. Conzen and Mark Donovan
Chicago Heights
Information-Age Chicago, 1990
Commercial office buildings
under 10,000 sq ft
10,000–100,000 sq ft
100,000–1 million sq ft
over 1 million sq ft
Parks and forest preserves
Rail transit lines
Expressways
Waukegan
Barrington
Northbrook
Arlington Heights
Elgin
Schaumburg
Des Plaines
Skokie
Evanston
LAKE MICHIGAN
St Charles
Wheaton
Oak Park
CHICAGO
Oak Brook
Cicero
N
5 MILES
Aurora
Naperville
Oak Lawn
Orland Park
Joliet
Lansing
Matteson

information and the proliferation of commercial journals. Chicago businessmen who pioneered and came to dominate a new form of trade—MAIL-ORDER houses—also utilized this concentration. Montgomery Ward was first in the field, but Sears, Roebuck & Co. became even larger. This revolution in retailing used printed catalogs to reach out to individual customers in rural areas and created white-collar "factories" in the center city—office buildings full of CLERICAL WORKERS who processed orders that arrived by mail and filled them from huge warehouses situated on the river and the railroads.

The continuing vitality of the old core was most apparent in the central business district, known as the LOOP after 1882 when it was encircled by a cable car line. Chicago banks had expanded quickly after the Civil War; the city ranked second nationally in BANKING, manufacturing, wholesaling, and population by the end of the century. Large banks now joined the Board of Trade and the Stock Exchange to make LaSalle Street Chicago's financial center. The concentration of PUBLIC TRANSPORTATION on the Loop enhanced its retail potential too, as middle- and upper-class shoppers enjoyed easy access from outlying residential neighborhoods. The department stores moved from Lake Street to State Street when Potter Palmer developed the latter as a fashionable street in the late 1860s. Stores such as Marshall Field's and Carson Pirie Scott reached a new level of elegance, appealing to the prosperous clientele created by the city's expanding economy as well as to the growing tourist trade. To serve the tourist trade, the LOOP provided hospitality and entertainment for every taste—from the elegant Palmer House to the cheapest transient hotels, and from the best THEATERS to the infamous Levee, Chicago's VICE DISTRICT. TOURISM hit a peak in 1893, when Chicagoans hosted the WORLD'S COLUMBIAN EXPOSITION.

The growing demand for office space in the Loop led upward because of the constricted area. The SKYSCRAPERS of Chicago became the symbol of business success and set the architectural fashion for central business districts throughout the country. The Loop's clerical and managerial workers used public transportation to commute to a variety of residential neighborhoods. Districts of BOARDINGHOUSES and APARTMENTS for those without children and middle-class housing for families sprang up in a ring around the inner areas. CONSTRUCTION was the city's largest employer and real-estate speculation was still a major avenue to wealth. Some contractors, such as S. E. Gross, built large developments of single-family houses, comparable in scale to more recent SUBDIVISIONS.

To maintain their economic prominence, Chicagoans sponsored more transportation improvements, like the Chicago SANITARY AND SHIP CANAL, built in the 1890s to replace the obsolete Illinois & Michigan Canal. Like comparable projects, it boosted industrial development outside the city limits. The Chicago Outer Belt Line Railroad, completed in 1887, facilitated freight traffic and spurred manufacturing in CHICAGO HEIGHTS, AURORA, JOLIET, and ELGIN. Although outlying areas had always attracted industry, the implications for Chicago changed in the twentieth century. When the city limits reached already established communities such as OAK PARK and EVANSTON, Chicagoans found the path to expansion blocked. After 1900, outlying communities resisted ANNEXATION to Chicago, and the metropolitan area developed as an integral economic unit without political control or social unity. The limits on Chicago's development were set.

After 1920, the suburbs grew faster than the city. New transportation, the car and the truck, encouraged the suburbanization of people and industries and reversed the century-old pattern of increasing concentration. Railroads spurred suburban development, but always along their rights-of-way. Cars and trucks allowed industries and people to disperse throughout the area. This provided the large tracts necessary for the single-floor factories that utilized continuous-flow automated technologies.

As deconcentration increased, however, the metropolitan economy also experienced new competition. Detroit monopolized the most important new industry of the early twentieth century—AUTOMOBILES. Even more significant were long-term shifts in regional development; the Midwest stagnated as the West and the South boomed. After 1920, cities in the Sunbelt enjoyed the advantages in location and transportation that previously had stimulated Midwestern economic growth. Chicago businesses reeled during the GREAT DEPRESSION of the 1930s and then boomed because of WORLD WAR II defense contracts, but the regional shift determined the long-term trend in economic growth and hence in population, and in 1990 Los Angeles surpassed Chicago as the second city in population and wholesaling.

Chicago's economy did not fall behind for lack of leadership or INNOVATION. Businessmen and politicians fostered transportation improvements such as the Mississippi-Illinois Waterway to accommodate modern barge traffic. Chicago port facilities modernized, although, like many economic functions, they did so by moving out of the center of the city. After the Cal-Sag Channel between Calumet Harbor and the Illinois River opened in 1922, Calumet Harbor replaced the Chicago River as the city's port. Chicagoans also embraced new technologies and developed MIDWAY AIRPORT in the 1920s, making Chicago the breakpoint for cross-country air traffic as it was for water and rail. The country's largest airline, United, headquartered in Chicago. To maintain the country's busiest airport after World War II, Chicagoans developed the larger, more modern O'HARE.

The building of the interstate highway system in the 1950s and 1960s helped the area's economy initially, because the first EXPRESSWAYS paralleled existing forms of transportation and reinforced older metropolitan areas. Transcontinental bus lines routed through Chicago, and the largest company, Greyhound, established its headquarters in the city. The Chicago area also became the country's leading trucking center. The interstate system intensified the attraction of suburban locations for industries, however, especially south of the city, where the major east-west and north-south routes met.

Between 1920 and 1970, the Chicago area retained most of its traditional industries. In 1954, it even surpassed Pittsburgh, the old leader, in iron and steel manufacturing, producing one-quarter of the nation's output. Production remained high in machinery, primary metals, printing and publishing, CHEMICALS,

---

Chicago has experienced three fundamental phases of economic development, reflected in the geography of its changing land use. Before the Civil War, Chicago sprang up as a highly successful merchants' town at the base of Lake Michigan, its future assured by the opening of the Illinois & Michigan Canal and the first railroad tracks laid westward. The commercial heart of the town developed along the Chicago River, which offered easy transshipment between lake vessels, canal boats, and train cars. Wholesale and shipping businesses crowded South Water Street, financial services located on Lake, Dearborn, and Randolph Streets, and lumber dealers lined the North and South Branches of the river. Between the Civil War and the Second World War, Chicago developed into a manufacturing city of staggering proportions, and industry of all types spread across the urban area. Most plants clung to the waterways and the proliferating railroads which crisscrossed the city without hindrance. By the turn of the twentieth century, the cheap, marshy lakeshore lands of the South Side attracted a disproportionate amount of heavy industry. For all its diversity, Chicago's manufacturing pattern was dense, urban-oriented, and tied firmly to the central city. In the last half of the twentieth century, as the region experienced significant amounts of industrial decentralization and outright loss, Chicago's metropolitan economy turned markedly to service provision and restructuring for the Information Age. This was aptly reflected by 1990 in the highly bifurcated pattern of office space: a vast concentration of commercial offices in the Loop business district offset by a widespread scatter of office parks and commercial space in the suburbs, tied closely to the expressway network as it had evolved by then. The geography of office development is the obverse of the old industrial pattern.

This cartogram captures Chicago's industrial dominance in the United States even as factories started moving to the suburbs and the sunbelt and the city's traditionally important industries like railroads and farm equipment began to decline. Creator: Chicago Plan Commission. Source: Chicago Historical Society.

FOOD PROCESSING, and fabricated metals. The consumer ELECTRONICS industry expanded greatly, as firms such as Motorola, Zenith, and Admiral captured a significant share of the market for radios and televisions. The first big loss, however, was meatpacking. The industry had been decentralizing since the turn of the century, as Chicago companies shifted to multiple plant locations in western cities, closer to the feed lots. The Chicago stockyards closed in the 1960s.

Although the area's industrial economy remained strong, the city's did not. Companies closed aging factories in the city and shifted WORK to new suburban plants. The McCormick Reaper Works was demolished in 1961; production was taken over by a new plant south of HINSDALE. Many new industries, such as Sara Lee's frozen foods, began in the suburbs. As jobs became more plentiful outside the city, people migrating to the Chicago area often settled in the suburbs, bypassing the city entirely. This was only true, however, if the migrants were white; because of discrimination, AFRICAN AMERICANS were restricted to the city. Out migration accelerated after 1950, when the city's population peaked at 3.6 million people. White people followed the jobs, as Chicago's share of the area's manufacturing dropped from 71 percent to 54 percent between 1947 and 1961.

The history of the Loop reflected both the struggle to remain competitive and the process of deconcentration. Financial institutions stayed on LaSalle Street, though not all retained their dynamism. The Chicago Board of Trade stayed on top of the national futures market by creating innovative contract markets in new fields such as financial instruments. Chicago banks, however, serviced the Midwest, and they grew slowly, in step with the sluggish regional economy. Beginning in the 1950s, many corporations moved their headquarters out of the skyscrapers to suburban "campuses." Headquarters thrive on quick access to air transport, and O'Hare drew them out of the Loop to the northwest suburbs. Most notable was Sears, which left after trumpeting its success by building the world's tallest skyscraper. The Loop's tenuous economic situation is reflected in the building booms and busts since World War II, which left some of the world's most innovative skyscrapers often half empty.

The Loop's retail functions also ebbed. Marshall Field's and other Loop department stores opened their first branches in the suburbs in the 1920s. City officials replaced the cluttered and decaying South Water Street with Wacker Drive in the 1920s, but new building in the Loop virtually ceased for decades while North Michigan Avenue became the Magnificent Mile. Suburban competition became intense in the 1950s with the opening of shopping malls. Loop retail trade declined, but the Loop continued to attract conventioneers after the construction of McCormick Place Convention Center. Loop Hotels, theaters, and museums drew tourists to the lakefront of the central city.

Since 1970, the character of Chicago's metropolitan economy has been transformed; both manufacturing and wholesaling play a lesser role than in the past. Chicagoans hoped to gain international commerce with the opening of the ST. LAWRENCE SEAWAY, but the ocean-going trade was not as successful as projected. Furthermore, foreign competition undercut many manufacturing companies. Older plants in Chicago closed first; newer ones in the suburbs followed. Some corporations, even giants such as International Harvester, failed. Both central city and suburbs suffered, as the area lost almost all railcar and agricultural machinery production and most of its consumer electronics industry. The steel industry declined precipitously but has since rebounded; at the end of the century it employed, however, only one-third as many workers as it did in the 1970s. A high-tech corridor has developed in the western suburbs, but most of the new industries are centered elsewhere.

The service sector is the source of most new growth for the metropolitan economy. The old central city is almost totally dependent on business services and tourism for its vitality. Where the river empties into the lake, a ferris wheel replaces the grain elevator as a symbol of what makes the city great. The diversity of the area's economy remains a strength, but its future, like its past, will depend on national and international economic trends. Chicago was geographically well situated to become the capital of the Midwest. It retains this position, but the old dream of dominating the continent has died.

Susan E. Hirsch

See also: Agriculture; Commuting; Global Chicago; Land Use; Metropolitan Growth; Places of Assembly; Railroad Supply Industry; Retail Geography; Trade Publications

Further reading: Cronon, William. *Nature's Metropolis: Chicago and the Great West.* 1991. • Marsh, Barbara. *A Corporate Tragedy: The Agony of International Harvester Company.* 1985. • Mayer, Harold M., and Richard C. Wade. *Chicago: Growth of a Metropolis.* 1969.

Economics, Chicago School. *See* Chicago School of Economics

Ecosystem Evolution. When Chicago's first human inhabitants arrived at the end of the last ice age, they encountered a LANDSCAPE much different from what the Europeans observed 11,000 years later. Mastodons and woolly mammoths inhabited an evergreen spruce forest similar to what can be found in Alaska today. Over the succeeding millennia, the CLIMATE warmed, the spruce forest gave way to deciduous forest and then to prairie, and the large Pleistocene mammals went extinct.

Climate, never constant, drove these changes. Cyclic variations in the Earth's orbit around the Sun, affecting the amount of solar radiation reaching the Earth, are a primary driver of climate change and of the glacial-interglacial cycle. Because of the constantly changing climate, ecosystems are in continual flux, as plants, animals, and other organisms must continually adjust their ranges to regions of suitable climate.

Geologists refer to the last 1.8 million years as the Quaternary period, a time when great continental glaciers advanced and then retreated 20 or more times. Rather arbitrarily, the Quaternary period is divided into the Pleistocene and Holocene epochs. The old idea was that the Pleistocene was the time of the ice ages, and the Holocene was the "postglacial" period; actually, the Holocene is but one of many interglacial periods that have characterized the Quaternary. The Holocene began approximately 11,500 years ago, when the last continental glaciers very rapidly began to melt away. The glaciers left behind characteristic deposits from which geologists can interpret the glacial history. Glacial ice is always flowing forward and always melting backward. The flowing ice continually transports rocks, pebbles, sand, and other material forward. Whenever a glacier stabilizes for a time at the same position, the transported material accumulates into hilly *moraines*, several of which occur in the Chicago region.

The starting point for the development of ecosystems in the Chicago region is the retreat of the glaciers at the end of the last ice age, the *Wisconsin glaciation*. During the maximum of the Wisconsin GLACIATION, the LAKE MICHIGAN lobe of the great Laurentide ice sheet, which covered much of Canada and the northern United States, advanced over the entire Chicago region. The ice sheet entered northeastern Illinois about 30,000 years ago during the Marengo Phase of the Wisconsin glaciation, and it reached its southernmost extent near Shelbyville in central Illinois about 24,000 years ago. At this time, glacial ice covered the entire Chicago region. The outer edge of the ice sheet advanced and retreated several times before finally disappearing from Illinois. By about 18,000 years ago, the active ice sheet retreated into the Lake Michigan basin, although stagnant, melting ice remained behind. The ice then rapidly readvanced to the prominent Valparaiso moraine in the western Chicago region. After retreating from the Valparaiso moraine, the ice margin made a series of minor advances and retreats, building the Lake Border moraines just north of Chicago about 17,000 years ago, after which the Wisconsin glacier finally retreated from Illinois. Thus, time zero for development of post-Pleistocene ecosystems in the Chicago region is about 17,000 years ago.

History of Lake Michigan

Much of the city of Chicago lies on beach and lake sediments deposited by Lake Michigan and its predecessor glacial Lake Chicago. After the Wisconsin glacier retreated from the Chicago region, it still occupied and dammed the northern end of the Lake Michigan basin, forming glacial Lake Chicago. This lake, which covered most of present-day Chicago, was higher than modern Lake Michigan. Its outlet was westward across the Valparaiso moraine via the modern Des Plaines and Illinois River valleys. The Chicago outlet consisted of the southern Calumet Sag Channel and the northern Des Plaines channel, now occupied by the DES PLAINES RIVER and the Chicago SANITARY AND SHIP CANAL. As the glacier repeatedly advanced and retreated in the Lake Michigan basin north of Chicago, the level of glacial Lake Chicago fluctuated as different outlets to the east were opened and closed. The Glenwood and Calumet beaches were formed during this time. When glacial ice finally melted completely from the basin about 12,000 years ago, the lake fell because the heavy weight of the ice had depressed the land surface in the northern part of the basin, producing a northern outlet lower than today's. This outlet was located in northeastern Lake Huron, where water drained through Lake Nipissing and into the Ottawa River. The land depressed by the glacial ice gradually uplifted, a process called *isostatic rebound*. As the northern outlet isostatically rose, the level of the confluent Lakes Michigan and Huron rose to a level higher than today, until the lake eventually spilled out southern outlets at Chicago and southern Lake Huron. This high lake level, called the Nipissing stage, was reached about 5,500 years ago and lasted about 1,000 years. The Toleston beach formed during this time. The outlet at the southern end of Lake Huron eroded downward more rapidly than the outlet at Chicago, so that by about 4,500 years ago, the Chicago outlet was no longer active. Lake and beach sediments from the Nipissing high stage cover much of the city of Chicago, and terrestrial ecosystems developed on these sediments after the Nipissing stage.

Ecosystem Development

Following the retreat of the glaciers, vegetation invaded the newly ice-free terrain. From about 18,000 to 16,000 years ago, open tundra-like vegetation with scattered spruce (*Picea*) TREES covered the landscape. Both white spruce (*Picea glauca*) and black spruce (*Picea mariana*) were present, as was larch (*Larix laricina*). These trees are all common today in the boreal forest or taiga of Canada. Although the glaciers had retreated, the climate was still quite cold. About 16,000 years ago, the spruce forest became denser, and closed forest developed. This spruce forest lasted for about 1,000 years, until about 15,000 years ago, when climate warmed and deciduous trees became more abundant, including balsam poplar (*Populus balsamifera*), black ash (*Fraxinus nigra*), and ironwood (*Ostrya virginiana* or *Carpinus caroliniana*). Balsam fir (*Abies balsamea*) also was present, as was spruce, although not as abundantly as before.

This late-Pleistocene forest of spruce and deciduous trees is unusual in that a forest of similar composition does not occur anywhere today. The implication is that the climate was unlike any climate in North America today. The presence of spruce suggests cool summers, whereas the deciduous trees imply relatively warm winters. Thus, the climate may have been more equable than it is now. Although the Laurentide ice sheet, which still existed to the north, may have kept the summers cool, it may also have blocked arctic air masses from extending into the Midwest during winter.

About 13,000 years ago climate apparently cooled again, and spruce became more abundant and black ash less common. During this time birch (*Betula*) and alder (*Alnus*) were also important components of the vegetation. Then from about 12,000 to 11,500 years ago, the vegetation changed very rapidly as climate suddenly warmed at the transition from the Pleistocene to the Holocene.

In the earliest Holocene, the conifers—spruce, fir, and larch—disappeared, and a deciduous forest dominated by black ash, elm (*Ulmus*), and oak prevailed. Other deciduous trees also occurred, including sugar maple, basswood, ironwood, hickory, and walnut (*Juglans*). The abundance of elm and ash, trees that favor wet SOILS, implies a very wet climate. After about 10,000 years ago, the climate became drier, and some limited areas of prairie developed in the Chicago region. This dry period may have lasted about 1,000 years, but conditions apparently became wetter again, because elm increased after about 9,000 years ago. About 6,000 years ago, the climate again became drier, and the modern mosaic of prairie and woodland began to develop. Elm and other fire-sensitive trees decreased in abundance, and oak became the predominate tree on the landscape. The driest time of the Holocene was from about 6,000 years ago to about 3,000 years ago, after which the climate again became somewhat cooler and wetter, although not as wet as in the early Holocene. However, prairie persisted because of its great propensity for burning and because the Native Americans provided a constant source of ignition. Some evidence of cooler climate is evident in the wetlands of the Chicago region. Larch reappeared in the region within the last 1,000 years, for example, at Volo Bog.

Vegetation

At the time when the first Europeans entered the Chicago region, the predominant vegetation was a mosaic of prairie, oak woodland, and savanna, with distinctive vegetation on sand dunes adjacent to Lake Michigan. Soils, TOPOGRAPHY, and firebreaks strongly controlled the vegetation pattern. Before European settlement, fire was a major influence. Every year the copious prairie vegetation dried in late summer, becoming highly flammable, and fires,

The Chicago Area before Human Transformation

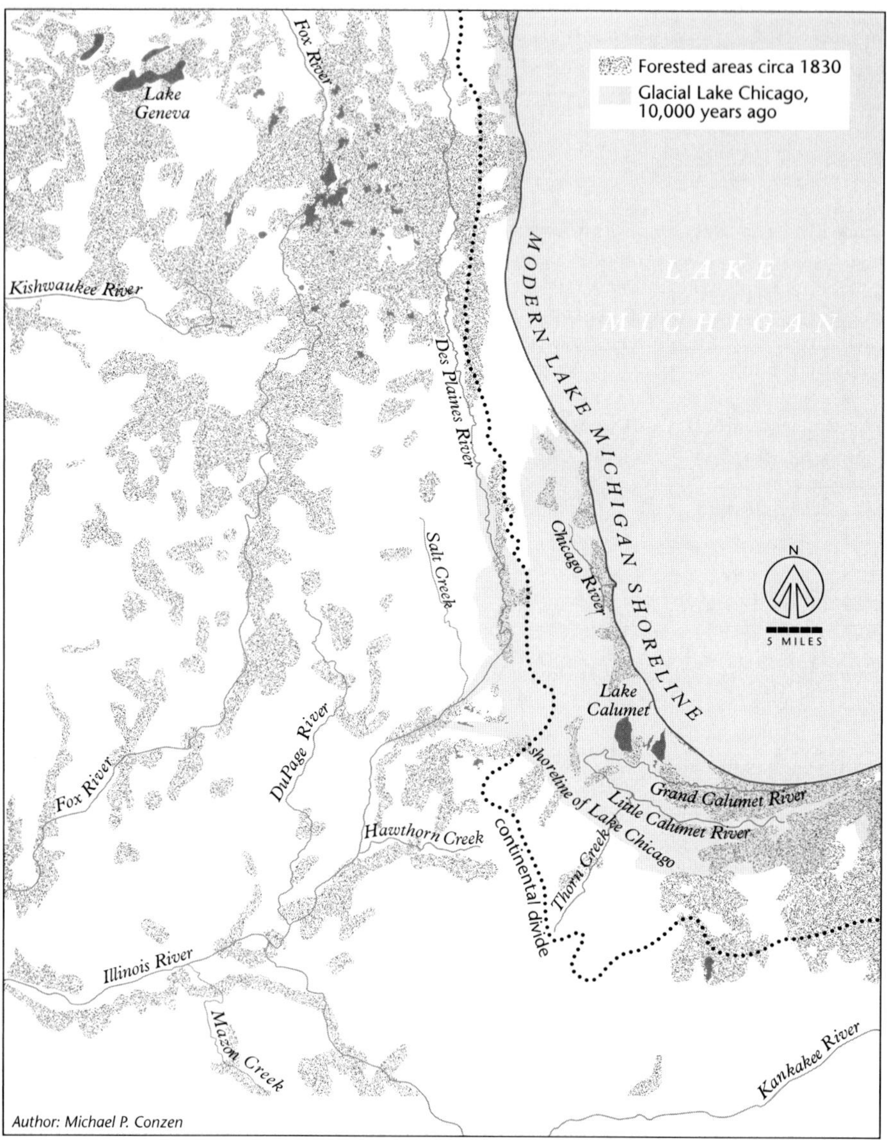

The region destined to be covered by metropolitan Chicago took natural form following the retreat of the North American ice cap 10,000 years ago. Meltwaters from the glacier's Lake Michigan Lobe, pent up for a time behind morainic ridges deposited at the ice sheet's margins, formed glacial Lake Chicago and drained southwestward, scouring what is today the lower Des Plaines valley. As ice receded and water drained away, Lake Michigan remained behind, contained within its modern shoreline. The area straddles what turned out to be a permanent low-lying continental drainage divide between the basins of the Great Lakes and the Mississippi River. The numerous lakes and marshes of the region represent the retreating glacier's messy legacy. By the early nineteenth century a tall-grass prairie environment covered much of the area, with thin strips of forest colonizing sandy beach ridges and shallow valley bluffs.

mostly set by NATIVE AMERICANS either accidentally or purposefully, occurred annually. These fires carried easily through the prairie and burned into adjacent woodlands. As a result, the woodland vegetation was dominated by fire-resistant trees and occurred in areas protected from fire by rougher topography or water bodies—rivers and lakes.

Native Americans had many reasons to burn the prairie vegetation, including making the prairie easier to walk through, removing cover that might hide enemies, lighting backfires to remove the immediate danger of wildfires, and especially for hunting. "Tallgrass" prairie occurred in Illinois and in the Chicago region. The dominant grasses were big bluestem (*Andropogon gerardii*), Indian grass (*Sorghastrum nutans*), and prairie dropseed (*Sporobolus heterolepis*), with large forbs such as prairie dock (*Silphium terebinthinaceum*) and rattlesnake master (*Eryngium yuccifolium*). Wet prairie with grasses such as prairie cordgrass (*Spartina pectinata*) occurred in more poorly drained areas.

On the loamy glacial moraines that cover most of the Chicago region, bur oak (*Quercus macrocarpa*) was the most common tree in woodlands, with lesser amounts of white oak (*Quercus alba*) and black oak (*Quercus velutina*). Bur oak has thick bark that makes it resistant to fire, and it resprouts if burned. Groves of bur oak occurred in more protected areas throughout the Chicago region. The early land surveyors described much of this vegetation as "scattered" or "scattering" timber or as "oak openings." The trees tended to be scrubby. In some places they might have been widely spaced with a grassy understory, but they often occurred in clumps with shrubby undergrowth of oaks and hazel (*Corylus americana*).

The vegetation pattern clearly shows the effects of fires emanating predominantly from the west. Strips of woodland were wider on the east sides of lakes and rivers. Broad bands of woodland occurred east of the FOX RIVER from AURORA to the Wisconsin border and east of the Des Plaines River in LAKE COUNTY. Much of the area in Lake County on rolling moraines and east of the larger lakes was forested. In areas more protected from fire, especially immediately east of the larger rivers, forests of oak and hickory (*Carya*) predominated. In the areas best protected from fires, trees quite sensitive to fire such as sugar maple (*Acer saccharum*) and basswood (*Tilia americana*) occurred. Particularly notable was the "Big Woods" east of the Fox River where the city of AURORA is now located. Early pioneers used this term for forests of large trees with a continuous canopy, in contrast to the scrubby, open, frequently burned woodlands that were more common in the region. Depending on exposure to fire, a continuum existed from bur oak savanna or scrub to oak-hickory forest to maple-basswood forest.

The plain of glacial Lake Chicago on which much of the city lies was prairie, but paralleling Lake Michigan were sand DUNES with black oak scrub having an understory of hazel, blueberry (*Vaccinium*), and other shrubs. Cottonwood (*Populus deltoides*) and jack pine (*Pinus banksiana*) also occurred on the dunes, and a few white pine (*Pinus strobus*) occurred in LAKE COUNTY. The dunes are still preserved at Illinois Beach State Park in LAKE COUNTY and Indiana Dunes National Lakeshore in northern Indiana.

Henry Chandler Cowles of the UNIVERSITY OF CHICAGO was one of the first plant ecologists in North America, and his research published in the *Botanical Gazette* in 1899 and 1901 on the succession of vegetation on the Lake Michigan dunes was seminal to the embryonic science of ecology. He documented a succession that begins with dune-forming plants such as beach grass (*Ammophila breviligulata*), sand cherry (*Prunus pumila*), willows (*Salix*), and cottonwood; followed by dune capture, with such plants as red-osier dogwood (*Cornus sericea*) and choke cherry (*Prunus virginiana*); and finally dune stabilization, with either black oak or jack pine. With long-term suppression of fires, Cowles noted an eventual succession to forest with shade-tolerant, fire-sensitive trees, particularly sugar maple. In contrast to sugar maples, oak seedlings do not survive in dense forest shade. In the past, occasional ground fires kept the forest more open and encouraged reproduction of oaks and hickories. Large oaks have thick bark and are quite resistant to ground fires, whereas sugar maples are much more sensitive. With fire exclusion, sugar maple is increasing at the expense of oak throughout Illinois.

Not only was the vegetation of the late Pleistocene much different from that of the present, so was the fauna. Arctic animals of today such as lemmings (e.g., *Synaptomys borealis*), caribou (*Rangifer tarandus*), and musk ox (*Ovibos moschatus*) occurred in the Midwest in the tundra-like vegetation that existed immediately after the glaciers retreated. Other large animals, the *megafauna,* went extinct at the end of the Pleistocene. American mastodon (*Mammut americanum*), woolly mammoth (*Mammuthus primigenius*), giant beaver (*Castoroides ohioensis*), Harlan's musk ox (*Bootherium bombifrons*), and stag-moose (*Cervalces scotti*) all occurred in the Chicago region. According to fossil finds, mastodon was particularly common. After the extinction of these animals, white-tailed deer (*Odocoileus virginianus*), elk (*Cervus elaphus*), and bison (*Bison*) survived. Large predators—wolves, cougars, and bears—also inhabited the region. Although early explorers described "large" herds of bison, these herds generally contained a few hundred animals, nowhere near the size of the populations of millions in the Great Plains to the west. The tall-grass prairie habitat was probably not ideal for bison, and hunting pressure from the relatively large Native American population was probably intense. Scientists are divided as to the degree to which hunting by early Americans or rapid environmental change at the end of the Pleistocene were the causes for the extinction of the megafauna.

The orbit of the Earth is an ellipse, and therefore the distance from the Sun varies throughout the year. At the beginning of the Holocene, 11,500 years ago, at the termination of the Wisconsin glaciation, the Earth was closest to the sun in July and farthest in January. Today, the opposite is true, with the Earth farthest from the Sun in summer, closest in winter. This seasonal difference is at least partly responsible for the continuously changing climate during the Holocene. However, shorter-term variations also occurred, and scientists are just beginning to recognize and understand these. The El Niño–La Niña cycle is one of these, but others are also apparently present. Thus, we can predict with total confidence that climate will change and that ecosystems will respond. The addition of greenhouse gases to the atmosphere—carbon dioxide will soon double from its preindustrial level—is a warming force. Although the levels of greenhouse gases have fluctuated during the Quaternary period, they are exceeding any levels the Earth has experienced during the last 2 million years. The exact nature and cause of natural climatic variation and of its interaction with anthropogenic greenhouse warming is a matter of great scientific debate and even greater consequence. Although the modern ecosystems of the Chicago metropolitan area are much modified by humans, the plants and animals that can occur in the region are still dependent on the climate, and the flora and fauna will change as the climate does.

Eric C. Grimm

See also: Great Lakes System; Lacustrine System; Plant Communities; Riverine Systems

Further reading: Baker, Richard G., Louis J. Maher, Jr., Craig A. Chumbley, and Kent L. Van Zant. "Patterns of Holocene Environmental Change in the Midwestern United States." *Quaternary Research* 37 (1992): 379–389. • Hansel, Ardith K., David M. Mickelson, Allan F. Schneider, and Curtis E. Larsen. "Late Wisconsinan and Holocene History of the Lake Michigan Basin." In *Quaternary Evolution of the Great Lakes,* ed. P. F. Karrow and P. E. Calkin, 1985, 39–53. • King, James E. "Late Quaternary Vegetational History of Illinois." *Ecological Monographs* 51 (1981): 43–62.

Ecuadorians. The Ecuadorian presence in Chicago dates back to the mid-twentieth century. In 2000 there were 8,941 Ecuadorians in Chicago, making them the fifth largest Latin American group in the city. Chicago joins New York, Miami, and Los Angeles as the four U.S. cities with the largest number of Ecuadorians.

Ecuadorians have dispersed throughout the West and North Sides of the city, primarily in Logan Square, Albany Park, Uptown, and Lake View. There are smaller concentrations in Irving Park, Belmont Cragin, Edgewater, and West Ridge. More recently, there has been an expansion to the suburbs, particularly Skokie, Glenview, Des Plaines, Morton Grove, and Elgin.

Ecuadorians have come to Chicago primarily in two waves. The first, approximately 1965–1976, originated primarily in the provinces of Guayas, Pichincha, Chimborazo, Cotopaxi, and Azuay. Ecuadorians arriving during this period worked mainly in factories, but also in service industries and eventually in retail. Ecuadorian businesses created by this first wave include several travel and courier agencies, restaurants, and food and clothing stores. Housed primarily but not exclusively on Milwaukee, Division, and 26th Streets, these enterprises cater primarily to Latinos. The second large wave of immigration took place in the 1990s. Coming from the highland provinces of Azuay and Cañar, these Ecuadorians relied on networks of family and friends to secure jobs in the restaurant and hotel industry for men, and in the housekeeping and garment industries for women.

Ecuadorian organizations include the Ecuadorian Civic Society, founded in 1959, the Ecuadorian Lions Club, the Federation of Ecuadorian Entities, the Social Association of Azuay, the Cotopaxi Foundation, the Alausí Foundation, and the Civic Society of Cañar. Religious organizations such as the Cristo del Consuelo and the Committee of Jesus of the Great Power have helped to preserve Ecuadorian religious traditions. Additionally, there are folkloric dance groups and several sports teams organized with the assistance of the Los Andes Sports and Social Club. Their presence in the city is most visible on Sunday afternoons, when the park on Wilson and Lake Shore Drive is visited by hundreds of Ecuadorians participating, as players or spectators, in soccer and volleyball tournaments.

Important annual events organized by the Ecuadorian community include Ecuadorian week around August 10, involving cultural exhibits, a picnic, and a parade that starts on Montrose and California and heads west, ending at Pulaski. Several music festivals, charity balls, beauty queen competitions, and fundraisers are held throughout the year.

Amalia Pallares

See also: Americanization; Demography; Multicentered Chicago

Further reading: "A Profile of Nine Latino Groups in Chicago." Latino Institute. October 1994. • "Latinos Face to Face/Latinos Cara a Cara." Latino Institute. 1995.

Edgewater, Community Area 77, 7 miles N of the Loop. Although it was an elite nineteenth-century suburb, Edgewater was not recognized as distinct when scholars laid out the community areas in the 1920s. Instead, Edgewater was merged into Uptown. In the 1970s, however, Edgewater's property owners persuaded the city of Chicago to make a rare change in its community area maps and recognize Edgewater as a separate entity.

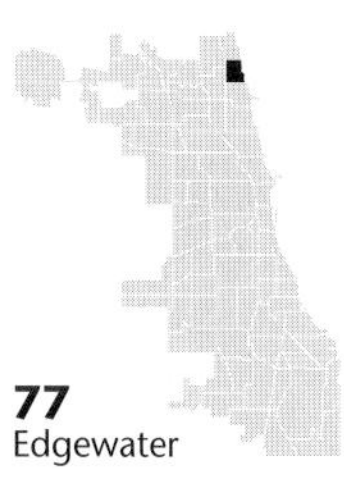

Few people lived in the Edgewater area before the late nineteenth century. Scattered settlers farmed celery. Edgewater's residents were mostly German and Irish. Swedes gathered along Clark Street in an area they called Andersonville.

John Lewis Cochran (1857–1923) purchased land near Lake Michigan in the town of Lake View in 1886. There he developed a subdivision he advertised as "Edgewater." He first

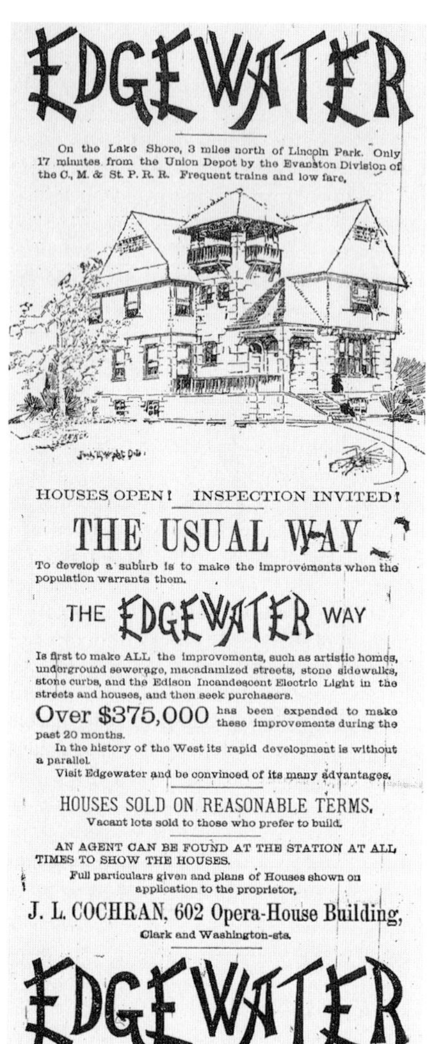

Advertisement for the Edgewater subdivision, 1888. Source: Chicago Historical Society.

built mansions on the lakefront for wealthy families and later had smaller houses built to the west. In contrast to other suburban developers, Cochran installed improvements such as sidewalks, sewers, and streetlights before customers moved in. Cochran also founded the Edgewater Light Company to ensure that his buyers could use the most modern conveniences. Cochran's final task was to provide adequate transportation to the area. He persuaded the Chicago, Milwaukee & St. Paul RAILROAD to open a stop on Bryn Mawr Avenue and was instrumental in the creation of the Northwestern Elevated Railroad Company, which in 1908 opened up a connection through to Howard Street. The availability of transportation encouraged the erection of APARTMENT buildings, a development Cochran had not intended. This strip of "common corridor" buildings and RESIDENTIAL HOTELS, concentrated between Winthrop and Kenmore, increased Edgewater's population density.

During the twentieth century, Edgewater solidified its status as one of the most prestigious residential areas in Chicago. In 1898, the exclusive Saddle and Cycle Club relocated to Foster Avenue, on the lakefront. The Edgewater Beach Hotel (1916) and the Edgewater Beach Apartments (1929), finished in sunrise yellow and sunset pink, served as local landmarks. Residential Edgewater's wealth reinforced the glamour of recreational Uptown.

During the city-wide housing crisis of the 1940s, these apartment buildings were subdivided into smaller units. The area began to become overcrowded and landlords collected increasing rents while allowing their properties to deteriorate. When building resumed, more large apartment buildings replaced older ones. Along the Winthrop-Kenmore corridor, most new structures were four-plus-ones. Along Sheridan Road, most of the old mansions were razed and replaced with high-rises, giving the street the feel of a canyon.

These developments disturbed some Edgewater residents. They regarded the Winthrop-Kenmore corridor as an eyesore that attracted transients, the ill, and the elderly. Single people who would not stay long in the area rented the Sheridan Road high-rises. Alarmed at the prospect of social and physical blight, property owners created the Edgewater Community Council in 1960. The ECC sought a variety of local improvements. For example, in conjunction with the Organization of the Northeast, they arranged a moratorium on the opening of new residential health care facilities. During the 1970s, ECC's strategy shifted to separating its identity from Uptown, which Edgewater residents regarded as the source of their plight. The opening of the Edgewater branch of the CHICAGO PUBLIC LIBRARY in 1973 was a major victory in this battle, which culminated in 1980 when the city government ratified the separation of Edgewater from Uptown by designating it Community Area 77. The success of the rehabilitation was reflected in LOYOLA UNIVERSITY's increasing involvement in Edgewater. Although it had been oriented to ROGERS PARK, by the late 1970s Loyola began encouraging its faculty and students to recognize, and even to live in, Edgewater.

At the same time, the smaller commercial strips within Edgewater promoted their own distinctive flavors. What began as a promotion of "CHINATOWN North" on Argyle Street evolved as Edgewater's population shifted to include diverse Asian Americans. Among the shop owners on Argyle were VIETNAMESE, THAI, JAPANESE, KOREANS, INDIANS, PAKISTANIS, and also Spanish-speakers, GREEKS, and ALBANIANS. Along Clark Street, merchants revived Andersonville's SWEDISH past during the 1960s, successfully marketing the area as a clean and friendly place to shop for curiosities. Later, merchants from other ethnic groups and enterprises run by lesbian women supplemented Andersonville's Swedish flavor.

Amanda Seligman

See also: Community Organizing; Gays and Lesbians; Housing for the Elderly; Housing, Single-Room Occupancy; Neighborhood Succession; Studying Chicago

Further reading: Marciniak, Ed. *Reversing Urban Decline: The Winthrop-Kenmore Corridor in the Edgewater and Uptown Communities of Chicago.* 1981. • Pacyga, Dominic A., and Ellen Skerrett. *Chicago, City of Neighborhoods: Histories and Tours.* 1986.

Edison Park, Community Area 9, 13 miles NW of the Loop. Edison Park lies in the far northwest corner of Chicago, a little more than a mile west of the CHICAGO RIVER, along a METRA commuter line. The area has changed from a home to various Indian groups to a farming community to a RAILROAD suburb to a Chicago neighborhood. At each transition, new residents and LAND USES have confronted old ones, reshaping the landscape.

The wooded areas along the river provided summer camps for NATIVE AMERICANS before the 1830s, when GERMAN farmers staked claim to the land. Among this group were members of the Ebinger family, who regularly met Native Americans who continued to move along the old trail (now Milwaukee Avenue) near the farms. A tavern along Milwaukee Road served both farmers and Indians as they traveled in the vicinity and on their way to Chicago. An Evangelical church and cemetery were among the institutions founded by these farmers.

After the arrival of the railroad in the early 1850s, developers tried to breathe life into two paper suburbs that today are part of Edison Park: Canfield and Ridgelawn. It was not until the 1890s that Edison Park grew, claiming to be the first Northwest Side community with electricity. Area residents organized as a village in 1896 and touted artesian WATER, a volunteer fire company, a HOTEL, a large railroad depot, and dozens of large houses. Located between two successful railroad suburbs, PARK RIDGE and NORWOOD PARK (later annexed to Chicago), Edison Park joined the competition. By 1910, there were 300 residents.

New residents and established farm families created a park district and a grammar school (part of Maine Township), improved roads and WATER PROVISION, and established new churches and clubs. Residents often traveled to JEFFERSON PARK on the railroad for shopping. In addition, several RELIGIOUS INSTITUTIONS established homes for children on former farmland.

One problem that area residents faced was the distance to a high school. Living in Maine Township, area students had to travel many miles to the new Maine West High School. Residents decided to annex to Chicago in 1910, so their children could attend Carl Schurz High School (accessible by rail). The village trustees disbanded the government and Edison Park began the slow process of integration into the city.

After WORLD WAR I, Edison Park experienced a major building boom. Businesses and industry began locating nearby and automobile travel made the area attractive to workers. Chicago BUNGALOWS and Dutch colonials soon outnumbered the older, larger houses. Second-generation immigrants, many of them ROMAN CATHOLIC or Lutheran, moved into the area as the population grew over 400 percent to 5,370 in 1930. Little farmland remained, and the Ebinger name was memorialized in the name of the new local school.

During the 1950s, builders constructed brick bungalows on remaining empty lots in the neighborhood. The neighborhood had an ITALIAN flavor, with ethnic grocery stores and bakeries in the business center. The construction of the Kennedy and Edens EXPRESSWAYS, the O'Hare RAPID TRANSIT LINE, and the Tri-State TOLL ROAD have diffused the importance of the railroad line to Edison Park residents. Residents in recent years find WORK, LEISURE, and shopping opportunities in all directions, both within the city and in surrounding suburban areas.

Ann Durkin Keating

See also: Agriculture; Annexation; Metropolitan Growth

Further reading: Scholl, Edward T. *Seven Miles of Ideal Living.* 1957.

Education. *See* Schools and Education

Egyptians. Egyptian immigrants began to arrive in Chicago during the mid-1950s. The initial immigrants were mostly urban, Christian professionals who left Egypt because they were dissatisfied with President Gamal Abdel Nasser's policy of forced nationalization. Nasser's regime also encouraged emigration as a solution to Egypt's overpopulation. Beginning about 1960, a small number of Egyptians who were funded by the Egyptian government came to Chicago for graduate studies in engineering and other professional fields, and many elected to remain in the Chicago area following the completion of their degrees. Although Egyptian immigration was facilitated by the 1965 Immigration and Nationality Act, which welcomed educated professionals to the United States, the numbers of Egyptian immigrants to the Chicago area remained relatively low until the period immediately following the June 1967 Arab-Israeli War. As jobs became more scarce in Egypt, the number of both Coptic Christian and MUSLIM Egyptian immigrants to the Chicago area increased markedly. Since the early 1970s, a steady wave of Egyptian immigrants pursuing graduate education and employment opportunities has continued to arrive in Chicago each year.

The Bureau of the Census generally underestimates the number of Arab Americans living in the United States. Several Chicago Arab American organizations estimated that Egyptians constituted just over 10,000 of the 150,000 Arab Americans in the Chicago area in 1998. Many Egyptians in Chicago work as engineers for companies such as Commonwealth Edison and BP Amoco, which has offices in both Chicago and Egypt. Other professionals are employed by Internet and technology companies.

Unlike some other Arab American groups, Egyptians have neither congregated in particular neighborhoods nor maintained an institutional presence in the Chicago area. Egyptians are represented, however, by some umbrella Arab American organizations, such as the Arab American Action Network, a social service organization established on the SOUTH SIDE of Chicago in 1995, and the Arab American Business and Professional Association, a national organization for business networking incorporated in 1985 with a branch office located in Buffalo Grove.

Many Egyptian Muslims worship at the Islamic Cultural Center of Greater Chicago (ICC), founded in NORTHBROOK in 1974. At the ICC, Egyptians join Muslims of other ethnicities, most predominantly BOSNIAN Muslims. St. Mark's Coptic Orthodox Church, founded in an apartment in EVANSTON in 1967, moved to BURR RIDGE in the late 1970s. St. Mary's Coptic Orthodox Church, the second Coptic church established in the Chicago area, built a home in PALATINE during the mid-1990s.

Daniel Greene

See also: Demography; Lebanese; Multicentered Chicago; Palestinians; Religious Geography; Syrians

Further reading: *Meeting Community Needs, Building on Community Strengths.* 1998. • Zaghel, Ali Shteiwi. "Changing Patterns of Identification among Arab Americans: The Palestinian Ramallites and the Christian Syrian-Lebanese." Ph.D. diss., Northwestern University. 1976.

Eight-Hour Movement. When the Chicago labor movement emerged in 1864, the eight-hour day quickly became its central demand. Exhausted by 12 to 14 hours a day of WORK, six days a week, workers throughout the city and state organized to secure a law limiting the workday to eight hours. In 1867, the Illinois legislature passed such a law but allowed a huge loophole that permitted employers to contract with their employees for longer hours. Trying to eliminate that option, Chicago labor called for a citywide STRIKE that began on May 1, 1867, and practically shut down the city's economy for a week. When the strike collapsed, the law collapsed with it and workers were left unprotected.

In the 1880s, the issue resurfaced and became the key demand of a movement that shook the city and the nation. In 1884, the Federation of Organized Trades and Labor Unions—predecessor of the American Federation of Labor—urged American workers to observe an eight-hour day beginning May 1, 1886. Implying direct rather than legislative action, the eight-hour movement united skilled and unskilled workers of all nationalities. Chicago ANARCHISTS, trade unionists, and the KNIGHTS OF LABOR, despite the coolness of their national organizations, actively promoted and profited from the movement, and made Chicago its national center.

In the midst of that scheduled agitation, the bomb exploded at HAYMARKET, giving the movement its martyrs and diverting and defeating the larger movement of which it had been a part. After HAYMARKET, the eight-hour day became one among a menu of issues promoted by the labor movement, rather than the key catalytic goal around which a movement organized. Under pressure from newly stable labor institutions, different industries gradually decreased hours, giving workers more time for LEISURE activities. The eight-hour day finally became a reality in 1938, when the NEW DEAL's Fair Labor Standards Act made it a legal day's work throughout the nation.

John B. Jentz

See also: Chicago Federation of Labor; Strikes; Unionization

Further reading: Nelson, Bruce C. *Beyond the Martyrs: A Social History of Chicago's Anarchists, 1870–1900.* 1988. • Roediger, David R., and Philip S. Foner. *Our Own Time: A History of American Labor and the Working Day.* 1989. • Schneirov, Richard. "Political Cultures and the Role of the State in Labor's Republic: The View from Chicago, 1814–1877." *Labor History* 32.3 (Summer 1991): 401–421.

Elburn, IL, Kane County, 43 miles W of the Loop. Named Blackberry Station when the Chicago & Northwestern RAILROAD built through the area in 1854, the village incorporated as Elburn in 1886. Once largely rural, the area's population began rapidly expanding in the 1990s. The 2000 population was 2,756.

Craig L. Pfannkuche

See also: Kane County

Further reading: Joslyn, R. Waite, and Frank W. Joslyn. *History of Kane County, Illinois.* 2 vols. 1908.

Elderly, Housing for the. *See* Housing for the Elderly

Electricity. *See* Gas and Electricity

Electronics. Chicago companies and their employees have long stood as leading players in the American electronics industry. For much of the twentieth century, the major consumer electronics products—that is, devices that manipulate the motion of electrons through such media as vacuum tubes and semiconductors—were radios and televisions, and the Chicago region was a major manufacturing center for these goods. During the latter part of the century, as the production of these devices moved overseas, Chicago's general preeminence in the American electronics industry faded, despite the importance of several area companies in the growing digital computer and telecommunications sectors.

By the time tens of thousands of Chicago residents and visitors examined the exhibits of machines and devices at the Electricity Building on the grounds of the WORLD'S COLUMBIAN EXPOSITION in 1893, electric lighting and TELEPHONE technologies were already well established, and it was obvious that electrical devices would become an increasingly important part of modern life. But it was not until the 1920s that radios—the first major consumer electronics products—began to be produced (as well as purchased) in large numbers by Chicago-area residents. One of the leaders in the field of early radio technology was Western Electric, the huge manufacturing and research arm of AT&T, based in suburban CICERO. During the 1910s, Western Electric researchers pioneered the development of the high-vacuum electronic tube, the condenser microphone, and air-to-ground radio communication. Such technologies were quickly put to use in the new radio equipment industry.

During the 1920s and 1930s, the production of radios was a major economic activity in the Chicago area, which was one of the centers of this new industry. By the end of the 1920s, about a third of the radios being made in the United States were manufactured by Chicago-area companies and their employees. At the end of the 1930s, about 12,000 local residents worked in radio and phonograph factories, which had an annual output valued at about $75 million.

During WORLD WAR II, many of Chicago's radio manufacturers turned to the production of electronics equipment for the military. The Zenith Radio Corporation, one of the city's leading radio makers since the 1920s, joined Western Electric and other firms in efforts to produce new radar equipment. Several of these manufacturers affiliated themselves into a trade organization called Radar-Radio Industries of Chicago, Inc., an association of area companies that together employed over 40,000 people, who made over half of the electronics equipment manufactured in the United States during the war. Another local electronics manufacturer turned military contractor was the Galvin Manufacturing Corporation (which would become Motorola after the war), which had been specializing in the production of radios for AUTOMOBILES. During the war, Galvin supplied the military with two-way portable radios known as walkie-talkies.

From the end of World War II through the beginning of the 1970s, Chicago-area companies and their workers continued to be leaders in the consumer electronics industry, which now entered the age of television. By 1949, local factories owned by Zenith and other companies employed about 40,000 people making televisions; roughly 40 percent of domestic output came from the Chicago area. By the early 1960s, the production of all kinds of electronics and communications equipment accounted for a total of about 140,000 area jobs—which made electronics the city's leading manufacturing sector. At that time, the Chicago area made nearly half of the consumer electronics goods produced in the United States, and area companies such as Zenith, Admiral, and Motorola were widely recognized as industry leaders.

As the electronics industry matured and moved into the computer age, Chicago's status as a leading manufacturing center declined. Competition from overseas cut into the profits of local makers of radios and televisions, forcing many of them to shrink or fold. One of the most dramatic chapters in this story was the fall of Zenith, the leading television manufacturer, which still employed over 12,000 area residents as late as the early 1970s. Zenith lobbied vigorously for protection from international competition but received little and was forced to cut jobs and move production out of the area. By the end of the twentieth century, a crippled Zenith had been purchased by a South Korean company, and its survival was uncertain. The fate of this one company was representative of the Chicago area's declining importance as a maker of consumer electronics products. By the early 1990s, there were still about 69,000 area residents with jobs making a wide range of "electronic and other electric equipment," but area companies now accounted for under 5 percent of national output—a far cry from the roughly 45 percent they had made a generation earlier.

In the late twentieth century, as the electronics industry began to use semiconductors to produce smaller and more sophisticated computing and communications equipment, a few Chicago-area companies and their workers played a part. Zenith, as it attempted to move into more profitable fields, became a major computer products maker during the 1980s. But the most important Chicago-area company in the new electronics industry was Motorola, which after changing its name from Galvin in 1947 had made a successful reconversion back from military to civilian production. As its headquarters moved from Chicago to suburban FRANKLIN PARK and then SCHAUMBURG, Motorola was growing into a large corporation that stood as one of the leaders of the U.S. electronics industry. As the manufacture of car radios and televisions became less profitable, the company managed to find success with new products. In the early 1990s, Motorola stood as the world's third-leading producer of the semiconductors and microprocessors, which were at the heart of the computing industry; it also sold nearly half of the world's cellular phones and dominated the market for electronic pagers. By the late 1990s, Motorola employed roughly 25,000 Chicago-area residents, making it one of the region's leading sources of jobs. Although Motorola's rapid rise had begun to falter somewhat by the beginning of the twenty-first century, it and a few smaller firms in the area continued to represent Chicago in what had become a highly competitive and dynamic global industry.

Emily Clark
Mark R. Wilson

See also: Broadcasting; Gas and Electricity; Global Chicago; Innovation, Invention, and Chicago Business; Schooling for Work

Further reading: Barrett, John Patrick. *Electricity at the World's Columbian Exposition.* 1894. • Gillespie, Richard. *Manufacturing Knowledge: A History of the Hawthorne Experiments.* 1991. • Kandlik, Edward. "Chicago Portrait—Electronics and Electrical Equipment." *Commerce* 61.10 (November 1964): 18–19, 43–45.

Elevated. *See* L; Rapid Transit System

Elgin, IL, Kane County, 35 miles NW of the Loop. The future site of Elgin was well known to the POTAWATOMI, for here the FOX RIVER could be forded at many times of the year, and there was good fishing in the shallows. Hezekiah Gifford apparently gave Elgin its name after the 1833 BLACK HAWK WAR. By 1837, it already had a bridge and a mill or two, and was beginning to enjoy a certain importance as a stage on the coach route from Chicago to the lead mines of Galena. In 1849, the Galena & Chicago Union Railroad reached Elgin, which later would be served by RAILROADS running along both banks of the Fox River, linking the growing town to Chicago and other urban centers. Elgin showed great promise in the 1850s, and in 1856 the Elgin Academy was founded. The town continued to thrive during the 1860s, both as a center of military production during the Civil War and because industrial enterprises began to use the water power of the swiftly flowing Fox River.

The most important venture founded at this time was the Elgin National Watch Company, organized to rival the American Waltham Watch Company of Waltham, Massachusetts.

From its small beginnings in 1864 it eventually became for a time the world's largest watch-manufacturing complex, spreading the name of Elgin across much of the industrialized world. In 1866 Gail Borden founded a condensed-milk factory, whose product also became widely known. Other Elgin industries included a large shoe factory and a number of grain mills. The population of Elgin grew from 5,441 in 1870 to 17,823 in 1890, when the city was divided into seven wards and had expanded far out from its origins by the ford, especially on the timbered east bank of the river. In 1872 it attracted a major state institution, the Northern Illinois State Mental Hospital.

During the twentieth century, Elgin has continued to thrive modestly. For a time during the 1920s it was one of the centers for a great network of interurban trains, which linked together the towns of the Fox River Valley and their neighbors to the east. This remarkable system might have continued to grow and to serve the region well, but it was dismantled during the great expansion in automobile travel in the 1950s.

Today the town extends well beyond the original nucleus, with growth along Interstate 90 to the north. Most of its heavy industries have disappeared, but it enjoys a quiet prosperity as a center for commuters and, increasingly, for companies such as Motorola and Bank One. Redevelopment of the downtown area has included the Grand Victoria Casino.

David Buisseret

See also: Economic Geography; Gambling; Mental Health; Metropolitan Growth

Further reading: Alft, E. C. *Elgin: An American History, 1835–1935.* 1984. • Alft, E. C. *South Elgin: A History of the Village from Its Origin as Clintonville.* 1979.

Holiday Inn of Elk Grove Village–Centex Industrial Park, 1968. Photographer: Curt Teich & Co. Source: Curt Teich Archives, Lake County Discovery Museum.

Elk Grove Village, IL, Cook and Lake Counties, 20 miles NW of the Loop. Elk Grove Village differs from many other suburban towns in that it did not emerge as a nineteenth-century market town, or around a railroad depot; indeed, it did not come into existence as a center of settlement until around 1940, roughly at the place where Touhy Avenue intersects with route 53.

This was in the southeastern corner of the old Elk Grove township, which took its name from the huge grove that is now the Ned Brown Forest Preserve. Bounded on the west by Salt Creek, and on the east by the line of the present Arlington Heights Road, this forested area attracted not only Potawatomi hunters, but also, from the mid-1830s onwards, Yankee settlers. The open prairie areas often tended to be marshy, but the early Yankee farmers were joined in the late 1840s by Germans, and together they eventually drained much of the area round the future site of Elk Grove Village.

No railroad traversed this part of the country, and it remained very rural right down to the Second World War; indeed, it is only on the map of 1941 that we begin to discern the development of a little town. At that time the future O'Hare Airport, a mile or so to the southeast, was beginning to emerge as a center for the manufacture of Douglas transport aircraft; eventually it would become the major hub of United Airlines, which would make its headquarters in Elk Grove Village.

All this lay in the future in 1941, and as late as 1956, when Elk Grove Village was incorporated, the population numbered only 125. After that development was rapid. Following a plan proposed by the Centex Corporation of Dallas (Texas), curvilinear streets were laid out, and by the late 1950s and 1960s a whole suburb came into being, complete with schools, churches and shopping centers; in 1958 this growth was much encouraged by the construction of the Northwest Tollway, cutting across the northern edge of the town.

The Northwest Tollway also clipped off the northern section of the old grove. But in general the Elk Grove Forest Preserve, established in 1924, succeeded not only in resisting such encroachments, but even in recovering land previously lost. By 1994 the great grove had largely recovered its historic outline. By 2000 Elk Grove Village had reached the limits of territorial expansion, with 34,727 inhabitants.

David Buisseret

See also: Built Environment of the Chicago Region; Suburbs and Cities as Dual Metropolis

Further reading: Buisseret, David, and James A. Issel. *Elk Grove Village and Township.* 1996. • Wajer, Mary Hagan. *Elk Grove: The Land and the Settlers, 1834–1880.* 1976.

"Old Main," Elmhurst College, 1943. Photographer: Curt Teich & Co. Source: Curt Teich Archives, Lake County Discovery Museum.

Elmhurst College. Elmhurst College was founded in 1871 as a private, all-male proseminary of the German Evangelical Synod of the Northwest (a precursor of the United Church of Christ) to provide professional training for theological students and parochial-school teachers of the Church. This remained the college's mission until 1919 when the school reorganized and expanded into the Elmhurst Academy and Junior College. Subsequent changes in the 1920s phased out the two-year program and initiated the bachelor of arts program. Since becoming a four-year institution the college has maintained its affiliation with the United Church of Christ while expanding enrollment to over 2,700 residential and commuter students.

Susanne Schmitz

See also: Colleges, Junior and Community; Protestants; Religious Institutions; Universities and Their Cities

Further reading: Cutright, Melitta J. *An Ever-Widening Circle: The Elmhurst College Years.* 1995.

Elmhurst, IL, DuPage County, 16 miles W of the Loop. Elmhurst shares the agricultural roots of its DuPage neighbors, but also served as an elegant center for great estate owners during the late nineteenth century and was DuPage's largest city in the 1920s.

York Township's early residents came mainly from New York or Europe to live along Salt Creek; Germans, such as Frederick Graue, settled in the north near the Elmhurst-Addison boundary, and those of predominantly English ancestry resided in the south near today's Butterfield Road. The village remained bilingual for decades.

Gerry Bates, referred to as Elmhurst's founder, brought a sense of community to the area when his Hill Cottage Tavern opened in 1843 as inn, stage stop, and local gathering place. In 1849 the Galena & Chicago Union Railroad arrived, and the community was officially named Cottage Hill, after the tavern. York Street became the village's main thoroughfare. In 1850 School District No. 1 was organized, with both English and German spoken in the classroom. The German Evangelical Synod of the Northwest established a proseminary in 1871, which later became Elmhurst College.

Thomas Barbour Bryan, a Virginia-born lawyer, purchased a thousand acres from Bates and built a country house. His contributions to the town led residents to refer to him as "The Father of Elmhurst." In 1862, he organized the first Protestant church as an Episcopal lay reader (St. Mary's Roman Catholic Church was founded the same year). Bryan's brother-in-law, Jedediah H. Lathrop, joined with other estate owners in planting a large number of elm trees along Cottage Hill, from which Elmhurst acquired its present name in 1869.

Swenson's Greenhouse, 5 York Street, Elmhurst, early twentieth century. Photographer: Unknown. Source: DuPage County Historical Museum.

The Fire of 1871 brought wealthy refugees to Elmhurst and marked the onset of Elmhurst's gilded age, an era of elegant socializing that lasted into the twentieth century. By the turn of the century, what is now the site of York High School had served as both the Elmhurst Golf Club and the original Hawthorne racetrack (relocated to Cicero).

Elmhurst was incorporated in 1882, serving not only these wealthy estate owners, but also farmers, local businessmen, and owners of area industries. In 1883 Adolph Hammerschmidt and Henry Assman founded Elmhurst-Chicago Stone Company near the village's western limits to quarry dolomite limestone.

During the 1920s Elmhurst became DuPage's largest city, with paved streets, a city planning commission and the founding in 1926 of the Elmhurst Memorial Hospital. The city-manager form of government was adopted in 1953. Elmhurst grew as a railroad suburb with many urban amenities, including Elmhurst College (whose campus is an accredited arboretum), the Lizzadro Museum of Lapidary Art (1962), the Elmhurst Art Museum, a public library, a park district, the Wilder Park conservatory (1923), the Elmhurst Historical Museum (1956), and the Elmhurst Symphony Orchestra (1960). Though essentially landlocked by the 1990s, Elmhurst engaged in ongoing redevelopment.

Jane S. Teague

See also: Metropolitan Growth; Planning Chicago; Suburbs and Cities as Dual Metropolis

Further reading: Russell, Don. *Elmhurst: Trails from Yesterday.* 1977. • Thompson, Richard A., ed. *DuPage Roots.* 1985.

Elmwood Park, IL, Cook County, 10 miles W of the Loop. Elmwood Park, once an open prairie with rich black loam soil and clay subsoil, sits at the southeastern section of Leyden Township between Chicago and the Des Plaines River. Native Americans made tools and constructed mounds along the river's bluffs. In the 1840s farmers came to the area, which was then known as Orison. The Chicago & Pacific Railroad laid tracks in Leyden Township in 1870. The tracks ran diagonally across the township along Old Army Trail or Grand Avenue, with a train station at 75th Avenue. Local speculators bought many of the smaller farms and subdivided the land for residential development. As farming gave way to home construction, Orison became known as Elmwood Park.

Local landowners were instrumental in extending the Grand Avenue streetcar line west past Harlem Avenue to 72nd Court in 1905. They understood that transportation was key to land development, and farmland and open prairie soon became rows of streets improved by street lighting, water, and sewers. Elmwood Park was incorporated as a village in 1914. Merritt Marwood, descended from one of the first farm families, served as the first mayor.

Elmwood Park experienced its greatest boom in population between 1920 and 1928. During this boom, new churches, a village hall, and a school were erected to serve the expanding village. Westwood, a 245-acre subdivision developed by John Mills and Sons Construction Company, contained 1,679 residential lots and 146 commercial sites. The Circle Parkway, a diversion from the standard grid just north of Grand Avenue, provided space for village functions as well as retail space.

Population expanded again after World War II, increasing from 13,689 in 1940 to 18,801 a decade later. The village built a high school and a new reservoir to accommodate this growth. Elmer Conti was elected the first village president in 1953, after Elmwood Park adopted a village manager system. A civic center was built on the Circle Parkway in the 1970s, and a new library was completed nearby in 2002.

Tina Reithmaier

See also: Built Environment of the Chicago Region; Government, Suburban

Further reading: Elmwood Park, Fourth of July Committee. *Elmwood Park Reflections.* 1976. • Elmwood Park, Golden Jubilee Celebration Committee. *Village of Elmwood Park Golden Jubilee, 1914–1964.* 1964. • Elmwood Park. *Elmwood Park.* 1959.

Elwood, IL, Will County, 41 miles SW of the Loop. Area residents incorporated the village in 1873 and established a Baptist church five years later. Elwood grew modestly until World War II, when the federal government built a 3,000-acre munitions plant with 12,000 jobs. An explosion at the plant killed 48 workers in 1942.

Erik Gellman

See also: Will County

Eminent Domain. Eminent domain is the right of government to take private property for a public purpose through condemnation and payment of fair value. A government can delegate powers of eminent domain to qualified common carriers, utilities, hospitals, and universities. An eminent-domain action can elicit a counteraction by rival claimants and affected businesses and citizens. Prime examples of eminent-domain controversies in Chicago were *A. Montgomery Ward v. Chicago* (1890–1911), *Chicago v.* Illinois Central Railroad

(1919), URBAN RENEWAL on the South and West Sides in the 1950s, the site searches for McCormick Place and the Chicago campus of the UNIVERSITY OF ILLINOIS in the 1950s, and mayoral control of Chicago's airports in the 1990s.

The public was effectively cut off from access to the south lakefront between the 1850s and 1920s by the 10-track mainline of the Illinois Central. The Lake Front Ordinance of 1919 provided some relief, but too little and too late. By 1940, the city's worst slums festered on the NEAR SOUTH SIDE. Fighting for their survival, affected hospitals and universities lobbied in Springfield and Washington to delegate powers of eminent domain to themselves and to add slum prevention and eradication to eligible public purposes. The resulting state legislation between 1941 and 1953 served as models for the National Housing Acts of 1949 and 1954, and produced the Lake Meadows, Prairie Shores, and HYDE PARK A & B residential developments.

Pierre de Vise

See also: Built Environment of the Chicago Region; Housing Reform; Land Use; O'Hare Airport; Real Estate; Waterfront

Further reading: Banfield, Edward C. *Political Influence.* 1961. • Corliss, Carlton J. *Main Line of Mid-America: The Story of the Illinois Central.* 1950. • Hirsch, Arnold R. *Making the Second Ghetto: Race and Housing in Chicago, 1940–1960.* 1983.

Employment. *See* Unemployment; Work

Englewood, Community Area 68, 7 miles S of the Loop. Before 1850, Englewood was an oak forest with much swampland. In 1852 several RAILROAD lines crossed at what became known as Junction Grove, stimulating the beginning of what we know today as Englewood.

The earliest settlers to Englewood were GERMAN and IRISH workers. They worked initially on truck farms, the railroads, and later at the UNION STOCK YARD. By 1865 Junction Grove was ANNEXED to the Town of LAKE and then Chicago in 1889. In 1868 Henry B. Lewis, a wool merchant in the LOOP and Board of Education member, suggested a new name, Englewood, deriving from his association with Englewood, New Jersey. Also in 1868, developer L. W. Beck gave 10 acres to Englewood for the Cook County Normal School (later Chicago State University), a teacher's college serving the Chicago region. Normal Park developed around the school, paving the way for incoming middle-class homebuyers. In the 1870s Englewood High School was opened.

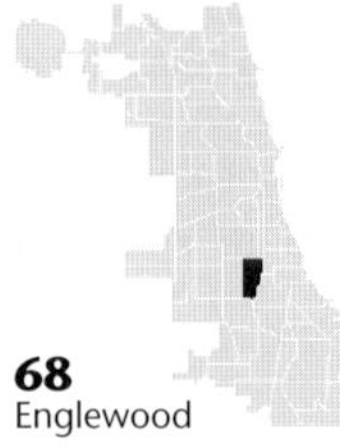

The first religious mission to the area was begun by the Presbyterians, but the first church was St. Anne's ROMAN CATHOLIC Church, established in 1869. In the 1870s PROTESTANTS of every variety established churches. By 1880 Germans, Irish, and SCOTS were the largest ethnic groups, but were supplanted at the turn of the century by Poles and other Eastern European immigrants. By 1887 horsecar lines connected Englewood to downtown, followed by electric trolleys in 1896 and the Elevated line in 1907. By 1922, 2,900 street railways, Elevated, and suburban trains serviced Englewood daily.

The construction of APARTMENT buildings in the 1910s and 1920s created problems of density and economic segregation. By 1920 the population soared to 86,619 and Englewood's SHOPPING DISTRICT at Halsted and 63rd was the second busiest in the city. In 1929, SEARS developed a $1.5 million store here. The GREAT DEPRESSION years did not affect the operation of the larger stores, but many smaller ones suffered and several banks in Englewood closed.

The 1940s witnessed a decline of REAL-ESTATE values in Englewood. Buildings were 40 years old, and the expanding BLACK BELT population from the east resulted in rapid turnover. Materials necessary to redevelop Englewood were scarce owing to WORLD WAR II, and later practices of REDLINING and disinvestment sealed Englewood's future as a low-income community with a declining housing stock. In 1959, a CHICAGO SUN-TIMES writer interviewed a banker about lending in Englewood. His reply illuminates attitudes among lenders at the time. "When a lender makes a loan on a house, he looks at the total financial position of the borrower. The rate is determined by risk. The Negro has to pay a *higher rate* because he is not as secure in his job."

While some economic gains by AFRICAN AMERICANS gave them the opportunity to purchase some of the larger houses in Englewood, many low-income residents rented in more crowded conditions. In 1940 blacks constituted just 2 percent of the population, but this increased to 11 percent in 1950, 69 percent in 1960, and 96 percent by 1970. In 1960 the population peaked at over 97,000 people, despite the exodus of 50,000 whites. Public works projects such as the Dan Ryan EXPRESSWAY and patterns of housing abandonment and deterioration led to a massive loss of housing stock. Further, attempts at restoring the SHOPPING DISTRICT through public funds have been unsuccessful. This is due in part to competition from shopping centers built in the 1960s not far away (such as Evergreen Park and Ford City). By the 1970s, Sears and Wieboldt's had closed, and Chicago State University had moved to 95th Street in ROSELAND. By the end of the century about 100 shops were still operational, with over 75 percent managed by KOREAN and PAKISTANI merchants. Englewood's population declined to 59,075 by 1980 and to 40,222 by 2000. Despite the 200 housing units built by the Antioch Baptist Church and some publicly funded apartments for elderly and handicapped persons, few communities in Chicago have lost as much population or housing stock in the twentieth century.

Clinton E. Stockwell

See also: Contested Spaces; Meatpacking; Public Transportation; Suburbs and Cities as Dual Metropolis

Further reading: Hill, Barbara Rector. *Englewood, 1912–1950: In Celebration of Chicago's Sesquicentennial.* 1988. • Pacyga, Dominic A., and Ellen Skerrett. *Chicago, City of Neighborhoods: Histories and Tours.* 1986. • Sullivan, Gerald E., ed. *The Story of Englewood, 1835–1923.* 1924.

English. The English presence as an identifiable ethnic group in Illinois has received little attention, in part because intermarriage, mobility, and a lack of ethnic institutions have led to their being virtually indistinguishable from native-born white PROTESTANTS after a generation or two. Yet, whether pioneer or entrepreneur, the English and their descendants have been a significant presence in Chicago since the early nineteenth century.

Great Britain's victory over France in the Seven Years' War (1756–1763) resulted in the cession of all FRENCH claims to property in North America east of the Mississippi River, opening a vast area of land to traders and settlers. The English flocked especially to the region eventually known as the Old Northwest, which included what later became the state of Illinois, mostly gravitating to AGRICULTURAL occupations.

The opening of the Erie Canal in 1825 spurred westward migration to the GREAT LAKES region, and, by 1850, Illinois could claim more English-born residents than any other state except New York and Pennsylvania. English-born inhabitants constituted 3 percent of Chicago's population by 1890. Trying to maintain a bit of the old country's traditions, members of Chicago's English community formed, in the spring of 1847, the Saint George's Society of Illinois, for both benevolent and social purposes.

As with Scotland and Wales, emigration from England to the United States generally declined during the twentieth century. American employers had little need for skilled English labor since emigration from Southern and Eastern Europe provided a cheaper workforce. More recently, English immigrants to these shores have tended to be well-educated professionals. Although in recent years there has been an upsurge of interest in ethnic heritage among SCOTTISH Americans, no comparable English equivalent is readily apparent in Chicago.

June Skinner Sawyers

See also: Australians; Demography; Welsh

Further reading: Berthoff, Rowland. *British Immigrants in Industrial America, 1790–1950.* 1953.

• Erickson, Charlotte J. *Invisible Immigrants: The Adaptation of English and Scottish Immigrants in Nineteenth-Century America*. 1972.

Entertaining Chicagoans.

Beginning with the earliest dances at Sauganash Tavern in 1833, Chicago's entertainment history divides into three phases. From the 1830s through the 1870s, entertainment reflected the informality and rough egalitarianism of a largely male frontier city, with few controls over audiences and few formal boundaries between social classes or high and low art forms. A second phase began slowly in the 1850s and was visible by the 1870s, when entertainment mirrored the complexity and stratification of a big city. Amusements underwent a process of refinement by which theaters tried to cater to middle-class tastes, and formal distinctions appeared between popular and high art. As decorum became a watchword in amusements, middle-class women entered genteel forms of amusement but found themselves more isolated from an expanded set of sensual attractions aimed at men of all classes. A third phase began at the turn of the century and reached fruition in the 1920s, when Victorian culture disintegrated as both sexes were drawn to livelier, heterosocial amusements rooted in the entertainments of the lower classes.

Chicago's nineteenth-century theatrical life exemplifies the first phase. In the 1830s and 1840s Chicago was a male frontier town. The scarcity of women diminished controls of class, family, and culture, leading to a rowdy, egalitarian, male-dominated theatrical life. Initial amusements were transient, mounted for short periods by traveling showmen in temporary quarters. The first THEATER opened in the vacant Sauganash Tavern banquet hall in 1837 as a makeshift affair, with rude sets and rude chairs, "all on the level floor, where all men sat in a spirit of equality." Similarly, the Rialto opened as the city's first permanent theater in the spring of 1838 in an old auction house on Dearborn Street. Like its predecessor it was "a den of a place, looking more like a dismantled grist-mill than a temple." No theater lasted long until the 1840s and 1850s.

Early theaters featured a wide variety of entertainments. Performances were long, from 7:30 p.m. until midnight, and theatrical bills consisted of a drama, a farce, and an afterpiece. This left room for a mix of attractions for every taste—romantic melodramas and comedies—punctuated by song and dance in and out of blackface. Shakespeare was the most frequently performed playwright in the city, appearing in the same milieu as circus acts, dancers, singers, minstrels, and comics. Often, the same performer went from Shakespeare or melodrama to popular songs on the same bill. At a benefit for the Rialto Theater, an actor performed Macbeth but between plays sang "Tam O'Shanter." At another benefit, an actor followed a melodrama with Andrew Jackson's campaign song, "The Hunters of Kentucky."

Men of all classes composed the early theater audiences. Respecting few controls over their behavior, they played an active role in the evening's entertainment, often surpassing what transpired on stage. Men did not go to the theater to sit quietly and take in the performance. Rather, they went to socialize, to drink and smoke, and to roam about the room. They also partook of the prostitutes who used theaters to advertise their wares. Stimulated by alcohol, male patrons stamped and yelled, and, as actor Joseph Jefferson noted, "in those days the audience used to throw money on the stage, either for comic songs or dances," and he gladly drew out his turns. The gallery gods and the mixed assemblage of men standing in the pit ruled the stage. As the *Chicago American* complained, performers appealed to rowdy audiences by ad-libbing "obscene witticisms which, while they catch the laugh of some, are very offensive to ladies and gentlemen in their attendance." This democratic male theatrical culture, reflective of the expansion of rights for free white males in the early republic, led one newspaper to declare, "it was not wholly proper for ladies to attend, and patronage came largely from the transient element of society." PROTESTANT clergy also found these theaters obscene, and the acting profession low and vicious. In this atmosphere, theaters could neither attract the city's elites nor make consistent profits.

The first phase of entertainment gave way after midcentury to a separation of high and low cultural appetites. During the 1850s and 1860s, theater managers struggled to control audience behavior and place their theaters on a solid paying basis. They did this by refining theatrical life to make it suitable for middle-class women. The Rice Theater (Randolph near Dearborn), for example, opened in 1847, burned down in 1850, and lacked stable profits. In 1853 John B. Rice redecorated to lend the theater an air of cultivation. To control rowdy male patrons, he transformed the pit, the area most associated with unruly mobs, into a parquette with the addition of comfortable seats and added elegantly furnished boxes. Financial difficulties forced Rice to give way to J. H. McVicker, whose new theater in 1857 cost $85,000 and was a major step in the attempt to legitimize the acting profession and uplift the drama. Located on Madison Avenue between Dearborn and State, McVicker's was bigger and more grandiose than its predecessors. Program notes for 1858 suggest attempts at gentility, with the parquettes for gentlemen and the admonition "no improper characters allowed in the theater"—an allusion to prostitutes and rowdies. In response, the press hailed McVicker's in 1859 for bringing "a better class of entertainment" in keeping with "the artistic tastes of the public."

Theaters also began to fragment along class lines. McVicker's attracted refined members of society and as such was the only theater to remain performing during the CIVIL WAR. In 1863 it offered Chicago's first matinee specifically intended for an audience of women and children. The nighttime offerings showed signs of change too. In contrast to the Rice Theater's long evening of mixed bills, McVicker's program started at 8 p.m., ended earlier, and featured only one drama. Moreover, after the Civil War, McVicker's separated Shakespeare's plays from mixed bills of raucous entertainment and gave the evening entirely to an appreciation of the dramatist's work. McVicker's thus exemplified the trend toward the formal distinction between high and low theater. It also showed that theaters could attract middle-class women

Sauganash Hotel, engraving, 1884. Artist: L. Braunhold. Source: Chicago Historical Society.

by removing sensuality, alcohol, rowdy audience participation, and PROSTITUTION. By the 1880s McVicker proudly linked Chicago theater with "a severer regime of good taste and decorum," adding that "the theater keeps pace with civilization."

By refining some of the city's drama with an emphasis on bourgeois decorum, theater managers made it possible by the 1870s and 1880s for women to become the mainstay of the matinee audience. Melodrama proved the backbone of popular theater, for it dramatized the official values of late-nineteenth-century Chicago by emphasizing that self-control and female refinement formed the basis of American civilization and progress. Attracting both men and women, melodrama featured male heroes who rescued virginal heroines. The hero's will set him apart from villains either poor and vicious or rich and decadent. By drawing on his internal morality to depose external authority symbolized by the villain, the hero demonstrated an allegiance to the refined heroine, the private family, and sexual restraint. To appeal to large female audiences, melodrama examined the demands of home and family and punished those women who strayed from its bounds.

Even blackface minstrelsy, the most popular male form of nineteenth-century amusement, showed a gradual evolution toward greater formalism and sentimentality. Dating from the 1840s, blackface singers and dancers appeared on the same bills as Shakespeare. As part of an industrializing, controlled world, white men blackened their faces to indulge in forbidden carnal impulses associated with blacks. Minstrels portrayed northern "Zip Coons" as self-indulgent, incapable of self-control and willpower, while plantation slaves were shown as happy because they lived subservient to white owners. In both cases, black men were the opposite of whites, whose producer values working- and middle-class audiences saw as their own. By wearing the mask, whites could act out the dangerous impulses they denied themselves as they struggled to uphold self-control and gentility.

By the 1870s, as part of growing specialization, minstrelsy was housed in its own separate theaters or appeared for a run at North's Theater. It also increasingly harkened nostalgically to a sentimental rural past free of industrial conflicts. Greater emphasis was placed on sentimental ballads and virginal belles, and with its sensual implications diminished, it was considered more suitable for white women.

Encamped in open spaces downtown, circuses dramatized the battle between civilization and nature. Once circuses regulated prostitutes and the carny atmosphere, they attracted family audiences. Featuring the struggle between beasts and animal trainers and equestrian daredevils, the circus enacted the progress of morally and physically courageous men and women over nature. The use of three rings in the 1880s and the elevation of circus owners to big businessmen symbolized the taming of nature, the growing power of hierarchical economic institutions, and the taming of audiences. A variant, Buffalo Bill's Wild West Show, proved a major Chicago attraction from the 1880s through WORLD WAR I, as it enacted the triumph of white American civilization, rooted in white womanhood, the private family farm, and the RAILROAD over primeval nature, wild animals, and savage races.

If Chicago entertainment showed a gradual evolution toward genteel amusements and high culture where bourgeois men and women could attend together in a decorous atmosphere, the fragmentation of amusements also permitted the expansion of more sensual attractions that were part of a rowdy male amusement world. While the middle and upper classes after midcentury adhered to Victorian notions of privacy and female refinement that limited where men and women could go together, men of all classes continued to enjoy a double standard. Men of all classes could enjoy rougher public amusements linked to SALOONS, where they could indulge in liquor, sports, POLITICS, and bawdy entertainment. Women who frequented these establishments were deemed prostitutes by moralists. Because GERMANS drank in family settings with women and children, the German beer garden eventually proved an exception to this pattern.

Staged in concert saloons, "variety" specialized in the rough male elements linked to the alcoholic intimacy and uproarious crowd behavior that had come to be excluded from more orderly theaters and considered too disreputable for respectable women. Variety featured song, DANCE, comedy, and waiter girls who served liquor and performed for the enjoyment of males. Because of the mixture of sex, alcohol, and audience participation, connoting unruly male passions, concert saloons had a poor reputation. Burlesque also occupied a low place of amusement. When Lydia Thompson's British Blondes appeared at Crosby's OPERA House in 1869 and 1870, they created a sensation; even middle-class women wanted to see their half-clothed verbal send-ups of current affairs. After editor Wilbur F. Storey attacked the troupe, however, a scandal erupted. As a symbol of the dangerous sexual impulses that the theater struggled to erase, the erotic burlesque female thereafter was cast from reputable middle-class amusements and appeared on stages specifically designed for male patrons only.

Public DANCE HALLS also challenged values of WORK, order, and restraint. Back in 1833 everyone had danced at the Sauganash Tavern, but after the Civil War, because many halls were in red-light districts and served alcohol, public dancing in Chicago assumed a notorious reputation. With saloons, brothels, and GAMBLING dens, the Levee lured men of all classes who enjoyed the rough equality and anarchic behavior of a legal VICE DISTRICT. As a result, the middle and upper classes organized their intimate activities, such as dancing, in the privacy of their homes or the carefully restricted world of society dancing master's halls and balls, while members of the working class enjoyed their dances as part of the benefits and celebrations of ethnic communities aimed at the entire family, thus safeguarding young women.

This divided world of amusements gave way to a third phase of entertainment around the turn of the century, as new entertainments,

Aragon Ballroom interior, ca. 1926. Photographer: Raymond Trowbridge. Source: Chicago Historical Society.

Balaban & Katz

Founded in 1916 by West Siders Sam Katz and Barney and A. J. Balaban, by 1925 the Balaban & Katz chain of motion picture theaters had constructed theaters of unprecedented size and splendor across the Chicago region, enjoyed a monopoly from Minneapolis to St. Louis, and set the national standard for luxury and profitability. "B&K" achieved this dominance by taking advantage of new technologies and shifts in population. Of their famous picture palaces—the Central Park (1917), Riviera (1918), Tivoli (1921), Uptown (1925), and Chicago (1921)—all but one were located in outlying areas of the city, newly served by the "L" and home to growing numbers of prosperous middle-class consumers. B&K attracted these patrons not with the quality of its films but with opulent surroundings, extravagant service, full-scale musical stage productions, and the pioneering use of air conditioning. These strategies influenced film exhibition nationwide.

In 1925 B&K merged with Famous Players–Lasky Studio to become the cornerstone of the national Publix chain. Its success lasted until 1946, when federal action dismantled vertical integration in the film industry.

Geoffrey Klingsporn

rooted in a new heterosocial ethic, stood poised to become regular parts of urban life. The demand for new forms of amusement lay in a psychic revolt against the feminization and rationalization of urban life during the late nineteenth century. The growth of a model of success based on money, consumption, and pleasure enabled rich and poor to shape entertainment. Rising wage rates enabled children of new immigrants to seek relief from mechanized jobs and entree to a wider American world through participation in cheap amusements. Similarly, white-collar workers turned to LEISURE to express their individualism outside corporate offices. At all levels, young women now worked outside the home and sought after-work leisure traditionally enjoyed by men. With time and some money to explore personal identity apart from family, they helped transform courting and youth culture and deeply influenced modern entertainment.

Electricity helped cheap amusements meet the growing demand for leisure. After 1900, AMUSEMENT PARKS emerged to offer new informal pleasures to mass audiences. Opened in 1904, Riverview Park (Belmont and Western) used electric streetcars to bring patrons and electricity to power the rides. White City (63rd and Cottage Grove) opened in 1906 as "the city of a million electric lights," at the terminus of "L" and streetcar lines. With fantasy decor, large grounds, and mechanical rides, amusement parks provided only pleasure, not education or uplift. Set apart from daily life, these parks offered patrons the chance to enjoy new machines as pleasure not utility, test themselves versus machines that dominated urban life, and burlesque urban experience. Surviving Riverview's Scenic Railway, a roller coaster built in 1907, riders triumphed over the noise and confusion of the industrial city and its machines. The jouncing rides also fostered informal sexual encounters as they threw young men and women into each other's arms. Release not restraint reigned. Rules of class and ethnicity temporarily suspended, people yelled, laughed, and shed their dignity, thus merging into a heterogeneous urban public. Perhaps this new informality explains why AFRICAN AMERICANS were denied entrance to all but the black-owned Joyland Park (33rd and Wabash), opened in 1923.

VAUDEVILLE, with its aura of consumption, was also designed to welcome a mixed-sex audience and depended on PUBLIC TRANSPORTATION to bring heterogeneous audiences. New vaudeville circuits refined low-class variety in order to attract women and children. Luxurious decor and decorous treatment gave everyone a sense of wealth and comfort. Ushers treated all white women as ladies, while the variety of acts reflected the diversity of city life: circus and minstrel acts, ethnic comedians, and dancers satisfied all tastes. Vaudeville also interpreted the material world of technology, money, and enjoyment for urban audiences, redefining success to mean enjoyment of wealth rather than its pursuit. Like all the new urban amusements, vaudeville proclaimed its respectability in order to attract women and families, but it also promised a new vitality and personal freedom distinct from Victorian codes of propriety. Singers like Eva Tanguay and Sophie Tucker, for example, offered thrilling glimpses of female sexuality. Chicago's vaudeville theaters were the second stop on the national circuits, and by the 1910s the Majestic and the Palace featured only headliners.

As the second major market in the country, Chicago played an important role in American movie history. Chicago's role initially involved production. William Selig built Polyscope, the world's first movie studio, in Chicago in 1897. By 1907 his studio, at Irving Park Road and Western Avenue, was the country's largest. Founded the same year, Essanay grew out of the partnership of George K. Spoor and

A short five blocks east of the epicenter of "the Stroll," the Plantation Café's bright neon sign at 35th and Calumet Streets suggested black Chicago's continuing engagement with the Deep South. Photographer: Unknown. Source: Chicago Historical Society.

cowboy star "Broncho Billy" Anderson. The Motion Picture Patents Company, to which both studios belonged, prospered with stars like Gloria Swanson, Francis X. Bushman, and Charlie Chaplin. California's better weather, however, combined with a court ruling that declared the company's exclusive right to motion pictures unconstitutional, shifted FILM production away from Chicago by World War I.

Moralists found the impact of the "nickel theater" extremely troubling. A mass art form because of electricity, the MOVIES were introduced as educational devices, but they soon became cheap pleasure machines when they opened in working-class areas as nickelodeons. The movies' reach threatened traditional notions about sex and class. Women went unchaperoned, young couples petted in the dark, and immigrant children saw dramas of crime, sexuality, and challenges to authority. These themes discouraged middle-class patronage and spurred the reform efforts of civic groups and SETTLEMENT HOUSE workers concerned that movies promoted vice among city migrants, especially women. By the 1910s Chicago had the nation's first censorship agency, a POLICE board that prescreened films. The reform effort was part of a larger fear of new amusements in the Progressive era. Fearing the spread of decadence from the rich and vice from the poor, an anxious middle class sought to uplift movies and make them more respectable. Movie men responded by hiring uniformed ushers to keep order and removing objectionable films. MOVIE PALACES, many built by Balaban and Katz, such as UPTOWN's Riviera and Uptown, the LOOP's Chicago and Oriental, and the SOUTH SIDE's Paradise, connected movies to success rather than to vice. Quality improved too. Films became longer playlets, historical dramas, and socially conscious movies. By the 1920s, stars became guides to personal behavior, fashion trends, and new styles of sexual interaction, just as the palaces themselves represented the height of mass urban luxury.

Dance halls followed a similar path. Linked to vice, they only slowly gained public acceptance. By 1900 saloons opened annexes for dancing to meet the demands of young working-class women eager for inexpensive places to meet members of the opposite sex apart from parents. Worried about the dangers to young women, reformers during the 1910s banned alcohol, censored close-hold ragtime dances, and opened city halls. These reforms alerted entrepreneurs to the dance hall's commercial potential. Working closely with reformers, the Karzas Brothers opened the Trianon Ballroom in 1922 at 62nd and Cottage Grove Avenue with a no JAZZ policy and floor spotters to police the crowd. In 1926 they opened Uptown's ARAGON BALLROOM. Both spots attracted a lower-middle-class and working-class clientele. Free from disreputable associations, ballrooms used luxurious palatial designs to uplift sex into romance.

As with other amusements, the pursuit of decorum and the fear of sex led to rigid racial segregation. But in the twentieth century, even the well-to-do sought ways to break down the cultural barriers that had set them off from the lower classes. Cabarets allowed affluent men and women to interact in new ways in settings of public anonymity. Initially, saloons cleared away tables, put in dance floors, and hired performers to form cabarets. Cabarets stressed informal, intimate entertainment on the floor and among the tables, breaking down barriers between performer and audience, and spurring guests to express themselves. Cabarets relied on the dance craze of the 1910s to become public meeting grounds for men and women who sought intimacy in new ragtime dances such as the Turkey Trot and Bunny Hug that arose out of black dance and lower-class pastimes. Cabarets were also the first public places to permit women to drink. To offset the danger in women's new behavior, cafes stressed their reputable character. The Edelweiss Gardens presented "Dining, Dancing and Entertainment" in "the most charming environment" and hired high-class ballroom acts, as did the Sherman Hotel's College Inn. The Movie Inn (17 N. Wabash) opened in 1915 to meet the demand for public dancing. Its booths named for movie stars, the Inn attracted players from Essanay studio but ran into trouble when gigolos appeared in the afternoon squiring married women. Fearful of mixing between women performers and audiences and the expression of body impulses in the ragtime dances, moralists protested afternoon dancing but lost in court when reputable venues objected.

By the 1920s Chicago nightclubs symbolized big-city lawlessness and the moral rebellion of PROHIBITION. As speakeasies, they came under the control of criminals like Al Capone and Bugs Moran. The attraction of risk, public intimacy, and the chance to see lively entertainment and rub elbows with celebrities made clubs popular. Nightlife was so popular that ROADHOUSES, often run by the mob, opened in incorporated areas from STICKNEY to NILES so urbanites and suburbanites might enjoy a night out. Uptown's ballrooms and clubs abounded. The Green Mill (Broadway and Lawrence) presented top acts like Sophie Tucker and Joe E. Lewis. TOWERTOWN, north of the river, had dives for the underworld and transients who filled the furnished rooms west of Clark, clubs for nearby Gold Coasters, and arty bohemian GAY spots. In the Loop, Friars Inn, Ciro's, the Hotel Morrison's Terrace Room, the Blackhawk, and many more enlivened nightlife by allowing women to drink, dance, and socialize on the same level as men.

Black Chicagoans participated in this entertainment upsurge, but in a separate amusement zone on the STROLL along 35th and State Streets. While Chicago's amusements elsewhere represented a new, wider public sphere, white skin remained a prerequisite for admission. African Americans found themselves excluded entirely in the most intimate of

Benny Goodman and Orchestra, Congress Hotel, 1935. Photographer: Unknown. Source: Chicago Historical Society.

entertainments or, in the case of theaters, segregated to balconies. They sued theater owners, but their major action was to build their own theaters, saloons, and cabarets, starting with the Pekin, the nation's first black-owned theater, opened in 1905 by Robert T. Motts. By the early 1920s, numerous places existed for black workers to dance or see a show on the Stroll. Among the cabarets and dance halls were the Dreamland Cafe, Lincoln Gardens, the Entertainer's Cafe, the Sunset, Plantation, and the Apex. For migrants from the South, clubs helped ease the transition between rural mores and city culture.

With the SOUTH SIDE'S cafes and dance halls booming, Chicago was America's jazz capital during the twenties. Musicians from New Orleans and other parts of the country followed their audiences to the city as part of the "GREAT MIGRATION." King Oliver's Dixie Syncopators (with Louis Armstrong), Carroll Dickerson's Orchestra, Earl Hines, Zutty Singleton, Ethel Waters, Alberta Hunter, Bessie Smith, clarinetist Jimmie Noone, and many more played all over the South Side. White slummers bent on losing their inhibitions in "black and tans" soon followed, as did the many white jazzmen who sought to learn the new expressive music from the artists who had created it.

From 1900 to the 1920s, Chicago enjoyed an explosion of popular culture. Movies, amusement parks, vaudeville, cabarets, dance halls, and music deeply influenced the Jazz Age. The new amusements redefined success to include pleasure and consumption, and as mixed-sex institutions they also created new ways for men and women to court, establishing greater equality for women in leisure activities. Technology, long the bane of the working class, was glorified as an agency for human pleasure. It was considered dangerous for blacks and whites to mix too intimately, so African Americans were kept outside the influence of assimilation that immigrants enjoyed. Segregated from white amusements, black Chicagoans pioneered their own. Their creative revenge was jazz, and Chicago became a capital of the new music. The GREAT DEPRESSION of the 1930s brought this explosion to a momentary close. Entertainments would reopen in different forms after 1934, when repeal of PROHIBITION and the NEW DEAL restored people's spirits, but the outline of modern amusements had already been established in Chicago in the preceding decades and over the preceding hundred years.

Lewis A. Erenberg

See also: Bands, Early and Golden Age; Creation of Chicago Sports; Lectures and Public Speaking; Street Life; Theater, Ethnic; Underground Economy

Further reading: Readers who seek further information on Chicago's early theaters should consult the exhaustive A. T. Andreas, *History of Chicago,* vols. 1–3 (1884). Julia Foulkes, "The Theatre Ascends as Chicago Grows: 1837–1871" (unpublished paper, Loyola University Chicago, 1990), provides the best analysis of early Chicago theater. She builds on Lawrence Levine, *Highbrow/Lowbrow: The Emergence of Cultural Hierarchy in America* (1988), which traces the shift in male and class undifferentiated theaters to more genteel theaters at the end of the century. Robert Allen, *Horrible Prettiness: Burlesque and American Culture* (1991), ties the growth of a more genteel theater culture to the increasing presence of women, while tracing the delights and dangers of burlesque theater. John Kasson, *Rudeness and Civility: Manners in Nineteenth-Century Urban America* (1990), traces the development of controlled audience behavior through the movies, vaudeville, and the concert hall.

For early-twentieth-century dance halls and amusements, see Kathy Peiss, *Cheap Amusements* (1986), which traces the shift to heterosocial entertainments to the new leisure patterns of working-class women. John Kasson, *Amusing the Million: Coney Island at the Turn of the Century* (1978), shows how amusement parks in New York became special types of parks, devoted to pleasure rather than uplift. On a related theme, Lauren Rabinovitz, *For the Love of Pleasure: Women, Movies, and Culture in Turn-of-the-Century Chicago* (1998), traces the idea of female spectatorship at the movies. For more on the growth of movies, see the pathbreaking books by Lary May, *Screening Out the Past: The Birth of Mass Culture and the Motion Picture Industry* (1983), and Robert Sklar, *Movie-Made America: A Cultural History of American Movies* (1975). For censorship of early films, see Kathleen D. McCarthy, "Nickel Vice and Virtue: Movie Censorship in Chicago, 1907–1915," *Journal of Popular Film* 5, no. 4 (1976).

Chicago nightlife is an open field. There are pieces of the story in Perry R. Duis, *Challenging Chicago: Coping with Everyday Life, 1837–1920* (1998). For jazz and cabarets in Chicago during the 1920s, William H. Kenney III, *Chicago Jazz: A Cultural History, 1904–1930* (1993), is indispensable. Harvey Zorbaugh, *Gold Coast and Slum: A Sociological Study of Chicago's Near North Side* (1929), offers an early Chicago School of Sociology approach to the role of cabarets, dance halls, and nightlife zones in Chicago. For the development of New York nightlife, which bore a number of similarities to its development in Chicago, see Lewis A. Erenberg, *Steppin' Out: New York Nightlife and the Transformation of American Culture, 1890–1930* (1984).

Environmental Politics. The city represents collective human effort to impose a BUILT ENVIRONMENT upon the natural one. In constructing these artificial habitats, power relationships are played out in spatial terms. The political economy of capitalist societies facilitates this process through its primary institution, private property, but the public sector has been intimately involved in building cities in three important ways. First, frameworks of LAW and POLITICS defined LAND USE patterns in Chicago from the first plat of 1830 to the present ZONING ordinances. Second, precedents of common law formed a basis for interventions by local government in the private sector to regulate activities that were deemed to have detrimental effects on the land as well as the air and the WATER. Over the course of the nineteenth century, these restrictions grew into elaborate PUBLIC HEALTH, plumbing, and BUILDING CODES, complete with inspectional bureaucracies to administer and enforce them. And since then, state and national governments have taken up the challenge of ameliorating the harmful impacts of urban pollution and sprawl. Third, initiatives of city hall built an INFRASTRUCTURE of complex technological networks in addition to providing an array of services such as garbage collection, street cleaning, and WATER SUPPLY. Taken together, environmental politics go a long way toward explaining not only the topography of the urban environment but also the quality of life within it. Some of the most critical challenges facing Chicago at the close of the twentieth century are the result of public policies that helped produce an exploding metropolis of toxic postindustrial slums in the midst of exclusive garden suburbs.

The political formation of urban space in metropolitan Chicago is set within a larger ecological context of the GREAT LAKES region. The city's location at the southwest corner of LAKE MICHIGAN was both its greatest economic asset and worst environmental liability. As historian William Cronon has brilliantly demonstrated, this "nature's metropolis" acted like a great entrepôt, gathering in the wheat, timber, and cattle of the Great West and shipping it out to expanding national markets. In the post–CIVIL WAR era, Chicagoans became increasingly adept at processing these raw materials into manufactured products: biscuits, FURNITURE, dressed beef. But a strategic location on the banks of the CHICAGO RIVER came at the price of erecting a city upon a low-lying marshland that was difficult to drain and protect against flooding. Local authorities soon attempted to engineer the environment to lift Chicago out of the mud and to supply its residents with a pure source of drinking water. Municipal politics would grow out of this dynamic tension between the demands of urban growth and the limits of environmental degradation below acceptable standards of community and human decency. Shifts in the balance of power between local and national levels of the federal system also helped define a series of distinct eras of environmental politics in Chicago.

From the founding of the city in the mid-1830s to the present, the political formation of urban space divides into five broad periods. During the initial stage of city building, land speculation and development dominated, engendering a "segmented" form of government. The reign of the property owners was expressed in long, thin ward boundaries, which empowered them to make decisions about the pace and cost of infrastructure improvements. An influx of GERMAN and IRISH immigrants brought a new era of rapid urban expansion and boss rule. A politics of growth characterized the second period, from the inauguration in 1863 of a WARD SYSTEM based on ethnic and class divisions to 1889, the pivotal year of the great ANNEXATION and the creation of the Sanitary District of Chicago. A third era of metropolitan integration followed until 1927, when the U.S. Supreme Court seized control of Chicago's sanitation system. The long-running court battle over the city's water management policy was emblematic of the policy dilemmas stemming from the ever-wider environmental impacts of the industrial city on the GREAT LAKES region. With the coming of the NEW DEAL in 1933, these problems of federalism were resolved to a large extent by a new partnership between the national government and city hall. During the next 40 years, Washington funneled huge sums of money for environmental improvement projects through the local party bosses. They, in turn, spent these funds in ways that promoted personal and partisan goals at the expense of their working-class constituents. A final, fifth period began in the early 1970s, when the national government took more direct responsibility for improving the quality of our air, water, and land. The dawning era of environmental protection encouraged federal bureaucracies and nongovernment organizations (NGOs) to hold city hall to account not only for pollution but also injustice in the distribution of its toxic health effects on poor neighborhoods and minority groups. Although national initiatives have begun to address the imbalance between urban growth and ecological limits, the forces of metropolitan sprawl and spatial segregation remain predominant in defining the quality of the environment in the various districts and suburbs of the Chicago area.

From 1830 to 1863, the site of Chicago was transformed from frontier outpost to boomtown, complete with all of the infrastructure needed to support a commercial entrepôt. For a brief time, a booster spirit of voluntary cooperation prevailed to launch Chicago as a contender for the crown of metropolis of the Great West. Early efforts focused on linking and extending markets by constructing ship harbors, RAILROADS, canals, TELEGRAPHS, and other technologies of a commercial economy. By the mid-1840s, the boosters had just about finished putting this machinery of capitalism into place, signaling a more competitive phase of urban development. Seeking to privatize the city building process, elite land speculators created what historian Robin Einhorn describes as a segmented form of government. Reflecting Jacksonian fears of partisan favoritism, they reduced city hall's role to that of a mere administrative agency while devolving decision-making power over environmental improvements to the property owners. The two key policy tools in the resulting creation of a new urban form were ward boundaries that reflected REAL-ESTATE values rather than social ones, and special assessment taxes that paid for individual paved STREETS, sidewalks, gaslights, and water mains. Urban space during the regime of the big property owners began to undergo a radical reorganization by economic functions of land use and by social categories of class and ethnicity. Settlement patterns tended toward geographic sprawl within the constraints of available TRANSPORTATION technologies. This process tended toward a physical and social bifurcation between the riverfront and industrial slums, on the one hand, and the lakefront and residential suburbs, on the other.

Representing a triumph of privatism, the segmented form of government achieved success by avoiding not only partisan conflicts but also policy decisions on an accumulating list of citywide problems. Issues affecting the whole community, such as building BRIDGES, supplying water, and soliciting aid from Washington for harbor improvements—issues that had been previously addressed by a frontier spirit of cooperation—could no longer be resolved within the public arena. After 1848, moreover, swelling numbers of German and Irish immigrants produced a more complex urban society with diverse special-interest groups pursuing conflicting agendas of city building. Large property owners, for example, wanted to protect their investments with tough fire codes, the very regulations that could price most would-be homeowners out of the market.

Provoking several ethnocultural clashes, including the so-called LAGER BEER RIOT, the segmented system finally collapsed under the weight of the centralizing pressures occasioned by the CIVIL WAR. The economic boom triggered by the sectional conflict tripled the population of Chicago within a single decade to 300,000 inhabitants. Two of the most pressing needs created by rapid growth called for planning large-scale environmental improvements: a water management system to safeguard the public health and an urban transit network to move people from home to work within the expanding borders of the metropolis. Mounting pressure for citywide solutions to these and other unresolved issues culminated in 1863 in a reform CHARTER that strengthened the powers of the central authority. Equally important, the new municipal government restored partisanship to public policy formation by redefining ward boundaries according to social categories of class and ethnicity rather than according to land values. But by vesting most decision-making power in the city council, this form of government would fuel the rise of a ward-based system of machine rule.

Under the regime of the ward bosses from 1864 to 1889, the politics of growth played a large part in the construction of landscapes of inequality between riverfront slums and lakefront districts. Despite the Great FIRE OF 1871, Chicago's population doubled each decade, making it the fastest-growing big city in the western world. Just trying to keep up with the incredible pace of this expansion in terms of installing the basic infrastructure of the modern city proved a herculean task. In this era of the horse railway, neighbors could be close geographically but live in totally different worlds in terms of the quality of their air, water, and ground. Whether or not property owners could afford the modern amenities of the built environment further divided the rich and poor into separate spheres. While the middle classes could afford commuter fares, the working classes were forced by poverty to live close enough to their jobs to walk to WORK.

War-fed prosperity turned the Chicago River into a polluted industrial corridor, but the city council completed the process of turning it into an open sewer. Empowered to build a citywide system of water supplies and sanitary sewers to protect the public health, aldermen instead ran the waterworks like a private business to maximize profits. They rejected progressive plans to divert the city's wastes away from the river and lake through a network of intercepting sewers. At the same time, continuation of special tax assessments to pay for most infrastructure improvements deepened the gulf between working-class districts hugging the industrial corridor and middle-class enclaves stretching along a shoreline of homes and parks.

This reordering of urban space into landscapes of inequality took place inside and beyond municipal boundaries. For example, both the exclusive residential community of HYDE PARK on the lakefront and the heavily industrial area of the stockyards on the South Branch of the river were located just south of the city line at 39th Street in the "suburbs." Although they grew up alongside each other with only a few miles in between, they were truly worlds apart. Hyde Parkers made effective use of the public authority to create a buffer zone of protected parks and boulevards that defended their homes against the poor immigrants flocking to the mecca of jobs, Packingtown. In sharp contrast, the city government of Chicago completely failed to stop the environmental degradation that endangered the lives of the families living in "the BACK OF THE YARDS." In spite of special powers to regulate the slaughterhouse district, city hall consistently put the profits of the meatpackers ahead of the health and safety of their workers.

The breakneck pace of Chicago's expansion and the shortsighted policies of city hall combined to produce a series of environmental and public health crises, each worse than the last. The two often went hand-in-hand, because sewage regularly found its way from the Chicago River into Lake Michigan, contaminating the city's drinking supplies and raising morbidity and mortality to EPIDEMIC proportions. The root of the problem lay in decisions to empty the sewers' human and animal wastes into the river rather than follow the example of cities like London in bearing the extra costs of diverting them away from the populated area. Using the shallow waterway was inherently risky, since normal weather conditions such as rainstorms and spring thaws often overcame the city engineer's efforts to keep the flow of the river permanently reversed away from the lake.

With the water intake cribs sitting just a few miles out, the aldermen's management of the environment put Chicago's health at risk from a ghastly stew of bacteriological diseases, including cholera, typhoid fever, diarrhea, and diphtheria. Physical and social segregation maintained a barrier between well-to-do and working-class Chicagoans, protecting the affluent from high-mortality airborne diseases such as TUBERCULOSIS. But the shield of spatial exclusion was illusory, as contaminated drinking supplies came right into their homes through unseen pipes buried underground. The great flood of 1885 marked a turning point, a crisis that galvanized the middle and upper classes into an irresistible force of public health reform. The Citizens' Association, an elite businessman's group, took the lead in pressuring city hall to support reform legislation that embodied broader metropolitan and regional perspectives on the environment.

In 1889, the politicians decided to go along with plans to create a separate agency, the Sanitary District of Chicago. They realized that this special tax district to build a 30-mile long sanitary channel was ready-made for PATRONAGE jobs and contract kickbacks. Party bosses wrestled control of the agency away from reformers by 1891, quickly transforming its goals from the public health of the community into a grandiose scheme of commercial development, an Atlantic-to-the-Gulf ship canal. Diverting funds from cleaning up the riverfront wards, party leaders installed interceptor pipes only in the lakefront wards. The political formation of geographies of inequality was reflected in sewer outfalls that dumped the human wastes of the well-to-do in the middle of the residential districts of the working classes. In similar ways, the toxic smoke generated by the city's factories, ferryboats, and locomotives was viewed by the professional politicians more as a lucrative source of graft than a public nuisance that should be abated by the administration.

The year 1889 was pivotal in the history of environmental politics in Chicago for a second reason, the great annexation. Increasing its size fourfold to 168 square miles and its population to over a million people, the enlarged boundaries also created a new set of political dynamics between urban growth and ecological limits, center and periphery, city and suburbs. On the one hand, the additional territory revived competition between the outer and the inner wards for infrastructure improvements. Fulfilling demands for service extensions in new subdivisions at the city's edge often came at the expense of the older, built-up areas where the original utilities dating back to pre–Civil War days badly needed upgrading and replacement. In addition, this competition coincided with the early phases of AFRICAN AMERICAN migration from the South. These demographic trends helped tip the balance of infrastructure improvements heavily in favor of the mostly white fringe districts. This lack of distributive justice in turn contributed to the consolidation during the early twentieth century of a new form of spatial segregation, the "BLACK BELT." Unlike previous neighborhoods defined by class and ethnicity, this kind of racial zone was imposed from the outside, forcing African Americans to live within separate and unequal areas.

The great annexation coincided with a second kind of political fragmentation. Before 1890, Chicago's outlying areas usually found municipal absorption advantageous, bringing better urban services and lower taxes. Subsequently, however, an array of powerful inventions such as electric light and power, trolleys, automobiles, and TELEPHONES allowed each suburban enclave to build its own network of urban technologies. The suburbs no longer needed to join the central city in order to enjoy all the conveniences of modern life. In 1892, EVANSTON's resounding rejection of annexation by a three-fourths majority heralded a new era of open political battle between the city and its collar communities. Symbolized by Frank Lloyd Wright's ARCHITECTURE, an emerging suburban ethos contained the seeds of an antiurbanism that would eventually mature into a virulent politics of physical segregation and social containment.

On the other hand, Chicago's metropolitan scale strengthened the resolve of a new generation of "Progressive" reformers to restore a broader, more inclusive sense of the city as a community. Rejecting the cruel determinism of social Darwinism, they envisioned urban society in holistic terms as a family household or organic body. These new perspectives gave birth not only to a conservation movement on the national level but also to social environmentalism on a local level. Urban Progressives believed that by making changes in the physical surroundings of the city, they could effect commensurate improvements in its social conditions and civic life. Moreover, they shared an optimistic faith in experts to solve contemporary problems with the potent tools of science and technology. In Chicago, affluent women often stood in the forefront of efforts to build bridges between the classes with liberal concepts of the public welfare that embodied democratic ideals of social and environmental justice. In 1889, Jane Addams and Ellen Starr moved into the HULL HOUSE in the riverfront district of infamous ward boss John Powers. Mary McDowell soon established a similar social settlement in Packingtown and joined the political campaign for what she referred to as "municipal housekeeping." Less well known was Annie Sergel, who organized the Anti-Smoke League to eliminate the air pollution that enveloped the city in a suffocating pall of black soot and noxious gases. The municipal reformers of the Progressive era achieved considerable success in strengthening the structure of city hall's regulatory powers over the environment and professionalizing the administration of its enforcement agencies, such as the smoke inspection and the health departments.

Chicago's long-running battle with the national government over the Great Lakes was emblematic of the new directions of environmental politics in the period leading up to the GREAT DEPRESSION. Under the reign of the party bosses, the sanitary district needed to take huge quantities of water from Lake Michigan in order to keep afloat its pretentious scheme for a deepwater ship canal. Lowering the Great Lakes by as much as six inches, the Sanitary District soon attracted attention from Canadians, who vigorously objected to the resulting economic and ecological damage to the entire region. Assuming the posture of conservationists, Canadian officials exerted unrelenting pressure on Washington to force Chicago to stop its damaging "diversion." Between 1900 and 1927, however, local politicians defied every attempt by the federal government to get the city to reduce its gluttonous consumption of water by building sewage treatment plants. Frustrated by this recalcitrance, the U.S. Supreme Court finally took over the management of the Sanitary District, gradually bringing it into compliance with the limitations set for the city's withdrawal of water from the Great Lakes. The coming of the New Deal would complete this process of integrating the metropolis into larger webs of regional and national interdependence.

From 1933 to 1970, a new federal partnership between the national capital and the city halls of America helped underwrite a massive public investment in the urban environment. Money flowed through municipal agencies to upgrade highways and sewers, build airports and subways, and replace slum districts with housing projects. In Chicago, this brief era of the urban nation reinforced not only the power of the party bosses but also the existing patterns of social exclusion and physical segregation. The mayor and the aldermen used funds earmarked for slum clearance and PUBLIC HOUSING to construct a second ghetto of high-rise APARTMENTS. They also perverted transportation planning by drawing the routes of EXPRESSWAYS to act like a racial Berlin wall. In the post–WORLD WAR II period, direct federal support to the working classes for inner-city renewal was small compared to the size of indirect subsidies to the middle classes for suburban development in the form of low-cost mortgages, free expressways, and cheap gasoline. By 1970, racial and class discrimination in the political formation of urban space had the ironic effect of ensuring the ascendancy of a suburban nation.

Informed by the science and the ethics of ecology, a new generation of reformers emerged in the postwar period seeking to place the city within a dynamic context of the larger natural world. In 1970, the creation of the U.S. Environmental Protection Agency and the celebration of the first Earth Day announced the coming of age of a politics of ecology. The commitment of the federal government to cleaning up the air, water, and ground was matched by the determination of many NGOs to hold local authorities to account for discriminatory practices that helped create and maintain geographies of exclusion and segregation. Of course, many other NGOs were formed out of less noble motives, especially those devoted to selfish "not-in-my-backyard" interests, or "NIMBYs," as they became known. Collectively, the NGOs helped persuade Washington to establish higher standards of environmental quality, enforce tighter regulations on public and private polluters, and allocate greater amounts of money for upgrading the urban infrastructure. In Chicago, the Tunnel and Reservoir Plan, or "DEEP TUNNEL," mushroomed into the single most ambitious and costly public works project ever to attempt to solve the area's chronic problems of storm runoff flooding basements and raw sewage contaminating Lake Michigan.

At the same time, Congress opened the doors of the federal courts to suits by NGOs against local units of government that perpetuated unfair patterns of resource allocation for public housing and urban services among the city's various neighborhoods. The Chicago PARK DISTRICT and the CHICAGO HOUSING AUTHORITY were the two agencies most directly implicated in the ensuing judicial assault on the city's politics of environmental RACISM. In both cases, the court found public officials guilty of discrimination intended to maintain and widen the gap in the quality of life between the white and black areas of the city. In 1969, for example, U.S. District Judge Richard Austin ruled in the landmark *Gautreaux v. Chicago Housing Authority* that site selection for new construction must begin to reverse the agency's previous patterns of segregation. Stubbornly resisting his decree by refusing to build any additional units for almost a decade, city hall was eventually dragged into compliance by a determined federal jurist. Besieged from the top and the bottom, the local political regime learned that it could no longer afford to make decisions affecting the environment while blatantly disregarding democratic ideals of equality and justice.

After 1970, the political formation of urban space took place within hostile arenas increasingly filled with state and national lawmakers who called for the containment of the city's social and environmental problems within municipal boundaries. Chicago, for instance, lost its grip on the statehouse to an insurgent coalition of legislators from suburban and rural districts. Despite new levels of ecological concern, a suburban majority has continued to support public policies that promote settlement patterns of geographic sprawl and high energy consumption. The state legislature has supported continued suburban growth through substantial appropriations for additional roads and highways outside of the city, while rejecting proposals for more equitable funding to support city SCHOOLS losing resources to those growing suburbs. Affluent districts have played the self-serving politics of NIMBY to place an unfair burden of health risks from toxic wastes and industrial sites upon impoverished and minority areas. The new perspectives of ecology have illuminated the interconnectedness of the built and the natural environments, the center and the periphery, and the rich and the poor. Yet contemporary society shows few signs of departing from traditions of POLITICAL CULTURE that express power relationships in spatial terms of exclusion and segregation.

Harold L. Platt

See also: Contested Spaces; Demography; Environmentalism; Environmental Regulation; Flood Control and Drainage; Industrial Pollution; Planning Chicago; Suburbs and Cities as Dual Metropolis; Waste, Hazardous; Waste Disposal

Further reading: A focus of historical inquiry on the environment is relatively new; even more recent is the emergence of the urban environment as a distinct subfield of study. These developments are traced in Richard White, "American Environmental History: The Development of a New Historical Field," *Pacific Historical Review* 54 (August 1985): 297–335; and Martin V. Melosi, *The Sanitary City* (1999). Questions of environmental justice and the city have only just begun to be addressed by historians. For insight on the state of the profession's belated interest, see the special issue of *Environmental History* 5 (April 2000) on urban environmental justice, including the essay by Harold L. Platt, "Jane Addams and the Ward Boss Revisited: Class, Politics, and Public Health in Chicago, 1890–1930," 194–222. The single best case study remains Andrew Hurley, *Environmental Inequalities: Class, Race, and Industrial Pollution in Gary, Indiana, 1945–1980* (1995), despite problematic conclusions about intentionality.

Sources on the history of environmental politics in Chicago can be conveniently grouped in the chronological periods used in this essay. Key secondary sources on city building and environmental history are William Cronon, *Nature's Metropolis: Chicago and the Great West* (1991); Robin Einhorn, *Property Rules: Political Economy in Chicago, 1833–1872* (1991); and Ann Durkin Keating, *Building Chicago: Suburban Developers and the Creation of a Divided Metropolis* (1988). For the period of rapid industrialization from 1863 to 1889, see Christine Meisner Rosen, *The Limits of Power: Great Fires and the Process of City Growth in America* (1988); Michael H. Ebner, *Creating Chicago's North Shore: A Suburban History* (1988); and Harold L. Platt, "Creative Necessity: Municipal Reform in Gilded Age Chicago," in *The Constitution, Law, and American Life: Critical Aspects of the Nineteenth-Century Experience*, ed. Donald G. Nieman (1992), 162–190.

For the following era of political fragmentation and metropolitan integration extending from the annexation to the New Deal, see Maureen Flanagan, "The City Profitable, the City Livable: Environmental Policy, Gender, and Power in Chicago in the 1910s," *Journal of Urban History* 22 (January 1996): 163–190; Harold L. Platt, "'Invisible Gases': Smoke, Gender, and the Redefinition of Environmental Policy in Chicago, 1880–1920," *Planning Perspectives* 10 (January 1995): 67–97; and Thomas Lee Philpott, *The Slum and the Ghetto: Neighborhood Deterioration and Middle-Class Reform, Chicago, 1880–1930* (1978). For the succeeding two periods of the federal partnership to 1970 and the current era of ecology, consult Eileen McMahon, *What Parish Are You From? A Chicago Irish Community and Race Relations* (1995); Roger Biles, *Richard J. Daley: Politics, Race, and the Governing of Chicago* (1995); and Terrence Kehoe, *Cleaning Up the Great Lakes: From Cooperation to Confrontation* (1997).

Environmental Regulation. Many kinds of laws regulate private activity in order to promote PUBLIC HEALTH and welfare. Since its incorporation in 1833, Chicago's Common Council has passed ordinances that limit some private activities and encourage others. Residents have elected and paid officers to police their private use of public resources.

Chicago's pre–Civil War residents understood that everyone's air, WATER, and public space could be damaged by the disorderly behavior of just a few people, so they established mechanisms for regulation. An elected commissioner removed stuck wagons and dumped timber which blocked streets, an engineer prepared residents for FIREFIGHTING, and a pound keeper removed stray dogs and pigs that were running at large.

Despite this activity, Chicago's growing population suffered decreasing environmental quality. People and animals eliminated onto the ground, and residents believed that the resulting smelly miasmas caused disease. The Common Council appointed public health officers who cleaned out dirty outhouses and stables, and outlawed the disposal of slaughterhouse offal in the city. In 1852 the Illinois legislature incorporated a municipal water company, which pumped clean drinking water from Lake Michigan. In 1855 the legislature created a Board of Sewerage Commissioners, which attempted to eliminate miasmas by interring a comprehensive network of drainage pipes and by requiring landowners to raise the surface of their lots by several feet.

After the CIVIL WAR, Chicago grew rapidly, and the council struggled to solve the environmental problems caused by the density of LAND USE. The Chicago FIRE OF 1871 showed that ordinances limiting wood construction were unenforced and that the WATER SUPPLY was inadequate to prevent this great environmental threat. That year, city physician John H. Rauch argued that sewers should be built in the most populous wards, which were poor. In the antebellum period, Chicago had balanced private property rights and public services by generally extending sewers, water pipes, and paved streets to residents who paid for them.

Rauch anticipated Jane Addams's position in the 1890s: rich and poor alike had a right to the parks, garbage pickup, and street cleaning that created urban environmental quality.

The Illinois legislature helped solve Chicago's problems by creating two municipal corporations. In 1869 the PARK DISTRICTS began to tax residents, issue bonds, condemn land, and build a park system of boulevards and green spaces. In 1889 the Sanitary District of Chicago established plans to make permanent the reversal of the CHICAGO RIVER so that the city's wastewater flowed toward the Mississippi, away from the reservoir of Lake Michigan. In the 1890s Congress expanded federal regulation by requiring the Army Corps of Engineers to prevent obstructions to navigable waters; the local federal officer began requiring Chicago to apply for permits to dump wastes in the river and lake.

When the Sanitary District reversed the river in 1900, it protected Chicago's water supply but economically injured Great Lakes shipping companies and electricity generating companies at Niagara Falls. In response, the secretary of war regulated the district by issuing a permit limiting the amount of water diverted from the Great Lakes; Chicagoans questioned whether this limit protected their drinking water, so they began chlorinating it. In the 1990s Chicago continued to violate the permit and the Supreme Court's enforcement order by diverting excess water illegally.

Advocates in the Progressive era called on government to pass more environmental regulations. Women organized in a campaign of municipal housekeeping and successfully advocated city ownership of garbage incineration. Women also organized for smoke abatement and promoted ordinances requiring the installation of smokestack technology which reduced particulate emissions. In step with the national conservation movement, the Illinois legislature created the Cook County FOREST PRESERVE District to preserve open space on the urban fringe; a Special Parks Commission created scores of PLAYGROUNDS AND SMALL PARKS in the inner city.

During the GREAT DEPRESSION, the federal government put thousands of people to work building the lakefront parks designed in the BURNHAM PLAN and improving the inner-city parks. These attractive amenities brought people out of their segregated neighborhoods and into contact while SWIMMING and playing. In 1947 the Park District developed a race relations manual for its police force, which instructed officers to preserve access to the parks for all races and ethnic groups.

Illinois has struggled to provide Chicago residents with clean air that meets federal standards established with the Clean Air Act of 1970, notably by initiating vehicle emissions tests in 1985. In the late 1980s, environmental justice activists on the SOUTH SIDE forced the federal Environmental Protection Agency to acknowledge that regulations have improved environmental quality in wealthy neighborhoods more than in poor neighborhoods. In the 1990s, the quest for environmental quality traveled indoors, as the CHICAGO HOUSING AUTHORITY reduced pesticide use, removed asbestos insulation, and abated lead paint.

During the 1990s, citizens had the opportunity to speak to expert administrators at hundreds of public hearings hosted by city, county, state, and federal agencies. This access increased in 1992, when Chicago created a Department of the Environment, which brought many scattered functions into one agency. Residents cannot recall these expert administrators by vote, as occurred in the small city government of early Chicago, but residents increasingly hold them accountable to local opinion.

Betsy Mendelsohn

See also: Environmental Politics; Environmentalism; Industrial Pollution; Infrastructure; Waste Hazardous

Further reading: Flanagan, Maureen A. "The City Profitable, the City Livable: Environmental Policy, Gender, and Power in Chicago in the 1910s." *Journal of Urban History* 22 (January 1996): 163–190. • Melosi, Martin V. *Garbage in the Cities: Refuse, Reform, and the Environment, 1880–1980.* 1981. • Rapsys, John R. *Toward a Brighter Future: EPA Region 5: The First 25 Years, 1971–1995.* 1996.

Chicago Wilderness

In the 1970s, the Illinois Natural Areas Inventory identified the 610 highest-quality forests, prairies, and wetlands surviving in the state. The high-quality lands surviving in Illinois represented seven-hundredths of 1 percent of the original. Most high-quality unpreserved lands in the Chicago area were subsequently acquired by state, county, and local conservation agencies. Major initiatives to restore and maintain conservation lands have brought the conservation agencies in the Chicago region to the forefront of the development of the discipline of ecological restoration and management. There is said to be more grassland and forest acreage under restoration in metropolitan Chicago than in any other area—urban or rural—in the Midwest.

In 1995, the Chicago Region Biodiversity Council ("Chicago Wilderness") was formed. This collaboration of over one hundred organizations includes research and education institutions; federal, state, and local agencies; not-for-profit groups; and others. Their mission is to create a culture of conservation for the Chicago region, centered on the region's 200,000 acres of conservation land.

Stephen Packard

Environmentalism. "Environmentalism" describes both the political movement to protect and improve the environment and the philosophy that has inspired that movement. Although it has roots in much earlier efforts, including nineteenth-century conservation and antipollution movements, not until the affluent post–World War II era did environmentalism become a mass movement. It has drawn most of its energy from the middle class, which has demanded relief from polluted water and air, and the development and protection of amenities such as recreational space. Another thread of environmentalism has been concerned with wilderness preservation and the protection of biodiversity. The movement gained momentum in 1962 with the publication of Rachel Carson's *Silent Spring,* which exposed the ravages of pesticides. Celebrated by a rally at the Civic Center Plaza and by thousands of Chicago-area students who collected trash around their schools, the first Earth Day in 1970 marked the arrival of environmentalism as a mainstream political force. By the mid-1970s, the federal government had passed a series of critical environmental laws, including the Wilderness Act (1964), Clean Air Act (1970), Clean Water Act (1972), and Endangered Species Act (1973).

Chicagoans have long been interested in improving their environment. As early as 1854 residents gathered to protest against a cholera EPIDEMIC caused by a poor sewage system and to demand a cleaner, more healthful city. Over the next two decades a sanitary reform movement led to the construction of new sewers, the raising of city STREET GRADES to prevent standing WATER, and the reversal of the CHICAGO RIVER'S flow to keep sewage from entering LAKE MICHIGAN. In the 1860s businessmen supported the creation of urban parks, knowing that residents appreciated their beauty and ability to revive health. This early effort led to the creation of Chicago's landscaped parks, including JACKSON, WASHINGTON, and LINCOLN. After the turn of the century, INDUSTRIAL POLLUTION gained more attention from activists. The Anti-Smoke League, for example, worked to force railroads to reduce their smoke emissions, and laborers complained about the stench from the famously polluted "Bubbly Creek" which ran through Packingtown. Others took a broader approach to environmental improvement by supporting urban PLANNING. Daniel Burnham based his famous 1909 *Chicago Plan* on a vision of an orderly, beautiful city, full of parks and inspiring vistas.

Chicagoans have also long expressed concern for environments outside the city itself. In 1922 Will H. Dilg helped create the Izaak Walton League, a conservation organization for outdoors enthusiasts. Headquartered in Chicago, the league attracted support mostly from the Midwest, but it very quickly became the first national environmental organization with a mass membership. An avid fisherman, Dilg made the league the most influential organization supporting wetlands protection. In an early accomplishment, the league pressured Congress into creating an extensive wildlife refuge to protect the upper Mississippi River. Chicago activists also played a crucial role in the preservation of the INDIANA DUNES. As early as 1914 the Chicago Conservation Council worked to preserve the spectacular dunes. Since that time Chicagoans have worked to create and expand the Indiana Dunes State Park (1923) and the Indiana Dunes National Lakeshore (1966).

With increases in average income, vacation time, and automobile ownership in the 1950s, more and more Chicagoans traveled to nearby natural areas for rest and recreation. The woods and waterways of Wisconsin became favorite destinations. By one estimation in 1959 about a quarter of Chicago-area residents stayed overnight in that state's VACATION SPOTS. Many of those residents chose state parks as destinations, and pressure from its southern neighbors forced Wisconsin to increase spending on recreation and preservation, a trend that has been followed around the nation.

The protection of Lake Michigan has been a focal point of Chicago's activism since the 1960s. With industrial pollution threatening the area's beaches, fishing, and drinking water, activists demanded government action. In 1967 the CHICAGO TRIBUNE began a "Save Our Lake" campaign which gained wide support for immediate action, particularly in cleaning up the pollution from the CALUMET REGION.

Chicago environmentalists have worked through a range of interest groups, some concerned with global issues, and others more regional in their focus, such as Citizens for a Better Environment, concerned with pollution and PUBLIC HEALTH issues since its 1971 founding, and the OPENLANDS PROJECT, which has worked to preserve recreational space. Some local environmental groups have focused on more specific issues, such as the North Branch Restoration Project, aimed at preserving and restoring the natural ecology within the Cook County FOREST PRESERVE. Since the 1970s Chicagoans have also worked for environmental justice, attempting to halt the practice of siting toxic waste primarily in minority neighborhoods.

David Stradling

See also: Air Quality; Ecosystem Evolution; Environmental Politics; Flood Control and Drainage; Waste, Hazardous

Further reading: Engel, J. Ronald. *Sacred Sands: The Struggle for Community in the Indiana Dunes.* 1983. • Hays, Samuel P. *Beauty, Health, and Permanence: Environmental Politics in the United States, 1955–1985.* 1987. • Kehoe, Terence. *Cleaning Up the Great Lakes: From Cooperation to Confrontation.* 1997.

Epidemics. During the nineteenth century, Chicago suffered fearsome though sporadic epidemics of disease. Cholera ravaged many American and European cities in the middle of the nineteenth century, and Chicago did not escape. The threat of a cholera epidemic provoked the creation of the Chicago Board of Health in 1835. Except for a few years in the 1860s, when the city council refused to fund it—a penny-wise policy reversed by a rash of contagion in 1867—the board has safeguarded the city's health with great effort and general success ever since.

Cholera kept reappearing, however. In 1852 and again in 1854, when it killed 1,424, cholera destroyed young and old, often within hours of their first symptoms. Another 210 died in 1854 from "diarrhea" and 242 more from "dysentery," either of which might actually have been cholera. Diagnoses differed, but the symptoms were similar. No one knew exactly what caused it, though personal and public cleanliness seemed to help, and impure WATER began to be identified as the principal transmitter.

Chicagoans died from other fast-moving contagions as well: dysentery killed 1,600 between 1854 and 1860; scarlet fever, over 1,200 between 1858 and 1863; smallpox, 283 in 1864. The Great FIRE OF 1871 also contributed: high mortality from exposure and low resistance to contagions struck down many burned-out survivors.

Cholera returned in the summer of 1873, killing 116. The Board of Health measured the duration of the disease, from first symptoms to death, at about eleven hours. It "struck hardest where sanitary laws were not observed," the board's reports stated, particularly south of 37th Street and west of State Street, an area "densely populated, principally by foreigners, consisting of GERMANS, SWEDES and POLES." Cleanliness, or lack of it, was the key: "Those who observed sanitary laws, attended to the disinfection of stools, and who were prompt in calling a physician, with few exceptions recovered, and the occurrence of a second case in such families was rare. On the other hand, when the stools were not cared for, and the vomit permitted to remain on the floor, and the bedding (principally feather beds) used without having been properly cleaned and where no attention was paid to ventilation or personal cleanliness, several cases would generally occur, and as a rule, prove fatal." Public conditions were equally noxious and threatening. Odors, or "miasmas," were widely believed to cause disease, and in Chicago, the slaughterhouses were "diffusing the odors of animal putrefaction throughout the city," especially in summer. In the North Branch of the CHICAGO RIVER, "the water remaining standing with the yearly accretions is, during the hot months converted into a cess-pool, seething, boiling and reeking with filth, which fills the north wards of the city with mephitic [noxious] gases." The South Branch had become "fully as foul."

But 1873 proved to be the low point. The aftermath of the Great Fire brought major, if gradual, improvements in PUBLIC HEALTH and, therefore, in the city's demographic stability. Miles of sewerage drained the city more effectively, and residents were required to "connect dwellings with sewers." Chicago's cholera days were over, and its death rate fell below New York's and Boston's. By 1881 the Board

Children at the Municipal Tuberculosis Sanitarium, 1923. In the 1920s physicians recommended exercise and fresh air as the best means to prevent and cure tuberculosis. Photographer: Unknown. Source: Chicago Historical Society.

of Health claimed that Chicago had the third-lowest death rate in the world among cities over 500,000.

Yet with germ theory still undeveloped, other contagions abounded. Deaths from diphtheria and whooping cough soared in the late 1870s; scarlet fever accounted for over 10 percent of deaths in Chicago in 1877. These so-called "childhood diseases" continued to kill, joined in summer months by "cholera infantum" and other gastrointestinal infections resulting from spoiled food and impure water. Something diagnosed as "inanition"—lethargy probably resulting from malnutrition—killed 314 in 1881. But most devastating was the smallpox epidemic that killed 1,180 in late 1881 and 1,292 in early 1882. The population rose too fast for vaccination programs to keep up with it. Each year from 1871 to 1881 the city removed the carcasses of 1,500 horses and tens of thousands of dogs from the streets, while 70 teams tried to cope with "the garbage, ashes, and rubbish daily accumulating." But tugboats and RAILROADS belched smoke, the stockyards still stank, and privy vaults infected water wells in many a backyard. The Board of Health lamented that "the great and rapid influx of population has caused a dangerous overcrowding in all the poorer districts.... Thousands of small houses and cottages arranged for one family are now packed with a family in each room," especially in neighborhoods of newly arrived Europeans. Chicago's doubling of population in the 1880s, much of it from Europe, had its downside. Overcrowding produced deaths from TUBERCULOSIS as well as from sanitary-related contagions.

The city simply had to conquer disease or stop developing. In 1891, bronchitis and pneumonia killed 4,300, typhoid fever 2,000. Every year in the early 1890s, 10,000–12,000 children under five died in Chicago. But the close of the nineteenth century brought control of disease, in a series of steps. Voters overwhelmingly approved the creation of the Sanitary District of Chicago in late 1889, and in January 1900 the city opened the SANITARY AND SHIP CANAL, permanently reversing the flow of the river, sending sewage and refuse away from LAKE MICHIGAN and southwestward toward the Mississippi. Pasteurizing of milk began in 1909, and chlorinating of the city's WATER SUPPLY, in 1912. Tens of thousands received diphtheria vaccination, slowly eliminating that disease. Death rates from every contagious disease fell dramatically. The city's death rate—often above 20 per 1,000 in the years before 1894, seldom topped 15 thereafter. By 1930 it fell to 10.4.

Truly disastrous epidemics were rare in the twentieth century. Like the rest of the world, Chicago suffered from the influenza epidemic of 1918–19. In just one month, October 1918, 10,249 Chicagoans died of flu, bronchitis, or pneumonia (different diagnoses but closely related infections), which was four or five times higher than normal. About 20,000 perished in 1918 and 1919 combined. No one knew how to stop the virus, or indeed what a virus was, or that it caused the flu. After filling many graveyards, it subsided.

Tuberculosis deaths slowly declined in the 1920s except among newly arrived AFRICAN AMERICANS, and after WORLD WAR II, antibiotics reduced that one-time leading killer to a rarity. By then, polio threatened annually to ravage the city's youth. It too receded, as a result of the Salk and Sabin vaccines of the mid-1950s. Sexually transmitted diseases became a major target of the Board of Health in the 1960s and 1970s, when about 40,000 cases of gonorrhea appeared each year. But they were seldom fatal. AIDS (acquired immune deficiency syndrome) was, however, killing hundreds annually after 1980—almost 1,000 in 1993 alone; it became Chicago's last epidemic of the twentieth century.

Walter Nugent

See also: Children's Health; Demography; Hospitals

Further reading: Beatty, William K. "When Cholera Scourged Chicago." *Chicago History* 11 (Spring 1982). • Report[s] of the Board of Health of the City of Chicago. 1870–.

Eritreans. Between 1965 and 1991, an estimated 750,000 Eritreans fled the Horn of Africa—roughly one-quarter of the country's population—in the wake of war, famine, political unrest, and persecution. Some of these REFUGEES made their way to the United States, with the bulk arriving in the 1980s. By 2000, approximately 30,000 Eritreans lived in the United States, with fewer than 800 in Chicago. A precise count has been difficult in part because prior to 1993, outside Eritrea itself, Eritreans were identified as ETHIOPIAN.

The main cause for the Eritrean exodus was the 30-year war of liberation (1961–1991) fought against Ethiopia. Following more than a half century of Italian colonialism (1882–1941) and a decade of British administration (1941–1952), Eritrea was ceded to Ethiopia by the United Nations. By the 1960s an armed nationalist movement had emerged, first in the form of the Eritrean Liberation Front and later the Eritrean Peoples Liberation Front (EPLF). Most Eritreans who resettled in the United States identified with one of these fronts, and a significant number were veterans of the conflict.

The Chicago Eritrean community began with less than a half-dozen students who arrived in the 1960s and early 1970s and grew significantly in the 1980s with the resettlement of refugees. The vast majority settled in UPTOWN, with pockets in EDGEWATER. ROGERS PARK, SKOKIE, EVANSTON, and WHEATON. Many Eritreans found work as TAXI drivers and parking attendants; others opened their own businesses, including RESTAURANTS, garages, and auto repair shops.

Distrust caused by political conflict and differences in social experience (education, gender, religion, region of origin) created challenges for the small Chicago community. The Association of the Eritrean Community in Chicago was formed in 1985 to help bridge these differences and solidify national unity. However, political identities have proven tenacious. The Chicago community has a chapter of the Peoples Front for Democracy and Justice (the ruling Eritrean political party, formerly the EPLF), and, in 2001, a chapter of the Eritrean Liberation Front–Revolutionary Council was founded. The National Union of Eritrean Women holds regular meetings and activities. The most fertile common ground has been found in Orthodox Christian, PROTESTANT, and ROMAN CATHOLIC congregations. SOCCER teams, who play in an annual Eritrean Tournament in the United States, have helped build cohesiveness. Eritreans also create community in informal spaces, celebrating life events, holidays, culture, and language. Overall, Eritreans in Chicago have struggled to balance their intense, active commitment to Eritrea with the need to develop firm institutions and community resources. Aside from personal relationships, Eritreans are generally isolated from the larger Ethiopian community, particularly since the border war of 1998–2000.

Tricia Redeker Hepner

See also: Demography; Multicentered Chicago

Further reading: Hepner, Tricia Redeker. "Backward Glances and American Chances: Eritrean Communities, Political Identity, and Transnational Activism in the US." Eritrean Studies Association First International Conference Proceedings, Asmara, Eritrea. Forthcoming. • Woldemikael, Tekle M. "Eritrean and Ethiopian Refugees in the United States." *Eritrean Studies Review,* vol. 2. 1997.

Erosion. *See* Shoreline Erosion

Erring Women's Refuge. In 1863, 24 white, middle-class, PROTESTANT women opened the refuge, which found a permanent home two years later at 3111 South Indiana. Challenging the legal and social inequity of the double standard of sexual morality which punished women—but not men—for extramarital sexual relations, they provided PROSTITUTES the support and resources necessary to leave the sex industry: education, job training, obstetric care, and the influences of Christian motherhood. The philosophy of the home was revolutionary for its time, stressing the reformability of prostitutes and the transforming spiritual power of women. By 1890 the mission of the refuge had changed. The word "Erring" was dropped and the institution became a home for delinquent girls.

Mary Linehan

See also: Chicago Area Project; Juvenile Justice Reform; Vice Commissions; Young Women's Christian Association

Further reading: Chicago Erring Women's Refuge for Reform. *Annual Reports.* Chicago Historical Society and Newberry Library. • Linehan, Mary. "Vicious Circle: Prostitution, Reform, and Public Policy in Chicago, 1830–1930." Ph.D. diss., University of Notre Dame. 1991.

Essanay Studios. *See* Film

Estonians. Estonian-speaking immigrants formed one of Chicago's most active ethnic communities in the decades after WORLD WAR II. Tracking their settlement before the 1920s, however, is complicated. Until the United States officially recognized Estonian independence in 1922, all immigrants from what would become Estonia were counted as RUSSIANS on census and immigration records. Based upon language, however, immigrants from Estonia could have been either Estonians, GERMANS, Russians, or even SWEDES.

Immigration from Estonia occurred as a result of economic changes and ethnic conflicts within the Russian Empire. Until Estonia achieved its independence after WORLD WAR I, a German elite dominated its economy and cultural life, while imperial authorities instituted a policy of "Russification." With opportunities for economic advancement and cultural expression limited, Estonians—primarily young men, many of whom were unskilled workers, farm hands, or sailors—left their homeland. SOCIALISTS and nationalists also fled after the failed 1905 revolution. In 1930, immigrants such as these organized Chicago's first Estonian association.

WORLD WAR II and the Soviet conquest of Estonia uprooted thousands of Estonians and forced them into exile across the globe. These wartime REFUGEES—also known as "Displaced Persons" or "DPs"—included women as well as men, and tended to be skilled workers or middle class professionals, such as Arthur Vššbus, who taught at Chicago's Lutheran School of Theology. Chicago's Estonian Americans guaranteed that upon arrival Estonian DPs would have housing and jobs, without which they would not have been allowed into the country. This assistance created a community which in 1970 numbered approximately 1,600 first- and second-generation Estonians, dispersed throughout Chicago's North and Northwest Sides, CRYSTAL LAKE, and WOODSTOCK.

Estonian DPs carried with them the determination to preserve their culture and end the Soviet occupation of their homeland. In 1948 Chicago's Estonians, among the most culturally and politically active in the United States, established the Chicago Estonian Society, followed by various other associations, drama troupes, folk dance groups, choirs, an Orthodox and three Evangelical Lutheran congregations, and even Boy and Girl SCOUT Troops. In 1967, Chicago's Estonians founded the Estonian House in unincorporated Prairie View in Lake County, which has since served the community as a place for church services, concerts, lectures, plays, a weekend school, and festivals such as St. John's Day (Midsummer) and Estonian Independence Day (February 24). Throughout the COLD WAR, Chicago's Estonians, in cooperation with HUNGARIANS, LATVIANS, LITHUANIANS, POLES, and UKRAINIANS, drew public attention to Soviet control over Eastern Europe, holding downtown parades and demonstrations on Daley Plaza.

The Soviet Union's collapse and the restoration of Estonian independence in 1991 eliminated much of the urgency behind the activities of Chicago's Estonian Americans. Faced moreover with a high rate of marriage outside the group, geographic dispersion, and upward social mobility, the missionary zeal of Chicago's Estonian Americans began to subside.

Bernard Maegi

See also: Demography; Eastern Orthodox; Multicentered Chicago

Further reading: Granquist, Mark. "Estonian Americans." In *Gale Encyclopedia of Multicultural America,* vol. 1, *Acadians–Iranian Americans,* ed. Judy Galens, Anna Sheets, and Robyn Young, 1995, 486–498. • Parming, Tsnu. "Estonians." In *Harvard Encyclopedia of American Ethnic Groups,* ed. Stephan Thernstrom, 1980, 339–343. • Pennar, Jaan, ed. *The Estonians in America, 1627–1975: A Chronology and Fact Book.* 1975.

Ethiopians. Chicago's Ethiopian community took root in the early 1980s, largely in the UPTOWN, EDGEWATER, and ROGERS PARK neighborhoods. Community leaders estimated roughly 4,500 Ethiopians resided in Chicago in 2000, with additional small enclaves in EVANSTON, ELGIN, and WHEATON. An estimated 200,000 people of Ethiopian descent lived in the United States in 2000, with Washington DC, Minneapolis, and Atlanta the three largest Ethiopian centers.

Before 1980, Chicago's few Ethiopians were mostly students. Beginning in the late 1970s and continuing through the late 1990s, Ethiopia experienced periods of repression by the country's military regimes, full-scale civil war, and external war with Eritrea and Sudan. This violence triggered massive outflows of REFUGEES, mostly to other African countries. A portion of emigrants found their way to the United States, and, between 1978 and 1998, 37,000 Ethiopians immigrated to the United States under refugee status, while another 56,000 immigrated through other legal channels between 1986 and 1998.

Among the refugee waves in the 1980s and 1990s, the earliest had relatively high levels of education and many had university training in Ethiopia. However, continued conflict through the 1990s and increased rural exodus meant lower education levels and fewer skills for more recent immigrants.

A tragic car accident in Chicago in 1984 involving the death of an Ethiopian immigrant exposed the lack of community resources to aid newcomers. Soon after, several Ethiopian residents founded the Ethiopian Community Association of Chicago (ECAC), initially located in Rogers Park. From its volunteer roots, the ECAC has slowly grown into a substantial organization, helping immigrants from not only Ethiopia but also other African and Middle Eastern countries negotiate the difficulties of adaptation to an urban environment. The ECAC has focused its efforts on housing, job placement, and employment training.

Beyond the ECAC, the Ethiopian Evangelical Church in Rogers Park and the Ethiopian Orthodox Church in Evanston remain important congregations in Chicago's Ethiopian community. The Ethiopian SOCCER League connects the Chicago community with Ethiopian Americans in other cities through summer competition and social events. Five Ethiopian RESTAURANTS in Chicago also serve as informal networking sites.

Chicago's Ethiopian immigrants, like other recent African immigrants, have had to adapt to Chicago's sometimes painful patterns of race relations but often resist America's historic racial categories. Instead, discussion of continuing internal struggle in Africa animates local political discussion and generates some tension between Chicago's Ethiopian community and its ERITREAN and SUDANESE communities.

D. Bradford Hunt

See also: African Americans; Demography; Multicentered Chicago; Religious Geography

Further reading: Bhave, Maya. "'Making It': The Social and Economic Experiences of Ethiopian Immigrant Women in Chicago." Ph.D. diss., Loyola University. 2001. • Ethiopian Community Association of Chicago. "Meeting the Challenge: Building a Community Together." 1996.

Ethnic Music. At the beginning of the twenty-first century, the label Ethnic Chicago evokes, on the one hand, a city with a long history of immigrant communities and shifting patterns of interaction between ethnic groups and, on the other, a New Ethnicity, in which identities are hybrid and multicultural, often forged from revivalism, tourism, and the invention of ethnicities that have little or nothing to do with immigration in recent generations. If the multiple meanings of Ethnic Chicago have changed over time, they have nonetheless persisted and even intensified during the city's history, revealing that cultural difference has provided a fundamental vocabulary for constructing self-identity, at the local and at the city-wide level. Music has been an indispensable part of the vocabulary of cultural difference, and music inevitably participates in the expression of ethnic identity. The history of Ethnic Chicago, therefore, is inseparable from the city's ethnic music history.

In this discussion, *ethnic music* (or *musics* plural) functions as a larger term used to describe the ways in which music (1) expresses historical differences and (2) constructs identities in a modern, urban society. In a community of new immigrants, for example, ethnic music that preserved culture, language, customs, FOLKLORE, and social and family interaction from the old country would have great importance because it embodied the memory of the past. Ethnic music assumes different forms in religious communities based on denominational distinctiveness, expressing the cohesiveness of belief systems. Certain working-class musics are imbued with ethnic functions, not only the workers' choruses of late nineteenth-century European immigrants, but the popular DANCE music of working-class ethnic suburbs. Ethnic musics stretch across stylistic boundaries between folk, religious, and CLASSICAL MUSICS. In the second half of the twentieth century, ethnic musics increasingly blur cultural and musical boundaries, reformulating ethnic and racial differences in Chicago.

Ethnic music connects a community to a selected component of its past, but it does so to give meaning to the present. Thus, ethnic music should be understood as changing, not static, as Polish American music, rather than as POLISH music, as MEXICAN American music that encodes migrations between Chicago and local cultures in Mexico, rather than simply as Mexican music. In particular, this discussion will look at the ways in which ethnic musics have shaped Chicago's urban landscape and continue to do so, especially as new immigrant groups from East and South Asia and from Latin America settle in Chicago, transforming, but by no means eliminating, the ethnic landscape shaped by generations of immigration from Europe.

The ethnic music history of Chicago unfolded during four phases that both reflect the city's broader ethnic history and respond to changing musical influences. During the initial historical phases, ethnic differences accumulated as new immigrant groups settled in the city and laid the groundwork for neighborhood structures; in the later phases, ethnic music underwent transformation, crossing cultural borders with musical mainstreams and other ethnic and racial communities.

Phase 1. Immigrant music

The first phase begins with the settlement of Chicago and takes place during a period of about 50 years, until the 1870s and 1880s. The music of Chicago's new communities expressed the character of the immigrant groups that settled them, that is, the character of a music culture transplanted to Chicago. Immigrant music depended on the retention of languages, musical instruments, and institutions that immigrants brought with them. The immigrant music cultures of German- and English-speaking communities dominated this phase.

Phase 2. Ethnic music: diversification and institution formation

Various factors precipitated the second phase of ethnic music history. American immigration escalated during the final decades of the nineteenth century, and new immigrant groups, notably from Southern and Eastern Europe, established themselves in Chicago. The FIRE OF 1871 and the WORLD'S COLUMBIAN EXPOSITION of 1893 also initiated widespread reconfiguration of Chicago's ethnic culture. When communities transform music that connected them to the past to practices adapting to the present, immigrant music becomes ethnic music; in other words, the music of GERMANS or ITALIANS in the New World becomes German American or Italian American music. Community institutions were increasingly important, as ethnic churches, social and fraternal organizations, and labor groups fostered ethnic musical activity.

Phase 3. Ethnic music: breakdown of European dominance

The third phase began roughly at the time of WORLD WAR I and continued through WORLD WAR II. During this phase immigration from Europe underwent several transformations, increasing in diversity after the collapse of the Russian, German, and Austro-Hungarian empires, but also responding to new immigrant quotas in the 1920s. Asian and Latin American immigration also grew during this phase, but the greatest impact on the ethnic music culture of Chicago was the GREAT MIGRATION and the growing presence of AFRICAN AMERICAN music in the city. Ethnic musical life in Chicago diversified during this phase, but it also fragmented, as established ethnic communities (e.g., the Central Europeans) dominated fewer areas of the city's public culture, while new communities enjoyed greater attention. Moreover, radio and the recording industry began to shape the ethnic music of this phase.

Phase 4. Multiculturalism and postethnic music

Since WORLD WAR II ethnic music in Chicago has responded to growing multiculturalism and ethnic border-crossing. After the war new ethnic groups (e.g., those fleeing the Communist states of Eastern Europe, such as POLES and YUGOSLAVS) and a New Ethnicity (from Latin America and Asia) replaced the more established European communities, and this process shows no signs of abating even as a new century begins. Musical

Hull House Dance and Rhythm Festival in the Hull House courtyard, ca. 1920s. Photographer: Wallace Kirkland. Source: University of Illinois at Chicago.

institutions within ethnic communities often survived by adopting hybrid repertories. The musical differences between ethnicity, race, and religion have also blurred, and in particular African American music undergirds what is most distinctive about the American influences in postethnic musics in Chicago.

Institutions for the Preservation of Ethnic Music

Social organizations and musical institutions have historically provided the most significant bulwark for the preservation of immigrant and ethnic music. The institution serves as a context with the requisite resources for preservation (e.g., a CHORAL library for an ethnic singing society), and it connects musical activities to other contexts in the community. Two basic types of institution dominate ethnic musical life: the organization or ensemble that is primarily musical, and the institution for which music is only one of several social activities.

Ethnic choruses have one of the oldest histories in Chicago. For German-speaking ethnic communities in the nineteenth century, first men's singing societies such as the Germania and then mixed choruses with men's and women's voices were staples of musical life. German singing societies in Chicago participated in national and international networks such as the North American Singing Union (Nordamerikanischer Sängerbund), and the city regularly served as the site for singing contests and festivals. At the beginning of the twenty-first century, German singing societies still thrive, and the DANK-Haus in the LINCOLN SQUARE neighborhood continues to serve as a center for rehearsals and performances.

For ethnic communities from Southeastern Europe, the *tamburitza* instrumental ensemble functions as a focus for social functions, especially among SERB and CROAT Americans. Young tamburitza players usually train in the local PARISH, but many parishes build affiliations with national tamburitza organizations (e.g., Pittsburgh's Duquesne University Tamburitzans) as well as with teachers in Europe.

By the turn of the present century, ethnic musical ensembles had both consolidated and professionalized their activities. Most ensembles no longer serve a specific parish but rather represent the ethnic group as a whole in Chicago. The Polish Lira Ensemble actively promotes Polish song and dance with performances in both Polish and non-Polish venues, especially in ethnic festivals. The JEWISH Halevi Choir draws upon several Jewish vocal traditions, ranging from a SACRED tradition connected to the synagogue to a secular repertory combining Eastern European Yiddish songs and Mediterranean Sephardic songs. At the beginning of the twenty-first century, the ethnic musical ensemble, thanks to its professionalization and the availability of public arts funding, commissions new compositions, therefore providing the basis for a modern and American ethnic musical tradition.

Religion and Interethnic Sites of Ethnic Music

Religion provides frameworks for stability and hybridity within ethnic communities. BUDDHIST traditions in Chicago, for example, cut across sectarian, ethnic, and generational differences, creating new opportunities for interethnic musics within Asian American communities. The Midwest Buddhist Temple, with its fundamentally *zen* framework, is a mainstay of the JAPANESE American tradition. The Midwest Buddhist Temple supports a *taiko* ensemble, which attracts participants from throughout the city, and in particular its activities draw together Japanese from different generations, including Japanese- and American-born. *Taiko* is a percussion ensemble, largely comprising drums, which embody a complex aesthetic of Japanese and Buddhist principles. The *taiko* ensemble at the Midwest Buddhist Temple serves as a musical path to encountering Japanese Americanness.

Theravada Buddhism in Chicago lends itself to much more extensive ethnic diversity. Its religious services are open to single ethnic communities, but they more often attract a mixture from the South, Southeast, and East Asian New Ethnic communities. The musical traditions that dominate *Theravada* Buddhist services do not derive from common historical, or even common linguistic, roots, but rather emphasize the improvisatory chant traditions, which utilize mantras in the shared sacred language of Buddhism, Pali, or a common vernacular, even English in the most ethnically mixed communities.

Islam in Chicago provides one of the most complex sites for interethnic musics. The ethnic histories included by Islam range from Balkan communities (historically, the first MUSLIM community in nineteenth-century Chicago was BOSNIAN), to the new presence of South Asians from PAKISTAN and North India, to the growing numbers of Black Muslims. Within Islam there are canonic sacred vocal practices that unite all Muslims, notably the recitation of the *Qur'an* and the *adhan*, or call to prayer. Islam, however, tolerates extensive local differentiation, which means that local musics in Chicago ALBANIAN communities may have little to do with those of Chicago LEBANESE or PAKISTANI communities. With the growth and diversification of Muslim communities in Chicago, shared musical and sacred practices yield new forms of interethnic musics, such as those connected with the ecstatic form of Islam known as Sufism, especially those that attract Black Muslims and Southeast Asian Muslims to South Asian musical genres, such as *qawwali.*

Technologies of Ethnic Music

Ethnic music moves between oral and written traditions, and it circulates because of the ways in which different media inscribe and disseminate it. Its histories, therefore, depend on technologies of ethnic music, which govern the production and consumption of music. MUSIC PUBLISHING was the most important technology for ethnic music in nineteenth-century Chicago. For Central European choral traditions, the German American press was essential, not only because it published anthologies of folk songs constituting the canon of German nationalism, but also because local publishers expanded German-language repertories for American consumption. The *Chicagoer Arbeiter-Zeitung,* for example, regularly published workers' songs in the late nineteenth century, adapting that tradition to the labor movement in Chicago during the period between the HAYMARKET Riot and World War I. The CZECH American publisher Vitak-Elsnik, which was active in Chicago and later in its suburbs from the 1920s into the post–World War II period, was the most important publisher of ethnic popular dance music.

Recording technologies have been fundamental for the maintenance and transformation of ethnic music in Chicago. Recordings in Chicago of Polish Highlander music performed in the 1920s by immigrants from the Tatra Mountains remained the standard for an earlier authenticity throughout the twentieth century, especially because these recordings traveled back and forth between Chicago and Poland. Ethnic records and ethnic BROADCASTING both thrived in Chicago during the first half of the twentieth century. Within the ethnic communities and diasporic landscapes of the new ethnic groups, ethnic radio and cassette culture enhance the local mediation and consumption of music. As technologies of ethnic music, radio and cassettes lend themselves to micro production of a two-hour radio program, with sponsors from the community, or distribution at low cost, thereby responding to changing musical tastes and markets. Recording and publishing technologies, finally, have made it possible for Chicago to export its ethnic musics to the world, from Francis O'Neill's volumes of IRISH music to CHESS RECORDS' recordings of BLUES and JAZZ.

Ethnic Popular Music

Ethnic popular musics are notable for the ways they cross ethnic borders and mark a wide variety of social activities as ethnic and, especially, postethnic. Ethnic popular musics have hybrid texts in which numerous ethnic traditions are identifiable. Their connections to any single ethnic community are never so esoteric as to hinder their appeal to other communities and the mainstream popular culture. Ethnic popular musics, finally, usually employ musical styles from other popular musics, and they

Polish Mountaineers celebrate their regional music and culture in this 1965 parade at 46th and Wolcott in the Back of the Yards neighborhood. Photographer: Joseph Topor. Source: Chicago Historical Society.

make extensive use of instruments from other popular musics.

Whereas diverse popular musics have been shared by Chicago's historically significant Central and Eastern European ethnic groups, the most widespread style is POLKA. As a dance style highly dependent on performance, polka provides a context in which different European American communities gather to experience a common repertory, albeit a repertory in which specifically German, Czech, or Polish traditions can be expressed. Chicago polka BANDS are mobile, and most bands play for numerous ethnic groups and community functions. Chicago polka styles have been very influential beyond Chicago, significantly shaping American ethnic popular music as a whole.

In Chicago's Hispanic communities, *mariachi* is one of the clearest examples of ethnic popular music. Historically an urban, MEXICAN style, mariachi now connects Mexicano, Tejano, PUERTO RICAN, and Central American communities in Chicago. In the 1980s and 1990s mariachi has broken through into mainstream popular culture and become the emblematic Hispanic music for public events. Depending on its functions, mariachi music therefore represents ethnicity in different ways, ranging from a more localized Mexicanness to a much more expansive Hispanicness with which non-Mexican Hispanics can identify.

In Chicago's South Asian communities, INDIAN film music, *filmi sangit,* functions as an ethnic popular music that crosses linguistic borders and is widely available in Indian and Pakistani video and grocery stores. Film music, however, has historically been imported, and its functions depended largely on mediated consumption. In the 1990s a new South Asian popular music became popular in Chicago, *bhangra,* a hybrid style that mixed elements from Indian film and classical music, HINDU (*bhajan*) and Muslim (*qawwali*) religious genres, ROCK 'N' ROLL, and AFRICAN AMERICAN popular music, especially hip-hop and funk. *Bhangra,* though performed primarily by a generation of South Asian Americans born in the United States, has widespread appeal, proffering a cultural, class, and religious unity in the ethnic community that had been impossible in India and Pakistan.

At the beginning of the twenty-first century, ethnic music is inseparable from GLOBAL networks. Just as certain ethnic musics have participated specifically in processes of change and dissemination unique to Chicago, these have exerted an impact on ethnic musics elsewhere in North America and abroad. The polka, following paths of musical change specific to Chicago's European ethnic communities, has undergone globalization, further contributing to the consolidation of a postethnic tradition. The blues, also a musical tradition whose history is inseparable from Chicago's urban history, possesses a truly transnational presence.

Already at the beginning of the twentieth century, Irish music in Chicago was exerting its presence as a globalized canon for the expression of ethnicity. Undertaking a number of recording and transcribing projects, a Chicago police captain, Francis O'Neill, gathered FOLK MUSIC, especially instrumental and dance tunes, from the city's large immigrant Irish community. Motivated by the desire to preserve, O'Neill published his collections of Irish folk music in Chicago, and they were soon available also in Ireland, where, during the 1920s and 1930s, they rapidly became the standard folk-music canon. At the beginning of the twenty-first century, O'Neill's publications remain the canon of Irish traditional music in Ireland and elsewhere in the world, giving a

Chicago inflection to the Celtic Revival during the century's final decades.

Globalization, for its part, spurred by increased mobility and new technologies, has transformed both ethnicity and ethnic music, and three new processes are notable: (1) the formation of new ethnic mainstreams, (2) postethnic culture and musics, and (3) diaspora. The development of musics in a larger Hispanic American community exemplifies the first process. Hispanic American music combines traditions from numerous Mexican, Central American, and Caribbean musics, as well as South American genres. The result is an ethnic mainstream for all Spanish-speaking ethnic groups. Postethnic musics result from the blurring of ethnic and racial boundaries and, most important of all, the active choice of and affiliation with ethnic musics that best suit an individual's cultural needs. Musicians with European ethnicity may actively participate in African American or Asian American ensembles, which in turn perform both inside and outside African American and Asian American contexts.

As Chicago's ethnic musical landscape responds to the formation of new ethnic communities, diaspora has become one of the most important global influences on the city's ethnic musics. Diaspora stimulates processes of exchange moving in several directions. Ethnic groups return to former homelands and accumulate new musical resources, such as the pilgrimage musics that Mexican Americans bring with them after a pilgrimage to Guadalupe. The teaching of Indian classical dance, *bharata natyam,* fully integrated into the South Asian diaspora connecting Chicago's suburbs to India and Pakistan, depends on teachers from India and other American diaspora communities. Musical exchange between Chicago's Polish Americans and Poland continues to reflect the diasporic structure of postmodern Polish ethnicity in Chicago. For ethnic communities, such as those with Balkan roots, diaspora even influences the ways in which music, drawn from diaspora sources, organizes ritual—for example, in the weddings of Albanian and MACEDONIAN Americans. At the beginning of the twenty-first century, ethnic music continues to proliferate in Chicago, acquiring not only new forms and contexts, but interacting with global historical forces in new ways.

Philip V. Bohlman

See also: Americanization; Chicago Sound; Demography; Multicentered Chicago; Pacific Islanders; Record Publishing; Sacred Music

Further reading: Bohlman, Philip V., and Otto Holzapfel, eds. *The Land without Nightingales: Music in the Making of German-America.* 2002. • French, Florence, ed. *Music and Musicians in Chicago.* 1899. • Grame, Theodore C. *Ethnic Broadcasting in the United States.* 1980.

Ethnic Theater. *See* Theater, Ethnic

Evanston, IL, Cook County, 12 miles N of the Loop. On the shore of LAKE MICHIGAN just north of Chicago, the area that is now Evanston was home to POTAWATOMIS until the 1830s, when they were moved west to Iowa. During the 1840s the area became thinly settled by farmers from upstate New York and elsewhere in the eastern United States and by GERMAN-speaking immigrants from the region where today the Netherlands, Belgium, Luxembourg, and Germany converge.

On August 11, 1853, the embryonic NORTHWESTERN UNIVERSITY purchased and surveyed more than three hundred acres of swampy land, which is now central Evanston. Northwestern held its first Evanston classes two years later. Two other educational institutions also opened that year: the Garrett Biblical Institute and the Northwestern Female College. Incorporated as a village in 1863, the town (named in honor of John Evans, a central founder of Northwestern) grew slowly through the 1860s.

The Chicago FIRE OF 1871 led thousands of well-to-do Chicagoans, fearing another fire, to build homes in Evanston. To meet their needs an influx of servants and tradesmen swelled Evanston's population. The village of North Evanston merged with Evanston in 1874, and in 1892, residents of South Evanston voted to join with Evanston.

Evanston's AFRICAN AMERICAN community, which predated the CIVIL WAR, also grew. Most African Americans were employed as domestic servants or manual laborers until the opening of light manufacturing on Evanston's west side, which drew its workforce both from African Americans and POLISH immigrants.

During the first two decades of the twentieth century a building boom of large APARTMENTS was stimulated by RAPID TRANSIT access to Chicago's LOOP. In the 1920s a REAL-ESTATE boom led to the development of northwest Evanston as a wealthy enclave. By the 1940s Evanston had become the home of numerous national organizations and nationally known firms.

By the 1960s Evanston's African American population had become largely concentrated in the city's west and south-central neighborhoods. Immigrants from HAITI and JAMAICA began arriving in sizeable numbers, as did a large number of former residents of Chicago's HYDE PARK neighborhood.

Growing racial tensions led to conscious efforts to ensure racial balance in the Evanston Public Schools. The opening of the Old Orchard Shopping Center in adjacent SKOKIE in the early 1960s drained vitality from Evanston's central business district. Many retail shops were replaced by RESTAURANTS, making Evanston one of metropolitan Chicago's premier dining centers, a development anticipated in 1972 when the city dropped a ban on the sale of alcoholic beverages that had its antecedents in an 1855 temperance amendment to Northwestern's charter.

Town-gown conflicts had surfaced periodically since 1874 because of the tax exemption that was granted to the university by the Illinois State Legislature in 1855. In the late 1990s, high property taxes and high rents threatened to diminish Evanston's long-standing attraction for middle-class residents. A joint Northwestern-Evanston Research Park failed to fulfill its promises of new jobs and renewed economic vitality. Despite these and other less formidable problems, Evanston remained at the turn of the twenty-first century one of Chicago's most stable and attractive suburbs.

Patrick M. Quinn

See also: Annexation; Economic Geography; Prohibition and Temperance; Seminaries; Suburbs and Cities as Dual Metropolis

Further reading: Ebner, Michael. *Creating Chicago's North Shore.* 1988. • Perkins, Margery Blair. *Evanstoniana: An Informal History of Evanston and Its Architecture.* 1994. • Sheppard, Robert D., and Harvey B. Hurd. *History of Northwestern University and Evanston.* 1906.

Evergreen Park, IL, Cook County, 12 miles S of the Loop. Evergreen Park is bordered by the city of Chicago on the north, east, and south, and OAK LAWN to the west. Two large CEMETERIES dominate the northwestern part of the village. The community's 13 churches give rise to its slogan "The Village of Churches."

As early as 1828, a GERMAN farming family had settled in the area of what is now Evergreen Park. In the succeeding decades, other German immigrants arrived. Kedzie Avenue and 95th Street crisscrossed the farmland and provided access to markets.

The first RAILROAD (now the Grand Trunk Railroad) came through the area in 1873. In 1875, the community built its first SCHOOL just west of 95th and Kedzie. The school and the stores that began to cluster around this intersection defined the community's main business area. Nearby, an optimistic REAL-ESTATE developer, smitten with a vision of the Arc de Triomphe area of Paris, laid out a star-shaped park with eight streets radiating from it. The evergreen trees planted in the park inspired the village's name.

In 1888 St. Mary's Cemetery opened, and mourners traveled by train from Chicago. RESTAURANTS and taverns sprang up to provide meals for cemetery visitors. Within five years, the village had become a recreation center that attracted hundreds of Chicagoans to its picnic groves, beer gardens, and DANCE HALLS. While dependent on Chicagoans, Evergreen Park incorporated in 1893 to eliminate the threat of ANNEXATION to the city of Chicago. The first of the village's 13 churches was established in 1893.

In the early decades of the twentieth century, as Chicago's SOUTH SIDE became more settled, DUTCH truck farmers moved out to Evergreen Park. A second large cemetery was established in 1910.

Although the village's population was only 705 in 1920, a 30-year growth spurt began in 1930. The Little Company of Mary Hospital opened that year, and the next year, the Western Avenue street railway reached Evergreen Park. Between 1945 and 1953, the village's population more than tripled. In 1951, the Drury Lane Theatre opened and in 1952, Evergreen Plaza, a pioneer shopping mall. Although there are some commercial areas are along 95th Street and Kedzie Avenue, Evergreen Park is predominantly residential, with little industry. The Little Company of Mary HOSPITAL is the village's largest employer, and the sales taxes generated by the mall form the bulk of the village's income.

Evergreen Park's population peaked in the 1970s at almost 26,000, dropping to 20,821 (88 percent white) by 2000. Most of the village's residents commute to Chicago or elsewhere to work.

Betsy Gurlacz

See also: Entertaining Chicagoans; Religious Geography; Shopping Districts and Malls

Further reading: Local History Files. Evergreen Park Public Library, Evergreen Park, IL.

Congress Parkway passing through the U.S. Post Office, 1959. Photographer: N. K. Benedict. Source: Chicago Historical Society.

Expressways. Expressways have reshaped the Chicago region perhaps more than any other twentieth-century force, creating new BUSINESS centers and dramatically expanding residential settlement.

Increasing automobile travel in the 1910s and 1920s gave new urgency to the arterial improvements recommended in the 1909 *Plan of Chicago.* In 1927, the Chicago Plan Commission laid out a system of limited-access highways radiating from the LOOP, including a route along Avondale Avenue next to the Chicago & North Western Railway (the route later used for the Kennedy Expressway) that was defeated in a 1928 bond issue vote. Lakefront recreational improvements became subordinate to construction of Lake Shore Drive as a traffic-carrying parkway. Its limited access and diamond interchanges made the section from Belmont to Foster a forerunner of the urban freeway when it opened in 1933.

Although the GREAT DEPRESSION slowed urban growth and limited civic spending, auto use continued to grow and in 1940 the city council approved a system of superhighways radiating from downtown Chicago that is nearly identical to what was eventually built. WORLD WAR II postponed all CONSTRUCTION, but postwar growth soon made those improvements imperative. Long-distance traffic, particularly intercity trucks, presented the most pressing needs, and the Chicago area's first expressways were easy-to-build approaches to the urban area. The Kingery Highway (originally called the Tri-State Highway) opened in 1950 as part of a long-planned metropolitan bypass, and connected with the Bishop Ford Freeway (known as Calumet Expressway until 1996). Milwaukee-bound traffic was relieved with the opening of the Edens Expressway (now I-94) in 1951.

Urban expressways provided greater challenges. A West Side superhighway, heir to the *Plan of Chicago*'s vision of a Congress Street arterial axis, had been tied to transit improvements with the creation in 1939 of the city's Department of Subways and Superhighways. Funding agreements between the city, county, and state finally fell into place in the late 1940s and construction began on the Eisenhower (originally Congress) Expressway, which opened in sections between 1955 and 1960. This project included construction of the north-south portion of Wacker Drive. COOK COUNTY Chairman Daniel Ryan engineered passage of a massive bond issue in 1955, expediting construction of other expressways.

Meanwhile, the state created the Illinois State TOLL HIGHWAY AUTHORITY (originally Commission) to plan bypass routes for northeastern Illinois. Construction of the Tri-State, East-West, and Northwest TOLLWAYS began in 1956 and all opened in 1958. To connect Chicago with the new Indiana TOLL ROAD, the Chicago (originally Calumet) SKYWAY opened in 1958.

By the time Congress created the Interstate Highway System in 1956, nearly all Chicago-area expressways were laid out, but federal funding pushed construction into high gear. The Kennedy Expressway opened in 1960, linking the Loop to the new O'HARE AIRPORT and the Northwest Tollway (I-90). The Dan Ryan Expressway opened to 95th Street in 1961–62. The abandoned ILLINOIS & MICHIGAN CANAL provided a convenient right-of-way through the city for the Stevenson Expressway (I-55), opened in 1964. Much of cross-country Interstate 80, skirting the south edge of the metropolitan area, opened at the same time.

Most of the urban routes were built next to RAILROAD embankments, but others were criticized for dividing and blighting neighborhoods. Mike Royko's 1971 biography of Mayor Richard J. Daley, *Boss,* claims that the Dan Ryan Expressway route was shifted to reinforce the border between Daley's native BRIDGEPORT and the BLACK BELT to the east. The approved route was indeed shifted in 1956, from next to the Chicago & Western Indiana Railroad (400 West) to run next to the Rock Island Line

Chicago-Area Expressways in 2003

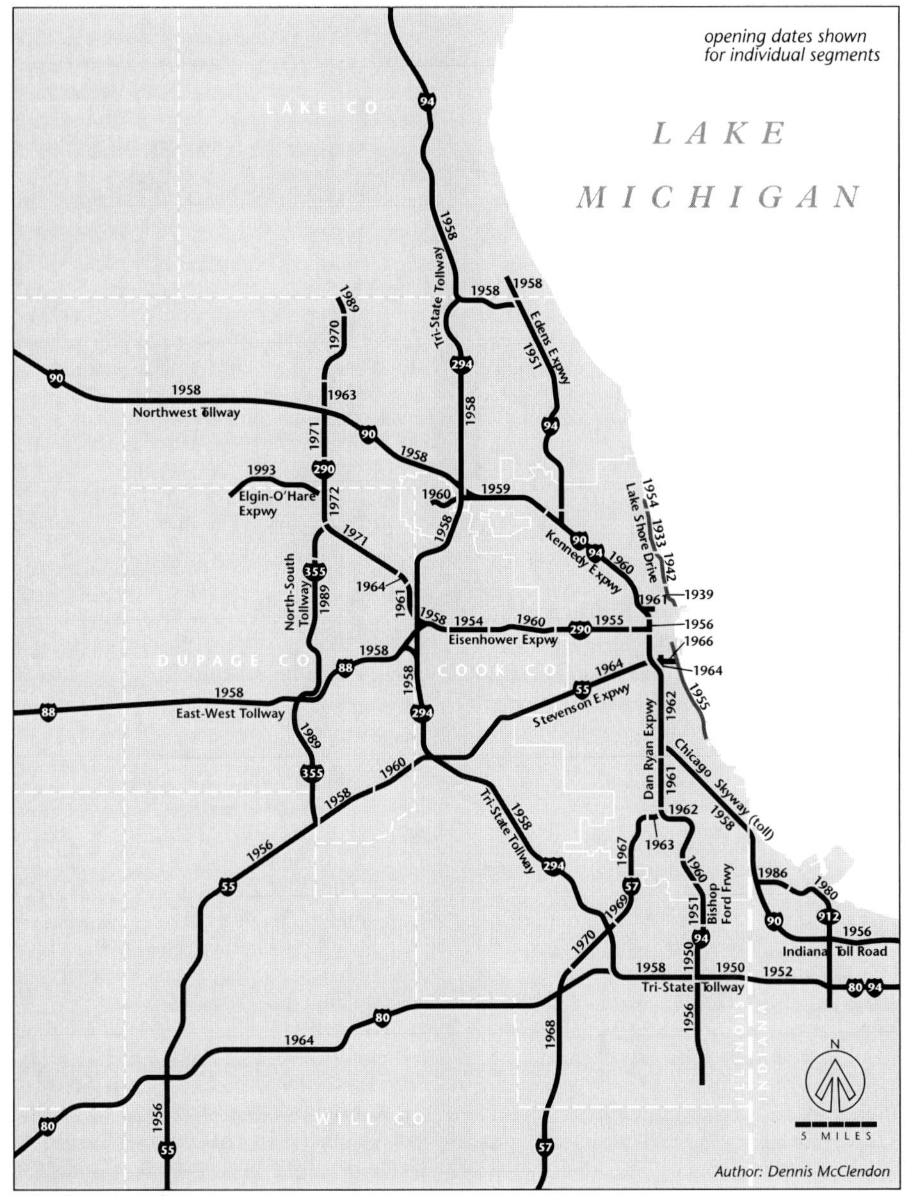

The region's first expressway links were easy-to-build segments through open areas serving heavy traffic to the east and to Milwaukee. A toll road network to bypass the city was built in three years, whereas construction of the city's first superhighway through the dense West Side took nearly a decade. Construction was accelerated after the Interstate Highway program made federal funding available. Radial expressways, intended to make central Chicago more accessible from the suburbs, proved "two-way streets" by also drawing businesses and residents outward. Extension of the metropolitan expressway network virtually stalled in the 1990s, and a combination of indecision and relentless urban development has precluded additional links along several logical corridors, such as the Fox Valley in Kane County.

at State Street, though the change might have been for the official reasons of "better alignment and traffic distribution," since it eliminated an inelegant four-block jog along 36th Street.

The design of Chicago expressways was straightforward, graced by neither the architectural detailing found along Lake Shore Drive nor the soaring ramps built on California freeways. Although early plans called for landscaped parkways, Interstate-era landscaping was minimal. Chicago did pioneer the use of median RAPID TRANSIT lines, which were built along the Eisenhower, Dan Ryan, and Kennedy expressways. The Kennedy also includes reversible lanes to carry rush-hour loads that are heavier in one direction than the other, an idea first tried on North Lake Shore Drive, but removed in the late 1970s. The Dan Ryan includes express lanes that bypass local exits, making one of the world's widest roads, with 14 lanes in one section.

A few additional routes continued to open in the 1970s: the Eisenhower Extension (I-290) was completed from ELMHURST to SCHAUMBURG in 1971, and I-57 (the Dan Ryan West Leg) opened in segments between 1967 and 1970. The Crosstown Expressway (I-494), planned to extend west from the Dan Ryan Expressway along 75th Street, then north along Cicero Avenue to the Kennedy Expressway, was never built, however. Community protests over the loss of housing and businesses, which a decade earlier might have been ignored, now coincided with growing environmental concerns, national doubts about urban expressways, and a changing political landscape in Illinois. After the death of Mayor Richard J. Daley in 1976, the project was traded for increased transit funding and other road projects.

These high-speed links reshaped the region as dramatically as had the railroads a century earlier. The Edens Expressway stimulated rapid development of the Skokie valley. Though designed for long-distance traffic, both the Northwest and East-West Tollways facilitated access to areas such as OAK BROOK and Schaumburg, previously undeveloped areas not served by commuter railroad lines. Although the network's radial pattern still seemed to be focused on the Loop, circumferential routes such as I-294 made these new outlying business locations convenient to O'HARE AIRPORT, new manufacturing and distribution facilities, and the decision makers and workers who increasingly lived in suburban areas.

This suburbanization created the need for additional suburb-to-suburb links, and the North-South Tollway (I-355) opened in 1989 through central DUPAGE COUNTY. The first section of the ELGIN-O'Hare Expressway followed in 1993. Continued expansion of the system has stimulated ongoing debate about the role such highways play in development.

Dennis McClendon

See also: Burnham Plan; Commuting; Economic Geography; Land Use; Planning Chicago; Streets and Highways; Transportation

Further reading: Christopher, Ed J., and Maryanne A. C. Custodio. "A History of the Northeastern Illinois Expressway System." *Chicago Area Transportation Study Working Paper* 97-04. 1997. • Condit, Carl W. *Chicago, 1930–1970: Building, Planning, and Urban Technology.* 1974.

Fairs. *See* County Fairs

FALN. *See* Fuerzas Armadas de Liberación Nacional (FALN)

Family Planning. People have long taken measures to control their fertility. Through the use of abortion, withdrawal, breastfeeding, and abstinence as well as condoms, douches, and pessaries, nineteenth-century Americans dramatically reduced their fertility rates. Chicago was known as a source of contraception and abortion providers because of its massive concentration of medical practitioners and commercial resources. Some believed, however, that the use of birth control disrupted the social order and promoted illicit sexual behavior. By the 1870s, coalitions of physicians, politicians, and lay reformers obtained the passage of "Comstock laws" restricting contraceptives, in addition to federal, state, and city statutes banning most forms of abortion.

By the early twentieth century, a new generation challenged the prohibitions against contraceptives, drawing upon socialist, PUBLIC HEALTH, and eugenic agendas. The earliest birth control advocates looked simultaneously toward improving women's health and liberating female sexuality by eliminating fears of unwanted pregnancy and the dangers of illegal abortion. In 1916, Margaret Sanger, a nurse by profession and socialist in politics, visited Chicago as part of her nationwide campaign to abolish Comstock laws and urge the establishment of local contraceptive CLINICS. Her speech, delivered near the stockyards to an audience of 1,200 people, inspired the creation of the Illinois Birth Control League. Despite opposition from Chicago's commissioner of health, Herman N. Bundesen, the league opened its first birth control clinic in 1923. Under the direction of HULL HOUSE resident Rachelle Yarros, the clinic provided married women primarily with the doctor-prescribed diaphragm. Similar facilities quickly spread across the city. By 1936, the decision to legalize pregnancy preventatives under the supervision of physicians in *U.S. v. One Package* reflected the growing acceptance of contraception.

By the early 1940s, birth control assumed a different image, as Sanger's national organization took on a new name to become the Planned Parenthood Federation of America. The feminist undertones of "birth control," the term coined by Sanger in 1914, were replaced by the less radical message of "family planning," which emphasized the family more than women's health or sexuality. Married couples were expected to have only *planned* children, and those who failed were often held responsible for expanding relief rolls and juvenile delinquency. "Family planning," however, also increasingly meant help for those unable to bear children. In response to couples' demands for assistance, in 1944 Planned Parenthood in Chicago opened an infertility clinic, one of the first of its kind in the nation.

Although "family planning" continued to earn popular approval, by the time oral contraceptives came on the market in 1960, many restrictions against contraception and abortion remained. Throughout the sixties, Chicago proved a hotbed of reform in both areas. The decision by the Illinois Public Aid Commission (IPAC) in 1962 to provide contraceptive information to all welfare recipients, regardless of marital status, provoked bitter criticism. ROMAN CATHOLICS condemned state support of contraception, and voices from the black community later charged that such initiatives represented an implicit attack on large families among AFRICAN AMERICANS. Nevertheless, by 1965 the commission voted to make information available to single and teenaged welfare recipients, despite the forced resignation of IPAC chairman Arnold Maremont. Seven years later, *Eisenstadt v. Baird* (1972) legitimated the right of the unmarried to obtain contraceptives.

Chicagoans also challenged abortion restrictions. By lobbying for legislative reform and providing thousands of illegal abortions through the militant "JANE" organization, they helped pave the way for the passage of *Roe v. Wade* (1973), which secured the right to abortion for women throughout the nation.

Debates over birth control persist. The 12-year battle in the 1980s and 1990s surrounding elective abortion in COOK COUNTY HOSPITAL indicates the lack of consensus regarding the procedure. Disputes over the distribution of condoms in Chicago's public high SCHOOLS in the 1990s further reveal how competing views of "appropriate" sexual behavior inform the meaning of birth control and its use.

Rose Holz

See also: Birthing Practices; Feminist Movements; La Leche League

Further reading: Brodie, Janet Farrell. *Contraception and Abortion in Nineteenth-Century America.* 1994. • Gordon, Linda. *Woman's Body, Woman's Right: A Social History of Birth Control in America.* 1976. Revised and updated edition. 1990. • Reagan, Leslie J. *When Abortion Was a Crime: Women, Medicine, and the Law in the United States, 1867–1973.* 1997.

Farming. *See* Agriculture

Federal Art Project. The Federal Art Project (1935–1943) was the best known of several NEW DEAL programs that provided employment for ARTISTS during the GREAT DEPRESSION. National director Holger Cahill aimed to foster cultural democracy by erasing the divide between fine and applied ART and making art a part of daily life for the public. Influenced by John Dewey's pragmatic philosophy—which emphasized learning by doing and understood art as a process of human relations rather than a material object—Cahill incorporated education and research as well as art making into the FAP.

In Chicago, Cahill's liberal notions met challenges from right and left. The first local director, painter and gallery-owner Increase Robinson, was more conservative and elitist. Her insistence on high professional standards meant fewer artists could qualify for the project. Whereas Cahill never sought to influence subject matter, Robinson specified "no nudes, no dives, no pictures intended as social propaganda." She also avoided hiring members of the Artists Union and neglected two key parts of the national project, children's classes and community ART CENTERS. After the union filed charges against Robinson with Cahill in 1938, she was removed. The subsequent directors, George Thorp and Fred Biesel, proved more sympathetic to a broader range of artists and programs. In 1940 the project came under fire again when the *Chicago Tribune* pronounced much of the art "incompetent and ugly" and permeated with "communistic motifs."

The FAP's legacy endures in Chicago. Numerous works remain in SCHOOLS and other public buildings, and the South Side Community Art Center, the only surviving FAP center in the country, continues to serve the city's AFRICAN AMERICAN community.

Diane Dillon

See also: Art, Public; Federal Writers' Project; Progressive Education

Further reading: *After the Great Crash: New Deal Art in Illinois.* Exhibition catalog. 1983. • Mavigliano, George J., and Richard A. Lawson. *The Federal Art Project in Illinois, 1935–1943.* 1990. • Smith, Clark Sommer. "Nine Years of Federally Sponsored Art in Chicago, 1933–1942." M.A. thesis, University of Chicago. 1965.

Federal Writers' Project. The Illinois Writers' Project, based in downtown Chicago, distinguished itself as one of the most accomplished state offices of the Federal Writers' Project and the Writers' Program that succeeded it. These programs were part of a larger national effort from 1935 to 1943 to employ artists and writers who might otherwise have been unable to work during the GREAT DEPRESSION. The Illinois office, directed by NORTHWESTERN UNIVERSITY professor John T. Frederick, included Nelson Algren, Richard Wright, Jack Conroy, Willard Motley, Frank Yerby, Saul Bellow, Margaret Walker, Arna Bontemps, Sam Ross, and Louis "Studs" Terkel. Its official publications included a massive guide to Illinois and smaller guides to localities, as well as studies of subjects ranging from BASEBALL to industry.

The project also afforded writers time to work on their own. Wright, for instance, worked on the landmark novel *Native Son.* Algren wrote his breakthrough novel, *Never Come Morning,* while employed by the project.

Writers on the project also influenced one another. Conroy, Algren, and other established figures advised novices like Terkel and Walker (and intimidated Bellow, who remembers that he "rather looked up to" the veterans, who "rather looked down on" him). Several AFRICAN AMERICAN writers on the project staff participated in the SOUTH SIDE Writers Group, which extended the momentum of the Harlem Renaissance of the 1920s, as Bontemps put it, "without finger bowls but with increased power." Many of the project's writers, white and black, shared a commitment to social realism and the left politics of the Popular Front.

Carlo Rotella

See also: Chicago Black Renaissance; Federal Art Project; Fiction; Great Depression; Literary Careers; Literary Cultures

Further reading: Federal Writers' Project. *Illinois: A Descriptive and Historical Guide.* 1939. • Mangione, Jerre. *The Dream and the Deal: The Federal Writers' Project, 1935–1943.* 1972. • Sporn, Paul. *Against Itself: The Federal Theater and Writers' Projects in the Midwest.* 1995.

Feminist Movements. Feminist movements promote gender equality and oppose the perpetuation of gender discrimination in economic, political, legal, and social structures. In Chicago, such feminist organization began with the Woman SUFFRAGE Party ofCOOK COUNTY, incorporated in 1912 with Charlotte C. Rhodus as president and dedicated to securing total political equality for women. Another early element of the feminist movement in Chicago was the birth control movement. Chicago-area feminists argued that the lack of legal, easily accessible birth control information and devices discriminated against women. The Chicago WOMEN'S TRADE UNION LEAGUE (CWTUL) demanded birth control information as a democratic right for all women and disseminated such information through its birth control committee, headed by Rachelle Yarros. Yarros and the CWTUL persuaded the Chicago Woman's Club to organize a birth control committee in 1915. In the 1920s, the Parents' Committee worked to defeat laws then being proposed to prevent licensed physicians from dispensing birth control information. In 1923, the committee tried to set up a CLINIC in Chicago where poor women could receive such information, but the Chicago Health Department refused to issue the requisite license. The committee turned instead to promoting birth control centers that functioned inside doctors' offices and founded the Illinois Birth Control League to set up such facilities, which eventually became Planned Parenthood centers.

Feminist ideals also inspired a series of WOMEN'S WORLD FAIRS (1925–1928), where women exhibited their achievements in the arts, literature, science, and industry. The fairs showcased women's accomplishments, but they also served as a venue in which women could inform each other about careers and jobs.

Feminist movements waned in Chicago thereafter, as they did across the country, reviving during the 1960s with new movements seeking to use law and legislation to overturn institutionalized political and economic inequality. In 1963, Chicagoan Esther Saperstein introduced a bill into the state legislature to create a Commission on the Status of Women in conjunction with comparable national legislation. In 1967, feminists met in Chicago to organize chapters of the National Organization for Women, whose recently adopted Bill of Rights called for passage of the Equal Rights Amendment, maternity rights in employment and Social Security benefits, equal job training opportunities, and women's right to control their reproductive capacities. Chicago women also organized chapters of the National Women's Political Caucus, the Women's Equity Action League to help women file discrimination charges, and the National Black Feminist Organization (renamed the National Black Feminist Alliance) to fight both racism and sexism.

The 1960s also produced a new-wave feminist movement called Women's Liberation, which argued that women suffered both personal and political oppression in a male-dominated society. In 1965, women at the UNIVERSITY OF CHICAGO organized one of the country's first campus groups focused on this issue. Chicago feminists then founded the CHICAGO WOMEN'S LIBERATION UNION (CWLU) to raise women's consciousness of their oppression, and from 1974 until its demise in 1981 the National Black Feminist Alliance was such a consciousness-raising group for AFRICAN AMERICAN women in Chicago. The CWLU argued that fighting women's oppression required radical alteration of prevailing economic, social, and political structures. The CWLU and other feminist organizations at the time also proposed to operate in a women's cooperative, "democratic" style as opposed to what they called a men's competitive style.

The feminist movements of the 1960s also concentrated on achieving reproductive and sexual freedom. Feminists demanded affordable child care, birth control and abortion on demand, more attention to women's health needs, rape crisis centers, and women's shelters. Their efforts resulted in the municipal Rape Treatment Center Act of 1974, which established rape treatment centers in city HOSPITALS. Feminists were also prepared to defy the law, forming an underground organization ("JANE") to provide abortions when they were still illegal in Illinois.

Economic equality was also a goal of feminist movements from the 1960s onward. Unlike many women's movements earlier in the century, which had often favored protective labor legislation for women, the new feminist organizations emphasized gender equality in the workplace. The Coalition of Labor Union Women was formed in Chicago in 1974 to give union women access to leadership positions denied in the male-dominated union structure, to help union women overturn discriminatory insurance rates and pension benefit deductions, and to secure maternity leave. Women Employed worked in Chicago to fight hiring and job discrimination for nonunion women. The Feminist Writers Guild, organized in the 1980s, sought similar equality of access for female writers.

Feminist collectives, some of them lesbian or at least closed to men, and periodicals also emerged. Periodicals included *Womankind,* published in the early 1970s by the Chicago Women's Liberation Union; *Mountain Moving,* published later in the decade by the Mountain Moving Collective in Evanston; *Sister Source,* subtitled "a midwestern lesbian/feminist newspaper," and published briefly in the 1980s; and *Catalyst: Chicago Womyn's Paper* (1980). The collectives and these periodicals were a manifestation of some Chicago-area feminists' desires by the late twentieth century to free women from male domination in a patriarchal society by removing themselves as much as possible from control by men in all areas of their personal and public lives.

Maureen A. Flanagan

See also: Civil Rights Movements; Family Planning; Gay and Lesbian Rights Movements; Politics; Sanitary Commission

Further reading: Cott, Nancy. *The Grounding of Modern Feminism.* 1987 • Payne, Elizabeth. *Reform, Labor, and Feminism: Margaret Dreier Robins and the Women's Trade Union League.* 1988. • Schultz, Rima L., and Adele Hast, eds. *Women Building Chicago: A Biographical Dictionary.* 2001.

Fenianism. Fenianism, a form of militant Irish American nationalism, arose after the failed 1848 rebellion in Ireland amid the nativism and poverty facing Famine-generation IRISH in America. The Fenian Brotherhood, a secret society formed in New York in 1858 to promote Irish independence, found a home among the roughly 20,000 Irish immigrants living in Chicago on the eve of the CIVIL WAR. Initially, the brotherhood spread slowly because of its condemnation by the ROMAN CATHOLIC church as a secret society, factional disputes between American and Irish branches of the movement, and the reluctance of many

Irish to endorse the Fenians' advocacy of violence.

The American CIVIL WAR provided the great spur to Fenianism in Chicago, as elsewhere. Amid calls to arms to defend the Union, Chicago Irish American leaders such as the JOURNALISTS John and William Scanlon rallied Irish nationalism to Fenianism. In turn, soldiers invoked Fenianism to recruit Irish regiments by linking the fight against the South with the struggle against England and promising that the training in the Union army would provide the means for Fenian strikes against British interests. The Chicago chapter, or "circle," of Fenians even proposed declaring war on England in 1864. The denunciation of the secret society by Chicago Bishop James Duggan in 1864 hardly tempered the brotherhood's militancy.

The numbers of Fenians in Chicago remain elusive. During the war, the Chicago "circle" of Fenians met regularly twice a week, and in 1866 it raised $10,000 for an invasion of Canada. The Fenians from Ireland who plotted an invasion of British Canada in 1865 claimed that 3,000 "officers from Chicago alone" would join the expedition.

Fenianism came apart almost as fast as it had formed. Factionalism wracked the movement, as did political ambitions among its leaders. William Scanlon moved his *Irish Republic* newspaper first into the REPUBLICAN PARTY column and then in 1868 to New York to support the presidential candidacy of Ulysses S. Grant. Most Fenians remained DEMOCRATS by habit if not interest. Abortive raids on Canada in 1866 and 1870 dimmed Fenianism's star. Fenianism lingered into the 1880s, but its day had passed by 1871. Former Fenians in Chicago joined their compatriots across America by transferring their allegiance to other Irish liberation movements, especially the Clan-na-Gael, which succeeded the Fenian Brotherhood as the dominant Irish nationalist society in Chicago and the United States.

Randall M. Miller

See also: Americanization; Fuerzas Armadas de Liberación Nacional (FALN); Garveyism; Polish National Alliance; Racism, Ethnicity, and White Identity; Zionism

Further reading: Funchion, Michael F. *Chicago's Irish Nationalists, 1881–1890.* 1976. • Miller, Kerby A. *Emigrants and Exiles: Ireland and the Irish Exodus to North America.* 1985. • Pierce, Bessie Louise. *A History of Chicago,* vol. 2, *From Town to City, 1848–1871.* 1940.

Fermilab. In 1966, a 6,800-acre site in what was then Weston (now eastern BATAVIA), won the competition for a federal project called the National Accelerator Laboratory (NAL). Continuing Chicago's tradition of scientific discovery that began with Enrico Fermi's first self-sustaining nuclear chain reaction at the UNIVERSITY OF CHICAGO in 1942, NAL became an international center for physics research with the highest energy accelerator in the world.

Fermilab's Accelerator Ring: Metropolitan Chicago's Largest Circle

Though underground, the accelerator ring can easily be discerned from above because of a twenty-foot berm of earth on the ground above the ring. (Imagine a very skinny, four-mile-around bagel.) Many people assume the berm's purpose is to absorb radiation from the machine, but it's really there because [founding director Robert Rathbun] Wilson was an aesthetic sort of guy. After all the work of building the accelerator, he was disappointed that he couldn't tell where it was. So when the workmen dug out holes for cooling ponds around the accelerator, he had them pile up the dirt in this immense circle. To accent the circle, Wilson created a ten-foot-wide canal around it and installed circulating pumps that fire fountains of water into the air. The canal is functional as well as visual; it carries the cooling water for the accelerator. The whole thing is strangely beautiful. In satellite photos taken from three hundred miles above the earth, the berm-and-waterway—looking like a perfect circle from that height—is the sharpest feature on the northern Illinois landscape.

Lederman, Leon, and Dick Teresi. *The God Particle.* 1993, 25–27.

Physicist Robert Rathbun Wilson, NAL's first director, established offices in OAK BROOK in 1967. Wilson pushed an aggressive construction program to deliver the goal of a 200 GeV (billion electron volts) proton accelerator ahead of schedule and below the authorized $250 million budget. Moving onto the site in 1968, Wilson also addressed ENVIRONMENTAL and CIVIL RIGHTS concerns affecting the project. Wilson achieved his goal in March 1972 with the circulation of the proton beam around the Main Ring, the four-mile accelerator enclosed within an underground tunnel. Hundreds of proposals for experiments using this powerful instrument poured into NAL from physicists around the world. In 1974, NAL was dedicated and renamed the Fermi National Accelerator Laboratory (Fermilab).

By 1977 a team of physicists led by Leon M. Lederman produced a major discovery at Fermilab—the bottom quark, one of only six known quarks. Lederman became director in 1978 and won the Nobel Prize for Physics in 1988. From 1979 to 1983 the Energy Doubler/Saver, a ring of superconducting magnets, was installed beneath the Main Ring, transforming the accelerator into the Tevatron. An Antiproton Source was constructed from 1982 to 1985 under the leadership of John Peoples, Jr. Computing power was essential for the large teams working on these experiments, and by 1988 the Advanced Computer Project coordinated experimental data with analysis.

Peoples became director in 1989. During his administration, Fermilab played a critical role in the computing project that gave birth to the World Wide Web. In 1994–95 nearly a thousand physicists from around the world working on two Fermilab experiments discovered the top quark, the partner of the previously discovered bottom quark. The Tevatron, upgraded between 1993 and 1999 and enhanced with the Main Injector, remains the highest energy accelerator in the world.

Michael Witherell became director of Fermilab in 1999, taking the helm of an enterprise with a $300 million budget and over 2,000 employees. Managed by Universities Research Association for the U.S. Department of Energy, Fermilab has become the anchor of Illinois' east-west high-tech corridor.

Adrienne W. Kolb

See also: Argonne National Laboratory; Innovation, Invention, and Chicago Business; Manhattan Project; Warrenville

Further reading: Kolb, Adrienne, and Lillian Hoddeson. "A New Frontier in the Western Suburbs: Settling Fermilab, 1963–72." *Illinois Historical Journal* 88.1 (Spring 1995): 2–18. • Kolb, Adrienne. "A Brief History of Fermilab." 1999. • Westfall, Catherine, and Lillian Hoddeson. "Thinking Small in Big Science: The Founding of Fermilab, 1960–1972." *Technology and Culture* 37.3 (July 1996): 457–492.

Fibber McGee and Molly. *Fibber McGee and Molly* (1935–1956), created by Peoria natives Jim and Marian Jordan and writer Don Quinn, rated among the top five radio programs throughout the 1940s. Before moving it to Hollywood in 1939, NBC broadcast the weekly comedy from WMAQ-Chicago.

The good-natured, disorganized McGee, named for his tall tales, and his sensible, forbearing wife, Molly, interacted with colorful neighbors in domestic situations. Fibber's overflowing closet exemplified the show's humorous take on daily life. Regularly dramatizing current events such as wartime rationing, the show served as a semiofficial propaganda vehicle during WORLD WAR II. Its cancellation reflected television's growing prominence.

Spencer Downing

See also: Broadcasting; Entertaining Chicagoans; Leisure

Further reading: Dunning, John. *Tune In Yesterday: The Ultimate Encyclopedia of Old-Time Radio, 1925–1978.* 1976. • Stumpf, Charles, and Tom Price. *Heavenly Days: The Story of Fibber McGee and Molly.* 1987. • Wertheim, Arthur Frank. *Radio Comedy.* 1979.

Fiction. Chicago fiction has been written from practically every imaginable aesthetic approach: popular potboilers, deterministic naturalism, grim realism, postmodern surrealism, lyrical understatement, high modernism, magical realism. But whatever the particular writer's style, certain themes resonate throughout fictional treatments of Chicago: the challenge of building an individual identity in a vast, alienating city; conflicts between and within classes, genders, and ethnic and racial groups; the corrosive effect of urban life on traditional moral values; and the sheer, potentially overwhelming reality of Chicago as a set of ever-changing urban spaces—STREETS, ALLEYS, parks, beaches, RAILROADS, EXPRESSWAYS, THEATERS, SALOONS, salons, offices, banks, factories, churches, temples, SCHOOLS, UNIVERSITIES, SKYSCRAPERS, APARTMENTS, BUNGALOWS, slums, and prairies. In these spaces Chicagoans live and work, and writers of Chicago fiction work to tell the stories of the city.

Aspects of fictional technique appear even in the earliest autobiographical and historical narratives about Chicago, such as Juliette Kinzie's *Wau-Bun: The "Early Day" in the North-West,* and historians now agree that many of Chicago's founding narratives are more interesting as fiction than accurate as history. Later histories, whether of the boosterish or urban exposé variety, make similar use of fictional methods and suspect stories. The CHICAGO SCHOOL OF SOCIOLOGY used sophisticated narrative techniques in the production of case studies examining Chicago's slums and SETTLEMENT HOUSES, while Chicago novelists absorbed and deployed the techniques of sociological research. Chicago, in no small part because of the historical reality of its connection to organized CRIME and political corruption, also has a long history of depiction in popular fictional narratives, from nineteenth-century DIME NOVELS to the numerous mystery and detective series set in the city, most prominently Sara Paretsky's chronicles of feminist private eye V. I. Warshawski. NEWSPAPER columnists granted the editorial freedom to invent characters as a means of exploring the city have also created lasting fictional depictions of Chicago. Finley Peter Dunne's barkeep-philosopher Mr. Dooley and Mike Royko's Milwaukee Avenue Everyman Slats Grobnik endure as representative fictional Chicagoans of their time.

But when discussing Chicago and fiction, most of the focus belongs on serious attempts in prose narrative—novels and short stories—to capture the essence of the city, its spaces, and its people. As Carl S. Smith has demonstrated, this project was from the beginning fraught with both aesthetic and ideological challenges, as the booming Chicago of the nineteenth and early twentieth centuries seemed to belong to some new world, a world not particularly amenable to the rules of narrative prose fiction as then practiced. Neither high-flown romance nor genteel realism could grasp a place grown from frontier outpost to world city in the course of two generations. Chicago has challenged fiction writers to contemplate new industrial methods and new urban spaces like the skyscraper; observe violent conflict between capital and labor; think about the moral drama of immigration from the Midwestern hinterland, the far reaches of Europe, and the world; and face the irreducible conflict between an urban culture centered on making money and traditional values placed on high art, civic service, and family virtue.

The earliest Chicago fiction often dealt with historical events such as the Great FIRE OF 1871 or the HAYMARKET AFFAIR, but writers such as Henry Blake Fuller addressed the fundamental divide in Chicago culture: the conflict between Philistine moneymaking and traditional cultural values embodied in ART, music, literature, and other refined pursuits. Fuller's *The Cliff-Dwellers* and *With the Procession,* along with Frank Norris's *The Pit,* examine the contradictory and occasionally overlapping roles of the businessman and the ARTIST in a city newly created by cutthroat real-estate speculation and shameless civic boosterism.

While fiction writers approached the challenge presented by Chicago in a variety of styles, Chicago fiction soon became strongly associated with realism and naturalism. Along with the plain-language poets of the CHICAGO LITERARY RENAISSANCE, writers such as Upton Sinclair and Theodore Dreiser, with their close attention to the details of everyday life and the new arrangements of space and power within the city, laid the foundation for a Chicago school of fiction. This tradition focused not only on the city but on the people most excluded from the city's bounty. In Sinclair's *The Jungle,* the story of LITHUANIAN immigrant Jurgis Rudkus and his extended family being ground up by stockyards capitalism and the city (until enlightened by Socialism) has created an enduring connection in the popular imagination between Chicago and its now-defunct MEATPACKING industry. The novel's exposé of unsanitary and dangerous conditions in the packing plants also helped President Theodore Roosevelt pass the Pure Food and Drug Act. This real-world influence of a work of fiction was not the conversion to Socialism that Sinclair had hoped to cause, but it did demonstrate the power of fiction to influence American politics. While Sinclair wrote *The Jungle* with the melodramatic plot tricks and ornate style learned in his career as a writer of popular novels, Dreiser's plain and direct language and relative artlessness reflects his background as a JOURNALIST (one shared with many writers of Chicago fiction). Dreiser's *Sister Carrie* depicts the native Midwestern immigrant parallel to Sinclair's Lithuanians, and Dreiser's depiction of Carrie Meeber's successful if by conventional standards immoral life in the big city created a scandal and blazed a trail for other writers to get beyond the idea that literature must depict the world as it should be rather than the world as it is.

Later writers, radicalized by the GREAT DEPRESSION, extended Sinclair's and Dreiser's naturalistic treatments of Chicago with the inflections of modernism and existentialism. Each prominent Chicago writer from this period staked out his own literal and figurative territory. James T. Farrell's *Studs Lonigan* trilogy and *Danny O'Neill* tetralogy, along with scores of short stories, depicted the conflict between the IRISH American working and middle classes on the SOUTH SIDE and the temptations of the city, as well as the dilemma of the Irish American writer who must choose between the values of his family and neighborhood and the wider world of thought and culture offered by the university and intellectual life. Richard Wright's *Native Son* depicted the grim emotional and physical realities of Chicago's racial segregation in the BLACK BELT, giving fictional life to characters representative of Chicago's AFRICAN AMERICAN community, both on its own terms and in relation to the dominant white community. Nelson Algren did the same for POLISH American immigrants of the near Northwest Side in his novels *Never Come Morning* and *The Man with the Golden Arm* (winner of the first National Book Award), as well as in many of his short stories collected in *The Neon Wilderness* and in his quasi-fictional prose poem *Chicago: City on the Make.* Farrell, Wright, and Algren elaborated a Chicago tradition focused on creating readerly identification with the outsider, giving a voice to the voiceless. In the work of each of these writers, Chicago itself acts as a sort of character, a potentially overwhelming force with the power to shape or deform the individual.

Perhaps the most prominent writer to emerge from postwar Chicago is the 1976 Nobel Prize laureate for literature, Saul Bellow. Much of Bellow's fiction is set outside of Chicago, but his long-term association with the city and the UNIVERSITY OF CHICAGO mark him as a figure to be considered. His National Book Award–winning *Adventures of Augie March* and *The Dean's December* can be read as a matched set, early and late in Bellow's career, depicting industrial and postindustrial Chicago. While *Augie March* treats Chicago as an energetic if flawed setting with limitless possibilities for intellectual growth and self-realization, *The Dean's December* depicts Chicago as a postindustrial wasteland, a nightmarish landscape of racial violence, empty materialism, and vapid power seeking. Bellow has, along with most writers in the Chicago fiction tradition, a critical attitude toward the city and its power structure, but his depictions of Chicago are differentiated by his emphasis on the intellectual or spiritual emptiness of the city, as opposed to the realist or naturalist emphasis on material causes for social problems and individual alienation.

Chicago fiction at the turn of the twenty-first century continues along the lines laid out over its first century and a half. Once, native Chicagoan Henry Blake Fuller attempted in fiction to make sense of the new urban environment created by the skyscraper, and Midwestern immigrant Theodore Dreiser showed the naive Carrie Meeber arriving in the bewildering city. Today, writers like Stuart Dybek, Sandra Cisneros, Harry Mark Petrakis, and Ana Castillo show the dilemmas facing both Chicago's bewildered native sons, as their neighborhoods are torn up to build EXPRESSWAYS, and newly arrived immigrants, alienated from the city by language and tradition. Whatever their métier or origins, writers of Chicago fiction continue to grapple with the fundamental dilemmas presented by city life in general and by the specifics of Chicago's urban spaces, history, and relentless change.

Bill Savage

See also: Chicago Black Renaissance; Literary Careers; Literary Cultures; Literary Images of Chicago; Multicentered Chicago

Further reading: Cappetti, Carla. *Writing Chicago: Modernism, Ethnography, and the Novel.* 1993. • Rotella, Carlo. *October Cities: The Redevelopment of Urban Literature.* 1998. • Smith, Carl S. *Chicago and the American Literary Imagination, 1880–1920.* 1984.

Field Museum. When the WORLD'S COLUMBIAN EXPOSITION closed in the fall of 1893, and its estimated 25 million visitors had gone home, all that remained standing on the fairgrounds was the Palace of Fine Arts. On June 2, 1894, in that building, the Field Museum of Natural History opened to a large and enthusiastic crowd. On opening day, the *Chicago Times* reported that the magic of the exposition had been captured in the new museum. "It was," the paper wrote, "all like a memory of the fair."

In fact, a natural history museum had been in the works for a few years. In 1891, Harvard professor Frederic Ward Putnam, in town to help oversee anthropological exhibits at the exposition, exhorted members of the COMMERCIAL CLUB OF CHICAGO to establish a museum using the objects that would be left over from the fair. An aspiring city like Chicago, Putnam argued, needed a major museum of natural history to compete culturally with East Coast cities, and Chicagoans agreed. When retail magnate Marshall Field offered a million-dollar check for the project, the Field Museum was born.

Directed by Frederick Skiff, the new museum divided natural history into four categories: botany, zoology, geology, and anthropology. This last category represented a new science, and it constituted some of the most extensive and attention-grabbing displays, curated initially by Franz Boas, America's most influential anthropologist.

While still in its JACKSON PARK location, the Field Museum (along with the ART INSTITUTE) underwent an important administrative change in 1903. Ownership of both institutions passed from the city to the newly constituted South

Interior of the Field Museum, Jackson Park, 1898–1916. Photographer: Unknown. Source: Chicago Historical Society.

Park Commission, one of three autonomous PARK DISTRICTS established as a Progressive-era reform.

The museum's collections quickly outgrew the space available in the old Palace of Fine Art, and in the early years of the twentieth century plans for a new museum building began to take shape. Members of the Field family provided much of the money, ensuring both the success of the project and also that the name would not change. Marshall's nephew Stanley Field not only contributed $2 million but went on to serve as museum president for 56 years.

The result of this PHILANTHROPY was a massive white marble building in GRANT PARK, closer to other downtown cultural institutions. The new Field Museum opened to the public on May 2, 1921.

In its current building, the museum houses over 10 million specimens. It has sponsored scientific expeditions around the world, and it publishes a scholarly research journal. Starting with a gift of $250,000 made by Norman Harris in 1911, the museum has also sponsored extensive outreach programs for schoolchildren. As a result, thousands of school groups troop through the galleries each year.

Since its founding, the Field Museum has evolved into one of the great natural history museums in the world. In this country only the American Museum in New York and the Smithsonian in Washington compete with it in terms of size, influence, and prestige.

Steven Conn

See also: Chicago Academy of Sciences; Leisure; Museum of Science and Industry

Further reading: Alexander, Edward. *Museums in Motion: An Introduction to the History and Functions of Museums.* 1979. • Conn, Steven. *Museums and American Intellectual Life, 1876–1926.* 1998. • Horowitz, Helen. *Culture and the City: Cultural Philanthropy in Chicago from the 1880s to 1917.* 1976.

Filipinos. After the Philippines became a U.S. colonial possession in 1898 following the Spanish American War, young male Filipinos came to Chicago, first as family-supported or government scholarship (*pensionado*) students, and later as self-supporting students who expected to both work and attend high school or college. In a pattern of chain migration, brothers, cousins, and friends followed, settling in enclaves on the NEAR WEST and NEAR NORTH SIDES. According to the United States census, Chicago's Filipino population grew from 154 in 1920 to 1,796 10 years later, dropping to 1,740 by 1940. Unofficial estimates, however, put Filipino numbers at approximately 5,000 during the 1930s.

Before WORLD WAR II, the typical Chicago Filipino was a high-school graduate with some college experience who found work in RESTAURANTS, clubs, and homes. Several hundred were employed by the U.S. Post Office as clerks and by the Pullman Company as bus boys, cooks, and club and dining car attendants. Few Filipino women (*Filipinas*) came to Chicago. In 1940, among those over the age of 20, men outnumbered women 21:1. Ninety percent married outside the ethnic community, as Filipinos typically married American-born daughters of European immigrant parents.

Although permitted unrestricted entry into the United States as "nationals" until the mid-1930s, Filipinos could not become citizens. In 1934, the Tydings-McDuffie Act promised the Philippines independence after 10 years, but also limited Filipino immigration to an annual quota of 50. After independence, Filipinos, like other Asians, were to be totally excluded.

Largely in recognition of Filipino valor during World War II, Filipinos became eligible for United States citizenship in 1946, and their annual quota was raised symbolically from 50 to 100 after Philippine independence on July 4, 1946. Between 1952 and 1965, however, most Filipinos came to the United States as nonquota immigrants under the family reunification provisions of the McCarran-Walter Act of 1952. Some were the newly married wives of pre-1934 "old-timers." By 1960 Chicago's Filipino population totaled 3,554: 2,143 men and 1,411 women.

After passage of the Immigration and Nationality Act of 1965, Filipino immigration to the United States surged. Occupational preferences enabled many professionals, especially NURSES and physicians, to qualify for entry. Over time, however, family reunification provisions became more significant in enabling the migration of extended family units. The Filipino population in Chicago numbered 9,497 in 1970, reached 41,283 in the Chicago area in 1980, and totaled 95,298 in the Chicago metropolitan area in 2000—32,266 in Chicago.

Although from a single nation, Filipino immigrants are simultaneously united and divided by provincial and language loyalties and have tended to form associations, in part, on the basis of these loyalties. In addition, ties deriving from occupation or profession, school attendance in the Philippines, voluntaristic commitment, religious affiliation, political belief, and personal interest have also spawned organizations. Throughout the twentieth century, "Philippine," "Filipino," and "Filipino American" clubs, societies, and associations have proliferated, providing individuals with identities beyond family, kinship, and friendship, as well as opportunities for recognition and leadership. At the same time, competition among multiple organizations has segmented Filipinos, fostering divisiveness and weakening group solidarity. To provide coordination and encourage unity, the Filipino American Council of Chicago, an umbrella association for Filipino organizations in the metropolitan area, was formed in the late 1940s under the leadership of Carmelito Llapitan, who, with others of his "old-timer" generation, purchased a former Swedish club building in 1974. The Dr. Jose Rizal Memorial Center at 1332 West Irving Park Road has since been the gathering place for many of the diverse organizations linked through the FACC.

Barbara M. Posadas

See also: Demography; Multicentered Chicago

Further reading: Posadas, Barbara M. "Crossed Boundaries in Interracial Chicago: Filipino American Families since 1925." *Amerasia Journal* 8 (Fall/Winter 1981): 31–52. • Posadas, Barbara M. *The Filipino Americans.* 1999. • Posadas, Barbara M., and Roland L. Guyotte. "Unintentional Immigrants: Chicago's Filipino Foreign Students Become Settlers, 1900–1941." *Journal of American Ethnic History* 9.2 (Spring 1990): 26–48.

Film. From the beginning, the film industry in Chicago had many supporters. The inaugural June 1907 issue of the Chicago-based trade magazine *Show World* proclaimed that "Chicago leads the world in the rental of moving picture films and in the general patronage of the motion view." Both of these claims were probably true of Chicago at the time. In the early film era Chicago very likely had more film theaters per capita than any other city in the United States, with five-cent theaters, or nickelodeons, opening early and often, as the Chicago election-day expression goes. The number of new nickelodeons grew each year from 1905 through World War I, and the opening of new film venues continued to play a significant, even anchoring role in commercial development in Chicago neighborhoods until the onset of the GREAT DEPRESSION.

The *Show World* commentator was also correct about the city's role in film distribution. Chicago was the home of the film exchange, or film rental house. The exchanges created a new niche in the industry, giving exhibitors access (through rentals) to a larger number of films than they could afford to purchase and allowing theaters to change their films frequently. By 1907 there were over 15 film exchanges in operation in Chicago, and they controlled 80 percent of the film distribution market for the whole United States.

Several film production companies were actively making moving pictures in Chicago and the suburbs during this time. William Selig, a former magician and theatrical troupe manager, was making and exhibiting films in Chicago by 1897. In 1907, the Selig Polyscope Company built a production facility at Irving Park Road and Western Avenue that covered three acres and employed over two hundred people. The other prominent production company with substantial Chicago facilities was Essanay, founded by George Spoor and Gilbert Anderson. Spoor, a moving picture exhibitor, and Anderson, a film actor, founded the company in 1907 and built a studio in UPTOWN on Argyle Street in 1908. Both Charlie Chaplin

Filming a movie set at the Selig Polyscope lot, Western and Irving Park, 1914. Photographer: Unknown. Source: Chicago Historical Society.

and Gloria Swanson worked at the Essanay studio in Chicago for a time.

After the organization of major film interests into the Motion Picture Patents Company in 1908, Chicago became the center of the independent movement, the effort to make, import, and distribute films while avoiding the use of patents held by the trust—or avoiding litigation from those whose patents they had violated. Carl Laemmle's Independent Motion Picture Company and several independent, antitrust importers and exchanges were located in the city. The films produced in Chicago and/or distributed by Chicago companies were increasingly important nationally and internationally as U.S. firms tried to compete with imported films for domination of film screens.

The stage for one of the popular Broncho Billy westerns, Essanay Studios, 1345 West Argyle, ca. 1910. Photographer: Unknown. Source: Chicago Historical Society.

Several "race film" companies (companies run largely by African Americans who made films for a black audience) were formed during the silent film era in Chicago as well. The Foster Photoplay Company, owned by William Foster, began producing films in 1912. The Ebony Pictures company began production somewhat later and made films throughout World War I and for some years after. Many race film production companies were founded and sought investors in Chicago but never actually made any films. All of the race film firms were profoundly undercapitalized and suffered from the lack of strong distribution networks. However, it is clear that Chicago was a significant market for these films, on several occasions bringing the highest grosses in the nation for them.

By the late teens those production firms who had not fled to California to avoid patent litigation left seeking better weather and more consistent sunlight. Chicago remained, however, an important distribution market in spite of these departures and even after the rise of the talkies in the late 1920s. South Wabash in the blocks from 800 to 1500 south had high-profile distribution offices for MGM, Columbia, Warner Brothers, Republic, Universal, RKO, and Paramount. Other film-related businesses gravitated to this "Film Row" to be where the market was; companies that made theater seating, film posters, and concessions had offices there. According to legend, Hollywood studios sent their toughest negotiators to the Chicago market, where audiences often produced large grosses for the studios.

Chicago was the original home of the largest theater chain in the studio era (1919–1952), the Balaban and Katz chain, started by two West Side exhibitors. Obtaining expansion capital in 1915 from Chicagoans in the retailing and taxi businesses, Balaban and Katz built increasingly large and elaborate "movie palaces" in which they showed movies and offered popular stage shows. The Chicago Theatre, the Oriental, and the Uptown were all Balaban and Katz movie theaters. Balaban and Katz affiliated with the Paramount studio to form one of the most powerful companies of the studio era, which ended after prolonged antitrust litigation forced studios to divest their theaters.

In the 1930s Chicago was the home of a regional branch of the (Workers') Film and Photo League. Nominally associated with the Workers' International Relief and the

COMMUNIST PARTY, the Chicago Film and Photo League made several short films and newsreels that dealt with labor issues in Chicago and other locales as well as slum conditions in Chicago. Extant films include Conrad (Nelson) Friberg's *Halsted Street* (1934), and Maurice Bailen's *The Great Depression* (1934), *Chicago May Day* (1936), and *Peace Parade and Workers' Picnic* (1936), each of which documents, at least in part, leftist demonstrations in the city as well as aspects of the cultural life of laborers.

In the 1980s Chicago again became a center of moving picture production. Illinois consistently ranked third or fourth among states in dollars spent in film production, much of it in Chicago. Several of the critical and popular successes of the 1980s were filmed in Chicago (*Ferris Bueller's Day Off; The Color of Money; The Untouchables; Planes, Trains, and Automobiles; When Harry Met Sally*), and several feature film directors and actors have returned to shoot films (either wholly or in part) in the Chicago area, including Dan Aykroyd and the Belushi family (*The Blues Brothers, About Last Night, Blues Brothers 2000*), John Hughes (*Sixteen Candles, The Breakfast Club*), and Andrew Davis (*The Fugitive, Chain Reaction*). This film and television production activity fostered local boosterism and the hope that film production in the city would continue to increase.

J. A. Lindstrom

See also: Economic Geography; Entertaining Chicagoans; International Alliance of Theatrical Stage Employees; Moving Picture Technicians, Artists and Allied Crafts; Movies, Going to the; Work Culture

Further reading: Carbine, Mary. "'The Finest Outside the Loop': Motion Picture Exhibition in Chicago's Black Metropolis, 1905–1928." *Camera Obscura* 23 (May 1990): 9–42. • Gomery, Douglas. *Shared Pleasures: A History of Movie Presentation in the United States.* 1992. • Rabinovitz, Lauren. *For the Love of Pleasure: Women, Movies, and Culture in Turn-of-the-Century Chicago.* 1998.

Film Censorship. From the earliest days of moving pictures, community leaders waged battles against their distribution. In 1907 Chicago became one of the first cities to censor MOVIES, when the city council empowered the chief of POLICE to issue permits to exhibitors. If denied a permit, a movie would either have to be cut to meet the censor's standards or removed from the theater. By 1909, both the Illinois Supreme Court and the United States Supreme Court upheld Chicago's code. The city also authorized a separate permit—colored pink—to designate those movies limited to adult viewing. That policy backfired when such permits advertised rather than penalized movies with salacious titles and material.

The city's censors also tackled issues far more incendiary, such as the controversy surrounding *The Birth of a Nation* in 1915. The explicit and crude RACISM of this landmark in moviemaking by pioneering director D. W. Griffith provoked the NATIONAL ASSOCIATION FOR THE ADVANCEMENT OF COLORED PEOPLE (NAACP), newspaper editorialists (especially at the CHICAGO DEFENDER), and religious organizations to call for its removal from Chicago theaters. Newly elected mayor William Hale Thompson rewarded his AFRICAN AMERICAN supporters with a ban on the film.

A few years later, in a revealing confrontation over censorship, Chicago convened a Motion Picture Commission from September 1918 through May 1919 to hear testimony from a variety of people associated with the medium. Although similar boards existed in other areas, Chicago's commission garnered attention because the city was the nation's second-largest movie market. The commission heard a diverse array of opinions regarding the role of movies in American life; and the proceedings marked the waning of civic censorship. Beginning in 1922, movie studios and producers began using a variety of organizations and codes to regulate movies in the hope of undercutting local efforts. Nonetheless, the city adopted a new code in 1922, one that remained in effect through the 1960s.

In 1961, in *Times Film Corp. v. Chicago*, the city's censorship code was once again contested and upheld. The United States Supreme Court ruled that municipal censors could screen and, therefore, prevent a movie from being shown if it was found "obscene." However, during the 1960s, community censorship laws slowly eroded under other legal challenges. By the early 1970s, Chicago's censorship board was no longer effective, and as in cities throughout the nation, Chicago residents could attend theaters that showed everything from the latest Disney movie to hard-core pornography.

Raymond J. Haberski, Jr.

See also: Entertaining Chicagoans; Free Speech; Vice Commissions

Further reading: City of Chicago Motion Picture Commission. *Report of the Chicago Motion Picture Commission.* 1920. • Couvares, Francis G., ed. *Movie Censorship and American Culture.* 1996. • Jowett, Garth. *Film: The Democratic Art.* 1976.

Film Criticism. Chicago's cinematic appropriation for movie sets inspired local film criticism. NEWSPAPER and radio journalists were the first to comment on films' merits. In the early 1900s, *Essanay News* printed film synopses to report a local studio's news, and more critical analyses emerged by the 1920s. Chicago COLLEGES developed academic programs in film criticism, attracting such scholars as Bruce Morrissette, and the UNIVERSITY OF CHICAGO Press issued titles in the series Books in Film Studies.

Gene Siskel and Roger Ebert were perhaps the best-known Chicago film critics. In the late 1960s, Siskel, a Chicago native, reviewed movies for the *Chicago Tribune,* and Ebert was the *Chicago Sun-Times*'s film critic. Their show, *Opening Soon at a Theater Near You,* debuted on Chicago public television station WTTW in 1975.

Debating movies' entertainment value, not their artistic intricacies, the pair rated each show thumbs up or down. Viewers understood Siskel and Ebert's commentary, and Chicago's Museum of Broadcast Communications honored them for making film criticism accessible to movie patrons. They won a Chicago Emmy Award and were inducted into the Chicago JOURNALISM Hall of Fame. A section of Erie Street was dedicated Siskel & Ebert Way. After Gene Siskel's death in 1999, *Sun-Times* film critic Richard Roeper joined Ebert on television.

Ebert and other Chicago critics have judged the Chicago Film Festival. Annually, the Chicago Film Critics Association honors movies and presents the Commitment to Chicago Award. As technology advanced, Chicago film critics analyzed not only movies shown in theaters but also videos and DVDs.

Elizabeth D. Schafer

See also: Art Criticism and Scholarship; Film; Film Censorship; Movies, Going to the; Public Broadcasting

Further reading: Bernstein, Arnie. *Hollywood on Lake Michigan: 100 Years of Chicago and the Movies.* 1998. • *Roger Ebert's Book of Film.* 1996. • Rosenbaum, Jonathan. *Placing Movies: The Practice of Film Criticism.* 1995.

Fine Arts Building, 410 S. Michigan Avenue. Originally known as the Studebaker Building (1885–1898), the Fine Arts Building was converted from a carriage assembly and showroom. Reopened after extensive renovation in 1898, it immediately became the hub of Chicago's Arts and Crafts movement as well as a headquarters for a burgeoning musical and LITERARY CULTURE. Scores of ARTISTS, sculptors, musicians, music teachers, and fine craftspeople rented studios and offices and opened small shops. Together, they organized an artist's collective known as the Fine Arts Shop, selling bound books, jewelry, and textiles. The ground floor consisted of a central atrium and three auditoriums, including a music hall. Many prominent literary publications occupied the building, including *The Dial* and Harriet Monroe's POETRY magazine. One group of artists occupying the top-floor studios, coveted for their capacious skylights, formed the Little Room, a social club whose founding members included painters and writers. Social activists contributed to the atmosphere as well, among them the Chicago Woman's CLUB and the Illinois Equal SUFFRAGE Association.

Derek Vaillant

See also: Art Colonies; Art Institute of Chicago; Literary Cultures; Literary Images of Chicago

Further reading: Duis, Perry. "Where Are They Now? The Fine Arts Building, 1898–1918." *Chicago History* (Summer 1977). • Peattie, Ella Wilkinson. *The Book of the Fine Arts Building.* 1911. • Pomaranc, Jean. *Fine Arts Building.* 1977.

Finns. After a visit to the United States in 1898 a Finnish journalist wondered why there were only four or five hundred Finns in Chicago, a figure that paled in comparison to the city's other ethnic groups. Chicago seemed a mere way station for Finns on their journey to the farmlands of Minnesota.

Coming primarily from rural northern Finland, immigrants in the 1880s had little interest in the urban factories of Chicago or WAUKEGAN. Those who found factory work along the CHICAGO RIVER settled among the SWEDES in the NEAR NORTH SIDE and WEST TOWN neighborhoods, where a small but scattered Finnish community began to form in the 1880s.

After 1900, however, immigrating Finns came largely from the industrial cities of southern Finland and were more likely to be attracted to factory work. By 1910 Chicago's Finnish population had risen from 500 to over 1,500, with nearly one-third of these new immigrants single women. The small Finnish community within Swede Town underwent growth in its businesses, churches, and voluntary associations.

Temperance halls like "Immigrants' Haven" established in 1893 served as social and educational centers offering a variety of activities, including band, choir, and drama. After 1903 labor halls offered similar fare. Activities at the Imperial Hall (SOCIALIST, later COMMUNIST) and Belden Hall (INDUSTRIAL WORKERS OF THE WORLD) appealed to labor activists and free thinkers. In the 1920s the Belden Hall group reorganized itself into the nonpolitical Finnish Progressive Society. Its Lincoln Auditorium at 4217 Lincoln Avenue served as a center for community activities for 30 years.

Organized in 1892, Chicago's small Finnish Lutheran Congregation struggled for over 50 years in rented facilities without a regular pastor, served primarily by the larger Finnish Lutheran Church of Waukegan. Congregationalists established the Finnish Mission Church in 1908, which remained active into the 1960s. In 1902 Swede-Finns (ethnic Swedes from the western and southern coastal regions of Finland) organized the First Finnish Baptist Church, which became Bethel Baptist Church in the 1930s. Approximately 30 percent of Finnish immigrants were Swede-Finns, who for reasons of language maintained their own temperance societies and fraternal organizations, and usually worshiped in Swedish churches.

By 1893 there were an estimated 100 Finns in Waukegan, most of whom worked at the American Steel and Wire Company. Despite its small size, the Waukegan community had an important Lutheran congregation, a famous Workers Hall, a large temperance hall, and one of the most successful Finnish consumer cooperatives in the country. Availability of DOMESTIC WORK attracted Finnish women to Waukegan, from where they COMMUTED on the North Shore INTERURBAN to work in the affluent homes in and near LAKE FOREST.

As the immigrant generation passed from the scene in the 1950s and 1960s, so also did many of the organizations they had created. Subsequent generations have carried the heritage forward, however, with participation in ethnic festivals and organizations like the Finnish-American Society of Illinois, Sibelius Male Chorus of Chicago, and the League of Finnish American Societies.

Chicago's Finnish community remained small, reaching an estimated peak of 4,000 in the 1930s and again during World War II when many Finns from Michigan and Minnesota came looking for work. The 2000 census counted 5,879 individuals in Cook County and more than 11,000 in the metropolitan area claiming Finnish first ancestry.

Timo Riippa

See also: Danes; Demography; Free Thought; Multicentered Chicago; Mutual Benefit Societies; Prohibition and Temperance; Protestants

Further reading: Arra, Esa. *The Finns in Illinois.* Trans. Andrew Brask. 1971. • Ilmonen, Solomon. *Amerikan Suomalaisten Historia II.* 1923. • Myhrman, Anders. *Finlandssvenskar i Amerika.* 1972.

Fire Limits. Fire limits were boundaries drawn around the center of a city within which buildings had to be constructed of brick or stone rather than wood. Ostensibly public safety measures—ways to prevent fires downtown—they also served as primitive ZONING codes by mandating expensive CONSTRUCTION techniques that in the nineteenth century were used for commercial rather than residential construction. They banned new wood construction and

Northwest corner of Monroe and LaSalle Streets, October 9, 1871. Photographer: Unknown. Source: The Newberry Library.

Aftermath of the Great Chicago Fire, 1871. Photographer: Unknown. Source: Chicago Public Library.

major repairs or improvements to old wood buildings. The Chicago Common Council enacted the city's first limit in 1845 and extended its area gradually, until in 1874 it covered the entire city. This transformed it from a zoning device to encourage commercial development into a general BUILDING CODE for the city.

The fire limit was administered by the council's Committee on Fire and WATER until 1861, when the Board of Public Works was created. These agencies received petitions to extend the limit to particular streets, remonstrances objecting to proposed extensions, and requests for individual exemption (like variances in the modern zoning process). Couched in the rhetoric of fire prevention, fire limit debates were a precursor to debates about zoning, which would not emerge until the 1920s.

After the Great Chicago Fire of 1871, the fire limit was the focus of a conflict between elites demanding extension over the whole city and working-class homeowners, particularly GERMAN immigrants on the North Side, who depended on cheap construction techniques. The full-city extension was defeated in 1872 but enacted after another major fire in 1874.

Robin Einhorn

See also: Balloon Frame Construction; Firefighting; Fire Limits in Chicago in the 1870s (color map, p. C2); Government, City of Chicago; Housing, Self-Built; Land Use; Lumber; Metropolitan Growth

Further reading: Rosen, Christine Meisner. *The Limits of Power: Great Fires and the Process of City Growth in America.* 1986. • Sawislak, Karen J. *Smoldering City: Chicagoans and the Great Fire, 1871–1874.* 1996.

Fire of 1871. On October 8, 1871, a fire began on DeKoven Street in a barn owned by Catherine and Patrick O'Leary. Fueled by a gale-force wind, this blaze grew into the Great Chicago Fire. Advancing northward for 36 hours, the inferno destroyed three and a half square miles in the heart of the city, leveling more than 18,000 structures. One-third of the city's 300,000 residents lost their homes, and at least 300 perished. Aided by an outpouring of charity from around the world, Chicagoans brought about a remarkable reconstruction; the city expanded as it rebuilt, and most visible signs of the destruction were erased within a year. Traditionally understood as the turning point of Chicago's early history, the Great Fire cemented the reputation of the rising metropolis as a place of opportunity, renewal, and future promise.

Karen Sawislak

See also: Architecture: The First Chicago School; Chicago Relief and Aid Society; Fire Limits; Fire Limits in Chicago in the 1870s (color map, p. C2); Planning Chicago; Progress of the Chicago Fire of 1871 (color map, p. C2)

Further reading: Sawislak, Karen. *Smoldering City: Chicagoans and the Great Fire, 1871–1874.* 1995. • Smith, Carl. *Urban Disorder and the Shape of Belief: The Great Chicago Fire, the Haymarket Bomb, and the Model Town of Pullman.* 1995.

Firefighting. From Chicago's incorporation in 1833, volunteer laborers protected the city from fire. Sanctioned by municipal ordinance in 1835, volunteer firefighters organized themselves into exclusively male companies and elected officers to lead them at fires. These community institutions reflected the class and ethnic diversity of the city. They also received support from their neighbors, local property owners, and INSURANCE companies. By 1853, over 500 Chicago volunteer firemen worked in 12 separate companies.

Volunteer firemen divided their demanding physical labor into two components: making hose connections and operating hand-pumped fire engines. Upon alarm of fire, they dragged their heavy apparatus to the scene of the fire. Hosemen established connections of riveted leather hose between fire engines and the city's burgeoning network of WATER pipes and hydrants. Enginemen, meanwhile, pumped levers or "brakes" attached to their engines in order to "throw" water onto the fire. Pulsing these brakes required intense physical strength and stamina. Few men could maintain the normal pace of 60 strokes per minute for very long, so a company's entire membership rotated in order to pour a steady stream of water onto the fire.

Intense competitiveness marked volunteer firefighters' service. The act of dragging apparatus to fires became an informal test of competence. Firefighters also competed to see which company could project water highest into the air. Firemen believed that winning such contests proved their manhood and their abilities as public servants. However, these formal and informal competitions sometimes exploded into violent confrontations between companies. Frequently such outbursts were expressions of ethnic and class tensions in the city, but just as often they resulted from the exuberant all-male culture of volunteer firefighters.

In the 1850s reformers took advantage of middle-class concerns over violence in the fire department. Along with business leaders, the insurance industry sought to replace the volunteer fire department with paid municipal workers operating steam fire engines. Reformers especially emphasized the efficacy of steam technology as a firefighting tool. However, such claims were dubious in the context of unreliable 1850s steam firefighting technology. In fact, when a steam engine was tested in 1856, three of the city's hand-operated engines defeated it by throwing water higher into the air. Although the city's volunteer firemen had proved their mettle, reformers pressed on. They remained impressed by claims that steam technology would improve work discipline and the moral order of the city.

In 1858, the city's volunteer fire companies elected a reformer, D. J. Swenie, as their chief. Swenie helped convince the city to establish a fire department staffed entirely by paid municipal employees. The new department consisted of four fire companies, each staffed by a captain, lieutenant, and engineer, and several pipemen, drivers, and stokers. The engineer received the highest salary; he earned almost $600 per year—more than three times the

Elmhurst Volunteer Fire Department, 1920. Photographer: Unknown. Source: DuPage County Historical Museum.

salary of the company captain. This discrepancy reflected how much the newly organized department depended upon steam fire engines. As the city expanded over the remainder of the century, expenditures on the fire department increased with the size of the population. As a result, the number of fire companies increased from 26 in 1870 to over 100 by century's end.

Over the same period of time, Chicago's fire department became increasingly rationalized and professional—both in its management and its use of innovative work techniques. For instance, the politically savvy Swenie—who was re-appointed chief in 1879 and served through 1901—sought to establish a merit system of hiring and promotions.

Even though Swenie removed the department from the influence of "POLITICS," his personal authority remained unchecked by written guidelines. Nonetheless, firefighters thrived. As in other cities, Chicago firefighters who remained on good terms with the chief and survived the job's many dangers could expect careers of extraordinary longevity. As late as 1900, 39 firemen who had fought the Great Chicago FIRE OF 1871 remained on the payroll.

In addition, the department adopted new work techniques and an expansive manual of drills. For instance, Swenie introduced "pompier" (or ladder) drills into the department. Using such ladder skills, firefighters scaled the sides of buildings in order to more effectively direct streams of water onto fires and to save lives. The chief also inaugurated the use of a training manual. This manual offered detailed guidelines on the proper care of firefighting equipment, ladder techniques, rescue skills, hose use, and departmental organization. By the end of Swenie's tenure, the Chicago Fire Department had adopted many of the reforms recommended by the most important professional organization founded by firefighters—the National Association of Fire Engineers.

During the twentieth century, the Chicago Fire Department continued this program of reform. The city introduced a drill school, and firefighters benefited from civil service legislation, better pensions, and a shorter workweek. In addition, the rank and file received vocal support from an increasingly activist and powerful insurance industry. As early as 1905, insurance companies began to recommend legislation for better fire prevention in cities throughout the nation that included provisions for civil service and increased firefighting budgets.

Firefighters' experiences continued to change as the city grew taller and more dangerous from the increased use of synthetic building materials. For instance, during the 1920s and 1930s, firefighters began to use primitive breathing apparatus to penetrate the dense toxic smoke generated by these new types of fires. It would not be until 1982, however, that use of such equipment became mandatory for all firefighters. Firefighters also became proficient in using a variety of new cutting tools, nozzles, and rescue skills. As WORK routines grew more complex, training grew increasingly standardized. Beginning in 1920, recruits received formal training at a drill

Fighting a fire on the Near North Side, 1948. Photographer: Unknown. Source: Chicago Historical Society.

school that broke firefighting work routines into 34 "evolutions" or training components.

During the 1960s, the fire department's membership and leadership grew increasingly diverse, as African Americans and women gained greater access to the department. African Americans had served in the professional department as early as the 1870s, but the terms of their service were limited. They worked in segregated fire companies, which typically served African American neighborhoods and were usually commanded by white officers. Beginning in the 1960s, the department stopped segregating companies by race, and increasing numbers of African Americans received promotions. Although the doors into the department slowly expanded for blacks, the all-male culture of firefighters continued to exclude women from the city's firehouses. The city hired female paramedics in 1974, but it was not until 1980 that the department allowed women to perform service as rank-and-file firefighters.

Mark Tebeau

See also: Government, City of Chicago; Police; Water Supply

Further reading: Bushnell, George D. "Chicago's Rowdy Firefighters." *Chicago History* 2 (1973): 232–241. • Einhorn, Robin L. *Property Rules: Political Economy in Chicago, 1833–1872.* 1991. • Teaford, Jon C. *The Unheralded Triumph: City Government in America, 1870–1900.* 1984.

Fitness and Athletic Clubs. Health, fitness, and athletic clubs are a rich part of Chicago's history because athletics, socializing, and business have always been interrelated. However, the concept of an "athletic club" or "health club" as most people know it today hardly resembles that of earlier times.

At the end of the nineteenth century, the most prominent athletic clubs were private, exclusive establishments founded by elite Chicagoans to foster business and social networking. Candidates seeking membership had to be voted in by existing members. Club facilities were not open to the general public.

Medinah Athletic Club swimmers Richard Connell and Elder Halverson at the club's pool, 1929. Photographer: Unknown. Source: Chicago Historical Society.

Founded in 1890 by three prominent business and professional men from Boston, the Chicago Athletic Association (CAA) erected its ornate clubhouse on fashionable Michigan Avenue in 1893. It was among very few big-city athletic clubs to survive the economic depression.

While the CAA was indeed an elite men's club, women were regular participants at the Wednesday night dinners and Sunday afternoon concerts and also flocked in on Ladies' Day, begun in 1893. Not until 1972 did the club open its membership to women, before a 1987 city ordinance required all clubs to do so. Nearly two decades passed before Mary Frances Hegarty was elected as its first woman president.

The Medina Athletic Club was built on North Avenue in 1929 for members of the Masonic order. Its greatest renown was its Olympic-sized swimming pool located on the 14th floor. A premier gathering spot for Chicago's elite and visiting dignitaries, it also had a shooting and archery range, miniature golf course, running track, billiards room, bowling alley, and two-story boxing arena. Women, although allowed access to the ballroom through a separate entrance and elevator, could not use any of the athletic facilities. Now the Hotel Inter-Continental Chicago, the building houses a new health club for hotel guests on the two levels below the swimming pool, the only remaining feature of its original use.

Belle Ogden Armour and Paulina Harriette Lyon founded the Woman's Athletic Club of Chicago (WAC) in 1898. Members of the CAA promoted and encouraged its creation. The United States' first private athletic club for women, it was intended to provide women with the same opportunities for exercise, relaxation, and friendship that were available in the men's clubs. The original clubhouse boasted a marble swimming pool, Turkish baths, a gymnasium, bowling alley, and running track. Members could partake in fencing and dance lessons and attend lectures on nutrition, literature, theater, and current affairs. The club also had a parlor, library, tea room, dining room, and hair-dressing and massage services. The WAC moved twice, ultimately erecting its own building at 626 North Michigan Avenue, today a Chicago landmark.

Chicagoans of lower social strata used parks and fieldhouses as their athletic locales at the turn of the twentieth century. Some fieldhouses, like Davis Square Park on the South Side, contained gymnasiums for men and women, meeting rooms, a public library, and a cafeteria. Parks all over the city provided playgrounds for children and sites for competitive sports events sponsored by the Chicago Park District, as well as corporate sports teams

Members of the Plzensky Sokol, an organization devoted to physical fitness and Czech culture, 1920s. Its clubhouse was at 1814 South Ashland in the Pilsen neighborhood. Photographer: Francis D. Nemecek. Source: Paul Nemecek.

seeking to challenge their commercial competitors.

The 1970s saw the proliferation of racquet sports enthusiasts, which prompted the opening of TENNIS and racquet clubs across Chicago, including the Midtown Tennis Club (1969), McClurg Court Sports Center (1970), Lakeshore Athletic Club (LSAC, 1972), and the Edens Athletic Club (1976). When the blizzard of 1979 collapsed the original LSAC on Fullerton Avenue, owner Jordan Kaiser decided to rebuild it as a "country club in the city," containing a pool, weight training, racquet courts, dining, spa services, a physical therapy clinic, and a 450-yard indoor track. Capturing the growing national fitness craze, LSAC became the largest health club in America in terms of both square footage and membership.

As the science of exercise physiology grew rapidly during the twentieth century, it became clear that regular, vigorous exercise that raises the heart rate for an extended period is necessary to prolong good health and avoid lifestyle diseases. Therefore, some activities which were commonplace in athletic clubs in the past, such as bowling, archery, shooting, and billiards, lost importance and popularity since they did not fit the recognized criteria of "health exercise." These were replaced by more rhythmic, regimented ways of exercising, including cardio machines like treadmills, stair climbers, stationary bicycles, and rowing machines, as well as aerobic dance classes, which exploded in popularity in the 1980s. Throughout the 1990s, group fitness instructors created new class formats that did not involve dancing, such as body sculpting, cardio boxing, and group yoga, the latter two replacing aerobic dance classes as the most popular group exercise formats in Chicago in the late 1990s.

In 1980, the East Bank Club was established on the east bank of the North Branch of the Chicago River as an exclusive club for upscale Chicago professionals, encompassing sports, health and fitness, socializing, dining, and spa services. National health club chains like Bally's Total Fitness, Powerhouse Gym, and World Gym also built large fitness clubs in communities throughout the Chicagoland area.

These joined the "neighborhood gyms" that emerged during the 1970s. The LINCOLN PARK and LAKE VIEW areas became home to several gyms, each finding its own niche. Weight training to improve aesthetic appearance and quality of life gained popularity among young people. Chicago Fitness Center was the first club in Chicago to offer both weight training equipment and martial arts classes in the same club.

Neighborhood gyms influenced the way clubs structured their membership fees and encouraged new members. While large chains typically charged new members an initiation fee plus monthly dues or encouraged long-term memberships, smaller clubs introduced a "no initiation fee/pay-as-you-go" concept.

Corporate fitness centers also emerged as businesses recognized that regular exercise increased productivity and reduced insurance costs and employee sick days. In addition to group exercise classes and athletic facilities, many corporate fitness centers also offered wellness programs, including smoking cessation, stress management, nutrition education, and health screenings. To keep employees motivated, incentive programs were established, whereby workout clothing and gear or club membership discounts were given to employees who adhered to a minimum number of workouts per week.

By the turn of the twenty-first century, the term "athletic club" became all but obsolete, whereas "health club" and "gym" typically referred to places offering exercise facilities. A few high-end health clubs that also foster networking and socializing still exist, but most gyms today serve the sole purpose of exercising, not dining or conducting business. Nearly all gyms have memberships of mixed gender and socioeconomic strata.

Tiffany L. Crate

See also: Baths, Public; Creation of Chicago Sports; Sports, Industrial League; Turnvereins; Young Men's Christian Association; Young Women's Christian Association

Further reading: Hilliard, Celia. *The Woman's Athletic Club of Chicago: A History—1898–1998.* 1999. • Kerch, Steve. "Classic Revival Finds Room on Michigan Avenue." *Chicago Tribune,* March 19, 1989. • Knobe, Bertha Damaris. "Chicago Women's Athletic Club." *Harper's Bazaar* 39 (June 1905): 537–546.

Flags and Symbols. Many municipal governments have adopted symbols such as city flag or seal, typically used on letterhead, city vehicles, brochures, water towers, and Web sites; Chicago has a special symbol just for vehicles. William B. Ogden, Chicago's first mayor, helped design Chicago's multifaceted seal in the 1830s. WEST CHICAGO adopted a much simpler one, depicting a locomotive, when it became a village in 1873. Well-established communities also have adopted symbols, especially on important occasions. Chicago, for instance, added another star to its flag after the 1933 CENTURY OF PROGRESS EXPOSITION. Some places have adopted a motto, or even a bird, tree, or flower.

Aside from notifying viewers that a building, territory, vehicle, or letter is "official," these symbols express pride in a community, its history, and its prospects, or boost the community to prospective investors. Several Chicago-area official seals take note of the NATIVE AMERICANS who first lived in the area—though not of their expulsion in the 1830s—and flags and seals often include dates of village or city founding. Commonly, they portray the economic foundations of the community. Befitting the "Crossroads of the Nation," CHICAGO HEIGHTS' official seal shows buildings and fields at a crossroads. A house and factory on either side of an elk's head on ELK GROVE VILLAGE's flag refer to the distinct industrial and residential districts of this planned community. Its Latin slogan, "Dignitatem Aedificatam in Terra," translates "On this land, we build with dignity." The virtues of the community are a favorite theme. TINLEY PARK's flag employs heraldic symbols for brotherhood, cleanliness, courage, growth, progress, and the village's enduring framework. The full meaning of such symbols may not be apparent without explanation. On Chicago's seemingly straightforward flag, five stripes represent the North, South, and West Sides, LAKE MICHIGAN, and the CHICAGO RIVER. Four stars stand for important moments in the city's history, and meanings have been assigned to each of the six points of every star. The first star, for example, represents FORT DEARBORN, while its points signify TRANSPORTATION, labor, commerce, finance, populousness, and salubrity. Like Fort Dearborn itself, each of these helps answer the question "Why is Chicago here?"

Christopher Thale

See also: Metropolitan Growth

Further reading: *Chicago Municipal Code*, chaps. 1–8. • Lindell, Arthur G. *Chicago's Corporate Seal.* 1962. • Scobey, Frank F. *The Story Behind West Chicago's City Flag.* 1967, 1985.

Flood Control and Drainage. The Chicago area is topographically dominated by the glacial Lake Chicago plain. This plain encompasses the CHICAGO RIVER, DES PLAINES RIVER, and the CALUMET RIVER. Early explorers discovered the Chicago PORTAGE, an area within Mud Lake that was only 15 feet above the level of LAKE MICHIGAN and on the watershed divide between the Mississippi River basin and the Great Lakes basin.

The Chicago area experienced many early drainage challenges. The natural condition was swampy. Chicago streets were poorly drained and muddy. The level of Lake Michigan was only two feet below the river banks, making subsurface drainage ineffective.

In 1834, the first attempt to solve the sanitation problem of Chicago included a drainage ditch dug down State Street and emptying into the Chicago River. Later, the city of Chicago raised streets, then buildings, 8 to 10 feet above natural ground level. This helped to drain the streets and to get the sewage to the river more efficiently, but the river could not cleanse itself of the sewage due to the high level of Lake Michigan.

The ILLINOIS & MICHIGAN CANAL, completed in 1848, flowed from present-day SUMMIT to LaSalle. From 1861 through 1870, the city of Chicago paid to operate the BRIDGEPORT pumps an additional 45 days per year to flush sewage from the Chicago River and away from the lake.

The 1872 flood diverted almost all the Des Plaines River flows into the Chicago River through the Ogden-Wentworth Ditch, causing significant pollution within the Chicago River when the sewage could no longer be sent downstream. A dam was constructed across Ogden-Wentworth Ditch to prevent future diversions of Des Plaines River flows.

In 1885, a large rainfall washed sewage and refuse out of Chicago and the Chicago River into Lake Michigan, polluting the city's WATER SUPPLY. The Illinois General Assembly authorized the establishment of the Sanitary District of Chicago in 1889 to implement the construction of the SANITARY AND SHIP CANAL to carry away waste from the city and to dilute it as it flowed downstream. Construction began in 1892, and flow through the canal began January 17, 1900. The North Shore Channel enlargement, begun in 1907 and completed in 1910, diverted more lake water to aid in dilution, and the Chicago River was enlarged in 1912. Construction of the Cal-Sag Channel began in 1911 and was completed in 1922, reversing the flow of the Calumet River away from Lake Michigan. A Supreme Court decree in 1933 ordered the construction of the Chicago River lock and controlling works, which was completed in 1938.

Areas outside the city of Chicago experienced many drainage alterations as well. The Illinois Farm Drainage Act of 1879 established the authority to create drainage districts, marking the beginning of a period of significant drainage modifications in agricultural areas. By 1929, 88 drainage districts covered 177,595 acres of the Chicago River, Little Calumet River, Des Plaines River, DUPAGE RIVER, and FOX RIVER basins. By 1971, 180 drainage districts were listed in an "Inventory of Drainage and Levee Districts" within COOK, DUPAGE, LAKE, MCHENRY, KANE, and WILL Counties.

As more land became developed with housing, streets and shopping areas, a greater amount of runoff from this developed ground ran to the sewers. The stormwater runoff mixed with sanitary sewage and became combined sewage. Suburban communities developed after WORLD WAR II realized the value of separate sewer systems to handle sanitary sewage and stormwater runoff. Suburban communities have installed countless miles of storm sewers to accommodate modern drainage needs, replacing the earlier systems provided by drainage districts.

Studies in the late 1960s recommended the Tunnel and Reservoir Plan (TARP), known as "DEEP TUNNEL," as a means to solve this problem. TARP tunnels include the Mainstem, Calumet, Des Plaines, and Upper Des Plaines systems, totaling 109 miles of tunnels. These tunnels capture sewer overflows that had been discharging into rivers and streams. TARP's three reservoirs, when completed, will provide significant flood control.

Flooding of rivers in the Chicago area is a natural phenomenon. Agricultural areas flood along with natural wetlands. The magnitude of these floods and the effects upon humans grew as the metropolitan area developed. Flood events of historical significance have occurred across the region during 1849, 1855, 1885, 1938, 1952, 1954, 1957, 1961, 1973, 1979, 1986, 1987, and 1996. Most record-setting flood stages and discharges in the region have been recorded since 1948.

Flood control and watershed planning in the Chicago region is managed by a group of federal, state, and local agencies. These include the U.S. Army Corps of Engineers, the U.S. Department of Agriculture, Natural Resource Conservation Service, the U.S. Environmental Protection Agency, the Illinois Department of Natural Resources, the Illinois Office of Water Resources, the Metropolitan Water Reclamation District of Greater Chicago, and storm water management agencies in each of the region's counties.

By the early 1980s several watershed plans were developed to address flood problems along the North Branch Chicago River, Upper Des Plaines River, Lower Des Plaines Tributaries, Poplar Creek, Upper Salt Creek, and the Little Calumet River. These plans will eventually implement 43.9 miles of channel modifications and 41,128 acre-feet (13.4 billion gallons) of floodwater storage facilities, including the Tunnel and Reservoir Plan. Flooding remains a serious problem along the main channel of the Des Plaines River and the Little Calumet River and many smaller streams. A 1998 estimate puts annual flood damages at $41,459,000 in the Chicago area, affecting nearly 20,000 homes and businesses.

Local, state, and federal agencies and individuals have become increasingly aware of the unmitigated impacts of urbanization on drainage and flooding. The Metropolitan Water Reclamation District implemented the first stormwater detention ordinance in 1972. This ordinance required new developments to detain a portion of the increased runoff and to restrict the outlet capacity of the detention basin to a predevelopment discharge. It has now become standard practice to provide stormwater detention within new SUBDIVISIONS to control the rate of runoff to predevelopment rates.

The 1986 flood was triggered by widespread regional rainfall with varying intensity and duration, which had been preceded by two weeks of nearly continuous rain falling across northern regions of the Des Plaines, North Branch Chicago, and Fox River watersheds. Flooding in rivers and streams across Lake, McHenry, northern Cook, northern DuPage, and northern Kane Counties resulted. The 1987 flood was generated by localized high-intensity and shorter duration rainfall which dropped up to 13 inches of rainfall in less than 24 hours, largely in Cook and DuPage counties. The 1986 and 1987 floods generated enough public awareness of the continued problems of drainage and flooding for the Illinois General Assembly to pass legislation authorizing the formation of countywide stormwater management programs.

Arlan R. Juhl

See also: Built Environment of the Chicago Region; Infrastructure; Landscape; Land Use; Riverine Systems; Water

Further reading: Barker, Bruce. *Lake Diversion at Lake Michigan.* Illinois Department of Transportation, Division of Water Resources, 1985. • Cain, Louis P. *Sanitation Strategy for a Lakefront Metropolis: The Case of Chicago.* 1978.

Flossmoor, IL, Cook County, 24 miles S of the Loop. Flossmoor, a small residential town in the southern suburbs, is to a great extent the creation of the ILLINOIS CENTRAL RAILROAD. The town is situated in the CALUMET RIVER watershed and lies in the TOWNSHIPS of Bloom and Rich.

Excavations at the Horton site (near Brookwood and Western) during 1966 and 1967 indicated NATIVE AMERICANS occupied the site in a large structure (about 30 feet wide) several hundred years ago.

The Illinois Central bought 160 acres in Flossmoor in 1893. The company's plan was to strip away the black dirt and use it as fill at the WORLD'S COLUMBIAN EXPOSITION, but the soil proved unsuitable. When the railroad later decided to sell its land, it received an unexpected boost.

In 1898 a group of investors conceived the idea of building a GOLF course in the area. They asked the Illinois Central to extend service beyond HOMEWOOD, then the southernmost stop on the COMMUTING line, and to erect a station close to the site of the proposed course. When the railroad agreed, the investors established the Homewood County Club (renamed Flossmoor in 1914). The venture was such a success that other country clubs soon followed, particularly Ravisloe, in Homewood (1901); Idlewild, in Flossmoor (1908); Olympia Fields, in OLYMPIA FIELDS (1915); and Calumet, in Homewood (1917).

The Illinois Central broke its land into lots, platted the SUBDIVISION in 1901, and in 1903 built a half-dozen houses. The U.S. Post Office selected the name Flossmoor from a list the Illinois Central had assembled through a contest to name the place. The railroad vigorously promoted Flossmoor, even running free-lunch excursions for prospective buyers from Chicago, and steadily built ridership by touting the country clubs and providing special services for golfers. Residential construction picked up after 1910, and by WORLD WAR I the upper-middle-class community was firmly established and included some of the railroad's executives. Electrification of the commuter train lines in 1926 further increased the desirability of the area.

Flossmoor incorporated as a village in 1924. Among the first local laws was an ordinance that prohibited industry within the town limits, thus guaranteeing the village's residential character. It also implicitly screened in new residents who worked elsewhere. By 1967, Flossmoor and neighboring Homewood were among a handful of suburbs where more than half the workers commuted to jobs in Chicago.

In the postwar period Flossmoor and Homewood formed some significant partnerships. Homewood-Flossmoor Community High School in Flossmoor opened its doors in 1959 and has proven exceptionally successful, winning Blue Ribbon Awards from the U.S. Department of Education in 1982–83, 1994–95, and 2001–2. A joint park district was incorporated in 1969.

Flossmoor's population at incorporation was 265, and by 1930 it had grown to 808. The village grew steadily through World War II and then in the 1950s surged 156 percent, to 4,624 in 1960. Population topped 8,400 in 1980 and reached 9,301 by 2000.

John H. Long

See also: Leisure; Metropolitan Growth; Suburbs and Cities as Dual Metropolis

Further reading: Adair, Anna B., and Adele Sandberg. *Indian Trails to Tollways: The Story of the Homewood-Flossmoor Area.* 1968. • League of Women Voters of Homewood, Flossmoor, and Olympia Fields. *Know Your Town: Homewood, Flossmoor, Olympia Fields.* 1967. • Wagner, Susan F. *A History of the Village of Flossmoor, 1851–1974.* 1974.

Folk and Traditional Dance. Social dancing in early Chicago was neither wild nor undisciplined, as frontier stereotypes suggest. The practice in New France was to conduct a ball with order and decorum, and even on the American frontier a dance customarily opened with a minuet. American fashions encompassed country dances in the French style—cotillions in square formations of four couples—and the English style—double-file sets of up to 15 couples. Dancers also did the jig and the four-hand reel. These dances have been maintained up through the twenty-first century in square dancing, contra dancing, and line dancing.

In 1834, the quadrille, a four-couple square DANCE, became popular, along with the waltz and the schottische. Specific dances such as the Prairie Queen Quadrille and the Chicago Glide were introduced in the early 1900s. While these particular regional dances have disappeared, the waltz and schottische were maintained and reintroduced by waves of European immigrants, including GERMANS, POLES, NORWEGIANS, and SWEDES, and continue to be danced at weddings, ethnic gatherings, and other neighborhood celebrations. Other folk dances such as the POLKA were brought to the region by Polish immigrants but became popular at weddings and other celebrations even by non-Poles.

Chicago's two world's fairs helped promote interest and awareness of ethnic folk dance as well as exotic dance. Ireland's Gaelic League's first American display of Irish dance costume occurred at the 1893 WORLD'S COLUMBIAN EXPOSITION.

Beginning as early as the 1920s, folk dance schools and programs were established both by ethnic groups and by those interested in maintaining or reviving older rural dance. Katherine Dunham, who later won international fame for

Latvian folk dancing at Hull House, 1951. Photographer: Victor T. Gorecki, Jr. Source: University of Illinois at Chicago.

her "Dunham Technique," began her teaching career with her "Negro Rhapsody" at the Chicago Beaux Arts Ball in 1931.

IRISH and SCOTTISH immigrants established dance schools from the 1920s on, often in family basements. Some of these schools, such as Trinity Irish Dance, have attained international visibility, others continue to serve a small local population and provide entertainment for festivals, cultural programs, and family celebrations. The Chicago Ethnic Arts Project conducted by the American Folklife Center in 1977 documented a wide variety of folk and social dance in Chicago, from KOREAN dance at the YMCA to JAPANESE classic and folk dance, Darlene Blackburn's traditional African dance troupe, Irish step dancing and social dancing, LITHUANIAN dancing at Saturday schools, NATIVE AMERICAN POWWOW fancy dress dancing, dance classes at the Polish Women's Alliance, DANISH dancing, YUGOSLAV dance, social dancing at a BLUES club on the SOUTH SIDE, Jewish social dance at a wedding, a "sweet sixteen" PUERTO RICAN dance party, and polka at Polonia Grove.

Several significant Chicago ethnic dance groups were established in the 1970s, '80s, and early '90s, including the MEXICAN Folkloric Dance Company, East INDIAN dance companies such as Natya, Nartan, and Kalapriya, and Alyo Children's Dance Theatre (an AFRICAN AMERICAN company). American country and square dancing have become a form of revived folk dance, promulgated by groups such as the Chicago Barn Dance Company (established in 1977) in order to maintain rural art forms.

Susan K. Eleuterio
Paul Tyler

See also: Folk Music; Theater, Ethnic

Further reading: Harnan, Terry. *African Rhythm American Dance: A Biography of Katherine Dunham.* 1974.

Folk Music. Folk music in Chicago is tied to the city's role as a national crossroads. In its neighborhood taverns, Chicagoans have embraced a variety of traditional music practices, from IRISH ceilidhs to down-home BLUES, from POLKA dances to hootenannies. Through regional recordings, radio BROADCASTS, sheet music publication, MUSICAL INSTRUMENT MANUFACTURE, and MAIL-ORDER marketing, the city has exported folk music throughout the United States and beyond.

In the mid-nineteenth century, Root & Cady, the largest local music publisher, disseminated the efforts of songwriter Henry Clay Work. His compositions, including "Kingdom Coming," "The Ship That Never Returned," and "Grandfather's Clock," entered informal tradition and still remain staples of rural performance. Other works, such as *O'Neill's Music of Ireland* (1903) and M. M. Cole's *One Thousand Fiddle Tunes* (1940), became templates for melodies disseminated—and adapted—throughout the country. Composer Thomas A. Dorsey's publishing firm fostered the growth and professionalization of GOSPEL, a folk-based art form. And the INDUSTRIAL WORKERS OF THE WORLD locally printed a union songbook from 1918 to 1933 that included topical songs often set to well-known melodies, a practice long employed in traditional music.

With the growth of commercial recording in the 1920s, Chicago's studios documented the ETHNIC MUSIC of Irish, ROMANIAN, and, in particular, POLISH emigrants. Karol Stoch, for instance, was a Polish mountain fiddler whose 1928–29 recordings recreated a regional rural style in a New World setting. Of greater fame, Chicago's polka musicians developed this native dance form, giving rise to a distinctive local sound.

In the 1920s, Henry Thomas and Blind Blake made recordings that drew on ragtime repertoires, field hollers, country reels, and minstrelsy. By the next decade, artists such as Memphis Minnie and Tampa Red explored and enlarged the domain of the blues. Chicago's most famous musical commodity, the urban blues codified by the amplified guitar and harmonica of Muddy Waters and Little Walter, respectively, represents not only a new creativity but a transformation of Mississippi folk melodies. Similarly, in his move from the Soul Stirrers to his own solo career, singer Sam Cooke serves as an example of the transfer of a folk-inflected gospel quartet style to pop music.

Hillbilly music in Chicago centered around the WLS's live *National Barn Dance,* which offered radio audiences cosmopolitan skits side-by-side with grassroots musicians such as Doc Hopkins and Bradley Kincaid. One of the show's clog dancers, Kentuckian Bill Monroe, returned to Chicago in 1946 to make his first bluegrass recordings with banjoist Earl Scruggs.

In the late 1950s, a folk revival characterized by an urbane approach to certain forms of American folk music ascended in national popularity. WFMT's *Midnight Special* began its broadcasts in 1953 while clubs such as the Gate of Horn, which opened in 1956, inaugurated a succession of nightspots devoted to this form of entertainment. The following year marked the founding of the OLD TOWN SCHOOL OF FOLK MUSIC. In subsequent years, other institutions, such as the UNIVERSITY OF CHICAGO Folk Festival (1961) and Flying Fish Records (1974), focused on the work of innovative artists rooted in traditional music—just a few pieces of Chicago's enduring yet evolving mosaic of folk music creativity.

Stephen Wade

See also: Chicago Sound; Entertaining Chicagoans; Labor Songs; Music Publishing; Record Publishing; WLS Barn Dance

Further reading: Brubaker, Robert L. *Making Music Chicago Style.* 1985. • Spottswood, Richard K. *Ethnic Music on Records: A Discography of Ethnic Recordings Produced in the United States, 1893 to 1942.* 1990.

Folklore. Chicago's folklore includes legends and stories, folk speech, names and expressions, material culture, FOODWAYS, traditions, beliefs, and folk arts. Many of these traditional genres are tied to historical events, characters, and places such as the Great FIRE OF 1871, Al Capone, Jane Addams's HULL HOUSE, the steel mills of SOUTH CHICAGO and northwest Indiana, and Chicago's swampy location at the base of Lake Michigan.

Chicago lore includes the word "CHICAGO," with its contested origins in Native American language. From before the time of the 1871 fire, Chicagoans have used legends and stories to explain both natural and man-made events and figures. The story of Mrs. O'Leary's cow is one of the most persistent of those legends, rooted in the belief that an IRISH immigrant's carelessness resulted in the fire of the century.

Other legends revolve around the exploits of Al Capone, one of the most notorious gangsters of the 1920s. Stories of Al Capone's deeds are told from Detroit to the outer suburbs of the city, and Chicagoans traveling abroad still encounter signs or sounds of the "rat-a-tat-tat" of a tommy gun when they name their home town.

Ghost stories and urban legends are a particularly ubiquitous form of folklore in metropolitan Chicago, with *Resurrection Mary* a favorite of the SOUTH SIDE, *La Llorona,* or the weeping lady of Mexico, found in northwest Indiana, and the *Hull House Devil Baby,* which tells about the former social workers' home on Halsted Street.

Stories of a ghostly, beautiful hitchhiker have shown up in Chicago since the running boards of the 1920s. Many Chicago-region teenagers relate a version of this ghost who lives in Resurrection CEMETERY on Archer Avenue and likes to go dancing, particularly on Halloween night. A movie character, Candyman, created by Hollywood writers in 1992 as a terrifying ghost who haunted CABRINI-GREEN, has also passed into legend, especially among AFRICAN AMERICAN children on the South and NEAR WEST SIDES of the city. A more recent urban legend also comes from a mix of popular culture and contemporary fears of urban life. Reports of a man dressed as Homie the Clown, a character from the television show *In Living Color,* driving a white van and kidnapping children throughout the metropolitan area, were collected from a variety of children in Chicago during the 1990s.

The Hull House "Devil Baby" is found mostly in the written folklore of Chicago. It is still possible, however, to find former residents of the old immigrant neighborhood on the NEAR WEST SIDE who know the cautionary tale of the young ITALIAN, Irish, or JEWISH girl who variously committed adultery, married an atheist, or married outside her faith, delivering a devil child to social worker Jane Addams at HULL HOUSE. MEXICAN immigrants across Chicago warn their children about *La Llorona,* the weeping woman of Mexico who is searching for her drowned children even in the waters of Lake Calumet.

Chicago folklore includes a variety of foodways, including Chicago deep-dish PIZZA; Chicago-style hot dogs made with cucumbers, onions, tomatoes, celery salt, mustard, and relish; and ethnic food customs, RESTAURANTS, stores, and traditions. Many suburbanites still come into the city to shop for specialty items or go to dinner at a neighborhood restaurant, though ethnic foods have gradually crept into chain stores as well. GROCERY STORES across the region carry *paczki,* a soft, donut-like, fruit-filled pastry used by POLISH immigrants to prepare for the hardships of Lent on Fat Tuesday but now eaten by many Chicagoans regardless of their ethnic heritage.

Folk customs include the territorial marking of PARKING spaces in the winter with everything from lawn chairs to dining room furniture. Official city traditions include dyeing the CHICAGO RIVER green on St. Patrick's Day. Unofficial neighborhood names often become official geographic markers such as Bronzeville, famous home of JAZZ and BLUES musicians on the South Side, MAXWELL STREET, for the old market on Halsted Street (which has now been "officially" moved by the city to Canal Street), and such areas as LITTLE ITALY, CHINATOWN, GREEKTOWN, and Little Vietnam, all named for the apparent majority of their residents.

One of the earliest groups created to study Chicago folklore was the Chicago Folklore Society, founded in 1891. Projects to document Chicago-area folklore include the Library of Congress American Folklife Center's study of ethnic traditions in 1977; Indiana University Folklore Institute's GARY Project in the late 1970s; the David Adler Cultural Center's research and documentation projects in the 1980s; and research by Indiana Traditions (Indiana University Folklore Institute) into LAKE and Porter County folk culture in 1998.

While the Chicago Folklore Society disappeared at the end of the twentieth century, grassroots folklore organizations have survived into the twenty-first century. The 1970s saw the rise of a number of groups devoted to folklore and folk culture, including the UNIVERSITY OF CHICAGO Folklore Society, which hosts an annual Folk Festival; the OLD TOWN SCHOOL OF FOLK MUSIC, which offers classes, workshops, and concerts on the North Side of Chicago; and the Fox Valley Folklore Society, which hosts a Folk Music and Storytelling Festival annually. Newer groups include the Chicago Association of Black Storytellers, founded in 1999, and the Illinois Folklife Society, established in 2000. This group includes folklorists, ethnomusicologists, and anthropologists who conduct research and coordinate public programming in folklore and folk culture in the Chicago area.

Susan K. Eleuterio

See also: Chicago Studied: Social Scientists and Their City; Crime and Chicago's Image; Flags and Symbols; Literary Images of Chicago; Street Naming

Further reading: Dorson, Richard. *Land of the Mill Rats.* 1981. • Scott, Beth, and Michael Norman. *Haunted Heartland.* 1985.

Food Processing.

LOCAL MARKET
REGIONAL AND NATIONAL MARKET

LOCAL MARKET. From its first days as a small settlement, Chicago has manufactured foodstuffs for its own and regional markets. The size and types of manufactories varied through time. Many small food producers have served Chicago's various ethnic communities with specialized products. Among the most important of these were alcoholic beverages, meat, baked goods, and candy.

Whiskey may have been the first manufactured "food" product. By 1812, members of the Kinzie clan had set up a still to sell their product from a shack. The first BREWERY was established in 1833, and GERMAN immigrants who arrived in midcentury brought forth many others. Names such as Berghoff, Gottfried, Schoenhofen, and Wacker were Chicago institutions. Like many other breweries throughout the country, all served the local populace. None became national brands like breweries in St. Louis and Milwaukee.

Given Americans' carnivorous propensities, meat processing was an important local industry. Archibald Clybourne's slaughterhouse, built in 1827 at the city limits, fed the immediate market. Clybourne sold his processed meat door to door in the 1830s, as did Sylvester Marsh. Food production was so localized that a contemporary claimed, "From 1832 to 1838 the incoming settlers consumed nearly all the products of those who had come before them."

George Dole's abattoir, begun around 1832, eventually not only served locals but began packing meat for the LAKE MICHIGAN shipping trade. The great national MEATPACKING industry thus was born. Nevertheless, sales to local customers by food manufacturers and processors who sold to wider markets would remain Chicago's pattern. Vienna Beef Company and many other packing companies located in the Randolph Street market area maintained retail outlet stores.

Candy companies followed a similar pattern. An 1857 survey shows 46 confectioners worked in the city, of whom 7 were large-scale manufacturers with wholesale markets. By the end of the century Chicago would become the largest producer of candy in the United States, a position it retained into the twenty-first century. A number of firms became national, including the Wrigley company (1891), Brach's (1904), and Curtiss Candy Company, maker of the Baby Ruth bar (1921). The Blommer Chocolate Company, a large regional wholesale chocolate manufacturer, maintains an outlet store to service local clientele. A number of other candy makers, such as Margie's Candies in the LOGAN SQUARE community area, remained small concerns dedicated to neighborhood clientele.

The manufacture and distribution of dairy products were always local. In 1911 there were 1,200 to 1,500 small dealers (most doing home deliveries with milk wagons) in the city receiving the milk of perhaps 5,500 regional producers. James Kraft, whose cheese-processing plant was located on Water Street, was one of them. As larger dealers perfected on-site bottling and an efficient distribution system, and with new pasteurization laws, the number of small dealers dropped. In 1935 there were 236 in the city, over half of whom received their milk from an average of just 5.4 farms. Two dealers, Borden and Bowman, accounted for over 58 percent of total purchases. The rise of centralized dairy businesses and national distribution systems beginning in the 1950s left only large producers selling to food stores. Hawthorne Mellody and Dean's Foods were preeminent, leaving only Oberweis Dairy of AURORA, revived in the last two decades of the twentieth century, as an artifact of the old home delivery business.

As the number of Chicago's food producers grew with rising population, their character changed according to ethnicity. German immigrants produced beer and pickles. By the mid-nineteenth century Chicago had 4 "pickle warehouses," 3 pickle makers (all with German names), and 14 vinegar manufacturers who catered to this new clientele. One B. Hyde even manufactured "Vermicelli and Maccaroni," showing the city's increasingly diverse citizenry.

Bakeries are one of the best indicators of ethnic change. By 1861 there were 59 where a generation before none had existed. Many of the bakers had German surnames, an indication of the large influx of Central Europeans. By the early twentieth century, bakers selling to the Chicago market included S. Rosen and Kaufmann's (JEWISH), Mary Ann (GREEK), and Baltic Bakery (LITHUANIAN) among many other small companies. Rosen's and Mary Ann transcended their neighborhood origins to achieve regional distribution. ITALIAN bakeries followed a similar pattern. As interest in Italian food became widespread throughout Chicago in the 1960s, Italian bread followed suit. Gonnella Baking Company, founded as a neighborhood place in 1886, became Chicago's largest producer of Italian bread and rolls.

Others, such as Fontana Brothers Bakery, remained in their ethnic enclaves. The cracker, sold from barrels in GROCERY STORES, was a staple American snack food. Cracker makers sold products to regional markets, but they also supplied the city's growing numbers of neighborhood grocery stores. By the end of the century, snack foods would be prepackaged, with national brands such as Uneeda Biscuits beginning to dominate store shelves. Local snack food companies such as Jays Foods (founded in 1927 as Mrs. Japp's) followed suit. Jays Potato Chips remains a major Chicago regional brand.

The arrival of other ethnic groups brought new food products to the local market. East European immigrants brought their food preferences with them—so did AFRICAN AMERICANS, Italians, and, later, MEXICANS. Emblematic of Eastern Europe were Vienna Beef and David Berg, both producing Chicago's singular all-beef hot dog; the Slotkowski Sausage Company, makers of Chicago's famous "POLISH" sausages, Leon's Sausage Company (UKRAINIAN), Daisy Meat Products (Bohemian), and many other small producers. Vienna Beef achieved national distribution. African Americans were served by Parker House Sausage Company's southern-style hot and mild links. Italian makers included Lucca Packing Company, Fabbri Sausage Manufacturing Company, and a host of neighborhood butcher shops.

Ethnicity remains a key to local food production. The CHINESE population required more "authentic" Chinese products. The Hong Kong Noodle Company established in 1914 in the "new" CHINATOWN on Wentworth Avenue was one such supplier. By the 1970s, with immigration from mainland China, new companies such as the Wah King Noodle Manufacturing Company and bakeries producing almond cookies, fortune cookies, moon cakes, and other specialties appeared, servicing both retail and restaurant markets. In similar fashion, the newer KOREAN (Lawrence Avenue), Arabic (North Kedzie Avenue), INDIAN (Devon Avenue), and Southeast Asian (Argyle Street) communities have brought forth bakeries and spice and sauce packers geared to local consumption.

As members of these groups moved out of their original neighborhoods, these goods followed them. Although the process is old, there is no better example than Chicago's Latino communities. The Mexican population grew rapidly after 1960. PILSEN soon sprouted tortilla factories such as Del Rey, Atotonilco, and Sabinas. As native Mexicans and Mexican Americans spread across the Chicago and Northern Illinois region, and as tastes for Mexican fare grew among many population segments, tortillas were to be found in many food stores, including chain supermarkets. Similarly, food processors and canners such as La Preferida Inc., once Hispanic-targeted, sold their beans, chiles, sauces and other "Mexican" products to the general public while maintaining their ethnic customer base.

Local processors like Bowman's Dairy had to rely on various forms of transportation not only to bring milk from farms, but also to distribute it to its consumers. At the turn of the century, Bowman's horse carts and milkmen were common sights on Chicago-area streets. Photographer: Unknown. Source: University of Illinois at Chicago.

Local markets also mean food distribution systems. The oldest systems were open-air markets and door-to-door STREET PEDDLING. A market at the corners of Lake and State Streets was superceded by a municipal market hall built in the middle of State Street in 1848. By 1850 population pressure led to three more market halls near the Loop area. However, continued dispersal of the citizenry spelled the end of central market halls. Except for the great MAXWELL STREET open-air market that flourished from the 1890s to 1980s, they were replaced by neighborhood grocery stores. Such establishments could better address local ethnic communities and served as the main distribution system for locally manufactured foodstuffs. Neighborhood grocers and meat markets were, in their turn, mostly eliminated by the spread of large supermarkets beginning in the years after WORLD WAR II. By 1990, multipurpose markets dominated the food retail business in Chicago. Dependent as they are on national and proprietary brands, these stores have provided venues for only a few locally produced, mainly fresh bread products and tortillas. Therefore, local manufacturers such as sausage makers have used smaller stores and factory outlet stores as their main distribution networks.

Ideas about food often move in cycles. New open-air retail markets replicated the city's earliest public markets. Rising interest in fresh foods led to the appearance of farmers' markets in the city in the late 1980s. During the growing season, local produce was trucked in and sold by farmers in various locations throughout the city. Daley Plaza in downtown Chicago became the scene of a weekly farmers' market, replicated on a smaller scale in other neighborhoods. In 1999, a popular "Green Market," selling only locally produced organic produce, was established in downtown Chicago.

Bruce Kraig

See also: Agriculture; Business of Chicago; Food Processing: Regional and National Market; Foodways; Retail Geography

Further reading: Andreas, A. T. *History of Chicago from the Earliest Period to the Present Time.* 3 vols. 1884. • Duis, Perry R. *Challenging Chicago: Coping with Everyday Life, 1837–1920.* 1998. • *Half-Century's Progress of the City of Chicago: The City's Leading Manufacturers and Merchants. History of Illinois*, pt. 1. 1887.

REGIONAL AND NATIONAL MARKET. As the leading city in one of the world's most productive agricultural regions, Chicago has long been a center for the conversion of raw farm products into edible goods. Best known for its dominance in MEATPACKING, Chicago has also been home to leading firms in other areas of the food processing industry, including cereals, baked goods, and candy, since the 1880s. At the end of the twentieth century, during which most parts of the industry became concentrated under fewer firms, food processors stood among Chicago's largest companies.

Lake steamer and grain elevator, 98th Street at the Calumet River, 1948. Photographer: Otho B. Turbyfill. Source: Chicago Historical Society.

In early Chicago, the most important food processing activity was grain milling. Before 1800 Catherine and Jean Baptiste Point DuSable had a pair of millstones and had constructed a bakehouse just north of the Chicago River. By the 1830s Chicago contained steam-powered flour mills and enjoyed a brief period of importance as a local milling center for spring wheat. But the great bulk of wheat handled by the city's booming grain trade was never milled locally: it was shipped east, to be processed in major U.S. cities such as Buffalo, or in Europe. After the CIVIL WAR, as wheat farming moved north and west, the national center of wheat flour manufacture shifted to Minneapolis. Meanwhile, other kinds of milling operations settled within close reach of Chicago. In 1910 the town of Argo (SUMMIT), southwest of Chicago, became the site of a new plant opened by the Corn Products Refining Company. By the 1930s this plant, manufacturing products with the Argo brand name, had become the largest corn refinery in the world.

The milling of oats served as the foundation for another of Chicago's leading companies. By the 1880s and 1890s, oatmeal producers in Chicago and around the Midwest had begun to form industrial combinations. Between 1901 and 1911, many of the industry's leading producers, then operating under the umbrella of groups such as the American Cereal Company and the Great Western Cereal Company, were absorbed by the Quaker Oats Company. This Chicago-based giant grew steadily, making big business out of oatmeal. At the close of the twentieth century, when it sold over $5 billion annually of a diverse range of products—including cereals, pastas, and Gatorade sports drink—Quaker, with its corporate headquarters in Chicago, was still an industry leader and one of the city's largest companies.

Compared to the highly industrialized milling and cereal business, bread in Chicago and elsewhere has been characterized by a more diverse range of producers. Even after the appearance of mechanized ovens, baking continued in the kitchens of individual households and in small shops. In 1880, most of Chicago's 280 bakeries were small, neighborhood retailers, and the number of small bakeries continued to grow until the 1930s. With the rise of mechanized bread factories, chain GROCERY STORES, and chain bakeries, more and more small bakers disappeared from the Chicago landscape.

Although bread baking saw significant consolidation over time, it was never as concentrated or industrialized as cracker and biscuit manufacturing, another business in which Chicago was a national leader. Between 1890 and 1898, Chicago lawyers A. W. Green and W. H. Moore led a series of cracker mergers

In 1954, Sara Lee marketed its pastries on this giant billboard near the Palmolive Building at North Michigan and Walton. Photographer: Hedrich-Blessing. Source: Chicago Historical Society.

that created the National Biscuit Company, which had its executive offices in Chicago until 1906. During its early years, this company (later known as Nabisco) controlled over 100 large bakeries—several of them in the Chicago area—which produced the company's well-known line of cracker and cookie brands, including Uneeda biscuits, Fig Newtons, and Oreos. In 1927, the Chicago region became home to another large cracker producer, the United Biscuit Company, based in ELMHURST. Renamed Keebler in 1966, this company has remained one of the region's largest. Another important baked-goods firm, the Sara Lee Corporation, takes its name from a Chicago bakery founded by Charles Lubin in 1949. By the end of the century, Sara Lee made clothing and meat products as well as frozen pies and cakes and had become an industry leader and one of Chicago's largest companies.

In the area of canned foods and processed meat and dairy products, Chicago firms have long been national leaders. By the 1880s, Libby, McNeill and Libby, a firm connected to Swift & Co., was packing 35 million cans annually, and several Chicago canners were filling large orders from European armies and navies. By 1918, Libby was the nation's second-largest canner. In the dairy industry, Chicago's strength was generated by its proximity to Wisconsin, a leading dairy state. Major dairy companies located in the city during the twentieth century included Beatrice Foods, which moved from Nebraska to Chicago in 1913, and Dean Foods, founded in 1925 by Sam Dean, a local dealer in evaporated milk. In processed dairy foods, the industry leader was James L. Kraft, who began selling cheese in Chicago in 1904. By 1930, Kraft had taken over much of the cheese distribution business from Chicago's meatpackers, and by 1960, processed cheese, Kraft's specialty, accounted for half of U.S. cheese production.

Throughout the twentieth century, Chicago and Illinois have dominated the American confectionery industry. William Wrigley, Jr., founded his Chicago-based chewing gum company in 1891, and several of his brands, including Juicy Fruit and Wrigley's Spearmint, rapidly became big sellers. The well-known Cracker Jack brand of snacks, popular at the 1893 WORLD'S COLUMBIAN EXPOSITION, were the creation of Chicago popcorn vendor F. W. Rueckheim. In the candy industry, some of America's best-known brands were produced in the Chicago area by companies such as M. J. Holloway (Milk Duds), and E. J. Brach. Another major candy firm, Tootsie Roll Industries, whose brands include Junior Mints and Tootsie Pop, has been located on Chicago's SOUTH SIDE since the 1960s.

For much of its history, Chicago has been an organizational center for workers in the food processing industries. In the 1880s, GERMAN bakers in New York and Chicago created the first bakers' unions in the United States. From 1904 to 1955, Chicago served as the headquarters of the Bakery and Confectionery Workers International Union, which claimed 28,000 members in 1920 and 80,000 in 1940. From the 1880s through the 1920s, Chicago bakers and baked-good distributors struck frequently, but with mixed success, in attempts to gain some power over hours, working conditions, and production. A major defeat in Chicago in 1922 was symptomatic of labor groups' lack of success in their confrontations with large bakery owners, but unions continued to have some power in the smaller retail shops.

Since the earliest days of the city, Chicago food processors have been subject to a variety of government regulations concerning food quality and monopolistic business practices. Rules for flour grading and inspection were established in Illinois in the 1850s. By 1880, Chicago was licensing its bakeries. In the first decade of the twentieth century, the federal Pure Food and Drug Act, along with new state and municipal rules, placed broader controls over the food industry; and federal oversight increased significantly during WORLD WAR I and WORLD WAR II. During the 1920s, Kraft struggled with the state of Wisconsin over cream skimming limits. In the realm of antitrust regulation, Quaker Oats was sued unsuccessfully in 1915 for alleged violations of the 1890 Sherman Act, and Beatrice was one of the companies investigated and regulated by the Federal Trade Commission between the 1930s and 1960s for alleged anticompetitive practices in the dairy industry.

As the twentieth century came to an end, Chicago-area companies continued to be important in the food processing business, but the city's status as an industry headquarters had been shaken by a recent rash of corporate takeovers and acquisitions. In 1985, the Chicago-based food giant Beatrice, one of the largest companies in the United States, was dismantled by investment bankers in a leveraged buyout. And in the 1990s, Quaker Oats suffered a $1.4 billion dollar loss on its Snapple drink brand. The massive capital flows involved in these kind of transactions, combined with changing consumer preferences, suggest a volatile landscape of food processing. But at the end of the 1990s, the stable strength of Midwestern agricultural production, along with the presence of major food processors such as Quaker, Sara Lee, Dean, Keebler, Tootsie, and Wrigley, indicated that Chicago would remain at the center of the industry.

Mark R. Wilson

See also: Advertising; Agriculture; Business of Chicago; Economic Geography; Railroads; Strikes; Unionization

Further reading: Connor, John M., and William A. Schiek. *Food Processing: An Industrial Powerhouse in Transition.* 2nd ed. 1997. • Gazel, Neil R. *Beatrice: From Buildup through Breakup.* 1990. • Thornton, Harrison John. *The History of the Quaker Oats Company.* 1933.

Foodways. At the end of the twentieth century, the multiethnic essence of Chicago's

Farm Security Administration photographer Edwin Rosskam in 1941 vividly captured Chicagoans' spiritual and physical needs with this photo of a storefront church and lunch wagon. Photographer: Edwin Rosskam. Source: Library of Congress.

foodways was reflected in one of its most familiar forms: the hot dog stand. Evolved from pushcarts manned primarily by Jewish immigrants in the early twentieth century, Chicago's hot dog stands now represent a virtual United Nations of cuisine. Next to yellow Vienna Beef signs, hot dog stands advertise Greek *gyros,* Italian beef sandwiches, Mexican burritos, Chinese *hom bao,* Middle Eastern *shawarma,* as well as pizza and hamburgers, themselves definitively American descendants of humble ethnic roots.

At the other end of the epicurean spectrum, the city's turn-of-the-century fine dining establishments also practice culinary transnationalism. Charlie Trotter's helped cement Chicago's reputation as one of the United States' restaurant meccas by winning multiple international awards for its "fusion" food, amalgamating global ingredients into creative dishes inspired by the city's architecture in both form and presentation. Surrounding Trotter in Chicago's culinary constellation were Rick Bayless's upscale Mexican Frontera Grill and Topolobampo, Arun's Thai cuisine, and a bevy of chic establishments serving every kind of international cookery, from Moroccan to Japanese to "pan-Latin."

All this does not necessarily represent anything new for Chicago's food scene. The city's ongoing roles as destination for migrants and major food distribution center have always placed food squarely at the center of Chicago's history and culture. The city's very existence was generated in the mid-nineteenth century by the exchange of commodities between the food producing regions of the rural Midwest and West and the hungry masses of the burgeoning nation.

As meat, grain, European immigrants, and American businessmen flowed into nineteenth-century Chicago, the city's taste for eating options varying in both price and ethnic diversity became clear. Fine dining establishments eschewed the city's gritty image by emphasizing Continental cuisine and service, importing oysters and lobster from the East, and comparing themselves favorably to New York's best. By the early to mid twentieth century, prompted by cultural trends toward "exoticism" and the growing numbers of immigrant businesspeople entering the fine dining market, the city's tonier watering holes began advertising their Chinese and Italian chefs and menus alongside their Continental and East Coast credentials.

By the early 1840s, business deemed Chicago a first-rate "expense account town," whose culinary and entertainment opportunities provided a respite from merchant travel in the uncivilized west. As the home of the Union Stock Yard, the city enjoyed a reputation as a mecca for high-quality, fresh beef. And Chicagoans continue to look with confidence to late-twentieth-century institutions like Morton's and Gene & Georgetti to continue the nineteenth-century culinary tradition of abundant quantities of red meat, red wine, baked potatoes, creamed vegetables, brandy, and cigars. In fact, it is the steakhouse that gives Chicago foodways their distinctively masculine character. While food is often thought of as a feminized cultural form, conjuring images of the comforts of home and mothers cooking family meals, Chicago foodways have a brawnier, more animalistic connotation, owing at least in part to the city's former glory as the center of the meatpacking world and to the ritual of the abundant steakhouse meal.

Meanwhile, the city's development from a commodity crossroads to a major industrial metropolis necessitated the growth of more modest food businesses to serve employees of the factories and stockyards. While home cooking continued to be most people's main source of sustenance, supported by neighborhood grocery stores, street peddlers, community gardening, and even livestock raising, the women who were largely responsible for this work were limited by tenement kitchens and work schedules that often failed to coincide with normal family mealtimes. As a result, large numbers of working-class Chicagoans ate out at neighborhood cafés, taverns, and lunch counters. These places reflected their patrons' ethnicities and cultural backgrounds. Many served as meeting places for union organizers and social clubs, employment and travel agencies, message centers, and informal banks. This custom continued into the twenty-first century in food businesses owned by new immigrants from places as diverse as Pakistan, Ethiopia, and Jamaica.

All of Chicago's neighborhoods and immigrant groups have contributed in their own way to a rich food culture in the metropolitan area. A case in point is the Italian food business community. Beginning in the 1850s, immigrants from Genoa entered Chicago's food business, as they did in other major American urban centers. Originally, they opened shops in the diverse wholesale markets ringing the city, relying on a network of Italian friends, relatives, and business partners who owned farms and transportation companies across the United States. Within 40 years, although Italians accounted for less than one percent of Chicago's population, they owned one-quarter of its fruit businesses and one-fifth of its restaurants. Of the 6,773 Italians living in Chicago in 1896, the Chicago City Directory listed 22 Italian saloonkeepers, 154 fruit merchants, 32 grocery store owners, and 38 confectioners, as well as several of the city's most respected fine dining establishments. By 1927, a survey of the Chicago Telephone Directory indicated that Italians owned no fewer than 500 grocery stores, 257 restaurants, and 240 pastry shops around the city, as well as numerous bakeries, delicatessens, fruit wholesalers, cafés, and pasta and cheese shops. Although these businesses were concentrated in Italian neighborhoods, they served other Chicagoans too. By the 1920s, non-Italian Chicagoans had discovered Italian food and helped to make it the most popular "ethnic" cuisine in America. Italian restaurants, and the generations of families that owned them, continued to play substantial roles in Chicago's food scene into the twenty-first century.

Other immigrants followed in a similar fashion. By the mid-twentieth century, the city and

Replica of Chicago's Water Tower made of Dunkin' Donuts, Chicago's 163rd Birthday Celebration, March 4, 2000, at the Water Tower. Photographer: Janice L. Reiff. Source: Janice L. Reiff.

its growing perimeter brimmed with GERMAN beer gardens, SWEDISH smorgasbords, Greek coffee shops, AFRICAN AMERICAN rib joints and chicken shacks, as well as a plethora of specialized bakeries, butchers, GROCERY STORES, and fishmongers, giving Chicago foodways a decidedly ethnic flavor. Many of these ethnic businesses found markets beyond their immediate communities, some growing into food industry giants such as Kraft Foods, Sara Lee Bakeries, and Oscar Mayer Meats. Yet the soul of Chicago foodways remains in its colorful, intimate neighborhood cuisines, from the remaining Italian restaurants in the once-bustling Taylor Street corridor, to the VIETNAMESE *pho* shops of the North Side's UPTOWN district, to the Michoacan *taquerias* of PILSEN and the LITTLE VILLAGE, to, of course, the hot dog stands that dot all the city's neighborhoods and reflect the city's global heritage.

Tracy N. Poe

See also: Commodities Markets; Economic Geography; Hotels; Housekeeping; Maxwell Street; Saloons

Further reading: Cronon, William. *Nature's Metropolis: Chicago and the Great West*. 1991. • Gabaccia, Donna. *We Are What We Eat: Ethnic Food and the Making of Americans*. 1998. • Poe, Tracy. "Food, Culture, and Entrepreneurship among African Americans, Italians, and Swedes in Chicago." Ph.D. diss., Harvard University. 1999.

Football. The first recorded football game in Chicago took place in 1879 at the White Stockings Park between Racine College and the University of Michigan, played under the SOCCER rules of the day. As the game evolved to allow running with the ball and scrimmage play, high-school students founded the Cook County Football League in 1885. Shortly thereafter, a group of former Ivy League players from Chicago formed an all-star team for an annual series of games with Cornell, the start of an east-west rivalry that extended beyond the football field. The new UNIVERSITY OF CHICAGO opened in 1892 and it sustained the eastern rivalry as it also vied for regional supremacy with Michigan, Wisconsin, and NORTHWESTERN. Chicago high-school teams claimed the national championship after defeating New York squads in successive years (1902 and 1903), 105–0 and 76–0.

By the turn of the century the YMCA, ethnic athletic clubs, and religious groups began fielding their own teams, bringing disparate factions somewhat closer in a common purpose. A neighborhood team from Normal Park, founded in 1898, evolved into the professional Chicago Cardinals by WORLD WAR I. By that time numerous independent sandlot, or "prairie league," teams, semipros, and professional teams proliferated in Chicago and the surrounding area. The Chicago Park District reported 196 games in 1914, and the Chicago Football League of 1919 included teams from JOLIET and as far as Dubuque, Iowa. Some teams were sponsored by politicians, employers or businessmen who saw value in promoting their names or products. The Staley Manufacturing Company's team, under George Halas, moved from Decatur, Illinois, to Chicago in 1921, and became the BEARS the next year.

WORLD WAR I rationing curtailed interstate travel and limited college play, but the nearby military teams thrilled Chicagoans. The Great Lakes Navy team defeated the Mare Island Marines 17–0 in the 1919 Rose Bowl, and George Halas won most valuable player honors.

Football enjoyed immense popularity in the 1920s as SCHOOLS, clubs, PARK DISTRICTS, fraternal organizations, churches, employers, and youth groups fielded teams, in conjunction with the multitude of independent neighborhood contingents. By that time football had become a highly commercialized activity, even at the high-school level, where teams engaged in numerous interstate contests. In 1934 the *Chicago Tribune* initiated its annual All-Star Game, in which collegians tested their skills against the pros. The Prep Bowl, an annual match-up between the champions of the Catholic and public high-school leagues, drew 120,000 fans to SOLDIER FIELD in 1937, the largest crowd ever to witness a football game in the United States. In 1940 Fenger High School played 13 games, more than the Big Ten colleges, including 3 within 10 days.

In the 1940s both the Chicago Park District and Catholic elementary schools initiated youth football competition based on weight classifications, providing seasoned players for the high schools, many of whom went on to star at Notre Dame or Big Ten colleges. The widespread interest in football prompted Arch Ward, sports editor of the *Chicago Tribune*, to start a new professional league, the All-America Football Conference, in 1944. Both the Chicago Rockets and Hornets franchises proved ill-fated and the AAFC eventually merged with the NFL.

Chicago semipro teams continued to compete in the Cook County Football League and in a Midwest regional association, but high-school football began to decline as urban problems, decreased school funding, and an emphasis on state championship play focused attention on suburban teams, starting in the 1970s.

The Chicago Fire of the World Football League started play in 1974, but survived only

Amos Alonzo Stagg and Football at Chicago

An 1888 Yale College graduate, Amos Alonzo Stagg was recruited by President William Rainey Harper to be on the original University of Chicago faculty as the first tenured football coach in America. The All-American rose to a position of considerable power in Harper's university thanks to his president's patronage and his pioneering work as entrepreneurial and football genius. Stagg was the leader of the second generation of American intercollegiate football, as he created influential formations and plays and led the move toward interregional games and football as mass entertainment. He was also a noted track, baseball, and basketball coach, and sometimes his player recruitment embroiled him with faculty. The 1924 conference gridiron championship proved Stagg's last; in 1933, at 70, he was forced by President Robert Maynard Hutchins to leave the university. He went on to have some success at College of the Pacific, retiring at 84.

Stagg's years as Chicago's football coach included several milestones. The University of Chicago pioneered the postseason "bowl" idea by sending its Maroons on a six-thousand-mile trip to sunny southern California in December 1894 to play Stanford—far from either campus and for no discernible educational purpose. In 1905, within 15 years of its founding, Chicago produced its first national football championship team (not to mention America's first Nobel Prize winner—Albert Michelson, in 1907). The Maroons' Old English "C" and the motto "Monsters of the Midway" were appropriated by George Halas's Chicago Bears after the abolition of the sport on the Midway.

Robin Lester

Stagg Field, University of Chicago, November 1927. Named after legendary Chicago coach Amos Alonzo Stagg, the now-demolished stadium eventually became as well known for the world's first self-sustaining nuclear reaction, which took place under its stands, as for the heroics of the teams that played there. Photographer: Howard Webster. Source: Chicago Historical Society.

a short time. The Chicago Bears Super Bowl championship of 1986 revived the city's football fortunes; but the game has yet to regain the widespread participation of its earlier heyday.

Gerald R. Gems

See also: Catholic School System; Clubs: Fraternal Clubs; Clubs: Youth Clubs; Great Lakes Naval Training Station; Leisure; Sports, Industrial League

Further reading: Gems, Gerald R. *Windy City Wars: Labor, Leisure, and Sport in the Making of Chicago.* 1997. • Lester, Robin. *Stagg's University: The Rise, Decline and Fall of Big-Time Football at Chicago.* 1995. • McClellan, Keith. *The Sunday Game: At the Dawn of Professional Football.* 1998.

Ford Heights, IL, Cook County, 26 miles S of the Loop. The village of Ford Heights sits on a rise of land that stretches northeast into areas along Deer Creek. Farmers came in 1848 and grew onion sets and maintained fruit orchards. Both black and white families farmed in the area before 1900.

After 1920, more residents came to live on newly subdivided land called the "Park Addition" on a farm road from CHICAGO HEIGHTS to Indiana. Acting together in 1924, 40 families successfully petitioned for electrical service. That same year, the main east-west road became a two-lane concrete highway designated as U.S. Route 30 in 1926, later known as the transcontinental Lincoln Highway. By the 1930s, the Park Addition had TELEPHONE service and was known as East Chicago Heights.

Early settlers included the family of Alberta Armstrong, whose grandmother was one of the first black residents. Also important and memorable was Isabella "Grandma" Greenwood. She and her husband, both born into slavery, built a small house in the village in 1893. Alberta Armstrong and others organized black and white women to raise funds for a fire truck, and by 1948 this group became the East Chicago Heights Citizens Association.

In 1949, East Chicago Heights incorporated with a growing AFRICAN AMERICAN population. However, then as now, the small size of its population, with little commercial activity, has limited the financial base for local government initiatives.

Such dilemmas were complicated by race. For decades, RACISM across the metropolitan area severely limited housing choices, and East Chicago Heights was a forced option. This fostered the success of the Sunnyfield subdivision in 1964 as a suburban place for middle-class black families but also brought families with limited resources to the village. In the 1960s, 63 acres with substandard housing were cleared in an URBAN RENEWAL project, leaving vacant land and the loss of over 60 families. New PUBLIC HOUSING further taxed village resources.

Once referred to as the "poorest suburb in America," the community has taken many steps to strengthen its future. In 1987, the village changed its name to Ford Heights.

Larry A. McClellan

See also: Gas and Electricity; Open Housing; Suburbs and Cities as Dual Metropolis

Further reading: Hayes, Jack. "The Poorest Suburb in America." *Chicago Reader,* September 18, 1987. • McClellan, Larry A. *A History of Ford Heights, Written and Compiled to Celebrate the 50th Anniversary of the Village Incorporated as East Chicago Heights in 1949.* 1999.

Forest Glen, Community Area 12, 10 miles NW of the Loop. Forest Glen is perhaps the most stereotypically suburban of Chicago's community areas. This well-to-do and well-kept area contains the prestigious Edgebrook and Sauganash neighborhoods. Many city administrators, upper-echelon POLICE and fire officials, lawyers, judges, and politicians live here. This secluded area lies on the city's far Northwest Side, and it is separated from surrounding portions of the city and suburbs by a ring of FOREST PRESERVES, parks, GOLF courses, and CEMETERIES. Here, the monotonous flatness of the Chicago lake plain gives way to very attractive heavily forested and gently rolling terrain. The North Branch of the CHICAGO RIVER forms part of the southern boundary of the area and wriggles from northwest to southeast through the community's eastern portion. The uniqueness of the area is further enhanced by a complex street pattern which, thanks to the serpentine wanderings of the river, departs markedly from the rigorous rectangular grid of most of Chicago's STREETS.

The woods to the east of the meandering river are thicker than those to the west since, from early times, the river protected the forest from fires blown eastward by the prevailing west winds. These flower-dappled woods once provided summer campgrounds and prime hunting territory for the MIAMI and POTAWATOMI Indians. Artifacts of their presence are still occasionally found here, and streets with Indian names invoke their memory. Indeed, the nearly two-and-one-half-square-mile area occupied by Sauganash and Edgebrook was once the preserve of Billy Caldwell, a colorful chief of the Potawatomi. Caldwell, whose Indian name was Sauganash (meaning Englishman), mediated the treaties between the Indians and the United States. In 1828, in recognition of his help, the federal government ceded Caldwell the tract of land.

As Chicago grew outward, more and more distant areas were drawn into the urban web, particularly with the expansion of commuter rail lines. RAILROAD stops at Forest Glen and Edgebrook encouraged commuter settlement by the 1880s. Residential development began in that decade when Captain Charles Hazelton founded the first church in the area, built a home which still stands, and subdivided 10 acres for additional development. Milwaukee Railroad executives created a residential retreat alongside a GOLF course at Edgebrook. Initially a part of JEFFERSON TOWNSHIP, this area was largely annexed to Chicago in 1889. The relative remoteness of Forest Glen from the city center and the limited TRANSPORTATION facilities probably contributed to its sluggish development. It was not until the 1920s that home building began in earnest.

By 1940, Forest Glen began to exhibit the character it shows today as a wealthy and powerful community of fine homes. By this time, the original residents of ENGLISH and SWEDISH stock were joined by neighbors whose nationalities were GERMAN, CZECH, and IRISH. ROMAN CATHOLICS founded new parishes alongside older PROTESTANT churches. The community reached its highest population of 20,531 in 1970. Mayor Richard J. Daley's insistence that city workers live in the city led many to live in Forest Glen.

At the end of the twentieth century, Forest Glen had a scattering of industry along the rail tracks and limited commercial facilities near major intersections on Cicero, Devon, and Lehigh Avenues. Even so, the area was overwhelmingly residential in character and most of the housing consisted of owner-occupied, single-family dwellings. Although there were virtually no APARTMENTS or townhouses, the housing stock was diverse. Within the community area, the various neighborhoods were rather stratified, with bungalows in Forest Glen, midrange housing in Edgebrook, and palatial dwellings in Sauganash. Homes in the area ranged from $150,000 to $300,000, but spacious and patrician older homes could fetch $500,000 or more. Some of these vintage homes have remained in the same families for generations.

The community is stable, comfortable, and wealthy relative to most of Chicago, and it holds an aura of political power. The population has retreated slightly from its 1970 high as younger residents have moved out to establish their own families. By 2000, the area continued as an overwhelmingly white, Roman Catholic community.

David M. Solzman

See also: Built Environment of the Chicago Region; Suburbs and Cities as Dual Metropolis

Further reading: Alexander, Lois Ann, et al. *Sauganash: A Historical Perspective.* 1999. • Chicago Fact Book Consortium, ed. *Local Community Fact Book: Chicago Metropolitan Area.* Based on the 1970 and 1980 censuses. • Solzman, David M. *The Chicago River: An Illustrated History and Guide to the River and Its Waterways.* 1998.

Forest Park, IL, Cook County, 9 miles W of the Loop. Forest Park extends from Harlem Avenue to the Des Plaines River and First Avenue on the west, and from Madison Street and the North Western Railway tracks on the north to Cermak Road on the south. The village's earliest inhabitants settled along the Oak Park spit, a high sand ridge along Des Plaines Avenue. In 1839, Leon Bourassa, a FRENCH Indian trader, purchased 160 acres along the DES PLAINES RIVER in present-day Forest Park, which was then part of Noyesville. Ferdinand Haase, a GERMAN immigrant, bought a 40-acre tract from Bourassa in 1851, which he eventually enlarged to 240 acres and turned into a popular park for residents and city dwellers. In 1856, the Chicago & Galena Union RAILROAD opened a shop and roundhouse at today's Des Plaines Avenue and Lake Street, bringing 25 men and their families to settle there. In the same year, John Henry Quick purchased a large tract of land in Forest Park and the east end of RIVER FOREST, and named the entire area Harlem after his hometown in New York.

Since the 1870s, Forest Park's main industry has been several large CEMETERIES—Jewish Waldheim (1870), Concordia (1872), German Waldheim (1873), Forest Home (1876), and Woodlawn (1912)—which cover most of the town's acreage. Forest Home, which merged with the adjacent German Waldheim Cemetery in 1968, has a long history of burials, as evidenced when two mounds containing Native American artifacts and skeletons were unearthed in 1900. Forest Home is also the final resting place for the four men hanged in 1887 for their presumed role in Chicago's HAYMARKET Riot. In 1893, these men were honored as martyrs to the labor movement with a large monument over their graves. In later years, a number of other prominent labor leaders, ANARCHISTS, SOCIALISTS, and COMMUNISTS were buried in the so-called Radicals' Row area of the cemetery.

LEISURE has also figured in Forest Park's history. An AMUSEMENT PARK that operated there from 1907 to 1922 featured a giant safety coaster that was the highest ride in the nation at the time. Other top attractions included a fun house, beer garden, casino, SWIMMING pool, and skating rink. The park closed in 1922. A thoroughbred racetrack was built by John

Condon in 1894, a year after the Hawthorne track. The track was unable to rebound following a fire in 1904. Between 1912 and 1938, the Harlem GOLF Course was located on the site, which is now occupied by the Forest Park Mall.

Incorporated as the Town of Harlem in 1884, the village was renamed Forest Park in 1907, as another post office named Harlem existed near Rockford. Historically composed of mainly Germans and ITALIANS, the town's ethnic composition has diversified in recent decades. Today, Forest Park enjoys a strong tax base—industrial and commercial—which includes a major shopping mall at Roosevelt and Des Plaines and bustling commercial life on historic Madison Street. As a result, low property taxes are fueling real-estate sales—luring empty nesters to Forest Park's CONDOMINIUMS as well as young people looking for affordable housing.

Jean Louise Guarino

See also: Horse Racing; Metropolitan Growth

Further reading: "History of Forest Park," scrapbook no. 1. (compilation of early newspaper articles). Forest Park Library, Forest Park, IL. • *The Chronicles of Forest Park, 1776–1976.* 1976. • *The Village of Harlem, Fiftieth Anniversary of the Settlement, 1856–1906.* 1906.

Forest Preserves. More than 153,800 acres of land is protected for conservation and recreation in the forest preserve districts of COOK, DUPAGE, LAKE, WILL, and KANE Counties as well as in the conservation district of MCHENRY COUNTY. Millions of people visit annually for picnics, BICYCLING, educational programs, or a walk in the woods. Endangered orchids, birds, and rare natural ECOSYSTEMS abound.

Forest Preserves were initiated by a 1913 statute authorizing the establishment of taxing districts, "To acquire . . . and hold lands . . . containing one or more natural forests or lands connecting such forests . . . for the purpose of protecting and preserving the flora, fauna and scenic beauties . . . restore, restock, protect, and preserve the natural forests and said lands together with their flora and fauna, as nearly as may be, in their natural state and condition, for the purpose of the education, pleasure, and recreation of the public." No similar preserves existed anywhere in the world at the time, but architect Dwight Perkins, the principal proponent of the preserve idea, believed that the preservation of nature would have important value for life in a growing metropolis.

Forest preserve districts are SPECIAL DISTRICTS within a single county that are distinct from other governmental entities. They are established by referendum and governed by boards comprising the same members as the county boards, except for DuPage County, which elects forest preserve commissioners separately. Funding comes primarily through property taxes and bonds. Conservation districts, authorized by a 1963 statute but prohibited in counties with fewer than a million people that already have forest preserves, are similar in purpose and organization. Conservation districts exist to acquire, develop, and maintain open spaces for recreational and conservation purposes and have developed primarily in rural areas.

Cook County organized the first forest preserve district in 1914 and within 13 years DuPage, Will, and Kane Counties had followed suit. Lake County passed a referendum in 1958 to establish a forest preserve district and McHenry established its conservation district in 1971. Since their establishments, forest preserve and conservation districts have continued to acquire land, accelerating efforts in the 1980s and 1990s under the pressures of urban sprawl. Will County has recently more than tripled its forest preserves, from 4,700 acres in 1984 to over 15,000 acres in 2001.

Preserve lands contain some of the Midwest's finest original forests, prairies, and wetlands. But the high-quality "remnants" are small—ranging in size from less than an acre to, at most, a few score acres. Most lands acquired for conservation had lost much of the original ecosystem through timbering, plowing, or grazing. The districts now restore and restock the natural flora and fauna, by gathering and planting seeds, controlling out-of-balance species, prescribed burning, restoration of natural hydrology, and other measures.

Forest preserves are also an important site of public education and recreation. Many offer nature centers and educational programs as well as designated areas for hiking, cross-country skiing, camping, picnicking, boating, fishing, and horseback riding. They also play an important role in maintaining the region's AIR QUALITY, flood control, property values, and other derivative benefits of nature.

Stephen Packard

See also: Environmental Politics; Openlands Project; Plant Communities; Waterfront

Further reading: Christy, Stephen T., Jr. "To Preserve and Protect: The Origins of the Forest Preserves." *Chicago Wilderness* (Winter 1999). • Stevens, William K. *Miracle under the Oaks: The Revival of Nature in America.* 1995. • Watts, May T. *Reading the Landscape.* 1975

Forest View, IL, Cook County, 9 miles SW of the Loop. Originally conceived by attorney Joseph Nosek as a haven for WORLD WAR I veterans, the village of Forest View received its name for the view of the FOREST PRESERVES just west of the incorporated area across Harlem Avenue. In the mid-1920s Nosek and others were forced to leave town by gangster Ralph Capone, and Forest View soon earned the nickname "Caponeville." Capone founded the Maple Inn, an infamous house of PROSTITUTION.

After Capone's influence waned, the effects of the GREAT DEPRESSION prevented Forest View from developing. Growth came in 1949 when Commonwealth Edison built a huge generating plant. Revenues from the plant gave the town a new lease on life, and the ANNEXATION of industrial land (part of the Clearing Industrial District) fueled further development after 1952. The village expanded from 50 homes to more than 250, and the proliferation of industry led some to refer to it as the trucking capital of the world.

The 2000 population stood at 778. Most people trace their ancestry to POLISH, CZECH, or GERMAN roots. Roughly 10 percent of the village's one square mile is residential; the 2-by-8-block residential area is a tiny oasis in the midst of industry.

Ronald S. Vasile

See also: Crime and Chicago's Image; Planning Chicago; Underground Economy

Further reading: "History of the Village of Forest View." In *Welcome to the Village of Forest View.* n.d. • Cordts, Michael. "Village Needs Sugar Daddy." *Chicago Sun-Times,* June 17, 1984. • Lait, Jack, and Lee Mortimer. *Chicago Confidential.* 1950.

Fort Dearborn. As a part of the 1795 TREATY of Greenville, the U.S. government acquired a parcel of land at the mouth of the CHICAGO RIVER from Native Americans. Strategically important, the PORTAGE area became even more so after the acquisition of the Louisiana Territory in 1803, and in that year Capt. John Whistler arrived in Chicago to build a fort named after Henry Dearborn, President Thomas Jefferson's secretary of war.

By 1808 the fort rose on a small hill of the south bank of the Chicago River, which wrapped along the LAKE MICHIGAN shoreline instead of emptying directly into the lake as it does today. The American soldiers and their families lived within the palisaded fort. To the south of the fort were the homes and businesses of the factor, interpreter, agent, merchant, and armorer. To the north of the river lived John Kinzie and other traders with British, FRENCH, and Indian ties.

In August 1812, the American force evacuated Fort Dearborn and was attacked along the lakeshore by area Indians as the contingent began its journey to Fort Wayne. After this attack, known as the Fort Dearborn Massacre, Native Americans burned the fort and the area was little inhabited until 1816 when the U.S. army returned to rebuild. Soldiers and traders returned to the area. The new fort was the center for military activity during the BLACK HAWK WAR, and area residents took refuge there as well. By 1840, the fort had outlived its

The barracks of Fort Dearborn, 1856. Photographer: Unknown. Source: Chicago Historical Society.

military usefulness, but it was not demolished until 1857.

A bronze marker in the pavement at Michigan Avenue and Wacker Drive marks the approximate site of the first and second Fort Dearborns.

Ann Durkin Keating

See also: Chicago in the Middle Ground; Demography; Fur Trade; Loop; Potawatomis

Further reading: Peterson, Jacqueline. "The Founding Fathers: The Absorption of French-Indian Chicago, 1816–1837." In *Ethnic Chicago: A Multicultural Portrait,* 4th ed., ed. Melvin G. Holli and Peter d'A. Jones, 1995. • Pierce, Bessie Louise. *A History of Chicago,* vol. 1. 1937. • Quaife, Milo M. *Checagou.* 1933.

Fort Sheridan. Designed by the Chicago ARCHITECTURE firm of Holabird & Roche, Fort Sheridan occupied over 600 acres along Lake Michigan in HIGHWOOD, Illinois, from 1887 to 1993. The land had been purchased in 1887 by the COMMERCIAL CLUB OF CHICAGO and donated to the federal government with the hope that the army would use the gift to create a military post near the city. Since the great STRIKES of 1877, members of the Commercial Club had supported the use of the army as a national police force for the protection of property and the suppression of labor unrest. After the HAYMARKET Affair of 1886, Commercial Club members were determined to bring a U.S. Army post to the city to have troops available immediately if needed. Fully supporting this plan was the CIVIL WAR hero and commanding general himself, Philip H. Sheridan. After Congress accepted the gift, over the objections of western senators whose local posts were being closed down, construction began in the spring of 1888. Soon afterward, President Grover Cleveland named the post in honor of General Sheridan.

Troops from Fort Sheridan responded only once to labor unrest, in 1894 during the PULLMAN strikes. In 1898, during the Spanish American War, Fort Sheridan became a mobilization, training, and administrative center and continued to house these functions through WORLD WAR II, when over 500,000 men and women were processed through military service at the fort. From 1953 to the 1970s, Fort Sheridan fought the COLD WAR by servicing and supplying all NIKE antimissile systems in the upper Midwest. After 1973 the post again housed administrative and logistical support services. In 1988 Fort Sheridan was among those slated for closure by the Base Realignment and Closure Commission and in 1993 the army post was closed.

After Fort Sheridan was slated for closure, residents of the area formed the Fort Sheridan Joint Planning Commission and developed a reuse plan with public participation. Environmental analysis identified landfills, pesticide storage areas, asbestos-containing material, PCB-containing transformers, unexploded ordnance, and a variety of petroleum products and metals in the soil and groundwater. Environmental cleanup began in 1993. Ninety-four buildings, including 64 designed by Holabird & Roche, are situated on the 110-acre Historic District, designated a National Historic Landmark in 1984. An Army Reserve base continues to use about 90 acres. The remaining property is divided between a golf course and a variety of ongoing commercial and residential developments.

Eleanor Hannah

See also: Contested Space; Glenview Naval Air Station; Great Lakes Naval Training Station; Historic Preservation; Lake County, IL; Planning, City and Regional; Waste, Hazardous

Further reading: Smith, Nina B. " 'This Bleak Situation': The Founding of Fort Sheridan, Illinois." *Illinois Historical Journal* 80 (1987): 13. • Sorenson, Martha E. *View from the Tower: A History of Fort Sheridan, Illinois.* 1985.

Fourth Presbyterian Church. In 1871 two churches merged to form Fourth Presbyterian Church. The new congregation worshiped at Superior and Rush from 1874 until 1914, when it moved to its current location on North Michigan Avenue's "MAGNIFICENT MILE."

Home to wealthy congregants and influential pastors, Fourth Presbyterian soon earned a civic and national reputation befitting its magnificent Gothic structure. Called "a social settlement with a spire," the church reached out to the poor in the nearby "Little Hell" neighborhood. It helped create the Presbyterian Hospital in 1884, and it seeded sister churches in the city's immigrant enclaves. Social activism continued during the twentieth century, as members tutored CABRINI GREEN children and Cook County JAIL inmates. In 1979 the church helped to create Atrium Village, an innovative mixed-income housing development.

Known throughout its history for preaching, community outreach, education, music, and the arts, Fourth Presbyterian Church has positioned itself as a model for mainline PROTESTANTISM in the new century.

R. Jonathan Moore

See also: Near North Side; Religious Institutions; Settlements, Religious; Social Gospel in Chicago

Further reading: Scroggs, Marilee Munger. *A Light in the City: The Fourth Presbyterian Church of Chicago.* 1990. • Wellman, James K., Jr. *The Gold Coast Church and the Ghetto: Christ and Culture in Mainline Protestantism.* 1999.

Fox. *See* Mesquakie (Fox)

Fox Lake, IL, Lake County, 46 miles NW of the Loop. When the Wisconsin glacier melted, it left behind a chain of lakes—Pistakee, Nippersink, Fox, Grass, Petite, and others—in the FOX RIVER Valley. Although some dairy and hay farming did occur, the area remained sparsely settled into the 1880s as the wet areas made travel difficult during most of the year.

Some large hunting and fishing lodges that were built along the eastern shores of the lakes in the 1880s were generally reached by steam launches based in MCHENRY. A visit by boat to Fox Lake's "Egyptian Lotus" beds became a popular excursion for vacationing Chicagoans in the 1890s.

The RAILROAD entered the chain of lakes in 1901 when the Milwaukee Road crossed the chain at its narrowest point between Pistakee and Nippersink Lakes on its way to Janesville, Wisconsin. A station built near the east side of the crossing called Nippersink Point became the center of the Fox Lake community. With rail access, the vacation trade mushroomed and numerous small resorts blossomed next to the large, older resorts such as the Bay View, the Illinois, the Waltonian, and the stately, 79-guest-room beauty, the Mineola. So much money flowed into the area from tavern licenses that area farmers paid no property taxes.

The county's leaders, living almost entirely in eastern LAKE COUNTY, soon ordered raids on the numerous unlicensed drinking and GAMBLING resorts around Fox Lake, adding the fines to the county's coffers. Unhappy with those actions, Fox Lake's resort leaders united their community to maintain local control through incorporation in 1907. The new government placed few restraints on its resorts and, with PROHIBITION-era enforcement at a minimum, Chicagoans flocked to enjoy the summer water amenities, drinking, and GAMBLING.

The war to control the lucrative Fox Valley beer and gambling trade came to Fox Lake with a vengeance on June 1, 1930, when three men friendly to anti-Capone interests were machine-gunned to death at the Manning Hotel and George Druggan, brother to mobster Terry Druggan, was wounded.

The permanent population of Fox Lake grew slowly between 1930 and 1950. The Depression-era trend of turning summer cabins into permanent housing expanded as soldiers returning from WORLD WAR II found affordable housing in a resort setting. The paving of Rand Road (now U.S. 12) through Fox Lake after the war allowed the village to remain a popular vacation destination for Chicagoans even as the permanent population grew.

Fox Lake began to modernize its INFRASTRUCTURE in the 1960s under five-term president Joseph Armondo, preparing the village for its present role as a middle-class residential community in a resort setting.

Today, Fox Lake is a haven for many water sports enthusiasts; the area remains one of the busiest aquatic vacation sites in the United States. While the renovated Mineola Resort and the Manning Hotel remain to remind the community of its past, the numerous commuter trains that end their runs at Fox Lake speak to the community's new residential identity.

Craig L. Pfannkuche

See also: Entertaining Chicagoans; Glaciation; Underground Economy; Vacation Spots

Further reading: *Fiftieth Year History of the Fox Lake Volunteer Fire Department.* 1958. • *The Fox Lake Region.* 1928. • *Preliminary Planning Report: Fox Lake, Illinois.* N.d.

Fox River. The Fox River of Illinois—not to be confused with the Fox River of central Wisconsin—arises in southern Wisconsin in a lake basin about 15 miles northwest of Milwaukee. From this point, the Fox flows southward for 185 miles (100 miles in Illinois) and drops 470 vertical feet to reach its confluence with the Illinois River. As the Fox enters Illinois, it passes through Illinois' chain of lakes and then meanders southward through LAKE, MCHENRY, KANE, and DUPAGE Counties. The Fox River is a major waterway with many small islands. Its steep valley has an average gradient of 3.6 feet per mile, and its strong flow made the stream a good source for industrial waterpower. This led to early industrial development with many dams and mills built on the stream. Now most of the old mill dams are gone, but they have been replaced by hydroelectric, FLOOD CONTROL, and navigation dams.

The Fox is a schizophrenic watercourse. Near its origins in Wisconsin it flows through bucolic rural areas and a chain of glaciated lakes in northern Illinois. Farther south, it drifts through Chicago's outermost manufacturing suburbs, tumbling over 15 dams, where it provides picturesque water frontage for industries and for parks and other recreational uses. Finally, south of OSWEGO as it approaches its confluence with the Illinois River near Ottawa, it leaps and rushes through a wild canyon filled with rare native plants and wildlife and reminders of Illinois' NATIVE AMERICAN heritage. The 28-mile stretch from YORKVILLE to Wedron is designated "The Historic Fox Valley Canoe Trail." This well-known, interesting, and demanding water trail includes the beautiful Fox River Dells in the 11-mile section from Sheridan to Wedron.

The Fox is also a stream under siege. For although its water quality is improving, the Fox valley has been engulfed by the land-hungry, sprawling Chicago metropolitan area. Today, riverboat casinos sit along the banks of the Fox, and the leading edge of Chicago's swelling urban development lies along Chicago's outer belt railway system amongst the ring of manufacturing suburbs that line the river. Formerly distinct suburbs such as ELGIN and AURORA are now being overwhelmed by intense development as more and more farmland is converted to suburban uses and the metropolitan region spreads relentlessly outward.

The Fox has recently been listed among the 10 most endangered rivers in America despite improving water quality. This is due to increasing threat from its many dams and from rapidly increasing sewage and sediment loads as development surges along its course. Dams are now understood to destroy stream health, and they create dangerous conditions that have led to many deaths by drowning. It now seems likely that despite their picturesque character and their role in local history, all 15 Fox River dams will eventually be removed. These measures and active citizen oversight seem likely to restore the Fox to its former glory.

David M. Solzman

See also: Economic Geography; Gambling; Industrial Pollution; Landscape; Riverine Systems

Further reading: Husar, John. "Scientists' Crusade against Dams Hits Close to Home." *Chicago Tribune,* March 2, 1999. • *The Riverine.* Newsletter for the Lower Fox River coalition. Lisle, IL. • Vierling, Philip E. *Illinois Country Canoe Trails* [Guidebook Number Two]. 2nd ed. 1994.

Fox River Grove, IL, Lake and McHenry Counties, 37 miles NW of the Loop. Into the 1860s, OJIBWA Indians chose the Fox River Grove region for their winter home. While the men trapped small mammals, women traded beadwork to farm families in exchange for potatoes or chickens.

In 1869, Frank Opatrny purchased 80 acres along the FOX RIVER not far from the Illinois & Wisconsin Railroad station in CARY. Opatrny's son Eman took over the land in 1900, building several cottages and a restaurant along a stretch of beach. Chicagoans were transported by livery bus from the Cary station. In 1902 Opatrny added a luxury hotel, Castle Pavilion, that featured windows from the 1893 WORLD'S COLUMBIAN EXPOSITION. Opatrny bought 100 additional acres in 1905 and erected new facilities, including six bars, shooting and photo galleries, and a racetrack.

In 1905 the Norge Ski Club purchased land in Fox River Grove and erected a ski jump. Large crowds came to see the jumping competitions, and in the 1950s the site was host to America's first international ski-jumping contest.

The town of Fox River Grove incorporated in 1919 and in the same year Louis Cernocky, Sr., a CZECH immigrant and harnessmaker, converted the Kosatka Hotel to Lou's Place, a Bohemian RESTAURANT and bar. Politicians such as Mayor Anton Cermak came from

Fox River dam at North Aurora, 1961. Photographer: John McCarthy. Source: Chicago Historical Society.

Chicago just to eat at Cernocky's restaurant. In 1922 Cernocky built Louis' Crystal Ballroom behind the restaurant. Dancers filled the eight-sided hall and heard big bands such as Glenn Miller's.

Cernocky's son, Louis, Jr., married Eman Opatrny's daughter Clara, and the pair purchased the Fox River Picnic Grove in 1942. The Cernockys sold the property to a developer, who died before he could build a resort hotel. From the late 1960s through the 1990s, the property remained unused. By the late 1990s the village had purchased most of the land for use as a public park as well as for conservation efforts.

While a small downtown shopping area was still considered the village's core, some of the main shops moved into Stone Hill Shopping Center at Routes 22 and 14 when it was erected in 1980. Building continued throughout the 1990s, and the 2000 population was 4,862.

Fox River Grove is home to Windy City Balloon Port, whose hot air balloons color the sky along the Fox River.

Marilyn Elizabeth Perry

See also: Creation of Chicago Sports; Entertaining Chicagoans; Leisure

Further reading: *A History of Fox River Grove Illinois.* 1951. • *McHenry County in the Twentieth Century, 1968–1994.* McHenry County Historical Society. 1994.

Frankfort, IL, Will and Cook Counties, 29 miles S of the Loop. The fertile lands along the shores of Hickory Creek, a tributary of the DES PLAINES RIVER southwest of Chicago, long attracted NATIVE AMERICANS. Following the BLACK HAWK WAR and the federal government's expulsion of POTAWATOMI from the area, Euro-American settlers from Indiana, Ohio, New York, Vermont, New Hampshire, and other eastern states and territories staked their claims in the area. Settlers formed agricultural communities stretching along the creek, from JOLIET eastward through WILL COUNTY.

By the second half of the nineteenth century, RAILROAD expansion was transforming the landscape and economy of northern Illinois, including the communities along Hickory Creek. With the arrival of several rail lines in the 1850s, settlements focused their commerce on villages that grew up alongside the tracks.

In 1855, workers for the Michigan Central RAILROAD laid track through Frankfort Township, linking the growing city of JOLIET and the agricultural communities along Hickory Creek with the railroad's main line in Indiana. In the same year, Sherman W. Bowen, a current alderman and future mayor of Joliet who owned 80 acres of land in Frankfort Township, laid out plans for a village along the tracks named Frankfort Station.

Within a year of the village's founding, a Detroit firm had built a grain elevator in the village, shipping local produce eastward along the Michigan Central cut-off line. During the following decades, Frankfort became a commercial center for local farmers, with banks, blacksmiths, cattle pens, slaughterhouses, hardware merchants, and manufacturers of agricultural implements. In 1887, the completion of the Elgin, Joliet & Eastern Railroad (Chicago Outer Belt Line), which ran through the south side of the village, tied Frankfort directly into Chicago's vast rail network.

Despite Frankfort's rail ties to the expanding metropolis of Chicago, the village remained a small community, surrounded by farms, with fewer than 700 residents in 1950. By 2000, while farmers and laborers continued to cultivate surrounding acres, Frankfort's population had risen to 10,391 and the village had been designated by the Northeastern Illinois Planning Commission as one of the fastest-growing communities in the region. Village authorities advertised Frankfort as both a local commercial center and a bedroom community for commuters to Chicago and Joliet. Officials and residents in Frankfort also sought to develop a local tourist economy by offering tours of the village's nineteenth-century architecture and developing a retail center and recreational trails through its historic district.

Sarah S. Marcus

See also: Agriculture; Planning Chicago

Further reading: *History of Will County, Illinois.* 1878. • Mayer, Harold M., and Richard C. Wade. *Chicago: Growth of a Metropolis.* 1969. • Sterling, Robert E. *Pictorial History of Will County.* 1975.

Franklin Park, IL, Cook County, 13 miles W of the Loop. Franklin Park has more than met the expectations of Lesser Franklin, who settled in the area in the 1890s. He envisioned an industrial center that would blend with residential neighborhoods. A century later, Franklin Park boasted over 1,200 industries and related businesses covering 60 percent of the community.

GERMAN farmers settled in the 1840s. By the mid-1870s the Atlantic & Pacific RAILROAD (Milwaukee Road tracks of the Chicago, Milwaukee, St. Paul & Pacific Railroad) laid tracks and built a station on Elm Street. The Minneapolis, St. Paul, & Sault Ste Marie (Soo Line) and the Indiana Harbor Belt railroads followed.

In the early 1890s Franklin, a REAL-ESTATE broker, purchased four farms totaling 600 acres. At the railroads' intersection he built the community's center. He named the town Franklin Park and enticed prospective buyers with parades along LaSalle Street in Chicago. He offered free Sunday train rides to the property. A pavilion was built on Rose Street where potential customers received free food and beer, heard speeches, danced, and participated in contests. Lot sales exceeded a million dollars.

The community was incorporated in 1892. Before the turn of the century the first industry was founded. Lesser Franklin donated land for an IRON foundry in 1900 and offered another parcel to the Siegel, Cooper Company to build a factory in 1905. Records from the 1923 foundry and school rosters listed the majority of workers and residents as POLISH, ITALIAN, and Slavic immigrants. WORLD WAR II and a national preparedness program brought Douglas Aircraft and Buick Motors into the area. By 1948, 40 manufacturing firms called Franklin Park home. During the next decade 155 new companies were added. The CHAMBER OF COMMERCE and the Northwest Suburban Manufacturing Association have continually supported the efforts of businesses.

Population increased from 3,007 in 1940 to 18,322 by 1960. Town government promoted industrial development with ZONING laws favoring their growth. A central alarm at the fire department gave both residents and industries access to heat- and smoke-detection systems. Water reserves provided large users with millions of gallons daily.

The village has remained in search of land for industrial expansion. In 1990 Franklin Park annexed 65 acres and was the fourth largest industrial area in Illinois. By 2000, population was at 19,434 with an Hispanic population around 38 percent. Most residents were blue-collar workers employed by the complex of industries. Good location and easy access to O'HARE AIRPORT cargo terminals, railroad freight terminals, major EXPRESSWAYS for routing, and spur tracks accessing the rear of buildings have made Franklin Park a desirable place for industry.

Marilyn Elizabeth Perry

See also: Economic Geography; Government, Suburban

Further reading: *The History of Franklin Park, Illinois in Words and Pictures: Centennial Commemorative Book, 1892–1992.* 1992. • Kunstman, John William. "The Industrialization of Franklin Park, Illinois." Ph.D. diss., Northwestern University. 1964. • League of Women Voters. *Know Your Town . . . Franklin Park, Illinois.* 1971.

Fraternal Clubs. *See* Clubs: Fraternal Clubs

Free Speech. Open (or free-speech) forums flourished in Chicago during the first half of the twentieth century, with several hundred thousand people participating at more than two hundred sites. Most participants were working people with little formal education; many were women, immigrants, or members of racial minorities.

The character of the forums varied widely. HULL HOUSE, Northwestern SETTLEMENT HOUSE, the Garrick Theatre, and the Abraham Lincoln Center featured staid, well-supervised LECTURES and debates, as did the dozens of forums sponsored by trade unions, churches, and synagogues. Less formal were the many ANARCHIST, socialist, INDUSTRIAL WORKERS OF THE WORLD, and other far left forums, the atheist and FREETHOUGHT forums, and the several "HOBO COLLEGES" scattered along the West Madison Street "Skid Road": the original Hobo College established in 1907, the later Knowledge Box, and another which eventually called itself the Social Science Institute.

The most influential and best-remembered forums were the least formal of all, and even went so far as to encourage heckling. These included such freewheeling outposts of the "soapbox culture" as the NEAR NORTH SIDE'S BUGHOUSE SQUARE (officially Washington Square Park), Jack Jones's Dill Pickle Club (often called "the indoor Bughouse Square") and its 1950s successor, Myron "Slim" Brundage's College of Complexes (billed as "the Playground for People Who Think"), and their SOUTH SIDE equivalent, the WASHINGTON PARK Forum, for decades known as the Bug Club.

Open forums, especially Bughouse Square, the Pickle, and the Bug Club, figure prominently in FICTION by prominent Chicago's authors. Writers as diverse as Carl Sandburg, Edna Ferber, Sherwood Anderson, James T. Farrell, Jean Toomer, Richard Wright, Alfred Kreymborg, Ben Hecht, Max Bodenheim, Emanuel Carnevali, Kenneth Rexroth, and Saul Bellow were habitués of these centers for free discussion and debate. Thanks to these writers' reminiscences, and to later journalistic accounts, some of the lost world of the open forum became a fixture of local legend.

Emphasis on the colorful, eccentric, and bohemian qualities of some forums has obscured their educational significance. Chicago writers and public intellectuals have affirmed, without disparaging their formal schooling, that their discovery of new ideas and intellectual controversy came to them via the open forums. Listeners at Dill Pickle gatherings, for example often numbered in the hundreds, coming to hear many of the foremost educators of the time. Also popular were such nonacademic speakers and debaters as attorney Clarence Darrow, psychoanalyst Franz Alexander, anarchists Lucy Parsons, Emma Goldman, and Voltairine de Cleyre, socialists Arthur Morrow Lewis and Scott Nearing, and African American radical Hubert Harrison.

By 1950, most forums had folded. Only a handful survived at the end of the twentieth century, most notably a one-evening-a-week remnant of the College of Complexes.

Franklin Rosemont

See also: American Civil Liberties Union; Haymarket and May Day; Literary Cultures

Further reading: Abrams, Irving. *Haymarket Heritage: Memoirs of Irving S. Abrams.* Edited by Phyllis Boanes and Dave Roediger. 1989. • Bruns, Roger A. *The Damnedest Radical: The Life and World of Ben Reitman, Chicago's Celebrated Social Reformer, Hobo King, and Whorehouse Physician.* 1987. • Fagin, Sophia. *Public Forums in Chicago.* M.A. thesis, University of Chicago. 1939.

Free Thought. Free thought embraced reason and anticlericalism, and freethinkers formed their ideas about religion independently of tradition, authority, and established belief. A product of the Enlightenment, free thought was deist, not atheist. In nineteenth-century Chicago, freethinkers, many of them immigrants from Europe, institutionalized irreligion.

Within Bohemian (CZECH) PILSEN, on the city's Southwest Side, the irreligious might have outnumbered the religious six to one, and they built an elaborate social network. The Congregation of Bohemian Freethinkers of Chicago, *Svobodna obec Chicagu,* founded in 1870, became a central community institution. That congregation published the largest Czech-language NEWSPAPER in the city. These freethinkers set up building and benevolent societies, maintained a school and a library, organized children's programs and adult lectures, and sponsored musical and dramatic programs. Their congregation offered secular baptisms for their children and secular funerals, in the Bohemian National CEMETERY, for their dead.

The Scandinavian Freethinker's Society, *Skandinavisk Fritænkere Forening,* founded in 1869, commemorated Tom Paine's birthday throughout the 1870s and 1880s. Native-born freethinkers formed the Liberal League in 1880; its members joined the Scandinavians as they celebrated Paine and his *Age of Reason.* Free thought appeared even within POLONIA, where the irreligious formed a society in the late 1880s and issued their own newspapers in the 1890s.

Free thought became disreputable in the minds of native-born elites, as it increasingly attracted a working-class audience after 1875. By the end of the century, free thinkers were becoming SOCIALISTS, and institutionalized free thought barely survived into the twentieth century.

Bruce C. Nelson

See also: Free Speech; Religious Institutions

Further reading: Goldberg, Bettina. "Deutsche-amerikanische Freidenker in Milwaukee, 1877–1890." M.A. thesis, Rühr-Universität Bochum. 1982. • Leiren, Terje I. *Marcus Thrane: A Norwegian Radical in America.* 1987. • Schneirov, Richard. "Freethought and Socialism in the Czech Community in Chicago." In *"Struggle a Hard Battle": Essays on Working-Class Immigrants,* ed. Dirk Hoerder, 1986, 121–142.

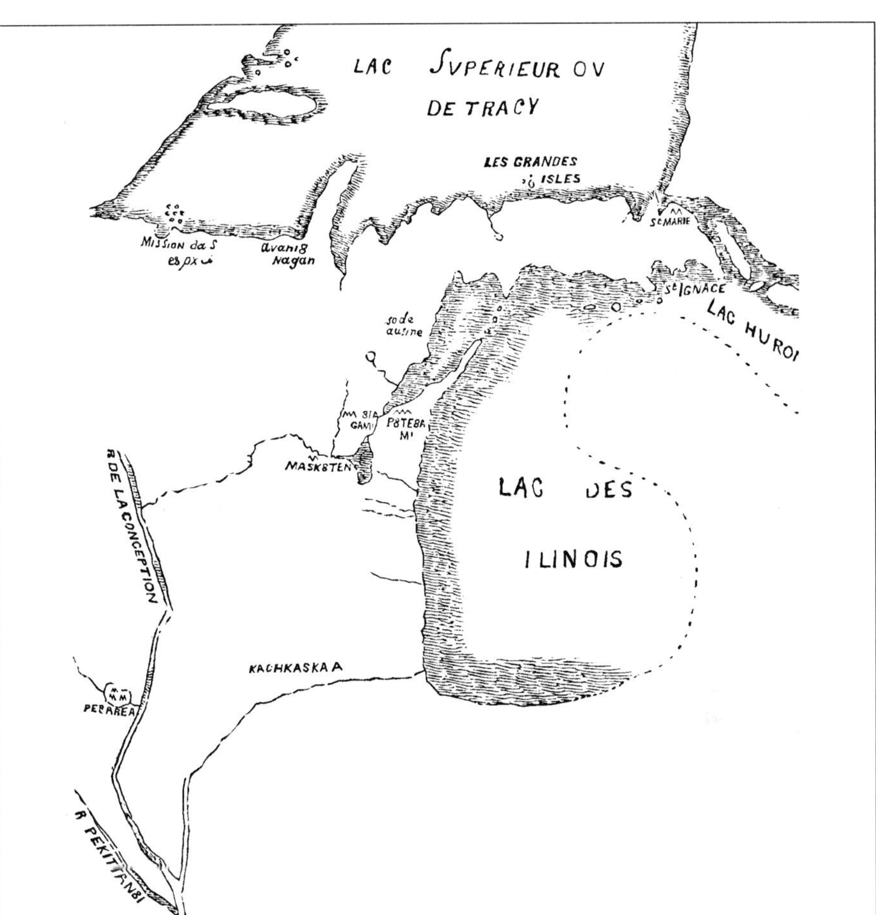

Marquette's map of his exploration and the Western Great Lakes. This reproduction shows only the central part of his original cartography. Marquette drew a continuous stream from the Illinois River to what is now called Lake Michigan, probably because he had passed during high water from the South Branch of the Chicago River through Mud Lake, into the Des Plaines River, and then to the Illinois River. Cartographer: Jacques Marquette. Source: The Newberry Library.

French and French Canadians. The French were the first Europeans to venture west of the GREAT LAKES region. *Coureurs de bois,* literally "wood runners," began to appear in the 1670s. In search of trade with NATIVE AMERICANS, these young men paddled their way along both the eastern and western shores of LAKE MICHIGAN and then up the creeks and rivers they discovered along the way. Seeking to earn a living, they consciously or unwittingly were extending France's domain in North America.

The French were latecomers to North America. During the Renaissance, while Britain, Holland, Spain, and Portugal conducted a systematic invasion of the Western Hemisphere, French kings had remained preoccupied with European politics. By the time that Jacques Cartier, in 1534, and Samuel de Champlain and Aymar de Chatte, in 1603, crossed the Atlantic Ocean, the only lands yet to be claimed were far north and lacking of either precious metals or arable lands—and therefore unattractive to their British rivals. Champlain founded Québec in 1608, Montréal in 1611. With the ascension to the French throne of Louis XIV in 1661, France began colonization in earnest. French expansion followed the waterways—the St. Lawrence River, Lakes Erie, Huron, and Michigan, then through the Fox and Illinois Rivers and on to the Mississippi.

Trader Louis Jolliet and Jesuit missionary Jacques Marquette pioneered French inland exploration in 1673 with a journey from the island of Mackinac down the Wisconsin and Mississippi Rivers to present-day Arkansas and back up the Illinois and CHICAGO RIVERS to Lake Michigan. But many individual entrepreneurs had already fanned out of the Mission of St. Ignace in what is now upper Michigan. Often linking their lives to Native American women, they created the first generation of the French presence in the Midwest.

This presence intensified when Robert Cavelier de La Salle and Henri de Tonti, plus 30 Frenchmen and a handful of Native American allies, built a settlement at Starved Rock. La Salle and his party eventually canoed their way down the Mississippi to the Gulf of Mexico, and, on April 9, 1682, they claimed all the North American continent for France—with the exception of the 13 British colonies and New Spain (Mexico).

In 1717, Illinois ceased to be part of New France (Canada) and was transferred to the government of Louisiana. Regardless of administrative jurisdiction, the Midwest remained an essential component of the French empire of North America, acting as a hinge between New France and Louisiana. The waterways between Lake Michigan and the Mississippi River were essential instruments of communication and remained essential to the FUR TRADERS who continued to venture southwest from Montreal and Quebec.

The Treaty of Paris (1763) marked the end of the French presence in North America, with France surrendering its territories between the

Atlantic and the Mississippi to Britain and transferring everything west of the Mississippi to Spain. A new distinction between French CANADIANS and French became clearer with the American Revolution and the separation between Canada, a British colony, and the United States. French cultural presence in the Midwest would all but disappear by the early 1840s, but the French in Canada, benefiting from a larger number and a cohesive grouping around the ROMAN CATHOLIC Church in a well-defined territory, retained a distinctively French culture.

During the second part of the nineteenth century, French Canadians migrating in the face of intense economic pressure at home made their way to the Kankakee area, where they founded the town of Bourbonnais. In the 1870s a large number of French Canadian families settled in the BRIGHTON PARK area of Chicago, where some of their descendants still remain.

Meanwhile, a few individuals, especially ARTISTS and persons in luxury trades, migrated from France to Chicago between the Franco-Prussian War and WORLD WAR I. Few because France avoided the severe economic crises that stimulated emigration from elsewhere in Europe, and it had its own colonies for the would-be emigrant. Interest in French culture was paradoxically maintained by Chicago society, who, in the 1890s, traveled extensively to France, where they bought the French art that would eventually enable the creation of the ART INSTITUTE's impressionist collection. This activity also led to the founding, in 1897, of the Alliance Française.

Charles J. Balesi

See also: Chicago in the Middle Ground; Demography; Miamis; Potawatomis

Further reading: Alvord, Clarence Walworth. *The Illinois Country.* 1920. • Balesi, Charles J. *The Time of the French in the Heart of North America, 1673–1818.* 1st ed. 1992; 3rd ed. 2000. • Eccles, William, J. *Canada under Louis XIV.* 1964.

Jolliet and La Salle's Canal Plans

With Father Jacques Marquette, Louis Jolliet traveled by canoe during the spring of 1673, first on the Wisconsin, then on to find the Mississippi River for Nouvelle France. They returned north on the Illinois River to the mouth of the Chicago River.

Jolliet made a careful notation of the physiography of the area, leading us to believe that he and his companions spent several days there. The Chicago PORTAGE fascinated Jolliet. He recognized the potential of a direct maritime link between the St. Lawrence estuary on the Atlantic Ocean and the Gulf of Mexico, writing to another Jesuit priest: "... it should be easy to go as far as Florida in a bark.... A canal would need to be cut across in only half a league of a prairie in order to enter from the lake in the River St. Louis (Illinois River) which discharges into the Mississippi."

Nine years later, in 1682, Robert Cavelier de La Salle and his men, in the course of his final—and successful—attempt to reach the mouth of the Mississippi, went through the Chicago Portage. La Salle did not favor the portage due to the unreliability of the depth of the water, which meant a possible six-mile trek overland (the path following present-day Archer Avenue). But he also believed that a canal could be easily cut, aware that the FRENCH had the technology, as demonstrated by the digging of the Canal du Midi, linking the Mediterranean Sea to the Atlantic Ocean.

Charles J. Balesi

Chicago's Mythical French Fort

There was never a FRENCH fort at Chicago. This persistent myth originated with a 1697 map that accompanied Father Louis Hennepin's account of his "adventures" with the La Salle expedition. This map showed a strangely shaped LAKE MICHIGAN with a river flowing into it at its southernmost point (roughly where the Dunes are) together with a fort. Hennepin had intended to show the St. Joseph River in Michigan with La Salle's new Fort Miami. Later cartographers, aware that no such southern stream existed, moved it all to the nearest river that actually existed, the CHICAGO RIVER—together with the fort. This solution was repeated in a whole series of French maps and even in English maps (Morden 1719, Popple 1733). Thus the erroneous idea of a fort at Chicago became widely accepted.

The missionary J. F. Buisson de St. Cosme, visiting the MISSION OF THE GUARDIAN ANGEL at Chicago in 1698, where he spent several days, wrote a long report describing the mission, the river, the prairie, the lake, the Miami villages, everything, but never mentioned a fort, because there wasn't any. The illusion of a Chicago fort had spread so widely that the official of the Ministry of the Marine in Paris, who years later, after the maps had become common, transcribed Buisson's report, made a surprised marginal note: "y a til un fort? aux Chicago" (is there a fort? at Chicago).

The idea of a French fort at Chicago even infected Americans. At the Treaty of Greenville (Ohio), in 1795, which forced the Indians to cede an area six miles by six miles around the mouth of the Chicago River, the representatives of the United States, none of whom had ever been to Chicago, also demanded in addition the "French fort." The Indians replied that not even the oldest among them had ever seen or heard of a fort at Chicago, but that the Americans were welcome to any fort they could find. This should have been the end of the question, but even today scholars overly impressed by all the old maps are sometimes convinced that the remains of a French fort must lie somewhere along the Chicago River.

Winstanley Briggs

Fuerzas Armadas de Liberación Nacional (FALN). The FALN (Armed Forces of National Liberation) is a clandestine organization committed to the political independence of PUERTO RICO from the United States. Between 1974 and 1983, the FALN claimed responsibility for more than 120 bombings of military and government buildings, financial institutions, and corporate headquarters in Chicago, New York, and Washington DC, which killed six people and injured dozens more. The purpose of these bombings was to protest U.S. military presence in Puerto Rico, draw attention to Puerto Rico's political relationship with the United States, and object to increased influence of U.S.-based corporate and financial institutions on the island.

On April 4, 1980, police arrested 11 FALN members in EVANSTON near NORTHWESTERN UNIVERSITY's campus. These members, as well as others arrested in Chicago in the early 1980s, were charged and found guilty of seditious conspiracy and sentenced to extensive prison terms in federal prisons throughout the United States. On August 11, 1999, President Bill Clinton offered clemency to 16 convicted FALN members on condition that they renounce violence. In September 1999, 11 prisoners were released, 2 had their fines remitted, and 1 had his prison sentence reduced. Clinton responded to criticism of his decision by explaining that the prisoners had already served extraordinarily long prison sentences for the crimes committed, and that none of the FALN members granted clemency had been convicted of any of the bombings or injuries and deaths associated with them.

Gina M. Pérez

See also: Fenianism; Polish National Alliance; Zionism

Further reading: Fernández, Ronald. *Prisoners of Colonialism: The Struggle for Justice in Puerto Rico.* 1994. • Torres, Andrés, and José E. Velázquez. *The Puerto Rican Movement: Voices from the Diaspora.* 1998. • Zavala, Iris M., and Rafael Rodriguez. *The Intellectual Roots of Independence: An Anthology of Puerto Rican Political Essays.* 1980.

Fuller Park, Community Area 37, 5 miles S of the Loop. Fuller Park is a neighborhood due south of COMISKEY PARK, the home of the American League Chicago WHITE SOX baseball team. One of Chicago's smallest community areas, this narrow two-mile strip lies between the Dan Ryan EXPRESSWAY and the Rock Island RAILROAD Metra lines to the east and the Chicago & Western Indiana Railroad to the west. The northern and southern borders are Pershing Road and Garfield Boulevard. The community derives its name from the small park named for Melville W. Fuller, Chicago attorney and U.S. chief justice.

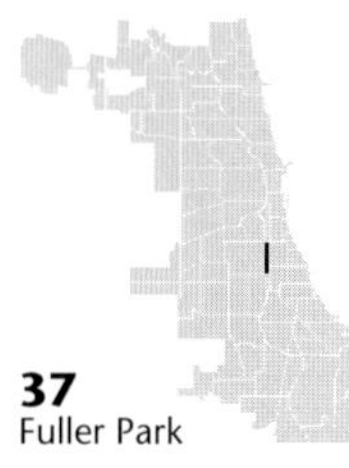

37
Fuller Park

After the CIVIL WAR, people of IRISH descent lived here, many of them employed either by the railroads or the stockyards. In 1871, a railroad roundhouse was built in the community by the Lake Shore & Michigan Southern Railroad. Because of the Great Fire in that year, residential growth increased in Fuller Park (then a part of LAKE TOWNSHIP) as developers built beyond the city limits to avoid expensive BUILDING CODES. Survivors of the 1870s include frame houses at 4463 South Wells and 4233 S. Princeton. In the mid-1880s, Chicago architect Henry Newhouse designed and built a series of modest Queen Anne–style houses at 5029–5045 S. Princeton.

In 1889, the Town of Lake was ANNEXED to the city of Chicago. GERMANS and AUSTRIANS joined the Irish as residents in the 1890s, and AFRICAN AMERICANS began moving into the community after 1900. In the early 1900s, a PUBLIC HEALTH movement among SETTLEMENT HOUSE leaders sought a plan to give residents access to light, air, and exercise. Consequently, Fuller Park opened in 1912, with a fieldhouse designed in classical Greek revival style by Daniel H. Burnham and Company.

By 1920, African Americans, MEXICANS, and Slavic workers had replaced the Irish and Germans. Fuller Park has always been home to the poor: in 1950, 24 percent of the community lacked indoor toilets. In the 1950s the community was overrun and split by the Dan Ryan Expressway, which displaced one-third of the population. The 1950s also saw the erosion of the local economy as trucking and interstate highways rendered the centralized UNION STOCK YARD unnecessary.

In the 1960s, the Union Stock Yard was in decline, eventually closing in 1971 and eliminating many jobs in the stockyards area. At the same time, thousands of southern African Americans migrated north each year and encountered a segregated housing market that restricted them to areas of the city's South and West Sides. Fuller Park saw its population change from 80 percent white in 1945 to 97 percent black in 1970, declining in total numbers from 17,174 in 1950 to 4,364 by 1990. From 1975 to 1990, there was a net loss of 41.5 percent of jobs in the stockyards area, including nearly 45 percent of all manufacturing jobs. Since 1969, no new housing, public or private, has been built in the community. In the same period, only 12 permits for commercial development were granted by the city. During the 1980s, Fuller Park received fewer bank loans for home improvement purposes than any neighborhood in Chicago.

While there are many longtime homeowners who either cannot or do not want to leave, over two-thirds of the community's 2,000-unit housing stock is rental. The poverty rate is over 40 percent and single mothers head a large number of families. Yet renewal efforts persist as the Neighbors of Fuller Park attempt to recover the neighborhood's rich architectural history. These efforts include the rehabilitation of the park, including its central fountain, courtyard, and fieldhouse. In the early 1990s, a SHOPPING CENTER was developed between the Dan Ryan Expressway and the Metra tracks just west of the ROBERT TAYLOR HOMES and adjacent to Garfield Boulevard.

Clinton E. Stockwell

See also: Housing Types; Playgrounds and Small Parks; South Side

Further reading: Chicago Historic Resources Survey. *An Inventory of Architecturally and Historically Significant Structures.* 1996.

Funeral Service Industry. The ubiquity of death has required people and institutions specializing in the handling of dead bodies and the supervision of rituals and activities connected with death. In Chicago, as in most cities, much of this work has been performed by undertakers and funeral directors, most of whom have operated relatively small businesses, often associated with particular religious or ethnic groups. The Chicago area is historically distinctive, however, in the sense that it has been a national center of the funeral service industry since that industry started to become more specialized and professionalized in the late nineteenth century.

During the city's first decades, Chicago families who required undertaking services often dealt with people for whom the funeral business was only a part-time affair. Starting in the 1830s, CEMETERIES were created around the city. These were staffed by men such as Henry Gherkin, a Prussian immigrant who was one of the first gravediggers in Chicago. During the period between the time of death and the time of burial, many Chicago families turned to undertakers, many of whom operated livery stables or other businesses when they were not handling the dead. As late as the 1880s, local undertakers such as Patrick Dingan, Charles Burmeister, and A. B. Russ engaged in a variety of businesses besides selling caskets and providing funeral services.

Chicago's growing population supported the emergence during the late nineteenth century of more specialized funeral service businesses, which formed associations to enhance their standing and authority. The professionalization of the American funeral service industry, which coincided with the rise of PUBLIC HEALTH regulatory activity during the late nineteenth century, was led by many individuals and institutions from Chicago. In 1868, the city's undertakers created a local group called the Chicago Association of Undertakers; this group sponsored the Illinois School of Embalming, which opened in Chicago in 1884. Other schools dedicated to "mortuary science" and the training of funeral service industry workers opened in the area over the following decades. By 1920, embalmers in Illinois were tested and licensed by the state. At the same time, many of the industry's national associations were headquartered in Chicago and nearby EVANSTON. The National Funeral Directors and Morticians Association, the descendant of a group formed in the early 1880s, settled in Chicago. Both the National Negro Funeral Directors Association and the JEWISH Funeral Directors of America were led by Chicagoans and chartered in Illinois in the 1920s and 1930s. For much of the twentieth century, Evanston was home to the headquarters of groups such as the Casket Manufacturers Association of America (founded 1912), National Selected Morticians (1917), the National Foundation of Funeral Service (1945), and Monument Builders of North America (1906).

The movement toward specialization and professionalization in the funeral service industry, though enhancing the authority of funeral directors and other specialists, did not mean that the business became standardized and homogeneous. In fact, providers of funeral services with strong ties to particular localities or ethnic groups continued to serve many Chicago families throughout the twentieth century, just as they had in earlier years. By the 1920s, AFRICAN AMERICAN entrepreneurs such as Daniel M. Jackson and Robert A. Cole ran large and successful funeral parlor and funeral INSURANCE businesses that served thousands of customers on the SOUTH SIDE and beyond. Mortuaries moved with ethnic populations from the city to the suburbs. Even the rise of national chains in the funeral service industry did not necessarily reduce the segmentation of the business along ethnic or religious lines. At the end of the twentieth century, for instance, Lloyd Mandel Levayah Funerals (based in SKOKIE), introduced a national chain of discount funeral service franchises, some of which were designed especially to handle the needs of Jewish families.

The constancy of death makes undertaking a relatively stable business, and several hundred funeral service businesses have been operating in the Chicago area at any given time for most of the last century. The industry has become somewhat more concentrated over time, but small-scale firms were still abundant through the end of the twentieth century. In the late 1940s, there were over 700 funeral service establishments in the metropolitan area. By the early 1990s, some 440 firms with an average of five employees each were doing a combined business of about $250 million a year.

Mark R. Wilson

See also: Birthing Practices; Demography; Mutual Benefit Societies; Schooling for Work

Further reading: Farrell, James J. *Inventing the American Way of Death, 1830–1920.* 1980. • Habenstein, Robert W., and William M. Lamers. *The History of American Funeral Directing.* 1955. • Weems, Robert E., Jr. "The Chicago Metropolitan Assurance Company: A Profile of a Black-Owned Enterprise." *Illinois Historical Journal* 86 (1993): 15–26.

Final assembly of a "pushback" theater chair at the Kroehler plant, Naperville, 1951. Photographer: Kroehler Furniture Co. Source: Chicago Historical Society.

Fur Trade. The fur trade was the economic mainstay of Chicago during the first third of the nineteenth century. FORT DEARBORN, which was established to protect U.S. interests in the fur trade, and the various trading posts formed the first stages of settlement preceding the land boom of the mid-1830s. Before that period, traders and travelers used Chicago mostly as a point of transit between the FRENCH and, later, the American settlements in the Mississippi Valley and the Straits of Mackinac. For a while, the wars between the Fox Indians and the French from the early 1700s to the 1740s closed access to the portage, and the line of communication shifted temporarily to the Wabash and Maumee Rivers south of Detroit. The flow of trade returned gradually to the more convenient location of Chicago, where the activity increased even more at the conclusion of the French and Indian Wars (1754–1763).

ENGLISH and SCOTTISH merchants, now settled in Montreal, took over control of the fur trade and allied themselves with the remaining French traders. They imported goods from London for the Indian trade: flintlock guns, gunflints, awls, trade axes, knives, metal kettles, glass beads, liquor, etc. They gave credit to the traders (*bourgeois*), a mixture of French, English, and Scots, who were stationed at various trading posts in the interior and who collected the furs from Indians and French MÉTIS. The most-traded furs included beaver, bear, black fox, deer, marten, and otter. French *voyageurs* continued to transport the goods and the furs in their bark canoes.

A number of small and large companies competed for the trade in the GREAT LAKES region. The North West Company, organized in 1779, worked mostly west of Grand PORTAGE on Lake Superior. The short-lived General Company of Lake Superior and the South, followed by the Michilimackinac Company with headquarters at Mackinac, included northern Illinois, the Mississippi River down to Cahokia, and the Wabash down to Vincennes in their operations.

The British monopoly thwarted efforts by the Americans to enter the fur trade in the Chicago area after the TREATY of Greenville of 1795, in which Indians ceded six square miles at the mouth of the CHICAGO RIVER to the United States. In order to break the British hold on the region, the U.S. government established Fort Dearborn in 1803 and opened a factory, or trading post. The factory system had been enacted by Congress in order to protect Indians from unscrupulous private traders and to regulate prices. The operations of the Chicago factory were successful in its early years, attracting good quality hatters' furs and shaved deer skins. The War of 1812 and the Fort Dearborn Massacre forced the closing of the factory. After it reopened in 1816, lack of financial support by the government and increased competition from the private sector gradually reduced its effectiveness until it was definitely closed in 1822 when Congress abolished the system.

The American Fur Company, established in 1808 by John Jacob Astor to compete with the powerful Canadian North West and Hudson Bay companies, practically took control of the fur trade in the United States following the War of 1812. It quickly became known for its ruthless practice of buying out or destroying the competition, as most private traders in Chicago soon found out. It appointed John Kinzie and Antoine Deschamps as its first agents in northern Illinois, and they reported to the company's headquarters on Mackinac

Island. Their field of operations covered northeastern Illinois and the Illinois River. In 1819, Jean-Baptiste Beaubien was brought in to assist Kinzie and eventually became head of the outfit. Gurdon S. Hubbard replaced Deschamps in 1823 but soon went on his own by purchasing all interests of the company in Illinois.

Astor formed an alliance with the Chouteau family in St. Louis in 1822. By extending the trade of his company to the Missouri River region and eventually all the way into the Rocky Mountains, he consolidated commercial connections between St. Louis, Chicago, and Mackinac. By the mid-1820s, Astor's American Fur Company dominated the economy of Chicago and, in consequence, its social life as well.

The opening of the Erie Canal in 1825 enabled Easterners to migrate in increasingly large numbers to the lands west of Lake Michigan. White settlements limited the supply of game for the Indians, who could no longer afford to pay their debts to the American Fur Company. By 1828, when Hubbard took over the business of the company in Illinois, the fur trade at Chicago was measured in hundreds instead of thousands of dollars. The Treaty of 1833, which extinguished all Indian land claims in Illinois, marked the end of the fur trade as a significant part of the Chicago economy. Diminishing profits convinced Astor in 1834 to sell his interest in the American Fur Company, which reorganized under Ramsay Crooks and moved its operations to the Far West. Fur trading disappeared from Chicago as the population boomed and land speculation became the rage.

B. Pierre Lebeau

See also: Chicago in the Middle Ground; Mesquakie (Fox); Potawatomis

Further reading: Haeger, John D. "The American Fur Company and the Chicago of 1812–1835." *Journal of the Illinois State Historical Society* 61 (1968): 117–139. • Peterson, Jacqueline. "Wild Chicago: The Formation and Destruction of a Multiracial Community on the Midwestern Frontier, 1816–1837." In *The Ethnic Frontier*, ed. Melvin G. Holli and Peter d'A. Jones, 1977, 25–71. • Quaife, Milo M. *Chicago and the Old Northwest, 1673–1835*. 1913.

Employees at the Tonk Manufacturing Company, once the nation's largest maker of piano stools, 1893. Photographer: Unknown. Source: Chicago Historical Society.

Furniture. Chicago's furniture industry expanded in the mid-nineteenth century by serving a regional rural market. Farmers in the city's hinterland prospered by selling their products in Chicago, and they purchased manufactured goods, including furniture, with their profits. Such markets, along with Chicago's own demands, fueled the westward expansion of all kinds of manufacturing.

RAILROAD connections gave Chicago access to LUMBER and the market, which it combined with a skilled immigrant labor supply, primarily of GERMAN and Scandinavian workers. In 1870, 50 percent of Chicago's cabinetmakers had been born in Germany, 10 percent in Scandinavia, while another 16 percent came from a mixture of other European countries. Immigrants were almost as well represented among furniture manufacturers in an industry where small craft shops and medium-sized firms still coexisted. YANKEES, nevertheless, usually owned the very largest companies.

Many furniture manufacturers were located on the West Side along the North and South Branches of the CHICAGO RIVER, near the neighborhoods of their workers and the lumber yards so well serviced by lake shipping and the railroads. They were also near industries producing byproducts of the MEATPACKING industry which were of use in furniture manufacture—hair, leather, and glue.

Chicago's dense concentration of modest-sized furniture plants made up an innovative center of specialty production, in which manufacturers made a wide variety of goods in response to changing and varied demand. In the 1880s, one Chicago firm ADVERTISED several thousand varieties of chairs, rockers, and cradles. Manufacturers depended on a core of skilled craftsmen to produce so wide a variety of goods, usually in small batches. Furniture makers were similar to other specialty producers—printers, foundries and machine shops, and millwork establishments.

The strong craft traditions and imported political values of the skilled furniture workers made them leaders in the labor movement. In the early 1870s, Chicago's German furniture workers founded the first local of what became a national American furniture workers' union. Rapid mechanization, using steam power and sophisticated new machines, stimulated labor organizing by changing, but not eliminating, the role of skilled workers in production. The concentration of the furniture workers in working-class neighborhoods near the factories contributed to labor's strength. Neighborhood organizations and communication networks supported the labor movement.

By the early twentieth century the structure of the industry had changed significantly. The severe depression of the 1890s destroyed many smaller craft shops owned by the foreign-born; and, as in the rest of American industry, a merger movement increased the scale and influence of larger companies. In 1900, Chicago's more than 100 furniture plants averaged about 70 workers per firm, well beyond the scale of craft production. In 1910, 200 furniture manufacturers had a workforce of over 10,000. Nevertheless, medium-sized firms still predominated, unlike the highly concentrated meatpackers or steel producers. Meanwhile, the extension of the railroad network and the growth of cities created a more integrated national market defined increasingly by urban tastes. Furniture manufacturers found it even more advantageous to be near urban centers of TRANSPORTATION, finance, and marketing.

Chicago's advantages in these areas made its furniture industry a national leader. In the early 1920s, Illinois ranked second only to New York in value of furniture produced, and Chicago dominated the state's furniture industry.

Taking advantage of Chicago's strengths in these areas, the city's furniture manufacturers became innovative leaders in national marketing. They published extensive catalogs, organized annual exhibitions for dealers, initiated installment buying, and sold extensively through Chicago preeminent MAIL-ORDER houses, Sears and Montgomery Ward. Symbolizing Chicago's importance was the opening of the American Furniture Mart in 1924. This architecturally significant building at 666 North Lake Shore Drive housed the nation's most important furniture trade shows for decades. In 1928 almost 6,500 dealers from around the country visited the Mart. In the 1920s manufacturers in the four states around Lake Michigan made the Midwest into America's largest producer of furniture by far. The region's furniture makers profited from a huge demand created by the housing boom of the decade.

Profound changes were, nevertheless, undermining the Midwest's primacy. After 1900, electricity powered ever more sophisticated tools, lessening the need for craft skills, while a decline of immigration shrank the supply of European craftsmen. Changing tastes increased the use of metal in furniture, and shaping metal required different kinds of workers and different machines. The GREAT DEPRESSION of the 1930s destroyed many firms. After WORLD WAR II, when trucks challenged railroads, furniture makers discovered that they could manufacture and market furniture in states like North Carolina, where labor was cheaper, unions were absent, and raw materials nearby. In the late 1970s, the Furniture Mart was sold for renovation into condominiums. By 1997, none of the top 25 manufacturers of household wood furniture were based in Illinois, whereas 15 of them were located in North Carolina and Virginia.

Chicago remains, however, a significant center of custom production and furniture design. Even before Frank Lloyd Wright, Chicago's architects, interior designers, and furniture makers worked together to define new styles. They still do today, drawing on Chicago's enduring significance as an innovative marketing and design center.

John B. Jentz

See also: Arts and Crafts Movement; Business of Chicago; Economic Geography; Innovation, Invention, and Chicago Business; Unionization

Further reading: Darling, Sharon. *Chicago Furniture: Art, Craft, and Industry, 1833–1983.* 1984. • Jentz, John B. "Artisan Culture and the Organization of Chicago's German Workers in the Gilded Age, 1860 to 1890," in *German Workers' Culture in the United States, 1850 to 1920,* ed. Hartmut Keil, 1988, 59–79. • Scranton, Philip. *Endless Novelty: Specialty Production and American Industrialization, 1865–1925.* 1997.

Gage Park, Community Area 63, 7 miles SW of the Loop. The area roughly from 49th to 59th Streets and from Leavitt to Central Park that now comprises Gage Park was once part of the vast Illinois prairie that extended to the Southwest Side of Chicago. In the 1840s GERMANS settled there as farmers, and in 1865 the area was incorporated as the town of LAKE, which was ANNEXED to Chicago in 1889. At that time, there were but 30 wood frame cottages in Gage Park, and no paved STREETS or PUBLIC TRANSPORTATION. Between 1900 and 1910, however, the electric trolley extended its service to Western and Kedzie Streets, contributing to a building boom. In 1911, the Bartlett Realty Company developed Marquette Manor, which became an economic stimulus for further neighborhood development. From 1905 to 1919, Western and Garfield Boulevards were laid out, and residential and industrial development escalated. The neighborhood was named after the Gage family, who owned much property in the area.

While PROTESTANTS tended to settle in CHICAGO LAWN (known more colloquially as MARQUETTE PARK), ROMAN CATHOLICS settled in Gage Park. Many came to Gage Park from nearby BRIDGEPORT and BACK OF THE YARDS. By 1920 there were 13,692 people in Gage Park, mostly Bohemian and POLISH, and mostly employees of the UNION STOCK YARD. The community supported three movie theaters, including the Colony, which was built in 1925 in classical Gothic style at 5842 South Kedzie. Slavic immigrants were lured to the area as national churches were created. St. Simon's was organized by Slavic Catholics in 1926 while LITHUANIANS organized the Nativity of the Blessed Virgin Mary PARISH in 1927, the largest Lithuanian parish outside Lithuania. Also in 1927, Poles organized St. Turibius Parish.

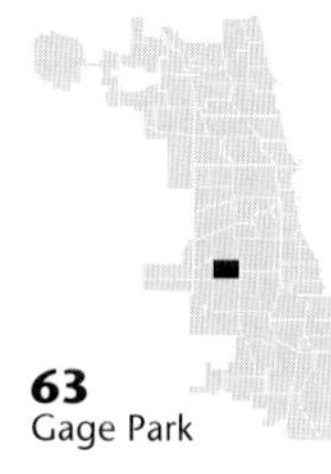
63
Gage Park

In 1922, Ben F. Bohac, a CZECH American, organized one of the largest SAVINGS AND LOAN INSTITUTIONS in Illinois, Talman Home Federal Savings and Loan at 51st and Talman Streets. Talman merged with the LaSalle National Bank in 1992. Bordered on three sides by railroads, Gage Park attracted other important employers, including Central Steel and Wire Company, Royal Crown Bottling Company, and World's Finest Chocolate.

In the 1960s, the Marquette Park–Gage Park area became a center of testing for OPEN HOUSING for AFRICAN AMERICANS. Martin Luther King, Jr., led a march to Marquette Park where he met violent resistance from counterdemonstrators, a minority of whom were sympathizers of the KU KLUX KLAN and the American Nazi Party. In 1972, Gage Park High School was integrated, despite much protest, including a boycott by white parents. In the 1970s and 1980s, several neighborhood organizations were formed to stabilize the area and to ease racial tensions: the Southwest Community Congress sought to improve race relations with bordering neighborhoods, whereas the Southwest Parish and Neighborhood Federation sought to curb real-estate BLOCKBUSTING tactics and to maintain middle-class stability in the community. A subsidiary, the Southwest Community Development Corporation, has sought to revitalize the area commercially.

Thanks to these efforts, Gage Park has retained its middle-class character, as it grows racially diverse. The 1990 census showed that the community included 26,957 residents, 70 percent of whom were white, 5 percent black and 39 percent Hispanic. Ten years later the population had grown to 39,193, of whom 79 percent were Hispanic and 7 percent African American. In 1993, the Orange Line Elevated RAPID TRANSIT line was finished, connecting the LOOP to MIDWAY AIRPORT, two miles from Gage Park. As a result, home values appreciated 70 percent, from an average of $50,000 in 1985 to $86,450 in 1996.

Clinton E. Stockwell

See also: Civil Rights Movements; Meatpacking; School Desegregation

Further reading: *Chicago Historic Resources Survey: An Inventory of Architecturally and Historically Significant Structures.* 1996. • Orr, Kathy. "Gage Park Again." *Daily Southtown,* December 20, 1996. • Pacyga, Dominic A., and Ellen Skerrett. *Chicago, City of Neighborhoods: Histories and Tours.* 1986.

Galleries. The beginnings of Chicago ART galleries are linked closely with the city's great mercantile tradition—some of the earliest galleries were located within department stores such as Marshall Field's and Goldblatt's. These and other early galleries, such as the W. Scott Thurber gallery, active in the 1910s, have since become known as "New York-style" galleries—spaces dedicated to the showing of paintings, prints, or small sculpture. In the years following World War II, a new model for galleries emerged in the form of a commercial studio that integrated art, ARCHITECTURE, and design. This so-called "Chicago-style" gallery tapped into indigenous sources such as the notion of art as social uplift that had been promulgated by the great Chicago industrialist-philanthropists in the late nineteenth century; HULL HOUSE, with its emphasis on social utility for the arts; and New Bauhaus (later INSTITUTE OF DESIGN) founder László Moholy-Nagy's philosophy of art training as a means to provide for a better society. A prime example was the Baldwin Kingrey Gallery in the Diana Court Building on North Michigan Avenue and Ohio Street which, backed by architect Harry Weese, opened in 1947. North Michigan Avenue and its immediate environs were the prime location for commercial art galleries from the 1940s until the 1980s. Pioneering spaces included Madeline Tourtelot's Gallery Studio, Benjamin Galleries, and the Frank J. Oehlschlaeger Studio, but Chicago's immediate postwar art scene in general was a small one, and most spaces were short-lived.

It was not until the mid to late 1950s that things began to change. Fairweather-Hardin, founded in EVANSTON in 1947, moved to the Michigan Avenue area in 1955. This gallery showed national figures but concentrated on artists in the local, postwar generation who had not yet established national reputations, including sculptor Richard Hunt. The Allan Frumkin Gallery, Richard Feigen Gallery, and Holland-Goldowsky (later B. C. Holland), all founded in 1957, brought international figures and the New York School to Chicago and were patronized especially by the postwar generation of art collectors, including Joseph Randall Shapiro, Edwin A. Bergman, and James Alsdorf. This generation of commercial galleries proved more viable, existing in various incarnations into the 1990s in Chicago or establishing a New York presence and continuing into the twenty-first century. Jan Cicero, Richard Gray, Rhona Hoffman, Donald Young, and Zolla/Lieberman, founded variously in the 1960s and '70s, pioneered and revitalized a former warehouse district now known as River North.

The opening of Phyllis Kind Gallery in 1967 as the home of the Chicago Imagists was a notable boost for the local population of ARTISTS, as well as a flashpoint for criticism of the city's fixation on this one particular style. Indeed, contemporary art galleries, and those showing to some degree Chicago artists, have always predominated in Chicago. The few longstanding exceptions include Alice Adam, who specializes in German Expressionism; Douglas Dawson Gallery, showing ethnographic arts; R. S. Johnson Fine Art, who focuses on works on paper; and R. H. Love Galleries, which specializes in American impressionism.

The 1980s and '90s saw an explosion in the growth of art galleries, many again short-lived, and most focusing on very recent contemporary art. Among the most notable were Feature, which relocated to New York in 1988, and the TBA Exhibition Space, which has allowed a variety of guest curators to organize topical exhibitions. In general, the gallery scene increased in depth, and in breadth, with spaces devoted to showing artists from various cultural backgrounds as well as media of all kinds opening their doors.

Lynne Warren

See also: Art Centers, Alternative; Art Institute of Chicago; Museum of Contemporary Art

Further reading: Warren, Lynne. *Art in Chicago, 1945–1995.* 1996.

Gambians. The first Gambians in Chicago came in the early 1970s for higher education opportunities not available at home. Most returned to Gambia after completing their degrees and assumed prominent positions in politics and business, while a small number remained in Chicago and began building a community. A steady flow of Gambian student migration has continued since the 1970s, and although most students continue to return home, a growing number have stayed to work and raise families. In addition, permanent settlers have attracted friends and other family members to Chicago in the 1990s. As a result of these migration patterns, the Gambian community in Chicago is on average relatively young, well educated, and highly professional. Gambians have entered a range of professions, including ACCOUNTING, teaching, medicine, and HOTEL management. The majority of Gambians live on Chicago's North Side in the UPTOWN area, although some have moved to the SOUTH SIDE and the suburbs. Community leaders estimated that the Gambian community in 2002 numbered between 100 and 200 people.

This small and cohesive community organizes celebrations for holidays like Ramadan, Christmas, and New Year's, while also meeting for important social events like naming ceremonies and weddings. Earlier Gambian migrants provide assistance and guidance to newcomers, and the community claims a tradition of providing financial assistance to members in times of birth, death, and illness. Building off the base of this social network, the Gambian Association of Chicago was founded in 1998 to promote mutual assistance and community building. The organization holds monthly meetings and fundraising events to support Gambians in Chicago and back home. It also organizes the Midwest Gambian Associations Conference every Labor Day weekend, bringing Gambian communities from Michigan, Minnesota, Wisconsin, Ohio, and Kansas together to coordinate fundraising and cultural activities, build a regional network, and discuss issues of interest. The conference invites distinguished guests to speak on major social, political, and economic issues facing Gambia and combines these activities with luncheons, dances, and a large SOCCER tournament.

Gambians in Chicago have also played a leadership role in building a larger Chicago African community. Gambian students in the 1970s were instrumental in organizing the African Student Union at the UNIVERSITY OF ILLINOIS AT CHICAGO. In addition, Gambians have played a strong leadership role in Africans on the Move, a nonprofit organization started in 1983 to deal with educational and political issues of interest to Africans. They have organized forums, celebrated holidays like African Liberation Day, and produced literature on current issues. Gambians maintain close ties with SENEGALESE and other African communities in Chicago.

Tracy Steffes

See also: Americanization; Demography; Multicentered Chicago

Gambling. Americans were tolerant of gambling when Chicago was founded, and Mark Beaubien's Sauganash featured it. But gambling seemed at odds with a commercial society's emphasis on hard WORK and self-discipline. Further, as gambling itself commercialized, crooked professional gamblers appeared. Affluent people began to class gambling with idleness and vice. The PROTESTANT clergy denounced gambling in the 1830s, and city officials, in the first of many crackdowns, jailed proprietors of two gambling houses.

Gambling appealed most to the poor and immigrants. Working-class men found an independence in gambling, in sharp contrast to their jobs, and risk taking and competition seemed to validate their masculinity. Bettors wagered on card games, checkers, backgammon, HORSE RACES, and prize fights. They played policy, a lottery-like game, and by the 1850s rowdy crowds gathered and gambled at rat and cock fights.

Gambling became a major business. By 1850, entrepreneurs had established hundreds of gambling houses, typically associated with SALOONS, especially downtown. Some houses were not only honest but elegant. Gambling on horses was common and was integral to racetracks. By 1866, "pool rooms" accommodated racing fans away from the track. Gambling payrolls, rents, and customers' purchases in adjacent businesses were important to the city's economy.

By the 1870s, gamblers combined into syndicates to handle big risks. The biggest gamblers, led by Mike McDonald, were important political contributors, and officials were reluctant to enforce laws against gambling. POLICE were often personally sympathetic to gambling, and many accepted payoffs. But campaigns against gambling found a few eager allies among politicians, and even the tolerant MAYOR Carter H. Harrison was pressured into crackdowns on the more open forms of gambling.

By 1900, three loosely organized syndicates controlled most commercial gambling. For the first time, big gamblers used violence in a struggle to control the specialized business of supplying racing news by TELEGRAPH, the strategic key to controlling lucrative off-track betting. Mont Tennes emerged as Chicago's most important gambler. While big gambling houses concentrated downtown, bookies and policy writers spread out into neighborhood newsstands, cigar and barber shops, and saloons. Promoters built racetracks beyond the city limits. In the 1890s, illegal casinos moved to the suburbs, a process accelerated by John Torrio in the 1910s.

Gambling was often associated with masculinity. Such male spaces as barber shops and saloons were sites for friendly wagers and headquarters for bookies and policy writers. Young working-class men threw dice on street corners, BASEBALL players challenged competitors, and side bets were an important feature of BOWLING tournaments. SOUTH SIDE housewives were important participants in policy, however, many patronizing policy writers who took their business door to door.

Opponents of gambling redoubled their efforts in the 1890s. School officials struggled to exclude gambling from extracurricular activities. Federal legislation restricted use of the mails and interstate commerce for gambling. Illinois lawmakers banned racetrack bookmaking and policy.

But gambling bounced back and expanded. Pari-mutuel betting on races was legalized in 1927. Policy, popular among AFRICAN AMERICANS, grew as they were forced into segregated neighborhoods in the early twentieth century. Black gamblers contributed to Bronzeville churches and charities and invested in its businesses. Bingo became popular, and during the GREAT DEPRESSION churches and charities sponsored it to raise funds, drawing many women as players. Meanwhile TELEPHONES facilitated the gradual decline of the male-dominated horse parlor.

The Torrio-Capone organization expanded its limited gambling operations, especially after PROHIBITION. Mobsters took over the slot machine business. In the 1940s, the mob forcibly took over the racing wire service, and some policy operations as well, though it never achieved total dominance. Mob gambling reached CHICAGO HEIGHTS, BROOKFIELD, GLENVIEW, and other suburbs by 1940. In 1959, the *Chicago Tribune* reported that 10,000 employees worked at 1,000 gambling establishments in COOK COUNTY. Postwar Chicago gangsters profited from gambling in many other cities.

But law enforcement began to rein in illegal gambling. Police reforms in the 1960s and subsequent federal law enforcement activity (notably Operation Greylord) discouraged corrupt protection arrangements. In the 1980s, federal authorities used antiracketeering laws and witness protection programs in successful prosecutions of illegal gambling executives. Mob gambling, now focused on sports, remained large enough to lead to point-shaving scandals. Mobsters have profited from video poker and extortionate lending to desperate people with gambling debts.

Meanwhile, the public had become more tolerant of gambling, and women were catching up to men as gamblers. The state of Illinois and licensed corporations have become the major organizers of gambling. Illinois began operating a state lottery in 1975, with sales over $1.5 billion in 2000. By then, 4 privately owned casinos and 10 off-track betting sites had been licensed in the Chicago region. With its image sanitized, "gaming" attracted many middle- and upper-income bettors.

Bingo and other gambling remains important for some churches and private schools, but competition has hurt revenues. Fantasy FOOTBALL and other games centered in leagues and taverns are popular as well. Internet gambling emerged and regulation is being discussed. Since the 1950s, Gamblers Anonymous and similar groups organized to help compulsive gamblers, who make up about one percent of the population.

Christopher Thale

See also: Creation of Chicago Sports; Crime and Chicago's Image; Mafia; Underground Economy

Further reading: Burnham, John C. *Bad Habits: Drinking, Smoking, Taking Drugs, Gambling, Sexual Misbehavior, and Swearing in American History.* 1993. • Haller, Mark. "The Changing Structure of American Gambling in the Twentieth Century." *Journal of Social Issues* 35.3 (1979): 87–114. • King, Rufus. *Gambling and Organized Crime.* 1969.

John "Mushmouth" Johnson and the Policy Racket

John "Mushmouth" Johnson was a black gambling-house proprietor who made a fortune controlling the city's policy racket and other gambling enterprises.

Johnson had little formal education before he took a job as a porter in a Chicago gambling house in the 1880s. Though not a gambler himself, he learned the business quickly and opened his own nickel gambling house on Clark Street. In 1890 he sold this establishment and opened a saloon and gambling house at 464 South State Street that remained in continuous business for 17 years until his death. Johnson protected his business through bribes to the police and contributions to politicians.

It was a mark of Johnson's success that he became a partner in the Frontenac Club, an establishment that catered only to wealthy whites. Johnson used his money to support "race advancement" causes in the black community, though his business was seen as disreputable by members of the older black elite. After his death in 1907, Johnson's wealth contributed to the establishment of a new black business elite when his surviving sister, Eudora Johnson, married rising black banker Jesse Binga in 1912.

Douglas Knox

Gangs. Chicago's first gangs developed along ethnic lines out of the volunteer fire departments during the antebellum period. With names like "Fire Kings," these outfits of young, often single working-class men competed against one another in departmental reviews, brawled in the streets, and conducted social events. "Running with the machine" was celebrated in the DIME NOVELS of the day as part of the culture of manly bravado. When the professionalization of FIREFIGHTING departments forced volunteer companies to disband, the locus of gang life shifted into SALOONS, where "political fixers" harnessed the energies of these men.

By the 1880s a thriving gang scene developed in BRIDGEPORT and BACK OF THE YARDS on the SOUTH SIDE. Several large IRISH gangs, such as the Dukies and the Shielders, exerted a powerful influence on the STREET LIFE around the stockyards, raiding peddlers, robbing men leaving work, fighting among themselves, and terrorizing the GERMAN, JEWISH, and POLISH immigrants who settled there from the 1870s to the 1890s. These gangs fought constantly among themselves, but they united as the "Mickies" to battle black gangs to the east. During this period, gangs became entrenched in the PATRONAGE networks of WARD machines. In Irish communities, the sponsorship of gangs by politicians and businessmen transformed them into "athletic clubs" like the Hamburg Club, Ragen's Colts, and the Old Rose Athletic Club. Based in saloons and clubhouses, and often claiming the membership of over a hundred men ranging from their late teens to early thirties, these CLUBS ensured the elections of their patrons by stuffing ballot boxes and intimidating voters.

By the early twentieth century, Polish and ITALIAN gangs were the most numerous in Chicago. Polish gangs located in the "Pojay" colony on the Northwest Side battled rival Polish groups across the river in the BUCKTOWN area and southward, where a different Polish gang occupied every block of Milwaukee Avenue down to the industrial area along the CHICAGO RIVER. These gangs also engaged in territorial skirmishes with Italian gangs of the "Little Sicily" neighborhood to their south. Usually identifying themselves by streets that served as hangouts, several of these Italian gangs reportedly had connections with "Black Hand" syndicates.

The involvement of Ragen's Colts in the RACE RIOT of 1919 established a pattern of white ethnic gang behavior that would affect the course of race relations in Chicago through the 1950s. Organized by DEMOCRATIC alderman Frank Ragen of CANARYVILLE, this gang attacked AFRICAN AMERICANS residing in a nearby BLACK BELT neighborhood after African American votes had helped lift REPUBLICAN "Big Bill" Thompson to victory in the municipal elections. Taking names like the Shielders and the Boundary Gang, white gangs patrolled the "color line" through the 1930s. These activities intensified with the accelerated migration of black southerners during WORLD WAR II, prompting the MAYOR'S COMMISSION ON HUMAN RELATIONS in 1946 to establish a Juvenile Bureau to investigate the role of youth groups in anti-black violence.

Partly as a defense against racial violence, which by the 1950s reached Chicago's Latino communities, African American, PUERTO RICAN, and MEXICAN gangs proliferated in the late 1950s. By the mid-1960s, several gang niches had developed throughout the city: black gangs like the Blackstone Rangers and Vice Lords pervaded the South and West Sides, respectively; PUERTO RICAN gangs such as the Latin Kings dominated the HUMBOLDT PARK area on the Northwest Side; and Mexican gangs like the Latin Counts filled the PILSEN area around 18th Street. Gang violence occurred both within and across racial and ethnic lines throughout this period, with recruitment drives accounting for many homicides.

The public image of gangs improved in the late 1960s, when some of the more powerful black and Puerto Rican gangs joined forces with political groups and community development organizations. In the black communities of WOODLAWN and NORTH LAWNDALE, the Blackstone Ranger Nation and the Conservative Vice Lords procured government and private grants to conduct job training and community improvement programs. The use of descriptors like "nation" and "conservative" represents the influence of the Black Power movement on these gangs. Despite significant accomplishments, these projects were discontinued amidst charges of fraud brought to national attention by Senator John McClellan's Permanent Subcommittee on Investigations. While gang leaders and community activists countered with allegations of harassment by the Gang Intelligence Unit of the Chicago POLICE Department and pointed to a reduction in gang fighting during the tenure of the program, such claims lost credibility in the early 1970s, when many gangs became involved in DRUG trafficking and violent recruitment efforts. African American gangs have been sporadically involved in ward-level POLITICS since this time, but the political thrust of the late 1960s seems distant in the context of the gang violence of the 1990s.

Although existing gangs have become entrenched as membership has extended across generations, the geography of Chicago gangs was changing by the end of the twentieth century. Asian youth gangs, many of whose members arrived in the United States in the 1970s and 1980s, have joined the spectrum of street gangs in Chicago. Gangs also have moved into surrounding suburbs and even extended their reach across the Midwest. In the 1990s, Chicago gang members traveled as far afield as North Dakota in order to sell drugs, often in partnership with their Chicago rivals. At the same time, Chicago gangs began to move into cyberspace by developing their own Web sites, some of which included secret chat rooms.

Chicago's gangs have also broadened their appeal by crossing gender lines. The CHICAGO CRIME COMMISSION estimated that females accounted for as many as 20,000 of the 100,000 gang members in the city at the turn of the century. In the past, girls and young women often occupied, or appeared to occupy, somewhat subservient roles within gangs. A study conducted in the late 1990s revealed, however, that increasing numbers of females were becoming full-fledged gang members and increasingly participating in gang-related violence.

Andrew J. Diamond

See also: Crime and Chicago's Image; Ku Klux Klan; Political Culture; Racism, Ethnicity, and White Identity; Tongs

Further reading: Horowitz, Ruth. *Honor and the American Dream: Culture and Identity in a Chicano Community.* 1983. • Spergel, Irving A., and G. David Curry. *Youth Gangs: Problem and Response.* 1991. • Thrasher, Frederic. *The Gang: A Study of 1,313 Gangs in Chicago.* 1927

Garbage. *See* Waste Disposal

Gardening. Initial horticultural efforts in Chicago focused upon orchard stock, available through itinerant tree peddlers working as agents for eastern nurseries. Ornamental TREES not native to the Midwest, such as white pine, were also available. The difficulty of shipping healthy specimens over long distances, however, soon encouraged regional nurseries. Among the most influential of Illinois' early nurserymen was John A. Kennicott, horticultural editor for Chicago's popular *Prairie Farmer* and whose Grove Nursery, in what is now Glenview, specialized in species appropriate for the GREAT LAKES region. Kennicott played a key role in organizing the Illinois State AGRICULTURE Society (1853) and the Illinois State Horticultural Society (1856), and in promoting better agricultural practices through public fairs, exhibitions, and university research.

City boosters encouraged ornamental gardening to demonstrate the city's cultural refinement. If Chicago was to thrive and assume a place on par with other cities, it needed to be more than simply an excellent place to do BUSINESS. Hence its motto, "Urbs in Horto" (City in a Garden), adopted in 1837. However, the pressure to open farms and establish businesses dominated. Horticultural literature consequently emphasized hardy plants requiring little care, many remaining popular regional varieties: bleeding heart, phlox, dianthus, feverfew, and heliotrope. Recommended shrubs were deciduous rather than evergreen: rose of sharon, spirea, flowering almond, lilac, and weigela. Nearly all were imports, because few wildflowers adapted well to domestication. Those that did included liatris, partridge pea, and false cowslip. Kitchen gardens were encouraged as well, with cold frames and hot beds to extend the growing season.

Most city gardens were modest enterprises, resembling rural counterparts in terms of plant varieties but on a smaller scale. The city's wealthier citizens, however, opted for a more ostentatious display, often with professional gardeners and private greenhouses. Fashionable imports, such as dahlias, a nineteenth-century favorite, required special care. John H. Kinzie, president of the Chicago Horticultural Society in 1847, boasted more than 50 varieties of dahlias in his garden. Although formal garden designs were seldom found outside city boundaries, the more natural "cottage" style popularized by Andrew Jackson Downing could be found in both city and countryside.

Chicagoans had unusual access to horticultural displays. The WORLD'S COLUMBIAN EXPOSITION of 1893 boasted a cavernous Horticulture Building, filled with exotic plants from all over the world. In front was Frederick Law Olmsted's naturalistic wooded island and lagoon. His design of suburban RIVERSIDE influenced Frank Lloyd Wright and others. The Chicago Park District CONSERVATORIES, replaced by a larger single facility at GARFIELD PARK in 1905, also presented numerous exotic displays. A new era of LANDSCAPE DESIGN, the "Prairie Style," exemplified by Jens Jensen, O. C. Simonds, and Walter Burley Griffin, meanwhile advocated landscaping with indigenous species for a Midwestern appearance.

A nationwide proliferation of garden CLUBS began in Philadelphia in 1904, with the North Shore Horticultural Society founded in LAKE FOREST only a year later. By 1928, some 30 clubs existed in the Chicago region. Annual downtown meetings spanned several days, with presentations ranging from "The Art of Japanese Floral Arrangement" to "Control That Insect." Local clubs usually met monthly.

Gardening was nonetheless a democratic pastime, as area businesses well understood. Vaughan's Seed Store, with two stores in Chicago and extensive greenhouses in WESTERN SPRINGS, was a conspicuous supporter of garden clubs but sought to reach a wider audience through its regular radio program on Chicago station WDAP. The needs of urban gardeners received particular attention, with shows such as "Landscaping the Small Home Grounds." The Chicago Park District made parallel efforts, issuing informative booklets about low-maintenance plants for the Great Lakes climate. During the two world wars, these efforts shifted to productive fruit and vegetable gardening.

Ellen Eslinger

See also: Chicago Botanic Garden; Housekeeping; Landscape; Leisure; Plant Communities

Further reading: Ernst, Erik A. "John A. Kennicott of the Grove: Physician, Horticulturalist, and Journalist in Nineteenth-Century Illinois." *Journal of the Illinois State Historical Society* 74 (1981): 109–118. • Miller, Wilhelm Tyler. *The Prairie Spirit in Landscape Gardening.* 1915. • Watson, Daryl. *Dooryard Gardens in Early Illinois: A Guide to Historic Landscape Restoration.* 1984.

Garfield Goose and Friends. A children's television show produced in Chicago, *Garfield Goose and Friends* captivated young audiences from the early 1950s until 1976. *Garfield Goose* was created by Frazier Thomas, who introduced the show in Cincinnati. After Thomas moved to Chicago in 1951, the show began appearing on Chicago television. From 1955 to 1976, it ran on WGN-TV, where it was one of the mainstays of the station's locally produced children's programming.

The show featured a puppet, Garfield Goose, who thought he was king of the United States. Frazier Thomas played the role of prime minister, and Roy Brown, who acted in other WGN-TV children's shows, was the puppeteer.

Philip T. Hoffman

See also: Broadcasting; Museum of Broadcast Communications

Garfield Park. Garfield Park, known originally as Central Park, was one of three large parks in Chicago's West Park System. The park was first formally laid out by William Le Baron Jenney in 1870 as an integral part of the city's emerging system of parks linked together by wide grassy boulevards, from which commercial traffic was excluded. As the residential population in the West Side increased through the late nineteenth century, there was increased demand for better facilities. With the retention of Jens Jensen as chief landscape architect for the West Park System, Garfield Park saw several major elements added within a short time. In 1907, the massive Garfield Park CONSERVATORY was completed according to Jensen's rigorous specifications. Shortly thereafter a pavilion, boat landing, refectory, and GOLF course were added, reflecting a distinct change in American LEISURE pursuits.

Max Grinnell

See also: Landscape Design; Park Districts

Further reading: Chicago Park Commissioners. *The West Parks and Boulevards of Chicago.* 1914. • Grese, Robert E. *Jens Jensen: Maker of Natural Parks and Gardens.* 1992. • *Prairie in the City: Naturalism in Chicago's Parks, 1870–1940.* 1991.

Garfield Ridge, Community Area 56, 10 miles SW of the Loop. Garfield Ridge, formerly Archer Limits, is a relatively young and well-ordered neighborhood of single-family houses along the western boundary of the city. It takes its name from Garfield Boulevard (55th Street), a main east-west thoroughfare, and a rather inconsequential topographic rise left behind in the retreat of glacial LAKE MICHIGAN. Limited agricultural development of the soggy prairies came in the nineteenth century. Industrial development, first around the area and then within it, prompted residential development after 1900. By 1950 residential development overtook the industrial as block after block filled with the middle-class brick BUNGALOWS that typify the area. Part of the farthest reaches of the city on the Southwest Side, once remote Garfield Ridge has over the last century steadily grown into its urban status.

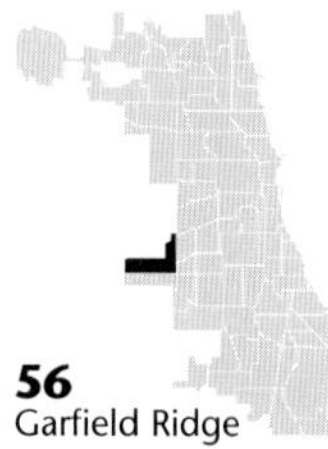

Speculators and farmers purchased the lands from the 1830s to the 1850s, but few stayed. Like NATIVE AMERICANS, whites at first just wanted to pass through, and did so on Archer Road, the ILLINOIS & MICHIGAN CANAL (completed 1848), and the Chicago & Alton RAILROAD (1850s). William B. Archer, I&M Canal commissioner, land speculator, and namesake of Archer Avenue, was among the earliest speculators, buying 240 acres adjoining present-day Harlem and Archer Avenues in 1835. In 1853, John "Long John" Wentworth, one-time mayor of Chicago, farmer, and fellow land speculator, purchased several tracts just to the east of Archer's holdings. A park that bears his name occupies ground once owned by Wentworth. Chicago ANNEXED the area in bits and pieces in 1889, 1915, and 1921.

Among the first to settle permanently were DUTCH farmers who specialized in market gardening, and in 1899 the Archer Avenue Reformed Church, formerly of SUMMIT, tended 275 parishioners. Intensive residential use began in the northeast section of the area, in what was known as the Sleepy Hollow neighborhood. More substantial growth came in the 1920s. During that decade, the population jumped from 2,472 to 6,050, with Eastern European immigrants, especially POLES, accounting for the bulk of the increase. The expanding industrial base around Garfield Ridge, in CLEARING and Argo (SUMMIT) especially, offered jobs and incentive to settle in the area. Archer Avenue, with its streetcar line, evolved into the main commercial corridor for the community. With the opening of the Chicago Municipal Airport (later MIDWAY) in 1926, the neighborhood's essential economic infrastructure was set in place. Nevertheless, the rural character of the area lingered. In 1936, residents commented on the still village-like appearance of the section west of Central Avenue, with dirt roads, farmhouses, haystacks, and grazing animals filling the landscape.

The pace of development slowed during the GREAT DEPRESSION years, but between 1940 and 1950 the population almost doubled from 6,813 to 12,900, and more than tripled to 40,449 during the following decade. Again, industrial growth, fostered in part by the activity at Midway Airport, led to residential growth, predominantly single-family houses that during the 1940s filled in the western portion of the community.

At the beginning of 1950 the community was entirely white. In 1960, Garfield Ridge maintained a high rate (almost 40 percent) of foreign-born residents, but for the first time included a sizable AFRICAN AMERICAN population (6.6 percent). Blacks lived exclusively in LeClaire Courts, a low-rise PUBLIC HOUSING project along Cicero Avenue just south of the Stevenson EXPRESSWAY, completed by the

Garfield Park, ca. 1885. Photographer: Unknown. Source: Chicago Historical Society.

Chicago Housing Authority in 1950 and expanded in 1954. Garfield Ridge's population peaked in 1970 at 42,998.

The decline of Midway traffic as airlines moved to O'Hare Airport led to declines in businesses, jobs, and population. Most of the residents who left were white, while lesser numbers of blacks and Hispanics, many as outmigrants from Little Village and Pilsen, took their places. Of the 36,101 residents of Garfield Ridge in 2000, 77 percent were white (more than one-third of Polish ancestry) and 12 percent were black; about 4 percent were Hispanic, predominantly of Mexican heritage. The African American community expanded beyond LeClaire Courts into surrounding middle-class homes.

In the 1990s, with the renewed interest and investment in Midway Airport and the arrival of rapid transit to downtown, the community continued on its path to urban maturity.

Jonathan J. Keyes

See also: Agriculture; Suburbs and Cities as Dual Metropolis

Further reading: *Local Community Fact Book* series. • Municipal Reference Collection. Harold Washington Library, Chicago, IL.

Garment Industry. *See* Clothing and Garment Manufacturing

Garveyism. "Garveyism" is the term used to describe the body of thought and organizational activities associated with Marcus Mosiah Garvey of Jamaica. In 1914, Garvey organized the Universal Negro Improvement Association and African Communities League (the UNIA). The basic organizing principle rested on the establishment of an international organization that constituted a government in exile for a revitalized African people in global dispersion from their homeland. The goals and principles appealed mainly to segments of the working class who sought a clearer identity along racial lines as well as a means to express their rising sense of group destiny, a nationalistic phenomenon observable around the globe in the aftermath of World War I.

Millions joined the UNIA globally; several thousands belonged locally. By 1920, the UNIA had several divisions in Chicago, located mostly on the South Side. Meeting weekly at Liberty Hall at 3140 Wabash, supporters extolled group pride, self-help, and solidarity. They also operated numerous small business enterprises on the South Side. Although Chicago Garveyites campaigned for a black congressional candidate in 1924, they usually avoided any involvement in American politics. The Chicago branch of the National Association for the Advancement of Colored People and Robert S. Abbott, owner of the Chicago Defender, headed Garvey's opposition within Chicago's African American community, led by middle-class men and women committed fully to enjoying the promise of American life.

Christopher R. Reed

See also: Civil Rights Movements; Fenianism; Mutual Benefit Societies; Nation of Islam; Zionism

Further reading: Clarke, John Henrik, ed. *Marcus Garvey and the Vision of Africa.* 1974. • Hill, Robert A., ed. *The Marcus Garvey and Universal Negro Improvement Association Papers.* 1983.

Gary, IN, Lake County, 25 miles SE of the Loop. Founded in 1906 on the undeveloped southern shore of Lake Michigan 30 miles east of Chicago, Gary was the creation of the U.S. Steel Corporation, which had been searching for a cheap but convenient Midwestern site for a massive new steel production center. The city was named after industrialist Elbert H. Gary, chairman of the board of U.S. Steel. Anticipating a large population of steelworkers, Gary Land Company, a U.S. Steel subsidiary, laid out a gridiron city plan, built a variety of houses and apartments, and advertised its new creation far and wide as the "Magic City" or the "City of the Century." Real-estate speculators and private builders came to control the new city's south side, however, where shoddy building of small houses and barrack-type apartments contradicted modern planning principles and dictated rapid slum development. Partially planned but partially abandoned to land speculators, Gary quickly came to be known as one of the new "satellite cities," or industrial suburbs, growing up in Chicago's widening orbit of economic influence.

The new Gary Works of U.S. Steel supplied the steel demands of the Midwest's expanding industrial economy in the early twentieth century. The city of Gary became home to a rapidly growing population of European immigrants, and, by the 1920s, southern blacks and immigrants from Mexico as well. The city's population grew to about 55,000 in 1920 and over 100,000 in 1930. Immigrants and their American-born children made up 45 percent of the population in 1930, while blacks constituted almost 18 percent. The mostly unskilled immigrant steelworkers came primarily from Southern and Eastern Europe—from Italy, Greece, Poland, Russia, and the Balkans—while the company's skilled workers and managerial staff were primarily English, Irish, German, or native-born. African Americans from the American South began migrating to Gary after the outbreak of World War I and the cessation of European immigration. In the 1920s, as immigration restriction became permanent, Mexican workers were imported by U.S. Steel to fill unskilled jobs in the mills. By 1930, over 9,000 Mexicans resided in Gary and nearby East Chicago, Indiana.

Throughout its first half century, Gary served as a testing ground for the assimilation and Americanization of European immigrants. By contrast, blacks and Mexicans were marginalized and isolated behind powerful walls of discrimination, segregation, and racism. Many of the city's American institutions—its schools, churches, workplaces, settlement houses, political system, and newspapers—focused on the struggle to Americanize the immigrant steelworkers and their families as soon as possible. Gary's nationally famous "work-study-play" or "platoon school" system, implemented by long-term school superintendent William A. Wirt, sought to Americanize immigrant children and prepare them for industrial work.

Gary's network of settlement houses and Protestant churches worked to Protestantize as well as Americanize the newcomers. However, Gary's immigrants established their own communal networks and ethnic institutions designed to retain language, culture, and custom. The conflict between native culture and immigrant newcomer was highlighted in the Great Steel Strike of 1919, when the mostly foreign-born steelworkers were depicted as radicals and revolutionaries—a portrayal used to justify mobilization of federal soldiers to put down the strike, ultimately delaying the unionization of the steelworkers until the late 1930s, when New Deal legislation protected union organizing efforts.

Gary grew substantially in the 1920s, as a native-born booster elite worked with U.S. Steel leaders to transform the city physically and plan its future growth. At the same time, ethnicity, race, and class shaped relationships among the city's diverse and socially fragmented cultures. Throughout the 1920s, the city's apparent economic prosperity remained dangerously dependent on a single industry, a condition that backfired during the Great Depression when the steel mills cut back production by 80 percent, unemployment soared, most banks failed, and the city government faced bankruptcy. The city was dominated politically by the local Republican Party until the 1930s, but an emerging New Deal political coalition prompted the ascendancy of a Democratic Party machine that retained power until well into the 1990s.

The economic demands of World War II revived the steel industry and pulled Gary out of the Depression. Wartime consensus shattered in late 1940s and after. Racial segregation and strife, labor problems in steel, industrial pollution, and political corruption (which had been persistent since the 1920s) earned Gary a national reputation as a troubled town. The city's population continued to grow moderately, reaching 133,911 in 1950 and

175,415 in 1970. But the composition of population was changing rapidly: African Americans made up 18 percent of the population in 1930, 29 percent in 1950, and 53 percent in 1970.

Population and politics were related. A succession of white ethnic mayors in the 1950s and 1960s ended in 1967 with the election of Richard G. Hatcher, one of the nation's first big-city black mayors. White flight to nearby suburbs had already begun in the 1960s, but Hatcher's election and subsequent confrontational style speeded the process considerably, paralleled now by white business flight as well. As descendants of European immigrants emptied out of the city, the population declined dramatically to 116,646 by 1990, while the proportion of African Americans rose to over 80 percent. With a secure black power base, Hatcher was reelected four times, an unusual record for big-city administrations, and served a total of 20 years as Gary's mayor.

Blacks anticipated better times under Hatcher, but disappointment gradually replaced political euphoria. The Hatcher years were accompanied by steel company disinvestment—Gary had over 30,000 steelworkers in the late 1960s but fewer than 6,000 in 1987. Hatcher also faced the consequences of national policy shifts as the urban development programs of the GREAT SOCIETY years began winding down under the Nixon and succeeding presidential administrations. Hatcher worked hard to reverse long-standing patterns of institutional racism and to initiate various economic development strategies, but the task was difficult given continued white political and business opposition to Hatcher's initiatives at the county and state level.

In 1987, another black Democrat with a less confrontational style, Thomas A. Barnes, ousted Hatcher and began two uneventful terms. In 1995, however, two black candidates divided the African American vote in the Democratic mayoral primary, permitting white attorney Scott King to win the mayor's office. Blacks continued to control the city council, which blocked many of King's proposals for governmental change and economic development. Created early in the twentieth century on a wave of optimism for the future, Gary came to exemplify in many respects the troubled state of urban America at the end of the century.

Raymond A. Mohl

See also: Economic Geography; Environmental Politics; Governing the Metropolis; Iron and Steel; Iron- and Steelworkers

Further reading: Catlin, Robert A. *Racial Politics and Urban Planning: Gary, Indiana, 1980–1989.* 1993. • Hurley, Andrew. *Environmental Inequalities: Class, Race, and Industrial Pollution in Gary, Indiana, 1945–1980.* 1995. • Mohl, Raymond A., and Neil Betten. *Steel City: Urban and Ethnic Patterns in Gary, Indiana, 1906–1950.* 1986.

Gas and Electricity. Gas and electric help supply the city's insatiable demand for energy. Until the 1930s, these two systems played a critical role in defining the urban environment. The "city lights" made Chicago distinctly different from more rural places. Its gas and electric services were developed as privately owned public utilities. To use the public STREETS for their networks of pipes and wires required a special franchise from city hall. The growth of utility companies took place within a context of government regulation and political conflict over the price, quality, and distribution of services.

Although gas lighting was introduced in the United States in 1816, Chicago had to wait until 1850 for this urban amenity. All of the gas supplied to the city was manufactured from COAL. This cheap and abundant fuel was placed in retorts and heated until it gave off a gas that could be used for illumination. The coal gas was stored in huge tanks until the evening, when lamplighters would make the rounds of the streets, starting open burners that produced a relatively feeble 12–15 candlepower. Compared to the alternatives of tallow candles or whale oil, however, gaslights were brighter, more convenient, and less prone to ignite fires. By 1860, the Chicago Gas Light and Coke Company had hooked up 2,000 customers in the city center to its 50 miles of underground pipes. In 1862 the PEOPLE'S GAS LIGHT AND COKE COMPANY started service, but a secret agreement established a duopoly that divided the city into noncompetitive zones. The result was high rates that kept gas lighting a luxury restricted to commercial and affluent residential districts. The cost of service, together with technological limitations such as dim illumination, excessive heat, and the risk of fire, continued to spur the search for better lighting.

In 1878, Chicago ushered in the electrical age with experimental demonstrations of arc lights, brilliant 2,000-candlepower devices that created a spark or arc of current across two carbon rods. While solving the problem of illuminating large public spaces, this technology was unsuitable for homes and shops. Two years later, Thomas A. Edison was the first to bring an incandescent light bulb to a point of commercial practicality. This invention was a revolutionary breakthrough because it produced light without a flame inside a fire-safe container. Equally important, parallel improvements in motors quickly led STREET RAILWAYS and RAPID TRANSIT cars to become the largest consumers of electricity. Light and power systems were sold just like steam engines as self-contained systems to individual customers. However, Edison and many of his competitors also imitated the model of the gas company by building central stations that offered service to everyone within limited distribution areas. The Chicago Edison Company, for example, initially sold only hardware, but, in 1888, it opened an electric station with a capacity to power 10,000 lights in the offices of the financial district around Adams and LaSalle Streets.

The years between 1878 and 1903 witnessed the "battle of the systems," a period marked not only by intense technological competition but by political conflict as well. In addition to the rapid growth of the electric industry, the gas business underwent a revolution of its own. New appliances and methods of making gas greatly improved its heating and illuminating qualities while dramatically cutting costs. As the expensive albeit preferred electric bulbs pushed gas lighting out of elite establishments and homes, the utility companies extended service pipes into working-class neighborhoods and began marketing energy for heating and cooking purposes. During this period, corruption and bribery of the city council became endemic as gas, electric, and transit promoters scrambled for the most advantageous franchises and lucrative service territories. In part, the reform movement known as urban progressivism was a response to this perversion of the

Samuel Insull: Electric Magnate

Born near London, Samuel Insull learned stenography and landed a job in 1881 as the personal secretary of Thomas Edison. Learning the electric lighting business from the ground up, Insull helped establish the manufacturing arm of what would become the General Electric Company in Schenectady, New York. In 1892, Insull became the president of the Chicago Edison Company, one of several electric companies in the city. Over the following decade, he mastered the unique economics of the electric utility BUSINESS and emerged as a national leader of the industry. Proclaiming that "low rates may mean good business," Insull developed a business strategy that encouraged the use of electricity among all types of energy consumers. This approach made him an innovator in the use of technologies, financial instruments, rate structures, and promotional campaigns to create a mass market for electric light and power. Moreover, he mounted a successful effort to establish a monopoly of central station service in Chicago for the renamed Commonwealth Edison Company.

Insull also became a pioneer in building larger, regional networks of power and related, holding company devices to maintain control of his sprawling utility empire. During WORLD WAR I, he was appointed chairman of the Illinois Council of Defense. In the 1920s, Insull was regarded as one of the nation's leading businessmen, a role which made him a perfect scapegoat for the GREAT DEPRESSION. Arrested and tried for securities fraud, he was acquitted in 1934 but remained a broken man until his death.

Harold L. Platt

Commonwealth Edison 14th Street Substation, 1905. Photographer: Unknown. Source: Chicago Historical Society.

political process. A wide range of women's and men's groups campaigned to clean up city hall and to impose a reasonable set of regulations on the utility companies that were providing what had truly become essential urban services.

Commonwealth Edison advertisement promoting electric lighting, ca. 1908. Source: Chicago Historical Society.

The arrival of Samuel Insull in 1892 permanently changed the history of public utilities in Chicago. Within 10 years, he established a virtual monopoly of central station electric service in the city under the corporate banner of the COMMONWEALTH EDISON COMPANY. Insull used low rates and marketing schemes to undercut the competition. After gaining key power contracts with the transit companies, he took a risk in 1902 when he installed the world's first modern turbogenerator at the Fisk Street Station. Over the following decade, this success encouraged him to integrate and expand suburban utilities into a unified network of power. He also worked to stabilize government-business relations through the creation in 1913 of a state-level utility commission. When the gas companies fell into financial difficulty during WORLD WAR I, Insull was called in to apply his business strategy of low rates, high technology, and metropolitan consolidation. In the late 1920s, he spearheaded efforts to lay a natural gas pipeline from Texas to the Midwest. The stock market crash brought about the collapse of Insull's securities empire. Energy demand briefly dipped during the ensuing GREAT DEPRESSION, but Chicago's utilities helped lead the way toward its economic recovery.

In the post–WORLD WAR II period, demand for energy in the form of gas and electric continued to soar. The Commonwealth Edison Company took a leadership role in becoming the first privately owned utility to operate a nuclear power plant. In April 1960, the Dresden Station began generating electricity, inaugurating a building program that would eventually make Chicago the metropolitan area most dependent on this form of energy in the United States. In the gas business, deregulation at the national level has meant increased competition at the local level. Similar trends in government-business relations are opening markets for electricity. At the same time, however, mounting environmental problems resulting from ever-increasing energy use have engendered a new set of technological challenges and political controversies.

Harold L. Platt

See also: Business of Chicago; Environmental Politics; Good Government Movements; Government, City of Chicago; Infrastructure; Interurbans

Further reading: Hughes, Thomas P. *Networks of Power: Electrification in Western Society, 1880–1930.* 1983. • Platt, Harold L. *The Electric City: Energy and the Growth of the Chicago Area, 1880–1930.* 1991. • Rice, Wallace. *75 Years of Gas Service in Chicago.* 1925.

Gas Stations. Gas stations have developed in Chicago and around the nation in response to the twentieth-century growth of the automobile. Early automobile owners bought gasoline in buckets, but innovations including the pump, underground tank, and drive-up service produced the first modern gas stations in the early 1900s. These early "split-pump stations" sold multiple brands of gasoline, but the 1911 breakup of the Standard Oil trust and new oil discoveries led to new marketing practices and corporate rivalry. Major oil companies sought to create brand loyalty among consumers by adopting distinctive corporate logos and slogans, standardized stations, and new services like oil checks and auto repair from the 1920s to 1960s. The gas station building itself reflected a corporate projected image, and ARCHITECTURE ranged from the functionalist modern to the truly fantastic, employing the talents of some of Chicago's top architects, including Frank Lloyd Wright, Mies van der Rohe, and Bertrand Goldberg.

The oil embargo of 1973 accelerated trends that changed the face of gas stations in Chicago. Faced with rising petroleum prices, major oil companies in Illinois, including Standard Oil of Indiana (Amoco), Shell, Clark, Arco, and Texaco, withdrew from some regions. At the same time, the gas shortages forced many independents out of business, accelerating the replacement of small neighborhood stations by larger, high-volume ones. In 1972, Illinois had 10,211 service stations but in 2001 only 4,653, despite an increase in gas consumption. In addition, companies began marketing price rather than service, a trend exemplified in the 1970s in the rise of self-service gasoline stations that sold gas for a few cents

Standard Oil gas station, Antioch, southeast corner of Main and Park, after 1914. Photographer: Unknown. Source: Lakes Region Historical Society.

less per gallon and offered none of the full-service amenities. Self-service grew slowly in Chicago because Illinois, for reasons of fire safety, was one of the last states to authorize self-service, and a Chicago city ordinance required stations to offer some full service until the early 1980s. Since then, self-service stations have taken over in Chicago and the suburbs.

Tracy Steffes

See also: Commuting; Land Use; Refining; Shopping Districts and Malls; Transportation

Further reading: Jakle, John A., and Keith A. Sculle. *The Gas Station in America.* 1994. • Vieyra, Daniel I. *"Fill 'er Up": An Architectural History of America's Gas Stations.* 1979.

Gated Communities. Strictly speaking, a gated community is any residential area which physically restricts the entrance of nonresidents. By this definition, gated communities have existed in Chicago and throughout the United States for over a century. Every hotel or apartment building with a doorman or a fence controls the flow of residents and nonresidents alike. Homeowners associations, meant to influence the appearance, population, and social character of the community, also have been used to restrict access.

Although each gated community and each neighborhood charter differs, most share a few common characteristics: physical barriers to entry and movement, the privatization and communal control of public spaces, and privatization of public services such as trash removal and police forces. Though more and more Americans are freely moving into these communities, they are not without controversy. Rosemont, a suburb of Chicago, illustrates some of the issues gated communities raise.

Rosemont is a paradox: the town's economy is entirely dependent on tourism, yet its citizens decided in 1995 to gate off half of the community, discouraging visitors from straying into residential areas. Residents of Rosemont, like residents of gated communities nationwide, saw several benefits of the move: freedom from crime and traffic, greater control of the makeup of the community, exclusivity, and the chance to form more tightly knit, old-fashioned neighborhoods. Opponents charge that gated communities are fundamentally anti-egalitarian and ultimately create more problems than they solve. Gating a community may decrease the fear of crime, but it does so by fostering the illusion that criminals are outside the community, which is often not the case. Gates also may create a fortress mentality, encouraging residents to exclude nonresidents from their lives and concerns. As one resident of the gated section of Rosemont explained, "We live in our own little world." Only time will tell if this is a blessing or a curse.

Patrick M. McMullen

See also: Land Use; Neighborhood Associations; Planning Chicago; Suburbs and Cities as Dual Metropolis

Further reading: Blakely, Edward J., and Mary Gail. *Fortress America: Gated Communities in the United States.* 1997. • Grunwald, Michael. "Gateway to a New America: Illinois Community Defends Its Barricade to 'Unwelcome' Outsiders." *Boston Globe,* August 25, 1997. • Stark, Andrew. "America the Gated?" *Wilson Quarterly* 22.1 (1998).

Gautreaux Assisted Housing Program. The Gautreaux Assisted Housing Program was created as a result of a series of class-action law suits filed against the Chicago Housing Authority (CHA) and the U.S. Department of Housing and Urban Development (HUD), beginning in 1966. The suits alleged that the housing authority deliberately segregated African American families through its tenant selection and site selection policies while HUD continued to fund such civil rights violations. One part of the settlement against HUD, reached in 1976, involved the use of Section 8 resources, including new construction and rent subsidies. The purpose of the program, named after Dorothy Gautreaux, the initiator of the original lawsuit, was to remedy past segregation by offering interested members of the plaintiff class, made up of African American residents of CHA public housing and those on the waiting list, an opportunity to find housing in desegregated areas throughout the metropolitan region.

In 1976, the Leadership Council for Metropolitan Open Communities, a private nonprofit fair housing organization, was contracted to run the program.

The Gautreaux Program ended in 1998 after meeting the target of 7,100 families placed, over half moving to affluent, white-majority suburbs. A number of longitudinal studies of Gautreaux families show a relatively high level of satisfaction with the program. There have been some racial incidents and some families have felt isolated from family, friends, and the larger African American community. But a far larger number, primarily those who have moved to the suburbs, seem pleased to be living in safer neighborhoods with quality schools and greater job opportunities. The relative success of the Gautreaux Program spawned similar efforts throughout the country as well as within the Chicago area. What began as a controversial experiment responding to a civil rights lawsuit has become an integral part of federal housing policy.

Paul Fischer

See also: Contested Spaces; Housing Reform; Open Housing; Suburbs and Cities as Dual Metropolis; Urban Renewal

Further reading: Hirsch, Arnold. *Making the Second Ghetto: Race and Housing in Chicago, 1940–1960.* 1983. • Kaufman, Julia E., and James Rosenbaum. "The Education and Employment of Low Income Black Youth in White Suburbs." *Educational Evaluation and Policy Analysis* 14 (1992): 229–240. • Rubinowitz, Leonard S. "Metropolitan Public Housing Desegregation Remedies: Chicago's Privatization Program." *Northern Illinois University Law Review* 12.3 (Summer 1992): 590–670.

Gay and Lesbian Rights Movements. The first known organization working for gay rights in the United States was founded in Chicago to bring homosexuals together as well as educate legal authorities and legislators. Henry Gerber applied on December 10, 1924, with six other men for a charter incorporating the Society for Human Rights, an enterprise modeled on German organizations.

While serving with the army in Europe following WORLD WAR I, Gerber had subscribed to German homophile publications and experienced the relative freedom for gay men in Weimar Germany. The society published two issues of its newsletter, *Friendship and Freedom*, financed almost entirely out of Gerber's pocket. But in 1925 the POLICE raided Gerber's home and arrested members of the small organization. While the charges against Gerber were eventually dropped, he lost his job based on a newspaper account of the raid. This effectively ended the Society for Human Rights. There is no documentation of another lesbian and gay rights organization in Chicago for another 30 years.

In the early 1950s, lesbians and gay men created groups such as the Daughters of Bilitis and the Mattachine Society—collectively referred to as "homophile" organizations. Local chapters of both groups existed in Chicago by 1955; these organizations attempted to secure social acceptance and understanding of lesbians and gay men through educational efforts. The Chicago chapter of the Mattachine Society engaged in few overtly political activities and functioned primarily as a social group. However, in 1964, several gay men and lesbians, led by Robert Basker and attorney Pearl Hart, reconstituted the organization as a more politically active group in response to escalating police harassment at gay bars. The new Mattachine Midwest monitored police harassment of gay bars, published a politically conscious newsletter, and by 1968 succeeded in securing ACLU support in defending gay men arrested by the police. This more activist-oriented Mattachine Midwest signaled a fundamental shift in how lesbians and gay men would organize politically.

Inspired by the Stonewall riots in New York, Henry Weimhoff, a former UNIVERSITY OF CHICAGO student, spearheaded the organization of the University of Chicago Gay Liberation Front. By February of 1970, Chicago Gay Liberation had absorbed the campus organization, organized a dance with over six hundred participants, and marched in an ANTIWAR demonstration giving the group important media exposure. In June of that year the Chicago Gay Liberation worked with other groups to organize Chicago's first Gay Pride Parade.

Over the course of the next two decades, the early activism of both Mattachine Midwest and Chicago Gay Liberation would lead to important political victories for gay men and lesbians in Chicago. In the late 1980s, a group of lesbian and gay business owners and activists—including Jon-Henri Damski, Lana Hostetler, Art Johnston, Rick Garcia, and Kit Duffy—led a successful lobbying effort which persuaded the city council in 1988 to pass the Chicago Human Rights Ordinance protecting lesbians, gay men, and bisexuals from discrimination in housing, employment, and public accommodation. In the wake of this successful campaign, the leaders formalized their partnership in the Illinois Federation for Human Rights, which became Equality Illinois. Equality Illinois successfully lobbied at the county level to extend protection against discrimination for lesbians, gay men, and bisexuals to all of COOK COUNTY in 1993. In 1997, EVANSTON became the first city in Illinois to provide this protection to transgender individuals, signaling new directions for CIVIL RIGHTS movements based on sexual identity. Five years later, transgender activists in Chicago successfully lobbied to add gender identity to the list of protections provided by the Chicago Human Rights Ordinance.

Carl Nash

See also: American Civil Liberties Union; Feminist Movements; Gays and Lesbians; Towertown

Further reading: Gregory A. Sprague Papers. Oral Histories, Chicago Gay and Lesbian History Project, Chicago Historical Society. • Katz, Jonathan. *Gay American History: Lesbians and Gay Men in the U.S.A.* 1976. • Onge, Jack. *The Gay Liberation Movement.* 1971.

Gays and Lesbians. As one of the busiest industrial centers and transportation hubs in the United States, Chicago at the beginning of the twentieth century attracted thousands of single women and men with new employment opportunities and nonfamilial living arrangements in the lodging-house districts of the NEAR NORTH and NEAR SOUTH SIDES. The anonymous and transient character of these neighborhoods permitted the development of Chicago's lesbian and gay subculture. During the early years of the century, much of this subculture was centered in the Levee, a working-class entertainment and VICE DISTRICT. Here, several SALOONS and DANCE HALLS catered to gay men and featured female impersonation acts. By 1911, the VICE COMMISSION of Chicago noted the presence of "whole groups and colonies of these men who are sex perverts," many of them working as DEPARTMENT-STORE clerks in the LOOP. The lesbian presence in the city was less visible during these years, in part because many working-class lesbians "passed" as men in order to gain access to better-paying jobs; Chicago NEWSPAPERS carried occasional sensationalized stories about local "men," many of them "married," who had been unmasked as women.

By the 1920s, a visible lesbian and gay enclave was well established in the Near North Side bohemian neighborhood known as TOWERTOWN. In the tearooms and speakeasies of this district, lesbians and gay men from throughout the city and the Midwest met and socialized with local ARTISTS and with heterosexuals bent on obtaining a glimpse of gay life. The Dill Pickle Club on Tooker Alley hosted group discussions and debates on homosexuality and lesbianism, while the Bally Hoo Cafe on North Halsted featured male and female impersonation acts, as well as a contest for cross-dressed patrons. In 1930, *Variety* estimated that there were 35 such venues on the city's Near North Side. Gay men also gathered along Michigan Avenue and on Oak Street Beach and mingled with lesbians, hobos, and political radicals in BUGHOUSE SQUARE. Yet while these public spaces played an important role in the construction of Chicago's lesbian and gay community, private parties and personal networks remained the foundation of gay culture. One such network headed by Henry Gerber, a postal clerk and Bavarian immigrant to Chicago, founded the nation's earliest documented gay rights organization in 1924; the Society for Human Rights published two pamphlets before its members were arrested and the group disbanded.

With the arrival of southern black migrants during the GREAT MIGRATION, a lesbian and gay enclave also developed on the city's SOUTH SIDE. AFRICAN AMERICAN lesbians and gay men became regular fixtures, as both patrons and entertainers, in PROHIBITION-era cabarets, including the Plantation Cafe on East 35th Street and the Pleasure Inn on East 31st. In 1935 a black gay street hustler and NIGHTCLUB doorman, Alfred Finnie, launched a series of drag (transvestite) balls on the South Side. Building on the success of the interracial drag balls that had been held at the Coliseum Annex on the Near South Side since the 1920s, the Finnie's Ball became a celebrated Halloween event on the South Side, drawing thousands of gay and lesbian participants and heterosexual onlookers well into the 1960s.

After the repeal of Prohibition in 1933, the first bars catering exclusively to lesbians and gay men opened in Chicago. Among the best known were Waldman's, a gay male bar run by a married Jewish couple on Michigan Avenue near Randolph Street, and the Rose-El-Inn, a lesbian bar on Clark Street near Division. During the 1930s and 1940s, the Loop became an increasingly important meeting place for gay men; the theaters, RESTAURANTS, and bars of this district supplemented the Near North Side venues as gathering spots for both gay men and the soldiers and sailors who swarmed the city during WORLD WAR II. Lesbian bars on both the Near North and Near South Sides, especially those run by the lesbian entrepreneur Billie Le Roy, drew sizable crowds, as did the South Side's Cabin Inn, which featured a chorus line of cross-dressed black men. The residential and social concentration of gay men in the Rush Street area drew the attention of Alfred C. Kinsey in 1939 and provided a significant sample pool for his landmark 1948 study, *Sexual Behavior in the Human Male*.

During the 1950s and 1960s, the Near North Side and Near South Side remained important lesbian and gay neighborhoods, and new enclaves formed in OLD TOWN, HYDE PARK, and in the LAKE VIEW neighborhood near the intersection of Clark Street and Diversey Parkway. The gay leather community also coalesced during this period—first, around Omar's Grill in the Loop, and in the early 1960s at the Gold Coast, Chicago's first gay leather bar.

As Chicago's lesbian and gay population grew larger and more visible, municipal authorities launched vigorous campaigns to suppress it. Raids on lesbian and gay bars became more frequent, and thousands of women and men were arrested, both in the bars and on the streets, for being inmates of disorderly houses (a label the authorities applied to lesbian and gay bars) or for violating the municipal ordinance against cross-dressing. Although Illinois became the first state in the nation to legalize private, consensual, homosexual relations in 1961, the authorities remained intent on eliminating public expressions of homosexuality; the local media assisted in this endeavor by publishing the names and addresses of those arrested in raids.

Lesbians and gay men began to organize in response to police tactics. Earlier local chapters of the Mattachine Society and the Daughters of Bilitis, two national homophile organizations, had been short-lived and largely social, but in 1964 a more politically active Mattachine Midwest was founded. Under the leadership of Jim Bradford (a pseudonym) for most of the late 1960s, this group organized a 24-hour telephone information and referral line, published and distributed a monthly newsletter to local bars informing patrons of recent POLICE crackdowns, and with the help of lesbian attorney Pearl Hart and others, aided in the defense of gay men and lesbians who had been entrapped on morals charges or arrested in bar raids.

Following the June 1969 Stonewall riots in New York City, a more militant gay liberation organization formed at the UNIVERSITY OF CHICAGO. This group sponsored a citywide dance at the Coliseum Annex in 1970, the first public lesbian and gay dance (aside from the annual Halloween drag balls) held in Chicago. Shortly thereafter, the university group merged with the newly founded Chicago Gay Liberation (CGL) and led a successful picketing campaign to force the Normandy on Rush Street to become the first gay bar in Chicago to obtain a dance license and to permit same-sex dancing. A Women's Caucus and a Black Caucus formed within CGL to address the specific concerns of lesbians and black gay men, later breaking away to become Chicago Lesbian Liberation and the Third World Gay Revolution, respectively.

These groups and others organized Chicago's first annual Gay Pride Parade in June 1970. Later that year, moderate members of CGL established the Chicago Gay Alliance, which operated a short-lived community center on West Elm Street and lobbied for the passage of a local gay rights ordinance forbidding discrimination in housing and employment. (A bill was first introduced in 1974 but did not pass until 1988). Throughout the 1970s and early 1980s lesbian and gay bars, dance clubs, and bathhouses multiplied. A community library and archives (now Gerber/Hart Gay and Lesbian Library and Archives), FILM festival, bookstore, and numerous political organizations, publications, choruses, and athletic and religious groups were also founded during this period. By the early 1980s, a new gay and lesbian commercial and residential center had emerged along North Halsted Street in Lake View, and in August 1982 area merchants launched the Northalsted Market Days, an annual neighborhood street fair that soon rivaled June's Gay Pride festivities.

During the 1980s the gay community was devastated by Acquired Immune Deficiency Syndrome (AIDS). Thousands of local gay men succumbed to this disease, which also fueled a new wave of discrimination and hate crimes against gay men and lesbians. Inadequate public funding to fight AIDS led the Howard Brown Memorial Health Center, which had been founded in 1974 as a venereal disease clinic associated with Gay Horizons (now, Horizons Community Services), to redirect its services toward AIDS prevention and treatment. As community organizations distributed safer-sex pamphlets and condoms in bars, Dykes and Gay Men Against Repression/Racism/Reagan (DAGMAR) began a campaign of militant AIDS activism in early 1987. Merging with the activist group Chicago for Our Rights (CFOR) in 1988, DAGMAR eventually became the Chicago chapter of the AIDS Coalition to Unleash Power (ACT UP/Chicago) and launched a series of demonstrations to pressure pharmaceutical companies and local, state, and federal governmental agencies to provide quicker access to AIDS treatments and increased funding for research and education. In the 1990s other activist organizations, such as Queer Nation and the Lesbian Avengers, led protests against antigay violence and continued police harassment, organized "queer nights" at popular heterosexual nightclubs, and campaigned to raise awareness of lesbian health concerns, including breast cancer.

By the late 1980s, lesbians and gay men had begun to make inroads into traditional Chicago POLITICS. Mayor Harold Washington appointed the Advisory Council on Gay and Lesbian Issues in 1987, employing a full-time liaison to the lesbian and gay community. In 1991 this group founded the nation's first city-supported Gay and Lesbian Hall of Fame, honoring the lives and work of several community activists and organizations each year. Building on the passage of Chicago's Human Rights Ordinance in 1988, a COOK COUNTY ordinance was passed in 1993 and the city voted to provide domestic partnership benefits to municipal employees in 1997. With his 1994 victory in the Cook County Circuit Court race, Thomas R. Chiola became the first openly gay elected official in Chicago. Nancy J. Katz became the city's first openly lesbian official upon her 1999 appointment and subsequent election to the same court. Larry McKeon, a former mayoral liaison to the community, was elected Illinois' first openly gay state legislator in 1996, representing a district including ANDERSONVILLE, which had become the city's second major lesbian and gay enclave.

Chad Heap

See also: Gay and Lesbian Rights Movements; Metropolitan Community Church; Street Life

Further reading: Drexel, Allen. "Before Paris Burned: Race, Class, and Male Homosexuality on the Chicago South Side, 1935–1960." In *Creating a Place for Ourselves: Lesbian, Gay, and Bisexual Community Histories*, ed. Brett Beemyn, 1997. • Johnson, David K. "The Kids of Fairytown: Gay Male Culture on Chicago's Near North Side in the 1930s." In *Creating a Place for Ourselves: Lesbian, Gay, and Bisexual Community Histories*, ed. Brett Beemyn, 1997. • Oral histories, Chicago Gay and Lesbian History Project. Gregory A. Sprague Papers. Chicago Historical Society, Chicago, IL.

Geneva, IL, Kane County, 35 miles W of the Loop. Geneva is the seat of KANE COUNTY. Located along the FOX RIVER, it has been called Big Spring, LaFox, Herrington's Ford, and Campbell Ford. Charles Volney Dyer, a New York émigré, ultimately suggested "Geneva" after a town in his home state. Geneva was incorporated as a village in 1858 and as a city in 1887. Its founders were James and Charity Herrington of Pennsylvania, arriving in 1833.

The Herringtons purchased Daniel Shaw Haight's cabin at "Big Spring" soon after they arrived. Initially they traded with a nearby NATIVE AMERICAN village, whose residents were soon forced to move west. White settlers quickly replaced Native Americans.

James died in 1839, having already had the town platted along the river and secured as county seat. He also founded its first general store and tavern and had served as postmaster as well as sheriff. Charity died in 1879, having added a subdivision to the town under her own name along the railroad. Of their 10 children, James became the first mayor and Augustus a U.S. District Attorney.

Geneva's original plat designated wide streets appropriate to a commercial center and county seat. The town's development reflects changes in TRANSPORTATION and communication. Its first axis straddled the river, then in 1853 Geneva began moving west along the new axis of the Chicago & North Western RAILROAD. In the twentieth century, automobiles allowed Geneva to expand ever westward. The cross-continental Lincoln Highway passes north and west through town. In 1993 the county's primary judicial services moved to a new complex west of town.

Geneva's architecture is notably New England in character. Early townspeople were primarily YANKEES and New Yorkers, and tended to be well educated. One significant group known as the "Boston Colony" included lawyers, doctors, merchants, ministers, and teachers. SWEDES were the first immigrant population and their cultural impact continues to this day. Arriving with construction of the railroad, they became a crucial component in the industrial labor force. Later immigrants were ITALIAN, GREEK, and IRISH.

While Geneva has emerged primarily as a white-collar bedroom community, industry has played a significant role in its economy. Early industries included a creamery; glucose and reaper manufactories; Bennett Bros. "Geneva Belle" flour; and Howell Company's "Geneva" fluting and smoothing irons and tubular steel furniture. At the close of the twentieth century, industries included industrial electronics, railway supplies, publishing, and Burgess-Norton precision-machined parts.

Geneva's first research and development facility, Riverbank Laboratories, began at the home of Colonel George and Nelle Fabyan. During the two world wars its research and intelligence work contributed to U.S. military successes. Other research projects have included work on acoustics, Shakespeare, and fitness. Fabyan FOREST PRESERVES honors that legacy.

The city's historic district is listed on the National Register of Historic Places, and Geneva is widely recognized for its commitment to HISTORIC PRESERVATION.

Sherry Meyer

See also: Economic Geography; Metropolitan Growth

Further reading: *Combination Atlas of Kane County and 1871 Atlas and History of Kane County, Illinois.* 1872. • *Commemorative Biographical and Historical Record of Kane County, Illinois.* Vol. 2. 1888. • Ehresmann, Julia M., ed. *Geneva, Illinois: A History of Its Times and Places.* 1977.

Gentrification. Gentrification refers to trends in neighborhood development that tend to attract more affluent residents, and in many instances concentrated, upscale commercial investment.

Much of the city's gentrification has clustered in the North Side neighborhoods of LINCOLN PARK and LAKE VIEW, areas that have retained a large stock of older housing, adjoin LAKE MICHIGAN and its parallel chain of municipal parks, and permit short COMMUTING via mass transit to the downtown Loop. In the late 1950s the city of Chicago initiated a major URBAN RENEWAL project in Lincoln Park, which resulted in considerable housing demolition in the southeastern portion of the neighborhood, especially along North Avenue. Within a few years, however, plans for further clearance met resistance from homeowners and renovators seeking to retain the area's historic ambience. OLD TOWN was Chicago's first neighborhood to experience gentrification, as thousands of middle-class house-seekers bought and restored old single-family dwellings, two- and three-flat buildings, and coach houses.

Since the 1970s gentrification has spread to WICKER PARK and LOGAN SQUARE on the city's near Northwest Side, to River North, the NEAR WEST SIDE, and the SOUTH LOOP in central Chicago, and to the Gap in the DOUGLAS Community Area on the SOUTH SIDE. Much of the residential upgrading in these areas has been initiated by large-scale developers. In Wicker Park, the Near West Side, and River North, the conversion of industrial buildings to residential and commercial uses has been commonplace.

Larry Bennett

See also: Building Codes and Standards; Contested Spaces; Housing Types; Metropolitan Growth; Near North Side

Further reading: Bennett, Larry. *Fragments of Cities: The New American Downtowns and Neighborhoods.* 1990. • Suttles, Gerald D. *The Man-Made City: The Land-Use Confidence Game in Chicago.* 1990. • Taub, Richard P., D. Garth Taylor, and Jan D. Dunham. *Paths of Neighborhood Change: Race and Crime in Urban America.* 1984.

Georgians. Since the late nineteenth century, small numbers of people have immigrated to the United States from Georgia, a country located in the Caucasus Mountains of southwestern Asia. However, most members of Chicago's Georgian community did not arrive in the city until after the Republic of Georgia became independent, with the dissolution of the Soviet Union in 1991. Many are scientists or doctors who came to Chicago to take advantage of economic opportunities in the city; others drive TAXIS or work in CONSTRUCTION. Chicago's Georgians have not congregated in any particular neighborhood, and they have founded few ethnic institutions. Community members say that they have been too busy adjusting to life in America to devote much time to creating institutions. In 1994, members of the community sponsored a party for Chicago's Georgians, and Georgians meet informally to celebrate holidays such as Christmas and Easter and to socialize with fellow Georgian speakers. The most important ethnic institution has been the Argo Georgian Bakery on Devon Avenue, which serves familiar Georgian foods to patrons from both Georgia and Russia.

Emily Brunner

See also: Belarusians; Demography; Multicentered Chicago; Russians

Germans. Chicago's initial period of rapid growth in the mid-nineteenth century coincided with the acceleration of German immigration to the United States, and especially with the movement of Germans into the Midwest. Germans had been migrating across the Atlantic for two centuries, and during the peak period of mass migration (1820–1930) 5.9 million reached the United States. Flight from religious persecution first triggered emigration when German Pietists from the southwestern part of the German territory were attracted by the promise of religious tolerance in colonial Pennsylvania. Social and economic factors, however, stimulated greater movement. Population growth, inadequate agricultural production caused by partial inheritance, and delayed industrialization made emigration an alternative to downward social mobility. When the Great Plains opened up for settlement in the 1830s and '40s, the structures for immigration were in place, and Germans were ready to go. Many stopped in Chicago to earn some money before moving on to claim a homestead. Those with skills in demand in the city could—and often did—stay. From 1850, when Germans constituted one-sixth of Chicago's population, until the turn of the century, people of German descent constituted the largest ethnic group in the city, followed by IRISH, POLES, and SWEDES. In 1900, 470,000 Chicagoans—one out of every four residents—had either been born in Germany or had a parent born there. By 1920 their numbers had dropped because of reduced emigration from Germany but also because it had become unpopular to acknowledge a German heritage, although 22 percent of Chicago's population still did so.

Toward the end of the nineteenth century, the origin of Chicago's German population reflected the overall pattern of German emigration. Originating in the southwestern part of the territory in the 1830s, mass emigration had moved toward the middle areas by the 1850s and '60s and tapped the agrarian northeast (Prussia, Pomerania, Mecklenburg, etc.) with its large estates in the 1880s and '90s. Approximately 35 percent of Chicago's Germans came from the northeast, 25 percent from the southwest, 17 percent from the northwest, 11 percent from the west, and 12 percent from the southeast. A rather crude divide between north (Protestant) and south (Catholic) suggests a 55 percent ROMAN CATHOLIC German community, although the PROTESTANTS were more outspoken on political and community issues. By 1900, German JEWS probably numbered approximately 20,000.

Networks of German organizations built upon and reinforced an ethnic identity based on WORK, family life, and the ethnic neighborhood. This community took form in churches,

A class at a German Turnverein, mid-1880s. Photographer: Unknown. Source: Chicago Historical Society.

organizations and CLUBS, NEWSPAPERS, theaters, and political and cultural activities. It presented itself to the city at large in beer gardens, at fairs, bazaars, and picnics, and in parades through neighborhood streets. The people who constituted this community, however, were anything but a homogenous group. They not only varied by religion and origin but also by generation, class, gender, and political leanings. Sometimes they were able to unite across class, religious, and political lines to defend "Germanism"—the concept that they considered to be at the core of their ethnic identity.

By 1900, Chicago's Germans fell into four generational categories. The elders were the children of the midcentury immigrants who had been the community's pioneers. This second generation inhabited a functioning German American community with churches, CLUBS (Vereine), theaters, small businesses, and a vibrant German press. Similar in outlook to this group were young adults who had accompanied their parents to Chicago in the 1880s. Technically "first generation" immigrants, these men and women had grown up and attended SCHOOL in Chicago and were unlikely to recall specific firsthand experience in Germany. With their American education and access to local occupational niches secured by their fathers, the men were likely to work in skilled crafts and as small businessmen.

More familiar with German culture was a third group, those who had arrived in the great wave of German immigration in the 1880s. These young adults, less Americanized than the first two groups, reinvigorated the community's ties to German culture and formed the core of the turn-of-the-century ethnic community. Many established small businesses, often with an ethnic clientele. Raising their children in the ethnic community, these parents had spent their own youth in Germany and therefore might have been able to convey a sense of German "Heimat" (homeland culture) to these young Chicagoans.

The most recent arrivals from the 1890s constituted the fourth group, the least adapted to American culture and distinguishable from their predecessors by differences in both Germany and the United States at the time of their migration. They had left behind a much more industrialized Germany than earlier emigrants had and arrived in Chicago at a time when skilled work was harder to find in the city's increasingly mechanizing industries.

If generational distinctions help us to understand the diversity of experiences among German immigrants, a focus on class provides insight into the diversity of ethnic identity. By 1900 this community had developed a small elite and a small middle class. Two-thirds, however, were living in working-class households, which meant that the transformation of work processes around the turn of the century affected a large proportion of the community. As late as 1880 Germans had such a large presence among shoemakers, bakers, butchers, cigar makers, FURNITURE and wagon makers, coopers, and upholsterers that these more traditional crafts were considered "typically German." They also found employment as unskilled laborers in the textile and tobacco industries. By 1900, these sectors of the economy had become less important to German workers. In some cases new immigrants from Eastern and Southern Europe had moved into their jobs; in others, the factories had moved away from Chicago. But for many the major change was the shift from skilled to semiskilled work, as the skilled baker preparing bread and making cakes in the 1880s had given way to the machine tender in a bread or cracker factory 20 years later.

This class structure was mirrored in the community's institutional life. In 1849 the first German lodge was founded, followed four years later by the German Aid Society, later to be among the most prestigious organizations in the community. In 1865 the small German elite began to meet in the Germania Club, and the "Schwaben Verein," founded in 1878, still celebrated its "Cannstatter Volksfest" (country fair) in the 1970s. Choirs and gymnastic groups (Gesangs und TURNVEREINE), regional associations (Landsmannschaften), THEATER clubs, and charity organizations offered rich and varied programs for middle-class entertainment and LEISURE.

A parallel network of working-class associations had emerged by the 1870s. When German workers began to arrive in the 1850s, they brought with them radical ideas which had originated in the years preceding the thwarted revolution of 1848. They also brought practical

Schwäbischer Sängerbund, Lincoln Turner Hall, 1934. Photographer: Kaufmann & Fabry. Source: Chicago Historical Society.

organizational experience to translate these ideas into action, which took the form of Chicago's first unions as well as enlistment in the Union army to fight slavery. Joseph Weydemeyer, a good friend of Karl Marx's, introduced COMMUNIST ideas in the early 1860s during his brief stay in Chicago, and in the late 1870s German Social Democrats, expelled by Bismarck's anti-Socialist laws, supported the nascent SOCIALIST Labor Party and International Workingmen's Association. German workers founded and participated in workers' associations and local craft unions, national trade unions such as the International Labor Union, the KNIGHTS OF LABOR, and unions affiliated with the American Federation of Labor. Over-represented in Chicago industry, they were organized to an unusually high degree and thus helped to establish the organizational structures to be used later by an emerging national and multinational labor movement.

This political bent often distinguished working-class entertainment from similar festivals enjoyed by Germans regardless of class. Although both working-class and bourgeois associations followed the seasonal and Christian calendar with carnivals in February and Christmas bazaars in November, the workers spiced their festivities with POLITICS: a political speech, a preceding demonstration, or money collected in support of striking workers. The community's entertainment schedule as a whole suggests the range and diversity of activities: one newspaper's announcements alone for 1898 totaled 350 events, including concerts, parties, masquerade balls, elections of officers, political campaign meetings, bazaars, gymnastic shows, picnics, commemorations, and excursions. The season for formal dances lasted from November until February, with more than 50 different festivities just in January. On any given Saturday in February a German American in Chicago could choose from nine different masquerade balls.

Women participated in these community events, while at the same time creating their own institutions. Beyond organizing women's choirs and gymnastics groups, they created a lively female public sphere of charity organizations and women's clubs; in newspapers directed toward female readers they debated "women's issues" such as proper HOUSEKEEPING and children's upbringing. They also managed to support a large home for the elderly (Altenheim) in FOREST PARK, which was still functioning at the opening of the twenty-first century, and organized fancy charity balls where the German American elite could present itself to Chicago society. Their bazaars, fairs, and other fundraising activities broadened the base for community participation in addition to providing material support to ethnic institutional life. Although German women's activities paralleled those of other Chicago women's groups, these women had a strong sense of their own value system. They considered themselves to be the better housewives, and having a more professional grip on household management stood at the center of their ethnic identity.

The physical spaces for this multifaceted institutional life were found in the neighborhoods. The oldest, originally settled by people from Bavaria and Württemberg, was on the North Side. A newer, working-class neighborhood, settled by immigrants from the East Elbian provinces, was situated on the Northwest Side, between Chicago and Fullerton Avenues on both sides of the river, with North Avenue often referred to as the "German Broadway." Other, less prominent settlements were scattered throughout the Southwest Side. Gymnastics and choir halls, beer gardens, and excursion sites were important parts of German American everyday culture. Whole families met in brightly lit and comfortable pubs, and on Sundays women and children joined the men on excursions to the beer gardens.

Much of this activity attracted criticism from Anglo-American elites, and the German American response to this criticism provided occasions for political organization along ethnic lines. Language was a particularly salient issue. German-language teaching in the Chicago Public Schools dated back to the late 1860s, a result of the election of the well-known forty-eighter Lorenz Brentano as chairman of the school board in 1867. However, German-language programs always had a precarious existence and were the first to be cut when money was tight. German language in the public schools depended heavily on the ability of the German American community to mobilize votes for school board elections. Each of Chicago's German-language newspapers—the *Illinois Staats-Zeitung*, the *Chicagoer Arbeiter-Zeitung*, the *Chicago Freie Presse*, and the *Abendpost*—catered to a particular clientele, but each considered the maintenance of the German language to be of utmost importance to all German Americans.

Temperance and SUNDAY CLOSING laws touched a similarly raw nerve, attacking fundamental issues of German sociability and way of life. Initially framed as a conflict between Anglo-American whiskey drinking and German beer culture, the liquor issue became a proxy for deeper ethnic divisions. Germans who allegedly wandered through the streets on Sundays, shouting, singing, and intimidating churchgoers and other pious citizens, were a thorn in the flesh of temperance advocates and church officials. German working men and women, who could meet with friends and fellow workers only on Saturday afternoons and on Sundays for leisure and pleasure, regarded the Sunday closing laws as an attack on their culturally specific habits and an infringement on their personal liberties and constitutional rights. For these working-class German Americans, Sunday closing merged class and ethnic interests more than any other issue.

Given their numbers and heterogeneity, Chicago's Germans never assembled an ethnic constituency behind one ethnic cultural broker promoting group interests. Rather, German men participated in nineteenth-century Chicago POLITICS on all levels, in all parties, representing a diverse electorate. However, politicians also made recurring attempts to attract German American voters as an ethnic bloc. During the 1840s to '60s Germans were well represented as aldermen and public office seekers. Michael Diversey, BREWERY owner, generous supporter of Catholic churches (St. Michael's), community builder (New Buffalo on the NEAR NORTH SIDE), and alderman of the Sixth Ward in the early 1840s, was well known beyond his immediate community. Though not all Germans were against slavery, Chicago Germans in the 1850s and '60s—mainly out of opposition to the Kansas-Nebraska Act—supported the young REPUBLICAN PARTY in great numbers and thus helped Abraham Lincoln's rise to power. In 1892 they shifted party allegiance to support German-born DEMOCRATIC gubernatorial candidate John P. Altgeld. From the 1890s to the early 1930s, however, the more conservative German Americans tended to support Republican candidates, most prominently "Big Bill" Thompson, who sought their votes by standing behind them during the difficult WORLD WAR I years. In the early 1930s, when Chicago became Democratic, German Americans more or less followed suit with German Catholics in the lead supporting Cermak in the 1932–33 elections.

Anti-German sentiment during World War I took a heavy toll on the influence of Chicago's German Americans, and many chose to hide their ethnicity out of fear of persecution. During the first war years, German American community leaders tried to raise support for neutrality, but German military activities such as the sinking of the Lusitania and unrestricted submarine warfare discredited their position. Though Chicago escaped much of the severe anti-German hysteria, many German American associations thought it opportune to hide their heritage: The Germania Club became the Lincoln Club (then returned to the original name in 1921), and in many German church services (except for the Missouri Synod) and parochial schools, where the German language was already in decline, they chose to preach and teach in English. After the war, many Chicagoans regretted the loss of the beer gardens.

In the 1920s, German community leaders tried to resurrect ethnic culture, recognition of German contribution to American society, and the respectability of the old fatherland. Generally these efforts were in vain, since it was difficult to build on a German American population which had lost interest in ethnic issues. On some occasions such as German Day or May Festival, people continued to publicly demonstrate ethnic pride though with reserved enthusiasm. In the early 1930s, for the most part they chose to ignore the Nazis rise to power in Germany, but they also failed to speak out against it. To some German American leaders Hitler represented Germany's reclamation of power and thus a chance to restore respectability. Others, among them the politically astute Otto Schmidt, issued warnings about political developments in Germany, but these were soft voices, almost inaudible. When Germany became, once again, America's enemy, German Americans kept their ethnicity to themselves, and they were not very eager to revive it in the 1950s and '60s. Those who became politically, culturally, and economically active among Chicago's Germans in the late twentieth century were, for the most part, post–World War II immigrants who had not lived through the legacy of anti-German sentiments during two world wars.

For over 150 years generation after generation of German immigrants came to Chicago, constructing a multifaceted, vibrant ethnic community, while at the same time building a Midwestern city. If it seems sometimes difficult to outline their specific contribution to the city's development, it is because of their ubiquitous presence.

Christiane Harzig

See also: Americanization; Choral Music; Demography; Housing for the Eldery; Lager Beer Riot; Prohibition and Temperance; Saloons; Theater, Ethnic; Unionization

Further reading: Hofmeister, Rudolf A. *The Germans of Chicago.* 1976. • Keil, Hartmut, and John B. Jentz. *German Workers in Chicago: A Documentary History of Working-Class Culture from 1850 to World War I.* 1988. • Tischauser, Leslie Vincent. "The Burden of Ethnicity: The German Question in Chicago, 1914–1941." Ph.D. diss., University of Illinois at Chicago Circle. 1981.

Ghanaians. When Ghana, the West African nation formerly known as the Gold Coast, achieved its independence in 1957, the number of Ghanaians living in the Chicago area was small. During the following four decades, however, Chicago's Ghanaian community grew to between 10,000 and 15,000 people. The first wave of immigration came in the 1970s; opposition to military coups and other undemocratic regimes led many Ghanaians, especially students, to pursue educational and other opportunities in the United States. Economic hardships in the 1980s continued this trend, and the Ghanaian population in Chicago grew to approximately 5,000–7,000. Since the late 1980s, immigrants have often been family members of original migrants, and a growing portion have been winners in the United States Diversity Immigrant Visa Lottery.

While Chicago's first Ghanaian immigrants settled on the SOUTH SIDE, there has been an increasing presence in North Side neighborhoods such as UPTOWN. The largest suburban Ghanaian community is located in BOLINGBROOK. No matter where Ghanaians have established themselves in metropolitan Chicago, they have maintained strong ties to the local ethnic community and to Ghana. To nourish these connections, and to provide support for new immigrants, the original student migrants created the Ghana Students Union in the late 1970s. In 1984, this group became the Ghana National Council of Metropolitan Chicago, an umbrella group for 12 ethnic and professional associations based in Chicago. These organizations include Asanteman Association, Brong Ahafo Association, Ewe Association of Metropolitan Chicago, Fante Benevolent Society, Ga-Adangbe Association, Ghana Chicago Club, Ghana Northern Union, Ghana Nurses Association, Haske Society, Kwahu United, Okuapeman Fekuw, and Okyeman Association. All of Ghana's ethnic and religious communities are represented within these groups. The associations elect community leaders that reflect traditional offices in Ghana. For example, each has a chief and queen mother, who in turn have "linguists," or spokesmen, and subchiefs.

These groups and the National Council see their mission as twofold: to serve the Ghanaian community in Chicago and to educate Ghanaian American youth and the Chicago public about Ghanaian culture. They often serve as support groups for immigrants who have suffered a death in the family, helping with funeral arrangements and giving both psychological and financial assistance to the bereaved. In 1999, the council funded the Ghanaian national women's SOCCER team's trip to the World Cup in Chicago. Their most visible cultural event is the Ghanafest, started in 1988 and held each July in WASHINGTON PARK. The festival features a *durbar* (assembly) that all ethnic associations' chiefs and queen mothers attend. The festival also introduces Chicagoans to Ghanaian cuisine and handicrafts.

Ghanaians have created businesses that cater to their needs as well as those of other Africans and the wider Chicago community. These enterprises range from a Ghanaian RESTAURANT to travel agencies and CONSTRUCTION companies, from doctors' offices and beauty salons to a NEWSPAPER, the *African Spectrum.* The Sahara Soccer Club, a team of Ghanaian Americans, was founded in 1984. Ghanaian-owned markets sell African foodstuffs. Several area churches have predominantly Ghanaian congregations, including the Lakeview Presbyterian Church, which holds Sunday afternoon services in Twi, one of the most widely spoken Ghanaian languages.

Amy Settergren

See also: Americanization; Demography; Foodways; Multicentered Chicago; Nigerians

Further reading: "He's Their Man: A Pillar of the Ghanaian Community Gets a Little Help from His Friends." *Chicago Reader,* March 3, 2000.

Ghettoization. "Ghetto" is a term with a long history, originally referring to Jewish enclaves within European cities, which were physically separated from surrounding areas, but whose economic institutions often played an important role in the life of the greater city. In American cities, including Chicago, the changing dynamics of the process known as ghettoization have paralleled shifts in racial-ethnic composition and underscored the effects of major public policy breakdowns.

In the early twentieth century, the predominantly Eastern European JEWISH Maxwell Street area on the NEAR WEST SIDE, through the research of sociologist Louis Wirth, earned the appellation of "the ghetto." Unlike European ghettos, this community of indigenously controlled cultural institutions and businesses was in no explicitly physical or legal fashion segregated from the remainder of Chicago. By the 1920s, however, on the city's South Side, a cluster of adjoining neighborhoods were congealing into a Black Belt, whose long-standing character would give a new meaning to the term "ghetto."

The original South Side Black Belt formed in response to external pressures, including discriminatory real-estate practices and the threat of violence in adjoining white neighborhoods. By the 1950s, the CHICAGO HOUSING AUTHORITY's (CHA) project-siting practices further contributed to the concentration of AFRICAN AMERICANS in the old South Side Black Belt and in a second band of neighborhoods on the city's West Side. Since the 1970s, the withdrawal of major industries and other employers from Chicago's inner-city neighborhoods has resulted in a degree of economic indigence and racial segregation that has yielded a new term for very poor, inner-city African American neighborhoods: hyperghettos.

Larry Bennett

See also: Douglas; East Garfield Park; Gautreaux Assisted Housing Program; Grand Boulevard; Housing Reform; Near South Side; Neighborhood Succession; Racism, Ethnicity, and White Identity; Redlining; Restrictive Covenants; Subsidized Housing

Further reading: Drake, St. Clair, and Horace R. Cayton. *Black Metropolis: A Study of Negro Life in a Northern City.* 1945. • Hirsch, Arnold R. *Making the Second Ghetto: Race and Housing in Chicago, 1940–1960.* 1983. • Wirth, Louis. *The Ghetto.* 1928.

Gilberts, IL, Kane County, 41 miles NW of the Loop. Platted in 1855 as Gilbert's Station along the Chicago & Northwestern RAILROAD, the community served as a loading point for AGRICULTURAL commodities. Incorporated in 1890 as Gilberts, the village grew slowly until the proximity of Interstate 90 and the growth of nearby ELGIN brought increased development. Population in 2000 was 1,279.

Craig L. Pfannkuche

See also: Kane County

Further reading: Joslyn, R. Waite, and Frank W. Joslyn. *History of Kane County, Illinois.* 2 vols. 1908.

Girl Scouts. *See* Scouting

Glaciation. The physical LANDSCAPE and surface geology of the Chicago area are the legacy of the most recent of several continental glaciations. Although glaciers invaded the Chicago area repeatedly during the Quaternary period, the span of geologic time from about 1.8 million years ago to the present, the youngest, the Wisconsin-episode glacier, melted back into the LAKE MICHIGAN basin about 16,000 years ago. Deposits of earlier glaciations, found farther south in Illinois, are absent at Chicago. These older glacial deposits were eroded from the area during the Wisconsin glaciation.

As in earlier glacial episodes, the glacial ice that flowed into the Chicago area during the Wisconsin episode came from the northeast. Because the glacier flowed as a river of ice through the Lake Michigan basin before it entered Illinois, it is known as the Lake Michigan Lobe. It was one of many lobes that flowed away from the center of a continental ice sheet called the Laurentide Ice Sheet that formed in Canada about 75,000 years ago.

Fossil wood and SOIL remains found within and beneath the Wisconsin glacial deposits in northeastern Illinois reveal that a spruce forest was growing in the Chicago region when the glacier advanced out of the Lake Michigan basin. Radiometric dating of wood and soil samples indicates that the Wisconsin glacier reached Illinois about 30,000 years ago and spread out to its maximum extent, 180 miles south of Chicago in central Illinois, about 23,000 years ago.

The glacial sediments in the Chicago area consist predominantly of unsorted or poorly sorted mixtures of gravel, sand, silt, and clay (called till) deposited beneath or in contact with glacier ice, stratified sand and gravel (called outwash) deposited by glacial meltwaters in channels and fans beyond the glacier margin, and laminated clay and silt deposited in lakes that formed on top of or adjacent to the ice. The glacial deposits at Chicago date to the later phases of the Wisconsin glacial episode in Illinois. They record two of many readvance events during the overall retreat of the Lake Michigan Lobe from its maximum position in central Illinois.

Overlying Chicago's Silurian dolomite bedrock are a layer of outwash sand and gravel and a hard, silty till (Lemont Formation) that contains abundant gravel clasts derived from the local bedrock. These dense, hard-to-drill materials, called the "Chicago hardpan" by engineers and drillers, record a readvance of the Lake Michigan Lobe about 19,000 years ago. Overlying the Lemont till layer is a pebbly clay till (Wadsworth Formation). This uppermost till layer in the Chicago area records a glacial readvance about 17,500 years ago.

During the Wisconsin glaciation, large arcuate ridges called end moraines formed at the margin of the Lake Michigan Lobe. These moraines mark positions where the ice margin remained for tens to hundreds of years while glacier flow continued to deliver sediment to the leading edge. In the Chicago area, from oldest to youngest, are the Valparaiso, Tinley, and Lake Border moraines. Ice-marginal streams (like the glacial Fox and DES PLAINES RIVERS) and/or lakes (like glacial Lake Chicago) formed between the retreating glacier margin and older moraines. The city of Chicago is built on the flat plain of glacial Lake Chicago.

Ardith K. Hansel

See also: Ecosystem Evolution; Topography

Further reading: Hansel, A. K., and W. H. Johnson. "Fluctuations of the Lake Michigan Lobe during the Late Wisconsin Subepisode." *Illinois State Geological Survey Reprint,* 1993-F, 1992, p. 18. • Hansel, A. K., and W. H. Johnson. "Wedron and Mason Groups: Lithostratigraphic Reclassification of Deposits of the Wisconsin Episode, Lake Michigan Lobe Area." *Illinois State Geological Survey Bulletin* 104 (1996): 116. • Johnson, W. H., and A. K. Hansel. "Age, Stratigraphic Position, and Significance of the Lemont Drift." *Northeastern Illinois: Journal of Geology* 97 (1989): 301–318.

Glen Ellyn, IL, DuPage County, 22 miles west of the Loop. Deacon Winslow Churchill and family arrived from New York in 1834 to become the first landowners in the area that is now Glen Ellyn. New neighbors soon established a tavern and schoolhouse at the intersection of Indian trails known as Stacy's Corners. The nucleus of settlement shifted to the south when the railroad came through the village in 1849. Although no stop was planned for the area, Lewey Q. Newton deeded a right-of-way to the RAILROAD and offered to build a depot and WATER tank at his own expense if it would

permit a stop there. This became known as Newton Station. Within three years, the new postmaster named the town Danby after his birthplace in Vermont.

Religious services were conducted by circuit riders until the first Congregational church was established in 1862. Various PROTESTANT churches rose in the village and it would be more than 60 years before ROMAN CATHOLICS built St. Petronille and the Maryknoll Seminary.

In 1889 Thomas E. Hill and Philo Stacy arranged to dam the stream near town to form Lake Glen Ellyn, named for the glen in which it rests and a Welsh spelling of Hill's wife's name, Ellen. The following year, nearby mineral springs were discovered, and Chicago's infamous Madam Rieck purportedly moved her brothel to Glen Ellyn.

In 1891 Glen Ellyn, advertised as Chicago's newest suburb and health resort, became the town's official name. The large Lake Glen Ellyn Hotel opened in 1892, the same year much of the business district was destroyed by fire. Fourteen years later, the hotel was struck by lightning and burned to the ground.

In 1907 Glen Ellyn's first fire department was organized. By the end of the twentieth century, it would be known as the last all-volunteer fire organization in DuPage County. By WORLD WAR I, Glen Oak Country Club served the OAK PARK and Glen Ellyn communities, and in 1922 the first Glenbard high school was built.

In the late 1990s Glen Ellyn was home to an Illinois state center for the deaf and blind. The village operated Village Links, a GOLF course owned by the municipality and built in conjunction with a water retention project. Its PARK DISTRICT sponsored the world-famous Glen Ellyn Children's Chorus, established in 1964. The COLLEGE of DuPage, founded in 1967, had become a major area educational institution.

Jane S. Teague

See also: Metropolitan Growth; Suburbs and Cities as Dual Metropolis

Further reading: Thompson, Richard A., ed. *DuPage Roots*. 1985. • Weiser, Frederick S. *Village in a Glen: A History of Glen Ellyn, Illinois*. 1957.

Glencoe, IL, Cook County, 19 miles N of the Loop. The origin of Glencoe's name remains shrouded in a variety of competing narratives. The most likely of these is that it is a combination of the geographic features of the wooded bluffs upon which the original town planners settled and the maiden name of former Chicago MAYOR Walter Gurnee's wife. While there appears to be no direct connection with the Scottish town of the same name, the north suburban village adopted the elder town's seal when it incorporated in 1869.

In 1835 several pioneers, including Anson and Lisa Taylor, set up businesses on the land originally inhabited by POTAWATOMI. They profited from a commercial pier and an inn that served the stagecoach traffic on the Green Bay Road.

Along with several other investors in 1867, Gurnee purchased and subdivided the land near the railway depot on the Chicago and Milwaukee line that had been completed a decade earlier. As president of the RAILROAD company, Gurnee made a practice of buying land near stations on the route as sure investments. While he had planned to settle in Glencoe, financial insolvency forced him to return to his hometown in New York.

Upon Gurnee's failure, Alexander Hammond bought 520 acres and formed the Glencoe Company with plans for an exclusive residential community. The charter included the building of a school and a church and the hiring of a teacher and a pastor. After some early financial problems, the settlement had grown to 536 homes by 1885.

At the turn of the century, Glencoe began to deal with the same issues of municipal services that other North Shore communities were facing. In many cases, Glencoe teamed with its neighbors to meet the demand for amenities from its mostly middle-class inhabitants. In 1893, Glencoe received WATER from the pumping station in WINNETKA until building its own in 1928. A sewage system was constructed in 1900 and was connected to the Chicago Sanitary District canals by 1913. Electricity came to the village by way of the HIGHLAND PARK Electric Light Company in 1903.

Glencoe's growth followed the pattern of many Chicago suburbs, accelerating rapidly in the 1950s and 1960s. Its population peaked at 10,542 in 1970. Glencoe's DEMOGRAPHY remained predominately affluent and white. Along with some of its North Shore neighbors, the village became home to a significant number of Chicago's JEWISH population in the middle decades of the twentieth century. North Shore Congregation Israel was organized in 1920 and built its current grandiose synagogue on Sheridan Road in 1964.

In recent years, Glencoe's population has declined, falling to 8,762 in 2000—95 percent of whom were white—while incomes remained among the highest in the state and the country. In 1999 the median household income was $164,432. Partly due to the prestige of New Trier High School—the district's public school—the village remains attractive to families, with 46 percent of households having children under 18.

Adam H. Stewart

See also: Governing the Metropolis; Lake Michigan; Suburbs and Cities as Dual Metropolis

Further reading: Ebner, Michael. *Creating Chicago's North Shore: A Suburban History*. 1988. • *Seventy-Five Years of Glencoe History, 1835–1944*. 1945.

Glendale Heights, IL, DuPage County, 23 miles W of the Loop. Glendale Heights remained a prosperous AGRICULTURAL area until the late 1950s, when residential SUBDIVISIONS began to replace farmland. Early farmers made their way southwest to WHEATON for stores, schools, and churches. Hiram Blanchard Patrick, for instance, arrived in DUPAGE COUNTY from New York in 1843, acquired a thousand acres of land, and farmed in the area of Glendale Heights for 30 years before moving to Wheaton. During that time his brother joined him and purchased additional land, including all of section 36 of Bloomingdale Township. Milton Smith was another early resident—a founder of the Wesleyan Methodist Church in Wheaton and an active ABOLITIONIST, with a station of the UNDERGROUND RAILROAD in his home.

Prosperous farmland in this area developed rapidly. In the post–CIVIL WAR era, dairy farms sold milk to creameries and cheese factories. One cheese factory used 4,000 pounds of milk and made 135 pounds of butter and 280 pounds of cheese daily. After train lines were established, milk was transported to Chicago for processing.

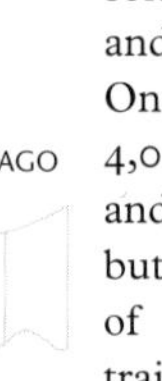

The ILLINOIS CENTRAL came through in 1888 with stops in Cloverdale and on Swift Road. The Great Western, built in 1887, stopped along Glen Ellyn and Bloomingdale roads. Army Trail Road served as a major thoroughfare from the days of the BLACK HAWK WAR. North Avenue became the first 40-foot-wide highway in the county in 1928. During the 1930s, the Civilian Conservation Corps made the road attractive by planting trees and shrubs along the boulevard.

With the exception of Glen Ellyn Countryside, which became Glendale Height's first subdivision in 1951, the area remained largely rural until 1958. In 1959 residents voted to incorporate as the village of Glendale. It was renamed Glendale Heights the following year. Until St. Matthew's ROMAN CATHOLIC Church was established in the early 1960s, Glendale Heights had no churches of its own. Through the twentieth century, Glendale Heights had no central business district or main street. A civic center was completed in the 1970s, and a library and a sports complex offer their services to the community. This ethnically diverse village contains the public Glendale Heights Polo Club, numerous parks, and the Glen Oaks HOSPITAL.

Jane S. Teague

Loading milk, Cloverdale, Illinois, postcard, ca. 1912–13. Photographer: Unknown. Source: DuPage County Historical Museum.

See also: Food Processing: Local Market; Metropolitan Growth; Suburbs and Cities as Dual Metropolis

Further reading: Thompson, Richard A. *DuPage Roots.* 1985.

Glenview, IL, Cook County, 16 miles NW of the Loop. Amid busy intersections, strip shopping centers, and corporate complexes, Glenview residents live in SUBDIVISIONS called Swainwood, Sunset Ridge, Bonnie Glen, Sleepy Hollow, and the Willows. To the east and west the community is bordered by 1,131 acres of FOREST PRESERVE. Recreational facilities include 480 acres of park land and an 18-hole public GOLF course. Glenview has been home to one of the area's last working farms.

Farmers first came to the area in the 1830s. John Kennicott arrived from New England in 1836 and became the first physician to practice in the area. Kennicott also ran a nursery, and in 1856 he had as many as 134 varieties of apple TREES along with various other trees and shrubs. His son, Robert, was a naturalist and explorer who traveled to Canada and Alaska under the sponsorship of institutions like the Smithsonian and the CHICAGO ACADEMY OF SCIENCES. The Kennicotts' 82-acre preserve, named the Grove and located on the village's west side on Milwaukee Avenue between Glenview Road and Lake Avenue, is a National Historic Landmark.

The village was originally called South Northfield. In 1872 the Chicago & Milwaukee RAILROAD laid a single track to the area and named the local station Glenview. A second track was added in 1892 to carry passengers to the 1893 WORLD'S COLUMBIAN EXPOSITION. In the 1890s members of the Swedenborgian Church purchased 40 acres of the Clavey farm, located at the northwest corner of Lake and Telegraph (later Glenview and Shermer Roads). They built Victorian-style homes, a clubhouse, school, and church in a secluded, wooded area which they named the Park.

In 1895 the village's residents adopted the name Glenview and in 1899 incorporated. Residents included the Swedenborgians, descendants of early YANKEE settlers, and GERMAN farmers. ROADHOUSES and inns served COMMUTERS and area residents. Two of these establishments, the Blue Heron roadhouse (later Eleanore's of Glenview) and the Glenview House, continued to operate into the twenty-first century.

In 1923 the Curtiss-Reynolds AIRPORT was built. The property was condemned in the early 1940s to make way for the GLENVIEW NAVAL AIR BASE, which eventually became the headquarters for the U.S. Naval and Marine Air Reserve Training Command. The base closed in 1995, and developers turned the site into a mixed residential and retail area. The base's golf course became part of Glenview Park District.

By 1950 the population was 6,142. In 1967 the UNIVERSITY OF ILLINOIS at Chicago purchased a five-acre parcel west of Greenwood and east of Milwaukee for use as a botanical laboratory and CONSERVATION area. Peacock Prairie, as it is called, is one of the last remnants of virgin prairie in the state of Illinois.

By 2000 there were 41,847 residents were living in the 13 square miles that covered Glenview. Kraft Foods, Zenith Electronics, and Scott, Foresman & Co. situated their headquarters here.

Marilyn Elizabeth Perry

See also: Built Environment of the Chicago Region; Metropolitan Growth; Religious Geography

Further reading: Dunbeck, Sylvia. *Great Views of Glenview: A North Suburban Village.* April 1987. • Glenview Area Historical Society. *Glenview at 75: 1899–1974.* 1974. • Glenview Bicentennial Commission. *Roots.* 1976.

Glenview Naval Air Station. During its relatively short history, Naval Air Station Glenview, as it was officially known, served several purposes. Created in 1929 as Curtiss-Reynolds Field, it was the result of the post–World War I fascination with flying. Aviation pioneer Glenn H. Curtiss and associates built it as part of a flight-training school, and the following year it was the site of the National Air Races.

The airport languished until its purchase by the navy in 1936. Little more than 200 acres in size, it functioned as a screening facility for pilot's school. During WORLD WAR II, the navy quickly bought 1,200 adjoining acres and announced that GLENVIEW would become its largest primary training base. A field in ARLINGTON HEIGHTS would serve as an initial training base. The navy invested $12.5 million in new hangars and over 12 miles of new runways.

Although Glenview ultimately produced 20,000 Navy pilots, it was best known for the training of aircraft carrier pilots. With no such ships to spare, Capt. Richard Whitehead suggested converting a pair of existing commercial ships by replacing everything above their hulls with flight decks and towers. Thus, the more than 20-year-old *Seeandbee,* once the largest passenger vessel on the Great Lakes, became the *U.S.S. Wolverine,* while the *Greater Buffalo* underwent a similar conversion to become the *U.S.S. Sable;* these were the only side-paddle-wheel aircraft carriers in naval history. Pilots took off from Glenview, used the BAHA'I Temple in WILMETTE as a visual landmark, and practiced landings and takeoffs on the ships, which were frequently stationed off the LOOP.

After the war, Naval Air Station Glenview installed some of the era's most sophisticated radar and thrived as a COLD WAR training facility. But the 1960s saw the beginning of a long, slow decline, with the base's air rescue capability emerging as an important factor in boating safety on LAKE MICHIGAN. In March 1993, Mayor Richard M. Daley suggested moving Air Force Reserve units from O'HARE to Glenview, but three months later the federal Defense Base Realignment and Closure Commission recommended that the facility be closed. Although some public officials fought to keep it open, many local interests welcomed the eventual conversion of its then 1,288 acres into housing and commercial LAND USES.

Perry R. Duis

See also: Built Environment of the Chicago Region; Fort Sheridan; Great Lakes Naval Training Station; Land Use; Transportation

Further reading: Duis, Perry, and Scott LaFrance. *We've Got a Job to Do: Chicagoans and World War II.* 1992. • Scamehorn, Howard Lee. *Balloons to Jets: A Century of Aeronautics in Illinois, 1855–1955.* 1957.

Glenwood, IL, Cook County, 23 miles S of the Loop. The suburban village of Glenwood is partly surrounded by Cook County FOREST PRESERVES. Glenwood's downtown, with its recently constructed but traditionally styled brick municipal building and relatively modest homes located along a grid of streets, seems far removed from the crowded sprawl of the surrounding suburban area.

Settlers in the 1840s called the area Hickory Bend. In 1871 the village of Glenwood was surveyed along the recently completed Chicago & Eastern Illinois RAILROAD. Glenwood served as a depot for local farmers and a home to workers employed in the railroad's nearby switch tracks, round table, and COAL yards. About 500 residents incorporated as a village in 1903.

Despite some unsuccessful subdivision activity in the 1920s, Glenwood remained a small village through the 1950s. However, nearly 3,000 homes were constructed between 1960 and 1980, when the village's population peaked at 10,538. In 2000 there were 9,000 residents in the village.

Glenwood's burst of growth in the 1960s and 1970s fostered a growing racial diversity.

In 1970 the village's residents were almost exclusively white, with fewer than 40 AFRICAN AMERICANS living in the community. By the 1980s large numbers of middle- and upper-middle-class blacks had moved to the south suburbs. Between 1980 and 1990, as the number of African Americans increased in the community, the white population defined. In 2000 there were around 4,600 white and 4,000 black residents in the village, as well as 450 Hispanics.

On average, the residents of Glenwood are somewhat more prosperous than those in the city of Chicago and in COOK COUNTY as a whole. Most of Glenwood's residents live in their own single-family detached homes. Of the 3,500 housing units in the village, fewer than 500 are rented. Unlike nearby suburbs where there has been a great deal of recent construction, there are relatively few new houses in Glenwood. Fewer than 200 houses were built in the village in the 1980s and 1990s.

Although freight train lines pass through the village, the nearest METRA rail stop is in neighboring HOMEWOOD, and fewer than 1 in 13 Glenwood residents takes PUBLIC TRANSPORTATION to work. The overwhelming majority drive to work, spending on average more than one hour per day COMMUTING.

The village is home to the privately funded Glenwood School, established in 1887 in Chicago by Robert Todd Lincoln and Oscar Dudley, with a later second campus in St. Charles. Today it is a residential school that emphasizes a military regime for boys and girls from broken or troubled low-income homes.

Glenwood is also the site of the Mount Glenwood CEMETERY, which is reputed to be the first racially integrated cemetery in the Chicago region. During the early twentieth century, African Americans traveled by train from Chicago to bury their dead in the cemetery. Notable black Chicagoans who are buried in Mount Glenwood include Elijah Muhammad, founder of the Nation of Islam, Fred Slater, Illinois' first African American circuit court judge, and Marshall "Major" Taylor, who in the 1890s was rated as the world's fastest bicyclist.

Ian McGiver

See also: Governing the Metropolis; Multicentered Chicago; Social Services

Further reading: Andreas, A. T. *History of Cook County, Illinois.* 1884.

Global Chicago. For most of human existence no city existed on the southwestern shore of LAKE MICHIGAN. Chicago arose there within the thinnest sliver of human time. But having been willed forth, Chicago became a prototypical American product, built from scratch and in a hurry, a timeball of urban dreams a mere 175 years old. And well before its own centennial, in its precocious size, itchy dynamism, and rough edges, Chicago had become what Frank Lloyd Wright called the "national capital of the essentially American spirit." As Chicago's material presence and power have grown, a parallel world has arisen to shape the outlook of its citizens, the reach of its physical prowess, and the outer bounds of its influence.

This essay maps that world by considering Chicago's role within the territorial economies of its region, the nation, and the globe, as well as its cultural institutions, intellectual creativity, and projected identity. Chicago redefined its spheres of influence, both internal and external, in five distinct but related stages.

New World Coming: 1780–1832

"Chicagou" came to life as one of several meeting points linking the diverse habitats of the GREAT LAKES with Indian portage routes to the vast Mississippi Valley. A nexus of periodic trade for centuries among Indian peoples, it acquired new meaning as European explorers, fur traders, and adventurers pounced on its regional advantages. As the FUR TRADE swelled in the late eighteenth century, Chicago formed as a loose community of Indian, FRENCH, and American traders distinguished by their long-distance ties, biracial households, and pragmatic cohabitation. It was a society dependent on consumer demand a continent and an ocean away, yet its isolation bestowed congenial self-governance upon its members.

This multiethnic world came under pressure from advancing colonial interests, reflected in the strategic establishment of FORT DEARBORN in 1803. As the fur trade declined and American settler interest grew, the small but relatively successful integrated community quickly succumbed to the relentless influx of white frontier opportunists intent on quickening the trade in European commodities and transforming the Middle West into a farmer's paradise. This world had no place for indigenes set in their ways.

Merchant Coming: 1833–1848

The city of Chicago was born on the promise of a canal capable of providing cheap transcontinental water access from LAKE MICHIGAN to the Illinois River, and whatever additional transport links might then follow. The ILLINOIS & MICHIGAN CANAL had a difficult birth, spanning a quarter century of planning, funding, and construction. Unlike the Erie Canal, Chicago's 97-mile-long waterway was built through a virtually unpopulated region, ahead of demand. Yet the canal's very imminence spurred settlement along its margins and brought hoards of speculators and capable businessmen to its Chicago terminus, many from New England and New York, with much-needed eastern capital in their pockets. Not surprisingly, then, Chicago's commercial links during the wait for the canal were primarily with the northeastern states of the Union. Most traffic came by lake, though intrepid travelers also journeyed overland through southern Michigan and northern Indiana.

A strange geometry of external relations paired this economic and cultural link to the east with political power emanating from the southern sections of Illinois, home to the governor and legislative influence over internal improvements. Little did these politicians realize how geographically lopsided the long-term benefits of canal construction would be, although Abraham Lincoln rightly stressed that any benefit for northern Illinois would indirectly aid the rest of the state. Had state representatives further south known how astounding Chicago's growth would be during the quarter century to follow, and how fatefully it would etch the social and political divide between the city and "Downstate," they would surely have hindered the canal's completion. As it was, Chicago at first developed as a terminal lake port awaiting the opening of transport avenues to the west and south, already savoring the prospect of huge increases in interregional trade. The immense confidence in the future shown by Chicago's fast-accumulating entrepreneurial class spurred speculative REAL-ESTATE bubbles of unprecedented scale, and this confidence spilled over into other BUSINESS activity.

The BUILT ENVIRONMENT of Chicago combined an odd mixture of boomtown flimsiness and incipient solidity. The former could be seen in the countless utilitarian homes and stores constructed of wood—going up by the score daily—while the latter characterized the proud new government structures, such as the courthouse, customs house, post office, and several elegant churches. Chicago built itself in the image of eastern cities of the day, full of Greek revival ARCHITECTURE and tall spires, as well as Federal-style commercial blocks that would have looked at home in Boston or Philadelphia. It was a merchant's town, focused on the business core strung along both sides of the main stem of the CHICAGO RIVER and benefiting from the federal government's financial help in straightening the river's mouth. Considering that the state canal commissioners (who controlled all canal land sales in the city environs) drew up and implemented the city plan—together with the canal works themselves, the river improvements, and the INFRASTRUCTURE provided by the establishment of federal services—one could be excused for regarding early Chicago as quite the government town. Such priming of the pump, together with the rush of private capital from outside, ensured the city's future.

Chicago possessed no clear urban margin. Land sales and lot SUBDIVISIONS were so lusty and widespread that houses and businesses tapered off indiscriminately into the countryside. Yet the place was too small and pedestrian-based to have suburbs. Chicago grew to more than 20,000 residents by 1848, a burgeoning community of new arrivals and transients preoccupied with getting and spending. Institutional development proceeded slowly, with a tilt toward commerce, especially among the NEWSPAPERS. Self-made men built mansions filled with imported exotica. More complete cultural refinement would come later.

For all the tenuous new wealth, when the canal opened and the first short railways were constructed, the physical world of Chicagoans was still decidedly local. The range of travel within a 24-hour period confined travelers to a sphere that barely penetrated the Illinois Valley and the southern districts around the base of Lake Michigan. The year 1848, however, was pivotal. The canal and first railroad west brought sudden agricultural bounty to the city from this new hinterland, and Chicago prospered as a transshipment center. This led to the formation of the Chicago Board of Trade and subsequently to its system of futures trading on wheat and corn deliveries. BALLOON FRAME CONSTRUCTION, strikingly associated with Chicago, forever changed Americans' access to inexpensive homes, and other auguries of an innovative urban environment began to make their appearance. Chicago had begun to define itself as a Midwestern metropolis, not just an Eastern reproduction.

Industrial Coming: 1848–1894

While the canal triggered Chicago's take-off to sustained growth, the concentration of long-distance RAILROADS during the 1850s, '60s, and '70s gave the city its regional power within the national economy. The railroads permitted Chicago to surpass the longer-established and proud city of St. Louis for control of trade in the great continental interior and the Far West and underwrote a dramatic industrialization of the metropolis that placed it at the forefront of American modernity by century's end. St. Louis was not the only rival; Chicago also eclipsed the older Queen City of Cincinnati and hobbled the chances of contemporary rivals such as Indianapolis and Milwaukee. St. Louis had seemed perfectly situated to serve as the central transfer point for the continental nation, but it was Chicago instead that fully grasped its own potential as the hub of western land routes and the industry-friendly water routes of the Great Lakes to the east. The radiating of trunk railroads from Chicago in all directions by the 1890s brought all manner of business to the city and gave its residents unparalleled choice in connecting with other places, making it a national center both economically and culturally. Chicagoans could now reach the bulk of the continental United States within 24 hours, a boast no other city's boosters could make.

The 1890 U.S. census listed Chicago as the country's second largest city (after New York), a fact surely attributable to Chicago's commercial ascendancy, but also to its strategic ANNEXATIONS of surrounding TOWNSHIPS during the year prior to the census. This happy conjunction of affairs was not unimportant in securing the epochal WORLD'S COLUMBIAN EXPOSITION for Chicago a mere two years later.

What the annexations only underscored, however, was the rapacious industrial development that Chicago and its outlying satellite communities had attracted by the 1890s. From the AGRICULTURAL MACHINERY industry (embodied by McCormick's reaper firm) of the late 1840s, to the giant MEATPACKING sector (the Armour and Swift companies) that emerged from the CIVIL WAR, and the manufacturing of complex machinery and railroad equipment (at George Pullman's Palace Car Company, for example) in the 1880s, Chicago industrialized on a gigantic scale. The economics of steelmaking came to favor a two-way system of IRON and COAL exchange through the Great Lakes shipping network that diffused the industry from Pennsylvania to the Middle West and to Chicago in particular. Railroads and steel undergirded a broad industrialization that transformed Chicago from a merchants' town into a metropolis of heavy industry with all its job-creating implications. Chicago became a factory city simultaneously for producer and consumer goods, which it could distribute in all directions. In 1848, Chicago had been dependent for most of its sophisticated manufactured goods on eastern imports; by the 1890s, Chicago competed with eastern centers in most categories of mass production. It was also becoming a BANKING center of national importance.

Physically, Chicago in this period developed a star pattern set within a giant wheel of satellite settlements. First, industrialization created a commuter city, a web of residential enclaves bordered by a latticework of industrial corridors, all woven together by mass transit sinews that thrust the city outwards in vectors along commuter railroad lines and selected STREETCAR routes. The railroads gave birth to bedroom suburbs strung like beads along lines out from the central city. These commuter spokes of the metropolitan wheel connected with outlying towns (WAUKEGAN, ELGIN, AURORA, JOLIET, and GARY) that had industrialized in their own right. Suburbs born on a grand scale were functionally dependent on Chicago in all but local governance, and outlying cities came within Chicago's daily orbit. A centripetal metropolitan world pulsating on a daily basis had begun to emerge.

The Great FIRE OF 1871 propelled Chicago's urban core into a modernizing mode. The center would be built with immense solidity (balloon frame wood construction had all too easily become kindling) and, increasingly, to a great height as tall buildings became technically feasible and businesses came to favor their operational efficiencies and symbolic potential. The core also gained culturally, as civic and business leaders began to create an institutional structure for arts, science, and letters through the founding of permanent performing companies (e.g., CHICAGO SYMPHONY ORCHESTRA, 1890), libraries (e.g., NEWBERRY LIBRARY, 1887; CHICAGO PUBLIC LIBRARY and CRERAR LIBRARY, 1897), museums (e.g., FIELD MUSEUM, 1894), and universities (e.g., UNIVERSITY OF CHICAGO, 1892) to humanize somewhat the raw face of this upstart behemoth. What kept the metropolis raw were the gross inequities of large-scale capital in an age of robber barons getting rich from abundant cheap labor sometimes made to work in scandalously unsafe conditions. The worker unrest of 1886 and the PULLMAN STRIKE of 1894 were explosive highpoints in a long struggle between labor and capital in Chicago that paralleled and punctuated its rise to industrial might.

Second Coming: 1894–1968

Chicago's meteoric rise to replace Philadelphia as the nation's second largest city conditioned Chicagoans to expect their city to catch up with and surpass New York in short order. And it was not simply a matter of uncontrolled boosterism. Using a heartland-rimland model of urban supremacy in the deployment of natural resources, a University of Chicago geographer confidently predicted just such an outcome in a 1926 address before the COMMERCIAL CLUB OF CHICAGO. While his predictions were not accurate, they reveal a recognition of the power of massive industrialization to propel the metropolis forward in size and complexity on the basis of coal, steel, and (later) petroleum. For the first two-thirds of the twentieth century, Chicagoans believed in the unfailing virtues of mass production in centralized facilities in central locations, and

Chicago's World—Within a Day's Travel

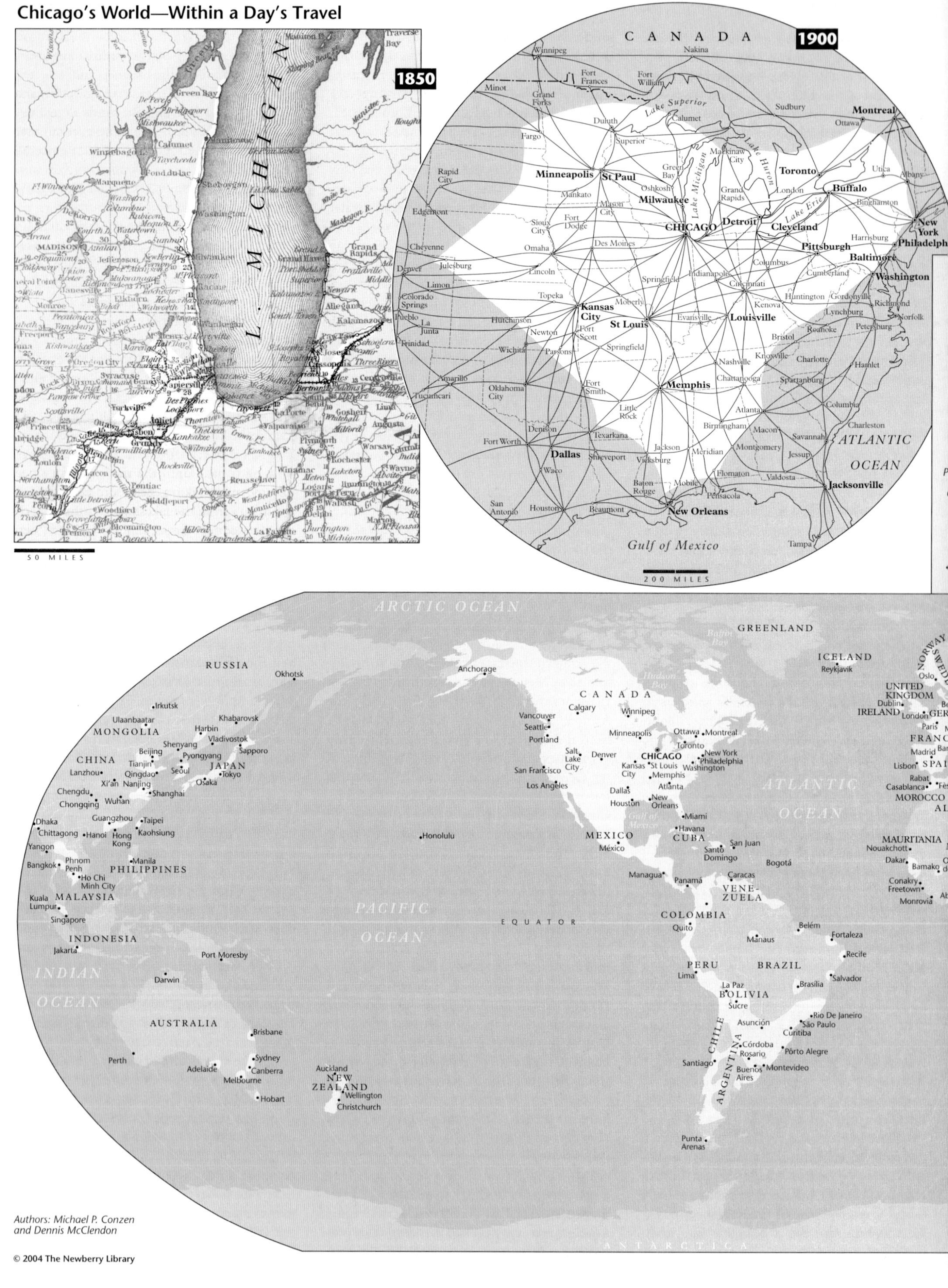

Authors: *Michael P. Conzen and Dennis McClendon*

shaped their city to proffer these conditions. Chicago became the great western anchor of a vast heavy-manufacturing belt stretching from Massachusetts to Illinois. To the west, north, and south lay the immense resource regions to supply it with raw materials—corn, wheat, cattle, LUMBER, iron ore, coal, and petroleum—with Chicago as consumer and funnel to eastern markets, as well as dispenser of manufactures to these staple-producing regions. From 1900 to 1970, Chicago functioned as a complete national-scale metropolis, with particular sway over a continental interior extending to the Rocky Mountains and beyond. By 1950, Chicagoans could travel to four continents in a single day's journey, thanks to planes and trains. New York had more international ties and better links with the national hinterland when only one extra-local connection was needed, but Chicago was its only serious competitor and trying hard to cut the margin.

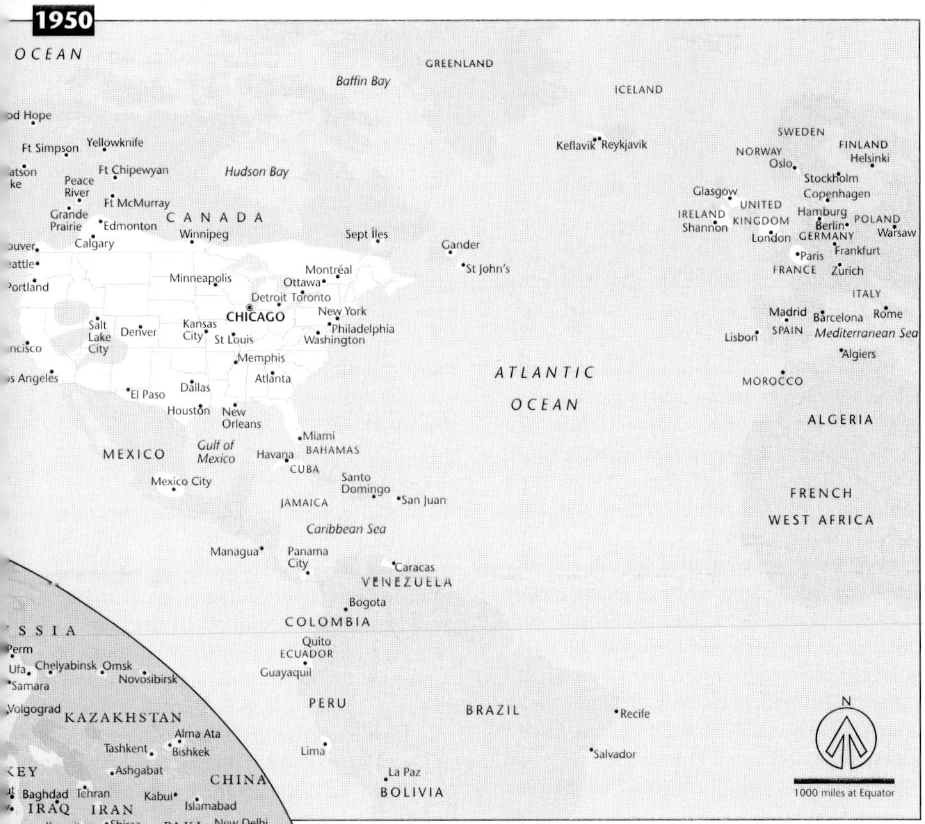

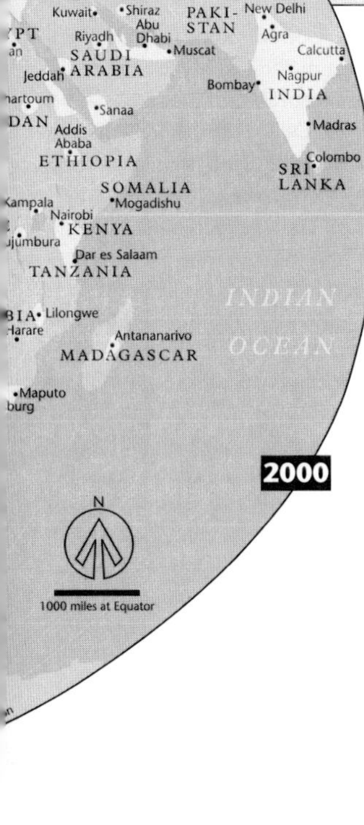

Chicago's relations with the wider world changed as its transportation links extended its geographical reach. The white areas on these four maps show how far a person could travel from Chicago by scheduled service in a 24-hour period, calculated for four dates at 50-year intervals since early in the city's history. In 1850, travel was restricted to lake and canal boat, stagecoach, and a single railroad line west of the city. Consequently, the zone of access with a day's travel reached little farther than Peoria, Milwaukee, and some other local centers within the region. By 1900, railroads had supplanted all other means of fast long-distance travel, and Chicagoans could reach most of the remainder of the United States and some parts of nearby Canada and Mexico within a day. In 1950, air service had joined railroads to extend 24-hour travel from Chicago (often in combination) to much of North and Central America, as well as some localities in Western Europe. By 2000, this combined reach, together with road service, had effectively expanded Chicago's reach to much of the rest of the well-populated world.

Chicago's world was enlarged socially, too, by the diversifying regions around the world from which it drew its new population elements. A ceaseless procession of new migrants piled into Chicago's growing factories. Eastern and Southern European immigrants streamed through East Coast ports of entry and headed straight for the capital of the midcontinent. Subsequently, AFRICAN AMERICANS headed north in unprecedented numbers from the penury of southern cotton fields. All added to an already multicultural city long dominated by YANKEES, IRISH, and GERMANS. For some from overseas, such as the SWEDES, LITHUANIANS, and DANES, Chicago became the second city for their ethnic community in the world, a veritable exclave of emigrants with new lives and new allegiances.

The world Chicagoans created in the region during this long period of industrial hegemony was characterized by rising densities in developed districts, infilling between the spokes, and aggressive expansion into the urban fringe, pushing it back until the metropolitan wheel became more like a giant crescent extending inland from the lakeshore. As the suburbs proliferated, an antiurban bias pitted them increasingly against the central city, socially and politically. The spread of the automobile offered individual freedom, until the next encounter with gridlock. Superhighways were inserted into the metropolitan frame, disrupting community life in the tight neighborhoods where EXPRESSWAYS were pushed through, while creating wholly new axes for urban development beyond the built-up zone.

Chicago flowered in this period as a center of literature, ART, design, and performance. From the novelists of the early-twentieth-century CHICAGO LITERARY RENAISSANCE to the rise of Chicago BLUES music, from the advent of the ART INSTITUTE to the rise of OPERA, BALLET, and the popularity of THEATER, Chicago invented, presented, and reconfigured its feisty urban culture to the world. Through boom and depression, peace and war, expansion and segregation, this cultural awakening created a canon of works that reflect the energetic, convoluted, contested social worlds of the time and something of the identity of the place. Above all, Chicago projected a hunger for and celebration of modernity, best captured in the technological wonders of the 1933 CENTURY OF PROGRESS EXPOSITION and the continuous record of architectural innovation from the earliest steel-skeleton SKYSCRAPERS to the Miesian lessness of slab-style architecture that culminated in the totemic Prudential Insurance Building.

But it was a fractured modernity, tolerating racial injustice, housing segregation, job discrimination, and political demagoguery. Urban PLANNING came of age, became bureaucratized, and, despite successive clarion calls for collaborative regional visions (beginning

Ticket counter for the Chicago, Burlington & Quincy Railroad's "Zephyr," Union Station, 1943. Photographer: Jack Delano. Source: Library of Congress.

most notably with Daniel Burnham), stopped, stupefied, at the municipal boundary. As suburbs prospered on Federal Housing Authority mortgage subsidies and became increasingly diverse in vision, social character, and environmental appeal, the central city inherited all the problems of an aging infrastructure, threatened tax base, and divided people. Moreover, the connected city was also the visible city: the 1968 Democratic National Convention gave the world an eyeful of America's social cleavages and provided a glimpse of Chicago's unsettled world.

Global Coming: 1969–2004

The world has been globalizing for centuries, but only since the 1970s has electronic connectivity gone meaningfully global for businesses and individuals. In this human environment, with its boundless competition for resources and markets, cities must strive to be global in their connections, if not always in assets and urban reputation. Chicago ranks with New York and Los Angeles as one of the world's 10 "alpha" cities in most inventories of global economic hipness. This status has been earned through a combination of old-fashioned, cumulative development of economic and social infrastructure critical to international operations, as well as through painful readjustments in the last three decades of the twentieth century to metropolitan deindustrialization, particularly severe in the central city. While industrial loss afflicted the "Rustbelt" as a whole, Chicago emerged tolerably well to compete in a new environment of diversified, globally positioned, high-tech industries, as well as to develop its financial and corporate services institutions. While losing much of its banking independence, Chicago sought to buttress its role as a home to international corporate headquarters. New York far outdistances Chicago in this field, but the move of the Boeing Company to Chicago in 2001 suggested the city's continuing viability at the highest levels of global business support.

In a world in which individuals can communicate via satellite signals with others almost anywhere in the world, the reach that a traveler can personally extend around the world in 24 hours remains a measure of social and societal significance. In 2000, such a traveler from Chicago could penetrate all six settled continents (although by no means reach all other important cities). Air travel has become an American norm for global and interregional movement, and Chicago's possession of strategic and busy (sometimes too busy) O'HARE INTERNATIONAL AIRPORT has been key to its global connectedness.

Whether or not Chicago has reached a stage of "postmodernity," the metropolitan crescent has become an ever-farther-flung web of regional settlement. Exurbs—residential subdivisions sitting amid cornfields with no visible support from nearby urban services—scatter across the countryside one hundred miles from downtown Chicago and send commuters to the outer fringes of the metropolitan employment web. Frequent direct daily express bus service connects residents of Madison, Wisconsin, and central northern Indiana with flights leaving from O'Hare Airport. Five million suburbanites inhabit the margins of Chicago, which struggles to retain and add to its own three million residents. This world is one of ever greater anonymity, congestion amid sprawl, efforts to maintain costly infrastructure, and strangely skewed or nonexistent conversations among communities, political and cultural, in the metropolitan web, as parochial worlds seek distance from one another's problems.

As Chicago's suburbs have aged, the central city has learned at least some lessons in recapitalizing the built environment. Something of a renaissance has taken hold in Chicago's public governance, approach to services, and official outlook on city viability and livability. That renaissance has been driven at least in part by DEMOGRAPHIC changes that occasionally transform minorities into majorities. But it has also been driven by a certain discipline imposed by global competitiveness to put on an attractive face for visiting conventioneers, TOURISTS, and other contributors to the urban economy. The city has become festooned with wrought-iron fences, median planters, and other elaborate street furniture, as well as spectacular nighttime lighting effects on tall buildings and other landmarks. GENTRIFICATION and new-town-in-town developments have penetrated large swaths of the once-tired urban core, crossed racial lines, and received municipal support through tax abatements and the effective PRIVATIZATION of neighborhood street parking.

Retrospect

Chicago's world has expanded exponentially over time, in physical, psychological, symbolic, and practical ways. The metropolitan "neighborhood" of greater Chicago has more people crammed in and strewn about than ever before; they move about with greater speed and frequency; there are vastly more things to acquire and aspire to; there is more choice of what to do and what to be interested in—and greater difficulty in comprehending the complexity of it all. Psychological time and distance and the pace of life have been redefined many times. Contemporary Chicagoans are worlds away from their predecessors, even those just a few generations back. Could Jean Baptiste Point DuSable, the I&M Canal Commissioners, Marshall Field, Jane Addams, Theodore Dreiser, and Anton Cermak possibly have imagined the character of Chicago as it existed at the opening of the twenty-first century? How much more difficult is it to realistically imagine the Chicago world they inhabited?

Michael P. Conzen

See also: Chicago Studied: Social Scientists and Their City; Commodities Markets; Commuting; Economic Geography; Food Processing: Regional and National Market; Land Use; Metropolitan Growth; Religion, Chicago's Influence on; Transportation; Wholesaling

Further reading: Belcher, Wyatt Winton. *The Economic Rivalry between St. Louis and Chicago, 1850–1880.* 1947. • Goode, J. Paul. *The Geographic Background of Chicago.* 1926. • Mayer, Harold M. "The Changing Role of Metropolitan Chicago in the Midwest and the Nation." *Bulletin of the Illinois Geographical Society* 17.1 (1975): 3–13.

Godley, IL, Will County, 55 miles SW of the Loop. Situated between Will and Grundy counties, Godley first developed as a coal mining town and incorporated in 1888. In 1988 Commonwealth Edison opened nuclear power plants in nearby Braidwood.

Erik Gellman

See also: Gas and Electricity

Further reading: Sterling, Robert G. *Pictorial History of Will County.* 1975.

Gold Coast, neighborhood in the Near North Side Community Area. "Gold Coast" refers to a stretch of expensive lakefront property occupied by the city's wealthiest residents. Because it was isolated from the downtown business district, only a few wealthy families, including the Cyrus McCormicks, the Potter Palmers, and the Joseph T. Ryersons, lived here before the construction of the Michigan Avenue Bridge in 1920.

The opening of the bridge brought the development of Michigan Avenue as a luxury shopping district. A new architectural form, the luxury apartment building, sprang up in the area, dispelling fears that apartment dwellers had to be poor. Some of Chicago's elite took up residence in new residential hotels such as the Drake. The district became the heart of the upper crust of Chicago society. Sociologist Harvey Warren Zorbaugh, who claimed that college boys returning from the East Coast dubbed the area the "Gold Coast," immortalized it in *The Gold Coast and the Slum.* The density of wealth in the Gold Coast buffered it against the deterioration that threatened other portions of the North Side in the 1950s. Developer Arthur Rubloff's projects, particularly the revitalization of the Magnificent Mile and Sandburg Village, sparked a new round of investment that protected the Gold Coast through the end of the twentieth century.

Amanda Seligman

See also: Metropolitan Growth; Studying Chicago; Urban Renewal

Further reading: Zorbaugh, Harvey Warren. *The Gold Coast and the Slum: A Sociological Study of Chicago's Near North Side.* 1929.

Gold Coast aerial view, 1929. Photographer: Underwood & Underwood. Source: The Newberry Library.

Golf. Upper-class Easterners and Midwesterners founded the first permanent golf courses and country clubs in the late 1880s. Metropolitan Chicago was ideally suited for golf. Its booming economy provided an economic and social elite with the leisure time and wealth to pursue the game, and its network of commuter railroads provided easy access to the proliferating number of suburban country clubs.

Stockbroker Charles Blair Macdonald, who learned to play while attending the University of St. Andrews in Scotland, played an especially important role in shaping the nature of the game both locally and nationally. After creating the nation's first 18-hole course in Belmont in 1893 for Chicago Golf Club, he sculpted a more challenging 18 holes for the club in Wheaton. Widely acknowledged as America's best, the new course hosted the third U.S. Open and Amateur championships in 1897; it was the venue for two of the first six opens as well as a third in 1911, when John McDermott became the first American-born winner. In 1907, the Chicago Golf Club hosted the ninth U.S. Women's Amateur Championship.

Macdonald joined members of four equally exclusive eastern clubs in December 1894 to form the United States Golf Association (USGA). He won the association's first U.S. Amateur in 1895 and, as an officer, was instrumental in making the USGA the acknowledged national governing body of golf.

Ironically, after Macdonald moved to New York in 1900, the Western Golf Association (WGA), founded by 15 Chicago clubs in April 1899 to protect "the best interests of the clubs of the Middle West," became the only challenger to the "eastern" USGA's authority over rules and competitions before admitting defeat in the 1920s. The WGA remained the nation's second most prestigious association, and, for many years, its Western Open and Western Amateur ranked only behind their USGA counterparts in importance. Thanks to Chicago's legendary amateur Charles E. "Chick" Evans, Jr., who won both the U.S. Open and Amateur in 1916, the WGA has made its greatest contribution by administering the Evans Scholars Foundation,

Golfers at Midlothian Golf Club, 1907. Photographer: Unknown. Source: Chicago Historical Society.

established in 1929 to fund college scholarships for caddies.

Following the nationwide golf boom of the 1920s, golf in Chicago, as elsewhere, suffered from the GREAT DEPRESSION and WORLD WAR II. Many private courses folded and war rationing brought equipment shortages, "fairway gardens," and transportation problems. Chicago, however, stood at the forefront of a new boom that began in the 1950s. George S. May's World Championship at Tam O'Shanter became the PGA tour's richest event and in 1953 the first golf tournament to be televised nationally.

By the 1990s new suburban residential golf communities lured wealthy baby-boomers while Chicago remained unequaled in the combined quality and quantity of its older private clubs—eight area clubs, more than in any other state, had hosted a total of 12 U.S. Opens. Chicago was now most significant as the leader in public-access golf. Public courses, many among the best in America, constituted well over half of the estimated 275 courses in the metropolitan area. The Chicago PARK DISTRICT owned six courses, including JACKSON PARK, which opened in 1899 on landfill from the World's Fair and was the first public course in the Midwest, and suburban municipalities and park districts operated several others. The jewels of public golf were often privately owned.

What Macdonald had done for the world of private golf, Chicago pro Joe Jemsek did for twentieth-century public golf. The son of Russian immigrants, Jemsek purchased St. Andrews Country Club in 1939, determined to provide private course conditions for public course players. He continued to buy, sell, and build high-quality public courses, capped by the opening in 1967 of Dubsdread, his fourth course at suburban Cog Hill in LEMONT. By the mid-1990s he owned seven courses, and similar "upscale" public courses were spreading throughout the country. Chicago courses of this type and those elsewhere benefited from a nationwide controversy over the restrictive membership policies of many private clubs, which, for example, cost Chicago Golf Club the 1993 Walker Cup. In 1991, Dubsdread became the permanent home of the Western Open, after it was moved from the all-male Butler National; earlier, local insurance executive James Kemper had secured the 1989 PGA Championship for his public Kemper Lakes in LONG GROVE, one of several area courses operated by Kemper Sports Management.

Despite the profusion of courses, however, metropolitan Chicago, with more than 850,000 golfers, was still well below the national average for courses per golfer.

Howard N. Rabinowitz

Further reading: Eberl, George. "Chicago: A Major American Home for Golf." *Golf Journal* 42 (May/June 1990): 25–29. • Rabinowitz, Howard. "Golf's Aspiring Autocrat [C. B. Macdonald]." *Golf Journal* 48 (May 1996): 36–39. • Wind, Herbert Warren. *The Story of American Golf.* 1975.

Golf, IL, Cook County, 14 miles NW of the Loop. Located near GLENVIEW, the village of Golf owes its existence—and its name—to its proximity to the Glen View Country Club, which was founded in 1897. Like other late-nineteenth-century GOLF clubs, Glen View had an elite membership which was drawn to its suburban location by either private or public TRANSPORTATION. Initially, Glen View was particularly difficult to reach, requiring "a long bumpy ride by horse-drawn public bus, carriage or horseback." One member, however, Albert J. Earling, president of the Chicago, Milwaukee & St. Paul RAILROAD, took his company's rails from his downtown office and arranged to have his private car switch to a siding near the club, where he was picked up by a carriage. Other members began using Earling's siding, which soon became a regular stop known as Golf.

A small settlement grew around the site and in 1928 was incorporated as the village of Golf. The Western Golf Association, the nation's second most important amateur golf association, after the United States Golf Association, soon moved its headquarters from downtown Chicago to the village's all-purpose post office. From there it ran tournaments and the Evans Scholars Foundation.

The village enjoyed a minor boom in the 1920s as the open farmlands once owned by John Dewes were bought by developers and subdivided into spacious residential lots. Growth then slowed, however, and by the 1990s the village was a half-mile-square, upper-middle-class enclave divided largely into half-acre lots with houses of stone facades and shingled roofs. "We're more like a small town somewhere in the middle of Kansas," as one longtime resident put it. Its population of 454 in 1990 was 98.9 percent white, with no blacks. It had a median age of 40.5, and its per capita income of over $48,000 placed it ninth out of 263 in the six-county Chicago area. Protected from the mushrooming growth of its surrounding northwestern suburbs, Golf's one concession to modern living was an upgrade of about 75 percent of the village's sewer and water system. Otherwise it remained a bastion of limited government. Most village officials are volunteers, and the village obtains essential services through contracts with its neighbors.

Howard N. Rabinowitz

See also: Government, Suburban; Leisure; Metropolitan Growth

Further reading: Hanley, Reid. "Token Players." *Golf Journal* (June 1997): 25–30. • Reich, Howard. "The Suburb That Growth Forgot." *Chicago Tribune*, January 16, 1993.

Good Government Movements. Renowned for its Democratic machine politics, twentieth-century Chicago has often seemed barren ground for good government reformers. Yet the good government movement has played a significant role in city politics, occasionally exercising considerable influence. Dedicated to honesty and efficiency and strongly suspicious of local party organizations, good government groups have endeavored to cleanse city hall and offer an alternative to rule by venal politicians.

The good government spirit, for example, manifested itself in the 1870s. Responding to the city fire department's ineffectiveness in fighting a devastating blaze in 1874, a group of concerned Chicago businessmen organized the Citizens' Association. According to its constitution, this organization sought "to insure a more perfect administration in our municipal affairs" and "to protect citizens . . . against the evils of careless or corrupt legislation." An organ for businessmen who sought "businesslike" government, the Citizens' Association would remain an active civic watchdog, dedicated especially to protecting the city treasury from the profligate and corrupt.

In the 1890s a new wave of disgust with Chicago city government spawned additional good government groups. A notorious band of aldermen known as the Gray Wolves were awarding public utility franchises in exchange for handsome bribes. Moreover, British reformer William Stead's If Christ Came to

Municipal election campaign poster, 1894. Source: Chicago Historical Society.

Chicago, published in 1894, embarrassed Chicagoans by exposing their indifference to the political corruption and social injustice in their midst. Organized in 1894, the Civic Federation of Chicago at first was intended to spark a wide-ranging civic revival and improve the political, philanthropic, educational, and moral health of the city. It became, however, primarily another fiscal watchdog, dedicated to honest and efficient government.

Recognizing the need for further action, reformers in 1896 organized the Municipal Voters League with the specific purpose of ousting the Gray Wolves from power. Headed by the energetic George Cole, this organization published the credentials of aldermanic candidates and the voting records of incumbents. It endorsed candidates who pledged to support the merit system of civil service and who promised to grant public utility franchises only to companies willing to adequately compensate the city. In the municipal elections of the late 1890s and early 1900s, the Municipal Voters League proved so successful in electing its approved candidates to the city council that muckraker Lincoln Steffens could proclaim that Chicago had a lesson to teach cities throughout the nation.

Other good government groups appeared in the early 1900s, most notably the City Club founded in 1903 and the Bureau of Public Efficiency organized in 1910 and headed by Sears magnate Julius Rosenwald. In 1911 University of Chicago professor Charles Merriam rallied reform forces in an inspiring but unsuccessful race for the mayor's office.

By the early 1920s, however, Republican Mayor William Hale Thompson had largely expunged the city's reputation for good government and the Municipal Voters League was only a shadow of its former self. Good government forces rallied momentarily in 1923, endorsing the successful mayoral candidate, William Dever. Yet after four years of honest, effective rule, Dever failed to win reelection, losing to Thompson. In the 1920s as in earlier decades, the panaceas of sober upper-middle-class good government reformers did not appeal to many working-class ethnics, who trusted their local ward boss more than the Civic Federation business leaders, and who found more solace in the corner saloon than in the high-minded settlement house. Moreover, the Great Depression of the 1930s took its toll on the good government movement. In 1932 the debt-ridden Bureau of Efficiency ceased its independent existence, merging with the still-solvent Civic Federation.

In succeeding decades, the Democratic party organization consolidated its grip on Chicago and was only periodically bothered by good government movements. From 1947 to 1955 Mayor Martin Kennelly served as an ineffectual good government front for the temporarily weakened Democratic organization, and in 1955 Charles Merriam's son Robert ran unsuccessfully for mayor as a reform alternative to the Cook County Democratic chairman Richard J. Daley. Alderman Mathias "Paddy" Bauler summed up the prevailing political climate of the mid-twentieth century when he observed, "Chicago ain't ready for reform yet." From the sidelines, businessmen in the Civic Federation continued to comment on the city's expenditures and urged a streamlined, efficient administration, but through the 1970s the Democratic organization ruled.

Jon C. Teaford

See also: Governing the Metropolis; League of Women Voters; Political Culture

Further reading: Roberts, Sidney I. "The Municipal Voters' League and Chicago's Boodlers." *Journal of the Illinois State Historical Society* 53 (Summer 1960): 117–148. • Steffens, Lincoln. *The Shame of the Cities*. 1904. • Sutherland, Douglas. *Fifty Years on the Civic Front*. 1943.

Goodman Theatre. The city's oldest and largest not-for-profit theater originated in 1922, when the parents of Kenneth Sawyer Goodman, a Chicago playwright who died of influenza while in the army in World War I, sent a letter to the trustees of the Art Institute proposing a theater at the rear of the museum as a memorial to their son. Three years later, a professional repertory company opened the auditorium, designed by Howard Van Doren Shaw.

After founding director Thomas Wood Stevens left in 1930, the professional company was dissolved, but the school of drama Stevens had established was continued and student productions took over the Goodman stage. In 1957, however, the newly hired John Reich, a Viennese teacher and director, mingled professional with student actors; and in 1969, Reich set up a fully professional THEATER COMPANY. In 1977, having divorced itself from the school (which moved to DEPAUL UNIVERSITY), the Goodman formed its own board, the Chicago Theatre Group.

The era of William Woodman, Reich's successor in 1973, was marked by the emergence of Chicago playwright David Mamet, whose *American Buffalo* had its premiere at Goodman's Stage 2 in 1975 in a production directed by Gregory Mosher, who would succeed Woodman as artistic director in 1978. In 1984 the Mamet-Mosher collaboration climaxed with the American premiere of the Pulitzer Prize–winning *Glengarry Glen Ross*.

With Mosher's departure to New York, artistic leadership in 1986 went to Robert Falls, a star of the city's burgeoning off-Loop theater scene. His tenure was highlighted by a landmark 1998 revival of Arthur Miller's *Death of a Salesman* and by plans for the theater to move in 2000 from the Art Institute to a new North LOOP complex on Dearborn Street.

Richard Christiansen

See also: Playwriting; Theater Training

Further reading: Goodman Theatre. *Again the Curtain Rises: A Pictorial History of Goodman Theatre Productions, 1925–1985.* 1985. • Ryan, Sheila. *At the Goodman Theatre: An Exhibition in Celebration of the Sixtieth Anniversary of Chicago's Oldest Producing Theatre, October 12, 1985–January 11, 1986.* 1985.

Goose Island, neighborhood in the Near North Side Community Area. William B. Ogden created Goose Island in the 1850s when he had a canal cut across the meandering path of the CHICAGO RIVER's North Branch approximately from North Avenue to Chicago Avenue. The WATERFRONT sites drew noisome industries, including tanneries, BREWERIES, and soap factories. Some IRISH factory workers took up residence on the island, which took its name from the geese they kept. In the 1890s, a few POLISH workers made their homes there, but Goose Island's 160 acres were primarily industrial.

In the late twentieth century, Goose Island's industries declined. Rising land values in the NEAR NORTH SIDE and nearby LINCOLN PARK prompted speculation over transforming the vacant factories into luxury residential lofts. In 1990, however, Mayor Richard M. Daley declared Goose Island the city's first Protected Manufacturing District.

Amanda Seligman

See also: Air Quality; Chemicals; Land Use; Leather and Tanning; Waste Disposal

Further reading: Winslow, Charles S. *Historic Goose Island.* 1938. Typescript. Newberry Library.

Gospel. Gospel music, a uniquely American style of religious song, can trace its roots to American FOLK MUSIC, African American spirituals, and early BLUES and JAZZ. Gospel lyrics resemble evangelism or sermonizing. The texts are drawn largely from evangelical hymns which are combined with melodies taken from popular musical styles of the early twentieth century.

In Chicago, Thomas Andrew Dorsey dominated the beginnings of gospel music. Dorsey, widely known as the "Father of Gospel Music," composed many of the most celebrated gospel songs, including "(There'll Be) Peace in the Valley (for Me)," "I'm Going to Live the Life I Sing About in My Song," and "Take My Hand, Precious Lord." Although Dorsey never claimed credit for creating the genre of gospel music, he stated that he coined the phrase "gospel songs" in the early 1920s, giving a name to the new musical style.

Dorsey was born at the turn of the twentieth century in a small, rural town outside Atlanta, Georgia. In 1919, in the midst of the GREAT MIGRATION of AFRICAN AMERICANS from the South to the cities of the North, he moved to Chicago. While much of his earliest musical training had been of a religious nature, Dorsey was also very familiar with blues and jazz, the new musical styles developing in the South. Shortly after settling in Chicago, Dorsey combined his knowledge of blues and jazz music with religious lyrics and began promoting his gospel songs.

In late 1931, Dorsey, Magnolia Lewis Butts, and Theodore Roosevelt Frye assembled the first gospel choir in Chicago at Ebenezer Baptist Church. The popularity of this choir

Promotional flyer for Spells Brothers Gospel Singers (no date). Photographer: Unknown. Source: Chicago Historical Society.

sparked the growth of gospel groups in African American churches throughout the city. Dorsey quickly moved on to form and direct a gospel choir at Pilgrim Baptist Church on South Indiana Avenue. He was the director of the Pilgrim gospel choir for nearly 60 years.

Dorsey was also instrumental in founding the National Convention of Gospel Choirs and Choruses (NCGCC), which was headquartered in Chicago. The NCGCC was held each year to teach choirs from all over the country how to sing gospel music. The first convention was held at Pilgrim Baptist Church in 1933 with Dorsey as its president. He remained president of the NCGCC until his death in 1993.

Other composers and performers who contributed to Chicago's role in the evolution of gospel music include Mahalia Jackson, Roberta Martin, Sallie Martin, and Kenneth Morris. Chicago was also home to many of the largest gospel MUSIC PUBLISHING houses. In addition to Dorsey's own publishing house, the Bowles Music House, Inc., owned by Lillian Bowles, and the Martin and Morris Music Studio, Inc., which was co-owned by Sallie Martin and Kenneth Morris, were also located in Chicago.

Gradually, new composers replaced the blues and jazz influences with more contemporary musical styles. Hip-Hop, RAP, and R&B influenced many late-twentieth-century gospel music composers. Since 1985, both traditional and contemporary gospel styles have been celebrated each summer during GospelFest, Chicago's annual salute to gospel music.

John Russick

See also: Chicago Sound; Ethnic Music; Religion, Chicago's Influence on; Sacred Music

Further reading: Boyer, Horace Clarence. *How Sweet the Sound: The Golden Age of Gospel.* 1995. • Harris, Michael W. *The Rise of Gospel Blues: The Music of Thomas Andrew Dorsey in the Urban Church.* 1994. • Heilbut, Anthony. *The Gospel Sound: Good News and Bad Times.* 1971.

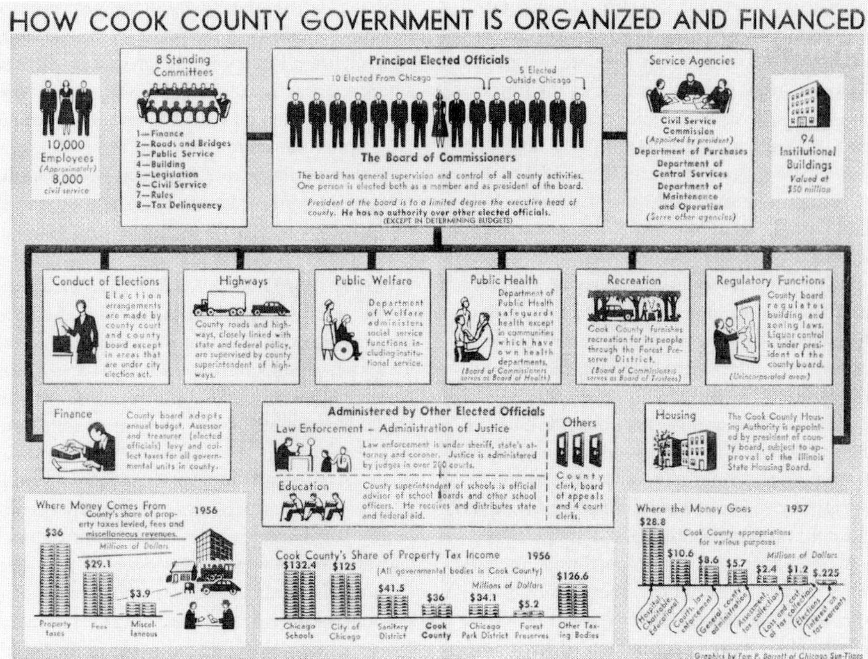

From *This Is Cook County,* published by the League of Women Voters in 1958. Creator: Tom P. Barrett, *Chicago Sun-Times*. Source: The Newberry Library.

Governing the Metropolis. To many people, particularly those interested in rational and efficient planning in local GOVERNMENT, metropolitan Chicago's numerous and diverse governmental bodies are hampered by considerable overlap in jurisdiction and, at times, seemingly unmanageable chaos. With 269 municipal (city and village) governments, 113 TOWNSHIP governments, 6 county governments, 558 SPECIAL DISTRICT authorities (including 306 public SCHOOL DISTRICTS), Chicago government seems to represent an inefficient use of its taxpayers' funds. This complex web of governance, however, is not unique; major metropolitan areas across the United States have comparable structures. Furthermore, the current system has roots and reasons dating back to the city's founding, yoking the city's present to its own and the nation's past.

Each of the four general categories of government units in the Chicago metropolitan area has authority over a separate jurisdiction. Municipal governments have the widest-ranging powers, providing, among other things, law enforcement, public HOSPITALS, and traffic supervision. TOWNSHIP governments provide services for small populations in unincorporated areas. The three principal functions of township governments are to maintain roads, assess property taxes, and administer general assistance programs.

The six county governments within the Chicago metropolitan area—COOK, DUPAGE, KANE, LAKE, MCHENRY, and WILL—have jurisdiction over decisions within their own county, including the upkeep of roads and the administration of budgets. As the largest county in the state, Cook County has many special powers as well as a unique form of administration, including a county board and a president with broad-ranging powers.

A multitude of special-purpose authorities deal with the issues and problems that cross city and county boundaries, such as parks, sanitation, and SCHOOLS. Each district body regulates a single area of activity, such as mosquito abatement districts and airport districts. Most have the authority both to levy taxes and to disburse funds within their jurisdiction.

The metropolitan area's governing agencies owe their inception to the powers of the Illinois State Legislature, the state's principal governing body. Like other states, Illinois has followed the general rule regarding local-state relations first articulated by Iowa Supreme Court Justice John F. Dillon in 1868. Dillon argued that "municipal corporations owe their origins, and derive their powers and rights wholly from the legislature," which means that in all matters affecting local government in Illinois, the state remains the final arbiter. In the early twentieth century, as cities grew in size, the issue of HOME RULE became more and more contentious between states and their largest cities. Illinois state law was specifically designed to limit the flexibility that larger municipalities—particularly Chicago—could exercise in governing their own jurisdictions. Many of the battles between state and city came down to a battle between the interests of rural legislators and those of urban officials. More often than not, states won. And if their victories came before the Illinois Supreme Court—itself dominated by men of rural backgrounds—they were usually upheld.

The 1970 Illinois Constitutional Convention reformed the 1870 constitution in a number of important ways. The new constitution permitted cities to exercise far more power than they had in the past, including more home rule authority. The 1970 convention also ruled that localities could join together to solve common problems, establishing a basis for metropolitan cooperation.

Although different local entities have different sources of funding (including state and federal dollars), property taxes provide the largest single funding source, particularly for counties, special-purpose districts, and school districts. Illinois ranks ninth in the country in the proportion of revenue it secures through property taxes. As of 1990, the property tax furnished 92 percent of the funding for public school districts and 63 percent of the funding for counties. Municipalities received 35 percent of their funding from property taxes and another 26 percent from local sales taxes. Accordingly, counties and school districts with large numbers of wealthy residents enjoyed more and better services than their poorer counterparts. In 1997, the extreme disparity in resources available to rich and poor school districts prompted Governor James Edgar to attempt a major reform of public-school funding patterns. He did not succeed.

Chicago governance has been influenced not only by local questions and specific personalities—especially powerful MAYORS—but also by the same broad influences found in virtually every American city. Though American laws and institutions borrowed liberally from English traditions, they evolved differently. The central governments of Great Britain and much of continental Europe consolidated their power over the course of the eighteenth and nineteenth centuries and have come to exercise a general hegemony over local authorities. The birth of the United States and its revolutionary rupture from Great Britain, on the other hand, gave colonists a reason to distrust centralized political authority from the start. Their distrust became embodied in the U.S. Constitution's emphasis on the rights of states and the protection of individuals.

As the nation's population grew, spread out, and established new settlements in the nineteenth century, questions of legal authority arose with increasing frequency. Legal precedent permitted citizens, sometimes groups of less than a few hundred, to incorporate themselves into towns and villages to pursue common projects and their own needs. The basic framework of a municipal corporation (a sovereign body of local residents) and the municipal CHARTER was adopted almost everywhere in the United States at different times and in slightly different ways, but state legislatures usually kept the lion's share of power for themselves.

Residents who had settled permanently in Chicago lobbied the state legislature for permission to incorporate themselves as a city in 1837. The legislature agreed, granting city dwellers a municipal charter that guaranteed them certain legal powers, including a municipal government with a mayor and common council, a municipal court, and limited taxing power over local residents. Demands for new charters arose as residents sought to exercise more power over local areas and as the city sought to extend the boundaries of its jurisdiction; additional municipal charters were granted in 1853, 1857, and 1861. But the 1870 Illinois Constitutional Convention reserved most authority over local matters to the state legislature, severely limiting what municipalities themselves could do. Chicagoans thus enjoyed fewer legal powers than city dwellers in states such as neighboring Wisconsin, whose state legislature had begun giving its larger cities more autonomy.

As the population of Chicago grew, more and more people moved from the downtown area to outlying districts. Small towns and villages, including HYDE PARK and EVANSTON, sprung up in the 1860s and 1870s. With the inception of rail lines fanning outwards from the core city, the growth of fringe (or suburban) areas increased measurably. In the 1870s and 1880s future neighborhoods such as RAVENSWOOD began developing along the rail lines. Some suburban areas, like AUSTIN and PULLMAN, grew as a result of the industries located nearby. By 1880 there were more than 35 outlying villages and towns in Cook County alone, and another 15 were added over the next two decades. Toward the end of the nineteenth century new villages took shape along the northern border of Chicago.

As the towns and villages bordering Chicago developed, they incorporated themselves and won their own municipal charters. At the same time, growing problems involving residents across multiple towns and villages necessitated broader governing bodies. But the Illinois Constitution did not permit localities the freedom to arrange cooperative agreements with other municipal governments, leaving regional governing bodies to deal with specific issues and problems. For instance, the Metropolitan Sanitary District of Chicago was created by the state legislature in 1889, and though its purpose was to direct Chicago-area sewage from LAKE MICHIGAN and thereby protect the local WATER supply, it eventually came to regulate the water supply for much of the region.

In the 1880s and 1890s, Chicago's population—like that of cities across the country—exploded, growing from 112,172 people in 1860 to 1,698,575 in 1900. The city sought to annex many of its adjacent territories, sometimes because residents of the adjacent areas wanted to secure the services provided by the city, other times because ANNEXATION just seemed to make sense for the region. Between 1837 and 1869, 25 square miles of land were annexed to the city.

Increasingly, though, adjacent areas resisted annexation. Sometimes their residents had fled the city precisely because they no longer wished to be a part of it; some even viewed the city as the den of all evil—including booze and bad politics. Efforts to annex Hyde Park succeeded in 1887 only to be overturned by the Illinois Supreme Court in 1888. A critical juncture was reached a year later when the proponents of annexation won a major victory in the state legislature. Overnight, the city of Chicago expanded from 43 square miles to 168 square miles, added 225,000 residents, and, with a population that now exceeded one million residents, became one of the largest cities in America.

Annexations continued over the next couple of decades. By 1925 the city of Chicago covered 200 square miles, with an estimated three million residents. But many suburbs continued to oppose annexation, and over the next 30 years only 20 square miles were added to the city's jurisdictional territory. The metropolitan region became dotted with more and more small municipalities. Township authorities came to govern those areas, such as EVANSTON, where a small number of residents had scattered across a large site.

By the 1930s, the Chicago metropolitan area was governed by more than one thousand different bodies. In addition to the governments of the city of Chicago and the nearby cities, villages, and towns, there were county governments and special-purpose districts, including PARK DISTRICTS, FOREST PRESERVE districts, and sanitary districts. To many local scholars, such as the renowned UNIVERSITY OF CHICAGO political scientist Charles Merriam, the increasing number of governing bodies seemed to pose a threat to order and efficiency in the region. Among other things, he observed, the population ringing Chicago was growing much faster than the city itself, making it hard to meet the needs of those residents. His suggestions for reform fell on deaf ears.

METROPOLITAN GROWTH continued over the next few decades. Where RAILROADS had once fed outward residential development and the growth of COMMUTING between suburb and city, now the newly constructed network of STREETS AND HIGHWAYS crisscrossing the region fed the process. Between 1940 and 1950, the city grew 6.6 percent, from 3,396,808 to 3,620,962, while Cook County grew by 11 percent, to 4,508,792.

The collar counties were growing even faster. With each new block of residents who settled outside the city came new needs, and with the growth of such needs, new municipalities were established along with new special-purpose districts and school districts. Nothing could stop the flow of residents, just as nothing could halt the proliferation of different governing bodies.

In the early 1950s, another effort was made in Chicago as in many American metropolitan areas to create order out of the patchwork quilt of disparate, sometimes overlapping forms of governance. Illinois State Representative Paul Randolph successfully persuaded the state legislature to create a commission, known as the Randolph Commission, to study problems of city governance. The main product of the commission was the 1957 creation of a state advisory agency for the region, the Northeastern Illinois Metropolitan Area Planning Commission, or NIPC. The legislature charged the commission to provide PLANNING assistance

County Boundaries in the Chicago Area

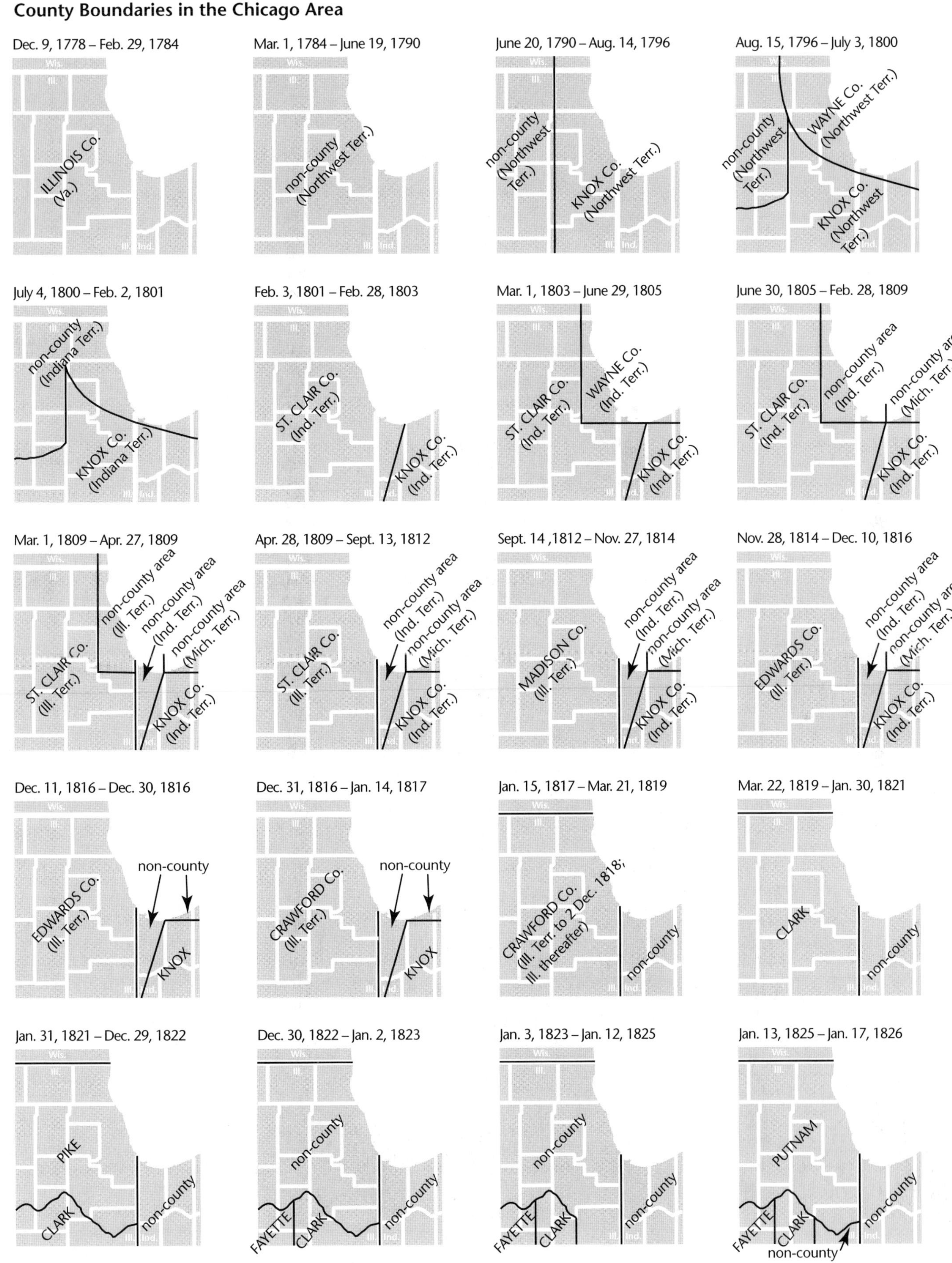

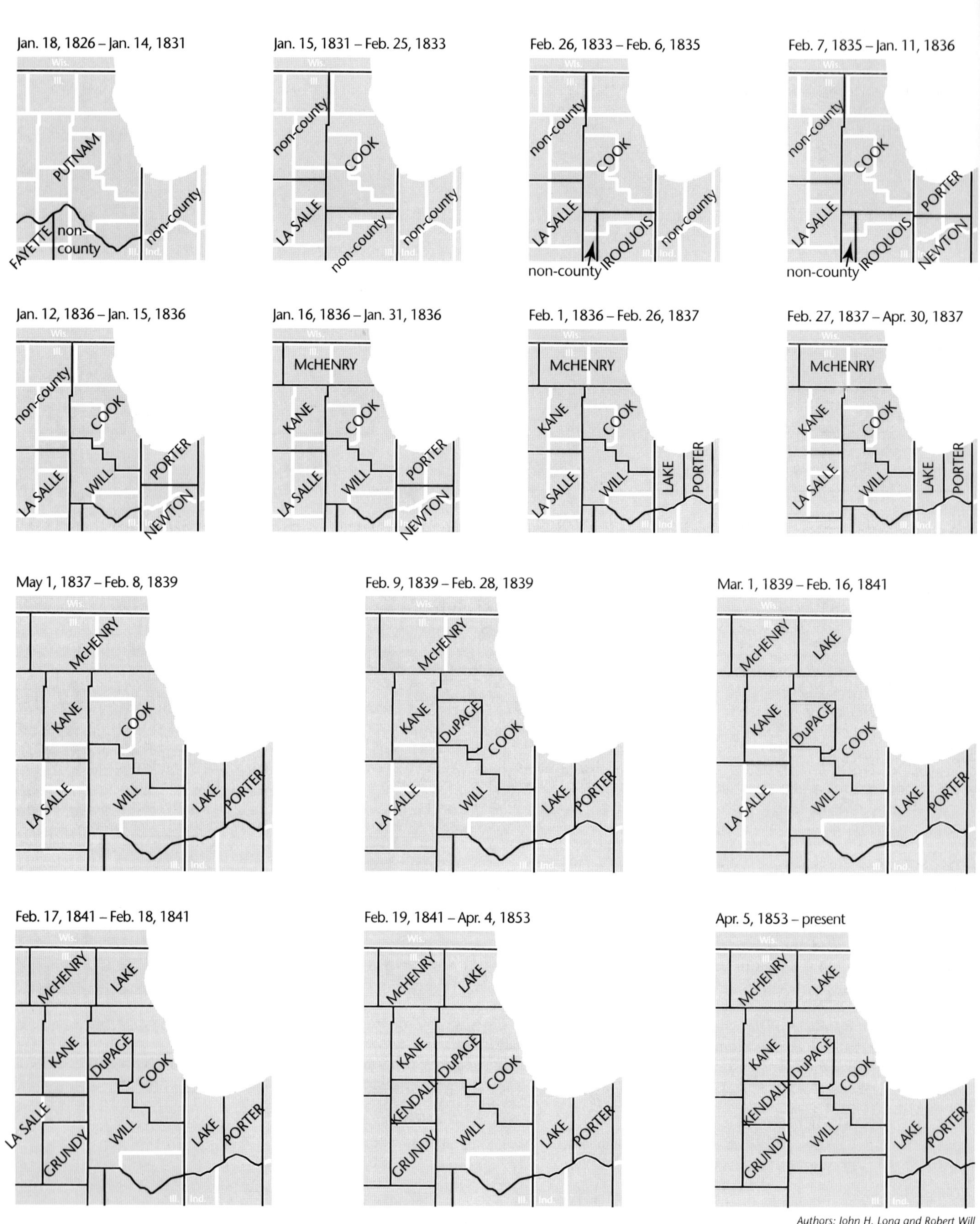

Authors: John H. Long and Robert Will

Counties are administrative subdivisions of their state, and, with few exceptions, state legislatures create them and make changes to their boundaries. In Illinois and Indiana, as in the rest of the United States, one of the important functions of counties has been the operation of the state judicial system. The county network usually blankets the entire state, including unpopulated areas, so that no place can be outside the jurisdiction of some sheriff or court. Additional responsibilities, many of which have grown in importance over time, have included probating wills, recording deeds and marriages, managing public health, conducting elections, and collecting taxes for the state, the minor civil divisions, and the special districts. Before the emergence of villages, cities, and similar units of local government in an area, counties provided the only local government.

Virginia was first to organize county government for what became the Chicago metropolitan region. In December 1778, based upon the land grant in its 1609 colonial charter, Virginia created Illinois County to cover the region between the Mississippi and Ohio Rivers. The federal government took control of that territory in 1784 and created the Northwest Territory to govern it. Subsequent authorities that were given jurisdiction over the Chicago area were Indiana Territory (1800) and state (1816) and Illinois Territory (1809) and state (1818).

Before the 1830s, county jurisdiction in the future Chicago area was uneven. Population initially flowed into Indiana and Illinois from the south; as a result, the network of counties in those states started at the Ohio River and spread northward in step with non-Indian settlement. Some counties (e.g., Pike and Putnam in Illinois) were extended far northward to cover all possible places, even though most of their territory had no settlers previously subject to the jurisdiction of the United States. Occasionally, there was no provision for county jurisdiction in the area. It was not until the 1830s, after a second wave of migrants heading westward from the Erie Canal (opened 1825) reached the southern end of Lake Michigan, that it became necessary to provide local county services. First was Cook County (1831), given responsibility for all of northeastern Illinois; second was Indiana's Porter County (1835), which brought United States–sanctioned government to northwestern Indiana where there had been no provision for such government since 1817. New counties were added as fast as new settlers poured into the area, and, by 1841, barely 10 years after the birth of Cook County, all but one of the counties of the Chicago area had reached their permanent configurations. The final boundary change (1853) shifted the southern line of Will County from the Kankakee River to the straight township and range lines of the federal Public Land Survey System.

The arrangement of boundaries and areas does not always tell the full story of how judicial and administrative jurisdictions worked. Sometimes state legislatures created counties without putting them into operation. In order to provide a minimum of governmental services, such an unorganized county (or occasionally a noncounty area) was "attached" to a fully operational county. Only two of the Chicago area's counties were temporarily attached: McHenry was created in January 1836 and was unorganized and attached to Cook for the following 13 months. Lake County (Indiana), created in February 1836, was unorganized and attached to Porter for a year. Records of marriages, real-estate sales, and other events in those counties (including Lake, Illinois, then part of McHenry) will be found in the archives of their hosts at the time, not in their own courthouses, because at the time they had no facilities or officials.

John H. Long

DenBoer, Gordon. *Illinois: Atlas of Historical County Boundaries.* Ed. John H. Long. 1997. Sinko, Peggy Tuck. *Indiana: Atlas of Historical County Boundaries.* Ed. John H. Long. 1996.

---

to the six-county region of Northeastern Illinois. But the commission was handicapped from the outset. Its initial mandate from the legislature was to provide technical assistance and to furnish comprehensive planning for the metropolitan area. But in 1961 the state legislature enacted proposals that involved master drainage for the metropolitan region and for areawide distribution of water, sewage, and drainage services, rejecting an NIPC-backed proposal that would have expanded the ability of areas, such as Chicago, to annex adjacent sites.

Evidence that many Illinois citizens were concerned about comprehensive planning for the metropolitan region emerged from the work of LOYOLA UNIVERSITY's newly created Center for Research in Urban Government in the mid-1960s. The center's most compelling work was done by Gilbert Y. Steiner, who identified three primary roadblocks to securing cooperation between the city and its nearby suburbs. The first was the disparity of tax revenues. Suburbs were typically flush in tax revenue to fund schools and other local needs; the city possessed few comparable resources. The second roadblock involved the growing difference in racial composition between city and suburb. Chicago was fast becoming populated by a large concentration of AFRICAN AMERICANS, many of whom did not wish to diminish their electoral strength in the form of broad metropolitan authorities. And third was the related difference in the political makeup of the city and its suburbs: Chicago was dominated by DEMOCRATS; the suburbs were a haven for more affluent REPUBLICANS. For these reasons, Steiner argued, it would be difficult to create a metropolitan authority, even for limited purposes.

Even Chicago-area businessmen got into the picture, forming the Committee on Urban Progress (COUP) in December 1963. The committee's conclusions—that "the chief obstacle to rational and farsighted control of urban expansion is political overlapping and fragmentation"—prompted Governor Kerner to propose the establishment of a commission designed solely to add structure to local POLITICS. In 1965, the governor's proposed legislation made it through the Illinois House of Representatives. It failed to pass the Senate.

It should not have been entirely surprising that efforts to overcome problems created by the fragmented nature of political authority in Chicago would stumble. There were prodigious obstacles to overcome. The state legislature remained dominated in the 1950s and 1960s by rural interests from downstate Illinois, and many of these interests opposed the expansion of the city's power, believing that it would simply add to the CLOUT already wielded by Mayor Richard J. Daley. Additionally, as geographer Malcolm Proudfoot argued at the time, "Chicago has been further weakened by the shortsighted antagonism and obstruction of many of its suburban residents, whose satellitic, not to say parasitic, municipalities form a continuous retaining wall of separate political and legal autonomy around the central city."

Still all was not lost. The 1970 Illinois Constitutional Convention considered a wide range of issues and eventually made key decisions that would affect matters of local governance. Its most important decision was to allow localities to engage in some forms of intergovernmental cooperation, granting broader powers to municipalities, such as the city of Chicago, and permitting localities to engage in important joint efforts. But in allowing the state to retain final authority, the convention in some ways simply re-inaugurated previous disputes over the range of municipal powers. The state legislature could still preempt local decisions.

Suburban development continued unabated throughout the two decades following the constitutional convention. DuPage and Lake Counties each grew by more than one-third between 1980 and 2000. Cook County, meanwhile, continued to lose residents until the 1990s. New development in northern Lake County reached out to markets that stretched across the state line, bringing residents from Wisconsin to shop and work in Illinois. This growth enriched the population of the area while accentuating old governmental divisions, particularly by widening the gap between rich and poor municipalities. In the late 1990s, Mayor Richard M. Daley tried to resolve lingering conflicts by bringing together mayors from neighboring cities to discuss issues of joint concern.

Chicago might not have the most rational administrative form, but it is one tailored to the fabric of American POLITICAL CULTURE and history. In fact, much of what happened throughout the history of Chicago governance reproduced the same general patterns set elsewhere in the United States. Some parallels were indicative of national movements, such as the effort by larger places to annex smaller ones at the end of the nineteenth century. Others simply mirrored the structural character of American government, which tended to favor decentralized political authority.

There are also ways in which the evolution of governance in Chicago differs sharply, if not always substantively, from governance elsewhere. The powerful personalities of many Chicago mayors, for instance, made the state legislature reluctant to grant the city home rule powers that might otherwise have been considered appropriate. In some instances, notably during the reign of Richard J. Daley from 1955 to 1976, the mayor of Chicago possessed sufficient political acumen to circumvent the legal basis of decentralized authority in the state. By holding two crucial offices simultaneously—mayor of Chicago and chairman of the Cook County Democratic Party—Daley was able to transcend the fragmentation of governance by centralizing power personally.

What gives coherence to the story of Chicago governance is its chronic incoherence. Then again, that very incoherence—that jumble of unintegrated factors and a cacophony of voices—may also be what gives the city its strength.

Anthony Orum

See also: Chicago Studied: Social Scientists and Their City; Court System; State Politics; Suburbs and Cities as Dual Metropolis; Taxation and Finance

Further reading: Keane, James F., and Gary Koch, eds. *Illinois Local Government: A Handbook.* 1990. • Keating, Ann Durkin. *Building Chicago: Suburban Developers and the Creation of a Divided Metropolis.* 1988. • Steiner, Gilbert Y. "Metropolitan Government and the Real World: The Case of Chicago." Center for Research in Urban Government, Loyola University. Vol. 1, no. 3 (January 1966).

Government, City of Chicago. In many respects, Chicago's government followed patterns common among nineteenth-century U.S. cities. As a commercial walking city, Chicago initially reflected the Jacksonian-era tendency for decentralized government with numerous officials elected on a frequent basis. Increasing government centralization and authority accompanied the city's rise as an industrial giant.

This development, however, was neither linear nor as pronounced as in some of the older American cities. Even as Chicago's government changed, it retained certain attributes from older forms of municipal organization, including a balance of power favoring the city council over the MAYOR; a large council elected by WARDS, with city services organized and delivered along ward lines; and various independent offices and jurisdictions across the metropolitan area, limiting centralized authority over policy and governance.

Ward-based elections and services have encouraged ethnic and neighborhood POLITICS, providing an obstacle to centralized government. Chicago initially had a board of trustees elected at large for annual terms. Its 1837 municipal CHARTER established a popularly elected mayor and Common Council, which in 1875 became the city council. As the city grew through ANNEXATION, the wards increased to 35 and the number of aldermen to 70. In 1923, the city was divided into 50 wards, each represented by one alderman elected for two-year terms. Aldermen have been elected on a nonpartisan basis since 1920, with a run-off election between the top two candidates if no one receives a majority in the first election. Since 1935, council terms have lasted for four years and elections have coincided with mayoral balloting.

By 1851, many offices appointed by the council had become elected, including clerk, treasurer, city attorney, and city marshal. Since 1907, the only officers elected citywide have been the mayor, clerk, and treasurer. Elections were also held in early decades for local officials, including tax assessors, justices of the peace, SCHOOL DISTRICT trustees, and POLICE constables. All of these became appointed positions. Only the public SCHOOLS reverted to some locally elected officials with the state education reforms of 1989 providing for election of local school councils. Boards of SPECIAL DISTRICTS providing such services as WATER and sanitation continue to be elected by districts; other governing bodies, such as the PARK DISTRICT board, are appointed by the mayor but, as with most of the municipal-area systems, are officially independent of city finances and authority.

The official powers of the mayor have always been weak, but there has been some centralization of authority over time. The term of office was increased from one year to two in 1863, nearly two decades after aldermen first enjoyed longer terms, and was extended to four years in 1907. From 1907 through 1995, mayoral candidates were chosen through a party primary system. In 1995, the state legislated a major change, providing for election of Chicago's three citywide offices in a manner similar to the election of aldermen—a nonpartisan election with a run-off between the top two vote getters if no candidate wins a majority. This system was suggested in the mid-1980s by local white politicians in reaction to the election by plurality of the city's first AFRICAN AMERICAN mayor, Harold Washington.

Through the nineteenth century, the mayor's power was mainly as a presiding officer over the council. Slowly, the office gained the authority to veto, to break tie votes in council, and to appoint commissioners. Executive authority over departments remained limited, however, as they operated independently of the mayor's office, with the council retaining authority over the city budget. In the crisis period after the Great FIRE OF 1871, the state legislature temporarily authorized expanded powers for the mayor, but by 1875 the factional politicians of the council reasserted their official authority from the city charter.

Decentralized decision-making frustrated business leaders and others with visions and interests beyond the local neighborhood and across the city or metropolitan region. Ironically, Chicago's decentralized system survived longer than in other cities in part because these

AN ACT

TO INCORPORATE

THE CITY OF CHICAGO.

PASSED MARCH 4, 1837.

Chicago:
PRINTED AT THE OFFICE OF THE CHICAGO DEMOCRAT.
1837.

The state legislature, which had incorporated Chicago as a town in 1833, approved Chicago's incorporation as a city four years later. Source: Chicago Historical Society.

interests developed informal policy-making structures to circumvent decentralized processes and divided government. These have ranged from outright bribery to the establishment of privately controlled bodies or interest groups to develop public policy, usually formed by business interests. The most famous of these is the Chicago Plan Commission, organized by business interests to fulfill the BURNHAM PLAN of 1909. Another was the Municipal Voters League, an organization of business reformers whose endorsed candidates won 59.4 percent of aldermanic races between 1907 and 1921.

More recently, decentralization has been mitigated by the informal concentration of power and influence in the person of the mayor. This is commonly recognized as the Chicago political machine, founded by Mayor Anton J. Cermak (1931–1933), developed by Mayor Edward J. Kelly (1933–1947), and perfected by Mayor Richard J. Daley (1955–1976).

Daley's control of DEMOCRATIC PARTY ward organizations permitted him to dominate the city council and thereby expand his authority. In 1956, state legislation removed the responsibility for initiating the city budget from the council and placed it in the mayor's office. This allowed the mayor, rather than council politicians, to establish the city's financial priorities. Daley also began to whittle away at independent sources of aldermanic authority, by, for example, taking over the "driveway permit" power (each minor construction permit required an individual bill passed by council) and professionalizing and centralizing ward services under his office. New state legislation also increased the mayor's authority over departments and the various URBAN RENEWAL agencies dealing with city PLANNING and CONSTRUCTION.

Later mayors, however, were less able to usurp the official power residing in the city council. Jane M. Byrne (1979–1983) was elected as a reformer but quickly recognized the need to ally with regular party leaders in the council. In Harold Washington's first three years of office, city council opponents marshaled a majority of votes to stymie his policy objectives and usher in the paralyzing "Council Wars." Only his veto power kept the council from completely ignoring his agenda until his supporters won a majority in special council elections in 1986. Mayor Richard M. Daley (1989–) has continued a functional aspect of his father's MACHINE POLITICS, using his campaign organization and network of fundraisers to offer advantages to selected aldermanic candidates.

Loomis Mayfield

See also: Good Government Movements; Governing the Metropolis; Home Rule; Political Culture; Taxation and Finance

Further reading: Chicago Home Rule Commission. *Modernizing a City Government.* 1954 • Fuchs, Ester R. *Mayors and Money: Fiscal Policy in New York and Chicago.* 1992. • Merriam, Charles E., Spencer D. Parratt, and Albert Lepawsky. *The Government of the Metropolitan Region of Chicago.* 1933.

Dolton Municipal Building, 1973. Photographer: Casey Prunchunas. Source: Chicago Historical Society.

Government, Suburban. Fragmentation is the dominant characteristic of suburban government. No single governmental unit rules Chicago's suburbs; instead, every type of local government authorized by the state exists. A multitude of municipalities as well as hundreds of SPECIAL DISTRICTS, SCHOOL DISTRICTS, and TOWNSHIPS share the responsibility for governing the vast population beyond Chicago's limits.

This proliferation of suburban governments was first evident in the last three decades of the nineteenth century. Under Illinois's permissive incorporation law, any community of at least 300 residents could opt for a municipal CHARTER. By 1880 the North Shore communities of EVANSTON, WINNETKA, GLENCOE, and WILMETTE already had incorporated, and other small municipalities were appearing across the metropolitan area. Moreover, in the late 1860s and 1870s the entire townships of LAKE, LAKE VIEW, HYDE PARK, CICERO, and JEFFERSON incorporated, ringing Chicago with suburban municipalities.

Yet these suburban governments generally could not match the level of services offered by the city of Chicago. Eager for improved WATER SUPPLY, sewerage, and fire and POLICE protection, the residents of many suburban municipalities voted to abandon independent status and consolidate with Chicago. Thus in the late 1880s the incorporated towns of Lake, Lake View, Hyde Park, and Jefferson all chose to join with Chicago, and in the early 1890s the incorporated villages of Washington Heights, West Roseland, Fernwood, ROGERS PARK, WEST RIDGE, and NORWOOD PARK all opted for ANNEXATION. At the close of the nineteenth century, many observers regarded the suburban units as only transitional governments, offering some services prior to their seemingly inevitable annexation to Chicago.

The birth rate of suburban municipalities, however, continued unabated, with the incorporation of 26 villages in COOK COUNTY between 1890 and 1900 and 14 more during the first decade of the twentieth century. By 1910 Cook County could claim 66 municipalities as well as 30 townships, and over 20 park commissions. Moreover, the number continued to rise. In the early 1930s there were 89 municipalities in Cook County, 195 independent school districts, and 57 separate park governments. Altogether 419 governments coexisted in Cook County.

During the early twentieth century, the level of satisfaction with suburban services rose, and contented suburbanites were not so willing to unite with Chicago. Many suburban residents valued the neighborly grassroots rule of the smaller outlying units and the freedom from big-city POLITICS and bureaucracy. Suburban municipalities could tailor local government to the social and economic desires of their residents. Upper-middle-class residential villages banned SALOONS, whereas some working-class municipalities welcomed them. Certain pristine villages excluded industry, whereas others protected tax-rich manufacturing concerns. Moreover, between 1914 and 1930 the elite communities of Glencoe, Winnetka, KENILWORTH, RIVERSIDE, and Wilmette opted for the reform scheme of city manager government then sweeping the nation. Efficient administration by a professional manager appealed to affluent residents dedicated to the values of corporate America. Meanwhile, Al Capone's gang took control of government in blue-collar Cicero. Whereas Winnetka won national recognition as a model municipality of exemplary professional administration, Cicero won even greater fame as a gangster refuge. It was, then, difficult to generalize about suburban government. Given the prevailing fragmentation, each segment of suburbia could pursue its own ends.

By the 1930s, however, criticism of the proliferation of suburban governments was mounting, as social scientists and good-government experts decried the division of responsibility and the supposed confusion which resulted. In 1933 scholarly investigators, led by UNIVERSITY OF CHICAGO political scientist Charles Merriam, published an indictment of the fragmented government of metropolitan Chicago and urged a program of reform to unify the region. Like most academic experts of the period, Merriam and his colleagues viewed township government as a ludicrous relic of a simpler rural past and eagerly awaited its demise. Moreover, the absence of cooperative PLANNING among the many municipalities seemed sure to bear bitter fruit. According to

Merriam and his colleagues, the solution appeared to be a transfer of authority to a central metropolitan agency and the consolidation of overlapping units of government.

Others criticized the inequity inherent in metropolitan fragmentation. Some units of suburban government enjoyed a much stronger tax base than other less fortunate units and thus could provide better services while imposing lower tax rates. In 1934 the poorest SCHOOL DISTRICT in Cook County had a per pupil valuation of taxable property of $906, whereas the figure for the wealthiest school district was $53,437. Given such figures, it was difficult to believe that all Cook County residents were receiving equal educational opportunities.

Proposals for metropolitan reform remained fashionable in academic circles for the next half century, but they had little impact on the structure of suburban government. The pattern of fragmentation persisted. By the 1980s the number of taxing units in Cook County had risen to 551, with 119 municipalities and 209 special districts, including 90 PARK DISTRICTS and 38 library districts. A statewide initiative to winnow the number of school districts had reduced the Cook County figure for these units to 152, but despite the complaints of the experts, the long-derided townships survived. Moreover, in adjacent DUPAGE and LAKE COUNTIES over four hundred governmental units enjoyed the power to levy taxes. During the second half of the twentieth century, the county governments expanded their responsibilities, seeking to coordinate the efforts of the many local units. But there was no far-reaching metropolitan reform. Municipalities remained jealous of their powers, and suburban authorities were ever suspicious of the motives of Chicago city officials. At the close of the twentieth century, the many suburban municipalities no longer appeared to be transitory units which would succumb to an inevitable consolidation of governmental authority. The fragmentation of suburban Chicago was an entrenched fact of political life.

Jon C. Teaford

See also: Governing the Metropolis; Metropolitan Growth; Taxation and Finance

Further reading: Keane, James F., and Gary Koch, eds. *Illinois Local Government: A Handbook.* 1990. • Keating, Ann Durkin. *Building Chicago: Suburban Developers and the Creation of a Divided Metropolis.* 1988. • Merriam, Charles E., Spencer D. Parratt, and Albert Lepawsky. *The Government of the Metropolitan Region of Chicago.* 1933.

Governors State University. Founded in 1969, Governors State University defines its mission as providing an academic home to those "traditionally underserved by higher education." The state institution has offered upper-level undergraduate courses and accredited master's programs to an older population of mostly working students: the average age of the 9,000 students in 2000 was 35, more than 70 percent of them women. The school has thus developed an extensive system of on-campus childcare while providing financial assistance to even its part-time students, who made up 80 percent of the student body in 2000.

Located 30 miles south of Chicago in UNIVERSITY PARK, the school's 750-acre campus is home to the Nathan Manilow Sculpture Park (named for an area developer), which began with one piece in 1969 and has since become one of the nation's most significant outdoor collections. The university assumed responsibility for the park after sponsoring a major exhibition in 1976. When the Illinois Board of Governors of Colleges and Universities disbanded in 1996 the university became subject to the oversight of its own newly constituted board of trustees.

Sarah Fenton

See also: Art, Public; Universities and Their Cities

Graceland Cemetery. Graceland Cemetery was founded in 1860 as a private, parklike resting place just north of Chicago's city limits. Now situated on 121 acres between Irving Park Road, Clark Street, Montrose Avenue, and the Howard RAPID TRANSIT, it holds the remains of many famous Chicago personalities. Graceland also showcases an expansive range of burial and ARCHITECTURAL styles, as several grave sites were designed by important architects and ARTISTS, some of whom are buried here as well.

Until midcentury, the city's lakefront cemetery was located in present-day LINCOLN PARK. When many feared that the burials would contaminate nearby LAKE MICHIGAN, the Chicago City Council decreed that all graves be moved to private CEMETERIES, including the bucolic Graceland.

Thomas Bryan, a successful businessman and civic booster, founded Graceland Cemetery. Early designs by H. W. S. Cleveland called for the cemetery's uniform appearance, without fences around individual plots. Ossian Simonds created a permanent plan that used native plants and naturalistic landscape techniques. The firm of Holabird & Roche designed the cemetery buildings, which fit into the natural landscape design.

Marshall Field, George Pullman, Ludwig Mies van der Rohe, and Potter and Bertha Palmer are among those buried in Graceland. Their resting places are marked respectively by a somber statue by Daniel Chester French, a stately column by Solon Beman, a streamlined headstone by Dirk Lohan, and a Greek temple by McKim, Mead & White. One of Louis Sullivan's outstanding works, the Getty tomb, as well as his own remains, are also in Graceland Cemetery.

Heidi Pawlowski Carey

See also: Landscape Design; Public Art

Further reading: Lanctot, Barbara. *A Walk through Graceland Cemetery.* 1988. • Sinkevitch, Alice, ed. *AIA Guide to Chicago.* 1993.

Graffiti. Inscriptions or drawings made on public surfaces such as buildings, fences, and sidewalks are generally called graffiti. In the early 1970s, a different kind of graffiti appeared when a group of inner-city youths began to spray paint their names and messages on the sides of New York subway trains, using strange lettering. The city considered these marks vandalism, and new ordinances prohibited this activity. But the "writers" persisted, replacing the markings as quickly as they were removed. As the lettering became more complex and gained some acceptance, the graffiti movement was born, soon to spread across the country.

Graffiti, also called spray can ART, appeared in Chicago in the 1980s. It began, as in New York, with "tags" featuring the writer's name, initials, or nickname; then it evolved into the "wildstyle," with names outlined and filled in with color, and finally into "pieces" (masterpieces)—large-scale, multicolored, complex compositions. There were and continue to be periods of official acceptance as graffiti art grows, and ARTISTS, who started in the streets, collaborate with traditional muralists on so-called permission pieces in community-based projects. These spray can–acrylic murals, by such muralists as Olivia Gude and "writer" Dzine, can be found in many Chicago neighborhoods, thus bringing graffiti art into the mainstream. City Hall's response to the phenomenon was the Graffiti Blasters program, established in 1993, limiting the sale of spray paint and spending millions to remove graffiti from more than 700,000 buildings. Graffiti art, now part of the hip-hop movement, is in profusion on the Internet, with dozens of vibrant Web sites.

Mary Lackritz Gray

See also: Art, Public; Free Speech; Street Life

Further reading: Chalfon, Henry, and James Prigoff. *Spray Can Art.* 1987. • Gude, Olivia, and Jeff Huebner. *Urban Art Chicago: A Guide to Community Murals, Mosaics, and Sculptures.* 2000. • Schoenberg, Nara. "Dispatches from the Graffiti Wars: Despite Mayor Daley's Attempts to Stamp It Out, Spray-Can Art Still Abounds." *Chicago Tribune,* December 13, 2001.

Grain Market. *See* Commodities Markets; Food Processing: Regional and National Market

Grand Army of the Republic. Founded in Illinois in 1866, the Grand Army of the Republic (G.A.R.) was the largest national organization of Union CIVIL WAR veterans. Chicago G.A.R. posts behaved in many respects like other nineteenth-century fraternal groups, but the organization was also a strong force for military pension reform.

The G.A.R. grew slowly at first, but in the 1880s membership climbed dramatically. The George H. Thomas post, the first in Chicago, was chartered in 1873 and remained the city's largest. By 1890 at least 13 had been chartered, including the John Brown post for AFRICAN AMERICAN veterans. The Grand Army Hall, a Civil War museum and G.A.R. meeting place, was a component of the CHICAGO PUBLIC LIBRARY building (1897) on Michigan Avenue.

Membership declined with the passing of Union veterans, but as late as 1914 Chicago had 23 posts with a combined roster of over two thousand.

David T. Thackery

See also: Clubs: Patriotic and Veterans' Clubs

Further reading: Dearing, Mary R. *Veterans in Politics: The Story of the G.A.R.* 1974. • McConnell, Stuart. *Glorious Contentment: The Grand Army of the Republic, 1865–1900.* 1992.

Grand Boulevard, Community Area 38, 5 miles S of the Loop. Originally called the Forrestville Settlement, the Grand Boulevard community became a part of HYDE PARK TOWNSHIP in 1861, and was ANNEXED with Hyde Park to Chicago in 1889. The area is bounded by 39th and 51st Streets to the north and south, and by Cottage Grove Avenue and the Chicago, Rock Island & Pacific RAILROAD tracks to the east and west. Until 1874 when the South Parks Commission lined with trees a thoroughfare they called Grand Boulevard (Now Dr. Martin Luther King Jr. Drive), the area was a combination of prairie and thick woods. The development of this street, situated at the center of the community, made it a popular carriage route on which many of Chicago's wealthy built elegant mansions. The population of the Grand Boulevard community grew steadily throughout the latter part of the nineteenth century, attracting not only the wealthy, but middle- and working-class American-born whites of IRISH, SCOTTISH, and ENGLISH origin, German JEWS, and a few AFRICAN AMERICANS.

38
Grand
Boulevard

Excellent TRANSPORTATION providing easy access to and from Chicago's Loop sparked the commercial and residential development of Grand Boulevard. Cable cars running along Cottage Grove Avenue reached 39th street by 1882 and 63rd street in 1887. East-west lines were also added. In 1896, the South Side "L" began stops in Grand Boulevard at 43rd, 47th, and 51st streets, around which small commercial strips of usually Jewish-owned businesses developed. By the turn of the century, good transportation and the construction of a large number of multiple-family dwellings transformed Grand Boulevard into a solidly middle- and working-class neighborhood, one of Chicago's most desirable.

There had been a small African American community in Grand Boulevard since the 1890s, but by 1920 blacks, many of them southern migrants, constituted 32 percent of the area's 76,703 residents. By 1930 African Americans in Grand Boulevard were 94.6 percent of the total population of 87,005. Like other areas of rapid racial transition in Chicago, Grand Boulevard experienced resistance and violence, but the influx of African Americans continued, and by 1950 blacks encompassed 99 percent of the community's 114,557 residents.

Grand Boulevard became the hub of "Bronzeville," the name the *Chicago Bee* gave to Chicago's SOUTH SIDE African American community. A thriving center of successful black businesses, civic organizations, and churches, Bronzeville was in every way "a city within a city." The large number of

African American residential neighborhood, 49th Street and Champlain, ca. 1925. Photographer: Webb. Source: Chicago Historical Society.

Bronzeville

In 1920 the African American population in Chicago was 109,894. REPUBLICAN-oriented Negro leaders like Alderman Oscar DePriest and Bishop Archibald Carey were referred to as "Race Men" because they were blasting the downtown establishment on behalf of African Americans seeking a piece of the sunshine pie.

The dominions that DePriest and Carey presided over were the Second and Third Wards on the SOUTH SIDE, which were alternately referred to as the "BLACK BELT" or "Black Ghetto" and occasionally "Darkie Town." Geographically, the Second and Third Wards were bounded by 22nd Street on the north and 51st Street on the south and Cottage Grove on the east and the Rock Island Railroad on the west. Many citizens of color resented having their neighborhoods referred to as the "Black Belt" or "Black Ghetto" by the major media.

James J. Gentry, a theater editor for Anthony Overton, the COSMETIC king and publisher of the *Chicago Bee,* suggested that they use his coined word Bronzeville to identify the community, since it more accurately described the skin tone of most of its inhabitants. Overton supported the idea and in 1930 his newspaper sponsored an unsuccessful Mayor of Bronzeville contest.

In 1932 Gentry left the *Chicago Bee* and carried his Mayor of Bronzeville idea to *Chicago Defender* publisher Robert S. Abbott. Abbott jumped at Gentry's idea. Charles Browning, the *Chicago Defender*'s promotional genius, developed the Mayor of Bronzeville contest into the newspaper's second most profitable promotion. The BUD BILLIKEN Club and Parade were and still are the *Chicago Defender*'s most successful promotions.

The mayoral contest attracted many of the high-profile business and professional leaders in Bronzeville. Thomas A. Dorsey, a mentor of Mahalia Jackson, was a candidate for the Mayor of Bronzeville, and Cora Carroll, a businesswoman, was the Mayor of Bronzeville in the 1960s.

Dempsey J. Travis

black intellectuals, politicians, sports figures, ARTISTS, and writers who made their homes in Bronzeville made it a cultural mecca, the central institution of which was the famed REGAL THEATER located at 47th and Grand Boulevard.

The Grand Boulevard community has also maintained a rich tradition of diverse religious institutions, housed in some of the city's most beautiful edifices. Irish ROMAN CATHOLICS established St. Elizabeth of Hungary at the corner of 41st and Wabash in 1881. Corpus Christi Catholic Church at 49th and Grand Boulevard followed later. Sinai Temple, was built on the corner of 46th and Grand Boulevard in 1915. Within a decade congregants moved out of the neighborhood in the wake of racial transition and the building was sold in 1944 to Corpus Christi to become a high school for African American Catholics. It was sold again in 1962 to form the Mt. Pisgah Missionary Baptist Church. Temple Isaiah at 4501 Vincennes Avenue, built in 1899 and the last major work of Chicago architect Dankmar Adler, became the Ebenezer Baptist Church in 1921.

Once a place of wealth and grandeur, Grand Boulevard has been more accurately characterized in the latter decades of the twentieth century by physical deterioration, poverty, UNEMPLOYMENT, and PUBLIC HOUSING. The loss of stockyard and steel mill jobs, as well as numerous black-owned businesses, has sent the community into a tailspin of economic decline. Along with a poverty rate of two thirds by the 1990s, Grand Boulevard contained the densest population of public housing in the country. Even with the demolition of some of its buildings in the late 1990s, the ROBERT TAYLOR HOMES, located primarily in Grand Boulevard, remained the largest public housing project in Chicago. Since the mid-1980s numerous individuals, as well as community-based organizations like Centers for New Horizons, have worked to address to the needs of Grand Boulevard and its people.

Wallace Best

See also: Multicentered Chicago; Religious Geography; Street Railways

Further reading: Bowly, Devereux, Jr. *The Poorhouse: Subsidized Housing in Chicago, 1895–1976.* 1978. • Holt, Glen E., and Dominic A. Pacyga. "Grand Boulevard." In *Chicago: A Historical Guide to the Neighborhoods: The Loop and the South Side.* 1979. • Reed, Christopher R., and Annie Ruth Leslie, "Grand Boulevard. In *Local Community Fact Book: Chicago Metropolitan Area, 1990,* ed. Chicago Fact Book Consortium. 1995. 1990.

Michigan Avenue at Grant Park, 1890. Photographer: Unknown. Source: The Newberry Library.

Grant Park. The area that became Grant Park at the turn of the nineteenth century was originally deeded to the commissioners of the ILLINOIS & MICHIGAN CANAL in 1835. The boundaries of the park were Randolph Street on the north, 12th Street on the south, Michigan Avenue to the west, and LAKE MICHIGAN to the east. This area (which by 1847 was called "Lake Park"), remained a mix of squatters' homes and refuse sites for over 40 years. Initially, the ILLINOIS CENTRAL RAILROAD ran parallel to the park in the Lake. Landfill eventually brought the railroad tracks into the park. Aaron Montgomery Ward brought suit against the city in 1890, demanding that they clean up the park and remove the many structures which had arisen over the past several decades.

The city later adopted a plan for the park which included a civic center and other buildings. Ward sued the city again, and only the new ART INSTITUTE building was constructed in 1893. The Chicago South Park Commission took responsibility for the area in 1896, bestowing the name Grant Park. The commission hired the Olmsted Brothers to develop a new design scheme for the park in 1903. Their plan, published in 1907, called for a more

Interstate Exposition Building on Michigan Avenue, 1880s. Photographer: Unknown. Source: Chicago Historical Society.

formalized park structure based upon French landscaping principles such as symmetrical spaces well defined by paths and plantings. Subsequent modifications to Grant Park, such as placing the commuter trains that ran through the park in a depression under street level and a well-developed program of park maintenance, helped make the area more amenable to Chicago residents and visitors.

Max Grinnell

See also: Creation of Chicago Sports; Landscape Design; Leisure

Further reading: Burnham, Daniel H., and Edward H. Bennett. *Plan of Chicago.* 1909. • Kurke, Mary A. "Public Park and Recreation Land Availability in the City of Chicago." M.A. thesis, Western Illinois University. 1976.

Graphic Design. Chicago's flourishing graphic design practice owes largely to the communication needs of a large industrial metropolis combined with the extraordinary growth of the PRINTING industry. Among the early designers in the 1890s were Will Bradley and J. C. Leyendecker, who did posters for the little MAGAZINES and commercial publications of the day.

The city's art schools played a major role in training early commercial designers. In 1899 Frederic Goudy began teaching lettering design at Frank Holme's newly founded School of Illustration, where Oswald Cooper came to study. Cooper epitomized a type of commercial artist known as a "lettering man," who was usually hired to provide lettering for advertisements and other printed matter. He was also in demand as a type designer and created many widely used faces such as Cooper Black.

The School of the ART INSTITUTE offered courses in commercial art before World War I, and in 1921 established a Department of Printing Arts. Its outstanding students included Robert Hunter Middleton, who epitomized the development of graphic design in Chicago from the mid-1920s through the 1950s. During Middleton's long tenure at the Ludlow Typograph Company, he designed almost one hundred typefaces, spanning a full range of traditional and modern styles.

The Society of Typographic Arts (STA), established in 1927, envisioned an ambitious program that included publications, exhibitions, and lectures. At the time there were no AFRICAN AMERICAN members, although Charles Dawson had established an active commercial art practice for black clients on the SOUTH SIDE. The Art Directors Club of Chicago, founded in 1932, made an overt push to bring contemporary European design tendencies to the attention of its members. In 1934, the club sponsored a course by the Austrian poster and advertising designer Joseph Binder, which influenced a number of Chicago art directors and illustrators, notably

The Society of Typographic Arts was Chicago's premier design professional organization from 1927 into the 1970s. The emblem shown here, designed by illustrator Elmer Jacobs, embodies STA's commitment to excellence in type as well as their more generalized embrace of modernism. Artist: Elmer Jacobs. Source: The Newberry Library.

Otis Shepard, whose billboard look for the Wrigley Company derived from Binder's style.

The most important force in bringing the principles and practices of European modern design to Chicago was the New Bauhaus, established in 1937 and renamed the INSTITUTE OF DESIGN in 1944. Its first director, Hungarian designer László Moholy-Nagy, placed ADVERTISING design within a more comprehensive "light workshop," which included PHOTOGRAPHY as well as typography, layout, and serigraphy. The workshop was headed by György Kepes, a fellow Hungarian who published the influential book *Language of Vision* in 1944.

By the 1950s the leading studios in the city included Whitaker-Guernsey and Tempo, and those of Everett McNear, and Morton Goldsholl Associates. Goldsholl employed Tom Miller, one of the few African American designers to work outside of Chicago's BLACK BELT during those years. Other African American designers at the time included Eugene Winslow and Fitzhugh Dinkins, both of whom had studied at the Institute of Design, and Leroy Winbush, whose firm, Winbush Associates, concentrated on window displays for banks. The bulk of the work for most of Chicago's design firms in the 1950s, however, was advertising, publications, and miscellaneous printed matter. Goldsholl carved out a special niche for corporate identity programs, packaging, and animated commercials. Several important magazines were also established in the 1950s: PLAYBOY, art directed by Arthur Paul; and the African American publications *Negro Digest*, *Jet*, and *Ebony*, products of Johnson Publishing, which were designed by African American art directors including Leroy Winbush, Herbert Temple, and Norman Hunter.

As early as the mid-1930s the Container Corporation of America, headed by Walter Paepcke, established a strong precedent for corporate design in Chicago. As director of the Department of Design, Egbert Jacobson dealt with logos, stationery, invoices, annual reports, and advertising, as well as the company's office interiors, factories, and trucks. In 1951 Paepcke, with the help of Jacobson and others, inaugurated the still ongoing series of Aspen Design Conferences. Also in the 1950s Ralph Eckerstrom headed Container's design department and brought to his job the tenets of the new Swiss design movement. In 1964 he and a group of partners started Unimark, one of the first international interdisciplinary design offices. Unimark, which grew quickly until its dissolution in 1979, became a training ground for many young designers, a number of whom continued to work in Chicago after they left the company. Jay Doblin, who joined Unimark while still director of the Institute of Design, established his own firm, Jay Doblin and Associates, in 1972, and developed a focus on what he later came to call "strategic planning," broadening from design into marketing and MANAGEMENT CONSULTING. Around the time Unimark began in the mid-1960s, several other offices, such as the RVI Corporation, headed by Robert Vogele, helped to establish Chicago as a major center of corporate design.

By the late 1960s, the work of RVI, Unimark, and the Container Corporation, along with the activities of other firms such as Design Consultants Inc. and the Design Partnership, had begun to give Chicago a national reputation for corporate design. In 1989 the Society of Typographic Arts changed its name to the American Center for Design (ACD) to acknowledge the broader range of design activities in which its members now engaged. Women in Design, a new organization established in 1978, sought more recognition for women through several exhibitions.

In the 1980s and 1990s a few of the smaller offices tried to carve out a niche for more expressive work but succeeded only to a modest degree. Although Chicago has remained a large and active center of graphic design practice, it was unclear at the beginning of the twenty-first century whether the city's designers could reassert a strong sense of identity similar to that which the city had from the 1920s to the 1970s.

Victor Margolin

See also: Artists, Education and Culture of; Book Arts; Industrial Art and Design

Further reading: Beck, Bruce, ed. *RHM: Robert Hunter Middleton, the Man and His Letters.* 1985. • *Fifty Years of Graphic Design in Chicago.* 1977. • Margolin, Victor. "Graphic Design in Chicago." In *Chicago Architecture and Design, 1923–1993,* ed. John Zukowsky, 1993, 283–301.

Gray Wolves. The 1890s Chicago City Council was notorious for corrupt political practices orchestrated by a faction of its aldermen known as the Gray Wolves. So named because they were viewed as preying upon the defenseless public, the Gray Wolves were led by First Ward aldermen "Bathhouse" John Coughlin and "Hinky Dink" Mike Kenna, and Johnny Powers of the Nineteenth Ward. These elected officials were not only skilled at trading votes for favors, but once in office they excelled in making municipal decisions to profit themselves financially.

The Gray Wolves operated successfully because in the late nineteenth century the city council awarded franchises to private businesses to build and furnish public services such as electricity, GAS, TELEPHONES, and mass transit. Entrepreneurs considered such franchises lucrative BUSINESS opportunities, so they cooperated with the Gray Wolves to manipulate the system in a practice dubbed "boodling." At times this meant businessmen simply bribed the aldermen for the franchise award. At other times, the Gray Wolves invented more spectacular profit-making schemes. In 1895, for example, they awarded a franchise to the Ogden Gas Company, which existed only on paper. The scheme was intended to force the existing franchise holder to buy up the rights of Ogden Gas, with the profits from the purchase to find their way into the pockets of the various conspirators. Such practices led a group of outraged Chicagoans to found the Municipal Voters League in 1896 with the expressed purpose of eliminating the Gray Wolves type of alderman from the council. In municipal elections over the succeeding years, the MVL had mixed success, but it did help to elect a number of more honest aldermen.

Maureen A. Flanagan

See also: Good Government Movements; Government, City of Chicago; Machine Politics; Privatization; Rapid Transit System; Traction Ordinances

Further reading: Flanagan, Maureen A. *Charter Reform in Chicago.* 1987. • Platt, Harold L. *The Electric City: Energy and the Growth of the Chicago Area, 1880–1930.* 1991.

Grayslake, IL, Lake County, 38 miles NW of the Loop. As the massive Wisconsin glacier melted from the Grayslake area over 12,000 years ago, it left fertile land coveted by YANKEE farmers, as well as numerous lakes and wetlands, which made movement in the horse and wagon era difficult.

In 1840, Massachusetts-born William M. Gray followed a difficult Indian trail from Chicago and settled at the southeast shore of an unnamed lake in western LAKE COUNTY. Two year later Gray purchased his claim along with the area covered by the lake which became known as Gray's Lake. Other farmers trickled into the area in the mid- and late 1840s as a plank road extending from WAUKEGAN to Belvidere (now Route 120) passed along the lake's south shore. Gray moved to Waukegan in 1845, where he engaged in mercantile activities.

Little development occurred in the area until the Wisconsin Central RAILROAD began building a line from Chicago to Fond du Lac, Wisconsin, in the early 1880s. A farmer whose land on the east side of the lake blocked the right-of-way refused to sell the railroad a strip of land, demanding instead that the whole farm be purchased. Subdividers purchased the farm, sold land to the railroad, and platted a community on the remainder in 1885. The railroad erected a station there in July 1886, naming it Grayslake. The community of 325 incorporated as a village on May 9, 1895, with local merchant George Thomson as president. In 1900 the Milwaukee Road Railroad constructed a branch line from LIBERTYVILLE Junction to Janesville, Wisconsin, along the south side of Grayslake, which gave village residents additional access to Chicago's products and amenities. Grayslake grew slowly, serving the needs of area farmers; the village population numbered only 736 in 1920.

As improved road construction following WORLD WAR I allowed the use of increasingly reliable automobiles, adventurous drivers discovered the beauty of Grayslake. Through the 1920s, moderately well-to-do Chicagoans built spacious houses along the lake.

Typical of the experience of other communities in the area, cheap land prices and easy rail TRANSPORTATION to the city served as a magnet to soldiers returning from WORLD WAR II who sought a less urban atmosphere to raise families. Chicagoans living mainly around Milwaukee Avenue in an area bounded by Fullerton and Cicero Avenues abandoned the city and found Grayslake a pleasant place to establish a suburban lifestyle. By 1950 the population had risen to 1,970.

In the late twentieth century, Grayslake officials embarked on an aggressive ANNEXATION policy. The community's boundaries now encompass the COLLEGE of Lake County, originally built in what was once a rural area and itself a spur to suburban expansion. The village population more than doubled in the 1990s, rising to 18,506 in 2000.

Craig L. Pfannkuche

See also: Glaciation; Motoring; Streets and Highways; Vacation Spots

Further reading: *Grayslake: An Historical Portrait.* 1994. • Mogg, Ruth. *Glimpses of the Old Grayslake Area.* 1976.

Great Depression. When the stock market crashed in October 1929, Chicago had a REPUBLICAN mayor, a virtually insolvent municipal government, and communities that were deeply divided along lines of race and ethnicity. When general prosperity returned in 1940, Chicago had an entrenched DEMOCRATIC machine, a fully solvent city government, and a population that, while still heavily segregated racially, had enthusiastically shared mass culture and mass movements. The transformations wrought by the Great Depression were the result of social protest movements and a growing sense that the government could and should affect the daily lives of average people in positive ways.

The Great Depression was particularly severe in Chicago because of the city's reliance on manufacturing, the hardest hit sector nationally. Only 50 percent of the Chicagoans who had worked in the manufacturing sector in 1927 were still working there in 1933. AFRICAN AMERICANS and MEXICANS were particularly hurt. By 1932, 40 to 50 percent of black workers in Chicago were UNEMPLOYED. Many Mexicans returned, responding to incentives like the free transportation offered from Chicago, or to the more coercive measures in Gary, Indiana Harbor, and South Chicago. Nor were white-collar employees necessarily safe. By February 1933, public school teachers were owed eight and a half months' back pay.

The city's difficulties were exacerbated by a fiscal crisis that had begun in the late 1920s. A 1928 property reassessment prevented the city from collecting taxes; it was immediately followed by a widespread TAX STRIKE. The financially strapped city could not afford to meet its own payroll, and by February 1, 1932, the city's emergency relief funds were totally exhausted. Traditional sources of help (RELIGIOUS INSTITUTIONS, benevolent societies, MUTUAL BENEFIT SOCIETIES) were often on the brink of financial ruin themselves. Neither private charities nor the city was equipped for such devastating hard times.

Many unemployed and frustrated workers took matters into their own hands. The Great Depression saw some of the most volatile STRIKES and protest movements in the city's history. Unions were often supported by the newly organized CONGRESS OF INDUSTRIAL ORGANIZATIONS. Organizing efforts were facilitated by mass culture, which provided a common ground to a disparate workforce. Workers united across race, ethnicity, and even across different industries. By 1940 one-third of the workers in Chicago's manufacturing sector were UNIONIZED. Active social protest movements extended outside of the workplace too. Unemployed workers, relief recipients, even

Unemployed men's club distributing cabbage to members and their families, October 1932. Photographer: Unknown. Source: Chicago Historical Society.

Parade of WPA workers along Madison Street near Wells, January 1939. During the Great Depression, the Works Progress Administration, the Civilian Conservation Corps, and other federal agencies provided jobs for many unemployed workers on projects designed to meet community needs, but there was always a demand for more jobs than were available. Photographer: Unknown. Source: Chicago Historical Society.

the unpaid schoolteachers held huge demonstrations during the early years of the Great Depression. Across the city, angry housewives protested retailers' misleading ADVERTISING and refusal to lower prices. In fact, it was a combination of public pressure and new state laws that ended the city's crippling tax strike. Although the degree of public unrest declined in later years, people's reliance on mass movements and national organization continued.

The Democratic Party was one key beneficiary of the public's new interest in POLITICS and mass reform movements. In Chicago, Democrat Anton Cermak unseated the Republican MAYOR by creating a broad coalition of Chicago's white ethnic groups in 1931. Edward Kelly, who became mayor after Cermak's 1933 assassination, expanded the coalition by appealing directly to blacks and to organized labor. Cermak's and Kelly's strong organization helped Chicago achieve national prominence as a city that could deliver a Democratic victory in tight elections, albeit with the help of shady voting practices.

Impressed with the dramatic returns furnished by the Chicago MACHINE, and with the dramatic social unrest caused by mass unemployment, Franklin Roosevelt encouraged agency heads to be generous with NEW DEAL funds in the city. Federally funded jobs and services reinforced the loyalty of many new voters, in spite of (and for some white voters because of) continued racial segregation. Meanwhile, Kelly's ability to reserve local funds for the repayment of teachers and for new PATRONAGE jobs ensured the strength of the Chicago Democratic machine. Federal funds also enabled the city to complete construction of Lake Shore Drive, landscape numerous parks, construct 30 new schools, and build a thoroughly modernized State Street Subway.

By the early 1940s, war production orders had effectively ended the unemployment and deflation that had marked so much of the 1930s. The Great Depression, however, had left its mark. Like much of the nation, Depression-era Chicago experienced stark poverty and a reorientation toward the Democratic Party. Like much of the nation, too, Chicago neighborhoods lost such landmarks as mom-and-pop stores and low-wattage, independent radio stations. White ethnic identity, while not entirely disappearing, was reconfigured with the loss of these institutions and the growth of a mass labor movement. African Americans now looked to the Democratic Party and the national government in their battles against segregation and discrimination. Indeed, the Great Depression transformed the daily lives, economic expectations, and political loyalties of most Chicagoans. The debates and unrest it engendered continued to frame political and social movements for the next 50 years.

Tracey Deutsch

See also: Economic Geography; Governing the Metropolis; Government, City of Chicago; Housekeeping; Public Works, Federal Funding for; Social Services

Further reading: Beito, David. *Taxpayers in Revolt: Tax Resistance during the Great Depression.* 1989. • Biles, Roger. *Big City Boss in Depression and War: Mayor Edward J. Kelly of Chicago.* 1984. • Cohen, Lizabeth. *Making a New Deal: Industrial Workers in Chicago.* 1990.

Great Lakes Naval Training Station. The largest single training facility for the U.S. Navy is a thousand miles from the nearest ocean. Great Lakes Naval Training Station, located in NORTH CHICAGO, formally opened in 1911 on land donated by the Merchants CLUB of Chicago. It was a product of the expansive nationalism of the era following the Spanish-American War, as well as aggressive self-promotion by Chicago businessmen and Illinois politicians. Ideally located at the nation's rail hub and near its population center, the camp gained great significance during WORLD WAR I, but reached its nadir when it was closed to new trainees between 1933 and 1935. Within a month after Pearl Harbor, the navy announced that a $33-million expansion would increase its recruit capacity from 10,000 to 45,000; by the end of 1942 75,000 were on base. During the course of WORLD WAR II, Great Lakes supplied about a million men, just over a third of all personnel who served in the U.S. Navy. With the Chicago, North Shore & Milwaukee INTERURBAN and Chicago & North Western stations adjacent to the base, sailors had ready access to Chicago's recreational opportunities.

AFRICAN AMERICAN seamen were trained at a base-within-a-base, Camp Robert Smalls, which was named for a CIVIL WAR hero and former slave. The segregated facility was hailed in its time as a major advance because it represented the first genuine training camp opportunity for African Americans. While many of those who passed through Camp Smalls were relegated to noncombat roles, in 1944 a group of African Americans nicknamed the Golden Thirteen became the first to enter the regular officer candidate school and receive commissions as ensigns.

Although scaled down after victory in 1945, Great Lakes remained an important naval facility and expanded again during the Korean War. By the late 1980s, however, it became the target of budget cutters who criticized its freshwater location. The number of recruits on base dropped to 18,000. In 1993, the Defense Base Closure and Realignment Commission instead decided that economy lay in centralization at Great Lakes. By 1997 the recruit ranks reached 50,000.

Not only did Great Lakes grow, but it marked two other milestones. In 1992 Rear Adm. Mack Gaston became the first African American commander of the base, and two years later, it began training women for the first time in its 83-year history.

Perry R. Duis

See also: Fort Sheridan; Glenview Naval Air Station; Lake Michigan; Public Works, Federal Funding for

Further reading: Duis, Perry, and Scott LaFrance. *We've Got a Job to Do: Chicagoans and World War II.* 1992. • Ebner, Michael. *Creating Chicago's North Shore: A Suburban History.* 1988.

Great Lakes System. The Great Lakes System comprises Lakes Superior, Michigan, Huron, Erie, and Ontario, plus hundreds of rivers and estuaries across the northern United States and southern Canada. The WATER in the system flows eastward from Lake Superior, six hundred feet above sea level, through the lakes into the St. Lawrence River, which empties into the Atlantic Ocean.

Increased precipitation and lower temperatures during the Pleistocene epoch 500,000 years ago resulted in the GLACIATION of North America. The accumulation of glacial snow and ice over thousands of years caused the earth to sink and form vast depressions which carved out the Great Lakes as the glaciers receded. The lakes and rivers underwent numerous changes in shape and flow as the system developed its present-day contours.

Humans arrived in the Great Lakes area 14,000 years ago and began a long history of exploiting the natural resources. The waterways were used as TRANSPORTATION routes to hunt and gather food. Early inhabitants mined the area's vast supply of copper for use in weapons and jewelry.

Today, fresh water ranks first among the system's resources. The United States and

The Great Lakes

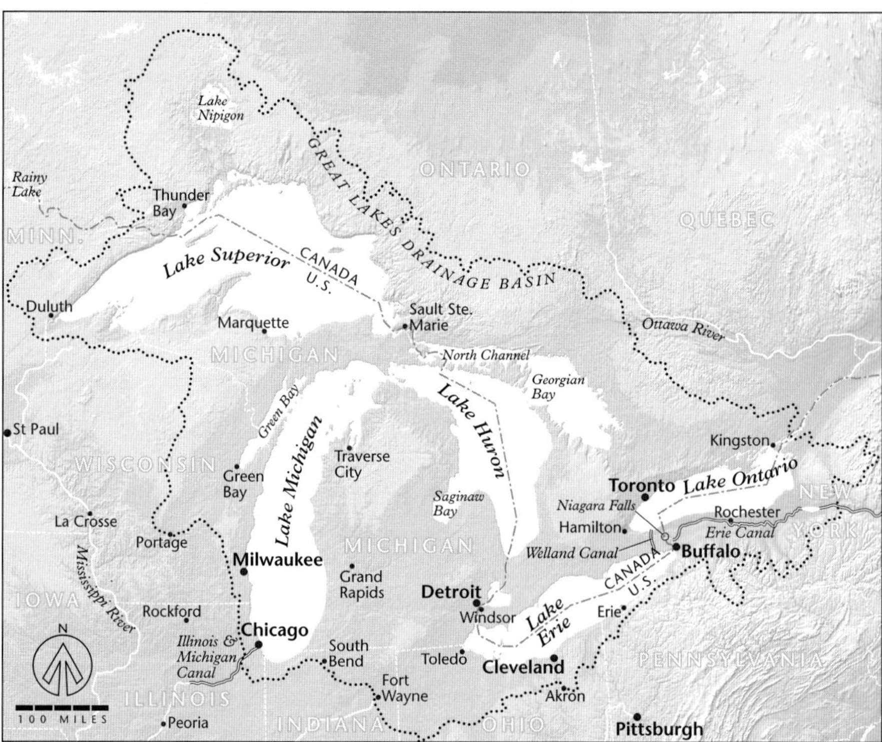

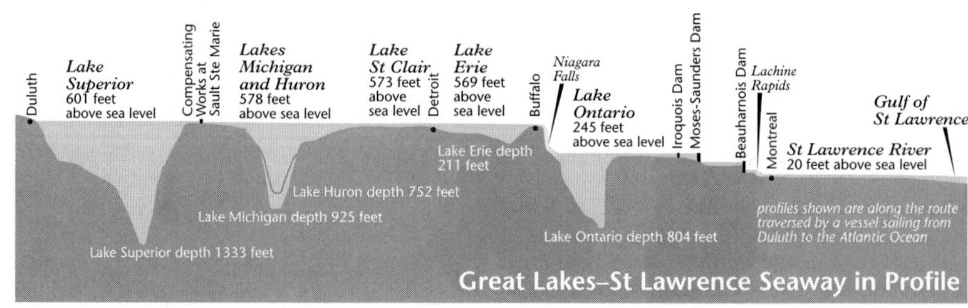

The Great Lakes drainage basin constitutes a huge natural resource region of major significance for Chicago's strategic position and historic growth. Rich with minerals, timber, and farmland, the region has provided an easy water highway for centuries, serving as the corridor for American westward movement and for subsequent industrialization. Situated at the southwestern margin of the region, with a fine harbor and easy access to rivers of the great Mississippi River basin, Chicago is the world's largest metropolis to sit astride a continental divide.

Canada work together under the Boundary Waters Treaty of 1909 and the Great Lakes Water Quality Agreement of 1978 to remedy pollution and other natural resource problems facing the area. Nevertheless, the Great Lakes continue to suffer from overfishing, water and air pollution, and increased recreational use.

Jerry L. Foust

See also: Lacustrine System; Lake Michigan; Portage; Riverine Systems

Further reading: Ashworth, William. *The Late, Great Lakes: An Environmental History.* 1988. • Rousmaniere, John, ed. *The Enduring Great Lakes.* 1980. • U.S. Environmental Protection Agency and Government of Canada. *The Great Lakes: An Environmental Atlas and Resource Book.* 1995.

Great Migration. The Great Migration, a long-term movement of AFRICAN AMERICANS from the South to the urban North, transformed Chicago and other northern cities between 1916 and 1970. Chicago attracted slightly more than 500,000 of the approximately 7 million African Americans who left the South during these decades. Before this migration, African Americans constituted 2 percent of Chicago's population; by 1970; they were 33 percent. What had been in the nineteenth century a largely southern and rural African American culture became a culture deeply infused with urban sensibility in the twentieth century. And what had been a marginalized population in Chicago emerged by the mid-twentieth century as a powerful force in the city's political, economic, and cultural life.

Although migration from the South had contributed to Chicago's black community since the 1840s, the city offered few opportunities to dissatisfied black southerners until WORLD WAR I. Chicago, like the rest of the North, offered freedom from legally sanctioned racial discrimination, but industrial employers turned away African Americans who approached the factory gates. Widespread beliefs about the aptitudes of racial and ethnic groups on the part of employers relegated East and South European immigrants to the least skilled jobs in industry, and African Americans had even fewer opportunities. Allegedly incapable of regular, disciplined WORK, they were virtually excluded except as temporary strikebreakers, notably in the MEATPACKING industry in 1904.

When World War I halted immigration from Europe while stimulating orders for Chicago's manufactured goods, employers needed a

Illinois Central Railroad Links to Chicago

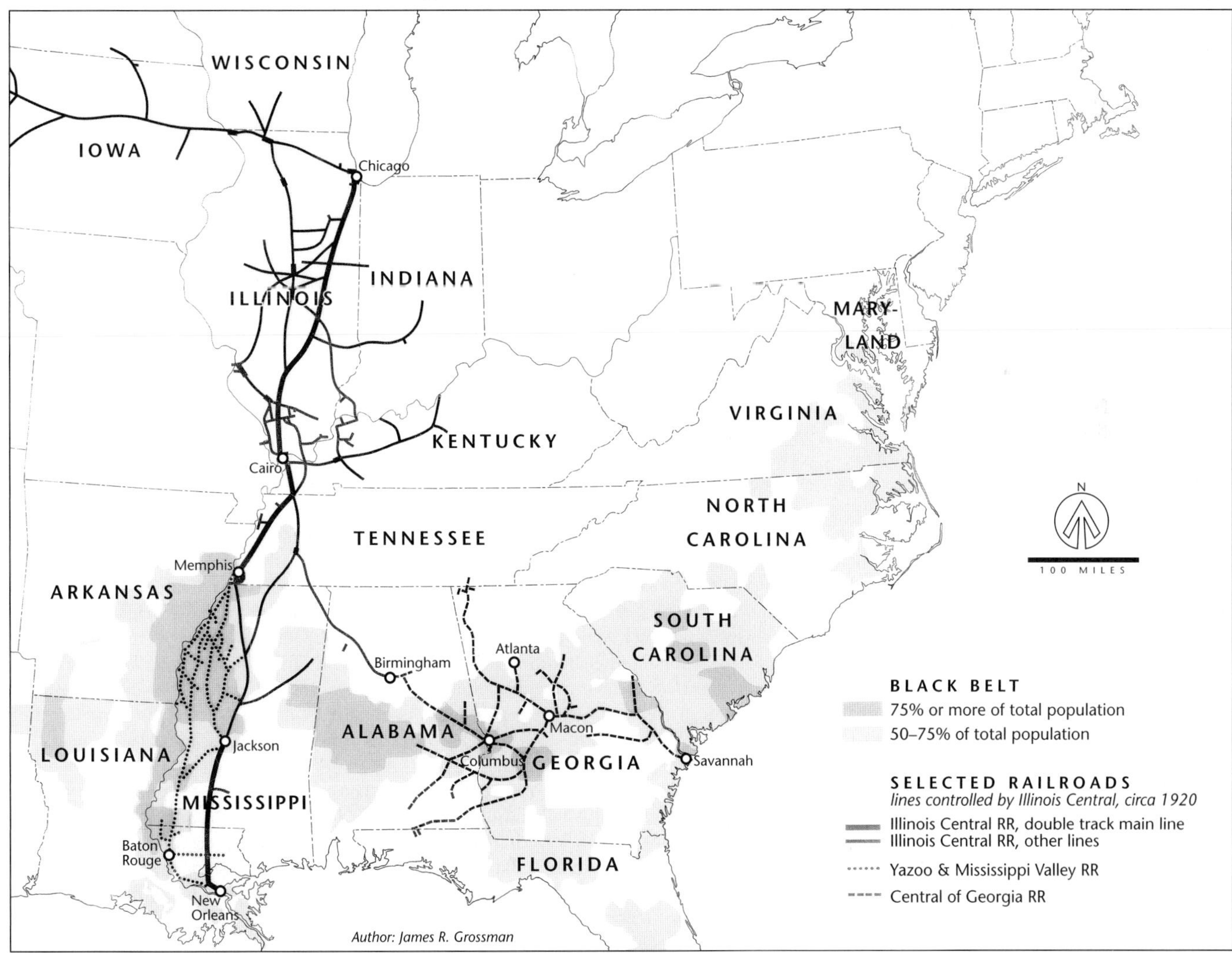

Before widespread automobile ownership, migration from the South generally followed water and rail routes. Chicago's popularity as a destination rested in part on the breadth of the Illinois Central Railroad network. By the time World War I opened employment opportunities for African Americans in northern cities, the Illinois Central and its feeder lines had penetrated many of the plantation regions where black population was most concentrated. Other railroad lines also offered access to Chicago from these and other parts of the South. Until 1916, black Chicagoans were likely to have roots in the upper South. Beginning in 1916, Chicago drew its African American population from the Deep South, especially Mississippi, Louisiana, Alabama, and western Georgia.

new source of labor for jobs assumed to be "men's work." Factories opened the doors to black workers, providing opportunities to black southerners eage to stake their claims to full citizenship through their role in the industrial economy. For black women the doors opened only slightly and temporarily, but even DOMESTIC WORK in Chicago offered higher wages and more personal autonomy than in the South. Information about these differences and about "the exodus" spread quickly through the South, partly because of the CHICAGO DEFENDER newspaper, which was so influential that many black southerners going to other northern cities went with images of Chicago. Equally important were the correspondence and visits that established "migration chains," linking Chicago with numerous southern communities, especially in Mississippi.

Migration ebbed and flowed for six decades, accelerating rapidly in the 1940s and 1950s. The expansion of industry during WORLD WAR II again provided the stimulus. This time, however, the invention of the mechanical cotton picker toward the end of the 1940s provided a push from the South that outlasted the expansion of Chicago's job market. By the 1960s Chicago's packinghouses had closed and its steel mills were beginning to decline. What had once been envisioned as a "Promised Land" for anyone willing to work hard now offered opportunities mainly to educated men and women.

The Great Migration established the foundation of Chicago's African American industrial working class. Despite the tensions between newcomers and "old settlers," related to differences in age, region of origin, and class, the Great Migration established the foundation for black political power, BUSINESS enterprise, and union activism.

The Great Migration's impact on cultural life in Chicago is most evident in the southern influence on the Chicago Renaissance of the 1930s and 1940s, as well as BLUES music, cuisine, churches, and the numerous family and community associations that link Chicago with its southern hinterland—especially Mississippi. To many black Chicagoans the South remains "home," and by the late 1980s increasing evidence of significant reverse migration, especially among retired people, began to appear.

James Grossman

See also: Chicago Black Renaissance; Demography; Iron- and Steelworkers; Multicentered Chicago; Packinghouse Unions

Further reading: Grossman, James R. *Land of Hope: Chicago, Black Southerners, and the Great Migration.* 1989. • Lemann, Nicholas. *The Promised Land: The Great Black Migration and How It Changed America.* 1991.

Great Society. Most twentieth-century presidents have tried to put a name on their disparate programs that would lodge in some warm corner of the public's mind. In this regard Lyndon Johnson both succeeded and failed: the name he chose, the Great Society, stuck, but in the long run it has shown itself to have a negative valence with voters, largely undeserved.

Johnson unveiled "Great Society" as the moniker for his domestic works, on April 23, 1964, in Chicago, at a fund-raising dinner for Mayor Richard J. Daley. The Chicago setting was appropriate. At the time both Johnson and Daley were much admired figures nationally, and they admired each other. The Great Society was supposed to fulfill a liberal agenda that had been roughly in place since the late 1940s and included such items as CIVIL RIGHTS, national health insurance, and federal aid to local public schools. Among the prime beneficiaries would be the kind of blue-collar urban MACHINE voters, black and white, that were Daley's core constituents; and the key actors in putting the Great Society in place would be practical-minded, administratively capable liberals like Daley and Johnson.

At the rational level, the Great Society has to be counted a big success. Thanks to a huge DEMOCRATIC landslide in the 1964 elections, Johnson was able to pass almost all of the programs he envisioned. At the opening of the twenty-first century, almost all of them were still going and quite popular. In particular it is impossible to imagine American politics and government without what was by far the biggest of the Great Society programs, Medicare.

At the level of perception, though, the big Great Society was dominated by the tiny War on Poverty, another Johnson slogan for a congeries of programs, aimed mainly at inner-city ghetto neighborhoods, which he had announced a few months earlier, in his 1964 State of the Union address. The War on Poverty was never popular with the public, and Mayor Daley especially disliked it. The main reason was that the best-known of the War on Poverty programs, Community Action, was based on the premise of funding neighborhood groups directly, rather than following the ancient political custom of allowing mayors, governors, and members of Congress to determine how federal money is spent in their jurisdictions. Daley felt that the Community Action Program, by circumventing city hall and funding independent groups (most notoriously the South Side GANG called the Blackstone Rangers), was contributing to the destabilization of the Chicago machine.

The Great Society poured enormous amounts of federal money into Chicago and created many new jobs. It was instrumental to the growth of Chicago's disproportionately government-employed AFRICAN AMERICAN middle class in the late 1960s and early 1970s. That it should in retrospect be primarily associated with one small, controversial program—and more broadly with the splintering of the Chicago machine and the national NEW DEAL coalition, and with the demise of the Democrats as a presidential party—is a calamity. But, as President Johnson's predecessor famously observed, life is unfair.

Nicholas Lemann

See also: Political Culture; Public Works, Federal Funding for; Subsidized Housing

Greater Grand Crossing, Community Area 69, 8 miles S of the Loop. As the name implies, Greater Grand Crossing encompasses several neighborhoods: Grand Crossing, Park Manor, Brookline, Brookdale, and Essex. The original Grand Crossing community consisted of the southeast corner of the present COMMUNITY AREAS. The entire area was annexed to Chicago in 1889 as part of HYDE PARK TOWNSHIP.

Development began after a train accident in 1853 that killed 18 people and injured 40 others. The accident occurred at what is now 75th Street and South Chicago Avenue when Roswell B. Mason, who was to become a Chicago MAYOR, secretly had intersecting tracks built for the Illinois Central across the rail lines of the Lake Shore & Michigan Southern RAILROAD. The intersection remained dangerous for many years after the 1853 accident, but industry developed around it as it became required for all trains to make a complete stop there.

Chicago REAL-ESTATE developer Paul Cornell thought that the area surrounding the intersection, although it was mostly prairie and swampland, would be ideal for suburban development because transportation to Chicago was assured via the railroads. Cornell began buying large tracts of land in 1855. Through the early 1870s he subdivided the area and offered lots for sale. Initially calling the subdivision Cornell, he changed the name to Grand Crossing after learning of an existing village named Cornell.

The early residents were of IRISH, ENGLISH, and SCOTTISH descent and developed railroad settlements in the southeast portion of Greater Grand Crossing, just south of Oakwoods CEMETERY. Factory workers, farmers, and craft workers of GERMAN origin followed in the 1890s, building frame cottages in what was the Brookline section of Greater Grand Crossing.

The WORLD'S COLUMBIAN EXPOSITION OF 1893 further stimulated growth. Single-family frame and brick homes, two-flats, and APARTMENTS began to appear in the area to accommodate the steady population increase between 1895 and 1912. There were improvements to INFRASTRUCTURE as well. The Calumet electric STREET RAILWAY at 63rd and Grand Boulevard (now Dr. Martin Luther King Jr. Drive) was extended to Cottage Grove and 93rd, and in 1912 the dangerous train intersection which had originally given rise to the community was elevated. White City, an AMUSEMENT PARK which opened in 1904, towered over the northern part of Greater Grand Crossing from Grand Boulevard, to Calumet Avenue and from 63rd to 67th Streets until it was closed in 1933. The structure was finally torn down in 1950 to make way for the Parkway Gardens, a PUBLIC HOUSING project.

Though there had been some industry in the area since the mid-nineteenth century, by 1920 the community, with a population of 44,538, was largely residential. By the 1930s people of SWEDISH and ITALIAN descent joined those of Irish and German origin. By this time, however, as AFRICAN AMERICANS came to the community in larger numbers, these ethnic groups along with native whites began to move out. During the decade of the 1950s, the black population of Greater Grand Crossing increased from 6 percent to 86 percent. Since 1980, the community has been 99 percent African American.

Apart from Parkway Gardens, there has been little construction in Greater Grand Crossing since the 1930s, and the community has undergone significant depopulation since the 1960s. In 1960 the population stood at 63,169. Between 1980 and 1990 the population dropped from 45,218 to 38,644. Although as of 1990 a fifth of the population, 56 percent of which were African American women, lived at or below poverty level, a third of the residents of Greater Grand Crossing were second- and third-generation property owners.

Wallace Best

See also: Built Environment of the Chicago Region; Economic Geography

Further reading: Chicago Fact Book Consortium, ed. *Local Community Fact Book: Chicago Metropolitan Area, 1990.* 1995. • Drury, John. "Historic Chicago Sites." Greater Grand Crossing clipping file, Chicago Historical Society. • Hutchinson, O. N. *Grand Crossing, 1871–1938.* Chicago Communities: Greater Grand Crossing, Special Collections, Harold Washington Library.

Greek Mothers' Club at Hull House, 1940. Photographer: Furla Studios. Source: University of Illinois at Chicago.

Greeks. Greek immigrants began arriving in Chicago in the 1840s. These were primarily seamen who came from New Orleans by way of the Mississippi and Illinois Rivers and became engaged in commerce on the GREAT LAKES. Some returned to their homeland with glowing tales of the Midwest and returned with relatives and friends. Such networks would stimulate significant migration, however, only after the Great FIRE OF 1871. The community of approximately 1,000 in 1882 drew considerably, for example, on the recruitment activities of Christ Chakonas, who became known as the "Columbus of Sparta." After coming to Chicago in 1873 he saw the moneymaking possibilities it offered and returned repeatedly to his native Sparta to recruit others. Many of these relatives and compatriots procured CONSTRUCTION jobs in rebuilding the city. Others became food peddlers or merchants on Lake Street, then the city's business center. When news of their success reached their hometown, a new wave of Greeks, many from neighboring villages in the provinces of Laconia and Arcadia, followed, giving the small community on the NEAR NORTH SIDE a distinctly Peloponnesian flavor. Chicago soon became the terminus for Greek immigrants to the United States and housed the largest Greek settlement in the nation until replaced by New York City after World War II.

Initially, Greek immigration to Chicago was primarily a male phenomenon. Young men and boys came to escape extreme poverty or, in the Turkish-occupied territory of Greece, to avoid being drafted into the Turkish army. The vast majority planned to return to the homeland with enough money to pay off family debts and provide marriage dowries for their daughters or sisters. And indeed, some 40 percent of the over 600,000 Greek immigrants to the United States had returned to their homeland by World War II, giving them one of the highest repatriation rates of immigrants in the United States.

Chicago's first Greek woman, Georgia Bitzis Pooley, arrived in 1885 as the bride of Captain Peter Pooley, who had earlier worked as a sea captain on Lake Michigan. Larger numbers followed after 1904, mostly as "picture brides." In keeping with Greek tradition, women seldom worked outside of the home, although Pooley played an active role in community affairs, especially education and charity. It was not until the GREAT DEPRESSION in the 1930s that Greek women, forced by economic constraints, sought employment outside the home.

Greek immigrants settled initially in the central city in order to be near their place of work, especially the WHOLESALE Fulton and South Water Streets markets, and to procure produce for their food peddling businesses. At the turn of twentieth century, Greeks began concentrating on the NEAR WEST SIDE at the triangle formed by Halsted, Harrison, and Blue Island Streets, which became known as the "Greek Delta." There in the shadow of HULL HOUSE and amidst other European immigrants, they developed a seemingly self-contained ethnic enclave, with its web of church and school, businesses, shops, doctors, lawyers, fraternal lodges, MUTUAL BENEFIT SOCIETIES, and hometown associations, along with RESTAURANTS and the ubiquitous coffeehouses. The oldest extant Greek American newspaper, the *Greek Star,* was founded in Chicago in 1904 along with the *Greek Press* in 1913. By 1930, Chicago had become home to approximately 30,000 first- and second-generation Greek Americans.

GREEKTOWN on the NEAR WEST SIDE remained the focal point of Greek life in Chicago until it was displaced by the new UNIVERSITY OF ILLINOIS AT CHICAGO campus in the 1960s. Residents relocated to other existing Greek settlements such as RAVENSWOOD and LINCOLN SQUARE (Greektown North), and to older communities in WOODLAWN, SOUTH SHORE, and PULLMAN on the SOUTH SIDE and AUSTIN on the West Side. By the end of the twentieth century, large concentrations of Greek Americans could be found in other Chicago neighborhoods such as ROGERS PARK and West Rogers Park, EDGEWATER, FOREST GLEN, LAKE VIEW, SOUTH CHICAGO, HEGEWISCH, ASHBURN, and BEVERLY. The old Greektown BUSINESS community remained intact and had even expanded through GENTRIFICATION.

Despite coming from predominantly agrarian backgrounds, Greek immigrants moved quickly into mercantile activities. By the late 1920s, Greeks were among the foremost restaurant owners, ice cream manufacturers, florists, and fruit/vegetable merchants in Chicago. In 1927 the *Chicago Herald and Examiner* reported that Greeks were operating more than 10,000 stores, 500 of them in the LOOP, with aggregate sales of $2 million per day. One-third of the wholesale business in Chicago markets in South Water and Randolph Streets was conducted with Greek American merchants.

This immigrant community worshiped overwhelmingly in the Greek Orthodox Church, beginning in 1885 in rented facilities in cooperation with Slavic Orthodox brethren. A distinct Greek Orthodox house of worship was established in 1892, at Union and Randolph Streets, again in rented quarters, and later relocated to a Masonic hall at 60 West Kinzie Street, close to the wholesale market area where most Greeks were employed. In 1897, the first permanent Greek Orthodox church, Holy Trinity, was established in Peoria Street in the Greektown area. In 1923, Chicago was made a diocesan center of the Greek Orthodox Church in America with jurisdiction over the Midwestern states.

Greek Orthodox parochial SCHOOLS followed closely behind the establishment of churches. Holy Trinity created the first in the nation in 1908, Socrates Elementary School. Soon, a network of Greek schools sprouted up—some full day schools with a BILINGUAL English and Greek curriculum; others, afternoon and Saturday schools with only a Greek-language curriculum. While the vast majority of Greek children attended the Chicago Public Schools (except for those enrolled in Greek day schools), practically all Greek children attended afternoon (following public school attendance) and Saturday schools, where they learned the rudiments of the Greek Orthodox faith along with Greek language and culture.

After WORLD WAR II a new wave of immigration to the United States took place, with many Greeks coming to Chicago under the Displaced Persons Act. This immigration surge accelerated with the 1965 repeal of the National Origins Act, which enabled some 260,000 Greeks to enter the United States, many of them settling with relatives in Chicago. By 1990 the U.S. census counted more than 70,000 people in metropolitan Chicago claiming Greek ancestry, approximately one-third in the city and two-thirds in the suburbs. The 2000 census counted 93,140 people of Greek ancestry in the metropolitan region. Community estimates, however, ranged from 90,000 to 125,000. Suburban concentrations include ARLINGTON HEIGHTS, BERWYN, DES PLAINES, GLENVIEW, MORTON GROVE, PROSPECT HEIGHTS, OAK LAWN, PALOS HILLS, PARK RIDGE, and SKOKIE, which together accounted for 13,869 Greek Americans in 1990.

This movement to the suburbs reflects widespread success among Chicagoans of Greek descent. High rates of literacy and college attendance have helped Greek Americans move into medicine, law, education, POLITICS, and BUSINESS.

Andrew T. Kopan

See also: Americanization; Demography; Eastern Orthodox; Multicentered Chicago; Street Peddling

Further reading: Diacou, Stacy, ed. *Hellenism in Chicago.* 1982. • Kopan, Andrew T. "Greek Survival in Chicago." In *Ethnic Chicago: A Multicultural Portrait,* ed. Melvin G. Holli and Peter d'A. Jones, 1995, 260–302. • Kopan, Andrew T. *Education and Greek Immigrants in Chicago, 1892–1973.* 1990.

Greektown. In the late nineteenth century, Chicago's GREEK population began to coalesce in the area surrounded by Halsted, Harrison, and Blue Island Streets, where the campus of the UNIVERSITY OF ILLINOIS AT CHICAGO is now located. Greektown (also known as "the Delta") was the largest and best-known urban community of Greeks in the United States for much of the early twentieth century.

Max Grinnell

See also: Near West Side

Further reading: Kourvetaris, George A. *First and Second Generation Greeks in Chicago.* 1971. • Steiner, Edward A. *On the Trail of the Immigrant.* 1906.

Green Oaks, IL, Lake County, 32 miles NW of the Loop. Green Oaks originally incorporated as Oak Grove in 1960. Initial zoning prohibited all but single-family dwellings on lots between one and five acres. In 1989 the village annexed Lamb's Farm, a nonprofit commercial attraction that serves adults with mental disabilities. While land on the west side of the TOLL ROAD remained residential, Green Oaks began ANNEXING land east of the TOLLWAY in unincorporated Rondout for industry. Businesses included a concrete plant and a recycling plant.

Marilyn Elizabeth Perry

See also: Lake County, IL; Land Use

Further reading: League of Women Voters of the Libertyville/Mundelein Area. *Know Your Town.* 1990.

Greenwood, IL, McHenry County, 52 miles NW of the Loop. Settling on fertile prairies in the 1840s, YANKEE farmers named this area after nearby oak groves. For over a century, the community remained a collection of houses around an 1859 school and an 1895 general store. In 1995, fearing annexation the village of WONDER LAKE, residents voted to incorporate. The population was 244 in 2000.

Craig L. Pfannkuche

See also: McHenry County

Further reading: *McHenry County in the Twentieth Century, 1968–1994.* 1994.

Griffith, IN, Lake County, 27 miles SE of the Loop. Farmers came to the area of Griffith in the early 1850s after Congress passed the Swamp Land Act, and the State of Indiana offered swamplands for $1.25 an acre. Area residents, many of GERMAN descent, traveled to SCHERERVILLE for social affairs and Sunday services until 1891, when Jay Dwiggins and his brother Elmer of Chicago laid out the town. Construction of factories, houses, and a school soon followed. The Dwigginses advertised the town as "Chicago's Best Factory Suburb," as it had numerous RAILROADS crossing through it, including the Erie & Kalamazoo (later the Michigan Central), built in 1852; and the Michigan Southern, built in 1854.

While the town established a government in 1904, it remained small, with two SALOONS, a small foundry, a glove factory, and a population of 523 in 1910.

In 1913 developer Ernest de St. Aubin formed the Griffith Land Company. De St. Aubin moved with his family to Griffith from Chicago and oversaw the town's SUBDIVISION development until his death in 1928.

Growth was slow but steady, with residents attracted to jobs in the railroad industry, at the steel mills in GARY and EAST CHICAGO, and at the Standard Oil refinery in WHITING. In

1914 Griffith ANNEXED what later became the commercial district, on Ridge Road. Residents voted to launch a municipal water system in 1919, and in 1920 the Griffith Volunteer Fire Department took over the loosely organized FIREFIGHTING to meet growing urban needs. The city also saw the opening of the Griffith State Bank and several stores. The bank collapsed during the GREAT DEPRESSION, and the building was later used for a library.

In the 1920s, Louis Keen opened the town's second foundry. Business in Griffith expanded greatly around that time, and the population grew to 1,176 in 1930. Keen's foundry became a large employer in the thirties.

Griffith grew despite the Depression because there were still jobs at the numerous steel mills and the refinery. Ernest Strack started a grocery business in the thirties which later became LAKE COUNTY'S largest local grocery chain. Growth continued after WORLD WAR II as white veterans saw Griffith as a bedroom community to the industrial cities of Gary, East Chicago, and HAMMOND in northwest Indiana.

By 1960, the population reached 9,483 and it soared to a peak of 18,168 in 1970. The 1990s brought another housing boom around a commercial strip on Ridge Road, even as population dipped to 17,334 in 2000. Fifteen churches serve the city. Griffith's biggest employer is Packaging Corporation of America.

Jennifer Mrozowski

See also: Economic Geography; Iron and Steel; Refining

Further reading: Griffith Diamond Jubilee Corporation. *Seventy-five Years of Growing Together: Griffith Jubilee, 1904–1979.* 1979. • Moore, Powell A. *The Calumet Region.* 1959.

Grocery Stores and Supermarkets. Supplying Chicagoans with a basic necessity, the retail food industry has not experienced the rise, decline, and renaissance that other industries in the area have seen; instead, it has steadily grown with the population. It has seen the passing of the public market, the decline of small family-owned neighborhood groceries and farmers' markets, the rise of large chain store companies, and the development of the supermarket.

During the early 1800s, general stores supplied food as well as manufactured items like tools, boots, glass, and medicines to the soldiers at FORT DEARBORN and the several settlers who had come to trade with the Indians in the area. Baldwin & Parsons and Andrus & Doyle, among other merchants, also offered to exchange their manufactured goods for farmers' produce, most of which they then sold to the local market.

Most people got their daily food from a variety of sources. In 1839 the city council granted Joseph Blanchard the right to construct the city's first public market and to rent out stalls to local butchers, grocers, and produce dealers. The council prohibited the sale of retail proportions of meat, eggs, poultry, and vegetables anywhere else in the city during market hours. Such arrangements were a convenient way of assuring dealers of perishables that they would be able to find customers for their goods. The public market also provided customers a central place to purchase food and socialize. The city council authorized the construction of two more markets in the 1840s—one on the aptly named Market Street, and another on State Street in the city's first municipal structure, the Market Building.

Mid-nineteenth-century WHOLESALE and retail grocers typically handled only imported goods or those items that were impossible to manufacture or process cheaply at home. Flour, sugar, syrup, salt, tea, coffee, tobacco, spices, and dried fruit were some of the more popular articles they ADVERTISED.

The phenomenal growth of the city in the second half of the nineteenth century meant that city markets became less convenient to growing numbers of people. Rising REAL-ESTATE prices and the restrictive BUILDING CODES in the city center following the Chicago FIRE forced residents and small retailers out of the old market areas. Large wholesalers and commission merchants remained. Rather than individual customers buying from stall merchants and nearby grocers, turn-of-the-century markets consisted of retailers and jobbers haggling with wholesalers for goods to stock the retail stores in the surrounding neighborhoods.

The late nineteenth and early twentieth centuries were the age of the independent mom-and-pop store. As residents moved into neighborhoods segregated by class and ethnicity and into the suburbs created by the new STREET RAILWAYS and RAILROADS, small family-run stores sprang up to meet their needs. These new groceries, meat markets, vegetable stands, and bakeries typically reflected the ethnic DEMOGRAPHICS of the neighborhood—POLISH neighborhoods were served by Polish grocers, JEWISH neighborhoods by Jewish grocers. Stores often carried ethnic foods that were hard to find elsewhere and conducted BUSINESS in the native language of their customers. Workers followed this pattern as well. The bakers' union had separate locals for its GERMAN, Bohemian, Scandinavian, Polish, and ENGLISH members, while the meat cutters had separate German, Bohemian, Jewish, and AFRICAN AMERICAN locals.

Thousands of small neighborhood stores dotted Chicago's urban landscape until the 1950s. Families rarely owned any sort of refrigeration besides an icebox, so housewives shopped for food almost daily. This put a premium on convenience; the store had to be within walking distance of home. By 1914, some 7,400 groceries, 1,800 meat markets, and several hundred fruit and vegetable stands served the city. Except for those stores located where streetcar lines crossed, proprietors could expect only a few hundred regular customers. To protect themselves from the fierce competition that characterized their industry, Chicago's retail food store owners formed many associations over the years. Since the industry was notorious for its long hours, these associations often agitated for early closing and SUNDAY CLOSING rules. As early as 1855, retailers formed an Early Closing Association to give themselves time off in the evening. The Chicago Grocer and Butcher Clerks Protective Association joined with the Retail Grocers and Butchers Association in 1900 to pressure employers who refused to join the Sunday closing crusade, but their successes were short-lived until union contracts introduced in the 1920s, 1930s, and 1940s effectively set the hours of operation for the industry.

The rise of chain store companies in the years after World War I seriously challenged the dominance of the independent grocers. The Great Atlantic and Pacific Tea Company (A&P) established its first branch in Chicago just after the fire of 1871, but, until the 1910s, chain store companies sold mainly teas, coffees, and spices. In 1912, A&P introduced its "economy stores," which sold a full line of groceries at low prices on a cash-and-carry basis. Instead of maximizing the profit per item like the independent grocer, A&P and other chain stores sold a heavy volume for little above cost. With many stores in a single city, chains could afford NEWSPAPER space to advertise specials and encourage more trade. They also circumvented wholesalers by buying in bulk from manufacturers and purchasing facilities where they produced their own store brands. Chicago's large chain store companies, National Tea, A&P, and Kroger, acquired hundreds of stores during the 1920s. Chicago-based National Tea, for instance, grew from 41 stores in 1914 to more than 550 branches in the Chicago area in 1928, including 10 stores along just 12 blocks of North Clark Street. By 1933, chain stores accounted for only 20 percent of the grocery stores in the Chicago area, but they had 60 percent of the sales.

Independent grocers and wholesalers attempted to cripple the chain stores legislatively, but they ultimately failed. Independent store owners formed the Associated Food Dealers of Greater Chicago in 1936 to meet the chain threat through business education and political lobbying. Perhaps the most lasting legislative victory of the national movement against chain stores was the Robinson-Patman Act (1936), which attempted to outlaw wholesaler discounts and rebates to chains for bulk orders. The Federal Trade Commission prosecuted several large chains for violations of this act, but the suits did little to stop their growth. The most popular response of independents

This 1920 interior view of a Glen Ellyn grocery captures the environment of the small store that would, as the decade progressed, experience sharp competition from larger grocery chains. Photographer: Unknown. Source: Chicago Historical Society.

to the chain store threat was to form voluntary chains with Chicago's large wholesalers. This gave independents the bulk buying and advertising power of the chains while retaining individual ownership of the stores. The voluntary chains did not enjoy the benefits of the chains' centralized management, but, through affiliation, many found a way to compete with the major chains. The largest of these groups was the Independent Grocers Alliance (IGA). Other wholesaler-retailer voluntary chains included Royal Blue, Supreme, Centrella Stores, Certified Grocers, and Grocerland Cooperative. By the 1950s these voluntary chains counted more than two thousand Chicago-area stores among their members.

In the late 1930s, large supermarkets challenged the dominance of the small neighborhood stores, whether they were independent or a member of a chain. The supermarket took advantage of several developments to become a viable method of marketing low-priced food. The availability of nationally branded packaged foods allowed supermarkets to replace full-service clerks with self-service aisles and counters staffed by "checkout girls." Increased use of the automobile and home refrigeration encouraged customers to abandon daily trips to neighborhood groceries, meat markets, vegetable stands, and bakeries for weekly trips to the supermarket, where all their food needs were met under one roof.

The shift from the family-owned neighborhood store to the corporate-run chain and supermarket occasioned a change in labor relations as well. Chicago's meat markets had been thoroughly organized by the Amalgamated Meat Cutters and Butcher Workmen since the 1920s, but Retail Clerks International was not able to organize the industry's clerks until the late 1930s, when chain stores and supermarkets with many employees broke the familial ties of the small neighborhood stores. The Retail Clerks Union flourished only after the supermarket industry began to dominate food retailing in the 1950s.

In Chicago, chain stores consolidated their neighborhood stores by opening supermarkets only after independents like Hillman's and Dawson's Trading Post proved supermarkets to be successful. After WORLD WAR II, the industry shifted to fewer, larger stores. In 1933, the Chicago area had over 17,000 food stores. By 1954, the number had shrunk to 13,260 (the largest 700 stores accounting for half of the sales); in 1987, the number stood at a mere 3,638. National Tea was particularly slow in recognizing the importance of the supermarket trend, switching fully to self-service only in the 1950s. A recent arrival to the food store industry, Jewel Tea Company (an old door-to-door sales company), became a market leader in 1950s by remodeling the old Loblaw Groceterias chain and opening supermarkets in new suburban SHOPPING centers. In the 1960s and 1970s, the once dominant chains, A&P, Kroger, and National Tea, with their smaller, unprofitable supermarkets in the city center, failed to expand into the suburbs. They ultimately closed their doors. The giant new 100,000-square-foot suburban stores of the 1980s and 1990s utilized computer scanners to control inventory and cut labor costs and sold everything from drugs and milk to meat and flowers. Newer companies and older independent chains that had successfully converted to supermarkets, like Eagle, Jewel, and Dominick's Finer Foods, dominated the industry by the late twentieth century.

Paul Gilmore

See also: Food Processing: Local Market; Foodways; Housekeeping; Retail Geography; Retail Workers; Unionization

Further reading: Duis, Perry. *Challenging Chicago: Coping with Everyday Life, 1837–1920.* 1998. • Mayo, James M. *The American Grocery Store: The Business Evolution of an Architectural Space.* 1993. • Pierce, Bessie Louise. *A History of Chicago.* 3 vols. 1937–1957.

Groundwater System. For more than a century, groundwater has been used by industries throughout the Chicago region and for drinking WATER in most suburban areas. Wells have been drilled into sand and gravel near land surface and into the underlying bedrock. Any layer of rock or sediment that can yield useful quantities of water to a well is called an aquifer. Four main aquifers occur in northeastern Illinois: sand and gravel within the Quaternary glacial deposits at or near land surface, shallow bedrock composed mostly of dolomite of the Silurian System that underlies the glacial deposits, and two deeper bedrock aquifer systems composed mostly of sandstones of the Cambrian and Ordovician Systems. The uppermost of the deep bedrock aquifer systems is the more important and more heavily used. It comprises two different geologic units, the Glenwood-St. Peter and the Ironton-Galesville Sandstones, that are often grouped together with other rock layers and called the Cambrian-Ordovician Aquifer (COA). Water from the deepest bedrock aquifer, the Mt. Simon Sandstone, is generally too saline for domestic or industrial use, particularly in the southern and eastern parts of the Chicago region.

Cambrian and Ordovician rocks, including those that make up the COA, occur at land surface or directly below glacial deposits in parts of north-central and northwestern Illinois and into southern Wisconsin. In those areas, precipitation and surface water enter (recharge) the COA then flow laterally through the aquifer. Groundwater may also recharge the aquifer from other geologic units. Water entering the aquifer east of a line in western Boone, DeKalb, and LaSalle Counties flows eastward and southward toward Chicago; west of that line, groundwater flows generally west and south. In much of northern Illinois, the bedrock layers slope downward to the east-southeast, so that beneath Chicago the COA is buried by several hundred to more than a thousand feet of sediment and rock.

The earliest known withdrawal from the COA in Chicago was in 1864, when a well was drilled at the corner of Chicago and Western Avenues; water flowed out of this well without pumping and initially had enough pressure to raise water in the well about 80 feet above land surface. By 1900, many wells had been drilled into the COA, causing water levels to decrease beneath Chicago, JOLIET, and other major pumping centers. By the 1940s, more water was being pumped from the aquifer than was being recharged naturally. Although withdrawals by Chicago industry began to decline in the 1970s, drinking water withdrawals to serve a growing population continued to increase until groundwater usage peaked in 1979. By then, water levels had been lowered by as much as 850 feet in Chicago and other major pumping centers, causing an area of depressed water levels in the aquifer that extended throughout northeastern Illinois and into parts of southern Wisconsin.

After 1979, withdrawals from the COA decreased as other sources of drinking and industrial water were used, such as LAKE MICHIGAN, the FOX RIVER, and the other shallower aquifers. Concerns regarding elevated radium levels in the COA and other water-quality issues increased the use of other sources of water. Dramatic decreases in withdrawals occurred as some suburban counties began to receive drinking water from Lake Michigan in the early 1990s. Groundwater levels in the COA increased over 250 feet in and near Chicago between 1991 and 1995. Although groundwater levels are expected to maintain this recovery in the short run, continuing population growth in the Chicago region will require additional use of groundwater because withdrawals from Lake Michigan have reached the maximum allowed by international treaty. Future increases in pumping may again lower water levels in the COA and other aquifers now in use as withdrawals exceed the natural recharge rate.

James J. Miner
Richard J. Rice

See also: Ecosystem Evolution; Lacustrine System; Riverine Systems; Water Supply

Further reading: Leverett, F. *The Illinois Glacial Lobe.* 1899. • Suter, M., R. E. Bergstrom, H. F. Smith, G. H. Emrich, W. C. Walton, and T. E. Larson. "Preliminary Report on Ground-Water Resources of the Chicago Region." *Illinois: Illinois State Water Survey and Illinois State Geological Survey Cooperative Ground-Water Report* 1 (1959): 89. • Visocky, A. P. "Water-Level Trends and Pumpage in the Deep Bedrock Aquifers in the Chicago Region." *Illinois State Water Survey Circular* 182 (1997): 45.

Guatemalans. Prior to the 1980s, Chicago was home to a small number of Guatemalan professionals and students. The first large wave of Guatemalan emigration occurred in the early 1980s, when intellectuals, students, union organizers, and other activists fled a particularly violent period in Guatemala's 36-year civil war. Mostly middle-class and *Ladino* (of mixed Amerindian-Spanish ancestry), these refugees were soon joined by a second refugee group of Mayan *campesinos* (small farmers). Later that decade, Chicago became the destination for Guatemalan Mayans terrorized by their government's "scorched earth" policy. By the early 1990s, Guatemalans residing in Chicago included representatives from each of the 21 different Mayan ethnic groups, though a majority spoke Quiché.

Many were survivors of war trauma. In 1986, when the Marjorie Kovler Center for the Treatment of Survivors of Torture opened in UPTOWN, Guatemalans were among its largest client populations. Émigrés also created organizations such as the Atanasio Tzul Guatemalan Refugee Network, which helped REFUGEES from Guatemala settle in Chicago and strengthened alliances between Guatemalan-based organizations in different U.S. cities.

In the 1980s, the U.S.-based Sanctuary Movement offered critical protection to Central American refugees. A Sanctuary alliance of Chicago-based churches and synagogues provided aid and shelter to Guatemalans and SALVADORANS facing deportation. In 1982, Chicago's Wellington Avenue United Church of Christ was the second church in the country to declare sanctuary. In 1983 and 1984, the Chicago Religious Task Force on Central America created an "UNDERGROUND RAILROAD" and relocated Guatemalan refugees from Arizona to Chicago.

Many Guatemalan immigrants have sought assistance from community-based organizations such as Casa Guatemala, which was founded in 1984 and has offered adult literacy and English classes, workshops on immigration issues, legal counseling, and international support drives. Other Guatemalan community activities have revolved around youth groups, textile weaving, SOCCER leagues, traditional Mayan ceremonies, and religious observance. Our Lady of Lourdes and Our Lady of Mercy ROMAN CATHOLIC churches in ALBANY PARK had the largest Guatemalan congregations in the city at the close of the twentieth century. A reemergence of Mayan religious practices in Guatemala took root in Chicago as well.

A second wave of Guatemalans fleeing dire economic conditions arrived in Chicago in the mid-1990s and was reenergized by the devastation of Hurricane Mitch in 1998. Community-based organizations estimated 50,000–80,000 Guatemalans in Chicago by the end of the decade, while the 2000 census counted 19,444 in the metropolitan area.

The factionalism of the war and fear of drawing INS attention have discouraged Guatemalan immigrants from forming large residential clusters. Chicago's Guatemalan population has dispersed in Uptown, ROGERS PARK, LOGAN SQUARE, and Albany Park. Outside the city, most Guatemalans live in ELGIN. Middle-class and Ladino immigrants who arrived during the first wave often achieved their professional equivalencies. Mayan campesino immigrants, who form the majority of the Guatemalan population in Chicago and often have little or no formal education, work primarily in the city's RESTAURANTS and factories, or in the suburbs as gardeners and DOMESTIC WORKERS.

Two translations of the sacred Maya text the *Popol Vuh* (or *Pop-Wuj*) are in the collections at the NEWBERRY LIBRARY, including the earliest surviving manuscript copy. The second, in modern Spanish and Maya-Quiché, was presented to the library in 1966 by the Guatemalan ambassador.

Central American Independence Day on September 15 is a major holiday of Guatemalans. The summer celebration of the Cristo Negro, the patron saint of Guatemala, at Our Lady of Lourdes draws from the ceremony in Escipulas, Guatemala.

Heather McClure
José L. Oliva

See also: Demography; Hondurans; Multicentered; Nicaraguans

Further reading: Burnett, Carla. "Guatemala: A Tortured Society." M.A. thesis, University of Chicago. 1992. • Latino Institute reports. DePaul University, Chicago, IL.

Guineans. Although preceded by a small number of academics and professionals, the majority of Guineans migrated to Chicago in the 1990s from New York. Political corruption and economic stagnation led many Guineans to flee the military regime in Guinea and seek opportunities in the United States. They migrated first to New York, Boston, and Atlanta in the late 1980s, where they established sizeable communities, and have since moved to other American cities, including Chicago. Friends and family have followed, as immigrants have entered a variety of occupations, particularly TAXI driving and hairbraiding. Community members in 2002 estimated approximately 200 Guineans in Chicago.

The Guinean community gathers for MUSLIM holidays and informal social events throughout the year. In 1998, community members founded the Guinean Association of Illinois, which offers financial assistance to Guineans to meet the costs of illness or death. Members meet monthly to contribute funds and discuss social issues facing the community. The Guinean Association of Illinois is affiliated with Guinean associations in New York, Texas, Georgia, and other states, and the organizations contribute funds to one another in times of need.

Tracy Steffes

See also: Beninese; Demography; Ivorians; Malians; Multicentered Chicago

Gun Control. Since the early 1970s, Chicago and its suburban municipalities have taken a national lead in enacting firearms control legislation. Citizens' groups such as the Committee for Handgun Control, formed in 1973 and renamed Illinois Citizens for Handgun Control in 1982, have worked together with city politicians and POLICE to pass some of the nation's toughest gun control laws. Mayor Richard J. Daley was outspoken in his stand against gun rights activists, testifying before U.S. House subcommittees on gun violence in 1972 and creating a special court to process gun crimes. In response to rising gun violence by the end of the 1970s, several Chicago aldermen began exploring the idea of a freeze on handgun registration.

In 1981 the suburb of MORTON GROVE became the first municipality in the United States to ban the sale, transportation, and ownership of handguns. When a federal judge upheld the ban, the village attracted national attention. The National Rifle Association began a campaign in many states to push for legislation that would preempt gun regulations by municipal governments. The campaign was unsuccessful in Illinois. In 1982, Mayor Jane Byrne and the city council began to hold hearings on an ordinance proposed by alderman Ed Burke banning the further sale and registration of handguns in Chicago. Receiving strong support from Byrne and her allies, and coming in the wake of the assassination attempts on President Reagan and Pope John Paul II, the ordinance passed. All residents who purchased and registered their handguns prior to January 1982 were allowed to keep their weapons. Chicago became the first major city to enact a handgun freeze in United States history.

Soon other suburbs began passing gun control legislation. In the fall of 1982, EVANSTON banned handguns. In 1984, OAK PARK became the third municipality to ban handguns. The following year, Oak Park became a battlefield for national forces, as both the National Rifle Association and Handgun Control, Inc., poured resources into a referendum on repealing the ban, which failed narrowly. The impact of the Chicago freeze was felt far away, as Mayor Diane Feinstein of San Francisco began her own campaign for similar legislation. HIGHLAND PARK began restricting handguns in 1989.

In 1992, led by Mayor Richard M. Daley, the Chicago City Council voted to ban assault weapons. Contests over gun control continued in 1998, when the city and Cook County filed a lawsuit against gun manufacturers.

Eli Rubin

See also: Homicide; Prohibition and Temperance

Further reading: "Suburban Voters Get Direct Shot at Gun Control." *Chicago Tribune,* March 15, 1985. • "Town Takes New Aim at Enforcing Gun Ban." *Chicago Tribune,* May 12, 1985. • *On Target.* Newsletter of the Illinois Citizens for Handgun Control. Spring 1982.

Gurnee, IL, Lake County, 37 miles N of the Loop. The village of Gurnee hugs the banks of

the DES PLAINES RIVER, just west of the port city of WAUKEGAN. Prior to 1835 the area offered the POTAWATOMIS a convenient ford in the river as well as PORTAGE access between the Great Lakes and the continental interior via the Mississippi River system. In 1836 the area was designated as a stopping point on the Chicago-Milwaukee stage line, which crossed the river on a BRIDGE built at the site of the Potawatomi ford. The opening of the east-west MCHENRY-Waukegan TOLL ROAD made it an important crossroads in the area. Water-powered industries serving the needs of local farmers opened almost immediately, including a gristmill in 1835 and a sawmill three years later. These were followed closely by mercantile trade and taverns catering to the needs of coach passengers. In 1850, the area organized as Warren Township to prevent annexation by Waukegan, the larger neighbor to the east.

The arrival of the RAILROAD in 1873 not only linked Warren with the regional markets in Chicago, but also provided the first village of the township with its name. The depot at Warren was named for railroad land agent and former Chicago MAYOR Walter S. Gurnee, who purchased the right-of-way for the Chicago, Milwaukee & St. Paul line. The relatively quick rail trip to Chicago encouraged local farmers to produce for the growing urban population. The Bowman Dairy Company furnished the city with a regular "milk train," and a stockyard developed near the depot. The overwhelming importance of the train to local life shifted the physical location of the town's center from the stage line to the depot.

When Gurnee was incorporated in 1928, the village had only 200 residents. The village remained a largely rural, agricultural town on the Chicago periphery until well into the latter half of the twentieth century. In the 1960s the construction of a new toll road in the area, Interstate 94, brought Gurnee directly into a tighter orbit of Chicago. In 1976 Gurnee became home to Great America, one of the largest amusement parks in the Midwest, and 1991 the largest shopping mall in the Chicago area opened in Gurnee. The concomitant growth of local industry and suburbanization led to a veritable population explosion, from 7,179 in 1980 to 28,834 in 2000.

Mark Howard Long

See also: Food Processing: Local Market; Governing the Metropolis; Metropolitan Growth; Shopping Districts and Malls

Further reading: Haines, Elijah M. *Historical and Statistical Sketches of Lake County, State of Illinois.* 1852. • Lawson, Edward S. *A History of Warren Township.* 1974.

Guyanese. Early Guyanese immigrants came to the United States along with other West Indians to work in war industries during WORLD WAR II. Some settled in Chicago after the war, joined by other Guyanese immigrants who entered the country as DOMESTIC WORKERS, or as teachers and other professionals, during the 1940s. Some of these Guyanese immigrants joined or helped to organize the AMERICAN WEST INDIAN ASSOCIATION, which assisted West Indian immigrants in Chicago.

The McCarran-Walter Act (1952) placed a quota on immigration from West Indian colonies like Guyana, severely limiting the flow of immigrants. Guyanese immigrants began to come in greater numbers only after the Hart-Celler Act of 1965 liberalized immigration policy. Political and racial conflict in Guyana during the 1960s pitted Afro-Guyanese against Guyanese of Indian descent and inspired many Guyanese of both ethnic groups to flee the country. Some Guyanese were attracted by job opportunities, and the population grew gradually by means of chain migration.

Many Guyanese arrived in Chicago as students, attending such schools as Wilson Junior COLLEGE and ROOSEVELT UNIVERSITY. Others came as professionals, working in Chicago as teachers, engineers, ministers, nurses, and in other HEALTH CARE industry positions. Still others went into REAL ESTATE or established small businesses like Kader's West Indian RESTAURANT, which was a meeting place for the community for some years.

The Guyanese in Chicago have maintained an identity separate from other West Indians. The racial overtones of the political conflicts at home shaped the emergence of two largely separate Guyanese communities in Chicago. Indo-Guyanese lived mainly on the North Side, while Afro-Guyanese immigrants gravitated toward the SOUTH SIDE. Community leaders estimate that roughly equal numbers of Indo-Guyanese and Afro-Guyanese immigrants have settled in Chicago, totaling around 5,000 at the turn of the millennium.

Institutional division followed geographical segregation. In 1965, Afro-Guyanese residents formed the Guyanese of Illinois Away from Home, which aimed to help newcomers get established and to ensure survival of cultural traditions in Chicago. Also known as the Guyanese-American Association of the Midwest, the Guyanese of Illinois Away from Home was defunct by the turn of the millennium, though annual cultural events including performances at the FIELD MUSEUM and an annual Father's Day celebration survived, organized by a small group called Guyanese in Chicago. Founded in 1965 by members of the Indo-Guyanese community in Chicago, the Illinois Indian Guyanese Organization played a similar role for the Indo-Guyanese community, aiding immigrants and carrying on traditions like annual picnics and New Year's celebrations.

Chicago's Guyanese have organized celebrations for their national Independence Day, May 26. They also maintained strong ties with the homeland, sending relief funds for hurricanes and sending goods home for family members. At the end of the millennium, small numbers of Guyanese immigrants continued to arrive in Chicago while many others struggled to obtain immigration visas.

Robert Morrissey

See also: Demography; Multicentered Chicago

Gypsies. Gypsies live the world over as nations within nations. They call themselves the Rom and live by a strict religious and legal code known as Romania. Their mother tongue is Romany, a Sanskrit-derived language that reveals their Indian origins. Typically they resist working for others, preferring to be self-employed in occupations as varied as fortunetelling, used-car dealing, and traveling cinema operations. Their involvement with non-Gypsies is mainly economic. They have no interest in assimilating into any country in which they live and have preserved a strong ethnic identity.

Gypsies first came to Chicago during the large waves of Southern and Eastern European immigration to the United States in the 1880s until WORLD WAR I. They were following SERBIAN and HUNGARIAN immigrants who found work in the steel mills and factories of the city. The Gypsies, who had no interest in this type of employment, developed an economic niche playing music from the immigrants' home countries. Hired by immigrants to play at weddings, fairs, saint-day celebrations, birthdays, and other joyous occasions, Gypsy orchestras included instruments from Europe such as the cimbalom.

Two separate Gypsy subgroups settled in Chicago. The Machwaya came from Serbia and parts of the Austro-Hungarian Empire with heavy Serbian populations such as Croatia and Vojvodina. These Machwaya Gypsies spoke Serbian, had ties with the Serbian Orthodox Church, and played traditional Serbian music. They settled on the Southeast Side of Chicago, living on the outer edges of the immigrant Serb community.

The Kalderash followed Hungarian immigrants to Chicago. Like the Machwaya, they earned their livelihood playing music for the transplanted Hungarian community. The Kalderash spoke Hungarian and affiliated with the ROMAN CATHOLIC Church.

The respective religious ties to the Serbian Orthodox Church and the ROMAN CATHOLIC Church were practical for both groups. Baptizing babies and attending Easter services were the extent of the Gypsies' religious participation.

The Machwaya and Kalderash functioned as separate groups and had no significant dealings with each other. Both groups were illiterate and did not send their children to school. Instead children were trained to be musicians, often earning their own livelihoods in child orchestras or BANDS.

The Gypsies' illiteracy prevented them from establishing and cultivating the kinds of institutions usually associated with immigrant communities. There was no Gypsy church, aid organization, or newspaper in Chicago. This does not mean, however, that the Gypsy communities did not exchange information, offer assistance to one another, or observe their own religious practices. All of this was accomplished in a more informal way.

Both the Machwaya and the Kalderash emigrated to Chicago in family groups, not as single men. While music was the chief source of income for men and boys, the women earned money by reading palms. Fortunetelling parlors were operated out of their homes or at booths at community fairs.

There was no new influx of Eastern European Gypsies to Chicago until the 1970s. In 1974, a group of 102 YUGOSLAV Gypsies was

Gypsies on the South Side, 1941. Photographer: Russell Lee. Source: Library of Congress.

abandoned in the Arizona desert by a Mexican smuggler who had helped them enter the United States illegally. The American Gypsy community arranged legal help for this group and held a tribunal to determine where to settle them. Chicago was chosen because the new arrivals were Machwaya and because areas of downtown could accommodate more fortunetellers. Through intermarriage with the American Machwaya, these recent immigrants have become fully integrated into Chicago Gypsy life.

Marlene Sway

See also: Demography; Eastern Orthodox; Ethnic Music; Multicentered Chicago

Further reading: Sway, Marlene. *Familiar Strangers: Gypsy Life in America.* 1988.

Hainesville, IL, Lake County, 39 miles NW of the Loop. Elijah Haines platted a village along the Waukegan to McHenry stagecoach trail in 1846. Residents organized a village government the following year, making Hainesville the oldest incorporated community in Lake County. When the Milwaukee Road Railroad set its construction camp at Round Lake in 1899, Hainesville languished for almost a century. The population of 134 in 1990 grew suddenly, to 2,129, in 2000.

Craig L. Pfannkuche

See also: Government, Suburban

Further reading: Halsey, John J. *A History of Lake County, Illinois.* 1912. • Johnson, Joanne F. *Reflections of Hainesville.* 1976. • *Memories of Round Lake: 1908–1983.* 1983.

Hair Care Products. *See* Cosmetics and Hair Care Products

Haitians. At the end of the twentieth century the Haitian Consulate reported approximately 10,000–22,000 Haitians in the Chicago metropolitan area. Community leaders estimated closer to 30,000–35,000, including undocumented residents. Most were living on the South and far Southwest Sides of the city, with others residing on the North Side and in various suburbs.

Jean Baptiste Point DuSable, who might have been born in Haiti, arrived as early as the 1780s. At the World's Columbian Exposition in 1893 the Haitian Pavilion provided a speaking venue for Frederick Douglass. It is also reported that some Haitians lived in Chicago around 1917 during the American occupation of Haiti (1915–1934). Before the Immigration Reform Act (1965), however, the Haitian population of Chicago was negligible.

Haitians have immigrated to the United States largely since the mid-1960s, initially as expatriates from the government of François Duvalier, who held power from 1957 until his death in 1971. Haitians continued to leave the island in droves during the presidency of Duvalier's son, Jean-Claude, who held power until 1986. The newest wave of Haitians left Haiti after the coup d'état that ousted elected president Jean-Bertrand Aristide in 1991. Although the number is undisclosed, many found refuge in Chicago.

Haitiansin Chicago have maintained their diverse cultural traditions through a number of institutions: Roman Catholic and Protestant churches, a Masonic lodge, various ad hoc social and political organizations, and numerous professional organizations, including the Association of Haitian Physicians Abroad, the Haitian Nurses Association, and the Midwest Association of Haitian Women. Artistic groups, mini-jazz bands, and soccer clubs have also flourished in Chicago.

Concerns with the changing political situation in Haiti have continued to elicit strong national loyalties among Haitians in Chicago, most of whom maintain strong ties to their homeland. For this reason, they have tended to retain their Haitian citizenship, which, for many, is a badge of pride. Many express the desire to "one day" return to Haiti. Most send money to family members and friends in Haiti. Some send appliances, clothing, medicine, and other practical items through Haitian-run charitable organizations.

William Leslie Balan-Gaubert

See also: African Americans; Demography; Multicentered Chicago; Refugees

Further reading: Conway, Frederick J., and Susan Huelsebusch Buchanan. "Haitians." In *Refugees in the United States: A Reference Handbook,* ed. David W. Haines, 1985, 95–109.

Hammond, IN, Lake County, 20 miles S of the Loop. In 1851 Ernest and Caroline Hohman purchased 39 acres of land along the Grand Calumet River, where they operated a stagecoach stop. The area remained unsettled until 1869, when the George H. Hammond Company purchased 15 acres from the Hohmans for a slaughterhouse. Initially a small operation, the slaughterhouse prospered, employing 1,500 workers by 1895. Marcus Towle, one of Hammond's partners, platted the first subdivision, established the first newspaper and cemetery, and built an expensive hotel, a roller skating rink, and an opera house. He also created a variety of small industries to diversify the economy. When the city incorporated in 1883, Towle served as Hammond's first mayor.

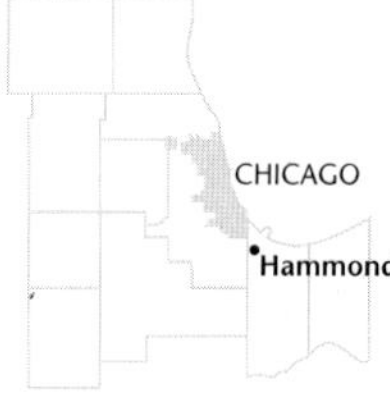

From its inception, Hammond was a German, working-class city, with a large percentage of homeowners among both skilled and unskilled workers. Local support for labor climaxed in 1894, when Hammond played a major role in the Pullman Strike. During the strike, local workers refused to handle Pullman cars, making Hammond the last stop for westbound rail traffic entering Chicago. City officials supported the strikers. But after violence erupted, federal troops occupied Hammond. On July 7, 1894, the troops shot and killed a local carpenter. Outraged, a mass meeting of citizens condemned President Grover Cleveland for having employed troops.

Support for labor diminished after 1901, when fire destroyed the Hammond Company and eliminated 1,500 jobs. The city faced a crisis. To attract new industries, local officials promised to protect capital from labor agitators. The promise allowed Hammond to attract new industries. The most significant came in 1906 with the arrival of Standard Steel Car Company, which employed 3,500 men. But the city never became as industrial as its neighbors Whiting, East Chicago, and Gary.

Instead, Hammond developed an impressive regional downtown with department stores, office blocks, and movie palaces. In addition, the 1920s produced a housing boom. A few of the new subdivisions south of downtown were exclusive, like Woodmar, which promised to move residents "out of the smoke zone and into the ozone" and provided work for local architects L. Cosby Bernard and Addison Berry. But most new homes were modest bungalows.

The Great Depression halted construction, which resumed at a fever pitch during the 1950s. By 1960, Hammond had no room for expansion. However, in 1966, the creation of River Oaks shopping mall in Calumet City challenged Hammond's 70-year history as a center for retailing. During the next decade, long-established family businesses closed and a wave of demolition gutted the once-prosperous downtown. Similarly, major industries closed, including American Steel Foundries in 1973, Pullman-Standard in 1981, and Rand McNally in 1981. Only Saint Margaret's Hospital and the First Baptist Church continued to prosper downtown.

From 1970 to 1990 Hammond's population declined 22 percent, from 107,983 to 84,236. In 1980, 47 percent of the workforce remained in manufacturing occupations, 40 percent in technical sales and service, and 13 percent in managerial and professional occupations. By 2000, the population of 83,048 remained 72 percent white, primarily of German, Polish, and Irish ancestry, while Hispanics and African Americans accounted for 21 percent and 15 percent of the population, respectively.

Joseph C. Bigott

See also: Economic Geography; Meatpacking; Railroad Workers; Shopping Districts and Malls

Further reading: Bigott, Joseph C. "With Security and Comfort for All: Working-Class Home Ownership and Democratic Ideals in the Calumet Region, 1869 to 1929." Ph.D. diss., University of Delaware. 1993. • Moore, Powell A. *The Calumet Region: Indiana's Last Frontier.* 1959. Reprinted with an afterword by Lance Trusty, 1977. • Trusty, Lance. *Hammond: A Centennial Portrait.* 1984.

Hampshire, IL, Kane County, 48 miles W of the Loop. A site called Henpeck, settled in 1839 along the Galena–Chicago Road north of the present village, was abandoned in 1874 when the Milwaukee Road RAILROAD bypassed it. Platted and incorporated along the railroad, the village is now in transition from an agricultural center to a suburban bedroom community. Population in 2000 was 2,900.

Craig L. Pfannkuche

See also: Kane County

Further reading: Joslyn, R. Waite, and Frank W. Joslyn. *History of Kane County, Illinois.* 2 vols. 1908.

Hanover Park, IL, Cook and DuPage Counties, 27 miles NW of the Loop. Ontarioville was the first name given to the village of Hanover Park, a town that straddled the COOK and DUPAGE COUNTY lines. In 1836 a stagecoach line carried townspeople along Lake Trail (also called Grant Highway and later Lake Street) as far as Galena. In 1872 the Chicago & Pacific RAILROAD (later the Chicago, Milwaukee & St. Paul) laid tracks on the property of Edwin BARTLETT after he donated more than seven acres for the construction of a depot.

Edwin Bartlett began setting down plans for the village in 1874 and by the 1880s the community was thriving as new homes were built in Bartlett's subdivision between the railroad tracks and Ontarioville Road. The little railroad stop became a connection to the larger world, with service extending to Omaha, Sioux City, and beyond.

Ontarioville's population was 250 in 1920, but when Lake Street became a major artery in the 1920s, a bypass skirted the town and an underpass went under the railroad tracks. Traffic and development were diverted away from the older section of town, in DuPage County. Slow development began on the Cook County side. In 1925 many people purchased lots in the new Grant Highway SUBDIVISION, but only a few homes were built before the GREAT DEPRESSION. In 1947 construction stalled again when the developers left town with the down-payment money.

There were so few commuters in 1955 that Ontarioville was taken off the schedule as a train stop. Nearby STREAMWOOD was expanding rapidly, and the Cook County portion of Ontarioville, afraid of ANNEXATION by its neighbor, incorporated as Hanover Park in 1958. Although the community wished to retain a rustic feel, it also hoped to prevent further encroachment of surrounding land by Streamwood. The village formed its own realty firm, Hanover Builders, to begin Hanover Park First Addition subdivision in 1959. The village also began to annex commercial property along Ontarioville Road in DuPage County.

North of Irving Park Road industries began to boom. Tradewinds Shopping Center on the northeast corner of Irving Park and Barrington Roads opened in 1968. A large annexation of DuPage County land took place in 1970, and by 1990 Hanover Park encompassed nearly five square miles. From a 1970 population of 11,916, the community nearly tripled by 1990 to 32,895.

The boundary between Cook and DuPage Counties produced an invisible dividing line for Hanover Park; now, the Elgin-O'Hare EXPRESSWAY physically divides the village.

Marilyn Elizabeth Perry

See also: Government, Suburban; Shopping Districts and Malls; Streets and Highways; Transportation

Further reading: Alft, E. C. *Hanover Township: Rural Past to Urban Present.* 1980. • Clipping file. Chicago Historical Society, Chicago, IL. • Feeley, Ralph. *From Camelot to Metropolis: The History of Ontarioville–Hanover Park.* 1976.

Hardware Manufacturing. American hardware manufacturing had its origins in the production of the agricultural implements and various tools that were produced in local nineteenth-century blacksmith shops. Prior to widespread advances in national and regional TRANSPORTATION and distribution systems, village blacksmiths fabricated nearly all of the tools used on area farms and many of those used in local manufacturing shops. So many different types of tools, gadgets, and devices were fabricated that the hardware manufacturing industry came to include the production of all sorts of contrivances not strictly defined in other metalworking trades or categories. The fabrication of nuts and bolts, shovels, hoes, rakes and forks, edge tools, handsaws and other hand tools, wood screws, wire nails, barbed wire, marine hardware, door locks, latches, table cutlery, and faucets, sinks, and other plumbing products can all be classified as hardware manufacturing. The assortment and adaptability of products manufactured by the hardware industry also lends the industry a distinctly American character.

With access to resources from its hinterland markets and its expanding base of foundries, Chicago was able to efficiently supply the metal and wire products necessary for the production of the materials and goods of the widening hardware industry. The emergence of Chicago as an industrial and manufacturing center in the years after 1860 occurred along with a national transition from an agrarian-based economy toward a multisector economy. These factors, coupled with Chicago's position as both a significant transportation and distribution node, meant that the economy of Chicago was particularly well suited for the establishment and expansion of hardware manufacturers. These manufacturers supplied the expanding array of tools, fasteners, and fixtures that helped the city of Chicago to become a leading center of manufacturing activity.

From modest beginnings several firms went on to become significant hardware manufacturers or distributors. Chicago-based McCormick Harvesting Machine Company began as essentially a hardware manufacturer, but as it achieved economic success and prominence it helped to define AGRICULTURAL MACHINERY as a distinctive industrial classification. Barbed wire was first developed and manufactured in DeKalb, Illinois, in 1874, although by the mid-1890s the vast majority of the barbed wire produced and exported from the United States was manufactured by the Chicago-based Consolidated Steel and Wire Company. Reacting to problems with conventional merchandise suppliers and distribution, Richard Hesse, the owner of a Clark Street hardware store, founded the Ace Hardware Corporation in Chicago in 1924. Hibbard, Spencer, Bartlett & Co. began as a nail manufacturer in Chicago in the 1850s but expanded its scope of operations and in 1932 introduced a product line of hand tools that were marketed under the brand name True Value. In 1962, Cotter & Co. acquired the wholesale hardware operations of Hibbard, Spencer & Bartlett and manufactured and distributed hardware under the True Value label. After merging with the American Hardware Supply Company and Coast to Coast, True Value became a principal division of the TruServ Corporation, headquartered in Chicago.

Timothy E. Sullivan

See also: Agriculture; Business of Chicago; Construction; Economic Geography; Iron and Steel

Further reading: Simmons, Edward C. "The Hardware Trade." In *One Hundred Years of American Commerce,* vol. 2., ed. Chauncey M. DePew, 1968, 633–641. • Kantowicz, Edward R. *True Value: John Cotter, 70 Years of Hardware,* 1986.

Harvard, IL, McHenry County, 63 miles NW of the Loop. In 1855 the Chicago & North Western Railway built toward Janesville, Wisconsin, from CARY. Calculating where trains from Chicago would have to stop for servicing in the days of wood fuel, Elbridge Gerry Ayer and two other North Western stockholders platted a community in southeastern Chemung Township on land that they had purchased without mentioning their RAILROAD affiliation. In April 1856, the railroad accepted Ayer's town plat as a station named Harvard. When the North Western's Kenosha-Rockford line entered Harvard in 1859, the railroad built engine-handling facilities there.

As railroad employment expanded, Harvard's population ballooned. In 1868 voters incorporated the community, and elected Ayer as president.

Bounded on the north by fertile corn-growing land and on the south by wet prairies called the Islands where masses of wild, fodder-quality hay grew, Harvard quickly became the center of a thriving dairy industry. The railroad cheaply transported fresh milk products to Chicago.

Hay-handling equipment manufacturer Hunt, Helm, and Farris (later the Starline Corporation) expanded job opportunities in the community when it arrived in 1883. By April 1891 Harvard had become so populous that voters acted overwhelmingly to form a city with ward divisions. The first mayor was N. B. Helm.

In 1939, the Kenosha Rail Line was torn out, marking the beginning of economic change in Harvard. The railroad's shift to diesel power in the late 1950s brought many layoffs. The Admiral Corporation, which opened a large radio assembly plant in 1947, expanded during the 1950s, but television usage and the success of Japanese ELECTRONICS forced the plant to close in the 1970s.

In 1942 the city instituted an annual celebration called Harvard Milk Days. A lavish parade down whitewashed streets presided over by a large plastic Holstein cow named Harmilda attracted thousands. Celebrations, aside, dairy farming declined as farmers found it easier and as profitable to supply metropolitan Chicago's supermarkets with produce. Many MEXICANS who came to work as temporary pickers and processors remained in Harvard as landscape laborers, significantly changing the community's population makeup.

With urban expansion overrunning eastern MCHENRY COUNTY in the late 1960s, Harvard's rural setting became a model to many who opposed that growth. They lobbied county government to adopt LAND-USE plans to preserve agricultural areas. Nonetheless, Harvard's rising property taxes coupled with resident demands for SHOPPING amenities and INFRASTRUCTURE improvements drove the city to ANNEX agricultural lands for industrial development. Harvard's leaders achieved their goal in 1996 when the Motorola Corporation opened a major cellular telephone manufacturing facility north of the city. However, in 2003 the plant closed.

Craig L. Pfannkuche

See also: Agriculture; Economic Geography; West Chicago, IL

Further reading: Behrens, Paul L. *The KD Line.* 1986. • *Harvard Area, 1829–1976.* 1984. • *History of McHenry County, Illinois.* 1885.

Harvey, IL, Cook County, 19 miles S of the Loop. In 1889 Turlington Harvey, a wealthy Chicago lumberman and banker, organized a REAL-ESTATE syndicate to promote the industrial suburb of Harvey, Illinois. The Harvey Land Association advertised in the nation's religious press, promoting the suburb as a temperance community offering steady work for skilled labor. To achieve this goal, the association induced a handful of manufacturers to establish factories in town. The ILLINOIS CENTRAL RAILROAD tracks divided the residential and industrial sections of the community.

The founders envisioned Harvey as a model town, a blend of capitalism and Christianity. The investors provided residents with a high quality of city services, similar to nearby Pullman. But unlike Pullman, Harvey encouraged home ownership by offering potential residents a variety of house plans. By 1900 the town contained 5,395 residents, a bank, and 11 industries. However, in 1895 residents voted by a slight majority to license SALOONS, ending the temperance experiment.

Throughout the first decades of the twentieth century, industrialists and local merchants functioned in tandem. By their efforts, Harvey acquired a fine public SCHOOL system with Thornton Township High School as its centerpiece. In the 1920s, industrialist Frederick Ingalls endowed a community hospital whose board brought together the prestigious members of the community. The development of a Young Men's Christian Association also united the interests of industrial outsiders and the local community.

During the 1920s Harvey's population grew from 9,216 to 16,374. The development produced a modest downtown and housing for various grades of industrial workers as well as finer residences for local merchants and white-collar commuters to Chicago. To a great extent, Harvey remained an evangelical PROTESTANT community. The first ROMAN CATHOLIC church, Ascension, established in 1899, was a small, predominantly IRISH parish. POLISH residents attended mass in nearby POSEN until 1914, when they established St. John the Baptist. Despite the growth of the Catholic community, Protestants retained control of the city thanks to the adoption in 1912 of a commission form of government, which replaced ward-elected aldermen with generally elected commissioners.

During the 1930s Harvey suffered an economic crisis. Two local banks closed, and the city could not maintain basic services, since most residents could not pay their property taxes. However, the high-school BASKETBALL team, led by Lou Boudreau, became state champions in an amazing run of victories.

Development resumed after World War II. In 1948 Sinclair Oil established a 38-acre technology-oriented research facility for developing new products. By 1960, Harvey's population reached 29,071, with many residents employed by local industries. In 1966, Dixie Square shopping mall opened on the western edge of the city, providing space for 41 stores.

From 1960 to 1980 Harvey changed dramatically as the AFRICAN AMERICAN population rose from 7 to 66 percent. The turnover led to racial violence at Thornton Township High School and to RACE RIOTS in 1969. Simultaneously, Harvey lost its industrial and commercial base. The closing of Dixie Square became a symbol of the city's escalating social problems. Many residents with HUD loans could not meet mortgage payments, leading to abandoned residences. Harvey's rates of crime, UNEMPLOYMENT, and poverty were among the suburbs' highest. The city struggled to redevelop industrial properties and improve its reputation as a residential city.

Joseph C. Bigott

See also: Economic Geography; Government, Suburban; Prohibition and Temperance; Racism, Ethnicity, and White Identity

Further reading: Gilbert, James. *Perfect Cities: Chicago's Utopias of 1893.* 1991. • *History: The City of Harvey, 1890–1962.* 1962. • Rahn, Carol. "Local Elites and Social Change: A Case Study of Harvey, Illinois." Ph.D. diss., University of Chicago. 1980.

Harwood Heights, IL, Cook County, 11 miles NW of the Loop. Harwood Heights has often been referred to as an "island" surrounded by the city of Chicago. It is often mistaken for part of the city instead of a suburb. Since Chicago rejected the suburb's bid for ANNEXATION in 1947, Harwood Heights has preferred to be on its own. And although it shares a library, a park district, and a high school with NORRIDGE, the community steadfastly holds to a separate identity.

In 1835 Israel Smith settled in the area, erecting his cabin on a ridge later known as Union Ridge. His father and brothers followed, and neighbors began referring to the land as "Smith's Ridge." When the Irving GOLF Club (now Ridgemoor Country Club) purchased Israel Smith's farm in 1908 the area remained rural without the conveniences of the city. Streetcar lines stopped 10 blocks short of the community. Residents were undaunted by their lack of services, since they did not want to pay taxes. Most presumed that Chicago would eventually annex their land as it had done with nearby NORWOOD PARK in 1893.

Farms were predominant in 1938 when Duro-Craft Homes developed the community's first SUBDIVISION on approximately six acres south of Foster Avenue and west of Harlem Avenue. Little more development came until after WWII. Without POLICE protection, sewers, paved streets, or streetlights, residents coped with muddy, rutted streets, and flooded basements. Hopeful that annexation to Chicago would improve their area, property owners were disappointed when Chicago rejected their bid. In 1947 they incorporated an area of four blocks square as a village, with approximately 500 residents. Herbert Huening, who had led the failed annexation effort, became the Harwood Heights' first president and conducted business in the first village hall, his basement. The origin of the town's name is uncertain, but some believe it results from combining parts of the names of Harlem Avenue and Norwood Park Township.

The village began expanding in the early 1950s by annexing land south of Lawrence. The area east of Harlem had been annexed by the end of the decade. Ridgemoor Country Club, although completely surrounded by Harwood Heights, was never annexed and remained unincorporated. In 1960 the population of the village totaled 5,688.

Harwood Heights has combined independent status with the convenience of the nearby city. It also has forged an important alliance with its other neighbor Norridge. Both work together to combat and street crime noise abatement issues with nearby O'HARE AIRPORT. Students from both communities attend Ridgewood High School. The 2000 census counted 8,297 residents, 92 percent of whom were white, 6 percent Hispanic, 4 percent Asian, and less than 1 percent African American. A large percentage of the population is of ITALIAN and POLISH ancestry.

Marilyn Elizabeth Perry

See also: Government, Suburban; Metropolitan Growth

Further reading: Clipping files are located in the local history room at the Eisenhower Public Library, Harwood Heights. • *Comprehensive Village Plan, Harwood Heights, Illinois,* and *Neighborhood Analysis, Harwood Heights, Illinois.* 1970. • McGowen, Thomas. *Island within a City: A History of the Norridge–Harwood Heights Area.* 1989.

Hawthorn Woods, IL, Lake County, 32 miles NW of the Loop.

The POTAWATOMI left the area of what is now Hawthorn Woods following a TREATY with the United States in 1829, and YANKEE farmers moved in. GERMAN immigrants followed in the 1850s, and later DUTCH farmers arrived. After the turn of the century, Chicagoans took weekend excursions to the area to walk on hiking paths through heavily wooded terrain.

In 1945 Matt and Germaine Larson purchased a forest farm located on Old McHenry Road. Oak, hickory, hawthorn, and elm TREES surrounded the farmhouse. In 1953 Matt Larson began development of the wooded area with sprawling ranch-style houses on large lots. Wanting to retain the rural atmosphere and to avoid the overcutting of trees, he stipulated that no trees could be removed without his permission. The houses were mainly cedar and redwood and all building materials had to meet Larson's approval. In 1967 a barn from the original farm became the village hall.

The town of Hawthorn Woods consisted of only 141 residents on 976 acres at incorporation in 1958. Incorporation came as a result of citizens wishing to protect their environment from the dense development proposed by Chicago builder Joseph Brickman. A limit on lot size for new development was set at a minimum of one acre.

The village grew to 6,002 by 2000; the majority of homeowners are white-collar professionals. Development has remained limited; only custom houses may be built in Hawthorn Woods. House styles range from historic farmhouses to mansions.

Marilyn Elizabeth Perry

See also: Government, Suburban; Lake County, IL

Further reading: "Hawthorne Woods." *Ela Township Centennial Guidebook.* 1965. • Loomis, Spencer. *A Pictorial History of Ela Township.* 1994.

Haymarket and May Day. On May 1, 1886, Chicago unionists, reformers, socialists, ANARCHISTS, and ordinary workers combined to make the city the center of the national movement for an EIGHT-HOUR day. Between April 25 and May 4, workers attended scores of meetings and paraded through the streets at least 19 times. On Saturday, May 1, 35,000 workers walked off their jobs. Tens of thousands more, both skilled and unskilled, joined them on May 3 and 4. Crowds traveled from workplace to workplace urging fellow workers to strike. Many now adopted the radical demand of eight hours' work for ten hours' pay. Police clashed with strikers at least a dozen times, three with shootings.

At the McCormick reaper plant, a long-simmering STRIKE erupted in violence on May 3, and police fired at strikers, killing at least two. Anarchists called a protest meeting at the West Randolph Street Haymarket, advertising it in inflammatory leaflets, one of which called for "Revenge!"

The crowd gathered on the evening of May 4 on Des Plaines Street, just north of Randolph, was peaceful, and Mayor Carter H. Harrison, who attended, instructed POLICE not to disturb the meeting. But when one speaker urged the dwindling crowd to "throttle" the law, 176 officers under Inspector John Bonfield marched to the meeting and ordered it to disperse.

Then someone hurled a bomb at the police, killing one officer instantly. Police drew guns, firing wildly. Sixty officers were injured, and eight died; an undetermined number of the crowd were killed or wounded.

The Haymarket bomb seemed to confirm the worst fears of business leaders and others anxious about the growing labor movement and radical influence in it. Mayor Harrison quickly banned meetings and processions. Police made picketing impossible and suppressed the radical press. Chicago NEWSPAPERS publicized unsubstantiated police theories of anarchist conspiracies, and they published attacks on the foreign-born and calls for revenge, matching the anarchists in inflammatory language. The violence demoralized strikers, and only a few well-organized strikes continued.

Police arrested hundreds of people, but never determined the identity of the bomb thrower. Amidst public clamor for revenge, however, eight anarchists, including prominent speakers and writers, were tried for murder. The partisan Judge Joseph E. Gary conducted the trial, and all 12 jurors acknowledged prejudice against the defendants. Lacking credible evidence that the defendants threw the bomb or organized the bomb throwing, prosecutors focused on their writings and speeches. The jury, instructed to adopt a conspiracy theory without legal precedent, convicted all eight. Seven were sentenced to death. The trial is now considered one of the worst miscarriages of justice in American history.

Many Americans were outraged at the verdicts, but legal appeals failed. Two death sentences were commuted, but on November 11, 1887, four defendants were hanged in the Cook County jail; one committed suicide. Hundreds of thousands turned out for the funeral procession of the five dead men. In 1893, Governor John Peter Altgeld granted the three imprisoned defendants absolute pardon, citing the lack of evidence against them and the unfairness of the trial.

Inspired by the American movement for a shorter workday, socialists and unionists around the world began celebrating May 1, or

Labor Unrest in Chicago, April 25–May 4, 1886

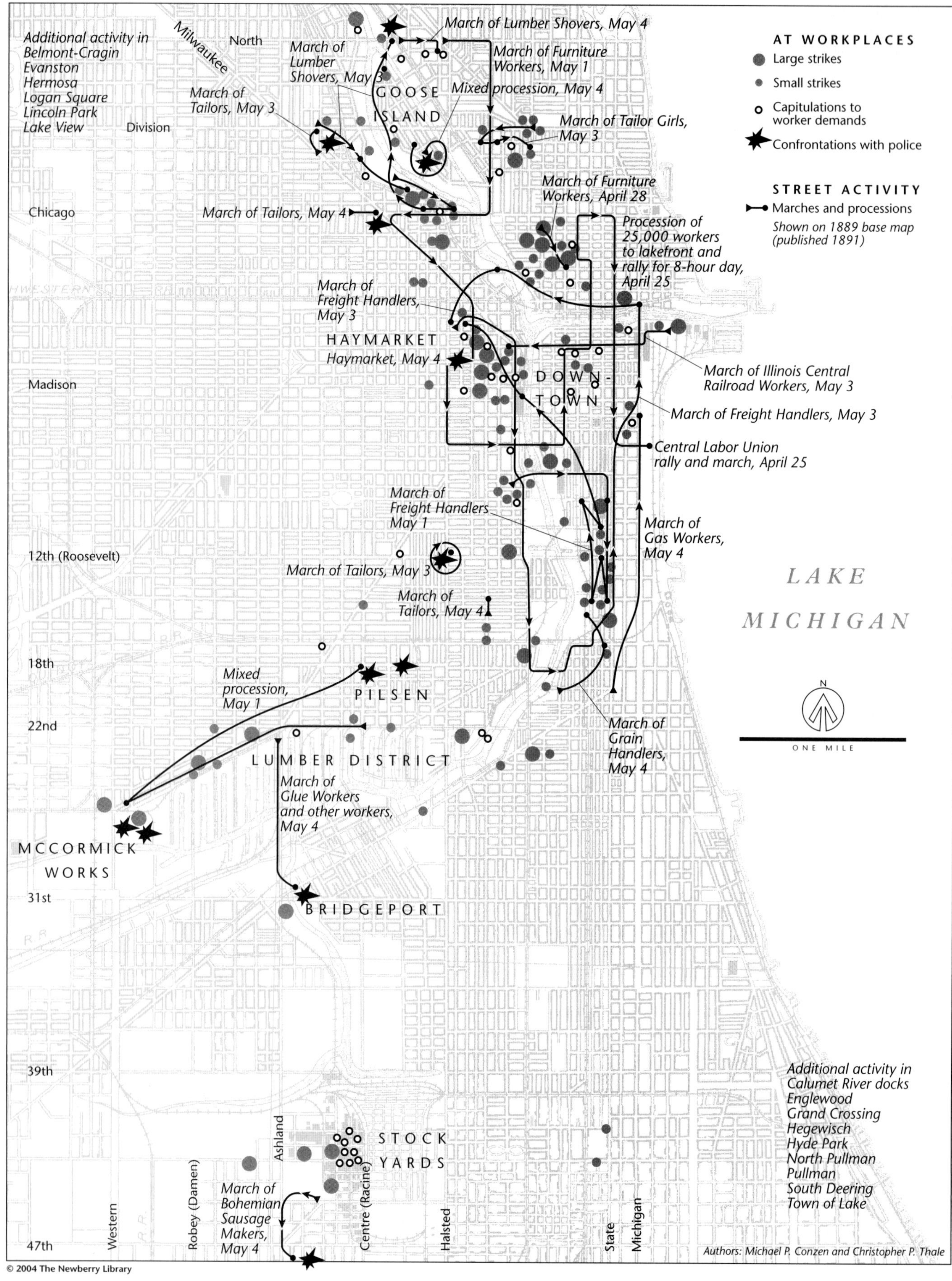

Workers throughout Chicago and its suburbs took part in the nationwide movement for an eight-hour day with strikes, meetings, and parades in early to mid-1886. Reflecting the city's economic and social geography, labor activity was concentrated in industrial areas along the Chicago River and in nearby working-class neighborhoods. Tens of thousands went on strike, and many strikers marched from workplace to workplace, displaying solidarity and summoning fellow workers to join them. On two separate days, thousands of railroad freight handlers marched for miles from one terminal to another. But worker processions were more often neighborhood affairs, centered on local employment concentrations and sometimes displaying ethnic clustering. To avoid strikes, many employers agreed to worker demands. Though most labor activity was peaceful, violent confrontations with the police also occurred. A clash on May 3 between workers and police near the McCormick Reaper Works (*left*) led to the call for a protest meeting at the Randolph Street Haymarket. The Haymarket (*upper center*) was the starting point for two parades and the scene of a May 4 protest meeting which ended in violence. In the aftermath, the eight-hour movement came to a resounding halt for the time being.

"May Day," as an international workers' holiday. In the twentieth century, the Soviet Union and other Communist countries officially adopted it. The Haymarket tragedy is remembered throughout the world in speeches, murals, and monuments. American observance was strongest in the decade before World War I. During the Cold War, many Americans saw May Day as a Communist holiday, and President Eisenhower proclaimed May 1 as "Loyalty Day" in 1955. Interest in Haymarket revived somewhat in the 1980s.

A monument commemorating the "Haymarket martyrs" was erected in Waldheim Cemetery in 1893. In 1889 a statue honoring the dead police was erected in the Haymarket. Toppled by student radicals in 1969 and 1970, it was moved to the Chicago Police Academy.

Christopher Thale

This poster, pasted on a wall in the San Telmo neighborhood of Buenos Aires, Argentina, recalls the significance of Haymarket in worldwide observances of May Day. Its caption reads "Another 1st of May in struggle." Photographer: Janice L. Reiff. Source: Janice L. Reiff.

See also: Contested Spaces; Free Speech; Global Chicago; Knights of Labor; Strikes; Unionization

Further reading: Avrich, Paul. *The Haymarket Tragedy.* 1984. • David, Henry. *The History of the Haymarket Affair.* 1936. • Schneirov, Richard. *Labor and Urban Politics.* 1998.

Hazardous Waste. *See* Waste, Hazardous

Hazel Crest, IL, Cook County, 22 miles S of the Loop. William and Carrie McClintock arrived in the area in 1890, purchasing 80 acres between Homewood and Harvey. They were impressed by the activity along the Illinois Central Railroad, especially with the upcoming World's Columbian Exposition.

McClintock platted and registered the land as South Harvey, anticipating benefits from the interest in and advertising for the planned industrial city of Harvey. However, South Harvey was fairly quickly annexed by the village of Homewood. By late 1895, residents organized a community church and led a successful campaign to deannex from Homewood. Carrie McClintock led a petition drive to change the name from South Harvey to Hazel Crest, after the many thickets of hazelnut bushes there.

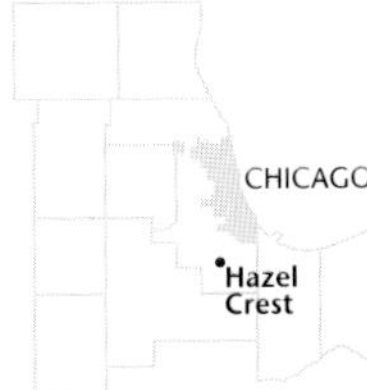

In 1910 the area had 310 residents, who voted to incorporate as Hazel Crest in 1911. Residents soon began municipal services, a volunteer fire department, a public school, and St. Anne's Roman Catholic Church.

Following World War I, the Illinois Central Railroad decided to raise the track level across the south suburbs and electrify its commuter line. In addition, in the 1920s and '30s, the IC built the Markham rail freight yards to the north of Hazel Crest. Polish, Italian, and Serbian yard workers moved to Hazel Crest.

With the rail yards, commuter access, and local enterprises, Hazel Crest continued its residential growth with a number of subdivisions, including Pottawatomie Hills. By 1960 there were 6,205 residents, with 14,816 by 2000. African Americans have come to dominate Hazel Crest's population, growing from 52 percent of the population in 1990 to 78 percent in 2000.

As with many suburbs, the village overlaps with a variety of other local governments, including four elementary and three high-school districts, three townships, and two community college districts, and it shares a library district with Country Club Hills. The community has a tradition of strong human services and was one of the first to have a Human Relations Commission.

Larry A. McClellan

See also: Governing the Metropolis; Railroads

Further reading: Baader, Geraldine M. "The Emergence of Hazel Crest." M.A. thesis, Governors State University. 1984. • Rocke, Verva Coleman, ed.; Lucile Ross and Ileane Breslin, co-eds. *Living in Hazel Crest, 1890–1990.* 1990.

Health. *See* Public Health

Health Care Workers. Efforts to organize health care workers in the United States, including the 100,000 workers employed in Chicago's 70 hospitals in the 1990s, have been hampered by long-standing divisions between doctors, nurses, and other hospital staff, as well as a series of U.S. Supreme Court rulings dividing hospitals into eight different bargaining units. Union organizers have also cited the increasing corporatization of American hospitals as an obstacle to organizing efforts.

Hospital organizing efforts surged nationwide in the 1970s but results varied from region to region. For example, in the late 1990s two-thirds of New York City's hospital workers were members of unions or professional organizations, while only 20 percent of their colleagues in Chicago were organized. Half of these were members of Local 73 of the Service Employees International Union (SEIU), accounting for 40 percent of the local's 25,000 members. Other workers, including occupational therapists, technical employees, office clerks, and skilled and semiskilled maintenance workers, have been organized by the American Federation of State, County, and Municipal Employees (AFSCME), the International Brotherhood of Electrical Workers, and the International Brotherhood of Teamsters. The most original feature of local health worker unionization in Chicago was a joint effort by Local 73 of the SEIU and Teamster Local 743 which resulted in the founding of the Hospital Employees Labor Program (HELP) in 1966. In its first five years, HELP concentrated on organizing low-paid service and maintenance workers, most of whom were African American. Later, nonservice and clerical workers were recruited.

Many nurses in the United States have traditionally preferred professional organizations over traditional union structures. Local nurses have been organized by the Illinois Nurses Association (INA), the local affiliate of the American Nurses Association (founded in 1901), and unions affiliated with the AFL-CIO like the SEIU, and AFSCME; as well as teachers unions such as the National Educational Association, the American Federation of Teachers, and the Chicago Teachers Federation. By the spring of 1999, 7,000 of Illinois' approximately 130,000 nurses, 70 percent of whom worked in the Chicago metropolitan area, were members of the INA.

Most doctors and their national organization, the American Medical Association, have traditionally opposed unionization. By 1999 only 30,000 of the nation's 680,000 doctors had joined unions. In the 1970s friction between doctors and INSURANCE companies stimulated interest in collective bargaining. In 1973, 15 Chicago-area doctors founded the Illinois Physicians Association (IPA), chartered by the AFL-CIO. However, organizers cited difficulties in mobilizing doctors to attend meetings and the IPA dissolved by 1979. Interest in collective bargaining by doctors, anxious to negotiate with health maintenance organizations over reimbursement amounts for medical procedures and drug coverage policies, rose once again in the 1990s. The Illinois State Medical Society voted to form a union in April 1999.

Keith Andrew Mann

See also: Cook County Hospital; Public Health; Work

Further reading: Budrys, Grace. *When Doctors Join Unions.* 1997. • Derber, Milton. *Labor in Illinois: The Affluent Years, 1948–80.* 1989. • Fink, Leon, and Brian Greenberg. *Upheaval in the Quiet Zone: A History of Hospital Workers' Union, Local 1199.* 1989.

Heat Wave of 1995. *See* Public Health

Hebron, IL, McHenry County, 58 miles NW of the Loop. YANKEES were Hebron's earliest settlers, though they eventually were joined by GERMAN, IRISH, DUTCH, and Scandinavian immigrants. The 1860 arrival of the Kenosha & Rockford RAILROAD allowed the township's farmers to ship livestock to Chicago's stockyards. Incorporated in 1895, Hebron remains primarily a farming community, with a population of 1,038 in 2000.

Brandon Johnson

See also: Agriculture; McHenry County

Further reading: *McHenry County in the Twentieth Century, 1968–1994.* McHenry County Historical Society. 1994. • Nye, Lowell A., ed. *McHenry County, Illinois, 1832–1968.* 1968.

Hebron, IN, Porter County, 45 miles SE of the Loop. An 1832 TREATY with the POTAWATOMI opened what is now Hebron to U.S. settlement, but only the 1863 arrival of the Pittsburgh, Chicago & St. Louis RAILROAD motivated significant growth. Incorporated in 1890, Hebron has become a bedroom community, a fact confirmed by the proliferation of SUBDIVISIONS and SHOPPING CENTERS there.

Brandon Johnson

See also: Lake County, IN

Further reading: *Charter Centennial (1890–1990), Hebron, Indiana: One Hundred Years.* 1990.

Hegewisch, Community Area 55, 16 miles SE of the Loop. Early maps indicate that a natural water passage existed from the present location of HAMMOND, Indiana, to the western banks of Wolf Lake through Hyde Park Lake. NATIVE AMERICANS settled on sand DUNES and traveled along this passage for trade purposes. Waterfowl also followed this natural route during migratory periods as the primary feeder to the Mississippi flyway.

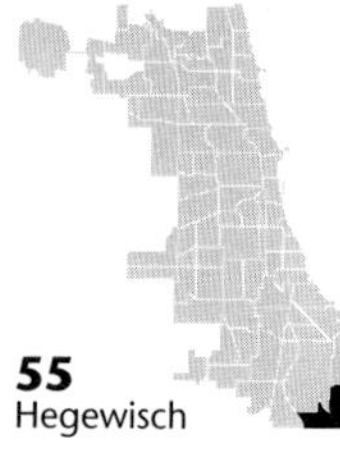

Immigrant laborers and other settlers built the first RAILROADS across this terrain into Chicago in the 1850s. Originally part of LAKE TOWNSHIP, it became part of HYDE PARK TOWNSHIP in 1867.

Adolph Hegewisch, president of U.S. Rolling Stock Company, hoped to establish "an ideal workingman's community" when he laid out the town along a rail line in 1883. He moved his company about 10 miles east to border the new town and announced plans to build two major canals as an incentive for other factories to locate near the town. The first canal would have shortened the CALUMET RIVER; the second would have stemmed from the first to connect Wolf Lake to LAKE MICHIGAN. Owing to a lack of capital, these plans never came to fruition, and the town of Hegewisch fell dramatically short of its estimate of 10,000 residents by 1885—only 500 names were listed in the town directory four years later.

In 1889, Hegewisch was ANNEXED to Chicago along with the rest of Hyde Park Township. Adolph died a few years later and the Rolling Stock Company became part of the Pressed Steel Car Company before World War I. During these decades, Joseph H. Brown and other industrialists developed steel mills in and around Hegewisch. New residents included many POLISH, YUGOSLAVIAN, CZECHOSLOVAKIAN, SWEDISH, and IRISH workers.

In 1935, attempts to organize workers for better pay, hours, and conditions affected the Hegewisch community. The CONGRESS OF INDUSTRIAL ORGANIZATIONS (CIO) created the Steel Workers Organization Committee (SWOC). In 1937, Carnegie-Illinois, a major subsidiary of U.S. Steel located in Hegewisch, signed a contract with the SWOC that limited hours, increased pay, and provided vacation time. The other "Little Steel" plants around the area did not follow suit, which prompted A STRIKE against Republic Steel and other plants in May. On Memorial Day, off-duty police officers hired by Republic opened fire on the nonviolent demonstrators, killing 10 and injuring hundreds. The violence succeeded in breaking the union until the emergence of the United Steelworkers in the 1940s. This event has since become known as the MEMORIAL DAY MASSACRE; a plaque commemorates the victims at 117th Street and Avenue O.

The steel mills in and around Hegewisch remained the mainstays of the community over the next half century. The Pressed Steel Car Company switched its manufacturing operation from railroad cars to Howitzer tanks and other vehicles during World War II. After the Vietnam War, steel manufacturing waned across America, Hegewisch included. After the closure of Wisconsin Steel in 1980, the population declined because of layoffs. However, the remaining residents focused new energies on community activism and successfully blocked plans for both a Calumet airport and designation of landfills in the area. In the 1980s, residents of Hegewisch initiated a renewal project that included successful lobbying for a METRA stop, a branch of the CHICAGO PUBLIC LIBRARY, and a $300,000 block grant to repair INFRASTRUCTURE. Since the 1960s, Hegewisch has balanced out some of its population losses with the relocation of a significant number of MEXICAN Americans into the area. Adjacent to the Bishop Ford EXPRESSWAY (I-94) and numerous railway lines, industry (including DMC, a major Midwest distributor of Ford automobiles since 1998) and nearby Indiana casinos constitute the employment base for the residents of Hegewisch.

Erik Gellman

See also: Economic Geography; Iron and Steel; Iron- and Steelworkers; Transportation

Further reading: Sellers, Rod, and Dominic A. Pacyga. *Chicago's Southeast Side.* 1998.

Hermosa, Community Area 20, 6 miles NW of the Loop. Hermosa is defined by RAILROAD tracks and embankments. The Chicago & North Western Railroad line forms its western boundary east of Cicero Avenue while the east and south borders are hemmed by two lines of the Chicago, Milwaukee & St. Paul Railroad (CM&SP). To the north, six blocks of Belmont Avenue were initially the tiny hamlet's main access into neighboring communities.

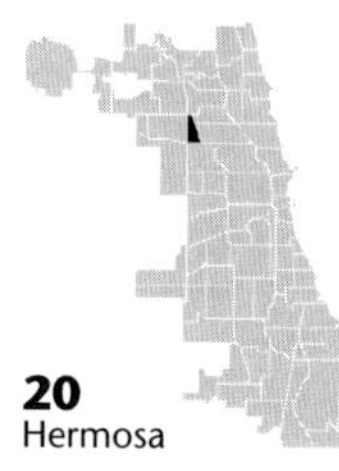

As early as 1875 the CM&SP had a depot in Hermosa, but it was not a regular stop until 1886. SCOTTISH immigrants settled here in the 1880s, calling the area of woods and prairie Kelvyn Grove after the eighth Lord Kelvyn. Not long after, GERMAN and Scandinavian farmers established themselves in the northwest and southern parts of what became Hermosa.

The Dreyer Company tried to establish a factory for locomotive works in 1882 where the two CM&SP lines intersected, but two years later when the building had still not been occupied, it was sold to the Laminated Wood Company. By 1886 a number of other companies, such as the Expanded Metal Company, the Eclipse Furnace Company, and a warehouse belonging to the Washburn and Moen Manufacturing Company, located along the rails.

To accommodate factory workers, REAL-ESTATE developers built in an area to the southwest, naming the SUBDIVISION Garfield after the recently assassinated president. One of the development companies, J. F. and C. P. Keeney, erected cottage-style houses and guaranteed each of the 150 home buyers that if they died before completion of the contract, their heirs would receive a free deed to the property. Keeney took a special interest in the community. He joined in local POLITICS, persuaded the railway to add a stop at Garfield, and then donated money for a depot, which was named after him. Chicago ANNEXED the area in 1889 under the name Hermosa, a name whose origin is disputed.

Although railroads brought some industry, and annexation slowly added municipal service and street improvements, accelerated growth did not occur until 1907 when streetcar lines extended along North, Armitage, and Fullerton Avenues. POLISH, IRISH, and ITALIAN populations moved into the SWEDISH and German community. The population stood at 15,152 in 1920, with construction booming in the vicinity of the newly created Kelvyn Park. Industrial growth along the railroads actually impeded residential construction, however.

Growth continued until the GREAT DEPRESSION. By 1942 frame and brick BUNGALOWS and two-flats predominated. Bordered by railroads, dead-end streets geographically isolated residents from adjacent communities but also gave them a sense of security. Many homes had 25-foot frontages, and this narrow distance between houses generated a neighborliness on the block.

Hermosa's population fluctuated only slightly from 1970 to 1980 but rose in the next decade from 19,547 to 23,131. Ethnically the area changed as Hispanics became the dominant group, growing from 31 percent in 1980 to 68 percent in 1990 and 84 percent in 2000. More than half of the Hispanic population were PUERTO RICAN, while most of the rest were MEXICAN.

Criminal activity concerned residents as early as the 1970s when the community's crime rate increased significantly. A 17.4 percent poverty rate in 1989 and an UNEMPLOYMENT rate of 10.9 percent in 1990 accounted for a decrease in home buyers and an increase in renters.

Working to prevent any further deterioration, residents banded together in block clubs, church groups, and other organizations. Groups such as United Neighbors in Action formed in 1982 to voice their concerns over proposed SUBSIDIZED HOUSING. To ensure safety and combat escalating GANG problems, some groups began policing their blocks. Kelvyn Park occupants joined together in the Kelvyn-Ken-Wel Community Organization to encourage redevelopment of two vacant properties where gangs were engaging in drug deals. Other projects included developing a neighborhood reinvestment program to encourage area banks to work with potential home buyers.

Marilyn Elizabeth Perry

See also: Economic Geography; Street Railways; Transportation

Further reading: Karlen, Harvey M. *Chicago's Crabgrass Communities: The History of the Independent Suburbs and Their Post Offices That Became Part of Chicago.* 1992. • Kruggel, Adam. "Federation Partnership Puts Community First." *National Training and Information Center Reports* (January, February, March 1997): 2, 4. • Skeris, Peter, and Maria T. Armendariz. *Hermosa: A Study of a Community in Transition.* 1971.

Hickory Hills, IL,

Cook County, 15 miles SW of the Loop. This predominantly residential community is in the northeast quarter of Palos Township, southwest of Chicago. Approximately half of the township is FOREST PRESERVE, with the three Palos communities (PALOS PARK, PALOS HEIGHTS, PALOS HILLS) and Hickory Hills in the eastern half. Originally, Hickory Hills was known informally as North Palos.

The Palos area had significant NATIVE AMERICAN settlement due to the resources and wildlife of the wooded hills and the Saganashkee Slough and trails through the area to the Chicago PORTAGES. Settlers from eastern states arrived as early as the 1830s, but the earliest individuals noted in local records (1858) were Mathias and Josephina Wachter.

Growth in the township was slow, with better options for farmers in areas without the hills and the slough. The whole area north of the Calumet feeder canal, lacked rail service.

The natural richness of the area had been recognized, and as early as 1916 the new Cook County FOREST PRESERVE District began purchasing land west and southwest of present-day Hickory Hills and Palos Hills. This has led to the acquisition over time of over 10,000 acres of preserve, the bulk of this being the western half of Palos Township.

During WORLD WAR II, the availability of land on the southern edges of the Hickory Hills area led to the development of cheap dwelling units, some of which served as housing for migrant workers employed in defense industries in the Chicago region. In 1951, the desire on the part of local residents to gain control over BUILDING CODES and to obtain some basic municipal services led to village incorporation. Incorporation also headed off concerns about the village of BRIDGEVIEW to the east, which was aggressively ANNEXING commercial land along Harlem Avenue.

The initial population was around 250, and the village enjoyed its "rural" living adjacent to the forest preserves. A number of residents maintained horse stables, and the community worked together on basic needs like local road repairs. By 1960, the population had grown to 2,707 as part of the great suburban growth of the 1950s. By 1980, the population had reached 13,778, and in 2000 it was 13,926.

In 1966, residents reorganized as the city of Hickory Hills. The new city replaced septic tanks with a sewer system and connected to Lake Michigan WATER.

Hickory Hills, named for its rolling hills and stands of hickory TREES, continues today as a residential community with three major SHOPPING DISTRICTS and one of the more than 20 GOLF courses in the southwest suburban region.

Larry A. McClellan

See also: Government, Suburban; Suburbs and Cities as Dual Metropolis

Further reading: Andreas, A. T. *History of Cook County, Illinois.* 1884. • Frale, Nanette. "Hickory Hills," *Hickory Hills Citizen,* April and May issues, 1980. • Venezio, Susan. "Hickory Hills: Rural Area to Urban Fringe, 1926–1976." Unpublished paper for Chicago State University, August 1976. Green Hills Public Library, Palos Hills, IL.

Highland, IN,

Lake County, 25 miles S of the Loop. Ohioans Michael and Judith Johnson settled in what came to be called Highland in 1847. According to legend, the Johnsons' son, Rod, found a flock of ducks frozen in the ice of the Little CALUMET RIVER one winter. Harvesting them with a stick, he earned enough money to buy 20 acres of land. Under Congress's Swamp Land Act of 1850, settlers could buy large tracts at $1.25 per acre if they agreed to drain the land.

A Philadelphia book publisher named Aaron Hart also bought up land in what became Highland, hence the name Hart Ditch, which channeled Plum Creek from DYER to the Little Calumet.

In 1883, the Chicago & Atlantic RAILROAD tracked through the area. The railroad surveyors, after surveying miles of swamp, called the sand ridge "Highlands." That year, a substantial landowner, John Clough, platted the town. The area for a short time bore the name Clough Postal Station for the purpose of MAIL DELIVERY, but the railroads surveyors' choice of Highlands won out.

Soon DUTCH settlers, who worked as tenant farmers, began moving to Highlands from nearby MUNSTER. They supplied much of the cabbage for the town's first industry, a kraut factory. A second kraut factory was also established, as well as a cement block company and a brick factory.

In the early 1900s several other railroads passed through, encouraging AGRICULTURE and other business. Highlands was incorporated in 1910, with a population of 304 people. In 1914 the first bank, the Farmers and Merchants Bank, was established, as well as a volunteer FIRE brigade. In 1927 Wicker Park was converted from pasture to a park commemorating the soldiers of WORLD WAR I. President Calvin Coolidge led the dedication.

Highland was dealt a serious blow by the GREAT DEPRESSION. Its lumberyard and bank failed, along with several other businesses. After WORLD WAR II the town's financial base began to change from agricultural to commercial. A modern dairy plant was built as well as a theater.

In the forties, Highland's population nearly doubled, and it exploded in the fifties, growing from 5,878 to 16,284 by 1960. Many of its new residents came from nearby industrial cities such as GARY, HAMMOND, and EAST CHICAGO. Highland benefited from the nation's attraction to the suburbs in the 1950s; Hammond considered annexing the town in the mid-1950s.

The central fire station was completed in 1972, and a more spacious post office opened in 1975. A new park, Main Square Park, was dedicated in 1981.

By 1980, the population reached a high of 25,935, and then dropped to 23,696 in 1990, remaining little charged. About 93 percent of Highland's residents in 2000 were white. The downtown area boasts a small business district, but most businesses are located along Indianapolis Boulevard and Ridge Road.

Jennifer Mrozowski

See also: Economic Geography; Food Processing: Local Market; Groundwater System; Lake County, IN

Further reading: Griffith Diamond Jubilee Corporation. *Seventy-five Years of Growing Together: Griffith Jubilee, 1904–1979.* 1979. • Highland, Indiana, Diamond Jubilee Committee. *Highland, Indiana, Diamond Jubilee, 1910–1985.* 1985. • Moore, Powell A. *The Calumet Region.* 1959.

Highland Park, IL, Lake County, 23 miles N of the Loop. Highland Park's bluffs, lake vistas, ravines, and accessibility to Chicago support the foresight of nineteenth-century developers who envisioned this picturesque suburb as a retreat for Chicago's affluent professionals.

Indian trails and mounds indicate that before the BLACK HAWK WAR, POTAWATOMI traversed the forested acres that became Highland Park. GERMAN immigrants founded two village ports, St. Johns (1847), and Port Clinton (1850), in hopes of opening hinterlands for trade.

By 1855, Walter S. Gurnee, former Chicago mayor, North Shore REAL-ESTATE speculator, and president of the Chicago & Milwaukee RAILROAD, took control of the Port Clinton Land Company and platted the area for residential settlement. Gurnee surmised that rail offered the best link to Chicago, and that residential development, rather than commercial, would succeed.

The city of Highland Park incorporated with about 600 residents, a school, a hotel, and a religious association in March 1869. Purchase or public consumption of alcohol was prohibited. To heighten the picturesque appeal of the area, developers hired landscape architects Horace W. S. Cleveland and William French to plat the streets. Prairie School architects left their mark on the summer and year-round estates of elite professionals who settled along the lake bluffs. Away from the water, developers built more modest homes for residents who provided services to the suburb.

Residents supported investment in a public library (1887) and ANNEXED the village of Ravinia, south of Highland Park, in 1899. By the turn of the century, Highland Park's population was 2,806, and socially, if not economically diverse. Institutions such as the Gads Hill Summer SETTLEMENT HOUSE encampment, the Railroad Men's Home, and Wildwood, a resort for German-Jewish families excluded from suburban country clubs, attest to this diversity. Unlike many of its suburban neighbors, Highland Park welcomed a sizable JEWISH population after WORLD WAR II.

The city experienced two growth spurts—in the 1920s, when the population grew by 98 percent to 12,203—and in the 1950s, when it leapt 52 percent to 25,532. Careful planning has protected the area's appeal by promoting its village character and building on its strengths of private and public amenities. The RAVINIA Music Festival is one such legacy that began as a recreational park and cultural center established in 1904 by A. C. Frost. Each summer, tens of thousands of visitors enjoy classical and popular concerts in a wooded outdoor setting, including performances by the CHICAGO SYMPHONY ORCHESTRA.

Derek Vaillant

See also: Architecture:The Prairie School; Golf; Landscape Design; Prohibition and Temperance; Suburbs and Cities as Dual Metropolis

Further reading: Ebner, Michael. *Creating Chicago's North Shore.* 1988.

High-School Sports. *See* Sports, High-School

Highways. *See* Expressways; Streets and Highways

Highwood, IL, Lake County, 24 miles N of the Loop. Highwood is a quiet North Shore residential community with lovely homes built from stone, brick, and masonry by local ITALIAN stonemasons. Highwood is also a community shaped by FORT SHERIDAN, whose business district was once so notorious for its bars and taverns that its nickname was "Whiskey Junction."

Highwood sits at the top of the Skokie ravine, the highest point between Chicago and Milwaukee. Along the Green Bay Trail, POTAWATOMI lived in the area until the 1833 Chicago TREATY.

IRISH and GERMAN immigrants were originally attracted to Highwood as CONSTRUCTION workers on the Chicago & Northwestern Railroad. Later area workers became the domestic labor force for the elite suburbs along Chicago's North Shore.

The 1886 HAYMARKET Riot led to the development of Fort Sheridan as a massing point for federal troops that could be used to put down urban disturbances. Employment on palatial North Shore estates and at Fort Sheridan became the primary source of income for Highwood residents.

The development of the fort affected Highwood's business district, which was soon filled with bars and taverns. Highwood's reputation led President Theodore Roosevelt to call it "the toughest town in America." Highwood set such an example that the federal government required legislation prohibiting new liquor establishments near military installations before they would consider enlarging GREAT LAKES NAVAL TRAINING STATION in NORTH CHICAGO. While Fort Sheridan helped introduce the liquor industry to Highwood, the fort alone could not sustain the area taverns. From EVANSTON to Kenosha, Highwood was the North Shore's only wet community. Patrons came from all North Shore communities to have a drink and find a home away from home.

While Highwood's business district was running wild, many of its residents embraced the temperance movement. Members of the Methodist Church and the Lutheran Church and local Baptists joined together to fight alcohol. Community members attempted to bring in an eminent temperance leader to open a Bible retreat in an area that is now the southernmost region of Fort Sheridan.

Highwood's ethnic makeup changed beginning in 1905 with the arrival of the first Italian immigrants. Italians brought the craftsmanship of stonemasonry and gardening. These skills were much sought after 1900 in wealthy communities up and down the North Shore.

Fort Sheridan served as a mustering-out base for WORLD WAR II soldiers, and with pockets full of money, those soldiers often made Highwood taverns their first stop upon being discharged. Highwood's business district flourished.

After World War II, residents began to tire of the effect the SALOONS had on Highwood's reputation. In the 1970s city officials began to push Highwood's bars to serve food. Within years, the community that had once been in the Guinness Book of World Records for the most bars now boasted many of the area's best RESTAURANTS outside the city of Chicago.

With the closing of Fort Sheridan in 1993, the community that provided blue-collar workers for North Shore and Fort Sheridan changed again. Once a four block by four block anomaly on Chicago's North Shore, Highwood doubled in size with the ANNEXATION of the Fort Sheridan subdivision.

Lisa Cervac

See also: Governing the Metropolis; Prohibition and Temperance

Further reading: Bernardi, Adria. *Houses with Names: The Italian Immigrants of Highwood, Illinois.* 1990. • Wittelle, Marvyn. *28 Miles North: The Story of Highwood.* 1953.

Hillside, IL, Cook County, 14 miles W of the Loop. Located in western COOK COUNTY,

Hillside occupies the center of a network of EXPRESSWAYS serving the Chicago region. Interstate 290 cuts through the village from east to west, with Interstate 294 and the Interstate 290 extension near Hillside's northwestern boundary. Providing access, but at the same time dividing the suburb into distinct sections, the expressway (and earlier the RAILROADS) contributed considerably to Hillside's development.

Settlement began in earnest in the 1840s as GERMAN Lutheran immigrants established farms and built Hillside's first school and church (Immanuel) at the corner of Wolf and 22nd Street. Even though most of Hillside's later development was north of 12th Street, Immanuel Lutheran Church and School were included within village limits, giving Hillside its distinctive shape.

Although farming was the major occupation in the 1850s, Marion Covell discovered a large deposit of limestone just a few feet below the surface of his property. The QUARRY that he began in 1854 continued to operate until the mid-1970s, supplying crushed stone for road-building throughout the Chicago region. Against the wishes of most village residents, the quarry was acquired by the John Sexton Company in 1979 and used as a sanitary landfill.

Beginning with Mt. Carmel in 1894, followed by Oak Ridge, Glen Oak, and finally Queen of Heaven in 1947, CEMETERIES also replaced active farmland just outside Hillside on its western and southern boundaries. Accessible from a station on the ILLINOIS CENTRAL RAILROAD and from a spur of the Chicago, Aurora & Elgin INTERURBAN that followed 12th Street, the cemeteries prompted the establishment of taverns, restaurants, monument companies, greenhouses, and floral shops. The village incorporated in 1905, adopting its name from the Illinois Central Railroad stop, which was called Hillside because the westbound trains had to go uphill at this point.

The 1920s saw the first concentrated residential development in the village as more farmland was sold and subdivided. St. Domitilla Roman Catholic Church and the Mater Dolorosa SEMINARY bought extensive properties there in the 1920s. Surrounded by open land for a time, these institutions were engulfed in a sea of residential construction after WORLD WAR II as Hillside's population doubled (from 1,080 to 2,131) from 1940 to 1950, then jumped to 7,794 in 1960. Adjacent to the newly completed Congress Expressway in 1956 was Hillside Shopping Center, an early regional shopping center soon surrounded by a Holiday Inn, Hillside Theaters, the High Point Tower office building, and the industrial park on Fencl Lane.

With the opening of newer, larger shopping centers and malls in the 1960s, Hillside Shopping Center's heyday was short-lived. Changes to the physical appearance of the mall as well as changes in its tenants and ownership could not reverse its decline. In 1997 most of the mall was demolished, making way for a large car dealership.

Patricia Krone Rose

See also: Built Environment of the Chicago Region; Shopping Districts and Malls; Transportation; Waste Disposal

Further reading: *Seventy-fifth Anniversary of Hillside, 1905–1980.* 1981.

Hindus. One of the earliest and still among the most famous Hindu visitors to Chicago was Swami Vivekananda, one of the few INDIAN delegates to the WORLD PARLIAMENT OF RELIGIONS. The "Hindu monk," as he came to be known, created an overwhelming impression. Vivekananda gained a considerable following among the elite; however, Chicago remained largely bereft of Hindus until the 1960s, when the first wave of Indian graduate students and professionals made their way to the United States.

Nearly all of Chicago's Hindus are of Indian descent, and most are concentrated in the northern and western suburbs. The Hindu Temple of Greater Chicago in LEMONT, with one *gopuram* (principal doorway) in the South Indian style and another building in the North Indian style, was established in 1986; its *pujari* (priest) claimed a following of several thousand people. The Sri Venkateswara Swami (Balaji) Temple in AURORA, which likewise attracts a large congregation, was built in the mid-1980s. Artisans and sculptors trained in India helped to adorn the elaborate edifice. There are also converted temples like the Manav Seva Mandir, or the Temple for Devotion to Humankind, which was formerly a KOREAN church.

The Hindu population of Greater Chicago, which numbers in excess of 50,000 people, is large enough to sustain a substantial number of other temples and cultural associations, and the social life of Hindus revolves largely around temples. Here Hindus gather to celebrate Hindu festivals and holy days (such as Diwali in the fall—also called Deepavali, Festival of Lights—and Holi in the spring). Chicago's Hindus also commemorate secular American holidays and even, as in the case of the ecumenical Ramakrishna-Vivekananda Center, Christmas. Weekly attendance at services is not expected, but each temple conducts two worship sessions (*aratis*) per day. As elsewhere in the Indian diaspora, more communitarian and fervent forms of worship are increasingly being embraced, as evidenced by the popularity of *satsangs,* the collective singing of devotional hymns. Various other Hindus, such as the followers of Satya Sai Baba, and the Arya Samajis, who forswear elaborate ritual, are also well represented, as are Jains, who share some religious and cultural traits with Hindus but nonetheless follow a separate faith with its own pantheon of deities and distinct religious practices. The Vishwa Hindu Parishad (VHP), a worldwide Hindu cultural organization that champions a militant resurgence of the faith, has won many adherents in Chicago.

Vinay Lal

See also: Religion, Chicago's Influence on; Religious Geography

Further reading: Burke, Marie Louise. *Swami Vivekananda in America: New Discoveries.* 1958. • Sheffield, Robin. "Home of the Gods." *Chicago Tribune,* December 29, 1994.

Hinsdale, IL, DuPage and Cook Counties, 16 miles W of the Loop.

Hinsdale, a commuter village along the Chicago, Burlington & Quincy RAILROAD, roughly encompasses the area between Kingery Highway, 59th Street, Interstate 294, and Ogden Avenue. The village sits on elevated prairie land. A valley runs east to west, splitting Hinsdale's morainic hills, some of which rise to over 70 feet above Lake Michigan.

Advertisement for Hinsdale, 1873. Artist: Unknown. Source: The Newberry Library.

Shortly after the BLACK HAWK WAR ended in 1833, a settlement developed north of present-day Hinsdale in an area along the Old Plank Road (Ogden Avenue) near the banks of SALT CREEK. This area, known as Brush Hill for its abundance of hazelnut bushes, grew into a thriving community of taverns, mills, and feed stores. By 1851 Ben Fuller had acquired most of Brush Hill, which he platted and renamed Fullersburg.

In 1858 Fuller petitioned the Chicago, Burlington, & Quincy Railroad to build a line through Fullersburg. Because of topographical problems, however, the line was built one mile south through Hinsdale's valley instead. In 1862 William Robbins bought 640 acres of what is now south Hinsdale. The tracks through Hinsdale were completed on May 20, 1864, and Robbins hired landscaper H. W. S. Cleveland to plat the village south of the tracks. Robbins planted elm and maple TREES along proposed streets and built a school.

Hinsdale was incorporated in 1873, with Judge Joel Tiffany as its first president. The Hinsdale LIBRARY Association was incorporated in 1887. During the 1890s Hinsdale installed a WATER pumping station, wood and brick-paved roads (1892), electric streetlights (1896), and a TELEPHONE exchange (1896). The Hinsdale GOLF Club set up links on Anson Ayres's property in the 1890s.

The Hinsdale Sanitarium was started in 1903. Improvements in the 1920s included Ruth Lake Country Club (1922), Madison school (1924), and the Hinsdale Theater (1925). The Woodlands, an area east of County Line Road, was annexed in 1917, and Fullersburg was annexed in 1923. In 1924, the Hinsdale Plan Commission was formed to consider ZONING ordinances. The colonial-style Memorial Building, which today houses village offices, was built in 1928, funded entirely by private donations.

From 1960 to 1975 Hinsdale arrived at its present borders by means of eight different ANNEXATIONS. In 1975 Hinsdale annexed Katherine Legge Memorial Park, which had been donated to the village by International Harvester. Since the 1980s, Hinsdale has restored many of its historic structures and builders have been encouraged to use the Georgian style of colonial architecture in keeping with the Hinsdale Plan of early civic leaders.

In 1870, 43 percent of Hinsdaleans were originally from the northeastern United States. The remaining 50 percent consisted of GERMAN, ENGLISH, and other northwestern European immigrants. In 2000 Hinsdale's population was 17,349, twice what it had been in 1950.

Tom Sterling

See also: Landscape Design; Planning, City and Regional; Suburbs and Cities as Dual Metropolis

Further reading: Sterling, Tom, and Mary Sterling. *Hinsdale and the World: One Hundred Years.* 1996. • Thompson, Richard A., ed. *DuPage Roots.* 1985.

Historic Preservation. Historic preservation is a diverse movement of private and governmental interests that identify and safeguard elements of the existing landscape, both built and natural, that they consider worth saving as a link to the region's past and to its architectural legacy.

The movement began as an effort to ensure the survival of individual buildings of special significance, but its concerns have been broadened, first to include districts and neighborhoods, then to encompass distinctive areas of the natural environment. It is now an integral element of urban planning and design.

Historic preservation gained popular support in Chicago in the 1960s when public concern over massive and indiscriminate destruction of Chicago's built environment developed in response to three trends: (1) government-sponsored "URBAN RENEWAL," which had resulted in wholesale destruction of some residential areas; (2) construction of high-speed, limited-access EXPRESSWAYS financed largely by federal highway funds, which slashed

The Garrick Building (known originally as the Schiller Building), on Randolph Street between Dearborn and State, was designed by Adler & Sullivan. Constructed in 1892, it was demolished in 1961 after an unsuccessful attempt to save it. Photographer: Arthur Siegel. Source: Chicago Historical Society.

through neighborhoods; and (3) the REAL-ESTATE boom in response to the demand for increased office space in the LOOP.

The proposed demolition of Louis Sullivan's Garrick Theatre on West Randolph Street rallied the first organized protest group. Despite petitioning and picketing, the building was torn down in 1961 to make way for a parking garage. In 1972 another historically and architecturally significant building by Sullivan and Dankmar Adler, the Stock Exchange Building on LaSalle Street, was lost. Other Loop buildings of historical significance were also threatened with demolition.

This threat to Chicago's architectural heritage brought about the formation of citizens' groups to educate the public and apply pressure to governmental departments and agencies to save the city's architectural legacy. The first was the Chicago Architecture Foundation (CAF), which grew out of the efforts of a group of architects in 1966 to save Glessner House, designed by H. H. Richardson and located at 1800 South PRAIRIE AVENUE, by purchasing it. CAF has since become a major force for architectural education in the city, training many volunteer docents and arranging popular tours of architectural highlights. Glessner House, now a separate museum, is the key structure in the city-landmarked Prairie Avenue District. It includes two other late-nineteenth-century houses and the Clarke House, reputedly the oldest house still standing in the city, which is now run as a house museum by the Department of Cultural Affairs of Chicago.

The Landmarks Preservation Council of Illinois (LPCI), which was established in 1971, is an advocacy group that lobbies for historic preservation projects. The LPCI has been closely involved with the disposition of FORT SHERIDAN in Lake County, which is a National Historic Landmark. It is being developed privately but with a commitment to preserve the buildings and character of the historic fort district.

Chicago has a wealth of impressive religious structures from the late nineteenth and early twentieth centuries. Ten have received recognition on the city's list of landmarks, but many more have been renovated by their congregations and now serve as important centers for their communities. During the 1990s a nonprofit organization, Inspired Partnerships, helped many of these communities maintain their buildings and in the process preserve an important part of the city's architectural and cultural legacy.

The city has had a Commission on Chicago Landmarks (CCL) since 1968. Now part of the city's Department of PLANNING and

The Henry B. Clarke House, one of the oldest buildings in Chicago, was built in 1836 and stood near Sixteenth Street and Michigan Avenue. After the 1871 fire, the structure was moved to 45th Street and Wabash Avenue (it is seen here at that site in 1934). The Clarke House was later moved to 1855 South Indiana, becoming part of the Prairie Avenue Historic District. Photographer: Chicago Daily News. Source: Chicago Historical Society.

National Historic Landmarks in the Chicago Metropolitan Area

NAME	ADDRESS	CITY/COUNTY	YEAR	HISTORICAL SIGNIFICANCE
Abbott (Robert S.) House	4742 South Martin Luther King Jr. Boulevard	Chicago	ca. 1900	From 1926 to 1940, home of Robert Abbott, publisher of the *Chicago Defender*
Adler Planetarium	1300 South Lake Shore Drive	Chicago	1930	First planetarium in the Western Hemisphere
Auditorium Building	430 South Michigan Avenue	Chicago	1889	Concert hall and opera house designed by Louis H. Sullivan
Bailly (Joseph) Homestead	West of Porter, IN, on U.S. 20	Porter County, IN	1822	Wilderness trading post
Carson, Pirie, Scott & Co. Store	1 South State Street	Chicago	1899–1906	Department store designed by Louis H. Sullivan, addition by Daniel H. Burnham
Charnley (James) House	1365 North Astor Street	Chicago	1891–1892	House designed by Louis H. Sullivan
Chicago Board of Trade Building	141 West Jackson Boulevard	Chicago	1928–1930	Commodity exchange
Compton (Arthur H.) House	5637 South Woodlawn Avenue	Chicago	1916	From the late 1920s to 1945, home of Arthur Compton, Nobel Prize–winning Univeristy of Chicago physicist
Coonley (Avery) House	300 Scottswood Drive	Riverside	1909	House designed by Frank Lloyd Wright
Crow Island School	1112 Willow Road	Winnetka	1940	Elementary school designed by Eliel and Eero Saarinen
Dawes (Charles G.) House	225 Greenwood Street	Evanston	1894	From 1909 to 1951, home of Charles G. Dawes, vice president of the United States
DePriest (Oscar Stanton) House	4536–4538 South Martin Luther King Jr. Boulevard	Chicago	1920	From 1929 to 1951, home of Oscar DePriest, the first African American elected to the House of Representatives from a northern state
DuSable (Jean Baptiste Point) Homesite	401 North Michigan Avenue	Chicago	1779	Location of settlement by Jean Baptiste Point DuSable
Farson (John) House	217 Home Avenue	Oak Park	1897	House designed by George Maher
Fort Sheridan Historic District	Fort Sheridan	Lake County	1889–1908	Military fort designed in part by Holabird & Roche
Glessner (John J.) House	1800 South Prairie Avenue	Chicago	1886	House designed by Henry H. Richardson
Grant Park Stadium (Soldier Field)	425 East 14th Street	Chicago	1924	Memorial to World War I soldiers
Grosse Point Lighthouse	2601 Sheridan Road	Evanston	1873	Maritime navigational landmark for Lake Michigan shipping corridor
Haymarket Martyrs' Monument	863 South Des Plaines Avenue	Forest Park	1893	Sculpture and monument commemorating 1886 Haymarket protest and struggle for eight-hour workday
Heurtley (Arthur) House	318 Forest Avenue	Oak Park	1902	House designed by Frank Lloyd Wright
Hull House	800 South Halsted Street	Chicago	1856	Settlement house established in 1889 by Jane Addams and Ellen Gates Starr
Illinois & Michigan Canal Locks and Towpath	Channahon State Park	Will County	1836–1848	Commercially significant canal linking Chicago to Mississippi River
Kennicott Grove	Milwaukee and Lake Avenues	Glenview	1856	From 1856 to 1866, home of Robert Kennicott, naturalist and explorer
Leiter II Building	403 South State Street	Chicago	1891	Early skyscraper designed by William Le Baron Jenney
Lillie (Frank R.) House	5801 South Kenwood Avenue	Chicago	1904	From 1904 to 1947, home of Frank R. Lillie, University of Chicago embryologist
Marquette Building	140 South Dearborn Street	Chicago	1893–1894	Early steel frame building designed by Holabird & Roche

National Historic Landmarks in the Chicago Metropolitan Area

NAME	ADDRESS	CITY/COUNTY	YEAR	HISTORICAL SIGNIFICANCE
Marshall Field & Co. Store	111 North State Street	Chicago	1892–1907	Location of retail firm of Marshall Field & Co.
Millikan (Robert A.) House	5605 South Woodlawn Avenue	Chicago	1907	From 1907 to 1921, home of Robert A. Millikan, Nobel Prize–winning University of Chicago physicist
Montgomery Ward & Co. Complex	618 West Chicago Avenue	Chicago	1907–1929	National headquarters for the country's oldest mail-order firm
Old Stone Gate, Union Stock-yard	Exchange Avenue at Peoria Street	Chicago	1879	From 1879 to 1971, main entrance to the Union Stock Yard
Orchestra Hall	220 South Michigan Avenue	Chicago	1904	Home of the Chicago Symphony Orchestra, designed by Daniel H. Burnham
Pullman Historic District	103rd–115th Street, Grove Avenue, RR tracks	Chicago	1880–1884	Model industrial town for production of railroad cars, planned by George M. Pullman; site of major strike in 1894
Reliance Building	32 North State Street	Chicago	1894–1895	Office building designed by Charles B. Atwood of Burnham & Root
Riverside Historic District	—	Riverside	1868–1869	Model community designed by Frederick Law Olmsted and Calvert Vaux
Robie (Frederick C.) House	5757 South Woodlawn Avenue	Chicago	1907–1909	House designed by Frank Lloyd Wright
Rookery Building	209 South LaSalle Street	Chicago	1885–1888	Office building designed by Burnham & Root; lobby remodeled by Frank Lloyd Wright
Room 405, George Jones Laboratory, University of Chicago	5700 block of South Ellis Avenue	Chicago	1929	Location where, on August 18, 1942, Glen T. Seaborg and colleagues first isolated pure plutonium
Sears, Roebuck & Co.	925 South Homan Avenue	Chicago	1905–1906	Office and printing facilities for Sears mail-order operations, once the country's largest
Shedd Aquarium	1200 South Lake Shore Drive	Chicago	1930	Surviving structure from Century of Progress Exposition; first inland saltwater aquarium in the United States
Site of First Self-Sustaining Nuclear Reaction	5600 block of South Ellis Street, University of Chicago	Chicago	n/a	Location where, on December 2, 1942, Nobel laureate Enrico Fermi achieved first controlled self-sustaining nuclear chain reaction
South Dearborn Street—Printing House Row Historic District	343, 407, and 431 South Dearborn; 53 West Jackson	Chicago	1883–1928	District includes four "Chicago School" buildings: the Manhattan (1891), the Fisher (1896), the Old Colony (1894), the Monadnock (1880–91)
Taft (Lorado) Midway Studios	6016 South Ingleside Avenue	Chicago	1885–1929	From 1906 to 1929, studios of sculptor Lorado Taft
Tomek (F. F.) House	150 Nuttall Road	Riverside	1907	House designed by Frank Lloyd Wright
U-505	Museum of Science and Industry, Jackson Park	Chicago	1929	German submarine captured June 4, 1944; displayed as memorial to 55,000 Americans who died at sea in World War II
Unity Temple	875 Lake Street	Oak Park	1907	Unitarian church designed by Frank Lloyd Wright
Wayside, The	830 Sheridan Road	Winnetka	1878	During the 1880s, home of social critic Henry Demarest Lloyd
Wells-Barnett (Ida B.) House	3624 South Martin Luther King Jr. Drive	Chicago	1889	From 1919 to 1929, home of journalist and civil rights advocate Ida B. Wells
Willard (Frances) House	1730 Chicago Avenue	Evanston	1865	Home of temperance movement leader Frances Willard
Williams (Daniel Hale) House	445 East 42nd Street	Chicago	ca. 1900	Home of Daniel Hale Williams, one of the first African American surgeons
Wright (Frank Lloyd) Home and Studio	428 Forest Avenue and 951 Chicago Avenue	Oak Park	1889–1898	From 1887 to 1909, home and studio of Frank Lloyd Wright

Source: National Park Service and other sources.

Development, it researches the background of properties or districts proposed for landmark status and recommends approval to the Chicago City Council, which then votes on granting such status. As of May 2002, 202 individual structures and sites and 34 districts had been officially recognized as landmarks.

These city designations are complemented by the list of National Historic Landmarks maintained by the National Park Service. In Chicago 32 buildings and sites had been identified by the close of the twentieth century, some of which, like the site of the first nuclear chain reaction on the UNIVERSITY OF CHICAGO campus, are not on the CCL list. There were also 11 listings in the Chicago suburbs, including the Frank Lloyd Wright Home and Studio in OAK PARK and the RIVERSIDE Historic District. The first National Historic Landmark in the area was the ILLINOIS & MICHIGAN CANAL locks and towpath in Will County, which was listed in 1964.

Within the network of parks created in the nineteenth century to ring the city—LINCOLN, HUMBOLDT, DOUGLAS, GARFIELD, WASHINGTON, and JACKSON Parks—there are important preservation projects, including the CONSERVATORY in Garfield Park and the receptory and stables of Humboldt Park.

The character of the city is closely tied to the openness and availability to the public of the lakefront. This was the centerpiece of the 1909 BURNHAM PLAN of Chicago. Although there have been breaches of the open lakefront concept—most notoriously with the siting of the convention center, McCormick Place, right on the lake—the preservation of public parkland for more than 15 miles of lakeshore is one of the glories of the city.

The one important landmark on the lakefront is NAVY PIER. Opened in 1916, its buildings fell into disrepair as lake shipping declined. The headhouse and east end buildings were given city landmark status in 1977, but only after a protracted fight over how to develop the space was the entire pier extensively rebuilt in the mid-1990s as a popular cultural and recreation center.

With increasing understanding that historic preservation is a way to connect the present with the past, more individuals and communities are undertaking their own preservation projects. Aging downtown areas have been rejuvenated by the restoration of an old theater, as in AURORA, or by the development of a district of nineteenth-century houses, as in GENEVA. Historic preservation has also been a factor in neighborhood revitalization, as in Lincoln Park in the 1960s and more recently in Bronzeville on Chicago's SOUTH SIDE.

One major preservation project that the city has undertaken directly is the restoration of the 1891–1895 Reliance Building at State and Washington. Its glass-dominated facade has fostered the claim that the building is a precursor of modern architecture. The building reopened in 1999 as the European-style Hotel Burnham.

Barbara Sciacchitano

See also: Architecture; Auditorium Theater; Church Architecture; Neighborhood Change: Chicago's Prairie Avenue, 1853–2003 (color map, p. C4); Planning Chicago

Further reading: Alice Sinkevitch, ed. *AIA Guide to Chicago.* 1993. • Bach, Ira J. *A Guide to Chicago's Historic Suburbs on Wheels and on Foot.* 1981. • *Chicago Historical Resources Survey: An Inventory of Architecturally and Historically Significant Structures.* Commission on Chicago Landmarks and the Chicago Department of Planning and Development. 1996.

Hmong. The first Hmong to migrate to Chicago came as REFUGEES from Laos after the ascension of the Communist group Pathet Lao in 1975. Hmong tribes, originally from southeastern China, had lived in the highlands of Laos for over a century, where they maintained a distinct ethnic identity. While some Hmong clans supported the Pathet Lao, others were recruited by the CIA and trained as a covert fighting force during the Vietnam War. With the ascension of the Communists, nearly one-third of the Hmong in Laos fled to refugee camps in Thailand and were resettled in the United States. Refugee resettlement agencies placed nearly 100,000 Hmong throughout the nation, but they began a massive secondary migration almost immediately to reunite with families. By 1990, the majority of Hmong in the United States lived in California, Wisconsin, and Minnesota, where they formed large, well-organized communities.

The nearly 3,000 Hmong that resettled in Illinois in Dixon, WHEATON, Ottawa, and Chicago faced a difficult adjustment to life in highly industrialized society. Hmong life in Laos was organized around clan ties and based on slash-and-burn agriculture. Formal education was limited, and, until Christian missionaries developed a written script in the 1950s, the Hmong had no written language of their own. Hmong refugees had few transferable occupational skills and limited English skills, and, in 1990, almost two out of three Hmong Americans lived below the poverty level. UNEMPLOYMENT has persisted, but many Hmong men have entered jobs as factory workers, janitors, light assemblers, and cleaners, and some Hmong women have carved out a niche in the handicraft market with *paj ntaub,* an elaborate needlework with colorful geometric designs.

Life in Chicago has generated changes in Hmong leadership, family structure, and cultural practices. While clan leaders still retain respect, new educated and professional leaders have emerged in the Hmong community based on their ability to bridge the cultural gap and provide useful information and services. In addition, families have been broken into smaller units, traditional gender relations have altered as a result of greater equality of women in the United States, and intergenerational relations have suffered from cultural divides between young Hmong and their parents. Furthermore, the conversion of many Hmong to Christianity, both through missionaries in Laos and conversion in the United States, has affected traditional cultural practices and divided the community. Traditional Hmong religion is based on the cult of spirits, shamanism, and ancestor worship and is central to traditional Hmong culture. Conversion to Christianity has meant that some Hmong no longer participate in traditional Hmong rites and identify primarily with their church communities.

Hmong in the Chicago area and across the country have developed strong networks of mutual assistance and lobbied for aid and SOCIAL SERVICES. In 1978, Hmong leaders founded the Association of Hmong in Illinois (AHMI) as a nonprofit organization to provide services for the Hmong community, including job counseling, youth programs, English-language training, and cultural programs. Amid clan divisions and organizational disagreements, a group broke with the AHMI in 1981 to form the Chicago Hmong Community Services (CHCS). The two organizations nonetheless worked closely to establish a Hmong community center and community programs. Hmong leaders also established Hmong Volunteer Literacy Inc. and the Moob Federation of America to assist Hmong refugees in metropolitan Chicago. While many of these organizations continued into the 1990s, the Chicago Hmong population began to migrate in large numbers in the mid-1980s to Wisconsin and Minnesota to reunite with families and take advantage of the services and opportunities offered by the larger Hmong communities there. By 2000, only a few hundred Hmong remained in the Chicago area, primarily Christian families.

Tracy Steffes

See also: Americanization; Demography; Laotians; Multicentered Chicago; Vietnamese

Further reading: Chan, Sucheng. *Hmong Means Free: Life in Laos and America.* 1994. • Thao, Paoze. "Mong Resettlement in the Chicago Area, 1978–1987: Educational Implications." Ph.D diss., Loyola University. 1994.

Hobart, IN, Lake County, 31 miles SE of the Loop. Hobart, one of LAKE COUNTY'S oldest communities, draws its origins from the arrival of three related families, the Siglers, Mundells, and Hursts. Nearby, ENGLISHman George Earle, who had invested heavily in Lake County land, was attempting to establish the town of Liverpool at the junction of Deep and CALUMET Rivers. Liverpool did not prove viable, and in 1845 Earle moved five miles up Deep River. Here he constructed a dam to power sawmills and gristmills. The resulting millpond became known as Lake George. Earle moved the post office from Liverpool in 1847 and recorded the plat for the new town in 1849, naming it for his brother, Frederick Hobart Earle, of Falmouth, England.

Although Hobart was on the Chicago-Detroit stage route (Old Ridge Road), it was the construction of the Pittsburgh, Fort Wayne & Chicago RAILROAD (later the Pennsylvania Railroad) in 1858 that transformed the settlement into a center for shipping LUMBER, bricks, milk, and agricultural products to the Chicago market. In 1882 the New York, Chicago & St. Louis Railway (now the Norfolk Southern) and in 1888, the Elgin, Joliet & Eastern were built, enhancing Hobart's position as a railroad hub.

Brickmaking was Hobart's most important industry in the nineteenth century. Small brickyards appeared in the 1850s. In 1863 Joseph Nash established the first large brickyard with an eye to the Chicago market. In 1886, the W. B. Owen brickworks converted from bricks to terra cotta building tile. Used for fireproof building construction, terra cotta found a ready market in Chicago and beyond. The Owen works was taken over by National Fireproofing Company in 1902 and operated until 1964. The Kulage Brick Works, which flourished from 1893 to the early 1920s, was another important brickmaker.

Hobart incorporated as a town in 1889. A volunteer FIRE department organized in 1891. The Hobart Light & Water Company, established in 1898, was one of the few municipally owned utility companies in the state. STREET RAILWAY service to Gary began in 1914.

In the 1920s, as nearby GARY boomed and new highways bypassed Hobart, the town lost its function as a retail and TRANSPORTATION center. It reincorporated as a city in 1923 and became a residential community for employees of area industries. From the late 1930s through the 1960s, Hobart continued to grow, primarily through the construction of single-family houses, while retaining its small-town character. A sewer moratorium halted growth until the 1980s, when it was lifted and home construction resumed. Two of the city's parks, Fred Rose Park and Pavese Park, as well as residential areas, border Deep River and Lake George. A dredging project to improve Lake George began in 2000.

Hobart's population in 2000 was 25,363. Major ANNEXATIONS in Hobart Township to the north in 1988 and Ross Township in 1992, including the Southlake Mall area along U.S. 30 to the south, have strengthened the town's potential for continued residential, commercial, and light industrial development.

Elin B. Christianson

See also: Built Environment of the Chicago Region; Economic Geography; Infrastructure; Quarrying, Stonecutting, and Brickmaking; Streets and Highways

Further reading: Pleak, Mariam, J. "A Short History of Hobart." *Hobart Gazette,* n.d. Mariam J. Pleak Memorial Library, Hobart Historical Society Museum, Hobart, IN.

Hobo College. To the HOBO population Chicago was "Big Chi," the place where thousands of migratory workers in the early 1900s hopped freight cars for jobs in the nation's harvest fields and logging camps. Amidst West Madison Street's missions, cheap eateries, bars, and other establishments that catered to the itinerants' needs, Ben Reitman, dashing physician, reformer, and ANARCHIST, founded a "hobo college" in 1908. There, men of the road gathered to swap stories and listen to lectures on everything from philosophy and politics to personal hygiene and vagrancy laws. For nearly three decades, the hobo college provided an educational experience to these men and fostered a spirit of fraternity among them.

Roger Bruns

See also: Bughouse Square; Near West Side; Street Life; Work; Work Culture

Further reading: Anderson, Nels. *The Hobo: The Sociology of the Homeless Man.* 1923. • Bruns, Roger A. *Knights of the Road: A Hobo History.* 1980. • Bruns, Roger A. *The Damndest Radical: The Life and World of Ben Reitman, Chicago's Celebrated Social Reformer, Hobo King, and Whorehouse Physician.* 1987.

Hoboes. Chicago became the "Hobo Capital of America" during the late nineteenth century, as migratory workers hopped freight trains headed to and from the nation's busiest RAILROAD hub. By the 1910s, authorities estimated that 300,000–500,000 transients passed through the city annually, with 30,000–70,000 of them present on any particular day.

Comprising primarily native-born single white men, this mobile community established a "hobohemian" district in Chicago. Its "main stem" occupied a stretch of West Madison Street from the Chicago River to Halsted Street, where inexpensive RESTAURANTS, SALOONS, flophouses, and employment agencies catered to hoboes' basic needs; a similar, segregated district on South State Street, between 22nd and 30th Streets, accommodated AFRICAN AMERICAN transients. Just south of the LOOP, State Street burlesque theatres provided hoboes with cheap entertainment, while the FREE-SPEECH forums of TOWERTOWN's Dill Pickle Club and BUGHOUSE SQUARE introduced them to ARTISTS, Wobblies, and other political radicals. During warmer months, hobohemia extended to the "open-air hotels" of GRANT and Jefferson Parks and to the ramshackle, "jungle" campsites that hoboes built behind the FIELD MUSEUM, creating an outdoor haven for their political and social nonconformity, including their unconventional, and often same-sex, sexual relationships.

From the 1920s, trucking, mechanized farming, and other economic and technological developments lessened the nation's dependence upon migratory workers, and their numbers began to decrease. NEW DEAL programs, including the Federal Emergency Relief Administration's Federal Transient Service and the Civilian Conservation Corps, mitigated a temporary upsurge in the transient male population, but these male-oriented programs offered little assistance to the growing population of women hoboes in Depression-era Chicago. By the end of the Second World War, as a more stationary HOMELESS population replaced the hoboes of West Madison Street, the city's "main stem" became its Skid Row.

Chad Heap

See also: Near West Side; Street Life; Unemployment

Further reading: Anderson, Nels. *The Hobo: The Sociology of the Homeless Man.* 1923. • Kusmer, Kenneth L. *Down and Out, on the Road: The Homeless in American History.* 2002. • Reitman, Ben L. *Sister of the Road: The Autobiography of Box-Car Bertha as told to Dr. Ben L. Reitman.* 1937.

Hockey. *See* Ice Hockey

Hodgkins, IL, Cook County, 14 miles SW of the Loop. TRANSPORTATION and stone QUARRIES have shaped the development of Hodgkins. In the late 1880s the Santa Fe RAILROAD came through this area and the Kimball and Cobb Stone Company opened a large limestone quarry. The town was named for Jefferson Hodgkins, president of the company, and was incorporated as a village in 1896.

ITALIAN Americansand others arrived in the 1890s to help build the Chicago SANITARY AND SHIP CANAL.

The quarry continued to dominate the local scene until the 1950s, although the economy diversified somewhat with the addition of numerous motor freight terminals.

Hodgkins has a growing MEXICAN population, almost 30 percent of the population of 2,134 in the 2000 census. Somewhat fewer than half of the residents live in three MOBILE-HOME parks. Proximity to Interstates 55 and 294 makes Hodgkins a natural distribution point, a fact recognized in 1995 when United Parcel Service opened a huge sorting facility here. In 1997 the Burlington Northern Santa Fe Railway established an intermodal freight facility at Hodgkins.

Ronald S. Vasile

See also: Business of Chicago; Cook County; Economic Geography

Further reading: Eicholz, Linda Buralli, and Janet Klotz Coleman. *Village of Hodgkins: One Hundred Years of Progress, 1896–1996*. 1996. • Zorn, Eric. "Small-Town USA Knows Its Own Mind." *Chicago Tribune*, June 23, 1990.

Hoffman Estates, IL, Cook County, 29 miles NW of the Loop. The unusual boundaries of Hoffman Estates derive from its drive to remain autonomous from neighboring SCHAUMBURG. The community began as Wildcat Grove, west of Roselle Road and north of Golf Road, a part of Schaumburg Township settled by GERMAN farmers which remained sparsely populated well into the twentieth century.

Gentlemen farmers purchased large tracts of land in the 1940s. In the early 1950s Schaumburg Township remained without incorporated towns or villages. Schaumburg Centre at Roselle and Schaumburg Roads was the nucleus of the township where 25 houses and small stores stood surrounded by farmland.

In 1954 Father and Son Construction, owned by Sam and Jack Hoffman, purchased a 160-acre tract of land east of Roselle Road between Golf and Higgins Roads. After purchasing an additional 600 acres, the Hoffmans had the first 40 acres rezoned into 10,000-square-foot home sites. The company offered affordable tract houses with various options to appeal to families seeking to live in the suburbs. Father and Son donated two park sites and four church sites and began construction on the first school.

Residents of Schaumburg Centre protested the tract development, desiring to keep sites at five-acre minimums. To stop development they began annexing land until they nearly encircled the Hoffmans' development and sought to incorporate. Outraged citizens living in what would become Hoffman Estates formed a homeowner's association. They filed a suit against Schaumburg Centre to overturn their ANNEXATIONS. The association lost and the two villages continued feuding.

In 1959, with approximately 8,000 residents, Hoffman Estates incorporated. They immediately began annexing land, the first parcel just south of Higgins and Roselle Roads. Next a 120-acre tract, already part of Schaumburg Centre, asked to be disannexed to become part of Hoffman Estates. Schaumburg Centre unsuccessfully challenged these annexations. By 1962, the size of the village doubled and included parcels north of the Northwest TOLL ROAD and the Paul Douglas FOREST PRESERVE. Ultimately, the village accumulated 4,080 acres of forest preserves, totaling one-third of its total area.

In 1963, Schaumburg moved ahead with plans for residential and commercial development, and Hoffman Estates formed the Industrial Inducement Committee. Two years later the Thomas Engineering Company moved in. Other plans were hampered when Poplar Creek Forest Preserve took over land that Hoffman Estates planned to use for industry. Hoffman Estates continued, however, with a five-year plan for commercial development on Roselle Road between Golf and Higgins Road. But Hoffman Plaza Shopping Center never equaled rival Schaumburg's development of Woodfield Mall.

In 1978 the village incorporated vacant land in Barrington Township for industrial development. In 1992 Sears, Roebuck & Co. relocated its 5,000-employee Merchandise Group to the 7,180-acre Prairie Stone Business Park, one of the largest corporate centers in the northwest suburbs. The park is also the site of Northern Illinois University's branch campus.

Between 1970 and 1990 population more than doubled, from 22,238 to to 46,561, growing to 49,495 in 2000. Most residents were white, with ethnic diversity rising slowly to 15 percent Asian, 11 percent Hispanic, and 4 percent black.

Marilyn Elizabeth Perry

See also: Economic Geography; Mail Order; Real Estate; Suburbs and Cities as Dual Metropolis

Further reading: Gould, Alice J. *Schaumburg: A History of the Township*. 1982. • *Hoffman Estates Community Profile*. Village of Hoffman Estates. 1996.

Holiday Hills, IL, McHenry County, 43 miles NW of the Loop. Originally a cluster of 1930s summer vacation cabins along the north shore of Griswold Lake, the area grew after the 1940s as Chicagoans began looking for a place to raise children in a country environment. The community incorporated in 1976 to obtain revenue-sharing dollars to improve their roads. The 2000 population was 831.

Craig L. Pfannkuche

See also: McHenry County

Further reading: "Holiday Hills." *Woodstock Sentinel*, March 2, 1976.

Home Rule. Throughout much of its history, Chicago has sought home rule, the power to determine its structure of GOVERNMENT and municipal policies without interference from Springfield. Illinois' constitution of 1870 prohibited special legislation regarding city government, and two years later the state legislature approved a general law for the government of municipalities. But the state's largest metropolis had special needs, and by the turn of the century Chicago leaders were clamoring for an exception to the prohibition on special laws. In 1904 they secured the necessary constitutional amendment, which provided that special legislation for Chicago would take effect only if approved by the city's voters. Exploiting this opportunity for a degree of home rule, a local convention drafted a new municipal CHARTER, but it was much amended in Springfield and defeated in a 1907 referendum.

Illinois' proposed constitution of 1922 included a home rule provision for cities, but the state's electorate overwhelmingly rejected the document. In a 1927 referendum Chicago voters supported home rule by a four-to-one majority, and throughout the late 1920s and early 1930s angry Chicagoans talked of secession from Illinois and separate statehood. A home rule commission in the 1950s produced many recommendations but little action. Finally, in 1970 Illinois adopted a new constitution which designated any municipality with a population greater than 25,000 as a home rule unit, securing for Chicago the power to handle most municipal matters without seeking permission from Springfield. With the assent of the local electorate, less populous municipalities could choose home rule status, and the first to do so were the Cook County communities of MCCOOK, BEDFORD PARK, ROSEMONT, COUNTRYSIDE, and STONE PARK.

Jon C. Teaford

See also: Governing the Metropolis; State Politics; Taxation and Finance

Further reading: Chicago Home Rule Commission. *Modernizing a City Government*. 1954. • Flanagan, Maureen A. *Charter Reform in Chicago*. 1987. • Lepawsky, Albert. *Home Rule for Metropolitan Chicago*. 1935.

Homelessness and Shelters. There have always been people in Chicago who could not find housing on a given night, going back to the days of FORT DEARBORN, with inevitable increases in the number of homeless during times of catastrophe, like the fire of 1871 or the depression of 1893.

The problem of large numbers of chronically homeless individuals, however, first developed at the close of the nineteenth century, a product of both Chicago's massive industrial growth and its position as the nation's RAILROAD hub. Chicago became the central way station for thousands of largely native-born, itinerantworkers taking skilled and unskilled jobs.

Finding shelter depends upon a poor person's cash reserves and, even more, the availability of low-cost shelter. Most low-income housing during the heyday of industrialization was provided by the private sector, and buildings like cage hotels (so-called because the small rooms were sealed at top and bottom by chicken wire) charged pennies a night. More than 100,000 people lived in these kinds of temporary quarters at the turn of the century. The police also let people sleep overnight in cells, providing the first municipal shelters. Progressive-era reformers, however, demanded that SOCIAL SERVICES be provided solely by trained practitioners, and restricted law enforcement to pursuing criminals.

The number of homeless grew enormously during the GREAT DEPRESSION. Emergency lodgings provided by both public and private agencies went from 1 million (an unprecedented figure) for the period October 1930 to September 1931 to 4.3 million between 1933 and 1934. The major policy change in this era shifted primary responsibility for handling this social concern from the private to the public sector, especially the federal government.

During the 1950s the number of homeless diminished substantially, in part because of a decreased need for itinerant workers, but also because of postwar prosperity. Most studies during this period focused on Skid Row (a term taken from Seattle) and the presence of alcoholism among this population; every study, however, showed that addicted drinkers made up a minority of Skid Row residents and of the homeless in general, and that poverty was more commonly the cause of their condition.

In the 1980s homelessness soared for a number of reasons: the recession of 1981–82; a shift to a high-tech economy that displaced low-skill workers; GENTRIFICATION that eliminated much of the low-income housing stock, such as single-room-occupancy hotels; and a drastic decline in federal support for housing.

Robert Slayton

See also: Economic Geography; Housing Reform; Housing, Single Room Occupancy; Residential Hotels; Unemployment; Work

Further reading: Anderson, Nels. *The Hobo.* 1923. • Bogue, Donald. *Skid Row in American Cities.* 1963. • Hoch, Charles, and Robert Slayton. *New Homeless and Old: Community and the Skid Row Hotel.* 1989.

Homer Glen, IL, Will County, 20 miles SW of the Loop. For 150 years after the first YANKEE settlers arrived, WILL COUNTY'S Homer Township remained essentially rural. In 1988, however, residents proposed a new municipality to provide services and control development in the township's suburbanizing eastern half. Township voters finally agreed to incorporate the 20-square-mile, 22,000-resident village of Homer Glen on April 3, 2001.

Elizabeth A. Patterson

See also: Government, Suburban

Further reading: Heinzmann, David, and Stanley Ziemba. "Homer Glen Takes Charge; Incorporation Entices Voters Wary of Growth." *Chicago Tribune,* April 4, 2001. • *History of Will County, Illinois.* 1878. • Richardson, Patricia. "It Takes a Village to Limit Growth: Upstart Homer Glen Wrestles with Sprawl." *Crain's Chicago Business,* September 10, 2001.

Hometown, IL, Cook County, 12 miles SW of the Loop. Joseph E. Merrion developed inexpensive duplex houses in Hometown after WORLD WAR II, targeting former GIs and their families. Hometown incorporated in 1953, and its population peaked at over 7,000 in 1958. In 1967, a tornado struck the town, destroying 86 homes and damaging 500 others. During the 1990s Hometown remained a close-knit community of fewer than 5,000 working-class residents.

Erik Gellman

See also: Built Environment of the Chicago Region

Homewood, IL, Cook County, 22 miles SW of the Loop. Central to Homewood's evolution from a whistle-stop farming center to a substantial suburb of a large city is its location on the ILLINOIS CENTRAL RAILROAD. There is no evidence of a NATIVE AMERICAN settlement in Homewood, but the Vincennes Trace (now Dixie Highway) ran through the town. The area drains into the CALUMET RIVER. Homewood lies in four TOWNSHIPS—Bloom, Bremen, Rich, and Thornton; it formally organized as a village in 1893.

Immediately after federal surveyors marked the section lines around Homewood in 1834, settlers bought land and started farms. In 1852, a year after the first store opened, the business district was platted as Hartford. The next year the Illinois Central Railroad commenced service with a stop called Thornton Station, because most passengers were traveling to or from nearby THORNTON. In 1869 the U.S. Postmaster General assented to a petition from local residents and officially changed the name to Homewood.

Through the nineteenth century the town grew slowly. Farmers shipped their produce to Chicago, and local businesses and some industry developed to serve their needs, including a flourmill that operated from 1856 into the 1880s. The population in 1900 was 352.

In the twentieth century, recreation began to draw visitors, some of whom became residents. Five early GOLF clubs still operate: Flossmoor Country Club, in neighboring FLOSSMOOR (organized in 1898 as Homewood Country Club, name changed 1914); Ravisloe (1901); Idlewild, in Flossmoor (1908); Olympia Fields, in OLYMPIA FIELDS (1915); and Calumet (organized in 1901 in Chicago, relocated to Homewood in 1917). The Illinois Central offered special schedules and created special stops just for golfers. That was the origin of the stops that became Calumet, Flossmoor, and Olympia Fields. The railroad attracted more new residents to both towns by selling REAL ESTATE in Flossmoor and, in 1926, by electrifying its commuter service. Homewood's population grew from 713 in 1910 to 1,389 in 1920 and 3,227 in 1930.

Relatively little direct benefit accrued from another recreational attraction, Washington Park Race Track, which opened in 1926 on grounds located west of Halsted Street just outside the village bounds. Few of the HORSE RACING aficionados who patronized the track shopped or ate in Homewood, because the Illinois Central built a spur line so passengers could ride directly between Chicago and the track. During the GREAT DEPRESSION, the Illinois Jockey Association helped Homewood pay for INFRASTRUCTURE built during the optimistic, prosperous 1920s. Washington Park went out of business after its grandstand burned in 1977; in 1992 Homewood bought the site and turned it into a commercial and retail development.

In the postwar period, Homewood and Flossmoor established institutional partnerships. Homewood-Flossmoor Community High School opened its doors in 1959, and a joint park district was incorporated in 1969.

The Great Depression and WORLD WAR II merely slowed growth. There were 4,078 people in 1940, but a surge pushed the total to 13,371 in 1960. Total population hit 18,871 in 1970 and since then has steadied between 19,000 and 20,000. By the 1970s, Homewood had become a virtual bedroom for Chicago—in 1967 Homewood and Flossmoor formed one of only three outlying suburban zones where half or more of the workers COMMUTED to jobs in Chicago—and the trend continued into the twenty-first century.

John H. Long

See also: Leisure; Metropolitan Growth; Suburbs and Cities as Dual Metropolis

Further reading: Adair, Anna B., and Adele Sandberg. *Indian Trails to Tollways: The Story of the Homewood-Flossmoor Area.* 1968. • Hinko, Michael J. *History of Homewood.* 1976.

Homicide. Most Americans probably associate Chicago, the city of the HAYMARKET bombing, the RACE RIOT of 1919, the LEOPOLD AND LOEB case, the ST. VALENTINE'S DAY MASSACRE, and the turmoil surrounding the 1968 Democratic National Convention, with high levels of violence. Some early-twentieth-century observers incorrectly termed the city the murder capital of America. But despite this reputation, trends in homicide in Chicago have been roughly comparable to those of other large cities and provide a rough measure of social tensions. Like other

Chicago Homicide Rates per 100,000 residents, 1870–2000

Year	Rate
1870	2.6
1880	5.4
1890	7.0
1900	6.0
1910	9.2
1920	10.5
1930	14.6
1940	7.1
1950	7.9
1960	10.3
1970	24.0
1980	28.7
1990	32.9
2000	22.1

urban centers, Chicago experienced surges in homicide between 1900 and 1925 and between 1965 and 1990 but decreases during the middle decades and the closing decade of the twentieth century. Throughout the last 140 years, Chicago violence has been concentrated in the poorest neighborhoods of the city, has disproportionately involved young men from minority backgrounds, and has typically involved Chicagoans who have been related to or acquainted with one another.

Nonetheless, lethal violence has changed in significant ways. During the decades after the CIVIL WAR, Chicago killers tended to be young, unmarried, poor men of IRISH decent. Since the start of the twentieth century, however, homicides have more often involved young AFRICAN AMERICAN men, reflecting poverty, dislocation, and discrimination in the city.

Jeffrey S. Adler

See also: Capital Punishment; Crime and Chicago's Image; Jails and Prisons; Police

Further reading: Adler, Jeffrey S. "'My Mother-in-Law Is to Blame, But I'll Walk on Her Neck Yet': Homicide in Late Nineteenth-Century Chicago." *Journal of Social History* 31 (1997): 253–276. • Block, Richard, and Carolyn Rebecca Block. "Homicide Syndromes and Vulnerability: Violence in Chicago Community Areas over Twenty-five Years." *Studies in Crime and Crime Prevention* 1 (1992): 61–87. • Lashly, Arthur V. "Homicide (in Cook County)." In *The Illinois Crime Survey,* ed. John H. Wigmore, 1929, 591–646.

Hondurans. Chicago's first Honduran immigrants began arriving during the early twentieth century. Some came to study at Midwestern universities and then settled in Chicago to practice medicine, engineering, or other professions. Primarily mestizos of mixed Indian and Spanish heritage, these immigrants established families and formed a community in SOUTH CHICAGO with other Hondurans who came to work in the steel mills. By 1960, several hundred Hondurans had settled in South Chicago, LITTLE VILLAGE (NORTH LAWNDALE), and HUMBOLDT PARK. Lacking formal ethnic organizations, families came together for informal gatherings in each others' homes.

As immigration increased in the 1970s and 1980s, Chicago's Hondurans began to pursue more formal associations, but with only modest success. Hondureños Unidos, established in 1970, dissolved after several years, and other organizational attempts proved equally ephemeral until La Sociedad Civica-Cultural Hondureña was founded in 1989. Committed to preserving Honduran culture and educating immigrants' children, the society provided scholarships, supported FOLK MUSIC, and sent donations of food and clothing to Honduras.

The last few decades of immigration have brought greater diversity as well as greater numbers to the Honduran community, including the arrival of many Garifuna, or Black Caribs, of mixed Indian and African descent. These late-twentieth-century arrivals were drawn by Chicago's employment opportunities. As the century drew to a close, many Honduran men were working in CONSTRUCTION or factories. Honduran women often found jobs as DOMESTIC WORKERS. Approximately 10 percent of Chicago's Honduran community were working as professionals. Many more had left professions in Honduras but were unable to practice in the United States.

WAUKEGAN was home to the largest Honduran community in the 1990s, but North and South Side neighborhoods with significant Honduran populations included LOGAN SQUARE, UPTOWN, South Chicago, WEST TOWN, ALBANY PARK, and NEW CITY. Although many Hondurans attend ROMAN CATHOLIC churches with other Spanish-speaking immigrant neighbors, they come together each year in early February to celebrate La Virgen de Suyapa, the patron saint of Honduras. Annually in September, Hondurans unite with Chicago's other Central American communities to celebrate Independence Day. In the late 1990s, Hondurans continued to arrive in Chicago, many migrating from the larger Honduran immigrant communities in New Orleans, New York, and Los Angeles, attracted by Chicago's reputation for higher-paying employment. The 2000 census counted 5,844 Hondurans in the metropolitan area, although community estimates ranged up to several times that number.

Kate Caldwell

See also: Costa Ricans; Demography; Guatemalans; Iron and Steel; Multicentered Chicago; Salvadorans

Horse Racing. Chicagoans have enjoyed horse racing since the early 1830s and by the 1930s had more tracks (six) than any other metropolitan area. In 1840 a jockey club was formed which built a harness course near Indiana and 26th four years later. In 1854 the Garden City track was opened, followed one year later by John Wentworth's BRIGHTON PARK. In 1864, Dexter Park was established at 42nd Street and Halsted, and in 1878 the West Side Driving Track was opened adjacent to Garfield Park for both harness and thoroughbred racing.

In 1883, 500 leading Chicagoans established the prestigious WASHINGTON PARK Jockey Club. Its $150,000 Washington Park Race Track at 61st and Cottage Grove opened the next year and became the Midwest's preeminent track. Opening Day and the running of the American Derby became major dates in the elite social calendar. The 1893 Derby, worth $50,000 to winner *Boundless,* was the second-richest race in nineteenth-century America.

Racing in turn-of-the-century metropolitan Chicago was very tenuous. In 1891, after horseman Edward Corrigan's lease expired at West Side Track, he relocated to his new

Derby Day, Washington Park Race Track, 1903. Photographer: Unknown. Source: Chicago Historical Society.

Hawthorne Race Track in STICKNEY to avoid political harassment. A syndicate of politically connected bookmakers who operated illegal off-track poolrooms, including Mike McDonald, promptly established the profitable outlaw GARFIELD PARK racetrack, which held races of questionable honesty, only to have reform MAYOR Hempstead Washburne close it in 1892. Gamblers George Hankins and John Condon opened the Harlem Race Track in that western suburb (later FOREST PARK) in 1894, but reformers pressured Washington Park to close the same year, and Hawthorne in 1896. In 1898, Washington Park and Hawthorne reopened, and a new track was started in WORTH, but all were closed when the state stopped all racing in 1905.

In 1909, Alderman Thomas Carey bought Hawthorne and, after trying unsuccessfully to hold races in 1909 and 1911, ran 13 days in 1916. In 1922, Hawthorne staged a two-week meet employing oral betting, expanding it to 25 days in 1923, the same year that Aurora Downs began operations. One year later the courts ruled that oral betting was legal, leading to the opening in 1926 of Lincoln Fields in CRETE and, in HOMEWOOD, a new Washington Park, which resurrected the American Derby.

In 1927, Illinois legalized and began regulating pari-mutuel betting. H. D. "Curley" Brown established ARLINGTON Racetrack but was supplanted one year later by businessman John Hertz to prevent a possible underworld takeover. The track operated the first all-electric totalizer in 1933 and introduced turf racing one year later. In 1940 control passed to Benjamin Lindheimer, who also operated Washington Park. In 1932 mob attorney Edward J. O'Hare converted the Hawthorne Kennel Club into the half-mile Sportsman's Park, owned by the Bidwells since 1943.

WORLD WAR II curtailed racing; Lincoln Fields closed in 1941 and Arlington in 1943, shifting its major races to Washington Park. In 1946, MAYWOOD Park introduced pari-mutuel betting on harness racing. Lincoln Fields reopened in 1954 (renamed Balmoral in 1955), with harness racing, and was operated after 1987 by a syndicate headed by Billy Johnson, who also had run harness racing at Sportsman's Park and Maywood Park since 1978.

In 1970, Marge Lindheimer Everett, manager of Arlington and Washington Park since 1960, admitted bribing Governor Otto Kerner to gain choice racing dates. In 1971, Madison Square Garden Corporation bought Arlington, the site, 10 years later, of the Arlington Million, the world's first million-dollar thoroughbred race. In 1983, Richard L. Duchossois's syndicate took over the track. After a 1985 fire destroyed its grandstand, it was replaced by a world-class facility in 1989, closed briefly in 1997, and reopened in 2000 by Churchill Downs Incorporated.

Steven A. Riess

See also: Creation of Chicago Sports; Gambling; Leisure

Further reading: Chicago Recreation Commission. *Chicago Recreation Survey*, vol. 2, *Commercial Recreation*. 1938. • Riess, Steven A. *City Games: The Evolution of American Urban Society and the Rise of Sports*. 1989. • Robertson, William H. P. *The History of Thoroughbred Racing in America*. 1964.

Horsecars. *See* Street Railways

Hospitals. The history of Chicago's hospitals begins with an almshouse established by COOK COUNTY as part of its responsibility to provide care for indigent or homeless county residents, and for sick or needy travelers. Located at the corner of Clark and Randolph streets, this public charity was in operation as early as 1835. It did provide medical attendance, but such places typically crowded the ill together with the healthy poor, the insane, and persons who were permanently incapacitated.

Unlike Cook County, the city of Chicago had no legal mandate to care for the sick poor, but its charter did charge it with guarding against "pestilential or infectious diseases." Cholera had hit the area in 1832, and smallpox and scarlet fever were familiar to many. By 1843 fear of EPIDEMIC prompted city officials to build the first institution devoted exclusively to medical care in Chicago, a small wooden structure located on the far northern border of the city. Ironically, it was built on land bought for a CEMETERY. This first "hospital," a frame structure at North Avenue and the lakeshore in what would become LINCOLN PARK, was designed to keep victims of contagious disease away from the center of population. Rebuilt after a fire, in 1852 it began to segregate smallpox cases from cholera cases, but when cholera threatened Chicago in 1854, the city council authorized a separate though only temporary hospital at 18th and LaSalle streets. The city kept the smallpox hospital at North Avenue and even built a two-story building there, but it perished in the FIRE OF 1871. Beginning in 1874, a series of new hospitals to isolate contagious diseases was built on the Southwest Side of the city, near the courthouse at 26th and California.

Institutions like the smallpox hospital and the temporary cholera hospital were not meant to be locations of general medical care, and as early as 1837 citizens were suggesting the city build a general hospital. It was not until a decade later, however, that both city and county officials worked with physicians from Rush Medical College to establish the first such hospital in the area, at North Water and Dearborn streets. Newly opened and seeking students, Rush College wanted a hospital to fill a need for clinical education. Rush provided the doctors, the county supplied the medicine, and the city paid for the building rental. However, it soon became evident that the accommodations were inadequate for the large number and variety of patients, and the hospital went out of business.

Rush physicians soon incorporated another general hospital, called the Illinois General Hospital of the Lakes, which opened in 1850 with 12 beds in the old Lake House Hotel at Rush and North Water Streets. The charge was three dollars per week per patient. The doctors asked the Sisters of Mercy, a ROMAN CATHOLIC order, to provide NURSING care, and in the spring of 1851 transferred control to the Sisters. With a new charter, the hospital was renamed MERCY HOSPITAL. Cook County supervisors paid Mercy to care for county patients. The oldest continuously running hospital in Chicago, it moved in 1853 to a new building at Wabash and Van Buren and in 1863 was relocated to its present campus at 26th and Calumet. Rush College retained the privilege of teaching medical students there until 1859, when Mercy switched affiliation to the Chicago Medical School (later known as NORTHWESTERN UNIVERSITY Medical School).

Medical sectarians, some with unorthodox therapeutic practices, founded their own hospitals, such as the Hahnemann Hospital, which opened in the early 1850s. Popular despite unyielding criticism from "regular" physicians, homeopaths held that disease could be cured using very small doses of medicines rather than the typically large amounts of strong, even potentially lethal drugs other doctors prescribed. Homeopathy had a large following in Chicago and elsewhere in the nineteenth century, and this was not surprising, since minimalist therapies such as theirs were usually easier on the body. Their support declining by the early twentieth century as scientific medicine became more accurate and effective, homeopathic medical colleges found improvement in MEDICAL EDUCATION difficult to implement, and their hospitals closed or adopted traditional techniques. During the mid-nineteenth century, however, homeopaths in Chicago held a strong hand. Friction between them and regular medical practitioners became a political battle in 1857, when the former sought representation on the medical staff of what was to be the new city hospital at 18th and LaSalle streets. The argument prevented the institution from opening until 1859, when Rush faculty members rented it for use as a private hospital. In 1862, the U.S. Army commandeered it for a military hospital, until the CIVIL WAR ended and the county leased it. Cook County finally had a relatively permanent hospital. As the number of charity cases grew, however, the old building proved too small, and County Hospital moved to new pavilions at the present site at Wood and Harrison Streets in 1876. Larger structures replaced these beginning in 1912, and these in turn were replaced in the first years of the twenty-first century.

In 1847 a Chicago physician built a private retreat for the insane just north of the city, and in 1854, when the county moved its almshouse to a site known as "DUNNING" 12 miles northwest of the city, an asylum was among the buildings constructed. Authorities transferred this asylum, the Cook County Hospital for the Insane, to the care of the state of Illinois in 1912, and the name changed to Chicago State Hospital.

Institutional efforts against TUBERCULOSIS began with the Chicago Tuberculosis Institute, which established the Edward Sanatorium in 1907. The Municipal Tuberculosis Sanitarium, funded by the city, opened in 1915 at Crawford and Bryn Mawr Avenues. To care for sick and injured sailors who worked on the GREAT LAKES, the federal government set up a hospital in 1852 on the grounds of Fort Dearborn. It later moved north of the city to what became the UPTOWN neighborhood. After WORLD WAR I, the United States Public Health Service established several large hospitals, forerunners of present-day VETERAN'S HOSPITALS. The Hines facility in MAYWOOD was among the largest.

Seen as part of a church's mission, religious hospitals were shaped by a charitable imperative and a desire to save souls while caring for the sick. Religious symbols and the presence of religious nursing orders provided constant reminders of spirituality. St. Luke's Hospital, a charity of Grace Episcopal Church on the NEAR SOUTH SIDE, began in 1865 in a small frame structure at 8th and State Streets, eventually moving into larger buildings on south Indiana and Michigan Avenues. The hospital remained at that site for almost a century, merging in 1956 with Presbyterian Hospital and Rush Medical College on the NEAR WEST SIDE. Lutheran pastor William Passavant established the 15-bed Deaconess Hospital at Dearborn and Ontario Streets in 1865. Destroyed by the 1871 fire, in 1884 it reopened at Dearborn and Superior as the Emergency Hospital, later named Passavant after its founder. In 1920, Northwestern University Medical School adopted Emergency as a site for clinical instruction. Methodist Wesley Memorial Hospital, established in 1888, joined Passavant as part of Northwestern's Chicago campus in 1941.

The Alexian Brothers, a Roman Catholic male nursing order originating during the bubonic plague of the thirteenth century, started a small hospital for males in 1866. Its first substantial building was at Dearborn and Schiller. After two years, Alexian moved to larger quarters at North and Franklin. It rebuilt after the fire, moving in 1896 to Belden and Racine and then to ELK GROVE VILLAGE in 1966. The Sisters of Charity began St. Joseph's Hospital in LAKE VIEW in 1868. It now serves the community from a modern high-rise building at Diversey Avenue near the lake. Other early Catholic hospitals were St. Elizabeth's, founded near Western and Division in 1887 by the Poor Handmaids of Jesus Christ, and St. Mary of Nazareth Hospital, established in 1894 by the Sisters of the Holy Family of Nazareth in the same neighborhood. St. Mary's served the POLISH-speaking immigrant community.

Early Chicago JEWS founded a hospital at LaSalle and Schiller in 1866. Like nearby Alexian Brothers, this institution fell victim to the fire, but Jewish Hospital did not rebuild immediately. The family of philanthropist MICHAEL REESE made large contributions, and the hospital bearing his name arose in 1882 at Ellis Avenue and 29th Street, becoming by 1950 the largest charity-sponsored hospital in Chicago, with 718 beds. The increasing population of Jews on Chicago's Near Southwest Side prompted the opening of Mt. Sinai Hospital near Douglas Park in 1919.

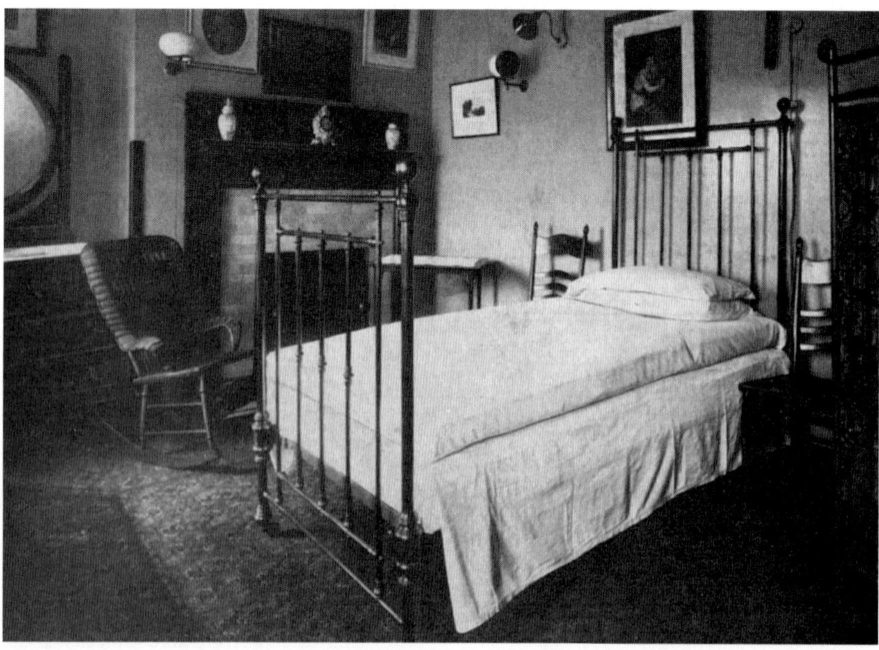

Private room, St. Luke's Hospital (no date). Photographer: Unknown. Source: Chicago Historical Society.

The influx of GERMAN immigrants into the Chicago area led to the 1883 founding of the German Hospital. It was renamed Grant Hospital during World War I. Baptists established the Chicago Baptist Hospital in 1891, and Methodists founded Bethany Methodist. By 1897, Lutherans had built Augustana, SWEDISH Covenant, the NORWEGIAN-American Hospital, and the Lutheran Deaconess Home and Hospital. Early twentieth-century Catholic groups started St. Anne's, St. Bernard's, and Columbus hospitals.

Several Chicago hospitals have aimed at specific types of patients. The Illinois Charitable Eye and Ear Infirmary began in 1858 under the direction of ophthalmologist Edward Lorenzo Holmes. In 1865, Mary Harris Thompson founded the Chicago Hospital for Women and Children, chiefly to serve widows and orphans of Civil War victims. Renamed the MARY THOMPSON HOSPITAL when she died in 1895, it opened on Rush Street, then moved to West Adams Street. Julia F. Porter endowed the Maurice Porter Memorial Free Hospital for Children in 1882 in memory of her son. In 1903 it took the name Children's Memorial. Joseph B. De Lee founded the Chicago Lying-In Hospital and Dispensary in 1895 in a tenement house on Maxwell Street in an effort to lower the high neonatal mortality rates. The Martha Washington Hospital advertised itself as a haven for alcoholics, and the Frances E. Willard National Temperance Hospital, named after the famous temperance advocate from Evanston, was for nondrinkers. It was dedicated to proving that diseases could be cured without the use of alcohol or alcohol-based medicines.

Until the mid-twentieth century, many Chicago hospitals refused to treat AFRICAN AMERICAN patients or employ black doctors and nurses. Daniel Hale Williams, one of the first African American surgeons in Chicago, organized PROVIDENT HOSPITAL in 1891 in an effort to ensure hospital services to African Americans in Chicago and to provide black health care workers a place to practice and learn.

Beginning in the last decade of the nineteenth century, groups of physicians and physician-entrepreneurs established for-profit hospitals such as the Lakeside Hospital, GARFIELD PARK Hospital, Westside Hospital, and Jefferson Park Hospital. Later examples of this type included North Chicago, WASHINGTON PARK, RAVENSWOOD, SOUTH SHORE, Washington Boulevard, BURNSIDE, Chicago General, John B. Murphy, and Belmont hospitals. Most of these were small and some lasted only a few years. Others became nonprofit

Technicians measuring blood counts, Wesley Hospital, 1951. By the 1950s, the clinical laboratory became a standard feature in hospitals, along with a new professional: the medical technician. Physicians' offices could not easily accommodate the new technologies, leading to an increased movement of diagnosis and treatment from private offices to the hospitals. Photographer: Unknown. Source: Chicago Historical Society.

institutions and continued to serve without investor ownership.

Reforms in nursing and a new understanding of the importance of cleanliness made the hospital a safer place for most patients by the end of the nineteenth century. Medicine began to incorporate developments in chemistry and biology, and aseptic surgery and clinical laboratories became effective tools in health care. Such changes in technology paralleled tremendous growth in population from immigration, which strained existing municipal services, including the provision of medical care. Hospital construction by both public and private agencies was one result. Tax-supported hospitals were built by the city, the county, the state, and federal government. Private hospitals included institutions owned or operated by medical schools, religious groups, individual doctors or groups of physicians, lay boards, and even companies such as RAILROADS. Especially in a city filling with immigrants, a hospital could be a place of comfort to particular beliefs, customs, languages, and races, as well as a site of medical care.

INSURANCE programs beginning in the 1930s encouraged hospital development, and as the Hill-Burton plan took effect after World War II, hospitals all over the United States were built or expanded. As the number of available beds increased, so did competition for patients among neighboring institutions. By 1950, with a population of 3.6 million, Chicago had 84 hospitals, including public and private sanatoria. The majority were nonprofit, receiving major funding from patient fees (often at least partly paid by insurance), donations, and endowments.

As government reimbursement programs initiated in the 1960s expanded to encompass so many patients that tax resources stretched thin, agencies demanded briefer hospital stays. New technologies allowed patients to be discharged earlier. Beds began to go unfilled and hospitals faced declining revenues. Many closed or consolidated, and the number of hospitals in Chicago fell to approximately 50 by the late 1990s. The advent of health-maintenance organizations (HMOs) was another factor in the loss of hospital income, since these organizations typically contracted for care at lower fees than traditional insurance paid. Hospital ownership began to consolidate as large corporations or associations sought economies of scale by purchasing formerly independent institutions.

Paul A. Buelow

See also: Clinics and Dispensaries; Medical Manufacturing and Pharmaceuticals; Mental Health; Public Health; Religious Institutions

Further reading: Bonner, Thomas N. *Medicine in Chicago, 1850–1950: A Chapter in the Social and Scientific Development of a City.* 2nd ed. 1991. • Chicago Medical Society. *History of Medicine and Surgery and Physicians and Surgeons of Chicago.* 1922. • Duis, Perry. *Challenging Chicago: Coping with Everyday Life, 1837–1920.* 1998.

Hotels. When Chicago was a small village in 1830, the American palace hotel ideal was literally being cast in stone on the eastern seaboard. Therefore, the typical developmental pattern of traveler accommodations that proceeded elsewhere from tavern to city inn and then, beginning in the 1820s, to luxury hotel took place in Chicago rapidly and on a large scale. The first three taverns, Caldwell's Tavern (built by James Kinzie), the Miller House, and Mark Beaubien's tavern, soon known as the Sauganash Hotel, arose at Wolf's Point at the fork of the Chicago River during 1829 and 1830. In 1831 Beaubien added a frame addition to his log building, establishing Chicago's first hotel. Chicago's first Tremont House followed in 1833, and, though modest, it was no doubt named for Boston's remarkable Tremont House (1829). The Lake House opened in 1836 across the CHICAGO RIVER from FT. DEARBORN near where the Wrigley Building stands today. It was an elegant three-story brick building costing $90,000, and it served as a center for social and political activity.

During the mid-nineteenth century, the building, destruction, and rebuilding of hotels continued, fueled by fire and burgeoning development. The Tremont House, Briggs House, Palmer House, Sherman House,

Grand Pacific Hotel as rebuilt after the fire, 1872. Artist: Unknown. Source: The Newberry Library.

Adams House, Matteson House, Massasoit House, and Metropolitan House were among the pre-1871 hotels that served the city in luxurious style. These five-, six-, and seven-story block masonry buildings offered amenities such as steam heat, GAS lighting, elevators, French chefs, and elegant surroundings. The Tremont House in particular, rebuilt for the third time in 1850, retained its position for many years as the city's leading hotel. Both Stephen A. Douglas and Abraham Lincoln spoke from its balcony to crowd-filled streets below, and, in 1860, the hotel served as the headquarters for the Illinois REPUBLICAN PARTY as it campaigned for Lincoln's presidential nomination. All of these hotels burned in the FIRE OF 1871. The Palmer House had been open only for a few months. Another hotel, the Grand Pacific, had been open only a few days.

The "Big Four" of the post-fire hotels included the Palmer House, the Grand Pacific, the Tremont, and the Sherman House. These buildings adopted the commercial palazzo style of architecture common to the grand hotel palaces of the East. All professed to be fireproof above all, but boasted grand lobbies, monumental staircases, elegant parlors, cafes, barber shops, bridal suites, dining rooms, ballrooms, promenades, hundreds of private bedrooms and baths, and the latest luxuries. Typical room charges ranged from $3.50 to $7 per day and included three to four meals. Guests incurred extra charges for private parlors, room service, fires in private fireplaces, and desserts taken to one's room from the dinner table. Hotels like the Grand Pacific and the Palmer House not only served transient visitors but also appealed to wealthy permanent residents who found in the palace hotel a convenient way to set up trouble-free elegant households. Hotels such as these served as models for other hotel construction, particularly in smaller American cities, where a luxury hotel symbolized and celebrated capitalist bourgeois values. Chicago also became a center for the hotel industry with three of the major hotel trade journals publishing from the city.

The architectural revolution that produced the SKYSCRAPER found its expression in Chicago's luxury hotels. First among these was Adler and Sullivan's AUDITORIUM BUILDING (1889), which featured a 400-room hotel in addition to the theater and 17-story office tower. A 400-room annex was added in anticipation of the 1893 WORLD'S COLUMBIAN EXHIBITION. The LaSalle Hotel (1908–9), one of the first of the new hotels to locate in the LOOP, soared 22 stories into the Chicago skyline and claimed 1,000 bedrooms. A Michigan Avenue hotel strip anchored by the nationally renowned Blackstone (1910) included the Congress (formerly the Auditorium Annex) and the Auditorium. These were soon challenged by hotel development in the prosperous North Michigan Avenue region, where the Drake (1918–20) and the Allerton (1923–4) offered quiet, elegant alternatives with a view of the lake. The economic boom and population growth of the 1920s and Chicago's increasing attractiveness as a convention city led to a perceived shortfall in hotel rooms, remedied by the 2,000-room Morrison Hotel and the newest rendition of the Palmer House, a Holabird & Roche creation built in 1923–25 whose 25 stories housed 2,268 rooms and for a very short time held the record as the world's largest hotel.

This title soon passed to the Stevens Hotel (now the Chicago Hilton and Towers), developed by the Stevens family of the Illinois Life Insurance Company and owners of the LaSalle. Opened in 1927, the Stevens occupied an entire city block on Michigan Avenue between Seventh and Eighth Streets. Its 3,000 guest rooms and supporting facilities such as ballrooms, restaurants, retail shops, and meeting rooms were designed according to principles of mass production and retailing perfected for the hotel industry by E. M. Statler. The hotel's size and unsurpassed convention facilities depended on continuing national prosperity for economic viability. The GREAT DEPRESSION of the 1930s sent the Stevens into receivership, as it did for hundreds of other hotel properties across the nation. Chicago's hotel boom had temporarily come to a halt.

Chicago's hotel industry continued to expand during the second half of the twentieth century. After WORLD WAR II, the growth of automobile travel led to the emergence

Edgewater Beach Hotel, 1930. Photographer: Curt Teich & Co. Source: Curt Teich Archives, Lake County Discovery Museum.

of dozens of new "motels" in the suburbs. Meanwhile, the rise of airplane travel created new clusters of hotels near O'HARE AIRPORT. By the end of the 1980s, the suburbs contained about 14,000 motel and hotel rooms. But the days of the large downtown hotels were far from over. Starting in the late 1980s, there was a new boom in luxury hotel construction and renovation in downtown Chicago. Huge new edifices such as the Hotel Nikko, the Four Seasons, and the 1,200-room Sheraton and Cityfront Center boosted the city's capacity to handle a large number of well-to-do BUSINESS travelers and tourists. Chicago's ability to attract and retain large national conventions—many of which were held at its enormous McCormick Place facility—fueled this expansion and helped the business of all the area's hotels. As the twentieth century came to a close, there were roughly 75,000 hotel and motel rooms in the Chicago area, and more space was being added to handle the roughly 25 million people a year who stayed as guests in and around the city.

Molly W. Berger

See also: Architecture; Built Environment of the Chicago Region; Places of Assembly; Tourism and Conventions

Further reading: Andreas, A. T. *History of Chicago.* 1884–1886. • Berger, Molly W. "The Modern Hotel in America, 1829–1929." Ph.D. diss., Case Western Reserve University. 1997. • Williamson, Jefferson. *The American Hotel.* 1930.

House Moving. In contrast to the present, when housing structures are seldom moved, Chicagoans in the 1830s, 1840s, and 1850s took advantage of the mobility of BALLOON FRAME structures without INFRASTRUCTURE connections. New arrivals could buy homes and then move them to a desired location. Chester Tupper, Chicago's first house mover, regularly moved structures on rollers down the middle of Chicago's early STREETS.

Only a very specific kind of building was easily moved. Shanties, log cabins, and structures made of brick or stone all posed particular problems for house movers. Balloon frame houses had none of these disadvantages. They were light, of flexible construction, and their frames were not sunk into the ground.

House moving was such a nuisance by 1846 that a group of Chicagoans asked that the city council not permit more than one building to stand in the streets of any block at the same time, or permit any one building to stand in the streets for more than three days. In 1855 Daniel Elston unsuccessfully petitioned the city council for permission to move a house across the Chicago River on the Kinzie Street Bridge.

There are several key reasons why house moving was so popular during these years. Early industrialization, which provided factory-made nails, and large-scale milling operations near Chicago facilitated house moving by making balloon frame construction possible. The lack of paved streets and the absence of utilities through the 1840s also facilitated house-moving.

Ann Durkin Keating

See also: Construction; Housing Types; Water Supply

Further reading: Bross, William. "What I Remember of Early Chicago," in *Reminiscences of Chicago during the Forties and Fifties,* comp. Mabel McIlvaine. 1913. • Gale, Edwin O. *Reminiscences of Early Chicago and Vicinity.* 1902.

House Numbering and Street Numbering. Numbering streets and buildings allows those not familiar with a building or home to locate it more easily. Early on, Chicago created a few numbered streets on the North and West Sides, but these did not last. By the 1860s, the city had numbered east-west streets on the SOUTH SIDE. Chicago's earliest building numbers were employed in the 1840s on Lake Street, the city's business center. Homes and businesses elsewhere were described in terms of street intersections, such as "on Kinzie Street, east of Dearborn." Use of house numbers spread slowly. During the CIVIL WAR, however, the U.S. Post Office began free door-to-door delivery of MAIL, contingent upon numbering of houses, and house numbering became common.

However, each "division" or side of the city had its own system, and many streets were numbered from the meandering rivers or shoreline, so that house numbers on parallel streets often failed to line up neatly. Beginning about 1881 on the South Side, house numbers on north-south streets were tied to the numbered east-west streets. Thus, for example, 2200 State was at 22nd Street. Here, numbering was much more regular than elsewhere.

Ordinary Chicagoans seem to have adapted to the fuzzy but familiar geometry of this house-numbering regime, but delivery workers and strangers found it confusing at times, and the confusion added to business costs. A campaign led by Edward P. Brennan resulted in a new house-numbering system in 1908, as well as to STREET-NAMING reforms. All buildings were numbered beginning at Madison and State Streets, making the business and retail heart of Chicago the center of the new system. The clean geometry of straight lines and right angles guaranteed uniformity in numbering. Throughout Chicago, the "twenty-four hundred block" is just west of Western Avenue, while the 3200 block is just west of Kedzie. House numbers rise by 800 every mile, or 100 per long block, except on the South Side, where numbered streets retained their uneven spacing from Madison to 31st Street (where the first three "mile" intervals are at 12th, 22nd, and 31st Streets).

Suburban areas gradually adopted house numbering as well, sometimes establishing their own systems, sometimes extending the city's. LAKE VIEW used the Chicago system on north-south streets but created its own scheme for east-west streets, with Western Avenue as its baseline. This scheme was continued when Lake View was annexed by the city in the late nineteenth century. Other areas annexed by the city were obliged to adopt the city's system. In the 1890s, OAK PARK, foreshadowing later changes in Chicago, adopted a numbering system based on 800 to the mile—with one hundred to each long city block—and using Chicago's State Street as its baseline.

Chicago's numbered street system has been extended far south into suburban communities, and some suburbs have adopted the city's house-numbering system. Others, however, emphasizing the uniqueness of their communities, adopted their own systems.

Christopher Thale

See also: Northwest Ordinance; Planning Chicago

Further reading: City directories provide street guides that explain house numbering in the nineteenth and early twentieth centuries. • Hayner, Don, and Tom McNamee. *Streetwise Chicago: A History of Chicago Street Names.* 1988. • The papers of the City Club of Chicago, Chicago Historical Society, contain extensive material on house-numbering and street-naming reform.

House of the Good Shepherd/Chicago Industrial School for Girls. Located at Grace and Racine, the House of the Good Shepherd officially opened in 1859, when four IRISH Sisters of the Good Shepherd arrived in Chicago from St. Louis to care for "abandoned women." Over time the sisters extended their care from those accused of PROSTITUTION or disorderly conduct to delinquent and dependent girls. After the turn of the century, most residents (over 400 at the end of the century) found their way to this ROMAN CATHOLIC institution through the JUVENILE COURT. Today, with public funding and major assistance from CATHOLIC CHARITIES, the House of the Good Shepherd shelters battered women with children.

In 1889 the Good Shepherd Sisters established the Chicago Industrial School for Girls to provide vocational training and religious instruction to dependent girls. After much controversy during the 1880s, this school at 49th and Indiana received regular support from the county. In 1911 Bishop James E. Quigley moved the girls to the grounds of St. Mary's Training School (for boys) in DES PLAINES so that sisters and brothers would live near one another. Refusing to give up their property, the Sisters of the Good Shepherd opened the Illinois Technical School for Colored Girls (both dependent and delinquent). They became the first nuns to serve AFRICAN AMERICANS on Chicago's SOUTH SIDE. In 1953, this "school-home" closed and became St. Euphrasia Day Nursery.

Suellen Hoy

See also: Children, Dependent; Convents; Religious Institutions; Schooling for Work; Social Services

Housekeeping. From all over the world, Chicago's many in-migrants have brought with them an immense variety in ways of keeping house. For every new household, there has been someone, usually a woman, who has negotiated the choices between old and new ways of eating, of housecleaning, and of purchasing household necessities. Having learned one set of skills—and housewifery was a highly skilled undertaking until well into the twentieth century—she had to learn another set that might be very different in Chicago. Thus, the pace of a family's assimilation to life in the city has owed in substantial part to mundane daily decisions by a housewife. To whose standards of cleanliness would she adhere? Where would she find the ingredients for her family's holiday dinner? Hundreds of thousands of Chicago women have pondered such issues over the generations and in this way have played a major role in shaping the character both of their families' lives and of the city's neighborhoods.

Some of those neighborhoods have constituted a particularly difficult challenge for a housewife—none more so than the famed Back of the Yards. Said two sociologists in 1911 of the area adjacent to the stockyards: "No other neighborhood in this, or perhaps in any other city, is dominated by a single industry of so offensive a character." The people who lived near the yards confronted filthy conditions: stench, decaying carcasses, pollution of many sorts. A plethora of packinghouses discharged their wastes into Bubbly Creek, a fork from the South Branch of the Chicago River that traversed Back of the Yards.

Postcard advertising cooking utensils manufactured by Illinois Pure Aluminum Company, Lemont, Illinois, 1913. Creator: Curt Teich & Co. Source: Curt Teich Archives, Lake County Discovery Museum.

Upton Sinclair described the problems vividly in The Jungle, published in 1906. His fictional Lithuanian immigrants, arriving in Back of the Yards, see housing worse than any they had heretofore encountered. Their landlady's home is "unthinkably filthy," with a "fetid odor" permeating the area. The thick swarms of flies, the terrible overcrowding—there is even a flock of chickens in the house—are all described in nauseating detail. The sociological report of 1911 stated that researchers had found one residence in the neighborhood in which a single water closet was provided for 47 persons.

With so many thousands coming to Chicago in the late nineteenth century, frequently to confront appalling housing conditions, it is not surprising that in 1889 this city gave birth to the American settlement house movement with Jane Addams's founding of Hull House. Addams, her Chicago colleagues, and those they inspired in other parts of the country, usually middle-class women, took up residence in homes in impoverished immigrant neighborhoods and tried to teach those in the vicinity about standards of cleanliness, among other things. Scholars still debate the extent to which the settlement house workers were busybodies—as opposed to being genuinely helpful—but what is incontrovertible is that thousands of working-class Chicago housewives were struggling and needed relief. Even if they were fortunate enough to live some place other than Back of the Yards, they might well be doing piecework at home, thus creating another set of challenges for maintaining a clean and pleasant domestic environment. In her memoir *Twenty Years at Hull-House,* Jane Addams left no doubt that she found the homes in the Hull House neighborhood as disturbing as Sinclair had found those in Back of the Yards: they were located on streets that were "inexpressibly dirty," suffered from "unenforced sanitary legislation," and were adjacent to "stables foul beyond description."

Dirt, diseases such as tuberculosis that correlate with unclean conditions, and demoralization—all these afflicted many homes at the same time that Chicago played host to the World's Columbian Exposition of 1893—the White City. The great fair, with alabaster buildings sited to create a pristine and orderly environment, stood in ironic contrast to the disorder and grime that plagued so many households in nearby areas. Most Americans cities contained stark contrasts between tenements and opulent households, but with the fair, Chicago flaunted its capacity to create an island of ideal beauty in a sea of squalor.

Such unhappy contrasts are part of the story of keeping house in Chicago, but they are not the whole story. Chicago came into being just as the first of many significant changes was taking place in household technology: the transition from open-hearth cookery to the stove. A dazzling array of further changes in the nineteenth century—the sewing machine and improved refrigeration, for example—were in place by the time of the world's fair and were featured in the fair's catalog. Moreover, displays at the White City's Electricity Building suggested possibilities for the future such as electric stoves, electrified pans, washing machines, and ironing machines.

In the nineteenth century working-class housewives struggled to maintain homes under highly adverse conditions while their middle-class sisters fretted about the "servant problem"—which became more intense as working-class white women began to enjoy employment options better paid and less stigmatized than domestic service. Middle-class women could look to technology for relief from their burdens. Working-class housewives would have to wait longer for relief from this quarter, because it was not until the 1920s that such consumer goods as household electrical appliances began to be widely disseminated throughout the society (owing both to lower prices and to the increasing use of installment buying).

Scholars who have studied domestic work have found that the women who waited upon other women and their families bore the heaviest housekeeping burden of all. At first Chicago servants were drawn primarily from the ranks of immigrants, and then as increasing numbers of African Americans began to move north, black women began to be the largest component of the domestic service workforce. Servants' days were long, they were poorly paid, and they could not count on being treated with dignity. Conflicts must have been common between middle-class housewives with their standards for how things should be done, and servants fresh off the boat or the farm with no notion of the niceties that might be expected in their new employment.

The trends of the twentieth century can be summarized briefly. Ever fewer households have employed servants, and those that have, have used them fewer days per week than in the past. Shrinking numbers of servants plus smaller families have meant that average household size has continued the decline it began in the early nineteenth century. Since ever more women have been gainfully employed outside the home, they have looked to technology and new products—and probably to their partners—to help with the demands of housekeeping. Hence homes have become both more mechanized and more commodified. All forms of household work have become deskilled as busy people increasingly use convenience foods or fast food for meals, while newer fabrics and clothing styles have simplified LAUNDRY and virtually eliminated ironing. Some things have remained constant: home is the place where children are reared, and home is still something people dream of owning, their most valuable possession if they are owners, and the place where newcomers mediate between old and new.

Glenna Matthews

See also: Boardinghouses; Foodways; Gas and Electricity; Grocery Stores and Supermarkets; Housing Types; Nursery Schools; Public Health; Work Culture

Further reading: Hoy, Suellen. *Chasing Dirt: The American Pursuit of Cleanliness.* 1995. • Katzman, David M. *Seven Days a Week: Women and Domestic Service in Industrializing America.* 1978. • Matthews, Glenna. *"Just a Housewife": The Rise and Fall of Domesticity in America.* 1987.

Housing for the Elderly. In the early nineteenth century there were no formal institutions in Chicago dedicated specifically to sheltering dependent elderly persons, although the county ALMSHOUSES gave rudimentary accommodations to destitute persons of all ages. In the 1880s reformers aiming to separate the elderly and disabled poor from the insane at the DUNNING and OAK FOREST poorhouses built the Home for Aged Couples, a two-story building for married residents. Nevertheless, public agencies continued to ignore the special needs of the elderly poor despite the fact that the proportion of those 60 years or older had climbed from 16.7 percent of the poorhouse residents in 1870 to 61 percent by 1908.

The Old Ladies' Home, created and governed in 1861 by a board of managers representing eight PROTESTANT religious groups, was the first private facility in Chicago to provide permanent residential care for the aged. After the Chicago Fire of 1871, the need for additional housing led to the construction of a larger facility with 80 single bedrooms and several public rooms, the Old People's Home at 3850 S. Indiana Avenue.

Facilities founded by other religious and ethnic groups followed. The Little Sisters of the Poor built residences serving the IRISH-ROMAN CATHOLIC population: Sacred Heart Home in 1876, St. Augustine's in 1882, and St. Joseph's in 1891. By 1905 they served 560 residents. During the 1880s, one SWEDISH and two GERMAN ethnic organizations sponsored homes. The Home for Aged JEWS was founded in 1891 at Drexel Avenue and 62nd Street to serve the German-Jewish community; and the Orthodox Jewish Home for the Aged, founded in 1899 at Albany and Ogden, served the Russian Jews. They were joined by DANES in 1891 (NORWOOD PARK), NORWEGIANS in 1896 (Norwood Park), and Bohemians in 1893. Religious sponsors included Episcopalians, who founded the Church Home for Aged Persons in 1890 in North KENWOOD and the Methodist Episcopal Old People's Home in 1898 in EDGEWATER. The Home for Aged Colored People was incorporated in 1898 at 610 W. Garfield Boulevard, but served only 15 residents in 1909. Many suburban homes were established including the Evangelical Lutheran Old People's Home (1892) in ARLINGTON HEIGHTS, the Presbyterian Home in EVANSTON, and the Scottish Home in NORTH RIVERSIDE.

These facilities owed their existence to the efforts of individual organizers motivated by distressed individuals within their own group. The word "home" indicated a substitute family providing care in pleasant surroundings. Most residents were in good health, longtime residents of the city, and "of good character." By 1912, private institutional care had become a widely accepted method of providing care for the aged poor, the first real effort in Chicago to treat the aged as a specific social group.

Until the 1950s, the CHICAGO HOUSING AUTHORITY provided no special housing for the elderly. In 1951, only 5 percent of the total CHA units were occupied by tenants over 65.

The first high-rise building designed especially for elderly residents, the Drexel Square Apartments, was part of the HYDE PARK–Kenwood URBAN RENEWAL Project. Another special building was in the Lathrop Homes, built in 1959. After 1961, eight federally financed buildings containing 1,009 apartments were designated for the elderly. Unlike most CHA housing, buildings for the elderly were constructed in all parts of the city, including three projects on North Sheridan Road. This does not mean that the projects were well integrated; most housed predominantly white or black residents, depending on location. Income limits were in force without the stigma attached to family projects.

In 1967, the Illinois Housing Development Authority (IHDA) was established to make construction loans and long-term mortgages to nonprofit and limited-profit entities for construction or rehabilitation of rental, cooperative, or CONDOMINIUM housing for persons of low or moderate income. IHDA received subsidies from the U.S. Department of Housing and Urban Development (HUD), enabling them to give developers low interest rates and preconstruction loans, which they were required to pass along to the tenant in the form of lower rent. In 1975 the Grace Street Housing off Lake Shore Drive was the first built for the elderly under this law.

In 1976 the 17-year CHA program for the construction of housing for the elderly, which totaled 46 developments with 9,607 units, was brought to an end. It was replaced in 1980 by the Chicago Housing Authority Scattered Sites Program, or the GAUTREAUX ASSISTED HOUSING PROGRAM, which used federal funds to provide scattered housing, managed by private firms. The CHA has also served as a landlord participating in the HUD subsidies.

All of these types of housing for the elderly, including IHDA managed facilities, private and publicly subsidized, have also been located in the suburban counties. In 1992, IHDA listed a total of 20,818 units in Chicago, of which almost 70 percent were HUD rent-subsidized and/or sponsored by nonprofit organizations, and 20,887 suburban units, of which 53 percent were subsidized. At the close of the twentieth century there were at least 26 religious- and ethnic-sponsored facilities in Chicago, 22 in Cook County, and 14 in the other suburban counties.

N. Sue Weiler

See also: Built Environment of the Chicago Region; Czechs and Bohemians; Housing Reform; Public Housing; Religious Institutions; Subsidized Housing

Further reading: Anderson, Arthur E. "The Institutional Path of Old Age in Chicago, 1870–1912." Ph.D. diss., University of Virginia. 1983. • Bowly, Devereux, Jr. *The Poorhouse: Subsidized Housing in Chicago, 1895–1976.* 1978. • Hancock, Judith Ann, ed. *Housing the Elderly.* 1987.

Housing, Mail-Order. The MAIL-ORDER house developed out of a need for inexpensive, sturdy homes. In 1906 the Aladdin Company of Bay City, Michigan, began to manufacture prefabricated houses. Aladdin quickly became the industry leader with its large variety of catalog houses.

In 1908, the Sears, Roebuck & Company entered the mail-order houses business. Richard Sears's original intent was to boost declining home furnishings sales. He believed that if a company sold an entire house, then it could sell all the items to go inside the house.

Sears competed with Aladdin for preeminence in the mail-order home market, but did not overtake Aladdin until the 1920s. The 1928 Sears catalog for *Honor Bilt Modern Homes* offered almost one hundred styles, a far greater number than any of its rivals. The company became the premier catalog retailer of prefabricated houses.

Sears's success was due to two strategies not utilized by Aladdin. First, not only could a buyer purchase the entire house and furnishings from Sears, but Sears would also finance the purchase with a home mortgage. Second, Sears owned the entire fabrication process from the LUMBER mills to the doors and windows factory.

Houses sold through the Sears catalogs were shipped directly to the buyers by RAILROAD. The mass of materials typically required a community with a rail siding where boxcars could sit while waiting to be unloaded. The precut materials were numbered and assembled according to a plan book, like a giant model.

Sears reportedly sold over 100,000 houses through mail orders between 1908 and 1940, eclipsing all of its competitors. In spite of the great number of houses sold, Sears ended their mail-order houses business just prior to World War II. The company had taken a great financial loss during the Great Depression, when over $11,000,000 in mortgages were liquidated.

Chicago-area communities that had large rail sidings during the first half of the twentieth century still contain Sears houses. West suburban Downers Grove has confirmed over 80 houses from a list of more than 200 potential ones. Many Chicago suburban communities like Elgin, Glen Ellyn, Villa Park, and Arlington Heights have inventoried their historic Sears mail-order houses.

Mark S. Harmon

See also: Balloon Frame; Consumer Credit; Housing Types

Further reading: Gowans, Alan. *The Comfortable House: North American Suburban Architecture, 1890–1930.* 1986. • Stevenson, Katherine Cole, and H. Ward Jandl. *Houses by Mail: A Guide to Houses from Sears, Roebuck and Company.* 1986.

Housing Reform. In 1878 the Chicago Board of Health published its first reports on overcrowding and lack of sanitation in the city's poor sections, where roughly half the population resided. Over the next several decades, health officials and reform-minded citizens continued investigating and publicizing the extent of squalid living conditions that existed in Chicago, in hopes of building momentum for change. Settlement workers from Hull House, in conjunction with the federal Department of Labor, surveyed their neighborhood in 1893. The City Homes Association sponsored Robert Hunter's extensive 1901 report; and in 1908, Edith Abbott, one of the founders of the University of Chicago's School of Social Service Administration, began a series of studies that she would continue intermittently for almost 30 years.

These surveys found numerous families packed into small houses and apartments built for single-family residence. Many slum blocks had no sewer connections, and unsanitary backyard privies provided the only toilet facilities; there was little or no indoor plumbing in many buildings occupied by several families. Those parts of the city to which African Americans were restricted, mainly the "Black Belt," a narrow strip running south from the Loop along State Street, were especially wretched. Yet in these areas slum landlords charged more than elsewhere, because discrimination limited blacks' rental options. Since many Americans in this era assumed that poor people were personally to blame for the bad conditions in which they lived, reformers, whatever their own beliefs, tended to downplay humanitarian rationales for change and to emphasize the health threats to the whole city when they reported on the slum conditions.

Leading Chicago citizens responded to these alarming reports by joining reform campaigns of various kinds. These included supporting regulatory legislation and trying to erect good-quality low-rent dwellings that could return limited but real profits for investors. Such efforts proved unable to supply housing that low-income families could afford, however. George Pullman built his famous model town in the 1880s in part to demonstrate that good housing could profitably be provided for factory workers. But, savvy entrepreneur that he was, Pullman failed because he had not factored in the impact of economic downswings and unemployment when designing his venture. Successful businessman Julius Rosenwald did turn a 6 percent profit on his Michigan Boulevard Garden Apartments built in the 1920s for African Americans, but rents were too steep for all but the best-paid black families. The so-called New Tenement law of 1902, which set minimum standards for space, ventilation, and sanitary facilities in new construction, also failed to produce significant improvement. Lack of enforcement was one problem with restrictive legislation, but even more basic was the same stumbling block that stymied the humanitarian builders: low-paid workers lacked the means to cover the cost of decent urban shelter. Insisting on decent standards simply priced housing beyond what low-income families could afford to pay.

Housing reformers also failed to confront segregation as a critical barrier to housing improvement. Over time many white families who started out in the slums did improve their financial situations, after which they moved to more pleasant neighborhoods. This option was not available to blacks, because property owners in middle-class neighborhoods used legal and extralegal means, including violence, to keep their distance from African Americans. Even economically successful blacks were trapped in sections of the city that became ever more dilapidated as more blacks migrated to Chicago and packed into the already crowded ghetto.

After decades of effort, housing reformers in the prosperous 1920s were dispirited to find large numbers of poor families still residing in bleak, deteriorated sections of the inner city. When private enterprise overlooked the slums during this high-growth era, Chicago reformers, along with their colleagues in other big cities, began to advocate government programs to construct subsidized accommodations for low-income people. They hailed the New Deal federal housing programs begun during the Great Depression of the 1930s, which produced four developments containing a total of four thousand units in rowhouses and low-rise apartment buildings. These were the Jane Addams Houses, the Julia C. Lathrop Homes, Trumbull Park Homes, and the Ida B. Wells Homes.

Unfortunately, public housing did not solve Chicago's housing problems. Few policy makers recognized the special problems faced

At the turn of the twentieth century, frame storefronts, like this one at 499 South Jefferson, included multiple housing units. Photographer: Unknown. Source: University of Illinois at Chicago.

MARTIN BOYER AND CO

☐ CONTINENTAL CASUALTY CO.

☐ TRANSPORTATION INSURANCE CO.

LIABILITY INSPECTION REPORT

ENTERED

SCRUTINIZED

ENGINEER K. Barron DATE 7-21-53 POLICY NO.

AGENT DATE OF EXPIRATION

NAME OF ASSURED Exchange National Bank as Trustee under Trust #3882 and Spector Realty Co as Agents.

BUSINESS ADDRESS 3616-18 S State St. Chicago, Illinois

LOCATION On the southside in a colored business and residential section.

1. Desirability of risk Poor (Fire trap)
2. Assured's interest: OWNER ☐ GENERAL LESSEE ☐ TENANT ☐ Trust #3882
3. Type of building Store and Apt bldg. Old brick Height 4 story
4. Occupancy of building Stores and small apts
5. Part occupied by Assured none
6. Occupancy of basement none (no basement)
7. Any undesirable business on premises? none Describe
8. Nationality of tenants Colored Class Poor Type of neighborhood Poor
9. Elevators: Number and type no ne Power
   Does Assured use operate control maintain elevators?
   Insured Company General condition
10. Assembly halls, lodge rooms, etc.: Is hall leased to general lessee or is it rented out directly by Assured for dances, etc. none
    Describe all purposes for which hall is used
    Dimensions of halls Capacity
    No. seats? Removable or permanent?
    Who maintains halls? Floor supports
11. Check the following for sub-standard condition. Describe conditions checked in detail.

Wiring is poor

	✓		✓		✓
Balcony railings		Chimneys, copings, cornices	Poor	Floor openings	
Stair handrails	Poor	Shutters and awnings		Roof	
Stair treads and supports	Poor	Radio aerials and masts		FIRE EXITS (adequate and marked)	Poor
Stair and hall lighting	Poor	Sidewalk and coal holes		FIRE ESCAPE SUPPORTS	Poor
Stair and hall covering		Sidewalk stairs		FIRE ESCAPES (Are they clear) ?	
Ceilings and walls	Poor	Sidewalk gratings		Roof drains piped to sewer	
Clothes poles		Vault lights		Window sills (loose objects)	
Clothes stands		Sidewalk XXXX	Poor	Gutters and downspouts	
Window lights	Poor	Yards and adjacent ways		Any other hazards	
Sky lights		Floor surfaces	Poor	*Give specific details.	

12. Any bowling alleys, billiard tables, swimming pools, shooting galleries or amusement devices?
    State if under control of Assured none
13. Signs: Owned by none Maintained by
    Type Condition Area

(OVER)

1953 inspection report for a building at 2358 South Indiana. Source: Chicago Historical Society.

by African Americans, and after World War II, public housing itself became a mechanism for more extreme segregation. Black Chicagoans seeking affordable housing were offered access only to grim high-rise apartment buildings in African-American neighborhoods where government had created a "second ghetto." In the 1960s, civil rights activists, including Martin Luther King, Jr., successfully challenged the racially motivated site-selection practices of the Chicago Housing Authority in what became known as the Gautreaux case. Yet, even as integrationists won victories in the courts, the political tide was turning against all public housing programs. In 1973 the Nixon administration announced a temporary freeze on federally subsidized housing programs, and relatively little building occurred in subsequent years.

During the 1980s and 1990s, the visibility of homeless people walking the streets of Chicago and other big cities in the United States stimulated renewed interest in housing reform. Ironically, many of the same problems that confronted earlier reformers persisted. Like their counterparts at the outset of the twentieth century, many middle-class Americans continued to focus on personal shortcomings of the poor in the explanations of why some people lacked decent shelter. Psychological explanations persisted, despite economic changes that generated high numbers of low-wage service jobs that left people unable to afford market-rate housing. Meanwhile, the legacy of decades of residential segregation left many African Americans residing in inner cities without easy access to employment opportunities in economically vigorous suburbs. And again, as with the creation of the second ghetto, Chicago's city government exacerbated the problem by approving redevelopment projects that destroyed inexpensive housing options, such as Skid Row hotels. As the twentieth century neared its end, housing reformers in Chicago struggled with these issues as they sought strategies for improving housing conditions that might fare better than those of previous generations of reformers.

Gail Radford

See also: Company Housing; Contested Spaces; Environmental Politics; Housing, Single-Room Occupancy; Infrastructure; Kitchenettes; Open Housing; Urban Renewal

Further reading: Hirsch, Arnold R. *Making the Second Ghetto: Race and Housing in Chicago, 1940–1960.* 1983. • Hoch, Charles, and Robert A. Slayton. *New Homeless and Old: Community and the Skid Row Hotel.* 1989. • Philpott, Thomas Lee. *The Slum and the Ghetto: Neighborhood Deterioration and Middle-Class Reform, Chicago, 1880–1930.* 1978.

Housing, Self-Built. Circumstances and entrepreneurs in Chicago have encouraged owners to build their own houses, but there are few American cities where this practice has also been so disparaged.

The once common practice of constructing your own house is fraught with difficulties, as Chicago humorist Ring Lardner caricatured in *Own Your Own Home* (1919). True self-builders (or owner-builders) undertake much of the physical labor themselves, often with the help of family or friends. Before the Civil War, newly arrived workers in Chicago frequently found they had to build their own houses because there was no excess housing stock.

Circumstances favored self-building in Chicago. For amateurs to attempt such a task they needed a simple construction technology, such as the balloon frame houses that were widely used in Chicago. Entrepreneurs helped make this technology available. From the early 1900s Sears sold house kits by mail. To compete, lumber dealers soon marketed house packages too.

While entrepreneurs catered to the self-builders, early-twentieth-century reformers condemned them. Self-building has been made to appear socially marginal and physically inferior. Later writers too have been critical on the grounds of health and aesthetics. In fact there has been more to praise about self-building than to condemn. Until the early 1950s many dwellings in the Chicago area were owner-built, 16 percent according to a 1949 survey. Some were inferior and unsafe, but most have been soundly built. Amateurs had little incentive to cut corners, and often built better than was necessary.

Self-building has long been concentrated in selected suburbs, especially after the city extended its fire limits in 1912 to include much recently ANNEXED territory on the SOUTH SIDE, including PULLMAN. In places such as STONE PARK, ROBBINS, and the fictitious community that Jessica North wrote about in *Arden Acres* (1935), which was reportedly based on a development located between 20 and 30 miles outside Chicago, self-building was routine. In places such as BLUE ISLAND and MELROSE PARK it was more scattered. Since WORLD WAR II, BUILDING CODES have become more common, and the cost of land with improvements such as utilities accounts for a growing proportion of housing costs. The opportunity to realize savings through sweat equity has diminished and, for lower-income families, suburban homes have actually become less affordable.

Richard Harris

See also: Built Environment of the Chicago Region; Housing, Mail-order; Planning, City and Regional; Zoning

Further reading: Christgau, Eugene F. "Unincorporated Communities in Cook County." M.A. thesis, University of Chicago, 1942. • Harris, Richard. "Chicago's Other Suburbs." *Geographical Review* 84.4 (1994): 394–410. • Stevenson, Katherine C., and H. Ward Jandl. *Houses by Mail: A Guide to Houses from Sears, Roebuck, and Company.* 1986.

Early frame two-flats, with separate entrance for each flat, ca. 1900. Photographer: Unknown. Source: University of Illinois at Chicago.

Housing Types. When white settlers arrived in northern Illinois, they brought with them accustomed common house forms. Few of these simple buildings remain within the city limits of Chicago. Fortunately, examples survive in scattered suburban locations, especially along the ILLINOIS & MICHIGAN CANAL and the FOX and DUPAGE RIVERS. Suburbs such as NAPERVILLE and LOCKPORT contain significant examples of the two forms which served as common houses for a majority of nineteenth-century Chicagoans.

The first dominant house form evolved from a very traditional hall-and-parlor house. The simplest type was a rectangular, two-room structure, roughly 12 or 14 feet by 24 feet, with gables facing to the sides. Since Chicago developed after the introduction of cast-iron stoves, these houses did not require large masonry fireplaces at the center of the structure, a dominant feature in earlier forms. Larger versions of this form contained a loft or second story that typically provided sleeping quarters for children. From 1830 to 1870, these buildings served as the first residences for urban and rural families throughout northern Illinois.

In suburban SOUTH HOLLAND, the local historical society operates two sites as museums, the Paarlberg and Van Ostenbrugge farms, which provide excellent examples of simple hall-and-parlor farm houses. The Murray house at NAPER SETTLEMENT in Naperville provides a more elaborate example of the form. This house contains four rooms on the first floor, as well as a formal entry hall. Larger than a simple farm house, the Murray house served as the residence for a middle-class LAWYER, who required space for entertaining and an office.

With time, most owners expanded the simple rectangular hall-and-parlor form. These additions altered the basic shape of the house into the form of a T. Sometimes called a wing-and-T, these structures became the dominant rural house form throughout the Midwest. They ranged from simple one-story, three-room houses to very elaborate structures that housed prosperous families. In a few suburban areas such as LEMONT, simple T-shaped houses served as the common house form.

However, throughout most of metropolitan Chicago, urban residents adopted a second form that differed from the traditional hall-and-parlor house. In all likelihood, settlers built cottage housing from the earliest years of settlement. While cottages were also rectangular, their gables faced the front and rear rather than the sides of the house. Consequently,

Urban cottages, two-flats, and storefronts on 44th and Wood Streets, Back of the Yards, 1959. Photographer: Clarence W. Hines. Source: Chicago Historical Society.

Ontario Flat Building, Sheridan Road near Irving Park Boulevard, 1903. Photographer: Unknown. Source: Chicago Historical Society.

simple one-story cottages contained a much different floor plan, with bedrooms lining one side of the house and parlor, dining room, and kitchen along the opposite side. Like the hall-and-parlor house, the cottage form contained a middle-class variant of two stories with a formal entry hall. These structures also located the private spaces for bedrooms on the second floor.

Frame cottages could be built and easily remodeled in great variety on the narrow lots that characterized much of urban Chicago. Consequently, they became the dominant urban house form by the time of the Chicago FIRE OF 1871. They accommodated all segments of the city's working class, including those who prospered. After the fire, brick cottages became common. As immigrant populations increased, the cottage form adapted to new demands in two significant ways. Old frame cottages often were raised on new brick foundations, converting one-family residences into APARTMENTS. In the most crowded sections of the city, these structures were moved to the rear of lots, allowing for new CONSTRUCTION at the front. The cottage also developed a variety of multiple-family types. The most common types were two-story structures that resembled two cottages placed one on top of the other. But variations of the cottage form could house six or more apartments.

By the great boom of the 1920s, many cottages had been expanded and modernized to include amenities such as plumbing, GAS, AND ELECTRICITY. Nevertheless, these structures appeared old fashioned and out-of-date. In newer sections of the city and suburbs, BUNGALOWS replaced cottages as the dominant common house form. Bungalows were more stylish and modern and were constructed with such amenities as central heating. Some scholars have suggested that the bungalow derived from influences outside Chicago, most notably California. Certainly, sections of the city, such as the VILLA DISTRICT (3600–3800 blocks of N. Avers, Hamlin, Harding, and Springfield), drew upon the Craftsman style. However, most Chicago bungalows were of traditional design. They followed the same floor plan as six-room cottages: parlor, dining room, and kitchen on one side of the house, bedrooms on the other. Basically, these bungalows were modernized cottages, placed on larger lots, with more stylishly designed roofs, higher quality millwork, and modern amenities. In the suburbs, many bungalows were frame. But common practice identifies the classic Chicago bungalow as a brick structure.

While most Chicagoans lived in common, traditional residences, greater affluence and a corporate economy led to the adoption of national styles of ARCHITECTURE by greater numbers of families in the city and suburbs. Whether Italianate in the 1870s, Victorian in the 1880s, or Colonial Revival in the 1920s, these structures were not indigenous to Chicago. The adoption of national forms of housing accelerated after WORLD WAR II, as most of the great suburban boom involved construction of ranch houses. However, pockets of traditional bungalow construction continued in the 1960s throughout lower-middle-class areas of the city and suburbs.

The most recent boom in new construction continues the trend by building house forms influenced by national trends. However, the GENTRIFICATION of inner-city neighborhoods and some suburbs has regenerated old forms. Many former cottages and TENEMENT buildings throughout the Near North have been transformed into high-priced single-family residences and CONDOMINIUMS. In these neighborhoods, old buildings have been torn down only to be replaced by new structures that, more or less, have facades resembling old Chicago cottages. Like the older structures, the form of these buildings is affected by the narrow lots that define the city's older residential neighborhoods.

During the past 15 years, traditional Chicago bungalows have also been remodeled. The desire to live in affluent suburbs like PARK RIDGE has led many homeowners to reconstruct one-story bungalows into much larger two-story structures. The same type of remodeling has occurred in less affluent sections of the city as well. In these neighborhoods, residents prefer to remodel traditional forms in familiar

Bungalows, from simple to more elaborate like the one pictured, were built across the region in the 1910s and 1920s. Photographer: Unknown. Source: Chicago Historical Society.

neighborhoods than to move to the suburbs. In either case, Chicago's landscape demonstrates a remarkable persistence of house forms.

Joseph C. Bigott

See also: Balloon Frame Construction; Built Environment of the Chicago Region; Metropolitan Growth; Rear Houses

Further reading: Bigott, Joseph C. *From Cottage to Bungalow: Houses and the Working Class in Metropolitan Chicago, 1869–1929.* 2001. • Glassie, Henry. *Vernacular Architecture.* 2000. • Philpott, Thomas Lee. *The Slum and the Ghetto: Neighborhood Deterioration and Middle-Class Reform, Chicago, 1880–1930.* 1978.

Hubbard Street Dance Chicago. This internationally acclaimed troupe combining balletic strength and discipline with JAZZ drive and showmanship was founded in 1977 by Lou Conte, a Midwesterner with considerable experience as a Broadway dancer and choreographer. He settled in Chicago in 1972 and opened the Lou Conte Dance Studio on Hubbard Street. From his best students, a group of four women began performing as the Hubbard Street Dance Company at senior centers and other local venues in 1977 and a year later Conte choreographed *The 40s,* a work which became the company's signature DANCE. The group featured dancers of great agility, strong musicality, and an exciting projection. The company grew steadily, giving its first downtown performance in 1981 and first going abroad in 1983, to Paris. An original company member, Claire Bataille, began choreographing with Conte in 1979. After 1982, Conte began to add works by such choreographers as Lynne Taylor-Corbett, Margo Sappington, Daniel Ezralow, Bob Fosse, and, most recently, Nacho Duato. The Twyla Tharp Project has added six of Tharp's works to the active repertory since 1990. In 1992, Conte altered the company name to reflect its close ties with Chicago, where in 1998 he opened a large new facility for the company.

Diana Haskell

See also: Ballet; Dance Companies; Dance Training; Modern and Postmodern Dance

Further reading: Catrambone, Kathy, ed. *Hubbard Street Dance Company: 10th Anniversary Commemorative Edition, 1978–1988.* 1988. • Cox, Ted. "Street of Dreams: Hubbard Dance Troupe Builds Its Reputation Step by Step." *Daily Southtown,* April 3, 1994.

Hull House. Hull House, Chicago's first and the nation's most influential SETTLEMENT HOUSE, was established by Jane Addams and Ellen Gates Starr on the NEAR WEST SIDE on September 18, 1889. By 1907, the converted 1856 mansion had expanded to a massive 13-building complex covering nearly a city block. The new structures included a gymnasium, THEATER, ART GALLERY, music school, boys' club, auditorium, cafeteria, cooperative residence for working women, KINDERGARTEN, nursery, libraries, post office, meeting and club rooms, art studios, kitchen, and a dining room and apartments for the residential staff. Attracting thousands of people each week from the surrounding neighborhood, the expanded Hull House complex provided space for the settlement's extensive social, educational, and artistic programs. Under Addams's skillful leadership, Hull House achieved recognition as the best-known settlement house in the United States and became the flagship of a movement that included nearly five hundred settlements nationally by 1920.

During its first two decades, Hull House attracted a remarkable group of residents, most of them women, who rose to prominence and influence as reformers on the local, state, and national levels. In the neighborhood, these residents established the city's first public PLAYGROUND and bathhouse, campaigned to reform ward politics, investigated housing, working, and sanitation issues, organized to improve garbage removal, and agitated for new public SCHOOLS. On the municipal level, they helped establish the first JUVENILE COURT in the United States, fought for neighborhood parks and playgrounds, agitated for branch libraries, and initiated housing reform. At the state level, Hull-House residents initiated and lobbied for protective legislation for women and children, child labor laws, OCCUPATIONAL SAFETY AND HEALTH provisions, compulsory education, protection of immigrants, and Illinois' pioneer MOTHERS' PENSION law. On the federal level, Hull House residents joined with settlement house leaders and reformers nationwide to fight for national child labor laws, women's SUFFRAGE, the establishment of a Children's Bureau, UNEMPLOYMENT compensation, workers' compensation, and the many other reforms that made up the Progressive agenda in the first two decades of the twentieth century.

Addams remained head resident of Hull House until her death in 1935. Hull House continued to be active on Halsted Street until the 1960s, when it was displaced by the UNIVERSITY OF ILLINOIS' new urban campus. Today it continues under the name of Jane Addams Hull House Association, an umbrella organization composed of several SOCIAL SERVICE centers across the city.

Mary Ann Johnson

See also: Feminist Movements; Juvenile Protective Association; Social Gospel in Chicago; St. Vincent DePaul Society

Further reading: Addams, Jane. *Twenty Years at Hull-House.* 1910. • Bryan, Mary Lynn McCree, and Allen F. Davis, eds. *100 Years at Hull-House.* 1990. • Hull-House Residents. *Hull-House Maps and Papers: A Presentation of Nationalities and Wages in a Congested District of Chicago.* 1895.

Humboldt Park, Community Area 23, 5 miles NW of the Loop. Chicago's HUMBOLDT PARK community, on the city's Northwest Side, centers on the 207-acre park named for the naturalist Alexander von Humboldt in 1869. ANNEXED to Chicago the same year, the sparsely settled prairie settlement experienced dramatic gains in REAL-ESTATE value during the early 1870s amid the avid promotion of parkside areas. In 1886 the STREET RAILWAY arrived, followed by branches of the Elevated Railway in the 1890s. Two-flat houses became popular between 1900 and 1920, together with new brick BUNGALOWS and one- and two-story frame dwellings. Later small APARTMENT buildings went up.

As the downtown business district expanded during the 1870s, Chicago's DANISH and NORWEGIAN communities extended northwest along the Milwaukee Avenue corridor, moving to Humboldt Park in considerable numbers during the 1880s and 1890s. By 1900 the Danish community stretched along North Avenue from Damen Street west to Pulaski, in a band six to eight blocks wide. Over two dozen Norwegian churches were located in and around the Humboldt Park and Logan Square areas.

Ethnic residential succession, from the waves of GERMANS and Scandinavians arriving during the last quarter of the nineteenth century through the presently dominant PUERTO RICANS, is evident in the use of the park itself, which quickly became a magnet for political and cultural activities. Statues (later transplanted elsewhere after the dissolution of the particular national community) were first raised by the Germans to Alexander von Humboldt (1892) and author Fritz Reuter (1893). In 1901, some 50,000 flag-waving, North Side Scandinavian Americans flocked to Humboldt Park for the unveiling of Sigvald Asbjornsen's statue of the heroic adventurer Leif Erikson. In 1904 POLES erected at the park's entrance an equestrian statue of Thaddeus Kosciuszko, a political exile who had served with distinction as a general in the American Revolutionary army. One hundred thousand Polish Americans gathered in June 1918 to celebrate the anniversary of the creation of the Polish army in France. Parades and other nationalistic events were regularly held at the statue's base at the peak of the Polish influx in the first two decades of the twentieth century.

During the 1920s and 1930s ITALIAN Americans and German and Russian JEWS, who had recently entered the community to take advantage of the newer and larger apartments, enjoyed the park's BICYCLING, boating, and SKATING facilities, as well as the rose garden and the prairie-style boathouse and shelter (designed in 1905 by Danish immigrant Jens Jensen). The more exotic Division Street locale offered sidewalk music and soapbox political oratory, a setting from which the writers Saul Bellow, Nelson Algren, and Studs Terkel emerged. By

1960 most of the Jewish residents of Humboldt Park had moved out, with many going to ALBANY PARK and NORTH PARK. Italians were the largest remaining European ethnic group, followed by Poles.

The next entrants were Puerto Ricans, who moved in from WEST TOWN and points east. The period 1950 to 1965 saw the first massive migration of Puerto Ricans to Chicago. In June 1966 a three-day riot erupted after a policeman shot and wounded a young Puerto Rican man in West Town. Community leaders rallied in the park to devise strategies to calm the crowds. Deteriorating economic conditions facing Puerto Ricans and incoming AFRICAN AMERICANS embodied many aspects of the national urban crisis while ethnic conflicts, especially those between young Puerto Ricans and Polish Americans, prevailed during the transition period. For Puerto Ricans the Division Street area (*La División,* in local parlance), with its stores and restaurants, has anchored settlement since the 1960s. Humboldt Park still remains the symbolic nucleus of Puerto Rican Chicago. Park thoroughfares have been renamed in honor of notables (such as former governor of Puerto Rico Luis Muños Marín and nationalist leader Pedro Albizu Campos), reflecting abiding concerns for the homeland not unlike those displayed in earlier years.

In smaller, but increasingly significant, numbers, MEXICAN immigrants joined the community mix; by 1980 they represented almost one-third of Humboldt Park's 29,000 Latinos (with Latinos constituting 41 percent of the total population). By 2000 Latinos were 48 percent of the population, and half were of Mexican origin. Meanwhile, the black population has steadily increased to equal the size of the Latino population. Most recently, the arrival of DOMINICAN immigrants in the northwestern section reflects the community's ongoing ethnic evolution.

David A. Badillo

See also: Contested Spaces; Landscape Design; Literary Cultures; Neighborhood Succession; Public Art

Further reading: Cutler, Irving. *The Jews of Chicago: From Shtetl to Suburb.* 1996. • Latino Institute. *Latinos in Metropolitan Chicago: A Study of Housing and Employment.* 1983. • Padilla, Felix M. *Puerto Rican Chicago.* 1987.

Humboldt Park. Humboldt Park began life as North Park in the 1860s on Chicago's Northwest Side as a tract of relatively flat land, with little local relief. In the 1870s William Le Baron Jenney crafted a LANDSCAPE plan, adding several lagoons and formal plazas. Oscar F. Dubuis followed this approach in the 1880s and 1890s. Landscape architect Jens Jensen added a formal rose garden and modified the lagoon in the western part of Humboldt Park to more closely resemble a river running through a tranquil prairie. In 1907 a boat landing and pavilion were added to the park, along with a music court for BAND concerts in 1913. Humboldt Park was transformed from an undistinguished marshy area into one where nearby residents could find a few minutes of respite amid the drudgery of the industrial metropolis.

Max Grinnell

See also: Landscape Design; Leisure; Park Districts

Further reading: Chicago Park Commissioners. *The West Parks and Boulevards of Chicago.* 1914. • Grese, Robert E. *Jens Jensen: Maker of Natural Parks and Gardens.* 1992. • *Prairie in the City: Naturalism in Chicago's Parks, 1870–1940.* 1991.

Hungarians. Chicago emerged as a primary destination for Hungarian immigrants at the end of the nineteenth century. From only 159 in 1870, Chicago's Hungarian population increased dramatically, to 1,841 in 1890, 7,463 in 1900, 37,990 in 1910, and 70,209 in 1920. These figures, however, do not always reflect the actual numbers of ethnic Hungarians (Magyars): some pre–WORLD WAR I figures include nonethnic Hungarians of the Austro-Hungarian Empire; post-WORLD WAR II data exclude ethnic Hungarians from the newly created Yugoslavia, Czechoslovakia, the enlarged Romania, and eastern Austria.

The first Hungarians reached Chicago in the 1850s as part of broader westward migration within the United States. The first arrivals were tradesmen, shopkeepers, artisans, and their families. Among them were also the emigrants of the 1848–49 Hungarian Revolution against the Hapsburg Empire. Escaping the retribution of the Austrian authorities, a handful of the Hungarian revolutionaries who were on their way to New Buda in Iowa stopped in Chicago and decided to settle in the city. Many of them were from the gentry, with formal education and therefore able to move into positions of civic leadership. Julian Kuné, a member of the Board of Trade, established Chicago's first private foreign language school. Some of the forty-niners went to fight in the American CIVIL WAR in Lincoln's Riflemen corps, organized by Géza Mihalótzy. The early immigrants were mainly men.

Hungarian immigration increased dramatically between 1889 and 1913, largely as an exodus from the countryside. Emigration overseas was the most intensive from the mountainous northeastern and southwestern regions which lay beyond the influence of Budapest, Hungary's major industrial center. Migratory traditions of villages and familial chain migration played a major role. These rural immigrants tended to form communities in the industrial South and West Sides of Chicago, where they could find a steady supply of jobs. Immigrants from Eastern Europe, Sweden, and Italy lived nearby.

The SOUTH SIDE housed four main Hungarian enclaves, in SOUTH CHICAGO, BURNSIDE, WEST PULLMAN, and ROSELAND. The earliest settlement was established in South Chicago in 1890 near the factories of the Illinois Steel Company. The area populated by Hungarians was known as the Bush (*Bozót*) and counted approximately 330 people in 1910. Hungarians gradually abandoned South Chicago and by the 1920s had moved to the industrial areas of EAST CHICAGO, GARY, and JOLIET.

In the 1910s Hungarians settled mainly in Burnside (Bronszajd), also called Triangle because it was bordered on three sides by the shops and tracks of the Illinois Central and Nickel Plate Railroads. Burnside became even more prominent in the 1920s with its numerous Hungarian stores, shops, and restaurants located near the intersection of Cottage Grove and 95th Street running just outside the Triangle. Hungarians, 25 to 40 percent of the residents on some streets, lived alongside people of UKRAINIAN, ITALIAN, and POLISH origin. West Pullman and Roseland also had large Hungarian groups working in the district's mills, RAILROADS, and large factories. In most families women went out to work in the factories to contribute to the family income. Some women stayed at home and made some money by doing sewing jobs. Others earned additional income by taking in boarders.

On the West Side, the factories of the Northwestern Railroad attracted immigrant workers. Although the Hungarians living on Crawford (now Pulaski), Madison, Lake, and Carroll were fewer than three hundred in the 1920s, it was the West Side settlement that became known as Little Hungary. A large Hungarian-owned factory, the Sinko Tool Company, was situated there and employed many skilled Hungarian workers.

Although WORLD WAR I and the restrictive U.S. immigration laws of the 1920s curbed immigration, Hungarians continued to arrive. The Trianon Treaty had deprived Hungary of two-thirds of its territory, leaving three and a half million Hungarians as an ethnic minority living outside the nation's new borders. Many decided to leave, and Hungarian Americans waged a steady campaign to raise the immigration quota. Ensuing years of chaos, revolution, counter-revolution, extreme nationalism, and anti-Semitism created many political refugees.

Immigrants coming from Hungary between the two wars were predominantly intellectuals and of urban background. They had little in common with the older working-class immigrants and tended to settle around LOGAN SQUARE and HUMBOLDT PARK. On the NEAR NORTH SIDE, Hungarians formed scattered enclaves around the edge of the old GERMAN community from North Avenue and Wells into LAKE VIEW and up Lincoln Avenue. They intermingled with the more prosperous Hungarian-speaking Germans and JEWS who ran stores, RESTAURANTS, trade companies, law offices, and banks in the region.

Although community building began with the creation of social clubs and MUTUAL BENEFIT SOCIETIES in 1892, the most important tool of ethnic cohesion was the PARISH. Hungarians founded the first PROTESTANT church in South Chicago in 1898. In WEST TOWN, the ROMAN CATHOLIC Parish of St. Stephen, King of Hungary, emerged as a major cultural center for Hungarians regardless of their religious affiliation. Hungarian language and cultural traditions were maintained by the Hungarian Cultural and Educational House (1969), which also published the literary periodical *Szivárvány*. In addition, events such as the annual grape festival helped to sustain Hungarian folk traditions. Women played active roles in the creation of sick-benefit societies. They were also highly visible in the communal and religious groups. The Scout Leaders of the Hungarian Scout Troop Association (1946), which is still active, have mainly been women. They, together with the Women's League of the Evangelical Church, have organized English-language classes for the newly arrived immigrants and Hungarian-language classes for the children of Hungarian Americans.

The post–World War II era brought more political refugees to the United States, with one thousand Hungarians taking up residence in Chicago under the Displaced Persons Acts of 1948 and 1950. After the suppression of the Hungarian Revolution of 1956, thousands of Hungarians, called fifty-sixers, sought refuge in the United States, with many settling in Chicago.

Yet the arrival of new immigrants could not stop the gradual dissolution of the Hungarian neighborhoods. Most Hungarians married outside the Hungarian community, and many South Siders moved to suburbs such as LANSING, CALUMET CITY, and BURNHAM. On the North Side, the last vestiges remained around Belmont, Clark, and Lincoln Avenues until the 1970s, when most Hungarian American families moved to SKOKIE, NILES, and NORTHBROOK.

Hungarians have participated in the growth and development of Chicago as entrepreneurs, designers, businessmen, ARTISTS, and scholars. László Moholy-Nagy, Marcel Breuer, and Albert Kner, formerly leading figures of the Bauhaus artistic tradition, became successful entrepreneurs by ingeniously combining art design with business. Conductors Sir George Solti and Fritz Reiner helped bring international fame to the CHICAGO SYMPHONY ORCHESTRA. Since the 1960s, Hungarian immigrants to the United States have been mainly professionals. A considerable number of scholars of Hungarian origin work at Chicago's institutions in medical research, computer science, engineering, and mathematics.

Eva Becsei

See also: Americanization; Austrians; Demography; Iron- and Steelworkers; Multicentered Chicago

Further reading: "Hungarian Americans." In *Gale Encyclopedia of Multicultural America,* vol. 1, 1995, 692–709. • Fejős, Zoltán. *A Chicagói Magyarok két nemzedéke, 1890–1940.* [Two generations of Hungarians in Chicago, 1890–1940]. Summary in English. 1993. • Schaaf, Barbara. "Magyars of the Midwest." *Chicago Tribune Magazine,* May 6, 1979.

Huntley, IL, McHenry and Kane Counties, 45 miles NW of the Loop. Platted beside the Galena & Chicago Union RAILROAD in 1851 by Thomas Huntley and incorporated in 1872, Huntley remained an agricultural village until the 1980s. Suburban sprawl and Sun City, a massive senior residential area on the village's south side, caused the population to grow from 2,453 in 1990 to 5,730 by 2000.

Craig L. Pfannkuche

See also: McHenry County

Further reading: *McHenry County in the Twentieth Century, 1968–1994.* McHenry County Historical Society. 1994. • Nye, Lowell A., ed. *McHenry County, Illinois, 1832–1968.* 1968.

Hyde Park, Community Area 41, 6 miles SE of the Loop. The development of the Hyde Park community began in 1853 when Paul Cornell, a New York lawyer, purchased 300 acres of property from 51st to 55th Streets. Always a shrewd investor, Cornell deeded 60 acres to the ILLINOIS CENTRAL RAILROAD in exchange for a train station and the promise of daily trips to the heart of Chicago's commercial core. The community continued to prosper over the next 30 years, as residential construction expanded and the TRANSPORTATION network grew dense. By the late 1880s, transportation options in the area included the Cottage Grove cable car and dozens of trains leaving from the South Park station at 57th Street to the LOOP.

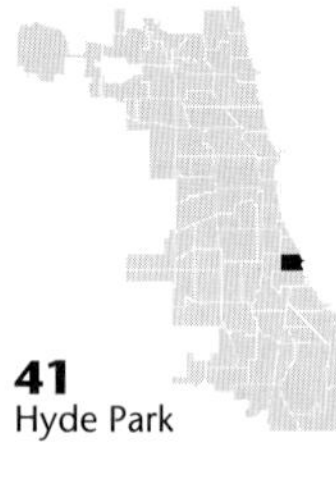

Despite such improvements, the transformation of the BUILT ENVIRONMENT of Hyde Park remained modest until two major events of the early 1890s. The first was the creation of the UNIVERSITY OF CHICAGO and the second was the WORLD'S COLUMBIAN EXPOSITION OF 1893. The University of Chicago emerged from the PHILANTHROPY of John D. Rockefeller, who was interested in launching an institution of higher learning in the Midwest, particularly one to serve the educational needs of the American Baptist community in Chicago. The university also benefited from the good will of Marshall Field, who donated a significant amount of land for the new campus. The Columbian Exposition stimulated the construction of hundreds of residential and commercial buildings in Hyde Park and WOODLAWN and the development of the South Side Elevated line, which reached southwards from the Loop to 39th Street by 1892 and finally reached the exposition in JACKSON PARK in the middle of 1893.

After a significant building slump immediately following the exposition, construction continued vigorously until the late 1920s. A variety of prominent architects worked in the area, including Frank Lloyd Wright, who designed both the Heller and Robie houses on South Woodlawn Avenue. Through the first two decades of the twentieth century, a mixed-use pattern of six-flat walk-up APARTMENT buildings interspersed with larger structures and a wide variety of commercial uses had become commonplace throughout Hyde Park.

During this period, the community also became increasingly ethnically diverse, as JEWISH residents became an important part of the area's social fabric. They began to set up a variety of social and civic institutions, including a Jewish community center and several synagogues. Many older Jewish residents preferred to live in the taller apartment buildings that were becoming commonplace throughout east Hyde Park, which was rapidly developing into a popular hotel and resort area. By the early 1930s, Hyde Park had over one hundred HOTELS, and the lakefront was home to almost a dozen of these increasingly elaborate and well-appointed structures, many of which were later converted into apartment buildings. Some of the older hotels built for the Columbian Exposition persevered, but others soon began to cater to a more transient population, a condition that would become problematic by the late 1940s.

Beginning in the early 1930s, concerns arose about certain community changes taking place in Hyde Park. Numerous studies were commissioned to examine the growing crime problem in the area, along with the citywide phenomenon of illegal residential conversions. While many in the community were concerned about the viability of an integrated community in light of a rapidly expanding AFRICAN AMERICAN population, other groups were concerned with the safety of the University of Chicago's campus and its physical plant, valued at many millions of dollars. In order to coordinate the efforts to help sustain and renew the community, the university in 1952 helped establish the South East Chicago Commission, which was charged with monitoring BUILDING CODE violations and local crime.

By the late 1950s, the first federally sponsored URBAN RENEWAL plan was underway in Hyde Park. The plan attracted severe criticism from within the community by those residents who were to be displaced by it and from outsiders, including Monsignor John Egan of the

Roman Catholic Church. The plan, which took almost a decade to execute, transformed many older densely built-up areas of Hyde Park into a state of semisuburbia. Along with the Columbian Exposition and the creation of the University of Chicago, Hyde Park's urban renewal was one of the most far-reaching and transforming events in the community's history.

Max Grinnell

See also: Architecture; Planning Chicago; South Side; Universities and their Cities

Further reading: Beadle, Muriel. *The Hyde Park–Kenwood Urban Renewal Years.* 1964. • Block, Jean F. *Hyde Park Houses: An Informal History, 1856–1910.* 1978. • Grinnell, Max. *Hyde Park, Illinois.* 2001.

Hyde Park Art Center. One of the oldest arts organizations in Chicago, the Hyde Park Art Center (HPAC) is notable because of the dedication of its volunteers and visible effectiveness of its education and exhibition programs. Founded in 1939 as the Fifth Ward Art Guild, HPAC began its commitment to community participation with the support of Senator Paul Douglas, author Helen Gardner, and University of Chicago art historian Ulrich Middeldorf. HPAC built a steady following of students and artists, particularly in the 1960s under the imaginative leadership of board member and collector Ruth Horwich and artist/curator Don Baum.

HPAC organized the first exhibitions of artists who came to be known internationally as the Chicago Imagists—Roger Brown, Christina Ramberg, and Jim Nutt among others—and achieved national recognition for its exciting exhibition openings and its support of emerging artists. The commitment to Chicago's cultural community continues in HPAC's exhibitions and through its education program, which was cited in 1996 by the President's Committee on the Arts and Humanities for outstanding work with at-risk youths.

Judith Russi Kirshner

See also: Art; Art Centers, Alternative

Further reading: Schulze, Franz. *Fantastic Images: Chicago Art Since 1945.* 1972. • Shaw, Goldene, ed. *History of the Hyde Park Art Center, 1939–1976.* 1976. • Warren, Lynne. *Alternative Spaces: A History in Chicago.* 1984.

Hyde Park Township. Between 1861 and 1889, Hyde Park Township, the area south of 39th Street and east of State Street, was an independent political unit separate from, and geographically larger than, Chicago. The township population grew more than fivefold between 1880 and 1889 (15,716 to 85,000). In 1889, Chicago annexed Hyde Park, which ceased to function as an independent political unit.

Ann Durkin Keating

See also: Annexation; Governing the Metropolis; Grand Boulevard; Hyde Park; Kenwood; Oakland; Pullman; South Deering; South Shore; South Side

Further reading: Keating, Ann Durkin. *Building Chicago: Suburban Developers and the Creation of a Divided Metropolis.* 1988.

Ice Hockey. Though the history of hockey reaches at least as far back as the sixteenth century, it was in Canada between 1840 and 1850 that the game was most fully adapted to the ice. From its early beginnings as a carnival event and club activity, ice hockey in Canada grew rapidly into leagues, then university teams, and finally, in 1886, the Amateur Hockey Association of Canada. In that same year a hockey exhibition at a Vermont carnival introduced ice hockey to the United States. Hockey in the United States was also organized first as a series of clubs and leagues, then as university teams, and finally, in 1896, as the United States Amateur Hockey League (USAHL).

Though most USAHL members lived in states bordering Canada, J. A. Tuthill's *Ice Hockey and Polo Guide* reported in 1898 that Chicago had a significant interest in hockey. The first clear institutional indication of Chicago's interest in ice hockey, however, came much later, when, in 1926, Major Frederick McLaughlin purchased an entire team from Portland, Oregon, and transplanted it in Chicago as the Blackhawks. Ice hockey came to Chicago because the National Hockey League wanted to expand, and McLaughlin's believed this "novelty" would justify his considerable investment.

Although the investment gradually paid off, other hockey programs were slow to follow. There were two short-lived Amateur Hockey Association teams: the Chicago Cardinals/Americans (1926–1927) and the Chicago Shamrocks (1930–1932). It was not until 1963, when the Elmhurst YMCA organized the first youth hockey program in Illinois, that a hockey tradition began to emerge from a growing number of city-sponsored outdoor rinks. Following the Elmhurst example, youth hockey emerged first in Lake Forest, Deerfield, Oak Park, Wilmette, Northbrook, and Chicago between 1963 and 1971. Early youth hockey was organized into "house leagues" in which youths (grouped from ages 8 to 18) competed intramurally, with occasional competitions between neighboring towns. Youth hockey was at first played on outdoor rinks. Only in the 1970s, after the Blackhawks captured their first NHL championship, were numerous indoor rinks built to accommodate the growing interest in hockey.

By 1972 local colleges including DePaul University, Lake Forest College, Northwestern University, and the University of Illinois at Chicago also had hockey teams. With the exception of UIC, these teams existed on a club basis and did not become affiliated with the NCAA. During the mid-1970s, Chicago was also home to two short-lived minor league teams, the Cougars and the Warriors.

The tremendous growth of hockey in Chicago during the early 1970s inspired the founding in 1975 of the Amateur Hockey Association of Illinois (AHAI), which is sanctioned by U.S.A. Hockey, Inc. With the possible exception of the Chicago Wolves, who came on the scene in 1994 as a franchise of the professional World Hockey Association and brought championships to Chicago in 1998, 2000, and 2002, the AHAI has been the most instrumental factor in the continued growth of hockey in Chicago. With 2,500 hundred members, the AHAI has supported hockey on all levels of play. In addition to seven age affiliations that range from pre-mite (age 3–5) to juvenile (17–18), the AHAI has also been instrumental in organizing hockey for girls and women. In 1998 the AHAI renewed its commitment to women's hockey by creating the Central States Hockey League, which boasts two "fifteen and under" teams and one "nineteen and under" team.

Seth Brady

See also: Creation of Chicago Sports; Skating, Ice; Sports, High-School

Further reading: Ferrington, S. Kip. *Skates, Sticks, and Men.* 1972. • Fishler, Stan, and Shirley Fishler. *Everybody's Hockey Book.* 1983. • Gems, Gerald. *Sports in North America: A Documentary History.* 1996.

Ice Skating. *See* Skating, Ice

Icelanders. Icelanders first came to the United States as Mormons in the 1850s. A much larger emigration, primarily to North Dakota and Minnesota, left a poor country beset with volcano eruptions and famine in the 1870s and 1880s. Until 1930 Icelanders were counted as Danes by the U.S. census, which by 1990 counted 40,529 Americans claiming some Icelandic ancestry; 111 of these lived in Chicago, with 6 more in Country Club Hills.

The first Icelanders came to Chicago in the late nineteenth century. Chester Hjortur Thordarson, for example, came via North Dakota to join his sister in 1884. The holder of over one hundred patents, he founded the Thordarson Electrical Manufacturing Company in Chicago. One of his employees, also from North Dakota, was fellow Icelander Arni

Helgason, who founded the Chicago Standard Transformer Corporation in 1928.

Icelanders have been less aggressive than other immigrant groups in organizing local societies, much less a national organization. Perhaps this is because they have neither been subjected to discrimination nor had a derogatory nickname. Approximately 20 local and state societies have formed, including the Icelandic Association of Chicago, founded in 1930. Membership in 1999 numbered about 90, with 35–40 percent able to speak Icelandic.

The main event of the year, an old Icelandic tradition, is the Thorrablót, a feast of special dishes and singing held from mid-January to mid-February. Its purpose is to celebrate the hope for an end to winter and the hope for an early spring.

Playford V. Thorson

See also: Demography; Multicentered Chicago

Further reading: Thorson, Playford V. "Icelanders." In *American Immigrant Cultures: Builders of a Nation,* vol. 1. 1997.

If Christ Came to Chicago. Written by the British journalist William T. Stead and published by Laird & Lee in 1894, *If Christ Came to Chicago* was an inflammatory exposé of Chicago's political corruption and the UNDERGROUND ECONOMY. Mixing radical religion and POLITICS, the text allegedly sold 70,000 copies on its publication day. Stead, the son of a Congregationalist minister and the editor of the *Review of Reviews,* previously had explored such themes in his "Maiden Tribute of Modern Babylon" in London's *Pall Mall Gazette* (1885) and *In Darkest England* (1890), coauthored with SALVATION ARMY founder William Booth. A color-coded map of the Levee district on the NEAR SOUTH SIDE precisely located the numerous brothels, SALOONS, and pawnbrokers, and an appendix enumerated the addresses, proprietors, and owners of the highlighted properties. Stead died on the *Titanic* in 1912.

Timothy J. Gilfoyle

See also: Crime and Chicago's Image; Machine Politics; Political Culture; Vice Commissions; Vice Districts

Further reading: Baylen, Joseph O. "A Victorian's 'Crusade' in Chicago, 1893–1894." *Journal of American History* 51 (December 1964): 418–434. • Stead, William T. *If Christ Came to Chicago! A Plea for the Union of All Who Love in the Service of All Who Suffer.* 1894; reprint, 1990. • Whyte, Frederick. *The Life of W. T. Stead.* 2 vols. 1925.

Illinois. The French adapted the word "Illinois" from a term the Illinois Indians used to identify themselves as "men." The Illinois spoke a Central Algonquian language nearly identical to the one spoken by the MIAMI Indians, from whom they separated just prior to meeting the Europeans. Archaeological analysis suggests that by the late 1630s the Illinois had moved out of Michigan and into northern Illinois and southern Wisconsin. They dominated this Illinois country, including the entire greater Chicago area. Tribal members divided themselves into groups no larger than two or three hundred during the winter months in order to promote hunting opportunities, and these winter encampments along various streams explain their residency in greater Chicago.

The Illinois living on the Illinois River across from Starved Rock met the FRENCH in 1673, when Father Jacques Marquette and explorer Louis Jolliet made their famous voyage. The French recorded the names of large summer villages, or subtribes, but a devastating population decline left only a few of these groups surviving into the eighteenth century: the Cahokia, Kaskaskia, Peoria, Michigamea, Moingwena, and Tamaroa. As the tribe lost population, it moved the center of its territory southwest and away from the Starved Rock area on the Illinois River; eventually the reduced Illinois located in the American Bottom, land on the east side of the Mississippi south of its confluence with the Missouri.

Conservative population estimates count perhaps as many as 13,000 Illinois during the period before 1673 and at least 12,000 when they encountered the French. Population decline accelerated dramatically during the next 160 years: they numbered about 6,000 in 1700 and just 2,500 in 1736. Warfare (particularly attacks from Iroquois raiders in the late seventeenth century), disease, Christianity and its insistence on one spouse, alcoholism, and emigration help to account for these losses. Most importantly, however, the tribe's military, economic, and religious dependence on the French explains why the Illinois suffered greater losses than more independent—and defiant—tribes like the Foxes. By 1800 the Illinois community numbered less than 100, and in March of 1833 it was reported that the last Kaskaskia Illinois elder had left the state with his relatives.

Influential tribal leaders included Rouensa, Chicago, and Jean Baptiste Ducoigne. During the late seventeenth century, Rouensa served as the Kaskaskia Illinois chief who, perhaps swayed by his teenage daughter Marie, converted to Christianity along with his wife and many other Kaskaskias. In 1725, Chicago, a Michigamea Illinois chief, visited Paris and the court of Louis XV. The city of CHICAGO, however, was not named for this chief; Frenchmen had referred to the site of the future city as "Chicagou" (variously spelled) since 1683. Jean Baptiste Ducoigne, a late-eighteenth- and early-nineteenth-century Kaskaskia Illinois chief who was related to Rouensa, supported the Americans during the American Revolution. Ducoigne formed a close personal relationship with President Thomas Jefferson (dining with him at the White House) and maintained his tribe's alliance with the Americans through the War of 1812.

The Peoria Illinois survived much more successfully than their kinsmen because they maintained greater independence. During the 1760s about 250 Peoria Illinois moved west of the Mississippi, eventually locating in Oklahoma, where they recombined with the Miami to form the Peoria tribe.

Raymond E. Hauser

See also: Chicago in the Middle Ground; Mesquakie (Fox); Native American Religion

Further reading: Blasingham, Emily J. "The Depopulation of the Illinois Indians." *Ethnohistory* 3 (Summer and Fall 1956): 193–224, 361–412. • Callender, Charles. "Illinois." In *Northeast,* ed. Bruce G. Trigger, vol. 15 of *Handbook of North American Indians,* ed. William C. Sturtevant, 1978, 673–680.

Illinois & Michigan Canal. Upon its completion in 1848, the Illinois & Michigan Canal joined the CHICAGO RIVER at BRIDGEPORT near Chicago with the Illinois River at LaSalle, 96 miles distant. The canal provided a direct WATER link between the Great Lakes and the Mississippi River, and helped to shift the center of Midwestern trade from St. Louis to Chicago.

Louis Jolliet first suggested the possibility of such a link in 1673 when he encountered the Chicago PORTAGE. The idea was taken up in 1822, when Congress made an initial land grant to Illinois for constructing a canal. Justus Post and René Paul made the first survey of possible routes. In 1830 the canal commissioners platted Chicago and Ottawa in the vain hope of raising sufficient money by selling land from a second land grant. The commissioners and private speculators platted numerous towns in the 1830s and 1840s, including LOCKPORT, JOLIET, Channahon, and LaSalle, as well as other towns that did not survive.

Canal construction began in 1836, but a depression over the following seven years brought the state to the brink of bankruptcy. The canal was finally completed after a financial and administrative reorganization in 1845. Much of the WORK was done by IRISH immigrants who lived and worked in transient work camps along the line of the canal. The project required the construction of 15 lift locks, five aqueducts, and four hydraulic power basins.

While the canal carried many travelers in the first few years after 1848, passenger traffic disappeared rapidly when the Chicago & Rock Island RAILROAD began competing in 1854. Commodity traffic continued to grow, however, particularly for heavy bulk items such as grain (the largest commodity), LUMBER, and stone. As many as 288 boats worked the canal in 1864, and the canal reached its peak tonnage of over a million tons in 1882. Tolls and land sales made it possible for the canal to pay off its debt in 1871, one of the few canals to do so.

Illinois Central Railroad steam locomotives at Randolph Street Station, 1893. Photographer: Unknown. Source: Chicago Historical Society.

The I&M Canal was the first inland canal to begin to shift from mule-drawn towlines to steam-propelled boats after 1871. Navigation became increasingly difficult as the state stopped investing in the maintenance of the canal. By the late 1890s commercial traffic had greatly diminished, and by 1914 it had all but ceased.

After 1900 interest in the canal shifted to recreational use. Canal excursion boats served a number of AMUSEMENT PARKS, such as Rock Run outside Joliet.

In 1935 the Civilian Conservation Corps in conjunction with the National Park Service restored some of the locks and started other projects for HISTORIC PRESERVATION and recreation. Although this work ended with WORLD WAR II, efforts to reuse the old canal right-of-way for this purpose were later revived, culminating in 1984 when President Reagan signed legislation creating the Illinois & Michigan Canal National Heritage Corridor, the first heritage corridor in the nation. The concept encouraged canal trails and nature preserves, and helped the downtowns along the canal by emphasizing economic development based upon history and historic preservation.

John Lamb

See also: Economic Geography; Historic Preservation; Initial Land Sales in Northeastern Illinois (color map, p. C1); Quarrying, Stonecutting, and Brickmaking; Transportation; Water

Further reading: Conzen, Michael P., and Kay J. Carr, eds. *The Illinois and Michigan Canal National Heritage Corridor: A Guide to Its History and Sources.* 1988. • Lamb, John. *A Corridor in Time: I&M Canal, 1836–1986.* 1987. • Putnam, James. *The Illinois and Michigan Canal: A Study in Economic History.* 1918.

Illinois Central Railroad. In the 1830s, Illinois began a program of internal improvements to open its prairie to AGRICULTURE and settlement. It was a failure, but in 1851 the state chartered the Illinois Central Railroad (IC) and selected a consortium of Eastern capitalists to construct and own the RAILROAD. Federal land grants of nearly 2,600,000 acres provided the economic incentive; the initial investment of $27 million came largely from British and Dutch interests.

The IC completed its "Charter Lines" (705 miles in Illinois) in September 1856. The "Chicago Branch" (from Centralia to Chicago) opened a year earlier, giving that city its most important link to the South. The trunk of the railroad extended from the Mississippi River at Cairo northwest to the Mississippi opposite Dubuque, Iowa. The company founded dozens of new towns in Illinois and made "colonization work" (attracting settlers from Europe and other parts of the United States) part of its corporate strategy.

Chicago quickly became the IC's principal terminus, with extensive freight, passenger, and suburban COMMUTER facilities. After the CIVIL WAR, the railroad expanded west to Sioux City, Iowa (by 1869), and south to New Orleans (by 1882). At the turn of the century, the IC System encompassed 5,000 miles of track, 800 locomotives, 700 passenger cars, nearly 33,000 freight cars, and over 33,000 employees.

Throughout the twentieth century, the IC remained a conservatively managed, reasonably modern, and consistently profitable railroad with Chicago as its center of activity. In 1926 the railroad completed electrification of much of its freight and passenger service in the Chicago area. By World War II, the IC had spent over $65 million on improvements to its facilities in the region.

After the war, the IC competed hard for its share of the declining freight and passenger business, embracing "piggyback" service (truck trailers on flat cars) and investing in track and support systems. In 1962, the company created a holding company, IC Industries, and diversified into REAL-ESTATE development, industrial goods, and consumer products. In 1972 the railroad merged with the Gulf, Mobile & Ohio Railroad to form the Illinois Central Gulf Railroad (ICG).

Loosened federal regulation in the 1980s permitted the railroad to again reinvent itself. Beginning in 1985, ICG sold nearly two-thirds of its railroad mileage in order to concentrate on the Chicago–New Orleans corridor. The company sold its Chicago commuter lines to Metropolitan Rail (METRA) in 1988. A year later, IC Industries spun off the rest of its railroad assets, which adopted the original "Illinois Central Railroad" name. The new IC was then purchased by New York's Prospect Group.

The Illinois Central Railroad profoundly affected the economic and physical development of Illinois and Chicago. It was the primary link between the Great Lakes and the Gulf of Mexico, providing access to the South for Chicago products and culture and a route north for millions during the "GREAT MIGRATION." In 1999 the Canadian National Railway acquired the IC, but its functions, routes, and franchise have remained important to Chicago's economy.

John P. Hankey

See also: Douglas; Hyde Park; Park Forest; Pullman; South Side; Transportation

Further reading: Corliss, Carlton J. *Main Line of Mid-America: The Story of the Illinois Central.* 1950. • Illinois Central Research and Development Bureau. *Organization and Traffic of the Illinois Central System.* 1938. • John F. Stover. *History of the Illinois Central Railroad.* 1975.

Illinois Institute of Technology. In 1940 Armour Institute of Technology and Lewis Institute were merged and reconstituted as Illinois Institute of Technology (IIT). Armour and Lewis Institutes had been chartered respectively in 1892 and 1895, established through funds provided by Philip D. Armour and the estate of Allen C. Lewis. Designed to provide training in various technical skills and in engineering for students from lower-income families, without regard to race, religion, or ethnicity, each had evolved into a research institution conferring undergraduate and graduate degrees in several fields.

IIT acquired its present form through a number of additional mergers and acquisitions. In 1938 Ludwig Mies van der Rohe and some members of the Bauhaus, the innovative school of ARCHITECTURE and design in Germany, came to Armour Institute, and in 1949 the INSTITUTE OF DESIGN, formerly the New Bauhaus, merged with IIT. The campus thereby became a leading academic center for professional training in architecture, design, and PHOTOGRAPHY, and played a significant role in the shaping of Chicago's skyline. The Stuart School of Management and Finance was established in 1969, and in the same year Chicago-Kent College of Law merged with IIT.

In 1999, full-time equivalent enrollment consisted of 1,505 undergraduates and 2,913 graduate students. The main campus, based on a plan by Mies, occupies 120 acres about three miles south of the LOOP. Chicago-Kent College of Law, the Institute of Design, and the Stuart School are located in the Loop. The Rice campus, acquired in 1986 and located in WHEATON, Illinois, offers undergraduate courses and degree programs to employed professionals.

IIT has always enjoyed close relations with industry and the business community of the Chicago area, and, beginning in 1936, added several research organizations to serve various technical needs of industry and government. Chief among these are the National Center for Food Safety and Technology, in the southwest suburbs, and IIT Research Institute (IITRI), headquartered on the main campus, which directs activities at 19 sites nationwide. Early experiments on magnetic recording begun by Marvin Camras as a student at Armour Institute were developed at IITRI into today's widely employed systems.

Wilbur Applebaum

See also: Douglas; Graphic Design; Innovation, Invention, and Chicago Business; Schooling for Work; Universities and Their Cities; Urban Renewal

Further reading: Macauley, Irene. *The Heritage of Illinois Institute of Technology.* 1978. • Peebles, James C. *A History of Armour Institute of Technology.* 1940.

Illinois Mathematics and Science Academy. The Illinois Mathematics and Science Academy (IMSA) was established by the Illinois legislature in 1985 and opened on September 7, 1986. The residentially based program in AURORA attracts 10th to 12th graders from throughout the state with special interests or talents in science and math, although other liberal arts and extracurricular programs are also offered. IMSA also serves professional educators through its "Center," which emphasizes the development of math and science pedagogy. The academy's achievements include producing the winner of the 1993 Westinghouse Talent Search and leadership in curriculum development.

Steven Essig

See also: Schools and Education

Illinois National Guard. The Illinois Militia (eventually the Illinois National Guard [ING]) first served in the BLACK HAWK WAR in 1832. As frontier threats faded, the antebellum militia offered volunteers excitement through military pomp and parade. The Illinois Militia nearly disappeared in 1865, after the volunteer regiments raised for the CIVIL WAR demobilized, but revived in time for 5,000 volunteers to celebrate the centennial in 1876. Civil War veterans reorganized this new militia just in time to serve during the RAILROAD STRIKE OF 1877. STRIKE service would be the most controversial of ING duties from that point on. But volunteer companies actually spent the overwhelming majority of their time training for war, hosting balls and LECTURES, performing in amateur theatricals, marching in military parades, fundraising, and lobbying for larger budgets and improved militia legislation at the state and federal levels. Achieving their goal of serving as the nation's reserve army, the ING served in Cuba in 1898–99, on the Mexican border in 1916, and in the American Expeditionary Forces in 1917–18. In the 1920s and '30s the ING continued to modernize and again provided trained personnel during WORLD WAR II. Since 1945, the ING has been fully integrated into the nation's military reserve and training system.

Eleanor Hannah

See also: Armories; Clubs: Patriotic and Veterans' Clubs

Further reading: Cooper, Jerry. *The Rise of the National Guard.* 1997. • Hannah, Eleanor. "Manhood, Citizenship, and the Formation of the National Guards, Illinois, 1870–1917." Ph.D. diss., University of Chicago. 1997.

Immigration. *See* Demography

Impresarios. Entrepreneurs have played a vital role in bringing performing arts to Chicago. Beginning with HOTEL and THEATER owners and continuing with managers of clubs, bars, stadiums, and concert halls, impresarios have transformed culture into entertainment, profit, and prestige. Chicago's first impresario was probably Harry Isherwood, who purchased a theatrical license in 1837. Florenz Ziegfeld (father of the famous Follies founder) founded Chicago Musical College (1867–) and imported musical talent as faculty and for his performance series. Uranus H. Crosby booked performers for his Crosby OPERA House (1866–1871).

The majority of early impresarios, however, were visitors from New York, such as Maurice Grau or Colonel James Henry Mapleson, who toured the country representing operatic companies or instrumental virtuosi. Seating over 4,200, Chicago's AUDITORIUM Theater was designed to attract just such traveling performances with promises of large paying audiences. (In the 1970s, the Auditorium's size made it an ideal ROCK touring venue.)

To minimize risk and return control to Chicago, PHILANTHROPISTS pooled their resources, sponsoring institutions with professional management. The Orchestral Association (1890–) manages the CHICAGO SYMPHONY ORCHESTRA. This practice created the impresario-manager—such as the Auditorium's Milward Adams. Later the city itself became a major presenter of summer music festivals in support of tourism and civic life.

Women often have been denied opportunities as impresarios. Exceptions include Ellen Van Volkenburg (theater), Merriel Abbott (DANCE), and Sarah Schectman (music)—who along with husband Harry Zelzer founded Chicago's Allied Arts. Increasingly, women have gained prominent roles in Chicago's cultural institutions. Carol Fox rebuilt the LYRIC OPERA, while Ardis Krainik made it one of America's most successful.

The association of elite society with high culture gave impresarios the opportunity to negotiate social hierarchies. Black entrepreneurs such as Robert T. Motts ran the South Side's Pekin Theater, and William Hackney sponsored All-Colored Composer's Concerts in prestigious Orchestra Hall (beginning 1914). Joe Segal established the Jazz Showcase in 1947, which helped elevate JAZZ to the realm of "art music" and confirmed Chicago's role in this history.

Mark Clague

See also: Classical Music; Entertaining Chicagoans; Outdoor Concerts

Further reading: Sherman, Robert L. *Chicago Stage: Its Records and Achievements.* 1947. • Upton, George Putnam. "Some Impresarios." In *Musical Memories,* 1908, 159–179. • Zelzer, Sarah Schectman, with Phyllis Dreazen. *Impresario: The Zelzer Era, 1930 to 1990.* 1990.

Improvisational Theater. It seems redundant to talk about the invention of improvisation. Improvisation is invention—a way of making things up spontaneously, out of whatever comes to hand, or to mind. Most of us improvise as a way of life.

What did have to be invented was a mechanism by which our everyday improvisations could be tapped, focused, and structured into theatrical art. That was achieved in Chicago in 1955, when David Shepherd and Paul Sills started an ensemble called the Compass Players. Set up in a HYDE PARK bar, just blocks from the spot where Enrico Fermi first split the atom, the Compass Players' experiments with improvisation opened a nearly limitless source of creative energy that continues to fuel every level of the American entertainment industry—television to theater, cabaret to commercials to film.

American comedy in particular has been transformed by concepts, techniques, and even attitudes pioneered in Hyde Park. The skit format that dominates television shows like *Saturday Night Live* owes much to the Compass; many of the artists who appear on those shows were trained by inheritors of the Compass approach. More broadly, alumni of the Compass—and of such successor companies as the legendary Second City—are consistently counted among the few who define the comic spirit of their times. Elaine May, Mike Nichols, Severn Darden, and Shelley Berman helped set the acerbic tone of the Kennedy era; John Belushi and Bill Murray embodied the gonzo surreality of the Vietnam years; Chris Farley's cartoonish excess made him a perfect clown for the 1990s.

But the method Sills and Shepherd pioneered has found applications well beyond comedy. Essentially a set of games designed for gaining access to all that is spontaneous, creative, and receptive in human nature, it is used in a variety of circumstances. Even Francis Ford Coppola—whose carefully burnished images would seem to suggest the antithesis of improvisation—has made the games part of his filmmaking process.

Revolutionary as the games have turned out to be, they weren't what David Shepherd had in mind when he arrived in Chicago in the fall of 1952. A radical scion of New York's fabled Vanderbilt family, he had developed a sharp distaste for the bourgeois amusements available on Broadway. He wanted to create an alternative, popular theater that would reflect the lived experiences of the mass of people. His inspiration was the commedia dell'arte, a genre that flourished primarily in sixteenth-century Italy. Commedia companies would travel from town to town performing plays for which no formal script existed—just a list of plot points, called a *scenario.* Actors playing stock characters were permitted to improvise dialogue (adding topical references, for instance) as long as they hit each point in the scenario. Shepherd meant to start a company that would perform scenario plays about contemporary society.

He soon hooked up with Paul Sills, a University of Chicago student who directed campus shows. Sills's mother, Viola Spolin, had been a drama supervisor with the WPA Recreation Project. In working with children, she had realized that she could bypass their resistance to acting by getting them to "play act" instead. For example, as Jeffrey Sweet recounts in his oral history, *Something Wonderful Right Away* (1978), "Spolin found that the [teenage] actors playing a romantic scene were shy about touching each other. Instead of saying 'Take her hand on that line' . . . she invented a game called 'Contact.' The rule of 'Contact' is that for every line he delivers, the actor must make physical contact with the actor to whom the line is addressed. . . . With this objective, the young performers soon forgot their shyness and focused their attention on meeting the challenge of the game."

Sills used the Spolin games as a way to build rapport within the Compass ensemble and also as a basis for the short improvisations that would follow each evening's scenario play. Created from audience suggestions, these witty, often topical skits were a big hit—too big for Shepherd, who saw his egalitarian dream theater being trampled by the college-educated professionals who queued up to see them. Short skits not only supplanted scenario plays at the Compass but throughout the entire improvisational movement as it developed over the next 35 years. Though some artists—including Sills and Shepherd—would continue to investigate other possibilities, there would be no strong challenge to what became the orthodoxy of the short skit structure until the beginning of the 1990s.

Since then, however, there has been an explosion in formal experimentation. Led by Del Close—a Compass alumnus who taught at Chicago's ImprovOlympic and epitomized the mystical (as opposed to pragmatic) strain in Chicago-style improvisation—many younger performers have carried out ambitious experiments with so-called "long form" structures. Thanks to the innovations of groups like Ed and Annoyance Theater, even the formerly staid Second City seems ready to reinvent improvisation.

Tony Adler

See also: Theater Companies; Theater Training

Further reading: Coleman, Janet. *The Compass.* 1990. • Spolin, Viola. *Improvisation for the Theater.* 1983. • Sweet, Jeffrey, ed. *Something Wonderful Right Away: An Oral History of the Second City and the Compass Players.* 1978.

Incorporation. *See* Charters, Municipal

Indian Creek, IL, Lake County, 30 miles NW of the Loop. Area residents incorporated in 1958 as a preventative against encroachment from their neighbor Vernon Hills. In 2000 Indian Creek encompassed the smallest area of any municipality in Lake County, with a population of 194.

Erik Gellman

See also: Government, Suburban

Indian Head Park, IL, Cook County, 16 miles SW of the Loop. The Potawatomi hunted and traveled along a trail (now Plainfield Road) en route to the Illinois River. Lyonsville developed as an agricultural community by the 1880s and was incorporated in 1959 as

Indian Head Park. Numerous golf courses help make this an attractive suburb for commuters on the Stevenson Expressway (I-55) and the Tri-State Tollroad (I-294).

Erik Gellman

See also: Cook County

Indiana Dunes. The Indiana Dunes are among the most significant landscapes in America—scientifically, esthetically, and politically. A remnant of their former glory, they survive as a jigsaw-shaped landscape of beaches, dunes, and wetlands largely preserved within the 2,182-acre Indiana Dunes State Park and the 15,139-acre Indiana Dunes National Lakeshore. What we now refer to as "the Indiana Dunes" were at one time part of an unbroken panorama of beach, dune, and wetland rimming the southern shores of Lake Michigan. Hunting, trapping, and logging depleted the Dunes of fur-bearers in the 1820s and of virgin oak and pine during the 1830s and '40s. The urban and industrial expansion of Chicago following the Civil War established the checkered pattern of factories abutting pristine natural settings that characterizes the Indiana Dunes today.

The Indiana Dunes are known as the "birthplace of ecology" in America because in 1899 University of Chicago botanist Henry C. Cowles published his classic paper on plant succession on the basis of field studies here. Many of Cowles's students and colleagues, such as Victor Shelford, Warder Clyde Allee, and Paul Sears, also did original research in the dunes, and became leaders of the new science of ecology.

For over a century "the dunes" have provided outdoor recreational opportunities for the Chicago metropolitan region, and inspiration to Chicago-area poets, literary naturalists, artists, landscape architects, and even playwrights, among them Carl Sandburg, Edwin Way Teale, Donald Culross Peattie, Frank Dudley, Jens Jensen, and Thomas Wood Stevens (whose 1917 dunes pageant played to an audience of 25,000).

The protracted battle to preserve the Indiana Dunes pitted several generations of socially conscious citizen environmentalists, with roots in Chicago and Gary settlement houses, against a powerful coalition of economic and political interests intent on industrializing the remaining Indiana shoreline. Chicago reformers associated with the settlement house movement initiated early attempts at Dunes preservation, culminating in the establishment of the Indiana Dunes State Park in 1923. In late 1966, Congress authorized establishment of the Indiana Dunes National Lakeshore, one of the nation's first urban parks, after a protracted lobbying campaign pitting industrial giants against a coalition of conservation groups led by the Save the Dunes Council. Senator Paul

Douglas of Illinois challenged Indiana's congressional representatives by supporting the park. Although compromised by Bethlehem Steel Corporation's preemptive leveling of centrally located high dunes, the establishment of the park represented a symbolic victory for Midwestern progressivism and the ideal of social democracy. At the dawn of the twenty-first century, INDUSTRIAL POLLUTION and urban sprawl continued to threaten the Indiana Dunes.

J. Ronald Engel

See also: Chesterton, IN; Environmental Politics; Environmentalism; Plant Communities; Vacation Spots; Waterfront

Further reading: Engel, J. Ronald. *Sacred Sands: The Struggle for Community in the Indiana Dunes.* 1983. • Franklin, Kay, and Norma Schaeffer. *Duel for the Dunes: Land Use Conflict on the Shores of Lake Michigan.* 1983. • Hurley, Andrew. *Environmental Inequalities: Class, Race, and Industrial Pollution in Gary, Indiana, 1945–1980.* 1995.

Patel Brothers grocery, 2542 West Devon Avenue, 1984. Photographer: Mukul Roy. Source: Chicago Historical Society.

Indiana University Northwest. The Indiana University Northwest campus originated in 1917 as a joint project of the Gary Schools and Indiana University, which offered extension courses in HAMMOND, GARY, and EAST CHICAGO. Instructors traveled from Bloomington and Chicago, and, by 1922, students could complete the requirements for an Associate of Arts degree. In 1932 Indiana University abandoned the Gary program to concentrate its extension work at the Calumet Center in East Chicago. Unwilling to allow Depression-hit Gary families to lose their opportunity to send their children to college, Gary Schools superintendent William A. Wirt opened Gary College.

In 1948 Indiana University assumed control of the struggling college, and the Gary Center of Indiana University grew rapidly in the 1950s. The city of Gary donated 27 acres of land in Gleason Park in 1955 and four years later the new campus opened. In 1963 the two Lake County campuses of Indiana University, the Calumet Center and the Gary Center, merged as the Northwest Campus of Indiana University, renamed Indiana University Northwest in 1968. The Northwest Center for Medical Education, a regional center of the Indiana University School of Medicine was added in 1972. By the end of the century, its 5,500 students attended the most ethnically diverse unit of the eight-campus Indiana University system.

Roberta Wollons

See also: Purdue University–Calumet; Universities and Their Cities

Indians. Though a few thousand Indians congregated on the West Coast by the early part of the twentieth century, the first major influx of Indians into Chicago awaited the arrival of graduate students and professionals eligible under the Immigration and Nationality Act of 1965. As with many other immigrant groups, the men arrived first, followed some years later by their families. The Indian population has grown steadily, though the increase owes less to the arrival of new professionals and more to the extended family system prevalent in India. By the end of the twentieth century, Chicago had the third-largest concentration of Indians in the United States. The 1980 census recorded 33,541 Indians in the Chicago metropolitan region; in 2000, the number had grown to 125,208. Many are professionals, particularly prominent in the sciences, medicine, the computer industry, and management. The number of Indian students at UNIVERSITIES remains large, but a working-class population is also emerging. As in other large cities, Indians are visible as TAXI drivers, shopkeepers, and GAS STATION owners.

Despite their affluence and professional status, Indians have never had a presence in Chicago POLITICS and have been relatively isolated socially. Many are, nonetheless, employed by the city and the state. They do not lack organizations: a pamphlet released in 1995 by the Vishwa Hindu Parishad, an organization that advocates pride in HINDU culture and the political ascendancy of Hinduism, lists nearly 70 Indian associations in the greater Chicago area, not including those catering to MUSLIMS. Several temples serve the Hindu community; there are two gurudwaras for SIKHS and one major Jain temple; and Indian Muslims frequent several mosques. Indian Christians and ZOROASTRIANS (Parsis) are also well organized. The ethnic, linguistic, and cultural divisions that prevail in India have been carried over with organizations such as the Bengali Association, the Bihar Cultural Association, the Tamilnadu Foundation, the Telugu Association, the Punjabi Cultural Society, the Maharashtra Mandal, and at least three Gujarati associations. Other organizations strive to evoke a more comprehensive notion of "Indianness": prominent among these are the Indian Classical Music Circle, which sponsors recitals by major Indian musicians, and the Chicago chapters of various professional organizations of Americans of Indian origin. Until the 1980s, no organization addressed adequately the problems encountered by Indian women, many of them unacquainted with legal and SOCIAL SERVICES. Apna Ghar was set up in 1989–90 to meet this need as a shelter for battered Indian women and counseling service.

A section of Devon Street, near the northwestern suburbs, provides a glimpse of Indian life. Indian RESTAURANTS proliferate, as do Indian GROCERY STORES, boutiques, and jewelry shops. Here, as elsewhere in the Indian diaspora, commercial Hindi films are extremely popular and may well be the element that cements Chicago's diverse Indian population into a more cohesive identity. The growing strength of Indians is indicated by the fact that in 1991 the "Little India" stretch of Devon was also designated Gandhi Marg (Way), which in turn prompted PAKISTANIS to press for the redesignation of an adjoining stretch to Mohammed Ali Jinnah Way in memory of the founder of Pakistan.

Vinay Lal

See also: Bangladeshis; Demography; Ethnic Music; Multicentered Chicago; West Ridge

Further reading: Rangaswamy, Padma. *Namaste America: Indian Immigrants in an American Metropolis.* 2000.

Indonesians. Indonesians started arriving in Chicago in 1883. Immigration to the United States has been slow, and they do not form a sizeable or recognizable community in the Chicago area. The community of fewer than 1,000 was scattered all over metropolitan Chicago in 2000. It encompassed Christians, largely of CHINESE descent, and MUSLIMS, who were likely to be of indigenous Indonesian ancestry. Many of the Christians came from affluent backgrounds, arriving in Chicago as students supported by their parents back home. Muslims have more often come on scholarships provided by the Indonesian government. Some have decided to settle in Chicago, having married Americans.

Asad Husain

See also: Demography; Malaysians; Multicentered Chicago

Industrial Art and Design. America's industrial design profession emerged during the GREAT DEPRESSION of the 1930s when manufacturers turned to appearance design to differentiate their products and boost sales. Architects, advertising ARTISTS, and theater designers sought employment as product "stylists" in the streamlined era. As the work of such designers became more valued, academic industrial design programs were established. Since design firms employed illustrators to draw product presentations and sculptors to model product forms, art schools often included product design in their curricula.

Since the 1930s, Chicago's manufacturers and merchandisers have provided rich opportunities for designers. The 1933–34 CENTURY OF PROGRESS EXPOSITION drew talented men to work for the exhibiting companies. Automotive designers from nearby Detroit transferred to Chicago-area employers. A typical career path for the first generation of product designers might have included a job at the 1933 fair or for a car manufacturer, then employment at Sears, Roebuck or Montgomery Ward, followed by work at a consultancy or for a manufacturer.

Anne Swainson formed the Bureau of Design at Montgomery Ward in 1931. In this powerful executive role, unusual for a female at that time, Swainson trained many product and package designers. The bureau designed thousands of products and their merchandising as well as set the standards for products purchased from suppliers. The bureau closed in the mid-1970s.

Sears, Roebuck opened Department 817, its Merchandise Testing and Development Laboratory, in 1934. John (Jack) R. Morgan left General Motors' Art and Color Section to head product design at Sears from 1934 to 1944 and then opened his own firm in Chicago. From 1935 to 1943, Jon W. Hauser worked in Detroit as an auto designer at General Motors and Chrysler and then was hired by Morgan to design for Sears. He worked for consultants Dave Chapman, Barnes & Reinecke, and Raymond Loewy before opening his own office in 1952, where he designed aviation and construction equipment as well as consumer products. Charles Harrison graduated from the industrial design program at the School of the ART INSTITUTE OF CHICAGO in 1954. Denied employment at major companies, Harrison, an AFRICAN AMERICAN, was hired by Henry P. Glass, his former professor, and then other small consulting firms. He was hired by Sears's Department 817 in 1961 and directed product design during the department's last decade until its closing in 1993. He then taught at the UNIVERSITY OF ILLINOIS AT CHICAGO.

Designers at major manufacturers directed internal staffs and hired consultants. Ivar Jepson, chief designer at Sunbeam, developed hundreds of household appliances from 1928 to 1965. His mixers and toasters became emblems of the American home. His successor, Robert Ernest, designed products for 40 years until Sunbeam closed its design department in the late 1980s. At Motorola, Herbert Zeller designed radios and televisions from 1950 to 1980. His successor as director of design, Rudolph Krolopp, designed cellular phones and communications systems for world audiences during his 1956–1997 tenure.

Jean Otis Reinecke came from St. Louis to manage displays at the Century of Progress, where he met James Barnes. In 1934 they formed Barnes & Reinecke, which designed top-selling, ubiquitous products such as Bell & Howell cameras, 3M tape dispensers, and Toastmaster toasters. During WORLD WAR II their design and engineering office swelled to 375 employees.

Melvin Boldt opened Mel Boldt and Associates in Chicago in 1948; in 1968 the firm moved to MOUNT PROSPECT. After Boldt's death in 1981, the firm continued until 1989. The Boldt office employed hundreds of designers who designed household appliances, jukeboxes, powerboats, televisions, and radios.

Chicago also figures prominently in design education. In 1937 the New Bauhaus was founded by László Moholy-Nagy, who had emigrated to Chicago after the influential Bauhaus in Germany was closed by the Nazis. Named the INSTITUTE OF DESIGN in 1944, the school became part of the ILLINOIS INSTITUTE OF TECHNOLOGY and today addresses design management issues for an international, technological age. Also in 1937, the University of Illinois at Urbana-Champaign began its industrial design program. The School of the Art Institute of Chicago maintained an industrial design program from 1946 to 1968. In 1965 the University of Illinois at Chicago opened its industrial design program. These schools have generated vital links to industry for faculty and students.

During World War II, Chicago designers served the war effort as civilians designing shortwave radios or as military cartographers and aircraft and naval equipment planners. The postwar tide of consumer goods produced by Chicago's manufacturers caused a surge in corporate design staffs and consultant firms.

During the 1980s, American corporations endured painful restructurings as the economy shifted from manufacturing to services. Manufacturing companies and retailers changed ownership, redefined their markets, and trimmed product lines in response to intense, global competition. Internal design staffs were disbanded and outside consultants provided more new product development services.

In the twenty-first century, lean corporate design departments outsource design and engineering needs. Midsize design consultancies perform varied tasks once done by large design organizations, in addition to meeting the new needs of global marketers. Firms provide services including strategic planning, consumer research, brand positioning, and computer-aided design critical to rapid new product development. In an economic environment that has moved much manufacturing out of the United States, the relative stability of the Midwest's diverse employment base has continued to attract corporate headquarters and production facilities to the Chicago area.

Victoria Kasuba Matranga

See also: Automobile Manufacturing; Electronics; Global Chicago; Graphic Design

Further reading: Heskett, John. "Mr. Sunbeam." *I.D.* (May/June 1994). • Mitarachi, Jane Fiske. "A Special Report on Midwest Design: The Chicago Area." *Industrial Design* (October 1956). • Pulos, Arthur J. *American Design Ethic: A History of Industrial Design.* 1983.

Industrial League Sports. *See* Sports, Industrial League

Industrial Pollution. Chicago's growth as a major manufacturing center forced its citizens to contend with staggering quantities of industrial waste. The impact of pollution on the population varied according to prevailing methods of WASTE DISPOSAL, the shifting geography of manufacturing, changes in the city's economic base, and specific political initiatives designed to reduce human exposure.

Early industrial activity concentrated along the South Branch of the CHICAGO RIVER, in part because the sluggish waterway provided a convenient repository for waste. During the nineteenth century this waste consisted largely of decaying organic matter—blood, grease, offal, and manure from slaughterhouses, MEAT PACKING plants, glue factories, tanneries, and fertilizer manufacturers. In addition, planing mills and sawmills sprayed copious amounts of wood dust into the air. The working-class populations that settled the adjacent residential districts suffered the most immediate effects, but prevailing winds from the southwest carried noxious stenches into the prestigious neighborhoods close to downtown Chicago. Citizen complaints prompted a more vigorous enforcement of PUBLIC HEALTH laws after 1860, the effect of which was to push the offending industries beyond the city limits into new industrial suburbs. Meanwhile, local officials turned to technological fixes to alleviate the continued threat that waterborne wastes posed to the city's drinking WATER SUPPLY. Repeated attempts to reverse the course of the Chicago River and to flush waste material away from the water-intake crib in LAKE MICHIGAN culminated in the completion of the Chicago SANITARY AND SHIP CANAL in 1900.

The rapid growth of the steel industry in the CALUMET REGION after the turn of the century shifted both the makeup and geography of industrial pollution. Steel mills in SOUTH CHICAGO, EAST CHICAGO, and GARY anchored a vast industrial complex along the southern Lake Michigan shoreline that also included oil REFINERIES, CHEMICAL plants, and over a hundred metal-fabricating factories. The steel mills discharged the largest quantities of waste. Skies glowed red at night from iron oxide particles spewed by open-hearth ovens. Slag from blast furnaces was used to fill swampy land and extend the lakeshore. Coal tars from coke plants and acids from finishing mills coated the Grand Calumet River. Although WATER quality in the southern tip of Lake Michigan showed a noticeable decline by the 1930s, rising levels of pollution during and after WORLD WAR II, a consequence of heightened industrial production, made the problem even worse. Slag debris fouled bathing beaches regularly and fish harvests of sturgeon, trout, and yellow perch declined precipitously. A preoccupation with the health effects of biological wastes deflected public attention from steel mill pollution through the 1950s. Not until the emergence of the environmental movement in the 1960s were manufacturers compelled by federal law to trap most pollutants prior to the release of waste into the air and water. Yet corporations dumped much of the captured waste into poorly designed landfills, as this method of disposal was not carefully regulated until the late 1970s.

The decline of heavy manufacturing in the metropolitan region did as much as the enforcement of federal regulations to reduce industry's contribution to air, land, and water pollution after 1980. Departing industries, however, often left their host communities to contend with abandoned toxic waste dumps and vacant contaminated buildings.

Andrew Hurley

See also: Contested Spaces; Economic Geography; Ecosystem Evolution; Environmental Regulation; Environmentalism; Iron and Steel; Leather and Tanning; Waste, Hazardous

Further reading: Colten, Craig E. *Industrial Wastes in the Calumet Region, 1869–1970: An Historical Geography.* 1985. • O'Connell, James C. "Technology and Pollution: Chicago's Water Policy, 1833–1930." Ph.D. diss., University of Chicago. 1980. • Wade, Louis Carroll. *Chicago's Pride: The Stockyards, Packingtown, and Environs in the Nineteenth Century.* 1987.

Industrial Workers of the World (IWW). Chicago has played a central role in the history of the Industrial Workers of the World (IWW). In January 1905 a group of radicals met secretly in Chicago, where they wrote an Industrial Union Manifesto and planned the founding convention of the IWW. Five months later, at Brand's Hall in Chicago, William D. "Big Bill" Haywood called to order "the Continental Congress of the Working Class," the labor radicals' challenge to the more cautious and craft-oriented trade unionism of the American Federation of Labor (AFL).

Thereafter the IWW retained an association with Chicago. Officials established the first national headquarters on West Madison Street, near the city's "Skid Row." Nearly all the national conventions met in Chicago, especially those most crucial to the IWW's history, such as in 1908 when a majority adopted syndicalism rather than political action as the path toward revolution. The funeral for the most famous IWW martyr, the SWEDISH immigrant roustabout and songwriter Joe Hill, was held in Chicago in November 1915, and the organization interred his ashes at Waldheim CEMETERY in suburban FOREST PARK near the graves of the HAYMARKET martyrs. When Bill Haywood died in Moscow in 1928, the Soviets returned half his ashes to Chicago for placement at Waldheim.

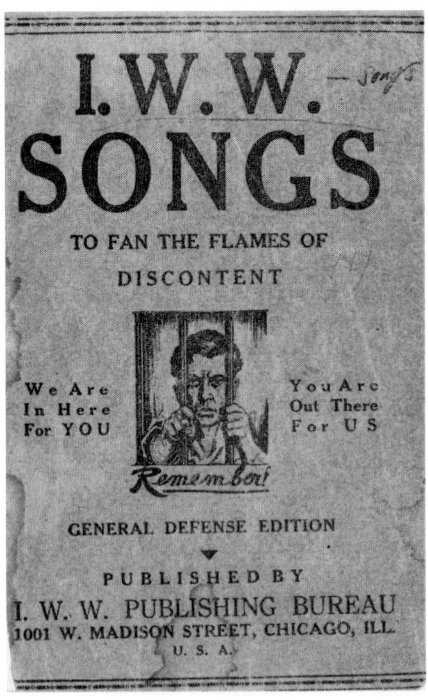

Cover of IWW songbook, 1918. In its various editions, the "Little Red Songbook" included organizing and protest songs written by such famous radicals as Joe Hill and Ralph Chaplin. Source: Chicago Historical Society.

The events most decisive to the IWW's decline also occurred in Chicago. In September 1917 U.S. Justice Department agents raided IWW national headquarters, seeking materials to prove IWW sedition and espionage during WORLD WAR I. And in 1918, the government tried over 100 IWW leaders in a federal courtroom in Chicago presided over by Judge Kenesaw M. Landis. The jury convicted all the IWW leaders, whom Judge Landis sentenced to long terms at the federal penitentiary in Leavenworth, Kansas. Thereafter, the IWW acted more as a legal defense organization than a fighting, revolutionary labor group. Even in its declining years, however, the IWW held national conventions in Chicago and kept its national headquarters there, moving to North Halsted Street, where it remained through the 1980s.

Melvyn Dubofsky

See also: Anarchists; Political Conventions; Red Squad; Unionization

Further reading: Dubofsky, Melvyn. *We Shall Be All: A History of the Industrial Workers of the World.* 1969. • Renshaw, Patrick. *The Wobblies: The Story of Syndicalism in the United States.* 1967.

Infrastructure. The term "infrastructure" has come to refer to almost every technological system in modern society. These systems are supplied by both the public and private sectors. The public sector supplies infrastructure at every level of government. In many cases, responsibility for services initially offered by private providers was assumed by the public sector. In recent years, that process has been reversed through "PRIVATIZATION."

Historically, the single most important component of Chicago's infrastructure is the ILLINOIS & MICHIGAN CANAL, the waterway that connected the GREAT LAKES and the Mississippi River drainage areas. When Illinois became a state in 1818, its northern boundary was moved to the north to include all the area that would benefit from the canal, but construction on the canal did not begin until 1836. Even before Chicago became a city, the CHICAGO RIVER became a federal harbor. A sandbar blocked the mouth of the river, and soldiers at FORT DEARBORN dug the first channel in 1828. The U.S. Army Corps of Engineers took over and completed the work in 1834; a pier built along the north side of this cut helped create Chicago's first harbor. Shortly thereafter, BRIDGES replaced the ferry that connected the north and south sides. The bridges

Water tower at Pullman, between 1890 and 1901. George Pullman built a private water supply system for his planned company town in 1886, but it was integrated into the Chicago municipal system after the area was annexed to Chicago in 1889. Photographer: Detroit Publishing Company. Source: Library of Congress.

were built by BUSINESS interests and landowners until 1856. The federal government constructed a lighthouse to mark the entrance to the harbor. By the late nineteenth century, the CALUMET RIVER and Lake Calumet emerged as the area's major port.

During the two glacial eras, much of what is now Chicago had been underwater. This flatness created Chicago's biggest problem before the CIVIL WAR—mud. In time, plank roads, RAILROADS, and interstate highways would be built on the former lakebed, but better drainage was critical. Primitive trenches dug in the streets proved to be a futile effort to address FLOOD CONTROL AND DRAINAGE. In 1852, the Illinois legislature created Chicago's Board of Sewerage Commissioners, which was formally charged with planning North America's first comprehensive sewer system, coordinating sewage and drainage. The board's chief engineer, Ellis Sylvester Chesbrough, called for an intercepting, combined sewer system that emptied into the river. Drainage was to be accomplished by gravity, but Chicago's flatness required the simple, but costly, expedient of having the city raise its level.

Chicago's first real highways were plank roads, removable oak planks placed across logs that had been laid on a firm foundation. These roads were 10 to 16 feet wide with a 4-foot shoulder and a drainage ditch. Many of the diagonal STREETS still in use today began as such roads, but they quickly reverted to regular roads, as maintaining the planks proved quite costly and evading the toll booths proved quite easy.

Chicago's first RAILROAD, the Galena & Chicago Union, made its maiden voyage in 1848, the same year the Illinois & Michigan Canal opened and TELEGRAPH service began. In the 1850s, Chicago became the western terminus for the most important eastern railroads and the eastern terminus for the most important western railroads. The Rock Island Railroad constructed the first railroad bridge across the Mississippi River, enhancing Chicago's position on the east-west trade route. The ILLINOIS CENTRAL RAILROAD (ICRR) effectively removed St. Louis from the north-south trade route. The ICRR's Chicago terminal was near the river on land east of where Fort Dearborn was located. The company built a breakwater in the lake on which it constructed a trestle. Following the FIRE OF 1871, the lake was filled past this breakwater, and GRANT PARK was created.

With the coming of the railroad, the city's population soared, roughly doubling every three years. Municipal WATER provision had replaced private provision, but even it was no longer adequate. Its intake point was close to the mouth of the river, so once the sewer system was complete, cholera and typhoid became regular visitors. Chesbrough convinced the city to construct new works with the intake point moved two miles into the lake. These works were begun during the Civil War. The intake was protected by a crib, a building roughly the size of Chicago's largest hotel. The pumping works were put on the beach just east of what would become Michigan Avenue. The tower built across the street to "beautify" the standpipe has become one of the city's best-known buildings. Chlorination began in 1912, and filtration began after World War II.

A series of dry summers in the 1850s required that Chicago River water be pumped into the Illinois & Michigan Canal to provide its summit level. This pumping effectively reversed the flow of the river, sending waste water away from the lake. In 1889, the Sanitary District of Chicago was created, and in 1900 the SANITARY AND SHIP CANAL was opened. It proved cheaper to dig a new canal than to enlarge the old one. As before, Chicago's growth put pressure on the system. Two additional canals were added, and, by the 1910s, the Sanitary District began experimenting with sewage treatment works. The Tunnel and Reservoir Plan ("DEEP TUNNEL") drafted in conjunction with the Northeastern Illinois Planning Commission and necessitated by the Federal Water Pollution Control Act of 1972, is nearing completion.

Unlike sanitation services, PUBLIC TRANSPORTATION remained privately owned until the creation of the CHICAGO TRANSIT AUTHORITY after WORLD WAR II. In the 1880s, Chicago had the largest cable car network in the country, but by the early years of the twentieth century, the 1,000-mile surface transit system had been electrified. A bus system replaced streetcars in the 1950s. In addition, there were 95 miles of elevated railways. Simultaneously, the development of the Commonwealth Edison network meant electricity rather than coal increasingly powered industry. The TELEPHONE and GAS utilities date from this same era.

At the turn of the century, one problem was that the old swing bridges across the river were open for ship traffic during half the daylight hours. One solution was the trunion bascule bridge, a type of drawbridge developed by Chicago Public Works engineers in 1899. The four-lane bridge constructed across the river at Michigan Avenue and the widening of that street between 1916 and 1922 created what became the MAGNIFICENT MILE. A second solution was the development of pedestrian and vehicular tunnels. The first pedestrian TUNNELS were dug just after the Civil War. These narrow, stone-lined shafts became STREET RAILWAY tunnels and remained in operation into the 1950s. A more adventurous tunnel system was begun in 1901 by private interests to move communication lines underground, but it soon became a system that served many downtown businesses. A 62-mile system of tracks lay 40 feet below the surface of downtown streets and brought all sorts of merchandise from downtown rail yards. The single most important commodity that moved on this system was coal. By the late 1950s, when coal was in decline, the system was sold to the city and reverted to its original purpose as a conduit for communication and other utility lines. It was largely forgotten until it flooded in 1992 and

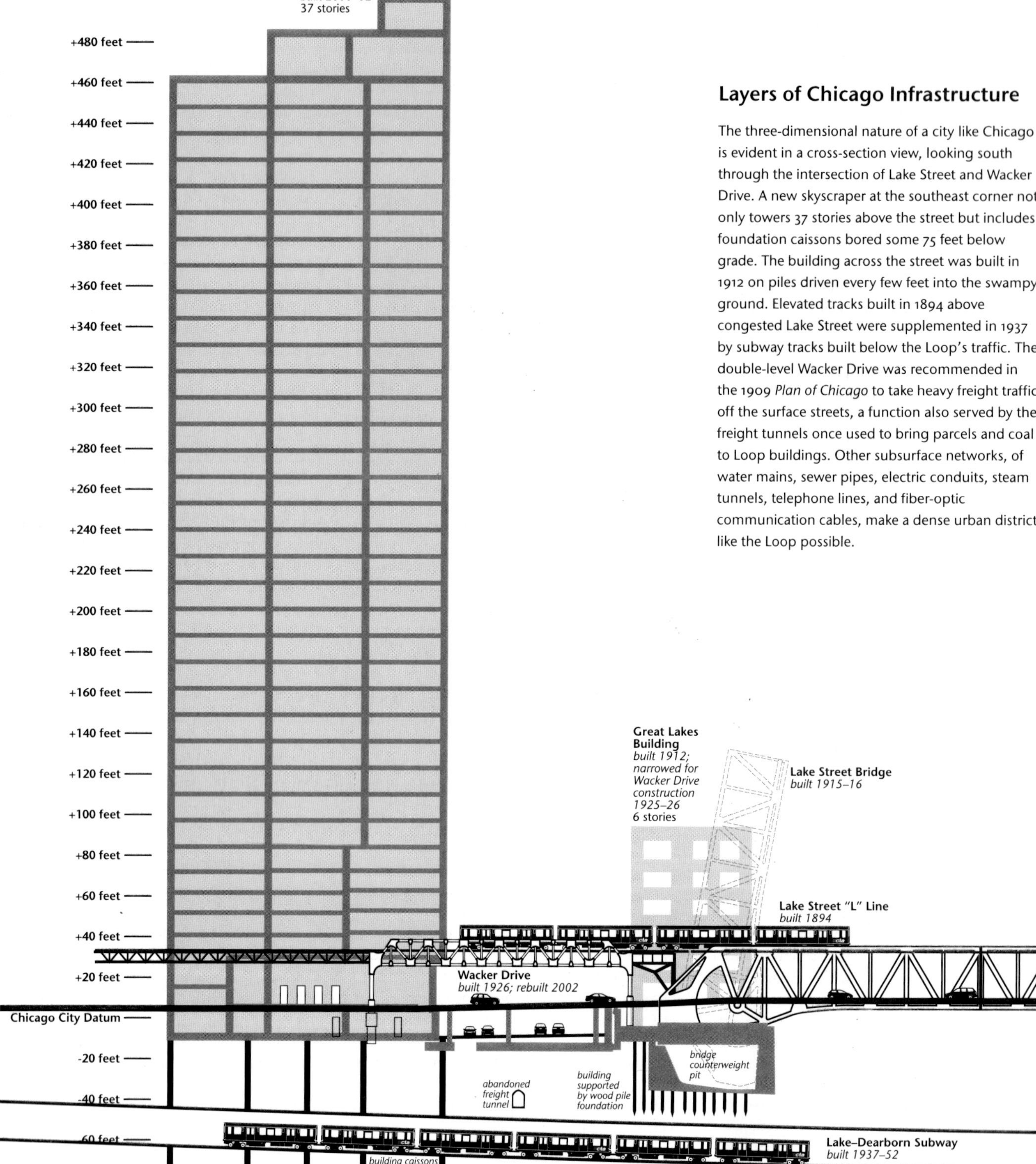

Layers of Chicago Infrastructure

The three-dimensional nature of a city like Chicago is evident in a cross-section view, looking south through the intersection of Lake Street and Wacker Drive. A new skyscraper at the southeast corner not only towers 37 stories above the street but includes foundation caissons bored some 75 feet below grade. The building across the street was built in 1912 on piles driven every few feet into the swampy ground. Elevated tracks built in 1894 above congested Lake Street were supplemented in 1937 by subway tracks built below the Loop's traffic. The double-level Wacker Drive was recommended in the 1909 *Plan of Chicago* to take heavy freight traffic off the surface streets, a function also served by the freight tunnels once used to bring parcels and coal to Loop buildings. Other subsurface networks, of water mains, sewer pipes, electric conduits, steam tunnels, telephone lines, and fiber-optic communication cables, make a dense urban district like the Loop possible.

closed much of the downtown district. Subways for RAPID TRANSIT were planned as early as 1902, but construction did not begin until the 1930s.

There were 12,000 automobiles in Chicago in 1910. By 1926, there were almost 350,000 cars and 18,000 trucks, with the result that the city spent over $500 million by 1930 to widen and resurface streets. Lake Shore Drive was constructed in the 1920s, and Chicago's first two "superhighways," the Edens and the Eisenhower, were completed before the passage of the Interstate Highway Act in 1956. Beginning with the Chicago Regional Planning Commission and continuing with the Chicago Area Transportation Study after 1958, businessmen and politicians planned a complete EXPRESSWAY system for the area. The Kennedy (1960), Dan Ryan (1962), and Stevenson (1966) completed the radial system. The Dan Ryan led to the Calumet SKYWAY, the only toll road inside the city, which opened in 1958. All but the Stevenson were built to carry rapid transit in the median. Public transportation for the city and suburbs became the responsibility of the REGIONAL TRANSPORTATION AUTHORITY.

The Kennedy led to O'HARE INTERNATIONAL AIRPORT. Initially, an airport was considered to be an adjunct of the city's downtown, much as the harbor and downtown rail terminals. As early as 1911 the idea of a lakefront airport was pursued. Such projects have been advocated at roughly 20-year intervals since then, and each time, financial considerations have caused it to be abandoned. The closest the city came was the creation of Meigs Field, which opened in 1948 and closed in 2003. The Works Progress Administration poured over $1 million in the 1930s into the construction of MIDWAY AIRPORT, which became America's busiest airport by 1932 and remained so until 1960. The development of jet aviation led to a demand for more space, and, in 1956, the city and the airlines prepared Orchard Field, what became O'Hare, for jets. Debate over the development of a third airport has continued to occupy politicians at the municipal, state, and federal levels.

Louis P. Cain

See also: Commuting; Land Use; Planning Chicago; Public Works, Federal Funding for; Street Grades, Raising

Further reading: Barrett, Paul, and Howard Rosen. *Public Works in Metro Chicago*. 1994.

Innovation, Invention, and Chicago Business. Joseph Schumpeter drew a compelling distinction between invention and innovation. Invention is the creation of something new, a new good or service, but what really matters for economic growth is innovation, the act through which these new ideas are successfully introduced to the market. Cyrus McCormick of Virginia improved upon his father's invention in the 1830s. He brought reaper production to Chicago in 1847 and introduced the machines to prairie farmers. Ray Kroc was not the inventor of fast food; he was the innovator. The market in which McCormick sold reapers was one that was just beginning to grow from local to national. The market in which Kroc sold hamburgers was one that grew from national to GLOBAL. What precipitated these changes were continuing improvements in TRANSPORTATION, production, and communication. Any examination of inventors and innovators in Chicago's BUSINESS history necessarily involves these improvements.

At incorporation, Chicago was still tied to the FUR TRADE, a business that avoids cities as readily as fur-bearing animals try to avoid people. Early businessmen John Kinzie, Gurdon Hubbard, and John Clark were involved in the fur trade, but they anticipated that something more substantial would arise at the mouth of the CHICAGO RIVER than a government fort and traders' cabins. An early innovator named George Dole arrived from Detroit in 1831. The following summer the firm of Newberry and Dole erected what is thought to be Chicago's first frame building used for business—specifically, the slaughtering and packing of cattle and hogs. While slaughtering for local consumption had taken place in Chicago for some time, Newberry and Dole were the first to pack meat for export. In 1839, the firm began shipping wheat from Chicago's first grain elevator, which was located at the north end of the Rush Street BRIDGE. Consequently, Dole is generally credited with being the father of Chicago's MEATPACKING industry as well as of its shipping, warehouse, and elevator systems. He innovated the market mechanisms that would make Chicago a major transshipment point.

William B. Ogden, another early innovator, arrived in Chicago in 1835 to manage property his brother-in-law and others had purchased. After selling roughly a third of the property at substantial profit, he moved into transportation. He played a major role in the completion of the ILLINOIS & MICHIGAN CANAL. He was the president of the Galena & Chicago Union Railroad and several other RAILROADS that became the Chicago & North Western Railroad, and of the National Pacific Railroad Convention held in Philadelphia in 1850. He also was the first president of the Union Pacific Railroad Company, the first mayor of Chicago, and the president of the Chicago branch of the State Bank of Illinois.

Ogden also played a role in bringing the McCormick Reaper Works to Chicago. Robert McCormick of Virginia first developed the reaper. His son Cyrus continued to work on the concept and moved to Cincinnati in 1845. Two years later, with Ogden's financial encouragement, he moved to Chicago to locate the firm at the heart of the emerging wheat-growing region. McCormick entered into a contract with Ogden in 1848 to distribute reapers to most of Illinois, Indiana, Michigan, Kentucky, and Tennessee. The McCormick firm developed a number of innovative business practices. It established agency relationships with local businessmen who promoted the use of reapers. It was one of the first enterprises to offer a written guarantee on every machine. It offered a free trial period during which dissatisfied customers could get a refund of the stated purchase price and offered credit as part of the terms of sale.

As more people and goods arrived to contribute to, and to benefit from, Chicago's growth, Ogden and others formed the Chicago Board of Trade in 1848 to promote Chicago's commerce. They promoted harbor improvements, tolls on the Illinois & Michigan Canal, and a land grant for the Illinois Central Railroad. From the beginning, the grain trade involved speculation. By the time farmers were able to harvest their crop and ship it as far as Chicago, water transportation on the upper Great Lakes was coming to an end for the winter. This meant that much of the grain would be shipped in the spring. The board facilitated the development of futures markets in which crops could be purchased well in advance of their delivery.

The Board of Trade, along with other Chicagoans, sought a resolution to the city's most serious problem—mud. In 1855, Ogden and the other members of the newly formed Board of Sewerage Commissioners planned a coordinated sewage and drainage system; Chicago became the first North American city to construct a comprehensive sewer system. The innovative plan, designed by Ellis Sylvester Chesbrough, called for an intercepting, combined sewer system that emptied into the river. Drainage was to be accomplished by gravity, but Chicago's flatness created a problem. This was resolved by the simple but costly expedient of having the city raise its level. As construction progressed away from the river, sewers were laid at the level necessary to accomplish gravity flow. Earth was then packed around them, and new streets were constructed above the sewers. Much of the fill was obtained by dredging the CHICAGO RIVER in order to lower and enlarge it. Building owners had to find a way to raise their property to the new level. George Pullman, who invented a technique for raising buildings during the enlargement of the Erie Canal in his native New York, moved to Chicago. Part of Chicago folklore is that guests in the Tremont Hotel were not disturbed when the building was raised about six feet.

Inevitably, the Chicago River became polluted as a result of the new sewer system. The pollution spread into the lake until it reached the WATER supply intake. By 1860, Chicago's sewerage commissioners, concerned with the offensive condition of the Chicago River, suggested diverting river water through the Illinois & Michigan Canal. It is customary to date the formal reversal of the Chicago River to 1871, when work was completed that deepened the canal and increased the pumping capacity at the BRIDGEPORT end. In fact, beginning some time in the 1850s, the river was reversed under normal conditions through the operation of the original Bridgeport pumps. From that time on, the city invested in additional works to keep sewage away from its Lake Michigan water supply. In 1889 voters approved the Sanitary District Enabling Act, which led to the construction of the SANITARY AND SHIP CANAL, essentially a larger version of the Illinois & Michigan Canal. Innovation continued into the twentieth century. In the 1970s, the Tunnel and Reservoir Plan, better known as "DEEP TUNNEL," included construction of larger sewers and underground reservoirs to hold storm water rather than allow it into the lake.

Grading grain, Chicago Board of Trade, 1948. Photographer: Gordon Coster. Source: Chicago Historical Society.

The Chicago River divided the city into three parts, impelling Chicagoans to become leading innovators in BRIDGE technology. The first bridge, constructed in 1832, was a fixed span that could not be opened and therefore was placed where it would not interfere with the part of the river used as a harbor. It ultimately was replaced by a series of drawbridges, swing bridges, and pontoon bridges that proved unsatisfactory. By the turn of the twentieth century, engineers determined that the trunnion bascule bridge, based on a seesaw principle, was the ideal solution to Chicago's bridge problems. That principle, built into the Tower Bridge in London, was modified to such an extent that bascule bridges came to be built in the "Chicago style."

While the railroad was not invented in Chicago, it was important to Chicago's economic development. By the late 1860s, rail connections were available from the Atlantic to the Pacific via Chicago, and the growth of the railroad network fostered commercial development. Because of its position on this network, Chicago became an important livestock market. Initially livestock were traded at Chicago and shipped live to Eastern markets, since that was the only way to assure fresh meat in those markets. By 1864, the livestock trade had grown so large that the burgeoning individual stockyards were considered a nuisance to the public and a costly burden to the railroads. Chicago encouraged the development of a new site by banning stockyard activity from the city limits. The "UNION STOCK YARD" opened for business in 1865. Nine railroad companies subscribed the vast majority of the $1 million cost, but every railroad entering Chicago was connected to the Yards.

Refrigeration was the critical innovation that transformed the livestock business. It changed MEATPACKING from a local business operating largely on a seasonal basis to a national business operating year-round and centered in Chicago. It contributed to a large increase in the operating scale of these firms by expanding the packers' operations beyond manufacturing into distribution and byproduct utilization. Around 1868, George Hammond of Detroit shipped eight tons of beef in a refrigerated car that had been designed for fruit shipments. While there were problems, HAMMOND was so confident of the technology's potential that he moved his operation to Chicago.

Gustavus Swift resolved the major marketing problems associated with shipping dressed beef. During the winter of 1877, Swift shipped a few carloads of dressed beef in regular cars with the doors left open so the cold air would keep the meat refrigerated. As a result of this experiment, Swift learned the advantages of shipping dressed beef in refrigerator cars, and he recognized this would require a major expansion in plant and equipment. When the railroads refused to produce refrigerator cars, Swift undertook the task on his own. Other packers began shipping refrigerated dressed beef east, often in Swift-built cars. Meat was shipped to refrigerated warehouses in big cities and distributed in smaller places in refrigerated "peddler" cars.

Such vertical integration, which contributed to the growth in the size of Chicago firms, was also pioneered by another meatpacker. In 1884, Armour & Co. purchased the Wahl Brothers glue works in Chicago and began funneling a large quantity of bones and low-quality hides into this plant. The same year, Armour hired a chemist to investigate the various alternative uses of animal wastes. Eventually, all the large packers were involved in such activities as soap production and selling hides to the leather industry and tails to the paintbrush industry. They also filled the bottom of the refrigerator cars with such goods as butter, eggs, and cheese. The large packers began buying the wastes of small packers; Armour, notes historian William Cronon, "built his empire on waste."

Like the meatpackers, the Pullman Palace Car Company innovated a new type of railcar. In 1859, George Pullman entered into a contract with the Michigan Central Railroad to fit two old passenger cars as sleeping cars. Pullman's initial car was like those on other lines; it consisted of a series of bunks and was used only at night. Four years later, he produced the first "Palace" car, one that could be used by day as well as for sleeping. Beginning in 1880, PULLMAN planned and constructed the model town that bears his name.

RETAILING was the bailiwick of one of Chicago's major innovators, Potter Palmer, who arrived from New York in 1852 and opened a dry goods store with several unorthodox practices. Other merchants largely rejected what has been termed the "Palmer system." Palmer insisted that his goods be displayed in an attractive manner, both in the store and in print advertisements. He allowed customers to take merchandise on approval and offered generous exchange provisions including a full refund. Perhaps just as importantly, he emphasized the continual introduction of new goods and, wherever possible, attempted to become their exclusive agent. In 1865, Palmer entered into partnership with Marshall Field and Levi Leiter. Palmer left the partnership in 1867; Leiter, in 1881. By then, the firm of Marshall Field & Co. had become a leading dry goods firm and a pioneer DEPARTMENT

STORE, the most complete retail establishment west of New York City. The Palmer system remained, in Field's phrase, "give the lady what she wants."

In 1865, Field, Palmer, and Leiter hired Aaron Montgomery Ward, who had quit his job in a Michigan general store and moved to Chicago. Two years later, he took a job as a traveling salesman for a similar firm in St. Louis. Living among the farmers, Ward got the innovative idea that through direct mail marketing he could make the goods enjoyed by city dwellers accessible to people living in small towns and on farms. He hoped to keep prices competitive by buying direct from manufacturers for cash and saving the expense of retail outlets and salesmen through MAIL ORDER. He also recognized his business location would have to minimize the cost of transporting the goods. He chose Chicago. The FIRE OF 1871 delayed the start of business until 1872, but Montgomery Ward & Co. proved an immediate success. The initial circular advertising the company's existence and the products it offered was one page; by 1886 the illustrated *Buyers' Guide* had grown to 304 pages. Success breeds imitation. Sears, Roebuck & Co., founded in Minneapolis in 1893, moved to Chicago two years later when shipping from Minneapolis proved impractical. Its 532-page catalog included housewares, saddles and buggies, and SPORTING GOODS, along with the watches and jewelry that reflected the firm's origins.

Another series of business innovations facilitated the extension of electric power throughout the Midwest. Samuel Insull, an Englishman who once served as secretary to Thomas Edison, believed electricity was a natural monopoly. In 1907, Insull, who had purchased most of the competing firms in Chicago, reorganized Chicago Edison as Commonwealth Edison and took the logic of his argument one step further. Using the holding company device pioneered on nineteenth-century railroads, he assumed control of entire territories by forming holding company upon holding company. Cash from the sale of stock in one company financed the next. At its zenith, Insull's Middle West Utilities Company controlled as much as one-eighth of the nation's electrical power and delivered it to 5,000 towns in 32 states and Canada. Among those who took advantage of electrification were Charles Yerkes, who put together Chicago's urban transportation system and introduced electric trolley cars, and Essanay Studios, which made motion pictures in Chicago before the FILM industry moved to Hollywood.

Chicago firms were also innovators in the emergence of the ELECTRONICS industry. In 1928, Paul Galvin started a small company that produced battery eliminators for battery-operated home radios, but, as that market dwindled, he became one of the earliest producers of car radios. The name "Motorola" comes from the conjoining of motion and radio. The company also produced walkie-talkies, a product line that Robert Galvin, the founder's son, followed while moving the company into the emerging field of electronics. As early as the 1950s, Motorola was innovating in the emerging field of cellular telephones. The company also produced two-way radios, pagers, and microchips. Motorola's 68000 series of microprocessors became the heart of the workstation market and the brains of the Macintosh computer.

In the twentieth century, automobiles, trucks, and air transportation pulled economic activity away from the confluence of lake and river. The suburbanization of business began as early as the 1920s, but the trend accelerated after WORLD WAR II, as the population also increasingly suburbanized. By 1970, half the population in the Chicago metropolitan statistical area lived in the suburban ring. The first pieces of what became the Interstate Highway System were the EXPRESSWAYS built as spokes out of the city, much as the railroads had been a century earlier. Falling transportation costs have allowed a corporation's headquarters to separate from its production facilities. A town like OAK BROOK, because of its easy access to an airport, is home to an amazing number of headquarters operations—and Ray Kroc's (McDonald's) hamburger "university."

Chicago's "hometown AIRLINE," United Airlines, like many other Chicago firms, is not native to the city. In the 1920s, Carl Fritsche of Detroit, in conjunction with Clement Keys of New York, determined to raise $2 million to start an air transport company in the hope Detroit would become to air transport what Chicago was to rail. National Air Transport's first flight was in 1926. In the fall of 1928, during a period of several air transport company mergers, Boeing and Pratt & Whitney created a holding company that adopted the name United Aircraft and Transport the following year. They wanted a connection between Chicago and New York and, in 1930, obtained National Air Transport, with whom United was doing cargo transfers at Chicago. The headquarters of United Airlines were located in Chicago because the airmail routes were established on the basis of the rail lines.

Many of Chicago's most vibrant, innovative enterprises in the twentieth century are oriented toward research. In the early 1920s, hospital administration and purchasing were developing specialties, and American Hospital Supply Corporation (AHSC), incorporated in Chicago in 1922, grew with those specialties and the highway system. Foster McGaw assumed leadership in 1946, and AHSC grew into a corporate giant with a national warehouse system. With the changes in the health care market in the 1980s, American merged with Baxter Laboratories.

Baxter got its start in 1929 when a Californian, Don Baxter, developed a baffle to prevent reflux in IV solutions under vacuum. Baxter became friendly with Harry Falk, who, in 1931, got financial assistance from his brother, Ralph Falk. Harry moved to GLENVIEW to begin sales. The small firm, through the leadership of William Graham, adopted a strategy of seeking specialty market niches and found several. In 1952, they were one of the first firms involved in the commercial marketing of human blood plasma. Four years later, Baxter agreed to help Willem Johann Kolff develop the market for the artificial kidney. Similarly, they worked with the University of Minnesota Medical School in developing the first heart-lung oxygenator, a key component of open-heart surgery.

A second successful health products firm is Abbott Laboratories. Many of the early medications were "nauseous mixtures," fluid-based concoctions. In 1888, Wallace C. Abbott began producing pills with measured doses in a room above his RAVENSWOOD pharmacy. His business soon expanded. The Abbott Alkaloidal Company was incorporated in 1900 and changed its name to Abbott Laboratories in 1915. The company introduced Nembutal, a sedative-hypnotic, in 1930, and a few years later Abbott scientists discovered Pentothal, an intravenous anesthesia.

The MANHATTAN PROJECT, a government research project that led to the development of the atomic bomb during WORLD WAR II, has left its legacy on research in Chicago. Although the project involved many scientists across the nation, the metallurgical laboratory of the UNIVERSITY OF CHICAGO developed the only known method for the production of plutonium-239. It was at the university that Enrico Fermi was successful in producing and controlling a chain reaction in December 1942. Atomic research remains the focus of considerable research at Chicago universities and sites such as ARGONNE NATIONAL LABORATORIES and FERMILAB.

Ray Kroc's hamburgers are now sold where McCormick's reapers once harvested. Yet for all the change, Schumpeter's dictum still holds—what really matters for economic growth is innovation. The continued health of Chicago business depends on its ability to attract innovators.

Louis P. Cain

See also: Consumer Credit; Dictionary of Leading Chicago Businesses, 1820–2000 (p. 909); Gas and Electricity; Global Chicago; Street Raising; Water

Further reading: This essay is based on themes developed in Louis P. Cain, "From Mud to Metropolis: Chicago before the Fire," *Research in Economic History* 10 (1986); and "A Canal and Its City: A Selective Business History of Chicago," *DePaul Business Law Review* (Fall/Winter 1998).

The two main sources for general information on the Chicago economy are A. T. Andreas, *History of Chicago from the Earliest Time to the Present*, 3 vols. (1884); and

Bessie Louis Pierce, *A History of Chicago*, 3 vols. (1937–1957). Among the other early general histories, Joseph Kirkland, *The Story of Chicago* (1892), has a good deal of information on business. Among the more recent histories, the two that emphasize Chicago's economy are William Cronon, *Nature's Metropolis: Chicago and the Great West* (1991); and Donald L. Miller, *City of the Century: The Epic of Chicago and the Making of America* (1996).

There is a large literature on the railroad industry. John F. Stover, *American Railroads* (1961), is a general survey. A much earlier work is William K. Ackerman, *Early Illinois Railroads* (1884). Wyatt Winston Belcher, *The Economic Rivalry between St. Louis and Chicago, 1850–1880* (1947), stresses the importance of Chicago's railroads.

A discussion of topographical and sanitation improvements, including the reversal of the Chicago River, can be found in Louis P. Cain, *Sanitation Strategy for a Lakefront Metropolis: The Case of Chicago* (1978).

An early three-volume history of the Chicago Board of Trade is Charles Taylor, *A History of the Board of Trade of the City of Chicago* (1917). A more academic approach can be found in Jonathon Lurie, *The Chicago Board of Trade, 1859–1905: The Dynamics of Self Regulation* (1979). A popular approach emphasizing the personalities involved is William G. Ferris, *The Grain Traders: The Story of the Chicago Board of Trade* (1988).

The authorized history of Marshall Field's is Lloyd Wendt and Herman Kogan, *Give the Lady What She Wants! The Story of Marshall Field & Co.* (1952). That of Sears is Boris Emmet and John Jeuck, *Catalogues and Counters: A History of Sears, Roebuck & Company* (1950). A more recent view is James Worthy, *Shaping an American Institution: Robert E. Wood of Sears, Roebuck* (1984).

The most comprehensive source on the meatpacking industry is Rudolf Clemen, *The American Livestock and Meat Industry* (1923). A short recent volume is Jimmy M. Skaggs, *Prime Cut: Livestock Raising and Meatpacking in the United States, 1607–1983* (1986).

Institute of Design. The landmark Chicago institution consecutively known as the New Bauhaus (1937–1938), the School of Design (1939–1944), and the Institute of Design (1944–present) offered the most important PHOTOGRAPHY program in the United States, becoming the seminal location for the education of the modern ARTIST-photographer from the 1930s through the 1960s.

The New Bauhaus opened in 1937 under the sponsorship of the Association of Arts and Industries with László Moholy-Nagy as its first director. Walter Paepcke and his company, Container Corporation of America, provided vital financial support in the early years. The school emphasized experimentation through an unconventional methodology based on the teaching principles developed at the Bauhaus in Germany. The school's goal was to train the "designer of the future" through a curriculum that gave equal weight to, and combined the basic elements of, ART, design, and photography. The hiring of Harry Callahan and death of Moholy-Nagy, in 1946, began a shift from the training of designers who used photography toward the training of artistphotographers.

Stephen Daiter

See also: Graphic Design; Illinois Institute of Technology; Industrial Art and Design

Further reading: Stephen Daiter Photography, Chicago Public Library, and Robert Henry Adams Fine Art. *Light and Vision: Photography at the School of Design in Chicago, 1937–1952.* 1994. • Travis, David, Elizabeth Siegel, and Keith F. Davis. *Taken by Design: Photographs from the Institute of Design, 1937–1971.* 2002.

Insurance. Chicago is not an "insurance town" on a par with Hartford or New York, but it still holds an important place in the history of the industry. While Eastern cities were home to pioneering life insurance companies, Chicago insurers spurred historic growth and innovation in fire and automobile coverage, safety standards, and insurance for AFRICAN AMERICANS. The insurance industry also helped to shape and reshape the physical city and played a crucial role in the aftermath of the Chicago FIRE OF 1871.

The first insurance agent in Chicago was Gurdon Hubbard, a FUR TRADER, investor, and speculator who arrived from Vermont in 1818. In 1834, Hubbard became the Chicago agent for the Aetna Insurance Company of Hartford, Connecticut, and this successful venture made him one of the city's most prominent mid-century businessmen. The Illinois Insurance Company, chartered in 1839, was the first insurance company to operate out of Chicago. The 1850s and '60s were a period of growth for Chicago insurance, as more national companies opened Midwestern offices and more Chicago-based firms were founded. By 1871, Chicago boasted 129 insurance companies, 14 of which were headquartered locally. Eighty-one were fire and marine insurers.

The Chicago Fire rocked the insurance world with the revelation that the industry was unprepared to meet such a massive calamity. Fifty-eight insurance companies were driven into bankruptcy by the fire. Even worse, thousands of policyholders were never compensated for their losses. While the venerable Gurdon Hubbard is said to have sold his own properties to meet the claims of some policyholders, in the end the industry paid the claims of only about half of the Chicagoans who had insurance policies.

The surviving insurance companies provided crucial capital for their policyholders to rebuild after the fire. But, by the most generous estimate, the insurance industry paid for less than a third of the total fire damage. Countless businesses and homeowners were denied their insurance claims and were never able to start over. Still, some contemporaries argued that the fire was a boon to the insurance industry because it wiped out the most poorly managed insurance companies, and that the new barrage of fire regulations made Chicago "the safest insurance field in the world." This claim seemed verified in the 1870s, as the insurance industry rebounded dramatically. The terrible losses of the Great Fire led insurance companies to pioneer fire-safety procedures with an eye to protecting their reserves against similar disasters. The Chicago Board of Underwriters, the industry's trade organization, created new institutions of fire safety in Chicago, including a fire patrol (1871) and fire inspectors (1886). The insurance industry also spearheaded fire-safety improvements at the UNION STOCK YARD in the 1880s.

Insurance company employees, July 1941. Photographer: Edwin Rosskam. Source: Library of Congress.

The GREAT MIGRATION of AFRICAN AMERICANS to Chicago during the First World War spurred the next major development in Chicago insurance: the creation of insurance companies to serve the black community. In the 1890s the life insurance industry's discriminatory practices had led to a proliferation of black-owned companies in throughout the South. Chicago's Supreme Liberty Life Insurance Company, founded by Arkansas native Frank Gillespie in 1919, was the first Northern black-owned insurance company. A tradition of saving for a dignified FUNERAL made Chicago's black community an enthusiastic and stable market for life insurance, despite its poverty. Black-owned insurance companies were one of the few sources of white-collar jobs for Chicago's African Americans, and some firms, like the Chicago Metropolitan Assurance Company (founded 1925), evoked nationalist sentiment by appealing to their policyholders' "race pride." However, the loss of African American customers to large insurers and the catastrophic black UNEMPLOYMENT of the 1980s ended the age of the independent black insurance company. Supreme Life was purchased by a national white-owned insurer, but Metropolitan Assurance was acquired in 1990 by the black-owned Atlanta Life Insurance Companies.

In 1931, the giant Sears, Roebuck, & Co. leapt into the insurance business with the creation of Allstate Insurance Company, based on the novel idea of selling auto insurance policies by MAIL ORDER. Recipients of the Sears catalog could simply clip a coupon from the book, mail it in, and receive an auto insurance policy by return post. After a few years Allstate switched from mail to the more traditional agent sales and acquired a life insurance branch, but auto insurance remained its specialty. In 1939 Allstate was the first company to tailor its rates to the characteristics of automobiles and their owners, such as make, mileage, and age. And, as with fire insurance companies in the previous century, Allstate's strategists realized their best chance for steady profits lay in improving safety. The company introduced rate reductions for good drivers in 1939, and by the 1950s Allstate offered grants to improve the training of driving instructors and began to pressure AUTOMOBILE MANUFACTURERS to make safer cars. In partnership with other insurers, Allstate has worked to persuade Detroit to install safety features, from standardized bumpers to airbags, in all passenger vehicles. As Chicago's largest insurance company, Allstate contributed to the relocation of jobs to the suburbs by moving its headquarters out of downtown Chicago, first to SKOKIE in 1953 and then to NORTHBROOK in 1967.

Kemper Insurance, Chicago's other major property and casualty company was founded in 1912 as Lumbermen's Mutual Casualty Company to provide workmen's compensation for Chicago lumberyard workers. In health insurance, Chicago's best-known institution is the Blue Cross Blue Shield Association, headquarters for the federation of nationwide health and hospital insurance plans. The Chicago area is also home to the insurance industry's national research arm, Underwriters Laboratories, Inc., which grew out of the old Chicago Board of Underwriters.

Chicago's skyline would not be the same without insurance companies. Insurers erected impressive Chicago landmarks like the Home Insurance Building (1884–85, by architect William LeBaron Jenney), the first SKYSCRAPER built using metal in its skeleton, and D. H. Burnham & Co.'s Insurance Exchange Building (1912). Two of Chicago's best-known (and most-criticized) skyscrapers, the Prudential Building and the John Hancock Center, bear the names of East Coast insurers. The landmark Standard Oil Building, currently Chicago's second tallest, in 2000 was renamed for the Aon Corporation. Aon, a giant insurance and brokerage company that adopted its name in 1987, resulted from the merger of Combined Insurance Corporation, founded by Chicagoan W. Clement Stone in 1919, and the Ryan Insurance Group, founded by Patrick G. Ryan in 1964.

Beatrix Hoffman

See also: Banking, Commercial; Firefighting; Lumber

Further reading: Allstate Insurance Company. *Allstate 50th Anniversary.* 1981. • Puth, Robert C. *Supreme Life: The History of a Negro Life Insurance Company.* 1976. • Weems, Robert E., Jr. *Black Business in the Black Metropolis: The Chicago Metropolitan Assurance Company, 1925–1985.* 1996.

International Alliance of Theatrical Stage Employees, Moving Picture Technicians, Artists and Allied Crafts. The International Alliance of Theatrical and Stage Employees, Moving Picture Technicians, Artists and Allied Crafts (known as the "IA") was established in 1893 to organize stagehand workers in theaters across the nation. After chartering locals in major cities such as Chicago, the IA expanded its jurisdiction by organizing theater projectionists who screened the short FILMS introduced during the late 1890s. As the motion picture industry developed over the next several decades, IA leaders began organizing workers in film production studios. Not surprisingly, the IA's aggressive posture and industrial orientation prompted numerous disputes with traditional craft unions whose leaders were also organizing theater and studio workers. These jurisdictional conflicts, which largely defined IA history through the 1940s, resulted in numerous costly STRIKES. Nonetheless, IA leaders remained committed to their jurisdictional claims, and by 1950, the IA's national dominance in studios and theaters was firmly established.

Although Chicago's history has been punctuated by the presence of IA locals and an important IA jurisdictional theater strike in 1935, the union's impact on the city pales in comparison to the impact Chicago has had on the IA. During the early 1930s, the IA came under the control of Chicago's infamous Capone-Nitti gang. For the remainder of the decade, Chicago mobsters engaged in racketeering while using violence and intimidation to silence theater and studio workers throughout the nation. And while racketeers' control of the IA ended in the early 1940s, Chicago's Capone-Nitti gang has left an indelible impression on the history of the union.

Laurie Pintar

See also: Crime and Chicago's Image; Movies, Going to the; Theater; Unionization

Further reading: Baker, Robert Osborne. *The International Alliance of Theatrical Stage Employees and Moving Picture Machine Operators of the United States and Canada.* 1933. • Dunne, George H. *Hollywood Labor Dispute: A Study in Immorality.* 1950. • Nielsen, Michael C. "Towards a Workers' History of the U.S. Film Industry." In *Critical Communications Review,* vol. 1, ed. Vincent Mosco and Janet Wasko. 1983.

International Amphitheater. Built to host the International Live Stock Exhibition when Chicago was hog butcher to the world, the amphitheater was commissioned in 1934 by Frederick Henry Prince, then head of the UNION STOCK YARD and Transit Company. Its original building stood at 42nd and Halsted Streets, on the east side of the Chicago Union Stock Yard, four miles from the LOOP.

Abraham Epstein's design became a prototype of future convention halls; when construction finished, Chicago's reign as a convention capital began. Among the amphitheater's many innovations were air conditioning and media space. Darkrooms sat only 30 feet from the speakers' platform; radio and television studios rested above; and coaxial cables allowed both the DEMOCRATIC and REPUBLICAN National Conventions to be seen nationwide for the first time in their history. The amphitheater hosted five presidential nominating conventions, including the famously riotous 1968 Democratic National Convention. In 1975, members of the NATION OF ISLAM convened there to appoint Wallace Muhammad successor to his father.

In the late twentieth century, amphitheater crowds were more likely audiences than conventioneers, witnessing performances by Frank Sinatra, the Beatles, the Ringling Brothers, and Elvis. Wrestling became the amphitheater's biggest draw in the 1980s; one of the last big matches hosted there featured future Minnesota governor Jesse Ventura. As convention business moved to newer venues in the suburbs or to McCormick Place, which was closer to downtown hotels, the sprawling complex became difficult to maintain. Built for $1.5 million, the building sold in 1983 to a REAL-ESTATE

Interurbans in the Chicago Region

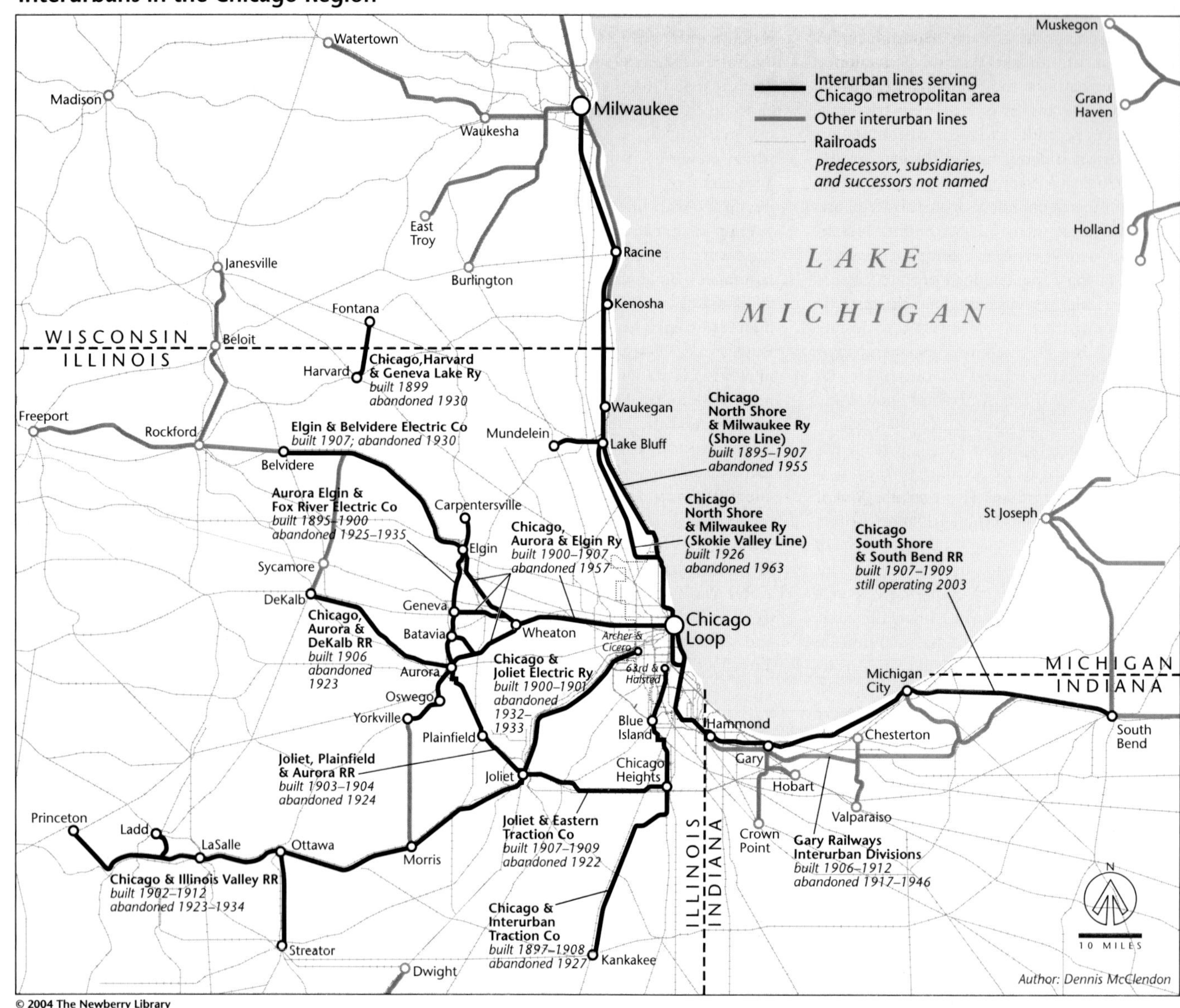

The promising new technology of electric traction prompted investors to build dozens of interurban lines linking small market towns to their trade areas and to each other. As a form of cheap "light rail" transport, this created a regional network partially paralleling the heavy railroads. Within two decades, most of the interurbans succumbed to competition from autos and from faster steam railroads forced by state regulations to lower their fares. Three lines radiating from downtown Chicago became major commuter lines, but they faced the dismal economics of commuter transport earlier than the steam railroads, which had other operations to subsidize them. Only the South Shore Line to South Bend, which moved substantial freight traffic through northwestern Indiana, survived until public subsidy for commuter operations became commonplace.

investor for $250,000. Over the next decade, it hosted too few large events to pay for its own upkeep and, on August 3, 1999, a backhoe began the formidable process of demolishing the amphitheater.

Sarah Fenton

See also: Economic Geography; Leisure; Meatpacking; Places of Assembly; Political Conventions; Tourism and Conventions

Interurbans. By 1910 a network of interurban electric railways connected many of the cities and towns of the Midwest. Enlarged STREET RAILWAYS, either alone or in short trains, operated over routes that utilized separate rights-of-way in rural areas and local streetcar tracks to reach downtown. Three interurbans once served Chicago's LOOP.

Closest to the typical Midwestern interurban was the Chicago, North Shore & Milwaukee RAILROAD. Constructed in sections from Milwaukee to EVANSTON between 1895 and 1908, it did not obtain operating rights through to the Loop over the Chicago Elevated Railway's Northwestern line until 1919. In 1926 it opened a new line through the SKOKIE valley between NORTH CHICAGO and Evanston. The original shore route was abandoned in 1955; the rest of the line followed suit in 1963 (the CHICAGO TRANSIT AUTHORITY's Skokie Swift rapid transit line still follows a short part of the route).

The Chicago, Aurora & Elgin Railway, like the North Shore line, reached the Loop via an elevated railroad, in this case the Garfield "L." Built between 1900 and 1907, this interurban stretched west from Chicago to ELGIN and AURORA. Unlike most interurbans, it was powered by an electrified third rail. When the Garfield "L" was removed to construct the Congress (Eisenhower) EXPRESSWAY, the line lost its connection to Chicago, and operations ceased in 1957. Today, the popular Prairie Path bike trail uses the old right-of-way.

To the south, the Chicago, South Shore & South Bend Railroad holds the distinction of being the nation's last surviving interurban. Opened in 1909 as a marginal line between the Chicago neighborhood of KENSINGTON, and South Bend, Indiana, its success was assured in the 1920s when it was rebuilt and obtained access to the Loop via the electrified ILLINOIS CENTRAL RAILROAD. The old familiar orange interurban cars were replaced in the 1980s, and since 1990 the line has been operated by the Northern Indiana Commuter Transportation District.

Ronald Dale Karr

See also: Privatization; Public Transportation; Railroads; Transportation

Further reading: Hilton, George W., and John F. Due. *The Electric Interurban Railways in America.* 1960. • Middleton, William D. *North Shore: America's Fastest Interurban.* 1970 [1964]. • Middleton, William D. *South Shore: The Last Interurban.* Rev. 2nd ed. 1999 [1970].

Invention. *See* Innovation, Invention, and Chicago Business

Inverness, IL, Cook County, 29 miles NW of the Loop. Inverness lies in the northwesternmost area of COOK COUNTY, surrounded by BARRINGTON, ROLLING MEADOWS, HOFFMAN ESTATES, SCHAUMBURG, and PALATINE. The village occupies six square miles of wooded, rolling hills. When Arthur T. McIntosh, a developer from KENILWORTH, first visited the area in the 1920s, the land reminded him of Scotland, and he named it after the capital of the Scottish Highlands.

While looking for a summer retreat for his family, McIntosh decided that this farmland was a perfect site for development. In 1926, McIntosh purchased the first of 11 farms. By 1939, McIntosh owned several dairy farms, grain farms, and a hog farm, as well as the Cudahy GOLF Course.

McIntosh and associate Way Thompson worked together to design and recreate a New England–like setting. They wanted to preserve Inverness's natural LANDSCAPE, so they set strict standards for construction. They designed roads that wove their way around the hills. Few of those roads led into or out of the village, providing Inverness with a certain exclusiveness and privacy while also protecting the quiet and natural setting from traffic from the neighboring towns.

The houses also followed the TOPOGRAPHY, for they were built upon the rises of the land. The first homes, built in the 1920s and 1930s, were mostly one-story buildings of the Cape Cod, Williamsburg, English Cotswold, and French Provincial styles. All lots were at least one acre in size. A "no fence" policy allowed the natural landscape to flow from lot to lot. Curbs and streetlights were prohibited in order to emphasize the Inverness landscape. To further add to the wooded setting, McIntosh planted thousands of TREES, including Norway pine, throughout the village.

Despite the GREAT DEPRESSION, McIntosh Company completed the first lot for sale in 1939. Those first homes, sold in the lofty price range of $9,000 to $20,000, established Inverness as an exclusive village. Though not initially successful, the population increased over time. Inverness began and remains a largely white enclave for the wealthy.

Inverness incorporated in 1962 and subsequently ANNEXED some bordering areas in an attempt to preclude any encroaching development. By 1970, Inverness had 1,674 residents. Beginning in the 1980s, more people began moving into Inverness, pushing its population up to 6,749 by 2000.

Though an independent community with its own village president, Inverness has, however, linked itself to the adjoining towns. With no industry other than its private country club, residents worked either in outlying communities or in Chicago. Route 68 provides residents access to the other suburbs while Route 14 leads into the city. METRA commuter rail service to downtown Chicago is available in neighboring BARRINGTON and PALATINE. Students attend classes in Palatine, while the police force is shared with Barrington. The fire departments of both Barrington and Palatine service Inverness.

Ronald Martin

See also: Built Environment of the Chicago Region; Government, Suburban; Landscape Design; Lincolnshire

Further reading: Women's Club of Inverness. *History of Inverness.* 1989.

Iranians. While the Iranian community of Chicago is not large, it reflects the diversity of Iran, with representatives of most of the major ethnic groups from that region, including the Azeri TURKS and the Kurds, as well as members of religious minorities, including the BAHĀ'ĪS and Iranian JEWS. However, most Iranians in Chicago are Persian-speaking Shī'ī Muslims. The majority of Chicago's Iranian community, estimated at the end of the twentieth century between 6,000 and 10,000 in the city and up to 30,000 in the metropolitan area, arrived in the wake of the 1979 Islamic Revolution in Iran.

Prior to the 1950s, given the strict controls put on emigration by the Iranian government, few Iranians came to the United States. However, Chicago had a special and unusual connection to Iran at the turn of the century, thanks to the growth of the Bahā'ī movement in Chicago. Several Iranian teachers of the new faith visited Chicago and other American Bahā'ī communities to help them learn the tenets of Bahā'īsm, most prominently Abd al-Fazl Gulpaygani, who stayed in Chicago between 1899 and 1901. In the period between World War II and the late seventies and early eighties, more Iranians began traveling to the United States, most on Iranian government scholarships to study medicine and engineering at American universities. Many of these students settled in this country once they completed their education, making major contributions in the technical and medical fields.

Beginning in 1979, Iranian immigration increased dramatically, consisting of large numbers of highly educated individuals. Though a majority of Iranians settled in California, many came to Chicago and began to set up a vibrant network of political, social, and cultural organizations. By the 1980s two Persian-language radio stations had emerged in Chicago. City publications in the 1990s included several Persian magazines and journals, such as the women's quarterly *Nimah-i Digar (The Other Half).* Through the sponsorship of such organizations as the Iranian-American Cultural Society, major Iranian singers and poets visit Chicago several times a year, drawing crowds of over 1,000. In addition, a popular Iranian film festival is held every October at the ART INSTITUTE OF CHICAGO. In order to perpetuate Iranian culture among American-born children of Iranian immigrants, several local centers offer courses in Persian, and private classes are conducted in various Iranian arts, including dance and music.

The Chicago area has boasted several world-respected medical professionals of Iranian heritage, as well as a significant number of famous Iranian writers and artists, including the sculptor Ario Mashayekhi. Most of the major universities in Chicago have Iranian scholars on their faculty. The majority of Iranians in Chicago live in the northern suburbs but are not concentrated in any particular area.

James S. Kessler

See also: Assyrians; Broadcasting; Demography; Multicentered Chicago

Further reading: Ansari, Maboud. *The Making of the Iranian Community in America.* 1992. • Sullivan, Zohreh T. *Exiled Memories: Stories of Iranian Diaspora.* 2001.

Iraqis. The Iraqi community of metropolitan Chicago reflects the ethnic and sectarian diversity of Iraq. Arabs, Kurds, ASSYRIANS, and Turkomans work to maintain their distinct ethnic identities in Chicago, holding to traditional family values, cultural practices, and language while also adapting to the norms of American society.

The largest and oldest Iraqi community in Chicago are the Assyrians, who number in the tens of thousands, making Chicago home to the largest Assyrian population in the United States. Assyrians are an ethnic minority in Iraq who claim a heritage dating back to the Assyrian Empire of Mesopotamia and whose homeland lies in northern Iraq, northwestern Iran, and southeastern Turkey. Chicago's first Assyrians, primarily Christian, arrived around the turn of the twentieth century and settled along the northern lakefront, establishing a community church in LINCOLN PARK. While a majority of the early Assyrians came from Iran, beginning in the 1960s a growing number of Iraqi Assyrians began to migrate to Chicago. In the mid-1970s, nearly 1,000 Iraqi-born Assyrians were resettled in Chicago as REFUGEES from the Lebanese Civil War, and throughout the 1980s and 1990s larger groups of refugees came to escape the Iran-Iraq War and the Gulf War of 1991. The new arrivals have sought residence along the lakefront in UPTOWN, EDGEWATER, ROGERS PARK, and nearby neighborhoods, while a growing number have moved to northern suburbs. Assyrians have entered a range of occupations from unskilled factory work to highly trained professional jobs. Many own small businesses. Assyrians have built a network of mutual assistance which reaches out to newcomers and have maintained strong ethnic identity through holiday celebrations that bring the entire community together, including Christmas, Easter, and Assyrian New Year.

Arabs constitute the majority in Iraq and the second largest group of Iraqi migrants to Chicago. Most of Chicago's estimated 6,500 Iraqi Arabs came to the United States in the late 1970s and early 1980s in search of economic opportunities. Highly educated MUSLIMS, these Arab migrants have entered a range of professional occupations and settled largely in NORTHBROOK and nearby suburbs. After the Gulf War, a new wave of Arabs migrated to Chicago from southern Iraq to escape political persecution. Many of these new arrivals were prisoners of war who were flown to the United States from Saudi Arabia, and a large portion were Muslim Shi'a who had staged a failed uprising against Saddam Hussein in 1991 and feared reprisal. Generally less educated than earlier Arabs, most new migrants work in factories or drive TAXIS and have settled on the North Side of the city. Iraqi Arabs celebrate Muslim holidays including Id Al-Fitr, Id Al-Adhha, and the Prophet's Birthday, and many attend a mosque in Northbrook that conducts daily prayers. Arabs were leaders in establishing the Iraqi-American Association, which has a membership of 3,000 predominantly Arab Iraqis and offers assistance to community members.

Kurds and Turkomans are ethnic minorities of Indo-European ancestry in Iraq and constitute small communities in Chicago dating from the aftermath of the Iran-Iraq War and the Gulf War. Kurds and Turkomans have both tended to settle in the northern neighborhoods of the city and in the suburbs, and most have taken jobs as factory workers or cabdrivers. Both groups are Muslim, but owing to their small size—less than 300 Kurds and 50 Turkomans—they attend the mosques of other communities. Each group maintains a distinct cultural identity and close ties with brethren outside of Chicago.

Asad Husain
Khoshaba Jasim

See also: Demography; Iranians; Multicentered Chicago; Syrians

Further reading: Korbel, Paul S. "Iraqi Americans." In *Gale Encyclopedia of Multicultural America,* 2nd ed., ed. Jeffrey Lehman, 2000. • Wolk, Daniel. "Assyrian Americans." In *Ethnic Handbook,* ed. Cynthia Linton, 1996.

Irish. From a few hundred residents in the 1830s, Chicago emerged as the fourth largest Irish city in America by 1860. Unlike their counterparts in New York, Philadelphia, and Boston, however, Chicago's Irish grew up with their city and exerted influence out of proportion to their numbers. Irish labor—first on the ILLINOIS & MICHIGAN CANAL (1836–1848) and later on the LUMBER wharves, RAILROADS, stockyards, and steel mills—contributed to Chicago's phenomenal growth from frontier town to urban metropolis. As Chicago became even more ethnically and racially diverse, the Irish continued to be well represented at the highest levels of the ROMAN CATHOLIC ARCHDIOCESE and city government, especially the POLICE force, FIRE department, and public SCHOOL system.

As a result of five potato crop failures beginning in 1845, Ireland lost nearly one million of its people to disease and poverty and 1.5 million more to emigration. After the famine, changes in inheritance laws and land-use patterns made emigration the only option for generations of young men and women. In sharp contrast to the migration of GERMAN, POLISH, and JEWISH families and ITALIAN men, Irish women often traveled alone or with groups of female relatives. Chicago's foreign-born Irish population peaked at 73,912 in 1900, but immigration continued steadily until the Immigration Act of 1924 reduced to 18,000 the number of Irish men, women, and children allowed into the United States each year. More restrictive quotas in 1929 and the GREAT DEPRESSION brought Irish immigration to a virtual halt until the 1950s. The last great wave of Irish migration to the United States, during the 1980s, included upwards of 36,000 undocumented immigrants, many university-trained men and women who settled permanently in Boston and Chicago. Because recent legislation has made it more difficult for them to obtain work permits and to adjust their status in the United States without incurring heavy penalties, they have taken jobs once reserved for unskilled immigrants: nannies, DOMESTIC WORKERS, bartenders, waitresses, and CONSTRUCTION workers.

Although the first wave of Irish immigrants to Chicago included many PROTESTANTS, they soon distanced themselves from their poorer, Catholic countrymen. In the 1850s and 1860s, for example, *Chicago Tribune* publisher Joseph Medill—the son of Ulster Presbyterians—routinely equated Irish with Catholic in his newspaper's coverage of city CRIME, poverty, POLITICS, and Irish nationalism. Yet the intended slur had just the opposite effect: it deepened the connection between ethnic identity, Catholicism, and nationalism. In the 1860s, Chicago was a hotbed of FENIAN activity. Significantly, the battle for Irish freedom did not divide ROMAN CATHOLICS into separate PARISHES as nationalism divided Chicago's POLONIA. On the contrary, parishes provided support through chapters of the Ancient Order of Hibernians, the Land League, and later, the Friends of Irish Freedom.

The Chicago Irish are perhaps best known for their political skills in winning elections and creating a multiethnic DEMOCRATIC machine. Never a majority among immigrants in the city, the Irish enjoyed a distinct advantage thanks to their knowledge of the English language and the British system of government. Chicago's twelve Irish MAYORS have governed for more than 80 years. Other legendary Irish politicians include "Honest John" Comiskey (father of WHITE SOX owner Charles Comiskey), "Hinky Dink" Kenna, "Bathhouse John" Coughlin, "Foxy Ed" Cullerton, and Johnny Powers (the nemesis of social reformer Jane Addams).

While politics and nationalism contributed to the high profile of Chicago's Irish, these tended to be male-dominated activities. The Catholic Church, on the other hand, with its extensive networks of parishes, schools, HOSPITALS, and charitable institutions, directly affected and involved the lives of thousands of Irish women and children as well as adult men. William Quarter, the first of nine bishops of Irish birth or descent to head the Chicago diocese since 1843, regarded Catholic institutions as essential to the well-being of immigrants and the larger city. At the same time he organized St. Patrick's for the Irish in 1846, he founded St. Peter's and St. Joseph's for the city's GERMANS. A pragmatic response to ethnic diversity, national-language and territorial parishes became distinguishing features of Chicago Catholicism. Moreover, CATHOLIC SCHOOLS contributed to the growth and development of the larger city. University of St. Mary of the Lake, dedicated on July 4, 1846, was Chicago's first institution of higher learning, and SAINT XAVIER Academy, founded by the Irish Sisters of Mercy in 1846, enrolled more Protestants than Catholics in its early years.

Irish women religious played a crucial role in Chicago Catholicism, staffing hundreds of parish schools in the diocese, financing academies, high schools, colleges, hospitals, and schools of NURSING. Agatha O'Brien, a working-class immigrant from County Carlow, Ireland, and her Mercy Sisters taught school, operated an employment bureau for Irish women, established Chicago's first ORPHANAGE, ran the city's first hospital, and nursed victims of the cholera EPIDEMIC of 1849. In 1851 they staffed the Illinois General Hospital of the Lake, incorporated as MERCY HOSPITAL in 1852. Along with St. Xavier's, predominantly Irish female religious orders founded BARAT COLLEGE in LAKE FOREST (the Religious of the Sacred Heart), Rosary College in RIVER FOREST and Mundelein College (the Sisters of Charity of the Blessed Virgin Mary). While these schools operated independently of the Archdiocese, they drew many of their students and faculty from local Irish parishes. The same held true for Chicago's two largest Catholic universities. Loyola University in ROGERS PARK traces its origins to the Jesuit parish of Holy Family in 1870, and DEPAUL UNIVERSITY began in 1898 in St. Vincent de Paul parish in LINCOLN PARK.

Since the 1840s, church building enabled Chicago's Irish Catholics to create community and leave their imprint on the urban landscape. While Irish parishes often looked to prominent Protestant and German American architects to create Gothic and Romanesque structures, they also patronized Irish and Irish American architects. Fifty years after its dedication as their mother church, St. Patrick's, built at Adams and Desplaines Streets in 1856, had become the old neighborhood parish for the Chicago Irish. Yet thanks to the genius of artist Thomas A. O'Shaughnessy, St. Patrick's was transformed, between 1912 and 1922, into the best-known example of Celtic Revival Art in America. Drawing inspiration from the ninth-century illuminated manuscript known as the Book of Kells, O'Shaughnessy created luminescent stained-glass windows and interlace stencils. Restored to their original beauty in 1996, O'Shaughnessy's designs continue to challenge conventional notions of Irish identity and sacred space.

Because they spoke English, the Irish had little need to create institutionally complete ethnic communities like Chicago's POLONIA or German Nord-Seite. However, for the vast majority of Chicago's Irish, estimated at nearly 300,000 by 1890, parishes remained the focal point of their lives and their neighborhoods. Staffed by priests and nuns of Irish birth and descent, these parishes played a vital role in mediating tensions between ethnic, Catholic, and American identities. While early Irish parishes were overwhelmingly working-class, by the 1880s middle-class parishes flourished in outlying neighborhoods such as Lincoln Park, LAKE VIEW, OAKLAND, HYDE PARK, ENGLEWOOD, and AUSTIN. In contrast to the national parishes of Chicago's Poles, Germans, Bohemians, LITHUANIANS, Italians, and SLOVAKS that remained clustered near industrial districts, the mile-square territorial parishes of the Irish kept pace with the development of Chicago, often following new streetcar lines and RAPID TRANSIT. In 1906, for example, the Chicago Irish claimed 83 of the city's 173 parishes. By the time the GREAT DEPRESSION of the 1930s halted new residential construction, Irish Catholics had built massive parish complexes along Chicago's boulevards as well as in new BUNGALOW belts and APARTMENT house districts. Although parishes established after World War II tended to be more ethnically diverse, many remained distinctly Irish.

Parishes and schools not only paralleled the growth of Chicago, they contributed to the social and geographic mobility of the Irish. Nowhere was this clearer than for the daughters of the famine generation. Amelia Dunne Hookway, for example, was born in St. Patrick's parish in 1858 and attended the high school run by the Daughters of Charity. She moved steadily through the ranks of the public school system, from classroom teacher in 1880 to her election as principal of the Howland School in the NORTH LAWNDALE neighborhood in 1896. As an independent wage earner, Amelia not only contributed to the Dunne family's prosperity, she also influenced their choice of residence in the city. Indeed, in a twist on immigrant migration patterns, JOURNALIST Finley Peter Dunne moved from neighborhood to neighborhood so that his sisters, Amelia, Kate, and Mary, could be near the schools in which they worked.

For Chicago's Germans, Bohemians, Poles, Italians, and Lithuanians, the ethnic press played a large role in keeping identity alive. With the exception of the *Chicago Citizen,* edited by firebrand nationalist John F. Finerty, and the *New World,* the official newspaper of the Chicago Archdiocese, the Irish relied on the daily papers that employed so many of their sons and daughters. International correspondent Margaret Buchanan Sullivan was Chicago's best-known reporter in the 1870s and 1880s. And in the 1890s, Finley Peter Dunne achieved national notoriety and literary fame as the creator of "Mr. Dooley," the saloonkeeper-philosopher of Archey Road. Irish American journalists also followed the activities of prizefighters John L. Sullivan and "Gentleman" Jim Corbett and labor leaders such as Michael Donnelly, a skilled butcher who led the drive to UNIONIZE the Amalgamated Meat Cutters and Butcher Workmen at the turn of the century; Margaret Haley, president of the CHICAGO TEACHERS FEDERATION; and John Fitzpatrick, head of the CHICAGO FEDERATION OF LABOR from 1905 to 1946. Chicago's Catholic labor priests and their outspoken bishop Bernard J. Sheil provided critical support for unions in the 1930s and 1940s and laid the groundwork for the BACK OF THE YARDS Neighborhood Council. Under the leadership of Saul Alinsky and Joseph Meegan, who had grown up in the Irish parish of St. Cecilia, this grassroots community group became a model for the nation. Irish Americans also played a prominent role in promoting racial justice, through such groups as Friendship House (1942) and the Catholic Interracial Council (1945).

Since the 1890s, the city's Irish have played a leading role in the cultural revival of traditional music and DANCE here and abroad. Francis O'Neill, a native of Tralibane, County Cork, Ireland, and chief of police in Chicago from 1901 to 1905, is widely credited with preserving Irish traditional tunes passed down orally for generations. He drew on the talents of fellow Chicago Irish policemen-musicians in compiling *O'Neill's Music of Ireland* (1903), still a standard reference work in Ireland and America. Among Chicago's best-known Irish musicians today is fiddler and composer Liz Carroll, the daughter of Irish immigrants, who has won the All-Ireland award twice since 1975. Likewise, Noel Rice's music students at the Academy of Irish Music (1994) have achieved acclaim both in the United States and Ireland. The popularity of Irish dancing also has soared, thanks to such innovators as Mark Howard, founder and artistic director of the Trinity Irish DANCE COMPANY (1990), and Michael Flatley, who grew up in Little Flower parish on Chicago's SOUTH SIDE and trained in the Dennehy School of Irish Dance. No longer confined to parish auditoriums, Irish traditional dance now attracts international audiences through such lavish productions as *Riverdance* and Flatley's *Lord of the Dance,* a mixture of Celtic mythology and ROCK and roll.

Equally important for the persistence of Irish ethnicity has been the scholarly work of the American Conference for Irish Studies (ACIS). Organized in 1960 by Lawrence J. McCaffrey of Loyola University, Emmet Larkin of the UNIVERSITY OF CHICAGO, and the late Gilbert Cahill of the State University of New York–Cortland, ACIS is now the nation's foremost interdisciplinary organization promoting the study of Irish and Irish American literature, history, language, political thought, culture, and art.

In addition to supporting the Irish American Heritage Center (1976) in the IRVING PARK Community Area of Chicago and Gaelic Park in suburban OAK FOREST, the Chicago Irish have preserved a sense of place and identity through their network of parishes. Although some of Chicago's historic Irish churches and schools have fallen to the wrecking ball, others have become well-known AFRICAN AMERICAN parishes. After more than 150 years, the Chicago Irish are still an influential ethnic

The Chicago Area's Iron and Steel Industry

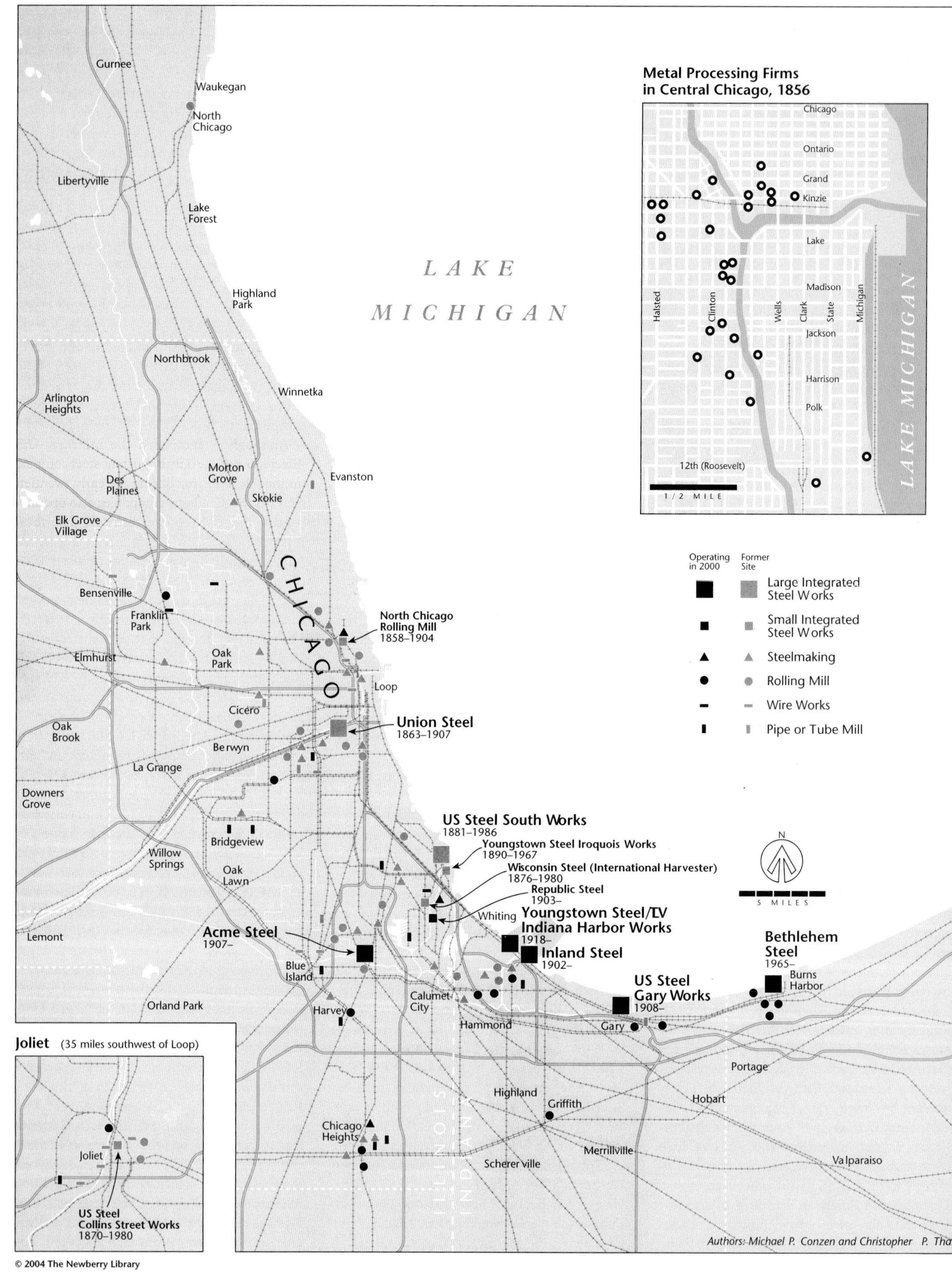

group, and their visibility is especially strong around St. Patrick's Day. Indeed, in recent years, the South Side Irish parade on Western Avenue has rivaled the traditional downtown parade in size and influence.

Ellen Skerrett

See also: Americanization; Church Architecture; Demography; Ethnic Music; Political Culture; Racism, Ethnicity, and White Identity

Further reading: Fanning, Charles. *Mr. Dooley and the Chicago Irish: The Autobiography of a Nineteenth-Century Ethnic Group.* 1987. • McCaffrey, Lawrence J., Ellen Skerrett, Michael F. Funchion, and Charles Fanning. *The Irish in Chicago.* 1987. • Skerrett, Ellen, ed. *At the Crossroads: Old Saint Patrick's and the Chicago Irish.* 1997.

Iron and Steel. Iron and steel mills have ranked among the largest economic enterprises in the Chicago region since before the CIVIL WAR. During the second half of the nineteenth century, the area became one of the world's leading centers of steel production. For much of the twentieth century, tens of thousands of area residents worked to turn iron ore into steel and shape steel into a variety of products. Only after the U.S. steel industry suffered a sudden decline in the 1970s did Chicago-area mills begin to shut down and lay off thousands of workers.

The emergence of a large iron and steel industry in the Chicago region during the nineteenth century was a function of entrepreneurial effort and geographical advantage. Mills could obtain raw materials from the vast iron ore deposits in the Lake Superior region relatively cheaply and easily. Because most of the iron ore used by the American steel industry during its rise was mined in Minnesota and Michigan, mills located along the GREAT LAKES were well positioned to enjoy lower costs than their competitors elsewhere, especially after 1924, when U.S. government regulators ended the "Pittsburgh Plus" pricing system that had protected Pennsylvania mills from competition.

As Chicago grew from small town to world-class city between the 1840s and the 1880s, the shape of the iron and steel industry was transformed completely. By the beginning of the 1850s, the city was home to several iron foundries, which melted preprocessed iron ingots and cast them into products such as stoves or boilers. But the first great iron-shaping enterprises in the Chicago area were mills that produced rails for the RAILROADS. The local pioneer in this field was Eber B. Ward, who used part of a fortune made in the Great Lakes shipping business to build Chicago's first rail-rolling mill in 1857. Located on the North Branch of the CHICAGO RIVER, Ward's plant was known as the North Chicago Rolling Mill Company. By 1860, when it employed about 200 men, it already ranked as one of the city's biggest enterprises; a decade later, it had expanded into a very large facility with 1,000 workers. In 1865, this mill experimented with rails made out of Bessemer steel ingots—the first such rails produced in the United States. At the beginning of the 1880s, Ward's company opened a sister mill at the mouth of the CALUMET RIVER on Chicago's SOUTH SIDE—the famous South Works. Meanwhile, several other mills had been established and became major rail producers. One of these was the Union Rolling Mill Company, built in 1863 on the South Branch of the Chicago River and employing about 600 workers by 1873. Another was the JOLIET Iron and Steel Company, which employed about 1,500 men soon after it opened in 1871. By the 1880s, these three companies together accounted for nearly 30 percent of the total U.S. output of steel rails.

In the final years of the nineteenth century, the steel industry in Chicago and around the country was simultaneously expanding and consolidating. By this time, Chicago-area mills sold large quantities of iron and steel products to the railroads and companies that built SKYSCRAPERS and BRIDGES, as well as to those that made goods such as pipe, containers, and wire. Dozens of area companies, from giants such as Pullman and Crane to much smaller firms, generated considerable local demand for steel. As local and national demand rose, mergers were thinning the numbers of steel producers. One of the first great mergers occurred in 1889, when most of the large Chicago-area mills—including NORTH CHICAGO, South Works, Union, and Joliet—combined to form a huge new entity, the Illinois Steel Company. The world's largest steel company, Illinois Steel not only owned multiple mills employing a total of about 10,000 men but also controlled iron mines, COAL MINES, and TRANSPORTATION systems. By the end of the nineteenth century, workers at the various Chicago-area mills owned by this company were turning out about a million tons of finished steel per year.

During the first part of the twentieth century, even after many of Chicago's largest mills were absorbed into a giant national corporation, the area's importance within the American steel industry continued to rise. The most important single development in the history of the industry occurred in 1901, when New York banker J. P. Morgan engineered the creation of U.S. Steel, the world's largest business enterprise. Illinois Steel (by then also known as Federal Steel, a holding company created by Chicago lawyer Elbert H. Gary in 1898) became part of this giant entity. U.S. Steel closed some of the Chicago-area mills, but the South Works—which employed about 11,000 people in 1910—stood as one of its largest plants. And in 1906, U.S. Steel built a huge new mill on south shore of Lake Michigan in what would become GARY, Indiana. By the 1920s, the Gary Works had 12 blast furnaces and over 16,000 employees, making it the largest steel plant in the country.

Although it dominated the industry, U.S. Steel was not the only important steel company in the Chicago area during the early twentieth century. Several local companies also operated large mills in the Calumet district and northern Indiana. Inland Steel, which was established in CHICAGO HEIGHTS in 1893, became a major player in the steel industry in 1901 when it decided to build a large new plant at Indiana Harbor. Inland Steel grew steadily through the 1930s, when the Indiana Harbor plant had four blast furnaces and over 9,000 employees. Another important local plant was the SOUTH DEERING facility of Wisconsin Steel, which supplied metal to International Harvester, its Chicago-based corporate parent. Other important steel companies in the area during the early twentieth century included Republic Steel, Acme Steel, Youngstown Sheet & Tube, and Interlake Iron. Together with the U.S. Steel plants, all of these smaller companies made the Chicago area an increasingly important center of steel production.

The growth of the steel industry during the early twentieth century was accompanied by serious conflict between companies and their employees. IRON- AND STEELWORKERS in the Chicago area had been forming associations since the middle of the nineteenth century. Starting in the 1870s, hundreds of them became members of the Amalgamated Association of Iron and Steel Workers, a national group. During the first part of the twentieth century, Amalgamated and other groups led organized efforts designed to win higher wages, shorter hours, and safer working conditions. Many steelworkers at this time worked 12-hour shifts, six or seven days a week, in hazardous environments. For the most part, STRIKES at Chicago-area plants between 1900 and 1920 ended in defeat for workers. The largest of these strikes occurred in 1919, when 90,000 Chicago-area workers led an industrywide,

Chicago's earliest metalworking industries were small in scale and located near the Chicago River in what is now central Chicago. The first steel mills and blast furnaces, supplying them with raw material, were not much farther out. As iron and steel works grew enormously in size, companies moved to remote sites with abundant—and cheap—land and water, mostly on the southern metropolitan fringe, with its ample harbors for lake-borne iron ore imports and proximity to coal supplies. Large plants were built in southeast Chicago and northwestern Indiana, where lonely sand dunes and swamps were transformed into vast industrial areas. Joliet and Chicago Heights emerged as lesser steel centers, and early wire mills centered in nearby DeKalb (not shown) and Joliet. Small steelmaking operations, rolling mills, and pipe and wire works were somewhat more widely scattered along the region's railways. By 2000 most steelmaking in the city of Chicago had ceased.

Illinois Steel Works, Joliet, between 1880 and 1901. Photographer: Detroit Publishing Company. Source: Library of Congress.

national protest coordinated by the American Federation of Labor (AFL) that sought union recognition and the 8-hour day. The strike temporarily halted steel production, but, after state and federal troops were called in, workers returned to their plants. A nationwide collapse followed soon thereafter. When the steel industry agreed to an 8-hour day in 1923, the change resulted more from public pressure and the efforts of U.S. president Harding than from the strength of organized labor.

During the 1930s, in the midst of the Great Depression and the reforms of the New Deal, steelworkers in the Chicago area and across the nation finally won substantial gains through unionization. The successful unionization efforts of the 1930s brought together tens of thousands of workers of various ethnic backgrounds. At the turn of the century, most steelworkers in the Calumet and Indiana mills had been immigrants from Southern and Eastern Europe. During the 1910s and 1920s, large numbers of Mexican and African American men found work in the mills. Often, area steel companies attempted to exploit ethnic differences among workers to fight unionization. For many years, steelworkers were divided by ethnicity and craft distinctions. But in the late 1930s, after New Deal legislation made unionization easier, workers were organized across the industry. In Chicago and elsewhere, Amalgamated joined the Steel Workers Organizing Committee of the Congress of Industrial Organizations (CIO) in launching a 1936 organization drive that won recognition by U.S. Steel in 1937. The most violent of the Chicago-area clashes accompanying this effort was the "Memorial Day Massacre," in which 10 people were killed by police gunfire during a strike outside the East Side plant of Republic Steel. But this incident did not prevent unionization, and, in 1942, steelworkers formed a powerful national union, the United Steelworkers of America (USWA). By the beginning of the 1970s, when the USWA counted 130,000 members in the Chicago region, the predominant ethnic groups in the mills were Mexicans and African Americans.

From the 1940s until the 1970s, the steel industry remained one of the Chicago area's leading economic sectors. Immediately after World War II, the United States was making over half the world's steel, and mills in Indiana and Illinois accounted for about 20 percent of total U.S. production capacity. Many of the large open-hearth plants established in the early part of the century continued to make huge amounts of steel. Between 1959 and 1964, Interlake and Wisconsin Steel became two of the first U.S. mills to install basic oxygen furnaces, which were faster and cheaper than the older open-hearth equipment. Meanwhile, a large new plant was built by Bethlehem Steel at Burns Harbor, Indiana. The last giant mill constructed in the Chicago region, the Bethlehem plant helped make the Illinois-Indiana region the geographical center of the U.S. steel industry at the end of the 1960s.

During the Cold War, when most Chicago-area steelworkers were represented by the USWA, relatively high wage levels did not prevent labor conflict. Between 1945 and 1959, there were five industrywide strikes. In 1952, about 80,000 Chicago-area steelworkers walked out for two months. An even more serious work stoppage occurred in 1959, when tens of thousands of workers in the Chicago area joined 500,000 steelworkers nationwide in a four-month strike to win changes in work rules, wage levels, and benefits.

During the 1970s and 1980s, the U.S. steel industry suffered a sudden collapse that threw thousands out of work. U.S. Steel and other

American steel companies that still depended upon large numbers of older, inefficient plants failed to withstand the combination of a decline in demand and the rise of international competition in the 1970s. The sudden decline of American steel stunned the employees of mills across the Chicago area. Between 1979 and 1986, about 16,000 Chicago-area steelworkers lost their jobs. Wisconsin Steel closed abruptly in 1980 after attempts at a financial bailout failed. South Works endured a prolonged shutdown before closing its doors in 1992. Inland Steel cut thousands of workers. Republic Steel dismissed half its employees. In 1984, it merged with LTV Steel, which declared bankruptcy in 1986. The closures left many steelworkers without jobs or health care and decimated communities in northwest Indiana and the Calumet district.

During the final years of the twentieth century, the Chicago region continued to be a leading center of production in an American steel industry that was much weaker and smaller than it had been before. By the mid-1980s, the area was home to several "minimills," small-scale plants that used sophisticated electric furnaces to recycle scrap metal. By the end of the 1980s, mills in Northern Indiana were making about a quarter of all the steel produced in the United States. While the region remained a center of steel production, the industry was no longer the powerhouse that had been a crucial part of the Chicago-area economy for over a century.

David Bensman
Mark R. Wilson

See also: Business of Chicago; Calumet Region; Economic Geography; Global Chicago; Poles

Open-hearth blast furnace, U.S. Steel Company's South Works, ca. 1952. Photographer: Unknown. Source: Chicago Historical Society.

Iron- and Steelworkers. As early as 1847, Chicago had six IRON foundries. Steelmaking in Chicago began in 1865. As steel production grew nationwide during the late nineteenth century, steel production in Chicago grew too. For decades, immigrants came to Chicago because of the high wages available in the mills. Steel companies specifically recruited many of them.

The first wave of immigrants to the mills, mostly SCOTS, IRISH, and GERMANS, came in the 1870s and 1880s. The second wave, of Slavic immigrants, mostly POLES and SERBS, first arrived in the 1890s and continued to come until the beginning of WORLD WAR I. The third wave, MEXICANS and AFRICAN AMERICANS from the South, began during World War I. The Europeans tended to settle in largely homogeneous ethnic neighborhoods near the mills along the CALUMET RIVER on the SOUTH SIDE, although the dominant group in particular neighborhoods has changed over time. These areas have prospered and declined along with the firms that ran the mills. African American employment in the Chicago steel industry increased sharply after WORLD WAR II, but hostility from white residents forced these workers to settle on the western and northern fringes of this area.

Around the turn of the century, the largest mills in Chicago were the South Works, built by the North Chicago Rolling Mill Company in 1880, and the Wisconsin Steel Works, built by International Harvester in 1902. When U.S. Steel formed in 1901, it took control of the South Works. Unable to expand its steelmaking operations in Chicago proper, U.S. Steel began work on building the city of GARY, Indiana, in 1906 so that it could continue to take advantage of the Chicago region's proximity to RAILROAD and barge routes. Other mills that took advantage of these same geographic conditions operated in Gary, JOLIET, even Milwaukee.

Chicago steelworkers played an important role in the industry's two most important STRIKES of the early twentieth century. The National Committee for Organizing Iron and Steel Workers, chaired by CHICAGO FEDERATION OF LABOR president John Fitzpatrick, began an organizing drive in Chicago during World War I. This push culminated in an unsuccessful nationwide steel strike in 1919. The industry's use of African Americans as strikebreakers during this dispute, particularly in Chicago and Gary, enflamed racial tensions among steelworkers for decades afterwards. In the late 1930s, the Steel Workers Organizing Committee of the CONGRESS OF INDUSTRIAL ORGANIZATIONS (CIO) began the first industrywide union organization since 1892. As part of this effort, employees at Republic Steel in Chicago participated in the unsuccessful

Little Steel Strike of 1937. Police attempts to keep demonstrators at bay resulted in the "MEMORIAL DAY MASSACRE."

Employees at the South Works were the first beneficiaries of U.S. Steel's attempt to improve safety in its mills, with a plan adopted throughout the corporation in 1906 as part of its WELFARE CAPITALISM efforts. Workers at Wisconsin Steel were among the first in the industry to belong to an employee representation plan (or ERP), which critics derisively referred to as a company union. Management used the ERP as a way to give workers limited collective bargaining rights without recognizing an outside union. Given the opportunity to join the CIO in the late 1930s and early 1940s, Wisconsin Steel employees repeatedly voted instead to maintain the ERP. Even though the National Labor Relations Board forced Wisconsin Steel to sever its ties to the ERP, it lived on for decades, having evolved into an independent organization.

As late as the 1970s there were 130,000 members of the United Steelworkers of America (AFL-CIO) in the Chicago-Gary area. In recent decades, iron- and steelworkers in Chicago have suffered a fate common to iron- and steelworkers across the nation. Wisconsin Steel went out of business in 1980. U.S. Steel closed the South Works in 1992. Plant shutdowns like these have devastated the economy of the entire South Side. They hurt not only steelworkers and their families but steel industry suppliers and other area businesses that depended upon the wages of steelworkers for their livelihood. Most of the iron and steel plants operating in Chicago at the turn of the century were small producers of specialty steel, not the basic steel producers of old that helped build the railroads, buildings, and automobiles of a bygone era.

Jonathan Rees

See also: Antiunionism; Economic Geography; Great Migration; Transportation; Unionization

Further reading: Bensman, David, and Roberta Lynch. *Rusted Dreams: Hard Times in a Steel Community.* 1987. • Cohen, Lizabeth. *Making a New Deal: Industrial Workers in Chicago, 1919–1939.* 1990. • Kornblum, William. *Blue Collar Community.* 1974.

Irving Park, Community Area 16, 7 miles NW of the Loop. Irving Park's past and present are tied to preservation of its historic houses. Building fine houses was the concept that businessman Charles T. Race decided upon after purchasing acreage in 1869 from Major Noble, whose father had bought the land in 1833. Race had intended to become a gentleman farmer, but his land was so close to the Chicago & North Western RAILROAD, he realized there would be more profit in beginning a settlement. After Race paid for a depot, the train line agreed to stop at the settlement, which was first called Irvington as a tribute to author Washington Irving, but was soon renamed Irving Park.

Race built himself a three-story brick house with basement and "French roof." Joined by associates, he organized the Irving Park Land Company, bought additional land, and subdivided it into lots. Advertisements promoted the area's easy access to downtown via hourly trains. Boasting an idyllic setting comparable to that of suburbs such as EVANSTON and OAK PARK, the ad pointed to Irving Park's "shady streets, fine schools, churches and stores," and homes of varied designs. The Irving Park SUBDIVISION was followed by Grayland, Montrose, and Mayfair.

The commuter suburb attracted many wealthy residents who sought larger homes of between seven and ten rooms, and amenities that included closets and drinking water from artesian wells. Race and his associates garnered a 600 percent profit on the land. Other residents who were less affluent came to the area to remove their families from the dangers of the city. Rich or middle-class, the population of Irving Park was generally native-born, PROTESTANT, and white-collar. They participated in community events and activities of a literary and musical nature. Both men and women were active in neighborhood organizations. The Irving Park Woman's CLUB formed in 1888 with an agenda of cultural and reform activities.

Suburban paradise was not without problems, however. In the 1880s heavy rains produced floods, and poor drainage turned unpaved streets to mud. In 1881 complaints were heard of raw sewage floating down Irving Park Road from the Cook County Poor House and Insane Asylum in DUNNING.

Although ANNEXATION of Irving Park into the city of Chicago as part of JEFFERSON TOWNSHIP occurred in 1889, in the 1890s streets were still unpaved and unlighted. As improvements were added, the main thoroughfare became a construction zone; STREETS were updated and PUBLIC TRANSPORTATION was created. A residential boom between 1895 and 1914 added more than 5,000 new buildings, of which 1,200 were multifamily residences. New structures changed the housing composition of the area, leading to concerns about community standards.

GERMANS and SWEDES had begun arriving around the turn of the century but in the 1920s were largely replaced by POLES and RUSSIANS. Population peaked at 66,783 in 1930, and commercial interests sprang up along the major roads, but until 1940, construction was mainly residential. Most notable architecturally were the bungalows of the Villa District; Old Irving Park with Queen Anne, Victorian, and Italianate houses farmhouses, and BUNGALOWS; and Independence Park with many homes of turn-of-the-century vintage.

A new emphasis on neighborhood unity and the preservation of area houses began in 1983 with the Old Irving Park Association (OIPA). The organization broke into two groups a year later, with the OIPA focusing on rehabilitating old houses, fund-raising for charity, helping needy residents, and sponsoring forums for political candidates.

The second association, the Old Irving Park Historical Society (OIPHS), began conducting an area house walk in 1985. They also worked on preservation. A number of structures have been cited as landmarks, including Carl Schurz High School and the Steven Race House. In the 1980s the Chicago Landmark Commission named 43 other buildings as potential landmarks.

Irving Park's population grew from 49,489 in 1980 to 58,643 in 2000. During those two decades the Hispanic population increased from 9 percent to 43 percent, and included immigrants from Central and South America along with larger numbers of MEXICANS and PUERTO RICANS. FILIPINOS and INDIANS predominated among Asians, who constituted 8 percent of the population in 2000.

Marilyn Elizabeth Perry

See also: Historic Preservation; Housing Types; Metropolitan Growth

Further reading: Drury, John. "Old Chicago Neighborhoods, XXII: Irving Park." *Landlord's Guide* (February 1949): 12–13. • Mayer, Harold. "Zoning Is Irving Park, Albany's Best Protection." *Real Estate* (June 28, 1941): 12–18. • Posadas, Barbara M. "Suburb into Neighborhood: The Transformation of Urban Identity on Chicago's Periphery—Irving Park as a Case Study, 1870–1910." *Journal of the Illinois State Historical Society* 76 (Autumn 1983): 162–176.

Island Lake, IL, McHenry and Lake Counties, 40 miles NW of the Loop. Platted as a summer cottage development around an artificial lake by 1936, Island Lake incorporated in 1952 following post–World War II expansion demands. While accepting growth, the community of small lots near the FOX RIVER has maintained much of its rural atmosphere. Recent residential developments brought the population to 4,449 in 1990 and 8,153 in 2000.

Craig L. Pfannkuche

See also: Lake County, IL; McHenry County; Vacation Spots

Further reading: *McHenry County in the Twentieth Century, 1968–1994.* McHenry County Historical Society. 1994.

Israelis. After the declaration of Israeli statehood in 1948, some of the first immigrants to Chicago from the area that became Israel were displaced PALESTINIAN Arabs—both MUSLIM and Christian. The exodus of Palestinians continued through 1967, when Israel began its occupation of the West Bank and the Gaza Strip.

In the late 1970s, after a devastating war and increasing economic pressures, many JEWISH Israelis began to look toward the United States. While the great majority of immigrants settled in the growing and extensively networked Israeli community in New York City, a significant number came to Chicago. These immigrants generally had a higher level of education than most Israelis and hoped to return to Israel within a decade. Some sought to take advantage of graduate and professional programs at Chicago universities.

The number of Israelis living in Chicago increased in the 1990s, probably to several thousand. Relationships between Chicago corporations—particularly technology companies such as Motorola—and Israeli firms has led to a rise in the number of Israelis located in Chicago for BUSINESS purposes. In 2000, over two hundred Illinois companies had business interests in Israel, and a large number of Israeli companies sent representatives to Chicago to stimulate trade.

Israelis living in Chicago mostly identify and form social networks with the Jewish community, often serving as language instructors for Hebrew schools and Jewish day schools. The Israeli Consulate for the Midwest is located in Chicago and provides some community services, such as Israeli House—a meeting place and program facility for Israelis in Chicago—and an annual Israeli film festival. Formed in 1997, Chicago Yisraelim is an organization for graduate students and young professionals in the city.

Adam H. Stewart

See also: Demography; Judaism; Multicentered Chicago; Zionism

Further reading: Cohen, Yinon. *Discrimination and Migration: Arab and Jewish Out-Migration from Israel and the Occupied Territories to the U.S.* 1994. • Rosen, Sherry. *The Israeli Corner of the American Jewish Community.* 1993. • Sobel, Zvi. *Migrants from the Promised Land.* 1986.

Funeral of Silvio Tosi, St. Anthony Catholic Church, West Pullman, 1929. Photographer: Unknown. Source: University of Illinois at Chicago.

Italians. Despite its interior location, in 1920 Chicago was the third-ranking city in the United States, after New York and Philadelphia, in the size of its Italian population. In 1970, Italian immigrants and their children in metropolitan Chicago totaled 202,373, accounting for some 3 percent of the area's inhabitants. In 2000 more than a half million residents of the region identified themselves as of Italian ancestry.

Italians began trickling into Chicago in small numbers in the 1850s, working largely as merchants, vendors, barbers, and other artisans. By 1880, there were 1,357 Italians in the city. Successful as SALOONKEEPERS and restaurateurs, some invested in REAL ESTATE and became wealthy. These early arrivals were predominantly from Liguria, with a sprinkling from other regions; among them were veterans of the Risorgimento, the movement for national unification of Italy. Imbued with patriotism for the newly unified Italy, they sponsored nationalist observances, including Chicago's first Columbus Day parade in 1868. In 1866, they organized a MUTUAL BENEFIT SOCIETY, Società di Unione e Fratellanza, and published a NEWSPAPER, *L'Unione Italiana* (1867–69).

In the late nineteenth century, mass migration from Italy accelerated. Chicago's foreign-born Italian population, 16,008 in 1900, peaked at 73,960 in 1930. These newcomers were predominantly peasants *(contadini)* from the southern regions, particularly Basilicata, Campania, and Sicily. Drawn to Chicago's market for RAILROAD WORKERS, these laborers were enrolled in work gangs by padrones (labor contractors), who shipped them to CONSTRUCTION sites throughout the country. As they gained stable employment in the city's PUBLIC WORKS and industries, women were sent for and families established. Many women worked in the sweatshops and factories of the garment industry.

Strongly attached to their places of origin *(campanilismo)*, *paesani* (townsmen) clustered in TENEMENTS, formed mutual aid societies named after patron saints, and maintained exclusive networks. Although the largest concentration of Italians by far was on the NEAR WEST SIDE, there were some 20 settlements scattered about the city and its suburbs. The older immigrant GERMANS, IRISH, and Scandinavians resisted these intrusions, but gradually gave way. For many years Italians encountered deep prejudice and discrimination in housing and employment. The Chicago press stereotyped them as violent criminals, paupers, and wage-cutters.

A growing middle class, composed of merchants, padrones, and professionals, sought to uplift their countrymen with patriotic exhortations and nationalistic celebrations. Italian newspapers proliferated that reflected the interests of the so-called *prominenti* (big shots), but only *L'Italia*, established in 1886, survived far into the twentieth century. Unity, however, evaded the Italians, who were divided by personal jealousies and regional antagonisms. By 1912, there were some four hundred competing societies, usually composed of *paesani*. Meanwhile, ANARCHISTS and SOCIALISTS sought—with sporadic success—to organize the immigrants along class lines. The Italian Socialist Federation with its organ, *La Parola dei Socialisti* (established 1908), was based in Chicago, but its adherents were a minority.

Although nominally ROMAN CATHOLIC, Italian immigrants generally were not devoted to the institutional church. The first Italian parish, the Church of the Assumption on the NEAR NORTH SIDE, was established in 1881. By 1920, there were 18 Italian national PARISHES in the Archdiocese of Chicago. Priests, however, often encountered indifference and anticlericalism among the immigrants. Papal opposition to Italian unification engendered strong anti-Vatican sentiments among nationalists, while radicals rejected all religious ideas. PROTESTANT denominations proselytized among Italians, but most *contadini* remained attached to the religious traditions of their *paesi*, above all to the patron saints whom they celebrated in elaborate *feste*. Italian women were especially devoted to maintaining traditional forms of piety. With time and understanding pastors, the parishes became important centers for community activities.

World War I marked a turning point in the history of Chicago Italians. The war, followed by restrictive legislation, cut off further immigration, thus stabilizing the foreign-born population. Because of labor shortages, Italians gained entry into factory jobs and other occupations. Paradoxically, wartime emotions inspired an increased sense of both Italian nationalism and American patriotism. Intensified anti-Italian prejudice and discrimination also caused a heightened ethnic consciousness. Fraternal orders such as the Sons of Italy in America now organized immigrants and their children on the basis of nationality. This growing ethnic identification coincided with the rise of Fascism in Italy in the 1920s, inclining most Chicago Italians—with the exception of a small but vigorous anti-Fascist element—to support Mussolini. The arrival of a squadron of Italian seaplanes led by the Fascist Italo Balbo in 1933 marked a high point of that enthusiasm.

Italian Americans remained largely blue-collar workers until well after World War II. But wages rose in the 1920s for factory workers, construction tradesmen, and truck drivers. Families were able to purchase houses, furnishings, and even automobiles. Chicago's Italians gradually began to move westward toward the suburbs. With the Great Depression of the 1930s, however, many Italians, along with others, lost homes and businesses and suffered long periods of unemployment.

Italian women and men constituted a substantial segment of the labor force in the clothing and garment industry and helped found the Amalgamated Clothing Workers of America. The International Hod Carriers and Building Laborers' Union of America, controlled by labor racketeers for much of its history, also had a large Italian membership in Chicago. Across a variety of industries in the 1930s, Italians engaged in labor struggles as members of the Congress of Industrial Organizations (CIO).

Reflecting their modest political clout, no Italian has won election as mayor of Chicago. Introduced to Chicago-style machine politics by Irish bosses such as Johnny Powers of the Nineteenth Ward, Italians initially traded their votes for jobs and other patronage. In the 1930s, the "Italian vote," which had fluctuated between the two parties, became solidly Democratic in support of Franklin D. Roosevelt and the New Deal. Since the 1950s, with rising economic levels, Italian Americans have increasingly abandoned their dedication to labor and the Democratic Party.

Although only a minority of Italians graduated from high school and very few from college until well after World War II, many rose to the middle class through business ventures in construction and commerce, particularly food and liquor merchandising. Prohibition in the twenties proved to be a bonanza for Italians who engaged in bootlegging. While Al Capone (born in Brooklyn) epitomized Chicago's big-time gangster, many families invested profits from the trade in booze to launch legitimate enterprises.

Capone became an albatross around the necks of Chicago Italians seeking respectability. The stereotype of the criminal and violent Italian was well established by the late nineteenth century. Numerous crimes attributed to the Mafia and *Mano Nera* (Black Hand) further reinforced the stereotype. However, it was the racketeering and mob wars of the twenties, perpetuated by innumerable movie and television versions, which made Chicago, crime, and Italians synonymous in the minds of many.

If Italian Americans sympathized with the Mussolini regime, events following Pearl Harbor demonstrated that their first loyalty was to the United States. Tens of thousands of men and women left to serve in the armed forces or work in defense industries. After the war, the educational and home mortgage benefits of the GI Bill facilitated their occupational and spatial mobility. Movement to the western suburbs was accelerated by urban renewal projects that demolished Italian neighborhoods to make way for public housing, highways, and the Chicago campus of the University of Illinois. While vestiges of old neighborhoods remained, by 1970 the majority of Chicago's Italians lived in suburbs such as Cicero, Berwyn, and Oak Park.

A few Italian inner-city parishes remain, but most were either dissolved or turned over to incoming groups. Religious and ethnic institutions administered by the Scalabrini Fathers, a missionary order for the Italian immigrants, became centered in the western suburbs: the Sacred Heart Seminary, the Villa Scalabrini Home for the Aged, and the Italian Cultural Center. Rather than the face-to-face contacts of old neighborhoods, Italian radio and television programs and a newspaper, *Fra Noi*, published since 1960, enable communication among far-flung audiences.

Although unity remained elusive, the Italian Welfare Council (established in 1945) addressed the educational, recreational, and social needs of Chicago's Italians. In 1952, the Council was succeeded by the Italian American Civic Committee, which as an umbrella organization sought to advance the interests of the ethnic group. Since 1952, it has sponsored the annual Columbus Day parade, combated defamation, and promoted Italians in business and public life. The persistence of associational activities is indicated by the estimated 150 Italian organizations with diverse professional, cultural, and political agendas. That the roots of Italian ethnicity in Chicago remain deeply buried in the soil of the *paesi* is demonstrated by the survival and revival of the religious festivals, which take place throughout the summer months.

Rudolph J. Vecoli

See also: Broadcasting; Demography; Housing for the Elderly; Madonna Center; Multicentered Chicago; Mutual Benefit Societies; Racism, Ethnicity, and White Identity

Further reading: Candeloro, Dominic. "Chicago's Italians: A Survey of the Ethnic Factor, 1850–1990." In *Ethnic Chicago: A Multicultural Portrait*, ed. Peter D'A. Jones and Melvin G. Holli, 1995, 229–259. • Vecoli, Rudolph J. "Chicago's Italians prior to World War I: A Study of Their Social and Economic Adjustment." Ph.D. diss., University of Wisconsin, 1962. • Vecoli, Rudolph J. "The Formation of Chicago's 'Little Italies.'" *Journal of American Ethnic History* 2 (Spring 1983): 5–20.

Itasca, IL, DuPage County, 21 miles W of the Loop. A large Victorian gazebo in Usher Park, a greenbelt area along the south side of Irving Park, symbolizes the essence of Itasca. Another green addition to the community was the 60-acre Spring Brook Nature Center, developed between 1966 and 1980. These leafy settings in central Itasca contrast with its fringes filled with industrial parks.

Elijah J. Smith, who founded Itasca, traveled to the Midwest in the early 1840s searching for a place to combine his two talents, farming and doctoring. He found rich soil and a tree-lined creek to start his farm. He learned that enough settlers had moved into the area to make his medical practice a success. Receiving title to 80 acres of land in 1843 and an additional 80 acres in 1845, Smith built a house and raised a barn to start a dairy business.

In 1846 a post office named Bremen was established. Later renamed Pierce, the town became known as Sagone in 1864. In 1873 the name changed again, first in error to Ithica and finally to Itasca.

The dairy business quickly replaced wheat farming, as a cheese factory was established as early as 1866. This business increased in 1873 when the Chicago & Pacific Railroad, later the Chicago, Milwaukee & St. Paul, established a line through Itasca. Smith donated land for the railroad's right-of-way and money to construct the station. Near the station he divided 80 acres of his land into lots.

In 1890 the village of Itasca incorporated. A decade later the population stood at 256. The community, which once consisted mainly of German speakers, evolved into one of predominately English-speaking people. More residents began commuting to Chicago and subdivisions replaced farms. Still cheese, butter, and milk remained a large part of the community's economy until the end of World War II. Since 1945 businesses such as a greenhouse, a lumber company, and a feed and coal store provided jobs when the dairy industry left the area.

In the 1960s construction moved from single-family residential to apartment complexes, industrial parks, HOTELS, and EXPRESSWAYS. In 1961 approximately four hundred acres located north of the railroad and on the western edge of the community were purchased by the Central Manufacturing District. The land was rezoned to a limited manufacturing use. In 1972 Ralston-Purina began development of the West O'HARE Industrial Park. ANNEXATION also gained Itasca hotels such as Nordic Hills.

While the center of Itasca remains quaint and old-fashioned with the rural look of yesteryear, the town's borders are dedicated to larger industrial and business complexes, including Hamilton Lakes, a 275-acre site, and the Spring Lake Business Park at Rohlwing and Irving Park Roads.

Marilyn Elizabeth Perry

See also: Agriculture; Built Environment of the Chicago Region; Land Use

Further reading: Fridlund, John, ed. *The History of Itasca: Centennial Edition.* 1990. • Greenblatt, Miriam. *The History of Itasca.* 1976. • Usher, Joyce M. "Itasca." In *DuPage Roots,* 1985.

Ivorians. While a small number of students came to Chicago in the 1970s and settled permanently as professionals, most Ivorians migrated to Chicago in the 1990s. The United States was not a popular destination for Ivorians before the 1980s, but economic and educational opportunities began to draw West Africans in that decade to New York and Washington DC. As those communities grew large in the 1990s, Ivorians began to migrate to Chicago, Atlanta, Boston, and other major cities in search of economic opportunities, particularly in hairbraiding and TAXI driving. Ivorians established a strong chain migration network, attracting friends and family to the city from New York and Côte d'Ivoire. In 2001, community estimates varied, ranging from 100 to 400 Ivorians in Chicago, most living on the North Side of the city in the ROGERS PARK area.

Chicago's Ivorian community is ethnically, culturally, and politically diverse. While this community lacks the ethnic tensions that exist at home, Ivorians in Chicago have organized along ethnic lines that correspond to regional differences in Côte d'Ivoire. Western Ivorians are the largest group in Chicago and in 1999 formed Organisation des Ressortissants de l'Ouest de la Côte d'Ivoire as a social and mutual aid organization. Northern Ivorians, who are more culturally similar to MALIANS than to people in the other regions of Côte d'Ivoire, are also well represented in Chicago and meet regularly. Eastern, southern, and central Ivorians constitute much smaller groups in Chicago and gather for social events and mutual assistance but are not organized as formally. The groups invite one another to parties, baptisms, and other events and also meet with other West Africans, including Malians, GUINEANS, and SENEGALESE. Ivorians in Chicago are also organized through political activity and discussion. The major political parties of Côte d'Ivoire, including the Ivorian Popular Front, Democratic Party of Côte d'Ivoire African Democratic Rally, and Rally of the Republicans, are represented locally and hold political meetings and fundraisers in Chicago.

Ivorians in Chicago have made several attempts to organize as a single community with moderate success. In the late 1980s, the earliest Ivorian migrants created the Association of Ivorians in Chicago as a social organization to bring all Ivorians together. The organization was initially successful and sponsored holiday celebrations and parties but dissipated in the early 1990s after suffering small misunderstandings and declining interest. More recent attempts have been made to organize the entire community for events like Independence Day (August 7).

Ivorians in Chicago are also leaders in creating a larger Ivorian diasporic identity. In 2000, they established IvoirEspoir (Hope of Ivory) as a nonprofit organization to raise money and awareness about HIV and AIDS in Côte d'Ivoire. Working closely with the Ivorian government, the organization raises money for AIDS education and treatment, including medical training, health CLINICS, and information dissemination. The organization has established additional chapters in Washington DC, and Atlanta and is rapidly expanding. It hopes to unite all Ivorians in the United States and raise global awareness about the AIDS crisis in Africa.

Tracy Steffes

See also: Beninese; Demography; Multicentered Chicago

IWW. *See* Industrial Workers of the World (IWW)

J

Jackson Park. Jackson Park, located south of 57th Street by Lake Michigan on Chicago's SOUTH SIDE, is the third largest of the city's more than five hundred parks and home to the famed MUSEUM OF SCIENCE AND INDUSTRY. Jackson Park was originally designed in the 1870s, but was little improved until 1890 when Frederick Law Olmsted laid out the WORLD'S COLUMBIAN EXPOSITION on the site.

Olmsted worked with Daniel Burnham to create the "White City," a fair laid out with white classical buildings surrounding reflecting pools, amid lagoons and a wooded island.

Today Jackson Park's facilities include an 18-hole GOLF course and golf driving range, SWIMMING beaches, new bathhouses, the Osaka Japanese Garden, and playing fields for activities as diverse as baseball, soccer, football, and lawn bowling. The "Golden Lady" (*Statue of the Republic*), a gilded scale replica of the huge sculpture that adorned the Court of Honor of the Columbian Exposition, graces this beautiful park.

David M. Solzman

See also: Hyde Park; Landscape Design

Further reading: Cromie, Robert. *A Short History of Chicago.* 1984. • Miller, Donald. *City of the Century: The Epic of Chicago and the Making of America.* 1996.

Jails and Prisons. Prior to the building of facilities specifically designed for detention and correctional confinement, trials and punishments were swift on the American frontier. Such methods as public flogging, the pillory, and short-term custody as well as the death penalty served as modes of censuring and punishing criminals in early Chicago. In 1831, revisions in the Illinois Criminal Code prohibited public whipping and the pillory, although flogging and pillorying continued inside Illinois prisons into the early twentieth century. In 1832, the newly chartered town of Chicago constructed an "estray pen" at the town square (Randolph and Clark) and a year later developed it into a log jail structure. COOK COUNTY and the town erected a courthouse in 1853, which included a basement jail, the jailer's dwelling rooms, the sheriff's office, and the city watch-house. This structure served the city until it was swept away by the Great Fire of 1871.

The House of Correction opened in 1871 on the city's far Southwest Side. This prison workhouse confined mainly individuals unable to pay fines: vagrants, drunks, petty thieves, pickpockets, counterfeiters, smugglers, and especially criminals preying on the growing commerce of Chicago's docks. Nearly all were poor; most had been imprisoned before. Moreover, it was common practice to imprison witnesses to crimes—often women and children—along with the accused against whom they were scheduled to testify.

During this period the POLICE stationhouse lockup—the "calaboose"—emerged as Chicago's standard form of custody for street criminals. Overused and filthy dens of despair, these "police prisons" finally gave way, by the late 1890s, to the improved construction and architectural design of the city's correctional

Exterior view of Bridewell Prison, West 26th Street and California Avenue, ca. 1903. Photographer: Unknown. Source: Chicago Historical Society.

facilities. A new addition to the County Jail in 1896 at Dearborn Avenue and Illinois Street included separate facilities for women and a section for juvenile offenders.

In the first quarter of the twentieth century, detention periods were becoming longer as a result of delays in the COURTS. The new County Jail, a Bastille-like structure at 26th Street and California, was termed obsolete on the day it opened in 1929 because it lacked adequate heating and had no separate facilities for female prisoners. Moreover, in 1928 all state executions were moved from the county jails to the state penitentiaries except in counties with populations over a million. The method of inflicting CAPITAL PUNISHMENT was likewise changed from hanging to the electric chair, leaving Cook County with the only county jail in the state eligible to maintain its own electric chair and carry out its own executions. The electrocution of James Dukes in 1962 was the last execution carried out at the Cook County Jail.

Subject to the politics of a one-term sheriff and an entrenched PATRONAGE system, the County Jail had to rely on a grossly untrained and underpaid jail guard corps. As a result, the wardens and supervisors yielded to the convenience of a "barn boss" system using particularly intimidating inmates for guard functions. This system inadvertently fostered the growth of GANG influence in the inmate population and jail operations. In 1967, a county civil service system was introduced to counter the political influence of patronage jobs and to better prepare officers to manage the jail. In 1974, the Illinois Department of Corrections opened the nation's first centralized training academy for correctional officers at SAINT XAVIER UNIVERSITY in MOUNT GREENWOOD.

The 1960s and 1970s were the years of the prisoner rights movement within the jails and prisons of America. Every aspect of correctional operations came under judicial scrutiny. The Cook County Jail was also racked by waves of disturbances, escapes, suicides, and murders of inmates. Three class-action lawsuits were filed alleging racial bias in inmate classification and housing and a lack of MENTAL HEALTH services. These lawsuits brought enormous changes in jail programs and staffing. A massive building program beginning in the 1970s yielded a new women's jail and the Cook County Juvenile Temporary Detention Center, which replaced the archaic Arthur J. AUDY HOME. A 1989 court mandate responding to overcrowding released 35,000 low-category inmates from the County Jail on individual-recognizance bonds. A new sentencing system of day-reporting and other community correctional alternatives to incarceration also reduced the prison population.

Now officially defined and readily recognized by the public and media as the Cook County Department of Corrections, it boasts "the largest (96 acres) single-site county predetention facility in the United States." It has 11 jail divisions, as well as a boot camp, an electric monitoring program for community correctional custody, a halfway house, and a substance-abuse program. It also contains the largest forensic residential psychiatric facility in Illinois and is developing gender-specific programs for female and male inmates.

Jess Maghan

See also: Almshouses; Homicide; Juvenile Courts; Juvenile Justice Reform

Further reading: Altgeld, John P. *Live Questions: Our Penal Machinery and Its Victims.* 1886. • Jacobs, James B. *Stateville: The Penitentiary in Mass Society.* 1977. • Mattick, Hans W., and Ronald P. Sweet. *Illinois Jails: Challenge and Opportunity for the 1970s.* 1969.

Jamaicans. The 1940s saw the first major influx of Jamaicans to Chicago. Like other West Indians, Jamaican men were recruited to work in war industries by the War Manpower Commission and the Farm Work Program, and eventually migrated to Chicago.

During the 1950s and 1960s, the number of Jamaicans seeking higher education in the United States increased, and schools like Chicago Technical College drew significant numbers to the city. Many worked part-time and attended school, often pursuing engineering degrees. Others came as trained professionals, especially in NURSING. Jamaicans also came as laborers to work in carpentry, DOMESTIC WORK, and various industries. Although many Jamaicans at first came individually and planned to stay only for a short time, many soon decided to settle permanently, and were joined by spouses and children. At the close of the twentieth century, community leaders estimated approximately 40,000 to 50,000 Jamaicans in Chicago.

Jamaicans apparently settled initially on the SOUTH SIDE. Because many found jobs such as HOUSEKEEPING on the North Side and in the northern suburbs, EVANSTON and ROGERS PARK also developed early and lasting colonies of Jamaicans. As the size of the Jamaican population in Chicago increased, especially through the 1970s and 1980s, Jamaicans spread out across the city and suburbs, with concentrations forming in areas like SKOKIE.

Jamaicans quickly organized strong community organizations. In 1944, they combined with other West Indian ethnic groups to found the AMERICAN WEST INDIAN ASSOCIATION to aid immigrants and provide a social and cultural organization. Under the umbrella of the AWIA, Chicago's Jamaicans hosted visiting dignitaries, raised relief funds to aid the victims of a 1951 hurricane in Jamaica, celebrated its island's independence from Britain in 1962, and helped to found the National Association of Jamaican and Supportive Organizations (NAJASO) in 1977. The next year, Chicago hosted the NAJASO National Conference.

After the breakup of the AWIA in the 1970s, the Jamaican American Association became the central organization for the Jamaican community. The Jamaican American Association has continued organizing community events (such as the annual *Carifete* on Midway Plaisance), sponsoring scholarships, and undertaking charity projects.

Religion and spirituality has played a significant role in the Jamaican community. On the South Side, many Jamaicans joined St. Edmunds Episcopal Church. In Evanston, Jamaicans in 1973 founded the New Testament Church of God, which had more than 300 members in the late 1990s. Rastafarians, practitioners of the religion founded in Jamaica and rooted in black nationalism, established their presence in Chicago in 1976 with the founding of the Development Unification of Brotherhood and Sisterhood.

Chicago's Jamaicans have retained their enthusiasm for cricket and SOCCER. They have participated in the organization of the United Cricket Conference, the West Indian Cricket Association, and a wide variety of cricket clubs, many of which have played in a WASHINGTON PARK summer league. The West Indian Jets Soccer Club, founded by Jamaican and other West Indians in 1970, represented Illinois in the 1977 USA Cup.

Jamaicans have maintained a strong relationship with their home island through support agencies and charity. Disaster relief has been a major focus dating back to the Chicago Committee on Jamaican Hurricane Relief in 1951. The Chicago Concerned Jamaicans, founded in 1988, has provided financial and material assistance to schools and libraries in Jamaica. The Jamaican Association of Health Care Professionals was founded in the late 1980s to provide assistance to clinics and hospitals in Jamaica. In 1994, a Permanent Committee for Disaster Preparedness was founded to help victims of floods and hurricanes.

RESTAURANTS, bakeries, and other small businesses have provided meeting places for the Jamaican community on the South Side and in Rogers Park and Evanston. In 1982, the Jamaican Consulate in Chicago began publishing a nationally circulated magazine, the *Jamaican American Caribbean Quarterly*, devoted to the affairs of Jamaicans in America. The consular office has also published a newsletter for the Chicago community, the *Jamaica Bridge*.

Robert Morrissey

See also: Demography; Multicentered Chicago

Jane. Jane, an underground abortion service in the years immediately preceding the Supreme Court's 1973 *Roe v. Wade* decision, is an example of radical FEMINIST initiative and alternative-institution building in the early years of the women's liberation movement. The project started as an abortion referral service in 1969 linked to a Chicago consciousness-raising group. Because abortions were illegal, Jane developed elaborate mechanisms to maintain secrecy and confidentiality while also providing follow-up support. To gain greater control over the process and ensure women's health and safety, they ultimately learned to administer the abortions themselves and provided more than 11,000 illegal abortions (with a safety record equal to that of the best HOSPITALS) until the Supreme Court decision made their service unnecessary.

Sara M. Evans

See also: Birthing Practices; Chicago Women's Liberation Union; Family Planning

Further reading: Kaplan, Laura. *The Story of Jane: The Legendary Underground Feminist Abortion Service.* 1995.

Japanese. Japanese Americans first settled in Chicago in the late 1890s, establishing small businesses such as RESTAURANTS and curio shops. While many Issei (first-generation) families arrived, increasingly stringent immigration restrictions after 1907 limited community growth. During the 1920s, about three hundred Japanese Americans lived in Chicago. Scattered across the city, this tiny community maintained contact through institutions like the Japanese Mutual Aid Society. A YMCA mission catered to Japanese students, although the organization closed during the 1930s. In addition, BUDDHIST and Christian churches and a Japanese school served the small population, which rose to about four hundred by 1941.

When WORLD WAR II broke out, hoodlums harassed a few Japanese-owned businesses, and the FBI rounded up and imprisoned community leaders. Still, the federal government chose not to intern Japanese Americans living outside the Pacific Coast area.

In 1942, federal authorities experimented with releasing a few Western Nisei (second-generation Japanese Americans) from internment camps to unrestricted areas in the East. The government deemed the climate in Chicago somewhat favorable and set up a field office there. Although the authorities and various private groups working with them initially envisioned placing Japanese Americans as DOMESTIC WORKERS, companies desperate for labor began to hire the arriving Nisei. Other interned Japanese Americans, most of whom had suffered frustrating economic discrimination in the West, flocked to Chicago.

Hard-working and usually well-educated, the Nisei resettlers experienced greater opportunities in wartime Chicago than they had ever known before, but also encountered significant discrimination. Japanese Americans discovered that many neighborhoods were closed to them and often settled in areas of racial transition between blacks and whites. Some HOSPITALS turned them away; most CEMETERIES refused them burial; and certain labor unions denied membership. Particular employers would not hire them at all, and others paid them less than white workers. At the same time, many managers favored them over AFRICAN AMERICAN employees.

The relative youth of the population (many Issei stayed in the camps throughout the war) also lent an element of instability to the resettler community. The Chicago Resettlers' Committee, which would later become the Japanese American Service Committee (JASC), formed to address this and comparable concerns.

By war's end, almost 20,000 Nisei and Issei had settled in Chicago, making it by far the most popular destination for resettlers. While thousands of Japanese Americans returned to the Pacific Coast after the war, the community in Chicago remained large into the 1960s. Institutions that had initially served the wartime resettlers endured, catering to the developing community. Discrimination lessened as well, with Japanese Americans joining whites in fleeing areas of racial transition during the 1950s and 1960s. While many Japanese Americans moved to the suburbs, they maintained their community connections through Chicago's Buddhist and Christian churches, the JASC, the Japanese American Citizens' League, and similar organizations.

In recent years, many of the aging Nisei have retired to the West Coast. But the Japanese American community in Chicago continues to support RELIGIOUS INSTITUTIONS, HOUSING FOR THE ELDERLY, and an annual Japanese festival on the North Side.

Charlotte Brooks

See also: Demography; Multicentered Chicago; Mutual Benefit Societies; Protestants

Jazz. Throughout the twentieth century, Chicago has played a leading role in the performance, recording, and artistic evolution of jazz. There are several reasons for Chicago's powerful musical influence. First, the city's industrial might attracted young workers from throughout the nation and the world during the first two-thirds of the century. Many of these younger people had discretionary income to spend on musical entertainment and arrived at the time of the GREAT MIGRATION of AFRICAN AMERICANS from the southern states. Their increased numbers created a new demand for cabarets, cafes, RESTAURANTS, DANCE HALLS, AMUSEMENT PARKS, and movie houses, particularly on the SOUTH SIDE, while also stimulating the market for musically accomplished entertainment there and in the city's "bright light" districts.

Ragtime pianists, important precursors of jazz, gravitated to the WORLD'S COLUMBIAN EXPOSITION in 1893, where they set in motion a grand procession of twentieth-century popular-music styles associated with Chicago. Whereas New York's Tin Pan Alley dominated the MUSIC PUBLISHING business, Chicago tended to attract performers rather than professional songwriters, and these musicians tended to excel at NIGHTCLUB work. As early as 1906, such influential performers as pianists Tony Jackson and Ferd La Menthe "Jelly Roll" Morton were experimenting with fresh improvisational possibilities that did much to transform ragtime into jazz. So too did Chicagoans listen to a series of cornetists/bandleaders, such as Freddie Keppard, Manuel Perez, and especially Joseph "King" Oliver. While most of the earliest Chicago pioneers were African Americans, a white group calling itself Stein's Dixie Jass Band performed at the Schiller Café in 1916. Several members of this BAND subsequently reorganized as the Original Dixieland Jazz Band, and in 1917 they played on the first jazz records ever made.

Chicago's magnetism proved especially powerful for musicians from New Orleans and the Mississippi Delta. Bountiful club work and, beginning in 1923, the possibility of making records, which did not exist in the Crescent City, proved irresistible. From 1917 to 1922, King Oliver's Creole Jazz Band, which performed at the Royal Gardens Café, later renamed the Lincoln Gardens Café, included such powerful instrumentalists as cornetist Louis Armstrong, clarinetist Johnny Dodds, and drummer Warren "Baby" Dodds. They traveled to the studio of Gennett Records in Richmond, Indiana, in order to record. New inexpensive and popular specialty labels such as Okeh, Paramount, and Vocalion responded to the swiftly growing markets for popular music by organizing active Midwestern field recording programs in Chicago. Between 1925 and 1928, Louis Armstrong with his Hot Five and his Hot Seven recorded some historic sides for Okeh in Chicago, as did Earl Hines, star pianist and bandleader at the Grand Terrace Café. Clarinetist Jimmy Noone cut influential records with his Apex Club Orchestra for the Vocalion label. These jazz and blues specialty labels issued what came to be called "race records" for the African American market, so that Chicago soon developed the reputation of being the nation's center of authentic BLUES and jazz recording. The Great Migration of southern musicians to Chicago continued, with the music of southern blacks captured on record during the 1930s, 1940s, and 1950s by such labels as Bluebird and CHESS.

The visceral excitement of the city's nightlife, when mixed with an increased awareness of the New Orleans jazz and VAUDEVILLE blues of Ma Rainey and Bessie Smith, led to the formation of many white jazz groups. A variety of recording groups formed around banjo player/tenor guitarist, raconteur, and bandleader Eddie Condon, cornetist Jimmy McPartland, clarinetist Frank Teschemacher, tenor saxophonist Bud Freeman, pianist Joe Sullivan, and drummer Dave Tough. This ensemble came to be known as the Chicagoans, and once the members moved to New York, their music was labeled Chicago Jazz by recording executives. Some of these jazz-crazed young musicians hailed from AUSTIN, and sometimes they referred to themselves as the AUSTIN HIGH GANG. Several young white Chicagoans hailed from center-city neighborhoods. Clarinetist and orchestra leader Benny Goodman went on to become the King of Swing in the 1930s and 1940s, most often with drummer Gene Krupa. Pianist Art Hodes built a long and successful career as a blues-influenced piano stylist, and cornetist Francis "Muggsy" Spanier made many important jazz records with his Ragtimers.

Most of the more ambitious members of the Roaring Twenties jazz scene in Chicago left for New York City late in the decade. The media and the music business increasingly centralized into national organizations run from New York, a trend that accelerated in the GREAT DEPRESSION. The Music Corporation of America, led by Chicagoan Jules Stein, was organized to book bands around the country on a national chain of dance halls. Radio stations, which BROADCAST live music in the 1920s, were nationalized into networks, while the record companies, led by Chicagoan Jack Kapp, reorganized in New York. Such influential musicians as Jimmy Noone, the Dodds brothers, Art Hodes, and Earl Hines continued to live and perform in Chicago, however, in part because racial bias closed the doors to most national media promotions.

The media, for example, transformed jazz into Big Band Swing beginning in the mid-1930s, but the blues was shaped as a more ethnic, specialty taste that was relatively less commercialized, less nationalized, and therefore more "authentic" in relation to Chicago's South Side. The Paramount, Bluebird, and CHESS labels recorded many of the leading blues singers in their Chicago studios. A Chicago school of immigrant blues pianists performed at South Side "rent parties" and led a national craze for boogie-woogie piano stylings during the Depression.

During World War II, a new and more urbanized blues style emerged in Chicago. The twenties sound of the solitary male vocalist singing in a southern, rural style while accompanying himself on the guitar melded with the jazz rhythm section, electrified instruments, and a more standardized pronunciation of the lyrics. As recorded in Chicago, this northern, urban blues style strongly influenced Berry Gordy, Jr., the first African American owner of a successful record company. Gordy created the Motown label in Detroit in 1959 and further mixed blues traditions with popular-song formulas to allow African American artists to cross over into the more lucrative popular-music markets.

The post–World War II years on Chicago's South Side brought a revolution in jazz. In the 1950s, avant-garde pianist/bandleader Sun Ra organized a jazz collective to promote performances and recordings of his Solar Arkestra. In 1961, a group of younger experimental musicians, aware of the decline of Chicago's jazz clubs and the history of racial exploitation in the music business and responding to a heightened interest in African-inspired cultural nationalism, further developed the idea of a musician-operated performance organization by forming what they called the Experimental Band. Reorganizing themselves into the ASSOCIATION FOR THE ADVANCEMENT OF CREATIVE MUSICIANS (AACM), such musicians as Anthony Braxton, Malachi Favors, Joseph Jarman, Roscoe Mitchell, Leroy Jenkins, Don Moye, and many others challenged the musical traditions and political parameters of jazz. The AACM grew from the musical traditions and deep political frustrations of Chicago's South Side. It advocated free, atonal music, arranged into multisectional units, and minimized the role of the individual soloist. The AACM's flagship ensemble, the Art Ensemble of Chicago, further defied the isolation of jazz from other art forms in its blends of experimental music with costumes, make-up, dance, pantomime, comedy, dialogue, and brief dramatic scenes.

At the dawn of the twenty-first century, Chicago presented a wide variety of jazz styles in clubs, concerts, and festivals, appealing to a broad spectrum of tourists and fans. With the help of recordings, many Americans still consider jazz in Chicago to be a vital expression of cultural diversity and downtown, cosmopolitan culture. Chicagoans have ample opportunities to experience jazz in clubs such as the Green Mill and through radio broadcasts, especially the nightly programming on public station WBEZ. The Chicago Jazz Festival on Labor Day weekend attracts tens of thousands of listeners each year to GRANT PARK. Chicago's musicians have made fundamental contributions to the musical, entertainment, and cultural dimensions of "America's original contribution to the musical arts."

William Howland Kenney

See also: Broadcasting; Chicago Sound; Civil Rights Movements; Douglas; Entertaining Chicagoans; Radio Orchestras; Record Publishing

Further reading: Kenney, William Howland. *Chicago Jazz: A Cultural History, 1904–1930*. 1993. • Radano,

Walter Dyett: Music Educator

Known as Captain Dyett for his service in the Illinois National Guard, Walter Henri Dyett fostered the growth of jazz and black musicians in Chicago. In 1922, putting aside medical school and violin, Dyett focused on teaching, arranging, and conducting orchestras. He led the Pickford Orchestra, Washington Park summer concerts, the DuSable-ites, the "Hi-Jinks," and many others. From 1931 to 1961, Dyett taught classical, military, and jazz music to more than 20,000 students at Wendell Phillips and DuSable High Schools. Jazz greats including Nat "King" Cole, Dorothy Donegan, Joseph Jarman, Dinah Washington, Johnny Griffin, and Mwata Bowden credit Dyett for their early musical training.

Kathleen Zygmun

Ronald M. *New Musical Figurations: Anthony Braxton's Cultural Critique*. 1993. • Travis, Dempsey. *An Autobiography of Black Jazz*. 1983.

Jazz Dance. "Jazz dance," an often contested term that generally refers to a fusion of European and African movement traditions performed to the rhythms of JAZZ music, has been a visible presence in Chicago since the early twentieth century—as both a social DANCE form and a theatrical art.

Jazz dance accompanied the northern migration of jazz music to Chicago in the period immediately following WORLD WAR I. As this new music thrived in the PROHIBITION era, jazz dancing turned up in cabarets, NIGHTCLUBS, and rent parties, especially on the city's SOUTH SIDE, and on VAUDEVILLE stages such as the Pekin, Regal, and Grand Theatres. During her company's Chicago engagements in the forties and fifties, Katherine Dunham further exposed audiences to popular jazz steps like the Charleston and the Black Bottom as part of her evening-length dance concerts.

By the 1960s, when jazz music had become less danceable, a new phase of jazz dancing, one which blended jazz-based vocabulary with BALLET and modern techniques, emerged on the Chicago scene. The founding of local DANCE COMPANIES like Gus Giordano Jazz Dance Chicago (1968), Joel Hall Dancers (1974), Joseph Holmes Dance Theatre (1974–1995), and HUBBARD STREET DANCE Chicago (1977) exemplified this trend. In the 1990s, the confluence of several events—the establishment of the Jazz Dance World Congress, held initially in Chicago, the relocation of the Jump Rhythm Jazz Project from New York to Chicago, and finally, the resurgence of swing dancing in local nightclubs—indicated Chicago's continuing role in the growth and development of jazz dance.

Anthea Kraut

See also: Entertaining Chicagoans; Modern and Postmodern Dance

Further reading: Ann Barzel Dance Collection. The Newberry Library, Chicago, IL. • Peterson, Bernard L., Jr. *The African American Theatre Directory, 1816–1960*. 1997. • Stearns, Marshall and Jean. *Jazz Dance: The Story of American Vernacular Dance*. 1968.

Jefferson Park, Community Area 11, 10 miles NW of the Loop. Jefferson Park continues to live up to its nickname, "Gateway to Chicago." Located at the northwest edge of the city, the community long has been an important TRANSPORTATION link and hub. Indian trails were already well traveled by traders and hunters when John Kinzie Clark built his cabin in the early 1830s. By 1836 a HOTEL had been erected, a SCHOOL DISTRICT established, and farmers, mostly ENGLISH, had settled. To get their produce to the Chicago markets they traveled on often mud-filled Indian trails. After 1849 farmers moved their goods more quickly on two plank roads, the North West Plank Road (later Milwaukee Avenue) and the Lower Road (Elston Avenue).

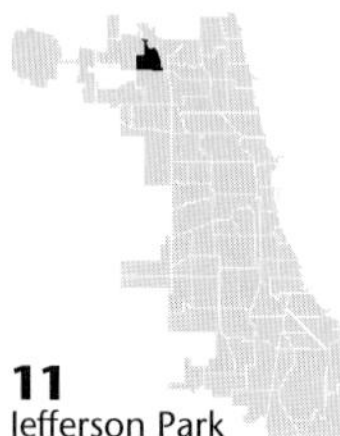

11
Jefferson Park

In 1850 the state formed JEFFERSON TOWNSHIP, named after President Thomas Jefferson, and in 1855 residents platted a village near Milwaukee Avenue and Higgins Road, naming it Jefferson. Farmers traveling to and from the city often stopped to water their horses, pick up supplies, or rest. In 1855 a resident recorded that the town consisted of approximately 50 buildings. When the Chicago, St. Paul & Fond du Lac RAILROAD (Chicago & North Western) laid tracks and built a depot near the town's center, population grew. The town of Jefferson was incorporated in 1872 and ANNEXED by Chicago in 1889. In 1884 an estimated 500 persons lived in Jefferson Township with most incoming residents POLISH and GERMAN immigrants. About this time the area became known as Jefferson Park.

By 1900 a web of STREET RAILWAY lines extended on Lawrence, Milwaukee, and Elston Avenues. With new means of transportation came an influx of laborers, artisans, and tradesmen. Immigrants of Polish, German, RUSSIAN, ITALIAN, CZECH, and SLOVAKIAN backgrounds brought ethnic diversity into the area. Growth mushroomed in the 1920s, bringing larger numbers of Germans, Poles, and Italians. By 1930 the population stood at 20,532. As the neighborhoods grew, Victorian graystones, A-frames, and BUNGALOWS predominated.

As plans for an EXPRESSWAY were implemented in the 1950s, some residents of Jefferson Park objected not only to the expressway, but also to a proposed tollbooth, until the 1956 Interstate Highway Act made tolls unnecessary. The Northwest Expressway (later the Kennedy Expressway) was completed in 1959, slicing diagonally through Jefferson Park and giving denizens an added means of transportation.

In 1970 the CHICAGO TRANSIT AUTHORITY (CTA) constructed a terminal in Jefferson Park that connected CTA and REGIONAL TRANSIT AUTHORITY bus routes, a Greyhound bus stop, a Chicago & North Western commuter railroad station, and an Elevated line. In the 1980s the Northwestern rapid transit line was extended to O'Hare Airport, running through Jefferson Park along a median strip of the Kennedy Expressway. But in spite of this access to transportation, relatively little industry developed in Jefferson Park. A complex of offices and small retailers located at the intersection of Higgins Road and Lawrence and Milwaukee Avenues, the original nucleus of the community, remained the center of activity.

In 1990 nearly half of the 23,649 population was of Polish descent. Many congregate at Copernicus Center, a Polish cultural and study organization, established in the former Gateway Theater. Asians and Hispanics also are a significant presence in the community. Although seniors constituted approximately 22 percent of the population in 1990, the end of the decade saw a trend toward younger residents. Transportation continued to attract newcomers: the METRA station served 10,000 commuters a day, and on weekdays 800 buses traveled Jefferson Park's main arteries.

Marilyn Elizabeth Perry

See also: Bungalow Belt; Metropolitan Growth

Further reading: Drury, John. "Old Chicago Neighborhoods: Jefferson Park." *Landlord's Guide* 38.3 (September 1947); and 41.8 (August 1950). • Karlen, Harvey M. *Chicago's Crabgrass Communities: The History of the Independent Suburbs and Their Post Offices That Became Part of Chicago*. 1992. • Posadas, Barbara M. "A Home in the Country: Suburbanization in Jefferson Township, 1870–1889." *Chicago History* 8.3 (Fall 1978): 134–149.

Jefferson Township. Between 1850 and 1889, the area west of Western Avenue between North Avenue and Devon functioned as Jefferson Township, an independent political unit separate from Chicago. In 1872 Norwood Park Township was created from the northwest corner of Jefferson. In 1889, Chicago ANNEXED the rest of the TOWNSHIP and it ceased to function as a separate political unit.

Ann Durkin Keating

See also: Avondale; Governing the Metropolis; Irving Park; Jefferson Park; Lincoln Square; Logan Square; Montclare; North Center; Norwood Park

Further reading: Keating, Ann Durkin. *Building Chicago: Suburban Developers and the Creation of a Divided Metropolis*. 1988.

Jewelers' Row. Jewelers' Row is centered at Madison and Wabash Streets in the LOOP. In 1912 the Mallers Building at 5 S. Wabash began to house jewelry manufacturers, wholesalers, and retailers. By WORLD WAR II, the most important Chicago firms, like Sherman Tucker and M. Y. Finkelman, had located there. Finkelman's son Marshall brought international fame to the Chicago jewelry trade in international gem markets and opened the Jewelers' Mall in the late 1980s at 21 N. Wabash. In the last two decades of the twentieth century, jewelers from Mexico, South America, and Southeast Asia brought new ethnic trends to Jewelers' Row. In 2002, plans to convert the 5 S. Wabash building into condominiums forced many jewelers to find new locations away from Jewelers' Row.

Eli Rubin

See also: Business of Chicago; Gentrification; Historic Preservation; Retail Geography

Further reading: "All That Glitters Is at 5 South." *Chicago Tribune*, October 16, 1995. • "Jewelers' Row."

Chicago Tribune, October 14, 1990. • "Mayor Leads Diamond Hunt." *Chicago Tribune*, October 30, 1985.

Jewish Community Centers. In the late nineteenth century, German JEWS established cultural, social, and recreational organizations, now known as community centers, to assimilate the Eastern European Jews who had followed them to America. They organized the MAXWELL STREET Settlement House in 1893 in the Jewish neighborhood on the NEAR WEST SIDE. In 1903 Orthodox and Reform rabbis supported the founding of the Chicago HEBREW INSTITUTE (CHI), whose extensive offerings celebrated Jewish culture while promoting AMERICANIZATION efforts. Its comprehensive sports program produced athletic champions who won attention and respect, helping to overcome the stereotype of Jews as cerebral but weak and cowardly. The Sinai Temple, with a new facility built in 1912, also won athletic prominence through its recreation center on the SOUTH SIDE. In 1921 the CHI changed its name to the Jewish People's Institute, and it followed the Jewish migration to the NORTH LAWNDALE district in 1926.

Gerald R. Gems

See also: Catholic Youth Organization; Religious Institutions; Social Services

Further reading: Cutler, Irving. "The Jews of Chicago: From Shtetl to Suburb." In *Ethnic Chicago*, ed. Peter d'A. Jones and Melvin G. Holli, 1981, 40–79. • Gems, Gerald R. "Sport and the Forging of a Jewish-American Culture: The Chicago Hebrew Institute." *American Jewish History* 83:1 (March 1995): 15–26. • Meites, Hyman L., ed. *History of the Jews of Chicago*. 1990 [1924, 1927].

Jews. Jews came to Chicago from virtually every country in Europe and the Middle East, but especially from Germany and Eastern Europe. Unlike most other immigrant groups, Jews left the Old Country with no thoughts of ever returning to lands where so many had experienced poverty, discrimination, and even sporadic massacres.

Jews began trickling into Chicago shortly after its incorporation in 1833. A century later Chicago's 270,000 Jews (about 9 percent of the city's population) were outnumbered only in New York and Warsaw. By the end of the twentieth century, approximately 270,000 Jews lived in the Chicago metropolitan area, but only about 30 percent of the entire Jewish population remained within city limits.

Chicago's first permanent Jewish settlers arrived in 1841 from Central Europe, largely from the GERMAN states. A few lived briefly in eastern cities before being attracted to the burgeoning city of Chicago. These early settlers included Henry Horner, whose grandson of the same name would become the first Jewish governor of Illinois. Many of these settlers started out as STREET PEDDLERS with packs on their backs and later opened small stores in the downtown area. From these humble beginnings they later established such companies as Florsheim, Spiegel, Alden's, Mandel Brothers, Albert Pick & Co., A. G. Becker, Brunswick, Inland Steel, Kuppenheimer, and Hart, Schaffner & Marx.

Chicago's first synagogue, Kehilath Anshe Mayriv (KAM), was founded at the corner of Lake and Wells in 1847 by a group of Jewish immigrants from the same general region of Germany. By 1852, about 20 POLISH Jews had become discontented enough to break off from KAM, and founded Chicago's second congregation, Kehilath B'nai Sholom, a more Orthodox congregation than the older KAM. In 1861, the second major secession from KAM occurred, and, led by Rabbi Bernhard Felsenthal, this splinter group formed the Sinai Reform Congregation, meeting in a church near the corner of Monroe and LaSalle Streets.

In 1859 the United Hebrew Relief Association (UHRA) was established by some 15 Jewish organizations, which included a number of B'nai B'rith lodges as well as several Jewish women's organizations. After the FIRE OF 1871, Jews moved out of the downtown area, mainly southward, settling eventually in the fashionable lakefront communities of KENWOOD, HYDE PARK, and SOUTH SHORE. Wherever they settled they established needed institutions, including MICHAEL REESE HOSPITAL, the Drexel Home (for aged Jews), and the social and civic Standard Club.

In the late 1870s Eastern European Jews, especially from RUSSIAN and Polish areas, started arriving in Chicago in large numbers. They came mainly from *shtetlach* (small rural villages or towns) and by 1930 they constituted over 80 percent of Chicago's Jewish population. They settled initially in one of the poorest parts of the city, the MAXWELL STREET area on the NEAR WESTSIDE. There they created a community with some resemblance to the Old World shtetl with its numerous Jewish institutions, including about 40 synagogues and a bazaar-like outdoor market that attracted customers from the entire Chicago area. They eked out a living as peddlers, petty merchants, artisans, and factory laborers, especially in the garment industry, where many men and women became ardent members, organizers, and leaders in a number of progressive unions.

The Eastern European Jews differed from the German Jews in their cultural background, language, dress, demeanor, and economic status and until mid-twentieth century the two maintained distinct neighborhoods and institutions. Friction also owed to differing religious practices, as the Orthodox newcomers encountered a German Jewish community increasingly oriented toward Reform JUDAISM.

A sense of kinship, however, along with the fear that poverty and the seemingly exotic culture of European Jews might provoke anti-Semitism, led Chicago's German Jews (like their counterparts in other American cities) to provide a foundation upon which the newcomers could build lives as Chicagoans. These institutions included educational (Jewish Training School, opened in 1890), medical (Chicago Maternity Center, 1895), and recreational (Chicago Hebrew Institute, 1903) facilities that offered practical resources while helping to speed up the AMERICANIZATION of the new immigrants. Julius Rosenwald, a prominent

Physical education class, Chicago Hebrew Institute, 1914. Photographer: Unknown. Source: Chicago Historical Society.

Band practice, Chicago Hebrew Institute, 1919. Photographer: Unknown. Source: Chicago Historical Society.

business executive and PHILANTHROPIST, was one of the chief organizers and financial contributors to these institutions.

Education and entrepreneurship provided many Jews with a route out of the Maxwell Street area by 1910. A small number joined the German Jews on the SOUTH SIDE; some moved into the north lakefront communities of LAKE VIEW, UPTOWN, and ROGERS PARK; more headed northwest into HUMBOLDT PARK, LOGAN SQUARE, and ALBANY PARK. The largest number moved west into the NORTH LAWNDALE area, which soon became the largest Jewish community in the history of Chicago, numerically and institutionally. By the 1930s, North Lawndale housed 60 synagogues (all but 2 Orthodox); a very active community center, the Jewish People's Institute; the Hebrew Theological College; the Douglas Library, where Golda Meir worked for a short while; and numerous ZIONIST, cultural, educational, fraternal, and SOCIAL SERVICE organizations and institutions.

After WORLD WAR II, increasing prosperity, along with government housing benefits to returning war veterans, allowed increasing numbers of Chicago Jews to fulfill their desire for single-family houses. Upwardly mobile Jews started moving out of their old communities into higher-status West Rogers Park (WEST RIDGE) on the far North Side. By the end of the twentieth century, West Rogers Park had emerged as the largest Jewish community in the city. More than 30,000 Jews were Orthodox and the rhythm of Orthodox life remained evident, from the daily synagogue prayer services to the numerous Orthodox institutions and the closing of Jewish stores on Devon Avenue for the Sabbath. Some of the recent 22,000 Russian Jewish immigrants also settled there. Other Jewish areas in the city included the APARTMENT and CONDOMINIUM complexes paralleling the northern lakeshore, and a small community in the Hyde Park area.

Many Jews joined the postwar migration to suburbia. Housing discrimination had limited suburbanization in early years, although in the early 1900s small numbers of Jews had moved into some of the suburbs that were open to them. The most concentrated movement of Jews into the suburbs followed World War II with the removal of restrictive housing covenants and increased affluence. Approximately 70 percent of the estimated 270,000 Jews in the Chicago metropolitan area in the 1990s lived in the suburbs, compared to just 5 percent in 1950. Most were concentrated in such northern suburbs as SKOKIE, LINCOLNWOOD, GLENCOE, HIGHLAND PARK, NORTHBROOK, and BUFFALO GROVE.

Although numerous Jewish institutions have been built in the suburbs, dispersal over wide areas has made it more difficult to supply certain services desired by Jews. These suburbanites are less dependent on totally Jewish institutions and services and there are no Jewish-oriented Maxwell, Roosevelt, Lawrence, or Devon commercial streets like the ones that once served their parents and grandparents so well in the dense Jewish neighborhoods.

While generally not facing the problems of poverty, prejudice, AMERICANIZATION, and German and Eastern European conflict that their immigrant ancestors experienced, the current Jewish population faces other problems involving Jewish identity, ethnic survival, policy toward Israel, and religious differences. Religious influence has declined through the years, but there remains a great diversity of religious feeling, ranging from the fervor of the Orthodox Hasidic to the humanistic Reform congregations. About 80 percent of affiliated Jews belong to Conservative or Reform movements, with the remainder belonging mainly to the once dominant Orthodox movement, which is concentrated in the city and the close-in suburbs.

Changing social and family values have accompanied a growing divorce rate, increasing assimilation, and a high rate of intermarriage. Chicago's Jewish community is now putting increasing emphasis on Jewish all-day elementary and high schools, of which there are about 30, Orthodox and non-Orthodox. The Jewish Federation of Metropolitan Chicago, a community umbrella organization funded by the contributions of almost 50,000 families annually, maintains or supports numerous educational, health, religious, cultural, and social welfare services that encompass many facets of Jewish life, both at home and abroad. It also maintains eight JEWISH COMMUNITY CENTERS serving the major Jewish areas. Hundreds of other fraternal, social, cultural, charitable, Zionist, and political organizations serve the community, including some with numerous local branches, such as B'nai B'rith, Hadassah, and Jewish War Veterans. The Spertus Institute of Jewish Studies houses an extensive library, mounts exhibitions of Jewish interest, and awards bachelor's and graduate degrees from its program in Jewish studies.

Irving Cutler

See also: Amalgamated Clothing Workers of America; Clothing and Garment Manufacturing; Demography; Israelis; Multicentered Chicago; Restrictive Covenants; Theater, Ethnic

Further reading: Cutler, Irving. *The Jews of Chicago: From Shtetl to Suburb.* 1996. • Meites, Hyman L., ed. *History of the Jews of Chicago.* 1990 [1924]. • *The Sentinel's History of Chicago Jewry, 1911–1986.* 1986.

Joffrey Ballet of Chicago. The Joffrey Ballet of Chicago, which gave its premiere performance in 1954 as the Robert Joffrey Ballet Concert, relocated to Chicago in 1995. An outgrowth of the American Ballet Center school cofounded by Robert Joffrey and Gerald Arpino in 1953, the company has gone through several name changes and two restructurings as well as a major change in its base of operations. The Joffrey was always a touring company that maintained its home base in New York City. By 1962, it had visited 400 cities in 48 states and was traveling with a small orchestra.

Arpino's ability to create fast-paced, exciting DANCES, while responding to socially relevant issues, brought the company to great heights of popularity. At the same time, Robert Joffrey was pursuing a course of recreating early-twentieth-century masterworks, including many works first performed by Serge Diaghilev's Ballets Russes. This dual approach to building repertory, along with its mission to tour widely, has given the Joffrey Ballet a reputation unlike any other DANCE COMPANY in the world. Its repertory contains works by 80 choreographers, and it practices a "no star–all star" policy within the ranks of its disciplined and dynamic dancers.

Diana Haskell

See also: Ballet; Modern and Postmodern Dance

Johnsburg, IL, McHenry County, 46 miles NW of the Loop. Immigrants from Germany's Eifel region named the area Johnsburg in the 1840s, after their church. In 1956, SUBDIVISION pressures led to the incorporation of a small area called Sunnyside. Fearing the growth of MCHENRY, neighboring residents supported ANNEXATION of their properties into Sunnyside in 1992 and successfully petitioned to rename the whole village Johnsburg. The 2000 population was 5,391.

Craig L. Pfannkuche

See also: Metropolitan Growth

Further reading: *McHenry County in the Twentieth Century, 1968–1994.* McHenry County Historical Society. 1994.

Joliet, IL, Will County, 35 miles SW of the Loop. In 1673 Louis Jolliet and Father Jacques Marquette paddled up the DES PLAINES RIVER and camped on a huge mound a few miles south of present-day Joliet.

In 1833 following the BLACK HAWK WAR, Charles Reed built a cabin along the west side of the Des Plaines River. Across the river in 1834 James B. Campbell, treasurer of the canal commissioners, laid out the village of "Juliet," a name local settlers had been using before his arrival.

The Juliet region was part of COOK COUNTY until 1836, when it became the county seat of the new WILL COUNTY. Just before the depression of 1837, Juliet incorporated as a village, but to cut tax expenses, Juliet residents soon petitioned the state to rescind that incorporation.

In 1845 local residents changed the community's name from "Juliet" to "Joliet." Joliet was reincorporated as a city in 1852. Soon, Joliet's TRANSPORTATION arteries included the Des Plaines River, a road that followed the Sauk Trail, the ILLINOIS & MICHIGAN CANAL (1848), and the Rock Island RAILROAD (1852), which ran through the business district. Today Joliet is served by several railroads, as well as Interstate Highways 55 and 80, which intersect a few miles southwest of the city.

The QUARRYING of limestone, with a bluish-white tinge, earned Joliet the nickname "City of Stone." The Illinois & Michigan Canal was both a consumer of stone in the building of locks, BRIDGES, and aqueducts and, after its completion in 1848, an artery for shipping stone to regional customers.

In 1858 the state of Illinois located a new penitentiary in Joliet, in part because of the abundance of stone for prison walls and cell houses. The Chicago FIRE OF 1871 spurred demand for stone and by 1890, Joliet quarries were shipping over three thousand railroad carloads of stone per month to Chicago and other cities.

The "City of Steel" emerged with the construction of the Joliet mill in 1869. The Bessemer converters installed at the mill in the 1870s were among the earliest used in the United States. While canal construction drew IRISH immigrants, the steel mill attracted thousands of southeastern Europeans. These new immigrants also found jobs on the railroad that serviced the steel mill, the Elgin, Joliet & Eastern Railway.

The city's large labor force and its steel mill attracted other industries. Wire mills, coke plants, stove companies, horseshoe factories, brick companies, foundries, boiler and tank companies, machine manufacturers, can companies, bridge builders, plating factories, steel car shops, and many others established businesses in the Joliet area. Other Joliet industries have ranged from the production of greeting cards and calendars to the bottling of Seven-Up, from the manufacture of Hart, Schaffner & Marx CLOTHING to the BREWING of beer. Pianos, windmills, wallpaper and barrels have been manufactured in Joliet, as have building materials, oil and CHEMICAL products, and Caterpillar scrapers. Joliet also became home of Joliet Junior College, the nation's oldest public community COLLEGE. Joliet's economy entered a period of decline in the late 1970s and by 1983 its unemployment rate stood at 26 percent.

During the 1990s, Joliet's economy rebounded. Millions of people visit Joliet's riverboat casinos and its new drag-racing and NASCAR tracks. The millions of dollars in new tax receipts have been used to revitalize the downtown City Center. Population leapt from 76,836 in 1990 to 106,221 in 2000.

Robert E. Sterling

See also: Economic Geography; Gambling; Iron and Steel; Jails and Prisons; Motor Sports

Further reading: Sterling, Robert E. *Joliet Transportation and Industry: A Pictorial History.* 1997. • Sterling, Robert E. *Joliet: A Pictorial History.* 1986. • Woodruff, George H. *The History of Will County, Illinois.* 1973 [1878].

Jordanians. Jordan's relationship with the area known as the "West Bank" makes defining Chicago Jordanians a complicated task. Wrested from the newly formed state of Israel by Jordan in the first Arab-Israeli War in 1948, the West Bank returned to Israel as an occupied territory in the Six Day War of 1967. Jordan, however, has continued to allow Palestinian REFUGEES and workers across its borders, granting them Jordanian passports. Most people migrating to Chicago with Jordanian passports in the second half of the twentieth century have actually been PALESTINIANS from the West Bank, generally identifying as Palestinians, not as native Jordanians.

The first community of Jordanians originally hailing from the current borders of Jordan began settling on Chicago's NEAR WEST and Southwest Sides in the late 1950s. Fleeing the hardships wrought by the first Arab-Israeli War, this fairly small group foreshadowed the community's labor practices for years to come. Some opened retail stores, often GROCERIES, while others earned degrees in business, medicine, and engineering. Many men returned to their families in Jordan after working or studying in Chicago for several years. While the vast majority of Jordanians are Sunni MUSLIM, most Jordanian migrants to Chicago, and to the United States generally, have been EASTERN ORTHODOX Christian.

By the mid-1960s greater numbers of Jordanians began arriving in Chicago, the result of more generous U.S. immigration laws coupled with the 1967 Arab-Israeli war. While most settled on the city's West and Southwest Sides, increasing numbers of the more affluent moved to nearby suburbs, especially OAK LAWN. Among these were some of the first congregants of St. George Antiochian Church, which has developed into one of the largest and most active Arab Christian institutions in the United States. By 1980, Chicago's Jordanian community had likely grown to several thousand people, their immigration accelerated by a Jordanian civil war (1970–71) and another Arab-Israeli war (1973).

Larger percentages of families, a growing number of them Muslim, marked the increased migration of Jordanians to Chicago beginning in the late 1980s. The overall growth and familial character of the new migrations has strained the community's informal social safety net, especially with the expanded immigration of Jordanians and Palestinians following the Persian Gulf War (1991). In the past, single male immigrants could be placed rather easily in a small Jordanian- or Palestinian-owned store. The large arrival of families has stretched the availability of jobs thin. While some Jordanians have arrived educated and entered the professions, many of the men have worked as TAXI drivers, in RESTAURANTS, or in automotive repair. Less-educated women have tended to work either at home or in DOMESTIC SERVICE.

In the late 1990s a study conducted by a consortium of area scholars and the Arab American Action Network estimated the population of Chicago Jordanians at near 30,000, approximately one-fifth of the area's Arab American population. While institutions like the Jordanian American Center and the Fuheis American Association have served the sociocultural needs of the Jordanian community specifically, Chicago Jordanians have tended to organize with the area's broader, and highly organized, Middle Eastern Arab community. They have especially associated with Palestinians, with whom they share a similar diasporic experience, and also LEBANESE and SYRIANS, with whom they share a common Arabic dialect and often political perspectives. Through organizations like the Arab American Action Network, the Arab American Business and Professional Association, the various Islamic Cultural Centers, and area churches and mosques, Chicago Jordanians have gathered with other Arabs to worship, celebrate holidays, network, and mobilize politically.

Stephen R. Porter

See also: Demography; Israelis; Multicentered Chicago

Journalism. From the expressly political NEWSPAPERS of the nineteenth and early twentieth centuries, to the birth and growth of radio and television journalism, through the advent of the alternative press and cable television, Chicago journalism has provided both the fertile ground for the growth of writers and the discourse from which enduring images of the city emerge.

The unprecedented growth of Chicago made its newspapers a vital part of creating a sense of the city for its inhabitants, most of them immigrants from Europe or other parts of the United States. Newspaper publishers such as Joseph Medill of the CHICAGO TRIBUNE, Wilbur F. Storey of the *Times,* and Melville E. Stone of the *Daily News* developed distinct approaches to journalism, methods that reflected competing ideas about the proper role of government and the very nature of the urban community of Chicago. While these and other mainstream daily newspapers have thrived or withered based on numerous factors, different journalistic approaches can be understood to represent different ideas about what most matters in the city, for the publisher and the audience. The diverse foreign-language press focuses on immigrant communities and issues of assimilation and acculturation. Local papers—in both neighborhoods and suburbs—deal with smaller-scale issues than those covered by the citywide papers. The North Side's alternative-press free weekly *Chicago Reader* presents extensive arts coverage as well as lengthy investigative reporting. *Streetwise*—sold by men and women struggling to emerge from homelessness—trains its editorial guns each week on issues of poverty, race, and social justice. *Crain's Chicago Business* and the *Chicago Daily Law Bulletin* attend to their specific beats, while various television, radio, Internet, and cable news outlets provide broader coverage. These varied points of view, taken together, create a sense of the entire city and demonstrate the diversity of Chicago journalism.

Many journalistshave created enduring literary and historical portraits of Chicago and its people. Late-nineteenth- and early-twentieth-century writers such as Finley Peter Dunne, George Ade, Eugene Field, Theodore Dreiser, Ben Hecht, Charles MacArthur, Carl Sandburg, and Ring Lardner all worked on various Chicago daily papers. Lardner helped to create the modern idiom and method of sportswriting, before moving on to write FICTION such as *You Know Me Al* (1916) and for the Broadway stage. Hecht and MacArthur helped to create some of the archetypical images of cutthroat—almost amoral—American journalism in their play *The Front Page* (1928). (The counter-image of the crusading reporter setting out to right injustices appeared in the 1948 film *Call Northside 777.* Based on a true story first reported by the *Chicago Times,* it features Jimmy Stewart as a reporter who helps to free a man who has spent 11 years in prison for a murder he did not commit.) These writers, like many others who read the papers but did not write for them, garnered the raw material for their fiction and POETRY from journalism reporting on Chicago's daily life, BUSINESS, games, crimes, and POLITICS.

Later, journalists like Lloyd Wendt and Herman Kogan, Robert Cromie, and others used their experience as print or BROADCAST reporters to write popular histories of Chicago. Mike Royko's *Boss* (1971), along with Len O'Connor's *Clout* (1975), are popular histories of midcentury Chicago and the internal machinations of the Cook County DEMOCRATIC PARTY.

The role of individual journalists, especially columnists like Royko and longtime television anchors and radio commentators, in the daily life of Chicagoans cannot be overestimated. The familiar faces, voices, and styles of these men and women function as part of the ongoing conversation about the city and its values. Writers give their opinions, and their readers and listeners weigh in, using the journalist's stance as a starting point for their own arguments in letters to the editor and among themselves. Radio interviews, especially those conducted by Studs Terkel on

Lloyd Lewis: A Chicago Journalist

Lloyd Downs Lewis was a journalist, historian, and major figure in a remarkable world of arts and letters that flourished in Chicago following World War I.

After 12 years as publicist for BALABAN AND KATZ, in 1930 he joined the *Chicago Daily News* as drama critic, becoming subsequently sports editor, managing editor, and a popular columnist. A gifted raconteur rich in friendships with the great literary, artistic, political, and sports figures of his time, Lewis was an ardent Chicagoan and Midwesterner with a voracious interest in the CIVIL WAR. His published work included *Chicago: The History of Its Reputation* (1929, with Henry Justin Smith); *Jayhawkers,* a three-act Broadway play coauthored with Sinclair Lewis (1935); and highly regarded biographies of Generals Sherman and Grant. His friends included Carl Sandburg, Sherwood Anderson, Frank Lloyd Wright, Sinclair Lewis, and Adlai Stevenson. Chicago's NEWBERRY LIBRARY was his second home; drawing on his personal contacts, he established the library's superb collection of modern (chiefly Midwestern) manuscripts.

Richard H. Brown

Although the familiar image of the Chicago journalist was established in Ben Hecht and Charles McArthur's famous play *Front Page*, journalists were involved in many tasks. In this 1961 photograph, seven *Tribune* journalists sit at the copy desk in the newspaper's press room. Photographer: Robert L. Foote. Source: Chicago Historical Society.

WFMT, brought both obscure-but-interesting and world-renowned figures into the workplaces, living rooms, and cars of any Chicagoan who cared to tune in. The growth of the talk radio format in the last decades of the twentieth century created a self-selected urban fireside conversation, where the fates of politicians and sports figures can be endlessly debated by journalists and their audience. In this way, journalism joins diverse Chicagoans in conversation and contention.

Furthermore, journalism creates a textual Chicago above and beyond the facts reported and the arguments begun or extended (arguments in Chicago never die, they just fade away). News about events in Chicago travel the wires and airwaves around the world and create an image of the city which enhances—and sometimes competes with—the reality of the place. The Great FIRE OF 1871 captured the world's imagination (and overshadowed the more deadly and destructive fire in Peshtigo, Wisconsin, on the same day), thanks in part to sensational newspaper coverage and photojournalism about both the fire itself and the city's seeming-miraculous rebirth. Al Capone came to be regarded as the quintessential American gangster and the worldwide symbol of Chicago because of both the spectacular violence of his criminal enterprise and the breathless journalism which detailed those crimes and his life (including stories reported by one victim of organized crime, corrupt *Tribune* reporter Jake Lingle, murdered in 1930). The AFRICAN AMERICAN–owned and –operated CHICAGO DEFENDER reported on Jim Crow and lynch law in the South in contrast to WORK available in Chicago; tens of thousands of African Americans came to Chicago in the GREAT MIGRATION, inspired by the *Defender*'s vivid depiction of Southern oppression and Northern opportunity. The 1968 Democratic National Convention was burned into the American consciousness through televised images of the "police riot" that greeted antiwar protesters and working journalists alike and the subsequent interview with a defiant Mayor Richard J. Daley by Walter Cronkite on CBS. Even sports journalism can help create the city's image, as Chicago BULLS star Michael Jordan, perhaps the greatest BASKETBALL player in history, finally supplanted Al Capone as the personification of Chicago across the world.

In whatever form—the daily or weekly paper, MAGAZINES, radio, broadcast or cable television—journalism functions as the daily conversation within which Chicagoans come to know their city and region at the same time as it presents an image of the city to America and the world.

Bill Savage

See also: Crime and Chicago's Image; Literary Careers; Literary Cultures; Literary Images of Chicago; Political Culture; Politics and the Press; Press: Suburban Press; Television, Talk; Trade Publications

Further reading: Farber, David. *Chicago '68*. 1988. • Grossman, James R. *Land of Hope: Chicago, Black Southerners, and the Great Migration*. 1989. • Nord, David Paul. "Read All about It." *Chicago History* (Summer 2002): 26–57.

Judaism. The handful of German JEWS who formed the first synagogue in the Midwest in 1847, Kehilath Anshe Mayriv (KAM), the Congregation of the Men of the West, were merchants and tradesmen. They were all nominally Orthodox Jews, though dissent and Reform raised their heads within the very first decade of the congregation's existence, producing defections in each direction, with the Reform impulse issuing in Sinai Congregation.

Jews from Eastern Europe arrived at the end of the century and the beginning of the 1900s. These Eastern European Jews were extremely varied: socialists, traditionalists, and everything in between. In the case of both GERMAN and East European immigrants, religious competence and commitment usually diminished after emigration from their homelands.

By the time of the WORLD'S COLUMBIAN EXPOSITION of 1893, Chicago's Jewish community was solid and growing. An ambitious presentation of Judaism to the general community at the great WORLD'S PARLIAMENT OF RELIGIONS was in many ways comparable to the introduction there of Eastern religions previously unknown to most Americans. A brilliant cadre of mostly liberal Jews presented their religious views as universal, rational, and, in many ways, as a quintessential American faith. Many, like Isaac Mayer Wise of Cincinnati (Chicago's rival for leadership in the Reform movement), believed that liberal Judaism was destined to win over the American people to its own ethical and noncreedal, intellectually defensible form of religion. The Columbian Exposition also witnessed the birth of Jewish FEMINISM in American Jewry, which issued in the creation of the National Council of Jewish Women, which, along with Hadassah, the Women's Zionist Organization, became the principal Jewish women's group in America.

MAXWELL STREET and subsequently NORTH LAWNDALE and DOUGLAS PARK became centers of Jewish institutional development. The famous Jewish People's Institute (1926–1955) was for decades a place where young people whose parents had come to Chicago in 1900 or slightly later could meet, court, and marry. The Hebrew Theological College (HTC), one of the great yeshivahs (rabbinical schools) of the nation, was located on the near West Side from 1922 to 1956, at which time it moved to SKOKIE, a near north suburb. The HTC instructed a generation of modern Orthodox rabbis (some of whom called themselves, only in Chicago, "traditional"), speaking English as well as Yiddish and observant of the Torah's

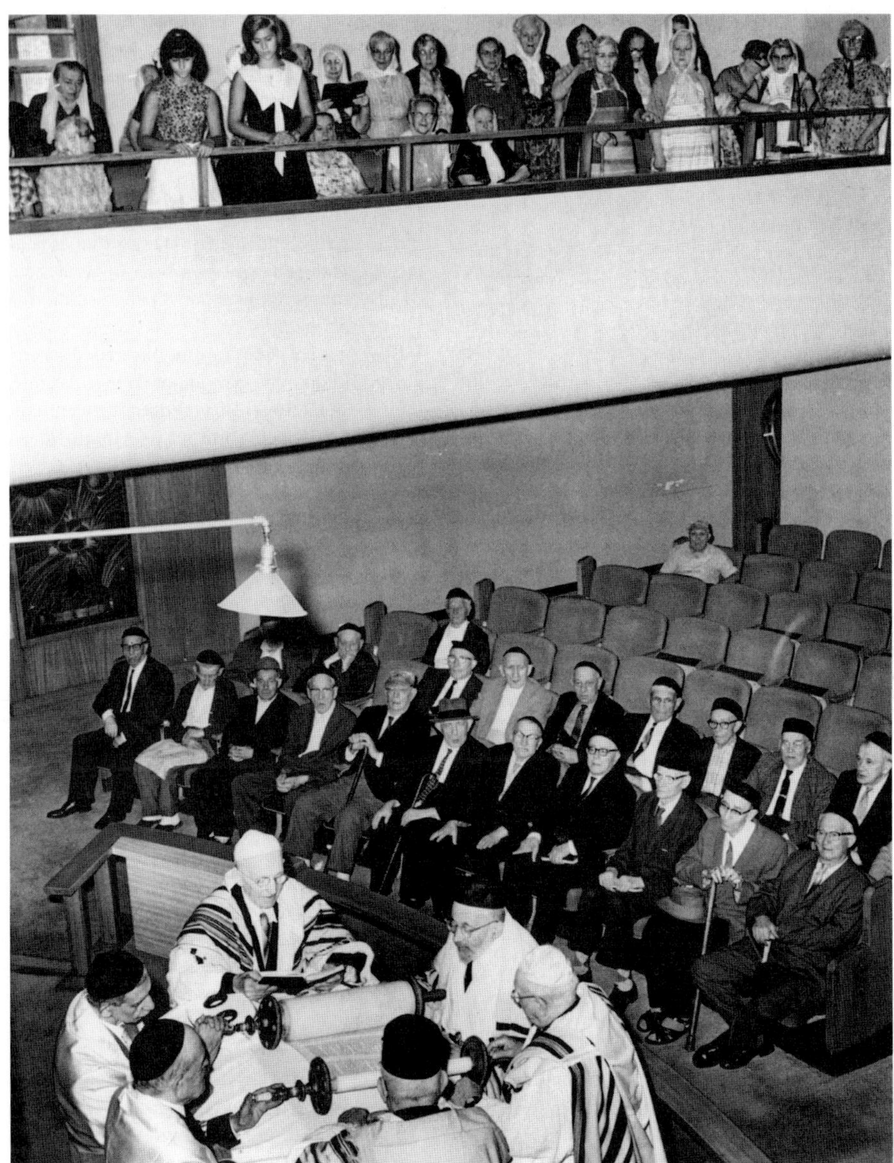

Religious services at Beth Moshav Z'keinim (Orthodox Jewish Home for the Aged), 1648 South Albany Avenue, 1964. The home opened in 1903 on the West Side after four years of organizational activity and fundraising, and was one of many Jewish institutions established in the Lawndale neighborhood during succeeding decades. While the home closed later in the century, successor institutions have been established by the Council for Jewish Elderly, founded in 1971. Photographer: Philip Weinstein. Source: Chicago Historical Society.

commandments; they filled the Midwest with an Americanized version of the ancestral faith. But it was left to less traditional communities to represent Judaism in the public imagination, largely through a remarkable group of Reform and Conservative rabbis in Chicago.

Rabbi Emil G. Hirsch, son of the former chief rabbi of Luxembourg, a famous European Jewish theologian, served Sinai Congregation from 1880 until his death in 1923. Far beyond the limits of Chicago, Hirsch spoke for a learned but profoundly radical version of classical Reform Judaism, and he taught at the new UNIVERSITY OF CHICAGO from its inception. Hirsch's lectures drew hundreds to his Sunday morning service, and his outreach to Jews of all streams and eddies in Chicago Judaism was unique.

Felix Levy, rabbi at Emanuel Congregation from 1908 until 1955, was partially responsible for transforming the Reform Judaism of Hirsch and his school into a more traditional version of peoplehood and faith. His advocacy of ZIONISM, of Hebrew, and a return to Halakah (legal Jewish norms of behavior) was the first clear statement of a Judaism in America that could respond to the demands of tradition as well as to the pragmatism and rationality of the American mind. Solomon Goldman, a Conservative rabbi at Anshe Emet Congregation from 1929 until his death in 1953, was a prolific author of original essays and interpretations of Jewish philosophy as well as president of the Zionist Organization of America. Saul Silber, rabbi of Anshe Sholom Congregation until his death in 1946, was president of the Hebrew Theological College, where he distinguished himself as the chief of a broad group of Orthodox scholars and teachers. Silber led religious Zionists to an important new role in Chicago's community affairs. Jacob Weinstein, rabbi of KAM from 1939 until 1967, was a leading spokesman for Judaism's mission of social action in American society. A fervent opponent of racism, he helped integrate HYDE PARK as a paradigm of solidarity and cooperation. He nudged the labor movement in the United States and in Israel toward egalitarian and humanitarian goals. Weinstein's disciples included Justice Arthur Goldberg and Judge Abner Mikva, as well as a host of younger rabbis and lay leaders in the Chicago and national communities.

Laymen have also been prominent in the task of Jewish continuity and renewal. B'nai B'rith was led by Chicagoans from the early days of Adolph Kraus until the present era of Philip Klutznick. PHILANTHROPISTS like Julius Rosenwald and Max Adler built museums that still recall their generosity.

Suburbanization and dispersion posed major challenges to Jewish institutional life and practice in the second half of the twentieth century. Formerly limited largely to several Chicago inner-city neighborhoods, Jews moved into the North Shore and northwestern suburbs in increasing numbers, depleting and sometimes abandoning older centers of Jewish population and creativity.

The new suburbs yielded new problems, including busy commuters, huge new congregations and schools, a vacuum of leadership, and conflicting religious goals. All of these, as well as the vicissitudes of the American economy and demanding overseas issues like the fate of Israel and Soviet Jews, transformed the nature of Chicago Jewry. Assimilation and intermarriage reached record proportions. Jewish education was at best haphazard, improvised, and poorly organized. Central institutions like the Jewish Federation of Greater Chicago grew in funds raised and in tasks undertaken but suffered a growing dispersion and sometimes even defection.

Jewish suburbia has yet to meet the challenges that the older population centers met. Will the varied, far-flung new Judaisms be loyal, creative, thoughtful, and compassionate, or will cultures be less nourishing to Jewish community and values? As a new century begins, indeed a new millennium, some Jews will continue to trust in the providence of God, though uncertain of their coreligionists' ability or willingness to cooperate in ultimately bringing the messianic age to America.

Arnold Jacob Wolf

See also: Americanization; Hebrew Institute, Chicago; Religious Geography; Religious Institutions; Roman Catholics

Further reading: Berkow, Ira. *Maxwell Street.* 1977. • Cutler, Irving. *The Jews of Chicago.* 1996. • Sklare, Marshall, and Benjamin Ringer. *Jewish Identity on the Suburban Frontier.* 1967.

Jungle, The. *The Jungle,* America's most influential proletarian novel, emerged from a seven-week investigation of Chicago's slaughterhouses. Researching the book in 1904, Upton Sinclair interviewed fellow SOCIALISTS, SETTLEMENT HOUSE officials, health inspectors, and the workers themselves, who smuggled him into MEATPACKING plants so he could view conditions firsthand. Within a year of its publication in book form *The Jungle* had sold more than 100,000 copies, and its revelations about contamination in the packing plants speeded passage of the 1906 Pure Food and Drug Act and Meat Inspection Act.

Dedicated to "the Workingmen of America," *The Jungle* tells the story of a LITHUANIAN immigrant family whose dream of success turns to a nightmare on the "killing floors" of the Chicago packinghouses. Jurgis Rudkus and his bride Ona are crushed by a series of blows that suggest parallels between the treatment of the livestock and the workers employed to process them. After the death of his wife and son, Jurgis quits the slaughterhouse and works at a variety of jobs, from strikebreaker to thief, discovering firsthand how democratic ideals have been betrayed by a citywide system of graft and corruption.

After Jurgis has lost everything—his family, his health, his hope—he discovers and converts to socialism. Many readers have found this resolution contrived, but it is integral to Sinclair's larger purpose: working-class liberation. His publisher's marketing campaign, however, emphasized the novel's alarms over the safety of the nation's meat supply while ignoring its critique of industrial capitalism. Sinclair himself recognized this fact, famously lamenting that he had aimed at the public's heart but hit it in its stomach.

The novel's unstable mixture of documentary naturalism and political polemic continues to trouble even those readers sympathetic to its Socialist politics. By rendering his characters as helpless victims, Sinclair denies them agency, and thereby distorts the rich histories of those who actually lived in and shaped the community known to its residents as the "BACK OF THE YARDS."

James Diedrick

See also: Americanization; Bridgeport; Chicago Studied: Social Scientists and Their City; Fiction; Literary Images of Chicago; Occupational Safety and Health; Packinghouse Unions; South Side

Further reading: Barrett, James R. *Work and Community in the Jungle: Chicago's Packinghouse Workers, 1894–1922.* 1987. • Rideout, Walter B. *The Radical Novel in the United States, 1900–1954.* 1956. • Sinclair, Upton. *The Jungle.* 1906.

Junior Colleges. *See* Colleges, Junior and Community

Junior Leagues. The Junior League of Chicago (JLC) was founded by Lucy McCormick Blair in 1911, inspired by a New York organization of the same name. Its purpose was to acquaint young society women with Chicago's industrial and social problems and train them as effective volunteers. The group's first project was to organize a suite of resting rooms where LOOP waitresses, who worked 10 nonconsecutive hours per day, could bathe, read, sew, or sleep between shifts.

Over the years and despite initial parental concerns about late hours and exposure to germs, the JLC created a large variety of programs to benefit immigrants, working mothers, sick and crippled children, battered wives, the military, seniors, crime victims, broken families, and drug abusers. Funds were often donated outright to benevolent institutions. The organization has also advanced the cultural climate of Chicago, providing music and art scholarships, initiating the ART INSTITUTE's Junior Museum and Docent Program, and creating the Express-Ways CHILDREN'S MUSEUM (renamed the Chicago Children's Museum).

At the opening of the twenty-first century, the JLC remained focused on developing the potential of women as trained volunteers, overseeing a multimillion-dollar budget and 2,100 members. Two other Junior Leagues in the metropolitan area (Evanston–North Shore and DuKane) operate independently.

Celia Hilliard

See also: Clubs: Women's Clubs; Gold Coast; Philanthropy

Further reading: Junior League of Chicago Archives. Chicago, IL.

Justice, IL, Cook County, 14 miles SW of the Loop. Justice grew along the route of Archer Avenue, which was a former Indian trail and one of the oldest roads in Cook County. Bordered on the northwest by the ILLINOIS & MICHIGAN CANAL, the community is divided into east and west portions by the Tri-State TOLLWAY. Two large CEMETERIES on the east side of Justice, as well as several smaller ones on the west side, further define the community.

In 1835 the I&M Canal commissioners began selling land in this area in order to help finance the construction of the canal. The earliest settlers were IRISH canal workers and GERMAN immigrants. Stagecoaches traveling along Archer Avenue linked the area with Chicago. When the I&M Canal opened in 1848, canal barges carried passengers and freight eastward to Chicago and westward to the Illinois River. By the 1850s, the Justice area was crisscrossed by Archer Avenue, La Grange Road, and the canal, as well as a RAILROAD running along the south side of the canal.

Settlement continued slowly in this area of farmlands. The population was supplemented by the arrival of German farmers after the CIVIL WAR.

By 1890 a small community stretched several blocks along the north side of Archer Avenue. Late-nineteenth-century and early-twentieth-century maps label this area as Mount Forest or Seafield.

In 1894 Bethania CEMETERY was established on the northeast side of the settled area. The presence of this cemetery and Resurrection Cemetery in 1904 stimulated economic growth. Picnic groves and taverns opened to cater to cemetery visitors from Chicago. In 1901, streetcars began running from Chicago to Joliet along Archer Avenue. Weekends and holidays brought crowds from Chicago to visit the picnic groves, taverns, and cemeteries. Three monument companies supplied headstones.

In 1911, the residents voted to incorporate as a village. (The source of the name Justice is unclear.) The original boundaries of the village zigzagged around Archer Avenue. Workers constructing the Calumet Sag Channel occupied an area along the eastern edge of the incorporated area, and in 1914, Justice deannexed this part of the village.

DUTCH truck farmers moved to the Justice area in the early decades of the twentieth century, and the village grew slowly. Its position at the intersection of Archer Avenue and La Grange Road made it a natural choice for the path of the Tri-State Tollway in 1958. This highway cut through the heart of the small village and divided the community into three areas. "Old Justice" lies north of Archer Avenue, and the TOLLROAD divides the southern part of Justice into east and west sections. The village of 12,193 people (2000) is governed by a mayor and six trustees.

Betsy Gurlacz

See also: Street Railways; Streets and Highways

Further reading: Untitled manuscript on Justice history. Justice Public Library, Justice, IL.

Juvenile Courts. Juvenile courts revolutionized the treatment of dependent, neglected, and delinquent CHILDREN. The world's first juvenile court, located in COOK COUNTY, opened in July 1899, and served as the model for this new social welfare approach that emphasized individualized treatment of cases instead of rigid adherence to due process, and probation over incarceration. The juvenile court also substituted the ideal of rehabilitation for retribution.

Located across the street from HULL HOUSE, Chicago's juvenile court symbolized the optimism of its famous neighbors and supporters, especially Jane Addams and Julia Lathrop. Within a generation, juvenile courts based on the Chicago model had been established in all the states except Maine and Wyoming, and in more than 20 foreign countries. By the end of the twentieth century, however, the initial faith in juvenile courts to reform wayward children had faded. Across the nation, including in Illinois, juvenile courts became increasingly indistinguishable from criminal courts.

David S. Tanenhaus

See also: Audy Home; Court System; Erring Women's Refuge; Juvenile Protective Association; Mothers' Pensions; Playground Movement

Further reading: Gittens, Joan. *Poor Relations: The Children of the State in Illinois, 1818–1990.* 1994. • Platt, Anthony. *The Child Savers: The Invention of Delinquency.* 2d ed. 1977. • Tanenhaus, David S. *Juvenile Justice in the Making.* 2004.

Juvenile Justice Reform. Chicago's juvenile justice system serves three distinct categories of children: delinquent, neglected, and abused. In the nineteenth century, children lived alongside adults in Illinois' poorhouses, asylums, and JAILS. Between 1855 and the Great FIRE OF 1871, convicted boys were sent to the Chicago Reform School. After the fire destroyed the building, they went to the State Reform School at Pontiac. In 1899 a coalition of "child-saving" reformers won a 30-year campaign for a separate juvenile COURT SYSTEM.

The Cook County Juvenile Court was the nation's first separate court for children. Under the principle of *parens patriae,* the state as parent, children's trials were informal hearings without legal counsel. In addition to the usual run of adult crimes, children could be charged with offenses such as truancy, incorrigibility, and sexual delinquency. But the creation of a distinct process for minors presented only a limited victory for the reformers. The court relied heavily upon institutionalization rather than the family preservation initially envisioned by reformers. On the court's twenty-fifth anniversary reformers lamented that it had become bureaucratic, unresponsive, and overburdened. A 1935 Illinois Supreme Court decision restricted its power to those cases that the state's attorney chose not to prosecute in adult court. A 1963 citizens committee report criticized the juvenile court for having limited and contradictory jurisdiction, overworked judges, and overburdened and underqualified staff, consisting predominantly of patronage appointees. In 1965 the state legislature overhauled the Illinois Juvenile Court Act, giving significant legal protections to minors, including the provision of a public defender. The 1967 U.S. Supreme Court *Gault* decision further extended the rights of accused juveniles to due process. During the next decade, however, public opinion demanded harsher treatment. A 1982 revision to the Illinois Habitual Juvenile Offender Act decreed that any juvenile aged 15 or older charged with murder, armed robbery, or sexual assault face prosecution in adult criminal court and, if convicted, commitment to the Illinois Department of Corrections.

While the scope of juvenile delinquency laws has been increasingly limited over the last three decades, the scope of child protection laws has greatly expanded. The 1975 Illinois Abused and Neglected Child Reporting Act gave the Illinois Department of Children and Family Services (DCFS) great latitude in interpreting the "child's best interest." The number of abused and neglected minors entering the court system has skyrocketed, with more and more entering DCFS custody for protection from neglect. Reformers argued that children removed to state care received minimal levels of treatment and often languished for years in "temporary" foster placements. Lawsuits filed in 1986 against the Cook County Guardian and in 1991 against DCFS resulted in sweeping changes in personnel and policies.

As the twentieth century drew to a close, Cook County Juvenile Court consisted of a huge complex on the city's Near West Side. In 1997 between 1,500 and 2,000 cases were heard every day, representing 25,000 active delinquency and 50,000 active abuse and neglect cases. The Arthur J. AUDY HOME was the largest juvenile jail in the world, housing 750 youths a day. Minority youths (95 percent) and males (90 percent) were disproportionately represented. Only 6 percent of delinquency cases involved serious violent offenders. Two-thirds of the court's caseload consisted of abuse and neglect cases, which reformers linked to increased rates of poverty, decline in high-wage jobs, and drastic cutbacks in welfare and SOCIAL SERVICES for families and children since the 1980s.

L. Mara Dodge

See also: Children and the Law; Children, Dependent; Juvenile Protective Association

Further reading: Ayers, William. *A Kind and Just Parent: The Children of Juvenile Court.* 1997. • Gittens, Joan. *Poor Relations: The Children of the State in Illinois, 1818–1990.* 1994. • Platt, Anthony M. *The Child-Savers: The Invention of Delinquency.* 2d ed. 1977.

Juvenile Protective Association. An offshoot of the campaign that established America's first JUVENILE COURT in Chicago, this women-led reform organization emerged in 1909 to stem the tide of 10,000 young offenders who passed annually through the city's court system. Headquartered at HULL HOUSE, the organization launched high-profile investigations of the dance halls and cheap theaters where working-class youths nightly congregated and, according to JPA literature, took their first innocent steps toward careers of immorality and crime. JPA president Louise de Koven Bowen persuaded municipal judges to create specialized courts for delinquent husbands and young male offenders, and JPA investigators filed thousands of criminal complaints during the 1910s against parents for contributing to the dependency or delinquency of children. A testament to the authority of middle-class women in Progressive-era moral reform—and a paragon of the era's intense interest in the "root causes" of crime—the JPA saw its political capital plummet during PROHIBITION and never regained its central place in criminal justice reform. By the twenties, the leading edge of child protection had shifted from the criminal courts to welfare agencies, and the JPA moved with it. Now located on the North Side (but still on Halsted Street), the JPA continues to serve as a vital center of SOCIAL SERVICE and advocacy on behalf of child and family welfare in Chicago.

Michael Willrich

See also: Children and the Law; Children, Dependent; Juvenile Justice Reform; Legal Aid

Further reading: Addams, Jane. *The Spirit of Youth and the City Streets.* 1909. • Bowen, Louise de Koven. *Safeguards for City Youth: At Work and at Play.* 1914. • Willrich, Michael. *City of Courts: Socializing Justice in Progressive Era Chicago.* 2003.

Kane County. Flowing south near the eastern boundary of KANE COUNTY, the FOX RIVER is the critical environmental factor in understanding the county's history. The river flows fairly swiftly through a narrow valley, and once provided power for early sawmills and gristmills at CARPENTERSVILLE, ELGIN, GENEVA, and AURORA. The river valley and the wide prairie beyond the river's west bank awaited primarily Yankee- and New York–born settlers who edged out of Chicago after 1832. Easy fording sites concentrated road traffic from Chicago to the northwest (U.S. 20), west (Illinois Route 38), and southwest (Ogden Road, U.S. 34).

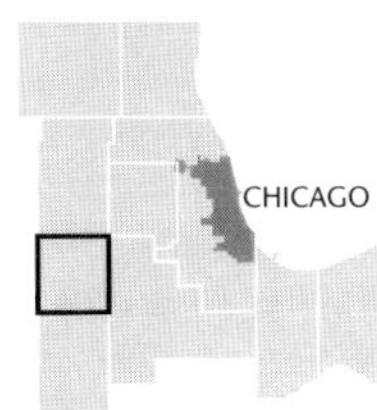

While much of the land between the DES PLAINES RIVER and the Fox River remained

part of COOK COUNTY after 1832, the 5,000 settlers along the Fox River Valley and scattered across the prairie to the western boundary of present-day DeKalb County found themselves within Kane County when it was created on January 16, 1836. (In 1837 DeKalb County separated from Kane County.) Kane County's name honored Elias Kent Kane, convention delegate at Kaskaskia in 1818, and U.S. Senator from Illinois until his death in 1835.

In 1836, three commissioners were chosen to govern the new county, with Geneva as the permanent county seat. As the county grew it built a succession of courthouses. The third, a limestone building designed by Chicago architect John M. Van Osdel, served the county from 1857 until 1890, when it was damaged in a fire.

Both the wealth of far-off Galena and developing AGRICULTURAL riches in the Fox River Valley spurred William Butler Ogden to drive his Galena & Chicago Union Railroad westward from Chicago. In 1849 the RAILROAD linked Elgin to Chicago. In 1853 the Galena Railroad crossed the Fox River at Geneva and pushed through Blackberry (now Elburn) toward Iowa.

At the same time, the Aurora Branch Railroad, precursor of the Chicago, Burlington, & Quincy Railroad, connected Aurora to Chicago via BATAVIA and Turner Junction (now WEST CHICAGO). The siting of locomotive building and repair shops at Aurora aided development of that city as an industrial center.

In 1850, the county was divided into fifteen 36-square-mile townships. Until the 1960s, TOWNSHIP government supervised much of the necessary road maintenance, area development, and social services. With growth sweeping the county in recent decades, many road services and much development planning and oversight have come into the hands of county officials. Township officials still handle immediate social assistance needs.

Early Kane County farmers produced milk and butter for Chicago's growing population. In 1865, the county became a dairy center to the world when Gail Borden chose Elgin as the site of his company that condensed milk for unrefrigerated shipment in cans.

After the CIVIL WAR, entrepreneurs embarked on a second wave of railroad building from Chicago through Kane County. The Chicago, Burlington, & Quincy sent a line toward Minneapolis from Aurora across the south end of the county in 1870 while the Milwaukee Road entered Elgin in 1873, building through Hampshire in 1875. The crossing of the Fox River south of Elgin by the ILLINOIS CENTRAL RAILROAD on its way to Galena and the Chicago Great Western Railway, crossing at ST. CHARLES in 1887, guaranteed Kane county farmers cheap and easy access to Chicago's markets.

Between 1860 and 1900, the county's population grew from 30,062 to 78,792, with the growth concentrated along the river. The population reached 125,327 by 1930, and continued to grow slightly even during the GREAT DEPRESSION. After WORLD WAR II, led by the construction of the massive Meadowdale housing project east of Carpentersville, the county's population increased to 208,246 in 1960, and continued to spiral upward to over 400,000 by the late 1990s.

Although the closing of Aurora's steel industries and locomotive shops and the withdrawal of the Elgin National Watch factory from Elgin in the mid-1960s hurt the county, the siting of the FERMI NATIONAL ACCELERATOR LABORATORY east of BATAVIA in 1968 brought an economic boost. By the mid-1990s gambling boats on the Fox River at Elgin and Aurora brought additional revenue to those communities.

Kane County's farm population remained stable from the 1960s to the late 1990s with about 80 percent of the county's 522 square miles dedicated to agriculture. Yet, with Interstate 88 reaching west from Aurora, Interstate 90 reaching northwest from Elgin, and COMMUTER rail expansion to GILBERTS, ELBURN, and MONTGOMERY contemplated, much more Kane County farmland may soon be overrun by the same sprawl of housing and business development that has flooded the space between the DES PLAINES and Fox Rivers.

Craig L. Pfannkuche

See also: Economic Geography; Streets and Highways; Suburbs and Cities as Dual Metropolis

Further reading: Duke, Kirsten. *Kane County Data Book.* 1993. • Joslyn, R. Waite, and Frank Joslyn. *History of Kane County, Illinois.* 1908.

Kelly-Nash Machine. The Kelly-Nash Machine dominated Chicago GOVERNMENT and the local DEMOCRATIC PARTY from 1933 to 1947.

Following the fatal shooting of MAYOR Anton Cermak in February 1933, longtime Cermak ally and Cook County party chairman Patrick A. Nash orchestrated the city council's appointment of Edward J. Kelly, chief engineer of the Sanitary District, to complete the mayor's term. Consolidating and refining Cermak's organization, these men shared political power in Chicago until Nash's death in 1943. Nash viewed POLITICS as a business where rewards equaled performance. He remained in the background praising and punishing machine members while tightening party control over the city.

Unlike Nash, Kelly was a gregarious mingler. A loyal New Dealer, Kelly produced huge majorities for Franklin D. Roosevelt and in return controlled NEW DEAL social and welfare programs in the city.

Kelly's terms as mayor were bathed in controversy. GAMBLING and organized crime ran rampant with little mayoral concern. But it was Kelly's progressive views on race, especially relating to housing, that led party leaders to consider him a liability. The very machine that he and Nash had nurtured forced Kelly's retirement from politics in 1947.

Paul Green

See also: Chicago Housing Authority; Machine Politics; Political Culture

Further reading: Biles, Roger. *Big City Boss in Depression and War: Mayor Edward J. Kelly of Chicago.* 1985.

Kendall College. In 1934, at the behest of the Scandinavian Conference of the Methodist Church, two SEMINARIES—one SWEDISH, the other DANISH-NORWEGIAN—came together to form Evanston Collegiate Institute, a junior college designed for students who sought a work-study program that would allow them to begin college debt-free. Many of those students found employment at the Washington National Insurance Company of EVANSTON, which also provided the school with substantial support. In 1950, the school was renamed in honor of the insurance company's founders, Curtis P. Kendall and his family. Kendall College became an accredited four-year institution in 1979. In 1985, a School of Culinary Arts and Hotel Restaurant Management opened at the college, along with seven specialized kitchens and an instructional restaurant called the Dining Room. The cooking and management program gained quick renown and received accreditation from the American Culinary Federation in 1988.

Sarah Fenton

See also: Colleges, Junior and Community; Schooling for Work

Kenilworth, IL, Cook County, 15 miles N of the Loop. In 1889 Joseph Sears planned a North Shore village in the image of the bucolic English countryside, which contrasted with his urban mansion on PRAIRIE AVENUE. He purchased 223 acres of woodland, pasture, and WETLANDS located between WILMETTE and WINNETKA, one of the last undeveloped tracts of farmland lying along Lake Michigan just north of Chicago. Much of the land was covered with native oak, hickory, and butternut TREES and overgrown with wild blackberry bushes. Its woodlands attracted serious botany students from NORTHWESTERN UNIVERSITY and its grassy pasture provided the neighborhood milk cows with daily forage. A settler's cabin from the 1830s still stood near

the lakeshore, though any Native American presence had long since vanished.

The Kenilworth Company's plan limited the number of building lots in the new village and used RESTRICTIVE COVENANTS to sell land to whites only. In 1896 Kenilworth incorporated and ordinances were adopted that required minimum-sized lots of 100 by 175 feet. The village name was taken from a town in the midlands of England. In 1899 the local women's CLUB selected, and the village adopted, street names such as Abbotsford and Essex, taken from Sir Walter Scott's novel *Kenilworth.* In 1920, when the nearby North Shore GOLF course went out of business, village residents bought the 40 acres west of the RAILROAD to ensure compatible development. No additional expansion of village boundaries was possible.

The Kenilworth Company built municipal features that made the village especially attractive to potential homeowners and protected the existing trees. Though in the 1960s Kenilworth lost many elms to disease, other mature specimen trees remain outstanding LANDSCAPE features. Commercial development was limited and today is found only along Green Bay Road, which parallels the railroad.

In 2000, Kenilworth's population was 2,494, small in comparison to its neighbors and relatively unchanged over time. For most of the twentieth century, houses there were among the most expensive along the North Shore. Residents traveled outside the village for employment. Kenilworth's good location and physical comforts attracted prominent residents, including utility magnate Samuel Insull in the 1920s and U.S. Senator Charles Percy in the 1960s and 1970s. Kenilworth remains a largely white community, although high income is the prerequisite, not race.

The village contains houses designed by a number of esteemed architects. Kenilworth has the largest collection of buildings by George W. Maher, a contemporary of Frank Lloyd Wright. Maher lived in Kenilworth and saw nearly 40 of his designs constructed between 1893 and 1926. He also fashioned the limestone pillars that mark the Sheridan Road entrances to the village and the town's central fountain. Consistent with the overall English theme of the village, Maher's buildings are strongly influenced by the English architects of the Arts and Crafts movement. Other designs reference the Prairie School. Maher's work plus Kenilworth's distinctive stone commuter train station built in 1890, its numerous Tudor revival residences, and the Old English–style street lamps continue to evoke the pastoral image of an earlier time and vision of community.

Jan Olive Nash

See also: Architecture: The Prairie School; Inverness; Lincolnshire; Suburbs and Cities as Dual Metropolis

Further reading: Ebner, Michael H. *Creating Chicago's North Shore: A Suburban History.* 1988. • Kenilworth Historical Society. *George Washington Maher in Kenilworth.* 1993. • Kilner, Colleen Browne. *Joseph Sears and His Kenilworth.* 1969.

Kensington. Born as a railroad town named Calumet Junction, Kensington grew up where the ILLINOIS CENTRAL and Michigan Central RAILROADS connected in 1852. The town grew slowly until, by 1880, 400 GERMAN, IRISH, Scandinavian, and YANKEE residents lived there, servicing the railroads and the population of farmers in the vicinity. Despite the presence of churches, stores, and schools, Kensington became notorious for its SALOONS, leading the DUTCH in neighboring ROSELAND to nickname it "Bumtown."

When George M. Pullman announced in 1880 that his model town would be built just north of Kensington, the small settlement boomed. BOARDINGHOUSES, taverns, and small stores opened to serve the construction crews and visitors to the site who, initially, took the train to Kensington and walked to PULLMAN. This close relationship between the two communities remained strong. Pullman workers lived in Kensington; Kensington businessmen lived in Pullman. Pullman workers relaxed in Kensington taverns and billiard halls; Kensington saloonkeepers delivered beer in Pullman. Kensington even figured prominently in the PULLMAN STRIKE. Its Eiche TURNVEREIN served as strike headquarters and its largest store, Secord and Hopkins, owned by Chicago MAYOR John P. Hopkins, offered credit and support to strikers and their families.

Changes in Pullman hiring policies and the opening of Illinois Terra Cotta brought ITALIANS to Kensington, which gradually became a center of SOUTH SIDE Italian life. Employment bureaus, travel agencies, and GROCERY STORES reflected the regional diversity within the Italian community. Nowhere was that diversity more apparent than in the three altars in San Antonio de Padua ROMAN CATHOLIC Church. The first altar, like the church itself, was named for the patron saint selected by the Venetians; the second was named for San Alessandro for the Calabrese; and the third named for the Virgin of the Rosary for the Sicilians.

When UNIVERSITY OF CHICAGO sociologists divided the city into community areas, they split Kensington among WEST PULLMAN, Roseland, and RIVERDALE. Roseland's Michigan Avenue business district grew south into Kensington's. Its Italian and POLISH populations linked it socially to Pullman's ethnic communities. By the 1960s, Kensington's unique identity was sustained primarily by the taverns that still lined its main streets, the Kensington police station, and St. Anthony's.

As industries began to close in the 1960s and 1970s, Kensington's population also began to change. MEXICANS and AFRICAN AMERICANS returned for the first time since the 1920s and, by the 1980s, African Americans came to dominate the community. The 5th District police station moved away, as did many of the stores along Michigan Avenue and 115th Street. The Salem Baptist Church located in the former St. Salomea building. In 1998, the last remnant of Kensington's nineteenth-century identity gave way as well. Led by members of Salem Baptist Church, precincts in what had once been Kensington voted themselves dry. As Chicago papers heralded what they called the Roselanders' victory, few appreciated that the residents of Kensington had finally achieved what the Roselanders had been hoping for for over a century. "Bumtown" was no more.

Janice L. Reiff

See also: Contested Spaces; Local Option; Prohibition and Temperance

Further reading: Andreas, A. T. *History of Cook County, Illinois.* 1884. • Greater Calumet Community Collection. Special Collections, Chicago Public Library, Chicago IL. • Vecoli, Rudolph J. "Chicago's Italians prior to World War I: A Study of Their Social and Economic Adjustment." Ph.D. diss., University of Wisconsin. 1963.

Kenwood, Community Area 39, 5 miles SE of the Loop. Kenwood, much like its bucolic counterparts to the north of the city, was settled in the 1850s by individuals seeking respite from the increasing congestion of Chicago. The first of these residents was Dr. John A. Kennicott, who built his home near the ILLINOIS CENTRAL RAILROAD tracks at 48th Street. He named the home Kenwood after his ancestral land in Scotland, and when the Illinois Central built a small depot near 47th Street, they named the station Kenwood as well. Shortly afterwards, the name Kenwood came to be applied to the area of land between 43rd Street and 51st Street, and from the lake west to Cottage Grove Avenue.

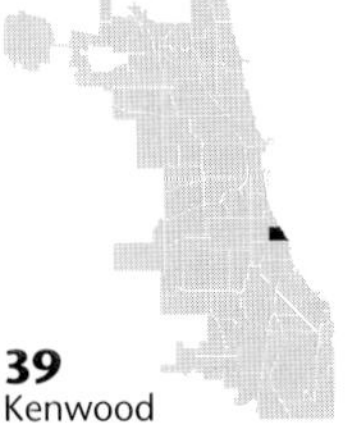

By the early 1860s, Kenwood was fast becoming a fashionable place for many of Chicago's most prominent residents. Enticed by the promise of increased TRANSPORTATION improvements (most notably the Illinois Central and, in the 1870s, horse railway lines), residents of note included Lyman Trumbull, the United States Senator; Norman Judd, President Lincoln's ambassador to Prussia; and William Rand, of the Rand McNally map corporation. In 1874, one publication dealing with Chicago suburbs stated that "Kenwood is the LAKE FOREST of the south, without the exclusiveness of its northern rival."

Kenwood continued to prosper through the 1880s and 1890s, and several new concentrations of large single-family homes began to emerge along Drexel Boulevard and between

45th and 50th Streets from Drexel Boulevard to Blackstone Avenue. The area had little retail development during this period, and most of it was concentrated along 47th Street. The area had few APARTMENT buildings, and wealthy residents continued to commission large homes in a variety of ARCHITECTURAL idioms, including the Prairie and Queen Anne styles. These residents included Martin Ryerson, the lumber merchant; Gustavus Swift, the meatpacker; and Julius Rosenwald, the chief executive of Sears, Roebuck & Co.

While Kenwood residents had a variety of transportation options for decades, the "L" finally reached the community in 1907, and the terminus of the Kenwood branch was built out to 42nd Place and the lake in 1910. This new RAPID TRANSIT facility attracted LOOP office workers to the northern part of Kenwood, and rooming houses and KITCHENETTE apartments proliferated. Numerous walk-up apartment buildings were constructed west of the Illinois Central tracks in the 1910s, and the population of the area increased to 21,000 by 1920. East of the railroad tracks some vacant land remained, but the late 1920s saw the addition of two impressive art deco elevator apartment buildings along with the increased popularity of the Chicago Beach HOTEL at Hyde Park Boulevard and Lake Michigan.

By the early 1930s there were signs of deterioration within the community, as the population of the area continued to grow significantly and was accommodated by the conversion of older homes into rooming houses and the subdividing of existing apartment units. As transient residents began to populate the northern half of Kenwood north of 47th Street, homeowners in the southern half began to gradually move elsewhere. This transformation accelerated from 1940 to 1960, as population increased 41 percent without new construction of residences. Conventional wisdom readily pointed to the influx of AFRICAN AMERICANS moving out of the BLACK BELT as the cause of community deterioration and blight in the area.

The late 1940s saw the creation of the HYDE PARK–Kenwood Community Conference, a group committed to maintaining a stable and integrated neighborhood in Kenwood. While much of the group's efforts were focused on the more pressing problems in Hyde Park, Kenwood benefited from the URBAN RENEWAL funds that became available in the late 1950s as well, and there were several housing projects developed as a result of their efforts in the community. Kenwood experienced a renaissance in the late 1970s, as several segments of the neighborhood were designated as historic districts by the city and new residential construction began to replace vacant lots. By the late 1990s, families were moving back into the area, and an educational partnership between the Chicago Board of Education and the UNIVERSITY OF CHICAGO resulted in the formation of a charter school.

Max Grinnell

See also: Contested Spaces; South Side; Universities and their Cities

Further reading: Abrahamson, Julia. *A Neighborhood Finds Itself.* 1959. • Hyde Park Historical Society. *Some Residential Structures of Historical and Architectural Significance in Hyde Park and Kenwood.* 1978. • *Kenwood District.* Commission on Chicago Historical and Architectural Landmarks. 1979.

Kenyans. The first Kenyan migration to Chicago might have occurred as early as the 1940s, when Kenyan scholars and students traveled under British passports to the United States. After Kenyan independence in 1963, small numbers of Kenyan students began arriving in Chicago, and many settled permanently because of the greater economic opportunities here. Kenyan student migration continued to grow through the 1980s and 1990s and was supplemented by the migration of political dissidents, professionals, and family members who were attracted to Chicago's growing Kenyan community. In addition, a sizable group of second-generation Kenyan Americans resided in Chicago by the end of the century. In 2001, community estimates counted 5,000 Kenyans in Illinois, the majority residing in metropolitan Chicago.

In the early 1990s, Kenyan students and expatriates in Chicago created the Organization of East Africans (OEA) to address an array of issues facing immigrants, including employment opportunities, adjustment to life in Chicago, and emergencies like death and illness. Comprising UGANDANS, TANZANIANS, and Kenyans, the OEA sponsored a variety of fundraising and social events. It pursued group health INSURANCE policies and investment opportunities and hosted community activities. Two of the largest annual events included Madaraka Day (June 1), which commemorates the beginning of self-government in Kenya, and Jamhuri Day (December 12), which marks the British withdrawal from Kenya and its official independence. While the OEA was a major force in the Kenyan community in the mid 1990s, activities declined steadily in subsequent years as it suffered financial difficulties and leadership problems. By 2000 the OEA was no longer fully operational but continued to conduct small and intermittent get-togethers at members' homes.

Although the OEA declined as an organizational force, the Kenyan community has continued to grow, with several new organizations emerging. Between 1998 and 2002, the Chicago Association for Kenyan Professionals (CAKP) and United Kenyans of Chicago (UKC) were founded. Both organizations serve the Kenyan nonimmigrant student population and a growing professional community. In addition, CAKP and UKC address issues that concern the community, including immigration, affordable housing, community involvement, job opportunities, and professional development. In 2001, Ushirika, which means "fellowship" in Swahili, was founded by a small group of Kenyan students from Chicago's MOODY BIBLE INSTITUTE. The group organizes monthly meetings dedicated to devotional and social activities. Since 2000, TopDonn Entertainment, a Kenyan-run entertainment business, has been hosting sizable monthly social events and activities for its largely African student membership. The Association of Kenyan Runners Abroad is another new organization designed to offer support and protection to Kenyan athletes in Chicago. Kenyan marathon runners are world renowned and have been extremely successful in the LaSalle Bank CHICAGO MARATHON.

Symon Ogeto
Tracy Steffes

See also: Americanization; Demography; Multicentered Chicago

Kildeer, IL, Lake County, 30 miles NW of the Loop. The first government land survey in 1837 indicates a cabin built by Hermann H. Pahlman near what is now Long Grove Road in Kildeer. The area consisted of rich, rolling, heavily forested land, with streams and small lakes. GERMAN farmers bought land from the U.S. government for $1.25 per acre. Ela Township was organized in 1849, named after an early landowner, George Ela. In 1852 a post office called Ela was installed in Quentin's general store, which was located in a trading center at the intersection of Rand and Quentin Roads.

Paved highways made commuting easier and brought weekend visitors and vacationers to surrounding lakes in the early 1900s. In 1958 Brickman Builders announced that they intended to build 16,000 single-family houses, 6,000 apartment units, a high school, four junior high schools, 29 elementary schools, a shopping mall, and an industrial park for a projected population of 60,000.

Local residents fought this development by incorporating as the village of Kildeer. To preserve their environment, a one-acre minimum on residential lots was established by the village government, along with narrow country-style roads, and severely restricted commercial development. In 2000 Kildeer's population was 3,460.

Clayton W. Brown

See also: Built Environment of the Chicago Region; Government, Suburban; Lake County, IL; Zoning

Further reading: Brown, Clayton W. *A Little Bit of History.* 1997.

Kindergarten Movement. In the United States, kindergartens originated in the 1850s, with the arrival of a small coterie of GERMAN émigrés devoted to the educational ideas of Friedrich Froebel, German creator of the kindergarten. Chicago was an early center of innovations linking the kindergarten to public schools, charity and SETTLEMENT work, and John Dewey's PROGRESSIVE EDUCATION reforms at the UNIVERSITY OF CHICAGO.

The Chicago founder was Alice Putnam, who began the first kindergarten study club in 1874. She became director of the Chicago Froebel Association Training School in 1880, which trained eight hundred kindergarten teachers over the next 30 years, and led the way in establishing free kindergartens for children of the poor.

Charity kindergartens in Chicago as elsewhere were linked to the settlement movement. Putnam's Chicago Froebel Association kindergarten classes constituted the first organized undertaking at HULL HOUSE. The kindergarten was viewed as an opening to the community, and Froebel's progressive principles of developing the whole child appealed to the values of the settlement workers.

Following the national trend, in 1892 the Chicago Board of Education voted to incorporate 10 privately sponsored kindergartens that had been operating in the public schools. The following year the kindergarten movement was recognized at the WORLD'S COLUMBIAN EXPOSITION with demonstration kindergartens in the Children's Building. Chicago emerged as the center of professionalization of the field when John Dewey began his progressive kindergarten experiment at the University of Chicago. In 1897, Dewey called a conference of Chicago kindergarten professionals from the settlements, the public schools, and Chicago Normal School, which effectively marked the transfer of kindergarten education into a legitimized field of university research and training.

Roberta Wollons

See also: Playgrounds and Small Parks; School Districts; Schools and Education

Further reading: Brosterman, Norman. *Inventing Kindergarten.* 1997. • Ross, Elizabeth Dale. *The Kindergarten Crusade: The Establishment of Preschool Education in the United States.* 1976. • Shapiro, Michael Steven. *Child's Garden: The Kindergarten Movement from Froebel to Dewey.* 1983.

Kitchenettes. The "kitchenette" initially described a newly constructed small APARTMENT in Chicago, first appearing around 1916 in UPTOWN, at a time when apartment construction in the city was increasing dramatically. It featured "PULLMAN kitchens" and "Murphy in-a-door beds" to conserve space, and connoted efficiency and modernity.

By the 1920s, and especially during the GREAT DEPRESSION, WORLD WAR II, and early postwar era, the term came to be associated with conversions by white and AFRICAN AMERICAN landlords and their agents of existing housing into smaller units, usually, although not exclusively, in the BLACK BELT and other areas occupied by African Americans. Single-family houses and houses meant for two and three families were converted to more intensive use. Brick buildings with medium and large apartments rented on a monthly basis were divided into one-room units, using beaver-board partitions. The resulting units were often rented out by the week as furnished rooms, although the amount of furniture offered was marginal. Entire families occupied single rooms, sharing with other residents an inadequate number of bathrooms and kitchens, exceeding the plumbing capacity, and leading to a serious deterioration in sanitary conditions. During the 1940s, more than 80,000 conversions of this type had occurred in Chicago, leading to a 52 percent increase in units lacking private bath facilities.

Kitchenettes of varying quality were rented by all races, including white World War II veterans and young families on the NEAR NORTH SIDE and elsewhere. But their rapid increase and clustering in the BLACK BELT made them more prominent in housing of African Americans. A federal study in the 1930s found that conditions in kitchenettes occupied by blacks in one SOUTH SIDE area were much worse than those occupied by whites. They had less space, sunlight, and amenities.

Poet Gwendolyn Brooks eloquently evoked the ambiance of these buildings in "kitchenette building," published in her first, award-winning collection, *A Street in Bronzeville* (1945).

Wendy Plotkin

See also: Boardinghouses; Housing Types; Land Use; Real Estate; Residential Hotels

Further reading: Drake, St. Clair, and Horace R. Cayton. *Black Metropolis: A Study of Negro Life in a Northern City.* 1945. • Hirsch, Arnold R. *Making the Second Ghetto: Race and Housing in Chicago, 1940–1960.* 1983. • Johnson, Charles. *Negro Housing: Report of the Committee on Negro Housing.* 1932.

Gwendolyn Brooks: kitchenette building

kitchenette building

We are things of dry hours and the involuntary
plan,
Grayed in, and gray. "Dream" makes a giddy
sound, not strong
Like "rent," "feeding a wife," "satisfying a man."
But could a dream send up through onion fumes
Its white and violet, fight with fried potatoes
And yesterday's garbage ripening in the hall,
Flutter, or sing an aria down these rooms
Even if we were willing to let it in,
Had time to warm it, keep it very clean,
Anticipate a message, let it begin?
We wonder. But not well! not for a minute!
Since Number Five is out of the bathroom now,
We think of lukewarm water, hope to get in it.

Brooks, Gwendolyn. "kitchenette building." In *A Street in Bronzeville*, 1945.

Knights of Labor. Founded in Philadelphia in 1869, the Knights of Labor spread to Chicago after the 1877 RAILROAD STRIKES. Initially viewed as an educational and political body by the local trade unionists who founded it, the Knights initiated some of the earliest labor organizing in the city's packinghouses, tanneries, garment sweatshops, and coal, lumber, and rail yards, and more generally among the IRISH. Under the motto "An Injury to One Is the Concern of All," the Knights sought to enroll all segments of the emerging industrial working class, including recent immigrants, AFRICAN AMERICANS, and women. The Knights did this by supplementing trade assemblies with "mixed" bodies, which could be formed on the basis of industry, sex, ethnicity, geography, or politics. With the advent of the movement for the EIGHT-HOUR day in 1886, the Chicago Knights mushroomed to approximately 27,000 members from only 1,900 the previous year by championing new methods of struggle, principally the boycott and sympathy STRIKE.

Local workers began to lose faith in the effectiveness of the Knights of Labor after a smashing defeat of its PACKINGHOUSE assemblies in fall 1886. The aftermath of the HAYMARKET Affair earlier that year and the ensuing government repression also stymied industrial organizing. To counter local government's antilabor bias, Chicago's labor activists looked toward electoral POLITICS, and in 1887, under the leadership of the Knights, the United Labor Party won 31 percent of Chicago's mayoral vote, the highest percentage achieved by any labor party in the city's history. But political mobilization did not translate into a flourishing union movement. Of the 116 new assemblies established in 1886, 61 percent had

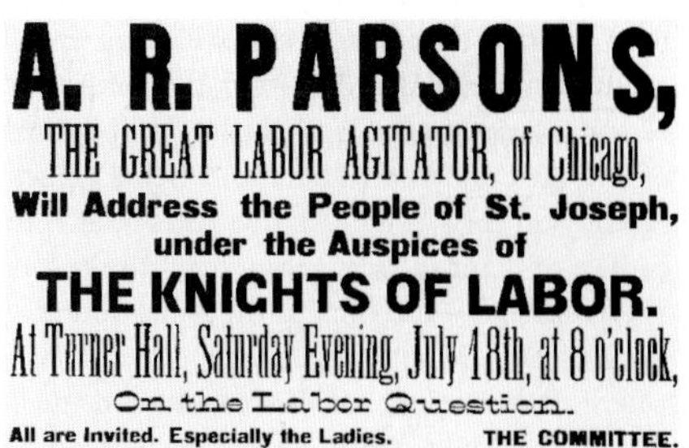

Labor leaders crossed the country supporting their causes and recruiting members. This flyer advertises a speech by Chicago's Albert Parsons in St. Joseph, Missouri. Source: The Newberry Library.

lapsed by 1887 and 80 percent by 1888. Yet despite the swift decline of the Knights, their principles of labor solidarity and their practice of inclusiveness would inspire subsequent labor movements, both in Chicago and across the nation.

Richard Schneirov

See also: Clothing and Garment Manufacturing; Meatpacking; Unionization; Work Culture

Further reading: Schneirov, Richard. *Labor and Urban Politics: Class Conflict and the Origins of Modern Liberalism in Chicago, 1864–1897.* 1998.

Koreans. Although Chicago's Koreans have only recently built a sizeable community, their roots go back until at least 1920, when the census counted 27 Korean residents. Many of these early immigrants had probably moved to the mainland after working on Hawaiian plantations; others came as students and stayed as ginseng merchants.

Chicago's Korean population began to increase rapidly in the 1960s, and reached approximately 10,000 by 1972. These included medical professionals, former students, Korean women married to American men, and former miners and nurses who had worked in Germany. Upon acquiring American citizenship, many sent for family members.

By the beginning of the 1970s, Koreans scattered across Chicago with a growing concentration in LAKE VIEW and LINCOLN PARK, and gradually increasing numbers in UPTOWN, EDGEWATER, and ROGERS PARK. A decade later, approximately 80 percent of Chicago's Koreans resided in nine adjacent community areas: ALBANY PARK, WEST RIDGE, LINCOLN SQUARE, Uptown, Edgewater, IRVING PARK, Lake View, NORTH PARK, and Rogers Park. By 1990 approximately 100,000 Koreans were residing in the metropolitan area, with growth concentrated especially in Albany Park.

The most distinctive feature of Korean economic life in Chicago has been the mushrooming of small BUSINESS establishments, which have provided entry points into the metropolitan economy. The first Korean-owned business, Diversey Cafeteria in Lake View, appeared at the corner of Diversey and Clark in the 1920s. In 1969, the first new Korean immigrant business, Sam-Mee RESTAURANT at 3370 North Clark, opened, followed by the opening of the Arirang Food Mart and Seoul Travel Agency on the same block two years later. The center of Chicago's Korean community—or "Koreatown"—emerged in the areas bounded by Pulaski, Montrose, Foster, and Clark, where the number of Korean-owned businesses increased from approximately 30 in 1978 to 428 in 1991, an estimated 70 percent of Chicago's Korean businesses.

Korean community life has evolved around ethnic churches and voluntary organizations. In the early 1970s, churches were the only ethnic institutions providing assistance and opportunity for association. As the community grew, Korean-language NEWSPAPERS (*Han'guk Ilbo, Chung'ang Ilbo, Hangyore Sinmun, Chicago Sinbo*), SOCIAL SERVICE centers (Korean American Community Services, Korean American Senior Center), more churches, and various voluntary associations emerged to provide services and information, while solidifying ethnic ties.

However, Chicago's Korean community is neither as harmonious nor united as it seems. As immigration has diversified, stratification and division have emerged despite the community's ability to maintain ethnic solidarity against the "outside" world.

Youn-Jin Kim

See also: Americanization; Demography; Multicentered Chicago; Mutual Benefit Societies

Further reading: Kim, Youn-Jin. "From Immigrants to Ethnics: The Life-Worlds of Korean Immigrants in Chicago." Ph.D. diss., University of Illinois at Urbana-Champaign. 1991. • Yoon, In-Jin. *On My Own: Korean Businesses and Race Relations in America.* 1997.

Kouts, IN, Porter County, 50 miles SE of the Loop. A trading post existed just southwest

of the town on the Kankakee River during the early nineteenth century when NATIVE AMERICANS controlled the region. Kouts developed around a RAILROAD station in the nineteenth century. The town has remained sparsely populated.

Erik Gellman

See also: Fur Trade

Ku Klux Klan. In the 1920s, when the Ku Klux Klan had more than two million members nationwide and was at the peak of its power and influence, Chicago had the largest membership (50,000) of any metropolitan region in the United States. At the time, the "Invisible Empire" was known for anti-Catholicism as much as for white supremacy and anti-Semitism, and Chicago had an abundance of all three targets. The Chicago Klan drew its primary support from lower-echelon white-collar workers, small businessmen, and semiskilled laborers, all of whom resented the growing influence of persons who did not meet the Klan's definition of "one hundred percent American." Beginning in 1921, various Kleagles (recruiters) set up more than 20 Klaverns (chapters) in the Chicago region, and the organization published a local periodical called *Dawn: A Journal for True American Patriots.*

The secret order's demise in Chicago was largely the result of the work of the American Unity League, a mostly ROMAN CATHOLIC organization which published a weekly newspaper, *Tolerance,* in 1922 and 1923 that printed the names, addresses, and occupations of thousands of Chicago-area Klansmen. The tactic worked, and by 1925 the Ku Klux Klan had almost disappeared from Chicago.

Kenneth T. Jackson

See also: Americanization; Racism, Ethnicity, and White Identity

Further reading: Jackson, Kenneth T. *The Ku Klux Klan in the City, 1915–1930.* 1967.

Kukla, Fran and Ollie. On October 13, 1947, puppeteer Burr Tillstrom brought an extraordinary troupe of performers already familiar to many Chicagoans to local television station WBKB. Joined by their front-of-stage friend Fran Allison, the Kuklapolitans—Oliver J. Dragon, Buelah Witch, Cecil Bill, Madame Ooglepuss, Fletcher Rabbit, Colonel Crackie, and Kukla himself—were welcomed into hundreds of thousands of American homes on network television shows of a variety of lengths and formats in the 1950s. Working without a script, the cast of *Kukla, Fran and Ollie* improvised conversations about everyday life laced with humor, astute commentary on current events, original music, and perennial features. Their nationwide following included children and adults; at the height of their popularity, the Kuklapolitans received 15,000 letters daily. The group continued to give occasional performances into the 1980s.

Phyllis Rabineau

See also: Bozo's Circus; Broadcasting; Ding Dong School; Garfield Goose; Mr. Wizard

Further reading: Adams, Rosemary K. "Here We Are Again: Kukla, Fran and Ollie." *Chicago History* 26 (Fall 1997): 32–51.

"L." Chicago's RAPID TRANSIT SYSTEM has been known as the "L" since before the first line opened in 1892. The peculiar Chicago spelling was used by all of the city's elevated railroad companies, and by local trade journals and NEWSPAPERS. Today, only 36 percent of the city's rapid transit system runs above the streets, but Chicagoans nonetheless say they are "taking the 'L.' "

Dennis McClendon

See also: Public Transportation; Rapid Transit

Further reading: Moffat, Bruce G. *The "L": The Development of Chicago's Rapid Transit System, 1888–1932.* 1995.

La Grange, IL, Cook County, 13 miles W of the Loop. Throughout the mid-nineteenth century, the expansion of the rail system around Chicago laid the framework for a sprawling metropolis. As RAILROADS reached into new areas, REAL-ESTATE developers bought land and built towns along the lines, offering affluent Chicagoans the chance to move out of the increasingly congested central city.

Like his fellow speculators, Franklin Dwight Cossitt sought to take advantage of middle- and upper-class Chicagoans' "suburban fever." In 1870, Cossitt purchased a 600-acre tract of farmland and uncultivated prairie adjacent to the recently completed Chicago, Burlington & Quincy line through western Cook County. Cossitt named his tract La Grange, after a Tennessee cotton farm that he had owned before the CIVIL WAR. A French word for "barn," La Grange had been the name of the ancestral home of Marquis de Lafayette, a Revolutionary War hero.

By planting hundreds of elm TREES, restricting the sale of liquor, building large single-family houses, setting aside property for schools and churches, contributing to the construction of a rail depot, and laying out a street plan that allowed for large lots, Cossitt wanted to distinguish his small, ordered village from what he saw as the overcrowded chaos of metropolitan Chicago. Emphasizing the contrast between suburban and urban physical landscapes, Cossitt advertised La Grange as a utopian retreat from the perceived dangers of the city. For investors in Cossitt's community, La Grange offered not only a cleaner, orderly, and more "natural" physical environment than Chicago, but also a seemingly less threatening population. Although La Grange's population, like that of many other railroad suburbs, represented a socioeconomic mix of upper-income professionals and lower-income service employees, many of its residents were native-born and few worked as industrial laborers. In contrast, the large concentration of foreign-born workers in Chicago contributed further to some Americans' image of the city as a dangerous, chaotic place.

The Chicago FIRE OF 1871 reinforced the image of La Grange (and other communities in COOK COUNTY) as a suburban sanctuary. By forcing refugees to seek shelter outside the city and by further convincing middle-class and wealthy Chicagoans that the city had become too dangerous, the fire accelerated the process of suburbanization and the expansion of the Chicago metropolitan area begun by the railroads, Cossitt, and other real-estate developers. By the end of the nineteenth century, when the suburban electric railway reached La Grange, the village had been incorporated within the expanding geographic entity of metropolitan Chicago.

La Grange continued to grow in the first decades of the twentieth century, both DEMOGRAPHICALLY and geographically, ANNEXING and developing surrounding land in order to accommodate a population that had risen from 6,525 in 1920 to 10,103 in 1930. Unable to find open and affordable land in Chicago, manufacturers like General Motors Corporation and Aluminum Company of America moved into La Grange during the 1930s and 1940s. In the mid-twentieth century, as the rates of suburbanization and exodus out of Chicago increased, the population of La Grange continued to rise, to nearly 17,814 by 1970. ZONING laws that restricted housing densities and placed limits on multiple-dwelling units prevented even greater population increases. By 2000, the population of La Grange had leveled off to 15,608.

Sarah S. Marcus

See also: Interurbans; Metropolitan Growth; Suburbs and Cities as Dual Metropolis

Further reading: Andreas, A. T. *History of Cook County, Illinois.* 1884. • Chamberlin, Everett. *Chicago and Its Suburbs.* 1874. • Cromie, William J., ed. *La Grange Centennial History.* 1979.

La Grange Park, IL, Cook County, 13 miles W of the Loop. In the late nineteenth century, residents of the Park—a small farming community in western COOK COUNTY—looked with alarm at the "blind pig" operating out of the home of a local stonemason. Horrified by their inability to stop the mason's unauthorized sale of alcohol or to control the behavior of his customers, local residents decided to incorporate. As an incorporated village, residents of La Grange Park could regulate the sale of alcohol, hire police to enforce temperance regulations, and control development within their community. La Grange Park joined several other rural communities in Cook County—including BARRINGTON (1865), PALATINE (1866), and ARLINGTON HEIGHTS (1887)—which incorporated primarily to control the sale of alcohol within their borders.

Unlike many suburban developers in the late nineteenth century, the founding residents of La Grange Park had little desire to promote the financial success of their community. While its citizens relied on neighboring LA GRANGE for shopping, transportation, banking, entertainment, and churches, La Grange Park remained a small, residential village. In 1900, eight years after the village's incorporation, only 730 people lived there, as opposed to the nearly 4,000 residents of La Grange. As late as 1940, the village claimed to be the only incorporated community in Illinois that lacked a railroad station, post office, street signs, parks, churches, or any significant business center. During the 1950s, however, village officials and citizens' associations actively pursued further housing and commercial development. The village's population more than doubled during the decade, from 6,176 in 1950 to 13,793 in 1960. Despite

South Side "L," 1893. Photographer: Unknown. Source: Chicago Historical Society.

this growth and increased economic diversity, La Grange Park remained a primarily residential community with a population of 13,295 in 2000.

Sarah S. Marcus

See also: Governing the Metropolis; Local Option; Prohibition and Temperance

Further reading: Cromie, William J., ed. *La Grange Centennial History.* 1979. • Keating, Ann Durkin. *Building Chicago: Suburban Developers and the Creation of a Divided Metropolis.* 1988. • Sonderby, Tina, and Laura Koranda. *La Grange Park: Reflections of the Past.* 1993.

La Leche League. The La Leche League is a voluntary association of women established in 1956 in a Near West Chicago suburb, to promote "good mothering through breastfeeding." During a time of rapidly changing parenting practices and gender roles, the league spread its message around the world through the organization of small discussion groups and the sale of millions of books and pamphlets, especially the best-seller, *The Womanly Art of Breastfeeding.* By offering a strong defense of traditional motherhood, combined with an assertion of female expertise in child rearing, the league contributed to the increased popularity of breastfeeding during the postwar era.

Lynn Y. Weiner

See also: Birthing Practices; Feminist Movements

Further reading: Weiner, Lynn. "Reconstructing Motherhood: The La Leche League in Postwar America." *Journal of American History* (March 1994): 1357–1381.

Labor Law. Labor law refers to the body of rules enacted by various governments that regulate the conditions of WORK and define the rights and obligations of employers, labor organizations, and employees. In Chicago, the law has determined the outcome of many struggles between capital and labor.

During the early twentieth century, the criminal COURTS often intervened in local labor disputes. Cook County state's attorneys used common and statute laws prohibiting conspiracy (technically, associated persons pursuing an unlawful end or accomplishing a lawful end by unlawful means) to prosecute strikers engaged in picketing and boycotting. Grand juries frequently charged unionists with conspiring to injure replacements and employers. In 1906 and 1907, the state twice prosecuted TEAMSTERS' union officials for conspiring to boycott the Montgomery Ward Company during a heated five-month STRIKE. Though neither trial ended in conviction, both financially weakened the CHICAGO FEDERATION OF LABOR (CFL) and discouraged labor militancy. Similar prosecutions continued to contain union power and labor militancy, with prosecutions haunting Chicago's most prominent union officers between 1910 and 1940.

Employers also restrained strikers by obtaining court orders. Between 1900 and 1920, Cook County judge Jesse Holdom repeatedly enjoined union pickets, often without a full hearing. In the 1920s, federal judge James Wilkerson became labor's nemesis, issuing broad injunctions during the 1922 railway shopmen's strike. Judges enforced their orders by holding violators in contempt, sending labor leaders to jail without a jury trial. Though lawyers like Clarence Darrow had some success defending unionists in court, such injunctions profoundly hindered efforts at organizing manufacturing workers.

But Chicago government often supported unions, and labor organizations held significant power in city government. In 1897, the powerful BUILDING TRADES Council pressured the Chicago Board of Education to pass a provision (later voided in state court) requiring contractors to hire union craftsmen. Labor's representatives on the Civil Service Board used their power to organize public employees, while unions of engineers, plumbers, teamsters, barbers, and moving picture operators obtained license laws that helped them govern their crafts. For example, the 1909 "Barber Shop Law" gave the Journeymen Barbers' Union effective control over who might legally cut hair in Chicago.

Because of labor's political strength, Illinois was among the first states to adopt laws protecting workers. In 1903, an alliance of unions and reform groups obtained a law limiting child labor. In 1909, the legislature passed the Health, Safety, and Comfort Act, which greatly reduced industrial accidents. A weak workers' compensation law followed two years later. These successes were limited, and labor did not obtain statutes addressing UNEMPLOYMENT, wages, or hours. However, in 1925, after much lobbying, labor unions finally gained a constitutionally valid state law limiting labor injunctions. Illinois law still prohibits state and county judges from enjoining workers engaged in peaceful picketing during a bona fide labor dispute.

Federal legislation during the GREAT DEPRESSION transformed industrial relations in Chicago, limiting judicial interference and encouraging UNIONIZATION. The Norris-LaGuardia Act of 1932 prohibited federal injunctions, while the National Labor Relations Act of 1935 (NLRA) established the right to organize and founded a National Labor Relations Board (NLRB) to oversee union elections. This new legal environment enabled committees affiliated with the CONGRESS OF INDUSTRIAL ORGANIZATIONS to organize operatives working in Chicago's MEAT PACKING and steel plants.

Over time, federal law became less friendly to labor. The 1947 Taft-Hartley Amendment to the NLRA overturned Norris-LaGuardia and freed federal judges to enjoin unions. The law also outlawed tactics such as the secondary boycott and other "unfair labor practices." Since the 1940s, judicial and administrative decisions have weakened federal support for unions. Some local commentators attribute the waning power of unions in Chicago to the vitiation of the NLRA.

Andrew Wender Cohen

See also: Antiunionism; Children and the Law; New Deal; Occupational Safety and Health; Work Culture

Further reading: Beckner, Earl R. *A History of Illinois Labor Legislation.* 1929. • Myers, Harold Barton. "The Policing of Labor Disputes in Chicago: A Case Study." Ph.D. diss., University of Chicago. 1929. • Staley, Eugene. *History of the Illinois State Federation of Labor.* 1930.

Labor Organizing. *See* Unionization

Labor Songs. Between 1865 and 1920 Chicago served as a center for working-class protest songs and poetry. Labor publications and organizations featured thousands of compositions by workers and their allies as they sought to rally workers.

In 1865, Charles Haynes, a blind musician, wrote one of the first modern labor songs. His "EIGHT HOUR Song" reflected labor's earnest temperament in this period:

Hear your leader's voices call you,
Hasten quickly on your way;
We must rally for the fight,
Stand for justice and for right,
Till the law for work be made 8 hours a day.

Most songwriters came from working-class backgrounds. William Creech, a machinist, frequently presented his work to working-class audiences. Shopkeepers, such as printers James and Emily Tallmadge, and local labor leaders, such as Gustav Lyser, a journalist and key figure in the GERMAN community's labor affairs, often contributed as well. In fact, the German community counted many skillful writers, among them Lyser and Robert Reitzel.

Songs appeared in NEWSPAPERS, songbooks, and broadsides, and at rallies, STRIKES, meetings, and socials. Literary and musical influences included folksongs, evangelical hymns, CIVIL WAR music, popular and sentimental POETRY, antebellum reform songs, romantic literature, and minstrelsy. Songs sometimes addressed less obvious labor concerns such as romance, religion, and nature. The majority offered social criticism and a prolabor message but also addressed specific issues: wages, hours, strikes, monetary reform, scabs, craft lore, socialism, gender roles, immigration, child labor. Chicago's own labor issues surfaced in songs such as "Boycott Armour" (1887):

The aged year was dying fast
As through Chicago's streets there passed,
A walking delegate carrying high,
A band with this new war cry:
"Boycott Armour!"

After 1900, mainstream unions moved away from broad-based social reform, as well as cultural activities such as music and poetry. Additionally, workers began seeking their entertainment from the burgeoning popular culture industry. Radicals, however, maintained and refined the labor song tradition, producing important work. The Chicago-based INDUSTRIAL WORKERS OF THE WORLD ("Wobblies") proved adept at the craft as their *Little Red Songbook* (1909) demonstrates. Communists and the new CIO unions in the 1930s diligently promoted labor music's potential. Singing at union gatherings would continue into the 1940s, as workers still sang Chicago "Wobbly" Ralph Chaplin's famous 1915 labor hymn: "Solidarity Forever! For the Union makes us strong." The days when labor songs permeated the labor movement, however, had passed.

Clark "Bucky" Halker

See also: Literary Cultures; Meatpacking; Unionization; Work; Work Culture

Further reading: Foner, Philip S. *American Labor Songs of the Nineteenth Century.* 1975. • Halker, Clark D. *For Democracy, Workers, and God: Labor Song-Poems and Labor Protest, 1865–1895.* 1991. • Industrial Workers of the World. *Little Red Songbook.* 1909.

The area historically known as "Mud Lake" as it looked in 1908, seen from the Kedzie Avenue Bridge along the South Branch of the Chicago River. Photographer: Unknown. Source: Chicago Historical Society.

Lacustrine System. The landscape that greeted early settlers to the Chicago area was filled with lakes, sloughs, and wetlands. These WATER bodies were the legacy of the last period of continental GLACIATION (the Wisconsin glaciation) which came to an end about 12,000 years ago. The lobe of glacial ice more than one-half-mile thick which had scoured out the LAKE MICHIGAN basin melted away and left a huge lake called Lake Chicago. The surface of this glacial lake lay 60 feet higher than the current level of Lake Michigan, and it overlay much of the future Chicago area. The lake was dammed behind ridges of glacial debris (moraines) that roughly paralleled the current shore of Lake Michigan and marked the farthest extent of the ice movement.

This huge glacial lake was short-lived and underwent numerous changes of size and level, but while the lake was in existence, it deposited silts and clays on the lake bottom. These deposits had major consequences for the future character of the area. Ultimately, Lake Chicago created two drainage outlets which converged southwestward through the ringing moraine hills. Then, over a period of roughly 3,000 years, the lake waters drained away toward the Mississippi in a prodigious torrent with a flow greater than that of the Amazon. This enormous flow created the two so-called sag valleys south and west of Chicago and also produced the large valley occupied today by the much smaller Illinois River. Eventually the glacial lake drained down to the present dimensions of Lake Michigan, leaving large swampy areas on the surrounding plain caused by the clay deposits that held water near the surface.

Lake Michigan is the third largest of the GREAT LAKES in area, and its surface stands 582 feet above sea level. It is the only one of the Great Lakes to lie entirely within the United States. It is 307 miles long and 118 miles wide at its widest point and contains roughly 1,180 cubic miles of water. The lake comprises two main basins. The deep basin north of Milwaukee has a depth of 923 feet and reaches 341 feet below sea level. It has a rough bottom and is swept by strong currents. The southern basin, by contrast, is much shallower, with a relatively smooth bottom and slow-moving currents. A surface (littoral) current flows southward along the lake's western shore and carries sand toward the notable dunes at the lake's south end.

In addition to Lake Michigan, other much smaller vestiges of Lake Chicago remain. These shallow lakes include Lake Calumet, which once covered three square miles, and the smaller Wolf and George Lakes. But water was everywhere upon the land and many other sloughs and wetlands were also present. One wetland, called Mud Lake by American settlers, lay athwart the sub–continental divide southwest of Chicago, which separated the waters that flowed southwestward toward the Mississippi from those that flowed eastward into Lake Michigan. The ancient PORTAGE route that connected Lake Michigan and the CHICAGO RIVER with the DES PLAINES, ILLINOIS, and Mississippi Rivers went through this wetland area.

In addition to Lake Chicago remnants, the glacial moraines that ring the Chicago area themselves hold large numbers of small lakes. As the moraines were formed, huge chunks of ice lay helter-skelter along the ridge surface. When these ice blocks melted they gave rise to many water-filled depressions called kettles and small surrounding hills called kames. Such undulating, pond-filled, moraine landscapes are very attractive and have often been developed into prestigious suburban residential areas.

David M. Solzman

See also: Dune System; Ecosystem Evolution; Riverine Systems

Further reading: Atwood, W. W. *The Geology of Chicago and Its Region.* 1927. • Bretz, Harlen J. *Geology of the Chicago Region.* Parts 1 and 2. 1939; 1955. • Solzman, David. *The Chicago River: An Illustrated History and Guide to the River and Its Waterways.* 1998.

Lager Beer Riot. Chicago's first civil disturbance, on April 21, 1855, resulted in 1 death, 60 arrests, and the beginning of political partisanship in city elections.

On March 6, a "Law and Order" coalition swept city elections. The coalition was formed by anti-immigrant, anti-Catholic nativists (Know-Nothings) and temperance advocates who were interested in moral reform and public order. With most municipal services either privatized or organized at the neighborhood level, city elections in the 1840s and early 1850s had been nonpartisan contests of little interest to anyone except REAL-ESTATE owners. The extremely low voter turnout permitted this quietly mobilized coalition to win control of city hall with a thin base of popular support.

Once elected, Mayor Levi Boone and the new council majority hiked LIQUOR license fees while also shortening license terms from one year to three months. Expecting resistance, Mayor Boone "reformed" the city's POLICE force: tripling its size, refusing to hire immigrants, requiring police to wear uniforms for the first time, and directing them to enforce an old, previously ignored ordinance requiring the SUNDAY CLOSING of taverns and SALOONS. These were intentionally provocative acts aimed at GERMANS and IRISH accustomed to spending their LEISURE hours in drinking establishments.

Germans organized to resist the $300 license ordinance, raising defense funds for tavern owners arrested for noncompliance. Prosecutions clogged the city courts and attorneys scheduled a test case for April 21. This, in effect, scheduled the riot. A huge crowd assembled to support the defendants. Mayor Boone ordered police to clear the courthouse area, which resulted in nine arrests. An armed group from the North Side German community decided to rescue the prisoners, but Boone held them off by keeping the Clark Street drawbridge raised until he was able to assemble more than two hundred policemen. When the bridge was lowered and North Siders surged across, shooting began. Boone called in the militia, and the riot ended in minutes.

The riot mobilized Chicago's immigrant voters. In March 1856, a heavy German and Irish turnout defeated the nativists, causing the $50 liquor license to be restored. More important was the renewed attention to city elections on the part of political party leaders, ending the era of municipal nonpartisanship. Never again would city elections be of such limited interest that a small group of extremists could win surreptitiously.

Robin Einhorn

See also: Near North Side, Politics; Prohibition and Temperance; Racism, Ethnicity, and White Identity

Lake Barrington, IL, Lake County, 35 miles NW of the Loop. The Native Americans who lived along the banks of the FOX RIVER over three thousand years ago found the oak- and prairie-covered rolling hills interspersed with marshlands to be both a beautiful and hospitable area in which to live. The recent discovery of burials from that time suggest an established Indian presence in the Lake Barrington area.

With the exception of a few fur-trapping expeditions in the late 1700s, the area remained in the hands of various Indian groups until the end of the BLACK HAWK WAR in 1832. Soon after, farmers began drifting into the area and turned to dairying as a way to obtain income.

The area remained rural and minimally populated until after World War I, when Chicago businessmen began turning farms into estates. One family, the Criswells, owned over six hundred acres around Indian Lake about five miles north of BARRINGTON. Still, the area around Indian Lake remained fairly undisturbed because marshlands made travel difficult prior to the advent of hard-surfaced roads.

In 1946 Robert Bartlett purchased the Criswell property and began planning a heavily populated residential complex along Indian Lake, which he renamed Lake Barrington. This development frightened many owners of large estates. They hoped to maintain a minimum five-acre lot size, but Bartlett and some farmers fought for half-acre ZONING, a density level that they believed would bring the best return for their property while keeping a semirural atmosphere. Estate owners south of Lake Barrington disagreed and sought to incorporate themselves as NORTH BARRINGTON to protect their own zoning plan. Both Lake Barrington and North Barrington voted to incorporate independently from each other on October 31, 1959. Jorgen Hubschman, supporting Bartlett's views, became Lake Barrington's president.

With Bartlett's death in May 1967, zoning issues arose again as developers vied to purchase his holdings and construct high-density subdivisions similar to the one called Lake Barrington Shores, a condo development in the northeast corner of the village. By the early 1970s, a compromise concerning population densities allowed for the completion of Lake Barrington Shores, the ANNEXATION of a commercial area along U.S. Route 14 at Kelsey Road, and the imposition of less dense zoning regulations in the rest of the village, where one-acre lot sizes were required.

Once the community's residents settled their internal disputes over zoning, Lake Barrington sought to protect its plan from county zoning regulations that allowed for even more dense settlement than half-acre or larger lots. In 1988, Lake Barrington joined an already active association of neighboring communities called the Barrington Area Council of Governments which had the goal of resisting development and preserving the semirural status and affluent character of its member villages.

While the population growth from 300 in 1970 to 4,757 by the end of the century may seem rapid, given the 3,200-acre size of the village, Lake Barrington seems to have successfully resisted the wave of intense development that flowed around it in the last three decades.

Craig L. Pfannkuche

See also: Built Environment of the Chicago Region; Government, Suburban; Lake County, IL

Further reading: "Village of Lake Barrington: Community Information Guide and Map." Pamphlet. N.d. • Galo, Maria T. "Regional Guardian Arrives at the Crossroads." *Chicago Tribune,* March 30, 1998. • *Lake Barrington: A Passionate Past That Gave Its Community a Secure Future.* Pamphlet. N.d.

Lake Bluff, IL, Lake County, 30 miles N of the Loop. Lake Bluff is the most distant suburb on the North Shore. It was settled in 1836 by Catherine and John Cloes. First known as Dwyer Settlement, it was subsequently renamed Oak Hill (1848), Rockland (1859), and then Lake Bluff (1882).

Location on the TRANSPORTATION corridor connecting Chicago to WAUKEGAN and Milwaukee, first by stagecoach (1836) and then by rail (1855), proved paramount to development. Walter S. GURNEE, MAYOR of Chicago (1851–52) and speculator, foresaw this place as another railway suburb. His early vision went unfulfilled for another 40 years.

The Lake Bluff Camp Meeting Association (1874) took form instead, at a summer gathering place established by Methodists. The association's founders appreciated its assets: lovely beaches, a RAILROAD, and the cachet of North Shore. Guests summered in tents through 1882. The five-story Hotel Irving (1883) advanced its attractions, embracing worldly activities including art, bathing, boating, dancing, and other recreational pursuits.

Lake Bluff was becoming a residential suburb, with the construction of modest cottages, by the late 1880s. In 1895 the village incorporated and erected a two-story public school. Hastening its transformation, a fire in 1897 destroyed the hotel, and the camp meeting association dissolved two years later. Soon after followed the building of a commuter station (1904) and a graceful village hall (1905). When the nearby GREAT LAKES NAVAL TRAINING STATION, completed in 1911, sought to designate Lake Bluff as its postal address, civic leaders lobbied in opposition. The NORTH CHICAGO post office was chosen instead.

Citizens contemplated consolidation into LAKE FOREST in 1895, 1908, 1912, and 1930, although never proceeding to referendum. After 1900, Lake Bluff became the site for country-style estates constructed by prominent Chicago families (Armour, Clow, Durand, and Field) as well as the exclusive Shore Acres Country Club (1916).

Lake Bluff reflected the nationwide suburban trend after 1945. Population increased: 2,000 in 1950, 5,008 in 1970, and 6,056 in 2000. A large SUBDIVISION—comparable to developments elsewhere—known as the Terrace, to the east and west of Green Bay Road, started in 1961, contributing to Lake Bluff's largest population advance in any decade, 1,514 new residents from 1960 to 1970. Other subdivisions, on the former estate of Phillip D. Armour III along Green Bay Road, yielded the more distinctive Armour Woods and Tangley Oaks, designed to conserve woodlands and ponds.

At the end of the twentieth century, Lake Bluff encountered challenges as well as opportunities. Its traditional housing stock east of Sheridan Road was its cherished coin, heightening interest in HISTORIC PRESERVATION. Median home value for Lake Bluff in 1990 was $285,200—above comparable countywide statistics but lower than in nearby suburbs BANNOCKBURN, Lake Forest, and METTAWA. Knollwood, an unincorporated residential neighborhood west of Lake Bluff but within Lake Bluff's park and school districts, made unsuccessful petitions for annexation in 1978, 1982, and 1996. Lake Bluff did expand to the southwest, developing a commercial and light manufacturing district plus a retail complex featuring a modern supermarket. Knauz Motors, conducting business in Lake Forest since 1934, relocated all its new-car dealerships to western Lake Bluff by 2001. Correspondingly, the economic vitality in the original retail center diminished, stirring the village board to contemplate ambitious plans designed to foster downtown rejuvenation.

Michael H. Ebner

See also: Conservation and Preservation; Government, Suburban; Leisure; Protestants; Religious Geography; Suburbs and Cities as Dual Metropolis

Further reading: Mellinger, Barbara A. "History of Lake Bluff." Unpublished senior thesis, Cornell College, Mt. Vernon, Ia. 1978. • Nelson, Janet, Kathleen O'Hara, and Ann Walters. *Lake Bluff, Illinois: A Pictorial History.* 1995. • Vliet, Elmer B. *Lake Bluff: The First 100 Years.* Ed. Virginia Mullery. 1985.

Lake County Discovery Museum.

Located in WAUCONDA within LAKE COUNTY's two-thousand-acre Lakewood FOREST PRESERVE and operated by the Lake County Forest Preserve District, the Lake County Discovery Museum hosts a variety of programs and collections. Public programs at the museum, which was established in 1976, have ranged from displays of antique farming machinery to Civil War encampments to history lessons targeted to first and second graders. The museum's permanent collections include local history archives of Lake County; material on FORT SHERIDAN, the U.S. Army base that was located in Lake County from the 1880s until it closed in the early 1990s; and records of the 96th Illinois Infantry Regiment, which included volunteers from Lake County during the CIVIL WAR.

The museum's most notable collection is the Curt Teich Postcard Archives. Considered to be largest public collection of POSTCARDS in the world, the archives contain millions of postcards, including nearly 400,000 images of twentieth-century American life and culture. Of particular interest are thousands of views of towns and cities across the United States and in more than 80 other countries. Established by GERMAN immigrant Curt Teich, the Chicago-based Curt Teich & Co. operated from 1898 until 1978. The company's agents crossed the country, selling postcards and taking PHOTOGRAPHS to make new ones. Between the First and Second World Wars, Teich's Irving Park Road plant on Chicago's North Side sometimes printed several million postcards a day. Throughout its existence, the company maintained an archive of all of its postcards and its photographs. After the company closed, the Teich family sought a home where the vast archive would be preserved as a single collection. In 1982 they donated the collection to the Lake County Discovery Museum, which makes the collection available to researchers and visitors in person and on the Web.

Ian McGiver

See also: Leisure; Museums in the Park

Further reading: Harris, Moira F. "Curt Teich Postcards of Minnesota." *Minnesota History* 54.7 (1995): 304–315. • Keister, Kim, "Wish You Were Here." *Historic Preservation* 44.2 (1992): 54–61. • Pyle, Christine A., "The Curt Teich Postcard Collection in Wauconda, Illinois."*Pharmacy in History* 30.4 (1988): 192–194.

Lake County, IL.

The Illinois State Legislature organized Lake County on March 1, 1839, by partitioning MCHENRY COUNTY. The new county was bordered by McHenry County on the west, the Wisconsin Territory to the north, COOK COUNTY to the south, and LAKE MICHIGAN to the east.

Settlers pursued trading, farming, and manufacturing in the hinterland of Chicago's growing economy. Beginning in 1836, stagecoaches traveled Green Bay Road along a route paralleling Lake Michigan that connected Chicago and Milwaukee. WAUKEGAN, along Green Bay Road 40 miles north of Chicago, became Lake County's economic and government center because of its prospering harbor. Designated as the county seat, supplanting LIBERTYVILLE, Waukegan accounted for 20 percent of county residents by 1850.

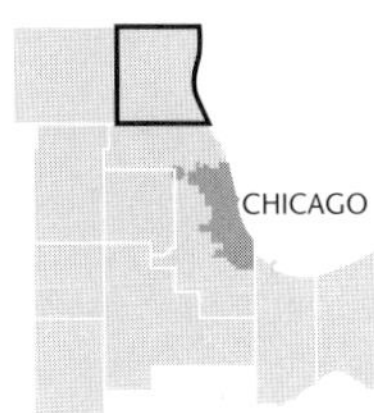

RAILROADS transformed Lake County. The earliest line, the Chicago & Milwaukee Railroad, commenced in 1855 and linked Chicago and Milwaukee via Waukegan. Even before its completion, Walter S. Gurnee (MAYOR of Chicago, 1851–52) promoted residential development that became Chicago's North Shore. Three North Shore suburbs—HIGHLAND PARK, LAKE FOREST, and LAKE BLUFF—were within Lake County. North Shore residents traveled to RAVINIA PARK, founded as an outdoor theater in 1904, for opera and symphonies.

The Elgin, Joliet, & Eastern Railroad (the Outer Belt Line), completed in 1891 as an intraregional freight carrier, linked Waukegan to Chicago's other satellite cities, spurring its industrial development. The Chicago, Milwaukee & North Shore Electric Railway (the North Shore Line), transported passengers and freight from 1899 until it shut down in 1963. These lines encouraged further industrial development at Waukegan and at NORTH CHICAGO, and also supported two federal defense installations, FORT SHERIDAN in HIGHWOOD (1887) and GREAT LAKES NAVAL TRAINING STATION in North Chicago (1911). The number of wage earners in manufacturing, mostly in Waukegan and North Chicago, advanced 71 percent (or 6,111) between 1900 and 1930. By 1925, Abbott Laboratories had relocated to North Chicago, terminating its Chicago operations.

Motor vehicles and new roads revolutionized travel by the 1920s. Early automobile traffic depended upon Sheridan Road, an outdated two-lane route along Lake Michigan, for north-south journeys. Work commenced on the Skokie Valley Highway (U.S. 41) in 1931 several miles west. When Lake County exceeded 100,000 inhabitants in 1930, its population included its first urban clusters—Libertyville and BARRINGTON—situated in its westerly reaches. The completion of the Skokie Valley branch of the North Shore Line in 1926 reinforced this westerward development.

A north-south segment of the Tri-State TOLLWAY (I-94) was completed in 1958 several miles west of U.S. 41, further accelerating westward growth, and enabling easy access to O'HARE AIRPORT and other metropolitan counties. DEERFIELD, GURNEE, and VERNON HILLS, all in close proximity to the tollway, attained significance as the county's most active centers for private-sector employment. Three enterprises—the Great America AMUSEMENT PARK (1976), the Hawthorne Center (1973) and Gurnee Mills (1991), each shopping malls—became major destinations. Waukegan's share of the countywide workforce declined by 9 percent between 1978 and 1998, although it retained primacy as the county's largest employment center. As of 2000, the five largest employers in Lake County were the GREAT LAKES NAVAL TRAINING STATION (23,000), Abbott Laboratories (15,300), Hewitt Associates (5,570), Motorola (5,000), and Kemper Insurance Companies (3,700). The region's first new rail COMMUTER line since 1926 opened in 1996 with eight stops in western Lake County.

The profound changes in Lake County during the second half of the twentieth century were an aspect of large-scale suburbanization within the nation's metropolitan regions. From 1950 to 2000, Chicago's population decreased 20 percent as Lake County's advanced 260 percent. The county was 97 percent white in 1950; by 2000 the county's population included 14 percent Hispanic, 7 percent African American, and 4 percent Asian residents. Waukegan, the sixth largest city in Illinois, has been the gateway for racial and ethnic minorities as it had been for white immigrants and their children decades earlier. The 2000 census classified 70

Loading ice at Loon Lake Ice House near Antioch (no date). Photographer: Unknown. Source: Lakes Region Historical Society.

percent of Waukegan residents as nonwhite or Hispanic.

The wealthiest county (median income of $67,675) in the state and ranked tenth nationwide based on data reported in 2000, Lake County is representative of the dual metropolis: persistent social isolation and intensified economic disparity. One in three county residents subsisting beneath the poverty line, based on data for 1990, lived either in Waukegan or North Chicago. Median home values ($136,000 for the county in 1990) reinforced stratification: in the county's wealthy southeastern communities (BANNOCKBURN, Deerfield, Highland Park, Lake Bluff, Lake Forest, and METTAWA), the aggregated figure was $384,140; the combined statistic for North Chicago and Waukegan was $67,700.

In the state's third most urban county, planning for future development has become a major political issue. Suburbanization has led to dramatic drops in farm acreage. Heightened environmental sensibilities prompted the formation of a Lake County FOREST PRESERVE District in 1958 and the adoption of a county LAND-USE plan in 1960 (updated four times through 2002.) Acreage owned by the Forest Preserve doubled between 1980 and 2000, to 22,273, roughly 6 percent of the county land mass, thanks to four referendums for land acquisition between 1991 and 2000. The daily journey to work in 2000 consumed 31 minutes for residents of the county; nationally it was 24 minutes and even in Los Angeles 28 minutes. The foremost contemporary issue, relentlessly contested by growth advocates and environmentalists, has been the proposed extension of Illinois Route 53 northward from Cook County into western Lake County.

Michael H. Ebner

See also: Economic Geography; Governing the Metropolis; Suburbs and Cities as Dual Metropolis; Transportation

Further reading: Ahmed, G. Munir. *Manufacturing Structure and Pattern of Waukegan–North Chicago.* 1957. • Cutler, Irving. *Chicago: Metropolis of the Mid-Continent.* 3rd ed. 1982. • Cutler, Irving. *The Chicago-Milwaukee Corridor: A Geographic Study of Intermetropolitan Coalescence.* 1965.

Lake County, IN. The retreat of the glaciers 25,000 years ago left a landscape of sand ridges and swamps 10 miles inland from the current shoreline of LAKE MICHIGAN. Consequently, the northern portion of Lake County offered few sites for productive AGRICULTURE. Fertile lands existed south of the CALUMET RIVER, where the Valparaiso Moraine rose 20 feet, creating a drier landscape that extended to the Kankakee River.

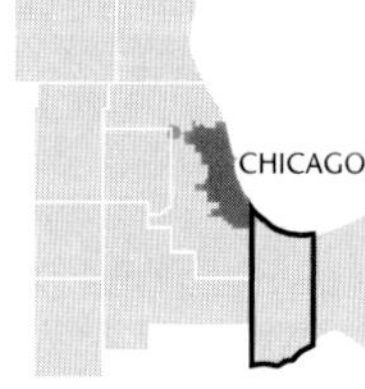

The POTAWATOMI hunted the region and established a number of trails, including the Old Sauk, the Calumet, the Toleston, and the Calumet River. With the arrival of the FRENCH, the trails provided a transportation corridor for the FUR TRADE between the St. Joseph and Kankakee Rivers. Located on high ground, they remain major TRANSPORTATION routes.

Settlers entered Lake County following TREATIES with the Native Americans in 1826 and 1832. Arriving from New York, Ohio, and southern Indiana, settlers squatted lands near the current towns of CROWN POINT, HOBART, and CEDAR LAKE. The sale of public lands did not occur until 1839. To protect their claims from speculators, 476 squatters formed a union in 1836. When sales occurred in LaPorte, the squatters traveled en masse to acquire legal title to their lands. Within two years of the sale, Crown Point became the county seat.

The agricultural portion of Lake County was 40 miles from Chicago, a distance requiring days of travel through difficult terrain. So the population rose modestly, from 1,468 in 1840 to 3,991 in 1850. Nearly all settlers south of the moraine were farmers. Fourteen percent were GERMANS who established small communities at ST. JOHN, SCHERERVILLE, Brunswick, Klaasville, Hessville, Hanover Center, and WHITING. Germans remained the county's largest ethnic group throughout the nineteenth century.

After 1850, the RAILROADS established various stations that provided farmers access to Chicago, where they could sell perishables like milk, fruit, and eggs. From these stations, farmers received cheap LUMBER and building materials, thereby ending the log-cabin era in Lake County. No longer isolated, farmers introduced refinements into everyday life, but the county did not develop an urban center. Crown Point lacked a rail outlet until 1865.

The railroads spurred industrial development among the sand ridges and swamps of North Township. By 1900, the industrial towns of HAMMOND, Whiting, and EAST CHICAGO contained 52 percent of the county's 37,892 residents. With the establishment of U.S. Steel's GARY Works in 1906, a large division existed between the industrial north and the rural south. Tensions were already evident during the PULLMAN STRIKE of 1894: North Township supported strikers while rural communities denounced the labor unions whose actions halted the shipments of perishable products to Chicago. Soon afterward, a few prominent citizens in HAMMOND unsuccessfully fought to relocate the county seat further north.

Rural and urban divisions increased once POLISH, SLOVAK, CROATIAN, and GREEK immigrants arrived to WORK in the rapidly expanding steel industry. The cities of East Chicago and Gary contained populations overwhelmingly foreign-born. As a consequence, the KU KLUX KLAN prospered in Lake County during the 1920s, drawing support from local PROTESTANT churches and from political leaders in Indianapolis. Anti-Catholic and antiunion, the Klan organized parades and rallies attracting thousands of supporters who called for "100 percent Americanism." Briefly, they were a force in county politics, until public scandal led to the imprisonment of the Klan's state leader, D. C. Stephenson.

Industrial growth fostered a series of REAL-ESTATE booms in North, Calumet, and Hobart Townships. By 1920 these townships contained 245,155 residents, roughly one-fourth of Chicago's suburban population. During the twenties, real-estate and commercial development accelerated. NEWSPAPERS in Hammond and Gary promoted a regional identity, boasting of prosperous industrial communities that offered employment and suburban residential opportunities. By 1930, immigrants and their children were a majority of the region's consumers, constituting three-fifths of all homeowners. General prosperity and the rise of a consumer-based economy reduced the tensions between the native and foreign born.

When the GREAT DEPRESSION ended prosperity, the industrial portions of Lake County embraced labor unions and the DEMOCRATIC PARTY. By WORLD WAR II, a better-educated, AMERICANIZED second generation replaced immigrants as the dominant segment of the population. During the war, employment opportunities increased rapidly for AFRICAN AMERICANS and MEXICAN immigrants. As minority populations increased in Gary and East Chicago, tensions surfaced once again between older residents and new arrivals. During the real-estate booms of the 1950s and 1960s, younger and more affluent residents, both white- and blue-collar, moved south to newer residential developments. These new developments profited from the construction of Interstates 80, 94, 90, and 65, which made regional COMMUTING possible from southern and western Lake County.

After 1968, racial tensions, plant closings, and the loss of jobs in the steel industry damaged severely the economy of northern Lake County. Economic decline destroyed thriving downtowns in Hammond and Gary. Lake County's total population fell 13 percent from 1970 to 1990, from 546,253 to 475,594. The industrial cities of Hammond, East Chicago, and Gary suffered the greatest loss, a drop of 29 percent. In contrast, the population outside these cities increased 12 percent, with housing units rising by 47 percent. In 1974, the opening of multimillion-dollar Southlake Mall near MERRILLVILLE, and later the Star Plaza Theatre entertainment complex, demonstrated clearly the movement in commercial development away from Hammond, Gary, Whiting, and East Chicago. By 1990, 51 percent of Lake County residents lived beyond the boundaries of these older industrial cities.

Currently, the region consists of striking contrasts. Gary and East Chicago contain dominant African American and Mexican American populations, with one-fourth of the population living below the poverty line. Further south, established suburban communities like MUNSTER, GRIFFITH, and HIGHLAND provide a high quality of housing. In 1990, Munster remained the wealthiest community per capita in Lake County. New growth, both residential and commercial, occurs south of the Valparaiso Moraine, especially in Merrillville, Schererville, St. John, and Crown Point. During the most recent real-estate boom of the 1990s, these communities built upscale housing. Nevertheless, Lake County and the Calumet region suffer from a reputation as a declining industrial district with little appeal for affluent, college-educated suburbanites. Even the newest upscale developments contain largely blue-collar populations.

Joseph C. Bigott

See also: Built Environment of the Chicago Region; Economic Geography; Expressways; Glaciation; Iron and Steel; Metropolitan Growth

Further reading: Ball, Timothy H. *Encyclopedia of Genealogy and Biography of Lake County, Indiana.* 1904. • Howat, William F., ed. *A Standard History of Lake County, Indiana, and the Calumet Region.* 2 vols. 1915. • Moore, Powell A. *The Calumet Region: Indiana's Last Frontier.* 1959.

Lake Forest College. In 1857, only two years after the completion of RAILROADS connecting Chicago to the string of towns stretching north along the shore of LAKE MICHIGAN, the city and the college of LAKE FOREST were simultaneously established 30 miles north of Chicago. Their Presbyterian founders hired Almerin Hotchkiss to draw up plans for a small, bucolic city with the school as its hub, and Lake Forest Academy opened to four boys in 1858, in the town's first building. The school's growth (including the addition of college-level courses in 1860) halted abruptly with the coming of the Civil War and the aftermath of the Chicago FIRE OF 1871. It reopened in 1876 to both men and women, focused increasingly on the liberal arts, and grew steadily over the next several decades. Enrollment ballooned after passage of the GI Bill, as Presbyterianism became less central to the school's identity. After several name changes, it officially became Lake Forest College with the renewal of its charter in 1965. Though their founders envisioned them as adjoined institutions, the college and city serve different needs: while the city of Lake Forest remains among the nation's wealthiest, 85 percent of the college's 1,270 students received financial assistance in the 2001–2 academic year.

Sarah Fenton

See also: Protestants; Universities and Their Cities

Further reading: Schulze, Franz, Rosemary Cowler, and Arthur H. Miller. *30 Miles North: A History of Lake Forest College, Its Town, and Its City of Chicago.* 2000.

Lake Forest, IL, Lake County, 27 miles N of the Loop. Lake Forest, a favorite retreat of Chicago's upper class, is tied to the network of suburbs north of Chicago along LAKE MICHIGAN regarded as the North Shore. Earliest white habitation, circa 1834, was for farming. The area was initially beyond Chicago's reach, but starting in 1855 railroads enabled daily commutation.

Presbyterians established Lake Forest in 1857. Almerin Hotchkiss's design resembled a park, featuring curvilinear lines. Incorporated in 1861, it attained high regard among wealthy Chicagoans by offering cultivated landscapes, abundant land, and the prospect of social order.

The founders simultaneously organized LAKE FOREST COLLEGE, anticipating its centrality in their community.

The population of 877 in 1880 advanced to 1,203 in 1890; it nearly doubled, to 2,215, in 1900. Chicagoans constructed country-style estates, often occupied seasonally (Cyrus H. McCormick, Jr.'s Walden; Louis F. Swift's Westleigh; and J. Ogden Armour's Mellody Farm). But the crowning glory was the Onwentsia Club, established in 1895 as a private country club.

Market Square was completed in 1917. This sublime commercial center designed by Howard Van Doren Shaw complemented the sumptuous private dwellings. Rectangular in form, it opened upon the railway station. Foreseeing the automobile age, the tree-lined square enabled access for motorists. Capitalized and operated privately through a land trust, it became a lasting civic expression. In 1978 it was listed on the National Register of Historical Sites as the nation's first planned shopping center.

Population reached 6,554 by 1930, with much of the growth occurring in the 1920s. Skokie Highway, completed in 1931, connected it to other population centers. Local services and facilities required attention: INFRASTRUCTURES for utilities; a new city hall; a professional fire department; the first free-standing post office as well as library; new schools (most notably a four-year high school); a youth center; a movie theater; a public GOLF course; and a modern HOSPITAL. To preserve the historic scale, a municipal ZONING ordinance was enacted in 1923. In 1926 voters approved the annexation of a largely uninhabited 10-square-mile expanse on Lake Forest's western boundary, tripling its size to 15 square miles.

Change accelerated in the second half of the twentieth century. Population surpassed 10,000 in 1960 and reached 20,059 in 2000. During these postwar decades the prevailing residential expression shifted from castles to ranch houses. While the east side remained mostly unchanged (save for new APARTMENT complexes), single-family homes in the southern and westerly reaches proliferated. Lake Forest also became a center of employment, especially in financial services: within its central business district, office space increased 286 percent (+327,731 square feet) between 1974 and 1999; private-sector employment citywide advanced 203 percent between 1978 and 1998, in part due to an office park acquired through further ANNEXATION. Local government again encountered challenges: vehicular congestion; WATER service; school construction; recreation (especially developing its beachfront); senior citizens; and cultural affairs. Advocacy for HISTORIC PRESERVATION and land conservation intensified. So did opposition to its governing regime, in place since the 1940s. Accelerated by the premium upon REAL ESTATE bearing a Lake Forest address, municipal officials enacted the nation's first building-scale ordinance in 1989 to regulate the demolition of residences and the construction of oversized replacements. For 1999, the average sale price of single-family homes was $821,316.

Michael H. Ebner

See also: Landscape Design; Shopping Districts and Malls; Suburbs and Cities as Dual Metropolis

Further reading: Arpee, Edward. *Lake Forest, Illinois, History and Reminiscences, 1861–1961.* 1963; rev. ed. 1991. • Dart, Susan. *Market Square, Lake Forest, Illinois.* 1984. • Miller, Arthur H., and Shirley M. Paddock. *Lake Forest, Estates, People, and Culture.* 2000.

Lake in the Hills, IL, McHenry County, 41 miles NW of the Loop.

Lake in the Hills was developed as a summer estate around artificial lakes in the 1920s, and investors began residential SUBDIVISIONS of the area in the 1940s. Incorporated in 1952, the rolling terrain is now a vast residential area. The village's population grew from 5,866 in 1990 to 23,152 in 2000.

Craig L. Pfannkuche

See also: McHenry County; Metropolitan Growth

Further reading: *McHenry County in the Twentieth Century, 1968–1994.* McHenry County Historical Society. 1994. • Nye, Lowell A., ed. *McHenry County, Illinois, 1832–1968.* 1968.

Lake Michigan. Lake Michigan is the third largest of the GREAT LAKES (22,400 square miles) and the only one located entirely within the United States. At least since 1670, when Marquette and Joliet crossed the Chicago PORTAGE, Lake Michigan has been Chicago's link to the wider world. A resource alternately treasured and plundered, the lake has served at various times as Chicago's dumping ground, a place from which to reclaim vital recreational space, and a source of drinking WATER. In 1818 the boundary of the new state of Illinois was adjusted 60 miles to the north so as to include the shore of the lake as part of the state's eastern boundary. Without this shift Chicago would not even have been located in Illinois.

Ben Hecht: Lake Thoughts

In 1921, the *Chicago Daily News* began running a column by Ben Hecht entitled "One Thousand and One Afternoons." Ruminating on life in general and on Chicago more particularly, Hecht considered the role of Lake Michigan in a Chicagoan's psyche:

During the summer day the beaches are lively and the vari-colored bathing suits and parasols offer little carnival panels at the ends of the east running streets. As you pass them on the north side bus or on the south side I.C., the sun, the swarm of bathers smeared like bits of brightly colored paint across the yellow sand and the obliterating sweep of water remind you of the modernist artists whose pictures are usually lithographic blurs.

Yet winter and summer, even when the thousands upon thousands of bathers cover the sand like a shower of confetti and when there are shouts and circus excitements along the beach, people who look at the lake seem always to become sad. One wonders why.

It is when one leaves the city and goes to visit or to live in another place where there is no lake that the lake grows alive in one's mind. One becomes thirsty for it and dreams of it. One remembers it then as something that was almost an essential part of life, like a third dimension. In some way one associates one's day dreams with the lake and falls into thinking that there is something unfinished, sterile about living with no lake at one's elbow.

Hecht, Ben. *1001 Afternoons in Chicago.* 1922; 1992, 231–234.

The lake's name is derived from the Algonquin word *Michigami,* meaning "great water." In the language of economics that great water functioned as an inexpensive medium of TRANSPORTATION and an integrated system of circulation for the communities within the Lake Michigan basin. As the market and hub for that basin, Chicago shaped the transformation of the coastal areas of Indiana, Wisconsin, and Michigan into discrete zones of economic activity. During the years between 1860 and 1900 hundreds of LUMBER schooners tied the frontier sawmill towns of northern Michigan and Wisconsin to the Chicago lumber market. During those same years steam-powered excursion and packet vessels linked Chicago with the small ports of southwestern Michigan and Door County, Wisconsin, unloading tourists and taking on crates of fresh fruits. NORWEGIAN, IRISH, and NATIVE AMERICAN fisherman fed Chicago and the region thousands of tons of whitefish and trout.

A less scenic transformation took place along the Little CALUMET and Grand Calumet Rivers. Giant bulk freighters united the IRON mines and stone QUARRIES of the North with the coal fields of the South in the steel towns at the southern end of Lake Michigan. In each case it was Chicago as a market, as a source of capital, and as a distribution center which shaped the shores of the entire lake. Chicagoans created the illusion that the pollution of sawmills could be segregated from commercial fishing, that AGRICULTURAL production existed in harmony with VACATION beach resorts, that the city was immune from the effluvium of metal fabrication.

Lake Michigan also has provided a respite from urban congestion. From the middle to the end of the nineteenth century vigorous young Chicagoans were attracted to the wild DUNES and beaches of the Near North and South Sides. SAILING was also popular, although it was not until 1875 that elite Chicagoans began to organize yacht clubs to facilitate the sport. Aaron Montgomery Ward's lawsuits and Daniel BURNHAM'S 1909 *Plan of Chicago* finally laid the foundation for a lakefront of parks, harbors, and beaches open to the masses of the city.

During the 1960s the fallacy of seeing Lake Michigan as a series of discrete zones of recreational, agricultural, and industrial use was revealed in the form of stinking piles of algae and alewives (four-inch-long silver fish). Choices had to be made among the numerous uses of the lake. Lawsuits against industrial and municipal polluters in the Calumet region during the early 1970s and a controversial ban on the use of phosphate detergents played a major role in stopping further deterioration of the lake. The 1972 federal Clean Water Act and the establishment of the Environmental Protection Agency helped to initiate a halting reversal of the lake's ecological deterioration.

Theodore J. Karamanski

See also: Chicago River; Environmental Politics; Global Chicago; Lacustrine System; Waterfront

Further reading: Mendes, Joel, Theodore J. Karamanski, and Philip Elmes. *The Maritime History of Chicago: A Guide to Sources.* 1990. • Quaife, Milo. *Lake Michigan.* 1944. • Wille, Lois. *Forever Open, Clear, and Free: The Struggle for Chicago's Lakefront.* 1972.

Lake Station, IN, Lake County, 29 miles SE of the Loop.

Lake Station, platted in 1852 along the Michigan Central RAILROAD, served as an important shipping center for AGRICULTURAL products. The town became part of the new suburb of East Gary in 1908. City boosters hoped to attract executives from GARY, but workers came instead. In 1977 East Gary was renamed Lake Station.

Peggy Tuck Sinko

See also: Lake County, IN

Further reading: Christenson, Susan. *From Lake Station to East Gary.* 1976.

Lake Township. Between 1850 and 1889 the area south of 39th Street, west of State Street, east of Crawford Avenue, and north of 87th Street constituted Lake Township, an independent political unit separate from Chicago. More than 10,000 new residents moved to the area, home of the UNION STOCK YARD, between 1870 and 1880. The incorporated government could not adequately provide services to this burgeoning population, and the area was ANNEXED to Chicago in 1889.

Ann Durkin Keating

See also: Fuller Park; Governing the Metropolis; Grand Boulevard; Meatpacking; New City; Townships; Washington Park

Further reading: Keating, Ann Durkin. *Building Chicago: Suburban Developers and the Creation of a Divided Metropolis.* 1988.

Lake View, Community Area 6, 4 miles N of the Loop. Over the past century and a half, the name Lake View has referred in turn to the first of Chicago's North Shore suburban developments, an independent TOWNSHIP, a city in its own right, and a COMMUNITY AREA within Chicago. All of the Lake Views have occupied land between two and eight miles north of Chicago's center. As one official incarnation of Lake View gave way to the next, it gradually transformed from a loose agglomeration of large parcels of land occupied by farms and estates into distinct neighborhoods housing many single young adults, childless married couples, and gay men.

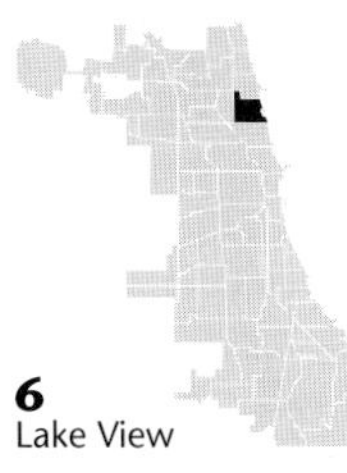

Lake View's early residents followed the lead of nearby LINCOLN SQUARE's first property owner, Conrad Sulzer. Farmers from GERMANY, SWEDEN, and LUXEMBOURG made celery Lake View's most important local crop. In 1854, James Rees and Elisha Hundley built the Lakeview House HOTEL near Lake Shore Drive and Byron Street as a resort for potential investors in local land. (According to legend, Walter Newberry stood on the hotel's veranda and, admiring its view, suggested that it be called "Lake View House.") Wealthy Chicagoans seeking summer retreats from the city's heat and disease bought up land in the eastern sector of the area. New RAILROAD lines prompted development of more residential land and added suburban characteristics to Lake View's resort atmosphere.

With increasing settlement came legal identity. In 1857, the area presently bounded by Fullerton, Western, Devon, and Lake Michigan was organized into LAKE VIEW TOWNSHIP; in 1872 residents built a town hall at Halsted and Addison; and in 1887 Lake View was incorporated as a city. In 1889, however, despite a controversial vote and the recalcitrance of Lake View officials, the city was ANNEXED to Chicago.

The urbanizing Lake View attracted not only new residents, but also visitors to its burgeoning commercial and recreational facilities. A baseball park at Clark and Addison later known as WRIGLEY FIELD (1914) attracted Chicagoans who lived outside Lake View. Wieboldt's DEPARTMENT STORE (1917) anchored a new SHOPPING DISTRICT at the intersection of Lincoln, Belmont, and Ashland Avenues. Southwestern Lake View's working-class residential character merged with that of neighboring NORTH CENTER, as factory workers sought homes near their jobs. They occupied such SUBDIVISIONS as Gross Park, which was laid out by Samuel Eberly Gross. Developers also built APARTMENT buildings to accommodate residents who could not afford homes such as those preferred by the old, suburban elite. In the mid-twentieth century, high-rise apartments and four-plus-ones (multiple-unit low-rises), both of which attracted single people and childless couples, were popular solutions to the growing housing problem.

The apparent changes in the family and architectural structures of Lake View alarmed some residents, who organized the Lake View Citizens Council in the 1950s to fight potential blight. LVCC quickly realized that Lake View was too well off for designation as a government conservation area, so it encouraged private redevelopment and rehabilitation instead. Residents and merchants used different strategies to preserve distinctive neighborhoods within Lake View. In the early 1970s, for example, East Lake View became known as New Town for its trendy shops and counterculture denizens. The elegant Alta Vista Terrace attained landmark status. A REAL-ESTATE frenzy during the early 1980s drove neighborhoods such as Wrigleyville into public view.

The physical preservation of Lake View, however, did not reconfigure the area into a family-centered community. While some of the new residents, such as World War II JAPANESE American refugees from California and the increasing Latino population, did arrive in family units, most of Lake View's new population were single, childless young adults. As early as the 1950s, an identifiable GAY male population resided in the Belmont Harbor area. According to the 1990 census, more than 22,000 residents of Lake View were between the ages of 25 and 44 and lived in "nonfamily" households.

Amanda Seligman

See also: Multicentered Chicago; Vacation Spots

Further reading: Andreas, A. T. *History of Cook County, Illinois, from the Earliest Period to the Present Time.* 1884. • Clark, Stephen Bedell. *The Lake View Saga.* 1985 [1974].

Lake View Township. Between 1857 and 1889, the area north of North Avenue, east of Western Avenue and south of Devon Avenue was an independent political unit separate from Chicago. The area population grew from 2,000 in 1870 to 45,000 in 1887, and under the weight of public service demands the TOWNSHIP annexed to Chicago in 1889.

Lake View town hall, built in 1872 at the corner of Halsted and Addison. Photographer: Unknown. Source: Chicago Historical Society.

Ann Durkin Keating

See also: Annexation; Edgewater; Governing the Metropolis; Lake View; Lincoln Park; Uptown

Further reading: Keating, Ann Durkin. *Building Chicago: Suburban Developers and the Creation of a Divided Metropolis.* 1988.

Lake Villa, IL, Lake County, 41 miles NW of the Loop. After the displacement of the POTAWATOMI, the earliest landowners in the area were farmers, who first bought the land from the government in the 1840s. The first local centralized place was Monaville, a crossroads hamlet southwest of what is now Lake Villa. Lake Villa itself began in 1883 as a project of merchant E. J. Lehmann, founder of the Fair DEPARTMENT STORE on State Street in Chicago. Lehmann bought land between Cedar Lake and Deep Lake and built a private resort and a sumptuous, 150-room HOTEL to entertain friends, guests, and vacationers.

Lehmann hoped to call the settlement "Lake City," but as there was already a town by that name in Illinois, the first post office in 1884 was called Stanwood. The name "Lake Villa" came into use after 1886.

Lake Villa was a station on the Wisconsin Central RAILROAD line built in 1887, providing convenient TRANSPORTATION to the resort from

Chicago. Lehmann's leadership ended in 1890, when he suffered a breakdown and was institutionalized. While some summer vacationers did pass through Lake Villa, the town itself grew slowly, incorporating in 1901. By 1910 the population was 342. While Grand Avenue (Route 132) was once the boundary between Antioch and Avon Townships, residents successfully petitioned to create Lake Villa Township in 1912, arguing that this change would end the need to travel more than six miles to vote on Election Day.

The village did not develop much of a commercial center to compare with nearby villages such as ANTIOCH and FOX LAKE. The Lake City Hotel burned in 1915. By the 1920s Lehmann's children had built expansive mansions on scattered estates, contributing to an image of the area as a wealthy enclave. Ice harvesting provided employment for some farmers and local residents in the winter. Lake Villa was also the location of the Allendale School, an institution for homeless boys founded in 1897. The Central Baptist Children's Home located itself on a Lake Villa estate in 1948.

In the 1950s a phase of suburban growth began. Developers subdivided the farmlands of many of the old mansions, including Ernst Lehmann's LINDENHURST Farm, which gave its name to what became a new neighboring municipality.

Lake Villa itself remained a small, settled village. There was some growth through new subdivisions in the mid-1980s. In 1990 the village population was 2,857. Population grew rapidly to 5,864 in 2000, as developers built thousands of homes, along with a strip mall and business center.

Lake Villa and Lindenhurst continue to have overlapping histories, sharing schools, churches, and the Lake Villa District Library. In 1995 the Lindenhurst–Lake Villa Chamber of Commerce was organized by expanding a preexisting Lindenhurst chamber.

The new North Central METRA line, providing service to O'Hare Airport and to downtown Chicago, opened in 1996 with a station at Lake Villa. This restored rail passenger service to the village for the first time since 1965. The station is a replica of the original 1886 station, which was torn down in 1974.

Douglas Knox

See also: Metropolitan Growth; Suburbs and Cities as Dual Metropolis; Vacation Spots

Further reading: Chatlien, Michael. *Timepiece: A History of the Lake Villa Area.* Videocassette. 1994. 53 min. • Trychta, J. K., ed. *Nine Decades: The Village of Lake Villa, Illinois, 1901–1991.* 1991.

Lake Zurich, IL, Lake County, 32 miles NW of the Loop. Cedar Lake was created in the 1830s by beavers who dammed an outflow stream from a lowland area. Seth Paine, believing that people could achieve happiness through communal living, settled land east of the lake in 1836. He dreamed of organizing a commune as described by the French philosopher Charles Fourier. Since some Swiss cantons were practicing Fourier's communal system, Paine named his settlement and the adjoining lake Lake Zurich.

In 1841 Paine constructed a communal store on his property and invited people from Chicago to come to the village he platted and live by Fourier's principles. Along with his Union Store, Paine constructed a shelter for HOMELESS Chicagoans, calling it the Stable of Humanity. He also welcomed escaping slaves and labored in the cause of the UNDERGROUND RAILROAD. By 1850, Paine's community numbered no more than 100 residents.

With skeptical neighbors refusing to join the commune, Paine returned to Chicago in 1852 to put into practice his belief that people would have to change their ideas about what constituted wealth before they could accept Fourier's vision. He opened the Bank of Chicago, basing its loan policy on humanitarian rather than profit principles. CIVIL WAR economics ended Paine's experiment, and Paine died in Chicago on June 6, 1872, barely remembered by Lake Zurich residents.

Although Rand Road (now U.S. Route 12), an important mail and stagecoach trail from Chicago to southern Wisconsin, ran through the community, Lake Zurich hardly grew during the late 1800s. In 1889, the Elgin, Joliet & Eastern RAILROAD (EJ&E) built its Chicago bypass line (from northern Indiana to Waukegan) through Lake Zurich. Believing that the railroad would bring development, community leaders incorporated Lake Zurich as a village in 1896, with Frank Clark as president.

Although large icehouses were built with a view to developing an industry, it failed to prosper because of poor TRANSPORTATION to Chicago's center, and the community's population rose to only just over 200 by 1900. In 1910, Justin K. Orvis persuaded residents to support the construction of a rail line linking Lake Zurich to the Chicago & North Western Railway at PALATINE. Passenger service on the Palatine, Lake Zurich & WAUCONDA Railroad (PLZ&W) began in 1912 after the railroad bridged the EJ&E.

The new line opened up Lake Zurich to summer picnic traffic and the community's reputation as a resort area blossomed. As Americans embraced the automobile, Rand Road became a paved highway in 1922, contributing to the demise of the PLZ&W. Auto trips to Lake Zurich's rental cottages increased dramatically in the 1920s, enhancing the community's reputation as a beautiful place to live.

Hearing such stories, many WORLD WAR II veterans moved to Lake Zurich to raise their families amid summer greenery. Most Lake Zurich summer cottages were winterized to make room for the expanding population; the community's 1936 population of 350 jumped to 3,800 by 1966. Although Lake Zurich's reputation as a summer resort for white-collar Chicagoans continued into the 1970s, by 2000 the community had gained the status of suburban bedroom community with a population of 18,104.

Craig L. Pfannkuche

See also: Metropolitan Growth; Streets and Highways; Vacation Spots

Further reading: Loomis, Spencer, and Gloria Heramb, eds. *Lake Zurich Centennial: One Hundred Years of a Midwestern Village.* 1996. • Loomis, Spencer. *Pictorial History of Ela Township.* 1994. • Whitney, Richard. *Old Maud: The Story of the Palatine, Lake Zurich, and Wauconda Railroad.* 1992.

Lakemoor, IL, Lake and McHenry Counties, 43 miles NW of the Loop. Platted in 1924 as a VACATION SPOT around Lily Lake, Lakemoor incorporated in 1938. Struggling over the issue of taxes, villagers voted to dissolve the incorporation in 1943. Requiring improved community roads and police protection, residents voted by a slim margin to reincorporate in 1952. Population in 2000 was 2,788.

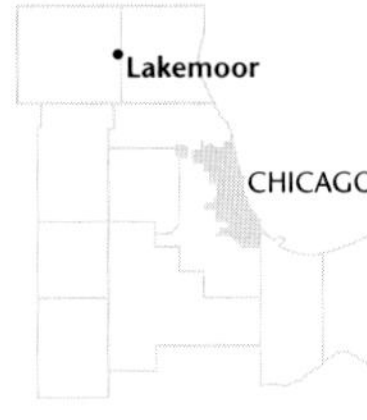

Craig L. Pfannkuche

See also: McHenry County

Further reading: Nye, Lowell A., ed. *McHenry County, Illinois, 1832–1968.* 1968.

Lakewood, IL, McHenry County, 45 miles NW of the Loop. Nestled along the south shore of CRYSTAL LAKE, this 1920s SUBDIVISION of large homes incorporated in 1933. Upscale housing development in the 1980s brought growth to the small community. Struggling to grow from its 2000 population of 2,337, the village battled neighbor Crystal Lake to annex commercial and residential properties.

Craig L. Pfannkuche

See also: McHenry County

Further reading: Nye, Lowell A., ed. *McHenry County, Illinois, 1832–1968.* 1968.

Land Use. The successful development of the Chicago metropolitan area is largely attributed to the region's strategic location at the southern end of LAKE MICHIGAN. This vital crossroads location has served the region's economy well in terms of production and the shipment of goods by all modes of transport. Chicago's locational advantage has

Illinois Central freight yards, from Randolph Street Bridge, before 1952. Photographer: Unknown. Source: Chicago Historical Society.

been exploited by land developers and INFRASTRUCTURE builders over time to produce the land-use pattern of today's metropolis.

Recognized as early as 1673 by Joliet and Marquette, the connection between the GREAT LAKES and the Mississippi River offered opportunities not only for exploration and trade, but also for REAL-ESTATE investment and speculation.

After Indian TREATIES cleared the way for large-scale settlement and investment, Chicago became a funnel for people, products, and investment dollars to the American West. Well-placed NATIVE AMERICAN trails and trading routes were transformed into shipping, rail, and highway routes, with settlements providing services. Early traders were joined by farmers, who set the stage for massive AGRICULTURAL and urban development.

Government sponsorship of the ILLINOIS & MICHIGAN CANAL and the marketing of canal lands encouraged the growth of Chicago and other canal towns from LAKE MICHIGAN to LaSalle-Peru. Chicago has always experienced boom and bust economic and development cycles. After rapid growth in the 1830s, there was the bust of 1837, followed by recovery. After the I&M Canal was completed in 1848, it was rapidly eclipsed by the development of more efficient RAILROADS, which added impetus to the following boom. Together, the WATER and rail systems that moved supplies and manufactured goods to the western frontier and agricultural products to eastern markets also provided the base for real-estate development. The developing pattern of land use was therefore largely oriented to the canal and rail corridors where warehouses, industries, and housing for canal and RAILROAD WORKERS were located.

It was during the period of extraordinary industrial development of the late nineteenth and early twentieth centuries that the "broad shoulders" image of Chicago was created. The IRON AND STEEL mills and the oil REFINERIES of southeast Chicago and GARY and along the industrial corridor following the original route of the I&M Canal (later the route of the SANITARY AND SHIP CANAL and the Stevenson EXPRESSWAY) became major land users that supported the region's economy and the development of worker housing.

Patterns of land use before rail transport were influenced by the location of landscape features such as rivers and ancient beach ridges, but much more profound was the influence of the surveyor's grid, which imposed a lasting square-mile pattern of roads and SUBDIVISIONS. The grid exists today, along with a pattern of COMMUTER rail corridors with nodes of bedroom communities radiating from the Chicago LOOP.

After WORLD WAR II, the square-mile surveyor's grid began to be filled in by the fashionable curvilinear style of subdivision development. Radial and circumferential EXPRESSWAYS, together with multilane arterial roadways, added further complexity to the pattern. Land use and real-estate development built on this pattern of the basic grid plus its overlays.

The region's world-famous PLANNING and urban design heritage have also influenced the history of land use and real-estate development. The company town of PULLMAN, the grand *Plan of Chicago* offered by Burnham and Bennett in 1909, the reservation of lakefront parkland and outlying FOREST PRESERVES, the prototypical curvilinear suburb of RIVERSIDE, the post–WORLD WAR II bedroom community of PARK FOREST, and the conservation community of Prairie Crossing in the 1990s all provided national models for progressive real-estate development and urban design.

The natural attractiveness of certain areas provided another stimulus for real-estate development. The cottages and resorts in the lake district in the northern part of the region gradually converted to full-service communities. Similarly, wealthy city dwellers seeking the country experience led the development of suburban GOLF courses reachable by commuter rail service, around which grew suburbs such as FLOSSMOOR and OLYMPIA FIELDS. The stunning Lake Michigan shoreline miles north of downtown Chicago provided captains of industry and civic leaders with an elegant, verdant, and unpolluted residential setting.

The single largest real-estate force over the last 50 years has, of course, been the automobile, which made the countryside accessible for new homeowners, allowing escape from the ills of city living. Where housing went, jobs followed. Thus, older urban communities and suburbs began a period of emptying, and new investment occurred in outlying and newly developing communities. Scattered employment opportunities and regional SHOPPING centers developed throughout the expanding suburban fringe. City and suburban workers were, and still are, dependent upon the automobile for most suburban travel. Cultural attitudes toward land use, reflected by traditional ZONING ordinances, strongly enforced the low-density development patterns and highly segregated land uses.

The disinvestment of urban Chicago and older suburbs seemed to accelerate the "concentric growth phenomenon," which had been described by urban economists such as Homer Hoyt at the University of Chicago. It was easy to see a concentric pattern of inner core, older inner areas, newly developing areas farther out, and finally, open countryside. In the period between the 1960s and the 1990s this dynamic progression was even more apparent.

There have been two periods of public concern about the phenomenon of suburban "sprawl," that is, a dispersed pattern of new development that leaves behind older areas and creates new, loose patterns of land use dependent on the automobile. The first wave of concern was soon after World War II when expressways were constructed and suburban growth and the preference for owner-occupied single-family houses increased. As a response, in 1957 the Illinois legislature created the Northeastern Illinois Planning Commission (NIPC) as an advisory agency charged with coordinating development among the hundreds of local governments and taxing districts, developing regional plans, and providing research and technical assistance. In its Comprehensive General Plan, adopted in 1968, NIPC called for concentrating new development largely along the radial commuter lines focused on the Chicago LOOP, and for preserving wedges of open space and low-density development between the radial corridors. However, Illinois' legal framework for planning, zoning, and real-estate TAXATION has encouraged a multiplicity of jurisdictions competing for tax revenues, thereby exacerbating sprawl. This does not encourage intergovernmental cooperation, long-range planning for public investment, compact development patterns, or resource conservation.

According to NIPC, the explosion of land consumption continued dramatically between 1970 and 1990 with a 40 percent increase in developed land area in the region, while the region's population increased by only 4 percent. More than four hundred square miles of farmland were consumed during this period. Major new development was being experienced in the counties lying just outside the six-county metropolitan area. Other metropolitan areas across the United States were observing the same phenomenon. Therefore, there was an increasing awareness in the 1990s that this growth pattern represented a very real threat to the long-term sustainability of communities and the metropolitan region. Planners in the northeastern Illinois region, as in many other regions, began to call for "smart growth" in order to promote mixed land uses, preservation of usable open space, and viable TRANSPORTATION systems. Federal and state governments were similarly taking up the charge.

Also during the 1990s, Chicago began to experience major new investment in the central part of the city and in other locations as well. Loft conversions, new high-rise apartments and condominiums, new townhouse developments, and infill on individual lots began to bring new vitality back to the city. Local school improvements and reduced crime rates further supported reinvestment in older cities and towns. Some of the older but more desirable suburbs were also experiencing the "teardown" phenomenon, where historic homes were purchased and demolished in order to build larger structures.

Federal initiatives to clean up rivers and streams have left shorelines attractive amenities for residential and commercial development, replacing their use for industry and disposal of waste. Similarly, techniques for cleaning up and redeveloping old industrial sites ("brownfields") were tested successfully by federal, state, and local agencies. This further added to the prospects for rejuvenation of older areas.

At the end of the twentieth century, there were signs of acceptance of new forms of real-estate development and land use. It remains to be seen whether these will become dominant forms and whether the region will find effective means to further a regional vision as it increasingly operates within a GLOBAL economy.

Richard D. Mariner

See also: Built Environment of the Chicago Region; Contested Spaces; Economic Geography; Environmental Politics; Fire Limits in Chicago in the 1870s (color map, p. C2); Gentrification; Governing the Metropolis; Neighborhood Change: Chicago's Prairie Avenue, 1853–2003 (color map, p. C4); Planning Chicago; Urban Renewal

Further reading: Cronon, William. *Nature's Metropolis: Chicago and the Great West.* 1991. • Mayer, Harold M., and Richard C. Wade. *Chicago: Growth of a Metropolis.* 1969. • Northeastern Illinois Planning Commission. *Strategic Plan for Land Resource Management.* 1992.

Landscape. Chicago's landscape is characterized by a flatness which reflects its underlying geology, many layers of sedimentary deposits laid down over the eons when the site lay beneath shallow seas. When these limestone layers were raised above sea level, the resulting plateau was cut by rain waters draining southward. The result was a low dissected plateau similar to the hilly terrain that exists today in the northwestern corner of Illinois.

The great ice sheets of the glacial age then pushed southward from Canada and rearranged the landscape, leveling the hills, filling in the valleys, excavating Lake Michigan's basin, and leaving debris of soil and rocks in a series of moraines that marked pauses in the retreat of the ice sheets. These recessional moraines ringing today's LAKE MICHIGAN dammed up the melt WATERS and created a series of great glacial impoundments that eventually became the GREAT LAKES. Before reaching their current configurations, however, the glacial lakes underwent a series of dramatic fluctuations. Lake Chicago emerged at one high point, covering an area larger and deeper than today's Lake Michigan. Eventually, melting water poured over the moraines, creating a spillway that drained Lake Chicago down to the current lake level.

After the rush of melt waters subsided, the spillway emerged as the divide between the Mississippi River and Great Lakes drainage basins, serving as a key PORTAGE location and later emerging as a major transportation corridor. It is clearly marked on most maps by the ILLINOIS & MICHIGAN CANAL, the SANITARY AND SHIP CANAL, and several RAILROADS. The old bed of Lake Chicago, flat, low-lying, and encrusted with heavy clay SOILS, became the site of the city of Chicago. It was poorly drained by short, sluggish rivers: the CHICAGO and the CALUMET. The higher moraine, drained by the DES PLAINES, DU PAGE, FOX, and Kankakee Rivers, all sources for the Illinois River, became sites for varied farms which supplied the city with food and provisions. AGRICULTURAL villages ringing Chicago grew into suburbs, often taking names to emphasize their increased elevation: ARLINGTON HEIGHTS, MOUNT PROSPECT, and, where the moraine swings eastward to meet the lake, HIGHLAND PARK.

The old lakebed itself was crossed by a series of former beaches and spits which offered better drainage because of their sandy soil. These sites were often marked by different vegetation as the glaciers retreated and a warm-summer, continental climate returned to the area. These ridges and beaches then became animal traces and NATIVE AMERICAN trails, later turning into pioneer roads. Some survive as modern thoroughfares.

When the ice sheets left the Chicago area for the last time about 13,000 years ago, a tempestuous weather pattern set in which further softened the landscape. Depressions were filled in with wind-driven soil while the melt waters

View from Cary Station Hills overlooking Fox River Grove, 1920. Photographer: Curt Teich & Co. Source: Curt Teich Archives, Lake County Discovery Museum.

flowing southward sorted out sands and gravel deposits which became resources for the later building of the city. Huge chunks of ice were left behind as the ice retreated.

Sometimes buried in the process, then slowly melting, they created depressions which became ponds and lakes. These pockets, and others created by the retreat of the ice and the rush of the melting waters, gradually filled with vegetation, turning into wetlands, sloughs, and peat bogs and covering much of the landscape, even on the higher elevations of the moraine.

The vegetation that reclothed the region in the postglacial period included wetlands and dry lands. The dry lands divided again into woodlands and grasslands, which nineteenth-century Americans respectively labeled groves and prairies. Grasslands came first and supported an array of large mammals: mastodons, mammoths, bison, elk, and their predators, like saber-toothed tigers and human beings. It was the latter, the early big-game hunters, who probably saw an advantage in encouraging the natural prairie fires which, started by lightning, kept the grasslands largely free of shrubs and trees. These fires maintained a prairie landscape in a climatic region that should have reverted to a forested region in due time. Indeed, the great forest extended from the north and the east up to the fringes of the Chicago area in historic times, but a prairie peninsula reached eastward to touch the Great Lakes at the site of FORT DEARBORN. Groves of oak and hickory dotted the prairie sea like islands when Americans first arrived, offering prime sites for pioneer settlement.

These nineteenth-century Americans settlers took on the massive task of changing the vegetation and altering the landscape to support their way of life. They looked upon the lands and the rivers as tools and resources. Trees were cut for LUMBER and fuel, the grasslands turned into pastures and fields, and Old World plants and animals replaced the native flora and fauna. Wetlands were drained and lowlands filled to make better use of the land. In the city of Chicago, the surface was raised to improve drainage, the shore line was filled in to gain land, the river was channelized and straightened, and its flow was reversed by deepening the canal in the spillway and placing a low dam at its mouth. New lagoons, ponds, and harbors were dug to help control storm waters or to create park lands and recreational areas.

The motto of the early city was "City in a Garden," and lots were made deep enough so that sidewalks and houses could be set back from the STREETS, creating "parkways" and "front yards" to display lawns and flower beds developed from imported plants. The use of the government land survey to create a grid of STREETS, rectangular blocks, and lots created a formal geometric urban plan, much more textured than but fully compatible with the pattern of farms and fields surrounding the city. The park movement in the latter half of the nineteenth century, the subsequent creation of a greenbelt of FOREST PRESERVES, and the OPEN LANDS movement in the twentieth century have created, preserved, or recreated various types of alternative landscapes.

Gerald A. Danzer

See also: Built Environment of the Chicago Region; Ecosystem Evolution; Glaciation; Lacustrine System; Landscape Design; Plant Communities

Further reading: Bretz, J. Harlen. *Geology of the Chicago Region: Part I, General; Part II, The Pleistocene.* 2 vols. 1939, 1955. • Fryxell, F. M. *The Physiography of the Region of Chicago.* 1927. • Schmid, James A. *Urban Vegetation: A Review and Chicago Case Study.* 1975.

Landscape Design. When Europeans first visited the Chicago region, three aspects of Indian LANDSCAPE design gained their attention—portages, trails, and fires. The several portages in the region, permitting transfer between the GREAT LAKES and Mississippi watersheds, were important on a very large scale and inspired speculation regarding the development of the continent. The trails, usually along unrecognized remnants of glacial activity—former beaches, eskers, moraines—showed where the land could be traversed in all times, regardless of the wetness of the season.

Most apparent to the early explorers was the burning of the prairies, usually in the fallow seasons. This management technique had transformed the Illinois region from one of mixed forest and grassland into the easternmost edge of the extraordinary tall-grass prairies of the American Great Plains. Because the burning destroyed small woody plants, the continuous views through the few stands of trees reminded European travelers of landscaped parks, reinforcing their sympathy for what came to be called the picturesque.

Applying the Land Ordinance of 1785, the landscape was platted into TOWNSHIPS of 36 square miles, with square mile sections. Early settlers were struck by the extent of the prairie and the pliancy of the river—in fact some saw it as a marsh with diverse channels. TREES, whether cottonwoods along watercourses or oaks along glacial rises, provided some relief to the planarity of the land. The lake, as an inland sea, entered consciousness as the most dramatic and sublime element of the landscape. However, it was the prairie in its limitless horizon that was so new and exciting and baffling to settlers. The gridded town and bounded house site organized space in a familiar manner, but the limitless prairie remained unaccommodated as it remained uncomprehended. Meanwhile, as Chicago's population grew from about 4,000 in 1840 to more than a quarter million at the eve of the CIVIL WAR, the initial individuality of building sites gave way to streetscapes bounded by uniform setbacks, heights, and orientation to the street, as well as regularized street zones.

From the creation of such landscaped CEMETERIES as Oakwoods, GRACELAND, and Rosehill, to the initiation of a park and boulevard system linking the expanding city neighborhoods, to the conscious design of railroad-served suburbs such as LAKE FOREST and RIVERSIDE, professional landscape designers applied the most current ideas about the role of landscape design in the creation of urban civilizations. Civic leaders such as Paul Cornell and William Le Baron Jenney served with distinction on, respectively, the south and west parks commissions. They commissioned designers such as Frederick Law Olmsted, Calvert Vaux, Ossian Simonds, H. W. S. Cleveland,

Rustic bridge in Union Park on the Near West Side, 1870. Artist: Unknown. Source: The Newberry Library.

and Jens Jensen, among others, to design these large-scale open-space components for the city. The area was in effect zoned according to LAND USE patterns determined as much by the implications of landscape design as by the patterns and routes of the expanding commercial and industrial city. From Frederick Law Olmsted to Daniel H. Burnham, landscape and urban designers used parks and planned suburbs to shape elements of the city, describing the entire region as a comprehensive act of environmental design—city, suburb, parks, FOREST PRESERVES greenbelts, zones of TRANSPORTATION and development.

BURNHAM'S PLAN of 1909 is the greatest single act of landscape design ever offered as a guide for the city. Integrating all elements of the growing city as well as the region it affected, Burnham's plan sought to comprehend the entire region as an interrelated system of built-up and open spaces. As with earlier plans, the aesthetic of the picturesque—WATER either moving or in ponds, irregularly framed open spaces, wooded borders and points of transition from one zone to another, the development and exploitation of topographic elements as seemingly natural features in the environment—dominated. The immediate regions of the various fieldhouses or other focused elements of the parks were occasionally treated in a more formal manner associated with French or Italian landscape design. The most famous outcome of the Burnham Plan—the development of parks for almost the entire lakefront of the city—was matched by another, equally large-scale transformation of the city, the elevation and embankment of the vast network of rail traffic in the city. The increasing loss of life caused by rail crossings at grade led to the systematic, and still incomplete, raising of the tracks. Such embankments tended to create or reinforce neighborhood distinctions at a time when a large new wave of immigration from rural America as well as from around the world was significantly increasing the importance of place for ethnic communities.

In the late twentieth century, an ecological and environmental movement inspired by the writings of Aldo Leopold and Rachel Carson led to efforts to preserve and restore the landscape. Sites targeted ranged from the extremely polluted to the surprisingly pristine. Numerous large, abandoned industrial and transportation sites provided opportunities to reconsider the land. Some proposed restoration to a condition prior to human use or presence, while others discussed mixed uses through clean up and remediation. Meanwhile, many people benefited from the discovery that nature could be found in one's back yard or along the parkway as easily as at the seashore or in the mountains. Several institutions helped generate and respond to citizen interest. The MORTON ARBORETUM, in LISLE, continued to be one of the most important such facilities in the nation, with a distinguished staff developing and applying basic science. The CHICAGO BOTANIC GARDEN, in a Cook County FOREST PRESERVE north of the Skokie Lagoons, achieved broad public support for its multiple garden settings and extensive public programs. The cooperative extension of the UNIVERSITY OF ILLINOIS continued its century-old pattern of identifying and serving communities that were increasingly urbanized and suburbanized. Regional advocacy groups such as the OPENLANDS PROJECT and the local offices of national entities such as the Nature Conservancy demonstrated through their programs and members the broadly popular appeal of ENVIRONMENTALISM.

The population of Chicago declined in the 1960 census for the first time since the founding of the city. Although suburbanization had accompanied the entire history of Chicago, now the suburbs were about to become the preferred place of residence of the majority, who would transform the appearance of the region by using new political power to change public policy. Other factors also intertwined to change the face of the region. The pursuance of CIVIL RIGHTS, the venality of "BLOCK BUSTING" REAL-ESTATE brokers, and the development of a national system of high-speed limited-access highways changed the appearance of neighborhoods, the people in them, and their relation to the communities around them. The landscapes of abandoned and devastated communities contrasted with the GATED COMMUNITIES of others. High-rise APARTMENT buildings along the lakefront spoke of the power and success of the city, while high rises along EXPRESSWAYS suggested a warehousing of populations. Both phenomena demonstrated an urban vision described as "the tower in the park" and advocated by the Swiss French architect Le Corbusier and the German American city planner Ludwig Hilberseimer.

Kevin Harrington

See also: Architecture; Built Environment of the Chicago Region; Environmental Politics; Glaciation; Planning Chicago; Plant Communities

Further reading: Bluestone, Daniel. *Constructing Chicago.* 1991. • Burnham, Daniel H., and Edward H. Bennett. *Plan of Chicago.* 1909. • Mayer, Harold M., and Richard C. Wade. *Chicago: Growth of a Metropolis.* 1969.

Lansing, IL, Cook County, 22 miles SE of the Loop. As a result of its early DUTCH settlement, Lansing shares a heritage with SOUTH HOLLAND and MUNSTER, Indiana. Lansing includes areas known as Bernice, Cummings Corners, Seester, and Oak Glen.

Through the center of Lansing, running east–west, is a 25-foot-high elongated ridge of sand and gravel deposits that was once a prominent Indian trail and is now known as Ridge Road. This ridge formed the shorelines of the CALUMET and Glenwood stages of Lake Chicago. North and south of this ridge are deposits of clay that became the basis for the Lansing brickyards of the late 1800s.

Evidence of NATIVE AMERICAN occupation of the Lansing area abound, especially at the Hoxie Site, to the west of the village, which dates to around AD 1400. The POTAWATOMI, who were the last Native Americans to occupy the area, departed by the 1830s.

The 1843 arrival of the August Hildebrandt family began a period of GERMAN and Dutch immigration. These settlers were plagued by the lack of adequate drainage, which was a result of the Wisconsin glacier of 10,000 years earlier. In 1862 a drainage ditch was dug, relieving part of the problem.

In 1846, Henry, George, and John Lansing settled the area, coming from the state of New York. In 1850, Lansing's first business, the Union Hotel, was built. The Pennsylvania RAILROAD came through Lansing in 1856, followed later by the Grand Trunk Railroad. In 1865, Henry Lansing was named postmaster and John Lansing platted the town, which was incorporated in 1893. AGRICULTURE and brickyards dominated Lansing's economy in the late 1800s.

The industrial development of the Calumet region in the early twentieth century had a significant effect on the Lansing area. With the availability of jobs the population grew, and the first bank in Lansing was chartered in 1909, followed in 1910 by the first SUBDIVISION for homes. In 1911 TELEPHONE lines were strung and in 1912 electricity followed. A major improvement in TRANSPORTATION was the paving of Ridge Road with concrete in 1915. Considerable business developed in the 1920s, and in 1924 the Ford AIRPORT was built with one of the first passenger waiting rooms in the country.

During the GREAT DEPRESSION, Lansing lost a number of small businesses as well as the first Lansing State Bank. Camp Thornton was built by the Civilian Conservation Corps in a forest preserve to the west of Lansing. During WORLD WAR II the camp was used to house German prisoners of war, who worked for local farmers.

In the postwar period Lansing experienced a building boom, as large numbers of white ethnics moved in from Chicago. During the 1950s Lansing experienced its largest population increase, and the last remaining farmland was subdivided in 1964.

The expansion of the EXPRESSWAY system in the 1960s and '70s stimulated the growth of light industry, commerce, and population. The 2000 population was 28,332, of which 85 percent were white, with a growing number of blacks and Hispanics.

Dave Bartlett

See also: Chicago in the Middle Ground; Ecosystem Evolution; Quarrying, Stonecutting, and Brickmaking

Further reading: "Thornton Township, Cook County, Illinois." *Where the Trails Cross* 3.4 (Fall 1973). • Andreas, A. T. *History of Cook County, Illinois.* 1884. • Markman, Charles W. *Chicago before History: The Prehistoric Archaeology of a Modern Metropolitan Area.* Studies in Illinois Archaeology 7, ed. Thomas E. Emerson. 1991.

Laotians. Until the end of the Vietnam War in the 1970s unleashed a massive influx of REFUGEES, few Southeast Asians had migrated to the United States. Millions of VIETNAMESE, CAMBODIANS, and Laotians fled to refugee camps in Malaysia, Thailand, and Indonesia after the ascension of Communist regimes in 1975. The plight of these refugees attracted international attention when camps were overwhelmed and had to turn away new arrivals. Canada, Australia, and France began accepting refugees from the camps, and nearly one million entered the United States in the largest refugee resettlement program in the nation's history. Over 230,000 Laotians arrived in the United States between 1975 and 1992, including both lowland ethnic Lao and highland HMONG. Assisted by SOCIAL SERVICE organizations, Laotians settled throughout the nation and have since migrated within the United States, forming their largest communities in California, Texas, Minnesota, and Washington. Between 1975 and 1983, 3,500 Laotians settled in Chicago, primarily in the UPTOWN and ALBANY PARK neighborhoods, while many more settled in the suburbs of ELGIN, AURORA, Rockford, and JOLIET, where the availability of refugee programs and services facilitated community growth.

Laotian immigrants have faced a difficult process of adjustment to life in metropolitan Chicago. Many Laotians came from rural backgrounds, spoke little English, and had few transferable occupational skills and limited language skills and education. While a few Laotian businesses, particularly Lao GROCERIES, have been established in areas with large Laotian communities like Elgin, many Laotians have sought factory jobs that do not require English skills. Federal grants and social service agencies such as the YWCA's Refugee Project in Elgin have provided services to facilitate adjustment. In addition, the community has built its own organizations and programs. Drawing on informal networks of mutual assistance, Laotians in Chicago established Lao American Community Services (LACS) in 1984 to assist newcomers and preserve Lao cultural heritage. LACS provides a variety of services, including job training and placement, youth services, English-language instruction, citizenship classes, health care services, and counseling. It also brings the community together through cultural programming like classical Laotian dance classes and activities.

RELIGIOUS INSTITUTIONS serve important spiritual, social, and cultural needs and are at the center of vibrant Laotian communities in the city and suburbs. Most Laotians are BUDDHIST, and in Laos the temple, or *wat,* is the center of village life and Buddhist philosophy an important part of traditional values. Buddhism remains an important part of life in metropolitan Chicago for most Laotians, and Buddhist temples in Elgin, Rockford, and Chicago draw these communities together for holy days, chanting, and meditation. Some Laotians have converted to Christianity and established Lao churches in Rockford and Elgin. These churches serve as centers of small religious communities, offering services to members and creating differences with Laotian Buddhists that are not only religious but cultural. The Lao New Year in mid-April and funerals are the two events that bring together Laotians of all faiths.

Tracy Steffes

See also: Americanization; Demography; Multicentered Chicago; Religious Geography

Further reading: Hansen, Marty. *Behind the Golden Door: Refugees in Uptown.* 1991. • Rumbaut, Ruben G. "A Legacy of War: Refugees from Vietnam, Laos, and Cambodia." In *Origins and Destinies: Immigration, Race, and Ethnicity in America,* ed. Ruben Rumbaut and Silvia Pedraza, 1996.

Latvians. For the relatively small Latvian population in the United States, Chicago has always been an important cultural center. Latvians from the Chicago area often have been leaders within their national ethnic community and—in the last decade of the twentieth century—have played important roles in their homeland's return to independence.

Propelled by a desire for economic and political change from hardships in the Russian Empire, Latvians began arriving in Chicago in the late nineteenth century. The few hundred settled by the mid-1890s formed a mutual aid society (1892), the Zion Lutheran Church (1893), and other organizations. As in other American cities where they settled, Chicago's early Latvian community was generally divided between religious believers and political radicals. After a failed uprising in Russia's Baltic province in 1905, many radicals fled to the United States. In Chicago, the case of Latvian revolutionary Christian Rudowitz in 1908–9 helped set a precedent in extradition law. The Russian government wanted Rudowitz sent back to face a murder charge, but U.S. Secretary of State Elihu Root ruled that because the fugitive's crime had been committed as part of a political revolution, he could stay in America.

Latvia declared its independence in 1918. During the next four decades, emigration to the United States slowed to a trickle, although numbers are sketchy, since until 1930 the census grouped Latvians with RUSSIANS or LITHUANIANS. Around 3,830 Chicagoans claimed Latvian ancestry in the 1940 census.

After WORLD WAR II, tens of thousands of Latvian REFUGEES scattered across Western Europe could not return to their homeland, which was occupied by the Soviet Union. Many came to the United States, creating a vibrant exile community that established churches, schools, community centers, and other cultural institutions, as well as engaging in anti-Communist political activism. The first Latvian song festival in the United States was held in 1953 in Chicago, continuing a tradition begun in 1873 in the homeland that brings together hundreds of singers and dancers—plus thousands of onlookers—in a celebration of national unity that has continued into the twenty-first century.

In 1990 the census counted 7,000 Latvians in the Chicago area, most in middle- to upper-middle-class neighborhoods. Several were involved in pro-independence activities, and after Latvia regained its independence in 1991 with the collapse of the Soviet Union, many returned to help the nation's transition to democracy and a market economy. Kârlis Streips, a second-generation Latvian and Chicago native, by the late 1990s had become a popular television journalist in the Latvian capital of Riga. Ojārs Kalniņš, who grew up in Chicago, served as Latvia's ambassador to the United States from 1993 until early 2000, when he moved to Riga.

Andris Straumanis

See also: Cold War Anticommunism; Demography; Multicentered Chicago

Further reading: Akmentins, Osvalds. *Latvians in Bicentennial America.* 1976. • Kārklis, Maruta, Līga Streips, and Laimonis Streips. *The Latvians in America, 1640–1973.* 1974. • Straumanis, Andris. "Latvian-Americans." In *Gale Encyclopedia of Multicultural America,* ed. Judy Galens, Anna Sheets, and Robyn V. Young, 1995.

Laundries and Laundering. In 1909, when the Census of Manufacturers first included power laundries, Chicago had 226 establishments employing 6,601 wage workers, nearly 20 percent more than the number of employees in New York City, the second ranking city. Owners of these mechanized businesses competed with an even larger number of "hand laundries" run by individual entrepreneurs, many of them CHINESE immigrants. In addition, thousands of women took in washing or hired themselves out as day laundresses in middle-class homes.

Laundry was big BUSINESS in Chicago for a number of reasons. As in other urban areas, bourgeois standards of cleanliness were rising just as urban pollution made it increasingly difficult to get clean and stay clean. Because Chicago was located at the terminus of a number of RAILROADS, Chicago laundries handled the washing of large numbers of travelers and the HOTELS, trains, and boats that catered to them.

In contrast to many better-known Chicago industries, women workers predominated in laundries. They filled most of the "inside jobs," marking and sorting incoming laundry and handling finishing WORK: starching, ironing, folding, and packing. As mechanized washers came to replace the traditional washtub, men took over the steamy confines of the washroom. They also drove the delivery wagons that navigated the city's streets and serviced the suburbs.

Before the GREAT MIGRATION, Northern European immigrants filled the majority of laundry jobs. Laundry owners avoided hiring AFRICAN AMERICANS, confining these women to hand laundries and domestic service. The influx of large numbers of southern migrants in the 1910s and 1920s coincided with the widespread introduction of ironing machines which eliminated the high-paying jobs attractive to experienced workers. By 1920, perhaps 25 percent of Chicago's laundry workers were African Americans. For many of these women (and a smaller number of men), laundry work provided an important transitional step from agriculture and DOMESTIC WORK to factory employment.

Chicago was also a center of efforts by the American Federation of Labor and WOMEN'S TRADE UNION LEAGUE to organize laundry workers. The female majority of workers proved difficult both to organize and to keep in unions. In 1903, the city was rocked by its first major laundry STRIKE, which began with a walkout from the company laundry at PULLMAN. For the next 30 years, this strike and the many that followed achieved only minimal gains. Widespread, stable UNIONIZATION was finally achieved after the passage of the Wagner Act and the spread of CONGRESS OF INDUSTRIAL ORGANIZATIONS unions in the late 1930s.

Nationwide, the laundry industry began to go into decline in the 1930s, reeling from the effects of the GREAT DEPRESSION and the growing popularity of electric washing machines for the home. The industry currently survived into the twenty-first century largely in the form of linen services and shirt laundries.

Arwen Mohun

See also: Housekeeping; Work Culture

Further reading: Mohun, Arwen P. *Steam Laundries: Gender, Technology, and Work in the United States and Great Britain, 1880–1940.* 1999. • Siu, Paul C. P. *The Chinese Laundryman: A Study of Social Isolation.* 1987.

Law. As Chicago's businesses grew in the late nineteenth century, so too did the city's need for a cadre of capable lawyers to handle the myriad problems caused by industrial expansion. Over the next century, solo practitioners and small partnerships gave way to large and powerful regional, national, and even international firms. The sheer number of lawyers practicing in the city grew rapidly, from some five dozen in 1850 to over 4,300 in 1900, about 14,000 in 1970, and 29,000 in the early 1990s. Moreover, the ranks of Chicago lawyers gradually, and sometimes grudgingly, opened to include JEWS, AFRICAN AMERICANS, and women. Over this same period the kind of law that lawyers practiced changed and evolved. Abraham Lincoln, who served a brief apprenticeship, later practicing in Chicago and other Illinois courts while the other partner in his firm tended to office matters, would have been hard-pressed to recognize the activities of twenty-first century lawyers as having any connection to the practice of law as he knew it.

Perhaps the most revolutionary change in the practice of law in Chicago has been the emergence of the large firm as the most effective way to organize the day-to-day activities of lawyers. In the mid-nineteenth century, the practice of law was largely carried on by solo practitioners or small firms of fewer than five lawyers. The creation of the modern corporation and modern industry created new areas of legal concern, leading to changes in legal practice. Corporate and securities law emerged, and tort law developed in response to RAILROAD accidents. Large firms could meet corporate clients' diverse and extensive legal needs under one roof, typically by distributing the work to specialists within the firm. Growth occurred gradually. For example, in 1906 Holt, Cutting & Sidley consisted of 4 lawyers, 4 clerks, and a nonlawyer staff of 10, but by 1957 the firm (then known as Sidley & Austin) had 29 partners and 20 associates, and over the next few decades it grew to include hundreds of lawyers. Such firms began adding departments to deal with new areas of the law, such as the administrative law revolution that the NEW DEAL initiated. Large firms became dominant only after the middle of the twentieth century. In 1948, 6 of 10 Chicago lawyers were still solo practitioners, but only 1 in 5 was a solo practitioner by 1975; and almost as many worked in firms of more than 30 lawyers. Firms also expanded their client base from regional to national and even international. For example, after WORLD WAR II, the Chicago-based firm of Baker & McKenzie undertook to serve an international market by opening an average of one new office each year. By 2000, the firm had 60 offices in 35 countries.

The other radical change in the legal profession that occurred between the mid-nineteenth century and the twenty-first century was the integration of groups other than white Anglo-Saxon PROTESTANT males into the practitioners' ranks. The Illinois Supreme Court rejected Myra Bradwell's attempt to join the bar despite her passing the bar exam in 1869. However, in 1872, the Illinois legislature mandated that women be admitted to the bar. Members of other groups such as Jews, African Americans, and Eastern European immigrants were allowed to get a license but were not hired by the firms that controlled the most lucrative business. The Chicago Bar Association was open only to invited members and did not admit African Americans until 1945, when, after a two-year battle, it admitted Earl B. Dickerson to membership. By the end of the twentieth century, although white males still predominated at the senior partner level of elite law firms, the official policy of firms in hiring associates have evolved to value diversity of race, religion, national origin, and gender.

Lawyers also practice in different and more specialized areas of the law than did the general practitioner of the mid-nineteenth century, and, unlike most nineteenth-century lawyers, they are college educated and law school trained in these specialties. The New Deal inaugurated a new type of law practice in front of regulatory agencies such as the Securities and Exchange Commission. An entire segment of legal business grew out of the expansion of tort liability to allow recovery when manufacturers placed defective products into the stream of commerce. By the late twentieth century the computer revolution and the Internet had created yet a new area of legal practice, information technology, and made intellectual property a new battleground in the fight to control the fruits of this revolution. Law firms with ties to Chicago were leaders in developing the expertise to deal with all of these changes in the law, and many others.

R. Ben Brown

See also: Accounting; Children and the Law; Court System; Juvenile Courts; Labor Law; Legal Aid; Racism, Ethnicity, and White Identity

Further reading: *Celebrating the Chicago Bar Association and Its Members: 125th Anniversary.* 1999. • Heinz, John P. *Chicago Lawyers: The Social Structure of the Bar.* 1982. • Law Bulletin Publishing Company. *Century of Law: 1900–2000.* 1999.

League of Women Voters. Suffragists founded the League of Women Voters when they disbanded the National American Woman Suffrage Association in Chicago in 1920 following passage of national SUFFRAGE. The league is dedicated to fostering political training for all women, investigating political issues and candidates, holding open discussion forums, and, when deemed advisable, advocating specific legislation. Chicago-area women originally organized in a COOK COUNTY branch, and in WARD or neighborhood branches. These local leagues belonged to the Illinois League of Women Voters until 1946, when they affiliated directly with the League of Women Voters USA. By 1950, Chicago neighborhood leagues had consolidated into the Chicago League of Women Voters, which in the 1990s had 12 units meeting in city neighborhoods, while suburban women maintained local organizations of their own.

In the 1920s, local, Cook County, and Illinois leagues were headed by women active in metropolitan Chicago's suffrage and women's club movements, including Flora Cheney, Julia Lathrop, Jennie Purvin, Irene Goins, Louise de Koven Bowen, Agnes Nestor, and Rachelle Yarros. In the 1920s, the leagues worked to secure the national Sheppard-Towner Maternity and Infancy Act, child labor laws, the EIGHT-HOUR day for workers, and the right of women to serve on juries, a right denied to Illinois women until 1939. They helped secure a statewide permanent voter registration law in 1941, opposed passage of "subversive activities" laws in the 1950s, promoted equal housing opportunity in the 1960s, and made adequate funding of public education a priority for the 1990s. The league published guides for voters, including *Key to Government in Chicago and Suburban Cook County* and *Illinois Voters' Handbook.*

Maureen A. Flanagan

See also: Clubs: Women's club; Feminist Movements; Good Government Movements; Political Culture

Further reading: Illinois League of Women Voters Manuscript Collection. Chicago Historical Society, Chicago, IL. • Illinois League of Women Voters. *Forty Years of Faith and Works.* Pamphlet. 1961. Chicago Historical Society, Chicago, IL. • Young, Louise H. *In the Public Interest: The League of Women Voters, 1920–1970.* 1989.

Leather and Tanning. Commercial tanning preserved hides and skins through a labor-intensive chemical process. Pelts were carefully scraped of connective tissues at "beam houses," chemically washed of their hair and oils, pickled, and then safeguarded by a variety of "tanning liquors." After currying and finishing, workers removed defects and added crucial dyes and polishes before the leather was worked into a variety of semidurable goods such as boots, shoes, horse tack, and book bindings.

Chicago's proximity to oak and hemlock tanbark from Wisconsin, its serviceable WATER sources, substantial rail facilities, and especially the growth of the MEATPACKING industry made it particularly receptive to large-scale production from 1860 to 1900. While Boston remained the nation's premier supplier of finished leather goods, Chicago developed a widespread, but decentralized, tanning trade. By 1880, more than 240 firms tanned and finished leather goods and employed, on average, 16 workers each. Beginning in 1880, however, larger production facilities began to replace small-scale producers. The introduction of substantial processing equipment and the automation of the beam houses, which made finer "splits" of the epidermis, consolidated the WORK and aided in mass production. By 1890, the typical Chicago tannery employed slightly more that 24 people. While fostered by the packing industry, these larger tanners remained independent and spatially separated from their local source of skins.

Employees of these larger firms were more likely to be unskilled operators than tannery craftsmen. This shift was aided by the relative poor quality of Chicago's leather goods. Unlike Boston's national providers, Midwestern tanners furnished "heavy leather" for the coarser wares demanded by regional consumers. Freed from the need to compete with refined "eastern goods," Chicago tanners were able to implement machines that sacrificed quality for quantity. Leather-related industries in Chicago lagged in UNION membership. By 1887, while almost every Cincinnati tanner paid dues to either the American Shoe Workers Protective or the United Shoe Workers, only three of Chicago's factories were organized and those by the more docile Boot and Shoe Workers.

The concentration of production within a few large firms coincided with the leveling off and eventual decline of the tanning and leather industries. While Chicago's "heavy leather" production remained stable from 1890 to 1930, the relative slow growth in leather-working trades sapped the industry's vitality. Eventually, even the heavy leather producers revealed their vulnerability. By 1955, new synthetic materials, public opposition to the foul odors and water pollution generated from tanning, and the availability of cheaper leather from Latin America obliterated any notion of a true industry within the city. The closure of Chicago's meatpacking facilities added to these problems by increasing the cost of raw materials. By 1990, only small artisans working handbags, belts, and other modest wares represented this once vital profession.

David Blanke

See also: Business of Chicago; Economic Geography; Lumber; Railroads

Further reading: Hoover, Edgar M., Jr. *Location Theory and the Shoe and Leather Industries.* 1937. • McDermott, Charles H. *A History of the Shoe and Leather Industries of the United States.* 1918.

Leather workers manufacturing suitcases, ca. 1900. Photographer: Ed Stratton. Source: Chicago Historical Society.

Lebanese. Lebanon has one of the largest diasporas of the Arab world. Approximately as many Lebanese live outside their country of origin as inside, leading one historian of Lebanese emigration to remark that there are really two Lebanons: the Republic of Lebanon, and "the Lebanon of overseas" ("le Liban d'outre-mer"). Since the late nineteenth century, Lebanese have immigrated to Africa, Asia, the Americas, and Australia, with especially large numbers settling in the United States and Latin America. By the end of the twentieth century approximately 1.5 million Americans of Lebanese descent lived in the United States.

The Lebanese in Chicago trace their roots to one of two large waves of emigration out of Lebanon. The first—lasting roughly from the 1880s to WORLD WAR I—consisted of a large-scale exodus of peasants, artisans, and entrepreneurs from Ottoman Syria (of which Lebanon was a part) to the Americas. A small but enterprising group among them made their way to Chicago's WORLD'S COLUMBIAN EXPOSITION of 1893 to sell their wares on the Midway Plaisance. Many stayed on after the fair had closed to work as STREET PEDDLERS, in dry-goods retail, and the textile trade. They were part of the larger "SYRIAN" community in the greater Chicago area which, according to a 1913 estimate by a Syrian cleric, comprised over 3,000 people. The residential core of the Syrian-Lebanese community was located between 12th and 15th Streets and California and Kedzie Avenues.

As the community flourished on Chicago's West Side, its members established institutions consistent with religious and newly formed national solidarities. Lebanese Maronites, for example, founded their own club in 1948 which was instrumental in raising funds for an Eastern-rite church called Our Lady of Lebanon. In 1956, a priest was sent from Tucuman, Argentina, to lead the congregation, which proudly purchased its own building near Waller and Race Avenues, where it remained until moving to suburban HILLSIDE in 1973. Actor and comedian Danny Thomas (born Muzyad Yakhoob) attended Our Lady of Lebanon, and encouraged his fellow Lebanese to support his project for the building of St. Jude Children's Research Hospital in Memphis, Tennessee, which, since its establishment in 1962, has become the largest childhood cancer research center in the United States.

The second important wave of Lebanese emigration occurred as a result of the political and economic turmoil that plagued Lebanon for over a decade, beginning with the devastating civil war of 1975–76. Immigration to Dearborn (Michigan), Los Angeles, and Chicago rose dramatically as Lebanese sought refuge outside their war-torn country. This immigration was substantially different from the earlier one. While the first wave had been predominantly ROMAN CATHOLIC, this immigration was multisectarian and reflected a wide range of professional interests. Students, for example, came to Chicago to attend university and went on to work as engineers, doctors, and pharmacists. Several hundred among them returned to Lebanon in the late 1990s to assist in reconstruction programs implemented after the formal end of civil strife. Lebanese-owned retail stores, GROCERIES, and bakeries in Chicago are also a product of the second wave of immigration. In addition, numerous Lebanese RESTAURANTS have become popular since the 1970s, catering not only to the city's sizable Arab American community, but to Chicagoans' growing affection for Mediterranean food as well.

Sarah Gualtieri

See also: Demography; Foodways; Multicentered Chicago; Palestinians; Refugees

Further reading: Hourani, Albert, and Nadim Shehadi, eds. *The Lebanese in the World: A Century of Emigration.* 1992. • Naff, Alixa. *Becoming American: The Early Arab Immigrant Experience.* 1985.

Lectures and Public Speaking. Public speeches have served as ENTERTAINMENT and educational vehicles for Chicagoans since the city's earliest days. Nineteenth-century Chicagoans attended evening lectures as social events. City booster William Bross recorded stretches of almost nightly attendance at public lectures as part of his LEISURE schedule in his diary entries in the 1870s. Immigrant Hilda Satt Polacheck attended lectures at HULL HOUSE and a 1903 speech by Emma Goldman in a West Side neighborhood hall.

Several significant events in Chicago have related closely to public lectures. The HAYMARKET Riot of May 4, 1886, began as a worker's rally with speeches by area anarchists. Samuel Fielden had just begun to address the crowds of striking workers and supporters when the bomb was thrown. Daniel Burnham's 1909 *Plan of Chicago* stemmed from Burnham's lecture for the COMMERCIAL CLUB of Chicago on March 27, 1897. Inspired by the speech, Commercial Club members committed at least $80,000 to the publication of BURNHAM'S PLAN. Public lectures were also later used as a tool to promote the completed plan to Chicagoans.

Frederick Jackson Turner's 1893 address to the American Historical Association meeting held in conjunction with the WORLD'S COLUMBIAN EXPOSITION ranks among the most historically significant of all speeches held in Chicago. In "The Significance of the Frontier in American History," Turner noted an 1890 U.S. census observation that a line of westward advancement by white settlers, a "frontier," no longer remained in the American West. Believing the existence of this frontier to have been an essential component in shaping the American character, Turner pronounced that a formative period of American life had come to an end.

The geographic center of public speech in Chicago has historically been Washington Square Park, first established in 1842 and known as "BUGHOUSE SQUARE" by the 1890s. The park's soapbox orators approached topics ranging from gender relations to Communism. The park's reputation for FREE SPEECH was enhanced by the location of the Dill Pickle Club nearby in 1916. This informal club hosted such visitors as Eugene Debs, "Big Bill" Haywood, and Clarence Darrow in its lecture hall.

Chicago-area CLUBS have sponsored many notable speakers. In the wake of the devastation caused by the Great Chicago FIRE OF 1871, Chicagoans launched a number of clubs designed to cater to the city's elite society. Organizations like the Fortnightly (1873), specifically aimed at women, and the Chicago Literary Club (1874) offered an array of speakers to members. The cultural efforts of such clubs brought Chicago favorable press in national periodicals.

Although public lectures no longer serve as such a popular form of recreation, Chicago UNIVERSITIES, colleges, and educational institutions all sponsor lecture series, as do bookstores, churches, businesses, unions, and political organizations. Perhaps the largest current public-speaking venue is the Chicago Humanities Festival.

Lisa Krissoff Boehm

See also: Burnham Plan; Literary Cultures; Political Conventions; Settlement Houses

Further reading: Commercial Club of Chicago Papers. Chicago Historical Society. • Kirkland, Joseph. *The Story of Chicago.* 1892. • Polacheck, Hilda Satt. *I Came a Stranger: The Story of a Hull-House Girl.* 1991.

Legal Aid. Organized provision of legal aid began in 1886, when the Protective Agency for Women and Children was founded to protect young working women. Two years later, the Bureau of Justice was established to help immigrants and the poor. Led by wealthy Chicagoans and elite lawyers, both groups helped clients collect unpaid wages, fended off loan sharks, and pushed for reform legislation to protect immigrants and workers from blatant forms of exploitation involving the legal system. The two groups combined in 1905 to form the Chicago Legal Aid Society (later the Legal Aid Bureau of UNITED CHARITIES of Chicago). The organization, with a staff of 16 in 1915, gradually lost its reformist focus and concentrated on individual cases.

President Lyndon Johnson's GREAT SOCIETY program expanded and transformed legal aid. In 1965, a network of neighborhood legal service offices opened with federal funding, under the umbrella of United Charities and the city of Chicago. Differences in philosophy and willingness to challenge government agencies in court divided the more activist federally funded programs from older programs, and, in 1973, they were reorganized as the independent Legal Assistance Foundation of Chicago, funded, since 1974, mainly by the federal Legal Services Corporation.

During the 1970s, the Legal Assistance Foundation grew to about 90 lawyers, though subsequent funding cuts led to fluctuations in its size, and it turned to private sources to supplement its income. Despite efforts by conservatives to eliminate such agencies, the Legal Assistance Foundation pursued a reformist agenda. In addition to representing some 30,000–40,000 clients in their dealings with landlords, creditors, and government agencies, the organization pursued cases with broad impact on the rights of welfare recipients, the disabled, immigrants, prisoners, tenants, and victims of discrimination.

By 2002, the Legal Aid Bureau (part of the renamed Metropolitan Family Services) focused exclusively on family law cases involving poor children. Law schools and other organizations also aided indigent clients, including over two dozen Chicago-area groups which since 1983 have received funds from interest on lawyers' escrow accounts.

Legal aid groups rarely assisted criminal defendants in the early years, and though judges occasionally appointed counsel for the indigent, most poor defendants had no lawyer. In the 1920s, as justice system scandals erupted, many reformers worried that the rights of defendants without connections or money were often ignored. In 1930 Cook County appointed its first public defender to represent indigent defendants in courts of record, and similar agencies were later established to serve in other courts in Chicago and in the collar counties. Legal decisions since the 1960s extended the right of counsel, and the Cook County Public Defender's Office has grown. With 460 attorneys in 1996, it was one of Chicago's largest legal organizations.

Christopher Thale

See also: American Civil Liberties Union; Children, Dependent; Court System; Great Society; Social Services

Further reading: Katz, Jack. *Poor People's Lawyers in Transition.* 1982. • McIntyre, Lisa J. *The Public Defender: The Practice of Law in the Shadows of Repute.* 1987. • Smith, Reginald Heber. *Justice and the Poor.* 1919.

Leisure. Chicago's leisure pastimes have been a product of several factors. Early Chicago's ENTERTAINMENT reflected its rough-edged frontier character, but, as the village grew into a walking city, leisure options reflected its growing urbanity. After the FIRE OF 1871, Chicago became an industrialized radial city with a huge, heavily foreign-origin population. These factors had a major impact on working hours, discretionary income, the formation of subcultures differentiated by class, gender, race, and ethnicity, and changing spatial relationships, all of which helped shape the leisure patterns of metropolitan Chicago.

Leisure in Preindustrial Chicago

Recreation in preurban Chicago reflected frontier life. The FORT DEARBORN community was made up of soldiers, FRENCH CANADIANS, and NATIVE AMERICANS who enjoyed rural sports, GAMBLING, and drinking. They hunted wolves and wild fowl and honed their skills with marksmanship contests. At the time the town was founded in 1833, denizens sleighed, skated, danced, went to HORSE RACES, and attended monthly concerts of popular music. Mark Beaubien's Sauganash HOTEL was the most important recreation center in the early 1830s, with dancing, drinking, card playing, roulette, and storytelling.

Chicagoans in the newly established walking city worked six days a week, leaving just Sunday and holidays for rest, most notably New Year's Day, May Day, the Fourth of July, Thanksgiving, and Christmas. The city charter empowered the municipality to license, regulate, or prohibit entertainment to encourage wholesome recreation, promote safety and morality, and raise revenue. The government originally banned billiards, shuffleboard, baiting sports, card playing, and PROSTITUTION to discourage GAMBLING and restrain the flourishing male bachelor subculture that frequented SALOONS, poolrooms, and brothels, although the revised 1851 charter licensed BOWLING alleys and billiard parlors, while other vile amusements went on illegally. Prostitution flourished. By 1856, 1,000 women worked in 110 brothels. Lotteries were legal, gambling games were commonplace, and betting at the racetracks was popular. A temperance crusade against Irish and GERMAN drinkers resulted in stiffer licensing and SUNDAY CLOSING laws that culminated in the LAGER BEER RIOT.

American middle-class reformers in the 1840s initiated the rational recreation movement that sought to substitute moral amusements for the evil pleasures of the male bachelor subculture in order to uplift people, reduce crime, and improve public health. In 1858 evangelist Dwight L. Moody set up a YMCA branch in Chicago to develop muscular Christians. New sports were introduced, particularly BASEBALL, a simple team sport that would supposedly build morality, character, and health. One year after the CIVIL WAR, there were 32 teams sponsored by fraternal organizations, occupational groups, the companies, and neighborhood clubs. Businessmen like Marshall Field, who had earlier opposed baseball as deleterious to hard work, began to see it as a means to promote teamwork, discipline, sobriety, and self-sacrifice, and sponsored company nines. By 1870 civic boosters raised $15,000 for a professional baseball team, the White Stockings (Cubs), to enhance the city's image nationally.

Touring professional singers first appeared in Chicago in 1839, the Christy Minstrel shows were popular in the mid-1850s, and the first OPERA season occurred in 1853. In 1837, Chicago's first theatrical performances, starring the renowned Joseph Jefferson, were widely opposed as demoralizing and out of fear that the Sauganash Hotel where they were held might burn down. A weak economy further discouraged THEATER troupes. In 1847 the $11,000 brick Rice Theater was constructed, with patrons segregated by price and race, but it was surpassed by the $85,000 McVickers (1857) and by Crosby's Opera House (1865), with its 3,000-seat auditorium; all three were located in the heart of the city. Popular plays included the works of Shakespeare and Richard Sheridan and productions based on local topics and anti-southern themes.

Other occasional entertainment was provided by touring monologuists and illusionists, exhibitors of panoramas of events like the burning of Moscow, and circuses like Barnum's "Grand Colossal Museum and Menagerie," which charged adults thirty cents admission. There were also dime museums, whose exhibitions of freaks, wax reproductions of infamous crimes, and objects of historical curiosity were popular with the lower classes.

Ethnic groups had a significant impact on entertainment. GERMAN, IRISH, and Scandinavian immigrants brought their own amusements, which promoted a sense of peoplehood, especially in terms of language and culture. Germans brought to America an intense love of CLASSICAL MUSIC. In 1850, Julius Dyhrenfurth conducted Chicago's first symphonic concert, and in 1852 the Männergesangverein, the city's first male chorus, was founded. An important German theater was established at midcentury

Picnic Groves: Ogden's Grove

Ogden's Grove, Wright's Grove, Brand's Park, Hoffman Park, and Schutzenpark are among the picnic groves that dotted the Chicago metropolitan area well into the twentieth century. Many were located along rivers and streams, which provided a picturesque backdrop for summer outings. Popular especially among GERMAN immigrants, these groves were the scene of special events sponsored by churches, businesses, unions, and clubs. In July, 1869, the Desplaines Hall Workers Club sponsored a picnic in Ogden's Grove which was covered in the German-language *Der Westen:*

> Sunshine, woodland green and woodland shade, the sound of horns! on a Sunday afternoon, what more could a German heart possibly wish for?!—A good mug of beer!—
>
> "Fellow countryman," I asked the cashier as he accepted my 15 cents, "would you have a drop of beer, too?"
>
> "Oh, plenty!" answered the man from Holstein . . . "not to mention spirited company!"
>
> The Desplaines Hall Workers Club was having a picnic under the oak columns at Ogden's Grove. There was a large group with many women and children and there were so many other people there that all the tables and benches were taken.
>
> Cheerful groups everywhere, families and their friends taking of Sunday afternoon nectar, extra-strong coffee, and the ambrosia without which it wouldn't be complete in the form of "Stippels"-Topfkuchen [sweet bread made with yeasted dough that is similar to coffee cake] and buttered almond cake. There, in all the different dialects of the dear German homeland, chatting and blabbering . . . and groups of young and old men and boys drinking beer . . . Ha! The Germans like nothing better than a party under the oaks! The life our forefathers had in the woods still clings to us.

Keil, Hartmut, and John B. Jentz. *German Workers in Chicago: A Documentary History of Working-Class Culture from 1850 to World War I.* 1988.

"The Desplaines Hall Workers Club Picnics in Ogden's Grove." *Der Westen* (July 22, 1896): 206–208.

Col. Wood's Museum, West Randolph Street, 1865. Artist: Unknown. Source: Chicago Historical Society.

that staged German classics that reminded audiences of the Old World. New plays were written that taught how to cope with the New World. The Svea Society (1857) sponsored a Scandinavian theater where performances were often followed by dances. Tickets cost fifty cents.

The Germans and the Irish brought athletic traditions. The Irish emphasized boxing, which was part of their own male bachelor subculture and enabled them to fit in with the prevailing bachelor subculture. However, the Germans made a more distinctive contribution with the mainly working-class *turnverein*, which emphasized calisthenics and gymnastics and supported workingmen's interests. *Turnhalles* were community centers, often the largest building in the neighborhood, with a large gym and auditorium. By the 1890s there were 5,000 turners in 34 units, the most of any American city. They provided a model for the establishment of similar organizations by Bohemians, Poles, and Ukrainians.

Leisure in the Industrial Radial City, 1870–1920

Chicago's leisure patterns in the industrial radial era were influenced by industrial capitalism and its social structure, a heterogeneous population divided into ethnic communities, gender, changing spatial relationships, and a liberal enforcement of Sunday blue laws. The upper class had the greatest wealth and control of time. They used leisure activities for fun and social prestige by participating in and financing expensive high-status pastimes. Parties, clubs, and sports dominated their social calendar. Charity balls introduced debutantes and honored individuals. Parties were ostentatious multicourse meals at elegant hotels or luxurious mansions. Institutions of high culture like the Art Institute, founded in 1879, were established to promote civilization, boost Chicago's reputation, and enhance personal recognition.

Chicago's elites gathered in the Chicago Club (1869), where men socialized and did business, and the Fortnightly (1873), where women considered social issues and pursued educational topics. Sports clubs, like the Chicago Yacht Club, the Chicago Athletic Club, and the Chicago Women's Athletic Club were less prestigious but enabled its new rich members to gain status and participate in expensive sports. Fascination with English country life and the new sport of golf, which was enormously popular in Chicago, resulted in the establishment of suburban country clubs, beginning with the Chicago Golf Club (1893). These organizations were particularly attractive to elite women who enjoyed golf, tennis, and parties at the clubs. The elite was very involved in equestrian sports, and a few owned thoroughbreds and belonged to the prestigious jockey club that operated the elegant Washington Park Race Track, founded in 1884.

The middle class, which made up 31 percent of the workforce in 1900, generally believed in hard work, domesticity, sobriety, and piety, and wanted to employ free time for self-improvement and self-renewal. Middle-class men worked a five-and-a-half-day week and had sufficient income to pursue leisure activities. The new middle class of professionals and bureaucrats turned to their pastimes to demonstrate their creativity, self-worth, and manliness at a time when WASP birthrates were declining and culture seemed to be feminized by influential mothers and schoolteachers. Men formed organizations that sponsored hobbies like the Chicago Philatelic Society (1886), the Chicago Camera Club (1904), and the Chicago Coin Club (1905). They became active sportsmen, joining groups like the

Chicago's railroads expanded leisure space for Chicagoans and for Americans more generally. In this Chicago & Northwestern ad from 1887, a Boston agent encouraged New Englanders to go hunting and fishing in the areas north and west of the city along its route. Creator: Poole Bros., Printers and Engravers. Source: Chicago Historical Society.

The Lake View Cycling Club in front of its clubhouse at 401–403 Orchard Street (old numbering) in the 1890s. Photographer: Unknown. Source: Chicago Historical Society.

Chicago BICYCLE Club (1879), and became ardent ball fans. They had the time and money to attend White Stocking games played in midafternoon. The team did not have Sunday games until 1893, originally because of league rules and then because owner Albert G. Spalding incorrectly assumed that middle-class fans opposed public amusements on the Sabbath.

Middle-class women also had substantial leisure time, as they seldom worked outside the home and many had servants to perform household chores. They read FICTION, belonged to clubs, and shopped in downtown stores. Specialty shops and DEPARTMENT STORES like Marshall Field's made SHOPPING an enjoyable experience with tearooms, fine RESTAURANTS, and free delivery. Increasingly, younger women also participated in sports, encouraged by physicians and female physical educators who recommended exercise to improve health and beauty. Such "feminine" sports as golf, tennis, horseback riding, cycling, and ice SKATING proliferated. Even certain active sports like BASKETBALL became women's sports, modified by special rules designed to conform to current notions of women's physical abilities.

Low wages and long working hours limited turn-of-the-century working-class leisure opportunities. Less-skilled workers regularly worked 60 hours per week, while more-skilled workers typically worked 54 hours. Yet the limited remaining free time was important, providing opportunities for self-expression, status, and even POLITICS, with the EIGHT-HOUR DAY MOVEMENT.

Reflecting the immigrant character of Chicago (80 percent of Chicago's population in 1890 was of foreign origin), blue-collar recreation was ethnic, neighborhood, and family-based and tied to religious customs. ROMAN CATHOLIC immigrants observed a Continental Sunday Sabbath, with afternoons free for moderate pleasures that contested local blue laws, while JEWS observed the Sabbath on Saturdays and considered Sunday a working day. Traditional holidays were still observed, like the ITALIAN festivals that honored patron saints in a carnivalesque atmosphere, providing continuity with the Old World. Houses of worship also provided space for weddings, sports, and clubs, most notably the CATHOLIC YOUTH ORGANIZATION, founded in 1930.

Gender was important in socializing and family gatherings that focused on the dinner table. Women prepared traditional foods, and afterwards men and women socialized separately. The primary daily entertainment for working-class women was visiting with friends and neighbors at home, on the stoop, or in the street. Second-generation daughters were very closely supervised, at least until they were full-time wage earners, when they gained a little more freedom. Their brothers, by comparison, had far more liberty to hang out in the STREET or participate in neighborhood recreation. They played sports at ethnic social and athletic clubs, pool halls, bowling alleys,

Spending the day at the lakefront was a favorite experience for all Chicagoans. Here, a group of Italian American senior citizens spend the day at the Lake Michigan beach in St. Joseph's, Michigan, ca. 1940s. Photographer: Unknown. Source: University of Illinois at Chicago.

Recreation Facilities in Chicago's Loop

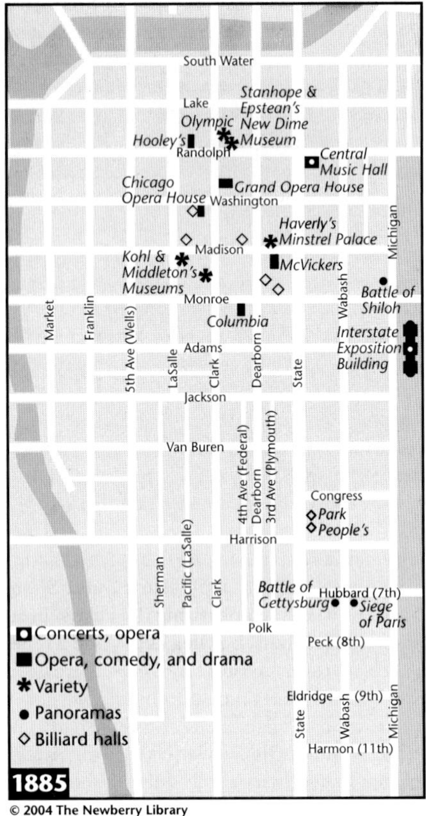

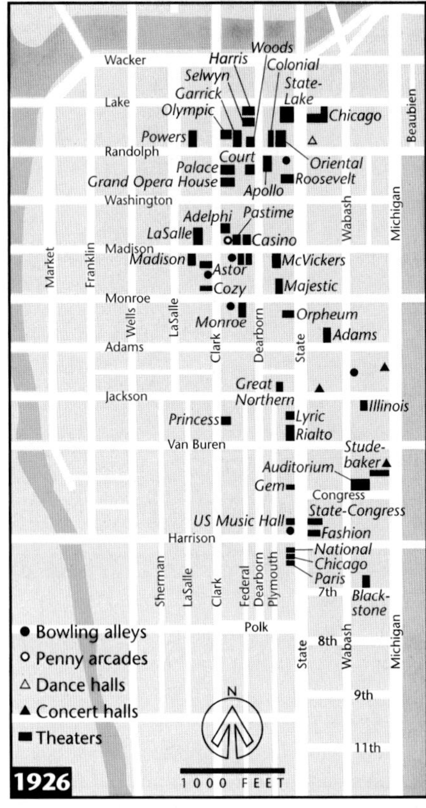

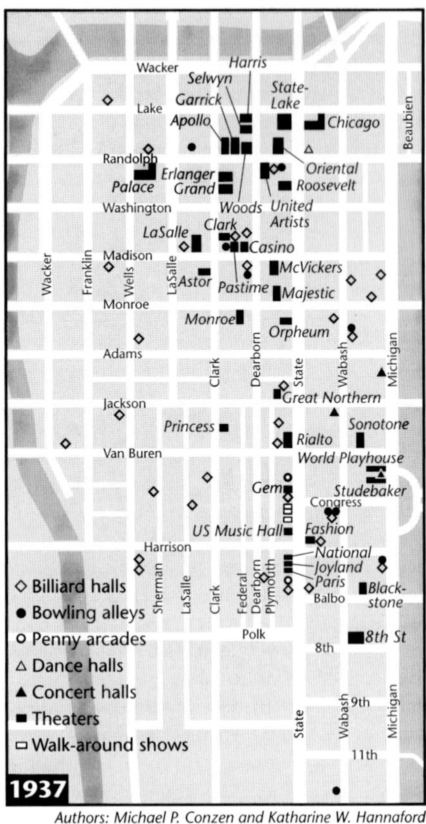

Authors: Michael P. Conzen and Katharine W. Hannaford

As Chicago more than doubled in population between 1885 and the 1920s, commercial entertainment expanded in number and variety to meet demand and concentrated in the central business district. In 1885, Chicago's downtown offered only a few major venues for music, drama, and variety performances, along with two panoramas, all examples of "passive" recreation. The majority of these were located north of Adams and east of LaSalle, away from the dense wholesale and financial districts. By 1926, downtown entertainment had become more varied, with penny arcades and bowling alleys adding a participatory element, and a secondary theater district had emerged, centered on South State Street. The pattern had further evolved by 1937, with a new attraction for men, billiard halls, finding locations throughout downtown.

boxing gymnasiums, or SETTLEMENT HOUSES, where reformers sought to use athletics to socialize inner-city youth into the values of the host society.

Adult men socialized away from crowded homes at fraternal CLUBS or SALOONS, often the only recreation site in their neighborhoods. By 1915 there was one saloon for every 335 residents in Chicago. German taverns were family institutions, well-lit beer gardens that provided wholesome entertainment. Most others, however, were "poor man's clubs," highly particularistic institutions where men drank, ate free lunches, played games, and gambled. Irish saloons, for instance, were modest, dimly lit "stand-up" taverns whose customers were encouraged to drink excessively.

Gambling and prostitution were rampant in Chicago. Illegal betting occurred at neighborhood saloons, resorts in the South Side VICE DISTRICT, and downtown gambling halls and poolrooms that served as off-track betting parlors. Men of all classes visited houses of prostitution, the most famous of which was the Everleigh House, where an evening could cost $50. The VICE COMMISSION identified 5,000 prostitutes working in 1,020 resorts in 1910. When Mayor Carter Harrison II closed the VICE DISTRICT shortly thereafter, prostitution moved into residential neighborhoods.

In the 1870s celebrated traveling companies boasting stars like Henry Irving, Ellen Terry, Lily Langtry, and Sarah Bernhardt played the McVicker's, the Academy of Music, and the Grand Opera House, where Chicagoans paid twenty-five to fifty cents to see them. VAUDEVILLE made its first Chicago appearance in the 1880s. Immigrants, who often brought with them a theatrical tradition, supported ethnic theaters in spite of weak scripts, inexperienced actors, and a limited audience base. The theater promoted their culture and ethnic pride, gained them respect from the host society, and helped newcomers become acclimatized to America. German theater dominated with *volkstheaters* and classical scripts. The English press reviewed an 1889 performance of Schiller glowingly, and a 1903 performance of Goethe's *Faust* drew 3,600 spectators to the AUDITORIUM THEATER.

Musical entertainment flourished between 1871 and 1920. Theodore Thomas first brought his chamber music orchestra to Chicago in 1869 and established the CHICAGO SYMPHONY ORCHESTRA in 1891. Certain dates were set aside for workingmen's concerts with reduced admissions. Popular vocal music emphasized light opera, and group singing was common at parties. There was growing interest in opera, and in 1885 over 100,000 enthusiasts attended the Chicago Opera Festival. The 4,300-seat Auditorium Theater, completed by 1890, had its first opera season in 1891 and continued to have opera every year through 1932, when the Civic Opera Company went out of business. CHORAL MUSIC was very popular with ethnic groups, especially Germans, Scandinavians, and POLES. The three major German singing societies in 1900 consisted of over 200 singing clubs, but interest sharply fell off during WORLD WAR I, when Chicagoans identified German culture as unpatriotic.

Dancing boomed in the early 1900s among all social and ethnic groups. In 1911, an average of 86,000 people nightly attended one of the 275 DANCE HALLS in Chicago, more than went to any other recreation. Especially popular with the most fashionable middle-class couples were cabarets, a type of nightclub influenced by the old beer gardens, public dance halls, and revues. Cabarets combined hot music, new dances, risqué shows, drinking, and smoking.

Ethnic leaders worried the second-generation would become debauched or meet the wrong people at public dances, so they organized dances at ethnic clubs and neighborhood halls. Their young men and women preferred modern commercial ballrooms with big bands but maintained a sense of ethnicity. They preferred accessible halls where their group dominated or controlled part of the floor. Rather than bringing formal dates, dancers often came in groups or met at the dance. The girls usually danced with neighborhood boys or other fellows from the same ethnic group. Many single immigrant men frequented taxi dance halls where they paid ten cents per tune to dance with women employed by the owner. By the late 1920s, Chicago had 36 taxi dance halls, which, along with cabarets, were often accused of demoralizing young people.

Silent MOVIES were a hugely popular entertainment based on a new technology. Chicago's first theaters in the early 1900s were five-cent nickelodeons, simple storefronts in working-class neighborhoods. By 1908 there were more than 340 in the city, and admission had reached ten cents. Moralists' concerns about conduct in the dark theaters and about subject matter resulted in the establishment of a film censorship code by 1909. The cinema boomed in the mid-1910s with the popularity of feature-length movies exhibited in elegant downtown and suburban theaters and accompanied by stage shows and large orchestras.

AFRICAN AMERICAN newcomers welcomed the leisure options available in Chicago which they in turn shaped in important ways. However, African Americans encountered prejudice at theaters, dance halls, YMCAs, public parks, beaches, and other entertainment venues. They had to rely heavily on their own institutions in the BLACK BELT to sponsor recreations and on entrepreneurs who established theaters, nightclubs, and baseball teams. The first notable African American nightspot was the 900-seat Pekin Theater at 2700 South State Street, established by policy kingpin Robert T. Motts to diversify his operations. It became a showcase for black musical talent. A stock company was established to perform dramatics, operettas, and comic operas. Admission was fifteen or twenty-five cents. The leading nightspots in the early 1910s were located on "the STROLL," State Street from 26th to 39th Streets. By 1920 as many as a thousand couples went to the Royal Gardens Café (459 East 31st Street) every Friday to dine, dance, and listen to JAZZ and BLUES music.

Black ballplayers were barred from playing in organized baseball. While African Americans did attend games played by the Cubs and WHITE SOX, most attended Sunday games played by local black semiprofessional teams like the Leland Giants, who were a source of community pride. In 1911 that club was supplanted by Rube Foster's AMERICAN GIANTS, which became a charter member of the Negro National League in 1920. The team played at Schorling Park (39th and Wentworth), adjacent to the ghetto, where adult tickets cost twenty-five cents.

William F. ("Buffalo Bill") Cody sitting in front of painted scenery, Old Cubs Park, 1916, before a performance. In 1893, his Wild West show played next to the World's Columbian Exposition and was one of its most popular entertainments. Photographer: Unknown. Source: Chicago Historical Society.

Other popular commercial entertainments of the time included museums, circuses, COUNTY FAIRS, and AMUSEMENT PARKS. Fairs often publicized agricultural and scientific achievements, most notably the Interstate Industrial Exposition, held downtown from 1873 until 1892. The WORLD'S COLUMBIAN EXPOSITION in 1893 attracted an estimated paid attendance of 21.5 million, who preferred the Midway's attractions to displays of technology or art. Buffalo Bill Cody's Wild West Show that summer played before 6 million spectators on a 14-acre site just across from the main entrance to the fair.

Major amusement parks included White City, established in 1905 at 63rd and South Park Way and emphasizing low-class pleasures like carnivals, bowling alleys, and a roller rink and roller coaster. By 1914 it provided year-round entertainment including two dance floors that accommodated five thousand people. It was partially destroyed by a fire in 1927 and went into receivership six years later. Riverview (1904–1967) was the North Side equivalent, with thrill rides, freak shows, dance halls, and a beer garden.

A much-needed park system was funded by the legislature in 1869. The new large parks

The Sans Souci Amusement Park, at Cottage Grove and East 60th Street, was one of Chicago's most popular attractions when this photo was taken in 1908. It was also a stop on that year's *Daily News* trolley trip, which introduced riders to Chicagoland landmarks and activities within reach of public transportation. Photographer: Unknown. Source: Chicago Historical Society.

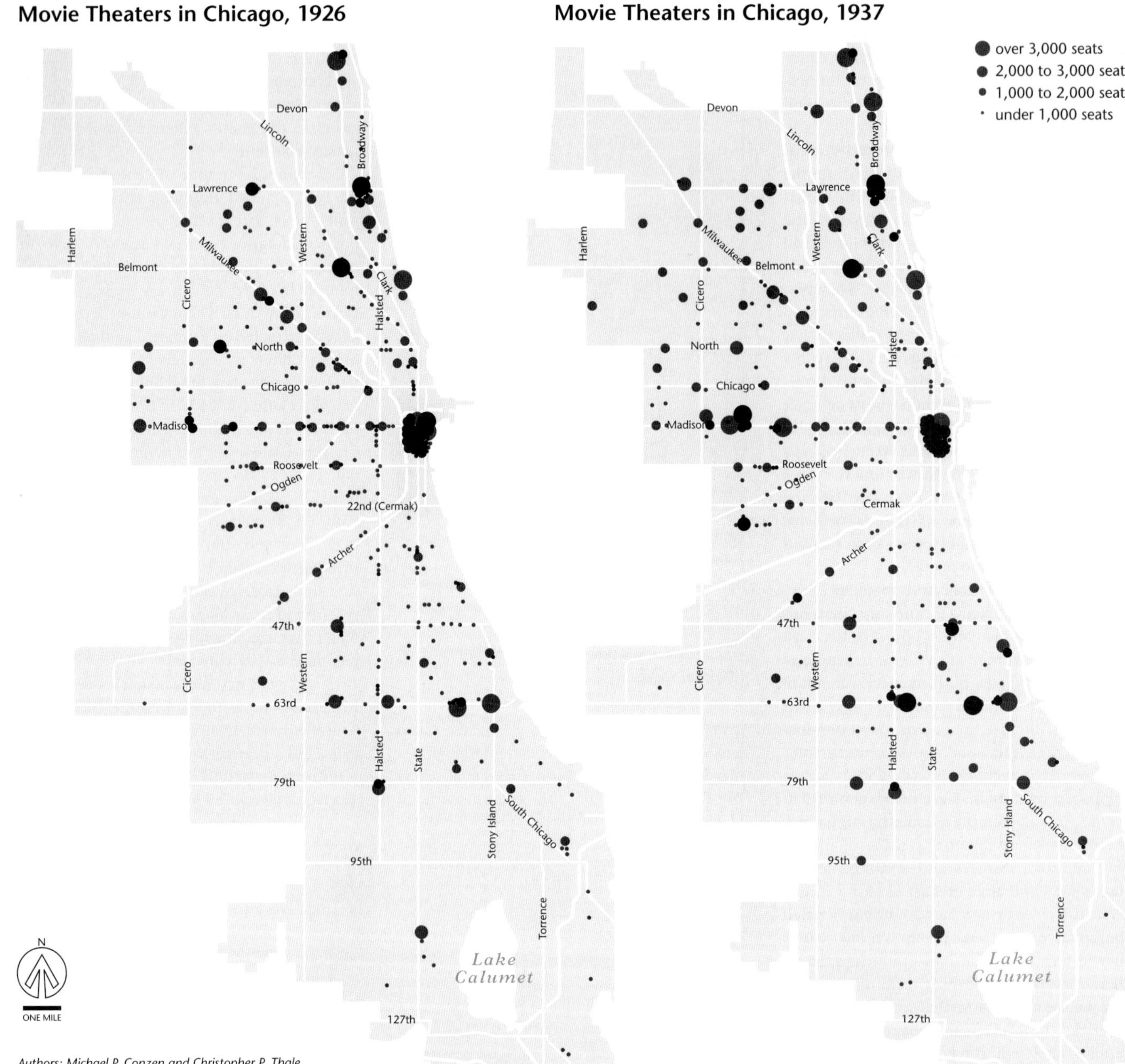

Authors: Michael P. Conzen and Christopher P. Thale

were JACKSON and WASHINGTON, south of the city; Douglas, Central (GARFIELD), and HUMBOLDT on the West Side; and LINCOLN PARK, the largest, at the city's northern border. These suburban parks, at first accessible only to middle-class residents of nearby communities and train riders, originally emphasized receptive recreation. But park goers wanted active recreation, and in the 1880s baseball diamonds and tennis courts were constructed. Lakefront beaches were opened for public use after 1895. Park space was also set aside for the Garfield Park CONSERVATORY and the LINCOLN PARK ZOO.

Unfortunately, the system lagged behind population growth. In 1899 one-third of the population lived more than a mile from any park. The suburban parks in the 1890s had become more accessible to better-paid workers once carfare on the expanding streetcar system dropped from fifteen to five cents, yet this was still too expensive for the poor. Reformers organized a small-park movement in the 1890s to alleviate the inner-city's need for play and breathing spaces, leading to the municipality funding neighborhood parks in 1904. The *Plan of Chicago* of 1909 stimulated future recreation by recommending the extension of Grant Park and the building of beaches, Municipal (NAVY) PIER (1914), FOREST PRESERVES (1914), and lakefront museums.

Leisure in the Interwar Era, 1920–1945

In the 1920s the average Chicagoan enjoyed a higher standard of living than ever before. By 1920 the blue-collar workweek had shortened by about 10 hours compared to 1914, plus wages had appreciated significantly, averaging about $1,000 a year for unskilled workers and $2,000 for skilled. During the GREAT DEPRESSION incomes plummeted, and workers enjoyed a lot of unwanted free time. The national standard of a 40-hour workweek was established in 1938 by the Fair Labor Standards Act.

In the 1920s leisure was heavily influenced by the greater freedom of young women who smoked, drank liquor, wore short dresses,

The cinema came into its own as a form of entertainment during the first two decades of the twentieth century, and movies took over and expanded the number of theaters downtown. As films came to be mass produced for screening, however, they were soon seen all over the city. By 1926 an explosion in the number of movie houses had occurred, bringing them to most city neighborhoods. The vast majority outside downtown were located on major arterial streets, studding the commercial shopping strips that lined them. Nevertheless, by far the largest concentration was in the Loop business core. By 1937, the geographical dispersion of the movie palaces had reached its apogee. Large theaters with over 3,000 seats could be found on West Madison, Belmont, Lincoln, and 63rd. The Loop's dominance, still intact, was by then already diminishing. Sixty-five years later, in 2002, the exodus of movie theaters to the suburbs that began after the Second World War was well advanced, and only 29 remained within the city of Chicago, a mere two in the Loop.

Movie Theaters in Chicago, 2002

Authors: Michael P. Conzen and Christopher P. Thale

danced the Charleston, and dated men with automobiles that provided privacy for dating couples as well as greater access to suburban recreational opportunities. During this decade ethnic peer groups mediated mass culture through sponsored dances, clubs, and sports. But by the 1930s white industrial workers were generally AMERICANIZED, and the ethnic factor was less prominent, although clubs, parades, and holidays were (and remain) significant.

There was a growing reliance on commercial entertainment by the 1920s. Blue-collar workers spent on average $22.56 a year on movies, more than the middle class and more than one-half of their amusement budget. Neighborhood theaters competed with downtown movie palaces with cheaper admission, films that reflected community tastes, and larger playhouses primed for a middle-class audience. In 1921 the city's largest cinema was the 3,000-seat Tivoli Theater (Cottage Grove and 63rd), which had a marble lobby and charged $1 admission. Sound was introduced in 1927, within three years all the big theaters had sound. Sound altered the ambience at neighborhood theaters, where audiences that in the silent era had been pretty loud quieted down to hear the actors. There was a movie seat for every nine Chicagoans during the Depression, when movies took in about one-third of all entertainment expenditures. Neighborhood prices for adults ranged from fifteen to twenty-five cents, half the price of downtown theaters. Sound films hurt the once-flourishing legitimate stage, which barely survived the early Depression, mainly with Broadway shows.

Radio became ubiquitous during the 1920s. Eighty percent of programming presented musical shows and comedy sketches. Nonprofit ethnic, religious, and labor stations supplemented commercial stations. The Radio Act of 1927 promoted station consolidation but did not kill ethnic programming, which in the mid-1930s accounted for 5 percent of local BROADCASTS. Families bought Victrolas, often on credit, so they could play their favorite music at home. Sales of ETHNIC MUSIC swelled as Italians bought records of Caruso singing operas, MEXICANS purchased recordings of Mexican music, and African Americans bought "race" records made by jazz and blues artists.

Nightlife flourished in the 1920s despite PROHIBITION and the demise of the workingmen's saloon. Illegal drinking became an exciting middle-class pastime at speakeasies. When Mayor William Dever closed many clubs in the mid-1920s, ROADHOUSES in CICERO, STICKNEY, and BURNHAM that offered liquor, sex, and gambling replaced them. Exotic "black and tan" nightclubs in the SOUTH SIDE ghetto, like the "Plantation Cafe," offered integrated audiences excellent music and the thrills of being naughty and dangerous by drinking illegal liquor, dancing to hot jazz, and rubbing shoulders with celebrities or gangsters. The center of the ghetto's nightlife shifted from the Stroll to 47th Street, where the first large commercial dance hall for African Americans, the Savoy, was opened in 1927, followed two years later by the 3,500-seat Regal Theater. These were a part of the "chitlin' circuit" of black theaters in the United States. Forty-seventh Street was home to the big bands in the 1930s and 1940s and RHYTHM AND BLUES music in the mid-1950s.

Chicagoans relied heavily on public resources for entertainment, particularly sites envisioned by the 1909 *Plan of Chicago.* The FIELD MUSEUM moved in 1921 to GRANT PARK, and next door the $6.5 million SOLDIER FIELD was opened in 1924 and completed five years later along with the John G. SHEDD AQUARIUM and, a year after that, the ADLER PLANETARIUM. Soldier Field was the site of the 1927 Dempsey-Tunney rematch, seen by 104,000, and the 1937 Austin-Leo high-school football championship, attended by over 110,000. In 1933 the MUSEUM OF SCIENCE AND INDUSTRY opened with popular presentations of scientific and industrial subjects. Museum attendance dropped off sharply during the Depression. Field Museum crowds dropped by one-third between 1933 and 1936, with 90 percent coming on free days. An exception was the CENTURY OF PROGRESS EXHIBITION of 1933 and 1934, which drew 40 million people. In 1934, BROOKFIELD ZOO opened, and 22 different PARK DISTRICTS were merged into the 5,416-acre Chicago Park District comprising 84 parks and 78 fieldhouses, along with golf courses and swimming pools.

The sports boom of the 1920s fell off during the Depression. The Cubs were a popular attraction, winning four pennants from 1927 to 1938; the BEARS began playing at WRIGLEY FIELD in 1921; and the BLACKHAWKS began playing in 1926 at the Coliseum, moving to the Stadium three years later. Boxing and horse racing were legalized in 1926, and several tracks soon opened, including Arlington Park in 1927.

Participatory sport also expanded. There were 55 metropolitan golf courses, including elite clubs whose initiation fees cost from $3,000 to $5,000. Bowling alleys and billiards halls boomed among the working class until the Depression, when one-third of the former and one-half of the latter closed.

Leisure in Metropolitan Chicago since 1945

The leisure activities of postwar Chicago were influenced by the same variables as in earlier periods, particularly a rising standard of living, along with technological innovations, fashions and fads, age, race, gender, and homesite. Two-day weekends were the norm along with increased VACATION time. By the 1980s, Chicagoans were spending about 6 percent of their income on leisure, double the 1901 proportion. Class became less important, although differences in taste remained significant. The upper middle classes who lived in fashionable neighborhoods like LINCOLN PARK and HYDE PARK and the wealthier suburbs were the main clients at theaters, concerts, golf courses, and college football games. Lower-class Chicagoans devoted relatively more attention to such sports as baseball, boxing, and horse racing, and to TV, whose rise hurt movies, radio, and reading. Race played a big factor, with differences in musical tastes and nightlife. Racial discrimination hindered opportunities, reflected by uneven park development in different neighborhoods. The feminist movement that emerged in the 1960s encouraged women to work, secure higher-paying jobs, become sexually liberated, and participate in sports, a sphere from which they had been largely absent since the early 1900s.

Crowd at Cicero's Hawthorne Race Track on Derby Day, 1924. Photographer: Unknown. Source: Chicago Historical Society.

Chicago enjoyed a rich nightlife, which flourished in the 1950s on Rush Street at NIGHTCLUBS like Mister Kelly's and at South Side blues halls which declined with the coming of ROCK 'n' roll. In the 1970s most of the remaining old clubs died in the wake of disco, urban decay, and the expense of booking name entertainers. Blues revived in the 1990s with new clubs on the African American South Side and especially with trendy North Side locales like BLUES and Kingston Mines. Jazz had a big following with places like the Green Mill in UPTOWN and the London House (360 North Michigan Avenue), a showcase for Ramsey Lewis, Oscar Peterson, and Stan Getz. Chicagoans had a choice of many comedy clubs, most notably the SECOND CITY. Eating out became an important recreation in the 1960s, with ethnic restaurants for the budget conscious as well as fine dining. Since 1980, Chicagoans have combined their love of music and cuisine in the annual Taste of Chicago lakefront festival.

High culture prospered in this era. In 1953 the LYRIC OPERA was organized, restoring a tradition of outstanding opera and, with the Chicago Symphony, making the city an internationally renowned center of classical music. DANCE COMPANIES and especially theater proliferated. By 1998 Chicago was home to about 50 theater companies, from community and experimental theaters and suburban dinner playhouses to LOOP theaters that charged Broadway prices for Broadway-style productions.

Interest in participatory and spectator sport has grown substantially. Especially since the 1970s, Chicagoans have taken advantage of public beaches, bicycle paths, volleyball courts, and SOCCER fields to improve FITNESS and to socialize. In the decades from the 1950s through the 1970s, the Blackhawks regularly sold out the CHICAGO STADIUM, and attendance at racetracks, Bears games, and major league baseball rose, the latter abetted by extensive TV coverage and the ambience of WRIGLEY FIELD. Interest in basketball was mainly at the collegiate level until the BULLS became popular in the 1970s and achieved fanatic support once they became title contenders in the late 1980s. The cost of attending sport events, however, rose dramatically in the 1990s, making them unaffordable for many Chicagoans.

Conclusion

Chicago's leisure patterns have been historically influenced by the city's growth and maturation. Leisure opportunities were a product of economic development, which shaped the social structure, income levels, and available free time and surplus income, on the one hand, and, on the other, of urbanization, which reshaped urban space and was accompanied by a booming population. Leisure patterns were further affected by entrepreneurs who commercialized recreation, by politicians who promoted public parks and festivals, and by immigrants and southern African Americans who brought with them their own cultural traditions and values.

Steven A. Riess

See also: Dance; Foodways; French Period in Chicago; Multicentered Chicago; Philanthropy; Places of Assembly; Playgrounds and Small Parks; Street Life; Theater, Ethnic; Waterfront; Work Culture

Further reading: Cohen, Lizabeth. *Making a New Deal: Industrial Workers in Chicago, 1919–1939.* 1990. • Gems, Gerald R. *The Windy City Wars: Labor, Leisure, and Sport in the Making of Chicago.* 1997. • Riess, Steven A. *City Games: The Evolution of American Urban Society and the Rise of Sports.* 1989.

Lemont, IL, Cook, DuPage, and Will Counties, 24 miles SW of the Loop. Lemont lies in the DES PLAINES RIVER Valley, on the south bank of the ILLINOIS & MICHIGAN CANAL. Few of Chicago's suburbs have been as strongly influenced by TOPOGRAPHY. The Des Plaines River at Lemont is deeply incised into surrounding glacial uplands. The village, established largely in response to impending development of the canal, was nestled between valley bluffs to the southeast and the river to the north. The I&M Canal, constructed along the south side of the river in 1848, left areas between the two waterways to be developed for industrial purposes. Lemont's downtown and residential districts grew between the canal and the valley walls.

The first attempt at settlement after the displacement of indians was the "paper town" of Keepataw, platted in 1836, followed by Athens in 1839. Lemont proper was not incorporated until 1873, on land previously occupied by the defunct Keepataw.

Early development was guided by farseeing commercial magnates such as Nathaniel Brown and Horace Singer, who along with other major landowners controlled both the residential district and the flatlands in the floodplain. When canal digging revealed "Athens marble" at shallow depths below the valley's floor, Lemont became famous for its QUARRIES. Used at first for the canal and local construction, the easily worked rock (a form of Niagaran dolomite) soon became a major export. Chicago's Water Tower is built of this stone.

Work in the quarries and on the area TRANSPORTATION links required a large labor force, supplied by European immigrants. The IRISH came first, followed in the 1880s by POLES, GERMANS, and Scandinavians. Each group left its mark, perhaps none more indelible than that of the Polish congregation led by Father Moczygemba. Sent in 1882 to minister to the Polish settlers, this priest established the cohesive residential community of Jasnagora that sits above Lemont today.

Life was not easy for the immigrant laborers, who struggled against low pay and poor working conditions. Employers quashed several STRIKES with the assistance of state militia between 1885 and 1893. Competition from better-quality, cheaper Indiana stone, along with labor conflict, contributed to the decline of the quarries. Lemont was rescued from stagnation, however, by a manufacturing base that included activities as diverse as dairying, soda and beer bottling, cement and tile making, and CLOTHING and shoe manufacturing. As the high-tech industry of its time, the Illinois Pure Aluminum Company (established 1892) provided a mainstay of employment for exactly a century. In 1922 the Globe Oil and REFINING Company opened what was then the largest refinery in the state.

Lemont became noted during the 1920s for an abundance of large institutional landholdings. FOREST PRESERVES, GOLF courses, CEMETERIES, and ecclesiastical retreats began to cluster nearby. After WORLD WAR II, these were joined by research installations such as the ARGONNE NATIONAL LABORATORY. More recently, the LITHUANIAN World Center and the HINDU Temple of Greater Chicago have added to the village's cosmopolitan flavor. Although they did not radically alter village life, these developments marked the start of a new era. Well into the 1960s, Lemont retained its identity as a small, spatially distinct canal town; with the growth of these religious and recreational functions, it began to attract people from throughout the Chicago area, and to merge with the expanding metropolitan fringe.

In the 1970s, Lemont suffered from industrial obsolescence and economic recession. At the same time, however, it drew on new resources from white-collar and professional families moving from Chicago to an expanding suburbia. With its inexpensive land and accessibility to employment centers, Lemont shared in the massive, area-wide growth of subdivision development.

Lemont moved to bring these subdivisions within its borders by actively ANNEXING land to the south. A greater population required more services, leading to the emergence of a new urban core on the southern edge of town. This new center was unabashedly modern in tone, with shopping malls and PARKING lots designed for an automotive public. No longer contained by its valley, Lemont shed the uniquely isolated character of the older village.

John D. Schroeder

See also: Business of Chicago; Glaciation; Metropolitan Growth

Further reading: Buschman, Barbara, ed. *Lemont, Illinois: Its History in Commemoration of the Centennial of Its Incorporation.* 1972. • Conzen, Michael P., and Carl A. Zimring, eds. *Looking for Lemont: Place and People in an Illinois Canal Town.* 1994.

Leopold and Loeb. On May 21, 1924, Chicago became the locale for an event long remembered as the "crime of the century" when 14-year-old Robert (Bobby) Franks was kidnaped and killed. On May 31, the case became even more notorious and the occasion for national reflection on issues of motivation, violence, and modern morality when Richard Loeb and Nathan Leopold, Jr., confessed to committing the crime.

Neither Loeb, who was 18 and already a graduate of the University of Michigan, nor Leopold, who at 19 had just graduated from the UNIVERSITY OF CHICAGO and was on his way to Harvard Law School, fit any ordinary profile of the criminal type. Their families were rich, respected, and socially well connected among Chicago's JEWISH business class. Because of their privilege and modern education, they were initially represented as Nietzschean supermen who killed for a thrill because they saw themselves as immune from banal conventions of right and wrong. But after their families hired Clarence Darrow, who mounted a defense to save Leopold and Loeb from the death sentence by using extensive testimony from prominent psychiatrists, the enormous publicity focused on the case introduced Americans to new ways of understanding crime which emphasized the troubled psyches and warped childhoods of the defendants.

Darrow's brilliant concluding remarks have become part of his legacy of eloquence, but may have had little to do with the fact that Judge John Caverly spared the lives of two of his most famous clients. Leopold and Loeb were sentenced to life terms. In 1936, Loeb died in Stateville prison after he was repeatedly slashed with a razor by a fellow inmate who accused him of making sexual advances. Leopold was paroled in 1958 after writing a set of memoirs devoted to his good works in prison. He died in 1971 in San Juan, Puerto Rico.

Paula S. Fass

See also: Crime and Chicago's Image; Homicide; Kenwood

Further reading: Fass, Paula S. "Making and Remaking an Event: The Leopold and Loeb Case in American Culture." *Journal of American History* 80 (December 1993): 919–951. • Gertz, Elmer. *A Handful of Clients.* 1965. • Higdon, Hal. *The Crime of the Century.* 1975.

Lesbians. *See* Gays and Lesbians

Levee. *See* Vice Districts

Lewis University. Lewis University originated as a ROMAN CATHOLIC high school for boys (Holy Name Technical School) in ROMEOVILLE, Illinois, in 1932. It soon attracted the interest and financial support of entrepreneur Frank J. Lewis and began adding college-level courses in 1934. Many of those courses involved aviation technology, and the school completed construction of its own airport in 1939. The U.S. Navy took over the campus from 1942 to 1944 and trained nearly 1,200 pilots there. After the war, the school reopened as a junior college, and in 1946 it became the Lewis College of Science and Technology. The high school was dropped altogether in 1949, and one year later women became a part of the student body. The educational order of the Christian Brothers assumed leadership of the college in 1960; it received accreditation two years later and, after adding several graduate programs, became Lewis University in 1973. Though it sold its AIRPORT to the Joliet Regional Port District in 1989, aviation remains a cornerstone of the Lewis University program.

Sarah Fenton

See also: Colleges, Junior and Community; Universities and Their Cities

Lexington Hotel. The history of the Lexington Hotel mirrors the fortunes of Chicago's once fashionable NEAR SOUTH SIDE. Completed in 1892 in time for the WORLD'S COLUMBIAN EXPOSITION, the HOTEL initially offered luxury APARTMENTS for permanent residents and temporary rooms for visitors. From 1928 to 1932 Al Capone made the hotel at 2135 S. Michigan Avenue his gangland headquarters, an association that the hotel's reputation never escaped. Eventually converted to a brothel and low-rent residential hotel, it closed in 1980. Despite its landmark status (1985), the building was demolished in 1995 after repeated unsuccessful attempts at renovation.

Jonathan J. Keyes

See also: Crime and Chicago's Image; Historic Preservation; Mafia

Liberians. Until the influx of REFUGEES fleeing the 1980 military coup began arriving in the United States, the Liberian community in Chicago consisted of a few scattered individuals who had come to the city for educational purposes. During the 1980s and 1990s, the community grew to approximately 1,000 households, comprising mostly refugees and former Liberian government officials. According to a coalition of local Liberian immigrants, the Organization of the Liberian Community, Chicago has become a destination for Liberians because it has an active community and because it is the location of the Midwestern Consul General of the Honorary Liberian Consulate.

Since the community is not concentrated in any particular neighborhood, except for some small pockets of settlement on the SOUTH SIDE, nor any occupational category, community life revolves around the yearly celebration of Liberian Independence Day on July 26 and on Liberian relief efforts. Many Liberian immigrants cooperate with the fundraising efforts of the Peace and Stability for Liberia organization, headed in the 1990s by former Illinois senator Paul Simon. Attempts in the early 1990s to organize a Liberian church met with little success. Although the community was thriving in the 1990s, most of its members still hoped to return to their country if the political situation there stabilized.

Tracy N. Poe

See also: Demography; Multicentered Chicago

Libertyville, IL, Lake County, 33 miles NW of the Loop. George Vardin settled on a low ridge of ground on the west side of the upper DES PLAINES RIVER along the Chicago-Milwaukee Road in 1835. Vardin thought that he could profit by platting a village on his farm site, and called his plat "Vardin's Grove." When a post office was established there in 1837, Vardin's Grove became known as Independence Grove. After postal authorities rejected that name, Archimedes Wynkoop rechristened the settlement as Libertyville.

When LAKE COUNTY was split from McHENRY COUNTY in 1839, some merchants worked to bring the county seat to Libertyville under the new name of Burlington. Their hope collapsed when WAUKEGAN took the honor and the name Libertyville was retained.

In the late 1860s, Ansel Brainerd Cook, later a sidewalk contractor and president of the Chicago City Council, constructed a large, porticoed house in Libertyville along the Milwaukee Road. The house, which still stands as Libertyville's centerpiece, was located on Cook's horse farm, which provided power for Chicago horsecar lines.

The Chicago, Milwaukee & St. Paul Railway built a line between Milwaukee and Chicago in 1872 which bypassed Libertyville. Walter C. Newberry, nephew of the founder of the NEWBERRY LIBRARY and a fellow Lake County REAL-ESTATE speculator and Chicago politician with Cook, persuaded Libertyville's merchants to fund a three-mile spur line into town in 1880. The resulting RAILROAD boom led Libertyville leaders to incorporate their community in 1882.

The architectural nature of Libertyville changed after a massive fire destroyed the business center in 1895 and the village board decreed that only brick buildings could be constructed in the downtown area.

In 1906, Samuel Insull purchased 160 acres south of the village. Unhappy with irregular electrical service in the area, Insull brought a number of rural generating plants together under the name of Commonwealth Edison in a successful experiment to improve reliability.

Insull acquired the Chicago & Milwaukee Electric line (renamed the Chicago, North Shore & Milwaukee), which had built a spur from Lake Bluff to Libertyville in 1903. Not only was this INTERURBAN line a major electricity consumer, but it also simplified Insull's COMMUTE from Chicago to his landholdings. By 1921, Insull's holdings around Libertyville grew to 4,445 acres, which he christened the Hawthorne-Mellody Farms.

In the mid-1930s, the GREAT DEPRESSION left Insull's empire in ruins, and portions of the Hawthorne-Mellody Farms were sold to successful Chicagoans such as John F. Cuneo, owner of Cuneo Press; and Adlai Stevenson, Chicago attorney and later two-time presidential candidate.

When suburbanization intensified in the 1960s, owners of estates around Libertyville, many carved from the Hawthorne-Mellody Farms, successfully resisted efforts to subdivide the area.

In 2000 Libertyville was a commercial center for over 20,000 residents who enjoy a suburban commuter lifestyle in spacious conditions thanks to the historic acquisitions of Cook and Insull.

Craig L. Pfannkuche

See also: Built Environment of the Chicago Region; Metropolitan Growth

Further reading: *Libertyville Illustrated.* 1993. • *The Past and Present of Lake County, Illinois.* 1877. • Turner, Elisha R. *The Growth and Development of Libertyville.* 1974.

Libraries.

COOK COUNTY LIBRARIES
SUBURBAN LIBRARIES

COOK COUNTY LIBRARIES. Chicago has been home to a great number and variety of libraries since its earliest days as a city. Religious, social, literary, and cultural associations developed in the 1830s and 1840s to provide for the enlightenment and spiritual needs of the growing population, and many developed and maintained small libraries charging members for the use of reading rooms and collections. In 1841, the Young Men's Association (later to become the Chicago Library Association) established a reading room open to the public on a fee basis. The library grew substantially over the next decades, reaching 30,000 volumes by 1871. It employed a full-time librarian to manage the collection and began to sponsor public lectures.

The 1850s and 1860s saw the establishment of dozens of professional, academic, religious, and ethnic libraries. In 1856–57 alone, the CHICAGO HISTORICAL SOCIETY, Board of Trade, Chicago Theological Seminary, Sigma Alpha Epsilon, Chicago Turngemeinde (GERMAN), old University of Chicago, CHICAGO

Academy of Sciences, Chicago Law Institute, Chicago Arbeiterverein (German), and Svea Society (Swedish) all established libraries in Chicago.

The fire of 1871 destroyed millions of books and leveled most of the city's libraries. A movement to establish free public library service, spearheaded by the Chicago Library Association, had begun in the late 1860s and was given impetus by the fire. In 1872, the Chicago Public Library was established, utilizing 8,000 books donated by British citizens. After the fire, some of the private libraries like the Chicago Historical Society rebuilt their collections, and new libraries sponsored by academic institutions, religious and social organizations, and professional groups opened as well. The Newberry Library, Ryerson Library at the Art Institute, Moody Bible Institute Library, Chicago Bar Association Library, University of Chicago libraries, and DePaul University Library were among some of the most prominent established before the turn of the century. In 1896, the Chicago Public Library, John Crerar Library, and the Newberry Library reached an agreement on collection development and responsibilities for specific areas of interest to each. John Crerar would collect in the biological, medical, and the physical sciences; Newberry Library, in the humanities: and the Chicago Public Library, in general literature and Chicagoana.

In the twentieth century, academic, professional, and other specialty libraries have continued to proliferate in Chicago to complement the growing public library system. Many of these libraries serve specialized needs, ranging from small company-sponsored libraries like the Illinois Bell Telephone Company library established in 1927 for employees, to larger libraries serving professionals in the city, like the American Institute of Baking Library, which opened in 1923 to provide technical resources to those in the baking industry. Elementary and high schools have opened libraries in growing numbers, and Chicago colleges and universities have established large research libraries.

The second half of the twentieth century has seen the growth of resource sharing and library collaboration. The Center for Research Libraries (CRL), founded in 1949 by 13 university libraries as the Midwest Inter-Library Center, has grown into a national consortium with hundreds of members and over 3 million volumes of rare research materials that it circulates to major research libraries, primarily colleges and universities. Large-scale, formal cooperation among libraries in Chicago emerged after the passage in 1965 of the Library System Act of Illinois, which authorized the construction of library systems—organizations of public and nonpublic libraries governed by autonomous boards of directors. The Chicago Library System, a consortium of 60 academic, 250 special, and 576 school libraries, provides cooperative system services, facilitates the sharing of resources among libraries, and develops library services in the city beyond the scope of individual member libraries.

Alice Calabrese

See also: Lectures and Public Speaking; Libraries: Suburban Libraries; Literary Cultures

Further reading: Chicago Library Club. *Directory of Libraries in the Chicago Area.* 1945. • Spencer, Gladys. *The Chicago Public Library: Origins and Backgrounds.* 1943.

SUBURBAN LIBRARIES. Small towns and villages surrounding major cities began opening public libraries as early as the mid-nineteenth century. In the late nineteenth and early twentieth centuries, women's clubs, churches, the YMCA, and other community groups were instrumental in starting and promoting publicly funded libraries, or in some cases establishing libraries that subsequently became tax supported. Some of Chicago's earliest suburban libraries were started by community organizations in Elgin, Evanston, and Waukegan.

From 1915 to 1919, Andrew Carnegie, through his "free library" program, endowed the construction of libraries across Illinois, including suburbs such as Blue Island, Glen Ellyn, and Park Ridge. When the Carnegie program ended in 1919, local organizations once again took up the challenge of finding funding for public libraries.

The Library Services Act of 1956 (LSA) initiated federal funding for libraries and had a significant impact on the growth of suburban libraries. The LSA was later reincarnated as the LSCA (Library Services and Construction Act) in 1964 and as the LSTA (Library Services and Technology Act) in 1996.

In Illinois, some LSCA funds were filtered through the Illinois State Library in grants called Project PLUS (Promoting Larger Units of Service). With the assistance of library systems, Project PLUS helped the Chicago suburbs build libraries to fill the noticeable gaps in suburban service. The grants enabled neighboring towns that were too small to support their own libraries to band together and form a library district encompassing several towns. For example, the Vernon Area Public Library District was started with a Project PLUS grant in 1974 to serve all or parts of the communities of Buffalo Grove, Lincolnshire, Long Grove, Prairie View, Riverwoods, Vernon Hills, and Vernon Township.

In many states, libraries belong to a library system that provides a variety of services to its members, including delivery of interlibrary loan materials between libraries, help with automation, and continuing education. The first library systems in Illinois, independent library-related entities with autonomous governing boards, were created in 1965. Three library systems serve the Chicago suburban area, North Suburban Library System to the north, Du Page Library System to the west, and Suburban Library System to the south.

Sarah Ann Long

See also: Chicago Public Library; Government, Suburban; Special Districts

Further reading: Baaske, Ian. "How Chicago Suburbs without Library Service Created Their Own." *Illinois Libraries* 80.3 (Summer 1998): 149–152. • Illinois Regional Library Council. *Illinois Libraries and Information Centers.* 1981.

Library, Chicago Public. *See* Chicago Public Library

Lily Lake, IL, Kane County, 44 miles W of the Loop. The lake in Lily Lake no longer exists. When the town paved its roadways in the 1930s, they drained the small lake to its south. Lily Lake began as a milk stop when dairy farmers shipped their products to Chicago on the Great Western railroad (established in 1885). In 1990 residents of Lily Lake grudgingly voted for incorporation to thwart a landfill plan. The population in 2000 was 825.

Erik Gellman

See also: Agriculture; Land Use

Lincoln Park, Community Area 7, 3 miles N of the Loop. During the nineteenth century, the inhabitants of the future Lincoln Park Community Area ranged from affluent residents focused on the park and the Loop, to German farmers and shopkeepers oriented to North Avenue, to industrial workers living near the factories along the North Branch of the Chicago River. Most of the early European residents were German truck farmers, whose products earned the area the nickname "Cabbage Patch." By 1852 the German community was well enough established to begin work on St. Michael's Roman Catholic Church, which was named for the patron saint of local brewer and land donor Michael Diversey. The city of Chicago made the southeastern portion of the area its cemetery in 1837, but the graves proved such a health hazard that the cemetery was moved and the land redesignated Lake Park in 1864. It was renamed Lincoln Park the next year for the assassinated president. This recreational center attracted such cultural institutions as the Chicago Academy of Sciences, the Lincoln Park Zoo, and the Chicago Historical Society. In 1863, Cyrus McCormick sponsored the opening of the Presbyterian Theological Seminary of the

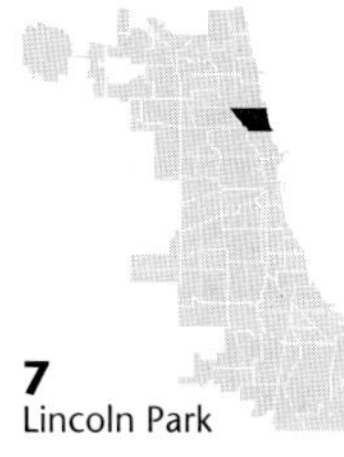

Girls' race at Adams Playground, 1919 North Seminary, Chicago Special Park Commission, 1907. Photographer: Unknown. Source: Chicago Public Library.

Northwest in northwestern Lincoln Park; the school was later renamed for its benefactor.

In 1871, the Great FIRE swept through the North Side, including much of Lincoln Park, and destroyed most of the structures there. Residents rebuilt swiftly, with many finding housing in temporary wooden shacks before the city extended FIRE LIMITS to the city boundaries in 1874. During the next decades, industrial plants such as furniture factories and the Deering Harvester Works concentrated along the North Branch of the river. ITALIANS, POLES, ROMANIANS, HUNGARIANS, and SLOVAKS worked in these factories and established the working-class character of west Lincoln Park. The eastern sector remained an enclave of families of middle-class commuters and expensive mansions fronting the park. Among the new institutions of the late nineteenth century was Crilly Court, an apartment complex designed by Daniel F. Crilly, who selected artists for tenants. In 1898, St. Vincent's College, renamed DEPAUL UNIVERSITY in 1907, opened near the McCormick Seminary. By the early twentieth century, Lincoln Park was firmly established as a residential neighborhood that hosted some of Chicago's major cultural institutions.

During the GREAT DEPRESSION, Lincoln Park's housing stock deteriorated as owners subdivided and neglected their properties. After World War II, residents of OLD TOWN, in the southeastern section of Lincoln Park, worried that their neighborhood hovered on the verge of becoming a slum. They formed the Old Town Triangle Association in 1948, which inspired residents of the mid-North neighborhood to create a similar organization in 1950. In 1954 the Lincoln Park Conservation Association was organized to cover the entire community area. LPCA pursued neighborhood renewal by encouraging private rehabilitation of property and the use of government tools such as federal URBAN-RENEWAL funds and enforcement of the housing code. In 1956, Lincoln Park was designated a CONSERVATION AREA, and in the 1960s the city began implementing its "General Neighborhood Renewal Plan." Although the LPCA had consciously tried to avoid the wholesale clearance that took place in HYDE PARK, it incurred the wrath of poor people who lived in the southwestern quarter of Lincoln Park. The Concerned Citizens of Lincoln Park argued that PUERTO RICANS and AFRICAN AMERICANS were being displaced from their homes and priced out of the renewing neighborhood. Developers bought land near the park and built high-rise APARTMENT buildings, to the consternation of LPCA, which had hoped to keep the district congenial to families.

In the last quarter of the twentieth century, land values increased dramatically, making it difficult for people and institutions in financial straits to remain in Lincoln Park. Most of the poor left. In 1973, the struggling McCormick Seminary sold its land to DePaul and moved to HYDE PARK. Single professionals and childless couples moved into the new high-rises and rehabilitated old houses. By the end of the twentieth century, the combination of public and private urban renewal efforts had made Lincoln Park one of the highest-status neighborhoods in the city.

Amanda Seligman

See also: Gentrification; Playgrounds and Small Parks; Seminaries

Further reading: Bennett, Larry. *Fragments of Cities: The New American Downtowns and Neighborhoods.* 1990. • Ducey, Michael H. *Sunday Morning: Aspects of Urban Ritual.* 1977. • Pacyga, Dominic A., and Ellen Skerrett. *Chicago, City of Neighborhoods: Histories and Tours.* 1986.

Lincoln Park. When Lincoln Park was named in 1865 to honor the assassinated president, the honor anticipated a more park-like setting than existed at the time. A cemetery at the site, active from the 1840s, did not cease burials until 1866, and graves were removed to more remote CEMETERIES for years afterward. Though the city had set aside land for a park, few improvements had been made, and the area's landscape appeared to contemporaries as a barren, sandy wasteland of wind-blown dunes and unstable shorelines.

The state created the Lincoln Park Commission as a SPECIAL DISTRICT, one of three Chicago-area PARK DISTRICTS, in 1869, with authority over lakefront land between North and Diversey Avenues. In the following decades workers excavated artificial ponds, mixed tons of clay and manure into the sand, and, after some failed experiments, largely stabilized the shoreline. By the end of the century many enduring features of the park were in place, including abundant greenery, fountains and statuary, winding walkways, BICYCLE PATHS, and the beginnings of the LINCOLN PARK ZOO (1868), Lake Shore Drive (1875), and the Lincoln Park CONSERVATORY (1892).

In 1895 the state legislature prepared the way for the park's expansion to the north by granting the commission the right to reclaim submerged lands along the lakeshore as far north as Devon Avenue. Lincoln Park joined in the consolidation of park districts that created the Chicago Park District in 1934.

In addition to recreational facilities and programs including beaches, picnic grounds, TENNIS courts, athletic fields, and summer THEATER, Lincoln Park has become home to the CHICAGO ACADEMY OF SCIENCES, which relocated in 1893 and reopened in 1999 as the Peggy Notebaert Nature Museum, and the CHICAGO HISTORICAL SOCIETY, which relocated in 1932.

Douglas Knox

See also: Leisure; Waterfront

Further reading: Bryan, I. J. *Report of the Commissioners and a History of Lincoln Park.* 1899.

Lincoln Park Zoological Gardens. The zoo began in 1868 with the donation of a pair of swans from the menagerie in New York's Central Park. With the arrival of these waterfowl, the development of a formal animal collection in Chicago's lakefront park began. The zoo's first director, Cyrus DeVry, was hired in 1888. His tenure lasted more than 30 years.

The early decades of the twentieth century saw the development of the Lion House (1912), with its great hall, and the Primate House (1927), home of one of the most famous gorillas, Bushman (1931–1951). This was a period of formal growth and organization for the zoo, by then a recreational destination and city treasure.

In 1945, Marlin Perkins came to the Lincoln Park Zoo and the two became synonymous, as is his name to this day with that of Mutual of Omaha and "Zoo Parade." More than almost any other individual, Perkins made zoos popular, recognizable, and an integral part of American life. He served as the zoo's director until 1962, helping to encourage the development of its first formal citizen support group, the Lincoln Park Zoological Society. One of the group's first efforts was the creation of the nation's first year-round Children's Zoo (1959), followed by the creation of the Farm-in-the-Zoo (1964), designed to show city dwellers something of the country life.

With Perkins's departure, zoo veterinarian Lester E. Fisher became the new director. Under his administration, nearly a dozen significant renovations, restorations, and new facilities were completed. Ultimately more than $40,000,000 was invested in the zoo's physical plant, including renovations to the Primate House, Small Mammal House, Bird House, and Children's Zoo and additions to the Farm-in-the-Zoo. The Kroc Animal Hospital and Commissary (1976) and the Great Ape House (1976) fulfilled long-standing needs. Also built were the Crown Field Administrative and Education Center (1979), the Blum-Kovler Penguin and Seabird House (1981), and birds of prey habitats (1989), as well as new facilities for large mammals and carnivores. In 1990, the Zoo Society reopened Café Brauer after massive renovations.

Following Fisher's retirement in 1992, political and financial issues surfaced that led to a re-evaluation of direction and management. In 1995, the Zoological Society assumed the zoo's management from the Chicago Park District, which remains the owner, and named Kevin J. Bell, Fisher's successor, as president and CEO.

Dennis A. Meritt, Jr.

See also: Brookfield Zoo (Chicago Zoological Park); Leisure

Further reading: Perkins, Marlin. *My Wild Kingdom.* 1982.

Lincoln Square, Community Area 4, 7 miles N of the Loop. The Lincoln Square Community Area has hosted a wide array of unrelated enterprises. The Ravenswood residential subdivision was so influential that its name at one time stood for the whole area. Only after the vacant commercial spaces filled up after World War II did local merchants promote Lincoln Square as a cohesive neighborhood with a shopping district at its heart.

Early commercial agriculture in the Lincoln Square area emphasized truck farming and the mass production of flowers, pickles, and celery. In 1836, Swiss immigrant Conrad Sulzer bought property near the present intersection of Montrose and Clark. Truck farmers, mostly of German and English descent, followed his example. They drove their produce in wagons down the old Little Fort Road (Lincoln Avenue) to market in Chicago. The celery crop gained such broad distribution that local growers proudly called the area the nation's celery capital. The Budlong brothers opened a successful pickle factory in 1857 and expanded into the flower business with the opening of Budlong Greenhouses in 1880. They employed Polish workers from Chicago on a seasonal basis. The increasing traffic along the old Little Fort Road encouraged the opening of many taverns for thirsty travelers.

Other investors promoted nonagricultural land use in Lincoln Square. Bowmanville, one of its first residential subdivisions, was developed in 1850 by a local hotel keeper who disappeared before his customers discovered that he did not own the land he had sold. Rosehill Cemetery, which occupies almost one quarter of the land in Lincoln Square, opened in 1859 around the site of Hiram Roe's tavern. The entrance faced the North Western railroad stop at Rosehill Drive as an encouragement to mourners and picnickers to make day-long outings to the area. In 1868, the opening of another flag stop about a mile south of the cemetery inspired the building of the Ravenswood subdivision, an exclusive commuter suburb that encompassed Sulzer's original property. Ravenswood's success encouraged other real-estate speculators to create more local developments, such as Summerdale and the Clybourn subdivision.

Electric street railways began running through Lincoln Square in the 1890s, and the Ravenswood Elevated opened in 1907. Both brought new residents to Lincoln Square. The area's farmland gradually began to fill up with bungalows, two-flats, and small apartment buildings; the names of two of the new developments, Ravenswood Gardens and Ravenswood Manor, traded on the area's residential history. Some land intended for residential use lay undeveloped until after World War II. Among the new residents were Greeks, whose many small businesses and St. Demetrios church (1929) set the stage for Lincoln Square to become the "new Greektown" when the old Greektown was displaced by the construction of the Congress (now Eisenhower) Expressway and the University of Illinois at Chicago. An industrial corridor developed along the North Western Railway tracks on Ravenswood Avenue. One of the largest of these interests was Abbott Laboratories, founded in 1888 by local physician and pharmacist Wallace Calvin Abbott (1857–1921).

The common use of the name "Ravenswood" reflected Lincoln Square's residential image. Beginning in 1949, the Lincoln Square Chamber of Commerce promoted its commercial identity. The intersection at Lincoln, Lawrence, and Western Avenues had never been as popular as other regional shopping districts, and the growing number of empty storefronts after World War II made some merchants worry about their ability to attract customers. In 1956, they erected a statue of the late president Abraham Lincoln, for whom the area and its major street were called. In 1978 they developed the Lincoln Square mall, a pedestrian plaza that required a controversial rerouting of local traffic. The chamber tried to evoke an Old World flavor with European-style shops and a lantern imported from Hamburg, Germany. Many of the empty storefronts did indeed fill in; an increasing number of proprietors, however, were not of European descent, reflecting the fact that Latinos and Asians in Chicago found the family-friendly housing of Lincoln Square as attractive as previous generations had.

Amanda Seligman

See also: Agriculture; Housing Types; Lake View Township; Metropolitan Growth

Further reading: Lake View–Ravenswood Historical Collection. Sulzer Regional Library, Chicago, IL. • Vivien M. Palmer Documents. Chicago Historical Society, Chicago, IL. • Zatterberg, Helen. *An Historical Sketch of Ravenswood and Lake View.* 1941.

Lincolnshire, IL, Lake County, 26 miles NW of the Loop. Lincolnshire is among the wealthiest communities in the Chicago metropolitan area. It is near the site of one of the earliest non-Indian settlements in Lake County, Half Day, now part of Vernon Hills.

Lincolnshire began as a subdivision of 280 acres into half-acre lots in 1955, promoted by developer Roger Ladd. The village incorporated in 1957. From the beginning it was marketed to relatively wealthy homeowners, many of whom were attracted by the rolling, wooded landscape along the Des Plaines River.

Lincolnshire remained a quiet residential community into the 1980s. Issues relating to the management of growth dominated village politics in the late 1980s and early 1990s, with a cautious approach predominating. Lincolnshire refused to annex two corporate office park developments in the mid-1980s.

Critics of the slow-growth policy noted that the village had to contend with increased traffic resulting from developments in neighboring communities, while the new tax revenues went to other villages. Lincolnshire later sought to annex the unincorporated community of Half Day, but in 1996 lost a court battle over ANNEXATION to rival Vernon Hills.

Lincolnshire did acquire its own commercial developments, including a Marriott Lincolnshire Resort near the 300-acre Lincolnshire Corporate Center, begun in 1983. The village built an imposing new village hall in 1993.

While the village had grown up without a center, trustees began working in the mid-1990s to develop a downtown anchored by a movie theater and retail and office space.

In 2000, almost all Lincolnshire residents were white and lived in single-family, owner-occupied homes with a median value of $425,200. Most households (83 percent) had two or more cars. Only 1 percent of residents reported incomes below poverty level.

Douglas Knox

See also: Inverness; Kenilworth; Lake County, IL; Metropolitan Growth; Suburbs and Cities as Dual Metropolis

Further reading: "A Lovely Town for Trees, Friends, and Fights." *Chicago Tribune,* May 21, 1994.

Lincolnwood, IL, Cook County, 10 miles NW of the Loop. Lincolnwood is an ethnically diverse, two-and-a-half-square-mile suburb. POTAWATOMI originally settled the wooded area, but vacated the land after the Indian Boundary TREATY of 1816. Rural development proceeded slowly on treacherous plank roads along present-day Milwaukee and Lincoln Avenues. Johann Tess, for whom the village was originally named, and his family came from Germany in 1856, purchasing 30 acres of barren land in the area. Population slowly increased, and the first commercial establishment, the Halfway House SALOON, was established in 1873.

The agrarian population grew after the establishment of a Chicago & North Western Railway station in nearby SKOKIE in 1891 and the completion of the North Shore Channel in 1909, which made the easily flooded prairie land manageable. More saloons and taverns soon appeared, specifically along Crawford and Lincoln Avenues. Because only organized municipalities could grant liquor licenses, 359 residents incorporated in 1911 and named the village Tessville. Tessville ANNEXED land throughout the 1920s, finally stretching to Central Avenue on the west and Kedzie Avenue on the east. During PROHIBITION, Tessville became a haven for speakeasies and GAMBLING facilities.

Tessville was long reputed for drinking and GAMBLING until the 1931 election of its longest-serving mayor, Henry A. Proesel, a grandson of George Proesel, one of the original American settlers. In 1932, Lincoln Avenue, formerly a plank TOLL ROAD, became a state highway. Proesel then worked with the federal government's Public Works Administration and hired the community's entire unemployed workforce to plant 10,000 elm TREES on the village streets. Most important, the community passed a liquor license law (1934) that limited the number of licenses allowable within the city limits and became a model ordinance for other communities. Proesel finally changed Tessville's image when he renamed the village Lincolnwood in 1936.

Lincolnwood's institutions, industries, and CLUBS continued to grow along with the suburb. The Bryn Mawr Country Club (1919), the East Prairie Welfare Club, later to become the Lincolnwood Woman's Club (1927), the Lincolnwood Afternoon Club (1953), and the American Legion Post #1226 (1952) helped create a sense of community in the village. School District 74 formed in 1938, and the Lincolnwood Public LIBRARY (1978) provided residents with quality education and offered much needed services. Bell & Howell's relocation to east Lincolnwood (1942) spurred growth and increased other industry relocation to the village. The Lincolnwood JEWISH Congregation (1958) and St. John's Lutheran Church (1942) served residents' religious needs.

Significant population growth in Lincolnwood occurred with the opening of the Edens EXPRESSWAY (1951). The village rapidly matured as a suburb, growing from 3,072 in 1950 to 12,929 in 1970. In 2000, Lincolnwood's ethnic composition was 75 percent white, highly educated, and had a median household income of $71,234.

Laura Milsk

See also: Germans; Prohibition and Temperance; Water

Further reading: Lamm, Shirley, W. "Lincolnwood, Illinois: A Thesis." Master's thesis, Northeastern Illinois University. 1969. • League of Women Voters of Skokie and Lincolnwood. *The Village of Lincolnwood.* 1973. • *Lincolnwood Seventy-fifth Diamond Jubilee Celebration, 1911–1986.*

Lindenhurst, IL, Lake County, 42 miles NW of the Loop. Lindenhurst began as a SUBDIVISION in LAKE VILLA Township in 1952. The land had been called "Lindenhurst Farm" by a prior owner, Ernst Lehmann, son of the wealthy Chicago DEPARTMENT STORE merchant who founded Lake Villa. Developer Morton Engle and his brothers bought the property in the late 1940s. Their company sought to market relatively inexpensive starter homes to war veterans. The company remained the primary developer into the early 1980s, building homes along with some small shopping areas and parks.

Lindenhurst was one of the first post–WORLD WAR II suburban-style developments in northwestern LAKE COUNTY. Most contemporaneous developments were in suburbs much closer to Chicago. The pace of building accelerated in the 1970s, and by 1990 the population was 8,038. This grew to 12,539 in 2000.

Most households consisted of married couples and their families living in owner-occupied homes. While residential growth outstripped business and commercial growth, the village made commercial ZONING a condition of some developments. In the 1990s the largest employer in the village was Victory Lakes Continuing Care Center, a retirement health complex.

While Lindenhurst began as an offshoot of Lake Villa, its more recent growth has been oriented toward the east, approaching Millburn (now part of OLD MILL CREEK) and GURNEE. Lindenhurst's planners and officials expected growth to continue, and sought to minimize the problems accompanying growth by securing boundary and ANNEXATION agreements with incorporated neighbors. The Lindenhurst Sanitary District began expanding its sewer capacity. New village and police buildings were constructed in the mid-1990s, along with a new Lake Villa District Library, which serves Lindenhurst. In addition, officials from neighboring SCHOOL DISTRICTS made efforts to coordinate their planning to deal with projected population increases throughout the region.

Though Lindenhurst's own corporate history is recent, a significant Lake County historic site came within its borders through annexation in the mid-1990s. The Lake County FOREST PRESERVE District acquired the historic Bonner Farm, dating to the 1840s, and planned to develop it into a historical museum to preserve part of Lake County's agricultural heritage.

Douglas Knox

See also: Built Environment of the Chicago Region; Suburbs and Cities as Dual Metropolis

Further reading: "It's Not on Cutting Edge, but Residents Like It That Way." *Chicago Tribune,* March 21, 1992.

Liquor Distribution. The AGRICULTURAL trade of the Midwest, particularly in grain and hops, made Chicago a natural choice for liquor manufacturing and retailing. The industry formed in close conjunction with Chicago's social evolution as it responded both to demand and to movements to limit the production, sale, and consumption of liquor.

Chicago's retail liquor trade began in 1827, when Samuel Miller and Archibald Clybourne established the Miller House, a store that doubled as the town's first tavern, serving a crude ale as well as some imported beer. By 1837, there were 10 taverns, 26 groceries, many of which sold liquor, and one brewery.

In 1860 Chicago had eight distilleries, but by the 1890s Peoria had emerged as the center of distilling in Illinois. Beer production, however, grew enormously, particularly after 1870. By the turn of the century, the city had over 50 BREWERIES, the great majority run by GERMANS. Because breweries depended on saloonkeepers for their livelihood, they tried to win the saloonkeepers' loyalty by such means as promising loans for remodeling or paying license fees. The brewers also became directly involved in the retail trade by opening their own SALOONS. By 1900, brewers dominated most of the barrooms of Chicago.

Ironically, organized efforts to restrict liquor spurred industry cooperation. In the early 1870s, the "Liberty League," made up of both dealers and saloonkeepers, was the first organization of liquor dealers in Chicago. In 1880, the Illinois Liquor Dealers Protective Association, the industry's first statewide lobby, was organized. Local interest groups formed at the same time, some at the neighborhood level, including the SOUTH SIDE Saloon Keepers Association and the HYDE PARK Liquor Dealers Association.

Even before PROHIBITION, the liquor industry faced problems. A 1907 act that allowed individual precincts and wards to enact their own prohibition laws led to the forced closure of saloons in two-thirds of the city. Grain conservation regulations during WORLD WAR I restricted production of alcoholic beverages, and anti-German sentiment made beer drinking unpopular. After passage of the Eighteenth Amendment enacting Prohibition, brewery owners desperately searched for prospective buyers of their establishments. Some brewers, aided by mobsters, continued to produce alcohol illegally. Others turned to the manufacture of nonalcoholic drinks or made ends meet by selling the raw materials that went into liquor production.

After Prohibition, persistent gangster connections and incursions by stronger national corporations into the Chicago market dashed the hopes of local liquor manufacturers for an economic resurgence. A handful of national companies dominated the distilling industry, and wine and beer production eventually became concentrated as well. By 1984, 94 percent of American beer was produced by six companies, none in Chicago.

In the 1930s, aluminum beer cans and nonreturnable bottles, coupled with widespread ownership of refrigerators, allowed consumers to drink cold beer at home. Packaged goods, sold in GROCERY and liquor stores, soon outstripped tavern sales. Drinking establishments remained but distanced themselves from the ethos of the old saloons. Federal and state legislation aimed to eliminate the "tied house." WHOLESALERS became the intermediary between beer, wine, and liquor producers and retailers (grocers, drug stores, taverns, liquor stores). In 1989, the Chicago Beer Wholesalers Association included some 30 wholesalers, each typically with a few dozen employees, each contracting with brewers to distribute exclusively in specified territories. Wine and liquor distribution became extremely concentrated in the 1980s and 1990s. The largest distributor, owned by William Wirtz, had some 1,500 employees in Illinois by 1999, and its operations extended into other states.

Sudhir Venkatesh

See also: Business of Chicago; Drugs and Alcohol; Food Processing: Local Market; Local Option; Teamsters; Underground Economy

Further reading: Duis, Perry R. *The Saloon: Public Drinking in Chicago and Boston, 1880–1920.* 1999. • Duis, Perry. "The Saloon in a Changing Chicago." *Chicago History* 4 (Winter 1975–1976): 214–224. • Skilnik, Bob. *The History of Beer and Brewing in Chicago: 1833–1978.* 1999.

In the 1890s, wagons such as these delivered beer to homes and businesses throughout the city and suburbs, even in areas considered "dry." Photographer: Unknown. Source: University of Illinois at Chicago.

Lisle, IL, DuPage County, 24 miles W of the Loop. The east branch of the DUPAGE RIVER, rich soil, rolling hills, and plentiful trees made the Lisle area an attractive site for farming. Migrants from New England, New York, Pennsylvania, and Ohio began arriving in 1832. In 1835, Alonzo B. Chatfield suggested naming the area for Lisle, New York. In the 1840s, several GERMAN-speaking farmers from the Alsace region of France settled in Lisle.

Lisle's location along major TRANSPORTATION routes transformed it from a traveler's way station into a commuter suburb and high-tech industrial destination. Initially, a stagecoach line between Chicago and Aurora carried mail to and from Lisle. In 1840, Mark Beaubien, one of Chicago's early residents, moved to Lisle, where he operated an inn. When the Southwest Plank Road (Ogden Avenue) extended from Chicago to Lisle's western edge in 1850, Beaubien collected the tolls from in front of his inn. In 1864, the Chicago, Burlington & Quincy RAILROAD extended its tracks through Lisle.

Educational and cultural institutions have occupied a central role in Lisle's history. In 1901, St. Procopius College and Academy, now known separately as BENEDICTINE UNIVERSITY and Benet Academy, relocated from Chicago. In 1922, Joy Morton, founder of the Morton Salt Company, established an arboretum at Lisle's northern edge. The MORTON ARBORETUM continues to draw over 300,000 visitors to Lisle annually and gives it the nickname "Arboretum Village."

Lisle's population grew slowly until the 1950s. In 1956, residents voted to incorporate as a village with a mayor and six trustees elected at large. The crossing of new EXPRESSWAYS, Interstates 88 and 355, at Lisle increased its attractiveness as a residential site for Chicago's COMMUTING population. Major Chicago builders developed SUBDIVISIONS of single-family houses, townhouses, and apartment complexes such as Four Lakes, Beau Bien, Green Trails, and Corporate Woods. Between 1970 and 1980, the village's population increased from 5,329 to 13,625; by 2000, Lisle had 21,182 residents.

The new highways brought major HOTELS and campus-style office complexes to Lisle in the 1980s. The Illinois Research and Development Corridor, a stretch of I-88 designated for high-tech companies, passes through Lisle. Lockformer, Molex, and Tellabs built company headquarters on Ogden Avenue. Lucent Technologies' Network Software Center, Unisys Conference Center, and the Interlake Corporation, among others, also located along I-88 and Warrenville Road. In 1994, Lisle's location and hotels helped rank the village as the third most popular meeting site in Illinois, following only Chicago and Springfield.

Patricia K. Kummer

See also: Economic Geography; Railroads; Streets and Highways; Suburbs and Cities as Dual Metropolis

Literary Careers. In nineteenth-century Chicago, rapid urbanization created a wealth of professional writing opportunities and accentuated the city's relative lack of established literary institutions. The 1830s frontier town provided little literary culture, and where professional writing did take place, it followed lines established in Boston, New York, and Philadelphia: "respectable" literary production targeted elite coteries of readers, while the urban penny press, DIME NOVELS, and sentimental FICTION gave writers profitable, but not necessarily prestigious, forums for work. So the writing of perhaps the city's first novel, *Wau-Bun: The "Early Day" in the North-West* (1856), had less to do with Juliette Kinzie's ambition to be a professional author than with her desire to convince elite Chicagoans of the crucial role the Kinzie family played in the city's founding. By the 1860s, changes in copyright laws, innovations in PRINTING technology, and an expansive railroad system had paved the way for a national literary marketplace, creating more favorable conditions for professional authorship. At a remove from major PUBLISHING houses in New York and Boston and unable to profit from short-lived, local publishing ventures, Chicago writers were slow to benefit from these developments. Moreover, established writers such as Henry Blake Fuller and Hamlin Garland remained pessimistic about the possibilities for improvement. To their way of thinking, Chicagoans were too absorbed by business and commerce to support an indigenous LITERARY CULTURE.

Although such concerns have led many Chicago authors to dramatize the conflict between art and commerce, the city's robust economy nonetheless provided job opportunities for emerging literary talent. Indeed, by the 1880s, Chicago had become a beacon for aspiring writers throughout the Midwest.

The most common place to begin a literary career was on one of Chicago's daily NEWSPAPERS. From midcentury onward, Chicago newspapers circulated throughout the Midwest, bringing an air of metropolitan sophistication to Main Street (as a paperboy in Galesburg, Illinois, Carl Sandburg could tell his customers' politics by the newspapers they subscribed to) and impressing would-be writers with the power of urban JOURNALISM. In addition to a ready-made audience, news reporting promised regular writing and congenial work conditions, and it did not require specialized training or education (certainly not college). During the 1880s and 1890s, George Ade, Ray Stannard Baker, Eugene Field, Finley Peter Dunne, William Payne, Opie Read, and Brand Whitlock, most of them drawn to the city from the surrounding hinterland, developed literary careers while earning between $12 and $35 a week. Dunne's "Mr. Dooley" columns and Ade's "Stories of the Streets and of the Town" represented the high end of a documentary style that portrayed Chicago's working and middle classes, its ethnic communities and country migrants, with sympathy and wit. Until the advent of standardized, nonliterary reporting in the 1920s, urban journalism continued to provide apprenticeships to notable Chicago writers, among them Sandburg, Theodore Dreiser, Floyd Dell, Ben Hecht, Ring Lardner, and Elia Peattie.

George Ade's first novel, *Artie* (1896), captured the character and lively vernacular speech of a young Loop office worker in a series of sketches first developed in Ade's feature column in the *Chicago Record,* "Stories of the Streets and of the Town." Artist: John T. McCutcheon. Source: The Newberry Library.

Beyond the dailies, Chicago's expansive foreign press and many specialized periodicals also provided employment opportunities. Clara Laughlin put in almost 20 years as a book reviewer and editor for the Presbyterian periodicals the *Interior* and *Continent* before focusing on her own fiction and travel writing in the early 1900s. Similarly, Sherwood Anderson's first published writings appeared in *Agricultural Advertising,* a trade journal directed toward advertisers and merchants. The particular interests served by such publications meant that much of the professional writing done in the city was not literary per se, but often commercial, religious, agricultural, or educational. Still, professional writing, no matter what the subject, instilled habits, developed skills, and acquainted writers with conventions that would serve them well in their careers as literary authors.

Chicago's white-collar professions, along with other circles of middle-class culture, yielded their fair share of writers. Joseph Kirkland, one of the city's most important writers during the 1880s, made his living as an attorney, as did poet Edgar Lee Masters, roughly 30 years later. Henry Blake Fuller and Hobart C. Chatfield-Taylor, both active participants in the late-nineteenth-century literary scene, benefited from family wealth. Edith Wyatt worked as a teacher and, like other turn-of-the-century women novelists, underscored the importance of cooperative, domestic values while downplaying the drama of individualistic career-making.

By the 1920s, the scope and opportunity for establishing a literary career in Chicago had broadened considerably. The popularity of Ring Lardner's baseball tales, published in the *Saturday Evening Post* and later collected in *You Know Me Al* (1916), demonstrated that a Chicago writer working with Chicago material could find success in the national market. On the other hand, Chicago's literary professionals also included poets, essayists, critics, and contributors to low- or nonpaying literary magazines such as Harriet Monroe's *Poetry* or Margaret Anderson's *Little Review.* As they had in the nineteenth century, writers still supported literary careers with money earned in nonliterary occupations. The difference in the 1910s, however, was the emergence of both a larger, diversified marketplace for literature and a heightened appreciation for creative writing done outside commercial literary structures. In the spirit of social and artistic experimentation, and perhaps rebellion, modernism and literary bohemianism fostered writing that was decidedly noncommercial. Moreover, beginning around 1900, institutions of higher learning like the UNIVERSITY OF CHICAGO created new career possibilities by paying writers and critics to teach and developing the study of literature as an academic discipline.

Amid the expansion and consolidation of the modern literary market, Chicago writing maintained its regional identity in part because its writers continued to enter the profession from the ground level. Though destined to be published in New York, the social protest novels written in the thirties and forties by James Farrell, Richard Wright, and Nelson Algren provide hard-bitten, autobiographical views of the city that were shaped by local writing experience. During the GREAT DEPRESSION, the FEDERAL WRITERS PROJECT, federally funded by the Works Projects Administration, paid Wright, Algren, Willard Motley, Jack Conroy, and Arna Bontemps, among others, to write about various aspects of Chicago culture. Other workshops, formal and informal, apprenticed aspiring local writers. For instance, Gwendolyn Brooks, who as a teenager published poems in the *Hyde Parker* and the CHICAGO DEFENDER, benefited from writing classes held at the South Side Community Art Center. Since World War II, Chicago writers have continued to parlay local writing experience and local material into national recognition, thus helping to build a vibrant, diverse urban culture.

Recent Chicago writing reprises some of these themes. Area writers still develop literary careers while working in a variety of occupations, and the proliferation of genres and subjects in both fiction and nonfiction has opened the market to greater numbers of professional writers. Though New York remains the nation's publishing headquarters, its relative importance as a literary center has diminished with the advance of transportation and communication technologies. In twenty-first-century Chicago, there should be plenty of room for small presses, literary journals, performance poetry, and finely wrought writing careers built from the ground up.

Timothy B. Spears

See also: Chicago Literary Renaissance; Poetry

Further reading: Duncan, Hugh Dalziel. *The Rise of Chicago as a Literary Center from 1885 to 1920: A Sociological Essay in American Culture.* 1964. • Fleming, Herbert E. "The Literary Interests of Chicago." *American Journal of Sociology* 11 (November 1905): 377–408; 11 (January 1906): 499–531; 11 (May 1906) 784–816; 12 (July 1906): 68–118.

Promotional poster for *Cavalcade of the American Negro,* a book published to accompany the Diamond Jubilee Exposition held in Chicago in 1940 to celebrate 75 years of freedom. During the Great Depression, the Federal Writers' Project employed many artists and writers, including the editor of this volume, Arna Bontemps. Artist: Cleo Sara. Source: Library of Congress.

Studs Terkel and Oral History

Studs Terkel is a Pulitzer Prize–winning author and Chicago activist.

See I call Nixon and myself "Neocartesians." "We tape, therefore we are." He did, and I do so. But to me, the tape recorder has become part of my life, but there's an irony connected with this [points to tape recorder] since I'm terrible technologically. I goof up; I can't drive a car. Don't mention the "wordprocessor" to me, "word process," and when you do, smile, because I don't know—I'm learning a typewriter. But I goof up on the tape, and yet, the tape recorder's my ally. Here I am, so when I press the wrong button, as I did, I lost Martha Graham and Michael Redgrave. I lost them. As I pressed the wrong button, I erased them, and so, this is part of my problem, but nonetheless, the tape recorder has helped me tremendously. . . .

My dream during the Depression and as a child of the Depression. . . . I wanted a job, as every young guy wanted a job, 9 to 5 job, security. What's more secure than a government job? So we took all kinds of examinations. There were these papers called Civil Service Journals. You could tell when exams are being held, and I took them all and finally passed one and went to Washington; that was part of it. But the dream is to have a 9 to 5 job, and instead I wound up on the stage doing soap operas, gangsters, but because I did have a job on the WPA of the New Deal.

Terkel, Studs. Interview with Timothy J. Gilfoyle, Loyola University, on the occasion of the 1995 Making History Awards, Chicago Historical Society.

Gilfoyle, Timothy. "A Chicago School of Literature—Gwendolyn Brooks and Studs Terkel." *Chicago History* (Spring 1997): 62–72.

Literary Clubs. *See* Clubs: Literary Clubs

Literary Cultures. Between 1875 and 1893 Joseph Kirkland read 15 papers at meetings of the Chicago Literary Club. Not just a lone pioneer on Chicago's fledgling literary scene, Kirkland was one of several elite Chicagoans committed to "uplifting" the city so that it more closely resembled older, more established centers of learning and culture such as Boston and Philadelphia. The Contributors Club, the Little Room, the Cliff-Dwellers' Club, and the Society of Midland Authors, as well as literary journals like the DIAL and *America,* strove in various ways to establish literature as a respectable civic art. Although some of these organizations remain active today, their mission to establish oases of learning and culture in Chicago's raw social climate belonged especially to the nineteenth century and paralleled the establishment of the city's great cultural institutions: the ART INSTITUTE, CHICAGO SYMPHONY ORCHESTRA, CHICAGO HISTORICAL SOCIETY, and the John CRERAR and NEWBERRY LIBRARIES. Yet after poet Harriet Monroe pressed for and received the commission to write the dedicatory poem at the 1893 WORLD'S COLUMBIAN EXPOSITION, she discovered that belles lettres ranked low on the list of artistic forms that Chicago's elite were willing to support financially. At the high point in the city's cultural uplift, Monroe's "Columbian Ode" barely sold, and the poet used the unsold copies to fuel the stove in her bedroom. In a city dominated by economic interests and lacking in literary traditions, even the most genteel efforts to boost literature's cultural importance had limited influence.

Nevertheless, Chicago's literary societies offered writers, intellectuals, and ARTISTS a much-needed sense of community, and a vision of what an urban culture of letters could be. The most promising of these organizations was the Little Room. Founded in the early 1890s, the Little Room brought together the artistic and professional elite in a membership that included reformer Jane Addams, sculptor Lorado Taft, architects Allen B. and Irving K. Pond, dramatist Anna Morgan, painter Ralph Clarkson, illustrator and publisher Ralph Fletcher Seymour, and at least five writers of considerable note: George Ade, Henry Blake Fuller, Hamlin Garland, Harriet Monroe, and Edith Wyatt. Deriving their name from a short story by Madeline Wynne in which a room magically disappears and reappears, the Little Roomers gathered in the

AUDITORIUM Hotel and the FINE ARTS BUILDING for afternoon teas and midnight dramas, all the while fostering an atmosphere of aesthetic playfulness and serious intellectual engagement that lasted until the club's demise in 1931.

During the first and most vital decade of its existence, the Little Room provided a forum for members to discuss social and aesthetic issues. Despite its trappings of privilege, the club did not simply promote ART for art's sake. Chicago's expansive economy and commanding physical presence precluded aesthetic detachment and, like many other middle- and upper-class Chicagoans, some Little Roomers worried about the city's lack of social order, and expressed their concerns in writing. Henry Blake Fuller, who felt more at home in European capitals and regularly lamented Chicago's lack of cosmopolitan culture, criticized the city's economic culture in what many critics consider to be the first realistic Chicago novel, *The Cliff-Dwellers* (1893). In her role as cofounder of HULL HOUSE, Jane Addams wrote sympathetically of the need to AMERICANIZE Chicago's immigrants. Writing columns for *News Record,* Ade wondered about the place of small-town and rural migrants in the ethnic urban mix, while Wyatt, also reflecting on the relation between Chicago and its hinterland, dramatized middle-class family life in the city. Inasmuch as these writers endorsed the genteel notion that literature had a vital if not moral role to play in civic culture, their own writings evidence their affiliation with cultural worlds that existed apart from the leisured space of the Little Room.

For instance, by 1900, Hull House featured a THEATER and had become a center for less conventional literary work: lectures, workshops, and classes, which beginning in early 1890s were provided under the auspices of the UNIVERSITY OF CHICAGO extension program. Not only immigrants, or their children, but also a wide range of artists and intellectuals made Hull House a vital creative community. Women in particular dominated Chicago's SETTLEMENTS, and their vision of what Addams called the "civic family," a culture of collaborative reform, pervaded Hull House. This perspective also informed novels about settlement work, like Elia Peattie's *The Precipice* (1914) and Clara Laughlin's *"Just Folks"* (1910). It also animated the 1912 establishment of the Little Theatre, an enterprise founded by English-born Maurice Browne, but guided by such women as Anna Morgan, Alice Gerstenberg, Mary Aldis, Lucy Monroe, and Browne's wife, Ellen Van Volkenburg. As home-focused novels like Edith Wyatt's *True Love* (1903) made explicit, Chicago literary women drew from their domestic experiences and imagined cultural alternatives to the models of individual accomplishment and economic success that male writers such as Theodore Dreiser typically emphasized in their writings about Chicago.

The gritty realism that characterizes the work of Dreiser, Richard Wright, Saul Bellow, and Studs Terkel, and which critics have dubbed the "Chicago School of Literature," found its earliest expression not in literary societies, but in nineteenth-century NEWSPAPERS. Beginning in the 1870s but especially in the 1890s, Chicago's large dailies nurtured a galaxy of talented reporters and promising writers. As part of the economic hurly-burly that was making the city internationally famous, Chicago's reporters attracted the recognition and readers that escaped Monroe's "Columbian Ode." While engaged in the business of writing, Eugene Field, Finley Peter Dunne, Brand Whitlock, Ray Stannard Baker, William Payne, Opie Read, Theodore Dreiser, George Ade, and others assembled in newsrooms and SALOONS, creating a literary culture rooted in vernacular realism and shaped by the conventions of urban masculine subcultures. The Press Club grew out of these gendered work conditions, and its weekly lunch meetings enabled reporters to swap stories and build social relationships. The Whitechapel Club, a more hard-boiled version of the Press Club, made a ritual of iconoclasm, once cremating the body of one its members on the shores of LAKE MICHIGAN. Ribald and creative in ways that barely resembled the Little Room's sense of humor, shenanigans like these exemplify the street-savvy reporting of Chicago JOURNALISTS. Women, too, wrote for Chicago dailies, but their contributions, typically to the arts and leisure sections, remained constrained by the conventional wisdom that reporting was essentially masculine work.

By 1910, a second generation of newspapermen was expanding the boundaries of what could go to press. Sometimes at odds with their publishers' tastes and opinions, editors such as Francis Hackett at the *Evening Post,* who directed the paper's influential supplement, the *Friday Literary Review* (founded 1908); Henry Justin Smith of the *Daily News,* who arrived in 1913; and Burton Rascoe, the literary editor at the *Tribune* in the late teens, lent a self-consciously literary element to newspaper writing. In succeeding Hackett at the *Review,* Floyd Dell encouraged contributors to write about themselves in their reviews.

As Finley Peter Dunne's popular Mr. Dooley columns of the 1890s suggest, the literary culture of the newsroom was often inseparable from politics. Exposed as youths to small-town skepticism, populism, and the home-grown radicalism of Robert Ingersoll, radicals like Dell or Carl Sandburg, who between 1900 and 1918 contributed POETRY and prose to Charles Kerr's *International Socialist Review,* brought their POLITICS with them to Chicago. There they discovered fellow travelers such as Edgar Lee Masters and Clarence Darrow.

Mr. Dooley Explains Our "Common Hurtage"

In the late 1890s, Finley Peter Dunne's newspaper columns in Irish dialect brought to life a fictional Bridgeport bartender, Mr. Dooley. During the Spanish-American War, Dunne used his sharp humor to critique a notion of imperialism based on the superiority of the Anglo-Saxon race, particularly for Chicagoans drawn from around the globe. Mr. Dooley extended a definition of Anglo-Saxon to include most of his ethnic neighbors:

> Schwartzmeister is an Anglo-Saxon, but he doesn't know it, an' won't till some wan tells him. Pether Bowbeen down be th' Frinch church is formin' th' Circle Francaize Anglo-Saxon club, an' me ol' frind Dominigo that used to boss th' Ar-rchey R-road wagon whin Callaghan had th' sthreet conthract will march at th' head iv th' Dago Anglo-Saxons whin th' time comes. There ar-re twinty thousan' Rooshian Jews at a quarther a vote in th' Sivinth Ward; an', ar-rmed with rag hooks, they'd be a tur-r-ble think f'r anny inimy iv th' Anglo-Saxon 'lieance to face. Th' Bohemians an' Pole Anglo-Saxons may be a little slow in wakin' up to what the pa-apers calls our common hurtage, but ye may be sure they'll be all r-right whin they're called on.

Since the mid-nineteenth century, Chicago had been home to a robust foreign-language press, and as the city's immigrant population expanded and diversified, so did the foreign periodicals. Because most of the ethnic writing published in nineteenth- and early-twentieth-century Chicago was written in native languages for specific immigrant groups, its influence on the mainstream, native-born audiences was slight. Within immigrant communities themselves, however, literary culture played a crucial role, serving as a source of ethnic pride and a social unifier. Theater was an especially popular venue since plays brought people together. Ethnic Chicagoans gathered in churches, NEIGHBORHOOD ASSOCIATIONS, and literary clubs (not unlike the genteel literary societies) to watch or act in plays about their native homes. In 1892, thousands of POLISH Chicagoans jammed the St. Stanislaus Kostka parish auditorium to see Helena Modjeska, a world-famous Polish actress, star in a drama written by a member of their own parish. Beginning in the 1860s and continuing until the 1950s, NORWEGIAN Chicagoans staged plays in Norwegian in order to preserve cultural traditions and their native language. Indeed, the world premiere of Henrik Ibsen's *Ghosts* took place in Chicago in 1882, and well into the twentieth century influential Norwegian social clubs made the production of Ibsen's work a touchstone of their ethnic identity.

Chicago writers Sherwood Anderson and Carl Sandburg mingled with radicals, unemployed workers, prostitutes, gangsters, and slumming Gold Coast socialites at the Dill Pickle Club on the Near North Side. The enterprising radical Jack Jones was the brains behind the basement cabaret, speakeasy, and theater located at 10 Tooker Place. His irreverent spirit is captured by the motto emblazoned on the club's door: "Step High, Stoop Low, Leave Your Dignity Outside." Photographer: Unknown. Source: The Newberry Library.

Chicago's increasingly expansive array of literary cultures owed much to the ongoing arrival of internal as well as foreign migrants. Drawn to the city from the provinces, aspiring writers found a variety of professional opportunities and a small-town, Midwestern ambiance that encouraged cultural mobility and allowed writers such as George Ade to mix into a variety of urban milieus. This social fluidity also made it easier to leave the city. During the first two decades of the twentieth century, recent arrivals like Ade, Dell, Dreiser, Hamlin Garland, Ben Hecht, Sherwood Anderson, Edgar Lee Masters, Maxwell Bodenheim, Susan Glaspell, Glenway Wescott, Margaret Anderson, and Ring Lardner took their LITERARY CAREERS elsewhere, usually to New York.

Indeed, transience itself was an important creative ingredient of the literary renaissance that took place during the 1910s and early 1920s. The bohemian neighborhoods that developed on the SOUTH SIDE around the buildings left over from the fair, and on the NEAR NORTH SIDE, among cheap rooming houses and restaurants near the Water Tower, encouraged social and artistic experimentation. In 1913 during their six-month residence in a makeshift studio on the South Side, Dell and his wife Margaret Curry hosted parties where Dell learned about Edgar Lee Masters from Theodore Dreiser. He in turn introduced Dreiser to Sherwood Anderson. Two years later, on the NEAR NORTH SIDE, Schlogl's restaurant and Jack Jones's Dill Pickle Club became sites for readings, plays, debates, and literary conversations that included Anderson, Bodenheim, Hecht, Masters, Sandburg, and various writers on staff at the *Daily News*.

By the mid-1920s, many of these writers had left Chicago. After their departure, according to sociologist Harvey W. Zorbaugh, TOWERTOWN became a popular destination for "egocentric poseurs, neurotics, rebels against the conventions of Main Street or the gossip of the foreign community, seekers of atmosphere, dabblers in the occult, dilettantes in the arts, or parties to drab lapses from a moral code which the city had not yet destroyed." Chicago's bohemia turned conventional, and its alternatives to traditional gender roles, sexual relations, and work habits became part of a broader transformation in social mores.

Yet the city's overlapping artistic circles had a positive impact on literary production itself. To the extent that the idea for the *Little Review* grew out of conversations editor Margaret Anderson had at Dell's soirees, or that submissions to *Poetry* were discussed over lunches at cheap North Side restaurants, these pathbreaking journals were the product of Chicago's decentralized literary cultures. While it may be true that literary modernism did not flourish in Chicago as it did in New York or in the salons of Paris, *Poetry* introduced readers to Ezra Pound's work, and the *Little Review* published work by Sherwood Anderson, William Butler Yeats, and Vachel Lindsay. The periodical *Chap-Book* and the exquisitely produced books that Herbert S. Stone and Ingalls Kimball published in the 1890s furnished a precedent for these artistic ventures, but the immediate impetus was the need to address the modernist revolution in literature and art. The diminutives shared in name by the Little Room, the Little Theatre, and the *Little Review* suggest that this search for expressive and social space, no matter how small, has been a crucial feature of Chicago literary history, as well as a manifestation of the Chicago writer's intense, sometimes embattled effort to make a home in the big city.

Especially for ethnic writers, this creative home has been the neighborhood. In his *Studs Lonigan* novels, the first of which appeared in 1932, James T. Farrell returned to the poor, IRISH-Catholic community of his youth. Deterministic and marked by a strong recognition of social inequity, Farrell's novels bear the imprint of his UNIVERSITY OF CHICAGO education. Yet the Chicago writer Farrell felt closest to was not the naturalistic Dreiser but

Chap-Book cover, 1895 (Will Bradley poster for Stone & Kimball). Chicago literary magazines of the 1890s were dressed in elegant and colorful covers by local artists who imitated French and English poster styles. Will Bradley was among the most successful at creating a personal style. Artist: Will Bradley. Source: The Newberry Library.

Sherwood Anderson, whose small-town worlds most resembled the close-knit neighborhoods of his youth. The connection serves as a reminder of the intimate, human scale that distinguishes even the grittiest urban fiction. For instance, in their novels of the 1940s and 1950s, Nelson Algren and Willard Motley give the streets an intimate cultural force while exploring the ethnic and class dynamics that distinguish one neighborhood from another. That radical politics often lay behind such renderings of ethnic and/or working-class landscapes is made vividly clear by Jack Conroy's participation in the FEDERAL WRITERS' PROJECT of the Works Progress Administration (WPA) during the GREAT DEPRESSION. Though already well known for writing proletarian fiction, Conroy was assigned to work in the FOLKLORE division, and went on to gather industrial folk narratives that documented methods of working-class resistance within the culture of factory work.

Also a participant in the Federal Writers' Project, Richard Wright helped initiate what Arna Bontemps, his colleague on the project, believed was a reawakening of the Harlem Renaissance. While in Chicago, Wright wrote "The Ethics of Living Jim Crow" and the stories that were published in his first book, *Uncle Tom's Children* (1938). Wright also laid the groundwork for the books that most explicitly engage his Chicago experience: *Native Son* (1940), *Twelve Million Black Voices* (1941), and *American Hunger* (1977), the continuation of his autobiography *Black Boy* (1945). Informed by Marxist politics and sociological theories developed at the University of Chicago, these books strongly express Wright's sense of being an outsider in white America. Though Wright had escaped the overtly racist South and found Chicago exhilarating, he struggled to find his place as an African American writer in an alienating urban culture. Nevertheless, Wright, Bontemps, and other writers associated with the project, such as William Attaway, Willard Motley, Margaret Walker, and Frank Yerby, invigorated the literary scene on the city's South Side. Gwendolyn Brooks, who grew up on the South Side, mixed with the WPA writers but drew from her own connections in the AFRICAN AMERICAN community in establishing herself as a preeminent Chicago poet and writer.

Whether or not this older Chicago, the city of neighborhoods and civic boosterism, will play a role in future literary cultures remains to be seen. Saul Bellow, perhaps the most distinguished contemporary writer to have emerged from this tradition, has remarked that American intellectual and cultural life has mostly migrated to the nation's universities. Where else is one more likely to find people talking about literature, or writing it? The list of Chicago writers, past and present, who at some point in their careers have found homes at academic institutions in the Chicago area is impressive: Maxine Chernoff, Leon Forrest, Robert Herrick, Robert Morss Lovett, Norman Maclean, Richard Stern, and even Saul Bellow. Moreover, universities and colleges have professionalized the culture of letters, making literary criticism an academic discipline and granting B.A.'s and M.F.A.'s to creative writers. In this regard, the quest to make literature a respectable civic art might well have succeeded.

Timothy B. Spears

See also: Chicago Black Renaissance; Chicago Literary Renaissance; Chicago Public Library; Clubs; Fiction; Literary Images of Chicago; Theater, Ethnic

Further reading: Bremer, Sidney H. "Willa Cather's Lost Chicago Sisters." In *Women Writers and the City: Essays in Feminist Literary Criticism*, ed. Susan Merrill Squier, 1984. • Cappetti, Carla. *Writing Chicago: Modernism, Ethnography, and the Novel.* 1993. • Smith Carl S. *Chicago and the American Literary Imagination.* 1984.

Saul Bellow on Chicago

From *The Adventures of Augie March* (1949): I am an American, Chicago born—Chicago, that somber city—and go at things as I have taught myself, free-style, and will make the record in my own way: first to knock, first admitted; sometimes an innocent knock, sometimes a not so innocent. But a man's character is his fate, says Heraclitus, and in the end there isn't any way to disguise the nature of the knocks by acoustical work on the door or gloving the knuckles.

From *Humboldt's Gift* (1975, describing the view from the Hancock Building): From the skyscraper I could contemplate the air of Chicago on this short December afternoon. A ragged western sun spread orange light over the dark shapes of the town, over the branches of the river and the black trusses of bridges. The lake, gilt silver and amethyst, was ready for its winter cover of ice.

Literary Images of Chicago. Near the beginning of Willa Cather's 1935 novel *Lucy Gayheart,* a young woman boards a Chicago-bound train. Having spent Christmas vacation in her small hometown on the western plains, Lucy is impatient to return to "the city where the air trembled like a tuning-fork with unimaginable possibilities." Lying in her dark sleeping berth, she pictures her destination: "Lucy carried in her mind a very individual map of Chicago: a blur of smoke and wind and noise, with flashes of blue water, and certain clear outlines rising from the confusion.... This city of feeling rose out of the city of fact like a definite composition,—beautiful because the rest was blotted out."

Lucy has created an image of Chicago that is inspired by the material city but also shaped by her aesthetic choices. Selecting and composing, she provides an apt figure of writers who have created lasting literary images of Chicago. Cities of fact are material places, made from steel and stone, inhabited by flesh-and-blood people. Cities of feeling are imagined places, made from words and images, inhabited by characters and traversed by the reader's mind. Chicago's writers, like Lucy, have drawn selectively upon the Chicago of fact to compose cities of feeling. Of course, these writers have also drawn upon other sources—they have read and responded to one another's work and to an enormous range of literary and intellectual influences—but the insistent fact of Chicago has inspired and sometimes defeated literary imaginations since the time of the city's founding.

Since the 1950s, most arriving travelers have seen Chicago from an EXPRESSWAY or from the air; in the late nineteenth and early twentieth centuries, though, the paradigmatic first view of Chicago was from the window of an arriving train. Carl Smith has shown how a variety of works—not only novels like Hamlin Garland's *A Son of the Middle Border* and *Rose of Dutcher's Coolly* or Theodore Dreiser's *The Titan,* but also the memoirs of Louis Sullivan and Frank Lloyd Wright—employ the entry by train to introduce the city.

The most celebrated such entry occurs in the first chapter of Theodore Dreiser's *Sister Carrie,* published in 1900, in which a young woman from Wisconsin named Carrie Meeber arrives in Chicago by train in 1889. She enters the prospective, expanding landscape of a city on the make:

> They were nearing Chicago. Signs were everywhere numerous. Trains flashed by them. Across wide stretches of flat, open prairie they could see lines of telegraph poles stalking across the fields toward the great city.... Frequently there were two-story frame houses standing out in the open fields, without fence or trees, lone outposts of the approaching army of homes.

That city is organized around its industrial INFRASTRUCTURE, indicated here by the converging rail lines that arrange the view. The processes of growth, exchange, and speculation shape the spokes of development radiating out from the region's central place. The city is growing into its role as the model of industrial modernity, and all aspects of urban life are inflected by Chicago's central function of collecting resources for processing into finished products to be circulated and consumed. Among those raw materials flowing from the hinterland into the city is Carrie, whose small-town training has made her a kind of half-baked urbanite aspiring to bigger things. Philip Fisher has traced the parallels between Carrie's prospects and those of Chicago, which are readable from the train's window in the landscape of a developing West Side that offers "a gigantic sketch of its own future." In Fisher's reading of the scene, Chicago "is the most compact and representative part" of an increasingly urban and industrial America, but the city also serves as an image of Carrie, "whose small, future-oriented self with its plans and expectations extending out into reality like trolley tracks and strings of gas lamps, the surrounding city magnifies and gives expression to."

Reaching Chicago, Carrie enters a web of social, economic, and cultural relations. Having entertained the advances of the traveling salesman Drouet during the train ride from Wisconsin, establishing the understanding that will underlie their affair, Carrie crosses a boundary into city life. She will soon learn to finesse the grinding processes of production and consumption as she moves from the "lean and narrow" constrictions of wage labor and neighborhood life to the "walled city" of privilege downtown, and she will do so by making both a more valuable commodity and a more efficient enterprise of herself. She will learn to bank on her unspoiled youth (a kind of futures trading), to capitalize on the sentimental appeal of the "emotional greatness" she projects on the stage as an actress, to preserve her worth as she trades Drouet for Hurstwood (a more accomplished man, although a married one) and then drops Hurstwood when he runs out of money and desire. As Carrie and Drouet approach Chicago in the novel's opening chapter, they exchange addresses: that is, they place themselves in relation to the landscape through which they are passing, thus offering an account of relations between themselves and the circulation of resources and meaning in the city. They are "nearing Chicago" in the fullest sense of the phrase—both a place and a way of being—a Chicago growing into its role as America's type of the modern industrial metropolis. The rail lines form the bones and arteries of a growing body, still awkward but on the upslope of its development: "It was a city of over 500,000, with the ambition, the daring, the activity of a metropolis of a million."

Like a functionary announcing the entrance of an important personage, a brakeman calls out "Chicago!" repeatedly as the train arrives at the station. The encounter fills Carrie with both anticipatory excitement and "a kind of terror." Taking leave of Drouet, struggling through the crowd on the platform, exchanging a "perfunctory embrace of welcome" with the "lean-faced, rather commonplace" sister who has preceded her to Chicago and who embodies hardworking thrift, Carrie begins to take the measure of city life: "Amid all the maze, uproar, and novelty she felt cold reality taking her by the hand."

Cold reality and Chicago literature took one another by the hand toward the middle of the twentieth century, as celebrated writers brought the hard facts and human consequences of neighborhood life to literary center stage. James T. Farrell, Richard Wright, and Nelson Algren were central figures in a flowering of Chicago realism that explored the social and literary consequences of the city's maturing as an industrial metropolis—in which the dispossessed bore the brunt of BUSINESS as usual. Their novels offer memorable images of the city: Farrell's Studs Lonigan passing from grimly rectilinear streets into the pastoral calm of WASHINGTON PARK in *Young Lonigan;* Wright's Bigger Thomas and Jake Jackson dreaming of grandiose possibilities as narrow horizons close tighter and tighter around them in *Native Son* and *Lawd Today;* Algren's near-hallucinatory views of the "L" from Sophie Majcinek's window in *The Man with the Golden Arm.*

But perhaps the most enduring, evocative images of midcentury Chicago can be found in the writing of Gwendolyn Brooks, who after WORLD WAR II succeeded Carl Sandburg as the city's preeminent poet. Like Sandburg, Brooks caught the inspiring temper of Chicago without becoming a booster or an apologist; like the neighborhood novelists, she made the daily lives of unglamorous people the subject of ambitious literature. Brooks won her initial reputation in the 1940s and 1950s with POETRY set in Bronzeville, the heart of the black SOUTH SIDE, as the GREAT MIGRATION made Chicago a crucial site in the transition

Gwendolyn Brooks, named Poet Laureate of Illinois in 1968, set much of her poetry on the South Side. The Mecca was an apartment complex demolished in 1951 as part of urban renewal. Designer: Muriel Nasser. Source: Chicago Historical Society.

of AFRICAN AMERICANS from Southern agrarianism to Northern urbanism. "We are now constructing the baby figure of the giant mass of things to come," concluded the sociologists Drake and Cayton in *Black Metropolis,* their massive sociological study of Bronzeville in that period. In her poetry, Brooks often considered the tension between possibility and constraint in this booming Black Metropolis.

A ballad entitled "Of De Witt Williams on His Way to Lincoln Cemetery," published in *A Street in Bronzeville* in 1945, exemplifies Brooks's spare, resonant style. Sketching a contradictory life—seedy but joyful, truncated but expansive, anonymous but exemplary—the poem begins and ends with a hymn-like summation that suggests an entire history of black migration, aspiration, and struggle against the limits imposed by others: "Born in Alabama / Bred in Illinois. / He was nothing but a / Plain black boy." Also repeated at the poem's end, the next lines—"Swing low swing low sweet sweet chariot. / Nothing but a plain black boy"—invoke the musical traditions of the black church to raise Williams's soul into the firmament, high above the mundane details of the life he led. If this man was insignificant, or encouraged to think of himself as insignificant (he was "nothing," "plain," a "boy"), he also merits a poetic funeral oration fit for an emperor. Edging sympathy with sharp irony, Brooks explores that framing paradox.

The poem's middle section maps an expressive landscape as it follows Williams's body, "Blind within his casket," down 47th Street, one of Bronzeville's main drags. It travels past the pool hall and the movie theater, underneath the "L," past the Warwick and the Savoy, DANCE HALLS "Where he picked his women, where / He drank his liquid joy." There is so much in these few spare lines. The tensions between constraint and release, pain and joy, blindness and a yearning glimpse of a higher place—all link the poem to the Chicago BLUES style also rooted in postwar Bronzeville. The southern echoes in a northern scene, not only the repetition of "Alabama" but also the reminder of field work in the image of Williams "picking" his women, open up a human geography characterized by continuity as well as change. The urgent sense that this landscape must be escaped (through movie fantasies, drunkenness, sensual pleasure, even death) clashes with an equally powerful sense of Williams's deep and genuine investment of himself in Bronzeville. We can believe both that the South Side might have killed him and that he delighted in being there. His passion for a street corner—he "loved so well" the northwest corner of 47th and Prairie Avenue—could indicate how impoverished his inner life was, or how rich it was, or, somehow, both.

If one can hear echoes of multiple traditions—not only the musical legacies of popular SACRED MUSIC and the BLUES, but also Wordsworth and the British poetic canon—one can also hear the "L" rumbling above the scene as Williams's casket travels beneath it. The "L" operates here, as it so often does in Nelson Algren's work, as a figure of all that delimits and constrains Williams's short life. The contradiction between the limitations on opportunity in Chicago and the expansive aspirations of even its most dispossessed inhabitants was never more pronounced than in postwar Bronzeville. At midcentury, many representations of the Black Metropolis still pursued a narrative line that tended up and out toward a better future, even if that tendency was frustrated by social constraint (as in Lorraine Hansberry's drama of social mobility and segregation, *A Raisin in the Sun*). "His lesions are legion. / But reaching is his rule," Brooks wrote of one of "the children of the poor" in *Annie Allen,* an image that captures the balance of protest and measured optimism in her understanding of the situation of urban blacks after World War II. Times would change: the urban crisis of the 1960s would inspire Brooks to take more militant political positions as well as to make formal experiments in her writing that drew her away from the ballad and the sonnet.

The urban crisis forced Chicago's writers, no less than its other citizens, to confront a changed city: it was no longer primarily a factory city, no longer primarily a collection of immigrant villages, no longer easily personified as the rising, big-shouldered young laborer immortalized by Carl Sandburg in his 1914 poem "Chicago." The literature of the 1970s, 1980s, and 1990s offers powerful images of the transformed metropolis in its maturity (or its dotage, in some versions), a multiplicity of imagined landscapes that suggests a complex city of feeling constantly being built and rebuilt. Prominent among them are Leon Forrest's elaborately textured vistas, David Mamet's acid-etched portraits in *The Old Neighborhood,* Li-Young Lee's encounter with poets floating paper boats in the gutter on the corner of Argyle and Broadway, Sandra Cisneros's watercoloristic word pictures of Mango Street, and Mike Royko's account of a day in the life of Richard J. Daley and his city in the first chapter of *Boss.*

Daley enjoys a special, often vexed status in the city's collective imagination, and not just because of his role in the political, social, and cultural upheavals that added up to an urban crisis in the 1960s. He remains the central character in Chicago's great transformational drama of the second half of the twentieth century: the dismantling of the old industrial city and the development of a new, postindustrial service city that makes traditional images of hog butchers and big shoulders seem quaint.

Daley appears intermittently in Chicago literature, perhaps most emblematically in Stuart Dybek's short story "Blight," collected in *The Coast of Chicago* (1990). In the story, an addled but soulful kid named Ziggy Zilinsky—who has been whacked in the head with a fungo bat and further bewildered by the effects of URBAN RENEWAL on his neighborhood—begins having visions of the mayor. In one such vision, Ziggy sees Daley riding in a limousine, sitting "in the backseat sorrowfully shaking his head as if to say 'Jeez!' as he stared out the bulletproof window at the winos drinking on the corner by the boarded-up grocery." The narrator, Dave, concedes that "Mayor Daley *was* everywhere" during the late 1950s and early 1960s: "The city was tearing down buildings for urban renewal and tearing up streets for a new expressway," and every sign announcing civic improvements prominently featured Daley's name.

Dybek, who grew up in PILSEN/LITTLE VILLAGE, has drawn upon late-twentieth-century Chicago to create a layered, dreamlike city of feeling in which his characters confront haunting survivals of the old city as well as casually surrealistic harbingers of the new. (Ziggy also claims to have spotted Daley picking through garbage cans.) "Blight" shows how Ziggy, Dave, and their friends in the neighborhood weather the transformation of inner-city urbanism in the 1950s and 1960s. They are buffeted and inspired by a variety of forces typical of the period: not only the designation of their neighborhood as an Official Blight Area, but also ethnic succession (in this case, a three-way encounter between POLES, Hispanics, and African Americans), the assimilation of immigrants and the arrival of new ones, the reverberating shocks of the Vietnam War and the urban crisis, and the potent countercultural influence of the beats, blues, and ROCK and roll.

By the end of the story, Dave has enrolled at a community COLLEGE to avoid being drafted. An English course taught by a professor known as the Spitter—whose Chicago accent turns the word "blithe" into "blight," causing Dave to observe that there "seemed to be blight all through Dickens and Blake"—inspires Dave to ride the "L" back to the old neighborhood. He has already described the view from the "L," one of Chicago literature's signature perspectives: "as my stop approached I'd look down at the tarpaper roofs, back porches, alleys, and backyards crammed between factories and try to imagine how it would look to someone seeing it for the first time." This time, Dave finds his way to the Carta Blanca, a bar where the MEXICAN songs on the jukebox sound suspiciously like the POLKAS that Polish customers once listened to, and there he has a curiously ecstatic experience that concludes the story:

> Then the jukebox stopped playing, and through the open door I could hear the bells from three different churches tolling the hour. They didn't quite agree on the precise moment. Their rings overlapped and echoed one another. . . . [S]omething about the overlapping of those bells made me remember how many times I'd had dreams, not prophetic ones like Ziggy's, but terrifying all the same, in which I was back in my neighborhood, but lost, everything at once familiar and strange, and I knew if I tried to run, my feet would be like lead, and if I stepped off a curb, I'd drop through space, and then in the dream I would come to a corner that would feel so timeless and peaceful, like the Carta Blanca with the bells fading and the sunlight streaking through, that for a moment it would feel as if I'd wandered into an Official Blithe Area.

A flash of insight charges the landscape of the old neighborhood with initially threatening but ultimately ecstatic possibility. The overlapping bells, like the overlapping musical genres on the jukebox (and the overlapping versions of Chicago created by its various writers), mark the overlapping of the neighborhood that was with the neighborhood that is and the neighborhood that will be—and the overlapping of all the different meanings each of those versions might have.

Without soft-pedaling the terror of feeling one's home TURF changing underfoot, "Blight" finds promise in the moment. That promise proceeds in part from a sense that the makings of ART reside in the stuff of daily life in Pilsen/Little Village. Dave has come to this moment by way of an English course, and the opportunities confronting him in "Blight" are explicitly literary, courtesy of Dickens, Blake, and the Spitter. One way or another, the familiar-yet-strange quality of neighborhood life in Chicago acts on Dave and his friends to inspire creative ambitions: they become musicians, poets, visionaries, storytellers, writers. (One of them, Deejo Decampo, even writes the first sentence of what promises to be a great Chicago novel, entitled *Blight:* "The dawn rises like sick old men playing on the rooftops in their underwear.") In Dave, especially, one can see the makings of the writer that Stuart Dybek became. The miraculous apparition of an Official Blithe Area at the story's end allows him to make the English visionary poet William Blake and the quintessential Chicago bossman Richard J. Daley speak in each other's voice—a fusion of ecstatic creativity and hard facts that recurs throughout Dave's narration, Dybek's writing, and Chicago literature.

Any survey of literary images of Chicago must select and compose, choosing a few exemplary scenes and failing to mention a thousand equally deserving ones. The images offered by Dreiser, Brooks, and Dybek were chosen for their literary significance and representativeness, but also because rail lines run through all of them. Chicago's literature, like the city itself, took shape around RAILROADS; trains run through its cities of feeling, carrying loads of meaning, just as trains still carry goods and flesh-and-blood passengers through the city of fact. Those connecting trains suggest a web of literary influences and linkages extending back from the present well into the nineteenth century; they also suggest a distinctive engagement with the city of fact that binds Chicago's literature to what Nelson Algren called "the thousand-girdered El" and all the hard realities it represents.

Carlo Rotella

See also: Chicago Black Renaissance; Chicago Literary Renaissance; Chicago Studied: Social Scientists and Their City; Fiction; Literary Cultures

Further reading: A reader wishing to know more about literary images of Chicago must, of course, seek them in the richly extensive and ever-changing literature of Chicago, which one could happily read for the rest of one's days without exhausting it. But one must start somewhere. A reader looking for texts with which to begin might try some of the novels, poetry, short stories, drama, and nonfiction discussed in the above essay: Nelson Algren, *The Man with the Golden Arm* (1949); Gwendolyn Brooks, *Blacks* (1987); Willa Cather, *Lucy Gayheart* (1935); Sandra Cisneros, *The House on Mango Street* (1984); St. Clair Drake and Horace R. Cayton, *Black Metropolis: A Study of Negro Life in a Northern City* (1945); Theodore Dreiser, *Sister Carrie* (1900); Stuart Dybek, *The Coast of Chicago* (1990); James T. Farrell, *Studs Lonigan* (1932); Leon Forrest, *Divine Days* (1992); Hamlin Garland, *A Son of the Middle Border* (1917); Lorraine Hansberry, *A Raisin in the Sun* (1959); David Mamet, *The Old Neighborhood* (1998); Mike Royko, *Boss: Richard J. Daley of Chicago* (1971); Richard Wright, *Native Son* (1940).

The scholarship that studies literary images of Chicago in relation to the historical city includes Sidney Bremer, *Urban Intersections: Meetings of Life and Literature in United States Cities* (1992); Carla Cappetti, *Writing Chicago: Modernism, Ethnography, and the Novel* (1993); Henry Claridge, "Chicago: 'The Classical Center of American Materialism,'" in *The*

American City: Literary and Cultural Perspectives, ed. Graham Clarke (1988); Carlo Rotella, *October Cities: The Redevelopment of Urban Literature* (1998); and Carl Smith, *Chicago and the American Literary Imagination, 1880–1920* (1984). Clarence Andrews' *Chicago in Story: A Literary History* (1982) provides an extensive listing, analytically annotated, of representations of Chicago from the nineteenth century through the 1970s. Finally, the recent fiftieth anniversary edition of Nelson Algren's prose poem *Chicago: City on the Make* (2001) bears mention: newly annotated by David Schmittgens and Bill Savage, it frames Algren's enduring imagery in useful historical context and recovers the provenance of Algren's increasingly obscure references. More of Chicago's most important writing should receive such loving treatment.

A reader interested in gathering literary images of Chicago might also turn to a number of collections of Chicago writing, among them *Port Chicago Poets: A New Voice in Anthology,* ed. Don Arthur Torgersen (1966); *Chicago Works: A Collection of Chicago Authors' Best Stories,* ed. Laurie Levy (1990); *New Chicago Stories,* ed. Fred L. Gardaphé (1990); *West Side Stories,* ed. George Bailey (1992); *South Side Stories,* ed. Steve Bosak (1993); *Chicago Stories: Tales of the City,* ed. John Miller and Genevieve Anderson (1993); and *Smokestacks and Skyscrapers: An Anthology of Chicago Writing,* ed. David Starkey and Richard Guzman (1999). In their pages, despite and perhaps because of the editorial predilections that underlie their various selections of Chicago writing, can be found a history of the city and of its representation on the page.

Lithuanians. Although the 2000 U.S. census counted 11,000 persons of Lithuanian first ancestry in the city, nearly 80,000 in the metropolitan area claimed some Lithuanian ancestry. Chicago's place in Lithuanian history rests on a broad base. Chicago Lithuanians played major roles in almost every stage of Lithuania's modern history as they struggled with the contradictions of assimilating into American culture while maintaining their ethnic identity.

Lithuanian immigrants began to come to the United States in significant numbers in the late nineteenth century when their homeland was still a part of the RUSSIAN empire. The majority of the first arrivals could not read or write. Most thought of making some money and then returning home, and therefore displayed little interest in buying land. Instead they sought work in mines and cities. After 1900 they came to Chicago in increasing numbers, settling first in BRIDGEPORT and then developing the Marquette Park (CHICAGO LAWN) area. Many found work in the stockyards. Census figures for this period are unreliable in judging ethnicity, but Lithuanians usually claim that Chicago had about 50,000 of their conationals by 1914, making it the largest urban settlement of Lithuanians in the world.

Lithuanian immigrants in Chicago received fame as residents of BACK OF THE YARDS, the setting for Upton Sinclair's muckraking novel THE JUNGLE (1906), in which Jurgis Rudkus, a goodhearted but naive young man, suffers at the hands of unscrupulous capitalists until he finds salvation in Sinclair's ideal of international socialism. In the years before WORLD WAR I, many immigrants from other regions studied this work in their English-language reading circles.

The early immigrants were mostly young men, who tended to live together in BOARDINGHOUSES. Once an immigrant had collected his basic stake, usually about five hundred dollars, he might return home or more likely send for a bride to come live with him in the new land. Many of those who returned home soon decided that they could not settle back into the rural communities there.

Lithuanian men first socialized in the taverns, where they could learn the ways of the city. There they drew their plans for churches—they were ROMAN CATHOLIC—and other community institutions, including SCHOOLS. The first Lithuanian PARISH developed around St. George's Church in Bridgeport (1892). The decision of the Sisters of St. Casimir to move from Scranton, Pennsylvania, to Chicago in 1911 provided staff for Lithuanian schools.

At the end of World War I Lithuania became an independent state, which together with new restrictions in American immigration laws, sharply reduced the flow of new arrivals. The children of the immigrants, having attended American schools and having become American citizens, participated actively in Chicago POLITICS, as both REPUBLICANS and DEMOCRATS, while working together on Lithuanian projects.

In 1935 a group of young Chicago Lithuanians made a major contribution to the culture of the homeland when they played BASKETBALL at a World Lithuanian Congress in Lithuania. Lithuanians took to the game enthusiastically. Chicagoans then helped Lithuania win the European basketball championship in 1937 and 1939. Basketball remains the most popular sport in Lithuania, and several Lithuanians have played in the National Basketball Association.

WORLD WAR II radically altered the makeup and purposes of Chicago Lithuanians, which according to community estimates numbered approximately 100,000 in 1940. That year Chicago Lithuanians organized the American Lithuanian Council to publicize their opposition to Soviet occupation. At the end of the war, Lithuanians in Western Europe, called "displaced persons" or "DPs," refused to return to their Soviet-ruled homeland. In 1949, the Supreme Committee for the Liberation of Lithuania supervised the formation of the World Lithuanian Community to keep alive Lithuanian culture amid emigration. Its "World Lithuanian Charter" insisted that "A Lithuanian remains a Lithuanian everywhere and always." In the 1950s the Supreme Committee and the World Lithuanian Community moved to the United States, and Chicago Lithuanians played major roles in both organizations.

Invigorated by the influx of new, younger émigrés, Lithuanian institutions in Chicago multiplied. The major Lithuanian NEWSPAPER in Chicago, *Draugas* (The Friend), published by the Marian Fathers since before World War I, enjoyed the largest circulation of any American Lithuanian newspaper; in 1951 it instituted an annual literary prize for Lithuanian writers. Other institutions include the Balzekas Museum of Lithuanian Culture (founded 1966), the Lithuanian Studies Center (1982), and the Lithuanian Foundation, a nonprofit organization established in 1962 to support Lithuanian education, science, and culture. In 1981 the Lithuanian World Community Foundation established an endowed chair in Lithuanian studies at the UNIVERSITY OF ILLINOIS AT CHICAGO. As they became more established in American society, Lithuanians also tended to move out of their original areas of settlement. In 1988 the Lithuanian World Community established the Lithuanian World Center in LEMONT.

Lithuanian culture in Chicago grew apart from the cultural life in Lithuania under Soviet rule; the language had already reflected these diverse paths even before the war. The major émigré organizations centered in Chicago were strongly Catholic, and they vigorously opposed Communist rule in their homeland, demanding that émigrés avoid Soviet institutions: relations with Lithuania should be limited to private contacts because contacts with officials of the Lithuanian Soviet Socialist Republic might compromise the U.S. government's policy of nonrecognition of Lithuanian incorporation into the USSR.

Younger émigrés, organized as Santara-Šviesa, a federation of two former student groups, took a more pragmatic position under the slogan "Face to Lithuania." To this end, Santara-Šviesa leaders, centered in Chicago, helped a basketball team of Chicago Lithuanians visit Lithuania in 1967, explaining that they wanted to learn more about actual conditions in Lithuania, to open the homeland up to foreign intellectual currents, and to confirm that there was in fact but one, united Lithuanian culture. In 1968 Santara-Šviesa began publishing a monthly newspaper in Chicago, *Akiračiai: Atviro Žodžio Mėnraštis* (Viewpoints: A Monthly for the Free Word), which challenged many aspects and beliefs of émigré life. Lithuanian intellectuals particularly remember the group for its smuggling books into Lithuania in the 1970s and 1980s.

When the Soviet system began to crumble in the late 1980s, Chicago Lithuanians enthusiastically supported Lithuanian independence. They contributed money and equipment to the national front organization in Lithuania, known as Sajudis, and lobbied vigorously in Washington. When Lithuanian politics began to divide into left and right, most Chicago Lithuanians supported the right, calling for a sharp break with Moscow and looking forward to establishing new, closer ties with their homeland. After Lithuania achieved international recognition as an independent state in 1991, many Chicago Lithuanians, although rather disappointed by limits on their rights to citizenship and property in Lithuania, chose to return there.

The life of Chicago's Lithuanians in essence grew closer to life in Lithuania. A number of young Chicagoans worked in the Lithuanian government in its first days of independence, and the World Lithuanian Community established institutional ties with the Lithuanian parliament. Many Lithuanian leaders came to Chicago to tap the intellectual and financial resources of the community. In 1998 Lithuanian voters elected a Chicago Lithuanian, Valdas Adamkus, as president of the Lithuanian Republic. Having fled Lithuania in 1944, Adamkus had made his way to the United States, and had graduated from the University of Illinois as an engineer. He was one of the founders of Santara-Šviesa. After long service as GREAT LAKES administrator of the Environmental Protection Agency, he retired in 1997 and returned to Lithuania. At the end of the 1990s, Chicago Lithuanians had closer ties to the homeland than at any other time in the century.

Alfred Erich Senn

See also: Americanization; Cold War and Anticommunism; Demography; Meatpacking; Multicentered Chicago; New City; Refugees

Further reading: Fainhauz, David. *Lithuanians in Multi-ethnic Chicago until World War II.* 1977. • Mockunas, Liutas. "The Dynamics of Lithuanian Emigre-Homeland Relations." *Baltic Forum* 2.1 (1985): 49–66. • Senn, Alfred Erich. "American Lithuanians and the Politics of Basketball in Lithuania, 1935–1939." *Journal of Baltic Studies* 19 (1985): 146–156.

Little Italy. Chicago's "Little Italy" developed in the NEAR WEST SIDE around Halsted and Taylor Streets near Jane Addams's HULL HOUSE in the late nineteenth century. Upon their arrival in the area, ITALIANS quickly established their own cultural, social, and religious institutions, such as Our Lady of Pompeii and the Holy Guardian Angel ROMAN CATHOLIC churches. While Italians were never actually a majority in the area, they maintained a strong presence in the commercial and political fabric of the area throughout the twentieth century.

Max Grinnell

See also: Demography

Further reading: Cipriani, Lisi. *Italians in Chicago and the Selected Directory of the Italians in Chicago.* 1933. • DeRosa, Tina. *Paper Fish.* 1980. • Holli, Melvin G., and Peter A. Jones, eds. *Ethnic Chicago: A Multicultural Portrait.* 1995.

Little Village. Known by its residents as the "MEXICO of the Midwest," Little Village, officially a part of the SOUTH LAWNDALE Community Area, has over the past 35 years joined PILSEN as a point of entry for Latino immigrants to Chicago. A gateway on 26th Street proclaims "Bienvenidos a Little Village." Neighborhood organizations like the UNITED NEIGHBORHOOD ORGANIZATION have sought to curb GANG violence and foster a sense of community solidarity. Little Village hosts the largest annual Latino parade in Chicago, drawing hundreds of thousands of spectators each September.

Erik Gellman

See also: Demography

Further reading: Adelman, William J. *Pilsen and the West Side: A Tour Guide to Ethnic Neighborhoods, Architecture, Restaurants, Wall Murals, and Labor History with Special Emphasis on Events Connected with the Great Upheaval of 1877.* 1977. • Padilla, Felix M. *Latino Ethnic Consciousness: The Case of Mexican-Americans and Puerto Ricans in Chicago.* 1985.

Local Option. "Local option" is a general term for laws that allow voters to decide if or how alcohol will be sold in their communities. The Illinois General Assembly established the principle of local LIQUOR control when it granted nearly complete licensing powers to county officials soon after statehood in 1818. The state's first local option law (1839) stipulated that a majority of voters in any county, justice's district, incorporated town, or city WARD could petition local authorities to stop granting liquor licenses. The law, ineffectual against Chicago's liquor traffic and thoroughly opposed by its political leaders, was repealed in 1841.

Some communities in COOK COUNTY feared Chicago's immoral influence, which they saw exemplified in the city's growing numbers of immigrant, non-PROTESTANT voters, its unwillingness to enforce its own liquor regulations, and its rapid industrialization and urbanization. They turned to prohibiting SALOONS and liquor sales as a way to keep the city's effects at bay. A community of temperate Methodists chartered NORTHWESTERN UNIVERSITY in 1851 with a four-mile dry zone around the school and in 1863 incorporated EVANSTON with a dry ordinance. WINNETKA and ENGLEWOOD followed in 1869, when both cities established schools with PROHIBITION provisos in their charters. The 1872 Towns and Villages Act, which gave city councils the power to license, regulate, and prohibit the selling or distribution of intoxicating liquors, provided towns the means to govern themselves on the issue, independent of Chicago's power. OAK PARK used this law to dry up in 1873, as did RIVER FOREST in 1879.

When Chicago began an aggressive ANNEXATION campaign in the 1880s, liquor again became a contentious issue. In 1889, HYDE PARK voters agreed to annexation if they could retain their local option laws, which required prospective saloonkeepers to obtain signatures of a majority of the property owners, tenants, and businesses on both sides of the street on the block where the saloon would be located. Although much of Hyde Park quickly allowed saloons in, the most wealthy, professional, and white residential areas fought protracted court battles over the next 30 years to remain dry. Other areas annexed by Chicago as dry territory by 1891 included part of CICERO, Fernwood, JEFFERSON, Town of LAKE, LAKE VIEW, NORWOOD PARK, WASHINGTON HEIGHTS, WEST RIDGE, and West ROSELAND.

By 1894 the Chicago City Council had adopted an informal agreement that aldermen could designate small residential portions of their wards "antisaloon territory." In 1907 the Illinois legislature passed a local option law that allowed voters to dry up whole precincts, not just residential districts, and it required only one-quarter of the voters to petition for the issue to be placed on the ballot. By 1909 nearly two-thirds of the city was dry. The remaining licensed saloons crowded into the slums, working-class neighborhoods, and the commercial LOOP district. Chicago's dry districts remained spotty until the Eighteenth Amendment initiated national PROHIBITION in January, 1920.

With the repeal of Prohibition in 1933, the state of Illinois included a local option proviso in its 1934 dramshop law. Like the 1907 law, it required only one-quarter of the voters in a Chicago precinct, or in an incorporated town, to petition to place prohibition on the ballot. As a result, a number of suburbs and city precincts remained dry after the 1934 and 1936 elections, including Evanston, Oak Park, River Forest, GLENCOE, Winnetka, KENILWORTH, WESTERN SPRINGS, WILMETTE, LA GRANGE, PARK RIDGE, WHEATON, MAYWOOD, and 47 of Chicago's 4,136 precincts.

By the early 1970s, some AFRICAN AMERICANS and Hispanic Americans began to protest the disparity between the number of bars in black and Hispanic versus white neighborhoods and the predominantly white suburbs, and they initiated local measures to minimize the number of liquor licenses. Since 1989, city council members have been able to place moratoriums on new liquor licenses in their wards, and as of 1995 the local option law has allowed voters to prohibit liquor sales at specific addresses. Chicago has become drier: by 2003 nearly one-fifth of Chicago's more than 2,700 precincts restricted the sale of alcohol.

A reverse trend occurred in the suburbs, which began to allow alcohol in, usually because of economic pressures to strengthen business districts with RESTAURANTS that serve liquor. Between 1972 and 1983, Evanston, Maywood, Oak Park, HIGHLAND PARK, Glencoe, Park Ridge, Wilmette, and Winnetka all lifted their bans on alcohol. River Forest followed in 1990.

Rachel E. Bohlmann

See also: Drugs and Alcohol; Public Health; Sunday Closings; Vice Districts

Further reading: Duis, Perry R. *The Saloon: Public Drinking in Chicago and Boston, 1880–1920.* 1983. • *Laws of the State of Illinois.* 1839–1997. • Pike, Claude O., ed. *The Chicago Daily News Almanac and Year Book.* Various years, 1932–1937.

Lockport, IL, Will County, 30 miles SW of the Loop. Lockport, located in the DES PLAINES RIVER Valley, grew initially as the headquarters for the ILLINOIS & MICHIGAN CANAL and as an AGRICULTURAL processing center. The agricultural promise of the area grew when a local farmer developed a steel plow in 1835.

The original town of the 1830s and 1840s was mainly populated by Yankees and a part of the town was called "Yankee Settlement." The other element was recently emigrated IRISH farmers and laborers. By the 1860s there was an increased number of GERMAN emigrants who were merchants and farmers. The late nineteenth century brought an influx of Scandinavians and a few AFRICAN AMERICANS who worked on the SANITARY AND SHIP CANAL. ITALIANS, mostly from northern Italy, worked in factories in the area. The town's population remained stable until the late 1980s when new residences were built for an influx of urbanites and close-in suburbanites.

Lockport was platted and named by the Illinois & Michigan Canal commissioners in 1837 as the canal headquarters. Chief Engineer William Gooding saw the water-power potential of the site, which is 40 feet higher than JOLIET four miles to the south. Gooding supervised construction of a headquarters and stone warehouse. The canal opened in 1848 and in 1853 Lockport residents incorporated as a town.

The canal grain trade dominated the town's early economy, and the 1858 arrival of the Chicago & Alton Railroad did little to change this. Hiram Norton oversaw an extensive canal operation devoted to grain shipping and processing. His water-powered flour mill was one of the largest in northern Illinois, and along with other hydraulic-powered production facilities and a number of canal boats, made him one of the wealthiest people in the 1860s.

The construction of the Sanitary and Ship Canal after 1895 halted the grain trade on the old canal and the Norton Company went bankrupt. The construction of the Calumet-Sag Channel north of Lockport, which began in 1911, cut off most of the water power to the town, and the remaining mills closed.

The area's economy revived after 1911 when the Texas Company decided to build its first REFINERY outside the Southwest on the northern boundary of Lockport. In addition, area RAILROADS began running commuter trains to Chicago and the 1901 opening of the Chicago & Joliet INTERURBAN Electric Railway encouraged COMMUTING between Lockport, Joliet, and Chicago.

In the 1980s, the closure of the Texaco refinery and other industrial plants in the area signaled yet another economic and social shift. History became a focus of commercial development. In 1968 the Will County Historical Society opened a canal museum in the old I&M Canal headquarters building. The Gayload Building, built in 1837 to store canal construction materials, was acquired by the National Trust for Historic Preservation and is now operated as a museum by the Canal Corridor Association. The old downtown was made a historical district in 1974 and Lockport began calling itself "The Old Canal Town." In the 1980s restaurants, antique shops, and specialty retailers opened in the historic district. In addition, population shifts in the metropolitan area drew residential developers to the area. The closing decades of the twentieth century brought not only history but also strip malls, fast-food outlets and other elements of urban sprawl. Population grew from 9,401 in 1990 to 15,191 in 2000.

John Lamb

See also: Commodities Markets; Economic Geography; Historic Preservation; Suburbs and Cities as Dual Metropolis; Water

Further reading: Conzen, Michael, and Adam Daniel, eds. *Lockport Legacy: Themes in the Historical Geography of an Illinois Canal Town.* 1990. • Lamb, John. *Lockport, Illinois: The Old Canal Town.* 1999. • LeBaron, W. *History of Will County.* 1878.

Logan Square, Community Area 22, 5 miles NW of the Loop. Logan Square is a large, densely populated community northwest of Chicago's LOOP. Long home to immigrant populations, it is now predominantly Hispanic. Logan Square is graced with a system of TREE-lined boulevards and squares, including the one for which the community is named. The area is bounded on the east by the CHICAGO RIVER and bisected diagonally by Milwaukee Avenue, one of Chicago's main commercial thoroughfares.

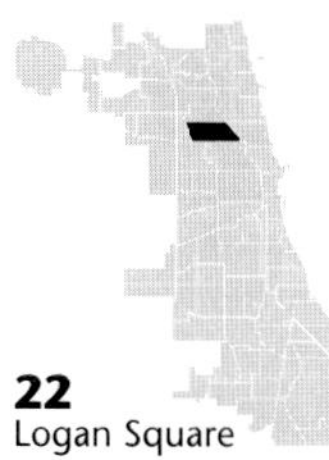

The open prairie that would become Logan Square lay beyond Chicago's borders in 1836, when New Yorker Martin Kimbell laid claim to 160 acres there. Other settlers soon joined Kimbell in what was then the town of JEFFERSON. Beginning in 1850, farmers in Logan Square and beyond could haul their produce to market along the North West Plank Road (later Milwaukee Avenue), which followed the path of an Indian trail angling northwest out of Chicago. Several years later, the Chicago & North Western Railway laid its tracks just west of the river. Industries soon followed. In 1863, Chicago annexed the territory east of Western Avenue and south of Fullerton. (This neighborhood—now BUCKTOWN—was known as Holstein for its population of GERMAN factory workers.) Six years later, the area just to the north (east of Western, between Fullerton and the river) became part of the city.

Logan Square grew more rapidly after the FIRE OF 1871. Because the area lay outside Chicago's FIRE LIMITS, moderately priced frame houses immediately appeared, especially in suburban Maplewood, south and west of the Chicago & North Western RAILROAD's new Maplewood station at Diversey Avenue, and along Milwaukee Avenue. By 1884, Maplewood's population had reached 6,000. (A second early subdivision, Pennock, in northwestern Logan Square, failed to thrive until the following decade.) With the extension of the Milwaukee Avenue STREET RAILWAY line to Armitage and then Belmont, German and Scandinavian immigrants increasingly moved northwestward into the area.

Chicago annexed the remainder of Logan Square in 1889. The "L" arrived the following year, and new homes quickly encircled the Fullerton and Milwaukee Avenue stations. Shortly thereafter, the city paved and planted the boulevard system, planned years before by the West Park Commission. The solid graystone two- and three-flats and substantial single-family houses of upwardly mobile Scandinavians and Germans soon lined Logan, Kedzie, and Humboldt Boulevards, and Logan and Palmer Squares.

After WORLD WAR I, Logan Square boomed. Even as earlier-arriving immigrants moved further out Milwaukee Avenue, POLES and Russian JEWS arrived to take their place. Construction of rental APARTMENTS and flats continued unabated. In 1925, developers claimed the last sizable tract of open land, the Logan Square Ball Park at Milwaukee and Sawyer.

Vibrant Logan Square began to fade shortly thereafter. Population fell gradually after 1930. Older frame residences on the community's industrial eastern edge deteriorated. In the late 1950s, construction of the Northwest (Kennedy) EXPRESSWAY effectively severed this district from the rest of Logan Square, prompting residents to depart. Construction of the Dearborn/Milwaukee subway (now the Blue Line) disrupted commercial life in central Logan Square in the following decade.

In the early 1960s, however, Logan Square saw the first signs of a resurgence that has lasted into the twenty-first century. In 1963, area residents formed the Logan Square Neighborhood Association, a group that has worked ever since to improve housing and community spirit. In the succeeding decades, young urban professionals purchased and rehabilitated many of the fine houses along the boulevards, obtaining recognition of the corridor as a National Register district in the 1980s. The oldest portion of Logan Square, the Bucktown neighborhood in the community's southeast corner, has become a haven for ARTISTS.

Today, Logan Square exhibits a vital ethnic and economic diversity. The population of Logan Square has fallen less rapidly than that of Chicago as a whole, thanks to an influx of Hispanics since 1960. By 1990, Hispanics made up almost two-thirds of Logan Square's population, comprising the largest PUERTO RICAN, CUBAN, and South and Central American populations in Chicago, together with a sizable MEXICAN community. Yet Polish can still be heard in the streets alongside English and Spanish. And while upper-middle-class professionals own the solid houses along the boulevards and new and rehabilitated townhouses in gentrifying Bucktown, the majority of Logan Square's residents continue to live in the community's many rental flats and apartments.

Elizabeth A. Patterson

See also: Annexation; Art Colonies; Neighborhood Succession; Public Transportation; Rapid Transit System

Further reading: Andreas, A. T. *History of Cook County Illinois.* 1884. • Chicago Fact Book Consortium, ed. *Local Community Fact Book: Chicago Metropolitan Area, 1990.* 1995. • Newspaper clippings in hardcopy and on microfilm. Municipal Reference Collection, Harold Washington Public Library, Chicago, IL.

Lombard, IL, DuPage County, 20 miles W of the Loop. Lombard shares its early history with GLEN ELLYN. Brothers Ralph and Morgan Babcock settled in a grove of trees along the DUPAGE RIVER. In what was known as Babcock's Grove, Lombard developed to the east and Glen Ellyn to west. In 1837, Babcock's Grove was connected to Chicago by a stagecoach line which stopped at Stacy's Tavern at Geneva and St. Charles Roads. Fertile land, the DuPage River, and plentiful timber drew farmers to the area.

Sheldon and Harriet Peck moved from Onondaga, New York, to this area in 1837. They claimed 80 acres of land which they farmed. In addition, Peck was an artist and primitive portrait painter who traveled to clients across northeastern Illinois. The Peck house also served as the area's first school and has been restored by the Lombard Historical Society.

In 1849, the Galena & Chicago Union RAILROAD ran two trains daily each way through Babcock's Grove. Farmers began to send their goods to Chicago along the railroad, quickly putting the stagecoach line out of business. Soon a post office, general store, and a hotel emerged near the train station. GERMAN farmers joined the early YANKEE and New York settlers.

Josiah Lombard, a Chicago banker, purchased 227 acres of land in 1868 and headed a group of capitalists who registered the first plat and spearheaded the incorporation of Lombard in 1869. Lombard hoped the area would develop as a commuter center. Stylish Victorian homes appeared on North Main Street, and the Lombard Historical Museum maintains a house museum in the style of one of these homes circa the 1870s. The Maple Street Chapel, which is now on the National Register of Historic Places, was constructed in 1870 to serve a growing population.

While commuters came, industry also developed. The Lombard train station was a "milk stop" for area farmers, and a cheese factory and creamery also operated for many years. Conflicts between farmers and commuters included temperance. After attempts to shut down SALOONS in Lombard were rejected numerous times in the nineteenth century, temperance advocates prevailed in 1911.

In 1910 William R. Plum, a retired Chicago lawyer, Civil War veteran, and Lombard resident, began collecting lilacs. The Plum garden became known as Lilacia, where over two hundred varieties of the flowering bush grew. In 1927, William and Helen Plum donated their estate to the village. The garden became a park, their home a public library. In 1929, the landscape artist Jens Jensen was hired by the Lombard Park District to design the park. The first Lilac Festival was held the following year and continues annually during May.

Between 1906 and 1957, the Chicago, Aurora & Elgin Railway provided passenger service on its INTERURBAN line. By 1920 the number of residents increased to 1,331. During the 1920s a new high school, a paving program, and the development of the Lombard Park District increasingly made Lombard attractive to new residents. The DuPage Theatre opened in 1928 with a starlit sky and gilded pillars. A significant population increase occurred after World War II. Throughout the fifties new homes and shopping centers were built, and by 1960 the population reached 22,561. Lombard remained primarily residential until the 1970s, when the 75-acre Yorkbrook Industrial Park and the 200-acre Clearing Industrial District were developed. The population reached 42,322 by 2000.

Elizabeth M. Holland

See also: DuPage County; Gardening; Landscape Design; Prohibition and Temperance

Further reading: Budd, Lillian. *Footsteps on the Tall Grass Prairie: A History of Lombard, Illinois.* 1977. • Fruehe, Margot. "Lombard." In *DuPage Roots,* ed. Richard A. Thompson, 1985, 191–199. • Knoblauch, Marion, ed. *DuPage County: A Descriptive and Historical Guide, 1831–1939.* 1948.

Long Grove, IL, Lake County, 29 miles NW of the Loop. The 1838 survey maps show large groves of oaks standing in bluestem prairie along the southern boundary of LAKE COUNTY, one of them labeled "Long Grove." Before 1840, a Yankee, John Gridley, settled at a minor trail crossing deep in Long Grove.

GERMAN immigrants to the area in the mid-1840s discovered that the open prairie had already been claimed and made their claims deep within the grove. A post office established in 1847 under the name Muttersholz ("Mother's Woods") highlights the area's strong German influence. By the early 1850s, immigrant families who had split from the ROMAN CATHOLIC parish at Buffalo Grove founded their own St. Mary's parish at Muttersholz. An Evangelical Lutheran congregation formed at the same time.

Recruitment during the CIVIL WAR and industrial opportunities in Chicago drained away most of the area's remaining YANKEE families, leaving German as the most commonly spoken language. Most families had their origins in the Rhineland and spoke in a "Plattdeutsch" dialect until nativist hostility to German culture during WORLD WAR I impelled residents to make greater use of English. Muttersholz became Long Grove once again. The cultural isolation of the small community, which had grown from 161 in 1870 to only 640 in 1960, deepened as the area's major roads, Routes 53 and 83, bypassed the still rural country crossroad.

Many of the community's young men who left to fight in WORLD WAR II stayed away, leaving behind old farms filled with German-crafted oak furniture and tools. When the Fanning family opened their Farmside Store in Long Grove in 1947, they found that well-to-do Chicagoans were interested in acquiring antiques from their resale store, and Long Grove quickly established a reputation as a center for the growing antique trade.

This commerce drew the attention of developers. In the early 1950s, area property owners formed an association to oppose a major development plan, countering with a village plat that would require a three-acre minimum lot size, with the aim of preserving the area's historic character. Following litigation between developers and the association, a referendum was passed in 1956, that incorporated the village of Long Grove. Guy Reed became the village's first president. After Reed's death in 1959, village president Robert Coffin pushed to retain the village's antique style through ordinances prohibiting neon signs and the development of convenience and chain stores. Any new business construction had to feature 1880s-style facades.

The hundreds of daily visitors who come to Long Grove's numerous craft and antique shops generate so much sales tax revenue that, as of the mid-1990s, no property taxes were levied and all municipal services were contracted. The low-density development objectives set forth in the villages 1973 comprehensive plan were reflected in the community's growth from 2,013 residents in 1980 to 6,735 in 2000.

Craig L. Pfannkuche

See also: Agriculture; Government, Suburban; Metropolitan Growth

Further reading: Michaelson, Mike. "One of a Kind." *North Shore Magazine,* July 1992, 81–94. • Park, Virginia L. *Long Grove Lore and Legend.* 1978. • Wittner, Dale. "Long Grove." *Chicago Tribune,* November 6, 1977.

Loop, The, Community Area 32. The Loop is the popular name for the Chicago business district located south of the main stem of the Chicago River. The name apparently derives from the place where the strands powering cable cars turned around on a pulley in the center of the city. The concept was extended to the ring of elevated rail tracks for rapid transit lines connecting downtown with the neighborhoods. Completed in 1897, this loop created an integrated intracity transportation system that helped insure the dominance of Chicago's historic core in the development of the metropolis. All of Chicago's nineteenth-century railroad depots were located at the edges of the central business district, creating a circle of stations around the hub of the city.

32
Loop

Jean Baptiste Point DuSable established a trading post on the north bank of the Chicago River in the late 1780s. Fort Dearborn followed on the opposite side in 1803–4. South Water Street, along the south bank, became a hub of activity in the 1830s, with Lake Street, a block to the south, soon picking up the character of a retail street. In the period of the walking city the Loop area accommodated all of the functions of the city near the main stem of the river.

The diverse nature of the population in the center city meant that most of Chicago's older ethnic groups can point to origins in the city's historic core. As early as the 1850s the area south and west from State and Madison Streets had a German character, although people of every background lived there, including Irish and African Americans. As the commercial district expanded toward the railroad stations, it pushed areas of blight, vice, and transient housing just ahead of it, often creating pockets of inexpensive housing just beyond the depots.

The Civil War brought rapid growth downtown encouraged by the use of streetcars, which first appeared along State Street in 1859. At the war's end Potter Palmer engineered the shift of retail commerce from Lake Street to State Street by erecting a splendid hotel, a large commercial emporium, and other mercantile buildings along State Street. This reorientation of the business district was well underway when the Fire of 1871 completely destroyed the central part of the city.

The fire destroyed most residential buildings, as well as historic church and school buildings, in the heart of the city. The rise of the skyscraper in the 1880s reinforced the trend toward commercial growth, creating a distinct character for the downtown district and establishing a skyline as the symbol for the entire city.

Improvements in transportation enabled the residents of the expanding city to maintain contact with the center. State Street's horsecars were replaced by cable cars in 1882, and these in turn yielded to electric trolleys in 1906. Gasoline buses joined the trolleys in 1927 and construction began on the State Street Subway in 1938. Until 1950 citizens of Chicago had two neighborhoods: their particular residential area and downtown, a common destination for work, recreation, government, and shopping. The number of passengers entering and leaving the Loop peaked in 1948, reaching almost a million per day in each direction, with a quarter of the total traveling by private automobile.

Clark Street at Jackson Boulevard, 1929. Photographer: Underwood & Underwood. Source: The Newberry Library.

After 1950 the outward pull of suburban development in the new automobile metropolis reduced the importance of the Loop in the daily lives of many Chicagoans. It no longer functioned as a second neighborhood for numerous citizens and retail sales downtown accounted for a much smaller portion of the metropolitan total. An extension of the central business district northward along Michigan Avenue kept a luxury shopping district close by, and a return of residential buildings downtown brought back aspects of the old walking city. Cooperation between the city government led by Richard J. Daley and business leaders, supported by a steady flow of state and federal funds, produced a building boom of unprecedented scale to provide offices for corporations, banks, and governmental agencies, as well as hotel rooms for visitors, and expanded facilities for cultural and educational institutions.

Gerald A. Danzer

See also: Architecture; Commuting; Entertaining Chicagoans; Magnificent Mile; Parking; Public Buildings in the Loop; Railroad Stations; Railroads and Chicago's Loop, circa 1930 (map, following p. 000); Shopping Districts and Malls

Further reading: Duis, Perry. *Chicago: Creating New Traditions.* 1976. • Holt, Glen E., and Dominic A. Pacyga. *Chicago: A Historical Guide to the Neighborhoods: The Loop and South Side.* 1979. • Johnson, Earl Shephard. "The Natural History of the Central Business District with Particular Reference to Chicago." Ph.D. diss., University of Chicago. 1941.

Lowell, IN, 42 miles S of the Loop. Tracing its origins to 1852 settlers, this south LAKE COUNTY community emphasizes its rural tranquility and proximity to urban areas as well as its recreational amenities, parades, and festivals. Its 7,505 residents (2000) work in local manufacturing and other industries or commute to jobs in Chicago, GARY, HAMMOND, or areas further south.

Steven Essig

See also: Economic Geography; Leisure

Further reading: *Lowell Centennial, 1852–1952.* 1952.

Lower West Side, Community Area 31, 3 miles SW of Loop. The Lower West Side has traditionally served as a point of entry to Chicago for working-class immigrants from a broad range of ethnic groups. The area is bounded on the south and east by the CHICAGO RIVER, and on the north and west by the Burlington Northern RAILROAD tracks. Though the area remained somewhat isolated for much of its history, its neighborhoods—especially PILSEN and Heart of Chicago—have been vibrant and dynamic enclaves for generations of Bohemians, GERMANS, POLES, and MEXICANS.

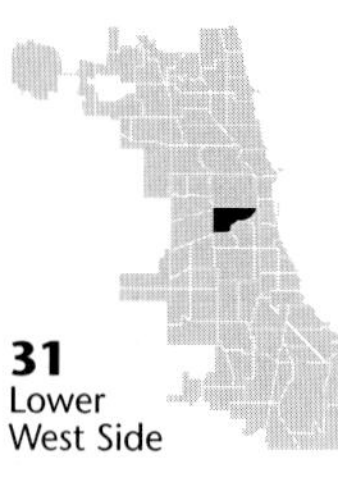

The oldest sector was settled predominantly by Bohemians displaced by the Chicago FIRE OF 1871 and was dubbed "Pilsen" after one of the largest cities in their homeland. Pilsen grew into a major manufacturing center and remained heavily industrial into the twentieth century. Germans and later Slavs worked alongside CZECHS AND BOHEMIANS in diverse industries: from Schoenhofen Brewery (18th and Canalport) and the LUMBER yards along the river to Chicago Stove Works Foundry (22nd and Blue Island) and McCormick Reaper Works (22nd and Western). Neighborhood residents UNIONIZED in the 1880s, founded ROMAN CATHOLIC and PROTESTANT churches, published newspapers in several languages, organized meetings of Freethinkers, and formed benevolent groups (Thalia Hall, 18th and Allport, 1892; Gads Hill Social SETTLEMENT HOUSE, 22nd and Robey/Damen, 1898) to aid newly arriving immigrants.

The area around Cermak Road and Damen (originally Robey) Street, lying between the Pilsen and SOUTH LAWNDALE neighborhoods, was known as Heart of Chicago. First settled by Germans and IRISH in the 1860s and 1870s, its population was largely Polish (with lesser numbers of SLOVENIANS and ITALIANS) by the turn of the century. Like their immigrant neighbors, Germans established their own schools, churches and newspapers. In 1889 they founded St. Paul Federal SAVINGS AND LOAN, which made homeownership possible for many generations of immigrants throughout the Chicago area. Like the Bohemians who moved to South Lawndale, many Poles moved westward from Pilsen as they

Arcades and theaters on South State between Van Buren and Congress, ca. 1912. Photographer: Unknown. Source: Chicago Historical Society.

accumulated resources, buying property in Heart of Chicago and establishing their own ethnic institutions. Some charitable associations and churches even returned to help poorer Pilsen neighbors through missions, including the Bethlehem Congregational Church missions (1890), which advocated temperance to their members, and Howell Neighborhood House (1905).

Until the 1930s the Lower West Side continued as a center of ethnic group development with fairly stable working-class populations. The hardships of the GREAT DEPRESSION and the housing crisis during WORLD WAR II, however, strained community and individual resources. In the 1950s many of the industries that formed the economic backbone of these neighborhoods closed their plants, including International Harvester; others relocated to the suburbs of Chicago.

Just as the prospects for Lower West Side residents began to look bleak, URBAN RENEWAL in the NEAR WEST SIDE coupled with the completion of the Stevenson EXPRESSWAY (1964) to revitalize the area. Mexican families, many of whom had lived on the Near West Side since the 1920s, resettled further south in Pilsen, while the Stevenson provided ready access to the LOOP and other parts of Chicago. As the MEATPACKING houses of the stockyards district shut down (1950s), many Mexican residents migrated north into Pilsen and Little Village. Throughout the 1960s and 1970s, Mexicans from the southwestern United States, PUERTO RICANS, and AFRICAN AMERICANS (many from NORTH LAWNDALE) also settled there. Like previous groups, Mexicans set up their own institutions and practices. Howell Neighborhood House became Casa Aztlán; Fiesta del Sol celebrations have been held since 1973; street parades annually celebrate September 16 (Mexican Independence Day); Benito Juárez High School was created in 1977; Mexican and Chicana/o ARTISTS painted several murals celebrating Mexican culture; Posada processions are held over Christmas; and the MEXICAN FINE ARTS CENTER MUSEUM opened in 1987.

Pilsen retains its character as a point of entry for poor and working-class migrants. RESTAURANTS and bodegas line its commercial center along 18th Street and evoke the residents' myriad homelands. Beyond the many regions of Mexico, new groups have come from other Latin American countries including El Salvador, GUATEMALA, CHILE, PUERTO RICO, and CUBA. Many continue to struggle against poverty and discrimination as LEGAL AID and MUTUAL BENEFIT SOCIETIES work to break these barriers, while others are following the westward drift of previous residents.

Gabriela F. Arredondo

See also: Agricultural Machinery Industry; Demography; Foodways; Metropolitan Growth; Religious Geography

Further reading: Casuso, Jorge, and Eduardo Camacho. *Hispanics in Chicago.* 1985. • Pacyga, Dominic A., and Ellen Skerrett. "Lower West Side." In *Chicago, City of Neighborhoods: Histories and Tours.* 1986. • Reichman, John J. *Czechoslovaks of Chicago: Contributions to a History of a National Group.* 1937.

Loyola University. Founded in 1870 by Father Arnold Damen, S.J., Saint Ignatius College was renamed Loyola University in 1909. The university began instruction at 1076 W. Roosevelt Road and in 1912 began a 10-year process of relocation to its Lake Shore Campus in ROGERS PARK. A downtown campus was established in the LOOP in 1914 and, after a move within that neighborhood in 1927, eventually relocated to the NEAR NORTH SIDE in 1946. To complement its liberal arts curriculum, Loyola established a LAW school in 1908, a medical school one year later, and a business school in 1922. The Chicago College of Dental Surgery merged with the university in 1923, closing 70 years later as part of a national trend. The medical and dental schools moved to MAYWOOD in 1969 to create a health care complex now called the Loyola University Medical Center.

The School of Sociology, which later evolved into the School of Social Work, was founded by Father Frederic Siedenburg, S.J., at the downtown campus in 1914. It included the first women to be admitted to Loyola. In 1966, undergraduate women—previously restricted to downtown programs—were given access to all courses on the Rogers Park Campus.

The university by its presence in Rogers Park has provided jobs and resources for the community and rendered assistance to the Rogers Park and EDGEWATER councils. The "Walk to Work Program" sponsored by the president's office has provided housing loans to faculty and staff to remain in the community. Nursing students have provided health assistance at St. Ignatius Church, and students have volunteered at various shelters in the community.

Loyola has continued to educate immigrant populations, earlier from Europe, and more recently from Asia and Africa.

In 1962, the university opened a campus in Rome, and the School of Business has offered summer programs in Athens, Bangkok, and Istanbul. In June 1991 the university acquired Mundelein College, which was adjacent to the Rogers Park campus, and in 1998, the board of trustees approved the purchase of the former Mallinckrodt College in Wilmette.

In 1970 the university legally separated from the Society of Jesus, placing it under lay control with an enlarged board of trustees.

Br. Michael Grace, S.J.

See also: Dentistry; DePaul University; Medical Education; Universities and Their Cities

Further reading: Garraghan, Gilbert J. *The Jesuits in the Middle United States.* Vol. 3. 1938. • Laub, Martin H. *A Hallmark of Leadership: The Presidents of Loyola University of Chicago.* 1994.

Lumber. Lumber, along with grain and MEATPACKING, was one of the "big three" commodities of nineteenth-century Chicago commerce. Through the second half of the nineteenth century, Chicago was the world's greatest lumber market. The city owed its status to geography, TRANSPORTATION, and population. Geography placed Chicago in close proximity to the dense forests of the Upper GREAT LAKES, rail and WATER transportation links made Chicago the natural hub for moving forest products, and the city's phenomenal population growth made it one of the single largest markets for lumber.

The commercial lumber business began in Chicago in 1833 with the arrival of a shipload of cottonwood boards from St. Joseph, Michigan. During the 1830s and 1840s the industry was largely focused on supplying the local market with building material. It was not unusual for farmers bringing a wagon of wheat across the prairie to Chicago to return home with a load of lumber for a frame house or outbuilding. The opening of the ILLINOIS & MICHIGAN CANAL allowed Chicago to emerge as a national lumber distribution center. The amount of lumber flowing into Chicago in 1848, the year the canal opened, was nearly double that of the previous year.

The Illinois & Michigan Canal transformed the Lake Michigan basin into a funnel through which the forest products of Wisconsin and Michigan were deposited in Chicago for sale throughout the western United States. During the navigation season a steady stream of logging schooners departed the mill towns of the north woods. During the 1860s and 1870s a northerly wind could bring as many as two hundred ships into the CHICAGO RIVER on a single day. The crowd of ships in the river would force open the numerous swing BRIDGES and bring downtown traffic to a maddening standstill. The destination of the lumber ships was the extensive lumber district that stretched out along the South Branch of the river all the way to the western margins of the city. "The timber yards are a considerable part of the city's surface," a British tourist remarked in 1887, "there appearing to be enough boards and planks piled up to supply a half-dozen States."

Numerous slips excavated into the banks of the river and extending for blocks into the district provided the lumber schooners with 12 miles of dockage space. Manpower in the form of burly lumber shovers unloaded the schooners. Working the docks of the district was a rite of passage for many immigrants to the nineteenth-century city. Lumber yards hired the fastest and cheapest workers they could find, so there was constant turnover among the stevedores. During the CIVIL WAR,

An 1886 *Harper's Weekly* engraving of Chicago's lumber district viewed from the West Side Water Works (near Ashland and Blue Island). The large factory on the top left is the McCormick Works at Western and Blue Island. Artist: Unknown. Source: Chicago Historical Society.

labor gangs of IRISH men not infrequently came to blows with AFRICAN AMERICAN lumber shovers over who had the right to unload a particular ship. In the RAILROAD STRIKE OF 1877, Bohemian lumber shovers spearheaded the upheaval that resulted in pitched battles with POLICE and a radicalization of workers in Chicago.

The decline of Chicago as the leading lumber market was tied to the exhaustion of the forests of the Upper Great Lakes region and changes in the economics of distribution. By 1900, Chicago lumber merchants, although heavily invested in the north woods, anticipated the decline and invested in southern pine lands. Into the 1920s leading companies such as Edward Hines kept the city a major market by stocking their Chicago wholesale yard with trainloads of southern yellow pine. Hines and other lumber merchants also developed new northern hardwood products from their Michigan and Wisconsin forest operations. Yet the manufacture of lumber for specialized products such as flooring, FURNITURE, and trim required new facilities which could be more cheaply be built near the source of the supply than at a central distribution center. RAILROAD and communication networks which allowed Chicago to access southern pine also encouraged the distribution of lumber directly from the mill site, saving on the costly transshipment to, and storage at, Chicago. By the end of the 1920s it was clear that the future of Chicago's lumber industry was in supplying the still considerable local market, the era of national significance having passed.

Theodore J. Karamanski

See also: Business of Chicago; Construction; Economic Geography; Food Processing: Regional and National Market

Further reading: Cronon, William. *Nature's Metropolis: Chicago and the Great West.* 1991. • Hotchkiss, George W. *History of the Lumber and Forest Industry of the Northwest.* 1898.

Luxembourgers. Immigrants from Luxembourg created one of Chicago's smallest but most self-conscious and enduring ethnic groups. Chicago's Luxembourgers also played a central role not only in the group's American history but in the modern history of Luxembourg itself. The first families from the tiny grand duchy (population 175,000 in 1839) arrived in Chicago about 1842, seeking on the American frontier the traditional agrarian life they could no longer sustain at home in the face of overpopulation and economic change. Many moved to more westerly farming frontiers, others pioneered farms in the woods north and west of Chicago, while still others found opportunity as laborers, artisans, and saloonkeepers within Chicago itself. New immigrants, increasingly job-seeking youths after the 1870s, continued to arrive through the 1920s.

Political changes within Europe make it difficult to determine exact numbers of Létzebûrgesch speakers in Chicago—the main basis for affiliation with the Luxembourg community—since Luxembourgers often appeared in the census as GERMANS, BELGIANS, or DUTCH. Best estimates suggest some 700 Luxembourg households in the Chicago region in 1880, and 2,500—or about 15,000 first- and second-generation Luxembourgers—by 1920 at their peak of local visibility. Though a minuscule proportion of Chicago's population, they formed the largest single concentration of the 50,000 Luxembourgers who emigrated to the U.S. between 1840 and the present.

Luxembourgers initially settled among German ROMAN CATHOLICS in the North Side's St. Michael PARISH beginning in the 1840s, near the stockyards by the 1870s, in southeastern Chicago's millgates by the 1890s, and near AURORA'S RAILROAD shops where they worked from the late 1850s. But the distinctive heart of Luxembourg Chicago lay "op der Rëtsch"—up on Ridge Avenue around its intersection with Devon. There numerous Luxembourg families laboriously cultivated vegetables for the Chicago market, specializing in celery. After 1880, they erected greenhouses for year-round industrial production of vegetables and flowers. Perhaps a hundred greenhouse clusters stretched from ROGERS PARK northwest through WEST RIDGE, NILES Center, and DES PLAINES, most in Luxembourg hands by 1919 when their growers' association numbered some 1,200 families. Urban development, speculation, competition from elsewhere in the United States, and the lure of less arduous urban occupations gradually undermined the industry after the 1920s, and with it the most important base of Luxembourg identity.

After 1870 Chicago's Luxembourgers were able to construct a rich ethnic life, shaped by growing nationalism in the homeland following effective independence in 1867, by their own increasing prosperity, and by their desire to distinguish themselves from a local German community often associated with labor radicalism. It found its focus in the parishes they founded, beginning with St. Henry's on Ridge in 1850; in MUTUAL BENEFIT SOCIETIES, particularly the Luxemburger Bruderbund, founded in 1886 and still in existence today; in the Luxemburg Independent Club, which emerged as their political voice in reaction to the 1886 HAYMARKET bombing; and in the annual Labor Day Schobermesse, or traditional fair, begun in 1904, showcasing their produce and inculcating a regionwide sense of ethnic identity.

One lasting consequence of their culture was the FOREST PRESERVE system, which "Rose and Carnation King" Peter Reinberg fostered during his 1914–1921 tenure as president of the COOK COUNTY Board of Commissioners. Another was their active manipulation of public opinion during WORLD WAR I to ensure that German-occupied Luxembourg gained a seat at the peace conference and permanent independence. Group organizations slowly waned after WORLD WAR II. The last Schobermesse was held in 1967. But social ties, encouraged by periodic grand ducal visits, continue to support among many Chicagoans of Luxembourg descent a sense of ethnicity that is largely symbolic but nonetheless significant.

Kathleen Neils Conzen

See also: Agriculture; Americanization; Demography; Multicentered Chicago; Religious Institutions

Further reading: Clark, Stephen Bedell, et al. *The Lakeview Saga.* 1985. • Ensch, Jean, et al., eds. *Luxembourgers in the New World: A Reedition Based on the Work of Nicholas Gonner, "Die Luxemburger in der Neuen Welt."* 1987. • Witry, Richard J., ed. *Luxembourg Brotherhood of America, 1887–1987.* 1987.

Lynwood, IL, Cook County, 25 miles S of the Loop. The village of Lynwood sits between State Route 394 and the Indiana state line. Settlement in the area has been light, and even after its incorporation in 1959, the 1960 census recorded only 255 residents.

The evolution of Lynwood can be seen in relation to the development of GLENWOOD to the west, LANSING to the north, and SOUTH HOLLAND to the northwest. All included large areas that were settled by "YANKEE," ENGLISH, and DUTCH farmers. Growing onions, beets, and soybeans, these farmers worked cooperatively to drain much of this land to increase its productivity. Scattered farms could be found in this part of Bloom Township in the late 1840s. In the 1990s, large tracts of this area were still in agricultural use.

Because of its easy access to Chicago and the industries of the CALUMET REGION, several attempts were made for large-scale residential developments seeking to bring thousands of homes into Lynwood. However, there was not a strong demand for housing in this part of COOK COUNTY, and for many years the village had problems with WATER and sewer services. By 1970, the community had grown to only 1,042 residents.

Other developers made further attempts to build in the community, which included the creation of Lake Lynwood in 1971. The population increased to 4,195 in 1980, and, with Lake Michigan water being pumped in and flooding controls underway, the village reached 7,377 residents by 2000. Parallel to this has been some modest commercial growth.

Although not directly affecting the development of Lynwood, two of its roads carry historical significance. The Glenwood-Dyer Road (in part Illinois Route 83) runs northwest/southeast through the center of Lynwood, following the path of an ancient trail that connected the old Sauk Trail at what is now DYER, Indiana, with the old Vincennes/Hubbard's Trail at a point near THORNTON, Illinois. At the south edge of the village, Route 30 follows the alignment of the old transcontinental Lincoln Highway, designated in 1922. Prior to that year, Lincoln Highway followed the Sauk Trail until meeting Dixie Highway (which was also the old route of the Vincennes/Hubbard's Trail) in SOUTH CHICAGO HEIGHTS.

Larry A. McClellan

See also: Metropolitan Growth; Streets and Highways

Further reading: Andreas, A. T. *History of Cook County, Illinois.* 1884. • Hayes, Charles. "Village Grows Optimistic When Sizing Up Its Future." *Chicago Tribune,* May 11, 1991. • Warren, Stewart. "Lynwood Springs from Farmers' Onion Fields." *Star,* June 20, 1993.

Lyons, IL, Cook County, 11 miles SW of the Loop. The marshy region at what is now 47th and Harlem separates waters that flow into the Great Lakes from those that flow into the Mississippi River. During wet seasons NATIVE AMERICANS could travel from the South Branch of the CHICAGO RIVER to the DES PLAINES RIVER through an area called Mud Lake.

The origin of the town name is uncertain; local lore suggests a relation to Lyon, France, another town at the confluence of two bodies of water. David and Bernardus Laughton established a trading post and tavern in the late 1820s near the confluence of SALT CREEK and the Des Plaines River. Construction on the ILLINOIS & MICHIGAN CANAL brought workers to the region. GERMAN farmers settled here, but growth was slow, in part owing to fear of prairie fires. A large BREWERY began operations in 1856, and two years later Lyons joined with other towns in petitioning for a RAILROAD to be built through their towns.

By the early 1880s, a thriving limestone QUARRY and lime kilns, a flour mill, and numerous taverns constituted the town's major commercial enterprises. Harvesting ice from the Des Plaines River provided seasonal employment. A ROMAN CATHOLIC church opened in 1876, and a Lutheran church served the large German community. By the 1880s POLISH immigrants arrived in significant numbers.

Formal incorporation came in 1888, and in 1897 the small town of Cooksville was transferred to Lyons from adjoining RIVERSIDE. In the early twentieth century one commentator referred to Lyons as "bibulous . . . the chosen abode of Bacchus and Terpsichore." A more restrained observer of the era characterized Lyons as "quaint" and traditional, and noted that there were "unlimited possibilities" for the development of the town.

Progressive-era reformers targeted the town for change, but in 1908 a vote to abolish SALOONS lost by a lopsided 244–14 margin. Not surprisingly, one of the most influential men in town was a brewer, George Hofmann, Jr. In 1908 he built a dam on the Des Plaines River in order to generate water power, and adjacent to the dam he erected the Hofmann Tower, the center of a park complete with boat rides on the river.

The paving of Ogden Avenue in 1914 expedited auto travel, and the Chicago & Joliet Electric Railway made the town even more accessible. AMUSEMENT PARKS and taverns continued, even during PROHIBITION. Residential development boomed after 1945, when most of the town's available land was converted to housing. The last amusement park closed in the 1970s, as did the red-light district.

The population of 10,255 in 2000 consisted of various ethnic groups, although there were relatively few AFRICAN AMERICANS. Lyons's reputation as a residential, blue-collar town has not diminished over the years, and there are still many taverns. METRA's Burlington Northern Santa Fe line provides easy access to Chicago. The Chicago PORTAGE National Historic Site, located in Ottawa Trail Woods, is a place where the Native American and FRENCH pasts mingle with the present. The Hofmann Tower remains a local landmark, and is on the National Register of Historic Places.

Ronald S. Vasile

See also: Entertaining Chicagoans; Fur Trade; Interurbans; Underground Economy

Further reading: Andreas, A. T. *History of Cook County Illinois.* 1884. • Benedetti, Rose Marie. *Village on the River, 1888–1988.* 1988. • *Lyons Diamond Jubilee, 1888–1963.* 1963.

Lyric Opera. From 1910 to 1946, seven OPERA companies—several merely different names for the same reorganized company—presented seasons at Chicago's AUDITORIUM THEATER and the Civic Opera House. All sunk in a sea of debt. From 1946 to 1954 the city had no resident opera company. Three people changed everything: Carol Fox, a student singer; Lawrence Kelly, a businessman; and Nicola Rescigno, a conductor and vocal teacher. With money from friends and Fox's father, the three formed the Lyric Theatre of Chicago in 1952. Their plan was to restore the city to the front ranks of international opera companies by building a roster of European singers whom the Metropolitan and San Francisco operas had overlooked or ignored. On February 5, 1954, the Lyric Theater presented its "calling card," a starry performance of Mozart's *Don Giovanni* at the Civic Opera House. The success of that production made possible a three-week season in autumn of 1954 consisting of 16 performances of 8 operas; 12 of those performances sold out the 3,600-seat theater. The inaugural season brought the American debut of the fiery American-born Greek soprano Maria Callas, as the title role in Bellini's *Norma.* Callas went on to even more rapturous successes here as Violetta in Verdi's *La Traviata,* the title role in Donizetti's *Lucia di Lammermoor,* and Cio-Cio San in Puccini's *Madama Butterfly,* among other roles. Italian singers and operas predominated in those early years. By 1956, when Fox took sole command of a rechristened Lyric Opera of Chicago, the company had been nicknamed "La Scala West."

By the late 1990s, Lyric boasted a greatly expanded repertoire, an imposing roster of world-class singers (including Catherine Malfitano, Renée Fleming, Dawn Upshaw, Jane Eaglen, Jerry Hadley, Ben Heppner, James Morris, and Bryn Terfel), and capacity houses for nearly every performance in seasons that extended from September to March. Ardis Krainik, who succeeded Fox as general director upon the latter's retirement in 1981, earned a reputation as a tough businesswoman and shrewd arts executive. She also won wide respect for the Lyric as a theater that took twentieth-century opera as seriously as the classics. The company's first integral production of Wagner's *Ring* cycle, in March 1996, was its most ambitious and, at $6.5 million, most expensive artistic endeavor to date. Her ambitious initiative "Toward the 21st Century," which included a retrospective of important American operas and world premieres commissioned by the Lyric, was a bellwether for similar programs at other U.S. companies. At Krainik's death in January 1997 she was succeeded by William Mason, the company's director of operations, artistic and production. As the Lyric entered the early twenty-first century, it remained internationally respected as a theater of high performance standards resting on an enviably secure financial base.

John von Rhein

See also: Classical Music; Entertaining Chicagoans

Further reading: Cassidy, Claudia. *Lyric Opera of Chicago.* 1979. • Davis, R. *Opera in Chicago.* 1966.

MacArthur Foundation. The John D. and Catherine T. MacArthur Foundation was created in 1978 through the bequest of John D. MacArthur, a Pennsylvania native who amassed a great fortune in the INSURANCE business and in real-estate investments in Florida. The bulk of his fortune, both company shares and real estate, was left to the foundation, whose endowment had surpassed $4 billion (with more than $150 million annual grant making) by 1998.

At its inception, the MacArthur Foundation attracted attention because it was a new, general purpose, nationally focused foundation with an asset base that almost immediately made it among the country's largest. The MacArthur Foundation was unusual in that the donor left no specific instructions as to the purpose of his philanthropic legacy. He simply named a number of business associates, old Chicago friends, and prominent academics as the board of trustees, whose job it has been to develop a systematic program of giving.

The MacArthur Foundation had become one of the largest and most important philanthropic foundations in the country by the end of its second decade. It focused on two major areas of giving: Human and Community Development (with special attention to Chicago and to Palm Beach County, Florida), and Global Security and Sustainability. But it was best-known to the general public for its MacArthur Fellows Program, popularly known as the "genius" awards—large prizes given without application to people of outstanding promise and performance in any field of endeavor.

Stanley N. Katz

See also: Philanthropy

Macedonians. The most intense period of Macedonian immigration took place before WORLD WAR I, and after a long lull, resumed in the decades after WORLD WAR II. In the first stage, thousands of Macedonians left the Old Country in the wake of the bloody 1903 Ilinden Uprising against Ottoman control, which ended with the ruin of some 200 villages and exposed many Macedonian men to conscription in the Ottoman army. The rest came as male labor migrants who sought to improve their families' grim economic fortunes by returning home with earnings from American factories. After World War I, with their home country divided between Bulgaria, Serbia, and Greece, the thousands of Chicago-area Macedonians recognized that they would not return to Europe. Reluctantly, wives and children joined their husbands and fathers, laying the groundwork for stable Macedonian communities in North America.

Prior to the creation of a Macedonian republic in 1944, most Macedonian immigrants viewed themselves as ethnically BULGARIAN and often referred to themselves as Macedonian-Bulgarians or simply Bulgarians. While immigration records failed to list Macedonians as a separate category, approximately three-quarters of those listed as Bulgarians were from the regions of Kostur and Bitola in Macedonia. These immigrants, and those from Bulgaria proper, typically settled together in the pre–World War II years, and established communities in Chicago and GARY as well as downstate in Madison, Granite City, and Venice, Illinois. In 1909 Grace Abbott, writing about the desperate poverty in which hundreds of these immigrants were initially living, estimated that 1,000 Macedonians and Bulgarians were living in Chicago.

Early in the century, Macedonians worked almost exclusively in heavy industry. Many found work in Chicago's rail yards. Others worked in slaughterhouses, tanneries, fertilizer factories, and steel mills. Chicago served as a transfer point for Macedonians heading to St. Louis, or to the Western states to find railroad and mining WORK. Prior to the formation of Orthodox churches in the 1930s, Macedonian immigrants found solace in cafes near their BOARDINGHOUSES, and in a number of MUTUAL BENEFIT SOCIETIES, the first of which was founded in Chicago in 1902.

Chicago Macedonians campaigned openly for the independence of their homeland. In 1910, several hundred members of the Bulgaro-Macedonian League paraded through the city's West Side and rallied at Bricklayer's Hall to protest Ottoman rule. In 1918 Chicago Macedonians held a "Great Macedonian Congress" to express hope that President Wilson's Fourteen Points would guarantee Macedonia a free homeland. In 1922, Macedonians in North America formed the Macedonian Political Organization (MPO) to campaign for Macedonian independence. Since the 1930s, Chicago and Gary have hosted the MPO's annual conventions on at least six occasions. In 1938 Bulgarians and Macedonians together founded St. Sophia Bulgarian EASTERN ORTHODOX Church on North Lawndale Avenue.

After World War II, Macedonian immigrants coming from the new republic or from northern Greece began to view themselves as ethnically Macedonian, and had fewer connections to the older generation. Macedonian Orthodox churches began to grow in the Midwest, Northeast, and Ontario, and in the 1960s the new generation of Chicago Macedonians, which was steadily making its way into the American middle class, founded Sts. Cyril and Methodins in Hinsdale, Illinois. The task of ascertaining the total number of Macedonians in Chicago is confused by the association of many with either the Bulgarian or GREEK churches, but Macedonians probably numbered fewer than 10,000 at the end of the twentieth century.

Gregory Michaelidis

See also: Americanization; Demography; Multicentered Chicago

Further reading: "Macedonians." In *Harvard Encyclopedia of American Ethnic Groups*, ed. Stephan Thernstrom, 1980. • Danforth, Loring M. *The Macedonian Conflict: Ethnic Nationalism in a Transnational World.* 1995.

Machine Politics. Urban political machines, built largely on the votes of diverse immigrant populations, dispensed jobs and assorted welfare benefits while offering avenues of social mobility at a time when local governments provided a paucity of such services. In the nineteenth and early twentieth centuries, Chicago sustained a strong two-party tradition that prevented the development of a centralized political machine. Neither the DEMOCRATS nor the REPUBLICANS succeeded in consolidating power citywide. Republicans prevailed most often in national elections; the Democrats won the majority of local contests; and both parties experienced considerable divisiveness that prevented any faction from establishing hegemony. Several Chicago MAYORS, most notably Carter H. Harrison (Democrat, 1879–1887, 1893), Carter H. Harrison, II (Democrat, 1897–1905, 1911–1915), and Republican William Hale "Big Bill" Thompson (1915–1923, 1927–1931) enjoyed loyal followings but failed to translate personal popularity into lasting organizational strength.

The potent Democratic machine that dominated Chicago POLITICS for nearly half a century formed under the leadership of Anton Cermak, a Bohemian immigrant of working-class origins. After the death of COOK COUNTY Democratic leader George Brennan in 1928, Cermak secured control of the party hierarchy and defeated Thompson in the 1931 mayoral campaign. He subsequently forced the party's dominant IRISH contingent to accept other ethnic groups into his "house for all peoples," bringing representatives from the GERMAN, POLISH, CZECH, and JEWISH communities into leadership positions. The life of the Democratic machine's George Washington was cut short in 1933 when Cermak became the unintended victim of an attempted assassination of president-elect Franklin D. Roosevelt.

After Cermak's death, the Irish seized control of the Democratic machine as party chairman Patrick A. Nash engineered the appointment of Edward J. Kelly as mayor. The KELLY-NASH MACHINE followed Cermak's lead, however, doling out PATRONAGE jobs, political appointments, and favors to a broad spectrum of ethnic groups. Kelly not only held the fledgling political machine together in its infancy but strengthened it by utilizing three important sources. First, he became a fervent supporter of Franklin D. Roosevelt's NEW DEAL and kept the city solvent through the liberal use of federal funds at a time when the GREAT DEPRESSION provided the most serious threat to the financial well-being of municipal governments. Second, he acquired additional financial resources from organized crime. By ignoring the operation of GAMBLING, PROSTITUTION, and other forms of VICE in the WINDY CITY, Kelly obtained from illegal sources the "grease" necessary to keep the machine operating. Third, he actively cultivated AFRICAN AMERICAN voters, and his success paid huge dividends in later years when Chicago's black population increased dramatically. Kelly won reelection in 1935, 1939, and 1943, but problems arose by 1947. Concerns about the number of scandals in municipal government (especially in the public school system) surfaced alongside a rising public outcry against the highly visible presence of organized crime in the city. But among the Democratic faithful, Kelly's greatest liability proved to be his uncompromising stand in favor of public housing and desegregated public SCHOOLS. The party leadership persuaded Kelly not to seek reelection in 1947 and replaced him with a figurehead, civic leader Martin H. Kennelly.

The Democratic machine endured Kennelly's presence in the mayor's office for two terms but then replaced him with a party regular, Richard J. Daley, in 1955. During Daley's prolonged tenure in city hall—he was reelected

Left to right: John Coughlin, alderman, First Ward; Anton J. Cermak, mayor; Herman Bundesen, health commissioner; J. Hamilton Lewis, U.S. senator; Al J. Hoover, municipal court bailiff; Michael Kenna, committeeman, First Ward; John J. Sullivan, Cook County Superior Court judge; Clayton Smith, recorder, Cook County, and chair, Democratic Party Managing Committee. Cermak's election as mayor in 1931 was attributable in large part to his use of incentives and threats to secure the support of different factions of the Democratic Party, including former rivals like Smith and Bundesen. As president of the Board of Commissioners of Cook County since 1922, and the dominant county Democratic leader after 1928, Cermak commanded considerable patronage. Rival Democratic leaders had expected to maintain Irish control of the party, although other ethnic groups (Poles, Germans, Jews) constituted larger proportions of the city's population. Some Irish ward stalwarts, such as Kenna and Coughlin, had long been allied with Cermak. Others fell into line as Cermak outmaneuvered his opponents and constructed a new, multiethnic, citywide Democratic "machine" that would be reinforced by his successors. Photographer: Unknown. Source: Chicago Historical Society.

The Era of "Hinky Dink" and "Bathhouse John"

"Hinky Dink" Kenna and "Bathhouse John" Coughlin created in the 1890s a First Ward political machine based on graft and protection money from the SALOONS, brothels, and GAMBLING halls of the Levee district, just south of the Loop.

Coughlin began his working life as a scrubber in LOOP BATH houses and opened the first bathhouse of his own in 1882. He prospered through connections with politicians, gamblers, and HORSE-RACING enthusiasts, who stimulated in him a lifelong habit of sartorial flamboyance.

Kenna, a small, quiet, discreet man, ran a saloon called the Workingman's Exchange, where he served generous quantities of beer along with free lunches. Unlike Coughlin he was personally frugal, and became quite wealthy through the business of POLITICS.

For over a decade Kenna and Coughlin together organized an annual First WARD Ball notorious for outrageous costumes and uproarious behavior. The ball, which among other entertainments featured songs whose doggerel lyrics were attributed to Bathhouse John himself, attracted thousands of people and raised large sums of money for the ward organization until pressure from reformers ended the event after 1908.

Before redistricting in 1923, each Chicago ward was represented by two aldermen. Coughlin was first elected to the city council in 1892, and Kenna joined him in 1897. Coughlin served as the sole First Ward alderman from 1923 until his death in 1938, with Kenna succeeding him until his own death in 1946.

Douglas Knox

A cartoon by John T. McCutcheon, in the *Chicago Tribune*, 1908. Artist: John T. McCutcheon. Source: Chicago Tribune.

five times prior to his sudden death in 1976—the machine reached its apogee. At a time when virtually no urban political machines survived, Daley steered the Cook County Democratic organization to one electoral triumph after another. The "last boss" controlled an estimated 35,000 patronage jobs, the use of which ensured party discipline and relegated the local Republican Party to insignificance. To a great extent, Daley managed to circumvent civil service regulations by repeatedly hiring the same loyal Democrats to "temporary" jobs that were not subject to the regulations. As government workers died or retired, the machine filled their positions temporarily pending civil service exams that were never given. A series of court decisions in the 1970s, culminating in the SHAKMAN DECREES, severely reduced patronage by first prohibiting the politically motivated firing of government workers and, several years after Daley's death, by outlawing politically motivated hiring practices. By the 1980s, the mighty Democratic patronage army shrank significantly, but during the Daley years civil servants who worked hard for the party at election time and precinct captains who produced healthy victory margins at the polls kept their patronage jobs and received other rewards.

Despite the conventional wisdom that political machines were hopelessly inefficient, Mayor Daley's reliable provision of services and apparent ability to balance the city's financial books led Chicago to be known as "the city that works." The years of his mayoralty saw the opening of O'HARE INTERNATIONAL AIRPORT, construction of the UNIVERSITY OF ILLINOIS branch campus, expansion of the city's interconnected EXPRESSWAY system from 53 to 506 miles, and a monumental building boom that revitalized the downtown LOOP area—and created, courtesy of the Democratic machine, a wealth of contracts and jobs for the CONSTRUCTION industry.

Long reliant upon the electoral support from a rapidly expanding black population, the political machine's prolonged success finally wavered because of DEMOGRAPHIC changes. Daley was an avid defender of residential segregation and an opponent of affirmative-action policies in GOVERNMENT, and his conservatism ran afoul of the CIVIL RIGHTS and black power movements. Daley's support among black voters dwindled in the 1970s, and wholesale changes came following his death in 1976. To succeed Mayor Daley, the Democrats chose Michael A. Bilandic, a colorless party functionary whose inept handling of a record-setting snowstorm led Chicagoans to question whether the machine could still deliver services efficiently. Unseating Bilandic at the first opportunity, the voters opted instead for Jane Byrne, a former machine regular who campaigned as a reformer but whose chaotic and ineffectual years in office enhanced the level of dissatisfaction with city government. Despite campaign promises to the contrary, Byrne ignored black political demands. The election of Harold Washington as the city's first black mayor in 1983 and his subsequent reelection four years later unequivocally ended Democratic machine rule in Chicago. Nor did the election to the mayoralty of Richard M. Daley, the eldest son of the deceased boss, indicate a resurrection of the machine in a new guise. As the younger Daley readily acknowledged, radically different demographics and the attendant alterations in the political calculus clearly made the machine politics for which Chicago became famous an anachronism by the end of the twentieth century.

Roger Biles

See also: Good Government Movements; Gray Wolves; Mayors; Political Culture; Privatization; Snow Removal

Further reading: Allswang, John M. *A House for All Peoples: Ethnic Politics in Chicago, 1890–1936.* 1971. • Biles, Roger. *Richard J. Daley: Politics, Race, and the Governing of Chicago.* 1995. • Erie, Steven P. *Rainbow's End: Irish-Americans and the Dilemmas of Urban Machine Politics, 1840–1985.* 1988.

Madonna Center. The Madonna Center was founded in 1898 as a ROMAN CATHOLIC mission to ITALIAN immigrants on Chicago's NEAR WEST SIDE. Its original name was Guardian Angel Mission, and it began as a tiny chapel in an abandoned parochial school. It was founded because Catholics feared that Protestant missionaries and secular institutions such as HULL HOUSE would weaken the immigrants' Catholicism. Soon its catechism class had approximately fifteen hundred students and one hundred volunteer teachers.

The mission's success, which inspired the construction of Holy Guardian Angel Church in 1899, rested in large part on the efforts of the Amberg Family. Agnes Ward Amberg directed the mission; her husband, William A. Amberg, provided financial support. Their daughter, Mary Agnes Amberg, became head resident in 1913, and together with her close friend Marie Plamondon operated the settlement for nearly 50 years.

The mission took on the functions of a SETTLEMENT HOUSE, offering classes in domestic science, sewing, and SCOUTING. In 1922, it moved into a substantial house on South Loomis Street and changed its name to the Madonna Center. The added space enabled the center to offer more athletic programs, children's clubs, a KINDERGARTEN, and a medical clinic.

Despite occasional conflict with Italian leaders, Amberg and Plamondon forged close ties with many of their neighbors. Unfortunately, the center's strength also turned out to be its weakness. When the neighborhood changed, the center failed to adapt. Amberg and Plamondon tried unsuccessfully to appeal to their new AFRICAN AMERICAN neighbors. The center closed permanently in 1962, upon Mary Amberg's death.

Deborah Ann Skok

See also: Catholic Charities; Jewish Community Centers; Multicentered Chicago; Salvation Army; Social Services

Further reading: Amberg, Mary Agnes. *Madonna Center: Pioneer Catholic Social Settlement.* 1976. • Lissak, Rivka. *Pluralism and Progressives: Hull House and the New Immigrants, 1890–1919.* 1989. • The Madonna Center Collection. Special Collections and University Archives, Memorial Library, Marquette University, Milwaukee, WI.

Mafia. "Mafia" is a word of uncertain origins and multiple meanings. A dictionary of 1868 defines it as a neologism denoting "bravado," while another of 1876 defines it as of Piedmontese origin, the equivalent of "gang." It is principally used, today, to refer to two criminal organizations, one in Sicily and one in the United States.

In Sicily, the organization is composed of *cosche*—a corruption of the word for "artichoke"—which control areas or activities and which form ties to politicians for protection and patronage. With each headed by a *capo* (*don* is merely a term of *rispetto,* or respect), but with some more powerful than others, the *cosche* form *consorteria* (alliances), which together are the *amico degli amici* (friends of ours), the *onorata societá* (honored society) of Sicily, or the "Mafia."

In the United States, the "Mafia" must be distinguished from the "Black Hand"—not a group, but a technique in the early 1900s of extortion (sending a "black hand" signifying death, if money is not paid)—and the Unione Siciliana, a fraternal organization, though widely infiltrated by gangsters, chartered by Illinois in 1895 and, after 1910, supervised by the Illinois Department of INSURANCE. According to the Federal Bureau of Investigation, the Mafia's membership in 1963 was approximately 5,000, including 2,500 in New York and 300 in Chicago. It comprised 24 *borgate* (families), headed by a *capo* (boss). The families were subdivided into *regime* (crews), headed by *caporegime* (captains). Not equal in wealth, power, or status, the families were under the jurisdiction of the *commissione* (national "commission"), which originated in cooperation among GANGS in the 1920s. In 1963, it included the bosses of four of the five families in New York and the bosses of the families in Buffalo, Philadelphia, Detroit, and Chicago. The families engaged in illegal activities—GAMBLING, narcotics, loansharking, hijacking, and labor racketeering—as well as legal activities such as WASTE DISPOSAL, RESTAURANTS and bars, vending machines, produce, trucking, and garment manufacturing.

The group was known by various names—in New York, La Cosa Nostra ("our family" or "our thing"), in Buffalo, "The Arm," and in Chicago, "The Outfit." It emerged in Chicago from the contest for supremacy in producing and distributing liquor in the 1920s. Composed of Sicilians or ITALIANS, its members formed numerous alliances with others. In Chicago, Alphonse Caponi ("Al Capone"), Anthony "Tony" Accardo, John "Jake" Guzik (a Polish JEW), and Llewellyn "Murray" Humphreys (a WELSHMAN), played key roles in the organization.

Today, the Mafia is a remnant of the 1963 organization because of prosecutions and civil suits, using, in particular, RICO, the racketeering statute, which authorizes long prison terms, the forfeiture of ill-gotten gains, and civil suits. Most families are little more than street gangs. Membership is down to 1,150, with 750 in New York and 50 in Chicago. The national commission, fearful of FBI surveillance, has not met since the late 1980s. The Mafia, which has never held a monopoly on organized crime in the United States, no longer has any special edge in an underworld teeming with Asians, RUSSIANS, and South Americans.

G. Robert Blakey

See also: Crime and Chicago's Image; Liquor Distribution; Mutual Benefit Societies; St. Valentine's Day Massacre; Underground Economy

Further reading: Jacobs, James B. *Busting the Mob.* 1994. • Nelli, Humbert S. *The Business of Crime: Italians and Syndicated Crime in the United States.* 1979. • President's Commission on Law Enforcement and Administration of Justice. *Task Force Report on Organized Crime.* 1967.

Magazines. The place of birth and death for thousands of magazine titles, Chicago has been home to influential publications such as the DIAL, *JAMA,* POETRY, *Esquire, Ebony, Bulletin of the Atomic Scientists,* PLAYBOY, and *O.*

The oldest continuing magazine founded in Chicago is PRAIRIE FARMER, started by agricultural reformer John S. Wright in January 1841. It relocated to Decatur in the 1970s and has become one of a number of allied publications with a combined circulation of over 600,000.

Other early Chicago magazines were short-lived, full of lofty aspirations for the new city, with titles such as *Garland of the West, Gem of the Prairie,* and *Free West.* The *Lakeside Monthly* (1869–1874), edited by Francis Fisher Browne, was the first magazine to portend Chicago's literary future. It was followed by the Browne-edited *Dial* (1880–1929),which encouraged modernist literary innovation and helped inspire the CHICAGO LITERARY RENAISSANCE. The *Dial* was the arbiter of culture for Chicagoans until it moved to New York City in 1918.

Gilded Age Chicago was home to *Little Corporal* (1865–1875), the first widely read national children's magazine. *Carl Pretzel's National Weekly* (1872–1893) was a humorous magazine written in a German-English dialect that featured serious social and political commentary. The *Arkansaw Traveler,* born in Little Rock but published in Chicago from 1887 to 1916, was one of the most popular humor magazines in the country. The *Chap-Book* (1894–1898) was the first Chicago magazine to publish quality POETRY. *American Field* began as a hunting and fishing magazine in 1874 before it turned to purebred sporting dogs.

Alliance (1873–1882) and *Ram's Horn* (1890–1910) were the most popular of hundreds of religious titles produced in the city. *Alarm; A Socialistic Weekly* (1878–1886), the leading English-language ANARCHIST journal in the United States, was produced in Chicago by Albert R. Parsons, one of the HAYMARKET anarchists. Chicagoans also produced a variety of technical, industrial, and trade publications which remained in print, although many are published elsewhere, at the beginning of the twenty-first century, including *American Printer* (1883), *Railway Track and Structures* (1884), *Boxboard Containers* (1892), *Rock Products* (1896), and *Telephony* (1901).

Chicago has been home to some of the most influential professional magazines in the nation. The *Journal of the American Medical Association,* now *JAMA,* began in Chicago in 1883. From a monthly of official proceedings, it became the world's most-read medical journal. Other such Chicago-based journals have included *Archives of Dermatology* (1882), *Journal of the American Osteopathic Association* (1901), the American Library Association's *Booklist* (1905), and *Journal of the American Dental Association* (1913).

In the twentieth century, the *International Socialist Review* (1900–1918), edited by A. M. Simons, published nearly all of the leading SOCIALISTS during their heyday. The religious *Moody Monthly* began as the *Institute Tie* in 1900. Chicago's literary renaissance was inspired by at least three magazines. The *Friday Literary Review* (1909–1916) was in reality a weekly newspaper supplement, but its editor, Floyd Dell, set a new standard for Chicago criticism. Harriet Monroe founded *Poetry: A Magazine of Verse* in 1912. Inspired by the *Chap-Book,* it introduced Carl Sandburg, Edgar Lee Masters, T. S. Eliot, Ezra Pound, Marianne Moore, William Carlos Williams, and other notable poets to Americans. Margaret Anderson's *Little Review* (1914–1929) was more sensationalistic than *Poetry,* introducing OAK PARK native Ernest Hemingway and James Joyce's *Ulysses* to Americans. Its serialization led U.S. postal authorities to seize four issues of the magazine and to convict Anderson and her associate editor, Jane Heap, on obscenity charges.

Other Chicago magazines have been equally unconventional. Arnold Gingrich and Alfred Smart launched *Esquire* as an oversized, slick men's fashion magazine in 1933. Its cosmopolitan style, humor, and drawings of scantily clad women led the U.S. Post Office to withdraw *Esquire*'s second-class mailing privilege during World War II. That act resulted in a landmark 1946 U.S. Supreme Court decision limiting postal censorship. Chicago native and one-time *Esquire* employee Hugh M. Hefner invented the centerfold and helped inspire the 1960s sexual revolution with *Playboy,* which first appeared in Chicago in 1953.

U.S. Catholic was founded in Chicago in 1935. *Ebony,* the world's leading black magazine, was a 1945 offshoot of *Negro Digest* (1942). Patterned after the original *Life, Ebony* was designed by publisher John H. Johnson to counteract negative black stereotypes prominent in white publications. With the smaller-sized *Jet,* introduced in 1951, and other titles, Johnson Publications was reaching half of all AFRICAN AMERICAN adults at the end of the twentieth century. The *Bulletin of the Atomic Scientists* was born over concern for the post–World War II nuclear arms race, in the cafeteria of the Stineway Drugstore on 57th Street near the UNIVERSITY OF CHICAGO in 1945. It has supported international cooperation and opposed government secrecy but remains best known for its Doomsday Clock, the universal symbol of the nuclear age.

Chicago, the metropolitan magazine for the Chicago area, was founded by Maurice English in 1954. The politically influential *Chicago Reporter* was founded by John A. McDermott in 1972 and funded by the Community Renewal Society, an agency of the United Church of Christ. *Crain's Chicago Business,* which chronicles local BUSINESS and labor, first appeared in 1978. *O, The Oprah Magazine* debuted in 2000 as part of a trend toward individual celebrity magazines. Prominent Chicago-based Internet magazines included *ePrairie, I-Street,* the *May Report,* and *Screen Magazine.*

Richard Junger

See also: Agricultural Journals; Journalism; Literary Careers; Literary Cultures; Literary Images of Chicago; Religion, Chicago's Influence on; Television, Talk

Further reading: Andrews, Clarence A. *Chicago in Story: A Literary History.* 1982. • *Gale Directory of Publications and Broadcast Media.* Previously known as *Ayer Directory of Publications* and *Rowell's American Newspaper Directory.* Various editions, 1869–2000. • Scott, Franklin W. *Newspapers and Periodicals of Illinois, 1814–1879.* 1910.

Wrigley and Tribune buildings, 1959. Photographer: Unknown. Source: Chicago Historical Society.

Magnificent Mile. Chicago's North Michigan Avenue, one of the city's most prestigious commercial and residential thoroughfares, extends northward from the LOOP to Oak Street and the Drake Hotel. Named the Magnificent Mile in the 1940s by developer Arthur Rubloff, it includes the Wrigley Building, Tribune Tower, London Guarantee Building, Palmolive Building, and the John Hancock Center.

The Magnificent Mile was proposed in Daniel Burnham's 1909 *Plan of Chicago,* and constructed in the 1920s. The avenue replaced the former Pine Street, which was lined with warehouses and factory buildings near the river, and large mansions and rowhouses as it passed through the neighborhoods of McCormickville and STREETERVILLE. Its most famous monuments, the Water Tower and Pumping Station, are among the oldest structures in Chicago.

Buildings constructed on the avenue during the economic boom of the 1920s were characterized by historicist architectural styles that ranged from Beaux-Arts classicism and Gothic revival to vertical-style modernism. As the buildings soared to new and unprecedented heights, each with a different stylistic elaboration and tower profile, there evolved a new definition of urban context and design compatibility.

A renewed surge of development occurred in the late 1940s after the GREAT DEPRESSION and war years amid escalating property values, growing rental demands, and liberalized ZONING laws that allowed for even greater building heights. Much of the interest in the avenue was due to a strategic marketing campaign initiated by Rubloff, who proposed a plan by the architectural firm Holabird & Root for the CONSTRUCTION of new buildings, the renovation of many existing ones, the addition of a park, and a more efficient traffic and PARKING system. Rubloff and a New York partner, William Zeckendorf, bought or gained management control of much of the property along the avenue, still at Depression-level prices, and proceeded to develop and promote it as the most prestigious address in the city, a distinction it continues to hold today.

John W. Stamper

See also: Architecture: The City Beautiful; Burnham Plan; Near North Side, Retail Geography; Shopping Districts and Malls

Further reading: Burnham, Daniel H., and Edward H. Bennett. *Plan of Chicago.* 1909. • Condit, Carl W. *Chicago, 1910–29: Building, Planning, and Urban Technology.* 1973. • Stamper, John W. *Chicago's North Michigan Avenue: Planning and Development 1900–1930.* 1991.

Mail car in service between 1895 and 1915 from Munn Post Office to local post offices on Clark, Madison, and Milwaukee routes. Photographer: Unknown. Source: Chicago Historical Society.

Mail Delivery. Government mail delivery in Chicago began in 1831 with the appointment of a FUR TRADER as the first postmaster. Prior to that time, letters and NEWSPAPERS had occasionally found their way to the military post at FORT DEARBORN, carried by military couriers on a route that linked Fort Dearborn with Fort Wayne, Indiana, and Green Bay, Wisconsin. In 1836, mail contractors instituted stagecoach service, taking advantage of postal subsidies to encourage passenger travel. The following year, the Chicago post office became a distribution center—testimony to the rapid expansion of the settlement and to its growing importance in the national postal network.

The local post office in the early republic was a beehive of activity. Here the leading men of the city met to read the newspaper, secure up-to-date market information, and discuss the affairs of the day. During the 1850s, private mail carriers supplemented the limited delivery facilities that the government provided. Yet most postal patrons had no choice but to visit the post office in person to pick up their mail. This changed in 1864, with the inauguration of free city delivery—and, with it, the modern postman.

Throughout the nineteenth century, the distribution of postal jobs and contracts was a major form of political PATRONAGE. Postmasterships were routinely awarded to newspaper editors with close ties to the party in power. During the CIVIL WAR, for example, the Chicago postmaster was John Locke Scripps, a founder of the *Chicago Tribune* and the author of a campaign biography of Abraham Lincoln.

Chicagoans figured prominently in the transfer of mail sorting from distribution centers to moving RAILROAD cars, an INNOVATION known as "railway mail." In 1864, Chicago postal administrator George B. Armstrong established a railway mail train on the route between Chicago and Clinton, Iowa. Armstrong had been anticipated in certain respects by William A. Davis, an assistant postmaster in St. Joseph, Missouri. Yet Armstrong got the credit and was soon appointed the first superintendent of the Railway Mail Service, a key element in the late-nineteenth-century communications INFRASTRUCTURE.

Chicago long remained the hub of the nation's railway mail network. To speed the movement of information across the continent, George S. Bangs instituted a special "Fast Mail" train in 1875 between New York and Chicago that was one of the technological marvels of the age. Bangs succeeded Armstrong as railway mail superintendent; like Armstrong, he had worked previously in the Chicago post office. A milestone in postal sorting occurred in 1924 with the construction in the city of an enormous railway mail terminal, hailed as the largest of its kind in the world.

Mass marketers such as Sears and Montgomery Ward relied on the Chicago post office to transmit their catalogs and magazine ADVERTISEMENTS. With the establishment in 1913 of parcel post, mass marketers also came to depend on it to transmit their goods. In this way, the Chicago post office—and, more broadly, the federal government—played a direct, enduring, and indispensable role in Chicago's economy.

Airmail service between New York and Chicago began in 1918. By the 1920s, it was possible, for an extra fee, to send a letter by air from Chicago to most of the major urban centers in the country. For several years, Chicago-bound airmail pilots landed at an airfield in suburban MAYWOOD. Early airmail pilots included Katherine Stinson, a female barnstormer celebrated for her daring and showmanship. By far the best known of these

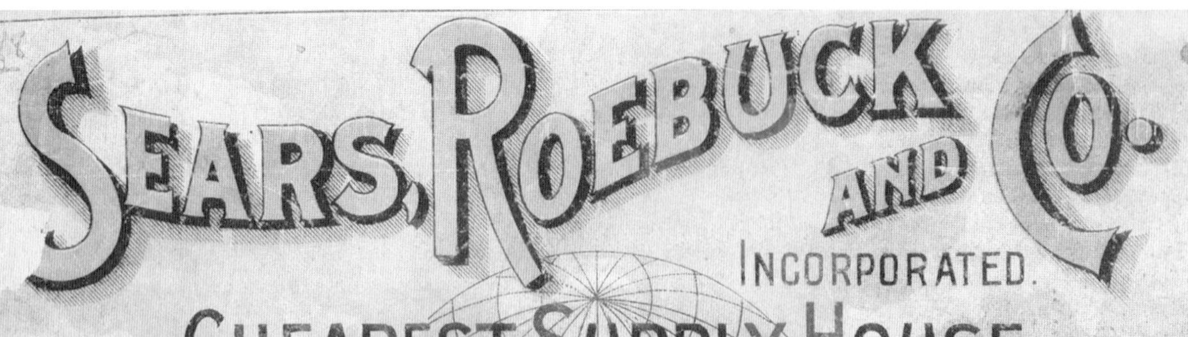

INCORPORATED.

CHEAPEST SUPPLY HOUSE ON EARTH

OUR TRADE REACHES AROUND THE WORLD

AUTHORIZED AND INCORPORATED UNDER THE LAWS OF ILLINOIS WITH A CAPITAL AND SURPLUS OF $ 450.000.00 PAID IN FULL.

REFERENCE BY SPECIAL PERMISSION
METROPOLITAN NAT'L BANK, CHICAGO
BANK OF COMMERCE "
NAT'L BANK OF THE REPUBLIC "
GERMAN EXCHANGE BANK, N. Y.

CONSUMERS GUIDE

CATALOGUE
No. 107

78 TO 96 FULTON
73 TO 87 DESPLAINES
AND 13 TO 31 W[illegible]MAN STREET.

CHICAGO [illegible]L, U.S.A.

aerial pioneers was the young Charles Lindbergh, who worked as an airmail pilot on the Chicago–St. Louis route prior to his celebrated solo flight across the Atlantic.

For most of the past century, the Chicago post office has been, along with the post office in New York, one of the busiest in the country. In the 1890s, it processed one-sixth of the nation's mail. By 1905, it employed 8,000 clerks and 1,800 letter carriers. The office has long furnished employment to large numbers of AFRICAN AMERICANS, who made up 65 percent of the workforce in 1966. In that year, Henry W. McGee became the first African American to be appointed Chicago postmaster, capping a 37-year career in the postal service.

The first Chicago post office was located in a store near the CHICAGO RIVER in the vicinity of Fort Dearborn. The first building to be designed specifically as a post office was completed in 1860; it burned in the Great FIRE OF 1871. Between 1879 and 1896, the post office was housed in an imposing government office building in the then fashionable Second Empire style. In 1905, it moved into an even more monumental Beaux-Arts edifice. Long a Chicago landmark, this building was hailed at the time of its construction as one of the largest and most expensive structures ever erected in the city. It was demolished in 1965, 33 years after the post office had moved out.

For much of the twentieth century, the Chicago post office was the largest postal distribution center in the world. At times, sorting methods failed to keep up with demand. In October 1966, a sudden increase in mail volume shut down the office for three weeks, delaying the delivery of 10 million pieces of mail. This notorious episode triggered a congressional investigation and hastened a full-scale reorganization of the postal system, which culminated with the establishment of the U.S. Postal Service in 1971.

Richard R. John

See also: Mail Order; Public Buildings in the Loop; Telegraph; Telephony

Further reading: Armstrong, George B., Jr., ed. *The Beginnings of the True Railway Mail Service and the Work of George B. Armstrong in Founding It.* 1906. • *Chicago's Main Post Office Building: The World's Largest.* Typewritten pamphlet, Collectors Club of Chicago. 1974. • Karlen, Harvey M., ed. *Chicago Postal History.* 1970.

Mail Order. Mail-order retailing became a big BUSINESS in Chicago. During the half century that followed the establishment of a mail-order company by Aaron Montgomery Ward in 1872, Chicago companies dominated the business of selling directly to consumers across the country by using catalogs and deliveries through the mail. Montgomery Ward and Sears, both based in Chicago, were the leaders of the early mail-order industry and became giant enterprises through catalog sales long before they began to open retail stores. Even after the 1920s, when the growth of the mail-order business slowed, Chicago companies continued to stand among its leaders. By the end of the twentieth century, when Wards went out of business entirely and Sears no longer issued giant catalogs, the city's mail-order industry was no longer the precocious adolescent it had been in 1900. Nevertheless, Chicago remained home to several leading companies in an evolving but still important sector of the economy.

Montgomery Ward & Co., the world's first giant mail-order enterprise, started in Chicago just after the FIRE OF 1871. Aaron Montgomery Ward, a native of New Jersey, arrived in the city just after the CIVIL WAR. He soon found a job with Field, Palmer & Leiter, the dry-goods WHOLESALER and retailer that would become Marshall Field & Co. Ward left town to work as a salesman in St. Louis and the South, but he soon returned. In 1872, when he was 28, he opened his own business. Ward's company tried to convince rural consumers to buy a variety of goods (including CLOTHING, FURNITURE, and HARDWARE) through the mail. It turned out that many farm families were willing and able to do so, especially after Ward initiated a policy of "satisfaction guaranteed or your money back" in 1875. Among Ward's first customers were members of the Patrons of Husbandry (or Grange), an AGRARIAN organization that liked the idea of circumventing local mercantile middlemen by buying directly from Chicago. Ward advertised by sending out a catalog, which started as a single page but expanded quickly, growing to 32 pages in 1874, 152 pages in 1876, and nearly 1,000 pages by 1897. By the 1880s, the growing volume of orders from this catalog led Ward to employ over a hundred Chicagoans as clerks; by 1897, this workforce was up to over a thousand. By that time, Ward's company had become Chicago's leading user of the U.S. mails, and annual sales had ballooned to about $7 million.

The heyday of the mail-order business occurred between the 1890s and the 1910s, when it was dominated by Montgomery Ward and Sears. During this period, these companies became two of the largest business enterprises in the United States. Wards, which opened several mail-order branches across the country during the first part of the twentieth century, was employing over seven thousand men and women in the Chicago area by 1910. By 1913, Wards was selling about $40 million worth of goods per year. Even more astounding than the rapid growth of Wards was the rise of Sears. The firm of Sears, Roebuck & Co., which settled in Chicago in 1895, was the creation of a Minnesotan named Richard W. Sears. After getting his start in the 1880s by selling watches through the mail, Sears (whose partner Alvah C. Roebuck started as a watch repairman) established a general mail-order company along the lines of Wards. Only a few years after its birth, Sears overtook Wards as the leading mail-order company. Like Wards, Sears issued giant catalogs and succeeded in attracting orders for a variety of goods from hundreds of thousands of rural consumers. By 1905, Sears had about nine thousand employees, and its annual sales approached $50 million. Much of Sears's success was overseen by Julius Rosenwald, who became a partner in the company in 1895 and became its president after Richard Sears retired in 1909. By 1914, when Sears had branches in Dallas and Seattle in addition to its central operation in Chicago, the company's annual mail-order sales had surpassed $100 million.

By the early part of the twentieth century, the mail-order retailing business—led by the Chicago giants—had become a major sector of the American economy, through which millions of rural consumers purchased a variety of goods. This development, which was part of a general trend in which commodity consumption by individuals and households was taking on greater economic and cultural significance, was both embraced and resisted. By 1919, Americans were buying over $500 million worth of goods a year from mail-order companies (roughly half of this business went to Wards and Sears alone). The millions of bulky mail-order catalogs sent from Chicago to points around the country had become important cultural documents, with significance that went beyond the purely economic. Particularly in rural areas, which were still home to half of the American population as late as 1920, the catalogs served not only as a marketing tool, but also as school readers, almanacs, symbols of abundance and progress, and objects of fantasy and desire. For many consumers, the kind of mail-order retailing pioneered by Wards and Sears offered a wider variety of goods (which ranged from the smallest items to entire houses), more generous credit terms, and lower prices than they could get from local merchants. Farmers' groups, which tended to favor the bypassing of economic intermediaries, were supporters of the mail-order business from the beginning. Local merchants, on the other hand, fought the national mail-order houses in both the economic and political arenas. Between the 1890s and the 1910s, U.S. postal policy became a battleground for retailers. The adoption of rural free delivery in 1898 and parcel post in 1913, both of which were enacted by Congress over the objections of local retailers and their allies, represented victories for the mail-order business and for Chicago.

The front cover of this 1898 Sears, Roebuck & Co. catalog celebrated its financial strength, its worldwide reach, and the products and regions on which the firm primarily depended for its business. Source: Chicago Historical Society.

Wards and Sears were not the only Chicago companies running successful mail-order enterprises during the early twentieth century. The Hartman Company, which sold FURNITURE by mail out of its central depot on Wentworth Avenue, filled about $13 million in orders per year by the early 1920s. Another Chicago furniture dealer that would eventually become one of the most important firms in the mail-order industry was Spiegel. This company's founder, the GERMAN-born Joseph Spiegel, started a home furnishings company in Chicago just after the Civil War. In 1904, Joseph and his son Arthur decided to move into mail order. By 1929, the Spiegel family's company (which by then sold women's clothing as well as furniture) was selling over $20 million in goods per year through the mail. A strategy of generous CONSUMER CREDIT, low prices, and high volume allowed Spiegel to accomplish the remarkable feat of expanding its operations during the GREAT DEPRESSION.

During the 1920s, facing slower growth in sales the Chicago mail-order giants decided to move into a new form of retailing by opening large numbers of stores around the country. Catalog sales continued, but Sears and Wards soon ranked among the world's leading chain stores. Led by Sears chief Robert E. Wood, this change represented a massive transfer of capital from mail-order to brick-and-mortar retailing. By 1929, only five years after opening its first store, Sears had over three hundred stores around the country; Wards had about five hundred. By the beginning of the 1930s, mail order was no longer the primary concern of the Chicago giants, which continued to grow and continued to stand among the country's leading companies.

During the second half of the twentieth century, the original Chicago mail-order giants and their catalog operations faltered, but other local companies prospered in what continued to be a major industry. By the 1970s, when the mail-order business accounted for about a third of U.S. postal revenues, most catalog customers lived in urban areas. By this time, the volume of Sears's annual mail-order business was about $3 billion, and that of Wards was close to $1 billion. But these mail-order sales (as well as those at the companies' stores) were no longer very profitable. During the 1980s and 1990s, both Wards and Sears stopped issuing their big catalogs. The death of Wards in 2000 was a final sign that the age of the Chicago mail-order giants was over. At the same time, however, the American mail-order business was expanding, and more specialized catalog firms in Chicago stood among its leaders. Spiegel, which in 1953 had chosen to pursue a different path from Sears and Wards by abandoning its retail stores, continued to operate out of headquarters in the Chicago area, where it employed about 4,000 local residents during the 1970s. In 1988, Spiegel acquired the "Eddie Bauer" retail stores and mail-order brand. By the 1990s, the company had about 20,000 employees worldwide and did over $3 billion in annual sales. Other leading mail-order specialists based in the Chicago region during the late twentieth century included Hammacher Schlemmer, the Quill Corporation, and the Reliable Corporation, which together sold hundreds of millions of dollars' worth of office supplies and equipment. At the opening of the twenty-first century, as some old mail-order catalogs were being replaced or supplemented with electronic versions, the city continued to be a leading hub in the industry.

Mark R. Wilson

See also: Clerical Workers; Global Chicago; Innovation, Invention, and Chicago Business; Philanthropy; Printing

Further reading: Emmet, Boris, and John E. Jeuck. *Catalogues and Counters: A History of Sears, Roebuck and Company.* 1950. • Rips, Rae Elizabeth. "An Introductory Study of the Mail Order Business in American History, 1872–1914." M.A. thesis, University of Chicago. 1938. • Smalley, Orange A., and Frederick D. Sturdivant. *The Credit Merchants: A History of Spiegel, Inc.* 1973.

Mail-order Housing. *See* Housing, Mail-order

Malaysians. Malaysians have been migrating to Chicago since the 1970s for occupational and educational opportunities. The first major wave of Malaysian students in the early 1970s was precipitated by political and economic tensions at home. Malaysians sought educational opportunities in the United States and other nations, forming small communities in the Midwest and larger ones on the West Coast and in New York. Chicago-area UNIVERSITIES continued to draw Malaysian students throughout the 1980s and 1990s as Malaysia developed economically, and some students found jobs with American companies and remained in the United States for a few years before returning to Malaysia. Malaysia's economic downturn in 1997 made study abroad more difficult, and the number of students declined. Professionals in technology fields, many of whom received education in the United States, have transferred to Chicago through their work with large international companies or have been drawn to the area in search of work opportunities, particularly after the 1997 downturn. Community leaders estimated the Malaysian population of metropolitan Chicago in 2001 at 600–700.

Malaysian professionals and families constitute the majority of Malaysians in Chicago. Geographically spread across the city and suburbs, the Malaysian community centers around the cultural activities of the Malaysian Club. Founded in 1999 for cultural preservation and to foster social and professional ties among Malaysians, the Malaysian Club holds about five events per year. Reflecting the ethnic diversity of Malaysia itself, the club celebrates holidays associated with Malay, CHINESE, and INDIAN culture, including Chinese New Year and Malay New Year. It is also active in city cultural events and with Chicago's Asian community, participating in events like Asian Heritage Month and the Chinese New Year parade.

Malaysian students constitute a separate and distinct group in metropolitan Chicago. Although dispersed across the state, Malaysian students are brought together by the Malaysian Student Department (MSD), one of three Malaysian government offices in the United States dedicated to assisting and supervising Malaysian students. The MSD office in EVANSTON covers the entire Midwest and sponsors several events each year for students in the region. The largest events include the National Day celebration, which celebrates Malaysian independence, the Midwest Games, which are a three-day sporting competition, and Ambassador Award Night, which recognizes the academic achievements of Malaysian students. Students have also formed Malaysian Student Associations at the ILLINOIS INSTITUTE OF TECHNOLOGY and the UNIVERSITY OF CHICAGO. These organizations seek to foster social ties and cultural awareness between Malaysian students and the university community. They hold events and offer a small social community to Malaysian students within the university.

Tracy Steffes

See also: Americanization; Demography; Multicentered Chicago; Singaporeans

Malians. Although a few came as students in the 1970s, most Malians in Chicago arrived in the 1990s. Famine and economic hardship in Mali in the 1970s and 1980s, exacerbated by a political coup and school closings in 1991, sent thousands of Malians to Europe and the United States. Malians, particularly large numbers of women, were drawn to New York and Washington DC by economic and educational opportunities. The rapidly growing New York community comprised largely Malian artists and *dioula* (traders) who began to seek new markets for their goods in the early 1990s. They traveled to summer festivals and began permanently settling in new cities including Chicago, Seattle, and Philadelphia. After the first Malians moved to Chicago, a large group followed from New York in the mid-1990s also seeking economic opportunities. They have been joined by a small number of Malian graduate students on United States government-sponsored scholarships and by family members using the green-card lottery system.

While there are a small number of professionals, most Malians in Chicago work as TAXI drivers, hairbraiders, or traders of African clothing, jewelry, and goods. Many also attend school but have to work full-time to finance their education. Women far outnumber men, largely because of women's success in carving out a niche in the hairbraiding business. Malians first settled on the North Side of Chicago in the ROGERS PARK area, but most have moved to the SOUTH SIDE of the city, where some own stores. Community members in 2002 estimated approximately 200 Malians in Chicago, and the community continued to grow rapidly as people migrated from New York.

The close-knit Malian community gathers regularly for birth parties and holidays, including MUSLIM and Christian holidays as well as Malian and American holidays. Malians come together informally for Thanksgiving, American Independence Day, and Malian Independence Day (September 22), among others. In addition, the community has organized a mutual aid organization to assist members in times of financial need. The Malian Association, created in 2001, is still in the process of building a strong organization but has the support of much of the community. It holds regular monthly meetings, at which members discuss issues facing the organization and the community and make financial contributions for use in emergencies like illness or death.

Malians in Chicago are also involved with other West African communities in Chicago, sharing many cultural, ethnic, and kinship ties with IVORIANS, BENINESE, SENEGALESE, GUINEANS, and other West Africans. National boundaries in West Africa were largely imposed by colonial powers and thus do not necessarily represent sharp differences among people. Many Malians regularly attend events and meetings of other West African organizations in Chicago, and, although these groups have largely organized along national lines, there is much fluidity among the organizations and talk of forming a larger West African organization in the city.

Tracy Steffes

See also: Americanization; Demography; Multicentered Chicago

Malls. *See* Shopping Districts and Malls

Management Consulting. Management consulting has a distinguished history in Chicago. Soon after Arthur Andersen, a professor of ACCOUNTING at Northwestern University, founded his eponymous firm in 1913, Arthur Andersen & Co. began to specialize in "financial investigations," the forerunner of the modern consulting study. By 2001, when Andersen Consulting reorganized as an independent public corporation named Accenture, it was the largest consulting firm in the world, with its headquarters still in Chicago. In 1914, Edwin Booz, a recent graduate of NORTHWESTERN in psychology, founded his firm, Booz Surveys, which would eventually become the international consulting firm of BOOZ ALLEN & HAMILTON, INC. Chicago's early dominance in consulting culminated in 1926 when James O. McKinsey, a leading expert on cost accounting at the UNIVERSITY OF CHICAGO, founded James O. McKinsey & Co. In 1939, two years after McKinsey's death, the original firm split into McKinsey & Company, the New York office, and A. T. Kearney & Co., the Chicago office, managed by Andrew "Tom" Kearney. All four of these management consulting firms—Accenture, Booz Allen, McKinsey, and A. T. Kearney—remained among the largest and most influential consultancies in the world.

The historical success of Chicago's consulting firms can be explained, in large part, by Chicago's small investment BANKING community prior to World War II. Instead of employing local banking staff, New York and Boston financiers hired Chicago consultants to analyze the management of the Midwestern companies in which they planned to invest. When NEW DEAL banking legislation, in the 1930s, prohibited banks from performing internal investigations, Wall Street bankers turned instead to the Chicago consulting firms to investigate East Coast companies. By the 1940s, the consultancies from Chicago dominated the national market, and, beginning in the late 1950s, these same firms expanded into Europe with remarkable success. Other nationally known Chicago consultants from the 1940s and 1950s included George Fry (a former partner of Booz, Allen, Fry & Hamilton) and George S. May, a notorious marketer who was investigated by the Kefauver Commission for his ties to Chicago gangsters.

By the early 1960s, the three leading consulting firms in the United States—McKinsey & Company, Booz Allen & Hamilton, and Cresap, McCormick & Paget (a spin-off from Booz Allen)—did more business in New York than Chicago. Their Chicago roots, however, were memorialized in the Cresap Laboratory and the Allen Center at Northwestern University. Chicago's industrial strength and its distance from Wall Street nurtured the development of consulting expertise that came to dominate the international market for managerial advice.

Christopher McKenna

See also: Business of Chicago; Innovation, Invention, and Chicago Business

Further reading: Higdon, Hal. *The Business Healers.* 1969. • McKenna, Christopher D. "The Origins of Modern Management Consulting." *Business and Economic History* 24.1 (1995). • O'Shea, James, and Charles Madigan. *Dangerous Company: The Consulting Powerhouses and the Businesses They Save and Ruin.* 1997.

Manhattan, IL, Will County, 37 miles SW of the Loop. Construction of the ILLINOIS & MICHIGAN CANAL after 1836, the Illinois Central RAILROAD in 1851, and a railroad stop in 1879 drew laborers to Manhattan (especially IRISH immigrants). In 1886, the village incorporated so that it could license SALOONS. The population of 1,117 in 1960 grew steadily to 3,330 in 2000.

Erik Gellman

See also: Transportation; Will County

Manhattan Project. The Manhattan Project, formally constituted in August 1942, was the code name for the federally funded research program to develop the atomic bomb. Fearing potential weapons applications of atomic research underway in Nazi Germany, President Franklin D. Roosevelt, in October 1939, authorized study on the feasibility of atomic weapons. Much of the theoretical research for the Manhattan Project was conducted at the Metallurgical Laboratory (Met Lab) at the UNIVERSITY OF CHICAGO, and at an affiliated site in the Western suburbs which would become the ARGONNE NATIONAL LABORATORY.

The Chicago Met Lab served as the hub of the nationwide Metallurgical Project, which was commissioned to study atomic theory and, if possible, to build a prototype atomic reactor. Under the leadership of Arthur H. Compton and Enrico Fermi, the Met Lab team built, and on December 2, 1942, successfully operated, the first atomic reactor, CP-1 (Chicago Pile-1), in an abandoned squash court under the grandstands of the since demolished Stagg Field at the University of Chicago. In February 1943 CP-1 was dismantled and rebuilt, as CP-2, at the more isolated Argonne site in LEMONT. The CP-2 experiments yielded continued technical assistance in the development of the bomb, which occurred mostly at other Manhattan Project sites in Hanford, Washington; Oak Ridge, Tennessee; and Los Alamos, New Mexico.

Once CP-1 had demonstrated the validity of theories that made the atomic bomb possible, the U.S. Army Brig. Gen. Leslie Groves took full command of the Manhattan Project in September 1942. The first successful detonation of an atomic weapon occurred in July 1945 near Alamogordo, New Mexico.

The Met Lab scientists attempted to influence postwar uses of atomic energy, both prior to and following the bombings of Hiroshima and Nagasaki. Before the close of WORLD WAR II, Met Lab committees led by Chicago scientists Zay Jeffries and James Franck attempted to warn government officials of the dangers of a postwar atomic arms race and the disastrous consequences of atomic warfare. At the close of World War II, Met Lab scientists including John Simpson and Eugene Rabinowitch founded the Atomic Scientists of Chicago and the monthly *Bulletin of the Atomic Scientists* in a continued effort to influence government policy regarding atomic energy and weapons.

Sean J. LaBat

See also: Fermilab; Innovation, Invention, and Chicago Business

Further reading: Hewlett, Richard G., and Oscar G. Anderson. *The New World: A History of the United States Atomic Energy Commission,* vol. 1, *1939–1946*. 1962. • Rhodes, Richard. *Making of the Atomic Bomb.* 1986. • Smith, Alice Kimball. *A Peril and a Hope: The Scientists' Movement in America, 1945–47*. 1965.

Manufacturing District, Central. *See* Central Manufacturing District

Maple Park, IL, Kane County, 50 miles W of the Loop. Several heated debates over incorporation culminated in the establishment of the town of Lodi in 1865. In 1880, the town changed its name to Maple Park. In 2000 Maple Park remained a small town of 765 residents on the border of KANE and DeKalb counties.

Erik Gellman

See also: Metropolitan Growth

Mapmaking and Map Publishing. Maps used by early Chicagoans were either the few manuscript maps on file at the local land office and courthouse, a few circulating hand-drawn copies, or printed maps imported from the east. Actual map PRINTING and publishing in Chicago before midcentury was highly intermittent, the first effort being Juliette Kinzie's sketch *Chicago in 1812,* which appeared in her *Narrative of the Massacre at Chicago* (1844). By 1853 the arrival of lithographers Henry Acheson and Edward Mendel served to anchor the BUSINESS firmly in the booming metropolis. From then on, maps were routinely manufactured as well as compiled and sold in Chicago itself, although maps published in the East continued to dominate the trade until after the CIVIL WAR.

Booksellers David B. Cooke, the Burleys, and Keen & Lee published maps in the mid-1850s, often in collaboration with Mendel or one of the other Chicago lithographers. Rufus Blanchard, who opened his Chicago Map Store in 1854, quickly entered the business of mapmaking and publishing, which he pursued until his death 50 years later. In the decade from 1861 to 1871, map publishers increased from four to six, and specialized services like map coloring and map finishing came to be separately advertised. The prolific Charles Shober joined the ranks of lithographers, and Warner and Higgins (later Warner and Beers) established their county atlas business in 1869.

Map publishing became even more specialized after the fire, a trend symbolized by the Lakeside Building, completed in 1873, which located several firms involved in all aspects of mapmaking under one roof. With the addition of Higgins, Belden & Co. and Alfred T. Andreas to the county and state atlas trade, Chicago became the premier subscription publishing center in the country, outstripping Philadelphia in cartographic output. Using newer printing techniques, George F. Cram & Co. (established 1869) and RAND MCNALLY & Co. (established 1868) turned out millions of reference atlases in a range of prices that radically loosened the New York grip on this market.

Between 1880 and the end of the century, the number of map and atlas PUBLISHERS in Chicago actually decreased from 11 to 10, but output soared. George A. Ogle emerged in the 1880s as a spirited successor to Alfred Andreas in county atlas PUBLISHING, continuing in this line until the 1920s. In the twentieth century, the leading figure in Chicago cartography has been Rand McNally & Co., also the nation's largest private mapmaker. After playing a pioneering role in the establishment of the automobile road map and road atlas in the years after World War I, Rand McNally dominated that branch of mapmaking until the demise of the promotional oil-company road map in the 1970s. Chicago also played a leading role in the production of globes, with Cram, Rand McNally, and later the Weber Costello Company and Replogle Globes all becoming major national producers.

Michael P. Conzen
Robert W. Karrow, Jr.

See also: Business of Chicago; Graphic Design; Motoring; Newberry Library

Further reading: Conzen, Michael P., ed. *Chicago Mapmakers: Essays on the Rise of the City's Map Trade.* 1984.

Mapping Chicago. The place name Chicago first appeared on French printed maps of North America in the 1680s, as "Riv[ier] Chekagou," "Portages de Chekagou," and "F[ort] de Chekogou." By the eighteenth century, most maps of North America showed a place called Chicago. The *New Map of the Western Parts of Virginia . . .* (1778), by the English Captain Thomas Hutchins, noted "River Chikago, Indian village and fort at the entrance."

Large-scale mapping of the Chicago region began with the surveys of the public lands in northeastern Illinois by the United States General Land Office. Besides marking the lines of the mile-square sections (which later became the routes of major streets and roads) these plats show watercourses and the extent of prairie and woodland. The first plat map of township 39 N., range 14 E., the six-mile square including the heart of Chicago, was surveyed in 1822. It shows FORT DEARBORN and cultivated land at what is now State and Madison.

In 1830 James Thompson surveyed and drew the first plat for the proposed town of Chicago. Thompson's original manuscript map and copies made from it directed the development of the city, dictating the layout of streets and the division of the land into saleable parcels. As the infant city underwent a land boom in the 1830s, printed elaborations of Thompson's basic map appeared—the first, by Joshua Hathaway, in 1834 and the second, a little later that year, by John S. Wright.

There followed a number of maps and plats of the city and additions, fueled by rapid population growth. Henry Hart's *City of Chicago,* published in 1853, was the largest and most detailed map up to that time and shows the footprints of individual buildings. The first land-ownership map of COOK COUNTY, including insets of dozens of outlying communities, was prepared by Walter Flower in 1861.

The Great FIRE OF 1871 and the rapid rebuilding of the city that followed were an additional impetus to city mapping, and in the last quarter of the century, city atlases began to appear. The earliest of these, *Peltzer's Atlas of the City of Chicago* (1872), shows STREETS, RAILROADS, property lines, and lot numbers in all subdivisions. Similar REAL-ESTATE atlases were published by H. R. Page (1879), Elisha Robinson (1886), and Greeley and Carlson (1884 and 1891–92). Fire INSURANCE atlases, which show the outlines of all buildings, name businesses, and are color coded to show CONSTRUCTION materials, made their Chicago debut in 1877 with Charles Rascher's *Fire Insurance Map of Chicago.* The Sanborn-Perris Map Company issued its first volume of Chicago fire insurance maps in 1894; more than 50 volumes had appeared by 1951, and updating of the printed maps by means of paste-on revisions continued into the 1970s.

The city's official mapping agency is now the Maps and Plats Unit in the Department of Transportation. The Department of Public Works had a separate department or bureau of maps at least as early as 1876.

Robert W. Karrow, Jr.

See also: Chicago Studied: Social Scientists and Their City; Northwest Ordinance

Further reading: Cobb, David A., and Marsha Selmer. *Illinois . . . Including Maps of Chicago.* Checklist of Printed Maps of the Middle West to 1900, vol. 4. 1981. • Library of Congress. *Fire Insurance Maps in the Library of Congress.* 1981.

Marathon. *See* Chicago Marathon

Marengo, IL, McHenry County, 56 miles NW of the Loop. Originally called Pleasant Grove, the village was settled along the Galena–Chicago Road after 1835 and prospered with the coming of the Galena & Chicago Union RAILROAD in 1851. An important commercial center for area farmers, the community incorporated as a village in 1857 and as a city in 1893. Slow but steady growth brought the population to 6,355 by 2000.

Craig L. Pfannkuche

See also: McHenry County

Further reading: *McHenry County in the Twentieth Century, 1968–1994.* McHenry County Historical Society. 1994. • Nye, Lowell A., ed. *McHenry County, Illinois, 1832–1968.* 1968.

Markham, IL, Cook County, 20 miles S of the Loop. Comprising five square miles, Markham is bordered by POSEN and MIDLOTHIAN to the north, HARVEY to the east, HAZEL CREST and COUNTRY CLUB HILLS to the south, and OAK FOREST to the west. Markham shares a history with all of these communities, especially Harvey, which contains the Markham Yards of the ILLINOIS CENTRAL RAILROAD.

Interstate 57 traverses the community, northeast to southwest, along a line which has both geological and historic significance. Markham is located on a lake plain formed by glacial Lake Chicago (12,000 BP). The Tinley Moraine follows the line of Interstate 57. NATIVE AMERICANS had long lived on the Tinley Moraine. Archaeologists have investigated the Oak Forest site, which was occupied in the 1600s.

Interstate 57 also runs along the route of an Indian Boundary Line. The POTAWATOMI ceded the lands northwest of this line to the United States government in the 1816 Treaty of St. Louis.

YANKEE farmers arrived in the mid-1830s, followed in the 1840s and 1850s by GERMAN and IRISH immigrants. The settlers bypassed the marshy areas which today are Markham's most celebrated natural features: the Old Indian Boundary Prairies. German immigrants planted 60 pine seedlings from the Black Forest, one of which survived until 1985 along the Old Indian Boundary Line, becoming the Lone Pine TREE symbol on Markham's city seal.

Both the Illinois Central and the Rock Island RAILROADS run near Markham, enabling farmers to ship their produce by rail. In the early twentieth century, new residents were drawn by railroad and industrial jobs found in northern neighbor Harvey. They built houses and incorporated Markham in 1925, naming their town in honor of Charles H. Markham, then president of the ILLINOIS CENTRAL RAILROAD.

AFRICAN AMERICANS moved into Markham during the second half of the twentieth century, as they took up the industrial jobs which European immigrants had held earlier in the century. By the 2000 census, 80 percent of Markham's population of 12,620 was African American, and 84 percent of homes were owner-occupied.

Dave Bartlett

See also: Economic Geography; Ecosystem Evolution; Glaciation

Further reading: "Featuring Bremen Township." *Where the Trails Cross* 7.1 (Fall 1976): 1–3. • Bluhm, Elaine A., and Gloria J. Fenner. "The Oak Forest Site." In *Chicago Area Archaeology,* 2nd ed., ed. Elaine Blum, 1983, 139–161. • *History of Oak Forest.* 1972.

Marquette Park. Residents of CHICAGO LAWN often refer to their neighborhood as Marquette Park, after the 300-acre park at Marquette Road (6700 South) and California Avenue.

Erik Gellman

See also: Community Areas; Park Districts

Further reading: Pacyga, Dominic A., and Ellen Skerrett. *Chicago, City of Neighborhoods: Histories and Tours.* 1986.

Mary and Leigh Block Museum. Established in 1980, the Mary and Leigh Block Museum of Art is designed to serve NORTHWESTERN UNIVERSITY's educational goals and to make its scholarly exhibitions and interpretive programs accessible to both students and the public. Founder Leigh Block, trustee and president of the ART INSTITUTE OF CHICAGO as well as a trustee of Northwestern University, joined with his wife Mary Block to assemble one of the finest personal ART collections in the United States. Elements of this collection form the basis for the permanent collection of the Block Museum, which includes over seven thousand works of art on paper, as well as monumental sculptures installed in a landscape garden environment.

The Block Museum sculpture garden, opened on June 3, 1989, was designed by Chicago architect John Vinci, whose other work includes restoration of the Stock Exchange Trading Room at the Art Institute and of the Frank Lloyd Wright studio in OAK PARK. The sculpture garden constitutes one of the Midwest's most significant groupings of modern sculpture, including such major ARTISTS as Jean Arp, Barbara Hepworth, Henry Moore, Jacques Lipchitz, and Joan Miro.

The collection of works on paper includes drawings, prints, and photographs dating from the fifteenth to the twentieth centuries. Especially notable is a large selection of contemporary prints and architectural drawings. Major Chicago-focused exhibitions have included *Second-Sight: Printmaking in Chicago, 1935–1995* (1996).

Ronne Hartfield

See also: Evanston; Smart Museum

Further reading: Mickenberg, David, ed. *BlockPoints: The Annual Journal and Report of the Mary and Leigh Block Gallery.* Vol. 1. 1993. • Silver, Larry, ed. *BlockPoints: The Annual Journal and Report of the Mary and Leigh Block Gallery.* Vol. 2. 1995.

Mary Thompson Hospital. The Chicago Hospital for Women and Children was founded in 1865 to provide medical care to indigent women and children and clinical training to women doctors.

The hospital's founder, Mary Harris Thompson, received her M.D. from the New England Female Medical College in Boston in 1863. Her first patients in Chicago were the wives, widows, and children of Union soldiers. Thompson's ability to care for them was limited by her inability to gain a hospital position. Neither of Chicago's two HOSPITALS permitted women to serve on their staffs, and one of them did not admit women patients. Thompson organized her own hospital.

The hospital depended upon the aid of wealthy Chicago women and the support of several medical men. The laywomen raised funds and managed all administrative work. The medical men became consulting physicians who aided Thompson in her medical and surgical practice. These doctors provided Thompson and her institution with the stamp of medical approval required because of a widespread prejudice against women physicians.

The hospital began training women doctors in 1871, when Thompson and William H. Byford established an affiliated medical school for women. Women medical students relied on the hospital for clinical observations and demonstrations. Graduates of the school, who seldom gained appointments in male hospitals, became interns, residents, and attending physicians in the hospital.

After Thompson's death in 1895, the hospital was renamed the Mary Thompson Hospital for Women and Children. It continued to provide otherwise unavailable clinical opportunities for medical women until 1972, when men were integrated into the staff. Financial burdens contributed to the closing of the hospital in 1988.

Eve Fine

See also: Medical Education; Women's Hospital Medical College

Further reading: Beatty, William K. "Mary Harris Thompson-Pioneer Surgeon and Hospital Founder." *Proceedings of the Institute of Medicine of Chicago* 34

(1981): 83–86. • Morantz-Sanchez, Regina Markell. *Sympathy and Science: Women Physicians in American Medicine.* 1985. • Roth Walsh, Mary. *Doctors Wanted: No Women Need Apply.* 1977.

Mass Transit. *See* Public Transportation; Rapid Transit System

Matteson, IL, Cook County, 26 miles S of the Loop. The village of Matteson is located along the METRA Electric commuter rail line and sits astride Interstate 57 and the Lincoln Highway. Although a largely residential community, the village is the site of several corporate office buildings and is home to the Lincoln Mall (1973), one of the largest shopping centers in the south suburbs.

In the mid-1850s, GERMAN settlers established the village at the junction of the recently constructed ILLINOIS CENTRAL and Michigan Central RAILROADS. They named the new community after then Illinois governor Joel Matteson. When Matteson was formally incorporated in 1889, there were fewer than 500 residents in the village, which served area farmers.

After the Second World War, Matteson grew steadily, reaching a population of 3,225 in 1960. By 1970 the village numbered 4,741, and then, with a boom underway, the population more than doubled, to 10,223 by 1980. In 2000 there were 12,928 people living in Matteson.

Population growth brought greater diversity. In 1970 the census listed only one AFRICAN AMERICAN in the community. By 1990, when the total population had climbed to 11,378 people, the 5,000 African American residents accounted for nearly half the population. In 2000, the 8,098 African American residents of Matteson outnumbered the village's white residents by nearly a two to one margin.

In the mid-1990s Matteson gained national media attention, and some notoriety, after the village board initiated an advertising campaign to actively seek new white residents so as to maintain the level of racial integration in the community. Critics noted that many of the African Americans who were moving into the community were wealthier and better educated than the white former residents. Village officials claimed that their attempts to attract white residents were simply efforts to maintain an integrated community and were similar to programs in other suburbs.

As Matteson has flourished over the last 50 years, there have been some substantial alterations in its geography. Originally platted on a 40-acre parcel near the intersection of the two rail lines, the village has grown tremendously with the ANNEXATION of several housing SUBDIVISIONS, and it now occupies more than 7 square miles of land. In 2000 there were some 4,712 housing units in the village, nearly two-thirds of them constructed in the last 30 years. Old Matteson, as the community's original center is sometimes called, has some of the feel of a traditional village, especially near Main Street and the railroad. However, most of the village's stores are located along the heavily commercialized Lincoln Highway and in two large shopping centers. In the late 1990s, Matteson officials created a "village commons" with a village hall and a bridge over Interstate 57.

Matteson is not the most exclusive of Chicago's south suburbs, but the median household income in the village is substantially higher than in either the city of Chicago or Cook County. More than 80 percent of the houses in the village are single-family. As is the case in other nearby suburbs, new houses tend to be more expensive than the smaller older residences.

Ian McGiver

See also: Shopping Districts and Malls; Suburbs and Cities as Dual Metropolis; Transportation

Further reading: Andreas, A. T. *History of Cook County, Illinois.* 1884.

Maxwell Street. For about one hundred years, Maxwell Street was one of Chicago's most unconventional BUSINESS—and residential—districts. About a mile long and located in the shadow of downtown SKYSCRAPERS, it was a place where businesses grew selling anything from shoestrings to expensive clothes.

Its immigrants arrived from several continents and many countries shortly before the turn of the century. First to come were GERMANS, IRISH, POLES, Bohemians, and, most prominently, JEWS, especially those escaping czarist Russia, Poland, and Romania. In the 1940s, Southern blacks worked in Maxwell Street's stores and entertained its crowds with Delta-style BLUES. Later, MEXICANS, KOREANS, and GYPSIES joined its teeming environment. From its own poverty-stricken homes came many famous—Arthur Goldberg, William Paley, Benny Goodman, Barney Ross—and infamous—Jake Guzik and Jack Ruby—people.

Goods on card tables and blankets competed with goods in sidewalk kiosks and stores. Sunday was its busiest day since the Jews worked on the Christian Sabbath, when stores were closed in most other parts of the city.

Merchants battled city officials to keep Maxwell Street alive despite its reputation for crime and residential overcrowding. Its eastern section was destroyed in the mid-1950s for the Dan Ryan EXPRESSWAY. In the 1980s and 1990s, virtually all of the rest was razed for athletic fields for the UNIVERSITY OF ILLINOIS AT CHICAGO. What remained of the market was moved several blocks to a place with none of the flavor of the old street.

Ira Berkow

See also: Czechs and Bohemians; Eminent Domain; Near West Side; Retail Geography; Street Peddling

Further reading: Berkow, Ira. *Maxwell Street: Survival in a Bazaar.* 1977.

May Day. *See* Haymarket and May Day

Mayors. Chicago's mayors from incorporation in 1837 through the Great FIRE OF 1871 were drawn from the upper reaches of the socioeconomic registers. Although Chicago was not old enough to have a patrician class equivalent to Boston's Back Bay Brahmins, these men were a representative sample of the social and commercial elite.

Chicago's first mayor, William B. Ogden (1837–1838), was a founding father not only of the city (because he wrote its first charter) but of the Chicago & North Western Railway, and was a principal in the nation's first transcontinental RAILROAD. He built the city's credit reputation as well as his own by keeping the city solvent during the depression of 1837. Also prominent in business was Chicago's third mayor, Benjamin Raymond, who founded the Elgin Watch Company. The city's fifth mayor, Francis Sherman, was a brick manufacturer, REAL-ESTATE investor, and a man whose wealth permitted him to retire at an early age and build the Sherman House HOTEL, a Chicago landmark. His successor, Augustus Garrett, ran an auction house and invested in real estate; his fortune was used to establish the Garrett Biblical Institute. The seventh mayor, Alson Sherman, established the first sawmill in Chicago, developed the LEMONT marble QUARRY, and

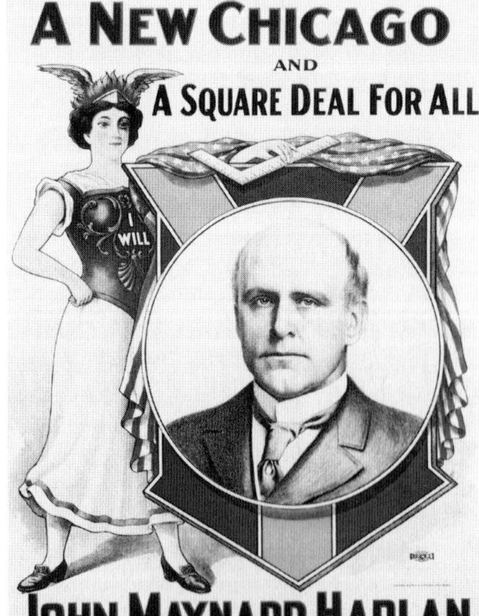

Campaign ad for mayoral candidate John Maynard Harlan,1905. Artist: Edwards, Deutsch & Heitman Litho. Source: Chicago Historical Society.

was one of the original trustees of NORTHWESTERN UNIVERSITY. One of the city's earliest MEATPACKERS, John Chapin, a New England Yankee and one of the founders of the Chicago Board of Trade, was the eighth mayor. The tenth, James Woodworth, acquired a comfortable fortune in land speculation, banking, and the milling of flour. His successor, Walter Gurnee, came from a well-to-do family and amassed a sizable fortune in his saddle and tanning business. Gurnee also founded the village of WINNETKA on land he had purchased and was at one time president of the Chicago & Milwaukee Railroad. As president of the Board of Trade, Chicago's eighteenth mayor, Julian Rumsey, was one of the primary movers behind implementing the stringent grain inspection that established Chicago's solid reputation in the national grain markets. He was also president of the Corn Exchange Bank. Even those mayors who were not part of the commercial elite ranked high in income and public recognition. Levi Boone, a descendant of Daniel Boone, and fourteenth person to occupy the mayor's chair, was first president of the Chicago Medical Society and a prosperous physician whose wealth came from canal lands and downtown real estate. Joseph Medill (1871–1873), was an owner, publisher, and editor of the CHICAGO TRIBUNE.

Mayor Medill's tempestuous administration, which included the unpopular enforcement of the SUNDAY CLOSING law, ended a period of relative tranquillity in the mayoralty and ushered in significant changes, including the "Mayor's Bill" of 1872, by which the legislature enlarged the mayor's powers of appointment. In 1875 a new city CHARTER lengthened the mayor's term from one to two years and expanded the office's powers. Because it was not clear whether the new charter extended the term of incumbent mayor Harvey Colvin, political chaos and near riots resulted when Colvin refused to give up the seat to the newly elected Thomas Hoyne in 1876. After a police cordon around City Hall prevented bloodshed, the court permitted Colvin to remain in office until a new election later that year.

The disputed mayoralty and the violent RAILROAD STRIKE OF 1877 brought about a sea change in mayoral politics as well as a shift in the social origins of its occupants. Thereafter men (and later one woman) of more humble origins began to occupy the office. The two Carter Harrisons, who served five terms each (1879–1887, 1893; and 1897–1905, 1911–1915, respectively), were not wealthy nabobs but professional politicians. GERMAN American Fred Busse (1907–1911), the first mayor to serve a four-year term, was a saloonkeeper politician and the first Chicago mayor without British ancestry. He died a pauper and bequeathed to his widow the life of a charwoman scrubbing floors to pay the rent. His successor William "Big Bill" Thompson (1915–1923, 1927–1931) practiced the politics of the "wide open town" to the delight of BOOTLEGGERS and gangsters. A mayor who accepted campaign funds from Al Capone and enriched himself from politics, Big Bill was a far cry from the civic-minded founding fathers and economic titans who ran the office in the nineteenth century.

After Thompson came a succession of plebes or former plebes such as a tanner's son, William Dever (1923–1927), who became a judicial careerist; the city's only foreign-born mayor, Anton Cermak (1931–1933), a COAL MINER and former firewood seller; sanitary district ax-man Edward Kelly, who built the KELLY-NASH MACHINE; Martin Kennelly, a self-made moving and storage company owner; and Richard J. Daley, a former stockyards cowboy out of working-class BRIDGEPORT.

Mayors began to resemble the voters more than had been the case in the nineteenth century. Whereas in the nineteenth century politics had often been a civic avocation, after the Great Fire it became a profession and a way of making of a living. Some did exceedingly well on the job. Big Bill Thompson left his widow $1.5 million in unmarked bills in his safety deposit boxes.

Although by charter Chicago government remains a "weak" mayor system, the office's powers have been strengthened over time, sometimes by formal and sometimes by extralegal methods. The mayor's authority and influence were considerably enlarged by the growth of the Kelly-Nash and Daley political MACHINE, 1933–1976. In addition, Daley took control of the city's budget from the city council, considerably enhancing his office's powers over those of the council.

Mayor Daley's death in 1976 broke a logjam of history that had slowed change in the city's governance. In 1977 Chicago picked its first non-IRISH mayor since 1933, Michael Bilandic of CROATIAN ancestry; in 1979 its first female mayor, Jane Byrne; in 1983 its first AFRICAN AMERICAN mayor, Harold Washington. The decade-long interregnum was punctuated by intensive ethnic-racial squabbling, including Chicago's "Ugly Racial Election" of 1983 and a stalemate dubbed "Council Wars" by a local comedian.

Assassination of Carter Harrison

Known as "the common man's MAYOR," Carter Harrison I (1879–1887, 1893) enjoyed riding through the city's neighborhoods mounted on his white horse and boasted that his office door was "always open." Ironically, this policy of easy availability would ultimately prove his demise.

Chicago was enjoying an unbounded period of celebrity on the evening of October 28, 1893, the night before the close of the WORLD'S COLUMBIAN EXHIBITION. Mayor Harrison's commitment to the world's fair had permitted Chicago to showcase its rise to modernity in the 20 years following the Great FIRE OF 1871. While enjoying a period of rest that evening after his dinner in the family mansion on South Ashland Avenue, the mayor was confronted by Patrick Eugene Prendergast, a deranged unemployed IRISH immigrant, embittered over failing to be appointed the city's chief attorney. Armed with a .38 caliber revolver, he shot Harrison three times at point-blank range. The mayor's wounds were fatal. Chicago was plunged into mourning. Even Clarence Darrow was unable to save Prendergast from the gallows.

Edward M. Burke

Mayor William Hale Thompson throwing first ball for the Whales, a Chicago Federal League baseball team, at Wrigley Field, 1915. Photographer: Unknown. Source: Chicago Historical Society.

Mayor Harold Washington honoring former Mayor Richard J. Daley on the 10th anniversary of Daley's death. Richard M. Daley sits to Washington's right; Abraham Lincoln Marovitz to his left. Photographer: Unknown. Source: Chicago Historical Society.

Other more substantive changes also occurred. Mayor Washington signed onto the SHAKMAN DECREES banning political hiring and firing, strengthening civil service regulations, and cutting into the vitals of the dying political machine. (Even so, "pinstripe patronage" survived the Washington years whereby a mayor can reward his political friends with consulting and vendor contracts.) Washington also opened city records by executive order and expanded contract set-asides for black and women contractors, policies that were continued by his successors.

Many of these changes have brought Chicago closer to the statutorily prescribed weak-mayor model. Nonetheless, because of tradition and practice, the Chicago mayor's office under an aggressive leader remains an office with considerable executive power, or what Chicagoans have dubbed "CLOUT."

The last mayor elected in the twentieth century, Richard M. Daley (1989–), son of Richard J., was reelected to a fifth term in February 2003 in the city's second nonpartisan election, which had replaced the partisan primary in February and general election in April. The new Daley, who carried more than 40 percent of the African American vote, was one of a new breed of pragmatic-minded mayors and built a national reputation for his leadership in school reform, with Chicago's model emulated by several other big city mayors.

Melvin G. Holli

See also: Chicago Mayors (table, p. 1001); Democratic Party; Governing the Metropolis; Government, City of Chicago; Political Culture; Republican Party

Further reading: Bradley, Donald S., and Mayer Zald. "From Commercial Elite to Political Administrators . . . Mayors of Chicago." *American Journal of Sociology* 71 (September 1965): 153–167. • Grosser, Hugo. *Chicago: A Review of Its Governmental History from 1837 to 1906*. 1906. • Holli, Melvin G., and Peter D'A. Jones, eds. *The Biographical Dictionary of American Mayors, 1820–1980*. 1981.

Mayor's Commission on Human Relations. The Mayor's Commission on Human Relations (1945 and 1946) grew out of the Mayor's Committee on Race Relations, appointed by Mayor Edward J. Kelly in 1943. Following RACE RIOTS in Detroit in 1943, the commission was established as public concern grew that Chicago could possibly be headed in the same direction. The primary responsibility of the commission was to evaluate race relations and devise ways of addressing civic concerns. The commission initially comprised a diverse and talented group of individuals that included Edwin R. Embree, president of the Julius Rosenwald Fund (a PHILANTHROPIC foundation committed to improving the conditions of AFRICAN AMERICANS and race relations); Charles S. Johnson, coauthor of the Chicago Commission on Race Relations report following the 1919 riots; Horace R. Cayton, coauthor of *Black Metropolis;* anthropologist Melville J. Herskovits; and urban sociologist Louis Wirth.

The commission attempted to develop a critical analysis of city policies and institutions. Two primary areas of concentration were the institutionalized segregation of blacks, reflected in the overcrowded SOUTH SIDE public SCHOOLS, and the lack of adequate housing for black families. The cumulative report issued in 1951, however, demonstrates that the commission became more concerned with crisis management—identifying problematic spots in the city and managing those crises that did arise—than with evaluating public policy. The commission defined "the race problem" largely as a neighborhood issue, pointing mainly to the irrational behavior of militant whites and teenage GANGS and the segregated mindset of blacks.

Charles E. Clifton

See also: Civil Rights Movements; Contested Spaces; Racism, Ethnicity, and White Identity; Urban Renewal

Further reading: *The People of Chicago: Five Year Report, 1947–51, of the Chicago Commission on Human Relations.* 1951. • *Race Relations in Chicago: Report of the Mayor's Commission on Human Relations for 1945.* 1945. • *Race Relations in Chicago: Report of the Mayor's Committee on Race Relations for 1944.* 1944.

Maywood, IL, Cook County, 11 miles W of the Loop. A planned community from the outset, Maywood lies on the west bank of the DES PLAINES RIVER, stretching from Roosevelt Road on the south to just beyond Augusta Street on the north. Maywood was originally part of a larger area known as Noyesville, named after one of Proviso Township's early settlers, who established the area's first post office in the mid-1830s.

In 1869, a group of Vermont businessmen formed the Maywood Company and purchased the village's original plat—a narrow, one-and-three-quarters-mile strip along the Des Plaines River. Company president William T. Nichols named the village after his daughter May, and immediately began subdividing the land and creating improvements necessary to "build up a neat, desirable suburb." In 1870, wide streets were laid out, 20,000 TREES were planted, and building commenced on the north side of the Chicago & North Western RAILROAD tracks, which bisected the community. In the same year, an advertisement boasted easy access to the city with regular train service, as well as a school, churches, post office, grocery store, HOTEL, and a beautiful park, as among Maywood's many amenities.

Since its incorporation as a village in 1881, Maywood's economic development has hinged on light industry, starting in 1884 with Chicago Scraper and Ditcher, a manufacturer of AGRICULTURAL MACHINERY. In 1885 Norton Can Works moved to Maywood, and by 1901 had become the American Can Company. Other industries subsequently attracted to the area located primarily within the factory district along the north side of the railroad tracks. Maywood gained a major institution in 1920 when the Edward Hines Jr. Memorial HOSPITAL was established for the care of war VETERANS. These businesses and their workers were served by excellent TRANSPORTATION, including the Chicago & North Western train (1870), electric STREET RAILWAYS (1893), and Chicago's RAPID TRANSIT SYSTEM. During the 1920s, Checkerboard Field (now Miller Meadow) provided air service.

In the 1970s several of Maywood's industries transferred out of the region, including the village's major employer, American Can Company. The village's retail base also declined, as Montgomery Ward and Sears, Roebuck DEPARTMENT STORES left the main shopping street, Fifth Avenue. Somewhat offsetting these losses, in 1969 Maywood had gained the LOYOLA UNIVERSITY Medical Center, including the Stritch School of Medicine.

In the 1990s, Maywood began to rebound from the economic decline of the previous decades. Trying to attract new industry and businesses, the village established a tax increment financing district on the former site of American Can Company, which was leveled in 1997. Economic change has been accompanied by DEMOGRAPHIC shifts, as Maywood's AFRICAN AMERICAN population increased from 3 percent in 1930 to 82 percent in 2000. Whites and Hispanics constitute 10 and 11 percent of the population, respectively, and live in the village's integrated northeastern section.

Jean Louise Guarino

See also: Cook County; Economic Geography; Metropolitan Growth; Suburbs and Cities as Dual Metropolis

Further reading: *Festival of Progress, Maywood, Illinois, Seventieth Year, September 23rd to October 1st.* 1938. Maywood Public Library, Maywood, IL. • *Maywood and Its Homes.* 1904. Maywood Public Library, Maywood, IL. • *Maywood, a Suburb of Chicago, As It Is in 1870.* 1870. Maywood Public Library, Maywood, IL.

McCook, IL, Cook County, 12 miles SW of the Loop. Permanent settlement in what is now McCook was slowed by marshy conditions and frequent flooding of the nearby DES PLAINES RIVER. The coming of RAILROADS in the 1880s spurred development. The village's name probably honors Santa Fe railroad director John James McCook.

Several QUARRIES began operating in the 1880s, and this dangerous and exhausting work attracted primarily youthful male laborers—first Eastern European immigrants, including POLES, CROATIANS, and ITALIANS, and later AFRICAN AMERICANS and MEXICAN Americans. The stone was shipped on the ILLINOIS & MICHIGAN CANAL and later on the SANITARY AND SHIP CANAL.

While the quarries continued to operate into the twentieth century, other industries began to play a role in McCook's development. In 1926 McCook incorporated as a village. In the middle 1930s the Electro-Motive Company, a subsidiary of the General Motors Corporation, opened a diesel engine plant. During WORLD WAR II, a large aluminum sheet mill provided airplane "skins," and other industries shifted to wartime production.

By 1976 McCook had over 60 manufacturing and commercial firms, and by 1999 that number had increased to 85. The McCook-Hodgkins quarry covers over six hundred acres and produces seven million tons of crushed stone per year. The 2000 population was 254.

Ronald S. Vasile

See also: Economic Geography; Water

Further reading: Wesby, Vernon, ed. *History and Progress of the Village of McCook.* 1976.

McCullom Lake, IL, McHenry County, 52 miles NW of the Loop. Beginning as a string of summer cottages along the north shore of a lake northwest of MCHENRY in the 1920s, McCullom Lake incorporated in 1955 to allow local control of lake maintenance and road improvements. The village has remained a moderate-income bedroom community, with a population of 1,038 in 2000.

Craig L. Pfannkuche

See also: McHenry County

Further reading: *McHenry County in the Twentieth Century, 1968–1994.* McHenry County Historical Society. 1994. • Nye, Lowell A., ed. *McHenry County, Illinois, 1832–1968.* 1968.

McHenry County. After the 1832 BLACK HAWK WAR, land-hungry New Englanders and western Virginians pushed out along Indian trails radiating away from Chicago in search of farm sites. To the north and northwest, they found a rolling, well-watered prairie interspersed with large oak groves. Finding access to COOK COUNTY government difficult, they petitioned for the formation of a more local county seat. The Illinois legislature approved the petition in 1836 and named the new county McHenry, after a leader of volunteers in the area during the Black Hawk War.

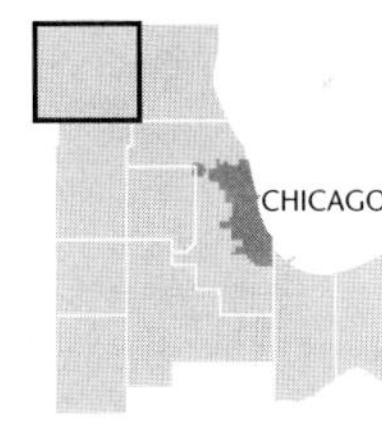

McHenry County stretched west from LAKE MICHIGAN to present-day Boone County and north from KANE COUNTY to the Wisconsin state line. Since the FOX RIVER flowed through the approximate center of the county and was easily fordable at the present site of McHenry, that village became the county seat.

The eastern side of the new county was settled earliest as most newcomers established homes along the Green Bay Trail. Farmers and speculators there found trips around numerous GLACIAL lakes and across wet prairies to McHenry too time consuming. In 1839 voters in eastern McHenry County were granted the right to form a new county (LAKE COUNTY.)

While the new boundary was supposed to be the Fox River, a survey put almost all of the river's valley in McHenry County. Although a courthouse already stood in the village of

McHenry, a more central location was demanded. In 1844 the county seat was removed to a midcounty location platted as Centerville and renamed Woodstock in 1845.

In early decades of the county's history, poor roads left residents isolated from markets. The county's most economically successful settlements (Crystal Lake, Marengo, and Richmond) were located along well-established Indian trails from Chicago. County voters established a township system of government in December 1849 to provide a better system for road taxation.

The introduction of railroads brought great changes. The Chicago & Northwestern Railroad blanketed the county. One line pushed west through Huntley and Marengo by early 1851. Two other lines were established in 1854. One ran diagonally across the county from the Fox River at Cary, reaching Harvard by 1855. The other ran north from Algonquin through the eastern McHenry County beyond Richmond. A fourth line graced the northern tier of townships by 1861. After 1900, a "Milwaukee Road" line would cross the northeastern corner of the county. Communities built in partnership with the railroad such as Harvard, Nunda (later Crystal Lake), and Cary prospered while non-rail communities such as Franklinville, Coral, Ostend, and Barreville faded from existence. Many Irish railroad laborers stayed and became farmers, cheaply shipping their produce to market. Chicago's demand for fresh milk products along with Gail Borden's milk condensing plants convinced farmers to try dairying. Railroad milk stations and cheese "factories" quickly appeared in all the county's townships.

Except for large numbers of vacationers who found the scenic Fox River relaxing, the county's population remained stable through the 1930s. World War II veterans, seeking to raise their new families away from urban settings, found the county's rail transportation perfect for commuting to city jobs. By the early 1960s, the Crystal Lake area experienced a flood of new residents. Large tracts of farmland disappeared beneath bulldozer blades and parking lots. Soon after, Algonquin, Lake in the Hills, Cary, and McHenry, all situated along the Fox River, faced similar transformations.

Shocked by this migration, farmers saw property taxes rising at a rate that made their enterprises unprofitable. Banding together with environmentally minded suburban residents, they decried the destruction of prime farmland and drew up a plan to preserve farming as a profession in the county. In 1979, the McHenry County Board adopted a land use plan with the primary goal of preserving agricultural lands. Successfully defending the program against court challenges initiated in 1980, the county strengthened the program in 1985 to preserve agricultural production in the county's western and northwestern areas.

The completion of a massive Motorola assembly plant near Harvard in 1996 shook the faith of the county's farmers that they could restrain the ever-growing pressure to expand development. Fearful that the municipal leaders of Huntley, Harvard, and Marengo would seek nonagricultural growth to pay for infrastructure modernization, McHenry County farmers have faced virtual extinction as once pastoral lands fall victim to continuing urbanization.

Craig L. Pfannkuche

See also: Annexation; Governing the Metropolis; Metropolitan Growth; Suburbs and Cities as Dual Metropolis

Further reading: *History of McHenry County, Illinois.* 1885. • *McHenry County in the Twentieth Century, 1968–1994.* McHenry County Historical Society. 1994. • Nye, Lowell A., ed. *McHenry County Illinois, 1832–1968.* 1968.

McHenry, IL, McHenry County, 46 miles NW of the Loop. In 1832 Major William McHenry led an expeditionary force through northern Illinois during the Black Hawk War. Settlement of the Fox River Valley began over the next few years, and on the river's west bank, at the site of an old Indian ford, the hamlet of McHenry developed.

The McLean, Wheeler, McCullom, and Boone families were influential in the community's early years. A sawmill, hotel, and ferryboat were in operation by 1837. Legislation creating McHenry County was passed that year, and the village served as county seat until 1844.

Gristmills started along newly dammed Boone Creek, and a wagon road entered town from the south in 1851. In 1864, the famed Riverside Hotel was built and still stands.

George Gage, who served as the region's first state senator (1854–1858), owned the lands west of the millpond, and was able to secure the route of the Fox Valley Railroad (afterward a branch of the Chicago & North Western) from Chicago in 1854. Consequently, Gagetown (later West McHenry) began to eclipse the older east side of town. Their rivalry can still be detected in the disjunct commercial pattern that characterizes McHenry.

The village incorporated in 1872. Though there were fewer than 800 inhabitants, commerce flourished. By 1876 there were seven churches and over 80 enterprises, including flour mills, harnessmakers, a pickle factory, a brewery, seven saloons, and a newspaper. The newspaper, the *McHenry Plaindealer,* was in publication from 1875 to 1985.

Over the next 50 years McHenry grew slowly. During the twenties the town became known as a resort destination. Bands played at local pavilions, trainloads of visitors arrived to tour the famous lotus beds, and summer cottages proliferated along the Fox River. A boatbuilding industry flourished; marine recreation still remains important.

With the advent of the automobile, State Route 120 crossed the Fox on a new two-lane bridge. The old wagon trail, now Highway 31, doglegged along the same route for a critical half mile before turning north toward Wisconsin. These configurations effectively relocated the city's commercial center to Route 120, and had the unintended side effect of isolating the original business districts (West Main, Riverside Drive, and Green Street).

A new wave of industry, including automotive components, electronics, and metalworking, swept into town after World War II. The Northern Illinois Medical Center, begun in 1956 as a 23-bed community hospital, evolved into a regional trauma center serving two states. Beginning in the late 1940s, subdivisions were annexed on all sides of the city. By this time, many residents were commuting to work in other localities, including Chicago. McHenry's population tripled from 2,080 in 1950 to 6,772 in 1970, and tripled again to 21,501 in 2000.

McHenry continues to grow in all directions. In 1995, the city's corporate boundaries leapt east of the Fox for the first time. The city now has seven separate commercial centers, but no distinct core. Traffic continues to be a problem, and the city's major scenic resource, the river, has insufficient access.

John D. Schroeder

See also: Annexation; Metropolitan Growth; Transportation; Vacation Spots

Further reading: *History of McHenry County.* 1885. • *McHenry County in the Twentieth Century, 1968–1994.* 1994. • Meyer, Barbara K., ed. *McHenry, 1836–1986: A Proud Past and Progressive Future.* 1986.

McKinley Park, Community Area 59, 4 miles SW of the Loop. McKinley Park has been a working-class area throughout its long history. This tradition began around 1836 when Irish workers on the Illinois & Michigan Canal took squatter's rights to small tracts of land. By the 1840s, a few farmers had purchased and drained land and sent the Irish squatters packing. One of the first attempts at town building, "Canalport," died stillborn, but Brighton was platted in 1840 and incorporated in 1851.

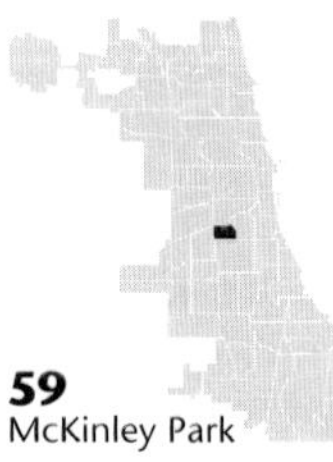

The completion of the Illinois & Michigan Canal in 1848 and the coming of the Chicago & Alton Railroad in 1857 spurred further

SUBDIVISION of the area. The rails amplified the TRANSPORTATION advantages of the area, and during the CIVIL WAR industries located along the waterways and the railroad. The Union Rolling Mill was founded in the early 1860s along the south fork of the CHICAGO RIVER and produced 50 tons of rails per day. Eventually, the firm became part of U.S. Steel.

Many steelworkers lived in the triangle formed by Archer and Ashland Avenues and 35th Street in an area called Mt. Pleasant. The name was probably ironic because of the adjacent steel mills, and because much of the area was swampy and undrained. Standing water bred hordes of mosquitoes and spring flooding was so severe that many houses were built on stilts. Not surprisingly, a portion of McKinley Park was called "Ducktown." Some landowners desperate to elevate their holdings invited scavengers to dump ashes and thereby fill low areas. Unfortunately the scavengers dumped not only ashes, but garbage as well. Thus the area was not only wet, but fetid. Even with these problems, McKinley Park was ANNEXED to Chicago in 1863.

The FIRE OF 1871 displaced numerous industrial operations and many relocated to this area. Within five years after the fire 11 factories opened—most in IRON AND STEEL—along with 27 brickyards. During this same period, MEATPACKING operations just to the south moved into high gear. The result was the creation of the solid working-class community that still exists today.

The packinghouses fouled the environment and dumped wastes directly into the south fork of the CHICAGO RIVER. Here the stream was such a hellish mess of decomposing material that it became known as "Bubbly Creek" because of the bubbles that constantly roiled its surface. The situation finally became so horrendous that the stream's upper reaches were filled in to rectify the problem.

If industries created pollution, they also created many good industrial jobs and led to a period of unprecedented growth and prosperity. Irish, GERMANS, SWEDES, ENGLISH, and native-born Americans filled the industrial jobs of the 1870s. Even after 1900, when POLES and other Eastern Europeans came to the area, English prevailed as the street language, and the area was the most American of all settlements in the stockyard districts. Transportation had always been poor, but the 1880s and 1890s saw improvement and extension of the car lines on Archer Avenue and on 35th Street. As time passed, steel mills and brickyards closed and industries changed, replaced by new activities. The CENTRAL MANUFACTURING DISTRICT was begun in 1905 on some 260 acres along the south fork. In the late 1990s it was still operating, Pepsi-Cola was opening a new bottling plant, and the Wrigley Company was still making chewing gum. Meanwhile, the CHICAGO SUN-TIMES was building a mammoth publishing and distribution plant west of Ashland along the Chicago River.

The beginning of the twentieth century led, after years of complaints by residents, to the creation of a park, which was named for President McKinley after his assassination. The 69-acre park now boasts a SWIMMING pool and ice-SKATING rink. It is the area's showplace and led to the naming of the entire community.

After years of declining populations, during the 1990s the population grew from 13,297 to 15,962, with MEXICANS joining the ethnic mix. Well-kept two- and four-flat buildings dominate the landscape, but new infill housing has begun to appear. Two stops on the CTA Orange Line RAPID TRANSIT have boosted property values and spurred development of a new restaurant, shopping mall, and drugstore.

David M. Solzman

See also: Economic Geography; Quarrying, Stonecutting, and Brickmaking

Further reading: The Chicago Fact Book Consortium, ed. *Local Community Fact Book: Chicago Metropolitan Area, Based on the 1970 and 1980 Censuses.* 1984. • Solzman, David M. *Waterway Industrial Sites: A Chicago Case Study.* 1966. • Solzman, David M. *The Chicago River: An Illustrated History and Guide to the River and Its Waterways.* 1998.

Meatpacking. The preparation of beef and pork for human consumption has always been closely tied to livestock raising, technological change, government regulation, and urban market demand. From the CIVIL WAR until the 1920s Chicago was the country's largest meatpacking center and the acknowledged headquarters of the industry.

Europeans brought cattle and hogs to North America, let them forage in the woods, and slaughtered them only as meat was needed. Commercial butchering began when population increased in the towns. Since beef was difficult to preserve, cattle were killed year round and the meat sold and consumed while still fresh. Hogs were killed only in cold weather. Their fat was rendered into lard and their flesh carved into hams, shoulders, and sides, which were covered with salt and packed in wooden barrels. Packers utilized hides, but blood, bones, and entrails usually went into the nearest body of running WATER. City government, understandably, tried to confine these operations to the outskirts of town.

Americans took their cattle and hogs over the Appalachians after the Revolutionary War, and the volume of livestock in the Ohio River Valley increased rapidly. Cincinnati packers took advantage of this development and shipped barreled pork and lard throughout the valley and down the Mississippi River. They devised better methods to cure pork and used lard components to make soap and candles. By 1840 Cincinnati led all other cities in pork processing and proclaimed itself Porkopolis.

Chicago won that title during the Civil War. It was able to do so because most Midwestern farmers also raised livestock, and RAILROADS tied Chicago to its Midwestern hinterland and to the large urban markets on the East Coast. In addition, Union army contracts for processed pork and live cattle supported packinghouses on the branches of the CHICAGO RIVER and the railroad stockyards which shipped cattle. To alleviate the problem of driving cattle and hogs through city streets, the leading packers and railroads incorporated the UNION STOCK YARD and Transit Company in 1865 and built an innovative facility south of the city limits. Accessible to all railroads serving Chicago, the huge stockyard received 3 million cattle and hogs in 1870 and 12 million just 20 years later.

Between the opening of the Union Stock Yard in 1865 and the end of the century, Chicago meatpackers transformed the industry. Pork packers such as Philip Armour built large plants west of the stockyards, developed ice-cooled rooms so they could pack year round, and introduced steam hoists to elevate carcasses and an overhead assembly line to move them. Gustavus Swift, who came to Chicago to ship cattle, developed a way to send fresh-chilled beef in ice-cooled railroad cars all the way to the East Coast. By 1900 this dressed beef trade was as important as pork packing, and mechanical refrigeration increased the efficiency of both pork and beef operations. Moreover, Chicago packers were preserving meat in tin cans, manufacturing an inexpensive butter substitute called oleomargarine, and, with the help of chemists, turning previously discarded parts of the animals into glue, fertilizer, glycerin, ammonia, and gelatin.

The extension of railroads and livestock raising to the Great Plains prompted the largest Chicago packing companies to build branch plants in Kansas City, Omaha, Sioux City, Wichita, Denver, Fort Worth, and elsewhere. To promote their dressed beef in eastern cities, they built branch sales offices and cold storage warehouses. When railroads balked at investing in refrigerator cars, they purchased their own and leased them to the railroads. Thus, Chicago's Big Three packers—Philip Armour, Gustavus Swift, and Nelson Morris—were in a position to influence livestock prices at one end of this complex industrial chain and the price of meat products at the other end. In 1900 the Chicago packinghouses employed 25,000 of the country's 68,000 packinghouse employees. The city's lead was narrower at the end of WORLD WAR I, but Chicago was still, in Carl Sandburg's words, "Hog Butcher for the World."

Government surveillance and regulation kept pace with the growth of the meatpacking industry. Even before Chicago ANNEXED the Union Stock Yard and packinghouse district (Packingtown), city government tried to control smoke, odors, and waste disposal. Livestock

Cattle pens, Union Stock Yard, ca. 1920s. From 1893 to 1933, there was no year in which fewer than 15 million head of livestock were unloaded at the stockyards. Photographer: William T. Barnum. Source: Chicago Historical Society.

raisers prevailed on state and federal government to investigate prices paid by the packers for cattle. At the behest of foreign governments, the U.S. Department of AGRICULTURE started inspecting pork exports in the early 1890s. Upton Sinclair's sensational novel THE JUNGLE (1906) led to the Meat Inspection Act, which put federal inspectors in all packinghouses whose products entered interstate or foreign commerce. Government inspectors began grading beef and pork in the 1920s; in 1967 Congress required states to perform the same inspection and grading duties in plants selling within state boundaries.

When the Armour, Swift, and Morris companies cooperated in a new National Packing Company and purchased some food-related firms, Charles Edward Russell warned about the existence of a "beef trust." His book *The Greatest Trust in the World* (1905) caused the federal government to start antitrust proceedings. Although the courts failed to indict, the National Packing Company voluntarily dissolved in 1912. In the Packer Consent Decree of 1920, the Big Three agreed to sell their holdings in stockyards, food-related companies, cold-storage facilities, and the retail meat BUSINESS.

Philip Armour and the Packing Industry

Philip Armour built Chicago's largest meatpacking company and was an important PHILANTHROPIST. Born on a New York farm in 1832, he spent time in the California gold fields before joining a provision firm and then a packing company in Milwaukee. The success of Chicago's UNION STOCK YARD (1865) convinced him that the future of meatpacking lay in that city. He and his brothers formed Armour & Co. in 1867 and started packing hogs in a rented plant on the South Branch of the Chicago River.

Armour purchased land west of the stockyards in 1872 and built a large pork plant. He and his family moved to Chicago three years later. By reinvesting profits over the next quarter century, Armour & Co. expanded its pork operation and added dressed beef, meat canning, and the manufacture of oleomargarine, glue, fertilizer, and other byproducts. It also acquired packing plants in Kansas City and Omaha, branch sales offices across the country, and refrigerated railroad cars to deliver chilled, fresh beef. Like other Chicago packers, Armour resisted trade unions and helped defeat strikes in 1886 and 1894.

A generous contributor to scores of organizations, his chief philanthropic interest lay in training young people. Armour Mission (1886), a nondenominational community center, sponsored classes and activities for children. Armour Institute (1893), later changed to ILLINOIS INSTITUTE OF TECHNOLOGY, taught engineering, ARCHITECTURE, and library science to high-school graduates at nominal cost.

Philip Armour died in January 1901. His son, J. Ogden Armour, succeeded him as head of the vast enterprise in Chicago.

Louise Carroll Wade

Meat packed in the canning rooms of Chicago's Union Stock Yard (here ca. 1890) was sold throughout much of the world. Photographer: Unknown. Source: Chicago Historical Society.

The packers faced challenges from their employees. First organized by the KNIGHTS OF LABOR, packinghouse workers in Chicago struck for the eight-hour day in 1886, but public reaction to violence in HAYMARKET Square ended that STRIKE. The Amalgamated Meat Cutters and Butcher Workmen of North America, an affiliate of the American Federation of Labor, made impressive gains in all the packing centers at the turn of the century. In the summer of 1904 this union led a long, bitter contest for wage increases. Some 50,000 packinghouse workers walked off their jobs. But in the end, only Jane Addams's intervention with J. Ogden Armour saved the strikers from total defeat. In response to renewed organizing during World War I and a demand for collective bargaining, President Woodrow Wilson established a federal arbitration process, and workers won temporary wage increases and the eight-hour day. When packers cut wages at the end of 1921, the Amalgamated called a strike which it soon rescinded. Thanks to the New Deal's pro-labor policies, Amalgamated membership revived in the 1930s and the CONGRESS OF INDUSTRIAL ORGANIZATIONS launched a new PACKINGHOUSE UNION. At the end of the decade, the large packing companies finally signed their first labor contracts. Postwar changes in the industry, however, minimized the impact of this victory.

Railroads centralized meatpacking in the latter half of the nineteenth century; trucks and highways decentralized it during the last half of the twentieth. Instead of selling mature animals to urban stockyards, livestock raisers sold young animals to commercial feedlots, and new packing plants arose in the vicinity. Unlike the compact, multistory buildings in Chicago, Kansas City, or Omaha, these new plants were sprawling one-story structures with power saws, mechanical knives, and the capacity to quick-freeze meat packaged in vacuum bags. Large refrigerator trucks carried the products over interstate highways to supermarkets. Many of the new plants were in states with right-to-work laws that hampered UNIONIZATION. Business in the older railroad stockyards and city packinghouses declined sharply in the 1960s. Chicago's Union Stock Yard closed in 1970, the same year the GREYHOUND CORPORATION purchased ARMOUR & CO.

At the end of the twentieth century, the meatpacking industry was widely dispersed but still under government regulation. Changing consumption patterns posed new challenges, as poultry and fish began to replace beef and pork in American diets.

Louise Carroll Wade

See also: Antiunionism; Back of the Yards; Business of Chicago; Economic Geography; Innovation, Invention, and Chicago Business; Packinghouse Unions; Public Health; Waste, Hazardous; Work Culture

Further reading: Barrett, James R. *Work and Community in the Jungle: Chicago's Packinghouse Workers, 1894–1922.* 1987. • Skaggs, Jimmy K. *Prime Cut: Livestock Raising and Meatpacking in the United States, 1607–1983.* 1986. • Wade, Louise C. *Chicago's Pride: The Stockyards, Packingtown, and Environs in the 19th Century.* 1987.

Medical Education. In nineteenth-century Chicago, a medical degree was not always needed to practice medicine. No licensing laws yet governed medical practice, and doctors commonly learned medicine by apprenticeship or by reading medical texts. Doctors who had obtained formal medical training in eastern medical colleges founded similar schools in their newly adopted city. These schools enabled local youth to afford medical education and provided founders and faculty with income from students' fees while enhancing their prestige and reputations, which helped them attract paying patients.

Chicago's first medical school, Rush Medical College, was founded by Daniel Brainard in 1843. Like most medical schools in the nation, it offered two 16-week terms. Instruction each week consisted of four daily lectures. The second term merely repeated the first term's lectures. Brainard attracted numerous skilled lecturers to Rush, including Nathan S. Davis, a founder of the American Medical Association. Dedicated to enhancing the status of the medical profession by reforming medical education, Davis advocated a "graded curriculum"—a medical course in which the second term built upon and extended the learning accomplished in the first.

Unsuccessful in his attempt to institute a graded curriculum at Rush, Davis established a competing school in 1859. The Lind University Medical School, later renamed the Chicago Medical College, eventually became the NORTHWESTERN UNIVERSITY Medical College. In addition to grading the curriculum, Davis increased the length of each term and established educational entrance requirements, a significant improvement upon the complete lack of such requirements in most U.S. medical colleges.

Though most of the students who attended Rush and the Chicago Medical College were Midwestern white males, these schools did accept and graduate a few AFRICAN AMERICAN medical students. Except for Mary Harris Thompson, who received her second medical degree from the Chicago Medical College in 1870, women could enroll but not graduate from either school in the nineteenth century. In 1871, the newly established WOMAN'S HOSPITAL MEDICAL COLLEGE, later renamed the Chicago Woman's Medical College, and then

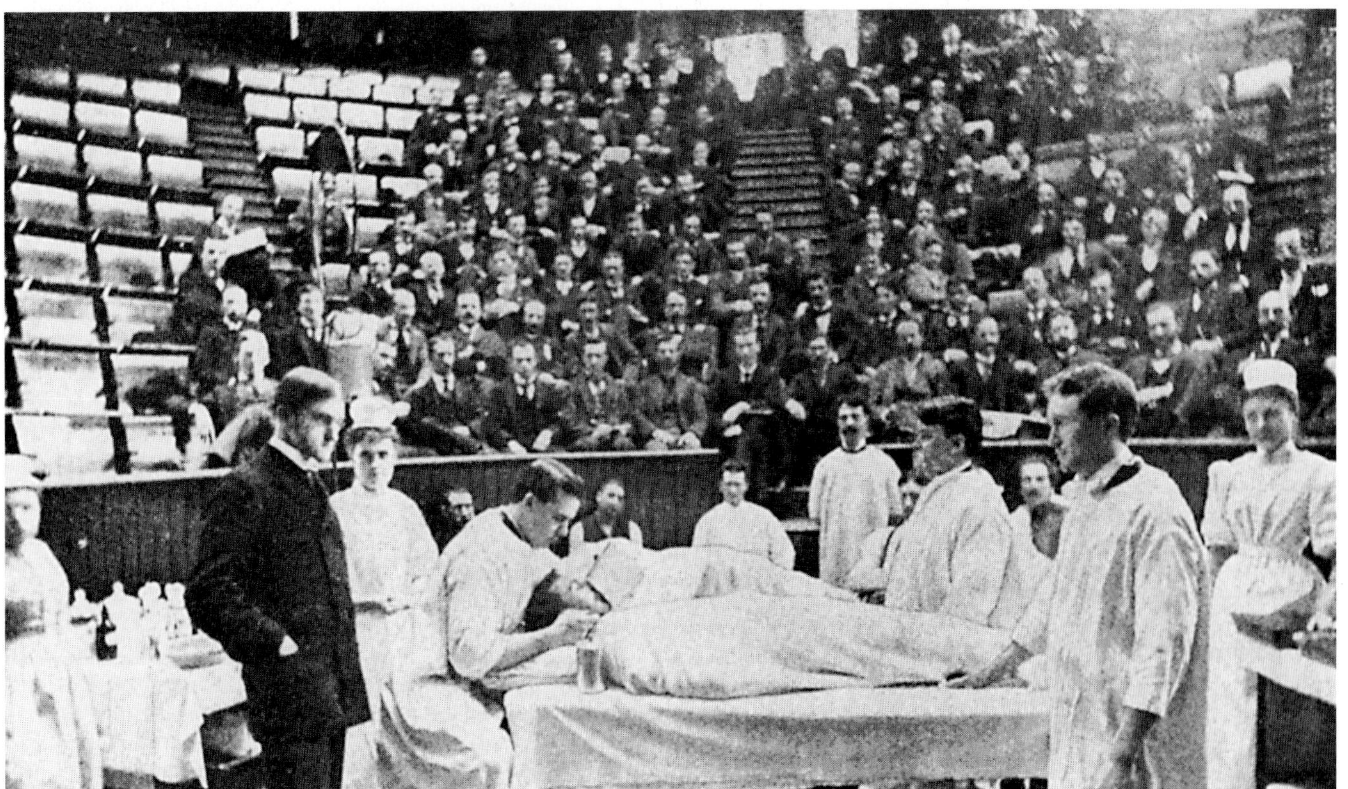

Surgical clinic at Rush Medical College, 1890s. Photographer: Unknown. Source: Chicago Historical Society.

the Northwestern University Woman's Medical School, provided Chicago women with access to formal medical education.

In 1881, several physicians established the College of Physicians and Surgeons. They aimed to improve the quality of medical instruction and to provide themselves with medical professorships. In 1897, this college affiliated with the University of Illinois and became the University of Illinois College of Medicine.

In addition to these "regular" medical colleges, several institutions trained practitioners in alternative medical practices. The most popular alternative, especially among well-educated segments of society, was homeopathy. Homeopathic theory held that drugs should be tested to determine their effects, that a drug which causes specific symptoms in a well person is the drug which should be used to cure those same symptoms in an unwell person (like cures like), and that a drug's potency is enhanced by a series of dilutions (the law of infinitesimals). The Hahnemann Medical College opened in 1860 and became coeducational in 1871. Except for the emphasis upon homeopathic therapeutics, instruction resembled that in Chicago's "regular" medical schools. Eclectic practitioners, another popular alternative, claimed to select the most effective forms of medical treatment from among all available therapies and avoided the depleting methods of bleeding and purging that characterized "regular" medicine. Their school, the Bennett College of Eclectic Medicine, opened as a coeducational school in 1868. Like their regular counterparts, Chicago's homeopathic and eclectic schools accepted a small contingent of African American students.

Throughout the second half of the nineteenth century, and especially after 1878, when state legislation required medical practitioners to possess medical degrees from approved medical schools with established standards, Chicago's medical schools gradually extended the length of each term, increased the number of terms required, and included lectures on a broader array of subjects. Pedagogical methods, however, did not change until acceptance of the germ theory of disease introduced laboratory-based training in bacteriology in the 1890s.

Despite these reforms, efforts to improve the general state of medical education in Chicago suffered in 1891, when political forces led John Rauch to resign as secretary of the State Board of Health. The weakened board was unable to control the spread of poor-quality medical schools. More than 20 new medical schools opened in Chicago in the 1890s and early 1900s. Many were short-lived and some were nothing more than diploma mills. Others, like the Harvey Medical College, which offered night classes, attempted to provide quality medical education to working-class men and women.

Home and Training School for Nurses, Hahnemann Hospital, 1909. Following larger trends within the medical profession, homeopaths established Hahnemann Hospital in 1871 to provide students with practical training. By the beginning of the twentieth century, Chicago had become the center for homeopathic medical education within the United States. The hospital also provided a course of instruction for nurses. Photographer: Unknown. Source: The Newberry Library.

By 1910 the situation had not improved, and Abraham Flexner's report on medical education in the United States labeled Chicago "the plague spot of the country." Subsequently, various reform efforts and the funneling of money from foundations and governments into certain schools led many schools to close, consolidate, or affiliate with UNIVERSITIES. Bennett Medical College joined with several other failing schools in 1910 and affiliated with LOYOLA UNIVERSITY, becoming the Loyola University School of Medicine. Rush Medical College affiliated with the UNIVERSITY OF CHICAGO in 1924. This union lasted until 1941, when the University of Chicago established its own medical school. Though Rush Medical College continued to exist as a corporate entity, it did not reestablish itself as a full-fledged medical college until the late 1960s.

Twentieth-century reforms in medical education led to remarkable standardization. All schools have similar premedical requirements, require four years of medical school attendance, offer a similar curriculum consisting of basic science and laboratory training in the first two years of medical education and clinical training in the last two years, and rely upon full-time, salaried faculty. Increasingly from the late nineteenth through the twentieth century, medical school education has been supplemented by additional clinical training obtained through HOSPITAL internships and residencies.

Eve Fine

See also: Nursing and Nursing Education; Public Health; Schooling for Work; Social Service Education

Further reading: Bonner, Thomas N. *Medicine in Chicago, 1850–1950: A Chapter in the Social and Scientific Development of a City.* 1957. • Chicago Medical Society. *History of Medicine and Surgery, and Physicians and Surgeons of Chicago.* 1922. • Davis, David J., ed. *History of Medical Practice in Illinois,* vol. 2, *1850–1900.* 1955.

Medical Manufacturing and Pharmaceuticals. Chicago's preeminence in both medicine and industry has made the city a manufacturing center for medical products. Practitioners and patients throughout the world depend on a vast array of supplies and drugs produced in Chicago-area laboratories and factories. Chicago INNOVATIONS read like a list of the twentieth century's greatest strides in medicine, including the development of antibiotics, blood transfusions, birth control, and AIDS drugs. While their products have saved or enhanced countless lives, the huge profitability of some Chicago medical and drug manufacturers has also embroiled them in controversies about the ethics of for-profit medicine.

Women workers at Baxter Laboratories, Glenview, Illinois, are shown here in 1942 banding bottles used by the armed forces for blood transfusions, plasma, and serum. Photographer: Howard R. Hollem. Source: Library of Congress.

Medical and Surgical Manufacturing

For most of the nineteenth century, American physicians designed their own surgical instruments or imported them from Europe. Chicago's Charles Truax & Co. revolutionized surgical instrument making in the 1880s by establishing simplified standard designs and applying the techniques of mass production to what had formerly been an individual craft. Charles Truax (1852–1918), who had opened a physician's supply store in Iowa in 1878, relocated to Chicago in 1884 to be near the city's growing numbers of physicians and medical colleges. Within five years, his surgical instrument sales had increased 20-fold. Truax responded to the new importance of antisepsis in medicine by creating the first line of "aseptic" surgical instruments that could be easily sterilized. In addition to its design and manufacturing innovations, Charles Truax & Co. (later renamed Truax, Greene) was known for its aggressive patenting and marketing practices. The company's 1893 sales catalog was over 1,500 pages long, and its products were so well known that physicians attending the WORLD'S COLUMBIAN EXPOSITION flocked to view Truax's Wabash Avenue headquarters. Charles Truax assured his place in medical history with the 1899 publication of his voluminous *The Mechanics of Surgery,* the first work to establish standard nomenclature for surgical devices.

By the time Truax & Co. dissolved in 1920, Chicago had become the leading center of medical manufacturing in the country. City directories listed a total of 74 surgical and dental instrument makers in Chicago at the turn of the century. The most important was V. Mueller & Co., manufacturer and retailer of medical devices, founded in 1898 by Vinzenz Mueller, a GERMAN immigrant. V. Mueller was particularly renowned for its ear, nose, and throat instruments. In addition to surgeon's tools, Chicago manufacturers produced medical items as diverse as artificial limbs, druggists' scales, and hospital clothing. Medline Industries, founded in Chicago in 1910 as a manufacturer of nurses' gowns, is today the largest privately held manufacturer and distributor of health care supplies in the United States; its more than 70,000 products include bandages, gowns, and wheelchairs.

But the true Chicago-area giant in medical manufacturing has been Baxter International, the top-ranked medical products company in the nation. In 1929, California physician Donald E. Baxter developed a method to produce safer intravenous solutions, which HOSPITALS had previously mixed themselves. With two partners, in 1931 he founded what would become Baxter Laboratories and soon opened a production site in a former garage in GLENVIEW. Baxter Labs invented the "Transfuso-Vac" in 1939, a device that allowed blood to be stored for up to 21 days, making blood banking possible for the first time. Skyrocketing demand for blood devices and solutions during WORLD WAR II forced Baxter to open temporary plants. Starting in 1953, Baxter enjoyed 24 consecutive years of more than 20 percent annual earnings growth as it introduced one revolutionary device after another, including the kidney dialysis machine, a blood oxygenator for open-heart surgery, and factor VIII blood products for hemophiliacs.

Baxter's success has been due to both its innovative research and development and its aggressive acquisition or elimination of competitors. The company's attempts to dominate the medical products industry began in the 1950s, when it purchased other major laboratories producing competitive plasma and blood products. Baxter presided over the largest health care industry merger of the 1980s, acquiring the Chicago-area distributor American Hospital Supply Corporation in 1985. This merger gave Baxter control over the distribution as well as development and manufacture of a huge array of medical supplies. In 1999, Baxter came under scrutiny for its role in the cancellation of an important cancer research trial by a small company, CellPro, that had developed bone marrow transplant technology to rival Baxter's. Baxter and partner's successful suit against CellPro for patent infringement forced the smaller company into bankruptcy and ended the trials of the rival technology, raising questions about contradictions between product monopoly and the needs of patients.

Pharmaceuticals

Chicago's first druggist was Philo Carpenter, who arrived in 1832 and opened a DRUG store on what is now Lake Street. Frederick Thomas, Chicago's first barber-surgeon, ran a retail drug business in the 1830s in addition to offering "bleeding, leeching and tooth-drawing." In 1844 the well-known homeopath David Sheppard Smith established a pharmacy in Chicago; his establishment soon became a national distributor of homeopathic medicines.

The founding of Rush Medical College in 1837 had made Chicago an important center of MEDICAL EDUCATION, and by 1859 the city boasted its own pharmacy school, the Chicago College of Pharmacy on Dearborn Street. The College of Pharmacy fell on economic hard times and briefly closed during the 1860s, but it reopened its doors on October 3, 1871, to a "large and enthusiastic class." After barely a week of lectures, the college and all its supplies were destroyed by the Chicago Fire. A fundraising drive enabled the college to open yet again in 1873 and to erect new headquarters on State Street. In 1896, it was absorbed by the UNIVERSITY OF ILLINOIS. Another pharmacy school, the Illinois College of Pharmacy, opened in 1886 and five years later joined NORTHWESTERN UNIVERSITY as its School of Pharmacy.

Pharmaceutical manufacturing also became an important part of Chicago's economy by the end of the nineteenth century. One of the nation's largest drug companies, Abbott Laboratories, originated in the city in 1888. That year, Wallace C. Abbott began producing "domestic granules," precisely measured amounts of drugs, in his apartment on the North Side. First incorporated as Abbott Alkaloidal Company in 1900 and renamed Abbott Laboratories in 1915, the company opened a manufacturing plant in NORTH CHICAGO in 1920. Abbott has been involved in some of the most important drug discoveries of the century. Abbott scientists developed the drug Pentothal in 1936, and in 1941 the company was one of five in the United States to begin commercial production of penicillin. During the second half of the century, Abbott's most important products have included new antibiotics, drugs for hypertension and epilepsy, and radiopharmaceuticals. In 1996, Abbott began worldwide sales of Norvir, a protease inhibitor for AIDS patients. Abbott has also marketed a number of highly controversial products, including the barbiturate Nembutal (later found to be addictive) and the infant formula Similac (criticized for its nutritional deficiencies compared to breast milk). In 1996, under pressure from consumer groups and the Federal Trade Commission, Abbott agreed to cease making unsubstantiated claims about the benefits of its nutritional supplement Ensure.

In 1890 an Omaha druggist named Gideon Daniel Searle relocated to Chicago, where he began producing drugs for syphilis and amoebic dysentery. He incorporated G. D. Searle & Co. in 1908, which throughout the century has developed such well-known products as Metamucil (for constipation), Dramamine (for motion sickness), Aspartame (an artificial sweetener), and the first birth control pill. In 1985, Searle became the pharmaceutical sector of the chemical giant Monsanto Corporation.

At the beginning of the twenty-first century, the Chicago-area's largest medical and pharmaceutical manufacturers were operating outside the city, with large campus headquarters and manufacturing facilities in the suburbs. Abbott, headquartered in suburban North Chicago and with 15,000 employees in Illinois, was named Chicago's number one company by the *Tribune* in 1999. Baxter International, with 4,000 Illinois employees, is in north suburban DEERFIELD.

Beatrix Hoffman

See also: Business of Chicago; Economic Geography; Mail Order

Further reading: Cody, Thomas G. *Strategy of a Megamerger: An Insider's Account of the Baxter Travenol–American Hospital Supply Combination.* 1990. • Kogan, Herman. *The Long White Line: The Story of Abbott Laboratories.* 1963. • Truax, Charles. *Mechanics of Surgery.* 1899.

Medical Societies and Journals. Chicago's oldest major medical association, the Chicago Medical Society (CMS), was founded by Levi Boone and other physicians in 1850 and was restructured in 1852 by Nathan S. Davis, a primary organizer of the American Medical Association in Philadelphia in 1847. The CMS organ, the *Chicago Medical Record* (later, the *Chicago Medical Recorder*), was not the first local journal—that honor belonged to the *Chicago Medical Journal,* which lasted from 1844 to 1889—but it appeared between 1891 and 1927, a crucial period in the development of the city's medical community. Other important Chicago journals include the *Surgical Clinics of North America,* originally a means to disseminate the findings of the Chicago surgeon John B. Murphy (1857–1916) and published since 1911, and the CMS publication *Chicago Medicine.* Long the largest local medical society in the world, the CMS successfully accommodated specialist societies like the Chicago Pathological Society (founded 1878) and the Chicago Neurological Society (founded 1898) by adopting in 1903 a federal-style organization in which specialized bodies conduct meetings but delegate policymaking to elected officers and financial matters to trustees.

Chicago's medical community has had great regional and national prominence as well. Chicago physicians dominated the Illinois State Medical Society soon after its establishment in 1840. Nathan S. Davis served, after 1883, as the first editor of the *Journal of the American Medical Association;* under the long editorship (1924–1949) of Morris Fishbein, another prominent Chicago physician, *JAMA* became the leading American medical journal. The American Medical Association has been headquartered in Chicago since 1902.

Christopher James Tassava

See also: Health Care Workers; Law; Medical Education; Trade Publications

Further reading: "150 Years of Medicine in Chicago." *Chicago Medicine* 103 (May 2000). • American Medical Association. *Caring for the Country: A History and Celebration of the First 150 Years of the American Medical Association.* 1997. • Bonner, Thomas N. *Medicine in Chicago, 1850–1950: A Chapter in the Social and Scientific Development of a City.* 1957.

Melrose Park, IL, Cook County, 12 miles W of the Loop. Melrose Park is one of Chicago's many pre–World War II suburbs that do not fit the mythology of suburban affluence.

Its origins may be dated to 1873, when the Melrose Land Company subdivided a large tract almost due west of Chicago, well beyond city limits. At first the company gave away a pair of 26-foot lots to anyone who agreed to build a dwelling valued at $500 or more. Within a year 50 people had accepted the offer. No services were provided, however, and settlement slowed. By 1880 the population was barely 200, and in 1882 only 38 votes were cast to establish the village of Melrose. The village grew steadily during the 1880s, however, adding 'Park' to its name in 1894. By the turn of the century it was home to 2,592 people.

Melrose Park evolved into an industrial suburb. Stagnating after 1900, it boomed after World War I. A number of manufacturers established or greatly expanded operations. These included National Malleable and Steel Castings, the American Brake Shoe and Foundry Company, and the Edward Hines LUMBER Company. At first, like other industrial suburbs, Melrose Park functioned almost as a self-contained entity. One of the larger companies in the early 1920s was Richardson's, manufacturers of asphalt shingles, roll roofing, and composition battery casing. In the mid-1920s three-quarters of its workforce of more than 500 lived within the village. During the 1920s the local demand for homes supported the activities of many small builders and at least one large one. In 1925 the Sol Bloch REAL ESTATE Improvement Company was building more than a hundred homes in Melrose Park and adjacent suburbs. It sold some for as little as $500 down, with the balance to be paid over a period of 7 to 12 years, while more substantial brick BUNGALOWS cost $8,500.

The opening of the huge Proviso freight yards in 1926 reinforced the character of Melrose Park as an industrial, working-class suburb. By 1940 the town offered 38 jobs for every 100 residents (including children), two-thirds of which were in manufacturing. These were higher ratios than for more diversified suburbs such as BLUE ISLAND, but lower than for industrial suburbs and satellites such as CICERO and CHICAGO HEIGHTS. Wartime growth sparked more of the same sort of development, notably through the construction of a Buick airplane motor plant along the Indiana Harbor Belt RAILROAD. Other businesses in Melrose Park after World War II included Zenith (which closed its factory in 1998), Alberto-Culver, a Ford AUTOMOBILE PARTS facility, and the headquarters of Jewel Food Stores. Melrose Park is also the site of the region's oldest AMUSEMENT PARK, Kiddieland, founded in 1929.

The ethnic composition of Melrose Park has included many ITALIANS, with smaller numbers of GERMAN, IRISH, and POLISH residents. Since 1894 the Feast of Our Lady of Mt. Carmel has been an annual Italian American celebration. In the latter part of the twentieth century many Hispanic immigrants were also attracted to Melrose Park by its jobs and inexpensive housing. In 2000, 54 percent of the village's population was Hispanic, while less than 3 percent was black.

Richard Harris

See also: Economic Geography; Housing, Self-Built; Stone Park, IL

Further reading: Christgau, Eugene F. "Unincorporated Communities in Cook County." M.A. thesis, University of Chicago. 1942. • Harris, Richard. "Chicago's Other Suburbs." *Geographical Review* 84.4 (1994): 394–410. • Keating, Ann Durkin. *Building Chicago: Suburban Developers and the Creation of a Divided Metropolis.* 1988.

Memorial Day Massacre. On May 30, 1937, striking Republic Steel workers and sympathizers attempted to establish a picket line at the front of the mill on Chicago's Southeast Side. The protesting marchers, including families from the surrounding community, halted when met by a line of Chicago POLICE officers in a field north of the mill gate. Following a short standoff, violence erupted; 10 protesters died and approximately 90 were injured while retreating from police clubs, tear gas, and bullets. The episode stands as one of the most violent in the history of U.S. labor organization.

Jonathan J. Keyes

See also: Business of Chicago; Congress of Industrial Organizations; Iron and Steel; Strikes

Mental Health. In 1847, Edward Mead, a general practitioner trained in Ohio, came to Chicago and founded the Chicago Retreat for the Insane. It was set afire by a patient and burned down, and it took 50 years for another private institution to be founded, in KENILWORTH. In 1851 the Illinois State HOSPITAL for the Insane (renamed Jacksonville State Hospital) was the first such state-sponsored institution in Illinois. Chicago State Hospital, known as "DUNNING" because of its location, was originally part of a county-sponsored poorhouse, a collection of freezing, filthy prison cells built in 1854. In 1912 it was transferred from the county to the state.

By the early 1900s psychiatry was still embedded in the practice of neurology, which had been introduced into medical school curricula in the 1840s. The Chicago Medical College had a chair of neurology and merged with NORTHWESTERN UNIVERSITY in 1891. Rush Medical College first set up a separate department of neurology in 1910. The College of Physicians and Surgeons joined the UNIVERSITY OF ILLINOIS in 1913. Neurologists in these medical programs focused primarily on managing the symptoms of patients' disorders rather than on theoretical investigations.

The State Psychopathic Institute in Chicago (founded 1907), a collaboration between the state and the University of Illinois Medical School, served as a clearing house for processing patients to the state hospitals. The care of psychiatric patients was essentially containment for the more seriously disturbed patients, but many languished at home in despair. The practice of diagnosis and treatment was rare in Chicago, dispensed mainly in neurologic programs and offices.

The development of psychiatry and what was then known as mental "hygiene" started in Chicago in the 1920s with the "guidance movement" for children's emotional problems and the attention to delinquency in adolescents and young adults. The judicial system turned for help to William Healy through the Juvenile Court of Cook County. The Institute for Juvenile Research (Juvenile Psychopathic Institute at its inception), headed by Healy, started the era of an organized interest in child and adolescent behaviors. This work was internationally known and respected in the new field of child psychiatry.

In the 1930s training and treatment CLINICS were becoming active at Chicago's medical schools. At the UNIVERSITY OF CHICAGO, psychiatry was a division in the department of medicine, while LOYOLA had a combined department of psychiatry and neurology. The University of Illinois had already separated psychiatry from neurology. MICHAEL REESE, in affiliation with the University of Chicago, had a mental hygiene clinic and trained residents.

Dr. Franz Alexander came from Vienna to the University of Chicago in 1930 as a visiting professor of psychoanalysis. A few years later he founded the Chicago Institute for Psychoanalysis, attracting a brilliant faculty of psychiatrists. The institute had unofficial affiliations with medical schools, Michael Reese's Psychiatric and Psychosomatic Institute, and some of the state hospitals. It also influenced the training at the Menninger Clinic in Topeka, and at universities in Cincinnati and Detroit.

The Illinois Neuro-Psychiatric Institute was established in 1942 under the auspices of the Illinois Department of Public Welfare and the University of Illinois. Its mission was the study of mental and nervous disorders and providing psychiatric training for practitioners. This facilitated the affiliation between psychiatric programs in the medical schools and the state hospitals.

WORLD WAR II occasioned a major shift. Psychiatrists in the medical corps treated large numbers of emotional casualties among the troops, and they returned as psychiatric practitioners in the state hospitals, medical schools, and in private practice.

In the late 1940s, general hospitals in Chicago began to set up psychiatric units. St. Luke's Hospital opened a unit and later merged into Rush-Presbyterian-St. Luke's Hospital; Michael Reese had several units; and Wesley and Passavant Hospitals had units that later merged with Northwestern Memorial Hospital. Other hospitals began to open psychiatric inpatient units, and clinic programs were available throughout Chicago.

The city of Chicago also exercised leadership in opening mental health clinics in some of the PUBLIC HOUSING projects for their surrounding communities through the Chicago Board of Health. The Illinois Department of Welfare was reorganized to improve the state psychiatric system. The state's zone system of care became the national model during the era of the GREAT SOCIETY's support of mental health programs.

At the end of the twentieth century, Chicago psychiatry reflected the state of American medicine with major research efforts in psychiatric treatment and research. Because of its labor-intensive requirements, psychotherapy treatment suffered from the limitations on visits imposed by the growing managed care programs.

Harold M. Visotsky

See also: Juvenile Justice Reform; Medical Education; Social Services

Further reading: American Psychiatric Association, "The Benjamin Rush Lecture." Annual meeting, 1970. • Grinker, Roy R., Sr. *History of Psychoanalysis in Chicago, 1911–1975.* In *Annual of Psychoanalysis,* vol. 23, 1995. • Rosen, George. *Madness in Society: Chapters in the Historical Sociology of Mental Illness.* 1968.

Merchandise Mart. When Marshall Field & Co. built the Merchandise Mart in 1931, it was the world's largest building and contained over four million square feet of floor space. It originally housed Marshall Field's WHOLESALE showrooms and manufacturing facilities, plus the showrooms of retail tenants. The Merchandise Mart centralized Field's wholesale trade on an unprecedented scale, introducing millions to the latest in home and commercial furnishings and other consumer wares. The Merchandise Mart boasted superior shipping and transport facilities and amenities including PARKING, RESTAURANTS, visitor lounges, a barbershop, and postal and TELEGRAPH offices. In 1945, with Field's wholesale business in decline, Joseph P. Kennedy purchased the Merchandise Mart. It remained Kennedy family property until sold to the Vornado Realty Trust in 1998. Designed by the famed firm Graham, Anderson, Probst & White, it still stands downtown along the CHICAGO RIVER. Though increasingly servicing commercial designers and architects rather than retailers, the Merchandise Mart remains an active wholesale showroom.

Michael Paul Wakeford

See also: Business of Chicago; Commercial Buildings; Retail Geography

Further reading: "Joe Kennedy Buys." *Time,* July 30, 1945. • "Storekeepers' Store." *Time,* January 13, 1936. • Marshall Field & Company. *The Story of the Merchandise Mart.* 1933.

Mercy Hospital. In 1852 the charter to Chicago's first HOSPITAL, the Illinois General Hospital of the Lakes, transferred its control to the Sisters of Mercy, who renamed it Mercy Hospital. Illinois General had been established in 1850 through the efforts of Nathan Smith Davis, a teaching physician on staff at Rush Medical College. Initially Rush medical students cared for patients at the new hospital, which was located at the Lake House Hotel on North Water and Rush Streets, until Davis employed the Sisters of Mercy.

The Illinois General Hospital of the Lakes, which had previously operated as a BOARDING-HOUSE, had been started with the proceeds from a lecture series. The trustees were unable to find permanent funds and turned to the Sisters with an agreement in 1851 that doctors would work for free with the privilege of giving clinical instruction to medical students. This transfer fulfilled the long-standing goal of the ROMAN CATHOLIC ARCHDIOCESE OF CHICAGO to erect a hospital operated by the Sisters in response to recent cholera EPIDEMICS and the continued poverty of many ROMAN CATHOLIC immigrants.

Mercy Hospital relocated to 26th and Calumet in 1863 and underwent its first expansion in 1869. Although many Chicago residents disparaged Mercy for its remote location in "the country," the move proved auspicious, as Mercy's new facility survived the Great FIRE OF 1871.

After extensive fundraising campaigns in the mid-1960s, new buildings were constructed in 1967 and the old complex razed. Though a board of trustees was established in the 1960s to give policy oversight, at the turn of the century the Sisters of Mercy continued to hold controlling sponsorship of Chicago's first Catholic and oldest continuing general hospital.

Wallace Best

See also: Convents; Medical Education; Religious Institutions

Further reading: Bonner, Thomas Neville. *Medicine in Chicago, 1850–1950: A Chapter in the Social and Scientific Development of a City.* 1957. • Clough, Joy. *In Service to Chicago: The History of Mercy Hospital.* 1979. • Coughlin, Roger J., and Cathryn A. Riplinger. *The Story of Charitable Care in the Archdiocese of Chicago, 1844–1959.* 1981.

Merriam Center (The Charles E. Merriam Center), 1313 E. 60th Street. Beginning in 1938, the Public Administration Building, located on the campus of the UNIVERSITY OF CHICAGO in HYDE PARK, was home to the International City Managers Association, the AMERICAN PLANNING ASSOCIATION, the Council of State Governments, the American Public Works Association, the Municipal Finance Officers Association, the Government Welfare Association, and the National Association of Housing Officials. In addition, 1313 was home to the Public Administration Clearing House, the Public Administration Service, and the Joint Reference Library.

The origin of the concept that there should be a building dedicated to public administration belonged to Louis H. Brownlow and UNIVERSITY OF CHICAGO political scientist Charles E. Merriam. Merriam student Beardsley Ruml, as executive director of the Spelman Fund (which had just merged with the Rockefeller Foundation), helped arrange a grant of $1 million in 1936 to the university specifically for the purpose of erecting a building. Designed by the architectural firm of Zantzinger & Borie, 1313 would be the last of the gray limestone neo-Gothic buildings to be built on the campus.

The Merriam Center embodied two central visions: (1) bringing together the headquarter staffs of professional state and local government-oriented associations in a single building, and (2) building a bridge between public administration practitioners and the university-based research community. The first vision was fulfilled in large part through the regular, direct contact of association staffs who worked at 1313. But efforts to establish on-campus connections between the theory and actual practice of public administration did not extend far beyond Merriam's personal influence.

The building was not without public controversy. An article, "Terrible 1313," published in the *American Mercury* in 1959, attempted to document that 1313 was the headquarters of an anti-American movement to introduce ZONING, BUILDING CODES, PUBLIC HEALTH laws, and other anti–private property initiatives. In 1979, the building was renamed the Charles E. Merriam Center for Public Administration. By 1995 none of the original associations remained; they had all moved their headquarters to larger, newer, and for the most part, more federally focused locations.

Howard Rosen

See also: Infrastructure; Planning, City and Regional; Universities and their Cities

Further reading: Brownlow, Louis. *A Passion for Anonymity: The Autobiography of Louis Brownlow.* 2 vols. 1958. • Karl, Barry D. "Louis Brownlow." *Public Administration Review* 39 (November–December 1979): 511–516. • Knack, Ruth Eckdish, and Howard Rosen. *Terrible 1313 Turns Fifty: The Golden Anniversary of the Merriam Center.* 1990.

Merrillville, IN, Lake County, 33 miles SE of the Loop. Known as "Downtown Northwest Indiana," the town of Merrillville, just south of GARY, embraces a large number of restaurants, banks, malls, and businesses typical of American suburbia in the late twentieth century.

In the mid-1830s, POTAWATOMI and MIAMI regularly visited the Merrillville area. Calling it McGwinn's Village, Indians would hold intertribal councils and conduct ceremonies and dances. Over 15 Indian trails crisscrossed the region, connecting with the Sauk Trail, a major east-west route through Indiana and into Illinois. In addition, the site comprised a NATIVE AMERICAN burial ground with over a hundred graves.

In 1835, as American settlers pushed west into Northwest Indiana, Jeremiah Wiggins purchased a claim just south of Turkey Creek and named it Wiggins Point. Other settlers arrived soon after, changing the name to Centerville because of its location in the county. In 1848, the post office renamed the settlement Merrillville, after residents Dudley and William Merrill. At that point, the village included a store, a blacksmith shop, a cheese factory, and the California Exchange Hotel. RAILROADS pushed through Merrillville in 1876 (later the Chesapeake & Ohio) and in 1880 (Chicago & Grand Trunk), opening links to the Chicago markets. Through WORLD WAR II, Merrillville was a typical Midwestern farming community.

Beginning in the 1950s, however, several phenomena combined to cause striking changes in the Merrillville landscape. First, as in other areas of the country, urban residents began their outward march to suburbia; in northwest Indiana, residents of the industrial cities of Gary, HAMMOND, and EAST CHICAGO began to buy new homes in central LAKE COUNTY. Next, the 1967 election of Richard Gordon Hatcher, Gary's first AFRICAN AMERICAN mayor, accelerated the white flight begun a decade earlier. Finally, Interstate 65 opened in 1968, connecting Interstate 80/94 in Gary to U.S. 30 in Merrillville.

Almost overnight, Merrillville experienced tremendous commercial and residential growth. Most of the retail and bank establishments relocated from downtown Gary and Hammond to Merrillville, as suburban malls and office complexes sprang up in the cornfields.

Efforts to incorporate Merrillville began in the 1950s but were unsuccessful until 1971, when Indiana's General Assembly passed legislation exempting only Lake County from the state's "buffer zone" law, which prohibited incorporation in areas within three miles of larger cities (such as Gary and neighboring HOBART).

Although Merrillville experienced a commercial and residential boom, little of that prosperity reached town government. In 1972 Indiana passed legislation freezing local budget increases to 5 percent per year. Merrillville's budgets quickly fell behind the inflation rate and the town struggled to maintain services. To compound matters, neighboring Hobart annexed a large portion of unincorporated Ross Township in 1994, which included the profitable Southlake Mall and other retail malls.

At the end of the twentieth century, Merrillville continued to serve as northwest Indiana's commercial hub. Its population stabilized and became more diverse, as African Americans and other minorities began to buy houses and attend schools. Several major road projects have been planned to ease traffic congestion near the malls.

Stephen G. McShane

See also: Economic Geography; Expressways; Governing the Metropolis; Metropolitan Growth; Shopping Districts and Malls

Further reading: Clemens, Jan. *A Pictorial History of Merrillville.* 1978. • Goodspeed, Weston A., and Charles Blanchard. *Counties of Porter and Lake Indiana.* 1882. • Moore, Powell A. *The Calumet Region: Indiana's Last Frontier.* 1959.

Merrionette Park, IL, Cook County, 14 miles S of the Loop. In contrast with communities that started as market towns, RAILROAD suburbs, or satellite industrial cities, Merrionette Park was an intentionally planned suburban development. Started in the early 1940s, it has remained a quiet bedroom suburb. It borders the Chicago neighborhood of MOUNT GREENWOOD and otherwise is surrounded by five CEMETERIES.

By 1943, Chicago developer Joseph E. Merrion built over 120 small single-family homes in this unincorporated area. Strong housing needs, coupled with a booming war economy, meant that working families were anxious to find affordable housing. Both during and after the war, Merrion responded to this need. Along with additional housing in Merrionette Park, Merrion built a major development that would become the small village of HOMETOWN and SUBDIVISIONS in what would become COUNTRY CLUB HILLS.

From the start, perhaps because of the wartime conditions, its somewhat isolated nature, its small size, and the dynamic of being only a residential place, this has been a demographically stable community, with many children returning as adults to live in the community.

The first residents formed the Merrionette Park Property Owners Association, which served for several years as a quasi-local government. About 60 percent of the residents participated, and by 1946 the association had negotiated WATER service from the city of Chicago, purchased a community school bus, put in streetlights, and organized social activities.

Population increases, however, multiplied the demand for services. In November 1946, the Executive Board of the Property Owners Association prepared a report detailing options for the community. It could continue as is, annex to Chicago, or become incorporated. The document led to the incorporation of Merrionette Park in 1947. The new village honored Joseph Merrion by maintaining the use of his name.

The village was landlocked, and, even with a new trailer park and new housing in the late 1940s, the 1950 population stood at 1,101. By 1970, the population was 2,303, declining to 1,999 in 2000.

As the village developed, its small size necessitated continued volunteer activity. The fire department remained voluntary. The police department started with the appointment of a chief in 1947 who supervised community volunteers who drove around the community with cardboard signs on their windshields reading "Police." Starting in 1951, the village's volunteerism extended to BASEBALL. In the 1990s, more than a thousand children from the village and surrounding communities were part of Merrionette Park Youth Baseball.

Into the late 1990s, Merrionette Park continued as a predominantly white community with a small percentage of African and Hispanic Americans. The financial stability of the village was strengthened when, in 1986, a small commercial core developed at the intersection of 115th Street and Kedzie Avenue. In 1997, Merrionette Park celebrated its 50th anniversary with a strong outpouring of support from past and present residents.

Larry A. McClellan

See also: Annexation; Government, Suburban; Metropolitan Growth

Further reading: *50th Anniversary, Village of Merrionette Park, August 16–17, 1997.* Fiftieth Anniversary Committee, Merrionette Park, IL. 1997 • "People of Merrionette Park, Shall We: 1. Continue . . . 2. Annex . . . 3. Incorporate." Mimeographed typescript, Village of Merrionette Park. November 25, 1946. • Nolan, Mike. "Tiny Village, Big Heart." *Daily Southtown,* February 2, 1998.

Mesquakie (Fox). The Mesquakies originally lived in the lower peninsula of Michigan, but in 1667, when the FRENCH first encountered the tribe, they were occupying villages along the Fox and Wolf rivers, near Lake Winnebago, in east-central Wisconsin. Mesquakie hunting parties ranged into northern Illinois, however, and in 1669 Jesuit priests reported that Mesquakie hunters encamped along the DES PLAINES RIVER in western Cook County had been mistaken for POTAWATOMIS and had been attacked by a war party of Iroquois. Although they continued to reside in Wisconsin, by 1700 Mesquakie hunters frequently descended the FOX RIVER Valley to hunt bison on the prairies of northern Illinois. Large numbers of Mesquakies also passed through the Chicago region in 1710 when part of the tribe temporarily moved to the Detroit region.

A military confrontation between the Mesquakies and French at Detroit in 1712 ushered in a quarter century of Mesquakie-French warfare, and although the Mesquakies returned to Wisconsin in 1712, Mesquakie warriors continued to scour the Chicago region attacking *coureurs de bois* and French-allied Indians. On December 1, 1715 a Mesquakie war party led by Pemoussa (He Who Walks) attacked a French expedition led by Constant Le Marchand de Lignery and in a series of skirmishes along the lakefront drove the French and their allies back toward Michigan. The warfare between the Mesquakies and French flared intermittently for over a decade, but Mesquakie war parties so disrupted the French FUR TRADE in northern Illinois and Wisconsin that the French sent several additional expeditions against the Mesquakie villages.

The French campaigns achieved some success, and during the summer of 1730 some of the Mesquakies attempted to abandon their villages in Wisconsin and pass through northern Illinois en route to joining the Senecas in New York. These Mesquakies descended the Fox River Valley just west of Chicago, crossed the Illinois River near modern Starved Rock, and traveled southeastward across the prairies where in early August they were intercepted by the French and their allies near modern Arrowsmith, in McLean County. The Mesquakies took refuge in a grove of trees on the prairie, and after a month's siege, they broke through the French lines but were attacked and defeated by their enemies, losing two hundred warriors and about three hundred women and children.

Following additional attacks upon their remaining villages in Wisconsin, in 1732 the Fox REFUGEES established a new, heavily fortified village on Pistakee Lake, northwest of Chicago, astride the modern boundary between Lake and MCHENRY COUNTIES. In October 1732, led by the war chief Kiala, the Mesquakies successfully defended this village against a large war party of French-allied Indians, but during the following spring they abandoned the village and returned to Wisconsin, where they sought sanctuary among the SACS at Green Bay. After 1733 the Mesquakies and Sacs lived together, first in Wisconsin, then in the lower Rock River Valley of northwestern Illinois, and finally in Iowa. A small village of Mesquakies reoccupied the Chicago region during 1741, but one year later they rejoined their kinsmen near Rock Island.

Today, tribespeople from the Mesquakie settlement near Tama, Iowa, form part of the modern NATIVE AMERICAN community clustered in Chicago's UPTOWN neighborhood.

R. David Edmunds

See also: Chicago in the Middle Ground; Native American Religion; Treaties

Further reading: Edmunds, R. David, and Joseph L. Peyser. *The Fox Wars: The Mesquakie Challenge to New France.* 1993.

Métis. The term Métis (MAY tee) refers to people of mixed ancestry, usually NATIVE AMERICAN and European. Historically, Métis people were important to Chicago and the GREAT LAKES region during the FUR TRADE era, especially during the eighteenth and early nineteenth centuries. Fur traders from Europe, Canada, and the Atlantic colonies and states frequently married Native American women living in the communities with which they traded. The Indians encouraged these marriages because they created diplomatic and kinship ties and facilitated cultural understanding between Natives and Euro-Americans. Fur traders' wives such as Catherine DuSable frequently became informal interpreters and often assisted with the business, as did their Métis children. Some of these women and many of the children became traders and fur trade workers themselves.

Métis people during the fur trade era generally spoke FRENCH and at least one Native language and were bicultural in other ways. This understanding of the cultures of both sides of their families gave them the ability to serve in many capacities as cultural mediators—as diplomats, interpreters, negotiators, tribal leaders, traders, guides, and so forth.

By the early nineteenth century, many of these mixed fur trade families had gathered in their own communities, including Chicago, Green Bay, St. Louis, Mackinac, Prairie du Chien, and Detroit. In these towns, Indian women, European men, and their Métis children created a culture that combined elements of Native American and European traditions in their values, language, domestic economy, music and other art forms, dress, marriage and kinship patterns, BUSINESS practices, and FOODWAYS. This locally produced culture together with the communities and the people who lived there are sometimes referred to as "Creole" (a term with a meaning different from that used in Louisiana). They maintained close contact with nearby Native American tribes, based on friendship, kinship, and trade relations. Most of the residents of these communities were ROMAN CATHOLIC.

Numerous biracial fur trade families, including Métis, Indian, and Euro-American members, were among the first families of Chicago. Between the 1790s and 1812, Billy Caldwell, Alexander Robinson, and members of the Beaubien, Ouilmette, Chevalier, Bourassa, Mirandeau, and LaFramboise families established Chicago as a fur trade center along with the Anglo Kinzie family and the AFRICAN AMERICAN Jean Baptiste Point DuSable. After the War of 1812, however, English-speaking settlers from the eastern United States began to migrate into northern Illinois, and by the 1830s this stream of migration increased to the point where the old French-speaking Métis and other Creole residents became a minority in their own town. The fur trade declined, as Indian tribes were removed west of the Mississippi. Thereafter, Métis people adapted in several different ways. Some who felt unwelcome in the culturally changing Chicago community joined their Indian kin in the West or migrated to Minnesota and Canada, where there was a Métis settlement at Red River. Others stayed on as inn- or tavern keepers. Some married newcomers, and many assimilated into the transformed economy and society.

Lucy Eldersveld Murphy

See also: Chicago in the Middle Ground; Native American Religion; Potawatomis

Further reading: Murphy, Lucy Eldersveld. *A Gathering of Rivers: Indians, Métis, and Mining in the Western Great Lakes, 1737–1832.* 2000. • Peterson, Jacqueline, and Jennifer S. H. Brown, eds. *The New Peoples: Being and Becoming Métis in North America.* 1984. • Sleeper-Smith, Susan. *Indian Women and French Men: Rethinking Cultural Encounter in the Western Great Lakes.* 2001.

Metra. Metra, the commuter railroad division of Chicago's REGIONAL TRANSPORTATION AUTHORITY, was created in 1983 as part of a general reorganization of the RTA following a succession of financial crises. Metra operates and oversees a 546-mile commuter RAILROAD system in Chicago and the suburbs.

Although the commuter railroad system dates from 1855 or 1856, it did not begin hauling commuters on a large scale until the 1870s. Prior to 1970 the commuter railroads as a group were in relatively sound financial shape, having benefited after WORLD WAR II from the rapid growth of suburbia and the modernization of their fleets. By 1970, however, costs were growing faster than revenues, and the RTA was created in 1974 to funnel tax revenues to the mass transit system, including the railroads. It subsequently bought several commuter lines in bankruptcy, upgraded track and equipment, and subsidized service. But when the RTA proved unable to control escalating costs, the state legislature created Metra to operate the commuter railroad system with RTA subsidies. By 1999, it was one of the largest commuter railroad networks in the world.

David M. Young

See also: Commuting; Public Transportation; State Politics

Further reading: Douglas, George H. *Rail City: Chicago USA.* 1981. • Grow, Lawrence. *On the 8:02: An Informal History of Commuting by Rail in America.* 1979. • Young, David M. *Chicago Transit: An Illustrated History.* 1998.

Metropolitan Community Church. The Metropolitan Community Church (MCC)—whose doctrine is mainstream PROTESTANTISM—has openly welcomed GAY AND LESBIAN parishioners since its founding in Los Angeles in 1968. The Good Shepherd Parish MCC, chartered in Chicago in 1970, was the first MCC congregation outside of California, an expansion that has produced more than 300 churches in 19 countries.

The Chicago congregation's initial meetings took place in founder Reverend Arthur Green's living room. They soon moved to the Broadway United Methodist Church and eventually began renting space from the Wellington Avenue United Church of Christ. The first MCC parish in Chicago has in turn nurtured others in the area, and MCC congregants can be found worshipping in BATAVIA, HINSDALE, HYDE PARK, EVANSTON, WAUKEGAN, and OAK PARK.

In 1987, the Good Shepherd Parish established an AIDS ministry outreach program at Illinois Masonic Medical Center. The parish has also been an active supporter of the Northside Ecumenical Night Ministry and the AIDS Pastoral Care Network.

Clinton E. Stockwell

See also: Gay and Lesbian Rights Movements; Religious Institutions; Settlements, Religious

Further reading: Metropolitan Community Church. *Only Believe: 25th Anniversary of Good Shepherd Parish.* October 1995.

Metropolitan Growth. The history of the Chicago metropolitan area is often told in geographic fragments—the histories of dozens of local areas, both inside Chicago and in suburbs. AUSTIN, BARRINGTON, SOUTH SHORE, UPTOWN, NAPERVILLE, WILMETTE, or HARVEY: all have their own histories, often told in isolation from one another. To tell the story of these geographic areas separately, however, denies the ways in which the Chicago metropolitan area operates as a whole. Few Chicagoans have lived self-contained lives within one suburb or neighborhood. And even the most self-contained residents are shaped by wider forces such as ethnicity, technology, religion, WORK, LEISURE, government, and the physical environment. Individuals live, work, worship, and play across the metropolitan area. Exploring Chicago's development on a metropolitan scale provides a historical and geographical context for the lives of Chicagoans.

Chicago's geographic location along a continental divide between the GREAT LAKES and Mississippi River drainage systems has long made the area a transportation nexus. TRANSPORTATION improvements which far exceeded the needs of metropolitan residents have fostered great mobility and physical expansion. Chicago's growth was tied to WATER and roads until the advent of the RAILROAD in 1848, and by the 1890s dozens of railroad lines crisscrossed the region. This spider web of tracks shaped settlement patterns. By the close of the nineteenth century, streetcars and rapid transit began a filling process that would connect contiguous settlement out from the LOOP. Highways and EXPRESSWAYS dramatically recast these settlement patterns in the twentieth century.

Chicago's explosive growth during industrialization has shaped metropolitan development down to the present. Factories located across the area, taking advantage of the many transportation lines. Chicago's opportunities drew hundreds of thousands of newcomers from the great waves of European emigrants in the nineteenth and early twentieth centuries. AFRICAN AMERICAN migrants from the South were drawn to Chicago between the 1910s and 1960s, and in the late twentieth century immigrants from around the world continued to take advantage of regional economic opportunities. Ethnic and racial diversity both resulted from metropolitan growth and contributed to its expansion.

While humans have inhabited this area for thousands of years, most of our local history begins with the POTAWATOMI presence in the eighteenth and early nineteenth centuries. Potawatomi farmed, hunted, and traded in this area, locating along trails and water routes. ALGONQUIN is alongside a Potawatomi trail between the CHICAGO RIVER and Lake Geneva. SUMMIT and PORTAGE PARK are among the sites that served as portage between rivers—here between the Chicago and DES PLAINES RIVERS. LISLE, ST. CHARLES, THORNTON, SKOKIE, PALOS HILLS, and OAK BROOK all have evidence of Potawatomi settlements along rivers within their current boundaries.

The 1833 Grand Settlement ended the BLACK HAWK WAR and substantial Potawatomi settlement in the metropolitan area. The U.S. government quickly sold this newly acquired territory to hundreds of farmers and speculators. Settlers from the American Northeast, as well as German immigrants, soon established farms. Along the same water routes and trails that the Potawatomi had exploited, they built mills, taverns, churches, schools, and stores. Graue Mill (Oak Brook), Hill Cottage Tavern (ELMHURST), Whiskey Point (BELMONT CRAGIN), Cass (DARIEN), Brush Hill (HINSDALE), the North Branch Hotel (NILES), and dozens of other settlements emerged to serve these farmers along the roads in and out of Chicago. Settlements grew along the route of the ILLINOIS & MICHIGAN CANAL, including BRIDGEPORT, ROMEOVILLE, Summit, LEMONT, and LOCKPORT.

GERMAN farmers came to dominate whole communities in northeastern Illinois by the 1840s. They composed an important part of early BLOOMINGDALE, ARLINGTON HEIGHTS, CALUMET CITY, CLEARING, CAROL STREAM, EDISON PARK, Skokie, DOLTON, LINCOLN PARK, NORTHBROOK, NILES, EDGEWATER, HARVARD, and HOFFMAN ESTATES. These Germans quickly established institutions—particularly churches and schools—which helped them to maintain their traditions. Within a few years after the CIVIL WAR, Niles Center (Skokie) had both German Lutheran and German Catholic congregations. German settlers founded both ELMHURST COLLEGE and NORTH CENTRAL COLLEGE in the mid-nineteenth century.

The first railroad arrived in the area in 1848. Soon Chicago grew as a national railroad center, and railroad stops spurred growth in virtually every direction of the metropolitan area. Farmers, industrialists, commuters, and those seeking leisure-time activities all took advantage of the speed and ease of rail travel. The railroad provided farmers with easy access to Chicago, as daily "milk runs" brought dairy products and farm produce into the city from across the metropolitan area. Lisle, Arlington Heights, CARY, FRANKFORT, Barrington, JEFFERSON PARK, and Harvard were centers for dairying and truck farming into the twentieth century.

Railroad settlements also shipped the raw materials of city building into Chicago. Bricks from NORTHBROOK, NORTH CENTER, PARK RIDGE, ROSELLE, WEST LAWN, Dolton, and WEST RIDGE, as well as limestone from Naperville and Elmhurst, were shipped into Chicago along the railroad, especially after the FIRE OF 1871. Ice harvesting relied on railroads to carry ice to Chicago from ROUND LAKE, ANTIOCH, CRYSTAL LAKE, and LAKE VILLA.

Stockyards developed along the rail lines in and around Chicago. While the opening of the Union Stock Yard in 1865 consolidated yards which had been located to the south and southwest of Chicago, outlying locations continued to operate across the nineteenth century, including Naperville, WEST CHICAGO, and HAMMOND. Agricultural processing industries also located near the rails: in Roselle, locally grown hemp was manufactured into rope; Argo established the largest corn-milling plant in the world in Summit; Gail Borden developed a condensed milk factory in ELGIN; and the Ovaltine Company established a factory in VILLA PARK.

Heavy industries also located along the railroad lines. Rolling mills on the Near North and Southwest Sides gave way to larger plants built at some distance from the city center, in areas like HEGEWISCH, Harvey, and SOUTH DEERING which had access to multiple rail lines. WAUKEGAN, ELGIN, AURORA, JOLIET, and GARY were labeled "satellite cities" by the turn of the nineteenth century and grew as industrial centers. The massive Pullman Company operations in Pullman, along the ILLINOIS CENTRAL RAILROAD; the Hawthorne Works of General Electric, located in CICERO; Inland Steel in EAST CHICAGO; and the South Works on the EAST SIDE all took advantage of easy rail and water transportation to obtain raw materials and ship finished products.

These industries drew new residents into and around the Chicago metropolitan area. Until after World War II, most industrial workers lived near work, or near a STREETCAR line which would quickly take them there. Alongside native-born migrants were immigrants from Germany and IRELAND in the early industrial era just before and after the Civil War, then Eastern and Southern Europeans joined the ranks of industrial workers by the turn of the century. In the 1910s and 1920s, MEXICAN Americans and African Americans came to work in industrial areas as wide-ranging as the LOWER WEST SIDE, Gary, and BENSENVILLE.

Leisure opportunities drew these workers from the suburb or neighborhood where they lived and worked. Sunday excursions to ballparks, cemeteries, picnic groves, and music halls were hallmarks of nineteenth-century Chicago.

Picnic groves, with hiking, biking, and dancing, developed along rail and INTERURBAN lines. In WEST GARFIELD PARK, picnic groves, a BICYCLE track, a HORSE RACE track, and greenhouses drew visitors from around the metropolitan area. Further from the city center, railroad excursions took Chicagoans to the Des Plaines River at SCHILLER PARK, WHEELING, and DES PLAINES. Dancing pavilions, picnicking, and camping attracted thousands during warm weather.

ROUND LAKE, FOX LAKE, Cary, ALGONQUIN, and Antioch all developed at the turn of the century as railroads and interurbans opened metropolitan access to the lakes and the Fox River. Resorts and cabin communities, along with facilities for day trips, helped to boom this resort area in the early twentieth century. An older German picnic grove along the North Branch of the Chicago River was transformed into an AMUSEMENT PARK called Riverview in 1904. In GREATER GRAND CROSSING, the White City Amusement Park opened in the same year. These parks drew residents from across the metropolitan area, along streetcar, interurban, rail, and elevated lines.

These resort sites each catered to different economic, and often different ethnic, clienteles. Wealthy Chicagoans were drawn to Lake Geneva and estate sites in DUPAGE, LAKE, and MCHENRY Counties. In contrast, the picnic groves and cottages along Bangs Lake drew blue-collar Chicagoans to WAUCONDA in the early twentieth century. Robert Ilg built a recreational park along a streetcar line in Niles for his workers that included two outdoor swimming pools and a replica of the Leaning Tower of Pisa. Illinois Bell and Montgomery Ward both established vacation enclaves for employees in rural WARRENVILLE.

Sometimes it was difficult to tell leisure-time activities from the search for a new home. In the 1870s and 1880s, developers of RIVERSIDE

Economic Origins of Metropolitan Chicago's Communities

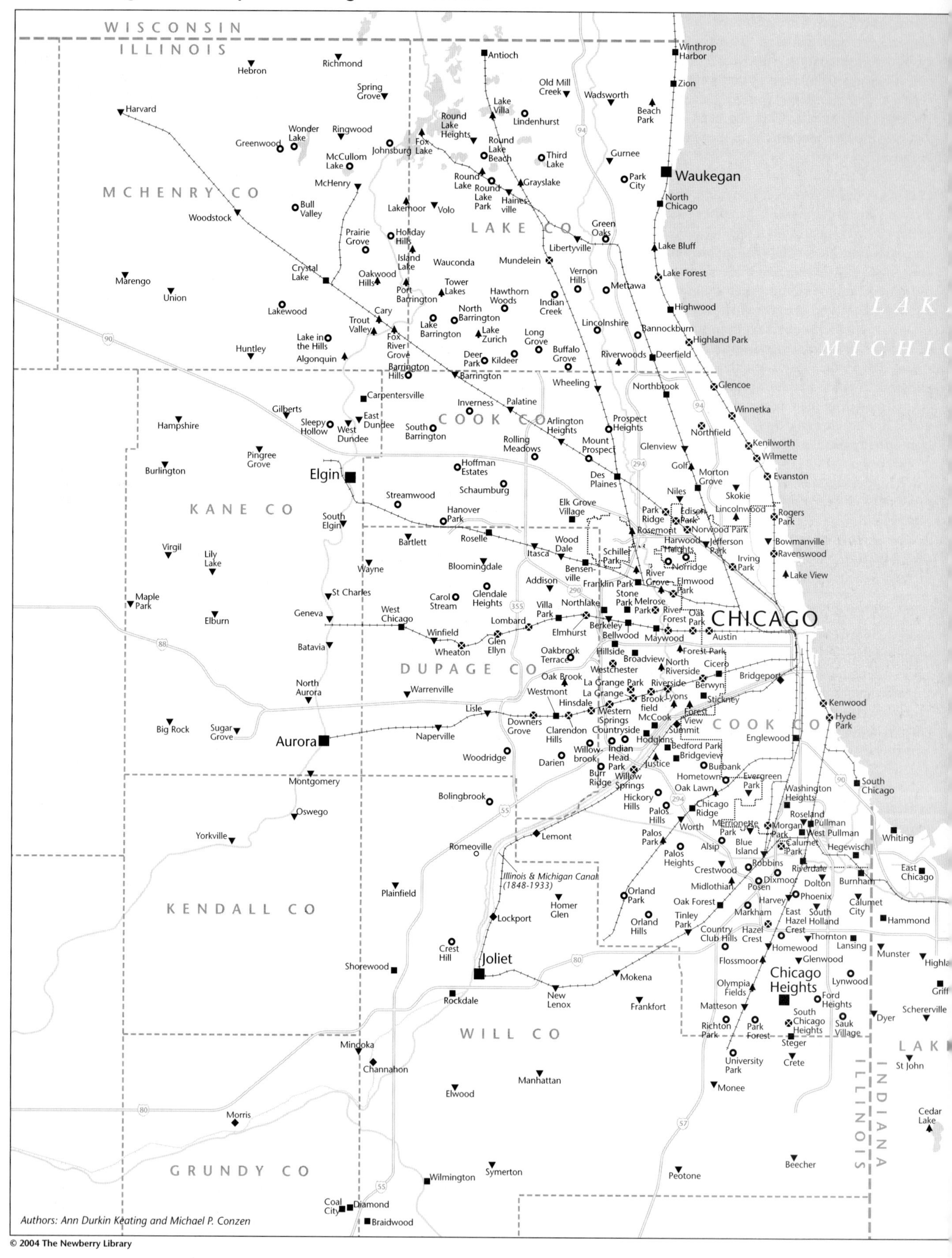

INITIAL IMPETUS FOR SETTLEMENT

- ■ Satellite cities
- ▪ Industrial suburbs
- ◆ Canal towns
- ⊗ Railroad commuter suburbs
- o Automobile commuter suburbs
- ▲ Recreational towns
- ▼ Agricultural trade centers

Commuter railroad lines in 2001
Expressways in 2001

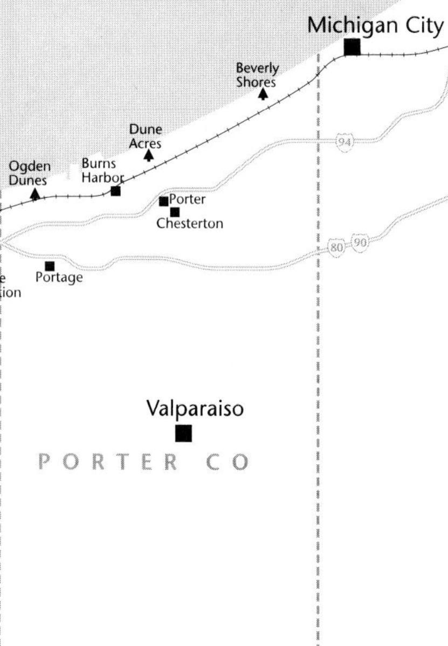

Bird's-eye view from the west, 1874, showing industrial and commuter suburbs. Artist: Unknown. Source: The Newberry Library.

The classification of community types displayed on this map is based primarily upon entries in this encyclopedia. Identifications reflect the initial impetus for clustered settlement beyond agricultural use, effectively the initial step in the urbanization process. Note the relationship between history and geography. Eight old industrial satellite cities ring the metropolis at a distance of about 25 to 40 miles, while old agricultural trade centers stud the region as a whole. Canal towns line the Illinois & Michigan Canal heading out of Chicago to the southwest, while communities that started as railroad suburbs line the major commuter railroad corridors. Later automobile-era suburbs fill in many of the interstitial spaces. Industrial suburbs of varying age appear with greater frequency on the near west and south sides of the metropolitan area, while recreational towns are more abundant to the north and northwest.

Land Subdivision and Urbanization on Chicago's Northwest Side

1851
John Boyd
J. Daly
Frederick Ebinger
Billy Caldwell Reserve
Robinson
F. Tanner
Parsonage
John Seybert
Dan. Dyre
Lewis Steegey
Northwest Hwy
Margaret Noble
Sporledor
Margaret Noble
John Robinson
Elijah Swift
Northwest Plank Rd
Geo. Bukerdike
M. Noble
F. Tanner
Talcott Rd
Russell Morton
Allison Abbott
Morton
N. Eckoff
A. Willson
William H. Bishop
Stanton M. Foycilous
R. Burrill
Patrick Thompson
Noble
Bishop
Higgins Rd
school
Patrick Thompson
J. Thornton
William H. Bishop
William Warbritton
Harlem Ave
James Rueland
Smith's Tavern
John H. Foster
A.K. Kinnear
H. Lanford
Hannah Scofield
Jedidiah Smith
W.W. Smith
Gus. Smith
W.W. Smith
Lucius B. Dean
John Harris
Rees Eaton
Jedidiah Smith
H.T. Byington
John Klein
INDIAN BOUNDARY LINE
C.R. Ball
I.G. Smith
N
Rebecca Denham
Jas. Bayres
Gus. Smith
Mary E. Clarke
ONE-QUARTER MILE
Sam Hoard
Knight
J. Shave
S.B. Cobb
Julius Wadsworth
Thos. Dyer
Hamilton Barnes

Parcels shown are the original government sales units, 1840–48

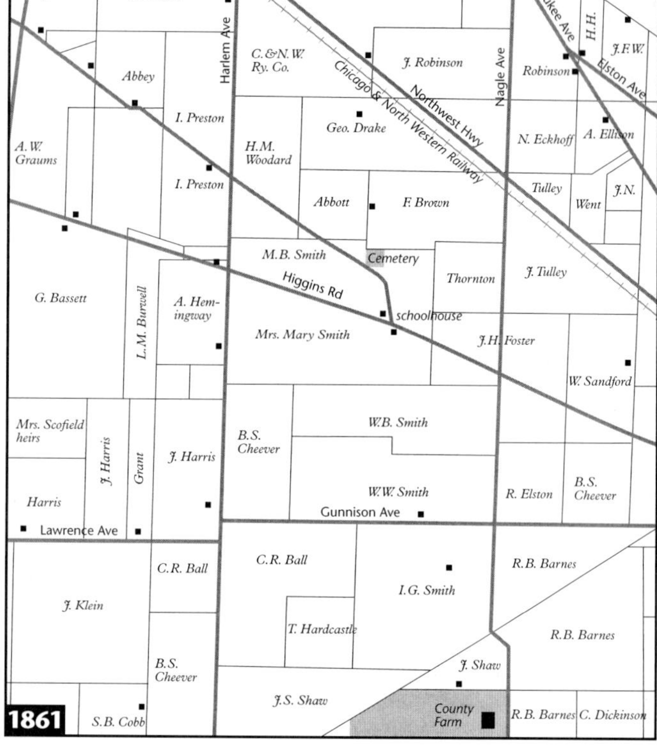

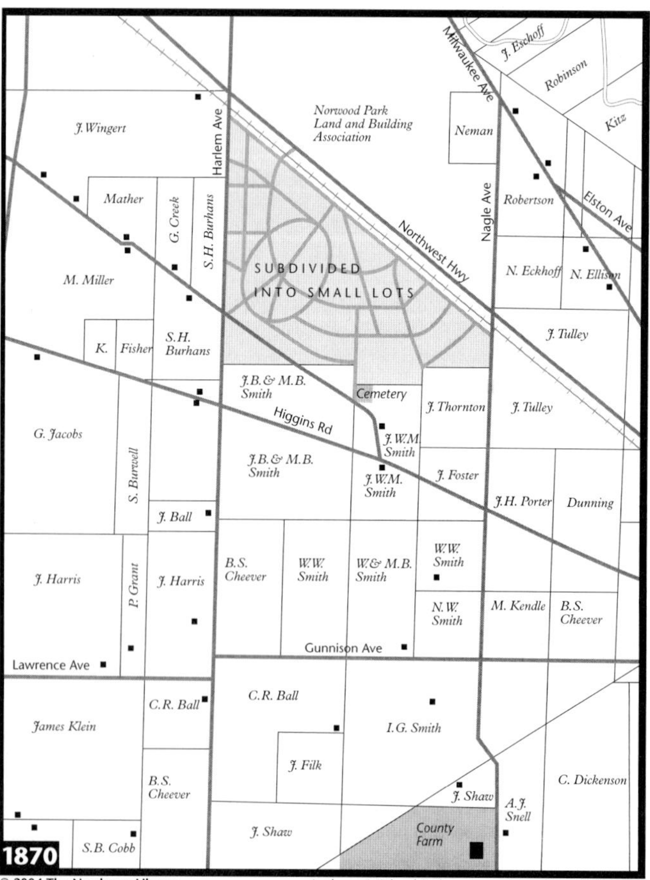

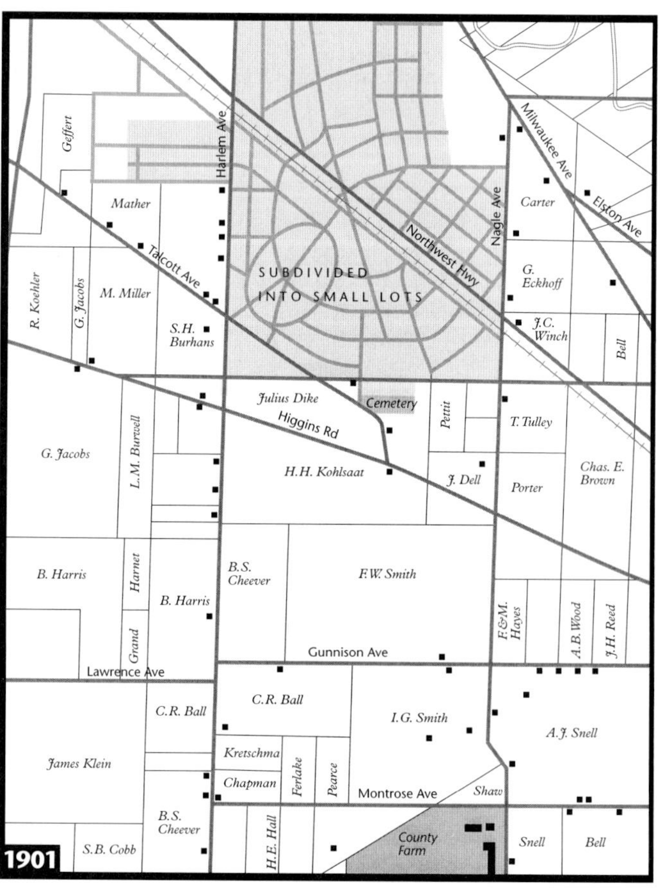

Authors: Michael P. Conzen and Ann Durkin Keating

These six maps trace the development of the Norwood Park area through initial land sale, farming, suburban enclave, and urban neighborhood. The 1851 map identifies the first owners of land parcels shaped by the rectangular national land survey system and reveals the permanent imprint of the Native American era with the reserve created for Billy Caldwell, the Indian Boundary Line, and the diagonal roads based on Indian trails. In 1861 new farmsteads revealed landholdings turning into productive farms served by a new railroad line from Chicago, and a county poor farm appeared. By 1870 a curvilinear suburban subdivision had been laid out around the train station, the beginnings of a residential commuter suburb still surrounded by farms. The 1901 map shows denser subdivision and an enlarged cemetery but still much continuity in rural land ownership, though non-farm residences were beginning to accumulate along well-traveled roads. By 1928 the area was being inundated with gridded urban subdivisions as Norwood Park was pulled closer within the orbit of the central city and became an urban neighborhood. Some of the open space was preserved for golf links and a forest preserve. By 1963, the Kennedy Expressway cut through the community, which had become fully built up by then, its one golf club having succumbed to residential redevelopment. Together, the six maps show changes in transportation that bound Norwood Park ever closer to Chicago, as well as the evolution of community institutions in the context of land-use competition within the area.

and Norwood Park built hotels, hoping to attract tourists who might then buy lots. During the 1890s, Lesser Franklin offered free Sunday excursions to his subdivision alongside a western railroad stop. Pavilions, parades, dancing, contests, food, and beer drew thousands and Franklin Park developed as a suburban town.

In the years after the Civil War, commuters, who often worked in professional and managerial positions in the Loop, found new and existing railroad settlements attractive as home sites. Unlike their working-class counterparts, these upper-middle-class Chicagoans had the money and time to commute to work.

Developers in railroad towns subdivided property and usually graded streets and paved sidewalks. Sometimes they began the process of providing other services (water, sewers, gas, and then electricity) to attract their affluent clientele. These suburban subdivisions were both inside and beyond the current Chicago city limits: Riverside, Morgan Park, Kenilworth, Elmhurst, Irving Park, Austin, Park Ridge, Beverly, Norwood Park, Rogers Park, Wilmette, La Grange, Western Springs, and Homewood.

Developments aimed at the lower middle class and working class began to emerge around streetcar and elevated lines in the late nineteenth and early twentieth centuries. Streetcar suburbs developed both within and outside city limits. North Center, Grand Boulevard, East and West Garfield Park, Albany Park, and Montclare were among the Chicago community areas developed in response to these changes. Outside the city, communities like Elmwood Park, Oak Park, Evanston, and Skokie grew along streetcar/elevated routes. In these areas with good transportation, apartment construction brought denser living, as property values soared.

By the 1920s, bungalows provided a housing alternative to cottages for successful working-class Chicagoans who like their wealthier counterparts sought suburban living both within and outside the city. Portage Park, Hermosa, Chatham, Brookfield, West Elsdon, Gage Park, and West Ridge grew after World War I, providing new housing in outlying districts for less affluent Chicagoans.

Settlements interspersed on the agricultural landscape dotted the Chicago metropolitan landscape in the early twentieth century. A variety of attractions, including jobs, picnics, and homes, drew individual Chicagoans to these areas. Railroads, distinctive physical amenities, and industrial sites helped to determine the locations of these communities. But other factors could also affect where settlements emerged and flourished, including temperance and government services.

Suburban government developed to meet the needs of geographically isolated settlements along railroad and streetcar lines. In the nineteenth century, suburban governments

Graue Mill, Oak Brook, 1964. Photographer: Curt Teich & Co. Source: Curt Teich Archives, Lake County Discovery Museum.

initially provided basic INFRASTRUCTURE services demanded by residents of railroad suburbs, such as running water and sewers. Over time, each suburban area developed a specific packages of services (and taxes) which attracted residents from the metropolitan area who sought those public benefits and the same level of TAXATION. Communities with the wealthiest residents had the broadest range of services and taxation.

Temperance also was a factor in the establishment of nineteenth-century municipalities. PROHIBITION of liquor drew like-minded residents to an area. It kept out taverns and restaurants that served liquor—establishments that might cater to people well beyond the confines of the immediate area. Temperance was also related to ethnicity and religion, as many ROMAN CATHOLIC immigrants, for example, looked askance at prohibiting alcohol. SOUTH HOLLAND, Barrington, and PALATINE were among the farming communities that incorporated in the mid-nineteenth century at least in part to restrict the sale and consumption of liquor.

Many early commuter suburbs also outlawed the sale of liquor as a way of signaling the sort of community that would emerge from the prairie. The developers of La Grange, RIVERSIDE, Beverly, MORGAN PARK, and Norwood Park all prohibited the sale of alcohol from the outset, setting a certain tone. Liquor restrictions in EVANSTON and WHEATON were tied to the location of WHEATON COLLEGE and NORTHWESTERN UNIVERSITY in these communities. Industrial suburbs Harvey, PULLMAN, and ZION touted temperance at the outset as a way of attracting both "right-thinking" workers and factory owners.

Interestingly, near many temperance towns, wet settlements grew. PHOENIX near Harvey, ROSELAND near Pullman, MOUNT GREENWOOD near MORGAN PARK, and LA GRANGE PARK near La Grange all supported SALOONS and taverns. In a few cases, a temperance town was established as an alternative to an area in which saloons operated. RIVER FOREST incorporated in 1880 because of the perceived threat of the saloons in nearby Harlem (FOREST PARK).

While much of the differentiation and sorting which took place among settlements across the metropolitan area provided more choices for residents, these same sorts of processes were used to keep whole classes of Chicagoland residents from portions of the metropolitan area. Expensive homes and property in exclusive subdivisions made a number of suburbs affluent bastions. While Chicagoans of more modest means could choose a less expensive area, wealth brought the widest range of choices. Kenilworth's developer intentionally drew residents from affluent city neighborhoods like Prairie Avenue. GOLF, along a northwestern railroad line, used incorporation to protect a very small upper-middle-class area of half-acre lots.

Outright discrimination based on race and ethnicity also played a growing role in the development of metropolitan Chicago. Before World War I, AFRICAN AMERICANS had little chance for industrial jobs in Chicago. With the end to the major tide of European immigration, however, African Americans came to Chicago to take jobs in the stockyards, steel industry, and elsewhere. They found few places where housing was open to them. By the 1920s, many new SUBDIVISIONS in Chicago had adopted RESTRICTIVE COVENANTS that prohibited property owners from selling property to African Americans (and to a lesser extent JEWS or Catholics). In some outlying areas, African Americans were restricted to certain parts of town. Morgan Park kept black and white homeowners segregated, as did Evanston.

Often arriving at the Twelfth Street Station of the Illinois Central, African Americans found that unlike European immigrants, they could not find housing adjacent to new jobs in the stockyards and other industries. Instead, African American settlement was largely restricted to a narrow band of the SOUTH SIDE, which began to expand with population growth in the 1920s, and a smaller enclave on the NEAR WEST SIDE. DOUGLAS, GRAND BOULEVARD, and WASHINGTON PARK were three of the first areas to experience racial change in Chicago. African Americans also moved directly to suburbs like Phoenix which offered southern migrants lots large enough to support a semirural lifestyle.

Highways and later expressways, overlaid on the nineteenth-century system of railroads and streetcars, shaped the course of twentieth-century development. AGRICULTURE, industry, homes, and leisure were all affected by these changes. The existence of a paved road (and later a limited-access highway) gave new locations advantage, especially in the post–World War II economy.

From the end of World War I to the development of the interstate EXPRESSWAY system after 1956, state and county highway departments surfaced roads and opened new connections across the metropolitan area. The paving of Ogden and North Avenues westward from Chicago out through DuPage provided ready automobile access to areas that had remained quite rural. Lincoln Highway connected isolated communities across the southern part of the metropolitan area.

The interstate highway system reworked the logic of growth. Places that had remained rural, or very small, were now drawn closely into the metropolitan web and grew in new ways. BOLINGBROOK, BLOOMINGDALE, DARIEN, CAROL STREAM, SCHAUMBURG, ROLLING MEADOWS, and ELK GROVE VILLAGE are among the suburban settlements which were born in the interstate highway era. Although farmers had worked the land on which these communities would be built, no concentrated settlements had borne these names. ARLINGTON HEIGHTS, which had been a small farming and industrial settlement in the nineteenth century, grew dramatically in the twentieth as businesses and homes took advantage of road improvements. Paving Rand Road in the northwestern part of the metropolitan area led to the decline of railroad resorts in the Fox Valley. However, it soon brought permanent residents who transformed summer cottages into year-round homes.

While much of the interstate growth displaced outlying farmland, it also required demolition of whole sections of built-up neighborhoods as well. The expressway system cut a large swathe from city neighborhoods in every direction from downtown. WEST GARFIELD PARK, JEFFERSON PARK, Douglas, and Grand Boulevard were among the areas that lost whole neighborhoods as the expressway system expanded in the late 1950s and early 1960s.

In contrast to the private development of railroads and streetcars, funding for the interstate system came from the federal government and was administered by the state highway department. Federal influence on the growth of the Chicago metropolitan area extended beyond the interstates. By the 1950s, federal insurance for homebuilding helped to boom outlying growth. GARFIELD RIDGE, HARWOOD HEIGHTS, FLOSSMOOR, LOMBARD, SCHILLER PARK, MORTON GROVE, Des Plaines, Park Ridge, PARK FOREST, and other areas grew dramatically as more and more Chicagoans could afford homes. The federal government's involvement made it more economical for many Chicagoans to purchase a home rather than rent. Coupled with the homeowner's deduction on income taxes, the insurance program underwrote the postwar development boom in suburban living.

Federal involvement, however, could also stifle development. The loan insurance programs of the Federal Housing Administration and the Veterans' Administration extended almost exclusively to new construction, in new subdivisions. Owners in older areas suffered as their property lost value. In addition, following discriminatory private practices established in cities like Chicago by the 1920s, the federal government "REDLINED" whole sections of Chicago as undesirable for their insured loan programs simply because African Americans lived there.

At the same time that federal home loan insurance programs were booming suburban areas, other federal dollars came to Chicago for URBAN RENEWAL and PUBLIC HOUSING projects. Whole sections of the NEAR NORTH SIDE, NEAR SOUTH SIDE, Near West Side, the LOOP, Douglas, Grand Boulevard, and EAST GARFIELD PARK were razed and redeveloped using over $150 billion in federal urban renewal funds. Despite the lower costs of building public housing on less expensive land in outlying areas and suburbs, the politically expedient decision was made to build most public housing in the metropolitan area on urban renewal land in a ring around downtown Chicago.

Interstate construction, suburbanization, and urban renewal accompanied major changes in Chicago's economy in the second half of the twentieth century. Industry had long propelled Chicago's growth, and its decline increasingly characterized the closing decades of the twentieth century. Deindustrialization affected many areas in Chicago but also had a profound effect on such suburbs as Cicero, MCCOOK, BEDFORD PARK, BELLWOOD, MAYWOOD, MELROSE PARK, NORTHLAKE, RIVER GROVE, WEST CHICAGO, ELGIN, Aurora, Waukegan, Joliet, ROMEOVILLE, BRIDGEVIEW, JUSTICE, Summit, CALUMET CITY, CHICAGO HEIGHTS, Harvey, SAUK VILLAGE, EAST CHICAGO, Gary, and Hammond. In Gary, steel industry employment dropped from over 30,000 in the late 1960s to less than 6,000 in 1987.

Deindustrialization had a less detrimental effect on areas which were able to develop their local economies in new directions. When the Kroehler FURNITURE Factory, which had been Naperville's largest employer for nearly a century, closed in the mid-1970s, it did not signal the decline of the community. Positioned to take advantage of new metropolitan growth along interstate highway corridors, Naperville moved successfully into service and light industry.

Metropolitan-area growth in the closing decades of the twentieth century came in high-technology industries and in the service sector. New urban centers emerged around substantial suburban shopping and commercial centers like OAK BROOK and SCHAUMBURG. Corporate headquarters, professional offices, hotels, theaters, and restaurants joined retail outlets to create what Joel Garreau has described as an "edge city." Often located at the junction of interstate routes, these new centers have further filled in the spider-web development created by the railroad in the nineteenth century.

These new suburban developments have drawn white-collar workers out from the Loop. Unlike in the nineteenth century, when white-collar workers commuted from suburban homes into the Loop, workers in the twenty-first century often commute from suburb to suburb. The dispersal of work locations has left white-collar workers increasingly reliant on automobile travel, in contrast to the railroad commutation of the nineteenth century. Their working-class counterparts, who in the nineteenth century lived near their industrial jobs, have also joined the ranks of commuters. High COMMUTING costs, both in time and money, are especially challenging for low-paid workers.

In the last three decades, a new wave of immigration has also affected metropolitan development. Both highly educated, high-skilled professionals and low-skilled, poorly educated workers are part of this new immigration. Immigrants from Asia and Latin America have settled across the metropolitan area, reshaping the landscape differently from earlier immigrants and migrants, but no less dramatically.

Ann Durkin Keating

See also: Built Environment of the Chicago Region; Economic Geography; Governing the Metropolis; Growth of the Chicago Metropolitan Area (map, preceding p. 543); Initial Land Sales in Northeastern Illinois (color map, p. C1); Local Option; Suburbs and Cities as Dual Metropolis

Further reading: Ebner, Michael. *Creating Chicago's North Shore.* 1988. • Mayer, Richard M., and Harold C. Wade. *Chicago: Growth of a Metropolis.* 1969. • Paycga, Dominic A., and Ellen Skerrett. *Chicago, City of Neighborhoods: Histories and Tours.* 1986.

Metropolitan Statistical Area. Metropolitan Statistical Areas (MSAs) reflect the efforts of the U.S. Office of Management and Budget (OMB) to map some popular images (such as New York as a metropolis, or "Greater Philadelphia") using urban census data. The first guidelines on the identification of MSAs (first called SMAs, Standard Metropolitan Areas) were issued in 1949. Since then, the standards have been regularly updated. The name of the units was changed to Standard Metropolitan Statistical Areas (SMSAs) just before the 1960 census, then to the present name in 1983.

The OMB has developed a series of criteria that formally define an MSA, including population magnitude and density, and characteristics of the labor force. The designation requires an urbanized county with a central city of at least 50,000, and surrounding municipalities that are socially and economically integrated with the center. Adjacent counties may be included in the MSA if they meet certain criteria of integration into the metropolitan area.

The sprawling Chicago urbanized area is populous enough to characterize a Consolidated Metropolitan Statistical Area (CMSA). A CMSA is a set of adjacent MSAs, called Primary Metropolitan Statistical Areas (PMSAs) in this context, related by economic and demographic criteria so as to constitute a super-MSA that resembles Jean Gottmann's abstract "megalopolis." The Illinois component of that area includes COOK, DUPAGE, MCHENRY, DeKalb, LAKE, KANE, Kendall, WILL, Grundy, and Kankakee Counties in Illinois, as well as Kenosha County, Wisconsin, and LAKE-PORTER Counties in northwestern Indiana, combined to form a three-state Chicago-Gary-Kenosha CMSA.

William Erbe

See also: Community Areas

Further reading: Gottmann, Jean. *Megalopolis: The Urbanized Northeastern Seaboard of the United States.* 1961.

Mettawa, IL, Lake County, 29 miles NW of the Loop. East of the DES PLAINES RIVER and west of present-day Interstate 94, tall trees and large lots continue to line the few main roads of Mettawa.

The village was named for a POTAWATOMI chief who resided there in the 1830s. IRISH farmers followed the Potawatomi into the area. After 1900 LAKE FOREST residents began hunting pheasants and picnicking in Mettawa's woods. In the early 1930s Harold Florsheim, shoe magnate, established Harham Farms.

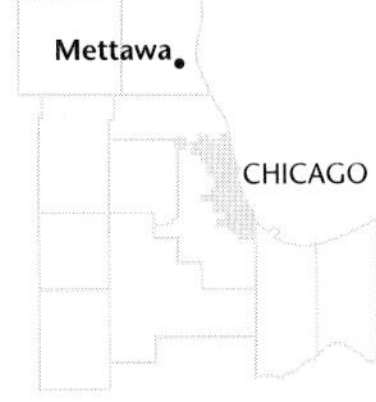

In 1938, Adlai Stevenson II constructed a metal house on his 70-acre property along the Des Plaines River. "The Farm" was eventually purchased by the LAKE COUNTY FOREST PRESERVE, along with the Daniel Wright Woods and the 490-acre MacArthur Woods FOREST PRESERV.

Mettawa incorporated as a village in 1960. In 1990 the population was 348 residents, of whom 20 percent owned horses. Only a mile wide and three miles long, Mettawa earned the distinction of being the wealthiest community in the six counties of the Chicago metropolitan area. The village has no stores, offices, or town hall and in 1994 there were only 189 homes. In the 1990s, however, Newton F. Korhumel won a suit to build a commercial development on the 125 acres he owns on Mettawa's east side on Highway 60 west of the Tri-State TOLLWAY.

Marilyn Elizabeth Perry

See also: Expressways; Suburbs and Cities as Dual Metropolis

Further reading: Clipping files. Vernon Area Library, Vernon Hills, IL.

Mexican Fine Arts Center Museum. The Mexican Fine Arts Center Museum (MFACM) is the first museum in the Midwest devoted to Mexican art and the largest Latino museum in the United States. Suggesting that Mexican culture is *sin fronteras,* the MFACM claims its subject matter from both the United States and Mexico.

In 1982 educators Carlos Tortolero and Helen Valdez founded the Center Museum "to conserve and preserve for our people." Influenced by the Chicago Freedom Movement, Malcolm X's call for political and economic autonomy, and by William Walker's community murals on AFRICAN AMERICAN history and culture, Tortolero dreamed of an arts institution led by Mexican arts administrators, ARTISTS, educators, and patrons. Finding new opportunities for Latino enfranchisement under Mayor Harold Washington, Tortolero and Valdez pursued their dream by producing exhibits and sponsoring over two dozen cultural events at community and downtown venues.

In January 1986 the Center Museum signed an agreement with the PARK DISTRICT to convert the Boat Craft Shop in Harrison Park into a museum, making the MFACM one of the city's MUSEUMS IN THE PARK. Since opening in PILSEN on March 27, 1987, the MFACM continued to grow, eventually housing a Permanent Collection Gallery, an education center, and a gift shop, Tienda Tzintzuntzan, that provides almost a quarter of the museum's income.

The Center Museum's exhibition season is devoted to four areas: the *El Día de los Muertos* exhibition, contemporary ART, traditional art, and Mesoamerican art and culture, including pre-Cuauhtemoc objects that assert the cultural authority of the region's indigenous people. The MFACM, however, is more than a museum. Devoted to visual arts exhibition and collection, performing arts, the professional development of Mexican artists, arts education, youth, and intercultural coalition building, the MFACM embodies the culturally based *centros* of the Southwest that have a history of educating and advocating for their communities, goals the Museum pursues in Chicago. In 1994, the MFACM inaugurated Del Corazon: the Mexican Performing Arts Festival and the Sor Juana Festival, a celebration of the art and activism of *mexicanas.* In 1998 the MFACM initiated the Yollocalli Youth Museum and purchased Radio Arte—WRTE 90.5 FM.

Karen Mary Davalos

See also: Art, Public; Civil Rights Movements; Ethnic Music; Lower West Side; Mexicans

Further reading: "The First 10 Years: 1987–1997 / The Tenth Year Anniversary." *Codice: Mexican Fine Arts Center Museum Newsletter* 1.1 (December 1997): 2–3. • Davalos, KarenMary. *Exhibiting Mestizaje: Mexican (American) Museums in the Diaspora.* 2001. • Nadanyi, Michele, and Mark Parry. "Case 26: Mexican Fine Arts Center Museum." In *Cases in Marketing Management,* ed. D. J. Dalrymple, L. J. Parsons, and J.-P. Jeannet, 1992.

Mexicans. The first major wave of Mexican migration to Chicago began in the mid to late 1910s, spurred on by the economic, social, and political displacements of the Mexican Revolutionary years and the rise in industrial and agricultural employment in the United States. Arriving through both direct and indirect routes, Mexicans worked as unskilled and semiskilled laborers in AGRICULTURE and heavy industry, including the Rock Island, Santa Fe, and Burlington railways; Inland Steel; U.S. Steel; Beetsugar Company; and the Armour and Swift packinghouses. The predominantly male Mexican workforce, and the "solos," migrated into Chicago from agricultural fields throughout the Midwest and from towns and villages in Texas and the Central Mexican states of Guanajuato, Michoacán, and Jalisco. Those who came were more likely from the middle class than from among the poorest peasants. Like many of the AFRICAN AMERICAN workers of the GREAT MIGRATION, some Mexicans were hired to break steel and PACKINGHOUSE STRIKES in the late 1910s and early 1920s, thus placing them in conflict with European workers.

Initially, *enganchistas,* labor recruiters, worked in Northern Mexico and parts of the U.S. Southwest to recruit Mexican laborers. Migration accelerated in the 1920s as word spread of ready WORK in Chicago and as industry successfully lobbied to exempt Mexicans from the restrictions of the 1924 Immigration Act.

Once arriving in Chicago, however, workers discovered that housing was substandard, crowded, and expensive. Much of the housing was owned by other immigrant groups who frequently charged Mexicans higher rents. Mexicans often responded by having more people living together in order to pay the expensive rents, thus compounding health and sanitation problems in already dilapidated buildings. Several men lived together in one or two rooms while families took in three or four boarders at a time. Many of those who worked on the RAILROAD, the *traqueros,* lived in boxcars along the tracks, their homes literally mobile as demand for workers rose and fell.

Mexican residential segregation, however, was not as pronounced as that of African Americans. *Colonias,* Mexican residential enclaves, sprouted within the industrial sectors of the CALUMET REGION, on the NEAR WEST SIDE, and in the BACK OF THE YARDS area. This

Deportation and Repatriation

On the eve of the GREAT DEPRESSION, Chicago was home to the largest MEXICAN community in the Midwest, with more than 25,000 Mexicans and Mexican Americans. This community consisted of families but also included large groups of single men. They worked in a variety of industries, including railroads, MEATPACKING plants, and steel mills. Mexican Chicago thrived during the 1920s, and the neighborhood Atlas Bank counted among its depositors some 600 Mexicans in addition to another 400 who regularly bought money orders. The Mexican community supported a business class who operated a variety of enterprises: fourteen RESTAURANTS, five pool halls, five GROCERY STORES, a barber shop, a shoe repair, four bakeries, a photograph gallery, a tailor shop, and a music shop.

Few of these businesses survived the Great Depression, when major industries commonly awarded preference to workers of European descent and marked Mexicans for layoffs. Mexico City newspapers reported vast UNEMPLOYMENT in Chicago and suggested that many of the unemployed were recent arrivals fleeing an even more deplorable situation in surrounding areas.

Many Mexicans refused welfare assistance even though starvation was imminent. Instead, many preferred voluntary repatriation to escape the difficult economic situation. As early as 1929, the local Chicago Spanish-language newspaper *La Raza* advocated repatriation for unemployed Mexicans. Chicago's Mexican consul Rafael Aveleyra also offered his good offices to assist his nationals and their children in securing transportation and relocating to Mexico.

Although repatriated Mexicans used various modes of transportation, including cars, buses, and trucks, public and private agencies preferred railroad transportation, because the trains were more reliable, delivered repatriates to the border, and offered a special discount rate of $15 per person. Most relief agencies in the United States preferred to pay a one-time train ticket fare rather than provide long-term assistance to Mexicans.

Chicago differed from other American cities and such neighbors as GARY, South Chicago, and Indiana Harbor in never mounting a public repatriation campaign against Mexicans. Discrimination by local POLICE and the COURT SYSTEM, and layoffs, however, induced many Mexicans to repatriate voluntarily. A conservative estimate reports that Chicago's Mexican community of 25,000 in 1929 declined to less than 16,000 by 1938.

Francisco E. Balderrama

largely male Mexican population lived amid several large Eastern and Southern European ethnic groups, including POLES and ITALIANS, creating both strife and occasional intergroup cooperation. Initially, Mexican male social life revolved around local pool halls, barbershops, and SETTLEMENT HOUSES. As the colonias expanded and more women arrived, Mexicans founded tortilla factories, RESTAURANTS, markets or *bodegas,* and several local NEWSPAPERS like *Mexico* (renamed *El Nacional* in 1930) and *El Ideal.* By the early 1930s they had founded local chapters of Mexican MUTUAL BENEFIT SOCIETIES, labor groups (including *El Frente Popular*), and fraternal organizations. *Mutualistas,* as these groups were called, entailed collective participation of individual members who paid dues into a general fund. Such funds were then used to help members through periods of UNEMPLOYMENT or workplace injury and often paid for funeral costs and sending the deceased back to Mexico.

Mexican religious life centered primarily around ROMAN CATHOLICISM, despite the growing presence of PROTESTANTS. Cordi-Marian nuns fleeing the anti-Catholic Cristero Revolts of the late 1920s in Mexico came to Chicago and worked with Mexicans in Packingtown, SOUTH CHICAGO, and the Near West Side. In South Chicago, Mexicans established the first local Mexican church, Our Lady of Guadalupe, in 1924. Rebuilt in 1928 at its present location at 91st and Brandon, the church continues to serve the Mexican community in the area, operating child care centers and a home for the elderly. On the Near West Side, Mexicans worshiped at St. Francis of Assisi, one of the few structures to survive the construction of the Kennedy EXPRESSWAY interchanges and the Chicago Circle campus of the UNIVERSITY OF ILLINOIS.

Mexicans organized neighborhood BASEBALL teams for both men and women and celebrated Cinco de Mayo and 16th of September festivals. Generational tensions erupted between Mexican parents and their children as the children learned English in SCHOOLS and took part in the spreading venues of mass culture, from JAZZ music and dances to movie houses. Mexican women increasingly took jobs outside the home, in garment factories, restaurants, and light assembly plants, while Mexican men stayed primarily in steel, MEATPACKING, and railroad industries. Mexican life in Chicago transcended the limits of metropolitan Chicago. Workers moved between Mexico, the Southwest (primarily Texas), and various parts of the Midwest. Those working in agriculture followed crops during the warm months; to save money, many spent winters working in industrial jobs in Chicago rather than traveling south.

The Crash of 1929 and the onset of the GREAT DEPRESSION froze these migrations. Considered the most expendable of workers,

Mexican workers in Willow Springs, 1917. Photographer: Unknown. Source: Chicago Historical Society.

Mexican laborers suffered disproportionately high rates of unemployment. Their plights, in the context of ongoing RACISM, fueled efforts to exclude and, ultimately, remove Mexicans from the United States. With the cooperation of the U.S. and Mexican governments, local civic organizations such as the American Legion of East Chicago rounded up hundreds of UNEMPLOYED workers and their families and placed them on trains bound for the U.S.-Mexico border. Forcible and voluntary repatriation drives focused on workers who "looked Mexican" and often ignored the citizenship of those who had been born in the United States. Others, conscious of their bleak prospects and the hostile social climate, voluntarily accepted the free train trip south. In the decade of the 1930s, the Mexican population in the Chicago area was cut nearly in half. By 1940 an estimated 16,000 Mexicans remained within Chicago.

Amid the tumult of the NEW DEAL and WORLD WAR II, those Mexicans who remained seized new opportunities for employment, mobility, and power to combat discrimination. Local non-publicly-funded aid organizations like the Immigrants' Protective League and the CHICAGO AREA PROJECT tried to provide relief when public funds were limited increasingly to U.S. citizens. In the late 1930s, building on labor traditions in Mexico and bolstered by the Wagner Act, some Mexican workers joined the CONGRESS OF INDUSTRIAL ORGANIZATIONS (CIO), not only to win better wages and working conditions but also to combat racism encountered at work.

Wartime industrial demands eased immigration restrictions, and Mexican migration into Chicago reached new heights. Between 1943 and 1945, over 15,000 *braceros,* "guest workers" under contract with the U.S. and Mexican governments, arrived in the city to work. Many of these stayed after their contracts ended or returned to Chicago in the years after the war. By the late 1940s, Mexican settlements outside the city grew as well. Long-standing settlements in AURORA, JOLIET, GARY, and BLUE ISLAND expanded, and newer populations sprouted in ARLINGTON HEIGHTS, BERWYN, and BENSENVILLE.

Despite a growing presence throughout metropolitan Chicago, Mexicans continued to face discrimination and renewed threats of repatriation as national programs like "Operation Wetback" sought to capture *braceros* who had overstayed their visas. While working to ensure economic stability, leaders of Chicago's Mexican communities supported the education of workers and the development of civic and community institutions like the Mexican Civic Committee, founded in 1943. As before the war, employers used Mexicans as strikebreakers. Inland Steel, for instance, imported 250 Mexican workers from Texas in May of 1947 to work in place of striking steelworkers. That those Mexican workers marched in solidarity with strikers and demanded transportation back to Texas attested to Chicago's growing working-class solidarity as well as the power of Mexican workers. In the 1950s, Chicago Mexicans went on to establish branches of CIVIL RIGHTS organizations already active in the Southwest, including the GI Forum and League of United Latin American Citizens (LULAC). The GI Forum fought for the rights of Mexican World War II veterans who were

Mexican Independence Day parade, Little Village, 1984. Photographer: Gregg Mann. Source: Chicago Historical Society.

too often denied GI benefits. LULAC sought to increase the numbers of Mexicans with U.S. citizenship and to secure the rights of Mexican Americans.

Such organizations neither represented nor actively lobbied for the growing populations of *indocumentados,* those Mexican nationals living in the United States without papers. By 1960, Chicago's primarily working-class Mexican community of nearly 56,000 was fractured along lines of citizenship, legal status, and language. As large numbers of PUERTO RICANS settled nearby, the Latino population in Chicago continued to diversify. Mexicans continued to live in the colonias of Back of the Yards and South Chicago, but with the construction of the University of Illinois at Chicago, those living in the Near West Side area moved south to PILSEN, *La Diesiocho* (named for the 18th Street commercial vein). In the mid-1970s, this colonia expanded past 26th Street and was known as *La Villita* (LITTLE VILLAGE) or *La Veintiseis.* Together these neighborhoods have become the fastest-growing areas of Mexican, and increasingly Central American, settlement in Chicago. More recently, Mexican-owned businesses ranging from shoe and clothing stores to travel agencies, CONSTRUCTION firms, and RESTAURANTS have sprouted along Cermak, attesting to the vibrancy and growing economic power of Chicago's Mexican population.

Ignited by the Chicano Movement in other parts of the United States, a thriving mural movement developed in the streets of Pilsen and *La Villita* as muralists brought ART to the streets while claiming those same streets with their paints. Mario Castillo's "Peace" mural, the mural on Casa Aztlán by Marcos Raya, Salvador Vega, and Carlos Barrera, and the newer nearly block-long mural on the Jose Clemente Orozco Community Center capture the flavor of Mexican life in Chicago. In 1987 the MEXICAN FINE ARTS CENTER MUSEUM opened, and its internationally acclaimed exhibits and collections have made it one of the premier institutes of Mexican art in the country.

Mexicans worked throughout the 1970s and early 1980s in groups like the Spanish Coalition for Jobs and the Latino Institute to improve housing and education while fighting the employment and social discrimination that many still faced. Political and community activists, including Juan Velazquez, Linda Coronado, Danny Solis, and Rudy Lozano, fought for institutions like Benito Juarez High School and founded a variety of organizations, including Centro de la Causa, Casa Aztlán, Mujeres Latinas en Acción, Pilsen Neighbors, and Latino Youth. More recent COMMUNITY ORGANIZING has highlighted the transnational aspects of Mexican life in Chicago by focusing on hometown associations like the Federation of Michoacán Clubs in Illinois. Such progress and struggles for empowerment remain central concerns for Mexicans in Chicago as Latino representation in local and state POLITICS becomes ever more visible. The 2000 census counted more than 530,000 Mexicans in the city of Chicago, with more than 1.1 million in the metropolitan area.

Gabriela F. Arredondo
Derek Vaillant

See also: Americanization; Demography; Multicentered Chicago

Further reading: Andrade, Juan, Jr. "A Historical Survey of Mexican Immigration to the U.S. and an Oral History of the Mexican Settlement in Chicago, 1920–1990." Ph.D. diss., Northern Illinois University. 1998. • Arredondo, Gabriela F. "'What! The Mexicans, Americans?' Race and Ethnicity, Mexicans in Chicago, 1916–1939." Ph.D. diss., University of Chicago. 1999. • Davalos, KarenMary. "Ethnic Identity among Mexican and Mexican American Women in Chicago, 1920–1991." Ph.D. diss., Yale University. 1993.

Miamis. The Miamis were originally an eastern woodlands, central Algonquian people for whom Chicago served as a vital way station. The Iroquois wars of the 1600s shattered the stability of the GREAT LAKES region, forcing most of the central Algonquian peoples (including the Miamis) into the REFUGEE zone of Illinois and Wisconsin, the *pays d'en haut.* Chicago was a temporary stopping point in their migrations. As the FRENCH offered military support and the Iroquois retreated back to their homelands in New York, the Miamis slowly returned eastward. Six separate groups constituted the Miamis around the year 1700: Atchatchakangouen (the Miami proper), Kilatika, Mengakonkia, Pepikokia, Piankashaw, and Wea. By 1800, only the Miami proper, the Piankashaw, and the Wea remained.

Believing that the Miamis had settled at Chicago permanently, the Jesuits founded the MISSION OF THE GUARDIAN ANGEL there in 1696. But the Miamis continued to migrate, and the mission probably ended sometime between 1703 and 1715. By 1710, roughly a third of the Miamis still resided at Chicago, with the majority at St. Joseph's, Michigan, and along the Wabash and Maumee Rivers to the southeast.

By the 1720s, the Miamis had resettled in Indiana. At the Treaty of Greenville in 1795, the Miami war chief Little Turtle defined tribal boundaries this way: "My forefather kindled the first fire at Detroit; from thence, he extended his lines to the head waters of Scioto, from thence, to its mouth, from thence, down the Ohio, to the mouth of the Wabash, and from thence to Chicago, on Lake Michigan." No other tribe represented at the treaty hearings challenged Chief Little Turtle's vast claims.

Chicago served as the site of another significant event in Miami history: the battle of FORT DEARBORN, in August 1812. In the second month of the war, the United States ordered the evacuation of Fort Dearborn. William Wells, Little Turtle's son-in-law, and 30 Miamis were to assist them. Dressed in Miami attire, his face painted black to anticipate death,

Wells and the accompanying Miamis, American soldiers, women, and children faced 400 hostile POTAWATOMIS. The Potawatomis killed 23 American soldiers, 2 women, 12 children, and 10 civilians.

In some survivors' accounts, the Miamis fought bravely on the side of the Americans; in others, they did not fight at all. Nonetheless, William Henry Harrison, commander of the Northwest Army, used the "massacre" at Fort Dearborn as a pretext to attack Miami villages throughout the Wabash region. With the wanton destruction of their villages, Miami chiefs Pacanne and Jean B. Richardville led the formerly neutral tribe into an alliance with the British.

The Miamis remained in Indiana until the United States government forcibly removed two-thirds of the tribe to Kansas in 1846 and 1847. Today, the Miamis live in northeastern Oklahoma and northern Indiana.

Bradley J. Birzer

See also: Chicago in the Middle Ground; Native American Religion; Treaties

Further reading: Barnhart, John D., and Dorothy Riker. *Indiana to 1816: The Colonial Period.* 1994. • Celeste, Sister Mary, R.S.M. "The Miami Indians Prior to 1700." *Mid-America* 16 (April 1934): 225–234. • Kinietz, W. Vernon. *The Indians of the Western Great Lakes, 1615–1760.* 1940.

Michael Reese Hospital. Among the many institutions destroyed by the Great Chicago Fire of 1871 was the HOSPITAL on LaSalle street (between Schiller and Goethe) established by the United Hebrew Relief Association. When Michael Reese, a wealthy REAL-ESTATE developer, died in 1877 his will provided sufficient funds to build a new hospital. An 1836 JEWISH immigrant from Bavaria, Reese had made a fortune in land speculation and silver mining by the 1850s. When the hospital was completed in 1880 Reese's heirs requested that it be named in his honor and that it serve all of Chicago without regard to race, creed, or nationality.

The original Michael Reese building, located on the corner of 29th and Groveland Avenue, was replaced in 1907 by another, larger building on the same site. The hospital's medical INNOVATIONS included Julius Hess's infant incubator (around 1915) and the first permanent incubator station for premature babies (1922). In 1946 Michael Reese Hospital along with a number of other area organizations formed the SOUTH SIDE Planning Board to refurbish the area surrounding the hospital, which had suffered considerable economic and physical decline. Like ILLINOIS INSTITUTE OF TECHNOLOGY and MERCY HOSPITAL, Michael Reese preferred URBAN RENEWAL to leaving the area altogether.

From the 1950s to the 1980s, Michael Reese hospital grew considerably, purchasing adjacent properties and constructing additional buildings. In 1998 the hospital's ownership shifted from Columbia/HCA Healthcare Corporation, of Nashville, Tennessee, to Doctors Community Healthcare Corporation, of Scottsdale, Arizona.

Wallace Best

See also: Douglas

Further reading: Gordon, Sarah, ed. *All Our Lives: A Centennial History of Michael Reese Hospital and Medical Center, 1881–1981.* 1981. • Hirsch, Arnold R. *Making the Second Ghetto: Race and Housing in Chicago, 1940–1960.* 1983.

Michigan City, IN, LaPorte County, 41 miles E of the Loop. Michigan City, Indiana, lies at the mouth of Trail Creek, on LAKE MICHIGAN's southeastern shore. Envisioned by nineteenth-century boosters as a commercial and transportation center, this small city is now best known as a tourist hub for the INDIANA DUNES territory.

When federal surveyors arrived in the Lake Michigan DUNES, they saw the low, swampy site at the mouth of Trail Creek as the ideal location for a major harbor at the end of the Michigan Road, then being built northward through Indiana. In 1831, armed with inside knowledge of the harbor plans, REAL-ESTATE speculator Maj. Isaac C. Elston of Crawfordsville, Indiana, began to buy land there. In 1832, Elston laid out the town of Michigan City. The first settlers arrived the following year. By 1836, the town's population had swelled to nearly 3,000.

Between 1837 and 1844, the town served as the principal grain market for northern Indiana. Several rail lines arrived in the 1850s, bringing their repair shops with them. The Haskell & Barker Car Company, established in 1852, quickly became the city's largest employer. The Northern State Prison began supplying local manufacturers with convict labor shortly after it opened in the early 1860s.

Harbor construction finally moved forward after the CIVIL WAR. In 1867 and 1868, the Michigan City Harbor Company built two piers and dredged a deep channel between them. With an infusion of federal funds, the harbor was soon ready to accept large vessels. Michigan City became one of Indiana's largest LUMBER markets. Industry boomed.

Michigan City's fortunes began to recede after 1900. Profitable convict labor was outlawed. The lumber trade gradually died out. The Michigan Central RAILROAD moved its rail shops at the close of WORLD WAR I, and the Haskell & Barker car works became Michigan City's sole large employer. Hoosier Slide, the town's once-towering sand dune, was completely mined out by the 1920s.

Fortunately for Michigan City, Lake Michigan tourism surged at about the same time. Though lake steamer excursions declined after 1915, when the Michigan City–bound EASTLAND rolled over in the CHICAGO RIVER, other modes of tourist transportation took their place. The Dunes Highway opened in 1923. Shortly thereafter, utilities magnate Samuel Insull upgraded the Chicago, South Shore & South Bend Railroad. Both the highway and the electric INTERURBAN provided Chicagoans with easy access to Michigan City and the dunes beaches. (They also provided Michigan City residents a convenient means of COMMUTING in the other direction.) Michigan City's lakeshore Washington Park, established in 1891 and improved in the 1930s, aimed to draw the tourist trade. The creation of the Indiana Dunes National Lakeshore in the 1960s fortified the tourism industry. By the end of the twentieth Century, downtown Michigan City, which had experienced decline in the face of URBAN RENEWAL, housed a popular outlet mall and a casino boat recently moored in Trail Creek.

Elizabeth A. Patterson

See also: Gambling; Leisure; Public Works, Federal Funding for; Quarrying, Stonecutting, and Brickmaking; Vacation Spots

Further reading: Greening, Elwin G., ed. *A Pictorial History of Michigan City, Indiana, 1675–1992.* 1992. • Nicewarner, Gladys Bull. *Michigan City, Indiana: The Life of a Town.* 1980. • Packard, Jasper. *History of LaPorte County, Indiana, and Its Townships, Towns, and Cities.* 1876.

Midlothian, IL, Cook County, 18 miles S of the Loop. Midlothian is bordered by CRESTWOOD and ROBBINS to the north, POSEN to the east, MARKHAM to the south, and OAK FOREST to the west, and shares a history with all of these communities.

Most of the surface of Midlothian is on the lake plain formed by glacial Lake Chicago as a result of the Wisconsin glacier (12,000 BP). In the southwestern corner, the Tinley Moraine passes through from northwest to southeast.

Evidence of NATIVE AMERICAN occupation in the area of Midlothian abounds, especially just south of town at the Oak Forest site. The site, on the Tinley Moraine overlooking a marshy area of glacial lake plain, dates to the 1600s. The POTAWATOMI were the last Native American occupants of the area. The Old Indian Boundary Line crosses to the southeast of the village. The Midlothian area and additional land to the northwest of this line were ceded in 1816 in the TREATY of St. Louis.

The early record of European occupation of the Midlothian area is the history of Bremen Township, which was first settled by YANKEE farmers in the early 1830s, followed by GERMAN and IRISH immigrants in the 1840s and 1850s. Midlothian was first called Rexford

Crossing and was a milk stop where the Rock Island line crossed Crawford Avenue.

The Midlothian Country Club was founded in 1898 on the rolling landscape of the Tinley Moraine. (The name Midlothian is a reflection of the SCOTTISH origins of the game of GOLF, in that it came from Sir Walter Scott's novel *The Heart of Midlothian.)* The country club, founded by George R. Thorne, president of Montgomery Ward and Company, attracted the elites of Chicago society and was the first golf club south of the city. The country club built the Midlothian & Blue Island RAILWAY to connect its clubhouse to the Rock Island Railroad at 147th street, and was unique in having the only railroad owned by a country club.

A small community developed around the station, with residential development beginning in 1915, an elementary school in 1919, and incorporation in 1927.

With the growth of population came the founding of the community's major religious congregations: St. Christopher ROMAN CATHOLIC in 1922, Midlothian United Methodist in 1925, Hope Lutheran and Concordia Lutheran in 1925. The Lutherans merged in 1973 as St. Stephen Lutheran Church. St. Christopher was the patron saint of travelers, and a tradition of blessing motorcycles developed at the Catholic church.

The GREAT DEPRESSION hurt many families in Midlothian, but attracted those who were employed and wanted better housing, such as Harry Raday, who served as mayor from 1961 to 1985. Midlothian has developed as a residential community, noted for its low taxes.

Midlothian was the home of the Highland Games from 1973 to 1981, a reminder of its Scottish name. Although the games became a major regional attraction, financial and legal problems caused their demise.

Dave Bartlett

See also: Entertaining Chicagoans; Protestants

Further reading: "Featuring Bremen Township." *Where the Trails Cross* 7.1 (Fall 1976): 1–3. • "Midlothian Golden Anniversary." *Midlothian Messenger.* 1977. • Markman, Charles W. *Chicago before History: The Prehistoric Archaeology of a Modern Metropolitan Area.* Studies in Illinois Archaeology 7, ed. Thomas E. Emerson. 1991.

Municipal Airport, 1929. Photographer: Chicago Aerial Survey Co. Source: Chicago Historical Society.

Midway Airport. Between 1932 and 1961, Chicago's Midway Airport, located on Chicago's Southwest Side between 55th and 63rd Streets and Cicero and Central Avenues, boasted the title of world's busiest airport. At its peak in 1959 the municipal airport served 10 million passengers. In competition with O'HARE Field, however, which had opened in 1955, passenger traffic through Midway plummeted 60 percent by 1961, as the modern, convenient, and jet-friendly runways of O'Hare lured away travelers. The venerable "Munie" faced apparent obsolescence before reinventing itself following the deregulation of the AIRLINE industry in 1978. By the 1980s and 1990s, Chicago's outmoded airport had reemerged as a haven for small carriers serving Chicagoans with competitively priced TRANSPORTATION.

Private aircraft were the first planes to take off and land from the square-mile parcel of land leased by the city of Chicago from the Chicago Board of Education. In 1926 the city began leasing the field for commercial purposes. A single cinder runway served airmail traffic, and was dedicated Chicago Municipal Airport on December 12, 1927, offering mail, express, and passenger service. Officials rededicated the facility as Midway to honor the Pacific air and sea battle of WORLD WAR II.

A bond issue funded construction of a passenger terminal and administration building in 1931, and federal grants in subsequent years covered major improvements in runway design, lighting, and safety and service features.

A 1941 court case ordered the Chicago & Western Indiana RAILROAD to reroute its tracks to permit new runway construction at Midway, marking the triumphant evolution of Chicago as a national transportation hub. Passenger air travel at Midway during the war years soared and reached 1.3 million by 1945. Subsequent partnerships between the city, the airlines, and new agencies such as the Federal Aviation Administration helped modernize service at Midway. The airport's south terminal served new overseas international flights and housed U.S. Customs operations.

At what should have been its greatest hour, Midway fell prey to technological changes in aviation. The requirements of supersonic air travel, such as longer runways, drew carriers to larger and more convenient O'Hare. The city of Chicago provided sustaining infusions of cash to Midway investing $10 million in renovation funds in 1968, and supported construction of the nearby Stevenson EXPRESSWAY as an artery to restore Midway's passenger supply. A few major carriers returned, but by 1976, only Delta Airlines continued to service the fallen giant.

Deregulation of the airline industry spurred entrepreneurship by new carriers and helped resuscitate the beleaguered airport after 1978. Upstart Midway Airlines formed to challenge major carrier dominance at O'Hare. It became the airport's flagship, supplying more than half of its passenger volume by 1990. Midway Airlines required reorganization, but the model inspired other carriers, such as Southwest Airlines. By the mid-1990s, Midway offered an alternative to O'Hare for cost-conscious travelers and families lured to the Southwest Side by competitive fares to popular destinations. Bolstered by construction of RAPID TRANSIT service to the LOOP, Midway has again become a vital circuit in Chicago's transportation system.

Derek Vaillant

See also: Airports, Commuter; Built Environment of the Chicago Region; Public Works, Federal Funding for

Further reading: Casey, John A. *Chicago Aviation and Airports: The First Forty Years, 1926–1966.* 1966.

Millennium Park. Millennium Park (constructed 1998–2004) is the 24-acre park, garden, underground PARKING garage, and cultural center located within GRANT PARK and bounded by Michigan Avenue on the west, Randolph Street on the north, Columbus Drive on the east, and Monroe Street on the south. Mayor Richard M. Daley conceived of Millennium Park as a collaborative public- and private-sector project to celebrate passage of the second millennium, cover the unsightly former rail yard and parking lot of the ILLINOIS CENTRAL RAILROAD, and complete the northwest corner of Grant Park in the spirit of Daniel Burnham and Edward Bennett's *Plan of Chicago* (1909).

City officials originally estimated the park, designed by Skidmore, Owings & Merrill, would cost $150 million, primarily for the garage and supporting foundation. Private-sector contributions from corporations, foundations, and individual donors were expected to pay for various "enhancements." A healthy economy, the organizational acumen of project director Ed Uhlir, and the talented fundraising of John Bryan, however, enlarged and transformed the project. Bryan and his executive team attracted more than 85 private gifts of $1 million or more, totaling over $145 million. Major funding came from the Pritzker Foundation, the Crown Foundation, Ann Lurie, the William J. Wrigley Jr. Foundation, the Robert R. McCormick Tribune Foundation, BP America Inc., the Bank One Foundation, and SBC Corp. An initiative to build a theater for mid-size music and dance companies added another $60 million in private donations, including a major gift from Irving and Joan Harris.

These PHILANTHROPIC contributions enabled Millennium Park planners to attract some of the world's leading artists and designers for certain enhancements in the park: a music pavilion, trellis, and bridge by architect Frank Gehry; a music and dance theater by architect Thomas Beeby; a garden by Kathryn Gustafson, Piet Oudolf, and Robert Israel; a fountain by Jaume Plensa; and a sculpture by Anish Kapoor. The enhancements also generated new expenses, which, combined with the addition of a $60 million renovation of the Grant Park North Garage and the underestimation of certain original costs, pushed the final price tag to approximately $475 million. Millennium Park was scheduled to officially open on July 24, 2004.

Timothy J. Gilfoyle

See also: Burnham Plan; Loop

Minooka, IL, Grundy and Will Counties, 44 miles SW of the Loop. Minooka incorporated in 1869 as a thriving town along the Rock Island RAILROAD. Originally called "the summit" by RAILROAD WORKERS because it represented the highest point along the Rock Island line, Minooka was renamed by early settler Dolly Smith, after a POTAWATOMI word purportedly meaning "good land" or "high place." In the late twentieth century, Minooka boomed thanks to proximity to Interstate 80 and chemical, oil, and power industry jobs opportunities along the Des Plaines River.

Erik Gellman

See also: Economic Geography

Mission of the Guardian Angel. The Jesuits established the Mission of the Guardian Angel at Chicago in 1696. Its short existence left no visible traces, and it has been placed everywhere from GOOSE ISLAND to WILMETTE. A contemporary account by J. F. Buisson de St. Cosme, a Seminarian missionary (member of the Seminary of Foreign Missions) from Quebec, locates it on the north bank of the Chicago River between Michigan and Rush, a "dry" area where the ancient Indian Green Bay Trail also began. This area was constantly transited by Indians using the trail, and Indian villages settled nearby: St. Cosme counted 250 MIAMI cabins in the vicinity.

This was a logical location for a mission: solid ground, easy access to the lake, the river, and the PORTAGE, great numbers of passing Indians and Indian villages nearby. And this is probably where the Mission of the Guardian Angel was located.

Infighting between Seminarian missionaries from Quebec and the Jesuits caused the end of the mission. In 1699, the royal governor, Count Frontenac, mediated an agreement: the Jesuits gave up their mission at Chicago but kept their huge mission to the Kaskaskia Illinois just across the Illinois River from Starved Rock. The Seminarians got the Mississippi Valley.

The Kaskaskia were, however, moving to the banks of the Mississippi on the Illinois side, some 65 miles south of the future St. Louis. The Jesuits had little choice but to follow. With Chicago gone and Kaskaskia deserted, northeastern Illinois was left without any missions.

Winstanley Briggs

See also: Chicago in the Middle Ground; French and French Canadians; Fur Trade; Roman Catholics

Further reading: A manuscript copy of St. Cosme's report is with the History Department of the Université Laval, St. Foy, Quebec.

Missionary Training Schools. Chicago has long been home to missionary training schools, Christian institutions that train committed believers to go forth and spread their message of "good news" to the city, the nation, and the larger world.

Chicago's most prominent institution has been MOODY BIBLE INSTITUTE (MBI). Founded by evangelist Dwight L. Moody in 1886, it began as the Chicago Evangelization Society. In 1900 MBI adopted its present name, and in the twentieth century became the self-designated "West Point of Christian service" for training "spiritual soldiers." By 1970, MBI claimed to train fully 15 percent of all Christian missionaries posted in foreign countries. MBI's commitment to evangelism only deepened as its centennial approached: publications, television, radio, music, and even an aviation training school all served the cause of spreading the Christian message. At the end of the twentieth century MBI enrolled around 1,500 students each year, many still dedicated to far-flung missionary endeavors.

Other missionary training schools have substantially affected city life. The Chicago Training School (CTS), an outgrowth of the Methodist deaconess movement, opened in 1885 to train women for missionary "field work." Lucy Rider Meyer played a key role in the early history of CTS, which had four students in its first graduating class. By 1886, CTS's growing success allowed it to move into new quarters at the corner of Dearborn and Ohio. Often referred to as simply the Training School, CTS rapidly expanded, soon turning out over 60 graduates a year for mission work both at home and abroad.

Other PROTESTANT missionary schools flourished for a time: the Baptist Missionary Training School, the City Mission Society, and the Chicago City Missionary Society. In 1868, Congregational and Presbyterian pastors' wives organized the Woman's Board of Missions of the Interior, which served as an administrative body to facilitate Christianity's expansion in the United States and around the world. It had great ambitions, seeking "to reach every church, approach and influence every member of each church, so that they may hear and obey the call to send the world of life to the ends of the earth."

R. Jonathan Moore

See also: Publishing and Media, Religious; Religion, Chicago's Influence on; Religious Institutions; Seminaries

Further reading: Hill, Patricia R. *The World Their Household: The American Woman's Foreign Mission Movement and Cultural Transformation, 1870–1920.* 1985. • Horton, Isabelle. *The Builders: A Story of Faith and Works.* 1910.

Mobile Homes. The mobile home evolved out of the travel trailer of the 1920s and 1930s and the house trailer of the 1940s and early 1950s. Conceived as a mobile and temporary form of shelter, it eventually became a primarily immobile and permanent form of housing. First used by VACATIONERS, itinerant travelers, and migrant workers, the mobile home gained greater recognition and legitimacy during World War II, when it was used as emergency housing for war workers. In the postwar period, it became a popular form of year-round housing for people on a limited budget. Today, once situated, most mobile homes do not move.

During the early years of the mobile home, production was concentrated in the Midwest. In 1942, Illinois ranked fourth among mobile home-producing states, behind California, Indiana, and Michigan. Chicago was the center of Illinois' mobile home industry. Reflecting the broad manufacturing base of the city and its strength in the areas of metalworking and machinery, the local mobile home industry included two of the largest early producers, Glider Trailer Company and Indian Trailer Corporation. Still, the local industry did not survive into the 1960s. The high cost of labor and factory space in Chicago and difficulties transporting the ever-larger mobile home units through the area compelled manufacturers to locate in other parts of the country.

Even as the local industry disappeared, the local popularity of mobile homes increased. Since the 1950s, the number of mobile homes in the Chicago metropolitan area has grown from around 8,000 to 17,000, with the greatest increases coming during the 1950s and '60s. During the 1960s and '70s, a larger number of small parks gave way to a smaller number of large parks, often capable of accommodating as many as 500 units. The majority are located outside the Chicago city limits, in CALUMET CITY and BLUE ISLAND to the south, LA GRANGE and COUNTRYSIDE to the west, DES PLAINES to the northwest, and GLENVIEW to the north. In Chicago itself, most mobile homes are located in the city's single mobile home park in the far SOUTH SIDE neighborhood of HEGEWISCH.

Despite the popularity of mobile homes, the Chicago metropolitan area has not been hospitable to them. Municipalities in the metropolitan counties generally restrict mobile homes to mobile home parks, and permission for a mobile home park is difficult to get. ZONING laws keep mobile home parks outside of residential neighborhoods. Since the late 1980s, some suburban mobile home parks have been crowded out by development, as park owners find more lucrative uses for their land.

Anna Holian

See also: Government, Suburban; Housing Types; Land Use; Zoning

Further reading: Wallis, Allan D. *Wheel Estate: The Rise and Decline of Mobile Homes.* 1991.

Model Cities. Model Cities, an element of President Lyndon Johnson's War on Poverty, was an ambitious federal urban aid program that ultimately fell short of its goals. Passed by Congress in 1966 but ended in 1974, Model Cities originated in several concerns of the mid-1960s. Widespread urban violence, disillusionment with the URBAN RENEWAL program, and bureaucratic difficulties in the first years of the War on Poverty led to calls for reform of federal programs. The Model Cities initiative created a new program at the Department of Housing and Urban Development (HUD) intended to improve coordination of existing urban programs and provide additional funds for local plans. The program's goals emphasized comprehensive planning, involving not just rebuilding but also rehabilitation, SOCIAL SERVICE delivery, and citizen participation.

In Chicago, Model Cities generated significant controversy, mostly over who would control the millions of new federal dollars. Congress gave some power over funds to elected officials, but it also required citizen participation in planning and implementation. In 1967, Mayor Richard J. Daley and his Department of Development and Planning quickly selected four deserving Model City neighborhoods: WOODLAWN, GRAND BOULEVARD, Lawndale, and UPTOWN. But at the same time, the mayor also moved to control neighborhood input. His office appointed politically connected citizen advisory councils for each area, intending them to act as rubber stamps for the city's plans. The attempt to sidestep real participation angered neighborhood activists and dismayed federal officials. After stormy community sessions, chairmen from two of the local councils resigned to protest the city's heavy-handed tactics.

A prominent community association known as The WOODLAWN ORGANIZATION (TWO) drew up its own Model Cities plan with federal encouragement. TWO's innovative proposal included a community health system, a neighborhood legal program, and a guaranteed minimum income program. But the city had no interest in TWO's ideas and instead proposed giving the new funds to existing city bureaucracies, including the CHICAGO TRANSIT AUTHORITY, the Board of Health, the Department of Streets and Sanitation, and the Board of Education, as well as the YMCA.

The fate of the two competing plans rested with federal officials, who had supported TWO as the legitimate community voice in 1968. But the new Nixon administration changed course, and HUD retreated from insisting on real citizen participation. The city outmaneuvered TWO and successfully won approval for its plan in the spring of 1969. As a result, Model Cities funds strengthened the Democratic machine but did little for communities. While city hall parceled out contracts and jobs ($38 million in 1969 and $53 million in 1970), it brushed aside neighborhood activists, leaving the targeted areas with few lasting gains.

D. Bradford Hunt

See also: Civil Rights Movements; Contested Spaces; Great Society; North Lawndale; South Lawndale

Further reading: City of Chicago. "Final Local Evaluation Report on the Model Cities Program of the City of Chicago." Municipal Reference Collection, Chicago Public Library, 1978. • Fish, John Hall. *Black Power/White Control: The Struggle of the Woodlawn Organization in Chicago.* 1973. • Protess, David L. "Community Power and Social Policy: Citizen Participation in the Chicago Model Cities Program." Ph.D. diss., University of Chicago. 1974.

Modern and Postmodern Dance. Modern dance drifted into Chicago on a June night in 1895 when the young Isadora Duncan, billed as the "California Faun," floated about to Mendelssohn's "Spring Song" as part of a VAUDEVILLE show at the Masonic Temple Roof Garden. Over one hundred years later, the postmodern Bill T. Jones/Arnie Zane Dance Company recalled the century and interrogated the future in "We Set Out Early... Visibility Was Poor" (1998) at the Arie Crown Theater. In the final moments of this production, two male soloists, one dark skinned, the other light, slowly repeated movement phrases taken from what were once racially distinct dance traditions. The difference between them remained visible but now as a part of one DANCE, on the same stage.

Chicago's first great modern dancers were Doris Humphrey, Katherine Dunham, and Sybil Shearer. Humphrey taught briefly in OAK PARK at the Humphrey School of Dance before leaving town to join the Denishawn Dancers in 1917. Dunham came to HYDE PARK in the late 1920s during a particularly vibrant period in Chicago dance history. While a student at the UNIVERSITY OF CHICAGO, she began forming a prototype of the Katherine Dunham Dance Company that would open on Broadway in 1940. After a two-year research project in the West Indies, Dunham created the fusion of Caribbean and AFRICAN AMERICAN movement that international audiences would later identify as American modern dance. Sybil Shearer "defected" from Manhattan to WINNETKA in 1943 after a triumphant debut at Carnegie Chamber Music Hall. She found a spare but fresh artistic environment in which to question the way modern dance was taught on the East Coast. Until her last performances in 1972, she refused to identify a "Shearer technique," insisting on making herself anew with each dance. Spectators came to Chicago from all over the nation to see what she would do next.

Modern dance in Chicago experienced a renewed period of growth, comparable to that of the late twenties, when Bruce and Judith Sagan created the Harper Theatre Dance Festival (1965–1975) in Hyde Park. Maggie Kast, Nana Shineflug, and Shirley Mordine introduced new approaches to dance making through their work as teachers and performers. Mordine founded the Dance Center of COLUMBIA

COLLEGE in 1969, as well as a DANCE COMPANY, providing major institutional support for the modern dance community. In 1972, the Muntu Dance Theatre began its investigation of African dance, music, and FOLKLORE, illuminating the Africanist presence that had always been implicit in twentieth-century modernism. Postmodern dance emerged from all of these sources. Among its most prominent representatives were the artists of the dance collective MoMING (1974–1990), Jan Erkert, Bob Eisen, Jan Bartoszek at the Chicago Cultural Center, Fluid Measure Performance Company, and XSIGHT! Performance Group.

Nancy G. Moore

See also: Dance Training; Improvisational Theater

Further reading: Ann Barzel Research Collection. Chicago Dance Collection, Newberry Library, Chicago, IL. • Barzel, Ann. "Dance in Chicago—An Early History." *American Dance* 2.1 (1986): 27–31. • Lyon, Jeff. "Oh, Did They Dance!" *Chicago Tribune Magazine*, January 28, 1996.

Mokena, IL, Will County, 27 miles SW of the Loop. The early residents of Mokena could hardly have imagined their small market center becoming part of a suburban fabric reaching southwest from Chicago.

In the early 1830s the McGovney and Van Horne families and others settled along the banks of Hickory Creek, a tributary of the DES PLAINES RIVER. In 1838 the post office of Chelsea was established for the community growing along the creek.

As with so many communities, the placing of a rail line reshaped settlement. By late 1852, the Rock Island RAILROAD had completed its line from Chicago through Will County, passing less than a mile north of Hickory Creek and Chelsea. Growth focused on the area platted in 1852 by Allen Denny around a rail stop on the Rock Island, and the settlement of Chelsea withered away.

The growth of Mokena paralleled that of many Chicago suburbs that began as railroad stops. One of the earliest buildings was the public SCHOOL, built in 1855. A Baptist Society formed in 1851, followed by a GERMAN United Evangelical congregation in 1862, St. Mary's German ROMAN CATHOLIC Church in 1864, and a Methodist church in 1867. This range of congregations, along with a German Lutheran church started in 1850 several miles to the east of town, reflects the presence of many German immigrants along with residents from various parts of the United States.

Mokena became the market center for a large farming area and by the late 1870s included five general stores, four blacksmith and wagon shops, three hotels, two butcher shops, seven SALOONS, and a variety of other businesses. When the village was incorporated in 1880, its population was 522; in 1940, it had increased to only 657.

Following WORLD WAR II, Mokena, as with so many outlying villages, rapidly came within the COMMUTING orbit of the expanding metropolis. It was accessible not only by rail and increasing commuter rail service, but also by good roads and, in 1968, by Interstate 80.

Mokena's population grew from 903 in 1950, to 1,643 in 1970, to 6,128 in 1990, to 14,583 in 2000. The small commercial core centered around the train stop became a lengthening commercial strip along Wolf Road.

Larry A. McClellan

See also: Agriculture; Metropolitan Growth; Suburbs and Cities as Dual Metropolis Transportation

Further reading: *History of Will County, Illinois.* 1976 [1878]. • Pitman, Florence. *The Story of Mokena.* 1963. • Quinn, Richard. "A Brief Illustrated History of Mokena." In *Mokena Centennial, 1880–1980.* 1980.

MoMing Dance and Arts Center. MoMing, a neighborhood center for DANCE TRAINING and avant-garde performance, was formed in 1974 by Jackie Radis, Jim Self, Susan Kimmelman, Eric Trules, Kasia Mintch, Tem Horowitz, and Sally Banes. Located at 1034 W. Barry in a building owned by the Resurrection Lutheran Church, the center continued for 16 financially turbulent years to provide local and visiting artists with a small-scale performance space suitable for experimental work informed by the visual arts. As the Harper Theatre Dance Festival had done with MODERN DANCE in the mid-sixties, MoMing introduced Chicago to the nation's leading postmodern choreographers, including Trisha Brown, Meredith Monk, and Bill T. Jones. After many financial crises, MoMing failed just after its most promising achievement—the 1989 festival "German Dance: Living Memories with a Future," conceived by Peter Tumbelston and Julie Simpson.

Nancy G. Moore

See also: Dance; Dance Companies; Entertaining Chicagoans; Hubbard Street Dance Chicago

Further reading: Ann Barzel Research Collection, Newberry Library, Chicago, IL. • Chicago Dance vertical files on MoMing, Visual and Performing Arts Division, Harold Washington Library, Chicago, IL.

Monee, IL, Will County, 32 miles S of the Loop. Strong local tradition ties the name of the village to the OTTAWA wife of Joseph Aubert de Gaspe Bailly. Marie and Joseph Bailly operated a FUR TRADING post now within the grounds of the INDIANA DUNES National Lakeshore in CHESTERTON, Indiana. Because of language difficulties, Marie was often referred to as "Mo-Nee" rather than "Ma-Rie." TREATIES in 1832 apportioned land to "the five daughters of Mo-nee, by her last husband, Joseph Bailly," including Raccoon Grove south of the present-day village. Settlers came in the mid-1830s to the edges of Raccoon Grove, farming the high ground of the Valparaiso Moraine.

In 1853 the ILLINOIS CENTRAL RAILROAD established a station at Monee. The town soon boasted a general store, a schoolhouse, and a grain warehouse with several elevators. By the 1870s, there were several small farm implements factories, four churches, and a massive wind gristmill.

Boosters hoped that Monee, midway between Chicago and Kankakee, would become a major city. Residents voted to incorporate as the village of Monee in 1874. In 1872 a GERMAN Baptist School Academy opened in a former BREWERY but survived only four years.

The Illinois Central depot was complemented in 1907 by a stop on the INTERURBAN line from Chicago to Kankakee. Monee also had a picnic ground and AMUSEMENT PARK at Raccoon Grove.

The small town center developed with the Illinois Central line at ground level. However, to lower the tracks, the railroads cut through the center of Monee in 1922, dramatically affecting train traffic that had previously gone uphill from both Chicago and Kankakee. The Illinois Central built a new depot down in the cut and four bridges were built to provide access around the community.

With an interchange on I-57, Monee has continued to grow as part of the southern expansion of the metropolitan region.

Larry A. McClellan

See also: Expressways; Suburbs and Cities as Dual Metropolis

Further reading: McClellan, Larry. "Monee: A High Point in the Southland Region." *Star,* November 1, 1998. • Milne, Muriel Mueller. *Our Roots Are Deep: A History of Monee, Illinois.* 1990.

Mongolians. Mongolian immigration to the United States was extremely limited until the 1990s. The first Mongolians to emigrate to the United States were the Kalmyk Mongols, a traditionally nomadic, pastoral group descended from the Western Mongols who left Central Asia in the seventeenth century for Russia. The Russian Revolution, the German invasion of Russia, and the dislocations of World War II caused many Kalmyks to flee across Eastern Europe. Politically classified as "stateless persons," many Kalmyks ended up in displaced persons camps in western Germany at war's end and were sponsored by American SOCIAL SERVICE organizations for resettlement in New Jersey and Pennsylvania. A handful of people from Inner Mongolia, part of China, also emigrated in the postwar period, but the independent nation of Outer Mongolia restricted emigration of its people to other Communist nations. In 1990, the Mongolian COMMUNIST PARTY, which had monopolized power in the country since its independence in 1921 and which was closely allied with the Soviet Union, moved toward democratic reform and political pluralism. The reforms opened up new opportunities for travel and emigration, and in the 1990s Mongolian immigrants established communities in Chicago, Denver, San Francisco, and Washington DC. By 2000, Mongolian community leaders estimated a Chicago population between 500 and 700.

Many of Chicago's Mongolians are students who came to Chicago to further their education and have chosen to stay in the United States after completing their schooling. Others have come in search of new personal or economic opportunities, and many anticipate their stay to be only temporary. A few Mongolian entrepreneurs have established small businesses, and there is a small professional community. Many Mongolians are well educated but face difficulties on the job market posed by limited English skills and illegal status, forcing them to enter trades and service industries, including rug and carpet cleaning, CONSTRUCTION, electrical trades, computers, food service, and custodial work.

Chicago's Mongolian community, while geographically dispersed, is an organized and active group with a strong network of mutual assistance. The Mongolian American Association, founded in 1998, aids newcomers from Mongolia, serves as an organizational center for the community, and sponsors social and cultural events such as concerts and speakers. It is affiliated with other Mongolian groups in San Francisco, Denver, and Washington, and by 2001 it boasted 250 members. Some Chicago Mongolians attend cultural events in Bloomington, Indiana, where a small community of Mongols is gathered around the Mongolia Society and Indiana University's Department of Central Eurasian Studies, the only program in the United States to grant a degree in Mongolian Studies.

Chicago's Mongolian community gathers each year in January or February to celebrate the Mongolian New Year. In addition, Mongolians hold a major celebration on the lakefront each year from July 11 to 13 in honor of the national holiday of Naadam. During the celebration, Mongolians compete in traditional sporting events and competitions that include archery, volleyball, WRESTLING, and BASKETBALL. The community also gathers frequently for parties, concerts, speeches, and other social events and such Mongolian cultural activities as a performance by a Mongolian artist or a visit by a Mongolian Buddhist Monk. The Mongolian community maintains ties with Tibetan BUDDHISTS in Chicago, and the groups sometimes celebrate holidays together.

Tracy Steffes

See also: Americanization; Demography; Multicentered Chicago

Further reading: Kotkin, Stephen, and Bruce A. Elleman, eds. *Mongolia in the Twentieth Century: Landlocked Cosmopolitan.* 1999. • Rubel, Paula G. *The Kalmyk Mongols: A Study in Continuity and Change.* 1967.

Montclare, Community Area 18, 9 miles NW of the Loop. First attracted by a rolling landscape, William Sayre in 1836 laid claim "by right of possession" to 90 acres in what is now the Montclare Community Area. Unable to gain title to the land because of an inaccurate government survey, he bought the acreage at the JEFFERSON TOWNSHIP land sales in 1838. A year later he married Harriet Lovett, daughter of another area settler, in the first marriage of the township. They set up HOUSEKEEPING in a newly built frame house in 1840.

Sayre and his neighbors cleared fields of hay and tended main crops of oats and corn. Farmers used Grand Avenue as their main thoroughfare to the downtown markets in Chicago, where many hawked their produce from wagons at the Randolph Street Market. The return home was sometimes dangerous: along the dark, lonely road, farmers faced the threat of robbery or by the 1880s risked having their wagons hit by a train.

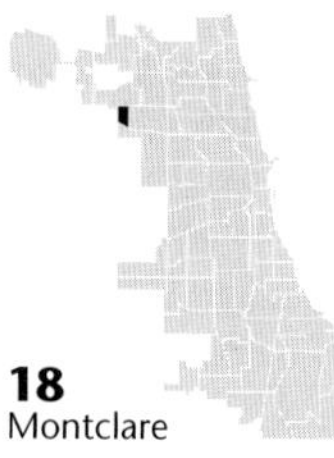
18
Montclare

In 1872 Sayre allowed the Chicago & Pacific RAILROAD Company right-of-way over his property, and Sayre Station was built on the farm. A year later another family farm in the area was platted by developers, who sold lots for $250 to $500. The town and the depot were named Montclare after Montclair, New Jersey.

In 1873 the rail line failed and was taken over by the Chicago, Milwaukee & St. Paul Railroad (CM&SP). As a result, the only form of COMMUTER transportation was a single daily train, reducing the desirability of the area. Lots remained vacant. Undaunted by a lack of new settlers, the some 120 residents went about their farming. Two schools were in evidence in 1884. Social activities focused on family, church, and Sunday School. Most residents were native-born, ENGLISH, or GERMAN.

Although Montclare was ANNEXED by the city of Chicago in 1889, the first spurt of growth occurred in 1912, when the Grand Avenue streetcar line extended service to the area. The Sayre family contributed acreage for community use in 1916, which, along with another piece of donated property, later formed Rutherford-Sayre Park. The park was divided down the middle by the railroad tracks that marked the town's southern boundary.

Settlement concentrated in the southeastern section near the depot, but was hampered until utilities and paved streets were added in the 1920s. Single-family structures, mainly standard BUNGALOWS, predominated in the area. Some residents found employment at light industrial plants along the CM&SP railroad lines that bounded Montclare on its eastern and southern edges; most workers crossed into neighboring communities where factories were more plentiful.

Housing extended north of Diversey Avenue in the 1930s, a combination of bungalows, ranches, and Tudor houses. Hugging Chicago's western edge, Montclare retained an identity more suburban than urban. Pre–WORLD WAR II commercial development was minimal; the only shopping was a retail strip at Grand and Harlem. In the 1960s the strip experienced decline and deterioration as stores left and newer shopping centers were built in nearby areas. But residential areas remained intact owing to good CONSTRUCTION and property upkeep by conscientious residents.

Population figures for 1970 showed 11,675, of which POLES, ITALIANS, and Germans were the majority. These numbers decreased to 10,573 in the 1990 census, with GREEKS, UKRAINIANS, LITHUANIANS, LEBANESE, and a growing number of Hispanics (11 percent) adding to the mix. In the late 1980s a few AFRICAN AMERICANS moved into the neighborhood, prompting racially motivated incidents that induced groups such as the Galewood-Montclare Community Organization to devote their efforts to reducing tensions. At the close of the twentieth century Montclare still had only 297 African American residents, but the Hispanic proportion stood at 38 percent.

Marilyn Elizabeth Perry

See also: Agriculture; Economic Geography; Street Railways

Further reading: Edwards, Brian. "Frontier Bargains: Tiny Montclare Offers Quiet Family Living Way Out West." *Chicago Tribune,* August 24, 1990. • Karlen, Harvey M. *Chicago's Crabgrass Communities: The History of the Independent Suburbs and Their Post Offices That Became Part of Chicago.* 1992, 163–166. • Melaniphy & Associates, Inc. *Chicago Comprehensive Neighborhood Needs Analysis,* vol. 2. 1982, 16–23.

Montgomery, IL, Kane and Kendall Counties, 38 miles W of the Loop. In 1834 the Chicago–Galena road forded the FOX RIVER at what became Montgomery. The site was a day's stagecoach journey from Chicago and a logical place for a travelers' inn. Elijah Pierce's tavern and Daniel Gray's mill soon faced each other across the river, each man having followed relatives from the east. Pierce followed his son-in-law, Jacob Carpenter, from Ohio, while Gray, a New Yorker, had earlier visited

his brother Nicholas's farm (now in Kendall County).

Blacksmith William T. Elliott arrived in 1834, serving travelers, settlers, and the remaining POTAWATOMI population. Stagecoaches delivered Montgomery's mail biweekly from NAPERVILLE, 10 miles distant. Montgomery's future looked bright until Samuel McCarty and a little civic chicanery diverted the stage coaches. When McCarty settled in AURORA in 1834, he found he had to travel to Montgomery to pick up his mail. Staking his own road from Naperville in 1836, with the promise of a month's boarding, he induced the stagecoaches to travel through Aurora.

Nevertheless, foundries, gristmills, and a reaper factory thrived on the river's millraces and dams, and Montgomery grew for three decades. Gray was Montgomery's catalyst. A visionary and entrepreneur, he was responsible for much of its earliest growth and industry and ultimately its platting. Originally "Graytown," Montgomery was renamed for Gray's home county in New York. Gray's mill stands as a historic landmark.

The arrival of the McCormick Works at Chicago doomed Montgomery's reaper plant. Likewise, the rail nexus at Aurora left Montgomery unable to compete. Population diminished, industry stagnated.

Relief started in 1880, when the Chicago, Burlington & Quincy RAILROAD constructed a station for livestock en route to Chicago's stockyards; by 1960 it was the largest worldwide. The rails also shipped Montgomery's produce and spring water to Chicago markets. In 1899 Riverview Park (later Fox River Park) opened. An AMUSEMENT PARK that drew crowds from as far as Morris and Chicago on express INTERURBANS, it was replaced in 1943 by United Wallpaper Company and then by AT&T. Lyon Metallic, Montgomery's first modern factory, moved from Chicago in 1906, drawing a reverse COMMUTE from Aurora and further stabilizing the economy.

Montgomery and Aurora have remained inextricably linked: along with NORTH AURORA, they form the Fox Valley Park District, and their students share a SCHOOL DISTRICT. As in the past, Montgomery's identity is closely tied to the Fox River and the quality of life it promises. Highways are drawing new populations to the valley at an unprecedented rate.

Though still a small town, Montgomery is rapidly growing, with a population of 5,471 in 2000. While Montgomery always straddled the river, it also came to straddle a county line, crossing south into Kendall County. Not everyone has favored more growth. An anonymous advocate for the Fox River ecosystem known as "The Fox" (later identified as James Phillips) began crusading in 1969, first protesting deadly INDUSTRIAL POLLUTION, then in 1999 standing alongside the Montgomery dam warning of suburbanization's threat to the river.

Sherry Meyer

See also: Agricultural Machinery Industry; Economic Geography; Meatpacking

Further reading: *Commemorative Biographical and Historical Record of Kane County, Illinois.* Vol. 2. 1888. • Giles, Wanda H., ed. *The History of Montgomery, Illinois, in Words and Pictures.* 1990. • Meyer, Sherry A. "The Historical Geography of Montgomery, Illinois, in Words and Images." M.A. thesis, University of Illinois at Chicago. 2000.

Monuments. *See* Art, Public, City as Artifact: The Above-Ground Archaeology of an Urban History, *and* War Monuments

Moody Bible Institute. One of the most successful world centers for MISSIONARY TRAINING, the Moody Bible Institute (MBI) began in 1889 from the joint efforts of Dwight Moody and Emma Dryer. Moody assumed leadership of the organization, which took his name in 1900 after his death. Its original intention was to train what Moody dubbed "gap-men" (filling a gap between ordinary people and professional clergy) to work among the "neglected masses of Chicago." Founded during the city's most dynamic period of growth, the institute was part of a national PROTESTANT effort to proselytize in urban areas where ROMAN CATHOLICS, JEWS, and nonadherents were fast becoming a majority. After Moody's death, the institute became known for its conservative fundamentalism and opposition to liberal theology and the SOCIAL GOSPEL.

A hundred years later, the institute had expanded into several impressive buildings on the NEAR NORTH SIDE. Training students in day and night schools, it has offered an array of courses, including Bible studies, SACRED MUSIC, and even aviation technology for missionary pilots. Besides a large publishing program and thriving AM and FM radio networks, MBI has produced hundreds of films and filmstrips through its affiliated Moody Institute of Science. Of its thousands of graduates, many have taken positions in churches and others have become foreign missionaries, although relatively few have made urban evangelism their commitment.

James Gilbert

See also: Publishing and Media, Religious; Religion, Chicago's Influence on; Settlements, Religious

Further reading: Getz, Gene. *MBI: The Story of Moody Bible Institute.* 1986. • Gilbert, James. *Perfect Cities: Chicago's Utopias of 1893.* 1991.

Morgan Park, Community Area 75, 13 miles S of the Loop. Since it was laid out in the 1870s by Thomas F. Nichols, Morgan Park's winding streets, small parks, and roundabouts have evoked images of an English country town. In 1869, the Blue Island Land and Building Company purchased property from the heirs of Thomas Morgan, an early English settler, and subdivided the area from Western Avenue to Vincennes Avenue that falls within the present community area of Morgan Park. Although the Chicago, Rock Island & Pacific RAILROAD laid tracks through the area in 1852, regular COMMUTER service to downtown was not established until the suburban line opened in 1888.

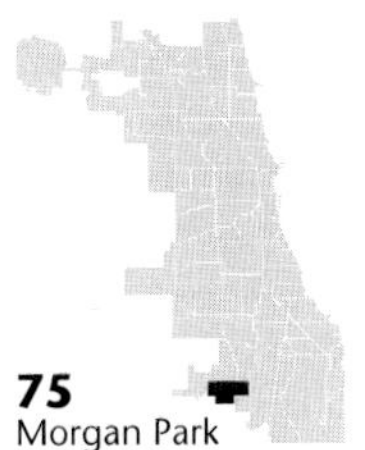

To spur residential development, the Blue Island company donated land and helped finance buildings for Mt. Vernon Military Academy (1873), the predecessor of Morgan Park Academy; Morgan Park Baptist Church (1874); and the Chicago Female College (1875). But the company's greatest success occurred in 1877, when the Baptist Theological Union agreed to relocate. By 1879 its well-regarded faculty included William Rainey Harper, who became the first president of the UNIVERSITY OF CHICAGO in 1891.

Reflecting its origins as a Baptist community, Morgan Park PROHIBITED the sale of liquor in the area between Western and Vincennes Avenues when it was incorporated as a village in 1882. Its middle-class character was further reinforced by the construction of main-line PROTESTANT churches, among them Methodist (1888), Episcopalian (1889), Congregational (1890), and Presbyterian (1891). Equally important was the completion in 1890 of a substantial brick structure for Esmond public SCHOOL and the imposing library donated by Charles Walker, president of the Blue Island Land and Building Company.

Despite these clear signs of growth, Morgan Park lost its bid to become the home of the University of Chicago, which settled in HYDE PARK. After the Baptist Theological Union left Morgan Park in 1892, its buildings were used as Morgan Park Military Academy.

Although Morgan Park cultivated an identity as a white Anglo-Saxon Protestant community, it also included a small settlement of AFRICAN AMERICANS as well as FRENCH immigrants. Beth Eden (1891) was the first of more than 19 churches organized by black families who lived in the segregated district east of Vincennes, near the main line of the Rock Island railroad. On the other side of the tracks near 117th Street, French ROMAN CATHOLICS who worked in the local Purington brickyard established Sacred Heart Church (1904).

The battle over ANNEXATION to Chicago in 1911, which sharply divided the community, dragged on in court until 1914. At a time when they were denied the franchise in national elections, women voted overwhelmingly in favor of annexation because it meant better police and fire protection as well as a new high school.

By 1920, 674 of Morgan Park's 7,780 residents were African American. The official report published in the wake of the city's 1919 RACE RIOT noted that, while whites and blacks in Morgan Park "maintain a friendly attitude," nevertheless "there seems to be a common understanding that Negroes must not live west of Vincennes Road, which bisects the town from northeast to southwest." Public institutions such as the new Morgan Park High School (1916) and the Walker Branch Library remained integrated.

But African Americans were not the only residents in Morgan Park to live on the periphery. Between 1930 and 1960, the community's population more than doubled, from 12,747 to 27,912, as new subdivisions were built up with homes. Whereas Morgan Park's mainline Protestants tended to live and worship in the oldest part of the neighborhood, the largely IRISH Roman Catholic parishes of St. Cajetan (1927) and St. Walter (1953) drew most of their congregations from the area west of Western Avenue. Reflecting the reality of urban segregation, African American Catholics established Holy Name of Mary (1940) at the east end of the neighborhood.

Racial integration in the larger Morgan Park area did not occur on a large scale until the late 1960s. By then, however, the west leg of Interstate 57 had effectively isolated the older black settlement east of Vincennes. Perhaps the greatest change to occur in Morgan Park involved the construction of nearly four hundred "section 235" SUBSIDIZED HOUSING units between 1969 and 1974, the largest number for any Chicago neighborhood.

With support from the BEVERLY Area Planning Association (1947), Morgan Park has marketed its historic homes, worked to keep their public schools integrated, and strengthened area shopping strips. The Walker branch library, enlarged and renovated in 1995, remains a showplace, and the Beverly ARTS CENTER'S new complex for the performing arts (2002) has sparked redevelopment at the intersection of 111th and Western Avenue. Morgan Park claims one of the city's pioneer African American communities, and, since 1979, its Irish American community has sponsored an event billed as the largest neighborhood-based St. Patrick's Day parade outside Dublin.

Ellen Skerrett

See also: Metropolitan Growth; Religious Geography

Further reading: Mayer, Harold M., and Richard C. Wade. *Chicago: Growth of a Metropolis.* 1969. • Pacyga, Dominic A., and Ellen Skerrett. *Chicago, City of Neighborhoods: Histories and Tours.* 1986.

Morgue. *See* Cook County Morgue

Mormons. Members of the Church of Jesus Christ of Latter-day Saints (or Mormons) began migrating from Missouri to Commerce (renamed Nauvoo), in western Illinois, in 1839. In its prime, Nauvoo rivaled Chicago in size and population, and Mormon activities, including the secret practice of polygamy among the church's hierarchy, attracted the notice of Chicago JOURNALISTS. Part of the correspondence between church founder Joseph Smith and the *Chicago Democrat's* John Wentworth became the denomination's Articles of Faith.

The Mormon presence in Illinois declined with Smith's death in 1844 and the forced departure in 1846 of most church members for what is now Utah. The Utah-based church resumed its proselyting activities in Chicago in the early twentieth century, however, and eventually built a temple, dedicated in 1985, in suburban GLENVIEW. While many Mormons who migrated to Chicago from Utah after WORLD WAR II lived in the suburbs, in the late 1970s the church undertook an aggressive missionary program in the city, which resulted in the racial integration of urban congregations. By the end of the twentieth century, metropolitan Chicago's 55 Mormon congregations included approximately 20,000 members.

Chicago is also important as a center for the Reorganized Church of Jesus Christ of Latter Day Saints, established in 1860 by Joseph Smith III, who united a wide array of dissident Mormon groups. In 1866 Reorganized church leaders moved their headquarters from Nauvoo to Plano, the church's flagship congregation until the 1880s. With 10 Reorganized congregations, metropolitan Chicago has become one of two or three "heartlands" of the Reorganized church. Renamed the Community of Christ in 2001, the church has remained separate from its Utah-based parent.

Brandon Johnson

See also: Religious Geography; Religious Institutions

Further reading: Launius, Roger D. *Joseph Smith III: Pragmatic Prophet.* 1995. • Launius, Roger D., and John E. Hallwas, ed. *Kingdom on the Mississippi Revisited.* 1996. • Shipps, Jan. *Mormonism: The Story of a New Religious Tradition.* 1987.

Moroccans. After Morocco won independence from France in 1956, limited numbers of its top young scholars turned from Parisian to American universities to obtain technology and science degrees. From the mid-1960s through 1980, Chicago's Moroccan population seldom exceeded 15, with only a handful making the city their permanent home. In the early 1980s, a new wave of Moroccan immigrants began arriving, many with the primary purpose of working, not earning a degree. Numbering at least several dozen by the end of the decade, some ran small retail shops while others opened RESTAURANTS catering to both Moroccans and non-Moroccans. The children of Chicago Moroccans provided the impetus for some parents to pursue Moroccan cultural activities and community ties more actively than had been done before.

By the late 1980s, Chicago's Moroccan community was becoming more geographically defined, organized, and religious in its orientation. Many settled in a large area on Chicago's near Northwest Side, still the community's center by the early 2000s. Several small Moroccan American organizations followed the lead of Chicago's Sister City Program with Casablanca, established in 1982, in promoting cultural, professional, and commercial ties with Morocco. An area mosque began serving as both a spiritual and secular gathering place, foreshadowing the increased centrality of Sunni Islam within the community by the late 1990s.

Developments in the 1990s contributed to the growth and complexity of the Moroccan community. Larger numbers of unskilled and less educated Moroccans came to Chicago as a result of tightened European Union immigration policies coupled with greater access to the United States. While the population of Moroccans in Chicago remained smaller than in New York City, Boston, and Washington DC, community estimates placed it somewhere above 1,000 by the early 2000s. Men from this larger wave of immigrants to Chicago found WORK as TAXI drivers, restaurant workers, and mechanics, while some women have had to adjust to employment as childcare providers and DOMESTIC WORKERS.

Moroccans have had limited association with Chicago's Arab and MUSLIM communities from the Middle East, instead turning toward other immigrants from the Maghreb, the term used for the western countries of North Africa. The Maghreb Assembly, an active organization since the mid-1990s, has worked to connect Moroccans of different socioeconomic statuses with each other as well as with ALGERIANS and Chicago's small population of Tunisians. It has aimed to help new immigrants adjust to Chicago's secular environment while remaining faithful to the tenets of Islam and their home cultures. The Maghreb Assembly sponsors a variety of activities, from meeting new arrivals at O'HARE airport, to setting them up with employment, housing, and SCHOOLS, to teaching English and computer skills at a mosque on the corner of Elston and Montrose Avenues. Religious activities, such as collective prayer and the feasts of Ramadan, have been central in unifying both Chicago Moroccans and other area North African Muslims. Several restaurants and cafés have served as informal gathering places for the men, while most women congregate in homes and their mosques.

Stephen R. Porter

See also: Demography

Morris, IL, Grundy County, 54 miles SW of the Loop. Morris was platted in 1842 and incorporated in 1850. Named for Isaac N.

TIMELINE AND YEAR PAGES

Timeline compiled by Sarah Fenton and Kendra Schiffman

History is not lived from A to Z. An encyclopedia, however, is organized that way, and this book, by presenting the story of metropolitan Chicago from "Abolitionism" to "Zoroastrians," is no exception. Hence a chronological scaffolding is in order, even if historical processes do not quite follow neat temporal divisions either. The following pages consist of two complementary overviews of Chicago history: a timeline of events followed by illustrated two-page spreads, or "year pages," featuring nine particularly significant years in the city's past. The timeline includes a selection of events discussed elsewhere in the Encyclopedia, as well as national and international events to provide a wider context. In addition to serving as a quick reference tool, the timeline can suggest connections between diverse topics and events. The year pages, which follow the timeline, not only provide a perspective on events that are mentioned in entries elsewhere in the Encyclopedia, but convey a glimpse of the complexity that could be found in a close investigation of any moment in Chicago's history. Both the timeline and the year pages are designed to stimulate consideration of relationships among processes, institutions, events, and people.

1630–1818

CA. 1630	Illinois Indians settle in northern Illinois
CA. 1670	French coureurs de bois first come to area
1673	Marquette and Joliet explore region, claim it for New France
CA. 1690	Miami refugees settle temporarily
CA. 1690	Potawatomi migrate from Wisconsin
1696–1699	Mission of the Guardian Angel
1701	Grand Alliance of French and Iroquois
1716	French use Chicago as base for war against Fox Indians in Wisconsin
1717	Illinois transferred from New France to the government of Louisiana
1717	Fox Wars
1754–1763	French and Indian Wars
1763	Treaty of Paris cedes French territory, including Canada, to Britain
1763–1764	Warfare drives Ottawa and Ojibwa tribes west to Chicago area
1776–1783	American Revolution
1779	DuSable trades at Michigan City
1783	Treaty of Paris: British cede land to American control
1785	U.S. Land Ordinance; rectangular land survey system
1787	Northwest Ordinance
1788	Ratification of U.S. Constitution by minimum number of states
1789	French Revolution
CA. 1790	DuSable settles in Chicago
1795	U.S. acquires land at Chicago in Treaty of Greenville
1800	DuSable sells holdings at Chicago River
1800	Indiana Territory formed from part of Northwest Territory
1803	Fort Dearborn established
1803	Louisiana Purchase
1803	Trader John Kinzie moves to Chicago
1808	Napoleon invades Spain
1808	U.S. bans importation of slaves
1808	American Fur Company in Chicago
1809	Illinois Territory established from part of Indiana Territory
1811	Burning of Prophetstown (IN)
1812–1814	War of 1812
1812	Fort Dearborn destroyed
1816	U.S. Army rebuilds Fort Dearborn
1816	Indiana statehood
1816	U.S. obtains canal corridor land in treaty
1818	Chicago's first chartered bank (closed 10 years later)
1818	Illinois statehood

1820–1846

	BUILT ENVIRONMENT	POLITICS AND PUBLIC ORDER	CIVIC CULTURE	POPULATION AND HEALTH
1820				
1821				
1822	○ IL gets federal land grant for canal			
1823				
1824				
1825		○ Billy Caldwell elected justice of the peace	○ First Baptist sermon preached in Chicago	
1826			○ Methodist mission established in Plainfield	
1827				
1828		○ Chicago elects first constable		
1829		○ First national election in Chicago		
1830	○ Original plat of Chicago		○ Methodists create Chicago Mission District	
1831	○ Ferry service across Chicago River begins	○ Cook County established ○ Chicago's first court of record ○ Govt. mail delivery begins	○ First Methodist Church established	
1832	○ First bridge spans Chicago River	○ Black Hawk War		○ Cholera epidemic
1833		○ Allied tribes cede IL lands ○ Chicago incorporates as town	★ Chicago Temperance Society ★ St. Mary's Roman Catholic Church ★ *Chicago Democrat* newspaper	
1834	○ First drawbridge built ○ Harbor improvements made		○ First Presbyterian Church established	
1835		○ Federal land office opens ○ Volunteer firefighters organized	★ Chicago Bible Society	★ Cook County Almshouse
1836	○ Construction of Illinois & Michigan Canal begins (completed 1848)	○ Kane County established ○ McHenry County established	○ Unitarians arrive ★ Lake House ★ Saloon Building	
1837	○ Lockport platted as I&M Canal hdqrs.	○ Chicago incorporates as city	★ St. James of the Sag Roman Catholic Church, Lemont	★ Chicago Board of Health
1838				
1839		○ DuPage County established ○ Lake County established ○ State's first local option law passed	★ *Juliet Courier* newspaper	
1840		○ First execution in Chicago	★ Chicago Anti-Slavery Society	○ Chicago pop. 4,470 ○ 8 counties pop. 39,246
1841		○ State local option law repealed	★ *Prairie Farmer* journal	
1842			★ Chicago Washington Temperance Society	○ City Tract Society begins feeding the hungry
1843			○ First Masonic lodge established ○ Roman Catholic Diocese of Chicago	○ First hospital ★ Rush Medical College (first medical school)
1844			★ Female Anti-Slavery Society	★ *Chicago Medical Journal*
1845	○ Woodstock platted	○ Joliet incorporated ○ First Sunday closing law passed ○ First city fire limit established	○ First Jewish minyan	
1846			○ Sisters of Mercy arrive ★ St. Patrick's Roman Catholic Church	

★ = Founding of

	ARTS AND EDUCATION	LEISURE AND SPORTS	WORK AND ECONOMY	INTERNATIONAL/NATIONAL
1820				○ Missouri Compromise prohibits slavery in North
1821				
1822				
1823				○ Steam travel on the Mississippi above St. Louis begins
1824				
1825				○ Erie Canal opens
1826				
1827			○ Clybourn builds slaughterhouse	
1828				
1829			○ Sauganash Tavern opens	
1830				○ Indian Removal Act ○ Steam railroads introduced in United States
1831				
1832			○ First drugstore	○ Andrew Jackson vetoes bank bill ○ First national Democratic Party convention ★ American Anti-Slavery Society
1833			○ First Chicago brewery opens ○ Commercial lumber business commences ○ Earliest Chicago printing press begins operation	
1834	○ First school of music ○ First professional theater performance			○ Whig Party forms
1835	★ Chicago Harmonic Society		○ First ship built	
1836				
1837	○ First local theater company forms		○ IL State Bank completed ○ Financial panic and depression begins (to 1843)	○ Abolitionist Elijah Lovejoy murdered
1838	○ First ballet performance			○ Cherokee Trail of Tears
1839			○ First bulk grain shipment ○ First city directory published	
1840	○ First brass band organized			
1841				
1842	★ Chicago Sacred Music Society	★ Washington Square Park		
1843				
1844	○ First Catholic school			○ First telegraph system (eastern United States)
1845	○ First volume of poetry published ○ First city school building			○ Potato famine begins in Ireland and Northern Europe
1846	★ St. Mary of the Lake University			○ Stephen A. Douglas elected to Senate ○ U.S.-Mexico War (to 1848)

1847–1867

	BUILT ENVIRONMENT	POLITICS AND PUBLIC ORDER	CIVIC CULTURE	POPULATION AND HEALTH
1847			★ German Lutheran Church–Missouri Synod ★ Quinn Chapel AME ★ *Chicago Daily Tribune* newspaper ○ First Jewish congregation	★ Chicago Retreat for the Insane
1848	○ Telegraph service begins ○ Plank roads built from Chicago (to 1854) ○ First railroad in Chicago	○ Second Illinois constitution ★ Federal Court in Chicago		
1849				○ First orphanages ★ Chicago Orphan Asylum ○ Cholera epidemic
1850	○ First omnibus ○ Gas lighting introduced	○ Townships organized ★ Pinkerton National Detective Agency	★ Xenia Baptist Church (later Olivet)	○ Chicago pop. 29,963 ○ 8 counties pop. 124,510 ★ Chicago Medical Society ★ IL General Hospital of the Lakes (later Mercy Hospital)
1851	○ First public water board		★ First Congregational Church	
1852	★ Board of Sewerage Commissioners ○ Michigan Central Railroad's Chicago connection	○ Waukegan incorporated		★ Mercy Hospital
1853		○ Aurora incorporated ○ New County Court House and City Hall		★ Chicago YMCA
1854		○ Elgin incorporated		○ Cholera epidemic ○ Dysentery epidemic (1,600 die by 1860)
1855		○ Lager Beer Riot ○ Chicago Police Department established		
1856	○ Street grade raising begins (to 1858) ○ IL Central Railroad Chicago branch		★ *Aurora Beacon* newspaper (later *Daily Beacon-News*)	
1857	○ Lake Forest platted	○ City destroys "Sands" lakefront brothel district ○ Fort Dearborn demolished ○ Naperville incorporated	○ St. James Episcopal Church completed	○ Board of Health eliminated ★ Chicago Relief and Aid Society ★ St. Vincent DePaul Society
1858	○ Rail link between Chicago and New York	○ Police uniforms introduced ○ First paid fire department		○ Scarlet fever epidemic (over 1,200 die by 1863)
1859	○ Street railways			★ Chicago Medical College (later Northwestern Univ. Medical School) ★ House of the Good Shepherd ★ Catholic Magdalen Asylum
1860		○ First national political convention ○ First post office building	○ Holy Family Roman Catholic Church completed	○ Chicago pop. 112,172 ○ 8 counties pop. 278,842
1861	★ Chicago Board of Public Works	○ Camp Douglas (closed 1865) ○ Lake Forest incorporated ○ Town of Hyde Park incorporated		★ Chicago Branch of the U. S. Sanitary Commission ★ Old Ladies' Home
1862		○ Race riot		
1863		○ New charter for Chicago ○ Will County established		○ First Sanitary Fair ★ Protestant Erring Women's Refuge ★ Soldier's Home
1864		○ Free mail delivery inaugurated	★ Des Plaines Methodist Campground	○ Smallpox epidemic (283 die)
1865		○ Funeral service for Lincoln held in Chicago		★ Angel Guardian Orphanage ★ Mary Thompson Hospital ★ St. Luke's Hospital
1866			★ *Skandinaven* newspaper	★ Cook County Hospital
1867		○ DuPage County seat moves from Naperville to Wheaton	★ St. Stanislaus Kostka Roman Catholic Church	○ Board of Health revived

★= Founding of

	ARTS AND EDUCATION	LEISURE AND SPORTS	WORK AND ECONOMY	INTERNATIONAL/NATIONAL
1847	★ Mozart Society ★ Rice Theater ★ Saint Xavier College		⚬ McCormick Reaper Works built	⚬ Abraham Lincoln serves term in U.S. Congress
1848			★ Board of Trade	⚬ California gold rush begins ⚬ Revolutions in Europe ⚬ Woman's Rights Convention at Seneca Falls, NY
1849			⚬ First building and loan association	
1850	⚬ First opera ⚬ First orchestra ★ Tremont Music Hall		⚬ First printer's union	⚬ Compromise of 1850
1851	★ Northwestern University	⚬ First baseball game		⚬ Temperance law in Maine
1852			⚬ IL free banking law ⚬ Potter Palmer arrives ⚬ Graue Mill built in Oak Brook	
1853	★ Wheaton College			
1854	⚬ First music published ⚬ First superintendent of schools		⚬ World's largest grain port ★ Chicago, Rock Island & Pacific Railroad	⚬ Kansas-Nebraska Act
1855	★ Chicago Theological Seminary	⚬ IL State Fair in Chicago	★ Chicago, Burlington & Quincy Railroad	
1856	★ Chicago Historical Society ⚬ Juliette Kinzie, *Wau-Bun: The "Early Day" in the North-West*	★ Union Baseball Club	★ Rand McNally & Co.	
1857	★ Chicago Academy of Sciences ★ Chicago Musical Union ★ McVickers Theater		★ North Chicago Rolling Mill Co.	⚬ Dred Scott case ⚬ Financial panic
1858	★ Mendelssohn Society	★ Chicago Base Ball Club ⚬ First lunch counters	⚬ Chicago connected to NYC markets by telegraph	⚬ Lincoln-Douglas debates
1859			★ Chicago & North Western Railroad	
1860				⚬ First "dime novel"
1861				⚬ Civil War begins ⚬ Unification of Italy
1862	⚬ Ordinance segregates public schools			⚬ Homestead Act ⚬ Morrill Land Grant Act
1863			★ First National Bank of Chicago	⚬ National Banking Act ⚬ Emancipation Proclamation
1864			★ Chicago Musicians' Protective Union ⚬ First Trades Assembly ★ R. R. Donnelley & Sons Printing Co.	
1865	★ Crosby's Opera House		⚬ First steel mill ⚬ Iron Molders International Union meets in Chicago ★ Union Stock Yard	⚬ 13th Amendment (abolishes slavery)
1866	★ Chicago Academy of Design ★ Great Western Light Guard Band		⚬ Borden builds condensed milk factory in Elgin	
1867	★ Chicago Academy of Music ★ Cook County Normal School		⚬ Citywide eight-hour strike ★ Pullman Palace Car Co.	

1868–1887

	BUILT ENVIRONMENT	POLITICS AND PUBLIC ORDER	CIVIC CULTURE	POPULATION AND HEALTH
1868	○ William Le Baron Jenney establishes architectural firm			○ First Jewish hospital
1869	○ Railroad link to Pacific ○ Water Tower and Pumping Station ★ West, South, and Lincoln Park Districts ○ Washington Street Tunnel completed ○ Riverside platted	○ Town of Cicero incorporated	★ Chicago Club	
1870	○ Palmer House	○ IL grants suffrage to black men ○ IL Constitutional Convention	★ Congregation of Bohemian Freethinkers	○ Chicago pop. 298,977 ○ 8 counties pop. 519,812 ★ Women's Hospital Medical College
1871	○ Great Chicago Fire of 1871 ○ Chicago River reversed ○ Illinois & Michigan Canal debt paid ○ Palmer House Hotel rebuilt	○ Cook County's first African American to hold elective office ○ First house of correction	★ Order of the Patrons of Husbandry (Grange)	
1872		○ Evanston incorporated ○ Town of Jefferson incorporated ○ First African American police officer ○ First woman admitted to state bar	★ *Cook County Herald (Daily Herald)* newspaper	
1873	○ Field & Leiter store		★ Polish Roman Catholic Union of America ★ Fortnightly Club	
1874		○ Fire limit expands to cover whole city ○ Fire south of downtown ○ Sunday closing repealed	★ Citizens Association of Chicago ★ Chicago Literary Club ★ Chicago WCTU	
1875	★ City Department of Buildings			
1876			★ Chicago Woman's Club	★ Chicago YWCA
1877			★ Commercial Club	★ Pacific Garden Mission
1878				
1879				
1880			★ Polish National Alliance	○ Chicago pop. 503,185 ○ 8 counties pop. 803,568
1881			★ Baptist Missionary Training School	★ College of Physicians and Surgeons (University of IL College of Medicine) ★ Michael Reese Hospital ○ Smallpox epidemic begins (2,472 die by 1882)
1882	○ Chicago City Railway (cable car system)	○ Elmhurst incorporated	★ Congregational Chicago City Mission (later Community Renewal Society)	★ Children's Memorial Hospital ★ St. Mary's Training School for Boys
1883	○ Hyde Park waterworks	○ Chicago bans street peddling on Sundays ○ Saloon licensing fee increases from $50 to $500 (1883–85)		★ *Journal of the American Medical Association*
1884			★ Presbyterian Hospital	
1885	○ Fine Arts Building ○ First skyscraper (Home Insurance Building)	○ IL Civil Rights Act passed ○ New City Hall and Court House		○ Salvation Army arrives
1886		○ Haymarket riot ○ Fire inspectors instituted		
1887	○ Fort Sheridan ○ Outer Belt Line Railroad	○ Town of Lake View incorporated		

★ = Founding of

	ARTS AND EDUCATION	LEISURE AND SPORTS	WORK AND ECONOMY	INTERNATIONAL/NATIONAL
1868	★ Lincoln Park Zoo		○ First shipment of refrigerated beef by railcar ★ Chicago Association of Undertakers	○ 14th Amendment (guaranteeing citizenship by birth; due process; equal protection)
1869	★ Oratorio Society			○ Transcontinental railroad
1870	★ *Art Review* ★ Loyola University	★ Chicago White Stockings baseball team (Cubs)		○ Franco-Prussian War begins ○ 15th Amendment grants suffrage to black men
1871		★ Lake Front Baseball Field	★ Joliet Iron & Steel Co.	
1872	★ Board of Education ★ Chicago Public Library ★ Apollo Musical Club (later Apollo Chorus) ○ First city atlas ★ Beethoven Society		★ Montgomery Ward & Co.	
1873	○ Interstate Industrial Exposition begins			○ Financial panic
1874	○ First kindergarten study club ○ State law forbids segregated education		★ Workingmen's Party of IL	
1875		★ Chicago Yacht Club		○ Civil Rights Act
1876			○ Spalding store	○ Philadelphia Centennial Exhibition
1877	○ Chicago Musicians' Protective Union folds		○ Knights of Labor local assembly ○ Railroad strike	○ End of Reconstruction
1878			○ Bell Telephone of Illinois begins service	
1879	★ Art Institute of Chicago ★ Central Music Hall	★ Chicago Bicycle Club ○ First recorded football game	★ IL Bureau of Labor Statistics	
1880	★ *The Dial* magazine ★ Chicago Musical Society		★ U.S. Steel South Works ★ Pullman (town)	
1881			★ *Breeder's Gazette* journal ★ Marshall Field & Co.	○ Garfield assassinated ○ Pogroms begin in Russia
1882		○ First vaudeville entertainment	★ Chicago Stock Exchange	○ Chinese Exclusion Act
1883		○ Chicago's first organized soccer league		○ Railroads adopt standard time
1884	★ Chicago Conservatory of Music and Dramatic Art	★ Washington Park Racecourse	○ Armour & Co. purchases glue works ★ Central Labor Union (anarchist) ★ IL School of Embalming ★ IL State Federation of Labor	
1885	★ Chicago Grand Opera Festival ○ Women admitted to Apollo Club			
1886	★ American Conservatory of Music ★ Chicago Kindergarten College		★ Gonnella Baking Co.	★ American Federation of Labor
1887	★ Newberry Library	○ Nation's first pro heavyweight wrestling championship		○ Interstate Commerce Act

1888–1904

	BUILT ENVIRONMENT	POLITICS AND PUBLIC ORDER	CIVIC CULTURE	POPULATION AND HEALTH
1888	○ Rookery		★ New Thought seminary and training school ★ Germania Club ★ Wesley Hospital	
1889	○ Auditorium Theater ○ Monadnock Building	○ Annexations (Chicago doubles in size) ★ Chicago Sanitary District ○ 35 wards in Chicago	★ Hull House ★ Moody Bible Institute ○ Over 60 convents in Chicago	★ Visiting Nurses Association
1890			★ City Press Association (later City News Bureau)	○ Chicago pop. 1,099,850 (second in United States) ○ 8 counties pop. 1,433,828
1891			★ Northwestern University Settlement	○ Bronchitis and pneumonia outbreaks (4,300 die) ★ Provident Hospital and Training School for Nurses ○ Typhoid fever epidemic (2,000 die)
1892	○ First elevated railways in Chicago ○ Telephone service between Chicago and New York launched		★ Chicago Commons ★ University of Chicago Settlement ○ First Greek Orthodox parish in Chicago ★ St. Vladimir's Russian Orthodox parish	
1893		○ Gov. Altgeld's Haymarket pardon	○ World's Parliament of Religions ○ First Chinese newspaper in Chicago ○ "Haymarket Martyrs" monument erected at Waldheim Cemetery ★ Civic Federation of Chicago	
1894		★ Chicago Political Equality League		★ Central Relief Association ○ Chicago's first public bath
1895	○ Marquette Building	○ First subsidized housing development built	○ *Hull-House Maps and Papers* ★ Chicago Zion Society	★ Amanda Smith Orphanage ★ Chicago Lying-In Hospital and Dispensary
1896	○ Grant Park	★ Municipal Voter League ○ William Jennings Bryan delivers "Cross of Gold" speech		
1897	○ Loop Elevated (Union Elevated Railway) opens	○ Yerkes bribes city council (1897–98)		
1898		○ First Cook County board of assessors elected	★ Polish Women's Alliance	★ Madonna Center
1899	○ Chicago Coliseum	○ World's first juvenile court established		
1900	○ City Beautiful movement begins ○ First pay telephones ○ Sanitary and Ship Canal		★ *International Socialist Review* ★ City Homes Association	○ Chicago pop. 1,698,575 ○ 8 counties pop. 2,141,817
1901		○ Oak Park and Berwyn split from Cicero Township		○ Robert Hunter, *Tenement Conditions in Chicago*
1902	○ First public auto parking garage ○ First trunnion bascule bridge	★ Tenement House Ordinance		○ Chicago becomes hdqrs. of American Medical Association
1903			★ City Club ★ Holy Trinity Orthodox Cathedral	○ Iroquois Theater fire (602 die)
1904				

★ = Founding of

	ARTS AND EDUCATION	LEISURE AND SPORTS	WORK AND ECONOMY	INTERNATIONAL/NATIONAL
1888			★ Abbott Laboratories	
1889			★ IL Steel Co.	
1890	★ Orchestral Association	★ Chicago Athletic Association	★ Building Trades Council ★ Chicago Ship Building Co. ○ First oil refinery	
1891	★ University of Chicago ★ Chicago Symphony Orchestra ○ Chicago's first of a continuous series of opera seasons		★ Wrigley Company ★ University of Chicago Press ★ Chicago Title & Trust Company	○ Basketball invented
1892	○ Interstate Industrial Exposition ends ○ Nation's first sociology dept. (University of Chicago)	★ Lincoln Park Conservatory		○ Chinese Exclusion Act extended ○ Ellis Island opens
1893	★ Armour Institute of Technology (IIT) ○ Art Institute building ○ Finley Peter Dunne begins "Mr. Dooley" columns ○ Henry Blake Fuller, *The Cliff Dwellers* ○ World's Columbian Exposition	○ Nation's first 18-hole course at Chicago Golf Club	★ Stone & Kimball	○ *Rerum Novarum* papal encyclical ○ National depression begins (ends 1897)
1894	★ Field Museum ○ Stone & Kimball's *Chap-Book* literary journal ○ William T. Stead, *If Christ Came to Chicago*	★ Paul Boyton's Water Chute (amusement park) ★ Garfield Park Conservatory	★ Chicago Stock Exchange building ○ Pullman Strike	○ Dreyfus affair
1895	★ Palette and Chisel Club ★ Caxton Club	○ Nation's first auto race	★ Arnold, Schwinn & Co. ★ Peoples Gas ○ Sears, Roebuck & Co. moves to Chicago	
1896		○ First state interscholastic basketball contest (girls' teams)	★ Chicago Federation of Labor	○ *Plessy v. Ferguson*
1897	★ Chicago Society of Arts and Crafts ★ Sherwood Music School ★ John Crerar Library ★ Chicago Teachers Federation			
1898	★ Little Room literary society ★ St. Vincent's College (DePaul University)	★ Woman's Athletic Club ★ Cardinals (as Morgan Athletic Club)	★ Curt Teich Company (postcard firm) ★ National Biscuit Co.	○ Spanish-American War
1899	○ Henry Cowles publishes study of Indiana Dunes ecology	○ First public golf course in Midwest ★ Jackson Park	★ Jewel Tea Company ○ First public employment office	○ U.S.-Philippine war begins
1900	★ Choral Study Club ○ Theodore Dreiser, *Sister Carrie*	○ One of every 10,000 Chicagoans owns automobile ★ White Sox baseball team	★ Abbott Alkaloidal Company ○ State prohibits employment of children under 14	
1901	★ Joliet Junior College	★ Midwest pro soccer circuit ○ Prizefight boxing banned	★ Chicago Federation of Musicians ○ McCormick adopts welfare capitalist programs ★ U.S. Steel ★ Walgreen's drugstore	○ McKinley assassinated
1902		★ McKinley Park	★ Chicago Flat Janitors' Union ★ Wisconsin Steel Works	
1903	★ Chicago Hebrew Institute		★ International Harvester	
1904	★ Ravinia Park ★ Orchestra Hall	★ Riverview amusement park	○ Garment workers' strike ★ Women's Trade Union League (national office in Chicago) ★ Spiegel mail-order firm ○ J. L. Kraft starts selling cheese in Chicago ○ Meatpacking strike	

1905–1919

	BUILT ENVIRONMENT	POLITICS AND PUBLIC ORDER	CIVIC CULTURE	POPULATION AND HEALTH
1905	○ Central Manufacturing District ○ 100,000 telephones in Chicago	○ Municipal courts replace justice of the peace courts	★ Rotary International ★ Abraham Lincoln Centre ★ *Chicago Defender*	
1906	○ Cable car system ends ○ Freight tunnels begin service	○ Saloon licensing fee increases to $1,000 ○ Gary incorporated	○ Bosnians establish first Muslim organization ★ *Englewood Economist* (later *Daily Southtown*) newspaper	
1907		○ IL local option law	★ Interdenominational Church Federation of Greater Chicago	
1908	○ "Brennan" street-naming system introduced		★ *Dziennik Związkowy* newspaper	○ Milk pasteurization ordinance
1909	○ *Plan of Chicago* ("Burnham Plan")		★ Pulaski Hall ★ St. Constantine parish (Greek Orthodox)	★ Juvenile Protective Association ★ United Charities of Chicago
1910		○ Chicago uses census tracts for the first time ★ Police Academy ○ Suffragist Party organized	★ Woman's City Club ★ Chicago branch of National Association for the Advancement of Colored People ★ Bureau of Public Efficiency	○ Chicago pop. 2,185,283 ○ 8 counties pop. 2,805,869
1911	○ Great Lakes Naval Training Station	○ Chicago Vice Commission publishes *The Social Evil in Chicago* ★ Court of Domestic Relations ○ IL mothers' pension law enacted		★ Infant Welfare Society
1912		○ Raids shut down Levee vice district ★ Woman Suffrage Party of Cook County	○ Baha'i Temple site dedicated	★ U.S. Children's Bureau ★ Chicago State Hospital ○ Chlorination of water supply begins
1913	○ Medinah Hall	○ IL forest preserve legislation enacted ○ Municipal suffrage for women adopted		○ First African American YWCA ★ *Journal of the American Dental Association*
1914	○ Fourth Presbyterian Church	★ Cook County Forest Preserve ★ North Shore Sanitary District		★ Welfare Council of Metropolitan Chicago
1915	○ Telephone service between Chicago and San Francisco launched	★ Cook and DuPage County Forest Preserve Districts ○ First African American alderman	★ Chicago Community Trust	○ Eastland disaster ○ First African American YMCA ★ Municipal Tuberculosis Sanitarium
1916			★ Chicago Urban League ○ Mundelein declares end of national parishes ★ Norske Club	○ New Cook County Hospital building
1917		○ Bombings of African American homes begins (to 1921)		★ Lions Clubs International ○ First school diphtheria immunizations ★ Julius Rosenwald Foundation
1918		○ Airmail service between Chicago and New York begins ★ Labor Party created in Chicago		○ American Dental Association moves hdqrs. to Chicago ★ Catholic Charities ○ Amanda Smith Orphanage closes ○ Influenza pandemic begins (kills 20,000 locally by 1919)
1919		★ American Communist Party ★ Chicago Crime Commission ○ Race riot	○ Associated Negro Press	

 ★ = Founding of

	ARTS AND EDUCATION	LEISURE AND SPORTS	WORK AND ECONOMY	INTERNATIONAL/NATIONAL
1905	★ Pekin Theater	★ Davis Square Park and fieldhouse o State bans horse racing ★ White City Amusement Park	o Household Finance creates first installment plan ★ IWW o Teamsters' strike	
1906	o Upton Sinclair, *The Jungle*	o White Sox defeat Cubs in World Series	★ U.S. Steel Gary Works	o Pure Food and Drug Act
1907	o Chicago begins film censorship ★ Green Mill nightclub	o Cubs win World Series	o ComEd forms from merger ★ Essanay Studios ★ IL Dept. of Factory Inspection	
1908	★ Umbrian Glee Club	o Cubs win World Series o First statewide high school boys' basketball tournament o World's first suspended roller coaster		
1909	o Film production begins in Chicago ★ *Friday Literary Review*		o Ten-hour-day law for women workers	o First Model T automobile
1910	★ Chicago Grand Opera Company ★ Federal Glee Club	★ Comiskey Park o First successfully lighted night baseball game, at Comiskey Park	★ Amalgamated Clothing Workers of America o Garment workers' strike (to 1911)	o Mexican Revolution ★ Boy Scouts founded by Chicago publisher W. D. Boyce
1911	o Chicago's first junior college ★ Junior League of Chicago	★ American Giants baseball team o First high-school soccer teams	★ IL Occupational Disease Act ★ IL Workmen's Compensation Act	
1912	o *Chap-Book* ceases publication ★ *Poetry: A Magazine of Verse* ★ Little Theatre		★ Foster Photoplay Co. ★ Kemper Insurance o Maxwell Street Market ordinance passed	
1913	o Lorado Taft sculpture, *Fountain of the Great Lakes* o Dalcroze eurhythmics introduced o Chicago's Armory Show o Public schools begin tracking for vocational education ★ Civic Music Association		★ Arthur Andersen & Co.	o 16th Amendment (federal income tax) o Federal Reserve Act o 17th Amendment (direct election of senators)
1914	o Edgar Rice Burroughs, *Tarzan of the Apes* ★ *Little Review* ★ Chicago Girl Scouts	★ Weeghman Field (later Wrigley) ★ Cook County Forest Preserve District	★ Tinkertoys ★ Booz Allen & Hamilton, Inc. ★ Goldblatts ★ Hong Kong Noodle Co.	o World War I begins
1915	★ Renaissance Society art museum		★ Yellow Cab Co.	o Joe Hill executed
1916	★ Dill Pickle Club ★ Arts Club o Carl Sandburg, *Chicago Poems*	★ Balaban & Katz movie theater chain ★ Original Dixieland Jazz Band		o Great Migration begins
1917	★ World Book Encyclopedia	★ Central Park movie palace (1,800 seats) ★ Chicago Tribune Silver Skates competition ★ King Oliver's Creole Jazz Band o White Sox win World Series	★ Stockyards Labor Council	o East St. Louis race riot o Russian Revolution o U.S. entry into World War I
1918	o *Dial* magazine moves to NYC ★ Goodman School of Drama		o Over 100 IWW leaders tried in federal court in Chicago o Lincoln Logs wood toy first sold	o Palmer Raids, Red Scare begin
1919	★ Social Science Research Council ★ National Association of Negro Musicians	o Thomas A. Dorsey arrives o Black Sox Scandal	★ Supreme Liberty Life Insurance Co. ★ Chicago Mercantile Exchange o Steel strike	o 19th Amendment (women's suffrage) o Nationwide steel strike o Prohibition (Volstead Act)

1920–1931

	BUILT ENVIRONMENT	POLITICS AND PUBLIC ORDER	CIVIC CULTURE	POPULATION AND HEALTH
1920	○ Michigan Avenue bridge opens	○ *American Bar Association Journal* moves to Chicago ○ Chicago Political Equality League disbands ★ League of Women Voters	★ Nation's first Ahmadi mosque ○ Over 200 convents in Chicago	○ Chicago pop. 2,701,705 ○ 8 counties pop. 3,575,209
1921			○ Chicago's first radio station (KYW)	★ Hines Veterans Hospital, Maywood
1922	○ *Wacker's Manual of the Plan of Chicago* ○ Calumet-Sag Channel completed ○ First sewage treatment plant		★ Gospel Tabernacle ★ Hebrew Theological College ★ Izaak Walton League	
1923	★ Chicago Regional Planning Association ○ First zoning ordinance	○ Chicago divided into 50 wards (was 35) ★ Indiana Dunes State Park	○ Preston Bradley begins radio ministry ★ IL Birth Control League	○ First birth control clinic opens ★ The Cradle Society (adoption agency)
1924	○ Niles Center (Skokie) grows tenfold by annexation (to 1926) ○ Union Station	○ Beer Wars begin (to 1930) ○ Leopold and Loeb murder ○ World's largest railway mail terminal opens	★ Our Lady of Guadalupe Church ★ Society for Human Rights (gay rights organization) ★ WGN radio ★ WLS radio	
1925			○ Robert McCormick becomes editor and publisher of the *Chicago Tribune* ○ Woman's World's Fair held in Chicago	
1926	○ Construction of double-decker Wacker Drive completed ○ Elks National Memorial Building		○ International Eucharistic Congress held in Chicago ★ WCFL radio ("Voice of Labor")	
1927	○ Chicago Municipal Airport (later Midway) ○ First gasoline-powered buses ○ Stevens Hotel ○ Tribune Building	○ Last Republican mayor elected ○ Real Estate Board promotes restrictive covenants ○ Cook County execution method changed from hanging to electrocution		
1928	○ 12,000 female operators employed by IL Bell in Chicago ○ 900,000 telephones in Chicago	○ Capone makes Lexington Hotel his hdqrs. (until 1932) ○ Tax strike	○ First national convention of Moorish Science Movement	
1929	○ Chicago Stadium ○ Rosenwald Gardens ○ Palmolive (Playboy) Building ○ Civic Opera Building ○ Michigan Blvd. Garden Apartments	○ St. Valentine's Day Massacre ○ U.S. Justice Department targets Capone		
1930	○ Stickney Water Reclamation Plant ★ Board of Trade Building	○ Police radios ★ Association of Real Estate Taxpayers ○ Community Areas created	★ Catholic Youth Organization	○ Chicago pop. 3,376,438 ○ 8 counties pop. 4,733,777
1931	○ Home Insurance Building demolished	★ Chicago Civil Liberties Committee ○ Tax strikes (to 1933)		

★ = Founding of

	ARTS AND EDUCATION	LEISURE AND SPORTS	WORK AND ECONOMY	INTERNATIONAL/NATIONAL
1920	○ *Encyclopaedia Britannica* moves hdqrs. to Chicago ★ Civic Music Student Orchestra (later Civic Orchestra)	★ Negro National League ○ American Giants win first Negro National League championship ★ Bears football team (as Decatur Staleys)		
1921	○ Pageant of Progress festival ○ Field Museum moves to Grant Park	★ Chicago Theatre ★ Figure Skating Club of Chicago ○ American Giants win Negro National League championship ★ Tivoli Theater, city's largest movie house (4,000 seats)		○ Sheppard-Towner Maternity and Infancy Act
1922	★ Chicago Association of Arts and Industries ★ Chicago Civic Opera ○ Chicago Grand Opera Company collapses ○ First independent ballet company ★ Morton Arboretum	★ Trianon Ballroom ○ American Giants win Negro National League championship ○ Louis Armstrong moves to Chicago	★ American Hospital Supply Corporation	○ Railway shopmen's strike ○ Partition of Ireland and Northern Ireland
1923			○ Steel industry adopts eight-hour day	
1924		★ Soldier Field ★ *WLS Barn Dance*	★ Ace Hardware ★ American Furniture Mart	○ National Origins Act
1925	★ Women's Symphony Orchestra ★ Goodman Theatre	★ Uptown Theater ○ Cardinals win NFL championship	★ Brotherhood of Sleeping Car Porters ★ Dean Foods ★ Dominick's grocery ○ IL limits labor injunctions	○ Scopes Trial
1926	★ Halevi Choral Society	★ Blackhawks hockey team ★ Aragon Ballroom ○ Wm. Wrigley purchases Cubs, renames ballpark ★ Harlem Globetrotters ○ American Giants win Negro National League championship ★ Sam 'n' Henry radio program (later Amos 'n' Andy) ○ Boxing legalized; IL Boxing Commission organized	★ James O. McKinsey & Co. ○ Largest street railway firm goes bankrupt	
1927	○ Mahalia Jackson arrives ★ Society of Typographic Arts ○ Frederic Thrasher, *The Gang*	○ Savoy Ballroom ○ State legalizes pari-mutuel betting ★ Lake Shore Athletic Club ○ American Giants win Negro National League championship ○ Dempsey-Tunney fight	○ Hawthorne experiments conducted at Western Electric ★ Helene Curtis Co.	
1928	○ Louis Wirth, *The Ghetto* ★ Regal Theater	★ Paradise movie theater	★ Motorola	
1929	○ Hutchins becomes president of University of Chicago ★ John G. Shedd Aquarium	★ Oak Park Conservatory ○ First disc jockey ★ First Bud Billiken Day Parade	○ "Spend Your Money Where You Can Work" campaign ○ Elementary education required for children under 14	○ Stock Market Crash
1930	○ Harvey Zorbaugh, *The Gold Coast and the Slum* ★ Adler Planetarium ○ Catholic school enrollment peaks	○ First soap opera	★ *Advertising Age* ○ Abbott Co. introduces Nembutal ○ Chicago becomes hdqrs. for United Airlines	
1931	○ Katherine Dunham presents *Negro Rhapsody* ballet ○ Little Room literary society closes ○ First gospel choir ★ DeVry Institutes	★ *Dick Tracy* comic strip	★ Allstate Insurance Co. ★ Baxter Laboratories ★ Merchandise Mart ★ Real Estate Research Corporation	○ Japan invades Manchuria

1932–1945

	BUILT ENVIRONMENT	POLITICS AND PUBLIC ORDER	CIVIC CULTURE	POPULATION AND HEALTH
1932		○ Democratic National Convention held in Chicago		
1933	○ Crawford Ave. renamed Pulaski ○ IL Waterway ○ Outer Lake Shore Drive	○ Cermak assassinated ○ Capone sent to prison		
1934	○ International Amphitheater	○ John Dillinger shot ★ Chicago Park District, from merger of earlier districts	○ Nation of Islam establishes temple	★ Chicago Area Project ★ Chicago's United Way/Crusade of Mercy
1935			★ *U.S. Catholic* magazine	
1936				○ Pregnancy preventatives legalized
1937	○ Ludwig Mies van der Rohe arrives	★ Chicago Housing Authority		
1938	○ Addams, Lathrop, and Trumbull Park housing projects		★ *Catholic Worker* newspaper	
1939		○ State permits women to serve on juries	★ Back of the Yards Neighborhood Council	
1940	○ Over one million telephones in Chicago	○ Chicago appoints nation's first African American police captain		○ Chicago pop. 3,396,808 ○ 8 counties pop. 4,890,674
1941	○ West Side Medical Center district ○ Orchard Field (site of future O'Hare International Airport) ○ Ida B. Wells Homes ★ IL Toll Highway Authority ○ Argonne National Laboratory			
1942	○ Cabrini Homes	★ Chicago Committee of Racial Equality		
1943	○ First subway ○ Master Plan of Residential Land Use of Chicago ○ Unified Traction Ordinance	★ Mayor's Committee on Race Relations	★ WBEZ radio	
1944			★ American West Indian Association ★ Midwest Buddhist Temple ★ Buddhist Temple of Chicago	
1945	★ Chicago Transit Authority		★ Atomic Scientists of Chicago, Inc. ★ *Ebony* magazine	

★ = Founding of

	ARTS AND EDUCATION	LEISURE AND SPORTS	WORK AND ECONOMY	INTERNATIONAL/NATIONAL
1932	○ Chicago's first Pulitzer Prize ○ J. Z. Jacobson, *Art of Today: Chicago, 1933* ○ Chicago Civic Opera ends ★ Art Directors Club ○ James Farrell, *Studs Lonigan*	○ First pinball machine	○ Chicago exhausts emergency relief funds	
1933	○ Century of Progress Exposition (1933 and 1934) ★ Museum of Science and Industry ★ National Convention of Gospel Choirs and Choruses	★ *Breakfast Club* radio program ★ *Esquire* magazine ★ Amateur Softball Association ○ First annual Negro Baseball League East-West All-Star Game	○ Homer Hoyt, *One Hundred Years of Land Values in Chicago* ○ Unemployed march to Springfield	○ United States grants Philippine independence ○ Repeal of Prohibition ○ National "Bank Holiday" ○ Hitler comes to power ★ Federal Deposit Insurance Corporation
1934	★ Brookfield Zoo	○ Blackhawks win Stanley Cup ○ First annual College All-Star football game begins		
1935	○ IL Writers' Project (until 1943)	★ *Fibber McGee and Molly* radio program	★ Committee for Industrial Organizations (later Congress of Industrial Organizations) ★ Fuller Products Co. ★ Leo Burnett Co.	○ Italy invades Ethiopia ○ WPA (to 1943) ○ National Labor Relations Act (Wagner Act) ○ Federal Writers' Project and Federal Art Project (until 1943) ○ Social Security Act
1936	○ Edith Abbott, *The Tenements of Chicago, 1908–1935*			
1937	★ New Bauhaus	○ Prep Bowl draws 120,000 to Soldier Field ○ Wrigley Field adds scoreboard, bleachers, ivy-covered outfield walls ○ Joe Louis becomes world heavyweight champion ★ Negro American League	○ Pullman recognizes Brotherhood of Sleeping Car Porters ○ Eight-hour day law for women workers ★ Chicago Teachers Union ○ Currency exchanges ○ IL becomes last state to adopt unemployment insurance law ○ Memorial Day Massacre (Republic Steel)	★ Packinghouse Workers Organizing Committee ★ Steel Workers Organizing Committee
1938	○ Arrival of Bauhaus designers ○ *Local Community Fact Book*	○ Blackhawks win Stanley Cup		★ Fair Labor Standards Act (40-hour work week)
1939	★ Hyde Park Art Center			○ World War II begins
1940	○ American Negro Exposition at Coliseum ★ IL Institute of Technology ○ Richard Wright, *Native Son*	○ First IL High School Association baseball tournament	○ Montgomery Ward employees unionized	
1941	★ Stone-Camryn School of Ballet ★ South Side Community Art Center			★ Fair Employment Practice Committee
1942	○ First self-sustaining nuclear chain reaction		○ Laborers recruited (from Western Hemisphere) to fill wartime labor	○ Internment of Japanese Americans begins ○ Second Great Migration begins
1943		★ All-American Girls Baseball League	★ United Packinghouse Workers of America	○ Chinese exclusion laws repealed
1944	○ Karl Shapiro, *V-Letter and Other Poems* (Pulitzer Prize winner) ○ New Bauhaus becomes Institute of Design			○ GI Bill
1945	○ St. Clair Drake and Horace R. Cayton, *Black Metropolis: A Study of Negro Life in a Northern City* ○ Gwendolyn Brooks, *A Street in Bronzeville* ★ Katherine Dunham School of Arts and Research ★ Roosevelt University		○ Chicago Bar Assoc. admits African Americans	○ First atomic bomb detonated ★ United Nations

1946–1962

	BUILT ENVIRONMENT	POLITICS AND PUBLIC ORDER	CIVIC CULTURE	POPULATION AND HEALTH
1946	★ South Side Planning Board			
1947	○ Developer Arthur Rubloff names Magnificent Mile ○ First parking meters		○ Nuclear "Doomsday Clock"	
1948	○ Meigs Field	○ U.S. Supreme Court declares restrictive covenants unenforceable	★ *Chicago Sun-Times* newspaper (from merger) ★ WGN-TV	
1949	○ Coaxial cable link to East Coast	○ Park Forest incorporated		
1950	○ Buses replace streetcars	★ Chicago League of Women Voters		○ Chicago pop. 3,620,962 ○ 8 counties pop. 5,586,096
1951	○ Edens Expressway opens ○ Coaxial cable link to West Coast			
1952	★ South East Chicago Commission			
1953	★ Chicago Community Conservation Board ○ First one-way streets			
1954			○ Marian Year tribute draws 260,000 to Soldier Field ★ Mosque Foundation ★ Chicago Educational Television Association ★ *Chicago* magazine	
1955	○ Eisenhower Expressway opens (in sections, through 1960) ○ Grace Abbott Homes		★ Daughters of Bilitis and Mattachine Society ★ WTTW-TV	
1956	○ *Planning the Region of Chicago* ○ Old Orchard Mall	○ Schaumburg incorporated	★ *Christianity Today* magazine ★ Sikh Study Circle (later Sikh Religious Society)	○ St. Luke's, Presbyterian, and Rush Hospitals merge
1957	★ Northeastern IL Planning Commission ○ Inland Steel Building ○ Chicago, Aurora & Elgin interurban ends service ○ Prudential Building		○ First mosque	
1958	○ Tri-State, East-West, and Northwest Tollways open ○ Calumet Skyway opens ○ Last streetcar service ○ Stateway Gardens Public Housing	★ Lake County Forest Preserve District		○ Our Lady of Angels school fire
1959	○ St. Lawrence Seaway ○ CHA's first Housing for Elderly ○ Freight tunnels abandoned	★ City Department of Air Pollution Control		
1960	○ Kennedy Expressway opens ○ Oakbrook Mall	○ Most police foot patrols end	○ Malcolm X founds *Mr. Muhammad Speaks* newspaper	○ Chicago pop. 3,550,404 ○ 8 counties pop. 6,794,461
1961	○ William Green Homes	○ "Freedom wade-in" at Rainbow Beach ○ IL first to legalize private consensual homosexual relations	★ Northwest Community Organization	
1962	○ Washington Park Homes ○ Dan Ryan Expressway opens ○ Robert Taylor Homes		★ Coordinating Council of Community Organizations	

★ = Founding of

	ARTS AND EDUCATION	LEISURE AND SPORTS	WORK AND ECONOMY	INTERNATIONAL/NATIONAL
1946	○ SAIC opens industrial design program ★ Chicago Youth Symphony		○ Chicago Employment Agency begins recruiting in Puerto Rico	○ Migration of displaced persons from WWII
1947	★ Jazz Showcase	○ Cardinals win NFL championship ★ *Kukla, Fran and Ollie* TV program	○ Peak of Chicago manufacturing employment	○ Taft-Hartley Act restricts unions ○ India-Pakistan partition and independence ○ Jackie Robinson reintegrates major league baseball
1948	★ 57th Street Art Fair ★ Exhibition Momentum (artists' group)			○ Israel founded ○ Mechanical cotton picker introduced ○ S. Africa institutes apartheid
1949	○ Nelson Algren, *The Man with the Golden Arm* ○ Institute of Design merges with IIT		★ Sara Lee Corp.	★ NATO ★ People's Republic of China
1950	○ Gwendolyn Brooks's *Annie Allen* awarded Pulitzer ★ Old Town Art Fair	★ Chess Records		○ Dawn of McCarthyism ○ Korean War begins
1951		★ *Garfield Goose* TV program ★ *Watch Mr. Wizard* TV program		
1952	★ Fromm Music Foundation	★ *Ding Dong School* TV program ○ American Giants disband ○ Negro American League ends	○ Steelworkers strike	
1953		★ Vee-Jay Records ★ *Playboy* magazine ○ First nationally televised golf tournament		○ Veterans Administration hospitals ban segregation
1954	★ Lyric Opera (as Lyric Theatre)	○ All-American Girls Baseball League dissolved	★ Johnson Products Co.	○ *Brown v. Board of Education*
1955	★ Chicago Opera Ballet ★ Compass Players	★ "Ann Landers" advice column ○ Chess releases "Maybellene" (Chuck Berry)	★ McDonald's (Des Plaines)	○ AFL-CIO merger ○ Warsaw Pact ○ Emmett Till murdered ○ Montgomery bus boycott
1956	○ WTTW initiates "TV College" ★ Chicago Children's Choir	○ Downtown St. Patrick's Day Parade revived		○ Interstate Highway Act
1957	★ Chicago Symphony Chorus ★ Old Town School of Folk Music	○ *WLS Barn Dance* ends		○ *Sputnik* satellite launched
1958		○ Vee-Jay releases "For Your Precious Love" (Jerry Butler and the Impressions)		○ European Common Market formed ○ Integrated circuit invented
1959		○ Nation's first year-round children's zoo ★ Second City theater company	○ Steelworkers strike	○ Cuban Revolution
1960	○ Archdiocese prohibits racial exclusion in schools	○ First Playboy Club ○ Cardinals (football team) move to St. Louis	★ McCormick Place Convention Center	○ OPEC founded ○ Independence for 17 African nations
1961	★ University of Chicago Folk Festival ★ DuSable Museum of African American History	★ *Bozo's Circus* TV program ○ Blackhawks win Stanley Cup	○ McCormick Reaper Works demolished	○ Fair Employment Practices Act
1962	○ Carl Sandburg named state poet laureate ★ Grant Park Symphony Chorus			○ Vatican II begins

1963–1979

	BUILT ENVIRONMENT	POLITICS AND PUBLIC ORDER	CIVIC CULTURE	POPULATION AND HEALTH
1963	○ Carl Sandburg Village ○ First condominiums established ○ O'Hare Airport	○ Fair housing ordinance passed	★ Openlands Project ★ WVON radio	
1964		★ Cook County Court System ○ Johnson introduces "Great Society" in Chicago	○ Associated Negro Press folds	★ IL Department of Children and Family Services
1965	○ Daley Center		○ Chicago Freedom Movement (to 1967) ○ Martin Luther King in Chicago ★ Operation Breadbasket	
1966	○ Stevenson Expressway opens ★ Chicago Architecture Foundation	○ Marquette Park violence against civil rights marchers ○ Humboldt Park rioting ★ Leadership Council for Metropolitan Open Communities		
1967	○ Chicago second to New York City in air pollution ○ Auditorium Theater renovated	○ Chicago receives "Model City" funds ★ Illinois Housing Development Authority	★ Chicago chapter of National Organization for Women	○ Swarm of tornadoes in downtown Chicago
1968	★ Commission on Chicago Landmarks ○ Federal funding for high-rise public housing ended	○ Riot at Democratic National Convention ○ West Side riots after King assassination ★ Black Panther Party		○ Record-setting snowstorm
1969	○ John Hancock Center	★ Chicago Women's Liberation Union ○ IL income tax adopted ○ Police kill Black Panther Party leaders	★ University of Chicago Gay Liberation Front	★ Jane (underground abortion service)
1970		○ IL Constitutional Convention	★ Chicago Gay Alliance ○ First annual Gay Pride Parade	○ Chicago pop. 3,369,357 ○ 8 counties pop. 7,612,314
1971	○ Woodfield Mall	○ Women elected to city council for the first time ★ McHenry County Forest Preserve District ○ Merrillville incorporated ★ Operation PUSH	★ Citizens for a Better Environment	
1972		○ Shakman decrees	★ *Chicago Reporter* monthly newspaper	
1973		○ Black Panther Party dissolves		★ Legal Assistance Foundation of Chicago
1974	○ Fermilab ★ Regional Transit Authority ○ Sears Tower	○ Women appointed as full-fledged police officers for the first time	★ Coalition of Labor Union Women ★ Donors Forum of Chicago ★ Islamic Cultural Center of Greater Chicago	
1975	○ First use of taxes to subsidize mass transit ○ Tunnel and Reservoir Plan ("Deep Tunnel") begins		★ Zoroastrian Association of Metropolitan Chicago	
1976	○ Water Tower Place			
1977				
1978			★ Center for Neighborhood Technology ★ John D. and Catherine T. MacArthur Foundation	
1979	○ State Street Mall	○ Chicago elects first woman mayor ○ Chicago School District declares bankruptcy	○ Pope John Paul II visits Chicago	○ Last public bathhouse closes

 ★ = Founding of

	ARTS AND EDUCATION	LEISURE AND SPORTS	WORK AND ECONOMY	INTERNATIONAL/NATIONAL
1963	○ Boycott for school desegregation	○ Zephyrs basketball team moves to Baltimore ○ Loyola basketball team wins NCAA championship		○ Kennedy assassinated ○ Civil Rights Act ○ March on Washington ★ Organization of African Unity
1964	★ Contemporary Chamber Players ○ School boycott ○ Exhibition Momentum disbands			○ Tonkin Gulf Resolution; United States escalates Vietnam War ○ Voting Rights Act
1965	○ University of IL opens Near West Side campus ★ Chicago Jazz Ensemble ★ Association for the Advancement of Creative Musicians			★ National Endowments for Arts, Humanities ★ Headstart Program ○ Immigration liberalized
1966	★ Hairy Who artist group ○ Imagists emerge	★ Bulls basketball team ○ First annual Division Street Puerto Rican parade ○ Indiana Dunes National Lakeshore ○ Vee-Jay closes		
1967	○ *Nommo* journal ○ *Wall of Respect* mural ★ Museum of Contemporary Art ○ Picasso sculpture unveiled at Daley Plaza	★ "Chicago" rock band ○ Riverview closes	○ Board of Education recognizes Chicago Teachers Union	○ War between Israel and Arab neighbors
1968	○ AfriCobra formed ○ Gwendolyn Brooks named state poet laureate ○ SAIC industrial design program closes	○ *Breakfast Club* radio program ends ○ International Polka Association moves to Chicago	○ United Packinghouse Workers of America merges with Amalgamated Meat Cutters ★ United Transportation Union	○ Assassination of Martin Luther King, Jr.
1969			○ First Chicago teachers' strike	
1970	○ Chicago Opera Ballet closes		○ Union Stock Yard closes	★ Environmental Protection Agency ○ Unix operating system unveiled
1971	★ Chicago State University	○ World's first $1 million thoroughbred race held at Arlington track ○ Chicago unveils 34 miles of bike routes ○ Soldier Field becomes home of the Bears	○ IL minimum wage law passed	★ Amtrak
1972	★ William Ferris Chorale ★ Chicago Botanic Garden	○ IHSA begins to add state meets for girls' sports ○ Rush-hour bicycle lanes open on Clark and Dearborn Streets		○ Demolition of Pruitt-Igoe public housing (St. Louis) ○ Watergate scandal begins
1973	★ *New Art Examiner* magazine ★ Chicago Opera Theatre ○ Regal Theater closes		○ Sears moves hdqrs. downtown from North Lawndale	○ End of democracy in Chile ○ Energy crisis ○ *Roe v. Wade*
1974	★ Smart Museum ★ Native American Educational Services (NAES) College ○ *History of the Packinghouse Worker* mural ○ *The Four Seasons* mosaic (Chagall) ★ MoMing Dance and Arts Center	★ Chicago Tribune Silver Skates competition ○ *Donahue* show moves to Chicago	○ Board of Trade, Mercantile Exchange begin trading in gold futures ★ National Coalition of Labor Union Women	○ NY City fiscal crisis
1975	★ Movimiento Artistico Chicano ★ Steppenwolf Theatre	○ Chess Records final closing ★ Sting pro soccer team ○ Siskel and Ebert debut on TV		
1976		○ Annual College All-Star football game in Chicago ends		
1977	★ Hubbard Street Dance Company	★ Chicago Marathon	○ Board of Trade begins trading in U.S. bond futures	
1978	○ Percent for the Arts Ordinance approved		★ *Crain's Chicago Business* newspaper	○ Airline Deregulation Act ○ Camp David Accords
1979	★ Windy City Gay Chorus ★ Randolph Street Gallery ★ Merit Music Program		★ United Food and Commercial Workers	○ Iranian Revolution

1980–2000

	BUILT ENVIRONMENT	POLITICS AND PUBLIC ORDER	CIVIC CULTURE	POPULATION AND HEALTH
1980	★ Gautreaux Assisted Housing Program ○ Rosemont Horizon	○ First women firefighters	★ United Neighborhood Organization	○ Chicago pop. 3,005,072 ○ 8 counties pop. 7,746,405
1981				
1982		○ Chicago first major U.S. city to ban handgun sales		
1983	○ 333 Wacker Dr. building ★ Metra ★ Pace suburban bus network	○ "Council Wars" (until 1987) ○ Six real-estate agencies sued for racial steering policies ○ First African American mayor	★ American Islamic College	
1984				
1985				
1986			★ Hindu Temple of Greater Chicago	
1987			★ Museum of Broadcast Communications	○ Provident Hospital closes
1988		○ Human Rights Ordinance	★ ACTUP Chicago	○ Mary Thompson Hospital closes
1989	○ North-South Tollway (I-355) opens ○ Navy Pier renovated			
1990			○ Archdiocese of Chicago closes 35 parishes and missions	○ Chicago pop. 2,783,726 ○ 8 counties pop. 7,865,702
1991				
1992		○ Assault weapons banned in city		
1993	○ Fort Sheridan decommissioned		★ Metropolitan Alliance of Congregations	
1994	○ United Center	○ First openly gay elected official		
1995	○ First municipal recycling system ○ Navy Pier opens 148-foot Ferris Wheel	○ Mayor assumes authority over schools	★ United Power for Action	○ Heat wave (739 die)
1996	○ City closes last municipal incinerator ○ Demolition of CHA high rises begins	○ CHA taken over by federal agency		
1997	○ Redevelopment of former Glenview Naval Air Station begins	○ Over 100 Chicago schools on academic probation		
1998				
1999			○ City News Bureau shut down	
2000				○ Chicago pop. 2,896,016 ○ 8 counties pop. 8,723,082

★ = Founding of

	ARTS AND EDUCATION	LEISURE AND SPORTS	WORK AND ECONOMY	INTERNATIONAL/NATIONAL
1980	★ Billy Graham Center at Wheaton College		○ Wisconsin Steel plant closes	○ Civil War begins in El Salvador ○ Refugee act regularizes refugee policy ○ Solidarity trade union founded in Poland
1981	★ New Tradition Men's Chorus ○ Stone-Camryn School of Ballet closes	○ Reinsdorf and Einhorn buy White Sox		○ Guatemalan civil war escalates ○ Personal computers introduced
1982	★ Chicago Children's Museum			○ AIDS given its name
1983	★ Gay Men's Chorus			
1984	★ Annual blues festival ★ City Dept. of Cultural Affairs			
1985	★ Annual GospelFest ★ Kohl Children's Museum	★ *Oprah Winfrey Show* ○ Michael Jordan joins Bulls	○ Printing unions strike *Tribune*	
1986	○ "Poetry Slam" at Green Mill ★ IL Mathematics and Science Academy	○ Bears win Super Bowl	○ State employees win collective bargaining rights	
1987	★ Mexican Fine Arts Center Museum ★ Terra Museum ○ U.S. secretary of education declares Chicago's public schools "the worst in America"			○ Palestinian intifada
1988	○ School Reform Act	○ Lights added to Wrigley Field		
1989	○ MoMing Dance and Arts Center closes	○ Phil Jackson begins coaching Bulls	○ Andersen Consulting spins off from Arthur Andersen & Co.	
1990		○ Original Comiskey Park demolished	○ Los Angeles surpasses Chicago in population and wholesaling	
1991		○ Bulls begin three-year NBA championship run ○ First game at new Comiskey Park		○ S. Africa repeals apartheid laws ○ Soviet Union breaks up ○ Yugoslavia fragments
1992			○ Sears moves hdqrs. to Hoffman Estates from Loop ○ U.S. Steel closes South Works	
1993		○ Michael Jordan retires		○ Graphical Web browser unveiled ○ Oslo Mideast peace process begins
1994		○ Golden Gloves boxing tournament admits women	○ Ty Inc. introduces Beanie Babies	
1995	○ Joffrey Ballet relocates to Chicago	○ Michael Jordan returns to Bulls ○ Chicago Stadium demolished		○ Oklahoma City bombing
1996	★ Ballet Theater of Chicago ★ National Vietnam Art Museum	○ Bulls begin second three-year NBA championship run		○ Welfare reform legislation
1997				
1998	○ Randolph Street Gallery closes	○ Michael Jordan and Phil Jackson leave the Bulls	○ First Chicago NBD merges with Banc One	
1999	★ Peggy Notebaert Nature Museum			○ New Deal banking regulations repealed
2000				

Chicago as an Indian Town

"Although every Indian town carried a tribal identity, the resident population included people connected with other tribes. They may have come to live in the village because of marriage alliances made during a trading visit. . . . Some were captives or slaves acquired during inter-tribal wars. There were frequently people of European and African heritage captured as children or adults. . . .

"Indian villages were the recognized home bases for their inhabitants, yet, unlike white settlements, were seldom fully occupied during the entire year. In the northern Great Lakes region, . . . the major fishing sites were the places regularly occupied during the spring to fall period of tolerable weather. To the south, . . . villages had their maximum population during the summer planting and harvesting seasons. . . . The village customarily split into smaller groups to depart for winter hunting camps, then moved to maple groves for sugar making in the early spring and often took in a short-term spring fish run before returning to plant corn and other vegetables and visit a major trading center. In mid-winter, an Indian village site might be entirely vacant or house only elderly people left behind with dried food supplies to serve as general caretakers during the four-month winter hunting season."

From Helen Hornbeck Tanner, *Atlas of Great Lakes Indian History*, 4–5

1795

Kentucky appropriates $2,000 to extend Wilderness Road from Crab Orchard to Cumberland Gap; Thomas Paine's *Age of Reason* U.S. bestseller

January: Naturalization Act requires five years residence for U.S. citizenship

June: Treaty of Amity, Commerce, and Navigation between United States and Britain ratified

ⓐ *Background:* Between the 1673 journey of Jolliet and Marquette and 1763, the French exerted colonial influence in the Illinois Country, an area that connected France's Canadian province with Louisiana, and that is shown in this geographically inaccurate 1795 map. At the end of the Seven Years' War in 1763, France surrendered all of its North American claims. Britain had conquered Canada; Spain received Louisiana. The Illinois Country, although nominally part of Britain's holdings, was far from its control, except through the influence it exerted through the fur trade. As part of the 1795 Greenville Treaty, the American government took land at sixteen strategic locations, including Chicago. Not until the end of the War of 1812, however, did the government begin to exert control over the region that would become Chicago.

ⓑ The Greenville Treaty set into motion a process which led DuSable to sell his Chicago holdings. Until then, Indian treaties with Great Britain and the United States had set the Ohio River as the boundary between areas of white and Indian settlement. Following Anthony Wayne's 1794 victory at the Battle of Fallen Timbers, Indians ceded over two-thirds of southern and eastern Ohio. In addition, they ceded "one piece of land six miles square at the mouth of the Chikago river, emptying into the south-west end of Lake Michigan, where a fort formerly stood." Within a decade, Fort Dearborn had been established.

ⓒ Chicago was on the periphery of the American empire, and decisions important to it were made far away. In this contemporary painting, the American military and Indians negotiate the Treaty of Greenville in Ohio.

ⓓ Despite this crude rendering, Jean Baptiste and Catherine Point DuSable had a considerable establishment on the north side of the main branch of the Chicago River just west of Lake Michigan. When sold in 1800, it included a 40-by-22-foot wood house, one horse mill, a pair of millstones, a bake house, tools, furniture, household goods, and livestock. —From A. T. Andreas, *History of Cook County*, 1884

ⓔ-ⓕ Exchanges between colonial powers and Native Americans included both trade items and culture. The DuSables were Roman Catholic, and the brass holy water font inscribed 1752 is among the very few religious objects recovered from eighteenth-century Chicago (discovered during the 1898 excavations for the Halsted Street Bridge). Native Americans exchanged furs for blankets, pots, and other metal objects, including items like this silver brooch, ca. 1799–1800 by Robert Cruickshank of Montreal and recovered at Chicago. Collections of the Chicago Historical Society.

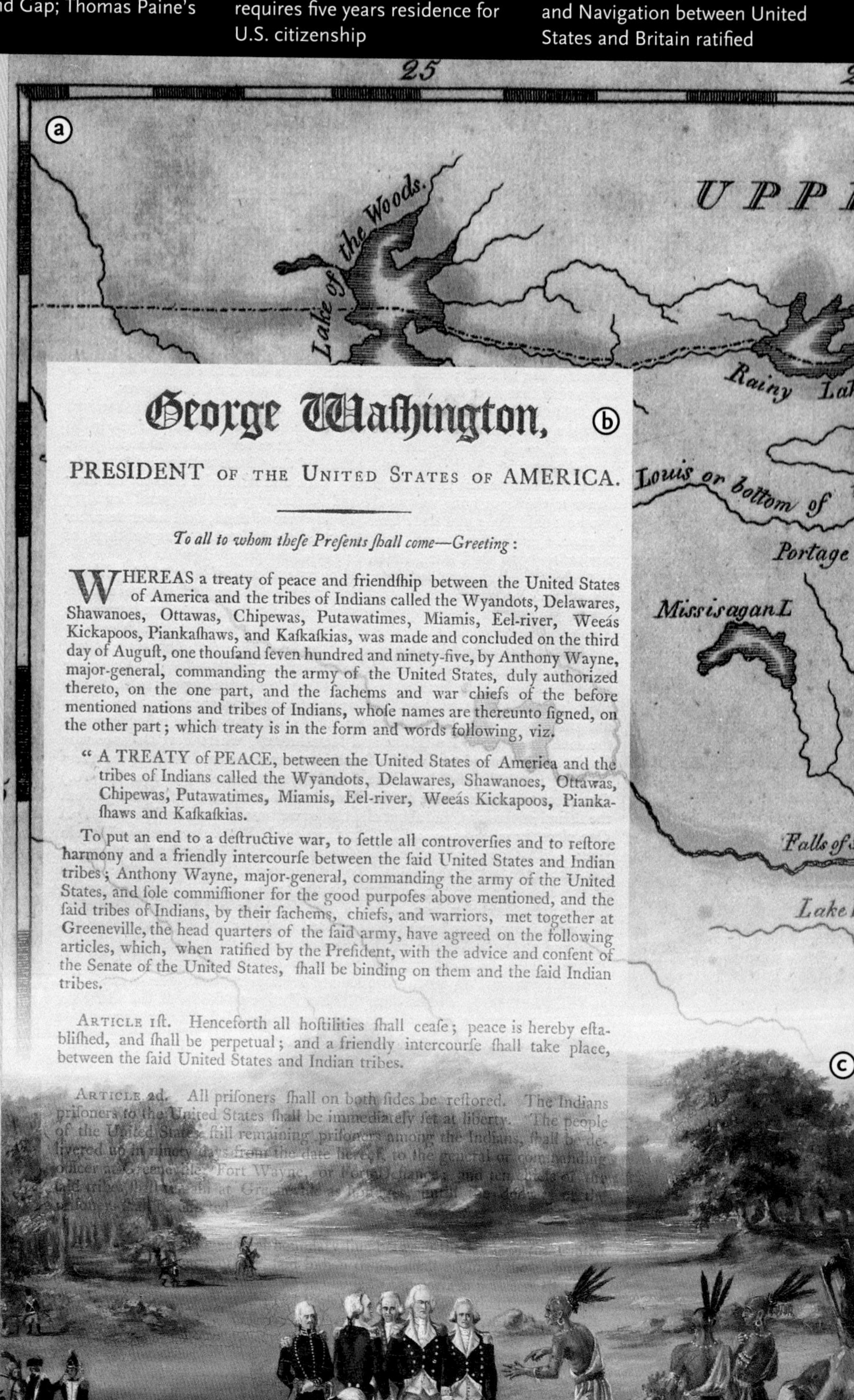

George Washington, ⓑ

PRESIDENT OF THE UNITED STATES OF AMERICA.

To all to whom theſe Preſents ſhall come—Greeting:

WHEREAS a treaty of peace and friendſhip between the United States of America and the tribes of Indians called the Wyandots, Delawares, Shawanoes, Ottawas, Chipewas, Putawatimes, Miamis, Eel-river, Weeás Kickapoos, Piankaſhaws, and Kaſkaſkias, was made and concluded on the third day of Auguſt, one thouſand ſeven hundred and ninety-five, by Anthony Wayne, major-general, commanding the army of the United States, duly authorized thereto, on the one part, and the ſachems and war chiefs of the before mentioned nations and tribes of Indians, whoſe names are thereunto ſigned, on the other part; which treaty is in the form and words following, viz.

" A TREATY of PEACE, between the United States of America and the tribes of Indians called the Wyandots, Delawares, Shawanoes, Ottawas, Chipewas, Putawatimes, Miamis, Eel-river, Weeás Kickapoos, Piankaſhaws and Kaſkaſkias.

To put an end to a deſtructive war, to ſettle all controverſies and to reſtore harmony and a friendly intercourſe between the ſaid United States and Indian tribes; Anthony Wayne, major-general, commanding the army of the United States, and ſole commiſſioner for the good purpoſes above mentioned, and the ſaid tribes of Indians, by their ſachems, chiefs, and warriors, met together at Greeneville, the head quarters of the ſaid army, have agreed on the following articles, which, when ratified by the Preſident, with the advice and conſent of the Senate of the United States, ſhall be binding on them and the ſaid Indian tribes.

ARTICLE 1ſt. Henceforth all hoſtilities ſhall ceaſe; peace is hereby eſtabliſhed, and ſhall be perpetual; and a friendly intercourſe ſhall take place, between the ſaid United States and Indian tribes.

ARTICLE 2d. All priſoners ſhall on both ſides be reſtored. The Indians priſoners to the United States ſhall be immediately ſet at liberty. The people

DuSable: A Regional Man

Jean Baptiste Point DuSable was a "free Negro," born into the French colonial empire in North America in the mid-eighteenth century. Questions about where he was born remain, but it is clear that by the 1770s DuSable was trading with partners who had connections in Montreal, Kaskaskia, and Cahokia. Historical records place DuSable as a trader at Michigan City in 1779, as a British prisoner at Fort Michilimackinac, and then as the British-appointed manager of a trading post north of Detroit in 1780.

DuSable negotiated between the colonial powers and the Potawatomi, Miami, and Chippewa with whom he traded. His wife, Catherine, was a Potawatomi whose family connections were important to this trade. By 1788, the couple had established a home at Chicago. They solemnized their marriage at a Roman Catholic church in Peoria (1788), and saw the marriage of their daughter Suzanne to Jean Baptiste Pelletier, and the birth of their granddaughter Eulalie (1790).

Sometime before 1800, Catherine died. DuSable sold his considerable holdings at Chicago and moved south to St. Charles, Missouri, where he died in 1818.

Ann Durkin Keating and Helen Hornbeck Tanner

August: Treaty of Greenville

September: Connecticut Land Company organized; purchases Western Reserve lands (now in Ohio)

October: U.S. gains rights on Mississippi River. Vancouver returns from four-year voyage mapping North American Pacific Coast

November: Future U.S. President James K. Polk born.

In 1812, a small settlement at Fort Dearborn was located on the south side of the Chicago River, near its entry point into Lake Michigan. When war erupted in June between the United States and Great Britain, Fort Dearborn was quickly threatened both by outside attack from the British and from internal dissension. The August 15 abandonment of the fort and the subsequent deaths of dozens of American soldiers and sympathizers at a scene called both the Battle of Chicago and the Fort Dearborn Massacre constitute the only military operation ever to take place at Chicago.

A frontier outpost, whose inhabitants included not only American soldiers and their families, but British allied traders, Indians, and long-established French traders, Fort Dearborn was built in 1803, named after the secretary of war Henry Dearborn. Each group of residents had extensive, intersecting networks beyond Chicago. For instance, the Potawatomi traveled, traded, and intermarried with other Potawatomi at Milwaukee and St. Joseph, along the Fox River, and south along the Illinois River. They traded with the British at Detroit and Michilimackinac, and with the French and Métis at Peoria, St. Louis, and River Raisin. They negotiated with American soldiers who came from Fort Wayne and Detroit.

When the War of 1812 broke out in June, the fragile society at Chicago was torn apart. Tecumseh called area Indians to ally with the British. Some did.

1812	Elgin Marbles to England; Beethoven composes Symphonies nos. 7 & 8	*January:* First Mississippi River steamboat arrives in New Orleans	*March:* Congress commits first foreign aid, to Venezuela after an earthquake; Congress authorizes first war bonds

ⓐ *Background:* At Fort Dearborn, the American soldiers and their families lived within the palisaded fort. To the south were the homes of the factor, interpreter, agent, merchant, and armorer. Indians in the area generally lived beyond the narrow confines of this map.

ⓑ Rebekah Wells was the niece of William Wells, the adopted son of the Miami Little Turtle. She married Captain Nathan Heald shortly after he was appointed commander of Fort Dearborn in 1811.

ⓒ The Healds were taken captive by the British following the battle on August 15. When a friend saw some of their belongings, including this distinctive hair comb, on sale in St. Louis, he assumed they were dead. He sent the items to Rebekah's family in Louisville. Months later, the Healds were released and made their way to Rebekah's family home. The comb remained among Rebekah's possessions until her death.

ⓓ John Kinzie was a skilled silversmith as well as trader. Items such as this silver cross, which he made in 1820, were among those traded with local Native Americans at Fort Dearborn.

ⓔ A young Victoire Mirandeau Porthier lived near Fort Dearborn in 1812, but left for Milwaukee before the massacre. She described herself in 1883: "My mother was an Ottawa woman; my father was a French-man. He was a good scholar, a very handsome man, and had many books. He taught us children to speak French, and We all learned to speak Indian. . . ."

ⓕ The Kinzie house, built by Jean Baptiste Point DuSable in the 1770s. John Kinzie moved here in 1804, and this house served as the base for his far-flung trading operations. Kinzie lived among the Potawatomi for long stretches, primarily in what is now Michigan. His wife, Eleanor, grew up among the Seneca as a captive.

ⓖ Black Hawk, a Sac leader traveling east to join Tecumseh's forces, arrived in Chicago just after the massacre. He later explained: "They had a considerable quantity of powder in the fort at Chicago which they had promised to the Indians; but the night before they marched, they destroyed it. I think it was thrown into the well! If they had fulfilled their word to the Indians, I think they would have gone safe."

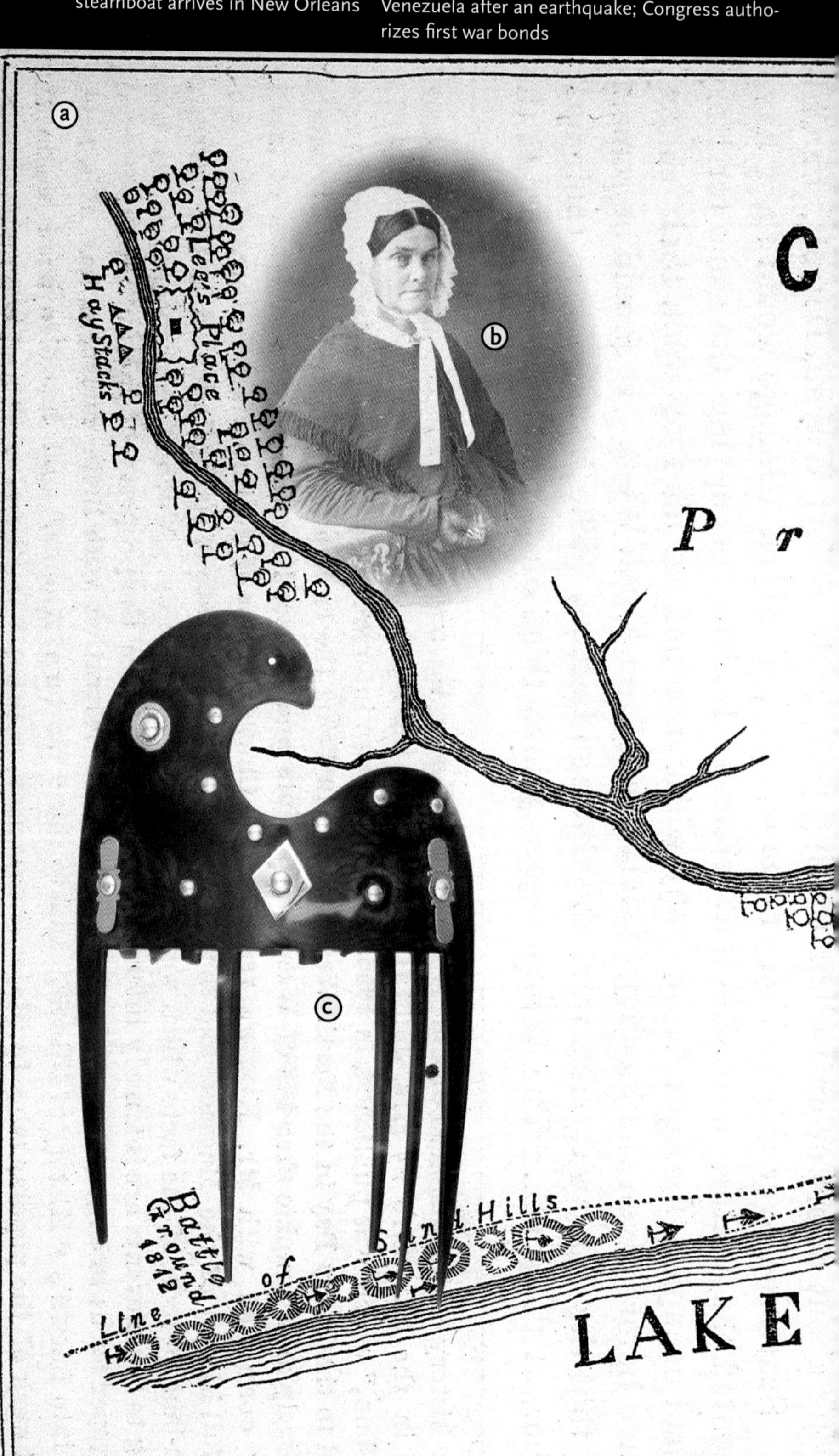

Captain Nathan Heald received an order of evacuation on August 9, and four days later Captain William Wells of Fort Wayne arrived with a Miami contingent to escort the evacuees. On August 14, Heald gave a growing number of Indians all of the fort's factory goods except arms, ammunition, and liquor. The following morning, the contingent headed south along the lakeshore. After about one and a half miles, they were attacked by a force of between 400 and 600 Indians. In under an hour 15 Indians and 52 members of the military contingent were dead. The remaining 41 returned to Fort Dearborn as prisoners, where several more lost their lives. The following morning the victorious Indians burned the fort and disbanded their prisoners.

Some of the prisoners taken by Indians were ransomed through agents at Peoria and St. Louis; others were held by the British at Michilimackinac and Detroit. Others spent months with Indian groups throughout the Midwest. Some of the French traders remained in the area. The Kinzie clan removed for a time back to Detroit. In 1816, the Americans returned, rebuilt the fort, and began to divest the area's Indians of their land.

Simon Pokagon, son of a Potawatomi participant in the events of August 1812, criticized their designation as a massacre: "When whites are killed it is a massacre; when Indians are killed, it is a fight."

Ann Durkin Keating

April: Louisiana admitted to union

June: United States declares war against Great Britain; Napoleon invades Russia

July: British attack on Sacketts Harbor on Lake Ontario; United States surrenders post on Michilimackinac

October: American forces defeat British at Ogdensburg, N.Y.

ESSENTIAL PARTS OF CHICAGO'S REGIONAL INFRASTRUCTURE APPEARED in 1848: the completion of the Illinois and Michigan Canal, the inception of the city's first railroad, the first telegraph connection, the founding of the Chicago Board of Trade. With approximately 20,000 people Chicago had not yet reached regional dominance, but these developments contributed to its future as a major world city and the leading metropolis of the Midwest.

The canal opened in April, after twelve years of intermittent construction, placing Chicago in the midst of a water route connecting the Gulf of Mexico and the Mississippi River to the Great Lakes and North Atlantic Ocean. Like the Erie Canal, and unlike other canal projects, it was a tremendous success, and remained so for several critical decades of Chicago's swift growth.

In January a telegraph line connected Chicago to Milwaukee, and by the end of the year Chicago was part of a network linking all the major Eastern cities. Business leaders welcomed the speed with which news from Eastern markets now reached them.

Overland transportation progressed more slowly. New wooden plank roads helped farmers bring their harvest to the city, but the roads were difficult to maintain. By the end of 1848 the Galena & Chicago Union Railroad track extended just 10 miles west. Within three years, however, Eastern rail lines arrived, and planning for the Illinois Central and other lines was underway.

1848

January: Discovery of gold in California

February: U.S.-Mexico Treaty of Guadalupe Hidalgo; Revolution in France; republic proclaimed

March: Chicago Board of Trade founded

ⓐ Chicago in 1848 was still a relatively small, raw, muddy city, growing at a pace that residents recognized would not always be graceful. On April 25, the *Chicago Daily Journal* published an engraving of improvements on the public square, showing the courthouse (1), with the Sherman House hotel looming behind it, the watch house (2), and jail buildings (3). The engraving was prepared from a daguerreotype, an early photographic process, and the *Daily Journal* editor, tongue planted firmly in cheek, noted: "It is proper to state, to prevent an erroneous impression, that 16 cows and calves, 10 horses and colts, and 30 or 40 dogs were driven out, and the gate-ways kept guarded, during the time the original picture was being taken. They were permitted to return, however, as soon as the artist left the ground."

ⓑ The 1850 manuscript census included several sheets for residents of canal boats. The boat captained by D. E. Oakley is typical in many respects. Most boat hands were men in their 20s and 30s from northeastern states; captains were sometimes older. Women often worked on the boats as cooks. Some of the larger boats included families with young children.

ⓒ Illinois and Michigan Canal administrators readily appreciated the speed of telegraphic communications as they sought to maintain the canal. In early December it was urgent for boats to exit the canal so that it could be drained before freezing weather arrived.

ⓓ *Background:* Chicago's first railroad depot, the Galena & Chicago Union, stood on Kinzie Street just north of the Chicago River. The telegraph poles suggest that this photo was taken several years after 1848. By the early 1850s the railroads had drawn nearly all passenger traffic away from the canal. Freight traffic by both canal and rail provided a significant boost to Chicago as an agricultural entrepôt, and the rapid development of the railroad network and of midwestern farms in the 1850s enabled Chicago's commodities market to grow to unprecedented levels of activity. The Board of Trade, little more than a club for businessmen in its first few years, began regulating the grading of grain by the end of the 1850s. Twenty years later its innovative futures market would begin to transform the economics of agricultural production and distribution.

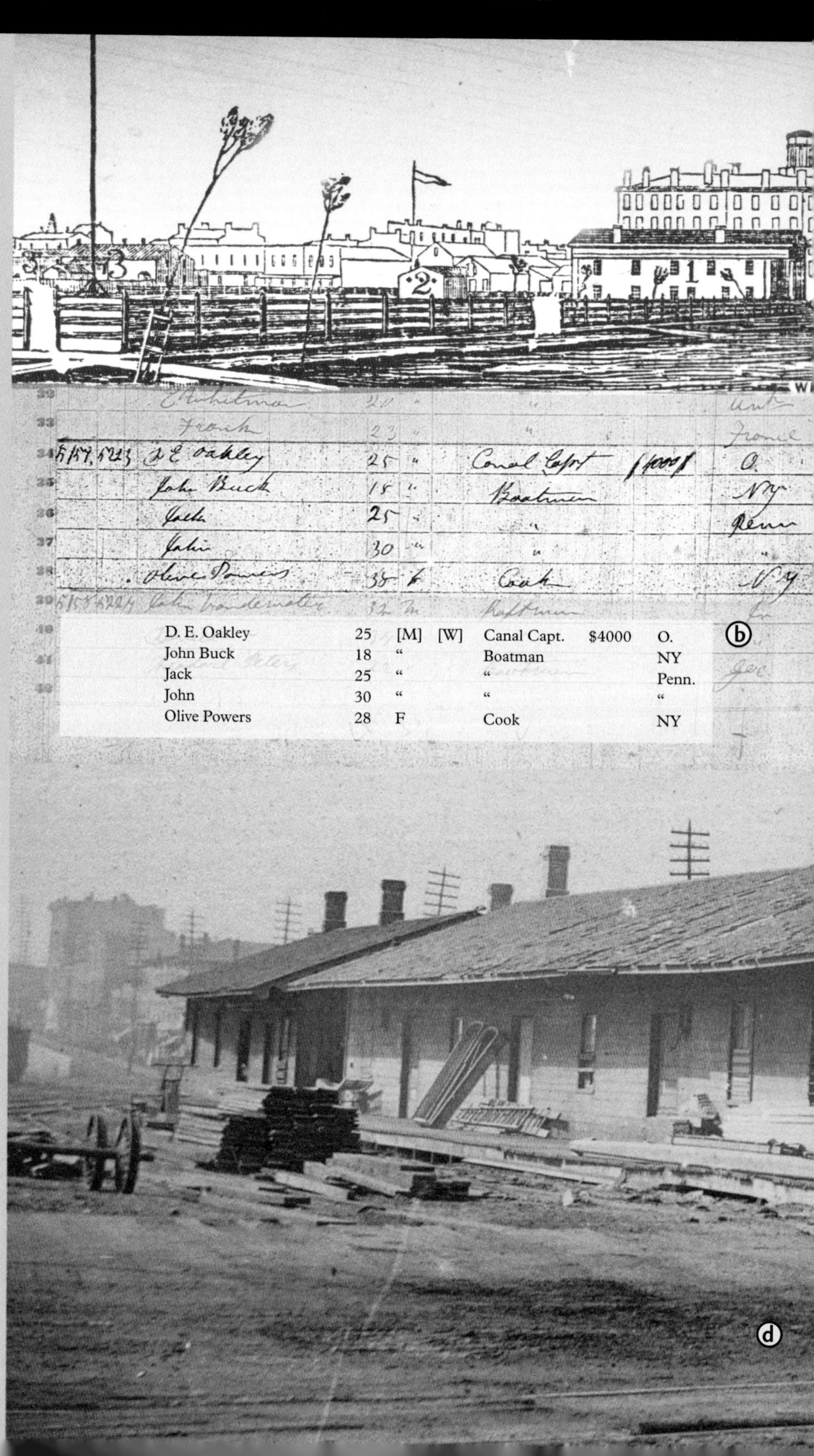

D. E. Oakley	25	[M]	[W]	Canal Capt.	$4000	O.
John Buck	18	"		Boatman		NY
Jack	25	"		"		Penn.
John	30	"		"		"
Olive Powers	28	F		Cook		NY

Within a decade Chicago would be the rail hub of the United States.

Transportation and economic developments fueled population growth. The Protestant Yankees who had predominated after displacing Indians in the early 1830s were joined by Irish, German, and other European immigrants, who would soon play a significant role in Chicago politics and culture. Religious, racial, and ethnic diversity have characterized Chicago since the 1840s; symbolic turning points include the establishment of Chicago's Roman Catholic diocese in 1843, the founding of Quinn Chapel, Chicago's oldest black church, in 1847, and the founding of Kehilath Anshe Mayriv, Chicago's first Jewish congregation, also in 1847.

While most enterprises were partnerships or family businesses, after 1848 the scale of industry and commerce began to change dramatically, and with it the city's class structure. Cyrus McCormick moved his reaper manufacturing business to Chicago from Virginia in 1847 and sought capital for expansion. With 33 hands in 1848, the McCormick firm was already one of the largest employers; two years later it employed 150, with continued growth. The later development of Chicago's vast stockyards and meatpacking plants, its lumber yards, its steel mills, its neighborhoods, its industrial workers and labor conflicts: all can be seen in retrospect as emerging from Chicago's turning point in 1848.

Douglas Knox and Michael Conzen

April: Official opening of the I&M Canal

May: Wisconsin statehood

July: Women's rights convention at Seneca Falls, N.Y.

October: Chicago's first locomotive *(Pioneer)* hauls materials to extend track

Ⓒ

Atlantic, Lake and Mississippi Telegraph.
ST. LOUIS AND CHICAGO LINE.
Office, 105 South Water Street.
ALL COMMUNICATIONS STRICTLY CONFIDENTIAL.
Chicago, Dec 7 1848
By Telegraph from Ottawa (Dec 7th
To C. B. Talcott

My boat is on Ottawa level will you have this break repaired so I can get through

D E Oakley.

In 1871, less than 40 years after its incorporation, Chicago had mushroomed from a pioneer outpost to a thriving and ever-expanding urban hub. Its modern incarnation was already obvious: a central business district, distinct industrial areas, and neighborhoods segregated by ethnicity and class. The city's preeminence as a transport center and processing site for resource extraction industries was established. Lured by the diverse economy, thousands arrived every year to see what opportunities Chicago might hold.

All this was interrupted the night of October 8. Fueled by a strong wind from the southwest, a fire that began in Catherine O'Leary's barn near DeKoven Street spread out of control. Ravaging the wooden cottages of the O'Learys' neighborhood, then feeding on the lumberyards on the South Branch of the river, the giant blaze moved steadily to the north. By the time the fire reached the central business district, it no longer needed wind or fresh fuel; the mile-wide holocaust had become a firestorm, propelling burning debris into the sky that began new blazes when it fell to earth. Commercial buildings touted as fireproof offered little more resistance than the wooden rookeries of the Irish ghetto. Bricks survived, but mortar dissolved, collapsing masonry walls. Through the city center, marble crumbled and iron melted. The main waterworks failed around 3:30 a.m.; the blaze leapt the main branch of the Chicago River soon after. For almost 20 hours more, the fire marched north, incinerat-

1871

January: German empire proclaimed

March: Indian Department Appropriations Act (IDAA) ratified; Paris Commune proclaimed, collapses in May

ⓐ *The City of Chicago as It Was before the Great Conflagration of October 8th, 9th, & 10th, 1871,* by William Flint. Chicago's population at the time of this bird's-eye view looking southwest from Lake Michigan was approximately 334,000.

ⓑ This Currier & Ives lithograph shows people fleeing across the Randolph Street Bridge. Thousands of people literally ran for their lives before the flames, unleashing remarkable scenes of terror and dislocation. "The whole earth, or all we saw of it, was a lurid yellowish red," wrote one survivor. "Everywhere dust, smoke, flames, heat, thunder of falling walls, crackle of fire, hissing of water, panting of engines, shouts, braying of trumpets, roar of wind, confusion, and uproar."

ⓒ Corner of State and Madison after the fire, 1871. Within a year, most visible traces of the destruction were gone, and Chicago expanded and improved as it was resurrected. This image shows how daunting the task was and how quickly the city set about rebuilding.

ⓓ The home of Patrick and Catherine O'Leary, their two children, and an Irish tenant family on DeKoven Street. Although the fire that started in the O'Leary barn left the house intact, it destroyed Mrs. O'Leary's reputation. Although the civic board empowered to investigate the cause of the Great Fire exonerated her, the popular imagination vilified her as a hag—a lurid example of all the laziness, drunkenness, and stupidity then commonly ascribed to the Irish.

ⓔ "Homeless Citizens Taking Refuge from the Flames among the Ruins," *Frank Leslie's Illustrated Newspaper.* Municipal authorities sought to nip in the bud any possible dependence, and mounted a program of rigorous screening for relief to weed out the "unworthy." Immigrant Chicagoans complained bitterly that administrators were limiting access to the relief fund through their failure to offer services in languages other than English, or to venture to the devastated North Side.

ing the homes of tens of thousands of German and Scandinavian immigrants. At the northern limits of the city, four and a half miles from the O'Leary barn, the Great Fire finally died.

The Great Fire has traditionally been understood as the turning point in Chicago's early history, the moment when the city proved its greatness. The fire led to critical shifts in land use, new forms of investment and finance, and innovations in technology and architecture. Chicagoans did rebuild their city, at a pace that can only be described as heroic.

Yet, the postfire months of 1871 were times of great hardship and social conflict. The poorest victims turned to public relief, gaining some sustenance from the gifts that flowed into the city from around the world and confronting a civic elite that believed that "zealous and promiscuous giving" would "corrupt the poor." A plan for a "fireproof" city drew fierce opposition from those who could not afford to rebuild in brick or stone. Housing shortages raised rents; a labor market glutted by new residents depressed wages. The Great Fire thus forced Chicagoans to confront the meaning of their city's social and economic fissures.

The Great Fire transformed the lives of Chicagoans and gave the city a lasting and special image as a place of renewal, progress, and great possibilities.

Karen Sawislak

April: Congress passes Ku Klux Klan Act, allows U.S. president to suspend the writ of habeas corpus in cases of secret conspiracy

November: New York Herald reporter Henry M. Stanley finds British explorer David Livingstone in Ujiji (Tanzania) in central Africa

THE END OF THE WORLD'S COLUMBIAN EXPOSITION IN LATE 1893, coinciding as it did with a severe national industrial depression, let loose destructive forces that shattered Chicago's grandiose expectations of an unlimited future. Unemployment and misery savagely struck the city. As Jane Addams wrote of her Hull House relief operations, "we all worked under a sense of desperate need and a paralyzing consciousness that our best efforts were most inadequate to the situation." During the winter, tens of thousands of workers lost their jobs; factories and businesses closed. The unemployed and homeless drifted through the city.

In February, the fiery British reformer William T. Stead proposed a new, cleansed vision of the city in his inflammatory book, *If Christ Came to Chicago.* Based on an 1893 conference that established the Chicago Civic Federation, the book attacked the wealthy, the powerful, the corrupt, and the immoral, often equating the four. Stead's jeremiad undercut the prestige of Chicago's builder/philanthropist elite who seemed unwilling to respond to the city's new social conditions. Their inertia during the Pullman Strike was even more damaging to their reputations. During the months of the strike, the city's merchant and manufacturing gentry provided little leadership. Rather, they seemed to sink from sentiments of largesse to shudders of fear in a few short months.

Like the city, the Pullman Palace Car Company benefited from the fair. Its

1894 *January:* *Edison Kinetoscopic Record of a Sneeze,* earliest extant copyrighted film | *March:* Coxey's Army departs Massillon, Ohio; arrives in Washington, D.C. on May 1 | *April:* ARU strike against Great Northern Railroad; predepression wages restored

ⓐ Stead's *If Christ Came to Chicago* opened with a foldout juxtaposing an image of Christ and the money changers with this map of the block bounded by Clark, Dearborn, Harrison, and Polk Streets in Chicago's First Ward. The map both illustrated many of the reform issues raised in the book and anticipated the use of mapping to present social information that informed the *Hull House Maps and Papers* and the Chicago School sociologists.

ⓑ The unrest at Blue Island sketched here in the *Chicago Tribune* led Attorney General Richard Olney to request federal troops to preserve order during the Pullman boycott. The investigation by the U.S. Strike Commission concluded that, in addition to 12 persons who died, the railroads lost at least $4,672,916; Pullman workers lost at least $350,000 in wages; and the 100,000 employees on the 24 railroads centering in Chicago lost wages of at least $1,389,143. In addition, "very great losses, widely distributed, were incidentally suffered throughout the country."

ⓒ U.S. regular troops on the lakefront, *Harper's Weekly*, July 21, 1894. This image by T. Dacy Walker, drawn from a photograph by J. W. Taylor, captures both the high visibility of army troops in Chicago and the skyline that the city had celebrated during the World's Columbian Exposition just a year earlier. The view is from Lake Park (Grant Park) looking south and west toward the Illinois Central train station. Altogether there were some 6,000 federal and state troops, 3,100 police, and 5,000 deputy marshals in Chicago during July 1894.

ⓓ Some of Chicago's unemployed took refuge in the abandoned buildings on the world's fair grounds. On January 8, 1894, the Manufactures and Liberal Arts buildings and the Peristyle burned, leaving only the twisted, underlying framework.

ⓔ The human costs of the depression and the Pullman Strike led to the organization in 1894 of three of Chicago's most famous settlement houses: Chicago Commons, Northwestern University Settlement House, and the University of Chicago Settlement House. Located at 140 Union Street, Chicago Commons served as home to Graham Taylor and other settlement workers and as a meeting place for neighborhood activities. It originally had belonged to a German-American family who had moved as industry replaced agriculture. After the Great Fire in 1871, it served as the office of the Northwestern Railway. Subsequently, the main house became a boardinghouse for lake seamen while the annex provided housing for eight "very poor Italian families."

end, however, brought an abrupt decline to profits. Pullman released workers and lowered wages while keeping rents high in the model town adjacent to the works where employees were encouraged to live. Encouraged by the American Railway Union (ARU), Pullman workers organized union locals and elected a grievance committee. When Pullman refused their demands for higher wages, lower rents, and union recognition, a strike began on May 11.

At first, Chicagoans supported the strikers, but when the ARU launched a national sympathy boycott, positions hardened. When local officials seemed unable to control the escalating disorder, president Grover Cleveland authorized the use of federal troops to guard mail shipments sent by train. When troops fired on strikers in Hammond, Indiana, on July 8, attorney general Richard Olney secured an injunction against the ARU, ensuring that the strike would be lost.

The violence and disruption of the strike seemed to mark the waning of the power of the city's former leaders. Together with the depression, it revealed how ill-equipped the city's institutions were to support the immigrants, industrial workers, and poor. The result was a new agenda for the city, unimagined in either the splendid summary of nineteenth-century culture at the world's fair or in Stead's plans for its reformation.

James Gilbert

July: ARU officers arrested for violating injunction

August: Sino-Japanese war

September: John Dewey begins teaching at the University of Chicago

October: Nicholas II ascends to throne of Russia

November: People's Party (Populists) win state, local, and congressional seats in off-year elections

ALTHOUGH MOST CHICAGOANS ENTHUSIASTICALLY GREETED THE END OF World War I in November 1918 and the subsequent return of local soldiers, they knew that the future held many unanswered questions. The influenza epidemic that attacked the city--and the world--had not been contained. Many had already perished; by the time the epidemic was declared finished, more than 20,000 Chicagoans would die. By mid-1919, production had already begun to decline, and employment along with it. Returning soldiers worried about whether they could reclaim their jobs. African Americans who had arrived during the war as part of the Great Migration feared that white soldiers would indeed claim jobs--and at their expense. And between 1919 and 1921 a brief spurt of immigration from Europe would add more newcomers to the mix.

Race and employment were the tinderboxes in Chicago in 1919. On July 27 a stone-throwing incident between white and black residents at the 29th Street beach led to the drowning of Eugene Williams, a young African American swimmer. His death erupted into a riot that ultimately claimed the lives of 23 blacks and 15 whites and left 537 wounded or maimed. In September, steelworkers around the country declared a strike that closed factories in Chicago and its suburbs and led to violent confrontations and large-scale arrests in Gary.

1919 *January:* Eighteenth Amendment (Prohibition) ratified *February:* First Pan-African Congress, organized by W. E. B. DuBois, meets in Paris *June:* Nineteenth Amendment (Woman Suffrage) sent to states for ratification

ⓐ *Background:* Soldiers parade through Gary, Indiana, while strikers look on. The steel industry's notoriously long hours and the antiunion policies of judge Elbert Gary, chairman of U.S. Steel's board of directors and the town's namesake, helped make the strike long and bitter. The call to strike on September 22 by union leadership charged "IRON AND STEEL WORKERS! A historic decision confronts us. If we will but stand together now like men our demands will soon be granted and a golden era of prosperity will open for us in the steel industry. But if we falter and fail to act this great effort will be lost, and we will sink back into a miserable and hopeless serfdom. The welfare of our wives and children is at stake. Now is the time to insist upon our rights as human beings."

ⓑ The White Sox scandal continued into 1921 when eight players were tried for fraud in an effort to make baseball respectable again. This criminal subpoena mandated left fielder "Shoeless Joe" Jackson's presence before the grand jury. Although the eight players were acquitted in 1921, baseball commissioner Kenesaw Mountain Landis, formerly a federal judge in Chicago, banned them from professional baseball.

ⓒ The 1919 mayoral campaign revealed significant cleavages in Chicago's body politic. Reform candidate Charles E. Merriam failed in his Republican primary challenge to incumbent mayor William Hale Thompson (pictured here voting in 1916). Thompson subsequently fought off five candidates in the general election. Many of Thompson's 259,828 votes (38 percent of total votes) came from German and African American voters, and his African American support drew considerable invective from Democrats in white neighborhoods on the South Side. Defeated by reformers in 1923, Thompson was reelected in 1927.

ⓓ World War I offered women many new opportunities, both paid and volunteer. One of the most popular volunteer agencies was the American Red Cross. In this 1918 picture, Red Cross volunteers address the domestic influenza epidemic by making the masks worn by hundreds of thousands of Chicagoans to avoid the spread of the deadly disease.

ⓔ National Guardsmen questioning an African American during the riots that traumatized the city in late July. The City Council briefly considered a proposal to avoid future confrontations by creating legally segregated residential districts in the city. Chicago was hardly unique: 26 American cities experienced race riots during the summer of 1919. Chicago's riots killed and injured more people than the others, but even its death toll scarcely compared to the 78 African-Americans lynched that year in the South.

FORTHWITH CAPIAS

State of Illinois, COOK COUNTY } ss. The People of the State of Illinois, To the Sheriff of said County, GREETING:

We Command You, that you take the body of

Joe Jackson

if to be found in your County, and safely Him keep so that you have Him before our Criminal Court of Cook County, Austin Avenue and Dearborn Street, in the City of Chicago, Forthwith, to answer unto the people of the State of Illinois, upon an indictment for

Obtaining Money and Goods by Means of the Confidence Game

lately preferred against by the Grand Jury of said Court.

And have you then and there this Writ.

Witness, WILLIAM R. PARKER, Clerk of our said Court, and the Seal thereof, at Chicago, in said County, this 20th day of OCTOBER A. D. 19 20

William R. Parker Clerk.

ⓐ ⓑ ⓒ

Local violence combined with national and international events to make Chicago a major target of attorney general A. Mitchell Palmer's attack on radicals. So wide was his net that the Industrial Workers of the World, headquartered in Chicago, and corporate leaders of firms like International Harvester and the packinghouses were all under suspicion, the first for advocating socialist and anarchist solutions, the second for trying to maintain their long-established commercial ties with Russia after the revolution.

If notions of Americanism were open to question, so, too, were civic pride and integrity. Throughout the summer, Chicagoans had celebrated their White Sox, seemingly the best team in professional baseball. But the Sox lost the World Series, and by the end of the year, Chicagoans--baseball fans and otherwise--knew about the bribes and the gamblers. Still another question loomed large for the future. On October 28, 1919, Congress passed the Volstead Act, providing for the enforcement of the Eighteenth Amendment to the Constitution that prohibited the manufacture, sale, or transportation of alcoholic beverages in the United States.

James R. Grossman

June: Allied Powers sign peace treaty at Versailles, create League of Nations

November: First steamer in Marcus Garvey's United Negro Improvement Association's Black Star Line sails

December: United States deports 249 resident aliens suspected of being Communists and anarchists to Russia

d

e

For many Chicagoans—at least for the 65 percent of the city's electorate who had cast their ballots for Franklin Roosevelt's reelection—1937 started on a note of cautious optimism. Although the Great Depression continued to exact a heavy toll, FDR's second term offered the possibility of expanded New Deal reforms that might help the region and its residents move toward better times.

Works Progress Administration (WPA) funds already paid artists to practice their crafts and researchers to survey the city. Public Works Administration (PWA) projects provided jobs and new housing. PWA funding and employees contributed to the Metropolitan Sanitary District's effort to upgrade the region's sewage system. Federal funds were also helping to improve the city's transportation network, from Lake Shore Drive to the expansion of Municipal Airport to accommodate larger passenger planes. Perceived governmental support helped to revitalize the labor movement, as workers, sometimes crossing racial boundaries, organized for better wages and working conditions. Early in the year, strikes among electrical workers and taxi drivers left the city dark and still. Groups as diverse as the Chicago Tunnel Transport workers, the employees of Fan-Steel and the Chicago Mail Order Company, and the waitresses at de Met's Tea Rooms staged sit-down strikes to achieve their goals. On Memorial Day, the entire nation was shocked when police injured

1937

January: Social Security taxes and benefits payments begin; FDR's second inaugural address points to "one-third of a nation ill-housed, ill-clad, ill-nourished"

March: Chicago celebrates 100th anniversary of incorporation

April: Basque city of Guernica bombed by Germans during Spanish civil war

Ⓐ *Background:* Images like this one and a Paramount newsreel shot at the scene of the confrontation between police and Republic Steel strikers on May 30 were used as evidence in the U.S. Senate's investigation of the incident. Although a local coroner's jury held the police blameless, the Senate and other investigative groups held that the ten deaths were both caused by the police and were avoidable. The newsreel, which was prohibited from being shown in Chicago, was used by the New York Police Department to demonstrate to officers what not to do in a similar situation.

Ⓑ As this 1928 announcement illustrates, the battle to achieve union recognition for the Brotherhood of Sleeping Car Porters began long before it happened in 1937. Excluded from most railroad unions because of their race and faced with the strong opposition of the Pullman Company, porters relied heavily on community support to build and sustain the union.

Ⓒ Joe Louis's victory over Jim Braddock in the eighth round was not only a matter of pride for Chicago's African American community, it was also a boost for the local economy. Of some 60,000 attending the fight, about 75 percent were visitors to Chicago. Included in the audience were governors, congressmen, a cabinet member, and diplomats. United Airlines flew six extra 21-seat planes to Chicago. The largest hotels were booked six weeks in advance; the few remaining hotel rooms were going for twice their usual cost.

Ⓓ The opening of the Outer Drive Bridge on October 5 and the president's visit provided depression-weary Chicagoans with an opportunity to celebrate despite worsening economic conditions at home and war threatening abroad. A parade down Michigan Avenue to the bridge included floats, Indian canoes, a covered wagon, horse-drawn carriages, a locomotive with tires, a man-powered hose cart, army units, American Legion and VFW posts, police, firemen, high-school and playground representatives, and other marchers organizers claimed exceeded 50,000. At the corner of the bridge where FDR spoke, he was greeted with airplanes, boats, hundreds of colored balloons, a fire tug spewing "geysers of water," and even more cheering Chicagoans.

Ⓔ Lathrop Homes, located at Diversey and the North Branch of the Chicago River, was one of three PWA housing projects built for white Chicagoans and leased to the new Chicago Housing Authority. In 1937, a fourth was being planned for African Americans. Reflecting the severity of Chicago's housing crisis, there were seven applicants for every one unit available.

90 strikers and killed four at a march targeted at Republic Steel. Unionization efforts spread and some unions, like the Brotherhood of Sleeping Car Porters, succeeded in gaining recognition and concessions from their employers.

FDR's decision to cut federal spending in response to improved economic conditions early in the year plunged Chicago and the nation into recession as the year waned. Unemployment climbed as federal jobs disappeared and businesses faltered, returning Chicago families to the frightening levels of need experienced in 1929–1930. Relief requests increased so sharply that payments had to be reduced to well below what the state had determined was necessary for a minimum standard of living. The impact on already suffering communities such as the African American neighborhoods where unemployment had previously reached as high as 50 percent was devastating.

By October, when Roosevelt came to Chicago to celebrate the completion of Lake Shore Drive and, belatedly, the centenary of the city's incorporation, politicians and voters were acutely aware of the need for solutions to end the depression. Few, however, fully appreciated the relevance of the president's topic that day: the threat to world peace posed by certain nations. The war he talked about avoiding would eventually break the depression and move Chicago, the region, the country, and the world in new directions.

Janice L. Reiff

May: FDR signs Neutrality Act

June: Illinois passes law providing unemployment insurance

July: Japanese and Chinese troops clash in North China, begin undeclared war; Farm Security Administration created

September: National Housing Act signed; Chicago Housing Authority created soon thereafter

As 1967 ended, Chicagoans anticipated a good year. The local economy was booming, supported by government defense contracts and Great Society social welfare expenditures. With over three and a half million people, Chicago was the nation's second-largest city, full of well-paying jobs for hard-working people.

But 1968 quickly turned sour. National antiwar organizations announced they would protest in Chicago during the August Democratic National Convention. Chicago-based comedian and civil rights activist Dick Gregory threatened convention-week protests if the city did not get an open housing bill and promote African American policemen to high-ranking posts.

On April 4, disaster struck when Martin Luther King, Jr., was assassinated. Three days before, the *Chicago Tribune* had editorialized against his support for striking Memphis sanitation workers, calling him "the most notorious liar in the country." In a memorial service at City Hall, Rev. Jesse Jackson indicted the political establishment, exclaiming, "The blood is on the chest and hands of those that would not have welcomed King here yesterday."

Despite pleas from the city's African American leadership, rioters filled the streets of Lawndale, looting and burning. Parts of the South Side also burned. During the conflagration, Chicago police, following the orders of superintendent of police James B. Conlisk, tried to use minimal force and avoid

1968

Unemployment rate 3.3%

January: Tet Offensive begins; North Korea captures USS *Pueblo*

February: 543 Americans killed, 2,547 wounded in one week in Vietnam

March: President Johnson announces he will not run for reelection

May: United States, North Vietnam announce peace talks; protests in Paris

ⓐ Protest organizer Tom Hayden, furious over a brutal, unprovoked police attack on Rennie Davis, voiced the protesters' frustration and anticipated what would happen: "This city and the military machine it had aimed at us won't permit us to protest. . . . Therefore we must move out of this park in groups throughout the city and turn this excited, overheated military machine against itself. Let us make sure that if blood is going to flow, let it flow all over this city. If gas is going to be used, let that gas come down all over Chicago. . . . If we are going to be disrupted and violated, let this whole stinking city be disrupted and violated."

ⓑ Using the good press of "The City That Works" and his political clout, Mayor Daley had persuaded the Democratic Party to hold their 1968 presidential convention in Chicago. A buoyant Daley boasted that the city knew how to throw a national political party convention—23 of the previous 56 had been held in Chicago.

ⓒ Protesters gather in Grant Park near Columbus and Balbo on August 28 preparing for a march on Michigan Avenue.

ⓓ The *Chicago Seed,* one of many underground newspapers that flourished in the late sixties, celebrated the Yippies, who organized a "Festival of Life" during the Democratic convention in Chicago. Joining them in Chicago were student supporters of candidate Eugene McCarthy ("Clean for Gene"), supporters of the assassinated Robert F. Kennedy, antiwar activists of all ages, various groups demanding that the Great Society fulfill its social promises, and local activists hoping to secure changes in Chicago.

ⓔ In the days after the assassination of Martin Luther King, Jr., in more than 130 cities, hundreds of thousands of black Americans let their anger and grief boil over into collective rage. In Chicago, more than 48 hours of rioting left 11 Chicagoans dead, 48 wounded by police gunfire, 90 policemen injured, and 2,150 people arrested. Some two miles of the commercial heart of Lawndale on West Madison were little more than charred rubble.

ⓕ Postconvention polls showed a great majority of Americans approved of the Chicago policemen's use of force and Mayor Daley's strong stand against disorder. Ironically, Mayor Daley, a political and economic liberal who believed that government had an obligation to foster a more equitable society, became a hero to Americans who shared few of Daley's core political beliefs.

unnecessary bloodshed. Once order was restored, however, mayor Richard J. Daley attacked Conlisk's approach: "I said to him very emphatically and very definitely that an order be issued by him immediately and under his signature to shoot to kill any arsonist . . . and to issue a police order to shoot to maim or cripple anyone looting any stores in our city." Later, the mayor backed away from his extreme position.

Nonetheless, four months later when the convention came, authorities wanted no disorder. Far from the cordoned-off International Amphitheater where Hubert Humphrey won the presidential nomination, protesters and police met in angry confrontations. The worst occurred August 28 after police stopped protesters from marching to the convention center. A crowd of some 10,000 ended up near Michigan Avenue and Balbo Drive. As protesters chanted "The whole world is watching" and television crews filmed, policemen beat hundreds of protesters bloody. Some 83 million Americans watching their televisions to see democratic process at work instead saw a street riot.

The violence poisoned Humphrey's bid locally and nationally. Unlike in 1960, Chicago's Democratic machine could not turn out enough votes. Illinois, like the nation, went Republican. By the end of 1968, Chicago had become a tragic symbol for a nation that had come undone.

David Farber

June: Robert Kennedy assassinated | *August:* USSR invades Czechoslovakia | *September:* First Boeing 747 rolled out | *October:* 541,000 U.S. troops in Vietnam; Mexico City Olympics | *November:* National Turn In Your Draft Card Day | *December:* Apollo 8 orbits the moon

At the start of 1983, Jane Byrne was Chicago's first woman mayor. By its end, Harold Washington, the city's first black mayor, occupied the chair. Between, it was decidedly not politics as usual in Chicago.

Helped by a bungled snow removal operation, Byrne had swept Michael Bilandic, mayor Richard J. Daley's successor, out of office in 1979. Her election presaged the rising discontent of many of the city's voters. Washington's candidacy activated the black community long neglected by and estranged from the regular Democratic organization to generate the excitement of a crusade among the city's reform groups.

On February 22, Washington narrowly beat Byrne and Richard M. Daley in the Democratic primary. For years, a Democratic primary victory had ensured victory in Chicago's general election, but not in 1983. Long-time Democratic stalwarts, many who feared Washington's promise to disassemble the political machine, threw their support to Republican Bernard Epton.

Although Epton had a strong record on civil rights as a state legislator, his campaign slogan, "Epton . . . Before It's Too Late," was widely perceived as playing on racial fears. Prejudices erupted openly during the campaign. Washington narrowly won the April 12 election with 51.8 percent of the vote.

The existing Democratic organization, however, refused to let Mayor Washington run the city. A bitter division in City Council pitted 29 white aldermen

1983 *January: Time* names computer "Man of the Year" | *March:* President Reagan reveals Strategic Defense Initiative | *April:* Space shuttle *Challenger* makes initial voyage | *June:* Sally Ride becomes first American woman in space

ⓐ Campaign headquarters like this one appeared all over the city in the months before the mayoral election. Election workers used these storefronts to coordinate campaign activities and as places where interested voters could come for information, campaign materials, and political conversation.

ⓑ The blue sunrise pictured on this campaign button served as the logo of the Harold Washington for Mayor campaign. Washington's campaign invigorated Chicago politics and attracted tens of thousands of new voters. Over 100,000 Chicagoans, many of whom were African American, registered to vote in the months before and after the primary and before the general election. These new voters were critical in the high-turnout, hotly contested elections.

ⓒ Map showing areas with substantial increase in poverty, 1970–1980. Tom Brune and Eduardo Camacho published *A Special Report: Race and Poverty in Chicago* in 1983 in which they documented that 1980 census data showed that one in five of Chicago's residents lived below the poverty line, an increase of 24 percent since 1970. This map, adapted from a more detailed presentation in their study, shows the parts of the city where the poverty rates increased by at least 10 percent. During the harsh winter of 1983–1984, public and private agencies were forced to address the problems of the city's homeless population, estimated then to be as many as 25,000.

ⓓ On May 2, 1983, 284 Roman Catholic bishops gathered in the Palmer House and adopted a pastoral letter calling for an immediate bilateral halt to the nuclear arms race. Entitled "The Challenge of Peace," its primary author was Chicago's archbishop Joseph Bernardin. Thousands of Chicagoans added their voices to the Catholic bishops' call with a Mother's Day Peace Festival in Grant Park on May 8. This action echoed mass demonstrations throughout Europe protesting the United States' deployment of nuclear weapons on the continent and President Reagan's Strategic Defense Initiative.

ⓔ On April 28, 1983, Judge Charles E. Freeman of the Cook County Circuit Court administered the oath of office to Harold Washington, who became Chicago's forty-second mayor. Breaking with tradition, Mayor Washington relocated the ceremony to Navy Pier from City Hall to include more Chicagoans in the festivities. Those who attended heard readings by Gwendolyn Brooks and Studs Terkel, performances by the Chicago Children's Choir and the Morris Ellis Orchestra, and Washington's rousing inaugural address.

against the 21 mostly black aldermen who supported Washington. The council, acquiescent to former mayor Daley, blocked administrative initiatives and undermined Mayor Washington's reform agenda. Chicago's "Council Wars" became infamous. Not until 1985 did Washington gain control of the council.

Political stalemate and continuing budget deficits led Standard & Poors to downgrade the city's bond rating. This was a blow to Chicago, still struggling to emerge from the national recession. The city experienced a steady loss of both middle-class residents and jobs. A June 12, 1983, *Chicago Tribune* article noted that the city had lost 123,500 jobs in the preceding decade. Polls showed that unemployment was the single greatest concern in all neighborhoods.

Although some suburban areas saw increases in corporate offices, population, and jobs in the early 1980s, in the city, political and economic realities stalled major projects. Elements of the business community were apprehensive about the Washington administration's commitment to balance downtown growth with neighborhood development. Yet measures such as a fee imposed on Loop construction to assist with neighborhood infrastructure improvements excited community and civic groups. They were delighted to be invited to the table and to have their ideas taken as seriously as those of business leaders.

Kathleen McCourt

September: KAL 007 shot down by Soviets

October: Bomb kills 241 U.S. soldiers in Beirut; U.S. invades Grenada; Chicago teachers go on 15-day strike

November: Jesse Jackson announces presidential candidacy

December: Lech Walesa awarded Nobel Peace Prize

"We have a clear vision of what our people can become, and that vision goes beyond mere economic wealth, although that is a part of our hopes and expectations.

"In our ethnic and racial diversity, we are all brothers and sisters in a quest for greatness. Our creativity and energy are unequaled by any city anywhere in the world. We will not rest until the renewal of our city is done."

—Harold Washington inaugural address, April 28, 1983

Growth of the Chicago Metropolitan Area

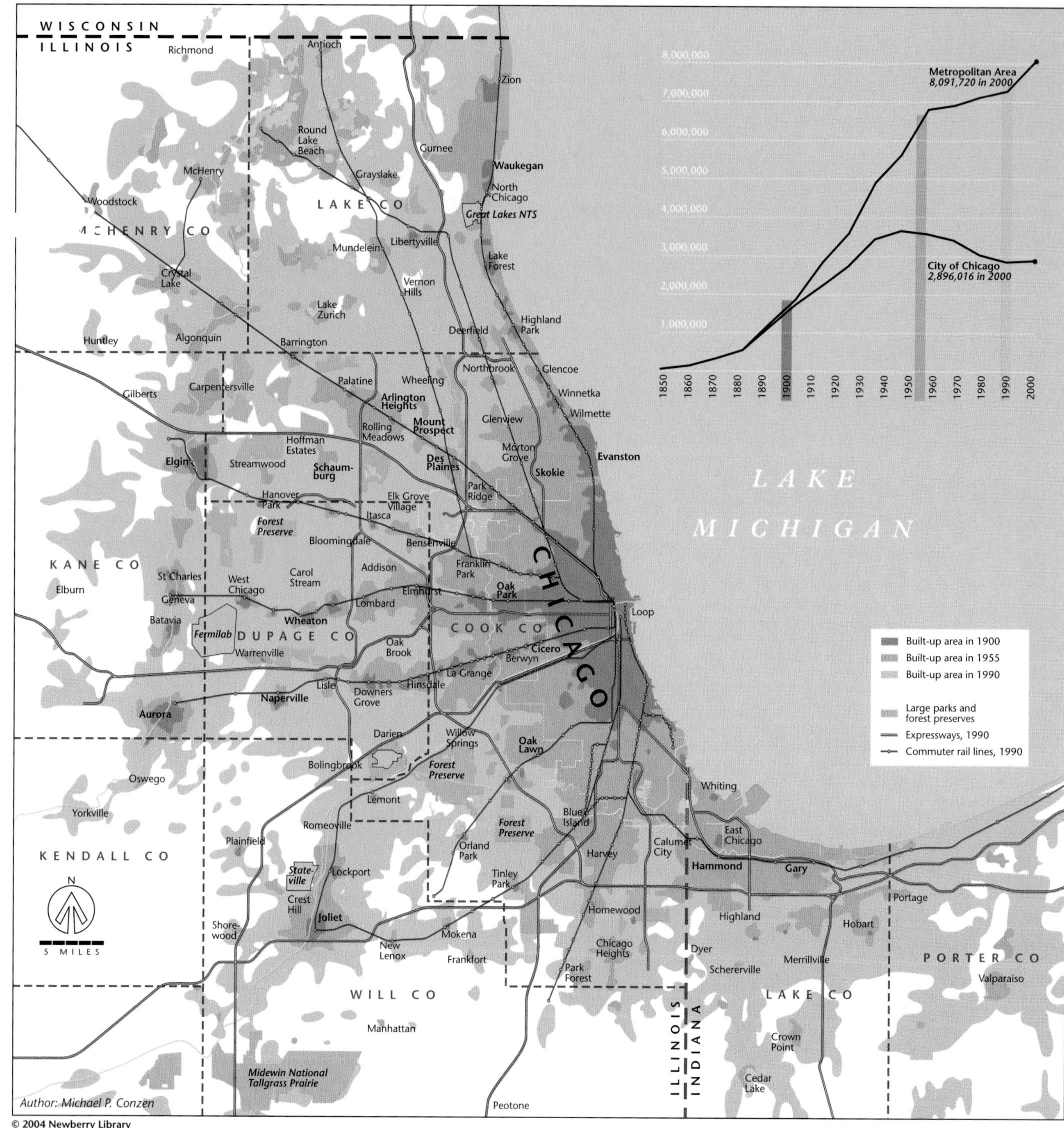

The growth of the built-up area of metropolitan Chicago can be summarized in three phases. Before 1900, streetcars and commuter railroad service conspired to create a fairly compact city together with small clusters of development around outlying railroad stations. Several satellite cities, such as Joliet and Elgin, studded the hinterland. By 1955, the railroad suburbs had proliferated and matured, creating a massive star-shaped metropolitan geometry, while widespread automobile ownership had encouraged the extension of the continuously built-up zone around the urban core. After 1955, construction of the expressway system permitted a vast decentralization of population and activity, filling in many of the interstices between the railroad axes radiating from the central city and producing a more rounded overall geometry. By the end of the twentieth century, there was hardly a farmer's field to be seen within 40 miles of the city center in any direction.

Morris, a commissioner for the ILLINOIS & MICHIGAN CANAL, the city became an important regional shipping center with the completion of the canal. A diversified industrial base has fueled the town's twentieth-century economy. Morris's population numbered 11,928 in 2000, up from 8,144 in 1970.

Brandon Johnson

See also: Economic Geography

Further reading: Conzen, Michael P., and Valerie M. McKay, eds. *Canal Town and County Seat: The Historical Geography of Morris.* 1994.

Mortality. *See* Demography

Morton Arboretum. The Morton Arboretum was founded in 1922 by Joy Morton, president of the Morton Salt Company. With Morton's estate at its core, the Arboretum encompasses 1,700 acres in LISLE. Its collection of living plants includes 3,300 different kinds of plants from around the world. The herbarium, the third largest in the United States, holds 165,000 preserved specimens. The library includes both circulating and rare book and print collections.

Charles Sprague Sargent, director of Harvard's Arnold Arboretum, helped to establish the Morton. He suggested the herbarium and the library, donated collection materials, trained personnel, and recommended landscape architect O. C. Simonds to lay out the Arboretum. Simonds, best-known for his naturalistic style, determined the informal placement of the living collections and the winding roads and paths throughout the property.

Initially, the Arboretum focused on enlarging its living and specimen collections and developing its educational programs. In the 1940s, under naturalist May Theilgaard Watts, the Arboretum established the first public education program in an American arboretum. During the 1950s, the Morton expanded its research programs in practical botany. Today, the Morton Arboretum supports research programs of local and national importance, including the study of TREES in the urban environment and the ecology of the Chicago region.

Riva Feshbach

See also: Conservatories; Ecosystem Evolution; Gardening; Landscape Design; Leisure; Plant Communities

Further reading: Morton Arboretum Archives. • *Morton Arboretum Quarterly.* 1965–1995.

Morton Grove, IL, Cook County, 14 miles N of the Loop. Morton Grove first gained national recognition through its greenhouses and later through its stance on GUN CONTROL. Fame, however, came as slowly as did settlement. ENGLISH immigrants moved into the Lehigh-Beckwith area in the 1830s, followed by GERMAN and Prussian families a decade later. In 1872 the Milwaukee RAILROAD laid a single-track line, setting up a flag stop in town. The approximately one hundred residents relied on truck farming or employment with local companies. They named their community Morton Grove for railroad financier Levi Parsons Morton, later vice president under Benjamin Harrison.

In 1889 new industry came with the Poehlmann Brothers Company greenhouse business. Renowned for its roses, the company received national attention when its Poehlmann Rose received first prize at the 1904 St. Louis World's Fair. The brothers operated three plants in Morton Grove, employing between 300 and 500 workers.

Between 1900 and 1930 the local economy depended on the wholesale florist business. Platz and Sons opened their greenhouse in 1904. In 1910 the Lochner family started a roadside stand selling vegetables and flowers, which prospered and led them to build a greenhouse 15 years later. The burgeoning floral business also benefited a local contractor who built greenhouses.

In 1892 the railroad completed a second track, a year after the first SUBDIVISION was built by George Fernald and George Bingham east of the tracks. Incorporated in 1895, the village covered 1,200 acres, with 600 more acres added by 1900. Four years later land along the North Branch of the CHICAGO RIVER and the SKOKIE marshes was designated FOREST PRESERVE property.

In the 1920s and 1930s Chicagoans came to play slot machines and GAMBLE at Morton Grove's numerous ROADHOUSES. The GREAT DEPRESSION hit the community hard, and the Poehlmann brothers went bankrupt. Twenty acres were purchased from the failing company by the Morton Grove Days Committee, land that later became Harrer Park. The remaining land was bought by Baxter Laboratories. Light industrial plants and research and development companies began operations in the area in the 1940s.

Morton Grove's biggest growth spurt occurred in the 1950s, when population rose by over 15,000 after the opening of the Edens EXPRESSWAY. In contrast to the 1920s, by the 1950s the village sought to develop a quiet suburban atmosphere, banning anything that would likely disturb the peace of the community. In 1981 Morton Grove became the first community in the country to pass an ordinance restricting the private possession of handguns within the village.

In 2000 the census counted 22,451 residents of Morton Grove, 74 percent white, 22 percent Asian, and 0.6 percent black; 4 percent were Hispanic. While other industries came into the area, greenhouse operations remained a constant, including Lochner's and Platz Flowers, a wholesale firm with an accompanying retail business named Jamaican Gardens.

Marilyn Elizabeth Perry

See also: Agriculture; Cook County; Government, Suburban

Further reading: Beaudette, E. Palma. *Niles Township, Niles Center, Morton Grove, Niles Village, and Tessville.* 1916. • Blythe, Robert W. "Morton Grove, Illinois, and 1950s Metropolitan Development." M.A. thesis, University of Illinois at Chicago. 1992. • Morton Grove Centennial Commission. *Morton Grove, Illinois, 1895–1995: Centennial Anniversary.* 1994.

Mothers' Pensions. Proponents of the original plan for mothers' pensions (also referred to as mothers' aid) intended to provide a universal subsidy to families with dependent CHILDREN but without an adult male income. Using the model of military pensions, they argued that a mother deserved a government pension in exchange for her service to the state through child rearing. Child welfare reformers, women's CLUBS, and JUVENILE COURT judges supported pensions as a vast improvement over existing options that sent families to the poorhouse, forced mothers to give up their children, or turned children into wage earners.

The Illinois state legislature passed the first statewide mothers' pension law in the United States in 1911. Only Kansas City and a few private charities scattered across the country had previously tried similar plans. The law did not mandate counties to implement mothers' pensions, but it legitimated the use of public funds for this purpose. Cook County's program became the largest and best-developed program in the state, as well as an important test case for other states to study.

The Cook County Juvenile Court administered the mothers' pension program and established its guidelines for operation. Early in its history, the administrators insisted that able-bodied mothers had to WORK for wages to qualify for a pension. Over half of all mothers who received a pension also worked for wages, thus defeating the program's original goal.

Limited local revenues in the early years of the GREAT DEPRESSION led to the decline of mothers' pensions, but they reappeared as the prototype for the Social Security Act's Aid to Dependent Children program.

Joanne L. Goodwin

See also: Chicago Relief and Aid Society; Feminist Movements; Relief and Subsistence Aid; Social Services; United Charities

Further reading: Bullock, Edna D. *Selected Articles on Mothers' Pensions.* 1915. • Goodwin, Joanne L. *Gender and the Politics of Welfare Reform: Mothers' Pensions in Chicago, 1911–1929.* 1997. • Leff, Mark. "Consensus for Reform: The Mothers' Pension Movement in the Progressive Era." *Social Service Review* 47 (1973): 397–417.

Motor Sports. In 1895 Chicago hosted America's first auto race, a road race running between Jackson Park and EVANSTON. The first major racing track in the Chicago area was the two-mile wooden-board Speedway Park in MAYWOOD, which hosted open-wheel Indianapolis-style racing from 1915 to 1918.

Small oval tracks flourished in and around Chicago. Raceway Park, a one-fifth-mile asphalt oval near BLUE ISLAND, opened in 1938 and by the 1950s was hosting more than 60 stock car races and 15 midget car races a year. During the 1940s, midget car racing also thrived as an indoor event at the International Amphitheater. Santa Fe Speedway, a quarter-mile clay oval near WILLOW SPRINGS, opened in 1953 with a program of races for midgets, sprint cars, stock cars, and motorcycles, and such events as tractor pulls, motocross, and demolition derbies.

Illegal teenage drag racing has a long history in Chicago, especially after World War II and through the 1960s. Organized drag strip competition was held at the U.S. 30 Dragstrip (in MERRILLVILLE, INDIANA) from 1957 until its closing in 1984.

During the 1940s and 1950s, SOLDIER FIELD was the most popular venue for big-time stock car and midget car racing, drawing crowds as large as 89,000. It was on the same racing circuit as the WAUKEGAN Speedway (1949–1979) and Rockford Speedway. This circuit produced Indianapolis 500 champs Pat Flaherty (1956) and Jim Rathmann (1960) and premier racing promoter Andy Granatelli. Soldier Field stopped hosting racing in 1968, but O'Hare Stadium (1956–1968), in SCHILLER PARK, sponsored the prestige races during the 1960s.

Chicago-area motor sports began to decline in the 1980s, as nationally televised big-track NASCAR racing and Indy Car racing drew fans away from local tracks. Santa Fe closed in 1996; Raceway closed in 2000. Motor sport racing revived in the late 1990s, when national racing organizations noticed huge television ratings for their product in the Chicago area. In 1998, the Route 66 Raceway complex opened in JOLIET and featured a 30,000-seat drag strip and 8,000-seat half-mile clay oval for sprint, stock, and truck racing. During 1999–2001, the Chicago Motor Speedway hosted NASCAR truck races in CICERO and Indy Car events. In 2001 the Route 66 Raceway complex opened Chicagoland Speedway for major NASCAR stock car races.

Robert Pruter

See also: Entertaining Chicagoans; Horse Racing; Leisure; Motoring

Further reading: Brown, Allan E. *The History of the American Speedway Past and Present.* 1984. • Cutter, Robert, and Bob Fendell. *The Encyclopedia of Auto Racing Greats.* 1973. • Pistone, Pete. "Chicago Owns a Racy Past." *Chicago Sun-Times,* August 20, 1999.

Chicago Times-Herald Race of 1895

America's first auto race was held in Chicago on Thanksgiving Day, November 28, 1895. The race was the idea of H. H. Kohlsaat, the publisher of the *Chicago Times-Herald.* Hoping to promote this new industry and sell more papers, Kohlsaat announced on July 9 "A Prize for Motors," with a $5,000 purse for "inventors who can construct practicable, self propelling road carriages." The race was originally planned to run from Chicago to Milwaukee, but bad roads north of Racine forced a shorter course, and it became a 54-mile course from Chicago to Evanston and back. The start/finish line was near the current Museum of Science and Industry.

So new was the idea of the automobile to Americans that there was no general term agreed upon to describe it, and the *Chicago Times-Herald* invited readers to coin a new word. Some of the terms considered were Horseless Carriage, Vehicle Motor, Automobile, Automobile Carriage, and Moto Cycle. On July 15, the *Times-Herald* declared "Moto Cycle" the winning term.

The official race was held on Thanksgiving Day in temperatures around 30 degrees Fahrenheit, with 6 inches of fresh snow and drifts of up to 24 inches. Almost 80 entrants had been promised, but only 11 agreed to run in such weather, and just six cars arrived at the start line. Only two entrants finished: the imported and modified Benz of Hieronymus Mueller & Co. of Decatur, Illinois, driven by son Oscar, and the Duryea, built and driven by J. Frank Duryea. The Duryea crossed the finish line first, 7 hours and 53 minutes later, with an average speed of 7 miles per hour. The official distance was 54.36 miles, and this was accomplished on 3.5 gallons of gas.

Keith R. Gill

Motoring. As a national TRANSPORTATION hub and merchandising center, Chicago played an important early role in the promotion of the automobile in the United States. Horseless carriages were showcased as novelties at the WORLD'S COLUMBIAN EXPOSITION in 1893, and on Thanksgiving Day 1895, the *Chicago Herald* staged a well-publicized test race through the city's streets. Six years later the first Chicago Automobile Show was held, yet only one out of every 10,000 Chicago inhabitants owned an automobile in 1900. For here, as elsewhere, automobiles were expensive and unreliable and consequently were mostly playthings of the rich.

Daniel Burnham and Edward Bennett's 1909 *Plan of Chicago* helped transform the automobile street from a promenade for the rich to a necessity of modern urban life. It was published just as new mass-produced cars such as Ford's Model T put automobile ownership itself within the reach of the middle and working classes. Autos flooded the LOOP, where the passenger cars driven by COMMUTING professionals competed for space with streetcars and commercial traffic. The automobile friendly Chicago Plan Commission gave high priority

After World War II, families could drive to places like Lake Pistakee in the newly established Chain O' Lakes State Park in Lake County and enjoy a vacation in cabins like these advertised on a 1948 postcard. Photographer: Curt Teich & Co. Source: Curt Teich Archives, Lake County Discovery Museum.

to elements of the BURNHAM PLAN that would relieve central city congestion, such as the widening of North Michigan Avenue (1920) and the construction of the double-decked Wacker Drive (1926). Lake Shore Drive was transformed from a pleasure drive into one of the nation's first limited-access highways.

In the 1920s, the automobile made it possible for the city's suburbs to expand away from their railroad-oriented cores, increasing suburban dependence on the automobile. Private automobile ownership rose steadily in Chicago, to one car for every eight inhabitants by 1930, but lagged behind state and national averages (around one for every five people). By 1990, there was about one car for every household in the city, but the average suburban household owned nearly two cars. In metropolitan Chicago, as elsewhere throughout the nation, the construction of the local system of superhighways during the 1950s and 1960s accelerated the suburban dispersal of residential districts, businesses, and services, rendering much of suburban Chicago almost entirely dependent upon the automobile and its INFRASTRUCTURE for their daily transportation needs. Motels and drive-in MOVIES and restaurants transformed the landscape, seas of parking lots spread out next to ice cream shops, book stores, and FOREST PRESERVES. Growing numbers of Chicago tourists drove to VACATION SPOTS such as the Wisconsin Dells, Interlochen, Michigan, and beyond. This trend showed no signs of abatement at the end of the century. From 1973 to 1993 in each of the six metropolitan counties, the average daily vehicle miles traveled, a rough measure of how extensively cars are used, significantly outstripped the growth of both automobile ownership and population.

James Akerman

See also: Automobile Manufacturing; Expressways; Leisure; Metropolitan Growth; Retail Geography

Further reading: Barrett, Paul. *The Automobile and Urban Transit: The Formation of Public Policy in Chicago, 1900–1930.* 1983. • Schafer, Louis S. "Yesterday's City: Chicago's Horseless Carriages." *Chicago History* 23.3 (Winter 1994–95): 52–64. • Sennott, R. Stephen. "Chicago Architects and the Automobile, 1906: Adaptations in Horizontal and Vertical Space." In *Roadside America,* ed. Jan Jennings, 1990, 157–169.

Mount Greenwood, Community Area 74, 14 miles SW of the Loop.

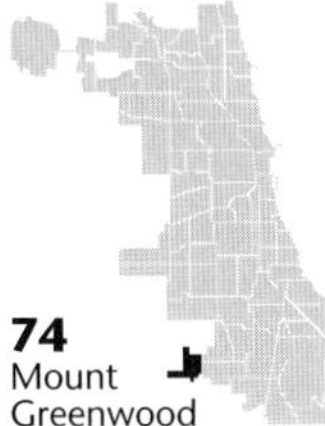

Mount Greenwood is a two-square-mile community area bounded by eight cemeteries and the suburbs of OAK LAWN, ALSIP, EVERGREEN PARK, and MERRIONETTE PARK. Because of the presence of CEMETERIES, the area was once known as Seven Holy Tombs.

GERMAN and DUTCH truck farmers were active in the area by the CIVIL WAR. In 1879, George Waite received a state land grant of 80 acres, and named the area Mount Greenwood after the presence of TREES on an elevated ridge. It seemed ideally suited for a cemetery.

By 1897 taverns and restaurants emerged on 111th and Sacramento Streets to serve mourners following funerals, which were all-day horse-driven affairs. Dog and HORSE RACING tracks were also close by, so that an assortment of customers patronized 111th Street. Irish SALOONS served corned beef and cabbage, while German saloons served sauerbraten and dumplings.

The first religious congregations in the community were Methodist and Reformed, respectively attracting German and Dutch PROTESTANTS. The Dutch and German populations were later joined by other European immigrant groups, including IRISH, WELSH, ENGLISH, POLES, LITHUANIANS, SWEDES, NORWEGIANS, and DANES.

In the early 1900s, Protestant temperance crusaders sought to close down the saloons and make the community dry like nearby Morgan Park. But the opposition succeeded in incorporating Mount Greenwood in 1907 as part of a strategy to remain wet. In 1927 Mount Greenwood voted for ANNEXATION to Chicago, hoping for improvements such as sewers, WATER mains, hard-surfaced streets, streetlights, and a new public SCHOOL, but such changes were slow to arrive. It was not until 1936 that the Works Progress Administration finally laid sewage systems and paved and lighted city streets. As late as the 1960s, the Mount Greenwood Civic Association was still fighting the city for curbs and gutters.

From 1930 to 1950, Mount Greenwood experienced its first spurt of residential growth, with population increasing from 3,310 to 12,331. These young families required new schools, parks, and public recreation areas. In the first years after WORLD WAR II, from 1945 to 1953, 4,000 new homes were built. But there was only one industry in Mount Greenwood, the Beverly Shear Company, and population declined from 23,186 in 1970 to 19,179 in 1990.

By the 1980s, Mount Greenwood was home to the last surviving farm in the city, which was developed as the Chicago High School for Agricultural Sciences. The magnet school stirred controversy in the late 1980s, when black students were bussed into the overwhelmingly white community. This led to a community protest and increased racial hostility. By 2000 the population had declined to 18,820, of whom 94 percent were white, with African Americans and Hispanics each under 4 percent.

Clinton E. Stockwell

See also: Entertaining Chicagoans; Infrastructure; Prohibition and Temperance; School Desegregation; Schooling for Work

Further reading: "The Tallest Fence: Feelings on Race in a White Neighborhood." *New York Times,* June 21, 1992. • Chicago Fact Book Consortium, ed. *Local Community Fact Book: Chicago Metropolitan Area, 1990.* 1995. • DeZutter, Hank. "The Last Farm in Chicago." *Chicago Reader,* August 15, 1981.

Mount Prospect, IL, Cook County, 20 miles NW of the Loop. YANKEE farmers established homesteads in what became the heart of downtown Mount Prospect after signing a POTAWATOMI treaty in 1833. New Englanders cleared and farmed the land until 1843. Many of these settlers, however, moved west for larger claims, and were replaced by GERMAN immigrants, who planted the roots of a small rural community.

By 1854, the Illinois & Wisconsin RAILROAD (later renamed the Chicago & North Western) ran through Mount Prospect, but it did not stop there until 1886. As a result, the remaining Yankee families who wanted access to broader markets moved to the neighboring railroad towns of ARLINGTON HEIGHTS and DES PLAINES. Meanwhile more German and IRISH immigrant families bought up the available homesteads.

In 1871, REAL-ESTATE agent Ezra Carpenter Eggleston built a four-block residential SUBDIVISION on farmland south of the railroad. Eggleston named the area Mount Prospect because the village sat on the highest point in Cook County. Eggleston went bankrupt, since the area failed to prosper until a RAILROAD STATION was established.

In 1900, the community still fell short of the three hundred people required for incorporation. A group of small businessmen known as the Mount Prospect Improvement Association pushed for official empowerment to solicit funds through TAXATION. In May 1917, the village immediately incorporated when a newborn infant became Mount Prospect's three-hundredth resident.

William Busse, a local storeowner, served as the first president from 1917 to 1929. During this period, Mount Prospect experienced business expansion and population growth that increased the number of residents to 1,225 by 1930. Although the area remained predominately farmland, a small industrial district appeared north of the railroad, which included a creamery, farm machinery retailers, a hardware store, a coal yard, and a general store.

The village's post–WORLD WAR II population growth was similar to neighboring communities with an influx of white, middle-class Chicagoans. During the 1950s, the population increased 370 percent to 18,906, prompting village officials to adopt a council-manager form of government. In this period of growth, the Randhurst Corporation opened an enclosed and air-conditioned mall, Randhurst Shopping Center (1962). The village also attracted new industry and light manufacturing with the addition of the Kensington Center (1974).

During the late 1970s, village president Carolyn Krause contested the Metropolitan Housing Development Corporation's efforts to rezone for the building of multifamily housing for minorities and the elderly. A federal agreement, however, allowed the construction of low-income housing on unincorporated land between Arlington Heights and Mount Prospect. Although village leaders continued to promote some light industry, they maintained Mount Prospect as a residential community made up primarily of middle-class white families. Most white-collar residents worked for large companies in the area, such as Centel, Mitsubishi Electronics, and Eastman Kodak, or commuted to Chicago. By 1992, the village's CHAMBER OF COMMERCE began a downtown revitalization campaign that sought to "keep the small in small town."

David MacLaren

See also: Economic Geography; Open Housing; Shopping Districts and Malls; Transportation; Zoning

Further reading: The Chicago Fact Book Consortium, ed. *Local Community Fact Book: Chicago Metropolitan Area, Based on the 1970 and 1980 Censuses.* 1984. • *Chicagoland's Community Tour Guide.* 20th ed. 1983/84. • Murphy, Jean Powley, and Mary Hagan Wajer. *Mount Prospect: Where Town and Country Met, An Illustrated History.* 1992.

Interior view of the Nortown Theater, 6326 North Western Avenue, 1960. Built in 1931 as part of the Balaban & Katz chain, the Nortown could seat over 2,000 patrons. Photographer: Unknown. Source: Chicago Historical Society.

Movie Industry. *See* Film

Movie Palaces. Balaban & Katz pioneered the movie palace as an exhibition strategy in Chicago. Barney and A. J. Balaban opened their first nickelodeon on the West Side in 1908; Sam Katz began four years later. In 1916 they teamed up, and with the support of Julius Rosenwald, president of Sears, opened the 1,800-seat Central Park in October 1917 on what is now known as Roosevelt Road. Success enabled B&K to open the 2,000-seat Riviera in UPTOWN a year later. Backers lined up, led by William Wrigley, Jr., and John Hertz, and in 1921 B&K opened the 3,000-seat Tivoli at 63rd and Cottage Grove, and the even bigger Chicago on North State Street. From this profitable core, B&K purchased and built some two dozen movie palaces in Chicago and then, later, added more throughout the Middle West. In October 1925, B&K merged with Paramount to form the most important movie company of Hollywood's Golden Age.

B&K made the movie palace a fundamental part of city life by carefully exploiting five nonfilmic factors. First, B&K located near fans who had just moved to what were then outlying districts. New mass transit made access simple. Only after these outlying theaters prospered did B&K build downtown.

Second, B&K fully exploited movie palace ARCHITECTURE. Chicagoans of the 1920s heralded B&K movie palaces as the most magnificent in the world. Eight-story vertical signs blazed day and night. Lobbies held as many people as the auditorium, in spaces gilded in gold and awash with mirrors. Sweeping promenades were lit by opulent chandeliers; auditoria were fashioned from models based on exotica from Spain, Italy, and France.

Third, B&K treated all patrons like royalty with obedient corps of ushers, uniformed in red with white gloves and yellow epaulets, maintaining quiet decorum as they guided patrons to their seats. Free child care, and galleries lined with paintings and sculpture, drew additional patrons.

Fourth, B&K always offered a live stage show in addition to movies. B&K so carefully nurtured local talent that, by the middle 1920s, it had become more famous for its impressive stage attractions, orchestras, and organists than for the movies. Shows celebrated fads and heroes, from Lindbergh to the Charleston to "Jazz and Opera" week.

Fifth, when B&K's Central Park opened, it represented the first mechanically air-cooled theater in the world. Drawing on the experience of Chicago's MEAT PACKING industry with cooling, Barney Balaban convinced the Kroeschell Bros. Ice Machine Company to cool movie house patrons and, in 1921 with the building of the Tivoli and Chicago, to dehumidify them as well. B&K constantly hung icicles from newspaper ADVERTISEMENTS; Chicago's Health Commissioner proclaimed their air purer than that of Pike's Peak; women in the final trimester of pregnancy were admitted free.

These five factors were widely copied and proved so influential that to understand how B&K accomplished this movie palace revolution is to understand how going to the MOVIES rose to dominate mass ENTERTAINMENT through the middle of the twentieth century.

Douglas Gomery

See also: Film; Innovation, Invention, and Chicago Business; Places of Assembly; Public Transportation

Further reading: Balaban, Barney, and Sam Katz. *The Fundamental Principles of Balaban and Katz Theatre Management.* 1926. • Gomery, Douglas. *Shared Pleasures: A History of Movie Presentation in the United States.* 1992. • *Variety.* Various issues, 1916–1930.

Movies, Going to the. Chicago helped launch the movie industry in the United States in the early 1900s, so it is no surprise that Chicagoans loved going to the movies. By the 1920s, Chicago had some of the most exquisite MOVIE PALACES in the world, and moviegoers could count on seeing several newsreels, a stage show, and the main feature for the price of admission.

The first movie palace built in the LOOP was the Chicago Theater at 175 N. State Street. The building was executed by the well-known

By 1941, moviegoing crowds had returned to the Regal Theater at 4719 South Parkway (Martin Luther King Drive). Opened in 1928, the Lubliner & Trinz theater seated 3,000 patrons in air-conditioned splendor as they watched films or listened to one of the theater's two orchestras. The *Chicago Defender* described the theater's interior as "an Oriental garden on a moonlight night." Part of a larger construction project that included the Savoy Ballroom and the South Center department store, the Regal helped make 47th Street's reputation as the Harlem of Chicago. The theater was demolished in 1973, but its legacy lives on in the New Regal Theater, the former Avalon Theater renamed in its honor. Photographer: Russell Lee. Source: Library of Congress.

movie theater architects Rapp & Rapp. Completed in 1921, the Chicago Theater seated 3,800 and featured a series of interior spaces inspired by the palace of Versailles. By the late 1930s, the Loop had the highest concentration of movie theaters within the city. Other prominent movie theaters included the McVickers at 25 W. Madison Street, the Oriental at 20 W. Randolph Street, and the RKO Palace Theater at 159 W. Randolph.

During this same period, grand movie theaters were built to serve neighborhoods throughout the city. The North, South, and West Sides were well served by theaters strategically positioned along major commercial arterials and TRANSPORTATION lines. The Paradise, at 231 N. Pulaski Road, was finished in 1928 and could seat 3,600 in its one-screen auditorium. The building featured a mansard roof and an interior lobby designed in the French Renaissance style. Other well-known neighborhood theaters included the Central Park at 3535 W. Roosevelt Road, the Tivoli at 6325 S. Cottage Grove Avenue (also by Rapp & Rapp), and the Southtown at 610 W. 63rd Street.

While the city had its share of movie palaces, many of Chicago's suburbs moved quickly to construct their own theaters. Perhaps the most dramatic of these was the Tivoli in DOWNERS GROVE, built in 1928. Designed as one of the first sound-equipped theaters in the United States, the interior was decorated in the French Renaissance style. This trend toward centrally located downtown suburban movie theaters would continue as other similar theaters were built in Kankakee in 1931 and OAK PARK in 1936.

The movie theaters of the period between World Wars I and II were often the most luxurious places the average person would ever visit. The exteriors of these buildings were elaborately detailed, transporting the patrons to a different time and place. Often eclectic, movie theaters of the day featured a mix of architectural influences, including Moorish, Spanish, Greek, and Persian. The interior spaces were often lavishly decorated with sculptures, oil paintings, and murals depicting various mythological events. Patrons were encouraged to enjoy these sumptuous surroundings while sitting on overstuffed chairs or sofas, often upholstered in silk or velvet. Men's and women's lounges also featured furniture for sitting and large framed vanity mirrors.

After World War II, the changing economic status of the motion picture industry and new leisure-time opportunities signaled the end of the movie palaces' reign at the top of Chicago's ENTERTAINMENT world. Very few movie theaters were built in the city of Chicago between 1950 and 1970, and quite a few of the neighborhood movie theaters were demolished in the 1970s and 1980s. New theater complexes began to be built again in Chicago in the late 1980s, and some of the old movie palaces in the Loop were restored as live entertainment venues.

Max Grinnell

See also: Leisure; Theater Buildings

Further reading: Hall, Ben M. *The Golden Age of the Movie Palace: The Best Remaining Seats.* 1975. • Naylor, David. *American Picture Palaces: The Architecture of Fantasy.* 1981. • Putnam, Michael. *Silent Screens: The Decline and Transformation of the American Movie Theater.* 2000.

Moving Days. The Chicago tradition of moving on the first of May or October can be traced to English and Dutch rural festivals. In parts of England, May 1 was known as "Pack Rag Day," the day on which servants would gather their belongings in a bundle and change their employers at hiring fairs. Michaelmas Day (September 29) or Old Michaelmas Day (October 10) was also a time when farmhands would change employment.

The tradition was also practiced in the Netherlands, where servants would change their employers at the fair at the beginning of May or November. Dutch immigrants brought this tradition to New York as May 1 became a traditional moving day in that city.

Mentions of May 1 as moving day in Chicago can be found as early as the 1840s. In the late nineteenth century as many as one-third of all Chicago households moved annually. It was a very unpopular event, with families facing greedy landlords, exorbitant rates charged by movers (known as expressmen), and the risk of breakage and loss of furniture and belongings.

In 1865 moving day was postponed until May 3, as President Lincoln's funeral cortege was passing through the city on the first day of that month.

In 1911, owing to the widespread unpopularity of a fixed moving day, the Chicago and Cook County real-estate boards allowed leases to be made at any time of the year. Despite these efforts, the first of May and October remain popular moving days in Chicago.

Emily Clark

See also: House Moving; Housing Types

Further reading: Duis, Perry. *Challenging Chicago: Coping with Everyday Life, 1837–1920.* 1998.• Wright, A. R. *British Calendar Customs, England.* 1940.

Mr. Wizard. Don Herbert began *Watch Mr. Wizard,* a popular science show for children, in 1951 on Chicago television station WNBQ, an NBC outlet known for innovative broadcasting in the early 1950s. Herbert demonstrated entertaining and magical experiments using everyday household materials, as his amazed young assistant exclaimed, "Gee, Mr. Wizard!" *Watch Mr. Wizard* introduced scientific principles to millions of children, won numerous awards, and became one of the most successful educational shows on commercial television. Herbert moved the show to New York in 1955, where it continued until 1965; it was revived briefly in 1971–72 and appeared on cable from 1983 to 1991.

Moving day, 1907. Photographer: Unknown. Source: Chicago Historical Society.

Kathy Peiss

Further reading: Dismuke, Diane. "Meet: Don 'Mr. Wizard' Herbert." *NEA Today* (April 1994). • Newcomb, Horace, ed. *Encyclopedia of Television.* 1997. • Turow, Joseph. *Entertainment, Education, and the Hard Sell: Three Decades of Network Children's Television.* 1981.

Multicentered Chicago. Chicagoans like to think of their home as "multiethnic," or as "the city of neighborhoods." Indeed, the celebration of neighborhood is one of the binding rituals of Chicago culture. The shelves of local bookstores are crammed with neighborhood guides of various sorts, and in the 1990s Mayor Richard M. Daley harnessed neighborhood consciousness to the marketing of tourism, officially defining certain well-known districts with banners, signs, and dramatic arches. When visitors come to the city one of the things they frequently ask to see is "Chicago's ethnic neighborhoods."

Yet every big city in America is a city of neighborhoods—forged by migration, work patterns, race, religion, and other factors in addition to ethnic culture. Boston, San Francisco, and many other cities have their own rich patterns of colorful locales. What, if anything, makes Chicago's multicentered settlement pattern distinctive? Answering that question requires setting aside notions of neighborhood geography and diversity that became widespread in the mid-twentieth century but have been challenged by recent scholarship. It requires looking beyond the notion of "neighborhood" itself, as that term has been commonly and vaguely used, and thinking about Chicago's many spatial subcommunities as changing manifestations of history and human initiative. It requires looking deeper into Chicago's past, recognizing how the city's growth fits into the long history of national urbanization, and defining certain features of Chicago's development that were unusual.

For many observers in the twentieth century, the most obvious factor shaping Chicago's social geography seemed to be its role as a magnet for newcomers, with each new group establishing a highly visible presence in some piece of the city, and the city overall growing as a mosaic of cultural tiles, a collection of discrete, long-enduring, slowly changing ethnic/racial cells. Chicago was touted as the city with more Poles than any other except Warsaw or, in a darker view, as the most segregated city in America. Social scientists of the "Chicago School" promoted the idea that such well-defined subareas were "natural," a product of physical and ecological processes governing urban growth.

In the past two decades, students of the city's history have noted limits to this vision of neighborhood development. With the important exception of the African American ghetto, Chicago's ethnic communities were never so well-defined or homogeneous as commonplace knowledge would have it. Even in Irish-dominated Bridgeport or the North

Side's LITTLE ITALY, there were always people from other backgrounds. The world of Jurgis Rudkus, in Upton Sinclair's THE JUNGLE, was centered in LITHUANIAN Catholic culture, but his neighbors were diverse, and his neighborhood was shaped as much by economic forces as by ethnicity. What's more, sociological assumptions about "natural areas" masked the dynamic qualities of ethnic and other neighborhoods—the enormous effort that Chicagoans invested in actively shaping their own communities: promoting them, sometimes defending them, and often moving them. Moreover, immigration and migration do not by themselves account for the pattern that has so vividly impressed visitors for more than a century: a great sprawling metropolis, including dozens of far-flung and constantly changing clusters, and scores of dispersed centers of employment and commerce. Chicago is more than an assembly of cultural chunks, its parts are ever changing, and its multicenteredness is rooted deep in the way it grew.

This is an essay about the variety of forces that have shaped not just the overall configuration of Chicago but the smaller spaces and communities in which Chicagoans have lived and worked. It is also about the variety of ways Chicagoans have imagined those subunits. Most residents, in the course of their daily lives, have had to deal with multiple roles and geographic elements, encountering the city as a complex and shifting array of focal points—places of WORK, worship, education, and amusement—rather than as a set of bounded cells. But there have been times and places where boundaries were important, and there has also been a history of "imagined communities" that resulted from the needs of government or information management or maybe the simple psychological need to simplify a hugely complicated LANDSCAPE. All of these kinds of subcommunities have a history in every big city and a distinctive history in Chicago.

The flow of people into Chicago and the local communities they created were conditioned by three characteristics of the city's particular history. First, Chicago grew in a setting that is relatively—but not entirely—flat, and one that has been shaped and reshaped by numerous natural and artificial waterways. On the one hand, flatness made outward growth easy; on the other, it presented an endemic problem of managing WATER: supplying it, disposing of it, trying to make it go to some places and not to others. Second, Chicago's most spectacular growth spurt occurred when the national economy was driven by RAILROADS, heavy industry, and European immigration. The city did not share in the long period of seaport growth that pushed East Coast cities and even inland ports like Cincinnati and St. Louis well on the way to big-city status. Moreover, Chicago's growth slowed when the centers of investment and production shifted westward in the second half of the twentieth century. Third, rapid growth offered extraordinary opportunities for both planning and conflict, and Chicago's landscape bears the marks of some of the most noble and some of the most invidious attempts at community building in American history.

Today's social geography is a product of the interaction of these three Chicago-specific characteristics, and today's Chicago bears the imprint of five prior phases of multicentered development. For convenience, they might be called periods of natural division, speculation and engineering, migrant clustering and industrial villages, cellular mapping, and elite community redevelopment. Each phase produced a new version of the multicentered city, occupying successively larger amounts of space. Furthermore, each phase was overlaid upon what came before, rather than neatly succeeding it, and the earliest still has influence on the twenty-first-century city along with the later four.

Natural Division, 1780–1830

The natural environment was paramount in shaping Chicago's earliest communities. The CHICAGO RIVER and its two branches divided the site of initial settlement into three parts, which by the early nineteenth century would be known as the North, West, and South "Sides." Native Americans who passed through and the European-descended people who settled permanently in the early nineteenth century built little clusters of dwellings in all three sectors of the area. A small group of civilians settled close to FORT DEARBORN in what is now the northeast corner of the LOOP. FUR TRADERS, tavern keepers, and mariners settled on the North and West Sides. Early Chicago contained several collections of huts, stores, shops, and warehouses strung out along the waterways. The British Kinzies on the North Side did not always get along with the mixed-blood LaFramboise clan down the South Branch, but they all built their houses close to the river that provided TRANSPORTATION for the community.

Yet water was a force for division as well as a focus of common activity. The river, sluggish and relatively narrow though it was, raised formidable obstacles to travel between the three segments of town. The first few decades of Chicago's history as a settlement are full of tales of ferries begun and abandoned, BRIDGES erected and then washed away in spring FLOODS. Even away from the river, the marshy, muddy quality of the site became a standing joke in early accounts of the town and a long-term problem for those trying to cultivate or build on the land. In these circumstances, glacial ridges and other scraps of high ground, stretching away from the village near the river's mouth, became the basis for roads and then linear farming settlements starting in the early 1830s. Thus, in addition to the early commercial center near the fort and the river's mouth, the high ground underlying the future Clark Street, Archer Avenue, and Cottage Grove Avenue provided the foundation for the first subcommunities in Chicago. Partly through historical accident, this first stage of development also inscribed lasting social distinctions on the landscape. The DuSable-Kinzie house, the largest and most opulent of Chicago's early dwellings, established a long tradition of affluent residences on the NEAR NORTH SIDE, while the "Hardscrabble" settlement of traders and fur company workers on the South Branch represented the first of a long line of economically marginal but proud communities in that vicinity.

Speculation and Engineering, 1830–1880

The hallmark of the second stage, from the early 1830s to the period of post-fire rebuilding in the 1870s, was an effort to reshape "natural" space, and the principal tools were political, economic, and technological. The initial events in this stage centered on the project to join the Mississippi and GREAT LAKES watersheds by means of a canal. That project, first envisioned in the seventeenth century, moved from long-term dream to near-term likelihood between the early 1820s and 1836. A series of surveys by state-appointed canal commissioners culminated in the platting of Chicago by James Thompson in 1830, a preparatory step to development. The federal government contributed by surveying northeastern Illinois into townships and sections, and granting more than 280,000 acres within the proposed canal zone in subsidy of that project. Long before there was much substantive evidence of either the canal or the town, the precision of surveyed lines and grids imposed a new matrix for the creation of speculative communities.

Speculation brought many new people to Chicago and created new roles for some old inhabitants. The most powerful actors in this new landscape of gridded space were of course those who had the means to deal in property, using either their own or other people's money. After the defeat of BLACK HAWK's rebellion in 1832, and especially after the opening of a federal land office in 1835, Chicago received a flood of investors, land dealers, and potential settlers. Old-timers like the Kinzies and newcomers like William B. Ogden scrambled to profit by platting "additions" to the original city or seizing control of potentially valuable "water lots" miles from the existing settlement—even in locations as far away as Calumet and SUMMIT. The formation of companies to build railroads expanded this pursuit, attracting attention to investment sites away from existing waterways. The timing of this speculative burst was full of implications for the city's future. When rail-based development came to older cities, even older interior cities such as Cincinnati or St. Louis, a large amount of capital and energy had already been invested in water-related facilities: levees, docks, shipyards, ropewalks, and the like. Remaking the fabric of the city to accommodate rail facilities involved either displacing or circumventing these established elements. Although Chicago also began its life as a water-oriented town, the process of fitting the city around a railroad skeleton began almost immediately and with few obstacles, either man-made or natural. In this sense, the city was "born modern"—and also born to sprawl.

Even before canal construction started, the speculative process created a development engine that radically accelerated Chicago's decentralization and shaped the building of neighborhoods for decades into the future. Land speculation, of course, including speculation in urban land, was an old practice. Investors in many other American cities had grown rich from buying undeveloped land and waiting for it to appreciate. But for individuals like John Jacob Astor in New York or Nicholas Longworth in Cincinnati, city land was a long-term investment, as development moved slowly outward from old mercantile cores. In Chicago, by contrast, both speculation and development went into hyperdrive and stayed there for several decades, with only a few short interruptions. Investors sought short-term gains (as well as long), bought in many places at once, and did not wait for urban growth but pushed it in directions they wanted it to go. Profit depended on promotion, and thanks to elaborately embellished and colored maps, Chicago's imaginary landscape raced far in advance of reality. Thanks to entrepreneurial innovations, the real city quickly caught up with the maps. Many successful promoters plowed their profits back into town building, constructing wharves and warehouses, and joining together to dredge the river and clear the large sandbar from its mouth. To finance such development in a capital-starved region, they created land companies as conduits for eastern investors. Outsiders, especially from New York, poured capital into this city as they never had into Cincinnati or St. Louis, and the urban development process was thus from the beginning tied into larger regional and national interests. Local entrepreneurs and builders spurred the growth process further through rapid adoption of INNOVATIONS like the BALLOON FRAME method of quickly erecting houses and commercial structures. Chicago's relatively flat landscape encouraged not only railroad but street railroad promoters, so that by 1880 it was not only the midcontinental hub of the rail system but also had local rail lines surpassed in mileage by only three of the older coastal metropolises. The whole process benefited, as older city growth had not, from federal largesse with land and federal policies of Indian removal. All of these refinements of the speculative process together were keys to Chicago's rapid sprawl to large size.

The result was that Chicago became not only the first of the nineteenth century's "instant cities" but also a city of instant neighborhoods. The engine of city building was also an engine of subcommunity development. Despite local rivalries, such as the one that led North Sider William B. Ogden to complain that "all the business is going over to the other side," the overall effect was to create dozens of new settlements, of many kinds, from the 1830s through the 1860s. A few of these were residential promotions aimed at the prosperous elite, first near the city, as in the Near North Side island of gentility cultivated by the Ogdens, McCormicks, and Farwells; then farther out along the rail lines, as in Paul Cornell's development of HYDE PARK or Henry AUSTIN'S investments in the suburb that bore his name. Other subcommunities were inadvertent creations near worksites along the river and the rails, such as the cluster near McCormick's reaper works or the dozens of later settlements around the stockyards. The overall effect was a sorting of space according to its developmental potential—for residential as well as commercial or industrial purposes—and this sorting produced new geographic reference points and categories. Especially in promoting middle- and upper-income residential areas, entrepreneurs worked hard to attach their own labels to the collective mental landscape, as in "Hyde Park," "OAK PARK," and "RAVENSWOOD." In other cases, new names arose from common usage, as in "McCormickville," "BACK OF THE YARDS," and the numerous "patches" that designated clumps of worker-immigrant settlement near major employment districts.

The arena of community-building activity was not at all the same thing as the built-up area or even the municipality. By the time of the FIRE OF 1871, "Chicago" included not only the continuously developed area within about a mile of the river's mouth but also a wide array of residential suburbs, manufacturing communities, QUARRY villages, rail yard settlements, and market-gardening centers that merged gradually into the sprawling hinterland becoming rail-linked to the city. Historian William Cronon has shown how Chicago's METROPOLITAN GROWTH was symbiotic with a dramatic transformation of the environment for hundreds of miles around. In a more deliberate way, Chicagoans were also transforming the environment in and close to the city. Partly through necessity, partly through competitive zeal, Chicago's elite moved quickly to use new technology in refashioning the city, creating what Cronon calls "second nature" not only on the former prairies of Iowa but also in the former marshes of downtown. Beginning in the 1850s the city undertook a decades-long project of raising the grade of its streets to allow for the building of sewers. Under the guidance of engineer Ellis Chesbrough, Chicago became an internationally known experiment in water management. First in planning for drainage, and then in the 1860s in the cutting-edge WATER SUPPLY system that drove a TUNNEL under Lake Michigan and set up the Water Tower and Pumping Station on the North Side, the city authorities began a century-long process that would remake the hydrological profile of an area hundreds of square miles in extent.

All the features of Chicago's early development—sudden and massive investment in a flat landscape, the codevelopment of city and rail lines, entrepreneurial zeal for both community building and huge technological systems—encouraged a multicentered pattern of growth. Chicago did not just spread outward from its core, it grew as a region, with many scattered centers developing simultaneously and in connection. Peripheral centers that were eventually annexed, such as ANDERSONVILLE or Bridgeport, were initially developed in the speculative boom of the 1830s. Even outlying parts of the metropolitan complex—the North Shore suburbs, the canal towns to the southwest, the industrial centers near Calumet—are almost as old as the city itself.

Migrants and Community Building, 1840–1930

Developmental ventures attracted migrants who further diversified the city's geography. Alongside the highly visible engine of speculative development and engineering, there was another engine of ethnic and religious community formation. This second engine was less noticed than the first, but it would ultimately shape at least as much of the city's geography. And like the speculative engine it continued working well into the twentieth century, as the arena of city building and community making expanded further outward. Canal, river, and railroad development gave birth to working-class and immigrant settlements, but the residents quickly became community builders in their own right. Near the old Hardscrabble area on the South Branch, the mostly IRISH laborers who dug the canal created the community called Bridgeport that would later attain legendary status in the city. Maritime workers on the canal, the river, and the lake fostered several raucous communities of BOARDINGHOUSES and SALOONS on both sides of the South Branch near downtown, the most notorious of which was called "Conley's Patch." GERMANS and Scandinavians who found work in the warehouses, shops, and BREWERIES of the Near North Side established two zones of settlement, one between the North Branch and Wells Street, the other near the lake north of Chicago Avenue. In each of these cases, churches, taverns, clubs, and stores quickly followed, creating local cultures in which German, NORWEGIAN, and Swedish mingled with

English and compelling the city to hire interpreters for elections and at tax time. All of these developments were well underway by 1850, when the city was barely a decade old, and each of these communities in turn spawned more centers of ethnic life as these early immigrants sought work, land, and housing throughout the area. Other settlements—of FRENCH, Danish, Polish, German JEWISH, and African American migrants—followed the same pattern in the 1840s and 1850s, so that by the CIVIL WAR Chicago was not only abloom with speculative additions, subdivisions, and suburbs but also displayed numerous overlapping ethnic clusters, each growing, each seeding its own centrifugal migration.

In the period between the fire of 1871 and the GREAT DEPRESSION, Chicago grew from a regional center to the second largest city in the country, the most important rail hub in the country, the seat of many of the largest heavy industrial plants, and the destination for hundreds of thousands of European immigrants. The so-called new immigration of Southern, Eastern, and Central Europeans transformed the social geography of Chicago and most other great cities in the United States between 1880 and 1920, but it left different landscapes in different places. Chicago was a prime destination for the new immigrants, receiving more of them than any other urban center except Manhattan and Brooklyn. Toward the end of this period some observers began circulating the idea that Chicago had more Poles than any city except Warsaw. This claim was not quite true: metropolitan New York City, whose two million immigrants nearly equaled the total population of Chicago by 1910, had more citizens of Polish birth, as it did for most other immigrant groups. But Chicago did have more Poles than any one of New York's five boroughs, and it had larger communities of CZECHS, Lithuanians, SWEDES, DANES, and LUXEMBOURGERS than any city in the country. What's more, the still-powerful cultural and institutional legacy of earlier immigrants—Irish, Germans, Scandinavians—made Chicago's blend of old and new hyphenated communities distinctive. New York City was the mecca of new immigrants; Milwaukee, a stronghold of old; Chicago had huge numbers of both.

The expansion of heavy industry and the flood of newcomers, combined with the building restrictions imposed after the fire, introduced new varieties of community building that affected the entire metropolitan area. On the edges of the old city, the super rich of the 1870s and 1880s promoted three new concentrations of mansions. They followed the leadership of Marshall Field on PRAIRIE AVENUE, Potter Palmer on Lake Shore Drive, and Samuel J. Walker along Ashland Avenue on the West Side. Meanwhile, prohibition of wooden frame buildings in the city's core encouraged new CONSTRUCTION at the outskirts to house the flood of working-class newcomers. The result was a wide belt of small dwellings stretching from the OLD TOWN area on the NEAR NORTH SIDE through the NEAR WEST SIDE to the stockyards, Bridgeport, and the BLACK BELT south of the Loop. Within this belt were many clusters, old and new. Beyond, stretching out along the still-growing STREET RAILWAY on Lincoln, Milwaukee, Lake, Taylor, and Ogden, were more clusters of new settlement housing slightly more prosperous immigrants and their descendants. On the far South Side, industrial satellites appeared at PULLMAN, in the steel complex at the mouth of the CALUMET RIVER, and eventually in the huge manufacturing district stretching southeast into Indiana.

In a pattern that echoed earlier themes, speculative developers like Samuel Gross fueled the engine of geographic mobility by tailoring clusters of new homes for various pocketbooks. Subsequently the engine of cultural creativity enriched the new spaces with churches, SCHOOLS, and other institutions that made them special places for this or that kind of people. By the late nineteenth century, observers could note the steeple-dotted skylines still evident today in older areas of ethnic settlement—steeples that serve as markers of the complex, overlapping, interpenetrating array of worshipping communities, the many languages and many architectures of devotion that Chicagoans created in this greatest surge of the city's growth. Especially for ROMAN CATHOLICS (then and now a large segment of the population), but to some extent for Lutherans and others, the proliferation of PARISHES and congregations provided the most important framework of spatial orientation and loyalty in the city for a century after the fire.

The same great surge of growth between fire and Depression produced another kind of community whose influence on the history of the city has been even stronger and more lasting than that of the immigrant clusters: the enormous and geographically isolated African American ghetto on the SOUTH SIDE. Popular accounts often trace the "Black Belt" to the GREAT MIGRATION of the WORLD WAR I era, but its history is far longer and more complicated. The three major areas of African American residence in Chicago, one in each division of the city, all trace their origins to tiny pre-fire settlements that once resembled those of many other migrants. They were primarily communities of manual workers who lived near rail yards, industrial centers, or wealthy neighborhoods where they could find employment as "hands" or as DOMESTIC WORKERS. The South Side community was always the biggest, and like other migrant settlements it had its institutions, most notably Quinn Chapel AME church in the early years. Even before the Great Migration, the explosive growth of the late nineteenth century brought many thousands of black newcomers to Chicago and boosted the population of the South Side community to well over 40,000 by 1910. In the following two decades, at least another 70,000 arrived from the South, swelling and crowding the South Side black community just as white resistance to African Americans as neighbors made it the most ethnically homogeneous and isolated district in the history of Chicago.

Cellular Mapping, 1880–1940

The growing complexity of Chicago's social geography was accompanied by a growing series of efforts at simplified description. Even in the 1850s newspaper articles occasionally exaggerated and caricatured the homogeneity and cultural isolation of Irish and German communities. In 1881, veteran reporter F. B. Wilkie, his tongue lodged firmly in his cheek, published an apocalyptic vision of Chicago in 1906. His city of the future was divided into two huge sections, "Teutonia" on the north and "Hibernia" to the south, separated by a 60-foot east-west wall down the middle of Madison Street. In addition, one very small section of English speakers called "First Ward" occupied the area of the Loop. Other journalists, then and later, played up the activities of street GANGS in defining and defending ethnic TURF, and all of these writings worked to produce one of the lasting myths of Chicago's geography: the notion of stable, segregated, homogeneous, cellular ethnic neighborhoods.

Astute writers (including Wilkie) knew that the reality of Chicago's social geography was more complicated, and recent scholarship has emphasized that complexity. With the notable exception of the African American (and for a time the ITALIAN) communities, Chicago's ethnic clusters were shaped more by the things that held them together than by lines that separated them. They were more centered than bounded. Locales were mixed, and most communities were dynamic—spreading, shrinking, hiving off pieces, changing with generations. To describe this dynamism, Robert Park, Ernest Burgess, and other scholars of the "CHICAGO SCHOOL" OF SOCIOLOGY popularized the idea of "NEIGHBORHOOD SUCCESSION," in which newer and poorer groups inherit neighborhoods left behind as more successful citizens seek better housing farther from the center.

Given all the evidence of complexity, the tendency toward cellular thinking becomes in itself a thing to be explained, and a piece of Chicago's distinctive version of multicenteredness. It was not just the journalists who contributed to the vision of an urban mosaic. Reformers, scholars, and officials played parts as well. Beginning in the 1890s, PHILANTHROPISTS, scholars, and SETTLEMENT HOUSE workers focused renewed public attention on certain "new immigrant" districts within the sprawling belt of worker housing. Florence

Kelley, Edith Abbott, and Sophonisba Breckinridge, in research that began at HULL HOUSE and continued using students from the UNIVERSITY OF CHICAGO's School of SOCIAL SERVICE Administration, produced a series of publications from 1895 to 1936 that graphically mapped conditions in many districts around the city. Although these researchers knew and appreciated the city's complexity, their color-coded maps and colorful descriptions of national cultures had the effect of attaching ethnic labels to the neatly delineated localities on their maps. The same sociologists who stressed "neighborhood succession" also helped to crystallize the notion of cells by promoting their idea that large cities are made up of "natural areas" separated by lasting physical boundaries. Robert Park, in what was probably a casual remark, produced a phrase that would take on a life of its own when he referred to a "mosaic of little worlds." In one of academia's most dramatic contributions to the imagined landscape of any city, these scholars established the "COMMUNITY AREAS" that have served as tools of both valuable analysis and misleading simplification since the 1920s.

Maxwell Street, 1941. Photographer: Russell Lee. Source: Library of Congress.

For some ordinary Chicagoans, other kinds of cellular thinking gained importance in this period, sometimes with tragic results. By the Depression, the South Side BLACK BELT was already the anomalous extreme case among Chicago's subcommunities. When a still larger migration came after WORLD WAR II, a similar community sprawled across the West Side, and by the late twentieth century Chicago's more than a million African Americans were probably the most segregated large urban population in the nation's history. These two black communities were at once the nearest approximation of the mythic mosaic cell *and* the geographic element against which many other communities defined themselves. The parallel institutions of the African American community—businesses, churches, entertainment centers—made it a vital matrix of innovation not only for black Chicagoans but for African Americans nationwide.

Yet the innovations fostered by the ghetto were double edged. As it grew, whites honed new methods of confinement. Some of these were political. A governing system based on 50 independent wards encouraged the building of the legendary DEMOCRATIC PARTY organization assembled slowly since the time of Cermak and perfected by Mayor Richard J. Daley. Thousands of political workers and city employees were bonded to precinct and ward organizations run by powerful aldermen, who spread largesse strategically within their ward limits and carefully monitored voter turnout within those same categories at election time. Until the 1960s this was a system dominated by white males, in which black participation was limited to those few wards where African Americans were the majority. For the huge proportion of Chicago's white population that was Catholic, parish boundaries became defensive lines as the growing African American population sought housing in new areas. A parallel process occurred with school districts, and all three kinds of areas—wards, parishes, school districts—became battlegrounds in the racial struggles that played a central role in Chicago's geographic evolution from the 1940s through the 1960s. When Martin Luther King declared, in 1966, that he had never encountered Chicago's kind of RACISM in the South, he was commenting indirectly on the passions engendered by battles over particular and multiple kinds of urban territory.

Elite Community Redevelopment, 1940–2000

Although Daniel Burnham, in the planning arena, and Anton Cermak, in the political, each had a broad vision of Chicago's future, it was the Depression crisis, more than any individual vision, that opened the way for those with money and power to remake the city. From the mid-1930s through the 1960s, the availability of federal subsidies allowed public agencies to "modernize" Chicago through slum clearance, the construction of EXPRESSWAYS, and the building of PUBLIC HOUSING projects, all of which had more extensive and dramatic (as well as controversial) consequences for Chicago than for most other large cities. Private actors—neighborhood groups, HOSPITALS, UNIVERSITIES, and developers—all played large roles in shaping the redevelopment process from the start. From the 1970s through the beginning of the twenty-first century, private initiatives, especially those of developers, outstripped public ones in clearance and redevelopment. The combined effect of both public and private activity was to erase whole areas of the older city, and to create a new armature for spatial thinking and investment. Elements of the city's geography that were once highly visible and widely known, such as "Little Italy," "GREEKTOWN," "MAXWELL STREET," were either vanished or vestigial by the end of the twentieth century. Prominent instead in the collective spatial consciousness are labels that had no meaning before the Depression: "CABRINI-GREEN," "River North," "The Gap."

Like the creation of Chicago in the early nineteenth century, the remaking of Chicago in the late twentieth involved a particular combination of vigorous local initiatives with large trends beyond the city. Just as the city's greatest growth spurt coincided with the rise of railroads and heavy industry, the post–World War II transformation coincided with the rise of interstate highways and a decentralized manufacturing economy. A truck-based growth pattern and a mass hunger for suburban housing led to a drain of both jobs and people from the city into an ever-expanding belt of suburbs. Throughout the second half of the century the suburbs grew at a faster rate than the city, which has suffered net population declines in every postwar decade except the 1990s.

The atrophy of Chicago's enormous rail facilities, steel mills, and MEATPACKING plants and the relocation of many factories to the distant suburbs were at the same time a stimulus to and a prerequisite for the redevelopment of space. And just as the greatest European exodus brought new residents to Chicago during its rise to Second City status, the greatest migrations of African Americans, Latinos, and Asians came during deindustrialization. Thus most of the European-born arrived when

Chicago was the gateway to the West and at the cutting edge of rail- and industry-based growth, and most of the late-twentieth-century migrants arrived when the leading edge of industrial growth had moved out of the city and to some extent out of the Midwest.

Two huge demographic trends—the shift of white Chicagoans to the suburbs and the rise of what scholars call a "spatial mismatch" between job creation on the fringe and the growth of a job-needy population in the core—set the stage for community building after 1950. Led by Mayor Richard J. Daley, postwar civic and BUSINESS figures focused on the drain of tax dollars and attacked the problem through large-scale PLANNING: creating O'HARE AIRPORT and ANNEXING it to the city, and clearing "blighted" districts. They also began a tradition of encouraging high-end private developments, from Arthur Rubloff's Carl Sandburg Village to the CONDOMINIUM and townhouse complexes on old railroad land near the Loop. These measures, which preserved more vitality in central Chicago than in most old industrial cities, were intertwined with other, more damaging policies. Alarmed by the drain of white population, city officials and private organizations cooperated in reinforcing racial segregation into the 1960s, most notably in building the "second ghetto" of high-rise public housing.

In the last decade of the twentieth century, the second Mayor Daley led yet another wave of elite redevelopment, intended in part to correct the unfortunate consequences of many earlier activities. The hallmark of this effort has been the rapid destruction of most of the high-rise public housing and the promotion of mixed-income communities instead. Like so many previous community developments, this one has been shaped by the continuing pressures of speculation in land, by shifts in the currents of migration, by a tendency to think big, by the vigorous and vocal involvement of local populations, and by intense controversy. And as in so many earlier steps, Chicago is distinctive—taking bigger actions than any other city, attracting national attention, and once again remaking its social landscape.

No single feature of Chicago's social geography is unique: not the flat setting, not the immigrants, not the industry, not the POLITICS, not the racial conflict or the urge to plan. It is in *how* and *when* the prominent features of Chicago's development came together, and how they interacted, that the city's distinctiveness lies. Between 1850 and 1930, in a city sprawling as no city ever had, Chicago produced hundreds of new communities, most of them tangled together physically but having clear and strong integrity in the minds of their residents. As the Irish and the Germans and the Italians and Jews moved outward—and, for so very long, the African Americans did not—both the real and the imagined localities exerted a powerful influence on the unfolding and changing meaning of "neighborhood" to the citizens. There has always been more than one Chicago in this location on the lake, and the metropolis that residents celebrate and visitors acclaim today is a product, a synthesis, not only of the many Chicagos of today, but of all those that came before.

Henry C. Binford

See also: Chicago Studied; Chicago's Ethnic Mosaic in 1980, 2000 (color maps, pp. C6, C7); Contested Spaces; Demography; Economic Geography; Mapping Chicago; Metropolitan Growth

Further reading: An exploration of Chicago's communities should begin with the development of Chicago's larger physical and economic setting. Two works by geographers are fundamental: Irving Cutler, *Chicago: Metropolis of the Mid-Continent,* 3rd ed. (1982); and Michael P. Conzen, "The American Urban System in the Nineteenth Century," in *Geography and the Urban Environment,* ed. D. Herbert and R. J. Johnston (1981). On the way metropolitan Chicago's earliest communities grew in this setting, see Edward Ranney et al., *Prairie Passage: The Illinois and Michigan Canal Corridor* (1998); and the fine series of books on the canal towns edited by Michael Conzen et al., *Studies on the Illinois and Michigan Canal Corridor* (1987–1994). Chicago's evolving relationship with an extended hinterland is the subject of William Cronon, *Nature's Metropolis: Chicago and the Great West* (1991).

The best starting place for study of entrepreneurial development is still Homer Hoyt, *One Hundred Years of Land Values in Chicago: The Relationship of the Growth of Chicago to the Rise in Its Land Values, 1830–1933* (1933). Also essential are Ann Durkin Keating, *Building Chicago: Suburban Developers and the Creation of a Divided Metropolis* (1988); and Michael H. Ebner, *Creating Chicago's North Shore: A Suburban History* (1988). Carl W. Condit provided a valuable if opinionated overview of twentieth-century growth in his two volumes entitled *Chicago, 1910–29: Building, Planning, and Urban Technology* (1973); and *Chicago, 1930–70: Building, Planning, and Urban Technology* (1974).

The shaping of small areas by European immigrants and Southern African Americans is a theme in many of the works already mentioned. Two useful gateways to more detailed information on settlement by particular groups are Melvin G. Holli and Peter d'A. Jones, *Ethnic Chicago: A Multicultural Portrait,* 4th ed. (1995); and Dominic A. Pacyga and Ellen Skerrett, *Chicago, City of Neighborhoods: Histories and Tours* (1986). Particularly valuable in showing how work patterns and class relations influenced communities are William Kornblum, *Blue Collar Community* (1974); and Lizabeth Cohen, *Making a New Deal: Industrial Workers in Chicago, 1919–1939* (1990). An old but excellent summary of the early growth of Chicago's African American community is to be found in St. Clair Drake and Horace R. Cayton, *Black Metropolis: A Study of Negro Life in a Northern City* (1945). Among many works on the twentieth century sharpening of racial lines and the building of the African American communities are Thomas Lee Philpott, *The Slum and the Ghetto: Neighborhood Deterioration and Middle-Class Reform, Chicago, 1880–1930* (1978); James R. Grossman, *Land of Hope: Chicago, Black Southerners, and the Great Migration* (1989); John T. McGreevy, *Parish Boundaries: The Catholic Encounter with Race in the Twentieth-Century Urban North* (1996); Arnold R. Hirsch, *Making the Second Ghetto: Race and Housing in Chicago, 1940–1960* (1983); Adam P. Green, *Selling the Race: Cultural and Community in Black Chicago, 1940–1955* (forthcoming); and Amanda I. Seligman, *Block by Block: Neighborhoods, Public Policy, and "White Flight" in Richard J. Daley's Chicago* (2004).

Insights on the ways Chicagoans both created a cellular model for thinking about the city and transgressed the imagined "boxes" in their everyday lives may be obtained from Harvey Warren Zorbaugh, *The Gold Coast and the Slum: A Sociological Study of Chicago's Near North Side* (1929); Albert Hunter, *Symbolic Communities: The Persistence and Change of Chicago's Local Communities* (1974); Perry Duis, *Challenging Chicago: Coping with Everyday Life, 1837–1920* (1998); Carl Smith, *Urban Disorder and the Shape of Belief: The Great Chicago Fire, the Haymarket Bomb, and the Model Town of Pullman* (1995); and Robin F. Bachin, *Building the South Side: Urban Space and Civic Culture in Chicago, 1890–1919* (2004).

Mundelein College. *See* Loyola University

Mundelein, IL, Lake County, 33 miles NW of the Loop. An 1850s settlement of ENGLISH millwrights three miles west of LIBERTYVILLE is said to have inspired the area's name of Mechanic's Grove. When the Wisconsin Central RAILROAD built through the area to Chicago in 1880, local farmer John Holcomb donated land for a station and village plat, which he named after himself. To honor the line's most notable stockholder, the railroad renamed the station after William Rockefeller in 1885.

Little changed in the tiny community until after the Chicago & Milwaukee Electric INTERURBAN terminated its LAKE BLUFF spur line there in 1904. Anticipating a boom, residents planned an incorporation referendum for January 1909. Although there were too few residents to meet the legal requirements, settlers around nearby Diamond Lake were included in the vote with the understanding that they could withdraw from the new village. The vote on January 25, 1909, was successful, with Sylvester L. Tripp being named president in March. Residents living around Diamond Lake withdrew shortly thereafter.

Meanwhile, Chicagoan Arthur Sheldon purchased a large holding on the east side of Rockefeller called Mud Lake. Hoping to prepare and sell home study business school courses, he erected large buildings and hired numerous staff, primarily women. Sheldon even persuaded villagers in mid-1909 to change Rockefeller's name to Area, an acronym for his company's motto: Ability, Reliability, Endurance, and Action.

Sheldon's business failed—perhaps as a result of WORLD WAR I—and his property fell vacant. By 1920 George Cardinal Mundelein, seeking to realize his dream of building a world-renowned theological SEMINARY, had purchased these holdings, renaming Mud Lake as St. Mary's Lake. In 1924, Area was renamed Mundelein in honor of the cardinal. As a grand complex of buildings rose, Mundelein played host to the 28th International Eucharistic Congress in 1926, which over 500,000 people attended.

The size of the crowds interested Samuel Insull, Chicago capitalist and electricity mogul, who attempted to organize a large, planned community with underground utilities and decentralized shopping centers. The failure of his economic empire and the GREAT DEPRESSION derailed his dream, and Mundelein's population grew to only 1,328 by 1940.

As suburbanization swept into LAKE COUNTY, Mundelein, which had been planned to accept growth, mushroomed from 3,186 in 1950 to over 12,000 in 1962. Even with such a population base, the Chicago, North Shore & Milwaukee Electric interurban ceased operating in January 1963.

Still, Mundelein's population continued to rise, from 17,053 in 1980 to over 30,935 in 2000. Community and other area leaders worked with METRA to acquire a rail COMMUTER route, which opened in 1996 as the Metra North Central Service line from Chicago through Mundelein to ANTIOCH.

Craig L. Pfannkuche

See also: Gas and Electricity; Roman Catholic Archdiocese of Chicago; Suburbs and Cities as Dual Metropolis

Further reading: "Mundelein." *Waukegan News-Sun,* October 2, 1995. • "Twenty-fifth Anniversary Edition." *Mundelein News,* June 27, 1968. • Purcell, Connie. *Memories of Mundelein.* 1984.

Municipal Charters. *See* Charters, Municipal

Munster, IN, Lake County, 24 miles S of the Loop. In 1850 most of the site of the future town of Munster lay under the turbid waters of Cady Marsh or was seasonally flooded by the Little CALUMET RIVER. But for centuries NATIVE AMERICANS, most recently the POTAWATOMI, had lived on the abundant fish, wildlife, and countless migratory birds found along the dry and sandy ridge. After 1840 a scattering of European American families moved in and as often drifted away. Beginning in 1845, a succession of innkeepers, among them Allen Brass and Johann Stallbohm, welcomed travelers to a rambling wooden structure beside Ridge Road.

DUTCH immigrants arrived in 1855, and by 1900 had established a tidy farm community. Jabaays, Kooys, Schoons, Jansens, and Bakkers raised potatoes, cabbages, beans, and flowers along the ridge for local families and regional wholesalers, and onion sets for the national market. Peter Klootwyck and town postmaster Jacob Munster operated small stores. Late in the century Aaron Norton Hart channeled through the ridge to the Little Calumet, drained Cady Marsh, and created hundreds of acres of valuable farmland. In 1927 Burns Ditch minimized the annual floods of the Little Calumet and made north Munster habitable.

The 7.5-square-mile Town of Munster was organized in 1907 with a population of 500. After 1920 growing numbers of COMMUTERS launched the suburban era. The GREAT DEPRESSION halted all growth until the late 1930s, when a war-induced regional housing shortage brought the working-class-oriented development of Independence Park, rows of brick duplexes, and even a few APARTMENT houses. By 1945 Munster was an uneasy mixture of small farmers, industrial workers, and well-to-do commuters.

Munster's suburban status was confirmed in the 1950s by the construction of 1,500 homes, which doubled the town's population to 10,313. The new residents were young, well educated, upwardly mobile, and family-oriented. They created a prosperous community of comfortable and occasionally grand houses. Modern public services were introduced. An industrial park attracted several large and small tenants. Farm stands were replaced by shops, banks, service stations, garden centers, and a lumberyard. Munster never developed a focused downtown, though a sizable mall was built beside Calumet Avenue.

The booming sixties and seventies saw the completion of Munster's transition into a suburban community. Though the town board continued to govern, a town manager was appointed, and municipal ordinances multiplied, along with streets and handsome trees, parks, and recreational areas. Long-empty South Munster filled with SUBDIVISIONS; Don Powers, one businessman among many, had developed almost two thousand homesites by 1990.

Excellent schools absorbed much tax revenue. Munster High School opened in 1966 and curricula were developed to serve a largely college-bound student population. As the century ended, Munster was a mature and prosperous suburban town, home to a well-educated and largely professional population of 21,511. A remarkable HOSPITAL complex dominated its skyline. A handsome ART CENTER stood beside the ridge. A second business park was attracting a variety of "clean" tenants. The farm village of 1920 had quite disappeared.

Lance Trusty

See also: Governing the Metropolis; Lake County, IN; Metropolitan Growth; Plant Communities

Further reading: Clipping file. Munster Branch, Lake County Public Library, Munster, IN. • Moore, Powell, A. *The Calumet Region: Indiana's Last Frontier.* 1977. • Trusty, Lance. *Town on the Ridge: A History of Munster, Indiana.* 1982.

Museum of Broadcast Communications. One of the earliest BROADCASTING museums in America, the Museum of Broadcast Communications opened to the public at 800 S. Wells in 1987. Bruce Dumont, a television and documentary producer for WBBM-TV, launched the museum both to preserve and to exhibit over 40 years of American radio and television history. In addition to 80,000 hours of programming in its archival holdings, the museum includes the A. C. NIELSEN, Jr., Research Center and the Radio Hall of Fame. In June 1993 the Museum of Broadcast Communications moved to the Chicago Cultural Center at the corner of Washington Street and Michigan Avenue.

Wallace Best

See also: Journalism; Public Broadcasting; Westinghouse Broadcasting

Further reading: "Museum Carefully Sifts History in a Hurry." *Chicago Tribune,* January 13, 1995. • *MBC History: Interview with Bruce Dumont.* Film. Produced by MBC. 1994.

Museum of Contemporary Art. The Museum of Contemporary Art (MCA), which opened in 1967, has evolved dramatically from an energetic organization supported by a dedicated group of Chicago collectors and patrons to a national institution presenting the ART of our time to an increasingly international public. The museum's opening occurred in an atmosphere of great artistic and social experimentation.

From its inception, the MCA focused on temporary exhibitions modeled on the example of a European *kunsthalle.* In 1974, the mission expanded to establish a permanent collection with works created after 1945. Joseph Randall Shapiro, a prominent collector of surrealism, provided the leadership to inspire other collectors and gather private resources to purchase and renovate a building on Ontario Street. Implicit in the MCA's mission was a commitment to vigorous performance and educational programs and an outreach mechanism designed to increase awareness of contemporary art. Building on the remarkable exhibitions in its early history—the first U.S. wrapping of a public building by Christo in 1969, a Robert Irwin exhibition in 1975, the first U.S. exhibition of Frida Kahlo in 1978, and a Magdalena Abakanowicz exhibition in 1982—and recognizing the necessity of a larger facility, in 1996 the MCA acquired the stunning site of the National Guard ARMORY between Lake Michigan and Michigan Avenue. Designed by Berlin architect Joseph Paul Kleihues, the new building clad in aluminum and Indiana limestone opened in June 1996 in a 24-hour summer solstice celebration.

Referencing the modernism of Mies van der Rohe as well as the tradition of Chicago ARCHITECTURE, the $46 million structure is among the largest in the United States devoted to contemporary art. Its 45,000 square feet of galleries, with a permanent collection boasting more than 5,600 works and a 300-seat auditorium and outdoor sculpture garden, is suitable for large-scale artworks, new media, and ever larger audiences.

Judith Russi Kirshner

See also: Art Institute of Chicago; Artists, Education and Culture of; Near North Side; Renaissance Society

Further reading: Neff, Terry Ann R., ed. *Collective Vision: Creating a Contemporary Art Museum.* 1996. • Warren, Lynne, ed. *Art in Chicago, 1945–1995.* 1996.

Museum of Science and Industry. The Museum of Science and Industry is one of the nation's oldest and largest institutions devoted to the display and exploration of scientific and technological advancements.

Though a community effort, the museum owes its founding primarily to the vision and PHILANTHROPY of Julius Rosenwald, one of Chicago's wealthiest merchandisers. In 1911, while vacationing with his family in Germany, Rosenwald visited the Deutsches Museum in Munich, a museum that focused on industrial and scientific processes and promoted visitor participation with the exhibits. Repeated contacts with the museum's director convinced Rosenwald that Chicago should have such an institution. In 1921 he proposed the idea to the COMMERCIAL CLUB OF CHICAGO. By 1926 the museum was incorporated, backed financially by a $3 million gift from Rosenwald and a city bond issue. At the time of his death in 1932, Rosenwald had contributed roughly $7 million in cash and stock donations.

The museum chose as its location the former Palace of Fine Arts Building in JACKSON PARK, the last structure left from the WORLD'S COLUMBIAN EXPOSITION of 1893 and former home of the FIELD MUSEUM of Natural History. Vacant since 1920, the building required extensive renovation, which began in 1929. Working toward an opening coincident with Chicago's 1933 "A CENTURY OF PROGRESS" World's Fair, the museum received its first visitors in June of that year with 10 percent of its space readied for visitation. As attendance and exhibition space grew throughout the 1930s, so too did its financial troubles. By the end of the decade, expenditures greatly outpaced revenues, endangering the museum's future.

A turning point in the direction and administration of the museum came in 1940, when the board of directors lured Major Lenox R. Lohr, the head of the National Broadcasting Company and former general manager of "A Century of Progress," to its presidency. Lohr quickly restructured the museum's organization and focus. Instead of relying on traditional in-house design, execution, and upkeep of the exhibits, Lohr hoped to attract industry-sponsored displays through increased attendance. In exchange for construction and maintenance costs, the museum would allow the sponsor to ADVERTISE in the exhibit. Exhibit space would be allocated to 10 percent to historical achievement and 90 percent to the present. Lohr's plan proved successful, although exhibit renovation did not occur at the rate he had originally envisioned. His legacy remains visible through the sustained popularity of the museum.

At the end of the twentieth century the museum's 350,000 square feet (approximately 8 acres), it presents over 2,000 exhibits in many fields, including technology, AGRICULTURE, TRANSPORTATION, energy, and communications. Educating as it entertains, the museum promotes learning through interactive, hands-on participation between the visitor and the exhibitions. Featured attractions include a working replica of a coal mine, the U-505 submarine, the Henry Crown Space Center, and Omnimax Theater. The museum began charging an admission fee in 1991. Nevertheless, attendance has remained high (approximately two million annually), ranking the Museum of Science and Industry as one of Chicago's premier TOURIST attractions and attesting to its role as an effective tool of mass education.

Jonathan J. Keyes

See also: Chambers of Commerce; Leisure; Museums in the Park

Further reading: Alexander, Edward P. *Museums in Motion: An Introduction to the History and Functions of Museums.* 1979. • Kogan, Herman. *A Continuing Marvel: The Story of the Museum of Science and Industry.* 1973. • Pridmore, Jay. *Inventive Genius: The History of the Museum of Science and Industry.* 1996.

Museums in the Park. Through an annual tax, Chicagoans provide for the maintenance and care of museums located in Chicago's parks. In 1903, voters approved the tax measure which had been proposed by the South Park District Commissioners. The commissioners declared that with this funding the institutions would be better able to serve more of Chicago's burgeoning population. These revenues benefit nine museums: the ART INSTITUTE OF CHICAGO, the FIELD MUSEUM of Natural History, the ADLER PLANETARIUM, the John G. SHEDD AQUARIUM, the CHICAGO HISTORICAL SOCIETY, the CHICAGO ACADEMY OF SCIENCES, the MUSEUM OF SCIENCE AND INDUSTRY, the DUSABLE MUSEUM of African American History, and the MEXICAN FINE ARTS CENTER MUSEUM.

Dennis H. Cremin

See also: Entertaining Chicagoans

Music Clubs. As hopes of prosperity inspired waves of migration from the South to the industrial North at the turn of the century, Chicago's position as the TRANSPORTATION hub and economic powerhouse of Middle America made it very attractive to musicians of all kinds. Through the "Jazz Age" and the "Roaring Twenties," Chicago established its reputation as a thriving, wide-open city, with an increasing number of entertainment options.

JAZZ was born in New Orleans. Chicago is where the music came of age, with Louis Armstrong's move to the city in 1922, when he joined King Oliver's band at the Lincoln Gardens Cafe, considered a milestone along the historical path of American music. Chicago became the center of black American culture, with jazz flourishing in clubs such as the Plantation and the Sunset, and later in the Grand Terrace and the Club DeLisa. In a variety of locations, Joe Segal's Jazz Showcase has remained one of the oldest jazz clubs in the world.

While the Mississippi Delta is celebrated as the cradle of the BLUES, the SOUTH SIDE Chicago clubs are where the music transformed itself and sustained its greatest popularity, from the boogie-woogie piano that flourished in the 1920s through the electrified, guitar-powered urban blues of the 1940s and 1950s. From neighborhood taverns such as Pepper's Lounge and Theresa's to "chitlin' circuit" palaces such as the REGAL THEATER, Chicago nightspots have enjoyed a storied reputation among blues fans.

Chicago has supported a varied and increasingly diverse array of music clubs, from 1960s and 1970s folk clubs such as the Gate of Horn, the Quiet Knight, and the Earl of OLD TOWN to sophisticated supper clubs such as the London House and Mister Kelly's. Through the latter half of the twentieth century, ROCK has been a mainstay of the Chicago club circuit, with dozens of clubs competing for the younger music audience. More recently, Chicago clubs have been an influential incubator in the development of house, techno, and other forms of dance music.

Don McLeese

See also: Aragon Ballroom; Dance Halls; Entertaining Chicagoans; Ethnic Music; Great Migration; Leisure

Further reading: Keil, Charles, Angeliki V. Keil, and Dick Blau. *Polka Happiness.* 1992. • Keil, Charles. *Urban Blues.* 2nd ed. 1991. • Kenney, William Howland. *Chicago Jazz: A Cultural History, 1904–1930.* 1993.

Music Publishing. Chicago's music publishing has mirrored the cultural history of the city and the nation through music for the church, school, popular entertainment, and the home, from the first piece of music in 1854, "The Garden City Polka," by Christoph Plagge, published by B. K. Mould, to the rise of GOSPEL music. The high point came during the CIVIL WAR, when patriotic songs like "The Battle Cry of Freedom" (1862) made Chicago a national center. Earlier, music had been issued primarily for a local market, but the Civil War songs made H. M. Higgins (1856) and Root & Cady (1858) nationally known. The Great FIRE OF 1871 ended this activity. For

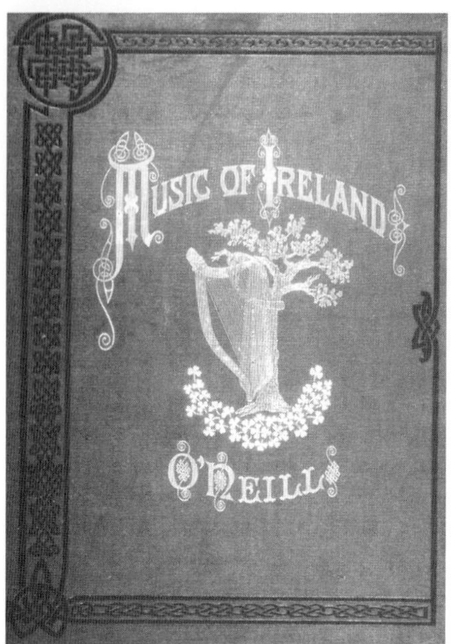

Title page of *O'Neill's Music of Ireland*, 1903. Designer: Unknown. Source: The Newberry Library.

the next 10 years little music was published. Among the pre-fire firms only Lyon & Healy (1864) survived.

In the 1880s inexpensive (five–ten cent) music began to be issued by the National Music Company (1882), Saalfield Brothers (1888), and McKinley Music Company (1891). Religious music became increasingly prominent, from publishers like Edwin O. Excell (1885), Hope Publishing Company (1894), and the Rodeheaver Company (1910). Clayton F. Summy was one of Chicago's longest-lived music publishers, specializing in teaching material, SACRED MUSIC, and works by Chicago composers.

With the popularity of VAUDEVILLE in the 1890s, Chicago became a center for popular song publishers, like Will Rossiter (1891), publisher of "The Darktown Strutters' Ball" (1917), and the Melrose Brothers Music Company (1920), publisher of "King Porter Stomp" (1924) and "It's Tight Like That" (1928).

As Chicago became a center of gospel music, it also became a center for publishing that music. The most notable firms were established by musician/composers: Dorsey House (Thomas A. Dorsey) and the Martin and Morris Music Company (Kenneth Morris and Sallie Martin).

Dena J. Epstein

See also: Business of Chicago; Musical Instrument Manufacturing; Publishing and Media, Religious

Further reading: Brubaker, Robert L. "Music Publishing." In *Making Music Chicago Style,* 1985. • Epstein, Dena J. *Music Publishing in Chicago Before 1871: The Firm of Root & Cady, 1858–1871.* 1969. • Thorson, Theodore W. "A History of Music Publishing in Chicago, 1850–1900." Ph.D. diss., Northwestern University. 1961.

Musical Instrument Manufacturing. After the Great FIRE OF 1871, Chicago quickly became a national center in musical instrument manufacturing, especially organs and pianos. Indeed, by 1910 Chicago manufacturers were supplying about half of all pianos sold in the United States, and one firm, W. W. Kimball Company, became the largest single producer of pianos and organs in the world. Although most of the early technological INNOVATIONS in piano design in the United States were by Eastern manufacturers, they share credit with the rising Midwestern firms for innovations developing the industrial magnitude of the trade. Significantly, the Chicago WORLD'S COLUMBIAN EXPOSITION in 1893 sparked a national marketing competition over the "best" piano between eastern and Midwestern manufacturers, generating valuable publicity for Chicago brands. By 1915 over 40 companies were producing pianos, organs, and other instruments; many had showrooms on Wabash Avenue, appropriately called. "Music Row." Familiar brands included Bush & Gerts, Cable, Cable-Nelson, Conover, Hamilton (Baldwin), Kimball, Lyon & Healy (originally renowned for harps), Steger & Sons, and Story & Clark. Kimball, along with Baldwin, pioneered modern dealership organization and aggressive sales techniques, and they as well as Cable were among the strongest corporations in the industry.

In the era before radio and sound MOVIES, self-playing instruments were a crucial part of the music industry. Chicago firms produced many brands associated with automatic pianos, notably Melville Clark, Kimball, and Gulbransen-Dickinson, whose famous "Gulbransen Baby" trademark rivaled Victor Talking Machine Company's "His Master's Voice" in familiarity. Furthermore, several Chicago companies specialized in manufacturing coin-operated, roll-activated electric music machines specifically designed for public entertainment. These "coin-pianos" and "orchestrions"—precursors of today's jukebox—often contained a variety of instrument sounds. Famous Chicago companies included Operators Piano Company, who made the Coinola, and the J. P. Seeburg Company, which, along with Wurlitzer, later dominated post–WORLD WAR II jukebox production. Seeburg was also a leader in producing "theater photoplayers"—automatic instruments uniquely designed to provide music and sound effects for silent movies—until sound movies destroyed this market in the late 1920s. Not surprisingly, Chicago was a manufacturing center for the actions and perforated music rolls for all types of automatic instruments. Chief companies were Gulbransen-Dickinson and the Q-R-S Company, the largest manufacturer of music rolls in the world, producing 10 million rolls annually by 1926.

Chicago's historical prominence in musical instrument manufacturing also included Frank Holton Company brasswinds (Holton had been first trombonist in Sousa's band), Lowry electronic organs, and Martin Band Instruments, one of the nation's oldest manufacturers. Chicago-based MONTGOMERY WARD & CO. and SEARS, ROEBUCK & CO. offered an impressive variety of musical instruments through their celebrated MAIL-ORDER catalogs, including accordions, banjos, mandolins, guitars, violins, harps, harmonicas, drums, brass and woodwind instruments, even pianos and organs. For generations, Ward and Sears provided Americans, especially in rural areas, with arguably the most important single source of instruments.

The music industry ceased to be dominated by the piano and organ trade after the GREAT DEPRESSION and WORLD WAR II, and Chicago lost its leadership as the musical instruments trade struggled against a wider variety of entertainment choices available in the postwar culture. Many old Chicago trademarks still in production at that time, such as Gulbransen, Story & Clark, Q-R-S, Holton, and Martin, have long since been sold to corporations in other states. Nevertheless, present-day Chicago-area firms still produce a variety of instruments, including fifes and song whistles, guitars, banjos, basses, mandolins, band and orchestral instruments, digital pianos, and synthesizers. Historically prominent names include Lyon & Healy harps, Lowry electronic organs, and W. H. Lee & Co., the largest maker of handcrafted orchestral string instruments in the United States.

Craig H. Roell

See also: Broadcasting; Entertaining Chicagoans; Movie Palaces

Further reading: "Chicago's Music Industry Is Huge." *Chicago Commerce* 24 (July 21, 1928): 7–9, 29–30. • Roell, Craig H. "The Piano Industry in the United States." In *Encyclopedia of Keyboard Instruments: The Piano,* ed. Robert Palmieri, 1994, 415–419. Reissued in 1996 as *Encyclopedia of the Piano.* • Roell, Craig H. *The Piano in America, 1890–1940.* 1989.

Muslims. The Muslim community of metropolitan Chicago reflects the ethnic and theological diversity of global Islam.

BOSNIANS, Arabs, and AFRICAN AMERICANS established Muslim organizations in the city prior to 1960. A Bosnian mutual aid and benevolent society, Muslimansko Potpomagajuce Drustvo Dzemijetul Hajrije of Illinois, established in the NEAR NORTH SIDE in 1906, appears to be the oldest Muslim organization in the United States. A subsequent Bosnian mosque on N. Halsted Street relocated in the 1970s to north suburban NORTHBROOK. This new mosque, called the Islamic Cultural Center of Greater Chicago, has served a multiethnic constituency, though not without some institutional struggle over its identity in the late 1980s and early 1990s.

Arab Muslims from Palestine began settling in Chicago in the early 1900s. Mostly entrepreneurs, they occupied a sociogeographic niche along the edge of the SOUTH SIDE'S African American community by the late 1940s. Political turmoil in the decades following the creation of Israel in 1948 brought more PALESTINIAN Muslims to Chicago, while many non-Palestinian Arab Muslims began arriving in the mid-1950s. The first local Arab mosque, now known as the Mosque Foundation (est. 1954), opened a new facility in southwest suburban BRIDGEVIEW in 1982, later adding two state-accredited schools for Muslim children. By the end of the twentieth century, Arab Muslims were attending various mosques throughout the metropolitan region, particularly on the city's North Side and in some suburbs.

Chicago has figured prominently in Islam's appeal to African Americans since 1920, the year Mufti Muhammad Sadiq, the first missionary to the United States from the Ahmadiyya Movement in Islam, relocated to Chicago. Sadiq established the first Ahmadi mosque in the nation, at 4448 S. Wabash Avenue, and Chicago served as the movement's national headquarters until 1950. Four Ahmadi mosques can be found in the region today, two predominantly African American, two predominantly Indo-Pakistani. The Moorish Science movement of Noble Drew Ali held its first National Convention in Chicago in 1928, and today at least three Moorish-derived mosques can be found in the city. Elijah Muhammad's NATION OF ISLAM originated in Detroit in 1930 but soon shifted its locus to Chicago's Temple No. 2 on the South Side. The movement split a few years after Elijah Muhammad's death in 1975, with Minister Louis Farrakhan continuing the ideology of the original Nation of Islam, and Imam Warith Deen Mohammed (Elijah's son) leading his group, the American Society of Muslims, into Islamic orthodoxy. At the end of the twentieth century over 20 African American mosques could be found locally, all but two within the city limits. The most impressive opened in 1987 at 47th and Woodlawn in KENWOOD, an independent mosque named Masjid Al-Faatir, built by another of Elijah Muhammad's sons with significant financial support from boxer Muhammad Ali.

During the four decades following 1960, Muslim Chicago grew from 5 mosques, all within the city limits, to nearly 70 mosques dotting the six-county region, about two-thirds of them within the city and one-third in the suburbs. Several prayer places have also been established in occupational settings. Diversity within the local Muslim community has increased dramatically since the 1965 changes in U.S. immigration policies. Indo-Pakistanis have made a particularly notable institutional impact in recent years: over half of the region's mosques serve predominantly Indo-Pakistani constituencies, and several of these mosques are located in suburbs with income levels above the regional median. Theological diversity has also increased: Sunni, Shi'ite, and Sufi groups can all be found, representing a range of orthodox and heterodox perspectives. Special-purpose organizations have proliferated as well, including two Islamic colleges, a council of local Islamic groups, several publishing and advocacy organizations, and an Islamic think tank.

Regular prayer constitutes one of Islam's foundational pillars. Five times daily, and during communal gatherings weekly on Fridays and at the two annual Eid festivals, devout Muslims face northeast from Chicago toward the sacred city of Mecca. The ritual gives concise expression to the ideal of Muslim unity in "submission" (the literal meaning of "Islam") to Allah ("God").

Paul D. Numrich

See also: Demography; Pakistanis; Religious Institutions

Further reading: Husain, Asad, and Harold Vogelaar. "Activities of the Immigrant Muslim Communities in Chicago." In *Muslim Communities in North America,* ed. Yvonne Yazbeck Haddad and Jane Idleman Smith, 1994. • Numrich, Paul D. "Facing Northeast in a Midwestern Metropolis: The Growth of Islam and the Challenge of the Ummatic Ideal in Chicago." In *History of Religion and Urban America: A Chicago Case Study,* ed. Virginia Lieson Brereton and Mark N. Wilhelm. Forthcoming. • Turner, Richard Brent. *Islam in the African-American Experience.* 1997.

Mutual Benefit Societies. Immigrant groups that entered cities like Chicago throughout the nineteenth and early twentieth centuries formed mutual associations that served many functions in their communities. First and foremost, these societies served immigrant economic needs. Before the creation of large INSURANCE companies, mutual benefit societies offered modest risk protection. For low fees organizations like the GrecoSlavonic Brotherhood, formed in Chicago in 1885, sold policies offering benefits to families when an insured member died or was injured. The LITHUANIAN Alliance of America even offered home mortgages to its members in Chicago.

Frequently these immigrant associations grew from local organizations that had performed comparable functions back home. Before coming to this country most groups had to form voluntary associations to meet the challenges of sickness and death and even foster new forms of job and educational training. ITALIANS, SLOVAKS, CZECHS, POLES, ROMANIANS, and other groups often brought small benefit organizations with them. In the early stages of settlement in America most of these societies consisted of members from the same homeland village. In time, however, these societies nationalized their membership by blending people from different regions and towns. By the 1920s the Sons of Italy in Chicago, for example, recruited members from all regions of the homeland. Similarly, in 1921 the CROATIAN Catholic Union was created from the merger of different local groups.

Once national fraternals became established, they were forced to find creative ways to sustain and increase their membership. Sometimes they undertook campaigns to improve the public image of their ethnic group. Law-abiding leaders of the Sicilian Union in Chicago attempted to rid their organization of any identification with organized crime and improve the standing of Italian Americans in the larger society by changing the organization's name in 1925 to the Italo-American National Union. Many organized programs throughout this century to preserve a sense of ethnic heritage and identity, something these organizations felt was indispensable for keeping their membership base. Thus, they established FOLK-DANCING groups, programs on homeland culture, and foreign-language instruction.

During the GREAT DEPRESSION mutual benefit societies attempted to help their members survive hard times. The SERB National Federation felt that social activities like ethnic group dances and theatrical productions could combat the "fatalism" of the 1930s. Local branches of this organization formed a tamburitza orchestra and weekly classes for the study of Serbian traditions. They also tried to help to the extent they could with economic problems. Although the Depression eventually overwhelmed their resources, nearly all societies distributed food to the needy at their local halls. In the aftermath of WORLD WAR II, Chicago's GREEK societies raised money and foodstuffs for war-ravaged areas of their homeland.

Mutual benefit societies also acted as agents of AMERICANIZATION. The UKRAINIAN Women's Alliance in Chicago attempted to promote a more active role for women in both the ethnic and larger community during the era of WORLD WAR I. Many mutual societies formed activities centering on American sports for their younger members. By the 1930s they were heavily involved in BOWLING leagues, BASKETBALL tournaments, and gymnastic tournaments. The central Illinois Jednota BASEBALL League taught another American game to second-generation Slovaks.

John Bodnar

See also: Americanization; Clubs: Fraternal Clubs; Ethnic Music; Theater, Ethnic; Turnvereins

Further reading: Cummings, Scott. *Self-Help in Urban America.* 1980. • Higham, John, ed. *Ethnic Leadership in America.* 1978.

N

NAES College. Native American Educational Services (NAES) College was established in Chicago in 1974 to promote the use of tribal knowledge, traditions, and values in higher education of NATIVE AMERICAN students. The only independent, Native-owned and -controlled college in the country, NAES College promotes an individualized and research-oriented educational program. The college directs students toward a single degree—a bachelor of arts in public policy—that encourages community leadership and development. In addition to its Chicago campus in the WEST RIDGE neighborhood, NAES College established campuses in the Twin Cities of Minnesota, on the Menominee Reservation in Wisconsin, and on the Fort Peck Reservation in Montana. NAES College allows students to remain at home to fulfill family and community responsibilities while completing their baccalaureate degree. Despite a 10 percent Native student graduation rate in most mainstream colleges, NAES College records a 70 percent retention rate through graduation.

Robert Galler

See also: Multicentered Chicago

Naper Settlement. Naper Settlement, the only nineteenth-century outdoor historic village in metropolitan Chicago, began in 1969 as a cooperative effort between the Naperville Heritage Society, a volunteer organization committed to HISTORIC PRESERVATION, and the city of NAPERVILLE to preserve examples of that city's heritage as an agricultural village before development completely transformed Naperville into a "technoburb." The 13-acre "living village" in downtown Naperville encompasses 27 historic relocated, recreated, or restored structures, including a Gothic revival church (1864), operational blacksmith and print shops, the first HOTEL built west of Chicago, and the Martin Mitchell house (1883), deeded to the city in 1936 and for many years Naperville's historical museum. A professional staff and nine hundred volunteers provide interactive exhibits six days a week to more than 93,000 visitors per year (1998), maintain over 20,000 historical artifacts, and conduct numerous educational programs and special events.

Harold R. Wilde

See also: Chicago Studied: Social Scientists and Their City

Naperville, IL, DuPage and Will Counties, 28 miles W of the Loop. Joseph Naper is credited with founding Naperville along the DUPAGE RIVER in 1831. He drew the first plat in 1842 and was elected the president of the board when the village of Naperville was incorporated in 1857.

Early families like the Napers, Scotts, Hobsons, and Paines came primarily from the Northeast; by the 1840s they were joined by Pennsylvanians, GERMANS, ENGLISH, and SCOTS. They built at least seven churches, four of which held most services in German.

Naperville became an important stop at the crossroads of two main stage routes that ran from Chicago to Galena and to Ottawa. By 1832, 180 residents had built sawmills, gristmills, stores, and the Pre-Emption House hotel. The town became the county seat when DUPAGE COUNTY was established in 1839.

Eight Naperville businesses contributed to the development of the Southwest Plank Road, which was completed in 1851 and connected Chicago, Naperville, and OSWEGO. These businessmen then opposed a Naperville right-of-way for the Galena & Chicago Union RAILROAD when its representatives came prospecting that same year. The Galena line went through WHEATON instead. But the town got a second chance when the Chicago, Burlington & Quincy Railroad ran its line through Naperville in 1864.

Naperville's growth for the next century was tied to this easy rail connection to Chicago. In 1870, NORTH CENTRAL COLLEGE (then North Western College) relocated to Naperville from PLAINFIELD to serve the community and members of the Evangelical Association of North America. Stone QUARRIES flourished, providing building materials for Chicago, especially after the disastrous FIRE OF 1871. The Stenger BREWERY shipped beer around the region. The Kroehler Manufacturing Company, which became Naperville's largest employer, shipped FURNITURE by rail into Chicago and its all-important markets.

Naperville organized as a city in 1890 and had a population of 2,629 by 1900. Between 1890 and 1920, residents began receiving city services such as water, sewers, electricity, and telephones. Naperville grew to 12,933 by 1960.

While the suburban boom began in the near western suburbs after WORLD WAR II, Naperville remained out of the range of this growth until 1954, when plans for the East-West TOLL ROAD were announced. The route, which skirted the northern edge of Naperville and included an interchange, linked the city to downtown Chicago via the just completed Eisenhower EXPRESSWAY. As a result of this new access, residential, retail, industrial, and service industries boomed in and around Naperville. The city grew to 50 square miles in 1993, with a population of 128,358 in 2000. Among municipalities in the metropolitan area only Aurora and Chicago itself were larger.

Many of the new enterprises attracted to the Naperville area were based in research and development. During the late 1950s and 1960s, ARGONNE NATIONAL LABORATORY, Northern Illinois Gas, Amoco Research Center, AT&T Bell Laboratories, and FERMI NATIONAL ACCELERATOR LABORATORY were established in or near Naperville. Harold Moser led the residential building boom with his first SUBDIVISION in 1956. By 1995, Moser had subdivided 8,000 building lots and had built 3,500 homes in Naperville.

North Central College, now Methodist-affiliated, continues to serve the Naperville community. The NAPER SETTLEMENT, established in 1969 under the Naperville PARK DISTRICT, has transported historic structures from across the area and serves as a focal point for the Naperville community. Beginning in the early 1980s, the Riverwalk revitalized the downtown area and today provides acres of park and paths.

Ann Durkin Keating

See also: Suburbs and Cities as Dual Metropolis

Further reading: Ebner, Michael. "Technoburb: The Growth of Naperville, Illinois, from a Small Town to a Midwest Technological Center." *Inland Architect* 37.1 (January 1, 1993). • Towsley, Genevieve. *A View of Historic Naperville*. Ed. Peg Sproul. 1979. • Wehrli, Jean, and Mary Lou Wehrli. *The Naperville Sesquicentennial Photo Album, 1831–1931*. 1981.

Nation of Islam, The. After a tumultuous beginning in Detroit, Michigan, the Nation of Islam (NOI) moved its headquarters to Temple No. 2 on the SOUTH SIDE of Chicago in the early 1930s. Elijah Muhammad and his wife, Clara Muhammad, organized the best-known nationalistic religious movement among Americans of African descent in the twentieth century.

Elijah Muhammad's teachings drew elements from the Bible and the Qur'an. Muhammad also taught that Africans were the earth's original people, and that AFRICAN AMERICANS, though still oppressed by the effects of centuries of slavery, would soon be restored to freedom. He demanded that Americans of African descent should be given a state of their own to separate from the white race and its evil. To blacks he taught that they needed to clean themselves up—work hard, avoid DRUGS AND ALCOHOL, avoid GAMBLING, and so on.

By the 1940s, thousands of black Chicagoans were attracted to the message. In 1960, the national spokesperson for the NOI, Malcolm X, founded the newspaper *Mr. Muhammad Speaks* in Chicago, which in a very short time became one of the most widely read

NEWSPAPERS in black America with a circulation of more than 600,000 nationwide.

In the early 1970s Elijah Muhammad built a mini-mansion in KENWOOD and bought the former St. Constantine Greek Orthodox Church in the SOUTH SHORE neighborhood as the new site of Temple No. 2. He died in 1975 and was succeeded by his son Wallace Muhammad. As Wallace, renaming himself Warith Deen Mohammed, sought to move the organization toward Muslim orthodoxy, the old Nation splintered. Louis Farrakhan began reviving its ideology and institutions in 1978.

Aminah McCloud

See also: Civil Rights Movements; Muslims; Religion, Chicago's Influence on

Further reading: Lincoln, C. Eric. *The Black Muslims of America.* 3rd ed. 1994. • Muhammad, Elijah. *Message to the Blackman in America.* 1965. • Muhammad, Elijah. *The Fall of America.* 1973.

National Association for the Advancement of Colored People (NAACP). The Chicago branch of the National Association for the Advancement of Colored People (NAACP) was organized in 1910 as a vigilance committee within a newly formed, biracial, national organization, the Committee on the Negro. Within Progressive-era Chicago, some of the most illustrious names in reform led the poorly supported group through its first decade as it strived to secure equal rights for AFRICAN AMERICANS. External and internal difficulties, both interracial and intraracial, stymied its development for several decades.

The growth of Chicago's NAACP branch reflected the changing class structure of black Chicago in the first half of the twentieth century. During the 1920s a more activist program replaced a passive one, and innovative, militant tactics were adopted, indicating that the branch was meeting the diverse needs of an African American population differentiated along lines of class, occupation, education, racial admixture, provenance, and ideology. In its first 50 years the branch led the fight in Chicago against housing discrimination, culminating in victory in 1940 in *Hansberry v. Lee,* which declared a single neighborhood's RESTRICTIVE COVENANTS unconstitutional. By 1948, dozens of other neighborhood covenants had been invalidated as a result of a coordinated national effort. The fight against de facto school segregation followed, along with support for fair employment practices legislation. By the mid-1950s, this activism had made the Chicago branch the largest NAACP branch in the country.

At the same time, however, the branch's aggressive CIVIL RIGHTS activities threatened the hegemony of Congressman William L. Dawson, a South Side political leader, who responded by neutralizing the organization. When the modern civil rights movement of the 1960s began, the Chicago NAACP was relegated to the sidelines of the struggle. During the 1970s, 1980s, and 1990s, the organization rebounded to play a meaningful role, although not a dominant one, in local civil rights advancement.

Christopher R. Reed

See also: Contested Spaces; Open Housing; Racism, Ethnicity, and White Identity; School Desegregation; Urban League

Further reading: Reed, Christopher R. *The Chicago NAACP and the Rise of Black Professional Leadership.* 1997.

National Association of Negro Musicians. The National Association of Negro Musicians (NANM), headquartered in Chicago, is dedicated to conserving concert music traditions within the AFRICAN AMERICAN community. Founded in 1919, NANM grew from concerns on the part of black artists, critics, and patrons that communal music traditions such as the spirituals were being corrupted by VAUDEVILLE and popular recordings from the early twentieth century. The association also championed the idea of innate artistic genius within the black race, making it an important advocate of African American contributions to national life and culture during an era of scientific RACISM and public derogation of blacks. NANM provided an anchor for a national training system for black concert musicians: universities, including Tuskegee and Hampton, as well as high schools, such as Dunbar (Washington DC) and Wendell Phillips (Chicago), worked closely with the organization, while association dues and outside grants underwrote scholarships and awards for young artists. Among those receiving association support early in their careers were vocalist Marian Anderson, songwriter Billy Strayhorn, OPERA singer Leontyne Price, and pianist Joseph Joubert. NANM boasted four local chapters by the 1940s. The group has maintained branches in cities and states throughout the country, and continues to be headquartered in Chicago, with two chapters still active locally.

Adam Green

See also: Chicago Defender; Classical Music; Ethnic Music

Further reading: Center for Black Music Research, Columbia College, Chicago. • Patterson, Willis Charles. "A History of the National Association of Negro Musicians (NANM): The First Quarter Century, 1919–1943." Ph.D. diss., Wayne State University. 1993. • Southern, Eileen. *The Music of Black Americans: A History.* 1981.

National Guard. *See* Illinois National Guard

National Negro Congress. The National Negro Congress (NNC), created in 1935, attempted to build a national constituency to pressure NEW DEAL administrators for labor and CIVIL RIGHTS. Over 800 delegates, 43 percent of them from Chicago and the rest from across the nation, representing 500 different organizations, filled the Eighth Regiment Armory on the Chicago's SOUTH SIDE for the inauguration of the NNC from February 14 to 16, 1936. A large crowd gathered outside the armory to listen to the proceedings on loudspeakers, and WCFL, "The [Radio] Voice of Labor," broadcast highlights of the event over the airwaves. The sessions included discussions concerning sharecroppers, interracial organizing, women and labor, the arts, business, and the war in Ethiopia. The *Chicago Defender* accurately assessed the event as "the most ambitious effort for bringing together members of the Race on any single issue."

The Chicago Council ranked among the most active NNC chapters. Charles Burton of the BROTHERHOOD OF SLEEPING CAR PORTERS held the leadership position until 1940, when Ishmael P. Flory, a more radical labor organizer, assumed the reins. The Chicago NNC protested against discrimination in the Cook County Nursing Home, demonstrated against POLICE brutality, aided CONGRESS OF INDUSTRIAL ORGANIZATIONS campaigns to organize steel mills and packinghouses, created tenants' leagues, and campaigned for increased AFRICAN AMERICAN employment. The congress disbanded in 1947 because of COLD WAR suppression, but many of its adherents remained lifelong activists.

Erik Gellman

See also: Congress of Racial Equality (CORE); National Association for the Advancement of Colored People (NAACP); Racism, Ethnicity, and White Identity

Further reading: Bates, Beth Tompkins. *Pullman Porters and the Rise of Protest Politics in Black America, 1925–1945.* 2001. • Cayton, Horace, and George S. Mitchell. *Black Workers and the New Unions.* 1939. • Wittner, Lawrence S. "The National Negro Congress: A Reassessment." *American Quarterly* 22.4 (Winter 1970).

National-Louis University. National-Louis University encompasses three colleges: the National College of Education, the College of Arts and Sciences, and the College of Management and Business. The oldest of these is the education unit, established in 1886 by Elizabeth Harrison, a participant in the mid-nineteenth-century KINDERGARTEN MOVEMENT. Harrison set out merely to provide the mothers of her kindergarten students with early-childhood teaching strategies, but her informal lessons grew into an institution: the Chicago Kindergarten College, as it was once known. From its first home in a few rooms of the ART INSTITUTE, this college came to admit more than five thousand students over the next decade, eventually offering one of the nation's first four-year bachelor of education degrees. The college moved north to EVANSTON in

1926. A gift from trustee Michael W. Louis transformed the by-then National College of Education into a university bearing his name in 1990.

Sarah Fenton

See also: Progressive Education; Schooling for Work; Universities and Their Cities

Native American Religions. Many aspects of Native American religion prior to European contact are lost to modern scholars, but archaeological evidence has opened windows onto various practices and their meanings. During the Burial Mound or Woodland period (ca. 500 BC–AD 1000) a person impersonating the deceased apparently simultaneously also represented the earth reborn during a combined mourning ceremony and ceremony of world renewal. Many burial mounds built during the middle and later part of the Woodland period reflect knowledge of a creation story featuring an Earth Diver who secured from beneath a primordial sea the mud from which the earth was then molded. The Calumet ceremony provides a clearer example of the adaptation of a mourning rite for community benefit. In the form of the Calumet of the Captain, this ceremony served to create a kin relationship between otherwise unrelated individuals of different Indian communities when one group adopted an individual from another group to symbolically reincarnate a deceased leader of the adopting group. During the seventeenth century this ceremony was utilized to facilitate trade and political relationships with the FRENCH.

By AD 1700 many Indians of the greater Chicago area organized community-level religious activities into medicine societies along the line of the more familiar OJIBWA Midewiwin or Medicine Lodge. The purpose of these societies ranged from associations of shamanistic curers to brotherhoods seeking long life and the prospect of reincarnation for their members, but all featured mourning observances. These organizations typically traced their origins to the time of creation and to events in the life of a demiurge or subordinate creator variously known as Manabush, Wenebojo, Michabo, and other names based on the concept of a Great Hare.

Indian acceptance of Christianity proceeded rapidly among the ILLINOIS or Iliniwek, beginning with missions of the French Jesuit fathers Jacques Marquette, Claude Allouez, and Jacques Gravier to the Kaskaskias and Peorias late in the seventeenth century. By contrast, resistance to European influences is epitomized by the conservatism of those Kickapoos who left the Illinois country in the second quarter of the nineteenth century and found their way to northern Mexico, where they have maintained their native language and preserved precontact religious beliefs and practices to the present day.

Native American religions attributed spiritual qualities and mental powers to all aspects of nature, from the earth and waters to the sky and winds and to all creatures dwelling therein. Principal among these were the birdlike thunderers, panther- and serpent-like water spirits, sun, moon, morning star, earth, fire, and four winds. There was a supreme being and a hierarchy of lesser divinities spoken of as spirits rather than as gods. The supreme being often retired early from his creative activities and left the details of creation and human relations to others.

The last major Indian religious movement important in the Chicago area before the era of removal was that of Tenskwatawa, brother of the Shawnee chief Tecumseh. Between 1805 and 1813 the teachings of this "Shawnee Prophet" spread throughout the Midwest and Great Lakes area in the form of a nativistic revival in reaction to the weakening position of the local native peoples in the face of white settlement. Tenskwatawa advocated renunciation of alcohol as drink and of cattle, sheep, pigs, and wheat bread as food—all of European origin. Cloth garments and iron tools were to be replaced by clothing of skin and implements of stone or wood, as used in the past, and fires were to be made by friction of wood on wood and not by flint and steel in the European manner.

The Shawnee Prophet provided an ideological dimension to his brother's efforts at political unification of area tribes to turn back the advance of white settlers into the Old Northwest. The name of Wabokieshiek, a Winnebago Prophet of mixed SAC and Winnebago ancestry, is similarly linked to the Sauk leader Black Hawk. Like Tenskwatawa, Wabokieshiek worked toward the renascence of precontact Indian values and ways of life, but the Winnebago Prophet's influence was much more limited. The BLACK HAWK WAR of 1832 took the course it did in part because of Black Hawk's acceptance of Wabokieshiek's mistaken prophecy that the POTAWATOMI and other tribes, backed by the English in Canada, would support Black Hawk's effort to return to Sac lands in the Rock River valley lost to the Americans in the disputed St. Louis Treaty of 1804.

Robert L. Hall

See also: Chicago in the Middle Ground; Treaties

Further reading: Hall, Robert L. *An Archaeology of the Soul: North American Indian Belief and Ritual.* 1997. • Radin, Paul. *The Winnebago Tribe.* 1970. • Ritzenthaler, Robert E., and Pat Ritzenthaler. *The Woodland Indians of the Western Great Lakes.* 1991.

Native Americans. Native peoples have always resided in the Chicago region, whether as indigenous residents prior to European invasion or as urban dwellers participating in the great metropolitan expansion during the nineteenth and twentieth centuries. They represent a continuing and unique strand of human experience throughout the life of the region.

The Chicago region served as home and trade center for various Native nations, including the POTAWATOMI, MIAMI, and ILLINOIS, once powerful nations that experienced dramatic decline in the face of European expansion into their territories. Warfare and disease substantially diminished their numbers as well as their economic and military power by the early 1800s, and through a series of TREATIES they were forced to cede their lands to the American government, which then opened the land to settlement. In this way, the Native presence was significantly diminished in the region, yet never entirely eliminated. Native families and individuals lived among the new, non-Native settlements throughout the remaining years of the 1800s.

During the 1900s, many Native Americans moved from reservations and other rural communities to Chicago in pursuit of jobs and other opportunities. This movement was fueled in part by the federal government's controversial "relocation program," which helped move thousands of people to major urban areas, including Chicago, during the 1950s and 1960s.

Once in Chicago, facing an alien culture and new way of life, Native people often sought the company and social support of other Native Americans. Social clubs began to form, and in 1953 the American Indian Center was established to serve the cultural and social needs of this growing, albeit still relatively small population in comparison to other ethnic groups in the city.

The Native American population in the Chicago area was nearly 40,000 at the end of the twentieth century, representing close to one hundred different tribes from across the United States and Canada. Native people live throughout the Chicago area with the highest concentrations in EDGEWATER, UPTOWN, ROGERS PARK, and RAVENSWOOD on the city's North Side. They have formed an extensive network of organizations and programs that address a wide range of community needs and interests from health and education to employment and the arts. Many of the organizations were formed during the 1960s and 1970s when CIVIL RIGHTS and social issues stood at the forefront of public consciousness, and federal resources were made available to encourage civic engagement. Its multitribal nature makes Chicago's Native American community a richly diverse one that crosses different cultural traditions and languages. This diversity makes the community a unique place to bring people together to learn about and address issues affecting Native people nationally.

Although many families are now in their third and fourth generations of urban life, they continue to maintain ties to tribal communities where they have both extended family and formal tribal membership that provides certain rights and privileges within the tribe. Several tribal communities (Oneida, Menominee, Ho-Chunk, OJIBWA) are located in Wisconsin within a half day's drive from Chicago, enabling members of those tribes, in particular, to sustain involvement.

Louis Delgado

See also: Demography; Mesquakie (Fox); Multicentered Chicago; NAES College

Further reading: Beck, David. *The Chicago American Indian Community, 1893–1988: Annotated Bibliography and Guide to Sources in Chicago.* 1988. • Straus, Terry. *Indians of the Chicago Area.* 2nd ed. 1990.

Aerial view, Navy Pier, ca. 1920–21. Photographer: Unknown. Source: Chicago Historical Society.

Navy Pier. Located just to the north of the mouth of the CHICAGO RIVER, Navy Pier endures as a 3,000-foot-long exclamation mark in the Chicago tradition of PUBLIC WORKS.

Municipal Pier (renamed in 1927 to honor navy veterans of World War I) represented a compromise between the hopes of Daniel Burnham in his *Plan of Chicago* for two recreational piers and the city's desire for a modern harbor facility. The design by architect Charles Sumner Frost offered a little of both, with twin two-story freight and passenger sheds along with classically designed buildings at the head and foot of the pier, including an auditorium. Resting on a foundation of over 20,000 wood pilings, the pier opened in the summer of 1916 at a cost of $4.5 million.

The pier has been a jail for draft dodgers in the summer of 1918; the site of two annual Pageants of Progress (1921 and 1922); a terminus for lake excursion ships; and a convention center.

During World War II, the U.S. Navy used the pier as a training center. Afterward, the pier proved a ready facility for the UNIVERSITY OF ILLINOIS. More than 100,000 students attended classes from 1946 to 1965.

The pier was in serious decline by the early 1970s. A refurbishing for the 1976 bicentennial revived interest in the pier, and in 1989, the Metropolitan Pier and Exposition Authority oversaw a $200 million renovation. The result is much as Burnham envisioned, with the pier again a site for recreation.

Douglas Bukowski

See also: Burnham Plan; Infrastructure; Leisure; Places of Assembly; Waterfront

Further reading: Bukowski, Douglas. *Navy Pier: A Chicago Landmark.* 1996.

Near North Side, Community Area 8, 1 mile N of the Loop. The CHICAGO RIVER and LAKE MICHIGAN form three edges of the Near North Side. The different uses that Chicagoans made of these bodies of WATER divided the Near North into an expensive residential strip in the east and an industrial, low-income area in the west. A residential and commercial corridor grew up around Clark Street, serving as a buffer between the two.

Illinois Central depot and grain elevators, south of the Chicago River, north of what would, when filled with land, become Grant Park, 1858. Photographer: Alexander Hesler. Source: Chicago Historical Society.

When, in the 1830s, New Yorker William B. Ogden saw the property that his family had bought on the Near North Side of the Chicago River, he was appalled by the swampy condition of the land. Nevertheless, rapidly increasing real-estate values and the possibility of industrial development along the river induced him to buy up large tracts of land there. He gave the Chicago Dock and Canal Company control of the land where in the twentieth century the Chicago North Pier was built. Ogden increased the amount of waterfront, manufacturing land by having a canal dug across a bend in the North Branch of the river, creating Goose Island. Residential patterns followed industrial use. Although Irish factory workers settled at the juncture of the river and its North Branch, an area called Kilgubbin or the Patch, Ogden's decision to bring the city's first railroad there in 1848 drove them northward along the river. Communities of German and Swedish farmers and merchants occupied the interior of the Near North Side. Finally, members of the McCormick family established an island of wealth when they built homes in the eastern quarter of the area, near to their Reaper Works located between Pine and Sand Streets, just north of the river.

In the 1850s, Chicagoans began to recognize the appeal of lakefront land. The sandy mouth of the river was not yet suitable for permanent building, but became the site of an aptly named vice district, the Sands. Ogden and other landowners took exception to its occupation by squatters and in 1857 persuaded Mayor John Wentworth to remove them.

The Fire of 1871 did not alter existing land use, despite destroying most of the structures on the Near North Side. Rather, it was Potter and Bertha Palmer's decision to build their mansion along the future site of Lake Shore Drive that began a century-long process in which the rich took over increasing portions of the Near North Side. Fashionable Chicagoans moved from Prairie Avenue and built mansions facing the lake, spreading out along Astor Street. The enterprising George Streeter claimed that the accumulating sand around his beached boat was outside the legal limits of Illinois, so he could govern it. Although he ultimately lost his case, that section remains Streeterville. The western district, meanwhile, was growing poorer and more disreputable. The increasing industrial pollution earned it the nickname "Smokey Hollow." In the 1880s a colony of Sicilians joined the Irish there. The area had a reputation for crime, and city police so feared "Death Corner" that they refused to investigate numerous murders there.

The 1920 opening of the Michigan Avenue Bridge, inspired by the Burnham Plan of 1909, secured the eastern sector of the Near North Side for the rich. The monumental bridge fostered a luxury shopping district on North Michigan Avenue. Investors built high-rise apartment buildings and sumptuous hotels. The central portion of the Near North Side became a district of rooming houses, segregating the elite from the concentrated poverty in the west.

The years after the Great Depression saw shifts in the balance between wealth and poverty on the Near North Side. City officials tried to erode the western slum by replacing part of it with the Frances Cabrini Homes. By 1982, the high-rise Cabrini Extension and William Green Homes constituted a new neighborhood—Cabrini-Green. Deterioration spread eastward, however, and the promise of public housing in Chicago was not fulfilled.

In the 1950s, the city turned to urban renewal. It cleared and sold the central strip between Clark and LaSalle Streets to developer Arthur Rubloff for Sandburg Village. Rubloff also spearheaded the revitalization of North Michigan Avenue under the banner of "The Magnificent Mile." The success of these developments spurred the erection of more high-rise apartments and new investment in the Near North Side. In the 1980s, the River North area became a center for art galleries. The Chicago Dock and Canal Trust, still controlled by William Ogden's descendants, made riverfront property available for new residential and commercial use with the Cityfront Center development. They redesigned old warehouses into a shopping mall called North Pier and built new skyscrapers. By the mid-1990s, expensive land encircled Cabrini-Green, but its residents were poor people determined to stay in their neighborhood. Mayor Richard M. Daley and other planners called for the demolition of part of the complex and its replacement with mixed-income housing.

Amanda Seligman

See also: Merchandise Mart; Multicentered Chicago; Museum of Contemporary Art; Navy Pier; Newberry Library; Planning Chicago; Retail Geography; Street Life Tourism and Conventions; Towertown; Tunnels

Further reading: Berger, Miles L. *They Built Chicago: Entrepreneurs Who Shaped a Great City's Architecture.* 1992. • Stamper, John W. *Chicago's North Michigan Avenue: Planning and Development, 1900–1930.* 1991. • Zorbaugh, Harvey Warren. *The Gold Coast and the Slum: A Sociological Study of Chicago's Near North Side.* 1929.

Near South Side, Community Area 33, 2 miles S of the Loop. The Near South Side has probably seen as dramatic change and redevelopment as any Chicago community.

The first settlers following the removal of the Indians were Germans, Irish, and Scandinavians who worked on the Illinois & Michigan Canal and then found work in the immense lumber district along the South Branch of the Chicago River. In the 1850s, railroads entering Chicago established shops and yards nearby and attracted related industries. The city limits were extended south to 31st Street in 1853, and horsecar lines through the area spurred development.

As the business district supplanted the fine houses lining Michigan and Wabash Avenues south of Jackson Boulevard, wealthy families built new mansions on Prairie, Indiana, Calumet, and Michigan Avenues south of 16th Street. By the time of the Chicago Fire of 1871, Prairie Avenue was the city's most fashionable street. A handful of grand mansions still stand in the 1800 block, including the John J. Glessner House, designed in 1886 by architect H. H. Richardson. Further south, Michigan Avenue and South Parkway (now Martin Luther King Drive) were lined with the homes of wealthy businessmen.

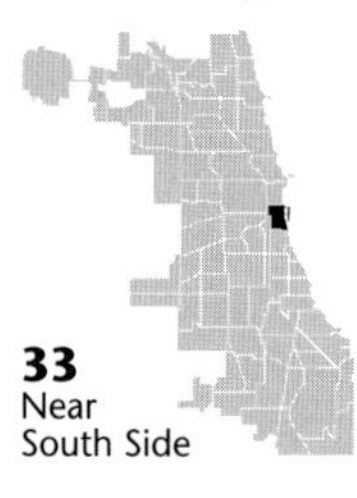

The fire spared the area, but displaced businesses found temporary quarters there, and former mansions became boardinghouses. Another large fire in 1874 destroyed Chicago's small original black neighborhood, in the South Loop, and it was reestablished west of State Street between 22nd and 31st Streets. Construction of the South Side Elevated Railroad in 1890–1892 brought rapid transit, and hotels and apartment buildings were built for the 1893 World's Columbian Exposition. As the area's character began to change, the wealthiest Chicagoans abandoned Prairie Avenue in the 1890s for the Near North Side, or moved further south, to Kenwood.

Wholesale houses, warehouses, and printing firms, displaced from the Loop, began moving to the area. A particularly dramatic transformation was Michigan Avenue between 14th and 22nd Streets. Grand houses lined the avenue at the turn of the century, but within a few years it had become "Auto Row," lined with elaborate terra cotta and plate-glass showrooms and garages.

Although the infamous "Levee" vice district around Cermak and State was officially closed in 1912, parts of the Near South Side continued to have an unsavory reputation. When black southerners began moving to Chicago in substantial numbers during and after World War I, many found housing in these low-rent areas west of State Street. As the Great Migration continued, housing discrimination confined blacks to a narrow "Black Belt" and century-old wooden houses became some of the nation's most shameful slums. The worst blocks were cleared in postwar urban renewal projects and public housing projects built in their place. At the end of the twentieth century, most of the area's residents lived in two CHICAGO HOUSING AUTHORITY complexes: the Harold Ickes Homes (1955) and the distinctive round Raymond Hilliard Center (1966).

Meanwhile, significant redevelopment projects have transformed the district's edges. During the 1920s and 1930s, Burnham Park and adjacent Northerly Island were created on landfill in Lake Michigan, and the FIELD MUSEUM OF NATURAL HISTORY, SOLDIER FIELD, the ADLER PLANETARIUM, and the John G. SHEDD AQUARIUM were built. The new landfill served as the site of the 1933–34 CENTURY OF PROGRESS EXPOSITION, and later the 1948 Railroad Fair. After WORLD WAR II, Northerly Island was offered as a site for the United Nations, then in 1947 became the site of Merrill C. Meigs Field AIRPORT, which closed in 2003.

The Railroad Fair and other trade fairs held on the site renewed interest in a permanent exposition hall, and in 1960 the first McCormick Place building opened on a controversial lakefront site at 23rd Street. When that building was destroyed by fire in 1967, pressure to rebuild quickly led to an even larger building on the same site. The complex was expanded with a second hall west of Lake Shore Drive in 1986, and a third mammoth building south of 23rd Street opened in 1997. Although some exposition-related businesses have located in the neighborhood, hoped-for HOTELS and retail revitalization had not materialized by the end of the twentieth century.

At the north end of the Near South Side, SOUTH LOOP residential development has expanded into the area. Construction began in 1988 on the second phase of DEARBORN PARK, a neighborhood built on the defunct rail yards between State and Clark Streets south of Roosevelt Road, and a decade later similar projects reached as far south as Archer Avenue. Development began in 1990 on Central Station, a mixed-use development on 72 acres of former rail yards and air rights east of Indiana Avenue between Roosevelt Road and 18th Street. Meanwhile, the success of residential loft conversions in nearby PRINTERS ROW has spread to buildings on Wabash, Michigan, and Indiana Avenues, making them residential streets again after 100 years.

Dennis McClendon

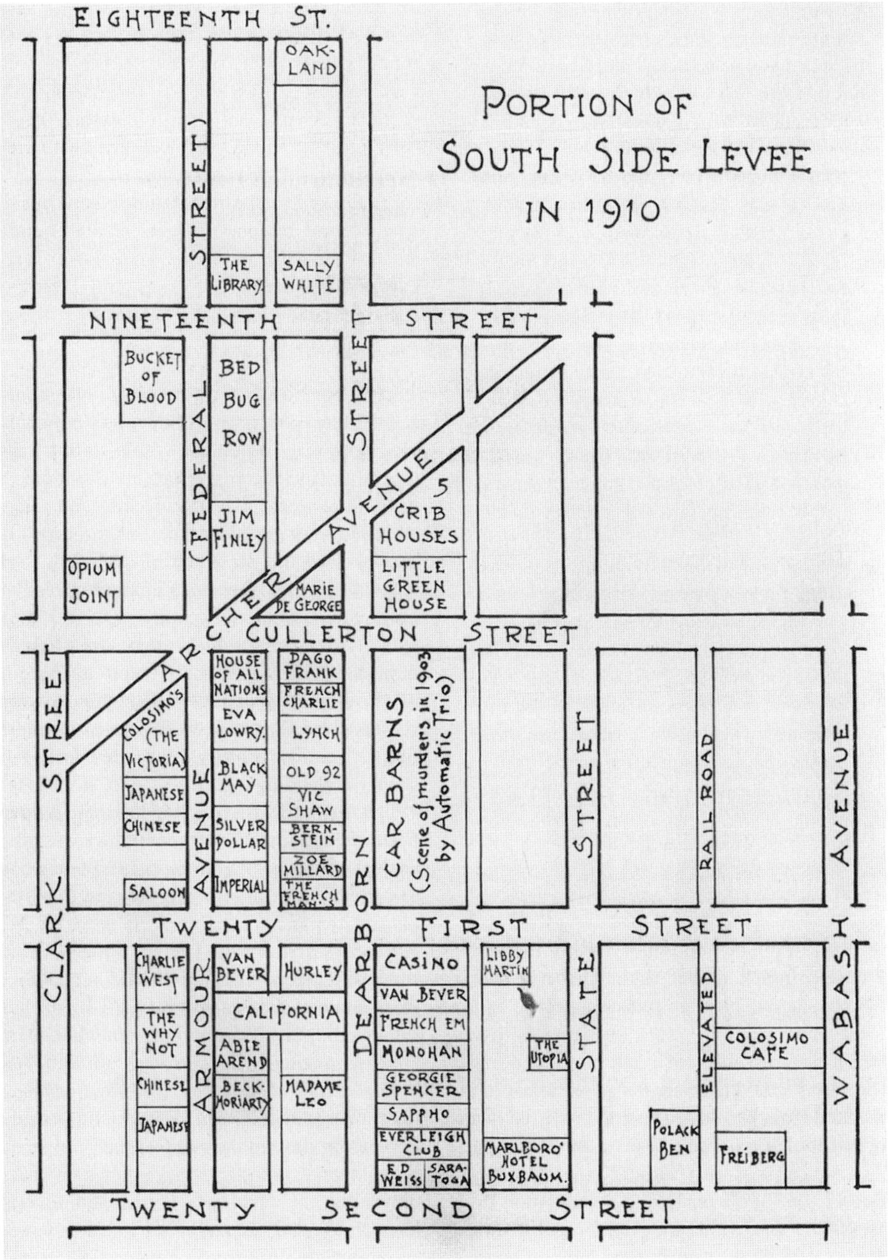

See also: African Americans; Community Areas; Contested Spaces; Multicentered Chicago; Neighborhood Change (color map, p. C4); Neighborhood Succession; Places of Assembly; Street Life

Further reading: Holt, Glen E., and Dominic A. Pacyga. *Chicago: A Historical Guide to the Neighborhoods: The Loop and South Side.* 1979. • Wille, Lois. *At Home in the Loop: How Clout and Community Built Chicago's Dearborn Park.* 1997.

PORTION OF SOUTH SIDE LEVEE IN 1910

Portion of the South Side Levee, 1910. Cartographer: Unknown. Source: Chicago Historical Society.

Near West Side, Community Area 28, 2 miles W of the Loop. The Near West Side

is bounded by the Chicago & Northwestern RAILROAD to the north, the Pennsylvania Railroad to the west, the South Branch of the CHICAGO RIVER to the east, and 16th Street at its southern edge. Between the 1840s and the early 1860s, the district was easily accessible from the Lake Street business district. At a convenient distance from the business center, the wealthy residents of Union Park sought to make the West Side an elite refuge from the daily commotion of the growing city. They created Jefferson Park (1850) and Union Park (1854) as small, safe public resorts.

By the 1870s a small middle class had gradually replaced the wealthy families around Union Park. But as early as the city's incorporation in 1837, the area already contained the seeds of what would come: residential areas divided along ethnic, economic, and racial lines. The first AFRICAN AMERICAN settlement in Chicago emerged around Lake and Kinzie streets in the 1830s. After 1837, IRISH immigrants settled in wooden cottages west of the river. The Irish were soon followed by GERMAN, CZECHS AND BOHEMIANS, and FRENCH immigrants. The section south of Harrison, bounded by Halsted on the west and 12th Street (later Roosevelt Road) on the south, would remain a port of entry for poor European immigrants. After the FIRE OF 1871, over 200,000 people took refuge on the Near

West Side, creating overcrowded conditions. Toward the end of the century, JEWS from Russia and Poland, along with Italians, replaced the Irish and Germans, with the ITALIANS settling between Polk and Taylor Streets, and the Jews southward to 16th Street. The center of the Jewish business community, the MAXWELL STREET Market, or "Jew town," came to life at the intersection of Halsted and Maxwell. A GREEK settlement known as the "Delta" developed between Harrison, Halsted, Polk, and Blue Island.

WHOLESALE trade businesses and manufacturers located on the north along an east-west axis in the 1870s and the 1880s. Lined with three and four-story buildings, many of which housed several business establishments, the area provided a dense center of employment opportunity.

In the middle of this rapidly changing area in 1889, Jane Addams and Ellen Gates Starr opened HULL HOUSE, one of the few institutions inclined to combine a policy of AMERICANIZATION with celebration of the neighborhood's ethnic diversity. African Americans were less welcome, relegated instead to the less comprehensive institutions that catered only to blacks.

Most institution building on the Near West Side emerged out of the efforts of individual ethnic groups to reconstruct cultural worlds left behind in Europe. The struggles among ethnic groups over urban space materialized in the construction and relocation of religious and educational institutions, along with the succession of SALOONS and small businesses. These tensions, sometimes marked by violence, along with economic mobility, led to an ongoing process of NEIGHBORHOOD SUCCESSION, as older groups were replaced by newcomers. Those who left sold institutions to groups who stayed behind, or to the newcomers. The home of Sacred Heart Academy (1860), for example, became the site of the Chicago Hebrew Institute (1903).

African Americans and MEXICANS moved into the Near West Side in larger numbers during the 1930s and 1940s. Approximately 26,000 African Americans lived there by 1940, with the number increasing to more than 68,000 by 1960, in part due to the "GREAT MIGRATION" of black southerners. On the West Side as a whole the African American community grew rapidly during the 1940s and 1950s, as residential opportunities remained largely limited to ghettoes on the South and West Sides. Rivalry between the two districts developed as a significant aspect of local African American neighborhood culture.

The second half of the twentieth century brought major alterations to the Near West Side. The Chicago Circle EXPRESSWAY interchange wiped out a significant section of "Greek town." The CONSTRUCTION of the UNIVERSITY OF ILLINOIS AT CHICAGO (UIC), resulted in the demolition of most of the Hull House complex, as well as the historic Italian neighborhood. Neither URBAN RENEWAL nor the construction of PUBLIC HOUSING, both of which began before 1950 and continued into the 1960s, could alleviate the poverty that had resulted from continued migration in the face of a declining economic base on the West Side. The riots after Martin Luther King's assassination in 1968 left a physical devastation on the West Side as a whole that reinforced existing images of the area as crime-ridden and bereft of hope.

Jane Addams: Halsted Street around 1890

When Jane Addams arrived in Chicago in 1889 with the intention of founding a SETTLEMENT HOUSE in one of Chicago's immigrant neighborhoods, she needed the help of Chicago reporters and businessmen to find a suitable location. Settling on a site somewhere near the junction of Blue Island Avenue, Halsted Street, and Harrison Street, Addams found a "fine old house standing well back from the street, surrounded on three sides by a broad piazza." She and Ellen Gates Starr furnished Hull House "as we would have furnished it were it in another part of the city."

Around Hull House was a neighborhood teeming with immigrants and their own institutions, like the imposing Holy Family ROMAN CATHOLIC Church just a few blocks away, built by IRISH immigrants before the FIRE OF 1871. But this was not a neighborhood of one immigrant group, and Addams understood this diversity just beyond her front porch:

> Halsted Street is thirty-two miles long, and one of the great thoroughfares of Chicago.... Hull-House once stood in the suburbs, but the city has steadily grown up around it and its site now has corners on three or four foreign colonies. Between Halsted Street and the river live about ten thousand Italians—Neapolitans, Sicilians, and Calabrians, with an occasional Lombard or Venetian. To the south on Twelfth Street are many Germans, and side streets are given over almost entirely to Polish and Russian Jews. Still farther south, these Jewish colonies merge into a huge Bohemian colony, so vast that Chicago ranks as the third Bohemian city in the world. To the northwest are many Canadian-French, clannish in spite of their long residence in America, and to the north are Irish and first-generation Americans. On the streets directly west and farther north are well-to-do English-speaking families, many of whom own their houses and have lived in the neighborhood for years; one man is still living in his old farmhouse.

Addams, Jane. *Twenty Years at Hull-House.* 1910, 77–78, 81.

University expansion toward the end of twentieth century once again reshaped the Near West Side, almost completely destroying the historical Maxwell Street Market and contributing to the gentrification that followed patterns established by other neighborhoods bordering the LOOP. With the increase in REAL-ESTATE values around UIC, and the construction of the new UNITED CENTER, parts of the Near West Side became increasingly attractive to middle-class and upper-middle-class Chicagoans interested in living near the downtown.

Myriam Pauillac

See also: Built Environment of the Chicago Region; Demography; Multicentered Chicago; Race Riots; Settlement Houses; Street Life

Further reading: Suttles, Gerald D. *The Social Order of the Slum: Ethnicity and Territory in the Inner City.* 1968. • Bryan, Mary Lynn McCree, and Allen F. Davis, eds. *100 Years at Hull-House.* 1990. • Rosen, George. *Decision-Making Chicago-Style: The Genesis of a University of Illinois Campus.* 1980.

Neighborhood Press.

See Press: Neighborhood Press

Neighborhoods.

See Community Areas; Multicentered Chicago

Neighborhood Succession.

Neighborhood succession refers to a process by which one previously dominant ethnic, racial, religious, or socioeconomic group abandons a residential area. In late-nineteenth- and early-twentieth-century Chicago, this process often involved the departure of descendants of YANKEES or early European immigrants (often ENGLISH, GERMAN, Scandinavian, and then IRISH) from neighborhoods that were then occupied by later immigrants such as Eastern and Southern European Catholics, GREEKS, or RUSSIAN and POLISH JEWS. However, for most of the twentieth century this process has been starkly defined by race.

The GREAT MIGRATION of AFRICAN AMERICANS beginning in 1916 combined with the exclusion of blacks from most neighborhoods to generate a persistent gap between the supply and demand of housing available for blacks. African Americans seeking housing became the main agents of neighborhood succession. Real-estate BLOCKBUSTERS played a significant role, as they sought to profit from white fears by encouraging black residents to settle on previously all-white blocks and then advising longtime residents to sell to avoid a supposedly impending drop in the value of their property.

Residential boundaries yielded in many cases only after contestation, often including violence. In some cases, resistant white homeowners and their allies in the REAL-ESTATE industry sought to limit change and contain black residents through the adoption of RESTRICTIVE COVENANTS. Although violence successfully maintained some boundaries, most eventually fell, especially after the Supreme Court declared restrictive covenants unenforceable in 1948. By the mid-1950s, the process of neighborhood succession was accelerating across the West and SOUTH SIDES, with whites moving steadily closer to the city's boundaries and into suburbia.

In the late twentieth century, the steady growth of the Latino population stimulated a change in the ethnic composition of some BUNGALOW BELT neighborhoods on the Southwest and Northwest Sides from white ethnic to majority or near majority Latino status, usually MEXICAN but often including PUERTO RICANS, CUBANS, and Central American groups as well.

Neighborhood succession can also involve shifts in socioeconomic class. Until the second half of the twentieth century, class change in Chicago neighborhoods was generally accompanied by a deterioration of the local housing stock. However, in recent decades, the growing phenomenon of GENTRIFICATION has transformed many once working-class areas into affluent neighborhoods.

Steven Essig

See also: Contested Spaces; Metropolitan Growth; Multicentered Chicago; Racism, Ethnicity, and White Identity

Further reading: Hirsch, Arnold R. *Making the Second Ghetto: Race and Housing in Chicago, 1940–1960.* 1983. • Jackson, Kenneth T. *Crabgrass Frontier: The Suburbanization of the United States.* 1985. • McGreevy, John T. *Parish Boundaries: The Catholic Encounter with Race in the Twentieth-Century Urban North.* 1996.

Nepalese. Estimated at approximately only two hundred individuals in the late 1990s, Chicago's Nepalese have been overshadowed by South Asian immigrants from INDIA, PAKISTAN, SRI LANKA, and BANGLADESH. While the community comprises a cross section of different ethnic groups, including Bahuns, Chhetris, and Tharus hailing from diverse areas of Nepal such as the Terai, Mid-Hills and Himalayan regions, most Nepalese in metropolitan Chicago tend to be *Newa Bhaay* (Newari)–speaking Newars from the Kathmandu valley.

Few, if any, Nepalese emigrated to the United States prior to Nepal's 1951 revolution because of the isolationist policies of Nepal's Rana oligarchy (1846–1951). Chicago's Nepalese began to arrive in the mid-1970s. Most immigrants have tended to be highly educated medical professionals, educators, and business executives. The majority of Nepalese found homes in Chicago's northern suburbs, but they have not concentrated in any particular area.

In the mid-1980s the Nepalese community began to establish a vibrant network of social, cultural, and charitable organizations. Besides celebrating cultural and religious occasions like Dasain, Tihar, and the Nepalese New Year, they have participated in local cultural events like Pacific Fest and ROGERS PARK interfaith community festivals. Nepalese Chicagoans have collaborated with the *Journal of Newar Studies* (*Newaah Vijnaana,* based in Portland, Oregon), and participated in the annual South Asian conference in Madison, Wisconsin. The community also has maintained contacts with many non-Nepalese people in Chicago who have been to Nepal as Peace Corps volunteers, nongovernment organization workers, and academics in various fields. More recently the various Nepalese associations have been active in charitable activities geared toward furthering development in Nepal. In June 1999 Chicago's Nepalese community hosted the annual meeting of the America Nepal Medical Foundation, which consists of medical professionals from the United States, Canada, and Nepal who channel volunteer personnel, medical supplies, and education materials to Nepal.

Gregory Price Grieve

See also: Demography; Multicentered Chicago

New Chicago, IN, Lake County, 29 miles SE of the Loop. Incorporated in 1908, New Chicago is part of the GARY metro area, located southeast of the intersections of I-65 and I-80/94. It numbered 2,063 residents according to the 2000 census, about 82 percent non-Hispanic white, the remainder mostly Latino.

Steven Essig

See also: Expressways; Lake County, IN

New City, Community Area 61, 5 miles SW of the Loop. University of Chicago sociologists established boundaries for COMMUNITY AREAS in the 1920s and subsequently named a large section of land around the Chicago stockyards New City. Yet the area designated as New City has never represented a single community.

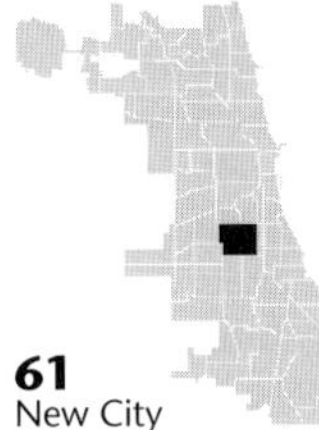

The UNION STOCK YARD opened for business on December 25, 1865, outside Chicago's city boundaries in LAKE TOWNSHIP. In 1889, this area was ANNEXED into Chicago. In its 105-year history, the stockyards and adjacent MEATPACKING district represented the key overlapping institutions for the diverse communities of New City. Although most residents worked for the stockyards or its auxiliary industries, these residents socialized in different spatial areas. Class and ethnic differences defined this area not as New City but by other separate designations; the most enduring of these appellations are the BACK OF THE YARDS and CANARYVILLE.

Inhabited by working-class immigrants, the Back of the Yards stretched to the west and south of the stockyards. IRISH and GERMAN workers moved into this area out of necessity after securing employment nearby; the lack of TRANSPORTATION gave these immigrants few alternatives to living within walking distance to the factories. During the 1880s, managers imported POLISH workers as strikebreakers. The hiring of these workers spurred an influx of Eastern European immigrants that changed the composition of the Back of the Yards. The older Irish and German working-class residents left the neighborhood by taking advantage of transportation improvements at the turn of the century. In an attempt to keep themselves ethnically segregated from the newer workers, these older residents moved to ENGLEWOOD and other neighboring districts. After WORLD WAR I, the neighborhood changed ethnic composition again due to the migration of MEXICAN American laborers into the neighborhood and AFRICAN AMERICAN workers who settled south of 49th Street. While Back of the Yards changed ethnic character over time, the working-class character of the neighborhood has remained consistent.

Settlers of Canaryville, to the east of the stockyards, worked as clerks, cattle buyers, and managers. This neighborhood began as a middle-class and largely German-based PROTESTANT community including the family of Gustavus Swift, one of the founders of the meatpacking empire. Soon after the establishment of Canaryville, lower-middle-class Irish ROMAN CATHOLICS moved into the neighborhood. While this neighborhood has also become more diverse over time, its residents still earn a higher average income than the other sections of New City.

New City reached its population apex during the 1920s, when the stockyards and other industries employed over 40,000 workers. After WORLD WAR II, the convenience of trucking routes replaced centralized train transport because butchers could purchase livestock directly from rural farms. All of the major packinghouses in New City closed between 1952 and 1962. In 1971, the stockyards followed suit. Since this time, new industry has gradually replaced the cattle-based trade. In 1984, Chicago selected these former factory sites as an urban enterprise zone. Enticed by these tax breaks, more than 100 companies moved into the area by 1991, employing over 10,000 workers.

Poor living conditions and a lack of public services made organizing a necessity and way of life for many working-class residents in New City. Despite its burgeoning population in the 1890s, few paved streets or sewers existed. The stockyards and meatpacking plants polluted without consideration of the workers who lived nearby. The tainted water supply of "Bubbly Creek" (a southern branch of the CHICAGO RIVER used to dump animal waste) and the stench of garbage heaps adjacent to the factories represented serious sanitation hazards. In response to these conditions, churches organized social services and Mary McDowell founded the University of Chicago SETTLEMENT HOUSE in 1894. In the 1930s, the organization effort became more effective and less paternalistic with the founding of the BACK OF THE YARDS NEIGHBORHOOD COUNCIL (BYNC). This organization applied community pressure on city officials to obtain school lunch programs, fluoride in its drinking water, and other badly needed services for its members. While the BYNC helped mainly white ethnics and members of the older Mexican American community area, other organizations coalesced in the 1970s to assist Latino and African American laborers. The Hispanic UNITED NEIGHBORHOOD ORGANIZATION and the African American Organization for New City have assisted New City residents with securing mortgages and home-improvement loans from banks and providing other basic social services that the older Catholic organizations provided before closing in the 1980s.

Erik Gellman

See also: Community Organizing; Economic Geography; Industrial Pollution; South Side

Further reading: Pacyga, Dominic A. "New City." In *Local Community Fact Book: Chicago Metropolitan Area, 1990,* ed. Chicago Fact Book Consortium. 1995. • Slayton, Robert A. *Back of the Yards: The Making of a Local Democracy.* 1986.

New Deal. Franklin D. Roosevelt's New Deal owed its significance to the severity of the GREAT DEPRESSION, a cataclysmic economic disaster that struck especially hard at America's large industrial cities. At the nadir of the Depression, Chicago's UNEMPLOYED numbered 700,000 people (fully 40 percent of the workforce). By 1932 the city's RELIEF expenditures reached $35 million annually, an amount supplemented by an estimated $11 million in private donations—but these totals fell far short of the need. The federal programs made available to the city created desperately needed jobs for thousands of Chicagoans, improved the INFRASTRUCTURE, and bolstered the local Democratic MACHINE.

New Deal relief agencies like the Federal Emergency Relief Administration and the Social Security Administration provided desperately needed assistance for the aged, infirm, and unemployable. Federally funded CONSTRUCTION projects put thousands of idle men and women to work and refashioned much of the cityscape: Works Progress Administration (WPA) and PUBLIC WORKS Administration expenditures resulted in the completion of Lake Shore Drive from Foster Avenue to Jackson Park, including the Outer Drive Bridge, as well as the State Street Subway. Federal government funds provided for the building of 30 new SCHOOLS and the city's first PUBLIC HOUSING projects. New Deal labor enlarged the city's antiquated municipal airport, landscaped acres of new parkland, resurfaced roads, and repaired sewers. The Home Owners Loan Corporation and the Federal Housing Administration provided emergency loans and underwrote mortgages so that increasing numbers of the middle and working classes could enjoy the benefits of homeownership. The WPA's Federal Project One provided jobs for unemployed ARTISTS, actors, musicians, and writers who met the criteria for relief.

Contrary to the belief that the New Deal helped to eliminate big-city political machines in America, much the opposite occurred in Chicago. Edward J. Kelly, who served as mayor from 1933 to 1947, immediately established himself as a fervent New Dealer who never missed an opportunity to remind voters of all the largesse secured by the city because of his good standing with the DEMOCRATIC administration in Washington. Roosevelt overlooked the graft and electoral irregularities rampant in the Cook County Democratic organization while Chicago turned out massive vote majorities for the president every four years. The New Deal's primary contribution to the Democratic machine lay in the financial windfall it provided for Kelly's administration during the hazardous Depression years. Using federal money for care of the indigent and unemployed, Kelly avoided having to cut city services or, most important, PATRONAGE rolls. At a time when a discredited REPUBLICAN PARTY could threaten the Democratic machine only in the case of the city's fiscal collapse, New Deal beneficence assured Chicago's solvency. With New Deal programs aiding an unprecedented number of AFRICAN AMERICANS and because of the Roosevelt administration's comparatively liberal record on race, Chicago's black voters (who also found much to admire in Mayor Kelly's record) switched allegiances from the Republican to the DEMOCRATIC PARTY.

Roger Biles

See also: Great Society; Kelly-Nash Machine; Political Culture

Further reading: Biles, Roger. "Edward J. Kelly: New Deal Machine Builder." In *The Mayors: The Chicago Political Tradition,* ed. Paul M. Green and Melvin G. Holli, 1987. • Biles, Roger. *Big City Boss in Depression and War: Mayor Edward J. Kelly of Chicago.* 1984. • Cohen, Lizabeth. *Making a New Deal: Industrial Workers in Chicago, 1919–1939.* 1990.

New Lenox, IL, Will County, 31 miles SW of the Loop. The village of New Lenox, like many of its neighboring communities, originated as a small AGRICULTURAL settlement along the shores of Hickory Creek, a winding tributary of the DES PLAINES RIVER southwest of Chicago.

For more than a century, POTAWATOMI and European traders and settlers had taken advantage of the waterway, and its surrounding groves and fertile lands, for food, TRANSPORTATION, and shelter. Farmers arrived in the 1830s after the federal government's forced expulsion of Potawatomi from the area.

In the 1850s, the Chicago & Rock Island RAILROAD (later the Chicago, Rock Island & Pacific) began offering service from Chicago through New Lenox to La Salle. George Gaylord, a merchant and grain dealer from LOCKPORT, laid out plans for a village at the site of the existing settlement along the rail line. Recognizing the importance of the railroad to the future of the community, residents named the village after the current superintendent of the Rock Island Railroad. Soon thereafter, however, the village adopted the name of the TOWNSHIP—New Lenox—which in turn had been named after Lenox, New York, the native home of the first township supervisor, J. Van Dusen. With the railroad as a commercial conduit, residents of New Lenox developed a strong economy based upon agricultural production, a grain elevator owned by the railroad, wagon shops, mills, blacksmiths, a hotel, and a butter factory.

As late as the 1930s, New Lenox retained its identity as an agricultural settlement. Authors of the *Federal Writers' Project Guide to 1930's Illinois* (1939) described New Lenox as a "community of small farms, poultry yards, and kitchen gardens." The guide also noted, however, the existence of small lots, owned by former urbanites who had moved out of the city and "back to the land."

Despite this suburban development and the official incorporation of the village in 1946, New Lenox remained a small community, with a population in 1950 of 1,235 people, 17 of whom were classified by the census as "rural/farm" residents. Twenty years later, Interstate 80 had been completed with an interchange near New Lenox, easing transport between the village and the surrounding metropolitan area; the population had increased to nearly 3,000, with 16 residents classified as farmers or farm laborers.

During the last decades of the twentieth century, the village's population boomed, doubling during the 1980s to 9,627, and reaching 17,771 in 2000. Although unincorporated acres of farmland surrounded New Lenox, the community thrived not as an isolated village, but as a suburb within the Chicago metropolitan region that incorporated much of WILL COUNTY.

Sarah S. Marcus

See also: Economic Geography; Expressways; Transportation

Further reading: Conzen, Michael P., Glenn M. Richard, and Carl A. Zimring, eds. *The Industrial Revolution in the Upper Illinois Valley.* 1993. • *History of Will County, Illinois.* 1878. • Sterling, Robert E. *Pictorial History of Will County.* 2 vols. 1975.

New Thought. New Thought, a mental healing cult closely related to Christian Science, first emerged in the 1870s. Its leaders promised that thought could shape reality, and that if one meditated upon a goal, that goal—be it health, spiritual enlightenment, or wealth—would be reached. This doctrine appealed to a wide range of Americans, from economically precarious white-collar workers hoping to "think" their way to success, to reformers who believed that elevated thoughts could save a nation mired in materialism and corruption.

Chicago played an early and significant role in the national growth of New Thought. By the 1880s Chicago boasted several New Thought publications and metaphysical "colleges" as well as dozens of New Thought teachers and healers. Between 1888 and 1895, the charismatic Emma Curtis Hopkins, perhaps the nation's most influential New Thought teacher, ran her New Thought SEMINARY and training school at 2019 S. Indiana. Almost every major New Thought leader came to Chicago to study with Hopkins, including Charles and Myrtle Fillmore, founders of the Unity School of Christianity. Hopkins's influential weekly column of New Thought bible studies appeared in the *Chicago Inter-Ocean.* Hopkins was admired by many of the city's most prominent FEMINISTS, including pioneering physician and publisher Alice Bunker Stockham and journalist and SUFFRAGE activist Elizabeth Boynton Harbert, and her ideas permeated the city's vibrant late-nineteenth-century feminist community.

Although New Thought reached its heyday before 1920, the movement's core ideas hold an ongoing attraction for Americans. New Thought doctrines have always appealed to people who hope to improve their social standing, and late-twentieth-century alternative healers and New Age practitioners revived interest in New Thought meditation practices. In the 1990s several Chicago-area New Thought churches continued to draw devoted adherents, including Johnnie Coleman's Universal Foundation for Better Living, the Unity Church of Chicago, the First Church of Religious Science, and the Ministry of Truth, which is devoted to the teachings of Emma Curtis Hopkins.

Beryl Satter

See also: Religion, Chicago's Influence on

Further reading: Braden, Charles S. *Spirits in Rebellion: The Rise and Development of New Thought.* 1963. • Satter, Beryl. *Each Mind a Kingdom: American Women, Sexual Purity, and the New Thought Movement, 1875–1920.* 1999.

New Zealanders. Like New Zealanders in other major urban centers of the United States, Chicago-area New Zealanders have assimilated relatively easily owing to their knowledge of English and comfortable economic status upon arrival. Thus, New Zealanders in the Chicago area do not constitute an extremely visible or residentially concentrated ethnic group, but instead have tended to be dispersed and scattered.

New Zealanders came to Chicago in significant numbers following WORLD WAR II. A handful of these postwar arrivals were war brides, women who married American servicemen stationed in the Pacific theater during World War II. Since the 1940s, most New Zealanders who have immigrated to the Chicago area have been drawn by opportunities for higher education or employment, notably in the finance, import-export, and entertainment industries. Members of the small New Zealander community estimated that approximately 40 New Zealanders were living in the Chicago area in 1999.

The New Zealand federal government has not maintained consistent representation in the Chicago area over the past 50 years, except for the positioning of an honorary consul general. This position, however, has generally been filled on a part-time basis by a figurehead, with representation of Chicago-area New Zealanders falling under the rubric of the New Zealand Embassy in Washington DC. In many cases AUSTRALIANS and New Zealanders have shared representation in one office, such as their CHAMBER OF COMMERCE, which closed in 1998 after cutbacks by the Australian federal government.

New Zealanders' primary community functions have been social. Because of their small numbers in the Chicago area, these social functions often take place in the Green Bay or Madison, Wisconsin, areas, each of which also have small New Zealander populations. Chicago's New Zealanders celebrate the founding of New Zealand on Waitangi Day (officially February 6) around the end of January (often in combination with Australia Day functions); ANZAC Day (Australian and New Zealander Army Corps Day), around April 25; and Haangi Day, an outdoor communal meal usually held in Green Bay in September.

Daniel Greene

See also: Americanization; Demography; Multicentered Chicago

Newberry Library. The Newberry Library is a privately endowed, independent research library, free and open to the public, concentrating in history and the humanities. The collections embrace Western civilization from the late Middle Ages to the end of the Napoleonic Era in Europe; from the Era of Discovery to the Age of Revolution in Latin America; and to modern times in North America. Within this framework are a variety of specialized collections, on such diverse topics as North American Indians and the history of printing.

The library was made possible by a bequest from the estate of Walter Loomis Newberry, an early Chicago pioneer involved in banking, shipping, REAL ESTATE, and other commercial ventures. Following his widow's death in 1885, Newberry estate trustees William H. Bradley and Eliphalet W. Blatchford established the library in 1887 on Chicago's NEAR NORTH SIDE and hired its first librarian, William Frederick Poole.

Poole was the dominant figure in shaping the library's noncirculating research and rare book collections and conceptualizing a facility to house them. The present building, designed by Poole and architect Henry Ives Cobb, opened in 1893 on West Walton Street.

The fifth Newberry librarian, Stanley Pargellis (1942–1962) broadened the library's mission, launching new scholarly outreach programs (e.g., fellowships, conferences, and the *Newberry Library Bulletin*) to publicize the library's holdings and encourage their use. Building on Pargellis's foundation, librarian Lawrence W. Towner (1962–1986) inaugurated

George A. Poole, a Chicago Collector

George A. Poole III, born in Chicago in 1907, attended the UNIVERSITY OF CHICAGO and graduated from Yale in 1930. He directed Poole Brothers, one of Chicago's three most important printing companies. Poole Brothers, originally a printer of transportation tickets and maps, came in these years to print *Advertising Age*, the *New England Journal of Medicine*, and many school texts.

Poole served on the boards of trustees of the NEWBERRY LIBRARY and the University of Chicago. His special interest was in fine printing, rare books, and library research collections. His own collection of rare manuscripts dating from the third to the sixteenth century was among the most notable of the mid-twentieth century. It is today at the Lilly Library at Indiana University. Among the collection's highlights is a stellar example of Carolingian script of which Poole often spoke in his later years. He also had a lifelong interest in the education of African Americans, notably in the South, where his mother's family had its origins. He was a trustee of and generous donor to Saint Augustine's College in North Carolina until his death in 1990.

Paul Saenger

Selected Chicago Daily Newspapers, English Language

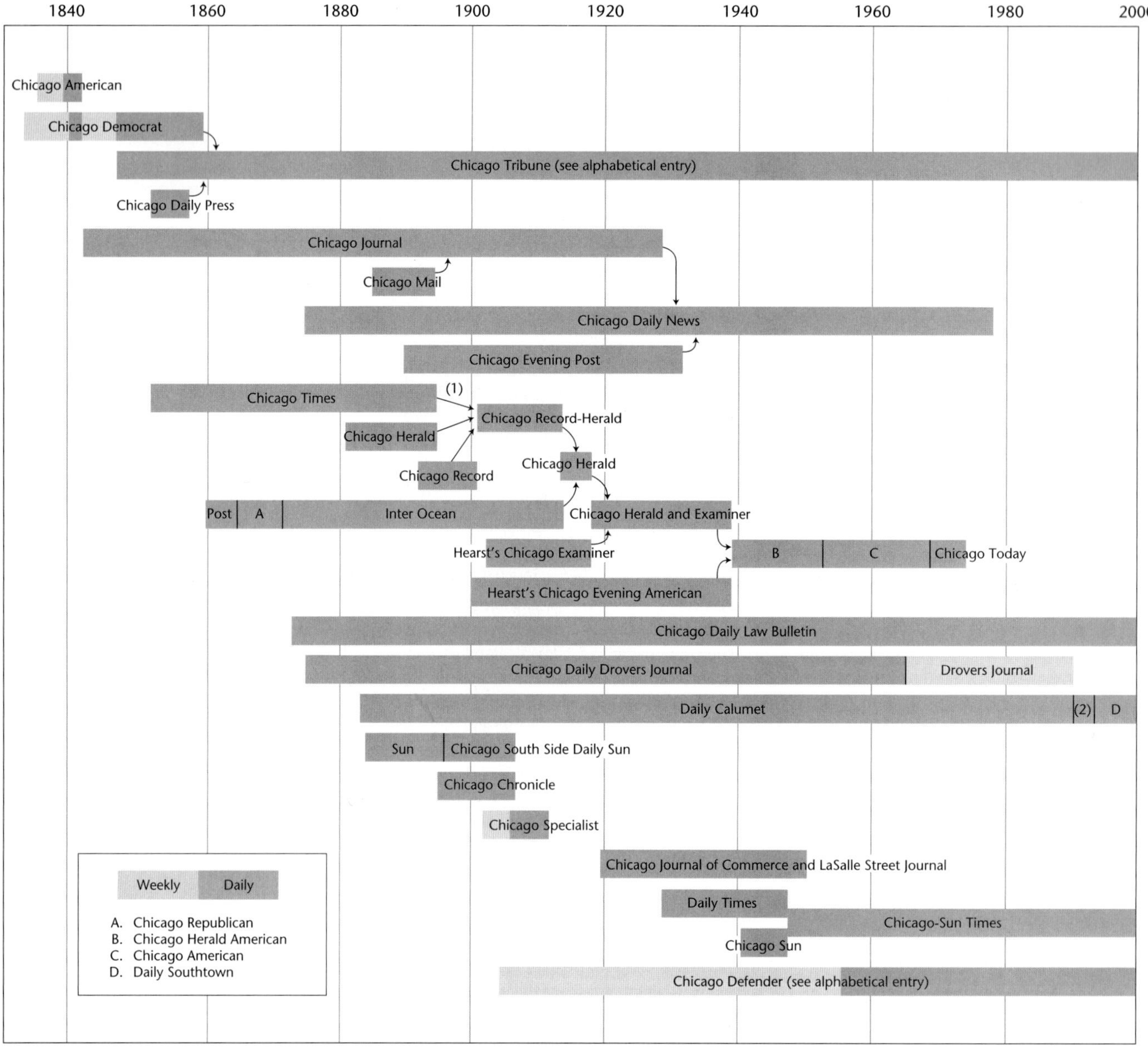

Notes:
(1) The *Chicago Times* and *Chicago Herald* merged in 1895 to form the *Chicago Times-Herald* (1895–1901).
(2) In 1990, the *Daily Calumet* became the *Southtown Economist* (1990–1993).

a series of new initiatives, including research centers in the fields of history of cartography, American Indian history, family and community history, and Renaissance studies.

The Newberry continued to widen outreach activities by establishing in 1994 its Center for Public Programs to coordinate a variety of humanities offerings, including exhibitions, seminars, lectures, and performances of the Newberry Consort.

Martha T. Briggs
Cynthia H. Peters

Further reading: Finkelman, Paul. "The Founding of the Newberry Library." *American Studies* 16 (Spring 1975): 5–22. • *A Guide to the Newberry Library Archives.* Comp. Martha T. Briggs, Alison Hinderliter, and Cynthia H. Peters. 1993.

Newspapers. Chicago's newspapers have nurtured four traditions: combative partisanship, competitive JOURNALISM, handsome design, and noteworthy reporters and writers, especially columnists. Moreover, Chicago newspapering has always been tamer than New York City's, as Rupert Murdoch learned when he unsuccessfully tried to import his New York Post sensationalism to the CHICAGO SUN-TIMES, which he owned briefly in the 1980s.

Chicago's first newspaper, the *Chicago Weekly Democrat,* was founded by John Calhoun in 1833 and bought by local politician "Long John" Wentworth three years later. It became a morning daily in 1840. Three Chicago businessmen, founded the Whig-later-REPUBLICAN morning *Chicago Daily Tribune* in 1847. Joseph Medill bought into the *Tribune* in 1855, gradually becoming its chief editorial force, gaining control in 1874, and directing it until he died in 1899.

The roots of suburban journalism in metropolitan Chicago lie in the founding of the *Juliet Courier* (later the JOLIET *Herald*) in 1939. The AURORA *Beacon* followed in 1846 and the WAUKEGAN *Gazette* in 1851.

Chicago's city newspapers grew steadily in the 1840s and 1850s, reaching 11 dailies and 22 weeklies by 1860. Although most pre–CIVIL WAR Chicago papers were short-lived, the *Chicago Journal* (1844), an afternoon Republican paper founded by J. Young Scammon, and the *Chicago Times* (1854), a morning DEMOCRATIC paper, survived the war and

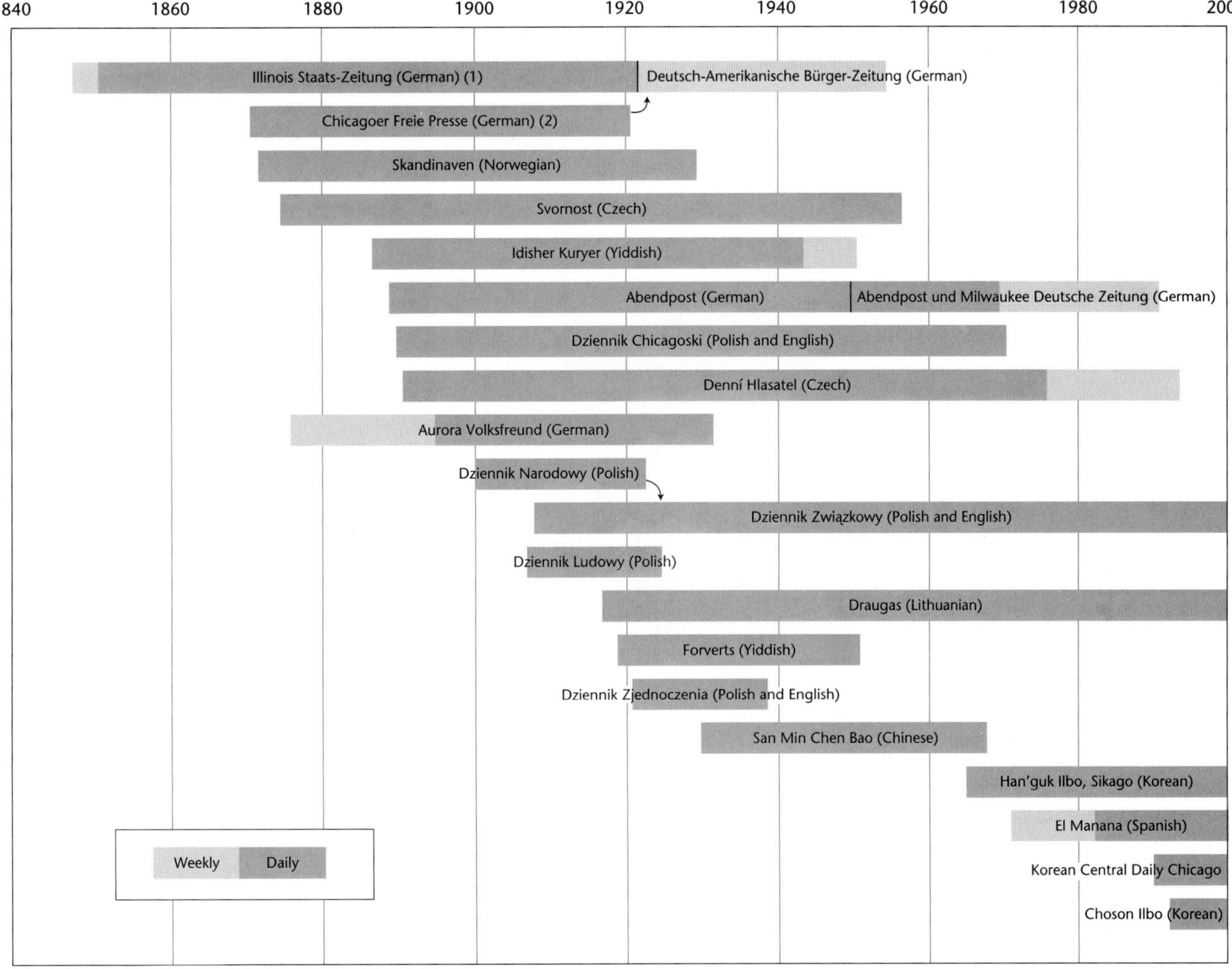

Notes:
(1) *Illinois Staats-Zeitung* published an evening edition: *Abendblatt* (German) (1891–1899).
(2) *Chicagoer Freie Presse* published an evening edition: *Abende-Presse* (German) (1896–1913).

flourished. The *Journal* became Democratic and in 1897 acquired Finley Peter Dunne's satirical Mr. Dooley columns, written in IRISH dialect.

The *Times* was sold in 1861 to Wilbur F. Storey, Chicago's most iconoclastic newspaper editor, who reasserted the paper's unpopular Democratic support for the Civil War. After the war, Storey, using the motto "to print the news and raise hell," turned the *Times* into an outspoken, eccentric reporter and critic of Chicago society. Storey edited the *Times* until his death in 1884; in 1895 the paper merged with the *Herald,* a daily founded in 1881, and became a Republican voice.

The morning *Chicago Republican* (1865), sporting the motto "Republican in everything, Independent in nothing," was edited briefly by Charles A. Dana and, in 1872, after passing the several hands, was renamed the *Chicago Inter Ocean,* an upper-class arbiter of cultural tastes. The *Inter Ocean* went into decline after 1895, when it became the property of Chicago traction boss Charles T. Yerkes, who used it as a tool in his political wars.

Melville E. Stone, believing that an evening penny paper could succeed in Chicago, founded the *Chicago Daily News,* on January 3, 1876. Although nonpartisan and specializing in bright, short news items, the paper was near death six months later, when Victor F. Lawson became its publisher and turned it around. In 1888, Stone left the paper to Lawson, who ran it with remarkable success until his death in 1925. The *Daily News* absorbed the *Journal* in 1929. A morning *Daily News,* started in 1881, was renamed the *Record* in 1893. It contained Eugene Field's humorous "Sharps and Flats" column, George Ade's "Stories of the Streets and of the Town" column, John T. McCutcheon's illustrations, and Ray Stannard Baker's stories about Chicago corruption.

In 1900, Chicago had nine general circulation newspapers when William Randolph Hearst's sensationalistic evening *Chicago American* appeared, followed by his morning *Chicago Examiner* (1902). The *American* upheld the raucous Hearstian/Chicago tradition of "The Front Page," even after it was sold to the CHICAGO TRIBUNE in 1956, renamed *Chicago Today,* and turned into a tabloid. *Today* died in 1974. The morning *Examiner* became the *Herald-Examiner* in 1918 and died in 1939, never able to overtake the *Tribune.*

The CHICAGO DEFENDER, *Tribune, Sun* and *Times,* and *Daily News* dominated twentieth-century Chicago newspapering. The weekly *Chicago Defender,* founded by Robert S. Abbott in 1905, was the nation's most powerful AFRICAN AMERICAN newspaper in its first two decades, covering RACISM sensationally, advocating rights for blacks, and offering a beacon of hope for migrants from the South. More moderate after the 1920s and more local after 1940, when John H. Sengstacke became editor, the *Defender* became a daily in 1956.

The weekly *Southtown Economist* first appeared as a SOUTH SIDE community paper in

Selected Daily Newspapers, Outside Chicago

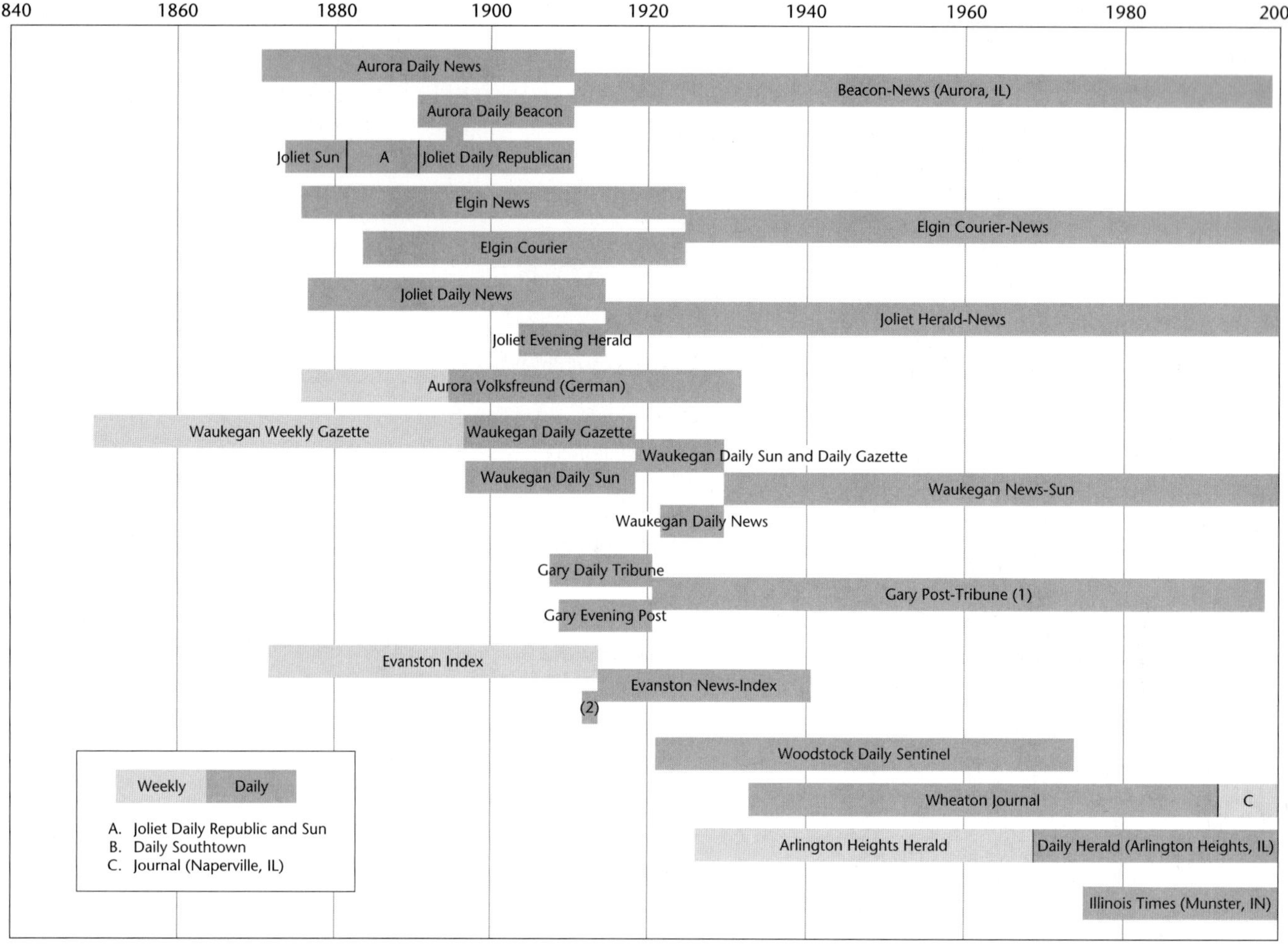

Notes:
(1) The *Gary Daily Tribune* and the *Gary Evening Post* merged in 1921 to briefly form the *Gary Evening Post and Daily Tribune* (1921–1923).
(2) The *Evanston Daily News* (1912–1914) merged with the weekly *Evanston Index* to form the *Evanston News-Index*.

1906, became a daily in 1978, was renamed the DAILY SOUTHTOWN in 1993, and in 1994 was purchased by Hollinger International, which by 2000 also owned the *Sun-Times,* the Pioneer Press (with 48 Chicago suburban papers), and the Star Newspapers (with 23 Chicago suburban papers). Meanwhile, the *Herald,* founded in Arlington Heights as a weekly in 1872, was made a daily in 1969 and in 2000 published 27 localized editions for suburban communities.

The *Tribune,* which under conservative Robert R. McCormick from 1911 to his death in 1955 dominated Chicago's morning field and the Midwest, was a pioneer in four-color printing. Sportswriter Ring Lardner wrote the *Tribune*'s "In the Wake of the News" column from 1913 to 1919; Bert Leston Taylor created and presided over the *Tribune*'s "Line o' Type or Two" from 1910 until his death in 1921.

Meanwhile, a second *Chicago Times* (1929) built Chicago's best news staff during its two decades. As WORLD WAR II approached, Marshall Field III founded the *Chicago Sun,* a NEW DEAL morning alternative to the isolationist *Tribune.* In 1947 the *Sun* acquired the *Times*'s news staff and presses, creating the tabloid *Sun-Times* in 1948.

The *Daily News*'s foreign news service began in 1898, carrying such noted interwar correspondents as Edward Price Bell, Paul Scott Mowrer, and Edgar Ansel Mowrer. The *Daily News*'s staff included reporter and critic Carl Sandburg and columnists Ben Hecht (1914 to 1922) and Mike Royko (1964 to 1978). When the *Daily News* died in 1978, Royko moved to the *Daily News*'s sister paper, the *Sun-Times.* He joined the *Tribune* in 1984, protesting Rupert Murdoch's purchase of the *Sun-Times.*

Richard A. Schwarzlose

See also: Political Culture; Politics; Press: Neighborhood Press; Press: Suburban Press

Further reading: Abbot, Willis J. "Chicago Newspapers and Their Makers." *Review of Reviews* 11 (June 1895): 646–665. • Murray, George. *Madhouse on Madison Street.* 1965. • Wendt, Lloyd. *Chicago Tribune: The Rise of a Great American Newspaper.* 1979.

Nicaraguans. Nicaraguan laborers probably trickled into Chicago along with MEXICANS and other Latin Americans in the 1940s. By the late 1950s, Chicago Nicaraguans and their consulate had established the Sociedad Civica Nicaraguense, which organized dances and social events for the small Nicaraguan population scattered across the city. Small numbers of students, doctors, and other professionals arrived in the 1960s and 1970s.

Events in Nicaragua in the 1970s and 1980s prompted the major influx of Nicaraguan immigrants to Chicago. In 1972, an earthquake destroyed Managua, exacerbating the already severe poverty among much of the country's rising population. In 1979, the Marxist Sandinistas overthrew Anastasio Somoza's government, sending him and many of his supporters into exile, and touching off an 11-year civil war between the Sandinista government and the anti-Communist Contras. Thousands of immigrants fled to America, through both documented (legal residency and political asylum) and undocumented channels, so it is difficult to know how many came to Chicago. Community estimates range in the low thousands. In 1997, the Nicaraguan Adjustment and Central

Newsboys were a common sight on Chicago's streets as Chicago's newspapers competed with each other for headlines and readers. Here, a newsboy sells the *Chicago Defender* near the Supreme Liberty Life insurance Building at 3501 South Parkway (later Martin Luther King Drive), March 1942. Photographer: Jack Delano. Source: Library of Congress.

American Relief Act allowed many undocumented immigrants from this period to gain lawful permanent resident status.

From the start of the conflicts in Nicaragua, the Chicago community divided sharply along political lines, and political activism provided the impetus for many community organizations. In 1976, anti-Somoza activists organized the Reconstruction Committee to support the revolutionary movement. In 1979, they formed Casa Nicaragua, a nonprofit organization which supported the Sandinista government. The group undertook staged rallies and presentations at churches and universities throughout the city, and published a newspaper (*El Pujil*) focusing on Nicaraguan issues. In 1979, the Chicago branch of the Nicaraguan Solidarity Committee organized to influence U.S. foreign policy in Nicaragua. In 1981, Nicaraguans in Chicago formed a local chapter of the "Pastor for Peace" movement, which protested against the U.S. embargo against Nicaragua and U.S. support for the Contras. The numerous pro-Somoza Nicaraguans, including both newcomers and many earlier immigrants, were less active in formal political organizations, although some of them found allies among the anti-Castro Cuban immigrants in Chicago.

Despite these strong divisions, some Nicaraguans put politics aside. In 1979 Sandinista and Somoza sympathizers cooperated to form a humanitarian organization, Mercy Donations for Nicaraguans, to send aid to refugees in Costa Rica. In the 1980s, the nonpolitical Nicaraguan Civic Society was founded as a member of the Central American Civic Society, an umbrella organization bringing together all of Chicago's Central American ethnic groups.

The Nicaraguan community's political divisions also receded in 1998, when Hurricane Mitch devastated the homeland. Nicaraguans of all political persuasions in Chicago united to raise funds and send aid to Nicaragua. Significantly, as a result of the hurricane, the United States in 1998 granted Temporary Protected Status to all Nicaraguan citizens in the United States without legal status, eliminating fear of deportation for undocumented immigrants.

Chicago's Nicaraguan community has for many years preserved its heritage with Independence Day (September 15) celebrations and annual summer picnics, where folk traditions such as *La Gigantona* have been preserved. The annual Nicaraguan religious holiday of *La Purísima*, celebrated each year at Queen of Angels in Ravenswood, has also been a major event.

Nicaraguans have settled throughout the city, largely in Hispanic neighborhoods. Community leaders identify substantial concentrations in suburbs like Schiller Park and Des Plaines, as well as on the South Side from 37th to 47th Streets, between Kedzie and Pulaski. The 2000 census counted 778 Nicaraguans in the city of Chicago and 1,465 in the metropolitan area. Given the number of undocumented immigrants from Nicaragua, however, community leaders estimated the population at anywhere from 2,000 to 6,000.

Robert Morrissey

See also: Cold War and Anti-Communism; Demography; Guatemalans; Multicentered Chicago; Refugees; Salvadorans

Nigerians. Chicago's 30,000 Nigerians constitute Chicago's largest African community. The first major influx of Nigerians to the Chicago area, and to the United States in general, occurred immediately preceding the outbreak of Nigeria's Biafran War, which lasted from 1967 to 1970. The Chicago Biafran refugee community raised money for relief supplies for the Biafran state, including medical supplies, food, and clothing. Many of the Biafran refugees who were eventually granted political-refugee status in the United States went on to settle in the Chicago area. Chicago's Nigerians have been an active and well-organized community ever since.

With the development of oil reserves in southeastern Nigeria throughout the 1960s and 1970s, an increasing number of Nigerian students found their way to American universities. After the war in Biafra ended, a period of considerable prosperity prompted the Nigerian government to fund scholarships for such students. At the same time, a series of military coups, interspersed with brief periods of civilian rule, generated a large population of expatriate Nigerian professionals, especially doctors, lawyers, and academics, who found it difficult to reenter Nigeria.

Nigerians shared something with Ghanaians that made integration into the American economy unusually smooth: the ability to speak English. Like immigrants from a variety of other countries, many Nigerians found initial work in transportation, often as taxicab drivers. A substantial number of these drivers went on to purchase their own "medallions," enabling them to go into BUSINESS for themselves.

Nigerian businesses and residents have concentrated mainly on the North Side. The number and variety of fruit markets and small stores on Broadway that carry large quantities of African foods indicate the Nigerian community's buying power. Such staples as *gari* (cassava flour), palm oil, dried fish, *egusi* (melon seeds), and yams can be found in many markets. More than just a place to shop, such markets also provide a place for new arrivals to make acquaintances. Little by little, these stores have been joined by other businesses, from law offices to INSURANCE agencies.

Religious diversity has been crucial to Chicago's Nigerian community, with a Nigerian Islamic Center on the North Side and Nigerian clergymen representing both ROMAN CATHOLIC and PROTESTANT denominations. Several of the city's churches have strong Nigerian representation, including the Faith Tabernacle Church on Grace and Broadway, and the Nigerian mass at Our Lady of Lourdes Parish.

Chicago's Nigerian community is particularly notable for its attempts to influence Nigerian politics. The crackdowns of the military regime in Nigeria during the 1990s limited the freedom of Nigeria's internal press, leading to an even greater expansion of Nigerian publications based in the Americas and Europe. Distance and security of life in Chicago have provided an outlet for an ongoing commentary on Nigerian affairs that would be difficult to conduct from within the country itself. Since 1990 alone, Nigerians in Chicago have published half a dozen periodicals, some of which remained in circulation at the end of the decade. In May 1995, representatives from Chicago met with representatives of other Nigerian communities in the first Nigerian–North American Conference.

Nigerians have influenced Chicago POLITICS as well. While much of the city's AFRICAN AMERICAN community came to the city during the GREAT MIGRATION of the mid-twentieth century, the arrival of immigrants from Nigeria and other African nations during the last 50 years has brought a new cultural dimension to the city. The Nigeria Festival Chicago is held every summer at the DUSABLE MUSEUM of African American History. Combined with similar patterns of immigration from the Caribbean and Latin America, the African presence has created within Chicago's black community a diversity comparable to that of the city's earlier European immigrants.

Charles Adams Cogan
Cyril Ibe

See also: Americanization; Demography; Foodways; Multicentered Chicago; Muslims

Further reading: Ugwu-Oju, Dympna. *What Will My Mother Say? A Tribal African Girl Comes of Age in America.* 1995.

Nightclubs. Chicago nightlife grew rapidly in the wake of the 1871 fire and then again in conjunction with the 1893 WORLD'S COLUMBIAN EXPOSITION. During this period the ragtime dance craze attracted exposition patrons to the entertainment area on the NEAR SOUTH SIDE. This infamous district, known as the Levee, was shut down in 1914 during MAYOR Harrison's reform administration, and nightlife establishments moved out into other areas of the city. Since the early decades of the twentieth century, nightclubs have been concentrated in three areas: the LOOP (on Randolph Street), the NEAR NORTH SIDE (on Rush Street), and the SOUTH SIDE (at State Street and Garfield Boulevard).

Beginning in the 1920s and 1930s, Loop HOTELS housed nightclubs catering to a general audience and featuring dancing to big bands, floor shows, and live radio BROADCASTS These included the Stevens Hotel's Boulevard Room, the Palmer House Hotel's Empire Room, and the Sherman Hotel's College Inn–Panther Room. Also located in or near the Loop were freestanding nightclubs such as Friar's Inn (343 South Wabash), the Blackhawk Restaurant (139 North Wabash), and Chez Paree (610 Fairbanks Court).

Located at State Street near Garfield Boulevard on the South Side, the Club DeLisa was the largest and most important nightclub in the AFRICAN AMERICAN community from the 1930s through the 1950s. At the Club DeLisa, Chicagoans could hear performers such as Count Basie and Joe Williams.

Opening in 1907 on the far North Side, the Green Mill (4802 North Broadway) remains the longest continuously operating nightclub in Chicago. Performers such as singer/comedian Joe E. Lewis and vocalists Ruth Etting, Billie Holiday, and Anita O'Day appeared there in the early stages of their careers.

One of the most exotic and colorful suburban nightclubs was the Villa Venice (2855 Milwaukee Road) in WHEELING. Its mobster clientele favored Parisian-style reviews with nude chorus lines, but they also supported appearances by JAZZ artists such as Eddie South and Milt Hinton.

In the western suburb of LYONS, Mangam's Chateau (7850 Ogden Avenue) offered popular entertainment with an outdoor dancing and dinner package.

In the southwest suburb of EVERGREEN PARK, the Martinique (2500 West 95th Street) was a popular restaurant and floor show venue for the far South Side.

Richard A. Wang

See also: Entertaining Chicagoans; Music Clubs

Further reading: Brubaker, Robert L. *Making Music Chicago Style.* 1985. • Kernfeld, Barry, ed. *The New Grove Dictionary of Jazz,* vol. 2. 1988. • Reich, Howard. "Hotter Near the Lake." *Chicago Tribune Magazine,* September 5, 1993.

Niles, IL, Cook County, 13 miles NW of Loop. In the early 1830s, GERMAN farmers flocked to the area around present-day Waukegan Road and Milwaukee Avenue, which came to be known as Dutchman's Point. John Schadiger and Julius Perren were the first, building an unusual house that had no windows and a single door. In 1837 John Marshall and Benjamin Hall erected the North Branch HOTEL, and the following year residents established the area's first schoolhouse.

By 1850 the North West Plank Road, later Milwaukee Avenue, allowed farmers to travel more easily to the markets of downtown Chicago. The TOWNSHIP of Niles formed in 1850; by 1884 the town, centered at Milwaukee, Waukegan, and Touhy Avenues, consisted of two stores, two HOTELS, one drugstore, three churches, three CEMETERIES, two SCHOOLS, and one doctor's office. In 1899, at the time of the village's incorporation, population was 500. The name of Niles was probably taken from the nationally distributed *Niles Register* newspaper.

After the turn of the century the Chicago Surface Lines STREET RAILWAY traveled down the middle of Milwaukee Avenue to Niles, bringing immigrants from Chicago. In the 1930s Niles's population of 2,135 included 800 POLISH orphans in St. Hedwig's ORPHANAGE.

In 1932 industrialist and inventor Robert Ilg constructed a recreational park for his employees. Although the Ilg Hot Air Electric Ventilating Company, later Ilg Industries, was located in Chicago, Ilg lived in Niles. He installed two SWIMMING pools and a water tower which he hid behind a half-size replica of Italy's Leaning Tower of Pisa. In 1960 the Ilg family turned over part of the park property to the Leaning Tower YOUNG MEN'S CHRISTIAN ASSOCIATION. The tower has since been restored and is a symbol of the community. In 1991 Niles and Pisa became sister cities.

Covering six square miles, Niles has no official downtown area, but considers Milwaukee Avenue its commercial center. In the 1950s the village ANNEXED an area at the northwest corner of the village, and construction of a commercial complex began soon afterward. The Golf Mill SHOPPING Center was dedicated in 1959. In 1989 approximately 1,100 businesses were active in the village, generating over $7 million in taxes.

Niles's population totaled 30,068 in 2000; 83 percent were white, 34 percent were foreign-born; 13 percent were Asian. More than a quarter were 64 or older. The only Chicago suburb to offer free BUS service to major shopping and recreational facilities, Niles transports more than 350,000 commuters annually. Residents have access to extensive services, ranging from senior citizen centers to six hundred park district programs to counseling services.

Marilyn Elizabeth Perry

See also: Cook County; Economic Geography; Metropolitan Growth

Further reading: Tyse, Dorothy C. *History of Niles, Illinois.* 1974.

Nommo. The Bantu term *nommo* denotes the magical power of words to cause change, which was the purpose of *Nommo,* the journal of the Organization of Black American Culture (OBAC) Writer's Workshop. Founded in 1967 amidst artistic and social ferment, OBAC sought to create a forum for black ARTISTS, writers, and critics. The literary journal that emerged developed within a shared set of ideals, concerns, and communal values, as *Nommo* gave form and substance to a new revolutionary black aesthetic. Nearly every 1960s black Chicago poet also wrote prose, and felt compelled to address issues, to take a stand.

Led by seminal critic and thinker Hoyt W. Fuller, artists and writers such as Johari Amini, Carolyn Rodgers, Jamila-Ra, Jeff Donaldson, Randson Boykin, Walter Bradford, and others came together with the younger generation, including Nora Brooks Blakely, daughter of acclaimed poet Gwendolyn Brooks. Brooks herself lent her considerable literary resources and prestige to the group, and several figures later attracted national attention, including poets Sterling Plumpp, playwright Sandra Jackson-Opoku, and Haki Madhubuti (Don L. Lee), founder of the Third World Press. Meeting first in the historic SOUTH SIDE Community Art Center and the DUSABLE MUSEUM, OBAC later settled into a home in the Abraham Lincoln Center. *Nommo,* like the CIVIL RIGHTS MOVEMENT, flourished throughout the next decade, bringing major figures like Amiri Baraka (LeRoi Jones) to Chicago as advisors. The Reagan years saw the waning of black artistic collectives throughout the United States, and Chicago was no exception, as *Nommo* closed its doors in 1987. An offshoot, Third World Press, continues to flourish, carrying on a rich legacy of bringing new and established AFRICAN AMERICAN writers to the public.

Ronne Hartfield

See also: Chicago Black Renaissance; Literary Cultures; Multicentered Chicago; Poetry

Further reading: Andrews, William, Frances Foster, and Trudier Harris, eds. *The Oxford Companion to African-American Literature.* 1997. • Gates, Henry Louis, Jr., and Nellie McKay, eds. *The Norton Anthology of African-American Literature.* 1997. • Parks, Carole A., ed. *Nommo: A Literary Legacy of Black Chicago (1967–1987).* 1989.

Norridge, IL, 15 miles NW of the Loop. Norridge shares 70 percent of its border with Chicago, but prefers not to be identified with the city that nearly annexed it in 1948. Its name is derived from the names of neighboring areas NORWOOD PARK and PARK RIDGE.

Farmers who bought acreage in the area in the 1830s built their cabins on scattered sites. The area was once called "Goat Village" because of a woman who raised goats in the eastern portion of town. Many called it the "Swamp" because of the muddy conditions and unpaved streets.

During the 1920s development was planned for an 80-acre SUBDIVISION from Ozanam to Olcott and Irving Park to Montrose. Residents SHOPPED in neighboring DUNNING until 1932, when a commercial strip was established along Irving Park Road.

In 1948 Norridge was about to be annexed to Chicago when a local improvement association moved to incorporate as a village, stymieing Chicago's efforts at ANNEXATION. The 1950s ushered in an era of growth and development, encouraged by the construction of a waterworks system, the paving of sidewalks, streets, and curbs, and the installation of storm and sanitary sewers.

In 1954 Norridge annexed land north from Montrose to Lawrence, and farms disappeared quickly. The same year the Norridge Youth Committee was established to promote athletic and social events. The Norridge Community PARK DISTRICT was established after the village purchased 22 acres between Wilson and Lawrence Avenues. The village grew from one-half square mile in 1949 to two square miles in 1958. Many new residents, predominately of ITALIAN and POLISH extraction, came from Chicago neighborhoods.

The Harlem-Irving Plaza brought in sales tax that led to decreased property taxes. Begun in 1955 with 45 stores, the center had 140 stores by the 1990s.

Although often compared to HARWOOD HEIGHTS because of their similar histories and their look-alike BUNGALOW and ranch houses, Norridge has more shopping and industry than its neighbor. Residents in the 1990s were still mainly of Polish and Italian heritage. The 2000 census counted 14,582 people, nearly 95 percent white, with small but growing Asian and Hispanic populations.

Marilyn Elizabeth Perry

See also: Governing the Metropolis; Infrastructure

Further reading: McGowen, Thomas. *Island within a City: A History of the Norridge–Harwood Heights Area.* 1989. • Mussen, Craig. "The History and Origin of Norridge, Illinois." Manuscript. 1979. Eisenhower Public Library, Harwood Heights, IL.

North Aurora, IL, Kane county, 36 miles W of the Loop. North Aurora is located on the FOX RIVER where it intersects with Interstate 88. In the early years four miles separated AURORA from North Aurora; they now abut each other. From the earliest days settlement straddled the river. The postal stop was known as "Schneider's Mills" until 1868, when it was officially designated "North Aurora"; the town was incorporated in 1905.

JohnPeter Schneider, a native of Frankfurt-on-the-Rhine, arrived in 1834, followed by other settlers attracted by the rich countryside with its river, woods, and farmland. The river provided water power, the woods lumber, and the land crops. Known as the "Big Woods" in the 1830s, the area provided lumber for numerous Fox River communities. The woods were quickly decimated, but not before Schneider had built a sawmill which established the settlement's economic foundation. In 1862 he added a grist mill. Around the same time, the North Aurora Manufacturing Company built a sash, door, and blind factory, then in 1874 a foundry. By 1875 a creamery was established, with cream cheese shipping as far as England.

This development related closely to the evolution of local transportation networks. Railroads passed through town in the 1850s, creating job opportunities and linking North Aurora's industries and commuters with the metro area. Early in the 1900s INTERURBAN rail lines connected North Aurora with communities up and down the Fox River valley, creating additional social, economic, and educational links. Since North Aurora had only one church until 1960, few stores and no public high school, worshippers, shoppers, and students alike relied on the interurbans, and later buses and cars, to reach congregations, shops, and schools in nearby towns.

Seeking managed growth, North Aurora updated its comprehensive plan twice in the 1990s to address its needs as a growing community and as part of an expanding region. In 1996, Oberweis Dairy relocated to North Aurora from Aurora to accommodate an ever-growing regional customer base. And coming full circle, North Aurora again supplied trees to the region—now from Marmion Military Academy's Christmas tree nursery.

Sherry Meyer

See also: Economic Geography; Lumber; Transportation

Further reading: *Combination Atlas of Kane County and 1871 Atlas and History of Kane County, Illinois.* 1872. • *Commemorative Biographical and Historical Record of Kane County, Illinois,* vol. 2. 1888. • Wiederman, Darrel, ed. *Schneider's Mill, North Aurora, 1834–1984.* 1984.

North Barrington, IL, Lake County, 34 miles NW of the Loop. At the end of the 1800s, the village of BARRINGTON served as a trading center for dairy farmers, whose herds roamed the oak-covered hills and marshlands north of the village. The marshlands prevented the spread of development that was occurring west of Barrington until the advent of hard-surfaced roads following World War I.

As estate development moved north of Barrington in the 1920s, dairy farming faded. In 1926 a SUBDIVISION including a private country club, the Biltmore, was developed. Believing that the subdivision was too densely populated, estate residents formed the North Barrington Association in 1934 to preserve the area's rural country atmosphere.

The GREAT DEPRESSION and WORLD WAR II halted development to the north of Barrington until the early 1950s. By then, the governments of Cuba Township (in which most of the North Barrington Association resided) and LAKE COUNTY began thinking of allowing home construction on half-acre lots. Residents heard that developments of such density were planned for nearby Indian Lake, renamed LAKE BARRINGTON by a developer. To the east, LAKE ZURICH, supporting high-density ZONING, was expanding west of Rand Road (U.S. Route 12) toward the Biltmore Country Club. To gain local control of zoning in order to stave off such development, which they believed would destroy the area's rural charm and decrease property values, North Barrington Association residents voted to incorporate. Incorporation was accomplished on October 31, 1959, the same day that Lake Barrington incorporated with a denser zoning plan. Richard Anderson became the first president of North Barrington.

For a time the Biltmore development was not a part of North Barrington, but after a struggle the club, with its somewhat higher population density, was annexed. Even then, in 1970 only 1,411 people were living in the village. By 1980, while other area communities experienced massive growth, North Barrington grew to just 1,475 residents.

As Lake Zurich expanded, North Barrington, to protect its low-density properties, annexed lands to the east called Wynstone. In 1985, W. Clement Stone presented a plan to turn 370 acres of that ANNEXATION into an exclusive GOLF course and residential area designed by the Jack Nicklaus Development Corporation. The plan was accepted as a buttress against expansion by Lake Zurich, and the residential portion quickly filled with expensive homes.

By the end of the century North Barrington contained about 2,500 residents on 2,950 acres. Because such low density provided a tax base for only minimal municipal services, North Barrington contracted out for POLICE, FIRE, and road services. An attempt was made to expand the completely residential tax base by approving an upscale shopping mall within the village east of Rand Road north of Lake Zurich, but opposition from long-term residents quickly developed and the plan was put on hold. Residents also struggled with the issue of the placement of cellular TELEPHONE towers in and around the community. The leadership of North Barrington continues to search for a balance between low-density rural charm and the need for revenue to provide basic municipal services.

Craig L. Pfannkuche

See also: Government, Suburban; Metropolitan Growth

Further reading: *The Founding of North Barrington.* Videocassette. North Barrington Village Hall. May 4, 1996. • Handley, John. "A Tale of Two Country Clubs." *Chicago Tribune,* April 30, 1994. • *The Village of North Barrington.* Pamphlet. N.d.

North Center, Community Area 5, 5 miles N of the Loop. Bounded on the west by the North Branch of the CHICAGO RIVER, North Center developed after industrialists' attention turned from the South Branch to the North Branch and working men and women began to settle near North Center's new factories and brickyards.

In the 1840s, John H. Kinzie and William B. Ogden owned most of the property in the North Center area. After trying unsuccessfully to market a few residential SUBDIVISIONS near the North Western Railway's stops, Ogden sold a large tract to John Turner, who moved out to a large farmhouse there after the FIRE OF 1871. Turner rented scattered, smaller tracts to GERMAN truck farmers. Most of the North Center area, however, remained uncultivated and undeveloped until the late nineteenth century.

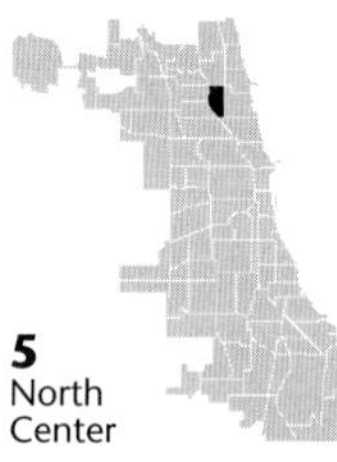

During the last quarter of the nineteenth century, Chicago's industrialists realized the potential of the river's North Branch. In 1880, the Deering Harvester Works opened at Fullerton Avenue and eventually expanded to encompass land in the North Center area. In the wake of the FIRE OF 1871, concern over the flammability of wood intensified the demand for brick buildings in Chicago. As the riverbanks yielded more and more suitable clay, brickyards and clay pits dotted the North Branch, earning the area the nickname "Bricktown." These industries provided work for skilled and unskilled laborers, who moved into the area to avoid the cost of TRANSPORTATION to their jobs. Early in the twentieth century, Ravenswood Avenue, which marks North Center's eastern border, became a light industrial corridor. Initially Germans and SWEDES, and later Kashubes, POLES, ITALIANS, HUNGARIANS, SLOVAKS, SERBS, and CROATIANS, working-class migrants set the unpretentious tone of North Center's residential areas—a striking contrast to the massive church complexes.

The last truck farmers did not give up farming until the first decade of the twentieth century, but in the 1890s the tie between WORK and residence in North Center began to break. New STREET RAILWAY lines and the opening of the Ravenswood "L" prompted a boom in residential development as far as Western Avenue. The combination of transportation and affordable homes enabled people who labored elsewhere in the city to COMMUTE to their jobs. The lots remained small and the inhabitants working-class. The growing number of residents whose economic subsistence did not depend on local industries increased public objection to the noisome, ugly clay pits along the river.

The clay pits did begin to shut down, but unfortunately for the protesting residents, the empty pits became dumping grounds for garbage. Land filled so haphazardly was not suitable for housing. One section of land owned by the Illinois Brick Company was filled in 1923 for the Mid-City GOLF Links at Addison and Western Avenues. The Chicago Board of Education acquired this land and in 1934 built Lane Technical High School there. During the GREAT DEPRESSION, one of Chicago's first PUBLIC HOUSING complexes, the Julia C. Lathrop Homes, was built on the river at Diversey, straddling North Center's boundary with LINCOLN PARK.

In 1879, members of the Krieger Verein, a German social CLUB, acquired the land around Belmont and Western for a family picnic grove. In 1905, owner George Schmidt transformed the grove into Riverview Sharpshooters Park and sought a clientele from around the city. Until Riverview Park closed unexpectedly after the 1967 season, the AMUSEMENT PARK'S concessions and rides brought millions of Chicagoans and Midwestern tourists through North Center. In the early 1980s, the Riverview Plaza shopping center and a district police office occupied the site of the old park.

Between 1940 and 1990, North Center's population declined from 48,759 to 33,010. Many white Chicagoans moved to suburbs, but people of Hispanic, KOREAN, and FILIPINO descent replaced some of them in North

Center. Like their predecessors, most of North Center's new inhabitants earned moderate incomes. In the 1990s, residents began to worry that they would be displaced by gentrification spilling over from neighboring LINCOLN PARK and LAKE VIEW. The popularity of newly designated neighborhoods like Roscoe Village provoked fears that longtime residents of North Center would no longer be able to afford their modest homes and small businesses.

Amanda Seligman

See also: Amusement Parks; Entertaining Chicagoans; Environmental Politics; Waste Disposal

Further reading: Drury, John. "Old Chicago Neighborhoods." *Landlord's Guide* (November 1948): 10–11. • Griffin, Al. "The Ups and Downs of Riverview Park." *Chicago History* 4.1 (Spring 1975): 14–22. • Vivien M. Palmer Papers, Chicago Historical Society, Chicago, IL.

North Central College. Plainfield College opened on November 11, 1861, with 40 students in a two-story frame house, 35 miles southwest of Chicago. Its founders were the Evangelical Association of America, and most students were from the surrounding area and of GERMAN descent. Much of the school's early faculty were educated at Oberlin College and, like Oberlin, Plainfield College was coeducational from its founding. With an eye toward growth, the school's board of trustees renamed it North Western College in 1864. Growth was unlikely, however, as the village of PLAINFIELD remained inaccessible by RAILROAD. North Western College thus moved northeast to NAPERVILLE in 1870.

The school struggled financially for several decades (fighting successfully to maintain accreditation throughout the 1920s), though its student body and course offerings continued to increase. In 1926, in part to differentiate the college from NORTHWESTERN UNIVERSITY in EVANSTON, the name was again changed. North Central College flourished for the rest of the century; in 1999 it served over 2,700 students from its 56-acre campus in Naperville's historic district, awarding bachelor of arts and science degrees in more than 50 majors and offering 6 graduate programs as well. Though still affiliated with the United Methodist Church, a successor to the Evangelical Association, North Central remains nonsectarian in hiring and admissions.

Margaret L. Frank

See also: Protestants; Universities and Their Cities

Further reading: Keating, Ann Durkin, and Pierre Lebeau. *North Central College and Naperville: A Shared History, 1870–1995.* 1995. • Roberts, Clarence N. *North Central College: A Century of Liberal Education, 1861–1961.* 1960.

North Chicago, IL, Lake County, 32 miles north of the Loop. Incorporated as a village in 1895, North Chicago was called South WAUKEGAN until 1901. Proximity to LAKE MICHIGAN and to Chicago made the area ideal for manufacturing. The fact that it was a temperance town with the motto "No SALOONS" was also a key selling point. However, workers grew impatient with the restrictions of temperance and demanded a change. By 1912 North Chicago possessed, in addition to its 15 industrial enterprises, no fewer than 26 saloons, all of which generated city revenue in the form of license fees.

Industry expanded rapidly in North Chicago. In 1892 the Washburn and Moen Manufacturing Company, headquartered in Worcester, Massachusetts, became the first industry to locate in North Chicago. The Illinois division of Washburn and Moen manufactured barbed wire. The Lanyon Zinc Oxide Company and the Morrow Brothers Harness Company, manufacturers of horse-collar pads, were two other major late-nineteenth-century industries to locate in North Chicago. The Chicago Hardware Foundry Company opened in 1900 and the National Envelope Company in 1905. The development of these industries in addition to others sparked a population boom in the area in the first decades of the twentieth century. From merely 20 residents in 1890, North Chicago counted 5,839 in 1920.

Companies like Washburn and Moen helped to stratify North Chicago along ethnic lines. The company transferred workers from the Worcester plant, and then added SWEDES, FINNS, and other Eastern Europeans. In the far north of North Chicago, SLOVAKS, who called the area "Kompanija," established Mother of God ROMAN CATHOLIC Church. More to the south, POLISH residents founded Holy Rosary Catholic Church, while GERMAN and IRISH residents also established schools and churches.

Into the 1950s North Chicago attracted more residents as the industrial base of the community continued to grow and included such companies as American Motors, Johnson Motors, Goodyear, Abbott Laboratories, and Ocean Spray. Further growth came with the expansion of the VETERANS HOSPITAL and the ANNEXATION of the GREAT LAKES NAVAL TRAINING STATION. The population reached 47,275 in 1970. As many plants began to close in the 1970s, jobs dwindled and the population decreased. Washburn and Moen, one of the city's largest employers in the 1950s, closed in 1979. Between 1970 and 1980 North Chicago lost 18 percent of its population. The drop in activity at the Naval Training Station after the Vietnam War further contributed to North Chicago's decline in population. By 2000 the population stood at 35,918.

Changes in North Chicago's racial makeup accompanied its decline in population. AFRICAN AMERICANS, who had lived in North Chicago since its inception, accounted for 34 percent of the city's population by the end of the twentieth century. The city also had become considerably poorer by the 1990s. Of the 261 municipalities in the six counties surrounding Chicago, North Chicago ranked 253rd in per capita income toward the end of the twentieth century. Much of North Chicago is federal land and untaxable, making the tax burden on private residents among the highest in Illinois. Abbott Laboratories remained one of North Chicago's largest taxpayers, but with the decline of other industries and the corresponding drop in commercial development and population, efforts to resuscitate the once-thriving community have met with difficulty.

Wallace Best

See also: Economic Geography; Prohibition and Temperance; Iron and Steel

Further reading: "North Chicago." In *Local Community Fact Book: Chicago Metropolitan Area, 1990,* ed. Chicago Fact Book Consortium, 1995. • Bateman, Newton, and Paul Selby, eds. *Historical Encyclopedia of Illinois and History of Lake County.* 1902. • Sayler, Carl E. "City of North Chicago." In *A History of Lake County, Illinois,* ed. John J. Halsey, 1912.

North Lawndale, Community Area 29, 5 miles W of the Loop. Today circumscribed by RAILROAD lines on three sides and extending north to within several blocks of the Eisenhower EXPRESSWAY, the West Side neighborhood of North Lawndale is home to some of Chicago's poorest black residents. In the past, North Lawndale boomed as a haven for refugees from the Great FIRE OF 1871 and then bustled as Chicago's JEWISH ghetto. The neighborhood's landscape was divided among two-flat APARTMENTS, Douglas Park, and massive industrial complexes. North Lawndale's prospects turned on its capacity to balance the needs of its industrial and residential populations.

In the early nineteenth century a portage trail extended through the prairie land from LAKE MICHIGAN to the DES PLAINES RIVER. After 1848 the region's DUTCH and ENGLISH farmers knew the route as Southwest Plank Road (later Ogden Avenue), an improved TOLL ROAD. The extension of the Chicago, Burlington & Quincy Railroad prompted further settlement in this portion of Cicero TOWNSHIP. After Chicago ANNEXED the eastern part of the township in 1869, the REAL-ESTATE firm Millard & Decker built a residential suburb. They advertised "Lawndale" as linking "in harmonious union the people of a community." The new western development's fireproof brick buildings attracted the people and businesses burned out by the fire of 1871.

In the late nineteenth century, many industrial workers settled in North Lawndale. The McCormick Reaper Works opened a plant in the neighboring LOWER WEST SIDE in 1873. The openings of a Western Electric Plant in nearby CICERO in 1903 and the headquarters of Sears, Roebuck & Co. in 1906 brought North Lawndale's population to 46,225 by 1910.

During the second decade of the twentieth century, Russian JEWS became North Lawndale's largest residential group. Eastern European Jews still living in the old Near West Side ghetto mocked those who left for having pretensions of upward mobility; accordingly, they called North Lawndale "Deutschland." Although not reaching the economic heights of the city's German Jews, North Lawndale's burgeoning population established their own small city of community institutions, including Mt. Sinai HOSPITAL, Herzl Junior COLLEGE (now Malcolm X College), several bathhouses, and a commercial strip on Roosevelt Road. One study found that in 1946, North Lawndale housed about 65,000 Jews, approximately one quarter of the city's Jewish population.

Fourteen years later, 91 percent of the neighborhood's 124,937 residents were black. AFRICAN AMERICANS began moving into North Lawndale in the early 1950s, some directly from southern states, others displaced from their SOUTH SIDE homes by URBAN RENEWAL projects. In response, white residents moved out to northern neighborhoods such as ROGERS PARK. Despite severe residential overcrowding, no new private housing was built in North Lawndale. Its physical decline was so severe that late in 1957 the city's Community Conservation Board recognized it as a CONSERVATION AREA.

In contrast to previous residents of North Lawndale, most new black residents could not find work in the neighborhood. North Lawndale's industries now employed people who COMMUTED to the neighborhood only for WORK. Consequently, the local consumer base became much poorer, and tensions grew between the whites who worked in North Lawndale during the day and the blacks who lived there. In 1966, the neighborhood's poverty prompted Martin Luther King, Jr., to pick North Lawndale as the base for the northern CIVIL RIGHTS MOVEMENT. Residents found King's visit highly symbolic: his stay attracted much attention, but little tangible change.

After King's assassination in 1968, however, the neighborhood did change. West Side residents rioted, and although commercial centers run by whites were the targets of physical attack, residential areas burned as well. Most of the large plants and small businesses left because they lost their insurance and feared repeated riots. International Harvester closed its factory in 1969, and Sears struck another blow when it moved its international headquarters to the new downtown tower in 1974. The community-based organizations King inspired—the Lawndale People's Planning and Action Council and the Pyramidwest Development Corporation—tried but failed to attract new industries to employ North Lawndale's residents and new housing to revitalize the neighborhood. During the last quarter of the twentieth century, North Lawndale's population dropped precipitously, from its peak in 1960 to 41,768 in 2000. Residents fled its increasing poverty, unemployment, crime, and physical deterioration, but hints of revitalization in the late 1990s suggested to some observers that the area was beginning to prosper.

Amanda Seligman

See also: Baths, Public; Community Organizing; Contested Spaces; Economic Geography; Mail Order; Neighborhood Succession; Suburbs and Cities as Dual Metropolis

Further reading: Cutler, Irving. *Jews of Chicago: From Shtetl to Suburb.* 1996. • Jefferson, Alphine Wade. "Housing Discrimination and Community Response in North Lawndale (Chicago), Illinois, 1948–1978." Ph.D. diss., Duke University. 1979. • Ralph, James. *Northern Protest: Martin Luther King, Jr., Chicago, and the Civil Rights Movement.* 1993.

North Park, Community Area 13, 9 miles NW of the Loop. North Park is a stable, quiet, tree-shaded, middle-income community where most homes are owner-occupied. It is located between Cicero Avenue on the west and the North Shore Channel on the east, the city limits and Devon Avenue on the north, and the North Branch of the CHICAGO RIVER on the south. The presence of the two streams provides a charming and unusual ambience for the area. Chicago's only waterfall (about four feet high) appears where the North Branch of the Chicago River tumbles into the North Shore Channel.

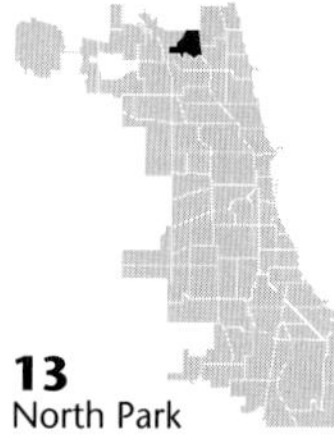

North Park's origins lie in 1855 when a village was platted in the newly organized JEFFERSON TOWNSHIP. The early residents were GERMAN and SWEDISH farmers who grew vegetables in fields laid out along the south bank of the North Branch of the Chicago River. CZECHS moved into the northwestern corner of the area after the Bohemian National CEMETERY was opened in 1877. They stayed only a short while, however, and began to move out of the area around 1900.

In 1893 the Swedish University Association of the Swedish Evangelical Mission Covenant purchased a large acreage in the area and donated about eight and a half acres along the river in the southeastern corner of North Park for establishment of a college. Construction at North Park College began in 1894 and the surrounding acreage was subdivided for homes. Within the next few years streets were laid out, sewer lines put in place, and board sidewalks installed. Nonetheless, development proceeded slowly; in 1910 the population numbered only 478. From 1910 to 1930, however, the area burgeoned, especially after the first two-flats and small apartments were built in the 1920s. The population tripled from 1920 to 1930 and the community was rapidly transformed from an area of prairie and woods to a mature residential community of BUNGALOWS and two-flats. The 1930s also saw development of a small industrial district in the northwest corner of the area along Peterson Avenue which, although declining, remains the only industrial activity in North Park.

Population grew rapidly during WORLD WAR II and in the postwar period and reached its high point in 1960. Like most city neighborhoods, North Park lost population through the next 20 years, but, unlike most others, North Park grew by over 6 percent from 1980 to 1990. Faculty, staff, and students of local colleges and universities often live in the area, as do employees of nearby Swedish Covenant HOSPITAL. This stabilizes the area, greatly reducing the turnover of homes. Others have also responded to the solid housing stock and the thriving family-oriented character of the neighborhood. In recent years Hispanics and a sizable number of KOREANS and FILIPINOS have joined the Swedes and Germans who long dominated the area.

The neighborhood is strongly supported by the presence of important educational and civic institutions. North Park College has now become NORTH PARK UNIVERSITY, serving a wider clientele than formerly. In addition, NORTHEASTERN ILLINOIS UNIVERSITY provides a wide-ranging curriculum and attracts students from throughout Chicago, as does Von Steuben magnet high school. The Municipal TUBERCULOSIS Sanitarium, built just after 1900 at the intersection of Pulaski and Bryn Mawr, was closed in 1974 and converted into senior citizen housing (North Park Village), a school for the mentally handicapped, and the North Park Village Nature Center, the only such facility in the city. A source of pride for area residents, this 46-acre preserve holds wetlands, woods, and savannas, and features 2.5 miles of hiking trails and a visitor center.

David M. Solzman

See also: Housing Types; Water

Further reading: The Chicago Fact Book Consortium, ed. *Local Community Fact Book: Chicago Metropolitan Area, Based on the 1970 and 1980 Censuses.* 1984. • Solzman, David M. *The Chicago River: An Illustrated History and Guide to the River and Its Waterways.* 1998.

North Park University. North Park University is located in a residential neighborhood along the North Branch of the Chicago River and includes North Park Theological Seminary. Founded in 1891 by the Swedish Evangelical Mission Covenant of America (currently the Evangelical Covenant Church), North Park describes itself as a "Christian Liberal Arts University" and retains close ties to the Covenant Church and the Swedish American community. In 1958 North Park expanded from a two-year college into a four-year program. During financial hardship in the late 1970s, trustees considered moving to a rural location in Wisconsin, but the 1990s saw recovery and expansion. In 1997, North Park became a university, combining its undergraduate college with the SEMINARY and new graduate programs. Full-time enrollment in 2000 was 1,300 students, and total enrollment approximately 2,300.

D. Bradford Hunt

See also: North Park, Protestants; Swedes; Universities and Their Cities

North Riverside, IL, Cook County, 10 miles W of the Loop. To many, the village of North Riverside is synonymous with North Riverside Park Mall. As a major retail hub located approximately 10 miles west of downtown Chicago, the mall attracts customers throughout western COOK COUNTY. Yet for most of its history North Riverside has had few connections with the property on which the mall is located.

Once the domain of the POTAWATOMI, the forested land along the DES PLAINES RIVER was purchased by a trapping and REAL-ESTATE firm in 1835. David A. Gage, treasurer of the city of Chicago, purchased approximately 1,600 acres along Harlem Avenue for his country estate. When Gage left office and the city treasury was found short of money, this property was turned over to the city of Chicago. Part of this land was used for the COOK COUNTY Home for Boys and later a TUBERCULOSIS sanitarium. For approximately one hundred years, the village necessarily grew to the west, near the Des Plaines River.

By 1900 onion farmers had settled in the area between Gage's former property and Des Plaines Avenue, and members of the Riverside Holiness Association (many of whom were Chicago businessmen who used the properties for summer retreats) had built homes between Des Plaines Avenue and the river.

At the time of incorporation in 1923, the Des Plaines River formed the western boundary of the village. The river in its forested setting brought recreational and retirement opportunities, including the Optimates Canoe Club, the SCOTTISH Home, the Melody Mill Ballroom, and the Riverside GOLF Club (founded in 1893). In 1926 the size of North Riverside more than doubled with the ANNEXATION of land west of the Des Plaines River. Residential construction boomed in the years after WORLD WAR II as new residents, many of whom were of Eastern European descent, moved into the new brick single-family homes. With manufacturing jobs available in nearby western suburbs, population peaked in 1970 at 8,097.

The construction of North Riverside Plaza shopping center in the early 1960s and the North Riverside Park Mall in 1975 brought increased commercial activity to the area. These retail properties have been invaluable; they now pay for over half of the village's operating expenses, making North Riverside an affordable community in which to live.

Patricia Krone Rose

See also: Entertaining Chicagoans; Leisure; Shopping Districts and Malls

Further reading: Maclean, John N. "Small-Town Virtues—and Low Taxes, Too." *Chicago Tribune*, December 29, 1990. • *North Riverside: Our 75th Year.* Commemorative Book of Village History, 1998.

Northbrook, IL, Cook County, 20 miles NW of the Loop. Prior to the establishment of a brick industry, Northbrook was a sleepy little settlement. In 1843 James M. Strode and Silas W. Sherman laid claim to 160 acres and eventually purchased enough acreage to own a substantial part of the town. In 1850 the Shepards arrived and set up a kiln in their home for brickmaking. They also opened a general store and a tavern, which became a stopover for travelers going to and from Chicago and Milwaukee. GERMAN farmers bought land in the area before the Civil War.

Following the FIRE OF 1871, brick replaced wood as a CONSTRUCTION material. When a farm near present-day Lake-Cook and Waukegan Roads was found to have excellent clay SOIL for brickmaking, the National Brick Company and the Illinois Brick Company began their businesses in Northbrook. Brickmakers established a residential settlement known as Bach Town. In 1872 a single track was laid and the Chicago, Milwaukee & St. Paul RAILROAD began to haul the bricks to the city for rebuilding. A second track was added in 1892. Brick production peaked between 1915 and 1920, when as many as 300,000 bricks were manufactured a day. The brick companies had closed by the 1950s.

In 1899, the ROMAN CATHOLIC Divine Word Missionaries purchased 337 acres, later adding over 400 more, and built St. Joseph's Technical School (later called Techny). The school operated for 12 years, instructing boys in the trades. A training center for missionary priests and brothers opened at the location in 1909.

In 1901, three hundred residents incorporated the village of Shermerville. The village had five SALOONS, a meat market, a coal and feed store, a general store, a harness store, a stonecutter, and a railroad station. Shermerville gained notoriety during its early years for boisterous gatherings at its inns and taverns. In 1923 the town's approximately 525 residents sought to change its image by changing its name to Northbrook.

In 1950 the population was 3,348; within a decade it more than tripled to 11,635, and grew to 33,435 by 2000. In the late 1960s developer J. Gould had an option to buy 300 acres of farmland adjacent to the village on Lake-Cook Road. His intention was to put up 2,300 apartments in 12-story high-rise buildings. Residents protested the development, which was nicknamed "Instant City" by newspapers. Another proposal to build a SHOPPING center resulted in Northbrook's ANNEXATION of the land. Northbrook Court, a 130-acre upscale mall, opened in 1976.

While Northbrook Court added to the village's tax base, large companies have also contributed. Northbrook became home to Allstate, United Parcel, and Underwriters Laboratories. Techny property has been annexed by Northbrook; plans for the 770-acre parcel include a mixed use of residential, commercial, industrial, and park land, and a GOLF course.

Marilyn Elizabeth Perry

See also: Cook County; Economic Geography; Quarrying, Stonecutting, and Brickmaking; Suburbs and Cities as Dual Metropolis

Further reading: Clipping file. Northbrook Library, Northbrook, Ill. • Pridmore, Jay. "A History and Lifestyle All Its Own." *North Shore,* August 1982, 97–108. • Randall, Frank A., Jr. *The History of Timber Lane and Nearby Shermer Road.* 1987.

Northeastern Illinois University. Established in the fall of 1961 on the North Side in NORTH PARK, Northeastern Illinois University's original purpose was to train elementary SCHOOL teachers for the city of Chicago. Under the governance of the Chicago Board of Education with support from the Ford Foundation, Chicago Teachers College–North, as it was called, began with 1,364 students under the leadership of Dean Roy N. Jervis. During the first decade of the school's existence, it underwent name changes to reflect transformations in its goals: in 1965, the school became Illinois Teachers College–Chicago North and, in 1971, Northeastern Illinois University, reflecting its expanded mission to train elementary and high-school teachers for the whole metropolitan region as well as students in the liberal arts and business.

At the opening of the twenty-first century, the university encompassed 330 faculty and over 10,000 students—7,000 undergraduates and 3,000 graduate students. It offers master's degrees in the liberal arts, education, and business. As a commuter college, Northeastern has drawn its students from the greater Chicago area; its diverse student population, representing over 40 ethnic groups, has mirrored the larger community. About 45 percent of the undergraduates attend part-time while holding jobs. Sixty-two percent of the student population is female, with 19 percent Hispanic, 12 percent African American, and 10 percent Asian.

Northeastern's Chicago Teachers' Center provides classroom instructional material and consultative services to teachers. Its Center for Inner City Studies offers degrees in African American Studies. Through various collaborations, the university also provides distance-learning courses to suburban communities in Cook, DuPage, and Lake Counties.

June Sochen

See also: Chicago State University; Universities and Their Cities

Further reading: Frederick, Duke. *Early Times at Northeastern: A Memoir.* 1978. • Northeastern Illinois University. "Review of Undergraduate Education." 1994–5. • Sachs, Jerome M. *Reminiscences about Northeastern Illinois University.* 1987.

Northfield, IL, Cook County, 17 miles NW of the Loop. Only 2.8 square miles in size, Northfield maintains a quiet suburban setting despite being intersected by the Edens Expressway and Willow Road. Industrial facilities are located on the eastern border along the Chicago & North Western Railway and the expressway. Nature lovers can bicycle on numerous paths that connect with pathways to the Skokie Lagoons and Erickson Woods. More than half of the residential properties are zoned for acre lot sizes. Northfield is one of the few communities allowing homeowners to have horses on their properties.

John Happ moved into the area from Winnetka some time after 1854, when the railroad lessened the demand for his services as a blacksmith. The German immigrant settled his family and his blacksmith shop to the west, where it was still rural. In the area that later became Northfield, other farmers settled near the Happs. The farming community grew at a leisurely pace through the remainder of the century.

In the 1920s electric utility innovator Samuel Insull built the Skokie Valley line of the North Shore interurban railroad, which came through the village. The town was originally incorporated in 1926 under the name Wau-Bun. But when Insull built a railroad station at Willow Road he called it Northfield. Village residents later adopted the name for their town.

In the early 1950s the Edens Expressway was built and the swampland to the east was dug out to become the Skokie Lagoons. The village grew rapidly during the 1950s. From 1930 to 1980 the population increased from 320 to 4,887, slowing down in the next decade to reach 4,924 by 1990. Housing types ranged from ranch-style and two-story frame houses to large estate houses.

In 1957 the Northfield Park District was established. It purchased property on both the north and south of Willow Road, providing a wooded backdrop for the heavily traveled two-lane road. Northfield has preserved that look in other respects by confining commercial and office buildings to eastern sections of the village. Residents shop primarily at two small strip areas. Very few multifamily dwellings are in evidence.

Northfield residents have for decades fought against widening the segment of Willow Road that passes through the village, and in the late 1990s successfully defeated a renewed attempt by the Illinois Department of Transportation to widen the road.

Marilyn Elizabeth Perry

See also: Agriculture; Metropolitan Growth

Further reading: Hobart, Mary B. *Northfield: A Friendly History.* 1961. • *Northfield.* Chamber of Commerce Community Guide. 1997–1998.

Northlake, IL, Cook County, 14 miles W of the Loop. Northlake, a town that attracted do-it-yourself carpenters, is in the process of rebuilding itself. It is seeking to rejuvenate sagging industry, revitalize business, and bring about redevelopment of older areas.

In 1939 the community consisted of farmland. The start of World War II brought industry to neighboring Melrose Park when the Buick defense plant was built on North Avenue. Housing for workers went up quickly as the Midland Development Company purchased acreage surrounding the plant. The housing complex was sandwiched between two railroad yards on its northern and southern edges. Midland built the shells and advertised "semi-finished" Cape Cod and ranch-style houses. Plant employees, eager to save money, liked the concept of adding their own skills to the completion of the houses. Buyers supplied paint and labor for the exterior, and installed electrical fixtures, heating equipment, and plumbing. By 1941 there were six hundred houses in the village. Midland reportedly ran a contest to name the city. The winner combined the names of two major roads in the community to form "Northlake."

The Proviso rail yards, built in 1929, ran through the south and west of the community, giving industry access to transportation, and major industry continued to draw new residents to the town during the 1940s. A vote to incorporate failed in 1944, but in an effort to keep Melrose Park from annexing them, residents voted to incorporate as the city of Northlake in 1949.

In 1953 the estimated population was 9,000. The Tri-State Tollway at the city's western border brought increased industry. One of Northlake's largest employers after 1957 was Automatic Electric, a telephone-switching equipment manufacturer later absorbed into AG Communication Systems Corporation. The company employed 14,000 workers in the early 1970s, roughly equaling the city's population, but by the early 1990s, the company had reduced its staff to 1,400, when it left Northlake altogether for a plant in DeKalb County.

Growth in the 1970s affected the infrastructure of the city in the 1980s. Between 1981 and 1988 city streets, sewers, and water lines were overhauled. Population in 1990 was at 12,505 with people of German, Irish, Italian, and Polish heritage and a large number of blue-collar workers. Over 16 percent of the population was Hispanic, and nearly 4 percent Asian. Most of the residential areas were located in the eastern section, while industry dominated the west.

In response to a 1994 land-use report citing Northlake as below the national average in open space, the city began renovating existing parks and opened a new 32-acre park, Centerpoint preserve.

Marilyn Elizabeth Perry

See also: Economic Geography; Housing, Self-Built; Infrastructure

Northwest Community Organization. During three decades of operation, the Northwest Community Organization served the West Town area of Chicago as "an organization of organizations," unifying churches, social service agencies, settlement houses, and neighborhood groups. NCO started through the initiative of nearly two dozen Roman Catholic churches in 1961 with the intention of reversing the physical decay of West Town and thereby keeping demographic change at bay. In its first two years of operation, NCO received critical assistance from the Industrial Areas Foundation.

With time, NCO's unfriendly, defensive posture softened and, by the 1970s, the organization enthusiastically embraced growing numbers of new neighbors from Puerto Rico and, later, Mexico. The group became involved with a wide assortment of issues involved with urban renewal, federally subsidized mortgages, employment training, building code

VIOLATIONS, arson fires, and governmental treatment of immigrants.

The Northwest Community Organization gained a reputation for its protest strategies, which included dumping accumulated garbage behind the tavern of a recalcitrant alderman, staging sit-ins at the mayor's office, taking complaints straight to utility company headquarters, and publicly identifying uncaring landlords.

Through the eighties, NCO continued its issue-based campaigns protesting, among other things, unfair distribution of Chicago's home-improvement loans, high utility rates, and sluggish toxic-spill clean-up. By the next decade, gentrification triggered yet another demographic transformation of West Town. Soon, leadership changes, a return to its church-based origins, and funding troubles caused the organization to became a casualty of change, and its insistent voice on behalf of racial and class diversity was silenced.

Thomas J. Jablonsky
Paul-Thomas Ferguson

See also: Environmentalism; Neighborhood Associations; Woodlawn Organization

Further reading: Lancourt, Joan E. *Confront or Concede: The Alinsky Citizen-Action Organizations.* 1979. • Northwest Community Organization Collection, 1962–1994. Chicago Historical Society. Chicago, IL. • Webb, L. Thomas. "Northwest Community Organization." In *Neighborhood Organization: Case Reports.* 1968.

Northwest Ordinance. The Northwest Ordinance of 1787 and the Land Ordinance of 1785 were designed to establish some order among western settlers. The Land Ordinance prescribed the division of the land into six-mile-square TOWNSHIPS. By 1820, townships had been laid out in the southern part of Illinois, and a solid band of them (the Bounty Lands) lined the northwest side of the Illinois River, working up toward the site of Chicago.

Meanwhile, the United Tribes had in 1816 agreed to cede to the federal government a corridor of land stretching southwestward from Chicago; between these Indian Boundary Lines a canal was to be built. During the early 1820s, townships were laid out in this corridor, to link up with the Bounty Lands. By 1830, the site of Chicago itself had been surveyed, as the eastern terminus of the canal corridor, and during the 1830s further surveys covered the whole of the future metropolitan area, west to the FOX RIVER and north to the Wisconsin border. In 1827, the federal government had assigned to the canal commissioners 286,000 acres within the canal corridor. From their headquarters in LOCKPORT, the commissioners then sold this land, so that between 1836 and 1848 they were able to construct the ILLINOIS & MICHIGAN CANAL, the basis for Chicago's emergence. As the city grew, its STREETS tended to develop on the section lines platted in 1830, so that the early surveyors in effect determined much of the outline of the modern grid. Indeed, the streets followed the grid so faithfully that in time the effect became wearisome, and in new suburbs like RIVERSIDE (platted in 1869) there was a determined attempt to set the streets out in more "natural," flowing lines.

With the adjacent metropolitan area now covered by the township-and-range grid, the surveyors' townships in many cases became civil townships, with names like Hanover, Lemont, and York, which survive to the present day. The townships for some years also had important administrative functions, but these withered over time, until today they are chiefly known for their role as SCHOOL DISTRICTS. As time went by, municipal entities emerged that overlapped the townships, more and more blurring their outlines. But these offspring of the Land Ordinance of 1785 had played an important role in early settlement, and continued in many cases as the origin of modern roads.

David Buisseret

See also: Land Use; Public Works, Federal Funding for; Real Estate; Subdivisions

Further reading: Northwest Territory Celebration Commission. *A Bibliography of Source Materials Concerning the Ordinance of 1787 and Northwest Territory.* 1937. • Onuf, Peter S. *Statehood and Union: A History of the Northwest Ordinance.* 1992. • Sable, Martin Howard. "The Northwest Ordinance of 1787: An Interdisciplinary Bibliography." *Bulletin of the Special Libraries Association, Geography and Map Division* (1987–1988): 149–151.

Northwestern University. On May 31, 1850, nine Chicagoans convened in a law office above a hardware store on the northern edge of the city's business district to found a university. Chief among them were the physician and REAL-ESTATE speculator John Evans, his brother-in-law, the commodities broker Orrington Lunt, and the prominent attorney Grant Goodrich. The other six included two lawyers, the owner of the hardware store, and the ministers of the three leading Methodist churches in the city. All nine were Methodists, yet they deliberately chose to found a secular university. In August 1853, with the financial support of John Evans, the founders purchased 379 acres of land located on LAKE MICHIGAN 12 miles north of Chicago. Here, during the winter of 1853–54, the university's financial agent Philo Judson laid out the streets of what would become the city of EVANSTON. In November 1855 the university held its first classes in a newly built three-story wooden building located on the northwest corner of Hinman and Davis Streets in what is today downtown Evanston. In 1869, Northwestern became one of the early universities to admit women students and opened its first permanent building, University Hall, which still stands as a signature campus landmark.

During the 1870s and 1880s, Northwestern became affiliated with several professional schools located in Chicago, including a law school and a medical school. It first fielded an intercollegiate football team in 1882, and later was a founding member of what became the Big Ten Conference. By 1890 Northwestern had grown rapidly, both in Evanston and in Chicago, but remained a relatively loose federation of semiautonomous colleges and schools until president Henry Wade Rogers (1890–1900) transformed it into a modern, fully integrated university.

During the presidency of Walter Dill Scott (1920–1939), Northwestern's enrollment substantively increased, additional faculty were recruited, and the university began to acquire a national reputation for academic excellence. Northwestern's professional schools in Chicago were brought together on the university's newly constructed campus on Chicago Avenue at Lake Michigan in buildings designed by James Gamble Rogers, who also designed many new buildings on the Evanston campus, among them Dyche Stadium (now Ryan Field), opened in 1926, and the Charles Deering Library, opened in 1933.

In the quarter century following the war, under the leadership of President J. Roscoe Miller (1949–1970), Northwestern substantially increased the size of its Evanston campus, constructing many new buildings on adjacent land reclaimed by filling in Lake Michigan. The university's academic programs were strengthened, the faculty was expanded, and enrollment was increased.

The last decades of the twentieth century saw Northwestern's J. L. Kellogg Graduate School of Management develop into one of the leaders in its field and the university's Materials Research Center emerge as a nationally recognized pioneer in applied specialized technology.

President Arnold R. Weber (1985–1994) stabilized the university's finances and enhanced the Evanston campus environment. Northwestern's relations with the Evanston community remained somewhat strained because of the university's exemption from property taxes as provided for in an amendment to its charter approved in 1855 by the Illinois State Legislature.

Patrick M. Quinn

See also: Innovation, Invention, and Chicago Business; Medical Education; Universities and Their Cities; University of Chicago

Further reading: Williamson, Harold F., and Payson F. Wild. *Northwestern University: A History, 1850–1975.* 1976.

Norwegians. Norwegian settlement in Chicago had its beginning in 1836 when a few families decided to remain in the city rather than continue on to the FOX RIVER settlement founded two years earlier southwest of

Chicago. Chicago was the third Norwegian settlement in America, after Kendall, founded in western New York State in 1825 by the pioneers of Norwegian emigration who that year arrived on the tiny sloop *Restauration.* Most of them moved to the Fox River settlement in the mid-1830s when group migration from Norway became an annual occurrence.

The first permanent Norwegian resident in the city was David Johnson, a sailor, who arrived in 1834. The ILLINOIS & MICHIGAN CANAL opened in 1848, providing employment to Norwegians and other immigrants. Norwegians played a significant role in shipping on the GREAT LAKES as seamen, captains, and SHIPBUILDERS as long as sailing ships dominated, into the 1870s. Captains and vessel owners became prominent within the ethnic community. Norwegian men found a special niche in the urban economy in the BUILDING TRADES and as tailors, while women who worked outside the home sought DOMESTIC WORK.

The pioneer Norwegians settled in "the Sands," the unhealthy area north of the CHICAGO RIVER where it empties into LAKE MICHIGAN. There in the late 1830s and 1840s they squatted on canal land, owning their primitive huts and shacks but not the ground on which they stood. In this close-knit community of families, with a much greater gender balance than in the city as a whole, the majority hailed from western Norway. Although transience renders an exact count impossible, it appears that more than 500 Norwegians lived in Chicago in 1850.

The building of warehouses, RAILROADS, and factories, added to the unsavory conditions, pushed Norwegians from their original settlement. Moving north and west from the center of town, they established a colony centering on Milwaukee Avenue in the sparsely settled district west of the North Branch of the Chicago River. The colony flourished and by the 1860s more than 60 percent of Chicago's 1,313 Norwegians lived there. In the 1870s Indiana Street (now Grand Avenue) became the center of the Milwaukee Avenue colony, with the fashionable WICKER PARK neighborhood to the north of this largely working-class district attracting the more prosperous members of the Norwegian community.

The third and final Norwegian colony—before Norwegians dispersed into the suburbs and outlying districts—developed farther west in the HUMBOLDT PARK and LOGAN SQUARE area. Movement of Norwegians out of the Milwaukee Avenue colony accelerated in the 1880s as more recent immigrants—mainly POLES, Polish and Russian JEWS, and ITALIANS—replaced Norwegian residents in these crowded, dirty, and smoky industrial river wards. By 1900 there were 41,551 Norwegian residents in Chicago, and by 1930, there were 55,948. Of these 63 percent lived in the Norwegian neighborhoods on the Northwest Side of Chicago. These were the golden years of Chicago's "Little Norway," the third-largest Norwegian population in the world, after Oslo and Bergen.

The Chicago colony was a major cultural and organizational center within the national Norwegian ethnic community. The NEWSPAPER *Skandinaven,* founded in Chicago in 1866, in time became the largest Norwegian-language journal in the world—no newspaper in Norway even came close—and it sought a national circulation. Victor Fremont Lawson, son of one of the founders, later became a major force in Chicago JOURNALISM as editor of the *Chicago Daily News.*

Other second-generation Norwegian men and women also found opportunities in the professions. The WOMAN'S HOSPITAL MEDICAL COLLEGE offered a unique opportunity for women, such as Helga Ruud, the first graduate in 1889, who was associated with the Norwegian-American HOSPITAL and the Norwegian Lutheran Deaconess Home and Hospital (now the Lutheran General Hospital at Park Ridge).

As Norway modernized in the early twentieth century, emigrants increasingly included engineers, architects, or others possessing technical or artistic skills. An elegant clubhouse on Logan Square suggested the status of this imported elite. As chief engineer of BRIDGES, Norwegian-born Thomas Pihlfeldt between 1901 and 1941 supervised the construction of no fewer than 55 bridges in Chicago. The many young men arriving after the turn of the century introduced an ethnic forte by arranging ski-jumping meets, in 1905 organizing Norge Ski Club. Knute Rockne, coming to the Logan Square community from Norway at age five in 1893, made a career as head FOOTBALL coach at Notre Dame.

Norwegian neighborhoods could be located by the CHURCH steeples, which symbolized their strong Lutheran identity. Religious practices adjusted to the new environment and an expanded congregational social role met the needs of compatriots. Baptists and Methodists, as well as other faiths, however, gained a following. Although Chicago became the center of Methodism for Norwegian American converts, fewer than five thousand Norwegian Americans had converted to the Methodist faith nationwide by 1900. At the close of the twentieth century, the Norwegian Lutheran Memorial Church on Logan Square was still conducting services in the Norwegian language to a church membership widely dispersed beyond the Logan Square community. Ethnicity persisted as a defining component for many of the nearly 84,000 individuals within the metropolitan area who in 2000 claimed Norwegian first ancestry.

Odd S. Lovoll

See also: Demography; Germans; Irish; Multicentered Chicago; Protestants; Swedes

Further reading: Lovoll, Odd S. *A Century of Urban Life: The Norwegians in Chicago before 1930.* 1988.

Norwood Park, Community Area 10, 11 miles NW of the Loop. Prior to Norwood Park's incorporation in 1874, the village had a country setting far away from the bustle of the city. Early developers hoped to create a resort, taking advantage of area woodlands and hills. The subdivision departed from the typical grid pattern, and instead, like Frederick Law Olmsted's RIVERSIDE, platted winding roads alternating with rectangular streets. One of the historic streets with old Victorian houses, the Circle, is shaped in an oval.

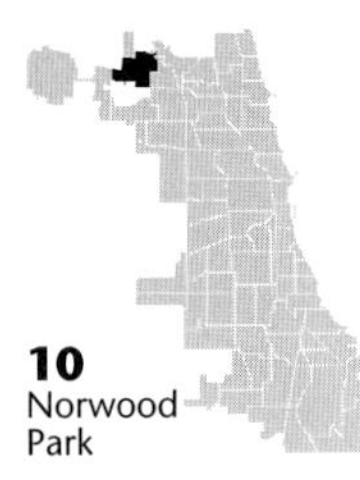

In 1833 Mark Noble became one of Chicago's prominent citizens when he purchased substantial acreage in NILES and JEFFERSON TOWNSHIPS. The frame house built that year by the Noble family, known today as the Noble-Seymour-Crippen house, is the oldest extant house in the city of Chicago.

ENGLISH farmers settled in the area in the 1830s. Over the years GERMANS became the major ethnic group, along with substantial numbers of POLES and Scandinavians. In 1853 the Illinois & Wisconsin RAILROAD, eventually the Chicago & North Western Railway, installed a rail line serving the area. For several months there was only one passenger, until other residents realized the advantages of railway travel to Chicago.

In 1868 the Norwood Land and Building Association created its curvilinear SUBDIVISION. Construction began on the Norwood Park HOTEL and an artificial lake in hopes that the area would attract Chicagoans seeking a resort atmosphere. Although the hotel attracted local residents for entertainment purposes, it never drew enough customers to be a success.

Following incorporation in 1874, the village prohibited the sale of liquor. The village's name followed Henry Ward Beecher's novel, *Norwood: Or, Village Life in New England.* The word "Park" was added after it was discovered that another post office in the state had the name of Norwood.

In 1893 the village of Norwood Park was ANNEXED to Chicago. Nine trains stopped in the town daily to serve residents commuting to the city. Although there were houses scattered around the village, most were built close to the railroad.

Improvements to roads such as Milwaukee Avenue, Northwest Highway, Foster, Devon, and Harlem in the 1920s led to easier travel and brought many newcomers to Norwood Park. Despite the hard times of the GREAT DEPRESSION the community continued to add homes and residents during the 1930s. In the 1950s the Kennedy EXPRESSWAY cut through Norwood Park, but was routed around the historic houses on the Circle.

Norwood Park is home to a number of institutions. The NORWEGIAN Old People's Home was built in 1896 on the site of the old hotel; a Passionist monastery (Immaculate Conception) in 1904; the DANISH Old People's Home in 1906. The Sisters of Resurrection (ROMAN CATHOLIC) founded Resurrection High School in 1913, Resurrection HOSPITAL in 1953, and Resurrection Retirement Community in 1977.

The population of 41,827 in 1970 declined to 37,669 by 2000. HOUSING TYPES are mixed in Norwood Park and range from nineteenth-century Victorian houses to post–WORLD WAR II BUNGALOWS, ranches, Georgians, and Cape Cods. Although most housing is single-family, CONDOMINIUMS gained in popularity in the 1990s.

Retail and service businesses line Northwest Highway, and Norwood Park has easy access to O'HARE AIRPORT, trains, and major highway TRANSPORTATION, but the village remains a mostly residential community, with no significant industrial base.

Marilyn Elizabeth Perry

See also: Annexation; Housing for the Elderly; Metropolitan Growth; Religious Institutions

Further reading: Andreas, A. T. *History of Cook County.* 1884. • McGowen, Thomas. *Island within a City: A History of the Norridge–Harwood Heights Area.* 1989. • Scholl, Edward T. *Seven Miles of Ideal Living.* 1957.

Nursery Schools. The growth of nursery schools, foster day care, and other formal institutions that cared for pre-school-age children in Chicago began in the late nineteenth century. Reflecting the customary guardianship provided by relatives, neighbors, and friends, early child care organizations emphasized easing the burdens of the poor or "abandoned" mother rather than meeting children's developmental needs. By 1897, SETTLEMENT HOUSES directed almost all of Chicago's 175 custodial nurseries. Of these, only the Chicago Orphan Asylum (COA), established in 1849, concentrated on child development.

By 1912, nurseries began to shift their focus away from Chicago's destitute in favor of working mothers who could not afford nannies, au pairs, or regular babysitters. During the GREAT DEPRESSION the NEW DEAL stimulated rapid expansion of institutional child care as the Federal Emergency Relief Administration (1933) constructed hundreds of nurseries to provide work for underemployed teachers, NURSES, and dieticians. The Lanham Act (1940) built on this national foundation, constructing more than 60 federal centers in Chicago alone, to curtail absenteeism by parents in war-related industries.

The withdrawal of federal financial support after 1945 and the evolution of child development practices led to a growing diversity of nursery service and after-school providers. Fewer than 23 federally sponsored "war nurseries" remained in Chicago by 1946, but the COA noted 40 new private institutions that focused first on child development rather than parental convenience. The 1960s saw a flurry of federal and state legislative activity intended to improve conditions and ensure proper ratios between children and caregivers as the need for and number of child care providers rose.

In 1965, Head Start, a cornerstone of President Lyndon Johnson's GREAT SOCIETY, extended the benefits of nursery schools to children living below the poverty line. By 2001, 18,000 children in Chicago had enrolled at more than 500 Head Start locations. Begun in 1967, the Chicago Parent-Child Project shared Head Start's goals and partnered with the federal government to provide educational opportunities to children ages three to seven.

As the number of women entering the workplace soared between the 1970s and the 1990s, the need for nonmaternal child care became more compelling. Many families remained on the waiting lists of crowded centers while others struggled to pay the average annual price of $3,000—a cost much higher than many parents could afford.

David Blanke

See also: Children, Dependent; Kindergarten Movement; Social Services

Further reading: Bremner, Robert H., ed. *Children and Youth in America: A Documentary History.* 1974. • Cauman, Judith. "What Is Happening in Day Care—New Concepts, Current Practice and Trends." *Child Welfare* 35 (1956): 22–27. • McCausland, Clare L. *Children of Circumstance: A History of the First 125 Years (1849–1974) of Chicago Child Care Society.* 1976.

Nursing and Nursing Education. Initially, Chicagoans received nursing care primarily from religious groups, which often established HOSPITALS to serve the poor. These included NORWEGIAN deaconesses, ROMAN CATHOLIC nuns, and nurses hired by PROTESTANT denominations to work on behalf of specific immigrant groups. Beginning in the 1880s, wealthy women, inspired by Florence Nightingale in Britain, began to form nondenominational nursing schools and visiting nurse organizations. Middle- and upper-class families engaged private duty nurses when ill. The poor alone went to hospitals in the nineteenth century.

Early schools of nursing were based in Chicago hospitals. Prominent among them were St. Luke's, PROVIDENT, and the Illinois Training School for Nurses. These schools followed the Nightingale model of incorporating science classes into nursing education combined with long hours of hands-on training in hospital wards. Hospitals hired only supervisory nurses; student nurses provided most care. Provident, structured like the other schools, was established in 1891 by the Chicago AFRICAN AMERICAN community in order to provide nursing education to black women who were excluded from other schools in Chicago and in the nation.

A small but significant trend to educate nurses in collegiate settings began during the

Visiting Nurse Association visit, ca. 1912–14. Photographer: Unknown. Source: Chicago Historical Society.

early 1900s. Initially, postgraduate courses in PUBLIC HEALTH were offered at local colleges such as the School of Civics and Philanthropy at the UNIVERSITY OF CHICAGO. The first baccalaureate degree program in nursing was initiated at LOYOLA UNIVERSITY in 1935. By the end of the century Chicago had seven universities offering bachelor's degrees in nursing, with some offering master's and doctoral degrees as well. In response to a nursing shortage in the 1950s, community colleges instituted associate (two-year) degree programs in nursing. Graduates were eligible to take the examination for registered nurses and served as hospital staff nurses. Baccalaureate graduates were to serve in leadership roles and public health.

In 1889, a group of wealthy society women created the Visiting Nurses Association (VNA), the third such organization in the country. Nurses were employed to provide free, scientific nursing care in the homes of the sick poor. During each of the following decades through 1920, the city's population grew by more than 600,000; as the population multiplied, so too did sickness. The VNA realized that the needs of the poor extended far beyond home visiting, and it then developed school nursing, industrial nursing, and day hospitals for babies. The VNA played a major role in creating what became the Chicago Lung Association. Two major organizations, the Infant Welfare Society and the Public Health Nurses of the Chicago Department of Health had their roots in the VNA. Local and national nursing leadership from 1903 into the 1930s was provided by Harriet Fulmer, Edna Foley, and Carrie Bullock (a VNA staff nurse who served as president of the National Association of Colored Graduate Nurses during the 1910s).

Chicago's nurses served in the Red Cross during WORLD WAR I and in the armed services thereafter. Staff shortages during wars led to new ways of delivering care. After WORLD WAR II, nurses led teams of lesser-trained assistants. Nursing units became specialized, and intensive care units were created beginning in the 1950s.

During the 1960s, nurses enjoyed unprecedented progress in upgrading salaries, working conditions, and employee benefits. At the beginning of the decade, no nurses had negotiated contracts with their hospitals. By 1970, more than 34 hospitals and agencies negotiated employment contracts with local bargaining units of the Illinois Nurses' Association. Considerable improvements in wages and working conditions resulted from these agreements, but, despite persistent shortages of trained nurses, pay has remained low relative to other professions.

Wendy Burgess

See also: Colleges, Junior and Community; Medical Education; Schooling for Work; Unionization

Further reading: Billings, John S., and Henry M. Hurd. *Hospitals, Dispensaries, and Nursing.* Papers of the International Congress of Charities, Correction, and Philanthropy, 1893. Repr. 1984. • Dunwiddie, Mary. *A History of the Illinois State Nurses' Association.* 1937. • Egenes, Karen, and Wendy Burgess. *Faithfully Yours: A History of Nursing in Illinois.* 2002.

Nursing Homes. *See* Housing for the Elderly

Oak Brook, IL, DuPage County, 17 miles W of the Loop. Oak Brook is located in the lower SALT CREEK drainage basin, where Salt Creek turns eastward toward the DES PLAINES RIVER. From the late 1600s to the early 1800s, the region was the location of the largest POTAWATOMI settlement in what is now DUPAGE COUNTY. OAK BROOK was then known as Sauganakka.

White settlers began arriving in the 1830s, following major Indian trails that are presently traced by Spring, York, and Butterfield Roads and Ogden Avenue. The Potawatomi, who had sold their land to the federal government, were moving out. Settler Elisha Fish arrived in 1834.

Families from New York, Pennsylvania, Ohio, Indiana, and Kentucky were attracted by the rich SOIL, clear streams, and abundant woodland. Residents called the area Brush Hill, and later Fullersburg, after Benjamin Fuller. Both names, owing to boundary changes, were shared with what is now HINSDALE.

Before the CIVIL WAR, some settlers maintained a way station on the UNDERGROUND RAILROAD in the gristmill of Frederick Graue on Salt Creek. Settlement continued after the war. Many of the newcomers were immigrants from Europe, mostly from GERMANY.

Over the next several decades, the area gradually changed from an agricultural settlement to a cluster of small estates. A significant event in this transformation was the purchase of land along Salt Creek by Frank Osgood Butler of Hinsdale in 1898. It was Butler's son Paul who was largely responsible for the development of Oak Brook as one of the nation's most affluent suburbs in the twentieth century. Butler, a business executive and sportsman, began acquiring neighboring farmland for investment purposes in the 1920s. Small parcels of farmland also were sold to other individuals who built homes on the sites.

In the mid-1930s, homeowners and farmers formed the Community Club, which helped unincorporated Oak Brook establish an identity separate from its neighbors, Hinsdale to the south and ELMHURST to the north.

Butler meanwhile had continued to accumulate land, hoping at some point to build a planned community. On part of his property, he established the multiuse Sports Core, which came to include nationally renowned GOLF and polo clubs. By 1958, when Oak Brook was incorporated, Butler owned much of the land within its boundaries.

Three factors had forced incorporation—completion of the nearby Tri-State and East-West TOLLWAYS, a change in ZONING along the tollways to commercial use, and the purchase of land by Marshall Field & Company for a proposed shopping center. The proposed shopping center was also claimed by neighboring Utopia (now OAKBROOK TERRACE) but was eventually annexed to Oak Brook. The Oakbrook Shopping Center opened in 1962 and became the commercial heart of the village.

Beginning in the 1960s, several luxury SUBDIVISIONS were built. In the years that followed, many nationally prominent corporations, such as Armour & Company, Eastman Kodak, and McDonald's, opened offices in Oak Brook. Development continued in the 1990s, including a major expansion of the shopping center.

Margaret Franson Pruter

See also: Built Environment of the Chicago Region; Shopping Districts and Malls

Further reading: Kinnavy, Susan, Audrey Muschler, and Pat Walker. *Oak Brook.* 1990. • Thompson, Richard, ed. *DuPage Roots.* 1985.

Oak Forest, IL, Cook County, 20 miles S of the Loop. The community's name came from the oak forests of the area, a portion of which remain as FOREST PRESERVES. Oak Forest is most widely known as the home of the COOK COUNTY Oak Forest HOSPITAL, an institution that has played a major role in the growth of the community. The older residential areas are immediately west and north of the hospital, with commercial areas along Cicero Avenue and 159th Street. These two major streets cross close to the community's COMMUTER station on the Rock Island RAILROAD. To the south and southeast of the hospital, ANNEXATIONS through the years have led to development surrounding the Oak Forest interchange of Interstate 57.

The original Oak Forest train station was primarily a milk stop used by YANKEE and GERMAN farmers of Bremen Township. In 1894 the

scene changed dramatically when the DuPont family purchased property on the east side of the tracks centered at about 155th Street. There they built what they claimed was the world's largest gunpowder magazine and factory. Most of the workers at the factory lived in BLUE ISLAND and commuted daily on the train. The entire complex blew up in 1906.

Of more lasting significance was the development of the hospital. The decision to locate a poor farm in the area was made in 1907 in response to the overcrowded conditions at the County Poor Farm in DUNNING on the Northwest Side of Chicago. The facility was completed in 1910 as the Oak Forest Infirmary, and accommodated close to 2,000 persons who were destitute because of poverty, mental illness, alcoholism, and other problems. Residents helped maintain farmland around the facility. By 1932, there were more than 4,000 patients, including over 500 with TUBERCULOSIS. Oak Forest Hospital continues to function today as an important part of the county's health care systems.

By the 1920s, several residential SUBDIVISIONS were underway, but in 1940 there were only 611 residents outside the hospital. While the hospital provided jobs and opportunities for business (like mortuaries), there were ambivalent feelings about the hospital. In the 1930s, some efforts were made to rename this small community "Arbor Park," but the new name did not stick. In 1947, the population grew to 1,618, and the residents voted to incorporate as the village of Oak Forest. Oak Forest experienced dramatic growth in the 1960s. A complex pattern of subdivisions emerged, helping to give the community its strange boundary. The population jumped from 3,724 in 1960 to 17,870 in 1970, but leveled off after the population reached 26,096 in 1980.

Significant commercial and industrial development accompanied this population growth.

Larry A. McClellan

See also: Transportation

Further reading: Centennial Book Committee. *1892–1992: The History of Oak Forest, Illinois.* 1992. • The Historical Committee. *The History of Oak Forest, Illinois.* 1972.

Oak Lawn, IL, Cook County, 13 miles SW of the Loop. Oak Lawn lies just outside the southwestern edge of Chicago, and is one of the largest municipalities in COOK COUNTY. The intersection of 95th Street (the village's main east-west thoroughfare) and Cicero Avenue is one of the county's busiest. A farming community until the mid-twentieth century, Oak Lawn is now home mainly to COMMUTERS.

Settlers established firms in the area in the 1840s and 1850s, attracted by a modest stream called Stony Creek (also spelled Stoney Creek) that meandered through a dense grove of black oak TREES. The area was variously known as Black Oaks and Black Oak Grove. By 1860, a schoolhouse and several farmhouses lined Black Oak Grove Road (95th Street). The nearest stores and post office were in BLUE ISLAND, some 10 miles away.

After the CIVIL WAR, GERMAN immigrants began settling in the area. A new post office opened in neighboring EVERGREEN PARK. The 1880s brought several changes to Oak Lawn. The Wabash RAILROAD connected the area with Chicago; the first SUBDIVISION was platted near the train station; and the community was formally called Oak Lawn for the first time. (It had briefly been called Agnes in the early 1880s, and was occasionally referred to as Oak Park.) Residents took the train to ENGLEWOOD to shop, and farm products and milk were sent to markets in Chicago.

A post office was established in 1882, and a portion of Stony Creek was enlarged to form Oak Lawn Lake, a recreational area. By 1909, the year of incorporation, the village's 300 citizens were scattered over 1.5 square miles. Some of these were DUTCH truck farmers who had arrived around the turn of the century. Incorporation meant that GAS lines could be installed, unruly visitors picnicking in the wooded areas along the creek and lake could be policed, and the city of Chicago would be less likely to annex the community. In 1911, the village's signature black oaks were replaced by electrical lines and poles.

An innovative plan begun in 1927 concentrated commercial development along major arteries and away from neighborhoods of single-family homes. Oak Lawn's population grew from 8,751 in 1950 to 60,305 in 1970s as white residents moved from Chicago's SOUTH SIDE to the suburbs. In 1953, the village changed from a trustee form of government to a managerial form. Several ANNEXATIONS increased the village's area to more than eight square miles. The village's rapid growth was checked briefly in 1967 by a tornado that killed 37 people and damaged or destroyed 900 buildings. In 1970, Oak Lawn became a HOME RULE unit, allowing the village greater latitude in determining municipal policy.

Commercial and retail businesses occupy about one-third of the village, mainly flanking 95th Street, with some industry in the southern and northwestern areas. The citizenry was 93 percent white in 2000. Although the community's largest employer is Christ HOSPITAL and Medical Center, most residents work in Chicago. Oak Lawn Lake is administered by the Oak Lawn Park District, and Stony Creek meanders through the Wolfe Wildlife Refuge on the village's south side.

Betsy Gurlacz

See also: Government, Suburban; Suburbs and Cities as Dual Metropolis

Further reading: *Black Oak and After: A Series on the History of Oak Lawn.* 1991. • *Oak Lawn, One Hundred Years: A Century of Growth.* 1982.

Oak Park, IL, Cook County, 8 miles W of the Loop. Joseph Kettlestrings bought 173 acres of timber and prairie land just east of the DES PLAINES RIVER in 1835. He erected a house on the stagecoach route from Galena to Chicago. The area was sparsely populated when the Galena & Chicago Union Railroad laid tracks parallel to the stagecoach route in 1848. Kettlestrings Grove slowly grew into the small village of Oak Ridge, which is now the northwestern portion of Oak Park.

By the end of the CIVIL WAR, the village was dotted with a market, a general store, a stationery business, and a small newspaper. The name Oak Ridge, already assigned to another post office in Illinois, was changed to Oak Park in 1872.

Oak Park grew dramatically after the FIRE OF 1871. James Scoville bought acreage once owned by Kettlestrings and subdivided the area near the RAILROAD station. The Cicero Water, GAS, AND ELECTRIC Light Company serviced the community, streets were paved, surface TRANSPORTATION lines established, and SUBDIVISIONS extended beyond the old stagecoach route later named Lake Street. The village was one of eight communities governed by the TOWNSHIP of CICERO. In 1902, however, Oak Park seceded from the township and incorporated as a separate municipality.

The extension of the Lake Street "L" to Harlem Avenue at the turn of the century linked Oak Park more closely to Chicago. It was one of only a few suburban stops in the system. The village's population rose to 10,000 in 1900 and increased to 40,000 by 1920. By the 1920s, the area around the elevated had developed into a regional SHOPPING DISTRICT and included Marshall Field's, Wieboldt's, and the Fair Store. Many of the older large homes in the central district were replaced by APARTMENTS and commercial and office buildings. Builders like Seward Gunderson and Thomas Hulbert developed homes south of Madison Avenue. The prairies north of Lake Street soon vanished, replaced by large homes, including many designed by Frank Lloyd Wright and E. E. Roberts. Wright established his studio in Oak Park in 1898 and designed the nearby Unity Temple, which is on the National Register of Historic Places.

Ernest Hemingway, Doris Humphrey, and Edgar Rice Burroughs are among those associated with Oak Park. Hemingway was born there in 1899, and the Hemingway Foundation has preserved his boyhood home and opened a small museum. Humphrey, who grew up in Oak Park, opened her first DANCE studio there before joining the Denishawn Company in 1918. The Doris Humphrey Society was established in Oak Park in 1989 to preserve her contributions to MODERN DANCE. Burroughs wrote 22 Tarzan books while residing in Oak Park from 1912 to 1919.

After World War II, Oak Park faced dramatic changes. Shopping malls along new EXPRESSWAYS drew business away from Oak Park's downtown. DEMOGRAPHIC change posed complementary challenges. By 1958, Oak Park's overwhelmingly Republican, mainline PROTESTANT, white population saw rising numbers of ROMAN CATHOLICS, JEWS, and fundamentalist Christians enter the village. This shift did not affect the community's high level of educational or economic attainment, but it sparked fears of a departure from Oak Park's traditional conservative values. By the early 1970s, ITALIANS and IRISH outnumbered the GERMANS, ENGLISH, and Scandinavians who had long predominated, and Catholicism had become a significant presence.

The ability of Oak Parkers to absorb new groups was soon tested again. Oak Park's eastern neighbor, Chicago's AUSTIN neighborhood, had long been characterized by tree-lined streets of gracious homes and small BUNGALOWS, with residents who had lived in the community for generations. Both communities, however, also had aging housing stock and weak ZONING and BUILDING CODES. Over 50 percent of Oak Park's housing comprised apartment buildings, most concentrated along its eastern border. Oak Parkers watched first-hand in the 1960s as Austin's residents fought desperately to defend their community from a destabilizing influx of AFRICAN AMERICAN home-seekers, with little success—resegregation was rapid and tumultuous.

Oak Park devised a different strategy, which would use planning to ensure that desegregation would not lead to resegregation. The village board created a Community Relations Commission charged with preventing discrimination, forestalling violent neighborhood defense mechanisms, and setting a high standard of behavior as the community prepared for imminent racial change. Village officials, often joined by clergymen, visited blocks to which families of color might move and carefully sought to control the fears and rumors generally associated with neighborhood succession. They identified white families who would welcome the newcomers. They encouraged African American families to disperse throughout the village to counter concerns of clustering and ghetto formation. In 1968, after lengthy and angry debate, and the passage of the federal Fair Housing Act, the village board passed an OPEN-HOUSING ordinance allowing officials to control many aspects of racial integration that otherwise were likely to lead to resegregation. REAL-ESTATE agents were banned from panic-peddling, BLOCKBUSTING, and the use of "for sale" signs. A community relations department would address rumors, monitor the quality of services and amenities throughout the village, and establish block clubs to promote resident cohesion and local problem-solving. The police force expanded by one-third, with a residency requirement whose impact was magnified because police generally lived in areas most likely to be threatened by resegregation. An equity assurance program for homeowners would reassure residents that they were financially protected against a downward spiral of property values. Leaders acted on a vision of Oak Park as a community strong enough to achieve integration, and able to challenge the Chicago pattern of block-by-block resegregation with a policy of managed integration through dispersal.

The most controversial policies involved racial STEERING. A group of residents led by Roberta (Bobbie) Raymond established the OakPark Housing Center, which retrained real-estate agents to prevent racial steering and encouraged black home-seekers to live throughout Oak Park. The center worked with the village to improve areas that white home-seekers or residents might find unattractive and steered whites towards these areas to limit the concentration of black residents in a particular neighborhood. A public relations campaign targeted white home-seekers across the country to promote an image of Oak Park as a multicultural, cosmopolitan middle-class community, close to the city, with good transportation and schools.

Despite these programs, during the 1970s the village experienced a net loss of 10,000 white Oak Parkers, coinciding with a net increase of only 5,500 black residents. Urbanologists' predictions that the ghetto would roll over Oak Park, however, proved inaccurate. Oak Park maintained its majority white population through extensive and white-oriented planning, and has remained an integrated village. Pockets of racial segregation have persisted, but the community has succeeded in maintaining a public culture that takes pride in racial diversity.

Tina Reithmaier
Camille Henderson Zorich

See also: Architecture: The First Chicago School; Historic Preservation; Suburbs and Cities as Dual Metropolis

Further reading: Goodwin, Carole. *The Oak Park Strategy.* 1979. • Guarino, Jean. *Oak Park: A Pictorial History.* 1988. • Halley, William. *Early Days in Oak Park.* 1933.

Oakbrook Terrace, IL, DuPage County, 17 miles W of the Loop. Oakbrook Terrace is located in the lower SALT CREEK drainage basin, lying west of the creek itself. It is a small residential and commercial city, covering approximately 1.8 square miles. For much of its existence, Oakbrook Terrace has lived in the shadow of its wealthy and prestigious neighbor, OAK BROOK, from which it adapted its name. The two neighbors have had a contentious relationship for decades.

NATIVE AMERICANS entered the area that became Oakbrook Terrace as early as five thousand years ago. When the last of these peoples, the POTAWATOMI, were forced to move westward in the early 1830s, white settlers, mainly of ENGLISH and later GERMAN extraction, established homesteads in the Salt Creek area. A combination creamery and cheese factory was built by Albert Knapp at what was called "The Corners" in 1873. The community that grew up around the Corners—now Butterfield and Summit Roads—came to be called Utopia in 1881. The area remained AGRICULTURAL well into the twentieth century.

Suburban growth began soon after WORLD WAR II, when the community was subdivided. Commercial development was started along two major east-west thoroughfares, Roosevelt Road and 22nd Street. At the time of its incorporation in 1958, Utopia included in its acreage the proposed site of a large SHOPPING center, but neighboring Oak Brook annexed the center and its commercial properties with state approval in 1959. That year, a disappointed Utopia changed its name to Oakbrook Terrace, indicating its proximity to the soon-to-be Oak Brook Shopping Center. Oakbrook Terrace attempted without success to regain control of the property from the village of Oak Brook in 1961.

Oakbrook Terrace experienced its greatest residential growth during the 1970s, when nearly half of its housing units were built. In the 1980s, the community rapidly developed its commercial areas, including construction of DUPAGE COUNTY's tallest office building, the 31-story Oakbrook Terrace Tower near Routes 38 and 83. Also during that decade, Drury Lane THEATRE, a popular dinner playhouse, was built. Lincoln Centre, a large office complex, was constructed along Butterfield Road in the 1990s. By 2000, when population reached 2,300, most of the city's available land had been developed for either residential or commercial purposes.

Margaret Franson Pruter

See also: Commercial Buildings; Suburbs and Cities as Dual Metropolis

Further reading: *1874 Atlas and History of DuPage County, Illinois.* Reprint, 1975. • Kinnavy, Susan, Audrey Muschler, and Pat Walker. *Oak Brook.* 1990. • Thompson, Richard, ed. *DuPage Roots.* 1985.

Oakland, Community Area 36, 4 miles SE of the Loop. Oakland is bounded by 35th and

43rd Streets, Lake Michigan, Cottage Grove, Pershing, and Vincennes Avenues. The entire area of the community is approximately one square mile.

Oakland originally grew out of the Cleaverville settlement. In 1851, industrialist Charles Cleaver purchased from Samuel Ellis 22 acres of swampy ground near 38th Street and Lake Michigan, and built a soap factory and company town that included a commissary, house of worship, town hall, and homes for workers. Part of the area was annexed to Chicago in 1863; the rest in 1889.

Residents were attracted to the area because of nearby Camp Douglas, the stockyards, and a commercial district that included popular saloons. The addition of a horsecar line in 1867 improved access to the city. In 1871 real-estate developers subdivided the area and renamed it Oakland. In less than five years the community became home to many of Chicago's elite. In 1881 transportation was greatly improved with an Illinois Central Railroad terminal at 39th and Cottage Grove. This area of commercial activity became known as the "Five Crossings." By the end of the century, more affluent residents moved out and were replaced by working-class Irish residents. Numerous single-family houses and apartments were constructed to accommodate the influx of immigrants.

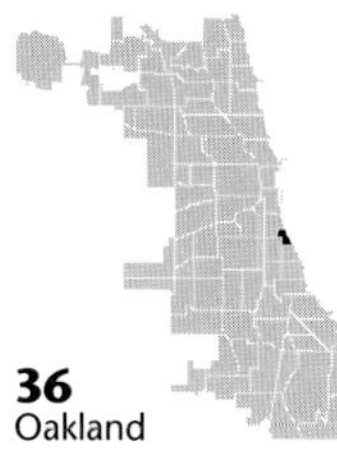

In 1905 the Abraham Lincoln Center was founded by Jenkin Lloyd Jones as a meeting place for people of various races, religions, and nationalities. Located at 700 Oakwood Boulevard, this historic landmark designed by Frank Lloyd Wright now serves as the home of Northeastern Illinois University's Center for Inner City Studies.

During the first wave of the Great Migration between 1916 and 1920 many African Americans settled in Oakland. During the 1930s Oakland experienced its greatest diversity, with a mixture of African Americans, Germans, Jews, English, Irish, Canadians, and Japanese. Racial tensions escalated as the African American population increased. Some white residents resorted to violence and restrictive covenants to prevent blacks from moving into Oakland, but such efforts proved unsuccessful, and by 1950 Oakland was 77 percent African American.

In the 1970s, Oakland experienced a declining economic base. Public housing projects such as Ida B. Wells, once the pride of the community, became crime-infested. The former Oakland Theatre located in the heart of Oakland near 39th and Cottage Grove became the headquarters of the notorious El Rukn street gang. The city of Chicago demolished dilapidated buildings, and vacant lots were left scattered throughout the community. Oakland's average income fell below the poverty level as middle-class residents moved further south.

During the 1990s, under the leadership of Robert Lucas, the Kenwood-Oakland Community Organization (KOCO) rehabilitated several buildings in the community and successfully pressured the city to invest in Oakland. Beginning in 1994, the North Kenwood–Oakland Conservation Community Council, led by Shirley Newsome, cosponsored the Kenwood-Oakland Parade of Homes, which helped the further development of single-family houses, townhouses, and rehabbed buildings.

Claudette Tolson

See also: Annexation; Community Organizing; Neighborhood Succession; South Side; Street Railways; Suburbs and Cities as Dual Metropolis; Urban Renewal

Further reading: Holt, Glen E., and Dominic A. Pacyga. *Chicago: A Historical Guide to the Neighborhoods: The Loop and South Side.* 1981. • Jones, LeAlan, and Lloyd Newman. *Our America: Life and Death on the South Side of Chicago.* 1997. • Travis, Dempsey. *An Autobiography of Black Chicago.* 1981.

Oakwood Hills, IL, McHenry County, 41 miles NW of the Loop. This community began as a group of summer homes along Andersen's Lake (now Silver Lake). Area residents, wanting to improve roads and control zoning, debated incorporation in the 1950s. Incorporated as Oakwood Hills in 1959, the village is a bedroom community for local workers and Chicago commuters. The 2000 population was 2,194.

Craig L. Pfannkuche

See also: McHenry County

Occupational Safety and Health. Much of Chicago's explosive nineteenth-century economic growth occurred in transportation and heavy industry. These two sectors were not only among the most profitable enterprises of the time, they were also among the most dangerous. By 1912, an estimated 2,000,000 American industrial workers were injured annually in the United States, and another 35,000 workers lost their lives each year. Since nineteenth-century legal doctrines held that employees assumed the risks for most freely contracted labor, the financial burden added to the emotional and physical toll these accidents took on industrial workers and their families.

Because of the large concentration of railroads and industrial corporations in Chicago, many journalists and social reformers focused on the city as a place where industrial workers, particularly immigrants, were most at risk. For example, William Hard's widely read article "Making Steel and Killing Men" focused on United States Steel's South Chicago plant, where 46 workers were killed and 368 employees became permanently disabled in 1906.

Alice Hamilton, a Chicago-area resident from 1897 to 1919, performed pivotal work in occupational health during her time in Illinois. Heavily influenced by her stay at Hull House, Hamilton worked to improve conditions for the immigrant poor by performing groundbreaking research in occupational health at Northwestern University, by reorganizing the Chicago Health Department in 1902, and by serving as the founding director of the Illinois Occupational Disease Commission in 1910. The IODC was the first such commission in the United States.

As Hamilton and other social reformers brought attention to problems surrounding occupational health and safety, industrial corporations began to suffer heavy losses in the courts and state legislatures. Sympathetic juries awarded healthy sums to injured workers suing their employers, and compensation laws increasingly placed the financial burden of occupational safety squarely on the employer. Illinois was one of the first states to pass such legislation, enacting Occupational Disease and Workmen's Compensation acts in 1911.

When it became evident that American industry had lost the battle over industrial safety in the courts, the press, and the legislatures, industrial corporations began to take an active role in preventing accidents. Representatives of some of the country's largest transportation and manufacturing concerns met in 1912 and decided to form the National Council for Industrial Safety, which became the United States' largest and most active safety advocacy organization of the twentieth century. The council organized in Chicago in 1913 and operated out of its downtown offices in the Continental and Commercial Savings Bank building; Illinois Steel's chief attorney, Robert Campbell, served as the council's first president.

Propelled by this early progress, as well as by the relative decline of U.S. employment in heavy industry, rates of industrial accidents and sickness gradually declined. Still, after conducting a survey of Cook County in the late 1940s, the United States Public Health Service found that despite improvements in manufacturing plants employing over 250 people, employees at smaller factories continued to be at risk. Moreover, they estimated that smaller plants employed almost half of the county's workers.

The landmark 1970 Occupational Safety and Health Act (OSHA) established national safety standards for private-sector employees and empowered the U.S. Department of Labor to oversee and enforce these standards. However, occupational health activists warned that OSHA lacked enforcement capacity and that additional contests would be fought in the legislatures and courts. One of these battles took place in Cook County in 1985, when executives of Film Recovery Systems, Inc., were convicted of murder after allowing workers to become fully exposed to cyanide in their recycling plant.

Tom Hafen

See also: Iron and Steel; Iron- and Steelworkers; Labor Law; Public Health; Work

Further reading: Aldrich, Mark. *Safety First: Technology, Labor, and Business in the Building of American Work Safety, 1870–1939.* 1997. • Hafen, Thomas. "Safe Workers: The National Safety Council and the American Safety Movement, 1900–1930." Ph.D. diss., University of Chicago. 2002. • Hard, William. "Making Steel and Killing Men." *Everybody's Magazine,* November 1907, 580–584.

Ogden Dunes, IN, Porter County, 29 miles SE of the Loop. Prior to the completion of Dunes Highway (Route 12) in 1923, the Ogden Dunes area remained largely undeveloped and was home to hermits and squatters, among them Chicagoan Alice Gray, known as "Diana of the Dunes." Dorothy Buell helped organize the Save the Dunes Council in 1952 and was a leader in establishing the INDIANA DUNES National Lakeshore, which surrounds Ogden Dunes.

Peggy Tuck Sinko

See also: Dune System; Lake Michigan; Leisure; Plant Communities

Further reading: Hoppe, David. "Child of the Northwest Wind: Alice Gray and 'Diana of the Dunes.'" *Traces of Indiana and Midwestern History* 9 (1997): 22–31. • Moore, Powell A. *The Calumet Region: Indiana's Last Frontier.* 1977. • Thomas, Joseph. *History of Ogden Dunes.* 1976.

O'Hare, Community Area 76, 14 miles NW of the Loop. The land constituting the O'Hare Community Area was only thinly developed before WORLD WAR II. The 1829 TREATY of Prairie du Chien gave two square miles around the DES PLAINES RIVER to Alexander Robinson, a SCOTTISH-OTTAWA interpreter who had aided whites escaping the FORT DEARBORN Massacre. In the early 1840s, a few families settled along what would become Higgins Road, while immigrants from GERMANY settled in the southwest section of the area, establishing a church and St. Johannes CEMETERY in 1849. The northeastern section was an unincorporated area called Orchard Place, named for the depot the Wisconsin Central RAILROAD opened there in 1887. Despite the railroad, however, few people settled in Orchard Place. A residential SUBDIVISION opened in the 1930s, but all traces of it vanished with the developments of World War II.

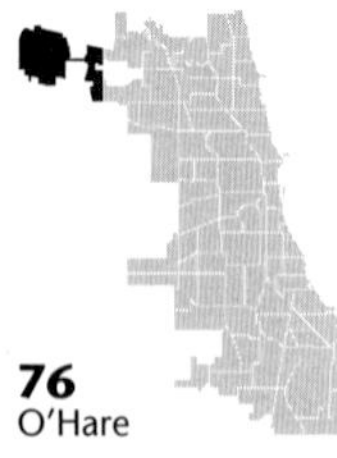

In 1942, Douglas Aircraft took over Orchard Place for the production of cargo planes. After war production ended, the facility became a commercial AIRPORT, and in 1947 the Chicago City Council picked it as the site for the city's new international airport (named for aviator Edward H. "Butch" O'Hare). All local facilities, except for St. Johannes Cemetery, were removed.

In order to consolidate its control over the airport area, Chicago ANNEXED it in March 1956, including the western edge, in DuPage County. Because legal incorporation required that annexed areas be contiguous with Chicago, the city council also annexed a narrow stretch of Higgins Road to connect the main body of the city with the airport. Concerned that this tie was too tenuous, Chicago overrode the objections of surrounding suburbs like SCHILLER PARK, annexing the FOREST PRESERVE areas named for Alexander Robinson and his wife in 1958 and exchanging Higgins Road for a wider stretch along Foster Avenue in 1961. The building of the Kennedy EXPRESSWAY in the late 1950s further reinforced the link between air travelers and the LOOP. The addition of such a large amount of land necessitated the creation of a new COMMUNITY AREA on the city's planning map, setting a precedent for the secession of EDGEWATER from UPTOWN.

The rapid success of the airport inspired a tremendous increase in nearby land values. Along the expressway, developers built a gleaming row of office towers occupied by businesses taking advantage of the proximity to other cities provided by the airport. High-rise APARTMENT buildings and a few small tracts of single-family houses and CONDOMINIUMS made the portion of O'Hare bisected by NORRIDGE a residential area in the 1960s. Employees of the airport and its airlines occupied many of these homes.

Amanda Seligman

See also: Airlines; Bensenville; Des Plaines; Franklin Park; Land Use; O'Hare International Airport; Real Estate; Rosemont; Transportation

Further reading: Chicago Fact Book Consortium, ed. *Local Community Fact Book: Chicago Metropolitan Area, 1990.* 1995. • Doherty, Richard P. "The Origin and Development of Chicago-O'Hare International Airport." Ph.D. diss., Ball State University. 1970.

O'Hare International Airport. In order to increase production of airplanes for World War II at a safe inland location, the Douglas Aircraft Company, the Corps of Army Engineers, the Civil Aeronautics Authority, Chicago Association of Commerce, and the Chicago Regional Planning Association selected a site on the outskirts of the Northwest Side of the city. The first C-54 Skymaster rolled off the line on July 30, 1943. Jennie Giangreco, the Windy City's answer to "Rosie the Riveter," dedicated this craft *Chicago.*

Simultaneously the city of Chicago was looking to expand air travel beyond MIDWAY AIRPORT. In 1944 Ralph Burke, city engineer, designated the Douglas Aircraft plant for use as an additional commercial airport. After retiring to private practice Burke developed a master plan for the airport, including its passenger terminals, highway access and, above all, provisions for later construction of a mass transit link to the Loop. Domestic commercial flights began on a small scale in 1955.

After Burke's death in 1956, Mayor Richard J. Daley selected C. F. Murphy Associates to continue the airport development. Led by partner Carter Manny, Jr., the firm designed a passenger terminal complex comprising four semiautonomous buildings linked by walkways. The terminals have long projections or "fingers" where passengers enplane and deplane. Mayor Daley and President John F. Kennedy dedicated the completed facility on March 23, 1963, formally naming it after the WORLD WAR II hero Lt. Comdr. Edward O'Hare.

In the ensuing decades air travel grew faster than many of the most optimistic long-term projections. In 1966, the Federal Aviation Agency employed I. M. Pei & Associates to design a new air traffic control tower. Seven years later a new HOTEL and multistory parking structure opened. Again Carter Manny, with the assistance of John M. Novack, led the design of both of these projects.

When the federal government passed the AIRLINE Deregulation Act of 1978, completing the transformation of flight into mass, long-haul transit, the resulting low, and sometimes idiosyncratic, fare structure greatly increased the number of travelers. In the 1980s this growth undergirded the demand for design and construction of new terminals, an internal surface mass-transportation system or "people mover," and the extension of a RAPID TRANSIT line (1984) to the airport. In 1983 Helmut Jahn of Murphy/Jahn designed a new terminal, meeting standards jointly set by the tenant (United Airlines) and the city Department of Aviation. Approximately five years later Perkins & Will completed a new international terminal. By the end of the century the array of buildings, transportation systems, and amenities at O'Hare constituted a city within a city.

David Brodherson

See also: Architecture: Second Chicago School; Economic Geography; O'Hare, Community Global Chicago; Planning Chicago; Transportation

Mayor Richard J. Daley and President John F. Kennedy at O'Hare Airport, March 1963. Photographer: Unknown. Source: Chicago Historical Society.

Further reading: Brodherson, David. "All Airplanes Lead to Chicago: Airport Planning and Design in a Midwest Metropolis." In *Chicago Architecture and Design, 1923–1993: Reconfiguration of an American Metropolis,* ed. John Zukowsky, 1993. • Cannon, Charles B. *The O'Hare Story.* 1980. • Doherty, Richard P. *The Origin and Development of Chicago–O'Hare International Airport.* 1970.

Oil Refining. *See* Refining

Ojibwa. Ojibwa people from the present Upper Peninsula of Michigan and northern Wisconsin began moving into the Chicago region in the 1760s as part of the tribal mobilization accompanying Pontiac's uprising (1763–64). A prominent leader known as Le Grand Saulteur, from the Sault Ste. Marie district, maintained a community at Chicago for several years. By 1810, the Ojibwa, known to Americans as "Chippewa," were a component of multitribal villages along the western side of Lake Michigan from the CALUMET RIVER of Indiana to the Manitowauk River in Wisconsin. Within this area, the Ojibwa became part of the group usually described as "The United Tribes (or Nations) of Chippewa, OTTAWA, and POTAWATOMI" in a series of peace and land cession TREATIES with the federal government during the period from 1816 to 1833. The final treaty called for the cession of their remaining territory in northeastern Illinois and Wisconsin. The treaty also abolished all their reservations in Illinois as well as southwestern Michigan, and provided for the natives' removal to land west of the Mississippi River. By that time, the United Nation was largely amalgamated and recognized as Potawatomi.

Helen Hornbeck Tanner

See also: Chicago in the Middle Ground; Demography; Native Americans

Further reading: Tanner, Helen Hornbeck, ed. *Atlas of Great Lakes Indian History.* 1987. • Tanner, Helen Hornbeck. *The Ojibwas.* 1992.

Old Mill Creek, IL, Lake County, 42 miles NW of the Loop. Located in north central LAKE COUNTY, five miles south of the Wisconsin border, Old Mill Creek remained a rural community well into the twentieth century. In the late 1830s, GERMAN and SCOTTISH settlers established the small agricultural community that would later become Old Mill Creek. Jacob Miller built a sawmill and gristmill along a tributary of the DES PLAINES RIVER, naming it Mill Creek. In 1838, the Strang brothers, originally from Scotland, traveled from Canada to Illinois in search of work on the ILLINOIS & MICHIGAN CANAL. They founded a small settlement near Mill Creek known as Strang's Corners, which served as the area's only commercial center. The name was later changed to Millburn, "burn" being the Scottish word for creek. The placement of the Chicago & Milwaukee RAILROAD several miles east of Millburn stunted the settlement's growth.

The village of Old Mill Creek was incorporated in 1959. In the 1950s, Chicago millionaire Tempel Smith, of Tempel Steel Company, purchased several thousand acres in Old Mill Creek and introduced large-scale grain cultivation. Smith also established Tempel Farms, where he bred Lipizzan horses, which he imported from Austria, Hungary, and Yugoslavia. Smith's large property holdings passed to his three children upon his death in 1980, and by the early 1990s, Tempel Steel and the Tempel Smith family owned close to 80 percent of the land in Old Mill Creek.

While suburban development took place to the south and west, Millburn and Old Mill Creek remained comparatively undeveloped. Most of the buildings in the almost 8,000-acre area were clustered in the 37-acre community of Millburn. In 1979, 18 of these were designated the Millburn Historic District and listed on the National Register of Historic Places. The buildings in the district date from the mid to late nineteenth century.

In 1994, a commission outlined a program for a planned community in Old Mill Creek that aimed to bring some 16,000 new residents to the village in the next two decades. The plan called for a "green belt" along the creek to surround the community, along with low-density, moderate-income housing, and a commercial office park. Concerned with the continued, rapid expansion of nearby LINDENHURST and GURNEE, residents of Millburn, which was then still unincorporated, looked to Old Mill Creek's strict ZONING laws to protect Millburn's country atmosphere. Residents thus elected in 1994 to be annexed to the village. The population of Old Mill Creek in 2000 was 251.

Elizabeth S. Fraterrigo

See also: Built Environment of the Chicago Region; Planning Chicago

Further reading: Christian, Sue Ellen. "The Lake Forgotten by Growth." *Chicago Tribune,* July 24, 1992. • Moore, Gary. "A Town in Waiting." *Chicago Tribune,* April 5, 1998. • Wagner, Robert. "Millburn Historic District." National Register Nomination Form. 1978.

Old Town, neighborhood in the LINCOLN PARK Community Area. During World War II, Chicago's Civil Defense Agency designated the triangle bounded by North, Clark, and Ogden Avenues a neighborhood defense unit. The neighbors in this residential section of "North Town" continued their association after the war, sponsoring annual ART FAIRS dubbed the "Old Town Holiday." The name Old Town, evoking a cozy, neighborly spirit, persisted when residents concerned about the area's physical deterioration formed the Old Town Triangle Association in 1948. OTTA's activities inspired URBAN RENEWAL throughout LINCOLN PARK.

During the 1960s, residents began to worry that OTTA's success undermined the insularity of their neighborhood. The rehabilitation of beautiful nineteenth-century houses and the increasingly popular art fair brought thousands of visitors to the area. Old Towners relished the presence of the Second City theater company and the OLD TOWN SCHOOL OF FOLK MUSIC. But when Wells Street, a commercial strip that cut through Old Town, enjoyed a boom of wealthy patrons of fashionable RESTAURANTS and stores, residents resented the noise, trash, and crowds. During the late 1960s, as Wells Street became a gathering place for hippies, some of the new shops failed and were replaced by stores marketing junky trinkets and pornography. Wells Street and Old Town resecured their status when Lincoln Park's urban renewal effort brought young professionals with money to the rehabbed cottages and new high-rises.

Amanda Seligman

See also: Community Organizing; Historic Preservation

Further reading: Callaway, John D. "Will Excess Spoil Old Town?" *Chicago Scene* 4.8 (August 1963): 21–23. • Commission on Chicago Historical and Architectural Landmarks. *Old Town: Preliminary Summary of Information.* 1975. • Pacyga, Dominic A., and Ellen Skerrett. *Chicago, City of Neighborhoods: Histories and Tours.* 1986.

Old Town School of Folk Music. The practice of self-made music has long served the OLD TOWN School of Folk Music. Founded as "the nation's first permanent school for the study of FOLK MUSIC and folk instruments," the school emerged from the urban folk revival of the 1950s. While appearing at the Gate of Horn, a NEAR NORTH SIDE night spot, musician Frank Hamilton began to conduct guitar classes in the OAK PARK home of folk aficionado Dawn Greening. The instructors, teaching different instruments, employed a group technique developed by West Coast–based singer Bess Lomax Hawes. Hawes encouraged her classes of informal adult learners to develop their personal musicality with a selection of uncomplicated songs they harmonized by ear. Performer Win Stracke, present at one of Hamilton's classes, was inspired to form a folk-music school based around this teaching method. Under Stracke's leadership, with Dawn Greening and Gertrude Soltker sharing administrative duties, and Hamilton instructing, the school officially began operations in December 1957.

Now housed in two permanent locations (4544 N. Lincoln and 909 W. Armitage), with scores of teachers and thousands of students, the school's fluid definition of folk music responds to evolving popular interests, with classes from tango dancing to IRISH fiddle, Beatles guitar to traditional banjo, African drumming to "Wiggleworms" music instruction for infants. With its long-standing hospitality to amateur players and professional performers alike, the school thrives, in the words of alumnus John Prine, "with no threat of a formal music education."

Stephen Wade

See also: Entertaining Chicagoans; Ethnic Music; Folk and Traditional Dance; Lincoln Square Music Clubs

Further reading: Cohen, Ronald D., ed. *"Wasn't That a Time!" Firsthand Accounts of the Folk Music Revival.* 1995. • Grayson, Lisa. *Biography of a Hunch: The History of Chicago's Legendary Old Town School of Folk Music.* 1992. • Weber, Bruce. "Folk Music with No Threat of a Formal Education." *New York Times,* November 18, 1997.

Olivet Baptist Church. Olivet Baptist Church is the oldest AFRICAN AMERICAN Baptist church in Chicago. It was organized first as Xenia Baptist Church on April 6, 1850, then became Zoar Baptist Church when it was formally incorporated three years later. Under the direction of the church's fifth pastor, Jesse F. Boulden, the church united with another black Baptist congregation and was named Olivet Baptist Church in 1861.

Olivet Baptist has been a wellspring of black leadership in Chicago since the nineteenth century. Many of the church's pastors have been influential in state, local, and national POLITICS. In 1869 Richard de Baptiste organized Illinois' first "Colored Convention" to fight for black CIVIL RIGHTS. Throughout his pastorate, Elijah John Fisher worked with Chicago's temperance activists to rid the SOUTH SIDE of SALOONS and VICE, and Lacey Kirk Williams remained a nationally prominent REPUBLICAN until his death in a plane crash en route to the GOP convention in 1940.

Olivet Baptist Church played a major role in the GREAT MIGRATION. Through the auspices of its Bethlehem Baptist Association and the *Chicago Defender,* Olivet stimulated the migration with the promise of jobs and housing. The congregation grew to an enormous size, estimated at approximately 10,000 in the 1920s, when it was hailed as "the largest PROTESTANT church in the world."

In recent years the size of Olivet's congregation has declined significantly. After the death in 1990 of Joseph Harrison Jackson, pastor of the church for 50 years, Olivet struggled to reclaim its former prominence in Chicago's African American community.

Wallace Best

Further reading: Drake, St. Clair. "Churches and Voluntary Associations in the Chicago Negro Community." Report of Official Project 465-54-3-386, Work Projects Administration. Chicago 1940. • Fisher, Miles Mark. "History of the Olivet Baptist Church." Thesis, University of Chicago. 1922. • Grossman, James R. *Land of Hope: Chicago, Black Southerners, and the Great Migration.* 1989.

Olympia Fields, IL, Cook County, 25 miles S of the Loop. The village of Olympia Fields developed from the Olympia Fields Country Club, for which it was named. Bounded roughly by Vollmer Road, 211th Street (U.S. Route 30 or Lincoln Highway), Crawford/Pulaski Avenue, and the eastern border of Western Avenue, the village lies almost entirely within Rich Township. The club is independent of the village, a part of unincorporated COOK COUNTY. Butterfield Creek drains the land into the Little CALUMET River. There is no evidence that Indians ever settled within the limits of the modern village. Elliott's AMUSEMENT PARK, which drew patrons from Chicago each summer from 1890 to 1913, occupied several acres northwest of where the ILLINOIS CENTRAL RAILROAD crosses Lincoln Highway. With that exception, the LANDSCAPE before twentieth-century development was farmland and woods.

In 1913, investors, attracted by the successes of country clubs in nearby Flossmoor and Homewood, began to buy land for a new club. Chartered in 1915, the club opened its first GOLF course the next year. First president Amos Alonzo Stagg chose the name Olympia Fields. The Tudor-style clubhouse, erected 1923–24, is on the National Register of

Historic Places. At its zenith, the club covered over a square mile and its facilities included a skeet range and a polo field west of the train tracks and four 18-hole golf courses to the east. The club hosted the U.S. Open in 1928 and 2003. Golf was so popular before the GREAT DEPRESSION that the Illinois Central scheduled "golf specials" from Chicago to Olympia Fields and other clubs.

An elite residential community centered on the club was part of the original investors' vision. Some families moved to the club for the summer and lived in canvas-covered "cottages," forerunners of the year-round homes on the grounds today. Residential lots on the western side of the tracks first sold in 1919, and by 1923 the Greek revival–style station at Olympia Fields was a regular stop for commuter trains. Population, however, remained slight. According to local lore, village incorporation was achieved in 1927 by counting railroad workers temporarily housed in cars on a nearby siding to meet the population minimum of 150.

The stock market crash of 1929 and the subsequent depression smothered growth until after WORLD WAR II. In 1944, the club sold two golf courses for residential development. Relatively few new residents joined the club, but the standards of an affluent, elite community have persisted. A mid-1950s ordinance was designed to make sure no two houses would look alike. Population surged from 160 in 1950 to 1,503 in 1960 and 3,478 in 1970, supported by ANNEXATIONS west of Kedzie Avenue. Institutional development followed: Tolentine Center (1958), originally an Augustinian SEMINARY and now the order's regional headquarters, Rich Central High School (1961), United Methodist Church (1964), and Temple Anshe Sholom (1964). As population grew (to 4,146 in 1980 and 4,732 in 2000), institutions kept pace. St. James Hospital (originally Osteopathic Medical Center) opened in 1976, as did the First Baptist and Assumption Greek Orthodox churches. Modest retail and commercial development, chiefly around the intersection of Lincoln Highway and Western Avenue, has been continuous since the 1950s.

John H. Long

See also: Leisure; Religious Geography; Suburbs and Cities as Dual Metropolis

Further reading: Dionne, Edward. *Olympia Fields: An Illinois Community's 50th Anniversary, 1927–1977.* 1977.

One-Way Streets. *See* Streets, One-Way

Open Housing. "Open housing" refers to the goal of a unitary housing market in which a person's background (as opposed to financial resources) does not arbitrarily restrict access. Calls for open housing were issued early in the twentieth century, but it was not until after WORLD WAR II that concerted efforts to achieve it were undertaken.

Many minorities in Chicago—especially MEXICANS, PUERTO RICANS, JEWS, and Asians—have suffered from a discriminatory housing market, but AFRICAN AMERICANS have been the most numerous victims. By the early twentieth century, white property owners and real-estate agents had devised mechanisms—most notably, RESTRICTIVE COVENANTS and discriminatory REAL-ESTATE practices—to ensure the residential segregation of the city by race.

The first major victory for open housing came in 1948 when in *Shelley v. Kraemer* the U.S. Supreme Court ruled that restrictive covenants were unconstitutional and therefore unenforceable. This decision was in part a result of agitation by black Chicagoans such as Earl Dickerson and Carl Hansberry.

In 1963, the Chicago City Council, after a heated debate, passed a fair housing ordinance prohibiting discrimination "against any person because of his race, color, religion, national origin or ancestry" in the quest for housing. (Subsequent versions extended protection on the grounds of sex, age, marital and parental status, sexual orientation, disability, source of income, and military discharge status.)

The dual housing market, in which whites can live anywhere they can afford but blacks and other minorities face restricted access, extended beyond the borders of Chicago proper. During the 1950s and early 1960s, white suburbanites often turned against pioneer black neighbors. In 1965, the American Friends Service Committee sponsored the North Shore Summer Project, which was designed to raise support for open housing in some of Chicago's most exclusive suburbs.

This project also served as an inspiration for the boldest charge for open housing in Chicago's history. In the summer of 1966, the Chicago Freedom Movement, an alliance between Chicago CIVIL RIGHTS forces and Martin Luther King's Southern Christian Leadership Conference, targeted Chicago's dual housing market and staged open-housing marches in all-white city neighborhoods and suburbs. The furor over these demonstrations led city leaders to support the creation of an organization dedicated to promoting open housing throughout metropolitan Chicago, the Leadership Council for Metropolitan Open Communities.

In 1968, the U.S. Congress passed a national fair housing law. The federal courts later upheld the suit of Dorothy GAUTREAUX and other public housing tenants against discriminatory policies of the CHICAGO HOUSING AUTHORITY (CHA), eventually ordering the CHA to issue rent subsidy vouchers to thousands of African American families so that they could live outside the inner city. In the past thirty years, African Americans and other minorities have moved into traditionally white communities throughout metropolitan Chicago. Nevertheless, a late twentieth-century report on open housing in the Chicago area concluded that "race and ethnicity (and not just social class) remain major factors in steering minority families away from some communities and toward others."

James Ralph

See also: Contested Spaces; Housing Reform; Neighborhood Succession; Redlining; Steering; Suburbs and Cities as Dual Metropolis

Further reading: Berry, Brian J. L. *The Open Housing Question: Race and Housing in Chicago, 1966–1976.* 1979. • Massey, Douglas S., and Nancy A. Denton. *American Apartheid: Segregation and the Making of the Underclass.* 1993. • Ralph, James R., Jr. *Northern Protest: Martin Luther King, Jr., Chicago, and the Civil Rights Movement.* 1993.

Metropolitan Housing Development Corporation (MHDC) v. Arlington Heights

The *MHDC v. Arlington Heights* case is significant because the Supreme Court allowed that there could be a violation of the 1968 Fair Housing Act without a finding of intent. The Seventh Circuit then held that in some circumstances there could be a violation of the Fair Housing Act when there is a racial impact or racial effect. In the *Arlington Heights* case a purportedly neutral zoning procedure and decision were determined to have a racial impact constituting a violation of the Fair Housing Act. The case has opened a large number of opportunities to build affordable open housing throughout the Chicago area and other parts of the country.

In 1970 the ROMAN CATHOLIC order Clerics of St. Viator agreed to let the Metropolitan Housing Development Corporation build an affordable housing development on vacant land adjacent to St. Viator High School. A petition was filed with the village to obtain necessary zoning and building approval for the development of Lincoln Green, which would be available without regard to race or national origins. Massive and bitter opposition by "anti-Viatorian advocates" ensued at a series of boisterous zoning and council meetings.

The village board voted against the development and the matter went to the U.S. District Court. After negotiating a settlement and protecting it from attacks by a neighboring municipality and homeowners nearby, integrated, affordable housing for families and seniors, called Linden Place, was built. At the time it was opened the mayor of Arlington Heights spoke of it as one of the best developments in Arlington Heights.

F. Willis Caruso

Openlands Project. Openlands Project was established in 1963 as a committee of the Welfare Council of Metropolitan Chicago "to seek preservation and development of recreation and conservation resources" in the Chicago metropolitan area. Occasionally, Openlands took on significant efforts beyond northeastern Illinois, such as the preservation of Beall Woods, a prime oak-hickory forest in southeastern Illinois. Among the central advocacy efforts in which Openlands played a key role during its first five years were groundwork for the Illinois Prairie Path, promotion of the McHenry County Conservation District, and support for preservation of the Illinois & Michigan Canal corridor.

Under the direction of founding chairman Jeffrey R. Short, Jr. (1963–1972), and Executive Director Gunnar A. Peterson (1963–1975), Openlands became an independent not-for-profit in 1968. Its mission has included educating citizens about conservation issues, advocating sound open-space policies, and serving as an incubator for new organizations that often evolved out of special programs. Friends of the Chicago River was organized as an Openlands committee in 1979 and became independent in 1988.

In 1982, the Canal Corridor Association (formerly Upper Illinois Valley Association) grew out of Openlands' efforts to create the first "National Heritage Corridor" along the route of the Illinois & Michigan Canal from Chicago to LaSalle-Peru. Since Congressional designation of the Illinois & Michigan Canal National Heritage Corridor in 1984, the association has provided leadership toward implementation of the legislation's goals for conservation, preservation, and economic development.

In 1978, the Corporation for Open Lands (CorLands) was formed as an affiliate of Openlands to provide technical assistance to local governments and private groups for land acquisition and preservation. By 2002, CorLands was responsible for the protection of over 10,000 acres throughout the metropolitan region.

Openlands has also addressed the quality and quantity of parkland in Chicago neighborhoods and in 1986 launched a formal urban program with an emphasis on urban forestry and the development of new community green spaces. TreeKeepers, a citizen action group, was formed in 1991 as a volunteer arm of Openlands to provide maintenance and grassroots advocacy for Chicago's urban forest.

In 1990, Openlands launched the *21st Century Open Space Plan,* which outlined an integrated regional framework for the organization's work. The plan called for the creation of a new generation of neighborhood parks and gardens in Chicago, a metropolitan network of greenways, and several large regional reserves, such as Fort Sheridan and the 19,000-acre Midewin National Tallgrass Prairie. Coauthored by Openlands and the Northeastern Illinois Planning Commission, the *Northeastern Illinois Regional Greenways Plan* was adopted in 1992 and by the end of the twentieth century included over 4,000 miles of linear parks and trails.

Gerald W. Adelmann

See also: Environmental Politics; Environmentalism; Forest Preserves; Planning Chicago

Opera. Like the other arts, opera was slow to develop as a part of Chicago's social and cultural identity. A small visiting troupe first brought opera to Rice's Theater in 1850. Ominously, the house burned down on the second night. Sporadic visits of Italian opera companies predominated through the Civil War era. In 1865, Uranus Crosby used his wartime distilling fortune to open Crosby's Opera House, which hosted touring opera companies until it burned down in the Fire of 1871.

Opera and the other arts exploded in Chicago in the 1880s. The city's sizeable German population contributed to the vogue of Wagner in the mid-1880s, and declining ticket prices made opera available not only to elites but to the socially aspiring middle class. The Chicago Opera Festival Association lobbied for a new permanent opera theater in Chicago, and in 1889 the Chicago Auditorium, an architectural and acoustical marvel, was opened downtown. It hosted touring companies until 1910, when the Chicago Grand Opera Company was opened as the city's first permanent resident company. It established the city as an operatic center of national prominence, thanks in large part to music director and conductor Cleofante Campanini's openness to experimentation and innovation and to the patronage of Harold and Edith McCormick.

Program cover, Chicago Opera House, April 26, 1889. Artist: Unknown. Source: The Newberry Library.

The dominating operatic personality in Chicago from 1910 to 1931 was lyric soprano and actress Mary Garden, who was appointed general director (or "directa," as she insisted on being called) after Campanini's death. The lavish season of 1921–22 included among its triumphs the world premiere of Prokofiev's *The Love for Three Oranges* but closed with a deficit, covered by the McCormicks, of over a million dollars, which ended the company. Support for opera was by then so widespread that a new organization,

Opera houses such as the Blue Island Opera House, featured in this 1908 postcard, provided venues for performances of all kinds and served as symbols of status and culture for the communities in which they were located. Photographer: Curt Teich & Co. Source: Curt Teich Archives, Lake County Discovery Museum.

Ernest Wolff brought his love of opera to friends, the nation, and to several generations of Chicagoans through his Chicago Miniature Opera Theater. It opened in November of 1936 with a staging of *Aida*. In 1938, Wolff and his puppets were recruited by the Gas Industries of America to perform at the 1939 New York World's Fair, where his theater performed *Rigoletto*, pictured here. After a hiatus for World War II, the Miniature Opera Theater found a home at Frederick Chramer's Kungsholm Restaurant in the former McCormick Mansion on Ontario at Rush. Both the restaurant and the theater closed in 1971. Some of the theater's puppets and sets are on permanent exhibit at the Museum of Science and Industry. Photographer: Unknown. Source: Chicago Historical Society.

the Chicago Civic Opera, was formed almost at once. Its president, the utilities magnate Samuel Insull, pursued a businesslike, populist policy designed to broaden the social and financial basis of opera's support. Like its predecessor, the Civic Opera toured nationally. Together, the two Chicago companies brought opera to 62 cities, large and small, between 1910 and 1929. The establishment of a permanent resident opera company in Chicago, together with the new venues of radio and the phonograph, democratized opera by making it available to a new and broader audience.

The Chicago Civic Opera moved into the Civic Opera House, a 45-story SKYSCRAPER of modern design at Madison and Wacker Drive, six days after the stock market crash of 1929. The GREAT DEPRESSION had a major impact on opera in Chicago, putting an end to the Civic Opera and summertime operas at RAVINIA Park, as well as making success impossible for subsequent companies in the 1930s. Opera was reborn in Chicago with the creation of the LYRIC OPERA (founded as the Lyric Theater) in 1952. Under Carol Fox (1956–1981) and Ardis Krainik (1981–1997), the Lyric found subscriber support in a broadening base of business and professional patronage. By 1989 every seat for every performance of the season had been sold before opening night. A growing commitment to new works led the Lyric to commission a major new work, William Bolcom's *McTeague* (1992).

Thomas Bauman

See also: Broadcasting; Chicago Opera Ballet; Classical Music; Dance Companies; Dance Training

Further reading: Davis, Ronald L. *Opera in Chicago.* 1966. • Dizikes, John. *Opera in America.* 1993.

Operation PUSH. Though often overshadowed by its founder, Jesse Jackson, Operation PUSH (People United to Serve Humanity) has been one of the most important social justice organizations in the United States since 1971.

The roots of Operation PUSH stretch back into the headiest years of the CIVIL RIGHTS MOVEMENT. When the Southern Christian Leadership Conference (SCLC) targeted Chicago in 1965, Jesse Jackson helped formally organize Chicago ministers to promote more employment opportunities for local AFRICAN AMERICANS. Operation Breadbasket enjoyed early success, and by the end of the 1960s it was the leading civil rights group in Chicago.

In 1971, Jackson broke with SCLC, and Operation Breadbasket became Operation PUSH. Despite precarious finances, Operation PUSH was active. It held rousing weekly meetings at its HYDE PARK headquarters to energize its supporters, which included both black and white Chicagoans. It pressured major companies to hire more AFRICAN AMERICANS and to extend business ties with the black community. And in 1976 it launched PUSH-Excel, a program designed to inspire inner-city teenagers across the country to work hard and to stay out of trouble.

Operation PUSH's fortunes have fluctuated since 1980. Though stalwart PUSH leaders like the Reverend Willie Barrow supervised its activities from its SOUTH SIDE headquarters, Operation PUSH declined during the 1980s with Jackson's pursuit of the presidency. In the mid-1990s, Jackson directed the merger of PUSH with the National Rainbow Coalition, a political organization he had founded a decade earlier, to form the Rainbow/PUSH Coalition. This new combination revived the traditional PUSH economic emphasis by launching "The Wall Street Project," a initiative that encourages leading financial firms and Fortune 500 companies to increase their minority hiring and inner-city investment.

James Ralph

See also: Community Organizing; Congress of Racial Equality (CORE); Coordinating Council of Community Organizations; National Association for the Advancement of Colored People (NAACP)

Further reading: Frady, Marshall. *Jesse: The Life and Pilgrimage of Jesse Jackson.* 1996. • House, Ernest R. *Jesse Jackson and the Politics of Charisma: The Rise and Fall of the PUSH/Excel Program.* 1988.

Ardis Joan Krainik and the Lyric Opera

Ardis Joan Krainik followed in the tradition of Chicago's great female opera company directors, a tradition that began with Mary Garden in 1921 and continued through the 27-year era of the company's cofounder (with Nicola Rescigno and Lawrence Kelly) and first general manager, Carol Fox. Krainik had served (from 1954) as supporting singer, chorus member, and, since 1960, assistant manager, before her appointment to the Lyric's top administrative post in 1981, following the retirement of Fox. Within months she recouped the theater's failing fortunes and put it in the black. Her shrewd business sense, artistic vision, and personal warmth were instrumental in establishing the Lyric as one of the world's leading opera companies, a prime American base for the foremost international singers, conductors, stage directors, and designers.

John von Rhein

Orland Hills, IL, Cook County, 23 miles SW of the Loop. A village of one and a half square miles, Orland Hills borders neighboring ORLAND PARK on the west and north and TINLEY PARK to the east and south. Driving through fast-growing Orland Township it is difficult to know when one has slipped from one of these villages into the other.

For countless centuries, the area of Orland Hills, as with much of the south metropolitan region, was predominantly open prairie. Large wooded areas and marshes existed to the north, but the immediate ground was prairie with small wetlands.

Along what would be the village's western edge, an ancient INDIAN trail led north into the rich hunting areas of the Saganaskie Swamp. The land of Orland Hills was first sold in 1836–37 to six men, most likely land speculators. There is evidence of established farms by the end of the 1850s.

With the exception of minor growth in the small village of Orland Park, Orland Township maintained a stable rural population for a hundred years. Throughout the south suburbs, however, growth exploded in the 1950s.

Part of this growth in the late 1950s was a small SUBDIVISION of a little over 100 homes at the intersection of 167th Street and 94th Avenue. Open farm country separated this subdivision from the villages of Orland Park and Tinley Park, which also were beginning to grow rapidly. To gain municipal services, the residents of this subdivision incorporated as the Village of Westhaven in 1961.

As with many small communities, Westhaven experienced a variety of financial and administrative difficulties in its early years. Initial growth was slow. Its first request for new housing permits came in 1970, nine years after incorporation. But that began additional new construction and land ANNEXATIONS. In 1971, the Wittich Memorial Church began work on a subdivision called Christian Hills.

In 1986, the name of the village was changed to Orland Hills so that it would be more closely and clearly identified as part of Orland Township and the Orland Park area. Commercial development along 159th Street and parts of 94th Avenue has emerged in the 1990s. During development several areas were preserved as wetlands and recreation, including a small lake.

From an isolated subdivision set in the midst of farmland about 40 years ago, Orland Hills grew to a population of 6,779 by 2000.

Larry A. McClellan

See also: Agriculture; Cook County; Government, Suburban; Metropolitan Growth

Further reading: McClellan, Larry. "How, Why Westhaven Became Orland Hills." *Star*, September 27, 1998.

Orland Park, IL, Cook County, 22 miles SW of the Loop. During the past 20 years, Orland Park has been one of the focal points for growth in the metropolitan region southwest of Chicago. Commercial growth has been dramatic, with Orland Square Mall and the surrounding blocks of business, especially along LaGrange Road (Route 45). The area is wholly oriented toward automobiles and its growth is supported by the continuing outward spread of residential SUBDIVISIONS.

Although it is a classic example of the American automobile-based suburb, Orland Park has a town center next to a RAILROAD commuter station. The center includes many of the early stores, a bank, and Twin Towers, formerly a Methodist church and Orland Park's only structure on the National Register of Historic Places. These are bordered by some of the village's original residential areas.

The beginnings of this community were somewhat to the east, in the area of the current commercial concentration. Known as the ENGLISH Settlement, the community centered on a grade school and a Methodist church. Settlers include Henry Taylor, who arrived in 1834, and Thomas Hardy, who came in 1836. They were followed by other immigrants from the British Isles—including the family of a 10-year-old named John Humphrey who arrived from England in 1848.

In the 1840s, LUXEMBOURGERS and GERMANS began to arrive. Their presence is commemorated in the original Hostert family log cabins now situated in a wooded park on the southern edge of the old village area.

The "father" of Orland Park was John Humphrey. When he was 21, he joined a wagon train going to California, later returning to work with his family. When the Wabash, St. Louis & Pacific Railroad completed its rail line through the area in 1879, Humphrey purchased a significant piece of land next to what was platted as the town center for the railroad stop. The Wabash had named its train stop Sedgewick, but the locals, with Humphrey's leadership, changed the name to Orland Park.

Humphrey participated in almost all aspects of the growth of the community. He was elected to the state house of representatives in 1870 and to the state senate in 1886. He was instrumental in the incorporation of the village in 1892, and served as its first president. In 1881, he had built the second house in Orland Park. This house has now passed into the hands of the Orland Historical Society.

From such beginnings, Orland Park grew in population from 366 in 1900 to 51,077 in 2000. While retaining its old commercial and residential core, the village has built an innovative municipal facility that sits between the old and new sections.

Larry A. McClellan

See also: Commuting; Metropolitan Growth

Further reading: "Orland Park." In *Local Community Fact Book: Chicago Metropolitan Area, 1990*, ed. Chicago Fact Book Consortium, 1995. • *The Orland Story: From Prairie to Pavement.* 1991.

Orphanages. The first Chicago orphanages, the Chicago Orphan Asylum and the Catholic Orphan Asylum, opened their doors in 1849 in the aftermath of a cholera epidemic. By 1890, there were 12 orphanages in the city. They split along ROMAN CATHOLIC and PROTESTANT lines. Chicago had no Jewish orphanages until the 1890s. Until then, JEWS tried to send orphans to institutions in Cincinnati, but some Jewish orphans lived in Protestant orphanages in Chicago. Almost all "orphans" in nineteenth-century Chicago orphanages had one parent living. They were places that single-parent families in financial crisis could safely keep their children. A few of them, like the Home for the Friendless, were gigantic, housing hundreds of children at a time.

Turn-of-the-century progressive reformers like Jane Addams attacked orphanages as places that warehoused children in unhealthy, overcrowded buildings. Reformers wanted children kept at home. Despite the complaints, new orphanages continued to be built between 1890 and 1920. Major institutions like the Marks Nathan Jewish Orphan Home opened around the turn of the century. By 1910, Chicago had more than 30 children's homes. While a few were small, most housed between 200 and 900 children.

Gradually, between 1900 and 1940, orphanages did respond to the reformers' challenge. By the 1920s, almost every major orphanage had moved from the center of the city to spacious suburban campuses. A few, like the Illinois Industrial School for Boys (now known as the GLENWOOD School for Boys), moved far south of the city. Most, however, moved northwest. St. Hedwig's, a Roman Catholic girls' orphanage, found a home in NILES Township. The Catholic Boys Asylum in the BRIDGEPORT neighborhood moved to DES PLAINES and became St. Mary's Training School for Boys. Hannah Greenebaum Solomon, a friend of Jane Addams, spearheaded the move of the Illinois Industrial School for Girls to PARK RIDGE.

In those same decades, the huge dormitories housing the children during the 1800s were gradually replaced by smaller "cottages" that tried to simulate a home setting. A few institutions run by progressive Protestants and

Jews shut down and became foster home placement centers. Still, more than 5,000 children remained in Chicago orphanages in the middle of the 1940s. ANGEL GUARDIAN, the largest Catholic institution, housed over 1,200 children during the GREAT DEPRESSION.

Orphanages declined in two stages after WORLD WAR II. Between 1945 and 1960, more than half the orphanages in the city, under pressure from welfare professionals, decided to either close down, turn their plants into HOUSING FOR THE ELDERLY or shift their focus to the psychotherapeutic treatment of small numbers of emotionally disturbed children. Then, in the early 1970s, the Illinois Department of Children and Family Services forced almost every orphanage still operating to shut down. Angel Guardian, still housing 400 children in the early seventies, closed in 1974. By the 1980s, only the most emotionally troubled adolescents lived in institutions. Compared to previous generations, the numbers were tiny.

Kenneth Cmiel

See also: Children, Dependent; Religious Institutions; Social Services

Further reading: Cmiel, Kenneth. *A Home of Another Kind: One Chicago Orphanage and the Tangle of Child Welfare.* 1995. • McCausland, Clare L. *Children of Circumstance: A History of the First 125 Years of the Chicago Child Care Society.* 1976.

Oswego, IL, Kendall County, 38 miles SW of the Loop. Settled in the early 1830s on the remains of a POTAWATOMI settlement, Oswego was quickly overshadowed by neighboring AURORA owing to the latter's position on the Chicago, Burlington & Quincy RAILROAD. Oswego is home to a Caterpillar Tractor Company plant.

Brandon Johnson

See also: Agricultural Machinery Industry

Further reading: Farren, Kathy, ed. *A Bicentennial History of Kendall County, Illinois.* 1976. • Hicks, E. W. *History of Kendall County, Illinois: From the Earliest Discoveries to the Present Time.* 1877.

Ottawas. Ottawas first made the Chicago region their home in the mid-1700s, when they and the Chippewas OJIBWAS joined the dominant POTAWATOMIS in making villages along the Illinois River and its tributaries. Intertribal wars had pushed the Ottawas from their earliest recorded villages on Manitoulin Island and the Georgian Bay in 1650, and they had moved eastward, occupying sites on the south shore of Lake Superior and east of LAKE MICHIGAN between 1650 and 1670. By 1670, Ottawas lived at the Straits of Mackinac and moved south into Michigan's Lower Peninsula, where the majority of Ottawas live today. Ottawas joined with Chippewas and Potawatomis in warfare against Chicago-area tribes in the late 1600s and early 1700s. This warfare left the Chicago region a disputed territory with rich natural resources harvested by several tribes, including the Ottawas. Between 1750 and 1783, a few Ottawas joined with the more numerous Illinois Potawatomis to build substantial villages and extend their control over the region. Ottawas from Michigan and Wisconsin traveled to the Chicago area to harvest rich RIVERINE resources including wild rice, game of various species, and Lake Michigan whitefish throughout the eighteenth and early nineteenth centuries.

By 1814, Ottawas and Potawatomis jointly occupied the Chicago village, and the Illinois River villages as well. Illinois Ottawas maintained ties to their Michigan and Canadian relatives by visiting the eastern villages and by hosting them for winter hunts. Ottawas from Michigan and Illinois joined Tecumseh's confederacy to fight the United States during the War of 1812. While the Ottawas and Chippewas in Illinois maintained distinct ethnic identities, they became socially and politically Potawatomis. United States officials called the Illinois River Indians the "United Nations of Chippewa, Ottawas, Potawatomie of the Waters of the Illinois."

The United States negotiated land cession TREATIES with the United Bands for Chicago area lands during the early 1800s, after purchasing the land where Chicago stands from Old Northwest Territory tribes at the 1795 Treaty of Greenville. Ottawas joined Potawatomis to sell the land immediately around Chicago in 1816. They and their Chippewa relatives sold more Illinois land in 1829 and 1832. Several bands who made these TREATIES kept small reservations where their villages stood. Most sold their reservations at the 1833 Treaty of Chicago and agreed to move west of the Mississippi River. By 1840, only the DeKalb County reservation of the Potawatomi chief Shabene (an Ottawa by birth) remained intact. The United Bands moved to a reservation at Council Bluffs, Iowa, between 1836 and 1838. Today, descendants of the Ottawas, Chippewas, and Potawatomis from Chicago live on a reservation near Mayetta, Kansas, and are known as the Prairie Band Potawatomis.

James M. McClurken

See also: Chicago in the Middle Ground; Native American Religion

Further reading: Baerreis, David, Erminie Wheeler-Voegelin, and Remedios Wycoco-Moore. *Indians of Northeastern Illinois: Anthropological Report on the Chippewa, Ottawa, and Potawatomi Indians in Northeastern Illinois.* 1974. • Edmunds, R. David. *The Potawatomis: Keepers of the Fire.* 1978. • Tanner, Helen Hornbeck. *Atlas of Great Lakes Indian History.* 1987.

Our Lady of the Angels Fire. On December 1, 1958, a parochial school fire killed 92 students and 3 nuns. The fire began in the basement of the 48-year-old building and billowed up an open stairway before fanning out into the second floor, trapping most victims in their classrooms and forcing others to jump from second-story windows.

No grand jury was convened despite a scathing report issued in 1959 by the National Fire Protection Association blaming the city and officials of the ROMAN CATHOLIC ARCHDIOCESE OF CHICAGO for educating children in "firetraps." Nor was the fire's cause officially determined. A 13-year-old former student's 1962 confession to arson was dismissed by a family court judge who ruled it was obtained improperly.

The tragedy's aftermath led to nationwide overhaul of fire safety codes for schools, including calls for automatic sprinkler systems, noncombustible construction, and fire alarms linked directly to the fire department. The fire was the nation's third-worst school disaster and Chicago's third-deadliest fire, trailing the Iroquois Theater fire (602 killed) and the Great Chicago FIRE OF 1871 (250–300 dead).

David Cowan

See also: Building Codes and Standards; Catholic School System; Firefighting; Roman Catholics

Further reading: Cowan, David, and John Kuenster. *To Sleep with the Angels: The Story of a Fire.* 1996.

Outdoor Concerts. Outdoor concerts have entertained, edified, and democratized the citizens of Chicago. When not merely providing a focus for summertime recreation, concerts have historically been tied to ethnic community celebration or progressive campaigns to uplift public taste, reform recreation, and instill patriotism. The development of spaces amenable to outdoor concerts, such as neighborhood and larger parks and open-air stadiums, offered increased opportunities to enjoy multiple forms of music, such as CLASSICAL, BLUES, JAZZ, pop/ROCK, and world music. More than mere entertainment, these concerts have reflected the struggles of urban residents to define the emerging civic culture of the city.

As early as 1851, citizens enjoyed outdoor concerts when the Great Western Band performed in Dearborn Park. After the CIVIL WAR, regimental BANDS filled the summertime air in squares, parks, private picnic grounds, and commercial summer gardens. Immigrant and ethnic groups, most notably GERMANS, Bohemians, and POLES, organized concerts to celebrate musical traditions, mobilize attention to issues, and express the vitality of their communities.

PHILANTHROPISTS and municipal officials helped sponsor public concerts in the 1860s in LINCOLN PARK, and these spread to the South and West PARK DISTRICTS. Concerts attracted thousands of patrons, ranging from members of the upper-middle class who arrived in carriages to "brawny young mechanics and bright-eyed young shop girls" who arrived via

From 1919 to 1931, when the Great Depression caused it to close, Ravinia in Highland Park was considered by many to be the summer opera capital of America. This 1931 photo captures operagoers at the park's main gate. Photographer: Unknown. Source: Chicago Historical Society.

PUBLIC TRANSPORTATION. Leading bandleaders like Hans Balatka and Johnny Hand conducted "popular" works ranging from Verdi to Wagner to Sousa. Concerts included waltzes, quadrilles, and, later, ragtime arrangements, for spectators wishing to dance.

As Chicago urbanized, concert audiences diversified and groups sometimes sparred over appropriate behavior. Park commissioners expected middle-class respectability to prevail but did their best to accommodate differences of musical taste among patrons. In the 1900s and 1910s, municipal outdoor concerts expanded as part of an effort to reform recreation among the residents of Chicago's industrial neighborhoods.

WORLD WAR I inspired many ethnic groups to organize outdoor concert rallies in parks and at SOLDIER FIELD to express love of their homelands *and* their loyalty to the United States. In 1914 the Civic Music Association promoted "music for the people" in the form of outdoor classical concerts. The association also sponsored "AMERICANIZATION" public sings in parks and at NAVY PIER involving thousands of children and their parents. Commercial AMUSEMENT PARKS like White City and Sans Souci featured regular outdoor concerts too.

Despite the persistence of ethnic community concerts, concerts increasingly catered to the population of Chicago-at-large. In the late 1920s, the *Chicago Tribune* inaugurated a "CHICAGOLAND Music Festival" by invoking a public identification with its imagined community of readers. By the late 1940s, the festival attracted tens of thousands of spectators and radio listeners. To bolster civic morale and aid UNEMPLOYED musicians during the GREAT DEPRESSION, James C. Petrillo, President of the CHICAGO FEDERATION OF MUSICIANS, helped initiate outdoor concerts in GRANT PARK, including an annual symphonic series begun in 1935. The WPA Federal Music Project helped sustain outdoor concerts by the Illinois Symphony Orchestra and the Chicago Women's Symphony Orchestra. The Grant Park Symphony and the Petrillo Bandshell were legacies of this public vision.

Racial segregation complicated the history of the outdoor concert as a democratic phenomenon. AFRICAN AMERICANS often avoided public concerts outside their own neighborhoods. But after the Depression, opportunities for blacks gradually increased. In the 1940s, the American Negro Music Festival annually brought classical and popular musical artists such as Roland Hayes, Louise Burge, Thomas A. Dorsey, and Dorothy Donegan to Soldier Field and COMISKEY PARK. By the 1970s and 1980s, popular tastes in commercial music helped sustain Chicagofest, which brought national pop, blues, and jazz performers to NAVY PIER. The Chicago Jazz, Blues, and GOSPEL Festivals followed, along with classical and popular concerts in Grant Park and other public city parks. At the opening of the twenty-first century, residents and visitors could enjoy a host of summertime concerts, featuring Celtic and Latin music, reggae, country, and OPERA.

Derek Vaillant

See also: Entertaining Chicagoans; Ethnic Music; Leisure; Places of Assembly

P

Pace. Horsecar lines served individuals in satellite cities such as JOLIET as early as 1874. Over the years the suburban STREET RAILWAYS were consolidated into increasingly larger companies like West Towns Railway, National City Lines, and United Motor Coach, but they were not able to influence suburban development or compete with the automobile.

Pace includes various suburban BUS systems which were consolidated in 1983 as the result of a state-mandated bifurcation of the RTA's suburban operations into bus (Pace) and rail (METRA) service. In 1998, Pace operated 232 bus routes in 210 suburbs with a fleet of 638 vehicles. Ridership that year was 39 million.

David M. Young

See also: Commuting; Transportation

Further reading: Sieroslawski, Jennifer. "Suburban Transit History." 1996. Pace files manuscript. • Young, David M. *Chicago Transit: An Illustrated History.* 1998.

Pacific Garden Mission. The oldest surviving and most visible Chicago RESCUE MISSION, the Pacific Garden Mission was founded in 1877 by George and Sarah Clarke in order to "keep crooked men straight." Located in the SOUTH LOOP in the middle of "Whiskey Row," the mission took its name from a former tenant, the notorious Pacific Beer Garden.

The mission has always coupled a simple evangelical Christian message with social outreach to the downtrodden, leading some to dub it the "HOBO Church." It has provided food, clothing, and the gospel to generations of Chicagoans. The famous "baseball evangelist," Billy Sunday, was saved at the mission's doors.

A "harbor for wrecked and ruined lives" throughout the twentieth century, the mission added in 1950 a radio program, *Unshackled!* which reaches more than a thousand stations worldwide with sentimental stories of ruin and redemption. A bright neon cross proclaiming "Jesus Saves" still pierces the night sky, announcing the mission's continuing ministry to Chicago's poor.

R. Jonathan Moore

See also: Protestants; Religious Institutions; Salvation Army; Social Services; Vice Districts

Further reading: Clarke, Sarah D. *The Founding of Pacific Garden Mission: Over Thirty-Five Years Contributed to the Master's Service.* 1914.

Pacific Islanders. "Pacific Islanders" is a census category used to describe culturally and geographically diverse migrants from thousands of South Pacific islands. The largest groups of Pacific Islanders in Chicago are Hawaiians, Samoans, Guamanians, and Chamorro, although there have also been Tongans, Maori, Tahitians, Fijians, and others at various times. Accurate statistics are difficult because Hawaiians, Guamanians, and Samoans are not subject to immigration controls as U.S. citizens and U.S. nationals. The census has recently begun to count them separately, but categorization can be difficult because centuries of migration to the islands have given them a multiracial character and blurred categories. The 2000 census identified more than 4,000 people in Chicago claiming at least partial Pacific Islander background, but community estimates were generally much lower.

While a small number of Hawaiian musicians might have migrated to Chicago as early as the 1920s, Pacific Islander migration remained extremely limited until after WORLD WAR II, when many JAPANESE from the islands left internment camps and settled in the city. In the 1950s, small numbers of Hawaiians in the military, AIRLINE, and entertainment industries began to settle in Chicago and attract friends and family seeking economic and educational opportunities. Popular Polynesian-themed clubs and RESTAURANTS, including Club Waikiki, attracted Hawaiian musicians to the area and encouraged Pacific Islanders already here to learn music and DANCE. June Rold's Dance Studio in DES PLAINES began to offer hula classes and formed a traveling dance troupe that would come to spawn a new generation of performers. In the 1960s and 1970s, Samoans and Tahitians began to migrate in larger numbers and found employment with many of the clubs and performance troupes. While Pacific Islanders have continued to migrate to Chicago and many have remained, a large number have also returned to the islands or migrated to the West Coast since the 1980s.

While many Pacific Islanders are not involved in the entertainment industry, music has been a primary way that the community has organized itself. Hula schools and entertainment troupes have proliferated in recent decades, and, although traditional music and dance have been shaped by Western audience expectations and commercial realities, they can be a form of cultural expression and source of community identity. Dance troupes perform at many public venues, including city parks and festivals. In addition, music has played a strong role in informal community gatherings. In the 1970s, Pacific Islanders created a ukulele club (revived in the late 1990s), a social club which met regularly for food and musical jam sessions. Music also figured prominently at annual summer Polynesian picnics in the 1980s.

A new movement to preserve authentic Hawaiian language and culture has sparked the creation of organizations in Hawaii and the mainland. In Chicago, Kupa'a Pacific Island Resources began in 1995 as a nonprofit organization dedicated to preserving and promoting Pacific Island cultures through educational programs and community events. Forming partnerships with the OLD TOWN SCHOOL OF FOLK MUSIC, public SCHOOLS, museums, and other public agencies, Kupa'a ("stand firm") offers both short educational demonstrations and longer classes. It sponsors annual cultural events and special concerts which draw large Pacific Islander audiences from around the Midwest.

Tracy Steffes

See also: Demography; Entertaining Chicagoans; Ethnic Music

Further reading: Fawcett, James T., and Benjamin V. Carino. *Pacific Bridges: The New Immigration from Asia and the Pacific Islands.* 1987. • Shore, Bradd. "Pacific Islanders." In *Harvard Encyclopedia of American Ethnic Groups,* ed. Stephan Thernstrom, 1980.

Packinghouse Unions. Chicago's important MEATPACKING industry experienced three successive waves of UNIONIZATION. The first two mass organizing campaigns ended in failure. The third effort gained momentum in 1937 and assumed institutional form as the United Packinghouse Workers of America (UPWA) in 1943. This union succeeded in organizing most workers in the stockyards and packinghouses.

Formed at the turn of the century, the American Federation of Labor's Amalgamated Meat Cutters and Butcher Workmen of North America (AMC) was the first national organization dedicated to the unionization of the meat industry. Its founders realized that control of the nation's packinghouses, especially those in Chicago, was essential to success. Between 1900 and 1904, the AMC built a powerful organization in the Chicago plants, especially Armour and Swift. Its strongest base of support lay with the skilled "butcher aristocracy," largely comprising IRISH and GERMAN workers. In sharp contrast to most trade unions, the AMC extended its organization into the ranks of the unskilled Central and East European immigrants who made up the majority of the workforce. Able to stabilize employment conditions, raise wages, and retain a modicum of control for the skilled elite, the AMC proved enormously popular among packinghouse workers. But a 1904 STRIKE proved disastrous to the union. Relying upon African American and immigrant strikebreakers, the

Workers trimming meat, 1892. Photographer: Unknown. Source: Chicago Historical Society.

packers destroyed the organization built up by the AMC.

The second wave occurred with the American entry into WORLD WAR I and the GREAT MIGRATION of southern blacks to Chicago. The wartime economic boom induced the CHICAGO FEDERATION OF LABOR (CFL) to mount an aggressive organizing campaign in the stockyards in 1917. Aided by sympathetic federal mediation, the Chicago Stockyards Labor Council (SLC) organized virtually all white workers but struggled to enroll the rapidly growing number of African American workers. The 1919 Chicago RACE RIOT doomed that struggle and led to the AMC's decision to leave the SLC. When the AMC struck in the winter of 1921, it did so without the CFL or black packinghouse workers not inclined to assist "the white man's union." As in 1904, the packing companies imported thousands of black workers to keep their plants operating. The AMC was thoroughly defeated.

During the 1920s, black workers continued to enter the city's packinghouses, eventually gaining positions as butchers on the killing floors. During the early 1930s, these workers took the lead in launching the organizations that later supported the CIO's Packinghouse Workers Organizing Committee (PWOC). PWOC succeeded in overcoming the ethnic and racial antagonisms that had plagued past organizing efforts. Active in both black and white neighborhoods, PWOC functioned as an important social and cultural institution in addition to its primary role as a union. When the UPWA was formed in 1943, it was headquartered in Chicago. The UPWA won a strike over wages in 1946 but lost a 1948 attempt to shut down the packing industry. Racial tensions did not surface after the 1948 strike, and the union was able to recover quickly. Throughout the 1950s it combined militant unionism with active involvement in the community-based struggle for racial equality.

Plant closings in the late 1950s and early 1960s decimated the UPWA. In 1968 it merged with the Amalgamated Meat Cutters, but by that time only a few small plants remained in Chicago. In 1979 a merger with the Retail Clerks created the United Food and Commercial Workers.

Rick Halpern

See also: Back of the Yards; Civil Rights Movements; Congress of Industrial Organizations; Work; Work Culture

Further reading: Barrett, James R. *Work and Community in the Jungle: Chicago's Packinghouse Workers, 1894–1922.* 1987. • Brody, David. *The Butcher Workmen: A Study of Unionization.* 1964. • Halpern, Rick and Roger Horowitz. *Meatpackers: An Oral History of Black Packinghouse Workers and Their Struggle for Racial and Economic Equality.* 1996.

John Kikulski and Chicago Labor

Born in German-occupied Poland in 1876, John Kikulski probably immigrated to the United States in 1891. He was naturalized and married in 1898. In 1904 Kikulski served one term as a director of the Polish National Alliance. He also served as president of the Polish Falcons from 1910 to 1912. In 1903 he ran for Sixteenth Ward alderman on the Independent Labor Party ticket and lost.

Active in the labor movement from the late 1890s on, Kikulski won election as president of Local 14 of the cabinetmakers and carpenters union in 1908. During WORLD WAR I, he worked as an organizer for the American Federation of Labor and helped to lead STRIKES at International Harvester and the Crane Company. In 1917 Kikulski joined the stockyards labor movement and gained his greatest success. Packinghouse workers elected him president of the largely Polish Local 554 of the Amalgamated Meat Cutters and Butcher Workmen and later secretary of the Stockyard Labor Council. Afterwards members voted Kikulski director of District 9 of the meat cutters' union. In 1919 he ran an unsuccessful campaign for city clerk as the Farmer-Labor Party candidate. Kikulski preached racial harmony and working-class unity, but saw the stockyard movement crippled by the RACE RIOT of 1919. Later that year he became entangled in Chicago's labor wars. Various factions accused him of embezzling money, but his working-class supporters remained loyal.

On May 17, 1920, two unknown assailants attacked and shot Kikulski in front of his home. He died four days later and received a hero's burial as mourners filled St. Hyacinth's Church beyond capacity. A procession of some two hundred automobiles escorted Kikulski's casket to St. Adalbert's Cemetery.

Dominic A. Pacyga

Pakistanis. The 2000 federal census counted over 18,000 Pakistanis in metropolitan Chicago, one of the largest concentrations of Pakistanis in the United States. Community estimates in the late 1990s, however, ranged from 80,000 to 100,000, most of whom were either Urdu- or Punjabi-speaking MUSLIMS. Like other South Asians, Pakistanis have commonly tended to settle in and around major urban areas, especially on the two coasts near New York and Los Angeles. Chicago and other inland cities such as Houston have also developed large and visible Pakistani communities.

Although Pakistani immigration to the United States dates back to Pakistan's independence in 1947, the greatest influx of Pakistanis occurred after the mid-1960s, when U.S. immigration policy toward South Asia became more relaxed. These early immigrants were generally well-educated and financially comfortable graduate students and professionals, such as doctors, engineers, and scientists, who emigrated for educational and economic opportunities. The political instability of Pakistan at the time and the rise of anti–South Asian sentiment in the United Kingdom accelerated the migration of Pakistanis to the United States. The decades of the 1980s and 1990s continued to bring educated Pakistani professionals to the United States, but a growing number of less-educated, middle-class immigrants also arrived, taking jobs as TAXI drivers and small business owners.

Although Pakistanis apparently have dispersed across Chicago's suburbs rather than concentrating in any single neighborhood, Pakistani presence has been most visible along Devon Avenue, the cultural and commercial center of Chicago's South Asian communities. Along this North Side street—where dozens of Pakistani RESTAURANTS and shops have nestled among other South Asian businesses—Pakistanis have celebrated their national independence day, August 14, with an annual parade. Pakistanis generally parade along the portion of Devon just east of Western Avenue that has been designated "Mohammed Ali Jinnah Way," in honor of Pakistan's founder and first head of state. On that same weekend, Chicago's INDIANS celebrate their independence day (August 15) along the portion of Devon that commemorates their nation's founder, Mahatma Gandhi. The peaceful side-by-side coexistence of Pakistanis and Indians in Chicago is a remarkable contrast to the strife that has riddled the two nations since their founding.

Chicago's Pakistanis have established a number of social and cultural institutions. Together with the city's greater Islamic community, Pakistanis have helped establish mosques and Islamic schools in and around Chicago, including the Islamic Foundation. Social and cultural associations have included the Pakistan Federation of America in Chicago and the Indus Society.

Ajay K. Mehrotra

See also: Americanization; Demography; Multicentered Chicago; West Ridge

Further reading: Rafi, Natasha. "Who Are the Pakistani Americans?" In *The Asian American Almanac.* 1995.

Palatine, IL, Cook County, 26 miles NW of the Loop. In the early nineteenth century, this was a rather swampy area, through which Salt Creek (then as now) passed. To the northwest was Deer Grove, so named for the numerous deer that it sheltered; "English Grove" lay due west, and Plum Grove about two miles to the south. Plum Grove was particularly important to the POTAWATOMI, who continued to visit

area burial sites after they were removed to Iowa in the 1830s.

Early settlers tended to choose these forested sites. Thus George Ela settled near Deer Grove in 1835, while Ben Lincoln and Ben Porter traveled from Vermont to Plum Grove. In 1853, the Illinois & Wisconsin RAILROAD was constructed across the township. A town emerged around the railroad depot, built just south of the Salt Creek swamp. Some people wanted to call it Yankton, but the name Palatine was adopted, after a town in New York.

By the time Palatine was incorporated in 1866, it was already a community of some size, with a Methodist church. While the earliest settlers were YANKEES, there was an influx of GERMANS beginning in the 1850s. By 1869 a substantial Lutheran church could be built. These Germans were mostly farmers, who joined the earlier settlers in bringing their produce to the Palatine depot for shipment to Chicago. Some commuters also began to settle in the little town, but it remained very rural down to World War II, in spite of the construction of the Northwest Highway in the 1930s.

All that changed in the 1950s, particularly with the construction of the Northwest TOLL ROAD in 1955, a couple of miles south of Palatine's southern boundary. The whole area was opened up to rapid automobile travel, and residential building accelerated. The streets were generally laid out in irregular patterns, to avoid the excessively rectilinear appearance of many of the suburbs nearer Chicago. By 1970 virtually all the land had been taken up, and the only large open area was the Palatine Hills GOLF Course, on the northwest edge of town. Beyond that lay the Deer Grove FOREST PRESERVE, a substantial remnant of the forested area that had drawn Indians and Europeans to these parts in the first place.

David Buisseret

See also: Metropolitan Growth

Further reading: Paddock, Stuart R., et al. *Palatine Centennial Book.* 1991.

Palestinians. Palestinians began migrating to Chicago in the late nineteenth century. They were a significant part of the contingent of "Syrian" Arab traders at the 1893 WORLD'S COLUMBIAN EXPOSITION, selling religious artifacts, textiles, and handicrafts from the Holy Land. Glowing reports of early trading successes at this and other fairs fueled the desire of Palestinians, SYRIANS, and LEBANESE to migrate to the United States and become traders. Arab migration to the United States and Chicago increased between 1890 and 1921, until overseas migration to the United States was halted by immigration quotas.

While Arabs from Palestine, Lebanon, and Syria were collectively referred to as "Syrians" by the American government and the American public, there were differences among them. The Syrians and Lebanese were largely Christians, while the Palestinians were largely MUSLIMS. Many of the former brought their families over before immigration quotas took hold; the Palestinians remained largely an all-male community until after World War II. As Muslims, Palestinians did not share in the dominant religious culture of the United States. They preferred to WORK hard, support their families back home, and retire in Palestine.

Early Palestinian immigrants lived either in all-male BOARDINGHOUSES near 18th and Michigan or behind their small retail shops on Chicago's SOUTH SIDE. From the beginning of the "GREAT MIGRATION" of black southerners to the North, Palestinians developed a trading niche in the emerging black communities on the South Side, selling food and dry goods as STREET PEDDLERS or shopkeepers. By the early 1970s, they owned nearly 20 percent of all small GROCERY and LIQUOR stores in Chicago, most located in AFRICAN AMERICAN communities, although Chicago's 30,000 Palestinians represented less than 1 percent of the city's population. By the 1990s, Palestinians had maintained this niche, but they also diversified into used-car dealerships, GAS STATIONS, auto repair shops, ethnic stores, and fast-food RESTAURANTS, remaining, however, primarily a community of small business entrepreneurs serving mostly "minority" communities. According to the 1990 census, more than 45 percent of employed Palestinians in the Chicago area worked in retail trade. The second largest concentration—some 14 percent—were professionals.

In the 1950s, Palestinians with families moved out of their boardinghouses and shops and into APARTMENTS and homes just west of Chicago's "BLACK BELT." By the 1970s, they formed a concentrated residential community in GAGE PARK and CHICAGO LAWN, on the South Side, and had established a business district with stores catering to Arab clientele. Chicago's largest concentration of Palestinians still lives in these areas and in the communities to the south and west of them. In the 1980s, many upwardly mobile Palestinian families moved to the southwest suburbs, bringing significant Palestinian populations to BURBANK, OAK LAWN, HICKORY HILLS, BRIDGEVIEW, ALSIP, and PALOS HILLS. Palestinians were the main contributors to a large mosque built in the 1970s in suburban Bridgeview.

Palestinian Christians established a presence in Chicago in the 1960s, settling in a widely dispersed area on the North Side between Belmont and Devon and Western and Pulaski. Like the earlier Muslim immigrants, the first Christian immigrants were males who brought their families over once they were financially established. Also concentrating in retail trade, they operated businesses on the North, South and West Sides of the city. Primarily Greek Orthodox by religion, Palestinian and JORDANIAN Christians share a church, St. George's, in CICERO. In the 1970s, a North Side Arab business enclave with shops catering to Arab customers emerged in ALBANY PARK. It has continued to expand as new waves of Palestinian immigrants, both Christian and Muslim, as well as IRAQI and Lebanese Arabs, settle on the North Side.

Palestinian migration to Chicago, Muslim and Christian, has increased steadily since the late 1960s. It comprises largely extended families from the West Bank, where ISRAELI military occupation since 1967 has stimulated extensive Palestinian emigration. A forced permanence was imposed on the Palestinian community in Chicago when Israeli laws denied residency and return rights to all Palestinians living outside the West Bank in 1967, as well as to those who subsequently remained out of the area for more than three years. This has enhanced a REFUGEE identity among Palestinians living in Chicago. By 1995 there were some 85,000 Palestinians in the Chicago metropolitan area, about half born outside the United States. Palestinians formed about 60 percent of the Arab population of the Chicago metropolitan area.

Louise Cainkar

See also: Americanization; Demography; Eastern Orthodox; Multicentered Chicago

Further reading: Cainkar, Louise. "The Deteriorating Ethnic Safety Net among Arabs in Chicago." In *Arabs in America: Building a New Future,* ed. Michael Suleiman, 1999. • Cainkar, Louise. *Palestinian Immigrants in the United States: Gender, Culture, and Global Politics.* Forthcoming.

Palmer House. Now in its fourth incarnation, the Palmer House HOTEL was long the pinnacle of grandeur and luxury in Chicago and was for decades the hotel of choice for visiting presidents, dignitaries, and businesspeople.

The crown jewel in the holdings of DEPARTMENT STORE mogul turned REAL-ESTATE developer Potter Palmer, the first Palmer House, with 225 rooms, opened in September 1870. Its furnishings alone cost $100,000, or half the construction cost. A second Palmer House was under construction nearby, but both buildings were destroyed by the FIRE OF 1871.

Palmer quickly rebuilt, employing calcium lights so workers could press on through the night. The resulting seven-story, $13 million HOTEL, opened in 1875, was filled with Italian marble and rare mosaics and was so ornate that it was alternately mocked and praised. That building—touted as the nation's only fireproof hotel—stood until 1925, when it was replaced with the $20 million, 25-story multitowered hotel that stands today.

Eclipsed in the 1980s by posh hotels on North Michigan Avenue closer to fine shopping, the Palmer House—a part of the Hilton

Hotel chain since 1945—continues to attract guests because of its proximity to the LOOP business district, the ART INSTITUTE OF CHICAGO, and downtown THEATERS. Too, its vast meeting spaces attract conventions. While its hotel rooms are standard upscale fare, the Palmer House's palatial lobby, conceived as a European drawing room, remains one of the most magnificent in the world.

Anne Moore

See also: Places of Assembly; Tourism and Conventions

Further reading: Berger, Miles L. *They Built Chicago: The Entrepreneurs Who Shaped a Great City's Architecture*. 1992. • Miller, Donald. *City of the Century: The Epic of Chicago and the Making of America*. 1996. • Schulze, Franz, and Kevin Harrington. *Chicago's Famous Buildings*. 1993.

Palos Heights, IL, Cook County, 17 miles SW of the Loop. Palos Heights is bordered by the Calumet Sag Channel on the north, Cook County FOREST PRESERVES on the south, PALOS PARK on the west, and CRESTWOOD on the east. Harlem Avenue, the main commercial thoroughfare, bisects the city, and is also the dividing line between Palos Township on the west side, and Worth Township on the east.

Little is known of the early history of this community; an 1851 map shows no farmhouses. The only road that ran through the area was 127th Street. A swampy area (later the route of the Calumet Sag Channel) stretched across the northern part of the Palos Heights region and may have discouraged development.

By the 1860s, the more level parts of the area were farmed by GERMAN and IRISH families, while the hills were used for pasture. An 1861 map shows that Harlem Avenue ran through the area, which was occupied by several farms. The east side of Harlem was divided into wood lots, to be used as sources of LUMBER and fuel by local farmers.

Ridgeland Avenue ran along the east side of the future townsite, according to an 1886 map, and 76th Avenue bordered the west side. The only indication of activity other than farming was a blacksmith shop on 76th Avenue. Near the northwest corner of town, train tracks ran to Chicago and Orland Park, although the nearest train station was in the Palos Park area.

It was not until 1901 that a SCHOOL DISTRICT was formed in the Palos Heights area. About this time, DUTCH farmers began to settle there.

While the area continued as farmland and pasture in the 1920s, the completion of the Southwest Highway in 1928 improved automobile access and led to development. In 1935, a REAL-ESTATE developer laid out a grid of streets flanking Harlem Avenue. The Harlem Heights subdivision featured quarter-acre homesites ("farmettes") that included tree saplings, grapevines, and incubated chicken eggs. Property deeds included racial RESTRICTIVE COVENANTS. Businesses sprang up along Harlem Avenue.

In 1937 the members of the growing community formed the Palos Heights Community Club, which was instrumental in the development of a public school and a fire department. Not until 1939 did Palos Heights acquire its own post office.

The building of SUBDIVISIONS continued throughout the 1940s and 1950s. In 1959, on the fourth try, Palos Heights was incorporated as a city. In that same year, TRINITY CHRISTIAN COLLEGE was established in the northeast corner of the city.

The last remaining farmland in Palos Heights was sold to subdividers in 1965. The Palos Community Hospital, the city's largest employer, opened its doors in 1972. There is no industry in the community. Palos Heights is governed by a mayor and eight aldermen. The city's first train station was under construction at the end of the century.

Betsy Gurlacz

See also: Agriculture; Cook County; Restrictive Covenants; Transportation

Further reading: Local history files. Palos Heights Public Library, Palos Heights, IL.

Palos Hills, IL, Cook County, 16 miles SW of the Loop. The northwestern part of Palos Hills lies on elevated and heavily timbered Mount Forest Island on the eastern side of the Valparaiso Moraine. The old Sauganash Swamp once covered the remainder of the area.

The earliest inhabitants were Indians during the Upper Mississippian and early historic periods. Archeological excavations reveal two Indian settlements: the Knoll Spring site near the Palos Hills Police Station, and another near 107th Street and Route 45. Indians remained in the area until the 1832 BLACK HAWK WAR.

The building of the ILLINOIS & MICHIGAN CANAL from 1836 to 1848 brought IRISH and GERMAN immigrants to the area. Farmers tilled the land and decimated the timber supply, sending much of it to Chicago via the canal. The first ROMAN CATHOLIC community, Sacred Heart Roman Catholic Church, was formed in 1872. To the south, PALOS PARK was incorporated in 1914. AGRICULTURE remained the principal occupation of the area until the 1940s.

During WORLD WAR II, the construction of the Dodge-Chrysler aircraft plant at 75th and Cicero attracted workers to the North Palos area, where they lived in substandard housing. Subsequent development of the factory site generated a demand for more housing, but also fostered disagreement on future growth.

Impetus for incorporation originated from ANNEXATION threats. Hickory Hills' annexation of streets in North Palos in order to establish a speed trap led to the formation of

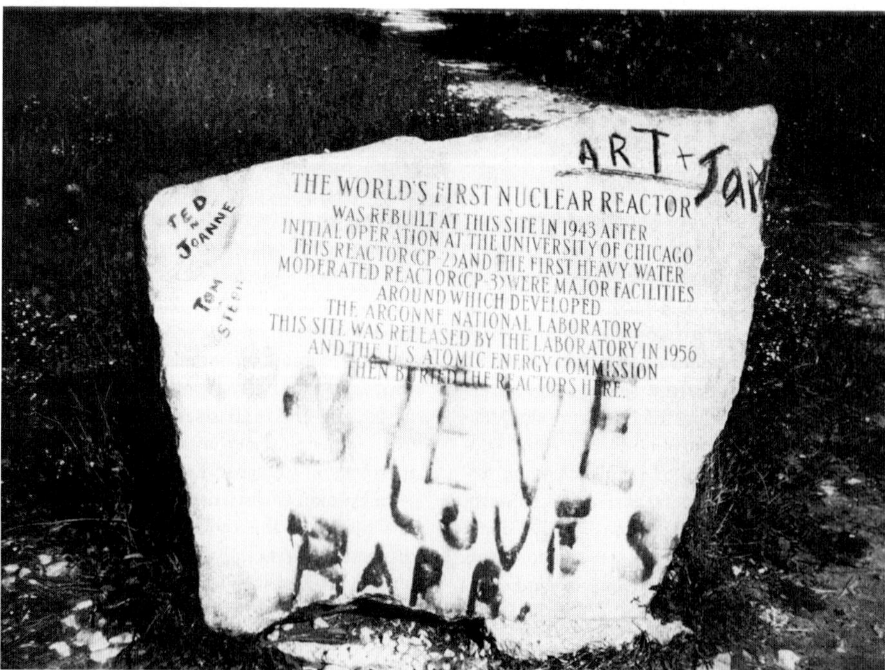

Stone marker commemorating an earlier site of Argonne National Laboratory in what is now Red Gate Woods, part of the Cook County Forest Preserve in Palos Hills. Photographer: Robert C. Long. Source: Chicago Historical Society.

the North Palos Community Council in 1957. The council fought street annexations, but ultimately was forced to choose between incorporation or continued annexation threats. In 1958 North Palos voted to incorporate as the city of Palos Hills.

Before 1963 city lots in Palos Hills were large, APARTMENTS were banned, and minimal services were provided. Thereafter planned growth allowed unit SUBDIVISIONS, leading to a building boom. By 1990 the community was white and largely middle-class, with strong public elementary and high schools, and Moraine Valley Community COLLEGE. Descendants of Irish, German, and POLISH immigrants constitute 50 percent of the population, with substantial numbers of ITALIAN and GREEK descendants. TRANSPORTATION needs are met by easy accessibility to the Stevenson EXPRESSWAY and the Route 294 TOLLWAY, as well as by METRA train service in the adjacent suburb of WORTH. The western border consists of 7,000 acres of the COOK COUNTY Forest Preserve.

William T. Corcoran

See also: Governing the Metropolis; Government, Suburban

Further reading: *History of the City of Palos Hills.* 1978. • *Palos Hills Fact Sheet.* Green Hills Public Library, 1992. • *Sacred Heart Parish Centennial Book.* 1972.

Palos Park, IL, Cook County, 19 miles SW of the Loop. The landscape of Palos Park—thickly forested hills—sets this village apart from other communities, just as its reputation as an ARTISTS' retreat did in the first half of the twentieth century. The village is surrounded on the north, west, and south by the Cook County FOREST PRESERVES, while Palos Heights lies to the east.

In the 1830s settlers from the eastern United States and Ireland began to farm the flatter ground west of what is Palos Park, while the hilly, wooded areas of Palos Park were used as sources of lumber and fuel. In the 1840s so many Northern IRISH settled here that the first post office was briefly named Orange. An 1851 map shows only one road—now La Grange Road—running to the west of the Palos Park area. The first RAILROAD came through in 1883 along the route of the present Southwest Highway and connected the area to Chicago.

In the 1890s Palos Park became known as a country retreat. Near the railway station, a group of well-to-do GERMANS founded a club called the Sharpshooters Association. The first subdivision of one- to ten-acre parcels was platted, attracting Chicagoans seeking fresh air and a respite from the crowds at the 1893 WORLD'S COLUMBIAN EXHIBITION. Artists, writers, retired theater and circus performers, and wealthy city dwellers built second homes in Palos Park. The community's position as an arts center was clearly in place by 1903 when the Palos Improvement Clubhouse was built. It seated 350, more than all the villagers combined.

In 1913 the railroad route was straightened, shifting slightly to the east, and in 1914 the villagers voted to incorporate as a village. In 1916 the Cook County Forest Preserve began buying land in the Palos Park area to ensure that it would remain a retreat for urban dwellers. This restricted the area of Palos Park from future growth and maintained the area's sylvan atmosphere.

Until midcentury, the village's population remained in the hundreds. The Calumet Sag Channel was completed across the north side of the small community in 1922. In 1928, the Southwest Highway opened along the old railroad right-of-way and improved access to the area. A handful of stores developed to serve the community, which continued to be dominated by artists and writers. Well-known people who sojourned in Palos Park included sculptor Lorado Taft, author Pearl Buck, and playwright Sherwood Anderson.

Slowly the summer and weekend homes were converted to year-round residences. The population rose as families from urban areas settled here, and the village became a bedroom community for people commuting to jobs in Chicago.

Palos Park's population (4,689 in 2000) contains few minorities and there is no industry in the village, although there is some commercial development along 123rd Street. The village is governed by a council composed of a mayor and four commissioners.

Betsy Gurlacz

See also: Art Centers, Alternative; Art Colonies; Leisure; Streets and Highways

Further reading: DeNovo, Nancy, and Geraldine DeNovo. *Palos Park, Seventy-fifth Anniversary, 1914–1989.* 1989.

Panamanians. Chicago's first Panamanians arrived shortly after WORLD WAR II as brides of American servicemen stationed in the Canal Zone. Following them were scores of young Panamanians seeking university degrees, a trend that has continued into the twenty-first century. Frustrated by limited economic opportunities at home, hundreds of less educated Panamanians began joining area family members in the 1950s and '60s. Women performed DOMESTIC WORK, while both men and women labored in light manufacturing companies, like Zenith. The first significant numbers of Afro-Panamanians settled mostly on Chicago's SOUTH SIDE in the 1970s. While many Panamanians from these early waves of immigration continued to hold blue-collar jobs, a growing number of men and women earned college degrees and entered professions like teaching, engineering, and ACCOUNTING. A small group of affluent Panamanian professionals migrated mostly to LAKE COUNTY in the 1980s, fleeing the instability of the Noriega regime.

Despite their economic, cultural, and spatial diversity, Chicago's Panamanians can be grouped geographically into three loosely defined communities: in the near-north suburbs, LAKE COUNTY, and on the South Side. Each community roughly affiliates itself with a corresponding organization. Two associations, one centered in Lake County and another in the near-north suburbs, have mostly Euro-Panamanian ROMAN CATHOLIC membership and primarily host celebratory events featuring Panamanian dances. The organizations usually affiliate with Central American groups but are also involved with broader Latino associations. The high cost of dance costumes, especially for women and girls, has prohibited some from performing with their troupes, making access to cultural expression an economic issue.

Many in the black Panamanian community belong to the African Methodist Episcopal Church and have embraced cultural traditions both similar to and somewhat distinct from those in the communities to the north. Members of this community operate a fundraising conduit for a museum in Panama dedicated to Afro-Panamanian culture. Until recently another South Side organization, now defunct, celebrated both Afro-Caribbean (mostly JAMAICAN) as well as Euro-Hispanic elements in *Antillano* culture, which had been brought to Panama by migrants from the Caribbean islands. Tensions arose in the late 1990s as the association complained of being excluded from events sponsored by the Lake County organization. As insufficient funding limited the amount of activities it could offer, the South Side group became effectively shut out from public forums of cultural expression. The organization in the near-north suburbs subsequently acted as a liaison between the two groups to ease tensions, and many community members on the South Side became active in the near-north association.

Area Panamanians have maintained active ties with other large Panamanian communities in New York City, Miami, and Panama. Those who cannot afford winter vacations to Panama, or whose resident status might make returning difficult, stay in touch with family and friends by phone, e-mail, and postal mail. However, many choose to live out their retirement in the warm climates of the American South, preferring its accessibility to their Chicago families over Panama.

Stephen R. Porter

See also: African Americans; Cubans; Demography

Paraguayans. The first community of Paraguayans to settle in the Chicago area began migrating in the middle 1960s from the provincial city of Caraguatay. Taking advantage of reformed U.S. immigration laws, a significant portion of Caraguatay's residents had migrated to Chicago, and especially New York, by 1980. Although many had worked in agriculture, some came to Chicago skilled in carpentry and metallurgy. All came seeking a better economic and political environment than Paraguay could provide. Chicago's Caraguatayan population numbered around 1,000 by the early 1970s and lived primarily in the city's northwest neighborhoods. The community's men created a labor niche for themselves in FURNITURE production and factory metalwork. The women, accustomed to household labor in Paraguay, often became DOMESTIC WORKERS in Chicago. By 1990 most of the community had left Chicago for New York City to join the large numbers of Caraguatayans there.

A smaller community of about 50 Paraguayan physicians and their families began settling in the northwest suburbs during the 1960s. Most of this group arrived as a result of a 1965 immigration law that accorded visa preference to those with professional skills acutely needed in the United States. Arriving with only temporary work visas, some of these young male and female doctors returned to Paraguay after their residencies and internships concluded. Others, however, successfully petitioned for permanent residency or citizenship and have remained in Chicago. While professional opportunity lured these Paraguayans to Chicago, the dictatorial rule of Alfredo Stroessner (1954–1989) drove them from Paraguay. Groups of other college-educated Paraguayans and students began joining the physicians in the 1970s, as Paraguay's political and economic climate wavered. Also settling in the northwest suburbs, some from this group entered the medical products sales force while others joined remaining Caraguatayans in the furniture business.

The Paraguayan community achieved its numerical zenith (approximately 2,000) and group activity during this wave of immigration in the 1970s and 1980s. Centro Paraguayo, a cultural organization, organized Paraguayan DANCE troupes of primarily women and children and hosted independence day parties. Its festivities often attracted Paraguayans from Detroit and New York City. A Paraguayan men's SOCCER team played regularly in area tournaments.

The number of Chicago-area Paraguayans has dropped and their group activities have waned in recent years. Most with Caraguatayan ties have left for New York, while the children of other Paraguayans have grown up, leaving their parents with fewer reasons to get together "as Paraguayans." Many Paraguayans have retired to Paraguay or the U.S. South with comfortable savings. While Paraguay's economic climate has remained unstable, its political environment has improved since the end of the Stroessner regime. Recent restrictions in American immigration policies have meant that fewer Paraguayans are entering the United States. Today, community activities are mostly restricted to groups of men watching the Paraguayan national soccer team play on satellite television at area sports bars.

Stephen R. Porter

See also: Demography; Multicentered Chicago; Refugees

Parish Life. Parishes occupied the center of a vital ROMAN CATHOLIC subculture in Chicago. They created neighborhoods of shared values and experiences. They also provided a haven for Catholics in the hostile PROTESTANT America of the nineteenth and early twentieth centuries. The ROMAN CATHOLIC ARCHDIOCESE OF CHICAGO initially organized parishes geographically, which laid the groundwork for building a network of churches with their respective members attending the nearby church. The English-speaking IRISH adapted to this arrangement. However, when other Catholic immigrant groups settled in Chicago, their foreign languages and different customs of worship made it difficult for them to move into these "Irish" parishes. The archdiocese agreed to allow each national group the opportunity to build temporary national parishes that would exist within territorial parishes. By allowing its followers to worship in their own traditions, the Catholic Church hoped to keep immigrants in the Catholic fold.

Expressions of Anglo-Protestant hostility to Roman Catholicism in public SCHOOLS encouraged many parishes to establish their own schools. In 1884, Catholic bishops gathered at the Third Plenary Council in Baltimore requesting that each parish support a school. The Chicago Archdiocese responded to this challenge by building the largest parochial school system in the world. While initiated as a response to nativism, these schools enabled non-English-speaking Catholics to pass on their language and customs to their children. CATHOLIC SCHOOLS reinforced for every generation the centrality of Catholicism to their identity in America.

As new immigrants arrived in Chicago and older groups moved toward the edges of the expanding city, Archbishop James Quigley (1903–1915) aimed to establish a parish for every square mile, ensuring the centrality of the local parish in the lives of its parishioners. National churches continued to be built within territorial parishes. However, the ethnic divisiveness that followed in the wake of WORLD WAR I prompted George Cardinal Mundelein, who came to Chicago in 1916, to curtail the establishment of national parishes. The xenophobia of the 1920s convinced Mundelein that Catholic ethnics should become AMERICANIZED. Catholic parishes became mini melting pots as ethnic groups moved up the economic ladder and out of immigrant communities. They joined the white English-speaking territorial parishes in the BUNGALOW BELT and middle-class neighborhoods. Irish, GERMANS, POLES, ITALIANS, and others forged a Catholic American identity.

Devotional Catholicism was also an important factor in shaping parish life. Catholicism had traditionally emphasized the importance of communal worship. To partake of the sacraments that were crucial to salvation, Catholics needed a priest and a parish. Other devotional practices such as novenas, Forty Hours Devotion, Stations of the Cross, Benediction, etc., encouraged public ceremonies and communal expressions of faith. Most parishes also supported a host of fraternal and charitable societies and sodalities. Some churches provided recreational facilities. Until Vatican II in the 1960s, white Catholics kept aloof from Protestants and inhabited a spiritual and social world from the cradle to the grave that centered on the parish.

In the wake of Vatican II and the movement of older white Catholic ethnic groups into the middle and upper classes and into a broader and highly educated world beyond a Catholic subculture, the parish is no longer a defining aspect of Catholic identity. Confident in their place in American society, practicing Catholics see the parish more as a place for spiritual nourishment than a refuge.

Eileen M. McMahon

See also: Religion, Chicago's Influence on; Religious Geography; Religious Institutions

Further reading: McCaffrey, Lawrence J., Ellen Skerrett, Michael F. Funchion, and Charles Fanning. *The Irish in Chicago.* 1987. • McMahon, Eileen. *"What Parish Are You From?" The Chicago Irish Parish Community and Race Relations, 1916–1970.* 1995.

Park City, IL, Lake County, 35 miles N of the Loop. Owners of four MOBILE HOME parks banded together to incorporate Park City in 1958 to block ANNEXATION from nearby WAUKEGAN. In the late 1970s, a federal housing lawsuit claimed that residents excluded nonwhites. Since that time, the minority population has increased, and single-family homes have emerged alongside trailer homes. In the late 1990s Columbia COLLEGE of Missouri opened a small branch campus in Park City.

Erik Gellman

See also: Lake County, IL

Park Districts. When Chicago officially incorporated as a city in 1837, it adopted the motto "Urbs in Horto," a Latin phrase meaning "City in a Garden." Despite this verdant slogan, the city had few public parks. Early residents succeeded in saving two small parcels of the lakefront as parkland. The few other small parks created during the 1840s and 1850s were donated or sold to the city at reduced rates by REAL-ESTATE developers. These speculators knew that a small square in the center of a residential development would boost the value of the entire subdivision. In 1849, real-estate speculator John S. Wright suggested a much more ambitious system of parks and interconnected pleasure drives. At the time, however, the city government had neither the administrative nor the legal means to realize this vision.

Concerns about the health threat posed by an unsightly North Side lakefront CEMETERY furthered the park movement in the 1850s and 1860s. Physician John H. Rauch realized that Chicago's WATER SUPPLY was being contaminated by cholera and other diseases because of poor burial conditions in the sandy low-lying site. Rauch, who also made a study of the world's most famous parks, led a crusade to convert the city cemetery into a public park. North Siders rallied behind the cause, and, in 1860, 60 acres were reserved as a pleasure ground. Five years later, after the assassination of President Abraham Lincoln, the park was named in his honor. Improvements were made in accord with an original plan by LANDSCAPE DESIGNER Swain Nelson.

In the late 1860s, Chicagoans rallied for additional parks, prompting the State Legislature to establish the South, West, and Lincoln Park Commissions in 1869. Each commission served its own jurisdiction and was responsible for improving one section of what was intended as a unified park and boulevard system. Reflecting Wright's suggestion of 20 years earlier, a ribbon of parks and pleasure drives encircling the city was envisioned.

LINCOLN PARK's early expansion included exhuming bodies and moving them to other cemeteries. Beginning in the 1880s, the park's boundaries were also extended through landfill projects. Lake Shore Drive was created as the boulevard linkage with the south parks. A boulevard connection with the west parks was also intended at Diversey Parkway. As the Lincoln Park Commission had less political autonomy or funding than the other two boards, however, it was unable to improve Diversey Parkway as a pleasure drive. Therefore, the boulevard system developed as a horseshoe rather than the ring that had been intended.

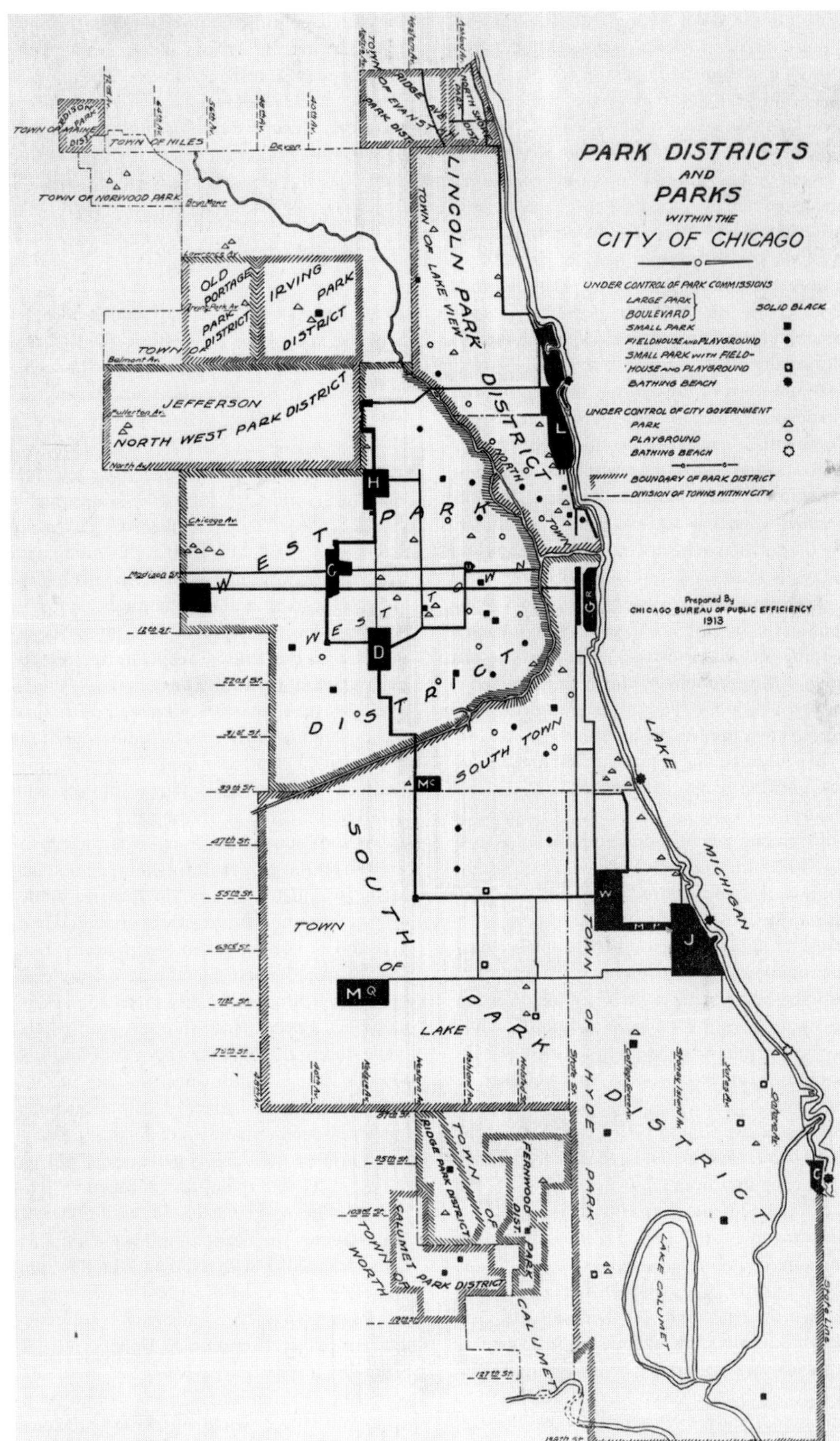

This 1913 map shows the several park districts which once served areas within the city of Chicago. Cartographer: Chicago Bureau of Public Efficiency. Source: Chicago Historical Society.

The South and West Park Commissions pursued ambitious plans, but exorbitant construction costs and problems with levying taxes after the Great FIRE OF 1871 resulted in phased projects. The South Park Commission hired Frederick Law Olmsted and Calvert Vaux to design what was originally South Park and is now considered JACKSON and WASHINGTON PARKS and the Midway Plaisance. Olmsted, who designed New York's Central Park, believed that parks should not only provide release from urban tensions but also serve as democratic places. His plan for Washington Park was largely realized. Jackson Park, however, had few improvements prior to its selection as site of the 1893 WORLD'S COLUMBIAN EXPOSITION. Olmsted worked with architect Daniel H. Burnham to transform the swampy area into the "White City." After the fair, the site's conversion back to parkland followed a third Olmsted plan.

The original West Park system was designed by Olmsted's friend and colleague, William Le Baron Jenney, the landscape designer, architect, and engineer who is now considered the father of the SKYSCRAPER. Composed of an ensemble of three large LANDSCAPES, the west parks are known today as HUMBOLDT, GARFIELD, and Douglas Parks. The renowned Prairie-style designer Jens Jensen created a second phase of improvements for these parks during the early twentieth century.

By the turn of the century, Chicago's population had increased to 1.7 million people. Nearly three-quarters of a million people lived in the central part of the city, more than a mile away from any of the existing parks. Social reformers launched a PLAYGROUND MOVEMENT for the creation of additional parks. In 1899 and 1903 the state legislature authorized the three park commissions to acquire property for new parks. The South Park Commission opened a system of 10 innovative neighborhood parks in 1905, which soon inspired similar parks in the West and Lincoln Park systems and in other cities across the United States.

In addition to the population boom, Chicago was growing geographically. In 1889, residents of townships encompassing 120 square miles surrounding the city voted in favor of ANNEXATION. As these areas were not served by the three park commissions, an 1895 law allowed the formation of additional park boards. Because of limited tax bases, these smaller park commissions had difficulty acquiring and improving land, and progress was made incrementally. Locally prominent architects such as Clarence Hatzfeld were hired for the design of fieldhouses in these parks. As many of the park sites were on flood plain areas along the North Branch of the Chicago River, they often had good natural features and needed only minimal landscape improvements. Between 1896 and 1930, 19 additional park districts were created, resulting in a total of 22 individual park commissions operating simultaneously in Chicago.

In the early 1930s, the GREAT DEPRESSION caused the bankruptcy of the individual park districts. In 1934, the 22 independent agencies were consolidated into the Chicago Park District. Over the next seven years more than $100 million of improvements were funded through the Works Progress Administration. Construction projects during this period included hundreds of new lakefront landfill acres and the reconstruction of Lake Shore Drive.

By the 1950s, the Chicago Park District was responsible for 169 parks totaling approximately 6,300 acres of land. More than 200 small play lots were operated by the city of Chicago. In 1959, the two agencies entered into a functional merger in which the park police were consolidated into the Chicago POLICE Department, the boulevards were transferred to the city of Chicago, and the city play lots were transferred to the Chicago Park District. At the opening of the twenty-first century, the Chicago Park District operated 547 parks totaling more than 7,300 acres of land.

Julia Sniderman Bachrach

See also: Conservatories; Leisure; Millenium Park; Playgrounds and Small Parks; Special Districts

Park Forest, IL, Cook County, 28 miles S of the Loop. The future Park Forest's first permanent white resident, Adam Brown, settled at the present corner of Sauk Trail and Chicago Road in 1833. John and Sabra McCoy established a farmstead in 1834 and, along with the Batcheldor family, were Methodist ABOLITIONISTS who offered their homes as stops for runaway slaves on the UNDERGROUND RAILROAD. The Batcheldor property became the largest part of the future Park Forest.

In 1852 the ILLINOIS CENTRAL RAILROAD was built along the northwestern border of the future Park Forest, and the Michigan Central Railroad came through in 1853 to intersect with the Illinois Central in neighboring MATTESON.

Chicago's south suburbs experienced expansive residential growth throughout the first half of the twentieth century. In the 1920s, developers planned to construct Indian Wood, a complete city centered on a newly built 18-hole GOLF course, on the as yet undeveloped Batcheldor land. Early speculation failed to attract buyers, and another attempt was made during the 1933 CENTURY OF PROGRESS World's Fair with little success. This was followed by another failed effort, this time a housing development marketed to AFRICAN AMERICANS around the existing golf course.

The successful plan for developing Park Forest came on the heels of World War II. On October 28, 1946, developer Philip M. Klutznick, along with Nathan Manilow and Carroll F. Sweet, held a press conference at the Palmer House in Chicago to announce that American Community Builders (ACB) planned to privately develop a new self-governing community in Chicago's south suburbs. The village would ultimately provide a variety of housing options for over 5,000 families, an extensive park system, one of the first major outdoor shopping centers in the country (based on the Plaza San Marco in Venice), and a town hall supporting all municipal functions with a village manager at its head. This announcement received national attention in the *New York Times* and *Collier's* magazine.

Park Forest was designed by Elbert Peets in the tradition of other planned communities such as Radburn, New Jersey, and RIVERSIDE, Illinois, to provide housing for veterans returning from the war, earning it the nickname "GI town." ACB placed advertisements in the *Chicago Tribune* to lure prospective residents to Park Forest. New tenants applied to live in the village and ACB screened applicants according to their income level, education, status as a veteran, and need. The first residents arrived in August 1948, and on February 1, 1949, Park Forest was incorporated as a village. By 1950, over 3,000 families had settled in Park Forest. The first black family took residence in 1959.

Park Forest was honored in 1954 as an "All-America City" for its citizens' help in the creation of Rich Township High School, and again in 1976 for racial integration and OPEN HOUSING initiatives. The population was 23,462 in 2000, when Park Forest received the Daniel H. Burnham Award for planning to redevelop the outdated shopping center into a traditional downtown. In 2003 meteorites landed in Park Forest and neighboring areas, in the first known meteorite fall in Illinois since 1938.

Todd J. Tubutis

See also: Planning Chicago; Planning, City and Regional; Shopping Districts and Malls

Further reading: *The Oral History of Park Forest: OH! Park Forest.* Park Forest Historical Society. 1982. • Randall, Gregory C. *America's Original GI Town: Park Forest, Illinois.* 2000. • Whyte, William H. *The Organization Man.* 1956.

Park Ridge, IL, Cook County, 18 miles NW of the Loop. Local legend claims that the suburb of Park Ridge contains the highest point in COOK COUNTY. While this is not true, the name is appropriate, reflecting the town's park-like setting along a gentle ridge.

The first residents of the area were the POTAWATOMI. After their removal under terms of the 1833 TREATY, YANKEE settlers from New England and upstate New York began trickling in and laying out farms. They honored their eastern heritage by calling the district Maine Township. Most prominent among these early people was Mancel Talcott, who built a log cabin and a bridge over the DES PLAINES RIVER near the present site of Touhy Avenue and served as postmaster.

Industry came to Maine Township in 1854 with the opening of George Penny's brickworks. When the Chicago, St. Paul & Fond du Lac RAILROAD (later the Chicago & North Western) began running shortly afterward, Penny arranged to have the trains stop by building his own station. The new community that grew up around the station was informally known as Pennyville, until Penny himself suggested the name Brickton.

By 1873 the population of Brickton was 405. The brick pits had been worked out, so when the residents voted to incorporate that year, the village was renamed Park Ridge. Over the next decades, as Park Ridge established its identity as a residential community, its leaders sought to develop the look of a traditional New England town, with large homes on wide lots and a profusion of trees. APARTMENTS were banned and industrial development discouraged.

Park Ridge experienced a major building boom during the 1910s and '20s. City dwellers discovered the pleasant surroundings and convenient commuter trains. From 2,009 in 1910, the population ballooned to 10,417 in 1930. Anticipating ANNEXATION pressure from Chicago, the village had reorganized as the city of Park Ridge in 1910. Maine East High School and the landmark Pickwick Theater date from this era.

The depression of the 1930s halted the boom. During the 1940s, some housing for war-industry workers was built. However, significant expansion of Park Ridge did not begin until the 1950s, as part of America's postwar suburbanization. The population rose from 16,602 in 1950 to 42,466 two decades later. Aiding the growth was the opening of nearby O'HARE AIRPORT, as well as the construction of two tollways and the Northwest (now Kennedy) EXPRESSWAY.

As its population grew, Park Ridge moved to increase its tax base by encouraging office development and allowing a limited number of apartments. Lutheran General HOSPITAL relocated from Chicago, and a second high school (Maine South) opened in 1964. In later years, as the community filled up its vacant land and property values soared, builders began to tear down small, older homes and replace them with huge new dwellings.

Park Ridge entered the twenty-first century as a mature, upper-middle-class residential suburb. The population continues to be largely white Anglo-Saxon PROTESTANT, but now with a significant number of POLISH ROMAN CATHOLICS. Concerns include maintaining the residential strengths of the community and alleviating the noise from O'Hare Airport.

John R. Schmidt

See also: Economic Geography; Quarrying, Stonecutting, and Brickmaking; Suburbs and Cities as Dual Metropolis

Further reading: Blouin, Nancy. *Park Ridge, Illinois: A Photo History.* 1994. • Park Ridge Chamber of Commerce. *Park Ridge, 1873–1973: A Century of Pride.* 1973. • Park Ridge Library has various clippings in its Heritage Room, as well as four videotapes of oral history interviews conducted from 1985 to 1987.

Parking. The early parking garages, constructed in the early twentieth century, were predominantly one-story structures located south of the LOOP. Some of the garages were horse stables, where automobiles were charged the same amount it cost to stable a horse.

The Hotel LaSalle parking garage, constructed in 1917, was the first high-rise parking garage in the Loop. Still standing at Washington and LaSalle today, the multicolored terra cotta structure was designed in the architectural tradition of the First Chicago School. The original ramp is still in use. The garage possessed complementary facilities such as a car-wash rack on each floor and a repair shop on the top floor.

In the 1920s, parking entrepreneurs Richard G. Lydy and Ben Kissel began buying old buildings in downtown Chicago on Franklin Street, Wells Street, and PRINTERS ROW, converting the obsolete structures into parking buildings. The 1930s brought about new parking-garage designs such as double-deck parking, more high-rise garages, and a growing number of parking lots. Parking rates were high and paid by businessmen, salesmen, the clients of doctors and dentists, and shoppers.

As the Loop developed, additional parking was created for the increasing number of people entering by car. The first parking meters were installed in 1947 on the upper and lower levels of Wacker Drive. The city built the first underground parking garages in the early 1950s and, in 1957, adopted the current ZONING ordinance to regulate privately owned parking facilities.

The 1970s brought parking policies that responded to federal air-quality standards. The city of Chicago, to attain higher air quality in response to EPA standards, banned private parking garages in the Loop. Over five thousand public spaces were eliminated between 1978 and 1983.

By 1997, there were 342 public parking garages and lots in the Chicago Central Area, which includes the Loop, Lakefront, SOUTH LOOP, River North, Upper NEAR NORTH, STREETERVILLE, and NEAR WEST SIDE areas.

The largest parking garage in the Chicago area is located at O'HARE AIRPORT.

Nasutsa M. Mabwa

See also: Architecture: The First Chicago School; Commuting; Environmental Regulation; Street Life; Transportation

Further reading: "Automobiles—Parking." Clipping file. Chicago Historical Society, Chicago, IL. • "Public Parking Facilities: Chicago Central Area, July 1997." City of Chicago, Department of Planning and Development, November 1998.

Parliament of Religions. *See* World's Parliament of Religions

Patriotic Clubs. *See* Clubs: Patriotic and Veterans' Clubs

Patronage. From the late nineteenth century until the 1931 election of Anton Cermak, the WARD was the locus of patronage POLITICS. After Cermak's election, the rise of the KELLY-NASH machine (later the Richard J. Daley machine) centered patronage politics in City Hall. Jobs, money, and insider contracts fueled these organizations, and the basic premise of political patronage in Chicago, as well as in the state government, was that "one hand washes the other." Job applicants and potential contractors were required to seek a written recommendation from local party officials before they would even be considered and were required to provide political work and financial support for the party. Failure to do so would result in firing or loss of contracts. This applied to most jobs and contracts, from the least skilled to the most professional. This system gave the party several resources: the ability to raise campaign money, an energetic army of campaign precinct workers, and enormous power over the selection and election of candidates. It also resulted in a bloated government workforce that was frequently more focused on campaign work and pleasing political sponsors than serving the public. The system of awarding noncompetitive, expensive contracts to the small circle of contributing political insiders often resulted in shoddy services and wasted tax money. Federal grants to city governments during Richard J. Daley's tenure as MAYOR provided an especially rich source of patronage.

Beginning in 1976 a series of federal lawsuits began to undercut the ability of officials to hire, fire and award government contracts on a partisan basis. The *Elrod* (1976), SHAKMAN (1983), *Rutan* (1990), *O'Hare* (1996), and *Vickery* (1996) cases established the principle

Pinstripe Patronage

"Pinstripe" patronage is a form of corporate and professional political favoritism that emerged in place of the more traditional patronage following successful litigation targeting the latter in the 1970s and 1980s. Patronage, a major cog of so-called MACHINE POLITICS, enabled "bosses" to dominate urban POLITICS from the nineteenth century until the 1950s, and in Chicago until the 1980s. In a series of rulings known collectively as the SHAKMAN DECREES the federal judiciary ruled that city of Chicago employees could not be fired or hired as political punishment or reward. These rulings went to the heart of the exchange model of political control, wherein bosses gave or withheld public employment in return for electoral support at the polls. After Shakman, Chicago political leaders shifted the emphasis of patronage to major ACCOUNTING and LAW firms, banks, and corporations by steering public business to those who helped maintain the regime in power.

Louis H. Masotti

that partisanship in hiring, firing, and contracting was an infringement of the First Amendment rights of citizens to hold political beliefs and act upon them. These cases have reduced some of the most blatant forms of patronage. Political patronage and insider contracting in local and state government have by no means been eliminated, but they have become more subtle.

David Orr

See also: Good Government Movements; Gray Wolves; Machine Politics; Political Culture; Privatization

Further reading: Bowman, Cynthia Grant. "We Don't Want Anybody Anybody Sent: The Death of Patronage Hiring in Chicago." *Northwestern University Law Review* 86 (Fall 1991): 57–95. • Hamilton, David K. "The Continuing Judicial Assault on Patronage." *Public Administration Review* 59.1 (January/February 1999).

Peddling. *See* Street Peddling

Peotone, IL, Will County, 39 miles S of the Loop. GERMAN and DUTCH settlers established Peotone around the Illinois Central RAILROAD in the late 1850s. The Rathje family built a large windmill in the 1870s to grind wheat into flour, and the mill became a site on the National Register of Historic Places in 1982. The town remained a small farming community throughout the twentieth century, with a population of 3,385 in 2000. Since 1970, there have been repeated proposals to build a third regional airport in the area.

Erik Gellman

See also: Transportation; Will County

Peruvians. According to census and survey data, the Peruvian community in Chicago numbered approximately 10,000 to 20,000 in the 1990s and included a range of social groups, from wealthy business executives and professionals to laborers and undocumented immigrants. In the same period approximately 750,000 Peruvians were living in the United States, largely in the New Jersey suburbs of New York City; in southern Florida, particularly in Miami; and in the area around Los Angeles. In Chicago most Peruvians have located on the Northwest Side, PALATINE, and WEST CHICAGO, where many Peruvians have intermarried with PUERTO RICANS.

Peruvians began emigrating to Chicago in the 1950s. Some arrived as college students and stayed in the country; others came as laborers or technicians, particularly for companies that already were operating in Peru during the free-market, open-economy regime of General Manuel A. Odría (1948–1956). Since then, Peruvians have come in different waves.

One of these waves took place during the regime of General Juan Velasco Alvarado (1968–1975), whose left-leaning government expropriated portions of the landed and industrial elite. Many of these families, along with professionals, technicians, and employees of American companies, moved to the United States. The largest wave of immigrants came in the 1980s, when Peru went into a state of quasi civil war. Hundreds of thousands of Peruvians left the country, most of them moving to the United States, either legally or illegally.

Efforts to recreate Peruvian culture in Chicago have included celebrations of the national Independence Day (July 28) with parades, dances, parties, and other activities. Chicago's Peruvians also venerate the "Procesión del Señor de los Milagros," a religious celebration of the Lord of the Miracles (Jesus Christ), in which the participants dress in purple garments. This October procession, along with parades and masses, takes place in PALATINE, where a Peruvian priest leads the festivities.

Sports, particularly SOCCER, have also played a central role. Many soccer clubs have also dealt with other aspects of AMERICANIZATION and social life, including providing job contacts and other information. These clubs have taken the names of traditional soccer clubs from Lima, such as Alianza Lima, Universitario de Deportes, and Sporting Cristal. All are active members of the Midwest chapter of the Association of Peruvian Institutions in the United States and Canada. Founded on May 25, 1990, this association constitutes the umbrella organization for Peruvians in the United States and Canada. The Midwest chapter was founded on December 3, 1994.

Chicago's Peruvian Arts Society ("Sociedad de Artes Peruanas"), publishes a bulletin titled *El Chasqui* (the Quechua name of the messengers during the Inca Empire), which contains information on the Peruvian community in Chicago.

José R. Deustua

See also: Demography; Multicentered Chicago

Further reading: Altamirano, Teófilo. *Exodo: Peruanos en el exterior.* 1992. • Altamirano, Teófilo. *Los que se fueron: Peruanos en Estados Unidos.* 1990.

Petroleum. See Refining

Pharmaceuticals. *See* Medical Manufacturing and Pharmaceuticals

Pharmacies. *See* Drug Retailing

Philanthropy. Philanthropy, the organized donation of money to charitable causes, has left an enormous and lasting legacy in Chicago. It has enabled the establishment of numerous educational and cultural institutions of national and international renown and has supported the development of a network of charities that have improved the health and social welfare of metropolitan area residents.

Over the past century and a half, philanthropy in Chicago has slowly undergone a major transformation. From 1850 to 1915 large donations by wealthy individuals in support of major institutions dominated the philanthropic landscape. Subsequently, philanthropy changed its course by spawning its own enduring charitable institutions, which have changed both the scope and character of giving. After WORLD WAR I, wealthy Chicagoans began endowing in perpetuity private philanthropic foundations as a way to create a stable, permanent flow of charitable resources that would continue the donor's philanthropic work long after his or her death.

Private foundations have not been the only philanthropic institutions that have challenged the earlier tradition of direct philanthropy by wealthy donors. Community funds and federated giving programs have allowed donors of more modest means to find flexible vehicles for their philanthropic efforts. Additionally, many Chicago-based corporations, among them several of America's largest BUSINESS enterprises, launched corporate philanthropic programs in the 1950s and 1960s.

Chicago's early philanthropic leaders were industrialists, merchants, and financiers who helped build the city, especially after the CIVIL WAR. Civic pride for the growing new city was certainly a key inspiration. Proud donors to the city's embryonic cultural institutions boasted that Chicago would become the "Athens of the West." Never afraid to use their charitable gifts to project their own personal ideals to the broader community, the city's donors also sought to instill culture in the working classes, offering them edifying pastimes that donors considered morally and culturally uplifting.

The early philanthropic emphasis was on building major cultural and educational institutions, which were seen as lasting contributions to the city's growth. Substantial donations launched the Chicago Atheneum, the FIELD MUSEUM OF NATURAL HISTORY, the ART INSTITUTE OF CHICAGO, and the CHICAGO SYMPHONY ORCHESTRA, as well as such quasi-scholarly institutions as the CHICAGO HISTORICAL SOCIETY and the CHICAGO ACADEMY OF SCIENCES. Educational institutions included NORTHWESTERN UNIVERSITY, founded by John Evans in 1851 to serve the people of the Northwest Territory; the UNIVERSITY OF CHICAGO, launched in part with a $600,000 gift from John D. Rockefeller in 1889; and the Armour Institute of Technology (now ILLINOIS INSTITUTE OF TECHNOLOGY), named after the legendary MEATPACKER at its founding in 1893.

Early philanthropy also focused on the enduring problems of poverty, health, and child welfare. SETTLEMENT HOUSES such as HULL HOUSE attracted notable female philanthropists

First Passavant Cotillion and Christmas Ball, 1949. By 1971 this annual debutante presentation had raised nearly two million dollars for the Passavant Hospital. Photographer: Unknown. Source: Chicago Historical Society.

and reformers like Jane Addams, Ellen Gates Starr, and Louise de Koven Bowen, who together made critical contributions to the eventual development of the field of social work. Not all social welfare philanthropy was maintained by women, however. The CHICAGO RELIEF AND AID SOCIETY, which was the city's largest charity after 1850, drew most of its support from the city's business leaders. In addition, numerous relief asylums and HOSPITALS attracted charitable aid from all quarters, as donors expanded their focus to include the city's most pressing problems.

By the 1920s approximately $80 million had been donated to charity in Chicago since the city's founding, with culture and education together garnering over $50 million. During the same period, health charities and hospitals raised around $10 million, child care attracted $2 million, relief organizations drew $1.3 million, and settlements attracted around $700,000. Around the turn of the century, there were several important individual gifts, such as the $8 million bequest from Marshall Field to endow the Field Museum and early gifts from Charles Hutchinson to the Art Institute. Walter Loomis NEWBERRY and John CRERAR endowed important private libraries. Between 1925 and the GREAT DEPRESSION Chicago philanthropy grew noticeably, as donations citywide totaled nearly $45 million. This short period witnessed the foundings of the SHEDD AQUARIUM, the MUSEUM OF SCIENCE AND INDUSTRY, and the ADLER PLANETARIUM.

Following a larger national trend that began in the east, Chicago's great individual donors gave way after World War I to a new philanthropic vehicle, the private foundation. Following the lead of Andrew Carnegie and John D. Rockefeller, who created the first foundations, wealthy Chicagoans gravitated toward institutional philanthropy. Large foundations with local, national, and international focuses emerged, not only changing the vehicle through which philanthropic funds were distributed, but also changing the character of philanthropy. While early philanthropic giving by wealthy individuals was profoundly shaped by the interests and values of the donors, foundation philanthropy gradually became the purview of professional staff who deliberate over formal grant requests. The new cadre of professional grant makers consolidated its control over philanthropic expertise though the formation in 1974 of the Donors Forum of Chicago, an association for the city's grantmaking professionals. Characterized by more formal grant-making rules and greater public reporting, this style of philanthropy has broadened the recipient pool to include a multitude of nonprofit organizations often working with disadvantaged communities.

Chicago's first major private foundation, the Rosenwald Fund, stands out because of its purposefully limited life span. Believing that permanent foundation endowments tend "to lessen the amount available for immediate use," Julius Rosenwald created a foundation in 1917 that was to be liquidated 25 years after his death. It ceased operation in 1948, a decade ahead of schedule, after spending $63 million, notably in support of AFRICAN AMERICAN education.

Several of Chicago's largest perpetual foundations were created in the 1950s during the national boom in foundation creation. Robert R. McCormick, the editor of the CHICAGO TRIBUNE for more than 40 years, created a trust in 1955 that began functioning nearly 35 years later as the billion-dollar Robert R. McCormick–Tribune Foundation. In 1948, the Joyce Foundation was created with a broad philanthropic mandate extending both within the city and beyond and assets that would grow to close to $950 million by 1998. The largest foundation in Chicago is the John D. and Catherine T. MACARTHUR FOUNDATION. John D. MacArthur left the Chicago area in 1960 for Florida, where he amassed an immense local real-estate portfolio to augment his insurance fortune. Upon his death in 1978, the assets passed to the foundation, which controlled over $4 billion in assets by the end of the twentieth century.

While business firms have always been part of the fabric of the city's philanthropic life through the gifts of their leaders, company-sponsored philanthropy has emerged as a critical ingredient in the city's charitable support system. Major Chicago-based firms such as Sears, Roebuck (1941), Allstate (1952), and Amoco (1952) have long-established corporate contributions programs. Unlike most other forms of institutional philanthropy, however,

Julius Rosenwald: Chicago Businessman and Philanthropist

Born in Springfield, Illinois, to a middle-class family of German Jewish immigrants, Julius Rosenwald began his career by going to New York to work as an apprentice in his mother's family's clothing business. In 1885, he returned to Chicago and opened his own clothing firm, which specialized in the sale of men's summer suits. At the suggestion of his brother-in-law, Rosenwald bought one quarter of the two-year-old Sears, Roebuck & Co. in 1895 for $37,500. A year later, he went to work for the MAIL-ORDER house. Presiding over Sears during a period of fantastic growth, Rosenwald amassed a fortune of more than $200 million.

A philanthropist and civic leader, Rosenwald sat on the boards of the UNIVERSITY OF CHICAGO and HULL HOUSE, but his main interest after 1910 was in assisting AFRICAN AMERICANS. Rosenwald helped spearhead the construction of black YMCAs in Chicago and throughout the nation, and he helped to build over five thousand primary and secondary schools for blacks in the South between 1913 and 1930. His most lasting act of philanthropy was the building of the Museum of Science and Industry, which he initiated and to which he, his estate, and his foundation gave over $11 million by the mid-1940s.

Peter M. Ascoli

corporate giving makes no claim to be entirely altruistic. Many of the largest corporations have long considered their philanthropic initiatives as important aspects of marketing and public relations.

Founded in 1915, the Chicago COMMUNITY TRUST was one of the earliest community foundations in the nation. One of its early leaders, Frank D. Loomis, spearheaded the national community foundation movement, which has spread this philanthropic vehicle to cities around the country. Loomis was also instrumental in launching the Community Fund, precursor to the Chicago's United Way/Crusade of Mercy in 1934. Under the leadership of Edward Ryerson, the fund raised $3.4 million in the city and suburbs in its first year to benefit 65 human service organizations. Over time, the United Way/Crusade of Mercy sought more effective ways to solve community problems and moved toward a more formal grant-making process, including more rigorous analysis of the capacities and relative effectiveness of organizations seeking funds. By 1998, fund-raising efforts succeeded in collecting $98 million, distributed to over 430 local service organizations.

On the eve of the twenty-first century, institutional giving in Chicago had grown to over $500 million, with more than a thousand foundations active in the city and suburbs. Through experimentation, change, and growth, major individual contributions in support of cultural and educational causes have branched out to a variety of forms of institutional giving, supporting hundreds of nonprofit organizations working in almost every field imaginable.

Peter Frumkin

See also: Charity Organization Societies; Relief and Subsistence Aid; Social Services

Further reading: Bremner, Robert H. *American Philanthropy.* 1988. • McCarthy, Kathleen D. *Noblesse Oblige: Charity and Cultural Philanthropy in Chicago, 1849–1929.* 1982. • Rosenwald, Julius. "Principles of Public Giving." *Atlantic Monthly* (May 1929).

Phoenix, IL, Cook County, 19 miles S of the Loop. Nestled between HARVEY and SOUTH HOLLAND, the area that became Phoenix was named by an early developer who had traveled in Arizona and enjoyed the city of that name. The development of this small community is tied to that of its neighbor, Harvey.

Harvey was established as an industrial, planned city with no SALOONS. By 1900 it boasted a population of 5,395 and industries employing 1,700. Many of Harvey's factories lay between the ILLINOIS CENTRAL RAILROAD and Harvey's eastern boundary at Halsted Street. Phoenix started during the 1890s as a small housing development for Harvey workers on the eastern side of Halsted Street in unincorporated territory. The SUBDIVISION was called "Phenix Park" (the spelling changed when the village was incorporated).

Along with a few houses, factories, and businesses, there were five saloons east of Halsted, which led to an ongoing controversy between Harvey's leaders and Phoenix's saloonkeepers. In 1900, to stop Harvey workers from patronizing Phoenix saloons, PROHIBITION forces sought to render Phoenix Park dry and annex Phoenix into Harvey. Residents of Phoenix Park, however, wanted to keep local control as an independent village. Understandably, they had the strong support of the saloon owners, who wanted to continue serving the workers from across the street in Harvey. In a controversial election on August 29, 1900, the "wet" forces won.

Phoenix grew slowly. Most of the early residents were of DUTCH and POLISH ancestry. AFRICAN AMERICAN families first moved to the village in 1915, and by 1920, there was a greater influx of blacks from Chicago and the South. Industry in Harvey and the RAILROADS, including the MARKHAM Yards of the Illinois Central, provided a strong employment base for these early residents of Phoenix.

The growing African American population in Phoenix led to the community's second great encounter with the city of Harvey. In 1960, Phoenix's 4,203 residents were for the most part segregated racially; white residents lived mainly in the southern part of town, and African Americans in the northern part. In votes by the white-majority administration of Phoenix and the administration of Harvey, the southern portion of Phoenix was deannexed to Harvey.

With the deannexation of the southern portion of Phoenix to Harvey, Phoenix lost 35 percent of its general revenue in taxes and commercial business. The remainder of the village's population was primarily African American. Since 1960 the African American population of the village of Phoenix has increased, standing at 94 percent of the villages 2,157 residents in 2000.

Larry A. McClellan

See also: Economic Geography; Prohibition and Temperance; Racism, Ethnicity, and White Identity; Suburbs and Cities as Dual Metropolis

Further reading: McClellan, Larry A. "History of Phoenix Reflects Sense of Community." *Star,* September 28, 1997. • Suggs, Ava, ed. *Phoenix, Seventy-fifth Anniversary.* 1975.

Photography. Since the invention of photography in France in 1839, amateur and professional photographers have created a rich visual heritage of life in Chicago. Aside from a few landscapes, the earliest photographs of Chicago are daguerreotype, ambrotype, and tintype portraits of the city's founding settlers made in the studios of professional photographers. The introduction of paper photographic prints made from glass negatives in the early 1850s made photographs more affordable and stimulated the growth of the photographic profession. In Chicago, the studios of Edwin Brand, John Carbutt, S. M. Fassett, Alexander Hesler, C. D. Mosher, and others sprang up in the 1850s and 1860s to meet the insatiable demand for carte-de-visite and cabinet card portraits.

These founders of Chicago's commercial photography industry also produced outdoor views of their frontier city in various antique formats, but the real mass market for city views came with the introduction in the mid-1860s of stereographic cards. Unlike cards made for albums, these dual-image photographs were viewed through a stereoscope that created a three-dimensional illusion. Immensely popular, stereo cards of local scenes were often published in sets and distributed nationally.

George Eastman's inexpensive and easily operated Kodak camera, introduced in 1888, revolutionized amateur photography. Chicagoans began to document every aspect of their lives. The availability of flexible roll film and the rise of the commercial photo finishing industry greatly increased photographic activity and awareness.

After the 1890s new technological innovations in the PRINTING industry made photographic reproductions in books, MAGAZINES, and NEWSPAPERS practical, and a new type of commercial photographer evolved for this new market. The introduction of factory-made gelatin dry plates had freed photographers from using the cumbersome wet plate negatives that had restricted photography to only the most dedicated few. The other great innovation was the introduction of halftone and other photomechanical printing methods and high-speed printing presses, which allowed photographs to be published easily and cheaply. Chicago became the major printing and publishing center in the West during the nineteenth century.

Commercial firms such as J. W. Taylor (1880s–1916), the Barnes-Crosby Company (1897–1960s), George Lawrence (1893–1908), Kauffman and Fabry (1910–1963), Raymond Trowbridge (1923–36), and the Hedrich Blessing Company (1930–) profited from a boon in REAL ESTATE and commerce. Unlike the early studio photographers who concentrated on portraits, they focused on ARCHITECTURE and ADVERTISING work.

Commercial photographers operating neighborhood-based businesses began to appear around the same time, supplying the photographic needs of everyday life as well as coverage of local ceremonies and events for community newspapers and local businesses. Examples are photographs made in the 1940s and 1950s in the LAKE VIEW and HYDE PARK

Ken Hedrich, 1936. The Hedrich Blessing firm, founded in 1929, became known for high-quality architectural photography. Photographer: Hedrich-Blessing. Source: Chicago Historical Society.

communities by Henry Delorval Green and Rus Arnold.

One of the richest sources of city views was the picture postcard, which was produced by major commercial photography firms as well as by neighborhood-based studios. First published for the WORLD'S COLUMBIAN EXPOSITION in 1893, picture POSTCARDS had instant success, much like stereo cards had earlier. Their greatest popularity lasted until the 1920s, a period during which America was changing from a rural to an urban society. Views promoting urban progress were produced in enormous numbers by commercial photographers like Chicago's Curt Teich, Barnes-Crosby, and Charles R. Childs companies.

A more conscious kind of documentary began to evolve as part of the burgeoning field of photojournalism. In the late 1880s a few investigative JOURNALISTS working for civic-minded newspapers and progressive SOCIAL SERVICE organizations saw photography as a new tool to awaken the public to the need for social reform in rapidly changing urban centers. In Chicago, photographers for organizations such as the Infant Welfare Society and the Visiting Nurse Association followed the example of social-reform photographers like New York's Lewis Hine by recording the difficulties of new immigrant groups in the city's slums.

This early documentary work engendered a torrent of photojournalistic images that gradually changed America from a literary into a visual society. This kind of documentary photography reached its zenith in the 1930s and 1940s in national publications such as *Life,* which was printed in Chicago, and local periodicals which covered both timely political and economic issues and the everyday life of average citizens in immensely popular human-interest picture essays.

While the new photojournalism attempted to cover daily events as they happened, a parallel movement in "official photography"—images that try to show things as they are supposed to be—was developing. Often the most interesting of these images were created by government agencies and commissions empowered with specific agendas. The most ambitious project of this kind undertaken on a national scale was the Farm Security Administration (FSA) photography project of the 1930s and 1940s. Eager to show that all segments of society, even previously neglected ones, were to be part of the national effort to end the GREAT DEPRESSION, most FSA photographers who came to Chicago focused on the city's growing AFRICAN AMERICAN population. The result combined photographic recording with powerful artistic statements.

During the postwar period the idea that photography itself was a medium worthy of appreciation grew steadily. New galleries sold photography as ART, and art museums (like the ART INSTITUTE in 1949) began to accept photographs for their permanent collections. By the 1960s a boom in photographic collecting, publishing, and exhibiting swept Chicago and the nation. During this prosperous decade, socially aware photographers found more support from the private sector than from public agencies. Reporting the social ferment of the 1960s and 1970s brought a resurgence in what some called "concerned photography." Unlike the "official photographs," these images were often powerful indictments of government itself and of society at large.

The wave of interest in photography continued into the 1970s as art schools, universities, colleges, and even high schools established formal photographic programs. Photography education opportunities in the Chicago area were especially plentiful, and thousands received training that had been unavailable only a generation earlier. The New Bauhaus/INSTITUTE OF DESIGN now at the ILLINOIS INSTITUTE OF TECHNOLOGY, the School of the Art Institute, COLUMBIA COLLEGE, the UNIVERSITY OF ILLINOIS AT CHICAGO, and various branches of the City College systems popularized a new kind of photography. These independent training centers concerned themselves more with artistic instruction than with political or economic study. Students were encouraged to look inward to express their personal view of the social landscape. This resurgence of interest in photography revitalized the commercial photography climate in Chicago and stimulated a flood of museum and gallery exhibitions, books, catalogs, and photodocumentary projects. The city's most lasting contribution was arguably as a national source of photographic educators and architectural photographers, together with its recognition of the importance of the medium of photography itself.

Larry Viskochil

See also: City as Artifact; Chicago Studied; Lake County Discovery Museum

Further reading: Hales, Peter Bacon. *Silver Cities: The Photography of American Urbanization, 1839–1915.* 1984. • Mayer, Harold M., and Richard C. Wade. *Chicago: Growth of a Metropolis.* 1969. • Viskochil, Larry A. *Chicago at the Turn of the Century in Photographs.* 1984.

Pilsen, neighborhood in the LOWER WEST SIDE Community Area. GERMAN and IRISH immigrants settled in this neighborhood in the 1840s, encouraged by the construction of the Southwestern Plank Road (a major route of trade from the hinterland into Chicago, which is now Ogden Avenue), the ILLINOIS & MICHIGAN CANAL (the South Branch of the CHICAGO RIVER forms the southern and eastern borders of the neighborhood), and the Burlington Railroad (the western boundary of Pilsen).

After the 1871 fire the McCormick Reaper Company (later International Harvester), lumber mills, garment finishing sweatshops, and railroad yard jobs defined the neighborhood. The creation of thousands of unskilled jobs in the 1870s induced many Bohemian immigrants to settle along Evans Street (18th Street). When one Bohemian resident opened a restaurant called "At the City of Plzen" to honor the second largest city in West Bohemia (now in the CZECH Republic), residents began to refer to the neighborhood as Pilsen. The subsequent naming of the post office as Pilsen Station institutionalized the moniker.

Lumber shover STRIKES in 1875–76 inspired a RAILROAD STRIKE IN 1877 (part of a national strike) that spread to all industrial workers in Pilsen. The 22nd U.S. Infantry marched into Pilsen in July to put down the strikers, killing 30 residents and injuring hundreds more. Pilsen workers also were involved in strikes in 1886 that culminated in the HAYMARKET Riot.

During WORLD WAR I, labor shortages in area industries induced over two dozen different immigrant groups to settle in Pilsen, including a modest number of MEXICANS. Due to liberal immigration law and the forced removal of Mexicans from the NEAR WEST SIDE to expand the UNIVERSITY OF ILLINOIS AT CHICAGO, Mexican migrants became predominant in the 1950s and 1960s. This ethnic shift spurred cultural changes in Pilsen, as Mexican ARTISTS decorated the neighborhood with colorful murals and mosaics.

The turnover from Eastern European to Mexican residents also shows continuities, especially Pilsen's tradition of strong working-class organization to control community space. Rubin J. Torres's neighborhood-based newsletter the *Crown* (1938–1998) supported and initiated youth CLUB activities; the Pilsen Neighbors Community Council, in addition to providing benevolent society functions, applied the COMMUNITY ORGANIZING tactics of Saul Alinsky to obtain city and industrial improvements; and community activists like Rudy Lozano, labor organizer and Midwest Director of the International Ladies Garment Workers Union, helped propel anti-machine politicians like Harold Washington into elected office and keep them there.

At the turn of the twenty-first century, Pilsen's residents have resisted attempts to gentrify their neighborhood, and have preserved the community as a gateway for Hispanic immigrants. During the first weekend in August, the Fiesta del Sol festival demonstrates the pride and determination of the residents of Pilsen to continue its rich working-class legacy.

Erik Gellman

See also: Clothing and Garment Industry; Demography; Economic Geography

Further reading: Baker, Anthony. "The Social Production of Space in Two Chicago Neighborhoods: Pilsen and Lincoln Park." Ph.D. diss., University of Illinois at Chicago. 1995. • Bartolozzi, Lorraine. "Community Study of the Lower West Side." 1930s, Lower West Side Community Collection, Box 1, Folder 11. Harold Washington Library Special Collections, Chicago, IL. • Schneirov, Richard. *Labor and Urban Politics: Class Conflict and the Origins of Modern Liberalism in Chicago, 1864–1897.* 1998.

Pingree Grove, IL, Kane County, 42 miles W of the Loop. Settled by the Pingree family from New Hampshire in the 1830s, the town remains one of the smallest in KANE COUNTY, with a population of 124 in 2000. In the 1870s, the construction of the Chicago & Pacific RAILROAD brought modest growth. At the end of the twentieth century the railroad no longer stopped in Pingree Grove, and the brick factory and dairy farm that once thrived there had long since shut down.

Erik Gellman

See also: Agriculture; Quarrying, Stonecutting, and Brickmaking

Pinkertons. The Pinkerton National Detective Agency, founded in Chicago in 1850, was long the nation's largest and most proficient private detective agency. For corporate America—notably RAILROADS, mines, and others involved in interstate commerce—it stood as an effective check on troublemakers within and without. To labor—particularly radical unions like the INDUSTRIAL WORKERS OF THE WORLD (IWW)—it was the most feared and hated agency in the land.

It took its name from founder Allan Pinkerton, who emigrated from Glasgow to Illinois, worked as a cooper at WEST DUNDEE (40 miles northwest of Chicago), then broke into law enforcement when he stumbled on a gang of counterfeiters. But it was Pinkerton's work for George McClellan, vice president of the ILLINOIS CENTRAL RAILROAD, that made his name. When President Abraham Lincoln gave McClellan command of the Army of the Potomac during the CIVIL WAR—and eventually all Union forces—the general made Pinkerton his intelligence chief.

Although less effective in gauging the Confederates' strength and intentions than he had been in apprehending Chicago's footpads (he absorbed McClellan's obsessive conviction that the Confederates outnumbered McClellan's troops), Pinkerton's association with McClellan and Lincoln made his name a national byword. Following the war, he returned to Chicago and built his agency into a goliath.

After suffering a stroke in 1869, Pinkerton delegated daily operations to his sons: Robert in New York developed the uniformed Pinkerton Protective Patrol, which provided "watchmen" for strikebound plants and mines (labor called them "strikebreakers"); while William in Chicago hewed to his father's emphasis on crime detection, symbolized by the company's slogan, "The Eye That Never Sleeps."

The agency could boast triumphs like James McParlan's infiltration of the Molly Maguires from 1873 to 1876, which resulted in the conviction and execution of 20 leading Mollies. But it had failures too: a misfired 1875 raid on a Missouri farmhouse in which Frank and Jesse James were supposedly hiding, which killed the James boys' eight-year-old half brother and left their mother with a severed arm; and the terrible day in 1892 when a raid on the Carnegie Steelworks in Homestead, Pennsylvania, killed three members of the protective patrol and seven strikers, while other Pinkertons were beaten and publicly humiliated by townspeople.

The Homestead debacle led to congressional investigations, in turn prompting 24 states to enact laws prohibiting armed mercenaries like the Pinkerton patrol from crossing state lines. Even before the legislators acted, the Pinkertons concluded that supplying watchmen in labor disputes was undesirable. The balance of power shifted back to Chicago and the detectives long favored by William, who came to be known as "The Eye," a reference both to his company's slogan and to his encyclopedic knowledge of the underworld.

J. Anthony Lukas

See also: Red Squad; Strikes

Further reading: Morn, Frank. *The Eye That Never Sleeps: A History of the Pinkerton National Detective Agency.* 1982.

Pizza. Modern pizza is reputed to have started in Naples in 1889 when Raffaele Esposito created the Pizza Margherita, with tomato, mozzarella, and basil replicating the colors of the Italian flag, for King Umberto I and Queen Margherita of Italy. From there, pizza spread across the world. Some late-nineteenth-century Chicago bakeries served pizza, in sheets or in small rolls. Early ITALIAN families served pizza on Taylor Street and the NEAR SOUTH SIDE.

Chicago-style pizza first appeared in the fall of 1943 with the opening of Pizzeria Uno. Many GIs had been introduced to pizza as they moved up the coast of Italy, and several Chicagoans anticipated that they would want more when they returned home. Restaurateur and bon vivant Ric Riccardo became partners with Ike Sewell, a LIQUOR salesman, and Sewell's wife, Florence, who had high-society connections in Chicago, in the new venture. Pizzeria Uno was located a few blocks from the well-known Riccardo's on Wabash at Ohio. Lou Malnati, Riccardo's associate manager, was brought over to help run the new establishment.

The Chicago style of pizza was marked by three characteristics: (1) enormous amounts of cheese and a thick, sweet pastry shell crust; (2) very high oven temperatures (600 degrees Fahrenheit) while baking, with plentiful amounts of cornmeal sprinkled in the pan to help insulate the bread; and (3) very long cooking times (50 to 60 minutes for a medium-sized pie). Such long cooking times allowed patrons time to consume many bottles of Chianti and Lambrusco while waiting.

NEWSPAPERS and visitors gave the new restaurant and its new pizza their enthusiastic support. Bolstered by the success of Uno, Sewall opened Pizzeria Due a few blocks away, and Chicago-style pizzerias spread throughout Chicago and the United States.

J. S. Aubrey

See also: Foodways; Restaurants

The Saloon Building was constructed in 1836 at the southeast corner of Lake and Clark Streets. It was the longest hall in Chicago and served as the site of political, religious, and cultural events, including the organization of a city government in 1837. Artist: Unknown. Source: Chicago Historical Society.

Places of Assembly. An important element of Chicago's transformation from a small military outpost to a world city has been the creation and appropriation of space for assembly. As the city grew in population and sophistication, it required an increasing amount of space available for public ceremony, celebration, religious worship, association, protest, trade, recreation, and entertainment. Whether in makeshift facilities, purpose-built structures, or open spaces, inhabitants and visitors have gathered as citizens, consumers, and members of various ethnic and religious groups.

In Chicago's earliest days the community could not support permanent facilities designed solely for assembly. When a large-scale enterprise required an enclosed space it was forced to provide for itself. When the circus came to town in 1836, for example, it pitched a tent on Lake Street. Most gatherings in the 1830s, '40s, and '50s, from theatrical events to town meetings, found space in other types of buildings: HOTELS, taverns, churches, and what were known as office blocks. The precursor to the modern office building, this multipurpose structure, with stores on ground level and flexible space above, often housed a "hall" which occupied one or two floors and was available for rental. Fraternal organizations like the Odd Fellows, ethnic organizations like the German TURNVEREIN, and religious groups like the YOUNG MEN'S CHRISTIAN ASSOCIATION often met in such spaces, which also served as sites for a variety of entertainments until dedicated THEATERS were built. The Saloon Building (1836–1871), located at Lake and Clark, offered the largest hall west of Buffalo for concerts, debates, dramatic performances, and political ceremony. In 1837, Chicago received its city charter under its roof and it served as city hall until 1842.

With its new official civic status in mind, Chicago's commercial and political leaders began to think of necessary improvements. One of the features the new city lacked was public space where citizens could meet on common ground. Throughout the late 1830s and 1840s, Chicago dedicated plots of land to public functions, including a public square—the future site of the city hall and courthouse. Here Chicagoans gathered as citizens for both everyday functions and ceremonies of state: over 125,000 people gathered to view Abraham Lincoln's body on its way home for burial in 1865.

Outside Chicago, churches, schoolhouses, county courthouses, and taverns and hotels like Stacy's Tavern in GLEN ELLYN (1846) and the Garfield Farm Tavern in GENEVA (1846) served the needs of small-town residents and farmers. At midcentury the city's surrounding counties operated agricultural fairs, starting with the Lake COUNTY FAIR (1851) in WAUKEGAN. These temporary places of assembly gathered people from great distances.

Chicago's need for more substantial and permanent gathering places grew as the city began its long history as a site of POLITICAL CONVENTIONS. In 1860 business leaders underwrote the cost of a temporary wooden convention hall known as the "WIGWAM" to attract the REPUBLICAN National Convention. DEMOCRATS followed suit in 1864, constructing a semicircular roofed amphitheater for its own convention. Political conventions as well as other large gatherings also found space in a new generation of theaters and halls, including Crosby's Opera House (1865) and the YMCA's Farwell Hall (1869), capable of holding 3,500 people. These buildings were swept away in the Great FIRE OF 1871.

More permanent was the Interstate Industrial Exposition Building, the city's first convention center. Constructed by W. W. Boyington in 1872, the glass and metal building with ornamental domes was based on exposition buildings in London and New York and was designed to house annual displays of industrial manufactures. It served a variety of other functions, as an ILLINOIS NATIONAL GUARD ARMORY, the first home of the CHICAGO SYMPHONY ORCHESTRA, and the site of national political conventions in 1880 and 1884, until it was razed in 1892 to make way for the ART INSTITUTE. Adler and Sullivan's AUDITORIUM BUILDING (1889), the site of the 1888 Republican Convention, could hold up to 8,000 people for meetings and had the added convenience of a hotel with 400 guest rooms on the premises.

A further addition to Chicago's growing supply of places of assembly was the Coliseum (1899–1983), a multipurpose meeting facility

The Wigwam, site of the 1860 Republican National Convention, corner of Lake and Market (later Wacker). Artist: Unknown. Source: Chicago Historical Society.

south of the LOOP capable of holding 15,000 people, a size rivaled only by Madison Square Garden in New York. The site of numerous political conventions, it also hosted a wide variety of gatherings, including BOWLING tournaments, automobile shows, and, in 1926, both the World Eucharistic Congress and the first Chicago BLACKHAWKS hockey game.

Old Farwell Hall, Madison Street between Clark and LaSalle, ca. 1880s. Photographer: Unknown. Source: Chicago Historical Society.

ARMORIES, built as bulwarks against the labor unrest of the late nineteenth century, often functioned as public places of assembly after 1900. North Pier (Pugh Terminal) was constructed between 1905 and 1920 as an exhibition center for wholesale products, and, to its north, Municipal Pier (now NAVY PIER) made its debut in 1916 as a commercial and recreational center, with RESTAURANTS, a DANCE HALL, and a huge auditorium.

Although multipurpose halls in the Loop, including the new Orchestra Hall (1905), continued to be available for rental to voluntary associations at the turn of the century, ethnic and fraternal associations erected purpose-built structures for their assembly needs: GERMANS led the way with the elaborate Germania Club (1888), POLES built Pulaski Hall (1909), and NORWEGIANS the Norske Club (1916). The Shriners built the city's most architecturally exotic place of assembly, the pseudo-Arabian Medinah Hall (1913), to host conventions, circuses, and concerts.

By 1890 regular rail service had spawned a ring of suburbs around the city. These centers required city halls and were able to support additional places of assembly, including public LIBRARIES like the Nichols Library in NAPERVILLE (1897), and, in the case of WOODSTOCK, an OPERA house (1889) which sheltered both a library and city hall as well as an auditorium. When RAVINIA was established in 1904 in HIGHLAND PARK, it offered a BASEBALL field and stands, a theater, a dining room, and picnic grounds.

In the city's early years Chicagoans had used open spaces for their games, but as the city grew these were increasingly difficult to find. A major center for sporting activity and other gatherings, the SOUTH SIDE included Dexter Park, the racetrack and exhibition space owned by the UNION STOCK YARD Company, which hosted stock shows, trotting events, and, in 1870, the games of the Chicago White Stockings. Wanderer's Cricket Club had its own grounds on the South Side, first at 37th and Indiana, moving to 71st and East End Avenue in 1909. In addition to its own matches, the cricket grounds also hosted many public high-school FOOTBALL games. Marshall Field, the UNIVERSITY OF CHICAGO's campus stadium, was completed by 1907. Renamed Stagg Field, after the university's famous coach, Amos Alonzo Stagg, in 1914, it served as the city's major football ground for nearly 20 years.

Facilities for BASEBALL multiplied as the game grew in popularity and became increasingly organized and professionalized. Seeking proximity to public TRANSPORTATION and cheap land, owners and managers of professional, minor league, and semiprofessional teams constructed ballparks across the city, moving frequently. Over more than 30 years the American League team played at six different sites on the West and South Sides. Minimal

The Coliseum at 1513 South Wabash, ca. 1908. It served as the city's major indoor arena until the opening of the Chicago Stadium in the 1930s. Photographer: Unknown. Source: Chicago Historical Society.

capital investment in the facilities, especially wood construction, made this mobility possible. Charles Comiskey, responding to an 1897 fire at New York's Polo Grounds, introduced an innovative concrete and steel stadium designed by Zachary Taylor Davis (1910). Davis was also responsible for the city's other perennial ballpark, Weeghman Field, constructed for the Chicago Whales, a Federal League club, in 1914. Located at Addison and Clark, this field was soon purchased by the Chicago Cubs and renamed Wrigley Field in 1926. As these "permanent" ballparks went up, the older ones were recycled for the use of other teams. The relocation of the White Stockings to Comiskey Park enabled Chicago's Negro League team, the American Giants, to purchase their old facility, South Side Park, located at 39th and Wentworth. Rechristened Schorling Park, it stood until 1940, when it was destroyed by fire. In an age of industrialization the names of these facilities, "park" and "field," had intentionally pastoral connotations, offering urbanites a retreat from the grid of the city into a carpet of green grass.

The city's parks, free and clear of development, were often the site of sporting events, and special facilities were constructed, like the Washington Park and Garfield Park Racetracks (1883, 1885) and the wooden Lake Front Baseball Field (1871, rebuilt 1883). Inspired by the combination of athletic, educational, and social facilities found in churches, YMCAs, synagogues, and settlement houses in the first decade of this century, public and private groups constructed neighborhood-based recreational facilities for urbanites. Several city parks were equipped with "park houses": public social centers with assembly halls, club rooms, swimming pools, and other athletic amenities for the use of neighborhood residents. Under the direction of Chicago School Board architect Dwight Perkins, public schools such as Carl Schurz High School (1908–1910) on the city's Northwest Side and New Trier High School in Winnetka (1901) took on some of the same functions, designed with gymnasiums, auditoriums, and sports fields for the use of the whole community. These attempts by public and private institutions to provide wholesome recreation facilities were motivated by a desire to compete with a rising number of commercial places of assembly, including an increasing number of saloons, nickelodeons, movie palaces, and vaudeville houses.

As part of a nationwide movement to erect community buildings as appropriate monuments to the dead of World War I, the Chicago Elks constructed the elaborate Elks National Memorial Building (1926). Increased demand for indoor meeting space was met by two structures (both 1928–29): the Civic Opera House and the Chicago Stadium. Traction magnate Samuel Insull presented one of the city's grandest meeting places, the Civic Opera House, in an innovative package, enclosing a 3,500-seat auditorium and a 900-seat theater inside a modern office building in the Loop. Less highbrow was the Stadium, as it was known, home to boxing, midget auto racing, political conventions, sports teams such as the Blackhawks and the Bulls, and musical performances of all kinds. Located on the Near West Side, the Stadium offered Chicagoans an alternative to the aging Coliseum.

In the 1920s the South Park Commission, inspired by the construction of the Rose Bowl

Dexter Park interior, 42nd and South Halsted, 1908. Photographer: Chicago Daily News. Source: Chicago Historical Society.

(1922) and the LA Coliseum (1923) and with an eye toward a bid for the Olympics, began construction on one of Chicago's greatest places of assembly, SOLDIER FIELD. The reinforced concrete structure cost more than $8 million and held over 100,000 people, making it the largest stadium of its day. Soldier Field has hosted everything from Army–Navy games to a reenactment of the burning of Mrs. O'Leary's Barn. Another major site for football was added in this period: NORTHWESTERN UNIVERSITY's Dyche Stadium (1926), home to Big Ten football games. A spurt of racetrack construction in suburban locations during this period responded to the repeal of the law against HORSE RACING in Illinois, which had lasted from 1905 until 1922. The earliest, AURORA Downs (1923), offered harness racing. Arlington Park (1927), located 22 miles northwest of Chicago, was joined by MAYWOOD Racetrack (1933) and Sportsman's Park in CICERO (1937).

Although the GREAT DEPRESSION slowed building construction, several additions or transformation to the city's places of assembly were made in the 1930s. On the South Side the aging Dexter Park Racetrack, destroyed by fire, was replaced by the INTERNATIONAL AMPHITHEATER (1934), an air-conditioned convention center with an attached hotel. It continued to host stock shows but also presented sports, ice shows, political conventions, and trade shows. In 1937, the 4,000-seat Chicago Arena, located in STREETERVILLE, opened its doors for roller and ice SKATING, boxing, WRESTLING, and other sporting events. Government-sponsored Works Progress Administration projects such as Lane Technical High School's Football Field (1930) and the Civic Center at HAMMOND, Indiana (1938), provided work and additional facilities to help structure the increased LEISURE time of the American public.

After WORLD WAR II, the emphasis turned toward economic development. To keep Chicago in the forefront of the burgeoning convention industry, the Metropolitan Fair and Exposition Authority built McCormick Place in the late 1950s on a lakefront site in Burnham Park. When this burned in 1967 it was replaced with another building on the same site in 1971. Two additional buildings, located across Lake Shore Drive and linked by covered passageways, were later added to meet the expanding demand for convention space. Renovated in 1995, Navy Pier again became a meeting center and the site of concerts and recreational activities.

The continuing importance of the city center as a place of assembly for all groups of the city's diverse population in postwar Chicago was marked by the design and use of civic space for ceremony, debate, and entertainment. Under Mayor Richard J. Daley the city received major new public, governmental spaces, most prominently the Daley Civic Center (1963–65), in the heart of the Loop. Adorned with a steel statue by Pablo Picasso, this space soon attained the status of the city's symbolic center, the site of the city Christmas tree and such ethnic events as the FILIPINO Independence Day Celebration.

The city's park spaces continued to be active places of assembly. GRANT PARK served as the site of protest during the 1968 Democratic National Assembly and throughout the early 1970s as young people gathered to protest the war in Vietnam. The lakefront and the lake itself also provided a locus of recreation and celebration, hosting Chicagoans during annual festivities on Venetian Night and the Fourth of July.

Throughout the postwar period, public officials, team owners, and private groups worked to upgrade Chicago's sports facilities. As other cities invested huge sums in new arenas and stadiums in the 1960s and '70s, Chicago facilities, especially Soldier Field and the Chicago Stadium, grew increasingly outdated in size and such amenities as the quantity and quality of luxury skyboxes. A major renovation in 2002–3 upgraded Soldier Field's ambiance, with special attention to skyboxes, but also transformed its facade with a controversial addition that towered above the classic colonnades. The Chicago Stadium was demolished in 1995.

Although they do not live up to the ambitious plans proposed in the 1960s and '70s, three new sports and entertainment facilities were completed: the UIC Pavilion (1982), Comiskey Park (1991), and the UNITED CENTER (1994). The UNIVERSITY OF ILLINOIS AT CHICAGO built its 100,000-square-foot center to house school sporting events as well as concerts, theater, and conventions, providing an alternative to the Stadium close to the Loop. Older, urban centers like the Coliseum and International Amphitheatre found it increasingly difficult to compete with these new facilities, forcing the demolition of the Coliseum and the sale and closure of the Amphitheatre in the 1970s and '80s. The ROSEMONT Horizon (1980, renamed Allstate Arena in 1999), with almost 20,000 seats, was designed to house college BASKETBALL as well as concerts, drawing people from urban, suburban, and exurban locations.

Paula R. Lupkin

See also: Architecture; Entertaining Chicagoans; Tourism and Conventions

Further reading: Hayner, Don, and Tom McNamee. *The Stadium.* 1993. • Riess, Steven. *City Games: The Evolution of American Urban Society and the Rise of Sports.* 1989. • Sutter, R. Craig, and Edward M. Burke. *Inside the Wigwam: Chicago Presidential Conventions, 1860–1996.* 1996.

Plainfield, IL, Will County, 35 miles SW of the Loop. The village of Plainfield lies in northwestern WILL COUNTY along the DUPAGE RIVER. Tracing its roots to the 1820s, Plainfield was the first permanent white settlement in Will County. Long considered a small town, Plainfield has experienced substantial growth since World War II, particularly in the 1990s.

FRENCH Canadian FUR TRADER Vetal Vermette, who stopped in the region briefly in 1823, returned later in the decade and established squatter's rights to the land.

In 1826, Jesse Walker, a Methodist preacher from Virginia, established an Indian mission in a forest south of present-day Plainfield. The mission was abandoned two years later, but James Walker, Jesse Walker's son-in-law, stayed behind and constructed a sawmill. The area soon became known as Walker's Grove, a permanent settlement which preceded Plainfield.

The Plainfield area played a significant role in the BLACK HAWK WAR of 1832. Settlers from the FOX RIVER Valley, fearful of Indian aggression, fled to Walker's Grove, and established a fort. James Walker served as captain for the local militia.

After the Black Hawk War ended, the community developed quickly. The first post office opened in 1833, and the town became a stop on the stagecoach line between Chicago and Ottawa. Chester Ingersoll and Squire Arnold laid out the town. Farming, milling, and manufacturing provided Plainfield with a strong economic base.

Incorporated as a village in 1861, Plainfield provided the first Union regiment from Will County for service in the CIVIL WAR. That same year, the Evangelical Association opened Plainfield College. Lured by TRANSPORTATION considerations, the college moved to NAPERVILLE in 1870 and eventually became NORTH CENTRAL COLLEGE. In the 1890s, Plainfield's own transportation systems were boosted when the Chicago Belt Line RAILROAD laid track through the village, helping it to become a major storage and shipping point for grain. Soon afterward, the JOLIET, Plainfield & AURORA interurban Railroad opened an electric line connecting those three communities.

In 1904, the Joliet, Plainfield & Aurora opened Electric Park to the public. Conceived primarily to promote travel on the fledgling railroad, Electric Park quickly became a popular VACATION SPOT. Lavish gardens flanking the banks of the DuPage River, as well as athletic grounds, bandstands, dancing pavilions, and a 5,000-seat auditorium featuring a large pipe organ, attracted vacationers, who relaxed in cabins featuring electric, GAS, and water service. But the railroad succumbed to financial difficulties in 1923, a victim of the automobile, and Electric Park ultimately closed in 1932.

After World War II, although some manufacturing took place, farming and gravel mining continued to represent the greatest sources of jobs and revenue for Plainfield. The increasing movement of Chicago residents to suburbia also contributed to the village's population.

On August 28, 1990, a devastating TORNADO rocked the Plainfield area. The twister killed 29 people and caused hundreds of millions of dollars in damage, destroying the west and south sides of town and Plainfield High School. Between 1990 and 2000, Plainfield's population, soared from 4,557 to 13,038.

Aaron Harwig

See also: Economic Geography; Entertaining Chicagoans; Metropolitan Growth

Further reading: *A History of Plainfield Then and Now.* 1976. • *Plainfield, Will County, Illinois, U.S.A.* 1980.

Planning Chicago. Everyone plans. Businesses contemplate markets and products, SOCIAL SERVICE agencies seek to improve service to their clients, workers think about retirement, politicians calculate their chances for reelection. In the language of urban history and policy, however, "planning" refers to efforts to shape the physical form and distribution of activities within a city. The objects of planning are sites and systems—the neighborhoods and places within which we carry on our lives and the networks that link the parts of a metropolitan area into a functioning whole. Planning shaped everything from PULLMAN and HYDE PARK to the Chicago park system and the web of highways that knit together the metropolitan region.

Planners divide into two groups. By far the most common are the "moneymakers"—the city builders (and rebuilders) of the private sector and private markets. From single individuals and households to the developers of entire new communities, they try to meet existing demand and support social patterns by intensifying the use of land. They put houses on vacant lots, subdivisions and industrial parks on cornfields, office towers on the sites of low-rise buildings. They work within the competitive framework of the REAL-ESTATE market, but the city they create is unified by common assumptions. In each generation, city builders have created vernacular neighborhoods and business districts that reflect prevailing tastes and market forces, whether GREATER GRAND CROSSING and AUSTIN in the nineteenth century, the BUNGALOW Belt of the early twentieth century, or the Edge Cities of the late twentieth century.

Less common but also influential are the "community makers" who are the focus of this essay. These government agencies, civic organizations, and owner-developers work with the conscious goal of altering social relationships and making "better" places through the planning of urban sites and systems. Some have concentrated on creating specific urban environments that are more socially harmonious and personally fulfilling than the market usually has provided. Other civic-minded community makers have searched for ways to make the city and its surrounding region function more efficiently. The story of planning in Chicago is thus the story of special places built from the ground up, such as RIVERSIDE or PARK FOREST; it is the story of places self-consciously rebuilt, such as Lake Meadows or the UNIVERSITY OF ILLINOIS AT CHICAGO; and it is the story of comprehensively designed support systems, such as parks and highways.

Community planning in Chicago has unfolded in four overlapping stages—eras in which particular planning concerns took center stage within the larger context of market-driven growth. In the first half of the nineteenth century, government actions constructed a spatial framework for the new city. From the 1850s to the early years of the twentieth century, the city and its environs were the location for a sequence of privately built, comprehensively planned, and idealized communities. From the later 1880s through the 1920s, the city experienced an unusual era when public and private interests coalesced around efforts to integrate the sprawling metropolis. And since the 1930s, metropolitan Chicago has witnessed gradual erosion and fragmentation of that civic vision as the goals of planning have become more specialized or limited.

Chicago's planning history offers a lesson that can be generalized to other American cities: efficiency is an easier goal than equity. Residents have found it relatively easy to agree and act on community needs that invite engineering solutions, for it has been possible to argue convincingly that canals, roads, sewers, and parks serve the entire population. Chicagoans have been less ambitious and less successful in shaping ideal communities that combine physical quality with social purpose. They have tried repeatedly to improve on the typical products of the real-estate market, but their experiments have faced often intractable issues of class and race. Success has usually required planning for narrowly defined segments of the middle class, while planning for socially inclusive communities at any large scale has built social conflict into the community fabric.

Drawing the Grid

Chicago got its start from the federal and state governments. FORT DEARBORN (1803) was a federal military outpost that helped the new nation assert its claim to the Northwest and protected American traders. Its location helped the commissioners in charge of the state-built ILLINOIS & MICHIGAN CANAL choose the mouth of the CHICAGO RIVER for its northern terminus. The small grid of STREETS that the commissioners platted in 1830 at the junction of the north and south branches of the river set the street pattern that private developers began to extend as early as 1834. Chicago's growth was also framed by the square-mile grid of the federal land survey, whose section lines would become major arterial streets as the city grew (Halsted Street, Chicago Avenue, and Roosevelt Road).

Local government also began to assume responsibility for basic INFRASTRUCTURE. Charter amendments in 1837 gave the city the power to directly supervise PUBLIC WORKS. The state

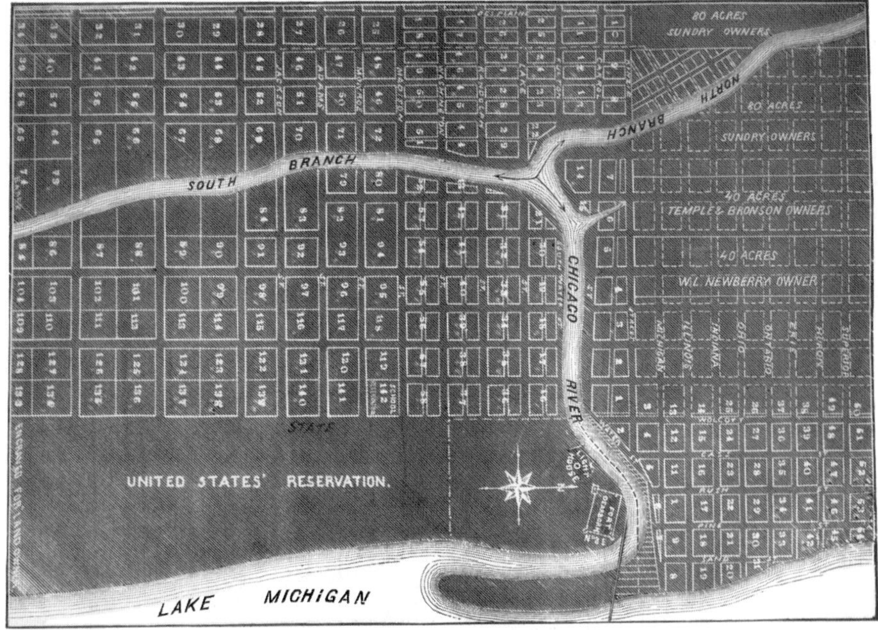

The original 1830 subdivision by the Illinois & Michigan Canal Commissioners is the area south of Kinzie Street (2 blocks north of the river). Map shows additions by 1835. Cartographer: Unknown. Source: The Newberry Library.

in 1851 authorized a public commission to build a WATER system with city funds and bond issues; in 1855 it added a sewerage commission. In 1861 a Board of Public Works took over management of WATER SUPPLY, sewerage, drainage, and streets. In the ensuing decades, water mains, sewers, and paved streets followed population outward into COOK COUNTY in a repeated process of catch-up (only developers of the most upscale suburbs commonly provide such necessary services).

Perfect Places

Chicagoans in the second half of the nineteenth century built a set of influential communities that embodied social purpose. As the city's new rail lines fanned outward over marshes and prairies and opened a seeming infinity of sites for community making, developers hurried to subdivide and profit from new neighborhoods and towns. Most efforts were simple grids with poorly graded streets and small lots. A few developments on the fringe of the industrializing city, however, pushed the envelope of the market beyond the simple provision of shelter and accessibility. Expressing Chicago's early exuberance and confidence, their goals were sometimes lofty—in some cases to allow harmonious relations between urban residents and their landscape, in other cases to promote compatible relations between workers and employers.

Chicago's planned residential communities along commuter RAILROAD lines were models for other nineteenth-century suburbs that sprang up outside Philadelphia, New York, and Boston. Their spacious design and attention to natural settings gave them continuing influence on community planners well into the twentieth century. In contrast, Chicago's industrial utopias moved quickly from admired experiments to examples of problems to avoid.

Following the initial examples of Llewellyn Park outside New York and Glendale near Cincinnati, Chicago's first planned suburbs represented attempts to think through and express a better relationship between people, their city, and their LANDSCAPE. In the 1850s, EVANSTON (1853) and the "pleasant woodland town" of LAKE FOREST (1856) matched UNIVERSITIES to upscale housing (and the strict morality of PROHIBITION in Evanston). Lake Forest and especially Riverside (1869) offered convenient access to the advantages of the city while being built with the natural landscape in mind. Upper-middle-class families who moved to the new towns enjoyed clean air, good water, picturesquely curving streets, large lots, parks, and public gathering places—all with a direct rail COMMUTE to the center of Chicago. They were escapes from the urban energy of the emerging downtown and close-in neighborhoods, but not from the city-region as an economic machine. Their residents gained quiet evenings and Sunday strolls along the lakeshore or the DES PLAINES RIVER, but they made their money oiling the gears of commerce.

Industrialist George Pullman intended his new town to serve the best interests of factory workers and factory production. Built on undeveloped land 10 miles south of the city, the town of Pullman offered new housing within walking distance of huge new factories. Like other company towns, its corporation was a paternalistic landlord that sought to manage the lives of its workers. Like more expensive suburbs, it also offered a version of the suburban ideal—clean air and water, an escape from flimsy speculative housing, and the opportunity for women to focus on home and family while men brought home a living wage. But the reform agenda of the 1880s collapsed during the bitter PULLMAN STRIKE of 1894; within a decade Pullman was another industrial neighborhood with good housing stock, not a suburban experiment for the working class.

HARVEY (1891), another new industrial satellite on the South Side of the city, was a less comprehensive version of Pullman. Having learned about some of the problems of a single-company town, lumber king Turlington Harvey laid out a city to which he invited factory owners and workers who shared the values of evangelical PROTESTANTISM. For a few brief years before the depression of the 1890s, Harvey flourished as a temperance town. Without the distractions of SALOONS OR GAMBLING, sober native-born workers and industrialists could share an interest in hard WORK, appearances by evangelist Ira Sankey, and lectures by Susan B. Anthony. In 1895, however, with Turlington Harvey's business in disarray, residents voted the town "wet." The vote ended the experiment with what historian James Gilbert has called a "religious, countercultural city," although the town's SCHOOLS and social services benefited from benevolent industrialists into the new century.

By the time the United States Steel Company laid out the new city of GARY in 1906, industrial corporations were wary of mixing social mission with worker housing. Designed for a population of 200,000, Gary had an ordinary street grid and privately owned housing. It gave over the lakefront to factories, railroads, and harbor. For the rest of the site, U.S. Steel acted like a giant tract developer with few overtones of paternalism, although title to lots did not transfer until houses were completed.

As Gary suggests, the "perfect communities" of the twentieth century have often been cities for industry rather than people. Chicago entrepreneurs in the 1890s invented the "industrial district." The UNION STOCK YARD and the Chicago Junction Railroad organized the Central District in 1890 and began to market its facilities in 1905. The company prepared land, assured rail service, put in utilities, graded streets, built standardized factory buildings, and leased space for factories and warehouses. The CENTRAL MANUFACTURING DISTRICT (which soon controlled several separate sites), the CLEARING Industrial District, and many others were subdivisions for industry. The thousands of industrial parks that dot the landscape of late-twentieth-century America are their direct heirs.

Metropolitan Planning

In the decades around the turn of the century, a widely shared metropolitan vision coalesced around the planning of systems to integrate the sprawling Chicago region. New York and Chicago epitomized the urban crisis of fin de siècle America, whose institutions seemed to be overwhelmed by waves of European immigration, increasing polarization of wealth, and the sheer complexity and congestion of the giant city. These challenges of headlong METROPOLITAN GROWTH called forth similar responses in both cities. Some Americans reacted with sweeping utopian or dystopian visions of the national future. Others searched for practical technological fixes such as electric lighting, improved sanitation, or electric streetcars and subways. Still others constructed ameliorative institutions such as SETTLEMENT HOUSES and began to lay the foundations of a modern welfare state with the social and economic reforms of Progressivism. And a significant minority worked to systematize the future growth of their cities, consolidating separate local governments into vast regional cities and developing regional plans for the extension of public services.

This story began in Chicago with the park system of the late nineteenth century. Although separate South, West, and LINCOLN PARK commissions (1869) served the three geographic divisions of the city, their investments and improvements worked together as a unified whole. Large semipastoral parks in the zone of the fastest residential growth allowed the poor and middle classes to enjoy temporary respite from the city. Broad boulevards connected the parks in a great chain from Lincoln Park to JACKSON PARK.

The ANNEXATION of 1889 tripled the area of the city; it took in established suburban communities and vast tracts of undeveloped land and set the stage for large public expenditures for water supply and sanitation. The Sanitary District of Chicago (1889) covered 185 square miles; its impressive regional accomplishment was construction of the SANITARY AND SHIP CANAL (1900) and the reversal of the Chicago River to carry the city's waste into the Illinois and Mississippi Rivers. Annexation also paved the way for a metropolitan vision that achieved full expression in Daniel Burnham and Edward Bennett's *Plan of Chicago* of 1909. Promoted by a civic-minded BUSINESS elite and widely embraced by middle-class Chicagoans, the "BURNHAM PLAN" was an effort to frame

Daniel Burnham: Highway Planning

Daniel Burnham is perhaps best known for his famous statement:

> Make no little plans. They have no magic to stir men's blood and probably will not themselves be realized. Make big plans, aim high in hope and work, remembering that a noble, logical diagram once recorded will never die, but long after we are gone will be a living thing, asserting itself with ever growing insistency. Remember that our sons and grandsons are going to do things that would stagger us.

In his 1909 Plan, Burnham applied this vision to the future of the Chicago region. He diagramed a system of encircling highways from Kenosha to Michigan City, with other roads running directly into the city. Burnham explained the importance of good roads for the future of the region more than a generation before the interstate highway system:

> It needs no argument to show that direct highways leading from the outlying towns to Chicago as the center are of necessity for both; and it is also apparent that suburban towns should be connected with one another in the best manner. Isolated communities lack those social and commercial advantages which arise from easy communication one with another. . . .
>
> While good highways are of great value to the terminal cities, they are of even greater value to the outlying towns, and of greatest value to the farming communities through which they pass. Good roads add an element of better living to an agricultural community; they afford ready communication with the city and reduce materially the cost of handling farm products of all kinds; and also they promote communication between farms. . . .
>
> At the earliest possible date measures should be taken for beginning what may be termed the outer encircling highway. Beginning at Kenosha on the north, this thoroughfare would run through . . . Woodstock, . . . DeKalb, Kankakee, . . . Valparaiso to Lake Michigan at Michigan City. . . . It is obvious that such a highway, properly built and adorned, would become a strong influence in the development of the social and material prosperity of the cities involved, and of all the farming communities along the entire route.

Burnham, Daniel H., and Edward H. Bennett. *Plan of Chicago*. 1909, 40–42.

the market (and the work of city builders) with a regional infrastructure of rationalized railroads, new highways, and regional parks to anticipate population growth. The plan knit downtown and neighborhoods, city and suburbs and surroundings, to a distance of 60 miles. It was to be implemented with public investments that would order and constrain the private market. The plan took the regional booster vision of the nineteenth century and transformed it into a concrete form and format for shaping a vast but functional cityscape.

Economically comprehensive as well as spatially unifying, the plan envisioned a Chicago that located management functions, production, and TRANSPORTATION in their most appropriate places. It assumed that the city would continue to be the fountainhead of industrial employment. Its vision of mutually supportive interests of business leaders and the mass of Chicago workers was naive in light of such failures as Pullman and the city's continuing record of labor-management conflict. However, it still offers a conceptual contrast to the decades after World War II, when URBAN RENEWAL and downtown redevelopment planned for the transformation of the economic base from manufacturing to services rather than the enhancement of the industrial economy.

From the early 1900s into the 1920s, Chicago benefited from a "civic moment" when business interest and civic interest seemed to converge, at least in the minds of privileged Chicagoans. Middle-class women as well as men took active roles in the discussion. Groups such as the WOMEN'S CITY CLUB battled for an accessible park system and for public access to the WATERFRONT. Although such organizations often opposed narrow economic development schemes floated by businessmen, they were important participants in the same planning discourse about the best ways to implement the vision of Burnham and Bennett.

The commercial-civic elite mounted a vigorous campaign to put the Burnham Plan into action. The city established a unique City Plan Commission—a miniature city parliament of 328 businessmen, politicians, and civic leaders—to monitor and promote implementation. Advocates tirelessly preached the gospel of urban efficiency with newspaper and magazine stories (575 in 1912 alone), illustrated lectures, a motion picture, and *Wacker's Manual of the Plan of Chicago*, a summary text that introduced the Burnham Plan to tens of thousands of Chicago schoolchildren.

Chicagoans acted in accord with many of Burnham's prescriptions. The city acquired lakefront land for GRANT PARK, a stately open space to set off and contrast with the growing skyline. Creation of the Cook County FOREST PRESERVE system implemented another set of recommendations. So did the extension of Roosevelt Road, improvement of terminals for railroad freight and passengers, movement of harbor facilities to Lake Calumet, and widening of North Michigan Avenue to allow expansion of the downtown office core.

As growth moved beyond the city limits, civic leaders in 1923 organized the semipublic Chicago Regional Planning Association. This effort to keep alive the planning vision of the 1910s was a forum for the voluntary coordination of local government plans outside the direct control of Chicago. Involving municipalities from three states, it had substantial success in coordinating park expansion and highways. However, the growing scale of the metropolitan area also introduced the erosive problem of suburban independence and competition for growth that would dominate regional planning in the United States in remaining decades of the century.

The Burnham Plan was certainly not perfect—it spoke to social issues indirectly at best—but it did place the question of good urban form at the center of the public agenda and held up Chicago as a model for wide-ranging thought about metropolitan futures. A publication entitled *Chicago's World-Wide Influence* (1913) trumpeted the importance of Chicago planning. Burnham and Bennett had tried out their ideas in San Francisco and followed with consulting work in other cities. The *Plan of Chicago* was also a template for more "practical" comprehensive planning in the 1920s.

Ironically, the *Plan of Chicago* and its implementation provided the context for New York to retake the lead in urban planning. The adoption of ZONING in Chicago (1923) followed New York's pioneering ordinance of 1916. The Regional Plan for New York (1929) not only dealt with the same issues as had Burnham and Bennett but added more careful attention to the patterns of LAND USE. By the 1930s, the Northeast had captured leadership in planning thought with Harvard University's graduate planning program, the reform-minded Regional Planning Association of America, the grand public works program of Robert Moses, and experimental communities such as Radburn, New Jersey, and Greenbelt, Maryland. The New York World's Fair of 1939 highlighted urban issues in a way that Chicago's CENTURY OF PROGRESS (1933) had not. Even *The City* (1939), the classic documentary film on issues of urban growth, used New England, Pittsburgh, New York, and Greenbelt to illustrate its ideas—not Michigan Avenue or Riverside.

1930–2000: Picking up the Pieces

Since the 1920s, the civic ideal has eroded in the face of RACIAL conflict, suburban self-sufficiency, industrial transition, and the daunting complexity of a huge metropolitan region. Like every other large American metropolis, Chicago has fragmented by race and place. At the same time, urban planning as a field of work began to splinter into poorly connected subfields. Advocates of PUBLIC HOUSING worked in the 1920s and 1930s for specific state and federal legislation. Proponents of improved social services became social workers and bureaucrats of the incipient welfare state. Engineers and builders of physical infrastructure concentrated on adapting a rail-based circulation system to automobiles, as with Chicago's Wacker Drive, Congress Expressway, and hundreds of miles of newly paved or widened thoroughfares. In Chicago and elsewhere, New Deal work relief programs reinforced the transmutation of comprehensive planning into a set of public works projects. City planners were left to effect incremental changes in private land uses by administering zoning regulations.

Chicagoans returned to the intentional creation of "better" communities with the help of the federal government after World War II. The Housing Acts of 1949 and 1954, the bases for an urban renewal program lasting until 1974, were intended as federal-local partnerships to rescue blighted city districts with exemplary reconstruction. But the politics of planning required that new or newly improved neighborhoods be homogeneous communities for single races or classes. This generation of neighborhood planning found it possible to bridge the chasms of class or race, but not both. The results were not necessarily bad, but they were neither as comprehensive nor as socially integrative as planning idealists might have hoped.

A central postwar imperative was how to keep white Chicagoans on the South Side in a time of heavy black migration and ghetto expansion. The city in the 1950s used urban renewal to clear low-rent real estate, attract new investment in middle-class housing, and buffer large civic institutions. A key example was the city's partnership with Michael Reese Hospital and Illinois Institute of Technology to create the new neighborhoods of Lake Meadows and Prairie Shores. High-rise apartments integrated middle-class whites and middle-class African Americans while displacing an economically diversified black neighborhood. The city and the University of Chicago worked together on a similar makeover of Hyde Park that preserved the university and a university-oriented neighborhood while building economic fences against lower-income African Americans. Federal funds also financed arrays of public housing towers, such as the Robert Taylor Homes, to hold black Chicagoans within the established ghetto.

Oak Park since the 1960s has offered an alternative approach to middle-class integration. Oak Park residents have used social engineering rather than land redevelopment to manage integration and harmonize some of the tensions of race and place. Working through private organization rather than municipal government, Oak Parkers have directly faced the problem of racial balance and quotas, marketing their town to white families and selected black families and steering other blacks to alternative communities.

The planned suburb of Park Forest (1948) tried to be inclusive by class (at least the range of the middle class). In so doing, however, it was solving a problem of the last century rather than directly addressing the issues of race and suburban isolation. The Park Forest plat reflected the best of midcentury suburban design, using superblocks to reduce the impact of automobiles and assembling the blocks into neighborhood units with neighborhood parks and schools. It also mixed single-family homes and two-story garden apartments so that upward mobility was possible within the same community. Park Forest has nonetheless gained increasing racial variety, emerging in the 1980s as another example of successful integration.

Park Forest, like Riverside, Evanston, and Pullman in the previous century, also assumed that men and women operated in separate spheres. Such communities turned inward on home and neighborhood for women and children while opening out to the workplace for men. This social vision would prove fragile as social customs changed and a majority of American women entered the workforce by the 1970s.

Chicago's South Shore neighborhood offers a twist on the Park Forest story. Efforts to replicate the Hyde Park experience of racial integration failed in the 1960s and 1970s, in part because of the contrast between middle-class whites and working-class blacks. Instead, it has gained as a broadly based African American neighborhood with the help of development efforts orchestrated by the community-oriented South Shore Bank (now ShoreBank).

In a less progressive variation on the Oak Park and South Shore examples, the private sector has increasingly controlled downtown redevelopment in the interests of business corporations and their professional and managerial employees. Through the 1960s, redevelopment initiative remained with the city because urban renewal put local governments in control of land acquisition. The University of Illinois campus in Chicago was built on lands acquired through urban renewal. In a variation on the Hyde Park / University of Chicago story, it transformed tracts originally intended for replacement housing into a pioneering public campus. As federal urban renewal funds dried up with the Housing and Community Development Act (1974) and the Reagan administration, however, the public sector lost most of its capacity to act directly. Efforts to leverage mixed-use development have met with success outside the Loop but left a gaping hole in the center of downtown during the 1990s.

Planning for regional systems, in contrast, has been more successful. Infrastructure planners can fall back on the rhetoric of technically sound proposals and sidestep direct confrontation with racial conflict. The Chicago Regional Plan Association issued *Planning for the Region of Chicago* in 1956. The Northeastern Illinois Planning Commission (NIPC) began work for a six-county region in 1957; it has issued and updated regional plans for water, open space, recreation, and land development. The 1962 plan of the Chicago Area Transportation Study (CATS) was a national model for transportation demand forecasting. CATS (now a federally recognized transportation planning organization) and NIPC have had the practical success of framing a regional road/rail system that reflects Burnham and Bennett's ideas and has kept the vast metropolis together.

Nevertheless, regional growth frameworks cannot themselves stem intraregional competition for jobs and upper-income residents. Mayor Richard M. Daley might admonish his suburban counterparts in 1997 that "we have to think of mass transit as a regional issue," point proudly to the continuing importance of downtown Chicago jobs, and convene meetings to discuss regional cooperation. Only the federal courts, however, have been able to override local isolationism on issues such as low-income housing.

Conclusion

Chicago's nineteenth-century planners assumed that good communities reflected and protected homogeneity—homogeneity of class as in Riverside and Lake Forest, homogeneity of culture as in Harvey. As exemplified in Pullman, their efforts foundered when faced with the differing values and expectations of workers and capitalists, native-born Chicagoans and immigrants, Protestants and Roman Catholics.

In the civic moment of the late nineteenth and early twentieth centuries, business interest and "civic" interest converged around the physical redesign of the metropolis. Much of the private sector was self-consciously public in rhetoric and often in reality. Middle-class women as well as men shared a vision of a reformed city that was implicitly assimilationist. The well-oiled economic machinery of the metropolis would have a place for everyone; improved housing and public services would help to integrate newcomers into the social fabric.

Even as the imposing *Plan of Chicago* was being so vigorously promoted, however, Chicago's growing black population was posing a challenge that lay outside the intellectual framework of physical planning. The congratulatory report *Ten Years Work of the Chicago Plan Commission* (1920) made no reference to the bloody race riot of the previous year. In the second half of the century, planning fractured into technical specialties and efforts to improve pieces of the metropolis—downtown, historic districts, new suburbs, and the occasional integrated neighborhood. In a time when everyone acknowledges the economic unity of city regions, the continuing challenge is to reinvigorate the civic-mindedness that has served Chicago well in the past and to craft political alliances and civic institutions to support physical efficiency and social equity across the entire metropolitan area.

Carl Abbott

See also: Built Environment of the Chicago Region; Contested Spaces; Environmental Politics; Governing the Metropolis; Planning, City and Regional; Special Districts

Further reading: Chicago's planned communities of the nineteenth and early twentieth centuries are the subject of Stanley Buder, *Pullman: An Experiment in Industrial Order and Community Planning* (1967); Janice Reiff, "A Modern Lear and His Daughters: Gender in the Model Town of Pullman," *Journal of Urban History* 23 (March 1997): 316–341; James Gilbert, *Perfect Cities: Chicago's Utopias of 1893* (1991); Michael Ebner, *Creating Chicago's North Shore: A Suburban History* (1988); and Raymond Mohl and Neil Betten, *Steel City: Urban and Ethnic Patterns in Gary, Indiana, 1906–1950* (1986). The context of market-driven development is described in Ann Durkin Keating, *Building Chicago: Suburban Developers and the Creation of a Divided Metropolis* (1988). Planning for the urban and regional support systems of parks, public utilities, and transportation is taken up in Louis Cain, *Sanitation Strategy for a Lakefront Metropolis: The Case of Chicago* (1978), and Daniel Bluestone, *Constructing Chicago* (1991). The topic is pursued for the twentieth century in John Stamper, *Chicago's North Michigan Avenue: Planning and Development, 1900–1930* (1991); Carl Condit, *Chicago, 1910–29: Building, Planning, and Urban Technology* (1973), and *Chicago, 1930–70: Building, Planning, and Urban Technology* (1974). Chicago's great plan can be studied in Daniel H. Burnham and Edward H. Bennett, *Plan of Chicago* (1909), and in Walter Moody, *Wacker's Manual for the Plan of Chicago* (1912). Maureen Flanagan, "The City Profitable, the City Livable: Environmental Policy, Gender, and Power in Chicago in the 1910s," *Journal of Urban History* 22 (January 1996): 163–192, explores the response of women's organizations to planning issues. The urban renewal era is dissected in Peter Rossi and Robert Dentler, *The Politics of Urban Renewal* (1961); Marvin Meyerson and Edward Banfield, *Planning, Politics, and the Public Interest: The Case of Public Housing in Chicago* (1955); George Rosen, *Decision-Making, Chicago Style: The Genesis of the University of Illinois Campus* (1980); and Arnold Hirsch, *Making the Second Ghetto: Race and Housing in Chicago, 1940–1960* (1983). The twentieth-century's experiments with racial integration are examined in Julia Abrahamson, *A Neighborhood Finds Itself* (1959); Harvey Molotch, *Managed Integration: The Dilemmas of Doing Good in the City* (1976); and Carole Goodwin, *The Oak Park Strategy: Community Control of Racial Change* (1979). Charles Hoch and Robert Slayton, *New Homeless and Old: Community and the Skid Row Hotel* (1989), and Gerald Suttles, *The Man-Made City: The Land-Use Confidence Game in Chicago* (1990), examine the fate of city neighborhoods in the era of megaprojects and headlong suburbanization. Downtown projects themselves are discussed in Suttles, *Man-Made City;* Ross Miller, *Here's the Deal: The Buying and Selling of a Great American City* (1996); and Larry Bennett, "Beyond Urban Renewal: Chicago's North Loop Redevelopment Project," *Urban Affairs Quarterly* 22 (December 1986).

The 1909 *Plan of Chicago* proposed recentering the business district on a new Congress Street axis, creating a new civic center where radial streets converge at Halsted and Congress. At the foot of Congress Street, a new cultural center in Grant Park would overlook a yacht harbor. Plate 129 from the *Plan of Chicago* (1909).

Planning, City and Regional. By tradition, the publication in 1909 of the *Plan of Chicago,* written by Daniel H. Burnham and Edward H. Bennett, marked the birth of both city and regional planning in the Chicago metropolitan area. Sponsored by the COMMERCIAL CLUB, an association of Chicago's most prominent business and professional leaders, the BURNHAM PLAN was Chicago's first comprehensive plan, although there were several important precedents. Burnham himself had previously written comprehensive regional plans for Cleveland, San Francisco, and Manila. As a prominent Chicago architect, he had also played an important role in the planning and construction of the WORLD'S COLUMBIAN EXPOSITION of 1893, remnants of which can still be seen in Chicago's HYDE PARK.

Burnham's call for an extensive lakefront park and a regional system of forest preserves was predated by Aaron Montgomery Ward's campaign to preserve GRANT PARK for public use and by the publication in 1904 of a report entitled "The Outer Belt of FOREST PRESERVES and Parkways for Chicago and Cook County." Although this latter document, edited by architect Dwight Perkins, was the first proposal for a regional network of parks, today's extensive system of parks along the shoreline of LAKE MICHIGAN and the 67,000-acre COOK COUNTY Forest Preserve system were both chiefly inspired by the Burnham Plan.

Also preceding the Burnham Plan were the efforts of the SANITARY AND SHIP CANAL Commission to reverse the CHICAGO RIVER by means of a system of canals and locks in order to protect Lake Michigan from contamination from sewer discharges. After 1899, sewage, whether treated or not, was carried by the Chicago River and the new canals into the Illinois and Mississippi Rivers.

The Burnham Plan was the first to recognize a Chicago metropolitan region encompassing southern Wisconsin and northwestern Indiana, but its main distinction was its comprehensiveness. In addition to parks, Burnham gave detailed attention to the LOOP and immediate environs and to the region's future highway system. Like others of his day, however, he failed to foresee the impact automobiles would have on American cities and their suburbs.

A companion document to the Burnham Plan was a textbook used for many years in Chicago public schools at the eighth-grade level. *Wacker's Manual of the Plan of Chicago: Municipal Economy,* written by Walter D. Moody and produced in six editions from 1911 through 1924, offered students a basic understanding of the history and function of cities and taught the importance of planning as a civic responsibility.

The publication of the Burnham Plan also led directly to the establishment of the Chicago Plan Commission and to a new department of city government, currently known as the Chicago Department of Planning and Development. Together, these two bodies have produced a number of important planning documents, including *The Comprehensive Plan of Chicago* (1966); *The Lakefront Plan of Chicago* (1972); and *Chicago River Urban Design Corridor,* volume 1, *Downtown Corridor* (1990); and volume 2, *North Branch Riverwalk* (1990).

Union Station, 1924. Photographer: Chicago Architectural Photographing Co. Source: Chicago Historical Society.

In 1923, the city planning movement was furthered by a group of citizens who established the Chicago Regional Plan Association. Its most prominent leader was Daniel Burnham, Jr. The new organization promoted planning at all levels of government throughout a Chicago region that included three counties in southern Wisconsin and three in northwestern Indiana. The first regional successor to the original Burnham Plan appeared in 1956, coauthored by Daniel Burnham, Jr., and Robert Kingery. Entitled *Planning the Region of Chicago,* this later document gave particular attention to the rapid growth then occurring in suburban areas and introduced chapters on industry, LAND USE, and WATER SUPPLY and sanitation.

Simultaneously, another civic organization, known today as the Metropolitan Planning Council, spearheaded the passage of state legislation creating in 1957 the first regional comprehensive planning agency, the Northeastern Illinois Planning Commission (NIPC). This new agency subsequently prepared a number of plans covering the six Illinois counties of Cook, DUPAGE, LAKE, KANE, MCHENRY, and WILL.

While NIPC plans are by state law only advisory, they have been used as a basis for federal agency reviews of applications from local governments seeking grants for parks, wastewater facilities, TRANSPORTATION improvements, and other PUBLIC WORKS. NIPC has produced a large number of regional plans and studies, including *Open Space in Northeastern Illinois,* Technical Report no. 2 (1962); *The Water Resource: Planning Its Use,* Technical Report no. 4 (1966); *Comprehensive General Plan* (1968, 1977); *Areawide Water Quality Management Plan* (1979); *Strategic Plan for Land Resource Management* (1992); *Northeastern Illinois Regional Greenways Plan* (coauthored with the Openlands Project, 1992, 1997).

The federal grant-making process also requires the existence of an approved long-range regional transportation plan and short-range capital program. To prepare these documents, a separate agency, the Chicago Area Transportation Study (CATS), was established in 1956 by means of a state and local government interagency agreement. The original CATS *Transportation Plan* (1962) proposed a network of new EXPRESSWAYS for the inner third of the six-county region.

A series of updated transportation plans followed and the CATS region was extended to include the six-county northeastern Illinois area. Currently, CATS and NIPC share responsibility for maintaining the region's long-range transportation plan. The latest update was prepared in 1997. Unlike the original Burnham Plan, today's regional transportation plans include highways, PUBLIC TRANSPORTATION, and bicycle transportation.

Today, each of the five counties outside Cook County also maintains its own comprehensive plan and, in some cases, separate transportation plans. Likewise, most of the region's 265 suburban municipalities maintain their own comprehensive plans, typically supplemented with capital improvement programs and ordinances regulating the use of private land and the protection of natural resources.

Lawrence Christmas

See also: Architecture: The City Beautiful; Infrastructure; Streets and Highways; Waterfront

Encountering the Prairie

Thousands of settlers entered the region after the 1832 BLACK HAWK WAR. Many came from eastern states in search of good farmland and other BUSINESS opportunities. Morris Sleight came to Chicago from Hyde Park, New York, in the summer of 1834, on a journey to Michigan and Illinois in search of land on which to settle. Sleight wrote to his wife to recount his travels and to convince her that a westward trip was worthwhile. On July 9, 1834, Sleight wrote to his wife from Chicago about a trip west to Naperville:

> I am highly pleased with Michigan, but I am delighted with Illinois. . . . The first view of a Michigan Prairie is delightful after passing the oak openings and thick forest, but the first view of an Illinois prairie is sublime. . . . A person needs a compass to keep their course, but the more I travel over them the more I like them. There is a great variety of flowers now on the prairies, but they tell me in a month from this time they will be prettier. I have sent you a few of them with Mr. Douglas which will be all faded by the time you get them, but they will be interesting to you as you will be sure they were picked from the prairies of Illinois. There is a number of other kinds on the dry prairies, some resemble sweet william, some pinks, sunflowers and almost every variety that grow in our gardens. . . . This is the best country I have ever seen for a poor man or a rich one, an industrious man or a lazy one. . . . It has the advantage of grist mills and saw mills, within half a mile, also a store and tavern and a thick settled neighborhood. As people build in the groves you cannot see many of your neighbors—I will not say houses yet, but cabins. In a few years I think I can say mansions.

Further reading: Bennett, Edward H., and Daniel H. Burnham. *Plan of Chicago.* Reprint, 1970. • Burnham, Daniel H., Jr., and Robert Kingery. *Planning the Region of Chicago.* 1956. • Moody, Walter D. *Wacker's Manual of the Plan of Chicago: Municipal Economy.* 2nd ed. 1916.

Plant Communities. The Chicago region, situated along the southwestern end of LAKE MICHIGAN, lies along the northeastern edge of the Tall Grass Prairie biome of the Midwest. The prevailing LANDSCAPE at the time of American occupation consisted largely of treeless meadows, which were named "prairie" by the FRENCH. The native Algonquian-speaking people of the region called the prairies *maskode,* the "burned over bare land." The prairies ranged in character from wet to dry, depending largely on the clay content of the SOIL and the proximity of a near-surface water table. While generally flat in comparison to the more dissected hill country of the eastern states, the Chicago region is relatively well disposed with gently rolling hills, particularly in the morainic regions that flank the lake plains. These hills were characterized in the better-drained areas by woodlands, mostly of open-grown oaks and hickories. Today, the word used to describe these timbered lands is "savanna" or "woodland." The native people referred to those places with trees as *mtigwaukee,* which meant the "place were the wood is." Everywhere in the wooded and grassy landscape, GROUNDWATER issued forth from the slopes as springs and seeps. Southward and westward from Chicago, the landscape was broken by large streams, with flat prairie bottoms and scattered stretches of tree-lined bluffs and backwaters.

The original plant communities of Chicago today are all but gone, the plants now consisting mostly of introduced weeds, crop plants, and ornamentals. Soon after European American settlement, changes in the human relationship with the landscape caused fundamental changes in plant composition. Cessation of fire, straightening of rivers, ditching, tiling, heavy grazing, and urban and suburban INFRASTRUCTURE have so modified the original structure of the land and its hydrology that our ability to piece together an understanding of an original order is profoundly compromised. Still, one can visualize for the Chicago region nine general kinds of native plant communities—aquatic, marsh, fen, bog, swamp, forest, savanna, DUNE, and prairie—and a ruderal community.

Aquatic

Aquatic plant communities were occasional throughout the region but were most abundant southeast and northwest of Chicago. They formed in the landscape in glacial potholes and in LACUSTRINE plains where there were no outlets. Since our region evaporates nearly or quite as much WATER as falls, aquatic communities are sustained by waters in excess of that provided by rain. Generally, these excess waters filtered down through vegetated ground into the underlying soil until they reached impervious material, then exited into aquatic communities as groundwater by way of springs, rills, or seeps. Along the major streams, aquatic plant communities developed in alluvial sloughs and ponds derived from surface melt or late winter runoff waters.

Marsh

Marsh plant communities generally occurred along the transition between aquatic communities and drier communities, or in large flats that were regularly inundated by shallow surface waters for much of the growing season. The marshes are best developed in lacustrine flats of the Lake Plain, and along the lower reaches of the DES PLAINES and Kankakee river drainages. A related community, with affinities to fens and wet prairies, is the sedge meadow, which developed in large, shallow, lacustrine flats, and was characterized by hummocks of sedges with many wildflowers interspersed among them.

Fen

Fens occurred in areas where the carbonate-rich glacial formations are such that bicarbonate-rich groundwater discharges at a constant rate along the slopes of kames, eskers, moraines, river bluffs, or even dunes, or in flats associated with these formations. Depending upon the circumstances, fens can occur where marl is at or near the surface or where mucks and peats are constantly bathed in minerotrophic groundwater; such areas can be wooded or open. Marly or mucky fens developed on open prairie slopes, commonly forming rills that flowed with constant rates of discharge 365 days a year. Related to these

Lotus beds, Spring Grove, McHenry County. Photographer: Charles R. Childs. Source: Chicago Historical Society.

hillside fens are the wooded seeps that occur sporadically on steep bluffs.

Bog

Bog, like most of the other terms used here to describe plant communities, is not a scientific term in the sense of referring to a standard, unique concept. Any quagmire of wet, mucky, hummocky ground was likely to have been termed a "bog" prior to the 1960s. Ecologists currently, however, tend to restrict the term "bog" to a hydric condition typified by saturated, acidic, usually organic substrates. Many of our peatlands are influenced significantly by waters rich in bicarbonates and can be called prairie fens. But as the cation exchange capacity damps off, bog-like conditions can begin to develop. For this reason, many of the floating peatlands northwest of Chicago can be called alkaline bogs.

Some peatlands actually float on a minerotrophic head of groundwater, with the deeper roots thus exposed to calcareous or circumneutral conditions where shallower-rooted species are imbedded in the upper sphagnum mat, probably in a more acidic environment. In large basins or in areas where the influence of minerotrophic waters is insignificant, characteristically acid bogs could develop. Related to the acid bog, often in sand flats or basins in the dune region, are floating sedge mats that rise and fall with the water table.

Swamp

Swamps are wetlands characterized by trees growing in large flats or basins that are poorly drained, with most of the water leaving through evapotranspiration. They developed in the backwaters of large, slow-moving rivers, such as along the Kankakee River or in associated wet sandy flats. They also occurred on the moraines in wet depressions and in the Lake Plains in large flats behind the high dunes. In sandy, poorly drained flats with a high water table, fire-dependent savanna-like swamps could develop. On the moraines, especially the Valparaiso and Lake Border moraines, there are shallow depressions ringed by oaks. In the broad low flats behind the high dunes of Lake Michigan lies one of the richest and most complicated forested systems in the region. It is characterized by a complex hydrology and is interspersed by gentle rises, shallow depressions, and hummocks, and consists of an inseparable mixture of wooded fen, bog, and moist forest.

Forest

Forests occurred just southeast of Chicago in northwest Indiana, where they developed on rises that are relatively well drained and physiographically located such that exposure to fire was infrequent. A relative of the forest occurred on the western bluff of Lake Michigan, north of Chicago in deep morainic dissections or ravines, but the ground cover vegetation was such that sporadic ground fires could creep down the slopes from the savannas on the higher, more level ground and nose slopes.

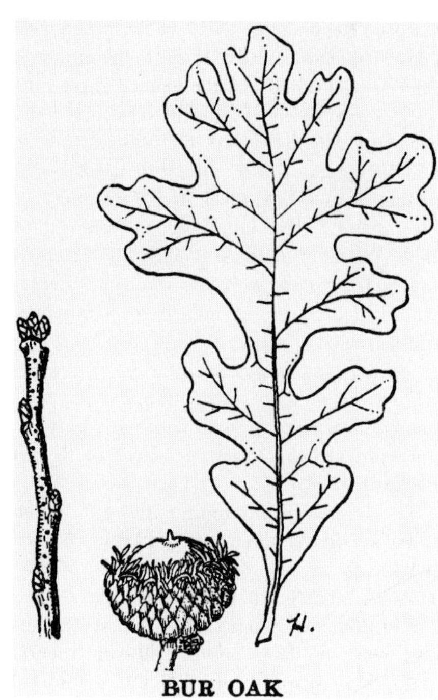

Drawings of a twig, acorn, and leaf of the Bur Oak (*Quercus macrocarpa* Michx.), from *Forest Trees of Illinois: How to Know Them* (1955), a publication of the Illinois State Department of Conservation. Artist: Unknown. Source: The Newberry Library.

Savanna

Savannas, as interpreted here, include those portions of wooded landscape in which structure was, to one degree or another, affected regularly by fires set by Native Americans in the thousands of years before European settlement. Generally, these communities were intercalated among the prairies and developed a ground cover vegetation that would carry at least occasional fires in the autumn, when the ambient prairies were wont to burn. The tree canopies of such savannas ranged in character from relatively closed and forest-like to very open with only scattered trees.

Most related to the forest communities are mesic savannas. These closed-canopy woodlands, dominated by maple and red oak, shaded a grassy ground cover capable of sustaining low, infrequent ground fires. Such savannas are best developed on north-facing and east-facing slopes in dissected or topographically complex portions of the moraines.

On the nearly level or gently undulating moraines are the open savannas of heavier soil characterized by open-grown trees of bur oak, which sometimes persisted only as multistemmed grubs. Such savannas have a well-developed grassy ground cover and carry substantial fires on a regular basis. These savannas developed on low mounds within the mesic or wet prairies, or in transitional zones between the lower prairies and the dry prairies of kames and eskers.

In sandy soils along well-drained ridges and old dunes, savannas were dominated by black oak, sometimes growing with white oak. Such savannas burned regularly and were closely associated with sand prairies, and the two communities have many species in common. Another kind of sand savanna developed along the southern shore of Lake Michigan on low dunes. A close association probably existed between the sand savannas and what once were pine savannas.

Dune

On the open sands of the foredunes of Lake Michigan there is a special habitat characterized by species that grow locally only in the shifting sands fronting the lake. In wet, interdunal flats (*pannes*), where sand has been blown out down to the water table, there is a plant community generally characterized by low sedge species and many beautiful flowers. A special form of panne surrounded by small forests of jack pine occurs near OGDEN DUNES, Indiana. Related to both the pannes and the prairie fens is a kind of wet alkaline prairie that otherwise developed in low flats behind the dunes.

Prairie

The prairies comprise those plant communities that are dominated by a diversity of perennial wildflowers growing in a perennial grass matrix, which forms a dry flammable mass in autumn. The prairie habitat included the regular autumnal fire, which, lacking an occurrence of dry lightning locally, was set annually by the Native Americans. Prairies developed on those substrates in which the above-ground perennial mass produced more fixed carbon annually than was likely to be grazed or decomposed. Chicago-area prairie communities ranged from wet to dry and dominated much of the landscape, intercalating among or blending insensibly with other communities.

To a Midwesterner, perhaps the first image evoked with the term prairie is that of the tall grasses of big bluestem grass and Indian grass in their full, late-summer development—"high as a man on a horse," interspersed with the rosinweeds, sunflowers, and asters. A wetter variant of the mesic prairie is more likely to be dominated by blue joint grass and cord grass, also with many wildflowers interspersed. In the drier prairies the grasses were somewhat lower in stature, dominated by little bluestem grass and side-oats grama. An important variant of the dry prairie is the sand prairie, in which the principal fuel species was commonly little bluestem grass. In many respects it seems scarcely to be more than an exaggerated opening in the sand savanna. Another variant of the prairie occurs on the dolomitic bedrock pavements exposed along the lower Des Plaines; it is characterized by a curious admixture of dry and wetland species.

In moist to wet acid sandy flats there occurred an amalgamation of plant species, interesting in that many of them have close relatives in the Atlantic and Gulf Coastal Plains. Such flats occur here and there throughout the moraines in the Lake Plain and in the sand districts along the Kankakee valley. Each such area has its own distinctive flora.

Ruderal

Most of our original communities are gone, but there are many tiny remnants here and there throughout the Chicago region, where seeds are created, cast, and grow. These tiny areas contain the germ material of sustained life, the genetic memory of Chicago, the stuff out of which the earth can make itself new with each passing year. But nearly all of the vegetated landscape today is dominated by a small number of ruderal plants that were not here two centuries ago. These plants are mostly Eurasian and well adapted to soils regularly disturbed mechanically and subject to heavy trampling or compaction, or to regularly tilled or destabilized fertile soils. These are the common weeds, such as dandelion, goat's beard, Queen Anne's lace, Kentucky bluegrass, and the sweet clovers. Then there are those areas of the region occupied by lawns and cultivated areas, which consist wholly of planted plants, without the capacity for the passing along of recombinant DNA, where evolution has stopped—and the earth can no longer renew itself and the ancient memory of Chicago has all but slipped away.

Gerould Wilhelm

See also: Climate; Dune System; Ecosystem Evolution; Glaciation; Topography

Further reading: Greenberg, Joel. *A Natural History of the Chicago Region.* 2002. • *Lichens of the Chicago Region.* Morton Arboretum, Lisle, IL. 1993. • Swink, Floyd, and Gerould Wilhelm. *Plants of the Chicago Region.* 1994.

Playboy. *Playboy,* a MAGAZINE aimed at the single American male, first appeared in December of 1953. Written and conceived by Hugh Hefner in his HYDE PARK apartment, the magazine featured a combination of articles on music, lewd jokes, short FICTION, and perhaps most striking, a nude photo of Marilyn Monroe.

Unlike other popular contemporary men's magazines, *Playboy* was directly concerned with addressing the issue of sex and sexuality. Each month, it instructed men in the delicate art of sophisticated seduction, with a strong emphasis on the role of conspicuous consumption. The corporation complemented the magazine with a worldwide network of Playboy Clubs, featuring attractive women serving men in a variety of amenable settings that often provided a wide range of LEISURE activities. The first Playboy Club opened in Chicago in early 1960, with the last of the remaining American clubs closing in Lansing, Michigan, in 1988. By the early 1970s, Hugh Hefner had moved most of Playboy's corporate activities to southern California, while production of *Playboy* magazine remained in Chicago.

Max Grinnell

See also: Entertaining Chicagoans

Further reading: Brady, Frank. *Hefner.* 1974. • Ehrenreich, Barbara. *The Hearts of Men: American Dreams and the Flight from Commitment.* 1983. • Weyr, Thomas. *Reaching for Paradise: The Playboy Vision of America.* 1978.

Playground Movement. Although the first sandlot opened in Boston in 1886, the playground movement didn't begin to develop until the mid-1890s, when PLAYGROUNDS were opened in nine major cities including Chicago. SETTLEMENT HOUSES or civic groups opened early play lots, often modest dirt lots, on land donated or lent by PHILANTHROPISTS. A wide coalition of child-saving reformers including social SETTLEMENT HOUSE workers, PROGRESSIVE EDUCATORS, and child psychologists urged municipal governments to construct playgrounds where the city's youth could play under supervised and controlled conditions. Playground reformers believed that supervised play could improve the mental, moral, and physical well-being of children, and in the early twentieth century they expanded their calls into a broader recreation movement aimed at providing spaces for adult activities as well. Municipally controlled parks and playgrounds included trained play leaders and planned activities as well as special facilities like gymnasiums, fieldhouses, and swimming ponds.

In 1898, the Municipal Science Club began studying Chicago's need for additional "breathing spaces," and in the following year the mayor created the Special Park Commission (SPC) to create municipal playgrounds in the city's most densely populated neighborhoods. Working cooperatively with the Board of Education and the three park commissions, the SPC urged elementary SCHOOLS to construct adjacent playgrounds and the park commissions to create new parks and playgrounds.

The South Park Commission became the most involved in this effort to create municipal recreation spaces and in 1902 opened the experimental McKinley Park with ball fields, a SWIMMING lake, and open-air gymnasium. In 1903 the South Park Commission embarked on an ambitious system of neighborhood parks that became a model for other American cities. The Olmsted Brothers LANDSCAPE DESIGNERS and D. H. Burnham & Co. architects were hired to design parks with running tracks, wading pools, playground apparatus, sand courts, and fieldhouses in beautiful landscape settings. Opened to the public in 1905, the first 10 parks drew over five million visitors in one year.

Julia Sniderman Bachrach

See also: Kindergarten Movement; Leisure; Park Districts

Further reading: Cavallo, Dominick. *Muscles and Morals: Organized Playgrounds and Urban Reform, 1880–1920.* 1981. • Mero, Everett B. *American Playgrounds: Their Construction, Equipment, Maintenance, and Utility.* 1908. • Tippens, William W., and Julia Sniderman. "The Planning and Design of Chicago's Neighborhood Parks." In *A Breath of Fresh Air: Chicago's Parks of the Progressive Era,* Chicago Public Library Cultural Center, 1989.

Playgrounds and Small Parks. The more than five hundred small parks and playgrounds that dot Chicago's neighborhoods are a distinctive legacy of turn-of-the-century progressive reform. The definition of a small park has changed over time, but most are less than four acres in size. Their function within the park system, their design, and their facilities provided a model for park reform across the United States and as far away as Europe and Japan.

A few small parks, like Union Park and the square that once occupied the City Hall site, were provided for in early city plats, but post–Civil War PLANNING emphasized large parks and boulevards as amenities for more affluent neighborhoods. By the 1890s, STREETS, empty lots ("prairies" in Chicago parlance), and occasional playgrounds adjacent to some public SCHOOLS provided the only recreational space accessible to most working-class residents. Reformers, drawing often on their own small-town backgrounds, argued that open space and fresh air were essential to childhood in a democratic society. They also regarded green spaces as necessary quiet refuges for adults bombarded with the noise and clamor of city life. Debates over the relative utility of contemplative versus recreational space, a recurring theme in park planning, were settled in 1904 by a compromise design of small parks which encompassed playgrounds and sports fields accompanied by landscaped areas for adults.

On the SOUTH SIDE, park commissioners added an additional innovation, which provided a focal element to many parks: the fieldhouse, designed as a year-round neighborhood center. Davis Square Park, for example, opened in 1905 near the UNION STOCK YARD on 10 acres of modestly LANDSCAPED land. Its fieldhouse contained gymnasiums for men and women, meeting rooms, a public library, and a cafeteria.

Organized park activity reflected both the turn-of-century concern with competition and strenuous exercise and a reform agenda to shape urban culture. Park personnel arranged gymnastics, athletic leagues, and other types of sports competitively, with strict rules. Recognizing the role ethnic culture played in the lives of working-class immigrants, parks reformers arranged for ethnic art, folk singing, and dancing. They also, however, scheduled plays, dances, and movies of a decidedly American flavor. During WORLD WAR I, park commissioners turned the parks over to the YMCA for AMERICANIZATION classes; more than one million Chicagoans attended these sessions.

The original concept of the neighborhood park called for meeting halls in which community issues could be discussed, an unintended harkening back to a FREE-SPEECH tradition established in Chicago's oldest extant small park. Washington Square Park, established in the 1840s, was the site of an immigrant gathering preliminary to the 1855 LAGER BEER RIOT. The parks continued to provide focal points for neighborhood organizations and activities. During World War I some accommodated labor union rallies. Although park commissioners subsequently prohibited such meetings, parks in working-class districts remained the hub of community activity. In the 1930s, Davis Square became the first headquarters of the BACK OF THE YARDS NEIGHBORHOOD COUNCIL.

After WORLD WAR II the small parks fell into decline. Other types of recreation attracted city residents, parks became less important to reformers, and the Chicago PARK DISTRICT saw itself as a provider of athletic leagues and other kinds of recreational services generally more appropriate to larger facilities. POLITICS and RACISM became increasingly visible, as the Park District remained a haven for PATRONAGE and parks became valued ethnic TURF and therefore sites of racial clashes. Increased gang activity and violence rendered some parks unsafe.

In the late 1980s the Chicago Park District began to revitalize the system, trying to return some of the parks to their original architectural and LANDSCAPE DESIGNS. Neighborhood residents demanded more say in park programs and policies, challenging centralized park authority. The Park District assisted the formation of community advisory councils which were given considerable input into playground rehabilitation. The problem of GANGS, however, continued to cripple some parts of the system. While the fieldhouses offered programs, street gangs controlled the streets leading to them.

Historically, small parks provided much-needed public space in Chicago's working-class districts. The showers and SWIMMING pools, TENNIS and BASKETBALL courts, meeting rooms, and assembly halls provided opportunities especially welcome in crowded low-income neighborhoods. Parks provided an important component of community, creating, along with the church, school, and SALOON, a social fabric that helped to define the very term "neighborhood."

Dominic A. Pacyga

See also: Baths, Public; Fitness and Athletic Clubs; Neighborhood Associations; Places of Assembly

Further reading: Cranz, Galen. *The Politics of Park Design: A History of Urban Parks in America.* 1984. • Gordon, Constance, and Kathy Hussey-Arnston, eds. *A Breath of Fresh Air: Chicago's Neighborhood Parks of the Progressive Reform Era, 1900–1925.* 1989. • McArthur, Benjamin. "The Chicago Playground Movement: A Neglected Feature of Social Justice." *Social Service Review* 49 (September 1975): 376–395.

Playwriting. Throughout most of the nineteenth century, Chicagoans watched plays authored by writers from other times and places. It was not until the 1890s, and the exploration of realism in Chicago's literary corners, that playwrights in the city began to reflect on the language, characters, and conditions of local life. George Ade, a newspaper reporter, penned several plays from work he originally published in the *Chicago Record.* In 1912 Maurice Browne and his wife Ellen Van Volkenburg launched the Chicago Little Theatre, a company that produced plays by local playwrights such as Cloyd Head and Mary Aldis.

Although subsequent decades saw mostly traveling productions of American and British classics at such LOOP theaters as the AUDITORIUM, the Harris, and the Selwyn, the GOODMAN was also producing plays for both adults and children, utilizing primarily the talents of its drama students along with professional guest artists. Many Chicagoans cite the children's shows at the Goodman as the origin of their love for the THEATER.

A major source of Chicago's modern playwriting tradition is the IMPROVISATIONAL process created by renowned theater teacher Viola Spolin, which was further developed by the Compass Players and expanded by its offspring, SECOND CITY. David Mamet, for example, wrote his first play, *Squirrels,* while working as a Second City busboy. Mamet's brutally insightful style set a distinctive tone that has influenced many younger scribes such as Rick Cleveland and Keith Reddin. Nicholas Patricca's plays are informed by a deeply spiritual and philosophical bent, while John Logan has often used historical events (such as the kidnapping of the Lindbergh baby) to explore human motivations and actions. The plays of Claudia Allen and Darrah Cloud have been naturalistic and lyrical, while Rebecca Gilman has explored issues like race and gender head-on. Charles Smith creates compelling drama, sometimes on an epic scale, from pivotal moments in AFRICAN AMERICAN history.

Organizations like Victory Gardens Theater, the Goodman, STEPPENWOLF, and Chicago Dramatists Workshop have all nurtured and developed Chicago writers, in some cases toward New York productions and national profiles. Victory Gardens was recognized in 2001 for its efforts when it received the Tony Award for Best Regional Theatre, as had Steppenwolf and the Goodman previously, furthering the nation's awareness of Chicago's role in new play development.

Andrea Telli
Richard Pettengill

See also: Literary Cultures; Theater Companies; Theater Training

Further reading: Pettengill, Richard. "Chicago Theater Voices, 1990." In *Resetting the Stage: Theater Beyond the Loop, 1960–1990,* exhibition catalog, 1990. • Ryan, Sheila. *At the Goodman Theatre: An Exhibition in Celebration of the Sixtieth Anniversary of Chicago's Oldest Producing Theatre, October 12, 1985–January 11, 1986.* 1985. • *Urban Voices: Chicago as a Literary Place.* Exhibition checklist and annotations, by Susan Prendergast Schoelwer, 1983.

Poetry. Chicago's long tradition as a center of poetic culture has two key aspects: Chicago has been a fertile ground for innovative poetic movements through publishing activity, and the city itself has provided a subject with which poets have grappled. The first volume of poetry published in Chicago was William Asbury Kenyon's *Miscellaneous Poems* (1845), although Benjamin Franklin Taylor (*Complete Poetical Works,* 1896) is generally considered Chicago's first significant poet. Chicago's poetry entered the national arena with Harriet Monroe's "Columbian Ode" (1893), a poem commissioned for the WORLD'S COLUMBIAN EXPOSITION. But Monroe is probably better known as the founder of *Poetry* magazine (1912), one of the nation's most important literary magazines, along with fellow Chicagoan Margaret Anderson's *Little Review.* Monroe and Anderson distinguished themselves and Chicago with their editorial daring and their support for new and innovative modernist poets such as Ezra Pound, James Joyce, and William Butler Yeats.

But Chicago's poetry scene did not focus only on international poetry: during the CHICAGO LITERARY RENAISSANCE, Carl Sandburg, Edgar Lee Masters, and other poets writing about Chicago and the Midwest reached national and international audiences. Masters, a disgruntled attorney, achieved his greatest renown with *Spoon River Anthology* (1915), a collection of monologues from beyond the grave spoken by the former citizens of a small Illinois town; this book's frankness helped establish a forthright use of the vernacular voice as a distinguishing feature of the Chicago poetic tradition. Sandburg's most important contribution, *Chicago Poems* (1916), featured the city's signature piece and one of the most frequently anthologized American poems, "Chicago." At least two phrases from this poem—"City of the Big Shoulders" and "Hog Butcher for the World"—remain emblematic of Chicago long after the closure of the

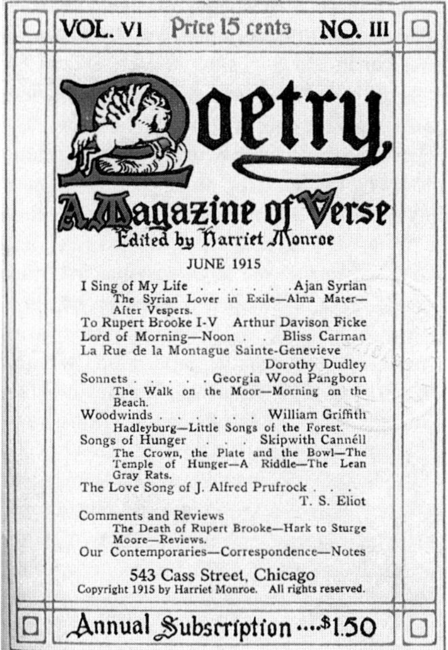

VOL. VI Price 15 cents NO. III

Poetry

A Magazine of Verse

Edited by Harriet Monroe

JUNE 1915

I Sing of My Life . . . . . . Ajan Syrian
The Syrian Lover in Exile—Alma Mater—After Vespers.
To Rupert Brooke I-V Arthur Davison Ficke
Lord of Morning—Noon . . Bliss Carman
La Rue de la Montague Sainte-Genevieve Dorothy Dudley
Sonnets . . . . . Georgia Wood Pangborn
The Walk on the Moor—Morning on the Beach.
Woodwinds . . . . . . William Griffith
Hadleyburg—Little Songs of the Forest.
Songs of Hunger . . . Skipwith Cannéll
The Crown, the Plate and the Bowl—The Temple of Hunger—A Riddle—The Lean Gray Rats.
The Love Song of J. Alfred Prufrock . . . T. S. Eliot
Comments and Reviews
The Death of Rupert Brooke—Hark to Sturge Moore—Reviews.
Our Contemporaries—Correspondence—Notes

543 Cass Street, Chicago

Copyright 1915 by Harriet Monroe. All rights reserved.

Annual Subscription $1.50

Cover of *Poetry: A Magazine of Verse*, June 1915. Source: The Newberry Library.

stockyards and the shift in Chicago's economy away from heavy industry.

The interaction between Chicago as a center of poetry publishing and the accomplishment of poets writing in and about Chicago continued, as George Dillon, an editor with *Poetry* magazine and author of *The Flowering Stone* (1931), became the first Chicagoan to win the Pulitzer Prize. *Poetry* continued to provide a focus for the city's poetic culture during the long period after the Chicago Renaissance when most of Chicago's literary reputation rested on its FICTION writers. Over the years, outstanding poets moved to Chicago as editors of the journal, including Karl Shapiro, a frequent dissenter from mainstream critical orthodoxy and winner of the Pulitzer Prize for *V-Letter and Other Poems* (1944), and John Frederick Nims, a formalist of exceptional wit and dexterity. Gwendolyn Brooks, Illinois' second Poet Laureate—after Sandburg—and one of the most important American poets of the twentieth century, has written with feeling and intelligence about the city, especially the AFRICAN AMERICAN experience in Bronzeville, since the 1940s. Her collection *Annie Allen* won the 1950 Pulitzer Prize.

In the 1950s and '60s two closely related literary journals, the *Chicago Review* and its Beat generation offspring, *Big Table,* played a major role in bringing a new generation of innovative poets to a sometimes skeptical, even hostile, reading public. The censorship drama which birthed *Big Table* out of the UNIVERSITY OF CHICAGO-sponsored *Chicago Review* was one aspect of the key split in Chicago (and American) poetry: the academic poets versus the performance poets. From the 1950s onward,

Poetry Slam

The term "poetry slam" was coined by Chicago native Marc Smith to describe the cabaret-style poetry show he began staging at the Green Mill Lounge in July 1986. Designed to encourage active audience participation, slams allow booing, cheering, hissing, finger snapping, and foot stomping as responses to the poems presented. A typical slam has an open-mike set for newcomers, a segment devoted to guest performances ranging from stand-up poetry to multimedia presentations, and a "slam competition."

Judged by randomly selected audience members, "slam competitions" loosely follow Olympic-style scoring. Poets perform for a maximum of three minutes, either solo or as part of an ensemble, and are rated between 0 and 10 for their performance skills and the quality of the text. Sometimes negative numbers are permitted.

Initially dismissed by mainstream POETRY circles as cheap entertainment, slams have demonstrated that the art of performance when combined with artfully written texts can enhance the general public's interest in poetic words. More than three hundred cities worldwide have active poetry slams. Each year the United States, Great Britain, and Germany hold national slam competitions attracting thousands of enthusiasts. Universities, high schools, and cultural centers use slams to spark student interest in poetry. Slams and slam poets have appeared on TV, in movies, and on the Internet.

Marc Smith

as an aspect of the growing academicization of LITERARY CULTURE in general, university patronage played a key role in providing a living and an intellectual home for many poets. Various Chicago-area universities employed accomplished poets such as Haki R. Madhubuti, Sterling Plumpp, Michael Anania, Reginald Gibbons, Susan Hahn, Mary Kinzie, Barry Silesky, A. K. Ramanujan, Elizabeth Alexander, Reginald Shepard, Martha Vertreace, Paul Hoover, and Maxine Chernoff. While these poets take a wide range of approaches to their craft—from politically engaged poetry about race and gender to an ornate late modernism—the term "academic poetry" has come to imply a formalized, erudite, even ivory-tower, aesthetic.

That academic environment has its counterpart, as performance-oriented poets, many of them working-class or people of color, thrive in the neighborhood SALOONS and arts organizations far from the libraries and seminar rooms of the university poets. Marc Smith's groundbreaking Uptown Poetry Slam at the Green Mill JAZZ club has spawned a high-profile nationwide performance-based poetry scene and has produced accomplished poets such as Tony Fitzpatrick, whose *Bum Town* (2001) is a worthy successor to Sandburg's *Chicago Poems* as an attempt to sum up the city in verse. The slam phenomenon has also generated a number of publishers which, along with *Poetry* and Chicago's academic poets and presses, perpetuate Chicago's role as a center of the writing, teaching, and publishing of poetry.

David Starkey
Bill Savage

See also: Literary Images of Chicago; Literary Cultures; Publishing, Book

Further reading: Monroe, Harriet. *A Poet's Life: Seventy Years in a Changing World.* 1938. • Smith, Carl. S. *Chicago and the American Literary Imagination.* 1984. • Starkey, David, and Richard Guzman, eds. *Smokestacks and Skyscrapers: An Anthology of Chicago Literature.* 1999.

Poles. The traditional Polish community in Chicago, an organization-rich ethnic settlement that developed in the years after the CIVIL WAR, reached maturity and almost complete institutional self-sufficiency before WORLD WAR I.

Polish Chicago, sometimes referred to as "POLONIA," has been shaped by at least three distinct immigration waves. The first and largest lasted from the 1850s to the early 1920s, and was driven primarily by economic and structural change in Poland. This immigration is often referred to as *Za Chlebem* (For Bread). Primarily a peasant migration, it drew first from the German Polish partition, and then from the Russian partition and Austrian Polish partition. Although restrictions during World War I and in the 1920s cut off this immigration, by 1930 Polish immigrants and their children had replaced GERMANS as the largest ethnic group in Chicago.

A second wave brought hundreds of thousands of Poles, displaced by WORLD WAR II and then by the Communist takeover of Poland. This second immigration reinvigorated many Polish-American institutions and neighborhoods. A small, economically stimulated immigration persisted throughout the postwar period. A third wave of immigration began in the 1980s, commonly referred to as the "Solidarity" immigration. These Polish immigrants came to Chicago as a result of the imposition of martial law in Poland (1981) and the decade-long struggle to bring democracy to the Polish Republic. Mainly professionals, ARTISTS, and intellectuals, these newest immigrants influenced the cultural and institutional life of Chicago's Polish community.

The first Polish emigrants to Chicago were noblemen who had fled Poland after the Polish-Russian War of 1830–1831. They arrived with ill-fated plans of establishing a "New Poland" in Illinois. Among these early settlers was John

Napieralski, believed to have been the first Pole in Chicago.

Polish Chicago's growth began in earnest after 1850. By the time of the Civil War, approximately five hundred Poles had created a small community on the Northwest Side; Anthony Smarzewski-Schermann, who emigrated to the United States around 1850 and earned his living as a carpenter before opening a GROCERY STORE on the corner of Noble and Bradley Streets, provided leadership for the young community. Peter Kiolbassa, who first fought in the Confederate army, but later served as a captain in the Sixth Colored Cavalry during the Civil War, also emerged as an important local leader. Kiolbassa organized the first Polish Society of St. Stanislaus Kostka in 1864. This organization prepared the community for the development of the first Polish ROMAN CATHOLIC parish in the city. The first Polish elected official in Chicago, Kiolbassa served in the state legislature (1877–1879), and as city treasurer (1891–1893).

The Polish settlement along the North Branch of the CHICAGO RIVER grew quickly. Many Polish Catholics attended St. Boniface Catholic Church. Here they met hostility from some of their German coreligionists who did not want their priest to attend to Polish religious needs. In 1867 the Polish community created its own Roman Catholic parish, St. Stanislaus Kostka, just a few blocks north of the German parish. The creation of the PARISH was central to the creation of Polonia. Since the midcentury arrival of large numbers of IRISH and German Catholic immigrants in Chicago, the creation of ethnic Catholic parishes provided both a stable institutional base for community and a status symbol that announced the importance of the new immigrant colony. St. Stanislaus Kostka became the first of nearly 60 Polish parishes in the archdiocese. In 1870, Bishop Thomas Foley invited the Polish Resurrectionist congregation to minister to Polonia's religious needs. Four years later the Resurrectionist Father Vincent Barzynski arrived to act as pastor of St. Stanislaus Kostka. Barzynski proved to be the great builder-priest of Polonia and remained pastor at St. Stanislaus Kostka until his death in 1899.

Kiolbassa paved the way for Polish participation in local elections, and others soon followed. By World War I, various other Polish Americans had entered POLITICS on both the DEMOCRATIC and REPUBLICAN tickets. Among the most important of these early politicians was John F. Smulski (1867–1928), a Republican who was elected city attorney in 1903 and state treasurer in 1906, and served on the West Side Park Board. Later important Polish politicians include Benjamin Adamowski, Roman Pucinski, and Dan Rostenkowski.

While the original Polish community located on the Northwest Side, other Polish settlements soon appeared. Poles joined their fellow Slavic immigrants on the NEAR WEST SIDE in the CZECH Catholic parish of St. Wenceslaus. Another Polish district appeared just west of 18th Street and Ashland Avenue, where in 1874 Poles founded St. Adalbert's parish. Other Polish settlements appeared soon after in BRIDGEPORT, MCKINLEY PARK, BACK OF THE YARDS, SOUTH CHICAGO, PULLMAN, and HEGEWISCH. These original core immigrant neighborhoods revolved around a heavy industrial base, whose jobs drew Poles to Chicago.

Immigrants from German Poland were soon joined by Poles from the Russian and Austrian partitions. By 1900, 23 Polish Catholic parishes were located throughout Chicago and its nearby industrial suburbs. None of these neighborhoods was exclusively Polish in ethnicity. Like other European ethnic groups at the time, Poles lived in diverse neighborhoods that were residentially integrated (by ethnicity, if not by race), but tended to be socially segregated. These ethnic groups developed their own churches, schools, and other institutions around which their social lives revolved.

The growth of Polonia was not without conflict. Questions of ethnic and religious identity often resulted in strife, including street battles in the early years. Many of these difficulties revolved around church ownership and the concept of parish. Sometimes these conflicts were a result of Polish regionalism transported to American shores. Within the community, nationalists battled with other Poles who were more focused on Roman Catholicism as a unifying factor. Rival fraternal groups emerged, such as the POLISH NATIONAL ALLIANCE (1880) and the POLISH ROMAN CATHOLIC UNION OF AMERICA (1873). Beyond the community, Poles protested against Irish and German domination of the American Catholic Church. One result was the growth of the independent church movement in the 1890s that led to the formation of the Polish National Catholic Church. Another consequence was the consecration of a Polish American Roman Catholic bishop, Bishop Paul Rhode of Chicago in 1908.

Like other immigrant groups, Polish Americans struggled over competing visions of the homeland. Poles in the United States often referred to their community as the "Fourth Partition." Many of their institutions worked for the liberation and reunification of Poland as well as for the well-being of the immigrant community. This was especially true of the large national fraternals such as the Polish National Alliance and the Polish Roman Catholic Union, as well as for the U.S. branch of the gymnastic and paramilitary group the Polish Falcons (1887). Polish women organized their own ethnic organizations, including the Polish Women's Alliance (1898), spearheaded by Stefania Chmielinska. All of these organizations aided the Polish independence movement by any means they could. In 1918 these efforts proved successful; Poland regained its independence as a result of negotiated settlements after World War I.

By the end of the nineteenth century, Polonia constituted the core of an almost institutionally complete ethnic community, with the parishes providing the base for much of this community development, along with institutions such as fraternal organizations, newspapers, and schools. Most of the large national fraternals located their headquarters near the intersection of Milwaukee and Ashland Avenues with Division Street. This neighborhood, home to the parishes of St. Stanislaus Kostka and Holy Trinity, quickly developed as the national capital of the American Polonia.

The major Polish newspapers also opened offices here, such as the DZIENNIK ZWIĄZKOWY (Daily Alliance), *Dziennik Chicagoski (Chicago Daily)*, *Naród Polski (The Polish Nation)*, and *Dziennik Zjednoczenia (Daily Union)*. Władysław Dyniewicz published the first Polish newspaper in Chicago, *Gazeta Polska (Polish Gazette)* in 1872. John Barzynski, brother of the pastor of St. Stanislaus Kostka Church, began publication of another Polish weekly, *Gazeta Polska Katolicka (Polish Catholic Gazette)* in 1874.

The parochial school provided another foundation for the creation and maintenance of the ethnic community. CATHOLIC SCHOOLS run by orders of Polish sisters such as the Felician Sisters, Sisters of the Holy Family of Nazareth, and others served Polonia. One Polish American order was founded in Chicago, the Franciscan Sisters of Blessed Kunegunda, by Josephine Dudzik (Sister Theresa) in 1894. These ethnic schools first taught classes exclusively in the Polish language, but quickly the archdiocese forced them to teach in both Polish and English. The main concern of the schools was the preservation of *Polskość* or Polishness among immigrant children. Another concern was to prepare the children for life in the United States. In addition to parochial grammar schools, Polish Chicago developed Catholic high schools run both as independent institutions and as part of parish structures. In 1890 the Resurrectionists opened St. Stanislaus College, the first secondary school opened by the congregation in the United States. In 1930 the school was renamed Weber High School. In 1952 the Resurrectionists established Gordon Technical High School. Polish parishes, such as St. Joseph in the Back of the Yards, also opened high schools.

The Catholic Church and the fraternals provided a layer of ethnically based SOCIAL SERVICE institutions. Polonia debuted its own HOSPITAL, St. Mary of Nazareth, in 1894 and established St. Joseph's Home for the Aged in 1898. St. Hedwig's ORPHANAGE opened in 1910. The Polish Catholic sisterhoods played a central function in these organizations. Polish Chicagoans created the Polish Welfare

A gathering in front of the headquarters of Kosciusko Guards, at Division and Noble Streets, 1890. Photographer: Unknown. Source: Chicago Historical Society.

Association (1922) to help Polish communities deal with juvenile delinquency and other social problems. Polish women, such as Stella Napieralska, performed important roles in social service institutions, such as Guardian Angel Day Nursery and Home for Working Women in Back of the Yards (1914). Polish Americans, in cooperation with Czech Catholics, opened St. Adalbert CEMETERY in Niles in 1872 and Resurrection Cemetery in JUSTICE, Illinois, in 1904. Thus Polish institutions provided for Polish Chicagoans from birth through death.

Chicago's Polonia also developed a significant class of small business owners. Milwaukee Avenue, Division Street, Archer Avenue, Ashland Avenue, Commercial Avenue, and West 47th Street provided some of the sites for this growing group of entrepreneurs throughout the late nineteenth and twentieth centuries. Many served a narrow ethnic clientele, but others reached beyond the ethnic community. In addition, a thriving Polish and East-European JEWISH business community developed in Polish neighborhoods. These businesses include the Goldblatt Brothers, Polk Brothers, and Meyer Brothers DEPARTMENT STORES. Along with the stores lining busy streets, a large group of Polish professionals, including doctors, lawyers, and journalists, served the immigrant community.

Polish Chicagoans also participated in the labor movement. Beginning with the 1904 strike, they took an active part in unionizing the stockyards. During the World War I era, John Kikulski, Alex Nielubowski, Stanley Rokosz, and Mary Janek led PACKINGHOUSE workers. Several Polish priests, especially the Reverend Louis Grudzinski, supported the labor movement and helped solidify Polish American support for UNIONIZATION. Poles also played important leadership roles in the 1919 steel STRIKE and in the CONGRESS OF INDUSTRIAL ORGANIZATIONS (CIO) drives of the 1930s and 1940s. Ed Sadlowski led a national reform movement of the United Steelworkers in the 1970s and 1980s.

Their experience in the labor movement and fraternal groups provided Polish Chicagoans with valuable organizational lessons which led to their involvement in neighborhood organizations. Polish institutions provided a solid base around which neighborhood associations could develop. Polish priests and lay people played crucial roles in their development. In SOUTH CHICAGO, Stephen Bubacz led the Russell Square Community Committee throughout its history (1938–1968). Father Edward Plawinski played a critical role in the BACK OF THE YARDS NEIGHBORHOOD COUNCIL (BYNC) in the 1940s. The Polish clergy of the Back of the Yards continued to play an important role in the BYNC well into the 1970s.

By World War I, the original core Polish neighborhoods had established a foundation for the expansion of the Polish community across the Northwest, Southwest, and Southeast Sides of the city. Polish Americans spread along Milwaukee Avenue northwest to HUMBOLDT PARK, LOGAN SQUARE, AVONDALE, JEFFERSON PARK, and eventually into the northwest suburbs. Poles moved out of Bridgeport and Back of the Yards into BRIGHTON PARK, GAGE PARK, WEST ELSDON, GARFIELD RIDGE, and the southwest suburbs. Poles in South Chicago moved south and east. By 1980 Hispanics and AFRICAN AMERICANS had largely replaced Poles in the older inner-city core neighborhoods. Many Polish Catholic parishes offered mass in Polish and Spanish, as well as in English. Icons of Our Lady of Guadalupe joined the Black Madonna of Częstochowa in churches across the city. Polish Chicagoans left old neighborhoods such as the Bush in South Chicago for newer settlements like Fair Elms on the EAST SIDE. They also moved beyond the city boundaries to NILES, PARK RIDGE, PALATINE, and NORTHBROOK. LANSING had the greatest percentage of Polish Americans in the area in 1980. In 1990, 65 percent of all Polish Americans in the Chicago area resided in the suburbs.

Polonia's move to the suburbs was not simply an example of upward mobility. Many suburbs were and are home to heavy industry and had long-established Polish American working-class communities. This movement does, however, reflect the pace of AMERICANIZATION. In the face of suburbanization, various organizations and leaders tried to maintain the older city neighborhoods and organized cultural institutions as community anchors. The Copernicus Center opened in the early 1980s near Milwaukee and Lawrence Avenues; and while the Polish Women's Alliance moved to Park Ridge and the Polish National Alliance moved its headquarters to the far North Side of the city, the Polish Roman Catholic Union and the Polish Museum remained in the original Polish settlement, and the Polish Highlanders Alliance built a new headquarters on Archer Avenue. Many of these associations are trying to assimilate the Solidarity immigrants into their organizational structures.

Chicago's Polonia has played a crucial role in the political, religious, educational, institutional, and cultural life of Chicago. Streets named Pulaski and Solidarity Drive are symbolic manifestations of the impact of Polish Americans. Although most Polish Americans are fully integrated into American society, Polonia remains a vital ethnic community because of the more than 150-year tradition of Polish immigration to Chicago.

Dominic A. Pacyga

See also: Church Architecture; Demography; Iron- and Steelworkers; Meatpacking; Multicentered Chicago; Polka; Racism, Ethnicity, and White Identity; West Town

Further reading: Pacyga, Dominic A. *Polish Immigrants and Industrial Chicago: Workers on the South Side, 1880–1922.* 1991. • Parot, Joseph. *Polish Catholics in Chicago.* 1981. • *Poles of Chicago, 1837–1937.* 1937.

Police.

Policing in the Nineteenth Century

Chicago elected its first constable in 1828, and COOK COUNTY its first sheriff in 1831, but these law enforcers worked part-time and did not patrol. Citizens victimized by criminals applied to a judge for a warrant, and the constable or sheriff "executed" the warrant, earning a fee. A night watch, of doubtful efficiency, was employed in 1839, to watch for fires, criminals, and drunks. A salaried city marshal was also authorized, to coordinate these disparate officials. Nine day police, added in 1853, managed traffic at depots and BRIDGES.

This decentralized, reactive police system was in keeping with traditional fears of despotic government and was well adapted to the concerns and sensibilities of merchants, professionals, and influential citizens. But disorder was more dangerous than a growing government presence. Commercial and industrial progress seemed increasingly hard to reconcile with rowdiness, drunkenness, or violence, while riots grew harder to control in a more sharply class-divided society.

The spark for establishing a centralized, bureaucratic, uniformed police came when the nativist American, or "Know-Nothing," Party won elections and raised SALOON license fees, precipitating the "LAGER BEER RIOT" of April 21, 1855, in which GERMAN and IRISH crowds fought the existing police and militia.

The city council quickly established the Chicago Police Department, organized into three precincts and commanded by Chief Cyrus P. Bradley. All of the first 80 recruits were native-born, and LIQUOR regulations were vigorously enforced.

Modeled on forces in London and New York, the new "preventive" police were salaried, full-time officials who patrolled day and night. Uniformed in 1858, they were highly visible representatives of public authority.

Police were soon arresting thousands of drunks, vagrants, and other "disorderly" people each year. Making one or two arrests each week, the average officer controlled much public "disorder" by warning offenders to move on. The mere sight of a police uniform was often sufficient to disperse beggars or kids playing in the street. Rarely debated, this policing affected many ordinary Chicagoans. It was not always welcome, especially in crowded neighborhoods with few opportunities for public recreation. Physical domination of the beat was essential in the face of challenges by rowdy young men and drunks. Police often made use of their clubs, their only weapons at first. Arrested people had to be pushed, dragged, even carried by wheelbarrow to the station house, sometimes while their friends attempted to "rescue" them. The patrol wagon, introduced in 1881, made arrests easier, but much violence remained. Strict legality was often ignored, and police settled fights on the street and disciplined youthful delinquents informally.

Police were ordered to regulate saloons and suppress VICE, but bribery and political interference discouraged enforcement, though police did restrict vice to specific areas and tried to impose outward order. Lurid corruption scandals ensued, though most patrolmen benefited little from graft.

During STRIKES and riots, beat officers were reassigned to large military formations, using clubs to drive off crowds. Police were employed to restore order on such notable occasions as the RAILROAD STRIKE OF 1877 and the HAYMARKET Affair (1886). Police proudly recalled Haymarket, regarding themselves as saviors of law and order, while many unionists condemned them as violent agents of BUSINESS interests.

Controlling crime and violence was but one among many police jobs. Police controlled traffic at BRIDGES, helped pedestrians cross downtown streets, and gave directions to strangers. They returned lost children, reported broken street lamps, and stopped runaway horses. Thousands of homeless people slept in station houses every year. Murder rates were low, and serious crime relatively rare. A detective unit was established in 1860, and a rogues' gallery in 1884. But dragnets, lengthy detentions of suspects without legal safeguards, and forced confessions were also employed.

Initially, the MAYOR and city council appointed officers. In 1861, control was placed in three commissioners, state appointed, later elected; the mayor and council regained control in 1875. The superintendent (as he was known after 1861) was often a weak leader. Despite centralized policies and practices, the captains who ran the precincts or districts were relatively independent of headquarters, owing their jobs to neighborhood politicians. Decentralization meant that police could respond to local concerns, but graft often determined which concerns got most attention.

Political connections were important to joining the force; formal requirements were few until 1895. After 1856, the department hired many foreign-born recruits, especially unskilled but English-speaking Irish immigrants. The first AFRICAN AMERICAN officer was appointed in 1872, but black police were assigned to duty in plain clothes only, mainly in largely black neighborhoods. Women entered the force in 1885 as matrons, caring for female prisoners. "Policewomen" were formally appointed beginning in 1913, to work with women and children. In 1895, Chicago adopted civil service procedures, and written tests became the basis for hiring and promotion. Standards for recruits rose, though policing remained political.

During a probationary period, police served an informal apprenticeship, but they received no formal training until 1910. Officers patrolled an average of 63 hours per week, much of it boring night patrol, and were on "reserve" at the station house, in case of emergency, for another 49 hours. Police, however, were better paid than most blue-collar workers and after 1861 could not be fired without cause. A police pension system began operation in 1887. Not surprisingly, cops held onto their jobs. Thrown together in a socially unique, sometimes vilified occupation, policemen developed a WORK CULTURE characterized by a strong sense of shared masculine identity.

Discipline, critics argued, was weak, and Captain Alexander Piper's famous 1904 investigation found police lounging on street corners, loafing in saloons, or simply absent from duty. Such complaints ignored patrolmen's grueling schedules and their thousands of arrests and services provided. Weak discipline was probably most evident in the inability of police administration to control excessive violence or graft.

Chicago's police were first to adopt a "signal service" in 1880, combining TELEGRAPH and TELEPHONE, to allow patrolmen on their beats to summon an ambulance or patrol wagon. Patrolmen were required to report hourly to ensure they were awake and on the job. A few "respectable" citizens were given keys to the signal system, which was also used as a field communications system for controlling crowds and riots. The practice of preventive patrol never matched its promise. Nonetheless, arrests declined, and some observers agreed that the streets—the patrolman's domain—were more orderly at the century's end.

Other law enforcement agencies had jurisdiction within metropolitan Chicago, including the county sheriff and the U.S. Secret

Policemen taking the sergeants exam, ca. 1904. Photographer: Unknown. Source: Chicago Historical Society.

Service, but far more important were suburban forces. In many outlying communities, law enforcement was still the province of constables, who provided limited, reactive policing. Some larger suburbs, such as the village of Hyde Park, the town of Cicero, and the city of Evanston, organized their own police forces. Many of these forces were poorly equipped or too small, one of the many reasons inducing some suburbs to seek annexation to Chicago in 1889. With the city's expansion, some 266 suburban officers were brought into the Chicago Police Department, which added other officers and built seven new station houses to cover the new territory.

1900–1960

The Chicago Police Department, by far the largest police agency in the region, grew from 3,314 employees in 1900 to 10,535 in 1960. There was little change in the pattern of arrests. In 1907, the average officer on a beat made 30 arrests per year, roughly half for disorderly conduct, drunkenness, or vagrancy. But bootlegging, scandal, and crime control received far more public attention.

A growing anti-vice movement pressured police into cracking down on the city's vice districts before World War I, but under Mayor William Hale Thompson (1915–1923, 1927–1931), Chicago was an "open town" for bootlegging and vice. Police were unable to overcome corruption and inefficiency to make arrests in gangland murder cases. A new administration from 1923 to 1927 attempted to suppress bootlegging, but the number of murders only rose.

Thompson's policies, along with fears of postwar "crime waves" and "auto bandits," led businesspeople and reformers to organize the Chicago Crime Commission and other anticrime groups, which were modestly effective in pressing for reforms. In 1929, the police department, with Northwestern University, established a crime laboratory, its most notable improvement in scientific policing since the adoption of fingerprinting in 1905. Formal police education, dating to establishment of the Police Academy in 1910, expanded from four weeks to three months of training in 1929.

The automobile brought changes in police practices as well. In 1906, a mounted squad was organized to control traffic, and by 1915 police used motorcycles to chase speeders. Police began issuing traffic tickets, rather than making arrests, in the mid-1910s. The department had begun to use cars for administrative purposes by 1908, and, in the 1920s, heavily armed detectives rode in squad cars. But communication was difficult until police began radio broadcasting in 1930. These changes, emphasizing the "war on crime," were responses to broad public concerns. They shifted attention from controversies surrounding the police and fostered the image of police as professional, scientific crime fighters. Nevertheless, foot patrol remained widespread.

Rank-and-file police groups organized to influence legislation and considered unionization during World War I. In 1944, the superintendent quashed a budding union. But police salaries remained relatively attractive, and schedules improved as reserve duty was reduced, then eliminated. By 1931 police worked a 48 hour week and enjoyed 15 days of vacation yearly. By 1960, their work week was 40 hours, though they still rotated shifts every month.

Police administration experts continued to criticize weak supervision and inadequate discipline. Widespread use of excessive force by detectives was exposed by a Presidential Commission in 1931, and violence also remained a crucial element in policing strikes. Public reaction to the "Memorial Day Massacre" of 10 steelworkers on May 30, 1937, and the growing power of industrial unions led to more restrained policies.

African Americans were better represented on the force than in other big cities and were slowly promoted, reaching the rank of captain—the first in the United States—in 1940. But black officers could not arrest white citizens, and black sergeants were never assigned to supervise white officers. Black citizens complained of arrests made for flimsy reasons, confinement of vice to black neighborhoods, and enforcement of de facto segregation on the beaches. The Race Riot of 1919 began when a white officer refused to arrest whites suspected in the fatal stoning of a black swimmer, and, after the riot broke out, police continued to fail to enforce the law evenhandedly.

After the 1890s, suburban communities increasingly incorporated to provide their own police and other services. By 1950, several larger suburbs had more than a hundred on their police payrolls. Most suburban police departments faced relatively few problems of crime and disorder and enjoyed substantial resources. In Cicero and some other suburbs, organized crime became well established, often controlling local police. As early as the 1920s, some criminals were escaping by car across municipal boundaries, and experts urged coordinating the hundreds of small agencies. Rudimentary metropolitan radio and teletype communication networks began to be developed in the 1930s. Constables still provided police services to many outlying areas. Other agencies with police roles included Cook County Sheriff's police, the state police, and the state militia.

National police agencies became more important in the 1920s. Prohibition brought Chicago a small number of federal agents, many corrupt, though federal agents managed to send gangster Al Capone to prison in 1932. New laws extended the federal government's criminal jurisdiction, and the FBI stepped into a highly visible enforcement role, tracking down John Dillinger in 1934 and providing local police with fingerprints, crime statistics, training, and the services of a crime lab modeled on Chicago's. From World War I on, federal agents spied on or suppressed antiwar dissidents, "enemy aliens," Communists, and other radicals.

1960–Present

Scandal over police involvement in a burglary ring prompted Mayor Richard J. Daley

Mounted police, July 1941. Photographer: John Vachon. Source: Library of Congress.

to appoint Orlando W. Wilson as superintendent of police in 1960. The nation's foremost expert on police administration, Wilson implemented an ambitious program of reorganization, emphasizing efficiency rather than ward politics. Wilson moved the superintendent's office from City Hall to Police Headquarters and closed police districts and redrew their boundaries without regard to politics. Hiring standards were raised, graft curbed, and discipline tightened, with a new Police Board overseeing it. Wilson updated the communications system, adopted computers and improved record-keeping, bought new squad cars, and eliminated most foot patrols. Police boasted of quicker response times to citizen calls. Police morale, and the public image of the police, rose.

Wilson also improved police relations with the black community. He recruited more African American officers, promoted black sergeants, and insisted on police restraint in racially charged conflicts. Wilson's retirement in 1967 came both as racial tensions intensified and disputes over policing grew more heated, and the example of his forceful leadership was not followed.

Mayor Daley signaled a change with his comment in April 1968 that police should "shoot to kill" rioters. Though Daley soon backpedaled, a new "get tough" tone was set. Its effects were evident when police confronted antiwar demonstrators during the DEMOCRATIC National Convention in August 1968. Rank-and-file officers were poorly deployed and supervised. Some attacked demonstrators, beat reporters, even clubbed passersby. Broadcast images of police clubbing demonstrators received favorable ratings from most Chicagoans, but police were defensive about extensive criticism.

On December 4, 1969, BLACK PANTHER PARTY leaders Fred Hampton and Mark Clark were shot and killed by officers working for the state's attorney. Though the police claimed they had been attacked by heavily armed Panthers, subsequent investigation showed that most bullets fired came from police weapons. Relatives of the two dead men eventually won a multimillion-dollar judgment against the city. For many African Americans, the incident symbolized prejudice and lack of restraint among the largely white police. The incident led to growing black voter disaffection with the Democratic MACHINE.

In 1976, the city was forced by court orders to agree to hire and promote more black officers. Growing black and Hispanic political clout was reflected in the appointment of African American Fred Rice as police superintendent in 1983 and in subsequent minority appointments. The number of bullets fired by police dropped considerably in the 1980s, reflecting better training and discipline. Disorderly conduct arrests, often a source of friction, declined from 52 percent of total arrests in 1982 to 23 percent in 1985.

Postwar courts increasingly restricted police discretion, restraining police search and interrogation practice. In 1985, a federal court ordered an end to police department "RED SQUAD" surveillance of radicals, minority organizations, and dissidents.

Federal affirmative-action rulings increased the presence of women in policing. As late as 1958, the force included only 85 women, many in stereotyped "policewoman" positions. Starting in 1974, women were appointed as full-fledged officers and assigned to regular patrol. By 1995, 18 percent of the department's sworn officers were female. Some 25 percent were black and 9 percent Hispanic, and a majority had at least some college education. Police were also unionized, something Mayor Daley had staved off. In 1981 the Fraternal Order of Police signed a contract with the city.

Growing use of computers in the late twentieth century meant that ordinary police officers were more tightly connected to citywide and indeed national institutions and networks of

Poster by Joseph Dusek for the DuPage County Centennial Police-Fireman Exhibition, Villa Park, June 4, 1939. Artist: Joseph Dusek. Source: Library of Congress.

information on drivers' licenses, outstanding warrants, and the like. Telephone communication made it increasingly likely that police would be summoned into citizens' homes.

But twentieth-century reforms generated unexpected problems. New technology and patrol practices, centralization, and elimination of political influences seemed to cut police off from city communities. Neighborhood patterns of crime and disorder were ignored, opening the door, many believed, to increasing crime and delinquency. As early as 1972, radio-dispatched patrol cars were unable to ensure rapid response to the growing volume of citizen calls for service, and radio motor patrol proved surprisingly problematic in curbing crime. Police began searching for methods to circumvent the burden of calls and to reach out to the city's neighborhoods. In 1992, the police department announced the Chicago Alternative Policing Strategy, aimed at bringing officers closer to citizens, returning decision-making to the neighborhood level, and encouraging initiative by beat officers. Community policing reversed decades of reformist thinking.

Postwar urban sprawl generated hundreds of suburban police departments, most small, but some, by the 1990s, with as many as 200 employees. Sheriff's police departments grew throughout the region, to patrol unincorporated areas and aid local police.

Federal law enforcement agencies, especially the FBI, have expanded their local role since the 1960s, notably against criminal organizations, drug traffickers, and corrupt public officials, including, among others, local police. The federal government has funded some local police activities, and federal, state, and local police have routinely cooperated in drug investigations and rounding up fugitives.

Christopher Thale

See also: Court System; Crime and Chicago's Image; Firefighting; Gambling; Homicide; Jails and Prisons; Political Culture; Prostitution; Racism, Ethnicity, and White Identity; Street Life

Further reading: Bopp, William J. *"O. W.": O. W. Wilson and the Search for a Police Profession.* 1977. • Haller, Mark. "Historical Roots of Police Behavior: Chicago, 1890–1925." *Law and Society Review* 2 (Winter 1976): 303–325. • Johnson, David R. *Policing the Urban Underworld: The Impact of Crime on the Development of the American Police, 1800–1887.* 1979.

Polish National Alliance. The Polish National Alliance (Związek Narodowy Polski) was simultaneously organized in Philadelphia and Chicago in 1880 by Polish exiles devoted to the twin goals of Polish independence and the assimilation of Poles into American society.

In contrast to the Polish Roman Catholic Union's religious goals grounded in Roman Catholic identity, the Polish National Alliance (PNA) argued that Poles everywhere had to unite into a single fraternal organization aimed toward the political liberation of the homeland. During World War I, the PNA was instrumental in raising more than five million dollars for war relief efforts in Poland. With the war's end, the PNA took an active role in Poland's newly restored independence.

During World War II, the PNA played a major role in the formation of the Polish American Congress. With more than 300,000 members at its peak after World War II, the PNA was the largest Polish American fraternal organization in the history of American Polonia. By the mid-1990s, the PNA's more than $300,000,000 in total assets supported thousands of Polish American scholarships, Polish studies programs, cultural endeavors, and social welfare projects for Poles across the United States. Throughout its history, the PNA has maintained its national headquarters in Chicago, where it administers a sizeable library collection of Polish Americana.

Joseph John Parot

See also: Americanization; Clubs: Fraternal Clubs; Fenianism

Further reading: Kruszka, Waclaw. *A History of Poles in America to 1908.* 4 vols. 1993–1999. This is an edited translation and new edition of Kruszka's *Historya Polska w Ameryce,* 13 vols, 1905–1908. • Parot, Joseph John. *Polish Catholics in Chicago, 1850–1920: A Religious History.* 1981. • Pienkos, Donald E. *PNA: A Centennial History of the Polish National Alliance of the United States of North America.* 1984.

Polish Roman Catholic Union of America. The Polish Roman Catholic Union of America (PRCU) is the oldest Polish fraternal organization in the United States. Founded in 1873 by the Reverend Vincent Barzynski and the Reverend Theodore Gieryk, it held its first convention in Chicago the following year, at Reverend Barzynski's St. Stanislaus Kostka Parish. Adopting as its motto "For God and Country," the group committed the PRCU to ethnic unity, mutual aid, insurance and death benefits, the care of "widows, widowers and orphans," and "absolute obedience to the bishops, and pastors anointed by them." Dominated by the clergy in its early years, the PRCU emphasized its Catholic character, especially in contrast to its more secular rival, the Polish National Alliance (PNA).

By the turn of the century, the PRCU, already 12,500 strong, had paid out more than one million dollars in death benefits. In the years that followed, in addition to providing war relief during both world wars, the PRCU dedicated itself to educational institutions, libraries, hospital work, home mortgage assistance, support for youth athletics and activities, cultural preservation projects, Polish and English language instruction, and its longstanding commitment to life insurance for Poles in Europe and America. Membership peaked in the mid-1950s, when the PRCU served more than 175,000 Polish Americans in some 1,075 lodges nationwide. At the close of the twentieth century it listed more than 300 lodges in the greater Chicago area and nearly three times that number in 23 states outside of Illinois.

Joseph John Parot

See also: Clubs: Fraternal Clubs; Mutual Benefit Societies; Roman Catholics

Further reading: Haiman, Miecislaus. *Zjednoczenie Polskie Rzymsko-Katolickie w Ameryce, 1873–1948.* 1948. • Parot, Joseph John. *Polish Catholics in Chicago, 1850–1920: A Religious History.* 1981.

Political Conventions. Chicago has been the nation's most popular political convention city, in part because of its geographic centrality. Between 1860 and 1996, Chicago hosted 14 Republican and 11 Democrat presidential nominating conventions, plus one notable Progressive Party assembly. Chicago's closest competitors for the most presidential conventions are Baltimore with 10, followed by Philadelphia's 9.

Chicago's first presidential nominating convention, the Republican National Convention of 1860, was held in the "Wigwam," a temporary two-story wooden structure. Last-minute backroom deals, plus a successful scheme to pack the galleries with holders of counterfeit tickets, brought unexpected victory to Abraham Lincoln.

Democrats convened for the first time in Chicago in 1864, when they nominated General George B. McClellan and passed an antiwar platform. Republicans returned to

Cross of Gold

"You shall not crucify mankind upon a cross of gold." With this indictment of the eastern establishment, William Jennings Bryan swayed the Democratic National Convention held in the Chicago Coliseum, July 1896. Bryan gained the nomination for president and secured a reform platform that called for a federal income tax and the minting of silver to stimulate the economy.

Chicago businessman and Illinois governor John Peter Altgeld made Bryan's victory possible. Angered over President Grover Cleveland's use of federal troops against the 1894 Pullman Strike, Altgeld challenged Cleveland's leadership of the Democratic Party. Altgeld authored the reform platform and prepared the revolt against the "gold standard" conservatives at the 1896 convention.

The Chicago convention marked a shift within the Democratic Party from the Northeast to the South and West. Chicago served as the financial and commercial hub of America's agricultural heartland, and Chicago reformers hoped to forge an alliance with western and southern agrarian reformers. The triumph of reform within the Democratic Party did not bring success at the polls. Bryan lost the presidential campaign, and Altgeld failed in his bid for reelection as governor of Illinois.

Bryan and Altgeld were colleagues of Chicago's William "Coin" Harvey, whose book *Coin's Financial School*, a fictional account of lectures on finance held at the Art Institute of Chicago, taught millions of Americans about the purported evils of the gold standard.

Bryan was an Illinois native and studied law at Chicago's Union College before moving to Nebraska, where he was elected to Congress in 1890.

Charles Postel

Illinois delegation parades for Adlai Stevenson, Democratic National Convention, 1952. Photographer: Unknown. Source: Chicago Historical Society.

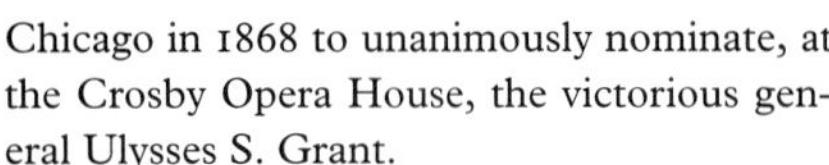

Chicago in 1868 to unanimously nominate, at the Crosby Opera House, the victorious general Ulysses S. Grant.

In 1880, Republicans convened in the Interstate Industrial Exposition Building on Michigan Avenue to nominate former speaker of the House of Representatives James A. Garfield, on the thirty-sixth ballot. Four years later, Chicago hosted its first double convention in the Interstate Industrial Exposition Building. Republicans nominated James G. Blaine, of Maine, secretary of state for the assassinated Garfield, on the fourth ballot. Democrats nominated New York governor Grover Cleveland, who became president. In 1888, Republicans met in the still-unfinished Civic Auditorium to nominate Senator Benjamin Harrison, of Indiana, on the eighth ballot. He lost the popular vote in the general election but beat President Cleveland in the Electoral College. In 1892, Democrats met in a temporary "Wigwam" in Lake Park to nominate Cleveland for a third time. He regained the presidency.

The 1896 Democratic convention, held in Chicago's first Coliseum on 63rd Street, was the most unpredictable of the nineteenth century, next to Lincoln's. William Jennings Bryan, just 36 years old, captured the hearts of delegates with his spellbinding "Cross of Gold" speech and won the nomination on the fifth ballot. He lost a dramatic election to business-oriented William McKinley.

In 1904, the Republicans gathered in the second Coliseum on South Wabash, to unanimously nominate President Theodore Roosevelt, who had assumed office after McKinley's assassination. In 1908, Republicans returned to the Coliseum to nominate Roosevelt's handpicked successor, William Howard Taft. Roosevelt challenged Taft in 1912, winning almost all the primaries, but was rebuffed by Republican leaders. Fearing violence from Roosevelt supporters, hundreds of Chicago police were on hand, and barbed wire was strung beneath the bunting of the podium. Roosevelt refused to drop out, and two months later the Progressive Party nominated him in the same building. New Jersey governor Woodrow Wilson won in November. In 1916, the Republicans returned to the Coliseum, again rejected Roosevelt, and nominated Supreme Court justice Charles Evans Hughes on the third ballot.

In 1920, the Republicans met again at the Coliseum. The convention was mired in a stalemate until a "senatorial cabal," meeting in "smoke-filled" rooms 408–10 of the Blackstone Hotel, selected Senator Warren G. Harding. The delegates ratified him on the tenth ballot.

Chicago hosted another double convention in 1932. First, Republicans glumly gathered in the new CHICAGO STADIUM during the depths of GREAT DEPRESSION to renominate President Herbert C. Hoover. Two weeks later, Democrats gathered in the same hall and selected Franklin D. Roosevelt over Al Smith on the fourth ballot. Roosevelt flew to Chicago to deliver the first-ever convention acceptance speech. In 1940 and 1944, Roosevelt was renominated for his third and fourth terms in the Stadium. Republicans challenged him in 1944 with New York governor Thomas E. Dewey, also nominated in the Stadium.

Republicans gathered in the Stockyards INTERNATIONAL AMPHITHEATRE in July 1952 to nominate General Dwight D. Eisenhower on the first ballot. The first national television audience was treated to a fistfight between delegates for Eisenhower and those for Robert Taft. Democrats convened in the same hall to nominate Illinois governor Adlai E. Stevenson II and returned four years later to give Stevenson a rematch with President Eisenhower. Republicans made their final appearance in Chicago in 1960, nominating Vice President Richard M. Nixon. After Chicago mayor Richard J. Daley's legendary role in swinging that year's close national election to John F. Kennedy, Republicans have declined to return to the city of their first presidential triumph.

The Democratic convention of 1968 was held at the Amphitheatre in the midst of the increasingly unpopular Vietnam War. When the party endorsed a prowar platform, violence between thousands of antiwar protestors and Chicago police broke out on Michigan Avenue in front of the Conrad Hilton Hotel. The events reached a national television and international audience and caused turmoil on the convention floor. The conflicts inside and out of the convention were contributing factors to Hubert Humphrey's narrow defeat in November to Richard M. Nixon.

A postcard of the Coliseum from the 1907 Republican National Convention. Between 1904 and 1920 the Coliseum hosted every Republican presidential nominating convention. Photographer: Unknown. Source: Chicago Historical Society.

Twenty-eight years passed before another presidential convention came to Chicago. Democrats renominated President William J. Clinton at the UNITED CENTER in 1996. While nominating and seconding speeches were but a sentence long at Chicago's first presidential nominating convention, they lasted all night 136 years later.

R. Craig Sautter

See also: Chicago Conspiracy Trial; Places of Assembly; Politics; Tourism and Conventions

Further reading: Congressional Quarterly. *National Party Conventions, 1831–1988.* 1991. • Sautter, R. Craig, and Edward M. Burke. *Inside the Wigwam: Chicago Presidential Conventions, 1860–1996.* 1996.

Political Culture. One stereotype of Chicago is probably true: people in the city are interested in POLITICS, and particularly in local politics. Where people in some other parts of the country might not even know who represents them in Congress, Chicagoans know not only who represents them, but why. They know which WARD formed his or her original political base and how particular ties within this base and beyond it served as a springboard to Congress. They know, in short, the details of how politics works in the city. Chicago voters also are famous for tolerating a certain amount of political corruption, in the nineteenth century and most of the twentieth. There is more to this than the city's legendary "MACHINE POLITICS." Sometimes, it seems corruption is tolerated for its sheer entertainment value, as in the "Greylord" judicial scandals of the 1980s, when the voters retained on the bench judges who were found to be letting lawyers pay for the right to hustle for clients in their courtrooms—in one case by actually stuffing wads of cash into the pocket of a coat on a well-placed coat rack.

This interest in the details of local politics may be a feature of American big-city politics generally. It was, after all, a Boston politician—the House Speaker Thomas P. "Tip" O'Neill—who famously explained that "all politics is local politics." The level of political engagement in New York City and San Francisco is also high. Yet in Chicago, it is widely felt that there is something special about the local political culture, a sentiment not confined to local residents. Outsiders have often marveled, chiefly at the skullduggery of the city's politics. "What kind of city is this?" asked an exasperated civil rights lawyer upon learning that the federal judge who refused to rule on whether Chicago's schools were segregated (which they were) was an old buddy of Mayor Richard J. Daley, placed on the federal bench because President John F. Kennedy probably owed the mayor his election. The idea that judicial qualifications involved friendship and politics more than legal acumen did not surprise Chicagoans.

The corruption of local politics has never been confined to the city itself. In the 1960s, DEMOCRATS were accused of manipulating electoral results in Chicago, but Republicans were suspected of doing the very same thing in the suburbs and downstate. In 1970, a University of Illinois political scientist, Daniel Elazar, was so perplexed by what he considered an outrageous tolerance for political corruption throughout Illinois that he developed an elaborate social theory to explain it, hinging on the various "migration streams" and political cultures of various parts of the state. Elazar's main point, however, was that corruption was not even remotely an "urban" phenomenon in Illinois. The "machine politics" that was so famously perfected in Chicago by Richard J. Daley, who was mayor from 1955 until his death in 1976, actually was a feature of politics throughout Illinois—including in the "downstate" areas whose residents prefer to see themselves as victims of Chicago's corruption.

For the last 25 years, urban historians have been chipping away at stereotypes about the "machines" that ruled many American big cities from the CIVIL WAR to WORLD WAR II. They have questioned the idea that cities were dominated by corrupt, financially profligate, and nonideological party organizations. In the old model, "machine politics" organized city politics in three ways: (1) it distributed PATRONAGE and other personalized services to individuals (called "divisible benefits" by political scientists), (2) it recognized the claims of diverse ethnic groups to the at least symbolic power of having their members slated for office on party tickets, and (3) it "humanized" urban bureaucracies by sending kindly "ward heelers" rather than inquisitorial welfare officials to "help" poor people, who in turn voted loyally for the party. Some versions of this older theory claimed that city dwellers, especially low-income immigrants and AFRICAN AMERICANS, had a "private-regarding" rather than "public-regarding" political ethos, and that this essentially moral failure prevented them from objecting to the corruption that affluent Anglo-Saxon "good government" types denounced as an affront to American democracy. In Chicago, where an organized political machine continued to exist much later than in comparable cities such as New York, some commentators have stressed the entertainment angle, describing local politics as a "spectator sport" in Chicago and citing the 1955 comment by the admittedly corrupt, but lovably candid, Alderman Mathias "Paddy" Bauler that "Chicago ain't ready for reform." In the reinterpretation of American big-city politics today, however, scholars argue that even the most flamboyant of the old-time bosses worked hard to keep taxes low and bond ratings high. Most historians of city politics now consider the idea that ward politicians were "welfare" providers to be little more than fantasy; they reject the old claim that ethnic coalitions were broadly inclusive; and they picture voters as generally rational and responsible in choosing their political leaders.

Indeed, surveying Chicago politics over the long term reveals a political history shaped, for the most part, by conflicts over substantive issues and by the representation of substantive interests. From Chicago's initial incorporation, as a town in 1833 and as a city in 1837, until the Civil War, the city's politics hinged on two efforts that would remain crucial even as other issues supplemented them later: building a physical infrastructure to make a rapidly growing city economically viable, on the one hand, and attracting outside investments in Chicago's development, on the other. The first goal required the city to build streets, bridges, sidewalks, schools, and the water works and sewer system. The second involved persuading the state and federal governments and private capitalists from the East to invest in the transportation links, especially railroad connections, that enabled Chicago to become the nation's primary market for corn, wheat, and lumber by the outbreak of the Civil War. Both efforts were the projects of a "booster" elite of eastern migrants, who had made very speculative investments in Chicago's real estate and therefore depended on the growth of the city's economy. Before the 1860s, these boosters dominated local politics. They served as mayors, in the city council, and on the independent boards that administered the water, sewer, and school systems. More of them were Democrats than Whigs, but the party distinction was unimportant in local politics, mainly because the boosters thought it was important to present a united front to the outside investors they were trying to attract.

The leading politician of the "booster" era was John Wentworth (known as "Long John" because of his height), who edited the *Chicago Democrat,* represented Chicago in Congress for six terms between 1843 and 1867, and served as mayor (for one-year terms) in 1857 and 1860. Almost alone among the city's political leaders at this time, Wentworth appealed to voters with a populistic, Jacksonian rhetoric attacking such "special privileges" of wealthy "monopolists" as the operation of state-chartered banks. Wentworth's opposition to the proslavery Southerners who increasingly dominated the national Democratic Party led him to join the Republican Party when it was formed in 1856.

The one truly explosive political issue in these years was liquor. As they would for the next few decades, battles over temperance legislation in the 1850s pitted much of the city's Yankee elite against large sectors of its immigrant working class (as early as 1850, 80 percent of the skilled and unskilled workers in Chicago had been born outside the U.S.). In 1855, the "Lager Beer Riot" resulted when anti-immigrant Know-Nothings won control of the city council and the mayoralty, hiked the liquor license fee from $50 to $300, and arrested tavern owners under an old but previously unenforced Sunday closing law. The North Side German community was particularly incensed and, after the riot and another city election, led the effort to get the license fee reduced to $100. Generally, however, city politics in this era did not involve broad social issues that mobilized the working-class electorate. From 1849 to 1854, city elections were nonpartisan contests with low voter turnout and little excitement. City government concentrated on building physical infrastructure, using privatized decision-making and financing procedures that minimized competition for resources and gave the politicians little patronage to distribute. These procedures allowed wealthier neighborhoods to get street projects they wanted without having to subsidize projects for poorer neighborhoods, where the streets were largely unpaved and the water and sewer facilities inadequate.

The outbreak of the Civil War in 1861 elicited overwhelming patriotic support for the Union cause in Chicago. Democrats and Republicans united in a Union Party until anger over the Emancipation Proclamation in 1863 helped the Democrats reorganize in opposition to some of the Lincoln administration's war policies. This opposition was fueled in the columns of the openly Copperhead *Chicago Times.* From the Civil War until 1932, Chicago had a two-party system, punctuated periodically by strong third-party showings.

The disaster of the Great Chicago Fire of 1871, and the fact that it was widely blamed on the cheap wooden buildings that enabled working-class families to afford homeownership in large numbers, prompted the organization of a Fireproof Reform Party led by Joseph Medill, the Republican editor of the *Chicago Tribune.* Medill and his party were dedicated to the passage of a fire limit ordinance that would ban wood construction in Chicago.

This effort failed, but the reformers were defeated in 1873 because of another disastrous policy: they renewed the temperance effort by enforcing Sunday closing of taverns. A proliquor People's Party, led by the North Side German Republican Anton Hesing (publisher of the *Illinois Staats-Zeitung*), won control of the city council and elected Harvey Colvin as mayor. Then, by manipulating the dates in the adoption of a new city charter, they managed to cancel the 1875 city election. Colvin's council allies were swept out of office in 1876, the

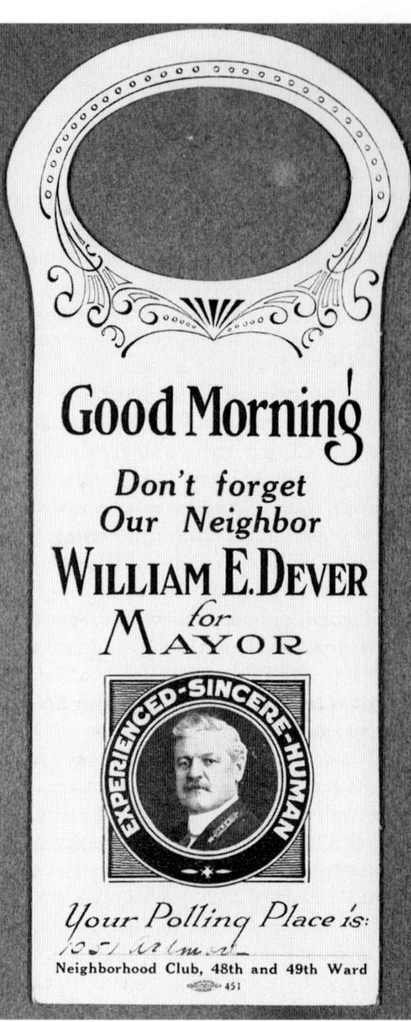

Doorknob flyer from William E. Dever's mayoral campaign, 1923. Source: Chicago Historical Society.

new council elected another mayor, and the rival administrations contested their legal legitimacy in court until yet another mayoral election was held. These shenanigans discredited the People's Party (despite the obvious entertainment value), but this time the regular politicians had learned their lesson. Liquor was removed from the agenda of Chicago politics. Democrats and Republicans both winked at liquor law violations to avoid alienating the Catholic, immigrant, working-class voters who viewed temperance crusades as insulting assaults on their cultural autonomy by Protestant elites. Not until the Al Capone era unleashed by national Prohibition would a mayor again try seriously to crack down on illegal liquor sales. Even in such extreme circumstances, the effort ended the political career of Mayor William Dever in 1927.

By the 1880s, meanwhile, the most important issues in city politics involved labor, and especially the role of the police during strikes. Trade union leaders and labor-oriented politicians first turned their attention to the police force after it was used to break the

Election flyer for mayoral candidate Carter H. Harrison, 1899. Source: Chicago Historical Society.

1867 general strike for the eight-hour day. City officials generally refused to use the police force to help employers to break strikes by disrupting picket lines or protecting strikebreakers, though there was one very spectacular exception to this generalization. From 1885 to 1889, police policy was shaped by the violently antilabor Inspector John Bonfield ("the club today saves the bullet tomorrow") and by a widespread fear of anarchism after the 1886 Haymarket Affair.

Union leaders and radicals in the city demonstrated their ability to mobilize working-class voters in the three-way race that launched the long mayoral tenure of its Democratic winner, Carter Harrison I. A popular figure known for his black felt slouch hat, galloping white horse, command of the languages spoken in many of the city's immigrant communities, and lack of interest in enforcing liquor and gambling laws, Harrison served four consecutive terms as mayor until 1887. Reelected to a fifth term in 1893, he hosted the World's Columbian Exposition before he was assassinated later that year. Four years later, his son Carter Harrison II was elected to serve the first of five mayoral terms of his own, 1897 to 1905 and 1911 to 1915. Harrison II added a "reformer" image to his father's repertoire of linguistic skill, tolerance of vice, and police neutrality during strikes, as the central issues of city politics shifted during the 1890s to the problem of corruption in the award of public utility franchises.

It was during the Harrison years that Chicago began to exhibit some of the characteristics of "machine politics" at the ward level, though not those of a citywide "machine." Republican "boss" William Lorimer built a base in the West Side Tenth Ward, led in the reorganization of the Cook County Republican Party into a network of precinct and ward clubs in 1893, and won election to Congress in 1894 and to the Senate in 1909—from which he was expelled in 1912 for bribing the state legislators who elected him. Among Democrats, the two Carter Harrisons enjoyed personal popularity, but their political bases comprised shifting coalitions of ward-based party leaders including the "Gray Wolves" of the city council, who capitalized on the private ownership of public utility companies by developing "boodling" schemes involving bribery or more elaborate forms of extortion.

Reformers responded to this corruption in 1896 by organizing the Municipal Voters League (MVL), dedicated to purging the boodlers from the council. In 1897 and 1899, candidates opposed by the MVL were defeated wholesale, though a few notorious boodlers survived, notably "Bathhouse John" Coughlin and Michael "Hinky Dink" Kenna of the First Ward (the downtown vice district) and Johnny Powers of the West Side Nineteenth (Powers is most often remembered today as the political nemesis of Jane Addams). The utility company issue came to a head as the "traction question" in 1906, when the council rejected municipal ownership of the streetcar system despite the fact that voters had elected Mayor Edward F. Dunne in 1905 in a campaign waged on the issue. Another referendum in 1907 endorsed a compromise that left the transit system in private hands in return for the service improvements that had made public ownership attractive in the first place. The significance of the mass transit issue was heightened by large annexations of suburban territory to Chicago in the 1880s and 1890s, which increased the population who depended on streetcars. These annexations also made it necessary to extend other city services. Suburbanites had voted to trade their political independence for the ability to enjoy Chicago's high-quality services, particularly its water and sewerage systems, in a politics that was the very opposite to urban-suburban relations today.

William Hale "Big Bill" Thompson, who was elected mayor three times between 1915 and 1931, symbolized the Roaring Twenties in Chicago. A clownish figure whose antics included a safari in search of tree-climbing fish, a political debate against a pair of caged rats, and a threat to punch the Prince of Wales in the nose if he ever dared to visit Chicago, Thompson was a "wet" Republican who counted Al Capone among his campaign contributors. He was attacked most vociferously, however, for his political overtures to the city's rapidly growing (and, before the New Deal, overwhelmingly Republican) African American community. Democrats actually hired a band to play "Bye, Bye, Blackbird" downtown in their 1927 campaign against him. Thompson was Chicago's last Republican mayor. His downfall did not result from either the racist attacks on him or his legendary toleration of organized crime. Like President Herbert Hoover, Thompson was a victim of the onset of the Great Depression, whose impact on Chicago's government was magnified by corruption. Decades of favoritism in the fixing of property assessments led the State Tax Commission to order the publication of Cook County's assessment rolls in 1928, revealing that, in 1927, property tax assessments ranged from a mere 1 percent of the actual value of real estate for some especially favored taxpayers to 105 percent of value at the other end. This was too outrageous even for Chicago, and especially for those taxpayers who were paying at the high end of the spectrum. The upshot was that the city of Chicago, Cook County, and the myriad of other "special taxing districts" that provided various city services (there were 27 overlapping governments in Chicago by 1933 and a whopping 419 in Cook County as a whole) received no property tax revenue from 1928 to 1930—the years in which the Depression began. With the city and other government bodies on the verge of default just as mass unemployment made relief measures urgent, Big Bill Thompson was forced into retirement.

In 1931, Anton Cermak built the modern Democratic machine. Beginning in 1933, the popularity of Franklin Roosevelt's New Deal, the movement of African American voters into the Democratic Party, and, later, the exodus of white middle-class voters to the suburbs destroyed the Republican Party as a viable force in Chicago. After Cermak died in 1933 (he was killed in Miami by a gunman aiming at FDR), Cook County Democratic chairman Patrick A. Nash and Sanitary District official Edward J. Kelly took control of the party. Kelly was elected mayor, and the Kelly-Nash machine maintained power in Chicago until 1947.

Using their control of the party, the machine was able to control the city, county, and other jurisdictions of the fragmented local government. The Kelly-Nash machine profited from federal money and patronage jobs in return for their ability to generate impressive electoral support for FDR. University of Chicago political scientist Harold Gosnell wrote a classic study of how this "machine" worked in 1937. In *Machine Politics: Chicago Model*, Gosnell located the heart of machine rule in the system of party governance based on elected ward committeemen. This system was created by a state primary law in 1910, but its legality was uncertain until 1935. Ward committeemen administer elections, choose candidates for backing by the organization in primaries, and supervise the work of precinct captains. This might sound decentralized (like having 419 independent government bodies), but the ward committee system was the basis for disciplined citywide (and countywide) Democratic machines when party leaders could control the access of the ward committeemen to patronage: jobs for their subordinates and policy-based favors to win business support (building permits, contract awards, favorable tax assessments). The ward committeeman system provided the organizational underpinning for the powerful machines built by Kelly and Nash (1933–1947) and Richard J. Daley (1955–1976). Daley introduced the further innovation of serving simultaneously as chairman of the Cook County Democratic Party and as mayor of Chicago.

The work of Democratic ward committeemen and the lack of Republican opposition guaranteed machine-endorsed candidates significant support in all elections, but the machine could not win elections by itself. Politicians still had to champion popular issues and policies to win electoral majorities, particularly in citywide elections. Party chairman Jacob Arvey's 1947 decision not to reslate Kelly for mayor was a clear illustration of the problem. Kelly had several liabilities. He alienated some ward leaders in factional struggles and lost favor with some voters through scandals, poor service provision, high taxes, and rampant organized crime. The crucial issue in 1947, however, was the fact that many white voters were angered by Kelly's support for desegregated PUBLIC HOUSING available to African Americans in all parts of the city. In 1946, hundreds of police battled hundreds of white demonstrators when a handful of African American families tried to move into the Airport Homes project, near MIDWAY AIRPORT. The project remained all-white, but Kelly pledged to continue to defend open public housing with force, a policy his successors, and particularly Richard J. Daley, abandoned. This retreat had had huge consequences, leading to the construction of the segregated high-rise towers that historian Arnold Hirsch has called Chicago's "second ghetto." By this time, moreover, divisive racial conflicts had become the main issue in Chicago's politics. Racially oriented politics became increasingly important through the Daley years, and climaxed in the 1983 election of Harold Washington, the city's first African American mayor.

Racial issues came to the fore in many American cities in the post–World War II era for obvious reasons. In-migration by African Americans (the massive "GREAT MIGRATION" between World War I and the 1960s) in addition to Hispanic and Asian American immigrant groups combined with out-migration by members of white ethnic groups ("white flight") to transform the DEMOGRAPHICS of many American cities, especially in the North. In Chicago for most of this era, the key racial issues involved conflicts between whites and blacks and revolved around the provision of three types of services: housing, education, and the police. Daley championed the interests of white voters on these issues in his long tenure as mayor. On housing and education, he risked the loss of federal funding to maintain segregated facilities. On the police, he refused to credit allegations of systematic RACISM and police brutality; after the 1968 riots that followed the assassination of Martin Luther King, Jr., he publicly proclaimed that police should "shoot to kill" all arsonists. Daley kept a tight control over African American ward politicians. In a system the black community called "plantation politics," he punished African American aldermen and ward committeemen who responded to the CIVIL RIGHTS concerns of their constituents in the 1960s, cutting off their patronage resources and replacing them with more pliable politicians.

The successes of the Daley regime were substantial. Like many other cities, Chicago experienced "white flight" from the 1950s to the 1970s, but a larger proportion of the white working-class and middle-class population remained in Chicago than in other comparable cities. This strengthened the local tax base and thereby underpinned the city's continued ability to offer high-quality services, making Daley's Chicago "the city that works." One reason many white residents stayed in Chicago was that they considered their interests protected at City Hall. Black voters supported Daley in his first election in 1955, in the primary in which he defeated the incumbent who had refused to protect blacks against white rioters in several housing project incidents. By the mid-1960s, however, African Americans had soured on Daley. Since he was unbeatable, black voters stayed away from the polls in large numbers. Daley's base increasingly consisted of white voters confident that Daley shared their cultural values and would protect their neighborhoods.

African American politicians found it very difficult to organize during the Daley years. The most powerful black politician in Chicago from 1942 until his death in 1970 was William L. Dawson, a ward committeeman and congressman who built a "submachine" in five SOUTH SIDE wards that delivered dependable Democratic majorities. After Dawson's death, however, Daley could not sustain "plantation politics." In 1972, Ralph Metcalfe, a loyal alderman in Dawson's organization who had won the congressional seat in 1970, became a hero in the black community when he launched a crusade against police brutality and survived Daley's attempts to destroy his career, though Metcalfe was not able to alter the system fundamentally.

Daley's death in 1976 changed the equation. While Daley had been mayor for 21 years, there were 6 different mayors in the next 13 years, culminating in the accession of Richard M. Daley in 1989. This political instability created opportunities that the African American community seized. Angered especially by the same old issues under Mayor Jane Byrne—white domination of housing, education, and police policies—the African American community organized a massive voter registration drive and, in a divisive three-way mayoral primary in 1983, elected Harold Washington over Byrne and Richard M. Daley. This caused an even more divisive general election, in which 79 percent of the city's white voters, most of whom were lifelong Democrats, voted for Republican

Council Wars

Within hours after Mayor Harold Washington had concluded his swearing-in speech in April 1983, one of the most dramatic moments in the city's history segued from thunderous applause and triumphant music at Navy Pier to the bitter realities of City Hall.

"Council Wars," which exacted havoc throughout most of the first term of Chicago's first AFRICAN AMERICAN mayor, pitted Mayor Washington against the "Vrdolyak 29," sobriquet for the all-white Chicago City Council's majority bloc, led by Alderman Edward "Fast Eddie" Vrdolyak of the Tenth Ward and Edward Burke of the Fourteenth.

Despite its reputation as a "boss-dominated" city, Chicago's governing structure is that of "strong council, weak mayor." The Vrdolyak 29 blocked the mayor's replacements of council committee chairs and appointments to the patronage-heavy PARK DISTRICT, CHICAGO TRANSIT AUTHORITY, Board of Education, City Colleges, and other key agencies.

Washington struck back by using the mayoral power of executive order to cut the city's payroll from an estimated 40,000 down to less than 30,000, erase the city deficit, balance the budget, and broaden freedom of information "as public policy." Chicago's bond rating leaped upward, enabling the mayor to push through a $100 million bond issue and the employment of Community Development Block Grants to resurface and repair five miles of city streets in each of the 50 wards. He also moved to improve housing for the poor, after-school and food pantry programs for the homeless, police-community relations, equity in Tax Increment Financing (TIF), and city economic PLANNING.

Council Wars ended in May 1986, when federal court-ordered special elections were completed in seven wards, remapped to reflect Chicago's black and Hispanic population growths. Washington supporters on the city council increased from 21 to 25—a tie with the 25 left from the Vrdolyak 29. With the mayor's tie-breaking vote activated, the council, on May 9, 1986, approved 25 mayoral appointments to 14 boards and departments.

Vernon Jarrett

Poster for Earl B. Dickerson, candidate to Congress, 1938. Artist: Unknown. Source: Chicago Historical Society.

Bernard Epton. White politicians organized the city council to oppose Mayor Washington, and the city's government was paralyzed for the next two years by what a local comic dubbed "Council Wars." A court-ordered remapping of ward boundaries increased the number of black and Hispanic aldermen, which broke the deadlock in 1986, but Washington died after his reelection the following year.

The centrality of racial politics to Washington's election and administration lies well within the main channels of Chicago's political history. But Washington's inability to organize party politics—partly because he refused to accept traditional levels of corruption—stands as an aberration. Whether he could have reshaped the city's political culture will never be known. His death derailed a movement that relied more on his charisma than on party loyalties. No mayor had faced the obstacles he encountered, with some aldermen trying to undermine his legitimacy by refusing even to refer to him by the title "mayor." Unable to win the support of most white Democrats beyond the lakefront, Washington relied on intense loyalty among black voters, support from Latino activists previously excluded from power, and a clean administration that won admiration from white liberals but made it impossible to maintain a well-oiled machine. His commitment to administrative reforms restored the city's financial health and eventually won grudging respect from the business community but weakened the party organization by thinning the ranks of patronage workers. He also left no political heir. The confusion that ensued after his death eventually brought Richard M. Daley into the mayor's office in 1989, the beginning of a new era in Chicago politics.

Robin Einhorn

See also: Good Government Movements; Journalism; Public Works, Federal Funding for

Further reading: For a foundational statement in the tradition of outsider outrage at the toleration of corruption in Chicago, see William T. Stead, *If Christ Came to Chicago* (1894). For the Illinois analysis, see Daniel J. Elazar, *Cities of the Prairie: The Metropolitan Frontier and American Politics* (1970). Civil rights lawyer Paul Zuber is quoted in Len O'Connor, *Clout: Mayor Daley and His City* (1975), 186.

For the skepticism about older interpretations of "machine politics," see Jon C. Teaford, *The Unheralded Triumph: City Government in America, 1870–1900* (1984); Eric H. Monkkonen, *America Becomes Urban: The Development of U.S. Cities and Towns, 1780–1980* (1988); Terrence J. McDonald, *The Parameters of Urban Fiscal Policy: Socioeconomic Change and Political Culture in San Francisco, 1860–1906* (1986); Stephen P. Erie, *Rainbow's End: Irish Americans and the Dilemmas of Machine Politics, 1840–1985* (1988); Ira Katznelson, *City Trenches: Urban Politics and the Patterning of Class in the United States* (1981); Terrence J. McDonald, "The Burdens of Urban History: The Theory of the State in Recent American Social History," *Studies in American Political Development* 3 (1989): 3–29; and M. Craig Brown and Charles N. Halaby, "Machine Politics in America, 1870–1945," *Journal of Interdisciplinary History* 17 (1984): 589–612. The older view was articulated especially influentially in Robert K. Merton, "The Latent Functions of the Machine," in *Social Theory and Social Structure: Toward a Codification of Theory and Research* (1949), and in Edward Banfield and James Q. Wilson, *City Politics* (1963), which makes the claim about "public-regarding" and "private-regarding" political cultures. See also Samuel P. Hays, "The Politics of Municipal Reform in the Progressive Era," *Pacific Northwest Quarterly* 55 (1964): 157–169, and, for Chicago specifically, John M. Allswang, *A House for All Peoples: Ethnic Politics in Chicago, 1890–1936* (1971).

For politics in the "booster era," see Robin L. Einhorn, *Property Rules: Political Economy in Chicago, 1833–1872* (1991); Rima Lunin Schultz, "The Businessman's Role in Western Settlement: The Entrepreneurial Frontier, Chicago, 1833–1872" (Ph.D. diss., Boston University, 1985); Don E. Fehrenbacher, *Chicago Giant: A Biography of "Long John" Wentworth* (1957); and Ann Durkin Keating, *Building Chicago: Suburban Developers and the Creation of a Divided Metropolis* (1988). General readers should not be put off by the title of Louis P. Cain, *Sanitation Strategy for a Lakefront Metropolis: The Case of Chicago* (1978), which tells an important and interesting story. Although many of its interpretations are now dated, Bessie Louise Pierce, *A History of Chicago,* 3 vols. (1937–1957), is a classic and useful work. For an influential recent gloss on the economy in this era, see William Cronon, *Nature's Metropolis: Chicago and the Great West* (1991).

On the politics unleashed by the Great Chicago Fire, see Karen Sawislak, *Smoldering City: Chicagoans and the Great Fire, 1871–1874* (1995). For a more detailed study, there is Christine Meisner Rosen, *The Limits of Power: Great Fires and the Process of City Growth in America* (1986). The People's Party is the main subject of John J. Flinn, *History of the Chicago Police from the Settlement of the Community to the Present Time* (1887; reprint, 1973). On the politics of liquor in later decades, see John R. Schmidt, "William E. Dever: A Chicago Political Fable," in Paul M. Green and Melvin G. Holli, eds., *The Mayors: The Chicago Tradition* (1987), and, in the same volume, John D. Buenker, "Edward F. Dunne: The Limits of Municipal Reform," and Douglas Bukowski, "Big Bill Thompson: The 'Model' Politician." Dunne, a one-term mayor who served from 1905 to 1907, tried to enforce higher license fees and Sunday closing but was unsuccessful. Thompson tried it in 1915, though by 1927 he was claiming to be "as wet as the Atlantic Ocean."

For the late nineteenth century, Richard Schneirov, *Labor and Urban Politics: Class Conflict and the Origin of Modern Liberalism in Chicago, 1864–1897* (1998), represents a quantum leap over earlier interpretations, though it reinforces some of the key points in Chester McArthur Destler, *American Radicalism, 1865–1901* (1946), and Ray Ginger, *Altgeld's America: The Lincoln Ideal Versus Changing Realities* (1958). For the Harrison years, see Edward R. Kantorowitz, "Carter H. Harrison II: The Politics of Balance," in Green and Holli, *The Mayors;* and Joel Arthur Tarr, *A Study in Boss Politics: William Lorimer of Chicago* (1971). For a dated but very entertaining gloss, see Lloyd Wendt and Herman Kogan, *Lords of the Levee: The Story of Bathhouse John and Hinky Dink* (1943). For the "traction question," see Paul Barrett, *The Automobile and Urban Transit: The Formation of Public Policy in Chicago, 1900–1930* (1983), and, for another crucial utility story, Harold L. Platt, *The Electric City: Energy and the Growth of the Chicago Area, 1880–1930* (1991). For the reformers, see Kenneth Finegold, *Experts and Politicians: Reform Challenges to Machine Politics in New York, Cleveland, and Chicago* (1995).

Inquiries into the formation of the Democratic machine in the Depression crisis must start with Harold F. Gosnell, *Machine Politics: Chicago Model* (1937), and Charles E. Merriam, Spencer D. Parratt, and Albert Lepawsky, *The Government of the Metropolitan Region of Chicago* (1933), supplemented by Roger Biles, *Big City Boss in Depression and War: Mayor Edward J. Kelly of Chicago* (1984). For the tax crisis, see Ester R. Fuchs, *Mayors and Money: Fiscal Policy in New York and Chicago* (1992), and David T. Beito, *Taxpayers in Revolt: Tax Resistance during the Great Depression* (1989). For electoral realignments, see Dianne M. Pinderhughes, *Race and Ethnicity in Chicago Politics: A Reexamination of Pluralist Theory* (1987). On the Daley machine, the best journalistic accounts are Mike Royko, *Boss: Richard J. Daley of Chicago* (1971), and Len O'Connor, *Clout: Mayor Daley and His City* (1975); and, more recently, Adam Cohen and Elizabeth Taylor, *American Pharaoh: Mayor Richard J. Daley, His Battle for Chicago and the Nation* (2000). Among many contemporary studies by political scientists, two are especially revealing on organizational questions: Milton L. Rakove, *Don't Make No Waves, Don't Back No Losers: An Insider's Analysis of the Daley Machine* (1975), and Thomas M. Guterbock, *Machine Politics in Transition: Party and Community in Chicago* (1980).

The literature on the Great Migration and African American politics is very substantial. Readers might start with James R. Grossman, *Land of Hope: Chicago, Black Southerners, and the Great Migration* (1989); Nicholas Lemann, *The Promised Land: The Great Black Migration and How It Changed America* (1991); and the classic and recently reprinted St. Clair Drake and Horace R. Cayton, *Black Metropolis: A Study of Negro Life in a Northern City* (1945). For the housing issue, see Arnold R. Hirsch, *Making the Second Ghetto: Race and Housing in Chicago, 1940–1960* (1983), and Hirsch, "Martin H. Kennelly: The Mugwump and the Machine," in Green and Holli, *The Mayors.* For African American voting and political organizing, see, especially, Paul Kleppner, *Chicago Divided: The Making of a Black Mayor* (1992); William J. Grimshaw, *Bitter Fruit: Black Politics and the Chicago Machine, 1931–1991* (1992); Pinderhughes, *Race and Ethnicity in Chicago Politics;* and, for a very good journalistic account, Gary Rivlin, *Fire on the Prairie: Chicago's Harold Washington and the Politics of Race* (1992).

Politics. Chicago politics is a national cliché, evoking images of a one-party system, dominated by a boss-controlled DEMOCRATIC political MACHINE whose crafty politicians dangle PATRONAGE before competing ethnic and racial groups in return for votes. As early as the 1871 municipal election following the tragic fire, the defeated People's Union accused the victorious "Fireproof" ticket of exhorting its supporters to "vote early and often." Indeed, no political, ethnic, class, or gender group in the city or its suburbs has escaped the lure of patronage politics or the stain of corruption. When reform REPUBLICANS captured control of the Common Council in the late 1890s, they behaved exactly as had the ousted Democrats. Republicans replaced all Democratic appointees with their own followers, a practice the Republicans had decried when done by Democrats. Democratic Alderman Johnny Powers did not find this strange: "To the victors belong the spoils," explained Powers.

Chicago women entered the fray upon obtaining municipal SUFFRAGE by Illinois law in 1913. In 1915, Mayor William Hale Thompson (1915–1923, 1927–1931) resisted the calls of a delegation of civic-minded women led by SETTLEMENT HOUSE head Mary McDowell to name an experienced woman to the new position of commissioner of public welfare. Thompson indeed appointed a woman, but rather than one with a background of work in public welfare, he chose a loyal Republican party worker, Louise Osborn Rowe. Within a year, Rowe was forced to resign after being charged with operating a kickback scheme in the welfare department.

No mayor has ever been convicted for illegal activities, but several have been enmeshed in dubious campaign practices and corruption scandals. Republican mayoral candidate Fred Busse (1907–1911) was accused of distributing jobs, money, and coal from his coal company in return for votes in the 1907 election. Thompson was persuaded not to run for reelection in 1923 amid a slew of scandals, including in the public SCHOOLS and charges of blatant political manipulation in the slating of nominees for circuit court judges. Mayor Ed Kelly (1933–1947) had been indicted for participating in payoff, bribery, and kickback schemes while serving as chief engineer of the Metropolitan Sanitary District. The charges against him were subsequently dropped. But even MAYORS who were personally honest have tolerated corruption. Mayor Martin Kennelly (1947–1955) cleaned up the school system and modernized city administrative practices but failed to attack political influence peddling in the POLICE department or to support his own appointee to head the Civil Service Commission when he attempted to control job patronage.

The policy of honest graft articulated in New York by Tammany Hall's George Washington

Marion Drake (*left*), Progressive Party candidate for alderman, 1914, having tea with Florence Catlin (*sitting*), an unidentified woman, and Margaret Dobyne. Drake ran against the notorious First Ward politician "Bathhouse" John Coughlin. Photographer: Unknown. Source: Chicago Historical Society.

Plunkitt—"I seen my opportunities and I took 'em"—seems to have been taken to heart in latter-day Chicago politics. Prominent aldermen, high-ranking municipal officials, even a mayoral press secretary have been accused, and in some cases convicted, of fixing city contracts, demanding payoffs and extorting bribes in return for jobs, and generally profiting personally from their positions of municipal authority.

This picture of Chicago politics is entertaining, and it is undoubtedly a part of the story. Yet the history of Chicago politics is more than a succession of colorful figures, corruption and scandals, ethnic TURF battles, and political failures. Chicago politics is also the story of urban growth in the United States. And it is the story of the struggle for democratic governance that took place within a federal legal system and political structure, the growth of the American political party system, the westward movement of white European settlers, shifting economic priorities, the dynamics of class and gender, and a population that grew and changed its contours as new immigrant and migrant groups poured into the city.

Chicago municipal politics began after European Americans defeated the last resistance of Native Americans in the BLACK HAWK WAR of 1832. The following year, Chicago received its first incorporation charter from the state legislature. Through the CIVIL WAR, as Chicago's white settlers struggled to establish a city on the western edge of the "frontier," Chicago politics was a contest between private interests and public needs. Money was needed to build an urban INFRASTRUCTURE of STREETS and sidewalks, sewer and WATER systems, SCHOOLS and shops. Capital investment had to be found to support new commercial activities to create jobs and guarantee economic growth. But Chicago had only a property TAX with which to finance such activities, and its residents were not eager to pay from their own pockets. Individuals exploited scarce public funds, as when in 1837 it was discovered that the COOK COUNTY School Commissioner had loaned the school fund, gathered through sale of federally donated land, to private REAL-ESTATE speculators who defaulted on the loans, leaving the city without sufficient funds to operate the schools. Chicago residents who wanted federal government aid for infrastructure projects were thwarted by others who preferred private development. This contest in Chicago reflected a national conflict between the political parties over whether there was a public need for federal government to foster development that should supersede private interests. Until the Civil War era, private interests largely prevailed.

An uneasy relationship to the state of Illinois also characterized early Chicago politics. U.S. cities receive powers of government from their states. State law regulates the relationship between cities and counties and the relationship of a city to other municipal authorities such as school boards, and it confers and limits a city's powers to tax and to finance municipal development. Historically, there has been a power struggle within the state. In 1839, the state legislature abolished the office of high constable for Chicago and did not inform the city for two months. Some Chicagoans sarcastically replied that they hoped to be informed more quickly should the legislature decide "to remove Chicago from the shore of Lake Michigan."

By the 1850s, growing social divisions in the city gradually inserted ethnic rivalry into Chicago politics. In 1855, older residents tried to regulate the leisure activities of the newer communities of GERMAN and IRISH immigrants by having the municipal government raise the cost of liquor licenses and require SUNDAY CLOSING of SALOONS. The resulting LAGER BEER RIOT forced the government to rescind its efforts, and henceforth the city's immigrant groups demanded a voice in municipal politics previously dominated by a small group of men who had governed the city in their interests.

The growing polarization within the Democratic and Republican parties along class and ethnic lines, along with an ongoing struggle between the city and the state over how much power Chicago should have to govern itself, characterized Chicago politics from the 1870s to the 1930s. These two elements fed upon each other as the city grew into an industrial metropolis and outpaced the legal restraints imposed by state law. The new state constitution of 1870 cancelled single-city CHARTERS, and in 1872 the legislature passed a Cities and Villages Act to apply to all incorporated areas with a population of 2,000 or more. This law suited the state's small homogeneous towns more than an industrial metropolis. From the early twentieth century, Chicago attempted to secure relief through a legislative grant of HOME RULE powers. But every such effort was thwarted by the historical distrust between city and state and distrust of Chicagoans for one another. Fearing Chicago's growing influence in the state, the legislature carefully restricted the city's home rule powers, refused to allow consolidation of the city and Cook County governments, and from 1900 until the 1940s limited Chicago's representation in the legislature by refusing to fulfill its legal obligation to redistrict the state.

Home rule efforts also foundered because they revived the ethnic and class conflict that had sparked political unrest in Chicago before the Civil War and that resurfaced when a group of prominent men attempted to control all RELIEF and rebuilding in the city after the FIRE OF 1871. Chicago workers accused these men of trying to control municipal government. These events, along with the street riots during the great RAILROAD STRIKE OF 1877, the fears engendered by the HAYMARKET massacre of 1886, and the pressures of massive immigration, divided Chicagoans even more along class and ethnic lines, and they perceived home rule as a question of "who ruled at home." Chicago politics then became a struggle among various groups in the city to control municipal government for their advantage.

The political struggle taking place in Chicago from the 1870s until the 1930s reflected the struggle within the United States to redefine the nature and purposes of democratic government. Rural Midwesterners, AFRICAN AMERICANS from the South, and increasing numbers of MEXICANS joined hundreds of thousands of European immigrants coming to Chicago seeking economic, political, and social opportunity. The poet Carl Sandburg celebrated Chicago's growth into the "City of the Big Shoulders" and "Hog Butcher for the World, Tool Maker, Stacker of Wheat, Player with Railroads and the Nation's Freight Handler." Others saw Chicago as the symbol of everything wrong with industrial capitalism. Englishman William Stead declared that "IF CHRIST CAME TO CHICAGO" he would weep at what he saw, and to Upton Sinclair, Chicago was a "JUNGLE" of human misery and exploitation.

Worker exploitation, extremes of wealth and poverty, and the corruption of both businessmen and politicians all existed in Chicago because neither federal nor local governments had the power to confront the worst aspects of economic and social injustices that were multiplying in the nation's cities. In the absence of such power, Chicago's political parties functioned as machines that promised to deliver favors in return for votes. Often these favors went to the immigrant poor who needed help finding a job or feeding the family, but these favors also went to businessmen who received potentially lucrative contracts from the city council. The parties were also machines for enriching the politicians, as in the 1890s when the notorious aldermanic ring of "GRAY WOLVES" sold municipal contracts and franchises to build street railways, haul garbage, or lay gas mains to the highest bidders.

Public outrage over such actions, as well as the exposés by writers such as Stead and Sinclair, produced a "progressive" reform movement in Chicago, but there was never any agreement about the desired ends of such reform. Business and professional men, supported by the Republican Party, stressed that all municipal reform should bring expertise and fiscal efficiency into government. They unsuccessfully supported the home rule charter of 1907, opposed municipal ownership and control of public utilities, sought business control of the public schools, and wanted to exploit the economic possibilities of the lakefront. They demanded an end to patronage politics, the election of professional experts rather than party politicians to public office, and a strong-mayor system that would weaken the power of the city council. The city's ethnic and immigrant groups, generally supported by the Democratic Party, opposed many of these ideas, arguing that they were designed to deliver city government into the hands of middle-class businessmen. Chicago's laborers, for example, sought municipal ownership as a way to control public resources. Ethnic voters supported a strong, ward-based city council as more democratic than a strong-mayor system. Unions opposed businessmen's ideas for the schools because they wanted school decisions kept closer to the people, but they also feared that business control of the school board would diminish the power the labor unions already wielded in school management.

Thousands of Chicago women worked through partisan political women's organizations, voluntary civic groups such as the Woman's City Club, and working women's organizations such as the Women's Trade Union League for progressive reforms to make the municipal government more responsive to the everyday needs of Chicago residents. These women called for putting public need ahead of private or even group interests. They demanded that the city provide more affordable housing, give teachers a greater voice in school decisions, provide a cleaner and more healthful urban environment—by building public beaches, preserving the lakefront for recreation, and instituting municipal ownership of garbage collection, for example—and pass new ordinances for fire prevention.

The political parties became the means for determining the outcome of the struggle over these issues, but not until the 1930s did the Democratic Party assume control of the city. Workingmen's parties and the Socialist Party attracted workers in the 1880s and 1890s. A small Labor Party ran candidates in the municipal elections of 1919. Progressive-minded men and women split from the regular Republicans to join the Progressive Party in 1912. Moreover, factional rivalry divided each party, and every municipal election was first a contest over who would control each party and then a contest among the parties to determine who would run the city. But the Democratic Party undercut all attempts to build a workers' party through patronage, promises to govern the city to the benefit of immigrants and the working class, and an alliance with the Chicago Federation of Labor. At the same time, the Republican Party became increasingly the party of the middle class and business and professional men. The city's African American residents, whose men were guaranteed the franchise after ratification of the Fifteenth Amendment in 1870, bucked this trend. They joined the party of Lincoln and secured election to a small number of countywide and state offices, elected their first alderman in 1915, and sent representatives to Congress on the Republican ticket.

Chicago women did not fit neatly into Chicago party politics. Neither Democrats nor Republicans made any serious overtures to securing the party loyalty of women, who, despite gaining municipal suffrage in 1913, remained largely excluded from Chicago politics. The parties refused to nominate women for municipal offices and male voters largely refused to vote for any woman who stood as candidate. Chicago women practiced party politics, but they were much more likely than men in the decades immediately following woman suffrage to vote for the candidate rather than the

Daley's Chicago

An Irish Catholic native of Chicago's Bridgeport neighborhood, Richard J. Daley attended parochial elementary and secondary schools and, after attending night classes for many years, received a law degree from DePaul University. He was elected a state representative in 1936 and a state senator in 1938; from 1941 to 1946, he served as senate minority leader. Following an unsuccessful run for Cook County sheriff in 1946, Daley returned to Springfield in 1949 as Governor Adlai Stevenson's state director of revenue. In 1950 he was elected Cook County clerk and in 1953 chairman of the Cook County Democratic Party. In 1955 Daley ousted incumbent mayor Martin Kennelly in a bitterly contested Democratic primary, then beat Republican Robert Merriam in the general election. He secured reelection five times, the last in 1975.

Mayor Daley enjoyed great success, particularly in his early years, in reshaping Chicago's landscape. He presided over an unprecedented building boom that created a spectacular downtown skyline, completed the city's expressway network, enlarged Chicago-O'Hare International Airport, and constructed the University of Illinois at Chicago–Chicago Circle. His attention to prompt and efficient service delivery made Chicago famous as "the city that works," and, by the 1970s, when the nation's metropolises were experiencing financial crises, his success at keeping Chicago solvent earned him a reputation as a fiscal genius. Based in part on his legendary machinations on behalf of John F. Kennedy in the 1960 presidential election, Daley became a powerful force in the national Democratic Party and a leading spokesman for urban interests in the 1960s and 1970s.

Despite Daley's continued electoral triumphs and many achievements, his forceful leadership often produced heated controversy. His autocratic manner was more efficient than democratic. The brutal suppression of dissent at the 1968 Democratic National Convention tarnished the city's image, as did his infamous "shoot-to-kill" order shortly after the rioting following the assassination of Martin Luther King, Jr. As Chicago's nonwhite population increased dramatically, Daley enjoyed little success mitigating the escalating racial tensions and aligned himself with conservative whites against civil rights groups. He resisted residential desegregation, refused to implement affirmative action procedures in the city's police department, defended the public schools' racially exclusionary policies, and used urban renewal funds to erect massive public housing projects that kept black Chicagoans within existing ghettos. Residents of white as well as black neighborhoods questioned Daley's decision to protect the city against suburban decentralization by revitalizing the Loop and North Michigan Avenue. His death and the subsequent dissolution of the Democratic machine unleashed forces of change long held in check, resulting in the election of Chicago's first black mayor, Harold Washington, in 1983.

Roger Biles

Ralph Metcalfe: Champion Sprinter and Free-Thinking Politician

After excelling as a student and a sprinter at Chicago's Tilden Technical High School and Marquette University (in Milwaukee, Wisconsin), Ralph H. Metcalfe competed in the 1932 and 1936 Olympics, held in Los Angeles and Berlin, respectively. In 1932, Metcalfe won the bronze medal in the 200-meter dash and took the silver in the 100-meter dash, losing to Eddie Tolan by a mere two inches. In 1936, Metcalfe again finished second in the 100-meter dash, with Jesse Owens winning the gold. Metcalfe teamed with Owens to win a gold in the 400-meter relay that year, helping to set a world record.

Following his athletic achievements, Metcalfe became the track coach and a political science instructor at Xavier University in New Orleans. He returned to Chicago and, in 1952, became a Democratic committeeman for the Third Ward; Metcalfe was elected alderman in 1955 and was reelected three times. In 1970, Metcalfe won a seat in the Ninety-second U.S. Congress, succeeding his mentor, the late William Dawson. Metcalfe began his career as a Daley loyalist but later broke with the mayor, becoming a strong and independent voice for his mostly African American constituency who felt ignored by the workings of the Daley machine. Metcalfe was elected to four terms in Congress and served until his death in October 1978.

Daniel Greene

SMASH TAMMANY!

DEFEAT

KELLY - NASH

MACHINE

ATTEND Shotwell Hall

1442 East 55th Street

Tuesday, 8:15 P.M. October 30, 1934

SPEAKERS

C. WAYLAND BROOKS

Congressman-at-Large

DAVID L. SHILLINGLAW

Board of Appeals

JAMES A. KEARNS

County Treasurer

LOUIS NETTELHORST

County Commissioner

EMMET BYRNE

Municipal Judge

WM. E. HELANDER

Municipal Judge

JOHN LEONARD EAST

Republican Committeeman, Fifth Ward

Republican poster, 1934 general election. Source: Chicago Historical Society.

party and especially to vote for any woman running for municipal office. Women also failed to control any important appointed municipal offices. When Mayor Thompson's commissioner of public welfare was forced to resign in 1916, the post remained vacant until the mayoral administration of William Dever (1923–1927). This was a particularly galling political defeat for women who had prized the creation of this office to address the problems of the city's neediest people. No woman was elected to the city council until 1971, when Marylou Hedlund and Anna Langford secured seats, and Jane Byrne (1979–1983) is the only woman ever elected mayor.

The ascendancy of the Democratic Party was not secured until Anton Cermak built a broad coalition of ethnic and working-class voters that secured his election to mayor in 1931. The Republican Party had meanwhile self-destructed, as progressive and liberal Republicans grew disgusted with the party's support of three-time mayor William Hale Thompson, whom they regarded as a practitioner of blatant ethnic politics. His campaigns of 1915, 1919, and 1927 included crude ethnic baiting and a willingness to switch sides on any issue when it suited his purpose. Thompson's 1931 renomination for mayor by party leaders was the last straw for Republican luminaries such as Charles Merriam, Julius Rosenwald, Jane Addams, and Louise DeKoven Bowen. They, and other liberal Republicans, threw their support to Cermak, whose ethnic and anti-Prohibition credentials also recaptured working-class and ethnic voters who had drifted into the Thompson camp when he championed ethnic interests and opposed Prohibition. This attraction to Thompson and the Democratic Party's support for labor issues and anti-Prohibition stance had helped guarantee that a Labor Party never took hold. The Democratic Kelly-Nash machine of the 1930s finished Cermak's work. It brought Chicago unions securely into its orbit and encouraged the city's African American voters to abandon a Republican Party that more and more was a party of the white middle and upper classes. No Republican has been elected mayor since 1931, and few Republicans have even made it into the city council.

The New Deal of the 1930s and the Great Society of the 1960s gave the Democratic Party access to new funds and programs for housing, slum clearance, urban renewal, and education, through which to dispense patronage and maintain control of the city. Mayor Richard J. Daley (1955–1976) also kept the city and party financially sound by exploiting the state's refusal earlier in the century to consolidate the city and county governments or to give the city more control over municipal services such as the public schools. Cook County, for example, remained responsible for providing and funding many social services and maintaining the only public hospitals so that the city has never had to bear their financial burden. Although the mayor appointed the Board of Education, the school system was independent of the municipal government and its funding kept separate from the municipal budget. This structure meant that the mayor's office could simultaneously exert influence on the schools and disavow any political responsibility for managing or funding the system. Mayor Harold Washington (1983–1987) used it to claim he had no responsibility for trying to settle the month-long teachers' strike that pushed back the opening of the 1987 school year by four weeks.

Mayor Daley and the Democrats also controlled Chicago politics by exploiting growing racial and class antagonisms. From the 1940s, growing African American and Hispanic populations competed for jobs, housing, and schools. Middle-class whites fled to the suburbs and the Democrats retained the support of ethnic, working-class whites by allowing de facto social and economic segregation in neighborhoods, housing, jobs, and schools. The selection of loyal black politicians for municipal posts that might provide jobs but offered little power kept African American voters loyal to the Democratic Party well into the 1970s. To make Chicago the "city that works," Daley courted the business community through contracts on new public works projects—much as the city council had done earlier in the century. He structured favorable real-estate and taxation arrangements and an urban renewal program that benefited the middle class and businessmen more than the urban poor.

As Chicago moved toward the end of the twentieth century, the brief surge of African American power embodied in Harold Washington's two elections ebbed, and Richard M. Daley was elected mayor. Chicago politics changed under the second Mayor Daley. He has maintained Harold Washington's initiatives in making Chicago politics and governance more inclusive as to race and gender and has fine-tuned the first Mayor Daley's idea of making the city's economic development its first priority. Yet, the exposés of sweetheart deals and contracts doled out to friends and supporters of the Democratic Party suggest that patronage politics is enough of a way of life in Chicago that it will never die.

Maureen A. Flanagan

See also: Environmental Politics; Governing the Metropolis; Political Culture; Public Works, Federal Funding for; State Politics; Ward System

Further reading: Biles, Roger. *Richard J. Daley: Politics, Race, and the Governing of Chicago.* 1995. • Einhorn, Robin. *Property Rules: Political Economy in Chicago, 1833–1872.* 1991 • Flanagan, Maureen A. *Seeing with Their Hearts: Chicago Women and the Vision of the Good City, 1871–1933.* 2002.

Politics and the Press. Chicago's first newspapers were firmly tied to the political parties of the 1830s, and for more than a century they continued to serve not simply as forums for political debate but as an inextricable part of the political process. "Long John" Wentworth's rise from editor of the *Chicago Democrat* (Chicago's first newspaper) to political powerhouse was atypical, however; more commonly newspapers were launched by politicians to support their aspirations or harass their opponents.

No faction could hope to be taken seriously without its own newspaper. Wentworth's office provided his paper with a steady stream of news, as well as patronage and political influence. Even the creation of well-financed newspaper firms such as the one resulting from the 1858 merger of the *Democratic Press* and the Chicago Tribune did not signal an era of political independence. The *Tribune*'s proprietors were every bit as committed to politics as traditional partisan editors such as *Staats-Zeitung* publisher and Republican boss Anton Hesing, and they played a key role in launching and giving shape to the national Republican Party.

It took decades for market forces to drive personal organs from the field. Well after the heyday of the partisan press had passed, dailies such as the *Republican* (est. 1895) still hearkened back to an earlier model of partisan journalism. The city's dominant newspapers were major political actors in their own right. The *Tribune*'s and *American*'s fervent support for their owners' political agendas is well known, but at the turn of the century independent papers such as the *Chicago Daily News* helped bankroll the Mugwump opposition.

They released staffers and funds to reform-oriented organizations such as the Municipal Voters League, which enjoyed the support of every major newspaper until beleaguered streetcar magnate Charles Yerkes bought the *Inter Ocean* to counter the flood of MVL-generated articles.

Newspapers were tied to political factions by sentiment, ownership, and mutual interest. Facing almost universal press opposition in 1891, Carter Harrison bought the moribund *Chicago Times* to provide DEMOCRATS (and himself) with a newspaper voice. Republicans were served by several newspapers, ranging from the *Inter Ocean* ("Republican in everything, Independent in nothing") to the *Tribune,* which while firmly Republican helped to drive corrupt Republican boss William Lorimer from the U.S. Senate. Even after civil service laws and other reforms brought an end to lucrative government PRINTING and patronage jobs, publishers continued to enjoy mutually beneficial relations with favored politicians. The *Tribune* and other newspapers received favorable property tax treatment and long-term leases of public land, city assistance in permitting newsstands on street corners (and barring those of competing papers), and other advantages.

By the 1940s the number of dailies had fallen sharply, and most newspapers sought larger audiences. But Chicago papers remained highly politicized, as the "Battle of the Colonels" suggested. While Col. Robert McCormick's *Tribune* warred against the NEW DEAL and U.S. entry into WORLD WAR II, Col. William Knox's *Daily News* was an equally fervent advocate of intervention to stop Hitler. While the *Daily News* and *Times* accused the *Tribune* of conveying German propaganda, the *Tribune* warned of the dangers of a dictatorship taking root in the United States. Marshall Field III launched the *Chicago Sun* in 1941 in order to break the *Tribune*'s hold as the city's only English-language morning daily. In the months leading up to the launch, supporters of Roosevelt's policies blanketed the city with buttons reading "Chicago Needs a Morning Newspaper" and handbills depicting a swastika atop the Tribune Tower.

Both the English- and foreign-language press gave voice to political leaders and to their constituencies, not as neutral forums for reporting news and opinion nor as political actors in their own right, but rather as facilitators for the intersecting political, ethnic, and class interests which most Chicago dailies continued to serve well past the conclusion of the Second World War. Many newspapers served as a forum for readers to debate political and social issues and forge community identities. Much of the commentary in labor papers such as the *Arbeiter-Zeitung* was contributed by readers involved in the myriad of community organizations that supported the paper. While CHICAGO DEFENDER publisher Robert Abbott was a staunch Republican, commentary in his paper ranged from Marxism to McCormick Republicanism. Such eclecticism was less likely in the foreign-language press, where larger immigrant communities were often served by competing newspapers, each tied to distinct networks of cultural, mutual aid, and political organizations.

Thus, Polish socialists, union locals, and other supporters owned shares in the *Dziennik Ludowy* (People's Daily), published from 1906 until 1925, and sent delegates to annual meetings to elect the editor and set policy. Readers not only owned the newspaper and provided its operating capital, they also sent in the reports of Polish American activities, working conditions, and strikes that filled much of the paper's pages. Competing Polish-language dailies were published by the MUTUAL BENEFIT SOCIETIES, the POLISH ROMAN CATHOLIC UNION, and the POLISH NATIONAL ALLIANCE.

Similar arrangements prevailed in most of Chicago's immigrant communities. Reader-shareholders removed several editors of the *Chicagoer Arbeiter-Zeitung* over editorial policies and relied on the newspaper and its staff to weld diverse community institutions into a coherent political movement. Government authorities recognized the paper's central political role in the aftermath of the HAYMARKET Affair when they raided the *Arbeiter-Zeitung*'s offices and ultimately hanged its editor and business manager. Chicago's many foreign-language newspapers were sites of heated political contestation, helping both to mold political perspectives and to mobilize and represent their communities' views in the larger polity.

The English-language community press had more modest aims, generally focused on securing the provision of city services. In the suburbs, community weeklies provided the only coverage of local government available to most readers, but they generally espoused political independence.

Today, the Chicago newspaper scene is dominated by English-language newspapers published by large corporations with no institutional or organic ties to political parties or other social forces. But this disengagement is a recent phenomenon, the result of professionalization and commercialization which have been underway for decades but which became entrenched only in the 1960s with industry consolidation and the replacement of individual proprietors with corporate executives more interested in profit margins than in political influence.

Jon Bekken

See also: African Americans; Chicago Sun-Times; Good Government Movements; Poles; Political Culture

Further reading: Bekken, Jon. "Working-Class Newspapers, Community and Consciousness in Chicago, 1880–1930." Ph.D. diss., University of Illinois. 1992. • Nord, David Paul. *Newspapers and New Politics: Midwestern Municipal Reform, 1870–1900.* 1981. • Schneider, James C. *Should America Go to War? The Debate over Foreign Policy in Chicago, 1939–1941.* 1989.

Politics, State. *See* State Politics

Polka. Polka music, which embodies both specific dances and cultural contexts, is the common secular music of Chicago's European ethnic communities. Because of its complex ethnic history and the nationwide presence of several Chicago ethnic groups, Chicago's role as a center for polka has been exceptionally significant throughout the twentieth century. Polka distinguishes the soundscape of Chicago and the suburbs with both local practices and extensive exchange, thereby allowing ethnic communities to use music to identify their own ethnic boundaries and to cross these to join other groups in the performance of ethnicity.

The history of polka in Chicago has unfolded in three distinctive phases: the 1880s until WORLD WAR I; the period between the World Wars; and the post–WORLD WAR II era. European immigrants and the confluence of ethnic musical styles in the first phase underwent extensive consolidation during the second, when Chicago became a center for publishing and recording ethnic music and for building large DANCE HALLS (e.g., the Trianon and ARAGON ballrooms). The CZECH American firm Vitak and Elsnic became the leading ETHNIC MUSIC publisher in North America during this phase but did so by diversifying its catalog for the entire ethnic spectrum. POLISH American musicians dominated the third phase, with the distinctive "Chicago style" and the growing centralization of national polka institutions in the city. At various points, the music has drawn upon extensive patterns of exchange among musicians from different ethnic groups in Chicago and the Midwest.

"Chicago style" polka (known also by such names as "dyno" or "honky" style) has a distinctive sound and performance practice. Clarinet, trumpet, and the button-box accordion are especially evident in the CHICAGO SOUND, and extensive improvisation—playing by ear rather than from arrangements—separates the performance practice of Chicago bands from those of other polka centers. Chicago polka musicians further specify their style by singing in ethnic languages, even with mixed texts. Polish American musicians shaped the core of Chicago style, notably Eddie Zima, Władziu ("Li'l Wally") Jagiello, Marion Lush, and Eddie Blazonczyk. By moving the International Polka Association to Chicago in 1968 and generating competitions, festivals, and conventions, Chicagoans contributed substantially to the growth and revival of the most widespread ethnic popular music in North America in the 1990s.

Philip V. Bohlman

See also: Music Publishing; Record Publishing

Further reading: Greene, Victor. *A Passion for Polka: Old-Time Ethnic Music in America.* 1992. • Keil, Charles, Angeliki V. Keil, and Dick Blau. *Polka Happiness.* 1992. • Spottswood, Richard. *Ethnic Music on Records: A Discography of Ethnic Recordings Produced in the United States.* 7 vols. 1990.

Pollution. *See* Air Quality

Polonia. The term "Polonia" originates from medieval Latin and came into common parlance during the second wave of POLISH immigration to the United States after 1945. It can refer either to a specific Polish community in America or to the entire community of Polish Americans. Since the mid-nineteenth century, Chicago's Polonia has been centered on the city's Northwest Side.

Wallace Best

See also: Back of the Yards; Black Belt; Hammond, IN; South Side

Further reading: Pacyga, Dominic A. "Polish America in Transition: Social Change and the Chicago Polonia, 1945–1980." *Polish American Studies* (Spring 1987). • Parot, Joseph John. *Polish Catholics in Chicago, 1850–1920: A Religious History.* 1981. • Zglenicki, Leon. *Poles of Chicago, 1837–1937: A History of One Century of Polish Contribution to the City of Chicago.* 1937.

Population. *See* Demography

Port Barrington, IL, McHenry County, 38 miles NW of the Loop. A VACATION SPOT developed along the Fox RIVER south of Island Lake in 1925, where residents enjoyed fishing and water sports almost from the backdoors of their cottages. Voting to incorporate as the village of Fox River Valley Gardens in 1969 to more easily provide municipal services, the community slowly grew to 788 by 2000. In 2002 the village adopted the name Port Barrington.

Craig L. Pfannkuche

See also: Government, Suburban; McHenry County

Further reading: *McHenry County in the Twentieth Century, 1968–1994.* McHenry County Historical Society. 1994.

Portage. Until the nineteenth century, water TRANSPORTATION provided the smoothest and often the fastest paths through North America. Connections between WATER routes, therefore, held special significance and importance. These connections often involved portages—the carrying of boats and equipment between navigable waters. In this region, portages often connected waterways which were part of the GREAT LAKES SYSTEM with those of the Mississippi River system.

Portages were made at various points between the DES PLAINES and CHICAGO RIVERS as well as between the CALUMET and Kankakee Rivers. One such portage over this continental divide was shown to French explorers Père Marquette and Louis Jolliet in 1673 on their return trip from the Mississippi Valley to Green Bay. This portage lay southwest of Chicago and involved the short and unprepossessing stream (now called the Chicago River) which drained swampland near the southwest shore of LAKE MICHIGAN. It was the portage to which this stream gave access that first focused human attention and motivated development in the Chicago area.

After the retreat of the last glacier from the basin of Lake Michigan, a large lake formed between the retreating ice and the moraines (depositional ridges) that marked the farthest reach of the glaciers. This lake eventually drained down to the current extent of Lake Michigan. However, the area around Lake Michigan was filled with bodies of clay deposited by the much larger glacial lake (Lake Chicago). These prevented water from sinking deeply into the ground and created a boggy, swampy landscape with many residual lakes and sloughs in the Chicago area.

One such wetland that early settlers called "Mud Lake" lay more or less across the low drainage divide that usually separated waters flowing east toward Lake Michigan from those that flowed southwest toward the Mississippi Valley. This wetland stretched roughly six miles from near what is now Damen Avenue to Harlem Avenue and formed the critical link between the Chicago River and the Des Plaines River to the west. Sometimes, in very wet weather, the waters of the Des Plaines mingled with those of the Chicago River and no portage was required. Most of the time, however, it was necessary for early travelers to pull out their canoes and carry them around this swampy area over the divide to deeper water.

This relatively short portage sparked the imagination of Louis Jolliet who, after passing through this route, exclaimed that it would take a canal across "only a few leagues of prairie" to link the Great Lakes and Mississippi Valley and create a stupendous inland water route through the heart of the continent. In 1803 the federal government built FORT DEARBORN at the mouth of the Chicago River to guard this portage route. Today the western end of the old portage is marked by the Chicago Portage National Historic Site, which commemorates the singular importance of this ancient passage.

David M. Solzman

See also: Chicago in the Middle Ground; Ecosystem Evolution; Landscape

Further reading: Cronon, William. *Nature's Metropolis: Chicago and the Great West.* 1991. • Miller, Donald. *City of the Century: The Epic of Chicago and the Making of America.* 1996. • Solzman, David M. *The Chicago River: An Illustrated History and Guide to the River and Its Waterways.* 1998.

Portage, IN, Porter County, 31 miles SE of the Loop. Before the State of Indiana created Portage Township in March 1836, the area then called Twenty Mile Prairie (denoting its distance from MICHIGAN CITY) had been visited by a succession of NATIVE AMERICAN tribes and, subsequently, travelers using a stagecoach path linking Detroit and FORT DEARBORN. Portage's first business establishment appears to have been a disreputable halfway house known as Carley's Tavern. Then came squatters, including Samuel P. Robbins and Jacob Wolf, who later amassed large farmlands. After the Michigan Central and the Baltimore & Ohio companies laid RAILROAD tracks across Portage in the mid-nineteenth century, the small villages of McCool, Crisman, and Garyton began to emerge. Portage residents supplied milk, livestock, produce, and sand to Chicago buyers. The area maintained its rural flavor for nearly a century, even after an INTERURBAN streetcar line linked residents to GARY, HAMMOND, EAST CHICAGO, CROWN POINT, and VALPARAISO. During world wars and other boom periods farmers could supplement their incomes by working at nearby steel mills such as the U.S. Steel Corporation's Gary Works.

During the 1950s many LAKE COUNTY urban dwellers, anxious to leave behind problems of pollution, crime, and racial tension, moved to Portage. Other newcomers in search of mill jobs from Kentucky, southern Illinois, and southern Indiana liked Portage's rural ambience and took advantage of inexpensive plots of land and trailer courts. In 1959 National Steel opened a mill along Portage's lakefront, and plans were afoot to construct a deep-water port nearby. Fear of ANNEXATION by Valparaiso or possibly even Gary led to incorporation in 1959. Progrowth land developers and CHAMBER OF COMMERCE officials persuaded voters to change Portage's status from town to city in 1968. The census of 1970 revealed that Portage's population had jumped from 11,822 to 19,127 in a decade despite drainage problems in the generally clay-based new SUBDIVISIONS, haphazard ZONING regulations, no clearly delineated downtown, and inadequate north-south thoroughfares.

Portage had 33,496 residents in 2000, including a significant MEXICAN American population. During the last third of the twentieth century Portage, unlike most northwest

Indiana cities, had a healthy two-party political competition. Three of Portage's first four mayors were DEMOCRATS, including Arthur Olson, John Williams, and Sammie Maletta, who defeated three-term REPUBLICAN mayor Robert Goin in 1987 and controlled city hall throughout the 1990s.

Throughout its short urban history, Portage has struggled for an identity. A 1961 promotional brochure bragged about Portage as a "City of Destiny" combining "Country Style Living with City Advantages." More recently, boosters have employed the slogan "Portage Pride" when citing the city's user-friendly hiking and bicycle trails, parks and recreational facilities, youth sports programs, jamborees, Elvis Fantasy Fests, and excellent school system. In 1997 *Times* reporter Joyce Russell dubbed Portage the "City on the Edge," a reference not only to its potential for self-sufficiency but to its nearness to LAKE MICHIGAN, the INDIANA DUNES National Lakeshore, BURNS HARBOR, and steel mills that still employ more residents than any other industry.

James B. Lane

See also: Governing the Metropolis; Iron and Steel; Mobile Homes

Further reading: "A History of Portage, Indiana." *Steel Shavings* 20 (1991).

Portage Park, Community Area 15, 9 miles NW of the Loop. Portage Park has long-standing connections to water. During wet weather, early Indian inhabitants could paddle their canoes from the CHICAGO RIVER to the DES PLAINES on a minor PORTAGE along present-day Irving Park Road. They were reported to have built a village on the top of an elevation west of Cicero and Irving Park Avenues. Another ridge two miles west near Narragansett formed the natural watershed between the Mississippi and Great Lakes drainage system.

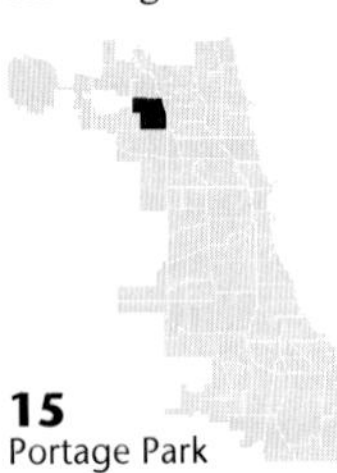

Following an 1816 TREATY, the Indians relinquished their rights to the land. E. B. Sutherland set up a tavern in 1841 along the North West Plank Road. By 1845 a post office was established and the following year Chester Dickinson bought the inn and job as postmaster. The inn's central location in JEFFERSON TOWNSHIP made it a popular stopping-off place for locals and it served as a temporary town hall. The township became part of the city of Chicago in an 1889 ANNEXATION.

Farming in the area proved to be difficult, as the land remained marshy, and ditchdigging was the only way to maintain dry property. Residential properties sprang up mostly in the northern and eastern sections. In 1912 neighbors formed the Portage PARK DISTRICT, and the following year the park district board of commissioners condemned 40 acres on the northeast corner of Irving Park Road and Central Avenue for the purpose of developing a park.

Initially the commissioners tried to raise money through a property tax. When residents objected that the tax was inequitable and that it might lead to corruption and graft, the assessment was invalidated in court. It was soon discovered, however, that the tax was an unnecessary measure, since park development was progressing without it. A portion of the park officially opened in midsummer 1916, and the Portage Park Citizen's Celebration Association formed to organize park events.

Visitors to the park that summer enjoyed a cool swim in a small sand-bottomed lagoon. In the coming years the park became a popular gathering place as other recreational facilities were added. In addition to the SWIMMING lagoon, TENNIS courts and BASEBALL fields were added, and in 1922 the fieldhouse was completed. A spectacular Fourth of July festival was held, complete with parade and athletic exhibitions. Attendance reached an estimated 40,000 persons, who came from numerous Chicago neighborhoods. In 1934 Portage Park was merged into the Chicago Park District.

With improved TRANSPORTATION and the inducement of the beautiful park, developers began building homes and urban dwellers flocked to the community. By 1940, its population had risen to 66,357.

Poor drainage that had created numerous problems of flooding over the years was finally corrected in the 1950s through the construction of an extensive drainage system. Late in the decade and early in the 1960s improved PUBLIC TRANSPORTATION and the Northwest (Kennedy) EXPRESSWAY connected residents to downtown Chicago. In the same period residents prevailed in their opposition to the proposed Crosstown Expressway.

Over the years activities remained centered on the park. A gymnasium was added. In 1959 the old pond was replaced by an Olympic-sized concrete pool. The swimming events of the Pan American Games were held there in the year that it opened, and the American Olympic team trials in 1972.

By 1990 the population had decreased to 56,513 and consisted mainly of residents of POLISH, ITALIAN, IRISH, and GERMAN descent. The main shopping center of the area was concentrated around "SIX CORNERS" (the intersection of Irving Park Boulevard, Milwaukee, and Cicero). The center of social and athletic events remained at the park, which had expanded to 36 acres and added eight tennis courts, an athletic field, a gymnasium with an indoor pool, and basketball courts by 1989. By 2000 population had rebounded to 65,340.

Marilyn Elizabeth Perry

See also: Creation of Chicago Sports; Flood Control and Drainage; Shopping Districts and Malls

Further reading: Clipping files. Chicago Historical Society, Chicago, IL; and the Portage-Cragin Branch of the Chicago Public Library, Chicago, IL. • Derx, Jacob J. G. "Portage Park: Yesterday and Today." *Portage Park Bulletin,* July 4, 1922. • Ryan, David Joseph. "The Development of Portage Park from the Earliest Period to the 1920s." Senior History Seminar, Northwestern University. May 24, 1974.

Porter, IN, Porter County, 34 miles SE of the Loop. In 1841, settlers of Fish Lake Township on LAKE MICHIGAN successfully changed the name to Porter Township, from which the town of Porter later took its name. Industry followed the construction of RAILROADS through the area. A number of brickyards were active in the late nineteenth century. By the end of the twentieth century, some residents worked at the Bethlehem Steel plant. Porter also features natural scenery as part of the INDIANA DUNES State Park and National Lakeshore.

Erik Gellman

See also: Economic Geography; Iron and Steel; Quarrying, Stonecutting, and Brickmaking

Portuguese. The first Portuguese immigrants to settle permanently in Illinois were probably Presbyterian converts from the Madeira Islands. A SCOTTISH pastor shepherded the Madeirans to the relative safety of Illinois's Morgan County after they were forced into exile in 1846. Few Portuguese settled in Chicago, however, before the Iberian nation's 1974 revolution. Between 1899 and 1910, only 166 immigrants of Portuguese origin reported Illinois as their final destination. By 1940, only 47 COOK COUNTY residents reported Portuguese ancestry in the U.S. census, a very small number when compared to the thousands who claimed Portuguese descent in maritime New England, New Jersey, California, and Hawaii.

Little is known about the Portuguese presence in Chicago before 1974. The government of Portugal sent an official contingent to the 1893 WORLD'S COLUMBIAN EXPOSITION to oversee an award-winning wine exhibit in the horticultural pavilion. Some Portuguese Jews fled their Iberian homeland for the United States in the 1940s to escape the danger fascism posed to the European continent, but only a few made the Chicago area their home. Only with the 1974 downfall of the right-wing regime instituted by Antonio Salazar in 1932 and maintained by his successor Marcelo Caetano did the majority of Portuguese citizens enjoy substantial freedom of movement within and away from Portugal. The somewhat modest influx of Portuguese into Chicago after 1974 consisted mainly of professionals, small business owners, and some laborers. These migrants have come from the Portuguese mainland as well as the Madeira and Azores Islands.

The increase of Portuguese immigrants that settled in the Chicago area after 1974 led leaders of this small ethnic community to organize the Luso-BRAZILIAN Club in the 1970s and the Friends of Portugal in the 1980s. Community leaders also petitioned to have the city of Chicago recognize the Portuguese community by flying the Portuguese flag over City Hall every June 10 to commemorate the death of famed Portuguese poet Luís de Camões in 1580. The 2000 census reported 2,417 people of Portuguese ancestry for Cook County, of whom 871 resided within Chicago's city limits.

Brandon Johnson

See also: Demography; Spaniards

Further reading: Pap, Leo. *The Portuguese-Americans.* 1981. • Poague, George Rawlings. "The Coming of the Portuguese." *Journal of the Illinois State Historical Society,* April 18, 1925: 101–135.

Posen, IL, Cook County, 18 miles S of the Loop. Posen's uniqueness is captured in a brief 1930s description of the village by the Works Progress Administration FEDERAL WRITERS' PROJECT: a community of industrial workers whose homes are surrounded by garden plots and small farms. Its homogeneous population (98 percent POLISH) reflects the enterprise of a Chicago REAL-ESTATE agent, whose 75 Polish salesmen sold 12,000 lots to their countrymen during 1893. Many of these lots were concentrated in an area south of Chicago, and the name Posen was chosen to remember the city of Poznan in Poland from which some of the residents had come.

The Poles who began settling in the area before 1893 joined DUTCH and GERMAN settlers to the east and south and west. More Poles came after 1893. After these residents petitioned the ROMAN CATHOLIC ARCHDIOCESE OF CHICAGO for a church of their own, a mission was established in 1894 with a Polish pastoral overseer. The mission became St. Stanislaus Bishop and Martyr Catholic Church, and in 1898 Father Serfino Cosimi came to serve the congregation.

Many of the new residents were industrial workers, not farmers, and immediately to the east, the new industries in HARVEY provided jobs. Although Harvey was a dry town, many taverns sprang up outside its limits. Temperance groups in Harvey wanted to annex the areas to the east and to the west in order to gain control and close down the taverns. To avoid this, some residents and tavern owners to the east incorporated as the village of PHOENIX. Similarly, the residents of Posen incorporated in 1900. Father Cosimi had played such a crucial role in the development of the church and the community that he was elected as the first village president for Posen soon after its incorporation.

The *Harvey Tribune-Citizen,* on January 26, 1901, argued that the only reason the village had incorporated was to collect license fees from its local tavern. While this was a major reason, it is also the case that Posen was a closely knit ethnic community seeking to maintain its own traditions.

Because the village was almost landlocked by the growth of Harvey, DIXMOOR, BLUE ISLAND, and MIDLOTHIAN, Posen's residential growth was slow in the 1920s. From a population of 343 in 1910, Posen grew to 4,730 in 2000. It reached roughly its present size in terms of land area and population during the 1950s and has seen the development of about 30 small industrial firms over the past 50 years. This predominantly Polish American community continues to be home for many families who have now lived there for three or four generations.

Larry A. McClellan

See also: Economic Geography; Local Option; Prohibition and Temperance

Further reading: "Village of Posen Founders Day, 1887–1987: Celebrating One Hundred Years." 1987. • Federal Writers' Project. *Illinois: A Descriptive and Historical Guide.* 1939. • McClellan, Larry A. "History of Posen Tied to Colombian Exposition." *Star (South Suburban)* November 30, 1997.

Postcards. The use of picture postcards has been so widespread in the twentieth century that few pause to think about their origins, or are aware that Chicago figured prominently in the history of postcards. Among the first picture postcards in the United States were those printed in 1893 for the WORLD'S COLUMBIAN EXPOSITION in Chicago. The set of 10 cards, produced by Charles W. Goldsmith, was decorated with artistic conceptions of the fair buildings. Since then, postcards have been unceasingly used as an inexpensive means of communication, as ADVERTISING, and to encourage tourism. Chicago was also the home of the world's largest-volume PRINTER of view and advertising postcards, the Curt Teich Company (1898–1978), and the prominent photographic postcard company C. R. Childs, which specialized in views of Chicago's neighborhoods and suburbs.

Katherine Hamilton-Smith

See also: Lake County Discovery Museum; Photography; Tourism and Conventions

Further reading: Carline, Richard. *Pictures in the Post: The Story of the Picture Postcard.* 1972. • Miller, George, and Dorothy Miller. *Picture Postcards in the United States: 1893–1918.* 1976. • Staff, Frank. *The Picture Postcard and Its Origins.* 1966.

Post Office. *See* Mail Delivery

Potawatomis. The first written descriptions of Potawatomi communities are from seventeenth-century FRENCH traders who first encountered the Potawatomis in Wisconsin. By the 1690s Potawatomis had migrated into the Chicago region, establishing small settlements along the CALUMET, CHICAGO, and DES PLAINES Rivers. Joined by kinsmen from southwestern Michigan during the first three decades of the eighteenth century, Potawatomis from the Chicago region occupied the FOX and Kankakee River valleys, gradually expanding as far south as Lake Peoria.

The Potawatomis at Chicago established close political, economic, and kinship ties with the French. French FUR TRADERS were welcomed into the Potawatomi villages, where their union with Potawatomi women produced growing numbers of mixed-blood, or MÉTIS, children. The Potawatomis at Chicago were much involved in the fur trade, first trading beaver pelts to the French, but also supplying traders with muskrat, raccoon, and otter pelts taken from the marshes along the Calumet and Kankakee Rivers. Throughout the colonial period they remained allied to the French, journeying to Montreal to assist the French in their wars against the British.

During the American Revolution, most of the Potawatomis at Chicago remained neutral, or even favored the Americans, while their kinsmen in Michigan were more pro-British. In the decade following the Revolutionary War, the Chicago villages remained aloof from the border warfare between NATIVE AMERICANS and settlers in Indiana and Ohio. They suffered a smallpox EPIDEMIC in 1794 and sent no warriors to the Battle of Fallen Timbers, but delegates from Chicago did participate in the Treaty of Greenville (1795).

In 1803 FORT DEARBORN was built at Chicago, but relations between the Potawatomis and the Americans deteriorated. Potawatomi war parties en route to attack the Osages in Missouri sometimes committed depredations in southern Illinois, and messengers from Tecumseh and the Shawnee Prophet recruited Chicago Potawatomis into their growing pan-Indian movement. In 1810 Tecumseh visited the Chicago region, recruiting additional warriors for his cause. Attempting to reduce the growing tension, federal officials escorted Main Poc, a chief from the Kankakee River, and Siggenauk (the Blackbird), a leader from Chicago, to Washington. Yet the chiefs remained suspicious, and Potawatomi hostility toward the government continued.

During the War of 1812 most Chicago Potawatomis favored the British, and on August 15, 1812, when federal troops abandoned Fort Dearborn, hostile Potawatomis led by Siggenauk and Mad Sturgeon attacked the garrison. More than 50 Americans and about 15 Indians were killed in the lakefront battle, which took place near modern Burnham Park.

Some of the American prisoners were rescued by friendly Potawatomis, including Black Partridge and Métis Alexander Robinson, who later relinquished the captives to British or American officials. Following the attack, many of the Chicago Potawatomis joined Tecumseh and the British on the Detroit frontier, or sporadically raided American settlements, but in 1813, after American officials built Fort Clark at Lake Peoria, Potawatomi attacks upon southern Illinois diminished. By late 1814 most of the Potawatomis at Chicago had abandoned the British and sought peace with the United States.

Following the War of 1812, the Potawatomis at Chicago were joined by significant numbers of OTTAWAS and Chippewas (OJIBWAS), and Métis leaders assumed a more important role. Particularly prominent was Billy Caldwell, a Métis elected as justice of the peace at Chicago in 1825. Many of the Métis were merchants who played key roles in the region's fur trade.

After 1816 the United States government distributed a major portion of the Potawatomi annuities at Chicago, and many tribespeople became more dependent upon these payments. To secure additional annuities, the tribe was forced to sell more land. Between 1816 and 1829, Potawatomi leaders from Chicago participated in six of the seven TREATIES in which the tribe gave up large sections of northern Illinois and adjoining regions of Wisconsin, Indiana, and Michigan. In turn, their reliance upon annuities drew the tribespeople into a closer relationship with the federal government, and in 1827, when hostility erupted between white settlers and Winnebagos in Wisconsin, Potawatomis from Chicago used their influence to keep their kinsmen in southern Wisconsin at peace. Five years later, Caldwell, Alexander Robinson, and Shabbona, a chief from a village west of the Fox River, rejected Black Hawk's invitation to attack the settlements and advised the SAC chief to return to Iowa. Following the meeting, Shabbona warned settlers of approaching Sac war parties, and late in June 1832 Caldwell led a party of Potawatomi scouts who assisted the U.S. Army against Black Hawk and his warriors.

After the BLACK HAWK WAR, pressure mounted on the Potawatomis to relinquish their remaining lands in Illinois and to remove to the west. In 1832 they gave up their claims to lands in eastern Illinois, and one year later more than 6,000 tribesmen assembled at Chicago, where they ceded their remaining lands in Illinois. In 1835 Billy Caldwell led the first Chicago emigrants west of the Mississippi. There they split into two small communities. Meanwhile, most of the remaining Chicago Potawatomis assembled at a camp on the Des Plaines River for the government's final removal effort. After a dispute with removal agents, many Potawatomis fled from the camp, seeking refuge among kinsmen in Wisconsin or Michigan. Finally, in September 1837 the remaining 450 Chicago Potawatomis left the camp and eventually joined with their kinsmen in the west. A few tribesmen, primarily Métis, remained on private tracts of land in northern Illinois, but after 1840 most Potawatomis were gone from the Chicago region.

R. David Edmunds

See also: Chicago in the Middle Ground; Demography; Miami; Native American Religion; Ottawas

Further reading: Clifton, James A. *The Prairie People: Continuity and Change in Potawatomi Indian Culture, 1665–1965*. 1977. • Edmunds, R. David. *The Potawatomis: Keepers of the Fire*. 1978. • Quaife, Milo Milton. *Chicago and the Old Northwest, 1673–1835*. 1913.

Powwows. The earliest powwows in the Chicago region are unrecorded, although a 1778 proclamation issued by George Rogers Clark forbidding powwow activity in the Kaskaskia area suggests that powwows preceded the area's first recorded ceremony in 1821. The gathering of two to three thousand Indians (largely POTAWATOMIS, OTTAWAS, and Chippewas) lasted over one month and was paid for by the United States government in the hopes of using the meeting to effect a TREATY extinguishing Indian land titles. Although the Indians were less than cooperative, a treaty did ensue, and the government sponsored another great powwow in 1833, lasting two weeks and resulting in a forced land sale by Chippewa, Ottawa, and Potawatomi. The last large powwow of the nineteenth century in Chicago, with about five thousand Indians attending, occurred in 1835, also with the support of the U.S. government, which this time wanted to provide Indians with their "annuity payment" and to begin the process of removal to reservations further west.

The only other substantial powwow activity recorded in the Chicago area in the nineteenth century took place as part of the 1893 WORLD'S COLUMBIAN EXPOSITION, which brought Indians to Chicago and housed them as exhibits.

The first powwows for Chicago's current NATIVE AMERICAN community were small social and cultural events generally confined to the community and a few friends. By the end of the twentieth century, powwows were being held frequently to educate Indians and non-Indians. Small powwows have been held within the community, while a larger event sponsored by the American Indian Center has occupied larger venues across the city, including NAVY PIER and the UNIVERSITY OF ILLINOIS AT CHICAGO. The Native American Educational Services (NAES COLLEGE) has also sponsored a major annual powwow.

Jerry W. Lewis

See also: Chicago in the Middle Ground

Further reading: American Historical Association. *Annual Report for the year 1944*, vol. 2 of 3, *Calendar of the American Fur Company's Papers: Part I, 1831–1840*. With a preface by Grace Lee Nute, reprinted from the *American Historical Review* 32.3 (April 1927). • Andreas, A. T. *History of Cook County*. 1884. • Cooke, Sarah E., and Rachel B. Ramadhyani. *Indians and a Changing Frontier: The Art of George Winter*. 1993.

Prairie Avenue. Prairie Avenue was an exclusive address for Chicago's elite in the late nineteenth century. This north-south boulevard, close to the lakefront, begins at 16th Street and continues to the city's southern limits. The sections between 16th and 22nd Streets and between 26th and 30th Streets were well known for grand homes.

The wealthy settled on Prairie Avenue after the CIVIL WAR because it was close to the LOOP, and it did not require its residents to cross the CHICAGO RIVER. The first large home on the upper portion of Prairie Avenue was built by Daniel Thompson in 1870. Marshall Field soon followed in 1871 with a grand home by Richard Morris Hunt. George Pullman's palace was constructed on upper Prairie Avenue in 1873. Mansions for other magnates were not far behind. This section of the avenue was dominated by Second Empire homes. The lower section of Prairie Avenue between 26th and 30th Streets began to attract wealthy residents in the mid-1880s, and this segment was made up of many Queen Anne and Richardson Romanesque houses.

Perhaps the best-known building on Prairie Avenue is H. H. Richardson's Glessner House on 18th Street. This imposing house, done in the architect's signature Richardson Romanesque style, was completed in 1887 for John Glessner, a farm equipment manufacturing executive, and his wife Frances. The structure is not set back from the lot line like most homes, and it appears fortress-like in its use of rugged granite for the exterior. Richardson's aim was to provide the family with a truly urban home that embraced a center courtyard and its interior spaces while shielding the inhabitants from the city street. As such, it caused a major stir among the Glessners' neighbors. But the design was prescient—Prairie Avenue was becoming a less desirable neighborhood in the late 1880s. Soot from the nearby RAILROAD was a major nuisance, and an infamous VICE DISTRICT was encroaching on the neighborhood.

Prairie Avenue became home to light industry and vacant lots in the mid to late twentieth century. Many mansions were torn down, others became dilapidated. In 1966, the Glessner House was purchased by a group of architects called the Chicago School of Architecture Foundation. The home is now a museum, and Prairie Avenue, although devoid of most of its mansions, was declared a historic district in 1978.

Heidi Pawlowski Carey

See also: Architecture; Built Environment of the Chicago Region; Historic Preservation; Housing Types; maps, pp. C4 and 772

Further reading: Harrington, Elaine, and Kevin Harrington. "H. H. Richardson and the Glessners." *Perspectives on the Professions* 3.4 (December 1983). • Hubka, Thomas C. "H. H. Richardson's Glessner House." *Winterthur Portfolio* 24.4 (Winter 1989): 209–229. • Molloy, Mary Alice. "Prairie Avenue." In *The Grand American Avenue, 1850–1920,* ed. Jan Cigliano and Sarah Bradford Landau, 1994.

Prairie Farmer. One of the leading farm papers of the Midwest, *Prairie Farmer* was the most influential force in the commercialization of Illinois AGRICULTURE. Headquartered in Chicago, the paper not only promoted scientific farming practices but also was dedicated to improving rural life through education, recreation, and better health practices.

First published in 1841 by the Union Agricultural Society, *Prairie Farmer* was the brainchild of founding editor John S. Wright. After a succession of owners, newspaperman Burridge D. Butler bought the paper in 1909. By 1931 Butler had absorbed *Prairie Farmer*'s competitors and expanded circulation to Indiana, Wisconsin, and Michigan by offering premiums, staging corn-husking contests, and landing the company plane in cow pastures. Butler purchased radio station WLS in 1928 to offer farm programming and produced the popular *Barn Dance* VAUDEVILLE show.

Butler saw his paper as the voice of the common farmer, and he conducted editorial campaigns against crime and deceptive marketing practices. The paper agitated for pro-farm legislation, and editor Clifford Gregory strongly supported the NEW DEAL. From a peak of 370,000 subscribers in 1950, circulation dwindled below 60,000 at the end of the century, a sign of the declining importance of farming as a way of life.

Susan Sessions Rugh

See also: Agricultural Journals; Broadcasting; Food Processing: Regional and National Market; Newspapers

Further reading: Bardolph, Richard. *Agricultural Literature and the Early Illinois Farmer.* 1948. • Evans, James F. *Prairie Farmer and WLS: The Burridge D. Butler Years.* 1969. • Lewis, Lloyd. *John S. Wright, Prophet of the Prairies.* 1941.

Prairie Grove, IL, McHenry County, 43 miles NW of the Loop. The village of Prairie Grove is located within Nunda Township in southeastern MCHENRY County. When the village incorporated in 1973, the rural locale's population of 434 residents was barely dense enough to qualify for incorporation. Since then land ANNEXATIONS, including manufacturing sites, have more than doubled the size of the village, which had a population of 960 in 2000.

Ian McGiver

See also: Agriculture; Economic Geography

Further reading: *McHenry County in the Twentieth Century, 1968–1994.* McHenry County Historical Society. 1994.

Prairie School of Architecture. *See* Architecture: The Prairie School

Preservation. *See* Historic Preservation

Press.

NEIGHBORHOOD PRESS
SUBURBAN PRESS

NEIGHBORHOOD PRESS. As Chicago expanded its boundaries in the late nineteenth century, absorbing formerly independent towns, community NEWSPAPERS shifted from covering local government and society to serving local retail shopping centers. Few papers devoted significant resources to news gathering, although several did subscribe to the Community News Service, which provided localized coverage of city GOVERNMENT. Editors served as civic actors, collecting complaints of poor city services and potholes from citizens and forwarding them to government officials for action (publishing reports on the conditions if complaints went unaddressed), as well as covering local groups, individuals, and events.

The 1920s saw dramatic growth in the community newspaper sector, as many job printers launched papers—several of which offered little more than an advertising salesman and an open invitation for press releases from local organizations. By 1929, some neighborhoods were served by three or four competitors, although the number of papers was halved with the onset of the GREAT DEPRESSION.

Community newspapers also included a handful of dailies. The *Daily Calumet* explicitly targeted the area east of Cottage Grove Avenue and south of 67th Street. Founded in 1873 as the *Enterprise,* the paper converted to daily publication as the *South Chicago Post* in 1883, changing its name to the *Daily Calumet* a few years later. A four- to eight-page evening daily, the paper's columns were devoted almost exclusively to local news and issues generated by its six editorial employees. It ceased publication in the 1980s.

In 1910 most community papers were independently owned, but by 1941 two-thirds were part of chains. Some chains were quite small, little more than zoned editions for distribution in adjacent communities. But others published dozens of papers, often as part of national media conglomerates.

Field Enterprises (publisher of the *Chicago Sun-Times*) launched the *Day* chain in 1966 to challenge Paddock Publications' 16 north suburban weeklies with a total market coverage Monday–Friday paper. The *Tribune* launched a free triweekly (the *Trib*) the next year in its own bid for suburban readers. Paddock, which responded by converting four of its papers to daily publication and redesigning them to appeal to younger readers, ultimately prevailed—buying out the *Day* in June 1970. By the mid-1970s, both Chicago dailies had retreated to publishing weekly suburban supplements. But the allure of the suburbs still beckoned, and by the 1990s the *Sun-Times* belonged to a publishing group that included the Pioneer and Star chains of community papers.

The twentieth century has seen a steady increase in the number of community newspapers published in the Chicago metropolitan area. In 1950, 181 such papers were listed in Ayer's directory, more than double the 82 listed in 1910. Few of the community papers published inside the city limits wield substantial clout; their influence, like their readership, is almost entirely local. Yet the number of papers continues to grow (the latest Bacon's directory lists more than 300 community papers in the greater Chicago area, the vast majority of which are published in the suburbs), driven by advertisers' needs for small-scale media and by a dense network of neighborhood groups which supply a steady source of news and a locus for community life. The suburban community papers play a more prominent role, helping to sustain local civic identities in a media environment dominated by the metropolis.

Jon Bekken

See also: Chambers of Commerce; Chicago Tribune; Daily Herald; Press: Suburban Press; Suburbs and Cities as Dual Metropolis

Further reading: Davis, Fred, and George Nollet. "The Community Newspaper in Metropolitan Chicago." M.A. thesis, University of Chicago. 1951. • Janowitz, Morris. *The Community Press in an Urban Setting.* 1952.

SUBURBAN PRESS. From erstwhile competitors to hometown chroniclers to rivals once again, Chicago's suburban NEWSPAPERS have persevered and prospered in their competition with the large downtown dailies.

The Chicago area's oldest and the sixth-oldest newspaper in Illinois is the JOLIET *Herald News,* born as the *Juliet Courier* on April 20, 1839, eight years before the founding of the *Chicago Tribune.* Early settlements along the Illinois and FOX RIVERS saw themselves as economic rivals to Chicago, and a hometown newspaper was considered essential to the success of an aspiring city. Thirteen JOLIET investors bought a PRINTING press and hired a Michigan editor, O. H. Balch, to publish the *Courier* in 1839. The paper went through a variety of owners and name changes until the *Joliet Herald* was merged with the *Joliet News* by Ira C. Copley in 1915. The *Herald News* remains a flagship publication of the Copley Press chain.

Copley Press also owns the *Aurora Beacon News,* founded as the *Aurora Beacon* by M. V. and B. F. Hall in June 1846. The *Beacon* began printing daily editions on September 6, 1856, in conjunction with the presidential election, and is considered the first suburban daily although the WAUKEGAN *Gazette* had published daily editions for a few weeks in 1854. The *Beacon* returned to a weekly format on April 30, 1857, but became a permanent daily in 1891. Copley bought the paper in December 1905, merging it with the *Aurora News* and three other AURORA newspapers into the *Daily Beacon-News,* which first appeared on January 2, 1912.

The *Geneva Republican* had its roots in the *Western Mercury,* which was founded in GENEVA in 1847. Its publication was suspended from 1851 until 1856, when it was renamed the *Kane County Republican.* The *Kendall County Record* was founded in YORKVILLE in 1864. Other early suburban newspapers were less successful. The "sound money" LAKE ZURICH *Banker* was published in 1856 until its editor was committed to an insane asylum. The (ELGIN) *Daily Dud* (1875) was produced by Dudley Randall, a one-time editor of the *Aurora Beacon.*

As Chicago affirmed its economic predominance over its area rivals during the 1850s, outlying newspapers began touting the advantages of suburban living. The EVANSTON *Suburban Idea* (1864) was one of the first papers to promote new COMMUTER settlements along Chicago's growing passenger RAILROAD system. It was joined by papers such as the RIVERSIDE *Gazette* (1871) and EVANSTON *Real Estate News* (1871–73), which quickly ceased publication when their settlements were populated.

Other suburban newspapers stressed local news and information that readers would not find in the Chicago dailies. The *Daily Herald* began in 1872 as the COOK COUNTY *Herald,* a weekly devoted to agricultural and business news for northwestern county residents. The paper was purchased by Hosea C. Paddock in 1889 and renamed the ARLINGTON HEIGHTS *Herald* in 1926. The *Elgin Daily Courier News,* founded as the *Elgin Daily Bluff News* in 1874, the DES PLAINES *Times* (1885), DOWNERS GROVE *Reporter* (1883), ELMHURST *Press* (1889), HARVEY *Star* (1890), *Waukegan News-Sun* (1892), HINSDALE *Doings* (1895), LAKE FORESTER (1896), GRAYSLAKE *Times* (1900), and *Daily Southtown,* founded as the ENGLEWOOD *Economist* in 1906, were all marketed toward residents who wanted to know about local events and save money shopping in their own communities and neighborhoods.

The railroads simplified newspaper distribution to the suburban communities along their lines, making newspaper chains an economic possibility. The first Chicago-area chain, the short-lived *Phoenix* (1877), was published at a home office in Joliet but had local editors in LOCKPORT, WILMINGTON, LEMONT, BRAIDWOOD, PEOTONE, and PLAINFIELD. Hosea C. Paddock created a PALATINE *Herald* to complement his *Cook County Herald* in 1898, but it was Ira C. Copley who perfected the chain newspaper idea in the Chicago area. Starting with the *Aurora Beacon News,* he created Copley Newspapers, formally organized in Illinois in 1928. By the end of the century the chain included 45 Illinois and California papers, including the NAPERVILLE-based Sun Publications chain, founded in 1935, along with dailies in Joliet, Elgin, and Waukegan.

Suburban newspaper chains flourished in the twentieth century. Life Newspapers began as the CICERO *Life* and BERWYN-STICKNEY-FOREST VIEW *Life* in 1927. The oldest semiweekly in Illinois, the BLUE ISLAND *Star,* founded in 1890, joined with the CHICAGO HEIGHTS *Star* to form Star Publications in the 1940s. The *Downers Grove Reporter,* which first appeared in 1883, started neighboring editions in the 1950s to form the Reporter/Progress chain. The B. F. Shaw Newspaper Group grew from the *Dixon Telegraph,* founded in 1851, to include the daily CRYSTAL LAKE *Northwest Herald,* founded in 1856, and *Kane County Chronicle,* founded in 1881, along with more than a dozen other suburban papers. The Pioneer Press chain grew from the BARRINGTON *Courier-Review,* founded in 1889, into a group of more than 40 daily and weekly papers.

Toll roads and freeways accelerated suburban growth after WORLD WAR II, touching off a new competition with the downtown dailies. A change in the ownership of the *Arlington Heights Herald* instigated an intense circulation war with suburban newspapers published by Field Enterprises, the owner of the *Sun-Times,* in 1968. A new generation of Paddock family members bought Field's suburban operations for $1 million one year later, nearly bankrupting themselves, but the *Herald* survived, becoming the *Daily Herald* in 1977. It became the third-largest circulating newspaper in Illinois in 1990.

Meanwhile, the *Sun-Times*'s ownership purchased the Star chain in 1983, the Pioneer Press newspapers in 1988, and the *Daily Southtown* in 1994 to form the largest suburban Chicago newspaper holding company, which at the end of the century was owned by Toronto-based Hollinger International. The *Chicago Tribune,* which saw a majority of its circulation base move to the suburbs during the 1960s and 1970s, began producing localized suburban editions in 1982, operating 11 suburban bureaus with more than 100 staffers to cover suburban news. By the 1990s, some suburban residents could chose from as many as five localized daily newspapers compared to the two local dailies available to Chicagoans.

Richard Junger

See also: Journalism; Metropolitan Growth; Press: Neighborhood Press

Further reading: Chicago Daily News. *Survey of Daily Newspaper Home Coverage in Metropolitan Chicago.* 1934. • Ebner, Michael H. *Creating North Shore: A Suburban History.* 1988. • Keating, Ann Durkin. *Building Chicago: Suburban Developers and the Creation of a Divided Metropolis.* 1988.

Presses, University. Like many of their counterparts elsewhere, Chicago-area UNIVERSITIES have established publishing companies to advance knowledge by disseminating works of scholarship and works of regional and general interest. The oldest university press in metropolitan Chicago is the University of Chicago Press, which was established in 1891 by William Rainey Harper as one of three divisions of the new UNIVERSITY OF CHICAGO and has grown to be the largest of American university presses. LOYOLA UNIVERSITY, Northern Illinois University, NORTHWESTERN UNIVERSITY, the UNIVERSITY OF ILLINOIS, and Southern Illinois University also established their own presses, joining the University of Chicago in active programs of book and journal publication. Since the city of Chicago has long provided a rich subject of study for scholarly authors, university presses in Illinois and elsewhere have published many books about the history, geography, sociology, ARCHITECTURE, music, and natural history of the city as well as FICTION, POETRY, and essays by Chicagoans.

Penny Kaiserlian

See also: Chicago School of Sociology; Chicago Studied: Social Scientists and Their City; Literary Cultures; Publishing, Book

Further reading: *Association of American University Presses Directory, 1999–2000.* 1999. • *University of Chicago Press Catalogue of Books and Journals, 1891–1965.* 1967.

Printer's Row. After the completion of Dearborn Street Station in 1885, this area on the NEAR SOUTH SIDE became the PRINTING center of the Midwest. The heart of Printer's Row—a two-block area between Congress Parkway and Polk Street along Dearborn—features examples of the First Chicago School of ARCHITECTURE, including the Duplicator Building (1886) and the Pontiac Building (1891). In the late 1970s developers began to convert printing centers such as the Donohue Building into loft-style apartments, and Dearborn Street Station was converted to retail space.

Erik Gellman

See also: Historic Preservation; South Side

Further reading: Bach, Ira J., and Susan Wolfson. *Chicago on Foot: Walking Tours of Chicago's Architecture.* 1987. • *Sweet Home Chicago: The Real City Guide.* 1993.

Printing. In the late nineteenth century, Chicago became a center for commercial printing in the United States second only to New York.

Chicago printers worked closely with magazine and catalog publishers; they had easy access to rail TRANSPORTATION; and they achieved a competitive position because Chicago was the point at which zoned shipping rates for bulky printed products increased. In the years after WORLD WAR I, Chicago's centrality in the industry developed into a regional industrial concentration greater even than that of the big eastern cities. By the end of the twentieth century, 4 of the 10 largest printing companies in the world were headquartered within 100 miles of Chicago. The internationalization of their operations since the 1970s, however, has included the exportation of the actual printing.

Before the widespread introduction of large power presses (ca. 1860), small printing houses were to be found in almost every American town. Markets outside major publishing centers were local or at most regional. Chicago was no exception. The city's earliest printer was John Calhoun, whose single press operated from 1833 to 1836 in printing the *Chicago Democrat* and a variety of occasional publications. There was nothing to distinguish Calhoun from hundreds of other printers in frontier towns. The early, rapid growth of Chicago, however, meant that already in 1846 there were eight printing offices and four NEWSPAPERS, making it the region's printing center. From 1850 to 1870, Chicago developed a fully integrated printing industry. Newspapers in 1860 reported 29 printing offices; the 1871 census listed 79 job printers in addition to the major newspaper offices. Seventeen binderies, 68 book stores, 5 manufacturers of printing supplies and machinery, and numerous print distributors served the industry on a regional basis. PUBLISHING houses fed the presses, led by A. C. McClurg, a general publisher, and by a variety of specialized publishers of textbooks, religious and trade literature, and catalogs. MAGAZINES were particularly important, even in these early years: some 20 new titles per year started in Chicago between 1860 and 1880. From the 1850s onward, RAILROAD printing became important because so many lines established headquarters or regional offices in the city. One early specialized railroad printer was RAND MCNALLY & CO., founded in 1868. Another Chicago specialty that began during this period was the printing of MAIL-ORDER catalogs.

The Great FIRE OF 1871 allowed printers to concentrate their works in the new central commercial district and on the NEAR SOUTH SIDE. Coinciding as this new construction did with technological advances in power presses, it also led to the creation of large-scale printing plants with skilled workforces and to the development of a characteristic tall and narrow loft-style building to house rows of presses in rooms with good natural light. Rand McNally, M. A. Donohue & Co. (1861), R. R. DONNELLEY & SONS (1864), and the W. F. HALL PRINTING COMPANY (1892) were among the large firms that grew up to exploit such economies of scale for long print runs of textbooks, magazines, and catalogs. Simultaneously, type foundries and printing press manufacturers opened in Chicago, although the great size and rapid growth of the industry meant that most machinery and type continued to be imported from the East. Barnhart Bros. & Spindler was for many years one of the largest Midwestern type founders. Two Chicago press manufacturers became leaders in their respective fields. The Miehle Company (1890) made fine, high-speed sheet-fed presses, and the Goss Company (1885) developed web presses for newspaper work. The final pieces in Chicago's complex printing industry were added just before World War I with the invention of new proofing presses by Robert Vandercook and the founding of the Ludlow Typograph Company, the city's only manufacturer of typesetting machinery. Theodore Regensteiner of the Regensteiner Printing Company pioneered in the introduction of color offset presses.

Locking up the press, ca. 1946. Rand McNally & Co.'s book manufacturing division used sheet-fed presses built by the Miehle Printing Press Company, a Chicago firm, for the production of atlases and textbooks. Here the stereotype plates for a book are locked into the press. Photographer: Unknown. Source: The Newberry Library.

The mature Chicago printing industry consisted of a fully integrated regional complex of suppliers and producers with extensive out-shipping to other regions and even worldwide. It was symbolized by the huge printing plants built at the south end of Dearborn Street and Plymouth Court near Polk Street for the Donohue (1883), the Donnelley (1897), and the Franklin Printing (1914) companies. Architectural gems of the present Printing House Row Historic District, these buildings are decorated flamboyantly with bas-reliefs and mosaics that portray the history and processes of printing from Gutenberg to Chicago.

Chicago's printing industry was a major field for labor and management organization. A price war broke out as early as 1840 and led to disputes about compositors' pay. The first printer's UNION in the city was founded in 1850 as a response to such wage concerns, and in 1852 the national union had recognized the Chicago Typographical Union as Local 16. Early organizing efforts achieved major wage-rate increases in the boom years of the 1860s, but these eroded in the slump after 1873. A union drive for a nine-hour day (part of a national effort) led the employing printers to form their own association in 1887, the Chicago Typothetae. Later in the same year these employers were instrumental in founding the United Typothetae of America at a convention held in Chicago.

The industry expanded well beyond the printing house district even before World War I. Printing supply and press manufacturing companies did not need to be as close to each other or to the shipping hubs as the printing plants at first did. Miehle and Goss put early plants west of the river; Ludlow's was in the Clybourn Avenue industrial corridor. Printers also located elsewhere as the need for larger plants developed. The Henneberry Printing Company opened a large plant at 22nd and

Clinton near the river in the mid 1890s, and it was vastly enlarged in the 1920s after the company was taken over by John Cuneo, becoming the city's second largest printer as CUNEO PRESS. But the symbolic leader of the industry was again the Donnelley Company, which built a vast printing plant designed by Howard Van Doren Shaw on 22nd Street near the lake between 1912 and 1929. Donnelley also opened one of the first regional printing plants of a Chicago firm at Crawfordsville, Indiana, in 1921.

The pace of regionalization quickened after WORLD WAR II, when the need to arrange large new offset presses on single floors led the industry giants to build plants in suburban SKOKIE (Rand McNally, 1952) and even farther afield (e.g., Miehle-Goss-Dexter in Rockford; Rand McNally in Kentucky; Donnelley in Indiana and downstate Illinois, and later in Kentucky and Tennessee). Smaller companies also multiplied within the region. The process of regionalization has continued into the twenty-first century. In 1927 almost all the region's printing was in the city; some 1,500 production facilities employed over 30,000 workers. In 1960 there were 2,100 printing establishments in the city (including the world's three largest at the time: Donnelley, W. F. Hall, and Cuneo), but another 1,550 plants were located in the metropolitan area. Total employment in the sector was close to 100,000. Further erosion of the urban concentration occurred in the late twentieth century, with the most rapid changes from the late 1970s onward. From 1977 to 1984, for example, the total number of firms in pre-press and press work (excluding newspapers) in the city dropped from 1,380 to 1,116, while jobs declined from 24,047 to 19,342.

Although Chicago has never been a major center for literary publishing, it was important in TRADE PUBLISHING and particularly in trade magazines and direct-mail sales from the 1860s onward. Starting in the 1920s, Chicago's large, versatile plants and edge in shipping rates lured major magazine accounts away from other regions. This aspect of its economy has continued to dominate the printing industry in Chicago. Industry giants like Donnelley and Rand McNally built their success on printing catalogs, magazines, MAPS, phone books, and textbooks, some published locally but most printed here for publishers outside the region. These Chicago companies have continued to serve huge bulk accounts even though the printing is now done with cheaper labor in their plants elsewhere in the region, in other regions, or abroad.

Paul F. Gehl

See also: Business of Chicago; Economic Geography; Printer's Row; Publishing and Media, Religious

Further reading: Brown, Emily Clark. *Book and Job Printing in Chicago.* 1931. • Kogan, Herman. *Proud of the Past, Committed to the Future.* 1985. • Regan Printing House. *The Story of Chicago in Connection with the Printing Business.* 1912.

Prisons. *See* Jails and Prisons

Privatization. Privatization of government services is defined as turning over responsibility for services from the public to the private sector. It can involve the sale of assets, volunteer activity, franchise agreements, or contracting with a private firm for the provision of a service, which is the most common form of privatization.

The city of Chicago, suburban municipalities, school and PARK DISTRICTS, and county governments have long contracted with private firms for public services, including public PRINTING, road building, and WASTE DISPOSAL. Local governments have also relied on other kinds of private providers, such as volunteer FIRE FIGHTERS, privately owned toll roads, and franchised streetcar and utility companies. Some of these arrangements still exist, but others encountered difficulties. For instance, STREET RAILWAY franchises involved massive corruption, and streetcars and BUSES eventually became unprofitable. Private charities were overwhelmed by the GREAT DEPRESSION. As these problems emerged and government financial and management capacity developed, many private providers were replaced by publicly operated bureaucracies.

Privatization emerged within the context of growing government activity in such fields as education, public safety, welfare, LIBRARIES, health, and TRANSPORTATION. As governments grew, reformers pushed to centralize administration, employ experts, and keep out POLITICS in order to promote efficiency and accountability. But in the 1980s and 1990s, privatization became an increasingly popular management tool for local officials responding to financial limitations, citizen demands for services, opposition to tax increases, and unfunded intergovernmental mandates. Under Mayor Richard M. Daley, the city of Chicago privatized a variety of services, including janitorial services, parking at O'HARE AIRPORT, PARKING enforcement, street resurfacing, engineering, purchasing, vehicle towing, and delinquent tax collections. According to city estimates, Chicago saved approximately $56.6 million from 1989 through 1995 through privatization and consolidation of services.

Supporters of privatization have traditionally argued that it improves the quality of services while lowering costs. Opponents, mostly employees and unions, have countered that any cost savings are the result of lower wages and benefits paid to employees of private contractors. In the 1990s, Daley attempted to overcome employee fears by adopting privatization on a case-by-case basis and structuring contracting to minimize layoffs. For example, the city privatized janitorial services gradually to allow time for the existing workforce to be reduced through attrition. City officials have also required contractors to give existing city employees first-interview rights.

Another criticism of privatization under Mayor Daley is that contracting with private firms is simply a way of evading the SHAKMAN DECREES, strict rules limiting the use of traditional political PATRONAGE hiring. Critics have labeled efforts to subvert Shakman and steer contracts to friendly firms "pinstripe patronage."

A series of investigative reports in the late 1990s uncovered contracting irregularities in Chicago that led to an upheaval in purchasing personnel and practices. Allegations of mob ties and subversion of minority-owned business regulations called into question Daley's emerging national reputation as a no-nonsense administrator of "GOOD GOVERNMENT." Daley's changes in contracting procedures and appointment of a private sector executive to oversee purchasing are too recent to evaluate, but they indicate a serious effort to remove the tarnish from the contracting process in Chicago.

Robin A. Johnson

See also: Government, City of Chicago; Government, Suburban; Machine Politics; Taxation and Finance

Further reading: The Civic Federation. *From Privatization to Innovation: A Study of 16 U.S. Cities.* 1996. • Donahue, John. *The Privatization Decision.* 1989. • Savas, E. S. *Privatization and Public-Private Partnerships.* 2000.

Progressive Education. Late-nineteenth-century Chicago, home of a new university and one of the first SETTLEMENT HOUSES, HULL HOUSE, was unusually receptive to new ideas. It is no surprise, therefore, that it became a major center for the development of progressive education, the ideology that would become a dominant form in American educational thought for much of the twentieth century. The movement had its roots in the thought of many people, but its major founders were Francis Parker and John Dewey, both of whom refined their educational ideas here.

Parker came to Chicago in 1883 as principal of COOK COUNTY Normal School and its Practice School. Before coming to Chicago, Parker had developed an approach to education that rejected rote learning and enlisted the natural curiosity of children in the schooling process. John Dewey was also dissatisfied with traditional forms of schooling and when he came to the UNIVERSITY OF CHICAGO in 1894, he enrolled his children in Parker's school. A frequent visitor at Hull House, Dewey was deeply influenced by Jane Addams's social concerns. With his wife, Alice, Dewey established a laboratory school at the University of Chicago in which he could evaluate new approaches to teaching. He was greatly aided in this enterprise by Ella Flagg Young, who had been

Crow Island classroom, Winnetka, 1940. Throughout the 1920s and 1930s, the "Winnetka Plan" served as a model of progressive education. It emphasized group and creative activities as well as individualized instruction designed to allow children to learn at their own pace. In this classroom, decorated with pictures and information about American Indians, students sit in a tipi while wearing costumes and weaving, activities designed to teach them about Native American culture. Photographer: Unknown. Source: Chicago Historical Society.

assistant superintendent of schools in Chicago before becoming a faculty member at the University of Chicago; she supervised the instruction in the lab school. Parker (whom Dewey thought of as "the father of progressive education") also joined the faculty at Chicago in 1901, shortly before his death.

Progressive philosophy was based on an optimistic view of human nature. Progressive SCHOOLS avoided the regimentation that characterized most schools of the era. The children who attended progressive schools learned in informal settings. These schools enlisted the spontaneous interests of the pupils and adapted the curriculum to the interests and needs of each child. The authoritarian approach was replaced by a more democratic mode and the ultimate goal, in Dewey's terms, was for the classroom to be an "embryonic community" that would provide a model for a more democratic larger society.

After Parker's death in 1902 and Dewey's departure from Chicago, their ideas continued to influence educational practices for many years. The school Parker founded and that bears his name is still in existence; so is Dewey's lab school. Young went on to become superintendent of schools in Chicago from 1909 to 1915. Carleton Washburne (whose mother had worked for Parker and who was also a friend of Dewey) served as superintendent of the suburban WINNETKA schools. In the 1920s and 1930s, under the leadership of Washburne, Winnetka became a much-visited model of how progressive practices could be implemented. With Flora J. Cooke (who had taught Dewey's son in the first grade at Cook County's elementary school) and Perry Dunlap Smith (a former student at Parker's school) Washburne founded the Winnetka Teachers College to prepare teachers to teach in the progressive tradition. After he left Chicago in 1904, Dewey devoted less of his attention to educational issues, but he continued to write about educational matters and served as president of the Progressive Education Association.

By the 1940s, progressive ideology and rhetoric (but not necessarily progressive practices) had become (in historian Lawrence Cremin's words) the "conventional wisdom" in American classrooms. In the cold-war atmosphere of the 1950s, however, educational progressivism came under serious attack. Progressive education was seen as endorsing Dewey's relativist ethics and as being insufficiently patriotic. Progressive curricula were held responsible for a lag in preparation for scientific and technological careers, culminating in the Sputnik crisis of 1957.

In the late 1960s and early 1970s, progressive ideas reemerged in the "open classroom" movement whose ideology was more closely tied to the romanticism of the 1960s than the ideas of Dewey and Parker. That movement proved to be short-lived. A new reaction against progressive ideology emerged with the recession and tax revolt of the 1970s, followed by the publication of the report *A Nation At Risk* (1983), which led to a new emphasis on basics, national learning standards, and improving results on standardized tests, all of which went counter to the ideas of Dewey and Parker.

Arthur Zilversmit

See also: Kindergarten Movement; Schooling for Work

Further reading: Campbell, Jack. *Colonel Francis W. Parker: The Children's Crusader.* 1967. • Cremin, Lawrence. *The Transformation of the School: Progressivism in American Education, 1876–1957.* 1961. • Dewey, John. *The School and Society.* Rev. ed. 1915.

Prohibition and Temperance. Organized expression of temperance ideas first appeared in Chicago in 1833 with the Chicago Temperance Society, a branch of the American Temperance Society, which attracted 120 members within a year. By 1847 Chicago had two Washington Temperance Societies, three tents of the Independent Order of Rechabites, three divisions of the Sons of Temperance, the Chicago Bethel (seaman's) Temperance Society, and the Catholic Benevolent Temperance Society.

Institutionalized temperance forces in Chicago soon turned to political processes. Primarily PROTESTANT organizations like the Washington Temperance Society joined the Good Templars (which organized both white and black lodges in Chicago) and the Catholic Total Abstinence Benevolent Association in fighting liquor licensing and urging statewide prohibition. Their efforts were partly responsible for the short-lived 1851 Illinois law which prohibited the sale of alcohol in quantities less than one quart, forbade consumption where sold, and banned the sale to minors under 18. All three points were repealed in 1853. These temperance forces also succeeded in pushing Chicago MAYOR Levi D. Boone to prosecute unlicensed saloonkeepers and in placing a referendum for statewide prohibition on the ballot in Illinois in June 1855. Although popular protest (known as the LAGER BEER RIOT) stopped Boone's reform efforts and voters rejected prohibition, Chicago temperance reformers enjoyed a brief period of political influence in the early 1850s.

Concern about the rising consumption of beer in the county generally, and in the city in particular, re-energized temperance work in Chicago immediately after the Civil War. In the 1870s and 1880s a number of new organizations appeared, including the WOMAN'S CHRISTIAN TEMPERANCE UNION (WCTU)

In 1908 the Cook County Woman's Christian Temperance Union organized a "dry" parade in Chicago that drew 6,000 marchers, according to the *Chicago Record Herald*. Under the campaign slogan "Let Illinois Go Dry," union leaders hoped to gain public support for the state's new local option law. A year after passage, the legislation had stimulated many downstate communities to prohibit the sale of liquor but found little support in Chicago's precincts. Photographer: Unknown. Source: Chicago Historical Society.

and the Citizens' League of Chicago for the Suppression of the Sale of Liquor to Minors. While both sought liquor law enforcement, the WCTU also pursued prohibitionist goals along with providing SOCIAL SERVICES that highlighted the problems women particularly faced from male intemperance. By 1889 the Chicago Central WCTU had established day care centers for children of working women, a medical dispensary, KINDERGARTENS and Sunday Schools, lodging houses, and a low-cost RESTAURANT, and had organized branches around the city and in the suburbs. New ROMAN CATHOLIC organizations, such as Erin's Hope Temperance and Benevolent Society and the Catholic Total Abstinence Union (CTAU), also organized in Chicago in this period. They pursued moral suasion and social-reform agendas but were not necessarily prohibitionist.

In 1898 the Anti-Saloon League (ASL), a group of Protestant clergy and laypeople (most of whom were men) committed to eradicating SALOONS and liquor traffic from the United States, organized in Illinois and by April 1900 claimed 18,000 members in 12 counties including metropolitan Chicago. Unlike the WCTU or the CTAU, the ASL's first agenda was the election of dry candidates. Aided by a sharp national increase in beer consumption between 1900 and 1913, their single-issue focus and pressure-politics approach worked: in 1907 the general assembly passed a LOCAL OPTION bill sponsored by the ASL that dried up two-thirds of Chicago precincts by 1909. In 1919 Illinois lawmakers ratified the Eighteenth Amendment to the United States Constitution, making the manufacture, sale, and transport of alcohol illegal in the state.

With the repeal of the federal amendment in 1933, the ASL effectively ceased to exist in Illinois and Chicago. Prohibition, however, fared somewhat better. EVANSTON, OAK PARK, RIVER FOREST, GLENCOE, WINNETKA, KENILWORTH, WESTERN SPRINGS, WILMETTE, LA GRANGE, PARK RIDGE, WHEATON, and MAYWOOD, plus 47 of Chicago's 4,136 precincts (or 1 percent), remained dry and only began gradually modifying their positions in the 1970s. Temperance, the individual decision to abstain from alcohol, also continued to interest Chicagoans. In 1937 an Evanston resident opened a chapter of Alcoholics Anonymous (AA), a loosely organized group begun by two alcoholics in Akron, Ohio, in 1935. By the end of 1949, the Chicago AA had 4,200 members. At the end of 1998, AA counted 75,000 members in the Chicago and suburban area, with more than 3,200 groups.

Alcohol consumption in the United States rose after 1960, and by the mid-1970s total annual consumption of absolute alcohol per capita was about two gallons, the highest level since the 1830s. Concern over the rising number of drunken-driving-related deaths led to state legislation raising the drinking age to 21 in 1980 and to the organization of Chicago-area chapters of Mothers Against Drunk Driving (MADD) in 1987. By the late 1990s, MADD had approximately one thousand members in a five-county area around Chicago (Cook, Lake, DuPage, McHenry, and Will).

Local temperance and prohibition work has also focused on using Chicago's 1934 local option law to dry up sections or locations in the city. For more than a decade Reverend Michael Pfleger, pastor of St. Sabina's, the largest AFRICAN AMERICAN Catholic Church on the SOUTH SIDE, led efforts to eradicate "nuisance" bars offering "adult" entertainment and prostitution as well as alcohol and billboards advertising alcohol to African Americans and Hispanics in their neighborhoods. In September 1997 and again in February 1998 the Chicago City Council passed ordinances to ban neighborhood billboards advertising alcohol and tobacco. Reverend James T. Meeks of the Salem Baptist Church in far South Side ROSELAND also led a working-class and poor African American community's struggle against the overpopulation of liquor stores and bars. In November 1998 voters in five ROSELAND-area precincts banned alcohol

Carter Harrison campaign poster, 1911 mayoral election. Source: Chicago Historical Society.

sales. As a whole, Chicago has become drier: in 1998 a total of 468 of the city's 2,450 precincts restricted the sale of alcohol.

Rachel E. Bohlmann

See also: Abolitionism; Drugs and Alcohol; Liquor Distribution; Sunday Closings; Vice Commissions

Further reading: Blocker, Jack S. *American Temperance Movements: Cycles of Reform.* 1989. • Pegram, Thomas R. "The Dry Machine: The Formation of the Anti-Saloon League of Illinois." *Illinois Historical Journal* 83 (Autumn 1990): 173–186. • Wiltsee, Herbert. "The Temperance Movement, 1848–1871." *Papers in Illinois History and Transactions for the Year 1937.* 1938.

Property Assessment. Throughout Chicago's history taxpayers and GOOD-GOVERNMENT groups have complained about inequitable property tax assessments. During the nineteenth century elected township assessors determined the value of taxable property in COOK COUNTY, and each assessor sought to lighten the tax burden in his TOWNSHIP through underassessment of REAL ESTATE. Inequity, moreover, was the norm, with favored property owners receiving inordinately low valuations. Much personal property, especially such intangibles as stocks and bonds, escaped taxation. To rectify these problems, in 1898 the Illinois legislature shifted control over assessment in Cook County to an elected, five-member county board of assessors. An elected, three-member board of review could revise assessments appealed by taxpayers.

Despite this shift of responsibility from the township to the county, many still criticized the assessment process. Among the most persistent critics were Catharine Goggin and Margaret Haley of the CHICAGO TEACHERS FEDERATION, who claimed that the underassessment of real estate and personal property deprived the public school system of needed revenues. Owing to the complaints of teachers and other groups, the Cook County Board of Commissioners in 1926 created the Joint Commission on Real Estate Valuation to consider the assessment problem. Meanwhile, an investigation of assessed valuations conducted by Prof. Herbert Simpson of NORTHWESTERN UNIVERSITY revealed gross inequities. The ratio of assessed value to sales value for LOOP property was two or three times that for property in outlying residential districts.

Moreover, assessments reflected the political influence of property owners. Whereas the home of the city's politically favored chief of detectives was valued at $500, the nearly identical house of his neighbor was assessed at $2,450. Confronted by such figures, in 1928 the State Tax Commission voided existing assessments and ordered a complete revaluation of Cook County. In 1932 the state legislature abolished the unsatisfactory county board of assessors and created in its stead the office of county assessor, concentrating authority over the assessment mechanism in the hands of a single elected official. Likewise, the three-member board of review yielded to a two-member board of appeals. During the 1930s, the county assessors were able to shift some of the tax burden to intangibles and correct some of the most flagrant abuses of the past.

But complaints persisted. During the 1970s and 1980s inflation in real-estate values resulted in sharply increased assessments, eliciting shrill protests from homeowners. Moreover, political favoritism and outright corruption tainted the assessment process. In 1980 some employees of the Cook County Board of Tax Appeals were indicted for accepting bribes to reduce valuations. Benefiting from the political advantages inherent in an office that determined the tax bills of 1.6 million parcels of real estate, Thomas Hynes, county assessor from 1979 to 1997, became a leading player in Cook County politics. Thus at the close of the twentieth century, there was no divorce between POLITICS and property assessment in Chicago, and taxpayers remained disgruntled and suspicious about the assessment process.

Jon C. Teaford

See also: Governing the Metropolis; Home Rule; Machine Politics; Tax Strikes; Taxation and Finance

Further reading: Simpson, Herbert D. *Tax Racket and Tax Reform in Chicago.* 1930. • Simpson, Herbert D. *The Tax Situation in Illinois.* 1929.

Prospect Heights, IL, Cook County, 21 miles NW of the Loop. Prospect Heights has a country-like atmosphere set amidst busy intersections, Palwaukee AIRPORT, and multifamily dwellings. According to local lore, Prospect Heights took its name from neighbors MOUNT PROSPECT and ARLINGTON HEIGHTS.

The east side contains commercial ventures and the airport. The west side encompasses two sloughs and houses on large lots with private wells. While RAILROAD lines in neighboring communities enticed Chicagoans to move to the northwest suburbs earlier, Prospect Heights remained in the shadows of settlement until the 1930s.

In 1830 a tract of one thousand acres located at Elmhurst and Willow Roads was home to the dairy farm of Hiram L. Kennicott. The farm's two hundred cows supplied milk and butter to Chicago markets. Kennicott was said to have lived in a "grand style": his home was nicknamed the Folly and housed tutors and governesses for his children.

Over a hundred years later, in 1935, the first houses were built along Elmhurst Road by developers Carlton Smith and Allen Dawson. They built low-cost homes and were nationally recognized for their early promotion of Federal Housing Administration financing. By the end of 1936, six two-story BUNGALOWS sat on large half-acre lots. The homes came with unfinished attics which could be used for later expansion. By 1945 there were 317 homes.

Sales were conducted from a garage at Camp McDonald and Elmhurst Roads. The building also served as a general store, meeting place, and post office. In 1937 a SHOPPING CENTER was erected at the corner by Smith and Dawson. Advertised as the Midwest's first planned "drive-in" shopping center, the four-corner hub became the town's center. In 1938, the small community formed the Prospect Heights Improvement Association (PHIA), which served both social and governmental needs. There were six hundred homes in the area by 1955. Proposals for incorporation garnered little interest from citizens until additional growth, the inability of the PHIA to control mounting problems, and the threat of ANNEXATION to other towns resulted in incorporation in 1976.

By the 1980s more that half of the city's housing was multifamily. At Euclid and Wheeling Roads, the development of the Rob Roy subdivision offered buyers townhouses set on a GOLF course. Another multifamily complex on the eastern fringes had a concentration of 110 buildings on 15 acres. This area of high density yielded a high rate of assault and battery cases. New single-family developments sprang up on the city's western border with Arlington Heights during the late 1980s and 1990s. The 2000 census tallied 17,081 residents, of whom 80 percent were white and 14 percent Hispanic.

Palwaukee Airport started in the 1920s on the border between Prospect Heights and WHEELING. In 1986 the two communities jointly purchased the airport, which is overseen by a commission with representatives from both communities.

Marilyn Elizabeth Perry

See also: Government, Suburban; Suburbs and Cities as Dual Metropolis

Further reading: Clipping files. Prospect Heights Library.

Prostitution. Chicago owes its reputation as a corrupt city in part to the history of one "vice" in particular—prostitution. Chicago's sex trade has been an adaptable industry and has undergone numerous transformations since the city's 1837 incorporation. In the middle of the nineteenth century, prostitutes labored in SALOONS, APARTMENTS, and rooming houses in and around the budding central business district, and in an enclave of brothels just north of the CHICAGO RIVER. However, as Chicago's prominence as a commercial center grew, so did its central business district, and disreputable resorts were eventually pushed in stages southward, out of the vicinity of reputable commerce. By 1900, the "Levee," bordered by 18th and 22nd Streets, State and Armour (Federal), was one of the nation's most infamous sex districts.

Twenty-second Street in the Levee district contained a variety of resorts ranging from the most extravagant brothels to small and unadorned houses of prostitution located in BOARDINGHOUSES and the back rooms of saloons. Some resorts provided male prostitutes for interested clients. So flagrant was Levee trade that Mayor Carter Harrison II appointed a commission to investigate vice conditions throughout the city. The 1911 publication of *The Social Evil in Chicago* prompted a flurry of reforms, including the closing of the Levee's most famous brothel, the exclusive Everleigh Club. Soon after, the U.S. state's attorney launched an attack on the Levee that quieted the once-thriving landscape of concentrated prostitution. The closing of the Levee in 1912 initiated important changes in the geography and institutions of sexual commerce in the city.

No longer based in brothels, prostitutes moved into the cabarets, NIGHTCLUBS, and other institutions of nighttime LEISURE that spread across the city during the 1920s. Many businesses evaded POLICE detection by relocating to the growing AFRICAN AMERICAN community on the city's SOUTH SIDE. Additionally, many sex entrepreneurs—saloonkeepers, club owners, HOTEL keepers, and sex workers—made arrangements with increasingly powerful vice syndicates to secure protection from police harassment.

Beginning in the 1920s, vice syndicates moved many saloons and houses of prostitution to the suburbs, where law enforcement was easier to control. Through the 1960s large houses of prostitution prospered on the outskirts of the city in CICERO, BURNHAM, STICKNEY, and CHICAGO HEIGHTS. Sexual commerce had not completely abandoned the city, however. Between 1920 and 1960, male and female prostitutes circulated in nightclubs within Chicago's South Side BLACK BELT and in bars and apartments throughout the city. Others worked the streets on the NEAR NORTH SIDE and intersections in commercial districts on the South Side.

In the last decades of the twentieth century, establishments linked to prostitution aggressively reentered the city landscape. In the early 1970s, massage parlors, peep shows, and bars featuring "live show girls" joined the street trade in areas like Rush Street on the Near North Side and Wells Street in OLD TOWN. During the late 1970s and the 1980s, urban redevelopment turned these pockets of sexual entertainment into districts with expensive condominiums and fashionable retail and dining. In the 1990s, GENTRIFICATION also displaced streetwalkers working on North Avenue west of Halsted. At the same time, new branches of the sex industry, including gentlemen's clubs and escort services, have packaged their services to appeal to a respectable clientele. However, women and men continue to work independently on the margins of the sex economy.

Cynthia M. Blair

See also: Crime and Chicago's Image; Near South Side; Underground Economy; Vice Districts

Further reading: Blair, Cynthia M. "Vicious Commerce: African American Women's Sex Work and the Transformation of Urban Space in Chicago, 1850–1915." Ph.D. diss., Harvard University. 1999.

Protestants. One can conceive of Protestantism as a movement within Christianity, the inspirer of various reform and educational agencies, an expression—at least in Chicago—of anti-Catholicism, or a gathering of denominations that were in some ways in competition with each other and in other ways could cooperate. Like most Americans, the telephone book's "Yellow Pages" classifies religions by denomination. So shall this article.

The chaos of Protestant sects and denominations acquires some outlines of order if one clusters the major ones. Thus the three leaders in colonial America—Episcopal, Presbyterian, and Congregational—were well poised to establish themselves at and after the birth of Chicago in 1833. The Episcopalians were the established church in the southern colonies, but Chicago benefited from the westward migration of the smaller Episcopal groups of the northeast. They were on the scene as early as 1834 and by 1837 had built their first church. John H. Kinzie, a prominent and wealthy son of a Chicago founder, was a major benefactor at St. James Episcopal Church, which was later to become the cathedral parish. Kinzie's interest is one indication of the tendency of the Episcopalians to attract wealthy residents.

They were not wholly united. Conflicts reflecting national church arguments took their toll. "High church" lovers of formality and incense berated "low church" majorities for being too informal. Both sides made accusations of each other and took their grievances to both churchly and secular courts. Such controversies did not prevent the majority of Episcopalians from staying united and establishing new parishes. Although they involved themselves in controversial court cases against each other, culminating in 1871, they united enough to build churches on a new and larger scale.

The Presbyterians were among the prime religious pioneers and newsmakers in the nineteenth century. Princeton graduate Jeremiah Porter arrived in 1833 as an agent of the American Home Mission Board of his church; within a year he gathered a flock and built First Presbyterian Church. But by 1837 it was torn over doctrinally complex issues that reflected national battles between Old School and New School factions. The conflict between antislavery forces and those that preferred not to take up the issue led to the founding of Second Presbyterian Church by those who resisted ABOLITIONIST preaching and work.

A celebrated incident in Chicago Presbyterianism occurred when the fashionable preacher

Swing Trial

One of the most celebrated heresy trials in American history was the Chicago Presbytery's 1874 prosecution of the popular Presbyterian preacher David Swing on charges of heterodoxy. Swing was well known for his repudiation of dogmatic religion and his relativist claim that religious expression cannot be understood apart from its culture. This reasoning infuriated theological conservatives like Francis Patton, professor at the Presbyterian Theological SEMINARY of the Northwest (now McCormick Theological Seminary) and future president of both Princeton University and Princeton Theological Seminary. Patton, who led the Presbytery's attack on Swing, argued that the preacher's logic might lead believers to consider doctrinal texts as culturally conditioned rather than absolutely valid.

Swing's acquittal by the Presbytery confirmed what many had already noticed: Chicago and the Midwest were successfully challenging the place of Princeton and East Coast theological conservatism as the dominant axes of American PROTESTANT thought and activity. Swing's exoneration sustained other Midwestern liberals in their continued disputes with protofundamentalists, until the latter retreated into separate denominational bodies in the 1920s and 1930s.

Brandon Johnson

Preston Bradley

The Michigan-born cleric, after brief service in Congregational and Presbyterian churches, early rejected the fundamentalism he learned at Chicago's MOODY BIBLE INSTITUTE and, with it, all Christian orthodoxy. He adopted what he called "Christian Unitarianism" and developed it as a form of liberal religious humanism. Bradley nurtured the North Side's Peoples Church into a major Chicago institution until it numbered four thousand followers. He spread his message over the radio to a claimed five million listeners. The civic-minded pastor served on the Chicago Public Library board for a half century after 1925; the Cultural Center in the historic library building perpetuates his memory and name. His Peoples Church saw rapid decline after he ended his long service there in 1976, but his influence continued. Long the city's best-known non-Catholic religious leader, Bradley parlayed a charismatic personality, masterly rhetoric, and a civic sense into a career that attracted the support of citizens who did not agree with his theology.

Martin E. Marty

Olivet Methodist Episcopal picnic, Garfield Park, 1900. Photographer: Unknown. Source: Chicago Public Library.

at FOURTH PRESBYTERIAN CHURCH, David Swing, started preaching what conservatives considered heresy between 1871 and 1875. This pathbreaking "modernist" spoke appreciatively of evolutionary theories and biblical criticism and preached gentle visions of God over against those of the more rigid Calvinists, whose doctrines struck him as harsh. Cleared by his presbytery of formal charges in 1874, he tired of fighting the Presbytery and founded an independent congregation that worshipped in the Central Music Hall, built for his services, and which attracted 5,000 to 7,000 people weekly.

The third of the dominant colonial groups, the Congregationalists, organized later as they moved out of their kin congregations, the Presbyterian churches, to form First Congregational Church in 1851. By 1871 there were 13 Congregationalist churches in Chicago, most of which took active roles in humanitarian and reform ventures in the rapidly growing city.

Their Chicago Theological SEMINARY was a leading school for training ministers. The appointment of Graham Taylor to the faculty in 1892 helped this seminary become a leader in the SOCIAL GOSPEL, just as the Chicago City Mission Society enabled the denomination to engage in efforts to deal with poverty and other urban miseries.

Two denominations that were growing strong in the East early in the nineteenth century prospered and helped transform the religious scene in Chicago from its beginnings. These were the Methodists and the Baptists. Jesse Walker represented a Methodist "circuit" as early as 1831, before Chicago incorporated, and the Methodists had their own house of worship as of 1834.

The Methodist Episcopal Church was a leader in the revival movement that aspired to attract converts and inspire the churches. Through revivals, Methodism came to be the largest (by 1848) of the English-speaking Protestant groups in the early decades of Chicago life. Methodists founded their first Sunday school in 1832 and encouraged efforts against the use of alcohol by founding the Chicago Washington Temperance Society in 1842. While most Methodists were English speaking, there were SWEDISH and other non-English-speaking Methodist missions.

The Methodists also had a heresy case, when Hiram W. Thomas, another early modernist and an adapter of Methodist teachings to currents of intellectual change, was pursued by orthodox stalwarts in the late 1870s. But he, like David Swing, resolved the issue by leaving the denomination, to found the Peoples Church of Chicago in 1880.

Chicago's Baptists prospered after the American Baptist Home Mission Society in 1833 sent Allen B. Freeman to represent them. They organized that year and began to build their first church in 1836. This denomination baptized through immersion, so new Baptists experienced the cold of LAKE MICHIGAN waters, their usual baptismal site.

Like the Methodists and Presbyterians, Baptists were to see long-lasting and, in the Baptist case, apparently permanent division into northern and southern bodies in the 1840s. While Chicagoans were in the northern group, they were not all united in passion against slavery, and their records give evidence of constant debate in the pre-CIVIL WAR years.

Like the Methodists, the Baptists also attracted some GERMANS and Scandinavians. This denomination favored expansion also by education. It was on the roots of a defunct seminary that Chicago Baptists, aided by funds from oil magnate John D. Rockefeller, founded the UNIVERSITY OF CHICAGO in 1892. Since the university was hospitable to all religions and to modernist theology, its activity inspired more conservative Baptists to found Northern Baptist Seminary in the twentieth century.

A third group that grew suddenly in the revivalist era on the frontier, the Disciples of Christ, developed in Chicago toward the end of the century. Conceiving of itself as a movement of Christian unity and resisting the idea of being a denomination, most of its members in Chicago favored the more moderate and eventually modernist wings of the movement and established a Disciples Divinity House at the University of Chicago, a signal of its cooperation with the Baptists and its choice to pursue modern intellectual currents in Protestantism.

To the colonial three and the frontier three, one would also add churches that appealed to immigrants from northern Europe. While some of these were Reformed, the majority were Lutherans from Germany and Scandinavia. Most were artisans, shopkeepers, and wage earners and were rarely as prosperous as Episcopalians, Presbyterians, and Congregationalists. By 1846 they had formed St. Paul's church, where what was to become the Lutheran Church–Missouri Synod was organized in 1847. But the choice to move in conservative Missouri's direction led to a split, and St. Paul's Reformed church was the consequence. It outpaced the Lutheran counterpart in growth and, at the time of the schism, attracted many of the more prosperous members.

St. Paul's members were of German stock. Scandinavian immigrants arrived in considerable numbers in the decade of St. Paul's founding, and in 1848 the NORWEGIAN Lutheran Evangelical members erected their first building. Lutherans, many of them German and Scandinavian, had formed 17 congregations by 1870 and within two decades were the largest Protestant group in the city. They were less involved in the dynamics of Chicago life, in part because they ministered in languages other than English and in part because it was not part of their ethos to be regularly involved in public affairs. Nor did most of them cooperate with non-Lutherans on causes such as antislavery before the Civil War or Sunday School and kindred movements after it.

Universalists, like the Baptists in some respects but preachers of "universal salvation," arrived in 1836 and had built by 1844, while Unitarians, who as liberals had split from Congregationalism, came in 1836 and built in 1840. Opposed by the orthodox, neither grew enough to compete numerically with the seven larger groups.

The most significant new element on the religious scene was the AFRICAN AMERICAN

Services at a storefront Baptist church, 1941. Photographer: Russell Lee. Source: Library of Congress.

church, which had deep roots among Chicago's free blacks. In the 1840s the Methodist Episcopal Church helped found Quinn Chapel, where a black preacher was active in 1847 in a congregation that had its own permanent building by 1854. Soon Bethel African Methodist Episcopal Church took shape, and in 1862 a merger of two congregations led to the founding of a new power, Olivet Baptist. While the members of such churches numbered in the thousands by century's end, the dramatic growth among the several Baptist and Methodist denominations, Pentecostal groups such as the Church of God in Christ, and many independents (including "storefront" congregations) occurred during the Great Migration northward of southern blacks during and after the two World Wars.

These congregations often bought edifices built by suburban-bound white congregations on Chicago's South and later West Sides. Taken together, they command the loyalty of the vast majority of Protestants within the city limits, while the large and well-off white churches dominate the suburbs, beginning with Oak Park and Evanston and eventually spreading through the metropolitan area. The relative weakness of ties between white and black, suburban and city churches, and the division into and within denominations have worked to inhibit Protestant influence.

What did unite Protestants? When Roman Catholic immigrants arrived in large numbers, especially after the famines in Ireland late in the 1840s, Protestants who argued with each other over doctrine and competed for souls could join forces against the "Roman threat," and did so. In the 1870s when mass revivals attracted thousands to Protestant affairs, these Catholic immigrants withstood efforts at conversion and remained a bloc that kept gaining numbers and acquiring political clout. And as the Protestant-based temperance movements gained momentum in the 1870s and 1880s, leaders portrayed Catholics as hard-drinking, wayward, irreformable, and clannish elements in the city.

More positive causes did also unite them, however. Many of these were reform and education movements, such as the Chicago Bible Society, organized in 1835, and the Chicago Anti-Slavery Society, formed in 1840. Four years later a Chicago Female Anti-Slavery Society, again largely Protestant, symbolized the initiatives of women in controversial causes and charitable activity. The Woman's Christian Temperance Union, for example, was founded by Methodists in 1874; under the leadership of Frances E. Willard it often set the pace among temperance movements nationally, while Chicago remained a stronghold.

Revivals also drew supporters across denominational lines. After the financial panics of 1857, Chicago, along with other cities, experienced a "laymen's revival" of prayer, devotion, and good works. On that scene came Dwight L. Moody, a Congregational layperson, who founded Sunday schools, attracted thousands to his local rallies while holding revivals elsewhere as well, and helped perpetuate his evangelistic work by founding the Moody Bible Institute in 1889. Three years earlier, another revivalist, professional baseball player Billy Sunday, was converted at the Pacific Garden Mission (founded for down-and-outers in 1877) and went on to stage extravagant revivals nationally, again finding Chicago a congenial base.

By no means do these few denominations cover all that Protestant church organization means. At the end of the twentieth century a Chicago Yellow Pages listed well over 100 denominations, each distinctive but in most cases housing internal varieties that confound definition. Few of these denominations are in open conflict with each other; most of the divisions are internal. Many are quite small. They are also extraordinarily diverse. What do the 16 members of the Netherland Reformed Congregationalist have in common with the tens of thousands of fellow Protestants who are members of the African Methodist Episcopal Church, or what do either of them have in common with the various Lutherans, still the largest of the Chicago area's Protestant families? (Greater Chicago is believed to have more Lutheran members than any other city in the hemisphere.) The only comprehensive way to define Protestants is to say that they are the Western Christian bodies that are not of the Roman obedience, or "under the Pope."

Still, there are some patterns of coherence, ones that go beyond simple categories of race. A fundamental fissure and source of tension occurred, often with Chicago as the testing ground, between two families or emphases. The one has come to be called "mainstream" and the other "evangelical." The former includes most of the denominations mentioned above, while the evangelicals include smaller or more recently formed denominations, such as the Assemblies of God, or are less concerned with denominational life.

At the time of Chicago's layperson's revival of 1858, most mainstream and evangelical Protestants would have been content to be called either "Protestant" or "evangelical." But the rise of modernism in positive response to theories of evolution and biblical criticism at the fledgling University of Chicago and elsewhere; the emphasis on a liberal social gospel designed to reconceive the industrial order to make it more congruent with "the kingdom of God"; and the decline of interest by mainstream Protestants in evangelism and revivalism led to an increasing schism.

That Chicago Protestantism had a major role in shaping the new evangelicalism is clear from the fact that Dwight L. Moody and Billy Sunday both called Chicago home. Add to them the twentieth century's greatest evangelist, Billy Graham—recalling that he got his start at Wheaton College, at a western suburban church, and at Youth for Christ rallies, many of them in Chicago—and it is credible to claim Chicago as the place of impulse behind much evangelism.

When tensions between fundamentalists and modernists grew so intense that denominations broke apart, it was in Chicago where centers of liberalism and modernism found their home: the University of Chicago and what became Garrett-Evangelical Theological Seminary were propagators. Meanwhile, Northern Baptist Seminary, Wheaton College, and Moody Bible Institute were flagships for the conservative group as it found its new name—fundamentalism—in the mid-1920s. While the most celebrated battle between fundamentalists and modernists—the Scopes Trial in 1925—took place in Tennessee, Chicago had a major role. Pitted against antievolutionist William Jennings Bryan was Chicago lawyer Clarence Darrow. And the Chicago Divinity School provided telephoned or written signals for Darrow and the proevolutionists.

The most influential magazines of the two factions are edited in Chicago. *The Christian Century* has been a liberal leader throughout the past century. The Billy Graham evangelicals founded a competitor, *Christianity Today*, which issues from CAROL STREAM, in the western suburbs.

There have been efforts to bring coordinated activity among Protestants, most notably through a Church Federation of Greater Chicago (CFGC), agent of many ecumenical causes. But the drain of funds, talent, energy, and personnel to the suburbs depleted the resources and lessened the credibility of the CFGC as a voice for Protestantism—especially as the evangelicals, most of whom did not participate in the ecumenical cause, prospered and most African American churches remain independent. So Protestant congregations are dependent on and speak for themselves or through their denominations, or they vie individually for visibility and clout, or they do not try to influence the metropolis.

The biggest change in Protestantism came with decline of the reasons to oppose Catholicism, thanks to the Second Vatican Council (1962–1965), which opened Catholicism to its "separated brothers and sisters." Vestiges of Protestant-Catholic holy wars subsequently disappeared.

This leaves Protestantism potent especially in its African American congregations in the city and its largely white suburban churches. Each may have spheres of influence nearby. Some may take part in coalitions for certain specific causes. But there seems to be little effort to bring together all the people called Protestant into a movement that sets out to influence—and succeeds in doing so, even in a small way—the dispersed Protestants and others in the metropolitan area.

Martin E. Marty

See also: Prohibition and Temperance; Publishing and Media, Religious; Religion, Chicago's Influence on; Religious Geography; Religious Institutions

Further reading: Hutchison, William R. *The Modernist Impulse in American Protestantism.* 1976. • Marsden, George M. *Fundamentalism and American Culture: The Shaping of Twentieth-Century Evangelicalism, 1870–1925.* 1980. • Sernett, Milton C. "When Chicago Was Canaan." In *Bound for the Promised Land: African American Religion and the Great Migration,* 1997.

Provident Hospital. In 1891, Daniel Hale Williams, a well-known black surgeon and graduate of Chicago Medical College, organized Provident Hospital and Training School for Nurses at 29th and Dearborn in the DOUGLAS Community Area on Chicago's near SOUTH SIDE. His aim was to provide this community with an institution of medical care in which AFRICAN AMERICANS would be welcome as patients and professionals. Williams attracted national attention in 1893 when he sewed up the lining of a human heart following a stab wound—an operation that had previously been considered impossible. In 1933 the HOSPITAL moved to 432 East 51st Street.

Situated in relatively poor communities for the 96 years of its independent existence, Provident was a private institution relying partly on patient fees for income. Since many patients were unable to pay the cost of services, the hospital also depended on welfare reimbursements and charity, both of which proved inadequate. Paradoxically, CIVIL RIGHTS legislation in the 1960s further reduced Provident's income, by enabling black patients to patronize other hospitals.

Provident Hospital was scheduled to close when in the 1970s a federal loan enabled the construction of a new facility, completed in 1981. Quickly falling into arrears, however, the hospital shut its doors in 1987. COOK COUNTY bought the building and opened it as a satellite medical facility in 1993.

Paul A. Buelow

See also: Medical Education; Nursing and Nursing Education

Further reading: Bonner, Thomas Neville. *Medicine in Chicago, 1850–1950: A Chapter in the Social and Scientific Development of a City.* 2nd ed. 1991. • Buckler, Helen. *Doctor Dan: Pioneer in American Surgery.* 1954.

Public Art. *See* Art, Public

Public Baths. *See* Baths, Public

Public Broadcasting. In 1953, local educational and civic groups lobbied for the creation of a noncommercial television channel in Chicago. With enthusiastic viewer support and sufficient financial backing, these organizations formed the nonprofit Chicago Educational Television Association and convinced the Federal Communications Commission to grant a license for an educational station. WTTW's first broadcast aired on September 6, 1955, from the Banker's Building. WTTW later relocated to the MUSEUM OF SCIENCE AND INDUSTRY as a "working exhibit" and increased its on-air schedule to 43 hours each week. WTTW provided local programming that resonated with Chicago's audiences at a time when New York producers controlled most of Chicago's commercial stations. Forty years later, the Chicago region would boast three public BROADCASTING stations: WTTW (Channel 11), WYCC (Channel 20), and WYIN (Channel 56).

Consistent with its educational mission, WTTW worked with the Chicago Board of Education to create "TV College" in 1956. Chicago's TV College was the first program in the country to enable students to receive college credit through "telecourses." Televised courses lessened the burden on city COLLEGES as enrollment soared during the late 1950s and 1960s. After 10 years, approximately 80,000 students had enrolled. By 1972, TV College consumed the lion's share of WTTW's air-time and production hours. William McCarter, then president of WTTW, decided to transfer TV College to WXXW in order to allocate more of WTTW's programming time to local issues. WXXW broadcasted on Channel 20 from September 1964 until it went off the air ten years later.

Channel 20 remained "dark" until February 1983, when its ownership transferred to Chicago's city colleges and the station was renamed WYCC. WYCC now broadcasts a

WTTW: The Beginning of Public Broadcasting

One day in the early 1950s, Edward L. Ryerson received a call from a friend in Boston, Ralph Lowell. Both men were highly respected community leaders. Lowell urged Ryerson to organize a not-for-profit organization and apply to the Federal Communications Commission for a license to operate an educational television channel, just as Lowell had done in Boston. Assured by Lowell that this would be good for Chicago, Ryerson created WTTW-TV (its call letters stand for "window to the world"), which was awarded Channel 11. Fortunately for WTTW, Lowell did not have friends like Ryerson in New York, Los Angeles, Washington DC, Philadelphia, and other large cities, so Chicago got a head start on September 6, 1955, by broadcasting its first program for viewers in homes circling a 60-mile radius of the LOOP.

When WTTW sought community support, 500,000 Chicago-area citizens responded. After a temporary start in the Bankers Building, WTTW found a home in the MUSEUM OF SCIENCE AND INDUSTRY. With a low budget, 43 hours of programming a week were developed within the first year, including televised college courses for credit. Within 5 years, 15,000 students had enrolled; within 10 years, 80,000 had enrolled. By the mid-1960s, WTTW had moved into its own quarters at 5400 North St. Louis Avenue, where architects Perkins & Will had designed a studio and headquarters on five acres of land.

Newton Minow

variety of programming, including locally produced series and PBS specials as well as college telecourses. Students taking telecourses for college credit make up 10 percent of WYCC's viewership. WYCC also telecasts a block of Spanish-language shows and produces and distributes Spanish programs to Telemundo. In partnership with the Illinois High School Association, WYCC broadcasts "The Seasons of Champions," exclusive coverage of all boys' and girls' championship events.

Located in MERRILLVILLE, Indiana, WYIN's inaugural broadcast aired on Channel 56 in 1987. WYIN focuses on local news and airs high-school FOOTBALL games. WYIN shares many of its viewers and much of its programming with WTTW.

Public television filled many of the gaps left by commercial broadcasters by providing educational programming and sharp analysis of local political and cultural life to large audiences without commercial sponsorship. In recent decades, however, decreased federal funding and increased competition from cable channels such as Discovery, Arts & Entertainment, and the History Channel challenged that financial model. Neither the Public Broadcasting Act of 1967 nor the creation of the Corporation for Public Broadcasting provided adequate funding for public television, even with viewers' contributions. Struggling to stay financially afloat, stations including WTTW bolstered corporate ties and adopted underwriting programs that allowed discreet mentions of corporate sponsors' participation during broadcasts. These relationships raised lingering concerns about public broadcasting's ability to stay true to its educational mission when insufficient funding forces stations to court corporate supporters.

WBEZ (91.5 FM) has been Chicago's public radio station since 1943, when it began under the auspices of the Chicago Board of Education. Thirty years later, WBEZ joined National Public Radio (NPR), and in 1990 the WBEZ Alliance gained control of the station from the Chicago Board of Education. WBEZ offers a variety of programming, including news, talk, JAZZ, and cultural content. WBEZ has won praise for its emphasis on international news and its ability to reach Chicago's international listening communities.

Listeners tuning to the far left of the FM dial will find a number of other noncommercial radio stations, including the UNIVERSITY OF CHICAGO's WHPK (88.5 FM), LOYOLA UNIVERSITY's WLUW (88.7 FM), NORTHWESTERN UNIVERSITY's WNUR (89.3 FM), NORTHEASTERN ILLINOIS UNIVERSITY's WZRD (88.3 FM), the MEXICAN FINE ARTS CENTER MUSEUM's WRTE (90.5 FM) and the College of DuPage's WDCB (90.9 FM).

Allyson Hobbs

See also: Colleges, Junior and Community; Political Culture

Further reading: "Chicago. Television Stations. General" and "Television Stations. WTTW." Clipping files. Chicago Historical Society. • "Future of Public Television." Roundtable discussion aired July 17 and July 19, 1982, on *Kup's Show.* Museum of Broadcast Communications.

Public Buildings in the Loop. In 1835, there arose at the northeast corner of Clark and Randolph Streets Chicago's first courthouse, a simple but dignified one-story structure. Its architecture reflected America's enthrallment with the Greek revival style, a fashion which stemmed from Thomas Jefferson's conviction that it was the only style appropriate for a republic. Four wooden Doric columns embellished the portico on the front of the red brick rectangular building.

Chicagoans demanded a far grander county courthouse and city hall as the city's population swelled over 30,000. The answer was a tall two-story classically inspired cupola-crowned edifice erected in 1853 from plans by John M. Van Osdel, Chicago's first architect. It stood in the center of the block bounded by Randolph, Clark, Washington, and LaSalle Streets, the site of all future Chicago city halls. The structure was enlarged by the addition of an Italianate third floor in 1858. It was the bell atop this building that sounded the alarm of the Great FIRE OF 1871, until the building itself was consumed.

Following the fire, Chicago commissioned a city hall and courthouse which consciously sought to surpass the one being built in Philadelphia and thus unequivocally proclaim the recovery of the metropolis. Designed by city architect James J. Egan in a vaguely Second Empire style, the mammoth limestone and granite structure took nearly a dozen years to construct and did not open until 1885. Standing on a rusticated two-story base, 35-foot-tall Corinthian columns rose to an elaborate entablature embellished with allegorical figures. Its cost—more than $5 million—precluded the completion of the vast dome with which the architect envisioned crowning the structure. And as soon as the gigantic edifice was considered complete, serious structural problems surfaced, while poor planning made for extremely difficult working conditions. Thus, between 1906 and 1911, barely more than 20 years after it was inaugurated, Egan's structure was replaced by the present City Hall and County Building, a restrained limestone Beaux-Arts composition by Holabird & Roche. Externally, its chief decorative element is its 75-foot-high attached granite Corinthian columns. Internally, its chief glory was the handsome wood-paneled City Council Chamber adorned with murals by Frederic C. Bartlett depicting major events in the history of Chicago. Gutted by a fire in 1957, this fine space was superseded by a bland modernist room devised by Paul Gerhardt, Jr.

No building more perfectly expressed Chicago's ambition in the nineteenth century to be the country's preeminent municipality than Henry Ives Cobb's Federal Building in the block bounded by Adams, Clark, and Dearborn Streets and Jackson Boulevard. Constructed between 1898 and 1905 to house the federal courts, the city's main post office, and various government bureaus, the Federal

Cook County building demolition, Washington and Clark, 1904–5. Photographer: Unknown. Source: Chicago Historical Society.

Federal Building, on the block between West Jackson and West Adams, South Clark and South Dearborn, before its demolition in 1965–66. Photographer: John McCarthy. Source: Chicago Historical Society.

Building was in the form of a Greek cross atop a high base which filled the entire block. Cobb's splendid Roman-inspired composition terminated in a majestic dome. More than $2 million was spent on the decoration of the building's interior, which was centered on a 300-foot-high octagonal rotunda whose 100-foot diameter made it larger than that of the Capitol in Washington. Cobb's building was demolished in 1965. Its site now forms part of the area occupied by the Chicago Federal Center, consisting of the 30-story Everett McKinley Dirksen courtroom building, the 45-story John C. Kluczynski office building, and a single-story post office. The architects for this uncompromisingly modernist complex were Ludwig Mies van der Rohe; Schmidt, Garden & Erikson; C. F. Murphy Associates; and A. Epstein & Sons. While the old Federal Building boldly proclaimed the Beaux-Arts tenets of the WORLD'S COLUMBIAN EXPOSITION of 1893, the structures of the Chicago Federal Center, with their glass and steel curtain walls, are an unmistakable expression of the aesthetics of the Bauhaus, which found a welcoming home in Chicago in the 1930s.

Completed in 1985, the State of Illinois Center represents the first distinctive physical presence of STATE POLITICS and government in Chicago. The salmon, silver, and blue color scheme and the 17-story atrium mark this postmodern design by Murphy/Jahn.

Shepley, Rutan & Coolidge designed the CHICAGO PUBLIC LIBRARY, now the Chicago Cultural Center, on Michigan Avenue between Washington and Randolph Streets. It opened in 1897. The edifice's restrained limestone and granite elevations, consisting of high arched windows on the lower level, with screens of Ionic columns above, owe not a little to McKim, Mead & White's Boston Public Library completed a decade earlier. The library's interior is one of Chicago's supreme Gilded Age spaces, a rich mix of white Carrara and green Connemara marble, mother-of-pearl, and a glass mosaic supplied by Louis Comfort Tiffany. Between 1977 and 1993, the building was renovated by Holabird & Root into rooms containing a popular library and areas for concerts and exhibitions.

Its successor, the Harold Washington Library Center at 400 South State Street, by Hammond, Beeby & Babka and A. Epstein & Sons, is a postmodern amalgam of elements and motifs reflecting the history of Chicago architecture. Completed in 1991, it is constructed of the materials—granite and red brick—favored by architects like Solon S. Beman and John Wellborn Root of the First Chicago School. The powerful Syrian arches of its entrances and the soaring arched openings above them are an unmistakable tribute to Henry Hobson Richardson's Marshall Field Wholesale Store and to Dankmar Adler and Louis Sullivan's Walker WAREHOUSE and their AUDITORIUM BUILDING. Even the seed pods which decorate the Library's Congress Parkway and Van Buren Street elevations have their antecedents in those which ornamented the elevator cage doors in Adler & Sullivan's Chicago Stock Exchange.

The library culminates in a daring architectural gesture, an enormous glass and steel winter garden, an acknowledgment of the architects of Chicago's early steel-framed skyscrapers, such as William Le Baron Jenney, Martin Roche, and William Holabird. But in a nod to the Beaux-Arts architects of the 1893 fair, particularly Daniel Burnham, the winter garden has been given a romantic postmodern fillip, for its corners and pediments are embellished with enormous classical acroteria.

David Garrard Lowe

See also: Architecture: The First Chicago School; Architecture: The Second Chicago School; Built Environment of the Chicago Region; Governing the Metropolis; Loop; Places of Assembly

Further reading: Condit, Carl W. *The Chicago School of Architecture: A History of Commercial and Public Building in the Chicago Area, 1875–1925.* 1964. • Hoffman, Donald. *The Architecture of John Wellborn Root.* 1973. • Lowe, David Garrard. *Lost Chicago.* 1975.

Public Health. Cholera, a disease dreaded for its distinctive symptoms and high mortality rates, prompted Chicago's first official public health action in early July 1832. Troops en route to the BLACK HAWK WAR brought cholera to Chicago, helping to spread what was already a worldwide pandemic. Victims experienced diarrhea, vomiting, and acute cramps that quickly caused severe dehydration, producing a bluish and puckered appearance and death within 24 hours. Chicago's 4,000 residents turned toward the state legislature for financial aid. Reactions to the EPIDEMIC reflected the prevailing view that disease originated from filth; that cholera spread by water remained unclear until English physician John Snow's observations in 1854, and the exact nature of the disease remained unidentified until German physician Robert Koch's findings in 1883. For three days, the local leaders required all men between the ages of 21 and 60 to clean up the streets and ALLEYS of Chicago, with penalties for noncompliance ranging from seventy-five cents to five dollars.

Because residents still skirmished with cholera, Chicago's 1837 charter included a Board of Health and a health officer. The officer's responsibilities included inspecting food markets, preparing death certificates, constructing a quarantine hospital, visiting residents with infectious illnesses, and boarding vessels to check for sickness. Once the immediate threat of cholera subsided in the mid-1850s, however, support for the board dwindled.

Public interest turned to solving the city's WATER and sewage problems. A wooden inlet that extended six hundred feet into LAKE MICHIGAN supplied Chicago with water until 1863, when the city council adopted a plan to build a two-mile TUNNEL under the lake to secure a cleaner supply. But the lake still functioned both as the main WATER SUPPLY and the main drainage depository. In 1855 the council asked the nationally acclaimed engineer, Ellis Sylvester Chesbrough, to devise a sewage solution. Chesbrough proposed creating an underground sewer system to drain into the CHICAGO RIVER and then into LAKE MICHIGAN. This plan necessitated a literal raising of the city's elevation, but the intolerable stench made the project worth the cost.

With financial pressures compounded by the Panic of 1857, Chicago eliminated the Board of Health entirely. The POLICE department assumed the board's duties and powers, until the reappearance of cholera in 1867 forced its reinstatement. Despite improvements in the WATER SUPPLY, and the re-creation of the Board of Health, the epidemic hit Chicago hard. Of the 1,561 cases reported, 990 persons died.

Although cholera retreated in the 1850s and 1860s, Chicagoans continued to suffer from infectious diseases such as scarlet fever, typhoid fever, and diphtheria. Until the bacteriological discoveries of the 1880s and 1890s, dirt remained the primary, though incorrect, explanation for disease. Consequently, public health policies focused on environmental issues, specifically garbage, sewage, and water.

The Great FIRE OF 1871 generated a series of potential public health threats. Leaving 93,000 people HOMELESS and vulnerable to disease, the blaze also leveled a significant portion of the city's medical INFRASTRUCTURE. Rush Medical College, the first medical school in Chicago, was completely destroyed, along with six HOSPITALS, over one hundred wholesale and drugstores, and the offices of four medical journals. Approximately two hundred physicians lost their homes, offices, libraries, and practices as a result of the fire. The WOMAN'S MEDICAL COLLEGE, which had opened its doors only the previous year, was also destroyed. The fire resulted in a permanent relocation for Rush, next to COOK COUNTY HOSPITAL. This proximity was considered advantageous, because internships and postgraduate residencies were becoming an integral part of a physician's professional education.

The CHICAGO RELIEF AND AID SOCIETY, an organization comprising private individuals and public officials, built temporary barracks to house the homeless and established several policies to prevent epidemic diseases. Sanitary officers conducted daily inspections of these makeshift quarters, and the city required a smallpox vaccination for anyone receiving relief. In spite of these efforts, smallpox, dormant since 1865, broke out. Over 2,000 people contracted the disease following the fire, and more than one-fourth of those infected died. Children under five were particularly susceptible to the disease, making their mortality rate the worst in Chicago's history.

Like the cholera outbreaks, the fire's threat to public health stimulated pressure to increase the powers of the Board of Health. In 1876 the city reorganized its GOVERNMENT and established a permanent Department of Health to grapple with public health concerns. But the department's formation did not mean that its future decisions would go uncontested.

The MEATPACKING industry proved particularly resistant to public health policies. From its inception, the industry dumped animal carcasses and chemicals into Lake Michigan and the Chicago River, subjecting not only workers but also the general public to health risks from a contaminated food and water supply. In attempting to clean up the meatpacking industry, Oscar Coleman De Wolf, the commissioner of health in the late 1870s and 1880s, instituted workplace inspections and attempted to move the slaughterhouses to the outskirts of the city. De Wolf's initiatives cost him his position after the 1889 municipal elections. Inside the meatpacking plants, packaging of spoiled meat and dangerous working conditions continued through the 1890s and 1900s. Upton Sinclair's exposé of the industry in THE JUNGLE, intended to draw attention to dangerous and unhealthy working conditions, resulted instead in the 1906 Meat Inspection and Pure Food and Drug Acts to protect consumers.

By the late 1880s Chicago's tremendous growth provoked the city to adopt another Chesbrough proposal, this time reversing the flow of the Chicago River to direct sewage from the river through a canal to the DES PLAINES RIVER, which eventually drained into the Mississippi. Upon completion in 1900, the Sanitary and Ship Canal's immediate impact was a lawsuit by Missouri, which remained unconvinced that the pollution dissipated prior to reaching its borders.

The Pure Food and Drug Act also generated attempts to regulate Chicago's milk supply. In 1909, Chicago became the first city in the United States to pass an ordinance requiring compulsory milk pasteurization. This law did not guarantee the city's residents access to safe, pure, and cheap milk, however, in part because of discrepancies between Illinois statutes and Chicago ordinances. The city passed stricter regulations than the state and had a larger inspecting staff. But Chicago still faced great difficulty enforcing its rules, because it could not command uniform standards from 12,000 dairies in four different states that supplied residents with milk. Nor was it able to exercise regulatory control over an interest group with power at the state level. Like its counterparts elsewhere in the nation, the Chicago Health Department found it difficult to assert local interests against other state forces. The city had always relied on the state for funds and support, but its particular urban public health ills put the city at odds with surrounding counties, who relied on the state to protect their interests. The conflict between the needs of city, county, and state became even more complex in the 1940s and 1950s, as METROPOLITAN GROWTH led to the establishment of autonomous health departments in suburban counties.

Private groups also worked to protect Chicago's public health. In 1889, Jane Addams founded HULL HOUSE, the first SETTLEMENT HOUSE in the United States, to attend to the needs of the surrounding immigrant community, including issues of health. In conjunction with Hull House, Addams founded a Visiting Nurse Association to supply NURSES to visit the working poor in their own homes. The association stationed nurses in 25 different districts in the city and supplied nurses for businesses like the Deering Reaper Works. Hull House also played an important role in shaping a national conception of public health issues through its surveys of working-class labor and living conditions. Alice Hamilton, who eventually became the nation's expert on industrial health, began her career at Hull House supervising these studies.

WORLD WAR I raised new public health issues. The war provoked the initial wave of the "GREAT MIGRATION," and AFRICAN AMERICANS who came to Chicago from the South were segregated into substandard and crowded living conditions, raising concerns about possible epidemics of contagious diseases. In reporting on the migration, Chicago's white daily NEWSPAPERS warned their readers that the migrants posed a threat both to themselves and to public health in general. The racial basis for these fears obscures a legitimate cause for concern: African Americans' living and working conditions imperiled their health. While TUBERCULOSIS death rates decreased for the white population of Chicago during the 1920s, the disease increased among African Americans. By 1930, 1,000 out of every 100,000 African Americans in Chicago died of the disease, compared to 400 for MEXICAN immigrants and 60 for the rest of Chicago's population. Although these numbers suggested an epidemic, racial biases kept Chicago's health department from taking extensive action. An unofficial policy maintained separate privately run medical institutions for African Americans, consisting of PROVIDENT HOSPITAL and the African American division of the Visiting Nurse Association. The health department's lax involvement also reflected medical knowledge at the time. The identification of the microbe that caused tuberculosis in the late nineteenth century had not led to a cure; treatment programs focused instead on individual prevention.

By 1932, public health encompassed not just regulations but also investigation, health education, licensing, and the construction of clinical programs. During the 1930s and 1940s, Chicago's programs ranged from milk regulations to the prevention and treatment of venereal disease. In 1955, Chicago became one of the first cities in the United States to introduce the Salk vaccine, and, facing a polio epidemic, the city's board of health instituted mass inoculations within the following year. During this period, one man's vision directed the board's public health policies. Herman Niels Bundesen, a Northwestern Medical School graduate, served as health commissioner from 1922 until his retirement in 1960. He lost his position as head only once, from 1927 to 1930, when he fell out of political favor with Mayor William Hale Thompson.

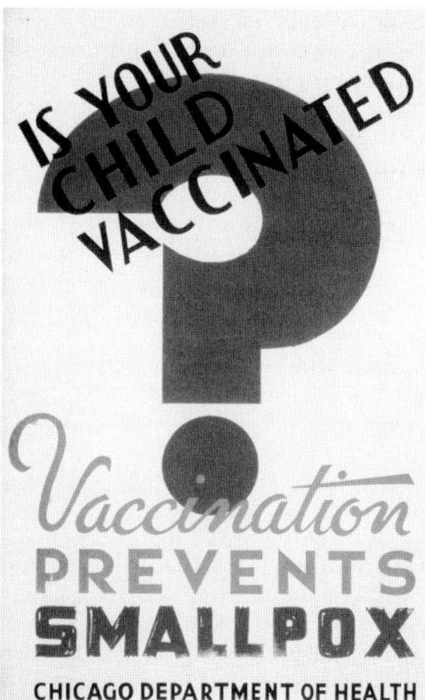

Designed by an artist working on the Illinois WPA Art Project in the late 1930s, this bold-red question mark drew the public's attention to the threat of smallpox. Promoting childhood vaccinations became an important strategy toward preventing outbreaks. The prevalence of the disease in the United States diminished in the twentieth century, and the World Health Organization declared in 1979 that it had been completely eliminated. Artist: Unknown. Source: Library of Congress.

Bundesen's programs sometimes met with resistance, particularly his 1922 campaign against venereal disease. Venereal disease had become an important issue in Chicago, as well as nationally, during World War I. Initially, Bundesen followed national guidelines that encouraged incarcerating suspected prostitutes to curb the spread of gonorrhea and syphilis among military personnel. He also resolved to fight the disease after the war with an aggressive program of distributing condoms in brothels, public restrooms, drugstores, and municipal CLINICS. Arguing that his tactics promoted immoral behavior, Chicago newspapers and medical journals condemned his proposal. Despite these disputes, Bundesen persisted and, in 1937, secured public support and national funding to conduct a comprehensive public health campaign against syphilis. This battle over contraception and public policy would reemerge in the 1980s and 1990s with regard to teen pregnancy and AIDS, engendering a debate among SCHOOL boards, public health officials, and the general public over the creation of health clinics within schools and the distribution of free prophylactics.

Chicago last revised its public health system in 1975. Bundesen's tenure had consolidated

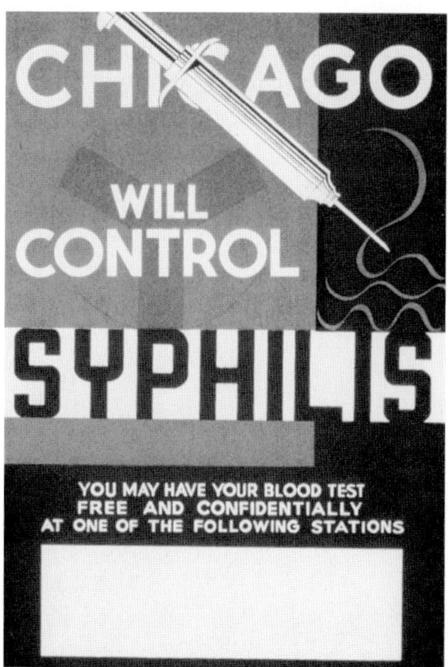

The Federal Art Project created tactful publicity to aid the Chicago Health Department's efforts to eradicate syphilis in the 1930s. Artist: Unknown. Source: Library of Congress.

policy making and management, and this last revision separated the two. A nine-member policy-making body, appointed by the mayor, constituted a new Board of Health. A new Department of Health administered programs and enforced regulations, reflecting the increased growth of programs and personnel. By 1986, Chicago employed almost 2,000 people to manage 6 neighborhood health centers, 12 maternal and child health clinics, a tuberculosis control program, a sexually transmitted disease program, 19 community MENTAL HEALTH centers, and an alcoholic treatment center hospital. In providing both education and treatment, these programs' roots extended as far back as the Visiting Nurse Association, but their specific methods and programs reflected late-twentieth-century public health concerns.

Pressures on Chicago's public health system continued as the century drew to a close. The shutdown of neighborhood hospitals in the 1980s placed increased demands on the public health care system. An increase in health maintenance organizations met some of these needs, but those most vulnerable, for socioeconomic reasons, remained at risk. In 1993, approximately 1.6 million people in Chicago were either uninsured, inadequately covered, or recipients of Medicaid. Although AIDS affected the city more gradually than in New York and San Francisco, by 1997 over 9,000 Chicagoans had died from this disease. Private organizations have taken the initiative in confronting AIDS. This new epidemic, coupled with the rising cost of health care, raises familiar questions about the power of public health authorities and how social understandings of disease influence the delivery of health care.

Jennifer Koslow

Heat Wave of 1995

On July 12, 1995, a dangerous hot-air mass settled over Chicago, producing three consecutive days of temperatures over 99 degrees Fahrenheit, heat indices (which measure the heat experienced by a typical person) around 120, high humidity, and little evening cooling. The heat wave was not the most extreme weather system in the city's history, but it proved to be Chicago's most deadly environmental event. During the week of the most severe weather, 485 city residents, many of whom were old, alone, and impoverished, died of causes that medical examiners attributed to the heat. Several hundred decedents were never autopsied, though, and after the event the Chicago Department of Public Health discovered that 739 Chicagoans in excess of the norm had perished while thousands more had been hospitalized for heat-related problems.

The patterns of heat wave mortality show that the disaster had a social as well as an ecological etiology. Over 70 percent of the victims were aged 65 and above; and AFRICAN AMERICAN mortality rates were roughly 1.5 times higher than those for whites. The heat wave deaths were concentrated in the predominantly African American community areas on the South and West Sides of Chicago, the places that also have high mortality rates and low life expectancy during normal times. The extreme weather helped to make visible some of the new dangers related to aging, isolation, and concentrated poverty in Chicago.

Eric Klinenberg

See also: Children's Health; Demography; Drug Retailing; Drugs and Alcohol; Environmental Politics; Medical Education; Occupational Safety and Health

Further reading: Bonner, Thomas Neville. *Medicine in Chicago, 1850–1950: A Chapter in the Social and Scientific Development of a City.* 1957. • Ginzberg, Eli, Howard S. Berliner, and Miriam Ostow. *Changing U.S. Health Care: A Study of Four Metropolitan Areas.* 1993. • Haas, Shirley. *150 Years of Municipal Health Care in the City of Chicago: Board of Health, Department of Health, 1835–1985.* 1985.

Public Housing. Public housing is one kind of SUBSIDIZED HOUSING found in the Chicago metropolitan area. Subsidized housing has included public and private initiatives, and the subsidies have been targeted at different classes. The CHICAGO HOUSING AUTHORITY and similar authorities in the suburbs have been responsible for public housing throughout the metropolitan area.

Ann Durkin Keating

Public Schools. *See* Schools and Education

Chicago grew by leaps and bounds and by 1890 was a sprawling metropolis, its residents held together by an intricate system of street railways. Public transit began with omnibus service on some major streets in the 1850s and quickly evolved into an extensive network of horsecar lines. Chicago's street railway companies adopted the cable car as an improvement to horsecar service, not as a separate network. Feeder cars pulled by horses were often attached to cable cars to be pulled downtown. Unable to cross movable bridges, the cable car systems took over or constructed three tunnels under the Chicago River. By 1890, the network was the world's largest, covering approximately 38 route miles and failing to penetrate only the southwestern and northernmost districts of the city. Beginning in 1892, electric traction quickly replaced the complicated cable technology, and Chicago's last cable car ran in 1906. It was this system, ultimately switching from streetcars to buses, that solved the problem of transporting hundreds of thousands of daily commuters to work across the vast face of the city.

Horse-drawn omnibus, ca. 1890s. Photographer: Unknown. Source: Chicago Historical Society.

Cable car, North Chicago Street R.R. Co., Clybourn Avenue, late 1880s. Photographer: Unknown. Source: Chicago Historical Society.

Chicago's Street Railways in 1890

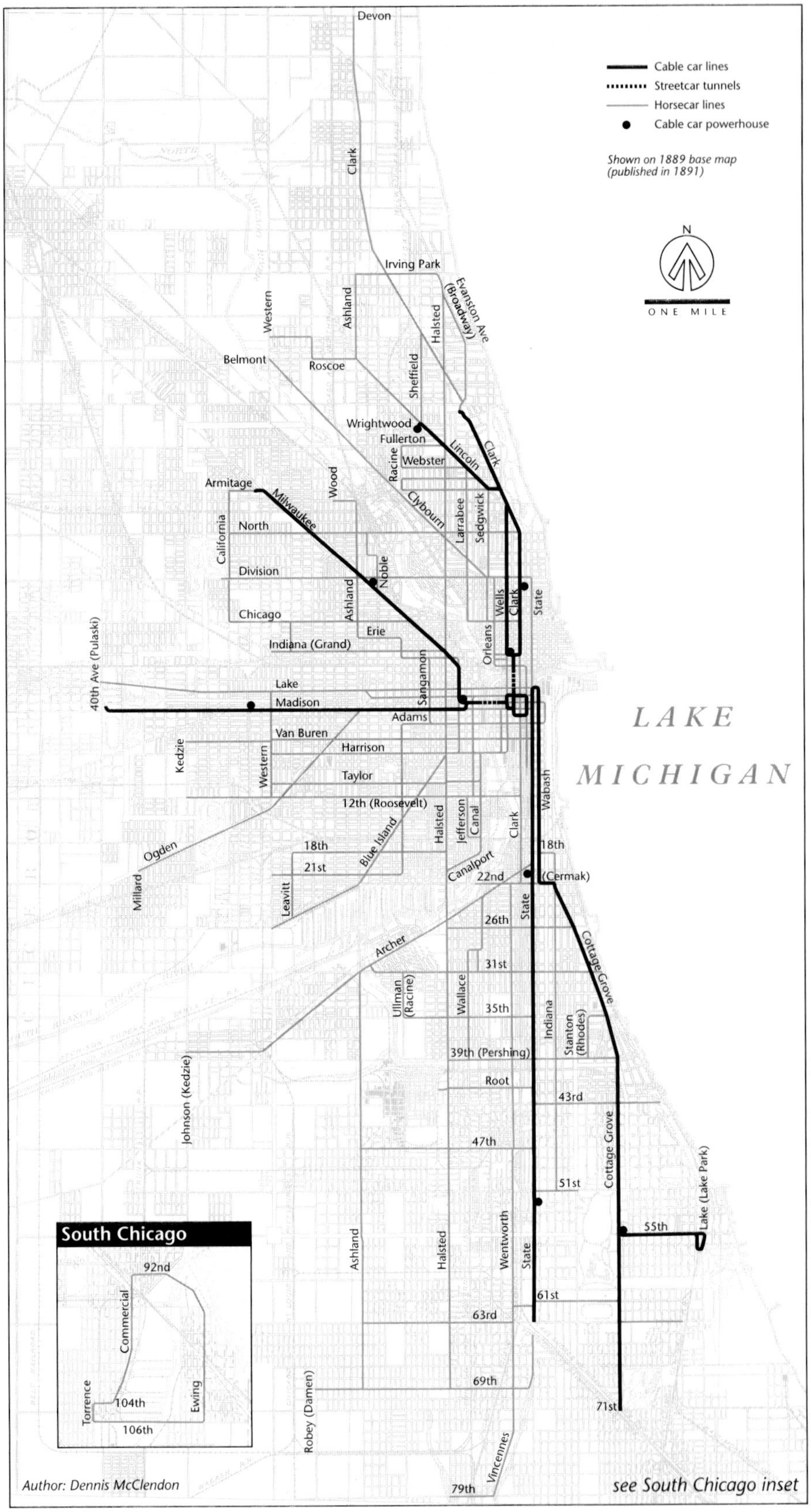

Cable car lines
Streetcar tunnels
Horsecar lines
Cable car powerhouse

Shown on 1889 base map (published in 1891)

N

ONE MILE

LAKE MICHIGAN

South Chicago

Author: Dennis McClendon

see South Chicago inset

© 2004 The Newberry Library

Public Speaking. *See* Free Speech; Lectures and Public Speaking

Public Transportation. Chicago before 1848 was a "walking city" whose inhabitants could easily get anywhere in town on foot or horseback. As population increased rapidly in the 1850s, the demand for public TRANSPORTATION arose. For nearly a century, private firms provided Chicagoans with transportation.

The first public transportation vehicles were omnibuses, which were horse-drawn carriages seating 20 to 30 people developed in France

Trolley bus, Central Avenue at Lake Street, 1930s. Photographer: Unknown. Source: Chicago Public Library.

Streetcar direct to World's Fair, 1933. Photographer: Unknown. Source: University of Illinois at Chicago.

in the 1600s. In Chicago, the first omnibuses in 1852 were nothing more than intercity stagecoaches put out of business by the newly arrived railroads and relegated to shuttling passengers between railroad stations. Omnibus operators probably filled seats with local commuters willing to pay a nickel to avoid walking. Cabs at the time cost 30 cents a ride and livery stable operators charged three dollars a day to rent a horse and carriage.

Poor drainage that turned Chicago streets into quagmires after a rain led to the replacement of omnibuses with street railways beginning in 1859. The earliest horsecars were little more than omnibuses fitted with steel wheels to run on rails spiked to the planks that covered streets.

In 1855–56 the mainline railroads began hauling local passengers to nearby summer resorts and offered them discounted or "commuted" fares to attract business. As the resorts grew, they became year-round settlements, or suburbs, and the residents who rode the trains to work each day in Chicago became known as commuters.

As Chicago's population continued to grow, reaching 1 million in 1890, the street railway company executives began looking for more efficient ways to carry the growing number of commuters. The use of small steam locomotives called "dummies" to pull streetcars was not successful, but after 1882 many horsecar lines were successfully converted to cable cars, and after 1890 to electric trolley cars. Increased traffic congestion in downtown Chicago in 1892 led to the construction of the city's first elevated railways. The Loop Elevated was opened in 1897.

Motor buses appeared during World War I but did not make much of an impact on public transportation for a decade. In 1958 the Chicago Transit Authority completed its program to replace streetcars with buses.

Public ownership of mass transit systems began in 1945 with the creation of the Chicago Transit Authority and developed on a piecemeal basis for the next 40 years as the privately owned companies got into financial difficulty because of dwindling ridership. The use of taxes to subsidize mass transit on an annual basis began in 1975 after the creation of the Regional Transportation Authority.

By the end of the twentieth century Chicago's public transportation system had grown into one of the largest in the world run by several public authorities. The commuter railroads consisted of more than five hundred miles of lines served by 130 locomotives and 970 passenger cars providing approximately 75 million rides a year. Pace carried 39 million riders on more than 600 buses and 300 paratransit vehicles. The Chicago Transit Authority, the largest of the public transportation systems in 1997, carried 287 million riders annually on approximately 1,900 buses and 130 million on 1,150 rapid transit cars.

The private automobile accounted for 79.7 percent of all commuter trips in the metropolitan area in 1990, and mass transit 15 percent. But the geographic distribution of these proportions suggests that availability of mass transit alternatives played a crucial role. Of the 774,000 people who entered downtown Chicago on an average day in 1980, only 202,582 came in private autos. Most of the rest rode buses, trains, or taxis.

David M. Young

See also: Built Environment of the Chicago Region; Metropolitan Growth; Rapid Transit

Further reading: Barrett, Paul. *The Automobile and Urban Transit: The Formation of Public Policy in Chicago, 1900–1930.* 1983. • Mayer, Harold M., and Richard C. Wade. *Chicago: Growth of a Metropolis.* 1969. • Young, David M. *Chicago Transit: An Illustrated History.* 1998.

Public Works, Federal Funding for.

From its earliest beginnings Chicago's public works infrastructure has intermittently been the focus of federal financial and technical support. Direct federal support has significantly shaped the city and region, but such support has not been a constant in the efforts to provide effective water supply, sanitation and wastewater treatment, transportation, solid waste disposal, flood control, parks, schools, and libraries. Funding for public works has come largely from area cities and villages using their own resources, leveraged by private investment and contributions from philanthropists and civic organizations. More recently, funding has come from special districts, and state and regional bodies.

Fort Dearborn, built near what is now Michigan Avenue and the Chicago River in 1803, arguably was Chicago's first public work. In 1833 Congress appropriated $25,000 to enable the U.S. Army Corps of Engineers to make harbor improvements and build a lighthouse. Another $30,000 in federal funds was allocated in 1838 for extending the channel. By 1869, Chicago's harbor was under the control of the corps. Federal involvement during the railroad era was mostly in the form of land grants, although Sen. Stephen Douglas (and others) argued effectively for additional federal aid to the Illinois Central Railroad.

Direct federal aid to Chicago (as well as other large cities) was negligible until the New Deal programs of the 1930s. Federal funds were used to complete construction of the last water crib in 1934, and a $5.5 million federal grant helped initiate construction of the city's South Water Filtration Plant in 1938. The Works Progress Administration (WPA) spent over $1 million on the construction of Midway Airport, which became the nation's busiest by 1939. WPA also helped pay for the construction of the Outer Drive, including the bridge over the Chicago River (part of the S curve), and the completion of Grant Park. Construction of Chicago's subway was partially funded through the Public Works Administration (PWA), which contributed $26 million of the $75 million total cost. The city was not the only area recipient of federal funds during the New Deal. The suburb of WINNETKA received $1.5 million, nearly half the total needed to depress the railway tracks running through the village in order to eliminate 10 grade crossings. Before 1938, more than 30 people had died in crossing accidents in Winnetka.

In the post–WORLD WAR II era, federal funding for transportation, URBAN RENEWAL, and PUBLIC HOUSING was significant. Federal funds contributed approximately 20 percent of the cost of improving O'HARE Field, which itself was on land purchased as surplus by the city from the U.S. Defense Department. From 1950 to 1970 some 40,000 units of public housing were built, largely with federal aid.

Federal resources have been instrumental in the construction of the Metropolitan Water Reclamation District's Tunnel and Reservoir Plan (TARP or DEEP TUNNEL). This project will eventually involve the construction of over 125 miles of TUNNELS, some as much as three hundred feet underground, and three enormous detention basins. Flood control in the Chicago region in the next century will depend largely on TARP.

Many city and regional transportation initiatives in the 1990s would not have been possible without federal support. Such projects as the extension of RAPID TRANSIT service to both O'Hare and Midway Airports depended on federal funds. The resurfacing of the Kennedy EXPRESSWAY and other major highway, bridge, and street projects in the 1990s were also the recipients of major federal funding.

Howard Rosen

See also: Environmental Politics; Governing the Metropolis; Government, Suburban; Political Culture

Further reading: Barrett, Paul. *The Automobile and Urban Transit: Policy Formation in Chicago, 1900–1930.* 1983. • Keating, Ann Durkin. *Building Chicago: Suburban Developers and the Creation of a Divided Metropolis.* 1988. • Mayer, Harold M., and Richard C. Wade. *Chicago: Growth of a Metropolis.* 1973.

Publishing and Media, Religious. Before the invention of radio and television, religious groups used print media to disseminate information, debate theological questions, and evangelize America's expanding population. Bible and tract societies distributed Christian materials, and colporteurs (mobile religious salesmen) sold books and evangelized across the city. But magazines and journals proved the most popular form of spreading the Christian message.

The middle and late nineteenth century was the golden age of religious publishing in Chicago. Because of Chicago's central location, many denominational headquarters have been located in the city, and virtually every PROTESTANT group had its own publication. The *Northwestern Baptist* journal, published in the early 1840s, was Chicago's first religious publication. The *Watchman of the Prairies,* also Baptist, soon followed in 1847 and was replaced six years later by the *Christian Times.* At midcentury, Congregationalists and New School Presbyterians created the *Herald of the Prairies,* and the Methodists began printing the *Northwestern Christian Advocate.*

Not to be outdone, Episcopalians had the *Church Record* in 1857 and then in 1862 the *American Churchman.* Presbyterians united behind the *Interior* in 1870. The first Quaker paper in the West, the *Herald of Peace,* began publishing in 1867. Seventh-day Adventists had the *Advent Christian Times* and Mennonites the *Herald of Truth,* both founded in 1864. GERMAN and SWEDISH Lutherans each had their own papers by 1870, as did Swedish and NORWEGIAN Methodists.

Not all religious publishing was Protestant. Spiritualists published the *Religio-Philosophical Journal* (1868–1870) and *News from the Spirit World* (1865–1895). ROMAN CATHOLICS published several periodicals, including the *Western Tablet* for the IRISH and the *Katholisches Wocheblatt* for Germans. In the 1870s Reform JEWS began printing the *Occident* and the *Reform Advocate.* Even individual congregations, such as the Salem Baptist Church and the local Swedenborgians, often undertook to publish their own magazines.

In the twentieth century, religious publications became more consolidated, but even more prominent, in Chicago. The *Christian Century,* under the early guidance of Charles Clayton Morrison, soon became the preeminent voice of mainline Protestantism. Evangelist Billy Graham helped to create a conservative Christian alternative, *Christianity Today.* First published in 1956, it soon became the most widely read religious magazine in America. Other important religious journals include *U.S. Catholic* and the NATION OF ISLAM's *Final Call.* Other kinds of religious media have enriched the city too. Many book publishers, like Thomas More and Moody Publishers, have located here. MOODY BIBLE INSTITUTE continues to be a pioneer in religious BROADCASTING through WMBI radio.

The "Sunday Evening Club" has long been a Chicago broadcasting staple. Founded in 1908 as a "club" so that it wouldn't sound too "churchy," the program began a weekly radio broadcast of an ecumenical religious service held in Orchestra Hall. High-profile speakers like Jane Addams, Reinhold Niebuhr, and W. E. B. Du Bois gained a wide audience and soon earned it the title of "The Nation's Pulpit." In 1956 the program made the transition from radio to public television, and it continues to offer weekly sermon installments.

R. Jonathan Moore

See also: Journalism; Religion, Chicago's Influence on; Religious Institutions

Further reading: Pierce, Bessie Louise. *A History of Chicago.* 3 vols. 1937–1957.

Publishing, Book. Book publishing in Chicago, a BUSINESS almost as old as the city itself, established its basic nature early on. Its initial growth and source of strength for a full century afterwards was tied to the city's rapid development as the nation's rail center—RAND MCNALLY got its start printing timetables, and the RAILROADS also made possible Chicago's early emergence as a distribution point for subscription titles, reference books, and school texts. Though for brief periods Chicago flourished as a writers' town, the trade book and MAGAZINE publishers they needed to support their efforts were never sufficiently numerous to keep them here. Nevertheless, the distinguished UNIVERSITY OF CHICAGO Press has maintained its position as the nation's largest university PRESS, and the metropolitan area's several specialty publishers have remained strong. By the 1990s, consolidation and technological changes in the book industry nationwide meant that the metropolitan area was no longer a center for any particular kind of publishing; on the other hand, changes in book distribution nationwide have enabled writers and small publishers in Chicago to compete with others around the country on an equal basis.

Chicago's first two publishers were printer Robert Fergus and bookseller S. C. Griggs. In 1839, Fergus issued the city's first regular directory, and in 1876 he began publishing the remarkable Fergus Historical Series, 35 titles chronicling the city's past. Griggs arrived in 1846, two years before the first railroad; a few years later his Literary Emporium on the Prairies had become the nation's largest domestic book agent. In 1872, he sold that business to concentrate on book publishing.

Rand McNally started in 1856 and soon began printing railroad tickets and timetables, which eventually led to guidebooks and MAPS, in which the firm pioneered both technologically and conceptually. Throughout its long history, Rand McNally often developed a substantial line of textbooks and occasionally a trade list; the latter included paperbacks for travelers in the 1870s and Thor Heyerdahl's *Kon-Tiki* in 1950. In the 1990s, it sold its printing business to confine its efforts to geography-related products.

When R. R. Donnelley & Sons was formally established in 1882, Richard Donnelley had been in both the PRINTING and publishing businesses in Chicago for nearly 20 years. One of his first ventures was the Lakeside Library, an 1870s series of inexpensive paperbacks. Though the name has been continued in the annual Lakeside Classics gift books, the firm has followed its founder's dictum that publishing and printing are separate activities, dedicating itself to being North America's largest commercial printer.

However, with some help from these giants, Chicago had become the largest publishing center west of New York City by the 1880s. In addition to the "DIME NOVEL" and subscription book publishers—Belford, Clarke was a major one—publishers of county histories like Benjamin F. Lewis flourished here. Chicago's significance as a literary center began at the same time. In 1880, the *Dial* was established in cooperation with A. C. McClurg (originally Jansen, McClurg & Company), successor to Griggs and still a leading wholesaler and retailer. While the *Dial* was becoming the nation's leading literary magazine, the city's NEWSPAPERS were drawing talents such as Eugene Field, George Ade, Theodore Dreiser, Floyd Dell, and Finley Peter Dunne, many of whom were attracted to the "Saints & Sinners Corner" in McClurg's Wabash Avenue bookstore. McClurg also published some Chicago writers, but his firm's most lucrative publishing venture came after his death, when in 1914 OAK PARK native Edgar Rice Burroughs brought them his *Tarzan of the Apes.* By 1933, the Griggs and McClurg bookselling operation had evolved into Kroch's & Brentano's.

Stone & Kimball, another noted venture, began in 1893 and quickly distinguished itself not only for the graphic and literary quality of its books but the elegance and enthusiasm with which it promoted them. Essential to this was the noted *Chap-Book,* a combination sales piece and literary journal. Contemporaneous were Way & Williams, which followed the tradition of fine printing, and a firm eventually known as Reilly & Lee, which in 1904 began publishing L. Frank Baum's Oz books and later Edgar Guest's popular poetry. In 1918, the P. F. Volland Company brought out the first of Johnny Gruelle's phenomenal Raggedy Ann and Andy series and other books for children.

A. N. Marquis was the city's first major reference book publisher; his *Who's Who in America* appeared in 1899. The *World Book Encyclopedia,* an easy-to-read general reference, was first published in Chicago in 1917. *Compton's Pictured Encyclopedia,* compiled by innovator Frank Compton, first appeared to considerable acclaim in 1922. Sometime earlier, SEARS, ROEBUCK had begun selling the *Encyclopaedia Britannica* through its catalog; in the 1930s, Sears moved *EB*'s editorial offices from New York to Chicago, where it became a major employer of editorial talent. After a few changes in ownership, it began evolving into an electronic information source in the 1990s.

The textbook business was led for nearly a century by Scott, Foresman & Co. In 1896 the company acquired *Robert's Rules of Order* from Griggs's firm and soon assumed national leadership through series such as the Elston Readers, first introduced in 1909, which evolved into the phenomenal Dick and Jane primers by the 1940s. In the 1920s, Row, Peterson published

ARTICLES OF AGREEMENT made this twentieth day of January, 1903, by and between Professor W. E. B. DuBois, of Atlanta, Georgia, party of the first part, and A. C. McClurg & Co., party of the second part.

WITNESSETH, That whereas the said W. E. B. DuBois is the owner of a manuscript entitled "The Souls of Black Folk" and desires to publish the same, Now, therefore, the said W. E. B. DuBois, in consideration of the agreement of said A. C. McClurg & Co., hereinafter contained, hereby gives, licenses, and allows to said A. C. McClurg & Co., its successors and assigns, the exclusive right of printing, publishing, and selling the aforesaid work, and any revisions of the same.

AND the said A. C. McClurg & Co., in consideration of the foregoing agreement, hereby agrees on its part as follows: That it will print and publish said manuscript at its own expense, at a retail price of one dollar ($1.00) net or one dollar and twenty cents ($1.20) net; that it will manage the sale of said book; see to the distribution of the usual editorial copies; give to said book a moderate amount of general magazine and newspaper advertising, and pay to the author a royalty of ten per cent (10%) upon the retail price of all copies sold over and above the first five hundred (500) copies sold.

A. C. McClurg & Co., further agrees to make and furnish to said W. E. B. DuBois statements of sales of said book and to pay any royalties due semi-annually, namely in February and June of each year; that it will present to said W. E. B. DuBois six (6) copies of the book immediately upon publication, and sell to him any additional copies desired at a discount of twenty-five per cent (25%) from the retail price of said book, said additional copies so purchased to be entitled to royalties.

It is understood and agreed that the book shall be copyrighted in the name of A. C. McClurg & Co., but that the ownership of the copyright will be vested entirely in said W. E. B. DuBois.

It is further understood and agreed that said W. E. B. DuBois will continue to intrust the publication of the book to A. C. McClurg & Co., so long as no proper ground of complaint shall be found against its management of the interests of said book; and if at any time said W. E. B. DuBois shall desire to remove the publication of said book from A. C. McClurg & Co., said W. E. B. DuBois shall then purchase from A. C. McClurg & Co., at a proper valuation, the electrotype and binder's plates.

WITNESS our hands, in duplicate, the day and year first above written.

W. E. B. DuBois

A. C. McClurg & Co.

Contract between W. E. B. DuBois and A. C. McClurg & Co. for *The Souls of Black Folk,* January 20, 1903. Source: The Newberry Library.

"Locking up a form" in the composition room of R. R. Donnelley & Sons, 1950. Photographer: Unknown. Source: Chicago Historical Society.

one of the first U.S. history texts to be used on both sides of the Mason-Dixon Line, and in 1939 Science Research Associates became a pioneer in the field of testing and guidance materials. Children's publishers included Albert Whitman & Company, which acquired its famed Boxcar Children series in 1942.

Evangelical publishing began in 1869 when Fleming H. Revell established a firm that could extend the ministry of evangelist Dwight L. Moody, his brother-in-law; one of the nation's premier religious houses for decades, it moved to the East Coast around 1910. Later, the Moody Bible Institute established its own press. One of its directors translated parts of the Bible into a version he called *The Living Bible* and in 1962 established Tyndale House Publishers to publish it. The firm later became the area's major evangelical publisher. In 1972, KAZI Publications was established to distribute and publish Islamic materials.

While the city's larger specialty publishers (Playboy Enterprises, Crain Communications, and Johnson Publishing Company) have published few books, some smaller specialty houses have been successful. By the 1990s, Third World Press had established itself as one of the nation's leading African American book publishers. The socialist Charles H. Kerr & Company was still around to observe its centennial in 1986; and Open Court, in nearby LaSalle, established in 1887 to publish scientific and religious books, also became a prominent publisher of textbooks and magazines for children.

More representative of late twentieth-century trends is the trade publishing firm established in 1947 by Henry Regnery; however distinctive, its nonfiction list was never very profitable, and 25 years later it became Contemporary Books, a publisher of sports titles and adult education material. In the early 1990s, it was acquired by the Tribune Company, which a few years later merged it into another acquisition, textbook house NTC Publishing. NTC/Contemporary was sold in 2000 to New York-based McGraw-Hill.

So although in 1900, it had looked as though trade publishing in Chicago could assume national leadership, this potential was ephemeral. By century's end, book publishing in Chicago was no longer even a major employer. The text and reference houses had moved or substantially contracted. Chicago's publishers were small-scale and specialized: Ivan R. Dee's nonfiction list, a revived Northwestern University Press, and Sourcebooks' popular compilations among them. Distributors such as the Independent Publishers Group capitalized on the growth of small independent publishers around the country. Various associations and a local book review tried to create a missing sense of community among Chicago-area publishers, but their dissimilar interests and geographic dispersion made that difficult. Chicago's various pieces of the book business may have been healthy, but its whole has never become greater than a sum of its parts.

Connie Goddard

See also: Literary Cultures; Music Publishing; Publishing and Media, Religious; Trade Publications

Further reading: Goodpasture, Wendell W. "Chicago Publishers through 75 Years." *Union League Men and Events* 31.2 (February 1955). • Regnery, Henry. *Creative Chicago: From the Chap-Book to the University.* 1993. • Tebbel, John. *A History of Book Publishing in the United States.* 4 vols. 1972–1982.

Puerto Ricans. Although a handful of Puerto Rican men and women moved to Chicago from New York in the 1930s, the first significant wave of Puerto Rican migration to Chicago began in the late 1940s. Unlike other newcomers, Puerto Ricans did not face legal barriers in moving to the United States. The Jones Act of 1917 conferred U.S. citizenship to all island and U.S.-born Puerto Ricans, which facilitated the large migration of Puerto Ricans to cities such as Chicago beginning in the late 1940s. Beginning in 1946 a private Chicago-based employment agency, Castle, Barton and Associates, recruited Puerto Rican men to work as unskilled foundry laborers and Puerto Rican women to serve as domestic workers in Chicago and suburbs such as Waukegan. Generally, single men and women moved to Chicago and sent for family members once they established stable jobs and residences.

These early migrants lived in various neighborhoods, including Woodlawn, the Near North Side, Lake View, Lincoln Park, Uptown, West Garfield Park, East Garfield Park, and the Near West Side. By the 1960s most Chicago Puerto Ricans were concentrated in Lincoln Park, West Town, and Humboldt Park and shared these neighborhoods with Mexican and Polish immigrants as well as African Americans. In Lincoln Park, Puerto Rican residents established a small, ethnic enclave along Armitage Avenue that included small grocery stores and businesses providing goods and services for Puerto Rican neighbors. By the mid-1960s, however, Puerto Rican and other low-income residents of Lincoln Park were displaced by urban renewal programs and the redevelopment of Lincoln Park. Puerto Rican residents relocated to West Town and Humboldt Park, where their concentration facilitated the creation of Chicago's first Puerto Rican *barrio,* or neighborhood, along Division Street, or, as residents frequently refer to it, *la Division.*

For Puerto Ricans in Chicago, Division Street plays a prominent role in the history of the development of their community. The annual Puerto Rican Parade, celebrated every June, ends with a procession down Division Street and is an important celebration of Puerto Rican cultural and national pride. Originally, this celebration commemorated *El Día de San Juan* (St. John's Day), an event organized by *Los Caballeros de San Juan* (the Knights of St. John), one of the first Puerto

Rican religious and social organizations in Chicago. *Los Caballeros de San Juan* was a key religious institution which, like the office of the Commonwealth of Puerto Rico, promoted integration of Puerto Rican migrants into mainstream Chicago life while maintaining cultural pride and integrity. In 1966 *El Día de San Juan* celebrations were renamed the Puerto Rican Parade and included new community institutions in the organizing of the annual festivities.

It was during this first Puerto Rican Parade on June 12, 1966, that one of the first Puerto Rican riots in the U.S. began, on Division Street. The riot, one of many urban disturbances across the nation in the 1960s, was a response to the shooting of a young Puerto Rican man by Chicago POLICE. Rioting continued until June 14. A key moment in the history of Puerto Ricans in Chicago, the Division Street riot drew attention to poverty and to strained relations between Puerto Ricans and Chicago's police department. At the same time it facilitated the creation of Puerto Rican community organizations such as the Spanish Action Committee of Chicago (SACC), the Latin American Defense Organization (LADO), and, in the early 1970s, ASPIRA Association and the Ruiz Belvis Cultural Center. A month after the riot, the Chicago Commission on Human Relations held open hearings which provided a forum for Puerto Rican and other Spanish-speaking residents of Chicago to discuss problems facing these communities such as discrimination in housing, hiring practices by the police and fire departments, and poor educational opportunities. As a result of these meetings, specific policy recommendations were proposed and implemented in the Puerto Rican community. The Puerto Rican community organizations which emerged from the riots also ensured that community concerns such as education, housing, health, and employment would be actively addressed and that Puerto Ricans would maintain a presence in city POLITICS.

Division Street continues to be an important part of Chicago's Puerto Rican community. The area remains a primary port of entry for new Puerto Rican migrants. It is also an ethnic enclave known as *Paseo Boricua* (Puerto Rican Road) with Puerto Rican stores, shops, and restaurants situated between the two 50-ton Puerto Rican flags that cross Division Street near the intersections with Western and California Avenues. Because no legal barriers prevent migration between Puerto Rico and the mainland, first- and second-generation migrants move freely and frequently between Chicago and Puerto Rico. The 2000 census counted 113,055 Puerto Ricans, 15 percent of Chicago's Latino population and second only to Chicago's Mexicans among the city's Latino communities. While new migrants continued to settle in the Division Street area, LOGAN SQUARE, BELMONT CRAGIN, and HERMOSA became increasingly popular neighborhoods for Chicago Puerto Ricans in the 1990s. That decade also witnessed the growth of Puerto Ricans living in Chicago suburbs such as NAPERVILLE and SCHAUMBURG as companies began to recruit highly skilled, bilingual employees to work in information technologies and consulting. This new migration of white-collar workers, however, contrasted sharply with the skills and employment opportunities of most Puerto Ricans in Chicago. In 1990, 60 percent of Puerto Rican men and women continued to work in manufacturing industries, as laborers, and in the service sector of the Chicago economy.

Despite their long history in the city, Chicago Puerto Ricans continue to maintain cultural, political, and economic links with Puerto Rico.

Gina M. Pérez

See also: Demography; Fuerzas Armadas de Liberación Nacional (FALN); Multicentered Chicago

Further reading: Maldonado, Edwin. "Contract Labor and the Origin of Puerto Rican *Communities* in the United States." *International Migration Review* 13 (1979): 103–121. • Padilla, Elena. "Puerto Rican Immigrants in New York and Chicago." Ph.D. diss., University of Chicago. 1947. • Padilla, Felix. *Puerto Rican Chicago.* 1987.

Pullman, Community Area 50, 14 miles SE of Loop. Once the most famous planned community in America, the oldest part of Pullman is notable for its role in American labor and PLANNING history. The town had its origins in the late 1870s as George M. Pullman looked for solutions to two problems. The first was where to build a new factory for his Pullman Palace Cars, the sleeping and parlor cars that were becoming increasingly popular with those traveling on the country's expanding rail system. The second was how to attract and encourage workers who would share his vision of American society. Pullman wanted to avoid the types of workers who participated in the turbulent 1877 Railroad STRIKE, or those he believed to be discouraged and morally corrupted by urban poverty and social dislocation.

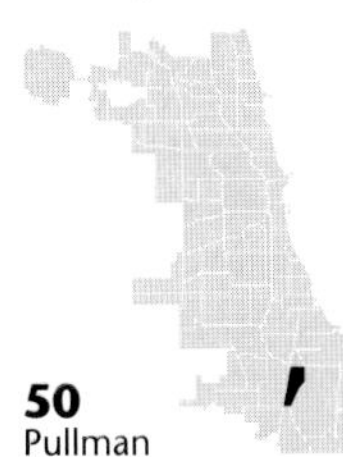

Although his primary manufacturing plant was located in Detroit, Pullman was a long-time Chicago resident. With the assistance of Colonel James Bowen, the Pullman Land Association quietly purchased four thousand acres near Lake Calumet in an area both thought had a bright industrial future. Pullman hired architect Solon Beman and landscape architect Nathan Barrett to erect a town designed to provide its residents with decent housing in a socially and physically healthy environment that would also generate a 6 percent profit for the Pullman Palace Car Company. Even before Pullman's first residents settled there in 1881, visitors came to admire its beauty, which stood in stark contrast to other working-class areas in industrial cities, and to marvel at the success of its social planning. Not only did Pullman workers live in brick houses, they and their families had access to schools, parks, a library, a theater, educational programs, and many other activities provided by the town. When state labor commissioners visited in 1884, they proclaimed it a successful venture, especially for the women and children, who seemed protected from the worst aspects of industrial America.

Not all observers viewed Pullman from the same perspective. In 1885, Richard T. Ely published an exposé in *Harper's Monthly* charging that the town and its design were un-American, a paternalistic system that took away men's rights as citizens, including the right to control their own domestic environment. When Pullman workers went on strike in 1894, protesting cuts in wages while rents and dividends remained unchanged, the strike captured a national audience. Commentators from across the nation debated the proper nature of the relationship between employers and employees, as well as the broader question of the political, social, and economic rights of working-class men and women.

By the close of the strike, even such bulwarks of Chicago's BUSINESS community as the *Chicago Tribune* and Swift & Co. publicly decried the suffering inflicted on law-abiding employees by an inflexible Pullman management. The Illinois State Supreme Court gave legal weight to this sentiment in 1898 when it ordered the company to divest itself of residential property in Pullman. By the end of the first decade of the twentieth century, Pullman had become another Chicago neighborhood, tied closely to the surrounding communities of KENSINGTON and ROSELAND.

In subsequent years, the Pullman community experienced changes familiar to other neighborhoods in the city: ethnic succession, the aging of housing stock, and changing employment opportunities that attracted residents away from the Pullman Car Works and into jobs elsewhere. Residents still perceived Pullman as a good place to live; neighbors maintained strong ties to each other, to their predominantly ITALIAN and POLISH ethnic communities, and to the neighborhood itself. Outsiders, however, saw old housing and vacant industrial land. Pullman's reputation fell most dramatically in the late 1920s and 1930s, when UNEMPLOYMENT and BOOTLEGGING activities made it seem to be a nascent slum. By then, Chicago sociologists had expanded the Pullman COMMUNITY AREA to include the largely unsettled area between the old historic town and 95th Street. In 1960, consultants to the South End Chamber of Commerce recommended that Pullman be demolished between 111th and 115th to make way for industrial expansion to benefit the remainder of the Calumet region.

Pullman residents fought this destruction. In 1960, they reactivated the Pullman Civic Organization to remove any signs of blight and to lobby to keep their neighborhood. Realizing that the community's own history could provide a valuable wedge in leading that fight, they founded the Historic Pullman Foundation in 1973. Pullman was designated a National Historic Landmark in 1971 and has received similar state and local designations. Pullman, the original showpiece community, retains much of its original architecture and spatial orientation and attracts thousands of visitors each year. In 1994, North Pullman residents, largely an African American population, achieved city landmark status for their area of Pullman as well. At the same time, they established a museum honoring Pullman porters. Since then, the city has joined the two separate districts into one Chicago landmark district.

The Pullman Car Works produced its last railroad car in 1981. A decade later the state of Illinois purchased a section of the plant, along with the Hotel Florence, the largest public building in Pullman, with the hope of creating a museum featuring the history of the community and the company. In December of 1998, a fire swept through the vacant clock tower and construction shops, putting the museum plans in doubt and creating a new challenge for the community and its residents.

Janice L. Reiff

See also: Brotherhood of Sleeping Car Porters; Economic Geography; Historic Preservation; Planning Chicago; Pullman Strike; South Side; Unionization

Further reading: Pullman Archives. The Newberry Library, Chicago, IL. • Reiff, Janice L. "Rethinking Pullman: Urban Space and Working-Class Activism." *Social Science History* 24.1 (2001): 7–32. • Smith, Carl. *Urban Disorder and the Shape of Belief: The Great Chicago Fire, the Haymarket Bomb, and the Model Town of Pullman.* 1995.

George Pullman and His Town

George Pullman established himself in Chicago in March 1859, as a building raiser and mover. He soon began converting railroad chair cars into luxurious sleeping vehicles. His first major sleeper, *The Pioneer,* appeared in May 1865, followed in February 1867 by the chartering of Pullman's Palace Car Company. For the next two and a half decades, Pullman expanded his operations and overcame his competitors until he controlled the industry. As a leading industrialist, he assisted in rebuilding Chicago after the 1871 fire, and helped found and support many of its social and cultural organizations. He also erected the Pullman Building in downtown Chicago and a home on Prairie Avenue.

After 1881, when Pullman opened the town of Pullman, Illinois, to house his construction plant and his workers, he was hailed as an enlightened employer who considered the best interests of his employees. This image was destroyed following the 1886 Haymarket Riot, and during a strike at the Pullman works between May and July 1894 which publicized his antilabor stance. Pullman's peers censured him for refusing to deal with strikers during the stoppage, while a subsequent government investigation revealed his unsympathetic treatment of employees.

Liston E. Leyendecker

Pullman Strike. The most famous and far-reaching labor conflict in a period of severe economic depression and social unrest, the Pullman STRIKE began May 11, 1894, with a walkout by PULLMAN PALACE CAR COMPANY factory workers after negotiations over declining wages failed. These workers appealed for support to the American Railway Union (ARU), which argued unsuccessfully for arbitration. On June 20, the ARU gave notice that beginning June 26 its membership would no longer work trains that included Pullman cars.

The boycott, although centered in Chicago, crippled railroad traffic nationwide, until the federal government intervened in early July, first with a comprehensive injunction essentially forbidding all boycott activity and then by dispatching regular soldiers to Chicago and elsewhere. The soldiers joined with local authorities in getting the trains running again, though not without considerable vandalism and violence. ARU president Eugene Victor Debs was arrested and subsequently imprisoned for disregarding the injunction. The boycott and the union were broken by mid-July, partly because of the ARU's inability to secure broader support from labor leaders.

While the use of an injunction for such purposes, upheld by the Supreme Court in 1895, was a setback for UNIONISM, and while most public sentiment was against the boycott, George Pullman attracted broad criticism and his workers wide sympathy. A federal panel appointed to investigate the strike sharply criticized the company's paternalistic policies and refusal to arbitrate, advancing the idea of the need for unions and for increased government regulation in an age of large-scale industrialization.

Carl Smith

See also: Antiunionism; Business of Chicago; Kensington; Pullman; Railroad Workers; Roseland; Welfare Capitalism

Further reading: Lindsey, Almont. *The Pullman Strike: The Story of a Unique Experiment and of a Great Labor Upheaval.* 1942. • Smith, Carl. *Urban Disorder and the Shape of Belief: The Great Chicago Fire, the Haymarket Bomb, and the Model Town of Pullman.* 1995. • United States Strike Commission. *Report on the Chicago Strike of June–July, 1894.* 1895.

Purdue University Calumet. Purdue University Calumet began as an extension to Purdue University, which opened in West Lafayette, Indiana, in 1874 on land granted to the state from the federal government; it was named for local businessman and benefactor John Purdue. In the late 1940s, this extension campus in Hammond, Indiana—the industry-heavy corridor 3 miles east of the Illinois border and 25 miles southeast of Chicago—began offering courses to students working toward a degree from Purdue's West Lafayette campus. Purdue Calumet has since become an autonomous degree-granting university, a commuter school whose five campuses served more than 9,000 students in the 2001 academic year, over half of them on a part-time basis and nearly 40 percent over the age of 25.

Sarah Fenton

See also: Indiana University Northwest; Universities and Their Cities

Quarrying, Stonecutting, and Brickmaking. From the city's beginnings through much of the twentieth century, the production of stone and brick was a major economic activity in the Chicago area. Millions of tons of limestone quarried from local sites have been used to create the area's BUILT ENVIRONMENT. Huge quantities of clay bricks and other basic CONSTRUCTION materials have also been produced by local companies over the years.

During the years when Chicago grew from a small town into a metropolis, quarries in COOK and WILL Counties were Illinois' leading producers of limestone and dolomite. By the 1850s, there were large limestone quarries southwest of Chicago, near the town of LEMONT along the ILLINOIS & MICHIGAN CANAL, employing as many as 300 men each. By 1900, quarries in Cook and Will Counties produced about \$2 million worth of limestone and dolomite a year, which accounted for over 6 percent of total U.S. output. As late as 1948, Chicago-area quarries—several of which were owned by the Material Service Corporation—were generating over a third of the limestone and dolomite produced in Illinois. By that time, most of the working quarries in the area were in suburbs to the west and south of the city, including ELMHURST, RIVERSIDE, LA GRANGE, BELLWOOD, MCCOOK, HODGKINS, and THORNTON.

After the stone was quarried, it still had to be processed and marketed. In the nineteenth century, stone-processing companies were among the largest of all Chicago-area enterprises. In many cases, stone was quarried outside the city and hauled into local "stone works" for cutting, polishing, and distribution. Just after the FIRE OF 1871, there were at least six stone works in the city that employed more than 200 men each. Among the largest of these companies were Singer & Talcott and Wenthe & Messinger, both of which were established during the 1850s. In the 1880s and 1890s, several local firms merged into larger organizations such as the Western Stone Company and the American Stone Company. By the 1890s local limestone had been displaced for building purposes by better-quality Bedford limestone from Indiana. Local quarries increasingly concentrated on supplying crushed stone for road construction and cement and lime production.

In Chicago's building materials industry, no less important than the quarrying and cutting of limestone was the production of brick. The city's brick factories, several of which came to be concentrated on the southern edge of the city in BLUE ISLAND, were among the largest in the nation. As early as the middle of the 1850s, there were over 20 large brickyards in the area, which transformed clay (abundant in local soils) into a total of nearly 100 million bricks per year. The use of brickmaking machines, introduced to Chicago in 1856 by M. O. Walker, allowed the output of individual yards to soar. The brickyard of Strauss, Hahne & Co. in Blue Island, established in 1863, was making over 25 million bricks per year by the 1870s. By the beginning of the 1890s, the metropolitan area was home to about 60 brickyards, which made a total of about 600 million bricks annually. Nearly half of this output came from the six largest yards, several of which were owned by local brick kings D. V. Purington and Frank Alsip. The Alsip-owned yard at Blue Island, which covered 150 acres, was one of the largest in the world at the time. By the beginning of the twentieth century, many of the area's yards were controlled by the Chicago-based Illinois Brick Company. When local brick production peaked in the 1920s, the Illinois Brick Company operated 10 yards with a total annual output of about 685 million bricks.

By the latter part of the twentieth century, the relative importance of quarrying and brickmaking in the local economy had declined. As the pace of the city's growth slowed, and as technological advances drove down the cost of brick and stone and the numbers of workers needed to produce them, these commodities no longer served as the foundation for many of the region's largest BUSINESS enterprises and workplaces. But stone and brick continued to be produced in the Chicago area, and the walls of thousands of local buildings and homes stood as evidence of the past vitality of the industry.

Mark R. Wilson

See also: Economic Geography; Soils

Further reading: Gutschick, Kenneth Anthony. "Building Material Industries of Metropolitan Chicago." M.S. diss., University of Chicago. 1950. • *Industrial Chicago,* vols. 1 and 2, *The Building Interests.* 1891. • U.S. Bureau of the Census. *Special Reports: Mines and Quarries, 1902.* 1905.

R

Race Riots. Chicago developed a reputation as a cauldron of specifically "racial" conflict and violence largely in the twentieth century. The determination of many whites to deny AFRICAN AMERICANS equal opportunities in employment, housing, and political representation has frequently resulted in sustained violent clashes, particularly during periods of economic crisis or postwar tension.

Chicago's most famous race riot of this type occurred between July 27 and August 3, 1919. The violence was precipitated by the drowning of an African American teenager who had crossed an invisible line at 29th Street separating customarily segregated "white" and "black" beaches. Soon, white and black Chicagoans, especially in the SOUTH SIDE residential areas surrounding the stockyards, engaged in a seven-day orgy of shootings, arsons, and beatings that resulted in the deaths of 15 whites and 23 blacks with an additional 537 injured (342 black, 195 white). The POLICE force, owing both to understaffing and the open sympathy of many officers with the white rioters, was ineffective; only the long-delayed intervention of the state militia brought the violence to a halt, and heavenly intervention in the form of rain was probably an important factor as well. The passions of this outbreak were rooted in pent-up tensions surrounding the massive migration of southern blacks during WORLD WAR I: sometimes hired as strikebreakers, their increased industrial presence was viewed by many white workers as a threat to their own livelihoods, fueling attempts to impose rigid physical boundaries beyond which blacks could not penetrate.

The aftermath of WORLD WAR II saw a revival of white attacks on black mobility, mostly on the city's South and Southwest Sides, but also in the western industrial suburb of CICERO. Aspiring African American professionals seeking to obtain improved housing beyond the increasingly overcrowded South Side ghetto, whether in private residences or in the new PUBLIC HOUSING developments constructed by the CHICAGO HOUSING AUTHORITY, were frequently greeted by attempted arsons, bombings, and angry white mobs often numbering into the thousands. The 1951 CICERO riot, in particular, lasting several nights and involving roughly two to five thousand white protesters, attracted worldwide condemnation. By the end of the 1950s, with black residential presence somewhat more firmly established, the battleground in many South Side neighborhoods shifted to clashes over black attempts to gain unimpeded access to neighborhood parks and beaches.

Since the mid-1960s, the nature of race riots in Chicago (as elsewhere) has significantly shifted. Although violent black/white clashes continued into the mid-1970s, the term's use shifted during the 1960s to refer to the uprisings of poorer blacks (or Latinos) protesting ghetto conditions, especially police brutality. Chicago has experienced several noteworthy outbreaks of this type, including the confrontation between police and the largely PUERTO RICAN communities of WEST TOWN and HUMBOLDT PARK during the summer of 1966, but most notably the massive 1968 West Side riots following the assassination of Martin Luther King. No clashes of this magnitude have occurred since (even following the 1992 Rodney King verdict in Los Angeles), but the continued salience of many of the protesters' expressed grievances—inferior housing, lack of meaningful employment, and inequitable law enforcement—suggests that the issues surrounding racial violence are by no means a finished chapter in Chicago history.

Steven Essig

See also: Bridgeport; Contested Spaces; Great Migration; Racism, Ethnicity, and White Identity; Washington Park

Further reading: Grossman, James R. *Land of Hope: Chicago, Black Southerners, and the Great Migration.* 1989. • Hirsch, Arnold R. *Making the Second Ghetto: Race and Housing in Chicago, 1940–1960.* 1983. • Tuttle, William M., Jr. *Race Riot: Chicago in the Red Summer of 1919.* 1970.

Racism, Ethnicity, and White Identity. If the grand jury investigating the white-on-black violence during the 1919 RACE RIOT in Chicago is to be believed, IRISH American GANGS played a central role in attempting to extend the bloodshed. Members of Ragen's Colts, one of the leading gangs, disguised themselves in blackface in order to set fire to POLISH and LITHUANIAN neighborhoods in the BACK OF THE YARDS area. Their hope was to draw the immigrant population into bloody reprisals against AFRICAN AMERICANS. Two years later, Ragen's Colts again mounted the barricades, hanging in effigy a KU KLUX

Klansman in the opening salvo of a successful campaign to isolate and drive from Chicago an organization known for violence against southern African Americans, but now focused on Roman Catholics and Jews as threats to American culture and society. In that incarnation, the Colts battled the forces of intolerance. Thus Ragen's Colts symbolized the bizarre extremes of racial intolerance and terror in early-twentieth-century Chicago.

The two faces of Ragen's Colts will almost inevitably strike contemporary readers as contradictory: at one moment deceptive, vile, and exclusionary and at the next campaigning against icons of hatred. However, such contradictions go to the heart of Chicago's history as well. In the city's past and present, two images contend. One emphasizes the astonishing cultural variety and vibrant cultural exchanges nourished in an atmosphere of tolerance. The other stresses how quickly and ruthlessly racial lines have been or can be drawn in the city sometimes called the nation's "most segregated," one that helped to teach Martin Luther King about a racism he had not encountered in the South.

To move beyond explaining away such contradictions as simply "paradoxes" requires coming to grips with the chilling extent to which processes of racial exclusion were part and parcel of building increasingly inclusive unities among European immigrants as *white* Americans. During the 1919 race riot, the blackface arson came in response to the lack of interest among Eastern European immigrants in brutalizing blacks. Some Poles argued that the riot was a conflict between blacks and whites, with Poles abstaining because they belonged to neither group. Indeed the Poles and Lithuanians might well have hated each other more than either group hated African Americans. Thus the racially disguised terror committed by the Irish American gang members was not only an act of racism. It was, perversely, also an act of inclusion, reaching out to newer Roman Catholic immigrants who did not have a secure place in U.S. systems of racial privilege and who did not sufficiently identify and act as whites. In that sense the arson served as a fit prelude to militant, but not interracial, protest against the Klan's attempts to restrict the white race to Protestant Anglo-Saxondom.

This essay traces the broader historical patterns through which dramatically inclusive new identities among whites formed in Chicago history. Such inclusive identities failed to expand further, and therefore challenge the color line, because inclusion itself was often based on drawing, extending, and policing color lines. In making this argument, it is tempting to rely on a firm distinction between race, as a relatively permanent boundary, and ethnicity, which was often breached as whites came together. Yet race is not a meaningful biological category; and ethnicity, far from a primordial attachment, is an imagined and constantly reimagined identity. Moreover, the firm distinction between race, as an identity imagined to be largely biological, and ethnicity, as an identity imagined to be based largely on culture, language, and history, came into being relatively recently. The "race relations cycle," which University of Chicago professor Robert Park and other "Chicago School" sociologists used to describe how immigrants and people of color assimilate into the dominant culture, used race to refer not only to African Americans and Mexican Americans but also to Italians, Slavs, and a multitude of other groups. This expansive use of race as a category fit well into an early twentieth-century context, when the relationship of Poles, Italians, and Lithuanians, for example, to American whiteness was far from clear. It was as a result of the process of drawing new European immigrants more fully into the white race that the Sicilian immigrant went from being a member of the Italian race to being a "white ethnic." The distinction between race and ethnicity therefore cannot explain why some, but not "other," residents of the United States were included in broadening white identities. Indeed the distinction itself needs to be explained by looking at patterns of inclusion and exclusion.

The sometimes hidden processes of building an overarching white identity through exclusion of people of color are old Chicago stories, dating back at least to the transitions that made Chicago a white city in the first place. In the early nineteenth century, William Cronon writes, Chicago was "a polyglot world." Potawatomi Indians controlled much of the land around Chicago and traded briskly with "Sacs, Foxes, French, Ottawas, English, Chippewas, Americans and others." But in 1833, when most remaining Potawatomis gathered in Chicago to negotiate with a U.S. government determined to strengthen its control of the Indian presence in Illinois, land in and around the city shifted into "Yankee" hands by virtue of a pair of treaties. Three years later, most Potawatomis had been removed west of the Mississippi River. "The hybrid cultural universe of Indians and Euroamericans that had existed in the Chicago area for decades was," Cronon continues, "finally to be shattered by different conceptions of property and real estate." The exclusions here carried great drama, but the ways in which the process created a new sense of being white and its importance among "French," "English," "Americans," and "others" also deserves attention. Deep connections between being white and possessing legally defensible rights to property developed as did a sense that whiteness mattered as much or more than specific national origins in making a new "American" race. By 1858, in his celebrated debates with Abraham Lincoln, Senate candidate Stephen A. Douglas heard supporters chant "white men" as he spoke. In arguing that, for example, Celtic people deserved full inclusion in the white race, Douglas emphasized to Chicagoans and other Illinoisans that Irish immigrants and other new arrivals were not black and were not Indian.

Chicago's history continued to feature dramas in which whites continued to create larger unities which themselves regularly became the basis for new exclusions. Even the very process of excluding became the basis for white identity. Irish immigrants whose loyalties before migration were often intensely local, for example, might have found themselves speaking Gaelic, building parishes, voting, frequenting bars, and supporting Irish nationalist causes together with migrants from other Irish clans and counties. Italian village and regional identities, although not lost, coexisted with broader identities as Italians and Italian Americans. Workplaces, such as the famously mixed stockyards and garment factories, threw populations together promiscuously. Neighborhoods did likewise, so that the well-studied Italian and Polish districts of the city, for example, were far from only Italian or Polish and sometimes contained only a minority of residents from the group that gave the area its ethnic name and identity. Catholic parishes, typically designed

IRISHMEN

ATTENTION!

Can you be sold out by the so-called silk-stocking element? It is a fact that cannot be disputed that the Republican nominee, John A. Roche, that your so-called representatives want you to support is an

ORANGEMAN!

Can you consistently and in honor to your nationality vote for a man who is pledged by his order (North Star Orange Lodge) to

DESTROY

all Catholic Institutions of a State or National character. Think well before you Vote.

This campaign poster captures some of the complexities of nineteenth-century ethnic politics in Chicago. The fusing of identities as "white" and "American" established a framework for difficult relations between Irish and African American Chicagoans. But Irish Catholic hostility toward "Orangemen" could be an even sharper political wedge. Source: Chicago Historical Society.

to serve what were visualized as distinct and bounded immigrant neighborhoods, often witnessed population changes and heard masses preached in both the language of the founding group and that of the newcomers. Some parishioners married across ethnic (but within religious) lines, often over sharp objections of parish priests.

These overlapping and wildly uneven processes of developing larger unities while keeping older ones were so complex as to defy easy categorization. Immigration historians have imposed some order on the processes by regarding "American" or "working-class American" as the largest unities being created. In doing so, historians of Chicago have been especially successful at avoiding any mechanistic emphasis on inevitable "assimilation" into a new nation. They have portrayed great dramas in which old values, new migrations, recrossings of oceans, economic change, and popular culture mattered greatly, in which cultures from various homelands both survive and are recreated in Chicago. Above all, they have shown that immigrants were actors, not objects, in the drama of AMERICANIZATION. Indeed in 1964 Rudolph J. Vecoli's essay on Italians in Chicago struck a first decisive blow against seeing immigrants to the United States as simply "uprooted" populations, desperate and acted upon. When Lizabeth Cohen and Roger Horowitz describe the "culture of unity" which made for the "working-class Americanism" underpinning union organizing in the 1930s and '40s, they emphasize that such interculturalism was in large part "carefully constructed" by immigrants and workers themselves. James Barrett's seminal work on "Americanization from the bottom up" similarly stresses the ways in which earlier generations of immigrants, and the institutions they built, imparted a sense of what it meant to be American to later arrivals. Often this process crossed lines between immigrant groups, with Irish priests, POLICE, and labor leaders, for example, shaping and limiting the process by which Eastern and Southern Europeans could become Americans.

But these complex dramas become still more fascinating when we realize that "American" and "working-class American" were not the only overarching unities being created across immigrant populations. So too were racial identities being made. During and after the 1960s, for example, Mexican Americans and PUERTO RICANS in Chicago developed what Felix M. Padilla calls a "situational" identity, enabling them to come together as "Latinos" for specific purposes and at particular times. However, the identity of "white American" was the critical one complicating the picture of cross-cultural relations in Chicago. In the major arenas in which cross-cultural contact occurred, the processes of learning and creating a sense of what it meant to be "Americans" and of what it meant to be white in the United States occurred together. Time and time again, becoming white accelerated, formed, and deformed the process by which immigrants from Europe became American.

The SETTLEMENT HOUSE, in which upper- and middle-class women mixed with immigrants and immigrants mixed with each other, is a case in point. The settlements, as historian Thomas Lee Philpott shows, practiced an "open-door policy" which reflected the fact that neighborhoods were mixed. "All the settlements," he added, excluded people for breaking rules, but "none of them drew any ethnic line." In Burnside, the 22-block area bordering on the neighborhood's settlement house included 22 national groups. Each group furnished settlement house members. In the 1920s, the UNIVERSITY OF CHICAGO settlement house serving BACK OF THE YARDS accepted, despite acute Polish-Mexican tensions, Mexican members and helped for a time to convince the neighborhood that they ought to be included in the "white race" and in the community. When the "Latin Club" of Italian and Mexican young men at HULL HOUSE fell into conflict, the Italians called for the exclusion of Mexicans as "nonwhite" in an incident illustrative of the complexities of racial categorizing of Mexican Americans in the city's history. Hull House leaders reaffirmed the policy of welcoming Mexicans. On the other hand, virtually all of the settlement houses made peace with Jim Crow policies, excluding or segregating African Americans. In 1915, Gads Hill Center on the LOWER WEST SIDE declared its blackface minstrel show a "great success." Polish and Bohemian actors and audience members did not always know English, but they could "enjoy the music [and] really attractive costumes" while learning about both Americanization and racial hierarchy. Young performers named Kraszewski, Pletcha, and Chimiclewski sang "Clare De Kitchen" and "Gideon's Band." Some of these immigrants might well have seen their residences burn in another "blackface performance," that of Ragen's Colts, four years later.

Mass movements of homeowners and visionary experiments in housing likewise brought together immigrant cultures and excluded African Americans. The Greater PULLMAN Property Restriction Association, which campaigned successfully in the 1920s to keep Pullman all-white and to extend greatly the all-white areas around it, "included Catholics, Protestants and Jews. They had names like Perlman, Korzeniecki, Birkhoff, Larocco, Hockstra, Teninga, Novak and Bezdek" as well as more "American" sounding ones. The exclusion of Jews and other new immigrant groups from buying in some limited areas might well have quickened their interest in joining movements to use "RESTRICTIVE COVENANTS" to prevent home sales to African Americans. To make "race" the focus of such campaigns cut against the drawing of exclusionary distinctions among Europeans.

A 1949 poem by Langston Hughes caught precisely the intent of restrictive covenants, compacts among white property owners to keep African Americans from moving into segregated neighborhoods:

In Chicago
They've got covenants
Restricting me—

However, Hughes also identified another dimension to housing discrimination. In their reaction to the possibility of integration, Hughes suggested, new European immigrants acted alongside the native-born white population:

When I move
Into a neighborhood
Folks fly.
Even every foreigner
That can move, moves.
Why?

In participating in the massive grassroots, if also real-estate-agent-sponsored, campaigns to enforce racially restrictive covenants in the second quarter of the twentieth century in Chicago, immigrants literally signed onto, and were accepted into, white racial identity. Coming from areas of Europe in which dividing the world into black and white people made little sense in daily life, and themselves often despised as "not quite white" on their arrival in the U.S., European newcomers and their children came to be more fully included in the white race precisely through the exclusion of African Americans.

In 1919, when the Reform Jewish / Christian Scientist businessman Benjamin J. Rosenthal built Garden Homes, Chicago's first model housing, he consciously strove to bring together "people of various nationalities" between State and Indiana below 87th Street. A third-generation Irish resident of the Homes would later recall that Rosenthal wanted to "show us turkeys and the polacks, lugans, dagoes and everybody else that we could all live together without knocking each others' heads in." Garden Homes was nonetheless "white only." The African American residents who broke the color line there in 1956 saw their home burn as a result of arson.

More intricate patterns of inclusion and exclusion characterized the ROMAN CATHOLIC Church and the unions in Chicago. The Church, as John T. McGreevy and others have shown, structured itself around the ethnic parish in the first half of the twentieth century. Interested both in Americanization and in maintaining ethnic lines, it was a model cultural-pluralist institution. The CATHOLIC YOUTH ORGANIZATION, founded in Chicago, brought together youth from various parishes and of various national origins without eroding ethnic and parish identities. Catholic high schools also increasingly fostered cross-cultural contact among whites. But ethnic exclusivity remained very strong at the parish level, in some ways increasing among priests worried about ethnic intermarriage in the 1920s and '30s. As McGreevy shows, segregation of African American Catholics into separate parishes occurred in this context, with the emphasis on autonomy as well as on exclusion. However, even early in the twentieth century, a sense of "Catholic whiteness" stretched across ethnic lines. As the Church abandoned national parishes and adopted a more integrationist stance after World War II, it failed to find a way to move many of its parishioners, and some of its clergy, to racial inclusion. The neighborhoods on which its parishes were based were increasingly defined as white, rather than simply by nationality.

Workplaces and unions are often and rightly seen as key sites of cross-cultural relations. Employers recruited labor from an astonishing range of national groups. Signs regarding safety on the job often appeared in several European languages, even at factories with ambitious Americanization programs. In some cases care was taken to isolate workers from others of the same nationality in an effort to divide the labor force. As a Wisconsin Steel superintendent put it, "We try never to allow two of a nationality to work together if we can help it. Nationalities tend to be clannish and naturally it interferes with work." Extremely heterogeneous work gangs cooperated to outwit management efforts to increase production and then retired to lunch with others of their own nationality.

Trade unions likewise often sought to bring workers together across ethnic lines. This unity was especially sought by radical labor organizations and those seeking to build broad industrial unions rather than narrow and often ethnically segregated craft organizations. The *Chicago Tribune* in 1885 was confident it could discredit the International Working People's Association by describing a dance which the organization sponsored: "Every variety of step might have been witnessed yesterday. The 'Bohemian dip,' the 'German lunge,' the 'Austrian kick,' the 'Polish ramp' and the 'Scandinavian trot.'" The prolabor Illinois Women's Alliance of the 1890s brought together organized labor, ethnically diverse sweatshop workers, and dozens of upper- and middle-class organizations, ranging from the Women's Christian Temperance Union to the Women's Homeopathic Medical Society. U.S. Commissioner of Labor Ethelbert Stewart had Chicago's slaughterhouses in mind when he wrote in 1905 on the labor union as "the first, and for a time the only, point at which [the immigrant] touches any influence outside of his clan.... By virtue of the intercourse ... clannishness is to a degree destroyed, and a social mixing along other lines comes into play." In the 1930s, a steelworkers' organizer reported his discovery of "Hungarian goulash, minestrone soup, lox ... corned beef [and] gefilte fish" in the course of his duties.

Some scholars, most notably the once Chicago-based sociologist Ira Katznelson, have argued that the world of labor also brought relatively great cross-cultural exchange where race was concerned. The "city trenches" that Katznelson identified divided workers by race largely via neighborhood boundaries, not in workplaces and unions. Such a view has obvious attractions. St. Clair Drake and Horace R. Cayton aptly observed in 1945 that "habits of thought ... characterize certain parts of the city as 'white' and others as 'Negro,'" whatever the overlapping concern with naming ethnic neighborhoods. Parks and beaches were likewise black or white. The "job ceiling" which kept work segregated was, on the other hand, more complex, with considerable mixing of African Americans and the Irish on lower rungs of the job ladder in the nineteenth century and of African American, Mexican, and European immigrant workers in the twentieth. Industrial unions, especially in meatpacking, at times fought hard for racial inclusion. Packinghouse union organizer Stella Nowicki echoed Katznelson's thesis in recalling, "We worked in the stockyards with blacks but when we came home, we went to lily-white neighborhoods and the blacks went to their ghetto." She then described vigorous union initiatives, from social events to campaigns to integrate major league baseball, to bridge "city trenches" off the job.

But inclusion on the job had very sharp limits. White-collar work in integrated settings, Drake and Cayton wrote, was broadly opposed by whites as a form of "social equality." Unions, especially in the crafts, often barred African American entry into jobs, and industrial unions frequently acquiesced or colluded in leaving skilled, high-paying manufacturing jobs in white hands. Wisconsin Steel and Western Electric, on the far Southwest Side, graphically showed the difficulties of imagining unity at work and exclusion residentially and illustrated the difficulties facing antiracist trade unionists. In the area near those plants, Cohen writes, white employees feared African Americans "as co-workers—to say nothing of as neighbors." Management in the factories, she adds, "respected community prejudice and did not hire blacks." In this instance, as in more formal actions to enforce residential segregation, the category "white" came to unite and include a variety of immigrant groups.

Both the exclusion of African Americans and the inclusion of new groups of often despised immigrant European workers as white were decisive in defining these cross-cultural exchanges. Through much of the twentieth century it was not clear that the "new immigrants" from Eastern and Southern Europe would be accepted as white or American. During the 1920s, a central character in James T. Farrell's *Studs Lonigan* would observe, "The Polacks and Dagoes, and niggers are the same, only the niggers are the lowest." In 1929, sociologist Harvey Warren Zorbaugh wrote that "while the Irish and Swedish had gotten on well as neighbors, neither ... would live peaceably with the Sicilian. There was considerable friction, especially among the children of the two races." Three European groups made two races—the white one to which Irish and Swedes belonged and the not-quite-white one which included Sicilians. The processes of inclusion and exclusion shaped the formation of white racial identity unevenly but enabled impressive progress toward inclusion among whites of those groups whom Ragen's Colts attempt to conscript into the white race in 1919.

In 1954, as pan-white unity reached new heights around issues of "property and real estate," an American Civil Liberties Union investigator was assigned to visit working-class saloons and to transcribe conversations on integration of the Trumbull Park Homes. "Well," one drinker argued, "if they get control over there it won't be long before they come here and our home will wind up in a nigger neighborhood and we will have to sell for little or nothing." This apt summation of what would become the logic of both "white flight" and "white backlash" reflected a complex identity. It was delivered in Polish, but by a Chicagoan who identified himself, and would have been seen, as a "white ethnic" and not a member of the "Polish race."

In his 1939 hit song "Ballad for Americans," African American artist and activist Paul Robeson sang of the promise of many becoming one, while maintaining diverse cultural practices. He sang of an "Irish, Negro, Jewish, Italian, French and English, Spanish, Russian, Chinese, Polish, Scotch, Hungarian ... Swedish, Finnish, Canadian, Greek and Turk, and Czech and double Czech American." The mysterious Czech and "double Czech," delivered in minstrel dialect, echoed the tag line ("Check and double check") of the much-protested racist radio comedy *Amos 'n' Andy*, a show that originated in Chicago. By reinjecting racism in concluding a litany of multicultural hope, Robeson reminded listeners that much remained to be done before African Americans achieved the inclusion the song heralded. If Chicago history is a guide, a further reminder may be in order: inclusion of most of the song's long list of groups involved their being recognized not simply as Americans but as white Americans and was inseparable from the forces that produced *Amos 'n' Andy*.

David R. Roediger

See also: Chicago in the Middle Ground; Chicago Studied: Social Scientists and Their City; Civil Rights Movements; Contested Spaces; Multicentered Chicago; South Side; Unionization

Further reading: On the early-nineteenth-century dramas of cross-cultural relations and exclusions, see William Cronon, *Nature's Metropolis: Chicago and the Great West* (1991). Important accounts of the role of immigrants themselves in building communities and identities include Rudolph J. Vecoli, "*Contadini* in Chicago: A Critique of *The Uprooted*," *Journal of American History* 51 (December 1964), and James R. Barrett, "Americanization from the Bottom Up: Immigration and the Remaking of the Working Class in the United States, 1880–1930," *Journal of American History* 79 (December 1992). For an attempt to apply these insights to issues regarding immigration and race, see Barrett and David R. Roediger, "Inbetween Peoples: Race, Nationality, and the 'New Immigrant' Working Class," *Journal of American Ethnic History* 16 (Spring 1997). Lizabeth Cohen's *Making a New Deal: Industrial Workers in Chicago, 1919–1939* (1990) usefully treats divisions and "cultures of unity" among workers. No historian has so brilliantly probed the complexity of whiteness and ethnic division in Chicago as the novelist James T. Farrell. See his *Studs Lonigan* trilogy (1993, originally 1932, 1934, and 1935). On the settlement houses and on housing discrimination, see Thomas Lee Philpott, *The Slum and the Ghetto: Neighborhood Deterioration and Middle-Class Reform, Chicago, 1880–1930* (1978). See also Arnold Hirsch's indispensable *Making the Second Ghetto: Race and Housing in Chicago, 1940–1960* (1983) and Langston Hughes, "Restrictive Covenants," in Arnold Rampersad and David Roessel, eds., *The Collected Poems of Langston Hughes* (1994), 361–362. John T. McGreevy's fine *Parish Boundaries: The Catholic Encounter with Race in the Twentieth-Century Urban North* (1996) informs discussion of Catholic interculturalism. I take "city trenches" from Ira Katznelson, *City Trenches: Urban Politics and the Patterning of Class in the United States* (1981).

Radio. *See* Broadcasting; Disc Jockeys

Radio Orchestras. As local radio matured during the 1920s, amateur entertainers were replaced by versatile, professional staff orchestras.

Eventually, stations owned and operated by major networks, including WMAQ (NBC), WBBM (CBS), and WLS (ABC), contracted with the CHICAGO FEDERATION OF MUSICIANS to have their own 45-piece orchestras. Working in various combinations as needed, staffers might perform a symphonic work one moment, then play on the *National Barn Dance* program the next. Enjoying stability and variety, many instrumentalists spent 30 or more years in radio.

A 1949 survey stated that musicians were the highest-paid station employees. Within a few years, those same figures imperiled most radio orchestras. The networks either let the union agreements lapse or bought their way out of them.

Only WGN (Mutual), under the same ownership as the *Chicago Tribune,* was financially able to maintain a band into the early 1960s—but by then it was only a quartet.

Christopher Popa

See also: Broadcasting; Entertaining Chicagoans; WLS Barn Dance

Illinois Central Railroad station, 1964. Photographer: Unknown. Source: Chicago Historical Society.

Further reading: Linton, Bruce A. "A History of Chicago Radio Station Programming, 1921–1931: With Emphasis on Stations WMAQ and WGN." Ph.D. thesis, Northwestern University. 1953.

Railroad Stations. Built by the Galena & Chicago Union Railroad in 1848, the city's first RAILROAD depot was of a simple board construction. The only ornamentation on the structure was a cupola over the second floor, which was used as a watchtower. The building was destroyed by the Great Chicago FIRE OF 1871.

The terminal railroad stations built in Chicago during the mid to late nineteenth century were somewhat more elaborate. The Central Depot, built in 1856 for the ILLINOIS CENTRAL and Chicago & Alton Railroads, was used until

Lake Shore & Michigan Southern Railroad station, 1872. Artist: Unknown. Source: The Newberry Library.

the early 1890s. While the building itself was a curious mix of architectural styles, it served as a precursor to the grandeur of future terminal stations in Chicago.

Other railroads soon followed suit, building many of their terminal stations along the fringes of the LOOP in order to maintain proximity to the increasing number of COMMUTERS who worked downtown. The Chicago & North Western Railway built their Wells Street Station (located on the site of the MERCHANDISE MART) in 1881 in an effort to consolidate their commuter passenger business at one location. The building was noted for its restaurants and spacious waiting rooms. The first Union Station was built the same year at the corner of Canal and Monroe Streets by the Chicago, Milwaukee & St. Paul and other associated railroads. Several other notable terminal stations were built within the next 10 years, including the Dearborn Street Station in the South Loop, the Grand Central Station at Wells and Harrison Streets, and the Central Station built by the Illinois Central at 12th Street.

While the first terminal station was a relatively simple affair, many of the terminal stations soon developed elaborate facilities for commercial and BUSINESS activity. Businessmen and travelers ate at the RESTAURANTS located in the downtown terminal stations. Soon space was set aside within the terminals for gift shops, shoe-shine stands, and even small book stands. The second LaSalle Street Station, built in 1902 at the corner of LaSalle and Van Buren Streets, featured a 12-story office building with a steel frame. The tenants of the building included the Chicago, Rock Island & Pacific Railroad and the Lake Shore & Michigan Southern Railroad.

As the first major phase of railroad terminal station construction concluded in the early 1890s, many outlying communities in the city and the nearby suburbs began clamoring for their own passenger stations. Given the land speculation that generally followed the entrepreneurial activity of the railroads, a new passenger station could be a potential boon to other local businesses. One such station was the Illinois Central Station at 57th Street in HYDE PARK. The station was built in the high Victorian Gothic style, and featured a large central pavilion area, along with canopies that sprawled around the entire building. The station also had restroom facilities and a restaurant frequented by local residents. While not every area was fortunate enough to have such an ornate building, certain architectural elements like cupolas, dormers, and long platforms were incorporated into many of the stations. Notable examples of this period in passenger station construction include the BEVERLY stations at 91st and 99th Streets and the MORGAN PARK stations at 111th and 115th Streets, all built to serve the Chicago, Rock Island & Pacific Railroad.

Scrubwomen at work, Union Station, 1943. Photographer: Jack Delano. Source: Library of Congress.

The culmination of downtown railroad terminal building came with the construction of two monumental buildings directly west of the Loop. The Chicago & North Western Station built in 1911 by the Chicago & North Western Railway featured a three-story waiting room decorated with bronze-trimmed marble. Union Station, the largest railroad station, was built in Chicago in 1925 at the corner of Canal and Adams Streets. This station was also noted for its impressive waiting room, which bore a strong resemblance to the Pennsylvania Station in New York.

After the 1920s, with passenger traffic waning, railroads built fewer stations in Chicago and its environs. Stations began to revert to the "decorated shed" model, often with a truncated platform and a tiny waiting area, if one was provided at all. Architectural details were no longer incorporated into these utilitarian structures. Interesting examples include the stations in HIGHWOOD and MOKENA. Where railroad stations had once been lively centers of activity within the surrounding community, they had returned full circle to their more spartan origins.

Max Grinnell

See also: Economic Geography; Transportation

Further reading: Bach, Ira J., and Susan Wolfson. *A Guide to Chicago's Train Stations: Present and Past.* 1986. • Mayer, Harold M. "The Railway Terminal Problem of Central Chicago." *Economic Geography* 21.1 (1945): 62–76. • Mayer, Harold M. *The Railway Pattern of Metropolitan Chicago.* 1943.

Railroad Strike of 1877. In late July of 1877, Chicagoans played their part in the first nationwide uprising of workers. On July 16, RAILROAD WORKERS in Martinsburg, West Virginia, walked off the job to protest a 10 percent wage cut leveled by their employer, the Baltimore & Ohio Railroad. STRIKES to protest cutbacks in the midst of a period of nationwide economic depression soon spread westward across the country. News of attempts to control boisterous crowds fueled worker protest and sporadic violence.

Chicagoans watched and waited as the Great Strike ran its course through Philadelphia, Pittsburgh, Louisville, and Cincinnati. While the city's SOCIALISTS envisioned an opportunity to spread their message about the evils of capitalism, elected officials and the mercantile elite resolved to maintain order, mobilizing citizen patrols and calling for the intervention of the ILLINOIS NATIONAL GUARD and the U.S.

Army. Tensions were heightened by lurid reports in the English-language press of "worker mobs."

From July 24 to July 28, this charged atmosphere kindled what one observer called a "labor explosion." In addition to walkouts and protests by RAILROAD workers, sympathetic actions by other wage workers brought the city close to a state of general strike. Escalating clashes between strikers and the POLICE culminated in a series of intense skirmishes on South Halsted Street, an area with a great concentration of immigrant wage workers in the railroad, MEATPACKING, and LUMBER industries. Thanks to a mass mobilization of "special" police by Mayor Heath, the mass arrest of protesters and socialist leaders, and the arrival of six companies of U.S. Army infantry, quiet was restored. At least 18 died in these clashes, and the fears of an uncontrollable class conflict spawned by this incident would long haunt the city and the nation.

Karen Sawislak

See also: Economic Geography; Haymarket and May Day; Knights of Labor; Lower West Side; Pullman Strike; Work Culture

Further reading: Foner, Philip S. *The Great Labor Uprising of 1877*. 1977. • Schneirov, Richard. *Labor and Urban Politics: Class Conflict and the Origins of Modern Liberalism in Chicago, 1864–97*. 1998.

George Pullman began manufacturing sleeping cars in Chicago in the 1860s. This is an exterior shot of one of the cars, during a celebration, in 1940, of the 90th anniversary of the first rail connection between Aurora and Chicago. Photographer: Unknown. Source: The Newberry Library.

Railroad Supply Industry. It is often said that the RAILROADS made Chicago, in the sense that the city's explosive growth was made possible by its position as a center of the national TRANSPORTATION network. What is observed less frequently is that Chicago made the railroads. Starting in the 1850s, the area was home to many manufacturers of railroad, track, and railcars. Not only the well-known Pullman Company, but several other of the area's leading economic enterprises, made a big BUSINESS out of providing railroads with the cars and supplies they needed to keep running. For much of the city's history, tens of thousands of local residents were employed in the industry, which ranked as one of the area's largest. Even after the rise of the automobile and the airplane, the railway supply business remained an important part of Chicago's economy; but, like the railroads, it declined considerably by the end of the twentieth century.

The manufacture and repair of railroad equipment and supplies became one of Chicago's leading industries during the decade before the CIVIL WAR, when the first lines began to reach the city. Both the railroads and independent companies operated major shops. By the 1850s, Chicago was home to several large railroad car makers, including the Eagle Works, the American Car Company, and the Union Car Works, which each employed about 300 men. At the same time, the railroad companies started to operate large production and repair shops in and around the city. In 1855 the ILLINOIS CENTRAL established shops along the lakeshore at the south end of the city; these works employed about 300 men in the 1850s. Another large establishment was the works of the Chicago, Burlington & Quincy, located in AURORA. By the 1870s, when the Aurora shops employed nearly 1,300 men, this might have been the region's largest single WORK site. Among the other large manufacturing sites in the area that supplied the railroad industry were the IRON AND STEEL mills, which started to make rails in the late 1850s. By the 1880s, Chicago-area steel mills were rolling nearly a third of all the rails made in the United States.

By the late nineteenth century, the railroad equipment and supply business was one of Chicago's leading industries. In 1880, four of the area's top eight manufacturing establishments in terms of wages paid were railroad company shops: a total of about 3,600 men were then employed at the shops of the Illinois Central; the Chicago & Northwestern; the Chicago, Rock Island & Pacific; and the Chicago, Burlington & Quincy. But it was the independent railcar makers that made Chicago the center of the U.S. rail supply industry. By 1890, the 12,000 men working in the metropolitan area on car construction and repair were evenly divided among the railroad companies and independents. By that time, the manufacturing operations of the independents alone constituted the area's sixth-largest industry. By 1900, two of the area's top 20 employers were independent railcar manufacturers: American Car & Foundry, which had about 1,500 workers in the Chicago area; and Pullman, which by that time employed about 6,000.

One of the world's leading manufacturers of railcars during the late nineteenth and early twentieth centuries, Pullman was the most important single company in the history of the railway supply business in America. This well-known enterprise was the creation of George M. Pullman, who began to experiment with the manufacture of specialty sleeper cars in Chicago during the 1850s and 1860s. In 1867, when there were already several dozen of Pullman's sleepers on the nation's railways, he formed the Pullman Palace Car Company. Although the new company was chartered in Illinois, it made most of its cars in New York and Michigan until the 1880s, when Pullman created a new company town a few miles south of Chicago. By the early 1890s, about 5,500 workers at the company's shops in the town of PULLMAN were making railcars at the rate of about 12,500 freight cars and 1,800 passenger cars per year. In 1894, after the company laid off hundreds of workers, Pullman became the center of a nationwide STRIKE that would become one of best-known labor disputes in American history. In the years after the strike, Pullman workers continued to turn out huge numbers of railcars. By the 1920s, the Pullman-Standard Car Manufacturing Company was the leading U.S. manufacturer of railcars, with an annual production capacity of close to 100,000 freight cars and hundreds of passenger cars.

Pullman was not the only important railcar manufacturer in the Chicago area. There were dozens of area firms in the railcar business during the late nineteenth and early twentieth centuries. After the all-steel freight car was introduced in the 1890s, several Chicago companies became leaders in this field. The American Car & Foundry Company was formed in 1899 in a merger of 13 companies, including Chicago's own Wells, French & Co. During the first part of the twentieth century, American Car & Foundry employed about 1,500 area residents. Even more worked for the Western Steel Car & Foundry Company, a major freight car producer based in HEGEWISCH, which was making about 100 cars a day by 1905, when its annual sales came to over $7.5 million. This level of output was matched by the Standard Steel Car Company, which built a new plant in HAMMOND in 1906 and became part of Pullman-Standard in the 1920s. Another leading firm during this period was the Hicks Locomotive & Car Company, which ran two large plants in CHICAGO HEIGHTS.

Several Chicago-area firms specialized in supplying railroad companies and other firms in the industry with goods other than finished railcars. One such company was Crerar, Adams & Co., a firm led by John Crerar and J. McGregor Adams, which during the late nineteenth century was one of the Midwest's leading suppliers of specialty railroad goods such as lamps and lanterns. Another important firm was Pettibone Mulliken Corporation, a Chicago company founded in 1880 that by the early twentieth century stood as a leading supplier of railroad track equipment such as frogs, crossings, and switches. Railroad cars across the nation stood on wheels manufactured by workers at the WEST PULLMAN plant of the Griffin Wheel Company, which made as many as 500 wheels a day in the 1900s and 1,000 a day in the 1920s. Other specialty manufacturers included Edward B. Leigh's Chicago Railway Equipment Company, a descendant of the National Hollow Brake Beam Company, founded in Chicago in 1887. During its first 20 years, this firm sold over six million brake beams.

Starting in the late nineteenth century, privately owned fleets of specialty cars—including sleepers, refrigerator cars, and tank cars—became an increasingly important feature of the U.S. rail system. Chicago-area companies were leaders in the production and operation of such cars. The fleet of luxury sleepers built and run by the Pullman Company, 8,000 of which were being used across the country by the 1930s, was particularly well known. No less important were refrigerator cars, which transformed the MEATPACKING industry. These cars, introduced in the 1870s, allowed packers to ship fresh meat to distant locations, giving them access to larger markets. Many of the larger packers owned and operated their own fleets of these cars: by the beginning of the twentieth century, Swift & Co. owned nearly 6,000 cars and Armour & Co. nearly 14,000. Some refrigerator cars were manufactured by the packers themselves; others by specialty firms; and still others by large freight car makers such as Pullman and American Car & Foundry. Another important specialty car was the tank car, which was used to transport oil or other liquids. During the early twentieth century, local manufacturers such as the General American Tank Car Company of EAST CHICAGO were among the leading American producers of tank cars.

By the early twentieth century, firms that leased freight cars to the railroads ranked among the most important kinds of enterprises in the U.S. rail transport industry. Chicago-based companies led the field. The Union Tank Car Company, a descendant of the Union Tank Line, created by John D. Rockefeller's Standard Oil Company of Ohio, moved its headquarters to Chicago in the 1920s. The first giant private car line in the United States, this company increased the size of its fleet from about 10,000 tank cars in 1904 to over 30,000 during the 1920s. Another large Chicago-based company that leased huge numbers of freight cars was the General American Transportation Corporation (later known as GATX). This company was founded in Chicago in 1898 by Max Epstein as the Atlantic Seaboard Dispatch Company, which started with 28 used cars. Although it specialized in leasing, General American soon began to manufacture some of its own cars—including innovative specialty cars such as glass-lined milk tank cars and nickel-lined compartments for holding acids—at its large shops in East Chicago, Indiana. By the 1930s, General American had passed Union Tank Car as the owner of the nation's largest private freight car fleet; in 1948, it owned and operated about 55,000 cars, including tank, refrigerator, and other freight cars.

The railroad equipment and supply industry continued to employ thousands of Chicago-area residents through the middle part of the twentieth century, but it declined sharply (like many other manufacturing sectors in the Midwest) after the 1960s. By the early 1990s, the production of railroad equipment employed fewer than 5,000 area residents—a small fraction of the numbers of Chicagoans who had been working in the industry a century earlier. What caused this shrinkage? As the railroad industry became less dominant within the transportation field and less profitable over the course of the twentieth century, several leading companies shut down their Chicago-area factories, along with many other plants across the country. By the 1980s, Pullman, American Car & Foundry, and GATX had all closed their Chicago-area manufacturing operations.

Because the late-twentieth-century decline of the railroad equipment manufacturing business in Chicago was part of a national trend, the importance of local firms within the national industry remained relatively high. In the early 1990s, workers at Chicago-area plants still accounted for about a fifth of the entire U.S. output of new railroad equipment. By that time, the leading local railcar maker was the Thrall Car Manufacturing Company of Chicago Heights, a division of the ELMHURST-based Duchossois Industries, Inc. Another area firm that continued to make cars was the Union Tank Car Company, by then part of the Marmon Group, a Chicago-based conglomerate. And ABC Rail Products, Inc., another firm based in the city, was selling about $240 million a year worth of railroad equipment such as wheels and track. Meanwhile, an Idaho-based company briefly used the old Pullman plant to make modest numbers of passenger cars, and GATX continued to be the leading U.S. lessor of tank cars. All of this activity amounted to a reasonably large economic chunk; but it was not comparable to what it had been at the height of the railway age, when Chicago was at the center of the railroad equipment and supply business, then one of the world's leading industries.

Mark R. Wilson

See also: Automobile Manufacturing; Economic Geography; Pullman Strike; Railroad Workers

Further reading: Buder, Stanley. *Pullman: An Experiment in Industrial Order and Community Planning, 1880–1930.* 1967. • Epstein, Ralph C. *GATX: A History of the General American Transportation Corporation, 1898–1948.* 1948. • White, John H. "Railroad Car Builders of the United States." *Railroad History* 138 (1978): 5–29.

Railroad Workers. Chicagoans began working on the railroad in 1848, when building began on the Galena & Chicago Union Railroad. By the 1870s, RAILROADS employed some 2,700 workers, about 9 percent of Chicago's labor force. Over 15,000 Chicagoans worked for railroads in 1900, and almost 30,000 in 1930.

Railroad workers ranged from unskilled freight handlers to locomotive engineers to those who built and repaired the rolling stock. In the early days of Chicago railroading, most engineers and conductors were native-born men. European immigrants built and repaired track, with the IRISH predominating early, followed by ITALIANS and, by the 1910s, ROMANIANS and MEXICANS. AFRICAN AMERICANS worked as Pullman porters and in other often segregated unskilled jobs, and, starting in the twentieth century, women were hired for some CLERICAL and TELEGRAPHY jobs, as car cleaners, and as on-train maids. Employment offices on Madison, Canal, and Halsted Streets recruited track laborers for jobs throughout the region.

Railroad workers put in long hours; a 1907 law restricted train crews to 16 hours WORK out of every 24. Well into the twentieth century,

Pullman Labor Day Parade, 111th Street and Pullman Avenue (later Cottage Grove), 1901. Photographer: Unknown. Source: Chicago Public Library.

work was unsteady and unsafe. One railroad worker in every 357 nationally died on the job in 1889. Though some track workers preferred their outdoor work to regimented factories, turnover was high. Railroads responded to this and to labor unrest by adopting bureaucratic forms of labor discipline and record-keeping and employee welfare programs well before other economic sectors.

Railroad workers dominated many Chicago and suburban communities. PULLMAN is the best-known example; others include AURORA, BLUE ISLAND, FULLER PARK, and BRIGHTON PARK. Chicago's BURNSIDE region, home to car building and repair shops and rail yards of several roads, was an industrial complex of 5,000 workers by 1910. Homeownership was common there. On the other hand, Cook and DuPage County track workers, most of them MEXICANS, lived in at least 26 company labor camps in 1928. Conditions in these camps, often consisting of boxcars, ranged from wretched to barely adequate. Despite this, residents frequently developed a strong community life, raised gardens, and held religious services.

As early as 1856, Chicago's railroad master mechanics established unions to represent their interests. Engineers struck for the first time, in 1863, against the Galena road. By the 1880s operating workers, in Chicago as elsewhere, had achieved a high degree of union organization and maintained relatively good pay and some job security. Chicagoans played a major role in the 1888 strike of the Brotherhood of Locomotive Engineers against the Burlington lines.

Chicago, home to several rail unions, was also at the center of other important rail STRIKES. Chicago rail workers and residents in the communities in which they lived participated in the "Great" RAILROAD STRIKE OF 1877, while, in 1886, thousands of unorganized railroad freight handlers struck for an EIGHT-HOUR DAY, as did track workers and switchmen. In the PULLMAN STRIKE of 1894, neighborhood residents in city and suburbs aided members of the American Railway Union (ARU) in their unsuccessful boycott of Pullman cars. Many joined in violence against railcars, strikebreakers, and POLICE in such diverse places as Blue Island, HAMMOND, and BACK OF THE YARDS. ARU president Eugene Debs was jailed in WOODSTOCK. Chicago rail workers of all skill levels participated in the expansion of unionism during and after WORLD WAR I, when the railroads were under federal control, a buildup which included the all-black Railwaymen's International Industrial Benevolent Association. In 1922, Chicago unionists were at the center of a national strike of some 400,000 repair shop workers, and, in 1925, the BROTHERHOOD OF SLEEPING CAR PORTERS launched what would be a successful effort to organize the Pullman Company's African American workforce of porters and maids.

During the 1930s, railroad workers took advantage of new federal legislation to join unions, many of which admitted African Americans for the first time. Newly UNIONIZED railroad workers enjoyed better pay, and railroad work grew increasingly safe. The U.S. Railroad Retirement Board provided railroaders with retirement benefits even before Social Security. Most unskilled employees and repair shop workers had unionized by 1941. Federal law mandated a 40-hour work week for nonoperating workers in 1949.

Railroad employment peaked in the 1920s, declined during the GREAT DEPRESSION, rose during World War II, and then dropped precipitously as railroads succumbed to competition from cars, buses, trucks, and airplanes. Meanwhile, railroad companies adopted diesel locomotives, track-laying machinery, and other innovations that cut their labor forces, often after bitter disputes with rail unions. Corporate reorganization and deregulation contributed to this job loss. Between 1920 and 1995, national rail employment dropped by 89 percent, although the proportion of white-collar and skilled jobs grew. Union membership remained high and pay scales were good, but the shock of downsizing damaged morale at some roads. CIVIL RIGHTS gains occurred slowly, just as overall rail employment was dropping. Pullman porters, for example, finally won their civil rights suit against the Pullman Company after the company had stopped operations. Chicago's railroad workers' neighborhood communities broke up, as central-city depots, yards, and shops were closed or reorganized and workers dispersed to homes distant from workplaces.

Christopher Thale

See also: Occupational Safety and Health; Railroad Supply Industry; Work Culture

Further reading: Harris, William H. *Keeping the Faith: A. Philip Randolph, Milton P. Webster, and the Brotherhood of Sleeping Car Porters, 1925–1937.* 1977. • Licht, Walter. *Working for the Railroad: The Organization of Work in the Nineteenth Century.* 1983. • Stromquist, Shelton. *A Generation of Boomers: The Pattern of Railroad Labor Conflict in Nineteenth-Century America.* 1987.

Railroads. Chicago is the most important railroad center in North America. More lines of track radiate in more directions from Chicago than from any other city. Chicago has long been the most important interchange point for freight traffic between the nation's major railroads and it is the hub of Amtrak, the intercity rail passenger system. Chicago ranks second (behind New York City) in terms of the volume of COMMUTER rail passengers carried each day.

The first railroad in Chicago was the Galena & Chicago Union, which was chartered in 1836 to build tracks to the lead mines at Galena in northwestern Illinois. The first tracks were laid in 1848, and then not to Galena but to a point known as Oak Ridge (now OAK PARK). The Galena & Chicago Union's terminal stood near the corner of Canal and Kinzie Streets.

Other railroads soon completed lines of track linking Chicago with the wheat fields of northern Illinois and southern Wisconsin. Later lines connected the city with Detroit, Cleveland, Cincinnati, New Orleans, St. Louis, Kansas City, Omaha, and St. Paul. Railroads were especially important as haulers of grain and livestock, which helped Chicago gain a primary role in the grain marketing and MEATPACKING industries.

Many of the railroads built west of Chicago had their corporate headquarters in the city, as well as yards and shops. Chicago became a center for the manufacture of freight cars, passenger cars (Pullman Company), and, later diesel locomotives (Electro-Motive Division of General Motors, in LA GRANGE).

Freight moving across the country is funneled through the railroad yards of Chicago, where it is classified and then transferred to the yards of other railroads within the metropolitan area. The largest of these yards include Proviso and BENSENVILLE on the western edge of the city, Clearing Yard in BEDFORD PARK, Barr and BLUE ISLAND Yards on the far SOUTH SIDE, and Corwith Yard near the Stevenson EXPRESSWAY. Although the nation's railroads now have been merged into just a few large systems, Chicago remains the hub where the tracks of one company end and those of another begin.

Until the 1960s the Chicago LOOP contained six major railroad terminals for intercity rail passenger traffic. Passengers traveling between the East and West Coasts often had half a day to spend in Chicago between trains and took advantage of the time by sightseeing. Journalists sometimes met trains arriving from New York or Los Angeles to spot the celebrities. The decline of intercity rail passenger travel brought about by the advent of jet AIRLINES led to the decline of the passenger train and the eventual consolidation of remaining services under Amtrak in 1971.

Hundreds of thousands of Chicago-area residents still commute to the Loop by train each day, now under the auspices of METRA, the publicly owned regional rail TRANSPORTATION authority. Twelve such commuter-train

Rail yards west of Loop, 1930s. Photographer: Mario Scacheri. Source: University of Illinois at Chicago.

Chicagoans Who Rejected the Railroad

While in retrospect technological innovation might seem preordained (or at least inevitable), those involved in the process are often initially blind to its advantages. In the 1830s, the future of Chicago seemed to rest on the proposed ILLINOIS & MICHIGAN CANAL, linking the GREAT LAKES and the Mississippi River. Chicagoans were unwilling to entertain a shift from a canal to a RAILROAD in 1834, when they wrote to the governor of Illinois:

> Our citizens are for a canal of some kind & they believe that it should *be undertaken by the state*—Rail Roads are out of the question with us, except, in those places where *canals cannot be obtained* for want of water to feed them or some other insurmountable obstacle.

The canal was finally completed in 1848, but it was only a few years before a rail line traversed the same corridor.

In the late 1840s, some area residents still questioned the need for a railroad. NAPERVILLE was growing at the convergence of several roads. Longtime resident Joseph Yackley remembered that when

> they built the Plank Road, it was left to Naperville whether or not they would have the Plank Road or the railroad. Surveys had been made by the railroad (now the Chicago & Northwestern) and if they had built it, they would have followed the present line of the Burlington to Naperville. But you know we had so much traffic at Naperville that the traders were afraid the railroad would take their business away from the[m], and finally decided that they would rather have the Plank Road than the railroad, so they let the Northwestern go [north through Wheaton instead] and took the Plank Road, expecting thereby to hold the traffic at Naperville, but they made a big mistake.

Naperville, however, was able to rectify its mistake by successfully courting the Chicago, Burlington & Quincy Railroad when it ran through the area in the 1860s.

Ann Durkin Keating

services extend outward along the radiating routes of Chicago's rail network. The Burlington Northern Santa Fe line to NAPERVILLE and AURORA carries the heaviest volume of passengers.

John C. Hudson

See also: Business of Chicago; Economic Geography; Metropolitan Growth; Pullman; Railroad Strike of 1877; Railroad Workers; map, p. C3

Further reading: Grant, H. Roger. *The Chicago and North Western Railway.* 1993. • Mayer, Harold M. "Location of Railway Facilities in Metropolitan Centers as Typified by Chicago." *Journal of Land and Public Utility Economics* 20 (1944): 299–315. • *Trains* 53.7 (July 1993). Article on the modern geography of railroads in Chicago.

Rainbow Beach. Dating back to the RACE RIOTS of 1919, Chicago has had a history of youth violence connected to the use of public parks and beaches. Rainbow Beach, extending from 75th to 79th along Lake Michigan in SOUTH SHORE, was one location where black and white youth vied for space. For decades a small enclave of AFRICAN AMERICAN families had lived near the STEEL mills of SOUTH CHICAGO. However, black families had for the most part refrained from letting their children use this public beach because of longstanding hostility from lifeguards and white bathers. As residential patterns changed during the 1950s and 1960s, tensions again began to mount among youth over the use of public space. On Saturday and Sunday, July 7 and 8, 1961, an interracial coalition of demonstrators, many of them members of the NAACP Youth Council, staged a "freedom wade-in" at Rainbow Beach. The coalition's objective was to use the direct-action civil demonstration methods employed by black and white students across the South to heighten public awareness and challenge de facto segregationist policies in Chicago. On Sunday, despite the presence of the POLICE, GANGS of white youth armed with stones attacked the demonstrators.

Charles E. Clifton

See also: Civil Rights Movements; Contested Spaces; National Association for the Advancement of Colored People; Racism, Ethnicity, and White Identity

Further reading: Bubacz, Stephen S. Diary, entries for July 1961. Stephen S. Bubacz Papers, University of Illinois at Chicago. • Hirsch, Arnold. *Making the Second Ghetto: Race and Housing in Chicago, 1940–1960.* 1983.

Rap. Blending a distinct vocal style with rhythms often borrowed from older recordings, rap (also known as hip-hop) began in New York City during the late 1970s. It soon spread to Los Angeles, and within a decade it had matured into a vibrant expression of urban, largely black, experience. New York and Los Angeles have continued to produce the lion's share of important rap artists, whereas Chicago has contributed little to the genre—little, that is, unless one counts "The Super Bowl Shuffle," a novelty hit recorded by the Chicago BEARS football team in 1985. Meanwhile, it became commonplace for serious rappers to cite the NATION OF ISLAM, a Black Muslim organization headquartered in Chicago, as a lyrical and ideological influence, a rap theme often resulting in controversy.

Rap is unique as a musical genre; all other urban genres of the century, including JAZZ, BLUES, and disco, have flourished in Chicago. House music, which, with its use of sequencers, synthesizers, and samples, is parallel to rap, arose in gay AFRICAN AMERICAN clubs in the West Loop as rap was taking shape.

During the second half of the 1990s, Chicago produced a few rappers of note, though this hardly equaled the impact made on both coasts. Chicago rap acts have originated from the city's South and West Sides and include Twista (formerly Tung Twista, known for his rapid-fire vocal style), Do or Die, and Crucial Conflict, which had a minor hit in 1996 with "Hay." The most important rap artist to emerge from Chicago, Common (formerly Common Sense), has introduced confession and introspection to a genre not known for exploring these softer sentiments. Common's success has fueled the ambitions of other local rappers, including Grav, Rubberoom, No I.D., and All Natural.

Mark Swartz

See also: Entertaining Chicagoans; Ethnic Music; Rhythm and Blues

Further reading: George, Nelson. *Hip Hop America.* 1998. • Rose, Tricia. *Black Noise: Rap Music and Black Culture in Contemporary America.* 1994.

Rapid Transit System. By the end of the nineteenth century Chicago's explosive growth had generated street traffic congestion that threatened to choke further expansion. Rapid transit enabled residential development to continue for several decades at a heady pace several miles from downtown in various directions.

New York built the world's first elevated railroad in 1868, but Chicago did not follow until 1892, when the Chicago & SOUTH SIDE Rapid Transit Company opened. Steam locomotives hauled passengers from Congress to 39th Street, along a right-of-way over the alley between State and Wabash. The line was extended to JACKSON PARK in 1893, and by 1910 branches had been built to ENGLEWOOD, KENWOOD, and the stockyards. Three other companies constructed elevated lines: the Lake Street Elevated Railway, which went into operation in 1893 from Market Street (now North Wacker Drive) west to California Avenue, reaching suburban FOREST PARK by 1910; the Metropolitan West Side Elevated Railroad, which began operating electric trains from downtown to LOGAN SQUARE in 1895, and by 1915 to Forest Park and Cicero, with branches to GARFIELD PARK, HUMBOLDT PARK, and Douglas Park; and the Northwestern Elevated Railroad, which opened from downtown to Wilson Avenue in 1900 and reached WILMETTE in 1912, with a branch to RAVENSWOOD. By 1898 all elevated lines had converted from steam locomotives to electric power.

In 1897 streetcar magnate Charles T. Yerkes, Jr., who owned the Lake Street "L" and the uncompleted Northwestern "L," completed the Union Elevated Railroad, a downtown LOOP connecting all four lines. The existing "L"s

Chicago's Rapid Transit Lines

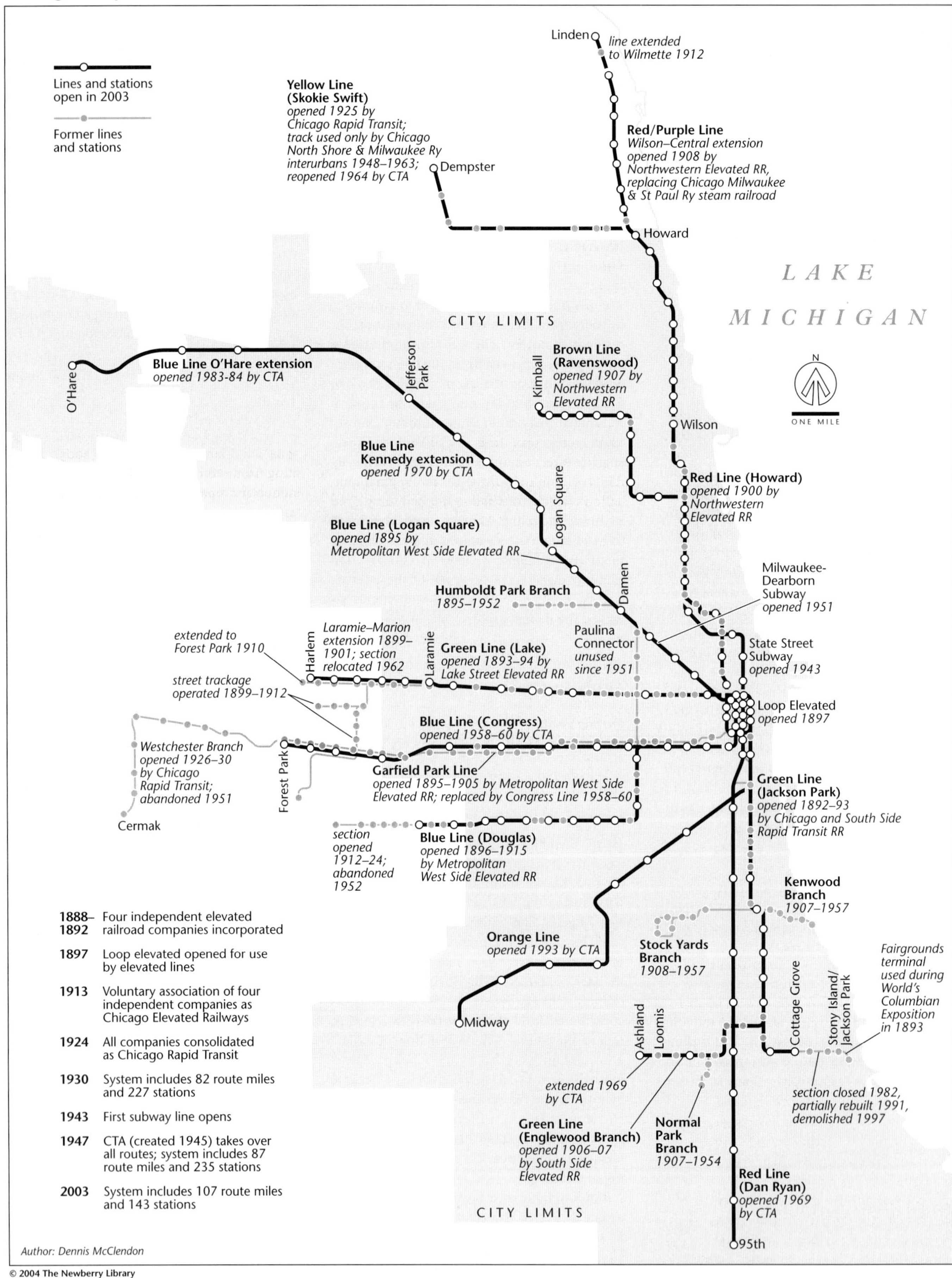

abandoned their individual downtown terminals and circled the loop. In 1911 the four Elevated companies were brought together under the Chicago Elevated Railways Collateral Trust, and in 1913 the trust finally provided through routing and transfers among the four "L" routes.

In 1947 the CHICAGO TRANSIT AUTHORITY (CTA) took over operation of the rapid transit lines. The CTA revamped the operation of the "L"s and closed stations with low ridership. Between 1948 and 1957 the Douglas Park and Humboldt Park lines, the outer end of the Garfield line, and the branches to Niles Center (restored in 1964 as the SKOKIE Swift), Normal Park, the stockyards, and Kenwood were abandoned.

Chicago's first subway had opened in 1943 under Clybourn, Division, and State Streets, 80 years after the London Underground and 46 years after the first U.S. subway in Boston. The busy North-South elevated line was rerouted through it, relieving congestion on the loop. A second subway under Dearborn Street was completed in 1951, enabling the CTA to abandon part of the Logan Square "L." In the 1950s the Garfield "L" was replaced by a rapid transit line in the median of the Congress (later Eisenhower) EXPRESSWAY. The Congress line inspired similar projects in other freeway medians. In 1969 the CTA opened a nine-mile extension via the Dan Ryan Expressway to the city's far South Side at 95th Street; in 1970 the Dearborn line was extended from Logan Square five miles to JEFFERSON PARK in the median of the Kennedy Expressway, and in 1984, to O'HARE AIRPORT. An entirely new line to MIDWAY AIRPORT opened in 1993. At the turn of the century the old elevated structures, some more than a century old, were being rebuilt, ensuring their survival well into the twenty-first century.

Ronald Dale Karr

See also: Economic Geography; Multicentered Chicago; Public Transportation; Street Railways; Transportation

Further reading: Barrett, Paul. *The Automobile and Urban Transit: The Formation of Public Policy in Chicago, 1900–1930.* 1983. • Central Electric Railfans' Association. *Chicago's Rapid Transit,* 2 vols. 1973–1977. • Cudahy, Brian J. *Destination Loop: The Story of Rapid Transit Railroading in and around Chicago.* 1982.

Four individual companies built elevated railroads to link outlying city and near-suburban neighborhoods between 1892 and 1930. Similar construction and equipment standards simplified the unified operation of the lines beginning in 1913, as did public ownership after World War II. The new Chicago Transit Authority closed several lightly patronized branches, reducing a 1947 system of 87 miles to 68 miles by 1958. Four significant extensions since 1969 brought the system to approximately 107 miles by 2003, with several placed innovatively along the median strips of expressways. The most recent, the Orange Line, was built in 1993 to link the neglected Southwest Side and a revivified Midway Airport to the Loop.

Ravenswood, neighborhood in LINCOLN SQUARE Community Area. Ravenswood, a residential subdivision in the township of LAKE VIEW, was designed to be one of Chicago's first and most exclusive commuter suburbs. In 1868, a group of REAL-ESTATE speculators formed the Ravenswood Land Company and purchased 194 acres of farm and wooded land eight miles north of Chicago. The company made a deal with the Chicago & North Western RAILROAD guaranteeing them a certain number of passengers if they would open a new stop. Hoping that the fee of $7.20 for a hundred rides would attract only wealthy residents, the company divided the property into large lots. The speculators hedged their real-estate gamble by building the Sunnyside Hotel adjacent to the village made up of the original 194 acres, so that potential customers might first come as visitors to a resort. By 1874, the original lone railroad COMMUTER had multiplied to 75.

The Ravenswood Land Company did not build houses, sewers, or sidewalks. Longtime Ravenswood residents interviewed in the 1920s recalled open ditches and muddy streets alongside the lovely lawns, houses, and TREES. Private subscriptions paid for some local improvements, but neighboring JEFFERSON TOWNSHIP would not permit Ravenswood's sewers to run through its land into the Chicago River. With the annexation of both Lake View and Jefferson Townships to Chicago in 1889, authority over improvements shifted to the larger municipality and Ravenswood got its sewers. The introduction of electric streetcar lines in the 1890s and the extension of the "L" in 1907 made the area accessible to less affluent residents, whose small houses, two-flats, and APARTMENT buildings filled in the gap between Chicago and its former suburb. The name Ravenswood, however, remained in popular use, even after the area was officially designated part of the LINCOLN SQUARE Community Area.

Amanda Seligman

See also: Infrastructure; Metropolitan Growth

Further reading: Andreas, A. T. *History of Cook County, Illinois, from the Earliest Period to the Present Time.* 1884. • Keating, Ann Durkin. *Building Chicago: Suburban Developers and the Creation of a Divided Metropolis.* 1988. • Zatterberg, Helen. *An Historical Sketch of Ravenswood and Lake View.* 1941.

Ravinia. The Ravinia Festival is a 36-acre international performance and education center in HIGHLAND PARK devoted to classical and contemporary music. Its open-air pavilion seats 3,350; the grounds can accommodate approximately 15,000.

Ravinia Park was founded in 1904 by an electric railway operator who hoped patrons would come to its open-air pavilion and amusements by INTERURBAN. In 1910, after the park went into receivership, patrons organized a campaign directed by Chicago philanthropist Louis Eckstein to purchase the grounds and establish the Ravinia Company (1911). Its reconstituted musical repertoire added OPERA, Eckstein's passion, for which the company gained acclaim. Bankruptcy forced the company's failure in 1931. Reorganized as the Ravinia Festival Association, it reopened on July 3, 1936. Eckstein's widow bequeathed the grounds to the festival in 1944, with the provision that it remain devoted to CLASSICAL MUSIC.

After fire destroyed the original pavilion in 1949, the festival expanded its scope to regain its international recognition. Walter Hendl, associate conductor of the CHICAGO SYMPHONY ORCHESTRA, served as the first artistic director (1959–1963). Esteemed music directors followed: Seiji Ozawa (1964–68), James Levine (1971–1993); Christoph Eschenbach (1995–2004); and James Conlon (from 2005). Benefiting from refurbished and newly constructed indoor and open-air performance spaces, the festival operates year-round. The Steans Institute for Young Artists (1988) attracts students and faculty worldwide.

Michael H. Ebner

See also: Amusement Parks; Entertaining Chicagoans; Outdoor Concerts; Philanthropy

Further reading: Ebner, Michael H. "North Shore: Patron of Ravinia Park." *Chicago History* 16.2 (Summer 1987): 48–63. • Weingartner, Fannia. *Ravinia: The Festival at Its Half Century.* 1985.

Real Estate. Few industries have been so closely connected to the development of the Chicago metropolitan region and the daily lives of its citizens as has real estate. In conjunction with governmental policies, regulations, and interventions, the real-estate industry has exerted enormous influence on the sociogeographical contours of the entire metropolitan area.

Chicago's real-estate activities divide into several branches, each with its trade, industry, or professional association. These include land assembly and SUBDIVISION platting, building, brokerage, property management, mortgage lending, land title INSURANCE, and appraisal and land value monitoring and research.

Nineteenth-Century Subdivision and Development

Chicago's early real-estate enterprise was marked by large-scale development and land speculation attending one of the world's fastest-growing cities. In less than the lifespan of one of Chicago's earliest residents, Emily Beaubien Le Beau (1825–1919), Chicago grew from fewer than 100 people into being the fourth-largest city in the world.

Most of Chicago's early builders and investors were attracted by the possibilities

Engraving of Calumet Harbor and South Chicago, from the *Land Owner*, 1873. Artist: Unknown. Source: The Newberry Library.

offered by canal building, the city's rapid growth after the Civil War, or its resurgence after the Fire of 1871. No other large city experienced such extensive and excessive subdivision platting and such volatile boom-and-bust cycles in land values. Fortunes were made and lost with each new cycle.

Subdividers fell into several categories of ownership and control: individuals, manufacturing companies, harbor and canal companies, improvement companies, land associations, syndicates, real-estate corporations, and real-estate companies. These early investors and developers shaped Chicago in many different ways. William B. Ogden, the first mayor of Chicago, was active in land sales connected with the Illinois & Michigan Canal, the Galena & Chicago Union Railroad, the Chicago Union Stock Yard, and the McCormick Reaper Company. John Wentworth, twice mayor of Chicago and three times congressman, facilitated the entry of the Illinois Central Railroad into Chicago and speculated in land in the Calumet Region and Garfield Ridge. Senator Stephen A. Douglas also speculated in Calumet land in the late 1840s, bought 70 acres of lakefront between 33rd and 35th Streets in 1852, and helped arrange a federal land grant to the Illinois Central in 1853. Potter Palmer bought three-quarters of a mile of State Street in 1867, built a score of buildings there, and bought land on the near north lakefront in 1882 for his mansion.

In the 1870s, the Pullman Palace Car Company and the Pullman Land Association bought nearly 4,000 acres for a factory and company town in Pullman, and Brown Steel Company built a company town in Irondale, now South Deering. During the same decade, the Calumet and Chicago Canal and Dock Company platted 6,000 acres in South Chicago, Calumet Heights, and the East Side. The firm of S. E. Gross targeted German buyers in bilingual ads for lots near horse-car and rail lines in the 1880s and near elevated lines in the 1890s, selling up to 500 lots a week in the land boom in the early years of that decade. In 1911, during another boom era, Bartlett Realty platted 600 acres in Archer Heights, Clearing, Gage Park, and Garfield Ridge. In 1918, the company created Greater Chicago, the city's largest single subdivision, in Roseland. Nine years later, it purchased 3,600 acres in what is now Beverly Shores, Indiana, to create a development that would rival Atlantic City.

This frenetic platting by individuals, land associations, and real-estate corporations resulted in excessive subdivision. Riverside was platted in 1871 for a population of 10,000, a target reached only briefly a century later. Harvey was subdivided in 1890 to shelter a population of 25,000, a figure achieved 70 years later. The subdivision boom lasted until 1926. Only when the Great Depression slowed population growth to a standstill did the extent to which the Chicago area was over-subdivided become clear. By 1935, there were enough lots in the region to accommodate a population of 15 million, about three times the population at the time and almost 40 percent more than the population at the end of the century.

Residential Finance

The success of subdivisions also depended on the highly interdependent building and

Samuel Eberly Gross's Subdivisions

As a real-estate developer in Chicago in the late nineteenth and early twentieth centuries, Gross built more than 21 SUBDIVISIONS and 10,000 homes. He developed working-class areas such as NEW CITY (near the stockyards) and middle-class subdivisions such as Alta Vista Terrace and Grossdale (now BROOKFIELD).

His success was due to a number of factors: his use of standardized house plans and mass-produced building materials; his location of subdivisions near existing or planned transportation lines; and his mastery of promotion and marketing—especially campaigns geared toward the working man and the immigrant.

Emily Clark

mortgage lending industries. Before the introduction of long-term mortgages in 1934, a response to the crisis of the GREAT DEPRESSION, other lending instruments facilitated building. Cyclical building booms were sustained by state banks before 1970. Eastern insurance companies financed the post–Great Fire boom of 1889–1892. "Shoestring" financing through the sale of real-estate bonds fueled the building boom of 1922–1928.

The Great Depression and WORLD WAR II put the brake on building until 1945. Housing legislation under the NEW DEAL replaced the familiar five-year balloon loan with the long-term mortgage loan. New housing programs sponsored by the Federal Housing Authority (FHA) and the Veterans' Administration (VA) were welcomed by the National Association of Home Builders, formed in 1942 to plan for postwar housing needs. The Mortgage Bankers Association of America (MBAA), created in 1914, was less receptive, fearful of competition from commercial banks and SAVINGS AND LOANS to serve the greatly expanded market for home loans. The MBAA relented with the advent of VA loans in 1944 and expanded its membership to commercial banks and savings and loans.

FHA housing programs also had another significant effect on the metropolitan area. Adopting the evaluations of the Home Owners' Loan Corporation (HOLC) and the best practices of the National Association of Real Estate Boards, FHA mortgage insurance was readily available only in areas where both the housing stock and population mix met well-defined standards. As a result, postwar housing development and expansion occurred predominantly in newer suburban communities and in more affluent white neighborhoods.

Land Title System

Several land title abstractors met in Chicago in 1907 to form the American Association of Title Men, renamed the American Title Association in 1923 and the American Land Title Association in 1962.

Ownership of real estate is conveyed by title. In COOK COUNTY, title is sometimes certified by the TORRENS system of land registration, but more often by title insurance, which guarantees against title defects and liens. Illinois is one of a few states which allow title to be held in a "blind" trust, where title is held by a trustee for the benefit of the holder. Chicago Title and Trust Company is Chicago's largest title insurer and trustee of BLIND TRUSTS.

Appraisal and Research

Inaugurating what would become the most reliable historical index of land values in the nation, George C. Olcott began his annual "Blue Book" of land values in 1910, establishing Chicago as a land value laboratory. Foremost of the resulting surveys is Homer Hoyt's *One Hundred Years of Land Values in Chicago* (1933). Hoyt documented the highly volatile boom-and-bust cycles, determining that peak land values had occurred in 1836, 1856, 1869, 1891, and 1925, and that troughs had occurred in 1842, 1865, 1878, 1898, 1920, and 1933.

Recent advances in computerizing data on asking and selling prices on house sales reported in Multiple Listing Services maintained by local Boards of Realtors greatly facilitate the task of monitoring changes in housing values. Continuously updated data on house asking and selling prices for different types of houses and locations allow the broker to identify housing suitable for buyers and the appraiser to determine the selling price of units comparable to the unit being appraised.

Post–World War II Developments

Large subdivision building resumed after World War II, with plans that included two "new towns" of the British model. In 1949, Philip M. Klutznick assembled 3,000 acres of cornfield on the southern edge of Cook County to build the planned new town of PARK FOREST. In 1967, Lewis Manilow built the sister town of Park Forest South, now UNIVERSITY PARK.

Other large postwar subdividers have included Sam and Jack Hoffman, who bought a 160-acre farm in 1954 to build HOFFMAN ESTATES; the central Texas Centex Corporation, which assembled 1,500 acres for the planned residential/industrial complex of ELK GROVE VILLAGE and Centex; and Hanover Builders and Three-H, who built several subdivisions in HANOVER PARK between 1961 and 1971.

Recovering from a 20-year moratorium on office building construction took longer. The completion of the Prudential Building in 1955 opened a new era of SKYSCRAPER building in the LOOP, topped out at the time by three of the world's tallest buildings.

In the 1970s, mortgage lenders in Chicago were accused of racial bias, as mortgage REDLINING, a term derived from the HOLC maps of the 1930s classifying certain neighborhoods as inappropriate for loans, became a big issue in the high-interest-rate era of the mid-1970s. Chicago's antiredlining activists were in the forefront of protests and lobbying which culminated in passage of the Home Mortgage Disclosure Act of 1975 and the Community Reinvestment Act of 1977.

Realtors, Urban Renewal, and Open Housing

Chicago serves as national headquarters for the National Association of Realtors (NAR), the Institute of Real Estate Management (IREM), and five other real-estate associations. Local brokers were prime movers in the founding of the National Association of Real Estate Exchanges in 1908, renamed the National Association of Real Estate Boards (NAREB) in 1916. NAREB the next year adopted "realtor" as the title for its members. Among its activities was the creation of ethical practices for realtors, including a commitment to not selling properties that would change the racial make-up of a community. NAREB took the name of National Association of Realtors in 1972. The Chicago affiliate changed its name from the Chicago Real Estate Board to the Chicago Association of Realtors at the same time.

NAREB's 1941 report "Housing and Blighted Areas" outlined a plan of federal-aided slum clearance which later inspired the National Housing Acts of 1949 and 1954. Local NAREB and IREM leaders including Holman Pettibone, Ferd Kramer, and Newton Farr helped guide Chicago's early renewal efforts. Pettibone worked hard to promote the "write down" formula which was later incorporated in the Illinois Redevelopment Act of 1947. Kramer, president of the Metropolitan Housing and Planning Council, managed Lake Meadows, a project funded by New York Life, and developed Prairie Shores. Farr, a past president of NAREB, served on the Committee of Six that oversaw the Hyde Park–KENWOOD Urban Renewal Project.

URBAN RENEWAL legislation in the 1950s gave Chicago HOSPITALS, UNIVERSITIES, and community boards the power of eminent domain to clear slums and build Sandburg Village, Lake Meadows, Prairie Shores, HYDE PARK A & B, and LINCOLN PARK I & II. New PUBLIC BUILDINGS included the Dirksen, Daley, and Thompson centers, the UNIVERSITY OF ILLINOIS AT CHICAGO, McCormick Place, and the Harold Washington Library.

Both NAR and IREM and its members were hard hit by STEERING/antisteering lawsuits brought by local OPEN HOUSING groups, culminating in the Supreme Court decision in *Gladstone, Realtors v. Village of Bellwood* (1979). The CHICAGO HOUSING AUTHORITY was found guilty of operating a racially discriminatory housing program and ordered to desist in the GAUTREAUX *v. Chicago Housing Authority* decision of 1969, expanded by the Supreme Court in its Gautreaux opinion of 1976.

Recent Trends

Population growth in the Chicago region slowed to a snail's pace in the last three decades of the twentieth century. As it did, the real-estate boom-and-bust cycles that punctuated Chicago's first century of rapid growth eased.

Overbuilding has persisted in some sectors, particularly in office space downtown, resulting in double-digit vacancy rates. But residential vacancy rates have fluctuated around a low 3 percent in the 1990s in both the city and the suburbs. Except for higher-priced neighborhoods on Chicago's North Side and North Shore, housing price increases have stayed within 1 percent of inflation through much of the 1990s. Chicago thus was spared the sharp boom-and-bust real-estate cycles experienced in California, Texas, and New England between 1983 and 1991 that resulted in the closing of hundreds of S&Ls in those regions.

Spurred by the region's prosperity, low interest rates, and the desirability of real-estate for investment, the closing years of the century witnessed a boom in the Chicago housing market. Developers converted downtown office buildings into residential units and built high-rise APARTMENT buildings, CONDOMINIUMS, townhouses, and single-family homes throughout the city. For the first time in almost half a century, Chicago's population increased. The suburban real-estate market expanded as well. Farmland was transformed into subdivisions of substantial homes. Properties like the former GLENVIEW NAVAL AIR STATION became new communities, seemingly overnight. As all the different elements of the real-estate industry contributed to these changes, they helped to reshape the metropolitan area as they had since the early years of land speculation.

Pierre de Vise

See also: Built Environment of the Chicago Region; Contested Spaces; Housing Reform; Housing Types; Initial Land Sales (color map, p. C1); Land Use; Planning Chicago; Restrictive Covenants

Further reading: Hoyt, Homer. *One Hundred Years of Land Values in Chicago, 1830–1933.* 1933. • Monchow, Helen Corbin. *Seventy Years of Real Estate Subdividing in the Region of Chicago.* 1939. • Randall, Frank A. *A History of the Development of Building Construction in Chicago.* 1949.

Real Estate Research Corporation.

Chicago's Real Estate Research Corporation (RERC) was one of the nation's first research and consulting firms for analyzing the REAL-ESTATE market. Founded in 1931 by James Downs it published a market newsletter for developers from 1938. RERC grew substantially after 1950, peaking with a staff of about 200. First Chicago Corporation bought the firm in 1970.

While much of RERC's work has involved land appraisals for the private development of projects such as shopping centers, HOTELS, and industrial parks, the firm has also reported on broad trends in URBAN RENEWAL and development. Private clients have included developers and groups like the State Street Council and the Chicago Central Area Committee; government clients have included city, county, state, and federal agencies.

RERC's founder, Downs, was well connected with Chicago DEMOCRATIC politicians and served as an important bridge between them and BUSINESS interests. As the city's housing and redevelopment coordinator under MAYORS Martin H. Kennelly and Richard J. Daley, Downs worked with leading figures such as Holman Pettibone of Chicago Title and Trust to develop state and city agencies to aid housing and urban development. He also served as liaison between the city and the UNIVERSITY OF CHICAGO during HYDE PARK'S URBAN RENEWAL in the 1940s, a project that foreshadowed national urban renewal efforts. Anthony Downs, a prominent political scientist at the Brookings Institution, took over as chair of RERC when his father retired in the mid-1970s.

Loomis Mayfield

See also: Built Environment of the Chicago Region; Planning Chicago; Shopping Districts and Malls

Further reading: Hirsch, Arnold R. *Making the Second Ghetto: Race and Housing in Chicago, 1940–1960.* 1983. • Obituary for James Downs. *Chicago Tribune,* Sept. 29, 1981. • *Who's Who in Chicago and Illinois.* 9th ed. 1950.

Rear Houses. Prior to 1890, frame cottages were ubiquitous residences for the working class in Chicago. Typically one-story, rectangular buildings of four to six rooms, these cottages often were built without permanent foundations of brick or stone. Resting upon cedar posts sunk below the frost line, most cottages sat on narrow lots, usually 25 by 125 feet. These narrow lots permitted a row of cottages to crowd one against another and still provide ample space within the interior of a city block.

During the 1880s in neighborhoods near the LOOP where land values rose dramatically, the crowding of two and even three cottages upon a single lot became profitable for immigrant homeowners. In districts where factories displaced residences, landowners purchased old cottages intended for demolition. Without permanent foundations or plumbing, these structures were raised and moved easily to another location, often the rear portion of a lot. In other instances, landowners moved older cottages from the front to the rear of their lots and then constructed larger brick buildings on the front of the lot.

Chicago's HOUSING REFORMERS universally condemned rear houses as dirty, miserable firetraps overrun with bugs and rats. In POLISH

Barns, garages, and houses along an alley, ca. 1900. Photographer: Unknown. Source: University of Illinois at Chicago.

and Bohemian neighborhoods on the West Side, rear houses appeared on one-fourth to one-third of all lots in the 1890s. With the increased construction of three-story brick tenements, these neighborhoods became notorious for dark, damp, and narrow passageways that prohibited adequate light and ventilation. On occasion, rear houses were raised on brick foundations, creating two floors. The new brick first floor sometimes contained primitive toilets or stables. The presence of numerous stables and inadequate sanitation compounded the problems of overcrowded lots. Without adequate space, great numbers of children played in dangerous passageways and foul ALLEYS. Despite BUILDING CODES, these conditions persisted.

In heavily populated districts like the BACK OF THE YARDS or the BLACK BELT on the SOUTH SIDE, rear houses presented a negligible problem since they appeared only occasionally. In industrial suburbs like EAST CHICAGO or CICERO, rear houses resembled their inner-city counterparts. But they appeared only in small, concentrated areas that housed the most recently arrived immigrants.

While rear houses remain common in older sections of Chicago, URBAN RENEWAL decreased their numbers. Refurbished rear houses also remain in a few GENTRIFIED portions of the city such as LINCOLN PARK. Ironically, housing once condemned as a social evil now offers a trendy address for a young, upwardly mobile population.

Joseph C. Bigott

See also: Built Environment of the Chicago Region; Housing Types; Planning Chicago

Further reading: Abbott, Edith. *The Tenements of Chicago, 1908–1935.* 1936. • Embree, Frances Buckley. "The Housing of the Poor in Chicago." *Journal of*

Political Economy 8 (June 1900): 354–377. • Hunter, Robert. *Tenement Conditions in Chicago.* 1901.

Record Publishing. Chicago's performers drive its record industry. While major labels maintain regional distribution offices in Chicago, their studios are in New York or Los Angeles. This vacuum creates opportunities for hundreds of independent labels run by local entrepreneurs. Many "indies" struggle, but some succeed.

Beginning in 1922, Brunswick (Iowa), Gennett (Indiana), Okeh (New York), and Paramount (Wisconsin), largely offshoots of Midwest piano manufacturers, recorded Chicago's leading BLUES and JAZZ talents, making the city a pioneer in "race records." In 1924, Marsh Recording Laboratories, based in Chicago, released the first electric recordings, on its Autograph label. By 1930, most jazz activity had moved to New York. Between August 1942 and November 1944, Chicago's James C. Petrillo, American Federation of Musicians president, enforced a wartime national recording ban.

After WORLD WAR II, Chicago-based companies such as Chance (1950), CHESS (1950), J.O.B. (1949), Delmark (1953), Parrot, United (1952), and Vee-Jay (1953), the largest black-owned label before Motown, mined the city's talent (especially blues, doowop, GOSPEL, jazz, and soul), forming the core of Record Row on South Michigan Avenue (1960s). Chicago's psychedelic bands appeared on Dunwich and USA, and Curtis Mayfield founded soul label Curtom (1968). Mercury, the city's last major label, closed in 1964. The 1970s welcomed blues and FOLK staples Alligator (1971), Flying Fish (1974), and Earwig Blues (1978), while Trax and D.J. International featured Chicago house music (1980s). In the 1990s, indies continued to accompany Chicago's performance scene. Cedille (1989) produces local CLASSICAL MUSIC artists, while Cajual and Dance Mania offer an array of dance and electronica.

Mark Clague

See also: Economic Geography; Music Publishing; Musical Instrument Manufacturing; Near South Side; Rhythm and Blues; Rock Music

Further reading: Kenney, William Howland. "Chicago's Jazz Records." In *Chicago Jazz: A Cultural History, 1904–1930.* 1993. • Pruter, Robert. *Chicago Soul.* 1991. • Rust, Brian. *The American Record Label Book.* 1978.

Red Squad. The arm of Chicago's law enforcement known alternately as the Industrial Unit, the Intelligence Division, the Radical Squad, or the Red Squad, had its roots in the Gilded Age, when class conflict encouraged employers to ally themselves with Chicago's POLICE against the city's increasingly politicized workforce. Following the HAYMARKET bombing, Captain Michael J. Schaack orchestrated a vicious campaign against anarchism, resulting in 260 arrests, bribed witnesses, attacks on immigrants and labor activists, and convoluted theories of revolutionary conspiracy. Continuing its use of both overt and covert tactics, such as surveillance, infiltration, and intimidation, Chicago's Red Squad in the 1920s under Make Mills shifted its attention from ANARCHISTS to individuals and organizations who the Red Squad believed to be COMMUNIST. Casting a wide net, the squad by 1960 had collected information on approximately 117,000 Chicagoans, 141,000 out-of-towners, and 14,000 organizations. After the 1968 Democratic National Convention, the Red Squad expanded its targets from radical organizations like the Communist and Socialist Workers Parties to minority and reform organizations, including the AMERICAN CIVIL LIBERTIES UNION, NATIONAL ASSOCIATION FOR THE ADVANCEMENT OF COLORED PEOPLE, National Lawyers Guild, and OPERATION PUSH.

After 11 years of litigation, a 1985 court decision ended the Chicago Police Department's Subversive Activities Unit's unlawful surveillance of political dissenters and their organizations. In the fall of 1974, the Red Squad destroyed 105,000 individual and 1,300 organizational files when it learned that the Alliance to End Repression was filing a lawsuit against the unit for violating the U.S. Constitution. The records that remain are housed at the Chicago Historical Society. The public requires special permission to access them until 2012.

Randi Storch

See also: Cold War and Anti-Communism; Free Speech

Further reading: Donner, Frank. *Protectors of Privilege: Red Squads and Police Repression in Urban America.* 1990.

Redlining. Redlining is the practice of arbitrarily denying or limiting financial services to specific neighborhoods, generally because its residents are people of color or are poor. While discriminatory practices existed in the banking and insurance industries well before the 1930s, the NEW DEAL'S Home Owners' Loan Corporation (HOLC) instituted a redlining policy by developing color-coded maps of American cities that used racial criteria to categorize lending and insurance risks. New, affluent, racially homogeneous housing areas received green lines while black and poor white neighborhoods were often circumscribed by red lines denoting their undesirability. Banks and insurers soon adopted the HOLC's maps and practices to guide lending and underwriting decisions. Further, the Federal Housing Administration, created in 1934, also used the HOLC's methods to assess locations for federally insured new housing construction.

Like other forms of discrimination, redlining had pernicious and damaging effects. Without bank loans and insurance, redlined areas lacked the capital essential for investment and redevelopment. As a result, after WORLD WAR II, suburban areas received preference for residential investment at the expense of poor and minority neighborhoods in cities like Chicago. The relative lack of investment in new housing, rehabilitation, and home improvement contributed significantly to the decline of older urban neighborhoods and compounded Chicago's decline in relation to its suburbs.

Redlining's negative effects remained largely unrecognized by policymakers until the mid-1960s. BANKING practices were the first to receive congressional scrutiny. The Fair Housing Act of 1968 prohibited housing discrimination and the Home Mortgage Disclosure Act of 1975 required the release of data on bank lending. Unsatisfied by the practical results of these laws, community activists in Chicago spearheaded further reform, leading the nation in identifying and addressing the redlining issue. In the early 1970s, the Citizens Action Program, a crossracial group of community leaders from the SOUTH SIDE, developed a strategy of "greenlining" by asking residents to deposit savings only in banks that pledged to reinvest funds in urban communities. Chicago organizers were also instrumental in lobbying Congress to pass the Community Reinvestment Act of 1977 (CRA), which required banks to lend in areas from which they accepted deposits. The law had limited effect until the National Training and Information Center in Chicago, led by Gale Cincotta, put public pressure on Chicago banks to lend to distressed neighborhoods. Cincotta's group successfully negotiated $173 million in CRA agreements from three major downtown banks in 1984, settlements that served as models for other cities.

The extent of progress in ending redlining in the INSURANCE industry remains an ongoing debate. In 1968, the President's National Advisory Panel on Insurance in Riot-Affected Areas found that insurance underwriting manuals explicitly instructed agents to use racial data in determining risk. While states passed laws prohibiting insurance redlining, federal legislation has never directly addressed the issue. Court cases, however, have forced change in both the banking and insurance industries. In the 1990s, prominent banks and insurance firms have settled several major lawsuits, agreeing to change their business practices to remove discriminatory policies and procedures.

D. Bradford Hunt

See also: Housing Reform; Metropolitan Growth; Open Housing; Racism, Ethnicity, and White Identity; Restrictive Covenants

Further reading: Jackson, Kenneth T. *Crabgrass Frontier: The Suburbanization of the United States.* 1985. • Squires, Gregory D., Larry Bennett, Kathleen McCourt, and Philip Nyden. *Chicago: Race, Class, and the Response to Urban Design.* 1987. • Squires, Gregory D., ed. *Insurance Redlining: Disinvestment, Reinvestment, and the Evolving Role of Financial Institutions.* 1997.

Refining. Chicago was not among the earliest locations of the petroleum industry, but when oil refining finally came to the area, it came with a bang. When the Standard Oil Company opened its new refinery in WHITING, Indiana, in 1890, the facility ranked as the largest refinery in the world. A century later, the Whiting facility still stood among the largest in the world, and the Chicago region remained an important refining center.

Refining came to the Chicago area at a time when an already robust oil industry was devoted to the production of illuminating oils such as kerosene. By the end of the 1880s, when the Standard Oil Company of Indiana was created as a new subsidiary of the giant corporation built by John D. Rockefeller, nearly $80 million had been invested in the American refining industry, which already employed over 11,000 men and generated over $85 million in products annually. Given this context, the new Chicago-area refinery being planned by Standard of Indiana was a kind of second-generation production plant, one that would be larger and more modern than its predecessors in Pennsylvania and Ohio. Initially, Standard of Indiana planned on building its new refinery at SOUTH CHICAGO, the terminus of a pipeline originating in the oil fields of Ohio and Indiana. But land costs, tax rates, and local opposition were high enough in South Chicago to lead the company to look elsewhere. It soon decided to begin construction at Whiting, located in northwestern Indiana along the shore of LAKE MICHIGAN. A little over a year after construction started in May 1889, the Whiting refinery went on line, and it began to turn crude oil into kerosene and other products.

The relative importance of the Chicago area within the oil industry was never greater than in the 1890s, immediately after the Whiting refinery began to operate. By the middle of that decade, the Whiting plant could process as much as 36,000 barrels of crude oil per day, and accounted for nearly a fifth of total refining capacity in the United States. By the end of the 1890s, about $6 million had been invested in the Whiting facility, which employed about 3,000 people, most of them European-born men.

During the early part of the twentieth century, as the oil industry began to focus upon the production of gasoline, the Whiting facility pioneered new refining technologies. In 1911, after the U.S. Supreme Court ordered the breakup of Rockefeller's oil trust, Standard of Indiana (based in Chicago) become an independent company. At the same time, the explosive growth of the AUTOMOBILE industry was causing the oil industry to expand quickly. During the 1910s, the value of the output of U.S. refineries increased by a factor of almost seven, and the number of workers in the industry quadrupled. Part of the industry's boom during the 1910s was attributable to technological innovations made at the Whiting refinery (which was now connected by pipeline to oil fields in Kansas and Oklahoma, as well as the older eastern fields). During the early 1910s, Standard of Indiana chemist and executive William M. Burton directed experiments at the Whiting plant that attempted to increase gasoline yields by processing (or "cracking") the crude oil at higher temperatures and higher pressures. These experiments proved successful, and Standard of Indiana collected $15 million in patent royalties between 1913 and 1920, as it and other oil companies used the new process to get more gasoline out of every barrel of crude.

By the middle part of the twentieth century, the Chicago region was home to several large refineries, and the employees of some of these plants took part in a national effort by oil industry workers to exert more influence over wages and the workplace. By the middle of the Depression, when Standard of Indiana employed about seven thousand residents of the Chicago area, the Sinclair Refining Company had about one thousand workers in its EAST CHICAGO refinery. During WORLD WAR II, more refineries sprang up around Chicago, and the local industry responded to a labor shortage by hiring hundreds of women. (At the Whiting refinery, about 15 percent of wartime employees were women.) In late 1945, just after the end of the war, refinery workers throughout the United States—many of them members of the Oil Workers International Union—were part of a major STRIKE that was intended to help workers achieve wage increases, industry-wide bargaining rights, and a closed shop agreement. Within the Chicago area, there were over 4,000 employees on strike at CALUMET-area refineries such as the one owned by the Socony-Vacuum Oil Company. Eventually, after President Truman authorized the U.S. Navy to seize some plants and the U.S. Department of Labor became involved in the dispute, many refinery workers in Chicago and the rest of the country were awarded a pay raise of about 18 percent.

During the second half of the twentieth century, as the U.S. refining industry became more concentrated in Texas, Louisiana, and California, the Chicago region became somewhat less important as an oil-processing center than it had been during the previous 60 years. Still, the area remained home to some large refineries. During the 1950s, refineries in the Chicago region were using about 175 million barrels of crude per year, which made the area the third-largest refining center in the United States. The Whiting plant, which used more WATER than the entire city of Chicago, now had a capacity of 200,000 barrels per day and employed over 7,000 local residents. Other large refineries in the area included the Sinclair plant in EAST CHICAGO; a Cities Service Oil Company refinery in East Chicago; a plant owned by the Pure Oil Company in LEMONT; and a Texas Company refinery at LOCKPORT. By the end of the twentieth century, when the Chicago region's share of total U.S. refining capacity had declined to about 5 percent, there were still large refineries on the metropolis's southern edges. Four local refineries—in BLUE ISLAND, Lemont, JOLIET, and Whiting—had a combined refining capacity of about 875,000 barrels per day. The largest of these plants was the one at Whiting—the same facility that had brought refining to Chicago in 1890. Now owned by BP Amoco (Standard of Indiana, long a huge multinational corporation, changed its name to Amoco in 1985; Amoco merged with BP just before the end of the century), the Whiting facility was still among the largest oil refineries in the United States.

Mark R. Wilson

See also: Gas Stations; Industrial Pollution; Motoring; Unionization

Further reading: Giddens, Paul H. *Standard Oil Company (Indiana): Oil Pioneer of the Middle West.* 1955. • Williamson, Harold F., and Arnold R. Daum. *The American Petroleum Industry: The Age of Illumination.* 1959. • Williamson, Harold F., et al. *The American Petroleum Industry: The Age of Energy, 1899–1959.* 1963.

Refugees. In popular usage of the word, refugees are those who seek refuge from economic, political, or social distress including war, famine, or civil strife. In that sense, Chicago has become home to many different groups of refugees—from NATIVE AMERICANS displaced by wars in the seventeenth century to the most recent political exiles from around the globe. Some of Chicago's largest immigrant groups, including IRISH, GERMANS, and POLES, came to Chicago to seek refuge from major economic and political dislocations at home.

Yet as an internationally recognized legal status that is new in the second half of the twentieth century, "refugee" has a more limited meaning. The 1951 Geneva Convention defined a refugee as one who is outside of one's own nation and is unwilling to return because of a "well-founded fear of being persecuted for reasons of race, religion, nationality, membership of a particular social group or political opinion." This definition distinguishes refugees from other immigrants as victims of human rights violations who lack the protection of their own governments.

Before the Immigration Act of 1924 established a system of immigration quotas based on national origin, the United States allowed virtually unrestricted entrance of non-Asians and thus had no need to differentiate between refugees and other types of immigrants. Between 1924 and 1946 refugees had to use regular immigration channels and fit within existing quotas. The magnitude of the refugee crisis after WORLD WAR II prompted the United

States to begin to admit refugees of "special humanitarian concern" through special acts of Congress and extension of the attorney general's parole authority. Admitted outside of regular immigration channels through ad-hoc policies and quota exemptions, refugees were still subject to strict limits.

Until the Refugee Act of 1980, which wrote into U.S. law the Geneva definition, only persons fleeing from Communist regimes were recognized as refugees. Under the 1980 legislation, public-private partnerships in resettlement were regularized and refugees granted special forms of assistance in recognition of the special hardships and trauma many have faced. In Chicago, several organizations, including Heartland Alliance, World Relief, and the Jewish Federation, aid in the resettlement of refugees. Working with local and federal support, these agencies find sponsors for refugees and help to get them established with homes, WORK, and SOCIAL SERVICES in the area.

Chicago has become one of the largest sites of refugee resettlement in the United States, but not all refugees come through the formal process of refugee resettlement. Some emigrate to the United States through other means and apply for asylum. Many individuals who could be considered refugees under the law find it easier to use regular immigration channels, including family reunification provisions. In addition, U.S. foreign policy has strongly influenced the way this country officially defines "political persecution"; some groups that could be considered refugees are not recognized for protection. For example, while the United States recognized NICARAGUANS as refugees who fled from the Sandinista regime, they did not recognize GUATEMALANS or SALVADORANS as refugees and often refused to grant asylum to people who fled torture or persecution by these U.S.-supported military regimes. Likewise, while CUBANS fleeing the Communist regime of Fidel Castro have been granted refugee status, HAITIANS have tended to be considered "economic migrants" despite evidence of persecution.

If "refugee" encompasses all migrants fleeing from persecution, regardless of legal status, Chicago has become home to hundreds of thousands of refugees over the course of its history. Some of the earliest known inhabitants in the area, including the MIAMI Indians, came to the region because they were pushed from their homeland by wars. In the nineteenth century, political domination by the Ottoman and Hapsburg Empires led to the persecution of ARMENIANS and ROMANIANS who then emigrated to Chicago. The Russian Revolution in 1917 produced a small wave of RUSSIAN refugees who fled the new regime. JEWS were targets of violence and discrimination by governments across Europe, and large numbers of Russian Jews in particular migrated to Chicago throughout the nineteenth and twentieth centuries. After World War II, Jews were among the earliest groups targeted for refugee status and protection by the United States government, and they joined a well-established community in Chicago. In addition, the Soviet occupation of Eastern Europe and imposition of totalitarian rule after World War II caused a surge of LATVIAN, ESTONIAN, UKRAINIAN, LITHUANIAN, Polish, HUNGARIAN, and Romanian émigrés.

In the 1960s and 1970s, Chicago became home to a large number of Cuban and Southeast Asian refugees as part of two major refugee resettlement projects by the federal government. In the 1950s, refugees from Cuba fled Fulgencio Batista's repressive regime. Immigrants in succeeding decades were the more conservative refugees from Communist Cuba. Although most Cubans settled in Florida and the southern coast, a growing number made their way to Chicago. After the fall of Saigon in 1975 and the ascension of Communist regimes in Southeast Asia, tens of thousands of VIETNAMESE, LAOTIAN, CAMBODIAN, and HMONG refugees migrated to Chicago from refugee camps in one of the largest resettlement projects in U.S. history. Assisted by SOCIAL SERVICE organizations, these communities rapidly organized networks of community support and services.

As political instability has plagued developing nations in the wake of decolonization and the COLD WAR, civil wars often targeting civilian populations have produced millions of refugees worldwide in the last few decades. Changes in U.S. immigration and refugee policies, which have expanded immigration quotas and dropped the preference for refugees fleeing from Communist regimes, allowed a broader range of refugees fleeing from Africa, Asia, and Latin America to settle in Chicago in the 1980s and 1990s. Civil wars and repressive political regimes in Africa have caused a surge of refugees who form growing communities in Chicago, including SUDANESE, LIBERIANS, NIGERIANS, ANGOLANS, CAMEROONIANS, SOMALIS, SIERRA LEONEANS, UGANDANS, CONGOLESE, ETHIOPIANS, and ERITREANS. Unrest in the Middle East and Eastern Europe has also produced a large number of refugees, as ethnic struggles for national control and shifting national boundaries have led to the persecution of political and ethnic minorities. ASSYRIANS, BOSNIANS, PALESTINIANS, IRAQIS, LEBANESE, CROATIANS, YUGOSLAVIANS, and refugees from the former Soviet Union have all migrated to Chicago in recent decades. Likewise, civil wars, military coups, and repressive political regimes in South and Central America have caused ARGENTINEANS, BOLIVIANS, DOMINICANS, URUGUAYANS, Nicaraguans, Salvadorans, Guatemalans, PERUVIANS, and Haitians to seek asylum in Chicago. Thanks to its cosmopolitan, multiethnic character and its strong network of social services and community organizations, Chicago remains an attractive destination for refugees around the globe.

Tracy Steffes

See also: Demography; Underground Railroad

Further reading: Haines, David, ed. *Refugees in America in the 1990s: A Reference Handbook.* 1996. • United Nations High Commissioner for Refugees. *The State of the World's Refugees, 2000.* 2001.

Regal Theater. The Regal Theater was a central mainstay of SOUTH SIDE public life from the late 1920s to the early 1970s. Built in 1928 and located in the heart of "Bronzeville" at 47th and Grand Boulevard (renamed South Parkway that year), the Regal catered specifically to the entertainment tastes of AFRICAN AMERICANS. Part of the Balaban and Katz chain, the lavish Byzantine edifice with its tall columns, plush carpeting, and velvet drapes hosted some of the most celebrated black entertainers in America. Cab Calloway, Louis Armstrong, Lena Horne, Dinah Washington, and Duke Ellington performed frequently at the Regal, and a few native Chicagoans like Nat "King" Cole got their professional start there. The Regal also featured motion pictures and live stage shows like the all-black cast *Carmen Jones,* which played in the mid-1950s.

Considered the apex of the entertainment world in Chicago, the Regal rendered a tremendous boost to the city's black culture and black economy. So important was the Regal Theater to the GRAND BOULEVARD community that when the Chicago Land Clearance Commission razed the theater in 1973, many businesses in the surrounding area went into decline.

Wallace Best

See also: Entertaining Chicagoans; Leisure

Further reading: "Once Majestic Regal Awaits Wrecker." *Chicago Tribune,* September 6, 1973. • Ottley, Roy. "Regal Theater, Frayed but Imposing, Tailored for the Community." *Chicago Tribune,* February 27, 1955.

Regional Planning. *See* Governing the Metropolis; Planning, City and Regional

Regional Transportation Authority. The Regional Transportation Authority was created amid controversy in 1973–74 to regulate, operate, and provide subsidies to PUBLIC TRANSPORTATION systems in the six-county Chicago metropolitan area. Because of a decline in transit riding after WORLD WAR II and high inflation during the Vietnam War, many of the systems were running deficits and were threatened with abandonment or service reductions.

The RTA's divisions include the older CHICAGO TRANSIT AUTHORITY, created in 1945, as well as the commuter RAILROAD system (METRA), and the suburban BUS network (PACE), both of which date from 1983. Prior to the RTA, the region's mass transit systems received no local tax subsidies and had operated entirely from the fare box revenues for 116 years.

The agency was narrowly approved by the voters in a referendum in 1974. A strong plurality in Chicago overcame opposition in the suburbs.

The RTA was able to stabilize the transit systems. By the end of 1997, the RTA oversaw one of the largest transit systems in the world, including a 769-mile rail system with 205 million passenger trips a year and a 363-route bus system handling 326 million passenger trips annually. RTA subsidiaries operated 2,100 assorted railcars and 2,894 buses.

David M. Young

See also: Governing the Metropolis; Privatization; Rapid Transit System

Further reading: Allen, John G. "From Centralization to Decentralization: The Politics of Transit in Chicagoland." Ph.D. diss., Massachusetts Institute of Technology. 1996. • Tecson, Joseph A. "The Regional Transportation Authority in Northeastern Illinois." *Chicago Bar Record,* May–June and July–Aug., 1975. • Young, David M. *Chicago Transit: An Illustrated History.* 1998.

State Board of Charities, 1908: *Left to right:* William B. Moulton, Julia C. Lathrop, William C. Graves, and H. G. Hardt. Photographer: Unknown. Source: Chicago Historical Society.

Relief and Subsistence Aid. When Chicago was founded in the 1830s, relief was based upon the religious ethic that the community had a moral obligation to provide. This ethic was manifested in two ways. First, the "poor laws," which were state laws administered by local officials, rested on the idea that resident poor had a right to resources drawn from the tax revenues of the locality. Second, RELIGIOUS INSTITUTIONS provided relief based upon the same ethic of local responsibility. Before the 1850s, church-based relief was provided by the local church or parish. In the 1850s, religious groups created organizations like the ST. VINCENT DE PAUL SOCIETY (ROMAN CATHOLIC) and United Hebrew Charities (JEWISH) to better meet the needs of those of their faith. Relief was given inside and outside of public and private charitable institutions, yet, insofar as relief meliorated want by meeting moral obligation, it remained part of a religious understanding of the poor and their relationship to the community.

After the CIVIL WAR, relief in Chicago shifted subtly from an approach informed by a religious ethic of duty to one that sought to use relief to reduce the numbers of the poor. Initially, in the years between 1870 and 1890, this new method of charity was based on the perception of the poor as a problem of "pauperism," which held that being poor was the product of moral lapses rather than a fact of social life. The CHICAGO RELIEF AND AID SOCIETY (CRA), understanding impoverishment in moral terms, restricted charity in order to teach lessons in proper living. The CRA thus distributed relief through bureaucratized methods in the hope that their approach would reduce the need for relief over the long term by forcing Chicago's poor to adopt self-reliant modes of conduct. After the crisis of the FIRE OF 1871, the CRA attempted to gain citywide control of relief by trying to bring Chicago's charities under its purview. This effort met with little success, however, because charitable organizations wanted to retain control over their resources. The CRA's approach to relief supplanted neither religious charitable organizations nor the poor laws. Yet, its existence signaled that a new approach to relief would be part of relief for decades, one that sought to alter the character and circumstances of the poor rather than simply to meet their basic needs.

After approximately 1890, the concept of pauperism, which stressed the moral dimensions of impoverishment, was replaced by the concept of poverty, which held that the structural economic forces of industrialization were responsible for widespread impoverishment. Jane Addams's approach to relief was the most visible manifestation of this new, Progressive definition of the origins of the poor. Addams

Emmanuel Church bread line for mothers, 1932. Photographer: Unknown. Source: Chicago Historical Society.

approached relief in two ways. First, her SETTLEMENT HOUSE, HULL HOUSE, gave the immigrant poor a resource to establish themselves economically, culturally, and socially. Second, Addams engaged in POLITICS in order to help reform conditions responsible for the poverty so prevalent in late-nineteenth-century Chicago. Other reforms of the Progressive era included MOTHERS' PENSIONS, which paid mothers to stay at home to nurture children, and the creation of a countywide welfare bureau to rationalize relief. By the 1910s and 1920s, relief was often delivered by professional SOCIAL SERVICE workers.

Although important figures in relief for a generation, women were increasingly finding productive careers in social services by this time. Again, despite new methods of relief, religious-based charitable organizations still provided relief out of moral obligation, though they too were centralizing their services. The SALVATION ARMY, an important and fundamentally evangelical Christian organization, distributed relief based on the religious ideal that the poor will always exist and will need humane care. Although Progressive reforms did not eliminate the existence of older charitable institutions, they formed a new approach to relief, one that stressed the elimination of the conditions that caused poverty.

The economic crisis of the GREAT DEPRESSION forced an alteration in methods of relief, one which shifted responsibility to higher levels of government and which resulted in the development of social service administrative bureaucracies. The Depression spurred the development of the concept of welfare, which legitimated a guaranteed level of subsistence, and hastened the creation of governmental mechanisms to ensure that right. Though governmental organizations increasingly assumed control of charitable resources, local charitable organizations did not disappear. To the contrary, the U.S. welfare state worked in partnership with local public and private organizations to deliver resources to the needy. Religious organizations, for instance, remain crucial providers of food and shelter to those who have fallen through the social safety net, though they now work ecumenically and with Chicago's Human Services department or with associations like the Chicago Coalition for the Homeless. The Personal Responsibility Act (1996) substituted state-level responsibility for federal welfare and made relief contingent upon productive labor rather than right of citizenship.

Relief and subsistence aid has depended upon the way in which Chicagoans have defined the problem of the poor. Since there never has been one, unitary way of understanding the problem, there has never been one mode of relief. Yet trends in relief are discernable. What began as a moral responsibility dictated by religious belief has become an aspect of the broader society's quest to eliminate poverty.

Scott Lien

See also: Catholic Charities; Great Society; Mutual Benefit Societies; Philanthropy; Schooling for Work

Further reading: Brown, James. *The History of Public Assistance in Chicago, 1833–1893.* 1941. • Coughlin, Roger J., and Cathryn A. Riplinger. *The Story of Charitable Care in the Archdiocese of Chicago, 1844–1959.* 1981. • McCarthy, Kathleen D. *Noblesse Oblige: Charity and Cultural Philanthropy in Chicago, 1849–1929.* 1982.

Annie McClure Hitchcock

Annie McClure Hitchcock (1840–1922) belongs to a generation of women about whose lives we can only know pieces. As Mrs. Charles Hitchcock, she settled into the fairly secure and comfortable lifestyle enjoyed by many middle-class women. But a small memoir that she wrote and her efforts in the wake of the Chicago Fire of 1871 provide glimpses of her as a person.

Annie McClure Hitchcock grew with the city. When she came to Chicago in 1844 it was so small that she remembered their house at the corner of Jackson and Sherman streets as being "way out on the prairie," where they "could look out over green fields down to the lake on the east and to the Chicago River on the west." She also witnessed the tempestuous politics of a young frontier city in such events as the lager beer riot of 1855. During those days Mayor Boone stationed armed guards around City Hall, and on the way to Sunday school young Annie McClure was forced to deviate from her usual route near City Hall by a bayonet-wielding guard.

The disastrous fire of 1871 spared the Hitchcock house, located in Hyde Park, but Annie McClure Hitchcock spent the months following the fire working to alleviate the suffering it had caused. She worked with Katharine Medill, wife of the mayor, to distribute clothing and bedding to those without. Her concern that many of the sufferers, especially women and children, were not being reached by the funds dispensed by the men of the Chicago Relief and Aid Society led her to undertake her own relief efforts in clear violation of the rules laid down by the society.

Maureen A. Flanagan

Emil Gustav Hirsch

Emil Gustav Hirsch came to the United States from Luxembourg in 1866. He received a Ph.D. from Leipzig University in 1876 and was ordained as rabbi. Himself a rabbi's son, Hirsch married a rabbi's daughter, Matilda Einhorn, in 1878. After serving congregations in Baltimore and Louisville, he led the Chicago Sinai Congregation from 1880 to 1923 and built it into the largest in Chicago. By 1900, Hirsch was rabbi for life and was the highest paid clergyman in the United States. In addition to being the founding director of the Jewish Manual Training School, he became founding editor of *Reform Advocate* in 1891 and was the first University of Chicago professor of rabbinical philosophy and literature by 1892. Hirsch authored several religious monographs and his honorary degrees included Hebrew Union College.

Hirsch advocated social justice, religious reforms, and attention to the plight of Russian Jews. Although Hirsch was a non-Zionist, he extended Sinai's pulpit to Louis Brandeis. Six thousand mourned at his funeral.

Richard Sobel

Religion, Chicago's Influence on. Chicago has been and remains a world-class religious center with GLOBAL influence. It has no major shrine or global headquarters and thus is not in a class with Rome and Jerusalem, Mecca or Benares. Nonetheless, for the past century and a half, it has served as a base for individual citizens and religious groups of many sorts who have sought to change the way moderns think about and pursue spiritual ends. Even when following more conventional lines, Chicagoans have had considerable influence on believers, both nationally and internationally.

The most vivid symbol of that centrality appeared in 1893. During the WORLD'S COLUMBIAN EXPOSITION, several enterprising Chicagoans invented and staged a WORLD'S PARLIAMENT OF RELIGIONS. This first modern spiritual "fair" exposed publics to representatives of world religions. One might picture the Parliament as a magnet that drew spiritual energies and people to Chicago and, immediately thereafter, propelled many to their home bases, ready to think differently from before about how religions thrive and interact.

Spiritual heirs of those original parliamentarians gathered a century later, again in Chicago, for a centennial observance in 1993. This observance not only led people to look backward to the good old days of 1893. It was designed to encourage them to look forward and outward, to give new impetus to interreligious exchange. This occurred at the end of a century in which religiously inspired conflict was killing people from Northern Ireland to South Africa, from the Middle East to the Asian subcontinent. The repeat observance was not as pathbreaking as the original had been, given that many of the 1893 participants had appeared more exotic to each other, as well as to Chicagoans and Americans at large. But the 1993 event did symbolize the interest Chicagoans have in seeing their city as a spiritual magnet and impelling force.

Most of Chicago's religious influences have been somewhat more traditional, but they have reflected enterprise and ambition. Two themes that vivified the Parliament have persisted. One seeks to promote interaction, to make the city a crossroads. The other has people presenting their own religions to others and to the nonbelieving world as being the true, or the best—which means something to which to be converted. The physical location of the metropolis helped and helps promote the former. Once lake traffic and RAILROADS poised Chicago as a place for the crisscrossing of influences; those who had ideas to try out on others could hardly avoid the city at the bottom of Lake Michigan, and they found it attractive.

The conversion efforts have been more visible and vivid. However much ROMAN CATHOLICS and others might have set out to win new members, in the United States people associate proselytizing, evangelizing, and converting with evangelical—generally "conservative"—PROTESTANTISM. The three best-known and most inventive modern Protestant evangelizers, Dwight L. Moody, Billy Sunday, and Billy Graham, began their decisive work in Chicago and, in the first two cases, made it their central base.

What was it about Chicago that led entrepreneurs of the spirit to embark on missions to convert there? Of course, it might have been pure coincidence that brought the three here. In the second half of the nineteenth century, Moody came as a young businessman who was soon found to be a success at "soul-winning." By the start of the twentieth century, Billy Sunday had left the baseball diamond, had been converted at the PACIFIC GARDEN MISSION, and had begun moving from a Northwest Side pastorate to a flamboyant set of missions nationwide. As the middle of the twentieth century approached, Billy Graham, the world's best-known evangelist ever, began his worldwide set of "crusades" during his years at suburban WHEATON COLLEGE. He became a pastor of a church in nearby WESTERN SPRINGS and gained wider reputation as a budding preacher in Youth for Christ, a movement that made news chiefly in downtown venues. In all three cases, one can write off the effects of coincidence by citing the accident of charisma and talent among such individuals. But they did find Chicago a most congenial metropolis.

So did their opposite numbers, the theological modernists. Late in the nineteenth century many of the traditional Protestant bodies produced a generation of critical and progressive thinkers. They used the new tools of biblical criticism to pursue the historical background of Christianity. They welcomed evolution, the scientific theory that so appalled conservatives. Their outlook on the future was optimistic; they would help "bring in the Kingdom of God." Chicago looked like a good place to start.

Many of the modernists influenced the theological world through the new UNIVERSITY OF CHICAGO, founded by Baptists but open to others. William Rainey Harper, the first president, and the dean of his university's Divinity School, attracted scholars and sent forth students to spread the modernist word. They helped force the issue of fundamentalism and modernism in the denominational battles of the 1920s. Chicago had a hand in the legal fray over the legitimacy of teaching evolution in the public schools in the Bible belt. In a famed trial in Tennessee in 1925, University of Chicago modernists coached the defenders of indicted teacher of evolution John Scopes, while Chicago fundamentalists backed William Jennings Bryan, lawyer for anti-evolutionists, against the legal attacks by Chicagoan Clarence Darrow, a liberal lawyer with a religiously agnostic outlook.

The clash of these two schools of thought represented but one of many events that helped color the religious scene nationally and beyond. Their leaders helped create an image different from the one Chicago has often presented. The city, known for its material achievements and its reputation as a sometimes cruel center of commercial and industrial competition, has also been recognized as a locale where spiritual endeavors have prospered, and a brief canvass of some of them will help focus this counterimage.

For many Chicagoans religion means and has meant RELIGIOUS INSTITUTIONS and what they represent and accomplish. Any survey of religious influences emanating from their city therefore must focus on the chronicling of church and synagogue life.

The beginnings of organized religion around the site of FORT DEARBORN during the 1830s were at the hands of English-speaking Protestants who pioneered in placing churches on the frontier. Before the end of the century these dominant Protestants found their place and position challenged by Protestants from the European continent—Lutherans and Reformed in particular—and then both kinds of Protestants found themselves outnumbered by Roman Catholics. Catholics had explored the Chicago region as early as 1673, but maintained no institutional presence after the closing of the MISSION OF THE GUARDIAN ANGEL in 1699. In the nineteenth century the first priest was assigned to Chicago in 1833, the year it incorporated. Chicago's Catholics were at first English-speaking, chiefly immigrants fleeing Catholic Ireland after devastating famines when potato crops failed. Immigrants from the European continent followed, speaking GERMAN, POLISH, and ITALIAN. Greeks, Russians, and others added EASTERN ORTHODOX churches to the mix. Immigrants stamped their ethnicity on Catholicism, a stamp that was widely observed by Catholics in other cities as they set out to cope with a new environment.

Chicago JUDAISM might not have had as much national influence as did Judaism in the New York area, and it developed no theological school to carry influence as did those that flourished in New York and Cincinnati. Yet Chicago became a center for the Midwest dispersion. By the 1880s, JEWS were well established in Chicago. These "Reform" Jews especially from Germany were called to welcome and accommodate poorer Eastern European Jews from ghettos and shtetls, refugees from pogroms that began in the Pale of Settlement along Russia's western border after 1881. The legacy: Chicago served as a model for other developing metropolises, most of them having ethnic and religious mixes that matched, on smaller scales, what the new Chicago immigrants were inventing.

After the Catholic immigrations, the greatest change came during and after the two world wars and in the prosperous postwar period, when AFRICAN AMERICANS by the many thousands migrated, especially from the rural South. They brought with them Methodist, Baptist, and later Pentecostal faiths associated with the South. They made their homes in the South and West Sides of the city, areas which most whites left. Catholicism and white Protestantism became increasingly suburban phenomena, although Catholic parishes persisted and Catholicism remained the majority faith in the city.

National leaders of the black churches made Chicago a base of operations at some stage or other of their career. These included Joseph Jackson, longtime president of the National Baptist Convention, U.S.A., Inc., and Martin Luther King, Jr., who made the city the northern base for efforts by the Southern Christian Leadership Council during the CIVIL RIGHTS struggle up to his death in 1968. In the middle of the twentieth century an innovation in African American religion came to be recognized worldwide. Elijah Muhammad built the NATION OF ISLAM (sometimes called "Black Muslims" in popular media) into a mass movement attracting thousands of African Americans to Islam and black nationalism.

The first Protestant churches were housed in impressive edifices expressive of the prosperity of leading members. Until the middle of the twentieth century, most of Chicago's elites were Protestant, and they helped subsidize great sanctuaries featuring, for example, Tiffany windows that have become landmark features in the city. Architecturally, however, it was Catholicism that turned the cityscape into a churchscape, and it is from Chicago Catholic experiments that influence spread. Wherever observers had vantages for looking at the skyline, they would see a crowd of steeples and domes, churches that often reflected the architectural styles of the old country or that aspired to make new statements by towering over the BUNGALOWS of the neighborhoods. The first

Dwight L. Moody: Heaven and Chicago

Chicago was the world headquarters for the evangelist Dwight L. Moody. During the World's Columbian Exposition in 1893, Moody and his associates ran a camp meeting in tents in Jackson Park that drew crowds of up to 150,000 people per week. He delivered his sermons worldwide, as well as publishing collections. Moody drew heavily on anecdotes and examples from Chicago and other cities that he preached in, as in this selection from "Heaven and Who Are There":

> Men who say that Heaven is a speculation have not read their Bibles. . . . My friends, where are you going to spend eternity? Your life here is very brief. Life is but an inch of time; it is but a span, but a fibre, which will soon be snapped, and you will be ushered into eternity. Where are you going to spend it? If I were to ask you who were going to spend your eternity in Heaven to stand up, nearly every one of you would rise. There is not a man here, not one in Chicago, who has not some hope of reaching Heaven. Now, if we are going to spend our future there, it becomes us to go to work and find out all about it. I call your attention to this truth that Heaven is just as much a place as Chicago.

Smith, Wilbur M., ed. *The Best of D. L. Moody: Sixteen Sermons by the Great Evangelist.* 1971, 199–200.

Billy Sunday outside the Moody Bible Institute, 1915. Photographer: Unknown. Source: Chicago Historical Society.

Catholic church building in America considered "modern" was St. Thomas the Apostle in HYDE PARK, designed by local architect Francis Barry Byrne.

When one reckons Chicago influence on religious architecture, however, the eye falls chiefly on buildings of Protestants and Jews that were designed by world-renowned architects who are identified with Chicago. The buildings they designed in Chicago might not have been their most noted, but by the force of their personality and the weight of their talents they called attention to their work here. These included Frank Lloyd Wright, who created a classic Unity Temple in OAK PARK; Mies van der Rohe, who planned a less-distinguished IIT chapel at Illinois Institute of Technology; Adler and Sullivan, who designed KAM Temple, which later became Pilgrim Baptist Church; and Louis H. Sullivan, who left a landmark in Holy Trinity Cathedral of the Russian Orthodox Church.

The Chicago influence has spread to other arts as well. One can make the case that "GOSPEL" and "soul," major African American contributions to religious music, originated in Chicago. Thomas Dorsey was the pioneer of gospel music, and singers like Mahalia Jackson helped carry it to the rest of the nation and much of the world. Long before that, Billy Sunday's musical partner, Homer Rodeheaver, influenced the kind of evangelistic gospel song popular in revivalistic Protestantism. NORTHWESTERN UNIVERSITY's school of music fostered world-acclaimed classical church music, for example through the compositions of Leo Sowerby. GIA Publications, under Catholic auspices, and Hope Publishing in Wheaton, an evangelical house, have encouraged and published music that shapes styles across the nation and wherever American religious influence spreads.

While Protestants, whatever their church polity, tended to depend on and encourage the lay initiative of congregations, which also meant that in most ways the congregations "owned" the properties, Catholic polity made provision for a different arrangement. This form, called "Corporation Sole," meant that all diocesan church properties of the parishes were legally under the "ownership" of the archbishop. These clerics became powerful presences in Chicago, often working with city hall (or criticizing it), just as in the neighborhoods priests and precinct captains tended to be partners of sorts. Some of the archbishops, usually named cardinal, were men of enormous personal power and the skill to wield it. Thus George William Cardinal Mundelein, archbishop from 1916 to 1939, who attracted a Eucharistic Congress to Chicago in 1926—an event that paraded the prosperity and numbers within Chicago Catholicism for the world, including mass gatherings of 125,000 people at SOLDIER FIELD—built a suburban campus in what became MUNDELEIN and presided over much parish building and growth during his tenure.

Other cardinal-archbishops became known not for Corporation Sole power but for scholarship (e.g., Albert Cardinal Meyer, archbishop from 1958 to 1965, who was influential at the Second Vatican Council, 1962–1965) and works of justice or examples of piety (e.g., Joseph Cardinal Bernardin, 1982–1996, the first of these hierarchs to become widely accepted as a mentor and example to non-Catholics of the city).

Religion in Chicago has not been housed only in church, synagogue, and mosque. The city has attracted and nurtured many

SEMINARIES and theological schools, some of them related to universities, as at Northwestern University and the University of Chicago; others "clustered," as in a Hyde Park coalition; and some in the form of a conglomerate or merger of many small theologates, as at the Catholic Theological Union, or a merger of half a dozen seminaries, as in the Lutheran School of Theology at Chicago. Priests and ministers from these schools have been at home with the changing city and have carried Chicago influences wherever they became pastors.

Roman Catholics in Chicago have often been innovators. One of the renowned inventions was the CATHOLIC YOUTH ORGANIZATION, a GREAT DEPRESSION–era creation of Bishop Bernard Sheil (1886–1959). Sheil was a very independent-minded auxiliary who, in the years from the Depression into the prosperous 1950s, put his main energies into raising funds for, administering, and publicizing a movement designed especially to hold the loyalties of young Catholics, mostly from the poorer neighborhoods, and to help them fill their lives. Sheil stressed athletic competition, especially BOXING.

At midcentury many analysts ranked the ROMAN CATHOLIC ARCHDIOCESE OF CHICAGO among the most inventive and influential in the Catholic world. Confronting a shortage of priests and nuns just before the Vatican Council II, the laity began to show new kinds of creativity. What came to be called "the apostolate of the laity" revealed Chicago influences, thanks to efforts by local people to promote new understandings of marriage, race relations, and support of organized labor. These "apostles" created literary fronts typified by the Thomas More Association, publisher and seller of books and magazines; St. Benet's bookstore; and various social justice movements and community-building agencies such as the Catholic Family Movement. Almost all of these had national influence.

Chicago has been an ecumenical center for what are called "mainstream" Protestant and Orthodox as well as "evangelical" styles. The only World Council of Churches Assembly—an event held roughly every seven years since 1948—to be held in the United States occurred at EVANSTON in the summer of 1954. On that occasion 502 delegates from 161 member churches were well hosted by Chicagoans and carried new ecumenical impulses to and from the city.

On the evangelical front, the National Association of Evangelicals, founded to gather church bodies that are somewhat more moderate than fundamentalists, has long been associated with WHEATON, sometimes dubbed "the evangelical Vatican," and later operated from suburban CAROL STREAM.

The largest and best known of the evangelical Protestant "megachurches," suburban WILLOW CREEK COMMUNITY CHURCH has had national influence and spawned many slightly smaller replications. Such independent congregations describe themselves as nontraditional and "user-friendly" and use contemporary techniques of market research and ADVERTISING to promote what members see as historical and biblical Christianity in a new package.

Two magazines symbolize the worlds these organizations embody, and from them the Chicago influence extends worldwide. The more liberal of the two, once quite modernist in outlook, is the *Christian Century*. The evangelical counterpart, founded in the 1950s in part to challenge the other magazine, is *Christianity Today*.

What many of the members of all these groups would consider to be marginal or esoteric, the innovative religions that have taken form in the United States, have had presences in greater Chicago, though it is not so strongly identified with these as are places like California. The Theosophical Society has a headquarters and publishes from Wheaton. The BAHA'I Temple in WILMETTE, while not the world headquarters of Baha'i, is such a distinctive building that it draws members of that faith and guests from around the world.

Among the once-marginal but now booming and well-known Christian movements developed in this century is Pentecostalism. Most historians associate Topeka, Kansas, and Los Angeles with its founding, between 1900 and 1906. But shortly thereafter the pioneers converged on Chicago, which is often seen as the third "birthplace" of the fastest-growing form of Christianity in many parts of the world. John Alexander Dowie led one of the most influential of the young Pentecostal movements and brought his healing movement and utopian impulses to north suburban ZION, which he founded in 1900.

Through all these influential experiments and changes, Chicago has retained the image of being the practical, material, competitive culture on one hand and, on the other, a place where the esthetic, spiritual, and often cooperative religious forces could come together to alter the city's harsh reputation and serve the people in it.

Martin E. Marty

See also: Missionary Training Schools; Moody Bible Institute; Publishing and Media, Religious; Religious Geography; Settlements, Religious

Further reading: Livezey, Lowell, ed. *Public Religion and Urban Transformation: Faith in the City.* 2000. • Seager, Richard Hughes. *The World's Parliament of Religions: The East/West Encounter, Chicago, 1893.* 1995. • Shanabruch, Charles. *Chicago's Catholics: The Evolution of an American Identity.* 1981.

Religious Education. *See* Catholic School System; Seminaries

Religious Geography. Wherever people have settled in metropolitan Chicago, they have built churches and synagogues, and eventually mosques, *gurdwaras,* and temples, of the various religions of the world. From their many countries of origin and from regions within the United States, they have brought diverse architectural styles, builders with unique technical skills, and sometimes even the building materials with which to recreate cultural forms expressing not only their religions but multiple dimensions of their heritage, including ethnicity, nation, region, race, and class.

The distribution of these places of worship across the space of metropolitan Chicago is part of a broader story involving the peopling of the region, its underlying economy, and the insistent sorting and re-sorting of social space. Long before the Great FIRE OF 1871, churches were scattered across the region, although the only concentration of more than a few churches was in the commercial district (now the LOOP) and the adjacent residential areas. After the fire, and following the international financial collapse of 1873–74, the organizational and geographic expansion of religion in Chicago reflected the growth, diversification, and distribution of the city's population, which in turn was tied to the growth and technological developments of its economy. Thus in the period of industrial expansion (the 1870s through the 1920s), religious organization accommodated immigrants from Europe and AFRICAN AMERICANS from the U.S. South who lived in areas determined by proximity to industrial jobs, by racial restrictions, and by the creation of more desirable residential areas in the "streetcar suburbs." In the period of industrial growth and consolidation (1930s–1960s), which included the rise of the automobile to dominance of local TRANSPORTATION, the suburbanization of religious organization reflected not simply the aggregate suburbanization of population but the fact that the suburbanization process was disproportionately white and Protestant. Finally, since WORLD WAR II and especially since the 1960s, the shape of religious organization has been commingled with the development of Chicago's postindustrial, information-based economy. The jobs clustered in suburbs, exurbs, and edge cities, combined with low-density housing far from Chicago's center, partially explain why former cornfields are now the sites not only of new Catholic PARISHES and Jewish synagogues but of HINDU and BUDDHIST temples, MUSLIM mosques, SIKH gurdwaras, and black and Hispanic PROTESTANT churches—some of them "megachurches."

Early Settlements

The effort to define one denomination's "religious space" began as early as Father Marquette's appointment as the first priest to the Illinois mission in 1673. Persistent contacts between ROMAN CATHOLICS and Native

Jewish Congregations on the Move in Chicago, 1849–2002

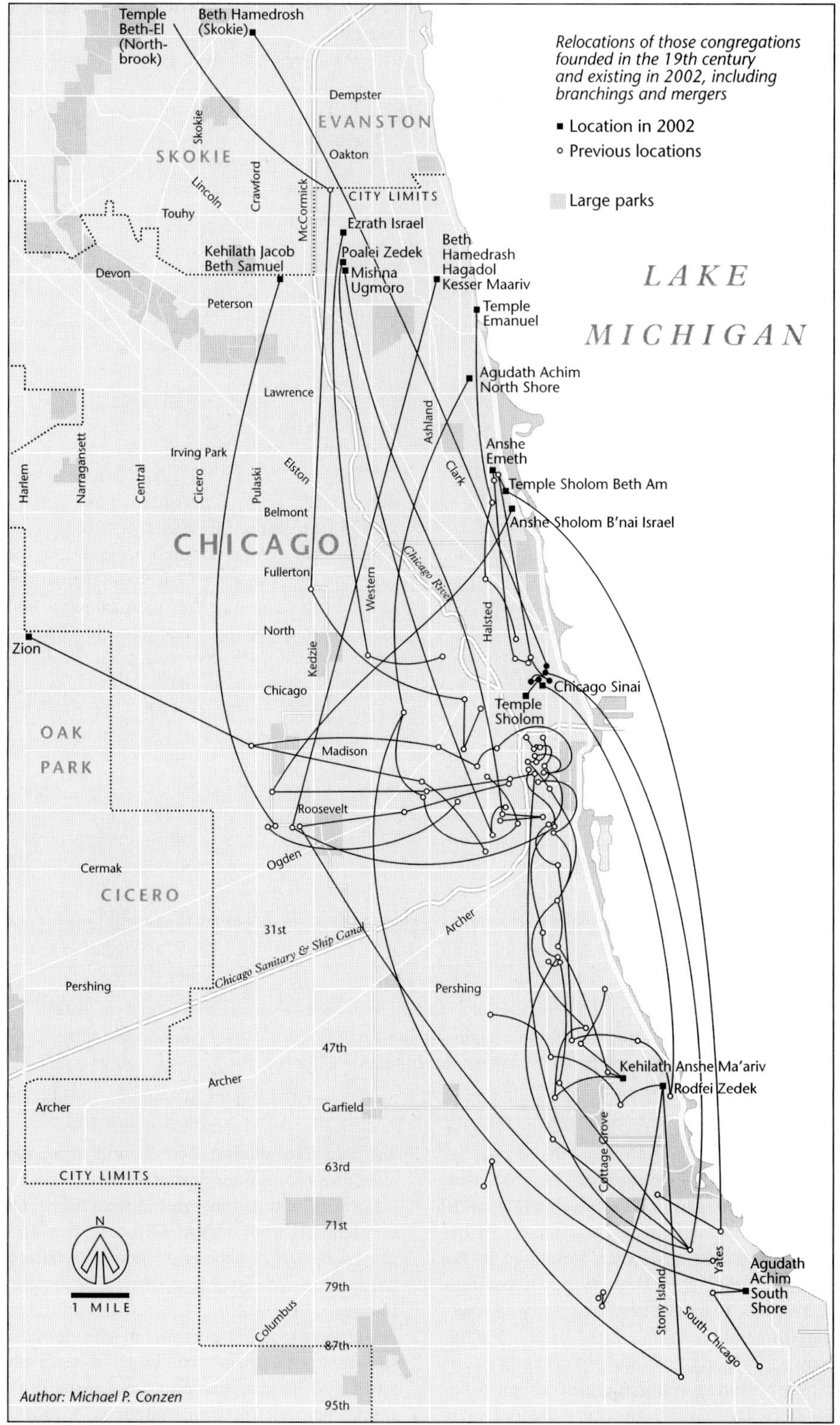

Americans continued down to the incorporation of Chicago in 1833. The first Baptist sermon was preached in 1825, and by 1830 the Methodists had created the Chicago Mission District. Of the congregations still in existence today, the first to be organized was First Methodist Church, which met for the first time in 1831 and built its first building in 1834. St. Mary's Catholic Church was organized in 1833 and erected a structure a few years later. By the middle of the century, Chicago's public square was flanked by five edifices (four Protestant and one Unitarian), whose size and imposing design represented religion's active presence in the public and commercial life of the young city. An equal number of churches, including Catholic St. Mary's, were built in the few blocks between the public square and Lake Michigan, and St. Peter and St. Patrick Catholic churches had been built in the western portions of the central area. The first Jewish congregation, Kehilath Anshe Mayriv, organized in 1847, met in space above Jewish-owned stores until 1851, when the congregation dedicated its first synagogue just three blocks south of the public square and its constellation of Protestant churches.

Most of the largest and most prestigious congregations in the civic and commercial center of the city succumbed to the escalating property values in the center and to the attraction of the new and prosperous residential areas nearby. Within 10 years of being built, all the churches on the public square except First Methodist (which remains on its site today) sold their properties and rebuilt in the fashionable residential areas along Lake Michigan south of the business center. Other churches abandoned their downtown locations for quieter areas west and north, notably St. James Episcopal Church and Holy Name Catholic Church, both of which moved north of the Chicago River, where large churches were built as the seats of their respective dioceses. This movement outward from the commercial district to residential areas presaged a pattern of locating congregations in residential rather than commercial or public areas, geographically expressing the association of religion with private more than with public life.

While the congregations meeting at the center of Chicago represented the greatest concentration of churches, Protestant and Catholic churches followed the expansion of residential areas away from the central business district. A notable German and Irish Catholic and German and Norwegian Lutheran presence

Chicago's Jewish congregations founded in the nineteenth century have had the longevity and complicated history of division and unification to illustrate the remarkable geographical mobility of the city's Jewish communities. Unlike Catholic churches, synagogues are local independent bodies free to locate and relocate at will. The patterns of synagogue location, when mapped, reveal a complex sequence of economic improvement and the quest for better housing and social acceptance within the spatial evolution of Chicago's neighborhoods. Early concentrations near downtown broke up as congregations moved south, west, and north. Eventually, the westward and southward migrating congregations abandoned their sectoral drift and relocated to northern neighborhoods and the suburbs beyond. Of these early congregations, only 3 remain on the far South Side and none on the city's West Side, whereas 12 remain on the North Side. Three forsook the city for suburban sites, where many congregations founded in the twentieth century are also to be found.

Churches of the Presbyterian Church (USA) in the Chicago Area

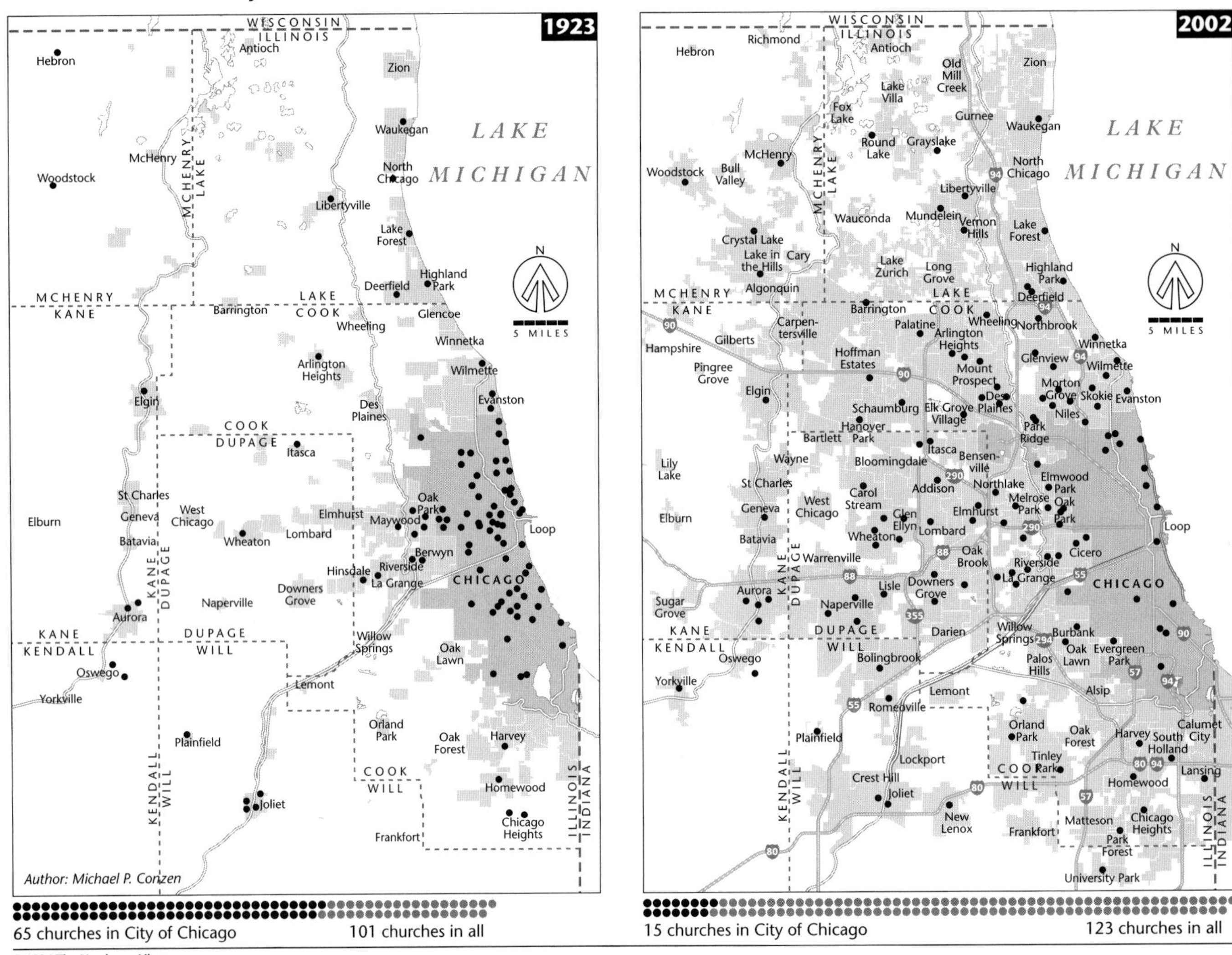

The changing distribution of Presbyterian churches at the metropolitan scale traces the suburbanization of a mainline Protestant denomination during the twentieth century. In 1920, the bulk of the group's churches in the region were located in the city of Chicago or in outlying satellite cities and the larger rural service centers. By 2000 the number of urban churches had significantly declined but was counterbalanced by new congregations established in the suburbs. This kept the metropolitan total almost constant over the period as a whole, even as overall membership steadily ebbed.

was felt in the years before the Chicago Fire—the predominantly German Lutheran Church–Missouri Synod was founded in Chicago in 1847—and heralded an increasing association of religion and ethnicity in the years to come. At the same time, Protestants and Catholics gathered and built churches in small farming villages, trading settlements, and open country scattered around what is now the metropolitan region. Of the 54 Roman Catholic parishes founded before the Chicago Fire of 1871, 37 were outside the city boundaries, though a few of these were in areas that would become Chicago neighborhoods through ANNEXATION in 1889. Not to be outdone, Methodist circuit-riding preachers, Lutheran pastors, and Congregational missionaries founded churches in settlements along the waterways, trails, and eventually rail lines that connected Chicago with its hinterland.

Early Industrial Expansion, 1870–1930

After the fire, religious activity kept pace with Chicago's tremendous population growth, from 300,000 in 1870 to 1.3 million in the early 1890s and more than 3 million by the onset of the GREAT DEPRESSION. Innovations in technology made large-scale manufacturing, wholesale and retail trade, and faster shipping possible, contributing to Chicago's rise as a transportation-oriented industrial and trading hub. This rapidly growing metropolis was increasingly separated into distinct districts, according to LAND USE, class, and ethnicity. Church construction followed this pattern into tenement districts and BUNGALOW BELTS. By the 1930s, "CHICAGO SCHOOL" SOCIOLOGISTS could point to distinct church "types" tied to community type—the "downtown church" of the central business district, the "institutional church" of the main development corridors, and "scattered parishes" confronting a rapidly changing socioeconomic matrix.

Because population growth was based on immigration and migration more than fertility, Chicago's religious geography reflected the patterns of settlement of its newcomers. Language and culture drew many of these newcomers together in ethnic neighborhoods, while RACISM and RESTRICTIVE COVENANTS ensured that African Americans and many JEWS would live and worship in ghettoes. National parishes—permitted if not encouraged by the leadership of the ROMAN CATHOLIC ARCHDIOCESE until 1918—anchored communities of Germans along the North Branch of the Chicago River, Irish west and south of the commercial district, and POLES in the southeast near the STEEL mills, southwest near the stockyards, and northwest along the AVONDALE industrial corridor. As these and other nationality groups rose to better-paying jobs, they built homes and churches further out. Protestants followed a similar pattern. German Lutherans often shared neighborhoods with German Catholics and built churches nearby. Immigrants from fiercely Protestant countries settled in neighborhoods defined by country of origin, such as the SWEDISH "ANDERSONVILLE" several miles north of the city center, and built clusters of churches specific to their country, such as Swedish Lutheran, Swedish Methodist, and Swedish Evangelical Covenant. Thus churches, synagogues, parochial schools, and HOSPITALS gave meaning and identity to places that were to make Chicago (like many other municipalities) a "city of neighborhoods."

Some of these neighborhoods were ghettoes. While many of the earliest Jewish settlers, mostly from Germany, were successful in business and able to live in the more comfortable neighborhoods near Lake Michigan, this was not the case with those who later fled the pogroms of Russian and Eastern Europe and provided cheap labor for Chicago's burgeoning industrial economy. By 1910, what Chicago School sociologists called the MAXWELL STREET Ghetto just southwest of the commercial district, close to factories and shipping centers on the Chicago River, was the site of more than 45 *shuls* (synagogues) and an elaborate infrastructure needed for religious observance of the 40,000 or more residents. However, after WORLD WAR I, most of these residents and synagogues moved to the NORTH LAWNDALE neighborhood, five miles west; a few pioneered into ROGERS PARK, ALBANY PARK, and LOGAN SQUARE and established congregations and other Jewish institutions there.

African American migration from the South slowly began to accelerate in the final decade of the nineteenth century. Excluded from most neighborhoods, black Chicagoans crammed into a narrow "BLACK BELT" extending south from the commercial district along State Street. By 1912 they had established 28 churches of nationally recognized denominations and an unknown number of independent congregations. The GREAT MIGRATION, beginning in 1916, brought even greater numbers, and by 1920 the black population had surpassed 100,000. By 1928 their churches—still mostly in the Black Belt—numbered at least 295. African American churches, most of which were located in an area five miles long and four blocks wide, accounted for some 20 percent of all churches in the entire Chicago region.

Industrial Consolidation, 1930–1960s

The geography of Chicago's religions continued to be shaped by developments in the industrial economy. Industrial jobs increased by more than 50 percent from 1929 to 1946, but these were concentrated in a roughly constant number of firms, mostly in SOUTH SIDE industrial districts served by ports and RAILROADS (although the advent of air transportation and the development of MIDWAY AIRPORT supported employment in light manufacturing in the western parts of the city and suburbs). The population of the city proper peaked in the early 1950s, but the suburbs continued to grow as the affordable automobile made it increasingly convenient to live there. The number of city churches increased only slightly, while the number of suburban churches grew rapidly.

The small change in the number and location of city church buildings, however, belied the profound change in the race, class, and religious denomination of the people worshiping in many of those buildings. Perhaps most dramatically, the Black Belt overflowed its boundaries as black migration continued, and black Chicagoans moved into the "Second Ghetto" of large-scale PUBLIC HOUSING projects, as well as other rental units and modest bungalows, in parts of the South and West Sides of the city previously restricted to whites. By the 1960s, black churches could be found throughout

Locational Stability: Saint Aloysius Parish, Chicago, in 1951

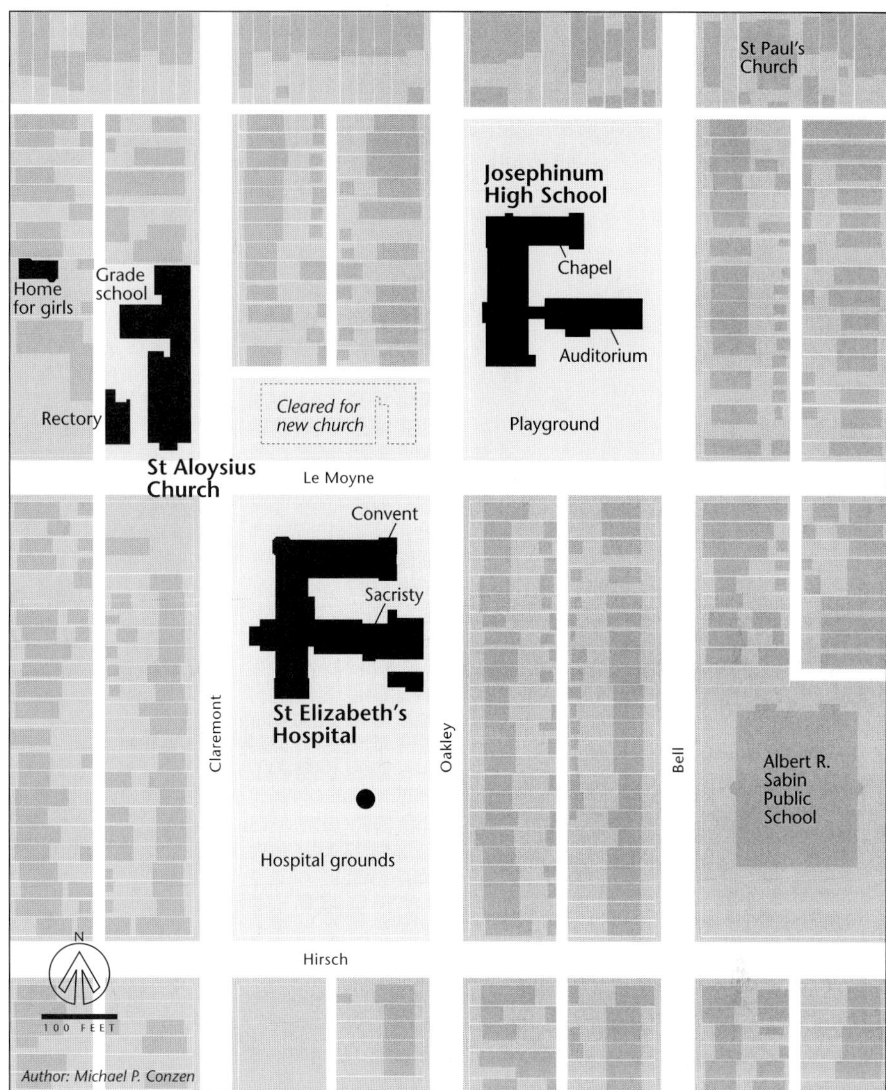

The locations of Roman Catholic institutions in Chicago demonstrate tremendous stability over time, being part of a religious organization with a centralized bureaucracy governing through a hierarchical and territorial system. The church-owned structures in Saint Aloysius Parish, on the city's near Northwest Side, illustrate how an ecclesiastical "precinct" has developed through the accumulation of activities and requisite buildings. Covering all or parts of four city blocks, the religious campus had come by 1951 to consist of the parish church, a rectory, a parochial grade school, Josephinum High School with chapel, St. Elizabeth's Hospital with sacristy and convent, and additional ground for a new church (since built). Different cultural groups have come and gone in the surrounding neighborhoods, but they have been substantially Catholic-oriented, so the parish has continued to serve a function in that location, despite great social change.

Religious Diversity on Chicago's Southwest Side in 2002

Chicago's religious geography is quite heterogeneous when viewed at the level of districts such as the Southwest Side east of Midway Airport. Many ethnic groups and their religious subgroups have passed through here at one time or another. The area's recent churchscape reflects accumulation and replacement involving a rich diversity of religions and denominations. Mainline Protestant churches founded by Lutheran, Episcopal, and Baptist congregations, for example, recall long-established residents of Chicago moving to the area when it was first built up. Roman Catholic churches and synagogues represent the addition of Irish and later Polish and Jewish residents in the area. Muslim and Pentecostal houses of worship signal the appearance of Arabs and African Americans and, more recently, Mexicans (who also support the Roman Catholic churches). The 2000 census revealed the increasing Mexican presence in the area, which correlates strongly with the appearance of Pentecostal churches in the district.

much of the SOUTH SIDE and West Side, often occupying buildings previously owned by white congregations. In the process commonly known as "white flight," or to sociologists as "NEIGHBORHOOD SUCCESSION," these white congregations moved with their members, either to other parts of Chicago, notably to the legendarily "white ethnic" Southwest Side and to the "Polish Corridor" of the Northwest Side, or to suburbs. The churches of the city were still tied to nearby industrial WORK opportunities for their members, but more and more of those members were minorities. By the same token, the growth of suburban churches reflects not only the "suburbanization of employment" but also the migration of white city dwellers from racially changing neighborhoods.

Large numbers of Jews also moved from racially changing neighborhoods as African Americans moved into Chicago's South and West Side neighborhoods during the 1950s and 1960s. Most dramatically, virtually all of the 110,000 Jews had left the Lawndale–GARFIELD PARK area by 1970, and all of the synagogues had either closed or moved to other neighborhoods or suburbs. Unlike their Protestant counterparts who scattered across suburbia, Jews clustered in a few North Side neighborhoods and suburbs, mainly to avoid the anti-Semitic sentiment prevalent in many areas and to build the infrastructure needed for the full observance of *halachah* (Jewish law). Particularly in the ALBANY PARK, ROGERS PARK, and WEST RIDGE neighborhoods and in suburban SKOKIE, LINCOLNWOOD, and BUFFALO GROVE, enough observant Jews settled to support not only Kosher groceries and restaurants but numerous Hebrew schools and such

Chicago's Non-Judeo-Christian Congregations, 2002

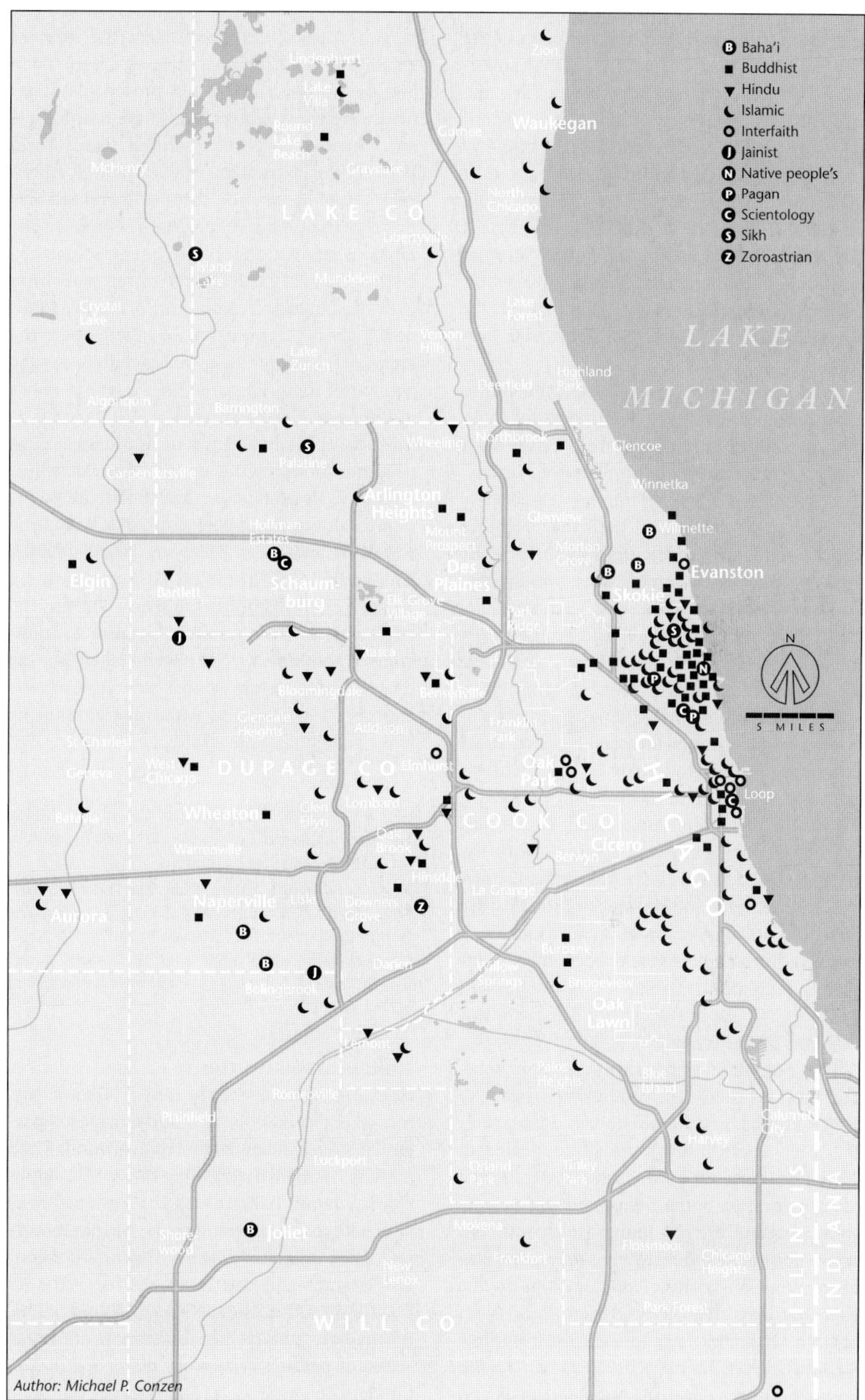

The most significant development in metropolitan Chicago's religious landscape has been the appearance and steady growth of non-Judeo-Christian congregations in the last decades of the twentieth century. Their geographical pattern indicates two dimensions: strong concentrations on Chicago's North Side, which represents the latest "port of entry" for recent immigrant groups establishing themselves in the region, and a widely dispersed metropolitan pattern in which many churches locate with easy access to the freeway network to draw adherents from a wide area.

institutions as the *beth din* (Jewish court), the *mikva* (ritual bath), and SOCIAL SERVICE agencies that strictly observe *halachah*. At the same time, more assimilated, liberal, and secular Jews were settling in comfortable lakefront neighborhoods and in some of the most affluent suburbs both north and south of Chicago.

Of all the religious groups, Catholics were most likely to stay and defend their PARISH neighborhoods, having been taught by priests and nuns that the parish is sacred space and that Christian community could best be built if people would buy their homes, send their children to CATHOLIC SCHOOLS, patronize neighborhood business, and work together to promote neighborhood improvement and shared codes of conduct. Thus the Southwest and Northwest Sides of Chicago remained not only "white ethnic" but hegemonically Catholic, with close cultural ties among parish members, blue-collar workers and their unions, and public servants such as POLICE, FIREFIGHTERS, and city government at the ward level. Even in the South Side and West Side African American neighborhoods, the Catholic church maintained parishes and parish schools to serve the small fraction of the black residents who were Catholic. In the areas of MEXICAN and PUERTO RICAN immigration like SOUTH CHICAGO and PILSEN, Catholic parishes replaced departing "white ethnics" with at least as many Spanish-speaking newcomers and, again, provided an institutional anchor for holding new communities in place. Despite Catholics' increasing achievement of middle-class status and their beginning participation in suburbanization after World War II, the Catholic Church remained more distinctly urban than suburban, more ubiquitously distributed throughout the city than any other denomination or faith, and a formidable presence in every city neighborhood.

Religion and Post-Industrial Sprawl, 1960s–2002

Although both Catholic and Protestant churches were founded in agrarian and trading settlements during the nineteenth century and in "streetcar suburbs" in the first half of the twentieth, it was not until the postwar decades that suburbanization became the dominant trend in religious geography. The religious hegemony of Chicago itself gave way, only in the 1970s, to multiple centers of religious concentration across the region and to the relocation of denominational authorities from downtown office buildings to office complexes far from the city center. The Evangelical Lutheran Church, for example, located its national headquarters near O'HARE AIRPORT in 1988, and the Northern Illinois Conference of the United Methodist Church soon moved to the same location from Chicago's Loop. By that time, a few suburbs that had access to open land and that were fortuitously located near the intersections of EXPRESSWAYS, rail, and air transportation routes were becoming "edge cities," which were home to the fastest-growing employers of the new technology and financial services sectors. While religious congregations did not necessarily locate within the edge cities, the rapidly expanding employment opportunities attracted new populations not only from Chicago but from other parts of the United States and the world. This dramatically altered the religious landscape, both in the city and throughout the metropolitan region. It became increasingly common for people to sustain long COMMUTES to worship either at places near expressways within Chicago (such as Old St. Patrick's in the Loop and Christ Universal Temple on the far South Side) or at automobile-oriented church complexes far from the city (such as Christ Church in Oak Brook or WILLOW CREEK CHURCH near Barrington).

Employers located in edge cities and other suburban locations have been powerful magnets to skilled immigrants from Asia, so it is no surprise that large numbers of Hindus, Buddhists, and Muslims immigrated directly to Chicago's suburbs and built their temples and mosques within driving distance of their homes. Other Asian immigrants who arrived with fewer skills settled in city neighborhoods where housing was cheaper and public transportation made a car unnecessary; they have set up religious centers in rented commercial space or have bought buildings formerly occupied by churches or theaters. By 2002 these immigrants to metropolitan Chicago had established some 24 Hindu temples, 33 Buddhist temples or worship centers, and 51 Muslim mosques, in both city and suburbs. With the exception of a few well-funded centers, however, the temples and mosques of the city are physically and financially marginal, while many of those in the suburbs and edge cities compare favorably with the elaborate churches and synagogues built in the city by European immigrants a century ago.

The economic attractions (not only jobs, but the new, low-density housing stock, the SCHOOLS, and the automobile-based shopping) that drew Asian immigrants also appealed to American-born city dwellers, escalating the deconcentration of the city population and the sprawl beyond the city limits. Jews continued their suburban exodus, leaving only a few Reform and Conservative congregations in the city, and one area (West Rogers Park) with enough Orthodox Jews to sustain a complete *halachic* infrastructure. The suburban Jewish population grew with the suburbs north and northwest of Chicago, and, while most migrants have been Reform, Conservative, or secular, the suburb of Buffalo Grove, some 30 miles northwest of the city, has attracted enough Orthodox to sustain an institutional infrastructure for *halachic* observance. Nevertheless, while a few Jewish congregations have prospered in suburbs south of the city, the rapidly growing DUPAGE COUNTY west of the city entered the twenty-first century with a population approaching one million, but only two synagogues.

Catholicism's growth in the Chicago suburbs, based partly on migration from city neighborhoods, has often taken the form of expansion of existing parishes, many of which had been established when present-day suburbs were rural villages. Although new suburban parishes have been formed since World War II, the expansion of suburban Catholicism tends to take the form of increased size rather than numbers of parishes. Moreover, the ranks of city Catholics have been replenished by the arrival of a half-million immigrants from Mexico, Poland, Ireland, and other predominantly Catholic countries. As of late 2002, the archdiocese counted 2.4 million adherents (36 percent of them Hispanic) in the 374 parishes of Lake and Cook Counties.

Much as Catholicism had dominated most neighborhoods of the early industrial workforce, so Protestantism had been the hegemonic faith in the streetcar suburbs and in the suburban expansion following World War II. The addition of Protestant churches as more and more farmland succumbed to commercial and residential expansion was thus a continuation of an old story; the novelty lay in sharing the suburban terrain with a growing Catholic church, with Jews, and with adherents to the many religions of the world.

Lowell W. Livezey
Mark Bouman

See also: Economic Geography; Judaism; Metropolitan Growth; Religious Institutions

Further reading: Cutler, Irving. *The Jews of Chicago: From Shtetl to Suburb.* 1996. • Drake, St. Clair, and Horace R. Cayton. *Black Metropolis: A Study of Negro Life in a Northern City.* 1945; 1962. • Livezey, Lowell W., ed. *Public Religion and Urban Transformation: Faith in the City.* 2000.

Religious Institutions. All large American cities can claim marks of a robust religious life, but several factors have made Chicago a particularly lively religious breeding ground. First, the city has benefited from a habit of religious charity dating back to the cholera epidemics of the 1850s, when temporary hospitals were set up by religious groups. The city contains the largest—and the most activist—ROMAN CATHOLIC ARCHDIOCESE in the United States, particularly notable for its nearly unbroken series of prelates who were either institution builders or whose social philosophies put them in the forefront of American reformist bishops. In the 1930s and 1940s, Chicago was arguably the headquarters of the Catholic activism that gave rise to organizations such as the CATHOLIC YOUTH ORGANIZATION (the founder was Bishop Bernard Sheil of Chicago), the Cana Conference (founded by Monsignor John Egan), the Christian Family Movement, and Young Christian Students. And it was in Chicago that the alliance between COMMUNITY ORGANIZER Saul Alinsky and the Catholic Church came to its fullest flowering.

PROTESTANTISM in Chicago has been unusually activist as well, no doubt partly to compete with Chicago's robust Catholicism, but also as a result of its early and intense alliance with sociology. Urban sociology as an academic discipline began in the teens and twenties at the UNIVERSITY OF CHICAGO; though the department of sociology ultimately became self-consciously secular, its early ties were religious and reformist. The first head of the department was Albion Small, a former minister, and one of the department members, Charles Henderson, doubled as university chaplain. In the early days the department had close ties with HULL HOUSE and with the Reverend Graham Taylor's SETTLEMENT HOUSE, CHICAGO COMMONS. (It is very likely, too, that sociological and reform activity at the University of Chicago helped stimulate the early 1914 establishment by Frederick Siedenburg of a department of sociology at Catholic LOYOLA UNIVERSITY.)

In the 1960s, Saul Alinsky, a former sociology graduate student at the University of Chicago, would attract an unusually large number of Chicago ministers and lay Protestant leaders to his organizing efforts. He often managed to build coalitions that included Catholics and Protestants, most notably in organizations like Organization for the Southwest Community and the WOODLAWN ORGANIZATION. The spirit of Alinsky's organizing went into the Urban Training Center (for prospective ministers and lay leaders, 1962–1975); UTC was the model for similar training centers in other American cities. Although UTC dissolved, its model for training urban religious workers has persisted in Chicago.

Nor was the activist ferment limited to white Christians. Chicago Judaism created religious social service institutions for the thousands of Eastern European JEWS who came to Chicago between 1880 and World War I; during and after World War I AFRICAN AMERICAN Protestants aided southern blacks who flocked to Chicago's SOUTH SIDE. Recent immigrant groups (e.g., BUDDHISTS, MUSLIMS, and HINDUS) have demonstrated a similar impulse to build religious institutions—temples, mosques, and schools especially—ensuring that Chicago would remain a city of lively faiths.

Here it might be well to define "religious institution." At the most obvious level these constituted houses of worship and other organizations that depended at least in part upon religious funding and were staffed and attended by persons with avowedly religious motivations. Religious discourse was likely to be a staple of these institutions as well. Most of the institutions mentioned in this article fit this description. However, "religious" institutions existed on a continuum, especially as the twentieth century advanced. As increasing prestige accrued to science, "objectivity," and professional expertise, some institutional leaders, such as Jane Addams at Hull House, tended to downplay their religious commitments even though those commitments probably persisted at deeper levels.

The institution building of Chicago's religious groups was accomplished in a relatively short span of time. In the first few decades after Chicago's incorporation as a city in 1837, religious leaders had all they could do to establish modest houses of worship. The first sign that a congregation was well established and acquiring wealth was its decision to employ an architect and invest in more expensive construction materials than wood or plain brick—thus, structures such as St. James Episcopal Church (1856–57; rebuilt 1875–1880); Holy Family (RCC; 1857–1860); First Baptist Church (1866); Union Park Congregational Church (1869–1871); St. Stanislaus Kostka (1877–1881); KAM Synagogue (1890–91; later Pilgrim Baptist Church); and Quinn Chapel (AME; 1891–1894). The next sign, in the case of a Protestant congregation particularly, might be a move to create a mission chapel elsewhere in the city, or a city mission to provide social and religious services in a poverty- or vice-stricken district. One such mission was the (Congregational) Chicago City Mission (1882), which continues today as the Community Renewal Society. Until the late decades of the nineteenth century, churches and synagogues tended to dispense charity in an ad hoc, informal manner, usually directed to needy members of the congregation rather than to city residents in general.

But the pattern in many congregations was toward wider outreach. In the decades immediately following the CIVIL WAR, cities, growing and industrializing at a dizzying rate, began to be conceived as religious "problems" (or more optimistically, "challenges") to an unprecedented degree. In the eyes of its religious leaders, the city presented immigrants and migrants from the country with temptations; even the more "innocent" pleasures of THEATER, concerts, shopping, and sports distracted city dwellers from religion. Grinding poverty too could separate people from their religious moorings.

Chicago religious leaders sprang into action, both denominationally and ecumenically. Brought to Chicago in 1858, the YMCA (and the YWCA after 1876) established Bible study groups, dormitories, employment bureaus, and recreational (especially athletic) facilities designed to encourage young men and women, fresh from rural America, to shun the attractions of the city. The YMCA and YWCA expanded into branches as well for work among particular immigrant groups, and the YMCA produced "railroad branches" aimed at teaching railroad employees arithmetic, vocational training, and penmanship. The WOMEN'S CHRISTIAN TEMPERANCE UNION, founded in Ohio in 1874, organized a branch in Chicago; eventually the international headquarters of the WCTU would be in the northern suburb of EVANSTON. In addition to advancing temperance, the Chicago WCTU also promoted women's rights, purity, honest municipal government, and labor arbitration. The SALVATION ARMY arrived in Chicago in 1885, and by 1892 it was providing social as well as evangelical services at its headquarters at Halsted and 12th Streets. The interdenominational Church Federation of Greater Chicago, founded in 1907, was strongly reformist in outlook and would become especially activist in the 1950s and 1960s.

Individual churches followed suit, establishing extensive Sunday schools, CLUBS, gymnasiums, dispensaries, vocational classrooms, facilities for the destitute, and missionary and devotional associations of various age groups, often separated by gender. Normally the physical plant of the church or synagogue had to be enlarged to accommodate all these functions. Some churches that engaged in this expansion self-consciously became known as "institutional churches," and their ministers and lay leaders typically embraced the "Social Gospel" of service to the sick and poor. Prominent institutional churches included All Souls Unitarian Church (1882) under Jenkin Lloyd Jones and Reverdy Ransom's (African American) Institutional Church and Social Settlement (1900). Though never labeled an "institutional church," wealthy FOURTH PRESBYTERIAN, by the time it moved into its new building on Michigan Avenue in 1914, provided a wide range of social and educational services. So did Moody Church, founded by Chicago's foremost evangelist, Dwight L. Moody. Jews expanded their scope of activities as well; when the Sinai Congregation built a new synagogue on the South Side in 1912, the building included a gymnasium, a pool, classrooms, and a social center. Chicago's Catholic churches offered meeting rooms for MUTUAL BENEFIT SOCIETIES, halls for socializing, gymnasiums, and BOWLING alleys.

In the 1920s a church's range of services became less visible than its drawing power—and the fame of its minister—through the mass media, especially the new medium of radio. In 1912, Preston Bradley, a former Presbyterian minister and skillful preacher, opened the long-lived, noncreedal, and liberal People's Church. Bradley's radio ministry, which began in 1923, attracted five million listeners in its heyday. On the other end of the Protestant theological spectrum, Paul Rader held forth at the nondenominational Gospel Tabernacle (1922–1933) and, like Bradley, conducted a successful radio ministry.

In addition to the churches and synagogues that offered multiple services and ministries under one or two roofs, there were institutions and agencies that were usually extracongregational and sometimes interdenominational creations. They fell into several categories, depending on what service they offered and their clientele. As in other cities, women (Protestant deaconesses, Catholic religious, and lay workers of all denominations) played a dominant role in founding, leading, and staffing these institutions.

One group of institutions served a fairly wide range of the needs of the poor, especially immigrant and migrant: Christian- or Jewish-sponsored or -supported settlement, neighborhood, or community houses; and rescue homes. The most prestigious SETTLEMENT HOUSES (HULL HOUSE [1889] and CHICAGO COMMONS [1894]) were officially unreligious, especially after 1913 when the National Federation of Settlements promulgated a policy against religious affiliation. But this left a number of lesser-known institutions: the Catholic Church's MADONNA CENTER (1898), under the leadership of Sr. Mary Agnes Amberg; several African American settlement houses in part supported by churches—the Emanuel Settlement, the Negro Fellowship League (1910), the Wendell Phillips Settlement (1907), the Clotee Scott Settlement, and the Frederick Douglass Center (1905); and the CHICAGO HEBREW INSTITUTE (1903; later the Jewish People's Institute). Rescue homes tended to be more evangelical and more conservative, with individual conversion their most important goal. But to effect a sound conversion, evangelicals also felt compelled to provide food and shelter, instruction, work placement, and sometimes jobs. The most prominent of these was the PACIFIC GARDEN MISSION (1877), where Billy Sunday was converted. Pentecostals too established a series of missions, the most famous on North Avenue dating from the earliest years of the twentieth century. A group called the Bible Work of Chicago, which arose in 1873 in the aftermath of the Great FIRE OF 1871, was eventually to be incorporated as the interdenominational MOODY BIBLE INSTITUTE (1889). The institute itself, a headquarters of conservative American evangelicalism from its founding, has been a lively player on the Chicago religious scene, operating radio WMBI and dispatching its students and staff to a variety of Sunday schools, Bible classes, RESCUE MISSIONS, street meetings, and other works of evangelization and mercy.

Young women alone in the city, in search of work or excitement, became an early and constant preoccupation of religious workers. Even more than young men, young women were perceived to be at risk in the city. Working in factories or domestic settings, they were often so ill paid as to be vulnerable to the temptations held out by PROSTITUTION or by more informal sexual arrangements. Thus, much attention was directed to prevention, through the provision of inexpensive supervised lodgings (especially YWCAs) or homes for rehabilitation once a young woman had "fallen." Chicago Catholics offered the Magdalen Asylum (1859), run by the Sisters of the Good Shepherd, and an associated industrial school for girls; Protestants ran the ERRING WOMEN'S REFUGE (1863).

Orphans and delinquent children also elicited a good deal of religious solicitude. Activities in this area were stimulated by COOK COUNTY's establishment of the world's first JUVENILE COURT (1899), and early on religious workers were involved in the activities of the court, sometimes as employees. Catholics especially were worried about losing their children to Protestant ORPHANAGES and foster homes and established numerous institutions of their own, such as the Angel Guardian (1865) and St. Joseph's Orphan Asylums, St. Mary's Training School for Boys (1882), and the Holy Family Orphan Asylum for POLISH and Bohemian children. African Americans had the Amanda Smith Orphanage and Industrial Home (Harvey, 1895–1918) and the Louise Juvenile Home (1905). The very old received attention from religious leaders; one of the best-known institutions of this type was the Drexel Home for Aged Jews (1893).

Because the activity of healing the sick and assisting the dying has so often been construed as inherently religious, Chicago religious institutions established a long tradition of HOSPITAL founding and operation. Most of these hospitals ministered to the indigent, often the indigent of all faiths or of no faith, and frequently there were waiting lists of people needing beds. The groups with traditions of sisters (Roman Catholic and Episcopalian) and deaconesses (especially Lutherans and Methodist) found themselves particularly able to staff these hospitals. In 1940 the archdiocese contained 25 Catholic hospitals. Prominent among them were Alexian Brothers' Hospital (1866), MERCY HOSPITAL (1852), and St. Joseph's Hospital (1872). The first Jewish hospital opened in 1868 on the Near North Side, with MICHAEL REESE HOSPITAL following in 1881. Mount Sinai opened in 1918, specifically for Eastern European Jews who had special dietary requirements. The Episcopalians had St. Luke's Hospital (1865) on Indiana Avenue; Chicago Presbyterians set up Presbyterian Hospital in 1884; Methodists established Wesley Hospital in 1888, depending on a nursing staff of deaconesses trained at the Chicago Training School for City, Home, and Foreign Missions; Lutherans set up the Norwegian Lutheran Deaconess Home and Hospital in 1897 on the North Side (relocated to PARK RIDGE in the 1950s and renamed Lutheran General Hospital). Late in the century, members of the SWEDISH Evangelical Covenant Church founded Covenant Hospital near their college and seminary in NORTH PARK.

The heyday of such multipurpose churches and church-sponsored SOCIAL SERVICE agencies was the 1910s and 1920s; the GREAT DEPRESSION effectively halted many of these efforts, and a number of them were never revived in the same form when prosperity returned. Not that religious concern for the poor ceased, nor the desire to instruct, convert, or provide wholesome entertainment. But after the NEW DEAL, government at the local, state, and federal levels took over many of religion's welfare tasks. Also, as roles such as social worker, nurse, and counselor (psychologist or psychiatrist) became professionalized, competitive salaries and advanced equipment raised the cost of operating these institutions. These new-style professionals frequently operated out of private and secular agencies and institutions, preferring a social scientific discourse over a religious one.

Yet certain religious institutional functions remained: soup kitchens and food pantries, shelters for the HOMELESS, advocacy for the poor and oppressed, organizations to fight racism and war. There remained the need for a ministry for persons unable to find their way through the labyrinth of public and private services or who belonged to portions of the population almost universally despised or feared—drug addicts, prisoners, youth GANGS. The interdenominational West Side Christian Parish (1952), an offshoot of the East Harlem Protestant Parish in New York, was established in Chicago by Archie Hargraves and Don Benedict and set itself these kinds of tasks. In the closing decades of the twentieth century, coalitions of churches, synagogues, and mosques, recognizing the failures of PUBLIC HOUSING and the diminished role of the federal government in affordable housing initiatives, have stepped into the housing breach. In the effort to foster ghetto businesses and sponsor housing for the poor, these institutions have often adopted a modified form of Saul Alinsky's community organizing efforts, now usually called "community development." Most prominently, since 1993 the Metropolitan Alliance of Congregations, comprising some three hundred churches, synagogues, and Islamic organizations, has organized for housing, regionalism, better TRANSPORTATION for poor people, and business reinvestment in the inner city and Chicago's older, deteriorating southern and southeastern suburbs. Reflecting an even more direct Alinsky heritage, in 1995 the Industrial Areas Foundation founded the congregation-based United Power for Action.

In the area of education, Protestant and Jewish efforts have focused mostly on part-time Sunday or religious schools and on forms of higher education: colleges, SEMINARIES, and MISSIONARY TRAINING institutions such as the Baptist Missionary Training School (1881). At the elementary school level most Protestants and Jews sent their children to the public SCHOOLS, whereas Catholics established parochial schools, ideally, one school per parish. Cardinal Mundelein's gift for administration resulted in a relatively centralized and systematized CATHOLIC SCHOOL SYSTEM. In recent decades the contrast between Jewish and Catholic education has become less stark: since World War II, Jews have established day schools through the high-school level, and Catholics, confronting the rising costs of full-time schooling and the dispersion of their population to the suburbs, have closed parochial schools and invested more in supplementary education through their Confraternities of Christian Doctrine.

Suburban developments have given rise to houses of worship, to charitable and welfare agencies (especially in the older, declining suburbs), and to religious schools. Suburbanization has presented its own problems for the establishment of religious institutions, however: except where religious-ethnic groups have settled in relatively dense communities, the dispersal and mobility of suburban populations has often made institution building difficult and unpredictable. Chicago-area Jews, for instance, have found it difficult to replicate the intimacy of the early communities of MAXWELL STREET and NORTH LAWNDALE. On the other hand, recently arrived HINDU and MUSLIM immigrants have dealt with the dispersion of their populations over the greater Chicago area by establishing many of their temples and mosques at prime locations along the main EXPRESSWAYS, thereby making them relatively accessible by car to both suburbanites and city dwellers.

Affluent suburban religious institutions, sometimes burdened with guilt about having "abandoned the city" or simply concerned for inner-city populations, have forged ties with "sister" churches and conducted various forms of mission to the city. In the 1970s, for instance, a Lutheran church in VALPARAISO sponsored a black family's move from CABRINI-GREEN housing to this almost all-white suburb. WHEATON Protestant churches, bolstered by the influence of the prominent evangelical college and its affiliated BILLY GRAHAM CENTER, have sponsored youth and other ministries in the city of Chicago.

Those religious groups that have arrived in substantial numbers only since the 1965 immigration legislation—Muslims (the largest), Hindus, BUDDHISTS, and others—have created a host of their own institutions. Some have taken a pan-Islamic or pan-Hindu stance; others have been more attuned to the particularities of ethnicity and place of origin. These groups, aided by a relatively high level of education and economic means, have rapidly replicated the behavior of their predecessors in Chicago, refurbishing old churches or schools or building new houses of worship (Hindus especially have lavished money and crafts skill on temples modeled after those in India and other homelands), caring for the indigent among their membership and sometimes joining in interfaith efforts such as soup kitchens and shelters, and performing multiple social and cultural functions. Most temples and mosques include community halls, kitchens, and auditoriums. The second generation has received particular attention: youth groups, religious and language classes, and summer camps and retreats (for Hindus there's a camping center in Ganges, Michigan). Whereas most of these groups have resorted to "supplementary" religious education scheduled on weekends or weekday evenings, Chicago Muslims when possible have established full-time schools K–12 teaching both secular and religious subjects. They have also founded the American Islamic College (1983).

For many observers, the coexistence of so much effective institution building is perhaps counterintuitive, especially in a "worldly" city like Chicago, the greater part of whose history has unfolded in the "secular" twentieth century. Yet the needs of so many Chicagoans—for ideals, ethical guidance, physical and mental healing, racial and economic justice, and simple food, shelter, and clothing—continue to elicit inherently religious responses. Government, businesses, PHILANTHROPIC foundations, and practical individuals are not always ready or able to go the extra mile. Religious institutions, with their claims to universality and their commitment to fairness—and their occasional disregard for what's possible—often try to do just that.

Virginia Lieson Brereton

See also: Catholic Charities; Church Architecture; Housing for the Elderly; Parish Life; Publishing and Media, Religious; Settlements, Religious

Further reading: Horwitt, Sanford D. *Let Them Call Me Rebel: Saul Alinsky—His Life and Legacy.* 1991. • Kantowicz, Edward R. *Corporation Sole: Cardinal Mundelein and Chicago Catholicism.* 1983. • Knupfer, Anne Meis. *Toward a Tenderer Humanity and a Nobler Womanhood: African American Women's Clubs in Turn-of-the Century Chicago.* 1996.

Religious Publishing. *See* Publishing and Media, Religious

Religious Settlements. *See* Settlements, Religious

Renaissance Society. The Renaissance Society, a noncollecting museum founded in 1915 at the UNIVERSITY OF CHICAGO, is Chicago's oldest contemporary ART museum. Named for the spirit of rebirth, the society sought to provide university students with a well-rounded education in the arts. Although located on the university campus, the museum has remained an independent institution.

Despite the controversies surrounding modern art following the ARMORY SHOW OF 1913, the society, from its inception, was quick to embrace modernism. Under director Eva Watson-Schutze (1929–1935), the society presented groundbreaking exhibitions of early modernists such as Pablo Picasso, Georges Braque, Marc Chagall, Jean Arp, Joan Miró, Wassily Kandinsky, Piet Mondrian, Henri Matisse, and Constantin Brancusi, as well as pivotal one-person shows of Isamu Noguchi, Alexander Calder, Fernand Léger, and Ludwig Mies van der Rohe. Since the appointment of Susanne Ghez as director in 1974, the society has increased its international reputation and scope, exhibiting conceptual, minimal, postminimal, and installation ARTISTS, who, in keeping with the original mission, question, redefine and expand the aesthetic boundaries of the visual arts.

Lisa Meyerowitz

See also: Galleries; Hyde Park; Museum of Contemporary Art; Smart Museum

Further reading: The Renaissance Society at the University of Chicago records, 1917–1981. Archives of American Art, Smithsonian Institution, Washington, DC. • Scanlan, Joseph, ed. *A History of the Renaissance Society: The First Seventy-five Years.* 1993.

Rent Control. In twentieth-century Chicago, skyrocketing rents have arisen as an issue in times of inflation and housing shortages. In response, for short periods, Chicago has adopted rent arbitration and rent control.

In 1919, the city council established a committee that, through 1921 in conjunction with the Chicago REAL ESTATE Board, arbitrated disputes over rising rents. The city council also called on the Illinois legislature to pass a law enabling cities such as Chicago to adopt rent control, an effort that did not succeed.

During WORLD WAR II, the entire nation, including Chicago, was required to participate in stringent rent controls imposed by the Office of Price Administration. When, in 1946, the federal program ended controls over HOTELS, including Chicago's substantial stock of RESIDENTIAL HOTELS, the Chicago City Council passed an ordinance returning these dwellings to rent control, only to be overturned by the Illinois State Supreme Court in January 1947. Federal rent control, having eased after World War II, ended in 1953 at the cessation of the Korean War.

In the 1970s, Chicago again found itself subject to federally mandated rent controls (August 1971–January 1973) under the Nixon administration's wage and price guidelines. Thereafter, high rents resulting from peacetime inflation, escalating property taxes, declining CONSTRUCTION, CONDOMINIUM conversion, and abandonment led Mayor Richard J. Daley, in 1976, to appoint a committee to consider rent controls. In 1977, the committee recommended against the adoption of controls.

In late 1979, the city council appointed a committee to consider an ordinance establishing rent arbitration. Neighborhood hearings revealed a growing tenants' rights movement. The 1980 hearings also featured arguments against rent control from the city's strong real-estate lobby, and the city council failed to adopt any form of rent control. The same ordinance was submitted in 1982 as part of a Tenants Bill of Rights, and again defeated in 1983. In 1987, the city council adopted a Tenants Bill of Rights that did not include rent control.

Wendy Plotkin

See also: Housing Reform

Further reading: Drellich, Edith B., and Andrée Emery. *Rent Control in War and Peace.* 1939. • Friedlander, Bernard, and Anthony Curreri. *Rent Control: Federal, State and Municipal.* 1948. • Plotkin, Wendy. "Rent Control in Chicago after WWII: *Prologue* 30.2 (Summer 1998): 110–123. Politics, People, and Controversy."

Republican Party. From the birth of the Republican Party in the mid-1850s through the end of the 1920s, Republicans had considerable success in Chicago POLITICS. Many of the city's MAYORS during that period came from the GOP, and many Republicans from the Chicago area exercised considerable influence in local, state, and national governments. From the 1930s through the end of the century, Republicans had little political influence within the city, but they enjoyed considerable strength in the growing suburbs.

Chicago elected its first Republican mayor—the veteran politician and newspaperman John Wentworth—in 1857, only one year after the party held its first POLITICAL CONVENTION in Illinois. In 1860, Chicago Republicans received a big lift as the city hosted the Republican National Convention. Local party members, led by CHICAGO *Tribune* publisher Joseph Medill, helped garner the presidential nomination for Illinois lawyer Abraham Lincoln.

Because the Republican and Democratic parties were built to compete in national and STATE POLITICS, it has not always been easy to identify clear differences between the two parties within the context of local politics. The positions that defined the Republican Party during the nineteenth century, such as its opposition to slavery and support for the gold standard and the tariff, did not always speak to the question of how its candidates would handle the governance of Chicago. Republicans generally were more apt to emphasize fiscal conservatism and anti-vice reforms than their Democratic counterparts. Such positions tended to attract the support of pietistic PROTESTANTS—including many ENGLISH, GERMAN, and Scandinavian immigrants—and many members of the middle classes and business elite.

Lincoln funeral procession entering Chicago's courthouse, May 1, 1865. Photographer: Unknown. Source: Chicago Historical Society.

In practice, Chicago's Republicans were often divided among two distinct factions: one that emphasized budget cutting and anti-vice reforms, and one that was more comfortable with the kind of PATRONAGE politics that prevailed in many large American cities. Indeed, many of the city's most successful Republican politicians were pragmatists who built patronage machines. John B. Rice, the city's Republican mayor during the late 1860s, was attacked by reform elements within his own party for failing to prevent city GOVERNMENT from becoming a spoils system. Politicians from the reform wing of the party, on the other hand, had trouble attracting enough voters from Chicago's diverse population. When *Tribune* owner Medill occupied the mayor's office in the early 1870s, he alienated many voters by choosing to enforce a law that ordered SALOONS to close on Sundays. More pragmatic Republican politicians were able to attract more support. One of the greatest of the city's Republican MACHINE POLITICIANS was William Lorimer, who during the 1890s built a strong political base from the city's West Side, which was populated by large numbers of working-class immigrants, including many ROMAN CATHOLICS. By avoiding the moralistic style that was the hallmark of the reform wing of his party, Lorimer managed to lure these voters and use their support to become one of COOK COUNTY's most powerful politicians.

The split between the reform and pragmatic wings of the Republican Party in the Chicago area continued into the early twentieth century, when it became clear that one reason for the division was the contrast between suburban and urban voters. Many of the area's most prominent reform-minded Republicans during this period drew their strength from suburban and middle-class voters. James R. Mann, a leading local and national Republican leader from the 1890s until his death in 1922, represented a SOUTH SIDE area that had formerly been the suburb of HYDE PARK Village. Another leading Republican reformer from the South Side was Charles E. Merriam, the UNIVERSITY OF CHICAGO professor who lost the city's 1911 mayoral race because his middle-class supporters failed to outnumber the working-class base of DEMOCRATIC PARTY candidate Carter Harrison II. A Republican who proved far more successful in Chicago politics was William Hale ("Big Bill") Thompson, the ex-cowboy who served as mayor from 1915 to 1923 and again from 1927 to 1931. Attacked by his own party's reform wing for being soft on vice and spoils, Thompson built a broad, ethnically diverse urban coalition while retaining the support of many business leaders, a pragmatic political formula similar to the one that would be used by Democrats to dominate city politics for the rest of the twentieth century.

Republican success in Chicago city politics ended during the GREAT DEPRESSION, when Democrats at the local and national levels built a powerful and diverse political base that included a majority of urban residents. Thompson lost his mayoral reelection bid to Democratic Party boss Anton Cermak in 1931; Cermak and his successor Edward Kelly quickly established a multiethnic Democratic political machine that reflected the changing DEMOGRAPHICS of the city. One of the greatest blows to the fortunes of the Chicago Republicans during the 1930s was the shift in party loyalties among AFRICAN AMERICANS. Before the Depression, most African Americans in Chicago voted Republican, and they were an important part of Thompson's machine in the 1910s and 1920s. But during the era of the NEW DEAL, they joined Kelly's winning Democratic coalition. For the rest of the century, no Republican won a Chicago mayoral election; after the 1950s, the party's political strength within the city was limited to small pockets of support on the far Northwest Side.

During the latter part of the twentieth century, the Republican Party remained a major political force in the Chicago region because of its considerable support in the suburbs. As the suburbs grew, the metropolitan area as a whole became a highly competitive political region. By the 1970s, the suburbs contained more voters than the city of Chicago; these voters were sending large numbers of Republican candidates into local, state, and national offices. As the twentieth century came to a close, Republicans familiar with the old political saying "fish where the fish are" were concentrating their efforts in the suburbs; within the city of the Chicago, they were faced with the prospect of a long wait.

Paul Green
Mark R. Wilson

See also: Cold War and Anti-Communism; Government, Suburban; Sunday Closings; Whigs

Further reading: Green, Paul, and Melvin Holli. *The Mayors: The Chicago Political Tradition.* 2nd ed. 1994. • Hansen, Lawrence N. "Suburban Politics and the Decline of the One-Party City." In *After Daley: Chicago Politics in Transition,* ed. Samuel K. Gove and Louis H. Masotti, 1982, 175–202. • Tarr, Joel Arthur. *A Study in Boss Politics: William Lorimer of Chicago.* 1971.

Rescue Missions. Religious people have always stepped in to help meet Chicago's social, economic, and spiritual challenges, forming missions to "rescue" their fellow citizens who have fallen into spiritual or material poverty.

Most Chicago rescue missions were active in the nineteenth century, starting in 1842, when the City Tract Society began feeding the hungry. Two years later Seamen's Bethel Church began ministering to sailors. The Chicago City Missionary Society began caring for the poor in 1853. A year later, the "Ragged School in the 'Sands'" began serving the poor living in shacks at the mouth of the Chicago River.

Presbyterians established the "Railroad Mission," where poor IRISH immigrants and AFRICAN AMERICANS were schooled together in a railroad car. Other efforts targeted newsboys and bootblacks, prostitutes, and SALOON frequenters. By 1871, Chicago had over 33 rescue missions.

The nonsectarian Armour Mission opened in 1886 at 33rd and Butterfield, shortly after the SALVATION ARMY began its ongoing mission to Chicago's poor. Both organizations revealed a trend toward interdenominational cooperation at century's end.

The PACIFIC GARDEN MISSION, perhaps the most visible Chicago rescue mission and the site of evangelist Billy Sunday's conversion, was founded in 1877 by George and Sarah Clarke in the South Loop. Named after the site's former tenant, the notorious Pacific Beer Garden, it sought to be "a harbor for wrecked and ruined lives" and soon became known as the "Old Lighthouse."

At the close of the twentieth century, Chicago's rich tradition of rescue missions was most visible in the Pacific Garden Mission, the Salvation Army, and the Chicago Christian Industrial League.

R. Jonathan Moore

See also: Protestants; Religious Institutions; Social Services

Residential Hotels. From the very beginning of Chicago's history, hotel managers have catered both to TOURISTS and to longer-term residents who paid by the week or month instead of by the night. Until 1930, people with comfortable incomes might move to Chicago and never live anywhere except in a HOTEL. A room or suite of rooms in a palatial hotel (for the rich) or a middle-priced hotel (for those of middle income) were luxurious, conveniently located, and cheaper than maintaining a private house in the city. Hotels gave Chicago residents an instant social position, and interaction with some of the wealthiest residents of the city. The famous Chicago architect Louis Sullivan lived in hotels most of his life. In the 1920s, the Chicago sociologist Day Monroe interviewed women physicians and businesswomen who could pursue their professional lives only because hotel life freed them from household duties.

Midpriced and palace-style hotels probably housed only about one-sixth of Chicago's hotel residents. Another one-third of the city's hotel residents lived in a widely varied class of dwellings called "rooming houses." A rooming house might range from a former single-family house to a three-hundred-room hostelry. Rooming house residents, half of them men, half women, and most of them young, worked as DEPARTMENT STORE clerks, secretaries, salesmen, or in journeymen construction BUILDING TRADES. Such work could not be counted on for every season of the year, so residents had to be within reasonable walking distance of multiple jobs. The NEAR NORTH SIDE was the city's most extensive rooming house district.

For people who were marginally employed in common labor jobs (from digging ditches to living in the off-season from field work or railroad construction) the only available homes were in hotel buildings disparagingly called "cheap lodging houses." Typically, half of a city's hotel homes were in such structures. In Chicago, the former Main Stem area on West Madison Street was nationally famous, although there were other cheap lodging house districts in the Near North and in several blocks in the racially segregated SOUTH SIDE.

During WORLD WAR I and WORLD WAR II, every type of residential hotel was filled to capacity with war workers. After 1945, however, many employers either closed or moved their factories to the edge of town. The cheap lodging house areas, especially, regained the reputation they had gained in the 1930s as "skid roads," known for large numbers of down-and-out men incorrectly assumed to be transients.

A postwar excess of lodging house rooms led city planners to see hotel districts as ideal for URBAN RENEWAL demolition. By the 1960s, the clearances were no longer eliminating excess rooms but rooms desperately needed for an increasingly fragile low-income population. Between 1973 and 1984 Chicago lost almost 23,000 hotel rooms, adding to a housing situation known as the "SRO crisis." Single-room occupancy and homelessness were often the only alternatives to hotel life at its cheapest levels.

Paul Groth

See also: Boardinghouses; Built Environment of the Chicago Region; Homelessness and Shelters; Housing, Single-room Occupancy; Near West Side

Further reading: Groth, Paul. *Living Downtown: The History of Residential Hotels in the United States.* 1994. • Hayner, Norman S. "The Hotel: The Sociology of Hotel Life." Ph.D. diss., University of Chicago. 1923. • Hoch, Charles, and Robert A. Slayton. *New Homeless and Old: Community and the Skid Row Hotel.* 1989.

Restaurants. Public dining has an important role in Chicago's social, cultural, and economic history. Types and numbers of eating establishments are tied to Chicago's growth from village to city. Dining outside the home may be divided into three broad categories: sit-down restaurants (from fine dining to "cheap" eateries); street food (including dining at public events such as ballgames and fairs); and a combination of these two, fast-food stands. Within these groups are varied establishments such as SALOONS of the PRE-PROHIBITION era, beer gardens, taverns, and cafeterias. All are or have been critical segments of the dining industry.

Because dining enterprises mirror the city's economic growth, their histories might be considered in two ways, "pull and push." Restaurants represent the centripetal forces that made the city the economic hub of the Midwest. Chicago's famed steakhouses testified to its hegemony in cattle shipping and meat processing. The city's historical core business area, the LOOP, has been an "economic catchment" center. Visitors to the Midwest's capital city and the necessity of feeding incoming hordes of workers made Chicago's eating places elements of a major industry. By 2000, the Chicago area's dining establishments did an

Interior of a restaurant with a primarily working-class male clientele, ca. 1895. Photographer: Unknown. Source: Chicago Historical Society.

estimated $10 billion in sales, second among U.S. metropolitan areas only to Los Angeles.

Types of prepared-food retailing businesses in the city followed this "pulling-in pattern" on three levels. Traditional sit-down, white-tablecloth restaurants became featured attractions for locals and visitors alike. The dining room of the Lake House HOTEL on Kinzie Street set the pattern in 1835. It used menu cards, napkins, and toothpicks and served oysters brought in from the East Coast. The many others that followed in the nineteenth century, from Henrici's to Rector's, made Chicago a destination restaurant city.

City shoppers and workers who packed downtown offices led to a boom in eating places. "Cheap Eats" restaurants first appeared in the 1880s, and many upscale restaurants and hotels served inexpensive lunches. Beginning in 1880 with H. H. Kohlsaat's "dairy lunch room," quick-service restaurants for midday meals sprang up. John Kruger began a small chain in the 1890s, dubbing them "Cafeterias." Soon, major chains such as Thompson's (with more than one hundred outlets), B/G Foods, Pixley & Ehlers, and many others were so numerous that the area around Madison and Clark Streets became known as "Toothpick Alley." Through proximity to WORK and shopping, city restaurants became magnets for urban populations.

Food stands and street vendors fall into the category of "petty consumption." Though important parts of the food economy, as cash businesses they are often underreported and hence an aspect of UNDERGROUND ECONOMY. Stands selling one of Chicago's paradigmatic foods, hot dogs, dot the city: an estimated 3,000 in present-day Chicago. None of the places are destination dining spots, but they are significant economic players by sheer numbers alone. By the end of the 1990s, the major purveyor of hot dogs in Chicago, the Vienna Sausage Manufacturing Company, was a business with some $98 million in annual sales. Neighborhoods into which immigrants moved and did business became identified with ethnic restaurants, particularly with fast-food (hot dog) stands.

Cafeterias and lunch counters were some of many INNOVATIONS in dining that "pushed out" across the country. Lunch counters, the ancestors of fast-food establishments, began in 1858 at Chicago's Rock Island RAILROAD Station. By 1900 the name "cafeteria" had spread across the country, carried along the TRANSPORTATION lines that flowed through the Chicago hub. Latter-day versions of this process are corporate fast-food dining places such as Chicago-area-based McDonald's. In 1997, McDonald's had sales of more than $33 billion worldwide, including $17 billion in the United States.

Fast food and cafeterias were not the only restaurant innovations that became national trends. Fred Mann opened a Chicago seafood restaurant in 1923 with a maritime decor that include fishnets, portholes, and waitresses dressed as sailors. An instant hit, other "theme" restaurants quickly sprang up across the country. The pattern was updated in the 1970s when Richard Melman and partners opened a series of casual dining restaurants in the Chicago area beginning with R. J. Grunts in 1971. The idea was quickly copied by national chains. By the end of the century, the company Melman founded, Lettuce Entertain You Enterprises, Inc., owned or licensed 70 restaurants across the United States and Japan. Like McDonald's, this and other dining enterprises have extended outward, thus enriching Chicago's economy and its reputation for dining.

Bruce Kraig

See also: Food Processing: Local Market; Foodways; Street Life; Street Peddling; Tourism and Conventions

Further reading: Drury, John. *Dining in Chicago: The Century of Progress Authorized Guide.* 1933. • Levenstein, Harvey. *Revolution at the Table: The Transformation of the American Diet.* 1988. • Shirecliffe, Arnold. "The Fascinating History of Early Chicago Restaurants." In *Chicago Restaurant Association Buyers' Guide,* 1945.

Restrictive Covenants. Restrictive covenants can limit a variety of options for homeowners, from landscaping to structural modifications to circumstances of sale or rental. Racially restrictive covenants, in particular, are

The Terrace Garden restaurant, located on the first floor of the Morrison Hotel at Clark and Madison in downtown Chicago, offered patrons live music and dancing with their lavish meals. In the 1920s when this picture was taken, the Morrison advertised itself as the focus of Chicago's downtown life. The restaurant was razed in 1965 for the construction of the First National Bank Building. Photographer: Unknown. Source: Chicago Historical Society.

contractual agreements among property owners that prohibit the purchase, lease, or occupation of their premises by a particular group of people, usually AFRICAN AMERICANS. Rare in Chicago before the 1920s, their widespread use followed the GREAT MIGRATION of southern blacks, the wave of housing-related racial violence which plagued the city between 1917 and 1921, and the U. S. Supreme Court's 1917 declaration that residential segregation ordinances were unconstitutional. The high court's subsequent dismissal of *Corrigan v. Buckley* in 1926 tacitly upheld these private, restrictive agreements and paved the way for their proliferation.

The Chicago REAL ESTATE Board (CREB) campaigned to blanket the city with such covenants and even provided a model contract, with a standard covenant drafted by Nathan William MacChesney, a member of the Chicago Plan Commission. In the fall of 1927, the CREB dispatched speakers across the city to promote the racial restrictions. Seen as the peaceful and progressive alternative to the violence that had earlier traumatized the city, restrictive covenants, within a year, according to the *Hyde Park Herald,* stretched "like a marvelous delicately woven chain of armor" from "the northern gates of HYDE PARK at 35th and Drexel Boulevard to WOODLAWN, Park Manor, SOUTH SHORE, Windsor Park, and all the far-flung white communities of the SOUTH SIDE." Two decades later, in the 85 square miles reserved for residential use in Chicago south of North Avenue, fewer than 10 were occupied by blacks, while 38, mainly in middle-class areas surrounding the BLACK BELT, were encumbered by these paper barriers. Even Al Capone's mother, Theresa, signed up to guarantee the "respectability" of the family home. White suburbanites could rest assured as developers in SKOKIE, PARK RIDGE, and EVANSTON wrote racial restrictions into the deeds on 1926–27 subdivisions. Restrictive covenants defined the white search for status and produced a "chilling effect" on potential black homeseekers.

In the end, Depression-era and wartime housing shortages probably did more to freeze Chicago's residential patterns than did the covenants. When challenged in 1938 by playwright Lorraine Hansberry's father, Carl, those covering the WASHINGTON PARK SUBDIVISION were ruled invalid (in *Lee v. Hansberry,* 1940). During WORLD WAR II, some local judges ruled against others on principled, as well as technical, grounds. Association with them soon became a political liability. Democrats defeated George B. McKibbin in the 1943 mayoralty after alleging that the Republican had signed just such a document; and in 1946, Richard J. Daley posed as the progressive, anti-covenant candidate in his race for sheriff. By 1947, the business and civic leaders framing the city's redevelopment program readily acquiesced in their prohibition. When the U.S. Supreme Court finally declared restrictive covenants unenforceable in *Shelley v. Kraemer* (1948), that decision did not so much dissolve an "iron ring" confining the city's black neighborhoods as much as it simply dissipated the legal clouds shadowing property already falling into black hands as a booming postwar housing market fostered mobility and racial succession.

Arnold R. Hirsch

See also: Blockbusting; Contested Spaces; Racism, Ethnicity, and White Identity; Real Estate; Redlining
Further reading: Long, Herman H., and Charles S. Johnson. *People vs. Property: Race Restrictive Covenants in Housing.* 1947. • Philpott, Thomas Lee. *The Slum and the Ghetto: Neighborhood Deterioration and Middle-Class Reform, Chicago, 1880–1930.* 1978. • Vose, Clement. *Caucasians Only: The Supreme Court, the NAACP, and the Restrictive Covenant Cases.* 1959.

Retail Geography. Retail geography has been a component of the evolving urban landscape of Chicago since the formal incorporation of the city in 1837. Historical records do not identify the first retailer in the city, but clearly the first major concentration of retail stores was located along Lake Street. Accounts of the Lake Street retail environment from the 1840s emphasized the rather slapdash construction of the stores and the rather coarse interactions between the dry-goods dealers and their customers. Despite the fact that Lake Street was one of the first streets in the city to be covered with wooden planks, travel up and down the STREET was at times quite difficult because of the heavy amount of animal and vehicular traffic in the area. The problem was exacerbated by bulky merchandise (such as building materials) that would extend beyond the wooden sidewalk into the main thoroughfare. By the mid-1850s, the intersection of Lake and Clark Streets was the nucleus of Chicago's retail environment. Here residents and travelers could find a bevy of goods ranging from ice skates to nails. Mirroring broader trends, several stores began to specialize in certain goods, such as haberdasheries and stores that only sold women's hats.

The South Water Street Market, located on the banks of the CHICAGO RIVER, emerged as an important center of activity for food distribution throughout Chicago. This WHOLESALE center was supplied by ships arriving from all around Lake Michigan. Photographs from the 1860s depict a scene much like the one found on Lake Street. Numerous carts and horses transported materials and goods from the ships to the wholesale retailers located on South Water Street, many of whom sold directly to mobile greengrocers who would later sell the produce from the back of their own horse-drawn carts. As the population of Chicago began to disperse, this type of mobile retail business became increasingly difficult, though it would persist in modified form into the twentieth century. By the early 1870s, the South Water Street Market was becoming an almost impossibly difficult place from which to transport goods around the city. Members of the local BUSINESS community, particularly those in the REAL-ESTATE industry, sought solutions from city leaders, but the question of South Water Street Market's future would not receive an official response until the early 1920s.

The next crucial development in the shifting retail geography in Chicago was the movement of the Field, Leiter & Co. store from

South Michigan Avenue between 111th and 115th in Roseland drew shoppers from all over Chicago's far South Side and the southern suburbs from the 1860s through the 1960s. This 1915 postcard illustrates why its range of stores attracted so much business in the mass transit era and why, with the wider use of automobiles, areas like this one with limited parking lost many of their customers to shopping malls. Photographer: Curt Teich & Co. Source: Curt Teich Archives, Lake County Discovery Museum.

Chicago's Retail Centers in 1948

Lake Street to the increasingly fashionable and business-friendly area developing along State Street. The development of State Street as a retailing mecca was aided by Potter Palmer, the Chicago mercantile king, who built an extravagant HOTEL at the corner of State and Monroe Streets and persuaded the city council to widen State Street. One contemporary observer, acknowledging PLANNING efforts in Paris, referred to Palmer's work as the "Haussmannizing of State Street." But most important to the retail community in Chicago was Palmer's role in persuading Field, Leiter & Co. to move into a rather ostentatious building on State Street.

It is difficult to overestimate the importance of Marshall Field on retail merchandising. Along with stocking dry goods in the Field, Leiter & Co. store at the corner of State and Washington, Field constantly maintained a stock of high-quality and cosmopolitan products, such as women's handbags and the latest fashions brought over from Paris. Field also helped maintain a loyal customer base through such innovative policies as a money-back guarantee and a competent and reliable delivery service. These customer-friendly policies were complemented by an almost astonishing array of ancillary services, such as children's playrooms, writing rooms, tearooms, and stenographic services. Marshall Field also kept a shrewd eye on the wholesale trade by contracting with the architect Henry Hobson Richardson to design a wholly modern wholesale goods distribution center at Adams and Wells Streets in 1885.

By the turn of the nineteenth century, most of the large-scale retail merchandisers had secured a place on the State Street corridor in the Loop. Along with Marshall Field's, Carson Pirie Scott and other large DEPARTMENT STORES had large and expansive emporiums that utilized large metal-framed display windows to showcase the wide variety of goods that they offered. Other prominent department stores included Mandel Brothers, the Boston Store, Rothschild's, Siegel, Cooper & Co., and the Stevens stores.

In the middle of the twentieth century, shopping in the Chicago region was still resolutely urban. It had developed around the historic business core of the city, which still accounted for an overwhelming proportion of total retail sales. It spread along major streetcar routes within the city, a seemingly endless string of family businesses, chain stores, and department store branches at key intersections. Beyond that, small retail concentrations were to be found in the downtowns of the region's satellite cities and the trackside business clusters of the railroad suburbs. The spread of the automobile at first simply reinforced this historic mass-transit-based pattern, because the plethora of city streets and slowly rising urban congestion limited the impact of the private car.

Once a common feature of many shopping areas, "dime stores" like this Grayslake store in the 1950s have disappeared from most neighborhoods. Their wide collections of goods, services, and conveniences are now found in ninety-nine-cent stores, grocery stores, drug stores, and large discount stores. Photographer: Unknown. Source: Grayslake Historical Society.

Arising at the same time as these magnificent edifices along State Street were the substantial retail centers in neighborhoods around Chicago. These retail businesses tended to reach their densest concentrations near TRANSPORTATION junctions, particularly near where the RAPID TRANSIT lines intersected with major STREET RAILWAY transfer stations. Two of the most important examples of this trend toward retail aggregation and clustering were 63rd and Halsted in ENGLEWOOD and Lawrence and Broadway in UPTOWN. As affordable and efficient transportation encouraged residential expansion around these increasingly popular areas, there was concomitant development within the retail environment. While many of these community and regional retail centers of activity would see their greatest flowering from the 1920s to the early 1950s, their presence within the urban environment was apparent by the first decade of the twentieth century.

In the years before WORLD WAR II, a new mode of retail geography began to develop in suburban Chicago. Older inner-ring suburbs that were intimately linked to the city by a network of interurbans also developed clusters of retail establishments at junctions of major transfer points. OAK PARK followed this pattern quite neatly, with a high concentration of major retailers at the intersection of Lake and Harlem Avenues, including a branch of Marshall Field's. At the same time, many other suburbs were building intricate and elaborately executed retail complexes that catered primarily to people with automobiles. One of the earliest such retail developments in the nation was Lake Forest Market Square in LAKE FOREST. Designed by the architect Howard Van Doren Shaw and constructed in 1916, this blend of retail and office space with residential APARTMENTS offered extensive PARKING facilities. The other early well-known retail development that catered to automobiles was the Spanish Court in WILMETTE. Built in 1926, this innovative development was also built with the understanding that many of its patrons would arrive by automobile.

Despite the increased competition from retail developments outside the city of Chicago, the downtown area maintained its dominant role as a major regional retail center of the first order. Even as late as 1958, it sold 8 times as many shopping goods as the largest regional center within the city (located at 63rd and Halsted) and had 10 times the total retail sales of this particular regional SHOPPING DISTRICT. While the downtown area maintained its position atop the city's hierarchy of retail centers, the central business district accounted for only 15 percent of all retail sales within the city of Chicago. Many of Chicago's neighborhoods were well served by a nexus of available retail options around major arterials, often including a small department store (such as a Wieboldt's or Goldblatt's) and a variety of other retail businesses.

Chicago's Retail Centers in 2000

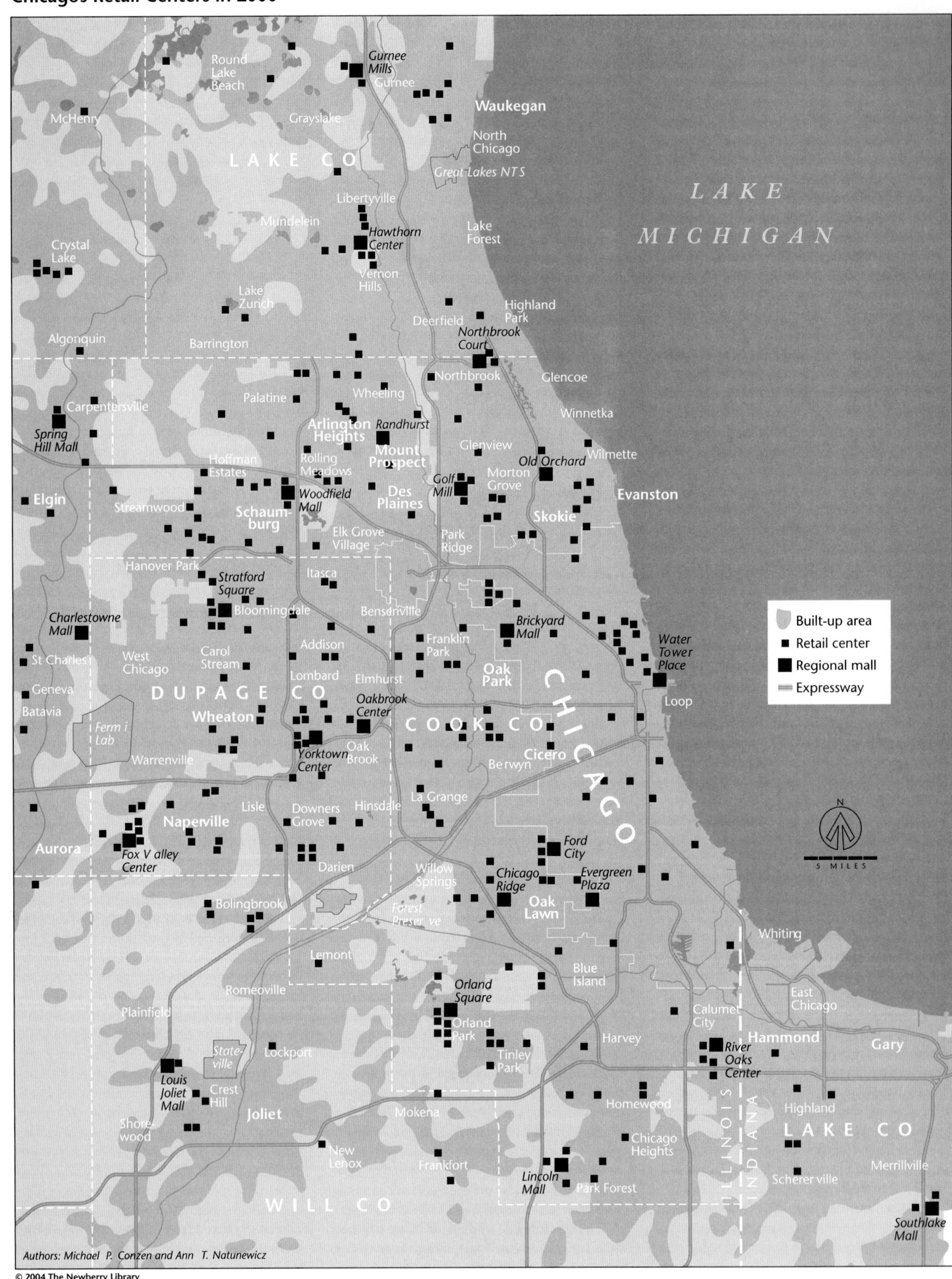

By century's end, shopping in metropolitan Chicago had been revolutionized. First, shopping plazas with off-street parking began the concentration of retail land use into favored nodes. Commercial strips incorporating such plazas also proliferated, especially along major arterial streets. But it was the building of the metropolitan expressways in the 1950s–80s that fundamentally realigned shopping locations for Chicagoans by providing widespread access to the new shopping malls and regional supermalls. By 2000 there were at least 23 regional malls within the contiguous built-up area. Most of the old commercial ribbons along major city streets atrophied, except where foot traffic remained strong, and downtown Chicago retail businesses faced severe competition from suburban competitors, leading a number of department stores to close in the urban core, having repositioned their sales space in the outlying malls.

Planned retail developments became increasingly popular after World War II in the Chicago metropolitan area, though few were built within the city for several decades. One of the most well-known planned retail centers was Evergreen Plaza, located right outside the city limits at 95th and Western. Evergreen Plaza was developed by real-estate mogul Arthur Rubloff, who had initially conceived of such a plan in 1936. When it was finished in 1952, Evergreen Plaza had approximately 500,000 square feet of retail space and 1,200 parking spaces. Cars could easily pull in off the street into the parking lot, and the plaza also featured a conveyor belt that transported GROCERIES from the supermarkets to a parking-area kiosk.

While many of these retail developments were built to accommodate a growing suburban population that was moving out to well-established suburbs in the metropolitan area, still other planned retail developments were built in conjunction with towns that were built totally from the ground up. PARK FOREST Plaza was a well-received example of this emerging retail complex style that sought to mimic a previous era in the history of town planning. At Park Forest Plaza, the architects Loebl, Schlossman, and Bennett placed a landscaped court amidst a circle of shops and surrounded the entire area with parking.

In the city of Chicago, many retailers in neighborhoods faced with widespread DEMOGRAPHIC shifts fell on increasingly hard times throughout the 1960s and 1970s. Former areas of robust retail spending, including many of those on the South and West Sides, found themselves plagued by arsonists, robbery, and a general decline in the socioeconomic makeup of their clientele. The city of Chicago attempted to alleviate the dwindling returns of these neighborhood retail centers by diverting automobile traffic from the main area of pedestrian traffic. While this policy might have been successful in OAK PARK (which created a small downtown pedestrian mall in 1974), it was met with resistance and apathy by shoppers and retailers alike along State Street, which was turned into a "pedestrian-friendly" street in 1979 and then restored to traffic in 1996.

Many of the city's formerly vibrant neighborhood retail areas continued on a downward spiral through the 1980s and 1990s. Planned retail developments such as Ford City on the city's Southwest Side seemed to siphon business away from surrounding neighborhoods rather than drawing nearby suburbanites into the area. Large-scale retail developments in the suburbs continued emerging throughout the late 1970s and early 1980s, with several notable examples, including the Old Orchard Mall in SKOKIE and Woodfield Mall in SCHAUMBURG, drawing city and suburban residents. Many of these malls began to offer a diverse set of amenities such as children's playgrounds, valet parking, and senior citizen days.

Another retail development, the "big-box" retail store, began to situate itself within both the urban and suburban fabric in the 1980s and early 1990s. Like many of their historical predecessors, these massive single-story structures were frequently located at significant transportation junctions, such as the confluence of major highways or freeway exits. While big-box retail developments remained popular through the 1990s in the city and surrounding suburbs, the LOOP has a seen a new influx of contemporary retailers, many of them occupying prime retail space along State Street. Along North Michigan Avenue, the much-heralded "vertical malls," such as Water Tower Place, remain popular and highly visible destinations for tourists, suburbanites, and Chicagoans.

Max Grinnell

See also: Economic Geography; Food Processing: Local Market; Magnificent Mile; Maxwell Street; Motoring; Retail Workers; Street Life; Street Peddling

Further reading: Berry, Brian. *Commercial Structure and Commercial Blight: Retail Patterns and Processes in the City of Chicago.* 1963. • Breese, Gerald William. "The Daytime Population of the Central Business District of Chicago." Ph.D. diss., University of Chicago. 1947. • Condit, Carl W. *Chicago, 1930–70: Building, Planning, and Urban Technology.* 1974.

Retail Workers. Chicago's explosive development in the wake of the CIVIL WAR propelled the city to preeminence as the leading manufacturing, TRANSPORTATION, and retail metropolis in the nation's interior, rivaled only by New York for much of the twentieth century. Retail giants Marshall Field & Co., Sears, Roebuck & Co., and Montgomery Ward all called Chicago home. These and other Chicago firms played leading roles in the creation of American consumer society; they also became leading employers of thousands of men and women in the city. By 1904, for example, Marshall Field's State Street store employed nearly 10,000 individuals.

Throughout Chicago's history, the variety of retail establishments demanded a diverse workforce, from individuals working alongside owners in specialty and neighborhood shops to the thousands toiling for large DEPARTMENT STORES with complex occupational hierarchies. Early retail clerks were primarily men who operated a small store from open to close and often slept on the counter to accommodate customers throughout the night. Beginning with the Civil War, retailers began employing women, a trend that continued with the emergence of large department and discount stores. From the early twentieth century, women have occupied a majority of retail positions, though men have continued to dominate supervisory jobs. Until the 1960s, when the federal government began enforcing equal opportunity laws, most employers practiced overt racial discrimination, refusing to hire persons of color for positions requiring contact with the public.

Retail workers faced poor working conditions and pay, especially before the passage of the Fair Labor Standards Act in 1938. Sales clerks served unusually long hours, toiling from 6 a.m. to 9 p.m. daily, plus a half-day on Sundays. Responsible for opening and closing the store, keeping shelves stocked, sweeping the sales floor, and devoting personal attention to each customer, retail workers toiled under sweatshop-like conditions. In an 1899 study, Annie MacLean of the UNIVERSITY OF CHICAGO went undercover to experience the life of a retail worker in a Chicago department store. MacLean reported that saleswomen were forced to stand the entire day, eat their lunches in cramped rooms, and survive on below-subsistence wages, prompting many to turn to PROSTITUTION. MacLean concluded that only UNIONIZATION would solve the problems of overwork and low pay.

Male retail workers in Chicago had attempted to organize as early as 1841, when downtown retail store and brokerage clerks banded together to form an Early Closing Association, forcing employers to adopt an 8 p.m. closing time. By the early 1890s, the Retail Clerks International Protective Association (RCIPA) boasted a local in Chicago, though organizers made more headway in GROCERY STORES than in dry goods establishments and department stores. Although the union officially demanded equal pay for women, the RCIPA failed to promote the organization of saleswomen, who made up a large chunk of the department store workforce by the 1920s.

Despite the low pay, poor work conditions, and indifference of organized labor, working-class white women flocked to retail occupations by the turn of the twentieth century. Sales

This 1873 engraving reflects the gendered landscape of the nineteenth-century retail environment. The clerks are all men; the shoppers, almost all women. Artist: Unknown. Source: The Newberry Library.

jobs offered white-collar respectability and pay commensurate with CLERICAL positions, while granting a degree of autonomy not available outside of NURSING and teaching. If the first half of the twentieth century represented the heyday of the American department store, it also witnessed the rise of the saleswoman as a legitimate profession in the eyes of the industry. Though still underpaid in comparison to men, saleswomen achieved a status according to which their skills in selling products and cultivating customer loyalty were recognized as central to their firms' success.

The increasing size of department stores and their workforces led to greater attempts at unionization in the 1930s, led by the newly formed United Retail, Wholesale, and Department Store Employees of America. Though unsuccessful at penetrating the huge emporiums on State Street, the union did organize the workers of MAIL-ORDER king Montgomery Ward in 1940, precipitating the most notorious labor conflict of WORLD WAR II. When Ward's chairman Sewell Avery refused to renew the union's contract in 1944, President Roosevelt's National War Labor Board authorized the U.S. Army to seize the company to guarantee the flow of consumer goods. The union then won a recertification election in a landslide. In the long run, however, retail unions have been unable to overcome employer resistance to organize sales clerks on a significant scale in Chicago.

In the post–World War II era, the changing nature of the retail industry reshaped the character of retail WORK. While in 1940 large, urban department stores featured active salespeople, by the end of the century major chains preferred smaller, suburban stores relying on television ADVERTISING and self-service displays. Although retail workers now benefited from federal minimum-wage and maximum-hour legislation, employers increasingly turned to a part-time, seasonal workforce to lower labor costs. While State Street and Michigan Avenue's "MAGNIFICENT MILE" still beckoned urban shoppers and tourists to Chicago, the city's retail workforce toiled primarily for companies whose headquarters were located elsewhere.

Daniel A. Graff

See also: Antiunionism; New Deal; Retail Geography; Work Culture

Further reading: Benson, Susan Porter. *Counter Cultures: Saleswomen, Managers, and Customers in American Department Stores, 1890–1940.* 1986. • Hendrickson, Robert. *The Grand Emporiums: The Illustrated History of America's Great Department Stores.* 1979. • Kirstein, George G. *Stores and Unions: A Study of the Growth of Unionism in Dry Goods and Department Stores.* 1950.

Rhythm and Blues. From the first decades after WORLD WAR II, Chicago was a major center for rhythm and blues, a new eclectic style of black-appeal popular music that grew out of BLUES and JAZZ. Operating out of "Record Row" (Cottage Grove between 47th and 50th), Chicago's independent record companies, including Chicago's Miracle (founded 1946), CHESS (founded as Aristocrat in 1947), Chance (1950), United (1952), and Vee-Jay (1953), helped to spread its popularity nationally and internationally.

Phil and Leonard Chess had achieved their original success with blues artists before becoming a major factor in the exploding R&B market with such guitarist/singers as Chuck Berry and Bo Diddley and such vocal harmony groups as the Flamingos and the Moonglows. Vee-Jay, founded by Jimmy Bracken and Vivian Carter, enjoyed success on both the R&B and pop charts with bluesman Jimmy Reed and with groups like the Spaniels and El Dorados. Many of these R&B artists crossed over to the pop charts and contributed significantly to the development of ROCK 'n' roll.

By the early 1960s, a relocated Record Row on South Michigan Avenue became the production, distribution, and marketing center for a new style of gospelized R&B called soul. The first notable Chicago soul-style record was Vee-Jay's "For Your Precious Love," a 1958 hit by Jerry Butler and the Impressions. Other notable Vee-Jay soul artists were Dee Clark, Betty Everett, and Gene Chandler. Led by producer Carl Davis, Chicago-based Okeh (Columbia's independently distributed R&B subsidiary) had huge success in the soul market with Major Lance, Billy Butler, Walter Jackson, and the Vibrations. Under Roquel "Billy" Davis, Chess produced hits for Etta James, Little Milton, the Dells, and Billy Stewart. George Leaner's One-derful (1962) specialized in southern-style "hard soul," featuring screamed lyrics, melisma (melodic embellishment), and rasping timbres. His most notable artists included Otis Clay, McKinley Mitchell, and the Five Du-Tones. These independent soul labels benefited from their policy of maintaining woodshedding practice studios and house bands that kept creativity high.

At Brunswick, Carl Davis produced major 1970s soul hits by Jackie Wilson, Barbara Acklin, Tyrone Davis, and the Chi-Lites. Curtis Mayfield, who with the Impressions had been one of Chicago's most significant R&B groups, helped pioneer the funk style of soul with his *Superfly* soundtrack, produced on his own Curtom label.

Although the city's record industry declined after the 1970s, Chicago continued to contribute to R&B. It introduced America in the 1980s to a dance-oriented version of R&B called house, a disco variant developed by club deejays at the Warehouse on the West Side. In the next decade, Chicago-based performers R. Kelly, Common (Rashied Lynn), and Crucial Conflict had national R&B hits.

Robert Pruter

See also: African Americans; Chicago Sound; Rap; Record Publishing

Further reading: Pruter, Robert. *Chicago Soul.* 1991. • Pruter, Robert. *Doowop: The Chicago Scene.* 1996. • Rowe, Mike. *Chicago Blues: The City and the Music.* 1981.

Richmond, IL, McHenry County, 54 miles NW of the Loop. Sheltering a well-maintained collection of two dozen beautiful Victorian-era homes, Richmond was founded in 1844 adjacent to a mill on the Nippersink Creek. Incorporated in 1872 to accommodate RAILROAD-related growth which never materialized, the community is now a mecca for antique collectors. Its population in 2000 was 1,091.

Craig L. Pfannkuche

See also: McHenry County

Further reading: *McHenry County in the Twentieth Century, 1968–1994.* McHenry County Historical Society. 1994. • Nye, Lowell A., ed. *McHenry County, Illinois, 1832–1968.* 1968.

Richton Park, IL, Cook County, 28 miles S of the Loop. Richton Park is a largely residential village located on the southern border of COOK COUNTY.

The village sits astride the Sauk Trail, a modern highway that follows the course of a NATIVE AMERICAN transportation route that ran from Rock Island on the Mississippi River across Illinois and Indiana to Detroit. By the late 1840s GERMAN migrants began farming in the area, then known as Thorn Creek.

After the arrival of the ILLINOIS CENTRAL RAILROAD in 1852, developers established a depot and platted a small agricultural village where the rail line crossed the Sauk Trail. In 1926, the Illinois Central Railroad electrified its suburban lines, with Richton as the last stop. Local residents incorporated the village, renaming it Richton Park. There was a brief burst of REAL-ESTATE development, but Richton Park remained a tiny community surrounded by farms heavily planted with asparagus.

When Chicago's suburban sprawl finally pushed into the area in the late 1960s and 1970s, the village's population boomed as it annexed new housing developments. There were 2,558 people living in the village in 1970. By 1980 the population had grown to nearly 9,403, and in 2000 the village had 12,533 residents.

Thousands of these new residents were AFRICAN AMERICAN. In 1970, virtually the village's entire population was white. By 1980, 7 percent of the population was African American, while persons of Hispanic descent made up about 4 percent of the residents. By 2000, 60 percent of Richton Park's residents were African American.

The geography of contemporary Richton Park bears little resemblance to the depot village that was platted on the mid-nineteenth-century prairie. The Sauk Trail is a commercial strip of mostly small businesses surrounded by housing SUBDIVISIONS. Although the PARKING lot of the up-to-date METRA station creates a central gathering place of sorts for commuters, nearly 5,000 of the 6,000 village COMMUTERS travel by automobile. They spend an average of 80 minutes in their cars each day getting to and from work, with the recently constructed nearby interchange on Interstate 57 providing ready, if at times somewhat congested, access to Chicago.

The residents of Richton Park are, on average, slightly wealthier than those living in the city of Chicago and Cook County as a whole. There are a substantial number of APARTMENTS in the village and one-third of the 4,500 households are made up of renters. But the majority of the village's residents live in their own single-family homes, which approach the median value for Chicago's south suburbs. Like many other south suburbs, Richton Park has attracted much new housing construction in recent years, and many of the newest houses are worth much more than the village's older, more modest homes.

Ian McGiver

See also: Economic Geography; Metropolitan Growth

Further reading: Andreas, A. T. *History of Cook County, Illinois.* 1884.

Ringwood, IL, McHenry County, 55 miles NW of the Loop. After the C&NW RAILROAD built through a large tree-ringed meadow, area residents platted a village there in 1854. Although little growth occurred for over a century, in 1994, fearing that they would lose their historic identity to an expanding JOHNSBURG, residents voted to incorporate. The population in 2000 was 471.

Craig L. Pfannkuche

See also: McHenry County

Further reading: *McHenry County in the Twentieth Century, 1968–1994.* McHenry County Historical Society. 1994. • Nye, Lowell A., ed. *McHenry County, Illinois, 1832–1968.* 1968.

River Forest, IL, Cook County, 10 miles W of the Loop. River Forest occupies two and a half square miles in western COOK COUNTY near its sister community of OAK PARK. Located along the eastern bank of the DES PLAINES RIVER, River Forest is noted for its many elegant houses designed and constructed at the turn of the century by, among others, Frank Lloyd Wright. The character of this era remains apparent and appreciated today, as River Forest enjoys some of the highest property values in the Chicago area.

OJIBWA, Menominee, and POTAWATOMI inhabited the River Forest area until the 1830s. In 1831, George Bickerdike and Mark Noble constructed a steam-powered sawmill on the Aux Plaines (now Des Plaines) River. Five years later, Ashbel Steele, coroner and later sheriff of Cook County, arrived, becoming the first permanent resident of Noyesville, a predecessor of River Forest.

Other settlers soon followed Steele to Noyesville, attracted by its proximity to Chicago. The area's fertile land, thick forests, and river location lent itself to farming and hog raising. A plank road constructed along present-day Lake Street in 1842 and the construction and opening of the Galena & Chicago Union RAILROAD in the late 1840s further helped to facilitate growth.

Two prominent families arrived in the 1850s and became the first subdividers of the area. The Henry Quick family arrived in Noyesville from Harlem, New York. Quick soon became a prominent landholder and lent his original hometown's name to the eastern portion of Noyesville as well as to Harlem Avenue. The David Thatcher family settled to the west and named their portion of the community Thatcher. The Quick clan donated land to the Episcopal church, while Solomon Thatcher (no relation to David) did the same for the Methodist and ROMAN CATHOLIC churches. These communities continued to grow over the next 30 years, helped by mass relocation after the Great Chicago FIRE OF 1871.

The temperance movement provided the spark for River Forest's incorporation in 1880. Feeling threatened by Harlem's saloonkeepers, community leaders quickly held an election in which voters approved incorporation. Opponents questioned the election's legality, but the Illinois Supreme Court upheld the results.

Ironically, community trustees approved licenses for two SALOONS to help provide revenue for city improvements. This money helped pay for the bricking of streets, electric streetcars and lights, the community waterworks, TELEPHONE service, and the public library.

With these urban amenities in place, River Forest became even more attractive and entered its period of greatest growth. Settlement once concentrated near Oak Park and the railroad fanned out north and west. From a population of 1,000 in 1894, River Forest's population exploded to 8,829 people in 1930. Reflecting the growth, CONCORDIA and Rosary Colleges located here in 1913 and 1918, respectively. Rosary College was renamed DOMINICAN UNIVERSITY in 1997.

After the 1930s, River Forest's rate of growth slowed as the community built out to its borders. Most expansion since then has occurred through the SUBDIVISION of estates. River

Forest's population hit its peak of 13,402 in 1970 and has remained fairly constant since then.

Aaron Harwig

See also: Architecture: The Prairie School; Government, Suburban; Infrastructure; Prohibition and Temperance; Protestants

Further reading: Hausman, Harriet. *Reflections: A History of River Forest.* 1975. • Historical Society of Oak Park and River Forest, Oak Park, IL.

River Grove, IL, Cook County, 11 miles W of the Loop. River Grove's past remains visible in the open spaces that make up approximately 50 percent of the community. The river and forest land, once home to the POTAWATOMI, was not officially opened for sale in River Grove until 1833, although special exceptions were made in private purchases from Indians. One such instance was that of half-FRENCH, half-Indian Claude LaFramboise, who, in the 1829 TREATY of Prairie du Chien, received land along the DES PLAINES RIVER that encompassed most of what would become River Grove. In 1833 Framboise sold the northern half of his land to his sister and the other half to Jesse Walker. Walker's share eventually passed to Walker's son-in-law, David Everett, who held Methodist services in his cabin. Triton COLLEGE is now on the site of Everett's land.

In 1834 Walker and Everett erected a BRIDGE that crossed the Des Plaines River along an Indian trail, later Grand Avenue. A stagecoach line using the trail and bridge took passengers from Chicago to Galena. In the 1840s the Spencer brothers built a HOTEL at the crossing to cater to travelers. The hotel and the settlement were named Cazenovia after the brothers' hometown in New York. The area east of the river was later named Turner Park.

In 1872 Richard Rhodes purchased land on the south side of Grand. He subdivided the 100 acres and put up six houses, calling the community Rhodes subdivision. A school and the First Presbyterian Church of River Park were established soon after. Both Rhodes and another SUBDIVISION west of the river, north of Grand near the railroad, were incorporated into River Grove in 1888. Altogether, this gave River Grove an estimated population of 200, four-fifths of whom were GERMAN.

Until the 1920s most newcomers into the area were German, predominantly Lutheran. Almost all were blue-collar workers, the majority working for the Milwaukee Railroad yards in FRANKLIN PARK. In 1920 Volk Realty established the Chicago Home Gardens subdivision north of the Oak Park County Club and west of ELMWOOD PARK. Village residents had electricity, GAS lines, and TELEPHONE service; a bank, movie theater, and Catholic church all were erected within the decade. Population rose to 484 in 1920 and by 1930 was at 2,741.

Triton College, on the village's southern border, opened in 1964. By 2000 River Grove's population had climbed to 10,668, with many of IRISH, POLISH, CROATIAN, and ITALIAN heritage and a growing number of Hispanics. River Grove's vast amount of unoccupied space includes 350 acres of FOREST PRESERVE, 290 acres of GOLF courses and cemeteries, 35 acres of public school property, and 6 acres of parkland.

Marilyn Elizabeth Perry

See also: Protestants; Streets and Highways

Further reading: Schacht, Sylvia Norten. *When River Grove Was Young, 1888–1938.* 1985. • Vercammen, Martha Ridge. *The Making of River Grove: A Centennial Publication.* 1988.

Riverdale, Community Area 54, 16 miles SE of the Loop. Riverdale became a community area by default, an industrial area bound by the ILLINOIS CENTRAL RAILROAD on the west, the city limits on the south, the Bishop Ford EXPRESSWAY on the east, and 115th Street on the north. Its first nonnative residents settled on the banks of the Little Calumet River in 1836, farming and operating a toll bridge across the river along the Chicago-Thornton Road. A second settlement grew up around the junction of the Illinois and Michigan Central Railroads at Kensington in 1852. Between the two at Wildwood, James H. Bowen of the Calumet and Chicago Canal and Dock Company built a summer home where Chicago's elites gathered in the 1870s and '80s. Until 1945, however, almost all of Riverdale's residents lived in the part of the KENSINGTON settlement south of 115th Street and around the original settlement at its far southwest edge.

Most of Riverdale's swampy land was used or ZONED for a wide range of manufacturing and industrial purposes. From the 1850s on, the RAILROADS that cut through the area claimed significant pieces of its land for rights-of-way and yards. The PULLMAN Land Association controlled significant acreage there along Lake CALUMET into the second half of the twentieth century. Riverdale was home to the Pullman Farm, fertilized by the sewage from the famous town, and the Pullman brickyards. Its largest industry began as the Calumet Paint Company in an abandoned church near both Pullman and the lake. By beginning of the twentieth century, Sherwin-Williams had purchased the plant and turned it into one of America's largest paint manufactories. Jobs there, along with those at Chicago Drop Forge, the Illinois Terra Cotta Works, and the Swift and Knickerbocker Ice plants, made Riverdale a place where far more people worked than lived until the end of World War II.

City, county, metropolitan, state, and federal agencies also controlled a substantial amount of land in Riverdale, and their actions shaped Riverdale's development. The Metropolitan Sanitary District (Metropolitan Water Reclamation District of Greater Chicago) located a sewage treatment plant there in the 1922 to service the growing communities nearby. Riverdale's most eastern region became part of the Beaubien FOREST PRESERVE. Governmental improvements on the Little Calumet and Lake Calumet and the construction of the Cal-Sag Channel shaped industrial development in Riverdale more generally.

Government actions also transformed Riverdale into a residential community when the National Housing Agency, the Federal Public Housing Authority, and the CHICAGO HOUSING AUTHORITY opened the massive Altgeld Gardens Housing Project in 1945. In 1954, the CHA built the Phillip Murray Homes nearby. The rapid transformation of Riverdale from an industrial area with 1,500 people in the 1940s into a residential area with 12,000 by the 1960s overtaxed the limited services available in the community. The fact that most of those residents were AFRICAN AMERICAN made sharing services with the nearby white communities problematic. Community leaders in ROSELAND spearheaded a drive against Altgeld Gardens even before it was built. Discriminatory practices in nearby HOSPITALS made it extremely difficult to get emergency health care there. In the 1960s, SCHOOLS became a battleground when district boundaries would have sent white students from WEST PULLMAN to Carver High School and black students from Riverdale to grade schools in West Pullman.

Riverdale's population reached its peak of 15,018 in 1970 after the construction of Eden Greens, one of the nation's first majority black-owned and -operated townhouse and apartment developments, in 1968. Eventually the project, sponsored by the Antioch Missionary Baptist Church and targeted for low- and moderate-income families, included one thousand units.

Since that time, Riverdale has lost both population and jobs. Industrial wastes from the factories that once operated there have polluted large tracts of land. By 1990 only 10,821 people lived there. Sixty-three percent of its households lived in poverty. Thirty-five percent of its workers were unemployed.

Janice L. Reiff

See also: Calumet Region; Economic Geography; Public Housing; Sanitory and Ship Canal; School Desegregation

Further reading: Andreas, A. T. *History of Cook County, Illinois.* 1884. • *Calumet Index.* Various issues. • *South End Reporter.* Various issues.

Riverdale, IL, Cook County, 16 miles S of the Loop. Riverdale shares borders with

Chicago to the northeast, DOLTON to the east and south, HARVEY to the southwest, DIXMOOR and forest preserves to the west, and CALUMET PARK to the northwest. The area north of 138th Street and east of Indiana Avenue, and across the Little Calumet River, is also known as Riverdale and was ANNEXED to Chicago in 1889. Riverdale shares a history with all these communities, and especially with Chicago and Dolton. The villages of Dolton and Riverdale were practically one community until each incorporated in 1892. Today Riverdale includes neighborhoods known as Highlawn and Ivanhoe.

The old Indian Boundary Line crosses through the northwestern part of the village. NATIVE AMERICANS ceded land to the northwest of this line in 1816 in the TREATY of St. Louis. The rest was ceded by the Treaty of Chicago in 1833.

The first settler in the Riverdale area after Indian removal was George Dolton, who settled where an old Indian trail (Lincoln Avenue) crossed the Little Calumet River in 1835 and operated a ferry with J. C. Matthews until 1842, when a toll bridge was built at what was known as "Riverdale Crossing."

Riverdale developed as a farming community at the river crossing. GERMANS and DUTCH came to the area in the 1840s and 1850s as farmers and lumbermen. In 1852 the ILLINOIS CENTRAL RAILROAD came through Riverdale, and by 1880 a total of six railroads crossed the area.

Industries that followed—including distilleries, lumber yards, ice houses, cattle pens, barrel makers, and a sugar refinery—attracted IRISH, SWEDISH, and Russian German workers to Riverdale. The dredging of the Little Calumet River and the construction of Cal-Sag Channel between 1911 and 1922 further stimulated industry. In 1918 Acme Steel Company located on the river and became a major force in the local economy. In 1919, the region's first artificial ice plant, the Federal Ice Refrigerating Company, built a plant in Riverdale.

In the mid-1920s the Illinois Central was electrified and elevated, resulting in improved COMMUTER service to Chicago. Residential expansion in the 1920s included the Ivanhoe subdivision. The GREAT DEPRESSION brought an end to residential construction, but WPA workers built sewers, curbs, and paved streets. The flight from the city after World War II resulted in renewed building until 1960. Ready access to Interstate 57 and 94 and two METRA commuter stations fostered residential development.

The early 1980s saw an influx of AFRICAN AMERICANS looking for better housing and schools. Riverdale's population was 15,055 in 2000, with a black population of 87 percent.

Dave Bartlett

See also: Calumet Region; Government, Suburban; Water

Further reading: League of Women Voters of Riverdale. *Spotlight on Riverdale.* 1958. • Thillman, Mary. *Celebrate the Centennial of the Village of Riverdale: A Century of Pride, 1892–1992.* N.d. • Zimmerman, J. F., comp. "History of Incorporated Municipalities of Thornton Township." 1938.

Riverine Systems. Compared to other areas of Illinois, the Chicago region boasts few rivers and streams. However, these rivers figure largely in the city's history. Chicago is located at the divide between the St. Lawrence River basin, draining to the North Atlantic, and the Mississippi River basin, draining to the Gulf of Mexico. Near SUMMIT, Illinois, only 10 feet of elevation separate these two basins where the CHICAGO and DES PLAINES RIVERS flow within a few miles of each other. The earliest European travelers across this PORTAGE immediately saw the potential for a continuous water route from the North Atlantic to the Gulf, influencing the growth of the city.

Chicago's riverine systems can be classified into three main groups, whose distribution reflects the last GLACIATION. The main rivers in the area—the Chicago, upper Des Plaines, and Calumet—all have gentle slopes. They run parallel to the shoreline of LAKE MICHIGAN before turning, either toward the lake or the Illinois River. These rivers lie in valleys inherited from the glacial landscape. Low ridges of rock debris or sand, left by the retreating glaciers and wave action in glacial Lake Chicago, follow the southern shoreline of the lake, directing the rivers in their intervening valleys. In contrast, the many steep ravines of the North Shore suburbs along Lake Michigan have a different origin. As the glacier retreated and the lake's level fell, streams flowing lakeward began to erode the newly exposed surfaces. The ravines thus created are continuing to erode toward their headwaters. Finally, on the edge of the Chicago region lie larger river valleys with steeper gradients that supported the development of water power. The Fox and Kankakee Rivers flow through substantial valleys carved from bedrock by huge torrents of water from the melting glaciers, while the lower Des Plaines flows through the old outlet of Lake Chicago. The canals connecting Lake Michigan and the Illinois River follow this outwash channel.

Since their establishment by glaciers, the rivers and their drainage basins have been highly modified for water power, navigation, sanitation, and flood control, affecting the patterns of settlement in the Chicago Region. Euro-Americans' initial settlement of the prairie country occurred along the spines of the chief watersheds during the early 1800s. Watercourses not only provided wood and WATER; they functioned as highways along which farmers could transport their goods from the countryside to cities. The rivers then became the first engines of industrialization, particularly along the FOX RIVER. Its steeper gradient made possible the first mills constructed in the region, in the 1830s. The post–Civil War decades saw water-power-dependent manufacturing expand dramatically with sawmills, foundries, machine shops, wool factories, and wagon and plow works.

As industrialization and urbanization intensified, so did pollution and flooding. By the end of the nineteenth century, the Chicago-area

One of Highland Park's characteristic ravines, 1912. Photographer: C. H. Warren & Co. Source: Curt Teich Archives, Lake County Discovery Museum.

waterways were open sewers, threatening PUBLIC HEALTH with typhoid and other water-related epidemics. Contamination of Lake Michigan by industrial and municipal sewage flowing into the CHICAGO RIVER was the main impetus for the construction of the Chicago SANITARY AND SHIP CANAL, which reversed the flow of the Chicago River. Completed in 1900, the canal flooded major portions of the Illinois River valley and polluted the river downstream to Peoria, killing virtually all of the fish and other aquatic animals for more than one hundred miles downstream. Despite the construction of the world's largest sewage treatment plant at STICKNEY, pollution has continued to be a major problem, exacerbated by the low gradient of the Chicago River and the paving of vast areas of wetlands and prairies. During large storms, runoff, with nowhere to seep into the soil, is concentrated into storm sewers, overflowing their capacity. The polluted runoff, mixed with sewage, reestablishes the river's old flow into Lake Michigan. To counter this problem, the Metropolitan Water Reclamation District has ultimately modified the riverine system, creating the Tunnel and Reservoir Plan (TARP), a parallel river system in enormous underground structures.

Daniel Schneider
Glenn Sandiford

See also: Calumet River System; Flood Control and Drainage; Illinois & Michigan Canal; Water Supply

Further reading: Bretz, J. Harlen. *Geology of the Chicago Region.* Part 1. 1939. • Ranney, Edward. *Prairie Passage: The Illinois and Michigan Canal Corridor.* 1998. • Sauer, Carl Ortwin. *Geography of the Upper Illinois Valley and History of Development.* 1916.

Riverside, IL, Cook County, 10 miles W of the Loop. Riverside, on the Des Plaines River, was designed in 1868 by Frederick Law Olmsted, the nation's most famous landscape architect. The innovative street plan and the striking open spaces are regarded as landmarks in American residential PLANNING.

In 1863 the Chicago, Burlington & Quincy RAILROAD was built through the area, and five years later a group of local investors decided to take advantage of both the railroad and the uniquely attractive site where it crossed the DES PLAINES RIVER. Forming the Riverside Improvement Company, they purchased a 1,600-acre tract of land along the river and hired Frederick Law Olmsted of New York to design an elite suburban community. Olmsted and his partner, Calvert Vaux, were already famous for creating Central Park in New York City. Their reputation, plus the lovely curvilinear streets, open spaces, and attractive village center they designed for Riverside, attracted Chicago's elite. By the fall of 1871 a number of large, expensive houses were occupied or under construction and an elegant HOTEL had opened.

Unfortunately for the developers, the Chicago FIRE OF 1871 drained away both CONSTRUCTION crews and capital from the village. The financial panic of 1873 compounded the company's troubles and it went bankrupt.

The demise of the improvement company brought new construction nearly to a halt for some time. A village government was established in September 1875 and Olmsted's original development plan remained in force. In 1893 several wealthy local residents formed an association and opened the Riverside Golf Club, one of the oldest GOLF clubs in the Chicago area. Frank Lloyd Wright, Louis Sullivan, William Le Baron Jenney, and several other prominent local architects drew the plans for houses that still stand in the village. A striking Romanesque village hall was built in 1895, and in 1901 the Burlington line constructed a charming stone RAILROAD STATION.

A major period of residential development came in the 1920s and late 1930s, when many modest houses were constructed on smaller parcels. The population grew to 7,935 by 1940 and comprised primarily small proprietors, managers, and professionals who were predominantly of Anglo-American and GERMAN American background. The remaining residential areas were developed during the post–WORLD WAR II boom and by 1960 no space was left. Population peaked at 10,357 in 1970 and dropped below 8,500 by the mid-1990s.

Riverside remains a beautiful, upscale suburban community, but one with a wider price range of homes than is found in the more uniformly wealthy suburbs along the North Shore. It includes small, well-maintained BUNGALOWS, larger comfortable houses from the 1920s and 1950s, and huge Victorian and early-twentieth-century mansions that attract architectural tours. The charming village center is replete with chic restaurants, cappuccino bars, and stores selling antiques and Victorian house fixtures. Riverside was fairly affluent and all white in 1940 and remained so at the end of the century. The only DEMOGRAPHIC changes that have occurred recently are the growing number of older residents and the influx of younger families of IRISH, POLISH, CZECH, and Scandinavian backgrounds, the wealthy children and grandchildren of Chicago's old ethnic working class. The entire village was designated a National Historical Landmark in 1970.

Joseph L. Arnold

See also: Architecture: The City Beautiful; Government, Suburban; Historic Preservation; Landscape Design; Planning Chicago

Further reading: Bassman, Herbert J., ed. *Riverside Then and Now: A History of Riverside, Illinois.* 1936. • The Frederick Law Olmsted Society of Riverside. *Riverside: A Village in a Park.* 1970. • Riverside Historical Commission. *Tell Me a Story: Memories of Riverside.* 1995.

Riverwoods, IL, Lake County, 24 miles NW of the Loop. Riverwoods is an island of tall trees in the midst of suburbia. Its founders, developers, and village officials have all sought to protect their environment.

POTAWATOMIS used what would become Riverwoods for their winter campgrounds. Still in evidence are the cuts on TREES where they tapped sap from maple trees to make syrup. In 1841 Jessie Leavensworth located near present-day Riverwoods Road and Deerfield Road.

In 1885 the Wisconsin Central RAILROAD added a spur line with a final stop near Deerfield and Milwaukee Avenue. By 1900 the area was a popular weekend destination. Visitors stepped from the train and were greeted by residents carrying balloons, ice cream, and refreshments. City dwellers then hiked out to the DES PLAINES RIVER, where they fished for black bass and walked along the banks where wildflowers grew in abundance. Then they might trek to Clybourn Park near the present-day Deerfield Road Bridge, where entertainment included a roller coaster, BOWLING alleys, beer stands, and a dance and roller-skating pavilion.

In the 1920s many Chicagoans and North Shore residents constructed summer cabins along the Des Plaines River. One buyer, Edward Ryerson, purchased a cabin on a 10-acre parcel along the river in 1928. In 1939 he bought Brushwood Farm, where he had an estate until 1966 when it was turned into FOREST PRESERVE land.

Louis Bouscaren, also drawn by Riverwoods' natural setting, built a vacation home and subsequently joined with neighbors to subdivide area property. Their association specified the responsibilities of property owners in maintaining the area, and when Bouscaren platted the South Riverwoods property he stipulated properties had to be more than one acre but less than two.

In the early 1950s approximately 40 families lived in Riverwoods. Residents banded together in 1955 to form the Riverwoods Residents Association. In 1959 they incorporated the village of Riverwoods in an effort to protect their wooded enclave and to keep out encroachment from other communities. The association also purchased 10 acres of woodland as a preserve.

In keeping with the idea of a natural setting, part of the village hall is housed in a log cabin built in 1929 and originally a meeting place for boy and girl scouts. The village of Riverwoods purchased the property in 1970 and constructed additions to the original building in 1979 and the early 1990s.

In 2000 the sleepy village had a population of 3,843 with no downtown and no shopping centers. Huge homes were being built in the 1990s on the few remaining open lots. In a quest to limit this trend and thereby prevent tree loss, the village worked toward ordinances to limit the size of new construction and additions.

Marilyn Elizabeth Perry

See also: Amusement Parks; Lake County, IL; Suburbs and Cities as Dual Metropolis; Vacation Spots; Zoning

Further reading: . . . *In the Beginning: The Village Hall, Riverwoods, Ill.* Riverwoods Residents Association. 1981. • *Living in Riverwoods.* Riverwoods Residents Association. 1973. • *A Village Remembered: Riverwoods after 25 Years.* Village of Riverwoods. 1984.

Roadhouses. Roadhouses thrived during PROHIBITION (1920–1933) in rural areas near Chicago, where law enforcement often was inadequate. By 1929 there were nearly 175 in operation. The growing numbers of automobiles and new roads made these previously remote establishments readily accessible. Roadhouses varied from small, sleazy taverns to big, fancy NIGHTCLUBS with name dance bands and floor shows. Many served food, but the big attraction was being able to drink illegal beer or LIQUOR.

Outlaw GANGS or syndicates distributed the illicit booze and controlled many roadhouses where recognized customers could get served. All roadhouses sold "set-ups," ginger ale or soda with ice, to customers who brought their own liquor in hip flasks. The Dells and Lincoln Tavern in MORTON GROVE, Villa Venice near GLENVIEW, the Purple Grackle east of ELGIN, Le Chateau near THORNTON, and the Triangle Café in FOREST PARK were among the biggest and best known.

Charles A. Sengstock, Jr.

See also: Crime and Chicago's Image; Dance Halls; Entertaining Chicagoans; Motoring; Underground Economy

Further reading: "The Dells." *Variety,* June 9, 1926, 44. • *Morton Grove: 100 Years, 1895–1995.* Morton Grove, IL, Centennial Commission, 1995, 34–35. • *Road House Survey of Cook County, Illinois, July 25–August 31, 1929.* Juvenile Protection Association, Chicago, IL, folder 106. Special Collections, University of Illinois at Chicago Library.

Robbins, IL, Cook County, 17 miles south of the Loop. Robbins is the oldest majority-black suburb in the Chicago area and one of the oldest incorporated black municipalities in the United States. Robbins is also characteristic of semirural black suburbs that developed in the United States during the GREAT MIGRATION.

Located in the bottomlands southwest of BLUE ISLAND, the area was largely farmland until 1910, when white REAL-ESTATE agents Henry and Eugene Robbins opened the first of several subdivisions, which they marketed to AFRICAN AMERICANS. As in many working-class subdivisions, lots in Robbins lacked paved streets, sewers, and other modern amenities. Robbins lots cost as little as $90 apiece.

The people who settled in Robbins were predominantly working-class African Americans who were willing to sacrifice urban services for land and a home of their own. Most were southerners who had preferences for homeownership, open space, tightly knit community life, and country atmosphere. At the same time, Robbins's location in the CALUMET REGION offered men access to factory jobs that many had left the South to obtain. DOMESTIC SERVICE and seasonal WORK canning and packing vegetables dominated women's paid labor. As workers near the bottom of the urban economy, some African Americans also favored homeownership in a suburb like Robbins because it allowed them to supplement wages with garden produce and small livestock. Many settlers cut costs even further by building their own houses and living without utilities. The result was a makeshift landscape that outsiders labeled a slum, but for many residents, the suburb represented a welcome compromise between North and South.

In 1917, residents of Robbins incorporated as a separate municipality, a bold step for a blue-collar community with almost no commercial tax base. Although city officials undertook modest improvements, the community's small tax base inhibited efforts to upgrade services. Robbins grew from 431 persons in 1920 to 1,300 by 1940. Residents established a newspaper, the *Robbins Herald,* plus many churches and small stores. Bessie Coleman, Cornelius Coffey, and Johnny Robinson were among those who created Robbins AIRPORT, a center for black aviation in the North. Robbins also became a popular recreation spot for black Chicagoans, who crowded its picnic grounds and nightclubs on summer weekends.

Population expanded to 4,766 in 1950 and 9,644 by 1970 (98 percent black), as developers opened new subdivisions and the village ANNEXED territory. Robbins was one of few places in the Chicago suburbs where African Americans could purchase homes without risking violence. In the 1960s, black developer Edward Starks opened the Golden Acres SUBDIVISION, which brought modern, suburban-style houses to the community.

As late as 1950, 22 percent of Robbins homes lacked indoor plumbing, and over 40 percent were considered substandard in 1960. Although the community paved streets and installed sewers in the 1950s, these costs, combined with plant layoffs in the 1970s, saddled the suburb with municipal debts. Economic woes notwithstanding, Robbins remained one of the few places in greater Chicago where African Americans with very limited resources could afford to buy a home of their own.

Andrew Wiese

See also: Cook County; Governing the Metropolis; Housing, Self-Built; Suburbs and Cities as Dual Metropolis

Further reading: Chicago Commission on Race Relations. *The Negro in Chicago: A Study of Race Relations and a Race Riot in 1919.* 1968 [1921], 138–139. • Rose, Harold M. "The All-Negro Town: Its Evolution and Function." *Geographical Review* 55 (July 1965): 362–381. • Wiese, Andrew. "Places of Our Own: Suburban Black Towns before 1960." *Journal of Urban History* 19 (May 1993): 30–54.

Robert Morris College. Named for a Philadelphia representative and businessman who reluctantly signed the Declaration of Independence and then tirelessly raised money for the Revolutionary army, Robert Morris College received its Illinois charter in 1965. For the next decade, the small school provided associate degrees in liberal arts and BUSINESS from its campus in Carthage, Illinois, 250 miles southwest of Chicago. In 1975, Robert Morris merged with Chicago's Moser School (a private business college founded in 1913) and made business and allied health the heart of its academic curriculum. After achieving accreditation in 1986, the school opened a series of branch campuses around Illinois: in Springfield, ORLAND PARK, NAPERVILLE, and BENSENVILLE. In 1998, the central branch of Robert Morris College moved into the landmark building at 401 South State Street in Chicago.

Sarah Fenton

See also: Loop; Schooling for Work

Robert Taylor Homes, neighborhood in the GRAND BOULEVARD Community Area. Upon completion in 1962, Chicago's Robert Taylor Homes became the largest PUBLIC HOUSING project in the United States. Built along two miles of State Street from 39th to 54th Streets in the Grand Boulevard and Washington Park community areas, the project comprised 28 16-story buildings mostly in U-shaped clusters of three, containing almost 4,300 apartments and 27,000 people.

This massive housing project was ironically named after Robert Taylor, an AFRICAN AMERICAN activist and CHICAGO HOUSING AUTHORITY (CHA) board member who in 1950 resigned when the city council refused to endorse potential building locations that would induce racially integrated housing.

Within forty years this neighborhood was being dismantled. Despite the structurally sound exteriors of the buildings and an academic study that found two out of three Taylor residents opposed to the demolition, the CHA had demolished half of the buildings by the year 2000.

Erik Gellman

See also: Housing Reform; Subsidized Housing

Further reading: Lemann, Nicholas. *The Promised Land: The Great Black Migration and How It Changed America.* 1991. • Venkatesh, Sudhir Alladi. *American Project: The Rise and Fall of a Modern Ghetto.* 2000.

Rock Music. When "rock 'n' roll" gained popularity in the 1950s, Chicago had long been a center for both BLUES and RHYTHM AND BLUES. Because rock owed much to both styles, the city played an integral role in the rock revolution. CHESS RECORDS, the independent label founded in Chicago in the late 1940s, played a critical part. Its roster included blues and R&B legends Muddy Waters, Howlin' Wolf, Bo Diddley, and Willie Dixon. Rock acts from Elvis Presley to the Rolling Stones borrowed from these artists. Chuck Berry, however, had a direct and immediate impact. In 1955 he released "Maybellene," the first in a string of rock classics, and became one of rock's few major AFRICAN AMERICAN stars.

Vee-Jay Records rivaled Chess. Founded by African Americans Jimmy Bracken and his wife Vivian Carter, the company rapidly emerged as major force in the industry. The owners received skillful assistance from Ewart Abner, Jr., and Calvin Carter, Vivian's brother. Vee-Jay's first hits came from R&B-based "doo-wop" vocal groups, a style at which Chicago artists excelled. The Dells, the El Dorados, and the Spaniels earned several hits in the mid-1950s. Chess doo-wop acts, particularly the Moonglows and the Flamingos, also had best-sellers.

While mainstream rock and roll temporarily stagnated at the end of the 1950s and into the early 1960s, some important local and regional scenes still flourished. Chicago continued to nurture and produce quality acts and recordings. Vee-Jay's Dee Clark, Gene Chandler, and Betty Everett enjoyed success in the early 1960s. In 1962 the label signed the Four Seasons, its first white group, and it also released the Beatles' first U.S. album.

Columbia-Okeh and ABC-Paramount also established Chicago bases. With Vee-Jay and Chess their efforts yielded "soul" music, a key part of rock in the mid to late 1960s. Jerry Butler's Vee-Jay releases established him as a leading purveyor of soul. Curtis Mayfield became a star songwriter, guitarist, vocalist, and producer-arranger. He and Carl Davis, an A&R director/producer at Paramount, created a "CHICAGO SOUND" that featured a more fluid, highly arranged, and orchestrated sound than the raw early R&B or the hard style that characterized southern soul music.

White rock acts performed a minor role in Chicago's early rock history. Those with hit recordings after 1965 relied on African American musical traditions. The Buckinghams scored several top-ten hits from 1966 to 1968 by employing a horn section, electric organ, and a vocal style that borrowed heavily from R&B, as did the Cryan Shames, Shadows of Knight, American Breed, and the New Colony Six. The city's most successful rock act of all time, "CHICAGO," also drew upon the city's JAZZ, blues, and R&B traditions. Their early recordings featured jazz-style horns, blues-infused guitar playing, and R&B vocals that defined "blue-eyed soul" in early 1970s. On later recordings the band discarded that style in favor of "light rock."

The city's fortunes as a key player in the rock world declined in the late 1960s. Chess and Vee-Jay failed to survive, while Paramount and Okeh closed their offices. Chicago's live music scene continued to flourish, but within industry circles the city's blue-collar credentials became a liability. Fewer Chicago artists got record contracts. Nevertheless, a few acts managed to do well. Cheap Trick mingled crafty songs with a big guitar sound, while the Chi-Lites offered polished and sweet R&B vocal arrangements. Styx's high-pitched vocals and pseudo-classical keyboards found a niche in radio's "album-oriented rock" format in the 1970s and early 1980s.

In the 1990s Chicago experienced a rock renaissance. Punk rock derivatives "alternative" and "grunge" provided the tonic for rock revival. Punk went mainstream, and the critical arbiters of taste deemed Chicago "hip." The Smashing Pumpkins and rich-kid-turned-Bohemian Liz Phair garnered acclaim and best-sellers in the '90s. Chicago's music scene had enough room for both heavy blues and heavy angst.

Clark "Bucky" Halker

See also: Disc Jockeys; Entertaining Chicagoans; Leisure

Further reading: Langer, Adam. "Glory Days." *Chicago Reader,* January 13, 1989. • Pruter, Robert. *Chicago Soul.* 1991. • Pruter, Robert. *DooWop: The Chicago Scene.* 1996.

Rockdale, IL, Will County, 36 miles SW of the Loop. Originally settled by SLOVENIAN and LITHUANIAN immigrants in the nineteenth century, Rockdale now includes a significant Hispanic population. Combining residences and industry, Rockdale incorporated in 1903. During the 1930s, the United States Navy built ships there along the DES PLAINES RIVER. More recently, the creation of the Des Plaines River Valley Enterprise Zone provided tax breaks for corporations to relocate in the area. The population in 2000 was 1,888.

Erik Gellman

See also: Economic Geography; Will County

Rogers Park, Community Area 1, 9 miles N of the Loop. Rogers Park ranks among Chicago's most diverse and populous neighborhoods. Between the late 1830s and his death in 1856 Irishman Phillip Rogers purchased approximately 1,600 acres of government land, part of which formed the basis of Rogers Park. In 1872 Rogers's son-in-law, Patrick Touhy, subdivided the land near the present-day intersection of Lunt and Ridge Avenues. By 1878 enough settlers had moved into the area to incorporate the village of Rogers Park. The number of residents increased steadily and further growth accompanied the village's ANNEXATION to Chicago in 1893. The 1915 annexation of the area north of Howard Street, east of the "L" tracks, and south of Calvary CEMETERY, variously known as Germania and South EVANSTON, brought Rogers Park and Chicago a new northern boundary.

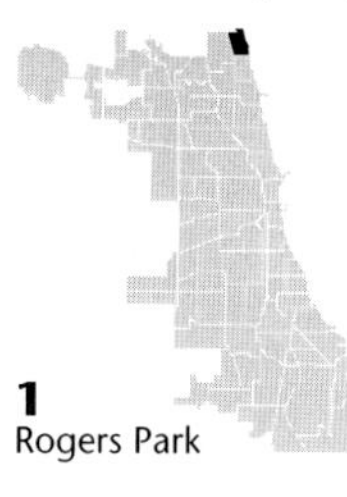

Rail connections between Rogers Park and Chicago date from the 1860s. Both the Chicago & North Western Railway and the Chicago, Milwaukee & St. Paul RAILROAD provided service to downtown Chicago. By the end of the nineteenth century large houses on sizable lots clustered between Greenview and Ridge Avenues and north of Touhy along Sheridan Road. When the Northwestern Elevated Railroad opened the Howard Station in 1908, population jumped dramatically. The construction of single-family houses slowed as subdividers built multiunit dwellings and the neighborhood's suburban qualities faded. Large APARTMENT building construction was most intense north of Howard Street and along the "L" tracks in the eastern portion of the community. Rogers Park became and remains primarily a renter community.

The intensive nature of apartment construction consumed almost all available land. Housing shortages during World War II encouraged the subdivision of large apartments into smaller ones. Population density increased especially in the area north of Howard Street. Deteriorating buildings brought lower rents and a more transient and poor population. Neighborhood concerns about congestion, poverty, and increased crime led to public-private partnerships to upgrade the housing stock, provide a variety of SOCIAL SERVICES, and stabilize the community. New construction in the neighborhood since the 1960s has consisted of moderately sized apartment buildings, townhouses, and nursing homes.

Neighborhood business activities, entertainment spots, and RELIGIOUS INSTITUTIONS are clustered on main streets and at TRANSPORTATION breaks. Commercial districts developed along Clark Street, Devon Avenue, and around the four neighborhood "L" stations. Until the

1980s entertainment venues were an important part of these districts. During the first half of the twentieth century Rogers Park possessed four large, elaborate MOVIE PALACES (the Howard, Adelphi, Granada, and Norshore Theaters), which ultimately succumbed to changes in the movie industry as well as different tastes among the viewing public. The neighborhood also has been home to a ballpark, a country club, and, most recently, a live-theater community. Finally, religious activity flourished as population grew and, although identified historically as a ROMAN CATHOLIC and JEWISH community, the neighborhood has always supported a variety of religious denominations.

Two institutions of higher education have been located in Rogers Park. The Jesuits purchased property in 1906 to expand the operations of St. Ignatius College, now LOYOLA UNIVERSITY CHICAGO. Mundelein College, now a part of Loyola, opened in 1930. Run by the Sisters of Charity of the Blessed Virgin Mary, Mundelein was Chicago's second Catholic women's college.

Over the years Rogers Park's population has grown increasingly diverse and older. The IRISH, GERMANS, and LUXEMBURGERS represented the major ethnic groups during the early years of community building. By the late 1960s the neighborhood had become home to RUSSIAN and Eastern European immigrants. The 1970s saw the movement of immigrants from Asia and the Americas as well as growth in the AFRICAN AMERICAN population. According to the 2000 census, 63,484 people lived in Rogers Park. Of these, 46 percent were white, 30 percent African American, and 6 percent Asian or Pacific Islander. A total of 28 percent were of Latino origin, 79 percent of whom were of MEXICAN ancestry. Thirty-four percent of those living in Rogers Park were foreign-born. Since 1960, Rogers Park has been home to a number of nursing and retirement homes.

Patricia Mooney-Melvin

See also: Demography; Housing for the Elderly; Kitchenettes; Metropolitan Growth; Railroads; Shopping Districts and Malls

Further reading: Mooney-Melvin, Patricia. *Reading Your Neighborhood: A Brief History of East Rogers Park.* 1993. • Palmer, Vivien M., comp. *Documents: History of the Rogers Park Community, Chicago, 1925–1930,* vol. 1. 1966. • The Rogers Park/West Ridge Historical Society and Museum. Chicago, IL.

Rolling Meadows, IL, Cook County, 24 miles NW of the Loop. In 1836 Orrin Ford became the first landowner in the area that is now Rolling Meadows, staking his claim of 160 acres in the tranquil forests and gently rolling terrain of an area known as Plum Grove. Other farm families followed, many traveling from Vermont. By the early 1840s settlers had built a dam across SALT CREEK and had laid claim to the entire Plum Grove area.

The community became part of newly formed Palatine Township in 1850 as GERMAN immigrants arrived. In 1862 they erected the Salem Evangelical Church, whose 40-foot-square church cemetery at the corner of Kirchoff and Plum Grove Roads still stood in 1998, a bit of history amid bustling traffic and a strip shopping center.

In 1927 H. D. "Curly" Brown bought 1,000 acres of what became Rolling Meadows to build a GOLF course and land adjacent to it for a racetrack. In the early 1950s Kimball Hill purchased the land intended for the golf course, and began home sales by advertising a floor plan of his basic house in the *Chicago Tribune*. Although the response was positive, officials in neighboring ARLINGTON HEIGHTS protested, hoping to buy the land themselves for estate homes. But prospective buyers of the Kimball Hill homes persuaded the Cook County Board for ZONING changes to allow Hill to proceed.

In 1953 the first families moved into the development, which Hill named Rolling Meadows. With a production schedule of 20 houses a week, 700 houses sold by 1955, mostly to blue-collar workers. Hill donated $200 per home for a school system, then built and equipped the first elementary school. He also founded the Rolling Meadows Homeowners' Association, donated land for parks, and funded the Clearbrook Center, a home for the mentally handicapped, which opened in 1955.

Rolling Meadows incorporated in 1955 as a city named for its gently rolling terrain, and soon began annexing land for future development. The town boomed during the 1950s and 1960s as businesses moved into the area. When Crawford's DEPARTMENT STORE opened in the 1950s it was the largest in the northwest suburbs (it closed in 1993). An industrial park opened on North Hicks Road in 1958, and Western Electric opened a facility in the 1960s which employed 1,500 workers. Developers inundated the area with APARTMENT buildings and by 1970 multifamily dwellings made up 35 percent of the total structures in Rolling Meadows. Ramblin' Rose North, renamed Meadow Trace, opened in 1966, followed by Three Fountains. Rolling Meadows complexes, however, suffered from a series of fires in the decade. This prompted the city to become more stringent in their BUILDING CODES, which had allowed for frame multifamily structures. Single-family housing continued to flourish in Rolling Meadows as developers utilized the natural wooded setting for the subdivisions of Tall Oaks, Dawngate, and Creekside.

By 2000 the population was 24,609, with 19 percent at Hispanic origin, 7 percent Asian, and 3 percent African American. The city had begun revamping commercial areas along Kirchoff Road. To the south on Golf Road, corporations such as 3Com, Helene Curtis, and Charles Industries established bases in what has become known as the Golden Corridor.

Marilyn Elizabeth Perry

See also: Built Environment of the Chicago Region; Economic Geography; Government, Suburban

Further reading: Perica, Esther. *They Took the Challenge: The Story of Rolling Meadows.* 1979.

Roman Catholic Archdiocese of Chicago. The history of ROMAN CATHOLICISM in Chicago has been shaped by the wider economic, political, and social realities of the city and metropolitan region. Conversely, the Church too has had a decisive impact on the shape of the city by its ownership of urban property, its provision of SOCIAL SERVICES, and the influence of its teachings on the men and women who live in Chicago. Even more, the Catholic Church has given a sense of communal solidarity to the many Chicagoans who have identified their neighborhoods by the name of their PARISH church. Often reinforced by ethnicity, this sense of identity has been characterized by joint participation in the creed, cult, and code of Roman Catholicism.

The juridical entity known as the Roman Catholic Archdiocese of Chicago is the chief organizational framework for Catholic life in Cook and Lake Counties. Defined according to Illinois law as a corporation sole, the Roman Catholic Archbishop of Chicago oversees thousands of employees, lay, religious, and clerical; owns millions of dollars' worth of prime city and metropolitan property; and most important, structures the spiritual lives of millions of Chicagoans. Through their spiritual and legal authority, as well as their own personal prestige, the bishops and archbishops of Chicago have exercised enormous influence. Although higher echelons of leadership in the Chicago Catholic Church have until recently been reserved for men, women and men have in many cases labored side by side in behalf of Catholic ideals and institutions. This includes not only the members of religious communities of men and women, but also lay people such as Christian Family Movement leader Patty Crowley.

The Founding Era: 1843–1879

The Diocese of Chicago, encompassing the entire state of Illinois, was formally separated from the Diocese of Vincennes by Pope Gregory XVI on November 28, 1843. By creating a separate diocese, church authorities acknowledged that the number of Catholics abiding in and near Chicago had risen sufficiently to sustain an independent ecclesiastical existence. Roman authorities appointed William Quarter as the first bishop of the new diocese. Quarter began to lay the groundwork for vigorous

High Mass at the International Eucharistic Congress, Soldier Field, 1926. Photographer: Kaufmann & Fabry. Source: Chicago Historical Society.

church life by creating parishes, establishing a seminary, and developing other educational institutions staffed by male and female religious communities. He also petitioned the legislature to establish the Chicago bishop and his successors as a corporation sole. This gave future bishops enormous power in arranging church affairs and developing the Catholic presence in the city. After Quarter's death the diocese suffered three decades of administrative instability, compounded by the loss of nearly a million dollars in church property in the FIRE OF 1871.

During this period portions of the diocese were clipped off to create separate ecclesiastical jurisdictions. The southern half of the state became the Diocese of Quincy in 1853. The Alton diocese (later Springfield) followed four years later and in 1877 the Diocese of Peoria was established. In 1880 Rome designated the Diocese of Chicago an archdiocese, raising it to preeminence among all dioceses in the region and establishing its bishop as an archbishop.

Ethnic Expansion: 1879–1915

Two bishops presided over this era of recovery and growth, Patrick A. Feehan and James Edward Quigley. The matrix of Catholic development in this epoch was the burgeoning industrialization of the city and the heavily Catholic immigration that provided its workforce. As Southern and Eastern Europeans augmented the existing core of IRISH and GERMAN Catholics, both Feehan and Quigley adopted a policy of ethnic accommodation that had a significant impact on the development of Chicago's neighborhoods. Both favored the ethnic parish as the chief means of attending to the spiritual needs of all these Catholic groups and allowed the building of numerous churches, schools, and social welfare institutions to respond to the distinctive needs of Catholic ethnics. Even though a western portion of the diocese would be lopped off by the creation of the Diocese of Rockford in 1908, the number of Chicago's churches increased from 194 when Feehan took over to 331 when Quigley died. Chicago's urban parishes flourished as an important spiritual, cultural, and educational component of Chicago's life.

Consolidation, Visibility, Clout: 1915–1965

Although the reigns of Feehan and Quigley provided administrative stability, the Chicago archdiocese still lacked a strong central administration and a means of providing locally trained clergy. Its impact on urban affairs was minimal or indirect. This would change with the advent of Archbishop George William Mundelein. Adept at using the trappings of office to emphasize his prestige and thereby to promote the cause of Catholicism in the city, Mundelein managed to bring harmony to the often fractious Chicago clergy; downplay, if not altogether stop, the balkanizing effects of the previous emphasis on ethnicity; and provide for the creation of a native clergy by building two magnificent SEMINARIES, Quigley on Chicago's NEAR NORTH SIDE and St. Mary of the Lake in MUNDELEIN. In 1924 Pope Pius XI named Mundelein Chicago's first cardinal. Two years later Mundelein welcomed the International Eucharistic Congress to the city, perhaps the single greatest religious gathering in the history of Chicago, with thousands of visitors crowding sessions at SOLDIER FIELD and on the seminary grounds in LAKE COUNTY.

Mundelein's successor, Archbishop Samuel A. Stritch, maintained Mundelein's administrative and financial structures but replaced his predecessor's imperial style with a more approachable and scholarly mode of leadership. After WORLD WAR II Stritch confronted the two-pronged challenge of AFRICAN AMERICAN migration into formerly all-white and Catholic neighborhoods and the concomitant movement of white Chicagoans to the perimeters of the city and suburbia. Stritch agonized over what he foresaw as the emptying of the city into the suburbs and attempted to cooperate with city officials to preserve certain Catholic institutions, especially HOSPITALS, as well as to stabilize neighborhoods through COMMUNITY ORGANIZATION. Stritch, a southerner, disdained "racial mixing." Nonetheless, as a series of embarrassing incidents of discrimination in archdiocesan parishes, schools, and Catholic neighborhoods erupted in the late forties and throughout the fifties, he became more aggressive in attending to cases of overt racism.

Stritch also responded to the needs of a growing ring of suburbs and to the movement of Catholics to these areas, as Chicago Catholicism began the shift from an urban to a suburban culture. He approved the construction of 72 new parishes, only 24 of which were in the city limits. In 1948, the counties of WILL, Kankakee, and Grundy were detached from Chicago to form the Diocese of Joliet. For reasons that remain a mystery locked in Vatican archives, Stritch was transferred to Rome in April 1958, where he died the following month.

Stritch's successor, Albert G. Meyer, also confronted Chicago's growing racial tensions and the particular response of Chicago's Catholic clergy, religious, and laity to racial change. In 1960, he ordered all-white CATHOLIC SCHOOLS to accept African American children and threw the weight of his office behind the long-lived efforts of such groups as the Catholic Interracial Council to effect changes in Catholic attitudes toward race and racial integration. In a 1963 National Conference on Religion and Race held in Chicago, Meyer firmly denounced racism as a "pathological infection."

Insisting on modern business techniques, updated technology, planning, and increased bureaucratic efficiency, Meyer implemented a major administrative reorganization of an archdiocese that had remained unchanged since the days of Mundelein. At Vatican Council II Meyer emerged as the de facto leader of the American bishops.

This period stretching from Mundelein to Meyer saw the emergence of Chicago as one of the leading Catholic cities in America. The nation's largest diocese, Chicago developed a leadership with a reputation for political liberalism, hearty commitment to social change, and liturgical innovation. Moreover, Chicago's clergy had relative freedom to pursue solutions to continually changing pastoral and social issues. This period also saw the waning of ethnicity as a powerfully defining feature of Chicago Catholic life. While ethnic identities persisted, and ethnic parishes continued to function, the effects of AMERICANIZATION were taking hold, especially as immigration restriction choked the flow of newcomers into the diocese. Even with the loss of Joliet the number of churches in this period grew from 331 to 457 and the number of diocesan priests from 524 to 1,344.

Tumult and Transition: 1965–1997

The deliberations of Vatican II brought sweeping changes to many of the time-honored externals of the Catholic faith. Liturgical changes reconfigured the interior of churches as altars were turned to face the people and Latin gave way to the vernacular as the tongue of worship. Catholic priests developed a new understanding of their role vis-à-vis their parishioners and built on old models of social action they had learned from the labor priests and interracial activists of the earlier era. At the same time, however, the Chicago clergy's traditional independent-mindedness ran into a major stumbling block in the person of the new archbishop, John Patrick Cody. A strong, at times authoritarian leader, Cody moved aggressively to deal with leftover clerical problems, centralize power in his own hands, and complete many of the administrative reforms begun by his predecessor. Cody's style did not sit well with many of the Chicago clergy, who organized the Association of Chicago Priests in an attempt to counterbalance his power. Committed to racial justice, Cody was a strong supporter of the efforts of African American parishes as well as joint racial endeavors.

Whatever internal problems Cody faced, he apparently remained on good terms with the city's leaders as well as with prominent factions in the area. He enjoyed a particular moment of triumph when he succeeded in bringing Pope John Paul II to the city in October 1979 for a historic mass in GRANT PARK and a visit to the city's Five Holy Martyrs Parish. Nonetheless, his leadership difficulties left him exposed when allegations of financial misconduct arose prior to his death in April 1982.

Cody's successor, Joseph Bernardin, brought a more irenic and collegial approach to archdiocese governance. Soft-spoken, gentle, and genuinely spiritual, Bernardin dispelled much of the rancor among the clergy generated by his predecessor when he introduced himself to his assembled priests by saying, "I am Joseph, your brother."

Recognizing Chicago's diversity, Bernardin widened the leadership circle by appointing auxiliary bishops representing the major ethnic groups in the city. He also appointed women to high-level administrative posts. One of the most ecumenical of Chicago's bishops, he cultivated warm ties with the city's other religious leaders. Despite his well-earned reputation for compromise and conciliation, Bernardin also won a reputation for his translation of religious values into firm principles. His "seamless garment" metaphor crystallized the Church's opposition to legalized abortion by linking it with a consistent defense of life in all its phases, including a rebuke of capital punishment.

Bernardin was compelled to deal with the effects of the DEMOGRAPHIC shifts that had been taking place in Chicago Catholicism since the end of World War II. In decisions marked by much controversy and public dispute, he closed or consolidated a large number of churches, many of them in areas populated largely by African Americans. The demise of many of these venerable institutions signaled more visibly than ever that Chicago's Catholic populace no longer claimed the city as its first locus of identity.

Bernardin also was compelled to deal with the maelstrom generated by revelations of sexual misconduct by clergy, more particularly misconduct involving minors. He himself was caught up in the turmoil when sensational allegations of this nature were made against him by a former seminarian who later recanted the accusations.

When Bernardin died on November 14, 1996, the entire city mourned. Lines stretched into the night to view his body in Holy Name Cathedral. Chicago media outlets kept up a steady commentary on his life and broadcast his moving funeral to millions. Across the city, PROTESTANTS, Catholics, JEWS, and others lamented his passing.

Bernardin's successor, Archbishop Francis George, OMI, was installed as Chicago's eighth archbishop and the thirteenth leader of the diocese in May 1997. A scholarly and articulate man, George was the first man born in Chicago to lead the diocese.

Steven M. Avella

See also: Catholic Charities; Catholic Youth Organization; Church Architecture; Convents; Mexicans; Neighborhood Succession; Poles; Religious Geography; Religious Institutions

Further reading: Avella, Steven M. *This Confident Church: Catholic Leadership and Life in Chicago, 1940–1965.* 1992. • Kantowicz, Edward R. *Corporation Sole: Cardinal Mundelein and Chicago Catholicism.* 1983. • Shanabruch, Charles. *Chicago's Catholics: The Evolution of an American Identity.* 1981.

Roman Catholics. There is probably no contemporary Catholic practice more revealing of its past and present than the *Via Crucis* (Way of the Cross), held each Good Friday in PILSEN since 1977. The procession begins in the shadow of the Dan Ryan EXPRESSWAY at Providence of God Church, founded in 1900 as Chicago's second LITHUANIAN parish. Moving west on 18th Street, it passes St. Procopius, the city's third Bohemian parish, established in 1875. After re-enacting the Crucifixion and Death at Harrison Park, *Via Crucis* ends after services at St. Adalbert, Chicago's third POLISH parish, formed in 1874.

Their Polish, CZECH, and Lithuanian predecessors would have had little trouble understanding the spiritual (and secular) concerns of the procession's participants: exploitation of undocumented workers; grinding poverty;

Good Friday parade, Pilsen, 1978. Photographer: Chicago Journal. Source: Chicago Historical Society.

Eastern Rite Catholics

Otherwise known as Eastern Catholics, Uniates, or Greek Catholics, Eastern Rite Catholics are Christians who give allegiance to Rome but adhere to those religious customs common to Eastern Orthodoxy. Most of the Chicago area's Eastern Rite Catholics are UKRAINIANS, though BELARUSIANS, Arab Melkites, ROMANIANS, LEBANESE Maronites, SYRIANS, and ASSYRIANS also worship in the area's Eastern Rite churches. The ROMAN CATHOLIC Church has not always embraced Eastern Christian traditions among Catholics and by the late twentieth century was pushing Eastern Catholic parishes to adopt Latin religious customs.

Brandon Johnson

Float from St. Philip Benizi's Church, ca. 1930s. Photographer: Unknown. Source: University of Illinois at Chicago.

drugs wreaking havoc on families; deportation; children killed in GANG violence. The suffering and sorrows of *las madres,* explicitly mentioned or alluded to at virtually every Station, brings to mind, moreover, "Serdeczna Matko"—Beloved Mother—Chicago POLONIA's leading Marian hymn. As Easter turns affliction into blessing and death into life, so too, *Via Crucis* is a way in which these contemporary Catholics, like their Eastern European antecedents, redeem their streets.

Few Chicago Catholics, however, would recognize the continuity between then and now so vividly present in Pilsen's *Via Crucis.* For some, it would be the blinders of race, for others, language, and still others, class.

IRISH and GERMAN immigrants constituted much of the Church's membership during its founding years. From 1844 to 1879, 22 territorial parishes (Irish) and nine German parishes were established. Like Catholics who would arrive later, these immigrants needed a tremendous array of what we now call SOCIAL SERVICES. Catholic nuns devoted their lives to providing this assistance. First to arrive, in 1846, the Sisters of Mercy were soon operating three SCHOOLS, running an employment bureau for working women, volunteering at a free CLINIC, and teaching literacy classes. Attending to many non-Catholics during the cholera EPIDEMICS of 1849 and 1854, they also took over what was to become MERCY HOSPITAL.

Nuns and other Catholic women attended to the needs of wave after wave of immigrants. They ran ORPHANAGES, HOSPITALS, HOUSING FOR THE ELDERLY, and day care centers. They worked with unwed mothers and tried to "rescue" female prostitutes. While almost never publicly challenging the male authority system—although some did not shrink from doing so privately—these religious women created for themselves an enormous sphere of autonomous or semiautonomous activity within the confines of an extraordinarily patriarchal ecclesiastical structure.

Above all, nuns taught school: without their labor and devotion, the CATHOLIC SCHOOL SYSTEM would not have existed. From its earliest days, building schools was central to Chicago's Catholic Church. In 1900, 76 percent of all parishes had schools; in 1930, 93 percent; in 1965, 95 percent.

The parish world in which these schools played such an integral role came to encompass almost every sphere of life. At Holy Family, on Chicago's NEAR WEST SIDE, boys' and girls' schools were established within months of the parish's founding in 1857. In 1878, the cornerstone was laid for Sodality Hall, which was necessitated by a staggering proliferation of sodalities and societies. In 1881, Holy Family's 4,267 families—20,320 persons—made it the largest English-speaking parish in Chicago. Working-class and poor Irish immigrants and their children built and maintained this Jesuit-run parish and its institutions.

The creation of this parish-based Catholic world rooted in the experiences of working people was duplicated across the city. St. Stanislaus Kostka, founded in the WEST TOWN area in 1867, is a Polish example. A grammar school was founded in 1874, and a large classroom building to house its growing enrollment was erected 15 years later. In 1890, a high school was established. In 1908, 5,438 families belonged to the parish and 4,500 children attended its schools. Dozens of societies and sodalities stood at the center of life in St. Stanislaus Kostka.

PARISH LIFE in Chicago meant the creation of "sacred space," the making holy of STREETS, ALLEYS, and neighborhoods. Radiating outward from resplendent and monumental churches, built primarily of the sweat and blood of DOMESTIC WORKERS, day laborers, butchers, and seamstresses, this sacralization of the profane developed through vivid and extraordinary events like the *Via Crucis* or an oldest child's first communion party—but more often through decades of daily life offered up to God. That parishioners of St. Stanislaus called their neighborhood *Stanislawowo* (the village of St. Stanislaus) epitomizes this sacralization.

Catholic parishes, however, were more than insular, defensive enclaves. They also were places where immigrants adjusted to the new and internalized social and individual values that facilitated an immensely significant, if in hindsight relatively moderate, upward mobility. By the 1880s and 1890s, Irish and German Catholics had begun their climb out of poverty, the Irish establishing parishes further south, the Germans, further north. Little of parish social and liturgical life, however, changed. As this upward and geographical mobility continued decade after decade, Chicago Catholics clung all the more tightly to a traditional parish life that both cushioned and camouflaged it. Catholic women bore the brunt of an antimodernist sensibility as the bedrock of Catholicism became their subordination within patriarchal structures and mentalities that assumed unchanging gender relations.

Irish Americans—and, to a lesser extent, German Americans—dominated the Catholic Church that Eastern Europeans and ITALIANS encountered when they arrived in Chicago. Eastern European parish building, again an essential component of working-class activity, was concentrated in four industrial districts: the NEAR NORTH SIDE, LOWER WEST SIDE,

Interior of St. Anthony's Church, 11530 South Prairie Avenue, West Pullman, ca. 1940s. Photographer: Unknown. Source: University of Illinois at Chicago.

BACK OF THE YARDS, and SOUTH CHICAGO. Much of the interethnic tension that could have resulted from such a situation was muted at the parish level because of the existence of nationality parishes, organized around language rather than geography. Conflict did, however, develop within clerical ranks, as Irish ecclesiastical rule deeply rankled.

In the secular world, the POLICE force had, more or less, become an Irish American—virtually synonymous with Catholic—organization. Irish American Catholics also commanded the higher ranks of the DEMOCRATIC PARTY and the recently formed CHICAGO FEDERATION OF LABOR. Single Irish American women were well on their way to doing the same in the teaching profession.

Even as class differentiation among Catholics increased, the creation of an all-encompassing Catholic world, largely based upon ethnic autonomy, continued apace. Catholics provided for themselves—partly because no one else would do it, partly because of virulent anti-Catholicism—much of what is now done by social welfare agencies. Orphanages, residences for single mothers, old-age homes, reform schools, hospitals, employment agencies, temporary relief, day care, SETTLEMENT HOUSES: nuns did much of this, but men's organizations (e.g., the Holy Name Society's Big Brothers) did other parts, and laywomen (e.g., the Catholic Woman's League) did the rest. Chicago Catholics also joined MUTUAL BENEFIT SOCIETIES at both the parish, diocesan, and national levels, read Catholic NEWSPAPERS, and attended Catholic colleges and universities.

George Mundelein, installed as Chicago's Catholic leader in 1916, sought to create an "American" Church. As the city's second native-born archbishop and a thoroughgoing AMERICANIZER, he slowed the creation of nationality parishes. He, moreover, appointed a central school board that severely limited the use of non-English languages in Catholic schools. There were substantial internal protests about both policies, yet little was said in 1917 when Mundelein ruled that St. Monica's, on the city's SOUTH SIDE, henceforth would be an entirely AFRICAN AMERICAN parish.

The official Chicago Church, although still comprising a working-class majority and committed, at least since *Rerum Novarum* (1893), to unions, had remained publicly neutral in most battles between capital and labor. At the parish level, some priests vocally supported or opposed STRIKES and union organizing, but pastors generally took a hands-off attitude best explained by their perceptions of the material conditions of their parishioners' lives. Despite the increasingly militant labor actions of working-class Catholics, especially in the packinghouses, steel mills, and farm equipment factories, this hands-off attitude did not change until the 1930s.

Under Mundelein's regime—ironic, since he ruled almost militarily—Chicago Catholicism's well-deserved liberal reputation emerged. Bishop Bernard Sheil, given free rein by Mundelein, best epitomizes that spirit. He was the initiating force behind the CATHOLIC YOUTH ORGANIZATION (CYO), which successfully attracted thousands of Chicago teenagers to its sports programs, of which BOXING was the most famous. In 1943, the Sheil School of Social Studies, which focused on adult education, opened at CYO headquarters. In 1954, Sheil vehemently attacked Joseph McCarthy at a time when most Catholics strongly supported the demagogic anti-Communist senator.

Most significant, Sheil's prolabor sentiments provided an umbrella under which dozens of Chicago labor priests and lay activists could function. He strongly supported the organizing of the CONGRESS OF INDUSTRIAL ORGANIZATIONS (CIO): his appearance on stage with John L. Lewis on behalf of the PACKINGHOUSE WORKERS in 1939 played an important role in their subsequent victory and typified his public endorsement of controversial strikes.

The emergence of the Chicago laity, many of them young men and women who began engaging the secular world in ways their parents never could have imagined doing, marked Chicago Catholicism as unique. In the Chicago CATHOLIC WORKER, the Association of Catholic Trade Unionists, Chicago Interstudent Catholic Action, and the Catholic Labor Alliance, they pursued the Church's social agenda. Later, they did the same, under, among others, the leadership of Monsignor Reynold Hillenbrand and Fathers Daniel Cantwell and John Egan, in the Young Christian Workers and the Catholic Interracial Council. The Christian Family Movement and the Cana Conference signaled the emergence of Catholic versions of companionate marriage and heterosociality.

By the end of the 1940s, Chicago Catholicism was on the brink of changes that would drastically transform it. Most important, industrial jobs, which had provided the basis for the creation of dozens of parishes and the social advancement of hundreds of thousands of Catholics, began disappearing. The stockyards and MEATPACKING plants began closing in the late 1950s; several International Harvester plants also shut down in the same decade. This flight of factory jobs to low-wage areas increased in the 1960s and the 1970s. During the 1980s, most of the remaining good-paying jobs in industry fled. This three-decades-long capitalist assault on the gains produced by the CIO devastated Catholic neighborhoods. This onslaught, moreover, established the context within which other questions played themselves out. That the context was seldom recognized made it no less real.

The changing racial composition of neighborhoods was the central urban issue from the 1940s through the mid-1960s. Not only did the experience of white Catholic ethnics tell them that racial change meant the destruction

Choir loft, Corpus Christi Catholic Church, 1942. Photographer: Jack Delano. Source: Library of Congress.

of their neighborhoods, but no one, including the Catholic Interracial Council, provided them with anything but moral platitudes as a solution during the early, critical years of social change. Therefore, often supported and sometimes led by their pastors, they repeatedly used violence to prevent African Americans from moving into their neighborhoods. Chicago's PUBLIC HOUSING, symbolic of a nation's failure to provide decent shelter for its poorest citizens, then was at least partially the result of the intransigent RACISM present in the ranks of the white Catholic working class.

This, though, is not the whole story. On the one hand, the parish as social organism led ordinary Catholics to see themselves and its boundaries as one and the same (and both as white). On the other, unlike readily mobile PROTESTANT and Jewish institutions that followed members out of inner-city neighborhoods, Catholic parishes, their priests, nuns, and not a few of their parishioners remained to serve the newcomers entering the community borders.

Suburbanization was obviously connected to racial change—one attraction of the suburbs was that they were white—but not identical with it. The social advancement that had accompanied Chicago Catholicism since its inception accelerated during the post–World War II boom as parish after parish was founded outside the city. While their founding often replicated the social processes undergirding the early establishment of city parishes, the low population density, the emphasis on the automobile, and the vast chasm between WORK and residence left behind "sacred space" as a central organizing principle. John Cardinal Cody's 1965 decision to prohibit the building of new Catholic schools in the suburbs further set these new parishes apart from their urban counterparts.

It is not surprising that few observers noted that Cody's ruling marked a significant retreat from Chicago Catholic tradition. Many other issues—both national and local—demanded attention, and Vatican II's spirit was then sweeping Chicago. That spirit, largely in result, not intention, in the long run, not the short run, often has been inhospitable to Chicago Catholicism's parish-based commitment to sacred space.

The devotions and piety encompassed by sacred space and the parish seemed embarrassingly primitive to the highly educated, perennially mobile, and relatively affluent white-collar elite that came to dominate lay affairs after Vatican II. Seemingly discomforted by the same sort of things, many Chicago clergy eagerly embraced developments that seemed quite "Protestant" and "evangelical"—yet simultaneously "New Age"—to both those raised in the pre–Vatican II tradition and those committed to sacred space.

MEXICAN, Central American, VIETNAMESE, and African immigrants found, then, a Church in the 1980s and 1990s that had changed from the one that had so welcomed previous waves of newcomers. Not only was it lukewarm to their desire for a sensuous faith ritualized in the language of their birth, but it also faced continuing budget deficits, a decaying infrastructure, and increasing demands for its limited resources. Declining Mass attendance and the close proximity of many inner-city parishes, moreover, made the decision to close and consolidate city parishes nearly "inevitable" in the words of one commentator. In ENGLEWOOD and WEST ENGLEWOOD on the city's SOUTH SIDE, one parish, St. Benedict the African, dedicated in 1990, replaced the dozen or so parishes that had previous existed. In that same year, archdiocesan officials closed 35 parishes and missions. These closings, while logical to officials responsible for the archdiocese's finances, often angered and bewildered those directly affected. It also often seemed as if the Church was surrendering sacred space at a rapid rate.

These issues will continue to engage the Chicago Catholic Church for the foreseeable future. What will remain at stake is the degree to which it will remember that many of its best aspects and most splendid accomplishments remain indelibly tied to the past and present of the streets and parishes of the *Via Crucis.*

Steve Rosswurm

See also: Jews; Religion, Chicago's Influence on; Religious Geography; Religious Institutions; Roman Catholic Archdiocese of Chicago; Settlements, Religious

Further reading: Kantowicz, Edward R. *Corporation Sole: Cardinal Mundelein and Chicago Catholicism.* 1983. • Shanabruch, Charles. *Chicago's Catholics: The Evolution of an American Identity.* 1981. • Skerrett, Ellen, Edward R. Kantowicz, and Steven M. Avella. *Catholicism, Chicago Style.* 1993.

Romanians. Romanians settled in Chicago in four waves. The first wave, numbering around 5,000 immigrants, came to AURORA and Chicago from Transylvania and Banat between the turn of the century and WORLD WAR I, fleeing ethnic persecution in the Austro-Hungarian Empire. Between the wars, another wave of immigrants arrived in Chicago. Beginning in 1948 and continuing through 1989, an estimated 20,000–40,000 emigrated or escaped from Communist Romania. Another wave of roughly 10,000 came following 1990, fleeing the harsh conditions under the neo-Communist Romanian government. During these latter two waves, many came from REFUGEE camps in Europe, aided by groups like InterChurch Refugee Immigration Ministries, CATHOLIC CHARITIES, and the Hebrew Immigration Aid Society in Chicago.

The early Romanian community in Chicago settled in relatively compact neighborhoods on the North Side, although some sparse settlements also dotted the SOUTH SIDE. The major community emerged in the "greenhouse" district (bounded on the east by Clark Street, on the north by Peterson Avenue, west by Ravenswood, and south by Cemetery Drive), where many former farmers could find work in vegetable gardens. By the 1910s, when an estimated 5,000 Romanians lived in Chicago, the community had spread out across the North Side to neighborhoods like ALBANY PARK, LAKE VIEW, LINCOLN PARK, and UPTOWN. Activity centered on the area around Fullerton and Clybourn where many Romanian-owned businesses and groceries served the community.

From their early WORK in AGRICULTURE, Romanian men moved into road CONSTRUCTION and other public works. Women worked predominantly in garment industries. A small percentage of Romanian workers joined unions and were active in the labor movement, some as members of the Romanian Workers' Club. Later generations moved into the professions, especially academia and engineering. Others have continued in construction trades, particularly hardwood flooring, and service jobs like DOMESTIC WORK.

These immigrants belonged mostly to the Romanian Orthodox Church, with smaller numbers belonging to Baptist and ROMAN CATHOLIC (Byzantine Rite) churches. In 1911, St. Mary's Romanian Orthodox Church parish was organized, and the first church building (1345 West Webster) was consecrated in 1915. St. Nicholas Catholic Church (4309 Olcott Avenue) was founded in 1913. The First Romanian Baptist Church (2622 North Ashland Avenue) was founded in 1914. After 1948, PROTESTANTS were allowed to emigrate from Romania in large numbers on account of their outspoken opposition to Communism. They established several Fundamentalist and Pentecostal churches, bringing the number of Romanian Protestant churches in Chicago to 12 at the end of the millennium.

In 1907, Romanians organized their first community group, *Speranta,* a MUTUAL BENEFIT SOCIETY. It was joined in 1909 by the *Emigrantul,* a cultural and beneficial organization. A Romanian-language NEWSPAPER, *Libertatea,* began publishing in 1911. In 1913, a fraternal organization, *Simion Barnutiu,* was founded, followed by youth CLUBS, political groups, and FOLKLORE societies like *Tineretului* (1916), *Independentsa* (1920), and *Caluseri* (1920s). The women's association *Credinta* was founded in 1916, and in 1918 the Romanian American Citizens Club organized to gain political recognition. In the early 1920s, Saint Mary's parish opened its "Coliba," or community center (2213 North Clybourn Avenue), which became the center of social and cultural life for the North Side community for many years. In 1939, the second Romanian Orthodox Church in Chicago, "Holy Nativity," was founded.

During the second half of the twentieth century, new community groups developed, especially among the Protestant population. Groups like Bucovina Mission helped Romanians settle in Chicago. Others, like the Romanian Missionary Society, Romanian American Alliance, and Romanian Freedom Forum were founded in the 1980s and '90s to organize for political rights and protest Communism in Romania. In 1998, the Illinois Romanian American Community united these groups together in a Chicago-wide alliance.

Mayor Richard J. Daley declared May 10, 1975, Romanian National Day. While the 2000 census found 11,871 Romanian immigrants and 25,050 residents of Romanian ancestry in the Chicago metropolitan region, community leaders estimated between 50,000 and 65,000 Romanians in the Chicago area.

Robert Morrissey

See also: Demography; Eastern Orthodox; Multicentered Chicago; Religion, Chicago's Influence on

Romeoville, IL, Will County, 29 miles SW of the Loop. Beginning in the 1830s, the planning and construction of the ILLINOIS & MICHIGAN CANAL generated development throughout the canal corridor southwest of Chicago. Anticipating increased commerce and rising land costs as a result of the canal, private speculators planned several towns in the area, including Juliet (later JOLIET) and Marseilles.

Civic officials also participated in the process of town creation. Acting under the mandate of the state legislature, a board of commissioners platted towns and sold lots to the public to generate funds for canal construction. Proposed town locations selected by the commissioners included a site north of Juliet; hoping to generate a rivalry with the neighboring village (and perhaps displaying their sense of humor), commissioners named the new town after Shakespeare's romantic hero—Romeo. In 1845, when the citizens of Juliet changed their town name to Joliet, in honor of Louis Jolliet, residents of Romeo responded by adopting the name Romeoville.

Expecting to profit from commerce and settlement along the waterway, REAL-ESTATE speculators began to purchase and develop lots in Romeo. The town's earliest inhabitants included many canal construction workers. Romeoville's economy, however, like that of other canal towns, depended on surrounding farms, including dairy operations. The town provided farmers with services, goods, and access to markets in which they could sell their produce. In the last decades of the nineteenth century and in the early twentieth century, mining in adjacent limestone QUARRIES supplemented the village's agricultural economy.

In the early twentieth century, industrialists were turning to Will County for development sites, building new factories near Joliet, LOCKPORT, and LEMONT. Unlike these towns, however, which were located on the flatter east side of the DES PLAINES RIVER, the center of Romeoville sat upon the bluffs on the west side of the river, less accessible both to the canal and to the major freight lines. While neighboring industrial centers expanded during the first half of the twentieth century, Romeoville's population decreased, dropping below 150 in 1950.

During the 1950s and 1960s, however, suburban development transformed Romeoville. Private developers purchased farmland along the west bank of the Des Plaines River for the construction of residential SUBDIVISIONS, which eventually were annexed as part of Romeoville. The village's population soared to more than 3,500 in 1960. Buoyed by this construction and ANNEXATION, as well as by the completion of Interstate 55 (Stevenson EXPRESSWAY), the population of Romeoville continued to rise, and by 1970 more than 12,000 resided in the village. The population and economy of Romeoville continued to expand, attracting retail and office developments away from the older central business districts. In 2000 the village had 21,153 residents.

By the 1990s, light and medium manufacturers had located in Romeoville, attracted by the village's proximity to Chicago and Joliet, the existing industry along the SANITARY AND SHIP CANAL, and numerous other TRANSPORTATION services. After reaching across the waterway and incorporating developed tracts along the eastern shore of the canal, the village boasted the second-highest industrial tax base by percentage within the Chicago metropolitan area.

Sarah S. Marcus

See also: Economic Geography; Metropolitan Growth; Suburbs and Cities as Dual Metropolis; Water

Further reading: Conzen, Michael P., and Kay J. Carr, eds. *The Illinois and Michigan Canal National Heritage Corridor: A Guide to Its History and Sources.* 1988. • *History of Will County, Illinois.* 1878. • Local history reference file. Fountaindale Public Library, Romeoville, IL.

Roosevelt University. In 1945, 68 professors from Chicago's Central YMCA College, protesting racial quotas imposed on applicants, walked out determined to found an institution of higher education based on principles of social justice, academic excellence, and equal opportunity. Named for President Franklin Roosevelt after his death in April, the new college was independent, nonsectarian, and coeducational. Eleanor Roosevelt, as well as Marshall Field, Albert Einstein, Thomas Mann, and Marian Anderson, joined the early advisory board. The first faculty included a number of notable European REFUGEES and minority scholars.

In 1946 the college purchased the deteriorating AUDITORIUM BUILDING on Michigan and Congress Avenues, and faculty spent time not only in class but also cleaning, painting, and repairing the grand old facility. In 1954, the Chicago Musical College (founded by Florenz Ziegfeld in 1867) merged with Roosevelt, which at that time also became a university. The university was rededicated in 1959 to honor the name of Eleanor as well as Franklin. In 1996, Roosevelt opened a second permanent campus in northwest suburban SCHAUMBURG.

Organized into colleges of arts and sciences, performing arts, education, business, and continuing education, Roosevelt University from the outset served international students, minorities, and first-generation college students, and pioneered in offering flexible class schedules for working adults. By 2004 the 65,000 alumni included the late Chicago mayor Harold Washington, jazz great Ramsey Lewis, jouralist and author Ira Berkow, and police chiefs Matt Rodriguez, LeRoy Martin, and Fred Rice.

Lynn Y. Weiner

See also: Loop; Universities and Their Cities

Further reading: Roosevelt University Archives. Chicago, IL. • Weil, Rolf. *Through These Portals: From Immigrant to University President.* 1991.

Roseland, Community Area 49, 13 miles S of the Loop. The village of Roseland had its origins in 1849, when a band of recently arrived DUTCH families built their homes along the Chicago–Thornton Road. Perched on the ridge west of Lake CALUMET between what is now 103rd and 111th Streets, High Prairie, as it was then known, took shape around the Reformed Church, the small truck farms, and the stores located on the road later known as Michigan Avenue. High Prairie prospered, its farms made profitable by Chicago to its north and the stockyards to the west. Its population grew, most often by additional Dutch settlers who, after 1852, arrived from the east at the Michigan Central RAILROAD station in nearby KENSINGTON.

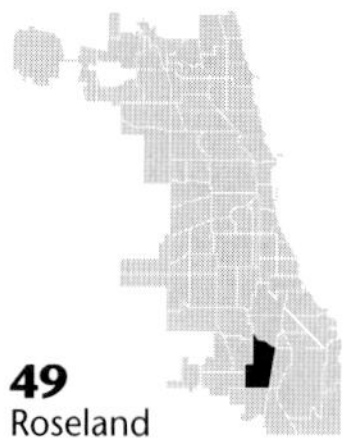

In 1873, James H. Bowen, president of the Calumet and Chicago Canal and Dock Company, suggested the name Roseland for the tidy village with its beautiful flowers. Residents agreed. Seven years later, Bowen initiated even more substantial changes when his company sold more than four thousand acres of land on Roseland's eastern edge to the Pullman Land Association for the Pullman Car Works and the town of PULLMAN. Within a decade, Roseland's and Pullman's fates had been inextricably merged along with those of the other communities that eventually grew in Pullman's shadow: Kensington, Gano, BURNSIDE, and WEST PULLMAN. Its Michigan Avenue stores served customers from all those communities. Pullman workers bought and rented homes from the Dutch who preceded them. By the 1890s, when all of Roseland was finally annexed to Chicago, it had become an ethnically and religiously diverse retail and residential community surrounded by a growing number of large industries.

The hiring policies of Pullman and other industries shaped Roseland's population and politics. The 1894 PULLMAN STRIKE created a larger community that transcended old town boundaries and left it with a legacy of political radicalism. Twice before WORLD WAR I, this Greater Pullman/Roseland district elected a SOCIALIST alderman. Local real-estate agents fought against this radicalism, selling an image of comfortable homes on tree-lined streets easily accessible to downtown Chicago by the Illinois Central and the Chicago & Eastern Illinois. By the 1920s, the community that was once a stop on the UNDERGROUND RAILROAD added whiteness to its list of advantages. Local REAL-ESTATE agents urged racially RESTRICTIVE COVENANTS on new developers and current homeowners. The South End Businessmen's Association even lobbied UNIVERSITY OF CHICAGO sociologists unsuccessfully to draw Roseland COMMUNITY AREA boundaries to exclude the small AFRICAN AMERICAN community of Lilydale, just north of the original High Prairie settlement on Michigan Avenue.

Strains between Roseland's diverse neighborhoods continued throughout the 1920s and '30s. Neighborhoods of residents whose religion committed them to temperance stood next to neighborhoods that manufactured alcohol for the Capones. The GREAT DEPRESSION and the end of PROHIBITION shattered the local economy as banks and building associations collapsed, workers lost their jobs, and the end of Prohibition stopped the profits from home brewing. Michigan Avenue became the site of vigorous debate and protest about Roseland's future as organizations from the Unemployed Citizens' Council to the Anti–Property Tax League sought support for their solutions.

WORLD WAR II returned prosperity to the community, but the debate over the nature of Roseland continued. The successful efforts of local businessman Donald O'Toole to construct housing for African Americans in nearby Princeton Park split Roseland apart. Spurred on by the *Calumet Index,* local leaders launched a 1943 petition drive to fight the construction of Altgeld Gardens in nearby Riverdale by the CHICAGO HOUSING AUTHORITY. More than 11,000 residents signed the unsuccessful petition. In 1947, Roselanders joined in the violence aimed at African American residents living in veterans' housing in Fernwood, one of Greater Roseland's oldest residential neighborhoods.

New housing development on Roseland's vacant edges brought a short-lived growth spurt in the 1950s and early 1960s. Changing industrial patterns, however, led to a decline in the community's economic fortunes. Production at Pullman and other local industries slowed. As jobs disappeared, workers followed their jobs to the suburbs. Joining them there were residents who feared integration. Despite sporadic efforts to create an integrated community and the commitment of several European ethnic communities to stay in place, the racial composition of the community area changed dramatically between 1965 and 1975. Its ECONOMIC GEOGRAPHY, however, changed more slowly. Greater Roseland continued to be home to the middle-class and elite on its edges; elsewhere it was home to successful working-class families.

The inflation of the 1970s followed by the collapse of the steel and automotive industries in the 1980s left many of Roseland's newest families without jobs. The virtually complete turnover of population meant that community institutions that had helped residents in earlier times no longer existed or were not established enough to carry the burden. Stores like the Peoples Store, which had accepted city scrip during the Depression, had also moved to the suburbs. The Pullman Company, which had loaned money to the local bank and juggled jobs to keep income in the community during the same decade, had closed its doors permanently. The out-of-state lending companies that financed more recent mortgages had little incentive to help individual lenders. By the mid-1980s, Roseland had become known for its high rates of HUD repossessions and was designated an Urban Homestead area.

Roseland has yet to recover from the effects of those decades of economic decline. The evolution and growing influence of community organizations, however, offer the possibility that Roseland might come to share in Chicago's new prosperity.

Janice L. Reiff

See also: Community Organizing; Contested Spaces; Economic Geography; Iron and Steel; Racism, Ethnicity, and White Identity; South Side

Further reading: *Calumet Index.* Various issues. • Rowlands, Marie K. *Down an Indian Trail in 1849: The Story of Roseland.* 1987. • *South End Reporter.* Various issues.

Roselle, IL, DuPage and Cook Counties, 24 miles west of the Loop. Elijah and Electa Hough moved from Massachusetts in 1836 to the area that would later bear the name of their youngest son, Roselle, an army colonel, a prominent Chicago businessman, and a driving force for Roselle.

As in much of DuPage County in the years before the Civil War, eastern migrants and German immigrants came to the area to raise livestock and grow corn, wheat, and other crops. The village was first platted and named Roselle in 1874.

Churches were among the few institutions these farmers had time for, and the strong German influence is clear. St. John Evangelical Lutheran Church and school were established in 1851, shortly after a Methodist church had been founded. By 1899, three area congregations had formed a Lutheran school district. Their first school was called Roselle Lutheran School, or the German School (because both English and German were taught there). In 1910, Trinity Lutheran congregation was formed and incorporated the German School.

Roselle Hough took a tack different from most other area farmers in the years after the Civil War. He chose to grow flax, not wheat or corn. Looking for opportunities beyond farming, Hough established the Illinois Linen Company, which manufactured linen and rope, and used his financial and political clout to persuade the Chicago & Pacific Railroad (Chicago, Milwaukee & St. Paul) to reroute through his land. Hough hired ex-convicts and ruffians from Chicago as laborers and built a hotel called the "Beehive" to house them. Their notorious drinking and fighting earned the town the nickname "Raise Hell."

By 1895 Roselle Hough had died, Roselle's soil was exhausted, and the flax mill had been shut down. The factory was converted to a tile and brick company, which closed five years later. The area reverted to farming, but Roselle as a whole continued to thrive into the twentieth century with grain, lumber, and gristmills, as well as access to the railroad "milk run."

The village of Bloomingdale was incorporated in February 1889, combining the present-day villages of Bloomingdale and Roselle, with boundaries identified on the plat of 1874. In 1922 municipal differences, such as a desire for a sewer and water system, led Roselle to incorporate as its own village.

The Roselle Park Club, built in 1898, was a popular recreation spot at the turn of the century. In 1926 Shriners from Roselle opened the Medinah Country Club. Eventually the land surrounding it became known as Medinah, and it was disassociated from Roselle.

Roselle grew quickly following the world wars. Subdivisions of single- and multiple-family dwellings were developed, and various light industries were established, including the Lynfred Winery. Roselle's population grew from 6,207 in 1970 to 23,115 in 2000.

Jane S. Teague

See also: Agriculture; Golf; Religious Geography

Further reading: Sanborn, Dorothy. *History of Roselle, Illinois.* 1968. • Thompson, Richard A., ed. *DuPage Roots.* 1985.

Rosemont, IL, Cook County, 14 miles NW of the Loop. Although of limited dimensions, Rosemont's boundaries accommodate a convention center, a performing arts theater, a major-events arena, and rows of hotels. Commercial success has come mainly from the vision of the village president, Donald Stephens, who came to the community in 1939. An insurance underwriter, he was first elected in 1956 and continued in office into the twenty-first century.

The Wisconsin Central Railroad (later the Soo Line) built a line through the area in 1857. The construction of a milk stop drew truck farmers, mostly of German heritage, who peddled produce in Chicago.

Parcels of Rosemont land were sold in Chicago at the 1933 Century of Progress Exposition. Construction began on two subdivisions, one on Thorndale, the other on Scott Street. Nearby Willow Creek frequently spilled its banks, flooding the area and making rowboats a necessity for homeowners. All of the Thorndale subdivision and part of the Scott Street subdivision would ultimately be torn down for expressway construction.

In 1942 the United States government built a Douglas Aircraft assembly plant for wartime production nearby. The facility had an airport and hangars. Following World War II, the city of Chicago bought the plant and in 1949 changed the name to O'Hare. The city had to go through Rosemont to install a water pipeline. In return, Rosemont received water from the city.

Des Plaines, Park Ridge, and Schiller Park all refused to annex what became Rosemont, so Rosemont incorporated, and Donald Stephens became the first village president in 1956. He expanded village boundaries, began commercialization, and worked to correct flooding problems. Stephens also faced personal difficulties when he was linked to crime-syndicate boss Sam Giancana and tried twice for political corruption. He was acquitted in both cases.

Near O'Hare Airport, Rosemont attracted hotels and various entertainment facilities. The Northwest Tollway, I-90, Tri-State Toll Road, and the I-190 spur crisscross Rosemont's small boundaries with easy on and off access. The Rosemont Horizon, an indoor entertainment complex, was built in 1979 and in 1999 was renamed Allstate Arena. The 1992 addition of Waterfall Park at the busy intersection of Higgins and River Roads offered visitors a waterfall and river walk along the Des Plaines River.

An estimated 3.4 million visitors came to Rosemont in 1996. Several new hotels were built in the late 1990s, and by 2000 the city offered 5,687 hotel rooms in 14 hotels. The 2000 population was just 4,224, of whom 79 percent were white, 35 percent Hispanic, 4 percent Asian, and 1 percent African American.

Marilyn Elizabeth Perry

See also: Places of Assembly; Suburbs and Cities as Dual Metropolis

Further reading: Lunde, Anne. "Rosemont History." In *The Village of Rosemont.* Reprint of an article for the *Suburban Times Newspapers,* April 30, 1986. • Reardon, Patrick T. "Everything's Coming Up Rosemont." *Chicago Tribune Magazine,* April 20, 1997. • Walsh, Mary A. "The Growth and the Need—A Geographical History in Story Form." In *A Jubilee of Joy,* 1982.

Rotary International. Founded in Chicago in 1905 by lawyer Paul Harris, Rotary International is an association of clubs whose members meet regularly for sociability, business contacts, and charitable activities. Harris began the club for businessmen who felt isolated in the big city. Early meetings "rotated" between members' offices. Soon Rotary began emphasizing service, and expanded to cities and towns across the country and throughout the world. Despite its big-city origins, Rotary became most associated in America with towns and suburbs, where clubs worked to strengthen communal solidarity. Recently Rotary has stressed its global mission, providing scholarships for study abroad and funding a worldwide fight against polio. Rotary has spawned many imitators, among them Lions Clubs International, organized in Chicago in 1917 and currently headquartered in the Chicago suburb of OAK BROOK. Rotary, with a 1997 membership of 1,213,748 in 28,736 clubs, has been headquartered since the 1950s in EVANSTON.

Jeffrey Charles

See also: Chambers of Commerce; Community Service Organizations; Governing the Metropolis

Further reading: Arnold, Oren. *The Golden Strand: An Informal History of the Rotary Club of Chicago.* 1966. • Charles, Jeffrey. *Service Clubs in American Society: Rotary, Kiwanis, and Lions.* 1993. • Walsh, James P. *The First Rotarian: The Life and Times of Paul Percy Harris, Founder of Rotary.* 1979.

Round Lake, IL, Lake County, 40 miles NW of the Loop. While the retreating Wisconsin glacier left an attractive environment for farmers who entered western LAKE COUNTY after the BLACK HAWK WAR of 1832, the numerous lakes and wet prairies there prevented easy movement to agricultural markets. Farmers traded at stage coach trail communities such as Hainesville, often exchanging dairy products and eggs for what they could not craft on the farm.

In the 1890s, when officials of the Chicago, Milwaukee & St. Paul RAILROAD extended a branch line from their Milwaukee–Chicago main line at LIBERTYVILLE Junction (later Roundout) to Janesville, Wisconsin, western Lake County farmers gained easy access to Chicago.

Landowners near Hainesville such as Amarias M. White knew that a RAILROAD STATION would increase property values. In a classic ploy, White offered the railroad free land in exchange for a station. He also drew up a town plat to show railroad officials that profitable traffic would come through his station site. White succeeded, and Round Lake, named after the nearby lake, not Hainesville, whose inhabitants failed to offer the railroad anything, became the area station on the "Milwaukee Road."

White's promise came true in 1901 when the Armour Company decided to harvest ice from Round Lake for their refrigerator car operations. They erected a massive ice storage building holding over 100,000 tons for shipment in spring and summer months.

In 1908 White and his partners acted to incorporate the station area. The proposed village population was too small to meet incorporation requirements, so area farmers were included in the village with the understanding that, once incorporation was successful, their farms would be disconnected. On January 7, 1909, Round Lake incorporated with White as village president. Soon after, those farmers who wished to disconnect were allowed to do so—an act which prevented present-day residents of the village from having any public access to their namesake lake.

A fire in 1917 destroyed the Armour operation in the village, although a dormitory housing winter ice cutters survived. Noticing vacation resorts which had sprung up around the lake, the Armour Company remodeled its dormitory into a rural summer retreat for company employees. The praise showered on the Round Lake environment by them helped bring a slow trickle of nonagricultural residential growth to the village.

With post–World War II expansion into the suburbs, Round Lake's Armour-era reputation as a rural refuge acted as a magnet for development. People began moving into the unincorporated area around the lake and demanding municipal services. The village of Round Lake failed to make those ANNEXATIONS. As a result new communities, using the words "Round Lake" in their corporate titles, arose. This resulted in a duplication of political hierarchies and village services which still exists.

Since the 1970s, Round Lake has embarked on an expansive annexation program. With ongoing development of those areas, Round Lake is expected to continue to grow.

Craig L. Pfannkuche

See also: Leisure; Meatpacking; Metropolitan Growth; Vacation Spots

Further reading: "Bicentennial Historical Journey through Lakeland." Lakeland Publishers, July 1, 1976. • Village of Round Lake. *Fifty Years Golden Jubilee: 1908–1958.* 1958. • Village of Round Lake. *Memories of Round Lake: 1908–1983.* 1983.

Round Lake Beach, IL, Lake County, 41 miles NW of the Loop. In 1930, land developer L. B. Harris noticed that only a small portion of Round Lake's shoreline had been built up since the coming of the RAILROAD in 1901. The lake's reputation as a resort area convinced him that the west side of the lake could be profitably developed even during the GREAT DEPRESSION. Charging as little as $295 for a summer home lacking electricity, WATER, and sanitary systems, Harris correctly believed that blue-collar Chicagoans would find his development attractive.

As the area's population increased, demands for municipal services grew. Residents voted to incorporate in January 1937 since the neighboring village of ROUND LAKE was unwilling to annex them. John J. Lynch was appointed the temporary president of a village whose name—Round Lake Beach—the state of Illinois refused to accept because of the prior existence of the village of Round Lake. After months of lobbying, the Illinois Secretary of State accepted the village name as sufficiently unique. Hans Roeh was elected village president at the end of April 1937.

Round Lake Beach's population ballooned as returning WORLD WAR II servicemen deserted the city for a suburban setting. The opportunity to have a home costing as little as $895 was a powerful attraction to those veterans. By the early 1960s, Round Lake Beach's population surpassed that of neighboring Round Lake and made "The Beach," as residents call the community, the largest population concentration in western Lake County.

At the same time, Round Lake Beach's leaders forged an aggressive ANNEXATION policy. They hoped that annexation northward to undeveloped Rollins Road, would, together with commercial development there, bring in enough sales taxes to pay the cost of upgrading the area's primitive INFRASTRUCTURE.

Upon reaching Rollins Road, the village borders quickly stretched from Fairfield Road eastward to State Route 83. This expansion meant that Round Lake Beach now encompassed the whole northern half of the lake.

As the area filled with homes in the 1970s, the envisioned commercial area along Rollins Road emerged. Later, to assure continued commercial growth and increasing sales tax receipts, Round Lake Beach instituted a Tax Increment Financing District at the northwest corner of Rollins Road and State Route 83. With the rapidly increasing population and the establishment of the new district, land there quickly attracted major shopping operations.

By the mid 1990s, area growth was so strong that METRA, which directs Chicago metropolitan rail commuter activity, added COMMUTER passenger service to the Wisconsin Central freight line which passes along the eastern edge of the various Round Lake communities. In late 1996, Round Lake Beach village officials proudly dedicated their station on that new line. The dreams of L. B. Harris, Round Lake Beach's first developer, had come to fruition.

Craig L. Pfannkuche

See also: Metropolitan Growth; Taxation and Finance; Transportation

Further reading: *Bicentennial Historical Journey through Lakeland.* Lakeland Publishers. July 1, 1976. • *Round Lake Beach: 50th Anniversary.* Lakeland Publishers. July 1, 1987. • *Silver Anniversary, Round Lake Beach.* Village of Round Lake Beach. 1962.

Round Lake Heights, IL, Lake County, 42 miles NW of the Loop. Originally called Indian Hills, the village is the only one of the four communities including "Round Lake" in its name not located along the lake. Upset with WATER distribution from ROUND LAKE BEACH, some residents fought for incorporation, succeeding on the third try in 1960. Round Lake Heights is now a bedroom community, with a population of 1,347 in 2000.

Craig L. Pfannkuche

See also: Government, Suburban; Lake County, IL

Further reading: *Memories of Round Lake: 1908–1983.* 1983.

Round Lake Park, IL, Lake County, 37 miles NW of the Loop. This third of a collection of villages to rise along the shore of ROUND LAKE began as a late-1930s site for inexpensive country residences. Its residents voted to incorporate in 1947 to help meet the need for improved roads and sanitary facilities. Its 2000 population was 6,308.

Craig L. Pfannkuche

See also: Lake County, IL

Further reading: *Memories of Round Lake: 1908–1983.* 1983.

Russians. "Russian" immigrants include two different groups: ethnic Russians and Russian JEWS. Historically, however, the term "Russian" was inconsistently used by U.S. immigration authorities to include such diverse groups as BELARUSIANS, UKRAINIANS, POLES, non-Russian Jews, and even GERMANS. Historians have therefore had difficulty determining precisely how many Russian immigrants have made Chicago home over the course of the city's history. While a majority of ethnic Russians and Russian Jews settled on the East Coast, Chicago became the largest center of Russian Jews and ethnic Russians in the Midwest.

Between 1861 and 1880, a small number of Russian Jews immigrated to Chicago's SOUTH SIDE, where they were left relatively unharmed by the Great FIRE OF 1871 but then badly hit by the fire of 1874. Russian Jews began arriving in Chicago in larger numbers during the 1880s to escape the persecution that had recently begun intensifying at home. By 1930, they constituted 80 percent of Chicago's Jewish population.

The Russian Jews who arrived in Chicago between 1881 and 1920 created a substitute for the culture of the *shtetl* in the densely populated area around MAXWELL STREET, where they created a thriving outdoor market. These immigrants worked largely in the CLOTHING industry; others became butchers, small merchants, or STREET PEDDLERS. After 1910, the immigrants who had given Maxwell Street its unique character began migrating toward Ashland, NORTH LAWNDALE, LAKE VIEW, and ALBANY PARK. By 1930, the population of Russian Jews in the Maxwell Street area had declined markedly, and after 1945 many began moving even further from the city's center, to the suburbs and to West ROGERS PARK, which remained the largest Jewish community in Chicago through the 1990s. Between 1969 and 1990, 23,000 Russian Jews and an estimated 500 ethnic Russian immigrants settled along Devon Avenue in West Rogers Park, as well as in Albany Park, GLENVIEW, NORTHBROOK, and MOUNT PROSPECT.

Ethnic Russians immigrating to Chicago in the early twentieth century settled most often in WEST TOWN, eventually earning the area around West Division, Wood, and Leavitt Streets the nickname "Little Russia."

The Russian Orthodox community organized around such institutions as Holy Trinity Orthodox Cathedral on North Leavitt, completed in 1903 after a $4,000 donation from the tsar. Between 1920 and 1924, many of those forced to flee in the aftermath of the 1917 Russian Revolution settled in Chicago. At the same time, a number of those who supported the new Soviet system returned to Russia to join the revolution. Still, many "reds" and "whites" continued to live side by side in Chicago. The "whites" gathered in Holy Trinity Cathedral while the "reds" met on North Western Avenue for mass, or in the Russian Workers Co-Operative Restaurant on West Division.

Throughout the 1920s, many ethnic Russians and Russian Jews worked on Chicago's West Side for McCormick Reaper (International Harvester), Western Electric, or Sears, Roebuck & Co. With large employers laying off workers in the early years of the GREAT DEPRESSION, the Russian-American Citizen's Club was organized in 1930 to lend a hand and voice to a growing number of unemployed workers. The Russian Independent Mutual Aid Society, a working-class fraternal society founded in 1914, incorporated in 1931 to provide benefits in cases of injury or death and to lend small sums of money to those hit hardest by an unforgiving economy.

Both ethnic Russians and Russian Jews have worked to preserve their own cultures while simultaneously adapting to life in the United States. The Russian Literary Society was founded in 1890. The short-lived Russian People's University (1918–1920) as well as various cultural festivals such as "Znanie" were created to preserve traditional Russian folk songs, literature, and dances. And though only a handful survived more than a few years, at least 19 NEWSPAPERS and 11 Russian magazines were published in Chicago after 1891. In 1973 the Friends of Refugees of Eastern Europe (FREE) began helping to ensure that local knowledge of Jewish heritage be remembered and shared. Other Jews from the former Soviet Union have maintained more of a Russian identity than a Jewish one, continuing to speak Russian and, together with ethnic Russians, Ukrainians, and Belarusians, supporting the publication of more than 10 magazines in Russian, including the biweekly *Zemliaki* (since 1996), the weekly *Obzor* (since 1997), and the daily *Svet* (since 1992). They have also organized language-specific libraries, POETRY readings, and choirs.

Katarzyna Zechenter

See also: Americanization; Demography; Eastern Orthodox; Multicentered Chicago; Mutual Benefit Societies

Further reading: Cutler, Irving. *The Jews of Chicago: From Shtetl to Suburb.* 1996. • Eubank, Nancy. *The Russians in America.* 1973. • Wertsman, Vladimir, ed. *The Russians in America, 1727–1975: A Chronology and Fact Book.* 1977.

S

Sac. Although oral traditions, linguistic evidence, and early FRENCH accounts suggest that the Sacs (or Sauks) originally inhabited the Lower Peninsula of Michigan, particularly the Saginaw Bay region, French Jesuits first encountered the tribe in 1669 in Wisconsin, where they occupied several villages closely associated with POTAWATOMIS and MESQUAKIES, near the head of Green Bay. Like the Mesquakies (or Foxes), Ho-Chunks (or Winnebagos), and other Wisconsin tribes, the Sacs periodically hunted southward around the southern tip of LAKE MICHIGAN, but there is little evidence that they ever erected any permanent villages in the Chicago region. Between 1712 and 1733, when both the FUR TRADE and intertribal relations in Wisconsin and northern Illinois were repeatedly disrupted by warfare between the French and the Mesquakies, the Sacs first attempted to remain neutral in the conflict, then split into two bands. One remained at Green Bay and the other relocated to the lower St. Joseph River in southwestern Michigan. By 1718, Sacs from the St. Joseph village regularly hunted along the Kankakee River northward to the PORTAGE between the Chicago and Des Plaines, while developing close ties to Potawatomis who also resided in the region. Ten years later, in an attempt to avoid the conflict between the

Mesquakies and French, the Sac villagers in Wisconsin temporarily abandoned their villages at Green Bay and joined their kinsmen on the St. Joseph River. In 1730, warriors from these combined villages reluctantly participated in the siege and slaughter of Mesquakies at a great battle on the prairie in Illinois, but following the battle most of the Sacs returned to Green Bay and used their influence to intercede in the Mesquakie survivors' behalf.

In 1733, Sac villagers at Green Bay provided refuge for the remaining Mesquakies in their village, and one year later, when a French expedition demanded they surrender the Mesquakies, the Sacs refused. After the resulting skirmish the Sacs and Mesquakies fled to Iowa. By 1738, the Sacs returned to Illinois, establishing Saukenuk, a major village at Rock Island. Saukenuk was occupied by the Sacs until 1831, when Illinois militia units forced the tribe to abandon the village and again retreat to Iowa. Black Hawk's attempt to reoccupy the village in 1832 caused widespread concern in Illinois and touched off the BLACK HAWK WAR, which ended any Sac occupancy of the Prairie State.

During the first third of the nineteenth century, Sac warriors and trading parties repeatedly passed through the Chicago region on "the Great Sac Trail," a track that led from Saukenuk, across northern Illinois to the southern tip of Lake Michigan, then eastward across southern Michigan to the Detroit region, and finally across the Detroit River to the British Indian Agency at Amherstburg. Sac war parties traversed this route to assist the British during the War of 1812, and in the postwar period they continued to pass through Chicago en route to Canada, where they would receive gifts from British Indian agents.

Today, a few Sac people form part of the modern NATIVE AMERICAN community in Chicago, but most live in either Kansas or Oklahoma.

R. David Edmunds

See also: Chicago in the Middle Ground; Native American Religion; Treaties

Further reading: Edmunds, R. David, and Joseph L. Peyser. *The Fox Wars: The Mesquakie Challenge to New France.* 1993. • Quaife, Milo Milton. *Chicago and the Old Northwest, 1673–1835.* 1913. • Wheeler-Voegelin, Erminie, and J. A. Jones. *Indians of Western Illinois and Southern Wisconsin.* 1974.

Sacred Music. Chicago's sacred music traditions have historically formed from a tension between mainline and sectarian religions. Mainline religions are those that attract large memberships who share belief and participate together in common religious and musical practices. The members of a mainline religious institution, as the common adage observes, "sing from the same songbook." Mainline musical practice has many possible meanings, but most reflect historical processes of consolidation. In sacred music history, sectarianism, on the other hand, arises from musical repertories and practices that (1) preserve, (2) express meaningful differences, and (3) resist the ideological domination of mainline religious organizations. Music functions, therefore, to give voice to sacred identities of difference.

At the same time, those identities have also depended on the city's diverse ethnic groups, the transformation of urban and suburban spaces, and the presence of the international and the global at local and neighborhood levels in the city. In the continuously changing interaction between populations and spaces, identity and belief, and consolidation and difference, sacred music has reflected and influenced Chicago's rich religious heritage.

During its history, Chicago has been home to numerous mainline sacred music traditions that have also played a significant role in shaping the North American sacred musical landscape. Among the earliest was a Lutheran mainstream that emerged from the interaction of the hymn and chorale traditions of Central and North European PROTESTANT immigrants in the mid and late nineteenth century. In twentieth-century Chicago, more than in any other urban center, GOSPEL music from both white and AFRICAN AMERICAN churches consolidated to form one of the most American of all Protestant musical mainstreams. Compositions by sacred musicians from Chicago served the entire city and country. Sacred MUSIC PUBLISHERS, which flourished in Chicago, and religious schools have historically channeled the mainstream flowing through the city's sacred musical landscape.

Sectarian musical traditions proliferated as new migrant groups established themselves in Chicago and as ethnic and cultural diversity responded to American multiculturalism. Whereas some sectarian musical traditions consolidated and entered the mainstream, others resisted and their sectarian qualities became even more extreme.

The first sectarian traditions were those of the ethnic groups that settled in Chicago in large numbers during the nineteenth century. Sacred musical practices in the ethnic church connected immigrants to the nation or region from which they came and therefore played an important role in maintaining ethnic identity. The Central and Northern European communities cultivated sacred traditions that were GERMAN, NORWEGIAN, or SWEDISH and only secondarily Lutheran. Ethnic sectarian traditions depended extensively on song- and prayerbooks published in Europe. Only later in the nineteenth century did repertories published in America supplant those of the immigrant generation to create a Lutheran musical mainstream. Even then, Lutheran musical traditions followed the separate channels opened by German and Scandinavian ethnic communities, with processes of consolidation and fragmentation constantly uniting and rediverting the Lutheran musical mainstream.

In the city's Jewish communities, waves of Eastern European JEWS practicing various musical traditions of the diaspora challenged the more mainstream Reform movement from Central Europe, creating several mainline musical traditions. Chicago was an early home to the publication of prayer- and songbooks for Reform Judaism, which was musically innovative and theologically liberal. One of the most important composers of new works for the synagogue was Max Jankowsky, whose compositions for Temple KAM Isaiah Israel have united American Jewish musical traditions across several denominational lines.

At the turn of the twentieth century, a new wave of initially sectarian traditions began to influence Chicago's sacred music: the spiritual repertories and performances of the African American church. The GREAT MIGRATION quickly multiplied the number and variety of black sacred practices, many of which had formed in the South as responses to white mainline churches, which in turn influenced the formation of mainline GOSPEL traditions in Chicago. African American traditions were improvisatory, requiring extensive congregational participation and empowering African American churches to adapt gospel to their own needs, while at the same time connecting each church service to the gospel mainstream. They also brought about a shift from stable repertories anchored in hymnbooks to oral traditions that stimulated musical change. As some African American traditions acquired more characteristics of the Protestant mainline sacred practices during the 1920s, a new gospel tradition began to take shape through the efforts of sacred music composers and performers such as Thomas A. Dorsey and Lucie Campbell. Drawing on evangelical hymnody for some resources, they introduced a performative context into black gospel.

During the second half of the twentieth century, sacred music traditions were enriched by new ethnic groups, especially from Latin America and Asia. Latin American influence on Chicago Catholic traditions was considerable, both because of the growing presence of Spanish in the Mass and because of the introduction of Hispanic repertories and instruments that created, for example, "mariachi Masses." Asian sectarian traditions, though sometimes Christian, as in many CHINESE and KOREAN neighborhoods, diversified the sacred music landscape by expanding the presence of MUSLIM, BUDDHIST, and HINDU musical practices. Sacred musical traditions from Asian religions are both ethnically localized, as in suburban South Indian Hindu temples, and interethnic, especially in Chicago's Muslim communities. Like the groups that preceded them, these new ethnic groups have introduced new patterns of musical sectarianism but also, as

Choir boys from Cathedral College of Sacred Heart walking out of the school and across the street to Holy Name Cathedral, 1909. Photographer: Unknown. Source: Chicago Historical Society.

in the case of the Midwest Buddhist Temple, have transformed the religious mainstream by contributing their own musical practices.

Despite their consolidating functions, mainline musical traditions also demonstrate dynamic histories. The music of Chicago's ROMAN CATHOLICS forms one of the most powerful forces undergirding acculturation, which should be understood as both a response to ethnic diversity and a religiocultural common denominator. The music of Catholic liturgy

THE

NORTH-WESTERN

HYMN BOOK.

A COLLECTION ADAPTED TO CHURCH, SUNDAY SCHOOL AND REVIVAL SERVICES.

COMPILED BY D. L. MOODY.

CHICAGO.

1868.

Title page of *The North-Western Hymn Book*, compiled by D. L. Moody (Chicago, 1868). Source: Chicago Historical Society.

during the nineteenth century offered immigrants with diverse linguistic backgrounds an experience all could share. Modern Catholic musical traditions, even in the post–Vatican II era, rely on the symbolic musical functions of the Chicago Archbishopric's centrality and other musical institutions controlled by the ROMAN CATHOLIC ARCHDIOCESE OF CHICAGO such as music education in Catholic schools.

Protestant evangelical traditions form a different type of musical mainstream. The evangelical hymn tradition, which stresses congregational singing of strophic hymns (hymns with multiple verses), most of them composed in the United States, first took shape during the eras of religious "awakening," or revival, at the end of the eighteenth century and then in the 1830s. Evangelical hymns depend on extensive participation and are thus musically accessible to the broadest possible public. Chicago played a very important role in the canonization of Protestant evangelical hymnody. Several of the most notable and influential hymn composers, including Ira D. Sankey and Philip Bliss, were active in Chicago, and Chicago publishers and institutions, such as the MOODY BIBLE INSTITUTE, contributed significantly to the dissemination of hymnbooks. Evangelical hymnody contains an essential mainline corpus for Protestants of European, especially English-speaking, heritage.

As Chicago underwent socioeconomic, ethnic, and racial transformations in the late twentieth century, sacred musical practices responded to a changing sacred landscape. Many mainline traditions remain connected to the urban center, especially the larger Catholic and Protestant churches in downtown Chicago. Certain sectarian traditions, especially in the larger ethnic communities, such as the MEXICAN and POLISH American PARISHES, have effectively entered the mainstream. The proliferation of sectarian African American religious music continues, especially in storefront churches. At the start of the twenty-first century the relation between mainline and sectarian sacred traditions is more dynamic than ever before.

The sacred landscape of Chicago also responds to the interaction between urban and suburban sacred musical traditions. Many ethnic and sectarian traditions have relocated themselves to the suburbs, although they may retain strong connections to an historical mother parish. The SLOVENIAN Catholic parishes that anchored Slovenian musical traditions after World War II are now distributed throughout several suburbs, with a spiritual center at St. Mary's monastery in LEMONT, even though St. Stephen's Church still provides occasional masses and concerts of sacred music in Slovenian. Coptic Orthodox Christian churches are entirely a suburban phenomenon, though many members, Arabic- and non-Arabic-speaking, live in the city. The core of Jewish musical practices, too, has shifted to the suburbs, although many synagogues consciously maintain the musical and theological traditions of a parent synagogue in the city. BOSNIAN and ALBANIAN Muslim communities have adapted well to suburban social structures.

The sacred landscape of Chicago's suburbs supports new religious institutions, which in turn undergird the music of new ethnic communities. The Hindu temple, an important component of the suburban sacred landscape, provides a site for consolidating Hindu sacred traditions, such as the repertories of *bhajans,* or hymns, that provide the basis for individual and congregational worship. It is in the suburban Hindu temple, furthermore, that schools of Indian classical dance, *bharata natyam,* thrive, combining instruction in music and dance with understanding sacred traditions of Hinduism, as well as rites of passage.

The new musical dynamics of Chicago's sacred landscape are remarkably global. Pilgrimage within and beyond the city has grown together with religious communities for whom pilgrimage is an essential component of self-identity. MEXICAN American Catholics, in particular, regularly undertake pilgrimage to Guadalupe. The ritual practices connected to the Guadalupe pilgrimage are bolstered by musical practices in Chicago's Mexican communities, giving pilgrimage an everyday aura. The abundance of miracles in Chicago's Catholic and EASTERN ORTHODOX communities has also unleashed new forms of pilgrimage, local and regional. Weeping icons of the Virgin Mary have been the most frequent contexts for miracles, and new musical practices transform these into sacred responses to warfare and poverty, especially within communities from the former YUGOSLAVIA and Orthodox Christian communities from the Middle East.

Through liturgy, performance practice, and repertory, the sacred musical traditions of Chicago have historically given voice to the common and the different—and the new that results from the blending of the two. In the late twentieth century, the musical traditions of Chicago's sacred landscape have demonstrated an increasing hybridity. These hybrid musical practices reflect new religious affiliations and new mainline traditions that have emerged from the fragmentation of older mainline traditions. They also promise that Chicago's complex sacred music history will continue into the future.

Philip V. Bohlman

See also: Ethnic Music; Multicentered Chicago; Religion, Chicago's Influence On; Religious Geography

Further reading: Bliss, Philip P., and Ira D. Sankey. *Gospel Hymns.* 1876. • Castillo, Ana, ed. *Goddess of the Americas/La Diosa de las Américas: Writings on the Virgin of Guadalupe.* 1996. • Epstein, Dena J. *Music Publishing in Chicago before 1871: The Firm of Root and Cady.* 1969.

Sailing and Boating. Before there were AIRPORTS, EXPRESSWAYS, and RAILROADS, Chicago was a water city. The city grew up at the crossroads of a vast inland waterway between the GREAT LAKES and the Mississippi River. Early Chicagoans exploited the waterways both for their BUSINESS interests and for recreation. Many had come from the east, bringing with them an avid interest in that most genteel East Coast pastime, yachting.

The Chicago Yacht Club, the city's first, was established in 1875 with 37 charter members. Today the club has locations at Monroe and Belmont Harbors and sponsors the annual CHICAGO TO MACKINAC RACE. Columbia Yacht club, also at Monroe Harbor, has traditionally used retired ships as floating clubhouses. Its current clubship is the 371-foot *Abegweit,* a former Nova Scotia ferry and the largest privately owned yacht on the Great Lakes. Many of the other yacht clubs along the lake offer junior sailing and community service programs such as the Burnham Park Yacht Club's Judd Goldman Adaptive Sailing Program for disabled sailors. Several clubs also sponsor "frostbite" sailing, for hearty souls who want to brave the frigid winter waters.

The yacht clubs sponsor highly organized sailboat racing. Series races and regattas are held on weekends. Less formal "beer can" races are held on Wednesday nights. Boats race around courses marked by buoys several miles out in the lake. There are also port-to-port races from Chicago to such cities as WAUKEGAN; MICHIGAN CITY, Indiana; and St. Joseph, Michigan. Racers compete in all weather, from May through October.

LAKE MICHIGAN boating is by no means the reserve of yacht club members. Sailboards, personal watercraft ("Jet Skis"), and small boats arrive on car tops and trailers, shoving off from beaches and boat launches all along the shoreline. Sport fishing also draws many boaters to the lake and to area rivers.

The Chicago PARK DISTRICT operates the second largest harbor system in the country. It can accommodate 5,000 boats in eight harbors: Montrose, Belmont, Diversey, Monroe, Burnham, 59th Street, and the Jackson Park inner and outer harbors. These harbors are part of a vast lakefront park system built on lakefill land. The Park District began a $35 million harbor improvement project in 1996 to upgrade aging boat slips and other facilities. The District offers public sailing classes through its "Rainbow Fleet" and sponsors the annual Venetian Night—a parade of boats festooned with lights and manned by costumed crews.

Many lakefront communities north and south of Chicago also have harbors, boat launches, and yacht clubs. NORTHWESTERN UNIVERSITY in EVANSTON has a very active sailing club, with a fleet of small Olympic-class boats.

Boating is also popular on inland waters. Canoeists enjoy the FOX RIVER, Skokie Lagoons, upper reaches of the Chicago River, and even the old commercial waterway, the ILLINOIS & MICHIGAN CANAL. Sailing, water-skiing, and fishing are also popular on inland lakes from Indiana to the Wisconsin border.

For those who do not own boats, there is a booming tour boat industry. Dozens of cruise ships, small tour boats, and water taxis ply lake and river from May to October.

Geoffrey Baer

See also: Leisure; Shipbuilding; Waterfront

Saint Xavier University. In 1846, Chicago's first ROMAN CATHOLIC bishop invited the order of the Sisters of Mercy, who had arrived in the United States from Ireland only three years before, to open a grade school for girls in Chicago. The result, Saint Xavier, was granted an Illinois charter in 1847. After its downtown campus was destroyed by the Great FIRE OF 1871, the school's patrons regrouped, and, by 1915, they were offering college-level classes for women. Saint Xavier opened an expanded campus in the MOUNT GREENWOOD neighborhood on the city's Southwest Side in 1956, and the college became coeducational in 1969. In 1998, Saint Xavier's 35 bachelor's degree programs served more than 4,000 students, approximately three-fourths of whom would become the first in their family to graduate from college.

Sarah Fenton

See also: Barat College; Universities and Their Cities

Saloons. The saloon in Chicago had its origin in two places. The oldest was the inn or tavern, a combination RESTAURANT, HOTEL, and drinking place. Much of the city's early social life revolved around such spots as the Green Tree, Sauganash, and the Eagle. A second type of drinking place evolved from grocers and provisioners who began to sell hard LIQUOR in wholesale quantities. At first, their sample rooms were literally places where customers could taste test the stock; long afterward, "sample room" became simply another name for saloon. By the late 1850s the term *saloon* had begun to appear in directories and common usage as a term for an establishment that specialized in beer and liquor sales by the drink, with food and lodging as secondary concerns in some places. Stops such as Stacey's Tavern in present-day GLEN ELLYN or the Pre-Emption House in NAPERVILLE were popular among farmers journeying to the city.

The rapidly growing ethnic population swelled the saloon ranks through the mid-nineteenth century, but during the early 1880s a growing overcapacity in the BREWERY industry began to force change. Overestimates of future growth, along with easy rail access to Chicago for St. Louis and Milwaukee brewers, left all of the producers scrambling for retail outlets. The answer lay in an adaptation of the British "tied-house" system of control. Brewers purchased hundreds of storefronts, especially on the highly desired corner locations, which they rented to prospective saloonkeepers, along with all furnishings and such recreational equipment as billiard tables and bowling alleys. Schlitz and a few others even built elaborate saloons, examples of which still survive in LAKE VIEW on North Southport Avenue. The Chicago City Council also contributed to the brewery domination by increasing the saloon license from $50 to $500 between 1883 and 1885 to pay for an expanded POLICE force supposedly made necessary by the barrooms. Relatively few independent proprietors could afford to pay such amounts.

The new realities of business not only transformed many saloonkeepers from entrepreneurs to employees but may have contributed to many of them turning to criminal involvement to supplement their incomes. Few Chicago bars honored the midnight closing hour, and some welcomed petty GAMBLING and PROSTITUTION. The need for protection from further legislation and the fear of tighter police enforcement drove saloonkeepers toward POLITICS. Many of the most colorful personages in Chicago's political history, including "Bathhouse John" Coughlin, Michael "Hinky Dink" Kenna, John Powers, and Edward F. "Foxy Ed" Cullerton, were barkeeps.

Politics was also a natural avocation for saloonkeepers because of the adaptable social nature of their business. In neighborhoods where literacy was low, the bar provided the principal place for the exchange of information about employment, housing, and the many tragedies that beset the city's poor; a savvy politician could turn his access to resources into votes. In slum districts, his place provided a safe for valuables, a telephone for emergencies, a NEWSPAPER for the literate, a bowl on the bar for charity collections. In factory districts, saloons became labor exchanges and union halls, as well as providing a place to cash paychecks. On busy streets and downtown, the saloon provided a restroom. And in all areas of the city, the purchase of a drink allowed access to the free lunch sideboard. This feature usually offered only cold foods, but competition could make it elaborate.

Saloons also varied by ethnic group. The IRISH preferred stand-up bars where whiskey was the drink of choice and women could obtain service only through the back door. GERMAN saloons were more brightly illuminated, more likely to serve restaurant food and beer at tables, and more oriented toward family patronage. Germans were often at odds with temperance forces over Sunday operation—illegal in Illinois but almost universal in Chicago—and over the operation of beer gardens in outlying neighborhoods. Other ethnic groups added their own features and their unique cuisines on the sideboard, while a few groups, most notably Scandinavians, JEWS, GREEKS, and ITALIANS, either preferred intimate social clubs or did little drinking in public.

The first decade of the twentieth century saw increasing accusations of saloon involvement in crime. Complaints about vicious DANCE HALLS and alliances with the so-called white slave trade led to passage of a $1,000 license rate in 1906, along with a moratorium on new permits. The latter created a license premium, a value on the transferable right to hold the permit that often reached $2,500 because of the desire of so many to enter the business and the brewers to dominate it. Saloonkeepers also saw their markets geographically limited. Aldermen from outlying neighborhoods had gradually eliminated liquor sales from their voting precincts since the 1890s, but in 1907 the General Assembly passed a LOCAL OPTION law that placed the process directly in the hands of the voters. Within two years nearly two-thirds of the city, including virtually all of the land annexed in 1889, was saloonless. By this time, the attack on the segregated prostitution of the Levee district had convinced the burgeoning middle class that the barroom was incompatible with residence districts. Many patrons drank downtown and telephoned for the delivery of liquor to their private sideboards.

Steinmetz Saloon, South Loop, 1898. Photographer: Unknown. Source: Chicago Historical Society.

The traditional saloon was declining many years before PROHIBITION. The automobile took patronage from what was clearly a pedestrian-streetcar institution. Nickelodeons competed for nickels. Increasing numbers of employers demanded abstinence during the workday. The city health department enacted regulations that eliminated the mustache towel and many features of the free lunch table. Finally, WORLD WAR I brought not only an attack on anything that seemed remotely German but also a temporary ban on brewing.

Prohibition killed the legal saloon in 1920, but over three thousand city speakeasies and dozens of suburban roadhouses, many of them once village taverns, serviced the demand for more secret illegal drinking. When Prohibition ended in 1933, the word "saloon" virtually disappeared from the public vocabulary. Owners instead chose the name "cocktail lounge" or "tavern."

Perry R. Duis

See also: Bootlegging; Drugs and Alcohol; Entertaining Chicagoans; Grocery Stores and Supermarkets; Political Culture; Public Health; Roadhouses; Vice Districts

Further reading: Ade, George. *The Old-Time Saloon.* 1931. • Duis, Perry R. *The Saloon: Public Drinking in Chicago and Boston, 1880–1920.* 1983. • Wendt, Lloyd, and Herman Kogan. *Lords of the Levee.* 1943.

Salt Creek. Salt Creek flows 48 miles from the northwest corner of COOK COUNTY through eastern DUPAGE COUNTY and back into Cook before meeting the DES PLAINES RIVER near LYONS. Early maps labeled the waterway the Little Des Plaines River, but the name Salt Creek came into use in the mid-nineteenth century after a wagonload of salt spilled into the river, according to local legend. Despite its name, Salt Creek has sufficient water flow to be classified as a river. The area was once a population center for the POTAWATOMI, but the arrival of American farmers in the 1840s brought new forms of development. Frederick Graue's gristmill, completed in 1852, served as an economic engine and as a station on the UNDERGROUND RAILROAD, and, later, as a working museum. For decades thereafter, Salt Creek provided power for mills, ice for refrigeration, and swimming holes for recreation. In the postwar years, however, partially treated municipal wastewater and increasing storm runoff caused extensive pollution. A major flood in 1987 caused $150 million in damage. Community cleanup efforts in the 1980s and 1990s began reversing long neglect of this significant resource.

D. Bradford Hunt

See also: Elmhurst, IL; Flood Control and Drainage; Riverine Systems; Water

Further reading: Dugan, Hugh G. *Village on the County Line: A History of Hinsdale, Illinois.* 1949. • Smallwood, Lola. "Goodwill Flows for Salt Creek." *Chicago Tribune,* June 17, 1998.

Salvadorans. Chicago's Salvadoran community dates back to the late 1920s, with a steady influx of families and individuals beginning in the 1950s. These immigrants were primarily middle- and upper-class students, military, and other professionals. By the 1970s, Chicago's several hundred Salvadorans had dispersed across the city and suburbs, with concentrations in North Side communities such as UPTOWN. Many attended St. Mary of the Lake, St. Sebastian, and other North Side ROMAN CATHOLIC churches. They formed an association of SOCCER leagues, and *futbol* continues to dominate the sports life of the community, as the Liga CASA (Central American Soccer Association) includes many Salvadoran teams.

Beginning in the late 1970s and continuing through the early 1990s, the civil war in El Salvador precipitated the second and much larger wave of Salvadoran immigration to Chicago. While earlier immigrants often had flown directly to Chicago from El Salvador, many wartime REFUGEES were forced to travel undocumented through Mexico and into the United States. While some continued north to Canada where legal status was more easily arranged, many joined family or friends in Chicago, unsuccessfully seeking political asylum in the United States.

The plight of Salvadoran refugees came to public attention through the effort of the Sanctuary Movement, which involved the decision of numerous churches and synagogues across the United States to openly defy U.S. immigration law by offering housing and aid to undocumented Central American refugees threatened with deportation. In 1982, Chicago's Wellington Avenue United Church of Christ was the second church in the country to declare sanctuary, housing Salvadoran and GUATEMALAN families. Chicago churches and synagogues subsequently formed the Chicago Metropolitan Sanctuary Alliance. The Chicago Religious Task Force on Central America relocated Salvadoran refugees by establishing an "UNDERGROUND RAILROAD" from Arizona to Chicago during 1983 and 1984, and other organizations, such as the American Friends Service Committee and CISPES (Committee in Solidarity with the People of El Salvador), worked to publicize and protest the U.S. government's unwillingness to grant asylum to these refugees.

The majority of Salvadorans, however, have sought aid from organizations within their own and other Latino communities. Centro Romero, named after Archbishop Oscar Romero, who was assassinated in El Salvador in 1980, offers a wide range of legal and SOCIAL SERVICES to the community, including English classes, after-school care for children, a domestic-violence prevention program, advice concerning labor discrimination, and information regarding immigration law. The concerns of Salvadorans also have been addressed by ethnic organizations, such as the Associación de Salvadoreños en Illinois and the Comité Cívico-Cultural Salvadoreño, which has published a magazine featuring local community events and individuals since 1990.

Chicago's Salvadorans remain dispersed across the city and suburbs among other Central and South American immigrants, especially Guatemalans, with concentrations in the North Side neighborhoods of ROGERS PARK, ALBANY PARK, LOGAN SQUARE, and EDGEWATER. There are also significant Salvadoran communities outside the city in WAUKEGAN and DES PLAINES. Only a handful of professionals were among the more recent arrivals, who often find employment at the city's RESTAURANTS, factories, and CONSTRUCTION sites. In the suburbs, many work as gardeners, DOMESTIC WORKERS, and nannies.

Salvadorans have brought to Chicago their native cuisine, such as the distinctive *pupusas* served in Salvadoran restaurants, and the celebration of such holidays as the festival of El Salvador del Mundo (Savior of the World) in early August and Central American Independence Day in September. BILINGUAL EDUCATION programs have facilitated the success of many Salvadoran children in Chicago's schools, but GANGS emulating the Salvadoran *maras* of Los Angeles provide evidence of the less positive effects of immersion in U.S. urban culture.

A reliable count of the Salvadoran community is unavailable owing to the large number of recent arrivals and the undocumented status of a sizable portion of the community. By the mid-1980s, between approximately 20,000 and 40,000 Salvadorans lived in the Chicago area. Many dream of returning to El Salvador, but the continuing difficulties regarding legal status make visits home impossible for many, and a more permanent return is often prohibited by the dependence of families in Chicago and in El Salvador on the immigrants' wages.

Kate Caldwell

See also: Demography; Hondurans; Multicentered Chicago

Further reading: Montes, Segundo. *Salvadoran Migration to the United States: An Exploratory Study.* 1988.

Salvation Army. The Salvation Army, an evangelical Christian social service organization known for its military structures and use of military idiom, was founded by William and Catherine Booth in 1865 to improve the spiritual and material condition of London's poor. In 1885, under the leadership of Captains William Evans, Hannah Simpson Evans, and Edwin Gay, the Salvation Army came to Chicago. Upon arrival, the small corps of Salvationists organized parades and meetings intended to attract both converts and detractors. Both numbers grew immediately.

City officials and the press initially objected to the Salvation Army's disruptive public activities. Relations improved as Salvation Army officers and volunteers provided valuable assistance to Chicago's needy during the panic of 1893 and the GREAT DEPRESSION, and most famously, to American soldiers serving in WORLD WAR I. The early decades of the twentieth century saw the Salvation Army move away from the fervent evangelism of its earlier days to focus on providing SOCIAL SERVICES. At the close of the twentieth century, Chicago's Salvation Army maintained nearly two hundred facilities, providing community members with food and shelter as well as job training and counseling.

Jonathan H. Ebel

See also: Protestants; Religious Institutions; Rescue Missions

Further reading: Blumhofer, Edith L. *Aimee Semple McPherson: Everybody's Sister.* 1993. • *The Salvation Army, 1885–1985: Chicago Celebrates 100 Years.* Metropolitan Divisional Headquarters of the Salvation Army. 1985. • Winston, Diane. *Red Hot and Righteous: The Urban Religion of the Salvation Army.* 1999.

Sandburg Village, neighborhood in the NEAR NORTH SIDE Community Area. Sandburg Village stands on the former divide between the slums of the Near North Side and the GOLD COAST. In 1961, the city accepted a $6,411,000 bid from a group of investors headed by Arthur Rubloff to erect high-rise rental APARTMENT buildings on cleared URBAN RENEWAL land located between Division Street and North Avenue along Clark and LaSalle. They named the complex for poet Carl Sandburg and the buildings for other literary luminaries. Although less expensive than those in neighboring Gold Coast, the apartments were far beyond the range of former residents. The new inhabitants were mostly middle-income, young professionals. Subsequent townhouses appealed to white families contemplating moving to the suburbs. In 1979, Sandburg Village converted to CONDOMINIUM ownership.

Amanda Seligman

See also: Gentrification; Land Use; Neighborhood Succession; Real Estate

Further reading: Berger, Miles L. *They Built Chicago.* 1992.

Sanitary and Ship Canal. This channel runs 28 miles between Damen Avenue and LOCKPORT, linking the South Branch of the CHICAGO RIVER to the DES PLAINES RIVER. With the construction of a series of locks, the Sanitary and Ship Canal permanently reversed the flow of the Chicago River in 1900. The canal was designed both as a TRANSPORTATION route and a means to improve WATER quality by sending Chicago's sewage south into the Illinois River instead of into LAKE MICHIGAN.

Ann Durkin Keating

See also: Environmental Politics; Illinois & Michigan Canal; Waste Disposal; Water Supply

Further reading: Cain, Louis P. *Sanitation Strategy for a Lakefront Metropolis.* 1978. • Hill, Libby. *The Chicago River: A Natural and Unnatural History.* 2000. • Solzman, David M. *The Chicago River: An Illustrated History and Guide to the River and Its Waterways.* 1998.

Sanitary Commission. Created in October 1861, the Chicago branch (later known as the Northwestern branch) of the United States Sanitary Commission was a privately funded effort to improve the morale, logistical support, and medical care of men serving in the Union Army during the CIVIL WAR. Judge Mark Skinner, a leading War DEMOCRAT, was the president, but as with most antebellum charities the officers relied upon "benevolent ladies" to handle the day-to-day operations of the organization. In the spring of 1862, the Chicago branch's operations were taken over by Mary A. Livermore and Jane C. Hoge, who quickly emerged as effective executives

Sanitary and Ship Canal construction cranes, 1895. Photographer: Unknown. Source: Chicago Historical Society.

and able fundraisers. Under their direction, the Chicago branch sent a steady stream of medical supplies and food to the front.

The Chicago branch also established several Soldier's Rests, where troops in transit were treated to coffee and sandwiches. In July 1863, a Soldier's Home was founded to house men too sick or wounded to return to their homes. To fund these activities Hoge and Livermore organized Sanitary Fairs in 1863 and 1865. These popular charity bazaars became a model copied in most northern cities and succeeded in raising hundreds of thousands of dollars for the war effort. The Chicago office became the funnel through which most aid from the Midwest reached the front. After the war the movement for women's SUFFRAGE in Illinois was spearheaded by the women who first came to public service as managers and nurses with the Sanitary Commission.

Theodore J. Karamanski

See also: Charity Organization Societies; Feminist Movements; Public Health; Social Services; Veterans' Hospitals

Further reading: Henshaw, Sarah Edwards. *Our Branch and Its Tributaries; Being a History of the Work of the Northwestern Sanitary Commission.* 1868. • Karamanski, Theodore J. *Rally 'Round the Flag: Chicago and the Civil War.* 1993.

Sauk Village, IL, Cook and Will Counties, 27 miles S of the Loop. This community in the southeast corner of COOK COUNTY has grown along the historic Sauk Trail and from thence comes its name. For centuries, the Sauk Trail served as a major route for travel from Detroit to the Mississippi River. Countless NATIVE AMERICANS, Midwestern settlers, and California gold seekers passed this way. In 1913, the Sauk Trail from the Indiana border to Vincennes/Hubbard's Trail in SOUTH CHICAGO HEIGHTS was designated as part of the Lincoln Highway. Thus this most important automobile road in American history literally became the "main street" for this quiet town. Sauk Village is now within the nationally designated Lincoln Highway scenic byway across Illinois.

The farmers who migrated here in the late 1830s were mostly of FRENCH and GERMAN descent. A small settlement emerged and received the name Strasburg, since some of these first residents were originally from Strasbourg (German *Strassburg*), on the French-German border. Some early records identify it as New Strasburg, and the post office first established in 1853 was Strasburgh. Tradition holds that the earliest church services in Bloom Township were held here, and in 1847 St. James Church was established. Rebuilt in 1871 and 1873 after lightning strikes, the current historic church structure on Sauk Trail at the Calumet EXPRESSWAY (Bishop Ford Freeway) dates from 1875 and serves now as a community center.

Major residential development came in the 1950s, and the village incorporated in 1957. Providing housing for workers in the industries of the region, the village went through periods of growth and stagnation related to the fortunes of area industries.

Since the 1970s, stronger involvement by the village government in development and the demand for affordable single-family housing led to new residential growth. In addition, several major truck terminal facilities have taken advantage of Sauk Village's location near the interstate highways.

Larry A. McClellan

See also: Economic Geography; Streets and Highways

Further reading: Michalek, Louise A. *A Look into the Past, Chicago Heights and Her Neighbors.* 1961. • *Sauk Village, 40th Anniversary of Incorporation, Commemorative Booklet, 1957–1997.* 1997.

Savings and Loans. Chicago's first building and loan association (called savings and loans after the 1930s) was established in 1849. Building and loan associations originated as part of the cooperative movement that began in England in the eighteenth century and came to the United States in the early nineteenth century. Building and loans originally were established for working-class people who wanted to buy homes but did not have access to banks. A group of people would deposit their savings into an association, then as the association gained enough money it would finance mortgages for its members. Unlike banks, building and loan associations made their investments based primarily on the interests of their members, rather than investing for the greatest return and security. Associations also tended to serve small groups or communities and did not offer many of the services banks did.

Chicago's small associations flourished in the 1880s, and by 1893, largely because of Chicago, Illinois ranked third in the nation in the number of building and loan associations, with 518. The impressive growth of Chicago's building and loan associations was steady between roughly 1880 and 1930, except for a portion of the 1890s. The 1890s was a period of depression and of "national" building and loan associations, many of which were based in Minnesota and Illinois. Because many nationals were fraudulent, associations across the country formed strong local, state, and national organizations that ran publicity campaigns and lobbied for legislation to ban nationals. Illinois passed such legislation in 1896.

Building and loan associations were most important to Chicago's working class, especially those who were members of ethnic communities. Commercial banks were rare in working-class neighborhoods. Although there were private ethnic banks, these often failed, did not receive as much public confidence as building and loans, and were banned in Illinois in 1917. Building and loan associations were especially popular among the ethnic groups that were hungriest for home ownership, namely the CZECHS, POLES, and ITALIANS. Even when commercial BANKING became more widely accessible after WORLD WAR I, many ethnic community leaders endorsed the local building and loan associations instead of nonethnic commercial banks, because they thought the associations promoted ethnic solidarity. By the end of 1918 there were 255 building and loan associations in Chicago, and the majority of them were part of ethnic working-class communities.

There was, however, tension between the ethnic and nonethnic associations, as the latter looked askance at the business practices of smaller and more community oriented ethnic associations. Efforts to get ethnic associations to change their business practices and join industry organizations met with mixed success. Many of the ethnic associations formed their own organizations, such as the American Czecho-Slovak, Polish American, SWEDISH, and LITHUANIAN Building and Loan Leagues, some of which eventually joined the Illinois League.

The GREAT DEPRESSION of the 1930s had a tremendous impact upon building and loan associations. Part of the reason they fared poorly, especially the ethnic ones, was that they had made many of their investments in the best interests of the community rather than profit. Many Chicago associations folded or were bailed out by the federal government. As a result of this crisis, the government took a much stronger role in the industry, both through regulation and by insuring customers' deposits. Associations that survived had to follow more stringent business rules and as a result became more similar to commercial banks. This was also the period when the associations came to be called savings and loans. The operation of S&Ls was still distinguishable from banks, but associations after WORLD WAR II made greater efforts to replicate the services of commercial banks.

In the post–World War II era, savings and loans continued to grow until the crisis of the 1980s. In an effort to make ailing S&Ls more competitive with banks and to allow them to deal with high inflation rates, the Ford, Carter, and Reagan administrations substantially deregulated the industry. To bolster their business, many associations began making high-risk/high-yield loans, but as these ventures often failed, the industry came crashing down. Deregulation had also made it easier for banking officials to engage in corrupt practices, which worsened the crash.

Although Chicago's institutions fared much better than those in the South and West, most savings and loans were in trouble, and publicity from the crash discouraged patronage. In its effort to save the industry, the federal government forced many of Chicago's associations to close or merge, producing fewer and larger S&Ls. The largest association to come out of this era was Talman Home Federal, which was forced to merge with two other institutions and emerged as the third largest savings and loan in the nation.

Talman's history is illustrative of the major changes that affected Chicago's S&Ls. It began as a Bohemian ethnic association, became more similar to a bank in the postwar era, merged with other S&Ls during the crisis of the 1980s, then merged with the LaSalle Bank, which in turn was purchased by Dutch giant ABN-AMRO. At the end of the twentieth century approximately 14 savings and loans still existed in the Chicago metropolitan area, but there were far fewer than before the 1980s, and their character was more similar to that of banks than was the case before the Great Depression.

Jeffrey A. Brune

See also: Business of Chicago; Consumer Credit; Housing Types; Mutual Benefit Society; Real Estate; Redlining

Further reading: Barth, James R. *The Great Savings and Loan Debacle.* 1991. • Bodfish, H. Morton, ed. *History of Building and Loan in the United States.* 1931. • Cohen, Lizabeth. *Making a New Deal: Industrial Workers in Chicago, 1919–1939.* 1990.

Schaumburg, IL, 25 miles NW of the Loop. Schaumburg differs from many of the other northwestern suburban towns in that it did not start around a RAILROAD depot. The area, which was very marshy, attracted its first settlers from eastern states in the mid-1830s. Trumbull Kent of Oswego County, New York, was the first YANKEE arrival. He was soon joined not only by other easterners but also by GERMANS, many of whom came from Schaumburg-Lippe, between Dortmund and Hannover. They settled along the Chicago–Elgin Road (Irving Park) and other local highways.

These farmers organized a German Lutheran congregation as early as 1840, and in 1847 they built their first church. A few years later there was a controversy over the name for the little town that was emerging near the church; some wanted it to be Lutherville, but in the end it became known as Schaumburg Center. It grew very slowly, for the area, though fertile, was swampy, and there was no railroad depot to open the communications with Chicago and stimulate rapid growth.

By the end of the nineteenth century the population of the whole township was only about 1,000. The township, which by 1900 boasted three cheese factories, continued to grow very slowly during the first half of the twentieth century, as did the little town.

The construction of the Northwest TOLL ROAD in 1956 wrenched Schaumburg from its isolation. Schaumburg-area farmers took an active role in industrial, commercial, and residential development. Soon a large number of streets, often at dizzying angles to avoid quadrilateral monotony, spread out from the old center, until by 1980 the population numbered 53,305 and the land was almost entirely built up.

I-290 came to border Schaumburg to the east, cutting it off from the forests and sloughs of the Ned Brown FOREST PRESERVE; to the north it extended as far as the old Algonquin Road, once an Indian trail and then the route of the Chicago–Galena stagecoach. In the northeastern area emerged Woodfield Mall, opened in 1971 and one of the region's largest shopping centers. It was not by chance that the mall developed close by both I-290 and the Northwest Tollway. While Schaumburg's dramatic growth came with the automobile, the community now has a rail depot and is a regional PUBLIC TRANSPORTATION center. Schaumburg today is a mature community, with a small industrial area in its southwestern section and a great variety of churches, schools, and open places. Its German origins are now muted, though they live on in road names like "Biesterfield."

While Woodfield defines Schaumburg to outsiders, residents have returned to the old crossroads at Plum Grove and Schaumburg Roads to develop a new town center in the 1990s. Local shopping, a public library, public recreational facilities, the government center, and a bandstand now provide residents with a service core.

David Buisseret

See also: Built Environment of the Chicago Region; Economic Geography; Shopping Districts and Malls; Transportation

Further reading: Gould, Alice. *Schaumburg: A History of the Township.* 1982. • Hurban, Renie. *Schaumburg: A Pictorial History.* 1987.

Schererville, IN, Lake County, 29 miles SE of the Loop. Because of the convergence of Indian trails, RAILROADS, and major highways in the Schererville area, the town adopted the slogan "Crossroads of the Nation." Many INDIAN (mostly POTAWATOMI) trails in Schererville connected with the Sauk Trail, the major east-west thoroughfare between Indiana and Illinois. The first American settlers arrived around 1840. Because the first railroad station was located on the John Reeder farm, the area became known as Reeder Station.

In 1846 Nicholas Scherer emigrated from GERMANY and arrived at ST. JOHN, Indiana, near the Reeder farm. His brother Mathias joined Nicholas and they opened a SALOON and hotel in St. John in 1849. By 1853 Nicholas began working for the State of Indiana, eventually becoming a swampland commissioner, administering lands under the federal Swamp Land Act of 1850. Two years later the Chicago Great Eastern Ohio (Panhandle) Railroad contracted with him to build railroad beds between Richmond, Indiana, and Chicago.

In 1866 Nicholas Scherer platted the Town of Schererville on 40 acres of land, purchased from the swampland mogul Aaron N. Hart. About 25 families constituted the population, the majority German Catholics. Other railroads crossed the new town, including the New York Central and the Michigan Central. Schererville boasted a public school, blacksmith shop, dairy, general store, grain elevator, icehouse, and cigar factory. In 1874, St. Michael the Archangel ROMAN CATHOLIC Church opened on land donated by Scherer.

Schererville maintained its rural character for the next hundred years. The town incorporated in 1911. Of particular importance was the development of the U.S. 30 and U.S. 41 junction. Businesses appeared around this intersection, most notably Teibel's Restaurant in 1929. In addition, the Ideal Section of the Old Lincoln Highway passed through the town. By the mid-1930s, the highways were paved and the junction's traffic grew. The town's population exceeded 700 persons.

Like its neighbors to the east and south, Schererville experienced explosive residential and commercial growth in the latter half of the twentieth century. In 1960 the town's population totaled 2,875 persons; in 1970 the census listed 3,663. Ten years later, however, the figure skyrocketed to 13,209, then catapulted to 20,155 in 1990, reaching 24,851 in 2000. According to a local REAL-ESTATE agent, most of the influx came from Illinois, as Chicago COMMUTERS took advantage of Indiana's lower taxes while remaining in close proximity to the LOOP. The U.S. 30–U.S. 41 junction saw exponential retail and commercial growth, as malls and SHOPPING centers sprang up in the vicinity. At the close of the twentieth century, Schererville had become a true Chicago suburb.

Stephen G. McShane

See also: Lake County, IN; Metropolitan Growth; Streets and Highways

Further reading: Goodspeed, Weston A., and Charles Blanchard. *Counties of Porter and Lake, Indiana.* 1882. • Howat, William Frederick. *A Standard History of Lake County, Indiana, and the Calumet Region.* 1915. • Moore, Powell A. *The Calumet Region: Indiana's Last Frontier.* 1959.

Schiller Park, IL, Cook County, 13 miles W of the Loop. Following the 1829 Treaty of Prairie du Chien, the federal government granted two square miles of land to Che Che Pin Qua, the son of a SCOTTISH trader and an OTTAWA Indian mother, known to whites as Alexander Robinson. This tract, most of which is in present-day Schiller Park, was given in recognition of Robinson's services in securing TREATIES and in helping settlers during the FORT DEARBORN Massacre. Robinson and his family are buried on Cook County FOREST PRESERVE property at Lawrence and River Roads.

The rich soil of the DES PLAINES RIVER basin drew farmers, hunters, and trappers. In 1881 William Kolze purchased 105 acres of land and built a house that became an inn called the White House. He served as honorary mayor of the unincorporated town, which was known as Kolze. In 1886 the Wisconsin Central RAILROAD bought a strip of Kolze's land and built a main track and a spur through the property.

North of Kolze's land was the community of Fairview, so named because of its scenic landscape. The railroad built a depot in Fairview that was first used by farmers.

The groves along the Des Plaines River near Kolze became popular spots for weekend excursions promoted by the railways. Trains brought Chicagoans first to the Fairview depot, then on the spur track right to the river. Hikers walked along the river to picnic grounds, dance pavilions, and SALOONS. The Schiller Liedertafel, a GERMAN singing society, frequented the area, and the picnic groves soon adopted the name of Schiller Woods.

The village incorporated in 1914 as Kolze, and was later named Schiller Park (1926). Although several areas were ANNEXED into the village during the 1920s and 1930s, few homes were built. In 1932, Julia Kolze, daughter-in-law of the founder, became the first woman village president or mayor in Illinois. Her avowed strategy was to employ kitchen table economics, running government on a budget the way she ran her household.

As the city of Chicago encroached upon nearby land, Schiller Park residents worried that their community would be annexed by the city. But although Chicago's PLANNING commission bought farmland for what became O'HARE AIRPORT and the Tri-State TOLLWAY, Schiller Park remained independent, annexing Soreng Manufacturing corporation (later Hostess Bakery) in 1949, as well as farmland for residential development in the 1950s.

The population of Schiller Park peaked in 1970 at 12,712 and stood at 11,850 in 2000. The largely white population were of German, IRISH, ITALIAN, and POLISH ancestry; 22 percent were Hispanic. In 1993 Anna Montana became the first woman president of Schiller Park since 1932 and was reelected in 1997. Like her predecessor Kolze, Montana set guidelines to eliminate debt and bring the community closer together, with its message of having a "small town feel with a world at its touch."

Marilyn Elizabeth Perry

See also: Entertaining Chicagoans; Leisure; Metropolitan Growth

Further reading: Demetros, Evelyn. "Schiller Park, Illinois: From Wilderness Settlement to Suburbia." Independent Study, Dakota Wesleyan University. 1974. • Ouland, June. *Plow Shares to Jet Fields: The Story of Schiller Park.* 1976. • Schiller Park, Illinois, Golden Jubilee, Inc. *A Short Historical and Pictorial Account of the Village of Schiller Park, Illinois.* 1964.

Schneider, IN, Lake County, 48 miles S of the Loop. Incorporated in 1915, Schneider has remained a tiny town, with 317 people in 2000. It is governed by a three-member town board and is located in rural southern LAKE COUNTY along Route 41.

Steven Essig

See also: Agriculture; Built Environment of the Chicago Region

School Architecture. The ARCHITECTURE of Chicago's SCHOOLS has been dominated by an often desperate need to find places for as many students as possible at the lowest possible cost. From the beginning of public education in the city, the public schools have had great difficulty in providing places for all eligible children. The result has been large classes and a strictly utilitarian architecture. The Chicago FIRE OF 1871 exacerbated the problem. One-third of the city's school buildings were destroyed and the remaining buildings were used as public shelters. It took three years before any replacement buildings were constructed.

An 1897 study emphasized the utilitarian nature of school architecture. Schools were generally three-story red brick buildings that resembled factories. They were poorly ventilated and poorly lighted and lacked adequate PLAYGROUNDS. Classrooms had blackboards on two sides and seats for 54–63 students.

The innovations of the "Chicago School" of architecture were first applied to public school buildings in 1905, with the appointment of Dwight H. Perkins as head of the schools' architecture department by a reform-minded board (which included Jane Addams). Perkins, an admirer of Louis Sullivan, had joined the innovative firm of Burnham & Root in 1888 and established his own practice in 1894. Throughout the 1910s and the early 1920s, Perkins was recognized as an innovative school architect, synthesizing the functionalism of the Chicago School with the social agenda and the aesthetics of the Arts and Crafts movement. His designs included Tilton Elementary (1908), Albert Lane Technical High School (1908–1910), and Carl Schurz High School (1908–1910), distinguished by its large, airy rooms flooded by daylight coming though banks of windows. Perkins's schools eliminated excess details and demonstrated a respect for natural materials. Like Addams, Perkins argued that schools should serve a broader purpose and function as community centers when school was not in session; gymnasiums and large auditoriums were always important elements in his designs. However, the reformers on the board were ousted in 1910 and Perkins was replaced by an unimaginative architect devoted to reviving classic forms.

Perkins's tradition of innovative school architecture was revived by his son, Lawrence, who worked with Eliel and Eero Saarinen to design the award-winning Crow Island School in WINNETKA (1940). By asking teachers how the new building could facilitate Winnetka's innovative, child-centered curriculum, Perkins produced an unusually attractive and comfortable environment. Each classroom had direct access to the outdoors and had its own workroom with a sink and its own bathroom.

Albert G. Lane Technical High School, 1962. Photographer: James Brink. Source: Chicago Historical Society.

The school included special rooms to support the Winnetka program of group and creative activities and a pioneer room in the basement where social studies classes could imitate the daily lives of early settlers.

New technologies for supplying artificial light and ventilation allowed postwar architects to experiment with new flexible configurations for school buildings, producing open-space schools. Without separate classrooms that required their own set of windows, these schools maximized the use of space. Buildings were divided into areas, each of which had easy access to a central learning center which included not only books but also television, filmstrips, and other technologies. LIBERTYVILLE's Butterfield School (1970) exemplified this trend. Teachers, however, preferred traditional, enclosed classrooms. When the national climate of opinion changed in the 1980s and more traditional approaches to education became dominant, open-space schools, like Butterfield, were turned into conventional schools, fitted with interior walls for separate classrooms.

Arthur Zilversmit

See also: Progressive Education

Further reading: Herrick, Mary J. *The Chicago Schools: A Social and Political History.* 1971. • Mayer, Harold M., and Richard Wade. *Chicago: Growth of a Metropolis.* 1969. • Sennott, R. Stephen. "Dwight Heald Perkins." In *American National Biography,* ed. John Garraty, 1999.

School Desegregation. School desegregation became an issue in Chicago during the years following WORLD WAR II, as the city's AFRICAN AMERICAN neighborhoods expanded and school officials adjusted boundary lines to assure that school districts remained as segregated as the housing market. CIVIL RIGHTS and black community groups demanded that the SCHOOLS be integrated and that funding disparities be addressed. Later, the federal and state governments challenged the city's schools to end segregationist policies. But desegregation remained a controversial issue in Chicago, and plans to achieve integration contributed to white migration from the city. When the Chicago Public Schools finally did undertake a court-ordered desegregation plan in the early 1980s, there were relatively few white students left in the system. This made meaningful desegregation almost impossible across the city's public school system.

Like other large northern cities, Chicago's population changed dramatically in the postwar period. The pace of suburbanization accelerated, drawing middle-class whites from the city. At the same time, by 1960 Chicago's black population reached over 800,000, almost a quarter of the total. In black neighborhoods schools were overcrowded, with many on double shifts. Class sizes were smaller in white schools than in black ones, even though more new buildings had been erected for black students.

School superintendent Benjamin Willis rejected calls for desegregation, and the portable classrooms added to black schools were derisively labeled "WILLIS WAGONS." In 1963 massive demonstrations were staged by students and parents to protest Willis's policies. Public outcries intensified in the wake of commissioned reports recommending dramatic steps to redress educational inequality. Threats by the U.S. Department of Health, Education, and Welfare to withhold federal funds until a desegregation plan was developed were thwarted by Mayor Richard J. Daley's intervention.

When Willis's term ended in 1966, James Redmond, his successor, attempted to develop integration plans that would send black students to predominantly white schools. Hostile demonstrations greeted such efforts on the city's Northwest and Southwest Sides. Redmond and other school leaders found themselves hampered by board members and local politicians reluctant to anger whites opposed to integration.

The failure of local initiatives led to federal and state intervention, resulting in a 1980 consent decree and court-mandated desegregation plan. But the movement of white students out of the system continued. Between 1970 and 1990 the white portion of the school population fell by nearly 75 percent. As the century drew to an end the vision of integrated schools remained elusive.

The loss of white students from the Chicago Public Schools can be explained partially by "white flight" from the city to suburban communities; but it also reflected a shift to private and parochial school education for many whites. By the 1990s, two-thirds of Chicago's white students attended private schools. The city's school-age population had become substantially divided between two types of schools, a majority black public system (with growing numbers of Hispanics) and a mainly white system of parochial and other private schools.

Despite the existence of a federally mandated office of desegregation compliance in the Chicago Public Schools, school desegregation has been quite limited in Chicago. Pockets of integration existed by the late 1990s; magnet schools on the city's North and Southwest Sides continued to attract many of the system's white students. But in vast areas of the city, children attended predominantly black or Hispanic schools. Despite some halfhearted efforts in the late 1960s and 1970s, Chicago never developed an exchange program between suburban and city schools, and suburban schools remained largely segregated as well.

John L. Rury

See also: Catholic School System; Civil Rights Movements; Contested Spaces; Racism, Ethnicity, and White Identity

Further reading: Herrick, Mary J. *The Chicago Schools: A Social and Political History.* 1970. • Orfield, Gary. *Must We Bus? Segregated Schools and National Policy.* 1978.

School Districts. Illinois state government granted local control over SCHOOLS in 1819, when the state set aside a section of land to finance public schools in each TOWNSHIP.

Elected local boards used the revenues to pay for teachers and school buildings.

In 1851 the state legislature transferred control of Chicago's school affairs to the city council, which hired the city's first school superintendent in 1854. The city's first high school opened in 1856 with 169 students. An 1857 reorganization created a board of education with 15 members appointed by the city council. The board's responsibility was broadened in 1863 when the state stipulated that each subdistrict in the city should provide free education in at least one school for children over five years old. In 1872 the mayor was given the power to appoint the board with the advice and consent of the city council.

In the largely unincorporated farmland outside of Chicago, a few schoolhouses were built by early settlers. With 180 residents, the settlement in NAPERVILLE opened its school with 22 students in 1831. The first school in OAK PARK was used as a Sunday school and a public meeting place in 1850. SKOKIE residents started their school in 1858.

In the post–Civil War period, districts in Chicago's six-county region were not yet bureaucratized, enrolled a small percentage of school-age children, operated few schools with grade levels, and maintained relatively low daily attendance. Of the 913 districts, one-fourth were in COOK COUNTY. While 97 percent of the districts operated some of their schools for more than 6 months, 17 districts had no school buildings. Only 10 percent of the 911 schools were graded, and almost half of the districts did not keep proper records.

In the tradition of local control, suburban districts have continued to be governed by independent school boards, which have the power to raise tax revenue, issue bonds, construct new buildings, approve union contracts, and oversee school operations. Each school board has seven members who are elected for four-year terms on a nonpartisan ballot. Chicago continues to maintain a unique governance structure, where the mayor directly appoints the five-member school board.

Local control and funding have tended to sharpen the socioeconomic differences between Chicago and the suburban districts. Chicago has a higher concentration of low-income students, who in 1990 constituted 79 percent of the total enrollment. In suburban Cook County, one out of five students came from low-income families. Racial and ethnic minorities also have had greater representation in Chicago schools. In 1995–96, Chicago schools had only 11 percent white students, compared to 63 percent in suburban Cook. Fifty-five percent and 31 percent of the students in Chicago were AFRICAN AMERICAN and Latino, respectively. The comparable figures for suburban Cook were 19 percent and 12 percent.

Disparity within suburban Cook County has also widened. In south suburban Cook during the early 1990s, 16 high-poverty districts generated only half the amount that the more affluent districts spent on a per-student basis. In response to these and other similar situations of funding inequity across the state, the legislature passed funding reform legislation in 1997 that, beginning in 1999, provided the poorest districts with additional state funds.

The Chicago Public Schools, the third-largest central-city educational system in the nation in 2000, has gone through three major phases of reform since the late 1970s. The three reforms can be broadly labeled as (1) state-directed accountability (1979), (2) parent empowerment (1988), and (3) a mayoral management model (1995).

The state expanded its involvement in Chicago in 1979, when the district declared bankruptcy. To impose fiscal discipline, the legislature created the School Finance Authority (SFA), jointly appointed by the governor and the mayor, to oversee and approve the district's budget. Although the district restored financial stability by 1988, the legislature granted the SFA new oversight authority over the implementation of parent empowerment reform and, after another financial crisis in 1993, expanded its purview even further.

In 1988, the state legislature adopted another major reform package, guided by a vision of parent empowerment and analogous to the principle of local control in the suburbs. Each of the system's 550 schools would be governed by a Local School Council (LSC), an elected body comprising six parents, two community representatives, two teachers, and the principal. LSCs hire (or fire) principals, establish school improvement plans, develop curricular focus, and set budgetary priorities. This systemwide decentralization was prompted by widespread frustration over teachers' STRIKES, an intense sentiment against the central bureaucracy, a strong grassroots movement that was encouraged by the election of the city's first black mayor, and coalition politics that cut across racial and income lines.

By the mid-1990s, policymakers and the public had grown increasingly frustrated by the lack of progress in student performance under the LSC reform. In July 1995, new reform legislation granted complete mayoral control over the school board and instituted a corporate management model in the Chicago Public Schools. Instead of the traditional school superintendent's office, the administrative core was now headed by the chief executive officer, overseeing the chief education officer, chief operating officer, chief fiscal officer, and chief purchasing officer. Schools with low test scores were subject to "probation" or "reconstitution," in essence shifting authority from the LSC to the central administration. In 1997, more than one hundred schools were placed on academic probation and seven high schools were reconstituted. The mayoral management model in Chicago soon spread to several cities across the nation.

Kenneth K. Wong

See also: Governing the Metropolis; Special Districts

Further reading: Herrick, Mary J. *The Chicago Schools: A Social and Political History.* 1971. • Pierce, Bessie Louise. *A History of Chicago,* vol. 2. 1940. • Wong, Kenneth K. "Toward Fiscal Responsibility in Illinois Public Education." In *Dilemmas of Fiscal Reform: Paying for State and Local Government in Illinois,* ed. Lawrence B. Joseph, 1996, 95–128.

Schooling for Work. The relationship between SCHOOLS and the preparation of the next generation of workers became a major issue in American education at the beginning of the twentieth century as the nation was transformed by new kinds of industry. In Chicago, a deep and bitter conflict over the relationship of schooling to the workplace revealed the conflicting class interests that were threatening to rend the city's social fabric. At the same time, the conflict demonstrated the issues that deeply divided two groups of reformers, both of whom thought of themselves as "progressives." One group, followers of Jane Addams and her associates at HULL HOUSE, saw themselves as humanitarians who wanted to use schooling as a tool for helping immigrants and the poor adapt to the new harsh industrial system while softening its rigors. Another group of progressives, largely composed of businessmen and concerned with social efficiency, wanted to modernize the schools to prepare workers for the new factories that were beginning to dominate the city's economy. Addams and her followers sought to maintain older, community values within a new system of production, while the social-efficiency progressives strove to prepare workers to fit into the rapidly developing, impersonal system of mass production without any effort to alter it. Both sets of reformers agreed that some form of vocational education was needed to increase the "holding power" of the schools—to make them more attractive to children who were likely to drop out because they lacked either academic interests or abilities.

The need for schools to adjust to the new industrial age was not at issue. Few people thought that the schools should merely replicate the traditional curriculum. As John Dewey pointed out in a series of lectures at the UNIVERSITY OF CHICAGO at the end of the nineteenth century, the rapid changes that industrialization brought with it required a radically different education. The new industrial society had disrupted the natural transition from childhood into the world of WORK. Children no longer learned about work through informally observing their parents, and, in Dewey's words, the school had become the legatee institution and needed to take on an expanded

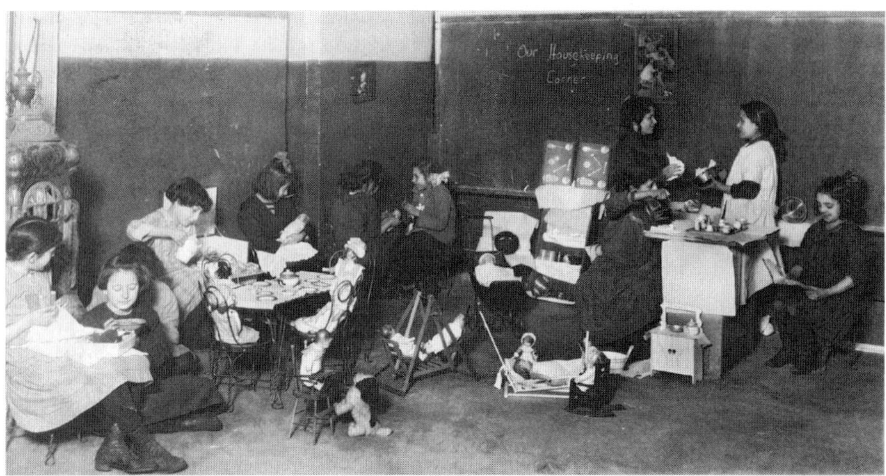

A class at the Chicago Hebrew Institute, 1915. Photographer: Unknown. Source: Chicago Historical Society.

role, providing an education that went well beyond the traditional three R's. For Dewey, this would not include preparing children for any specific occupation but rather for the ability to respond to new needs and new tasks. The study of occupations would be a central part of the curriculum in Dewey's laboratory school—important not as vocational training but as a way of helping children to understand the new industrial world around them.

At the same time, members of Chicago's powerful BUSINESS community also recognized that schools could play a crucial role in preparing the next generation of workers. They argued that schools should offer a vocational curriculum to future factory and office workers while, at the same time, inculcating the habits necessary for work. The schools also needed to undertake the essential task of AMERICANIZING the large number of immigrants who were increasingly providing the city's labor needs. For schools to socialize the children of immigrants and the poor, they needed to develop a curriculum that would keep them in school longer. A "practical" course of study which offered a path to employment was the answer.

At first, Chicago's businessmen agreed with educational reformers like Dewey and welcomed the idea of manual training in the schools. Giving children a basic knowledge of how to use tools was important. But by the early years of the twentieth century, as the demand for more highly trained labor became ever more imperative, they began to argue that the schools should go beyond manual training and teach actual trades. Impressed by the growing commercial competition from European nations and especially Germany, the Chicago COMMERCIAL CLUB (Chicago's most prestigious business club) commissioned former superintendent of schools Edwin Cooley to visit Europe to study their systems of vocational education. In the wake of his report of 1911, businessmen increasingly supported a differentiated system of vocational education, with the high schools preparing the "noncommissioned officers" of an industrial army and vocational schools furnishing the well-trained soldiers that modern industry required. The new vocational education, as differentiated from manual training, would "consist of the actual trade processes" and produce "articles of commercial value" under "conditions of the occupation outside the school." Such vocational programs would be gender-specific, preparing children for careers in a highly differentiated job market.

In 1912 the Chicago Public Schools adopted the new philosophy and introduced a differentiated curriculum, encouraging sixth graders to choose between an academic and an industrial track. The latter would lead to a two-year high-school vocational program. The Board of Education also established different kinds of high schools—technical schools with both two-year and four-year programs that prepared students for skilled laboring positions or technical colleges. In these schools even the "academic" subjects took on a workplace orientation. Instead of history, for example, they offered "industrial history." Overtly vocational education also infiltrated the general high schools, and by 1913, 16 of the city's 21 high schools had become composite high schools offering vocational courses in addition to academic work. The board also offered "continuation" courses in which children already in the workforce could improve their work skills and enhance their ability to find more highly skilled jobs. At the same time, again at the behest of businessmen, the board instituted a program of commercial courses—such as bookkeeping, typing, and business English—in the high schools. The commercial program eventually included more specialized courses in selling and advertising. By 1914, one-third of Chicago's high-school students were enrolled in day and evening commercial courses.

Although the radical shift in the program of the schools did not arouse immediate opposition, it led to a great debate and a political crisis in 1913. Supported by members of Chicago's business elites, former superintendent Edwin Cooley recommended that Illinois establish a state system of vocational education. Cooley's proposal would have established full-time vocational schools and, for youngsters already in the workforce, continuation schools, in a school system that would be fully separated from the regular public schools. The new program would be governed by independent boards, made up of men with practical experience in industry and commerce, and funded by a special tax. Promoters of the Cooley plan had an additional agenda; a major goal of the new venture would be to shape the ideology of the working class as a way of fighting radicalism, promoting the morality of hard work, and instilling such industrial virtues as punctuality.

The Cooley bill, introduced several times between 1913 and 1917, was strenuously opposed by Superintendent Ella Flagg Young (a disciple of Dewey), the CHICAGO TEACHERS FEDERATION, and the CHICAGO FEDERATION OF LABOR. First and foremost, opponents protested that the Cooley plan was undemocratic; it would lead to permanent class divisions by stifling social mobility. Opponents shared the opinion of the Illinois State Federation of Labor, which charged that the specialization it would encourage would prevent children from "acquiring the skills and training necessary to the continued development, or even proper maintenance of various trades and callings." Moreover, labor leaders saw the plan as an ill-disguised attempt to turn the public schools into institutions that would supply industry with a well-trained and docile (non-union) workforce. It would weaken trade unions by taking away their role in admitting new workers to apprenticeship programs. Unionists saw the new vocational schools as little more than potential "scab factories." Professional educators bristled at Cooley's assumption that vocational education, to be efficient, had to be "kept out of the hands of the old fashioned school master."

The critics were correct in pointing out that the new vocational education plan constituted a radical reorientation of public education. Horace Mann and the common school reformers of the pre–Civil War period had seen education as the great equalizing institution, bringing rich and poor, immigrants and native-born, together in the same classroom, where they would be offered equal opportunities for advancement. Dewey, too, saw the classroom as the basic unit for building a democratic community. For him, manual training was a gateway to understanding the modern industrial world, not preparation for a specific trade. Contrary to the educational reformers' vision, advocates of the new vocationalism would divide children at an early age; those who were thought destined for factory or clerical work would go to different schools from those who would be offered academic courses. The children of the poor and immigrants would be relegated to the dead-end vocational track.

Businessmen countered the argument that the new program was undemocratic by contending that offering children the chance to learn a trade fostered economic mobility and reduced potential class conflict. Indeed, preparing children for a specific trade was now a requirement for citizenship education. They also argued that in a separate school system men with practical experience (as opposed to educational credentials) could be hired to teach.

Although the business-minded reformers lost the battle over the Cooley bill, they were able to attain many of their objectives with the federal Smith-Hughes Act (1917). This provided funds for vocational education and, like the ill-fated Cooley bill, allowed states to establish separate vocational education boards. Under the auspices of Smith-Hughes, businessmen attained their primary goal—a program of training students for specific skills, directed by people of practical experience.

The divisions revealed by the Cooley bill resurfaced in 1923, when a new, efficiency-minded superintendent, William McAndrew, proposed a system of junior high schools. When teacher representatives asked him if the junior high schools would offer terminal programs for children not headed for high school, McAndrew was evasive, and it became clear that these new schools could easily become vehicles for tracking children of the laboring classes into vocational programs while the children of the higher classes were being prepared for high school (this, in effect, was what they believed had happened in the schools of Rochester, New York). McAndrew, who believed that teachers should follow orders rather than give advice, went ahead with his plans and tried to avoid further consultations with them. Instead, it became clear that he was eager to consult the businessmen who had supported the Cooley plan. The board adopted the new program, despite the opposition of many of those who had united to oppose the Cooley plan. Although the worst fears of the opponents were not realized by the junior high schools, the controversy was significant because it revealed once more the way in which the issue of schooling for work could uncover the tensions between business and labor in Chicago.

The Great Depression had a devastating impact on all aspects of Chicago's public schools, including its vocational programs. No major city in the United States was in worse financial condition when the crisis began. The impact of the national crisis was exacerbated by the high degree of corruption and racketeering that had infected the administration of Chicago's schools as well as persistent revenue battles between Chicago politicians and representatives of downstate Illinois. In 1933, faced with a devastating financial crisis, the Board of Education increased teachers' workloads, slashed their pay, and cut many programs, including most vocational courses. In 1936, however, while the schools were still suffering under the draconian cuts imposed by a highly politicized school board, a new attempt to promote vocational education revived the bitter battles that had been fought over the Cooley bill. William H. Johnson, who became superintendent after the death of the popular William J. Bogan, was a man who was distinguished largely for his personal ambition and his subservience to an economy-minded board. Faced with the continuing financial crisis, he saw that a new emphasis on vocationalism could be a money-saving proposition. First he cut back the number of "major" academic subjects that high-school students could take. He then boldly proposed allowing only 20 percent of Chicago public school students to enter academic programs and sending the others into vocational courses. Since the salaries of vocational teachers were heavily subsidized by the state and federal governments under the Smith-Hughes Act, replacing teachers of academic subjects with vocational teachers would relieve some of the financial pressure on the Board of Education.

Johnson's proposal was even more restrictive than the Cooley plan. It not only threatened the democratic ideal of equal access to academic opportunities, it also directly attacked teacher tenure. Like his predecessors Cooley and McAndrew, Johnson was a moralist who sought to use vocational programs as a way of shaping the working classes. After a great storm of popular protest, which included charges that the plan to use the educational system to sort students into occupational niches was a "fascist" device, Johnson claimed that his original proposal had been "misunderstood" and he withdrew the plan. The proposal indicated once more, however, that there were still those who saw public education as a way of sorting children into appropriate vocational categories, and, despite the failure of the Cooley and Johnson plans, this was, in fact, how vocational education often functioned in Chicago.

The increased use of vocational education as a sorting device was facilitated by the fact that during the Depression, the Chicago labor movement, which had been a leading force in opposing the creation of a dual track educational system, had abandoned its concern for such broad educational issues. Organized labor was in large measure co-opted by Chicago's powerful Democratic political machine. The Chicago Federation of Labor now concentrated on getting its share of political rewards by emphasizing such bread-and-butter issues as the salaries of school custodians and maintaining labor representation on the school board. It no longer supported the teachers' demand for increased school funds nor their campaign for a more democratic system of education.

The use of vocational education to sort children became central to a program for "prevocational" education in the upper elementary grades with the establishment of vocational centers for children who were 14 or older and still enrolled in the sixth grade. Beginning in 1913, these children were offered special vocational classes—one set for boys and a different set of courses deemed appropriate for girls. While the intent of the program was expressed in the language of John Dewey as appealing to the interests and needs of the child, in their actual operation, pre-high-school vocational schools became disproportionately the schools for children seen as lacking the intellectual abilities for the regular academic program. In addition, children who were troublesome for the schools—chronic truants and children who misbehaved—were increasingly shunted into these programs. As a result, of course, the reputation of the vocational programs suffered. Good students were discouraged by their parents from attending these schools, and they became virtually reform schools. By 1941 (a typical year), the average IQ of children attending the Chicago Public Schools' vocational centers was 79.

After World War II, it became clear that Chicago's vocational program (as in so many other cities) was highly segregated by race. The best programs with the best connections to the job market were in white neighborhoods. As late as the 1960s, Washburne Trade School, which accepted only students who had been granted apprenticeships by the notoriously racist unions of the building trades, had an enrollment that was 99 percent white. When, in the 1980s, pressured by a federal consent decree, Washburne finally opened its doors to minorities, a number of the skilled unions drastically cut their programs or withdrew completely from Washburne. African American youth were served by Dunbar Vocational Center (which was not promoted to high-school level until 1952) and other vocational schools that had inferior equipment and instruction. Dunbar's curriculum followed the highly segregated Chicago labor market by offering only programs leading to the less-desirable, lower-paid trades.

Deindustrialization dealt an even more serious blow to meaningful schooling for work in Chicago's African American neighborhoods. As the steel mills and meatpacking industry left the South Side, new industries did not replace them, and by the 1970s it was clear that there were few jobs for which even the most successful vocational programs could provide an entry. As unemployment in the vast ghettoes of Chicago climbed, schooling for work became ever less relevant to the young people

Commercial class, St. Joseph's Bohemian Orphanage, Lisle, 1922. Photographer: Curt Teich & Co. Source: Curt Teich Archives, Lake County Discovery Museum.

growing up in a community that was increasingly isolated from the rest of the metropolitan area.

Reformers who valued social efficiency eventually won the battles over vocational education in the Chicago Public Schools that had begun early in the twentieth century. While the best of the vocational programs succeeded in preparing workers for the industrial and commercial needs of the city, for many children, especially the poor, vocational education provided a relatively inexpensive way to meet the requirements of compulsory attendance laws.

After World War II, as the world became more and more reliant on technology, much of the focus on schooling for work shifted to community and junior COLLEGES and their vocational centers, administered by the City Colleges of Chicago. Malcolm X College, founded in 1911 as Crane Junior College and located on the West Side near Cook County and St. Luke's Presbyterian Hospitals, offered a large number of vocational programs in the health sciences, in addition to courses in computer science and the child care professions. Truman College, located in the UPTOWN neighborhood, advertised itself as the most "richly diverse" of any community college in Illinois. Building on an institution begun in 1956, Truman has served NATIVE AMERICANS and immigrants from Latin America, Asia, and Poland. It offered, among other vocational programs, NURSING, pre-engineering, CHEMICAL-industry technology, and child development. The City Colleges also established a number of job skills centers. The one established by Olive-Harvey College, located in the African American community in the Southeast Side's PULLMAN neighborhood, trained workers for entry-level jobs such as counter person, bank teller, nurse's assistant, and security guard.

The public school system was by no means the only source for vocational education in Chicago. From the earliest days, Americans have gone to school to prepare for specific careers by attending private, entrepreneurial schools, and in the dynamic economy of early-twentieth-century Chicago, these schools proliferated. By 1898 a Chicago directory listed schools as varied as the Chicago School of Assaying, the Chicago Nautical School, and at least four shorthand schools. Schools listed in later directories include several millinery schools, the Chicago School of Bookkeeping, as well as the Wahl-Henius Institute of Fermentology and the Zymotechnic Institute and Brewing School. While these schools differed in quality, their persistence indicates a continuing demand by Chicagoans for schooling directed toward preparation for specific careers.

Perhaps the best known of Chicago's entrepreneurial schools was founded in 1931 by Herman A. DeVry, a pioneer in developing motion picture projectors. With a loan from a friend, DeVry purchased a defunct school with 25 students and three employees. Its purpose was to train students for technical work in ELECTRONICS, motion pictures, radio, and, eventually, television. The DEVRY INSTITUTE has trained thousands of people and now awards college degrees as well as certificates. Purchased by Bell and Howell in 1967, the school rapidly expanded beyond its Chicago base and established campuses in several other states as well as Canada.

Schooling for work in Chicago also involved a great number of postgraduate institutions. Foremost among these were programs in teacher education, initially offered as part of the public school program. The metropolitan area also offered graduate training in LAW, medicine and NURSING, and business. Except for teacher and nursing education, these programs were quite different from most schooling for work in that they attracted mostly middle-class participants. And unlike precollegiate vocational education, they provided genuine opportunities for social mobility.

The story of schooling for work in Chicago is, of course, one aspect of a national problem. Vocational education has never been simply a way of preparing youngsters for work; it has

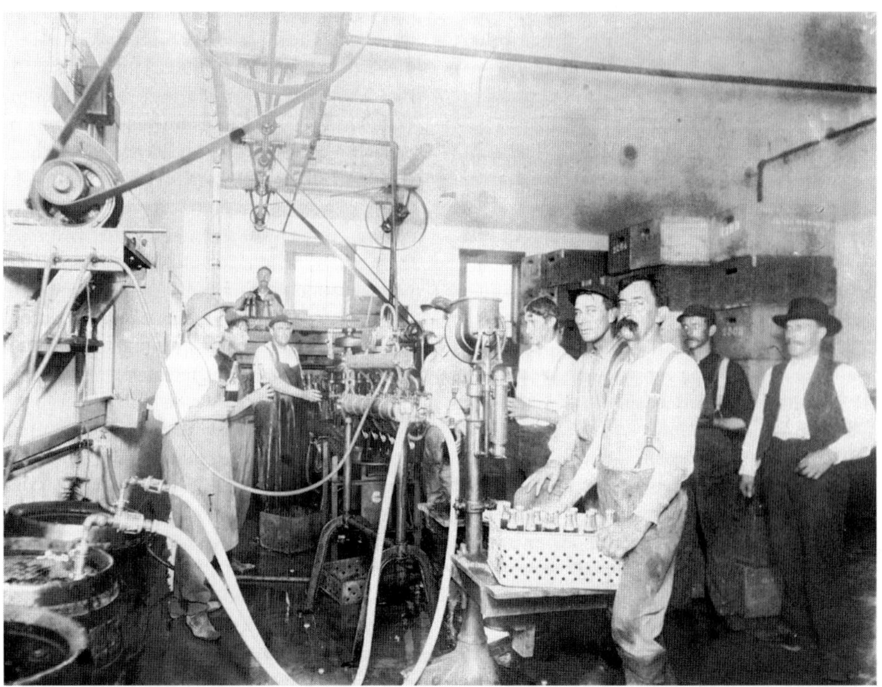
Siebel's brewing academy, ca. 1902–1904. Photographer: Unknown. Source: Chicago Historical Society.

also been called upon to serve children who are unmotivated or lack academic abilities in a system that requires them to be in school. The great pressures to deal with the second problem have meant that the first motive often has gotten lost. Another limit on schooling for work within the public school system has been finding the flexibility to deal with a rapidly changing job market. The Smith-Hughes Act compounded this by its emphasis on agricultural work and other trades that rapidly became irrelevant to the needs of employers. Absent the requirement of serving as a means of keeping unmotivated and frequently troublesome children in school, however, the Chicago City Colleges and the private, entrepreneurial schools were able to concentrate on preparing people for new jobs—and this they have done with notable success.

Arthur Zilversmit

See also: Antiunionism; Bilingual Education; Medical Education; Progressive Education; Seminaries; Social Service Education

Further reading: The most recent study of vocational education is Herbert Kliebard, *Schooled to Work: Vocationalism and the American Curriculum, 1876–1946* (1999). While this study emphasizes developments in Milwaukee, it offers valuable insights on the place of vocationalism in American schools. Another source for the study of the general history of vocational education in the United States is Marvin Lazerson and W. Norton Grubb's introduction to *American Education and Vocationalism: A Documentary History, 1870–1970* (1974). This volume includes a comprehensive analytical bibliography. The selections include an excerpt from the Cooley report and Dewey's criticism of it. Martin Carnoy and Henry M. Levin, *Schooling and Work in the Democratic State* (1985), establishes a context for the Chicago story. See also Edward Krug, *The Shaping of the American High School,* vol. 1, 1880–1920 (1964, 1969), and vol. 2, 1920–1940 (1972).

The role of politics in shaping the history of schooling for work in Chicago can be best studied in Julia Wrigley, *Class Politics and Public Schools: Chicago, 1900–1950* (1982), which gives a detailed account of the controversy over the Cooley bill and the Johnson plan; and David John Hogan, *Class and Reform: School and Society in Chicago, 1880–1930* (1985), which provides a fine discussion of the class issues involved in the struggles over the Cooley bill. On the intersection of class and race in Chicago school politics, see Ira Katznelson and Margaret Weir, *Schooling for All: Class, Race, and the Decline of the Democratic Ideal* (1985). A valuable but somewhat disjointed account of Chicago schools is Mary J. Herrick, *The Chicago Schools: A Social and Political History* (1971).

On John Dewey, Jane Addams, and the role of the Progressives, see Lawrence Cremin, *The Transformation of the School: Progressivism in American Education, 1876–1957* (1962), and *American Education: The Metropolitan Experience* (1988). For a different view of Progressive education, see Arthur Zilversmit, "Progressive Education: A Definition," in Zilversmit's *Changing Schools: Progressive Education Theory and Practice* (1993), 1–18. John Dewey's views on the role of manual arts as a liberalizing subject are found in his lectures at the University of Chicago, published as *School and Society* (1900; rev. ed. 1915; repr. 1956). A valuable introduction to Dewey's thoughts about the relationship of education to democracy is Robert B. Westbrook, *John Dewey and American Democracy* (1991). On Jane Addams, see Christopher Lasch, ed., *The Social Thought of Jane Addams* (1965). For a good account on the aims of those Progressives who were primarily interested in improving the efficiency of the schools, see David Tyack, *The One Best System: A History of American Urban Education* (1974), and Raymond Callahan, *Education and the Cult of Efficiency: A Study of the Social Effects That Have Shaped the Administration of the Public Schools* (1962).

There is little published material on the role of schooling for work in the elementary schools of Chicago, although this proved to be a crucial stage for the role of vocational education as a sorting device. William Joseph Quirk's M.A. thesis, "The Development of Chicago Prevocational Schools" (DePaul University, 1948) offers much useful material. See also Jon Francis Smith, "The Historical Development of the Vocational Elementary Schools of Chicago" (M.A. thesis, DePaul University, 1954).

A brief examination of Chicago schools in recent years (but before the most recent school reforms) is a series of articles reprinted from the *Chicago Tribune* under the title *Chicago Schools: "Worst in America"* (1988). For the impact of urban poverty and deindustrialization on the inner city, see William J. Wilson, *When Work Disappears: The World of the New Urban Poor* (1996).

Schools and Education. Beginning with modest structures in the early nineteenth century, Chicago's schools have performed an increasing variety of functions, from providing literacy to monitoring health and physical development, AMERICANIZING immigrants, and addressing problems of social and economic inequality. Education has meant not only reading, writing, and arithmetic but also vocational education and preparation for citizenship, including lessons about fairness and good behavior, moral purposes the schools have always served. This story of constancy and change has been fraught with conflict, as various groups have battled for control of education. Private and suburban schools have offered alternatives to public education, eventually creating a variegated institutional patchwork that mirrored the region's diverse population.

The region's first schools were established in the early 1830s, as the tiny settlement of Chicago began to expand. Eliza Chappell is often credited with being the city's first public school teacher, but a number of private schools existed earlier. Whether public or private, however, life in these institutions was often chaotic. Early schools were makeshift and rudimentary. Funds earmarked for public education reached only a fraction of the school-age population. One teacher generally supervised classes numbering a hundred or more, with students ranging in age from 4 to 17. Schoolhouses were adapted from existing structures and often served multiple functions. Chappell's school had originally been a store. "The schoolhouse opened, " her daughter wrote, "in a little log house outside the military reservation" (FORT DEARBORN), and was "divided by calico curtains into two apartments, one for a schoolroom and the other for lodging."

Dearborn School, Madison and State Streets; the school existed from 1845 to 1871. Photographer: Unknown. Source: The Newberry Library.

When Chicago received its CHARTER in 1837, volunteer examiners were appointed to oversee the schools, but funding remained meager. In 1845 an inspector reported schools housed in temporary quarters, crowded, poorly equipped, and foul-smelling, "well calculated to create in the minds of children a disgust for the school room and make the acquisition of knowledge an irksome as well as a difficult task." Even when the city built its first school building that year, it was derisively dubbed "Miltimore's Folly," after a teacher who had suggested its necessity. By 1850 less than a fifth of eligible children were enrolled in public schools. Larger numbers attended private and parochial schools, but thousands did not enroll at all, particularly older children. Public school classes remained large, often conducted in poorly maintained rooms and with inadequate materials. Under such conditions, teachers could barely maintain order and listen to students read. One student recalled a typical lesson as consisting of reading "a chapter of the bible in mock unison," and then shouting "at the top of our voices as rapidly as possible every word in 40 pages of coarse print in Kirkham's grammar." Only the most gifted and persistent students could advance beyond rudimentary literacy. Families that wanted and could afford better education usually hired private tutors.

This was the situation encountered in 1854 by John Dore, Chicago's first superintendent of schools. Appointed by the city council, Dore and his better-known successor, William Wells (1856–1864), who were from Massachusetts, struggled to reform the schools. They worked diligently for better-trained teachers, a longer school year, improved facilities, and age-graded classes. Class sizes fell below 70, regular examinations were instituted, and the rudiments of age grading appeared in schools. Individual seats and desks gradually replaced benches and tables in many classes, to eliminate what Wells described as "one of the greatest of all school evils . . . or whispering." To make instruction more appealing, Wells urged less emphasis on rote memorization and the use of "a variety of intellectual and physical recreations," particularly for younger children. Wells also reached out to the city's growing immigrant communities, particularly ROMAN CATHOLICS, to expand the schools' clientele. He established the city's first public high school and later added a normal school course for training teachers.

Chicago gradually developed a system of public education similar to those in large cities elsewhere in the country. Between 1860 and 1870 the public school population more than quadrupled, to more than 27,000, outpacing the city's growth. In 1872 the state legislature established a Board of Education, with members appointed by the mayor, to oversee all aspects of public education in the city. Within this governance arrangement, leaders sought to develop a complex system to deliver education, with graded elementary schools, specialized courses of secondary education, and postsecondary courses for high-school graduates. At the same time, continued friction existed between the city's different school systems. Private schools, particularly in Catholic PARISHES, remained a substantial presence in Chicago. GERMAN immigrants demanded instruction in their native language, and the IRISH and other Catholics objected to Protestant Bible readings in public schools. These issues helped fuel private school enrollments, and by 1900 more than 50,000 students were enrolled in the CATHOLIC SCHOOLS alone.

Still, the public schools expanded rapidly, thanks both to the city's rapid growth and improved attendance. Between 1870 and 1900, Chicago's population expanded by a factor of six, and the public schools by a factor of eight—to about a quarter million. School leaders scrambled to find seats and teachers for these students. In the 1880s, for instance, children often shared desks because of crowding; boys and girls were paired "for the sake of discipline." An absent child lost the seat, returning to sit on a bench until another child's absence created a vacancy. Basements often were used for classes, school supplies were limited, and many children continued to use old hard slates for writing lessons because expensive paper tablets were scarce.

The system struggled to improve instruction. Monthly records on attendance were collected, along with regular reports on topics ranging from discipline to academic performance. The Board of Education published curriculum guides and sponsored teacher institutes to improve instruction. A manual issued in 1879 urged the use of "slate work" as well as "oral work" in teaching arithmetic "to aid the teacher in securing *variety*" in instruction (emphasis in original). Methods were suggested for teaching mathematics and other subjects at each grade level. In 1880 corporal punishment, the foundation of the old system of harsh discipline, was finally dropped as a board-sanctioned practice in the public schools. In a growing number of schools it was possible to find classes conducted in German, in response to political pressure from the city's largest non-English-speaking ethnic group. Superintendent Albert G. Lane (1891–1898) was emblematic of leaders concerned both with improving the quality of instruction and the efficiency of district operations.

By 1900 there were more than five thousand teachers in the public schools. Thousands more taught in private and parochial schools. Over 80 percent of these teachers were women, most of them young, unmarried, and born in the United States. In 1897 the CHICAGO TEACHERS FEDERATION (CTF) was formed to advocate a uniform pay scale, teacher pensions, and better working conditions in the public schools. It claimed thousands of members and became one of the most influential teachers' organizations in the United States. Led for more than 30 years by Margaret Haley, the CTF was an advocate for improved school funding and teachers' rights.

The opening decades of the twentieth century were a tumultuous time in the history of Chicago's public schools. The CTF resisted the efforts of Superintendent Edwin Cooley (1900–1909) to centralize the district's administrative functions. The union also successfully fought legislation proposed by Cooley to create a separate vocational track for students outside of traditional high schools. The CTF was affiliated for a short time with organized labor before being attacked by the Board of Education under the leadership of Jacob Loeb. A two-year battle ensued over the right of teachers to organize, reflecting long-standing divisions in the city between labor and business interests. The arbitrary dismissal of CTF members led to passage in 1917 of the Otis Law, which included Illinois' first provisions for teacher tenure. The influence of the CTF declined thereafter, especially during the term of Superintendent William McAndrew (1924–1927), who established the city's first junior high schools and further expanded vocational education programs.

In the early twentieth century, Chicago was a major center of educational reform. Francis Parker (principal of the COOK COUNTY Normal School), John Dewey (professor and director of the UNIVERSITY OF CHICAGO Laboratory School), and Ella Flagg Young (innovative teacher and superintendent of the Chicago Public Schools) were prominent national figures in PROGRESSIVE EDUCATION, along with William Wirt in nearby GARY. Together with other reformers, they established new experiential curricula, community programs linked to the schools, and teachers' councils to provide a forum to discuss pedagogy and related issues. Superintendent Young (1909–1915) was an outspoken advocate of teachers and received strong support from the CTF during her term. She declared the centralization of administrative authority undemocratic and "un-American" and resisted board attempts to attack the CTF, twice threatening resignation.

At about the same time, reform influences gradually infused the schools. Following an exposé of lifeless drill in classrooms visited by Joseph Mayer Rice in the 1890s, teachers were encouraged to use object lessons and other progressive techniques. The district later established a Child Study Department to recommend ways of improving the welfare of students. Particular attention was given to exercise and children's physical development, major concerns of PUBLIC HEALTH reformers at the time.

As Chicago's immigrant population expanded, the schools were called upon to aid in its assimilation into American life. In 1886, the year of the HAYMARKET Riot, the *Chicago Tribune* editorialized that "it ought to be the first function of the public schools to teach loyalty, love of country, and devotion to American principles and institutions." The study of American history and "civics" had long been an integral part of the curriculum but received more attention as the numbers of foreign-born students grew. In 1897 school board president Daniel Cameron declared that the schools should impart "permanent admiration and loyalty" for the United States. Jane Addams, on the other hand, believed instruction should be less doctrinaire. "Give these children a chance to utilize the historic and industrial material which they see about them," she wrote, "and they will begin to have a sense of ease in America, a first consciousness of being at home." Addams helped provide for the education of thousands of immigrants at HULL HOUSE, and other SETTLEMENT HOUSES followed suit. Many classes were offered for adults on a wide range of topics, including American history and civics. In 1918, Frances Wetmore was appointed to direct "AMERICANIZATION" instruction for the public schools, moving her classes from the University of Chicago settlement and eventually serving thousands of aliens seeking citizenship. These offerings, which continued through the following decade, were later provided by the Works Progress Administration during the GREAT DEPRESSION.

Following WORLD WAR I, Chicago's public schools entered a period of enrollment stability at about 400,000 students, and an era of corruption and controversy over issues ranging from the curriculum to school finance. Republican mayor William Hale Thompson attacked Superintendent McAndrew for allegedly anti-American textbooks used in the schools. Thompson and his political allies used provisions allowing city control of non-teaching personnel to make the schools a source of PATRONAGE appointments. This marked the beginning of a long period of graft in the school system, as the appointment of political operatives continued under Thompson's DEMOCRATIC successors, particularly Edward Kelly. The state provided little support for education, and by the late 1920s the board was borrowing to fund basic programs. This ongoing financial mismanagement contributed to a fiscal crisis during the Great Depression, when the jobs of politically connected custodians and clerks were protected before those of teachers. In turn, teachers conducted occasionally raucous demonstrations to protest drastic cuts imposed by the board. By the time financial recovery measures were instituted, with help from the state legislature, public confidence in the city's schools had weakened significantly. Scandals over corruption and nepotism continued to plague the schools through the late 1940s.

Life in schools often reflected this malaise. Standards became increasingly uniform and more students went to high school, but classroom experiences often were rather mundane. Evidence of reform influence was difficult to find. Inspectors from New York's Columbia University in the early 1930s observed that most schools still practiced uniform drill exercises, even requiring children to read in unison. Although some teachers employed more imaginative and engaging teaching methods, traditional approaches apparently predominated. The district's rules were partly to blame, requiring time allotments for subjects which "too often . . . serve to delimit worthwhile experiences." In the high schools, investigators reported that the curriculum "seems to support too much the concept that education is something to be got, passed and recorded."

As high schools grew, students were both sorted and urged to intermingle. "Homogeneous grouping" was introduced, a practice later known as ability grouping or tracking, utilizing standardized tests. A student handbook for ENGLEWOOD High School explained that "those who can learn more quickly are not hindered by the slower pupils, while those that are slow are in classes by themselves." Some secondary schools also practiced limited segregation of boys and girls, to support "improvement in the scholarship of the boys," who were believed to lag behind girls developmentally. At the same time, spaces such as the lunchroom or cafeteria, where students could interact under supervision, were created to promote sociability. Student publications complemented schoolwide events such as dances and pep rallies, intended to encourage school spirit.

The region's private and parochial schools also expanded between 1920 and 1950. Catholic school enrollments grew by nearly 30 percent in the city and nearly tripled in the suburbs. Under the leadership of George Cardinal Mundelein and Samuel Cardinal Stritch, parishes scrambled to build schools to meet the demand, particularly for high schools. By the early fifties, nearly 200,000 students attended Catholic schools, about 70 percent of them in the city.

Suburban communities grew steadily after the World War I, and their school systems began to gain public favor. No longer isolated rural districts, they sought a quality of education equivalent to the best urban schools. Affluent school systems to the north and west provided new facilities and innovative curricula for a largely middle- or upper-class clientele. In WINNETKA, Superintendent Carleton Washburne became a celebrated champion of progressive education, and his schools featured imaginative courses of study and exemplary student support services. Other suburban districts adopted similar reforms, albeit to varying degrees. These educational systems did not have the politically charged atmosphere of city schools, and many saw them as havens of responsible innovation and community responsiveness.

In the 1940s the ongoing crisis over mismanagement of the Chicago Public Schools finally came to a head. Following an investigation by the National Education Association, regional accreditors threatened sanctions. This, coupled with the election of Mayor Martin Kennelly and passage of state legislation expanding the power of system administrators, signaled a new era. Herold Hunt's decision to move from Kansas City in 1947 to become superintendent marked an end to blatant political interference in the schools.

Hunt and his successor, Benjamin Willis, presided over a period of expansion in public education. In the wake of a postwar baby boom and a buoyant economy, they embarked on a building campaign that added significantly to the system's capacity. Enrollments surged, peaking at nearly 600,000 in the late sixties. At the same time, class sizes dropped significantly for the first time in decades, from about 40 to 32. New programs were added, from specialized vocational training to arts education, and new services were offered, such as free summer programs, expanded guidance counseling, and rehabilitation services. Salaries for teachers increased in the wake of a national shortage. But budgets were sound, and the system was generally free of political interference.

Important developments affected the experiences of schoolchildren. Audio-visual technology enabled teachers to introduce a new component into everyday instruction. By the end of the 1950s the Chicago schools owned thousands of educational films on a wide variety of topics, and every building had projectors. New science materials encouraging more "hands-on" experimentation were obtained with help from the National Defense Education Act. These included human anatomy models, microscopes, incubators, and "computer kits." In the 1960s new curricular models were adopted in a variety of subjects, ranging from the "new math" to "whole language" approaches to reading and writing instruction. By 1964 the system reportedly owned more than 75,000 "manipulative materials" and "visual aids" to assist education. These developments helped to reduce the emphasis on drill and memorization that characterized the schooling of earlier generations, even if older teachers often resisted new approaches.

At the same time, a new source of controversy came fully into view: racial inequality in education. Black Chicagoans had been aware of the disparities for decades, and in the mid-twentieth century the issues finally entered broader public discourse. By 1960 Chicago's AFRICAN AMERICAN population had surpassed 800,000, almost a quarter of the city's total—up from 14 percent just 10 years earlier. Vast areas of the South and West Sides became densely populated ghetto neighborhoods, and racial segregation was high. Schools in these areas were overcrowded, and some ran on double shifts, with children attending for just half a day. In poor inner-city areas the annual turnover of students exceeded 50 percent, and in some instances it approached 100 percent. Schools in these neighborhoods often fell into disrepair. "The broken windows were there," wrote one young teacher at DuSable

Timuel Black Attends School in the 1920s

My mother took me to school. The neighborhood had not begun to buzz yet. It was predominantly white, JEWISH, IRISH Catholic, pretty upper-middle class. And she took us, I transferred from overcrowded Willard, triple shifts, to Burke. . . . So I went to this [second grade] room and the teacher was flabbergasted. And the kids went on about their business. And a girl who I never will forget, Barbara Wilkes, moved over to share her book. And the teacher went berserk. The kids, Barbara started crying. And the kids and I'm mad at my Momma for putting me in this situation. You know, I was just very uncomfortable. Barbara didn't know what to do. And the teacher shouted, "Barbara what are you doing?" And the kids were startled. I was angry. And I was lonely. Now when I came home . . . My mother says, "Don't worry, baby. It'll be alright." My mother was that way. My Dad says, "What the hell, you put that child in a room with those crackers?" They were always doing that. They were always saying things with the Marcus Garvey movement. So, now, once the principal, you know, lets us know, lets everyone know that whoever comes to live in that neighborhood is going to go to school if they want to go to that school, things begin to settle down.

Black, Timuel. Interview with James Grossman and Jamie Kalven, February 2, 1996.

High School in the early seventies, "along with the torn window shades and broken desk tops, appendages to the badly lighted, worn central hallway." These conditions, he reflected, "encouraged failure and a sense of depression." Observations such as these led to calls for integration, and demands that inequities between black and white schools be resolved.

Professing belief in neighborhood schools, Superintendent Willis characterized the ferment over inequity as unwarranted interference in the province of professional educators. Public outcries intensified over his use of portable buildings, widely derided as "WILLIS WAGONS," to accommodate overcrowding at black schools. Demonstrations rocked the system in the early 1960s. External reports recommended dramatic steps to redress educational inequality but were ignored. After a somewhat histrionic resignation offer, Willis ended his superintendency in 1966 amidst growing acrimony.

James Redmond, Willis's successor, and the superintendents who followed him attempted to develop integration plans that would send black students to predominantly white schools. Hostile demonstrations on the city's Northwest and Southwest Sides erupted. The failure of board initiatives led to threatened federal intervention, resulting in a 1980 consent decree and SCHOOL DESEGREGATION plan. Meanwhile, the movement of students out of the system accelerated. Between 1970 and 1980 the white portion of the schools' population fell by nearly 60 percent, and by the early 1990s it had almost been halved again. White Chicagoans were moving to the suburbs or enrolling their children in private or parochial schools.

Suburban communities grew rapidly in the postwar period, and their school systems became widely acclaimed, especially in the years following 1970. These SCHOOL DISTRICTS engaged in building campaigns to keep up with rising demand, funded by an expansive local economy and an electorate willing to invest substantially in education. Some schools gained national attention, such as Winnetka's New Trier High School, frequently cited as an exemplary institution. Beginning in the early 1960s, studies noted the differences between schools in the city and the suburbs, arguing that their newer facilities, better funding and a largely middle- and upper-class clientele gave suburban districts a clear advantage. When the state launched the Illinois Goals Assessment Project (IGAP) to measure achievement levels in the early 1980s, suburban schools consistently outperformed most inner-city public schools.

Teachers in the Chicago area began to organize in the postwar years, like their counterparts elsewhere. City teachers were dissatisfied with salary provisions and the unresponsiveness of the Willis administration. In 1966 they elected the Chicago Teachers Union (CTU) as their bargaining agent and three years later conducted the first systemwide teachers' strike in Chicago's history. Even though it was settled quickly, following Mayor Richard J. Daley's intervention, it represented a new era in the relationship of teachers and the district. Strikes occurred frequently over the next two decades, as the union and administrators battled over such issues as salaries, job security, class sizes, and transfer policies. Similar conflicts occurred in suburban districts, albeit on a smaller scale, as teachers organized there also. An atmosphere of dissension became associated with the schools, particularly in the city, and it contributed to mounting public dissatisfaction with the state of public education.

In the 1980s public education in Chicago faced a variety of challenges. Declining enrollments and escalating costs led to a fiscal crisis in the late 1970s and the creation of the state-mandated Chicago School Finance Authority in 1980 to oversee the system's budget. Continuing money problems, recurring conflicts with the CTU, poor performances on standardized tests, and continuing white flight from the system contributed to a perception of failure. In the fall of 1987, U.S. Secretary of Education William Bennett declared Chicago's public schools the "worst in the nation."

Under the leadership of Mayor Harold Washington, a coalition of community groups, business leaders, and reformers helped to draft a series of proposals to transform the schools. Passed by the state legislature in 1988, the Chicago School Reform Act created a Local School Council for each of the system's

School Reform

The citizens of Chicago tax themselves heavily in the interests of public education, and as a body they are honest in their desire for good schools. Why then do their efforts terminate occasionally in such a miserable fiasco as that which has recently attracted the attention of the world? Any attempt to answer this question must carry the inquirer into that complicated and restless sea of social forces which perpetually surround and condition the public school.

—George S. Counts, *School and Society in Chicago*, 1928.

The year was 1928; three-quarters of a century later and the statement retains a contemporary rhythm. William Bennett, Ronald Reagan's ambitious secretary of education, proclaimed Chicago SCHOOLS "the worst in America" in 1987. With more than half the students dropping out, close to 10 percent chronic truants, and less than a third of high-school graduates reading on grade level, the system stood near collapse.

The causes of school crisis were various: the inequitable distribution of educational resources (for example, more than half of the poorest children and 80 percent of non-English-speaking students in Illinois attended Chicago schools in 1988, and yet Chicago operated on substantially less money per child than surrounding SCHOOL DISTRICTS); the stubborn power of a range of self-interested bureaucracies—central office, unions, departments—to work their will against the common good; an unresponsive, rigid classroom culture; and a sense that students are all-danger, all-deficit, all-dread.

The modern school reform movement was born of this disaster. While the spark was a teacher's strike—the ninth walkout in 18 years—the prairie fire consisted of mobilized parents and citizens who raised broader issues of education goals, standards, and accountability. By the time the strike ended, a powerful coalition had been forged and a new alignment of power and priority was on the horizon.

Legislation in 1988 created Local School Councils (LSCs) at each school, comprising six parents, two teachers, and two community representatives. LSCs were given real power: hiring the principal on a four-year performance contract (marking the end of principal tenure), drafting school improvement plans, and spending discretionary funds—half a million dollars in most elementary schools, three quarters of a million in a typical high school.

After the first few years some results were remarkable. LSCs spent most on teachers: three thousand new teachers were in the system as a result of local decisions. About one-third of all schools were making dramatic improvements in leadership, climate, and student achievements, while another third were making modest progress and the remainder were essentially stalled. More young AFRICAN AMERICAN and Latino principals had entered the system. Perhaps most important, school reform engaged the energies and hopes of tens of thousands of people—six thousand citizens convening officially every month to focus on the schools.

Legislation in 1995 kept LSCs in power but reasserted control of the central office by the mayor. His appointees took dramatic steps to streamline the system and to hold schools accountable to known standards. The central office began to take over failing schools.

The most hopeful initiative has been the creation of small schools, either as alternative schools, teacher-led or parent-led schools, charter schools, or whole schools devolving into several schools within a single building. These schools require teachers to be thoughtful, caring, reflective, and responsible, and they place children firmly at the center.

William Ayers

The Eagle, Juarez High School's yearbook, 1981. Source: Chicago Historical Society.

schools. Consisting of parents, community members, and educators, these councils became a new source of energy for schools and communities across the city. Chicago's school reform also helped to put the district back into the national limelight, as other urban school systems attempted similar reforms. Test scores in some schools improved, while others remained the same or even declined. But irrespective of test results, there was renewed public interest in the city's schools.

In 1995 yet another Chicago school reform bill was passed in Springfield, this time under the leadership of Mayor Richard M. Daley. Local school councils were retained, but the Board of Education was reconstituted and the superintendent was replaced by a chief executive officer. The system was relieved of oversight by the School Finance Authority and was given new powers to utilize resources. The result was a series of decisive moves to augment performance at poorly performing schools and to locate centers of excellence throughout the system. New contracts were negotiated. Public confidence in the system improved, although problems remained. Paul Vallas, a former city budget director, served as the system's first CEO; in 2001 he was replaced by Arne Duncan.

At the start of the twenty-first century, education in the Chicago area remains highly fragmented. The Chicago Public Schools have experienced radical changes in the last several decades, with profound demographic change followed by organizational modification and school reform. The suburban districts appear to enjoy substantial advantages, and the advent of new testing regimes and other means of comparing achievement levels make it difficult to ignore these differences. The region's private schools serve a largely white and affluent clientele, while urban schools, Chicago's in particular, are largely black and Hispanic. By 2000 more than three-quarters of Chicago's public school students were from low-income or poor families. Schooling is highly unequal across the region; overcoming these differences will be the great challenge of the future.

John L. Rury

See also: Governing the Metropolis; Progressive Education

Further reading: Herrick, Mary J. *The Chicago Schools: A Social and Political History.* 1970. • Sanders, James W. *Education of an Urban Minority: Catholics in Chicago, 1833–1965.* 1977. • Zilversmit, Arthur. *Changing Schools: Progressive Education Theory and Practice, 1930–1960.* 1993.

Scots. Although thousands of Scots crossed the Atlantic in the nineteenth century, the greatest wave of Scottish emigration to the United States came after WORLD WAR I and into the 1920s. These white and largely PROTESTANT immigrants assimilated easily into American culture: they already knew the language, and many were skilled laborers, craftsmen, or members of the professional or merchant class.

Chicago's Scots established their own organizations, from Burns clubs (after poet Robert Burns) to pipe bands, nurturing Scottish culture and perpetuating Scottish customs. PHILANTHROPIC groups were among the earliest immigrant societies within the Scottish American community. In 1846 Chicago Scots founded the Illinois Saint Andrew Society, the oldest charitable institution in the state. With over one thousand members in the 1990s, the society has continued to operate the Scottish Home in NORTH RIVERSIDE, Illinois, which in the late twentieth century had to abandon its policy of admitting only patients of Scots descent because of dwindling numbers.

Scottish immigrants played major roles in Chicago's early development. John Kinzie was probably Chicago's first English-speaking resident. Other early Chicagoans of Scottish birth or descent include trader Alexander Robinson; printer Robert Fergus, considered the father of the PRINTING industry in Chicago; detective Allan PINKERTON, whose house on West Adams Street was a stop on the UNDERGROUND RAILROAD; James MacLagan, pastor of the First Scotch Presbyterian Church. In the late 1890s many wealthy second- and third-generation Scottish Americans lived along fashionable PRAIRIE AVENUE or, further south, on Drexel Boulevard. As late as the early decades of the twentieth century, a cluster of churches, halls, and Masonic temples on the SOUTH SIDE, especially along 64th Street, catered to the Scottish American community.

Scots were particularly well represented in Chicago's MEATPACKING industry. The UNION STOCK YARD was built primarily by a combination of Scots, Scottish Americans, and Ulster Scots. Many of the cattle owners and drovers were themselves Scottish immigrants. In addition, a number of Chicago institutions have Scottish roots, including Encyclopedia Britannica and Carson Pirie Scott & Co.

Numerous Scottish place names dot the Chicago area, from INVERNESS and WEST DUNDEE to BANNOCKBURN and MIDLOTHIAN. Moreover, many Chicago streets honor Scottish places and people: Aberdeen Street, for example, is named after Scotland's third largest city, while St. Clair Street commemorates the life of General Arthur St. Clair, the Scots-born Revolutionary War hero. Yet another physical reminder of Scotland's impact on Chicago is the statue of Robert Burns, Scotland's national poet, that stands in GARFIELD PARK. Erected in 1906, it remains a source of pride for the city's Scottish American community.

June Skinner Sawyers

See also: Demography; English; Housing for the Elderly; Multicentered Chicago; Welsh

Further reading: Berthoff, Rowland. *British Immigrants in Industrial America, 1790–1950.* 1953. • MacMillan, Thomas C. "The Scots and Their Descendants in Illinois." In *Illinois State Historical Society Transactions,* no. 26 (1919): 31–85. • Rethford, Wayne, and June Skinner Sawyers. *The Scots of Chicago: Quiet Immigrants and Their New Society.* 1997.

Scouting. Chicago played a significant role in the development of youth scouting organizations. In 1909, the YOUNG MEN'S CHRISTIAN ASSOCIATION supported an informal scouting troop led by O. W. Kneeves which met at Hamilton Park. Chicago publisher William D. Boyce incorporated the Boy Scouts of America in 1910. Chicago's first official Boy Scout troops formed soon after in WOODLAWN. During the 1910s and 1920s, Chicago publishers issued a popular series of scouting adventure books. Juliette Low, who founded the American Girl Scouts in Georgia in 1912, traveled to Chicago two years later to organize local troops. Chicagoans also participated in the Campfire Girls.

Promoting citizenship and patriotism, scouts performed wartime service, assisted in peacetime relief work, and greeted such dignitaries as Charles Lindbergh. Chicago Boy and Girl Scouts learned wilderness skills and gained appreciation for the environment at camps near the city and in nearby states. The Owasippe Scout Reservation in Michigan, owned by the Chicago Boy Scout Council since 1911, is the nation's oldest scout camp. Originally militaristic in tone, camps gradually became primarily recreational and educational. As suburban populations grew, especially in the 1960s, scouting programs expanded,

Boy scouts whitewashing a metal barrel in an alley on the Near South Side as part of a Clean-Up Day sponsored by Eighteenth Ward alderman Carl T. Murray, 1915. Photographer: Unknown. Source: Chicago Historical Society.

sponsored as they were in the city, by communities, churches, and other organizations.

Both male and female Chicago scouts have engaged in career-oriented programs. The ARGONNE NATIONAL LABORATORY provided scouts access to science and engineering research. The Chicago POLICE Department, through the Explorers Program, offered teenaged scouts experience in LAW enforcement professions. Sea Scouts practiced naval management on ships affiliated with Chicago and suburban troops.

Chicago was the setting for various scouting milestones. Chicago hosted two national Boy Scout Council meetings, in 1951 and 1958. In 1985, a twenty-two-cent stamp celebrating American Boy Scouting's 75th anniversary was dedicated at Chicago. In 2002, Girl Scouts celebrated their 90th anniversary at NAVY PIER.

Chicago scouts came to represent the region's diversity. Chicago's ethnic residents joined scout troops or formed their own groups, such as the POLISH Scouting Organization. Troops began the gradual process of racial integration in the 1920s. In the 1990s, the Chicago Commission on Human Relations criticized the Chicago Area Boy Scouts Council's discrimination against a homosexual Eagle Scout. At the beginning of the twenty-first century, hundreds of thousands of boys and girls in the Chicago region participated in scouting through dozens of councils.

Elizabeth D. Schafer

See also: Americanization; Clubs: Youth Clubs; Fitness and Athletic Clubs; Sailing and Boating; Turnvereins

Further reading: MacLeod, David. *Building Character in the American Boy: The Boy Scouts, YMCA, and Their Forerunners, 1870–1920.* 1983. • Peterson, Robert W. *The Boy Scouts: An American Adventure.* 1984. • Wright, Katharine O. *Girl Scouting in the Great Lakes Region: A History.* 1938.

Second City Theatre. Opened December 16, 1959, at 1842 N. Wells St., the Second City cabaret THEATER was founded by a group of bright young artists, including many UNIVERSITY OF CHICAGO alumni, who had worked in such earlier, folded Chicago companies as the Playwright's Theatre Club and Compass Players.

Slyly named after a series of derisive *New Yorker* articles by A. J. Liebling, their theater quickly became a Chicago institution. The IMPROVISATIONAL theater techniques of the original artistic director, Paul Sills, fueled its satirical comedy revues.

Second City's success became a key factor in establishing the legitimacy of homegrown talent in Chicago theater and prepared the way for the major 1970s expansion of resident theater in the city. Its reputation expanded with engagements in New York and London, extensive tours, training and touring companies, a permanent Toronto base in 1973, and a new Chicago home at 1616 N. Wells Street in 1967.

Already noted in its early years for the theater and film successes of such former cast members as Alan Arkin, Barbara Harris, and Severn Darden, Second City's fame accelerated in the mid-1970s, when several Chicago alumni, including John Belushi and Bill Murray, became stars of TELEVISION's *Saturday Night Live.* Still more attention came from another TV offshoot by former Second Citizens, the 1980s series *SCTV.*

Second City's ownership shifted from cofounder Bernard Sahlins to Canadian Andrew Alexander in 1985. Its early hip, urban satire replaced by a broader base of humor references, the theater still uses a bare stage and a cast of five or six performers for each edition.

Richard Christiansen

See also: Acting, Ensemble; Theater Companies; Theater Training

Further reading: Sweet, Jeffrey. *Something Wonderful Right Away: An Oral History of Second City and the Compass Players.* 1994.

Second Chicago School of Architecture. *See* Architecture: The Second Chicago School

Seiches. A seiche (pronounced "saysh") is a sudden fluctuation of water levels on a lake or inland sea. The GREAT LAKES are among the few regions in the world where these potentially deadly events occur.

When a strong and rapid change in atmospheric pressure takes place on one side of a lake, usually associated with a line of thunderstorms, it can cause the water level to drop. As a result, the water level rises at the other end of the lake, in a motion that sometimes resembles a tidal wave. This sudden rise in water levels is potentially dangerous to swimmers, boaters, or anyone near the water.

Eight people drowned in Chicago's most tragic seiche, on June 26, 1954; a ten-foot wave swept seven people off the rocks at Montrose Harbor and an eighth from North Avenue Bridge. Since then, there have been numerous seiche scares and reports of smaller seiches, but none that caused similar damage or deaths.

Thomas G. Bobula

See also: Climate; Tornadoes

Seminaries. Chicago boasts more theological seminaries of more denominations than any other American metropolis. The original theological schools tended to be in the East, at Princeton, New Brunswick, Harvard, and Yale, and Catholic seminaries were similarly at home on the East Coast, for example in Philadelphia and Baltimore.

As populations and churches moved west, Chicago became a strategic center, "halfway to everywhere." At junctures of shipping and RAILROAD lines, it could send priests and ministers to the rest of the then West (now Midwest) and, eventually, into all the nation and the world.

Chicago came to prominence at a time when PROTESTANT magnates were in a position to help fund seminaries. The McCormicks funneled profits from their reapers to McCormick Theological Seminary, and John D. Rockefeller helped support the UNIVERSITY OF CHICAGO Divinity School, the only seminary fully integrated into a host university. Aside from the University of Chicago, which could not depend upon Baptist congregation funds the way more conservative schools could, Chicago's seminaries generally depended less on gifts from millionaires and more on members of ordinary congregations who wanted to assure a constant supply of educated and well-equipped clergy.

Religious denominations vary widely in their policies regarding clerical preparation. In some Baptist bodies, for example, a person without any special education can "get the call" and respond, becoming ordained and entering practice. In many storefront churches, the pastor has had no graduate seminary or college education.

Most clergy, however, are prepared at schools for postbaccalaureate students, schools that must meet standards of the Association of Theological Schools in the United States and Canada. Such schools may be completely defined and monitored by a host church body, as is St. Mary of the Lake, the ROMAN CATHOLIC ARCHDIOCESAN school, or by a cluster of agencies within a body, such as the Catholic Theological Union in HYDE PARK, supported by a number of religious orders. The schools may be denominationally associated but connected with a university, as Garrett-Evangelical is with NORTHWESTERN UNIVERSITY, or may be located near a university, drawing on and contributing to its resources, as the schools in the Hyde Park Cluster of Theological Schools are around the University of Chicago. Schools also may be integrated into university life and have little independent existence or relation to denominations, such as the University of Chicago Divinity School.

While historically the training of clergy began in high school for ROMAN CATHOLICS and after college for Protestants and JEWS, today many older matriculators, people of "late vocation," choose to be trained as clergy after years in another profession. For most Protestants, the course is three years, but almost always there is a year of internship at a congregation or some other religious agency. Chicago, with its hundreds of congregations, is an excellent laboratory for seminarians who gain practical experience doing field work or serving in teaching parishes. Technical training occurs in programs such as Clinical Pastoral Education, which involves HOSPITALS and other medical institutions around the city.

All these internship, field work, and clinical connections are dependent on Chicago institutions, just as they feed human resources and energies into these Chicago places. Many parts of theological education, however, could occur in any part of the country and the curriculum would look similar. A catalog of the Association of Chicago Theological Schools (ACTS) lists the disciplines as Biblical, Historical, Theological, Ethical, Religion and Society, World Mission, and Ministry Studies, along with History of Religions.

The same ACTS guidebook also points to a recent trend to recognize ethnic, racial, and other emphases. So one reads of AFRICAN AMERICAN, Asian, Cross-cultural, and Hispanic Studies; there are also Women's Studies, fields of MISSIONARY TRAINING at the Chicago Center for Global Ministries, Judaic Studies, and Urban and Public Policy Studies.

Chicago theological training has benefited from innovation, most visibly by William Rainey Harper, the founding president of the University of Chicago. Harper's writings, critical of substandard and antiquated theological education as he had observed it in the East, are often regarded as classics that shaped subsequent innovations. He demanded a confrontation between seminarians, too long hidden in ivory towers, and the city and its congregations, its slums, and its libraries. Similarly, Chicago Theological Seminary profited from the Social Gospel contributions of Graham Taylor and colleagues drawn around him, professors who taught their students to make use of sociology and other human sciences.

Clerical training today usually has an ecumenical accent. Not only Presbyterians attend McCormick Theological Seminary, or Lutherans the Lutheran School of Theology at Chicago, a merger of a number of long-independent Lutheran seminaries. Some of them formally connect curricula, as in the Hyde Park Cluster and at Northside Theological Institute, including Garrett-Evangelical, NORTH PARK, and Seabury-Western seminaries along with the Catholics' Mundelein Seminary and Trinity Evangelical Divinity School.

While approximately a dozen schools make up ACTS (the University of Chicago Divinity School not being among them), at various times as many as 30 seminaries or their academic equivalents have existed around the city. ACTS claims 2,500 students in its member schools, students who have access to 1.7 million volumes in libraries.

Flagship JEWISH seminaries are in New York and Cincinnati. Chicago's SPERTUS Institute of Jewish Studies is the largest nonrabbinical training school for Jewish learning in the Midwest. Its resources are of use to already ordained rabbis and for others who are exploring the rabbinate.

A registry of Chicago training centers for ministry is hard to assemble, in part because definitions of ministry and clergy differ from group to group and not all call their leaders clergy. Thus there is a School for Officers Training of the SALVATION ARMY, whose graduates serve a role analogous to clergy in other bodies.

Training of the clergy occurs in the context of faculties who engage in much of the research of the supporting churches. The research element has drawn the talents of world-renowned professors to Chicago, particularly to the university-related schools. But Chicago Theological Seminary has been most closely identified with the city through all its decades, using the city as a site for experiment and, through its seminarians and faculty, influencing the urban scene. While Chicago earlier helped shape the religious world through evangelism and similar endeavors, in recent decades it is no doubt through its powerhouse of seminaries that the influence continues.

Martin E. Marty

See also: Medical Education; Religion, Chicago's Influence on; Universities and Their Cities

Senegalese. Senegalese have immigrated to Chicago since the 1970s as students, wage laborers, and itinerant traders, often inhabiting the trader role during transition to the other two occupations. They have driven TAXIS and worked in HOTELS and retail establishments. Chicago also boasts a sizable population of Senegalese engaged in professional occupations such as engineering and ACCOUNTING. The number of Senegalese immigrants moving through Chicago increased dramatically following the implementation of structural adjustment programs in the 1980s and devaluation of the CFA currency in Senegal in the 1990s. The majority of Senegalese in Chicago had been young men, until the late 1990s, when women also began immigrating to open hair-braiding salons on the SOUTH SIDE, operate clandestine restaurants out of their homes catering to male traders, and attend universities.

Senegalese first moved to Chicago not from Senegal but from New York. These immigrants sought to expand their trade networks to more profitable markets less saturated with other West African immigrants. Although these Senegalese traders have specialized in African art, they have also obtained counterfeit designer goods such as tee shirts, sunglasses, and purses from KOREAN and INDIAN wholesalers. These traders sell goods in Chicago or they may send wholesale shipments for sale in other parts of the trade circuit in Washington DC, New York, and Atlanta or in Senegal. They send their remittances overseas to their households in Senegal and to religious organizations there.

The primary community association established by Senegalese immigrants is a MUSLIM religious association called Da'ira Tuba Chicago in ROGERS PARK. Members of this organization are disciples of the Murid *tariqa* (Arabic: a Muslim Sufi order). The Da'ira president and three of its original members were traders who immigrated to Chicago from New York in 1972. However, the majority of the current Da'ira members are recent newcomers from New York in search of better markets and better educational opportunities. The Da'ira has organized numerous activities in Chicago. Generally, the Murids gather weekly to chant the litanies of their *wali* (Arabic: friend of God or saintly leader) Cheikh Amadou Bamba. The disciples also collect contributions for the organization's development projects in its sacred capital, Tuba, Senegal. The Da'ira sponsors a yearly interfaith conference with the AFRICAN AMERICAN and Arab Muslim population in Chicago on August 13, which in 1997 the city of Chicago declared as Cheikh Amadou Bamba Day. The Da'ira also sponsors the visit of a Murid marabout, a spiritual leader, from Senegal and a number of Islamic scholars. Senegalese Muslims have also participated in the yearly prayer session at McCormick Place held on Korite, the holiday marking the close of Ramadan, the month of fasting during which the Qur'an was revealed. The Murid tariqa has also initiated an exchange program with the American Islamic College in Chicago.

Beth Anne Buggenhagen

See also: Americanization; Demography; Multicentered Chicago

Further reading: Buggenhagen, Beth Anne. "Body into Soul, Soul into Spirit: The Commodification of Religious Value in the Senegalese Murid Community in Chicago." M.A. thesis, University of Chicago. 1998. • Cruise O'Brien, Donal B. *Saints and Politicians.* 1975. • Diop, Momar Coumba. 1981 "Fonctions et activités des *dahira* mourides urbains (Sénégal)." *Cahiers d'études africaines* 81–83, XXI-1-3: 79–91.

Serbs. Serbian immigrants first came to the Chicago region along with thousands of other Southern and Eastern European immigrants from the 1880s to the 1910s looking for unskilled work in the region's booming heavy industries. Most Serbian immigrants in the United States and the Chicago area did not come from Serbia proper, but rather from parts of the Austro-Hungarian Empire, mainly Croatia, Slavonia, and Vojvodina. Peasant men made up the bulk of these early immigrants, with women following later. Serbian professional men, including journalists, lawyers, teachers, politicians, and priests, also constituted a small portion of this immigration.

Serbian immigrants settled mainly in the steel district of the Southeast Side in the CALUMET region, around WICKER PARK in the WEST TOWN area, in JOLIET, and in GARY, Indiana. Excluding the Wicker Park contingent, Serbian men largely earned their livings in the steel mills. The Wicker Park Serbs were mostly middle-class and served as local and national leaders in Serbian immigrant life.

The Chicago region's Serbian immigrants were Serbian Orthodox, an ethnic church that is part of EASTERN ORTHODOXY, and spoke Serbian, a Slavic language using the Cyrillic alphabet. These two aspects of Serbian culture served as the focal points of Serbian immigrant life. In 1905, the Wicker Park Serbs founded a church, Holy Resurrection, which briefly served as the seat of the Serbian Orthodox Church in North America. Holy Resurrection also served as the center for Serbian religious life in the Chicago region until Serbs founded churches elsewhere in the area.

Southeast Side Serbs founded St. Archangel Michael in 1919 and consecrated a permanent church building in 1927. St. Archangel Michael became the leading institution among working-class Serbs in the CALUMET REGION. By this time, Serbs in both Gary and Joliet had also founded churches. This flurry of church founding symbolized the recognition among Chicago-area Serbs by the outbreak of WORLD WAR I in 1914 that they would not return to their homelands and would become permanent residents of the Chicago area.

Serbian immigrants also founded a multitude of MUTUAL BENEFIT, fraternal, athletic, youth, and women's societies. By 1929, the Serb National Federation (SNF) had emerged to oversee this panoply of Serbian ethnic organizations in the Chicago region. The SNF provided sick and death benefits to its members, who often had no INSURANCE. More important, the SNF and its women's auxiliaries served as a local, regional, and national umbrella under which Serbian life formed. For example, the SNF and its related institutions organized CHORAL performances and commemorations of Serbian patriotic and religious holidays.

Serbian women also founded independent women's organizations. The leading national Serbian women's group with a strong presence in the Chicago area was the Circle of Serbian Sisters. Both Serbian churches in Chicago had these circles, which actively promoted immigrant support of the Kingdom of Serbia during World War I. After the war the Serbian Sisters of St. Archangel Michael raised funds to support the church and its varied activities.

Chicago's Serbs attracted national attention through material published by the local Palandech Press, founded by Serbian immigrant John R. Palandech. Palandech and his brothers published numerous local and national NEWSPAPERS and commemorative volumes. After World War I, Palandech, supported by the local Serbian middle class, wanted Serbs to unite with Croats and Slovenes to form Yugoslavia.

With the onslaught of the GREAT DEPRESSION in the 1930s, most working-class Serbs turned their attention to survival, as many found only seasonal work at the steel mills in the Calumet region, Joliet, and Gary. Concern over their own economic survival became mixed with fears for the fate of their homeland during World War II after Nazi Germany invaded Yugoslavia in 1941. The SNF and Chicago's middle-class Serbs focused much of their energy upon saving and defending Yugoslavia.

Communist ascendancy in post–World War II Yugoslavia sent tremors through Chicago's Serbian community. Many supported the king and wanted him to regain the throne, while a small minority supported Communism. The local Serbian Orthodox hierarchy split along similar lines. As a result of this split, in the 1940s and 1950s, the Chicago region also became a major focal point for COLD WAR anti-Communist agitation within the United States.

Not all Serbs, however, concerned themselves with the politics of their homeland. Most worked to improve their own lives in the Chicago region. With the growth in suburbs and prosperity in the 1950s, many Serbs moved from Wicker Park and the Calumet region to such suburbs as SOUTH HOLLAND, LANSING, and PALOS HILLS. Slowly, the local churches' strength withered as they lost parishioners to these suburbs. But with this suburban growth new churches were built to accommodate the shift in the Serbian population.

Peter T. Alter

See also: Clubs; Demography; Iron and Steel; Multicentered Chicago

Further reading: Blesich, Mirko. *The Serbian Who's Who.* 1983. • Prpic, George J. *South Slavic Immigration in America.* 1978.

Service Employees International Union (SEIU). In 1902, janitors, elevator operators, and window washers in APARTMENT buildings organized the Chicago Flat Janitor's Union, the nation's first union of building employees and the forerunner of the Service Employees International Union (SEIU). Most members were immigrants, and the union's leadership and membership crossed racial and gender lines from its inception. Goals included higher wages and better working conditions and, because janitors often lived in dank basement apartments in buildings where they worked, better living conditions. Supported by the CHICAGO FEDERATION OF LABOR and the American Federation of Labor, the nascent union of largely unskilled workers barely survived a 1905 attack by powerful LOOP building owners. Organizer and first international president William F. Quesse revived the union in 1912, securing alliances with other BUILDING TRADES unions by agreeing to limit the repair work janitors could perform and targeting smaller apartment buildings rather than downtown interests. TEAMSTERS' support proved crucial during a 1914 STRIKE, as they stopped deliveries of ice, coal, and milk. In the winter of 1917, following strikes that left some Chicago buildings without heat, the union's six thousand members (roughly 20 percent of them AFRICAN AMERICAN) and Chicago's REAL-ESTATE Board agreed to a citywide contract that included a closed shop, arbitration of disputes, and a ban on forcing wives of janitors to do janitorial work. In 1921, the Chicago Flat Janitor's Union became Local 1 of the new Building Service Employees' International Union, later the SEIU, an AFL union headquartered in Chicago until 1990.

Local 1's membership, with its diverse and geographically scattered workforce, grew into a potent political force. Beginning in 1917, Mayor "Big Bill" Thompson arbitrated several contract disputes and intervened to win pardons for union leaders convicted of charges by courts friendly to real-estate interests. From 1940 to 1960, the SEIU was led by President William McFetridge, a nephew of Quesse and a close confidant of Mayor Richard J. Daley. McFetridge modernized the union's administration, reduced fiscal corruption, and used his ties to city hall to negotiate steady wage increases with both public and private employers. McFetridge also invested the union's large pension fund in major Chicago real-estate developments, including Marina City. In the second half of the twentieth century, the SEIU began organizing HEALTH CARE and public sector workers, reaching 80,000 members in the Chicago area in 2000, roughly half of whom were women and one-quarter of whom were minorities.

D. Bradford Hunt

See also: Belgians; Unionization

Further reading: Beadling, Tom. *A Need for Valor: The Roots of the Service Employees International Union, 1902–1992.* 1992. • Jentz, John B. "Citizenship, Self-Respect, and Political Power: Chicago's Flat Janitors Trailblaze the Service Employees International Union, 1912–1921." *Labor's Heritage* 9.1 (Summer 1997): 4–23.

Set Design. Until the mid-1970s, set design originating in Chicago was hardly memorable, thanks to two strong inhibiting forces: fire and New York. A series of fires, ranging from the Great FIRE OF 1871, which destroyed nearly every THEATER BUILDING in town, to the Iroquois Theatre fire in 1903, resulted in city safety ordinances that severely limited where and how theaters could operate. As the "second city," Chicago had to wait to see Broadway productions until national touring companies were formed, usually with cut-down or simplified versions of the original New York sets. Well into the 1940s a restriction of a 5 feet 9 inches maximum of one dimension was imposed by the railroad baggage cars used to transport scenery. An influential exception was the pre-Broadway production of Tennessee Williams's *Glass Menagerie* at the Civic Theatre in 1944, with a locally built set designed by New Yorker Jo Mielziner.

The easing of fire codes in 1974 stimulated the emergence of THEATERS across the city, in storefronts, church basements, back rooms of RESTAURANTS, bars, and even bookstores. Set designers were forced to use ingenuity and creativity when faced with such factors as playing space as small as 10 feet square, limited budgets, and no fly space (a characteristic of all the storefronts and even the professional GOODMAN THEATRE before its new building was completed in 2000).

In its early days, LYRIC OPERA (founded in 1954 as Lyric Theatre) did little to enhance set design in Chicago, resurrecting old Chicago Civic Opera productions from the warehouse or borrowing sets from Italian OPERA houses, leading some critics to refer to Lyric as "La Scala West." In 1989, however, Lyric embarked on its "Toward the 21st Century" initiative, commissioning new productions and even new operas where set design gained wide attention. These included John Conklin's *The Ghosts of Versailles* (owned jointly by Lyric and the New York Metropolitan Opera) and John Boesche's projections for *The Voyage of Edgar Allan Poe.* David Hockney's *Turandot* and Boesche's *Tannhauser* brought revolutionary new designs to traditional operas.

New York is no longer an inhibiting force, and two Chicago productions transferred from Chicago to Broadway with great success—Kevin Rigdon's set for *Grapes of Wrath,* in 1988, and Mark Wendland's radical departure from Mielziner's classic set for *Death of a Salesman,* in 1999. As Chicago THEATER has gained more international recognition—especially Lyric Opera, STEPPENWOLF, and Goodman—"international" designers such as Michael Yeargan of Yale and Santo Loquasto have designed productions for all three companies.

Robert R. Boyle

See also: Dance Companies; Theater Companies

Settlement Houses. Settlement houses were important reform institutions in the late nineteenth and early twentieth centuries, and Chicago's HULL HOUSE was the best-known settlement in the United States. Most were large buildings in crowded immigrant neighborhoods of industrial cities, where settlement workers provided services for neighbors and sought to remedy poverty. The prototype, Toynbee Hall, opened in 1884 in an East London slum, and was home to an Anglican clergyman, his wife, and several young men from Oxford and Cambridge Universities. Unrelated middle-class women and men lived cooperatively, as "settlers" or "residents" who hoped to share knowledge and culture with their low-paid, poorly educated neighbors.

The settlement idea appealed to young Americans who wished to bridge the gulf of class, help the urban poor, implement "social Christianity," and understand the causes of poverty. Stanton Coit, who lived at Toynbee Hall for several months, opened the first American settlement in 1886, Neighborhood Guild on the Lower East Side of New York. In 1889, Jane Addams and Ellen Gates Starr launched HULL HOUSE in Chicago. As word of these experiments spread, other settlements appeared in New York, Boston, Philadelphia, and Chicago. Hull House inspired Charles Zueblin to organize NORTHWESTERN UNIVERSITY Settlement in 1891. The following year, Graham Taylor started CHICAGO COMMONS and Mary McDowell took charge of UNIVERSITY OF CHICAGO Settlement near the stockyards. By 1900, there were more than 100 settlements in America; 15 were in Chicago. Eventually there were more than 400 settlements nationwide. The most active and influential ones were in the large cities of the Northeast and Midwest.

Unlike their British counterparts, American settlements were in neighborhoods populated by recent European immigrants, few of whom spoke English. Thus the first outreach was to children and mothers, through day care nurseries, KINDERGARTENS, and small play lots. Mothers' CLUBS, English classes, and groups interested in arts, crafts, music, and drama followed. The early residents paid room and board, and volunteered as group leaders or teachers. As their numbers increased and programs expanded, the settlements incorporated and trustees raised money to purchase or build larger quarters. These structures accommodated gymnasiums, auditoriums, classrooms, and meeting halls, as well as living space and communal dining facilities for a dozen or more residents. Settlements welcomed meetings of trade unions, ethnic groups, and civic organizations. Some established country summer camps, and a few developed their music programs into serious schools. Many exchanged information through city federations, the first of which was established by the Chicago settlements in 1894. Approximately half of the American settlements, usually the smaller ones, had religious sponsors and comparatively small programs. The rest eschewed religious orientation because it was bound to offend at least some of their neighbors.

As settlement house residents learned more about their communities, they proposed changes in local government and lobbied for state and federal legislation on social and economic problems. *Hull-House Maps and Papers*

Maypole dancing, Chicago Commons Day Nursery (no date). Photographer: Unknown. Source: Chicago Historical Society.

Mary McDowell and Chicago Settlement Houses

Born in Cincinnati, Mary McDowell arrived in Chicago with her family in 1870. A devout Methodist, she worked with the WOMAN'S CHRISTIAN TEMPERANCE UNION in the 1880s, organizing youth groups and kindergartens. Upon completion of Elizabeth Harrison's training program, she became the kindergarten teacher at HULL HOUSE and founder of the settlement Woman's Club. In 1894 McDowell took charge of a small program near the stockyards which the Christian Union of the UNIVERSITY OF CHICAGO had started.

Over the next two decades, she secured independent funding for the University of Chicago Settlement, acquired a gymnasium and auditorium, and built a three-story building to accommodate the residents and programs. For the IRISH, GERMAN, Bohemian, and POLISH families living in the vicinity of the packinghouses, the settlement sponsored classes in English and citizenship, a woman's CLUB, youth groups, a KINDERGARTEN, and a PLAYGROUND.

McDowell gave staunch support to the striking PACKINGHOUSE workers in 1904 and 1921, was a cofounder of the National WOMEN'S TRADE UNION LEAGUE and an officer of the Chicago League, and was one of the initiators of the federal investigation of wages and working conditions for women and children. As a member of the City Waste Commission, she helped force Chicago to modernize its waste collection and disposal practices. And as head of Mayor William Dever's Department of Public Welfare in the 1920s, she investigated the shortage of low-income housing and helped secure the appointment of Chicago's first Housing Commission.

Louise Carroll Wade

(1895), a study of housing, employment and wages, prompted other settlements to survey their neighborhoods. The University of Chicago Settlement published three studies of family budgets and opportunities for youth. Having documented harsh working conditions and bad housing and sanitation, the settlements and their allies pressured city government to provide public BATHHOUSES, neighborhood parks and PLAYGROUNDS, branch LIBRARIES, better WASTE collection and disposal, and KINDERGARTENS and night classes in the public schools. The network of settlement supporters included civic organizations, women's clubs, businessmen's groups, and often trade unions. This same coalition supported settlement efforts to secure state laws regulating child labor, hours of WORK for women, and women's wages. The Chicago settlements and their allies won most of these reforms and, in addition, a local JUVENILE COURT, partial SUFFRAGE for Illinois women in 1913, and, on the federal level, the Children's Bureau and an investigation of wage-earning women and children. Although settlement residents had been admitted to the National Conference of Charities and Correction in the late 1890s, they nevertheless established a National Federation of Settlements in 1911 to coordinate their reform efforts and enhance their impact on public policy. Addams, McDowell, Taylor, and later Lea Demarest Taylor served as presidents of this organization.

Most historians agree that settlement house influence peaked about the time of WORLD WAR I. The war diverted attention from reform and Congress drastically restricted immigration. The first wave of AFRICAN AMERICANS out of the South changed settlement neighborhoods, and residents and trustees were slow to respond. Volunteers dwindled and staff members, now holding degrees from social work schools, demanded salaries and shunned group work in favor of casework, helping individuals adapt to trying circumstances. Community-chest fundraising restricted the autonomy of settlements in many cities. After World War II, most staff members refused to reside in the settlements. Trustees sold the older structures and found new locations for the settlement activities and programs. These settlements-without-residents called themselves neighborhood centers or community centers. URBAN RENEWAL and highway construction devastated some settlement neighborhoods; in others, the settlement clientele shifted with the arrival of many more African Americans; and newcomers from Mexico and the Caribbean challenged still others. The Johnson Administration's War on Poverty launched a vast array of social welfare programs run by government social workers who contracted work to the neighborhood centers or remaining settlements. When federal welfare spending declined in the 1970s and 1980s, neighborhood centers often had to merge to increase their efficiency. Belatedly, the National Federation of Settlements changed its name to United Neighborhood Centers of America in 1979.

In Chicago, Hull House was displaced by a new university campus; closure of the stockyards and packinghouses undermined the University of Chicago Settlement; a new EXPRESSWAY destroyed much of the Chicago Commons neighborhood; and the Chicago Federation of Settlements expired in the 1980s. However, the Chicago Commons Association (1948–) and Hull House Association (1962–), both loose federations of former settlements, neighborhood centers, and SOCIAL SERVICE agencies, perpetuate the names and at least some of the aspirations of the original settlement houses.

Louise Carroll Wade

See also: Americanization; Good Government Movements; Great Migration; Schooling for Work; Universities and their Cities; Woman's City Club

Further reading: Carson, Mina. *Settlement Folk: Social Thought and the American Settlement Movement, 1885–1930.* 1990. • Davis, Allen F. *Spearheads for Reform: The Social Settlements and the Progressive Movement, 1890–1914.* 1967. • Trolander, Judith Ann. *Professionalism and Social Change: From the Settlement House Movement to Neighborhood Centers, 1886 to the Present.* 1987.

Settlements, Religious. The well-known mainstream U.S. SETTLEMENT HOUSE movement was largely secular, or at least nondenominational. Inspired by the founding of Jane Addams's HULL HOUSE in Chicago in 1889, the settlement house movement aimed mainly at helping European immigrants adapt to the conditions of industrializing cities, and sought to minimize religious differences, discourage proselytizing, and differentiate between settlements and religious missions. Settlements combined a plethora of services and entertainments with commitment to social change, providing everything from union halls to gymnasiums and English classes and helping many individuals and poor communities. Yet, a bias against religious settlements meant that this variation was often less acknowledged and poorly integrated into the rest of the movement.

Settlement-type activity, embracing the same combination of services and reform, was actually frequently conducted under religious auspices. The YWCA, the ROMAN CATHOLIC Church, and the Women's Home Missionary Society of the Methodist Episcopal Church South, for example, all offered such reform work nationally. At times, settlements in the mainstream mold had churchly origins, as in the case of the Abraham Lincoln Centre, founded in Chicago in 1905, which began as a program of the Unitarian All Souls Church.

AFRICAN AMERICANS in particular spearheaded many religious settlement efforts in the late 1800s and early 1900s, often in response to black migration. Called "institutional churches," they ran the same extensive variety of activities as the settlement houses, combining welfare, employment, education, insurance, and SAVINGS AND LOAN services. The African Methodist Episcopal Institutional Church on South Dearborn in Chicago was established by Reverend Reverdy C. Ransom in 1900 to administer social work among what was then the largest black community in the city. And the OLIVET BAPTIST CHURCH, another example of religious settlement work in Chicago, had a membership of 9,069 in 1919.

Elisabeth Lasch-Quinn

See also: Chicago Commons; Hebrew Institute, Chicago; Madonna Center; Religious Institutions; Social Services

Further reading: Albert J. Kennedy Papers. Social Welfare History Archives, University of Minnesota. • Johnson, F. Ernest, ed. *The Social Work of the Churches: A Handbook of Information.* 1930. • Lasch-Quinn, Elisabeth. *Black Neighbors: Race and the Limits of Reform in the American Settlement House Movement, 1890–1945.* 1993.

Sewers. *See* Infrastructure; Water

Shakman Decrees. In 1969, one man made his stand against the Chicago political MACHINE. Michael Shakman, an independent candidate for delegate to the 1970 Illinois Constitutional Convention, battled against one of the most enduring traditions in Chicago's POLITICS: political PATRONAGE, or the practice of hiring and firing government workers on the basis of political loyalty. With many behind-the-scenes supporters, Shakman's years of determination resulted in what became known as the "Shakman decrees."

Shakman filed suit against the DEMOCRATIC Organization of COOK COUNTY, arguing that the patronage system put nonorganized candidates and their supporters at an illegal and unconstitutional disadvantage. Politicians could hire, fire, promote, transfer—in essence, punish—employees for not supporting the system, or more particularly, a certain politician. The suit also argued that political patronage wasted taxpayer money because public employees, while at work, would often be forced to campaign for political candidates.

In 1972, after an exhaustive court procedure and much negotiating, the parties reached an agreement prohibiting politically motivated firings, demotions, transfers, or other punishment of government employees. A 1979 ruling led to a court order in 1983 that made it unlawful to take any political factor into account in hiring public employees (with exceptions for positions such as policy making). Those decisions along with companion consent judgments—collectively called the Shakman decrees—are binding on more than 40 city and statewide offices.

Roger R. Fross

See also: Good Government Movements; Government, City of Chicago; Political Culture

Further reading: Freedman, Ann. "Doing Battle with the Patronage Army: Politics, Courts, and Personnel Administration in Chicago." *Public Administration Review* 48.5 (September–October 1988): 847–859. • Johnson, C. Richard. "The Seventh Circuit Symposium: The Federal Courts and the Community: Successful Reform Litigation: The Shakman Patronage Case." *Chicago-Kent Law Review* 64 (1988): 479–496. • Shakman, Michael L. "Shakman on Shakman: Chicago Is Ready for Reform." *Chicago Lawyer* 6.5 (May 1983): 2–3.

Shedd Aquarium. Planning for the John G. Shedd Aquarium began in 1924, when John Groves Shedd, second president of Marshall Field & Co., donated $2 million toward construction of a facility that he hoped would showcase "the greatest variety of sea life under one roof." The world's largest indoor aquarium opened more than five years later, in December 1929, along LAKE MICHIGAN, just south of GRANT PARK and east of the FIELD MUSEUM. Additional Shedd exhibit halls were completed in the early years of the GREAT DEPRESSION.

The aquarium's significance was not restricted to size or location. It opened with both freshwater and salt aquaria, then unheard of for an inland aquarium. The ARCHITECTS Graham, Anderson, Probst & White designed the aquarium in the Beaux-Arts style (one championed by Graham's mentor Daniel Burnham), with elements of classical Greek architecture to make it a better structural match with the neighboring Field Museum. Under Walter H. Chute (who served as its second director from 1928 to 1964), the aquarium pioneered the use of a railroad car to transport fishes and invertebrates collected for exhibition and study. The rotunda pool, with its lush plant growth, fish, and reptiles, remained an attraction for 40 years, until it was replaced by a huge cylindrical coral reef community tank. The R/V Coral Reef served as a collecting boat from 1971 to 1985, when it was replaced by a specially designed vessel, the Coral Reef II.

William P. Braker followed Chute as aquarium director, with a vision of an enlarged and more complete aquatic experience. Under Braker's leadership, a membership initiative in the 1970s began encouraging both TOURISTS and city residents to participate in aquarium activities. A volunteer program, implemented in 1975, provided aid to visitors and complemented the Helen Shedd Keith Aquatic Science Center. Invertebrates (including sea anemones) were added to the galleries in 1980; river otters in 1986.

The idea for a marine mammal exhibit, set aside in 1967 and considered anew in 1980, finally received state support in 1986. In April of 1991 the Oceanarium and its marine mammal pavilion opened to the public. Sea otters, dolphins, belugas, penguins, and harbor seals played in state-of-the-art exhibits replicating natural conditions. Public response to the Oceanarium exceeded expectations, and programming grew. The McCormick Tribune Reference Library was built to serve as a specialized regional resource on aquatic sciences.

In 1994, Ted Beattie became the aquarium's fourth director. The additions under his watch include the Amazon Rising exhibit in 2000. The aquarium also became one of the principal components of the city's vast Museum Campus, built to integrate three important lakefront institutions—the Field Museum, the ADLER PLANETARIUM, and Shedd Aquarium—by removing a section of Lake Shore Drive that had long isolated the buildings from one another. In 2001, annual aquarium attendance grew to nearly 2 million.

Dennis A. Meritt, Jr.

See also: Conservatories; Museums in the Park

Shelters. *See* Homelessness and Shelters

Shimer College. In the middle of the nineteenth century, Frances Wood Shimer and Cinderella Gregory journeyed west from New York State with plans to educate the frontier. They landed in northwestern Illinois in

1853 and founded Mt. Carroll Seminary, one of the nation's first preparatory academies for women. Early course catalogs list home economics and etiquette classes alongside "intellectual mathematics" and the study of electricity. In 1896, now 70 years old and seeking to ensure her school's survival, Frances Shimer allied it to the UNIVERSITY OF CHICAGO. The renamed Frances Shimer Academy of the University of Chicago began to provide college-level courses in 1909. The schools' association burgeoned in the mid-twentieth century when Shimer adopted a curriculum based on then Chicago president Robert Hutchins's belief that undergraduate education should have "no vocational aim" but should instead furnish "a common stock of fundamental ideas."

Shimer became an autonomous four-year college and began accepting men in 1951. The school thrived academically for the next two decades but ran into financial trouble in the early 1970s, filing for bankruptcy in the spring of 1977. A mayoral invitation to relocate from the isolated campus in Mt. Carroll to WAUKEGAN saved Shimer. The 60 students and 13 faculty members who remained packed up and moved the school themselves and voted to adopt a uniform salary structure, which at the end of the century was still paying its employees based on seniority instead of job title.

Sarah Fenton

See also: Progressive Education; Universities and Their Cities

Shipbuilding. Shipbuilding in Chicago has always been tied to the city's status as a port. When Chicago flourished as a port it was the site of a thriving shipbuilding industry. As the port has waned so has shipbuilding.

The first ship built in Chicago, the *Clarissa,* was begun in 1835. By 1847, 82 ships had been built in the city, the overwhelming majority of them schooners. Shipbuilding was of greatest importance in Chicago during the period 1850 to 1875, when Chicago was the busiest port city in the United States. Wooden ships, both steam and sail, made up the bulk of the lake commercial fleet. Shipbuilders were attracted to Chicago because of its busy port and the fact that it was the LUMBER center of America. Scores of shipyards were located both along the North Branch and the South Branch of the CHICAGO RIVER. The largest and most important shipbuilder was Miller Brothers & Co., located on the Chicago River just above the Chicago Avenue Bridge. The firm built steamships, tugs, canal boats, and schooners. When the shipping industry was booming the Miller Brothers dry docks, the largest on LAKE MICHIGAN, were constantly occupied with ships being rebuilt while carpenters were busy with one or more new ships. The busiest time of year for new ship construction

U.S. Navy minesweeper under construction at Henry C. Grebe & Co. shipyard on the west bank of the North Branch of the Chicago River, June 1952. Photographer: Louis F. Zimmerman. Source: Chicago Historical Society.

was in the late winter and early spring. Sailors idled by the close of shipping joined with the professional ships' carpenters and caulkers to finish new vessels before the navigation season began again in April.

William Wallace Bates, the most influential shipbuilder working on the Great Lakes during the age of sail, operated a shipyard in Chicago in the 1860s and 1870s. Bates turned out a series of clipper schooners renowned for their carrying capacity and speed. Even more important than new shipbuilding was the city's role as a place to repair or rebuild existing ships. With as many as five hundred vessels annually wintering in the Chicago River, the shipyards of the city were kept busy maintaining the fleet. The ship chandlers of the city were also extremely important, as they supplied sails and cordage to the bulk of the Lake Michigan marine.

The decline of wooden shipbuilding brought the decline of Chicago as a construction site. The Chicago River was too small to serve as a building site for the four- and five-hundred-foot-long steel ships demanded by the grain and iron ore trade in the late nineteenth and early twentieth centuries. Chicago River shipyards remained active by focusing on small boat or yacht construction. During WORLD WAR II the Henry Grebe shipyard, on the North Branch of the river, produced the last wooden ships built in Chicago-minesweepers for the U.S. Navy. By that time the servicing and construction of large vessels shifted with the bulk of the city's commercial traffic to the CALUMET Region.

The CHICAGO SHIPBUILDING COMPANY was the most important of the steel shipbuilding firms in Chicago. Founded in 1890 as a subsidiary of the Globe IRON Works of Cleveland, the company launched in its inaugural year the *Marina,* the first steel-hulled ship built on Lake Michigan. By 1899 the company was widely regarded as the most progressive and prolific shipbuilder on the GREAT LAKES. In that year, the company merged with the other large steel shipbuilders on the lakes to form the American Shipbuilding Company. Under the control of the new company the Chicago yards continued to produce new ships, although repair and conversion became an increasingly important part of their business.

Chicago shipyards produced vessels for federal service in the CIVIL WAR, WORLD WAR I, and World War II. With the advent of vessels over a thousand feet long, fewer and fewer ships were capable of meeting the needs of lake commerce. The American Shipbuilding Company limited its Chicago yard to smaller jobs such as scows and barges-taking advantage of Chicago's location at the meeting place of the Mississippi and Great Lakes waterways. The opening of the ST. LAWRENCE SEAWAY in 1959 promised a resurgence of the shipping industry in Chicago. Any resurgence was forestalled, however, by the limited size of the seaway's locks and by federal shipping policy. By the late twentieth century, shipbuilding had ceased to be an important activity not only in Chicago but on Lake Michigan.

Theodore J. Karamanski

See also: Business of Chicago; Economic Geography; ***Further reading:*** Karamanski, Theodore J. *Schooner Passage: Sailing Ships and the Lake Michigan Frontier.* 2000. • Wright, Richard J. *Freshwater Wales: A History of the American Shipbuilding Company and Its Predecessors.* 1969.

Shipping. *See* Transportation; Water

Shopping Districts and Malls. By the 1850s, Chicago's principal retail shopping district had emerged along Lake Street, paralleling the main branch of the CHICAGO RIVER and economically tied to the commercial shipping arriving at the river's mouth. Lake Street's retailing preeminence was short-lived. In 1867, Potter Palmer, who had previously sold his interest in a prospering dry-goods business on Lake Street, bought a substantial stretch of State Street running north–south at a short distance from the Lake Michigan shoreline. In the years just preceding the Great Chicago FIRE OF 1871, Palmer had begun to develop State Street, which in the years following the fire quickly surpassed Lake Street as the city's retailing center.

Among the principal establishments on prefire State Street were the Palmer House HOTEL and Field, Leiter & Co., the dry-goods business that Potter Palmer had founded on Lake Street. In the years following the fire, Palmer rebuilt his State Street hotel, and Marshall Field's emerged as a pioneering retail establishment. On the one hand, the scale of Field's operation was spectacular—employing as many as 9,000 people during peak shopping periods—but just as influential was Marshall Field's dedication to providing solicitous service to its affluent female clientele. Not only could such women count on home delivery of larger items, but

Shopping district in St. Charles, Illinois, 1929. Photographer: Unknown. Source: Chicago Historical Society.

Park Forest Centre

A shopping mall opened in 1949 south of Chicago in the visionary new planned suburb of Park Forest. The mall was one of the nation's first retail environments characterized by a group of small stores "anchored" by several large department stores and surrounded by acres of parking. Within a generation, these malls would emerge across the United States as powerful competitors to downtown shopping districts.

Traditional suburban downtowns lacked the parking facilities appropriate to the emerging automobile culture. Envisioning a shopping center that would function as both town hub and commercial facility, developers Philip Klutznick and Nathan Manilow placed Park Forest Plaza (later Centre) in the center of a new town. The mall was intended to serve Park Forest and surrounding communities, countering the insularity of the suburb by drawing in outsiders. Consumers, primarily women, would create a sense of community through shopping. Architect Richard Bennett designed the plaza for women, offering them a sense of adventure as they shopped in a center that was modeled on Venice and included a clock tower.

The Park Forest developers and design team went on to build some of the largest and most successful shopping centers in the Chicago area. Despite initial success and rapid expansion, however, the Park Forest Centre could not compete with newer regional malls built in the 1970s with easy expressway access.

Ann Durkin Keating

within the store customer lounges and dining rooms transformed shopping into a leisure pastime.

By 1900, State Street was lined with retailers from Lake Street south to Van Buren Street. The preeminence of the State Street retail corridor was assisted by the geography of the city's mass transit lines, which carried many streetcars, and later, elevated trains into Chicago's commercial core. Indeed, in 1897, when the elevated Union rail loop was completed in the downtown area, central Chicago had won its permanent designation as "the Loop."

Although State Street dominated the city's retail trade, in the burgeoning Chicago of the late nineteenth and early twentieth centuries other market areas also flourished. On the Loop's northern and western margins, the South Water and Randolph Street areas were centers for wholesale meat and produce sales. To the southwest of the Loop, the Maxwell Street Market offered every imaginable commodity, and given the straitened economic circumstances of its immigrant clientele, at very low prices. In the subsequent decades numerous neighborhood shopping districts emerged on the city's North, West, and South Sides. In some cases, these shopping areas grew from the intersections of major streets (for example, at Milwaukee and Chicago Avenues on the West Side). Other neighborhood shopping districts formed at transit terminal points, such as along Broadway north of the Wilson Avenue station. By the 1930s, an imposing commercial area along 47th Street served as the economic nucleus of the South Side "Black Belt."

As a racially segregated commercial district, 47th Street represented but an extreme example of a fairly common circumstance. In the early decades of the twentieth century, many of Chicago's neighborhood shopping districts catered, in large part, to one or another ethnic population.

By the 1920s, when Marshall Field's opened stores in Evanston and Oak Park, several commuter suburbs sported prominent retail districts. However, it was following World War II that State Street and the city's many neighborhood shopping districts began to lose large numbers of customers to newly built shopping complexes in Park Forest, Hillside, Skokie, and other outlying communities. By the 1970s, a new generation of regional shopping centers such as the mammoth Woodfield Mall in Schaumburg not only attracted visitors from across the metropolitan region but, in effect, functioned as suburban town centers complete with shopping, entertainment, and office facilities. Within Chicago, a number of developers responded to the rise of suburban shopping malls by assembling large parcels of land and building enclosed shopping complexes to compete directly with the new outlying facilities. Two such examples of suburban-like shopping centers within Chicago are Ford City and the Brickyard Mall, on the city's Southwest and Northwest Sides, respectively.

With the opening of the Michigan Avenue bridge in 1920, a second major downtown Chicago commercial district emerged along North Michigan Avenue. With the opening of Water Tower Place in 1975, Chicago returned to the retailing vanguard. Towering 74 floors above North Michigan Avenue, Water Tower Place included seven levels of retail shops, two department stores, restaurants, cinemas, offices, condominium residences, and a hotel. Along one side of its seven-story atrium, a bank of elevators offered eye-popping rides between levels. In a bow to the new realities of urban shopping, Water Tower Place also provided 667 underground parking spaces.

Following years of decline, in 1979, the State Street commercial corridor was closed to automobile traffic and its sidewalks were widened in an effort to create a more hospitable pedestrian environment. This revitalization scheme did not restore the street's vitality. In 1996 State Street was reopened to automobile traffic, and in a second campaign to rejuvenate the city's longstanding commercial hub, Victorian-style lighting and street furniture were added—in the hope of reminding the city's end-of-the-millennium population of the street's glories at the turn of the preceding century.

Larry Bennett

Pullman Arcade Building, 1885. The Arcade Building was home to the Pullman Bank, a library, a post office, a theater seating 1,000 people, and stores selling dry goods, groceries, boots and shoes, clothing, household goods and furniture, hardware, medicines, and other wares. Artist: Unknown. Source: The Newberry Library.

See also: Business of Chicago; Dictionary of Leading Chicago Businesses, 1820–2000 (p. 909); Economic Geography; Gold Coast; Metropolitan Growth; Retail Geography

Further reading: Drake, St. Clair, and Horace R. Cayton. *Black Metropolis: A Study of Negro Life in a Northern City.* 1945. • Mayer, Harold M., and Richard C. Wade. *Chicago: Growth of a Metropolis.* 1969. • Miller, Donald L. *City of the Century.* 1996.

Shoreline Erosion. Chicago's entire 28-mile LAKE MICHIGAN shoreline is man-made. The original sand DUNE and swale TOPOGRAPHY has been dramatically altered. Before American settlement, storms changed the shoreline, either by building up or eroding sand. Today, step-stone and rubble revetments and offshore breakers withstand wind, waves, and the freeze/thaw of the seasons. Even beach sand is held in place by groins or armored with revetments or sea walls.

Beginning in the 1830s, when a harbor and piers to protect the harbor entrance were built at the mouth of the CHICAGO RIVER, barriers have been constructed to protect the shoreline from erosion. Throughout the 1800s, Chicago's importance as a center of commerce required port facilities and RAILROADS to be constructed along the lakefront. To accommodate the ILLINOIS CENTRAL RAILROAD, breakwaters were built and the lake filled in, extending the lakefront from Michigan Avenue almost to its present-day shoreline.

Recreation, not commerce, dictated lakefront development by the turn of the century. Aaron Montgomery Ward's idea that the public has a right to Lake Michigan access helped spur the development of JACKSON, Burnham, GRANT, and LINCOLN Parks. Sand and swamp were replaced by fill, dredged harbors, marinas, GOLF courses, ball fields, and Lake Shore Drive.

High water levels in the 1980s eroded beaches, imperiled private property, and temporarily closed parts of Lake Shore Drive. Shoreline protection structures and the analysis of the effect of such structures on littoral transport processes will determine future erosion prevention activities.

Karen M. Rodriguez

See also: Flood Control and Drainage; Public Works, Federal Funding for; Waterfront

Further reading: Chicago Park District. *Shoreline Protection and Recreational Enhancement.* 1989. • City of Chicago, Department of Development and Planning. *Lakefront Plan of Chicago.* 1972. • U.S. Army Corps of Engineers. *Reconstruction Plans to Repair Chicago's Shoreline from Erosion and Storm Damage.* 1993.

Shorewood, IL, Will County, 39 miles SW of the Loop. In 1834, Jedediah Wooley, Jr., built a large sawmill along the DUPAGE RIVER, among the first of its kind in WILL COUNTY. In 1931, residents established the Shorewood Beach Improvement Association. In 1957, Shorewood incorporated to regulate trailers along the river. In the 1970s, Shorewood began a residential boom based on convenient access to interstates 55 and 80. The village grew from 1,749 in 1970 to 7,686 in 2000.

Erik Gellman

See also: Expressways; Mobile Homes

Sierra Leoneans. The first Sierra Leoneans to migrate to Chicago came as students in the 1970s and were attracted to the city by its educational opportunities and connections to family or friends in the city. Student migration continued through the 1980s and 1990s, and many students settled permanently, sending financial assistance home and encouraging others to migrate. When the civil war and violence in Sierra Leone escalated in the 1990s, a large wave of REFUGEES entered the United States through the sponsorship of relatives and friends. Community leaders estimate that the Sierra Leonean community in Chicago more than tripled during that decade, from an estimated 100 people in 1990 to between 300 and 500 in 2000. Recent refugees tend to be less educated than earlier migrants, who have high levels of education and have entered a variety of professional fields, including medicine, ACCOUNTING, NURSING, and engineering.

Sierra Leoneans in Chicago come from a variety of ethnic and religious backgrounds but have joined together to form an active and united community. The Chicagoland Association of Sierra Leoneans formed in 1996 as a nonprofit organization to bring Sierra Leoneans together as a community, socialize newcomers, and provide aid to Sierra Leoneans in Chicago and abroad. The organization engages in a range of fundraising activities and holds major events, such as an annual summer picnic at Montrose Beach and an Independence Day celebration on April 27 with Sierra Leonean food, music, and dancing. In 2001 a second Sierra Leonean organization was created when Tegloma established a chapter in Chicago. Tegloma, established in Washington DC in 1975, is the largest nonprofit, nonpolitical Sierra Leonean organization in the world and had 14 chapters in the United States and United Kingdom by 2001. Its name meaning "let's progress" in Mende, Tegloma is a cultural and philanthropic organization dedicated to assisting Sierra Leoneans around the world and promoting Mende culture, the culture of the largest ethnic group in Sierra Leone. The organization holds a variety of fundraising activities and demands commitment from its members, who include both Mende and non-Mende Sierra Leoneans as well as AFRICAN AMERICANS.

Tracy Steffes

See also: Americanization; Demography; Multicentered Chicago; Mutual Benefit Societies

Sikhs. Sikhism, founded by Guru Nanak, emerged in the sixteenth century as a distinct religion in the Punjab region of northwest India. A considerable diaspora of ethnic Sikhs has developed since the late nineteenth century, with significant settlement on the American West Coast beginning in the early 1900s.

Most of the first Sikhs to settle in Chicago came as university students in the 1950s. The Sikh Study Circle formed in 1956 around social and religious gatherings on the UNIVERSITY OF CHICAGO campus, drawing students from several Midwestern universities. In 1972 the group took the name Sikh Religious Society of Chicago and broke ground on a new *gurdwara* (a sacred facility housing the Guru Granth Sahib, Sikhism's scripture) in PALATINE in 1976. First services were held three years later. Six other Sikh religious centers opened in the region in the 1990s, as either *gurdwaras* or *deras* (mission outposts): WEST RIDGE in Chicago; OAK BROOK; ISLAND LAKE; MERRILLVILLE, Indiana; and two in Milwaukee, Wisconsin.

The initial wave of Sikh immigration to Chicago brought a largely professional population that eventually settled in affluent suburban areas, particularly northwest and west of the city. A more occupationally diverse and less affluent wave since the mid-1970s has settled around Devon Avenue on Chicago's North Side. American-born ethnic Sikhs have begun to exert leadership within the local community. These include Ravneet (Ravi) Singh, whose request to wear a turban while in U.S. military uniform was granted by federal law in 1987.

In addition to ethnic Sikhs, the Euro-American, convert branch of Sikhism represented by Yogi Bhajan's 3HO Foundation has also had a small presence in Chicago since the 1970s.

Paul D. Numrich

See also: Indians; Religious Geography; Religious Institutions

Further reading: Numrich, Paul D. "Recent Immigrant Religious Groups and the Restructuring of Metropolitan Chicago." In *Public Religion and Urban Transformation,* ed. Lowell Livezey, 2000. • Williams, Raymond Brady. *Religions of Immigrants from India and Pakistan: New Threads in the American Tapestry.* 1988.

Singaporeans. Singaporeans have been coming to the Chicago area for work and school since the late 1960s. While a small number of families have settled permanently, the majority of Chicago's Singaporeans remain for short periods on visas as students or professionals. While the number of Singaporeans has fluctuated over time, community leaders estimated that between 200 and 300 Singaporeans lived in Chicago in 2000.

Attracted to area universities for training in technical fields, Singaporean students have tended to major in areas like engineering, business, science, and technology. The Singaporean government sponsors some students to study abroad, requiring that they return to Singapore upon completion of their degrees for six years to work off their bond. Other students obtain private funding and often find jobs with American companies and remain in the United States for a period before returning to Singapore.

Working professionals sent to Chicago by their employers for a brief tenure have constituted a second distinct group of Singaporeans in Chicago. Generally young and single, they have established careers in technical fields like MANAGEMENT CONSULTING, communications, finance, information technology, and engineering. A growing number of these working professionals have settled permanently in Chicago for family reasons, enjoying the standard of living and the amount of time they are able to spend with their children.

The Singaporean community in Chicago is close and well organized. Contact Singapore, a government-sponsored international network, opened an office in Chicago in 2000 with the twin goals of recruiting skilled manpower for work in Singapore and assisting local Singaporeans. The organization sponsors community activities and maintains close ties to professional and student organizations across the Midwest. Professional Singaporeans living in Chicago have also established their own organization, Singapore Chicago Connection. Beginning as the Singapore-Malaysia Association in 1999, the organization reorganized as Singapore Chicago Connection with Contact Singapore sponsorship in 2001 but retains close ties to the MALAYSIAN community. The organization's primary purpose is to foster connections between Singaporeans, and it draws the community together for social activities and professional networking. It also serves as an information source for the community, keeping local Singaporeans abreast of local events and news from Singapore through its Web site and e-mail list. Singaporean students, while also connected to Contact Singapore and the Singapore Chicago Connection, have formed student organizations which sponsor their own events and activities. NORTHWESTERN UNIVERSITY Singaporeans and Friends and the UNIVERSITY OF CHICAGO's Singaporean and Malaysian Students' Union create small Singaporean communities at those universities.

The entire Singaporean community comes together for two major celebrations every year, the CHINESE New Year and Singapore National Day. Food plays a central role in these events and is culturally important for Singaporeans, who spend a lot of time and effort to obtain authentic food. Penang Malaysian Restaurant caters many Singaporean events and serves as a gathering place for Chicago Singaporeans.

Tracy Steffes

See also: Americanization; Demography; Foodways; Multicentered Chicago

Single-room Occupancy Hotels. "Single-room occupancy hotel" refers to various types of inexpensive housing for single, poor adults. SROs began to appear in Chicago in the late nineteenth century, in response to a large transient workforce that came in and out of Chicago on a seasonal basis.

The most common facility at the turn of the century was the cage hotel. These were lofts or other large, open buildings that were subdivided into tiny cubicles using boards or sheets

Starr Hotel, a Skid Row SRO later destroyed to clear land for Presidential Towers, 1954. Photographers: Lil and Al Bloom. Source: Chicago Historical Society.

of corrugated iron. Since these walls were always one to three feet short of the floor or ceiling, the open space was sealed off with chicken wire, hence the name "cage hotels." Heat, lighting, ventilation, and sanitary conditions were abysmal and owners could pack as many as 200 men on a floor. Estimates are that this form of housing provided shelter for as many as 40,000 to 60,000 people during the winter.

Of lesser privacy were dormitories—large open rooms filled with beds—and true flophouses, where a customer paid for the right to spend the night on the floor, out of the elements: literally, a place to flop. Prior to 1920, the population that lived in these places was varied. At the top of the SRO hierarchy were hoboes, transient workers, many of them highly skilled. These men preferred outdoor work and during the winter they holed up in Chicago. There were also tramps (men who traveled but did not work), and bums (men who lived in the SRO district full-time). The majority of the men in all these groups, however, wound up living in SROs because of their economic fortunes, rather than because of any social deviancy. Until recently this population was almost entirely male; it was also segregated, with AFRICAN AMERICANS confined to specific hotels and sections of the SRO neighborhood.

The SRO district, primarily along Madison Street east of Halsted Street on the NEAR WEST SIDE, was known as the Main Stem. By the 1920s the number of jobs available to skilled migrant workers was in serious decline, owing to the relatively complete settlement of the West. By the 1950s the SRO district had became known as Skid Row. While its popular image was of a haven for people with alcohol-related illnesses, data showed that most of the residents were instead much like their predecessors: poor, with no other affordable housing available to them. URBAN RENEWAL and redevelopment efforts eliminated much of this housing. In the 1980s, however, the homeless crisis led to the rediscovery of SROs, and several community groups began to maintain them.

Robert A. Slayton

See also: Homelessness and Shelters; Housing Reform; Unemployment

Further reading: Bogue, Donald. *Skid Row in American Cities.* 1963. • Hoch, Charles, and Robert Slayton. *New Homeless and Old: Community and the Skid Row Hotel.* 1989. • Solenberger, Alice. *One Thousand Homeless Men: A Study of Original Records.* 1911.

Sister Carrie. *Sister Carrie,* a novel by Theodore Dreiser published in 1900, tells the story of young Carrie Meeber, who comes to Chicago from rural Wisconsin. The book paints a rich portrait of turn-of-the-century Chicago. Carrie finds WORK in a shoe factory and boards with her working-class sister and brother-in-law. But soon she becomes the live-in mistress of traveling salesman Charles Drouet. During Drouet's absences she meets George Hurstwood, a married man who manages a fashionable bar. When Hurstwood's wife learns of the affair and throws him out, he steals $10,000 from his employer and tricks Carrie into fleeing with him to New York.

John Mack Faragher

See also: Chicago Literary Renaissance; Fiction; Loop

Six Corners, PORTAGE PARK Community Area. Six Corners is a commercially active area whose corners are formed by the three-way intersection of Irving Park Boulevard and Milwaukee and Cicero Avenues. Business interests began in 1841 with Dickinson's Inn, which located one block north of the intersection. The town hall for JEFFERSON TOWNSHIP was built on the site in 1862, and the area was ANNEXED into the city of Chicago in 1889. As residential SUBDIVISIONS extended to the area, commercialization began with Brenner's grocery, Bauer's bakery, and Fabish's restaurant. In the late 1870s, D. D. Mee's general store opened. A dairy farm and a cherry orchard occupied one corner until the coming of the Irving Park and Milwaukee Avenue STREET RAILWAY lines heightened retail development. A contracting and painting establishment opened in 1907, a dry goods store began operations in 1908, and German immigrant Emil Bengson followed with a coal and feed store, starting out with two horses and two dilapidated wagons. Business expansion culminated in a moving business which by 1915 employed 20 men with a number of trucks and moving vans.

In 1914 Jacob Derx began publishing the *Weekly Bulletin,* a local paper carrying neighborhood news and advertisements of area merchants. Six Corners became a booming retail center.

The architecturally elaborate Portage Theater was built in the 1920s. People came in droves to see a feature movie and listen to the theater's organ. In 1938, major retailer Sears, Roebuck & Co. became an anchor. By the 1980s, there were 150 stores at Six Corners. National chains had blended with established and family businesses into the 1990s.

Marilyn Elizabeth Perry

See also: Annexation; Movies, Going to the; Portage Park; Retail Geography; Shopping Districts and Malls

Further reading: Fitzgerald, Michael. "Six Corners, 150 Stores." *Chicago Sun-Times,* "Cityscape" (supplement), August 1988. • Howard, T. J. "A Three-dimensional Success: Six Corners' Commerce Is Built on a Strong Residential Foundation." *Chicago Tribune,* March 10, 1983.

Skating, Ice. During the nineteenth century, ice skating on Chicago's ponds, rivers, lagoons, and manufactured rinks was one of the city's most popular forms of winter recreation.

Competitive speed skating began to thrive in the 1890s, particularly among NORWEGIANS in HUMBOLDT PARK, who formed the Northwest Skating Club in 1890. The city pioneered women's competition in 1904 with a state meet at Humboldt Park that attracted 50,000 spectators. Speed skating subsequently spread into grade schools, and by the 1920s formal competition was conducted by the high schools, the CATHOLIC YOUTH ORGANIZATION, and the Chicago Park District. The city was also home to three major skate manufacturers: F. W. Planert & Sons, Nestor Johnson Mfg. Co., and Alfred Johnson Skate Company.

By 1923 metropolitan Chicago's winter landscape was dotted with more than six hundred outdoor rinks (more than in any other city) and was unrivaled in producing champion speed skaters, starting with four-time national champion Bobby McLean (1911–1914). Every Olympic Games from 1924 through 1998 had Chicagoans competing, notably Diane Holum, Ann Henning, Leah Poulos, and Andy Gabel. The CHICAGO TRIBUNE Silver Skates competition from 1917 to 1974 was the preeminent speed skating event in the United States, attracting up to 60,000 fans during its heyday in the 1920s and 1930s.

Figure skating as a professional sport in Chicago emerged when the Figure Skating Club of Chicago, with headquarters in the Chicago Arena (333 E. Erie), formed in 1921. The CHICAGO STADIUM began hosting shows such as the Ice Follies in the late 1930s. Chicago produced Olympic figure skating pairs Ronald and Vivian Joseph as well as David Santee and Calla Urbanski.

Picture Section
In 2 Parts Part 1

Chicago Sunday Tribune. THE WORLD'S GREATEST NEWSPAPER

November 30, 1930

THE DRAMA OF CHICAGO: A PAINTER VISUALIZES A GREAT CITY'S PULSING POWER—Two more water colors by Richard A. Chase, reproduced here, amplify the impressions of metropolitan vigor presented on this page last Sunday. In "State Street Bridge" is symbolized the city's conquest of an ancient barrier—the river—and more. Like a great back drop for this triumph is the vista in the background, of the old giving place to the new, of citadels of commerce rising to ever-loftier heights, of tremendous mass and power in this Chicago which to the world is a material expression of youth, virility, and restless, surging energy.

Richard Chase, *State Street Bridge,* watercolor, 1930. Artist: Richard Chase. Source: The Newberry Library.

By the first decade of the twenty-first century, figure skating and indoor speed skating were most often sponsored by suburban clubs such as NORTHBROOK and GLEN ELLYN.

Robert Pruter

See also: Creation of Chicago Sports; Ice Hockey

Further reading: Houghton, Bill, ed. *Speed Skating Handbook: 1998–1999.* 1998. • Lindberg, Richard C., and Biart Williams. *The Armchair Companion to Chicago Sports.* 1997. • Riess, Steven A. *City Games: The Evolution of American Urban Society and the Rise of Sports.* 1989.

Skokie, IL, Cook County, 12 miles NW of the Loop. Called Niles Center until 1940, Skokie emerged in the mid-1850s at the confluence of two Indian trails, one going north to Gross Point (Gross Point Road), and the other veering westward to what is now MORTON GROVE (Lincoln Avenue). Most of this area was wooded, with a marshy prairie extending down from the north. The POTAWATOMI maintained several villages along the banks of the North Branch of the CHICAGO RIVER, which bounds Skokie to the west.

Immigrants from GERMANY and LUXEMBOURG came in the 1850s, giving the area a strong German flavor, expressed by Lutheran (1867) and ROMAN CATHOLIC (1868) churches. By the 1870s a little town was emerging, and in 1888 the village of Niles Center was incorporated. Without rail connections to Chicago, farming remained the principal source of income for the area's residents until the 1920s. A flurry of land speculation occurred after 1925 when Samuel Insull built the Skokie Valley line of the North Shore Railroad (what became the Skokie Swift in 1964). Although the GREAT DEPRESSION thwarted the REAL-ESTATE boom, leaving many lots vacant in Skokie throughout the 1930s, by the late 1940s revitalization and rezoning efforts stimulated commercial and residential growth.

Skokie continued to grow with the completion of the Edens EXPRESSWAY in 1951, which provided greater access to Chicago; and the Old Orchard SHOPPING Center, opened in 1956, generated further commercial development in the area. During the 1950s and 1960s great numbers of houses were built, often using the streets laid out in the 1920s, and by 1970 the population reached 68,627.

Many of the new inhabitants of Skokie were Jewish people moving out of Chicago. They built a number of synagogues, which have continued to attract Jewish immigrants, most recently from Russia. In 1978, the American Nazis received court permission to march in Skokie. Although they ultimately marched in MARQUETTE PARK instead, the Nazis provoked thousands of counter demonstrators. To commemorate the Holocaust, of which many of Skokie's Jewish residents were survivors, a memorial sculpture was dedicated in the community's village center in 1987.

Since the early 1970s Skokie has attracted people from many parts of the world. The 2000 census reported that 21 percent of Skokie's population was Asian, with 6 percent Hispanic and 5 percent African American; thirty-seven percent were foreign-born. The village of Skokie was not only a great melting pot of nationalities, but also a center for nearly four hundred companies. Rand McNally and G. D. Searle & Company were longtime residents of Skokie, and although Bell & Howell has facilities in other suburban areas of Chicago, they are headquartered in Skokie. Although the population of Skokie had been dropping since reaching its peak in 1970, it stood at 63,348 in 2000, up from a decade earlier.

David Buisseret

"A city under one roof—the Masonic Temple, Chicago," 1894, showing the temple's height relative to buildings and monuments elsewhere. Artist: Unknown. Source: Chicago Historical Society.

See also: Demography; Economic Geography; Interurbans; Jews

Further reading: Buisseret, David, Rosemary Schmitt, and Richard J. Witry. *St. Peter Catholic Church, Skokie, Illinois: Building God's Community of Faith, 1868–89 to 1993–94.* 1994. • Strum, Philippa. *When the Nazis Came to Skokie.* 1999. • Whittingham, Richard. *Skokie, 1888–1988: A Centennial History.* 1988.

Chicago's Tallest Buildings since 1854

	YEAR	HEIGHT (FT)	STORIES	LOCATION
Holy Name Cathedral	1854	254	—	733 N. State Street
Chicago Water Tower	1869	154	—	800 N. Michigan Avene
Holy Family Church	1874	266	—	1080 W. Roosevelt Road
Masonic Temple	1892	302	21	State and Randolph, NE corner
The Tower Building	1899	394	19	6 N. Michigan Avenue
Wrigley Building	1922	398	29	400 N. Michigan Avenue
Chicago Temple	1923	568	21	77 W. Washington Street
Chicago Board of Trade	1930	605	44	141 W. Jackson Boulevard
Richard J. Daley Civic Center	1965	648	31	50 W. Washington Street
John Hancock Tower	1969	1,127	100	875 N. Michigan Avenue
Aon Center	1973	1,136	83	200 E. Randolph Street
Sears Tower	1974	1,450	110	233 S. Wacker Drive

Skyscrapers. The invention of the skyscraper in the late 1800s made possible the concentration of BUSINESS and services that have in turn made Chicago the great metropolis of the interior United States.

Chicago has been the site of many of the skyscraper's stylistic and technical advances. In the phenomenal growth years after the 1871 fire, an extraordinary pool of architectural talent known as the First Chicago School advanced the skyscraper form. The Home Insurance Building (1885–1931), utilizing a fireproofed metal frame, was Chicago's first skyscraper.

Early skyscrapers were clothed in historical styles, but eventually the form's distinctive skeletal metal frame was fully expressed, as in the Second Leiter Building (1891), which showed the wall becoming more glass than stone. The luminous Reliance (1895), with its continuous horizontal bands of window, ended all pretense of supporting walls, anticipating the glass curtain wall of the next century.

The late 1920s saw a flurry of art deco towers such as the Palmolive (1929) and Board of Trade (1930) in the distinctive telescoping setback Vertical style. Depression and war stopped tall building construction until the 1950s, when Mies van der Rohe's 860 Lake Shore Drive apartments (1951), with their glass

Home Insurance Building, LaSalle and Adams Streets, ca. 1905. Photographer: Unknown. Source: Chicago Historical Society.

and steel curtain walls, set the International Modernist agenda for the next two decades. Amid a barrage of imitators, the elegant stainless steel and green glass Inland Steel Building (1958) and the rusty Cor-Ten steel Daley Center (1965) stand out as masterful variations on the Miesian theme. The glass and steel box was also made plastic by the sculptural Lake Point Tower (1968), which was in fact based on a 1921 Mies design, while the pyramidal John Hancock Center (1969) broke from the right angle and the grid with its gigantic diagonal X supports running up and down the tower. Sears Tower, the world's tallest building from 1974 to 1997, crosses Mies with the telescoping setback.

By the 1980s postmodernists were creating visual excitement with all manner of historical references and contextual sensitivity. The graceful 333 Wacker (1983) gives and takes with the curve of the river, while the PaineWebber Tower (1990) revives a 1920s Saarinen design in scintillating contemporary garb. Chicago continues to be a living museum of the skyscraper, where the great architects of the world show their work.

Charles Laurier

See also: Architecture: The First Chicago School; Architecture: The Second Chicago School; Built Environment of the Chicago Region; Commercial Buildings

Further reading: Condit, Carl W. *The Chicago School of Architecture.* 1964. • Sinkevitch, Alice, ed. *AIA Guide to Chicago.* 1993.

Skyway. The Chicago (originally Calumet) Skyway is a 7.8-mile long EXPRESSWAY connection between the Dan Ryan Expressway and the Indiana TOLL ROAD, including a high-level bridge over the CALUMET RIVER.

When the terminus of the Indiana Toll Road was set at 106th Street and Indianapolis Boulevard, a diagonal route, adjacent to the Pennsylvania and New York Central RAILROAD embankments, was approved in 1954. Construction began in 1956 and the toll road opened in April 1958.

State law did not permit cities to build toll roads, so legally the facility is a toll bridge with long approaches. Traffic counts fell far short of projections as motorists used toll-free I-94 instead, and for decades the city was unable to repay the revenue bonds, even as tolls increased from twenty-five cents to two dollars. The roadway became self-sustaining in 1989 and was rehabilitated in the late 1990s.

Dennis McClendon

See also: Governing the Metropolis; Transportation

Sleepy Hollow, IL, Kane County, 38 miles NW of the Loop. Rolling, wooded, and serene, the village of Sleepy Hollow has no gridlike street pattern or even a main street. Floyd T. Falese designed the community in this manner after purchasing Sleepy Hollow Farm in 1953.

Falese built a house that he called "Singing Waters" on the 340-acre property, which featured two lakes and a waterfall. But it was not long before he acquired more land, gave up farming, and became a developer.

Falese hired an architect to devise a LANDSCAPE that followed a natural setting. Lakes were dredged and stocked with fish. No sidewalks were installed and no trees were cut down; lots were at least one-half acre. Bridle paths were established and horses were also allowed on a 25-foot apron along the road.

The first lots Falese offered for sale in the mid-1950s were east of Sleepy Hollow Road and bordered on the north by Illinois 72. Operating as the Falese Land Company, Falese advertised his new SUBDIVISION of custom-built houses as Sleepy Hollow Manor, "a retreat in the country for the common man's boss."

Falese intended to keep the area unincorporated to preclude interference by governing bodies who would impose high taxes and stringent BUILDING CODES.

But as the surrounding communities fanned out closer to Sleepy Hollow, residents began to debate ANNEXATION to WEST DUNDEE, and Falese decided to move for incorporation. In 1958 the village incorporated as Sleepy Hollow and Falese became the first village president. Eventually Falese's barn became the village hall.

By 1960 the town's population totaled 311. Within the next decade the village grew rapidly, increasing to 1,729 residents in 1970 and 3,553 by 2000. The town remained residential without business or industry for many years.

In 1979 the first annexation was a planned subdivision, Saddle Club Estates. In the 1980s

Windsor Development built the Deer Creek and Surrey Ridge subdivisions.

The town has no fast-food restaurants, no downtown, and little traffic. In a nod to Washington Irving's legendary town, the Headless Horseman is part of the village flag.

Marilyn Elizabeth Perry

See also: Government, Suburban; Kane County; Suburbs and Cities as Dual Metropolis

Further reading: Bullinger, Carolyn J., ed. *Dundee Township, 1835–1985.* 1985. • Provisional League of Women Voters. *Fox Valley Four.* 1971.

Slovaks. Immigrants began arriving in Chicago from Slovakia, which was then part of the Hapsburg Empire and governed by Hungary, in the 1880s. Most came from eastern Slovakia and emigrated in response to diminishing economic opportunities. Many Slovak immigrants intended to earn some money and return to Slovakia, and they went to industrial regions that promised plentiful jobs with relatively high wages. Although more than half of all Slovakian immigrants to the United States went to central Pennsylvania, a significant although immeasurable number migrated to Chicago. Entering the city with few marketable skills, they settled in neighborhoods in close proximity to the industrial jobs that attracted them to Chicago. These included SOUTH CHICAGO, PULLMAN and ROSELAND, WHITING, PILSEN, the NEAR WEST SIDE, HUMBOLDT PARK, and especially BACK OF THE YARDS. Initially, most Slovak men took jobs in RAILROAD yards, steel mills, factories, and stockyards. Women worked in light industry and in the stockyards, although most families preferred that married women not work outside the home. Women were also responsible for seeing to the needs of the boarders whom many Slovak families took in to augment their income.

After the original Slovak pioneers arrived in the 1880s, they sent word of the opportunities in Chicago to friends and family members in Slovakia, encouraging them to migrate to the city. These networks facilitated adjustment from rural Slovakia to urban industrial America. Increasingly, newcomers could also look to ethnic institutions, including fraternal societies, gymnastic clubs, and at least seven Slovak SAVINGS AND LOANS. Starting in 1893, Slovaks built a number of churches to minister to both the majority ROMAN CATHOLIC and minority Lutheran communities in Chicago. Eventually, there would be eight Roman Catholic Slovak PARISHES in addition to numerous Slovak Lutheran churches in the Chicago area. Most of the Catholic churches sponsored a parochial school, to which most Slovak Catholic parents preferred to send their children. Although Lutheran parents sent their children to public SCHOOLS, many Slovak Lutheran children attended biweekly after-school religion and culture classes at their churches. Since most Slovaks came to America with little sense of Slovak identity, these RELIGIOUS INSTITUTIONS served to reinforce and sometimes create a sense of belonging to a distinctive Slovak people.

This sense of Slovak identity, which was created despite Hungarian attempts to convince Slovaks that they were really Hungarian, was threatened after 1918, when the Hapsburg Empire dissolved and Slovakia became part of the new state of Czechoslovakia. CZECHS outnumbered Slovaks in Czechoslovakia as well as in Chicago, and Chicago's Slovaks feared that their distinctive culture would be eclipsed. This tension culminated in 1933, when Slovak leaders pulled out of the committee to create a national exhibit at the CENTURY OF PROGRESS fair that year. Slovak community leaders wanted the country to be called Czecho-slovakia, believing that the hyphen signified the equality of the Czech and Slovak portions of the nation. When the exhibit was eventually called the Czechoslovak pavilion, without a hyphen, Slovak leaders interpreted it as a symbol of Czech dominance and an insult to Slovaks in Chicago and Slovakia.

Chicago's Slovak institutions, like those of many ethnic groups, were hit hard by the GREAT DEPRESSION of the 1930s. The Dunaj Savings and Loan, the most important Slovak financial institution in Chicago, was a casualty of the Depression, and the *Osadné Hlasy,* the Catholic Slovak weekly NEWSPAPER, repeatedly begged readers to continue to patronize the Slovak businesses that advertised in the newspaper and whose prosperity was necessary for the paper's survival. Many Slovak institutions did survive the Depression: the churches and athletic clubs remained intact, and *Osadné Hlasy* continued to publish until 1963.

Ironically, economic catastrophe threatened Slovak institutions less than the subsequent increasing prosperity which allowed Slovak Americans to leave the working-class neighborhoods where their parents and grandparents had settled. As the younger generation moved to more prosperous neighborhoods in the city and suburbs, most of the Slovak Catholic churches closed. By the beginning of the twenty-first century, only one Catholic Church, St. Simon the Apostle, at 52nd and California, continued to offer Slovak-language Mass. The Lutheran churches, which always had more geographically dispersed congregations, fared better. Trinity Church, which had relocated to the IRVING PARK community area from WEST TOWN in the 1920s, moved northwest to its current location in the FOREST GLEN community area in 1950, and, later that decade, Sts. Peter and Paul Church relocated from 19th and Halsted Streets to RIVERSIDE, Illinois. The athletic societies have survived as social clubs, although their elderly members are no longer particularly involved in athletic pursuits.

After the fall of Eastern European Communist government and the breakup of Czechoslovakia, more Slovaks moved to Chicago, settling especially in GARFIELD RIDGE on the Southwest Side. St. Simon's Church continues to act as an important meeting place for these new Slovak immigrants.

Emily Brunner

See also: Americanization; Demography; Iron and Steel; Meatpacking; Multicentered Chicago

Further reading: Barton, Josef. *Peasants and Strangers.* 1975. • Stolarik, M. Mark. *Immigration and Urbanization.* 1989.

Slovenes. Although a few individual Slovenes came to Chicago before the CIVIL WAR, the bulk of the population arrived after the 1880s. Most settled in SOUTH CHICAGO, PULLMAN, and especially in JOLIET and around 22nd Street (now Cermak Road) in PILSEN, areas that were located near the industrial jobs that attracted Slovenian immigrants to Chicago. They generally had agricultural backgrounds and emigrated because of diminishing economic opportunities. Early immigrants were likely to be young men who later sent for wives and other family members. The largest contingent of Slovenian immigrants went to Pennsylvania and Ohio, and Cleveland remains the most important center of Slovenian culture in America. Chicago and Joliet do not rival Cleveland as the capital of Slovenian America, but because they were relatively early centers of Slovenian settlement, they have been home to the headquarters of Slovenian NEWSPAPERS and benevolent societies.

Chicago's and Joliet's Slovenes founded institutions that not only served their community and reinforced ethnic ties but also reflected some of the fundamental rifts that divided, and continue to divide, Slovenian Americans in the Chicago area and elsewhere. The most important conflict divided those who identified with the ROMAN CATHOLIC Church from those who thought of themselves as freethinkers. Many, although not all, of the freethinkers were SOCIALISTS. The most important Catholic institutions were the three Slovenian Catholic churches: St. Joseph's, founded in Joliet in 1891; St. Stephen's, founded in Pilsen in 1898; and St. George's, founded in South Chicago in 1903. Freethinkers maintained a community center on Lawndale Road, several blocks west of St. Stephen's Church and the affiliated Catholic institutions. The two groups had rival newspapers, community centers, and cultural organizations such as singing societies and sports teams. The two rival benevolent societies, the Catholic Kranjsko Slovenska Katoliska Jednota (KSKJ) and secular Slovenska Narodna Podporna Jednota (SNPJ), were both founded in the Chicago area and continue to be active in Chicago in the twenty-first century.

Many Slovenian institutions survived the GREAT DEPRESSION, and the St. Stephen's community received an infusion of energy after WORLD WAR II, when a small number of new immigrants came to the United States fleeing the Communist government in Yugoslavia, of which Slovenia had been a part since 1918. Their presence revitalized the Slovenian community but also reinforced the rift between Catholics and freethinkers. Many new immigrants condemned freethinkers and socialists for supporting Josip Broz Tito, the anti-Nazi partisan who eventually became the leader of Yugoslavia's postwar Communist regime. There was also some tension between newcomers and older members of the Catholic organizations, but for the most part newcomers aligned with the church, bringing a new sense of personal grievance to the old split between religious Slovenes and freethinkers.

In the late twentieth century, Pilsen and South Chicago lost their Slovenian flavor, as young people moved to the suburbs and members of the older generation died or moved closer to their children. St. George's remains an active Catholic Church, but the congregation is now largely Latino. In 1998, St. Stephen's was taken over by the Jesuits and the parish buildings converted into a high school. Many of the Slovenes who worshiped at St. Stephen's now attend church at the Slovenian mission in LEMONT, which is home to a Slovenian Catholic SEMINARY and has long been an important site for Slovenian Catholics in America. The Slovenian Cultural Center in Lemont has assumed many of the functions that the PARISH used to fulfill and now hosts language classes, a weekly after-church lunch, and other events. Freethinkers, who do not feel welcome at the Cultural Center, no longer have a central meeting place but continue to meet in SNPJ lodges in the city and suburbs.

Unlike South Chicago and Pilsen, Joliet continues to be home to a thriving Slovenian community. St. Joseph's Church retains its Slovenian identity, and several KSKJ lodges are active in Joliet and nearby suburbs. The KSKJ is headquartered in Joliet, and the Slovenian Women's Union also maintains its headquarters and a small Slovenian heritage museum in the town.

Emily Brunner

See also: Americanization; Demography; Free Thought; Multicentered Chicago; Yugoslavians

Further reading: Klemencic, Matjaz. "American Slovenes and the Leftist Movements in the United States in the First Half of the Twentieth Century." *Journal of American Ethnic History* 15.3 (1996). • Prisland, Marie. *From Slovenia to America: Recollections and Collections.* 1968. • Susel, Rudoph M. "Slovenes." In *Harvard Encyclopedia of American Ethnic Groups,* ed. Stephan Thernstrom, 1980, 934–942.

Smart Museum. Affiliated with the UNIVERSITY OF CHICAGO, the Smart Museum opened as a gallery in 1974 with a one-million-dollar bequest from the David and Alfred Smart family foundation. These patrons had also founded *Esquire* magazine here in 1933. Designed by Chicago architect Edward Larrabee Barnes, the building and sculpture garden provide approximately 9,600 square feet of display space. Founding director Edward A. Maser was appointed to oversee collections which range from ancient Greek vases and Chinese bronzes to medieval sculpture and Old Master paintings; from Frank Lloyd Wright furniture and Tiffany glass to modern sculpture by Degas, Matisse, and Rodin and twentieth-century paintings by Mark Rothko, Diego Rivera, and Arthur Dove. The original furniture and fixtures from Frank Lloyd Wright's nearby Frederick C. Robie residence are also housed in this collection.

In addition to serving as a university museum, where the collections are drawn upon for research and teaching, the Smart Museum has initiated important community outreach programs, including its Docent for a Day program, which became a national model for connecting museums to schools.

Ronne Hartfield

See also: Architecture: The Prairie School; Art; Mary and Leigh Block Museum

Further reading: Taylor, Sue, and Richard A. Born, eds. *The David and Alfred Smart Museum of Art: A Guide to the Collection.* 1990.

Smoke-Filled Room. The original smoke-filled room was in Chicago's Blackstone Hotel, where, according to an enduring legend, a small group of powerful United States senators gathered to arrange the nomination of Warren G. Harding as REPUBLICAN candidate for president in 1920.

Meeting at the Coliseum, the convention deadlocked on Friday, June 11. At a suite in the Blackstone, Republican leaders held a series of discussions late into the night. Though leaning toward Harding at that point, participants did not control the convention. But when the Associated Press reported that Harding had been chosen "in a smoke-filled room," the phrase entered the American political lexicon. Ever since, "smoke-filled room" has meant a place, behind the scenes, where cigar-smoking party bosses intrigue to choose candidates.

Christopher Thale

See also: Political Conventions; Political Culture

Further reading: Russell, Francis. *The Shadow of Blooming Grove: Warren G. Harding in His Times.* 1968. • Safire, William. "Smoke-Filled Room." In *The New Language of Politics: An Anecdotal Dictionary of Catchwords, Slogans, and Political Usage.* 1968. • Sinclair, Andrew. *The Available Man: The Life and the Masks of Warren G. Harding.* 1965.

Snow Removal. The winter of 1967 had been a relatively mild one in Chicago, with unusually warm temperatures. Early in the morning on Thursday, January 26, snow began to fall. By Friday morning, 23 inches of snow had fallen with drifts of up to 6 feet. Over the next week and a half, intermittent snow and cold temperatures persisted. SCHOOLS closed, PUBLIC TRANSPORTATION stalled, and city services were severely taxed. By the time the storm had ended, 75 million tons of snow had fallen on the city. It was the most severe snowstorm Chicago had experienced in the century.

In 1979, Chicago was again brought to a standstill with another unusually severe January snowstorm. And, once again, the effect on TRANSPORTATION and city services was debilitating. The city's inability—or reluctance—to remove parked cars made it virtually impossible to clear the streets of snow and implement an effective snow removal plan. Public criticism of the MAYOR for his handling of the situation was widespread, and many believed that it hastened his departure from office in the next general election.

The snowstorms of 1967 and 1979 underscored the public's dependence on—and expectation of—government to provide effective maintenance of the urban INFRASTRUCTURE throughout the year. Until the late nineteenth century there was little concern for street cleaning and maintenance, although as early as the 1850s Chicago had enacted laws requiring building owners or residents to keep their sidewalks free of ice, snow, and dirt. Injuries caused by ice and snow occasionally resulted in lawsuits against the city for negligence.

Rapid growth toward the close of the nineteenth century brought expanded municipal responsibilities, including the maintenance and cleaning of streets and sidewalks. Later, the increased use of automobiles and trucks as well as the motorization of vehicles for emergencies, WASTE DISPOSAL, and commercial delivery services meant that cities like Chicago had to ensure that streets were accessible all year round.

Streetcars used snow sweepers to remove snow from the tracks. In the downtown area and along city streets, snow was removed by hand, shoveled into horse-drawn wagons, and hauled to empty lots to be dumped. Improvements in motorized vehicles during World War I helped aid development of modern methods of snow removal in the 1920s. Street-cleaning and maintenance equipment were adapted to snow removal: shovels were attached to urban trains to clear rails and to trucks to remove snow from streets. During the 1930s, horizontal curved blades mounted on trucks could push the snow to one side of the street for more effective street clearance. Plowing, mechanical and hand loading, motor-driven clamshell buckets, and motor-driven trailer trains to haul snow away were common. The use of salt and chemicals for melting snow increased following World War II, though salt had been used as a deicer several decades earlier.

By the 1950s, with the growth of suburbs and expansion of the EXPRESSWAY system, snow removal became a larger component of STREET AND HIGHWAY departments across the metropolitan area. Snow removal and ice control programs have reflected improvements in equipment as well as improvements in predicting snowstorms.

Joel Mendes

See also: Climate; Infrastructure; Planning Chicago; Political Culture; Street Life

Further reading: Armstrong, Ellis L., ed.; Michael C. Robinson and Suellen M. Hoy, assoc. eds. *History of Public Works in the United States, 1776–1976.* 1976. • Mendes, Joel, and Howard Rosen, eds. *One Hundred Years of Public Works Equipment: An Illustrated History.* 1986.

Soap Operas. Broadcasting's most enduring genre emerged in Chicago's radio studios in the early 1930s, the outcome of an experiment to determine whether daytime network programming would attract audiences and sponsors.

Sharing the credit for the earliest soaps were Irna Phillips, a WGN staff writer, and the ADVERTISING agency team of Anne Ashenhurst and her eventual husband, Frank Hummert. Ms. Phillips's initial offering, *Painted Dreams,* the saga of Mother Moynihan and her extended family, debuted locally on WGN in October 1930. Following a dispute with management, Phillips left WGN in April 1932. Two months later her *Today's Children*—a thinly veiled remake of *Painted Dreams* in which the Moynihan clan became the Moran family—began airing on WMAQ. CBS brought *Painted Dreams* to the network in September 1933.

Meanwhile, Hummert and Ashenhurst introduced NBC network audiences to *Betty and Bob* (featuring a young Don Ameche as Bob) in October 1932, *Just Plain Bill* in March 1933, and *Ma Perkins* nine months later.

These 15-minute episodes soon came to occupy a central place in the culture of the American housewife. Advertisers flocked to them as readily as listeners, and their forever unresolved multithreaded plots provided a template for repeated imitation. Irna Phillips thus earned the title "Queen of the Soap Operas." The Hummerts' writing team churned out as many as 90 episodes weekly. Thanks largely to the soaps, the combined daytime revenues of NBC and CBS more than trebled between 1932 and 1939.

Only at the end of World War II did the soaps begin their irreversible exodus from the Chicago studios where they were born.

Rich Samuels

See also: Broadcasting; Television, Talk

Further reading: Barnouw, Erik. *A Tower in Babel.* 1966. • Dennison, Merrill. "Soap Opera." *Harper's* 180 (April 1940). • Lavin, Marilyn. "Creating Consumers in the 1930s: Irna Phillips and the Radio Soap Opera." *Journal of Consumer Research* 22 (June 1955).

Sparta A.B.A.

Extends Congratulations to the National Soccer League on their 25th Anniversary and our admiration to the "Herald-American" for their sponsorship of the Brooklyn-Hispano - National League All Stars game from which the entire receipts will go to the Wounded Veteran's Fund.

OFFICIALS

L. KOSTKA, President
J. SILOVSKI, 1st Vice-Pres.
A. MOTTL, 2nd Vice-Pres.
L. HLAVIN, Secretary
V. SNOBL, Financial Secretary
A. HRUSKA, Treasurer

OFFICIALS

CHAS. J. FENCL, Mgr.
R. PISKULE, Field Mgr.
J. TVRZICKY, Trainer

SPARTA A.B.A.—1945
ORGANIZED IN CHICAGO—1914

RECORDS

Chicago Soccer Leagues CHAMPIONS 1928-30-31-32-33-34-35-36-38

Peel Cup Winner 1928-29-30-31-32-33-37

National Cup Western Finalist 1927-29-33-36-38-39

UNITED STATES CHAMPIONS SEASON 1938-39

Page from *25th Anniversary Program* (1945) for the National Soccer League sponsored by Chicago's Sparta ABA (Athletic and Benevolent Association) Soccer Club, a Czech organization. Source: Chicago Historical Society.

Soccer. In the spring of 1883, the 39th Street Wanderers and the Pullman Car Works soccer teams kicked off at PULLMAN's Lake Calumet athletic field complex. Thus commenced the inaugural season of the city's first organized soccer league, the seven-team Chicago League of Association Football (CLAF). British and CANADIAN immigrants had played soccer in the city for years, but with the formation of CLAF, the city's extensive commitment to the sport gained national and international recognition.

CLAF flourished under the direction of its first president, Charles Jackson. In addition to the Wanderers and the Pullman clubs, other teams of British extraction included the HYDE PARK Blues, Hyde Park Grays, Campbell Rovers, McDuffs, Swifts, Calumet, and a team of miners from the BRAIDWOOD coalfields. Interest in the league grew as local papers reported on an increasing number of teams, roster lineups, and scores. These early teams played two seasons per year, competed in friendly challenge matches against soccer clubs from visiting cities, and played annually for the Jackson Challenge Cup trophy. In 1901, looking to capitalize on soccer's popular appeal, Charles COMISKEY established a Midwest professional soccer circuit with teams from Chicago, St. Louis, Detroit, and Milwaukee. Midway through the season financial support deteriorated, and the league folded. The game flourished despite this setback, and by 1904 another league, the Association Football League of Chicago, began play.

Just as organized soccer spread from England to the European continent and beyond, by 1912 soccer in Chicago parks had extended from ENGLISH immigrant communities to other European ethnic groups. The formation of the International Soccer League (ISL) in 1920 brought organization and regulation to these teams. Twentieth-century amateur teams in Chicago, such as the Sparta, Schwaben, Vikings, Green-White, Eagles, Kickers, and Maroons, descended from soccer clubs that came to prominence in the ISL. Known to late-twentieth-century fans as the National Soccer League, the ISL claims the title of the nation's oldest organized soccer league.

In 1911, brothers Archibald and Alexander Paterson introduced soccer into two Chicago high schools, Englewood and Lane Technical. Other than a brief decline in 1936—when financial constraints allowed only two schools to field teams—high-school soccer grew steadily more popular, and by the late twentieth century soccer was drawing more participants than any other high-school sport in the city. Local universities also sponsored soccer. As early as 1910 the UNIVERSITY OF CHICAGO played the University of Illinois, and by 1928 the latter offered soccer as a varsity sport. WHEATON COLLEGE has long been a preeminent collegian soccer power, having fielded a varsity squad since 1935.

Professional Chicago soccer debuted in 1967, and the following year saw the formation of the North American Soccer League (NASL). The Chicago STING captured two championship banners before the NASL folded in 1984. Professional soccer returned to the city in 1998 with the Chicago Fire, which won the league championship and the Dewar (Open) Cup in its inaugural season.

Since as early as 1905, when the Pilgrim Football Club from England played against a Chicago all-star team, international soccer clubs have often chosen Chicago as a major venue to exhibit some of the finest soccer talent in the world. Chicago clubs have played teams from London, Glasgow, Mexico City, Vienna, Prague, Budapest, Munich, Liverpool, Tel Aviv, Toronto, Uruguay, and Scotland. The memorable 1959 Pan-Am games saw the U.S. national team defeat Brazil and Mexico. Chicago hosted the 1994 World Cup and the 1999 Women's World Cup.

In 1924, Chicagoan Peter J. Peel took the first U.S. Olympic soccer team to Paris. Since then the city has contributed players, managers, and coaches to most U.S. Olympic and World Cup teams. Some of the greatest players of their time, such as Ben and Sheldon Govier (Pullman), Julius Hjulian (Chicago Wonderbolts and keeper in the 1934 World Cup), Gil Heron (Chicago Corinthians and the first black player in the Scottish First Division with Glasgow Celtic), Ed Murphy (Maroons, national team), Willy Roy (Hansa, national team, Sting), and

Brian McBride (national team), honed their skills on Chicago soccer pitches.

Although long ignored by mainstream press and media, soccer continues to be the most played sport in Chicago. Founded in 1916, the Illinois Soccer Commission coordinates over 600 women's and men's teams, while over 2,000 metropolitan Chicago youth teams compete in the Illinois Youth Soccer Association.

Gabe Logan

See also: Creation of Chicago Sports; Leisure; Sports, High-School; Sports, Industrial League

Further reading: Cirino, Tony. *U.S. Soccer vs. the World: The American National Team in the Olympic Games, the World Cup, and other International Competition.* 1983. • Illinois Soccer Commission. *Illinois Soccer Commission, 25th Anniversary, September 25, 1941, Hotel Sherman–Chicago.* 1941. • *Spalding's Official Soccer Foot Ball Guide.* 1907 through 1913–14.

Social Gospel in Chicago. The Social Gospel movement came to prominence nationally and dominated liberal PROTESTANT outreach in the first two decades of the twentieth century. While the formal expression declined in the 1920s, this movement has had profound influence on most later Protestant efforts to bring reform and spread justice in the United States. Chicago was host to many Social Gospel expressions, and Chicagoans had an influence on the national movement.

While the movement took many forms and is hard to define, it can best be seen as an effort to use biblical and church historical themes as standards by which to measure modern urban industrial capitalist societies. Supporters of the Social Gospel cause did not often act on their own politically, instead uniting with other progressive movements.

The UNIVERSITY OF CHICAGO Divinity School and a number of other SEMINARIES, including Chicago Theological Seminary and what is now called Garrett-Evangelical Seminary, were among the early leaders of the movement. The injustices, poverty, labor situation, and slums of Chicago provided a rich field for Social Gospel reform. Seminarians, in particular, carried the themes and strategies from their schools to the urban scene.

Notable among Chicago Social Gospel leaders was Graham Taylor, who in 1892 came to Chicago Theological Seminary, where he founded the nation's first professorship of Christian sociology. The founder of CHICAGO COMMONS, a SETTLEMENT HOUSE, Taylor chose to live in Chicago's slums in order to experience the need for change and guide others to become aware of urban problems. He wrote a regular column in the *Chicago Daily News* to enlarge his appeal to the city.

Many Protestant congregations in Chicago took up the Social Gospel cause. While Protestants were not as effective at reaching and serving Catholics as they were with other immigrant groups, they did work with Jane Addams at HULL HOUSE in addition to Chicago Commons. In many of the suburban congregations, pastors who carried Social Gospel ideas from seminary to PARISH met apathy or resistance from many of their middle-class parishioners.

During the prosperous 1920s it was ever more difficult to keep urban need in front of well-off Christians. But during the GREAT DEPRESSION and ever after, churches have worked out many Social Gospel impulses, although under other names and perhaps with less optimism.

Martin E. Marty

See also: If Christ Came to Chicago; Religion, Chicago's Influence on; Settlements, Religious

Further reading: May, Henry F. *The Protestant Churches and Industrial America.* 1967. • McGiffert, Arthur Cushman, Jr. "Sociological and Theological Frontiers." In *No Ivory Tower: The Story of Chicago the Theological Seminary.* 1965. • Wade, Louise C. *Graham Taylor, Pioneer for Social Justice, 1851–1938.* 1964.

Social Science. *See* Chicago Studied: Social Scientists and Their City

Social Service Education. Social service education in Chicago developed in response to the social dislocation resulting from industrialization and immigration in the nineteenth and early twentieth centuries. Significant numbers of immigrant families, sick, and homeless people required organized assistance and the qualified individuals to provide it. Before the development of government-sponsored social welfare programs, services were provided by SETTLEMENT HOUSE workers who focused primarily on social reform and by "friendly visitors" from church-related charitable organizations concerned with the distribution of alms to deserving individuals.

SOCIAL SERVICE educational institutions trace their origins to the demand for skilled professionals created by settlement houses and by private and public social agencies. Early social work educators sought to make benevolence scientific while continuing to focus on improving social conditions and individual well-being. An early question for each educational program was whether to affiliate with a university, which would make the education more academically than technically focused. Programs in Chicago moved more rapidly into UNIVERSITIES than did programs in other parts of the country. For example, the YMCA Training School, established in Chicago in 1890, became a college in 1913 and eventually the Aurora University School of Social Work. The CHICAGO COMMONS School of Social Economics, which began in 1895 with a series of lectures and conferences, ultimately became the School of Social Service Administration established at the UNIVERSITY OF CHICAGO in 1920. The Loyola School of Social Work, established in 1914 at LOYOLA UNIVERSITY, began with Father Frederic J. Siedenburg's Lecture Bureau, designed to educate ROMAN CATHOLICS working in helping professions. And the UNIVERSITY OF ILLINOIS AT CHICAGO Jane Addams School of Social Work began when the University of Illinois started offering courses in Chicago in 1947 to meet the demand from agencies and settlements for more social group workers.

A second and related question confronting programs was the extent to which they would emphasize research and social reform versus a more technically oriented casework approach. Early social work educators Edith Abbott and Sophonisba Breckenridge of the University of Chicago School of Social Service Administration advanced a reformist and state-building vision of casework, in which casework was viewed as the best forum for evaluating the success or failure of social policy and informing the development of social legislation. This highly influential vision led to the development nationally of educational curricula incorporating practice, policy, research, and social science theory relevant to a delivery of social services that remains in place today.

As both public and private social welfare agencies and institutions grew and developed in Chicago and the United States, the demand for well-prepared social workers grew as well. By the end of the twentieth century, there were 4 graduate social work programs in Chicago (at AURORA UNIVERSITY, Loyola University Chicago, University of Chicago, and University of Illinois at Chicago), 6 in Illinois, and more than 16 undergraduate programs statewide. Research and knowledge development about individual well-being, the causes of social problems, and the efficiency and effectiveness of social interventions continues to characterize these educational programs.

Jeanne C. Marsh

See also: Chicago Studied: Social Scientists and Their City; Medical Education; Seminaries

Further reading: Edith Abbott Papers. Special Collections, Joseph Regenstein Library, University of Chicago. • Shoemaker, L. M. "Social Work, Sociology, or Socialism?: Competing Visions of Social Work Education in New York, Boston, and Chicago, 1898–1930." *Social Service Review* (1991).

Social Services. The term "social service" (or social welfare) refers to the variety of programs made available by public or private agencies to individuals and families who need special assistance. Prior to the 1920s, Americans referred to these services as charity or relief, but they covered a wide range of services, including LEGAL AID, immigrant assistance, and travelers' aid. The new terminology corresponded to changes in the philosophy, approach, and organization of social work.

For most of our country's history, the social and economic insecurities that accompanied old age, UNEMPLOYMENT, disability, desertion, or death of the family wage earner had

Cook County Poor House, Oak Forest, postcard, 1908. Artist: Unknown. Source: Chicago Historical Society.

to be met by the family or local efforts. Religious and fraternal organizations, along with private and public welfare organizations, provided minimal forms of aid. Economically advantaged families purchased private insurance, and workers' families joined MUTUAL BENEFIT or aid societies for the death benefits they provided. The first major expansion in public provision came in the years between the American Revolution and Reconstruction, when state governments built asylums and ALMSHOUSES for dependent and delinquent CHILDREN, the disabled, and the mentally ill. Counties built poorhouses for the aged, infirm, and poor. The asylum movement did not replace but evolved concurrently with voluntary societies formed to aid a variety of constituents, including former slaves, the mentally ill, widows, immigrants, and juvenile delinquents.

By the 1890s, progressive social workers and industrial reformers introduced new ideas about social survey research, equitable access to social resources, and rights of social citizenship into the debates on social provision. They challenged the traditional perspective of a limited state as they developed plans for social insurance and expanded municipal services. Crucial to the widespread influence of these new ideas were the national organizations and their state affiliates that generated support for new legislation and policies. Groups as diverse as the National Conference of Corrections and Charities and the National Consumers League made the transition more feasible. By the 1920s, evidence of this new approach to social services could be found in newly legislated programs like workmen's compensation and mothers' aid programs; an expanded governmental infrastructure including JUVENILE COURTS and social service divisions; and greater coordinated benefits between public and private groups.

The GREAT DEPRESSION's economic crises led to a shift in Americans' ideas about government responsibility for economic security. The NEW DEAL infused federal funds into programs that affected banks as well as farmers, investors, and industrial workers. The Social Security Act of 1935 created a federal system of provision for the aged, unemployed, and categorically poor, funded by an employees' contributory tax. The U.S. social insurance system divided benefits between entitlements to workers in covered jobs and categorical aid (welfare) to those in uncovered sectors or unable to WORK. States retained considerable control over the expenditure of funds and administration of services for the categorical welfare programs. Historians generally agree that the infusion of federal funds through the New Deal programs averted a prolonged economic decline but did not pull the country out of the Depression. That credit goes to the war industry jobs that started at the end of the 1930s and in the first years of the 1940s.

The federal government continued to promote economic and social stability for a wide range of Americans following WORLD WAR II. Employment policies for returning veterans, low mortgage interest rates, and subsidies for national highways contributed to the era's economic expansion. COLD WAR politics provided a new rationale for CIVIL RIGHTS laws and economic opportunity policies. Presidents Kennedy and Johnson cultivated this approach most specifically with their education and antipoverty programs. Like the programs that proceeded them, the new services sought to ameliorate social problems created in part by economic and social inequality.

Chicago's development of social services fits prominently within the larger national trends. Public and private charities contributed to Chicago's early social services, but the private societies held the dominant role until Progressive-era programs altered the balance. Chicago's oldest and largest private charity, the CHICAGO RELIEF AND AID SOCIETY (CRAS), founded in 1857, considered its mission to assist the "worthy poor." That service base broadened by necessity when the 1871 fire destroyed many homes and left thousands helpless. The city of Chicago selected this established group to distribute approximately $5 million in donations, but it appeared that the CRAS might lose its autonomy in the push to coordinate the delivery of services. The concern revived in 1887 when the CRAS annexed Chicago's first CHARITY ORGANIZATION SOCIETY, but it managed to retain its autonomy by resisting efforts by charity organization societies to coordinate resources and investigate charity cases.

Chicago's social services comprised both public and private resources at the turn of the twentieth century. Public facilities included the COOK COUNTY HOSPITAL, the Juvenile Court, the Municipal TUBERCULOSIS Sanitarium, the County Agent's Poor Relief Department, and the DUNNING institutions (among them the poorhouse). Most of the poorhouse residents came from the ranks of the aged, the seasonally employed, and single mothers with young children. District poor relief offices dispensed "outdoor relief" to the desperately destitute in the form of bags of coal, baskets of groceries, and infrequent stipends. During severe economic downturns, the city of Chicago opened temporary BOARDINGHOUSES for unemployed men. These usually had auxiliary "employment bureaus" and wood yards where boarders worked off their stay.

Privately organized agencies provided a multitude of other services, such as homes for the aged, unwed mothers, orphans, working girls, and abandoned or dependent children. Child health services, KINDERGARTENS, and day NURSERIES received their earliest support from private organizations. However, the majority of private charities provided services only to a specific religious or ethnic group.

Proponents of a reformed and coordinated system of social services, including Jane Addams (HULL HOUSE settlement), Lucy Flower (Chicago Woman's Club), Charles Henderson (professor of sociology, UNIVERSITY OF CHICAGO), Julia Lathrop (first director of the U.S. Children's Bureau), and Julius Rosenwald (philanthropist) worked with others to found a new organization called the Central Relief Association, renamed the Bureau of Charities in 1894. This association took charge of relief efforts during the depression of 1893 and had 10 districts with 800 friendly visitors providing services in Chicago by 1897. In addition to a register of clients for better-coordinated services, the bureau broadened those it served through programs such as day nurseries, lending libraries, dental

Chicago & Northwestern Railroad pamphlet cover, ca. 1911. Source: Chicago Historical Society.

dispensaries, kindergartens, and a loan fund. In 1909, the Bureau of Charities joined with the Relief and Aid Society to form the UNITED CHARITIES of Chicago.

Between the 1890s and 1930, new ideas about the cause of poverty changed the substance and structure of social services in Chicago. Private and public charities continued to serve selective populations, but support for a wider range of publicly funded social programs gained prominence nationally and locally. The city's UNIVERSITIES and SETTLEMENT HOUSES formed the heart of the new initiatives. Charles Henderson led early investigations with his University of Chicago sociology students. He collaborated in social research projects with Graham Taylor at CHICAGO COMMONS, Mary McDowell at University of Chicago Settlement, and Jane Addams at Hull House. New methods of social investigation such as social surveys and statistical analysis produced new explanations for the causes of poverty, as social researchers investigated the relationships between environment, family structure, and local POLITICS on one's chances for economic and social opportunity. Although elite ideals of noblesse oblige and beliefs in individual failing as the cause of poverty would still remain, they competed in a new environment.

Some participants recognized the limits of the charity ideal of self-help after taking part in social investigations. Lathrop's research on county public charities for an 1893 federal study of urban slums led her to criticize sharply the county's poor relief office. Robert Hunter, another resident of Hull House, wrote *Poverty*, his treatise on the structural dynamics of economics, in 1904, shortly after his tenure as the organizational secretary for Chicago's Board of Charities.

The systematic analysis of social issues demanded specialized training for social workers. Settlement leaders believed that a coordinated course of study that involved students in methods of social investigation offered a significant improvement over the irregular training of settlement workers, friendly visitors, and poor relief investigators. Reformers from the settlements and the community joined with academics at the University of Chicago to develop a program of study in social work. Taylor gave the first series of lectures as early as 1895. The program expanded rapidly when Henderson, Lathrop, and Hunter also contributed lectures. Within a few years, students could take a program in social research at the Chicago School of Civics and Philanthropy. The school's Department of Social Investigation directed by Edith Abbott and Sophonisba Breckinridge, conducted the earliest social investigations of the Juvenile Court and trained AFRICAN AMERICAN social workers through the Wendell Phillips settlement. The School of Civics and Philanthropy joined the University of Chicago as the School of Social Service Administration in 1920 and continued the tradition of using scientific research to inform social work practice.

The justification for social provision began to change as well. One component of progressive reform sought to use state authority to decentralize the economic power of monopolies and to create greater access for Americans to the economic and social benefits of democratic capitalism. This created an opening for those reformers who wanted to expand individual rights to include government responsibility for and protection of citizens, specifically workers, immigrants, women, African Americans, and children. Reforms such as protective LABOR legislation, MOTHERS' PENSIONS, and child labor laws came out of this context and had early successes in Illinois because of the effective leadership of Chicago reformers.

African American residents of Chicago used public social services to the extent possible, but de facto residential segregation and pervasive RACISM remained a persistent obstacle. The African American community created numerous institutions to serve individual and family needs. Of dozens of local programs, the best funded were PROVIDENT HOSPITAL, the URBAN LEAGUE, and the YMCA. The Wendell Phillips and Frederick Douglass settlement houses offered community services within their neighborhoods as well as social work training. Ida B. Wells founded the Negro Fellowship League in 1910 as a resource for young men. A network of women's CLUBS, churches, and mutual aid societies raised funds for the Phyllis Wheatley Home, day nurseries, and homes for dependent children. However, the community's difficulty securing funds eventually made it difficult to maintain community control. The Urban League, formed in 1916, provided the first coordinated services to African Americans in Chicago and began to involve white philanthropists like Julius Rosenwald in the support of programs. The organization identified itself as a vehicle to create opportunities (usually meaning self-help through employment) for men and women and distanced itself from any charitable activity.

One significant result of the new directions taken in social services during the Progressive era can be found in the expansion of the public infrastructure for services. Chicago's initiation of a juvenile court in 1899—the first in the nation—offered an early example of the changes ahead. The Chicago Woman's Club drafted a juvenile court law in 1895, but questions of constitutionality stalled it before it reached the legislature. By 1898, a coalition of women's clubs, charities, lawyers, and child welfare advocates submitted a new bill and saw it through the legislature. In 1911, the COURT SYSTEM expanded again to accommodate two new programs, for mother-only families. The Cook County Municipal Court opened a new Court of Domestic Relations. Two-thirds of the cases heard involved abandonment and nonsupport of women and children. The court defined its purpose as a clearinghouse to receive complaints, find responsible parties, retrieve and disburse support funds, and refer families to appropriate agencies. The Juvenile Court also initiated a new branch to administer the new mothers' pension law that year.

The court's judge recognized the social service aspects of the law and included representatives of the social work community in the organizational plan. The mothers' pension division had its own director, investigators, and staff.

The era's changes led to a greater degree of planned and coordinated services. Several Chicago agencies had been associated with the state conference of Charities and Corrections since the 1890s, but the degree of expansion and change created additional layers of collaboration at the local level. In 1914 the Chicago City Council approved the creation of a Department of Public Welfare to conduct social research. The Welfare Council of Metropolitan Chicago, formerly the Chicago Council of Social Agencies, founded in 1914 by representatives of public and private agencies to anticipate needed reforms and coordinate research on issues, served as the liaison between local government, business, and philanthropic communities.

By the late 1920s, signs of economic dislocation appeared among Chicago's most vulnerable workers. Layoffs, first experienced by African Americans and MEXICAN Americans, increased the demand for temporary relief services. Unemployed transient men once again drew attention to the need for lodging houses. Although Chicago's settlements continued to provide social services to their neighbors, Hull House and Chicago Commons adapted their services to address also the needs of Mexican Americans and African Americans, whose numbers increased in the city during the 1920s and 1930s. During the winter of 1932–33, approximately 40 percent of the labor force in Chicago had no work. The network of public and private agencies tried to respond, but local efforts in Chicago were overwhelmed by demand. By 1933, federal PUBLIC WORKS programs started to mitigate the crisis by employing the unemployed on building projects. This infusion of federal funds staved off a deeper depression.

The influence of individual Chicagoans in Progressive-era social services and planning extended over several decades and beyond city and state borders. The economic crises of the 1930s and the expansion of the federal bureaucracy with New Deal programs brought many Chicago reformers to Washington DC. Charles Merriam began the Social Science Research Council (SSRC) shortly after his failed 1919 mayoral campaign. The SSRC organized the Commission on Recent Social Trends with the intent to design a national plan for development. The Depression and Franklin Delano Roosevelt's defeat of Herbert Hoover derailed Merriam's strategy, but only temporarily. Merriam's campaign manager for the Chicago mayoral race, Harold Ickes, became Roosevelt's secretary of the interior. He appointed Merriam to the National Planning Board. More specific to social services, Chicago reformers served on committees that would write the Social Security Act. Grace Abbott, past director of the U.S. Children's Bureau, served on the Advisory Council to the Committee on Economic Security and developed the child welfare provisions. Edith Abbott served on the advisory committee on public employment and public assistance.

The postwar economy created greater prosperity in employment and consumption for many Americans, and Chicago continued to attract those seeking work. It was a major destination for African Americans who left the South during and after the war as well as Mexican Americans who had begun migrating to Chicago in substantial numbers during 1920s. However, the expansion left behind many Americans. The elderly, mother-only families, the chronically ill, and racial minorities had disproportionate rates of poverty. Lyndon B. Johnson's GREAT SOCIETY programs focused on creating equality of opportunity through federal initiatives in health, education, and welfare. Programs for the aged, including Medicare, created a powerful "senior" lobby and made this component of the welfare state difficult to challenge. In contrast to the popularity of Medicare, the War on Poverty programs that intended to improve education, employment, housing, and health care in areas of concentrated poverty received a hostile reception from voters and local politicians.

Chicago's experience with Great Society programs varied. Politicians gladly accepted the federal funding attached to employment, housing, and model cities programs without sharing in the greater social goals to create opportunities for economic mobility. But federal officials never developed the state and local support of elected officials necessary for the successful implementation of programs. At the end of the twentieth century, new social problems emerged as a result of transitions in the postindustrial economy, stagnant or declining wages, drug trafficking, and a health care system in crisis. At the time that the country needed new solutions for these crises, support for government spending on social services declined precipitously and voluntarism increasingly filled the gap. The election of Ronald Reagan to the presidency in 1980 signaled a national groundswell of support for limited government spending and a turn away from the previous two decades of enlarged social programs. No political entity escaped these efforts to dismantle the welfare state. In Chicago and elsewhere, cutbacks in public funding resulted in a decline in some services and programs, an increase in nonprofit provision of services and in philanthropy, and greater state and local decision-making on the use of federal matching funds. The public and private collaboration that defined social services at the beginning of the century continued at the end of the century, as local governments contracted with private agencies to support numerous social services.

Joanne L. Goodwin

See also: Children and the Law; Clinics and Dispensaries; Occupational Safety and Health; Relief and Subsistence Aid; Religious Institutions; Social Service Education

Further reading: Abbott, Grace. *From Relief to Social Security: The Development of the New Public Welfare Services and Their Administration.* 1941. • Cook County, IL, Board of County Commissioners. *Charity Service Reports.* 1910–1927. • Patterson, James T. *America's Struggle against Poverty, 1900–1985.* 1981.

Socialist Parties. Socialists first attracted notice in Chicago during the depression of the mid-1870s, when the Workingmen's Party of Illinois, a group of immigrant, largely GERMAN craft unionists, coordinated marches of the unemployed to pressure the city government for relief and jobs. Building on the massive 1877 STRIKE wave that left at least 18 dead at the hands of Chicago's POLICE, the Workingmen's Party attempted to channel working-class anger into political gains. Renamed the Socialist Labor Party (SLP), the group achieved moderate success in the late 1870s, electing five aldermen, three state representatives, and one state senator.

The socialists' electoral success proved short-lived, however, as the mainstream parties co-opted elements of their platform and practiced voter fraud in immigrant-dominated wards. Disillusioned with the experiment in parliamentary socialism, many broke from the SLP in 1881 to form the International Working People's Association (IWPA), a "revolutionary socialist" organization dedicated to direct action and industrial unionism. The IWPA mobilized to support the burgeoning EIGHT-HOUR MOVEMENT, which exploded in May 1886 with mass strikes, police violence, and the infamous HAYMARKET Square bombing. Condemned as dangerous anarchists, eight IWPA leaders were convicted and sentenced to death for throwing the bomb. In the aftermath of the Haymarket incident, police repression destroyed the IWPA. The SLP endured as a minor political entity.

The efforts of early Chicago socialists proved more successful than their electoral record would suggest. Ethnic-based socialist clubs, rooted in the working-class experiences of the city's immigrant population and assisted by a thriving, multilingual socialist press, served as important vehicles of political education and mobilization. While helping to forge working-class consciousness within ethnic communities, however, the socialist clubs proved unable to overcome the multiple barriers separating them from the city's less radical native and IRISH workforce.

From the late 1880s, socialists played a small but vital role in the growth of the city's trade unions and progressive political coalitions. The creation of the Socialist Party in 1901 promised the greatest hope for socialists on a national level, bringing together native reformers, immigrant trade unionists, and tenant farmers. By the 1910s, the Socialist Party was a significant left-wing presence in many American cities, including Chicago, where a strong membership base supported at least 12 socialist NEWSPAPERS. Unlike elsewhere, however, Chicago's socialists failed to crack the dominance of the two major parties, despite drawing nearly 40 percent of the municipal vote in the 1917 elections.

WORLD WAR I and the Russian Revolution brought severe repression from federal and state government officials intent on preventing the contagion of Bolshevik radicalism from spreading to the United States. The Socialist Party's relationship to the emerging Soviet Union also caused internal conflicts, provoking a split which gave rise to the rival COMMUNIST PARTY. Officially linked to the USSR, the Communist Party assumed the socialists' cherished spot as the left flank of the labor movement in Chicago, proving instrumental in the rise of industrial unionism in the 1930s. The Socialist Party never recovered as a viable leftist political presence within Chicago, but the socialist legacy continued to live on in the global celebration of May Day as the international workers' day commemorating the Haymarket martyrs.

Daniel A. Graff

See also: Chicago Federation of Labor; Industrial Workers of the World (IWW); Politics; Unionization

Further reading: Nelson, Bruce C. *Beyond the Martyrs: A Social History of Chicago's Anarchists, 1870–1900.* 1988. • Schneirov, Richard. *Labor and Urban Politics: Class Conflict and the Origins of Modern Liberalism in Chicago, 1864–1897.* 1998. • Shannon, David. *The Socialist Party of America: A History.* 1955.

Sociology, Chicago School. *See* Chicago School of Sociology

Softball. Softball has complex and disputed origins. Some historians trace the game back to indoor BASEBALL, invented in Chicago in 1887 using a ball with a circumference of 17 inches, while other historians contend the game dates from 1895 in Minneapolis, where an outdoor game used a 13-inch ball.

Around 1907 indoor baseball in Chicago began to move outdoors, as the game rapidly became a staple for all age groups on the city's PLAYGROUNDS. That same year, Chicago's park, school, and church associations formally established "playground ball," with lengthened baselines and smaller ball sizes (12-inch and 14-inch).

Softball was established as a national sport at Chicago's CENTURY OF PROGRESS EXPOSITION in 1933, when the first national softball championships were held and the Amateur Softball Association (ASA) was formed. For the next seven years, the ASA held its championships in Chicago, with a Chicago men's team winning in 1933 and Chicago women's teams winning in 1933 and 1934. In 1934 the Windy City Softball League was formed to play slow-pitch 16-inch softball. Soon this game predominated in the city, pushing out the 12-inch variety.

But the 12-inch game—both slow and fast pitch—continued to thrive in the suburbs. AURORA became a softball hotbed: its Sealmasters won four ASA fast-pitch championships from 1959 to 1967 as well as the first world championship, held in Mexico City in 1966. In the slow-pitch division, Lilly Air, in Chicago, won a men's ASA title in 1984, and the Fox Valley Lassies won a women's ASA title in 1977. In 1976, the Illinois High School Association added women's fast-pitch softball to its athletic program.

Robert Pruter

See also: Clubs: Youth Clubs; Creation of Chicago Sports; Leisure; Park Districts

Further reading: Bealle, Morris. *The Softball Story.* 1957. • Cole, Terrence. "'A Purely American Game': Indoor Baseball and the Origins of Softball." *International Journal of the History of the Sport* 7.2 (September 1990): 287–296. • Gems, Gerald R. *Windy City Wars: Labor, Leisure, and Sport in the Making of Chicago.* 1997.

Softball, 16-Inch. When former president Jimmy Carter, a SOFTBALL enthusiast, was presented with a 16-inch softball during a 1998 Chicago visit, the unfamiliar object fascinated him. It's not surprising that he had never seen one before, because although thousands of games of 16-inch softball fill Chicago's parks every summer Sunday, the game is virtually unknown outside of the city.

Softball was invented in Chicago in November 1887. The exact dimensions of the first ball, crafted from BOXING-glove laces by creator George Hancock, is unknown. A 14-inch ball was used, however, in 1933 when 70,000 people saw the first major tournament game at the CENTURY OF PROGRESS EXPOSITION.

Eventually the 12-inch ball became the national standard, but Chicago embraced the softer 16-inch or "mush" ball. While its smaller cousin can be pitched fast or slow, the always slow-pitched Chicago softball makes for easier contact by the batter. Also, the softness of the ball allows for the game to be played barehanded.

Jacob Austen

See also: Baseball, Indoor; Creation of Chicago Sports; Leisure; Park Districts

Further reading: Claflin, Edward. *The Irresistible American Softball Book.* 1978. • Hevrdejs, Judy, and Mike Conklin. "A Convert." *Chicago Tribune,* October 30, 1998.

Soils. The soils of the Chicago region were formed by five universal factors: parent material, TOPOGRAPHY, organisms, CLIMATE, and time. Enormous continental glaciers crossed the land about 14,000 years ago like a grinding bulldozer, making soil parent material and moving it around into concentric ridges called moraines. These moraines acted as earthen dams holding lakes of melting ice that burst through in places. Sandy beaches formed around the lakes and later were shaped into DUNES by the wind. Flowing sheets of meltwater dumped sand and gravel in and around the moraines. Then the wind spread a blanket of dust from the Mississippi River valley, with a silty texture ideal for plants. The climate provided WATER to move through these materials and freezing and thawing to cause further weathering. Topography concentrated the water from high to low areas, above and underground. In turn, soil moisture and the warm seasons supported the plants and animals that worked to make the interconnected sponge-like fabric of the soil.

The glacial lakebed soils have a clayey subsoil with a thick, rich, dark topsoil, the product of wet prairies. Along the ancient shorelines, the drier, sandy beaches have a thin, moderately dark topsoil formed by a mix of prairies and TREES. In the city, many of the ridged moraines were eroded by the lakes and, like the Blue Island Ridge, exist as remnants. To the north, these ridges continue between the DES PLAINES RIVER and LAKE MICHIGAN, starting at North Avenue in OAK PARK. The soils on these ridges, in their thin, moderately light to dark colored topsoil and bleached white subsurface layer, show a record of forests as well as of widely spaced trees with prairies. The subsoil is clayey, very dense and very difficult to dig in, particularly when dry. Most of Chicago was built on the lakebed soils, which were too wet for the construction of a city, so the land surface was raised by repeated filling (including debris from the Great FIRE OF 1871). The deep canals dug for navigation, along with the sewers, helped to rid the city of water as more soil was covered.

Beyond the largest glacial expansion of Lake Michigan lies another ridge of moraines with soils similar to those on the inner moraines. These stand at the highest elevations and form a ring parallel to Lake Michigan, from VALPARAISO, INDIANA, to Wisconsin. The Des Plaines River runs on the east of this ridge until it turns southwest and cuts through it at WILLOW SPRINGS, exposing bedrock. The DUPAGE and FOX RIVERS define the western boundary. Along the rivers just above their valleys, there are sandy and gravelly soils from flowing meltwater. The valley floors have silty, dark colored soils eroded from upland prairies and deposited by postglacial floods. Beyond the "Valparaiso" moraines are broad, flat to gently sloping prairie soils, with dark, silty topsoil over clayey subsoil to the south and silty subsoil to the southwest. This zone is bounded by a far ridge that forms a semicircle from Kankakee to Ottawa to YORKVILLE. North of Yorkville, west of the Fox River, more ridges with gravelly to loamy soils continue to the north. Within this mix of morainal ridges, lakebeds and river valleys are scattered, very wet depressional environments with organic soils made up of decomposed plants and animals. These organic soils are black, contain fibers, feel greasy, and stain the hands.

Today, the most profound effects on the soil are human-induced and can be traced to urbanization and a loss of AGRICULTURAL knowledge. The soil is treated as a nuisance or at best a building material with no concern for its natural fabric. This artificially manipulated LANDSCAPE, ideal for the foundations of buildings and streets, is inhospitable for plants because the water cycle is short-circuited by altering the soil without rebuilding it. Nevertheless, there is hope, in new parks, the restoration of wetlands, and a growing desire to reduce unnecessary earthmoving in suburbia.

Donald J. Fehrenbacher

See also: Ecosystem Evolution; Glaciation

Further reading: Mapes, D. R. *Soil Survey of DuPage and Part of Cook Counties.* 1979. • Willman, H. B., and J. C. Frye. *Pleistocene Stratigraphy of Illinois.* 1970.

Soldier Field. During the 1920s, the South Park Commission constructed Soldier Field, the first great metropolitan-sponsored athletic structure, at the approximate site where the BURNHAM PLAN of 1909 had proposed a facility for sport and other great events. Originally known as GRANT PARK Stadium, it was soon renamed Soldier Field in honor of deceased WORLD WAR I servicemen. Architects Holabird & Roche won a competition to design a 100,000-seat U-shaped amphitheater which they modeled after the Parthenon, conforming to the adjacent FIELD MUSEUM's neoclassical style. In 1920 voters approved a $2.5 million bond issue, but CONSTRUCTION costs exceeded expectations, requiring additional $3 million bond issues in 1924 and in 1928, for a total cost of $8.5 million. Overruns were attributed to the difficulties of construction on reclaimed land, the elegant classical accouterments, and kickbacks to Park Board president Edward J. Kelly.

Soldier Field became the site of major events even prior to completion. In 1926 the International Eucharistic Congress attracted over 200,000 (later surpassed on September 28, 1954, when 260,000 attended the Marian Year tribute), and the Army-Navy FOOTBALL game drew 100,000. In 1927 the Dempsey-Tunney ("long-count") heavyweight championship rematch was attended by 104,000 fans who paid $2.6 million, a record BOXING gate. The largest sporting crowd was 115,000 for the 1937 Austin-Leo high-school football championship game. Soldier Field has been the home of the BEARS since 1971. In 2003 a controversial new 66,944-seat edifice was completed inside (and rising above) the old colonnades at a cost of $632 million.

Steven A. Riess

See also: Architecture: The City Beautiful; Creation of Chicago Sports; Leisure; Places of Assembly

Further reading: Duis, Perry, and Glen Holt. "The Classic Problem of Soldier Field." *Chicago Magazine* 27 (April 1978): 170–173. • Martin, Andrew, Liam Ford, and Laurie Cohen. "Bears Play, Public Pays; Soldier Field Tab Higher; Less Parkland and Revenue." *Chicago Tribune,* April 24, 2002.

Somalis. Although Somalis have been coming to Chicago as REFUGEES since the 1970s, and ethnic networks among the estimated 300 immigrants were reported to be strong at the twentieth century's end, there has been no formal organization that represents the whole community. This is due, in part, to the intense ethnic and clan divisions that followed refugees from the Somali civil war, which began in 1988. The United States' Operation Restore Hope in 1992 resulted in a wave of refugees to Chicago, mostly ethnic rebels seeking asylum from political persecution, while those connected with Somalia's governing regime went to Washington DC. Scholars and community leaders claim that some attempts at community organization were made at this time, but the intensity of clan and political conflict made consensus difficult. Nonetheless, in the late 1990s many Somalis of different ethnic affiliations lived in close proximity to one another on Chicago's Northwest Side, in the ALBANY PARK neighborhood along Kedzie Avenue.

Tracy N. Poe

See also: Demography

Soul Music. *See* Rhythm and Blues

South Africans. The first South Africans to migrate to Chicago were primarily academics and doctors in the 1960s. They established a network to recruit professionals in medicine and related fields which lasted several decades and attracted hundreds of professionals to Chicago. South African migration to Chicago increased in the 1970s as opposition to apartheid policies grew more violent, prompting many white South Africans to leave in fear or protest. A major surge of emigration occurred after the 1976 Soweto student uprising in particular, including a large group of JEWISH South Africans who established a community in the northern suburbs of Chicago and attracted others to the area. Small numbers of black students and political REFUGEES migrated, but emigration policies under apartheid made it difficult for most to leave; political refugees generally had to first move to other African nations. Migration continued throughout the 1980s and 1990s as South Africans left for political reasons, to reunite with families, and for professional opportunities. It peaked around the election of 1994, when large numbers of white South Africans, particularly Afrikaners, migrated for fear of changes that would occur as a result of the transfer of political power to the black majority. According to community estimates in 2001, Chicago's South African population boasted 2,000 to 3,000 people drawn from diverse ethnic groups and backgrounds and spread throughout the city and suburbs.

The South African community in Chicago comprises different groups and organizations that foster cultural awareness and promote community. Indaba, which means "discussion" in Zulu, is a major organization in this community. Established in the early 1990s, Indaba sponsors a number of community events and activities each year, including an annual summer *braai,* or barbeque. In addition, Indaba facilitates information exchange through a Web site and e-mail list, keeping South Africans abreast of both international and local issues and events. The South African consulate in Chicago maintains contact with many expatriates and hosts an annual Freedom Day party on April 27 as well as other events and speakers throughout the year. In addition, graduates from the University of Witwatersrand in Johannesburg have opened a Chicago alumni chapter which hosts events for members. In 2001, the South African United States Women's Action Group was created to promote awareness and understanding about South Africa among Americans. South Africans also meet in many other forums, including informal parties, religious worship and activities, rugby matches, and holidays.

South Africans have also created many ties with the city of Chicago in the interests of furthering business, educational, and cultural exchange between South Africa and the Midwest. The United States Midwest and South African Chamber of Commerce, formed in 2000 by American and South African businessmen working with the South African consulate in Chicago, aims to increase awareness and exchange between the areas. In addition, the Chicago Sister Cities International Program maintains an official relationship with Durban, South Africa.

Tracy Steffes

See also: Americanization; Demography; Multicentered Chicago; Zimbabweans

South Barrington, IL, Cook County, 30 miles NW of the Loop. A myriad of contrasts typifies the nature of South Barrington. Its southern edge bustles with corporate activity, while to the north estate-sized homes sit on sprawling acreage. Its diversity is reflected in the old farm buildings that have been converted to house the headquarters of a meat-processing company and a restaurant. Down the road on Illinois Highway 72, a large fiberglass pumpkin atop a silo greets visitors at Goebbert's Pumpkin and Farm Market. The community also has the distinction of having one of the largest nondenominational churches in the country.

Into the 1950s the area was still agricultural. In 1959 a group of property owners sought to form a village called Barrington Countryside in order to change ZONING laws to allow for quarter-acre lots. Other residents, including William Rose, who in 1957 moved his family onto farm property on Mundhank Road, fought the move. Within three days they had the necessary papers to incorporate as the village of South Barrington ahead of the other group. Later, zoning laws that the founders fought to maintain were changed, allowing for new minimum lot sizes of one and a half acres.

Following incorporation, Rose founded the Barrington Construction Company and bought up farm properties to build three SUBDIVISIONS: Sunset Ridge Farms, the Cove, and the Glen. In 1973 he purchased 17 acres on Barrington Road near the Northwest TOLL ROAD. The building on the property became the corporate offices for the Rose Packing Company, located in Chicago. Over the years Rose used farm buildings for the Millrose Brewing Company, which houses a RESTAURANT and a country store.

In the 1960s HOFFMAN ESTATES began annexing land adjacent to South Barrington. The two villages have continued ANNEXATION battles for land in the corridor along the Northwest Tollway.

A parcel of land in South Barrington was donated to the Audubon Society of Chicago by Alexander Stillman in 1976. The 80-acre Stillman Nature Center, a prairie preserve, is in tune with South Barrington's desire to maintain a tranquil setting amidst the commercial concerns growing up beside them. The village also has 45 private lakes and ponds.

In 2000 South Barrington's population stood at 3,760, with the village covering about seven square miles. Adding a different dimension to the region is WILLOW CREEK COMMUNITY CHURCH, an interdenominational church built in 1981 at the southeast corner of Barrington and Algonquin Roads. Weekend attendance grew to over 17,000 by 2000. A 30-screen theater complex went up on the northwest corner of Barrington Road at the Northwest Tollway in 1998.

Marilyn Elizabeth Perry

See also: Land Use; Plant Communities

Further reading: League of Women Voters of the Barrington Area, Illinois. *In and Around Barrington.* 1990. • Rose, William. *The Corridors of Time.* December 1984.

South Chicago, Community Area 46, 10 miles SE of the Loop. Situated at the mouth of the CALUMET RIVER, South Chicago first evolved as a rural settlement for fishermen and farmers. In 1833, speculators began buying up land, projecting that the area would become developed because it would connect outside shipping routes. The town was first named Ainsworth. Settlers included IRISH Catholics, who established St. Patrick's parish in 1857. South Chicago's location at the intersection of river and RAILROAD TRANSPORTATION routes fostered early growth.

Following the Great FIRE OF 1871, industry migrated south from Chicago proper. SWEDES, SCOTS, WELSH, and GERMANS provided skilled labor for the flourishing steel, grain, railroad, and LUMBER industries. The Brown IRON AND STEEL Company opened its doors on the Calumet in 1875, followed by the South Works of North Chicago Rolling Mill Company in 1880. A commercial area serving the growing number of workers developed around South Works at Commercial Avenue and 92nd Street. South Works provided the steel that fortified many of the city's landmarks, such as the Sears Tower and McCormick Place.

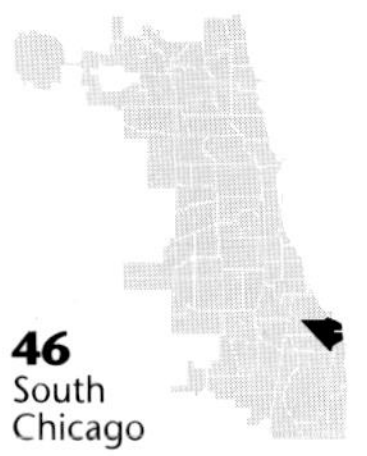

A part of the Township of HYDE PARK, South Chicago was annexed to Chicago in 1889. At the time of ANNEXATION, half of the area's residents had been born outside the country.

In 1901 the U.S. Steel Corporation acquired South Works. POLES, ITALIANS, AFRICAN AMERICANS, and MEXICANS entered the area before and after WORLD WAR I. African Americans tended to WORK as stevedores and, were generally segregated in small residential neighborhoods, including the oldest housing at the mouth of the river. A trend of ethnic succession developed: older, more established groups tended to migrate across the river to the better neighborhoods on the East Side, while newer groups settled in the original mill neighborhoods. One of these was known as the Bush. Bathed in the soot of the steel furnaces, the neighborhood became notorious throughout Chicago for its poor environmental and economic conditions. Workers in South Chicago established complex social bonds built on ethnic ties and work groups. The ROMAN CATHOLIC Church, the DEMOCRATIC PARTY precinct organizations, and later, the United Steelworkers International Union of America helped bridge the ethnic divisions.

In 1919 a major STRIKE against U.S. Steel erupted, involving some 365,000 workers nationwide. Though the strike proved unsuccessful, it drew recent, unskilled immigrants into union activities. Mexicans were first hired as strikebreakers in 1919, eventually becoming one of the largest, most stable Latino communities in the Midwest.

The GREAT DEPRESSION era witnessed intense battles over worker efforts to unionize. At South Works, union activists led by George Patterson captured the company-sponsored employee representation plan, and in 1937 won company recognition of the Steel Workers Organizing Committee as an independent bargaining representative. SWOC became the United Steelworkers International Union of America (USWA) in 1942. USWA Local 65, with headquarters on South Commercial Ave., emerged as one of the community's key power bases and played a role in larger civic affairs.

After WORLD WAR II, refugees from SERBIA and CROATIA came to South Chicago, and its racial and ethnic composition began to shift as the descendants of earlier European immigrants left for the south suburbs. By the 1980s, African Americans constituted almost half of the population, and Latinos, many recent immigrants from Mexico, nearly 40 percent. Concurrently, South Works endured a prolonged shutdown of its facilities. Though the union attempted to restore the mill's economic viability by agreeing to many concessions, USX, successor to U.S. Steel, closed South Works in April 1992, preferring to concentrate production at its larger, nearby Gary Works.

South Works' decline damaged local businesses. The South Chicago community reached out to city leaders to support redevelopment schemes, including a new airport, a plan to host the summer Olympics, and new enterprise zones, all without ultimate success. In 1998 urban planners began a new study of the area's potential for redevelopment. In 2002 the Solo Cup Company began construction of a new facility on the southern portion of the former South Works plant.

David Bensman

See also: Contested Spaces; Economic Geography; Iron- and Steelworkers; Unemployment

Further reading: Bensman, David, and Roberta Lynch. *Rusted Dreams: Hard Times in a Steel Community.* 1988. • Pacyga, Dominic A., and Ellen Skerrett. *Chicago, City of Neighborhoods: Histories and Tours.* 1986. • Squires, Gregory D., et al. *Chicago: Race, Class, and the Responses to Urban Decline.* 1987.

South Chicago Heights, IL, Cook County, 28 miles S of the Loop. Near the southern edge of COOK COUNTY, this small town grew around the intersection of the Sauk and Hubbard's Trails. Both had existed for hundreds of years as major routes for native peoples and early traders. The Sauk Trail ran from Detroit to the Mississippi River, and the Hubbard's Trail, from Vincennes, Indiana, to Chicago.

In 1833, Adam and Phoebe Brown, from Ohio, settled here with their young son Christopher. They eventually had nine children and operated a general store and inn on the northwest corner of the intersection of the two trails. The intersection remained in family hands for 70 years. Local traditions suggest that Brown's Corner was a stop on the UNDERGROUND RAILROAD.

Brown's Corner remained well known. By the end of the nineteenth century, the trails were wagon and coach roads, with Hubbard's Trail now better known as Chicago Road. In 1906, the Browns sold their inn to the Burgel family, who maintained it until 1968.

In 1907, residents in the immediate area joined with commercial interests around the old intersection and, meeting in the depot of the Chicago & Eastern Illinois RAILROAD, voted to become the village of South Chicago Heights. The first year's budget was $3,800, which was met by property taxes and three SALOON licenses at $500 each.

By 1910, the village had its own volunteer fire department and its first policeman. From 1913 into 1928, the original route of the Lincoln Highway came into the village from the east on Sauk Trail and then north on Chicago Road. The section along Chicago Road also was designated as part of the Dixie Highway in 1915. In 1926, this became Illinois State Route One.

This famous intersection had four GAS STATIONS, including the first in the region to sell "Gasolene." The last of the four replaced the old inn demolished in 1968. This was the "landmark" service station, which is now gone, along with the other three.

The village is landlocked, with CHICAGO HEIGHTS to the north and east, STEGER to the south, and FOREST PRESERVE land to the west. Housing is predominantly for workers in nearby business and industries, with the neighborhoods originally home for those of ITALIAN, POLISH, and GERMAN ancestry who worked in Chicago Heights. Today there is an area of newer, more expensive housing adjacent to the forest preserve land and strip commercial properties developed along Chicago Road. In response to a now aging population, the village has an attractive senior center.

Larry A. McClellan

See also: Streets and Highways; Transportation

Further reading: *90 Years of Growth and Development: Village of South Chicago Heights, Illinois.* 1997. • *The Past to the Present: 75 Years of Progress, 1907–1982.* 1982. • *The Past to the Present: Village of South Chicago Heights, Illinois.* 1976.

South Deering, Community Area 51, 13 miles SE of the Loop. South of 95th Street and west of the CALUMET RIVER, South Deering's development rested on steel. Following improvements by the federal government and the Calumet Canal and Dock Company, the Joseph H. Brown IRON AND STEEL Company located here in 1875. The surrounding settlement of steelworkers became known as Irondale. In 1903, community leaders renamed the area South Deering.

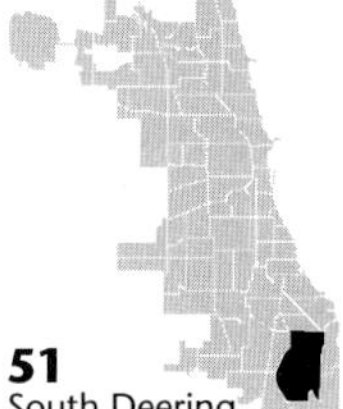

IRISH, WELSH, and ENGLISH workers arrived first, followed by SWEDES and GERMANS. Irondale was initially PROTESTANT; Irish ROMAN CATHOLICS worshiped in nearby SOUTH CHICAGO. After 1900, new settlers arrived from Eastern and Southern Europe, and MEXICANS came following WORLD WAR I. Founded by Irish workers at 105th and Torrence, St. Kevin's Roman Catholic Church developed as an ethnically diverse congregation.

International Harvester, an AGRICULTURAL MACHINERY manufacturer, acquired Brown's mill in 1902 and then announced the construction of a new facility, Wisconsin Steel, to produce steel for its tractors and combines. Gold Medal Flour Company, Illinois Slag and Ballast Company, and the Federal Furnace Company also opened here. As the local economy boomed, a number of improvement campaigns were launched, including the construction of Trumbull Park at 103rd Street and Yates.

New neighborhoods, including the Trumbull Park Homes and the Manors, were constructed in the 1930s and 1940s. Labor shortages during WORLD WAR II opened new opportunities for women in the workforce.

In 1953, an AFRICAN AMERICAN family moved into the Trumbull Park homes, sparking a decade-long period of violence and protest by white residents. African Americans had been working in the mill for some time in less desirable jobs, but they did not live in South Deering. CIVIL RIGHTS legislation in the 1960s banning discrimination in hiring and segregation in housing slowly brought African Americans better jobs and access to area housing.

In exchange for the workers' loyalty, Wisconsin Steel provided services such as supplying coal and electricity to local churches. Because most of Wisconsin Steel's production went to Harvester, rather than to the open market, management did not push production as much as at neighboring mills. When the Steel Workers Organizing Committee began to organize South Chicago mills in 1936, they faced difficulties at the paternalistic Harvester mill. Workers there voted to establish their own independent organization, the Progressive Steelworkers Union (PSWU), rather than affiliate with SWOC. In the 1960s and 1970s, the union's leadership enjoyed close relationships with both management and with the leader of the local DEMOCRATIC organization, Edward Vrdolyak.

Following a series of bad financial decisions, International Harvester stopped investing in Wisconsin Steel in 1969. Because closing the mill would have necessitated payment of large unfunded pension liabilities and shutdown benefits, Harvester sold the mill to EDC Holding Company, an assetless subsidiary of Envirodyne Industries, in 1977. The Progressive Steelworkers Union signed an agreement with Harvester releasing the company from all nonpension contractual benefits. When Envirodyne shut the mill without notice in March 1980, workers lost all benefits that were not covered by the Pension Benefit Guarantee Corporation. It appeared that Harvester had succeeded in avoiding $85 million in liabilities.

The community responded to its economic devastation in a variety of ways. At first they turned to traditional points of leverage in the Southeast Side: the churches, local politicians, and union officials of the steel communities. But as the UNEMPLOYMENT crisis intensified, people also turned to COMMUNITY ORGANIZING. New groups such as the UNITED NEIGHBORHOOD ORGANIZATION and the Save Our Jobs Committee emerged. The SOJC, led by Frank Lumpkin, a former Wisconsin Steel worker, filed a class-action lawsuit against IH (renamed Navistar) to recover the benefits surrendered by the PSWU contract. In 1988, Harvester settled the suit by agreeing to pay $14.8 million. While the settlement brought some satisfaction, it did not reverse South Deering's decline. Hundreds of families left, seeking jobs in Texas, Arizona, and California, or retiring to Mexico.

David Bensman

See also: Contested Spaces; Economic Geography; Hegewisch; Neighborhood Succession; Racism, Ethnicity, and White Identity; Work

Further reading: Bensman, David, and Roberta Lynch. *Rusted Dreams: Hard Times in a Steel Community.* 1988. • Pacyga, Dominic A., and Ellen Skerrett. *Chicago, City of Neighborhoods: Histories and Tours.* 1986. • Squires, Gregory D., et al., *Chicago: Race, Class, and the Responses to Urban Decline.* 1987.

South Elgin, IL, Kane County, 37 miles W of the Loop. Built around a gristmill dam on the FOX RIVER in 1847 and known as Clintonville, the community grew slowly. Following the establishment of the Elgin State HOSPITAL just north, the community incorporated as South Elgin in 1897. Rapid growth as a bedroom

community to ELGIN brought the community's population to 16,100 in 2000.

Craig L. Pfannkuche

See also: Kane County

Further reading: Alft, E. C. *South Elgin: A History of the Village from Its Origin as Clintonville.* 1979. • Tredup, Ralph. *South Elgin: 150 Years of Heritage, 1835–1985.* 1989.

South Holland, IL, Cook County, 20 miles S of the Loop. South Holland evolved from a nineteenth-century agricultural community of DUTCH immigrants into a twentieth-century COMMUTER suburb. Founded in 1846 and incorporated as a village in 1894, the community retained much of its ethnic and AGRICULTURAL heritage for over one hundred years. As farmlands were converted to housing developments and industrial parks, and as the population grew larger and more diverse, South Holland assumed a new role as a racially and ethnically diverse residential suburb.

The community began as an enclave of Dutch farmers. Attracted to the flat stretches of prairie in the CALUMET REGION, these settlers at first pursued self-sufficient farming, then soon moved into market gardening, supplying the burgeoning city of Chicago with fresh produce. In 1892, Dutch and GERMAN farmers began raising onion sets (small bulb onions ready for planting), and came to dominate the commercial production and distribution of this crop. Their efforts earned for South Holland the title "Onion Set Capital of the World." This crop and truck farming provided the economic base for the community through the 1940s. Though diminishing in importance after this point, agriculture continued to provide income for Dutch farmers and MEXICAN migrant workers into the 1960s.

The cover of a local history of South Holland, showing the transition from Dutch farmers to suburbanites. Designer: Unknown. Source: The Newberry Library.

Two faces of agriculture in South Holland. The Paarlberg house reflects the economic success achieved by many early settlers who owned and worked their own farms. The Mexican migrant worker's home demonstrates the shift to itinerant and seasonal labor recruited from outside the community. Photographers: Unknown. Source: The Newberry Library.

After WORLD WAR II, South Holland's role in the metropolitan system began to change. Chicagoans hoping to escape the troubles of urban life and developers wanting to satisfy their housing needs found the suburb a desirable location. Once again the open lands proved attractive as farms and farmers gave way to SUBDIVISIONS and families. Interstate Highways 57 and 94, which made the downtown easily accessible, further encouraged the transformation. The final assault on agriculture came as the local government turned to industrial parks as a tax base.

Though developers and former city dwellers altered the rural economy of South Holland, they did little to change the conservative character given to the community by its Dutch founders. Blue laws prohibiting certain businesses from opening on Sundays (first introduced in 1959), a ban on liquor sales, and ZONING restrictions that disallow APARTMENT buildings and CONDOMINIUMS have all helped to shape and maintain a religious, family-oriented lifestyle. This conservatism was most notably challenged in 1969 when elementary School District 151, a part of which resided in South Holland, was ordered by federal authorities to desegregate, the first school district in the north to be ordered to do so. Though the order roused some protest from South Hollanders, the issue passed without violence. The school district integrated later that year.

No longer reliant on agriculture and no longer predominantly Dutch, South Holland nevertheless holds onto its ethnic past. Tulip festivals capitalize on it and Dutch-denominated churches remind us of it.

Jonathan J. Keyes

See also: Contested Spaces; Expressways; Local Option; Prohibition and Temperance; School Desegregation; Sunday Closings

Further reading: Cook, Richard A. *A History of South Holland, Illinois [1846–1966].* 1966. • Hahn, Arvin William. *The South Holland Onion Set Industry.* 1952. • *South Holland, Illinois: Seventy-fifth Anniversary, 1894–1969.* 1969.

South Lawndale, Community Area 30, 5 miles SW of the Loop. "Bienvenidos a Little Village." Traveling under an arch stretching powerfully over 26th Street while heading west at Albany Avenue, a visitor is immediately aware that he or she has entered the MEXICAN and Mexican American enclave of LITTLE VILLAGE, *La Villita.* Situated between the Stevenson EXPRESSWAY at its southern limits and stretching roughly along Cermak Road to the north, with Western Avenue and Cicero as its east to west boundaries, South Lawndale was settled first in the aftermath of the FIRE OF 1871 by GERMANS and CZECHS (Bohemians). Successive groups such as POLES, and now Hispanics, have followed to take advantage of employment opportunities in nearby industry.

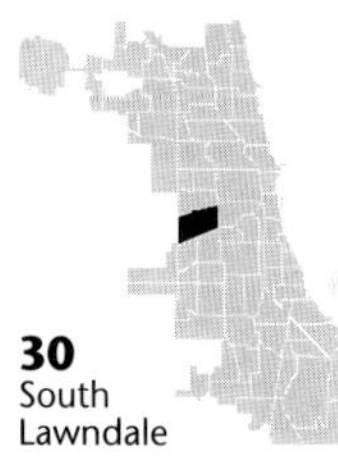

This blue-collar community area has experienced major economic dislocations since the late 1960s, with the closure of the huge International Harvester plant in the southeast quadrant and the Western Electric complex along its western boundary. The 1990 census recorded a disastrous unemployment rate of 14 percent. Residents have seen jobs disappear in the high-wage industrial sector, so they have sought employment in the service and public sectors. Job training for the economy of the twenty-first century is offered at the West Side Technical Institute, part of the City COLLEGES of Chicago.

By 2000, 91,071 people made their home in the area. Eighty-three percent were Hispanic, and nearly half were foreign-born. This represented an appreciable increase in South

Lawndale's Hispanic population, from 47 percent in 1980 and 4 percent in 1970. As the Hispanic population expanded, ethnic white neighborhoods disappeared as those residents migrated farther west out of the city. Over the last several decades, 40 percent of the total population has been under 20 years of age. With this youthful population, the local public SCHOOLS have been filled to capacity, and overcrowding has been exacerbated by the financial collapse of parochial schools.

The housing stock dates primarily to the period before WORLD WAR I. Only 5 percent of the 20,000 housing units standing in 1990 were less than 20 years old. However, commercial revitalization has begun to drive property values higher, with more than 1,600 businesses located along 22nd and 26th Streets. The median home value in 2000 was $105,000, compared to slightly less than $50,000 in 1990. Rental properties that averaged $360 per month in 1990 increased at least 50 percent in the following decade. While not a middle-class community, Little Village has struggled to remain affordable to the working families who attend half a dozen ROMAN CATHOLIC churches and sustain a thriving commercial life on 26th Street, or Calle Mexico, where a variety of restaurants, shops, and BANKING institutions provide services. The community also struggles to counterbalance the effects of GANG activity.

With more than five thousand inmates, the Cook County JAIL and the city of Chicago's House of Corrections add many non-Hispanics to the area's overall demographic profile. The Hispanic community has struggled for community-based political representation at least since the 1970s. By the end of the twentieth century, Latinos represented the community in the City Council, the Cook County Board, the Illinois General Assembly, and the U.S. Congress.

Christopher R. Reed

See also: Agricultural Machinery Industry; Court System; Economic Geography; Electronics; Political Culture; Schooling for Work

Further reading: Chicago Fact Book Consortium, ed. *Local Community Fact Books: Chicago Metropolitan Area.* For the years 1990, 1980, 1960, 1950, and 1938. • Little Village Chamber of Commerce. 1999 Business Directory.

South Loop, neighborhood in the NEAR SOUTH SIDE Community Area. The South Loop was one of Chicago's first residential districts, which recent redevelopment has again transformed into a residential neighborhood.

Working-class immigrants, primarily IRISH, initially settled south of the young city near the river while the well-to-do built houses along Michigan and Wabash Avenues. RAILROADS entering Chicago in the 1850s established passenger stations and freight houses at the southern edge of the business district. The Chicago FIRE OF 1871 spared the area, but displaced LOOP businesses found temporary quarters there. Another fire, in 1874, ended the area's remaining residential character.

By 1900, railroad tracks filled the area from State Street to Clinton Street, serving freight depots and passenger stations—Central, Dearborn, LaSalle Street, and Grand Central—that marked the southern edge of the central business district. An infamous VICE DISTRICT flourished around the stations, including the brothels mapped in *If Christ Came to Chicago* (1894). As Chicago became the nation's PRINTING center, high loft buildings filled the narrow blocks near Dearborn Station, convenient both for printing salesmen and express shipments.

The decline of passenger trains left the rail yards vacant, while changes in the printing industry had emptied out PRINTERS' ROW. The 1973 Chicago 21 Plan reflected BUSINESS leaders' worries about the derelict South Loop and called for construction of an urban new town there.

Downtown businessmen organized a corporation to build such a community, on 51 acres of Dearborn Station rail yards, and residents moved into DEARBORN PARK in 1979. Middle-class residents were attracted to an integrated neighborhood in the heart of the city, and a second phase was built south of Roosevelt Road after 1988.

Pioneering architects and developers had recognized the potential of loft buildings on Printers' Row, and those were converted to APARTMENTS as Dearborn Park was being built. Redevelopment spread west to the river when River City opened in 1985, and then east and south with residential conversions along Wabash and Michigan Avenues. In 1992 construction began on Central Station, a 72-acre redevelopment project on former ILLINOIS CENTRAL rail yards east of Michigan Avenue south of Roosevelt Road.

Dennis McClendon

See also: Gentrification; Metropolitan Growth; Near South Side; Neighborhood Succession; Railroad Stations; Urban Renewal

Further reading: Cassidy, Robert. "Laying the Groundwork for Chicago's New-Town-in-Town." *Planning* (August 1977). • Wille, Lois. *At Home in the Loop: How Clout and Community Built Chicago's Dearborn Park.* 1997.

South Shore, Community Area 43, 9 miles SE of the Loop. A 1939 description of South Shore stating that it was "predominately middle class—upper middle class, to be sure, but not social register," offers an apt though antiquated characterization of this SOUTH SIDE community. Though the class gap among its residents has at times run quite wide, for most of its history South Shore has been a solidly middle-class enclave. The area, bounded by 67th and 79th Streets to the north and south and by Stony Island Avenue and Lake Michigan to the east and west, was mostly swampland in the 1850s when Ferdinand Rohn, a GERMAN truck farmer, utilized trails along the area's high ground to transport his goods to Chicago.

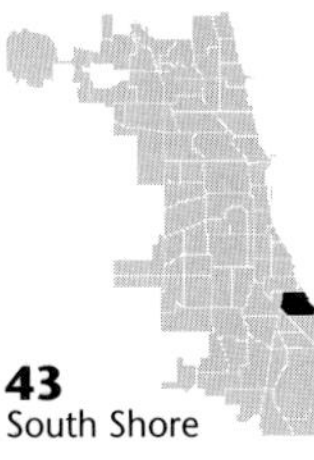

Before the community came to be known as South Shore in the 1920s, it was a collection of settlements in southern HYDE PARK TOWNSHIP. The names of these settlements—Essex, Bryn Mawr, Parkside, Cheltenham Beach, and Windsor Park—indicate the British heritage of the ILLINOIS CENTRAL RAILROAD and steel mill workers who had come to inhabit them. Most of these settlements were already in place when the Illinois Central built the South Kenwood Station in 1881 at what is now 71st and Jeffrey Boulevard.

As with many SOUTH SIDE Chicago communities, the two events that sparked commercial and residential development were ANNEXATION to Chicago in 1889 and the WORLD'S COLUMBIAN EXPOSITION in 1893. The location of the fair in nearby JACKSON PARK prompted the sale of land and building lots and subsequently housing explosion. White PROTESTANTS fled neighboring WASHINGTON PARK as immigrants and AFRICAN AMERICANS moved there. In 1905 these former residents of Washington Park built Jackson Park Highlands, an exclusive residential community ensconced within South Shore. In 1906 they established the South Shore Country Club, a posh 67-acre lakeside playground, which excluded blacks and JEWS.

A housing boom in the 1920s generated not only a large increase in the area's population, but also greater diversity among its residents and in housing stock. Between 1920 and 1930 the population of South Shore jumped from 31,832 to 78,755. Many of these new residents were IRISH, SWEDISH, German, or Jewish and had followed native white Protestants from WASHINGTON PARK to live in South Shore's high-rises, single-family homes, and apartment houses. Institutions built in South Shore during these years reflected the community's growing diversity. By 1940 South Shore contained 15 Protestant churches, 4 ROMAN CATHOLIC churches, and 4 Jewish synagogues.

As African American families moved to South Shore in the 1950s, white residents became concerned about the neighborhood's stability. The South Shore Commission initiated a program they called "managed integration," designed to check the physical decline of the community and to achieve racial balance. The initiative was largely unsuccessful on both counts. Although residential and commercial decline did coincide with an increase in the African American population (69 percent by 1970 and 95 percent by 1980), it had more to do with real-estate "REDLINING" and commercial

Golfers at South Shore Country Club, 1908. Photographer: Unknown. Source: Chicago Historical Society.

disinvestment. In the early 1970s, a collaboration between the Renewal Effort Service Corporation (RESCORP) and the Illinois Housing Development Authority resulted in two rehabilitation programs called "New Vistas." When in 1973 the South Shore Bank attempted to relocate to the Loop, the federal Comptroller of the Currency denied their petition to move under pressure from local activists. These local activists became the new management of the bank in 1973. The bank's reinvestment in South Shore led to both residential and commercial revitalization.

By the late 1990s South Shore had reemerged as a solidly middle-class African American community. Although the commercial strips on 71st and 75th still struggled, developers built a shopping plaza at 71st and Jeffrey. The cultural life of the area has been enhanced since the Park District purchased the waning South Shore Country Club in 1972, converting it into a cultural center. The New REGAL THEATER opened in 1987 on 79th Street and remained open until 2003. Perhaps still not "social register," South Shore remained a choice destination for those desiring a congenial middle-class community on Chicago's South Side.

Wallace Best

See also: Community Organizing; Multicentered Chicago; Neighborhood Succession; Suburbs and Cities as Dual Metropolis

Further reading: "The South Shore Commission Plan: A Comprehensive Plan for Present and Future by the Residents of South Shore." Municipal Library of Chicago, 1967. • Chicago Fact Book Consortium, ed. *Local Community Fact Book: Chicago Metropolitan Area, 1990*. 1995. • Pacyga, Dominic A., and Ellen Skerrett. "South Shore." In *Chicago, City of Neighborhoods: Histories and Tours*, 1986.

South Side. The boundaries of Chicago's South Side have shifted over time and varied according to the diverse spatial and cultural perspectives that influence how Chicagoans label sections of the city. To a considerable extent the section is a state of mind: the South Side is that part of the city that houses people who consider themselves South Siders. To the east, LAKE MICHIGAN and the Indiana state line have provided enduring points of demarcation. Roosevelt Road (12th Street) provides a stable northern border. Chicago's expanding city limits have provided a dynamic, but readily identifiable southern boundary. The greatest uncertainty lies along the western edge, in part because neither a natural nor even an artificial dividing line provides a meaningful marker. A contemporary perspective informed by historical circumstances points to the railroad tracks just east of Western Avenue, a marker that would have to be bent to accommodate a few blocks of westward drift to take in the BEVERLY and MORGAN PARK Community Areas.

Chicago South Side has long had a distinct identity. Often identified in the second half of the twentieth century with the city's AFRICAN AMERICAN population, it has actually accommodated remarkable diversity.

The South Side boasts its own major league BASEBALL team, the Chicago WHITE SOX, and once provided a home to the Chicago AMERICAN GIANTS of the Negro National Leagues and the CARDINALS of the National Football League. It long has served as the location for much of the city's convention business, first with the Chicago Coliseum and the INTERNATIONAL AMPHITHEATER, and later with the massive McCormick Place exhibition complex. The South Side has also provided a fertile site for creative energy, from the fiction of Upton Sinclair, James T. Farrell, and Richard Wright to the POETRY of Gwendolyn Brooks, the paintings of Archibald Motley, Jr., the sculpture of Lorado Taft and Henry Moore, the GOSPEL music of Thomas A. Dorsey and Mahalia Jackson, the BLUES of Muddy Waters.

Neighborhoods developed south of the Loop as early as the 1850s. After the Great FIRE OF 1871, the South Side expanded quickly as both the rich and the poor left the city's center.

The late 1860s and 1870s also saw the movement of industry away from the Loop. In 1865 the UNION STOCK YARD opened in LAKE TOWNSHIP, south and west of downtown Chicago. The PULLMAN Palace Car Company brought its plant and model city to HYDE PARK TOWNSHIP in 1880. One year later Illinois Steel began operations at its massive South Works in SOUTH CHICAGO, also in Hyde Park Township. Chicago ANNEXED both of these townships to the city in 1889, creating much of the South Side in the process.

Development was directly connected to TRANSPORTATION technologies and their expansion. The ILLINOIS CENTRAL RAILROAD opened its first Hyde Park station at 51st and Lake Park Avenue in 1856. The expansion of horse-drawn streetcars and later cable cars (1880s) and electric trolleys (1890s) proved to be a boon to developers. From 1890 to 1892, the South Side "Alley L" began to make its way south from the Loop to JACKSON PARK in time for the WORLD'S COLUMBIAN EXPOSITION (1893).

The pattern of affluent residents moving outward from the central city was set early in Chicago's history. Wealthy white PROTESTANTS originally lived in the southeast quadrant of the Loop, but moved south along the lakefront, leaving behind an area increasingly devoted to industry, WHOLESALING, and the expanding VICE DISTRICT. The upper crust settled along PRAIRIE AVENUE. By the 1870s and 1880s, elegant houses lined Prairie Avenue from 16th Street to 22nd Street (Cermak Road). Other prosperous residential districts developed farther south in KENWOOD and HYDE PARK. Hyde Park was especially transformed by the Columbian Exposition and by the opening in 1892 of the UNIVERSITY OF CHICAGO along the Midway Plaisance just west of Frederick Law Olmsted's Jackson Park.

American-born, white, middle-class families also pushed south along the boulevards, populating large sections of the NEAR SOUTH SIDE, DOUGLAS, and GRAND BOULEVARD COMMUNITY AREAS. They were soon joined by other groups, especially middle-class IRISH ROMAN CATHOLICS and German JEWS. The Irish founded the parish of St. James on 26th and Wabash Avenue in 1855. In 1889 the Christian Brothers established De La Salle Institute at 35th Street and Wabash Avenue in the Douglas Community Area. Among its graduates are five Chicago MAYORS.

German Jews also came to Douglas. In 1881 Michael Reese HOSPITAL opened its doors at 29th Street and Cottage Grove. In 1889 the Standard CLUB, an elite Jewish men's organization, moved to 24th and Michigan Avenue. Kehilath Anshe Mayriv (KAM) Synagogue moved in 1890 to 33rd and Indiana Avenue.

Other European ethnic groups also made their way to the South Side. GERMAN Catholics and Protestants spread across the area. Working-class Irish communities appeared in BRIDGEPORT, CANARYVILLE, and BACK OF THE YARDS. After 1880, large numbers of POLES,

Chicago's Prairie Avenue Elite in 1886

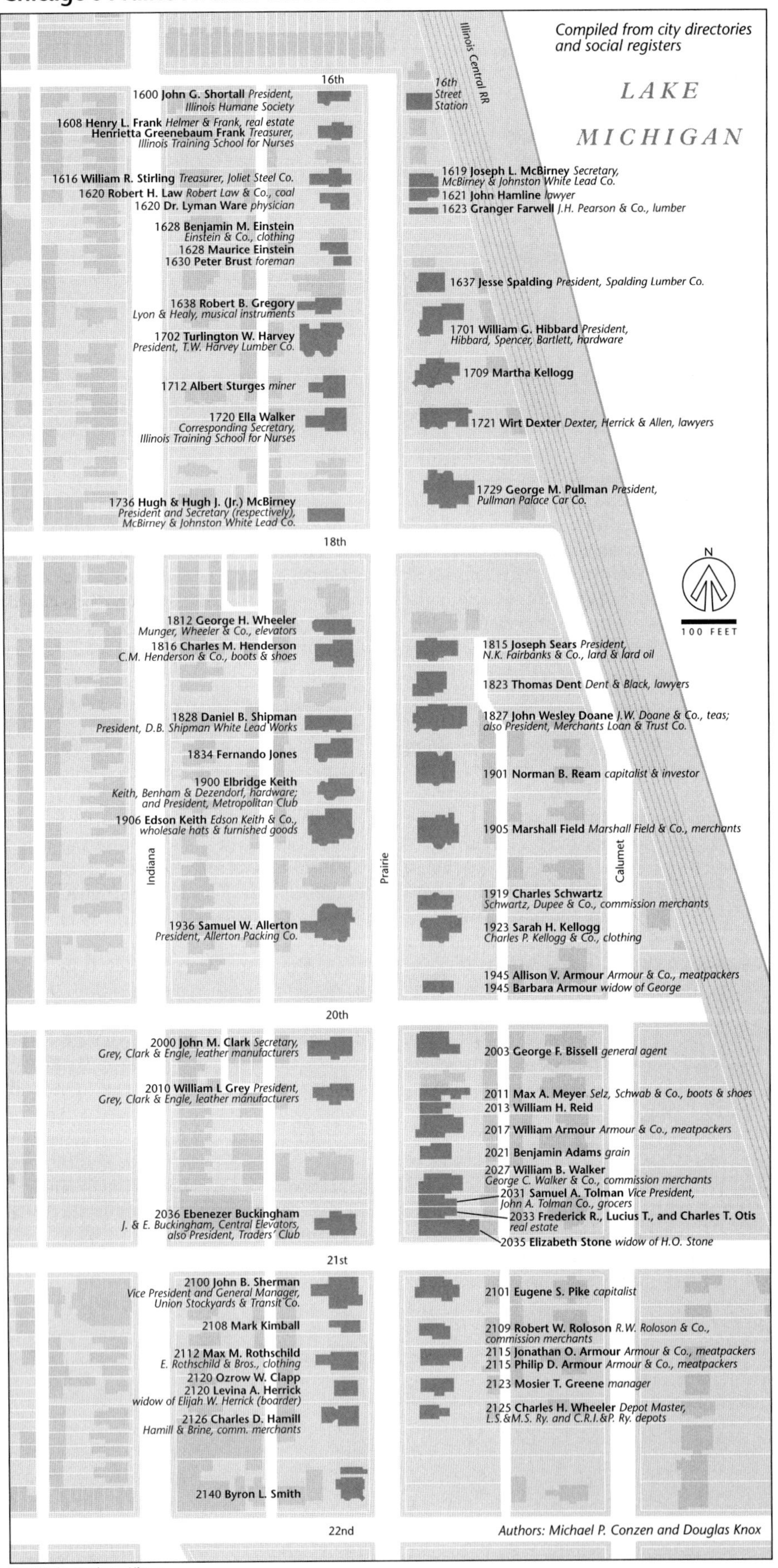

LITHUANIANS, CZECHS, SLOVAKS, East European Jews, and other immigrants from Southern and Eastern Europe settled near the stockyards. These groups also followed the Irish, Scottish, WELSH, Scandinavians, and GERMANS to South Chicago and SOUTH DEERING near the rapidly expanding steel mills and to other manufacturing centers.

South Side African American residents and institutions date back to the decades preceding the CIVIL WAR, although a concentrated settlement emerged only toward the end of the nineteenth century. More growth took place between World War I and the 1920s, when new employment opportunities in northern industry opened the doors for what came to be known as the GREAT MIGRATION.

Residential segregation, rooted in nineteenth-century patterns, emerged in full force during the war era. With few exceptions, African Americans found themselves confined to a narrow strip south of the Loop between State Street on the east and Wentworth Avenue to the west. White residents moved farther south to WASHINGTON PARK, Hyde Park, and SOUTH SHORE. As population pressures increased, African American families pushed south of 39th Street (Pershing Road) toward Garfield Boulevard (5500 South) into Grand Boulevard and Washington Park, and east across State Street toward Cottage Grove. These predominantly white middle-class neighborhoods that included parts of the Douglas, Grand Boulevard, OAKLAND, Kenwood, and Hyde Park Community Areas resisted black residential encroachments. To the west of the BLACK BELT lay the predominantly

---

Following the destruction of elite villas on South Michigan Avenue in the Great Fire of 1871, the four blocks of Prairie Avenue between 17th and 22nd Streets developed as one of Chicago's finest neighborhoods, attracting many of the city's newly wealthy. By 1886 the district sported some 70 of the region's tycoons in manufacturing, commerce, real estate, law, and finance. At the top of the heap were the families, and homes, of George Pullman, manufacturer of luxury railroad cars; Marshall Field, the department store prince; Philip D. Armour, the meatpacker; and John B. Sherman, vice-president and general manager of the Union Stock Yard. They built commodious homes of ebullient forms, urbane but cheek by jowl in the manner of the day, creating an opulent streetscape that rivaled those of European cities. As the twentieth century dawned, and industry crept closer to the district, Prairie Avenue's social elite became restless and one by one departed for quieter climes, some moving to newer city neighborhoods such as Kenwood and the Gold Coast, but most choosing the low-density suburban havens of the North Shore. In little more than 30 years, Prairie Avenue had risen to the social pinnacle and just as quickly fallen from grace, leaving behind a remarkable architectural legacy no longer valued until it was almost all gone.

Bigger Thomas: A Tale of Two Neighborhoods

Richard Wright came to Chicago in 1927, one of thousands of African AMERICAN MIGRANTS from the South. Living on the South Side, Wright saw first-hand the dramatic racial and class divides which separated blacks and whites. He described this chasm through the eyes of his character Bigger Thomas in *Native Son* (1940). *Native Son* opens with Bigger Thomas awaking to a huge black rat in the single room in DOUGLAS which he shared with his brother, sister, and mother. Later, Bigger journeys south into Kenwood, an all-white affluent neighborhood, in search of work. Bigger chose to carry a knife and gun with him:

> He was going among white people, so he would take his knife and his gun; it would make him feel that he was the equal of them, give him a sense of completeness. Then he thought of a good reason why he should take it; in order to get to the Dalton place, he had to go through a white neighborhood. He had not heard of any Negroes being molested recently, but he felt that it was always possible.

So armed, Bigger Thomas walked south to 46th Street. He saw that the

> houses he passed were huge; lights glowed softly in windows. The streets were empty, save for an occasional car that zoomed past on swift rubber tires. This was a cold and distant world; a world of white secrets carefully guarded.

Richard Wright. *Native Son.* 1940.

white ethnic working-class neighborhoods of Bridgeport, ARMOUR SQUARE, FULLER PARK, Canaryville, and ENGLEWOOD. Here too blacks were not welcome.

As World War I came to a close, social, residential, political, and economic pressures reached a peak. In July 1919, a RACE RIOT broke out resulting in 38 deaths and hundreds of injuries. While rioting took place across the city, most of the injuries and deaths occurred on the South Side where the black and white Chicagoans lived and worked in close proximity.

The 1920s witnessed the development of what is often called the Black Metropolis, or Bronzeville. Centering on the intersections of 35th and State Streets and 47th Street and Grand Boulevard (King Drive), Bronzeville developed as an institutional, social, cultural, and economic center of black urban life. The *Chicago Defender* emerged as spokesman for this community as well as its ambassador to the rest of black America. Large mainline churches such as OLIVET and Pilgrim Baptist and Quinn Chapel African Methodist Episcopal drew thousands of worshipers each Sunday morning. JAZZ clubs, and two decades later blues clubs, provided a musical signature for both the South Side and Chicago as a whole.

The 1920s also saw the further dispersal of the population. White families made their way to the Southwest Side and to outlying parts of the South Side. Chicago's BUNGALOW BELT emerged, forming a wide ring around the city. These single-family free-standing structures modeled on Prairie School ARCHITECTURE were intimately tied to yet another transportation system, the private automobile. During the 1920s well-established ethnic groups, such as the Irish, Scandinavians, and Germans, pushed out of the older core neighborhoods to these newer middle-class and lower-middle-class developments. They were followed in turn by Poles, Lithuanians, and other Eastern and Southern Europeans.

In Back of the Yards, Bridgeport, and South Chicago, the Polish and other East European ethnic communities developed a wide range of social, cultural, and economic institutions including parishes, parochial schools, fraternal organizations, banks, SAVINGS AND LOANS, and other businesses. By the end of the 1920s these European ethnic groups were joined, particularly in South Chicago and Back of the Yards, by MEXICAN immigrants.

After WORLD WAR II, cars and roads opened neighborhoods and suburbs not easily accessible by PUBLIC TRANSPORTATION. The result was a housing explosion on the periphery of the city and in the suburbs. The South Side also saw more residential development on its edges in Jeffery Manor, South Deering, EAST SIDE, and HEGEWISCH. The result was white flight and the expansion of the South Side's African American neighborhoods well beyond the confines of the old Black Metropolis. This process provoked considerable conflict, as race riots broke out across the South Side, most notably in the Trumbull Park Homes in South Deering and in Englewood. Especially after 1960, the South Side witnessed a great expansion of the Mexican community from its base in Back of the Yards, South Chicago, and the West Side's PILSEN neighborhood. Other Hispanics also settled on the South Side, including a small PUERTO RICAN community.

Older South Side neighborhoods, especially the traditional Black Belt, also saw new housing in the 20 years after 1945. This housing was for the most part PUBLIC HOUSING built and administered by the CHICAGO HOUSING AUTHORITY. Dearborn Homes, STATEWAY GARDENS, and ROBERT TAYLOR HOMES replaced much of Federal Street. The new campus of the ILLINOIS INSTITUTE OF TECHNOLOGY (IIT), designed by Ludwig Mies van der Rohe, replaced another part of the old Federal Street slum. Private housing developments also appeared as Prairie Shores and Lake Meadows were constructed in the 1960s along the lakefront south of 26th Street. New and restored housing also appeared in Hyde Park, Kenwood, and Beverly. URBAN RENEWAL took various forms, but the South Side's landscape was most dramatically affected by public housing; institutional expansion in the form of IIT, the University of Chicago, and various hospitals; and the construction of the Dan Ryan and Stevenson EXPRESSWAYS. The new South Side, however remained very familiar to Chicagoans, as it retained its segregated housing patterns and huge pockets of poverty and wealth.

What the South Side could not retain was its industrial base. In the mid-1950s Chicago faced its first postindustrial crisis as the major MEATPACKING companies began to close their production facilities. By 1964 most of the large packers had disappeared. The Union Stock Yard finally closed its doors on August 1, 1971, after nearly 106 years of operation. The late 1970s and early 1980s saw the further decline of the city's industrial base, especially among the steel mills on the Southeast Side. The closing of Wisconsin Steel in 1980 signaled the end of Chicago's dominance of the steel industry. U.S. Steel's South Works closed, after more than a hundred years of operation, in 1993. Empty factories and warehouses symbolized the shift in Chicago's employment base from manufacturing to the service industries.

The South Side, however, has continued to attract investment. By the 1990s over a hundred firms had located at the site of the old Union Stock Yard. This industrial park is the most successful in Chicago even though employment levels remain well below those of the meatpacking industry at its height. A variety of neighborhoods have provided sites for new upscale housing, including DEARBORN PARK (which has expanded from the SOUTH LOOP south of Roosevelt Road), Central Station (along the lakefront south of Roosevelt Road), Bridgeport, Hyde Park, Kenwood, the Gap, and CHATHAM. CHINATOWN has spread beyond its earlier boundary along Archer Avenue with the development of Chinatown Square. In 1991 the Chicago White Sox began to play in a new COMISKEY PARK across the street from the old stadium. With its neighborhoods, parks, museums, and UNIVERSITIES, the South Side continues to play an important role in the social, cultural, political, and economic life of the city.

Dominic A. Pacyga

See also: Contested Spaces; Creation of Chicago Sports; Economic Geography; Iron and Steel; Metropolitan Growth; Neighborhood Succession; Places of Assembly

Further reading: Drake, St. Clair, and Horace R. Cayton. *Black Metropolis: A Study of Negro Life in a Northern City.* 1945. • Holt, Glen, and Dominic Pacyga. *Chicago: A Historical Guide to the Neighborhoods: Loop and South Side.* 1979. • Pacyga, Dominic. *Polish Immigrants and Industrial Chicago: Workers on the South Side, 1880–1922.* 1991.

South Side Community Arts Center. *See* Artists, Education and Culture of

Southerners. Although the GREAT MIGRATION of AFRICAN AMERICANS to the North is generally more widely known, white southerners also left in droves between WORLD WAR I and the 1970s. Chicago and other Midwest locales—both urban and rural—provided destinations for most Appalachian migrants, estimated at approximately 3.2 million between 1940 and 1970.

Like many other American migrants and also like foreign immigrants, white southerners moved partly in response to changes in labor markets. As first World War I and then national policy halted immigration, personnel managers in Chicago eagerly invited upland southerners, who had empty stomachs and pocketbooks but strong backs. Mine operators used their profits from World War II to mechanize, leaving thousands of unemployed and underemployed miners. Harlan County, Kentucky, lost one-third of its population—more than 24,000 people—between 1940 and 1960.

Although migration ebbed and flowed with the health of the economy, white southern newcomers found it easier to find jobs than to forget home. As a result, migrants sojourned for years, frequently refusing, unlike African Americans, to move permanently. Harsh Chicago winters were always difficult, and winter factory slowdowns only clinched the decision to return south frequently. Many migrants who wintered in Chicago returned south in the spring to put in a crop and come back after harvest. In UPTOWN, home to a particularly large community of Appalachian migrants, school attendance among southern migrant children in the 1950s was highest in November and lowest in April.

Perhaps because white southerners were reluctant to view Chicago as a permanent home, some were apparently willing to tolerate what other Chicagoans considered deplorable living conditions. During the 1960s, as a stagnating economy prevented newcomers from passing through port-of-entry communities and into more stable ones as had their predecessors, attention on the "hillbilly problem" increased, especially in Uptown.

Their ambivalence about a permanent move also meant that southern white migrants planted their culture in Chicago only gradually. But over time music and churches sprouted in the North. Taverns in Uptown and in the 3000 block of West Madison Street advertised "LIVE HILLBILLY MUSIC" in neon, while WLS BROADCAST the new music across the airwaves. Meanwhile, other migrants began organizing southern churches in the city. Chicago in 1950 had 9 Southern Baptist Convention churches; nine years later, there were more than 70.

But if southern Appalachian migrants received attention—and scorn—in the media, census data reveal that between 1955 and 1960, almost twice the number of people left western Tennessee than eastern Tennessee, most of them bound for Chicago. Migration was not a hegira from the hills but rather from the upland South.

Census data also demonstrate that white southern migrants to Chicago and other Midwestern destinations enjoyed household incomes that were just slightly less than those of native white Midwesterners. By the 1980s, retiring migrants were faced with another decision, whether to live out the winter of their lives in the North or return to their southern home. For many, the choice was difficult.

Chad Berry

See also: Demography; Multicentered Chicago; Yankees

Further reading: Berry, Chad. *Southern Migrants, Northern Exiles.* 2000. • Borman, Kathryn M., and Phillip J. Obermiller, eds. *From Mountain to Metropolis: Appalachian Migrants in American Cities.* 1994. • Guy, Roger. "Diversity to Unity: Uptown's Southern Migrants, 1950–1970." Ph.D. diss., University of Wisconsin–Milwaukee. 1996.

Spaghetti Bowl. The Circle Interchange, or Spaghetti Bowl, as it was dubbed by radio traffic reporters, was built in stages from 1955 to 1962 to connect three major EXPRESSWAYS west of the Loop—today the Eisenhower, Kennedy, and Dan Ryan. The interchange, a series of expanding concentric circular patterns of ramps, quickly became one of the nation's most heavily used traffic nexuses. The complex also lent its name to the UNIVERSITY OF ILLINOIS campus built nearby, which for a time was known as the Chicago Circle campus.

David M. Young

See also: Commuting; Near West Side; Transportation

Further reading: Chicago Area Transportation Study. *1995 Travel Atlas for the Northeastern Illinois Expressway System.* 1998. • Condit, Carl W. *Chicago, 1930–1970: Building, Planning, and Urban Technology.* 1974. • Mayer, Harold M., and Richard C. Wade. *Chicago: Growth of a Metropolis.* 1969.

Spaniards. Immigrants from Spain established a small but vibrant community in Chicago. Rural poverty and population pressure encouraged growing numbers of emigrants to leave Spain through the late nineteenth and early twentieth centuries. Though most went to Latin American countries, several thousands moved to American cities. By the 1920s a small number of Spaniards had settled in Chicago, attracted to the area by jobs in steel mills and other industries. However, with the national quota system prescribed by the 1924 immigration legislation, immigration from Spain declined dramatically, as Spain's quota was set at just 131 immigrants per year. Substantial numbers of Spanish immigrants began settling in the Chicago area only after the elimination of the quota system in the 1960s.

Spanish immigration increased gradually in the 1950s and more rapidly in the 1960s. Many of these immigrants found employment as teachers, professors, doctors, or engineers; others opened small businesses and RESTAURANTS. A smaller number of working-class Spaniards have also found jobs in carpentry and other trades in Chicago. Significant numbers of Spaniards came to Chicago to pursue higher education, but most have remained in the city only until completing their degrees.

Spaniards did not settle in one particular neighborhood or parish in Chicago, but they remained connected socially and culturally through the activities of a community organization, the Spanish Association of the Midwest. Founded in 1976, the Spanish Association organized programs to promote the culture of Spain and to unite and support Spanish immigrants and persons with Spanish heritage living in Chicago. Meeting regularly at local Spanish restaurants such as Café Iberico, the group has hosted a film series, endowed scholarships for study in Spain, and organized a local Spanish SOCCER team. Other activities have included regular concerts and performances by Spanish artists, an annual summer picnic, and the annual October 12 "Dia de la Hispanidad," commemorating Columbus's voyage to America.

At the end of the millennium, the Spanish Association of the Midwest had 120 families in its membership. Community leaders estimated approximately 500 Spaniards spread across the Chicago metropolitan area.

Robert Morrissey

See also: Demography; Iron and Steel Workers; Multicentered Chicago; Roman Catholics

Special Districts. Special districts are units of government superimposed on the traditional units (municipalities, TOWNSHIPS, and counties). As independent governments, they may have the power to levy taxes and issue bonds. The boundaries of special districts may cut across the boundaries of other districts and local governments, resulting in a layered public sector of considerable complexity. The number of layers may vary even within a single municipality, and in some suburban areas there are as many as 15 different governmental units levying property taxes.

While the number of special districts has been growing steadily throughout the United States since the 1950s, Illinois has consistently had more special districts than any other state. In the six-county greater Chicago region, there were 353 special districts (other than SCHOOL DISTRICTS) in 1962. This number grew to 621 districts in 1992. In Indiana, the special district device has been used much less. There were only 36 special districts in Lake County, Indiana, in 1992, fewer than in any of the six Illinois collar counties.

Special districts have generally been established by local referendum, with enabling legislation from the Illinois legislature. Unlike general-purpose governments that exercise multiple functions, most special districts are dedicated to a single purpose. Although school districts may receive the most public attention, other districts provide FIRE protection, LIBRARY facilities, SOIL conservation, mosquito control, and other services. Special districts may be created in response to demands for services that existing governments cannot or will not provide.

The district device has great territorial flexibility, since boundary lines need not follow municipal, township, or county borders. Districts may achieve economies of scale and avoid problems of coordination between general-purpose jurisdictions that share a need for services. The municipalities of HOMEWOOD and FLOSSMOOR, for example, are covered by a single PARK DISTRICT. Districts may cross county lines, as in the case of the AURORA Sanitary District, which covers parts of DUPAGE and KANE Counties. Districts may also define smaller areas within municipalities, as is the case with the Ridgeville and North East (or Lighthouse) Park Districts within the city of EVANSTON.

In addition to their geographic versatility, special districts provide a powerful public-sector fiscal tool. The Illinois Constitution that was in effect from 1870 to 1970 narrowly limited the debt that municipalities could acquire. Special districts proliferated partly as a way to evade these constraints, since they could issue their own bonds, levy their own taxes, and provide services independently of the limits on existing governments. While the state constitution of 1970 adjusted these limits and sought to encourage intergovernmental cooperation, the number of special districts has continued to increase.

Park districts were among the earliest special districts created by the state. Special legislation in 1869 authorized the formation of three park districts in Chicago; these districts and several small park districts merged in 1934 to form the Chicago Park District. In 1893 the legislature passed general legislation to enable the creation of park districts on local initiative. There were approximately 50 such districts in Cook County by 1930, and 100 by 1990. In the six-county region the numbers have also grown rapidly in recent decades, from approximately 94 park districts in 1962 to 193 in 1992.

The 1909 BURNHAM PLAN envisioned a system of "outer parks" outside the city of Chicago. The state passed enabling legislation for FOREST PRESERVE districts in 1913, with the restriction that there could be just

Among the many special districts, the Metropolitan Pier and Exposition Authority directed the redevelopment of Navy Pier, seen here in 1961, before that work began. Photographer: Unknown. Source: Chicago Historical Society.

one district within a county, and the district boundaries could not cross county lines. The COOK COUNTY and DUPAGE COUNTY Forest Preserve Districts were formed in 1915, followed by Kane County in 1926, WILL COUNTY in 1927, and LAKE COUNTY in 1958. The MCHENRY COUNTY Conservation District was formed in 1971 under different legislation, but its functions are similar to those of forest preserve districts.

The Metropolitan Water Reclamation District of Greater Chicago (MWRDGC) is one of the largest and most capital-intensive special districts in the region. It was also among the earliest, created as the Chicago Sanitary District in 1889 by the Illinois legislature in response to complaints by Chicagoans that sewage in the CHICAGO RIVER was contaminating LAKE MICHIGAN, the city's WATER supply. The district was limited to Cook County.

The North Shore Sanitary District came into being in 1914, after the Lake County suburbs had not been permitted to join the Chicago district. After 1938, numerous small collector sanitary districts were formed in unincorporated parts of Cook County to collect sewage to be treated by the MWRDGC. Such districts may also purchase water from adjacent municipalities and resell it to district residents. In 1992 there were nearly 60 sanitary districts in the six counties.

The REGIONAL TRANSPORTATION AUTHORITY and its semi-independent service boards (the CHICAGO TRANSIT AUTHORITY, the Metra Commuter Rail Division, and the PACE Suburban Bus Division) are among the largest special districts. The RTA district consists of the entire six-county region. By the size of its revenues and expenditures, the CTA alone was the largest special district in the region in 1992.

As suburban population density increased after WORLD WAR II, people wanted urban services, but they did not always want urban government to provide them. The existing governmental structure was not authorized to provide many urban services. Special districts could provide services in unincorporated areas and small municipalities without resort to incorporation or ANNEXATION.

Fire protection districts were authorized by enabling legislation in 1927. There were 121 in 1962, and 153 in 1992 in the six-county region. The BARRINGTON Countryside Fire Protection District is an extreme case of multiple jurisdictions, as its territory encompasses parts of Cook, Lake, Kane, and McHenry Counties. It also includes parts of the municipalities of BARRINGTON HILLS, SOUTH BARRINGTON, LAKE BARRINGTON, and INVERNESS. Moreover, the fire station is not located in the district, but in the nearby municipality of BARRINGTON.

Illinois first authorized library districts in 1943. By 1992 there were 118 library districts in the six-county region, 66 of them outside Cook County. New suburban residents have wanted library services comparable to those that they previously enjoyed in larger communities. To bypass municipal inaction, library districts have been formed in municipalities, sometimes including adjacent unincorporated territory to serve residents who want library facilities but not municipal government.

There were also 13 mosquito abatement districts in the six-county region in 1992. Other categories included AIRPORT, CEMETERY, civic center, drainage, HOSPITAL, PUBLIC HEALTH, soil and water conservation, street lighting, and tuberculosis sanitarium districts.

Special districts may be governed by elected boards or by boards appointed by elected officials. Board members often receive no compensation (as in the case of park district commissioners) or only a nominal salary (as in the case of forest preserve district commissioners). While the special district device may promote efficient provision of services, a wide range of choices, and maximum local control, the proliferation of special districts may also represent a fragmentation of government and a minimizing of citizen participation. The varying boundaries and numerous layers of local governments create fragmented communities of participation and contribute to the relative invisibility of special districts in public consciousness. Voter turnout in special district elections is usually much lower than in municipal elections.

Donald F. Stetzer

See also: Governing the Metropolis; Planning Chicago; Suburbs and Cities as Dual Metropolis; Taxation and Finance

Further reading: Bollens, John C. *Special District Governments in the United States.* 1957. • Illinois Commission on Intergovernmental Cooperation. *Legislator's Guide to Local Governments in Illinois: Special Districts.* 1992. • Keane, James F., and Gary Koch, eds. *Illinois Local Government: A Handbook.* 1990.

Spertus Institute of Jewish Studies.

Spertus encompasses three institutions devoted to the preservation of Jewish history and culture: the Spertus Museum, the Asher Library, and Spertus College. Founded in 1924 as the College of Jewish Studies to instruct teachers for the Jewish schools and clubs then multiplying around Chicago, the college received accreditation in 1971. By 2002 it served primarily as a center for graduate education, granting both master's and doctoral degrees in Jewish studies. The library and museum opened in 1967, and the three institutions moved together from their original location on East 11th Street to South Michigan Avenue in 1974. The largest museum devoted exclusively to Jewish culture outside of New York and California, the Spertus Museum maintains a collection of more than 10,000 artifacts and houses the nation's first permanent exhibition on the Holocaust.

Sarah Fenton

See also: Jews; Judaism; Seminaries; Universities and Their Cities

Further reading: Cutler, Irving. *The Jews of Chicago: From Shtetl to Suburb.* 1996.

Sporting Goods Manufacturing.

Sports are played for recreation and personal FITNESS, while sporting events are prominent entertainment and BUSINESS enterprises. Sports and sporting activities consistently attracted Chicagoans, and the types of sporting goods manufactured and activities pursued by the residents of Chicago provide insight into shifting social and economic conditions. In the late nineteenth and early twentieth centuries, as income levels began to rise, the citizens of Chicago and the nation experienced expanding levels of prosperity, which allowed them to turn to sporting activities in their LEISURE time. Time away from WORK helped create and expand the market for sporting goods manufacturers. With names like Spalding, Wilson, Brunswick, Schwinn, and Kiefer, Chicago has been home to many of the most recognizable brands in sporting goods manufacturing.

Chicago's physical expansion and DEMOGRAPHIC dynamism have stimulated demand for an increasingly wide range of sports equipment. GERMAN American immigrants pushed the Chicago School Board to initiate a gymnastics program in 1885. By 1914, every one of the city's public high schools had gymnasiums and physical fitness programs. The popularity of archery, handball and racquetball, SWIMMING, TENNIS, GOLF, BOWLING, weightlifting, roller-skating, and BICYCLING all depended upon the availability of space as well as affordable equipment. Space became more available as public parks began to be not merely public gardens but also locations that increasingly encouraged recreational and fitness activities. In 1895, the city of Chicago opened its first public beach, in LINCOLN PARK. Five years later, there were 26 golf courses and a number of public outdoor swimming pools in the metropolitan area. Equipment became more affordable as escalating industrialization encouraged mass production, resulting in falling prices in this industry as in others.

The emergence of the sporting goods industry is closely linked with the growth of organized sport teams, especially professional BASEBALL. Although early sporting goods equipment was crudely fabricated and locally supplied, one Chicago-based manufacturer shaped and redefined the industry with its aggressive marketing strategy. Chicago had the economic advantage in the manufacture of balls and gloves with its plentiful supply of hides and leathers, a byproduct of the MEATPACKING industry. After opening a sporting goods store in 1876, Albert Goodwill Spalding (1850–1915), in partnership with his brother and brother-in-law, manufactured baseball gloves and, beginning in 1878 and for the next hundred years, was the exclusive supplier of the "official baseball of the National League." While still one of the early star players of professional baseball, Spalding was one of the first players to wear a baseball glove, a glove that was, of course, manufactured and sold by A. G. Spalding & Brothers. Soon, professionals and amateurs alike were using the

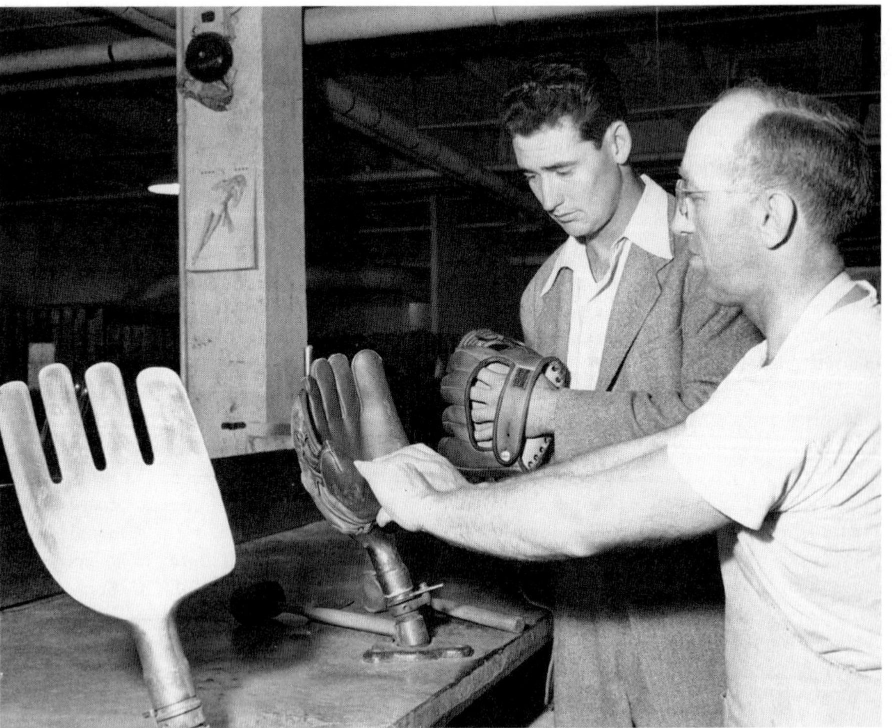

Famed Boston Red Sox outfielder Ted Williams watches Frank Stawinoga work a new model of baseball glove on the shaping form at the Wilson Sporting Goods factory, 1949. Photographer: Unknown. Source: Chicago Historical Society.

equipment made and distributed by Spalding, and his name became synonymous with baseball and other sporting activities. As a player, manager, promoter, and manufacturer, Albert Spalding helped establish baseball as a national pastime. By the time the press began referring to Spalding as baseball's "Big Mogul," he had branded himself the "father of American baseball." By the late nineteenth century, Spalding had a virtual monopoly on sporting goods equipment.

Another sporting goods manufacturer that profited from the proximity of the byproducts of Chicago's stockyards was the Ashland Manufacturing Company, founded in 1913. In 1914, Thomas Wilson was named the new president of Ashland. In 1916, the company was renamed the Thomas E. Wilson Company and in 1931 became the Wilson Sporting Goods Company. Even though Thomas Wilson left the firm in 1918, as a brand name Wilson has remained one of the most familiar trade names in sporting goods manufacturing. From its origins on the SOUTH SIDE of Chicago, Wilson manufactured a diverse line of balls, racquets, athletic footwear, golf clubs, and other sporting goods and, with its early acquisition of knitting mills, significantly expanded its product line into the production of jerseys and uniforms. Wilson has been innovative and aggressive in both its manufacturing activities and in its marketing campaigns. It was among the first American manufacturers to rely on celebrity consultants and had endorsements from such prominent sporting figures as Knute Rockne in FOOTBALL, Gene Sarazen and Sam Snead in golf, "Lefty" Gomez and Ted Williams in baseball, and Jack Kramer in tennis.

Along with baseball, another emerging national pastime in the late nineteenth century was cycling. The popularity of bicycles can be understood by their use not only in sporting events but also for recreational activity and as a means of basic TRANSPORTATION. By the late 1880s, bicycle races had become familiar events in Chicago and helped to promote the general use of bicycles. By the late nineteenth century, there were approximately 300 firms manufacturing bicycles in the United States and, even though many of these manufacturers were based in New England's Connecticut Valley, there were 101 Chicago-based manufacturers by the mid-1890s. The popularity of cycling allowed Spalding to diversify its product line to include bicycle manufacturing in 1894. In 1895, GERMAN immigrant Ignaz Schwinn (1860–1948) founded a bicycle manufacturing partnership with Adolph Arnold, as Arnold, Schwinn & Co. The firm became Schwinn & Co. in 1908. From its first production facility in downtown Chicago, it became one of the most recognizable names in the industry and for decades accounted for at least a quarter of bicycle manufacturing in the United States.

The oldest manufacturer of recreational and leisure-time products in the United States is the Brunswick Corporation. Brunswick originated in the 1840s as a Cincinnati-based carriage and cabinetry maker which manufactured billiard tables. The company moved to Chicago in 1848 and was, by the 1880s, when the firm had diversified its product line to include bowling pins and bowling balls, one of Chicago's most well known and successful manufacturers. Another prominent sporting figure and sporting goods manufacturer from Chicago is Adolph Kiefer. In 1946, the former Olympic swimmer and spokesman established Adolph Kiefer & Associates, which has over the years not only designed and manufactured sporting goods but also promoted and enhanced aquatic sports and safety.

Timothy E. Sullivan

See also: Creation of Chicago Sports; Playgrounds and Small Parks; Turnvereins

Further reading: Duis, Perry R. *Challenging Chicago: Coping with Everyday Life, 1837–1920.* 1998. • Kogan, Rick. *Brunswick: The Story of an American Company from 1845 to 1985.* 1985. • Levine, Peter. *A.G. Spalding and the Rise of Baseball: The Promise of American Sport.* 1985.

Sports. *See* Creation of Chicago Sports

Sports, High-School. The first sport that Chicago-area SCHOOLS adopted for competition was BASEBALL. The earliest match-up on record took place between two academies in 1868, in the midst of the nation's post–Civil War baseball rage. The model for high-school competition was the amateur baseball club, in which boys in a school would form a club, elect officers, organize a team, and issue challenge matches to schools and amateur teams.

FOOTBALL became a high-school activity in the early 1880s, and by this time the model for competition had shifted to the colleges, and this model prevailed as other sports were adopted. High-school competition was largely of the sandlot variety at this time, but by the end of the 1880s both baseball and football had became full-fledged sports, with uniforms, schedules, and laid-out fields.

In 1889–90, Chicago students formed one of the pioneer interscholastic leagues in the country—the COOK COUNTY High School League—which embraced all Chicago and suburban public high schools. The league conducted its first track-and-field and football championships in 1889 and its first baseball championship in 1890. The Cook County League high schools subsequently adopted a variety of other sports, including TENNIS (1894), indoor baseball (1895), girls' basketball (1895), boys' BASKETBALL (1900), SWIMMING (1906), cross-country (1908), SOCCER (1910), and GOLF (1911).

By 1898, abuses (principally the use of ringers) caused by haphazard growth and student control prompted the Cook County League to establish a regulatory Board of Control. In 1904, under the urging of Superintendent Edwin G. Cooley, the board passed radical new regulations removing all student representatives from positions of management. The Cook County League continued, however, to be plagued by conflicts over eligibility, the use of paid coaches, and traveling restrictions.

In 1913, three important high-school athletic conferences formed that would dominate high-school athletic competition in the area for decades—the Catholic League, the Suburban League, and the Chicago Public League. Other important leagues soon followed, notably the Northern Illinois Conference (which included ELGIN, AURORA, and JOLIET) in 1916, the South Suburban League in 1927, the West Suburban League (in DUPAGE COUNTY) in 1924, and the Northwest Suburban League in 1925. The parochial schools organized themselves into the Private League in 1935.

UNIVERSITIES also played central roles in the growth of high-school sports. The UNIVERSITY OF CHICAGO sponsored major interscholastic track-and-field meets (1902–1933), tennis tournaments (1895–1932), and basketball tournaments (1917–1930). NORTHWESTERN sponsored swim meets (1914–1930) and indoor track (1910–1930).

In 1909, the Illinois High School Association (IHSA) took over the state basketball tournament—first held the previous year at OAK PARK High School. By the late 1920s, the IHSA decided that the national competitions sponsored by universities and athletic clubs were inimical to the education process. From the perspective of high-school administrators, control lay appropriately within the scope of the schools rather than colleges or private clubs. From 1927 to 1930, the IHSA led the National Federation of High School Associations in a campaign to shut down virtually all national meets. The IHSA had shared supervision of the state track-and-field, tennis, and GOLF meets with the University of Illinois since 1926, but in 1934 the IHSA took these over completely. The first baseball state championship took place in 1940 and was taken over by the IHSA the next year. The IHSA also added state championship competitions in swimming (1932), wrestling (1937), cross-country (1946), and gymnastics (1958).

The most notable high-school competition in Chicago was the Prep Bowl, which began in 1927 and pitted the Public League football champion against the Catholic League champion annually in SOLDIER FIELD. At the height of its popularity in the late 1930s, the bowl drew more than 100,000 fans.

The post–World War II baby boom caused a tremendous upheaval in high-school athletics. Many new leagues were added in the Chicago area—notably the Mid-Suburban

Victorious DuSable High School basketball team carrying coach Jim Brown in 1954. The team reached the state finals, the first all–African American team to do so, only to lose to Mt. Vernon High School in a game that still provokes debates about questionable officiating. Photographer: Unknown. Source: Chicago Historical Society.

(1963), South Inter-Conference Association (1973), Central Suburban (1975), and DuPage Valley (1975).

Though the IHSA had sponsored "postal" state meets (in which schools would compete intramurally and mail in times and results) for girls in various sports for decades, it was not until the 1970s that Illinois caught up with surrounding states by adding interscholastic competition for girls. In quick succession, state meet competition was added in tennis (1972), track and field (1973), BOWLING (1973), golf (1975), swimming (1975), volleyball (1975), SOFTBALL (1976), basketball (1977), gymnastics (1977), and cross-country (1979). Later, the IHSA added state meet competition in soccer (1988) and WATER POLO (1999). The IHSA also broadened state meet competition for boys, adding state championships for soccer (1972), football (1974), volleyball (1992), and water polo (1999).

Robert Pruter

Armour football squad, 1896. Photographer: Unknown. Source: Chicago Historical Society.

See also: Creation of Chicago Sports; Fitness and Athletic Clubs; Schools and Education; Sports, Industrial League

Further reading: Gems, Gerald R. "The Prep Bowl: Football and Religious Acculturation in Chicago, 1927–1963." *Journal of Sport History* 23.3 (Fall 1996): 284–302. • Gutowski, Thomas W. "Student Initiative and the Origins of the High School Extracurriculum: Chicago, 1880–1915." *History of Education Quarterly* 28 (Spring 1988): 49–72. • Whitten, Charles W. *Interscholastics.* 1950.

Sports, Industrial League. Chicago BUSINESSES began fielding athletic teams as early as the 1860s, when employees banded together to form BASEBALL teams for interdepartmental play and to oppose their commercial competitors. By the 1890s the Brunswick-Balke-Collender Company employed traveling all-star teams to promote its billiards and BOWLING equipment. In the 1880s the model town of PULLMAN featured the most comprehensive industrial recreation program in America. Designed to foster wholesome recreation and company loyalty, the program served as a model for companies nationwide. By the 1890s at least four different baseball leagues organized by occupation competed in the city, followed by even more commercial bowling leagues.

Ongoing labor discontent prompted employers to expand such offerings and to coordinate their recreational programs with public agencies in order to use the facilities of the city's parks and PLAYGROUNDS. At least 60 industrial baseball leagues competed in Chicago, and the city hosted the Union Printers international tournament in 1909. Many industrial teams turned semipro and some became fully professional as employers realized the promotional value of winning teams and employees capitalized on their athletic abilities. The Chicago BEARS, for example, started as an industrial team in downstate Decatur.

By the 1920s industrial sports offered opportunities to the numerous AFRICAN AMERICANS working in the stockyards and to the increasing number of women in the workforce. Western Electric's Hawthorne Works had 28,000 members in its athletic association by 1923, and it provided 14 sports for women. Its 20th annual track and field meet in 1930 attracted 10,000 spectators. Such programs offered working-class women a complement to the noncompetitive play days favored by physical educators in the schools.

Chicago women garnered numerous national championships in track, BASKETBALL, SWIMMING, SOFTBALL, and bowling. By the 1930s, the latter two had become extremely popular for both men and women. By 1937, 225 firms fielded 1,700 bowling teams, and 264 companies sponsored almost 1,000 softball teams.

The American COMMUNIST PARTY tried to counter the efforts of capitalists with its own

Olympics, held in Chicago in 1932. Labor UNIONS, too, offered their own programs as an alternative to the employers. The Chicago Association of Street, Electric Railway and Motor Coach Employees constructed a $1 million building, while the Amalgamated Clothing Workers had their own gym and a comprehensive sports program for its 16,000 members.

Such programs continued throughout World War II to maintain morale on the homefront and to encourage FITNESS. TENNIS and GOLF attracted white-collar workers, as evidenced by the 128 teams in the industrial golf association.

The GRANT PARK Recreation Association catered to Loop employees, offering competition in five sports. By 1968 it hosted 682 softball teams. Four years later, 30 industrial softball leagues for men and another 5 for women competed in the city's parks. Another 43 teams played in women's volleyball leagues.

Some companies have continued to maintain their competitive sports programs. In addition, in the 1980s, many firms began to emphasize executive fitness and employee wellness programs, shown to reduce absenteeism and lower employers' health care costs.

Gerald R. Gems

See also: Creation of Chicago Sports; Leisure; Welfare Capitalism

Further reading: Chicago Recreation Commission. *The Chicago Recreation Survey, 1937*, 5 vols. 1937–1940. • Diehl, Leonard J., and Floyd R. Eastwood. *Industrial Recreation: Its Development and Present Status.* 1940. • Pesavento, Wilma J. "Sport and Recreation in the Pullman Experiment, 1880–1900." *Journal of Sport History* 9.2 (Summer 1982): 38–62.

Spring Grove, IL, McHenry County, 54 miles NW of the Loop. Platted around a gristmill in 1845, this hamlet stagnated even after the Milwaukee Road RAILROAD appeared in 1900. Incorporating in 1902 in anticipation of growth that finally materialized in the 1980s, Spring Grove today contains residential, light industrial, and agricultural areas and hosts a noted annual storytelling festival. Population in 2000 was 3,880.

Craig L. Pfannkuche

See also: McHenry County

Further reading: *McHenry County in the Twentieth Century, 1968–1994.* McHenry County Historical Society. 1994. • Nye, Lowell A., ed. *McHenry County, Illinois, 1832–1968.* 1968.

Sri Lankans. The first major wave of Sri Lankan migration to Chicago began in the late 1960s and comprised primarily medical professionals who took advantage of United States immigration preferences to pursue educational and professional opportunities. This first generation of migrants, composed of both Tamil and Sinhalese families, settled permanently in Chicago and created a strong community, attracting friends and relatives as tensions in Sri Lanka escalated. The outbreak of civil war between the Sinhalese majority and Tamil minority in 1983 caused a large wave of Tamils to leave Sri Lanka for Canada, the United States, Britain, and Australia, and subsequent ethnic violence and unrest has caused an influx of REFUGEES from all ethnic groups. Most refugees in the United States have settled in the large Sri Lankan communities found in California and New York. Chicago's much smaller community has continued to attract professionals, students, and kin of earlier migrants as well as more recent migrants seeking economic opportunities. In addition, a second generation of Sri Lankan Americans have reached adulthood in Chicago.

Chicago's Sri Lankan community is extremely diverse, with a range of ethnic groups, religions, and classes represented. Community estimates vary widely, suggesting 1,000 to 2,500 Sri Lankans in Chicago at the beginning of the twenty-first century. Sinhalese BUDDHISTS constitute the majority, complemented by many Tamil HINDUS, some of whom are involved in Tamil cultural activities, including Chicago Tamil Sangam, which sponsors cultural activities and performances for INDIAN and Sri Lankan Tamils. There is also a growing MUSLIM community that meets informally and a sizeable number of Sri Lankan Christians. The majority of Chicago's Sri Lankans are professionals, but a growing number of nonprofessionals have entered a range of occupations including TAXI driving and service industries.

Efforts to organize as a community have been complicated by this diversity and by the political tensions in Sri Lanka. An attempt to organize a formal Sri Lankan association in the late 1970s failed as a result of these pressures. However, the Sri Lankan community in Chicago has escaped much of the political conflict and tension that exists in Sri Lanka and in Sri Lankan communities in many other cities. This is due in large part to the large first wave of migrants, who created strong and lasting personal and professional relationships across ethnic groups before the war and who have exerted a strong influence on the development of the community since. Recent migrants have felt these tensions more strongly, as have some Tamils, who have maintained their own community and organized separate holidays and events.

While there are many different groups within the larger community that meet socially throughout the year, most of the Chicago Sri Lankan community comes together a few times each year for holidays including Sinhalese-Tamil New Year (mid-April), Christmas, and New Year's, as well as occasional summer picnics and parties. In addition, special cultural events, such as performances by visiting Sri Lankan drama and dance troupes, draw the community together.

Tracy Steffes

See also: Americanization; Demography; Multicentered Chicago

St. Charles, IL, DuPage and Kane Counties, 35 miles W of the Loop. The site of St. Charles was well known to the POTAWATOMI, who established two summer camps near the shallows where they forded the FOX RIVER and fished. Later settlers also were attracted by the varied nature of the country, with prairie to the west and extensive woods on both sides of the river to the north. They also prized the creeks that ran into the Fox River for mills and used rock outcrops in the area for building stone.

By 1836 a BRIDGE and dam had been built, and a little town was growing up around them on both the east and west banks. It was at first called Charleston, but as there was already a town in Illinois with that name, it was changed to St. Charles. Most of the early settlers came from New England, and the YANKEE influence remained strong throughout the nineteenth century.

From 1849 to about 1859 St. Charles was served by the St. Charles Branch RAILROAD. But regular rail service did not come until 1871 when the Chicago, Saint Paul & Kansas City Railroad established a depot, ushering in a period of economic growth. Some new industries, like the cheese factory and the milk condensery, processed local farm produce; but others, like the IRON works, paper mill, piano factory, and cut-glass factory, took advantage of St. Charles's WATER power and strategic location. Factory work drew many hundreds of SWEDISH immigrants, along with substantial numbers of LITHUANIANS, BELGIANS, and DANES.

By the end of the nineteenth century the built-up area of the town extended for about half a mile in each direction from the Fox River crossing, and the woodland to the north was also being cleared for farms and outlying houses. The coming of the automobile in the 1920s drew St. Charles into the expanding Chicago market. The population grew from 2,675 in 1900 to 6,709 in 1950. But the town did not experience the explosive postwar growth of some of the towns to the east, and as late as 1970 did not extend for more than a mile each way from the historic center. The 1980s and 1990s saw the development of new residential SUBDIVISIONS on both sides of the river and to the north and south. The population reached 27,896 in 2000.

There have also been major economic changes, as factories have given way to a variety of service-based enterprises. Still, St. Charles

St. Charles bridge over Fox River, 1932. Photographer: Unknown. Source: Chicago Historical Society.

retains evidence of its past, not only in the many early buildings at the center of town, but also in names like Ferson's Creek, named for a Yankee settler, and Brewster and Norton Creeks, called after the mills that once lined their banks.

David Buisseret

See also: Agriculture; Metropolitan Growth; Musical Instrument Manufacturing

Further reading: Badger, David Alan. *St. Charles of Illinois.* 1985. • Pearson, Ruth. *Reflections of St. Charles: A History of St. Charles, Illinois, 1833–1976.* 1976.

St. John, IN, Lake County, 31 miles S of the Loop. Early GERMAN settlers named St. Johns (the s disappeared in the early twentieth century) as a tribute to John Hack, one of its first settlers. German Catholics supported BILINGUAL EDUCATION and establishment of the first ROMAN CATHOLIC church of LAKE COUNTY in 1842. In the late twentieth century the town attracted Chicago commuters, with population growing from 1,757 in 1970 to 8,382 in 2000.

Erik Gellman

See also: Metropolitan Growth

St. Lawrence Seaway. The canal system that enables ships to travel 2,342 miles from the mouth of the St. Lawrence River in Canada via the GREAT LAKES to Chicago dates from 1842, when the British built a system of four "bateau" canals for canoes around the rapids at Montreal. The link between the St. Lawrence and the Great Lakes was a complex undertaking because the canals would have to raise ships 230 feet to bypass Montreal and 327 feet to bypass Niagara Falls.

New York State, fearful that British Canada would control trade by building a canal around Niagara Falls, completed the Erie Canal in 1825 connecting the Hudson River to Lake Erie. British Canada completed the Welland Canal in 1829 to permit small ocean-going ships to enter the Great Lakes, bypassing Niagara Falls. The locks on the St. Lawrence were enlarged in 1847, permitting the *Dean Richmond* in 1856 to sail from Chicago to Liverpool with a load of wheat. Chicago's role as an international seaport dates from that sailing.

The limited dimensions of the canal locks restricted international traffic until 1901, when Canada completed the enlargement of both systems to handle ships 270 feet long and 55 feet wide, allowing the new steel-hulled ocean steamers access to the lakes.

The construction of the modern St. Lawrence Seaway was a joint project between the United States and Canada begun in the 1940s and completed in 1959 at a cost of $470 million. The seven locks on the 190-mile St. Lawrence section and eight on the 26-mile Welland Canal were each built 766 feet long, 80 feet wide, and 30 feet deep to accommodate ocean ships.

The seaway never quite lived up to its proponents' expectations, however. Although traffic increased steadily from 18.4 million metric tons in 1960 to 57.4 million tons in 1977, it began to decline thereafter. The larger ships built for transoceanic and lake traffic could not negotiate the seaway's locks. Overseas traffic to and from Chicago via the seaway declined from 4.3 million short tons in 1977 to 1.9 million by 1996.

David M. Young

See also: Calumet River System; Global Chicago; Illinois & Michigan Canal; Water

Further reading: LesStrang, Jacques. *Cargo Carriers of the Great Lakes.* 1985. • Mayer, Harold M. *The Port of Chicago and the St. Lawrence Seaway.* 1957. • Rice, Mary Jane Judson. *Chicago: Port to the World.* 1969.

St. Valentine's Day Massacre. Posing as POLICE officers conducting a routine raid on February 14, 1929, four men entered a warehouse at 2122 N. Clark Street, used by George "Bugs" Moran and his GANG to store LIQUOR. The impostors lined up six gang members and a hanger-on against a wall, produced machine guns from under their overcoats, and opened fire.

The prime suspect was Al Capone, head of Chicago's crime syndicate. Moran's North Side gang, the largest obstacle to the Capone organization's power in metropolitan Chicago, had hijacked Capone's liquor shipments, competed in protection rackets, and murdered Capone allies. Law enforcement officials could not prove any involvement by Capone, who was in Miami at the time. No one was ever tried for the killings.

The raid's cold-blooded efficiency left the public in shock, and the St. Valentine's Day Massacre came to symbolize gang violence. It confirmed popular images associating Chicago with mobsters, crime, and spectacular carnage. The site of the warehouse, razed in 1967, continues to draw tourists from around the world.

Christopher P. Thale

See also: Crime and Chicago's Image; Prohibition and Temperance; Underground Economy

Further reading: Ruth, David E. *Inventing the Public Enemy: The Gangsters in American Culture, 1918–1934.* 1996. • Schoenberg, Robert J. *Mr. Capone.* 1992.

St. Vincent DePaul Society. Founded in Paris in 1833, the Society of St. Vincent de Paul is an organization of ROMAN CATHOLIC laypersons dedicated to charity work. The Reverend Dennis Dunne, pastor of St. Patrick's Church, brought the society to Chicago during the economic depression of 1857 in order to help his parishioners. Within seven years it spread to nine other parishes in the city. In Chicago, as in the rest of the United States, the society was primarily IRISH in composition until the mid-twentieth century.

The society provided a number of basic services. Society members, all men, would visit the poor in their homes to offer material aid and spiritual comfort. The society also handed out grocery tickets, which the poor could use

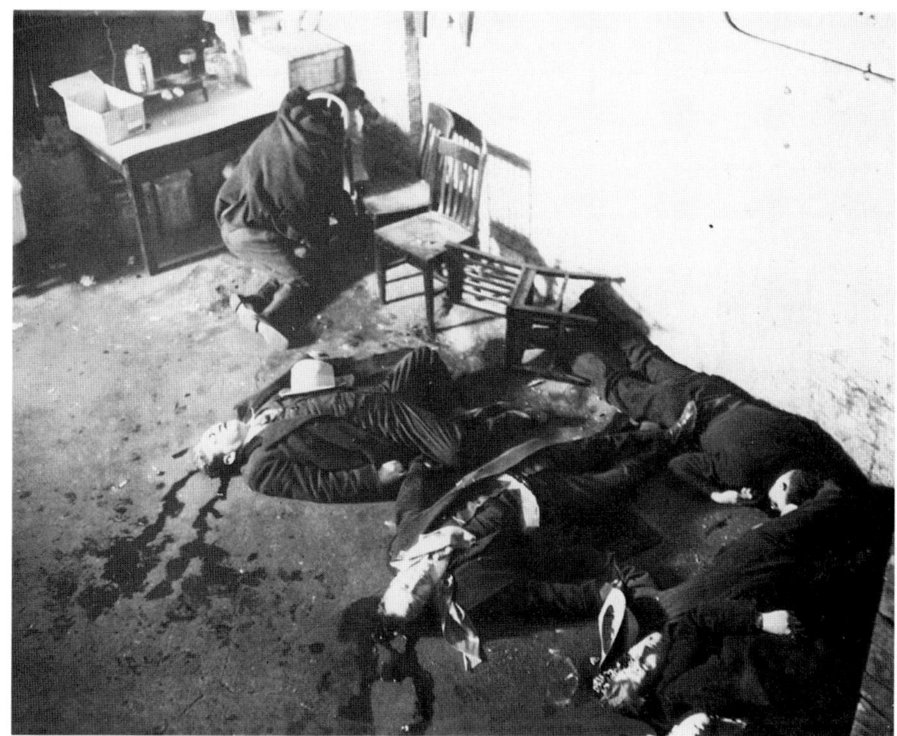

St. Valentine's Day Massacre, 1929. Photographer: Jun Fujita. Source: Chicago Historical Society.

to buy food. It paid for parochial schooling and Catholic funerals. Finally, it sent representatives to other Chicago CHARITIES, such as the CHICAGO RELIEF AND AID SOCIETY and the Charity Organization Society, to prevent discrimination against Catholics.

Around 1900, the Society of St. Vincent de Paul began to cooperate more with Chicago's non-Catholic agencies. It adopted many of the professional standards of the day: it kept more records, centralized fundraising and administration, and increased coordination with other Catholic charities. It helped its poor gain access to Catholic HOSPITALS and found Catholic probation officers for children in the JUVENILE COURT.

Yet at a time when many other charities were hiring professional social workers, the society continued to use volunteers. It created a Women's Auxiliary in 1913. Volunteers saved money, so much so that the society was able to grow to almost four times its original size. By the GREAT DEPRESSION, it had grown to the extent that it could administer a federal program. In 1933, Cardinal George Mundelein convinced Franklin Roosevelt that the society should handle the distribution of federal relief funds to poor Catholics in Chicago.

During the 1960s, the Vatican II conference of renewal for the Catholic Church prompted the society to revise its rules. It admitted women to full membership for the first time and urged members to exhibit greater concern for social justice. In the midst of these changes, the society continued into the twenty-first century to practice many charitable activities just as it did during the nineteenth century. It still gives food vouchers, and members still visit the poor in their homes and in institutions. In Chicago, it also operates thrift shops and soup kitchens. Finally, the society remains dedicated to the principle of serving Christ by helping those in need.

Deborah Ann Skok

See also: Catholic Charities; Philanthropy; Relief and Subsistence Aid; Religious Institutions; Social Services

Further reading: Jones, Gene D. L. "The Chicago Catholic Charities, the Great Depression, and Public Monies." *Illinois Historical Journal* 83, no. 1 (Spring 1990): 13–30. • Katz, Michael B. *In the Shadow of the Poorhouse: A Social History of Welfare in America.* 1986. • McColgan, Daniel T. *A Century of Charity: The First One Hundred Years of the Society of St. Vincent de Paul in the United States.* 2 vols. 1951.

Stadiums. *See* Places of Assembly

State Politics. Despite its huge and diverse population, enormous industrial might, and key location as a major center for national and international trade, Chicago has not dominated state GOVERNMENT in Illinois. Instead the city has held a unique position of power and influence in a state where regional POLITICS has enjoyed a robust tradition. From the beginning, and perhaps more than in any other state, Illinois legislators have sought benefits such as canals, roads, prisons, and universities for their own particular region, a tendency made apparent early on when the capital was relocated three times in the state's first three decades. State party organizations have been weak, and only Stephen A. Douglas in the 1850s and Richard J. Daley in the 1960s have been able to assemble strong statewide MACHINES. Political power has traditionally rested in city halls and county courthouses where local party organizations select candidates, control decisions on key issues, distribute PATRONAGE to party faithful, secure patronage-rich statewide offices, and form alliances to increase local portions of state expenditures. In the pre–CIVIL WAR era, the issue of slavery gave DEMOCRATS an edge over their WHIG rivals.

Between the CIVIL WAR and the GREAT DEPRESSION, however, the REPUBLICANS held the upper hand in the legislature because of the party's strength in the prosperous northern and central sections of the state and its successful resistance to any reapportionment scheme that would have further strengthened Chicago's numbers in the Illinois legislature. Following WORLD WAR II, Democratic strength grew in Chicago to such an extent that some downstaters became alarmed that the giant city, with its legions of foreign-born citizens, blacks, and notorious political bosses, would dominate the statehouse. However, Chicago political leaders, all Democrats since the 1930s, were never strong enough to secure statewide offices without considerable support from allied downstate Democratic organizations and a good share of the state's independent voters.

The remarkable growth of Chicago following the Civil War convinced downstate legislators that the city needed to be controlled. Historian John Keiser has noted that "Chicago towered over the state like Gulliver in Lilliput, while the Lilliputians of downstate spent much of their time shooting darts at the giant and attempting to tie it down." By 1870, Chicago already held 12 percent of the state's population, a figure that leaped to 35 percent by 1900, and 44 percent by 1930. After 1900 the state had no reapportionment for the Illinois General Assembly or the U.S. congressional delegation until 1947 because downstaters feared that a legislature dominated by Chicagoans might enact liberal, prolabor legislation. The state's congressional districts were realigned in 1947 only because Illinois lost a seat in the U.S. House of Representatives, but still COOK COUNTY and Chicago, with more than half the state's population, had only 19 of the state's 51 state legislative districts. Almost two decades later, the partisan deadlock over reapportionment led to a court-ordered at-large election in 1964 in which all 177 members of the Illinois House were elected from a ludicrously long ballot sheet.

Indifference and hostility by the legislature regarding the unique problems of Chicago led to overlapping governmental and taxing bodies, creating inefficiencies and producing a climate where professional politicians could advance their personal interests. Chicago's

"Downstate"

"Downstate" defies any single definition. For some Illinoisans, downstate begins at the southwest city limits of Chicago. Others would claim that any area north of I-80 is "outstate," and that downstate does not really begin until one reaches Bloomington.

Nor is there agreement on "Southern Illinois." Most believe it begins south of Springfield, but hardcore Southern Illinois residents don't claim any territory north of Carbondale.

All of this is beside the point, however, because "downstate" is a state of mind more than a state of geography. Although acres of corn and beans will never be confused with Michigan Avenue, the plain fact is that Chicagoans and downstaters *think*—and speak—differently.

While Chicago is a great city of ethnic neighborhoods, the small towns and rural areas of downstate are somehow more *personal,* with a bit of the frontier spirit remaining. People know their neighbors—and their neighbors' problems. Church groups, BOWLING leagues, Farm Bureau, and ROTARY all promote a more tight-knit sense of community and a "oneness" often absent from the fast-paced anonymity of life in a big city.

POLITICS is often the sport of downstate Illinois and is taken very seriously. Chicagoans—with a mayor elected for life—make do with the BULLS, BEARS, CUBS, BLACKHAWKS, WHITE SOX, and Chicago Fire.

Downstaters both fear and envy Chicago. Downstaters are convinced that Chicago gets "their" highway money and "their" school funds. Chicago equals big city, big city equals CRIME, noise, traffic, welfare, and poverty. Forgotten—except to the occasional tourist—are the architectural wonders of the nineteenth and twentieth centuries, LAKE MICHIGAN, the exchanges that buy and sell downstate's agricultural produce, the ART INSTITUTE, the CHICAGO SYMPHONY ORCHESTRA, the LYRIC OPERA, the parades, festivals, and the sheer wealth and exuberance of America's "most livable" big city.

Of course, to combine all the strength of Chicago with the quiet beauty of Southern Illinois (which is geographically and spiritually closer to Mississippi than it is to Chicago) is to realize that Illinoisans have the best of all worlds, and that Teddy Roosevelt was right when he said almost a hundred years ago that Illinois is the most American of all the states.

James R. Thompson

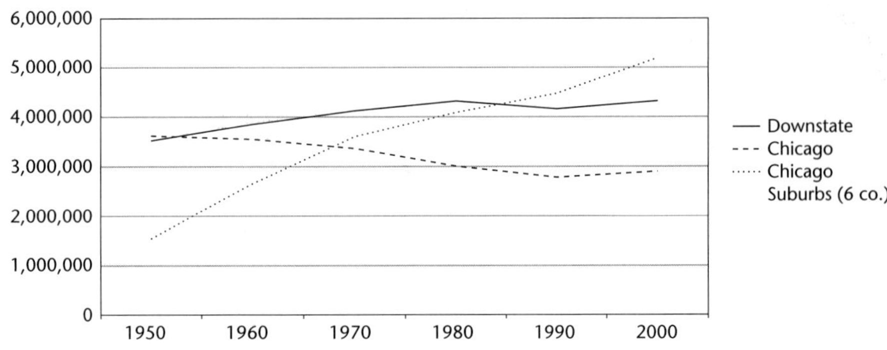

Illinois population in Chicago, suburbs, and downstate, 1950–2000. Source: U.S. Census.

under-representation in the state's capitol also left many important city functions in the hands of state government. Chicago's efforts to secure "HOME RULE" were successfully fended off by downstate politicians, and the state constitution of 1870 created a unique cumulative voting mechanism for electing representatives to the Illinois House: each district sent three representatives to Springfield, with voters casting their three ballots for one, two, or three candidates. While providing minority party representation in even the most partisan legislative districts, this unorthodox system tended to create a class of professional politicians who frequently broke ranks with the party to support an issue dear to their districts. A new state constitution in 1970 provided a measure of relief on reapportionment, and home rule for Chicago and other municipalities. The unorthodox system of cumulative voting was not abandoned until 1981.

Regional divisions, ethnic and racial tensions, intense partisan rivalries, conflicting special-interest groups, and political corruption have characterized the complex POLITICAL CULTURE of Illinois, which, because of its diversity, many political observers consider to be the state most resembling the nation as a whole. Perhaps Illinois state politics is so complicated because there is so much of it. Historian Cullom Davis notes that the Illinois political fabric comprises more units of government than any other state, including 102 counties, nearly 1,300 cities and villages, and more than 1,400 townships, all overlapped by no less than 2,500 SPECIAL DISTRICTS responsible for fire protection, airports, libraries, parks, water and sanitation, community colleges, and even mosquito abatement. In addition, the state has more than 960 school districts. Perhaps because of the numerous conflicting currents and agendas, the strength of the major political parties statewide remained remarkably balanced through the 1970s and early 1980s, with the Republican and Democratic Parties each holding almost exactly 30 percent of registered voters.

Beginning in the 1970s, Chicago's suburbs located in Cook and the surrounding "COLLAR COUNTIES" (LAKE, MCHENRY, KANE, DUPAGE, and WILL) emerged as a third major center of regional political power. In the 1980s, cities like JOLIET and Kankakee, traditionally considered downstate, were suddenly viewed as part of the Chicago metropolitan area as the suburban frontier sprawled outward.

As Chicago and many of Illinois' rural counties and smaller cities continue to lose population, the rapid growth of the largely Republican suburbs has caused Chicago's Democratic political leaders to look increasingly downstate to check the rising suburban power and hold on to the city's share of the political spoils. At the same time, the suburbs, particularly to the south of the city, have become more ethnically and racially diverse, enabling Democratic gains in traditional strongholds of the suburban Republicans.

Despite the economic interdependence of Chicago, the suburbs, and the rest of the state, regional animosities remain characterized by notions of difference and distance. Many Chicagoans still view the downstaters as unsophisticated country folk; downstaters often consider the big city to be inhabited largely by hoodlums, slickers, and welfare recipients. Meanwhile many suburbanites increasingly locate the poverty of southern Illinois and the problems of the inner city beyond their concerns. Chicagoans, including suburbanites, seldom venture into the southern parts of Illinois and find it difficult to believe that this state's capital exists some two hundred miles south of the LOOP; at the same time many downstate view Chicago, and its increasingly affluent suburbs, with distrust and disdain, consider St. Louis, Missouri, as their most important urban center, and root for the Cardinals rather than the Chicago CUBS.

Michael J. Devine

See also: Charters, Municipal; Governing the Metropolis; Metropolitan Growth; Taxation and Finance

Further reading: Davis, Cullom. "Illinois: Crossroads and Cross Section." In *Heartland: Comparative Histories of Midwestern States,* ed. James H. Madison, 1988. • Gove, Samuel K., and James D. Nowlan. *Illinois Politics and Government: The Expanding Metropolitan Frontier.* 1996. • Jensen, Richard J. "Sectionalism in Illinois Politics." In *Illinois: Its History and Legacy,* ed. Roger D. Bridges and Rodney O. Davis, 1984, 12–22.

Stateway Gardens. Built in 1958, the 33-acre site between 35th and 39th Streets along State Street in the DOUGLAS COMMUNITY AREA replaced the Federal Street slum area with all-black public high-rise housing. By the 1970s, municipal neglect and budget cuts created opportunities for GANGS to gain control

Initial Land Sales in Northeastern Illinois

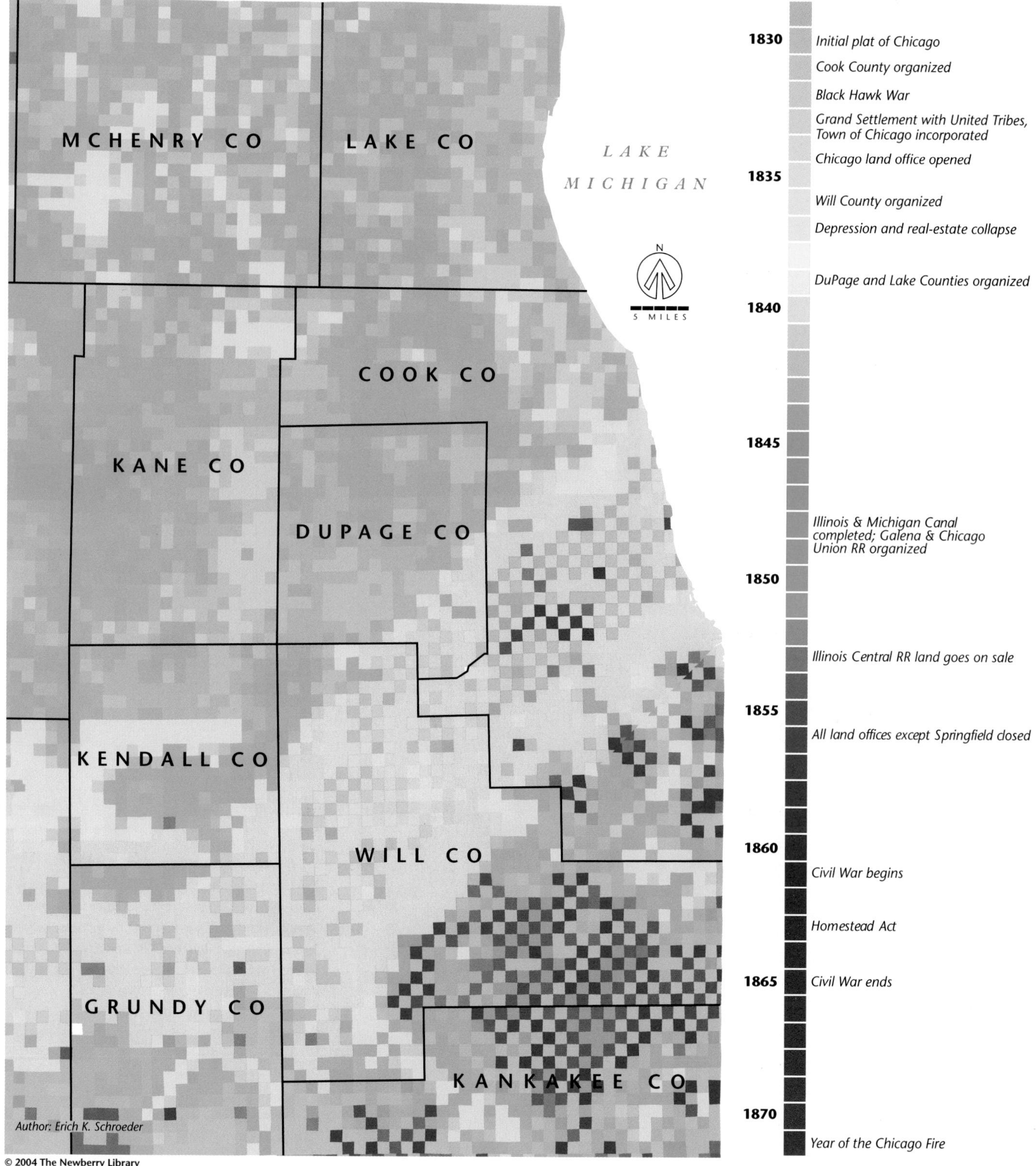

Initial Land Sales in Northeastern Illinois

Northeastern Illinois was colonized by settlers from the United States beginning in the 1830s, following the survey and sale of canal lands within the canal corridor to private interests. The checkerboard pattern of sales in this diagonal yellow zone reflects the difference between early land purchases from the state canal commissioners (yellow and buff hues) and later acquisitions from the federal government (green and blue hues). Most of the remainder of the region was purchased by individuals during the 1840s, except for the Illinois portion of the Kankakee Marsh district in the southeast portion of the map, which was not completely sold off until the 1850s and '60s. This pattern of differential timing in initial land sales strikingly demonstrates the impetus given to agricultural settlement by the Illinois & Michigan Canal.

Progress of the Chicago Fire of 1871

OCTOBER 8
8:30 pm–midnight

OCTOBER 9
midnight–6:00 am
6:00 am–noon
noon–6:00 pm

OCTOBER 9–10
6:00 pm–4:00 am

Firebrands carried aloft
Origins of separate fires
Paths of fire expansion

Fullerton
Lincoln
FIRE BURNED OUT DURING RAINFALL EARLY OCTOBER 10
LINCOLN PARK
Centre (Armitage)
Clark
CEME-TERY
Halsted
North
Division
LAKE MICHIGAN
Mahlon Ogden residence not burned
State
Wells
Water Tower not burned
Chicago
Kinzie
7:00 am
2:30 am
7:00 am
piers not burned
Chicago River
1:30 am Court-house
Madison
12 midnight
Area burned by fire on October 7
11:30 pm
Harrison
10:00 pm
2:30 am
blocked by railroad tracks
Area burned by 1874 fire
8:30pm O'Leary's stable
1000 FEET
12th (Roosevelt)
Author: Michael P. Conzen

Fire Limits in Chicago in the 1870s

Progress of the Chicago Fire of 1871

The Great Chicago Fire was not one fire, but a succession of nine separate fires started by flying brands carried from earlier burning sites, which then melded into one relentless inferno. It all started in the O'Leary barn on a rear alley of DeKoven Street on the Near West Side at 8:30 p.m. on October 8, 1871. Amid firefighting difficulties and official confusion, the fire spread north and eastward. Ninety minutes later a burning brand, caught in the updraft, sailed over and landed on Bateham's Mills to the north, starting a second fire. Brands from there started other fires across the river near and in the business district, and by 2:30 a.m. a flying brand started a fire on property north of the river. Given the prevailing winds, the coalescing fires burned most of the western portion of the city center and a swath of the North Side heading north-northeast to the lakefront by 6:00 a.m. the following day. By then it was unstoppable. Over the next 22 hours the fire finished off the business district, the lakefront harbor, and a large wedge of the North Side as far as Fullerton, by which time rain helped the fire burn itself out.

City limits in 1871
Built-up area in 1871
Area burned in fire
"Fire Limits" *area where 1872 ordinance restricted building materials*

Lincoln Park
ESTROYED BY FIRE
Business District
LAKE MICHIGAN
State
N
ONE MILE

Railroads and Chicago's Loop, circa 1930

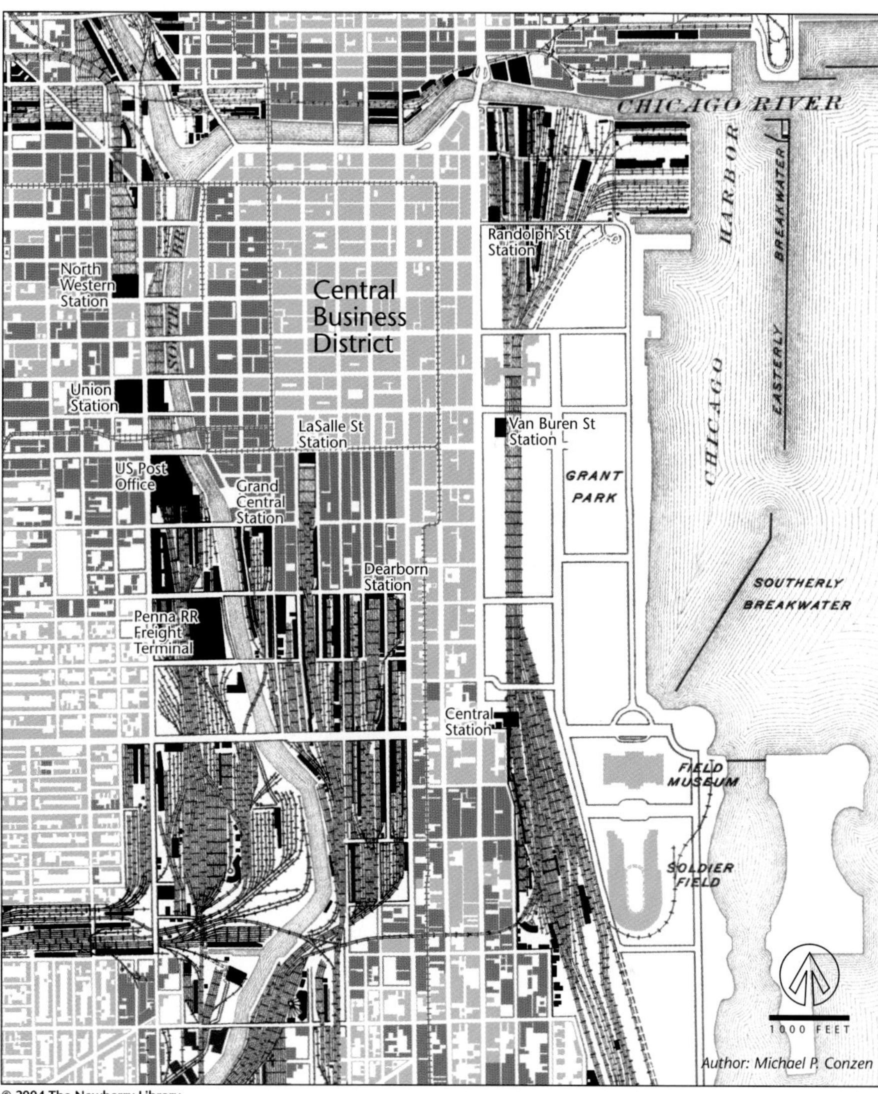

Railroad Facilities | Warehouses | Other Buildings

Fire Limits in Chicago in the 1870s

The Chicago Fire of 1871 burned less than a quarter of the built-up area of the city. It destroyed the business district, residential blocks immediately to the south and southwest, and a good portion of the North Side east of the North Branch of the river, but missed virtually the whole South Side and most of the vast West Side. In 1872, "fire limits" were established within which new construction was to be of brick or stone. The limits were drawn, however, so that much of the North Side could again be built up with wooden structures, a concession to the meager resources of many residents. Notwithstanding the new regulations, many replacement buildings across the city continued to be built of wood, making the fire limits a hollow act of city governance.

Railroads and Chicago's Loop, circa 1930

As the nation's single most important transportation hub, and as the key commercial pivot between the East and the great West, Chicago developed an extraordinary concentration of railroad terminals and related warehousing districts around its central business core. This map captures the pattern in 1930, when a great deal of urban manufacturing shared space with warehouse quarters (purple) adjacent to the railroad stations, yards, and riverfront and lakeside docks and elevators (black). The combination of these facilities created a complete collar five to eight blocks deep encircling the business district (dense brown), except on the eastern flank where Grant Park (white) was laid out between the Illinois Central tracks and Chicago Harbor.

Neighborhood Change: Prairie Avenue, 1853–2003

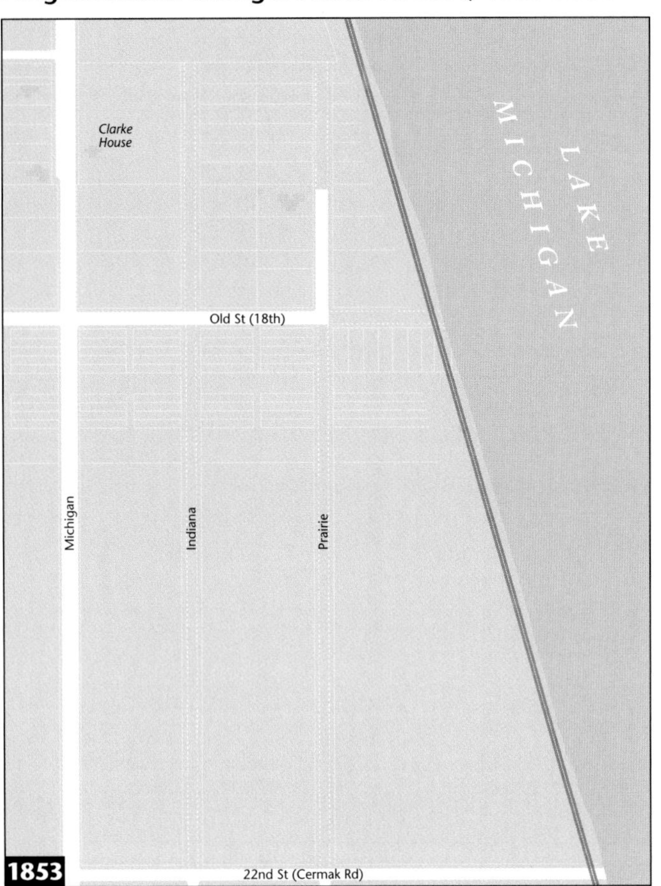

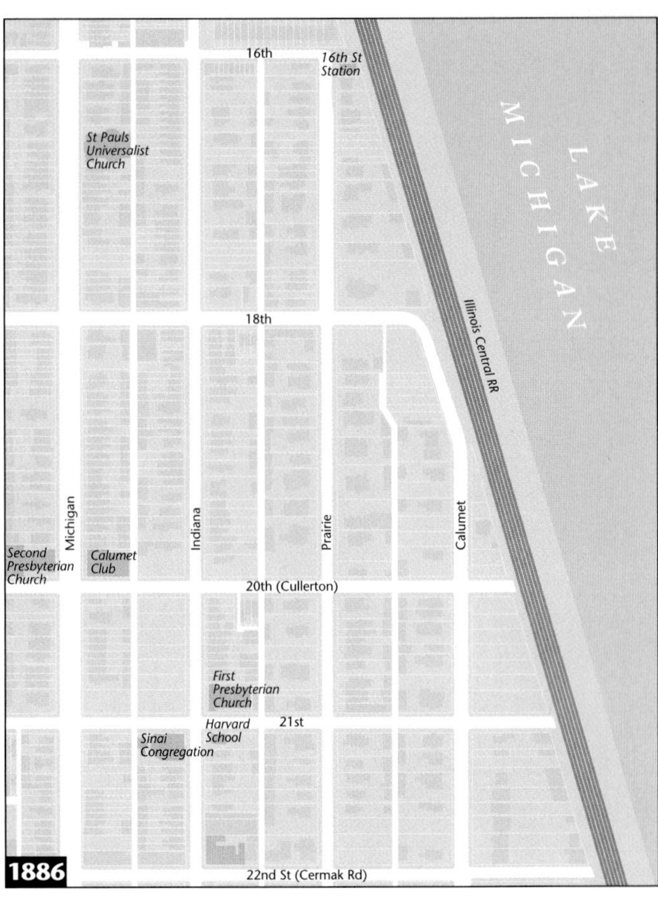

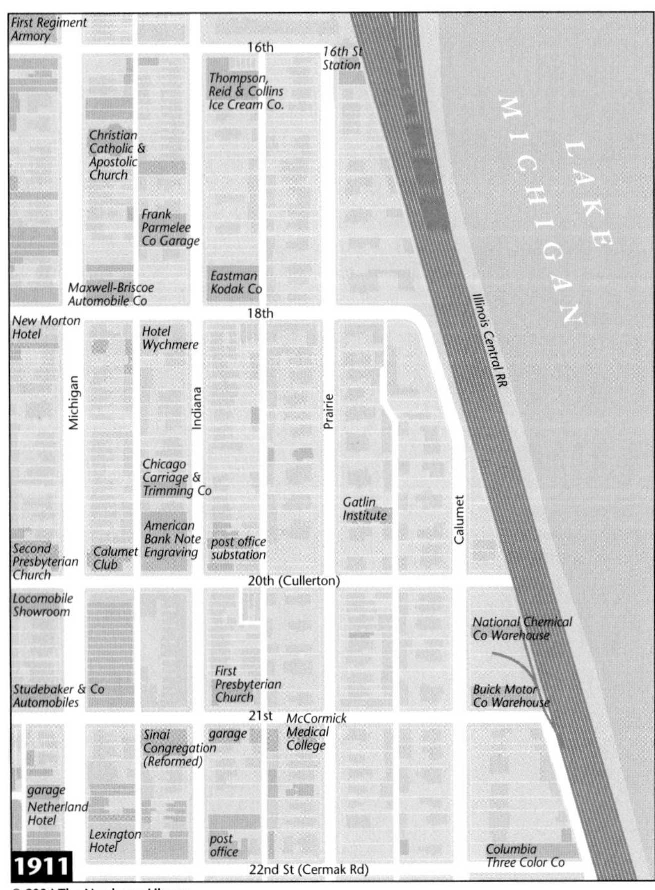

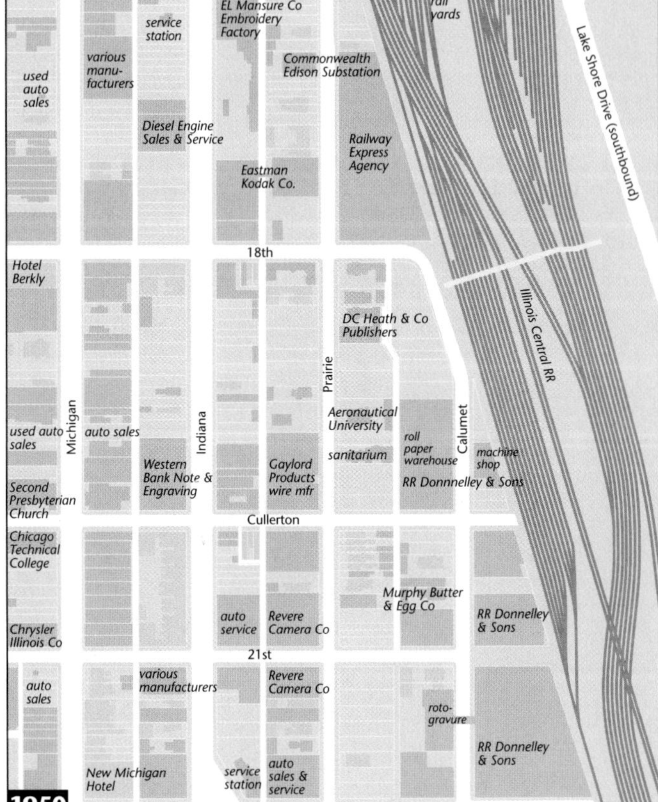

Neighborhood Change: Prairie Avenue, 1853–2003

From elite section to factory district and back to upscale neighborhood, Prairie Avenue and its environs have seen massive cycles of urban investment, decay, and revalorization. In 1853 the area was only partly subdivided in anticipation of residential development, being almost a mile beyond the southern edge of town. Just one grand villa had been built. By 1877, following the Great Chicago Fire, the 11-block area had largely filled up with mansions on Prairie and Calumet Avenues, while Indiana Avenue received a more mixed stock of row houses and detached residences. By 1886, Prairie Avenue was home to many of the city's richest families, and every mansion had its own carriage house. By 1911 the spread of manufacturing close to the South Side railroad yards brought warehouses and factories to the margins of the Prairie Avenue district, and the elite began to depart. A few mansions were converted for boarders or for nonresidential uses or knocked down for more factories. By 1950 large industrial structures dominated the district, and the sites of many former mansions stood vacant. As of 2003, the area was again being transformed. Deindustrialization and urban congestion pushed manufacturing from the area. Some factories were demolished, others converted to trendy loft apartment buildings. The few surviving much-neglected mansions were restored or renovated and declared a city historic district, while new infill housing colonized the vacant spaces in between.

Chicago's Ethnic Mosaic in 1980 and 2000

(pp. C6–C7)

Chicago's residential space has always been socially fluid, and frequently contested. Early Yankee, Irish, and German neighborhoods dissolved as established residents gained wealth and shifted to newer housing at the expanding urban fringe. Older neighborhoods drew newer migrant Swedes, Dutch, Italians, Russians, and Poles. Each of these groups filtered through city neighborhoods, shifting slowly outward. African Americans partly followed this pattern, subject to the limitations of formal and informal residential exclusion. A large Mexican community and a smaller Puerto Rican one initially settled neighborhoods between white and black districts and, subsequently, areas formerly occupied by Poles and other Eastern Europeans. Chinatown emerged significantly in the twentieth century, but other Asian groups have settled in Chicago only recently, mostly on the North Side.

It is difficult to represent the complexity of ethnic space in Chicago systematically on a single map. Here, for 1980 and 2000, census tracts are colored for the most numerous group in each tract, based on the five U.S. census population files that include data on ethnic identity. While not completely compatible, these data permit nevertheless a mapping of the most prominent groups in terms of the areas they chiefly occupy. All of the groups that are numerically preeminent in at least one tract are shown by an individual color tint. Letter symbols identify smaller groups in tracts where they represent at least 1 in 10 residents. Members of other groups are also present in various localities, but at densities of less than 1 in 10.

Between 1980 and 2000, Chicago's ethnic mosaic shifted significantly but along a predictable spatial trajectory. Mexican Americans and African Americans in particular increased their presence. Chinese Americans had notably enlarged their community. Germans had almost faded from the map area, diluted and assimilated into the general suburban population. This occurred to some extent also with Italians and Irish (though they kept a suburbanizing presence on the Southwest Side), while Czechs and Lithuanians, by falling below the 10 percent concentration level, have dropped off the map. New groups to concentrate sufficiently to be shown included Asian Indians, Armenians, and Assyrians, while other Asian, African, and Latin American groups made an appearance as small groups significantly present in a few tracts.

Chicago's Residential Patterns According to Census Racial Categories in 2000 *(p. C8)*

In a city renowned for its strong patterns of racial segregation, it is notable that the margins between racial groups in geographical space are sometimes quite blurred. This map displays the population of the metropolitan core in units of 200 people by racial categories used by the U.S. census. For 2000, the population of each group within each census tract was determined as so many dots, which have been placed within each tract area. The pattern exhibits strong racial segregation in several places but also countless locales in which people of various races were found together.

Residential buildings | Industrial/Commercial buildings | Institutional buildings | Park

Authors: Michael P. Conzen, Douglas Knox, and Dennis McClendon

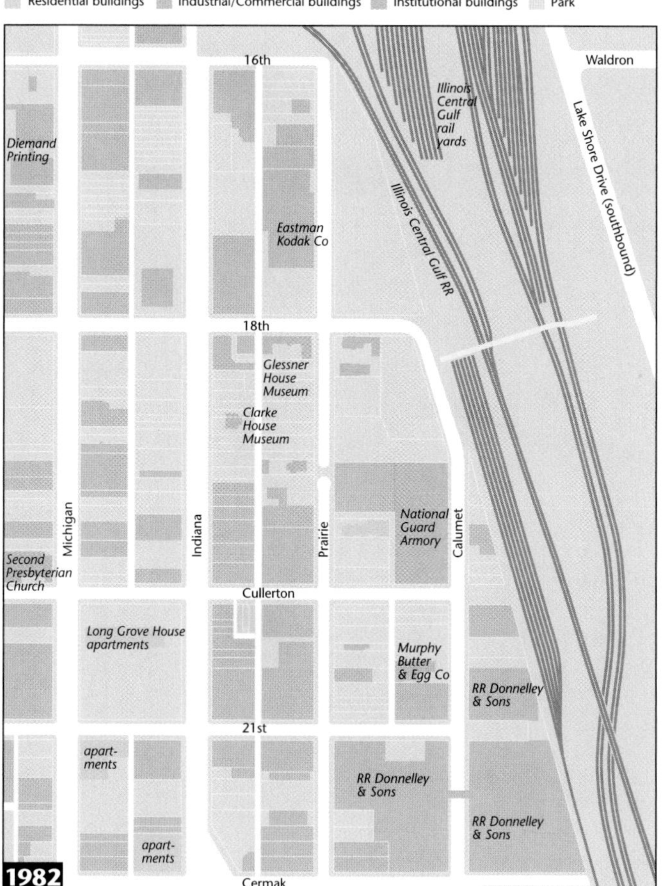

Chicago's Ethnic Mosaic in 1980

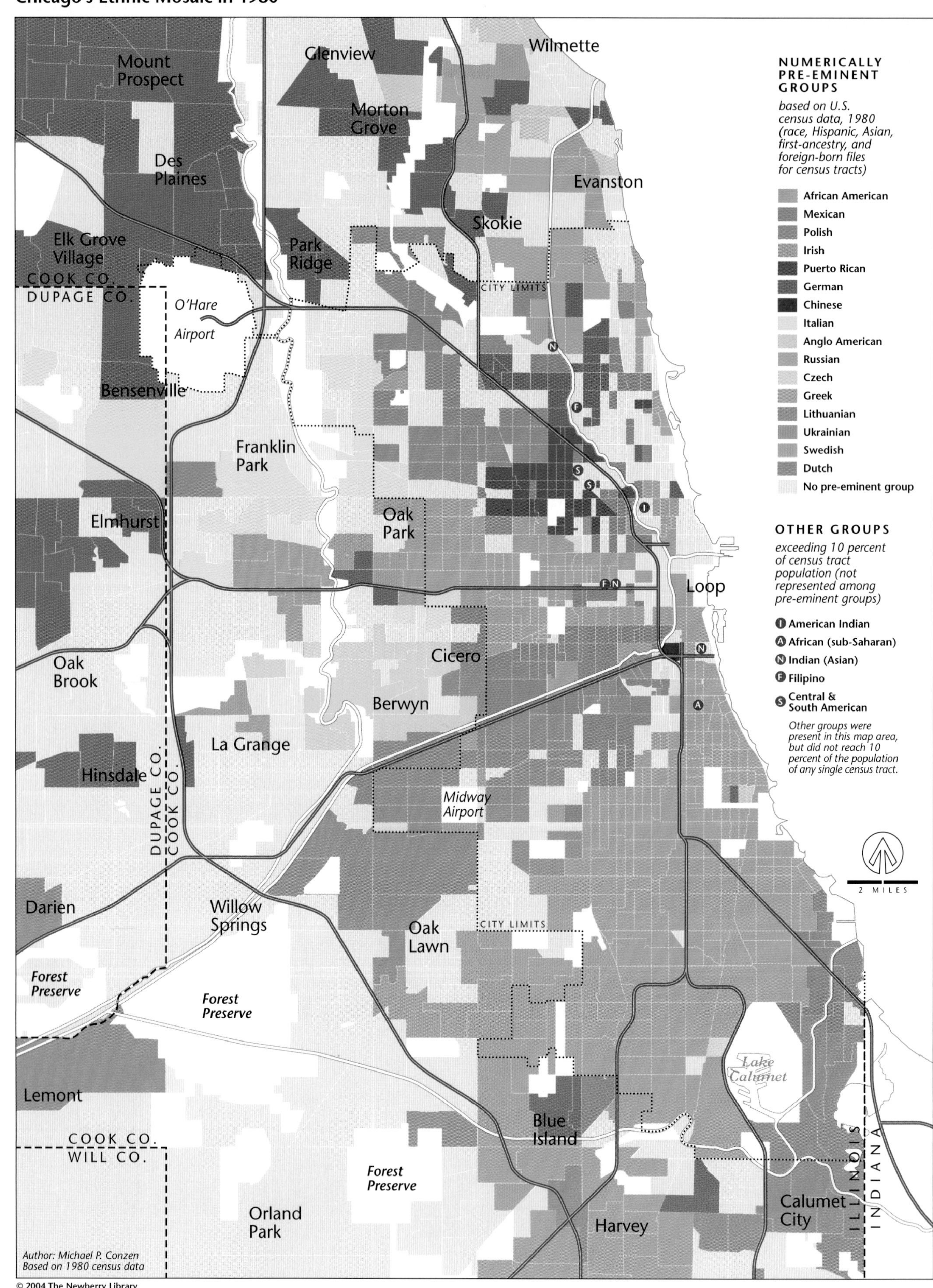

Chicago's Ethnic Mosaic in 2000

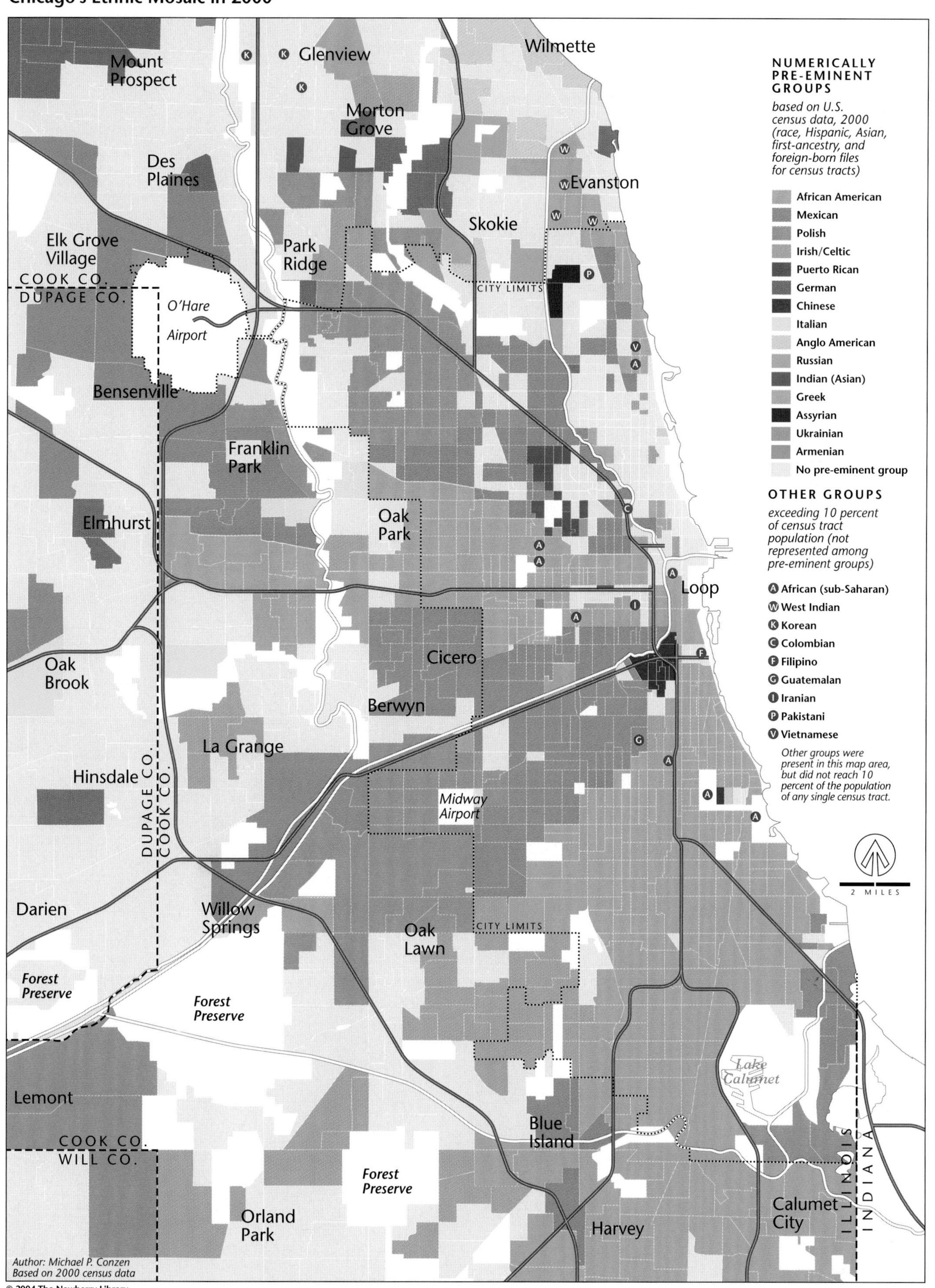

Chicago's Residential Patterns According to Census Racial Categories in 2000

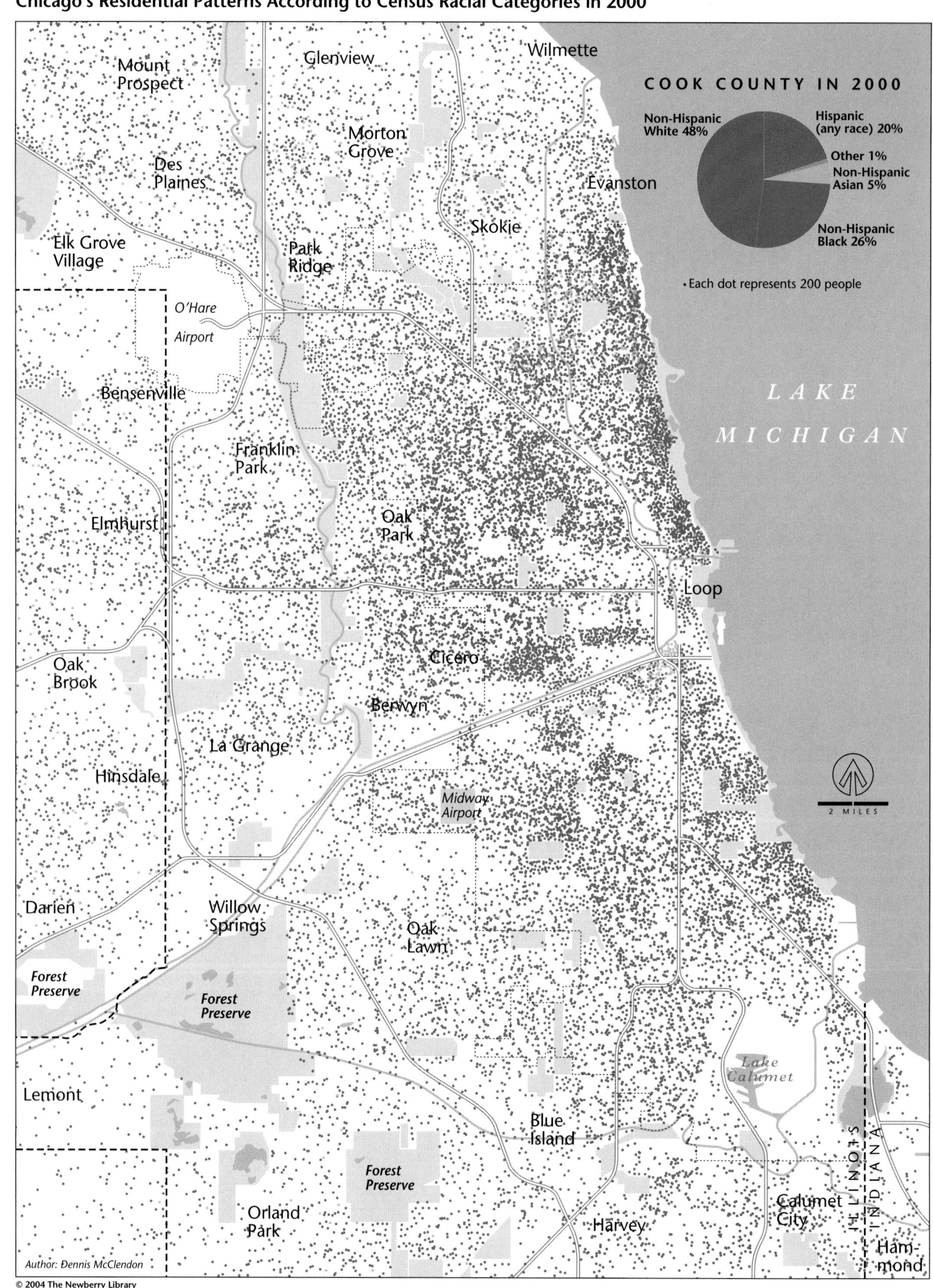

over the project's UNDERGROUND ECONOMY. In 2001 the CHICAGO HOUSING AUTHORITY began the process of demolishing the existing 1,644 units and replacing them with new mixed-income low-rise housing.

Erik Gellman

See also: Public Housing; South Side

Further reading: Downey, Sarah, and John McCormick. "Razing the Vertical Ghettoes: Mayor Daley Plans to Rescue His City's Squalid Public Housing by Destroying It." *Newsweek,* May 15, 2000. • Pacyga, Dominic A., and Ellen Skerrett. *Chicago, City of Neighborhoods: Histories and Tours.* 1986.

Steel. *See* Iron and Steel

Steel- and Ironworkers. *See* Iron- and Steelworkers

Steering. Racial steering refers to the practice (illegal since 1968) engaged in by some property owners, brokers, and managers of steering white home and APARTMENT seekers into white areas, while steering equally creditworthy black prospects into black and racially changing areas. Antisteering, sometimes called benign steering by critics, refers to efforts by municipalities and housing groups to combat illegal steering by lawsuits and managed integration programs.

The Leadership Council for Metropolitan Open Communities and the South Suburban Housing Center are lead agencies in antisteering litigation, and OAK PARK and PARK FOREST have the best-known managed integration programs.

Two developments in the late 1960s set the stage for antisteering efforts. In January 1966, Martin Luther King, Jr., chose Chicago for a national campaign against housing bias. After a summer of riots, arson, and marches, Mayor Richard J. Daley agreed to convene the Conference on Religion and Race. The resulting summit agreement led to the formation of the Leadership Council to act as a housing bias watchdog agency. In Washington, five years of CIVIL RIGHTS legislation culminated in the Fair Housing Act of 1968, which made it unlawful to deny to sell or rent a dwelling solely on account of race, and declared neighborhood integration a national goal.

In 1975, the Leadership Council, the village of BELLWOOD, and five residents accused two brokers of steering black home buyers into a racially changing 12-by-13-block area in Bellwood, thereby denying the buyers the benefits of living in an integrated neighborhood, and inducing lower property values and erosion of the tax base. The district court denied the plaintiffs standing to sue, a decision reversed on appeal. The Supreme Court, in *Gladstone, Realtors v. Village of Bellwood* (1979), decided that the village and homeowners in a racially changing area have standing to challenge steering practices as indirect victims of housing bias.

The Leadership Council had been denied standing to sue in *Bellwood.* Testing remedies were expanded in *Havens Realty Corp. v. Coleman* (1982), in which the Supreme Court said that housing groups and black testers (people who pose as buyers, both black and white, to monitor practices) given false information may sue. Thus empowered, the Leadership Council sued six real-estate agencies in southwest and northwest Cook County in 1983. The following year, the South Suburban Housing Center and nine South Cook County suburbs sued the South Suburban Board of Realtors.

In addition to antisteering suits, suburbs facing racial change have also used techniques of benign steering and managed integration. These include the monitoring of racial turnover by water meter readers, benign steering marketing, marketing to whites only, the enforcement of strict housing and occupancy codes by annual inspections, the regulation and licensing of "for sale" signs, and the banning of overnight street PARKING.

Realtors have opposed most schemes of managed integration. The National Association of Realtors countersued the plaintiffs in the South Suburban Center suit of 1984, charging their managed integration techniques violated the Fair Housing Act. In 1997, the court exonerated the managed integration practices of the plaintiff suburbs and dismissed most other complaints by plaintiffs and counterplaintiffs.

Pierre deVise

See also: Blockbusting; Housing Reform; Neighborhood Succession; Open Housing

Further reading: DeVise, Pierre. "Housing Discrimination in the Chicago Metropolitan Area." *De Paul Law Review* 32.2 (1985): 492–513. • Goodwin, Carole. *The Oak Park Strategy: Community Control of Racial Change.* 1979.

Steger, IL, Cook and Will Counties, 29 miles S of the Loop. Columbia Heights, platted along the Chicago & Eastern Illinois RAILROAD and the Vincennes/Hubbard's Trail, was an industrial town named after the WORLD'S COLUMBIAN EXPOSITION of 1893. Later known as Steger, it became a growing suburb sitting astride the COOK–WILL County line.

In 1893, John Valentine Steger opened a piano factory on 20 acres of land alongside the railroad. The railroad town also boasted a second factory, a general store, a post office, and a burgeoning housing stock. With 324 residents, the village incorporated in 1896. John Steger agreed to pay $400 toward election costs if the name was Steger rather than Columbia Heights. Steger won and Columbia Heights was no more.

John Steger played an instrumental role in the town's development. Along with the factory, Steger planned a residential SUBDIVISION. Learning from the mistakes of George PULLMAN, he encouraged homeownership and independent commercial development.

Serving two terms as village president, Steger oversaw development of a volunteer fire department, WATER and sewer facilities, and a unique system of underground pipes which provided steam heat for workers' homes from the heating plant of the factories.

He also recruited GERMAN craftsmen, developed assembly-line manufacturing of pianos, and designed special railcars for shipping them. By 1920, Steger was the "piano capital of the world," producing more than a hundred a day. Phonographs were also manufactured there.

John Steger engaged with the industrial leaders of Chicago, joining the Union League CLUB and serving on bank boards. In 1910 the Steger Building was completed at the corner of Jackson and Wabash in the LOOP as his administrative and display center. Designed by Benjamin Howard Marshall, this 19-story structure still stands.

After Steger's death in 1916, the factories continued until closing in 1926. Having depended on one major manufacturer, the village was particularly vulnerable during the GREAT DEPRESSION. However, the remarkable collection of buildings continued to be a key employment center. In 1930 a macaroni factory started in one of the old buildings, and several years later local craftsmen joined together to manufacture radio cabinets in another. At its height of activity, their Steger Furniture Company employed close to 700. Following other uses over time and a major fire, the buildings were demolished in 1972–73. By the end of the century, a small strip commercial area, a large Kmart, and a huge expanse of asphalt parking lot covered the site.

Along with the growth of some light industries and new stores, the village lost much of its original town center and became increasingly an automobile-oriented suburban area. In 1990, a large annexation to the east doubled the land size of the village.

Larry A. McClellan

See also: Furniture; Infrastructure; Musical Instrument Manufacturing

Further reading: *Happy Birthday, Steger, Celebrating 100 Years.* Newsprint. Village of Steger, 1996. • Steger Historical Society. *Steger: A Pictorial History of Steger, The Early Years.* Vol. 1. 1995. • Wozny, John W. *John Valentine Steger: The Man and His Town.* 1995.

Steppenwolf Theatre. In its rise from a humble hometown start to international fame, Steppenwolf became a Chicago cultural icon, symbolic of the heights of high-profile achievement to which a locally based THEATER could climb.

Founded in 1975 and originally housed in the 88-seat basement auditorium of a ROMAN CATHOLIC church and school in north suburban HIGHLAND PARK, the scrappy, ambitious ensemble of young actors, including several alumni of Illinois State University, made their first, sensational impression with intense, highly physical interpretations of gritty contemporary drama.

Moving into Chicago in 1980, the company achieved major breakthroughs when several of its hit Chicago productions—*True West, And a Nightingale Sang, Balm in Gilead,* and *Orphans*—transferred to much-applauded engagements in New York's off-Broadway theaters, effectively launching the big-time stage, screen, and television careers of ensemble members Gary Sinise, John Malkovich, Laurie Metcalf, John Mahoney, Kevin Anderson, and Joan Allen. This success was followed by a 1985 Tony Award as outstanding regional theater and a 1990 Tony for best play of the 1989–90 Broadway season for director Frank Galati's adaptation of John Steinbeck's novel *The Grapes of Wrath.*

In 1991, Steppenwolf moved into a new $8 million, 500-seat theater at 1650 N. Halsted Street, and in 1998, in a first for a theater organization, it received a National Medal of Arts, which cited its outstanding contributions to the excellence, growth, support, and availability of the arts in the United States.

The company, grown to more than 30 members, concentrated on larger-scale dramas in its new theater complex. Significantly, though its star members no longer lived in Chicago, they regularly returned to the home base for theater engagements.

Richard Christiansen

See also: Acting, Ensemble; Entertaining Chicagoans; Theater Companies

Stickney, IL, Cook County, 8 miles SW of Chicago. Until about 1900 most of the village of Stickney was covered by Mud Lake, a large marshy area stretching from Chicago to LYONS. Across Mud Lake ran a historic PORTAGE trail between the CHICAGO and DES PLAINES RIVERS. Mud Lake began to recede with the construction of the ILLINOIS & MICHIGAN CANAL in 1836, and by 1900 the SANITARY AND SHIP CANAL had left it relatively dry. Developers moved quickly to build on the reclaimed land, and early residents of what is now Stickney included GERMAN and DUTCH farmers.

The village is named for Alpheus B. Stickney, a RAILROAD executive who played a central role in establishing the Clearing Industrial District. The village's story is closely linked with the history of Stickney Township, organized in 1901. In 1913 the village of Stickney was established from Stickney Township land. The early years of the village were marked by peculiar venues for official meetings: the organizational meeting was held at Hawthorne racetrack, and subsequent meetings took place in the waiting room at Mount Auburn CEMETERY. In 1919 most residents worked as truck farmers or in the QUARRIES near town.

Neighboring CICERO and BERWYN boomed in the 1920s, and Stickney also expanded.

Around 1920 Al Capone and other criminals moved into Stickney, establishing brothels and speakeasies. To some extent village government was complicit: at the funeral of a famed gangster in 1924, Stickney police served as an honor guard. Illegal GAMBLING operations persisted until at least the 1950s. By the late 1930s Stickney's population stood at about 2,000, and the town was known more for its taverns than anything else.

Stickney's population increased after WORLD WAR II, reaching 6,239 by 1960. With much vacant land remaining, the village allowed bondholders to take over land with unpaid taxes, and home construction peaked in the 1950s. The residential area is concentrated in the western end of town. In 1949 Commonwealth Edison began construction of a coal-powered generator power plant that straddled Stickney and its neighbor Forest View. Stickney has collaborated with FOREST VIEW on many projects, including the formation of the Stickney–Forest View Library District in 1953.

Stickney has achieved a measure of fame (or infamy) for its sewage treatment plant, the largest in the world. Operated by the Metropolitan Water Reclamation District of Greater Chicago, the plant, opened in phases since 1930, takes up 40 percent of the village's land and is its largest employer. While many would find little cachet in living in a town with the world's largest sewage treatment plant, the village has taken aggressive steps to ameliorate the impact of the facility.

Within a land area of less than two square miles, residents enjoy the safe, quiet streets and close-knit ties with neighbors. Many of Stickney's 6,148 residents in 2000 were of Polish, Mexican, German or Czech ancestry. Spacious Mount Auburn Cemetery, founded in 1895, has a sizable number of CHINESE burials.

Ronald S. Vasile

See also: Crime and Chicago's Image; Economic Geography; Gas and Electricity; Water

Further reading: "Our Township Government: Stickney's History from Indians to Skyscrapers." 1942. • Cohen, Laurie. "Suburb Clears the Air: We're Close-Knit and We Like It." *Chicago Tribune,* January 12, 1991. • Village of Stickney. *Stickney's Golden Jubilee, 1913–1963.* [1963]

Sting. Chicago witnessed several attempts for professional SOCCER to gain a toehold in the local scene before the Sting, founded in 1975 by wealthy COMMODITIES trader Lee Stern, achieved this with North American Soccer League championships in 1981 and 1984. These were the first titles won by a Chicago pro franchise in any sport since the BEARS FOOTBALL crown in 1963. The Sting, coached by Willy Roy and fortified with a few top European players, was a perennial league contender. The 1981 campaign attracted major media attention and consistently drew crowds of 20,000 or more for the first time in Chicago soccer. The Sting stopped playing after the 1984 season when the league suspended operations in the wake of the financial collapse of several franchises.

Mike Conklin

See also: Creation of Chicago Sports

Stockyards. *See* Meatpacking; Union Stock Yard

Stonecutting. *See* Quarrying, Stonecutting, and Brickmaking

Stone Park, IL, Cook County, 13 miles W of the Loop. One of the smallest and poorest of

Chicago's suburbs, Stone Park also has one of the most distinctive histories. It boasted a population of 636 and an area of 0.4 square miles when incorporated in 1939. Stone Park grew rapidly during the 1950s and 1960s, reaching a population of 4,429 by 1970 and growing to 5,127 by 2000. In 1987 it ranked 258th in per capita income out of 262 communities in the six-county Chicago area.

As was common elsewhere, settlement began before the suburb was incorporated. Professional builders avoided the area, which had no BUILDING CODES or municipal services. Land was cheap during the 1930s. Property taxes were a fraction of Chicago's. "Reliefers" (people receiving welfare relief during the GREAT DEPRESSION) dug wells and built their own homes, using secondhand materials or the sorts of garage kits sold by Sears and local LUMBER dealers. Lacking an industrial base, the municipality was poor and slow to provide services. With no storm sewers, the area was vulnerable to FLOOD damage. During the floods of 1950, about one-third of all homes—then numbering 375—had to be evacuated. The pace of development then picked up, with more than half of the area's housing stock constructed during the 1950s.

Its size and poverty also made Stone Park vulnerable to organized CRIME, for which it became notorious. Local lore suggests that Al

Capone ran a BREWERY here during PROHIBITION, while the hometown boy and gangland criminal Rocco Pranno made Stone Park his base in the 1960s. For a time Pranno's brother controlled all political offices in the town, while Pranno himself ran a crime syndicate from his office table at the Club D'Or on North Mannheim Road.

Since the 1960s Stone Park has transcended its gangland image. Like other interwar suburbs, including adjacent MELROSE PARK, it has become a destination for a new generation of immigrant workers looking for inexpensive housing. Modest homes have been well-maintained, improved, and extended. While the district was once home to many ITALIANS, and remained the site of the Italian Cultural Center, 79 percent of the population was Hispanic in 2000.

Richard Harris

See also: Built Environment of the Chicago Region; Crime and Chicago's Image; Housing, Self-Built; Underground Economy

Further reading: Christgau, Eugene F. "Unincorporated Communities in Cook County." M.A. thesis, University of Chicago. 1942. • Harris, Richard. "Chicago's Other Suburbs." *Geographical Review* 84.4 (1994): 394–410. • Sakamoto, B. "A Tiny Town Outlasts Its Gangland Roots." *Chicago Tribune,* April 7, 1990.

Streamwood, IL, Cook County, 29 miles W of the Loop. For over a century, farmers, many German immigrants, worked the land now known as Streamwood. A stagecoach line along Lake Street and a tavern along present-day Route 20 served early residents from the 1830s. In the 1950s Streamwood stepped out of its role as farm country and emerged as a rapidly growing community looking to engulf neighboring unincorporated towns.

SUBDIVISION development came in 1956 when Maxon Construction built 21 preassembled houses on concrete slabs. The houses, shipped from Indiana by National Homes Corporation, were already packaged with insulated walls, ceiling, roof sections, and framing. The factory also installed doors, windows, screens, and inside trim. A local contractor and a construction crew living in trailers on the site poured the foundations, shingled the roofs, sided, wired, painted, and installed the plumbing. Assembly was completed in less than two weeks and led to nicknames like "Plywood City" and "Mudville."

New residents often came from the same Chicago neighborhoods and rented with an option to buy. Many were skilled tradesmen and salesmen. New occupants faced an insufficient well system, and their cars were often stuck in muddy driveways.

Young families predominated. In 1958 Woodland Heights School opened with six classrooms to accommodate two hundred children. When this quickly became insufficient for the burgeoning population, four hundred children took classes in split shifts, and mothers who marched in front of the school to discourage buyers were arrested for disorderly conduct. The town's continued success was doubtful. Streamwood SHOPPING Center, built in 1962, was condemned because of extensive water damage resulting from its construction on unstable ground. It took years to fix the problems and for the center to reopen.

Despite this problematic start, population surged to 18,176 by 1970. The village, which had incorporated in 1957, grew in size to nearly six square miles. Industries located on the southeast side. Builders parceled off their acreage and donated land for schools, a village hall, and a pool.

In 1989 Westview Shopping Center opened, two-thirds of which is in Streamwood, the remaining third in HANOVER PARK. In 1990 Streamwood Oaks GOLF Course opened its nine holes to the public, adding another amenity to the once struggling community.

Although ranch-style housing was still available, new housing was predominantly two-story colonials with clapboard siding. "Mudville" had changed its face, with the only mud being at the bottom of 15 acres of conservation wetlands at the Oak Ridge Trail subdivision. By 2000 there were 36,407 residents of Streamwood.

Marilyn Elizabeth Perry

See also: Construction; Cook County; Metropolitan Growth

Further reading: Alft, E. C. *Hanover Township: Rural Past to Urban Present.* 1980. • Church, Everett. *Historical Chronology of the Village of Streamwood.* 1994. • Feeley, Ralph. *From Camelot to Metropolis: The History of Ontarioville–Hanover Park.* 1976.

Street Grades, Raising. In the late 1850s, the streets on most of the SOUTH SIDE and parts of the North and West Sides were raised by an average of between four and five feet, though in some places by as much as eight feet. This was done in two stages, in 1855–56 and 1857–58, for the purposes of facilitating drainage and accommodating the city's sewerage system. The most spectacular aspect of this effort, and the one that drew commentary from tourists, was the raising of existing buildings to the higher grades.

Low, flat, and on a clay and loam soil that absorbed little moisture, Chicago lacked natural means of drainage. It also was impossible to install underground sewers steep enough to drain their contents into the CHICAGO RIVER without raising the streets. The first phase of grade raising seems to have been an effort to drain rainfall. The second was part of the larger project of building the sewer system, designed by engineer Ellis Sylvester Chesbrough for the city's Board of Sewerage Commissioners and constructed beginning in 1856.

While the street raisings were public projects, raising buildings to the higher grade was left to individual property owners. Frame structures were relatively easy to raise, though many were not raised (houses in some parts of the city are still below grade), but the raising of large brick HOTELS, banks, and other business buildings was a technological feat in the 1850s. George M. Pullman, of sleeping car fame, made his initial reputation in Chicago raising buildings.

Robin Einhorn

See also: Flood Control and Drainage; Infrastructure; Innovation, Invention, and Chicago Business; Landscape; Water

Further reading: Cain, Louis P. *Sanitation Strategy for a Lakefront Metropolis: The Case of Chicago.* 1978.

Street Life. If anything has characterized the history of Chicago's street life, it has been disagreement, as each generation of urbanites has had to answer the same questions: How are public and private spaces defined and used? What should constitute proper conduct? Which of many competing uses should predominate? And which prevails, people or technology? Yet, at the same time, those same streets have functioned as a place for unifying celebration.

The Pre-Horsecar Era

The history of Chicago's street life has been shaped largely by changes in predominant forms of TRANSPORTATION. Before the mid-1850s Chicagoans walked or used private horse-drawn vehicles. The lack of effective paving and sidewalks made it difficult to use the streets for any purposes. Most people tolerated the mud and dust because they had no choice but to walk the largely unpaved streets to get to WORK. Even well-to-do men angrily petitioned city officials that the lack of sidewalks forced their wives to traipse through a thick coating of spring mud to get to church or to shop. Many women would not have used the downtown district at all had it not been for a group of young "crossing sweepers"—often HOMELESS youth—who swept brick crosswalks that had been installed at the corners. During the 1850s the elevation of the STREET GRADE to improve sewer flow also inhibited street life because it was done on a piecemeal basis by individual property owners. Those who lifted their buildings to the new level also elevated their sidewalks, leaving pedestrians to climb up and down tall ladders simply to walk down the street.

From the beginning, the borders between private and public use of the streets frequently blurred. Inadequate fencing allowed farm animals to wander, forcing the county to erect an estray in the courthouse square. And when

View of block on Lake Street between Clark and LaSalle during street raising, 1850s. Artist: Unknown. Source: The Newberry Library.

early ships arrived carrying a miscellany of unconsigned merchandise, their captains set up impromptu retailing areas along boat docks and adjacent streets.

When street and sidewalk conditions finally improved, Chicagoans began to use them as places to spend idle time. A summer's eve stroll on Michigan Avenue became a favorite way for middle- and upper-class "saunterers" to catch the lake breezes. But the proper citizenry of the city had a difficult time with a second group who used the streets for recreation. The press and city leaders condemned what appeared to be intentional idleness among a less desirable social stratum. Known in the 1850s as "corner puppies," these "loafers" whistled, made rude comments, or grabbed at women passing on the sidewalk. By midcentury, Chicagoans were avoiding such dangerous parts of town as "the Patch" and "Kilgubbin" (Goose Island), in part because the inhabitants appeared to be so menacing.

The development of the omnibus, an urban version of the stagecoach, began a series of subtle changes in the perception of the street. Patrons could not only travel longer distances in the same amount of time they used to walk, they also enjoyed a voluntary separation from the life of the street, much in the manner of the very wealthy who utilized private carriages. Omnibus riders became more interested in getting home as quickly as possible and began to regard any nontransportation uses of the street as obstacles. In 1857, Mayor "Long John" Wentworth temporarily stopped businesses from invading the sidewalks with merchandise displays and signs, although by the late 1860s it had once more become commonplace for advertisers to cover the exterior walls with billboards and hang banners from wires strung over streets.

Despite the dominance of workaday uses, there were many efforts to use the streets for unifying public celebrations. Some were impromptu. For instance, before railroads provided all-weather links to the outside world, crowds greeted the arrival of the first ship from the East, which signaled the end of the long winter isolation. Other events were more carefully planned. From the 1830s and 1840s there were parades on the Fourth of July and St. Patrick's Day. Political parties also used the streets for torchlight parades that unified the ranks and demonstrated their strength to the opposition. An inaugural speech delivered from the tall steps of City Hall traditionally followed each mayoral election. Within a few years of the introduction of the telegraph in 1848, news of wars and elections would cause crowds to gather outside newspaper offices for public postings of telegraphic reports. During the Civil War, the city reverberated to the sound of military marches, and torchlight parades accompanied departing units to depots. The same streets hosted victory celebrations and such mournful events as the funeral procession for Lincoln.

The Golden Age of the Street

The post-fire decades ushered in the era of most intensive street life, as one observer's view of excitement became another's description of a nightmare. Increasing volumes of human and vehicular traffic, squeezed into a public space that couldn't easily be widened, brought unprecedented congestion. At the same time, the growing anonymity of city life and the general inability of an understaffed city police force to control what went on in the streets created what amounted to laissez-faire conditions. Different social groups continued to compete for control of the same space. Those who might be described as "destination travelers" became a more clearly defined group; their principal use of the street was in getting from one place to another with maximum efficiency. These included travelers moving between hotels and railroad stations, as well as commuters who rushed to work and back home either on foot or on omnibuses and horsecars. The introduction of cable cars in the 1880s and electric trolleys the following decade increased the intrusion of technology on the street, especially during rush hours. The construction of the "L" system between 1892 and 1907 aided this quest for efficiency by creating a whole new layer of street above the surface traffic. Its downtown structure assumed the name "Loop," which had originally described a square of streetcar tracks.

Late-nineteenth-century street life also contributed to the mixed images of Chicago, especially as it was portrayed in illustrated national magazines and in travelers' accounts. After the fire of 1871, civic leaders were proud to point out how the busy streets reflected rebuilding and rebirth. At the same time, illustrations of the bloody railroad strikes of 1877, the 1886 Haymarket Affair, and 1894 Pullman Strike focused on street confrontations and provided a quick stereotype of the instability of society in the mushrooming city. Likewise, the street created an instant impression on such foreign visitors as Rudyard Kipling, who

St. Patrick's Day Parade, 1949. Photographer: Unknown. Source: Chicago Public Library.

disdainfully described the "collection of miserables" who daily passed through "turmoil and squash." In 1900, Scottish author William Archer proclaimed that "New York for a moment does not compare with Chicago in the roar and bustle and bewilderment of its street life." Similarly, many of Chicago's greatest writers—especially those of rural origin—wove

Horse-drawn buggy wrecked in collision with Aurora, Elgin & Chicago interurban train, Wheaton, 1909. Photographer: Unknown. Source: DuPage County Historical Museum.

their fascination with the energy and variety of the public spaces, especially downtown, into their works. This is evident in the arrival scenes in novels such as Theodore Dreiser's *Sister Carrie* (1900). Sherwood Anderson's *Marching Men* (1917) described the way in which the working poor displayed their misery as they tramped the streets or rode the cars. Chicago-born Henry Blake Fuller's *The Cliff Dwellers* (1893) described the view from a SKYSCRAPER as if through the eyes of a bird of prey looking from its nest down at the street. Street life was also prominent in shorter forms of literature. George Ade drew inspiration from peddlers and passersby for his aptly titled column "Stories of the Streets and of the Town," which ran in the Chicago *Record* (1893–1900). And of course, the "painted women" of Carl Sandburg's "Chicago," as well as "Clark Street Bridge" and other pieces among his lesser-known POETRY, celebrated workaday street life.

In the real world, street life—and expectations about it—became as specialized as the neighborhoods that contained it. Downtown, the display windows of DEPARTMENT STORES invited pedestrians to pause and ponder, and by the 1880s strangers' guidebooks provided tourists with suggested routes and maps to enable them to wander in search of "the sights." Police, meanwhile, remained vigilant for "mashers," an updated version of corner puppies, who might make the Loop shopping visit unpleasant for women. Outside of downtown, COMMUTING patterns concentrated traffic along certain main streets that linked downtown and the sprawling neighborhoods. Major outlying SHOPPING DISTRICTS appeared where these heavily used destination travel corridors intersected, such as at 63rd and Halsted, or Lincoln and Belmont.

Out in the neighborhoods the patterns of street life varied by class. The levels of poverty and congestion in the adjacent housing usually determined the extent of the residents' dependence on the public places for their daily survival. For those at the bottom of the social scale, the street was home. After the FIRE OF 1871, living in public places had become part of the survival strategy for tens of thousands of temporarily homeless victims, many of whom wandered the city for months. During the depression that began two years later, the first generation of tramps (mobile nonworkers) and HOBOES (mobile seasonal workers) arrived in Chicago because it was the hub of the nation's growing rail network. By the end of the century thousands of UNEMPLOYED men populated three Skid Row districts that ringed the downtown. Here, day labor agencies did their hiring curbside, while the local street life consisted of the denizens of cheap RESTAURANTS, barrooms, pawnshops, used-clothing stores, and a variety of hotels ranging upwards of "nickel flops." Amidst them on the sidewalks and streets were such noisy "redeemers" as the SALVATION ARMY band and the Gospel Wagon of the PACIFIC GARDEN MISSION. It was easy for the more affluent Chicagoans to conflate idlers with the poor, who utilized public spaces as a necessary last resort for survival.

Each step up the economic ladder allowed participation in street activities to become more voluntary. Just above the transients, the tenement neighborhood provided somewhat more permanent dwellings, although conditions still forced a blurring in the distinctions between private and public. The street functioned as a verbal communication conduit within largely nonliterate communities, as well as a place to work and play. Sweltering nights saw much of the population sleeping on the sidewalks, and evictions cast newly homeless families and their meager possessions onto the curbstones. By 1868 there were already enough homeless youth peddling papers on the streets to justify the creation of the Newsboy's and Bootblack's Home, and their ranks grew. Greedy adults also snatched the earnings of large numbers of immigrant juveniles who had been imported during the 1870s to become street musicians.

Mass-produced subdivisions—reached by streetcar and "L"—allowed a further move up the social scale by making affordable such BUNGALOW neighborhoods as ENGLEWOOD, with its world of small porches, vegetable gardens, and modest fences. Further up the income scale, the lawns and ornamental fences in such substantial middle-class areas as RAVENSWOOD divided neighbors from the street and each

Traffic on Dearborn and Randolph, 1909. Photographer: Unknown. Source: Chicago Historical Society.

other, while children played in parks rather than on the streets. Here, also, neighborhood improvement associations pressured residents to maintain peace and order and beautify their private property, and residents joined private Bicycle clubs. Finally, at the top of the social scale, residents of such elite neighborhoods as Prairie Avenue and Astor Street utilized streets primarily for such symbolic activities as the annual opening-day parade to the Washington Park Race Track or for efforts toward public beautification. The wealthy rode in private carriages, ate lunch at downtown Clubs, and conversed by Telephone or at teas, not on the curbstone.

The level of independence from the street not only helped to determine one's social class, but that same space was often the meeting place or interface between social classes. More affluent Chicagoans, who could ride through tenement districts on streetcars, the "L," and commuter trains, came in contact with the poor largely through the street trades. Peddling, which involved an amazing variety of goods and services, was the source of economic survival for some and a convenience or annoyance for others. Adult immigrants realized that a minimum financial investment and hard work could provide an entree into capitalism and the means to avoid working for someone else. Successful vendors positioned themselves amidst the flow of likely customers. "Shoeshine boys" and news vendors knew where to find male commuters, while fakirs, who sold generally useless trinkets, occupied spots just outside department stores where mothers, who might have felt a bit of guilt at their personal spending, might be tempted to buy something for their children. Similarly, Teamsters maintained street stands near the retailers of furniture and other large items, while hacks cruised near the depots and hotels. Street trades on the edge of legitimacy and beyond also knew the importance of location. Years of contact with the street brought an understanding of the flow of traffic: a location outside of train stations, for instance, was ideal to collect donations from sympathetic rural travelers. Streetwalkers (Prostitutes), who peddled sex in public places, and their customers mutually discovered places where they did not draw unnecessary attention to themselves.

Other types of vendors learned the most productive routes through residential neighborhoods. Street Peddlers bought food that was often near the end of its shelf life from wholesalers and carried it to poorer districts that were too far from marketplaces for housewives to visit in person. Such mobile services as knife and scissors grinders alerted neighborhoods of their presence by the sound of a bell. Recyclers of various kinds also worked their way through the neighborhoods. Rag pickers, metal buyers, and other kinds of scavengers resold their findings at a profit because bottles, cloth, and even castoff cigar stubs could be recycled into new products. The specialties that developed in this economic street life mirrored the city's ethnicity, with Italians dominating in produce sales, Greeks in confectionaries, Jews in recycling trades, Dutch in scavenging, and Germans in handyman services. But what was a convenience to the working class was a nuisance to the more affluent, who valued privacy and wanted peddlers banned from their neighborhoods.

This hierarchy of class and privacy explains much about the nature of street life, but superimposed over the story were the temporal rhythms that determined the ebb and flow of activity. In the predawn hours hundreds of workers bought and sold produce at the Randolph and South Water Markets, while lamplighters turned off gas jets and crews from the city and the Municipal Order League watered and swept the surfaces. The morning rush hour saw factory workers walk to work as well as thousands of vehicles cross the Bridges into the Loop. Women shoppers began to appear on the streets later in the morning, while the noon hour saw thousands of downtown employees and shoppers pour out of buildings in search of lunch. In the midafternoon, women shoppers left downtown to be home when their children returned from school. Then began the evening rush hour of streetcars and pedestrians. Workers walking home along "Dinner Pail Avenue" (Milwaukee Avenue) near Chicago Commons settlement house were so numerous that they raised clouds of dust.

The character of street life changed after the dinner hour. Out in the patchwork of ethnic neighborhoods, children played in the roadway while their parents conversed on stoops and curbstones. Some workers left for all-night factory shifts. In warm weather, middle-class Bicycle riders took to the outlying streets. But the deepening darkness also increased the fear of crime. Chicagoans thought many tough neighborhoods were safe enough to pass through in the daytime but dangerous at night. Newspapers reported frequent muggings near the ends of streetcar lines and at open bridges and described the night as dominated by criminal elements. Downtown, there were sharp contrasts. Diners and theatergoers filled the "bright light" Randolph Street district late into the night, while the nearby Levee hosted a lively street life around the clock. But after the cleaning crews departed, the large office blocks became what one newspaper called the "loneliest place in Chicago."

The life of the street reflected other cycles of life, including age and seasonality. Cold weather drove indoors all but the heartiest peddlers of necessities, while others restocked with holiday merchandise. Transit lines utilized closed-side equipment, heated by stoves, instead of the open-style cars which brought summer riders close to the sounds and smells of the street. The street also meant different things to people who were near the beginning or the ending years of life. The street was a microenvironment of socialization where youths set their own rules and learned the ways of the world. Their games and songs were a part of city FOLKLORE. Youth GANGS, however, had already begun battling for domination of neighborhood TURF by the mid-nineteenth century. At the other end of the spectrum, aged CIVIL WAR veterans came to the Loop post office to collect their monthly pension checks, and many elders sold newspapers or worked at such jobs as "baby watcher" outside of outlying department stores.

The New Age of the Street

By the turn of the century several factors were already beginning to transform the streets and create a more restrictive attitude toward them. First, a variety of reform efforts attacked inner-city street life as the locus of the city's social problems. Middle-class reformers joined economic elites to separate the poor from public places. Curfew and truancy laws were aimed not only at eliminating child labor but also at keeping children off the streets; the Special Park Commission created dozens of inner-city PLAYGROUNDS with the same goal. Reformers also became increasingly hostile to STREET PEDDLERS, condemning them as PUBLIC HEALTH hazards, loiterers, and as disorderly and intrusive obstructions to the flow of traffic. New health laws banned outdoor dining and the vending of perishable food to avoid contamination from dry clouds of airborne horse manure.

At the same time, decades of urban growth had fostered the process of sorting urban functions by LAND USE (wholesale, retail, residential), social class, and ethnicity. The heterogeneous urban mixture of the mid-1800s had given way to a pattern of more homogeneous districts of social classes and neighborhoods. Citywide antinoise laws were aimed at silencing obtrusive peddlers and imposing quietude and order on middle-class neighborhoods as well as the Loop. In 1913 the city began an effort to push all street trades out of middle-class areas and into the MAXWELL STREET district. At the same time, the enforcement of antiloitering laws gradually drove the transient population into Skid Row districts to the north, south, and west of the Loop. The goal of these efforts was a more orderly street life that was confined to what were deemed appropriate districts.

Finally, the efficiency of crowd control during the WORLD'S COLUMBIAN EXPOSITION inspired Chicagoans to believe that they could impose a similar sense of beauty and order on the rest of the city. Infrastructure innovations included newly designed bridges and the elevation of steam railway tracks to remove crossing hazards. But nothing symbolized the desire for aesthetic and efficient streets more than Daniel BURNHAM'S *Plan of Chicago* (1909). Its emphasis on traffic flow countered the traditional working-class social uses of the street. The plan's impressionist-style illustrations by Jules Guerin emphasized the celebrational city as if viewed on a warm Sunday afternoon. Meanwhile, a series of statues financed by the Benjamin F. Ferguson Fund stressed the streets' artistic rather then survival possibilities. Beauty and efficiency, which were supposed to contribute to the economy by making workers happier and more contented, also represented a triumph of the middle- and upper-class view of what street life should be.

Burnham's plan, with its unimpeded traffic flows, also represented a transition into the automobile age, which dramatically changed the relationship between Chicagoans and their streets. The auto not only benefited from the growing disdain for the street by providing the kind of isolation from street life that had once been enjoyed by only the wealthy, but cars and trucks also accelerated other changes. Their gradual displacement of horse-drawn vehicles in turn displaced animals—along with manure and dead carcasses—which had been a familiar part of street life. Drivers also demanded speed and the elimination of peddlers, plodding wagons, playing children, or any other street use that interfered with getting from here to there. By the 1920s the growing volume of fast-paced traffic produced intersection hazards that encouraged the introduction of mechanical traffic signals; this, in turn, resulted in the displacement of hundreds of traffic officers, another familiar part of street life. Even then, auto fatalities, which had already soared to 302 in 1918, included many pedestrians. The extension of Ogden Avenue from Chicago Avenue to Armitage at LINCOLN PARK symbolized a new attitude. In the quest for an efficient way to link the West and North Sides, the roadway slashed thought existing neighborhoods and scaled Goose Island with a lofty bridge. That same attitude that almost any part of the built city might be expendable was present in early plans for wide, limited-access roadways. The idea of the street as a place for getting from here to there was about to triumph.

But hints of the former uses of the street would not disappear. During the GREAT DEPRESSION the public ways once again became a means of survival. Jobless thousands flocked to Chicago in search of work but ended up utilizing the street as an employer of last resort. Some of the newly homeless sold apples; others took jobs on government PUBLIC WORKS projects that built hundreds of miles of new infrastructure. All of that ended during WORLD WAR II, when the streets once more assumed a unifying and celebrational role. Downtown State Street became an outdoor museum of military equipment, while the LaSalle Street side of City Hall became "Victory Square," scene of patriotic rallies. Out in the neighborhoods, civilian defense exercises, flagpole signs, and memorial shrines promoted unity, as did the countless parades that wound through every part of the city.

After V-J Day—when the streets were once more used to celebrate—and the period of postwar recovery of the national economy, the street became a barometer of another kind of urban transformation. Pundits predicted that URBAN RENEWAL, high-rise APARTMENTS, air conditioning, and television would kill off neighborhood street life. The newspaper box, for instance, displaced hundreds of human vendors, in part because the general decline in public transit ridership put so many former pedestrians into autos. The idea of the street as employer of last resort survived in impoverished neighborhoods. Peddlers elsewhere became such a rarity that the visit of the once-ubiquitous scissors grinders now became the subject of great excitement. During the 1950s the press began to note a loss of neighborhood social life that had traditionally grown out of public places. The front porch or stoop, which had fostered neighboring on warm evenings, had begun to give way to air conditioning and television. And in the poorest neighborhoods, high-rise PUBLIC HOUSING completely destroyed the role of the street in the community.

The EXPRESSWAY system, which removed much of the traffic from the major city thoroughfares, represented the near triumph of the idea of the single-use street: the only possible function was as a place for cars to drive. (Chicago managed to create an ingenious exception by routing rapid transit down the otherwise-useless median strip.) Neighborhoods that lay in the way were now regarded as irrelevant piles of rubble-to-be, and the older transient districts were flattened to make way for superhighways. Meanwhile, at the other end of the auto commute, the mass production of a limited number of house designs in booming suburbia was reflected in the mass creation of quiet residential streets. Juvenile trees matched tricycles and other juvenile transportation equipment. Sociologists noted that cul-de-sacs favored neighborliness. Even the temporal rhythm of the suburban street was different. Rush hour dominated the clock, although the shopping centers that displaced older commercial streets were now open evenings.

Meanwhile, the street life of downtown Chicago fell into decline, as the boast that State and Madison was the "world's busiest corner" disappeared during the 1960s and '70s. Loop department stores were displaced in part by suburbia and the rise of North Michigan Avenue as the high-end street for strolling and window shopping. As downtown streets began to empty out after dark and the Loop took on the unwarranted reputation of being unsafe, movie distributors helped to drive away the street life. They had formerly released new films in downtown theaters weeks before they arrived at outlying screens; when they began distributing them everywhere at once, the

Loop THEATER crowds disappeared. In 1968 the term "streets of Chicago" took on connotations of disorder similar to those of 1877, 1886, and 1894. In desperation, the city rebuilt State Street into a mall, a misplaced suburban model that failed to bring people back.

But even during this nadir, there had been a few hopeful signs. Mayor Richard J. Daley had revived the downtown St. Patrick's Day Parade in 1956, an important symbolic gesture, while CHINESE, Germans, Greeks, Poles, and others also used the streets for celebrations. Triumphs achieved by Chicago sports franchises, as well as the symphony, astronauts, and other dignitaries, prompted massive parades. Meanwhile, newly arrived Latin American and Asian ethnic groups were quietly bringing with them their own celebratory processions and parades, as well as a strong tradition of street trading. And the TAXICAB industry continued to allow the kind of low-capital entry into American entrepreneurship for immigrants that street trades have always provided to newcomers.

Neighborhood block parties and the gradual return of outdoor dining were the first signs of the manner in which the booming economy of the late 1980s and 1990s and a gentrified inner city would bring about a revival of activity. New office towers and the conversion of factories and warehouses into apartments nurtured a revival of center-city dining. But contemporary street life only hints at the rich variety of activities that were once there. What returned was closer to the "city beautiful" of the Burnham Plan than it was to the workaday intensity of the late nineteenth century. Chicagofest, followed later by Taste of Chicago, the Blues and Gospel Music Festivals, and a patchwork of neighborhood festivals, represented a highly selective new form of Disneyfied street life, carefully planned, advertised, predictable, sanitized, and policed.

During the late 1990s, many of the last remnants of the old street life were threatened. Police removed the homeless from Lower Wacker Drive, while GENTRIFICATION nibbled away at the old south and west transient districts. The demise of SRO hotels and the charities that supported their tenants resulted in the removal of most of the transients, many of whom had been dumped from state institutions. Meanwhile, campus expansion at the UNIVERSITY OF ILLINOIS AT CHICAGO brought an end to the storied Maxwell Street Market, while the city launched a crackdown on ethnic food vendors, proclaiming them a nuisance and health hazard.

Perry R. Duis

See also: Art, Public; Contested Spaces; Leisure; Public Transportation; Underground Economy

Further reading: There is no comprehensive study of Chicago street life, but readers may piece together the story from a number of works that chronicle its constituent parts. Milo Quaife, *Chicago Highways, New and Old* (1923), places city streets in the context of early roads, while a city publication, *Chicago Public Works: A History* (1973), is a useful introduction to the physical history of the street. Many of the entries in a book of travelers' accounts, Bessie Louise Pierce, *As Others See Chicago: Impressions of Visitors, 1673–1933* (1933), deal with how the conditions and uses of public places struck visitors. Perry R. Duis, *Challenging Chicago: Coping with Everyday Life, 1837–1920* (1998), discusses a number of related topics and provides a framework of private, semipublic, and public space in which the reader may view street life.

Public transportation has been a principal function of the street, and R. David Weber, "Rationalizers and Reformers: Chicago Local Transportation in the Nineteenth Century" (Ph.D. diss., University of Wisconsin–Madison, 1971), details the struggle between riders and the private carriers. Paul F. Barrett, *The Automobile and Urban Transit: The Formation of Public Policy in Chicago, 1900–1930* (1983), is a classic study of how the automobile challenged the streetcar and the "L."

The street has always served as a home and employer of last resort for the urban poor. Charles Hoch and Robert Slayton, *New Homeless and Old: Community and the Skid Row Hotel* (1989), analyzes the Skid Row lifestyle and the impact of decline of cheap housing. Survival through the street trades is the subject of Carolyn Eastwood, *Chicago Jewish Street Peddlers* (1991), while Ira Berkow, *Maxwell Street: Survival in a Bazaar* (1972), deals with some of the famous personages whose roots went back to the famous street of peddlers' carts and hucksters. Gilbert Gorman and Robert E. Samuels, *The Taxicab: An Urban Transportation Survivor* (1982), is an excellent analysis of another variant of street trading.

Maxwell Street musician, 1959. Photographer: Clarence W. Hines. Source: Chicago Historical Society.

Street Musicians. Many cities encourage, or tolerate, street musicians as local color that enhances the culture. Historically, Chicago has not been one of them. Instead, POLICE and city officials have generally treated street musicians as panhandling pests, beggars with guitar cases. Moreover, it takes a hardy soul to sing for a living against the screech of the downtown subway or the winds of the Michigan Avenue Bridge.

MAXWELL STREET was long the city's hotspot for street BLUES, until URBAN RENEWAL and the expansion of the UNIVERSITY OF ILLINOIS AT CHICAGO claimed much of the prime territory. From Muddy Waters and Howlin' Wolf to Hound Dog Taylor and Maxwell Street Jimmy, the market earned renown as what author Ira Berkow termed "the most important area in the most important city for modern blues in America."

The administration most friendly to street musicians was that of Mayor Harold Washington, who authorized a licensing system in the mid-1980s that allowed buskers to ply their trade for a token fee of 10 dollars. By the late 1990s, however, street musicians were once again subject to misdemeanor arrest for solicitation of public funds.

Don McLeese

See also: Contested Spaces; Ethnic Music; Street Life; Street Peddling

Further reading: Berkow, Ira. *Maxwell Street*. 1977.

Street Naming. The street names of Chicago offer a rich record of the city's spatial and social development. In 1830, southern Illinois mapmaker James Thompson created Chicago's first official map. Commissioned by the federal government to bring order to the city, Thompson platted the small downtown area bounded by Kinzie, Jefferson, Washington, and Dearborn streets. Departing from the tradition of naming streets for their destination, Thompson initiated the enduring practice of naming streets after figures of national and local significance.

Fight for 40th Street

In 1913, as part of an effort to eliminate duplicate street names, the city council named the West Side 40th Street after Peter Crawford, an early Cicero Township landowner. In 1933, MAYOR Edward Kelly sought to consolidate his ties to Polish voters by renaming Crawford Avenue to honor Count Casimir Pulaski, a POLISH hero of the American Revolutionary War. Business owners at the intersection of Crawford and Madison, one of the city's major SHOPPING DISTRICTS, protested. Pulaski's supporters countered that such objections masked anti-Polish prejudice. Crawford's proponents obtained a temporary injunction against the change, but in April 1935, the Illinois Supreme Court upheld the city council's right to select street names.

Crawford's backers did not give up. Angry residents tore down "Pulaski Road" signs, and the Postal Service continued to deliver mail addressed to Crawford Avenue. In 1937, Illinois passed a law that the city council must change a street name on the request of owners of 60 percent of its frontage. So in 1938 some property owners submitted petitions for the restoration of the name Crawford Avenue to Pulaski Road, while others asked that Haussen Court, which was less than two blocks long, be renamed for Crawford. Neither petition had enough signatures to require city action.

In 1949, owners of businesses along Pulaski Road filed a final round of petitions for Crawford. Although these signatures were valid, the city council refused to act. Property owners sued city officials for dereliction of duty. The second Crawford Avenue lawsuit culminated in 1952, when the Illinois Supreme Court ruled in favor of the name Pulaski.

Amanda Seligman

In the decades that followed, explosive urban growth, annexation, and the popular political favor of honorary street naming resulted in multiple streets of the same name and streets known by several different names. In 1901, building superintendent Edward P. Brennan confronted the confused state of affairs. He suggested that Chicago be ordered as a large grid with a uniform street numbering system, and proposed State and Madison Streets as the city's primary north-south and east-west axes. In 1908, the "Brennan" system was officially adopted by the city council and became the basis of modern Chicago's street naming system.

Over the next decades, Brennan's system incorporated not only the principle of having street address numbers register distance and direction, but also the ideas that all portions of the same street should go by a uniform name and that north-south streets should be named alphabetically as one moved west from the Chicago/Indiana border. Led by Brennan and Howard C. Brodman, superintendent of the city's Department of Maps and Plats, the city council and business community continued through the 1930s to replace duplicated street names in order to simplify navigation and economize postal service and merchandise delivery. Of the more than a thousand streets within Chicago's city limits today, the greatest number—more than 170—bear the names of real-estate developers. English towns and Chicago's former mayors and aldermen have provided the next most popular sources of names.

Michael Paul Wakeford

See also: Built Environment of the Chicago Region; Subdivisions

Further reading: Bike, William S. *Streets of the Near West Side.* 1996. • Hayner, Don, and Tom McNamee. *Streetwise Chicago: A History of Chicago Street Names.* 1988. • Vogel, Virgil J. "The Indian Origin of Some Chicago Street Names." *Chicago Schools Journal* (March/April 1955): 145–152.

Street Numbering. *See* House Numbering and Street Numbering

Street Peddling. As early as 1847 the city of Chicago established official markets where peddlers could set up their wares on the sidewalk, occupy stalls in the street, or park wagons at the curb. Street peddling was largely the occupation of immigrant JEWISH, ITALIAN, and GREEK populations who settled in the city's NEAR WEST SIDE in the 1870s through the early 1900s. Street peddlers would set up stationary locations along streets with trolley lines and well-traveled routes to peddle their wares. In these congested streets, food items, notions, and other merchandise were peddled by pack or wagon. The dense immigrant neighborhoods, which were serviced in this same manner, received virtually all the essentials for daily living from street peddlers.

Public markets relocated street peddling from congested areas where it hindered traffic and also regulated the wares that were peddled. Chicago's longest-standing open-air market, the MAXWELL STREET Market, was created by a city ordinance in 1912 for licensed peddlers to operate seven days of the week. The Maxwell Street Market was relocated to Canal Street in 1994, and continued into the new century.

The variety of street trades has ranged from the peddling of food items, produce, and flowers; scrap paper, rags, and iron; to used merchandise, fix-it services, and entertainment. The most colorful street peddlers have often been the musicians, and Chicago is noted for its BLUES traditions among street musicians.

Although street peddling had a continued presence in Chicago in the twentieth century, its florescence was affected by changing marketing habits, social patterns, and public policy. The Municipal Code of Chicago defines a peddler as "... any individual, who going from place to place, shall sell, offer for sale, sell and deliver, barter or exchange any goods, wares, merchandise ... from a vehicle or otherwise." In the 1990s, the term "peddler" was changed to "vendor," and vendors were organized and licensed by the city to operate in designated locations or territories. These areas have included such public spaces as outside of MUSEUMS, where vendors sell food from trailers; along State Street, where fruit or hot dogs are sold under canopied carts; in ethnic neighborhoods, where pushcart peddlers sell ethnic confections; along popular streets, where vendors sell beneath magazine kiosks; or in busy city streets, where newspapers or various merchandise and food items are marketed to vehicular traffic.

Street peddling has provided an important service to Chicago residents and continues to operate as an economic option for entrepreneurs. The economic viability of street peddling can be seen in the legacy of successful Chicago businesses like Vienna Beef, Flukey's Hot Dogs, and the former Mages Sporting Goods, all of which started with the peddling of wares on Chicago's streets.

Lori Grove

See also: Business of Chicago; Foodways; Grocery Stores and Supermarkets; Retail Geography

Further reading: Duis, Perry R., and Glen E. Holt. "Chicago as It Was: When That Great Street Was Every Street." *Chicago Magazine* 26.6 (1977). • Eastwood, Carolyn. "A Study of the Regulation of Chicago's Street Vendors." Ph.D. thesis, University of Illinois at Chicago. 1988. • Eastwood, Carolyn. *Chicago Jewish Street Peddlers: Toehold on the Bottom Rung.* 1971.

Street Railways. Chicago had one of the largest street railway systems in the world before it was replaced by BUSES in the 1950s. In 1929 on the eve of the GREAT DEPRESSION, red streetcars operated by Chicago Surface Lines (CSL) were a familiar sight on arterial streets and carried almost 900 million riders—more than the city's other transit systems and automobiles combined. Yet within 30 years the streetcars were gone.

Omnibuses, large carriages seating up to 30 people, first appeared in Chicago in 1852 to haul travelers between the new RAILROAD STATIONS and HOTELS. The first street railway, or horsecar line, opened in 1859. Horsecars, which typically seated 20 passengers on benches, were pulled by one or two horses along rails laid on the streets. They survived on lightly used lines until 1906.

Soon after the introduction of the city's horsecar lines, their owners began looking for some sort of mechanical traction system to replace them. Not only did the horses last only a few years in heavy service, but the estimated 6,600 horses owned by the street railways in the 1880s dumped a considerable amount of manure and urine on the streets. Many horses

This 1959 photo of a huckster and his cart at the corner of 47th and Wood suggests the wide variety of shopping experiences available at that time. People could buy from peddlers, walk to their local stores, or drive to shopping malls located further away. Photographer: Clarence W. Hines. Source: Chicago Historical Society.

were killed in the Chicago Fire of 1871, and an influenza-like equine epizootic decimated the surviving horses the following year.

The street railway systems in 1867 tried replacing horses with small steam locomotives called "dummies," but the public objected to the smoke, noise, and sparks they generated. Chicago City Railways (CCRY) on the South Side in 1882 acquired cable car technology from San Francisco. The CCRY cable line on State Street proved so successful that Chicago's street railways eventually built more than 80 miles of lines—one of the largest such systems in the world.

Large steam engines mounted in central power plants pulled miles of cable through channels dug into the streets. The cable car operator, or gripman, applied power to the car by attaching his grip to the continuously moving cable.

Charles J. Van Depoele demonstrated an electric streetcar system in 1883 at the Chicago Exposition of Railway Appliances, and Frank J. Sprague built the first successful electric streetcar system, in Richmond, Virginia, in 1888. Chicago's street railways began converting from cable cars to streetcars after 1890, a task completed in 1906. Electric cars were cheaper to operate than cable cars, were larger, and could accommodate more passengers. From 1864 the city had streetcar companies on the West, North, and South Sides, and a number of minor ones in outlying areas. Charles T. Yerkes bought the West and North Side systems in the 1880s and began consolidating them—a task not completed until after 1900. By 1920 there were two major systems and three minor ones. These five companies operated in areas that had been suburbs before they were annexed to Chicago in the late nineteenth century. They also owned subsidiaries that ran smaller operations in the suburbs.

The conditions that were to prove the street railways' undoing appeared long before the turn of the century. Traffic congestion in the Loop slowed overcrowded streetcars to a crawl. Public disenchantment was aroused by the corruption of traction magnate Charles T. Yerkes, of the city council's infamous "Gray Wolves" faction, and even of property owners who had to give their consent before streetcar lines could be built in front of their land. Beginning in 1907, the city and then the state began to regulate and tax street railways. The city and state continued the 1859 cap on fares at five cents despite inflation that drove up costs, and taxed profits at a 55 percent rate. The railways, which had been highly profitable in the last decades of the nineteenth century, had difficulty after 1907 raising capital to modernize or expand.

Although the automobile did not become a factor in commuting in Chicago until the middle 1920s, the city's largest street railway, the Chicago Railways Company operating on the North and West Sides, filed for bankruptcy in 1926—a time at which ridership was at record levels and nearly three years before the onset of the Great Depression drove the remainder of the railways into bankruptcy. When it proved impossible to reorganize the street railways as a private enterprise, the state created the Chicago Transit Authority to buy them.

The last suburban streetcar ran on the West Town's system in 1948, and Chicago's last streetcar operated June 22, 1958, on the Clark-Wentworth line. The street railways were the victims of their own high costs, increased use of the automobile, overregulation, and population migrations to the suburbs. The street railways, which suffered declining profits after 1907 because of city and state regulation, did not have the money to build new lines into the suburbs.

Charles Tyson Yerkes and Street Railways

A street railway and financial speculator from Philadelphia, Charles Yerkes came to Chicago in 1882 to pursue his business interests. Over the next 15 years, he would not only amass a fortune of almost $30,000,000, but also arouse a civic crusade to depose him.

Yerkes played a crucial role in modernizing and integrating the city's public transit system. After gaining control of two of the three main street railway companies covering the North and West Sides, he converted the horsecar lines first to cable and then to electric traction. The advent of rapid transit allowed him to extend the tracks from less than 75 miles to 575 within a decade. In 1897, he built the elevated loop around the central business district.

At the same time, however, Yerkes was gaining the unenviable reputation as Chicago's most notorious "robber baron." He cheated his stockholders and partners, insulted newspaper editors, bribed city officials with impunity, and retaliated against customers who complained about inadequate services and broken-down equipment. As public opinion mounted against him, he attempted to force a bill through the state legislature in 1897 that would give the transit companies a 50-year extension on their franchises. This issue formed the first common cause among civic-minded groups in Chicago. Uniting Yerkes' opponents, the battle for municipal reform was fought in the state capital and the city hall over the next two years. Finally defeated, the traction magnate sold out, went to London, and helped build its subway system.

Harold L. Platt

The bankrupt CSL system, which included all five of the streetcar companies, was acquired by the new Chicago Transit Authority in 1947 for a bargain-basement price of $75 million. Its investors lost $110 million on the transaction.

David M. Young

See also: Economic Geography; Governing the Metropolis; Interurbans; Metropolitan Growth; Rapid Transit System; Taxation and Finance; Transportation

Further reading: Barrett, Paul. *The Automobile and Urban Transit: The Formation of Public Policy in Chicago, 1900–1930.* 1983. • Weber, Robert David. "Rationalizers and Reformers: Chicago Local Transportation in the Nineteenth Century." Ph.D. diss., University of Wisconsin. 1971. • Young, David M. *Chicago Transit: An Illustrated History.* 1998.

Streeterville, neighborhood in the NEAR NORTH SIDE Community Area. Early maps of Chicago showed little but lake immediately north of the CHICAGO RIVER and east of Pine Street (Michigan Avenue) where Streeterville is now located. Sand and silt accumulated north of a 1,500-foot pier built at the mouth of the river in 1834 and was nicknamed "the Sands." The arrival of squatters on the Sands and the emergence a VICE DISTRICT alarmed investors in lakefront property. In 1857 they persuaded MAYOR "Long John" Wentworth to clear out the trespassers.

Confrontations between squatters and lakefront property owners recurred after 1886, when George Wellington Streeter (1837–1921) stranded his boat on the Sands. "Cap'n" Streeter claimed that his grounded ship created this land, which was therefore outside of Illinois' jurisdiction. Streeter's brashness endeared him to local newspapers, which delighted in reporting on his "Deestric of Lake Michigan." A series of eviction attempts escalated into gun battles and landed him in prison. Finally, in 1918 the court ruled Streeter's claims invalid. Some of Chicago's most expensive land and famous buildings, including the John Hancock Center and Water Tower Place, now stand on the formerly CONTESTED site.

Amanda Seligman

See also: Dune System; Lake Michigan; Land Use; Magnificent Mile; Real Estate; Shoreline Erosion

Further reading: Stamper, John W. "Shaping Chicago's Shoreline." *Chicago History* (Winter-Spring 1985–86). • Tessendorf, K. C. "Captain Streeter's District of Lake Michigan." *Chicago History* (Fall 1976).

Streets and Highways. Geography was a major factor in the pattern of Indian trails that intersected at the confluence of the CHICAGO RIVER and LAKE MICHIGAN, and that pattern carried over into the auto age with the EXPRESSWAY system.

Indian trails, largely paths that meandered to avoid obstacles, skirted the southern shore of the lake and then radiated in all directions. European settlers arriving after 1830 tried to straighten the trails, but stagecoaches in some cases found it more expedient to use the beaches along the lake than rutted trails inland.

The first attempts by government to build hard-surfaced roads occurred in the 1840s when Chicago covered some of its streets with planks, and toll plank roads were built in outlying areas. When they quickly deteriorated, Chicago turned to a parquet-like, wood-block paving system that persisted into the twentieth century.

Dirt roads built and maintained by TOWNSHIPS were predominant in suburban areas until the 1920s, but Chicago in 1861 created the Board of Public Works, the first agency in Illinois with a professional staff to build roads. A limited-access scenic parkway along the lakeshore was built to connect Chicago with then-suburban HYDE PARK in 1869–70, and after concrete paving was developed in the twentieth century the parkway became the nucleus of Lake Shore Drive, the precursor of the expressway system.

Gradually after about 1890 pressure on the state to build hard roads increased as a result of lobbying by recreational BICYCLISTS, farmers who needed to move crops to market, and, eventually, motorists. The state's inventory of roads in 1905 counted only 7,864 miles of improved roads in Illinois—1,900 of them in Chicago. The high cost of street CONSTRUCTION forced the city after 1900 to impose driver and auto license fees to finance them.

Systematic planning for public roads in Chicago began in 1910 when the Chicago Plan Commission was created to implement the plan of Daniel Burnham and Edward Bennett, which put heavy emphasis on avenues and thoroughfares. At the time there were fewer than 10,000 automobiles registered in Chicago. The state did not begin a public road program for the suburbs and rural areas until after WORLD WAR I and did not levy a gasoline tax for roads until 1929—by which time auto registrations in Chicago were increasing at a rate of 32,000 vehicles a year. The federal highway program for rural and suburban roads began about the same time.

In 1941, Illinois became one of five states to create a toll highway authority based on the early success of the Pennsylvania Turnpike. WORLD WAR II intervened before anything could be built in Illinois, but during the war various local agencies began planning an expressway (freeway) system.

Construction on the $1.1 billion system, which took 18 years to complete, began after the war, with the suburban Edens and Calumet Expressways. They cost about $1.6 million per mile. In 1949 the city began building the Congress (later Eisenhower) Expressway on the West Side. It cost $183.5 million, took 11 years to complete, and was unique in that it included a RAPID TRANSIT railway line in the median strip.

The passage by Congress of the Interstate Highway Act in 1956 shifted the bulk of the cost of freeways (90 percent) to the federal government and enabled the city and county to continue their ambitious road building. Until then, the expressways had consumed all available transportation funds, prompting the state to create the Illinois State Toll Highway Commission to build the Tri-State, Northwest, and East-West TOLL ROADS in the suburbs. The Tri-State was built as a beltway around the city linking interstate highways in Indiana and Wisconsin.

The culmination of the road-building art in Chicago was the Dan Ryan Expressway—a 14-lane road with a two-mile-long bridge over the South Branch of the Chicago River and adjacent RAILROAD yards on the SOUTH SIDE. It cost $282.7 million, or $25.7 million per mile to build.

Public opposition to expressway construction by the 1970s forced the city and state to cancel plans to build a crosstown freeway on

K-Town

Residents of NORTH LAWNDALE Community Area sometimes refer to the western part of their neighborhood as "K-Town" because so many STREET names there begin with the letter K. For several miles west of Pulaski Road there are stretches of north-south streets all starting with the same letter. This naming practice arose because of the ANNEXATIONS of 1889, which brought approximately 133 square miles and many duplicate street names within Chicago's boundaries. John D. Riley, superintendent of the city's Bureau of Maps, prepared a plan in which each mile west of the Indiana-Illinois border was assigned a successive letter of the alphabet, starting with A; streets within each mile were to begin with that letter. The city council rejected the proposal for the eastern sections of the city, but did apply it to some western streets in 1913. K-Town thus marks the eleventh mile from the Indiana state line.

Amanda Seligman

the West Side and the state to abandon a proposal for a freeway in the FOX RIVER Valley 30 miles west of the Loop in the early 1990s.

By the 1990s, the Chicago metropolitan area had 54,600 miles of streets and roads, including 2,500 miles of expressways, 17,300 miles of highways and arterial streets, and 34,800 miles of local streets. Almost 80 percent of all COMMUTING was done by automobile.

David M. Young

See also: Chicago in the Middle Ground; Metropolitan Growth; Tollway Authority; Transportation

Further reading: Condit, Carl W. *Chicago, 1930–70: Building, Planning, and Urban Technology*. 1974. • Quaife, Milo M. *Chicago's Highways Old and New: From Indian Trail to Motor Road*. 1923. • Young, David M. *Chicago Transit: An Illustrated History*. 1998.

Streets, One-Way.

One-way streets in Chicago took on citywide significance with the passage of the Uniform Vehicle Code of 1931. Prior to this ordinance, different traffic laws had prevailed in the various municipal corporations of the city such as Lincoln Park, South Park, and West Park. While the "one-way designation" was henceforth available to the city council, not until the early 1950s did they avail themselves of this traffic-fighting weapon in any widespread manner. Throughout the late 1940s, aldermen proposed studies of the LOOP area for the purpose of implementing a system of one-way streets to ease traffic flow, signaling a spread of this method from its original use in governing alley traffic. This plan came to fruition in 1953 with the creation of main arteries with two adjacent streets designated as one-way streets, notably Ohio/Ontario and Superior/Huron Streets, which served to move traffic in and out of the NEAR NORTH more efficiently. Combined with the use of the "through street" designation, and a prohibition on left turns, one-way streets in downtown Chicago were an integral part of the city's response to a massive increase in the number of automobiles descending on the offices and shops of the Loop.

One-way designations spread quickly from commercial districts, marked by an explosion of one-way proposals scattered throughout the city, though this growth seemingly lacked coherence. Traffic combined with a PARKING crunch in many neighborhoods; streets in older residential areas simply had not been designed to handle automobiles, whether in motion or parked. A one-way designation could double the number of available parking places, and to the residents of dense, APARTMENT-filled blocks, this was an important consideration as ownership of automobiles skyrocketed. ROGERS PARK saw numerous proposals filed, referred, passed, amended, or rejected. In many cases streets had one-way designations applied and removed several times in the span of five years. For example, some portion of W. North Shore Street was the subject of a one-way proposal in 7 of 10 years during the 1950s. This situation was not stabilized until the late 1960s, when the grid of residential areas such as Rogers Park assumed the form familiar to its modern-day residents.

The number of "one-way" proposals peaked at 224 in 1970–71, thereafter suffering a gradual but steady decline, with only 98 such motions entertained in 1995. Significantly, a growing proportion of the motions were to rescind the one-way designation. Where a solution to traffic problems had been the primary concern of urban planners in the immediate postwar years, by the 1990s new PLANNING doctrines were ascendant that placed a priority on making streets friendly to pedestrians. The paramount example of this shift was south State Street's return to two-way traffic in an effort to revitalize a once-active area. Many downtown streets remain one-way, but the legacy of the "one-way" is the maze of narrow, car-filled streets confronted by Chicago residents each night as they return home.

Christopher Miller

See also: Commuting; Planning Chicago; Streets and Highways

Further reading: Condit, Carl. *Chicago, 1910–1929: Building, Planning and Urban Technology*, 1973. • Condit, Carl. *Chicago, 1930–1970: Building, Planning and Urban Technology*, 1974. • Journal of the Chicago City Council. Harold Washington Public Library Center, Chicago, IL.

Strikes. Perhaps no city in the United States exceeded Chicago in the number, breadth, intensity, and national importance of labor upheavals in the period between the CIVIL WAR and 1919. Overall, there have been six important strike waves or labor upheavals in Chicago history that were notable for their social impact.

On May 2, 1867, Chicago's first Trades Assembly (formed in 1864) sponsored a general strike by thousands of workers to enforce the state's new EIGHT-HOUR-day law. Though the one-week strike was unsuccessful, it capped a four-year mobilization of local workers that encouraged political parties to incorporate labor demands into their platforms and appeals.

In July 1877, Chicago workers struck again as part of a nationwide RAILROAD STRIKE. Though lacking unions, thousands of working men, women, and teenagers thronged the streets, marching from factory to factory behind brass bands calling employees out to strike. At the height of the conflict, POLICE and militia forcibly dispersed crowds of IRISH, Bohemian, and GERMAN strikers while the U.S. army waited in readiness. By the time the strike had been suppressed, 30 workers lay dead and 200 were wounded. The strike was significant, not just for the class bitterness it engendered, but for the unprecedented participation and solidarity of workers across skill, gender, and ethnic lines. Meanwhile, as the only group supporting the strikers, SOCIALISTS emerged as the voice for local workers, and Chicago became the nation's strongest center of socialism.

In 1886, Chicago was the center for another labor upheaval. Approximately 88,000 workers in 307 separate strikes demanded the eight-hour day that year, most of them on May 1. Industry was paralyzed, and the city "assumed a sabbath like appearance." The HAYMARKET Affair of May 4 triggered widespread antilabor repression. Moreover, the failure of the movement to spread much beyond Chicago made it easier for employers who competed in national markets to ignore labor demands.

As the tide of the great upheaval receded in the late 1880s, the character of strikes began to change. Until then, strikes often mobilized large numbers of immigrant men, women, and children within ethnic communities such as Irish BRIDGEPORT and Bohemian PILSEN. Easily replaced unskilled workers, in particular, relied on crowd actions to intimidate strikebreakers. To avoid riots and capture the vaunted "labor vote," 1880s politicians such as Mayor Carter Harrison began to restrain police from intervening in strikes called by well-connected local unions. As the mass strike subsided, craft unions spread among skilled workers employed by small-scale employers in local and regional markets. A metropolitan unionism took hold particularly among the BUILDING TRADES, the building service workers, and the TEAMSTERS. For the most part, strikes were not spontaneous but were called, coordinated, and supported by the strike funds of permanent unions and aided by a hands-off attitude of the police.

Strike of messenger boys, 1902. Photographer: Unknown. Source: Chicago Historical Society.

By the turn of the century, labor was a recognized interest in local politics and Chicago had became a "union town."

The most important early attempt of the new unionism to penetrate the domain of corporate-run industry came in 1894 when the American Railway Union, an industrial union founded by Eugene V. Debs, mounted a boycott of the nation's Pullman railway cars. With much of the nation's transportation at a standstill, a federal court granted the railroads an injunction declaring the strike illegal, and President Grover Cleveland dispatched 2,000 federal troops and over 5,000 U.S. marshals to Chicago, precipitating widespread violence. Despite a general strike by 25,000 Chicago unionists, the ARU was crushed.

In the aftermath of the PULLMAN STRIKE employers increasingly resorted to injunctions to bring in the federal government on their side in strikes, especially sympathy strikes and boycotts. A particular object of the courts' ire was the Teamsters union, which in the early part of the century used its control over the distribution of local goods to support and spread local unionism via the sympathy strike. In the 1910s, the struggle for union recognition by workers in the emerging corporate-run, mass-production sector of the economy precipitated renewed upheavals. In 1919, workers in Chicago's packinghouses, steel mills, and ready-made CLOTHING and agricultural equipment industries engaged in tumultuous strikes marked by RACE RIOTS and government repression. The defeat of these strikes unleashed a powerful employer counterattack in the form of an open shop movement that kept strikes to a minimum during the 1920s.

In the late 1930s, workers in basic industry finally won union recognition. Congressional legislation stopped the courts from issuing labor injunctions during strikes and enforced the right of workers to be represented by the union of their choice. For the first time, large numbers of AFRICAN AMERICANS and Eastern European immigrants and female semiskilled industrial workers were organized in permanent industrial unions under the wing of the CONGRESS OF INDUSTRIAL ORGANIZATIONS. But victory was achieved amidst a series of bitter strikes, notably the Little Steel Strike of 1937 in which police shot to death 10 strikers in the "MEMORIAL DAY MASSACRE." Local industrial workers were also heavily involved in the great nationwide wave of strikes in 1946.

From the end of WORLD WAR II through the early 1970s strikes continued to be widespread, but with the acceptance of collective bargaining they did not precipitate social upheavals nor did they generate the enormous class hostility that they had earlier. In the 1970s, the postwar liberal accord between capital and labor began to unravel. The strength of labor weakened as automation and the export of jobs overseas by corporations took its toll in heavily UNIONIZED Chicago. Industrial work increasingly gave way to service-sector WORK that was largely nonunion. Then, following the example of President Ronald Reagan in the 1981 Air Traffic Controllers Strike, private employers, especially those facing GLOBAL competition and deregulated markets, returned to the union-busting tactics of their forebears. Since then, with the exception of public-sector unions such as the CHICAGO TEACHERS UNION, strikes have been scarce in Chicago.

Richard Schneirov

See also: Antiunionism; Contested Spaces; Iron- and Steelworkers; Packinghouse Unions; Railroad Workers; Work Culture

Further reading: Barrett, James R. *Work and Community in the Jungle: Chicago's Packinghouse Workers, 1894–1922.* 1987. • Lindsey, Almont. *The Pullman Strike: The Story of a Unique Experiment and of a Great Labor Upheaval.* 1942. • Schneirov, Richard. *Labor and Urban Politics: Class Conflict and the Origins of Modern Liberalism in Chicago, 1864–1897.* 1998.

Stroll, The. The Stroll was the name given to State Street between 26th and 39th Streets. In the 1910s and 1920s, thanks to the publicity efforts of the CHICAGO DEFENDER, it was the best-known street in AFRICAN AMERICA, rivaled only by Seventh and Lenox Avenues in Harlem.

The Stroll was where the action was. This section of State Street was jammed with black humanity night and day. In the evening the lights blazed and the sidewalks were crowded with patrons attending the JAZZ clubs and those just gazing at all the activity. During daylight hours it was a place to loiter, to gossip and watch the STREET LIFE. Black Chicagoans were on show and they dressed up and acted accordingly. There were women on the Stroll but it was a place that displayed an aggressively masculine ethos.

The opening of the hugely successful Savoy Ballroom at 47th Street and South Parkway in 1927 created a new center of black nightlife that effectively killed off the Stroll.

Shane White

See also: Dance Halls; Douglas; Entertaining Chicagoans; Grand Boulevard

Further reading: *Chicago Defender.* Various issues. • White, Shane, and Graham White. *Stylin': African American Expressive Culture from Its Beginnings to the Zoot Suit.* 1998.

Subdivisions. From the city's beginnings, land was one of Chicago's most attractive commodities, and sales and speculation in REAL ESTATE were among the earliest trades to flourish. Local citizens as well as East Coast and foreign investors rode the cycles of speculative booms and busts, winning and losing fortunes with each wave of trading activity.

The original 1830 plat at the inland fork of the CHICAGO RIVER measured only three-eighths of a square mile. This kernel followed the survey system of the 1785 Land Ordinance, which divided new territories into mile-square sections, creating a uniform rectangular grid that shaped all later development. By 1834, new subdivisions—parcels of land divided into smaller blocks that were in turn divided into lots—were already laid out north of this core.

A large grant of land was given to the state of Illinois in 1822 to finance construction of

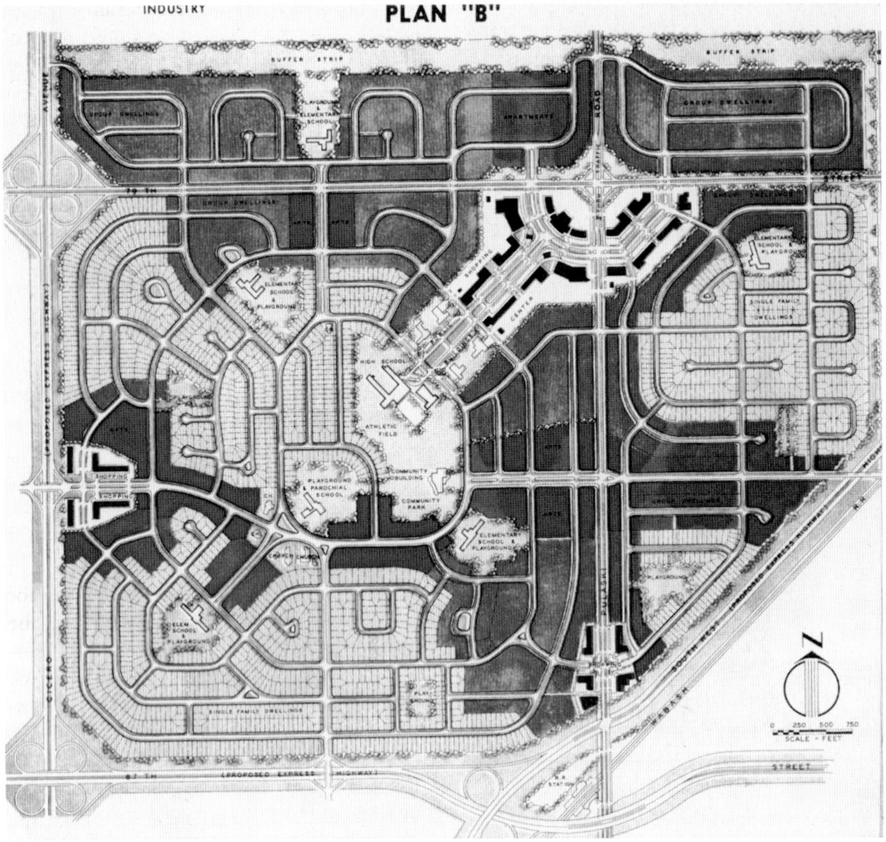

Chicago Plan Commission diagram for a "well-designed subdivision," 1943. Creator: Chicago Plan Commission. Source: The Newberry Library.

the ILLINOIS & MICHIGAN CANAL. A period of wild speculation ensued, setting the pattern for the future: each new TRANSPORTATION project stimulated a speculative frenzy and swelled the supply of subdivided acreage.

New transportation technology also encouraged subdivisions at increasing distances from the city core. Beginning in 1848, RAILROAD connections led to new development at stations along their radial routes. Soon the horse-drawn omnibus and then the STREET RAILWAY fostered subdivision development along their routes. Subdivisions both north and south along Lake Michigan such as LAKE FOREST and HYDE PARK, which began as summer retreats for the wealthy, increasingly evolved into commuter suburbs, as did outlying settlements to the west. By 1857, the subdivided area of Chicago embraced more than 24 square miles, and by the end of the CIVIL WAR Chicago's suburban belt extended more than 40 miles from the center.

Periodic depressions after the Civil War interrupted but did not stop development, which was spurred by the introduction of electric trolley service in the 1880s, the elevated RAPID TRANSIT in the 1890s, and preparations for the 1893 WORLD'S COLUMBIAN EXPOSITION. Distance from the center, proximity to industry, the provision of utility connections and other improvements, and the use of restrictions, BUILDING CODES, and ZONING contributed to the creation of subdivisions differentiated by class and race.

The "L" encouraged the filling-in of older subdivisions with new houses, APARTMENT buildings, and industries, urbanizing the inner suburbs through the 1920s. Another wave of subdivision activity in that decade, stimulated by increased auto ownership, produced building lots for three times the existing population. These were absorbed after WORLD WAR II, when federal homeownership programs and highway funds underwrote suburbanization on a massive scale. Continued growth of residential subdivisions, EXPRESSWAY construction, and the emergence of high-tech industries have converted some of Chicago's far-flung suburbs into a ring of edge cities that compete economically with the center.

The survey grid dominates the subdivision landscape, but Chicagoans have also supported influential innovations in subdivision design. These range from Frederick Law Olmsted and Calvert Vaux's RIVERSIDE (1868) to the planned new town of PARK FOREST (1948), and include the ideas on paper submitted to the 1913 City Club model suburb competition.

Carolyn Loeb

See also: Metropolitan Growth; Northwest Ordinance; Planning Chicago; Planning, City and Regional; Transportation

Further reading: Keating, Ann Durkin. *Building Chicago: Suburban Developers and the Creation of a Divided Metropolis.* 1988. • Mayer, Harold M., and Richard C. Wade. *Chicago: The Growth of a Metropolis.* 1969.

Subsidized Housing. Mention Chicago's subsidized housing and most people think of PUBLIC HOUSING: specifically, imposing rows of CHICAGO HOUSING AUTHORITY (CHA) high-rise buildings. Yet before the creation of the CHA in 1937, PHILANTHROPISTS and private organizations developed subsidized housing. And as early as 1934, Congress established the principle of federal subsidization of home ownership through intervention in mortgage markets.

If the definition of subsidized housing includes homes built by philanthropists willing to make only a modest profit, or no profit, there were four early subsidized housing developments in Chicago. The first, constructed on the West Side in 1895, was Francisco Terrace, designed by then 28-year-old Frank Lloyd Wright. The developer, Edward Waller, planned to earn only 3 percent, or one-half of the then going rate, on his investment. The apartments were rented for $12 a month, mostly to newlyweds of modest means. This 44-unit "model tenement" stood at 255 North Francisco until being demolished in 1974.

The next large-scale endeavor was the Garden Homes, constructed in 1919 by Benjamin J. Rosenthal, a REAL-ESTATE developer and civic leader. In *Reconstructing America* (1919) he asked, "Can a workman be efficient if he is crowded in a badly lighted, unclean house in a congested neighborhood? Can he be happy if he is obliged to occupy living rooms unfit for human habitation?" The answer was no for Rosenthal, so he purchased six blocks of land at 87th and State Streets and built 133 detached houses and 21 double ones. Their architecture is reminiscent of English cottages, and the project is based on England's "garden city" developments. Rosenthal originally sold the houses for $5,700.

The city's largest philanthropic housing developments are the Michigan Boulevard Garden Apartments, at 47th and Michigan, and the Marshall Field Garden Apartments in OLD TOWN, both built in 1929 and both modeled after the Dunbar Apartments built by John D. Rockefeller, Jr., in 1926 in New York City's Harlem.

The Michigan Boulevard Garden Apartments were built by philanthropist Julius Rosenwald, who controlled Sears, Roebuck. Covering a square block, the buildings enclose an enormous central landscaped courtyard. Rosenwald built the development of 421 units to provide sound housing for AFRICAN AMERICANS and to relieve the tremendous overcrowding due to the extensive racial segregation of Chicago. The development also

Philanthropist Julius Rosenwald funded the construction of the Michigan Boulevard Garden Apartments in 1928 for African Americans on the South Side. This 1951 photograph shows several of the buildings and the well-maintained public spaces. Photographer: Mildred Mead. Source: Chicago Historical Society.

included 14 stores along the 47th Street side of the property, four of which were occupied by black-owned businesses, and a nursery school. Rosenwald invested $2.7 million in the project, receiving only a 2.4 percent return during the first seven years.

The Marshall Field Garden Apartments were at the time the largest moderate-income housing development in the country, with 628 units. This experiment, built by Marshall Field III, aimed not only to provide housing at a reasonable cost but also to provide a catalyst for renewal of the surrounding area. Like the Michigan Boulevard Garden Apartments, the buildings are five-story walk-ups, here in a two-square-block site. Both developments have the feeling of college quadrangles. The project originally included 20 stores, a parking garage for 288 cars, and the progressive Marshall Field School for Children. The tenants had their own newspaper, theater groups, and many clubs. Because of the GREAT DEPRESSION rents had to be lowered, and the development never lived up to the initial modest financial expectations, was never enlarged as planned, and did not stimulate the hoped-for revitalization of the area. Both the Michigan Boulevard and the Marshall Field Garden Apartments remain viable, after several changes in ownership and various renovations through the years.

Dearborn Street looking north to Stateway Gardens, 1959, showing the kind of buildings razed to make way for high-rise housing. Photographer: Clarence W. Hines. Source: Chicago Historical Society.

CONSTRUCTION of subsidized housing resumed after WORLD WAR II. The Depression and the war had created the most severe housing shortage in Chicago's history, especially for poor people. In 1948 the CHA created the Chicago Dwellings Association as a private corporation to construct housing for moderate-income families. In 1953 it built the 318-unit Midway Gardens, at 60th and Cottage Grove, and several smaller developments. Other nonprofit developers included the Community Renewal Foundation and the Kate Maremont Foundation, which by 1963 had purchased the Michigan Boulevard Garden Apartments. The efforts of these groups met with mixed results at best, and new initiatives were few and far between.

By the 1960s new federal legislation provided mortgages at subsidized rates to for-profit developers whose projects met federal cost and low-income tenancy requirements. These programs resulted in the construction of developments such as South Commons at 26th and Michigan Avenue in DOUGLAS, as well as others in WOODLAWN, HYDE PARK, KENWOOD, and the NEAR WEST SIDE. This housing met with mixed success, but as the mortgages were paid off toward the end of the twentieth century, some of the buildings were converted to market-rate housing.

The grand experiment of the last third of the twentieth century involved rent vouchers, issued initially under Section 23 of the U.S. Housing Act of 1965 and later under the Section 8 program. They fall into two categories; project-based subsidies attach to all or a designated group of apartments in a development; "finders keepers" certificates can be used by a tenant for any apartment that passes a Section 8 inspection and whose landlord agrees to participate in the program. Section 8 tenants pay 30 percent of their income for rent, after certain adjustments for factors like family size; the majority of the rent is paid by the federal government. However, there are enough vouchers available to help only a fraction of the families with incomes low enough to qualify. Also, many landlords decline to participate for one reason or another, and many apartments do not pass Section 8 inspections.

At the turn of the century, CHA was demolishing much of the housing it had built, especially high-rises, and constructing fewer new units, many in mixed-income developments. The majority of the displaced tenants have received Section 8 certificates, leaving them at the mercy of the market and discriminatory rental practices. The city's efforts to provide housing assistance have been channeled into various programs to aid organizations or developers in constructing new or rehabilitated single-room occupancy housing for potentially HOMELESS people and programs to assist middle-income first-time home buyers. The latter programs fit neatly into the most widespread forms of public subsidy for private housing across the United States—inexpensive mortgages insured through Federal Housing Authority and Veterans Administration programs and the mortgage tax deduction. Since the 1950s, these public subsidies have helped expand home ownership and increase housing values across the metropolitan area.

Devereux Bowly, Jr.

See also: Company Housing; Housing Reform; Housing for the Elderly; Housing, Single-Room Occupancy

Further reading: Bowly, Devereux, Jr. *The Poorhouse: Subsidized Housing in Chicago, 1895–1976.* 1978. • Condit, Carl W. *Chicago, 1910–29: Building, Planning, and Urban Technology.* 1973. • Werner, M. R. *Julius Rosenwald: The Life of a Practical Humanitarian.* 1939.

Suburban Government. *See* Government, Suburban

Suburban Libraries. *See* Libraries: Suburban Libraries

Suburban Press. *See* Press: Suburban Press

Suburbanization. *See* Metropolitan Growth

Suburbs and Cities as Dual Metropolis. Chicagoans inhabit a dual metropolis, experiencing daily reminders of decay and glitter, despair and aspiration. As of 2000, the region encompassed 293 municipalities (263 in Illinois) spread over 4,401 square miles in COOK, DUPAGE, KANE, LAKE, MCHENRY, and WILL Counties, plus the northwestern Indiana counties of Lake and Porter. What sociologists refer to as spatial mismatch is among the region's dominant and most entrenched characteristics: technologically oriented job opportunities requiring high skill levels, mostly concentrated along suburban corridors; poorly educated, underemployed labor pools, more often than not in the most socially isolated locales within central cities; and disparities in TRANSPORTATION networks, inhibiting opportunities for links between residence and WORK. The poorest residents of inner cities, contentiously labeled an "underclass," suffer disproportionately from the compound effects of their environs as one affliction builds upon another.

Replete with the starkest of contrasts, the contemporary metropolis—whether measured residentially or occupationally—is indicative of national political structures and an economic system that too often proves disdainful of the inner city, its depleted resources, and its most beleaguered inhabitants. A quandary with deep historical roots, the imbalance intensified during 1980s. Historian Richard C. Wade foresaw as early as 1982 that the Reagan administration's policy—an artifice with the positivist label "new federalism"—deepened imbalances between tax-rich municipalities and their poorest neighbors. Federal spending on cities diminished from 15 to 6 percent of the national budget between 1980 and 1990; the nation's central cities accounted for 43 percent of Americans below the poverty line in 1991, up from 27 percent in 1959. The ratio of median family incomes between metropolitan Chicago's richest and poorest communities in 1989 was nine to one; in 1960, it had been roughly five to one. The United States Conference of Mayors itemized the accumulating urban afflictions in 1986: population loss, impoverishment, racial concentration, deindustrialization, UNEMPLOYMENT, HOMELESSNESS, crime; poor schooling; and high taxes. European urban experts visiting American cities expressed puzzlement upon encountering conditions comparable to those in the Third World.

Cabrini high-rises, 1959. The Chicago Housing Authority completed this "Cabrini Extension" in 1958, alongside the Frances Cabrini Homes, which had been built in 1941–42. With the construction of the William Green Homes in 1962, the complex became known as simply "Cabrini-Green." Photographer: Betty Hulett. Source: Chicago Historical Society.

Historian Kenneth T. Jackson has argued that a single process—population deconcentration—has shaped American metropolitan areas during the twentieth century. (The category of suburban is avoided, wherever possible, because it confuses as much as it explains.) While the foundation of American demographic patterns was constructed in the nineteenth century, in the final third of the twentieth century the process accelerated.

Two fateful statistical benchmarks reached in 1990—both widely reported and assessed—underscored the consequences of sustained deconcentration. First, Chicago's total population fell below 3 million for the first time since 1920; between 1970 and 1990, the city lost 17 percent of its population as its collar-county suburbs advanced 24 percent. Second, Chicago's share of metropolitan private-sector employment dropped to slightly under 40 percent for the first time; it was 56 percent in 1972. In 1992, Sears, Roebuck attracted attention when it relocated corporate headquarters from Sears Tower, affecting five thousand employees. Their destination was a newly constructed, horizontally organized 1.9-million-square-foot facility (as of 2002 expanded to 2.4 million square feet) in the northwestern suburb of HOFFMAN ESTATES.

Embodying the bleakest circumstances of the dual metropolis is Census Tract # 3805 on Chicago's SOUTH SIDE. Lying four miles south of the LOOP, the area includes the CHICAGO HOUSING AUTHORITY'S ROBERT TAYLOR HOMES. Constructed between 1960 and 1962, this complex included 28 identical high-rise buildings until 2000, each 16 stories, with a total of 4,415 apartment units. The Taylor Homes, like the adjacent STATEWAY GARDENS to the north, was part of a wider public policy intended to contain the increasing black population within existing ghettos. The second wave of the GREAT MIGRATION increased Chicago's black population from 277,731 to 1,102,620 between 1940 and 1970. Only 8 percent of the city's population in 1940, black Chicago constituted one-third of the city by 1970. Exacerbating the physical isolation of this area was the completion of the Dan Ryan EXPRESSWAY in 1962 immediately to its west, sealing its isolation from jobs, facilities, and white residents on the other side of the 10-lane highway. The census of 1990 documented the grim statistics of hyperpauperization: 100 percent of the census tract's 2,169 residents were AFRICAN AMERICAN; 89 percent lived below the poverty line, as contrasted with 64 percent for the surrounding area; 89 percent of the families were headed by a female; 58 percent of the civilian labor force was unemployed (versus 11 percent citywide); 44 percent were under the age of 13; and 6 percent of all adults had graduated from high school.

KENILWORTH, in turn, exemplifies the glitter and aspirations of the dual metropolis. In 1990, it ranked as the wealthiest place in the metropolis (per capita income of $69,814). It was also the nation's ninth richest community and had one of the highest proportions (163 per 10,000 adults) of listings in *Who's Who in America;* 83 percent of its adult population held at least a bachelor's degree and 98 percent had graduated from high school. Situated in the northeastern corner of Cook County, Kenilworth is one of the eight suburban municipalities known compositely as the North Shore, all linked to Chicago by a RAILROAD operating since 1855. The rush-hour COMMUTE by rail covers 16 miles in 32 minutes. Such places—whether on Philadelphia's Main Line or north of New York City in Westchester County—amounted to classic suburbs. Cultural homogeneity reinforced by RESTRICTIVE COVENANTS—white PROTESTANTS only—defined what Kenilworth's founder envisioned. Contrived as a sociological island, it was purposefully designed to resist the sweeping social and cultural changes unleashed by the economic transformation of the nineteenth century. By 1990, only 60 of Kenilworth's 2,562 residents were nonwhite. The median housing price exceeded $500,000.

FORD HEIGHTS, in spite of its classification as a suburb, represents a textbook case study of decay and despair. Twenty-five miles from Chicago in southern Cook County, it was identified in 1990 as the nation's poorest suburb. Known until 1987 as East Chicago Heights, it deliberately altered its name, (unsuccessfully) hoping to annex an adjacent unincorporated site upon which Ford Motor Company operated a factory. Between 1980 and 2000, the population of Ford Heights declined from 5,437 to 3,456. Ninety-six percent of its residents were African American. Per capita income (adjusted for inflation) declined 22 percent between 1979 and 1989, to $4,660, compared to Chicago's $12,889 and Kenilworth's $69,814. Unemployment in Ford Heights approached 40 percent, and only 30 percent of its housing stock was privately owned. In 2000, it registered the nation's highest percentage of single-mother households (34 percent).

NAPERVILLE, 30 miles west of Chicago, is a widely cited example of population deconcentration in large American metropolises. As recently as 1950 it looked like a commuter suburb and stood 91st among Illinois municipalities in total population. Today its characteristics defy traditional assumptions about urban and suburban. Labels for such places include boomburb, edge city, technoburb, and totalized suburb. These communities are situated 30 to 40 miles from their original urban centers. People work, live, and pursue many of their LEISURE activities in some 200 of these settings scattered across the United States (e.g., Bellevue, Washington; Gwinnett County, Georgia; Overland Park, Kansas; and Tysons Corner, Virginia).

Notable within the dual metropolis for its combination of burgeoning population and affluence, Naperville was singled out in 1992 as having the lowest poverty rate (1.5 percent) among cities nationwide with populations of at least 50,000. Whatever label is attached to this locale, its rudimentary ingredients included location along interstate highways, ease of access to major airports, reliance upon automobiles, excellent public SCHOOLS, university research centers in close reach, and rapid economic development led by assorted technology-related and retail enterprises. Naperville's corporate roster includes BP Amoco Research Center, Dow Jones & Co., Lucent Technologies, Nalco Chemical Company, and Nicor. Nearby are ARGONNE NATIONAL LABORATORY and FERMI NATIONAL LABORATORY.

Naperville ranked fourth in population (ahead of Peoria and behind Aurora) statewide in 2000. It is the largest city in DuPage County (and its oldest, founded in 1831), with a population of 128,358 in 2000 (its municipal bounds have spilled over into Will County). It experienced the second biggest surge (growing by 43,007, or 50 percent) among the 20 largest municipalities within the collar counties over the preceding decade; surpassing 100,000 in 1994, it was the 10th-fastest-growing city in the nation since 1990. In new-home CONSTRUCTION it ranked first among the collar counties as of 1982; in physical size, it expanded from 5.8 square miles in 1960 to 31 square miles, the result of nearly 400 separate annexations. But in its demographic attributes, unlike so many places conventionally portrayed as suburbs, Naperville changed notably. Among its 5,272 residents in 1940, 99.9 percent were white. In 2000, nonwhites accounted for 15 percent of its total population. Asians constituted the largest nonwhite proportion (9.6 percent), while African Americans accounted for 3 percent of the population.

Metropolitan Chicago's deconcentration is hardly a contemporary phenomenon. From 1860 to 1910, the city's population increased 20 times, to nearly 2.2 million; New York City's, by contrast, grew sixfold. By 1910, Chicago's population exceeded Berlin's (2 million) and was making inroads upon Paris (2.9 million). Although Chicago's physical size had expanded significantly between 1880 and 1900, from 43 to 169 square miles, as a result of consolidation and ANNEXATION, thereafter its growth stagnated. Suburbs—among them EVANSTON and Oak Park—rejected annexation during the 1890s. Their residents demonstrated a determination to set apart their communities politically and culturally.

The LOOP, since its completion in 1897, symbolized Chicago's magnetism. Drawing on major advances in the technology of electrified railway transportation realized in the late

1880s, the elevated line encircled the central business district and connected it to the South, West, and North Sides. The district pulsated. Each workday, according to a 1910 study, approximately 650,000 commuters journeyed to the Loop. During the evening rush, it was estimated in 1916, 100,000 passengers used the trains between 5 and 6 p.m. Street-level space was at a premium. The top cost per front foot, at the corner of State and Madison—possibly the world's busiest intersection—was $10,000 in 1910. Ten years later it was almost $25,000. Correspondingly, rents for downtown office space soared, increasing 15 percent in 1902 and again in 1903. Between 1905 and 1911 the city, county, and federal governments each erected major downtown office structures. LaSalle Street was the financial center. The Loop was also close to a complex of newly opened edifices housing renowned cultural institutions, including the AUDITORIUM (1889), the ART INSTITUTE (1893), the CHICAGO PUBLIC LIBRARY (1897), Orchestra Hall (1904), and the FIELD MUSEUM of Natural History (1920).

Among the multiplicity of forces encountered in the Loop, none caused more chaos than the competition among drivers of motorized vehicles, horse-drawn wagons, and streetcars. They battled for access to public roadways, a problem confounded by the proliferating number of automobiles. A 1907 traffic survey reported 1,421 automobiles entering the district via the Rush Street bridge in a 12-hour period; eight years later the figure reached 10,158. By 1911, to contend with this morass, approximately 85 POLICE officers were assigned to daily traffic duty; PARKING time was limited beginning that year to 60-minute intervals and in 1915 was reduced to 30 minutes. Traffic lights were introduced, with only limited success, in 1916. A survey in 1919 revealed 130,000 vehicles—motorized and horse-drawn—entering the Loop daily. Yet whenever Chicago's aldermen deliberated on the question of imposing new restrictions on parking, proprietors of small businesses feared the loss of valued customers.

William A. Wieboldt realized the predicament caused by congestion in the Loop. In 1917 he established a major retail operation—the eight-story Wieboldt Department Store—situated at the intersection of Lincoln, Belmont, and Ashland Avenues—entirely outside the central business district. Sears first opened neighborhood branches in 1925, and Marshall Field's launched its suburban stores in 1929. Recognizing audience demands in outlying neighborhoods, local movie theaters—the Pastime on West Madison, the Tivoli at Cottage Grove and 63rd Street, Schumacher's in the BACK OF THE YARDS—commenced their operations during that decade. Wholesale and manufacturing enterprises also required less costly, more expansive sites away from the Loop. Notable relocations included Western Electric (1903), Sears, Roebuck (1904), Montgomery Ward (1906), and Edward Hines Lumber (1906). SOUTH CHICAGO emerged as a major center for heavy manufactured products, and by 1916 commerce along the CALUMET RIVER exceeded that on the CHICAGO RIVER by five times. Ten years before, the proportion had been equal. Another mark of the decentralization of economic activity was the founding of GARY, INDIANA, in 1906 by the United States Steel Corporation. Just beyond the eastern boundary of Illinois at the southernmost tip of LAKE MICHIGAN, it was the nation's first instant industrial city, although its fortunes were linked to Chicago's transportation network and labor supply.

Daniel H. Burnham embodied the hopes inspired by Chicago's monumental progress since the FIRE OF 1871. He had risen to fame as chief of construction for the WORLD'S COLUMBIAN EXPOSITION of 1893. In 1906, in the culminating assignment of his career, he was retained by the Merchants Club of Chicago to formulate a comprehensive design for future growth. The heralded *Plan of Chicago,* written in collaboration with Edward H. Bennett, appeared on July 4, 1909, and caused an international sensation. (The Merchants Club and the COMMERCIAL CLUB merged in 1908, hence the Commercial Club is credited with having sponsored the plan.) BURNHAM'S PLAN combined fanciful aspiration and practicality; its focus was the metropolis, not the city alone. After Haussmann's plan for Paris of 1853–1859, Chicago amounted to the next step in the progression toward a comprehensive urban design. Distinguishing the work of Burnham and Bennett was the attention to the city in the age of rapid, mechanized mobility. Some of their recommendations were fulfilled, notably the preservation of the lakefront as a central space for culture, recreation, and leisure. Also enduring, although in less dramatic terms, was the attention to traffic patterns on streets and waterways. Other objectives remained unfulfilled, none more regrettable than their call for a unified commuter-rail terminal facility.

But the deconcentration of Chicago's population, as the authors of the *Plan of Chicago* recognized, could not be denied. Between 1900 and 1910, the population of the city and the six-county region increased nearly 30 percent. Lake County, Illinois, was the fastest-growing county in the metropolis; its population increased 60 percent to Cook's 31 percent. During the following decade the population of Chicago increased 24 percent, but the average growth of the combined northern and western suburbs was 100 percent. Significant advances in population registered in WINNETKA (113 percent), Oak Park (105 percent), WILMETTE (58 percent), and Evanston (49 percent). Starting in the mid-1920s, major corporations offering well-paid employment departed from Chicago—including Abbott Laboratories (to NORTH CHICAGO), G. D. Searle (SKOKIE), Jewel Tea Company (BARRINGTON), Motorola (FRANKLIN PARK)—to fulfill their needs for enlarged operating expanses.

A 1947 census bureau study of the redistribution of population within American metropolises pinpointed a multiplicity of causal factors: improved mass transit; the cachet of a suburban address; the deconcentration of industry; and technological advances such as TELEPHONE and electrical services. But the primary cause—"a factor of great importance," claimed Thompson—was the automobile. The marriage between suburb and automobile was consummated during the 1920s: vehicle registration nationwide reached 8 million in 1920 and 26 million by 1929.

Following the Second World War, the suburban trend—Chicago's and across the nation—seemed a self-fulfilling prophecy. Families coveting security after 15 exhausting years of depression and war often realized their quest in suburban communities. A record 2.2 million marriages occurred during 1946, and 20 percent more babies were born that year than in 1945. The federal government also exercised an important influence. Many new homes were situated on the metropolitan periphery, constructed inexpensively and with federally subsidized mortgages. Housing starts between 1946 and 1955 doubled compared with the preceding 15 years. A suburban life inspired two-car families as well as rising numbers of women remaining in the postwar labor force; *Glamour* (1953) linked home ownership to two-income households. New car sales nationwide soared from 69,500 in 1945 to 2.1 million in 1946 and 5.1 million in 1949; Chicago's automobile count increased from 428,000 in 1945 to 765,000 in 1953. Highway construction burgeoned, reaching $2 billion in 1949 and $4 billion by 1955 across the United States.

As early as 1943, the federal government urged large metropolises nationwide—including the governments of Chicago and Cook County—to devise plans for a postwar system of modern highways. The culmination was the Interstate Highway Act of 1956, which spurred a transcontinental network of superhighways stretching 42,500 miles and costing $60 billion. The resulting complex of metropolitan expressways in and around Chicago proved pivotal. These included the Bishop Ford Freeway (begun 1953 and completed 1956); Edens Expressway (1951–1958); Tri-State TOLLWAY (1953–1958); Eisenhower Expressway (1954–1960); East-West Tollway (1958–1972); Kennedy Expressway (1958–1960); Dan Ryan Expressway (1961–1962); and Stevenson Expressway (1964–1966). Residents of Naperville, appreciating the benefits of securing improved ties to Chicago, campaigned unabashedly to place the route

This 1968 image shows the dividing line between suburban and agricultural areas in Buffalo Grove, where Levitt & Sons developed the subdivision in the foreground. Photographer: Hedrich-Blessing. Source: Chicago Historical Society.

of the East-West TOLLWAY just north of its boundary.

Postwar deconcentration of retailing underscored consumer proclivities first evident during the 1920s. The proliferation of suburban malls (42 of them built in the 1950s around Chicago) affirmed the preference for living and shopping in automobile-dependent suburbs. To the consternation of businesses in the central business district, Chicago's segment of metropolitan revenue derived from retail sales—measured in the billions—dropped from 71 percent in 1949 to approximately 40 percent in 1972. Correspondingly, receipts in downtown MOVIE PALACES dropped as early as 1947. Woodfield Mall opened in the northwestern suburb of SCHAUMBURG in 1971. Its 2.3-million square feet featured four major DEPARTMENT STORES, 230 smaller retail establishments, and 11,000 parking spaces spread over nearly 200 acres. Malls became civic space, featuring artistic performances and civic meetings as well as consumer-oriented pursuits.

Woodfield Mall, Schaumburg, 1973. Photographer: LeRoy L. Mick. Source: Chicago Historical Society.

At the beginning of the twenty-first century, meaningful prospects existed for addressing Chicago's metropolitan future. They centered in an abiding faith in our capacity as a democratic nation to foster renewal and change, with the suburban majority discovering compelling reasons to recast its sensibilities on a regional scale. One project took aim at alleviating the spatial mismatch. Originally advanced by the mayor of Schaumburg in 1997 and endorsed by other municipalities along the northwest suburban corridor, it anticipated shortages in the private-sector workforce. This unprecedented plan would expand the reach of the CHICAGO TRANSIT AUTHORITY rail line into the northwest suburbs, with suburban stations strategically situated at Hoffman Estates and Woodfield Mall. The CTA outlined a more comprehensive design in 2002 to extend itself beyond the city in other directions as well.

During the 1990s, several Chicago-based not-for-profit organizations—the Chicago COMMUNITY TRUST, the CIVIC FEDERATION, the John D. and Catherine T. MACARTHUR FOUNDATION, and the Metropolitan Planning Council—worked to advance regional solutions. More often than not, their ally was the Northeastern Illinois Planning Commission. A public agency created by the state of Illinois in 1957, it identifies salient regional issues but lacks legislative authority for implementation. ("We're like the United Nations except that we have no army—and more governments," an NIPC representative observed in 1993.) Because of the leverage resulting from its philanthropic resources and its sustained commitment to the future of Chicago, the MacArthur Foundation emerged as a champion of regional initiatives rooted in consensus. Favorites included enlarged transportation systems, metropolitan LAND-USE planning, augmenting the stock as well as dispersing the locations of affordable housing, and metropolitan government as well as tax structures.

But disagreement surfaced about how to implement policy objectives. Activists—urban and suburban—envisioned political action and welcomed the likelihood of needier communities contesting for the prerequisites savored by their prosperous neighbors. Whether by means of consensus or contention, the desired end might culminate in a series of political and economic imperatives—involving the public and private sectors, diverse neighborhoods and communities, giant corporations, small enterprises, and labor unions—at the local, state, and even national levels.

Legal scholar Gerald E. Frug has raised the possibilities of interlocal political institutions. The Puget Sound Regional Council, founded in 1991 to encompass four counties constituting metropolitan Seattle, is a singular example. Constituencies, in addition to the 4 counties, include 70 municipalities, 3 public authorities, and 2 state agencies. The problems it contends with—in the areas of transportation, economics, and growth management—are caused mainly by population deconcentration. In other metropolises, initiatives take varied forms, among them Minnesota's Fiscal Disparities Act (1971), Oregon's Urban Growth Boundaries (1973), the South Coast Air Quality Management District in Southern California (1976), and the Georgia Regional Transportation Authority (1999). Chicago's programmatic strategy, embodied in Metropolis 2020, is by contrast decidedly ad hoc.

"Metropolitan" is a contested word in the glossary of American urban history, a continuous source of fractious debate. Reaching back to the very inception of the American nation-state, the lack of provision for cities in the federal system created by the Constitution has rendered their status perpetually unresolved. Viewed through skeptical eyes, "metropolitan" is regarded pejoratively, invoking images of people furtively escaping into their local suburban enclaves. Their expectation: eluding the intricacies associated with their daily lives as citizens of the metropolis. Alternately, this key word also can take its form as a set of programmatic solutions. Their goal: diminishing rather than perpetuating the disparities between the neighborhoods and communities that separate the citizens who inhabit the dual metropolis.

Michael H. Ebner

See also: Governing the Metropolis; Metropolitan Growth; Planning Chicago; Planning, City and Regional; Racism, Ethnicity, and White Identity

Further reading: Of great value, because it frames issues globally, is Sir Peter Hall, *Cities in Civilization* (1998). Provocatively reconceptualizing the American metropolis is Peter Marcuse, "The Ghetto of Exclusion and the Fortified Enclave: New Patterns in the United States," *American Behavioral Scientist* 41.3 (November/December 1997): 311–326; Marcuse updates, to the end of the twentieth century, the specter of people striving to fashion metropolitan lives on sociological islands apart from everyday realities, a notion first explicated in the context of the Industrial Revolution by Robert H. Wiebe, *The Search for Order, 1877–1920* (1967). William Julius Wilson, *When Work Disappears: The World of the New Urban Poor* (1996), and Douglas S. Massey and Nancy A. Denton, *American Apartheid: Segregation and the Making of the Underclass* (1993), explore the ramifications of the dual metropolis. Kenneth T. Jackson's classic *Crabgrass Frontier: The Suburbanization of the United States* (1985) must be read in tandem with Robert Fishman, *Bourgeois Utopias, The Rise and Fall of Suburbia* (1987), and Margaret Marsh, *Suburban Lives* (1990). Still indispensable is Warren S. Thompson, *Population: The Growth of Metropolitan Districts in the United States, 1900–1940* (1947). For an informative rhetorical analysis of the American metropolis, turn to Zane L. Miller, "Pluralizing America: Walter Prescott Webb, Chicago Sociology, and Cultural Regionalism," in *Essays on Sunbelt Cities and Recent Urban America*, ed. Robert B. Fairbanks and Kathleen Underwood (1990), 151–176. For a critical appreciation of how journalists and scholars assay the contemporary American metropolis, consult William Sharpe and Leonard Wallock, "Bold New City or Built-Up 'Burb'? Redefining Contemporary Suburbia,"*American Quarterly* 46.1 (March 1994): 1–30. Joel Garreau, *Edge City: Life on the New Frontier* (1991), has exerted strong influence on how issues of growth and change affect the fringe of the metropolis but must be augmented by Robert Fishman, "The American Metropolis at Century's End: Past and Future Influences," *Housing Policy Debate* 11.2 (2000): 199–213. Framing cities and suburbs in a broad context are Elaine Tyler May, *Homeward Bound: American Families in the Cold War Era* (1988); James T. Patterson, *Grand Expectations: The United States, 1945–1974* (1996); Jon C. Teaford, *Cities of the Heartland: The Rise and Fall of the Industrial Midwest* (1993); and Derek Bok, *The State of the Nation: Government and the Quest for a Better Society* (1996). James T. Lemon, *Liberal Dreams and Nature's Limits: Great Cities of North America since 1600* (1996), devotes an expansive chapter to Chicago circa 1910. Focused on metropolitan policy issues are Richard C. Wade, "The Suburban Roots of the New Federalism," *New York Times Magazine*, August 1, 1982, 20–21; Jon C. Teaford, *Post-Suburbia: Government and Politics in the Edge Cities* (1996); and Robert J. Waste, *Independent Cities: Rethinking U.S. Urban Policy* (1998). Four studies examine important dimensions of the altered metropolis: Lizabeth Cohen, *A Consumer's Republic: The Politics of Mass Consumption in Postwar America* (2002); Robert M. Fogelson, *Downtown: Its Rise and Fall, 1880–1950* (2001); Gerald E. Frug, "Beyond Regional Governance," *Harvard Law Review* 155.7 (May 2002): 1766–1836; and Peter O. Muller, "The Suburban Transformation of the Globalizing American City," *Annals of the American Academy of Political Science*, no. 551 (May 1997): 44–58. Also instructive is Neil Harris, *Cultural Excursions: Marketing Appetites and Cultural Tastes in Modern America* (1990). Harold Henderson contributed four informative articles to the *Chicago Reader* probing the debates over regional strategies: "Cityscape: Who Planned This Mess," March 12, 1993; "Up against Sprawl," September 6, 1996; "The Great Divide," January 31, 1997; and "The Future Is Theirs," January 25, 2002. Deeply informing Chicago-area research is the Chicago Fact Book Consortium, ed., *Local Community Fact Book: Chicago Metropolitan Area, 1990* (1995), and its predecessor volumes. Between 1989 and 1994, the *Chicago Tribune* issued a series entitled "Home Guide," profiling each of the 263 incorporated municipalities in the collar counties; for an alphabetized listing, consult "End of a Series," *Chicago Tribune*, August 20, 1994.

Subway. *See* L Rapid Transit System

Sudanese. At the end of 2001, an estimated 350 to 450 Sudanese were living in and around Chicago. Southern Sudanese immigrants began to arrive during the mid-1980s, when civil war broke out in the Sudan between the Islamic northern government and the primarily Christian and African traditionalist southern region, a conflict compounded by the drought of 1984–85, the worst in a hundred years. They constituted a relatively small and scattered group around the city throughout the 1980s and 1990s, but in 2001, two episodes accelerated the growth and organization of the Sudanese community. The first was the initiative taken by senior Sudanese immigrants to form the Sudanese Association, an effort which culminated in June 2001. The second was the arrival of a set of southern Sudanese REFUGEES popularly known as the Lost Boys of the Sudan, who began living in metropolitan Chicago in March 2001. While they neither form nor represent the entire Sudanese community, these young men are responsible for mobilizing a Sudanese presence that was less conspicuous prior to their arrival; as a result, they have significantly characterized the Sudanese impact on Chicago.

Displaced from the Sudan in 1987–88 by the ongoing civil war, the "Lost Boys" spent the intervening years before coming to America living in refugee camps in Ethiopia and Kenya. In 2000, the U.S. Department of State arranged to bring some of these southern Sudanese to the United States, including 150 to Cook and DuPage Counties. Most of the young men brought to metropolitan Chicago originated from the Dinka tribe of the southern Sudan; some are Nuer and Mora. Their ages ranged mainly from 18 to 26, and they were exclusively men. Most southern Sudanese girls were compelled to stay behind in Sudan, and comparatively few made it to the camps; however, about three-quarters of the 68 girls initially sent to the United States lived in nearby Michigan.

Most of the men came to the United States to take advantage of work and education opportunities. Many planned to go back to the Sudan eventually to participate in the southern political cause; some would settle in Chicago permanently in order to provide financial support to family at home and to foster local awareness about the conditions in Sudan. The men clustered principally on the city's North Side in ROGERS PARK, EDGEWATER, and RAVENSWOOD/ALBANY PARK. The "Lost Boys" brought with them various skills, including ACCOUNTING, engineering, carpentry and masonry, crop and animal husbandry, social and humanitarian work, and teaching. Yet they could not always apply this experience to corresponding jobs in Chicago, and the majority of Sudanese men began work in food service, retail, HOSPITALS, HOTELS, and airport security. Others secured more specialized positions, particularly those with relevant educational and vocational backgrounds. St. Augustine's College and Truman College in UPTOWN offered various levels of schooling, from GED preparation to college degree programs, and Seabury-Western Theological SEMINARY in EVANSTON periodically hosted

Sudanese clergy studying for advanced degrees.

Southern Sudanese strongly identify with their Christian heritage: almost all are Episcopalian, a few are ROMAN CATHOLIC. Local Episcopal and Catholic churches became their earliest centers of worship and community networking. These include St. Paul's by-the-Lake in Rogers Park, the site of a weekly social gathering; Church of the Atonement in Edgewater; St. Nicholas in Evanston; and St. Luke's in Evanston. Sudanese Chicagoans are committed to retaining their African heritage, and they find ways to solidify their communal identity through various cultural activities. In particular, the southern Sudanese observe May 16, a holiday commemorating the day in 1983 when southern Sudanese separatists first organized against the northern government.

Elizabeth E. Prevost

See also: Demography; Multicentered Chicago; Protestants

Further reading: Editorial. "Sudan's 'Lost Boys' Find Chicago." *Chicago Tribune,* July 5, 2001. • Lyman, Rick. "Sudan's 'Lost Boys' Survive Trek, Find a Future." *Chicago Tribune,* May 17, 1992. • Madhani, Aamer. "New Life in U.S. Stifled When There Are No Jobs: Sudan Refugees Learn Economic Reality." *Chicago Tribune,* November 7, 2001.

Suffrage. Full suffrage became a political issue for Chicago in the 1860s. On the eve of the CIVIL WAR, Illinois was one of seven Midwestern states that denied the vote to AFRICAN AMERICAN residents. After the Fifteenth Amendment enfranchised African Americans in Illinois in 1870, black Chicagoans moved slowly into POLITICS and political officeholding. Chicagoan John Jones, who had led the fight to remove all state and local restrictions on African Americans, was elected to the COOK COUNTY Board of Commissioners in 1871, the first black man to hold elective office in the state, and John W. E. Thomas of Chicago was elected to the state legislature in 1876.

Chicago women did not win complete suffrage until 1920. The first women's organization to raise the suffrage issue directly was the Chicago Sorosis Club, founded by Mary Livermore, Myra Bradwell, and Kate Doggett in 1868. Almost upon its founding, the Sorosis confronted the issue of whether to concentrate on securing women's rights alone, or to promote a universal suffrage that included black suffrage and rejected any property or education requirements for voting. The dilemma split the Sorosis, as it did the national suffrage movement, and any united effort for suffrage disappeared in February 1869 when both sides held woman suffrage conventions and each group formed its own association.

A group of middle-class and professional women revived organized suffrage activity in the mid-1880s when they founded the Cook County Suffrage Association. Then, when the rift in the national suffrage movement over whether to seek national or state-by-state suffrage healed in the 1890s, the Chicago-area movement gained significant momentum. In 1894, the Chicago Woman's Club organized the CHICAGO POLITICAL EQUALITY LEAGUE to work for suffrage and named Celia Parker Woolley as president of this new group. In 1901, Catharine Waugh McCulloch, who had attended the 1896 DEMOCRATIC PARTY national convention as a member of the National Woman Suffrage Association, led a small movement to secure women taxpayers' right to elect TOWNSHIP officials who assessed and collected taxes. Suffragist women thereafter expanded their focus to securing municipal suffrage for all women as the means to protect their homes and families in the city. They seized upon Chicago's attempt to write a new municipal CHARTER in 1906 to demand that any new charter legislation include municipal suffrage for all women. When the proposed charter failed to include municipal suffrage, around a hundred women's organizations, including working-class and immigrant women, waged a successful campaign to urge male voters to defeat the charter when it was put before Chicago voters in late 1907. In 1910, many of the most active suffragists organized their own Suffragist Party.

Although white, middle-class Chicago and Cook County women organized the early woman suffrage campaign, from 1907 the movement crossed class, race, and ethnic boundaries. Restaurant worker Elizabeth Maloney led the Self-Supporting Women's Equal Suffrage Association. Glove-worker Agnes Nestor journeyed to Springfield in 1909 to lobby for suffrage, along with the leader of the Jewish Chicago Woman's Aid, Flora Witkowsky. Women's clubs of the city's SETTLEMENT HOUSES distributed suffrage leaflets and sold buttons declaring "Votes for Women" on one side and "WOMEN'S TRADE UNION LEAGUE" on the other side. When the SOCIALIST PARTY held its national convention in Chicago in 1908, Chicagoan Corinne Brown led socialist women in organizing a separate meeting to establish women's organizations to pursue suffrage. In 1913, Ida B. Wells-Barnett organized the ALPHA SUFFRAGE CLUB of African American women. Chicagoan Mary Fitzbutler Waring was a leading African American campaigner for woman suffrage, while Chicagoan Mary C. Bryon was named one of the few African American organizers in the National American Woman Suffrage Association. Thousands of working women joined the Wage Earners' Suffrage League organized by Emma Steghagen.

The first major suffrage victory came in 1913 when the Illinois legislature gave all women of the state suffrage for local and national elections. Because a woman's citizenship was still tied to her husband's citizenship by a national law of 1907, many women still could not vote. Nevertheless, more than 150,000 Chicago women registered to vote in the spring of 1914. Many Chicago-area women remained unwilling to settle for anything short of full political equality, so the campaign continued. When full suffrage came with the national amendment in 1920, Chicago played its final role in the woman suffrage movement, hosting the meeting disbanding the National American Woman Suffrage Association and replacing it with the LEAGUE OF WOMEN VOTERS.

Maureen A. Flanagan

See also: Civil Rights Movements; Clubs: Women's Clubs; Feminist Movements; Political Culture; State Politics

Further reading: Buechler, Steven. *The Transformation of the Woman Suffrage Movement: The Case of Illinois, 1850–1920.* 1986. • Flanagan, Maureen A. "The Predicament of New Rights: Suffrage and Women's Political Power from a Local Perspective." *Social Politics: International Studies in Gender, State, and Society* (Fall 1995): 305–330. • Hendricks, Wanda. "Ida B. Wells-Barnett and the Alpha Suffrage Club." In *One Woman, One Vote: Rediscovering the Woman Suffrage Movement,* ed. Marjorie Spruill Wheeler, 1995, 263–276.

SPECIMEN BALLOT

WOMAN SUFFRAGE BALLOT

(Authorized by an order entered March 13, 1912, by County Judge John E. Owens)

For use in all of the City of Chicago and Town of Cicero

FOR the Extension of Suffrage to Women

AGAINST the Extension of Suffrage to Women

J.H.MYERS Clerk Election Commissioners

Woman suffrage sample ballot, 1912. Source: Chicago Historical Society.

Sugar Grove, IL, Kane County, 43 miles W of the Loop. The POTAWATOMI called this area Sugar Grove because of the preponderance of sugar maples (now the Bliss Woods FOREST PRESERVE). Farmers from Ohio and New York arrived in the 1830s. Incorporated as a village in 1957, Sugar Grove grew to 3,909 residents in 2000 thanks to its convenient commuter location just south of Interstate 88.

Erik Gellman

See also: Agriculture; Kane County; Toll Roads

Summer Theater. The typical THEATER season in Chicago lasts from mid-September until late July, when THEATER COMPANIES present audiences with the latest psychological drama, love story, or memory play. In the summer, theaters in the city lighten their fare and produce musicals or comedies, often drawing a different kind of theatergoer. Summer audiences consist of more families and people who generally do not attend productions during the regular season.

Even though the regular season traditionally ends with the warm weather, patrons of the dramatic arts are still able to find opportunities to attend plays well into the summer months. The GOODMAN THEATRE frequently extends its season-ending musical to accommodate tourists and other visitors to the city. STEPPENWOLF THEATRE often ends its season by bringing back original ensemble members such as Laurie Metcalf or Gary Sinise, who have since moved on to successful Hollywood careers. From 1986 to 1996, the International Theatre Festival biannually brought theater groups from around the world to Chicago. Bailiwick Repertory's annual Pride Performance Series, which focuses on GAY AND LESBIAN themes, began in the summer of 1989 and now extends well into Bailiwick's regular run.

Other theater companies in the Chicago area present productions exclusively in the summer, and exclusively outdoors. The Chicago PARK DISTRICT's Theater on the Lake, located at Fullerton and the lakeshore, was established in the early 1950s. The OAK PARK Festival Theatre has played to audiences since 1975. Playwright David Mamet played in the Festival Theatre's first production, Shakespeare's *A Midsummer Night's Dream.* Subsequent seasons drew local actors William H. Macy and Joe Mantegna, now well-known movie actors, to the Oak Park stage. These outdoor theaters bring the Bard of Avon and classic plays to a broad audience who often bring their children and extended families to enjoy the "magic of outdoor theater at night."

Andrea Telli

See also: Entertaining Chicagoans

Further reading: Voedisch, Lynn. "Lite Theatre: A Guide to Breezy Entertainments on Local Stages." *Chicago Sun-Times,* June 2, 1989.

Summit, IL, Cook County, 12 miles SW of the Loop. Aptly named, Summit sits on the gentle rise separating the CHICAGO RIVER from the DES PLAINES. Various Indian tribes traveled for centuries through a mass of trails and portages that crossed the swampy interfluve. A hint of the original landscape can be found in the Chicago PORTAGE National Historic Site, on Harlem Avenue in LYONS, just north of Summit.

Father Jacques Marquette and Louis Jolliet first used that portage during their return from the Mississippi in 1673. In the early 1830s Russell Heacock built an inn and farmed in the area. Summit is located along the ILLINOIS & MICHIGAN CANAL, and in 1845 canal commissioners sold area land to defray construction costs. Peter Kern bought much of what would become Summit in 1851. His children sold most of this land to Frederick Petersdorf and John Wentworth.

From the start, Summit was marked by an extremely diverse ethnic mix. Native-born settlers, lured by frontier opportunities, were joined by Irish canal workers by the late 1830s. The GERMANS followed shortly thereafter. From the 1880s to the early 1900s, the flow of immigration became a flood as POLES, CROATS, SLOVAKS, RUSSIANS, ITALIANS, and the DUTCH all arrived. A few AFRICAN AMERICAN and MEXICAN households were present at the turn of the century, and the first GREEK family arrived in 1910. Incorporated in 1890, Summit's population was 547 in 1900; it rose to 4,019 by 1920.

The early settlement was known for the quality of its produce, and large shipments of vegetables were sold in Chicago. In those early days, the village formed around Lawndale and Douglas Streets on the north side. As population increased, the business district grew along Archer.

Since the mid-nineteenth century, Summit has been served by several major RAILROAD lines running through the valley; its importance as a rail junction increased when the Indiana Harbor Belt Railroad entered from the east along 63rd Street. The I&M Canal was replaced by the larger SANITARY AND SHIP CANAL, completed in 1900.

South of the village, in 1907, the Corn Products Refining Company began building what would become the largest corn-milling plant in the world. Summit annexed this area in 1911. Called Argo after one of the firm's products, this area continues to pull development in its direction.

After WORLD WAR I, manufacturing and services diversified in Summit. The *Des Plaines Valley News* began in 1913, and in 2000 was one of the last independent suburban newspapers. Between 1916 and 1922, the Elgin Motor Car Company produced over 8,000 automobiles. Food processing companies, functionally related to the Argo plant, were established. The rail yards transferred meat products from the Chicago stockyards. In the 1950s, the canal was filled in at Summit, so the land could be used for the Stevenson EXPRESSWAY.

Restricted at the start of the century to the home, shops, or—if widowed—to maintaining rooming houses, women now take a leading part not only in Summit's civic affairs, but in business and politics. In 1995, this was exemplified by the election of Summit's first female mayor.

John D. Schroeder

See also: Automobile Manufacturing; Demography; Food Processing: Local Market; Food Processing: Regional and National Market; Transportation

Further reading: Summit Bicentennial Commission, Heritage Committee. *Summit Heritage.* 1990.

Sun-Times. *See* Chicago Sun-Times

Sunday Closings. In Chicago, the policy of Sunday closing, requiring commercial venues to close on the traditional Christian day of worship, was tied to three questions that had moral overtones for many Americans during the nineteenth and early twentieth centuries: alcohol consumption and licensing, regulation of labor, and LEISURE. The city's first Sunday closing law, in 1845, prohibited any "tippling house" from opening on the first day of the week. Chicago's law resembled the state's 1845 Sunday law, which prohibited open tippling houses and the sale of alcohol on Sundays and stipulated that anyone who disturbed the peace and order on Sundays by labor (works of necessity and charity excepted) or amusements would be fined. Shipyard and RAILROAD WORKERS who loaded and unloaded passengers and goods were exempt, as were Sunday travelers, and the law allowed a person to hold a different day sacred and consider Sundays a regular workday.

The city and state's closing laws, however, proved unpopular with Chicago's IRISH and GERMAN immigrants. German Americans, for example, were accustomed to attending beer gardens with family entertainment on Sundays. When MAYOR Levi Boone attempted to enforce the law in 1855, the ensuing LAGER BEER RIOT left the Sunday law a dead letter in the city. Less than two decades later, Mayor Joseph Medill attempted to enforce the Sunday closing law at the request of a group of PROTESTANT temperance advocates. His unsuccessful campaign mobilized Chicago's Irish and German voters against the law, and the city amended it in 1874. The new city ordinance allowed businesses to open on Sunday providing all doors and windows that opened onto public streets were closed or covered. The city law provoked contention over whether it superseded the state Sunday closing law, and in 1909 the Illinois Supreme Court affirmed that the state law was operative in Chicago. By that time the movement for PROHIBITION had gathered momentum in the state. Although the city allowed Sunday drinking by the mid-1870s, it prohibited selling goods on sidewalks on Sundays, and in 1883 the city banned Sunday STREET PEDDLING.

In 1887 the Chicago clerks union initiated agitation that led to the introduction of state legislation to require all businesses, factories, and other places of employment to close on Sundays. The city's butchers, who desired a six-day workweek, joined the movement. The vast majority of the bill's supporters, however, were native-born Protestant ministers and temperance workers who sought the suppression of Sunday commerce to ensure a concomitant suppression of vice. With citizens and police routinely ignoring existing laws, it was impossible to stem the tide of Sunday consumption. The 1887 bill and a second in 1889 failed to pass in the legislature. By 1890 professional BASEBALL games and THEATER performances were commonly held in Chicago on Sundays.

The most spectacular struggle over Sunday closing in Chicago occurred when city organizers sought federal support to host the WORLD'S COLUMBIAN EXPOSITION in 1893. Effective petitioning by Protestant church leaders ensured a Sunday closing requirement in the fair's 1892 enabling legislation. The fair's directors filed suit and won a partial victory. Although the fair opened on Sundays, no machines were allowed to operate and most exhibits remained closed.

Two state laws, both enacted in the 1930s, defused some of the moral and labor questions that had sustained the state's 1845 Sunday law. The 1934 Liquor Control Act, passed in the wake of Prohibition, prohibited alcohol sales on Sundays unless allowed by local government. The second law, enacted in 1935, specified that employees receive a day of rest each week and advance notice when required to WORK on Sundays. By 1963 the last section of the 1845 Sunday law, which forbade disturbances of the peace on Sunday, had been repealed. In its place the state prohibited specific activities, including HORSE RACING and automobile sales.

Rachel E. Bohlmann

See also: Entertaining Chicagoans; Local Option; Woman's Christian Temperance Union, Chicago Central

Further reading: Laband, David N., and Deborah Hendry Heinbuch. *Blue Laws: The History, Economics, and Politics of Sunday-Closing Laws.* 1987. • Pettibone, Dennis Lynn. "Caesar's Sabbath: The Sunday-Law Controversy in the United States, 1879–1892." Ph.D. diss., University of California, Riverside. 1979. • Sawislak, Karen. *Smoldering City: Chicagoans and the Great Fire, 1871–1874.* 1995.

Supermarkets. *See* Grocery Stores and Supermarkets

Swedes. During the early decades of Swedish immigration, Chicago served as a gateway to settlement in agricultural areas of the Midwest. Overpopulation and the comparatively late industrialization of the Swedish economy persuaded over one million Swedes to permanently emigrate between 1845 and 1930, attracted by available agricultural land and an expanding American labor market in cities such as Chicago. By 1910, one-fifth of all people who were born in Sweden lived in the United States. Only Ireland and Norway lost a higher proportion of their population in the migration to America.

Most Swedish immigrants were young, PROTESTANT, and literate, originating from rural areas of southern Sweden. Chicago's first Swedish settlement emerged in 1846, when immigrants destined for the Swedish religious colony in Bishop Hill, Illinois, decided instead to settle in Chicago. The Swedish community in Chicago subsequently grew to become the largest in the United States. The Swedish presence in Chicago can be divided into four distinct phases: early establishment between 1846 and 1880; mass migration and dispersal from 1880 to 1930; maturation and decline between 1930 and 1960; and modernization after 1960.

In 1848, only 40 Swedes lived in Chicago, and that population grew slowly. Many of these earliest settlers came to WORK on the ILLINOIS & MICHIGAN CANAL. Although the Swedish settlement remained small for the next two decades, reaching 816 people in 1860 and 6,154 in 1870, it represented the largest single cluster of Swedes in the United States. During the 1870s, the Swedish population in the city doubled, outnumbered only by the GERMAN, IRISH, and British immigrant groups. These early Swedish settlers established three distinct ethnic enclaves. The largest emerged north of the CHICAGO RIVER on the NEAR NORTH SIDE and became known as Swede Town; a second, smaller enclave developed on the SOUTH SIDE in DOUGLAS and ARMOUR SQUARE; and the third grew on the West Side in NORTH LAWNDALE. Smaller settlements emerged in WEST TOWN and the NEAR WEST SIDE.

Most Swedish men worked in skilled trades, such as CONSTRUCTION and metalworking, or in factory jobs at the McCormick Reaper Works, the UNION STOCK YARD, or the Pullman Palace Car Company. Like their Irish counterparts, most Swedish women who worked outside the home found employment as domestic servants in American households. Within the Swedish enclaves, Swedes established a network of churches and secular associations, the earliest of which were the St. Ansgarius Church (1849), the only Episcopal Swedish church in Chicago, the Immanuel Lutheran Church (1853), and the social club Svea (1857). Chicago became an important center of the Swedish American press. The Lutheran NEWSPAPER *Hemlandet* (1855) relocated to Chicago from Galesburg, Illinois, in 1859, and was rivaled by the more secularly oriented *Svenska Amerikanaren* (1866). Both newspapers reached Swedes across America and in Sweden.

After 1880, the Swedish population in Chicago exploded. Waves of new immigrants were drawn by the city's expanding economy. During the 1880s, the Swedish-born population in Chicago increased by roughly 233 percent to more than 43,000 people. By 1930 there were 65,735 Swedish-born Chicagoans and more than 140,000 children of Swedish immigrants. Networks of friends and relatives eased the transition to urban life, helping newcomers find housing, jobs, and social connections.

After the 1880s, Swedes relocated to newer settlements away from the older enclaves in the central districts of the city. By 1920 Swedes dominated the North Side neighborhoods of LAKE VIEW, ANDERSONVILLE, and NORTH PARK; and West Side neighborhoods of AUSTIN and BELMONT CRAGIN. On the South Side, Swedes settled primarily in HYDE PARK, WOODLAWN, ENGLEWOOD, WEST ENGLEWOOD, SOUTH SHORE, GREATER GRAND CROSSING, EAST SIDE, MORGAN PARK, and ROSELAND. Swedes were least likely to settle in areas dominated by GREEKS, CZECHS, HUNGARIANS, RUSSIANS, POLES, YUGOSLAVIANS, and ITALIANS; instead, they settled near Germans, Irish, and NORWEGIANS, groups whose earliest arrival in Chicago coincided with their own.

In these widely dispersed areas, Swedish immigrants created lively ethnic communities, building new churches and social organizations. The variety of churches established—Augustana Lutheran, Mission Covenant, Free Church, and the Swedish branches of the SALVATION ARMY and Methodist and Baptist churches—reflected denominational movements among the Swedish people. Through worship, music, and socials, churches served as important cultural hubs to Swedes in the city, and many single immigrants met their spouses through these churches. Secular CLUBS developed in neighborhoods after the establishment of the mainline Swedish churches, when the Swedish population was large enough to sustain a variety of organizational interests. Singing and sports clubs, fraternal lodges, temperance and educational organizations, professional associations, and Swedish branches of trade unions all added to the diversity of Swedish life in Chicago.

Churches and secular organizations started benevolent institutions to assist sick, unemployed, widowed, orphaned, and aging immigrants, the largest of which became Augustana Hospital (1882) and Swedish Covenant Hospital (1886). Although most Swedish children attended public SCHOOLS, the Swedish churches augmented this education by providing Swedish-language summer programs. The Mission Covenant Church transferred its college and SEMINARY to Chicago in 1893, naming it NORTH PARK COLLEGE and Theological Seminary after the neighborhood in which it was located. Most Swedes continued to work as skilled, semiskilled, and DOMESTIC WORKERS, but an ever increasing number achieved success in business and professional endeavors. Per Samuel Peterson (1830–1903), after whom Peterson Avenue is named, began the Rose Hill Nursery in 1856 and by 1900 he supplied most of the trees along the streets of Chicago. The American-born son of Swedish immigrants,

Swedish Old People's Home, Norwood Park, 1925. Photographer: Unknown. Source: Chicago Historical Society.

Charles R. Walgreen (1873–1939), founded his first Walgreen's drugstore in Chicago in 1901. Immigrant Frederick Lundin (1868–1947) won seats in the Illinois state senate in 1894 and the U.S. House of Representatives in 1908. He played an instrumental role in the successful MAYORAL elections of William Hale Thompson in 1915 and 1919 and the creation of Thompson's PATRONAGE system.

Until 1960, Swedes ranked as Chicago's fifth-largest foreign-born group, behind Poles, Germans, Russians, and Italians. By then, however, Chicago's Swedish community was shrinking and growing older. Swedish-born settlers declined from 65,735 in 1930 to 16,674 in 1960. International depression and world war disrupted Swedish immigration, and a modernizing Swedish economy improved conditions there and diminished the need to leave for better opportunities elsewhere. Swedish organizational membership flattened during these years and more associations adopted English as their official language as fewer newcomers arrived from Sweden. The importance of preserving the historical record of Swedish immigrants in Chicago and the United States was realized by a new generation, and with this in mind, the Swedish Pioneer Historical Society was founded in Chicago in 1948.

By 1970, slightly more than 7,000 native-born Swedes resided in the city. With the ease of trans-Atlantic travel, most modern Swedes living in Chicago were on short-term business assignments, studying abroad, or married to Americans. The vast majority were highly educated and fluent in English well before settling in Chicago. Despite declining numbers, the Swedish ethnic heritage in Chicago lived on. In the 2000 census, more than 123,000 residents of the metropolitan region cited Swedish as their main ethnic identity.

Preservation of ethnic heritage was carried on by the Swedish American Historical Society (formerly the Swedish Pioneer Historical Society), the Swedish American Museum Center (1976), the Central Swedish Committee and its member organizations, and the Center for Scandinavian Studies at North Park University (1985). The Andersonville neighborhood remained an important Swedish American center, yet it lacked the dense clustering of Swedish residents of an earlier time. As third- and fourth-generation Swedish Americans dispersed residentially, the work of Swedish fraternals, churches, and foundations that did not depend upon residential clustering became even more important in reminding Chicago of the important role Swedes played in shaping the city's history.

Anita Olson Gustafson

See also: Americanization; Demography; Ethnic Music; Multicentered Chicago; Prohibition and Temperance

Further reading: Anderson, Philip J., and Dag Blanck. *Swedish-American Life in Chicago: Cultural and Urban Aspects of an Immigrant People, 1850–1930.* 1992. • Beijbom, Ulf. *Swedes in Chicago: A Demographic and Social Study of the 1846–1880 Immigration.* 1971. • Nordahl, Per. *Weaving the Ethnic Fabric: Social Networks among Swedish-American Radicals in Chicago, 1890–1940.* 1994.

Swimming. Chicago's elite athletic clubs and YMCAs pioneered competitive swimming in Chicago during the 1890s. The Chicago Athletic Association, the city's principal athletic club, opened its pool in 1893, formed its first competitive swim team shortly thereafter, and hosted the nation's second annual Amateur Athletic Union (AAU) indoor and outdoor championships in 1897.

Chicago's first great swimmer, H. Jamison Handy, won a bronze medal in the breaststroke as a member of Central YMCA Olympic squad in 1904. Handy improved the crawl with an underwater exhaling technique that brought him record-setting national championships between 1906 and 1909.

The UNIVERSITY OF CHICAGO completed its first swimming pool in 1904 and hosted the first intercollegiate contest in the Midwest—a dual meet with the University of Wisconsin—the following year. NORTHWESTERN UNIVERSITY built its first pool in 1910 and, with largely local swimmers, soon became one of the best programs in the nation.

By the 1920s, many ethnic associations and SETTLEMENT HOUSES had also built swimming pools and established competitive swim programs. The Chicago HEBREW INSTITUTE, which built its first pool in 1915, was noted for its strong women's program.

Among Chicago's high schools, the COOK COUNTY League conducted its first swim meet in 1906, and the Illinois Athletic Club (IAC) inaugurated an annual interscholastic meet in 1908. New Trier (WINNETKA) built the country's first indoor high-school pool in 1913; many other Chicago area schools soon followed. In 1932, the Illinois High School Association (IHSA) inaugurated a state high-school swimming meet.

In 1912, Bill Bachrach became swimming coach at the IAC, which dominated competitive U.S. swimming for the next decade. The IAC continued to produce champions up through the 1920s, including freestyler Johnny Weissmuller, one of the world's all-time greatest swimmers. When the AAU began sponsoring women's swimming competition in 1916, Bachrach worked assiduously with female swimmers. His most notable protégées were two 1924 Olympic champions, backstroker Sybil Bauer and freestyler Ethel Lackie. By the late 1920s, though, the Illinois Women's Athletic Club (IWAC), founded by Bertha Severin in 1918, was dominating women's swim competition. IWAC member Jane Fauntz competed in the 1928 Olympics in the breaststroke and in the 1932 Olympics in springboard diving.

The Lake Shore Athletic Club (LSAC), founded in 1927, succeeded the IAC as Chicago's preeminent producer of swimmers,

How to Dress at the Bathing Beaches

A city ordinance published in the *Daily Calumet*, 1919.

General

Suitable Bathing Dress Required—No person shall swim or bathe in the waters of Lake Michigan adjacent to the city, or in any part of the harbor, or in any public bathing beach in the city, unless such person be clothed in a suitable bathing dress. No all white or flesh or colored bathing suits, nor suits that expose the chest lower than a line drawn on a level with the arm pits shall be worn at bathing beaches, and all bathers at such bathing beaches shall, as to dress, observe and conform to the following minimum requirements.

Men

Men must wear suits with skirt effect or shirt must be worn outside of trunks, except when flannel knee pants with belt and fly front are worn, and in all cases trunks must not be shorter than four inches above the knee (top of the patella) and the skirt or shirt must not be shorter than two inches above the bottom of the trunks.

Women

Ladies' blouse and bloomer suits may be worn with or without skirts, and with or without stockings, provided the blouse has one-quarter arm sleeve or close-fitting arm holes and the bloomers are of a pattern that is full and not shorter than four inches above the knee (top of the patella). Ladies' jersey knit suit may also be worn with or without stockings, provided the suit has skirt or skirt effect with one-quarter arm sleeves or close-fitting arm holes, trunks not shorter than four inches above the knee (top of the patella) and the bottom of the trunk.

Life Guards

Life guards must wear scarlet shirts with blue flannel pants, fly front and white belt, and the shirt must bear the words "Life Guard" in white three inch block letters.

Penalty

Any person violating the provisions of the ordinance shall, upon conviction thereof, be fined not less than five dollars nor more than twenty dollars for each offense.

Bathers on Oak Street Beach, July 1941. View is looking west across Lake Shore Drive. Photographer: John Vachon. Source: Library of Congress.

winning three national titles during the 1930s and earning the club international prestige. In 1941, Adolph Kiefer (a former LSAC swimmer) led the Chicago Towers Club to the national title. The LSAC became a women's swim power in 1933, when it inherited a team of great swimmers from the defunct IWAC—including Olympic breaststroker Dorothy Schiller.

After World War II, Chicago's private athletic clubs largely retreated from sponsoring AAU teams. The Chicago Town Club, located in the Sheridan Hotel on Michigan Avenue, emerged as a national power in the late 1940s and produced two Olympic freestylers, Jackie LaVine (1948 and 1952) and Jody Alderson (1952).

From the 1930s through the 1950s, Chicago consistently ranked second to California as a producer of world-class swimmers and divers because of the talent produced in Chicago-area high schools. Top swim powers were Maine (Des Plaines), Lane Tech (Chicago), New Trier (Winnetka), Evanston, and Fenwick (Oak Park). During the 1960s, Hinsdale Central dominated state competition, producing Olympian John Kinsella. In 1975, the IHSA added women's competition.

Robert Pruter

See also: Creation of Chicago Sports; Fitness and Athletic Clubs; Leisure; Sports, High-School; Young Men's Christian Association

Further reading: Gems, Gerald R. "The Rise of Sport at a Jewish Settlement House." In *Sports and the American Jew*, ed. Steven A. Riess, 1998, 152–153. • Hyatt, Chauncey A. "Interscholastic Swimming in the Middle West, 1915–16." *Intercollegiate Swimming Guide, 1916–17.* 1916, 111. • Pieroth, Doris H. *Their Day in the Sun: Women of the 1932 Olympics.* 1996.

Swiss. Swiss immigrants come from a small country yet belong to four different ethnic groups and speak either German, French, Italian, or Romansch. They have remained nearly invisible as they are often taken for German, French, or Italian. Most are either of the Reformed or Roman Catholic faith. Coming from a long-established democracy, the approximately 400,000 Swiss estimated to have resided in the United States between 1820 and 1990 easily blended into American life. In 1870 there were some 1,500 Swiss in Chicago out of 8,980 in Illinois; in 1930, 4,230 out of 7,315. In the 2000 census more than 20,000 people in the greater Chicago metropolitan area reported some Swiss ancestry.

The occupational status level of Chicago's Swiss resembled that of Americans at large. A 1915 membership roster of a Chicago Swiss organization listed among its 389 members some 30 professionals, among them 6 merchants, 5 owners of factories, 5 hotel owners, and 4 physicians, as well as 19 laborers. The rest were engaged in numerous lower- and middle-class occupations. This paralleled the general status of Swiss in the United States, of whom about 40 percent were middle class in 1915.

Among Chicago's first Swiss were William Haas and Andrew Sulzer, who established Chicago's first brewery in 1833. Swiss actively involved in Chicago's civic life have included Conrad Sulzer, an early official and benefactor of Ridgeville and Lake View; Brigadier General Hermann Lieb, editor of the *Chicago Democrat* and Cook County Clerk from 1873 to 1877; surgeon Henry Banga, a pioneer of antiseptic methods at Michael Reese Hospital; Albert Ochsner of Rush Medical College, chief surgeon at Augustana Hospital; surgeon Nicholas Senn, also at Rush, donor of a building for medical research and of two European medical collections, now part of the John Crerar Library. Rudolph Ganz, president of the Chicago Musical College from 1933 to

1954, greatly enhanced Chicago's musical life. Physician Elisabeth Kübler-Ross, author of *On Death and Dying* (1969), pioneered new approaches to the terminally ill.

Chicago's Swiss established several organizations—at times divided along ethnic lines—to further social cohesion, preserve the national heritage, and provide mutual help. A *Grütli Verein* was organized in 1856, a Swiss Club in 1888, a Swiss Men's Choir in 1869, a Swiss Benevolent Society in 1872, a French Swiss Benevolent Society in 1888, and in 1927 a Swiss American Historical Society. Several of those organizations had also special singing, gymnastics, and Alpine wrestling sections. Metropolitan Chicago has been and remains a favored destination of Swiss newcomers to the United States. Today many of them are not immigrants, however, but professionals temporarily relocating to pursue their careers.

Leo Schelbert

See also: Americanization; Demography; Multicentered Chicago; Mutual Benefit Societies

Further reading: Schelbert, Leo. "Some Glimpses of the Past: The Swiss Benevolent Society of Chicago, 1872–1972." In *100th Annual Report of the President,* Swiss Benevolent Society of Chicago, 1971, 10–19. • Schelbert, Urspeter, ed. *Swiss Colonists in 19th Century America.* 1995. Reprint of *Geschichte und Leben der Schweizer Kolonien,* ed. Adelrich Steinach. 1889.

Symerton, IL, Will County, 44 miles SW of the Loop. Since its incorporation in 1904, Symerton has remained a small AGRICULTURAL town. Over half of its housing was built before 1939, and the 2000 population was 106.

Erik Gellman

See also: Will County

Syrians. The first wave of "Syrian" immigrants to the United States came from a part of the Ottoman Empire known as *bilad al-Sham,* an area that included the current Syria, Lebanon, Jordan, Palestine, and Israel. Faced with overpopulation, declining local industries, and punishing debt, "Syrians" (as the inhabitants of *bilad al-Sham* called themselves) began to make the journey to the Americas in large numbers at the close of the nineteenth century.

Included in this first wave was a pioneering group of Syrians bound for the WORLD'S COLUMBIAN EXPOSITION OF 1893. They were officially part of the Ottoman contingent on the fair's Midway Plaisance and—along with other peoples from the Middle East and North Africa—enticed fairgoers to buy their handmade wares. News of the fair's success and of work opportunities in and around Chicago reached family and friends in Ramallah, Damascus, Zahle, and other Syrian towns, prompting many to emigrate.

Like their counterparts in Latin America, most Syrians in Chicago worked initially as STREET PEDDLERS. They sold curios from the "Holy Land" such as rosaries and holy water, but quickly began to add items like buttons, thread, and handmade lace to their packs. Successful peddlers channeled their savings into dry-goods RETAIL and WHOLESALE supply stores, while a few wealthier merchants catered to luxury tastes in fine linens, kimonos, and carpets. Syrian women were especially active in the peddling trade, and were also sought after as seamstresses in Michigan Avenue businesses owned by well-to-do Syrians.

The early Syrian community in Chicago consisted mainly of Melkites (Greek Catholics). In 1894 they founded St. John the Baptist Church at 323 South Franklin Street, which was one of the first Arabic-speaking parishes in the United States. By 1910, the parish had grown to over 350 people and was able to buy a building of its own on South Washtenaw. The new St. John's became the center of community activity for the next half century, serving as a place of worship and meeting place for its Maronite, Orthodox, and Melkite constituents. Syrians in Chicago also supported voluntary associations and a lively Arabic-language press.

The Immigration Act of 1924 severely limited the number of Syrians allowed entry into the United States. By this time, geographic Syria had been divided up into mandates administered by France and Britain. The struggle for the independence of their homelands galvanized many members of the diaspora, although an equal number—particularly second-generation Syrian Americans—were assimilating into the American mainstream and losing touch with the culture and concerns of their parents and grandparents. In Chicago, St. John's lost many of its members as they moved to the suburbs and joined ROMAN CATHOLIC churches closer to their homes in BERWYN, ELMHURST, OAK PARK, and RIVER FOREST. Others broke away from St. John's for different reasons, such as to form their own Eastern-rite churches like St. George Antiochian Orthodox and Our Lady of Lebanon.

The 1960s and 1970s marked a turning point for the Syrian community in Chicago, as a new wave of immigrants from the independent Arab states reinvigorated the diaspora politically and culturally. This wave differed significantly from the first in that it comprised largely students and professionals, many of whom had left during the unrest brought on by the wars with Israel. While their presence enriched the Arab communities here, it deprived the Arab world of some of its most talented citizens—so much so that this period is commonly referred to as the "Arab brain drain." The majority of the immigrants who came to Chicago during this period were PALESTINIAN and JORDANIAN. At the end of the twentieth century these immigrants played leading roles in the Chicago Arab American community, 3 percent of whom were estimated to be of Syrian descent.

Sarah Gualtieri

See also: Demography; Eastern Orthodox; Iraqis; Lebanese; Multicentered Chicago

Further reading: Haddad, Safiyah Fahmi. "Socialization and Cultural Change among Syrian-Americans in Chicago." Ph.D. diss., University of Chicago. 1964. • Hitti, Philip. *The Syrians in America.* 1924. • Naff, Alixa. *Becoming American: The Early Arab Immigrant Experience.* 1985.

T

Taiwanese. Separating Chicago's ethnic Taiwanese community from the broader CHINESE American community is a delicate task involving an understanding of Chinese history, politics, ethnicity, and culture. Between 1950 and 1980, roughly half of immigrants labeled Chinese by U.S. authorities arrived via Taiwan. Many identified themselves as ethnically Taiwanese, claiming cultural roots to the island originally known to westerners as Formosa; others were "mainlanders" who had retreated to Taiwan following civil war in the 1940s. Before 1970, most Taiwanese arrived in Chicago as graduate students and then stayed to accept professional jobs. Efforts to organize the community often originated with students, who formed the Taiwanese Association of Chicago (1956) and the Taiwanese Student Association (1957). Later, the North American Taiwanese Professors Association (1980) and the Taiwanese United Fund (1985) were founded in Chicago.

The bulk of Taiwanese immigration took place in the 1970s and 1980s, after the 1965 Immigration Act raised quotas to 20,000 migrants per year. (The quota survived the U.S. government's derecognition of the Republic of China in 1979.) Since 1980 the proportion of Taiwanese relative to other Chinese ethnicities has shrunk as immigration from the mainland has surged. The majority of Taiwanese were concentrated in the west, northwest, and north suburbs.

The Taiwanese have long been closely attuned to the political tensions between the mainland People's Republic of China and Taiwan's government, the Republic of China. Since 1976, the *World Journal,* a daily NEWSPAPER with ties to the Kuomintang party that ruled Taiwan from 1949 until 2000, has been widely available; in 2000, circulation reached 30,000 in the Midwest. The weekly *Pacific News* and *Taiwan Tribune,* also distributed in Chicago, provided outlets for opposition party news. As in Taiwan, most Taiwanese in Chicago supported complete independence for Taiwan during the conflicts of the second half of the twentieth century, while a small minority has supported unification with China. But voices were also heard among Chicago's Taiwanese in opposition to the Kuomintang's martial law, imposed from 1949 to 1987. The shift to democracy and the Kuomintang's defeat in 2000 reduced factors pushing Taiwanese to emigrate to the United States.

Divisions between Taiwanese and mainland Chinese in the Chicago area have been social and economic as well as political. Language is often one barrier; Taiwanese largely speak Taiwanese and Mandarin, while Cantonese is the predominant mainlander language. Class is another; Taiwanese who migrated between 1950 and 1980 often arrived with high levels of education and readily found professional jobs. Location is a third; the Taiwanese largely avoided Chicago's CHINATOWN and instead sought campus and suburban settings.

Divisions widened in the 1980s when the Taiwanese community in Chicago became more assertive in differentiating itself culturally from the mainland community. A network of nine suburban Chinese-language schools was created to stem the loss of language among succeeding generations. The Formosan Association of Public Affairs, founded in Los Angeles in 1982 to lobby Congress for Taiwanese independence, has a chapter in Chicago. In May 1999, the city celebrated its first Taiwanese American Heritage Week. By the start of the twenty-first century the largely middle-class and suburban Taiwanese had developed a cultural identity distinctive from their mainland brethren.

D. Bradford Hunt

See also: Cold War and Anti Communism; Demography; Koreans; Multicentered Chicago

Further reading: Ng, Franklin. *The Taiwanese Americans.* 1995.

Tanning. *See* Leather and Tanning

Tanzanians. The Tanzanian presence in Chicago is a relatively recent phenomenon, and the few Tanzanians who live in the city form a modest community. During the early 1980s a drought in Tanzania caused serious economic distress, inducing some people to seek opportunities and financial stability elsewhere. These educated immigrants began to come in appreciable numbers in 1986, when 370 Tanzanians emigrated to the United States. The majority of those who have arrived since have chosen to live in Chicago.

Many of the city's Tanzanians are students and professionals who came to Chicago to pursue an advanced degree or work for an employer who sponsored their entry into the country. Many Tanzanians in Chicago work as technicians, executives, and managers. Sometimes individuals have left families and friends behind to gain a foothold in their careers and then return home a few years later. More men than women have made the trek to the United States, and at the end of the 1990s most were between 20 and 44 years of age.

Because their stay in Chicago is often relatively short and focused on personal pursuits, Tanzanians participate in few collective undertakings around the city. Like KENYANS, their East African neighbors, they are less visible than some West African groups and their cultural impact is therefore more subtle. Most Tanzanians are scattered across the North Side, with a few in HYDE PARK, clustering around the UNIVERSITY OF CHICAGO and the nearby Lutheran School of Theology. Efforts to bring people together in a social or cultural setting have included student gatherings at the end of the year to socialize and build networks. On the last Sunday of every month, the Lutheran School of Theology holds worship services in Swahili, the official language of Tanzania. Religion plays an active role in the lives of many, as roughly 40 percent of the Tanzania's population is Christian, 30 percent MUSLIM, and 30 percent followers of ethnic faiths. Some Chicago churches, such as Zion Lutheran and Augustana Lutheran, have small Tanzanian memberships. Heritage Books, located on Granville Avenue, is a hub of information on Tanzanian culture and history.

Tramayne M. Butler

See also: Demography; Multicentered Chicago; Protestants

Tap Dance. Tap, a hybrid DANCE form deriving from both African and IRISH cultures and distinguished by its rhythms, has a long history in Chicago, one made apparent by a resurgence of the genre in the last decades of the twentieth century. Paralleling the international growth of tap dance, Chicago's revival grew out of an alliance between an older generation of AFRICAN AMERICAN tap dancers and a younger generation of rhythm tappers. Individual artists like Jimmy Payne, a tap performer and teacher in Chicago since the 1940s, provided living links to the VAUDEVILLE and Broadway tradition, while forums like the Chicago Human Rhythm Project, an annual tap festival begun in 1990 by Lane Alexander and Kelly Michaels, fostered awareness and collaboration between artists and audiences of various backgrounds. At the close of the century, leading Chicago tap companies included the Especially Tap Company, Steppin' Out, Rhythm I. S. S., and the Jump Rhythm Jazz Project.

Anthea Kraut

See also: Dance Companies; Jazz Dance

Further reading: Ann Barzel Dance Collection. The Newberry Library, Chicago, IL. • Ts'ao, Aimée. "Tap Resurgence Blows into Windy City." *Dance Magazine* 71.7 (July 1997): 26.

Tax Strikes. Between 1931 and 1933, Chicago and COOK COUNTY experienced one of the largest tax strikes in American history. The instigators belonged to the Association of Real Estate Taxpayers (ARET), which had been founded in 1930 by several wealthy REAL-ESTATE owners.

The chief demand of ARET was that local and state governments obey a long-ignored provision of the Illinois Constitution of 1870 requiring uniform TAXATION for all forms of property. John M. Pratt and James E. Bistor charged that the failure to assess such personal property as furniture, cars, and stocks and bonds was not only illegal but left owners of real estate with excessive burdens. ARET's program also included support for sweeping rate reductions in the general property tax and retrenchment in local governmental spending.

ARET functioned primarily as a cooperative legal service. Each member paid annual dues of $15 to fund lawsuits challenging the constitutionality of real-estate assessments. The radical side of the movement became apparent by early 1931 when ARET called for taxpayers to withhold real-estate taxes (or "strike") pending a final ruling by the Illinois Supreme Court, and later the U.S. Supreme Court. Mayor Anton Cermak and other politicians desperately tried to break the strike by threatening criminal prosecution and revocation of city services.

ARET's influence peaked in late 1932, with a membership approaching 30,000 (largely skilled workers and small-business owners.) By this time, it had a budget of over $600,000 and a radio show in Chicago. But it suffered a demoralizing blow in October 1932 when the U.S. Supreme Court refused to hear a case it had brought. Buffeted by political coercion and legal defeats, and torn by internal factionalism, the strike collapsed in early 1933.

David T. Beito

See also: Government, City of Chicago; Property Assessment

Further reading: Beito, David T. *Taxpayers in Revolt: Tax Resistance during the Great Depression.* 1989. • Murphy, Marjorie. "Taxation and Social Conflict: Teacher Unionism and Public School Finance in Chicago, 1898–1934." *Journal of the Illinois State Historical Society* 74 (Winter 1981): 242–260.

Taxation and Finance. The history of local taxation in northeastern Illinois is largely a tale of growing disenchantment with the property tax and of the search for alternate sources of revenue. From the 1830s on, Chicago's city GOVERNMENT levied a property tax, and by the close of the nineteenth century Chicagoans paid additional property levies to fund the SCHOOLS, the LIBRARIES, and the sanitary and PARK DISTRICTS, as well as the county and townships. Throughout the nineteenth and early twentieth centuries, special assessments for sidewalk, STREET, and sewer improvements supplemented the property tax. Chicago relied more heavily on such assessments than other large cities in the United States, expecting the holders of abutting property to shoulder the costs of construction and paving.

During the late nineteenth century, criticism of the property levy mounted, focusing not on the weight of the tax burden but on the inequity of the system. An increasing amount of wealth was in the form of stocks, bonds, and bank accounts, and because these forms of property were less visible to assessors than buildings or land, they largely escaped taxation. Assessors could not be sure of their existence, and taxpayers failed to list them. Consequently, the tax burden fell more heavily on REAL ESTATE. Moreover, taxpayers complained that PROPERTY ASSESSMENT practices were unfair. Seemingly identical properties were assessed at markedly different values, with some real estate paying far less than its just share.

To supplement the much-criticized property levy, late-nineteenth-century municipalities turned to license fees. In Chicago receipts from licenses rose more than eightfold during the 1880s and by 1890 totaled $3.1 million compared with $5.2 million raised through the municipal property tax. SALOON licenses produced most of this revenue, with each LIQUOR retailer paying $500 per year for the privilege of quenching Chicagoans' thirst. Dry suburbs such as EVANSTON, however, could not profit from these lucrative fees and thus paid a price for their moral scruples. During the first four decades of the twentieth century, the property levy remained the chief source of local revenues, despite an uninterrupted flow of criticism. To guard against excessive taxation, the Illinois legislature adopted in 1901 the Juul Law, which limited the aggregate rate of all city, district, county, and township property taxes to no more than 5 percent of the assessed valuation. This was the beginning of a history of state-imposed tax limits. During the following decades, the much-amended law became so complicated that supposedly only one person in Illinois fully understood its complexities. In any case, the Juul Law did not enhance municipal revenues but seemed only to compound the confusion about local finances.

Hard times during the 1930s heightened the cries for revenue reform as local governments found it increasingly difficult to meet their obligations. Though the city of Chicago did not default, COOK COUNTY, the Sanitary District, the Cook County FOREST PRESERVE District, and the West PARK DISTRICT all fell into arrears on their debt payments. Seeking to provide employment through PUBLIC WORKS projects, the federal government became a new source of revenue, from 1935 to 1946 contributing $17 million for the construction of Chicago's subway and $5.7 million for a water filtration plant.

During the second half of the twentieth century, new tax levies weaned the local governments of the Chicago area from their excessive reliance on the property tax. In 1955 the Illinois legislature authorized municipal councils to impose a sales tax to be collected by the state and then returned to the municipality where the sale was made. Within a decade virtually every incorporated community in the state had adopted the tax. Answering complaints that shopping centers in unincorporated areas were stealing business from stores in sales-tax municipalities, in 1959 the Illinois legislature extended the privilege of imposing the sales tax to counties. Cook County soon adopted the new levy, thereby ensuring that sales in both incorporated and unincorporated areas were subject to a local tax. Henceforth, the sales tax was generally second only to the property levy as a source of tax revenue for the city of Chicago. Some suburban municipalities relied even more heavily on this new impost. In SCHAUMBURG, site of the region's largest SHOPPING MALL, the sales tax proved so lucrative that by the 1970s the municipality did not find it necessary to impose a property tax.

Other new nonproperty levies also boosted the fiscal capacity of local governments. In 1955 Chicago adopted a gross receipts tax on public utilities, which would become a source of substantial revenue. When Illinois adopted a state income tax in 1969, one-twelfth of the annual receipts was reserved for local governments. Ten years later Illinois abolished the corporate personal property tax, and to compensate local governments for the loss of revenue, lawmakers in Springfield established another scheme for distributing state receipts to localities. SCHOOL DISTRICTS remained heavily dependent on the property tax, though a complex state-aid formula, intended to narrow the funding gap between rich and poor districts, ensured a flow of state revenues to school authorities. By the mid-1980s the state of Illinois paid anywhere from 3 percent to 70 percent of the total funding for Cook County's individual school districts.

During the 30 years following WORLD WAR II, federal grants to local governments proliferated, especially benefiting the city of Chicago. In 1972, amid much ballyhoo, Congress adopted a revenue-sharing scheme, distributing federal money to all municipalities, counties, and townships. Federal revenue-sharing, however, never had a dramatic impact on local finances and the program ceased in 1986. In the long run, state revenue-sharing through the distribution of state income tax receipts proved more significant than the federal program.

A careful manager of funds, Mayor Richard J. Daley was able to gloat about Chicago's financial stability in the mid-1970s when New York City and other urban giants stood on the brink of bankruptcy. But following Daley's death, even Chicago faced some bad financial news. By 1979 the city school system was in dire financial straits, and that same year the city's bond rating dropped, sending a signal to investors that Chicago was not as sound financially as the late mayor had boasted.

Yet the various governments of the Chicago area remained solvent. The property tax survived, and complaints about it continued. But nonproperty taxes and state sharing played a larger role in local government finance during the late twentieth century than they had in earlier decades.

Jon C. Teaford

See also: Governing the Metropolis; Home Rule; Politics; Special Districts; State Politics; Suburbs and Cities as Dual Metropolis; Tax Strikes; Toll Roads

Further reading: Fairbanks, Robert P., and Glenn W. Fisher. *Illinois Municipal Finance: A Political and Economic Analysis.* 1968. • Fisher, Glenn W., and Norman Walzer. *Cities, Suburbs, and Property Taxes.* 1981. • Merriam, Charles E. *Report of an Investigation of the Municipal Revenues of Chicago.* 1906.

Taxis, Liveries, and Limousines.

Companies offering livery and carriage service appeared shortly after the founding of the city of Chicago. As early as 1853, the Parmelee TRANSPORTATION Company was organized to cater to RAILROAD passengers. A short-lived electric cab venture opened on Chicago's STREETS in 1899 with 100 vehicles. Entrepreneur Charles A. Coey opened the city's first public PARKING garage for the horseless carriage in 1902 and soon afterward opened the city's first auto livery business. In 1909, six or seven companies operated about 100 rigs, many of which were equipped with the latest "taximeter" technology to reduce disputes between drivers and "fares." It could be argued, however, that the taxicab did not take off until John Hertz popularized the service by painting cabs a highly distinctive shade of yellow. Responding to public complaints that fares were too high, he expanded his fleet and cut rates in half, and started the Yellow Cab Company of Chicago in 1915. Competitor Morris Markin started the Checker Cab Manufacturing Company in 1922.

Despite repeated calls to regulate the industry in the 1910s, by the early 1920s the taxi business remained a largely unregulated one controlled by AUTOMOBILE MANUFACTURERS and owners of large consolidated fleets.

Independents, including veterans, would challenge Yellow and Checker's dominance after WORLD WAR II. Moreover, controversy arose over cabdrivers adding to LOOP congestion.

An oversupply of cabs and poor economic conditions in the 1930s and 1940s laid the groundwork for UNIONIZATION and regulation. A successful strike by the TEAMSTERS in 1937 was followed by a quarter-century of strong union presence in the industry. During this period, controversy also swirled around the competition offered by drivers of "jitneys" in the SOUTH SIDE Black Belt (who served a population often ignored by standard taxicabs), large numbers of unemployed war veterans who drove illegal cabs, and the unregulated and inexpensive suburban cabs that frequently solicited business in the outlying neighborhoods of the city.

In 1999, there were six thousand licensed taxicabs in Chicago. Owing to rapidly increasing labor costs and financial problems in the industry after World War II, drivers no longer belonged to fleets, but leased cabs and affiliated themselves with associations. Cabs have continued to cruise for fares in the Loop and NEAR NORTH SIDE entertainment districts during peak hours, but most Chicagoans have to call central dispatchers to summon a car to their location. Yellow and Checker, still quite formidable as driver associations, compete with associations such as American-United and Flash Cab.

Joshua M. Lupkin

See also: Commuting; Public Transportation

Further reading: Barrett, Paul. *The Automobile and Urban Transit: The Formation of Public Policy in Chicago, 1900–1930.* 1983. • Gilbert, Gorman, and Robert E. Samuels. *The Taxicab: An Urban Transportation Survivor.* 1982.

Taylorism. The scientific management movement pioneered by Frederick Winslow Taylor at the turn of the twentieth century left an indelible mark on Chicago's industrial landscape. Taylorist principles inspired changes in labor processes in local BUSINESSES as diverse as the great steel mills, the stockyards, and CLERICAL and retail offices. Henry Ford's observation that cattle entered the killing floor in the Chicago stockyards in one piece and emerged after having been cut into numerous parts and packaged for distribution was part of the inspiration for the assembly lines used in his Detroit auto works. In 1927, researchers inspired by Taylorist methodology began experiments in worker productivity at the Western Electric Company in nearby CICERO. That research led to the discovery of the Hawthorne effect, which holds that productivity increases when workers are aware that they are being observed.

Keith Andrew Mann

Between 1924 and 1933, Western Electric conducted a large study of worker productivity at its Hawthorne Electrical Works in Cicero. With a team from Harvard Business School, the company created test environments in the plant to evaluate their impact on productivity, in addition to studying external influences such as home life, upbringing, and diet. Between 1928 and 1930 alone, researchers interviewed some 21,000 employees. Photographer: Curt Teich & Co. Source: Curt Teich Archives, Lake County Discovery Museum.

See also: Iron and Steel; Meatpacking; Welfare Capitalism; Work

Further reading: Braverman, Harry. *Labor and Monopoly Capital: The Degradation of Work in the Twentieth Century.* 1974. • Chandler, Alfred Dupont. *The Visible Hand: The Managerial Revolution in American Business.* 1977.

Teamsters. Teamsters are workers engaged in commercial road TRANSPORTATION, though the word also refers generically to members of the International Brotherhood of Teamsters (IBT), a labor union. Before 1945, most teamsters worked locally, driving "teams" of horses throughout Chicago. By the late twentieth century, national road networks enabled an interstate trucking industry employing many long-haul drivers.

Around 1900 teamsters began organizing labor unions. By 1905 the IBT had established a joint council in Chicago, with 45 affiliates and 30,825 members. These locals were militant, assisting other unions in their struggles for recognition. In 1905, teamsters aided striking employees of Montgomery Ward & Co. When other businesses rallied to Ward's defense, the dispute spread quickly. Unionists battled replacement drivers for 105 days, leading to 21 deaths. After the employers' victory, some locals deserted the IBT, forming a rival Chicago Teamsters' Union (CTU).

Critics dogged the teamsters' leadership. Charges of graft in 1904 and 1905 toppled union president Albert Young and delegitimized the striking drivers. In the 1920s and 1930s, businessmen attacked officials for alleged corruption, coercion, and gangsterism, while radicals like William Z. Foster charged them with selfishly thwarting mass unionism. Such accusations continued through the following decades.

The teamsters survived these allegations and remained influential in Chicago labor circles. After reincorporating the CTU locals in 1937, the IBT expanded by organizing transportation, CLERICAL, RETAIL, and manufacturing workers. William A. Lee of the bakery drivers local served as CHICAGO FEDERATION OF LABOR president from 1946 to 1984, even though the AFL-CIO had expelled the IBT in 1957.

Andrew Wender Cohen

See also: Strikes; Unionization; Work Culture

Further reading: "Union Teamsters' Forces in Chicago." *Chicago Tribune,* April 30, 1905. • Commons, John. "Types of American Labor Organization—The Teamsters of Chicago." *Quarterly Journal of Economics* 19 (1905). • Poole, Ernest. "How a Labor Machine Held Up Chicago, and How the Teamsters' Union Smashed That Machine." *The World To-Day* 7.1 (July 1904): 896–905.

Telegraph. The telegraph, which received its first practical demonstration in 1844, came to Chicago in 1848. Telegraphy made possible instant communication with the East Coast, and eventually with the entire country. Daily NEWSPAPERS began publishing next-day accounts of speeches, elections, and battles, all furnished by telegraph. During the FIRE OF 1871, a telegram from the mayor brought FIRE-FIGHTING equipment from Milwaukee; when it was over, citizens lined up at a makeshift Western Union office to inform alarmed friends and relatives that they had survived.

Chicago quickly became the eastern terminus of "western" communication and by the

1880s was the nation's second city in sheer volume of messages. The telegraph in turn promoted Chicago's economic growth. It proved critical in managing the long-distance RAILROAD routes which made Chicago a vital link between the Midwest and the East Coast. Chicago companies, serving far-flung markets by rail, could coordinate their operations by telegraph. Small-town storekeepers could obtain price information or place orders with their Chicago suppliers. In 1858 the Chicago Board of Trade began receiving market news from New York City by telegraph, while the board's grain and COMMODITY prices, now telegraphically disseminated, propelled it to national prominence as a grain market. Traders could complete deals by telegraph.

Chicago's resources, and its importance as a center of national telegraphic activity, made it the home of Western Union's central division, and the city attracted and fostered a wealth of engineering and entrepreneurial talent. Chicago became a center for manufacturing telegraphic (and later telephonic) equipment when the predecessor of the Western Electric Company relocated from Cleveland in 1870.

Most railroad stations served as telegraph offices, so residents of most neighborhoods and suburbs could send important messages anywhere in the metropolis. To get in touch with a group of employees near suburban RIVERSIDE, for instance, George PULLMAN instantly proposed sending a telegram. On the other hand, EVANSTONIANS seeking information on the Great Chicago Fire were frustrated because the local telegraph office was closed.

In 1869 private line service became available in Chicago, and the American District Telegraph Company soon offered affluent Chicagoans a home service allowing them to summon a firefighter, private policeman, or messenger. Telegraphic communication with other Chicagoans was facilitated by the company's network of neighborhood offices and messengers.

In 1865, the Chicago Fire Department contracted to build fire alarm boxes employing telegraphic signals. Located throughout the city, they allowed citizens to report fires quickly. In 1880 the Chicago POLICE Department began using call boxes on the streets. Citizens could report crimes, though only after obtaining keys to the boxes, which were selectively distributed; relatively few crime reports were made. More important, the boxes facilitated official communication among the police. Patrolmen were obliged to make hourly "duty calls," and were thus subject to stricter supervision. They could also summon a patrol wagon in the event they made an arrest. The call boxes used an innovative combination of telegraphic signaling for routine messages and the telephone for unusual messages, a design adopted by police departments throughout the country.

The telegraph diminished in relative importance as TELEPHONY grew more widespread. By 1940 Chicago had more than one million telephones in use, and 90 percent of fire alarms were telephoned to the Fire Department. Portable two-way radios finally rendered police call boxes obsolete, while other forms of telegraphy were largely superseded by more advanced electronic communications.

Christopher Thale

See also: Business of Chicago; Economic Geography; Firefighting; Police

Further reading: Andreas, A. T. *History of Chicago.* 1884–1886. • Reid, James D. *The Telegraph in America.* 1879. • Tarr, Joel A., with others. "The City and the Telegraph: Urban Telecommunications in the Pre-Telephone Era." *Journal of Urban History* 14.1 (November 1987).

Telephony. The telephone came to Chicago in 1877, just a few months after a small group of Massachusetts investors had decided to commercialize Alexander Graham Bell's remarkable invention.

Had circumstances been different, it is conceivable that Chicago—rather than Boston—might be remembered today as the cradle of the telephone industry. As the home of Western Electric, a leading manufacturer of electrical equipment, the city boasted a large number of technically trained tinkerers who were familiar with the latest developments of electrical science. One of the most prolific of these inventors was the HIGHLAND PARK resident Elisha Gray. In the mid-1870s, Gray devised a method of voice transmission that embodied several of the key principles of telephony. Unfortunately for Gray, his patent application reached the government a mere two hours after a similar application of Bell's. Bell's patent would soon become the single most valuable patent to have been issued by the federal government.

Gray's misfortune helped to guarantee that the history of telephony in Chicago would long be dominated by firms that traced their lineage back to Bell. These firms included the Chicago Telephone Company, the dominant Chicago firm at the turn of the twentieth century, and Illinois Bell, which absorbed Chicago Telephone in 1920. Both of these companies were pillars of the "Bell System," the national telephone network that was coordinated after 1900 by American Telephone and Telegraph (AT&T). The Bell System remained the backbone of the American communications infrastructure from the 1870s until the court-mandated breakup of AT&T in 1984. Following the Bell breakup, Illinois Bell became part of Ameritech, which, in 1999, was acquired by SBC Communications, a telecommunications firm based in San Antonio, Texas.

The first half century of telephony in Chicago was a period of rapid, and, indeed, often extraordinary growth. In 1878, the first Bell company began operations with a mere 75 telephones. By 1905, the total had increased to 100,000; by 1930, to 1.26 million. In per capita terms, this translated into one telephone for every 3.7 inhabitants, one of the highest ratios in the world.

In the early years, the telephone was primarily used to facilitate communications within a city or metropolitan area. Long-distance telephony was expensive and posed a variety of technical challenges. Telephone service to New York from Chicago began in 1892; to San Francisco, in 1915. Not until the 1960s—following the standardization of area codes and the advent of long-distance direct dialing—would it become common to call friends or family members who lived in another region or state. International telephony was even more unusual, and remained somewhat exotic until the rise in the 1970s of MCI and other competitors to AT&T.

Though the telephone in its early years was primarily a business tool, many middle-class families embraced it as well. Residential expansion was especially rapid in the 1890s, when a number of independent firms challenged the Chicago Telephone Company's dominant position in the downtown LOOP. Women used the telephone extensively to place orders for household goods, spearhead a variety of public-spirited reforms and converse with family and friends. Women also worked in large numbers as telephone operators; in 1928, Illinois Bell employed 12,000 female operators in Chicago alone. Operators were essential to the proper working of the system, since, prior to the introduction of the telephone dial in the 1920s, every telephone call made on a Bell telephone required the intervention of an operator to complete the connection.

For Chicagoans who lacked the inclination or means to subscribe to telephone service, the "nickel-in-the-slot" pay telephone provided a welcome alternative. Beginning around 1900, such devices could be found in thousands of drugstores, HOTELS, and other public places. A favorite of bookies and gangsters, they have been immortalized in dozens of Hollywood movies.

In subtle yet significant ways, the telephone reordered the urban landscape. By providing an alternative to face-to-face interaction, it helped to render obsolete the swarms of messenger boys who had previously clogged streets, stairways, and elevators. In this way, it lifted a major constraint upon the development of the SKYSCRAPER. In addition, it encouraged BUSINESS owners to separate the factory floor from the corporate headquarters, hastening the creation of the modern central office district.

Chicago has long been a center for the manufacture of telephone equipment. In the late nineteenth century, leading firms included Western Electric—long the exclusive supplier of Bell System telephones, switchboards, and related devices. For much of the twentieth century, Western Electric's Hawthorne Works in CICERO was one of the largest and most technologically advanced suppliers of telephone equipment in the world. Also important were the many firms that served Bell's competitors. These firms helped spearhead a short-lived but vigorous "independent" or non-Bell telephone boom around the turn of the century, and sponsored a number of lively Chicago-based trade journals, including the *American Telephone Journal* and *Telephony*. Telephone manufacturers in the Chicago metropolitan area in the late twentieth century included Motorola, a major supplier of cellular equipment based in SCHAUMBURG, and U.S. Robotics, a producer of modems and related devices.

One of the strangest chapters in the history of Chicago telephony unfolded in 1992, when, following a bizarre sequence of events, millions of gallons of water engulfed the basements of dozens of downtown buildings. This accident had been caused when construction workers unintentionally poked a hole in a segment of a long-forgotten network of underground TUNNELS that bordered the CHICAGO RIVER. Built almost a century earlier by upstart telephone entrepreneurs, these tunnels remained long after the firm had failed—a dramatic, if unfortunate, legacy of Chicago's early telephone pioneers.

Richard R. John

See also: Electronics; Global Chicago; Infrastructure; Innovation, Invention, and Chicago Business; Work

Further reading: Brooks, John. *Telephone: The First Hundred Years*. 1976. • Hounshell, David A. "Elisha Gray and the Telephone: On the Disadvantages of Being an Expert." *Technology and Culture* 16 (April 1975): 133–161. • Mahon, Ralph L. "The Telephone in Chicago, 1877–1940." Typescript. SBC Communications Archives, San Antonio, TX.

Television. *See* Broadcasting; Chicago School of Television

Television, Talk. During the final quarter of the twentieth century, Chicago became the center for production of nationally syndicated talk television, highlighted first by Phil Donahue, then Oprah Winfrey, Jenny Jones, and Jerry Springer. Phil Donahue began modern talk television from Dayton, Ohio, and then moved to Chicago. Expanding through the 1970s, he became the nation's number one host with an innovative style that saw him climb into a coffin to interview a mortician, run footage of a woman giving birth, and banter with phone-in callers who voted on the morality of an anatomically correct male doll. Through it all Donahue was ever walking into the audience, pointing his microphone to his nearly always female fans, and asking what they thought.

Donahue's success was emulated by others, notably Oprah Winfrey. By 1990, Winfrey far outdistanced Donahue, setting records for ratings and advertising time sold. She had come to Chicago from Baltimore in 1983, joining *A.M. Chicago* on WLS-TV. Soon she went national, surpassing Donahue by 1986 and, from her Chicago base, becoming one of the most popular and wealthy personalities in TV history. From her Chicago-based Harpo studios came not only her daily talk show but also miniseries and documentaries. Winfrey's intuitive ability to sympathize with guests (often to the point of tears) upped the ante of talk TV sensationalism. Imitators, led by Chicago-based Jenny Jones and Jerry Springer, pushed even further, featuring lewd shouting matches and bawdy (staged) brawls.

Douglas Gomery
Chuck Howell

See also: Advice Columns; Broadcasting

Further reading: Carbaugh, Donald A. *Talking American: Cultural Discourses of Donahue*. 1988. • Priest, Patricia Joyner. *Public Intimacies: Talk Show Participants and Tell-All TV*. 1996. • Shattuc, Jane. *The Talking Cure: Women and Daytime Talk Shows*. 1996.

Temperance. *See* Prohibition and Temperance

Tenements. Chicago's tenements were not like those made famous by Jacob Riis in New York City—six- or seven-story walk-up apartments, occupying almost all of their lots and built next to other structures of the same nature. Chicago's sprawling growth and decentralized employment magnets such as the stockyards and the steel mills meant that low-income housing districts were scattered, not concentrated as in lower Manhattan. Nevertheless, an exploding population of poor migrants, occupying hastily built and shoddily modified dwellings, gave the city large districts of crowded and unsanitary rental structures targeted by reformers as a danger to PUBLIC HEALTH and morals.

After the 1871 FIRE, the prohibition of wooden frame buildings in the city's core encouraged construction at the outskirts to house the flood of working-class newcomers. The result was a wide belt of small dwellings stretching from the OLD TOWN area on the North Side through the NEAR WEST SIDE to the stockyards, BRIDGEPORT, and the BLACK BELT south of the LOOP. A second stage of tenement evolution occurred with the arrival of immigrants from Southern and Eastern Europe between 1880 and 1914. Desperately poor families, clustering near WORK sites and people who shared their religious and ethnic backgrounds, fostered subdivision of already crowded dwellings and construction of cheap "REAR HOUSES."

Fear of epidemics and the specter of "New York conditions" fed Chicago's movement for tenement reform. After 1880, the city's health department had authority to inspect and to approve construction plans for tenements and workshops, but population growth and the proliferation of tenements overwhelmed official monitoring. Beginning in the 1890s, SETTLEMENT HOUSE workers and scholars focused public attention on certain districts within the sprawling belt of worker housing. *Hull-House Maps and Papers* (1895), Robert Hunter's *Tenement Conditions in Chicago* (1901), and Edith Abbott and Sophonisba Breckinridge's *The Tenements of Chicago, 1908–1935* (1936) reviewed housing conditions and the mixed results of reform.

Rear houses off an alley in the Near West Side community area, near Hull House, ca. 1910. Photographer: Unknown. Source: University of Illinois at Chicago.

Replacing old tenements with innovative low-income housing became a new goal. In the late 1920s, Sears magnate Julius Rosenwald and the Marshall Field family sponsored two large privately subsidized apartment projects, replacing demolished tenements on the NORTH and SOUTH SIDES. Chicago HOUSING REFORMERS praised these efforts but pointed out the limitations of private action in dealing with the huge number of tenements. Chicagoans Abbott, Jane Addams, and Harold Ickes helped to shape the NEW DEAL program of federally subsidized slum clearance and PUBLIC HOUSING which steadily transformed the landscape of Chicago after 1934. By 1970, private redevelopment and public URBAN RENEWAL had demolished most of the nineteenth-century tenements, though the problem of housing the poorest Chicagoans persists.

Henry C. Binford

See also: Economic Geography; Kitchenettes; Subsidized Housing; Suburbs and Cities as Dual Metropolis

Further reading: Abbott, Edith. *The Tenements of Chicago, 1908–1935*. 1936. • Bowly, Devereux, Jr. *The Poor House: Subsidized Housing in Chicago, 1895–1976*. 1978. • Philpott, Thomas Lee. *The Slum and the Ghetto: Neighborhood Deterioration and Middle-Class Reform, Chicago, 1880–1930*. 1978.

Tennis. Chicagoans began playing tennis soon after the game reached America from Britain in 1874. Cost initially limited participation to the wealthy, but, as facilities became more accessible through clubs, parks, schools, etc., tennis's popularity soared. In 1897 five courts, all grass, were installed in LINCOLN PARK. Second-generation courts were mostly clay, cheaper to build and maintain. During the NEW DEAL one federal jobs program paved more than 330 Chicago parks courts with asphalt, creating precursors of today's low-maintenance all-weather hard courts. Tennis peaked in popularity during the 1970s, the decade when Chicago-based Wilson Sporting Goods saw its tennis volume exceed that of GOLF. Students from Chicago won nearly every one of the state high-school tennis tournaments, from their inception in 1912 through World War II. Since the war, the state championships have been dominated by Chicago's suburbs, most notably HINSDALE during the 1970s. In 1997, despite the conversion of some courts to skating rinks, Chicago Park District courts totaled about 700.

Chicago has contributed much to American tennis. The RIVER FOREST Tennis Club hosted the U.S. Lawn Tennis Association's national clay court championships every year from 1935 through 1965. George Lott began tennis at Chicago's WASHINGTON PARK and became the world's leading doubles player of the 1930s. Marty Riessen won the state high-school singles championship four times for Hinsdale, 1957–1960, and became a leading professional in both singles and doubles. Andrea Yeager of LINCOLNSHIRE turned pro in 1979 at age 14 and was ranked second in the world at 16, before being forced from competition by injury at 19.

John H. Long

See also: Creation of Chicago Sports; Leisure; Sports, High-School

Further reading: Campell, Nelson. *100 Years of Courtship: The Story of the Western Tennis Association's First Century, 1895–1995*. 1995. • *The Chicago Recreation Survey, 1937*. 5 vols. 1937–1940. • *The History of the Wilson Sporting Goods Co., 1913–1996*. 1996.

Terra Museum of American Art. As late as the mid-1970s, there was no museum devoted solely to American ART within a four-hundred-mile radius of Chicago. Daniel J. Terra located a site in EVANSTON to house and display his own extensive private collection, and, after major renovation, the Terra Museum of American Art opened in the spring of 1980. Five years later, Terra commissioned the renovation of three North Michigan Avenue properties into a unified museum, and in 1987 the museum began operation in the heart of Chicago's elegant SHOPPING DISTRICT, with over 60,000 square feet of newly designed galleries, a bookstore, education facilities, and administrative offices. Taking the success of the Chicago institution to France, Terra and his wife Judith Terra founded the Museum of American Art in Giverny, France, in 1992.

The Chicago collection comprises extensive representations of American impressionist work, including works by John Singer Sargent, Maurice Pendergast, William Sydney Mount, George Caleb Bingham, Winslow Homer, and James Abbott McNeill Whistler, among others. The Terra also has presented traveling exhibitions of rarely seen work by AFRICAN AMERICAN artists. In 2003 the Terra Foundation board voted to close the museum the following year, to loan parts of the collection to the ART INSTITUTE, and to refocus the foundation's efforts on research and education programs.

Ronne Hartfield

See also: Art Institute of Chicago; Museum of Contemporary Art

Further reading: Neff, Terry A., ed. *A Proud Heritage: Two Centuries of American Art; Selections from the Collections of the Pennsylvania Academy of the Fine Arts, Philadelphia, and the Terra Museum of American Art, Chicago*. 1987.

Thais. Thai immigration to metropolitan Chicago has mirrored national immigration patterns for this Southeast Asian population group. Few Thais came prior to the liberalization of U.S. immigration laws in 1965, but steady increases since the 1970s made Thais one of the 10 largest Asian groups in the region by the end of the twentieth century with more than 6,000 counted by the 2000 census.

Thai NURSES, among the first to arrive locally, hosted community gatherings in their homes during the early years and were instrumental in organizing the first notable public event—commemoration of the king of Thailand's birthday in December 1965. Community leaders founded the Thai Association of Greater Chicago in 1969, which incorporated as a nonprofit organization in 1982 and changed its name to the Thai Association of Illinois in 1989. The Thai Association serves both cultural and advocacy functions for the local Thai community, highlighting each year by sponsoring a celebration of the king's birthday.

Three occupational clusters have predominated among local Thai immigrants in recent decades: RESTAURANTS, sales and service, and professional fields, especially in medicine. Important professional organizations include the Thai Nurses Association of Illinois (1982), the Thai Engineer Association of Illinois (1988), and a local branch of the Thai Physicians Association of America (1978). Two charitable organizations with specific geographical ties to Thailand have also emerged: the Thai American Southerner Association of Illinois (1975) and the Thai Northerner Association of Illinois (1984).

Most Thais practice Theravada BUDDHISM, Thailand's national religion. Thai monks, the focal point of Theravada piety, visited Chicago as early as 1972. Local Thai leaders established the Thai Buddhist Center in 1974, which evolved into the first Thai temple, Wat Dhammaram (legally known as the Thai Buddhist Temple, incorporated 1976). Wat Dhammaram occupied a former Christian church in WEST TOWN between 1976 and 1983, when it relocated to a former public elementary school near 75th Street and Harlem Avenue in unincorporated southwest Cook County. In the early 1990s the temple opened a striking new multipurpose hall dedicated to Queen Sirikit of Thailand. Four more Thai Buddhist temples have opened since the mid-1980s: Buddhadharma Meditation Center in HINSDALE and Natural Buddhist Meditation Temple of Greater Chicago in BURBANK (both established 1986), Wat Phrasriratanamahadhatu in UPTOWN (1993), and Dhammakaya International Meditation Center of Chicago in JEFFERSON PARK (1997). Two local Thai Christian congregations exist, both of which meet in FOREST PARK: the Thai Community Church of Chicago (1988) and the Thai Presbyterian Church of Chicago (1992).

As in other U.S. metropolitan regions, Thai settlement has dispersed throughout greater Chicago. Substantial residential presence can be found on the city's North Side and in northern and southern suburban COOK COUNTY, with DUPAGE COUNTY claiming the next highest number of Thais. Some Thai physicians have located their practices in nearby states, particularly Michigan, though they maintain ties to the Chicago region.

Paul D. Numrich

See also: Demography; Foodways; Multicentered Chicago; Religious Geography

Further reading: Codman-Wilson, Mary Louise. "Thai Cultural and Religious Identity and Understanding of Well-Being in North America: An Ethnographic Study of an Immigrant Church." Ph.D. diss., Northwestern University. 1992. • Numrich, Paul David. "Americanization in Immigrant Theravada Buddhist Temples." Ph.D. diss., Northwestern University. 1992.

Theater. The first public professional performance in Chicago took place in 1834, three years before Chicago incorporated as a city. It cost fifty cents for adults, twenty-five for children, and was staged by a Mr. Bowers, who promised to eat "fire-balls, burning sealing-wax, live coals of fire and melted lead." Somehow, he also did ventriloquism. Other traveling showmen passed through over the next two years; a circus pitched its tent on Lake Street in the fall of 1836. But it was not until 1837 that the first local THEATER COMPANY—the Chicago Theater—was established.

Harry Isherwood co-managed this pioneer ensemble. Though famously dismayed to see a flock of quail crossing a rain-pelted wooden sidewalk on his first morning in town (a sign, he thought, that Chicago was not yet ready for culture), Isherwood and his partner, Alexander McKinzie, nevertheless obtained an amusement license from the city council. They took over the recently abandoned dining room of the Sauganash HOTEL, and—sometime in late October or early November—began offering plays, including such titles as *The Idiot Witness, The Stranger,* and *The Carpenter of Rouen.* The bill changed every night and the season lasted about six weeks, after which the company went on tour.

When they returned to Chicago in the spring of 1838, Isherwood and McKinzie set the company up in an old wooden auction house known as the Rialto. There was opposition to their presence: a formal petition cited the risk of fire; moral objections were made as well. Even so, the city council voted to grant the troupe a new license. On September 3, 1839, two Chicago Theater shows—*The Warlock of the Glen* and *The Midnight Hour*—became the subjects of Chicago's first published theater review.

The ensemble members included Joseph and Cornelia Jefferson and their nine-year-old son, also called Joseph. The child sang comic songs, filled out crowd scenes, and played the Duke of York. He grew up to become one of the iconic performers of his time, a stage comedian widely, intensely, and fondly identified with several roles, especially that of Rip van Winkle. His connection with Chicago is memorialized in the Joseph Jefferson awards, given annually for distinguished work in local professional theater.

The Chicago Theater did not outlast its 1839 season, and Chicagoans went back to relying for the most part on touring shows and circuses. A nonprofessional Thespian Society was formed by local men in 1842 and flourished—according to the story—until somebody stole their sets.

The next great leap took place in 1847, when John B. Rice, newly arrived from Buffalo, New York, contracted with a local alderman to build a theater near the corner of Randolph and Dearborn Streets. Rice's Theater opened on June 28 with a comedy called *The Four Sisters* in which Mrs. Henry Hunt (later known as Louisa Lane Drew, a founder of the Barrymore dynasty) played all the title roles. According to newspaper accounts, both the play and the place were enthusiastically received.

Rice's Theater attracted major stars of the time, including Edwin Forrest and Junius Brutus Booth. Built of wood, it burned during the summer of 1850 but was replaced within six months by a new brick structure. John Rice sold his theater in 1857 and began a successful political career, serving as mayor of Chicago from 1865 to 1869. Eighteen fifty-seven was also the year McVicker's Theatre opened, under the management of James H. McVicker, an actor and former employee of Rice's who went on to own a chain of theaters in cities around the United States.

For the Chicago theater community as for everyone else, the Great FIRE OF 1871 was both devastating and opportune. James McVicker took a leading role in the rebuilding, as did David Henderson. A Scottish-born newspaperman turned entrepreneur, Henderson built the Chicago Opera House, ran several other theaters, and produced a series of musicals with exotic Levantine settings (*The Arabian Nights, Sinbad the Sailor, Ali Baba*) that not only revived the Chicago stage but earned the city a reputation as an American theatrical hub into the 1900s.

If the affluent downtown crowds were looking for exotica (not to mention erotica, as purveyed by the likes of Lydia Thompson and her British Blondes, who brought burlesque to Chicago in 1869), the new immigrants in the neighborhoods were longing for something familiar—and found it in their own theaters. A GERMAN-language company was operating as early as 1852. Others followed fairly quickly. A Yiddish theater scene developed at the turn of the century and even produced a few mainstream stars. The best-known of these was Muni Weisenfreund, who became Paul Muni on Broadway and in Hollywood. Muni first appeared onstage in 1908, at the age of 13, in a theater his parents operated near the MAXWELL STREET Market.

Another grassroots phenomenon, the proudly amateur "little theater" movement, found a

One of many "little theaters" in Chicago during the 1910s and 1920s, the Dill Pickle Club featured plays by Strindberg, Ibsen, O'Neill, and Ben Hecht. The low-budget productions featured homemade sets and amateur actors. Along with jazz dances, art shows, and lectures, theater productions drew an eclectic audience of bohemians, young working people, and adventure-seeking middle-class Chicagoans. Source: The Newberry Library.

strong foothold in Chicago in the first quarter of the twentieth century beginning with the amateur theater established in 1899 at HULL HOUSE. Maurice Browne, the father of the movement, opened his influential Little Theatre of Chicago in 1912. Practically all of what would come to be significant about Chicago theater in subsequent years was born in SETTLEMENT HOUSE and community venues. Viola Spolin, for instance, was working for the Works Progress Administration in a neighborhood setting when she began the investigations that led initially to her groundbreaking theater games—and then to modern American improvisation in all its forms. Later, in the mid-1960s, Robert Sickinger's noncommercial Hull House Theatre provided a training ground for a number of important Chicago theater artists, including playwright David Mamet.

Although commercial theater flourished in Chicago after World War I, very little of it was local in origin. The city was entertained mainly by touring shows from Broadway. The only consistent exception was the GOODMAN THEATRE, founded in 1925. Indeed the most celebrated theatrical figure of this period was not a playwright, director, designer, or actor but a critic: Claudia Cassidy of the CHICAGO TRIBUNE earned her billing as Chicago's "dragon lady" in part by attacking the shoddiness of traveling productions.

The situation changed fundamentally in 1955, when two friends from the UNIVERSITY OF CHICAGO—Paul Sills and David Shepherd—started the Compass Players. Sills and Shepherd had already worked together on a repertory company called the Playwrights

Good Shepherd Community Center, rehearsal for Langston Hughes play, 1942. Photographer: Jack Delano. Source: Library of Congress.

Theatre Club, producing 24 plays in just two years; but now they were trying something new. Shepherd had a vision of a modern form of commedia dell'arte (Italian IMPROVISATIONAL THEATER) that would bring a lost immediacy back to the stage as it attacked current issues, assumptions, and even its own audience. Sills, a son of Viola Spolin, had inherited the technique for making Shepherd's vision possible. They formed an ensemble, taught Spolin's theater games to its members, and opened at a bar in Chicago's HYDE PARK neighborhood, doing plays and sketches built on improvisation.

The Chicago Compass lasted only a year and a half, but it led directly to the SECOND CITY (1959) and indirectly to dozens if not hundreds of other improvisation-based companies and concepts, both onstage and in other media. It can be considered Chicago's first truly indigenous theater and—after Spolin—perhaps its single most significant contribution to the performing arts.

The 1960s and '70s saw an explosion of homegrown theater in Chicago. Consciously or not, young ensembles followed the Compass strategy of performing in unorthodox, inexpensive settings—back rooms, vacant storefronts—away from the mainstream commercial venues in the city's downtown LOOP area. Paul Sills himself helped initiate the so-called off-Loop trend by locating one of his post–Second City experiments, the Body Politic Theater, in a former bowling alley on what was then considered a seedy strip of Lincoln Avenue. The Kingston Mines, Victory Gardens, Organic, St. Nicholas, and Wisdom Bridge theaters were some of the more vivid to come out of this period.

STEPPENWOLF THEATRE arrived a step behind these companies, as part of the off-Loop's second wave, and became by far the most successful of them all. Justly lauded for rough, muscular productions of contemporary American plays—Sam Shepard's *True West* in particular—Steppenwolf launched (and was, in turn, launched by) the careers of ensemble members such as John Malkovich, Gary Sinise, Joan Allen, and Laurie Metcalf. Though still conceived to be an actor-run theater, as it was when it was founded, Steppenwolf's scope, prestige, and relative wealth have brought it the stature of a regional institution.

In the 1990s the city of Chicago focused on redeveloping the north end of the Loop (appropriately, the area where both the Sauganash Hotel and Rialto once stood) as a theater district. The Goodman relocated to Randolph and Dearborn in 2000, but otherwise the area is tenanted for the most part with corporate theaters offering outsized, elaborate Broadway-cum-Disney-style shows. Third- and fourth-wave off-Loop companies continue to work out of storefronts in neighborhoods throughout the city.

Tony Adler

See also: Entertaining Chicagoans; Playwriting; Set Design; Theater Training; Theater, Ethnic

Further reading: Andreas, A. T. *History of Chicago from the Earliest Period to the Present Time.* vol. 1. 1884. • Smith, Sid. "Entertainment Center: How Chicagoans Have Been Amused Since 1847." *Chicago Tribune,* May 17, 1997. • Sweet, Jeffrey. *Something Wonderful Right Away: An Oral History of the Second City and the Compass Players.* 1978.

Theater Buildings. Fire and the threat of fire have had a profound effect on the history of THEATER in Chicago. By influencing the number and type of structures available for theatrical performance, fire ultimately has affected the nature of repertory and even ACTING style in this city. In this context, the history of Chicago theater buildings divides into three general periods: burning buildings, restrictive fire codes, and small storefront theaters made possible by the repeal of those codes in 1974. It is in this last period when intimate venues helped encourage a naturalistic acting aesthetic that has sometimes been called the Chicago Style. At the end of the twentieth century, Chicago appeared to be entering a new era of building and renovating larger theaters while maintaining a fairly constant number of small theaters with ever-changing tenants. The near future of theater in the city seemed quite diverse, both architecturally and in terms of repertory.

Time and again in the mid-nineteenth century, theaters were built, burned down, quickly built again (with promises of being fireproof), and burned again. From the first Chicago theater, built by John Blake Rice in 1847 and rebuilt following a fire three years later, through the Great FIRE OF 1871 and until the end of the century, fire kept Chicago's theaters in a state of constant regeneration not unlike the surrounding Illinois prairie. The final straw came during a holiday matinee on December 30, 1903, when the burning of the Iroquois Theater killed 602 patrons. This fire inspired nationwide ordinances ensuring that all public exit doors must open outward. Locally, it led to fire codes that were so restrictive they severely limited theatrical growth in the city for three-quarters of a century. Small groups in particular found it difficult to fashion performing spaces out of storefronts and warehouses without running afoul of regulations involving fire curtains and multiple exits. When those BUILDING CODES were finally relaxed, the half-dozen small theaters that sprang to life led the off-Loop theater movement to develop an intimate style of performance that gained considerable renown. In spite of, or perhaps because of, the cramped nature of these venues, the acting was often astonishingly powerful.

Chicago's more imposing theater buildings include Dankmar Adler and Louis Sullivan's ornate AUDITORIUM Theater, the Goodman Memorial Theatre, Crosby's Opera House, McVicker's Theatre, and Steele MacKaye's grandly designed but never built Spectatorium. Late in the twentieth century, the Oriental and Chicago theaters, both built as movie houses in the 1920s, were refurbished to house theatrical productions. Two neighboring theaters, the

McVicker's Theatre, before the fire of 1871. Photographer: Unknown. Source: Chicago Historical Society.

Harris and the Selwyn, both built in 1922, were extensively renovated and used by the GOODMAN THEATRE Company, beginning with the 2000–2001 season. All of these were built in the LOOP. Other notable theaters built in the past quarter century include the Apollo (1978) and the Royal George (1986), both on Lincoln Avenue, the STEPPENWOLF (1991) on Halsted, and, on Navy Pier, the Chicago Shakespeare Theater (1999), which is unusual in its towering seating area, which, although indoors, was inspired by the Globe. Of course, no one knows for certain what the Globe looked like, since it, too, burned to the ground. With the threat of fire and restrictive fire codes largely a thing of the past, Chicago has become a city of smaller venues scattered far and wide and larger buildings and renovations clustered in and around the Loop.

Scott Fosdick

See also: Architecture; Fire Limits; Places of Assembly; Public Buildings in the Loop; Set Design

Further reading: Lowe, David. *Lost Chicago.* 1975. • Wolfe, Gerard R. *Chicago in and around the Loop.* 1996. • Young, William C. *Documents of American Theater History,* vol. 1, *Famous American Playhouses, 1716–1899.* 1973.

Theater Companies. Chicago's position as the prime city of the Midwest has made it both a necessary stopover on the itinerary of any touring production and a home for a thriving resident THEATER community. From the start, this resident theater movement took root in small houses scattered across the city. Jane Addams established an enterprising amateur theater in her HULL HOUSE in 1899 out of the belief that good plays were good for the community. In 1912, the poet Maurice Browne and his actress wife Ellen Van Volkenburg founded a seminal though brief-lived community theater organization, the Chicago Little Theatre, seating only 91 persons, in the FINE ARTS BUILDING. Its motto, a template for future Chicago companies, was "Create your own theater with the talent at hand."

These early theaters and most of their successors in the twenties and thirties, however, took their cues from plays and players in the European and East Coast mold. The successful founding of the SECOND CITY comedy cabaret in 1959 helped focus attention on talents and techniques that were unique to the city. Encouraging local actors to develop scenes through IMPROVISATION, Second City created its own kind of theater, without copying work that had originated elsewhere.

In 1963, when road tours provided generally second-rate copies of Broadway originals, a first-rate homegrown theater company emerged with the opening of Hull House Theatre in the Jane Addams Center at 3212 N. Broadway. Here, director Robert Sickinger's agenda included using and developing native talent. Though small in seating capacity, it was ambitious in its selection of cutting-edge work and devoted to presenting the work of Chicago artists. Hull House helped set the pattern for development of Chicago theater companies in the rest of the century.

The mushrooming growth of homegrown, homemade theater reached its climax in the mid-1970s, with the opening of several small companies that proved training grounds and taking-off points for young directors, actors, designers, and PLAYWRIGHTS. These troupes included Victory Gardens, Northlight, Wisdom Bridge, the Body Politic, St. Nicholas (founded by playwright David Mamet), Remains, Organic, and STEPPENWOLF theaters.

However different their productions, these theaters shared certain key elements. They were founded and staffed by young persons just out of school and eager to find recognition. They were housed in 150- to 250-seat auditoriums in buildings that had never been designed as theater spaces. Warehouses, bowling alleys, ballrooms, church halls, and retail shops were all converted to theater use by the youthful companies who established these revamped spaces as their bases of operations.

Patterns of growth also were similar. Often started with amateur talent and focused on the work of a particular director or writer, the theaters edged into professional status as their audiences and revenue grew. Unlike their counterparts in other cities, however, these companies stayed out of the high-rent downtown districts. Instead of a large theater company in a center-city cluster of high-profile edifices, Chicago offered a swarm of small, enterprising "off-Loop" theaters, many of them in North Side neighborhoods on the fringes of downtown. GOODMAN THEATRE, the city's largest resident company, joined this movement by creating a Stage Two (later evolving into the Goodman Studio), on which new works by Chicago-based writers (Mamet, Scott McPherson, Rebecca Gilman) were often showcased.

Budgets and financial rewards for the younger companies were small, but the risks of survival were not overwhelming either. It was possible to flop and move on to the next show, without fear of one failure closing down the whole operation.

Some theaters of high quality moved from itinerant wayfarers to established companies with their own multimillion-dollar homes. Steppenwolf, formed around a hub of aggressive young actors in the mid-1970s, built its own complex on the NEAR NORTH SIDE in 1991, and the Chicago Shakespeare Theater, which had started out performing in a North Side pub, in the autumn of 1999 moved into a theater designed according to its specifications on NAVY PIER.

The lure of Broadway, movie, and television success continued to draw talent from the city, but as the city's theater companies grew, so did the talent pool and the range of theatrical styles. Theater artists who supplemented their income with work in FILM and TV productions shot in the city chose to remain and to keep Chicago as their home base. Even some of those who had moved away and found TV or film fame often returned to perform on the small stages where they had first worked.

A few important off-Loop theaters—Remains, St. Nicholas, Wisdom Bridge, the Body Politic—failed when the original leadership was gone or when financial resources faltered. Other companies—Victory Gardens, Northlight—maintained leadership strength and financial viability into the twenty-first century.

Behind them was an always changing, always growing group of small new young companies, each one struggling to establish its niche, make its mark, and break out of the pack.

Richard Christiansen

See also: Arts Funding; Dance Companies; Theater Buildings; Theater Training

Further reading: Dedmon, Emmett. *Fabulous Chicago.* 1953.

Theater, Ethnic. The ethnic THEATER was an important Old World institution reinvented in immigrant neighborhoods. In 1849, GERMAN immigrants established a German theater that enacted the classic German repertoire, especially Schiller. By the late 1890s, Chicago had 11 German theaters, often performing new works by German American PLAYWRIGHTS analyzing contemporary political and working-class issues. Critics rated German productions superior to the American stage.

The local SWEDISH theater had its origins in the Svea Society (1857). A POLISH theater began in 1873 but was not professionalized until 1908. SETTLEMENT HOUSES, notably HULL HOUSE, helped nurture ethnic theater, especially among ITALIANS and GREEKS. There were several Yiddish theater companies, including the Weisenfreunds, starring Paul Muni. In 1905, Robert T. Motts opened the 900-seat Pekin, billed as "the only Negro owned theater in the world." Its Pekin Stock Company gained renown for their song and DANCE performances.

The ethnic theater provided inexpensive entertainment, helped maintain ethnic culture, and helped show the broader society that a particular group deserved respect. It declined in the 1920s amid a steep decline in immigration, as the second generation looked more to VAUDEVILLE, film, and other popular amusements. Although Yiddish theater persisted in Chicago, it tended to be increasingly nostalgic.

In the 1920s, AFRICAN AMERICAN cultural revitalization spawned numerous small theaters in cities across the country, including the Skyloft Players and the Ethiopian Art Theatre in Chicago. Initially these theaters produced plays from mainstream repertoires, but they soon devoted themselves to developing and producing works by African American playwrights. In the 1930s, the Federal Theatre Project boosted African American theater when it established a black theater unit in the Chicago. In the 1960s and 1970s, African American theater blossomed in the city as part of the nationwide Black Arts movement and the widespread interest in COMMUNITY ORGANIZING. A number of small African American community theaters were formed and several of them persist, including the highly regarded ETA theater on the SOUTH SIDE.

Poster for Great Northern Theatre, WPA Federal Theatre Project, ca. late 1930s. Source: Library of Congress.

Hispanic theaters began staging their own productions and hosting professional touring groups during the 1920s. These enterprises declined during the GREAT DEPRESSION, however, when UNEMPLOYMENT forced many of Chicago's MEXICAN Americans to move to Mexico. Chicago's Hispanic American theater was reborn in the 1960s and 1970s when a number of new community theater groups were established.

Financial survival is an ongoing struggle for Chicago's small, community-based ethnic theaters. But the same force that keeps ethnic theater lively keeps it on the margins of the city's mainstream arts movements. In order to remain distinct and vibrant, ethnic theater needs to address the issues of a culture within a culture and before an audience that fully understands the complexities and nuances of that culture.

Steven A. Riess
Ian McGiver

See also: Entertaining Chicagoans; Ethnic Music; Nommo

Further reading: Kanellos, Nicolas. "Fifty Years of Theatre in the Latino Communities of Northwest Indiana." *Aztlan* 7.2 (Summer 1976): 255–265. • Naeseth, Henriette. *The Swedish Theater of Chicago, 1858–1950.* 1951. • Peterson, Jane T. "Pride and Prejudice: The Demise of the Ethiopian Art Theatre." *Theatre History Studies* 14 (1994): 141–149.

Theater, Improvisational. *See* Improvisational Theater

Theater, Summer. *See* Summer Theater

Theater Training. Theatrical companies in nineteenth-century Chicago generally were run by actor-managers dedicated to bringing the established plays of the day to audiences in the city. As the actor-manager system of theatrical organization gave way to the director's THEATER that emerged around 1900, new venues for theatrical training appeared. Young Chicago businessman Kenneth Sawyer Goodman envisioned offering theater workshops through the ART INSTITUTE OF CHICAGO, allowing drama students to learn alongside professionals. After Goodman's death in 1918, these workshops became a reality when his parents funded a dramatic department at the Art Institute in his honor.

The early years of the Goodman School of Drama were marked by the creativity and tenacity of two men, David Itkin and Maurice Gnesin. Itkin arrived at the GOODMAN THEATRE from Russia in 1929. He soon began directing plays both at the Goodman and the DEPAUL UNIVERSITY Department of Drama. In 1931, Maurice Gnesin became head of the Goodman School of Drama, and under his direction it began to resemble an academic theater department. For the next 25 years Gnesin and Itkin developed the mission and curriculum of the school. Both men felt that the best way to train young actors was to immerse them in productions alongside professionals in the repertory company. Alumni who trained under Gnesin and Itkin included Geraldine Page, Karl Malden, and Sam Wanamaker. Bella Itkin, David's daughter, would also go on to have a significant impact on theater training at the Goodman School. Under her direction, and based on the vision of Charlotte Chorpenning, the children's theater at the Goodman was used as a training ground for students who acted and produced plays that were as enjoyable to adults as they were to the children who came to see them.

In the late 1950s, John Reich came to the Goodman and advanced Gnesin and Itkin's training traditions by hiring professional guest artists to work with the students. More recent alumni of the school include Joe Mantegna and Linda Hunt. Although the Board of Trustees of the Art Institute voted in 1975 to close the Goodman School of Drama, it reemerged three years later to become one of the colleges of DePaul University.

Theater training was also occurring outside of the Goodman/DePaul theater curriculum. In the 1940s and 1950s, the UNIVERSITY OF CHICAGO played host to a "band of students" that included Ed Asner, Mike Nichols, and Elaine May. In the 1950s and 1960s, the

Department of Theatre and the Department of Oral Interpretation (later renamed Performance Studies) at NORTHWESTERN UNIVERSITY came to prominence and remain important forces in the training of Chicago actors and theater professionals. In the 1970s and 1980s, Illinois State University's theater program, with a curriculum designed to "push characters to the extreme," trained many of the actors who formed the STEPPENWOLF THEATRE Company ensemble.

Several Chicago-area theaters also have sponsored classes. The Body Politic's founder Jim Shiflett often used Viola Spolin's theater games as the basis for his instruction. The St. Nicholas Theater Company, founded by David Mamet, used theater classes as revenue raisers. In the suburbs, the Piven Theatre Workshop has been training budding thespians for over 25 years. Founded by Byrne and Joyce Piven, it offers classes based on "story theater," a directorial method developed by Paul Sills, Spolin's son. The workshop's impressive list of alumni includes John and Joan Cusack, Aidan Quinn, Lili Taylor, and the Pivens' children Shira and Jeremy.

Andrea Telli

See also: Improvisational Theater; Theater Companies

Further reading: Bloom, Arthur. "Chicago Theater Then. . . ." In *Urban Voices: Chicago as a Literary Place.* Exhibition catalog. 1983. • Ryan, Sheila. *At the Goodman Theatre: An Exhibition in Celebration of the Sixtieth Anniversary of Chicago's Oldest Producing Theatre, October 12, 1985–January 11, 1986.* 1985.

Third Lake, IL, Lake County, 39 miles NW of the Loop. In 1959 the residents of a subdivision on the north side of the Third Lake, once known as Chittenden Lake, incorporated to control the pollution of its namesake and limit further development. Further development emerged in the early 1980s on the southern edge of the lake. Third Lake is the North American headquarters for the Free Serbian Orthodox Church.

Erik Gellman

See also: Environmental Politics; Lake County, IL

Thornton, IL, Cook County, 21 miles S of the Loop. Thornton shares boundaries with SOUTH HOLLAND to the north, GLENWOOD to the south, and HOMEWOOD and EAST HAZEL CREST to the west. COOK COUNTY Forest Preserves are to the east and south. The northern part of Thornton is traversed east to west by the Tri-State Tollway (I-80/I-294). Halsted Street (Route 1) is part of Thornton's western border and has an interchange with I-80. The first RAILROAD (later the Chicago & Eastern Illinois, now the Union Pacific) came to Thornton in 1869. At one time there was a depot in Thornton, but there is no longer passenger service.

Thornton has been shaped by its geologic past. The western part contains 400-foot-deep sedimentary deposits of dolomite and was first quarried by Gurdon Hubbard in the mid-1830s. The Thornton QUARRY is one of the largest commercial stone quarries in the world, operated by Material Service Corporation since 1938.

Ten-mile-long Thorn Creek flows through the village from the south into the Little Calumet River. In the early years, Thorn Creek was about 40 feet wide and 4 to 6 feet deep; noted for its clear spring-fed water, it was navigable to Thornton.

Evidence of NATIVE AMERICAN occupation of the Thornton area abounds, especially along Thorn Creek. The Hoxie Site to the east of Thornton dates to around AD 1400.

The village of Thornton is the oldest settlement in Thornton Township, and both are named after William F. Thornton, one of the commissioners of the ILLINOIS & MICHIGAN CANAL. The first white settler was William Woodbridge in 1834.

The town was first platted in 1835 by John H. Kinzie. In 1836, Kinzie, Hubbard, and John Blackstone established a sawmill on Thorn Creek which provided the lumber for the first school in that same year. In 1852, John S. Bielfeldt, a GERMAN immigrant, established a BREWERY that was operated by his family until PROHIBITION. During Prohibition the brewery continued to produce beer and was sometimes raided by federal agents. The Frederick brothers bought the brewery and operated it in the 1940s. A LITHUANIAN immigrant, Ildefonsas Sadauskas, owned it in the early 1950s. Later the site housed a restaurant and other small businesses.

The GREAT DEPRESSION had a profound impact on Thornton. The bank closed in 1934 and moved to BLUE ISLAND. During 1939–40 the Works Projects Administration created the public library and constructed sidewalks, curbs, and sewers in the village. In the 1930s the Civilian Conservation Corps operated Camp Thornton in the Sweet Woods FOREST PRESERVE. The camp, which later housed German POWs during WORLD WAR II,was last used by the Girls SCOUTS until 1988.

Thornton's population has been stable for years at around 3,000, with its housing in great demand. Like much of the surrounding area, Thornton attracted a large number of Germans in its early years. Later, many Eastern Europeans arrived to work in the quarry, living south of the quarry in an area that became known as "hunkeyville."

Dave Bartlett

See also: Economic Geography; Toll Roads

Further reading: "History of Thornton, Illinois." In *Where the Trails Cross,* vol. 3, no. 4. South Suburban Genealogical and Historical Society, South Holland, IL. • Andreas, A. T. *History of Cook County, Illinois.* 1884. • Markman, Charles W. *Chicago Before History: The Prehistoric Archaeology of a Modern Metropolitan Area.* 1991.

Tibetans. Tibetans began arriving in Chicago in 1992. After Chinese forces invaded and occupied Tibet in the 1950s, provoking an uprising in 1959, thousands of Tibetans fled into exile in Nepal, India, and Bhutan, seeking religious and civil rights. In 1989, the Tibetan U.S. Resettlement Project, a nonprofit coalition of Tibetans-in-exile and American supporters, persuaded the U.S. Congress to grant one thousand visas for Tibetan exiles as part of the Immigration Act of 1990. Chicago was one of several destinations for Tibetan immigrants using these visas. One hundred arrived between 1992 and 1994.

The Chicago chapter of the Tibetan Resettlement Project was instrumental in assisting the newcomers, as were voluntary agencies like the Jewish Federation of Metropolitan Chicago. With the help of sponsors, Tibetans settled on the North Side, with the majority living near Foster and Sheridan. In 1993, the Tibetan Resettlement Project was reorganized as the Tibetan Alliance and continued to assist with English-language tutoring, visa processing, health care, and employment.

Many Tibetan immigrants arrived in Chicago with advanced education and had little trouble finding jobs. Although spared poverty and unemployment, however, they were unable to secure jobs commensurate with their education level because many employers would not recognize their degrees from NEPALESE and INDIAN universities. Many found employment in data entry and housekeeping positions.

Starting in 1996, after the initial 100 Tibetans were settled, the process of family reunification added to the size of the Tibetan community. Although some left Chicago for other cities, the number of Tibetans in Chicago grew to roughly 200.

In Chicago, Tibetans have sought to preserve their culture and heritage through organizations like the TIBET center, which was founded in 1999 as a cultural center for the entire Midwest. With a library and research center, cultural programs like Tibet Festival, lectures about Tibetan medicine and astrology, and language classes, TIBETcenter has established itself along with the Tibetan Alliance as a focal point for the community.

In addition to their cultural associations, in the mid-1990s the Tibetans formed the

Chicago Nomads SOCCER team, which competes annually in a tournament against other Midwestern Tibetan teams. The Tibetan Children's Dance group was formed in the 1990s.

The Chicago Tibetan community practices Tibetan BUDDHISM and at the turn of the millennium was in the process of raising money to build its first temple. The community hosts visiting monks frequently. In 1993 and 1999, H.H. the Dalai Lama visited Chicago and gave audiences to the Chicago Tibetan community. As part of its religious calendar, the community celebrates the July 6 birthday of H.H. the Dalai Lama as well as "LOSAR," the Tibetan New Year. The community also annually commemorates the March 10, 1959, Tibetan uprising against the Chinese.

Robert Morrissey

See also: Demography; Multicentered Chicago

Tinker to Evers to Chance. Along with third baseman Harry Steinfeldt, the trio of shortstop Joe Tinker, second baseman John Evers, and first baseman Frank Chance formed the legendary infield of the championship Chicago CUBS teams of the early 1900s. The slick combination of Tinker to Evers to Chance, celebrated in a famous poem by JOURNALIST Franklin P. Adams, is credited with perfecting the modern double play. All three were later inducted into BASEBALL's Hall of Fame.

David M. Oshinsky

See also: Creation of Chicago Sports; Leisure

Further reading: *The Bill James Historical Baseball Abstract.* 1986. • Voigt, David. *American Baseball,* vol. 2. 1970.

Tinley Park, IL, Cook and Will Counties, 23 miles S of the Loop. There is much evidence of NATIVE AMERICAN residents in the area of Tinley Park, especially at the Oak Forest site to the east of town. The site, on the Tinley Moraine, overlooking a marshy area of glacial lake plain, dates to the 1600s. The 1816 Indian Boundary Line crosses to the southeast of the village.

After the John Fulton family from New York arrived in 1835, a community developed, with the early names of the "ENGLISH Settlement" and Yorktown. As large numbers of GERMANS arrived in the 1840s it became known as New Bremen, after their port of departure. Bremen Township was organized in 1850. The Chicago, Rock Island & Pacific RAILROAD arrived in 1852 and became an important asset in the area's early growth and economic development. In 1892 the village was incorporated and named Tinley Park, in honor of Samuel Tinley, Sr., the longtime Rock Island station master.

Tinley Park developed as an AGRICULTURAL service center. In 1869 a grain elevator opened, and a Dutch-style windmill was constructed in 1872. In the 1890s a soft-drink bottling plant opened and operated until the 1940s. TELEPHONE service began in 1898 and a municipal WATER system was built in 1899. In 1905 the Diamond Spiral Washing Machine Company built the first factory in Tinley Park. In 1909 an electric utility was created by local businessmen.

The village had a population of 300 by 1900 and grew very slowly until WORLD WAR II. After the war young families from Chicago were attracted by the affordable housing. From 1950 the population doubled every decade until 1980, and Tinley Park was one of COOK COUNTY's fastest-growing communities; 80 percent of the housing stock has been built since 1970. In recent years larger, more expensive houses have been built and the village continues to annex land. Tinley Park became the home of the World Music Theater and has experienced major commercial growth as industrial and office parks located along the I-80 corridor. The village is committed to "controlled growth," however, with the goal of maintaining a livable community. Population had grown to 48,401 by 2000.

Tinley Park's residents have included John Rauhoff, who created Ironite, an additive for waterproofing cement which was important in the building of Hoover Dam. John Poorman invented an improved chicken brooder. The Bettenhausen family produced famous Indianapolis 500 drivers.

Tinley Park has been working to preserve its history. The area of the old 1892 village has been designated a historic district, where property owners are encouraged to restore and preserve their historic buildings and homes. The Carl Vogt Building is listed on the National Register of Historic Places and has been restored and is now used for commercial purposes. The Tinley Park Historical Society has renovated the Old Zion Landmark Church for use as its museum and headquarters.

Dave Bartlett

See also: Metropolitan Growth; Transportation; Will County

Further reading: "Featuring Bremen Township." *Where the Trails Cross* 7.1 (Fall 1976): 1–3. • Schwertfeger, Krista A., and Gail D. Welter. "Tinley Park." In *Local Community Fact Book: Chicago Metropolitan Area, 1990,* ed. Chicago Fact Book Consortium. 1995. • Tinley Park Chamber of Commerce. *Tinley Park, Illinois: A World Class Community.* 1995.

Togolese. Togolese immigrants are among Chicago's most recent arrivals. From a few scattered members in the 1970s, the Togolese community in Chicago grew rapidly in the 1980s, when closer ties between the United States and Togo, along with the emergence of a free-trade zone, made mastery of the English language and an American education more valuable. During Togo's transition to democracy in the late 1980s and early 1990s, political REFUGEES reinforced the Togolese presence in Chicago. By the late 1990s, approximately 300 Togolese lived in the city and 500 in Illinois.

The earliest Togolese to arrive in Chicago were probably from the former British Togoland protectorate. Togo was a German colony from 1884 until WORLD WAR I, when joint British-French forces invaded and annexed its western half to Britain's Gold Coast colony. In 1956, the people of British Togoland voted in a United Nations plebiscite to join with the soon-to-be independent nation of Ghana. Thus, many of these early "Togolese" immigrants would now consider themselves GHANAIANS. In Chicago, Togolese from the south often join Ghanaian community groups.

In 1991, a coalition of the region's earliest Togolese residents founded the Association of Togolese in Chicago (ATC). The association had an original core of fewer than 100 members and modeled itself on the much larger associations of Chicago's NIGERIANS and Ghanaians. Its primary goal was to provide assistance for new Togolese immigrants, especially in the areas of housing and job placement. The Togolese community grew increasingly active in the city's political life, and by the beginning of the century the president of the ATC had become a member of the Mayor's Advisory Board for African Affairs. During summer months, the ATC held picnics with popular SOCCER matches against teams from other Francophone African communities.

Beginning in the 1980s, the Togolese community settled mostly on the city's North Side, in UPTOWN, LAKEVIEW, and EDGEWATER. The fruit markets and stores in these neighborhoods began carrying extensive African foods and publications, all of which attested to the cumulative buying power of a growing African community in Chicago. The Equator Club began inviting bands from the Democratic Republic of Congo to perform to packed crowds in the late 1990s, including Pepe Cale, Les Quatres Etoiles, Diblo Dibala, and Rochereau. In December 1997, the Togolese singer Afia Mala performed at the House of Blues, and the concert hall included Papa Wemba and Salif Keita in its 1998 AfroFest. Togolese women also introduced elaborate West African coiffures to residents of the Midwest. When West African braids became fashionable in the 1980s and 1990s, hair styling became a skill that could guarantee quick employment and, in some cases, small-business ownership. Many of the Togolese scholars visiting or teaching on Chicago's North Side were drawn there by the Africana collection at NORTHWESTERN UNIVERSITY, the largest such collection in the world.

Charles Adams Cogan
Nourou Yakoubou
Ben Kokouvi Mensah

See also: Demography; Multicentered Chicago

Toll Roads. Toll roads, or turnpikes, date from the early years of the American republic. Several plank toll roads built in the Chicago area beginning in 1848 were put out of business within a few years by the RAILROADS. The idea lay dormant until the growth of automobile use and the success of the Pennsylvania Turnpike in 1940 revived interest in toll roads.

The construction of a $1.1 billion system of five freeways in Chicago and COOK COUNTY following WORLD WAR II consumed most available TRANSPORTATION funds, so the state in 1953 created the Illinois State Toll Highway Commission to build an EXPRESSWAY system in the suburbs. Federal subsidies were not available until after the adoption of the Interstate Highway Act by Congress in 1956.

By then, the tollway commission had already sold $415 million in bonds to be repaid by future toll revenues to build the 83-mile Tri-State Tollway, a beltway between the Indiana and Wisconsin state lines, the 76-mile Northwest Tollway to the Wisconsin state line north of Rockford, and the 28-mile East-West Tollway to AURORA. Chicago had independently proceeded with construction of the 7.8-mile Chicago SKYWAY to Indiana Toll Road's western terminus.

The Skyway initially was a money loser, especially after completion of the parallel Interstate 80 freeway bypassing Chicago. Bondholders several times successfully obtained court orders raising Skyway tolls to cover interest on the $101 million in bonds sold to build the road, and the city was forced to subsidize Skyway maintenance programs. By the 1990s Skyway traffic had increased, primarily owing to motorists trying to avoid congestion on I-80, to the point that the road was turning a profit.

The Toll Highway Authority, as it had been renamed, sold additional bonds in 1970 to build a 69-mile extension of the East-West Tollway to Sterling, Illinois, and in 1989 a 17-mile north-south tollway through DuPage County. As the twentieth century closed, the TOLL AUTHORITY was negotiating to extend that road south into WILL COUNTY to connect with I-80, the transcontinental interstate road between New York and San Francisco.

The tollway system was originally designed as an extremely limited-access roadway along which not all interchanges had four-way access and egress. Since 1970, however, commuter traffic on the tollways has increased considerably, forcing the authority to expand interchanges and add new ones.

David M. Young

See also: Built Environment of the Chicago Region; Commuting; Public Works, Federal Funding for

Further reading: Chicago Area Transportation Study. *1995 Travel Atlas for the Northeastern Illinois Expressway System.* 1998. • Quaife, Milo M. *Chicago's Highways Old and New from Indian Trail to Motor Road.* 1923.

Tollway Authority. Encouraged by the success of other states with toll roads to serve growing intercity traffic, the Illinois General Assembly created a Toll Highway Commission in 1953. The commission became the Illinois State Toll Highway Authority in 1968.

The original routes consisted of the Northwest Tollway, now I-90, from ROSEMONT to South Beloit; the Tri-State Tollway, a bypass route running south and west of Chicago as I-294, continuing north to the Wisconsin border as I-94; and the East-West Tollway, now I-88, from HILLSIDE to AURORA. Construction began in late 1956 and the 187-mile system, costing approximately $459 million, was opened in sections in 1958.

The system was initially geared to intercity traffic, with widely spaced interchanges and several "oasis" service plazas. The new highways both encouraged and served suburban development, however, and soon became Chicago-area COMMUTER routes. When the system opened, approximately 70 percent of traffic was long-distance. By the end of the twentieth century tollway officials estimated 70 percent was commuters.

In 1971, ground was broken for the East-West Tollway (now I-88) extension west of Aurora across northern Illinois to near Moline, which opened in sections in 1974. The North-South Tollway (I-355), built to serve suburb-to-suburb traffic, opened in 1989 from I-55 to ADDISON, where the route continues as I-290 and Illinois Route 53 through SCHAUMBURG to BUFFALO GROVE. Proposed extensions—south to I-80 and north into LAKE COUNTY—have stimulated debate over whether highway construction induces development that would not otherwise occur.

Dennis McClendon

See also: DuPage County; Expressways; Toll Roads; Transportation

Further reading: Illinois State Toll Highway Authority. *Illinois Tollway: Concise History.* 1989.

83rd Street Toll Plaza, Tri-State Tollway (I-294), 1964. Photographer: Casey Prunchunas. Source: Chicago Historical Society.

Tongs. Tongs are fraternal secret societies that once represented CHINESE immigrants lacking their own surname or native place groups. At the turn of the century, Chicago's On Leong Tong helped create the CHINATOWN at Cermak and Wentworth Streets.

Nineteenth-century tongs monopolized the Chinatown VICE trade, and their protection rackets forced most Chinese to join a tong. Social conflict in Chinatowns resulted in numerous tong feuds until U.S. officials started to crack down on the organizations in the 1890s. The emergence of a significant American-born population by the 1930s and 1940s further eroded tong strength. While these traditional organizations tried to capitalize on America's anti-Communist policies in the 1950s and resurgent Chinese immigration after the 1960s, they never regained their early-twentieth-century importance in Chinese American communities.

During the 1970s, the Hip Sing Tong encouraged Chinese American merchants to establish a second Chinese community around Argyle Street. Today, organizations like On Leong and Hip Sing have dropped "tong" from their names and disavowed the "soldiers" who once defended their interests. However, police allege that the nation's tongs maintain ties to youth GANGS and play a role in organized crime.

Charlotte Brooks

See also: Clubs: Fraternal Clubs; Cold War and Anti-Communism; Mafia; Underground Economy

Further reading: Kwong, Peter. *The New Chinatown.* 1987. • Tsai, Shih-shan Henry. *The Chinese Experience in America.* 1986.

Topography. Metropolitan Chicago's topography is almost entirely a product of GLACIATION.

Only in scattered outcroppings is the underlying bedrock exposed in the form of low, isolated hills. The bedrock layers under the city of Chicago include massive reefs of limestone that are several hundred million years old, but they cannot be seen except in rock QUARRIES such as the giant pit along the DES PLAINES RIVER at MCCOOK. At the other extreme are the human-created landforms of the Chicago region. Mostly the result of solid-waste dumping over the years, some of these mountains of trash (which now are grass-covered hills) rise 175 feet above the surrounding surface.

Chicago's flat topography is the result of its origin as a lake bottom. On at least three occasions between 14,500 and 4,000 years ago, glacial Lake Chicago, as this temporary enlargement of LAKE MICHIGAN was known, rose and fell. The balance was determined by the size of the glacier that blocked drainage to the north and the depth of the Des Plaines River outlet through the bedrock layers near LEMONT. Glacial Lake Chicago was at its maximum extent about 12,500 years ago when it covered what is now the entire city of Chicago.

The various levels of glacial Lake Chicago are marked by beach features such as spits and bars that formed along the temporary lake's margins. On the north side are the WILMETTE Spit (Ridge Avenue, Wilmette); Rose Hill Spit (Ridge Avenue, EVANSTON); and Graceland Spit (prominent near Graceland Cemetery at Clark and Montrose). On the SOUTH SIDE, former beach lines are encountered along Ashland Avenue at 63rd (West Englewood) and 95th Streets (BEVERLY) and in EVERGREEN PARK. Farther south and east the Toleston, Calumet, and Griffith Spits represent successively older beaches corresponding to successively higher lake levels that can be seen traveling south on Highway 41 from either GARY or HAMMOND.

Like present-day beaches, these ancient features consist of almost pure sand. In contrast are the glacial moraines that formed at the margins of the stagnant or retreating ice sheets and which consist of unsorted boulders, sand, clay, and pebbles. Prominent among them is the morainic ridge known as BLUE ISLAND which was surrounded by the waters of glacial Lake Chicago. It extends from Dan Ryan Woods (87th and Western) nearly six miles south to the Calumet Sag Channel in Blue Island.

Some of the Chicago-area moraines are part of the Lake Border morainic system and their shape generally parallels that of the present shoreline of the lake. Green Bay Road in GLENCOE follows the crest of the HIGHLAND PARK moraine. The Deerfield moraine (Waukegan Road) separates the east and west forks of the North Branch of the CHICAGO RIVER. The PARK RIDGE moraine is crossed by Milwaukee Avenue and Northwest Highway in NILES and Park Ridge.

Still higher (and older) are the Tinley and Valparaiso morainic systems, whose outline also parallels that of Lake Michigan, but about 15–20 miles to the west. Rolling topography associated with the Valparaiso moraine occurs in a wide swath around the southern end of Lake Michigan and includes the hills of such communities as BARRINGTON, WHEATON, and MONEE. The Tinley moraine occupies a similar swath, about six miles closer to Lake Michigan, and includes FLOSSMOOR, WESTERN SPRINGS, and ARLINGTON HEIGHTS.

This entire complex of features—Lake Michigan, the beach ridges, and moraines—lies at a higher elevation than the Upper Illinois River valley. The city of MORRIS, where the Des Plaines and Kankakee Rivers join to form the Illinois, lies about 75 feet below the level of Lake Michigan. Crossing the drainage divide between the Des Plaines–Illinois–Mississippi system to the west and the Chicago River–Lake Michigan–St. Lawrence River system to the east thus involves "stepping up" in elevation even though the drainage divide itself is barely noticeable.

John C. Hudson

See also: Ecosystem Evolution; Landscape; Plant Communities; Riverine Systems; Waste Disposal; Water

Further reading: Willman, H. B. *Summary of the Geology of the Chicago Area.* 1971.

Tornadoes. Tornadoes, nature's most evil wind, have been no strangers to the Chicago area. Over the last one hundred years, the metropolitan area has experienced numerous tornado-related deaths.

From the 1960s into the 1990s, severe weather and tornadoes have increased in frequency in the far western and southwestern suburbs, for obscure reasons. One theory suggests that cooler winds from LAKE MICHIGAN collide with hot air coming up from the southwest, giving extra lift to thunderstorms in a corridor from AURORA to JOLIET and south toward Kankakee. However, tornadoes can occur anywhere in the Chicago area. The downtown area and the lakefront are not immune to tornado activity. On a gray and windy day in April 1967, a swarm of tornadoes struck the area, killing 58 people. OAK LAWN was hit particularly hard. The tornado then skipped across the SOUTH SIDE of the city, crossing the Dan Ryan EXPRESSWAY at rush hour, and hitting the lakefront near 79th Street.

On June 13, 1976, a wild twister looped through the LEMONT area, killing two people and remaining on the ground for more than an hour. More recently, the PLAINFIELD and WILL COUNTY tornado on August 28, 1990, left 29 people dead and caused $165 million in damage. It is believed to have been the most powerful tornado to strike the U.S. during the month of August. The Lemont area was struck again in March 1991, with minor damage.

Thomas G. Bobula

See also: Climate; Seiches

Torrens Title. Torrens Title is a simplified system of transferring title to land which was introduced by Robert Torrens in South Australia in 1858. The method involved filing a judicial proceeding that determined the owner of the land, which was recorded on an Original Registration Certificate maintained by the Torrens administrators. Under this system, the state guarantees title. An examination of the registrar's records could quickly determine the status of title, a substantial improvement over past systems.

The Chicago FIRE OF 1871 destroyed COOK COUNTY REAL-ESTATE records. As Chicago and Cook County were expanding rapidly, providing an adequate verification of title was difficult. In 1897, the Illinois legislature provided an answer by establishing the first Torrens Title Act in the United States.

The Torrens Act was welcomed by real-estate interests, who used it heavily to promote expansion and development. By 1937 approximately 20 percent of the 1,300,000 parcels of land in Cook County were held in the Torrens system.

The use of the Torrens system began to decline during the 1930s; by then, 60 years of public records were available to private insurance companies, who competed vigorously with the Torrens system. Only 163 new registrations were filed from 1967 to 1977. Attorneys preferred the fast, efficient title insurance company methods to the slower administrative processes of the Torrens system. Also in the late 1970s the practice of selling mortgages to a secondary market became widespread, but institutional investors would not accept a Torrens certificate as a guarantee of title.

In view of the declining use of the Torrens system, in January 1992 the Illinois legislature began the process of phasing it out.

John T. Durkin

See also: Built Environment of the Chicago Region; Business of Chicago

Further reading: 1985 Illinois *Revised Statutes,* chap. 30, secs. 45–148. • 1991 Illinois *Revised Statutes,* chap. 30, sec. 1481. • Turano, Guerino J. "Torrens in Cook County 1897–1997: A Tearless Requiem." *Title Issues* 1.3 (n.d.).

Tourism and Conventions. Always a place of commerce and spectacle, Chicago from its infancy played host to major conventions and to individual travelers. As early as 1847, Chicago hosted a meeting of American BUSINESS and political leaders that brought 20,000 to a city whose population was only 16,000.

The city's central location in the United States, access, large meeting areas, and ample hotel rooms over the years created a spot unequaled for efficient gatherings, and by the 1990s, industry-specific conventions such as the HARDWARE or housewares show generated $5 billion annually for the local economy.

MAKING CHICAGO INTERESTING AND ATTRACTIVE

The James Simpson-Field Museum expedition of the Roosevelts will add a world famous collection of Central Asian exhibits to the museum.

The new Zoological Garden will attract thousands of visitors.

Reg. U S Pat. Off., Copyright, 1926, by The Chicago Tribune.

The Civic Opera produces opera unexcelled in the world.

In this series of drawings that originally appeared first in the *Chicago Tribune* and then in *Opera Topics*, cartoonist John T. McCutcheon celebrated some of Chicago's most famous sites for tourists and locals alike. Artist: John T. McCutcheon. Source: The Newberry Library.

While conventioneers or businesspeople come for a reason—to meet or to study an INNOVATION—such visitors typically branch out and enjoy the city's shopping, cultural, entertainment, or sports offerings.

From 1850 on, political, industrial, commercial, religious, and sports conventions have been held regularly in Chicago. Even in the beginning, business leaders underwrote infrastructure costs for such events, knowing that upfront spending brought even greater returns when visitors arrived and opened their wallets and purses for the city's plentiful goods and services. Local and federal funds were used as well, and by the 1960s, under the guidance of Mayor Richard J. Daley, convention halls, highways, and the airports had been built, expanded, or modernized, creating one of the world's most modern and functional meeting centers.

Temporary outdoor stages were among the first structures built to accommodate conventions. Permanent structures followed: the WIGWAM was built to attract the 1860 REPUBLICAN Convention, and by the turn of the century, the vast, turreted Coliseum became home to large gatherings and political conventions. The Republican Party chose the Coliseum for its gathering three times from 1908 through 1916.

In 1960 the McCormick Place Convention Center was opened. While the hall was not an instant success, when it burned seven years later, it was quickly rebuilt and expanded. Two more halls were added in later years, creating 2.1 million feet of space. Thirty years later, the UNITED CENTER was built as a sport and entertainment showcase; it was also home to the 1996 DEMOCRATIC National Convention.

While conventions typically have been a boon to the city, some have proved to be a public-relations disaster (e.g., television cameras captured Chicago police beating students protesting the Vietnam War during the 1968 Democratic National Convention).

For decades, Chicago tourism was limited to domestic travelers, typically honeymooners, businesspeople, or residents from smaller Midwestern cities and rural towns who came to shop and marvel at the city's manifestations of power and wealth: PRAIRIE AVENUE mansions, grand European-style HOTELS, massive grain elevators, and endless train yards. Later, GOLD COAST homes, the Sears Tower and other SKYSCRAPERS, and the trading floors of the Chicago Board of Exchange provided the same power to awe.

But before 1900, writers and visitors from Europe either praised the city for its rapid growth or dismissed it as a mishmash of wealth and poverty. The WORLD'S COLUMBIAN EXPOSITION of 1893 boosted the city's image, but some observers noted that the magnificent and orderly fairgrounds were temporary, while the city's problems with grime and poverty appeared to be permanent. Domestic visitors were not put off by the city's extremes, however, and before its close, 12 million total attendees had come for the fair. In a single day set aside to celebrate Illinois, more than 540,000 came.

The CENTURY OF PROGRESS EXPOSITION in 1933 provided a similar occasion for visiting Chicago, as well as a bright glimmer of hope in the midst of the GREAT DEPRESSION. Again, observers noted the forward-looking fairgrounds compared with the grim reality of Chicago's slums. Even so, visitors flocked to the fair: more than 39 million attended over the course of a year.

By the 1950s, most tourists came from a 500-mile radius and were friends or family of area residents. It wasn't until the late 1980s that Chicago blossomed as a world-class destination, its image fueled by top-flight retail stores lining North Michigan Avenue, major one-of-a-kind shows at the ART INSTITUTE OF CHICAGO and other museums, BLUES and JAZZ clubs, dazzling ARCHITECTURE, lake and river cruises, fine dining, gallery districts, discount shopping in the suburbs, historic WRIGLEY FIELD, as well as the opportunity to see in action BASKETBALL legend Michael Jordan.

Guides like this one from Rand, McNally & Co. published in 1890 advertised Chicago and introduced visitors to the city's sights. Designer: Unknown. Source: Chicago Historical Society.

The increase in domestic and international tourists had a major economic impact on Chicago in the 1990s, causing a boom in hotel building, restaurant openings, and services geared to travelers.

By 1995 tours of ethnic neighborhoods and their cultural institutions were added to many itineraries. Certain neighborhoods such as PILSEN, with a large MEXICAN population, began courting tourists with walking maps and periodic festivals and ethnic fare timed with cultural holidays.

Anne Moore

See also: Entertaining Chicagoans; International Amphitheater; Leisure; Places of Assembly; Political Culture

Further reading: *Crain's Chicago Business.* Various articles on conventions by Jeff Borden and Joanne Cleaver and on tourism by Anne Moore. 1994–1998. • Lowe, David. *Lost Chicago.* 1993. • Mayer, Harold M., and Richard C. Wade. *Chicago: Growth of a Metropolis.* 1969.

Tower Lakes, IL, Lake County, 36 miles NW of the Loop. Tucked into the southwest corner of LAKE COUNTY, Tower Lakes is a 1.1-square-mile village that encompasses two artificial lakes, Tower Lake and North Lake. The area was mostly farmland until 1923, when D&B Partnership created the lakes and subdivided the property. A favorite weekend spot for Chicagoans, the village was incorporated in 1966. Population stood at 1,310 in 2000.

Marilyn Elizabeth Perry

See also: Leisure; Metropolitan Growth; Vacation Spots

Further reading: The League of Women Voters of the Barrington Area, Illinois. *In and Around Barrington.* 1990.

Towertown, neighborhood in the NEAR NORTH SIDE Community Area. Towertown was Chicago's bohemia in the early twentieth century. Lacking precise boundaries, the district took its name from the Water Tower, which stood to its north and east on Michigan Avenue. An ART COLONY took root in Towertown when Anna and Lambert Tree built Tree Studios to tempt ARTISTS to stay in Chicago after the 1893 WORLD'S COLUMBIAN EXPOSITION. The concentration of artists, writers, and poets attracted bookshops and COFFEEHOUSES, the most famous of which was the Dill Pickle Club. Soapbox orators gathered in BUGHOUSE SQUARE to debate the issues of the day. GAYS, lesbians, and experimenters in free love took refuge among Towertown's radicals. By the mid-1920s, rising property values driven by the luxury shopping district on nearby Michigan Avenue were pricing out many of the artists. Towertown became a tourist attraction, further alienating its bohemian denizens. By the GREAT DEPRESSION, the art colony had dispersed.

Amanda Seligman

See also: Gentrification; Literary Cultures; Magnificent Mile; Poetry

Town of Pines, IN, Porter County, 37 miles E of the Loop. Town of Pines contained only 798 residents as of the year 2000, the overwhelming majority of them white. It is located near the INDIANA DUNES on Lake Michigan's south shore.

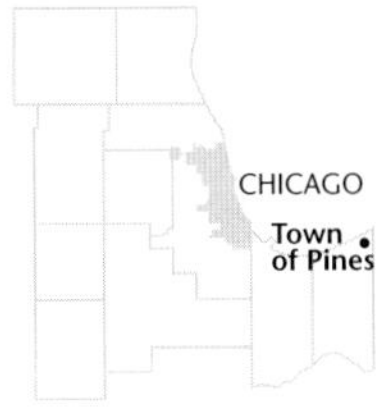

Steven Essig

See also: Lake County, IN; Metropolitan Growth

Townships. The federal government surveyed the Chicago area, as part of the Northwest Territory, into townships ordinarily of 36 square miles (each square mile identified as a "section"). These survey townships eventually became political entities: as a result of a new state constitution, in 1850 counties in the metropolitan area organized townships, which became responsible for basic governmental functions such as roads and taxes. In the mid-nineteenth century, the townships ringing Chicago—LAKE VIEW, JEFFERSON, Cicero, LAKE, and HYDE PARK—incorporated in order to provide more services to their increasingly suburban constituents. However, incorporated townships proved too unwieldy and most were ANNEXED into Chicago in 1889. Townships continue to provide basic services in many suburban areas.

Ann Durkin Keating

See also: Governing the Metropolis; Government, Suburban; Northwest Ordinance

Further reading: Keating, Ann Durkin. *Building Chicago: Suburban Developers and the Creation of a Divided Metropolis.* 2002.

Toy Manufacturing. Throughout the twentieth century, Chicago was home to the leading manufacturers of toys, from Lincoln Logs and Tinkertoys to Pac-Man machines and Beanie Babies. Toy manufacturers thrived in Chicago for the same reasons makers of other products did: rail, WATER, and air transport provided a cheap means to receive raw goods and to ship finished products to WHOLESALERS and retailers worldwide. The city's abundant labor supply also contributed to the area's attractiveness as a manufacturing base.

By 1900, manufactured toys were designed to be smaller versions of the machinery, conveniences, or building materials used by adults: cars, trains, cabs, and tractors were molded from cast iron, fitted with clockwork engines, and stamped with a real brand name at such firms as Hafner Manufacturing Company, whose plant was on the NEAR WEST SIDE. By 1907, Hafner was handling huge orders for the look-alike mechanical toys—especially their model trains, the American Flyer line—pouring in from New York wholesalers and local merchants such as Montgomery Ward & Co.

So great was the demand for realistic toy cars that in 1923 Freeport-based Structo Manufacturing Company turned from making Erector Set–style building toys to making model-kit vehicles such as a toy Model T, which came with a real hand crank and shifting gears. Similarly constructed trucks and tractors filled out the Structo line, which flourished for decades.

A special variety of miniature toy got its start in Chicago, when publisher Charles O. Dowst saw a Linotype machine at the WORLD'S COLUMBIAN EXPOSITION and lit on the idea that such a machine could be modified to stamp out tiny metal charms. From there, Dowst founded Tootsietoys, the company that made tiny charms and novelties, including the prizes found in boxes of Cracker Jack. Dowst was the first to create a die-cast miniature car; he later made a replica of the Model T Ford, then General Motors cars and Mack trucks. Makers of those cars and trucks often requested a look-alike by Tootsietoys and used the miniatures as marketing gimmicks.

Chicago was also the birthplace of some famous wooden toys. Tinkertoys—still a popular building toy—were created in EVANSTON by Charles H. Pajeau, who poked holes on the rim of a wooden sewing spool and created an ingenious building joint, allowing wooden spokes to be connected in a variety of directions. Pajeau first exhibited his invention—as a windmill—in a storefront during a New York toy fair in 1914 and never lacked for buyers after that time. By the 1960s two million Tinkertoy sets sold annually. The product was then owned by another company, but Pajeau ran the Toy Tinkers Company from EVANSTON until 1952.

Lincoln Logs, first made out of notched redwood in 1918, were invented by John Lloyd Wright, the architect's son, and marketed along with other sturdy, functional wood toys under the Red Square Toy Company name. The company was bought in 1943 by Playskool Corporation, another toy giant with roots in Chicago, which still markets Lincoln Logs.

Metal toy makers were caught in a squeeze for raw goods during WORLD WAR II—when certain materials were rationed or became exorbitantly expensive—and an industrywide consolidation over several decades left Chicago with few local toy manufacturers by the 1960s. Also, toy makers turned to plastic by the 1950s, rendering much of the Chicago manufacturers' equipment obsolete.

Some toy makers live on in the area. Chicago-based Radio Flyer Inc., for example, markets a toy-sized version of its distinctive red wagon, though the manufacturing of that toy is done overseas.

The making of coin-operated amusements took off just as toys made from metal and wood began their decline. Chicago-based Lion Manufacturing Corporation created, in 1932, the first pinball machine, the Ballyhoo—which sold 50,000 in less than a year—and spawned a new company, Bally Manufacturing Company, which is still based here.

While Bally was the biggest, two other Chicago-area companies, Williams Electronics and D. Gottlieb & Co., were also major makers of hand-operated games, and, once again, Chicago became a major center for the manufacture of goods for amusement.

Of the three, Bally reigned supreme because of steady innovation. Bally created the first electric slot machine in the 1960s, and, only ten years later, it embraced a variety of the newest technologies to create the best-selling arcade games of the late twentieth century: Space Invaders and Pac-Man.

By 1994, miniatures came back into fashion with the arrival of Beanie Babies, made by OAK BROOK–based Ty Inc. The soft, beanbag animals came tagged with amusing names like Cubbie the Bear, Patti the Platypus, or Bronty the Brontasaurus. Such was the craze for the little limited-edition creatures that collectors bid up $5.95 items to prices as high as $5,000.

Anne Moore

See also: Bicycling; Business of Chicago; Century of Progress Exposition; Transportation

Further reading: Achilles, Rolf. *Made in Illinois: A Story of Illinois Manufacturing.* 1993. • Cross, Gary. *Kids' Stuff: Toys and the Changing World of American Childhood.* 1997. • Rozek, Dan. "Big Beanie Business." *Chicago Sun-Times,* October 11, 1998.

Traction Ordinances. Passed in February 1907 by the Chicago City Council, the traction ordinances represented the culmination of 15 years of public debate over mass transit policy. The settlement between the city and the surface line companies contained several major components, including a continuation of private ownership, plans to finance major service improvements, broad new regulatory powers for the local government, and the creation of a supposedly neutral body of experts to help settle disputes, the Board of Supervising Engineers. While promising immediate relief for the long-suffering straphanger, the agreement ended up contributing to the decline of public transit and the rise of the automobile as the preferred mode of transportation.

The roots of the controversy lay in Chicago's tremendous growth in size and population following the great ANNEXATION of 1889. A powerful new technology, the electric trolley, seemed to offer a solution to increasing problems of crowding and congestion, but corrupt politicians and unscrupulous transit operators frustrated hopes for rapid gains in the quality and cost of services. Demands for better PUBLIC TRANSPORTATION, as well as other public services, were significant components in the rise of a series of political reform movements collectively known as "progressivism." Public discourse on transit policy focused attention on the most notorious STREET RAILWAY owner, Charles Tyson Yerkes, and a group of equally disreputable aldermen called the "GRAY WOLVES" for their predatory behavior. In 1897, the reformers defeated Yerkes' scheme to win a 50-year franchise from the state legislature, and he sold out two years later. Popular agitation made transit policy a pivotal issue in municipal elections, with candidates demanding either stiff city regulations or public ownership of the companies. After a number of proposals along these lines failed to achieve political consensus, financial leaders and conservative reformers cobbled together the settlement embodied in the 1907 ordinances. By severely narrowing policy options for the future of mass transit, they undermined its economic viability and literally helped pave the way for the automobile.

Harold L. Platt

See also: Chicago Transit Authority; Commuting; Motoring; Political Culture; Rapid Transit System

Trade Publications. The story of the Chicago trade press is a complicated one. It is a yarn of free enterprise—with entrepreneurs launching MAGAZINES, NEWSPAPERS and newsletters because an industry, profession, or BUSINESS needed information. Yet it is also a tale of closed associations, far removed from capitalism—with organizations starting their own periodicals to offer news, features, and research to their memberships.

Chicago has long been a major center for the publication of specialized business periodicals; more than 200 were still published in the city in 2000. The majority were published by independently run corporations, large and small, such as Crain Communications, Real Estate News Corporation, Talcott Communications, Trend Publishing, Luby Publishing, and Jacobsen Publishing. But a large minority are published by associations headquartered in Chicago, including the American Medical Association, the American Bar Association, the American Library Association, and the American Marketing Association. Indeed some of the most widely circulated specialized business periodicals are published by these organizations.

On the entrepreneurial side, the story of Crain Communications, Inc., illustrates many of important principles of Chicago trade publishing in both the nineteenth and twentieth centuries. G. D. Crain, Jr., who moved his small company to Chicago from Louisville, Kentucky, in 1916, was a master of launching publications and acquiring MAGAZINES. *Advertising Age,* the best known of the tabloids that he launched, started in Chicago in 1930 but has since moved to New York City. Many of the properties Crain acquired were and continue to be based in Chicago. In 1967, Crain Communications purchased American Trade Magazines, publishers of *American Drycleaner* and the *American Laundry Digest;* those publications remain in the city. But Crain—like a number of trade publishers—discovered that Chicago alone could not be its sole base of operations. The acquisition which signaled that move was the acquisition of Detroit-based *Automotive News* in 1970.

In 2000, Crain remained a privately owned company with nearly all stock owned by family or active employees; the family also controlled the management of the company. The company itself was on strong financial footing, with 30 publications and two radio stations (in Florida) and more than 900 employees. It ran its operations out of 17 different offices in the United States and abroad, including two offices in Chicago. The Rush Street facility is the home of the corporate human resources as well as *Business Insurance* (circulation over 50,000), *BtoB* (circulation over 50,000), *Crain's Chicago Business* (circulation over 50,000), *Modern Healthcare* (a weekly with a circulation over 80,000), and *Modern Physician* (circulation over 30,000); the other, on

North Dearborn, is the headquarters of the American Trade Magazines' smaller circulating properties—*American Clean Car, American Coin-Op, American Drycleaner,* and *American Laundry News.* Crain's corporate activities for administration, accounting, and circulation are now based in Detroit.

The other segment of trade publishing in Chicago is based in associations. Chicago is home to many professional and trade associations. Most organizations only publish one or two periodicals, but some of the larger associations, such as the American Library Association, the American Medical Association, and the American Bar Association (ABA), each publish a variety of journals, magazines, and newsletters. One of the largest and best known is the *ABA Journal* (established 1915, published since 1920 in Chicago), a slick monthly designed to cover LAW and the practice of it. With a circulation of almost 400,000, it is the most widely read magazine on law in the nation.

Chicago's trade publishing picture differs considerably from many other cities. Because of the diversity of the economic base of Chicago, the trade press has never been dominated by a single industry, business, or association. The *Chicago Daily Hide & Tallow Bulletin, Bowling Center Management,* and *JAMA* have all called Chicago home.

Kathleen L. Endres

See also: Journalism; Medical Societies and Journals; Printing; Publishing, Book

Further reading: Baird, Russell, and A. T. Turnbull. *Industry and Business Journalism.* 1961. • Endres, Kathleen L., ed. *Trade, Industrial, and Professional Periodicals of the United States.* 1994. • Goldsborough, Robert. *The Crain Adventure: The Making and Building of a Family Publishing Co.* 1992.

Transportation. By the 1880s residents of Chicago could rightly claim that their city was the RAILROAD mecca of America. Chicago was served by nearly a score of long-distance rail carriers and several switching and terminal companies. Forty years earlier Chicagoans had seemed sanguine about the future of WATER transport, whether on the GREAT LAKES, inland rivers, or canals. The advent of steam-powered vessels after the War of 1812 had significantly shortened the travel time between destinations on navigable bodies of water and the city was advantageously situated at the mouth of the CHICAGO RIVER on the southwestern shore of LAKE MICHIGAN. Moreover in the 1840s, prospects looked good for construction of a strategic "ditch," the ILLINOIS & MICHIGAN CANAL, to link the Chicago and Illinois Rivers and hence connect Lake Michigan and the Mississippi River system. This 96-mile canal opened in 1848.

Chicagoans correctly perceived transportation as both a cause and an effect of urban development and they strove to enhance their facilities. Better transport, however, meant more than better waterways. Caught up in the fad of plank roads during the 1840s, residents endorsed placement of wide wooden planks across timber stringers to create a solid surface over the muddiest stretches of road. By the early 1850s there were seven such thoroughfares. But the continual expense of upkeep and the failure of privately owned plank-road companies to generate profits dampened interest.

Although barely visible in the Middle West, by the 1840s the Railway Age had already dawned. Public support contributed to making Chicago a railroad hub. Backing took the form of franchises, subscriptions to railroad securities, and grants of REAL ESTATE for rights-of-way and facilities.

Chicagoans saw their first iron horse in 1848. On October 10, 1848, a 2-4-0 type steam locomotive, appropriately named *The Pioneer,* began to pull cars laden with construction supplies and workers over the advancing line of the Galena & Chicago Union Railroad. Spearheaded by several Chicago businessmen, including Walter Newberry, William Butler Ogden, and Charles Walter, the company formed

First broached by Louis Jolliet in 1673, the idea of a canal at the base of Lake Michigan did not materialize until 1836–1848, when the Illinois & Michigan Canal was built. Its vital function was to unite the waters of the Great Lakes with those of the Mississippi Basin. The canal was the crucial catalyst for the early growth of Chicago, after which railroads confirmed the city's centrality within the nation. The federal land grant to help build the canal with the proceeds of land sales (the first such aid in the nation) stimulated farm settlement in northeastern Illinois, while the canal itself spurred town growth along its route. Twice as many towns were founded by overzealous promoters as could ultimately survive, so half remained mere "paper towns." Water power and minerals added industry to the commercial base of many of the canal towns, and all benefited from the steady stream of farm produce, lumber, and other necessities moved on the canal in the early 1850s. Despite losing much traffic to the railroads after 1855, the canal remained important for bulk movements until the end of the century. The only major American canal to pay off its construction debts and make a profit, it was succeeded by a modern replacement, the Illinois Waterway.

The Historic Illinois & Michigan Canal Corridor in 1851

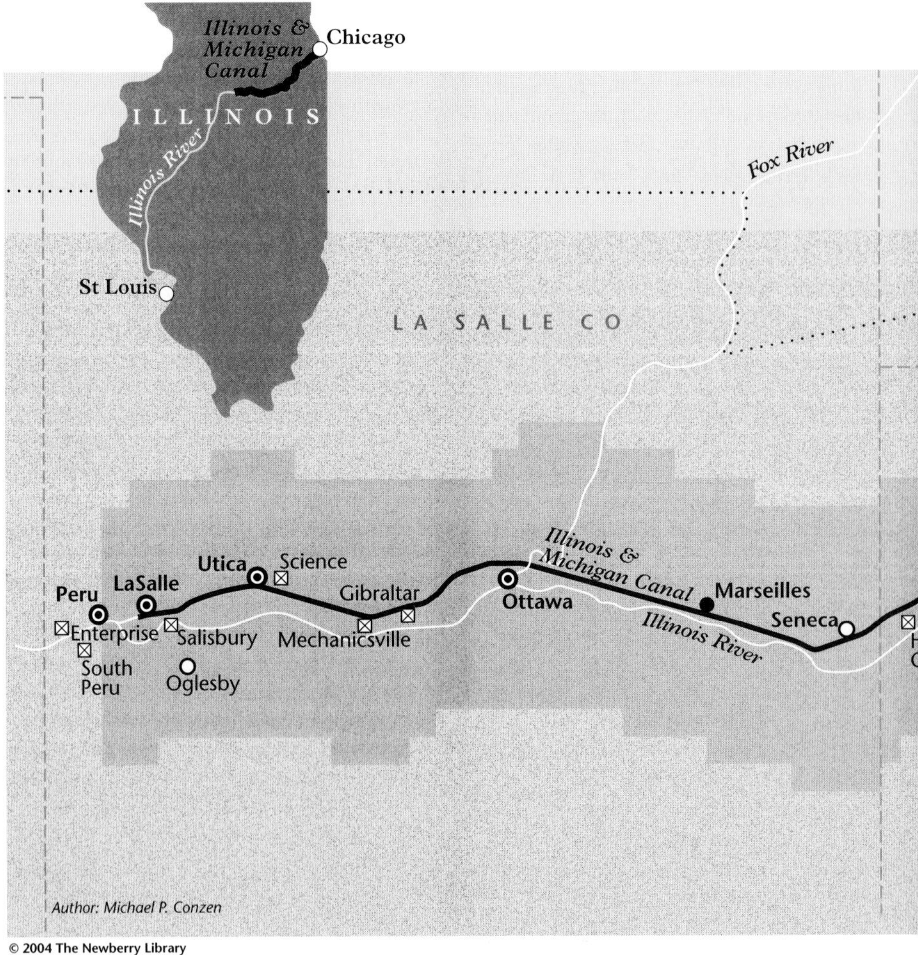

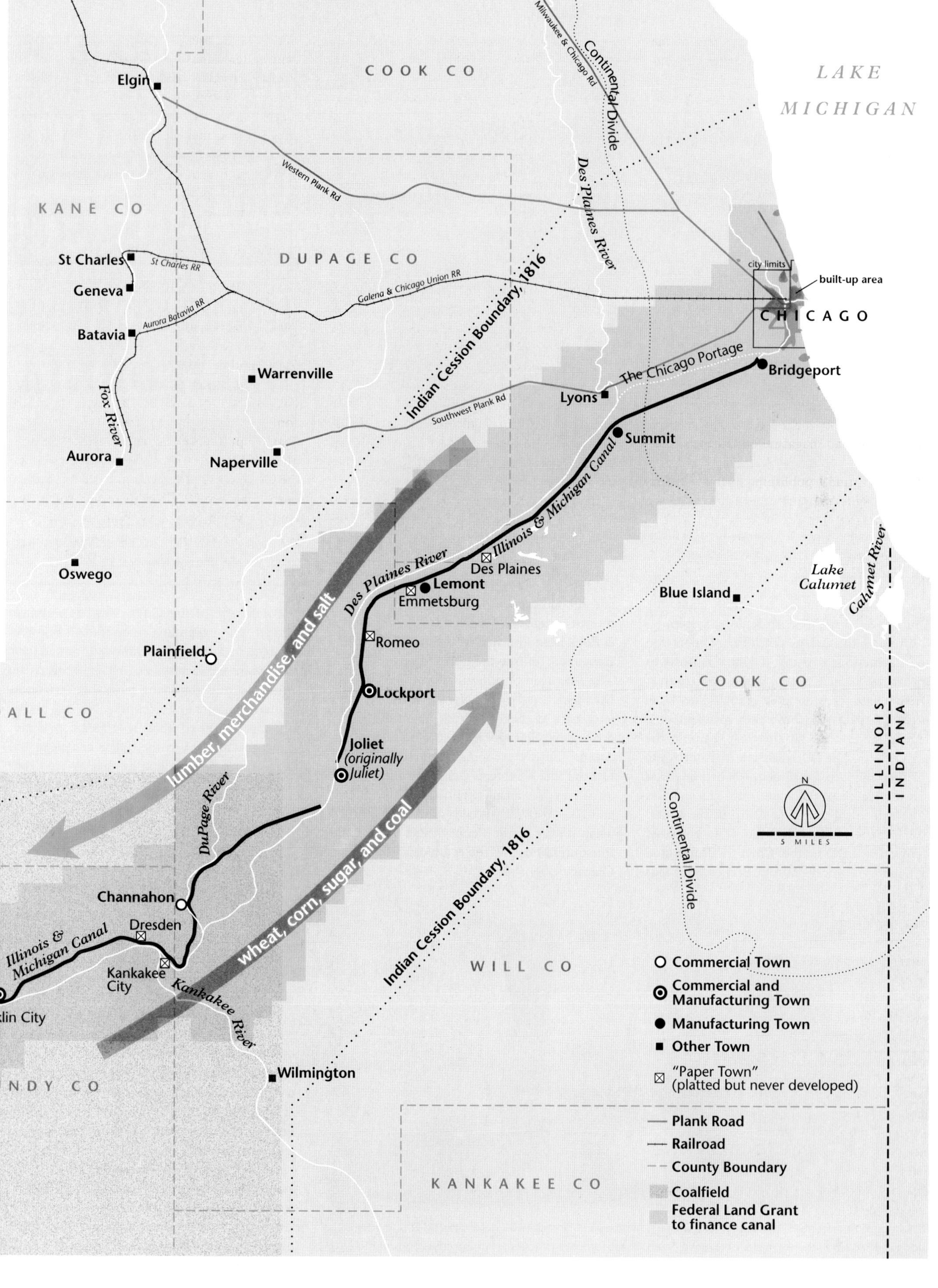
LAKE MICHIGAN
COOK CO
KANE CO
DUPAGE CO
DALL CO
UNDY CO
WILL CO
KANKAKEE CO
ILLINOIS
INDIANA
CHICAGO
city limits
built-up area
Elgin
St Charles
Geneva
Batavia
Aurora
Oswego
Warrenville
Naperville
Plainfield
Lyons
Bridgeport
Summit
Lemont
Emmetsburg
Des Plaines
Romeo
Lockport
Joliet (originally Juliet)
Blue Island
Channahon
Dresden
Kankakee City
nklin City
Wilmington
Lake Calumet
Calumet River
Fox River
Des Plaines River
DuPage River
Kankakee River
Continental Divide
Milwaukee & Chicago Rd
Western Plank Rd
St Charles RR
Galena & Chicago Union RR
Aurora Batavia RR
Southwest Plank Rd
The Chicago Portage
Illinois & Michigan Canal
Indian Cession Boundary, 1816
lumber, merchandise, and salt
wheat, corn, sugar, and coal
N
5 MILES
Commercial Town
Commercial and Manufacturing Town
Manufacturing Town
Other Town
"Paper Town" (platted but never developed)
Plank Road
Railroad
County Boundary
Coalfield
Federal Land Grant to finance canal

Reopening of the Illinois & Michigan Canal at Bridgeport, 1871, after the channel had been deepened. Artist: Unknown. Source: Chicago Historical Society.

Advertisement for the Chicago & North Western Railway, with daily trains to California and beyond, 1869. Source: Chicago Historical Society.

the core of that future corporate giant, the Chicago & North Western Railway System.

Although the Galena & Chicago Union won the distinction of being the first railroad to turn a wheel in Chicago and Cook County, it soon lost its monopoly status. The Illinois Central (IC), the first recipient of a federal land grant, rapidly took shape in the early 1850s. The IC created a monster route for that era with a wishbone-shaped line that ran the length of the state from Chicago and Dunleith in the north to Cairo in the south. Other carriers followed. Extant Chicago-based companies include the Chicago, Burlington & Quincy (formerly Aurora Branch Railroad) and the Chicago, Rock Island & Pacific (formerly Chicago & Rock Island). The Burlington & Rock Island pushed westward to the Mississippi and later into the trans-Mississippi West. The Michigan Southern (soon to become the Michigan Southern & Northern Indiana, and later part of the New York Central system), arrived in Chicago from the East in 1852. Another future component of the New York Central, the Michigan Central, appeared that same year. But an all-rail link between Chicago and New York City was not forged until 1858, when a unit of the Pennsylvania system, the Pittsburgh, Fort Wayne & Chicago, opened its Chicago extension.

By the eve of the Civil War, 11 railroads served the expanding metropolis. Boosters claimed that a hundred trains daily served their city. More significant was Chicago's role as the principal transshipment point between eastern and western rail networks. No city before or since assumed such a strategic position. Chicago emerged as the major beneficiary of a transportation geography that favored railroad termini over places that had been heavily dependent upon water navigation.

Chicago continued to strengthen its position as America's premier railroad hub with the

Chicago in 1950 was at the height of its power as the railroad center of the United States. Fully 37 long-distance railroad lines, operated by 21 independent railroad companies, fanned out from Chicago in all landward directions, connecting with all corners of the nation and the settled portions of Canada. This was the pay-off for the efforts of the city's business leaders a century before to ensure that practically all trunk railroads passing through northeastern Illinois terminated in the city of Chicago. One local corporation, the Elgin, Joliet & Eastern Railway, was later formed to create a huge belt line that circumnavigated the metropolitan area, handling traffic between locations on the periphery and diverting some through traffic around the congestion of the urban center. Shown but not individually identified are numerous short lines within the urban area built to exchange freight between the trunk railroads and to service metropolitan industry.

The *Pioneer* powered the first rail trip in the Chicago metropolitan area, between the city and Elmhurst in 1848, along the first leg of the Galena & Chicago Railroad. The locomotive is now part of the collections of the Chicago Historical Society. Photographer: Unknown. Source: Chicago Historical Society.

Chicago's Railroad Pattern in 1950

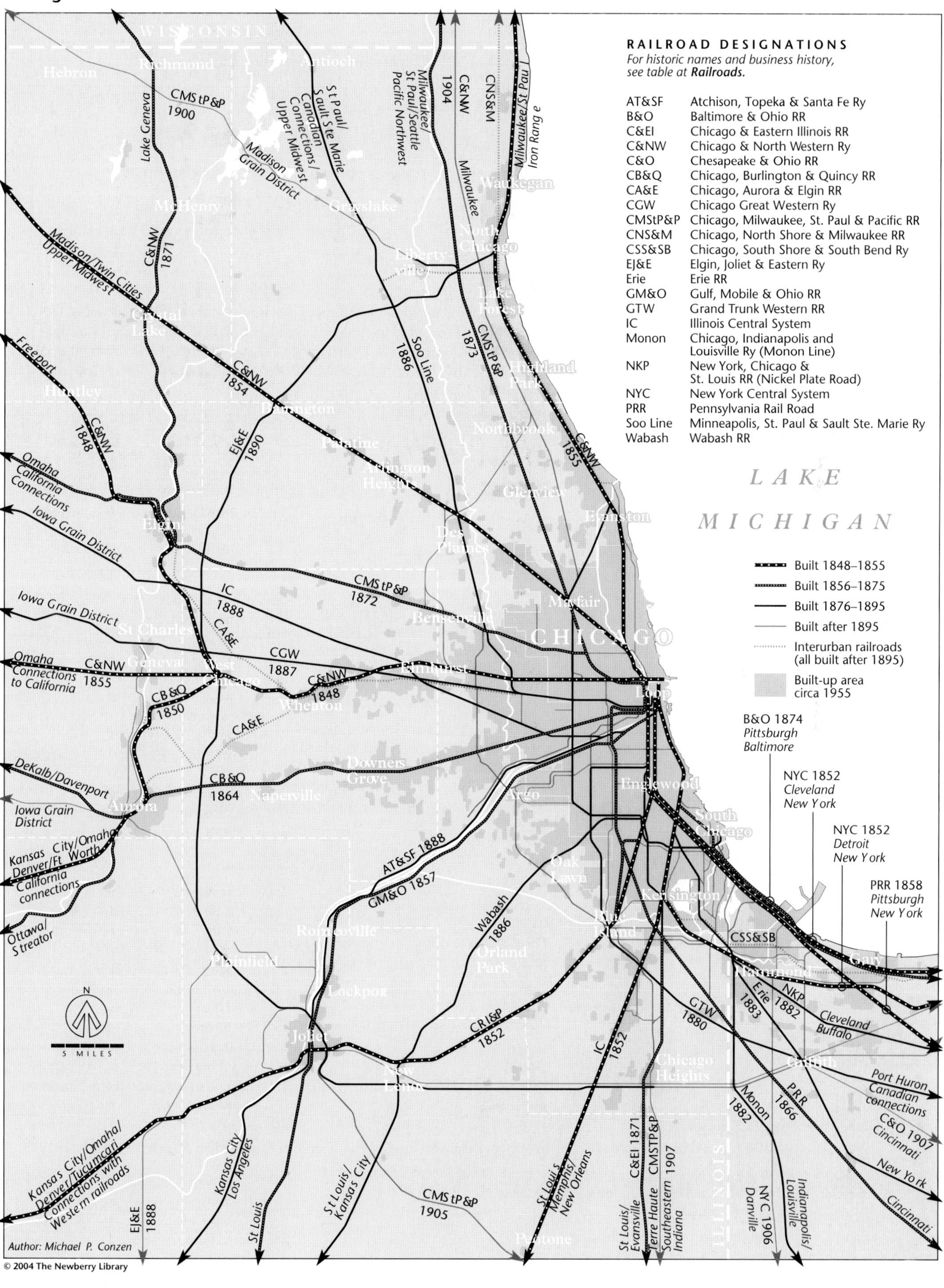

Development of Railroad Lines from Chicago

RAIL LINE ON MAP	DATE OF LINE	HISTORICAL SIGNIFICANCE
Alton Chicago & Alton Railroad (1861)		
St. Louis	1857	First route between Chicago and St. Louis.
AT&SF Atchison, Topeka & Sante Fe Railway ("The Santa Fe") (1859)		
Kansas City–Los Angeles	1884	Headquartered in Chicago after 1904; connected Chicago with Southwest.
B&O Baltimore & Ohio Railroad (1827)		
Pittsburgh–Baltimore	1874	First significant railroad in the United States; built line to expand B&O's eastern network into Chicago.
CB&Q Chicago, Burlington & Quincy Railroad (1856)		
Kansas City, Omaha–Denver / Ft. Worth / CA	1850, 1864	Aurora Branch RR built initial 13-mile track from Aurora to West Chicago in 1850, a line extended westward to the Mississippi River by 1855 and renamed Chicago, Burlington & Quincy. Route from Chicago to Aurora built in 1864. CB&Q thrived in nineteenth century by bringing agricultural goods from Illinois, Iowa, Missouri, and Nebraska to Chicago.
Iowa Grain District	1871	
Ottawa–Streator	1871	
CGW Chicago Great Western Railway (1892)		
Iowa–St. Paul	1887	Self-described "Corn Belt Route" served upper-Midwest agriculture.
C&EI Chicago & Eastern Illinois Railroad (1877)		
St. Louis, Evansville	1871	Served as strategic bridge line and was called "an All-American average railroad."
CMSTP&P Chicago, Milwaukee, St. Paul & Pacific Railroad ("The Milwaukee Road") (1874)		
Milwaukee–St. Paul	1873	Known as "The St. Paul" in the nineteenth century and "The Milwaukee Road" in the twentieth, this railroad connected Midwestern farmers and passengers with Chicago. It pioneered the grain elevator and painted its cars a distinctive bright orange. Overexpansion into the Pacific Northwest and Southern Indiana after 1905 led to largest bankruptcy in U.S. history in 1925.
Omaha–CA	1873	
Terre Haute–SE Indiana	1904	
Madison–Grain District	1900	
DeKalb–Davenport	1905	
C&NW Chicago & North Western Railway (1859)		
Omaha–CA	1848	The Galena & Chicago Union (GCU, 1848) built the region's first railroad, from Chicago to West Chicago in 1848, extended to Freeport and the Mississippi River by 1855. In the "Great Consolidation" of 1864, the well-managed GCU merged with (and took the name of) the smaller C&NW, which owned a line to Madison. Rapid post–Civil War expansion created a large railroad serving upper-Midwest and Great Plains agriculture.
Freeport	1853	
Madison–Twin Cities	1854	
Milwaukee–St. Paul	1855	
Milwaukee	1904	
C&O Chesapeake & Ohio Railway (1868)		
Cincinnati	1907	Major coal hauler from Ohio Valley to Chicago.
CRI&P Chicago, Rock Island & Pacific Railroad ("The Rock Island") (1866)		
Kansas City, Omaha–Denver–Tucumcari	1852	The Chicago and Rock Island Railroad (1851) reached Joliet in 1852 and in 1854 became the first Chicago railroad to cross the Mississippi River.
EJ&E Elgin, Joliet & Eastern Railway (1887)		
	1890	Outer Belt Line served freight connections around city.
Erie Erie Railroad (1895)		
New York	1883	Suffered from stock manipulation in 1860s; specialized in freight traffic to Northeast.
GTW Grand Trunk Western Railroad (1900)		
Port Huron/Canada	1880	Important freight link to Ontario; absorbed by Canadian National system after 1923.
IC Illinois Central Railroad (1851)		
St. Louis–Memphis–New Orleans	1852	First railroad financed by a federal land grant, the IC completed route from Chicago to Cairo in 1856. During the twentieth century, the IC served as a major route for southerners migrating to Chicago.
Iowa Grain District	1888	

Development of Railroad Lines from Chicago (Cont.)

RAIL LINE ON MAP	DATE OF LINE	HISTORICAL SIGNIFICANCE
Monon Monon Line Railroad (1956)		
Indianapolis–Louisville	1882	Major carrier of Indiana building stone and coal to Chicago.
NKP New York, Chicago & St. Louis Railroad ("The Nickel Plate") (1881)		
Cleveland–Buffalo	1882	Known for fast, low-cost freight traffic along Great Lakes trunkline.
NYC New York Central System (1853)		
Cleveland–New York *Detroit–New York*	1852 1852	Lines built by Michigan Central and Michigan Southern, arriving into Chicago one day apart in 1852; NYC was chief rival to PRR as passenger and freight carrier to New York.
PRR Pennsylvania Railroad (1846)		
Pittsburgh–New York	1858	Premier carrier to East Coast; 1905 Broadway Limited reached New York in 18 hours.
Soo Minneapolis, St. Paul & Sault Ste. Marie ("The Soo Line") (1883)		
St. Paul/Sault Ste. Marie/Canada	1886	The Soo Line connected upper-Midwest farmers first with Canada then with Chicago after 1909 lease of Wisconsin Central line into Chicago built in 1886.
Wabash Railroad (1877)		
St. Louis–Kansas City	1886	Under Jay Gould, Wabash connected main Toledo–Kansas City line with Chicago.

opening of the first route to the Pacific in 1869, and with subsequent transcontinental arteries. The city witnessed other linkages that bolstered commerce; for example, completion of the Minnesota & Northwestern (Chicago Great Western) between Chicago and St. Paul in 1887 offered new avenues of trade.

Chicagoans also encountered the great monuments of the Railway Age—urban terminals. Unlike St. Louis, where all trains entered and departed a true "union" station in 1894, six major depots served Chicago by the early twentieth century. With the exception of the Chicago & North Western terminal on Wells Street (replaced by a massive structure on Madison Street in 1911), Chicago's RAILROAD STATIONS served more than a single carrier. A process of replacement terminals continued throughout the era of heavy train travel. In 1924 the last major terminal to open was Union Station, located on Adams and Canal Streets. This facility, which replaced an 1881 depot, became a bona fide union station in 1971, when the quasi-public National Railroad Passenger Corporation (Amtrak) assumed most intercity passenger operations. COMMUTER trains, which had served the greater Chicago area since the 1850s, continued to use this facility and several other stations, albeit greatly modified ones.

When travelers patronized a Chicago railroad terminal, they frequently used local transport, which after the Civil War progressed from horsecar to cable car to electric trolley and elevated train (the "L"), and ultimately included the BUS. Just as the city boasted of being the railroad capital of America, its intracity transport facilities could also be described in superlatives. For instance, the largest, and on the whole the most important, cable system in the nation was the Chicago City Railway, which operated from 1882 until 1906 along the principal commercial streets.

While convenient surface transport pleased railroad officials, they hardly welcomed the growth of Chicago as one of the nation's aviation centers. A steady and at times rapid expansion continued after 1925, especially in the late 1950s, when the jet airplane began to replace the passenger train as the most popular form of long-distance intercity transport. Merrill C. Meigs Field was joined first by Chicago MIDWAY AIRPORT and then O'HARE INTERNATIONAL AIRPORT.

Similarly, the automobile caused massive dislocations for existing forms of transportation. The sting of auto competition led to abandonment of two of Chicago's most significant electric INTERURBANS by 1963: the Chicago,

Swimming races in the Chicago River, such as this one in 1908, were popular in the early twentieth century. They were emblematic of the sharp decline in river commerce and the dramatic improvement in the quality of river water after its 1900 reversal. Photographer: Unknown. Source: Chicago Historical Society.

Cable cars, electric trolleys, hansom cabs, electric automobiles, and pedestrians share the corner of State and Madison, around 1905. Photographer: Unknown. Source: Chicago Historical Society.

Aurora & Elgin; and the Chicago, North Shore & Milwaukee, both products of the "interurban madness" of the early twentieth century. Steam railroads, too, were forced to revamp their commuter operations to cope with increased automobile traffic after World War II owing to ever-improving roads, EXPRESSWAYS, and interstates. The most notable response came in the mid-1950s with the introduction of double-deck equipment and "push-pull" trains on the North Western. Financial difficulties, however, forced commuter roads to back creation in 1974 of the REGIONAL TRANSPORTATION AUTHORITY to finance service in the six-county Chicago region.

Taxpayer involvement in commuter service paralleled events in intracity transport. By 1945 the city's private transit companies, the Chicago Surface Lines and the Chicago Rapid Transit Company, could no longer economically survive. They were replaced in 1947 by the CHICAGO TRANSIT AUTHORITY, a state-chartered organization, which was charged with operating the RAPID TRANSIT, trolley, and bus lines on the basis of revenues earned. The bus routes of the Chicago Motor Coach Company were added to the system in 1952. As with intercity passenger trains, the private sector wanted no part of hauling people. Yet freight was sought and Chicago retained its status as *the* American railroad center. Moreover, the city gained the distinction of being a national AIRLINE and motor transport hub.

H. Roger Grant

See also: Global Chicago; Public Transportation; Public Works, Federal Funding for; Railroads and Chicago's Loop (map, p. C3); Street Railways; Streets and Highways; Toll Roads

Further reading: Bach, Ira J., and Susan Wolfson. *A Guide to Chicago's Train Stations: Past and Present.* 1986. • Conzen, Michael P., and Kay J. Carr, eds. *The Illinois and Michigan Canal: National Heritage Corridor.* 1988. • Grant, H. Roger. *The North Western: The Chicago and North Western Railway System.* 1996.

Horsecars such as this one operated into the early 1900s. Photographer: Unknown. Source: Chicago Historical Society.

Treaties. The Chicago area was directly affected by five of the approximately 370 ratified treaties between the federal government and American Indian nations signed from 1778 to 1871. Indian treaty making ended by law in 1871, but an additional 73 "agreements" containing similar provisions were ratified up to 1911. Treaties involving the Chicago area were signed in 1795, 1816, 1821, 1829, and 1833.

The Treaty of Greenville, Ohio (1795), ceded to the federal government the southern two-thirds of present-day Ohio, ending the allied Indians' long battle to maintain the Ohio River as the boundary between areas for white and Indian settlement, a boundary set by the Treaty of Fort Stanwix in 1768. The treaty also ceded 16 tracts at strategic locations on the water transportation routes of the Northwest Territory, including three in present-day Illinois: (1) the mouth of the CHICAGO RIVER, where FORT DEARBORN was erected in 1803; (2) the PORTAGE area between the Chicago and DES PLAINES RIVERS; and (3) the mouth of the Illinois river.

Following the War of 1812, the regional band of OTTAWA, Chippewa, and POTAWATOMI ceded to the United States a strip of land extending directly southwest from points 10 miles north and 10 miles south of the mouth of the Chicago River. Through this Treaty of St. Louis (1816), the government acquired control over the Chicago River corridor linking LAKE MICHIGAN and the Mississippi River. At Chicago, Ottawa, Chippewa, and Potawatomi representatives signed a treaty August 29, 1821, giving up land in southwestern Michigan and also gave permission to build a road from Detroit to Chicago, completed in 1835.

The pioneer farm of Antoine Ouilmette, now a lighthouse site in WILMETTE, marked the corner of an area extending westward to the Rock River ceded by the Treaty of Prairie du Chien (Wisconsin, 1829). Other treaty provisions granted sections of land along the Chicago and Des Plaines Rivers to several people of Indian heritage, including Billy Caldwell, Alexander Robinson, and Archange Ouilmette, Potawatomi wife of Antoine.

The famous Treaty of Chicago (1833) brought an estimated three thousand Indians, traders, government officials, army troops, land speculators, and adventurers to the small village to witness the dramatic proceedings whereby the Potawatomi ceded the last of their Illinois and Wisconsin lands and their last reservations in Michigan. Indians began the demanded removal to land west of the Mississippi river, or fled to Wisconsin and Canada before the treaty was ratified in 1835.

Helen Hornbeck Tanner

See also: Black Hawk War; Chicago in the Middle Ground

Further reading: Kappler, Charles J., comp. and ed. *American Indian Treaties.* 1972. • Prucha, Francis Paul. *American Indian Treaties.* 1994. • Royce, Charles C., comp. "Indian Land Cessions in the United States." *Eighteenth Annual Report of the Bureau of American Ethnology for 1896–97, Part II.* 1899.

Trees. "What can be finer than the White Elm?" "Let the whole avenue consist of noble elms, arching beautifully overhead." Addressing the Illinois Horticultural Society in 1882, horticulturist John Warder was referring to the American elm then beginning to influence the character of countless young towns of the Midwest as it became queen of the STREET trees. In addition to its attractive vase shape, its tough branches and capacity to tolerate street-side soil adversities were valuable attributes.

For many decades, the American elm reigned as a splendid dominant feature of Midwestern streetscapes. In the middle of the twentieth century, disaster struck in the form of Dutch elm disease. A vascular fungus decimated the elm populations of hundreds of cities and towns in the Midwest, including many in the Chicago region. Insecticide application and prompt removal slowed attrition. The disease has continued to destroy American elms, but remnant arcades persist in metropolitan Chicago.

Following WORLD WAR II, suburban developers and residents looking for quick shade planted whole communities with silver maple and Siberian elm. In older Chicago communities, however, the American elm remained the predominant street tree (45 percent) as late as the 1970s. Norway and silver maples were half as common, followed by ash at 12 percent. Far behind were oaks, remnants of naturally occurring groves, and scattered plantings of honey locust and linden. Less common were catalpa, ginkgo, sycamore, hawthorn, mulberry, cottonwood, pin oak, willow, horse chestnut, hackberry, and crabapple.

The past two decades have seen a marked increase in diversity in street tree planting in both Chicago and its suburbs. Hybrid trees of maples, elms, and lindens contribute special toughness and stress tolerance. Oaks are increasingly being planted. Recent extensive tree planting has enriched the Chicago streetscape. Downtown Chicago has a rich matrix of honey locust, augmented generously with well-chosen newcomer trees.

George H. Ware

See also: Forest Preserves; Landscape; Landscape Design

Further reading: Schmid, James A. *Urban Vegetation: A Review and Chicago Case History.* 1975 • Warder, John A. "Trees for the Park, the Avenue and the Street." *Transactions of the Illinois State Horticultural Society,* n.s. 16 (1882): 186–192. • Warder, John A. "Street Trees for Prairie Towns." *Transactions of the Illinois State Horticultural Society, 27th Annual Meeting* (1883): 1–5.

Tribune. *See* Chicago Tribune

Trinity Christian College. Trinity Christian College in Palos Heights, Illinois, is a private, four-year liberal arts college founded in the Reformed tradition.

In the late 1940s, synods of the Christian Reformed Church investigated the desirability of creating junior colleges to complement Calvin College (Michigan). Richard Prince, principal of Chicago Christian High School, and Harold Dekker, of "The Back to God Hour" radio program, led the Chicago effort, and in 1959 the first trustees purchased the Navajo Hills Golf Course in PALOS HEIGHTS to serve as its site. The constitution drew from those of the Free University of Amsterdam and Calvin College.

Trinity's mission evolved in the ensuing years. It became a four-year college, conferring baccalaureate degrees in 1971, while also creating professional programs in business administration, NURSING, and education. Enrollment grew from 37 students in 1959 to over 600 in 1997, shifting from a predominantly Dutch Reformed orientation toward greater ethnic, racial, and sectarian diversity.

Jeffrey Webb

See also: Dutch; Protestants

Further reading: Lucas, Henry Stephen. *Netherlanders in America: Dutch Immigration to the United States and Canada, 1789–1950.* 1955. • Pace, Robert C. *Education and Evangelism: A Profile of Protestant Colleges.* 1972. • Ringenberg, William C. *The Christian College: A History of Protestant Higher Education in America.* 1984.

Trinity International University. Trinity International University, in DEERFIELD, is a private, four-year liberal arts college and SEMINARY founded in 1897 in the evangelical Christian tradition.

Organized by the Evangelical Free Church, Trinity operated on the model typified by MOODY BIBLE INSTITUTE in Chicago. Each offered short-term MISSIONARY TRAINING courses, though Trinity merged with Trinity Seminary and Bible Institute of Minneapolis in 1946, and began to confer the baccalaureate degree in 1954.

The college and seminary separated in 1974, when the college also severed its ties to the Evangelical Free Church. These associations were restored 10 years later, and in 1993 Trinity established a branch campus in Florida at the former Miami Christian College.

Trinity has been noted for its contributions to conservative PROTESTANT theology, and for the prolific matriculation of its graduates into professional Christian ministry.

Jeffrey Webb

Further reading: Hanson, Calvin B. *The Trinity Story.* 1983. • Marsden, George. *Understanding Fundamentalism and Evangelicalism.* 1991.

Trolleys. *See* Street Railways

Trout Valley, IL, McHenry County, 39 miles NW of the Loop. Trout Valley was originally the site of a massive horse-breeding farm owned by John Hertz of Chicago TAXI and auto rental fame and, later, a Curtiss Candy Company farm. Residential development began in 1953. Residents on large lots opposed to CARY's development plans voted to incorporate in 1996. Population was 599 in 2000.

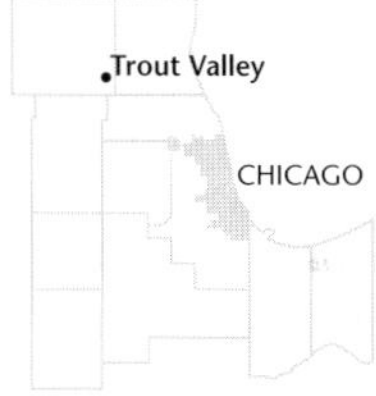

Craig L. Pfannkuche

See also: McHenry County

Further reading: Cary Historical Group. *Cary Me Back: 1893–1993.* 1993.

Tuberculosis. Tuberculosis is an infectious disease of the lungs and other organs. Once considered incurable, the disease caused its victims to slowly waste away, which was why it was called "consumption." With a mortality rate of approximately 18 per 10,000 people, tuberculosis was a leading cause of death within the city of Chicago at the turn of the twentieth century.

Early attempts at controlling tuberculosis in Chicago focused on home sanitation, PUBLIC HEALTH education, and isolation of the patient. Private HOSPITALS took a few tuberculosis patients, but public facilities to care for consumptives were not available. In order to raise public awareness, the Visiting Nurses Association and physician Theodore Sachs spearheaded an antituberculosis movement in the early 1900s. This eventually resulted in the passage of state legislation, the Glackin Tuberculosis Law, in 1909, giving the city of Chicago the ability to raise funds for the treatment and control of tuberculosis through a special property tax. In 1915, the Chicago Municipal Tuberculosis Sanitarium opened and remained in operation until the 1970s.

Mortality rates from tuberculosis declined slowly in Chicago in the early twentieth century with disparities in mortality rates due especially to race. As a result of overcrowding and poverty, AFRICAN AMERICAN and immigrant communities were hardest hit. While mortality rates for whites were decreasing, racially restrictive hospital admittance and public health policies led to an increase in mortality for the black community. Finally, midcentury drug therapies effectively controlled tuberculosis. Tuberculosis remained under control in Chicago until the 1980s, when the spread of AIDS created a community of individuals susceptible to the disease.

Susan Vieweg

See also: Demography; Epidemics

Further reading: Bonner, Thomas Neville. *Medicine in Chicago 1850–1950.* 1957. • McBride, David. *From T.B. to AIDS: Epidemics among Urban Blacks.* 1991. • Rothman, Sheila. *Living in the Shadow of Death.* 1995.

Tunnels. Chicago has been able to use tunnels to solve various INFRASTRUCTURE problems, thanks to an easily excavated layer of blue clay underlying the city. Even deeper flood control tunnels have been cut through bedrock, as part of the DEEP TUNNEL project.

Water Tunnels

WATER intakes just offshore proved inadequate soon after their construction in the 1850s, as the river carried raw sewage into LAKE MICHIGAN. Engineer Ellis Chesbrough, who designed the city's sewer system, proposed a tunnel two miles long to a new water intake further out in the lake.

Beginning in 1864, a crew tunneled from the shore, joined later by another crew tunneling from the intake crib in the lake. Two shifts a day mined by hand the clay and occasional gravel deposits, with the spoil carried away by small mule-drawn railcars. A third shift of masons lined the five-foot-diameter tunnel with two layers of brick. The two tunnels met in November 1866, less than seven inches out of alignment.

This tunnel supplied water to the new Chicago Avenue pumping station and water tower. By 1874, a second tunnel was dug to the same intake crib, and a diagonal tunnel under the city delivered water to a pumping station near Cermak and Ashland. Today the city has 65 miles of WATER SUPPLY tunnels, including several lake tunnels extending as much as four miles underwater.

Chicago's Freight Tunnels, circa 1930

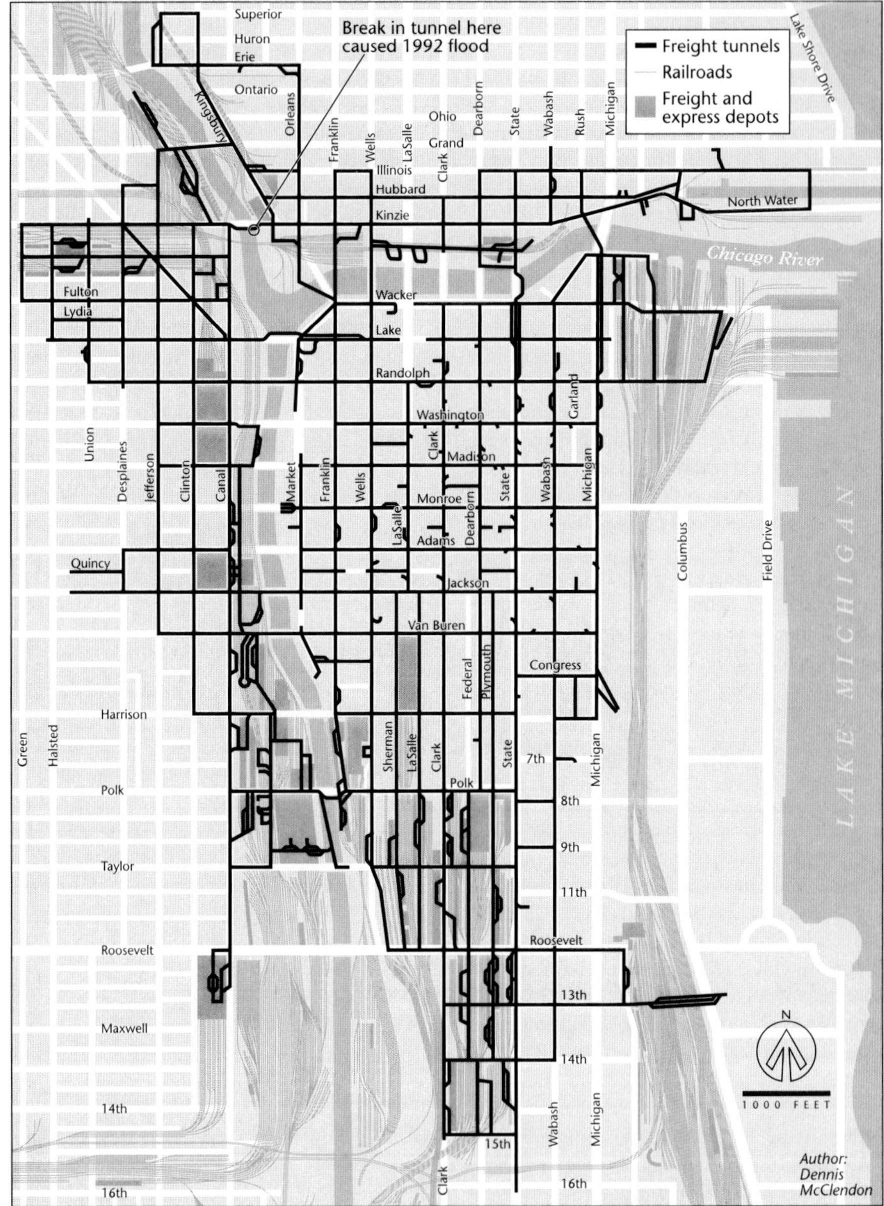

Built from 1900 to 1909, the freight tunnel network extended under nearly every downtown street, with short spurs into building basements for delivery of coal or freight and removal of ash from furnaces. Numerous connections and sidings at railroad freight houses were used to transfer freight and coal shipments. Temporary trestles into Grant Park allowed excavation spoil to be used for park expansion. Most of the freight tunnels are still in place and, though abandoned as a transport system in 1959, many came to be used to carry utility and communication lines.

River Tunnels

The low BRIDGES crossing the CHICAGO RIVER were frequently opened for the passage of masted vessels, cutting off street traffic to the North and West Sides. City officials began discussing tunnels under the river as early as 1844. The 1,605-foot Washington Street tunnel opened January 1, 1869. North Side access was made easier with construction of the LaSalle Street tunnel (1869–71), 2,000 feet long. The tunnels were a valuable escape route during the FIRE OF 1871, which quickly consumed the wooden BRIDGES. These first two tunnels served private vehicles and pedestrians; they carried no horsecar lines. However, in the 1880s the cable car companies took over the two tunnels, because cables could not cross drawbridges, and in 1891–92 built a third street railway tunnel just north of Van Buren Street, 1,514 feet long.

Although the tunnels had been some 18 feet under the riverbed when built, reversal of the

Chicago River in 1900 exposed them. They were closed with the end of cable car operation in 1906. Wider, deeper replacements were built underneath the original tunnels and opened to electric streetcar service in 1911–12. To avoid steep grades at either end, the new LaSalle Street tunnel was built in dry dock, of steel plate, and lowered into a trench in the riverbed.

The Van Buren Street tunnel was closed to regular traffic in 1924. The LaSalle Street tunnel closed in 1939 to allow subway construction, and the Washington Street tunnel was closed in 1954.

Freight Tunnels

A network of freight tunnels under most downtown streets once carried freight from railroad terminals, packages from DEPARTMENT STORES, coal to LOOP office buildings, and ash and excavation spoil to fill in the lakefront.

In 1899, an independent TELEPHONE company was given a franchise to lay telephone cables under downtown streets. Whether it was the company's original intent, or a later inspiration, construction began in 1900 of tunnels large enough to carry a narrow-gauge (two-foot) electric railroad. Freight service began in 1906, and the approximately 60-mile network was largely complete by 1909. Shipments arriving at railroad freight houses were reloaded on the small tunnel cars, which were lowered by elevators to the tunnels and towed to their destinations. Tunnel trains carried coal to basement boiler rooms and carried ash away for disposal.

By the 1930s, motor trucks proved more efficient than the freight tunnels. Subway tunnels constructed in 1939 at the same level cut off important parts of the network, and Loop buildings shifted to coal delivery by truck and then to natural GAS. The freight tunnels were abandoned in July 1959.

Today, some sections of the tunnels are used for utility and communication lines. In April 1992, one of the tunnels under the Chicago River near Kinzie Street was punctured, flooding most of the system and two dozen downtown buildings with open tunnel connections.

Subway Tunnels

Beginning in 1938, federal financing from the Public Works Administration facilitated construction on nine miles of RAPID TRANSIT subways. Route No. 1, under Clybourn Avenue, Division Street, and State Street, and Route No. 2, under Milwaukee Avenue, Lake Street, and Dearborn Street, were unfinished when the U.S. entered World War II. The city was able to finish the State Street Subway by October 1943. The Dearborn Subway opened in February 1951.

Contractors experienced with sewer CONSTRUCTION dug the subway through blue clay, about 43 feet below street level. Station mezzanines were constructed by excavating from street level and reconstructing the street on overhead steel supports, a technique known as "cut-and-cover" construction. As had been done earlier with the LaSalle Street streetcar tunnel under the Chicago River, tubes constructed in dry dock were lowered into a trench in the riverbed and connected to the State Street tunnels at both ends.

The Dearborn Subway was extended in 1958 under the new Congress Parkway, and the line to Logan Square was extended in 1970 using cut-and-cover construction under Kimball Avenue to reach the Kennedy EXPRESSWAY extension.

Dennis McClendon

See also: Innovation, Invention, and Chicago Business; Street Railways

Further reading: Chicago Department of Public Works. *Chicago Public Works: A History.* 1973. • Moffat, Bruce G. *The Chicago Tunnel Story: Exploring the Railroad "Forty Feet Below."* 2002. • Piehl, Frank J. "Our Forgotten Streetcar Tunnels." *Chicago History* (Fall 1975).

Turf. "Turf" is the city's physical space, overlaid by the symbolic and practical claims of its users and residents. For example, early in the twentieth century, several largely IRISH enclaves existed on the city's South and Southwest Sides, even as the South Side BLACK BELT was taking shape and the West Side JEWISH ghetto emerged. It is probably due to this residential patterning that youth GANGS began to protect local turf, that is, physically intimidate outsiders who ventured onto their home ground. In the contemporary city, some gangs continue to defend turf, but to regulate the marketing of illegal products. Politicians also seek to protect or expand their turf in the neighborhoods occupied by constituents.

Larry Bennett

See also: Crime and Chicago's Image; Machine Politics; Politics

Further reading: City of Chicago, Department of City Planning. *Historic City: The Settlement of Chicago.* 1976. • Thrasher, Frederic M. *The Gang.* 1927. • Venkatesh, Sudhir Alladi. "The Gang in the Community." In *Gangs in America,* ed. C. Ronald Huff, 1996.

Turks. Turks constitute a small proportion of Chicago's population, with an estimated total of 5,000 individuals in the 1990s. As a whole, they form a highly educated segment of society, many working in the medical and engineering professions.

Though the largest portion of the current Turkish community descends from post–WORLD WAR II immigration activity, the first Turkish speakers, mostly young men, arrived around the turn of the century, seeking employment in heavy industry. However, calculating the number of Turks who arrived in the United States in general and Chicago in particular prior to WORLD WAR I is difficult. Since they came from the Ottoman Empire, an extensive, multiethnic state, they were often grouped by immigration officials with other Ottoman subjects, including GREEKS, BOSNIANS, ARMENIANS, Kurds, and JEWS, many of whom also spoke Turkish. This ambiguity was compounded further when the officials, confronting a language unlike any they normally dealt with, often changed the names of the Turkish men to something more comprehensible to the English-speaking world. Thus records are difficult to trace on this early group. Of the total of 291,435 Ottoman immigrants recorded by U.S. immigration between 1900 and 1920, best estimates place the Turkish contingent at between 45,000 and 65,000. Most of these were young men from villages in the Anatolian plateau, leaving the Ottoman Empire illegally and planning on staying in the United States for a limited period. A small group of 100 such men sailed into Detroit on the cargo ship *Gulcemal* in 1914, many of these men moving on to Chicago. The majority of these early immigrants actually returned to their homes in Anatolia during or shortly after the end of World War I, but several, including a number of men in Chicago, married American women and stayed.

Shortly after the founding of the Turkish Republic in 1923, Turkish immigration was severely curtailed, with an official quota of 100 Turks allowed into the United States per year, although there were exceptions for spouses of U.S. citizens and certain specialists, such as medical professionals. Beginning in the 1950s, a number of highly educated Turks, this time including women, arrived to enroll in American universities, such as the UNIVERSITY OF CHICAGO and NORTHWESTERN, or to serve in skilled professions, particularly medicine and engineering. Like the first wave of immigrants, many of these students and professionals married into the community and remained in Chicago.

Unlike some immigrant communities, the Turks in Chicago have not tended to reside in certain areas of the city, but in general are scattered through the northwest, including significant groups in NAPERVILLE and HIGHLAND PARK. To serve the needs of the Turkish community, the Turkish American Cultural Alliance was founded in 1964 and by 1968 had opened a cultural center on Harlem Avenue, including a mosque and a weekend Turkish-language school. In addition, Chicago has also been the site of a Turkish consulate since 1948.

James S. Kessler

See also: Demography; Multicentered Chicago; Muslims

Turnvereins. Like their counterparts here and abroad, Chicago's Turnvereins grew out

Turnvereins in Northern Illinois joined together in the 1910s to build a camp in Cary. Turners and their families could vacation there, staying in tents and, later, cabins, and take advantage of lake swimming, boating, hiking, and other athletic activities while getting away from the city. This 1919 postcard shows members participating in an open-air gymnasium. Photographer: Curt Teich & Co. Source: Curt Teich Archives, Lake County Discovery Museum.

of the nineteenth-century liberal GERMAN effort to unite the numerous independent German states into one nation. The Turnvereins were designed to train patriotic citizens of the new republic—not just physically through gymnastics, but also morally and intellectually.

The defeat of the German Revolution of 1848 sent a wave of political exiles abroad, reinforcing the liberal and radical groups already in the United States. Drawing on such immigrants, Chicago's Turners founded their first organization in the mid-1850s.

The political culture of Chicago's Turners changed with the aging of the generation of 1848 and the arrival of new groups of German immigrants. By the late nineteenth century Chicago's Turnvereins ranged from elite clubs to hotbeds of SOCIALISM.

Like German American ethnic culture, Chicago's Turnvereins declined amid the twentieth century's two world wars and the slackening of German immigration. At the end of the twentieth century Turnvereins in AURORA and ELGIN continued to promote cultural education and physical exercise.

John B. Jentz

See also: Creation of Chicago Sports; Fenianism; Fitness and Athletic Clubs; Leisure

Further reading: Barney, Robert K. "Forty-Eighters and the Rise of the Turnverein Movement in America." In *Ethnicity and Sport in North American History and Culture*, ed. George Eisen and David K. Wiggins, 1994, 19–42. • Pumroy, Eric L., and Katja Rampelmann. *Research Guide to the Turner Movement in the United States*. 1996. • Wagner, Ralf. "Turner Societies and the Socialist Tradition." In *German Workers' Culture in the United States, 1850–1920*, ed. Hartmut Keil, 1988, 221–239.

Ugandans. Ugandan immigration to Chicago has taken place in four waves. The first, in the 1960s, comprised primarily students who came to study at the UNIVERSITY OF CHICAGO, LOYOLA UNIVERSITY, and the ILLINOIS INSTITUTE OF TECHNOLOGY. The second wave occurred in the 1970s, as REFUGEES fled Idi Amin's regime. Lutheran and ROMAN CATHOLIC church organizations helped political figures like former Ugandan cabinet member Luyimbazi Zake settle in the Chicago area during this period, establishing Chicago's reputation as a destination for Ugandans seeking asylum. The connection between religious organizations and the Ugandan community remained strong in the late 1970s and early 1980s, when the third wave of immigration brought seminarians and clerics to Chicago to study and serve as pastors for African congregations. Since the 1970s, Ugandans have studied at Mundelein SEMINARY and provided clerical leadership to Catholic and PROTESTANT congregations. In the post-Amin era, people have once again been free to travel in and out of Uganda, encouraging a fourth, economically driven immigration of students and young families.

By the late 1990s, according to leaders of the Chicago-based Midwest Chapter of the Uganda North American Association, the city had developed a reputation as the "Black Republic" of the United States, not only for its concentration of Ugandan immigrants, who at the end of the century numbered about 500, but for the cooperation among African immigrant organizations in addressing the political, legal, economic, and social concerns of refugees, immigrants, and naturalized citizens of African origin.

The tight-knit Ugandan community celebrates weddings and funerals together, as well as the June 3 Ugandan Saints' (or Martyrs') Day. Unlike other African communities such as the LIBERIANS and ANGOLANS, Chicago's Ugandans do not celebrate their Independence Day, owing to what community leaders call "negative associations." Over 60 percent of Chicago's Ugandans are Catholic, and Saints' Day was frequently celebrated at the Ugandan St. Charles Lwanga parish on Garfield Boulevard near the Dan Ryan Expressway, until the church closed in the early 1990s. The holiday is also observed at the various Episcopalian, Lutheran, and Evangelical Protestant churches to which the remaining members of the immigrant community belong.

An estimated 85 percent of Ugandan Chicagoans speak English and Luganda, the language of the Buganda province. They tend to be clustered occupationally in the medical, legal, computer, and civil service or religious professions, although newer, younger immigrants may be students or work in blue-collar jobs. Homeowning Ugandans are concentrated in the south suburbs such as SOUTH HOLLAND, PARK FOREST, CHICAGO HEIGHTS, and COUNTRY CLUB HILLS, while apartment dwellers flock to the pan-African neighborhoods of UPTOWN and EDGEWATER. Although members of the first and second waves of immigrants have traditionally thought of themselves as temporary residents of the United States, later waves have established a strong permanent community, approximately 40 percent of whom had become naturalized American citizens by the end of the twentieth century.

Tracy N. Poe

See also: Demography; Multicentered Chicago

Ukrainian Village, neighborhood in the WEST TOWN Community Area. In the aftermath of the FIRE OF 1871, GERMAN immigrants developed the area bounded by Division, Damen, Chicago, and Western. After the first of wave of UKRAINIAN and RUSSIAN immigration from 1880 to 1910, however, Ukrainians outnumbered other ethnic groups in the neighborhood. By 1930 estimates placed the Chicago Ukrainian population between 25,000 and 30,000, and the majority resided within this small, 160-acre tract.

In contrast to WICKER PARK, Ukrainian Village began as a predominately working-class neighborhood. Many of the area's first residents were craftsmen employed to build the mansions of their wealthy Wicker Park neighbors. Ukrainian Village came to boast many ornate churches, including SS. Volodymyr and Olha, St. Nicholas Ukrainian Catholic Cathedral, and Holy Trinity Orthodox Cathedral, designed by Louis Sullivan.

Although Mayor Jane Byrne designated Ukrainian Village an official neighborhood on January 18, 1983 (the first such designation in the city's history), steady outmigration throughout the latter portion of the twentieth century depleted the Ukrainian population. By 1990, only 2,500 people living in the Ukrainian Village claimed to be of Ukrainian descent, and many of the residents were young white professionals with no Ukrainian heritage. The cultural impact of Ukrainians on this neighborhood, however, was still apparent at the end of the century, evidenced by many institutions, including churches, the Ukrainian Cultural Center, and the Ukrainian National Museum.

Wallace Best

See also: Church Architecture; Eastern Orthodox; Roman Catholics

Further reading: "Ukrainian Village: Ethnic Enclave 'Discovered' by Well-to-Do Outsiders." *Chicago Sun-Times,* February 12, 1982. • Kuropas, Myron. "Ukrainian Chicago." In *Ethnic Chicago,* ed. Melvin G. Holli and Peter d'A. Jones, 1995. • Pacyga, Dominic A., and Ellen Skerrett. *Chicago, City of Neighborhoods: Histories and Tours.* 1986.

Ukrainians. According to the 2000 census, 45,036 residents of the Chicago metropolitan area consider themselves to be of Ukrainian ancestry. Most trace their ancestry back to one of four waves of immigration from what is now western Ukraine and eastern Poland.

The first wave of Ukrainian immigration began in the 1880s and lasted until World War I. It originated among impoverished peasants in eastern Galicia and Subcarpathia, regions of the Austro-Hungarian Empire which had been governed previously by Poland and Hungary but came under Austrian rule by the late eighteenth century. Most of these immigrants identified themselves not as Ukrainians but as Rusyns ("Ruthenians" in English), the customary designation in the Austrian empire. Many immigrants also continued to use more regional identities (Hutsuls, Lemkos or Boykos). Immigrants of this wave originally belonged to the Uniate or Greek Catholic Church, created by Poland's Eastern Orthodox Church in response to the Counter-Reformation. Many immigrants found themselves excluded from the Roman Catholic Church in America and joined the Russian Orthodox Church, which sought to reconvert Uniates. Their descendants gradually began to identify themselves as Russians. Some joined either the Blessed Mother of God parish, Chicago's first Greek Catholic parish, founded in 1902, or St. Nicholas Greek Catholic Church, which was founded in 1905. Soon this church became the center of a Ukrainian neighborhood surrounding the 2300 and 2400 blocks of Chicago Avenue, which has since become known as Ukrainian Village.

A second wave of immigration began after the Austrian empire's collapse. Like the earlier wave, it originated in eastern Galicia and Subcarpathia. However, many second-wave immigrants were educated and had participated in the Ukrainian independence movement that emerged after the Austro-Hungarian and Russian empires collapsed. Although they originated in a region that was now divided between Poland, Romania, Czechoslovakia, and Hungary, these immigrants identified themselves as Ukrainians. By 1930, there were approximately 25,000 to 30,000 Ukrainians in Chicago.

A third wave of immigration began after World War II. This brought an estimated 7,000 to 8,000 wartime refugees from the former Galician-Subcarpathian region, most of which was annexed to Soviet Ukraine in 1939. Although relatively small in number, this wave was considerably better educated than previous waves, and was actively involved in a movement to form an independent Ukrainian state. The network of civic organizations (credit unions, schools, youth groups, choral and dance ensembles) founded or managed by members of this third wave soon began to dominate community life in the Ukrainian Village neighborhood, complementing Chicago's seven Ukrainian Catholic churches, five Ukrainian Orthodox churches, two Carpatho-Rusyn Greek Catholic churches, and one Carpatho-Ruthenian Orthodox church. By the late seventies, Chicago was home to the United States' largest, most concentrated and best organized Ukrainian community with its own professional organizations, senior citizens' home, radio programs, publications, and summer resorts.

A fourth wave of immigration began in the late eighties and originated in the former Soviet republic of Ukraine. Some of these immigrants have integrated into the existing Ukrainian community and have joined churches and civic organizations. Most have not. Not only do they have little time for participating in diaspora organizations, they find that local political and civic leaders are ill-equipped to help them fend for themselves in a new system. Like their predecessors, however, some enterprising recent immigrants have established new businesses and have helped the local community to forge closer ties to newly independent Ukraine.

With almost 14,000 located within city limits and more than 45,000 living within the greater Chicago metropolitan area in 2000, Ukrainian Americans have grown increasingly dispersed in the last two decades, moving further from the West Town neighborhood where they were once concentrated. Just under 2,500 persons living in West Town claimed Ukrainian ancestry in 1990. They were far outnumbered by recent Latin American immigrants, who have constituted West Town's majority population since 1980. Chicago's Ukrainian population now lives outside the Ukrainian Village neighborhood, primarily in Cook, DuPage, and Lake Counties. Nevertheless, this neighborhood's churches, shops, schools, and associations remain the center of community life for Chicago Ukrainians and are often visited by touring performance groups from newly independent Ukraine. Not only is Ukrainian Village the center of associational life for numerous professional and youth organizations, it is also the site of an annual festival. Local organizations as well the Ukrainian Institute of Modern Art and the Ukrainian National Museum host frequent talks, performances, and exhibits by local groups as well as by newly independent Ukraine's leading artists and intellectuals.

Alexandra Hrycak

See also: Belarusians; Czechs and Bohemians; Demography; Hungarians; Lithuanians; Multicentered Chicago; Poles

Further reading: Kuropas, Myron. "Ukrainian Chicago." In *Ethnic Chicago,* ed. Melvin G. Holli and Peter d'A. Jones. 1995. • Markus, Daria, ed. *Ukrainians in Chicago and Illinois.* 1989.

Underground Economy.

The underground economy involves the exchange of goods and services which are hidden from official view. Examples of such activities range from babysitting "off the books" to selling narcotics. Over time, the underground economy has changed as lawmakers redefine what is legal or what is to be taxed. How far "underground" an activity is depends not only on its legal status but also on the capacity of government to enforce laws and/or collect taxes. The underground economy serves willing customers. However, the fact that it is hidden from official view may impose unique costs on participants (e.g., bribes), create opportunities for monopoly, reward a suboptimal scale of operations, or even encourage violence.

Early Chicago's underground economy was limited, for relatively few economic activities were licensed or regulated. Social and economic change led Americans to demand tighter regulation of personal behavior and, later, economic activity. Shortly after the city's founding, some Chicagoans, especially affluent ones of native stock, expressed worry over gambling, vice, and alcohol; the first temperance society was founded in 1833. Nineteenth-century Chicago also attracted disproportionate numbers of young men, many unattached, and many business travelers. In conditions of urban anonymity, commercial gambling, sex, and drinking thrived, despite the law. City officials were reluctant to alienate voters, visitors, or underground entrepreneurs who cultivated them with political support and outright bribery. There were sporadic raids and arrests but no serious attempt to close illegal businesses until the turn of the twentieth century, when the old Levee vice district was closed. On the other hand, proposals for legal, regulated PROSTITUTION made no headway.

By the late nineteenth century, the illegal sector of the underground economy consisted of hundreds of small, mostly owner-operated businesses, primarily brothels and gambling houses. Prostitution was a multimillion-dollar business, and gambling was even more lucrative. Gambling houses thrived in and near the downtown, and specialized VICE DISTRICTS radiated out from rail stations at the edges of the Loop, making little effort at secrecy. Protection from POLICE raids was absolutely essential, and a handful of politicians arranged this.

Meanwhile, the underground economy broadened as businesses whose products were legal evaded new regulations aimed at controlling the emerging industrial economy. For example, despite the enactment of an ambitious BUILDING CODE by the 1870s, vast numbers of small contractors and landlords continued to erect structures and operate them in violation of the code. An 1893 state law prohibited employment of children under 14 in manufacturing, and the law was soon extended. Authorities claimed that 8,543 underage children worked in industry in Illinois cities in 1900. Enforcement was difficult because enforcement agencies were understaffed. Child labor declined most rapidly in large enterprises targeted by inspectors, such as MEATPACKING. Compulsory schooling helped as well, though smaller businesses such as garment makers continued to hire children.

Other products, once legal, became illegal. In 1897, state law restricted opiates, which had been available in ordinary drugstores. Subsequent legislation tightened up access to narcotics, and druggists, drug companies, and doctors gradually conformed to the law. The demand for these DRUGS was intense, and new entrepreneurs appeared. By the 1920s, illegal drug importers and wholesalers were well organized. Small-scale retailers sold to friends and acquaintances, often in established vice areas.

A similar process drove the manufacture and sale of alcoholic beverages underground during national PROHIBITION (1920–1933). Prohibition was the greatest achievement of the constellation of movements to regulate personal behavior deemed immoral. BOOTLEGGING quickly became the largest source of illegal income and jobs. Gross receipts from Chicago BREWERIES, beer distributorships, and LIQUOR importing were estimated at $60 million in 1927.

Bootlegging shows how a business's illegal status could transform its character. The absence of legal property rights to most illegal businesses, and the participants' unwillingness to rely on the police, led to violence. At first bootlegging in Chicago was conducted by numerous independent operators, but it was eventually organized into a cartel that divided sales territories, raised prices, and reduced consumer choice and product quality. Illegal entrepreneurs devoted extraordinary energy and ingenuity to arranging political protection, guarding against hijacking, and murdering rivals. While great wealth was possible, imprisonment was likely and a violent death was not uncommon.

Slot machines, seized in an effort to curtail gambling in Chicago, are destroyed with hammers, 1907. Photographer: Unknown. Source: Chicago Historical Society.

Al Capone's free lunch for the unemployed, 935 South State Street, 1930. Photographer: Unknown. Source: Chicago Historical Society.

Ordinary jobs in this sector were relatively undesirable. Employees were drawn from impoverished neighborhoods, and, in spite of above-average incomes for those neighborhoods, they suffered from violence and arrest, enjoyed few benefits, and (with a few exceptions) had low status. Women recruited by cheap brothels daily risked becoming infected with sexually transmitted diseases.

Class, race, and ethnicity helped determine where illegal businesses located. For instance, when the old vice areas were forced out of the LOOP in the 1910s, sex businesses moved into immigrant and AFRICAN AMERICAN neighborhoods. Because they were politically weak or represented by politicians linked to vice interests, these areas had difficulty keeping out vice. Some illegal businesses were more welcome than others. "Policy" (known elsewhere as the numbers game) was a major source of jobs and of investment capital in African American neighborhoods. Similarly, some less affluent suburbs welcomed or at least tolerated illegal enterprises because they contributed to local tax revenues and created jobs. By contrast, residents of well-to-do areas were more vigilant in enforcing the law, especially Prohibition.

Since the 1930s, the underground economy continued to change as TAXATION and government regulation grew, while its illegal sector began emphasizing new activities. During WORLD WAR II, the federal government rationed hundreds of items and controlled prices. In Chicago and elsewhere, a black market quickly emerged to sell goods in limited supply. More important, the federal government paid for the war by taxing the incomes of most wage and salary earners. After the war, extensive taxation remained, to pay for the war debt and the enlarged size of the federal government, including the military. In the 1970s, the IRS estimated that Americans failed to report at least $100 billion in income, most of it legal income. Other taxes were evaded as well.

Tens of thousands of Chicagoans work for cash that they may not report—babysitters, lawn care workers, even garment workers. Typically they work in small-scale businesses or are self-employed. Some are moonlighting; some are seriously exploited. Tax evasion peaked in the early 1980s, diminishing as the federal government cut tax rates.

Some workers and businesses operate underground to avoid government regulations. For instance, when licensed TAXI cabs failed to provide adequate service to SOUTH SIDE African American neighborhoods in the 1930s and 1940s, unlicensed jitney cab operators filled the gap, plying their trade openly on the streets until MAYOR Martin Kennelly ordered a crackdown. In 1980, an estimated half of all Chicago home-remodeling jobs were completed without required permits. Unlicensed child care providers have met a growing demand for services, evading official requirements concerning facilities.

Beginning in the 1930s, the illegal sector changed as the syndicate formerly headed by Al Capone declined and new syndicates arose. After Prohibition, this syndicate, with its centralized organization and substantial capital, expanded its suburban gambling operations and in late 1940s muscled its way into the independent "policy" gambling operations, dominated by African American entrepreneurs. This "traditional" syndicate lost ground, however. Demand for prostitutes' services diminished, competition from the state lottery and legalized casinos cut into gambling and policy revenues, and courts imprisoned mobsters for tax and other violations.

On the other hand, the demand for narcotics and other controlled substances rose, and the illegal drug business expanded. In the 1950s and '60s, street GANGS such as the Blackstone Rangers began selling illegal drugs. Despite aggressive and successful federal prosecutions beginning in the 1970s, large street gangs remained in the drug business. Their activities spread throughout poor neighborhoods, where legitimate jobs are scarce. Some customers are local, but many came from elsewhere. In more affluent city neighborhoods and suburbs, drug dealing takes different forms, off the street, embedded in social networks where it is very difficult to police.

Perhaps the most unusual part of the underground economy was JANE, a group founded in 1969 by feminists in HYDE PARK to provide abortions. Illinois had banned abortions in 1867, but initially recognized broad exceptions to the ban. As definitions of legal "therapeutic" abortion narrowed and official surveillance increased, abortion providers dwindled in number. Jane was a loosely organized group, operating out of conviction rather than the profit motive. Four years after its founding, the U.S. Supreme Court decriminalized abortion, making it again officially part of the "regular" economy.

Government enforcement capacity grew substantially in the twentieth century, but the underground economy will likely continue to exist. Even with strong public support for law, some enterprises will always engage in illegal activity to meet demand and make a profit. Enforcement is especially difficult when politically effective constituencies are divided over what to define as illegal.

Christopher Thale

See also: Building Trades and Workers; Chicago Crime Commission; Children and the Law; Political Culture; Politics; Work

Further reading: Haller, Mark. "Bootlegging: The Business and Politics of Violence." In *Violence in America*, vol. 1, *The History of Crime*, ed. Ted R. Gurr, 1989. • Johnson, David R. *Policing the Urban Underworld: The Impact of Crime on the Development of the American Police, 1800–1887.* 1979. • Witte, Ann D. "Beating the System?" In *Exploring the Underground Economy*, ed. Susan Pozo, 1996.

Underground Railroad. As the terminus of most Underground Railroad routes originating in Illinois towns bordering the Mississippi and Ohio Rivers, Chicago was a hub of antislavery activity. Workers provided lodging or transportation and were sometimes personally involved in rescue efforts. Participants included physician C. V. Dyer, wealthy merchant John Jones, women's rights advocate Mary Richardson Jones, pharmacist Philo Carpenter, early black homeowners Joseph and Anna Hudlun, educator Eliza Porter, members of the Liberty Association vigilance committee, detective Allan Pinkerton, businessman Henry O. Wagoner, attorneys L. C. Paine Freer and Calvin DeWolf, and pastors and members of Quinn Chapel AME, OLIVET BAPTIST, First Presbyterian, and First Baptist Congregational churches.

Prior to the Fugitive Slave Act of 1850, enslaved AFRICAN AMERICANS who began their perilous journeys in Missouri, Kentucky, and Tennessee found Chicago to be a relatively safe destination. Although the Illinois Black Codes denied them full citizenship rights, they opened businesses or hired out their services performing tasks for which they had been uncompensated while in bondage.

After passage of the Fugitive Slave Act slavecatchers abducted black people even if they had certificates of freedom. Black and white ABOLITIONISTS converged on the Chicago Common Council to protest Senator Stephen A. Douglas' support of this bill. Subsequently many black Chicagoans emigrated to Canada where they could be protected under British law.

Glennette Tilley Turner

See also: Civil Rights Movements; Great Migration

Further reading: Illinois Writers' Project. "Negro in Illinois" Papers. Vivian G. Harsh Research Collection, Chicago Public Library, Chicago, IL. • Muelder, Hermann R. *Fighters for Freedom: The History of the Anti-slavery Activities of Men and Women Associated with Knox College.* 1959. • Turner, Glennette Tilley. *The Underground Railroad in Illinois.* 2001.

John and Mary Jones: Early Civil Rights Activists

John and Mary Jones arrived in Illinois in 1844 and found a wide range of laws which restricted the freedoms of African American residents. The couple worked tirelessly in Chicago during the late 1840s and 1850s against slavery and the Illinois Black Laws. A few years after the abolition of slavery and the end of the Black Laws in 1865, John Jones was elected a Cook County commissioner and fought segregation in public SCHOOLS. In 1955, their granddaughter Theodora Purnell described Mary Jones's role:

> She was mistress of the home where Nathan Freer, John Brown, Frederick Douglass and Allen Pinkerton visited. She harbored and fed the fugitive slaves that these men brought to her door as a refuge until they could be transported to Canada. In fact she stood at my Grand-father's side—her husband John Jones—when their early Chicago home became one of the Underground Railway Stations. She it was who stood guard at the door when these pioneer abolitionists were in conference—with the slaves huddled below in her basement.
>
> She was a pioneer in the initial Suffrage Movement and was hostess to Susan B. Anthony, Carrie Chatman Catt, Emma Chandler and Mrs. John Brown.

Letter by Theodora Lee Purnell, September 2, 1955. John Jones Collection, Chicago Historical Society.

Unemployment. Great turbulence, marked by periods of economic dislocation and grassroots movements for social insurance programs, has characterized Chicago's unemployment history. In 1819, Illinois enacted poor laws that provided for overseers of the poor. However, recurrent panics brought unemployment and poverty so severe as to require municipal attention. In the depression of 1857, 20,000 Chicago workers and their dependents faced starvation, and relief was inadequate. On Christmas Day, in the depression year of 1873, POLICE dispersed crowds of unemployed begging for food at the RELIEF AND AID SOCIETY.

Four years later, during the "great" RAILROAD STRIKE, unemployed workers joined strikers to battle police and U.S. troops. The

American Federation of Labor Convention in Chicago in 1893 resolved that the government had a duty to provide jobs when economic conditions, like then, made them difficult to find. In the spring of 1894, Jacob Coxey, an Ohio businessman and reformer, organized the jobless into "Coxey's Army" and led a march on Washington DC. Declaring Coxey a "demagogue," the Chicago Tribune (April 24, 1894) editorialized that "action must be taken at once to suppress" his movement. That call was followed by two decades of intermittent violence and confrontation between Chicago police and the unemployed. During these same years, however, police stations provided shelter to hundreds of thousands of homeless people, many of them unemployed workers.

In 1899, Illinois became the fifth state to establish a State Employment Service. Compulsory unemployment insurance became an objective of reformers. A committee at the University of Chicago sponsored by the American Association for Labor Legislation called in 1912 for a state or national unemployment insurance program.

Labor's agitation for the abolition of unemployment was the strongest in Illinois, where the Illinois Federation of Labor and the powerful Chicago Federation of Labor, under the progressive leadership of John Fitzpatrick, formed the core for a local, state, and national labor party movement. In the spring of 1919, Chicago leaders ran state and local tickets on a reform manifesto called "Labor's Fourteen Points," which demanded full pay for the jobless and comprehensive social insurance.

Unions also attempted to set up their own system of unemployment insurance between 1919 and 1928, as the Amalgamated Clothing Workers of America and the International Ladies' Garment Workers' Union adopted progressive unemployment insurance plans. The depression of 1920–22 terminated these "Chicago Plan" developments, but the unions managed to pay reduced unemployment insurance through the mid-1930s.

The stock market crash of 1929 brought new turmoil and organization. Almost half a million in Illinois were unemployed by the end of 1930. By mid-1932, the Communist-led Chicago Workers Committee on Unemployment had organized 25,000 jobless in 60 locals to fight for jobs and adequate relief. They marched on relief stations in the city and in industrial suburbs like Melrose Park. Early in 1933, the unemployed planned a statewide hunger march to Springfield. More than a thousand relief demonstrators from Chicago and Rockford formed a cavalcade of automobiles and trucks ultimately repulsed by state police.

Despite this burgeoning right-to-work movement, there was no nationwide organization of the unemployed until April 1936, when the Workers Alliance of America was formed, merging with the Unemployed Council, the Unemployed League, and some independent organizations. The alliance's protest activities served to support increased appropriations for the New Deal's work programs, such as the Works Progress Administration (WPA), created by executive order of the president on May 6, 1935.

The Wagner-Peyser Act (1933) established the federal-state system of public employment services and the Veterans' Employment Service. The Social Security Act of 1935 mandated unemployment insurance in the United States. Illinois was the last state to adopt the unemployment insurance law in 1937.

Unemployment nationally dropped to an all-time recorded low of less than 2 percent during World War II. Postwar national economic stabilization policies prevented massive unemployment, but joblessness remained a major problem, especially as the burden of

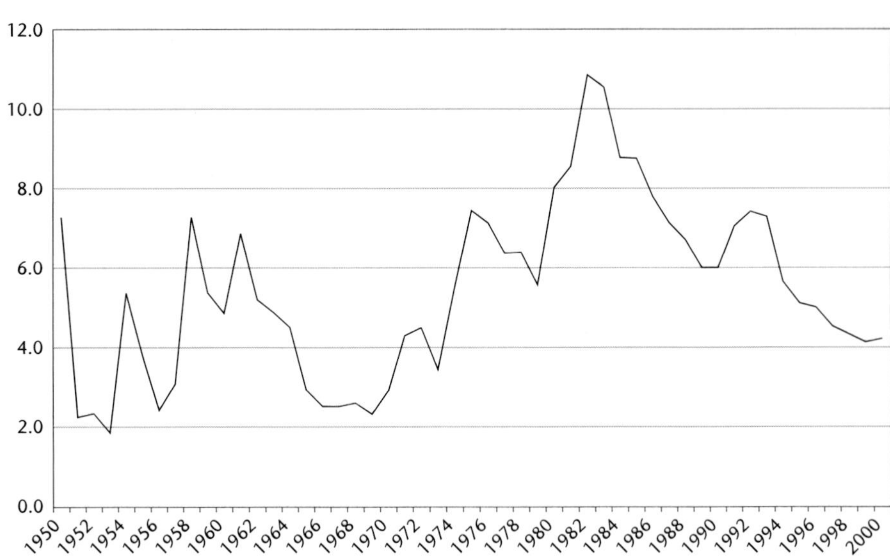

Chicago area unemployment, 1950–2000. Sources: Illinois Department of Labor and Illinois Department of Economic Security.

Thousands of unemployed demonstrating near Monroe and Sangamon, 1932. Photographer: Keller. Source: Chicago Historical Society.

unemployment shifted. Relatively fewer workers were out of work, but for longer spells, and young people and minorities were increasingly affected. Their plight was cited as a major factor behind rioting during the 1960s; federally funded jobs programs mitigated the problem but failed to solve it. Limited education, inadequate transportation, and persistent hiring discrimination have brought substantial long-term unemployment to many minority communities, causing high poverty rates, housing abandonment, and other problems. Economic downturns in the 1970s and 1980s exacerbated these problems, which, coupled with technological innovation and foreign competition, devastated some long-established Chicago industries and the industries dependent on them. The unemployment rate in GARY in 1990, for instance, was 17 percent. In September 2002, 261,600 workers were unemployed in metropolitan Chicago, or 6.3 percent of the civilian workforce.

Alan Harris Stein

See also: Business of Chicago; Iron- and Steelworkers; Packinghouse Unions; Railroad Workers; Work; Work Culture

Further reading: Folsom, Franklin. *Impatient Armies of the Poor: The Story of Collective Action of the Unemployed, 1808–1942.* 1991. • Nelson, Daniel. *Unemployment Insurance: The American Experience, 1915–1935.* 1969. • Rosenzweig, Roy. "Organizing the Unemployed: The Early Years of the Great Depression, 1929–1933." *Radical America* 10 (July–August 1976).

Union, IL, McHenry County, 53 miles NW of the Loop. Platted in 1851 as a station on the Galena & Chicago Union RAILROAD, the village failed to prosper. Incorporated in 1897, Union remained a small trading center. It is home to the MCHENRY COUNTY Historical Society and the Illinois Railway Museum. The population in 2000 was 576.

Craig L. Pfannkuche

See also: Transportation

Further reading: *McHenry County in the Twentieth Century, 1968–1994.* McHenry County Historical Society. 1994. • Nye, Lowell A., ed. *McHenry County, Illinois, 1832–1968.* 1968.

Unionization. Chicago's historic reputation as a "labor town" is somewhat misleading. Workers have built some of the strongest organizations in the country, but unions have often struggled for life against well-organized, militant employers, and racial and ethnic diversity has shaped the movement's character as much as the dynamics of social class. How do we explain the broader patterns of labor organization in terms of the city's distinctive characteristics? What factors contributed to the rise, changing character, and decline of the movement, and what are its prospects at the dawning of a new century?

With the shifting composition of its working-class population and the diversity of its metropolitan economy, Chicago has presented both enormous challenges and special advantages for labor organizers. Heavy immigration from the mid-nineteenth century through the early 1920s, and then again in the postwar era and especially after the Immigration Act of 1965, required labor to carry its message in diverse languages to people from vastly different cultures. Likewise, the GREAT MIGRATION of black southerners, immigration from Mexico and other Latin American nations, PUERTO RICAN migration, and the influx of East and South Asian immigrants in the late twentieth century have forced organizers to confront race issues for most of the movement's history. Yet racial and ethnic minorities have often played key roles in building and transforming the movement.

The city's largest employers in the late nineteenth and first half of the twentieth century were building CONSTRUCTION and maintenance companies, RAILROADS, and a range of manufacturing concerns characterized by increasing concentration in a few large firms—slaughtering and MEATPACKING, metalworking, garment manufacturing, IRON AND STEEL production, LUMBER and woodworking, electrical manufacturing, and a variety of FOOD PROCESSING factories. Chicago also built a large PRINTING and PUBLISHING industry and, as a corporate, legal, and medical center, claimed an increasingly large population of white-collar and technical workers beginning in the late nineteenth century. Such variety led to the conventional wisdom that "anyone can make a living in Chicago," but it also required that any successful labor movement embrace a diverse range of workers. Immigrants and workers of color often have been more difficult to organize, not because of any intrinsic qualities, but because they have tended to be among the least skilled and the poorest paid—and as such particularly vulnerable in periods of economic crisis and employers' offensives.

One of the Chicago movement's distinctions, then, was that well into the mid-twentieth century it generated considerable power amid this social, cultural, and occupational complexity. Another was the movement's division between conservative and often corrupt elements, concentrated disproportionately in the Building Trades Council, and progressive, often radical elements. In the late nineteenth century the radicals were represented above all by the GERMAN-speaking Marxists; in the early twentieth century, by the mainstream labor progressives around CHICAGO FEDERATION OF LABOR (CFL) president John Fitzpatrick; and in the GREAT DEPRESSION and war years, by the activists involved in the creation of the new CONGRESS OF INDUSTRIAL ORGANIZATIONS (CIO) unions. Such progressives provided the movement with an aggressive, innovative leadership that helps to explain organized labor's relative success in Chicago. They were particularly important in expanding the movement to those otherwise left behind—women, the unskilled, and racial minorities.

John Fitzpatrick and the CFL

John Fitzpatrick played a prominent role in the struggle to oust gangsters from the Chicago Federation of Labor (CFL), gaining support from middle-class progressives and reformers throughout the city. Elected president of the CFL in 1904, he held this office, with one brief interruption, until his death of a heart attack in 1946.

Born in Ireland, Fitzpatrick immigrated to the United States in 1882. He worked for three years in the stockyards before apprenticing as a blacksmith, joining the International Union of Journeymen Horseshoers, and smithing for more than a decade, during which time he became increasingly active in the local labor movement.

Fitzpatrick's most intense activism was during WORLD WAR I. Under his leadership, the CFL oversaw mass organizing drives in the steel and meatpacking industries and supported the effort to UNIONIZE female teachers and clerical workers. Fitzpatrick welcomed all workers into the CFL, utilizing their organizational talents and muting the inevitable factional disputes that arose. Thoroughly committed to the interests of the working class as a whole, Fitzpatrick made the CFL one of the more dynamic and powerful local labor bodies in the country.

Rick Halpern

As elsewhere, skilled workers led the move to permanent organization. In the 1850s and 1860s, printers, shipwrights and caulkers, iron molders, machinists and blacksmiths, and others established craft unions that were often linked to some of the earliest national organizations. By the late 1860s Chicago workers supported more than 20 unions aimed at higher wages and shorter working hours; a lively newspaper, the *Workingman's Advocate;* numerous producers' cooperatives; and a network of EIGHT HOUR Leagues which organized in municipal, state, and congressional elections, winning both city and state eight-hour laws. As with later legislative successes, however, the laws worked only where unions were strong enough to enforce them, a rare scenario during the 1873–77 depression.

Until the 1880s, the city's unskilled—IRISH, Bohemian, and POLISH lumber shovers, brickyard workers, coal heavers, and construction and track laborers—found their voice only sporadically, often in violent STRIKES and riots, as in the 1877 RAILROAD STRIKE. The "Great

Upheaval" of the mid-1880s brought a dramatic expansion of unionism among virtually all occupations, including craftsmen. The big breakthrough, however, came in the organization of the Irish and other unskilled workers in the ranks of the Knights of Labor, by far the largest and most important late-nineteenth-century labor reform movement. As craftsmen poured into the Knights' trade assemblies and laborers into its mixed assemblies, the movement grew from 2,300 in 1882 to more than 40,000 by 1886. Led by Elizabeth Rodgers, the Knights also organized thousands of women. Working together, the radical Central Labor Union's German and Bohemian socialists and anarcho-syndicalists, the immigrant and native-born craftsmen in the mainstream Trades and Labor Assembly, and the Knights created perhaps the strongest and most radical movement in the United States. They sponsored labor newspapers in various languages, a vibrant cooperative movement, and a United Labor Party which seemed poised to win control of the city government. More than 40,000 joined a general strike for the eight-hour day in May 1886, and throughout the world Chicago became a great symbol of labor solidarity.

A number of factors explain the destruction of this movement. First, a series of crushing defeats, particularly among the unskilled in the stockyards and elsewhere, reversed the movement's expansion. Second, internal conflicts, especially within the Knights of Labor, eviscerated the movement's vitality. Finally, the radical socialist and anarchist wing, especially strong in Chicago and a key to the organization of unskilled immigrants, was decimated in the political repression following the events at Haymarket Square in 1886. By 1887 many of the radicals were in prison, blacklisted, or dead, while the Knights had shrunk to 17,000 members.

A new movement emerged in the 1890s. While the Knights lost 75 percent of their membership between 1886 and 1887 and the revolutionary organizations were badly disrupted, many of the craft unions survived. The new American Railway Union emerged to organize both skilled and unskilled in the early 1890s. Greater federation through the formation of the Building Trades Council (1890) and the Chicago Federation of Labor (CFL, 1896) brought more planning and coordination and an era of effective sympathy strikes. Thus, the movement emerged from the historic defeat of the Pullman Boycott in 1894 and the depression of the 1890s with renewed strength. At the turn of the century, organization spread once again to the less skilled—in the stockyards and steel plants, in machine shops, in candy, garment, and box factories, among scrubwomen, waitresses, and teachers. By the end of 1903, 245,000, more than half of the city's workers, were affiliated with the CFL, including 35,000 women in 26 different occupations. Strikes mushroomed amid new calls for a shorter workday. Federation leaders claimed that theirs was the "best organized city in the world."

Yet much of this movement, particularly among the unskilled, had been destroyed by 1905. In the building and metal trades, among transport owners and garment manufacturers, and elsewhere, well-organized employers declared their establishments open shops and waged war on the city's unions. Spectacular lockouts in the midst of heavy unemployment in 1904 weakened organization among the skilled and extinguished it among immigrant laborers in meatpacking and other factories around the city. Except for the clothing and garment industry, where strikes in 1909 and 1910 led to the expansion of the International Ladies Garment Workers Union (ILGWU) and the foundation of the Amalgamated Clothing Workers of America (ACWA) in 1910, new organization was minimal until World War I.

The CFL attracted national attention again from 1917 to 1919, spawning successful national organizing drives in both steel and meatpacking and launching the Cook County Labor Party, the linchpin for the national labor party movement of the postwar years. Again, a combination of mainline progressives around CFL president John Fitzpatrick and secretary Edward Nockels with syndicalists and other radicals associated with William Z. Foster provided much of the leadership for these movements, and they made special efforts to integrate immigrant and African American laborers. Political repression in the form of the Red Scare (1919–1922), however, along with unemployment, the Race Riot of 1919, and a powerful employers' open-shop drive employing court injunctions, lockouts, and blacklists, shattered the movement. While organization persisted under fire throughout the 1920s in the building trades, among other craftsmen, and on the railroads, most of the breakthroughs among the unskilled in basic industries were eradicated by 1922, and political innovation stagnated for most of the next decade.

One important community of workers was largely absent from this movement even at its height. While it reached out to unskilled immigrant women as well as men, Chicago's labor movement largely excluded or segregated African Americans. There were important exceptions, as in the garment and meatpacking industries, but on the eve of World War I, more than a third of the CFL's constituent unions excluded blacks entirely or segregated them into Jim Crow locals. Many other unions practiced more subtle forms of discrimination. The cynicism among black workers that grew from such experiences created a serious problem once the massive migration of the war years and the 1920s created a large black labor force in meatpacking, steel, and elsewhere. The ultimate destruction of promising

A parade of women support strikers on West Jackson Boulevard near Morgan Street, 1910. The United Garment Workers strike began in September of that year and continued until early February of 1911, shortly after an agreement was signed with Hart, Schaffner & Marx but while over 20,000 garment workers were still on strike against their employers. Photographer: Unknown. Source: Chicago Historical Society.

organizations in basic industry during the 1919–1922 era can be explained largely in terms of postwar unemployment and another aggressive open-shop campaign, but the unions' unsuccessful efforts to integrate the black migrants helps to account for the relative weakness of Chicago unions during the 1920s and the early Depression years. Industrial organization emerged in meatpacking, steel, AGRICULTURAL MACHINERY manufacturing, and elsewhere only in the late 1930s and during WORLD WAR II, when the new CIO unions stressed CIVIL RIGHTS in strenuous organizing campaigns among African Americans, MEXICANS, and other minority workers. In turn, these workers provided some of the strongest bases of support for the new industrial unions. Yet some building trade unions continued to discriminate long after the civil rights legislation of the mid-1960s and were forced to integrate only through federal government pressure and protests from the Coalition of Black Trade Unionists and other local groups.

The story of Chicago's building trade unions represents many of the strengths and weaknesses of Chicago labor. Strong craft organizations flourished in a decentralized industry where technological limits and a series of building booms created a persistent demand for skilled manual labor. By the end of the nineteenth century more than a score of unions had federated into a powerful Building Trades Council (BTC), which coordinated a complex range of work rules and crippling sympathetic strikes on sites throughout the city. Federated contractors copied the model, launching lockouts in 1900 and 1921, but union control persisted. In some trades, union power came along with graft and collusion. Most building trades became closely allied with the emerging DEMOCRATIC political MACHINE and several with organized crime. Throughout most of the twentieth century, conservative leaders from the building trades excluded women and minorities from their lucrative apprenticeship programs and dueled with progressive elements in the CFL.

The initiative for the new CIO unions of the late 1930s and the World War II era lay in some of the older and more progressive AFL unions, notably the ILGWU and ACWA, which had completely organized the clothing industry by the mid 1930s; and among radical rank-and-file organizations, notably affiliates of the Communist Trade Union Unity League, in steel, farm implement, furniture, and electrical manufacturing and in meatpacking and other food processing plants. By 1939, the Packing House Workers Organizing Committee (PWOC, later the United Packinghouse Workers of America—CIO [UPWA]) had organized the giant Armour plant and built a membership of 7,550, or about 40 percent of the Chicago industry's workers. As in packing, the Steel Workers' Organizing Committee (SWOC, later the United Steel Workers of America—CIO [USWA]) had one major breakthrough in the late 1930s—U.S. Steel and its subsidiaries in 1937. In May of that year, however, SWOC faced a major setback in its campaign to organize the independent "Little Steel" firms when police killed 10 workers and wounded dozens of others in the "MEMORIAL DAY MASSACRE" at Republic Steel. This violence and a return of unemployment in the period from 1937 to 1939 slowed the organizing, and SWOC ended the 1930s with a membership of less than 21,000, about one-third of the region's steelworkers. Other CIO beachheads were established when the Farm Equipment Workers (FE) won representation rights at the giant INTERNATIONAL HARVESTER plant (6,300 workers) and the United Electrical Workers (UE) won contracts in a number of electrical manufacturing plants.

As late as the beginning of the Second World War, Chicago's labor movement was still dominated by the AFL unions, which had a 1939 membership of over 330,000 compared to the CIO's 60,000. The new industrial unions benefited, however, from a massive increase in defense production and federal policies that facilitated union formation and expansion during World War II. USWA District 31 grew from 18,000 in 1940 to 100,000 in 1945 and the UPWA, FE, and UE all experienced comparable expansion, as did the ILGWU and ACWA.

Following a massive strike wave in 1946–47 involving more than 2.5 million workdays lost, labor relations stabilized, but union fortunes remained uneven in the postwar period. Mayor Richard J. Daley's tenure (1955–1976) is often thought of as a golden age for organized labor, and, in fact, with the economy booming and collective bargaining largely accepted by employers, most unions thrived. The politically well-connected building trades prospered most. In the midst of a sustained boom in building construction, construction journeymen enjoyed a 250 percent increase in real wages between 1945 and 1980. Signs of trouble emerged as early as the late 1950s, however, with the gradual decline of manufacturing employment, a trend that accelerated in the next two decades. Moreover, the high-wage, unionized manufacturing industries were declining just as large numbers of African Americans and Latinos were entering the city's labor force. Major strikes reemerged in the late 1960s and 1970s, and the labor movement was clearly in decline by the time of Daley's death in 1976.

In the same years, however, changes in state law and in Chicago's occupational structure and the racial and ethnic composition of its population led to a dramatic transformation. As older manufacturing-based unions like the UPWA, USWA, and the garment workers' unions declined as a result of technological change and low-wage competition abroad, government and service workers created a new movement. Public employees poured into the American Federation of State, County, and Municipal Employees (AFSCME), and health care and service workers, into the Service Employees International Union (SEIU). These industries included large numbers of women, African Americans, and Latinos. By 1980 nearly half of all Chicago truck drivers were black or Latino, while minority representation in the Teamsters warehouse and other locals tended to be much higher. In the same years, SEIU Local 73, with 18,000 HEALTH CARE WORKERS, became the largest AFL-CIO local union in the state.

Women have been active in the city's labor movement at least since the formation of the Chicago Working Women's Union (CWWU) in the mid-1870s and were instrumental in efforts to organize the clothing trades and other industries with substantial female labor forces. The growing proportion of women in the labor force after World War II, however, together with the shift in the city's occupational WORK structure from industrial to service and CLERICAL jobs, the rise of feminism over the past three decades, and the subsequent struggles for women's rights, all have created a larger and more important role for women in the local movement during the second half of the twentieth century. Chicago activists have also played important roles in the national movement. A long legacy of women's activism—from the CWWU, through the Knights and the WOMEN'S TRADE UNION LEAGUE, to CIO industrial unions and early efforts to organize clerical and service workers—made Chicago the natural birthplace of the National Coalition of Labor Union Women (CLUW) in 1974. CLUW has pursued not only better wages and working conditions but also broader social issues and the special needs of working women, including child care.

The challenges facing Chicago labor are those facing workers throughout the United States—and the same ones they have faced in the past. Will unions be able to integrate wage earners from vastly different backgrounds on the basis of class solidarity? Can they develop new forms of organization and protest better suited to the technological and occupational facts of the twenty-first century than the old craft or industrial unions and the traditional strike? Answers to these questions will emerge within the context of Chicago's historic reputation as a labor town, its progressive political heritage, and the striking diversity of its working-class population.

James R. Barrett

See also: Antiunionism; Business of Chicago; Iron- and Steelworkers; Packinghouse Unions; Pullman Strike; Work Culture

Further reading: Derber, Milton. *Labor in Illinois: The Affluent Years, 1945–80.* 1989. • Newell, Barbara.

Agnes Nestor and the WTUL

Agnes Nestor was a founder and officer of the International Glove Workers Union of America (IGWU) and president of the Chicago Women's Trade Union League (WTUL). Born in Grand Rapids, Michigan, Nestor moved to Chicago in 1897 and worked as a glovemaker. She led women in a successful strike by Chicago glovemakers in 1901. This strike spurred the formation of the IGWU, which secured higher wages and better conditions for workers in Chicago and the nation. Nestor was president of the IGWU from 1913 to 1916 and vice president from 1916 to 1939.

Nestor also organized overworked and underpaid women workers in Illinois through the Chicago WTUL, which she headed from 1913 to 1948. Her most important achievement, however, was the 1909 state law limiting work for women to 10 hours per day. She led the successful lobbying effort against fierce opposition from Illinois businessmen. Nestor also believed that workers needed education to counteract their mind-numbing labor, and she developed programs of courses through the WTUL and the Chicago Federation of Labor. She served on many government advisory boards and helped to craft the Smith-Hughes Act of 1917, which provided the first federal aid for vocational education.

Susan E. Hirsch

Chicago and the Labor Movement: Metropolitan Unionism in the 1930s. 1961. • Schneirov, Richard. *Labor and Urban Politics: Class Conflict and the Origins of Modern Liberalism in Chicago, 1864–1897.* 1998.

Union Stock Yard. The Union Stock Yard opened on Christmas Day 1865. Operated by the Union Stock Yard & Transit Co., the 475-acre market located at Exchange and Halsted Streets in the New City Community Area consolidated several small stockyards. In the mid-1870s major packers located next to the stockyard and remained until the late 1950s.

The stockyard owed its origins to innovations in railroad transportation. In turn, direct sales from breeders to packers, the emergence of interstate trucking, and the resulting decentralization of the meat industry brought its decline. The market closed on August 1, 1971, after handling more than one billion animals. By the end of the century the stockyard site was home to the city's most successful industrial park.

Dominic A. Pacyga

See also: Back of the Yards; Meatpacking; Packinghouse Unions

Further reading:Holt, Glen E., and Dominic A. Pacyga. *Chicago: A Historical Guide to the Neighborhoods: The Loop and South Side.* 1979. • Wade, Louise C. *Chicago's Pride: Packingtown and Environs in the Nineteenth Century.* 1987.

United Center. The United Center opened on West Madison Avenue in 1994, replacing the Chicago Stadium as the home of the Bulls (National Basketball Association) and the Blackhawks (National Hockey League). In addition to professional and college sports, the United Center has hosted figure skating, circuses, concerts, and the 1996 Democratic National Convention.

Blackhawks owner William Wirtz and Bulls owner Jerry Reinsdorf provided $175 million to build the arena, which seats between 20,500 and 25,000 depending on the event. At 960,000 square feet, the United Center was the largest arena in the United States at the end of the 1990s.

Daniel Greene

See also: Leisure; Near West Side; Places of Assembly; Political Conventions

United Charities. United Charities of Chicago (UCC), one of the city's most visible charitable organizations, is a direct descendant of Chicago's first citywide charity association, the Chicago Relief and Aid Society (CRA), founded in 1850–51 and reorganized in 1867. The CRA attempted to bring most charitable organizations under its purview after 1871, but it enjoyed limited success because many associations did not wish to cede decision-making authority to a centralized body.

In 1894, during a severe depression that increased the depth and breadth of poverty, the Central Relief Association was formed to give Chicago's poor an alternative to the CRA, which was roundly criticized for parsimonious relief efforts and for its contention that poverty reflected moral rather than economic or social problems. The Central Relief Association, renamed the Chicago Bureau of Charities (CBC) in 1896, understood poverty as a product of a flawed social and economic system as opposed to a manifestation of moral lassitude and thus sought to provide a broader range of social services than mere relief. It also began to use its resources to reform the economy and society.

In 1909, the CRA, succumbing to criticism, merged with the CBC to form United Charities of Chicago. UCC elaborated on the CBC tradition of working simultaneously to reform economic and social conditions and to provide services to the needy. It developed a systematic approach to giving, designed to eliminate need through cooperation and improved methods of social provision. By the 1920s, UCC deemphasized economic reform, instead stressing social services designed to help people cope with a rapidly changing society and engaging in public policy study and advocacy.

Since the creation and augmentation of the American welfare state during the Great Depression of the 1930s, UCC has become an important partner with many levels of government and other service agencies, providing direction and expertise to the social service effort throughout metropolitan Chicago. UCC operates an array of social services, including legal aid, family counseling, and help for the aged, helping thousands of persons and families cope with crises every year.

Scott Lien

See also: Catholic Charities; Charity Organization Societies; Philanthropy; Relief and Subsistence Aid

Further reading: Bowen, Louise de Koven. *Growing Up with a City.* 1926. • Kusmer, Kenneth L. "The Functions of Organized Charity in the Progressive Era: Chicago as a Case Study." *Journal of American History* 60 (December 1973): 657–678. • McCarthy, Kathleen D. *Noblesse Oblige: Charity and Cultural Philanthropy in Chicago, 1849–1929.* 1982.

United Neighborhood Organization. Established in 1980, the United Neighborhood Organization of Chicago (UNO) is a service organization that aims to empower and improve the quality of life for Chicago's low-income Latino residents, focusing primarily on the issues of education, citizenship, and homeownership. UNO's organizers, including Daniel Solis, hoped it would become a voice for Chicago's Latino community.

UNO's voice in Chicago's public schools has continued to grow since the group began lobbying for the West Side Technical Institute in 1986. Eventually the school opened in 1996 to provide job training for West Side residents. The organization also promotes parental involvement in schools and has influence in issues such as school board membership and public school repairs.

Amidst the environment of immigration reform in the mid-1980s, UNO began to organize citizenship and voter registration initiatives that by 1996 had generated over 36,000 new voters in Chicago. In 1986, Congress passed the Immigration Reform and Control Act (IRCA), which gave amnesty in the form of temporary residency to millions of immigrants who had been living in the United States prior to 1982 and allowed them to apply eventually for U.S. citizenship. In 1987 and 1988, almost 120,000 illegal immigrants in Chicago applied for amnesty under IRCA, many taking advantage of local amnesty sign-up locations and information sessions often coordinated by UNO. In 1992, UNO began sponsoring citizenship drives to help eligible immigrants apply for citizenship by fingerprinting and photographing applicants and helping them fill out application forms. UNO also helps coordinate large swearing-in ceremonies and encourages new citizens to contribute to their communities by registering to vote and investing in homes.

Amy T. Peterson

See also: Americanization; Hondurans; Mexicans; Neighborhood Associations; Nicaraguans; Puerto Ricans; Salvadorans; Social Services

Further reading: Jackson, David. "Give Us Your Tired, Your Poor, Your Votes: Drive for New Citizens Creates New Democrats." *Chicago Tribune,* August 27, 1996. • Poe, Janita. "Potential Citizens Begin Task: Cicero Drive Attracts 200." *Chicago Tribune,* September 12, 1994, Metro West section, 1.

U.S. Cellular Field. *See* Comiskey Park

Universities and Their Cities. Locating the University of Illinois, a public university, in Urbana in 1867 left the work of college founding in Chicago to religious denominations and to local boosters and patrons. Methodists opened NORTHWESTERN UNIVERSITY (1850); Presbyterians founded LAKE FOREST COLLEGE (1857); the Evangelical Association (later the United Methodist Church) founded Plainfield College (1861; moved to Naperville in 1870 and renamed NORTH CENTRAL COLLEGE in 1926); Wesleyans founded WHEATON COLLEGE (1860); and Baptists established the first UNIVERSITY OF CHICAGO (1857–1886). ROMAN CATHOLICS established SAINT XAVIER (1846), BARAT (1858; merged with DePaul, 2001), St. Ignatius (1870; renamed LOYOLA UNIVERSITY, 1909), St. Vincent's (1898; renamed DEPAUL UNIVERSITY, 1907), and Mundelein (1930; merged with Loyola, 1991).

New graduate, professional, and extension divisions fulfilled late-nineteenth-century university aspirations. The reborn University of Chicago (1892) opened schools of commerce, education, law, and medicine. Northwestern opened a school of commerce (1908) and a graduate division (1910). DePaul and Loyola added professional divisions to retain Catholic students but offered little graduate work. Lake Forest, facing intensified competition, decided to focus on the liberal arts and to sever its loose affiliations with several professional schools located in Chicago. Private dominance confined public higher education to Chicago Normal College (1867), administered by the Chicago Board of Education—a competitor for extension students with University College of the University of Chicago. Crane Junior COLLEGE, Chicago's first public two-year college, opened in 1911 and grew to three branches during the GREAT DEPRESSION.

Chicago's private universities celebrated their urban location. "Urban universities are in the truest sense national universities," argued University of Chicago president William R. Harper, because "the great cities represent national life in its fullness and its variety." Private universities proffered scholarship and service to the city in return for political and philanthropic support. Professors examined Chicago's growth, SETTLEMENT HOUSE life, immigrant family structure, educational structure, and criminal justice system; they advocated political reform, urban planning, PUBLIC HEALTH measures, economic development, and efficient public and nonprofit administration.

Direct service complemented applied scholarship. Nearly a quarter of University of Chicago professors and 15 percent of Northwestern professors participated in reform movements between 1892 and 1919. Harper served on the Chicago school board and chaired an 1898 school commission advocating a professionalized school superintendency. Philosophy professor George Herbert Mead and education professors Charles H. Judd and Ella Flagg Young, later Chicago's school superintendent, continued the battle. The PROGRESSIVE EDUCATION theories of John Dewey, founder of the University of Chicago's Department of Education, reverberated through Robert Havighurst's 1964 evaluation of the Chicago SCHOOLS, in Edgar Epps's school board membership in the 1970s, and in Anthony Bryk's and Gary Orfield's 1980s initiatives on behalf of public school reform.

In the 1890s, Northwestern and the University of Chicago established settlement houses in WEST TOWN and near the stockyards in the NEW CITY community area, respectively. Sophonisba P. Breckenridge and Edith Abbott, mainstays of the Chicago School of Civics and Philanthropy, which merged with the University of Chicago, maintained close ties to Jane Addams and HULL HOUSE. Charles R. Henderson, after helping to found the Bureau of Charities with fellow University of Chicago sociologist Albion Small, oversaw its professionalization as the UNITED CHARITIES of Chicago and led movements for workers' compensation and prison reform. University of Chicago sociologist Robert E. Park was president of the Chicago URBAN LEAGUE.

Alderman Charles Merriam, a University of Chicago political scientist, exposed corruption and promoted city planning, social welfare, and criminal justice. But he failed to win the 1911 mayoral election or the 1919 Republican mayoral primary. Other University of Chicago professors held elective office: philosopher T. V. Smith was a state senator; economist Paul H. Douglas was Fifth Ward alderman and U.S. Senator.

University of Chicago faculty shifted from local improvement to national service between the world wars, including work on Herbert Hoover's failed attempts at national social planning and NEW DEAL social welfare legislation. Northwestern, under President Walter Dill Scott, filled the local void by embracing applied research at its professional schools. Chicago's heretofore indifferent philanthropists responded by funding a downtown professional school campus.

Postwar demand for higher education led the University of Illinois to open a two-year satellite at NAVY PIER in 1946. A move to the Harrison-Halsted campus as the four-year University of Illinois at Chicago Circle (1965) began a rise to university status that would include 15 colleges and schools offering doctoral work in 58 specializations. "Circle" became the UNIVERSITY OF ILLINOIS AT CHICAGO after merging with the University of Illinois Medical Center in 1982. Strong demand for teachers led to the opening of Chicago Teachers College–North in 1961. This college, renamed NORTHEASTERN ILLINOIS UNIVERSITY, together with the original South Side college (renamed CHICAGO STATE UNIVERSITY) and with public, upper-level Governors State (1971), became comprehensive universities in 1971 over sporadic downstate and private college opposition. The City Colleges of Chicago—Crane's new name—grew to eight two-year units by 1975 before downsizing to seven in 1993.

ROOSEVELT UNIVERSITY (1945) refrained from discrimination in admitting minority students, a frequent practice at other private colleges. Elsewhere, relations with contiguous minority communities deteriorated as universities expanded or attempted to "stabilize" their neighborhoods. Constructing the Chicago Circle campus meant destroying ethnic neighborhoods and several Hull House buildings; similarly, racial tensions increased during the 1950s in HYDE PARK—an early URBAN RENEWAL site. DePaul, Loyola, and Roosevelt expanded via suburban satellites but retained a basic commitment to Chicago. By the end of the twentieth century, over 30 of the region's 114 universities and colleges had downtown locations.

Steven J. Diner
Harold S. Wechsler

See also: Chicago School of Sociology; Chicago Studied: Social Scientists and Their City; Schooling for Work; Social Service Education

Further reading: Diner, Steven J. *A City and Its Universities: Public Policy in Chicago, 1892–1919.*

Old University of Chicago

The first, or "Old," University of Chicago was established in 1857 by Illinois Senator Stephen Douglas as a Baptist mission school. Though not himself a Baptist, Douglas was willing to support an institution of higher learning that could promote the cultural and commercial growth of Chicago. The university stood on 10 acres at Cottage Grove Avenue near 35th Street, directly across from Douglas's "Oakenwald" estate. The university offered college courses as well as programs in medicine and law. The newly formed Baptist Union Theological Seminary held its first classes there too, but moved to suburban MORGAN PARK in 1877 after a series of financial setbacks. The University of Chicago could not meet its growing debt, and was forced to close in the spring of 1886.

Robin F. Bachin

1980. • Rosen, George. *Decision-Making Chicago-Style: The Genesis of a University of Illinois Campus.* 1980. • Storr, Richard J. *Harper's University: The Beginnings.* 1966.

University of Chicago. The University of Chicago opened in 1892 under the auspices of the American Baptist Education Society. Baptist oil magnate John D. Rockefeller provided the initial funding for the nonsectarian, coeducational institution modeled on the graduate research universities of Germany. Rockefeller and William Rainey Harper, the first president of the university, hoped the school would be a force for Christian moralism in the Midwest at the same time that it developed and promoted modern scientific research.

Retail merchant Marshall Field donated 10 acres in HYDE PARK for the campus and later sold additional lands as the university expanded. Architect Henry Ives Cobb designed the Gothic revival campus in the image of Oxford and Cambridge, with the enclosed quadrangles creating a feeling of insularity and detachment from the surrounding city. The board of trustees hoped the design would foster a tight-knit community of scholars.

The university initially drew students primarily from the Midwest; most were children of small merchants and professionals. Women, many in graduate school, constituted over half of the students by the first years of the twentieth century. This generated concern among many trustees and administrators, who considered limiting women's admissions or ending coeducation altogether. Alumnae and faculty members successfully lobbied for women's continued access to the university.

Harper hired some of the most distinguished scholars from colleges and universities across the nation and the world. John Dewey and George Herbert Mead helped establish the philosophy department. Scholars like Albion Small, and later Ernest Burgess and Robert Park, built one of the most influential sociology departments in the nation, as the "CHICAGO SCHOOL" pioneered research in immigration, race and ethnic studies, and urban community studies. Faculty worked closely with Chicago reformers such as Jane Addams, Graham Taylor, and Mary McDowell, who became head resident of the University-sponsored SETTLEMENT HOUSE in Back of the Yards. The university played a central role in linking the emerging disciplines of the social sciences with urban reform activities and municipal government.

To expand of the university's role in the city, President Harper launched the University Extension Program, modeled on the British program and on the American Chautauqua movement. Nonenrolled students, particularly adults in other parts of the city, could take courses part-time and off-site. Harper also sought university affiliation with other institutions in the city, including Rush Medical College, the Chicago Theological SEMINARY, and the Chicago Manual Training School.

Robert Maynard Hutchins, who became university president in 1929, eliminated intercollegiate FOOTBALL and revamped the undergraduate curriculum. His 1931 "New Plan" consolidated departmental structure, introduced general survey courses, and inaugurated comprehensive examinations. Hutchins also launched the "Great Books" program, which brought together university faculty with city elites to read and discuss classic texts of Western civilization. Librarians and public school teachers were trained to lead discussions, making the program more accessible and widely available across the city and the nation.

Departments in the physical sciences gained distinction throughout the 1940s and 1950s. In 1942 a team of scientists led by physicist Enrico Fermi initiated the first self-sustaining nuclear reaction under the football stands at Stagg Field, as part of the MANHATTAN PROJECT. Research in subatomic physics provided a new partnership between the federal government and the university that shaped the future of scientific research.

After a postwar boom in student enrollment, applications declined in the 1950s, largely as a result of changing neighborhood conditions in Hyde Park. Economic and demographic changes, particularly the increasing presence of AFRICAN AMERICANS in Hyde Park, led many white residents to leave the neighborhood. Many property owners subdivided homes and became absentee landlords, often neglecting building upkeep and maintenance. To revitalize the neighborhood, the university worked with local residents to create the Hyde Park–KENWOOD Community Conference in 1949. Members promoted urban renewal policies to address issues of crime, poverty, racial integration, and PLANNING. Several thousand residents were displaced in the process, but the partnership between the university and local residents became a model for promoting interracial and economically stable urban communities.

The University of Chicago's international stature is symbolized by the large number of faculty who have won Nobel Prizes. The university maintains a strong presence in city affairs and public policy and provides expertise in areas as diverse as legal aid, tax policy, housing, education, and medicine.

Robin F. Bachin

See also: Chicago Studied: Social Scientists and Their City; Northwestern University; Social Service Education; Universities and Their Cities; Urban Renewal

Further reading: Diner, Steven. *A City and Its Universities: Public Policy in Chicago, 1892–1919.* 1980. • McNeill, William H. *Hutchins' University: A Memoir of the University of Chicago, 1929–1950.* 1991. • Storr, Richard J. *Harper's University: The Beginnings.* 1966.

Robert Maynard Hutchins and the University of Chicago

Robert Hutchins spent his adolescent years in Oberlin, where his father, a Presbyterian minister, taught in the School of Theology. After attending Oberlin for two years, he served in the U.S. Army Ambulance Corps (1917–1919), graduated from Yale, and became secretary of the Yale Corporation in 1923. In 1925 he graduated magna cum laude from the Yale Law School and was appointed acting dean and associate professor of the Law School two years later. At the age of 30, he became the president and ultimately chancellor of the University of Chicago, posts he held for over 20 years.

Hutchins's greatest contribution to higher education was his realization of a rigorous and unique program for undergraduates in which required acquaintance with the intellectual tradition and its methods took center stage. He placed learning at the center of college experience and in so doing challenged the elective system and the standards of other institutions. He fought for a separation between graduate and undergraduate curricula and was among the first to advocate earlier entrance to college. Under his watch, the University of Chicago became a unique community of scholars and learning, free of trivial trappings characteristic of other universities. After leaving the University of Chicago, Hutchins became the guiding force at the newly created Ford Foundation in the mid-1950s, headed the Fund for the Republic, and founded the Center for the Study of Democratic Institutions at Santa Barbara, which he led until his death in 1977.

Leon Botstein

University of Illinois at Chicago. The University of Illinois at Chicago (UIC) originated in 1982 with the consolidation of the two urban campuses of the state's flagship university: the University of Illinois at the Medical Center and the University of Illinois at Chicago Circle. The former, which became the West Campus of UIC, combined a handful of separate institutions over the years, giving it roots reaching back to 1858. The Circle or East Campus opened in 1965, drawing on more recent beginnings (1946) when a two-year undergraduate division opened on NAVY PIER to serve returning war veterans.

By 1998 UIC enrolled 25,000 students in 15 colleges, making it the largest university in the Chicago area. A major economic engine, it employed about 12,000 people with a budget of approximately a billion dollars. By the turn of the century, one of every 73 Chicagoans over age 21 was a UIC graduate.

The oldest building on campus, HULL HOUSE, erected in 1856, has been restored as a memorial to Jane Addams. By 1889, when Addams moved into the old Hull mansion to create a pioneering settlement house, the University of Illinois had been founded downstate (1867) and three private institutions were functioning in Chicago: the Charitable Eye and Ear Infirmary (1858), the Chicago College of Pharmacy (1859–1861, 1869), and the College of Physicians and Surgeons (1882). The Chicago Dental College, established in 1892, formed another root for UIC.

In 1896 the Chicago College of Pharmacy became part of the University of Illinois, beginning the state university's presence in the city. Gradually, between 1897 and 1943 the other private institutions became colleges in the university. In 1925 the General Hospital opened as the university's teaching and research facility. The state legislature then created the Medical Center District in 1941, with the university's health colleges and hospital forming key components. With the addition of schools of NURSING (1951), public health (1970), and the associated health professions (1979), UIC became one of the few universities in the nation with a full complement of six health science colleges.

Meanwhile, the original two-year Undergraduate Division at Navy Pier enjoyed widespread community support and a drive started in 1953 to create a four-year program in the metropolitan area. As university officials were considering various sites, Mayor Richard J. Daley offered the city's assistance in land acquisition in 1959, preferring a site near the LOOP and connected to both the new EXPRESSWAYS and the public transit system. The selection of the Harrison-Halsted site in 1961 stirred up opposition in the neighborhood, but in 1965 classes opened in modern buildings designed by Walter Netsch. By the time the campus underwent a major renovation in 1994, the original four colleges of the Circle Campus (architecture and art, business administration, engineering, liberal arts and sciences) had multiplied to include schools of education, graduate studies, social work, and urban planning and public affairs.

Gerald A. Danzer

See also: Dentistry; Maxwell Street; Medical Education; Near West Side; Universities and Their Cities

Further reading: "Campus City, Chicago." *Architectural Forum* 9 (1965): 21–44. • Rosen, George. *Decision-Making Chicago Style: The Genesis of a University of Illinois Campus.* 1980.

University Park, IL, Will and Cook Counties, 31 miles S of the Loop. This village, one of the region's few planned communities, was known as Wood Hill, Park Forest South, and finally University Park.

In the late 1950s, Woodhill Enterprises purchased land south of PARK FOREST for a large subdivision. Building began in 1961, but by 1967 Wood Hill had only 240 homes. Residents created a homeowners association, which fostered a community identity.

In 1966 Nathan Manilow, one of the developers of Park Forest, started to purchase land around Wood Hill. Park Forest had been a model for PLANNING in the 1940s, and Lewis Manilow, son of Nathan, formed New Community Enterprises (NCE) to build "a whole new town." Major partners included Illinois Central Industries and United States Gypsum Company.

NCE supported the incorporation of Park Forest South in 1967 with projections for 100,000 residents. Under the federal New Communities Act of 1968, Park Forest South was designated as one of 15 such "new communities." Planning included space for residential, commercial, and industrial development and addressed the needs of education, recreation, and faith communities. Racial integration was a goal from the beginning, and Park Forest South became a leader in support of OPEN HOUSING.

GOVERNORS STATE UNIVERSITY opened in 1969, and the ILLINOIS CENTRAL RAILROAD made its first commuter extension in 40 years to Park Forest South. Plans for wooded preserves and recreation areas were addressed, building on recreation area set-asides and major land donations by the Manilow organization.

The creativity and energy of the developers and village leadership led to great hopes for their "whole new town." In 1970, the state of Illinois allocated $24 million for the GSU campus. In 1971, HUD guaranteed $30 million in loans to bring the vision to reality.

The developers modernized the WATER and sewage treatment facilities and in 1970 initiated the first elementary school, the first apartment complex, and Governors Gateway Industrial Park.

However, difficulties arose in the economy, in the requirements and lack of resources from HUD, in the projections for growth, and in other areas, leading to suspended development in late 1974. For over two years, intense activity at public and private levels untangled many of the problems. The new town, intended for 100,000, adapted to a slow-growth plan anticipating an eventual 20,000 to 25,000 residents. The 2000 population, however, was 6,662, up slightly from the previous decade.

New town planning remains evident. The industrial park next to I-57 is integral to the village, and residential areas continue to offer open space, bikeways, and additional development. The new town heritage includes the Nathan Manilow Sculpture Park, a monumental internationally recognized outdoor sculpture park at GSU developed by Lewis Manilow to honor his father.

In its own way, University Park succeeded as a planned community, with racial diversity and economic solidity on the edge of the developed south suburbs.

Larry A. McClellan

See also: Built Environment of the Chicago Region; Planning Chicago; Public Art

Further reading: McClellan, Larry. *Park Forest South/University Park: A Guide to Its History and Development.* 1986.

University Presses. *See* Presses, University

Untouchables. The U.S. Justice Department created a special unit in 1929 to combat Al Capone's illegal alcohol operations. Department leaders chose for its head Eliot Ness, a Chicago-based PROHIBITION Bureau agent with a reputation for diligence and honesty. For his team Ness handpicked nine Bureau agents, choosing young, unmarried men with strong records and unquestioned integrity.

For two and a half years, the unit harassed the Capone organization and collected evidence for prosecution. Relying on information from anonymous tips, paid informants, wiretaps, and other surveillance, the agents raided and destroyed over two dozen BREWERIES and distilleries, including one whose capacity Ness estimated at 20,000 gallons of alcohol per day.

Cultivating favorable coverage, Ness invited reporters to accompany the group on raids. After he publicly denounced a large bribe offer early in 1930, a *Chicago Tribune* reporter gave the group its popular identity—"the Untouchables."

The unit's work helped secure prohibition-related indictments against Capone and others. But federal prosecutors believed that tax-evasion charges constituted a stronger case against Capone, and he was never prosecuted for the prohibition violations.

David E. Ruth

See also: Crime and Chicago's Image; Mafia; St. Valentine's Day Massacre; Underground Economy

Further reading: Ness, Eliot, with Oscar Fraley. *The Untouchables.* 1957.

Uptown, Community Area 3, 6 miles N of the Loop. Only sparsely settled in the nineteenth century, Uptown has become one of the densest and most ethnically diverse residential areas of Chicago. In 1861 GRACELAND CEMETERY was opened in what is now the southwest quarter of Uptown, and soon became a

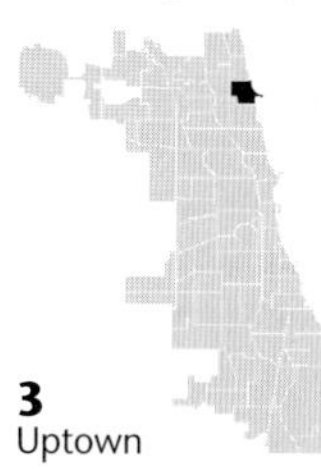

Schloesser & Co. (John W. Schloesser) grocery store at 4633 North Broadway in Uptown, 1908. Photographer: Unknown. Source: Chicago Historical Society.

destination for outings. GERMAN and SWEDISH immigrants operated scattered farms. The Cedar Lawn (1869), Buena Park (1860), Sheridan Park (1894), and EDGEWATER (1887) developments in LAKE VIEW TOWNSHIP brought middle-income and wealthy residents to the area. Land speculator John Lewis Cochran's (1857–1923) Edgewater set a building pattern for the area that fostered a broader mix of classes. Along the lakefront he favored mansions, but west of Evanston Avenue (Broadway) he encouraged multifamily housing. Cochran convinced the Chicago, Milwaukee & St. Paul RAILROAD to stop at Bryn Mawr Avenue and two decades later was instrumental in the building of the Northwestern Elevated Railroad Company tracks near his developments. These routes made Uptown one of Chicago's most populous residential centers.

A commercial boom in the first quarter of the twentieth century ushered in days of glamour. To compete with the LOOP and WOODLAWN, the Central Uptown Chicago Association promoted the area's shopping and recreational opportunities with images of New York City; the main thoroughfare became "Broadway" and the area, "Uptown." Loren Miller's DEPARTMENT STORE (later Goldblatt's) anchored the SHOPPING DISTRICT. Revelers visited the ARAGON BALLROOM (1926), the Riviera Theater (1919), the Uptown Theater (1925), and the Marine Room of the tony Edgewater Beach Hotel (1916). Thousands of worshipers flocked to the People's Church and tuned their radios to hear the sermons of Unitarian minister Preston Bradley. For a decade (1907–1917), Essanay Studios made Uptown the heart of the American FILM industry. Luxury APARTMENT buildings and HOTELS appeared along Winthrop and Kenmore Avenues.

Uptown's fortunes changed during the GREAT DEPRESSION. The extension of Lake Shore Drive to Foster Avenue in 1933 made it possible for shoppers to bypass Uptown for places further north. During the housing crisis of WORLD WAR II, the large rooms of the luxury apartments along the Winthrop-Kenmore corridor seemed ideal for conversion into more profitable smaller accommodations. Some landlords neglected their property or did not require long-term leases or security deposits, which made Uptown accessible to recent migrants and Chicago's poor. In the 1950s, whites from Appalachia, JAPANESE Americans from California, and NATIVE AMERICANS from Wisconsin, Minnesota, and Oklahoma settled in Uptown's affordable but deteriorating housing. In addition, the state of Illinois channeled released MENTAL HEALTH patients to Uptown's small apartments and halfway houses.

The changes in Uptown's economy, population, and housing stock drew the attention of residents, business owners, COMMUNITY ORGANIZERS, and public officials. Longtime residents and commercial institutions created the Uptown Chicago Commission, which successfully sought designation as a CONSERVATION AREA (1966). The federal government made Uptown a MODEL CITIES Area. New residents joined community organizations, including Jobs or Income Now, sponsored by Students for a Democratic Society; Slim Coleman's Heart of Uptown Coalition; and the Uptown HULL HOUSE's Organization of the Northeast. Wary of the land clearance that had accompanied URBAN RENEWAL in HYDE PARK and LINCOLN PARK, they wanted to improve local conditions while keeping Uptown within the means of the poor. They protested the building of Truman COLLEGE (1976), which displaced several hundred residents.

Dozens of SOCIAL SERVICE organizations opened to serve the needs of Uptown's diverse poor, including the American Indian Center, St. Augustine's Center for American Indians, the Lakefront SRO Corporation, a federal Urban Progress Center, and the Edgewater-Uptown Community Mental Health Center. Uptown continued to attract immigrants from Central America, Asia, Africa, and the Middle East into the twenty-first century.

Residents of Uptown who wished to distance themselves from its image of poverty and blight discovered a new way to protect their interests; they changed the public identification of their neighborhoods. Residents of the northern half of Uptown rediscovered the name "Edgewater" and in 1980 achieved recognition as a distinct COMMUNITY AREA, halving Uptown's population. Homeowners in Buena Park (the area between Graceland Cemetery and the lake) and Sheridan Park (between Graceland and St. Boniface Cemeteries), won recognition as historic landmark districts. The secession of these prosperous neighborhoods reinforced Uptown's reputation as an area of diversity amid faded glamour.

Amanda Seligman

See also: Contested Spaces; Dance Halls; Entertaining Chicagoans; Historic Preservation; Housing Reform; Kitchenettes; Lake View; Movie Palaces

Further reading: Gitlin, Todd, and Nanci Hollander. *Uptown: Poor Whites in Chicago.* 1970. • Hansen, Marty. *Behind the Golden Door: Refugees in Uptown.* 1991. • Warren, Elizabeth. *Chicago's Uptown: Public Policy, Neighborhood Decay, and Citizen Action in an Urban Community.* 1979.

Urban League. Throughout the twentieth century, the Chicago Urban League has advanced racial democracy, although moderate methods and an elite orientation have circumscribed its approach to black POLITICS. Founded in 1916 as an affiliate of the National Urban League (NUL), the Chicago branch was neither a mass-membership nor community-based organization. Its interracial board's first president was UNIVERSITY OF CHICAGO sociologist Robert Park, and it set a lasting pattern by drawing its initial funding largely from local corporations and individual BUSINESS leaders. Its staff, led by T. Arnold Hill, formerly an NUL organizer, comprised mainly black social workers who provided services to newly arrived black southerners seeking employment and housing. The organization did yeoman work placing AFRICAN AMERICANS into jobs and attempting to break the job ceiling in industrial and white-collar WORK. However, the league's "Stranger Meetings," where black club women secured

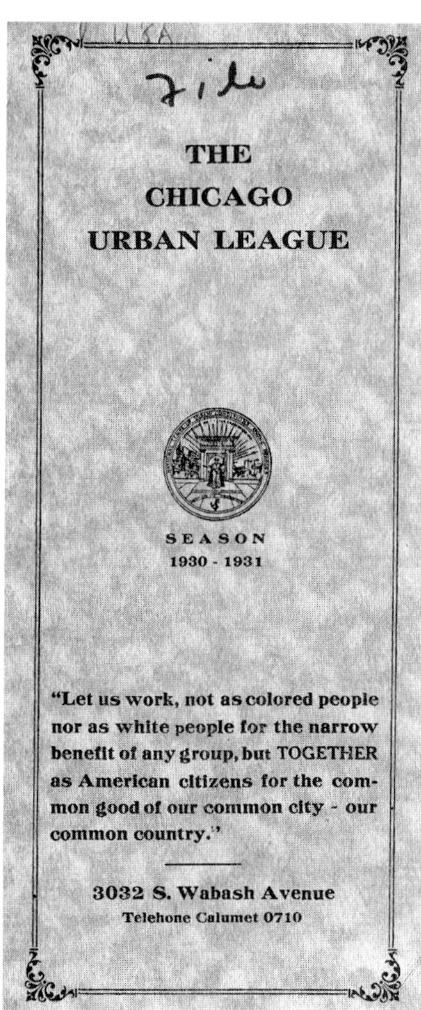

Chicago Urban League pamphlet, 1930–31. Source: Chicago Historical Society.

pledges from migrants to maintain appropriate public dress and deportment, reinforced the social distance between middle-class SOCIAL SERVICE providers and their poor and working-class clients.

After the 1919 RACE RIOT, white business and political leaders blamed the violence partly on the interaction of "unadjusted" black newcomers with whites in public spaces and workplaces. Their hope that the Urban League could hasten adjustment dovetailed with concern among African American elites that migrants provoked white RACISM through offensive habits brought from the rural South.

The Chicago branch experienced periodic organizational instability in a new environment of black protest activity after 1930. During the GREAT DEPRESSION, the league became useful again to the city's elite as an acceptable alternative to COMMUNIST-inspired resistance by unemployed and homeless blacks. After a reorganization in 1947, activist Sidney Williams became the new executive secretary. Williams's public opposition to violence against blacks seeking fair housing earned him the enmity of conservative board members. His subsequent removal in 1955 reinforced the league's role as a moderate race relations agency constrained by its conservative board. Executive Director Edwin Carlos "Bill" Berry made Chicago the Urban League's largest affiliate by 1958. Although aggressive—he called Chicago America's most segregated city—he retained traditional Urban League methods of lobbying and negotiations with elites during the 1960s.

In keeping with its traditional approach, today's league emphasizes the need for black citizens to "prepare" for the opportunities wrested from business and political officials. It endorsed self-help for poor blacks during the conservative 1980s and 1990s, continuing its long history of teaching unemployed workers habits desired by potential employers.

Preston H. Smith II

See also: Civil Rights Movements; Great Migration; National Association for the Advancement of Colored People (NAACP)

Further reading: Strickland, Arvarh. *History of the Chicago Urban League*. 1966.

Urban Renewal. Following World War II, and continuing into the early 1970s, "urban renewal" referred primarily to public efforts to revitalize aging and decaying inner cities, although some suburban communities undertook such projects as well. Including massive demolition, slum clearance, and rehabilitation, urban renewal proceeded initially from local and state legislation, which in Illinois included the Neighborhood Redevelopment Corporation Act of 1941 (amended in 1953), the Blighted Areas Redevelopment Act of 1947, the Relocation Act of 1947, and the Urban Community Conservation Act of 1953. The earliest emphasis was placed on slum clearance or "redevelopment," which was followed by a focused effort to conserve threatened but not yet deteriorated neighborhoods.

The new legislation had three primary functions. First, it expanded the city's power of EMINENT DOMAIN and enabled it to seize property for the new "public purposes" of slum clearance or prevention. Second, it pioneered the "write-down" formula which permitted the city to convey such property to private developers at its greatly reduced "use" value after the municipality subsidized its purchase and preparation. Last, the state provided assistance in relocating site residents—an absolute necessity in a time of severe housing shortages to enable the clearance of crowded, inner-city sites. The federal Housing Acts of 1949 and 1954, and their later amendments, mirrored the Illinois initiatives, providing a national framework and greater financial resources for the renewal effort. The clear intent was to offer public assistance to the private sector in the hope of heading off an urban crisis.

As early as 1943 a Chicago Plan Commission survey had found 242,000 substandard housing units within a 23-square-mile zone of "blight," with the most desperate conditions extending in a sweeping arc south and west of the LOOP. Another 100,000 such units were scattered across Chicago in "non-blighted" areas. Such conditions, combined with the decentralizing pull of the burgeoning suburbs, threatened to ravage the city's tax base, deplete the stock of middle-class consumers, and raise the cost of basic city services such as POLICE and FIREFIGHTING. Worried about rising taxes, declining property values, and their traditional source of shoppers and workers, Loop interests such as Marshall Field & Co. and the Chicago Title and Trust Company moved swiftly to design plans to enhance the downtown. Within weeks of his 1947 inauguration, Mayor Martin H. Kennelly received a housing program and legislative package that had gestated in Loop boardrooms.

Major institutional interests on the SOUTH SIDE, such as the ILLINOIS INSTITUTE OF TECHNOLOGY (IIT) and MICHAEL REESE HOSPITAL, also faced the daunting prospect of surviving within rapidly deteriorating neighborhoods. Even before WORLD WAR II, they had recommitted themselves to the area, and, in 1946, they joined other local interests to create the South Side Planning Board (SSPB). Staking out a planning interest of seven square miles from Cermak Road south to 47th Street and from Michigan Avenue west to the Pennsylvania Railroad, their efforts—along with those of their Loop counterparts—enticed the New York Life INSURANCE Company to finance the Lake Meadows development. Michael Reese HOSPITAL soon followed with its own Prairie Shores complex; IIT expanded its campus from 7 to 110 acres; MERCY HOSPITAL decided to remain and grow in the area; and South Commons was developed as a middle-income housing enclave.

The UNIVERSITY OF CHICAGO took the initiative in the urban renewal of HYDE PARK, as it did with the conception and enactment of the Illinois Urban Community Conservation Act of 1953, a law precisely tailored to the institution's needs. Proceeding in stages throughout the 1950s under earlier redevelopment acts and through the South East Chicago Commission (SECC), the university responded forcefully to a process of racial transition that had been accelerated by clearance projects to its north. The city approved a general renewal plan for Hyde Park–KENWOOD in 1958 after the SECC had removed the worst pockets of "blight" and prevented precipitous "white flight." By 1970, the university and various public agencies had invested some $100 million in the area—an amount augmented by an additional $300 million in private funds.

The largest renewal site north of the Loop provided space for Carl Sandburg Village

Polk Street before construction of the University of Illinois at Chicago, looking westward from 1020 West Polk, ca. 1957. Photographer: Unknown. Source: University of Illinois at Chicago.

between Division Street and North Avenue and, roughly, Clark and LaSalle. Most of the displaced residents were unmarried white renters without deep roots in the neighborhood. Demolition proceeded in 1960–61, with Arthur Rubloff & Co. beginning CONSTRUCTION the next year. At its completion in 1969, the combination of high-rise towers and townhouses encompassed 3,166 units. At the same time on the NEAR WEST SIDE, Mayor Richard J. Daley tried to protect the Loop, fight decentralization, and enhance Chicago's image by building a campus of the UNIVERSITY OF ILLINOIS in the Harrison-Halsted area. Sparking considerable grassroots protest, the project displaced thousands of individuals and hundreds of businesses in an old, largely ITALIAN community before it opened in 1965.

Concern with protecting and enhancing Chicago's core also generated a construction boom within the Loop itself. Beginning with the opening of the Prudential building in 1957, a 20-year burst of activity nearly doubled downtown office space; the federal government, COOK COUNTY, and the city of Chicago each added massive administrative centers.

The neighborhoods, however, experienced a different kind of transformation. While whites were among those uprooted in Hyde Park and on the North and West Sides, urban renewal in this context too often meant, as contemporaries noted, "Negro removal." Between 1948 and 1963 alone, some 50,000 families (averaging 3.3 members) and 18,000 individuals were displaced. Old neighborhoods disappeared, and new ones faced increasing racial pressures. Although some urban renewal sites were redeveloped for institutional expansion or middle-class housing, displaced AFRICAN AMERICANS received little benefit from the program. The city tried to contain the expansion of African American living space, in part, by using densely packed, centrally located high-rise PUBLIC HOUSING. Segregation became public policy, as the courts acknowledged in deciding the 1966 suit brought by CHICAGO HOUSING AUTHORITY (CHA) resident Dorothy GAUTREAUX. In 1969, federal district court judge Richard Austin found that 99 percent of the residents of CHA family housing were black, and that 99.5 percent of such units were confined to black or racially changing areas. Rather than solve the urban crisis, urban renewal had set the stage for its next phase.

Arnold R. Hirsch

See also: Contested Spaces; Planning Chicago; Redlining; Subsidized Housing

Further reading: Condit, Carl W. *Chicago, 1930–1970: Building, Planning, and Urban Technology.* 1974. • Hirsch, Arnold R. *Making the Second Ghetto: Race and Housing in Chicago, 1940–1960.* 1983. • Mayer, Harold M., and Richard C. Wade. *Chicago: Growth of a Metropolis.* 1969.

Uruguayans. Although some Uruguayans came to Chicago for the WORLD'S COLUMBIAN EXPOSITION of 1893 and the Eucharistic Congress of 1926, very few settled in Chicago permanently before 1940. The first influx of Uruguayan immigrants to Chicago included a small number of scholars, students, and professionals who arrived in the period following World War II. New BUSINESS relationships between Chicago and Uruguayan companies prompted the formation of the United States–Uruguay Alliance of Chicago in 1951 and attracted a small number of Uruguayan businesspeople and travelers to Chicago. By 1959, Chicago's Uruguayans had attained sufficient visibility to prompt Mayor Richard J. Daley to declare August 25 (Uruguay's Independence Day) Uruguay Day in Chicago.

The bulk of Chicago's Uruguayan population arrived starting in 1967 and continuing

Vacant property razed to make way for the University of Illinois at Chicago, 1962. Photographer: Larry Hemenway. Source: Chicago Historical Society.

through the 1970s, when a guerilla war, military dictatorship, and economic troubles in Uruguay prompted many to leave the country. A few were leftist dissidents who feared imprisonment, torture, or "disappearance" at the hands of the authoritarian military regime. Most, however, came to seek opportunity and escape an economic depression that had begun in the 1950s and was exacerbated by the civil strife of the 1960s and 1970s.

Many of the working-class Uruguayan immigrants of the 1970s came individually rather than in families and took jobs initially as carpenters, mechanics, and in food service. They settled throughout the North Side and in some SOUTH SIDE neighborhoods such as Heart of Chicago along with the city's growing Hispanic population. Many eventually started their own businesses—RESTAURANTS, auto shops, and small firms. Highly educated professionals, doctors, students, and businessmen also continued to arrive in Chicago, creating a marked elite within the community.

Uruguayans socialized together during the 1970s with frequent picnics at Le Bagh Woods, Che-che-pin-qua Woods, and Horner Park. In 1976, the community formed a SOCCER team, *Charruas* (named after the indigenous people of Uruguay), which allowed them to practice their national passion in their new city. Community leaders point to soccer's important role in the life of the community, bringing Uruguayans together frequently to compete and to watch and support their national team.

In the early 1980s, Uruguayans established Operación Gurí ("young boy"), to provide aid to needy children and schools at home in Uruguay. For several years, the group was the center of community activity, organizing annual picnics on August 25 and other cultural activities. Operación Gurí fundraising events included Uruguayan film festivals and *folklorico* productions, at which the traditional *Candombe* and tango dances were performed. Another important cultural institution, the weekly radio program *Chicago Esquina Tango,* aired Saturday afternoons beginning in the early 1980s through 1999. Although Operación Gurí ended in the 1990s, and no major organization immediately replaced it, the community remained active, with picnics and celebrations on August 25, as well as informal contacts and social life.

At the turn of the millennium, community leaders estimated a slowly increasing population of roughly 500 Uruguayans in Chicago, with an additional 100 or 200 living in the suburbs. Persistent economic problems in Uruguay contributed to continued immigration, especially among the young.

Robert Morrissey

See also: Demography; Multicentered Chicago; Refugees

V

Vacation Spots. In Chicago, as elsewhere in the United States, it was well into the twentieth century before the vacation became truly commonplace. It took innovations in TRANSPORTATION (steam, rail, auto, and air service), labor policies (EIGHT-HOUR day, stable wage structures, paid vacations), economic development, and city, state, and national recreation initiatives to make the vacation widely attainable.

Nineteenth-century vacations demanded large resources of time as well as money, and only Chicago's elite enjoyed these in abundance. Prominent families, such as the Palmers, Armours, and Fields, regularly fled urban clamor and climatic extremes for the woods, mountains, seaside, and lakeshore. They circulated among exclusive resorts in Europe and the New England coast in summer (Bar Harbor, Maine and Newport, Rhode Island) and flocked to Florida's private beaches in winter.

For middle-class professionals, getting away in the 1870s meant camping at summer colonies on the urban fringes, such as LAKE BLUFF and New Buffalo, Michigan, or a pilgrimage to the INDIANA DUNES. More distant vacation destinations remained too expensive for middle-class Chicagoans.

Increasingly, the nearby woodlands and pristine waters of the Wisconsin, Michigan, and Indiana shores of LAKE MICHIGAN beckoned Chicagoans seeking recreation and repose amidst natural beauty. Hunters, anglers, and boaters drawn to the strenuous life took to the woods and waterways, camping in tents or in rugged shelters in proximity to rural agricultural and logging settlements.

During the 1870s and 1880s, wealthy Chicagoans started forming private corporations to purchase plots of Michigan and Wisconsin WATERFRONT for summer cottages. These "resorts" tended to be modest in scale and amenities, embodying notions of rustic, family-centered recreation. Chicago mothers often presided over these summer colonies at Mackinac Island, Benton Harbor, and South Haven, Michigan, and Green Lake and Lake Geneva, Wisconsin, supervising their children while their husbands labored in the city. By the 1920s, AFRICAN AMERICAN professionals from Chicago and other Midwestern cities had begun developing Idlewild, a resort community in northwestern Michigan.

As the industrial city grew, health activists celebrated the moral benefits of vigorous activity in the fresh air and contributed to an emerging view of the vacation as a necessary antidote to urban life. Middle-class sufferers of physical and mental ailments "took the cure" at fresh-air spas, mineral springs, and wilderness retreats and sanatoriums in Wisconsin, Michigan, and downstate Illinois. Religious organizations sponsored "camp meetings" combining recreation with spiritual education and fellowship.

Soaring population in the 1880s and 1890s increased demand for affordable, accessible, and stimulating getaway opportunities. Railway and steamship lines joined forces with commercial developers to create vacation resorts for consumers seeking speedy and inexpensive access to lively surroundings where they could unwind with their families or meet members of the opposite sex.

By the turn of the century, resort HOTELS and campgrounds serving Chicagoans of various incomes were transforming sleepy encampments and lake ports such as Holland, Michigan, into bustling vacation spots. Thousands of Chicagoans traveling as families, church

Resorts: Summer Journey to Saugatuck

Trips across the lake to towns like Saugatuck, St. Joseph, South Haven, and Michigan City were popular with Chicago workers in the early twentieth century. Day, weekend, and even week-long trips to these resorts were easily made by ship from downtown Chicago. Hilda Satt Polachek, a young Jewish woman who worked in the knitting trades and was an active participant at HULL HOUSE, spent the 1911 summer working at the Forward Movement Park in Saugatuck, Michigan. The camp provided vacations for deaf, crippled, and blind children from Chicago. Polachek described her journey:

> It was an overnight trip from Chicago to Michigan, but we were as excited as if we were going to cross the ocean. For some of us it was the first vacation away from Chicago. We had reserved state rooms, one for the boys and one for the girls. There were four bunks in each room. There was little or no sleeping that night. We stayed up on deck, watching the lapping water as the big ship went skimming along. There was a small orchestra on the boat and we danced for a while. We were young and life was beautiful. . . .
>
> Our first view of the Forward Movement Camp was a sight I can never forget. The lake was blue and calm that morning and the sandy beach seemed endless. . . . The angry whitecaps that I had often seen in Chicago during the stormy weather were hidden in the bosom of the lake. The clouds had been stored in ethereal bags; it was a perfect day!

Polachek, Hilda Satt. *I Came a Stranger: The Story of a Hull-House Girl*, ed. Dena J. Polachek Epstein. 1991, 111–113.

congregations, ethnic societies, and neighborhood groups might visit on a Fourth of July weekend.

Increasing access to automobile ownership in the 1910s radically transformed the vacation landscape. Middle-class Chicagoans discovered "autocamping": Vacationers drove into the countryside and slept in their cars or pitched tents by the roadside or in municipal campgrounds on the outskirts of rural towns. Between 1920 and 1930 the total acreage of state and county parks almost doubled, and Chicagoans headed for Starved Rock, Chain O'Lakes Park, and the Indiana Dunes. The autocamps, which offered rustic shelters not much larger than cars themselves, gave way to cabins with amenities such as running water and eventually to motels and motor courts in the 1930s and 1940s.

The post-1945 boom in production, prosperity, and improved benefits packages for workers expanded vacation budgets and options. Loaded into station wagons and recreational vehicles, Chicagoans took to the new interstate highway system in record numbers.

Over 7 million people visited state parks in Illinois in 1950. By 1970 total visits nearly tripled, increasing to approximately 20 million. In 1950, 3.2 million people visited state parks in Wisconsin. These visits more than quadrupled by 1999, when Wisconsin state parks hosted 14.1 million visitors annually. Overnight visits to state parks also soared: in 1970, over 6 million people camped overnight in Michigan's state parks, compared to the 700,000 people who did so just 10 years earlier.

By the end of the twentieth century, competition in the TOURISM and AIRLINE industry, along with Chicago's national status as an air hub, had increased middle-class access to national and international travel. Chicagoans traveling beyond the GREAT LAKES region have been especially partial to California and Florida.

Derek Vaillant

See also: Eastland; Forest Preserves; Leisure; Metropolitan Growth; Motoring; Park Districts

Further reading: Amory, Cleveland. *The Last Resorts.* 1952. • Bateman, Newton. *Historical Encyclopedia of Illinois.* 1908. • Bogue, Margaret B., and Virginia A. Palmer. *Around the Shores of Lake Superior: A Guide to Historic Sites.* 1979.

Valparaiso, IN, Porter County, 41 miles SE of the Loop. Valparaiso, the county seat of Porter County, Indiana, is at best an hour's drive south and east from Chicago's LOOP. The roads are often so clogged, however, that the trip can take somewhat longer.

Traffic flows both ways. Many residents of Valpo, as it is familiarly known, work in Chicago or frequently take advantage of its cultural and other opportunities, while many Chicagoans are drawn to the small-town security and other amenities of Valpo and environs. Valparaiso means "Vale of Paradise." The name is Spanish but the pronunciation is American, Val-pah-ray'-zo. Tradition says that the name was suggested by sailors who served under Commodore David Porter, a hero of the War of 1812 for whom the county was named. His ship, the *Essex,* was lost in a famous battle at the harbor of Valparaiso, Chile.

The land where Valparaiso now stands was purchased by the federal government in 1832. Among the first settlers of the new acquisition was Thomas Campbell, who scouted the area near the Sauk Trail. Some 80 years later the nation's first transcontinental highway, U.S. 30, was constructed following the route of this old Indian trail through Valparaiso.

In 1834 J. P. Ballard built the first house in what became the town of Portersville, its name until christened Valparaiso in 1837. After Porter County was established by the Indiana General Assembly in 1836, the first county board of commissioners, meeting in Ballard's kitchen, selected Portersville as the county seat.

Portersville was created by land speculators. The town site, centered on a public square that was donated to the county, was carved into lots that sold for an average price of $100. It took only three years for the Portersville Land Company to sell every lot in town.

The area was heavily wooded with oak, ash, maple, birch, and pine TREES. Wild fruit, nuts, and game were plentiful. Sawmills were quickly started. Settlers concentrated on farming and trade. Benjamin Harrison, who later became president, often hunted and fished here.

The city has experienced steady growth. Its population in 2000 was 27,428, although the Valparaiso Post Office service area embraces nearly 70,000 inhabitants. In the decade of the 1990s about 2,000 residential building permits were issued.

Residential growth has been accompanied by new and expanding industrial development. For example, the Hoosier Bat Company has provided BASEBALL bats to Cubs slugger Sammy Sosa and others, while Urschel Laboratories, founded in 1910, designs and manufactures food processing equipment sold worldwide.

Valparaiso is widely known as the home of VALPARAISO UNIVERSITY and its magnificent chapel. One of its noted citizens, the late Orville Redenbacher, is honored each year on the first Saturday after Labor Day by the city's annual Popcorn Festival.

Mel Doering

See also: Agriculture; Sporting Goods Manufacturing; Streets and Highways

Further reading: "Where Reality Meets Ideal." *Valparaiso Times,* June 27, 1999. • Neeley, George E. *Valparaiso: A Pictorial History.* 1989. • *Porter County Sesquicentennial, 1836–1986.* 1986.

Valparaiso University. The Valparaiso Male and Female College was founded in 1859. It later became the Northern Indiana Normal School and then Valparaiso University (VU). By 1907 it was the second largest university in the country, second only to Harvard. (The UNIVERSITY OF CHICAGO was third; state schools had not yet become the giant institutions of today.) Since 1925 VU has been operated by the Lutheran University Association. Its Chapel of the Resurrection, the nation's largest collegiate chapel, attracts visitors from far and wide.

Mel Doering

See also: Protestants; Valparaiso, IN

Further reading: Albers, James W. *From Centennial to Golden Anniversary: The History of Valparaiso University from 1959–1975.* 1976. • Baepler, Richard P. *Flame of Faith, Lamp of Learning: A History of Valparaiso University.* 2001. • Strietelmeier, John. *Valparaiso's First Century: A Centennial History of Valparaiso University.* 1959.

Vaudeville. From 1880 to 1910 this form of popular entertainment stood atop the show business world. In 1882 C. E. Kohl and George Middleton opened the first acknowledged vaudeville entertainment in Chicago, their West Side Museum. In 1883 the pair opened the Clark Street Museum; a year later they leased the Olympic Theater, hiring George Castle to manage it. By 1895, Kohl and Middleton were making so much money they leased the Chicago Opera House; three years later they acquired the Haymarket. In 1900, Kohl bought out Middleton's leases and later with George Castle built the Majestic, acquired the Academy of Music, took over the Star, and opened Chicago's first Palace theater. But this company never went national, instead selling out to the Orpheum Circuit. Headquartered in San Francisco, Orpheum, along with the Keith-Albee Circuit, dominated "big time" vaudeville. (There was also the cheaper "small time" vaudeville and, for an even lower price, burlesque houses.)

Chicago always trailed only New York in vaudeville stops. Its largest theaters seated about 2,000 patrons, with the most important including the Academy of Music (on South Halsted), the Haymarket and the McVickers's (both on West Madison), and the Majestic (on West Monroe, renamed the Shubert in 1945). There were two dozen more during the heyday of vaudeville, including the Olympic, the Folly, Howard's, the International, the Metropolitan Music Hall, the original Palace, Sid Euson's, Trocadero, the Alhambra Hippodrome, the Colonial [the former Iroquois], the Empress, the Julian, the Marlowe Hippodrome, the Star Hippodrome, the Willard, and the

Wilson Avenue (the best-known of the outlying "suburban" houses, but only one among many). The Pekin (at 2700 South State Street) was in a special category as the lone black-owned and -operated vaudeville house. The beginning of the end of the vaudeville era came in 1921 with the opening of Balaban and Katz's Chicago theater, which offered both movies and live entertainment for the same price as the vaudeville-only shows. By 1930 pure vaudeville had died, crushed by Hollywood.

Douglas Gomery

See also: Entertaining Chicagoans; Leisure; Movies, Going to the; Theater; Theater, Ethnic

Further reading: Allen, Robert C. "B. F. Keith and the Origins of American Vaudeville." *Theatre Survey* 21 (November 1980): 105–115. • Duci Bella, Joseph R., ed. *Theatres of Chicago.* 1973. • Slide, Anthony. *The Encyclopedia of Vaudeville.* 1994.

Venezuelans. Although Chicago has never attracted many Venezuelan immigrants, a small but viable community has resided in the city beginning in the 1950s. Chicago's earliest Venezuelans included Chico Carrasquel, WHITE SOX star shortstop and, in 1951, the first Latin American to play in the Major League All Star Game. He joined only a handful of other Venezuelans living in the city during the 1950s.

Venezuelan migration to Chicago accelerated during the 1970s and 1980s. Many came as university students with the support of a major Venezuelan scholarship sponsored by the Fundación Gran Mariscal de Ayacucho. Although most returned to Venezuela after their studies, this temporary student population constituted a substantial segment of the community up through the turn of the millennium. Economic crises in Venezuela during the 1980s prompted many businessmen and professionals to seek jobs in the more secure markets of U.S. cities. A handful of musicians and political expatriates also added to the Chicago Venezuelan community. The 2000 census counted 600 Venezuelans in Chicago with nearly 1,400 in the metropolitan area.

Not concentrated in any single neighborhood or parish, the diverse Venezuelan community in Chicago has spread across the city and suburbs. In the early 1980s, Venezuelans in Chicago founded a community organization aimed at bringing together this disparate group. ASOVEN-Chicago, the Asociación de Venezuela en Chicago, became a social and cultural haven for the Venezuelans, sponsoring parties and cultural events throughout the 1980s and early 1990s. ASOVEN organized an annual July 5th picnic to celebrate Venezuelan Independence Day and hosted Christmas parties and Easter celebrations. These festivities became opportunities for Venezuelans to maintain such ethnic traditions as playing with *perinolas* and eating *hallacas.* Though ASOVEN ceased to function in the mid-1990s, members of the Venezuelan community continued to gather for frequent parties and picnics.

Robert Morrissey

See also: Colombians; Demography; Multicentered Chicago

Chico Carrasquel

After beginning his professional baseball career at the age of 17 in Caracas, Venezuela, Chico Carrasquel played for the WHITE SOX from 1950 to 1955. In 1951 he was the first Latin American to play in the Major League All-Star Game. His first challenges as an immigrant and a baseball player included the language barrier: management wanted all the Latin players to speak in English.

Luis Aloma was a pitcher—a Cuban guy—so he spoke English and he helped me, because in those days I didn't understand anything in English. . . . Today, the Latin players have [translators, etc.]. In those days, in the 40s and 50s, we don't have help. They say, "Go to hell." Nowadays, you look at the lineup, it's a lot of Latin players, but in those days, what the hell, just one or two, so they say you have to speak English. . . . They told Hector Rodriguez to speak English and he said, "The only thing I know is, well, if he wants me to talk English, I know how to say 'Chicago White Sox.'" I played shortstop, he played third base, and all game, what he said was, "Chicago White Sox, Chicago White Sox." And I said, "Hector, please say something different." He said, "Chico, they want me to speak English, the only thing I know is 'Chicago White Sox.'" Nellie Fox, Billy Pierce, Minnie Minoso, they tried to help me and I got along with them real good. . . .

I remember those days, we were having a hard time. I hit a home run, and the pitcher, oh, they called me dirty names, and I said, "Why?" I remember, they said "Hey! Chico, you South American son of a bitch!" . . . Latin players and black players were the same. If somebody was white and hit a home run, that was okay, but Latin players, that's a different story. . . .

In those days, in the 50s and the end of the 40s, the Spanish players, they said, "Oh, we can't go. That's for the white people, that's for the black people." . . .

If we played good ball, the fans at Comiskey don't care if you were black, or white, or a Latin player, because you played good. We got a chance to show those people and they recognized.

Robert Morrissey

Vernon Hills, IL, Lake County, 30 miles NW of the Loop. W. D. Coon and Theodore Mills established the foundation of this community when they started a two-hundred-acre farm in 1851. In 1885 railroad tracks were laid, enabling farmers to move their crops via the Soo Line RAILROAD.

The community remained agricultural until the 1950s, when developers Quinn Hogan and Barney Loeb bought land from nurseryman Gordon Clavey to build homes and a GOLF course. Naming their corporation Vernon Hills, they built 24 houses and some APARTMENT buildings. The village incorporated in 1958 with 123 residents. A HOTEL and Vernon Hills Country Club were completed in 1960. Tourists and prospective home buyers stayed at the hotel, where they received a weekend membership to the club's golf course. But Vernon Hills's period of prosperity ended when bankruptcy forced Hogan and Loeb to sell to the original owner, Gordon Clavey.

Although there were 1,050 residents in Vernon Hills in 1970, the community had no commerce. In 1971 Vernon Hills annexed a parcel of land off Illinois Highway 60 and Milwaukee Road after developers approached the village with a SHOPPING center proposal. The result was the 1.2-million-square-foot Hawthorne Center. Tax revenues from the shopping center removed the burden of property taxes from residents, and Vernon Hills blossomed in the next decade. By 1980 the census tallied 9,827 persons, increasing to 20,120 in 2000.

From the 1950s to the 1980s the community concentrated on residential development; after 1980, commercial buildings were increasingly added through ANNEXATIONS. In 1986 the village annexed an area that became the Corporate Woods business park and Centennial Crossing residential development.

In 1988, Vernon Hills annexed the 1,200-acre section of Hawthorne-Mellody Farms that had once belonged to John F. Cuneo, a prominent Chicago businessman. The former Cuneo Estates continued to house a museum and gardens, but the annexed land was developed into 2,100 residences, an 18-hole golf course, and several retail business lots.

After a battle with neighboring LINCOLNSHIRE, Vernon Hills annexed the village of Half Day in 1994, linking the southeast corner of town to everything north and giving the community a new boundary line of Milwaukee Avenue and Route 45.

Vernon Hills continued to look for additional space in the 1990s with annexations occurring nearly every year; by 1998 it had expanded to eight square miles, In 2000 it annexed a site that had been a Navy pilot practice area in 1945 and a Nike antiaircraft missile base from 1955 to 1969.

Marilyn Elizabeth Perry

See also: Lake County, IL; Suburbs and Cities as Dual Metropolis

Further reading: League of Women Voters of the Libertyville/Mundelein Area. *Know Your Town: Green Oaks—Libertyville—Mundelein—Vernon Hills.* 1990.

Veterans' Clubs. *See* Clubs: Patriotic and Veterans' Clubs

Veterans' Hospitals. Beginning in the early 1800s, the government of the United States government opened institutions called marine HOSPITALS for the medical care of merchant seamen. Originating on the Atlantic seaboard, these institutions eventually were built at major cities on inland waterways as well. Administered by what came to be called the U.S. PUBLIC HEALTH Service, marine hospitals, as well as Soldiers' Homes, the U.S. Naval Home in Philadelphia, St. Elizabeth's Hospital in Washington DC, and occasionally active-duty Army and Navy hospitals, provided medical care for veterans of the armed forces on an as-needed basis.

When approximately 200,000 discharged U.S. soldiers in need of further hospitalization began to return from WORLD WAR I, the necessity to expand hospital care for veterans became apparent. In the Chicago area, sick and injured veterans were sent to the old Marine Hospital in the LAKE VIEW community on the North Side and to United States Public Health Hospital No. 30, which was the commandeered Cooper-Monatah HOTEL building at 47th and Drexel on the SOUTH SIDE. Needing more beds on the South Side, the Public Health Service also took over Jackson Park Hospital at 75th and Stony Island Avenue.

In 1921 the new Veterans' Bureau (renamed the Veterans' Administration [VA] in 1930) consolidated veterans' affairs and the following year assumed control of Public Health Service hospitals serving veterans. Largest of the Chicago-area Veterans' Hospitals, the Edward Hines, Jr., Hospital opened in MAYWOOD in 1921. LUMBER magnate Edward Hines, Sr., donated more than a million dollars for this hospital as a memorial to his son, who had died in France. Marshal Foch of the French Army came to Chicago for its dedication. Five years later, the NORTH CHICAGO Veterans' Administration Hospital opened near the GREAT LAKES NAVAL TRAINING STATION about 40 miles north of the city.

Although they had fought America's enemies alongside white soldiers, AFRICAN AMERICAN veterans found segregation and unequal treatment in some veterans' hospitals, and doors were totally closed to them at others.The Harding administration built a federal hospital for black veterans in Tuskegee, Alabama, in 1923, but it was not until 1953 that the VA officially ordered an end to segregation in all its hospitals.

Just after WORLD WAR II, the Hines Hospital was first in the VA system to affiliate with a local medical school to enhance medical care while providing clinical education for medical students. Large numbers of veterans after World War II and the Korean War, along with a drive to expand MEDICAL EDUCATION, prompted construction of two VA hospitals within Chicago's borders. The West Side VA Hospital was built in Chicago's Medical District in 1953, and the VA Research Hospital (later known as Lakeside Hospital) arose on the Chicago campus of NORTHWESTERN UNIVERSITY in 1954.

At the beginning of the twenty-first century, approximately 170 VA hospitals provided general medical and SOCIAL SERVICES to both male and female veterans: acute care in cases of serious injury or sickness, rehabilitation in cases of disability, nursing homes, and domiciles for indigent veterans. The same demographic and economic forces affecting other hospitals in the last decades of the twentieth century had an impact on VA hospitals. The two Chicago VA hospitals merged into the VA Chicago Health Care System in 1996, and the North Chicago VA Hospital, which had been slated for closing, merged with the Great Lakes Naval Training Center Hospital.

Paul A. Buelow

See also: Clubs: Patriotic and Veterans' Clubs; Cook County Hospital

Further reading: Amey, Dorothy M. *Veterans' Administration Health Care: Planning for Future Years.* 1984. • Chicago Medical Society. *History of Medicine and Surgery and Physicians and Surgeons of Chicago.* 1922. • U.S. Congress. House. Committee on Veterans' Affairs. *Medical Care of Veterans.* 90th Cong., 1st sess., 1967. Committee Print 4.

Vice Commissions. In March 1910 Mayor Fred Busse appointed 30 Chicagoans to solve a vexing problem of public policy. Should PROSTITUTION remain a regulated business in segregated VICE DISTRICTS, such as the Levee at 22nd and Dearborn? Or, should the districts be outlawed, scattering prostitution throughout the city?

At first, the Chicago Vice Commission members—including Frank Gunsaulus, Ellen Martin Henrotin, Julius Rosenwald, and Graham Taylor—favored segregation. As typical Progressive-era reformers, however, they set out to thoroughly investigate the question. Commissioners spoke to civic, religious, and neighborhood organizations, POLICE officers, and prostitutes. They concluded that segregation and regulation had failed and that the vice districts must be permanently abolished.

Their report, published in 1911 as *The Social Evil in Chicago,* also included a statistical section, which attempted to define and quantify prostitution in the city, and 96 recommendations for improvement. They estimated that 5,000 professional prostitutes worked in Chicago, serving over 5 million men every year. These women were older and had longer careers than conventional wisdom suggested. Prostitutes were not necessarily unintelligent but they were uneducated and unskilled and had few other opportunities for economic advancement.

The most radical finding of the Vice Commission was the connection drawn between low wages and a woman's choice to prostitute. Women's earnings averaged six dollars a week, 40 percent less than the commission deemed necessary for independent living, while the average prostitute earned approximately 25 dollars per week. Though their findings clearly pointed to the need for minimum-wage legislation, businessmen on the commission refused to acknowledge a connection between wages and vice, and none of the commission's recommendations called for such action. Most relied on education and legislative action, the traditional progressive responses, to diminish the demand for sexual commerce.

The commission called for a new city bureau to investigate and prosecute prostitution. After the city refused to establish such an agency, anti-vice leadership passed to a private organization, the Committee of Fifteen. Studies sponsored by the committee erroneously concluded that most prostitutes were AFRICAN AMERICAN, leading to police persecution of young black women during the 1920s.

The Chicago Vice Commission also led to a 1913 Illinois Vice Commission, which forcefully concluded that poverty was a principal cause of prostitution and that businesses had a responsibility to pay a living wage.

The Committee of Fifteen did not meet the expectations of the Chicago Vice Commission and few of their recommendations were ever enacted. Nonetheless, the commission was a step toward minimum-wage legislation in Illinois. The 1911 report, though temporarily banned from the mails as obscene, circulated around the world and influenced vice commissions in 43 cities.

Mary Linehan

See also: Erring Women's Refuge; Police; Prohibition and Temperance; Underground Economy; Work Culture

Further reading: Chicago Vice Commission. *The Social Evil in Chicago.* 1911. • Connelly, Mark Thomas. *The Response to Prostitution in the Progressive Era.* 1980. • Linehan, Mary. "Vicious Circle: Prostitution, Reform, and Public Policy in Chicago, 1830–1930." Ph.D. diss., University of Notre Dame. 1991.

Vice Districts. A nineteenth-century Chicagoan looking for a prostitute could easily find one in any of the city's wide-open vice districts. Like GAMBLING houses until they were dispersed by raids in 1894, brothels and streetwalkers clustered in these areas partly because they were convenient for customers, but mainly because of selective law enforcement. Public officials and many private citizens viewed PROSTITUTION as a necessary evil that should

South State Street vice district, 1944. Photographer: John Vachon. Source: Library of Congress.

be segregated into a few poor neighborhoods to protect the rest of Chicago.

Pockets of vice formed as early as the 1850s. The notorious lakefront brothel district called "the Sands" was destroyed by city officials in 1857, but prostitution continued to thrive and expand on the southern edge of what is now the LOOP. Smaller districts developed in the NEAR WEST SIDE and NEAR NORTH SIDE. Intermittent raids through the late nineteenth and early twentieth centuries aimed not at closing the brothels but at maintaining a flow of bribes to POLICE, politicians, and politically connected crime bosses. Raids also helped to preserve a modicum of public order within the districts and to control their borders. In 1897, for instance, Mayor Carter Harrison, Jr., ordered police to clean up a section of South Clark Street in which prostitutes were visible from a new trolley line. In 1903, he began sweeping vice away from the southern LOOP, while leaving intact the newer Levee district between 18th and 22nd Streets.

The policy of tolerating vice districts was challenged on moral and practical grounds in the 1910s, most notably by the Chicago VICE COMMISSION, which pointed out that the policy had failed even to keep vice contained. In response, raids virtually shut down the Levee in 1912. Vice was already scattering throughout Chicago anyway, into "call-house flats" and other covert locations, dependent on a communications network of pimps, TAXI drivers, and saloonkeepers. The automobile and the telephone helped free prostitution from geographic limits.

Prostitution boomed in the BLACK BELT in the 1910s and 1920s, and was also common in parts of the Near North Side, UPTOWN, and LAKE VIEW. Not nearly as compact or flagrant as the Levee, these districts owed their existence to corrupt police and ward politicians. The area around Clark Street and Chicago Avenue emerged as the main vice district of Chicago in the 1940s and 1950s, protected by organized crime. Strippers and "B-girls" solicited openly in the bars. Similar districts grew in tolerant suburbs such as CALUMET CITY and CICERO. The Clark Street vice district declined in the 1960s and 1970s because of URBAN RENEWAL and efforts to control police corruption. Nevertheless, pockets of prostitution persisted in certain suburban areas with little interference.

Peter C. Baldwin

See also: Crime and Chicago's Image; Street Life; Underground Economy

Further reading: Duis, Perry R. *The Saloon: Public Drinking in Chicago and Boston, 1880–1920.* 1983. • Lindberg, Richard C. *To Serve and Collect: Chicago Politics and Police Corruption from the Lager Beer Riot to the Summerdale Scandal, 1855–1960.* 1998. • Peterson, Virgil W. *Annual Reports on Chicago Crime, 1953–1969.* Chicago Historical Society.

Vietnamese. Persons of Vietnamese origin began moving to Chicago in significant numbers in the mid to late 1970s. Several hundred Vietnamese REFUGEES were resettled in Chicago following the fall of Saigon in 1975. While the largest number were resettled during the late 1970s and early 1980s, refugees from Vietnam continued to be placed in the metropolitan area through the early 1990s under special U.S. government resettlement programs for former South Vietnamese detention camp detainees and Amer-Asians born to Vietnamese women and U.S. military personnel. As they have become established in the city, many Vietnamese have sponsored family members from Vietnam to join them in Chicago. The 1990 census enumerated 4,640 persons of Vietnamese ethnicity living in the city of Chicago and 8,053 in the larger metropolitan area. A decade later, the Illinois Bureau of Refugee and Immigrant Services estimated approximately 10,000 Vietnamese living in the city of Chicago, and another 8,000 elsewhere in the metropolitan area.

Beginning in 1975, the voluntary resettlement agencies active in Chicago began placing most Vietnamese refugees in a few North Side neighborhoods, including UPTOWN and ROGERS PARK. Continuing into the late 1980s and early 1990s, many of the former reeducation camp detainees and Amer-Asians were also resettled in Uptown and vicinity by these agencies. Vietnamese living in the city of Chicago remained residentially clustered in Uptown, Rogers Park, and ALBANY PARK. Within the rest of the metropolitan area, Vietnamese residents have spread out, with the largest numbers living in the north and west as opposed to the southern suburbs.

The substantial residential presence in the Uptown neighborhood stimulated a concentration of Vietnamese commercial establishments. Since the late 1970s, ethnic CHINESE originating from Vietnam and ethnic Vietnamese have opened scores of RESTAURANTS, grocery stores, gift shops, hair salons, video shops, and other businesses targeted to a Southeast and East Asian clientele in the vicinity of Argyle and Broadway Streets. Significantly, the growth of Vietnamese businesses in this neighborhood has also revitalized a long moribund and physically deteriorating inner-city RETAIL district.

Persons of Vietnamese origin have established a variety of ethnic institutions in the Chicago area for the purposes of social support and the maintenance of their cultural heritage. Most of these institutions, including MUTUAL BENEFIT SOCIETIES a CHAMBER OF COMMERCE, and veterans' organizations are based in Uptown or elsewhere on the North Side. The Vietnamese Association of Illinois, with its offices on Broadway, has provided advocacy and SOCIAL SERVICES to the population since its establishment in 1976. Among other institutions, several Vietnamese temples and churches have contributed to religious pluralism in the Chicago area. There are five Vietnamese BUDDHIST temples in the region as well as two VIETNAMESE ROMAN CATHOLIC congregations. A couple of Baptist churches located in Uptown have established Vietnamese-language ministries.

Mark E. Pfeifer

See also: Cambodians; Demography; Multicentered Chicago

Further reading: Hung, M. H., and D. W. Haines. "Vietnamese." In *Refugees in America in the 1990s: A Reference Handbook,* ed. David W. Haines, 1996. • Zhou, Min, and Carl Bankston. *Growing Up American: How Vietnamese Children Adapt to Life in the United States.* 1998.

Villa District, Irving Park Community Area. The Villa District is an architectural study of BUNGALOWS. Its boundaries are the alley east of Pulaski Road, Avondale Avenue, Hamlin Avenue, and Addison Street. Most of the houses were built between 1907 and 1922.

Albert Haentze and Charles M. Wheeler purchased the land in 1907, when RESTRICTIVE COVENANTS were already in place determining lot lines and spacing. The bungalows were designed in the "Chicago" and "California" styles with numerous variations. The simple American Foursquare was a boxlike structure with a broad front porch inspired by Prairie school ARCHITECTURE. Other styles included elements of colonial or Tudor design.

The houses sat on parklike landscapes and sold for from $4,000 to as much as $20,000 for mansion-sized houses. Any number of combinations went into the exterior, such as clapboard, brick, shingles, and stucco. The interior was typically long and narrow. Although Haentze and Wheeler sold most of their vacant Villa property in 1913, subsequent building followed the same patterns.

The Villa Improvement League was begun in 1907 by area builders to foster community participation and preserve the uniqueness of the neighborhood. In 1923 the league enhanced the Villa District by building six-foot-tall rock structures crowned with flower boxes on every street corner.

Between 1986 and 1991, residents planted 120 TREES to replace those killed in the 1960s epidemic of Dutch elm disease. In 1992 the Villa's 126 homeowners bought their own SNOW equipment to clear their streets. Named a National Historic District, the picture-perfect, tree-lined streets of the Villa District lend a quiet suburban quality to the heart of the city.

Marilyn Elizabeth Perry

See also: Historic Preservation; Neighborhood Associations; Subdivisions

Further reading: Commission on Chicago Historical and Architectural Landmarks. "The Villa District: Preliminary Summary of Information." May 1982. • Prosser, Daniel J. "Chicago and the Bungalow Boom of the 1920s." *Chicago History* (Summer 1981): 86–95. • Roberts, Gary. "Villa Neighbors Find Life Easy." *Portage Park Times,* September 10, 1992.

Villa Park, IL, DuPage County, 18 miles W of the Loop. The village of Villa Park sits in east-central DuPage County, flanked by Addison, Elmhurst, and Lombard. Villa Park represents a good example of Chicago suburban development in the early twentieth century.

The Potawatomi primarily inhabited the Villa Park region before the 1830s; some Ojibwa and Ottawa Indians also shared the land. When the Black Hawk War Treaty drove these tribes west in 1833, other farmers came from New England, New York, and Germany, drawn by the open, fertile land and wild game.

To deliver their surplus farm goods to market, settlers improved St. Charles Road in 1843, while the Galena & Chicago Union Railroad began service in 1849.

In 1900, Florence Canfield and Louis Meyer, two area farm owners, sold land to the Chicago, Aurora & Elgin Railway, setting in motion the chain of events that would transform the area into a bustling suburb. The INTERURBAN began service in 1902, providing passenger travel, newspaper and milk delivery, and even funeral TRANSPORTATION to CEMETERIES in eastern Cook County.

In 1908, the Chicago REAL-ESTATE firm of Ballard and Pottinger purchased and subdivided a parcel of land near the rail line into 203 one-acre lots for homes, naming the development Villa Park. Two years later, Ballard and Pottinger developed another subdivision directly west of Villa Park named Ardmore. The Villa Park and Ardmore subdivisions united in 1914. The new incorporated community began life as the village of Ardmore, displeasing some in the Villa Park side of town. They led the call for a public referendum, and in 1917 voters changed the village's name to Villa Park.

The young community received a business boost in 1917 when the Wander Company, manufacturers of the chocolate drink Ovaltine, constructed a plant in the village. Villa Park's proximity to Chicago, combined with its ready access to farmland and strong transportation services, attracted residents as well as businesses. By 1920, Villa Park had nearly tripled its initial population of 300; in 1930, over 6,000 residents called Villa Park home.

Villa Park continued to grow in the 1930s and 1940s. After World War II, the development of suburbs, including Villa Park, exploded. Many of the village's original lots were subdivided to accommodate additional homes. Even the closure of the Chicago, Aurora, & Elgin Railway in 1957—the catalyst for Villa Park's birth and development—failed to hinder the community's growth.

Nearly all of Villa Park's schools expanded in the 1950s to accommodate the throngs of students. In 1959 Willowbrook High School opened to alleviate massive overcrowding at nearby York High School, enrolling 1,950 students. Further growth required an addition at Willowbrook only three years later. Between 1950 and 1970, Villa Park grew from 8,821 to 25,891 residents.

Eventually, the widespread growth in DuPage County landlocked Villa Park and its suburban neighbors. In 2000, Villa Park was a mature suburb, maintaining a population of 22,075. While still desirable, Villa Park's assets have transformed radically from those that attracted settlers a century ago.

Aaron Harwig

See also: Economic Geography; Government, Suburban

Further reading: Martin, Irene S. "Villa Park." In *DuPage Roots,* ed. Richard Thompson. 1985. • *Recollections: Story of Villa Park, IL.* 1976.

Virgil, IL, Kane County, 47 miles W of the Loop. Nineteenth-century settlers traveled the Oregon and St. Charles Road to Virgil. Residents of Virgil in the early twentieth century witnessed the town at its peak with a general store, bank, and creamery. Later, many of these business sites near Route 64 were dormant. As part of the townspeople's resistance to change, they succeeded in blocking a planned landfill by incorporating in 1990, with a population of 319.

Erik Gellman

See also: Agriculture; Kane County

Visitation and Aid Society. Founded in 1888, the Visitation and Aid Society was a politically progressive, lay-operated Roman Catholic charity that established a cooperative church-state welfare system serving delinquent or dependent juveniles, families, and prisoners in Cook County. Nationally, it was an important welfare lobby, publishing a journal, the *Juvenile Record* (later, the *Juvenile Court Record*), which tracked social policy developments in North America and Europe. Leaders included Timothy Hurley and William Onahan, who, under V&A auspices, helped to found the world's first JUVENILE COURT and to quell interreligious rivalries by cooperating with Protestant and Jewish charities. In 1911, the V&A's work was assumed by the St. Vincent de Paul Society.

James P. McCartin

See also: Catholic Charities; Children, Dependent; Social Services

Further reading: Hurley, Timothy. *The Origin of the Illinois Juvenile Court Law.* 1907. • Walsh, John Patrick. "The Catholic Church in Chicago and the Problems of Urban Poverty, 1893–1915." Ph.D. diss., University of Chicago, 1948.

Volo, IL, Lake County, 41 miles NW of the Loop. Formed at the junction of the Chicago—Lake Geneva and Waukegan—Woodstock stage trails in the 1840s, the settlement was originally called Forksville. The community failed to prosper when RAILROADS bypassed the

area. Fearing aggressive expansion by neighboring LAKEMOOR, residents incorporated in 1993 after a series of court hearings. The 2000 population was 180.

Craig L. Pfannkuche

See also: Lake County, IL

Further reading: Bateman, Newton, Paul Selby, and Charles A. Partridge. *Historical Encyclopedia of Illinois and History of Lake County.* 1902.

Wadsworth, IL, Lake County, 41 miles N of the Loop. The Wadsworth area was not settled as early as many other communities in Lake County. Green Bay Road bypassed it to the east while the plank road to the county's interior from the lake port of WAUKEGAN ran south of the area. It was not until the mid-1840s that land-seeking YANKEES followed the upper reaches of the DES PLAINES RIVER to the area's great oak groves and meadows.

Early farms were not prosperous; meadow SOILS were often mixed with thick bands of clay deposited over 13,000 years ago by the receding Wisconsin glacier. Many of the larger meadows were originally massive holes filled with the muck and sediment from glacial drainage. Farmers still find 10,000-year-old spruce logs and the bones of mastodons under their fields.

In 1873, the Chicago, Milwaukee & St. Paul RAILROAD completed the construction of a line between Milwaukee and Chicago which ran along the east bank of the Des Plaines River. Hoping to increase his land's value, local farmer John Lux platted a village site in 1874. The "Milwaukee Road" accepted the plat as a station stop, naming it Wadsworth after Elisha Wadsworth, a major Milwaukee Road stockholder.

Although a post office opened in Wadsworth in 1874, the station was primarily used as a milk collection point for the area's numerous large dairy farms for Chicago delivery. Because of the large amount of clay found in the area, two drainage tile factories and a brick factory came into operation near the station by 1886.

Since much undeveloped land still remained around Wadsworth in 1958, Tempel Smith, owner of Tempel Steel Company of Chicago, decided to purchase five thousand acres next to the original village for Tempel Farms, home to a troupe of noted Lipizzan horses.

Although Wadsworth's population was only 558 in 1962, most residents feared the ANNEXATION of the land surrounding Wadsworth, including Tempel Farms, into an aggressively expanding Waukegan. In, 1962 Wadsworth's residents voted to incorporate their village, and elected Albert Heiser the first village president. Heiser and the village trustees strongly favored retaining the village's spacious AGRICULTURAL landscapes. Wadsworth's population did not reach 1,000 until 1980.

Because construction around the source of the Des Plaines River caused seasonal flooding, village leaders supported the development of a new 450-acre wetland along the bank of the river to act as a natural FLOOD CONTROL basin. The pioneering project was completed in 1997 and has kept the scenic upper Des Plaines basin from needing channelization.

With their lands protected by estate ZONING, the 2,500 people living in Wadsworth at the end of the twentieth century have maintained a spacious rural lifestyle similar to that which existed in the 1870s.

Craig L. Pfannkuche

See also: Glaciation; Land Use; Suburbs and Cities as Dual Metropolis

Further reading: "Our Town: Wadsworth/Gurnee." *Waukegan News Sun,* November 5, 1990. • Cermak, June, ed. *Bridge to the Past.* 1977. • Dolan, Laurie, ed. *Wadsworth Village Hall: Dedication.* 1985.

War Monuments. The first war monuments in most Chicago-area communities were erected in CEMETERIES and dedicated to the 22,436 COOK COUNTY men who fought in the CIVIL WAR. Typical were the Chicago Soldiers and Sailors Monument in Rosehill Cemetery and the GERMAN veterans statue in St. Boniface Cemetery, which depict enlisted men standing guard over the graves of their comrades. In the lakefront parks of Chicago, numerous heroic equestrian bronzes commemorate heroes of the Civil War: Ulysses S. Grant, John A. Logan, and Abraham Lincoln. Hundreds of thousands of Chicago-area residents thronged to the parks for the dedication of these larger-than-life monuments.

Twentieth-century Chicagoans have taken a more circumspect approach to commemoration. Save for Leonard Crunelle's monument to AFRICAN AMERICAN doughboys on King Drive, the emphasis on WORLD WAR I commemoration was to produce so-called "living monuments" that could contribute to the community. Rather than glorify either war or the warrior, Chicagoans built utilitarian structures such as SOLDIER FIELD (1926) and NAVY PIER (rededicated in 1927), which over time ceased to be thought of as memorials at all.

WORLD WAR II produced an explosion of small, ad hoc memorials in virtually every neighborhood in Chicago. Street-corner memorial plaques and neighborhood honor rolls expressed community solidarity. After the war many of these memorials were gradually removed, casualties of changing neighborhoods and callously implemented street improvements.

The 1980s brought a new wave of war memorials. The opening of the Vietnam Veterans Memorial in Washington DC in 1982 sparked a national movement to come to terms with America's COLD WAR military campaigns. At the same time, suburban villages founded or transformed by the post–World War II boom sought symbols that rooted residents in the American experience and bound them together as a community. Like almost all memorials, the monuments of the 1980s and 1990s were the result of the efforts of veterans groups anxious that their sacrifice be not forgotten.

Theodore J. Karamanski

See also: Art, Public; Clubs: Patriotic and Veterans' Clubs

Further reading: Bodnar, John. *Remaking America: Public Memory, Commemoration, and Patriotism in the Twentieth Century.* 1992. • Karamanski, Theodore J. "Memory's Landscape." *Chicago History* 26.2 (Summer 1997): 54–72.

Ward System. Chicago has been divided into municipal legislative districts called wards since its first municipal CHARTER in 1837, which created six wards. Except for the single alderman allotted to wards Three and Five until 1839, each ward elected two members of the Common Council. The number of wards increased repeatedly in the nineteenth century to accommodate growth in population and territory, eventually stabilizing at 35 wards after the major ANNEXATIONS of 1889. In 1923 the current system was adopted, with one alderman representing each of 50 wards. State law requires that ward boundaries be redrawn after each federal census to ensure roughly equal representation by population size. In the 1970s and 1980s there were five court-ordered partial redistrictings to redress the underrepresentation of racial and ethnic minorities.

Chicago is unusual in having maintained its ward system while many cities were experimenting with at-large voting systems, smaller councils, and nonpartisan elections. Besides being a device of representative government, wards have organized residents' access to city services and, for an earlier generation, shaped the ward-and-precinct structure of political parties. In some cases, wards have developed localized cultural identities akin to those of neighborhoods.

Douglas Knox

See also: Government, City of Chicago; Machine Politics; Political Culture; Politics

Further reading: Karlen, Harvey M. *The Governments of Chicago.* 1958. • Pierce, Bessie Louise. *A History of Chicago.* 3 vols. 1937–1957. • Sparling, Samuel Edwin. *Municipal History and Present Organization of the City of Chicago.* Bulletin of the University of Wisconsin, no. 23, May 1898.

Warrenville, IL, DuPage County, 29 miles W of the Loop. Warrenville began as a mill center, developed as a VACATION SPOT along an INTERURBAN line, and has become a center of research and suburban development. Its development has long been tied to NAPERVILLE to the south, and to the natural springs in the area.

The Warren family traveled two miles north from Naperville along the DUPAGE RIVER in 1833 to claim land near a spring at McDowell Woods. The family established a LUMBER business, a house (one of the oldest still in the county), and a BOARDINGHOUSE for sawmill workers. A gristmill, built in 1847, attracted farmers from as far as Galena. A nearby dam provided a recreational spot, as well as a baptismal font for churches.

The Second Baptist Church, Warrenville's first congregation, was founded as a branch of Naperville's First Baptist Church in 1836. During the 1850s Warrenville Academy served the Baptist congregations in Warrenville, Naperville, and surrounding communities. Its students included Bertha Honoré, later known as Mrs. Potter Palmer.

Warrenville's connection to Naperville strengthened in 1849, when the Chicago-Southwest Plank Road linked both communities. Bypassed by earlier RAILROADS, Warrenville finally became a stop along the Chicago, Aurora & Elgin Railway between 1902 and 1959. Its station provided a second town center, and was remodeled as the city hall and police station in 1970.

The interurban link helped to make Warrenville an attractive, but convenient retreat from city life. Except for BOOTLEGGING activity during PROHIBITION, Warrenville was considered a quiet VACATION SPOT. Illinois Bell opened a rest home for TELEPHONE operators in 1916, familiar today as the Warrenville Cenacle retreat facility. Similarly, Montgomery Ward established a vacation home for employees in 1918.

Warrenville continued to be a center for recreational activities into the late twentieth century. In the 1970s Mount Hoy, nicknamed Mount Trashmore, was created by combining refuse and soil into a hill that became popular for tubing. Blackwell FOREST PRESERVE, a popular recreational area, excavated land to create Silver Lake in 1977. The remains of the Warrenville Mammoth were discovered in the site of the lake.

Only since the 1960s has Warrenville grown as a suburban community, reaching a population of 13,363 in 2000. With the opening of the toll road I-88 to the south of the community, businesses such as Northern Illinois Gas and Amoco Research Center located in Warrenville. Residential subdivisions began to appear, and Warrenville was finally incorporated as a village in 1967. In the 1980s the city established a tax-increment financing district to help pay for the development of the 650-acre Elmhurst-Chicago Stone Company QUARRY. It was one of the last large, undeveloped properties under a single ownership in the county.

Jane S. Teague

See also: Suburbs and Cities as Dual Metropolis; Toll Roads; Waste Disposal; Welfare Capitalism

McCormicks

From Cyrus McCormick (1809–1884) to his grandnephew Brooks McCormick (1917–), the McCormick family has been a force in the business, cultural, and philanthropic life and history of the Chicago metropolitan area for over 150 years.

Cyrus McCormick relocated his reaper work to Chicago from Virginia in 1847. The reaper's market was on the plains and prairies of Chicago's growing hinterland. Cyrus McCormick became one of the richest businessmen in the city.

The merger in 1902 of the McCormick Harvesting Machine Company and the Deering Harvester Company into International Harvester Company (now Navistar International Corporation) would solidify McCormick and his descendants' lock on the market of farm implements for nearly 150 years. McCormicks have also been involved in the banking, investment, news media, and real-estate businesses.

Family influence has spanned Chicago and its suburbs. Cyrus's descendants would occupy "McCormickville" on Chicago's GOLD COAST, country estates in the North Shore suburb of LAKE FOREST (Harold Fowler and Edith Rockefeller McCormick's Villa Turicum, built in 1911; Nettie Fowler McCormick's House-in-the-Woods, built in 1916; Cyrus H. McCormick, Jr.'s "Walden," built in 1896), and the western suburbs of WARRENVILLE (Chauncey and his son Brooks McCormick's St. James Farm, built in 1903 and purchased by the McCormicks in the 1920s) and WHEATON (Robert R. McCormick's Cantigny, built in 1896 by Joseph Medill).

Marriages of the McCormicks with other bluebloods such as the Rockefellers and the Deerings have allowed large philanthropic donations to many Chicago cultural and nonprofit organizations such as NORTHWESTERN UNIVERSITY, the FIELD MUSEUM OF NATURAL HISTORY, the LYRIC OPERA, the ART INSTITUTE, the LINCOLN PARK ZOO, the NEWBERRY LIBRARY, and the CHICAGO HISTORICAL SOCIETY.

Kevin Davis

Washington Heights, Community Area 73, 12 miles S of the Loop. Located on the far SOUTH SIDE of Chicago, Washington Heights, is bounded by 89th and 107th Streets and two RAILROAD lines at roughly Ashland Boulevard to the west and Stewart Avenue to the east. The COMMUNITY AREA includes the settlements once known as Brainerd and Fernwood. From the 1830s to the 1860s, the area was populated mostly by farmers. After the 1860s, railroads dominated the economy of the region, beginning in 1864–1865 when RAILROAD WORKERS temporarily settled in the area.

SUBDIVISION followed the arrival of the railroad. In 1866 Willis M. Hitt and Laurin P. Hilliard bought the land from 103rd to 107th Streets from farmers and subdivided for development along 103rd street from Loomis to Racine. In 1869, the Blue Island Land and Building Company purchased and subdivided 1,500 acres between 99th and 107th Streets. By 1874, Washington Heights had enough residents to incorporate. In 1883, the Fernwood subdivision was registered between 99th and 103rd Streets. Fernwood lay to the southeast of Washington Heights, and had over 185 houses by 1885. The Brainerd subdivision, named after an early farm family, was developed from 87th to 91st Streets, but owing to a lack of transit, there were only six houses standing by 1885. In 1890 Washington Heights and Brainerd were ANNEXED to the city of Chicago, and in 1891 Fernwood was annexed and designated as part of Washington Heights.

By 1900 "the heights" area of Washington Heights had developed separately as a settlement for upper-income residents and was renamed BEVERLY. The Washington Heights Community Area grew to nearly 18,000 people by 1930. Brick BUNGALOWS constructed from 1920 to 1950 defined the residential character of Washington Heights. In this period, the community was made up of white ethnics including GERMANS and SWEDES, but mainly IRISH, many of whom had moved to Washington Heights from South Englewood and GREATER GRAND CROSSING for better housing.

After WORLD WAR II, Washington Heights experienced racial succession as AFRICAN AMERICANS began to settle just east of Halsted. By 1960, African Americans constituted 12 percent of a population of 29,793. REAL-ESTATE firms practiced BLOCKBUSTING tactics to scare whites to sell their homes "before property values went down." White families did move, but property values remained steady. A journalist wrote in 1969: "The economic level of the new residents is no different from that of the old. Neither are the social values. . . . But many whites are running scared." By 1970, the population of Washington Heights peaked at 36,540, 75 percent black. A decade later the community had declined to 29,843 people, 98 percent black. Throughout the change, Washington Heights has retained its essentially middle-class character, as over three-fourths of the population own homes and incomes are well above the city median. Washington Heights also boasts the Woodson Branch of the Chicago Public Library at 95th and Halsted. Its Vivian Harsh Collection is the second-largest collection of African American history and literature in the Midwest.

Clinton E. Stockwell

See also: Contested Spaces; Metropolitan Growth; Neighborhood Succession

Further reading: Chicago Fact Book Consortium, ed. *Local Community Fact Book: Chicago Metropolitan Area, 1990.* 1995. • *Chicago Historic Resources Survey: An Inventory of Architecturally and Historically Significant Structures.* 1996.

Washington Park, Community Area 40, 7 miles S of the Loop. Washington Park takes its name from the recreational area situated along the eastern border of the community, stretching from 51st to 60th streets along Cottage Grove Avenue. The western edge of Washington Park is the Chicago, Rock Island & Pacific Railroad. Low-lying and swampy prior to being dredged in 1884, the western portion of Washington Park was settled by Irish and German railroad and meatpacking workers in the 1860s and 1870s. By the 1890s German Jews had begun to settle in east Washington Park, a small number of African Americans had moved into the working-class district south of Garfield and west of State Street, and affluent American-born whites settled on the wide avenues that ran northward from the area into Chicago. This amalgam of ethnicities and classes made Washington Park an early example of neighborhood diversity and suburban development.

Transportation routes stimulated rapid growth in Washington Park during the latter part of the nineteenth century. By 1887 cable cars reached 63rd on State Street, and 67th on Cottage Grove. The "L" train reached beyond 55th Street by 1892, and in 1907 extended the length of Washington Park into the Woodlawn area. The wide boulevards in the Washington Park area also contributed to the growth of the community. These avenues attracted wealthy Chicagoans, who built mansions and elegant apartments on Grand Boulevard (now Dr. Martin Luther King Jr. Drive), and Calumet, Indiana, and Michigan Avenues. The boulevards, along with the cable cars and the elevated trains, provided easy access to Chicago's central business district, making Washington Park an attractive location for the working class of the western section, as well as for the wealthy and middle-class residents of the eastern portion of the area.

A boom in the construction of apartments around the turn of the century played a role in the racial transition of Washington Park. As Chicago's African American ghetto expanded southward during the Great Migration, blacks gained entrance into the large number of apartments in Washington Park, many of which had been converted into kitchenettes. Native whites, German Jews, and other ethnic groups moved to points south and north in Chicago, and Washington Park was transformed into a largely black neighborhood (92 percent) as early as 1930. The area's racial transition was rapid and punctuated with violence. A stark example of conflicts to follow, Washington Park, along with the Grand Boulevard community, became a hotbed of racial tension during the Race Riot of 1919.

The cultural and religious institutions of Washington Park have reflected the area's racial transition and its predominately black population. St. Anselm Church, built in 1909 by Irish Catholics and celebrated in the James T. Farrell trilogy, *Studs Lonigan,* became a black parish in the early 1930s. Greek Orthodox residents built SS. Constantine and Helen also in 1909 at 61st and Michigan. In 1948, the building was taken over by the Church of St. Edmund, an Episcopal congregation that had been formed in Washington Park in 1905 and was entirely African American by 1928. B'nai Sholom Temple Israel at 5301 S. Michigan was sold to black Baptists and became Bethesda Baptist Church in 1925. St. Mary's African Methodist Episcopal Church at 52nd and Dearborn was established in 1897 and is the oldest black congregation in the area. The DuSable Museum of African American History (1961) is a Washington Park landmark, having moved to the area in 1973. This nonprofit institution devoted to the collection and preservation of African American history and culture is one of the largest African American museums in the country.

In more recent years Washington Park has been associated with poverty, urban blight, and public housing. The area has contained one of the highest concentrations of public housing in the United States, and along with the Washington Park Homes (1962), contains roughly a third of the largest housing complex in the world, the Robert Taylor Homes (1962). The presence of industry in Washington Park has been negligible; nor is there any significant commercial center. Since 1950, and due in part to the initiatives of the Chicago Land Clearance Commission, the population of the community has declined, down from nearly 57,000 in 1950 to 14,146 in 2000. As the twentieth century drew to a close, nearly half of Washington Park residents lived below the poverty level.

Wallace Best

See also: Rapid Transit System; Religious Geography; South Side; Street Railways; Suburbs and Cities as Dual Metropolis; Urban Renewal

Further reading: Chicago Fact Book Consortium, ed. *Local Community Fact Book: Chicago Metropolitan Area, 1990.* 1995. • Cutler, Irving. *Chicago: Metropolis of the Mid-Continent.* 3rd ed. 1982. • Pacyga, Dominic A., and Ellen Skerrett. *Chicago, City of Neighborhoods: Histories and Tours.* 1986.

Washington Park. Washington Park's 372 acres stretch west from Cottage Grove Avenue between 51st and 60th Streets. In 1870 noted landscape designers Frederick Law Olmsted and Calvert Vaux centered their prairie-based design on a 100-acre greensward called the South Open Green. Surrounding the green were curvilinear walking trails, trees, and shrubs to create an element of the picturesque within the park. The designers also planned more formal spaces, including a bandstand and refectory, a promenade, carriage roads, and gathering spots for picnics.

The Great Chicago Fire of 1871 destroyed the building that housed Olmsted and Vaux's blueprints. The South Park Commission hired landscape designer Horace W. S. Cleveland in 1872 to execute the plans as best he could, though financial setbacks as a result of the fire and the 1873 depression made the commissioners scale back their plans. Cleveland carried out the plans for the greensward, walking paths, carriage drives, and some shrub and tree plantings, and enhanced the site with more formal flower plantings that were less expensive than the alterations to the landscape proposed by Olmsted and Vaux. Architect Daniel H. Burnham designed stables, administrative offices, and the refectory for the park.

Washington Park often was the scene of racial tension and conflict as the demographic composition of its users began to change. The African American population north and east of the park began expanding during and after World War I. Many blacks who tried to use the park reported threats and intimidation, primarily from white gangs. Still, black semiprofessional baseball teams played each other on the baseball fields at Washington Park through the 1920s. In the 1930s, park commissioners added new facilities, including swimming pools and a wading pool. By the 1990s, Washington Park boasted some of the premier aquatics facilities in Chicago.

Robin F. Bachin

See also: Contested Spaces; Leisure; Park Districts

Washington Park Subdivision, neighborhood in the Woodlawn Community Area. If the Washington Park neighborhood had rectangular rather than ragged edges, it would include the Washington Park Subdivision. Just south of the eponymous Washington Park, the Washington Park Subdivision is instead a three-by-eight-block portion of northwestern Woodlawn.

The prestigious Washington Park racetrack occupied the southern two-thirds of the subdivision from 1884 to 1905, when the city outlawed betting. By 1912, developers had built new housing in the SUBDIVISION, but several prominent commercial recreation facilities continued to attract visitors to Woodlawn until the GREAT DEPRESSION. Revelers could visit the White City AMUSEMENT PARK, watch movies at the Tivoli Theater and the Woodlawn Theater, or dance at the Trianon Ballroom. The Sans Souci Amusement Park, a beer garden with a band shell, was remodeled into the tony Midway Gardens by architect Frank Lloyd Wright in 1914. WORLD WAR I and PROHIBITION dampened Midway Gardens' potential, however, and after a stint under the ownership of the Edelweiss Brewing Company, the site became a garage and car wash before being demolished in 1929.

Between 1928 and 1940, the newly residential subdivision was the center of a legal battle over the expansion of the BLACK BELT. Alarmed by the prospect of poor blacks moving into Woodlawn through the corridor between Washington Park and the middle-class black West Woodlawn, the Woodlawn Businessmen's Association and the UNIVERSITY OF CHICAGO cajoled landlords in Washington Park Subdivision into signing RESTRICTIVE COVENANTS under whose terms property owners agreed that if enough other owners complied, none of them would rent or sell homes to nonwhites. With the onset of the GREAT DEPRESSION, however, landlords found fewer whites who would pay the rent they wanted and instead began subdividing their apartments and renting to blacks. The covenant's organizers sued to prevent the Hansberry family from occupying 6140 S. Rhodes. Despite the legal action, African Americans continued to try to occupy the western half of the subdivision. In 1940, the U.S. Supreme Court held, in *Lee v. Hansberry*, that the areawide covenant was unenforceable. Shortly thereafter, blacks moved into the Washington Park Subdivision and the rest of Woodlawn, while most of the white population moved out. In 1950, over 99 percent of the subdivision's population was black.

Amanda Seligman

See also: Community Areas; Horse Racing; South Side

Further reading: Holt, Glen E., and Dominic A. Pacyga. *Chicago: A Historical Guide to the Neighborhoods: The Loop and South Side.* 1979. • Plotkin, Wendy. "Deeds of Mistrust: Race, Housing, and Restrictive Covenants in Chicago, 1900–1948." Ph.D. diss., University of Illinois at Chicago. 1999.

Waste Disposal. Early Chicago's wastes included ashes from wood burned by households and businesses, droppings of horses on streets and in stables, and relatively small amounts of food wastes, newspapers, and the like. Most of it appears to have been readily biodegradable. In 1849 the city of Chicago appointed its first city scavengers. Wastes were often dumped in marshy areas on the city's edge. In Chicago's flat terrain, the transformation of lowlands into city blocks suitable for development often involved raising the level of the land through dumping of wastes, which also eliminated standing water. Many Chicago buildings and streets now rest on as much as a dozen feet of nineteenth-century refuse. The mouth of the CHICAGO RIVER was transformed by landfilled refuse, and debris from the Great Fire, along with much ordinary refuse, was used to extend Lake (now GRANT) PARK.

Though residents protested the odors, rats, and insects at dumps, ENVIRONMENTAL REGULATION was very limited. The city sanitation services often performed poorly, leaving wooden garbage boxes overflowing, especially in immigrant neighborhoods where residents lacked CLOUT. Reformers at HULL HOUSE pressured the city to improve collection in the 1890s, and Jane Addams served as a local garbage inspector for several years.

Chicago's industries generated enormous quantities of waste. City ordinances limited land dumping of MEATPACKING wastes after 1878, but packers dumped refuse liberally into the waterways, a practice tolerated because the industry was so important to the city's economy. "Bubbly Creek," a fork of the CHICAGO RIVER, was so named because of the bubbles rising from decomposing slaughterhouse wastes. Tanneries, distilleries, and other industries dumped wastes into the North Branch of the Chicago River and the CALUMET RIVER. IRON AND STEEL mill wastes were used to extend the lakefront of southeast Chicago and northwestern Indiana.

Industrial wastes grew in the early twentieth century. Steel mills often dumped slag on adjacent lands, where in some cases residences were built. Oil, CHEMICAL, and steel industries dumped into waterways, especially on the Southeast Side. Chicago's LAKE MICHIGAN water supply was largely but not completely protected from these wastes by reversing the flow of the Chicago River and by digging canals which diverted wastes away from the lake.

Only slowly did the problems created by careless waste disposal methods begin to be addressed. Slag from U.S. Steel's Gary Works was used in cement making and fertilizer production. Pressure from the Metropolitan Sanitary District (now the Metropolitan Water Reclamation District of Greater Chicago) led to neutralization of sulfuric acid discharged into the Calumet by Sherwin-Williams, because it damaged sewage treatment equipment. Unfortunately, cleanup and treatment sometimes created further problems. Sewage treatment, begun in 1922, generated sludge which was dumped on land. And though public pressure was occasionally effective in addressing careless waste disposal, often there were no barriers to unsafe practices. The advent of nuclear energy added to the hazards. Between 1945 and 1963, for instance, radioactive thorium wastes were used as landscaping fill, deposited in ordinary dumps, or discharged into the DUPAGE RIVER.

In 1905, the city was disposing of 1,614 tons of refuse each day, and clay pits and QUARRIES near the city began to fill up. Former dumps were often used for SCHOOLS or parks, including the land on which SOLDIER FIELD is built. Chicago experimented again with incineration and other disposal methods, but most wastes were still dumped. By 1954, the city had no more new sites outside of Lake Calumet. In 1963, Chicago exported almost three million cubic yards of wastes to 72 active suburban dumps, which also served booming suburban populations.

The amount of household refuse grew enormously in the late twentieth century as the region's population grew and an affluent society indulged in waste-generating practices. Ashes virtually disappeared from municipal refuse as COAL was replaced by other heating sources, but Americans disposed of growing quantities of nonreturnable cans and bottles, corrugated food packaging, and plastics. By 1988 the typical Chicagoan threw out a ton of garbage per year.

In Chicago, household wastes were picked up by a department long known as a source of PATRONAGE jobs for politicians. To cut costs in the 1980s, plastic garbage carts replaced metal garbage cans—long a symbol of machine politics in Chicago, where aldermen handed them out to residents with their names stenciled on the side. Businesses, apartment owners, and most suburban GOVERNMENTS contracted with private haulers. Private haulers were once the domain of small operators, including many AFRICAN AMERICANS. At times they were subject to extortion by mobsters. In the 1970s and '80s, however, a few large companies came to dominate the business, benefiting from superior access to landfills and better finances and organization. The biggest companies owned and operated landfills and incinerators.

To accommodate the growing volume of wastes, the city turned to incineration in the 1950s. From the early 1960s until 1980, Chicago burned most of its garbage. But scientists and the public grew increasingly concerned over smokestack emissions, especially from plastics and other complex substances. In addition, incinerator ashes contained toxic chemicals. In 1996, faced with prohibitive costs for up-to-date pollution controls, the city closed down its last municipally operated incinerator. State subsidies to incinerators were eliminated, and private incinerators in schools, HOSPITALS, apartment buildings, and single-family residences began to shut down in the

1970s, leaving only a few hundred by the 1990s.

The result was to increase dependence on landfills for city, suburban, and industrial wastes. But by midcentury, the long-term environmental hazards of landfills had become well known, especially contamination of underground WATER SUPPLIES. Sanitary landfill techniques to avoid these problems—including lining the site and monitoring "leachate" to ensure toxic substances do not leak into the water table—were known by the 1940s, but Chicago was reluctant to adopt them because of their higher costs. State regulations mandated sanitary landfills by 1966, but they were poorly enforced at first. Many older landfills in the region pose threats to water supplies.

Within the city, landfills opened or expanded only in the sparsely populated Lake CALUMET REGION, much of it marshlands not suitable for industry or residences. Hundreds of acres of Lake Calumet itself have been filled in with Chicago refuse, and by the 1990s, the Southeast Side's Tenth Ward had over 25 square miles of landfill. Though the city had protected its Lake Michigan water supply, it paid little heed to the effect of landfilling on Calumet-area birds, fish, or GROUNDWATER.

By the 1980s and 1990s, sanitary landfill techniques had become the norm. Small operations could not meet the new standards, and vocal opposition from neighbors and environmental groups limited landfills to those that could plan far in advance and build expensive facilities. By 2000, the 9 counties of northeastern Illinois had only 14 landfills, most of them huge suburban facilities. While earlier dumps had consisted of quarries or marshes, filled to ground level and abandoned, many "landfills" were now small mountains of wastes, stretching hundreds of feet into the air, with pipes protruding to vent escaping methane. New features on the region's flat landscape, these landfills, when shut, are often converted to use as golf courses or parks. Locating new landfills in the region became increasingly difficult, and public officials and landfill operators began sending refuse downstate.

Fly dumping, or dumping without a permit, became a serious problem in the 1980s, as landfill costs grew and regulations proliferated. Relatively small private companies found it advantageous to dump illegally, targeting especially minority neighborhoods. The most infamous case involved a two-block area near Kildare and Roosevelt where a company owned by John Christopher dumped CONSTRUCTION debris that rose to more than five stories. Christopher was a key figure in the federal government's "Silver Shovel" investigation into corruption related in part to fly dumping.

The growing costs of landfill and potential disappearance of suitable sites created a sense of crisis in the late 1980s. A few communities adopted user fees to give householders incentives to curb waste generation. The Illinois legislature began limiting what items could be placed in landfills. The law banned putting yard waste—roughly one-fifth of municipal wastes—in sanitary landfills in 1990 and obliged local governments to recycle. Chicago embarked on a unique "blue bag" recycling system in 1995, in which recyclables are placed in special blue bags, tossed into the garbage truck with other wastes, and sorted later. The program was criticized for low participation rates and for breakage of bags, resulting in "mixed" waste that could not be genuinely recycled. In most suburbs, recyclables were placed in special containers and picked up by a separate truck.

Garbage in an alley in the Back of the Yards neighborhood (no date). Photographer: Unknown. Source: Chicago Historical Society.

Government pressure also brought changes in handling of industrial wastes. In the late 1970s, courts ordered an end to the dumping of untreated pollutants. The practice of dumping dredging spoils, which are often toxic, into Lake Michigan finally ended in 1967 and was replaced with landfilling. Under heavy regulation, specialty companies dispose of hazardous wastes, which are typically landfilled in specially designed sites or burned in special incinerators. Controversy continues over the long-term safety of these procedures.

Past waste disposal practices have left a legacy of dangers to PUBLIC HEALTH and safety. Cleaning up old disposal sites, or "brownfields," with wastes ranging from old cars to benzene, has become a major challenge, especially for the federal government's "Superfund," which attempts to clean up and redispose of hazardous wastes at the worst sites. As of 2000, the Chicago area had more than 240 Superfund sites, about one-third in the city itself.

Christopher Thale

See also: Dutch; Ecosystem Evolution; Environmental Politics; Hazardous Waste; Industrial Pollution; Water

Further reading: Clippings on "refuse disposal." Municipal Reference Collection, Harold Washington Library, Chicago, IL. • Colten, Craig E. "Chicago's Waste Lands: Refuse Disposal and Urban Growth, 1840–1990." *Journal of Historical Geography* 20.2 (1994): 124–142. • Melosi, Martin V. *The Sanitary City: Urban Infrastructure in America, Colonial Times to the Present.* 2000.

Waste, Hazardous. The production of hazardous waste accompanied the development of industry in Chicago. From slaughterhouse activities in the nineteenth century to metal-based factories in the twentieth, the byproducts created by these various industrial enterprises resulted in extensive health threats. Lead-containing dust, asbestos, and unsafe levels of arsenic and cyanide were just a few of the toxins generated. Until the 1920s, however, health officials focused their attention on bacteriological dangers rather than the byproducts of industrialism. Even then, they framed the discussion in terms of industrial waste's risk to WATER rather than to human life. The environmental movement began to address these hazardous waste sites starting in the late 1940s with the mandate for using sanitary landfills, but the absence of a standardized classification system for industrial waste stymied its efforts. The reinvigoration of the environmental movement in the late twentieth century led Illinois to prohibit open waste dumping in 1966. In 1969 Chicago compelled industries to pretreat pollutants prior to release.

CHEMICAL and steel companies remained important sources of employment in Chicago until the 1960s, when hundreds of factories began to relocate to other regions. Those that relocated at that time, before there were legal constraints upon abandoning wastes, left many toxic, vacant areas in their wake. By the end of the twentieth century, over two hundred of the worst historical waste sites were being monitored and cleaned up through federal legislation. Thousands of other active sites that generated, transferred, stored, or disposed of hazardous wastes (or were more recent recipients of this waste) were under federal or state scrutiny.

Don Coursey

See also: Environmental Politics; Environmental Regulation; Industrial Pollution; Public Health; Waste Disposal

Water. Chicago's unusual wastewater disposal history was conditioned by the location of the city at the juncture of LAKE MICHIGAN and the CHICAGO RIVER. Initially, the city used the lake to supply water and to dispose of wastes. Beginning in the 1850s on an informal basis, and in 1871 on a formal basis, Chicago flushed its wastewater into the Mississippi River drainage system by reversing the flow of the Chicago River. With continued growth, sewage treatment works became necessary to conserve the lake water quality.

Before its natural topography was altered, the Chicago River reached the DES PLAINES RIVER during the wet seasons via a shallow lake across the divide between the GREAT LAKES

Water Quality in the 1830s

When Caroline Palmer Clarke arrived in Chicago in 1835, she wrote to her sister-in-law describing the city. A few years later, Clarke would settle into her new home, which remains one of the oldest houses in Chicago, now located in the Prairie Avenue Historic District.

I am thus far much better pleased with Chicago than I expected. . . .

I had expected to find the water very hard, but am as much disappointed in that as any one thing. The Lake water, which they use for almost every purpose, is as pure and good tasted as any I ever saw in my life. It is soft and washes perfectly well. To be sure they have the trouble of bringing it, but that costs only a *shilling* a *barrel*, which is nothing you know where they are in such a great way of doing business as they are here at Chicago.

Caroline Palmer Clarke to Mary Clarke Walker (sister-in-law), dated Chicago, November 1, 1835. Chicago Historical Society.

"The Great Chicago Sewer," Bridgeport, 1871. The city's sewage system dumped directly into the Chicago River, whose course was fitfully reversed, beginning when the Illinois & Michigan Canal was enlarged that year. Artist: Unknown. Source: The Newberry Library.

and Mississippi River drainage systems. The first regional PUBLIC WORK proposed was a canal crossing the Chicago PORTAGE, to create a permanent, navigable waterway between the Atlantic Ocean and the Gulf of Mexico. When completed in 1848, the ILLINOIS & MICHIGAN CANAL was fed by the Des Plaines and Calumet Rivers and by the South Branch of the Chicago River through a lift wheel at BRIDGEPORT.

A second topographical feature that contributed to the shaping of Chicago's wastewater strategy was that, during wet seasons, the flat, nonporous terrain turned to mud. In 1852, the Illinois legislature empowered sewage commissioners to install sewers in the most densely settled areas of Chicago.

The board's plan, designed by chief engineer Ellis Sylvester Chesbrough, called for an intercepting, combined sewer system that emptied into the river. Chicago's flatness created problems. These were resolved by the costly expedient of raising Chicago's level. The new sewers were laid at the level necessary to accomplish gravity flow. Earth was then packed around them and new streets were constructed above the sewers. Much of the fill was obtained by dredging the Chicago River in order to lower and enlarge it. Inevitably the river became heavily polluted. The pollution spread from the river into Lake Michigan until it reached the WATER SUPPLY intake.

The river was probably first reversed during several dry summers in the 1850s. To maintain the summit level in the canal, the Bridgeport lift wheel was run continuously, and lake water was pulled through the river. By 1860 Chicago's sewerage commissioners were considering a permanent reversal.

As conditions in the river worsened, other civic leaders agreed. An 1865 report recommended the canal be deepened over the 26-mile stretch between Bridgeport and LOCKPORT, and additional pumps were to be added at Bridgeport. These new works, completed in 1871, formally reversed the flow under normal conditions and transformed the canal into an open sewer whose current diluted impurities. The Sanitary District of Chicago (now the Metropolitan Water Reclamation District of Greater Chicago) was created at the end of the century as the Chicago metropolitan area quickly outgrew the canal's wastewater-carrying capability.

The Sanitary District Enabling Act of May 29, 1889, was a direct result of the Drainage and Water Supply Commission's recommendation to create a regional government for solving water supply and wastewater problems. The enabling act provided for the construction of the Chicago SANITARY AND SHIP CANAL to collect sewage and discharge it, diluted with Lake Michigan water, into the Des Plaines River. It was cheaper to build a new canal than enlarge the old one. Section 23 set the channel's capacity at 10,000 cubic feet per second, the Chicago River's maximum measured flood flow. Over time, the district annexed contiguous areas. The two largest additions, the North Shore and Calumet areas, were added in 1903. The North Shore (1910) and the Calumet-Sag (1922) Channels were constructed to serve these areas.

In 1895 a federal commission investigated the new channel's potential effect on lake and harbor levels. Its report claimed that the district's proposed diversion of 10,000 cfs would lower the level of the GREAT LAKES by six inches. From this point forward, overestimates would fuel the long-running "lake levels controversy."

The concern with lake levels, which was more likely the result of climatic variation than Chicago's diversion, was undoubtedly influenced by the fact that several Great Lakes states brought lawsuits to restrain Chicago from diverting any water at all. The inclusion of Canada in these suits, through the International Waterways Commission, gave impetus to the effort. The IWC argued that the growth of industry, combined with continued population growth, would put significant pressure on the sewage-handling capabilities of the channel system. All the critics, as well as many within the district, agreed that some form of sewage treatment would eventually prove necessary in addition to (if not in place of) the open sewers.

While these suits were pending, the main channel was constructed in three distinct sections: an earth section between Robey Street (now Damen Avenue) and SUMMIT, an earth and rock section between Summit and WILLOW SPRINGS, and finally a rock section from Willow Springs to Lockport. When completed, the rock section was 40 percent larger than the other two. This proved to be the determining factor in selecting a size for the Calumet-Sag Channel, which reached its confluence with the main channel at the Sag, the north end of the rock section.

Residents of the Illinois River basin, into which the main channel emptied, objected to receiving Chicago's wastewater. St. Louis believed the wastewater posed a threat to its Mississippi River water supply. On January 2,

Skokie Marsh, in an undated photograph. The lowland area in western Winnetka, Glencoe, and Highland Park was known as the Skokie Marsh, which connected to the North Branch of the Chicago River. It was transformed into the Skokie Lagoon by the Civilian Conservation Corps in the 1930s. Photographer: Fred M. Tuckerman. Source: Chicago Historical Society.

1900, the district quietly removed the dam at the main channel's northern end, and two weeks later, on January 17, the dam at Lockport opened. That same day, Missouri petitioned the U.S. Supreme Court to enjoin the state of Illinois and the Sanitary District of Chicago from discharging sewage into the new canal, a suit that was ultimately unsuccessful.

Chicago quickly felt the beneficial effects of the new channel. The typhoid death rate fell by almost 80 percent, and there were similar decreases for other waterborne diseases. Within 10 years, however, it was clear that the critics were correct: the channels were too small to handle the growing volume of domestic and industrial wastes. Consequently, during the 1920s, the district began to construct the major treatment works that became the foundation of its wastewater strategy. The U.S. Supreme Court limited the annual average net diversion from Lake Michigan to successively lower levels over an eight-year period, ultimately reaching a level of 1,500 cfs. This decision reinforced the district's shift from a strategy based on open sewers to one based on wastewater treatment. The Calumet sewage treatment works had been placed in operation in 1922, followed by the North Side works (1928), the West Side works (1931), and the Southwest works (1939). These plants were enlarged and additional plants added (Hanover Park, John E. Egan, and O'Hare) as continued regional growth increased the quantity of wastewater needing treatment. By 1970 Chicago had the largest wastewater treatment facilities in the world.

Three important problems persist. First, the lake levels controversy remains. Since the channel system still receives the treated effluent and overflow, it is necessary for some diversion to provide a current. When drought conditions in the 1980s hampered navigation on the Illinois and Mississippi Rivers, suggestions that the Chicago diversion be increased were opposed on the basis of the potential reduction in lake levels.

Second, pollution continues to affect the area. In 1969, the Sanitary District adopted an ordinance that forced pretreatment of industrial pollutants at their source. It prohibited discharges into Lake Michigan and reduced those into the waterways. Although more than 90 percent of the district's wastewater is treated, a heavy rainfall or quickly melting snow still can force the district to open the floodgates and let raw sewage escape into the lake, violating the spirit, if not the letter, of this law.

A 1972 federal law required areawide planning to control water pollution. The Tunnel and Reservoir Plan (TARP), prepared by the Northeastern Illinois Planning Commission with Sanitary District expertise, provided a solution to the third problem, the lack of efficient natural drainage in such a flat region. The majority of the district has combined sewers carrying both waste and storm water. Heavy rainstorms can overload the combined sewer systems so that the sewers overflow into the district's waterways and flood low-lying areas. Phase 1 of TARP, the antipollution phase, which went into operation in 1985, involved the construction of 10 miles of tunnels to capture the overflow. Phase 2, the antiflooding phase, calls for an additional 21 miles of tunnels plus three large reservoirs.

From the initial reversal of the river, to the creation of the Sanitary District, to the planning mandated by federal law, as the city's human and business populations grew, the underlying objective of Chicago's wastewater strategy has been to protect and conserve the area's Lake Michigan water supply.

Louis P. Cain

See also: Deep Tunnel; Flood Control and Drainage; Infrastructure; Landscape; Metropolitan Growth; Special Districts

Further reading: Cain, Louis P. "Separating Wastewater from the Water Supply in a Lakefront City: Conserving Chicago's Water Resources." In *Water and the City: The Next Century,* ed. Howard Rosen and Ann Durkin Keating, 1991. • Cain, Louis P. "The Search for an Optimum Sanitation Jurisdiction: The Metropolitan Sanitary District of Greater Chicago, A Case Study." *Essays in Public Works History,* no. 10 (July 1980). • Cain, Louis P. *Sanitation Strategy for a Lakefront Metropolis: The Case of Chicago.* 1978.

Water Polo. Water polo originated in England in 1874 and arrived in Chicago in 1893, when Englishman John Robinson became Swimming instructor at the Chicago Athletic Association. As codified by Americans in 1897, water polo involved a semi-inflated ball and was a far more brutal game than that played in Europe. In 1911, Chicago amateur club teams dropped the softball style and switched to the European style, which started a decade of innovation by Chicago teams. Top hall of fame and Olympian water polo players developed by the Illinois Athletic Club (IAC) were Harry Hebner, Perry McGillivray, and H. Jamison Handy.

For much of the twentieth century, amateur clubs in New York and Chicago dominated the sport: from 1906 to 1960, 31 of the 43 national championships in the indoor competition were won by Chicago-area teams, most of them from the IAC. During the 1950s and 1960s the city supported a thriving league of amateur clubs. During the 1960s, however, Chicago lost its preeminence in water polo, as teams from California began to dominate the sport. The IAC won its last national title in 1960, and the Mayor Daley Youth Foundation team was the last Chicago club to win a national title, in 1967.

The University of Chicago and Northwestern University formed water polo teams not long after building swimming pools, in 1904 and 1910 respectively, each winning several unofficial Big Ten titles before ending their programs in the early 1940s. Water polo had been briefly popular in Chicago-area high schools around 1900, but died out until 1969, when a boys' state championship was inaugurated by the Illinois Swimming Association (ISA). In 1980 the ISA introduced a girls' state tournament. The Illinois High School Association took over sponsorship of the boys' and girls' state water polo championship tournaments in 2002.

Robert Pruter

See also: Creation of Chicago Sports; Fitness and Athletic Clubs; Leisure; Sports, High-School

Further reading: Bell, Taylor. "Making Major Ripples." May 18, 1997. • Menke, Frank G. *The Encyclopedia of Sports*. 6th rev. ed., rev. Pete Palmer. 1977. • Smith, James R. *The World Encyclopedia of Water Polo*. 1989.

Water Supply. In 1851, Chicagoans responding to recurrent cholera epidemics organized the city's first public water board, which hired William J. McAlpine to design a municipal water supply system. The water commission began laying pipe within areas in which the threats of fire and disease were thought to be highest, including the central business district and the residences of some of the wealthiest and poorest Chicagoans. Public hydrants protected the district from threat of fire and were used by those unable to afford direct connections to their homes.

At first, the commission laid water pipe solely with regard to public health and safety. By 1864, however, the commissioners refused to extend water pipes into areas that would not yield a sufficient income in water rents. Property holders willing to advance the money to cover the extension of water service pipes and mains could pay to have the water system extended to their property.

The wealthiest residents had water connections as a matter of course. The poorest residents who lived in the central portions of the city generally had access to a single tap within the building in which they were living because of municipal regulations. Because of the cost of water connections, some middle-class residents forewent these improvements to keep costs down in the purchase of their homes. Other middle-class families, more secure financially, sought out subdivisions in which water connections—and other service improvements—were already in place.

Early on, the annual water rents and revenue from tap water permits provided a significant and increasing income. By 1878, the waterworks ended its fiscal year with a surplus, and the commissioners retired some of the bonds that had financed the original construction. However, the commission spent more money on extending the system than on retiring debts through the turn of the century.

Outside the city limits, residents turned to township governments and small village boards with their water demands. One reason for the massive 1889 annexation was the high quality of water provision within Chicago. It took decades for Chicago's water department to service the vastly increased territory within the confines of the city. The water department had the difficult task of integrating many small systems into one large one, as well as extending service into areas which previously had not received water. By 1902, only Rogers Park, Norwood Park, and Austin, former suburban settlements on the extreme edges of the city, remained outside the boundaries of water extensions. While no further major annexations took place, by 1990 Chicago's water department was providing water to 90 suburban communities, as well as the city itself.

Lake Michigan remains the main source of water in the metropolitan area. In 1900, the Sanitary District of Chicago completed the 28-mile Sanitary and Ship Canal to reverse the flow of the Chicago River away from Lake Michigan, thereby improving the quality of lake water. Canada as well as neighboring states opposed the diversion of Lake Michigan water, and Supreme Court decisions limited the amount of Lake Michigan water that could be diverted into the Sanitary and Ship Canal (1930) and the water supply for Illinois communities (1967). As a result, the amount of water which any community in the state may draw from Lake Michigan is regulated by the Illinois Department of Transportation's Division of Water Resources. Because of these legal limitations on Illinois' use of Lake Michigan water, new allocations come at the expense of existing users and contribute to the continuing highly charged debate about water in the Chicago area.

Ann Durkin Keating

See also: Governing the Metropolis; Government, Suburban; Housekeeping; Infrastructure

Further reading: Cain, Louis P. *Sanitation Strategy for a Lakefront Metropolis*. 1978. • O'Connell, James C. *Chicago's Quest for Pure Water*. 1977. • Rosen, Howard, and Ann Durkin Keating, eds. *Water and the City*. 1991.

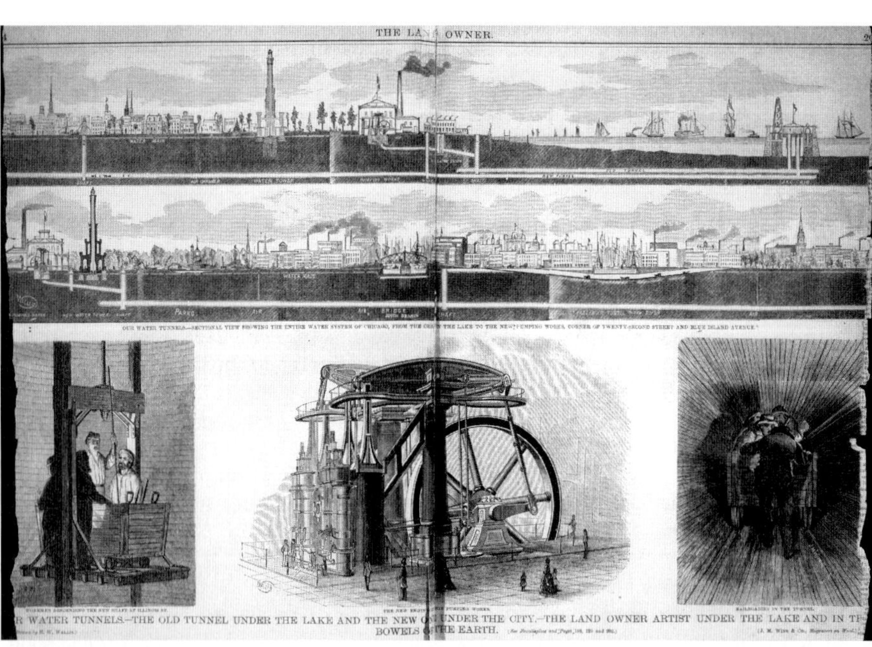

Sectional view of water system, from lake crib to pump works, 1871. Artist: Unknown. Source: The Newberry Library.

Waterfront. Metropolitan Chicago's expansive waterfront includes a portion of the shores of Lake Michigan and the banks of the Chicago, Des Plaines, Calumet, Fox and DuPage Rivers and their tributaries. It also includes built areas and connective systems such as the Illinois & Michigan Canal and the Sanitary and Ship Canal. This collective waterfront has been used for commerce, industry, and leisure.

Chicago's position on a mid-continental divide between the Great Lakes and Mississippi River systems facilitated the city's early economic growth.

Early developments reflected the massive industrial growth of the city, and Chicago's waterfront was primarily devoted to commerce and industry. Near the end of the nineteenth century, concerns over cleaner water and environments and changing industrial patterns marked a move toward increased leisure use of Chicago's waterways. By the close of the twentieth century, the shores of Lake Michigan and those of the river systems had become less polluted, providing increased recreational opportunities.

In the early part of the nineteenth century, Chicago's riverine waterways flowed relatively clear, encouraging leisure pursuits such as fishing, swimming, hunting, walking along the waterfront, and boating. By midcentury, however, people interested in such activities needed to travel away from the city center and the polluted Chicago River, whose use as Chicago's harbor and primary industrial site exacted a devastating toll.

In contrast, Lake Michigan, the city's source for fresh WATER, increasingly became the reserve of leisure activities. By the middle of the nineteenth century, promenading along the lakefront to breathe in the healthful lake air became a popular activity. Within the city, the lakefront was spared much of the heavy industry and instead hosted some of the city's early green space and residential use. There were notable exceptions near the heart of the city, such as the ILLINOIS CENTRAL RAILROAD line that was run in the 1850s along the lakefront. Despite the obstructed view and increased pollution, people continued to flock to the lakeshore to promenade, fish, boat, and ICE SKATE in the area between the shore and the piers. After the Great Chicago FIRE OF 1871, this area was filled in by debris from the conflagration.

Just prior to the fire, the city began to create its large park system with plans that included modifications to the lakefront. Professional BASEBALL was played adjacent to the lake near Michigan Avenue and Randolph Street. To the south, at Adams Street, the Inter-State Industrial Exposition of 1873 featured a Crystal Palace–styled building that hosted annual fairs, conventions, and other forms of entertainment over the next two decades. The building defined the lakefront as a cultural center and presaged the city's lakefront fairs. During those years, SAILING attracted recreational craft onto the lake at the new yacht clubs and harbors along the shores of Lake Michigan.

Another significant boost to the lakefront came from the WORLD'S COLUMBIAN EXPOSITION, which led to the development of the east side of Jackson Park. After the exposition, a number of architects and planners made designs for Chicago's lakefront, calling for a permanent "White City" to be built there. In 1896, the city began extending Grant Park into Lake Michigan with landfill, a project that became a model for much of the lakefront.

Away from the city, the lakefront was increasingly dotted with large industrial developments in the latter part of the century. By 1900 the lake's shore was divided into discrete zones of recreational, residential, agricultural, and industrial uses.

Industrialization and pollution quickly became impediments to recreational activities on the waterways. Concern over water quality, especially preserving Lake Michigan's water, became one of the city's top priorities. Efforts to keep the lake's WATER SUPPLY from contamination by the Chicago River led to the reversal of the river's flow with the deep cut of the ILLINOIS & MICHIGAN CANAL in 1871 and the construction of the SANITARY AND SHIP CANAL at the turn of the century. The creation and expansion of Calumet harbor in the latter part of the nineteenth century marked an improvement for the Chicago River, at the ecological expense of Lake Calumet and the CALUMET RIVER.

The construction of Municipal Pier in 1914 was just one of the projects that reshaped the lakeshore. Photographer: Unknown. Source: Chicago Historical Society.

In 1909, Daniel Burnham and Edward Bennett published their comprehensive plan for Chicago. The BURNHAM PLAN, adopted by the city, prescribed the expansive recreational development of the lakefront and the Chicago River. Included was a plan for the construction of a pier in the lake, eventually known as NAVY PIER.

The CENTURY OF PROGRESS fairs of 1933 and 1934 were built on landfill just south of Grant Park. The GREAT DEPRESSION limited the original plans for extensive landfill activity. Yet the NEW DEAL created an opportunity to make other improvements, such as the construction of Lake Shore Drive. These improvements helped make the lakefront the focal point for citywide celebrations and a core of cultural institutions that now include the ART INSTITUTE OF CHICAGO, the FIELD MUSEUM, the SHEDD AQUARIUM, the ADLER PLANETARIUM, and the Grant Park Music Festival.

Subsequent changes to Chicago's waterfront have increased its recreational uses. When, in 1973, Mayor Richard J. Daley mused that he would like to see the day when people fished and grilled their catch on the river's shore, the idea seemed far-fetched. However, this scenario has become possible with increased

Clarendon Avenue Beach, 1916. The beach was created in response to a private beach just to its north at Wilson Avenue. Purchased in 1912, the beach was opened to the public in 1915. By 1929, some two million people had visited the two-block-long beach. Photographer: Special Park Commission. Source: Chicago Public Library.

Chicago's Lakefront Landfill

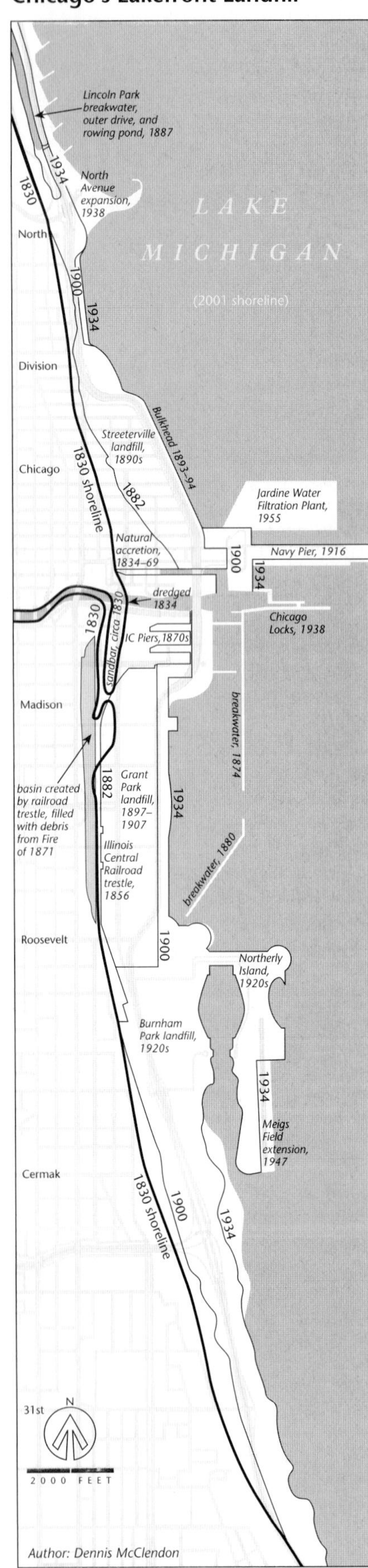

In some places, Chicago's downtown shoreline lies a half-mile east of where early European settlers found it, the result of landfills created for private profit and public improvements. The Chicago River was given a direct entrance to the lake, and in 1852 the Illinois Central Railroad was allowed to enter the city on an offshore trestle, entrapping a basin that soon became a polluted backwater and which was filled in with debris from the fire of 1871. Groins built to protect the river mouth caught sand currents from the north in the Streeterville area, where landowners also undertook landfill operations. Lincoln Park was expanded into the lake beginning in the 1880s, while Grant and Burnham Parks were greatly enlarged by landfill, as suggested in the 1909 *Plan of Chicago*. The *Plan* also recommended a chain of offshore islands, of which only Northerly Island was actually built.

environmental awareness, sewage treatment, and the work of special interest groups such as the Friends of the Chicago River. In a symbolic gesture reflective of this activity, the city in 1989 dedicated the Chicago Water Arc, which shoots water over the Chicago River from McClurg Court.

Dennis H. Cremin

See also: Economic Geography; Environmental Politics; Lacustrine System; Outdoor Concerts; Park Districts; Places of Assembly; Planning Chicago; Public Works, Federal Funding for; Shoreline Erosion

Further reading: Cronon, William. *Nature's Metropolis: Chicago and the Great West.* 1991. • Solzman, David M. *The Chicago River: An Illustrated History and Guide to the River and Its Waterways.* 1998.

Wauconda, IL, Lake County, 37 miles NW of the Loop. In 1836, Justus Bangs was attracted to land on the south side of what is now called Bangs Lake along a horse trail from Chicago to Janesville, Wisconsin. Lacking good TRANSPORTATION, the beautiful, fertile area could not profitably support farming. To obtain the cash to improve his land, Bangs contracted to carry mail between Chicago and Janesville through his informal settlement until 1845, when the trail was improved to allow stagecoach travel.

By 1839, Andrew Cook, a Bangs family friend, had erected a cabin near Bangs and helped construct a log schoolhouse. By the mid 1840s, Cook fired local clay into brick for a substantial home that still stands near the southwest shore of Bangs Lake. In 1850 Bangs and Cook platted a village to aid in the sale of area land. They called the unincorporated town Bangs Lake, although others called the community "Wauconda" at the suggestion of a local schoolteacher impressed with an Indian character from a romance novel of the time.

Slow growth prevented the incorporation of the village of Wauconda until 1877. Robert Harrison became its first president.

Although Wauconda's population was only 368 in 1910, the community had achieved some prominence as a VACATION SPOT for blue-collar Chicagoans enjoying the waters of Bangs Lake. Numerous summer homes ringed the lake and a small commercial center developed.

While Rand Road, the old mail route to Janesville, now Route 12, remained a muddy or snow-clogged track, residents searched for a way to ease travel to Wauconda. In 1910 Justin Orvis and Robert Wynn touted the construction of a traction rail line from PALATINE to FOX LAKE. As grain prices rose, Wauconda citizens quickly contributed almost $20,000 for the line. Construction began immediately from Palatine, but economic and engineering difficulties delayed the entry of the restructured steam line, the Palatine, LAKE ZURICH & Wauconda (PLZ&W), into Wauconda until mid-1913. The RAILROAD hauled agricultural products, local passengers, and numerous summer vacationers from Chicago to Bangs Lake and the many picnic groves along the line. Still, the underfunded and poorly constructed line did not help develop Wauconda; the community's population grew to only 550 by 1939.

The hard surfacing of Rand Road in the 1920s (which doomed the PLZ&W) and the movement of large numbers of World War II veterans into the area by auto were the main factors which brought expansion to Wauconda. Wauconda's 1946 population of 650 almost doubled by 1952. Many of the new residents were ex-soldiers from Chicago's West and Northwest Sides, living in converted summer cottages. Wauconda remained a popular vacation destination into the 1960s, and its beaches were memorialized in the 1980 movie "Blues Brothers." Its permanent population rose to over 2,200 by 1956 and 5,662 in 1974 as the community became a suburban residential area. The village attracted many additional residents in the 1990s, a population of 9,448 in 2000.

Craig L. Pfannkuche

See also: Metropolitan Growth

Further reading: *Wauconda.* Wauconda Chamber of Commerce. 1980. • Whitney, Richard. *Old Maud: The Story of the Palatine, Lake Zurich and Wauconda Railroad.* 1992. • Wishik, Tony. "Wauconda." *Wauconda Herald,* August 17, 1977.

Waukegan, IL, Lake County, 36 miles N of the Loop. FRENCH traders were familiar with the Waukegan area as early as 1650, and explorers Louis Jolliet and Jacques Marquette encamped there in 1673 on their journey to find the Mississippi River. By 1725 traders established the Little Fort trading post, which existed until 1760. Thomas Jenkins of Chicago constructed a two-story frame structure on LAKE MICHIGAN in 1835 (on the site of the old trading post), and by 1841 Little Fort was established as the county seat of Lake County. In March 1849 residents approved the name Waukegan, the POTAWATOMI equivalent to Little Fort.

The phenomenal growth of Waukegan, located 36 miles north of Chicago and 60 miles south of Milwaukee, can be attributed to industry, Lake Michigan, and the RAILROADS. Toward the middle of the nineteenth century, Waukegan became a thriving center of industry with enterprises that included ship and wagon building, flour milling, sheep raising, pork packing, and dairying. The most successful of these early Waukegan industries was the brewing of malt liquors. By the late 1860s William Begley's Waukegan Brewing Company sold throughout America and beyond. It was also in the 1860s that a substantial GERMAN population developed in the area. At mid-nineteenth century, Waukegan harbor was one of the busiest on the GREAT LAKES, with nearly a thousand ships sailing per year. Growth was further stimulated by the construction of the Chicago & Milwaukee Railroad by 1855, which was followed by the ELGIN, JOLIET & Eastern Railroad systems. These railroads became indispensable to the larger industries which appeared in Waukegan in the later part of the century: U.S. Sugar Refinery, Washburn and Moen Wire Mill (U.S. Steel Corporation), U.S. Starch Works, and Thomas Brass and IRON Works.

Trolley service reached Waukegan by 1896 and the first electric service by way of the Chicago & Milwaukee Electric INTERURBANS by 1899. Further infrastructural improvements occurred between 1900 and 1910, spurring middle-class residential development. Jack Benny, Ray Bradbury, and Otto Graham are among the community's most famous former residents. Churches built by ROMAN CATHOLICS, Congregationalists, and Baptists, along with SHIMER COLLEGE (1853), remain Waukegan's chief religious and educational institutions.

Though largely a residential community throughout the twentieth century, Waukegan also continued as an industrial center with companies such as Abbott Laboratories, Fansteel, Anchor Glass, Baxter International, and National Gypsum. In the latter twentieth century, SHOPPING DISTRICTS and financial, governmental, and legal services have added to that industrial core. The near north historic district, which includes houses in the Victorian, Prairie School, Greek revival, and Italianate styles, was placed on the National Register of Historic Places in 1978. The population of Waukegan was 67,653 in 1980, and 87,901 by 2000. The small AFRICAN AMERICAN population in Waukegan that had existed since the 1870s had grown to nearly 20 percent of the total population by 2000.

Wallace Best

See also: Breweries; Economic Geography; Liquor Distribution; Transportation

Further reading: Bateman, Newton, and Paul Selby, eds. *Historical Encyclopedia of Illinois and History of Lake County.* 1902. • Dorsey, Curtis L. "Black Migration to Waukegan and the Conditions Encountered up to 1933." M.A. thesis, Northeastern Illinois University. 1974. • Osling, Louise, and Julia. *Historical Highlights of the Waukegan Area.* 1976.

Wayne, IL, DuPage and Kane Counties, 33 miles W of the Loop. Wayne is an equestrian oasis in far western DUPAGE COUNTY, with homes and barns on large lots.

In May 1834, a stream of settlers moved into Wayne Center (believed to be named after Maj. Gen. Anthony Wayne). The first RAILROAD arrived in 1849, and Solomon Dunham arranged for an inn, a general store, and a house to be built east of the tracks, where he became station agent and postmaster for a second settlement area, Wayne Station. By 1861, all the land in the township had been settled, with business districts in both locations.

Three railroads etched their way through the township by 1888, followed by the electric INTERURBAN Chicago, Aurora & Elgin Railway in 1903, which also provided electricity for streetlights. Only a few industries, including a hemp mill and the Morton Sand and Gravel Company, located in Wayne.

Instead, Wayne became an equestrian center. Mark Wentworth Dunham, Solomon Dunham's youngest son, inherited his father's farm in 1865 and founded a horse-importing and breeding business. In the 1920s, this large estate was subdivided, and Solomon Dunham's red brick farmhouse became home to the Dunham Woods Riding Club.

Wayne residents ran the community through a private association between 1945 and 1959. The association fostered long-range PLANNING, preservation of open lands, and support of a police force. The Women's CLUB operated the streetlights until 1951. Despite the expansive development taking place in surrounding communities, Wayne wished to retain its rural flavor. Into the closing years of the twentieth century, the village did not have postal delivery service, property was ZONED for large lots and equestrian use, and fox hunts were given right-of-way over vehicular traffic. In 1995 the Illinois Historic Preservation Agency named the village a Certified Local Government, making it eligible to apply for federal matching funds for HISTORIC PRESERVATION projects.

Jane S. Teague

See also: Agriculture; Metropolitan Growth; Suburbs and Cities as Dual Metropolis

WBBM. This radio (and later television) station has long been Chicago's link to CBS. WBBM-AM went on the air in November 1923; WBBM-FM followed in December 1941. WBBM-FM long duplicated the AM broadcast, but as FM ascended in popularity in the late twentieth century it tried a number of different music formats. WBBM-AM pioneered all-news broadcasting.

WBBM-TV began as WXBK in 1940, affiliated with Balaban and Katz, but in 1953 was sold to CBS in a complex swap whereby CBS took over WBBM-TV, and ABC took over WLS-TV. WBBM's McClurg Court studios have long been a Chicago fixture.

Douglas Gomery

See also: Broadcasting; Disc Jockeys; Entertaining Chicagoans

Further reading: "Chicago's Channel 2." *Broadcasting,* August 6, 1951, 62. • Sternberg, Joel B. "A Descriptive History and Critical Analysis of the Chicago School of Television: Chicago Network Programming in the Chicago Style from 1948 to 1954." Ph.D. diss., Northwestern University. 1973. • WBBM station file. Library of American Broadcasting, University of Maryland, College Park, Maryland.

WCFL. WCFL was the nation's first and longest-surviving labor radio station. Created by the CHICAGO FEDERATION OF LABOR in 1926, WCFL initially was listener-supported. During its first decade it offered entertainment, labor, and public affairs programming designed to serve the labor movement and working-class communities.

By the 1940s WCFL had become more commercially oriented. It featured sports in the 1950s and '60s and, from 1966 to 1976, challenged WLS for Chicago's ROCK MUSIC title. The labor federation sold the failing station in 1978. As ownership changed again and ratings declined, WCFL went from talk to adult music to religious formats and, in 1987, ceased operations entirely.

Nathan Godfried

See also: Broadcasting; Unionization

Further reading: Godfried, Nathan. *WCFL: Chicago's Voice of Labor, 1926–78.* 1997. • McChesney, Robert W. "Labor and the Marketplace of Ideas: WCFL and the Battle for Labor Radio Broadcasting, 1927–1934." *Journalism Monographs* 134 (August 1992): 1–40.

WCTU. *See* Woman's Christian Temperance Union

Weather. *See* Climate

Welfare Capitalism. From the earliest factories to the mature industrial state, employers have frequently augmented cash payments to workers with noncash compensation. Utilizing a clever assortment of auxiliary benefits, welfare capitalists have attempted to achieve BUSINESS goals by innovative management of labor relations. While no American city became its hub, Chicago firms have presented prime examples of each phase of welfare capitalism.

During the Gilded Age, the classic expression of welfare capitalism was the Pullman Palace Car Company. PULLMAN'S picturesque village featured a theater, library, three churches, and recreational facilities. Hundreds of company-owned dwellings were deliberately set apart from workshops, and no saloonkeeper was permitted to tempt tired and thirsty workmen. Workers were discouraged from appearing publicly in informal attire, and company inspectors imposed fines for disorderly HOUSEKEEPING. George Pullman hoped his model community would nurture business virtues, defined as dedication, neatness, promptness, and sobriety. These in turn would encourage employee loyalty, control alcohol use, reduce labor turnover, and generally build labor tranquility. "Clean living" would bring good profit.

But in 1894 Pullman's dream of a placid, classless village was dashed by a bitter STRIKE. The walkout showed that social programming alone could not inoculate a firm against disruption. Meanwhile, other firms also strived for industrial peace. In 1901 the McCormick Harvesting Machine Company hired Gertrude Beeks, a protégé of Jane Addams, as the full-time "social secretary" of its works. Her appointment signified the arrival of welfare capitalism as a profession and its linkage to the Chicago SETTLEMENT HOUSE movement.

Beeks's assignment was nebulously defined as doing "betterment work." She organized Sunday outings, a CHORAL group and operetta, and an employees' loan fund. In 1919 the McCormick company added an employee representation plan, a common feature among large welfare capitalist firms of the time. In combination, McCormick programs were intended to blur the distinction between worker and manager, to bind employees to the firm, and most emphatically, to deter UNIONIZATION.

The peak of enthusiasm for welfare capitalism was in the 1920s, and in that era the Western Electric Company was widely respected as a model employer. Its executives concluded that settlement houses did not fully meet the needs of female employees at its Hawthorne Works. So it offered BASEBALL, TENNIS, BOWLING, and GOLF, all of which were very popular with both office and factory women, as were holiday festivals and community dances. Dozens of firms aimed similar programs at young working women.

Though the GREAT DEPRESSION restricted the growth of welfare capitalism and transformed its character, it did not destroy it. Stock purchase and profit sharing declined, as did certain recreational and educational programs. In 1935, company unions became an illegal practice. But after World War II, welfare capitalism reemerged, with Sears, Roebuck & Co. in the leading position.

Sears had long practiced traditional welfare capitalism. But a new chief and the impact of the Depression modified its strategy. Grounded in social science techniques, the modernized Sears program emphasized profit sharing and stock ownership, employment security, and equalitarian personnel policies. The updated version of welfare capitalism appeared in other firms and in other "fringe benefits," but it generally remained faithful to the historic goals of encouraging workforce stability and eradicating unionism.

Stuart Brandes

See also: American Plan; Americanization; Anti-unionism; If Christ Came to Chicago; International Harvester Co.; Pullman Strike; Social Services; Sports, Industrial League

Further reading: Brandes, Stuart D. *American Welfare Capitalism, 1880–1940*. 1976. • Buder, Stanley. *Pullman: An Experiment in Industrial Order and Community Planning, 1880–1930*. 1967. • Jacoby, Sanford M. *Modern Manors: Welfare Capitalism since the New Deal*. 1997.

Welsh. The Welsh have left a light trace on Chicago. Although the city was once home to one of the largest Welsh populations in urban America, the relatively small number of Welsh and the scattered geography of their residences and businesses meant that they never developed a strong ethnic community, as did some other small but geographically concentrated immigrant groups. This was typical of the Welsh. They tended to pass through cities like New York, Philadelphia, and Chicago en route to agricultural areas or coal and iron towns. For one moment, however, the Welsh did make their presence felt in Chicago—during the WORLD'S COLUMBIAN EXPOSITION of 1893.

The first wave of Welsh immigrants to the Midwest came in 1840–1855. Most continued their rural way of life, farming in Wisconsin, Iowa, or Minnesota. Racine rather than Chicago was their main port of entry. In 1850, there were more Welsh in rural Waukesha County, Wisconsin, than in the entire state of Illinois. The first Welsh chapel in Chicago relied on preachers from Wisconsin to supply services in the Welsh language. By 1870 the city had 565 Welsh-born residents and its rural-industrial hinterland nearly 2,600 more, including skilled IRON WORKERS at SOUTH CHICAGO rolling mills and COAL mining families in western Illinois. Chicago's Welsh population peaked around the turn of the century, when over 1,800 immigrants provided sufficient leadership and enthusiasm for a surge in Welsh American ethnic consciousness.

The Columbian Exhibition of 1893 spurred quiescent Welsh organizations, such as the Cambrian Benevolent Society, and Welsh-born businessmen, such as Pullman executive Samuel Job, to display Welsh culture in its most refined light. Aiming to match the grand scale of the World's Fair, the Welsh mounted an International Eisteddfod (aye-STETH-vod), a competitive literary and music festival, on the Fair grounds. CHORAL performances reportedly drew crowds of 6,000 to the Festival Hall. Despite the participation of prominent figures such as the Unitarian minister Jenkin Lloyd Jones, competitions for composing traditional Welsh verse were far less popular, reflecting the waning significance of the language and the irrelevance of antique literary forms to most Welsh immigrants and their children. The costumed procession of Druidic bards at the Eisteddfod's opening ceremony received most notice in the Chicago press. To the Welsh themselves, the event signaled their arrival on the national stage as respectable Americans whose ethnic heritage, encapsulated in musical excellence, made them the right sort of immigrants.

This period also saw a flowering of Welsh American institutions in Chicago, including the newspaper *Y Columbia* (serving largely as a publicity organ for the Eisteddfod), the Kymry Society, and the Madoc Lodge of the Order of American True Ivorites. Of the city's six Welsh chapels, the Calvinistic Methodists' mother chapel, Hebron (1852–circa 1988), proved the most durable, maintaining at least occasional Welsh-language services until the early 1980s. Although the chapels were social centers for the dispersed Welsh community, their shifting locations to western suburbs mapped the assimilation of their members into the unhyphenated American middle class.

Anne Kelly Knowles

See also: Demography; Ethnic Music; Protestants; Multicentered Chicago; Scots

Further reading: Edwards, Hywel Teifi. *Eisteddfod Ffair y Byd: Chicago, 1893* (The World's Fair Eisteddfod: Chicago, 1893). 1990. • Hartmann, Edward G. *Americans from Wales*. 1983. • Monaghan, Jay. "The Welsh People in Chicago." *Illinois State Historical Society Journal* 32 (1939): 498–516.

West Chicago, IL, DuPage County, 30 miles W of the Loop. Although travelers arrived in West Chicago as early as the 1830s, Alonzo Harvey is credited as the community's first settler in 1842. The site developed a reputation as the first Illinois community created as the result of the RAILROADS.

Chicago's first railroad, the Galena & Chicago Union, arrived in 1849 with plans to extend toward Elgin. Immediately, the surrounding towns of ST. CHARLES, BATAVIA, and AURORA added branches (the latter becoming the Burlington railroad), intersecting in what is now West Chicago. Water and fuel facilities for the locomotives and an eating house and hotel for travelers were built. In 1853, a three-stall roundhouse and a mill for repairing rails were added.

In 1855, John B. Turner, president of the G&CU, platted his acreage and donated land for a Congregational church, naming the town Junction. Two years later, Joseph McConnell and his wife, Mary, platted a second portion of town just north of Turner's plat. Grateful for Turner's donation of land to the Congregational church, they recorded their plat as the Town of Turner in his honor.

Many of the first residents of Turner were New Englanders of ENGLISH or IRISH heritage who migrated west as RAILROAD WORKERS. GERMAN immigrants predominantly sought farmlands. In 1873 Turner Public School opened. It was renamed Northside School in 1887 when a second school (Southside) was built.

During the 1880s, factory sites were offered free of charge to attract businesses to "Chicago's Coming Great Manufacturing Suburb." In 1894 the Bolles' OPERA House Block was built for traveling shows and other community events. Turner was renamed West Chicago in 1896 to help prospective industrialists visualize the town's location and to sound more industrial and metropolitan; it was reincorporated as a city in 1906.

Numerous businesses, including Belding Engineering Company (1878), Turner Brick Company (1892), Borden's milk condensing plant (1906), and three woodworking plants, established there. From 1918 to 1964 the stockyards in West Chicago provided a stopover point for livestock being shipped east from western grazing lands. In 1928, Route 64 and a private AIRPORT (paved and used in WORLD WAR II by the federal government; later known as DuPage County airport) were built.

Christ the King SEMINARY, a Spanish-style structure at Routes 59 and 64, housed the Franciscan brothers until converted to a convalescent center in the mid-1970s. Originally opened as Illinois Institute in 1853, Wheaton Academy moved to West Chicago in 1944, where it remains the oldest high school in continuous operation in the county.

As railroad transportation declined, the town changed. In the 1970s, the city government acquired the 1912 C&NW depot to develop for community purposes. In the 1980s, West Chicago became known as the fastest-growing industrial and manufacturing center in the county. With the tracks removed and land sold for commercial use, there are few hints of what was once a prominent and prosperous railroad community.

Jane S. Teague

See also: DuPage County; Economic Geography; Transportation

Further reading: Scobey, Frank F. *A Random Review of West Chicago History.* 1976. • Thompson, Richard, ed. *DuPage Roots.* 1985.

West Dundee, IL, Kane County, 37 miles NW of the Loop. West Dundee mixes historic charm with newer commercial and residential development. Over the years there have been efforts to merge West with EAST DUNDEE, the village just across the Fox RIVER: a 1956 referendum was approved by East Dundee but rejected by West Dundee. These roles were reversed in a 1962 referendum. Each town's retention of individuality dates back to their early days, when West Dundee's SCOTTISH and ENGLISH heritage kept it apart from its GERMAN neighbors.

In 1835 Elder John and Nancy Oatman established a tavern and a store that became the core of the community. Others settlers came, and in 1837 they held a lottery to determine who would name the town. Alexander Gardiner won and named the town Dundee in honor of his Scottish hometown. In 1843 Scotsman Allan PINKERTON, later the renowned detective, set up business as a cooper. The town was incorporated in 1867.

West Dundee was hemmed in from development for years. The river formed a natural eastern barrier. To the north and west, the D. Hill Nursery, founded in 1855 by William Hill, specialized in fruit TREES. The business grew to include evergreens, some of which were sent to Chicago for the WORLD'S COLUMBIAN EXPOSITION in 1893. Expanding to 900 acres, the nursery survived the GREAT DEPRESSION by running a cattle feed operation that continued through WORLD WAR II. Some of the thousands of seasonal workers traveled to work from Chicago by electric car, while the majority lived on the nursery grounds.

In the 1950s a segment of the Hill property was sold and turned into the Highlands SUBDIVISION, which was ANNEXED into West Dundee in 1956. The community also annexed property west of Illinois 31 in 1957, Royal Lane in 1960, and the Old World subdivision in 1966. The nursery eventually sold all of its land and moved to McHenry County. Plans for the Spring Hill Mall on Hill's land began in 1973 and the project was completed in 1980. The 1.1 million-square-foot mall's retail sales boosted West Dundee's economy and created an estimated 1,600 jobs by 1982. New subdivisions were built to the west of Spring Hill.

With a 2000 population of only 5,428, West Dundee has managed to keep its quaintness and small-town feeling intact. Designated historical sites, include some of the elegant houses on Oregon Avenue. Restored buildings include structures reported to have provided refuge for slaves on the UNDERGROUND RAILROAD.

Marilyn Elizabeth Perry

See also: Government, Suburban; Metropolitan Growth; Shopping Districts and Malls

Further reading: Bullinger, Carolyn J., ed. *Dundee Township, 1835–1985.* 1985. • Provisional League of Women Voters. *Fox Valley Four.* 1971.

West Elsdon, Community Area 62, 8 miles SW of the Loop. Before the early twentieth century, the area now designated West Elsdon was a marshy remnant of an ancient lake. The Grand Trunk RAILROAD tracks gave definition to the eastern boundary of the area in 1880. Among the early settlers were GERMAN farmers and IRISH RAILROAD WORKERS.

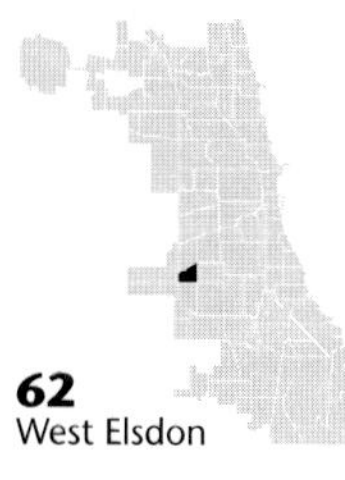

The area became part of Chicago with the ANNEXATION of the town of LAKE in 1889. A small hamlet of railroad workers called Elsdon grew up around car shops built by the Grand Trunk Railroad near 51st Street and Central Park, in what is now neighboring GAGE PARK. The railroad eventually opened passenger stations at 51st, 55th, and 59th Streets, but most residential development remained east of the tracks, as the land in West Elsdon was swampier and unimproved.

By the 1920s, people were settling in the area in greater numbers. Population grew from 855 in 1920 to 2,861 in 1930. The development of the nearby Kenwood and Clearing Industrial Districts and the opening of Chicago Municipal Airport (MIDWAY AIRPORT) in 1927 just to the west made the area an attractive place to settle. The new residents were primarily POLISH and CZECH, with smaller numbers of ITALIAN, YUGOSLAVIAN, and LITHUANIAN immigrants. The ROMAN CATHOLIC ARCHDIOCESE OF CHICAGO established St. Turibius parish in 1927 to serve the growing Catholic population. An elementary school was established with the church, and Lourdes High School was built in 1936.

During the 1920s, Crawford Avenue (Pulaski), 55th Street, and other streets were paved, sewers were installed, and two public SCHOOLS were built. Though some street improvements were made in the section west of Pulaski during the 1930s, the GREAT DEPRESSION economy suspended growth for a time. The area remained rural, and as late as 1938 cows and goats still grazed along 55th Street.

During World War II growth resumed, and the West Elsdon Civic Association organized itself to lobby for street improvements and other community goals. West Elsdon grew from a population of 3,255 in 1940 to its peak of 14,215 in 1960. Almost all of the new building consisted of detached single-family brick houses, and West Elsdon became an extension of the BUNGALOW BELT.

Many new residents were second-generation or established first-generation immigrants, sometimes moving from the BACK OF THE YARDS or other Southwest Side neighborhoods. They were drawn by the prospect of owning a house in a quiet residential area. Predominately Polish, many were part of the "white flight" from neighborhoods to the east.

West Elsdon residents played a central role in the history of racial segregation in Chicago during the Airport Homes RACE RIOTS in 1946, the first of a series of PUBLIC HOUSING riots in Chicago. "Airport Homes" was the name of the site in nearby WEST LAWN established by the CHICAGO HOUSING AUTHORITY to provide temporary housing to returning veterans and their families during the postwar housing shortage. Residents of West Lawn and West Elsdon rioted and succeeded in intimidating a few black war veterans and their families from joining white veterans in the homes.

The West Elsdon Civic Association became one of the first vocal political enemies of the CHA and its first executive secretary, Elizabeth Wood. Opposition to public housing remained strong in the area. In the early 1970s the West Elsdon Civic Association was an active participant in the "No-CHA" citywide coalition opposing scattered-site public housing in predominantly middle-class white neighborhoods.

In the half century following WORLD WAR II, West Elsdon remained a quiet, blue-collar white community with a high rate of homeownership. Several processes brought changes in the 1990s. As the older white ethnic generation aged, new families with young children moved to the area. MEXICAN residents increasingly settled in the eastern part of West Elsdon. As the number of children classified as Hispanic increased in the public elementary schools in the early 1990s, the number of black children admitted from other communities under a SCHOOL DESEGREGATION consent decree rapidly declined.

In 1993 the CHICAGO TRANSIT AUTHORITY began RAPID TRANSIT service to the LOOP on its Orange Line, with a station at Pulaski on the northern edge of the community. This brought suburban-style retail development on Pulaski, and raised property values nearby.

Douglas Knox

See also: Contested Spaces; Racism, Ethnicity, and White Identity; Transportation

West Englewood, Community Area 67, 8 miles SW of the Loop. West Englewood was swamp and oak savanna when white settlers first came to the area in the late 1840s. These homesteaders were predominately GERMAN and SWEDISH farmers. Development followed as RAILROADS began crisscrossing the area. In February 1852 the Michigan Southern & Northern Indiana Railroad began rail service to the region. The Rock Island Railroad and the Wabash Railroad also laid track in the area by the close of the 1850s. The rail stop and the adjacent area of railroad switch tracks, junctions, and scattered farms became known as Chicago Junction, and later Junction Grove. New residents arrived following job opportunities with the railroads and the Chicago stockyards just to the north of the district. These workers, mostly IRISH and German immigrants, lived in the area of Junction Avenue, now 63rd Street, from Indiana Avenue to Halsted Street. Farther west, a small AFRICAN AMERICAN population was located at 63rd Street and Loomis Boulevard.

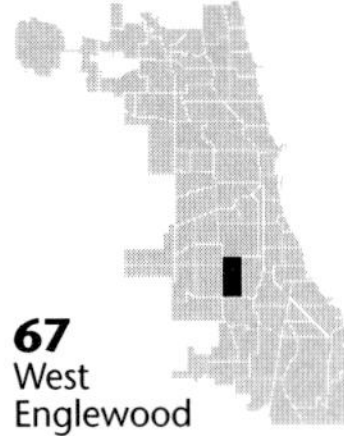

In 1865, Junction Grove became part of the incorporated town of LAKE. In 1868, Henry B. Lewis, a wool merchant on South Water Street, and a member of both the Cook County and Town of Lake boards of education, suggested the name of Englewood (after Englewood, New Jersey), since the area was heavily wooded. Displaced survivors of the Chicago FIRE OF 1871 and others seeking to escape urban congestion prompted a slow building boom in an area that became known as West Englewood in the early 1870s. Chicago ANNEXED the area in 1889, and by 1896 streetcars connected the community to downtown Chicago. During this time sidewalks were built, single-family frame houses were constructed, and in 1907, the Englewood branch of the "L" was extended into West Englewood to Loomis Boulevard.

The aftermath of WORLD WAR I saw an influx of ITALIAN immigrants to West Englewood. The railroads and stockyards continued to be important employers, and residents had the employment opportunities of the entire city only a local train ride away. A transit bus barn at the corner of 74th and Ashland became a leading employer in the area. The community's commercial and retail strip ran along 63rd and Ashland Avenue south to 75th street.

By 1920 the community totaled 53,276; Germans, Irish, and Italians were most numerous among the foreign-born. In the 1930s the population of West Englewood continued to grow as more African Americans moved into the area, an influx that accelerated in the 1940s and 1950s with migrants from the rural South. The greatest demographic shift occurred between 1970 and 1980, when the African American population increased from 48 to 98 percent.

The 1970s saw the decline of West Englewood's economic prosperity. The closing of the CHICAGO TRANSIT AUTHORITY bus barn and the loss of stockyard and railroad jobs hit the community hard. For the first time since its founding, West Englewood population declined, after peaking at 62,069 in 1980. Many residents followed jobs to the suburbs. In 1990, West Englewood's population was 52,772, 98 percent African American. Behind the outward bleakness of closed retail shops and gang GRAFFITI, only 14 percent of the population had an income of $50,000 or more, and little more than a quarter of the residents had high-school educations.

Under MAYOR Harold Washington's administration, many abandoned homes and vacant buildings were demolished, and repairs were made on sewage lines and major streets. The West Englewood United Organization was organized by three area churches to provide financial and advisory assistance to homeowners in the community and to provide summer programs for neighborhood children. In addition, Neighborhood Housing Services, a national network of neighborhood improvement programs, began to address some of the problems of the community.

West Englewood is home to the highly rated Lindblom Technical High School, known for its massive neoclassical facade.

Franklin Forts

See also: Community Organizing; Meatpacking; Neighborhood Succession; Railroad Workers; Rapid Transit System; Street Railways

West Garfield Park, Community Area 26, 5 miles W of the Loop. Before 1873, most people who saw the farms scattered on the square mile west of the future GARFIELD PARK were on their way somewhere else. The Barry Point Road (Fifth Avenue) headed southwest to LYONS. Truck farmers going to Chicago and stagecoaches traveling west to Moreland (AUSTIN) and OAK PARK took the ELGIN Road (Lake Street). The West Chicago Park Commission established three West Side parks in 1870, naming the one in the middle "Central Park." In 1873, the North Western Railway built its shops north of Kinzie, initiating the area's urbanization. Several thousand employees and their families, mostly Scandinavians and IRISH, built the village of Central Park south of Kinzie. The local school was named after G. W. Tilton, superintendent of the RAILROAD shops. Residents from as far south as Harrison Street bought their groceries on Lake Street.

Although the village was primarily residential, it also offered recreation. Central Park, renamed for the assassinated President Garfield in 1881, featured an administrative building

with a gilded dome, exhibit houses for exotic plants, picnic groves, and a BICYCLE track. HORSE-RACING fans went to the Garfield Park Race Track, founded as a gentlemen's club in 1878 and converted for GAMBLING 10 years later. Taverns catering to spectators lined Madison Street. The Garfield Park track, however, could not compete with the prestigious Washington Park course or the Hawthorne track. In 1892, the Chicago POLICE raided the Garfield Park track three times. During the last raid, a horseman shot two police officers and was himself killed, sealing racing's fate there. Various spectator shows, including Buffalo Bill's Wild West Show, appeared in the arena before it was demolished in the early twentieth century to make way for homes.

The demise of the seedy racetrack opened space for new housing and commerce. A policemen's syndicate sold its members homes on Wilcox Street, nicknamed "Uniform Row." The establishment of the Sears plant in neighboring NORTH LAWNDALE drew new residents to the southeast quarter of the area. Lake Street, shadowed by the "L" built in 1893, went into decline and Madison Street took its place as the district's commercial heart. Entrepreneurs opened DEPARTMENT STORES, MOVIE PALACES, and HOTELS in the newly advertised "Madison-Crawford district" after 1914. Merchants so valued this identification that they led a 19-year fight against the renaming of Crawford Avenue as Pulaski Road, even though Peter Crawford's farm had been in the area of present-day SOUTH LAWNDALE. West Garfield Park's rise was tempered by bank closures, deprivation, and neglect during the GREAT DEPRESSION and World War II, but residents and businesspeople emerged into the postwar years ready to restore its standing.

During the 1950s, however, changes in the West Side prompted some residents to reevaluate that commitment. The new Congress (Eisenhower) EXPRESSWAY displaced residents from the neighborhood's southern sector. Others homeowners feared that West Garfield Park would experience the same rapid racial change underway in EAST GARFIELD PARK and North Lawndale. In 1959, when a black family bought a house on the 4300 block of Jackson, white homeowners formed the United Property Group, which opposed further sales to AFRICAN AMERICANS. The Garfield Park Good Neighbors Council, by contrast, gave a friendly welcome to black homebuyers. These groups unsuccessfully petitioned the state to build the new UNIVERSITY OF ILLINOIS campus in Garfield Park, hoping to prevent further population change, create a racial buffer zone, and stimulate the local economy.

Middle-class black families did move into the area. Like the whites who were abandoning their homes, they built small organizations and block clubs intended to maintain their new neighborhood. They could not, however, prevent the increasing rolls of absentee landlords from neglecting and overcrowding their apartment buildings. During the early 1960s, West Garfield Park was increasingly stigmatized as a poor, disorganized community by observers who did not see its block-by-block variations or its struggling, unpublicized organizations. Rioting that centered on the Madison-Pulaski intersection in 1965 and 1968 hastened the departure of the remaining white businesspeople from West Garfield Park and further damaged its image.

In the 1970s, OPEN-HOUSING laws provided Chicago's black middle class with an avenue of escape from the city's increasing poverty and physical decline. In their absence, the area's economic base eroded further, leaving the West Side vulnerable to illegal drug traffic and accompanying crime. Nevertheless, a few organizations dedicated themselves to turning around West Garfield Park. Most notable among these was Bethel New Life, which hoped to enshrine the West Side's past with an oral history project and ensure its future with new and rehabilitated housing.

Amanda Seligman

See also: Community Organizing; Conservatories; Humboldt Park; Race Riots

Further reading: Hawkins, Michael Ryan. "The West Side History Project: Tours #1–4, 1928." 1993. Harold Washington Library Department of Special Collections. • *Local Community Fact Book* series. • Seligman, Amanda. "Block by Block: Racing Decay on Chicago's West Side, 1948–1968." Ph.D. diss., Northwestern University. 1999.

West Lawn, Community Area 65, 9 miles SW of the Loop. West Lawn is west of CHICAGO LAWN, from which it is divided by the Grand Trunk RAILROAD tracks. Developers subdivided the land northeast of 67th Street and Pulaski as part of a more extensive promotion of Chicago Lawn in the 1870s. The rail station at 63rd and Central Park attracted settlement primarily to the east of the tracks, while the marshy land of West Lawn remained unsettled.

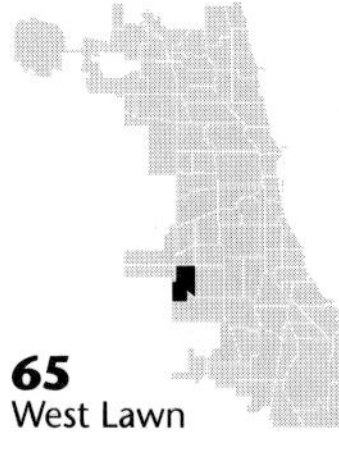

A brickyard and an artesian well were briefly active on land northwest of 67th and Central Park in the late nineteenth century, but both projects were soon abandoned, leaving a cold, dangerous pond that served as a SWIMMING hole and ice-SKATING rink before it was filled in during the early twentieth century.

With the growth of the industrial district in Clearing to the west and the extension of a horse-drawn STREET RAILWAY on 63rd Street through West Lawn to Clearing, the population grew to 2,544 by 1920. The area east of Pulaski and north of 63rd street was settled with single-family houses by 1930, when the census reported 8,919 people in West Lawn, primarily GERMAN, IRISH, CZECH, POLISH, and ITALIAN, with a small LITHUANIAN immigrant population. Residents were factory, clerical, and professional workers.

Institutional development followed the growth in population. The ROMAN CATHOLIC parish of St. Nicholas of Tolentine began as a mission in 1909, with a small church and school building. Four PROTESTANT churches were established between 1923 and 1931.

In anticipation of rising REAL-ESTATE values, streets were paved and other improvements made on the vacant land west of Pulaski during the 1930s. The GREAT DEPRESSION, however, suspended growth, and special assessments and delinquent property taxes discouraged building. In the early 1940s, an observer standing on Pulaski near 67th Street saw paved but vacant streets to the west contrasting with unpaved streets full of new houses to the east.

Growth resumed with WORLD WAR II. The nearby Chicago Municipal Airport (MIDWAY) expanded. Industrial development in the southwestern corner of West Lawn and in neighboring CLEARING attracted new residents. A factory at Cicero Avenue and 77th Street produced bomber engines during the war and was adapted for Tucker, and, later, Ford AUTOMOBILE MANUFACTURING after the war.

In 1946 the CHICAGO HOUSING AUTHORITY constructed housing in West Lawn for returning veterans. Residents of West Lawn and WEST ELSDON, to the north, however, actively prevented racial integration during the Airport Homes RACE RIOTS at 60th Street and Karlov in 1946.

Population grew rapidly in the decades after World War II, from 14,460 in 1950 to 27,644 in 1970. This growth in part resulted from a white ethnic migration out of neighborhoods undergoing racial change. With a growing Catholic population, the parishes of St. Mary Star of the Sea (1948) and Queen of the Universe (1955) were formed from parts of the St. Nicholas of Tolentine parish. Parish schools grew rapidly, with enrollments peaking in the early 1960s.

The Ford City Shopping Center opened in 1965 on the site of the then-abandoned Ford auto factory on Cicero Avenue. Manufacturers such as Tootsie Roll and Sweetheart Cup built near Ford City to take advantage of rail access. Richard J. Daley COLLEGE, a regional Federal Records Center, and an army reserve base also located west of Pulaski and south of 72nd.

Pulaski and 63rd Street continued to develop as a local retail center and public space. In 1986 the West Lawn branch of the CHICAGO PUBLIC LIBRARY opened near the corner, becoming one of the busiest branches. Also in 1986 the Balzekas Museum of Lithuanian Culture moved into the defunct Von Solbrig Hospital building at 65th and Pulaski.

While political, COMMUNITY AREA, and neighborhood boundaries often crosscut each other, West Lawn became the heart of the Thirteenth Ward, a conservative, white DEMOCRATIC stronghold. No ward in the city gave a smaller percentage of votes to Harold Washington in the 1983 and 1987 mayoral elections.

Since the 1970s, younger MEXICAN families have been attracted to the area, and some Arab families and businesses have followed the 63rd Street retail corridor westward from Chicago Lawn. The revival of activity at Midway Airport and the opening of the CTA Orange Line in neighboring areas have raised residential property values and brought renewed attention to the area from other parts of the city.

Douglas Knox

See also: Automobile Manufacturing; Contested Spaces; Parish Life; Public Housing; Transportation

Further reading: Fremon, David. *Chicago Politics Ward by Ward.* 1987. • Hirsch, Arnold. *Making the Second Ghetto: Race and Housing in Chicago, 1940–1960.* 1983.

West Pullman, Community Area 53, 14 miles S of the Loop. When UNIVERSITY OF CHICAGO sociologists created the West Pullman COMMUNITY AREA in the 1920s, they merged several existing communities. The first was KENSINGTON, a town established at the junction of the ILLINOIS CENTRAL and Michigan Central Railroads in the 1850s that grew rapidly in the 1880s along with the new town of PULLMAN that adjoined it. The second was the former village of Gano, first offered by Cincinnati developers in the 1880s and populated by Pullman workers anxious to own their own homes and escape from the corporate control of the company town. West Pullman, launched as an industrial and residential SUBDIVISION in 1891 by the West Pullman Land Association (WPLA), was the largest of the identifiable communities and home to the working-class families whose livelihood depended on the factories the WPLA had recruited to its industrial district. Stewart Ridge emerged at the turn of the century when the WPLA put size and building restrictions on its most desirable property to attract a wealthier class of resident. Those who created the new community area of West Pullman also incorporated large adjacent tracts of vacant land into it.

By the 1920s, the area of West Pullman had developed into a residential community of over 20,000, with a large industrial base, several retail areas, SCHOOLS, parks, and a variety of other institutions. Mechanics, laborers, and their families lived in the neighborhoods closest to Pullman and surrounding the West Pullman industrial area, where they worked at International Harvester, Whitman & Barnes, Carter White Lead Paint, and the other factories that had located there. Ethnic pockets flourished. Joining Gano's GERMANS and Scandinavians were ITALIANS, POLES, HUNGARIANS, LITHUANIANS, and, later, ARMENIANS, all of whom built their own churches and other ethnic institutions. Different neighborhoods also reflected the great economic diversity that marked West Pullman. Corporate officers lived in large homes in Stewart Ridge; the area's poorest lived in small homes that were already a quarter of a century old and boasted no modern conveniences. And there were a growing number of families who could afford the newer homes being built on the edges of the older neighborhoods.

Developers who built many of those homes put a new kind of restriction on their property, one that prohibited AFRICAN AMERICANS from living anywhere in their subdivisions. In doing so, they contributed to a growing effort to keep West Pullman white, at least outside of Kensington, which had some 170 African American residents in 1930. Employers helped. International Harvester, for example, did not hire African Americans at its West Pullman works until mandated to do so during World War II. In 1933, after an African American woman bought a two-flat near 120th and Stewart, irate neighbors exploded a black powder bomb at the house, reflecting what the *South End Reporter* identified as high "public indignation." A decade later, West Pullmanites joined in the battle against the CHICAGO HOUSING AUTHORITY's Altgeld Gardens in nearby RIVERDALE and against smaller projects built in Greater ROSELAND.

West Pullman's population fell during the GREAT DEPRESSION, but it boomed in the years following WORLD WAR II. Land originally offered by the WPLA and re-offered in the 1920s finally found purchasers anxious for a new home with the conveniences offered by the increasingly middle-class community area and its excellent TRANSPORTATION links to the LOOP, the industrial CALUMET REGION, and the far south suburbs. By 1960, over 35,000 people called West Pullman home, all of them white.

Beginning in the 1960s, some of the vacant land on West Pullman's western edges finally opened to African Americans. Built on formerly restricted land, Maple Park offered comfortable new homes to black Chicagoans anxious to find the same kinds of homes, services, and connections European Americans had found in West Pullman earlier. Gradually, African Americans began moving into other West Pullman neighborhoods as well. By 1980, 90 percent of West Pullman's 45,000 residents were black.

Like other racially changing neighborhoods, West Pullman was victimized by predatory lenders in the 1970s. In the 1980s, its residents lost both industrial and professional jobs, making UNEMPLOYMENT the community's single biggest problem. Additionally, the numerous factories that had closed in West Pullman left a toxic legacy behind. Lead from the paint factories and contaminants from other factories created health problems for residents and led to the designation of part of the industrial district as an EPA brownfield.

The city, the federal government, and private investors, thanks to the ongoing efforts of neighborhood and community organizations, have finally begun to correct some of the intentional and accidental harm done to the community, with measures that include cleaning up toxic wastes and recruiting new industries and businesses. As they do, West Pullman continues to be a large community area rich with institutions and marked by economic diversity.

Janice L. Reiff

See also: Contested Spaces; Demography; Economic Geography; Environmental Politics; Industrial Pollution; Restrictive Covenants; South Side

Further reading: Chicago Plan Commission. *Housing in Chicago Communities: Community Area Number 53.* 1940. • Melaniphy and Associates, Inc. *Chicago Comprehensive Neighborhood Needs Analysis, West Pullman Community Area.* 1982. • West Pullman Land Association. *West Pullman and Stewart Ridge, Chicago, Illinois, 1892–1900.* 1900.

West Ridge, Community Area 2, 9 miles N of the Loop. West Ridge, also called West ROGERS PARK or North Town, lies nestled between Ridge Avenue and the North Shore Channel. POTAWATOMI established villages in this area in the seventeenth century but were forced to abandon their claims in a series of TREATIES between 1816 and 1829. Indian Boundary Park (1922) is situated along the northern boundary of the 1816 Indian cession. During the 1830s and 1840s GERMAN and LUXEMBOURGER farmers settled in the area and a small community known as Ridgeville grew up around the intersection of Ridge and Devon Avenues.

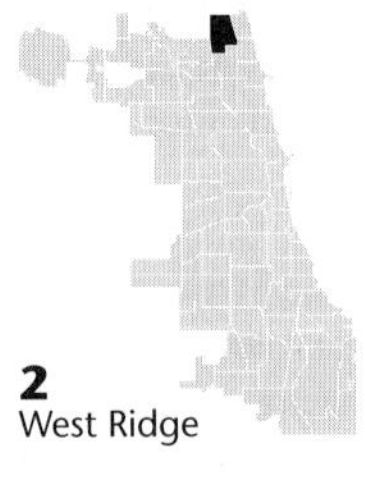

During most of the nineteenth century West Ridge remained relatively rural. St. Henry's ROMAN CATHOLIC Church served as both the religious and social center of the community. West Ridge was home to two CEMETERIES, Rosehill and St. Henry's, and Angel Guardian ORPHANAGE. Truck farms, greenhouses, and the open prairie characterized much of the area. Disagreements with Rogers Park about taxes for local improvements led to the incorporation of West Ridge as a village in 1890.

Despite local controversy over ANNEXATION to Chicago in 1893, proponents prevailed and West Ridge became part of Chicago. Unlike in Rogers Park, annexation did not bring immediate growth. The number of residents remained under 500 until after 1900. No prominent business districts existed, as community members relied on either Rogers Park or EVANSTON for their goods and services.

The pace of growth quickened in West Ridge after 1900. Brickyards formerly located along the North Branch of the CHICAGO RIVER moved into the area of present-day Kedzie Avenue to take advantage of the sand and natural clay deposits. The construction of the North Shore Channel of the Sanitary District of Chicago in 1909 increased the amount of clay available. Scandinavian and German workers moved from other parts of Chicago to find jobs in the expanding brickyard operations, and workers' cottages appeared in the western part of the community. REAL-ESTATE interests began to market West Ridge both locally and nationally.

The end of WORLD WAR I triggered a real-estate boom. Brick BUNGALOWS and two-flats became the dominant residential structures in the neighborhood. APARTMENT buildings also appeared, but relatively poor TRANSPORTATION facilities in the area before 1930 limited the demand for large multiunit buildings. By the end of the 1920s Park Gables and a number of Tudor revival apartment buildings clustered around Indian Boundary Park. A TENNIS club built in the Tudor revival style opened at 1925 W. Thome. A business district along Devon Avenue also developed during this period as the area's population swelled from about 7,500 in 1920 to almost 40,000 by 1930 and local residents looked to their own community for goods and services.

Unlike many Chicago communities, West Ridge grew steadily during the 1930s. Population growth and economic development, however, did not alter the overwhelming residential character of the community. The area possesses no manufacturing establishments and its economic base remains primarily commercial in orientation. Population growth necessitated more housing units and larger, multiunit structures appeared. One of the largest residential construction projects in Chicago during the 1930s, the Granville Garden Apartments in the 6200 block of Hoyne Avenue, was built in 1938 to help meet the need for housing.

The end of WORLD WAR II sparked a final surge of growth which began to level off by the end of the 1960s. A large number of JEWS moved to West Ridge from other parts of Chicago and were joined by a steady stream of Russian and Polish Jews. Although the pace of growth has slowed since the 1960s, West Ridge has been a popular destination for many ethnic groups, and its commercial centers cater to Jews, Middle Easterners, INDIANS, PAKISTANIS and KOREANS. As of the 2000 census, 73,199 people resided in West Ridge, of which approximately 46 percent were not native born.

Patricia Mooney-Melvin

See also: Agriculture; Metropolitan Growth; Quarrying, Stonecutting, and Brickmaking; Suburbs and Cities as Dual Metropolis

Further reading: Chicago Fact Book Consortium, ed. *Local Community Fact Book: Chicago Metropolitan Area, 1990.* 1995. • Palmer, Vivien M. comp. *Documents: History of the West Rogers Park Community, Chicago, 1925–1930,* vol. 2. 1966. • The Rogers Park/West Ridge Historical Society and Museum. Chicago, IL.

West Town, Community Area 24, 3 miles NW of the Loop. Chicago's West Town community area, located on the city's near northwest side, is perhaps best understood as an amalgam of several distinct neighborhoods. With its official boundaries roughly corresponding to Bloomingdale on the north, Kinzie on the south, the CHICAGO RIVER'S North Branch to the east, and a shifting western boundary that goes as far as Kedzie, West Town has long sustained a strikingly diverse population mix.

Most of the area east of Wood Street was within the original 1837 city limits. Workers came to the area in the late 1840s to build RAILROAD lines. Other settlers were attracted to factories near the river.

By the turn of the twentieth century, GERMANS and Scandinavians tended to live in the north and northwestern sections, particularly near WICKER PARK, while POLISH immigrants settled around Division and Ashland Streets, an area that eventually became known as "Polish Downtown." Russian JEWS tended to live near HUMBOLDT PARK to the west, while ITALIANS concentrated on the southeastern portions, particularly along Grand Avenue. The UKRAINIAN community settled in the section between Chicago and Division, Damen and Western—popularly known as UKRAINIAN VILLAGE—and their presence there is still marked through such institutions as the Ukrainian Institute of Modern Art as well as a number of architecturally imposing churches, including the St. Nicholas Ukrainian Catholic Cathedral and the Holy Trinity Orthodox Cathedral, the latter designed by Louis Sullivan.

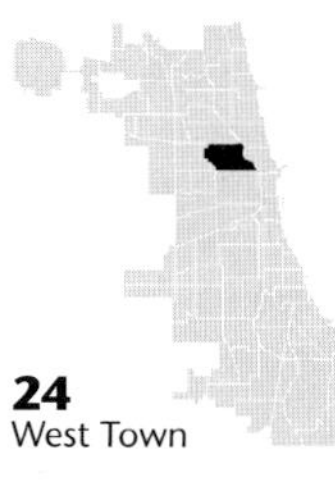

In the second half of the twentieth century, West Town became a primarily Latino "port of entry" neighborhood. First, PUERTO RICANS moved westward toward Humboldt Park, and then MEXICANS concentrated in areas east of the Ukrainian Village. By 1990, Mexicans formed the dominant Latino group. Their presence is reflected in the SHOPPING DISTRICT along Chicago Avenue, particularly east of Damen. AFRICAN AMERICANS have settled in the area since the 1930s but became particularly numerous in the 1970s with the construction of the Noble Square Cooperative project as well as other SUBSIDIZED HOUSING in the vicinity. In the late twentieth century, black ARTISTS and other more affluent blacks moved in as part of the overall evolution of Wicker Park as a "hip alternative" area catering to musicians and artists. The African American percentage of the community area population stood at a solid 10 percent during the last two decades of the twentieth century.

At the turn of the twenty-first century, West Town was changing again. The influx of artists, students, and other younger "bohemian" populations drew more affluent residents, particularly in the BUCKTOWN section north of North Avenue. This gentrification subsequently spread to the southeast areas along Milwaukee Avenue and Halsted, with RESTAURANTS, nightclubs, and shops near the cultural landmarks and institutions created and sustained by earlier residents. The various Latino groups remained a clear majority into the early 1990s but fell to 47 percent by 2000. Lower-income residents of West Town have moved to areas further north and west to escape the area's rising REAL-ESTATE values.

Steven Essig

See also: Art Colonies; Multicentered Chicago; Work Culture

Further reading: Pacyga, Dominic A., and Ellen Skerrett. *Chicago, City of Neighborhoods: Histories and Tours.* 1986.

Westchester, IL, Cook County, 13 miles W of the Loop. Except for a handful of old farmhouses scattered throughout the village and a few streets named after GERMAN farmers who once owned the land, little remains of the nearly 150-year history of farming in the area that became Westchester. The village name, the vast majority of street names, and a few homes built in the 1920s provide clues to the founders' plans for a model English-style town, which was thwarted by the GREAT DEPRESSION.

Plans for the village of Westchester began when utilities tycoon Samuel Insull and associates purchased approximately 2,200 acres of farmland in 1924. A native of London, Insull wanted the new suburb to be a model English town. The planned extension of the GARFIELD PARK RAPID TRANSIT line from Chicago made this location ideal for suburban development. Westchester incorporated in 1926. Several REAL-ESTATE developers directed the construction of paved streets, sidewalks, sewers, and street lamps, plus the laying of water mains and the planting of parkway trees. The all-English street names chosen by Insull and the construction of houses and apartments of brick, stucco, and hand-hewn timbers set Westchester apart from many other Chicago suburbs. Completion of the rapid transit line to 12th St. (Roosevelt Road) in 1926 and to 22nd St. (Cermak Road) in 1930 enabled prospective buyers to view properties in Westchester.

Construction came to a halt in the 1930s as many properties were tied up in contract and tax delinquencies. The clearing of these delinquent properties after WORLD WAR II initially caused construction here to lag behind other nearby suburbs. Westchester's biggest gain in population occurred between 1950 and 1960 as the village grew from 4,308 to 18,092, and the few English-style houses that had been built before the Depression were surrounded by Georgians, ranches, and split-levels. With the removal of the rapid transit line and the building of EXPRESSWAYS in the 1950s, transportation in the postwar era shifted its focus. Westchester's proximity to the Eisenhower Expressway (Westchester's northern boundary) and to the Tri-State TOLL ROAD (near the village's western boundary) became increasingly important to village residents.

In the 1980s, some of the remaining farmland became the Westbrook Corporate Center, a cluster of five 10-story office buildings near Cermak Road (22nd Street) and Wolf Road. This expanded the commercial tax base of the almost entirely residential village. Residential construction south of the Westbrook development in the 1990s has used up all but one tract of open land within the village—the 85-acre Wolf Road Prairie, which has been spared development, largely through the efforts of the Save the Prairie Society, active in Westchester since 1975. An Illinois State Nature Preserve, this prairie is but a small, rare remnant of the vast prairies that once covered much of Illinois.

Patricia Krone Rose

See also: Conservation and Preservation; Gas and Electricity; Metropolitan Growth; Suburbs and Cities as Dual Metropolis

Further reading: Miscellaneous articles and newspaper clippings. Westchester Public Library, Westchester, IL. • Petersen, Clarence. "'A Good Place to Live' Still Has Some Drive." *Chicago Tribune,* May 6, 1989.

Western Springs, IL, Cook County, 15 miles W of the Loop. Western Springs, located along the Chicago, Burlington & Quincy RAILROAD between Chicago and Aurora, encompasses roughly the area between Willow Springs Road, Ogden Avenue, Interstate 294, and 55th Street. Named for local mineral springs on the southwest side of town, Western Springs originally consisted of flat prairie land with a swamp on its western border.

By 1834, after the BLACK HAWK WAR, farmer Joseph Vial had built a cabin along what is now Plainfield Road south of Western Springs. This cabin served as a stagecoach station, hotel, general store, and post office for the entire area.

The CB&Q Railroad built a line through Western Springs in 1863, filling in much of the west-side swamp in the process. In 1870 the Western Springs Land Association, consisting of promoter Thomas Clarkson Hill, William Page, and two sons of Phillip F. W. Peck, bought the three tracts that make up the area for $105,000.

A large number of early residents were Quakers, and deeds often prohibited the sale of alcohol. In 1872 Hill moved to the area from Chicago, and the community began organizing to attract more COMMUTERS. Residents built a wooden schoolhouse (1872) and a post office (1873). Over time, with increased commuter settlement, Western Springs came to look less and less Quaker.

In 1885 the Grand Avenue School replaced the wooden schoolhouse, and the office of village marshal was created as a combination policeman, dogcatcher, and groundskeeper. In 1886 the Friend's Church (razed in 1958) was built on the corner of Walnut and Woodland. That same year Western Springs incorporated as a village on February 30, 1886, and elected T. C. Hill as its first president.

After the spring dried up in 1890, the village hired engineers Edgar and Benezette Williams to build the village waterworks system, including the famous WATER tower. Constructed using NAPERVILLE stone, the tower stood 112 feet high. Replaced in 1962, it became a museum in 1970 and entered the National Register of Historic Places in 1981.

Western Springs added many improvements over the years, including a fire department (1894), electric plant (1898), TELEPHONES (1899), a PARK DISTRICT (1923), and a library (1926). The village expanded south of 47th Street, ANNEXING the SUBDIVISIONS of Forest Hills (1927), Springdale (1955), and Ridgewood (1973). Spring Rock Park was created in 1931, and four more parks followed in 1945.

Tom Sterling

See also: Local Option; Prohibition and Temperance; Religious Geography; Restrictive Covenants

Further reading: *Western Springs: A Centennial History of the Village, 1886–1986.* 1985.

Westinghouse Broadcasting. This pioneering radio set manufacturer began operating a radio station in Chicago in 1921. On Armistice day, Westinghouse placed KYW-AM, its fourth station, on the air from KYW's transmitter located on the roof of the Commonwealth Edison Building. Live broadcasts from the AUDITORIUM THEATER commenced the following Monday, enabling 1,300 "radio homes" in the Chicago area to hear OPERA. But profits proved elusive, and in 1934 Westinghouse moved KYW-AM to Philadelphia and did not re-enter the Chicago market until late in 1956, when it purchased WIND-AM. In 1988 Westinghouse sold WIND-AM and purchased WMAQ-AM from NBC, and in 1996 it merged with CBS and Infinity Broadcasting. By 2002, Westinghouse owned seven radio stations, not including WMAQ, which went dark in 2000.

Douglas Gomery

See also: Broadcasting; Entertaining Chicagoans; WBBM

Further reading: "KYW-Station File." Library of American Broadcasting, University of Maryland, College Park, MD. • Bliss, Edward, Jr. *Now the News: The Story of Broadcast Journalism.* 1991. • *Broadcasting Yearbook.* Various editions, 1931–.

Westmont, IL, DuPage County, 19 miles W of the Loop. Easy access to TRANSPORTATION is central to Westmont's story. In 1834 two stage routes passed through the area, one along Ogden Avenue and the other down Naperville Road. The Chicago, Burlington & Quincy Railroad began stopping in Westmont (then Bushville) in 1864.

While neighboring towns were settled by the wealthy, Westmont grew through the efforts of working people. In 1872, following the Chicago Fire, William Gregg found the region to have good clay for brickmaking and started the Excelsior Brick Company. He built his factory on the highest point of the RAILROAD so that after bricks were loaded onto a railcar, the load was easily shuttled downhill to the city. In the 1870s Excelsior employed 120 people and produced 70,000 bricks a day. CZECH, POLISH, and ITALIAN workers came and lived in the settlement that was soon named Greggs. Two schools and a depot were built. Gregg invented a triple-pressure brick machine, which manufactured bricks able to withstand 100,000 pounds of pressure without cracking. The boom period lasted until after 1900, when the brickyard closed down and many workers left.

In 1919 Arthur McIntosh bought land in Westmont and offered working-class Chicagoans an opportunity to own property for five dollars down and small monthly payments. By 1923 the McIntosh subdivision had more than 1,800 people, many either AUSTRIAN, Polish, or GERMAN immigrants or their children. Newcomers first lived in tents and shacks, and had no paved streets or utilities. Before long, however, they constructed modest cottages.

In 1921 the village was incorporated as Westmont, but during PROHIBITION acquired the nicknames "Whiskey Hill" and "Wet Mont," as liquor flowed in the community. People in neighboring towns frequented the area where the illegal trade continued.

Population grew to 2,733 in 1930; and as late as 1939, 35 percent were foreign-born. Development escalated in the post–WORLD WAR II days; brick houses became fashionable in a large development called Blackhawk Heights. By the 1960s a large number of laborers and skilled tradesmen had moved into the area to take jobs at Western Electric and International Harvester.

In 1990 renters dominated the housing market, totaling nearly 50 percent, with single-family houses beginning to replace apartments. Car dealerships were prevalent along Ogden Avenue and generated 40 percent of the sales tax revenue in 1994. Westmont's population had grown to 24,554 in 2000, with 12 percent Asian, 7 percent Latino, and 5 percent African American.

Marilyn Elizabeth Perry

See also: Built Environment of the Chicago Region; Economic Geography; Foodways; Quarrying, Stonecutting, and Brickmaking

Further reading: Knoblauch, Marion, ed. *DuPage County: A Descriptive and Historical Guide, 1831–1939*. 1948. • Thompson, Richard A., ed. *DuPage Roots*. 1985.

WGN. Its call letters standing for "World's Greatest Newspaper," WGN, a clear-channel radio (and then TV) station, was not actually started by its longtime owner, the Tribune Company, but was purchased by the NEWSPAPER giant soon after it went on the air in June 1924. In 1934 WGN talent and executives helped create the Mutual Radio Network; recently it has attracted thousands of listeners with a middle-of-the-road music/talk format. WGN-TV signed on in April 1948. After short-term affiliations with both CBS and DuMont, channel 9 programmed as an independent, non-network station. It took this strategy national as a "superstation" in November 1978.

Douglas Gomery

See also: Bozo's Circus; Broadcasting; Business of Chicago; Entertaining Chicagoans

Further reading: Feder, Robert. "WGN to Celebrate 60 Years on the Air." *Chicago Sun-Times,* June 17, 1984, 2, 4. • WGN station file. Library of American Broadcasting, University of Maryland, College Park, Maryland.

Wheaton College. Organized in 1853 by Wesleyan Methodists, Illinois Institute was rechartered in 1860 as Wheaton College. Jonathan Blanchard came from Knox College to become Wheaton's first president, separating the school from any denominational support. At this time, Wheaton was the only school in Illinois with a college-level women's program. Blanchard used the school as a platform for ABOLITIONISM, anti-Masonic advocacy, and his national presidential campaign on the American Party ticket in 1884.

The conservative theological stance of emergent fundamentalism became a defining characteristic of the college after Charles Blanchard succeeded his father as president in 1882. Accreditation and enrollment growth, however, would await the administration of James Oliver Buswell, an outspoken Presbyterian who became the nation's youngest college president in 1926. Buswell's tenure was characterized by expanding enrollment (from approximately 400 in 1925 to 1,100 in 1940), a building program, strong academic development, and divisiveness over faculty scholarship and personalities. During WORLD WAR II, Wheaton expanded its campus, adding a library, a student center music building, a chapel, new dormitories, and food service facilities to meet the needs of increasing enrollment, which surpassed 1,600 by 1950.

By the late 1940s, Wheaton emerged as a fortress of PROTESTANT evangelicalism. National and international recognition was in large measure due to the stature of its best known alumnus, Billy Graham. Over the next half century, enrollment growth and more selective admissions accompanied athletic success, additional and improved facilities, and expanded programs. Sites in the Black Hills of South Dakota and northern Wisconsin augmented the 80-acre WHEATON campus. By 2000, approximately 2,300 undergraduates complemented the 250 graduate students enrolled in the Psy.D. and nine M.A. programs.

The lifestyle and theological identification of Wheaton College with Evangelical Christianity, while independent of any denominational affiliation, remains its signature.

Thomas O. Kay

See also: Religion, Chicago's Influence on; Universities and Their Cities

Further reading: Bechtel, Paul M. *Wheaton College: A Heritage Remembered, 1860–1984*. 1984. • Cairns, Earle Edwin. *V. Raymond Edman: In the Presence of the King*. 1972. • Coray, Edward A. *The Wheaton I Remember: Memoirs*. 1974.

Wheaton, IL, DuPage County, 25 miles W of the Loop. Erastus Gary arrived in 1831 to develop a farm and mill on the west branch of the DUPAGE RIVER in WARRENVILLE, several miles west of present-day Wheaton. Gary's neighbors from Connecticut, brothers Jesse and Warren Wheaton, claimed nearly a thousand acres of nearby land in 1838–39. Other settlers from New England soon followed. The settlement was formally incorporated in 1859, and by 1880 the population approached 1,000. The community became the county seat in 1867 following a decade-long contest with Naperville that resulted in a successful midnight raid on the NAPERVILLE courthouse for the county records. In 1887, Wheaton began a long-term PROHIBITION of the sale of alcohol.

A Wesleyan Methodist congregation organized in 1843 was the first formal church in the community. The Wesleyans opened Illinois Institute in 1853, which became WHEATON COLLEGE in 1860. Methodists formed their own congregation in 1853, and Jonathan Blanchard organized a Congregational church (temporarily subsuming the Wesleyans) in 1860. Baptists, ROMAN CATHOLICS, Lutherans, Episcopalians, and others followed shortly thereafter. Following WORLD WAR II, many new congregations were formed as the population of the community increased rapidly over the succeeding decades from its 1940 level of 7,400.

In 1874 local residents built one of the first public schools in the county that included grades 1–12. Additional grammar schools were built as the population increased: Holmes, Whittier, and Lowell, each in a different quarter of the town. A new high school was added in 1925, Wheaton North in 1964, and Wheaton South (Wheaton-Warrenville) in 1973.

Wheaton was becoming a suburban community. The Galena & Chicago Union RAILROAD arrived in 1849, on land donated by Warren Wheaton, whose name identified the local station. COMMUTER service became a regular feature of the community. The establishment of the banking house of Gary and Wheaton, a new courthouse, the Adams Memorial Library, and construction of residences and places of business gave evidence of a growing, prospering community at the end of the nineteenth century. In 1902 a second railroad, the Chicago, Aurora & Elgin electric line, connected Wheaton to the Fox River Valley until 1957.

Wheaton was the site of summer residences for some wealthy Chicagoans, offering a course for HORSE RACING and the Chicago GOLF Club (the first 18-hole golf course in the United States). The community was also home to several persons of national note: Judge Elbert Gary (founder of U.S. Steel and the city of GARY, Indiana), Senator C. Wayland Brooks, John Quincy Adams (financier and philanthropist), Edwin Hubble (astronomer), Grote Reber (radio astronomer), Red Grange and Vic Gustafson (football players), and Margaret Mortenson Landon (author of *Anna and the King of Siam*). Wheaton College, the Billy Graham Center, the Theosophical Society in America, and World Evangelical Fellowship help make Wheaton a metropolitan religious center.

Thomas O. Kay

See also: DuPage County; Interurbans; Protestants; Religious Geography

Further reading: Burnham, Graham. *Wheaton and Its Homes.* 1892. • Moore, Jean. *From Tower to Tower: A History of Wheaton, Illinois.* 1974. • Moore, Jean. *Wheaton, Illinois: A Pictorial History.* 1994.

Wheeling, IL, Cook County, 23 miles NW of the Loop. FOLKLORE attributes Wheeling's name to the rumble of wagon wheels bumping down the community's dusty main road, but the village was actually named for Wheeling, West Virginia. The continuous stream of wagons did give rise to numerous eateries along Milwaukee Avenue, earning the area a nickname of "Restaurant Row," a name it continued to carry into the 1990s.

By 1836, Milwaukee Avenue, then known as Des Plaines Valley Road, had become a stagecoach route between Chicago and Green Bay, Wisconsin. This prompted Joseph Filkins to build a tavern and hotel at the corner of Dundee Road and Milwaukee Avenue.

Along with the surrounding GERMAN farming community, another hotel, a blacksmith shop, a HARDWARE store, and a school spurred population growth in the 1840s. Napoleon Periolat started a BREWERY in 1850 which operated until 1910 and was followed by more HOTELS and restaurants.

Because of Wheeling's location along the DES PLAINES RIVER, and its numerous restaurants and taverns, Chicagoans flocked to the area on weekends. In the 1880s the popular sport of BICYCLING prompted races between Wheeling and Chicago with as many as a hundred participants. In 1886 a line of the Wisconsin Central RAILROAD came through town, stopping at a station just south of Dundee Road.

Wheeling had formed a TOWNSHIP government in 1850. When RAILROAD WORKERS and laborers began frequenting Wheeling's SALOONS, often creating disturbances on the streets, local officials seeking the authority to maintain law and order opted to move for incorporation. In 1894, the newly formed village immediately began regulating the dramshops.

In 1917 the Knights of Columbus built the Columbian Country Club, later called Windsor, Bon Air, and finally Chevy Chase. The country club and 18-hole GOLF course changed ownership in the 1930s and operated as a GAMBLING establishment. Gambling plus big BAND music were also the attractions at Red Mary's Wheeling Inn. Regardless of the town's notoriety, it was these establishments and the good-quality restaurants that enabled Wheeling's residents to survive the GREAT DEPRESSION.

Between 1950 and 1970 Wheeling grew from 916 to 14,746 residents. Manufacturing burgeoned during this period with the addition of 86-acre South Wheeling Industrial Park and the arrival of companies such as Acco International, makers of office supplies.

In 1984 Wheeling ANNEXED the 131-acre Arlington Country Club. Along with its neighbor, the city of PROSPECT HEIGHTS, Wheeling purchased Palwaukee AIRPORT from the Priester family in 1986. The METRA North Central Service opened service through the area in 1996 and built a station for commuters off Wheeling Road just south of Dundee. The population in 2000 was at 34,496 21 percent of whom were Hispanic and 9 percent Asian.

Neighboring suburbanites and Chicagoans have continued to frequent RESTAURANTS along Milwaukee Avenue. In 1990 village eateries totaled 40, including the prestigious French restaurant Le Francais, Bob Chinn's Crabhouse, Hackney's Restaurant, Don Roth's, and the 94th Aero Squadron.

Marilyn Elizabeth Perry

See also: Entertaining Chicagoans; Government, Suburban; Local Option; Prohibition and Temperance; Streets and Highways; Underground Economy

Further reading: McConnell, Shirley Ward. *A Century to Remember.* 1964. • McIntyre, Barbara K., and Robert L. McIntyre, eds. *Wheeling through the Years: An Oral History of Wheeling, an Illinois Village.* 1987. • Oaks, Glenn, ed. *Wheeling Diamond Jubilee, 1894–1964.* 1964.

Whigs. From the mid-1830s to the mid-1850s, opponents of the DEMOCRATIC Party organized under the banner of the Whigs. In the national political arena, Whigs distinguished themselves by promoting a national bank, higher tariffs, and more federal spending on TRANSPORTATION infrastructure; they also tended to support temperance and other moral-reform laws. In Chicago, as in the nation as a whole, this platform often landed Whigs in second place, behind Democrats who promised less intrusive government.

The Whig party attracted some of early Chicago's leading businessmen and lawyers, including John H. Kinzie, George W. Dole, Benjamin W. Raymond, Justin Butterfield, and Jonathan Y. Scammon. Competitive in city politics for a decade, Whigs won 4 out of 10 mayoral elections between 1837 and 1846. From 1838 to 1843, Chicago was part of a large U.S. Congressional District represented by John T. Stuart, a Whig from Springfield. The city's Whigs advanced their views in the *American* NEWSPAPER and its successors, the Chicago *Express* and the Chicago *Daily Journal;* they also staged rallies, barbecues, and parades.

By the late 1840s, the influence of Chicago Whigs was waning. As more European immigrants settled in the city, the pro-temperance, nativist flavor of the traditional Whig platform became more of a political liability. Meanwhile, it was apparent that partisan divisions at the national level did not necessarily translate to meaningful differences in the everyday practice of city POLITICS. From 1847 to 1854, Whigs and Democrats did not contest city elections, which became nonpartisan during these years. After the American Whig party collapsed in the mid-1850s, many of Chicago's former Whigs joined a new party: the REPUBLICANS.

Thomas F. Schwartz
Mark R. Wilson

See also: Mayors; Political Culture; Prohibition and Temperance; Yankees

Further reading: Einhorn, Robin. *Property Rules: Political Economy in Chicago, 1833–1872.* 1991. • Pierce, Bessie Louise. *A History of Chicago,* vol. 1. 1937.

White Flight. *See* Neighborhood Succession; Racism, Ethnicity, and White Identity

White Sox. With roots in Sioux City, Iowa, and St. Paul, Minnesota, the White Sox came to Chicago in 1900 to play in the new American League. Owned by Charles Comiskey, a former minor league owner and major league star player from Chicago's West Side, the White Stockings—shortened to White Sox by local sportswriters—opened their season in a makeshift ballpark at 39th Street and Wentworth. The team captured the American League pennant in 1901. Attendance was high; fans appreciated the exciting style of White Sox BASEBALL as well as the twenty-five-cent admission charge—half the price of a Chicago CUBS ticket. In 1906, the Sox (93–58 and dubbed the "Hitless Wonders" for their American League–low batting average) upset the more established Cubs (116–36) in the World Series. Four years later, the team settled in its "permanent" home, COMISKEY PARK, at 35th and Shields.

Comiskey was a genius at spotting talent. In the WORLD WAR I era, he created an apparent dynasty by signing established stars like Eddie Collins and "Shoeless Joe" Jackson, as well as new talent like George "Buck" Weaver. Yet Comiskey alienated many players with his tightfisted, petty behavior. He kept their salaries low, deducted World Series bonuses from their paychecks, and even required them to launder their own uniforms. In 1919, player resentment boiled over. When the White Sox lost the World Series to the underdog Cincinnati Reds, rumors surfaced that several Sox players had taken bribes from gamblers to "throw" the games. In the end, eight players—including Jackson, pitcher Ed Cicotte, first baseman "Chick" Gandil, and shortstop "Swede" Risberg—were banned permanently from organized baseball.

The "BLACK SOX" SCANDAL rocked the nation, the major leagues, and especially the team. Many fans blamed Charles Comiskey, who knew far more about the scandal than he cared to reveal. There would be no more pennants for Comiskey, who died a broken man in

1931. The team featured individual stars like batting champion Luke Appling in the following years, but it rarely played winning baseball. The White Sox did not shed their losing image until the early 1950s, when General Manager Frank "Trader" Lane acquired exciting new talent, including pitcher Billy Pierce, shortstop "Chico" Carrasquel, second baseman Nellie Fox, and outfielder Orestes "Minnie" Minoso, the team's first AFRICAN AMERICAN player. In 1959, a group of investors led by Bill Veeck took control of the team. That year the "Go Go" White Sox, managed by Al Lopez, captured the American League pennant with superb pitching, defense, and speed, but lost the World Series to the Los Angeles Dodgers.

Although the White Sox contended for the pennant in 1964 and 1967, lean years lay ahead. Veeck gutted the farm system and traded away talented young prospects. Attendance plummeted; poor play was compounded by fears that the neighborhood surrounding Comiskey Park was no longer "safe." Veeck responded with typical showmanship, hiring "witches" to change the team's luck and outfitting his players in hideous softball uniforms. Even popular announcer Harry Caray departed the White Sox for the Cubs in 1982.

The 1980s opened with a ray of hope. Veeck and his partners sold the White Sox to Jerry Reinsdorf, a REAL-ESTATE developer who owned the Chicago BULLS, and Eddie Einhorn, a television sports producer who had once sold hot dogs at Comiskey Park. Stocking the team with solid veterans like Carlton Fisk and Greg Luzinski, the new owners brought a division title to Chicago in 1983. But the erosion of fan support and media coverage continued, leading to fears that Reinsdorf and Einhorn would move the White Sox to another city. In response, the Illinois legislature provided funding for a new ballpark. The new park opened in 1991 across the street from the old stadium, which was demolished in favor of a parking lot.

David M. Oshinsky

See also: Creation of Chicago Sports; Leisure

Further reading: Lindberg, Richard C. "Chicago White Sox: Second Class in the Second City." In *The Encyclopedia of Major League Baseball: American League*, ed. Peter Bjarkman, 1993.

Whiting, IN, Lake County, 16 miles SE of the Loop. In 1889 the Standard Oil Company decided that it needed a REFINERY west of Cleveland to serve its growing kerosene and lubricant trade in the interior of the country. Company officials selected a site south of downtown Chicago on Lake Michigan filled with large sand ridges and populated by some 50 GERMAN families who hunted, fished, and supplied lodging and meals to the many sportsmen who used the area. The settlement of Whiting itself dates to 1871 when a post office was established at the place where "Old Pap Whiting," a conductor on the Lake Shore RAILROAD, had wrecked his train.

The refinery altered the remote outpost forever as it brought construction teams, SALOONS, stores, workers, and immigrant families to the town. Shortly after the commencement of construction BOARDINGHOUSES sprouted at both entrances to the refinery. In a short while 119th Street became the chief center of commerce and trade. At the corner of 119th and Front Streets Henry Schrage sold food and clothing and distributed the mail. The first stage of the refinery was completed on September 2, 1890, and the facility was altered and expanded many times after that.

Refinery jobs proved especially attractive to immigrants and led to the creation of a community marked by ethnic diversity. The workforce soon consisted of Americans, CROATIANS, FINNS, Germans, HUNGARIANS, IRISH, POLES, RUSSIANS, and SLOVAKS, who were probably the largest ethnic group to settle in the town. As in most industrial plants of the time, native-born skilled workers held the best jobs, and unskilled toilers, like Croatians and Slovaks, did the hot, dirty task of cleaning the refinery stills.

Standard Oil of Indiana dominated the life of the town throughout the twentieth century. Its Industrial Relations Plan, created in 1919, gave workers stock-purchase plans, health insurance, retirement programs, and a community center complete with gymnasium and pool which still serves the community. Families who benefited from these plans valued them greatly and many households even in the 1990s continued to receive Standard Oil pensions. During the GREAT DEPRESSION the company attempted to employ as many workers as possible, even if for only a few days a week.

A turning point in the life of Whiting came in 1956 when an explosion started a fire at the plant so massive that it could be seen from downtown Chicago. The damage caused the company to modernize the facility in a way that reduced the demand for employees and led to layoffs in the early 1960s. Families accustomed to good benefits and stable employment were now angered enough to support a union outside the control of the company for the first time: the Oil, Chemical and Atomic Workers. Nevertheless, levels of employment continued to drop. The population fell from 10,880 in 1930 to 5,137 by 2000, with most of the loss coming after 1950. As the children of the first immigrant wave left to find work elsewhere, MEXICAN Americans moved in to take what positions were available.

John Bodnar

See also: Demography; Plant Communities; Unionization; Welfare Capitalism

Further reading: Federal Writers' Project, Indiana. *The Calumet Region Historical Guide*. 1939.

Wholesaling. Given that Chicago long ranked as America's "second city," it is not surprising that it has served since the mid-nineteenth century as a major wholesaling center. Like most cities, Chicago has been a place for the exchange and distribution of commodities and information. Some of the most important actors in this urban economy have been wholesalers—that is, merchants who specialize in connecting the producers of commodities with the retailers who sell them to final users. Chicago wholesalers have been among the leading distributors and marketers of all sorts of goods, including LUMBER, grain, dry goods, HARDWARE, and metals. Although the power of merchant middlemen has declined in many industries during the years since Chicago was founded, at the beginning of the twenty-first century the city remained a wholesaling capital.

Chicago's wholesale trade grew rapidly after the ILLINOIS & MICHIGAN CANAL was completed in 1848, and this growth was boosted even further by the completion of major RAILROAD links to the city during the 1850s. By the eve of the CIVIL WAR, when the volume of the city's annual wholesale trade was estimated at no less than $32 million, Chicago had become one of the most important centers in North America for the distribution and marketing of lumber and grain. Leading Chicago lumber merchants like Charles Mears built fortunes during the city's early years by serving as wholesalers of forest products, sorting and grading lumber and collecting commissions by connecting producers and consumers. Meanwhile, grain elevator owners and merchants were making the city into one of the world's most important sites for the marketing of corn and wheat. The Chicago Board of Trade, one of the city's most important institutions, served as a regulator and promoter of the wholesale trade in grain.

During the latter part of the nineteenth century, when Chicago continued to serve as a major center for the distribution of farm products, the city's merchants became some of the world's leading wholesalers of manufactured goods. By 1900, there were nearly 3,400 wholesale dealers in the city, and the volume of the annual wholesale trade handled by Chicago firms stood at about $1 billion. The city's greatest wholesalers at this time were the companies led by Marshall Field and John V. Farwell, both of which sold dry goods such as textiles and clothing. Marshall Field & Co., which by the later twentieth century would be known only as a DEPARTMENT STORE retailer, was once one of the world's leading wholesalers. By the early 1880s, when Field's partner Levi Leiter left the

South Water Street was the city's primary wholesale produce market until it was relocated in 1925 for the construction of Wacker Drive. Photographer: Unknown. Source: Chicago Historical Society.

company, its annual sales totaled about $4 million in the retail department, and $22 million in wholesale. The company's wholesale division, headed by John G. Shedd, purchased most of its goods from dealers in New York City and sold them to retailers throughout the Midwest by sending out catalogs and traveling salesmen. In 1887, Shedd's division moved into an enormous new Chicago wholesale store, designed by the architect H. H. Richardson and containing about 12 acres of floor space and 1,800 employees. Only slightly smaller than the wholesale operations of Marshall Field & Co. were those of the company owned by John V. Farwell, a veteran of the Chicago dry-goods trade. By the 1880s, when Field and Farwell reportedly ranked as two of the three leading wholesalers in the United States, the latter company was selling $20 million worth of goods a year to retailers around the country.

Field and Farwell were not the only important firms during the wholesaling heyday that was occurring in Chicago during the late nineteenth and early twentieth centuries. In the field of dry goods, other major Chicago wholesalers included Mandel Brothers and Carson Pirie Scott. Among the city's leading dealers in GROCERIES were Henry Horner & Co., which started wholesale operations in 1856, and William M. Hoyt & Co., which also started before the Civil War and which was selling over $5 million worth of groceries a year by the early 1890s. The city's leading JEWEL merchant at this time was Henry A. Spaulding, who opened a business in Chicago in 1888. One of the most important firms in the DRUG industry was one headed by Robert Morrison and Jonathan Plummer, who moved their business from Richmond, Indiana, to Chicago in 1876. By the 1910s, when it became the Fuller-Morrison Company, it employed 38 traveling salesmen and ranked as one of the largest drug wholesalers in the United States. No Chicago wholesaling company during this period was more prominent within its industry than the hardware-dealing firm of Hibbard, Spencer, Bartlett & Co., which grew out of a business established in the city during the 1850s by William G. Hibbard. By 1903, when the company moved into a new 11-story building at the foot of State Street BRIDGE, it was one of the leading hardware wholesalers in the country, a position it retained through the first half of the twentieth century.

Although the aggregate volume of the city's wholesale trade has grown considerably over the years (from virtually zero before 1848 to $6 billion by 1929 to nearly $200 billion a year by the end of the twentieth century), the history of wholesaling in Chicago is not one of steady expansion across all industries. In fact, for a variety of reasons, wholesalers of certain kinds of commodities have lost economic power over time. In several industries, the growth in the size of manufacturers on the one side and retailers on the other squeezed out independent wholesalers. The urbanization of the American population, which reduced the geographical scope of large markets, boosted the rise of department stores and chain stores that could bypass middlemen by buying in bulk directly from manufacturers. Meanwhile, many of the merchants who served rural markets were being pushed out by large MAIL-ORDER firms, including Chicago's own Montgomery Ward and Sears. At the other side of the supply chain, some of the large industrial corporations that began to appear in the late nineteenth century (including Chicago MEATPACKERS such as Swift & Co.) began to dispense with wholesalers by creating their own distribution and marketing departments.

In Chicago, one of the most notable transformations of the commercial sector during the early twentieth century was the decline of the great dry-goods wholesalers. At Marshall Field & Co., as late as 1906, about two-thirds of the annual sales volume of $73 million came from the wholesale department. Over the next two decades (when the company was headed by John Shedd, the former wholesale division chief), Field's continued to attempt to make money from the wholesale trade. In an effort to gain a steady supply source for its wholesale operations, Field's bought about 30 textile mills during this period; and during the late 1920s, it began to build the Merchandise Mart, the huge Chicago structure—intended as a wholesaling center—that became the world's largest building when it was completed in 1931. But despite these considerable efforts, Field's was unable to keep its wholesaling operations profitable, and they ended entirely during the GREAT DEPRESSION. At John V. Farwell & Co., wholesaling ended even earlier, in 1925. Carson Pirie Scott & Co., which (like Field's) had a growing retail business, closed its wholesale department in 1941.

Although some of Chicago's leading wholesale dealers were pushed out of business before WORLD WAR II, wholesaling remained an important part of the city's economy during the latter part of the twentieth century. The numbers of wholesaling firms in the Chicago area and the aggregate volume of their BUSINESS continued to grow, and the city remained home to leading wholesalers of commodities such as hardware, groceries, paper products, and metals. During the Depression, the number of Chicagoans employed in various aspects of wholesale commerce declined from about 140,000 to about 120,000. But by the 1950s, about 175,000 local residents worked for roughly 11,000 Chicago-area wholesaling firms, which did a total of about $20 billion in annual sales. Only New York City was a more important American wholesaling center. By the early 1990s, when the Chicago area's roughly $190 billion in annual wholesale trade accounted for about 6 percent of the national total (down from 8 percent in 1929), the metropolitan area was home to about 18,000 wholesaling firms with 260,000 employees.

During the latter part of the twentieth century, one of the city's leading wholesalers was

Ryerson Tull, Inc., the descendant of an old Chicago firm founded by Joseph T. Ryerson before the Civil War. During the Depression, the Ryerson company merged with Inland Steel and served as the processing and distribution arm of that leading Chicago metals producer. By the end of the twentieth century, this operation had evolved into Ryerson Tull, a processor and distributor of metals with about 5,000 employees worldwide and $3 billion in annual sales. An even bigger Chicago wholesaler with deep roots in the city was the Truserv Corporation, an enormous dealer-owned cooperative hardware company that was a descendant of the old firm of Hibbard, Spencer & Bartlett. Truserv's leading competitor, the Ace Hardware Corporation, was also a homegrown Chicago company. Among the most important of the other wholesaling firms headquartered in the Chicago region at the beginning of the twenty-first century were W. W. Grainger, Inc., a dealer in machinery; Anixter International, which specialized in wire; Boise Cascade Office Products and United Stationers, Inc. (both sellers of paper products); Topco, a distributor of groceries; and the Chas. Levy Company, one of a handful of MAGAZINE wholesalers remaining in the United States.

Mark R. Wilson

See also: Commodities Markets; Food Processing: Regional and National Market; Retail Geography

Further reading: Cronon, William. *Nature's Metropolis: Chicago and the Great West.* 1991. • Currey, J. Seymour. *Manufacturing and Wholesale Industries of Chicago.* 3 vols. 1918. • Porter, Glenn, and Harold Livesay. *Merchants and Manufacturers: Studies in the Changing Structure of Nineteenth-Century Marketing.* 1971.

Wicker Park, neighborhood in the WEST TOWN Community Area. Bounded by Ashland and Western Avenues to the east and west, Bloomingdale and Division Streets to the north and south, Wicker Park became, in the aftermath of the FIRE OF 1871, the abode of Chicago's wealthy Germans and Scandinavians. Uninhabited, and on the western edge of the city, the area provided an alternative to a population who had already been spurned by the Anglo-PROTESTANT establishment residing on Chicago's lakefront.

The FIRE OF 1871 also influenced the architecture of Wicker Park. Having witnessed the vulnerability of wood construction, many Wicker Park residents built large mansions made almost entirely of brick and stone. By the 1890s the area was an architectural showplace, possessing houses in a variety of styles, including Victorian Gothic and Italianate. Many of these houses circled the four-acre park after which the community was named.

Not everyone who settled in Wicker Park, however, was wealthy and resided in a large house. By the late nineteenth century, Bell Avenue had become home to working-class AFRICAN AMERICANS and Eastern Europeans who lived in the small cottages dotting the street. Labor activists also resided in that section of Wicker Park, including the martyrs of the HAYMARKET Affair.

By 1930 Wicker Park began to undergo a dramatic racial and class transition. The wealthy GERMANS and Scandinavians abandoned their mansions, while the area's poor and working-class residency grew. POLES drew the area into the "Old POLONIA" of surrounding West Town. Further changes came in the 1950s when a large Spanish-speaking population began to emerge. This transition coincided with a post–WORLD WAR II housing shortage, and many of the mansions were divided into multifamily units and rooming houses. By the 1960s and 1970s, Wicker Park was a predominately poor and working-class neighborhood with a large Hispanic population.

Efforts to revitalize Wicker Park in the early 1980s initiated another wave of changes to the neighborhood. Young white professionals bought many of the old houses and restored them to single-family residences. GENTRIFICATION stirred racial and class tensions, as it displaced much of the area's poor and mostly Hispanic population. By the 1990s, however, Wicker Park had achieved a level of cultural and racial heterogeneity. And with commercial development along Division and North Avenues, the neighborhood had become again one of the most desirable in Chicago.

Wallace Best

See also: Contested Spaces; Housing Types; Park Districts

Further reading: "Wicker Park Restored to Its Former Elegance." *Chicago Tribune,* July 13, 1986. • Pacyga, Dominic A., and Ellen Skerrett. *Chicago, City of Neighborhoods: Histories and Tours.* 1986. • Sommers, Nicholas. *The Historic Homes of Old Wicker Park.* 1979.

Wigwam. The site of the 1860 REPUBLICAN National Convention, the Wigwam was built in little more than a month entirely of wood, on Lake Street near the Chicago River. The hall was packed with more than 12,000 delegates and spectators, and the multitude of enthusiastic supporters of Abraham Lincoln in the galleries helped to stampede the Republican delegates toward the dark-horse candidate from Illinois. The building was used for political and patriotic meetings during the 1860 election and at the outbreak of the CIVIL WAR. Subdivided into several stores, the rectangular building functioned as a retail space until its removal sometime between 1867 and 1871. Its name derived from the antebellum custom (especially in New York) of calling a political campaign headquarters a "wigwam."

Theodore J. Karamanski

See also: Places of Assembly; Political Conventions; State Politics

Further reading: Karamanski, Theodore J. *Rally 'Round the Flag: Chicago and the Civil War.* 1993. • Sautter, R. Craig, and Edward M. Burke. *Inside the Wigwam: Chicago Presidential Conventions, 1860–1996.* 1996.

Will County. Less than two hundred years ago, the land that is now Will County was covered by prairie. POTAWATOMI farmed, trapped, and traversed the area, which was at the crossroads of their land trails and river routes. In the late seventeenth century, European FUR TRADERS also began to take advantage of the abundance of muskrat, beaver, and other creatures. Trade slowed substantially by the 1820s, as hunting and the enclosure and tilling of the soil depleted the fur supply.

While the fur trade waned, the population expanded. In 1826, Jesse Walker established the area's first permanent white settlement, Walker's Grove, near the present town of PLAINFIELD. While Walker worked as a missionary to Potawatomi, most newcomers relied on agriculture, milling, and trade for their subsistence.

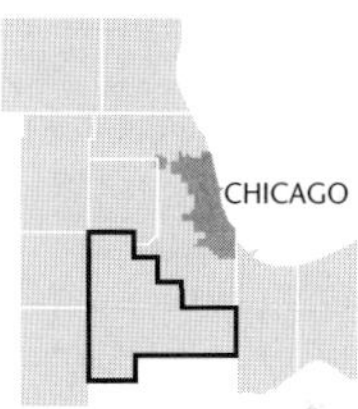

Responding to their expanding population and to the inconvenience of day-long trips to and from Chicago for legal transactions, settlers soon demanded separation from COOK COUNTY. On January 12, 1836, the state of Illinois responded to the residents' petition and formed the County of Will, combining parts of Cook and Iroquois Counties. The Illinois legislature named the county for Conrad Will, a member of the first nine general assemblies, who apparently never resided in the Will County area.

Later that year, the three commissioners of the Will County board held their first meeting in the county seat of Juliet (later JOLIET). The commissioners divided the county into electoral, road, and SCHOOL DISTRICTS, appointed surveyors for the first county road, discussed the possibilities of canal construction, and fixed the price of tavern charges at twenty-five cents for a meal, twelve-and-a-half cents for lodging, and six-and-a-quarter cents for a drink.

Despite their legal separation from Cook County, residents of Will County maintained economic and social ties with their neighbors in Chicago. Even before 1834, when Joliet served as a stopping post on the first coach route running west from Chicago, travel paths linked the two regions. On July 4, 1836, less than a year after county formation, workers broke ground for the 96-mile-long ILLINOIS & MICHIGAN CANAL between the Illinois and CHICAGO RIVERS, initiating the final link in a continuous water route from the East to the Gulf of Mexico.

Even before the canal was opened in April 1848, laborers and developers flowed into Will County, especially the canal towns of Joliet and LOCKPORT, hoping to profit from commercial activity along the waterway. Some even predicted that the canal would turn Joliet into the nation's center for livestock and grain exchange. When commercial traffic along the canal ceased in 1915 owing to competition from railroads and the deeper Chicago SANITARY AND SHIP CANAL (opened in 1900), Joliet continued to serve as the county's hub of settlement, commerce, and industry.

In the mid-nineteenth century, mining augmented the county's economy. In 1864, while drilling for water, William Henneberry unintentionally hit a rich vein of coal. Soon thereafter speculators arrived, and by the early 1880s COAL MINING had reached its peak in Will County, with seven companies operating mines, employing 2,180 men and producing 700,000 tons of coal annually.

Although coal mining began to ebb in the 1890s, limestone QUARRYING boomed. By the 1880s, Joliet had adopted the nickname Stone City, shipping tons of limestone to Chicago for use in the construction of the Water Tower and residences and businesses throughout the city.

In the early twentieth century, the economic base of the region again began to shift. Motivated by diminishing space for industry around Chicago and by the opening of the Sanitary Canal, manufacturers turned to Will County for development sites. In 1911, a Texaco oil refinery opened north of Lockport, followed by other REFINERIES in LEMONT and south of Joliet in the 1920s. During WORLD WAR II, military production contributed to the further industrialization of areas within Will County. As the demand for labor increased, the number of residents soared. Between 1920 and 1930, the AFRICAN AMERICAN population in Will County more than doubled, and nearly doubled again by 1950 to reach 5,886.

Like many other industrial areas in the Rust Belt, Joliet suffered from changing economic conditions in the 1970s and 1980s. While the population of Joliet fell during these decades, areas like Lockport, ROMEOVILLE, and Joliet's suburbs expanded rapidly. As the county's population grew, the unincorporated area between Joliet and Chicago's southern contiguous suburbs continued to shrink. The TRANSPORTATION ties that had linked the town of Chicago with the communities of Will County—walking paths, wagon roads, canals, rail lines, and highways—now ran within a single, expanding metropolitan region.

Sarah S. Marcus

See also: Economic Geography; Suburbs and Cities as Dual Metropolis; Water

Further reading: Conzen, Michael P., and Kay J. Carr, eds. *The Illinois and Michigan Canal National Heritage Corridor: A Guide to Its History and Sources.* 1988. • *History of Will County, Illinois.* 1878. • Sterling, Robert E. *Pictorial History of Will County.* 2 vols. 1975.

Willis Wagons. "Willis Wagons" was the pejorative term for portable SCHOOL classrooms used by critics of Superintendent of Schools Benjamin C. Willis (1953–1966) when protesting school overcrowding and segregation in black neighborhoods from 1962 to 1966. In December 1961, the Board of Education approved Willis's plan to buy 150 to 200 of the 20 x 36-foot aluminum mobile school units and install them at existing schools and on vacant lots. Besides installing the portable units, officials accommodated swelling ghetto pupil enrollments with double-shift schedules, rented commercial space, and much new school construction. Black parents, neighborhood organizations, and civil rights groups also urged authorities to permit black children to attend white schools with empty seats. Willis and the school board, however, resisted, preferring traditional neighborhood-based schools and refusing to reconfigure boundaries. Blacks countered with sit-ins, boycotts, and marches. The WOODLAWN ORGANIZATION claimed that it coined the "Willis Wagons" label in its one-day boycott of Carnegie School, May 18, 1962. The boycott protested the arrival of six portable units to house students until a new school building opened in late 1963. Personalizing school segregation and overcrowding dramatized these issues and later drove Willis from office. But the portable units and segregation both predated and outlived Willis's administration.

Michael W. Homel

See also: Civil Rights Movements; Coordinating Council of Community Organizations; Great Migration; Neighborhood Succession; School Desegregation

Further reading: Fish, John Hall. *Black Power/White Control: The Struggle of the Woodlawn Organization in Chicago.* 1973. • Ralph, James R. *Northern Protest: Martin Luther King, Jr., Chicago, and the Civil Rights Movement.* 1993.

Willow Creek Community Church. In 1975 leaders of Son City, a successful youth program at PARK RIDGE's South Park Church, decided to create a new ministry for unchurched adults. A door-to-door survey of the local community taught them why people stayed away from church. Incorporating contemporary music, drama, and multimedia technology, the new congregation first met on October 12, 1975, in PALATINE's Willow Creek Theater. Within two years worship services grew from 125 to 2,000 people. In 1981 the evangelical church moved to its current location in SOUTH BARRINGTON and continued to increase in numbers and size on its sprawling campus. By 2000, it drew 15,000 for weekly services.

Led by Pastor Bill Hybels, Willow Creek Community Church became famous as the prototypical "megachurch," widely imitated—and criticized—for its entertaining worship style and use of modern marketing strategies. "Seeker services" deliberately target the curious and the unchurched, while members worship at believer-oriented New Community services. To connect people to the church, Willow Creek has hundreds of small groups, devoted to everything from Bible study to singles' fellowship to car repair. The affiliated Willow Creek Association publishes curriculum materials, runs leadership seminars, and encourages thousands of affiliated churches, extending its influence nationwide.

R. Jonathan Moore

See also: Moody Bible Institute; Protestants; Religion, Chicago's Influence on; Religious Institutions

Further reading: Hybels, Lynne, and Bill Hybels. *Rediscovering Church: The Story and Vision of Willow Creek Community Church.* 1995. • Pritchard, G. A. *Willow Creek Seeker Services: Evaluating a New Way of Doing Church.* 1996.

Willow Springs, IL, Cook and DuPage Counties, 17 miles SW of the Loop. The TOPOGRAPHY of the DES PLAINES RIVER Valley favors Willow Springs as a place of rustic beauty. Known for its ravines, much of what is now Willow Springs is known to geologists as Mt. Forest Island, a large upland moraine left by ice age glaciers thousands of years ago. Archaeological evidence indicates that Native Americans hunted and buried their dead here. Canal boats later stopped at the area's springs, hence the town's name.

In the late 1830s the ILLINOIS & MICHIGAN CANAL commissioners built Archer Avenue to connect Chicago with LOCKPORT. Canal construction began in 1836. One of the contractors was George W. Beebe, from Montreal, who also kept a BOARDINGHOUSE for canal diggers. After the canal was completed, Beebe opened a popular tavern on Archer Avenue.

The cutting of timber for use by the Canal Commission and later the RAILROADS served as the major industry in the mid-nineteenth century. The Joliet & Chicago railroad arrived after 1854, and Willow Springs became a favorite picnic place for Chicagoans, who flocked to "Lake Willow Springs" (actually a five-hundred-foot-wide section of the Des Plaines River) toting "multitudinous kegs of beer," according to one source.

In 1873 Chicagoan Henry Dietrich and others purchased three hundred acres and laid out the Mt. Forest SUBDIVISION near Willow Springs. In the fall of 1883 the Chicago, St. Louis & South-Western Railroad came through the town, the forerunner of today's METRA line.

In the 1870s and 1880s ice harvesting from the Des Plaines River was a major enterprise in Willow Springs. The construction of the SANITARY AND SHIP CANAL from 1892 to 1899 brought a new generation of canal workers to the Willow Springs area, including many ITALIANS. This led to the village's incorporation in 1892, with the towns of Mt. Forest and Willow Springs combining their names to form Spring Forest. In 1937 the name was changed to Willow Springs.

Willow Springs developed a reputation as a place with numerous SALOONS, and the onset of PROHIBITION in 1920 did little to curb the liquor trade. Speakeasies, moonshiners, and PROSTITUTION were all common. Cook County Sheriff's Police were the only law in town until Willow Springs established an independent police department in 1952.

The 1940 census showed only 948 people, with 246 homes and 35 businesses. A post–WORLD WAR II housing boom brought new residents and improved services. By 1970 the population stood at 3,318. Since then Willow Springs has experienced an expanding housing market, with average home values soaring to over $235,000 by the late 1990s.

Most villagers trace their descent to POLISH, GERMAN, Italian, or IRISH origins, with very few AFRICAN AMERICANS and Hispanics. The town is cognizant of its connection to the I&M Canal, hosting the annual I&M Canal Rendezvous and maintaining a bike trail along the canal. Interstates 294 and 55 run through Willow Springs, and Metra's Heritage Corridor line stops here, enhancing transportation options for residents. A significant percentage of the village is owned by the Cook County Forest Preserve, providing residents with an outstanding recreational resource.

Ronald S. Vasile

See also: Glaciation; Lumber; Metropolitan Growth; Transportation; Water

Further reading: Andreas, A. T. *History of Cook County, Illinois.* 1884, 816, 819. • Chamberlin, Everett. *Chicago and Its Suburbs.* 1874, 411–412. • *The History of Willow Springs: 1892–1992.* 1992.

Willowbrook, IL, DuPage County, 18 miles SW of the Loop. Into the twentieth century, farms dominated the Willowbrook area. The construction of Route 66 on Willowbrook's south side led to the development of RESTAURANTS and GAS STATIONS. In 1946 the "Nationally Famous Chicken Basket" opened, attracting drivers along the busy highway by installing a rooftop SKATING rink complete with professional ice skaters. Inside, big-name bands played music while customers peered out picture windows to watch helicopters take off from Hinsdale AIRPORT. Dell Rhea bought the restaurant in 1963, renaming it Dell Rhea's Chicken Basket.

Ridgemoor Homeowners Association, east of the Marion Hills SEMINARY, led the drive to incorporate. In 1960, the village of Willowbrook was created to prevent development of low-cost two-bedroom homes. The community had only 167 people living in 37 houses. The name of the village came from the willow trees along an area creek.

Suburban growth came in the 1970s, drawing industry and retail. Industrial parks include Willowbrook Executive Plaza, a 105-acre park built in 1975 on the site of Hinsdale Airport. Many of the firms located in these parks are high-tech electronics and plastics-related firms. In addition, motels, stores, and shopping centers have turned Route 83, the village's main artery, into a bustling thoroughfare. Four shopping centers, the largest a quarter of a million square feet, are located in Willowbrook.

In the 1980s, a swampy area was transformed into Willow Pond. Cleanup and tree plantings, a rock-laden shoreline, and lighting enabled the pond to be used for recreational activities such as skating. In 1990 the village was 60 percent multifamily occupied. Single-family residences included two-story, ranch, and split-level homes. The 1980 population of 4,953 grew to 8,598 in 1990 but increased by less than 400 in the 1990s. The 2000 population was 85 percent white, 10 percent Asian, 4 percent Hispanic, and 2 percent African American.

Marilyn Elizabeth Perry

See also: Built Environment of the Chicago Region; Retail Geography; Streets and Highways

Wilmette, IL, Cook County, 14 miles N of the Loop. The village of Wilmette is named for Antoine Ouilmette, a FRENCH-CANADIAN fur trader who settled in Chicago in 1790 on the north bank of the CHICAGO RIVER. Ouilmette and his part-POTAWATOMI wife, Archange Chevallier, moved to the LAKE MICHIGAN shore of present-day Wilmette around 1826. Ouilmette was instrumental in convincing local Indians to sign the 1829 TREATY of Prairie du Chien, which gave the federal government title to much of northern Illinois. In appreciation, the government deeded 1,280 acres, encompassing much of present-day WILMETTE and part of EVANSTON, to Archange and her children.

By 1848, the Ouilmette family had sold off their entire parcel of land to farmers and developers such as John G. Westerfield, who in 1857 built pickle and vinegar factories, marking the beginning of commercial development in the area. Other early industries included a cooperage, a tavern, a brick kiln, and an icehouse. In 1854, the Chicago, North Shore & Milwaukee RAILROAD extended its tracks to WAUKEGAN through Wilmette. Residents however, were unable to pool the funds needed to build a station along the line until 1869. Wilmette incorporated as a village in 1872, observed yearly on September 19 as Charter Day.

In 1880, Wilmette had 419 residents. From that point, the village experienced tremendous population growth, encouraged by increasing train service. By 1900, the population had reached 2,300. The influx strained public services, and Wilmette residents considered ANNEXATION by neighboring EVANSTON. The proposal, however, was defeated in 1894 by a referendum vote of 168 to 165. Annexation of land to Wilmette began in 1912 and continued throughout the first half of the century. The neighboring village of Gross Point was annexed in two parcels in 1924 and in 1926 as a result of its bankruptcy.

The most controversial annexation came in 1942, when Wilmette laid claim to "No Man's Land," an unincorporated strip located on the northern border of the village. A lack of ZONING restrictions had encouraged the development of entertainment establishments that were open on Sunday, but a 1932 fire had destroyed the strip as neighboring fire departments refused to assist the unincorporated area. The area did not regain commercial success until it opened in 1968 as the Plaza del Lago shopping center. Wilmette has opened several additional shopping centers, including Edens Plaza (1956), which encouraged westward residential settlement. The village is also home to the BAHA'I House of Worship (1953), the first such temple to be built in North America.

Wilmette's population peaked in 1970 at 32,134. The population of Wilmette consistently has been over 90 percent white, a percentage that declined in the late 1990s with an increase of Asians in the village. The economic status of the residents has remained among the highest in the Chicago area throughout the twentieth century. In 1980, the median income was $41,640, the fifth highest in the country, and by 2000 the figure had increased to $106,773.

Adam H. Stewart

See also: Government, Suburban; Local Option; Metropolitan Growth; Retail Geography; Suburbs and Cities as Dual Metropolis

Further reading: Ebner, Michael. *Creating Chicago's North Shore: A Suburban History.* 1988. • Holley, Horace. *Wilmette Story.* 1951.

Wilmington, IL, Will County, 49 miles SW of the Loop. Settlers of what was originally called Winchester ran gristmills on the Kankakee River. Local ABOLITIONISTS rebuked travelers looking for fugitive slaves and harbored runaways before the CIVIL WAR. In the early 1900s, COAL MINING predominated. During WORLD WAR II, workers from the nearby JOLIET Arsenal settled in Wilmington. In recent years, industry has declined, but new commuter residents have been attracted to Wilmington's water recreation opportunities. The population in 2000 was 5,134.

Erik Gellman

See also: Economic Geography; Quarrying, Stonecutting, and Brickmaking

"Windy City." Chicago's exposed location between the Great Plains and the GREAT LAKES—and the wind swirling amidst the city's early SKYSCRAPERS—lend credence to the literal application of this famous nickname dating from the late 1800s, but it is a favorite observation of tour guides and reference books that in fact Chicago's climate is not distinctively windy. (The same moniker is shared by Wellington, New Zealand, where it is more precisely meteorological.)

The power of the name lies in the metaphorical use "windy" for "talkative" or "boastful." Chicago politicians early became famous for long-windedness, and the Midwestern metropolis's central location as a host city for POLITICAL CONVENTIONS helped cement the association of Chicago with loquacious politicians, thus underlying the nickname with double meaning.

FROM THE WINDY CITY.

JUDGE FOOTE'S CIVIL RIGHTS(?) DECISION.

Political Notes—Social Items—Personal Mention—Numerous General Notes.

[THE GAZETTE is on sale in Chicago by Geo. J. Smith, No. 108 East Harrison Street; A. H. Dorsey, No. 97½ Van Buren Street; Hon. Albert Jones, No. 468 State Street; Grant & Co., 410 State Street; Lucas', No. 861 W. Kinsey Street, near Oakly; P. W. Brooks, No. 213 Second Street; Thomas Buck, No. 54 Fourth Avenue.]

CHICAGO, Ill., Sept. 17.—A political meeting was held at 164 Fourth avenue, last Sunday, to arrange for holding the county convention.—In a recent Civil Rights case, Judge Foote decided against the bill, and at once dismissed the case, stating that the law was wrong in every respect. This action is an insult to the colored people as well as to the Legislature that made the law. The decision will not produce the desired effect, when the source of it is considered. The weakness and inabilty of the Judge (?) were the motives of this decision.—Miss Hattie Warner was married Thurs-

Cleveland Gazette, September 19, 1885. Source: Ohio Historical Society.

Perhaps even more important, however, is early Chicagoans' boosterism, or self-promotion. During the mid-1800s nearly any city could (and did) proclaim itself the ascendant "Metropolis of the West." Boosters' arguments emphasized the superabundance of their locale's natural advantages and the inevitability of its preeminence, boasting that in fact they had no need to boast. Such was the "windiness" of Chicagoans, as they sought to secure investment, workers, and participation in projects of national scope such as the building of RAILROADS and the provision of CIVIL WAR matériel. Early uses of the term appear in Cleveland (1885) and Louisville (1886) newspapers, and the 1885 appearance of the label in a headline suggests the possibility that this was not its initial invocation. It may well have been Chicago's urban rivals who coined a nickname, in derision, which has come to be adopted with pride.

Jonathan Boyd

See also: Chicago

Winfield, IL, DuPage County, 27 miles W of the Loop. While along an early stagecoach line and the first RAILROAD out of Chicago, Winfield remained in the shadow of its neighboring towns, WEST CHICAGO, WHEATON, and NAPERVILLE. Until the 1920s, Winfield primarily was a center for GERMAN-speaking farmers. Suburban growth came with the TOLL ROADS after 1960.

Before the village of Winfield was officially established, the area was associated with Gary's Mill, a LUMBERING settlement established in the 1830s by Erastus, Jude, and Charles Gary, two miles northeast of Warren's Station. Although a James P. Doe of New Hampshire received a land grant in the area in 1845, he did not have it platted as the Town of Fredericksburg until 1853. The following year, however, it appeared on railroad maps as Winfield.

Stagecoach-related business and significant freight shipping for the region were largely responsible for Winfield's early growth. When a railroad was established in Naperville in 1864, the bulk of the freight business at Winfield was lost.

New Englanders predominated in Winfield's 1850 census. By 1860, half the residents were German, with some DUTCH and some FRENCH from the Alsace-Lorraine region. The Winfield Creamery was one of the largest businesses at this time. The first public school opened in 1856, but St. John's parochial school was preferred when it opened in 1882, and the public school remained a one-teacher school until 1939. Enrollment in the public school climbed after World War II.

An acre of land donated by Julius Warren in 1867 became the site for St. John the Baptist ROMAN CATHOLIC Church, school, and rectory. The church remained German-speaking until World War I and has continued to serve the community in an expanded facility. In 1925, the Winfield Community Church became the town's first PROTESTANT congregation.

In 1897 Jessie P. Forsythe's rest home was established. In 1909 it became the Chicago-Winfield TUBERCULOSIS Sanitorium, and since 1964 it has been the site of Central DuPage HOSPITAL, a nonprofit, acute care facility.

Cantigny Museum and Gardens is located in nearby unincorporated DuPage on the estate of Robert McCormick. The Kline Creek Farm, an 1890s farmstead living-history museum on 200 acres of FOREST PRESERVE, is adjacent to the village's first GOLF course community. Barely maintaining its rural flavor amid encroaching suburban sprawl, the village installed its first traffic light in 1990. In 2000 there were 8,178 residents.

Jane S. Teague

See also: Agriculture; DuPage County; Streets and Highways

Further reading: Spanke, Louise. *Winfield's Good Old Days: A History*. 1978. • Thompson, Richard ed., *DuPage Roots*. 1985.

Winfield, IN, Lake County, 39 miles SE of the Loop. Recently incorporated, Winfield had a population of 2,298 in 2000. However, thousands more people live in a nearby unincorporated area known as Lake of Four Seasons. RESTRICTIVE COVENANTS regulate property usage in this GATED COMMUNITY, where all amenities are private.

Ann Durkin Keating

See also: Governing the Metropolis

Further reading: McMichael, Verna Yeager. *Winfield Township, Lake County, Indiana*. 1998.

Winnetka, IL, Cook County, 16 miles N of the Loop. In 1836, Erastus and Zeruah Patterson established the Patterson Tavern along the Green Bay Trail, which connected Chicago to Fort Howard in Green Bay, Wisconsin. Eighteen years later Charles E. Peck and Walter S. Gurnee, president of the newly formed Chicago & Milwaukee RAILROAD, platted three hundred acres in New Trier Township along the western shores of Lake Michigan. The town was named Winnetka, a NATIVE AMERICAN word thought to mean "beautiful place." That year, the Chicago & Milwaukee began servicing Winnetka and other shoreline communities north of the city. In 1869, Winnetka was incorporated as a village, and Charles Peck donated land now known as the Village Green east of Winnetka's main business district.

The village began making municipal improvements in the 1870s. A 119-foot-tall brick WATER tower constructed near the lake served as a local landmark until 1972. In 1900, the Municipal Electric Utility Plant began operating. Profits from this village-owned utility funded the complete construction of Winnetka's village hall and also helped pay the salaries of local teachers during the GREAT DEPRESSION.

In 1890, social activist and Winnetka resident Henry Demarest Lloyd helped found the Winnetka Town Meeting, providing a forum for residents to hear such speakers as Jane Addams and Clarence Darrow. In 1915, the village formed the Winnetka Caucus to maintain citizen control over Winnetka's future. Winnetka continues to operate under this system.

The arrival in 1899 of the Chicago & Milwaukee Electric RAILROAD (later the Chicago, North Shore & Milwaukee) provided an additional link between suburb and city. Chicagoans looking to escape the crowded city were attracted to Winnetka's lakefront location and commuter services. Between 1880 and 1920 Winnetka's population grew ten-fold. Intent on maintaining its suburban repose, Winnetka elected to become dry in 1912. In 1917, the village council appointed a commission to formulate a comprehensive PLAN for village development. In 1921, the commission published the Winnetka Plan, which emphasized the goal of maintaining Winnetka's quiet character.

The plan also stressed the need for grade separation of the railroad tracks. By 1937, 31 people had been killed at railroad crossings in Winnetka. Concerned that elevating the tracks would divide the community, Winnetka opted to have them lowered instead. Between 1938 and 1943, workers under the Public Works Administration excavated the roadbed and lowered the North Western and North Shore lines' rights-of-way. Winnetka's track depression is a unique feature among North Shore suburbs.

Hailing from Winnetka, Secretary of the Interior Harold Ickes proposed draining the adjacent Skokie wetlands as a NEW DEAL project. Civilian Conservation Corps workers spent 10 years on the massive land-reclamation project that created the Skokie lagoons.

In 1955, the North Shore INTERURBAN line abandoned its passenger service to the communities along the lakeshore. Since the 1960s, Winnetka's population has remained below 13,000. At the close of the twentieth century, Winnetka was an affluent, predominantly white (97 percent) community whose members work primarily in professional or managerial occupations.

Elizabeth S. Fraterrigo

See also: Gas and Electricity; Government, Suburban; Lectures and Public Speaking; Suburbs and Cities as Dual Metropolis

Further reading:Dickinson, Lora Townsend. *The Story of Winnetka.* 1956. • Ebner, Michael H. *Creating Chicago's North Shore: A Suburban History.* 1988. • Harnsberger, Caroline Thomas. *Winnetka: The Biography of a Village.* 1977.

Winthrop Harbor, Lake County, 42 miles NW of the Loop. Winthrop Harbor has the distinction of being the northeasternmost point in Illinois. While J. H. Van Vlissingen made plans for development in 1883, Winthrop Harbor was not platted until 1899, when the Winthrop Harbor and Dock Company assumed ownership of more than two thousand acres. The village was incorporated in 1901, shortly before the 1902 incorporation of its southern neighbor, ZION.

Although Winthrop Harbor was intended for industrial development, the community remained primarily rural and residential throughout the twentieth century. There are few multiunit dwellings in Winthrop Harbor, the vast majority being single-family, detached homes. Industry is located outside Winthrop Harbor in Zion, WAUKEGAN, and NORTH CHICAGO.

In 1989, the Illinois Department of Natural Resources opened the North Point Marina, the largest on the Great Lakes. The marina includes a 240-acre FOREST PRESERVE. Though still not returning projected profits, by the late 1990s North Point Marina had boosted the economy of the small rural community, adding revenues for state and village governments.

The population of Winthrop Harbor has always been small compared to its neighboring Lake County towns. The village did experience an increase in population, however, during the 1990s. Between 1990 and 2000 the population of Winthrop Harbor grew from 6,240 to 6,670, as the area became increasingly popular as a VACATION SPOT and location for second homes. The residents of Winthrop Harbor have historically been white. According to the 2000 Illinois census, 0.6 percent of Winthrop Harbor residents were AFRICAN AMERICAN, 1.9 percent Asian, and 4.5 percent Hispanic.

Wallace Best

See also: Economic Geography; Sailing and Boating; Suburbs and Cities as Dual Metropolis

Further reading: Bateman, Newton, and Paul Selby, eds. *Historical Encyclopedia of Illinois and History of Lake County.* 1902. • Halsey, John J. *A History of Lake County Illinois.* 1912, 589.

WLS. Radio station WLS—for "world's largest store"—was started by Sears, Roebuck & Co. in 1924. Four years later, Sears sold it to the *Prairie Farmer* newspaper, which made its *Barn Dance* a national hit. As a clear-channel station, WLS could be heard throughout the Midwest and beyond. In 1960 ABC purchased WLS and changed its format to top 40. By 1990 ABC still owned WLS, but its format had switched to talk. The television station, WENR, came to ABC when it merged with the Paramount Theater chain; its first broadcast was in September 1948. Long headquartered on North State across from the Chicago Theater, channel 7 became most famous for its local "Eyewitness News."

Douglas Gomery

See also: Broadcasting; Disc Jockeys; Entertaining Chicagoans

Further reading: WLS station file. Library of American Broadcasting, University of Maryland, College Park, Maryland.

WLS Barn Dance. Although nearly forgotten today, this variety program begun in 1924 ranked as America's most popular country music radio show through the 1930s and 1940s. By 1931 increased power meant a BROADCAST could be heard throughout the United States and Canada. In 1932 it moved to the Eighth Street Theater; a year later it was renamed *The National Barn Dance,* when the NBC network nationally broadcast a segment. Stars included Gene Autry, George Gobel, Red Foley, Homer and Jethro, Lulu Belle, and Scotty. Lack of success on TV signaled the end in 1957, but limited editions survived until 1971 (finally on WGN radio).

Douglas Gomery

See also: WLS

Further reading: Baker, John C. *Farm Broadcasting: The First Sixty Years.* 1981. • Evans, James F. *Prairie Farmer and WLS: The Burridge D. Butler Years.* 1969.

WMAQ. This longtime NBC outlet went on the air in 1922, when it was owned by the *Chicago Daily News.* In 1929, WMAQ-AM moved to the just-opened Daily News building and, two years later, once NBC purchased it, to the new MERCHANDISE MART studios. From there NBC originated many notable programs, none more infamous or popular than *Amos 'n' Andy.* The clear-channel radio station survived the coming of TV, but in March 1988 it was sold to WESTINGHOUSE and became noted for its all-news format. WMAQ-TV began on Channel 5 as WNBQ in September 1948; the call letters were changed in August 1964.

Douglas Gomery

See also: Broadcasting; Entertaining Chicagoans; Newspapers

Further reading: "WMAQ-Station File." Library of American Broadcasting, University of Maryland, College Park, MD. • *The Story of WMAQ.* 1931. Lawrence J. Gutter Collection of Chicagoana, University of Illinois at Chicago.

Woman's Christian Temperance Union. The Woman's Christian Temperance Union (WCTU), the nation's largest women's organization during the late 1800s, attracted over 150,000 mostly PROTESTANT, middle-class members by 1900. The WCTU provided thousands of Christian women with a perceivably riskless transition into the secular world of women's associations.

Among the numerous Chicago WCTUs organized, the first, the Chicago Central Union, led by Frances Willard between 1874 and 1877, was the most prominent. Matilda Carse succeeded Willard, and under her guidance the union launched two day nurseries, a mission for wayward girls, Sunday and industrial schools, two medical dispensaries, an employment bureau, and a low-cost lodging house and restaurant.

The WCTU was a forerunner of social settlements in many areas of social reform. KINDERGARTENS, girls' sewing and cooking classes, and recreational and residential facilities were components of the Central Union's agenda prior to the founding of HULL HOUSE.

The Chicago Central Union reached its zenith of activity during the 1880s and 1890s. The WCTU national headquarters, located in Chicago until 1900, lent the prestige of national leaders to local affairs. Frances Willard, who remained a local member while president of the national WCTU until her death in 1898, undoubtedly attracted many women to the Chicago group. During the early decades of the twentieth century, as the Central Union declined, its projects were administered by the Cook County WCTU, established in 1901 and still active.

Nancy Daffner

See also: Prohibition and Temperance; Settlement Houses

Further reading: "Twelfth Annual Meeting of the Central Union of the W.C.T.U." Newspaper clipping in Frances Willard scrapbook no. 29. Frances E. Willard Library, Evanston, IL. • Bordin, Ruth. *Woman and Temperance: The Quest for Power and Liberty, 1873–1900.* 1981. • Minutes of the Woman's Christian Temperance Union of Chicago, Illinois, 1874, 1878–1881, 1883, 1886. Chicago Historical Society, Chicago, Ill.

Activists in the Woman's City Club's campaign against litter, 1940. Photographer: Chicago Park District. Source: Chicago Historical Society.

Woman's City Club. The Woman's City Club of Chicago was founded in 1910, before women could vote, to initiate and coordinate the participation of women in Chicago's civic affairs and to promote the welfare of the city. The club's original officers and directors were clubwomen, SETTLEMENT HOUSE workers, and UNIVERSITY OF CHICAGO professors, including Ellen Henrotin, Jane Addams, Ruth Hanna McCormick, Louise de Koven Bowen, Mary McDowell, and Sophonisba Breckinridge, with Mary H. Wilmarth as its first president. The members were primarily middle-class and working women from the city and surrounding suburbs, and the club grew from 1,200 members in its inaugural year to over 4,000 in 1920.

The club had its greatest impact on municipal affairs during its first decade. Dedicated to investigating municipal problems, the club demanded from city government enhanced health, environmental, and sanitary conditions, funding for the public schools, safe and affordable housing, and parks, beaches, and recreational facilities. The club helped lead woman SUFFRAGE drives, and after Illinois women received the local suffrage in 1913, organized voter registration drives and citizenship classes for women. The club also supported the activities of union women, sought to ameliorate troubled race relations in the city, and worked to secure more honest municipal government.

Although its influence in municipal affairs waned after woman suffrage, the club continued to investigate municipal affairs, often working with the LEAGUE OF WOMEN VOTERS and other women's organizations to obtain state and local legislation for women and children and to support women's equal citizenship.

Maureen A. Flanagan

See also: Clubs: Women's Feminist Movements; Good Government Movements; Juvenile Justice Reform; Political Culture; Chicago Women's Liberation Union

Further reading: Flanagan, Maureen. "Gender and Urban Political Reform: The City Club and the Woman's City Club of Chicago in the Progressive Era." *American Historical Review* (October 1990): 1032–1050.

Women's Clubs. *See* Clubs: Women's Clubs

Woman's Hospital Medical College. In 1870, after failing to gain acceptance for women in Chicago's male medical colleges, Mary H. Thompson and William H. Byford, a faculty member of the Chicago Medical College, established a women's medical school in connection with Thompson's Chicago Hospital for Women and Children. The Woman's Hospital Medical College of Chicago encountered many hardships during its early years. The college faced financial difficulties, and women doctors confronted opposition and resentment from much of the male medical profession.

Faculty members, who loaned money to the school to purchase a school building in 1877, eased the financial woes of the college. In the 1880s, the school's reputation and enrollment increased substantially. In 1892, the faculty sought and secured an alliance with NORTHWESTERN UNIVERSITY, believing that the relationship would enhance their school's respectability, ensure its longevity, and secure funding to improve teaching and laboratory facilities.

Northwestern University, however, refused to invest money in the women's medical school.

As resources diminished and other medical schools in Chicago and in the nation began accepting women, the school's ability to meet students' educational needs was threatened and enrollment declined. In 1902, the Northwestern University Woman's Medical School was closed.

Ironically, the demise of the Woman's Hospital Medical College resulted from its success: by educating women as physicians and proving that women could become physicians, it convinced other medical schools to remove obstacles to the MEDICAL EDUCATION of women.

Eve Fine

See also: Hospitals; Medical Education

Further reading: Beatty, William K. "Mary Harris Thompson—Pioneer Surgeon and Hospital Founder." *Proceedings of the Institute of Medicine of Chicago* 34 (1981): 83–86. • Morantz-Sanchez, Regina Markell. *Sympathy and Science: Women Physicians in American Medicine.* 1985. • *Woman's Medical School, Northwestern University: The Institution and Its Founders.* 1896.

Women's Suffrage. *See* Suffrage

Women's Trade Union League. The Chicago Women's Trade Union League (WTUL) was one of the most active branches of a national organization that aimed to organize women workers into trade unions, lobby for protective legislation and woman SUFFRAGE, and promote vocational education. Its membership included both working-class women and upper-class "allies" who supported the organization financially. Led by an unusual and at times uneasy mix of civic reformers including Jane Addams and Mary McDowell and trade unionists including Agnes Nestor and Mary Anderson, the WTUL held its meetings in HULL HOUSE from its inception in January 1904 until 1908, when it moved to the offices of the CHICAGO FEDERATION OF LABOR. In addition to supporting STRIKES of women workers, WTUL programs included musical and dramatic CLUBS, a national publication edited in Chicago by Alice Henry, educational programs such as English-language classes and instruction on parliamentary procedure, and a visiting physicians program.

Under the leadership of Margaret Dreier Robins, an upper-class woman who devoted her professional life to the organization, the Chicago WTUL deepened its alliance with the Chicago Federation of Labor, promoted the leadership of working-class women, and played a key role in the 1910–11 garment workers' strike. In addition to providing food relief to strikers and their families through a system of commissaries, the WTUL helped draft the agreement ending the strike for workers at CLOTHING manufacturer Hart, Shaffner & Marx, where women workers had sparked the citywide strike. The WTUL also played a role in efforts to organize DOMESTIC WORKERS, office and department store workers, TELEPHONE operators, and women PACKINGHOUSE workers.

Although the WTUL carried on until the 1950s, it became a less vital organizing force by the mid-1920s, especially after its national office moved from Chicago to Washington DC in 1929.

Tobias Higbie

Further reading: Dye, Nancy Schrom. *As Equals and as Sisters: Feminism, the Labor Movement, and the Women's Trade Union League of New York.* 1980. • Nestor, Agnes. *Woman Labor Leader: An Autobiography of Agnes Nestor.* 1954. • Payne, Elizabeth Anne. *Reform, Labor, and Feminism: Margaret Dreier Robins and the Women's Trade Union League.* 1988.

Women's World's Fair, 1925. The Women's World's Fair of 1925 was held April 18–25 in the American Exposition Palace. It attracted more than 160,000 visitors, and consisted of 280 booths representing 100 occupations in which women were engaged. The fair was the idea of Helen Bennett, the manager of the Chicago Collegiate Bureau of Occupations, and Ruth Hanna McCormick, a leading clubwoman and Republican politician. Women publicized and ran the fair; its managers and board of directors were all women.

The fair had the double purpose of displaying women's ideas, work, and products, and raising funds to help support women's REPUBLICAN PARTY organizations. The booths at the fair showed women's accomplishments in the arts, literature, science, and industry. These exhibits were also intended as a source for young women seeking information on careers. Among the exhibitors at the fair were major corporations, such as Illinois Bell TELEPHONE Company and the major national and regional NEWSPAPERS. Local manufacturers, banks, stores, and shops, area hospitals, and women inventors, artists, and lawyers set up booths demonstrating women's contributions in these fields and possibilities for employment. Women's groups were represented by such organizations as the WOMEN'S TRADE UNION LEAGUE, Business and Professional Women's Club, the Visiting Nurse Association, the YWCA, HULL HOUSE, the Illinois Club for Catholic Women, and the Auxiliary House of the Good Shepherd. The 1925 fair raised $50,000 and was so successful that it was held for three more years.

Maureen A. Flanagan

See also: Century of Progress Exposition; Clubs; Feminist Movements; Suffrage; World's Columbian Exposition

Further reading: Woman's World's Fair. *Scrapbook* and *Souvenir.* Chicago Historical Society.

Wonder Lake, IL, McHenry County, 56 miles NW of the Loop. Situated on the west side of an artificial lake, residents of the Sunrise Ridge SUBDIVISION incorporated as Wonder Lake in 1974 to obtain local control of BUILDING CODES and ZONING, and police services. The village remains a slowly expanding bedroom community with a population of 1,345 in 2000.

Craig L. Pfannkuche

See also: Governing the Metropolis; McHenry County

Further reading: *McHenry County in the Twentieth Century, 1968–1994.* McHenry County Historical Society. 1994. • Nye, Lowell A., ed. *McHenry County, Illinois, 1832–1968.* 1968.

Wood Dale, IL, DuPage County, 19 miles W of the Loop. Before 1834 the Winnebago made a yearly hunting trip to this area from Wisconsin, burning the prairie to facilitate the trapping of pheasants, rabbits, and deer. In 1834 Hezekiah Dunklee, with Mason Smith, cleared a heavily forested area for planting which became known as Dunklee's Grove. Soon after, GERMAN immigrants purchased these lands for their own farms.

When the Chicago & Pacific RAILROAD came through the area in 1873, farmer Frederick E. Lester donated land for a train depot. Clustered around the depot, the agricultural settlement was known as Lester's Station, and a SUBDIVISION platted near the train station was named Wooddale. Later subdivisions advertised land as ideal for chicken farms. Following incorporation as a village in 1928, Wooddale changed the spelling of its name to Wood Dale to distinguish it from another Illinois town of the same name.

Travel into the area was improved in 1916 with the paving of Wood Dale Road from Lake Street to Irving Park Road, but it was air travel that later spurred nonagricultural development in the area. An AIRPORT on Thorndale Avenue between Central Avenue and Route 83 was used as a navy emergency training field during WORLD WAR II. In 1950 part of the airport was leased to the MOODY BIBLE INSTITUTE to train missionaries to become pilots and mechanics. The institute purchased the entire airport three years later and changed its name to Moody Airport. Eventually annexed by Wood Dale, the airfield became Klefstad Industrial Park.

Proximity to O'HARE AIRPORT, as well as to TOLL ROADS and EXPRESSWAYS, made Wood Dale an ideal site for industrial development in the late twentieth century. Large corporations such as Motorola, Mitsubishi, and NEC built facilities in Wood Dale. A 225-acre industrial site called Chancellory Business Park housed more than 50 companies in 1990 and Wood Dale's industrial base spanned 700 acres, an increase from just 35 acres only 10 years earlier. Industrial revenues helped to create a water park complex and a new city hall.

Marilyn Elizabeth Perry

See also: Agriculture; DuPage County; Economic Geography

Further reading: Mittel, Mary Lou. "Wood Dale." In *DuPage Roots,* ed. Richard A. Thompson, 1985.

Woodlawn, Community Area 42, 7 miles SE of the Loop. Surrounded by Oakwoods CEMETERY (1853), JACKSON PARK (1869), the Washington Park Race Track (1884), and the Midway Plaisance, the residential neighborhood of Woodlawn prospered when it could attract commercial enterprises within its limits.

Woodlawn Park's first residents were DUTCH farmers who arrived in the 1850s. The population hovered between 500 and 1,000 until 1890. Woodlawn's farmers sent their produce to merchants in nearby Chicago on the ILLINOIS CENTRAL RAILROAD, which opened a station on Junction Avenue (63rd Street) in 1862. By 1889, when Chicago ANNEXED Woodlawn along with the rest of HYDE PARK TOWNSHIP, residents had created several active civic organizations, including a Citizen's Improvement Club and the Woodlawn Businessmen's Association.

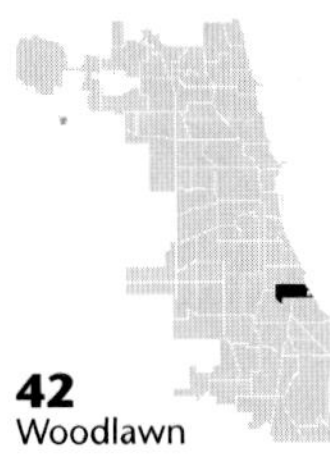

The decision that Jackson Park would host the WORLD'S COLUMBIAN EXPOSITION of 1893 brought 20,000 new residents and entrepreneurs to Woodlawn. In the subsequent building boom, developers landscaped Jackson Park, created the Midway, expanded the Elevated east along 63rd Street, and constructed large apartments and tourist hotels.

When the fair's closing dispersed the tourists, economic depression threatened Woodlawn's future. Local boosters promoted two commercial centers: the WASHINGTON PARK SUBDIVISION, with its AMUSEMENT PARKS, racetrack, and beer gardens; and 63rd Street, where dozens of specialty shops attracted "L"-riding Chicagoans throughout the 1920s. The rest of Woodlawn was residential. UNIVERSITY OF CHICAGO faculty found the neighborhood congenial. When betting was outlawed in 1905, apartment houses replaced the racetrack in Washington Park. West Woodlawn, a trapezoidal subdivision in the southwest part of the neighborhood, attracted middle-class AFRICAN AMERICANS with the means to buy homes outside the nearby BLACK BELT.

The combination of racial succession and economic decline distressed local businessmen and officials of the University of Chicago, who organized to preempt the movement of poorer blacks east through the Washington Park Subdivision. In 1928, local landlords agreed to a joint RESTRICTIVE COVENANT to keep nonwhites out of the subdivision. But the GREAT DEPRESSION made the higher rents blacks paid for illegally subdivided apartments a temptation to landlords. A lawsuit decided in the U.S. Supreme Court in 1940 found the covenant invalid, ratifying a DEMOGRAPHIC transformation already underway. In addition, 63rd Street's businesses began to fail, and taverns replaced furriers. In 1946 the Chicago Plan Commission designated Woodlawn eligible as a conservation area, but no plan was implemented. By 1960 Woodlawn had deteriorating, crowded housing and few commercial attractions to support a population that was 89 percent African American.

In contrast to West Woodlawn's middle-class homeowners, Woodlawn's new residents were recent southern migrants and refugees from redevelopment elsewhere in Chicago. They brought with them anger at being displaced and channeled their energy in two directions. Many young men joined two new street GANGS, the Blackstone Rangers and the East Side Disciples. In 1959, other residents, in a coalition of churches, block clubs, and business owners, invited Saul Alinsky's Industrial Areas Foundation into Woodlawn to organize the community against external control. Led by Rev. Arthur Brazier and then Leon Finney, the Temporary Woodlawn Organization (later renamed The WOODLAWN ORGANIZATION, or TWO) initiated a series of well-publicized protests against overcrowding in public SCHOOLS, slum landlords, exploitative local merchants, and a University of Chicago plan to expand south into land occupied by recent arrivals. In the late 1960s, TWO gained national notoriety for participating in the MODEL CITIES program and using a War on Poverty grant to train gang members for jobs.

Despite TWO's organizational capacity and persistent proposals for economic renewal programs, Woodlawn's economy did not recover. Most white business owners, fearing repeats of the riots that devastated the West Side, left the neighborhood after the assassination of Martin Luther King, Jr. A rash of arsons destroyed a reported 362 abandoned buildings between 1968 and 1971. UNEMPLOYMENT, poverty, and crime climbed. Those who could afford to, moved out: Woodlawn's population declined from a high of 81,279 in 1960 to 27,086 in 2000. But the neighborhood's tradition of sophisticated civic action continued. In the early 1990s, community leaders began to bring private development, commercial enterprises, and a bank back to Woodlawn.

Amanda Seligman

See also: Community Organizing; Gambling; Gentrification; Great Society; Horse Racing; South Side; Transportation; Willis Wagons

Further reading: Fish, John Hall. *Black Power/White Control: The Struggle of the Woodlawn Organization in Chicago.* 1973. • Schietinger, Egbert Frederick. "Racial Succession and Changing Property Values in Residential Chicago." Ph.D. diss., University of Chicago. 1953. • Spray, John C. *The Book of Woodlawn.* 1920.

Woodlawn Organization, The. The WOODLAWN Organization, a premier example of the organizing style of Saul Alinsky, gained national prominence in the 1960s as a militant protest organization. In struggles with its SOUTH SIDE neighbor, the UNIVERSITY OF CHICAGO, and with the city administration, TWO developed tactics that empowered Woodlawn residents and advanced TWO's goal of "black self-determination." As TWO developed, it engaged in less controversial activities. Unable to halt neighborhood deterioration in the seventies, TWO continued to provide service programs and survived to become a major player in the rebuilding of a new Woodlawn neighborhood at the end of the century.

John Hall Fish

See also: African Americans; Community Organizing; Contested Spaces

Further reading: Brazier, Arthur. *Black Self-Determination: The Story of the Woodlawn Organization.* 1969. • Fish, John Hall. *Black Power/White Control: The Struggle of the Woodlawn Organization in Chicago.* 1973. • McCallister, Brent Hall. "From Protest to Program: The Conservative Evolution of the Woodlawn Organization." B.A. thesis, Princeton University. 1998.

Woodridge, IL, DuPage and Will Counties, 23 miles SW of the Loop. The village of Woodridge is located in south-central DUPAGE COUNTY. The conception and growth of Woodridge reflects the massive suburban development that took place outside Chicago after World War II. In less than 40 years, Woodridge progressed from sprawling farm fields to a densely populated, largely residential community.

Native Americans maintained a strong presence in the Woodridge area until 1833, when the conclusion of the BLACK HAWK WAR forced all Indian communities out of Illinois. The POTAWATOMI represented the largest of these tribes; OJIBWA, OTTAWA, and SAC Indians also inhabited the area. The groups regularly held intertribal gatherings on a site near 71st Street and Woodridge Drive, north of the Indian Boundary Line.

Pomeroy Goodrich, a Vermont-born farmer, settled in the Woodridge area before the Indians moved west, building the first log cabin and coexisting with the neighboring tribes. In 1841, William Greene, originally from New York, established one of the first farms, at today's Hobson and Greene Roads. Many GERMAN-speaking farmers also arrived from the Alsace-Lorraine region of France. The Woodridge area remained a farming region throughout the next century, largely untouched by the advent of the RAILROAD, which influenced the growth of many DuPage communities.

This relative seclusion disappeared in the 1950s as the booming postwar economy promoted construction of new homes, while improvements in highway design and construction decreased travel times to and from Chicago and opened up new areas for development. Surety Builders planted the seeds of Woodridge in 1958 by developing a plot of land southeast of 75th Street and Route 53. This development, situated on a ridge overlooking wooded areas surrounding the DUPAGE RIVER, inspired the name "Woodridge." Veterans receiving loans insured through the GI Bill found Woodridge attractive, purchasing a majority of the homes. When residents approved incorporation overwhelmingly in August 1959, 459 people called the fledgling community home.

Developers realized Woodridge's potential and snatched up open farmland to construct more homes. The Winston Hills SUBDIVISION, developed by Winston-Muss Builders, opened to the north of Woodridge in 1964, expanding the village's population to 5,300, while the Woodridge Center development, annexed in 1972, doubled Woodridge's land area. This growth, however, inadvertently contributed to sectionalism in the village. The opening of Woodridge Drive in 1974 helped alleviate this problem, joining the subdivisions via a convenient north-south thoroughfare.

The growth of services reflected Woodridge's expansion. Woodridge School District 68 constructed six schools between 1961 and 1976, while Community High School District 99 opened DOWNERS GROVE South High School to accommodate Woodridge students. The village's first shopping center opened in 1965, while voters approved the establishment of a library in 1967 and the Woodridge Park District in 1969 to preserve quickly disappearing land. Wilton Industries, then a division of Pillsbury, located in the village in 1977 and represented the birth of an industrial base in Woodridge.

Woodridge continued its growth and development through the 1980s and 1990s reaching a population of 30,934 in 2000. Seventy-fifth Street became the commercial center of the village, while the opening of the North-South Tollway (Interstate 355) in 1989 created greater residential and industrial opportunities.

Aaron Harwig

See also: Agriculture; Economic Geography; Expressways

Further reading: Kagann, Joel, and Laurie Kagann. "Woodridge." In *DuPage Roots,* ed. Richard Thompson, 1985. • Woodridge Local History File. Woodridge Public Library, Woodridge, IL.

Woodstock, IL, McHenry County, 51 miles NW of the Loop. Woodstock was originally

called Centerville to attract the seat of MCHENRY COUNTY government in 1842. The Centerville site was chosen instead of CRYSTAL LAKE or MCHENRY when Alvin Judd donated a two-acre public square for county offices. The square became the hub of a village plat recorded in 1844 by George Dean. In 1845, Woodstock adopted its current name after the Vermont birthplace of early settler Joel Johnson. Woodstock incorporated as a village in 1852 with Alvin Judd as president. The Greek revival–style courthouse that stands next to the square was built in 1857; it is now privately owned.

In 1855 the Chicago & North Western RAILROAD passed through Woodstock. allowing farmers to send their dairy production quickly to Chicago. The Borden Company opened a dairy processing plant, one of the world's largest. The building is later became the home of the Claussen Pickle Company.

Because of increasing population following the CIVIL WAR, residents voted to give Woodstock city status in 1873, with John S. Wheat becoming mayor.

In January 1895, a federal court in Chicago sentenced Eugene V. Debs, president of the American Railway Union, to jail in Woodstock for his activity in the 1894 PULLMAN STRIKE. The square was filled with over 10,000 onlookers when he was released in November of the same year.

Woodstock's economic strength grew in 1896 when city officials donated empty factory buildings to Thomas Oliver for the manufacture of the noted Oliver Typewriter. In 1910, the Emerson Typewriter Company moved to Woodstock and began producing Woodstock typewriters. By 1922, about half the world's typewriters were made in Woodstock.

Besides the jail, built in 1887, a combined city hall, library, firehouse, and theater was built on the square in 1890. Jane Addams and Leo Tolstoy spoke in the building, known as the Woodstock OPERA House, on different occasions. The theater was also used by students from the private Todd School for Boys in Woodstock, including the notable Orson Welles, who was a student between 1926 and 1931. Wells hinted at his experiences at the school and opera house in his 1946 movie *The Stranger.*

As the city vacated the opera house, the building became home to the Woodstock Players, a group that provided young graduates of Chicago's GOODMAN THEATRE School with valuable professional experience in the late 1940s and early 1950s. Shelly Berman, Tom Bosley, Paul Newman, Geraldine Page, and Lois Nettleton performed regularly at the opera house, which is still in use after a major restoration in 1977.

Industrial activity generally declined in Woodstock after WORLD WAR II. Yet, with reliable rail COMMUTER transportation, the area became a destination for new residents fleeing Chicago's congestion. Residential construction boomed after the 1960s, bringing with it both economic prosperity and a lamented loss of a rural atmosphere. The revitalization of Woodstock's square, prominent in the 1993 movie *Groundhog Day,* displayed this growing prosperity. Population grew from 14,353 in 1990 to 20,151 a decade later.

Craig L. Pfannkuche

See also: Agriculture; Economic Geography

Further reading: *History of McHenry County, Illinois.* 1885. • *McHenry County in the Twentieth Century: 1968–1994.* McHenry County Historical Society. 1994. • Nye, Lowell A., ed. *McHenry County, Illinois, 1832–1968.* 1968.

Work. In the late nineteenth century, booming Chicago struck visitors as the "purest kind of commercial city," a place devoted to work and moneymaking. More than its notoriety for CRIME, corruption, and political MACHINES, work has defined Chicago in popular and literary imagery, shaped the city's character, and served as the fulcrum of its history. As the city grew, work in Chicago underwent dramatic transformations, both in the type of industries that dominated and in the organization of work itself. Especially in the late nineteenth century, Chicago was both shaped by and helped to foment a nationwide revolution in work that first undermined and then remade the democratic promise of America. People flocked to Chicago to find work and fought there over what work should be. The changes wrought by large-scale corporate manufacturing and trade provoked battles over the character and control of work that spilled over into broader political fights over democracy, citizenship, and the rights of workers.

At first the work of Chicago was trade and—nearly equally important—speculation in REAL ESTATE and in the city's future as the great metropolis of the frontier. Chicago's commercial and, eventually, industrial power depended on its linkages to the hinterland and other cities, first by lakes, rivers, and canals, then roads and RAILROADS, which consolidated Chicago's central position until the ascendance of air power and interstate highways after WORLD WAR II. Although trade and TRANSPORTATION remained key, in the mid-nineteenth century small factories first began processing the products of the prairie—packing pork, sawing LUMBER, or milling flour—and then started making grain harvesters, FURNITURE, and CLOTHING for farmers and frontier towns. From 1870 to 1930, Chicago grew rapidly from bustling trading center to quintessential industrial complex, Carl Sandburg's "Hog Butcher for the World," "City of the Big Shoulders."

As the nation's transportation hub, Chicago also became the Midwest's primary labor market for rural and small-town job seekers and immigrant workers—at first from Germany, Ireland, and Scandinavia, then from Southern and Eastern Europe. Beginning in World War I, they were joined by large numbers of AFRICAN AMERICANS from the South and, after 1965, by Latinos and Asians.

From its early days, Chicago was a place where everything happened fast. The town grew with amazing speed, generating jobs in CONSTRUCTION and the manufacture of construction materials, but there was a high priority on doing things quickly and grandly in every other endeavor as well. This emphasis on speed and scale also encouraged businessmen to find faster, simpler ways to get things done, resulting in the standardization of products from grades of grain to sizes of lumber. Chicago's success lay partly in the ability of its businesses to make nature abstract in ways that transformed products of farms and forest more readily into commodities for the market. Chicago's grain merchants turned discrete bags of grain from specific fields into a standard type passing through the city's new grain elevators, financed in part by contracts for future delivery that formed the basis for a new financial services BUSINESS.

Typical of most early-nineteenth-century American industry, Chicago's earliest manufacturing took place in artisan workshops and manufactories where skilled craftsmen, aided by laborers or apprentices, dominated production. Manufacturers in Chicago, with rail access to abundant southern Illinois COAL, turned to steam power for larger factories after the CIVIL WAR. As they did, they initiated changes in the nature of factory work and the relationship between those who owned the factories and those who worked there.

Chicago's competitive environment fostered a search for production methods that were faster and less expensive. Anxious to cut costs, businesses sought ways to trim the cost of labor. One important step was elaborating the division of labor. Dividing a job, such as building a house or butchering a pig, that had previously been executed by a master craftsman, made it possible for employers to hire unskilled workers at lower wages. Equally important, it shifted control to the employer, who adopted a variety of strategies to respond to labor market supply, technological opportunities, and worker resistance.

In Chicago, major industries such as construction, MEATPACKING, garment making, and machinery manufacture followed distinctive courses. Although large contractors rather than master carpenters dominated Chicago building construction as early as the 1840s, carpenters were still skilled tradesmen who supplied their own extensive tool chests. In 1833 BALLOON FRAME construction opened up the potential for increased reliance on factory mass production of building parts like sashes and doors. Even at the work site, contractors turned to piecework, fragmenting the work into specialties that required little training and offering lower pay tied to output. In meatpacking, the "disassembly line" arrived in Chicago soon after its introduction in Cincinnati. The industry relied on the line to fragment labor-intensive production and to organize meatpacking on a much larger scale than had previously been possible. The scale of operations, combined with the pressures of cost cutting and environmental complaints, fostered the growth of ancillary industries that used what otherwise would have been waste—"everything but the squeal." In the men's clothing industry, boosted by Civil War uniform contracts, small contractors would bid for work from "jobbers" who cut the cloth and then turned it over to workers at home or in small shops for different stages of sewing; competition among these workers based on price made for classic sweatshop conditions. There could be up to 150 separate operations divided among many workers in sewing a man's coat. By the late nineteenth century, major men's clothing retailers consolidated many sweatshops into larger factories to gain more control over quality, although contractor sweatshops persisted. At the McCormick reaper factory, company president Cyrus McCormick, Jr., in 1886 installed new pneumatic molding machinery to displace the skilled iron molders and their union, thereby securing management control. The machines turned out poor-quality castings, however, and nearly tripled labor costs in the short term.

Beef-dressing floor at Armour & Co., 1952. Photographer: Studios of Williams & Meyer. Source: Chicago Historical Society.

As the new factory system challenged the craftsman's control, the foreman—and, to a lesser extent, labor brokers and employment agents—assumed new importance. The foreman—with his arbitrary and discriminatory power over hiring and firing, especially of pro-union workers or blacklisted "troublemakers"—was the key figure in the "drive system" that pushed workers to work faster, continuously, and more dangerously. His power provoked worker rebellions small and large.

Before the new factory system, hours of work were usually long, but work was sporadic and often paced by workers themselves. Until the 1930s, it was not unusual for Chicago factory or other manual workers to put in 10 hours or more a day, 6 days a week, with 12-hour days common in many industries, including steel. Yet the opposite condition was equally problematic: work continued to be irregular and unreliable. Many industries in the nineteenth and early twentieth centuries were seasonal, with meatpacking jobs more available in the winter and construction jobs in the spring through fall. Even within the seasons, work was erratic. For example, a few

Construction workers, Chicago Daily News building, at Madison, Washington, Canal, and the Chicago River, 1928. Photographer: Unknown. Source: Chicago Historical Society.

PACKINGHOUSE workers were given steady jobs and, in return, were expected to show fervent loyalty to management. Most workers, however, did not know how much work they would have. They would show up outside the gates of the stockyards and wait to be called, then perhaps end up working very long hours early in the week but few or no hours at the end. Uncertain business cycles, panics, and depressions precipitated widespread cuts in wages for many and threw others out of work, forcing them to rely on limited private charity. During boom periods, workers in factories experienced extremely high turnover, as many expressed their frustrations and hopes by quitting. Immigrant workers complained that work in Chicago was harder than back home, and historians debate how much better off financially, if at all, immigrants were here, especially with employers' persistent efforts to drive down wages. Even when productivity soared, workers struggled to gain their share. At McCormick Reaper and its successor, International Harvester, for example, wages and benefits grew on average 0.1 percent a year during the nonunion period but 3.85 percent a year when workers were organized into unions.

Historians often describe the change in work in late-nineteenth-century Chicago as an homogenization of labor toward a low common denominator comparable to the homogenization of nature and standardization of products by Chicago's industries. As mechanization increased in factories, semiskilled machine operator positions grew in numbers, threatening the skilled workers, sometimes providing better jobs for unskilled workers, and complicating relationships between workers. But the intensified commodification of labor did not eliminate all distinctions. Employers maintained elaborately differentiated wage scales and increasingly designated certain jobs or departments within a factory as primarily the province of particular ethnic groups or genders. At a time when roughly two-thirds of Chicago factory workers were immigrants, employers pursued a variety of strategies to mix and separate different ethnic groups to the employers' advantage. While some divisions reflected skills and labor market supply and demand, they were primarily part of a management strategy to control workers, discourage their organization into unions, exploit entrenched social discrimination, and create individualistic motivations to work harder. Just as Chicago gained fame as a center of unionism and worker radicalism in the middle and late nineteenth century, the city's business leaders were equally notorious for their adamant opposition to UNIONIZATION or other worker organization.

Workers did not submit meekly to the changes imposed on their work. They protested wage cuts and demanded the EIGHT-HOUR day; they also challenged, from different perspectives, the legitimacy of the new industrial capitalist order. With the agitation about chattel slavery in the South and the Civil War vividly in their minds, nineteenth-century workers denounced the "wage slavery" to which they were subjected. Native-born American workers and union leaders commonly adopted a "labor republican" outlook, arguing that employers were robbing workers of the fruits of their labors while the emerging wage labor system denied their manhood and their rights as citizens. They called for a cooperative commonwealth of producers that would include farmers and some small businessmen. Immigrants, especially skilled GERMAN workers, brought with them socialist ideas about state ownership as a solution to the growing power of corporate industrialists. The influential Chicago ANARCHISTS, who supported insurrectionary action over POLITICS, did not share the labor republican ideology but envisioned a future society that more resembled the cooperative commonwealth advocated by rural populists.

Unions fought for short-term gains, especially to restore wage cuts or to reduce hours of work. They also fought to maintain control of the shop floor, often through informal restrictions on output and the labor market, through closed union shops or union label campaigns. The movement for an eight-hour day, in which Chicago workers played a leading role, was not just an effort to reduce hours of hard-driven toil. Leaders saw it as a critical step to restore lost citizenship and to transform the wage labor system. Chicago unions were politically active, strongly influencing local political parties and usually securing neighborhood POLICE neutrality in conflicts from the 1860s through the early 1880s. After the post-HAYMARKET collapse of the Great Upheaval of 1886, when the police and government more clearly acted against workers and for employer interests, unions tried forming labor parties but failed to displace the Democrats.

During the 1890s, unions increasingly turned away from attacks on the wage system to advocate a living wage that would guarantee workers an "American" standard of living, improved conditions at work, and regulation of the labor market. They found allies among some upper-class reformers, such as members of the Chicago CIVIC FEDERATION, who joined with unions in support of legislation to protect women workers and exclude children from industry. As unions and reformers found common ground on regulation, employers enacted their own strategy to regulate markets by combining smaller firms into large corporations and oligopolies—from U.S. Steel and International Harvester to the group of dominant meatpackers. This strategy protected business from ruthless competition, but it further reduced workers' power. Powerful literary works like Upton Sinclair's *The* JUNGLE demonstrated that loss of power to readers around the world by identifying the "beef trust" as the chief oppressor of Jurgis Rudkus and his fellow workers.

In the early decades of the twentieth century, while many skilled trade unions moved toward a practical-minded "business unionism," efforts to build broad-based industrial unions in industries such as meatpacking, steel, RAILROADS, and farm implement manufacture were dramatic but short-lived. Labor republicanism died out, but socialist ideas had wide appeal among workers, and into the 1920s the leaders of the Chicago labor movement advocated a labor party and industrial democracy as a response to corporate power. During the 1930s, Chicago workers finally succeeded in forming broad-based industrial unions in steel, meatpacking, farm implements, and other sectors. They also became linked to both the NEW DEAL ideas of economic regulation and government provision of social welfare and the local DEMOCRATIC machine, setting a pattern of reform and accommodation with a system their predecessors had reviled that persisted with modest changes throughout the century.

By 1880, Chicago was, after New York, the second most important manufacturing center in America. Factories in Chicago were, on average, larger than elsewhere. By 1900, three of the nation's 14 giant factories employing over 6,000 workers were in Chicago. In most cases, the big factories also employed the most advanced mechanization of work.

But Chicago was more than a center of manufacturing and trade in the natural products of the Midwest. From efforts to sell goods that both reflected and spread a new era of industrial capitalism into farms and small towns, Chicago became the center of new techniques in mass marketing, ADVERTISING, and CONSUMER CREDIT, epitomized by the giant catalog merchandisers, Montgomery Ward and Sears, Roebuck. Their MAIL-ORDER catalogs, warehouses, and centralized sales staffs displaced not only many traveling salesmen but also small-town retail shops. The scale of these industrial and commercial enterprises, along with the broad coordinated networks formed by the railroads, contributed to further changes in management and the growth of a white-collar bureaucracy to administer large, complex enterprises.

Initially, men dominated the office workforce, but after the 1880s, the invention of the typewriter and the proliferation of business colleges opened certain jobs to women. At the same time, managerial strategies of dividing tasks and reducing required skills were extended from factories to offices. In nearly every case, women were paid substantially less than men who had previously done the same work. Gradually, lower-level office work was redefined as women's work, while men continued to dominate the upper ranks. Office jobs greatly expanded women's place in the labor market, which had previously been limited to extensions of what were seen as women's natural domestic and maternal roles. In 1870, two-thirds of female workers in Chicago were domestic servants. Over the next 30 years the number of women working in clothing manufacture rose dramatically. The growth of Chicago women in CLERICAL and sales work—especially in large DEPARTMENT STORES like Marshall Field's—was faster than in the nation as a whole. Even as women entered factories, their work was distinct from and less well paid than that of male workers. In 1900, DOMESTIC WORK was still the principal female occupation reported in the census, and many women still toiled at home tending to their families, taking in paid but unrecorded work, and managing the boarders common to working-class households.

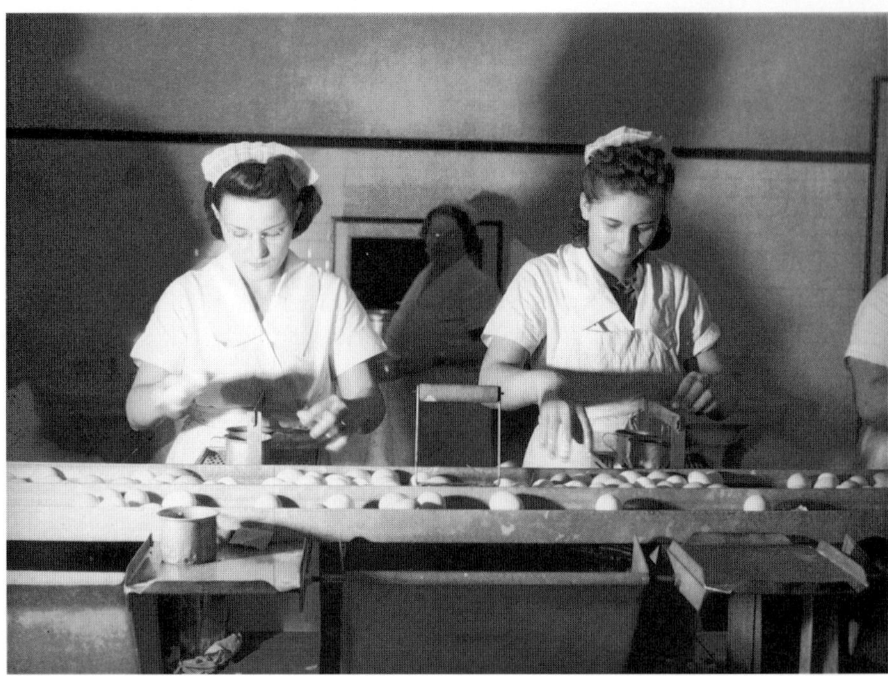

Women working in an egg-breaking plant, Chicago, July 1941. Egg breaking to provide processed egg products (as compared to shell eggs) was well established before World War II. The demand for dried eggs for lend-lease and military needs during the war meant an increased need for egg breakers. Photographer: John Vachon. Source: Library of Congress.

The less than 2 percent of Chicago's 1890 population who were African American also worked primarily in domestic and personal service jobs. One of the most prestigious of such jobs was working as a railcar porter for the Chicago-based Pullman Company. Although African Americans were regularly denied regular jobs in factories, they were frequently hired to break strikes, as employers manipulated racial hostilities to stymie worker demands. When strikes ended, blacks often lost their jobs, and smoldering RACISM worsened.

Despite these conflicts—and many unions' prohibitions against African American members—blacks and whites sometimes did cooperate to improve working conditions. For example, black men made up roughly half of the RESTAURANT and HOTEL waiters in late-nineteenth-century Chicago. Like their white counterparts, black waiters were upset by job insecurity, pay inequities, and factory-like discipline. Excluded from white unions, however, blacks either identified with employers or formed their own unions. In 1890, an interracial Culinary Alliance struck with some success, only to watch employers fan racial tensions and bring in women strikebreakers—although until then women were not common in the trade. During World War I, when European immigration declined precipitously and employers turned to the rural South for workers, African Americans made important breakthroughs into industry. Between 1915 and 1920, blacks tripled their ranks in Chicago factories, especially meatpacking, when factory work surpassed service as the primary employment of black men. The formation of the BROTHERHOOD OF SLEEPING CAR PORTERS in 1925 was pivotal for the entire black community, but the organization of the multiracial industrial unions during the 1930s had an even broader impact on black workers' lives.

Although many Chicagoans continued to work in small stores and workshops or in the informal economy, by 1920 more than 70 percent of manufacturing wage earners worked for corporations employing 100 or more workers, a third for firms employing more than 1,000. The big corporations with their large factories, warehouses, and offices dominated the local economy and had the largest impact on changes in work. Most big companies continued to control workers with proven tools: strikebreakers, private detectives and spies, divisive tactics, deskilling technology, and the legal apparatus of the state. Partly in hopes of reducing both worker turnover and discontent, during the early decades of the twentieth century employers also moved toward more bureaucratic administration, scientific management, and efforts to motivate workers with more than the threats of the old drive system. Centralized management, used increasingly by most big companies, brought tighter financial accounting and, in the spirit of Frederick Winslow TAYLOR's "scientific management," a closer evaluation of individual workers.

George PULLMAN's model town and factory south of Chicago in 1880 had been one of the most prominent early examples of paternalistic control in the guise of providing for workers' welfare, but modified versions of the strategy grew increasingly common as corporations consolidated economic power and sought new ways to fight unionization. In 1901 McCormick/Harvester adopted "welfarism," including profit-sharing, pensions, and sickness and accident benefits, as a way to fight unions, win public approval, limit legal liabilities, and fend off antitrust action and other government regulation. In 1919, partly in reaction to a postwar strike wave, Harvester introduced its Works Council, a prominent example of the company-controlled unions that several major Chicago employers adopted in the 1920s, when Harvester, U.S. Steel, Armour, Swift, and Western Electric espoused what often was called "WELFARE CAPITALISM" or "the AMERICAN PLAN."

Companies sought innovative ways to increase productivity, reduce turnover, and resist unions. Western Electric, one of many firms that made Chicago a national leader in electronics manufacturing in the decades after 1920, initiated research on how adjustment of various physical factors, such as lighting, influenced work at its giant Hawthorne Works in CICERO. Instead, researchers found that the social organization of the work group and the attention given workers by researchers were both more important than physical variables. This study laid the foundations for a new school of centralized personnel management that gradually supplanted the foreman in organizing and controlling work.

Welfare capitalism and employee unions faltered in the GREAT DEPRESSION, but they provided additional legitimation for workers' belief that companies should treat them more fairly. Although many believed that the Depression demonstrated the failure of capitalism, a larger number were interested simply in a fairer, more moral capitalism regulated by a federal government that provided more economic security and better working conditions. The new industrial unions of the CONGRESS OF INDUSTRIAL ORGANIZATIONS, as well as some American Federation of Labor craft unions, provided a voice for workers in the mass-production industries. They readily joined the labor movement during the Depression and World War II, despite continued resistance from employers that at times turned bloody, as in the Memorial Day 1937 police attack on Chicago's striking Republic steelworkers.

Demand for war material during WORLD WAR II combined with labor shortages caused by troop mobilization opened industrial jobs for new workers, especially women, who were expected to return home after the war. Anxious to avoid strikes, the federal government pushed companies to recognize unions. In the postwar years, strong domestic demand kept UNEMPLOYMENT low, and newly established unions raised wages and expanded benefits, including pensions and health insurance, which were tied to jobs rather than universally provided. Union contracts and government social safety nets combined to reduce the hardship for workers during recessions, and unionization provided new protection from arbitrary managerial decisions, especially through the use of seniority to determine jobs and grievance procedures to resolve disputes. Union contracts often set the standard for pay, benefits, and even personnel systems that nonunion companies felt forced to approximate. Mechanization and fragmentation of work continued on its established trajectory, further undermining many manual skills, but employment was steadier and more lucrative for most workers than in the past.

In 1947, manufacturing employment in the city of Chicago peaked at 667,407 workers. It began to drop sharply in the 1950s, before stabilizing in the 1960s at roughly one-half million. Manufacturing employment plummeted in the 1970s, falling to 147,000 by 2000. Chicago, whose boosters had long boasted that someone who couldn't find work there couldn't find work anywhere, began to consistently register unemployment rates higher than the national average.

Industries closed or dispersed to new locations. The largest companies found it easiest to relocate, leaving small suppliers stranded without their traditional customers. Many manufacturers relocated to the suburbs, seeking cheaper land and taking advantage of the new interstate highway system. By 1965, more than half of manufacturing jobs in the metropolitan area were located in the suburbs, jobs that made the Chicago metropolitan area home to the nation's largest concentration of manufacturing jobs in 1970. Suburban Chicago manufacturing employment continued to expand until the early 1980s. Other businesses, however, relocated factories to the Sunbelt. Meatpacking moved west, leading to the closing of the famed packing plants and stockyards in the mid-1960s. From the 1960s onwards, when foreign competition began to cut into sales and employment in industries like steel, apparel, and consumer electronics, manufacturers increasingly located operations in foreign countries. In many cases, employers fled to escape unionization and to pay lower wages. The loss of central-city manufacturing jobs hurt African Americans hardest, as sociologist William Julius Wilson showed in his studies of the social devastation of concentrated poverty in Chicago's neighborhoods.

In the latter part of the twentieth century, Chicago's remaining factories were smaller, and major companies increasingly subcontracted production work to smaller firms. In the 1990s, suburban-based Sara Lee exemplified the trend in announcing that it no longer intended to manufacture the products it sold. Manufacturing productivity increased as businesses invested in technology, including computers, and refined the organization of work, with measures including adoption from the Japanese of just-in-time production. Although manufacturing at the end of the twentieth century remained more important in Chicago (18 percent of all jobs) than for the national economy as a whole (15 percent), Chicago was no longer the manufacturing powerhouse it had been a century earlier. The limited career ladders of the nineteenth-century factory and office have been almost entirely displaced by requirements for formal education as a prerequisite for more-skilled and better-paid jobs. Debates about the future of work in Chicago increasingly focused on the adequacy of its educational system, even though most service and retail economy jobs demand little skill. Services, including HEALTH CARE, business services, finance, and RETAIL WORK had become the mainstays of employment in Chicago, each roughly providing as many or more jobs than manufacturing. While Chicago remains comparatively highly unionized, the labor movement is not the dynamic force it once was, even if it does raise questions about deindustrialization, globalization, inequality, and living wages.

Although efforts to preserve and nurture manufacturing in the central city continue, Chicago business and political leaders at the close of the twentieth century are more concerned with Chicago as part of a regional economy and its prospects as a "GLOBAL city," a center of corporate administration, professional services, finance, government, communications, UNIVERSITIES, and culture. But there are questions about whether Chicago could become part of a rarefied elite with London, New York, and Tokyo and about what that would mean for most Chicago workers. The economic transformations of globalization since the early 1970s have brought increasing economic inequality and less stable employment to both Chicago and the country as a whole. Although work is still more predictable than it was for most Chicagoans a century ago, there is increasing dependence on contingent (contract, part-time, or temporary) work at all skill levels and less job security even for white-collar employees. Once identified with companies like Swift and Armour that slaughtered cattle by the millions, Chicago—or rather suburban OAKBROOK—is now more identified with McDonald's, whose global workforce flips burgers by the billions. While Chicago is the headquarters of many global corporate leaders,

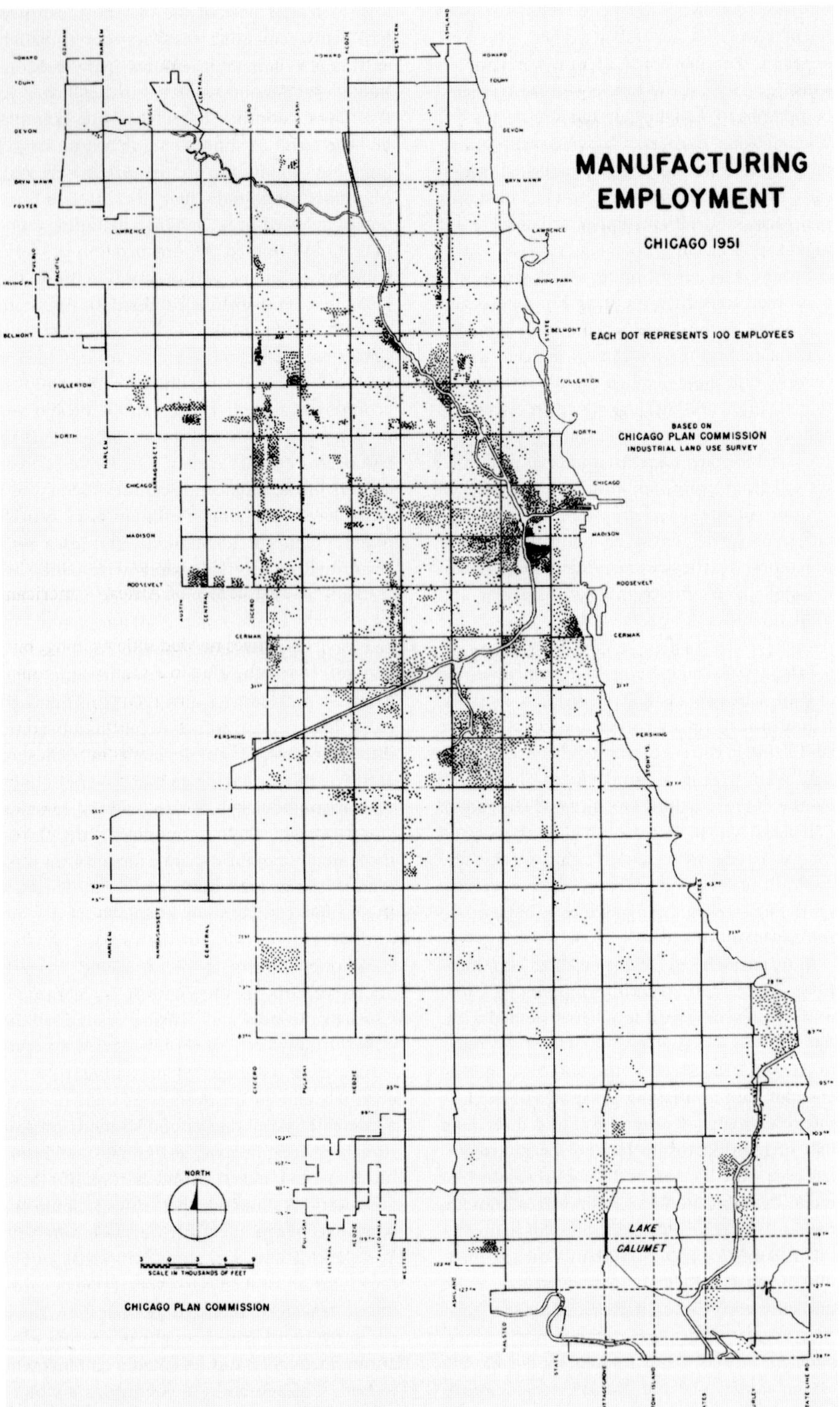

Manufacturing employment in Chicago, 1951. Creator: Chicago Plan Commission. Source: Chicago Historical Society.

their employment—like that of technology giant Motorola—is spread throughout the world, not concentrated in the corporate backyard as was true of their predecessors. In a similar fashion, even many of the biggest Chicago banks and businesses (like Amoco) are owned and controlled by companies outside the city and even the United States. Not only have workers never regained the control over their work that union leaders in late-nineteenth-century Chicago thought was essential for a citizen of a democratic republic; increasingly, local political leaders and business executives do not appear to control the city economy as they once did. As far as the future of work in Chicago is concerned, the "City of the Big Shoulders" has become the "metropolis of the big question mark."

David Moberg

See also: Antiunionism; Commuting; Economic Geography; Leisure; Socialist Parties; Work Culture

Further reading: Cohen, Lizabeth. *Making a New Deal: Industrial Workers in Chicago, 1919–1939.* 1990. • Montgomery, David. *Workers' Control in America.* 1979. • Schneirov, Richard. *Labor and Urban Politics: Class Conflict and the Origins of Modern Liberalism in Chicago, 1864–97.* 1998.

Work Culture.

When 18-year-old Carrie Meeber, the title character of Theodore Dreiser's novel *Sister Carrie* (1900), steps off the afternoon train from Wisconsin onto the streets of Chicago, she enters a world of seemingly endless WORK possibilities. An industrial behemoth, Chicago bristled with crowded factories, bustling stockyards, brimming grain elevators, a rapidly growing labor force, and most of all, complex cultures of work.

What Carrie saw was a remarkable diversity of opportunities shaped by the unique geography of the city. The centrality of Chicago to shipping and TRANSPORTATION routes by WATER and land made possible and profitable businesses of all kinds—and a correspondingly wide variety of workplaces. Carrie's brother-in-law Sven cleans refrigerator cars at the stockyards; her friend Drouet is a "drummer"—a traveling salesman; and his acquaintance Hurstwood is a well-to-do RESTAURANT manager. Carrie finds her first job punching eyeholes into shoes at a factory on Van Buren street. Their choices within this cornucopia of employment possibilities were determined by a combination of gender, age, education, ethnicity, race, and marital status.

Work cultures, that mix of practices and ideologies arising from the interactions of people with their work environments, have been shaped in Chicago above all by diversity—diversity of employment opportunities, population, and housing. The ways in which people find jobs, the rhythms of employment and UNEMPLOYMENT, the size of the workplace, the process of getting to and from work, how the workday is organized, power relationships and hierarchies, how workers learn and manage their tasks, how they socialize and organize family life, how informal worker behavior interacts with sanctioned authority and rules—all these things constitute work culture. There are many different work cultures, reflecting the differences between skilled and unskilled labor, professional, white-collar, and service work, and workers' identities by race, gender, age, and ethnicity. Work cultures have also changed as the nature of work has transformed over the past 150 years.

During the city's infancy a FUR TRADING culture developed through interactions between POTAWATOMI and white traders. Intermarriage and custom led many whites to adopt Indian ways while never losing sight of the controlling hand of the American Fur Company. At the same time, white influence and trade goods altered traditional patterns of work and life for NATIVE AMERICANS. A mixture of frontier autonomy, native culture, entrepreneurial values, and financial dependence thus coexisted uneasily in one of the earliest work cultures of the city.

Throughout the nineteenth century, work for a huge pool of floating and unorganized labor was shaped by transience. The reliance on the products of nature for profit—AGRICULTURE, livestock, ice, and LUMBER—required men to move according to the rhythms of the seasons. They planted in the spring, harvested crops or timber in the fall, cut ice in the winter, and shepherded cattle and pigs through increasingly narrow roads into the city for processing and sale. Uncontrollable forces like drought or fire could instantly create or destroy opportunities for employment.

Transient laborers tended to be white, unmarried men. Answerable to a gang boss, men would work for a season, collect their pay, and move on to the next opportunity. This was not usually a life for families. Transient laborers often lived in cheap BOARDINGHOUSES, able to pick up and follow work wherever it appeared.

One of the transient job opportunities in mid-nineteenth-century Chicago was lumber production. LAKE MICHIGAN lumbermen hired Chicago laborers on seasonal contracts, specifying work from sunrise to sunset daily. Workers were to bring their own axes and pay their passage to the timber fields across the lake, where they would haul logs, push them through blades, and stack lumber. In return, they received room, board, and from $100 to $200 yearly; on occasion their wives and children would be hired to do the "inside" work of cooking and cleaning. During hard times—such as the 1857 panic—these workers would be precipitously fired, or offered store credit in place of currency for wages.

The nature of work in shops was very different. Through the early decades of the nineteenth century, workshops were small, with craftsmen hiring a few skilled handicraft workers at a time. Apprenticeship and later employment were personalized and individualized, as cabinetmakers, upholsterers, machinists, and others created items from design to finished product.

The coming of the canals by the 1840s and then the expansion of the first RAILROADS by the 1850s increased the market range for the city from a few hundred miles to the length and breadth of the country, while providing the means to transport people and goods to and from far distances. Chicago became the nexus of a huge organization of products: lumber from Michigan, Wisconsin, and Minnesota; ores from Illinois, Minnesota, and Colorado; pigs, cattle, and grains from the Mississippi Valley. After the calamitous FIRE OF 1871, the local economy experienced an unprecedented building boom, which led to work for timbermen, carpenters, laborers, and painters, and a concomitant need for local stores and services.

The growing demand for labor coincided with the influx of immigrants. Reflecting national patterns, the first waves of foreign immigrants to Chicago in the 1850s and 1860s included IRISH, GERMAN, and Scandinavian newcomers. From the 1870s through the beginning of the twentieth century, people from Eastern and Southern Europe—Bohemians, LITHUANIANS, ITALIANS, RUSSIANS, GREEKS, HUNGARIANS, AUSTRIANS, POLES, and Eastern European JEWS—flooded into Chicago looking for opportunity and work. Often unskilled and with limited English, these workers found work in the giant factories, particularly in the stockyards, ironworks, and steel industries. CHINESE came in lesser numbers and looked especially to LAUNDRIES as opportunities for self-employment. By the 1890s, three out of four Chicagoans were either immigrants or the children of immigrants.

Irish Canal Workers

Much of the work on the Illinois & Michigan Canal between 1837 and 1848 was done by hand. While canal laborers included Yankees, southerners, Native Americans, African Americans, Germans, English, and French Canadians, most were Irish immigrants. Hundreds of poor Irish men journeyed to the region to take up this backbreaking, low-wage work. Their poverty, foreignness, and Catholicism isolated them, as did the remote and often isolated construction sites. In 1838, canal workers rioted over wages, and local property holders such as James Brooks expressed their concern:

> Since the Commission of the outrages by the Irish at my work on the canal on the 19th and 20th inst. and the course that has been pursued in relation to the matter, I conceive that it would be unsafe for me at this time to go upon my work. And if it were safe for me to go upon my work I am unable at present to do so, on account of the injury received from the Irish. I have a large amount of property on and about my works, which is exposed to the rapacity of the Irish, and I have no men who can, or who dare to take measures to preserve my property.

"Letter from James Brooks to the Canal Commissioners Concerning Irish Rioters." In *The Illinois and Michigan Canal, 1827–1911: A Selection of Documents from the Illinois State Archives*, ed. Robert E. Bailey and Elaine Shemoney Evans, 1998, 37.

But the city's newcomers were not only from distant lands. Tens of thousands of people from American small towns and farms sought the excitement and possibilities of life in the big city, creating a pool of migrants. Theodore Dreiser's fictional Sister Carrie came from "Columbia City"—a small town in Wisconsin, a state sending a multitude of migrants to Chicago. Young people from farms and rural towns in Minnesota, the Dakotas, Iowa, Michigan, and Indiana also turned to Chicago as an attractive alternative to what they perceived to be a dreary and limited future on the countryside.

From the South during the 1890s came the first significant numbers of AFRICAN AMERICANS. A majority of these black migrants, barred from higher-paying factory jobs, found work in domestic service or day labor. As industrial labor opened during the 1910s, the GREAT MIGRATION from the South would bring thousands more blacks and establish the city as a leading center of African American life.

Factory operatives needed little training, but they did have to be able to endure long hours in rough conditions. The majority of these workers were white male immigrants, except in the garment trades, which welcomed women. Factory workers found an increasingly impersonal life as "hands" or "operatives" laboring monotonously on a minuscule part of the production of an item for 10 to 14 hours, six days a week. The individualized and personal work culture of artisans faded as industry grew. By the end of the century, factories had become huge places of business. In 1880 over 75,000 Chicago workers labored in industries including MEATPACKING, CLOTHING production, IRON AND STEEL, the manufacturing of foundry, machine, and agricultural implements, beer and liquor processing, FURNITURE manufacture, and PRINTING. By 1920, 70 percent of workers in manufacturing trades were employed by companies of 100 workers or more, and one-third of these worked in establishments with over 1,000 employees. The personal relationship between upper management and workers became increasingly distant as the size of companies grew.

The plant foreman set the daily pace. His authority was absolute. He could raise or decrease the speed of work, determine pay, and assign hours and tasks of labor. He represented factory management to the operatives under his command and had the power to hire and fire at will. For his workers, the workday offered very little autonomy or sense of empowerment.

Finding work could be a complicated business. In Upton Sinclair's 1906 novel *The Jungle*, Jurgis Rudkus, a Lithuanian immigrant to Chicago, gets his first job by joining the morning crowd outside a Packingtown factory; a "boss" picks him out for the task of sweeping out cattle entrails on the killing floor of the plant. Similarly, Jurgis's cousin-in-law Marija Berczynskas wanders in and out of smaller factories in the district until she is hired by a "fore-lady" to paint cans of smoked beef. People could also find work through "intelligence" or personnel agencies, SALOONS and hiring halls, labor unions, newspaper advertisements, and employers' organizations. Kin and ethnic networks provided a time-honored resource for finding a job. Italian and Greek immigrants could also find work through the *padrone* system of labor agents steering them to unskilled work—for a price.

The cost of this unregulated industrial growth included the pollution of home and workplace. Workers labored long hours in unsafe conditions, sometimes standing all day in noisy, crowded, filthy, overheated and unventilated rooms, always with the threat of dire poverty should injury or illness or unemployment stop a paycheck. There was no safety net.

Industrial workers, especially if they were white, tended to live near their jobs, in the shadow of the mills, stockyards, or factories. Within these neighborhoods, institutions like SALOONS brought men together with offers of fellowship, food and drink, and such essential services as check cashing and mailing addresses. Women, barred by custom from the world of the saloon, often instead found friendship, education, and social services through the neighborhood SETTLEMENT HOUSES, such as HULL HOUSE or CHICAGO COMMONS, which proliferated around the turn of the century. Other community institutions such as churches, barbershops, ethnic newspapers, MUTUAL BENEFIT SOCIETIES, corner stores, and fraternal organizations preserved ethnic cultures and racial identities at the same time that the forces of "AMERICANIZATION" were at work.

By the late nineteenth century, many Chicagoans looked to unions and labor federations to win influence over their working conditions. STRIKES and lockouts could be violent, as indicated by labor disorders among stevedores, lumberyard workers, RAILROAD WORKERS, and stockyard laborers during the 1870s and 1880s. The growing success of labor legislation within the context of union activism—particularly minimum wages, maximum hours of work, unemployment compensation, and safety standards—changed the hierarchy of industrial relations as government regulatory agencies became influential participants. Factory inspectors, pioneered by Florence Kelley, attempted to enforce new LABOR LAWS meant to protect the health and well-being of workers from indifferent company policy. At the same time, some workers resisted the new protective labor legislation. Chicago women who worked as elevated railroad ticket agents, for example, protested in 1911 when their hours were cut from 12 to 10 a day because of a new law limiting the hours of women's employment.

Racial segregation kept the relatively few black factory workers in more distant parts of the city, forcing them to find daily transportation to and from their work and blocking channels of social interaction that might have reduced racial barriers. Until 1916 black factory workers were few and far between, though some did find employment on the killing floors of the stockyards or in the steel mills. More commonly, black men worked as unskilled day laborers, restaurant waiters, Pullman porters, bootblacks, and hotel redcaps, while black women filled the laundry trades and other forms of DOMESTIC service. Like industrial workers, unskilled laborers and service workers faced uncertain job security, as slack times led to staff reductions with no notice. Moreover, black employees of HOTELS, restaurants, and the railroads found themselves employed in places which would deny them and their families and neighbors service as customers.

Some of the 48 saloons near the stockyards, Ashland Avenue, 1907. Photographer: Unknown. Source: The Newberry Library.

White and educated native-born men more easily found employment possibilities in business and the professions. By the 1950s, studies of such new postwar suburbs as Chicago's PARK FOREST suggested that the culture of white-collar work for men had transformed. The workplaces of large corporations in business, government, and industry were staffed by bureaucratic "organization men" who evidenced a "group-mindedness" characterized by values of security and safety rather than initiative and risk. They identified their well-being with that of the company, and so long hours at work, and the belief that the company would reward loyalty with lifetime employment, fostered an environment of conformity that marginalized individual initiative and creativity.

The corporate environment at midcentury included few women or blacks. For women, there had always been a much smaller choice of jobs. With some notable exceptions, only the poorest of married women worked for wages before the middle of the twentieth century, while single women in most ethnic groups worked at least briefly. Poor women found jobs in garment, millinery, and shoe factories, or as DOMESTIC servants or laundry workers. Some turned to PROSTITUTION. Hilda Polacheck, a Polish Jew whose family had immigrated to Chicago in 1892, left school at the age of 14 to work in a knitting factory on State Street. Six days a week for over 10 hours a day she operated a machine—one of 400 in a huge room—until she was fired for attending a union meeting. Hilda next worked at a shirtwaist factory, sewing shirt cuffs for 10 hours a day. Her description of this job as "deadly monotony" typified the difference between the earlier culture of artisans who could take pride in their work and newer conditions for industrial laborers.

Native-born white women also found opportunities in emerging occupations, such as the professional fields of education and librarianship and the white-collar areas of clerical and DEPARTMENT STORE work. Wages were consistently lower for women than for men, and UNIONIZATION far less frequent.

Jobs defined as women's work went through tremendous changes in the twentieth century. CLERICAL WORK, for example, once the domain of men, became feminized by the end of the nineteenth century after the invention of the typewriter and through the twentieth century grew to become the single largest job category for women of all races. Montgomery

Labor Day parade, Main Street, Glen Ellyn, postcard, 1909. Photographer: Unknown. Source: DuPage County Historical Museum.

Ward—a MAIL-ORDER firm whose workers had no direct public contact—employed the most black clerical workers in the country by 1920, when over 1,000 African American women worked for the Chicago company. As the size of office staffs enlarged, new management techniques originally developed for factories began to affect the lives of office workers. Domestic service, which at one time included a population of workers who lived in the homes or businesses of their employers, became more of a day job, increasingly perceived as temporary. Restaurant waitressing also grew as a category of low-paid, often transient unskilled work for women.

As the great urban department stores like Marshall Field's appeared during the second half of the nineteenth century, department store sales work also became a woman's profession. Managers trained "shopgirls" to become "professional" saleswomen skilled in everything from etiquette to merchandise. At Marshall Field's a personnel department was described as "a conscientious mother" working to influence the workers in the niceties of behavior and saleswomanship. Managing the business was a large-scale enterprise; by 1904, the workforce at Marshall Field's could reach 10,000 in a store which served up to a quarter of a million customers a day.

The work culture of this particular occupational group developed to express three identities of the saleswoman: worker, woman, and consumer. These identities, reflected through a set of unwritten rules followed on the job, illustrated the complexities of women's lives where private and public identities intersected. The interactions among managers, saleswomen, and customers—which favored skills of social interactions and initiatives—allowed these RETAIL WORKERS a relatively autonomous working environment.

Many of these workers were called "women adrift"—the term for unmarried women living outside of traditional family life before the 1930s. They created a kind of "working girls" subculture in the city, challenging Victorian prescriptions for behavior, influencing popular culture, and ultimately changing social mores. This heterogeneous group of women—young and old, black and white, native-born and immigrant—lived in BOARDINGHOUSES, both supervised and unsupervised, and later in APARTMENTS and furnished rooms. They patronized restaurants, DANCE HALLS, and theaters. This population of workers was sharply delineated by race; boarding homes, for example, were often segregated, as were working girls' clubs. For example, in Chicago the Eleanor Clubs served white women, while the Phyllis Wheatley Home had a black clientele.

For most married women, the ideal was a one-wage-earner family economy. For middle-class women—both black and white—voluntary participation in civic culture through organizations like church, women's CLUBS, and school organizations like the Parent-Teacher Association constituted a kind of unpaid work which contributed to the community environment. Additionally, the HOUSEKEEPING and child care they provided constituted unpaid labor for their families, although many through the 1920s relied on domestic servants as they organized household work.

More often, however, a man's salary was insufficient to support his family. Women often supplemented family income by such "off the books" homework as midwifery, keeping boarders and lodgers, doing laundry, selling goods door to door, or by manufacturing garments or other goods at home. Hilda Polacheck, for example, describes how women and children labored around kitchen tables in crowded West Side tenements to make cloth flowers for women's hats during the late 1890s.

Children have long been part of the work history of the city. As part of the family economy, children labored on farms and in rural areas. In the city, in the era before schooling became a longer part of life, children often left SCHOOL at the age of 14 or much earlier and hawked NEWSPAPERS, labored in sweatshops, traveled as messengers, or peddled goods on the streets. Their earnings were sometimes critical for family sustenance.

With the advent of the twentieth century, industrial work culture began to change. Scientific management came to many big corporations, such as the PULLMAN Palace Car Company, where from 1913 to 1919 efficiency experts brought modern techniques of manufacturing to the shop floor. As the century progressed, new standards of technology and factory organization greatly reduced the need for physical labor in the plants. Women and black men began to work in factories previously barred to them, although the type of work available was often still segregated by race and gender.

The population of the workforce changed along with the city. As new suburbs developed after the streetcar lines were built in the late nineteenth century, many city workers lived further away from downtown; by 1913 some 123,000 suburban passengers arrived and departed the city daily, riding on 746 trains. The construction of such highways as the Kennedy and the Eisenhower EXPRESSWAYS further accelerated suburban growth and a COMMUTER culture. Work itself migrated to the new suburbs, as some large corporations left Chicago's downtown and as a high-technology corridor developed in suburban COOK and DUPAGE Counties. Computer technologies and wireless communications developed in the 1980s and 1990s allowed some workers new freedom of place, as they were able to work from home or on the road as well as in an office. Piecework, once the province of the factory or home worker, became high tech.

Further decline of industrial manufactures occurred in the later twentieth century, as professional, technical, and service industry occupations increased. The growth of multinational corporations meant that many more professional and white-collar workers now found that job security and work definitions could be determined by distant executives from abroad instead of by a local foreman or manager; HEALTH CARE WORKERS saw the rise of Health Maintenance Organizations in the last two decades of the century change the nature of even professional workers' autonomy and decision-making power.

Additionally, the population of workers transformed. New immigrants arrived from PUERTO RICO, CUBA, MEXICO, Central America, Asia, and Africa. Child labor by the 1940s was no longer as accepted as it was earlier because of new legal requirements for longer schooling as well as changing cultural conceptions of childhood. Even more significantly, during the second half of the twentieth century the labor force participation rates for women in every age group under 65 increased, especially as married women began to work at higher rates. As more married women and mothers of young children entered the workforce, debates about policies on child care, extended school hours, and such conditions of work as flextime were raised across a variety of occupations.

Since Chicago's earliest years as a fur trading outpost on the Midwestern prairie, the city's work culture has reflected the tremendous diversity of its people and its economy. Strongly shaped by geography and characterized by a remarkably varied population, Chicago's story has been no less than the larger saga of American economic and social development—continually changing and reflecting complex interactions between people and their workplaces. If the industrial city witnessed by Carrie Meeber at the end of the nineteenth century has vanished, still new forms of work and work culture have developed which just as surely shape the lives of Chicagoans and reflect the continuing evolution of the city itself.

Lynn Y. Weiner

See also: Business of Chicago; Eight-Hour Movement; Schooling for Work; Welfare Capitalism

Further reading: The work culture of Chicago can be approached through numerous works of history, economics, sociology, and fiction. Perry Duis, *Challenging Chicago: Coping with Everyday Life, 1837–1920* (1998), presents a nice overview of modernization. For a picture of a pivotal era, see Susan Hirsch and Robert Goler, *A City Comes of Age: Chicago in the 1890s* (1990). A standard work for understanding the impact of geography and the environment on the city's economic growth is William Cronon, *Nature's Metropolis: Chicago and the Great West* (1991). For definitions of work culture, see both Martin Blatt and Martha Norkunas, *Work, Recreation, and Culture: Essays in American Labor History* (1996), and Eileen Boris and Nelson Lichtenstein, *Major Problems in the History of American Workers* (1991). Studies which look at specific occupations, populations, or occupational groups in Chicago include Joanne Meyerowitz, *Women Adrift: Independent Wage Earners in Chicago, 1880–1930* (1988); Lizabeth Cohen, *Making a New Deal: Industrial Workers in Chicago, 1919–1939* (1992); William H. Whyte, Jr., *The Organization Man* (1956); Melvin Holli and Peter d'A. Jones, eds., *Ethnic Chicago: A Multicultural Portrait* (1995); Jacqueline Jones, *Labor of Love, Labor of Sorrow* (1985); and Susan Porter Benson, *Counter Cultures: Saleswomen, Managers, and Customers in American Department Stores, 1890–1940* (1986). On the settlement house movement and its importance for workers, see Jane Addams, *Twenty Years at Hull-House* (1910); Hilda Satt Polacheck, *I Came A Stranger: The Story of a Hull-House Girl* (1991); and Anne Meis Knupfer, *Toward a Tenderer Humanity and a Nobler Womanhood: African American Women's Clubs in Turn-of-the-Century Chicago* (1996). An account of industrialism, race, and unionization is given in Rick Halpern, *Down on the Killing Floor: Black and White Workers in Chicago's Packinghouses, 1904–1954* (1997), and of course a fictional rendering of stockyard work is given in Upton Sinclair's *The Jungle* (1906). Other fictional accounts of work life in Chicago abound, including Theodore Dreiser, *Sister Carrie* (1900). Daniel Nelson's *Managers and Workers: Origins of the Twentieth-Century Factory System in the U.S., 1880–1920* (1995) explores the transformation of the factory through the lens of worker-manager interactions. Finally, Chicago's oral historian Studs Terkel presents invaluable testimonies about the nature of daily life for working people in his various books, excerpted in *My American Century* (1997).

World War I. World War I (1914–1918) had a profound impact on Chicago both before and after the American war declaration on April 6, 1917. Illinois provided more than 300,000 recruits for the United States military during the war. Several thousand recruits from Chicago, and elsewhere, were trained at the officers' training camp at FORT SHERIDAN and at the GREAT LAKES NAVAL TRAINING STATION, both located north of Chicago along LAKE MICHIGAN.

The war inflamed and altered Chicago's ethnic landscape. The city's large GERMAN and IRISH communities tended to sympathize with the Central powers: Germany, Austria-Hungary, Turkey, and Bulgaria, or at least favored American neutrality. Chicago's Germans, the city's largest immigrant group, vociferously opposed Washington's growing sympathy for the Entente powers: Great Britain, France, and Russia. Prominent Chicago German Americans, such as meatpacker Oscar Mayer, city plan commission member Charles Wacker, and CHICAGO SYMPHONY ORCHESTRA director Frederick Stock, as well as the Germanophile Irish American congressman Fred Britten, were well placed, and vocal, opponents of an American alliance with the Entente.

German Americans, however, failed to keep the United States neutral. German attacks on American shipping and revelations of a German initiative to secure a Mexican alliance in return for a promise of returned territory in the Southwest silenced many opponents to war with Germany. Once the United States entered the war, German Americans, as well as their culture, fell under growing suspicion. German-sounding foods were renamed: sauerkraut became "liberty cabbage"; frankfurters became "hot dogs." Chicago institutions were anglicized as well, with the Germania Club becoming the Lincoln Club, and the Bismarck Hotel the Hotel Randolph. Frederick Stock took a brief leave of absence from the Chicago Symphony Orchestra to apply for naturalization. Zealous to ensure domestic security, private organizations such as the American Protective League monitored Chicago's Germans and detained draft dodgers in occasional "slacker" drives.

The war also insinuated itself into Chicago POLITICS. Mayor William Thompson plied German and Irish voters by advocating American neutrality and courted Chicago ANTI-WAR Progressives such as SETTLEMENT HOUSE worker Jane Addams and UNIVERSITY OF CHICAGO professor Charles Merriam. Following

Children standing in front of an anti-German sign posted in the Edison Park neighborhood, 1917. Photographer: Unknown. Source: Chicago Historical Society.

Charles W. Folds, president of United Charities of Chicago, affixes a Liberty Loans poster in 1918. Photographer: Chicago Daily News. Source: Chicago Historical Society.

the declaration of war, Thompson allowed antiwar groups such as the People's Council of America for Democracy and Terms of Peace to meet in the city. The mayor drew further attention by spurning the visiting Marshal Joseph Joffre, of the Entente forces, as well as by his cold reception of Liberty Bond salesmen at the beginning of the first war loan drive. Thompson's dubious patriotism was a factor in his 1918 loss to Congressman Medill McCormick in the Illinois REPUBLICAN primary for the United States Senate. The same election also witnessed future mayor Anton Cermak's defeat in the race for Cook County Sheriff, after he ran on a stoutly anti-German platform in a county dominated by heavily German Chicago.

World War I's most significant long-term impact on Chicago involved economic adjustments, especially in the labor force. The war shut off immigration and siphoned native-born labor into the war effort. Many Chicago employers turned to women and AFRICAN AMERICANS, hiring them for jobs previously reserved for white men. These new opportunities, mainly in heavy industry, stimulated the GREAT MIGRATION of African Americans from the South to Chicago and other northern cities.

Sean J. LaBat

See also: Americanization; Cold War and Anti-Communism

Further reading: Bukowski, Douglas. "Big Bill Thompson: The 'Model' Politician." In *The Mayors: The Chicago Political Tradition*, ed. Paul M. Green and Melvin G. Holli. Rev. ed. 1995. • Holli, Melvin G. "The Great War Sinks Chicago's German *Kultur*." In *Ethnic Chicago*, ed. Melvin G. Holli and Peter d'A. Jones. Rev. and exp. ed. 1984. • Luebke, Frederick C. *Bonds of Loyalty: German Americans and World War I*. 1974.

World War II. Between September 1939 and December 7, 1941, Chicago was the scene of a vigorous debate over whether Americans should become involved in the European War. *Chicago Tribune* publisher R. R. McCormick led the isolationists, while *Daily News* publisher Frank Knox and *Sun* publisher Marshall Field III articulated the interventionist viewpoint. But after Pearl Harbor, it became impossible for anyone to escape the impact of World War II. By D-Day in 1944, the average Chicago block had given seven residents to the military. Those who remained at home attended massive rallies and bought heroic amounts of bonds, endured food rationing, and grew victory gardens. The neighborhood was the building block of these home front activities that almost immediately enveloped every family. Twenty thousand elected block captains held ceremonies for those departing for the military and erected small shrines for those who did not return. Neighbors joined to hold civilian defense drills as well as drives to collect scrap metal, paper, rubber, and grease for conversion into nitroglycerine.

The war instantly reshaped the workplace. The city's diversified industrial base made it second only to Detroit in the value—$24 billion—of war goods produced. Over 1,400 companies produced everything from field rations to parachutes to torpedoes, while new aircraft plants employed 100,000 in the construction of engines, aluminum sheeting, bombsights, and other components. The Douglas-Chicago plant on the site of present-day O'HARE Field turned out 654 C-54 Skymaster transports in 25 months. Just over half of all military ELECTRONICS used in the war came from 60 local plants. Although Chicagoans frequently worked double shifts to aid the effort, such production levels created labor shortages that brought the physically disabled, the elderly, and tens of thousands of women into the workplace. War jobs also attracted 60,000 AFRICAN AMERICANS from the South and an equal number of JAPANESE Americans who were released from desert detention camps. Round-the-clock training programs at high schools and UNIVERSITIES provided these new war workers with necessary skills.

Chicago also played a very visible role as a crossroads city. GREAT LAKES NAVAL TRAINING STATION provided boot camp for a third of those who served in the U.S. Navy, while FORT SHERIDAN became an important army training facility. GLENVIEW NAVAL AIR STATION turned out 20,000 carrier pilots, who trained on two old lake ships that had been converted into aircraft carriers. A similar number of officers graduated from NORTHWESTERN UNIVERSITY's Naval Midshipmen's program. There was also specialized training in electronics, meteorology, naval machinery, foreign language, and espionage. Tens of thousands of other military personnel who were passing through the city by rail enjoyed the hospitality of the USO, as well as the Chicago Servicemen's Centers at 176 W. Washington and in the AUDITORIUM BUILDING, the latter serving 24 million meals by the end of the war.

On V-J Day, August 14, 1945, it was all over. Chicagoans joined the nationwide victory celebrations, but only a few people then knew that on December 2, 1942, scientists had created the first sustained nuclear reaction. Ironically, as public and pervasive as the war effort had been, these first steps toward creating the weapon that would end it had taken place in deep secret under the grandstands at the UNIVERSITY OF CHICAGO's Stagg Field.

Perry R. Duis

See also: Great Migration; Manhattan Project; World War I

Further reading: Duis, Perry R. "No Time for Privacy: World War II and Chicago's Families." In *The War in American Culture: Society and Consciousness during World War II*, ed. Lewis A. Erenberg and Susan E. Hirsch, 1996, 17–45. • Duis, Perry R., and Scott

LaFrance. *We've Got a Job to Do: Chicagoans and World War II.* 1992. • Schneider, James C. *Should America Go to War? The Debate over Foreign Policy in Chicago, 1939–1941.* 1989.

World's Columbian Exposition, May 1 to October 30, 1893. Organized to commemorate the 400th anniversary of Columbus's landfall in the New World, the World's Columbian Exposition became a defining moment in Chicago's history and the history of the United States as a whole.

When the World's Columbian Exposition opened, only 22 years had passed since the Chicago FIRE OF 1871; only 28 years had passed since the end of the American CIVIL WAR. In the interval, the era of Reconstruction had given way to a Gilded Age characterized by frenetic industrial growth, mass immigration, and class violence as evidenced by Chicago's 1886 HAYMARKET Square bombing. With many Americans wondering if sectional conflict had given way to class conflict, American political and economic leaders followed the example of their peers in Europe and turned increasingly to the medium of the world's fair to provide the cultural cement for their badly fragmented societies. The first world's fair, London's Crystal Palace Exhibition of 1851, had been championed by the British government to counter the spread of political radicalism and to tout the global expansion of the British Empire. The success of London's imperial show inspired Britain's continental rivals to organize fairs of their own. The United States followed in 1876 with a world's fair in Philadelphia, but this exposition lost money and left many Americans wondering if the exposition movement would ever take hold in the United States. Chicago's World's Columbian Exposition cast all doubts aside.

Momentum to celebrate the Columbian quadricentennial began building in the early 1880s. By the close of the decade, civic leaders in St. Louis, New York City, and Washington DC joined their counterparts in Chicago and announced that they were interested in hosting a fair that, in a time of great economic uncertainty, held the promise of generating commercial profits as well as increasing REAL-ESTATE values. Exposition backers also were also motivated by the prospect of securing greater prestige for themselves and for their cities. By 1890, it was clear that the U.S. Congress would have to decide where the fair would be held and that the principal contenders, by virtue of their superior financial resources, would be Chicago and New York. New York's financial titans, including J. P. Morgan, Cornelius Vanderbilt, and William Waldorf Astor, pledged $15 million to underwrite the fair if Congress awarded it to New York City. Not to be outdone, Chicago's leading capitalists and exposition sponsors, including Charles T. Yerkes, Marshall Field, Philip Armour, Gustavus Swift, and Cyrus McCormick, responded in kind. Furthermore, Chicago's promoters presented evidence of significant financial support from the city and state as well as over $5 million in stock subscriptions from people from every walk of life. What finally led Congress to vote in Chicago's

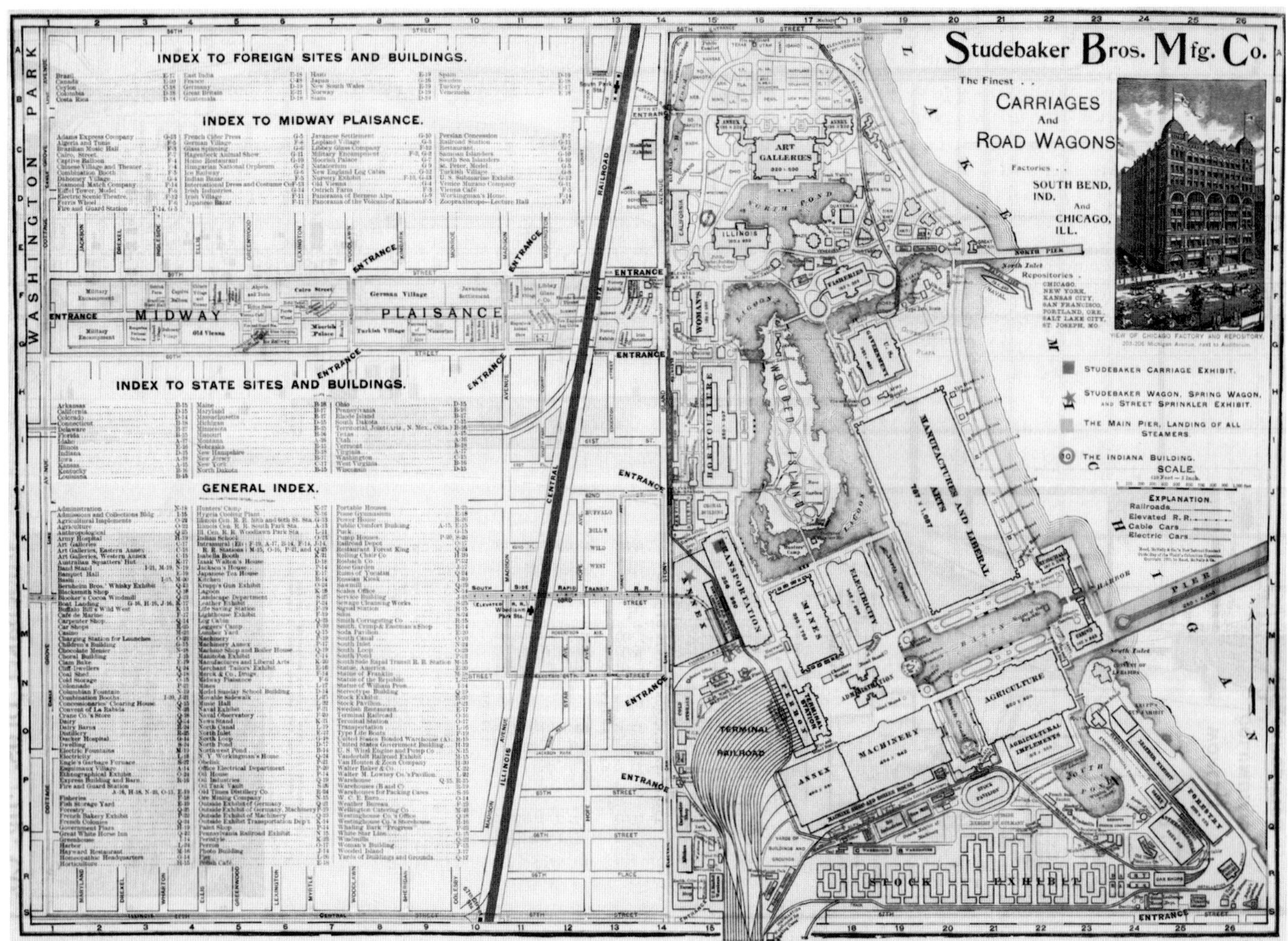

Many Chicago mapmakers published maps of the grounds, often folding them into guidebooks or producing vest-pocket editions. Numerous exhibitors customized maps to direct fairgoers to their displays. This illustration shows Rand, McNally & Co.'s standard map of the grounds, adapted into an advertisement for the Studebaker Brothers Manufacturing Company. The reverse side of the sheet featured a map of downtown Chicago highlighting the location of Studebaker's showroom. Cartographer: Unknown. Source: Chicago Historical Society.

This exhibit of produce from Los Angeles County in the Horticultural Building combined several of the fair's most prominent themes and representational strategies. By piling oranges high, the installation at once conveyed a sense of California's natural abundance and its conversion into an economic resource. By imitating the Liberty Bell, the display made ordinary commodities look extraordinary and reinforced the fair's patriotic message. The exhibit also exemplified the exposition's culture of simulation and repetition, as it was one of three Liberty Bells on view: the original was transported from Philadelphia for display in the Pennsylvania Building (a replica of Independence Hall) and another copy occupied the plaza in front of the Administration Building. Photographer: Unknown. Source: The Newberry Library.

The Court of Honor was the architectural showpiece of the exposition. At the right is the Columbian Fountain, designed by Frederick MacMonnies. Machinery Hall is visible behind it, and the Agricultural Building appears at the left. The ensemble of neoclassical palaces and Venetian waterways set a tone of imperial splendor and aesthetic sophistication, which Chicago's fair supporters hoped would counter the city's reputation as a commercial center lacking in refinement and high culture. Photographer: Charles Dudley Arnold. Source: Chicago Historical Society.

favor was banker Lyman Gage's ability to raise several million additional dollars in a 24-hour period to best New York's final offer.

Euphoric over their accomplishment, Chicago's powerful exposition backers had no time to rest. Although Congress pushed back the opening of the exposition to 1893, major battles lay ahead, especially over the selection of a site. Many downtown commercial interests favored a central location, but struggles over property rights and traffic congestion forced the exposition corporation, headed by Harlow N. Higinbotham, and the national exposition commission, headed by Thomas W. Palmer, to settle for JACKSON PARK, a marshy bog seven miles south of the Loop.

To hasten the process of construction and exhibit selection, exposition authorities vested responsibility in Daniel H. Burnham, the exposition's director of works, and George R. Davis, director-general. Both drew inspiration from earlier fairs, especially the 1889 Paris Universal Exposition with its famed Eiffel Tower. And both sought ways to make the Chicago fair distinctive.

For Burnham, ARCHITECTURE and sculpture would be to the Chicago fair what engineering had been to the Paris exposition. With the help of his partner, John W. Root, who died suddenly in 1891, Burnham assembled a stunning array of artistic and architectural talent to design the fair's main, palatial exhibition buildings on grounds that landscape architect Frederick Law Olmsted envisioned becoming a public park that would rival Central Park in New York City. Major outdoor sculptures included works by Augustus Saint-Gaudens, Frederick MacMonnies, and Daniel Chester French. The major buildings and their architects included Administration, by Richard Morris Hunt; Agriculture, by Charles McKim, William Mead, and Stanford White; Electricity, by Henry Van Brunt and Frank Howe; Horticulture, by William L. Jenney and William B. Mundie; Fisheries, by Henry Ives Cobb; Machinery Hall, by Robert Peabody and John Stearns; Manufactures and Liberal Arts, by George B. Post; Mines and Mining, by Solon Beman; and Transportation, by Dankmar Adler and Louis Sullivan. With the exception of the latter, which boasted Sullivan's long-remembered Golden Door, all these buildings were decidedly neoclassical, lathered with plaster of Paris, and painted a chalky white, thus bestowing the moniker of "White City" on the main exposition buildings. The White City's neoclassicism provoked a long-lived debate among architects. Sullivan, for one, would decry the pernicious effects of the fair on American architecture, while others praised the "civilizing" and uplifting effect that Burnham's Beaux-Arts plan would have on the public architecture of squalid American cities.

The Street in Cairo, modeled on the Rue de Caire at the 1889 Paris Exposition, was the most popular ethnographic attraction on the Midway. The Islamic architecture and Egyptian visitors formed a colorful stage set, where tourists could buy exotic souvenirs and ride on donkeys and camels. The scene was further enlivened by daily performances of local spectacles such as "The Arrival from Mecca" and "The Wedding Procession." This pen-and-ink drawing was made by John T. McCutcheon, a staff artist for the *Chicago Record.* Artist: John T. McCutcheon. Source: Chicago Historical Society.

Ida B. Wells: African Americans at the World's Columbian Exposition

Ida B. Wells grew up in the post–Civil War South and became a fierce opponent of lynching. She came to Chicago in 1893 to protest the exclusion of African Americans from exhibits at the World's Columbian Exposition. The Haitian building stood in as a center for Americans of color. Frederick Douglass, the noted abolitionist and advocate for equal rights, represented the Haitian government at the fair. Wells described Haiti's pavilion as "one of the gems of the World's Fair, and in it Mr. Douglass held high court."

Wells and Douglass wrote and published *The Reason Why the Colored American Is Not in the World's Columbian Exposition.* As Wells described it, the pamphlet

> was a clear, plain statement of facts concerning the oppression put upon the colored people in this land of the free and home of the brave. We circulated ten thousand copies of this little book during the remaining three months of the fair. Every day I was on duty at the Haitian building, where Mr. Douglass gave me a desk and spent the days putting this pamphlet in the hands of foreigners.

Ultimately, the fair officials offered to sponsor a special day for African Americans. Wells and many other African Americans considered Negro Day little more than a gesture and were reluctant to participate. Frederick Douglass, however, took the opportunity to spotlight the problems that people of color faced in the United States. Douglass died in 1895, but Wells moved permanently to Chicago and became involved in a wide range of civic and club activities.

Duster, Alfreda M., ed. *Crusade for Justice: The Autobiography of Ida B. Wells.* 1970.

While Burnham was developing his blueprint for the exposition grounds and buildings, Davis and his team of directors tackled the equally monumental task of giving form to the millions of exhibits that would go on display. For assistance with classifying exhibit material, Davis relied on the advice of America's foremost taxonomist, the Smithsonian Institution's G. Brown Goode, who conceptualized the fair as a veritable encyclopedia of civilization.

What exactly did "civilization" mean? Part of the answer came from the monumental exhibition palaces stuffed to overflowing with technologies of industrial and agricultural production as well as exhibits of fine art that surrounded the Court of Honor. Another part of the answer was provided by negative example through exhibits and concessions arranged along the Midway Plaisance, a mile-long avenue that ran at a right angle to the White City and blended education with amusement.

The inspiration for the Midway came from the 1889 Paris Universal Exposition, where the French government and prominent anthropologists turned representations of the French colonies into living ethnological villages featuring people from Africa and Asia. To lend anthropological legitimacy to their enterprise, Chicago's exposition directors placed the Midway under the nominal direction of Harvard's Frederic Ward Putnam, who had already been chosen to organize an Anthropology Building at the fair. Putnam envisioned the Midway as a living outdoor museum of "primitive" human beings that would afford visitors the opportunity to measure the progress of humanity toward the ideal of civilization presented in the White City. All of the ethnographic villages and most of the other attractions on the Midway, however, were commercial ventures organized by entrepreneurs who obtained concessions through the Ways and Means Committee of the World's Columbian Commission. By opening day, the Midway boasted an African village and a massive Streets of Cairo concession along with other ethnological shows. But the Midway, in addition to providing a serious

The world's first Ferris wheel was erected at the center of the Midway. Built on speculation by George W. Ferris, a bridge builder from Pittsburgh, the ride was the fair's most prominent engineering marvel. The wheel rose to 264 feet, surpassing the Eiffel Tower, and offering breathtaking views of the fair and the city. This lithograph, based on a watercolor painting by H. D. Nichols, is from a portfolio of prints that accompanied a deluxe edition of Hubert Howe Bancroft's *The Book of the Fair.* Artist: H. D. Nichols. Source: The Newberry Library.

This postal souvenir features a view of the Woman's Building juxtaposed with a portrait of Bertha Honoré Palmer, president of the Board of Lady Managers. Picture postcards were broadly popularized for the first time at the exposition, where they were sold from vending machines. In general, images of fair officials and of the buildings were among the most frequently reproduced icons of the fair, appearing in a wide range of visual media, from magazines and books to souvenir badges and spoons. Artist: Unknown. Source: Chicago Historical Society.

educational component to the fair, had become its AMUSEMENT center as well. With its wheel designed by George Ferris revolving high above the fairgrounds, its notorious—at least by Victorian standards—belly dancers, and its varied cuisine, the Midway's multiple fascinations challenged the White City's unity and dignity. Indeed, the Midway Plaisance is perhaps best understood as a cultural hothouse that generated many novel mass cultural forms (Riverview Park and Coney Island, for instance, were direct offshoots of the Midway) that would lend a distinctive character to American culture as it evolved over the course of the twentieth century.

As tensions between the White City and the Midway Plaisance made clear, the World's Columbian Exposition reflected broader struggles in American society over the future course of American society and culture. Concerns about the power of the exposition to shape the future were also apparent in the struggles fought by AFRICAN AMERICANS and women over their representation at the fair.

The whiteness of the White City became increasingly offensive to African Americans as plans for the fair unfolded. In response to the determination of African Americans to show the world their accomplishments since emancipation, exposition directors insisted that African American proposals for exhibits be approved by all-white state committees. Most such requests were rejected out of hand. In response to requests from African Americans that they receive a role in planning the fair, exposition authorities appointed a St. Louis school principal to the position of alternate on the national commission. Enraged by the politics of exclusion and tokenism, some African Americans, led by Ida B. Wells, urged African Americans to boycott the fair. Frederick Douglass, who served as Haiti's representative at the exposition, disagreed and urged African Americans to participate as fully as possible. When exposition managers set aside a special "colored American" day (white ethnic groups had their own days as well), Douglass seized the occasion to insist that Americans live up to the Constitution and their promises of social justice for former slaves. But the fair, through its racist policies, had already helped pave the way for national acceptance of the separate-but-equal doctrine that would become the law of the land in 1896.

Since the act of Congress that originally awarded Chicago the fair mandated that a Board of Lady Managers be created as part of the exposition's governing structure, it was clear that white middle-class women would have more success than African Americans in securing measure of representation at the fair. But it was not clear how women would be represented. Some women argued that exhibits prepared by women should be displayed in the major exhibition palaces alongside those organized by men and judged accordingly. Others pressed and won their case that women should have a separate building for their exhibits. Bertha Honoré Palmer, president of the Board of Lady Managers, lent her considerable talents to organizing exhibits for the Woman's Building, which was designed by Boston architect Sophia Hayden and located near the point where the Midway Plaisance joined the main exposition grounds.

The World's Columbian Exposition defined American culture. Its World's Congress Auxiliary presented lectures and discussions by prominent political activists and intellectuals about subjects as wide-ranging and pressing as religion and science, labor, and women's rights. Historian Frederick Jackson Turner gave his famous paper on the significance of the frontier in American history to a meeting of historians held in conjunction with the fair. Henry Ford saw an internal combustion engine at the fair that fired his dreams about the possibility of designing a horseless carriage. For millions of visitors, the electrical illuminations of the fair were a source of wonder and excitement about the possibilities of illuminating America's farms and cities. Whether they saw the fair firsthand or experienced it through POSTCARDS or accounts in newspapers and magazines, most Americans regarded the World's Columbian Exposition as a cultural touchstone and remembered it for the rest of their lives.

Multiple tragedies marked the end of the fair. A smallpox EPIDEMIC that originated at the fair in midsummer spread throughout the city by early autumn. Then, just before the gala closing ceremonies were to be held, MAYOR Carter Harrison was assassinated. Finally, shortly after the fair's close, a fire swept through the fairgrounds, destroying many of the buildings.

The fair was gone, but not its influence. It lifted the spirits of over 20 million people who paid to visit the exposition just as the Panic of 1893 hit. Furthermore, many of the exhibits found their way into museums around the country, including the Smithsonian Institution and the Philadelphia Commercial Museum. Chicago's FIELD MUSEUM owed its origin to the fair and opened in 1894 in the former Palace of Fine Arts, a building that would later be reconstructed to become the MUSEUM OF SCIENCE AND INDUSTRY. And the building that had housed delegates to world's congresses would become the ART INSTITUTE OF CHICAGO. On another level, the triumph of the World's Columbian Exposition revivified the American world's fair movement and set a standard against which every subsequent exposition would be measured. Forty years later, the promoters of the CENTURY OF PROGRESS EXPOSITION made clear their indebtedness to the 1893 fair when they triggered the opening of their exposition with a beam of starlight that left Arcturus the same year that the World's Columbian Exposition had illuminated Chicago's skies.

Robert W. Rydell

See also: Architecture: The City Beautiful; Burnham Plan; Business of Chicago; Entertaining Chicagoans; Global Chicago; Racism, Ethnicity, and White Identity

Further reading: Badger, Reid. *The Great American Fair: The World's Columbian Exposition and American Culture.* 1979. • Harris, Neil, Wim de Wit, James Gilbert, and Robert Rydell. *Grand Illusions: Chicago's World's Fair of 1893.* 1993. • Rydell, Robert W. *All the World's a Fair: Visions of Empire at America's International Expositions, 1876–1916.* 1984.

World's Parliament of Religions.

While a reprise of the original World's Parliament of Religions in the centennial year of 1993 drew some attention, it was the one held during the WORLD'S COLUMBIAN EXPOSITION of 1893 that made history. Promoters of the exposition welcomed all kinds of satellite programs that helped bring people to Chicago, just as ambitious religionists took advantage of the crowds that came. The liberal Presbyterian minister John Henry Barrows was a major influence on the 17-day event. He saw the occasion as an opportunity to liberalize Christianity, encourage interreligious activities, and show forth the splendors of Jesus and the Christian faith. The Parliament's notable speakers included James Cardinal Gibbons for ROMAN CATHOLICISM, Isaac Mayer Wise for JUDAISM, Mary Baker Eddy for Christian Science, Annie Besant for Theosophy, and reformer Frances Willard. Some of the participants later toured the United States, striving to help establish or renew institutions connected with their religious outlooks.

Martin E. Marty

See also: Protestants; Religion, Chicago's Influence on

Further reading: Seager, Richard Hughes, ed. *Dawn of Religious Pluralism: Voices from the World's Parliament of Religions, 1893.* 1993. • Seager, Richard Hughes. *The World's Parliament of Religions: The East/West Encounter, Chicago, 1893.* 1995

Worth, IL,

Cook County, 16 miles SW of the Loop. Southwest of Chicago, Worth is bounded on the south by the Calumet-Sag Channel. Its early history is tied to that of ALSIP to the east and PALOS HILLS to the west. Its incorporation was simultaneous with that of CHICAGO RIDGE on its northern border.

At the end of the last glacial period, two great torrent valleys were shaped by the vast flow of water as the glaciers melted and receded. Today, the Cal-Sag Channel follows the path of one of these valleys. Part of the CALUMET RIVER is in the eastern part of this torrent valley, along with a tributary, Stony Creek. The western half contained the Saganashkee Slough, a huge swamp area that reached from the DES PLAINES RIVER eastward, at times reaching to the bend in the Calumet River (southeast of present-day BLUE ISLAND).

FRENCH explorers and traders traveling through the region in the seventeenth century used this route for a PORTAGE as an alternative to the South Branch of the CHICAGO RIVER. In the 1820s and 1830s, some Illinois legislators also considered this option in the planning for the ILLINOIS & MICHIGAN CANAL, but preferred to place the end of the great canal at Chicago rather than at the mouth of the Calumet River.

By 1848, the Calumet River had been dammed below Blue Island to divert some of its flow into a canal that fed WATER from Stony Creek and the Saganashkee Slough into the Illinois & Michigan Canal.

Permanent settlement began in the 1830s, and parts of Worth and Alsip grew in an area known as Lane's Island. Named for an early family, the area was higher ground between the Saganashkee Slough and Stony Creek. The community experienced small but steady growth through the second half of the nineteenth century, with both farming and other employment spurred by the establishment of a train stop for the Wabash, St. Louis & Pacific RAILROAD in 1882. A market center began to develop along what is now 111th Street to serve the farmers in the immediate area. A racetrack brought Chicagoans to Worth, and more commuters settled there.

In the period from 1911 to 1922, the Metropolitan Sanitary District constructed the Cal-Sag Channel connecting the Sanitary and Ship Canal with the Calumet region. This construction led to a boom in development and employment in Worth. To control growth and provide municipal services, the community voted to incorporate in 1914. The community took the township's name, which had been selected in 1850 to honor William Jenkins Worth, a general in the Mexican War.

From its start as a small village of 240 in 1920, Worth's population reached a plateau of more than 11,000 by 1970, and has become well integrated into the southwestern suburban fabric. Both historically and today, the heart of the village is found where the Wabash line intersects with Harlem Avenue and 111th Street.

Larry A. McClellan

See also: Glaciation; Horse Racing; Planning Chicago; Transportation

Further reading: "Some History of Lane's Island" and "The Bishop Family (and Store) of Worth, Illinois." In *Where the Trails Cross* 16.2 (Winter 1985). • "The Story of Worth: Fifty Years as a Village, 1914–1964." *Worth Palos Reporter,* August 27, 1964. • Andreas, A. T. *History of Cook County, Illinois.* 1884.

Wrestling.

Chicago's wrestling tradition began in 1887, at Battery D Armory, where Evan "Strangler" Lewis beat Jack Carkeek for the first recognized professional heavyweight wrestling championship in the United States. In 1911, 30,000 fans in COMISKEY PARK watched the most famous pro wrestler of the era, as world champion Frank Gotch beat challenger George Hackenschmidt. The city produced a national champ, Charlie Cutler, in 1914–15. During the 1920s, however, the pro sport developed into a mere exhibition, which attracted large crowds, notably at the Coliseum. From the 1930s through the 1950s, the CHICAGO STADIUM hosted famous matches featuring such pros as Gorgeous George and Jim Londos. Professional wrestling BROADCAST from the Marigold Gardens and the INTERNATIONAL AMPHITHEATER attracted an audience in the 1950s. In the suburbs, pro wrestlers competed at town fairs. Local professional wrestling essentially died out during the 1960s.

Amateur wrestling in the 1890s thrived in athletic clubs and colleges, which included wrestling matches as part of their athletic carnivals. After 1900, wrestling grew as a separate sport, under sponsorship of YMCAs, SETTLEMENT HOUSES, and ethnic clubs. The Chicago Hebrew Institute produced several national champions, notably 1920 Olympic medalist Fred Meyer. The GREEK Olympic Athletic Club and SWEDISH-American Athletic Association also had top teams. Chicago's PLAYGROUNDS began sponsoring a wrestling tourney for boys in 1911. A local organization, the Amateur Athletic Federation (AAF), for many years ran a citywide tournament.

The UNIVERSITY OF CHICAGO first competed in intercollegiate wrestling in 1910, NORTHWESTERN UNIVERSITY in 1915. The Chicago Public League introduced high-school competition in 1926, dominated for decades by Tilden Tech under coach Bob

Hicks. Proviso, in 1931, was the first suburban school to adopt the sport and under coach Lou Slimmer won many state titles after a state tournament was begun in 1937. Northwestern University sponsored a national high-school tournament in 1929–30. Chicago-area wrestling Olympians included Jack Riley (New Trier), Terry McCann (Schurz), and Bob Pickens (EVANSTON).

The Midlands Tournament, a premier college event, was founded in the Chicago area in 1963 and has been held at Northwestern University since 1972. The first U.S. Freestyle Senior Open was held at Northwestern in 1969, with the Mayor Daley Youth Foundation winning its first of five titles. Following the formation in 1970 of an amateur sponsoring group, the Illinois Kids Wrestling Federation, an extensive club program for all age groups blossomed in park districts, middle schools, and YMCAs, particularly in the suburbs.

Robert Pruter

See also: Armories; Creation of Chicago Sports; Fitness and Athletic Clubs; Leisure; Sports, High-School

Further reading: Chapman, Mike. *Encyclopedia of American Wrestling.* 1990. • Gems, Gerald R. "The Rise of Sport at a Jewish Settlement House." In *Sports and the American Jew,* ed. Steven A. Riess, 1998. • Sherrill, Rob. *Mat Madness: 60 Glorious Years of Illinois High School Wrestling.* 1996.

Wrigley Field, 1950. Photographer: Unknown. Source: Chicago Historical Society.

Wrigley Field. A mecca for BASEBALL fans, a Chicago landmark, and the heart of "Wrigleyville," fabled Wrigley Field originated in 1914 as home of the Chicago Whales in the short-lived Federal League. When that league folded in 1916, owner Charles Weeghman bought the National League Chicago CUBS, moving them from the West Side to his new ballpark at Clark and Addison Streets. Following purchase of the team by William Wrigley, Jr., in 1920, the park became Wrigley Field in 1926. A second deck was added in 1927–28; bleachers, the famous manually operated scoreboard, and ivy-covered outfield walls in 1937; and lights in 1988, 40 years after they were standard elsewhere.

Rich in legends, redolent with nostalgia, and superbly maintained, Wrigley Field is known nationwide as a site for baseball as it once was and as many would like it still to be: a game played on natural grass, chiefly in the daytime, in intimate surroundings that link players and fans, in a residential neighborhood rather than a sea of parking lots. Rumbling by the right-field stands, "L" trains link baseball with its yesterdays and the Cubs with their legions of North Side fans.

Successfully marketing "Beautiful Wrigley Field" and "The Friendly Confines" as an attractive place to spend a carefree afternoon in the sun, the Wrigleys and the TRIBUNE COMPANY (owners since 1981) have found it unnecessary in the modern era to mount a consistently good team. Built for baseball, the park proved an unsuitable home for football's Chicago BEARS, who played there until 1970. At the beginning of the twenty-first century, about to become the oldest ballpark in baseball, Wrigley Field had become a model for a new generation of baseball-only parks in other cities.

Richard H. Brown

See also: Comiskey Park; Creation of Chicago Sports; Lake View; Leisure; Places of Assembly

Further reading: Golenbock, Peter. *Wrigleyville: A Magical History Tour of the Chicago Cubs.* 1996. • Hartel, William. *A Day at the Park: In Celebration of Wrigley Field.* 1994. • Lowry, Philip J. *Green Cathedrals: The Ultimate Celebration of All 271 Major League and Negro League Ballparks Past and Present.* 1992.

Writers. *See* Journalism; Literary Careers; Literary Cultures

WTTW. *See* Public Broadcasting

WTUL. *See* Women's Trade Union League

Y

Yankees. Yankees, Americans of English descent via New England or New York, began moving to Chicago in the 1830s and infused it with a peculiar dynamism. For a century they dominated BANKING, INSURANCE, LAW, education, medicine, RAILROADS, merchandising, ARCHITECTURE, mainstream JOURNALISM, PHILANTHROPY, high society, and progressive reform. Their BUSINESS leadership required fashioning complex organizations of cooperating strangers that involved identifying talent, trusting expertise, and winning the confidence of investors back East, especially those from Boston. No city, not even Boston, was as attractive to ambitious young Yankees as Chicago, the destination of Walter Newberry in 1833, William Butler Ogden and Jonathan Scammon in 1835, John Wentworth in 1836, Charles Farwell in 1844, Stephen Douglas in 1847, Henry Farnam in 1850, Potter Palmer in 1852, George Pullman and Lyman Gage in 1855, Dwight Moody and Marshall Field in 1856, Mary Livermore and Frances Willard in 1857, Wilbur Storey in 1861, William LeBaron Jenney in 1868, John Root in 1871, Gustavus Swift in 1875, Lorado Taft in 1886, Frank Lowden, Frank Gunsaulus, Richard Sears, and Clarence Darrow in 1887, Jane Addams and Ellen Gates Starr in 1889, Charles Dawes in 1895, and L. Frank Baum in 1897. Others, like Daniel Burnham in 1855, came as children. In the 1890s a whole slew came with William Rainey Harper to the new UNIVERSITY OF CHICAGO.

Yankee POLITICAL CULTURE emphasized civic mindedness and encouraged organizations to abolish slavery, destroy the rebellion, uproot political corruption, install efficient civil service, and create SCHOOLS to identify and train the needed talent. The old Puritan strains, which called for temperance laws and saw the IRISH Catholics as the antithesis of Yankee values, provoked working-class and ethnically based political opposition that the overwhelming financial resources of the Yankees could never completely vanquish.

By the 1890s, Chicago's Yankees identified education as the key to uplifting the working class—and everyone else—to a higher stage of practical efficiency and political morality. Their triumph was the UNIVERSITY OF CHICAGO, designed and led by Yankees such as Harper, Harry Pratt Judson, James Tufts, Max Mason, and Robert Maynard Hutchins.

The Yankees were leaders in Chicago's Congregational, Methodist, and Baptist churches and were well represented in Presbyterian and Episcopalian ranks. Representative was Frank Lowden, an Iowa farm boy, graduate of NORTHWESTERN Law School and a leader of the bar. Marriage to Pullman's daughter brought him into the top ranks of business and POLITICS. Active in Central Church (where Gunsaulus, a Congregationalist, preached a modernized SOCIAL GOSPEL), he became a patron of the arts and worked tirelessly with his mostly Yankee friends and associates to promote the city and the state.

The golden era of the Yankees in Chicago peaked in the 1890s. After that some, including Baum, Dewey, and Lowden, left town, while low birth rates and a dearth of new arrivals from the northeast meant the Yankee factor would slowly diminish and merge through intermarriage. The University of Chicago brought newer Yankee arrivals, such as Edith Abbott in 1902 and her sister Grace in 1907, Paul Douglas in 1920, and Hutchins in 1929. What did not diminish was the sense of a Yankee ethic—values and virtues that remained deeply embedded in Chicago's leading institutions.

Richard Jensen

See also: Demography; Innovation, Invention, and Chicago Business; Prohibition and Temperance; Protestants

Further reading: Jensen, Richard J. *Illinois: A History.* 1978, 2001. • Schultz, Rima Lunin. "The Businessman's Role in Western Settlement: The Entrepreneurial Frontier, Chicago, 1833–1872." Ph.D. diss., Boston University. 1985.

A Yankee Recollection

When Judge Henry W. Blodgett arrived in Chicago as a young boy in 1831, his family located on the east branch of the DuPage River in what is now Naperville. Writing over 60 years later, Blodgett remembered that the Potawatomis lived in the country around his family:

> [T]he band of the tribe of which Half-Day or Ap-ta-ke-sic was the chief, had free range for hunting, trapping, and fishing over the territory between the Fox River and Lake Michigan extending north as far as, or further than where Racine is now located, and south nearly, if not quite, to the Kankakee River.
>
> The special hunting grounds of Ap-ta-ke-sic and the members of his family were upon the east branch of the DuPage, although their corn fields were on the Des Plaines River near the mouth of Indian Creek, not far from the site of the present village of Half Day in Lake County.
>
> It was not long after we got into our log cabin before we had visits from the old chief and members of his family, and my father being a blacksmith, had frequent calls to mend their traps and guns, so that we all became quite intimate with them. . . . At that time, Ap-ta-ke-sic was probably about forty-five or fifty years old. He was a man of fine figure and presence, over six feet in height, straight, well proportioned, with clear bright eyes and a pleasant face and manner.

Letter from Judge Henry W. Blodgett to Hon. A. H. Burley, Waukegan, January 23, 1893. Chicago Historical Society.

Yemenis. Yemenis have a rather small ethnic presence in Chicago, even within the metropolitan area's other Arab communities. The first immigrants possibly arrived in the late nineteenth century, but it is more probable that they arrived in the 1920s. Finding only low-status jobs in service enterprises like RESTAURANTS and LAUNDRIES and in factories, Yemeni immigrants had difficulty generating sufficient income to establish institutions or businesses or to maintain a viable community.

As late as the end of the twentieth century, there were few Yemeni-owned or -managed commercial establishments in Chicago. The small number that can be documented gathered along Lawrence Avenue between Kedzie and Pulaski. Here, as in other locations (such as Brooklyn, New York, and South Dearborn, Michigan), the first Yemeni-owned and -operated enterprises were COFFEE shops and liquor stores. Neither are characteristic of Yemeni culture, and it is likely that the coffee shops represent an economic activity borrowed from the larger and more affluent LEBANESE and PALESTINIAN communities. The range of economic activities which developed in other centers of Yemeni emigrants has not developed in Chicago.

Chicago never acquired a critical mass of Yemenis sufficient for it to become a preferred destination, like South Dearborn, Brooklyn, or California's San Joaquin Valley. By 1990, the census reported approximately 2,000 Yemenis in Chicago (many of whom were not permanent residents), and there is little reason to suspect any undercount.

Manfred Wenner

See also: Americanization; Demography; Multicentered Chicago

Further reading: "The Arab Population in the Chicago Metropolitan Area." Arab American Action Network. N.d. • Sabbagh, Georges, and Mehdi Bozorgmehr. "The Settlement of Yemeni Immigrants in the United States." In *Sojourners and Settlers: The Yemeni Immigrant Experience,* ed. Jonathan Friedlander, 1988. • Zanayed, Salameh. "The Arab Community in the Greater Chicago Area: A Demographical Study." Unpublished essay for the Chicago Commission on Human Relations Advisory Council on Arab Affairs. N.d.

YMCA. *See* Young Men's Christian Association

Yorkville, IL, Kendall County, 45 miles W of the Loop. Yorkville was settled permanently in 1836 but was not incorporated as a village until 1887. Located on the FOX RIVER, the city increased in local importance with the arrival of the Chicago, Burlington & Quincy

RAILROAD in 1870. Smaller retail stores satisfy the bulk of the community's contemporary economic needs and nearby AURORA provides employment for many of Yorkville's citizens.

Brandon Johnson

See also: Metropolitan Growth

Further reading: Farren, Kathy, ed. *A Bicentennial History of Kendall County, Illinois.* 1976. • Hicks, E. W. *History of Kendall County, Illinois: From the Earliest Discoveries to the Present Time.* 1877.

Young Men's Christian Association. The Chicago Young Men's Christian Association was founded in 1853 as an interdenominational PROTESTANT evangelical group devoted to the spiritual and social needs of young white-collar workers. In the 1860s and 1870s, under the leadership of evangelist Dwight Moody, the Y departed from its initial mission to young men and took on more general evangelical work, including noon prayer meetings for the public and the distribution of relief to the poor. The city's first YMCA building, Farwell Hall (1867), named after benefactor and dry-goods merchant John V. Farwell, contained a library and parlor for the use of its members but lacked the features for which the Y is best known: dormitories and a gymnasium. Instead, its revival hall and offices served as a center for practical Christian work in Chicago, housing such groups as the WOMEN'S CHRISTIAN TEMPERANCE UNION.

In 1879 special programs for young boys and a gymnasium and baths were introduced by popular demand. Tract distribution and relief work were dropped in favor of new, more popular methods of evangelism, including the employment of popular White Stockings star Billy Sunday as spiritual leader from 1883–1887.

These changes were spearheaded by a new set of leaders drawn from Chicago's mercantile elite, including James Houghteling, Cyrus H. McCormick, Jr., and John V. Farwell, Jr. In the last quarter of the nineteenth century, the organization grew in size and scope, establishing branch buildings for RAILROAD WORKERS at junctions (beginning 1879), for college students (1891), and for the general population on the West Side (1887) and in HYDE PARK (1895). Athletics became an integral part of the YMCA's character-building mission, and an expanded physical and athletic program included rental of an outdoor athletic ground and a BASEBALL park in the 1880s.

In 1893, construction began on a new 13-story building on LaSalle Street, the "Central" YMCA, which included a BOWLING alley, SWIMMING pool, and gymnasium. Young white migrants could find rooms at the YMCA HOTEL (1916), located just south of the LOOP.

In the 1910s the YMCA began to offer English classes and AMERICANIZATION programs and worked with industry leaders like Sears, Roebuck to provide recreation facilities for its workers. Although racial discrimination in public accommodations was illegal in Illinois, the YMCA claimed that custom demanded separate facilities for blacks and whites. With seed money from Sears executive Julius Rosenwald, the AFRICAN AMERICAN community erected a building on South Wabash Street in 1913 that served as the welcoming center for newcomers, offering temporary accommodation, job placement, and other services.

During the 1920s, the YMCA planned an expansion campaign that would put a modern, fully equipped building with residences, gymnasium, and educational facilities in every city neighborhood; and the camping program for boys, initiated as early as 1899, acquired its first permanent facilities, including Camp Hasting (1923) in Lake County and Camp Martin Johnson (1925) in Michigan. In this period, the Chicago Y's initial programs in business education blossomed, resulting in the creation of a formalized, accredited program known as the Central YMCA College, which later became the basis for ROOSEVELT UNIVERSITY. Chicago also became a national center of education for Y staff workers with the construction of a training school, later named George Williams College (1915), on the SOUTH SIDE.

Although the GREAT DEPRESSION placed a severe strain on YMCA resources, new branches were established and school and camp programs were often offered without charge. Membership became more inclusive; in 1931 the requirement for affiliation with an evangelical church was dropped, and by 1933 women were admitted on an equal basis. The Protestant faith remained central to the YMCA's programs until 1947, when leaders enacted a policy designed to encourage people of all faiths to practice the customs of their own religions.

In the postwar years the Y again adapted to changing conditions, renaming itself the YMCA of Metropolitan Chicago to describe its changing role as both an urban social welfare agency and a middle-class suburban athletic center. Several inner-city branches were refashioned to tackle UNEMPLOYMENT and HOMELESSNESS. In the suburbs, the Metropolitan Y recognized the need of growing communities for family-based activity centers and built seven new buildings in the 1950s. These branches, tied administratively to the city, differed from the independent suburban Ys established in the early twentieth century. The post–World War II suburban expansion of the YMCA of Metropolitan Chicago was part of a concerted effort to address the region's social, physical, educational, and spiritual needs as a whole.

Paula R. Lupkin

See also: Religious Institutions; Settlements, Religious; Social Services

Further reading: Dedmon, Emmett. *Great Enterprises: 100 Years of the YMCA of Metropolitan Chicago.* 1957. • Hopkins, Howard C. *History of the YMCA in North America.* 1951. • Lupkin, Paula. "A Temple of Practical Christianity." *Chicago History* 24 (Fall 1995): 22–41.

Young Women's Christian Association. In 1876, a group of female reformers established the Young Women's Christian Association of Chicago to promote the religious, moral, and intellectual welfare of young self-supporting women. The reformers' concerns were safe provisions and moral guardianship. Yet the association circumscribed its initial membership according to race and religion. In 1877, the association refused to admit AFRICAN AMERICAN women. It later discriminated against JEWISH and Catholic applicants.

By the 1890s, the expansion of services necessitated larger accommodations, which included a library, gymnasium, employment bureau, auditorium, and over 180 sleeping rooms. Although the association served both permanent and transient boarders, it attempted to create a homelike setting in which young women could engage in edifying recreations. Concerned about the dangers of low wages, commercial amusements, and opportunistic men, the YWCA established literary societies, LECTURE series, Bible study, glee clubs, and classes.

Older women volunteered for the association's Travelers' Aid, which assisted young girls at the train stations. Although they provided lunches, medical care, and even money, their primary intent was rescue and protective work. It was not until 1912, however, that they assisted African American girls, whom they referred to African American women. African American women established their own YWCA in 1915.

During the 1920s, the Ys began their own democratic experiments, offering classes in citizenship as well as expanding board representation to the girls. Some girls also attended the summer industrial class at Bryn Mawr College in Pennsylvania. Nonetheless, accommodations at Chicago's four YWCA residencies varied tremendously by the late 1920s. The most luxurious residence, the Harriet Hammond McCormick YWCA, had laundry facilities, a SWIMMING pool, and beauty parlor. Some girls could not afford the cost of this YWCA, which was more expensive than many BOARDINGHOUSES.

Although the Chicago YWCAs emphasized world fellowship in the 1930s and 1940s, they grappled with segregated residencies and summer camps. Competing concepts of integration continued through the late 1950s.

Anne Meis Knupfer

See also: Americanization; Jewish Community Centers; Religious Institutions; Settlement Houses; Social Services

Further reading: Bycer, Alene Merle. "The Voluntary Association in Transition: A Case Study of the YWCA of Metropolitan Chicago." Ph.D. diss., University of Chicago. 1981. • Meyerowitz, Joanne J. *Women Adrift: Independent Wage Earners in Chicago, 1880–1930.* 1988. • Mjagkij, Nina, and Margaret Spratt, eds. *Men and Women Adrift: The YMCA and the YWCA in the City.* 1997.

Youth Clubs. *See* Clubs: Youth Clubs

Yugoslavians. Beginning in the last half of the nineteenth century, significant numbers of South Slavic migrants from Croatia, Serbia, Slovenia, Bosnia, Macedonia, and Montenegro arrived in Chicago. From 1918 (the year the Treaty of Versailles created the Kingdom of SERBS, Croats, and SLOVENES) to 1991 (the year Yugoslavia disintegrated), these immigrants were lumped together and labeled Yugoslavian by a U.S. government supportive of Yugoslav nationalism. As well, non-Slavic Chicagoans unable to differentiate the various ethnicities often used the term. However, pre-1918 immigrants had already built substantial ethnic communities in Chicago, and post-1918 migrants retained their separate ethnic identities. They rarely self-identified as Yugoslavian. Those who came to the United States often did so to escape the various Yugoslav regimes and therefore had little interest in Yugoslav nationalism. A handful of institutions on Chicago's Southwest Side, including the Yugoslav Hall, attempted to serve as a gathering point for both SERBS and CROATIANS and had some success until the early 1990s. Between 1991 and 1995, when independence movements broke apart Yugoslavia, tensions among Chicago's South Slavic communities increased, though not to the point of violence.

D. Bradford Hunt

See also: Bosnians; Macedonians

YWCA. *See* Young Women's Christian Association

Z

Zambians. The first Zambians in Chicago probably came as students in the 1970s and 1980s. After Zambian independence in 1964, the government began to send large numbers of students to Europe and the United States for education. While many returned to Zambia, others settled permanently, and when the economic situation deteriorated in Zambia in the mid-1980s they encouraged friends and family to emigrate. Most Zambians emigrated to Europe, particularly Great Britain, although several hundred settled in the United States and established small communities in Washington DC, Chicago, New York, New Jersey, and Indiana. The Zambian community in metropolitan Chicago, estimated by community members to be at 90, is thus one of the largest in the United States.

Most Zambians in Chicago migrated in the mid to late 1990s and were drawn directly to Chicago by networks of family and friends. The Chicago Zambian population is generally young and well educated; most are under the age of 35 and nearly all are high-school graduates, while many also have some college education. Some migrants face obstacles in obtaining jobs commensurate with their level of education because the United States does not recognize their degrees obtained at home. Others have a difficult time because of their legal status and as a result take odd jobs, drive TAXIS, or work in childcare. Many Zambians live on the North Side of the city, particularly in the ROGERS PARK neighborhood, while some have settled in the suburbs of MOUNT PROSPECT, DES PLAINES, and WILLOWBROOK.

In 1997, Zambians in Chicago formed the organization Pamodzi, which means "together" in Nyanja, a common Zambian language. Pamodzi offers aid to community members and serves as a social and cultural center bringing the community together for social events and holidays, including Christmas, New Year's, and Independence Day. For the Independence Celebration, held on October 24, community members pool their resources to rent a hall for music, food, and dancing, and they invite other groups of Africans and Europeans to join them. In its first few years, Pamodzi hosted several social events which sought to bring Zambians together with Americans and other immigrant groups in Chicago. In addition to the important role it plays as a social and cultural center of the Zambian community, Pamodzi offers assistance to recent migrants and raises money to help cover the cost of funerals.

Tracy Steffes

See also: Demography; Multicentered Chicago

Zimbabweans. The first major wave of Zimbabwean migration arrived in Chicago during and after the War for Independence in the 1970s. The changing political and economic situation prompted many white Zimbabwean families to migrate first to South Africa and Britain and then increasingly to the United States and Australia. In the United States, Zimbabweans were drawn to the warmer climates of the South and to regions with established SOUTH AFRICAN communities. These early migrants share a distinct cultural identity, many of them identifying as Rhodesians and claiming a cosmopolitan heritage inflected with British influences. While some maintain contact with the United States branch of Rhodesians Worldwide, which circulates a newsletter and meets once a year, this group has been slow to organize as a community in Chicago and meets only occasionally for speakers or holidays, including the Unilateral Declaration of Independence Day (November 11).

A second and distinct group of Zimbabwean students began to migrate to Chicago in the 1980s and has increased in number in the 1990s. Zimbabwe boasts a high literacy rate and good primary-school system but has a limited and extremely competitive university system, which has prompted many Zimbabweans to seek educational opportunities abroad, particularly in business and technical fields like engineering and information technology. While earlier student migrants generally returned home after completing their degrees, more students in the 1990s chose to remain in the United States because of the economic situation in Zimbabwe and the job opportunities available here. Some have been joined by family members and friends, but the majority of Zimbabweans remain students and young professionals, both black and white. This group is not organized formally but tends to gather socially for SOCCER, parties, and cultural events like Zimbabwean musical performances at summer festivals.

The generational and cultural differences, combined with the small number and geographical dispersion of Zimbabweans, have made it difficult for Zimbabweans in Chicago to find one another and organize as a single community. Some efforts have been made to organize meetings and holiday events in order to build a social basis for more formal organizing, but these efforts have been only modestly successful and reached only a small part of the estimated 80–100 Zimbabweans in the area. Many Zimbabweans in Chicago maintain close ties with the large and well-organized community in Indianapolis which holds annual Independence Day celebrations (April 18) and other events, including the first Annual Zimbabwe Business Convention and Exposition in 2002, which drew Zimbabweans from around the region.

Tracy Steffes

See also: Demography; Ethnic Music; Multicentered Chicago

Zion, IL, Lake County, 41 miles N of the Loop. On New Year's Day 1900, John Alexander Dowie announced to the church he had established in 1896, the Christian Catholic

Apostolic Church, that he planned to build a utopian city on a tract of land at the extreme northeastern edge of Illinois. When Zion City was incorporated in 1902, 5,000 inhabitants joined the Christian utopia. Named after the mountain upon which Jerusalem was built, Zion City was to be communitarian and theocratic, a place of Christian cooperation, racial harmony, and strict fundamentalist morals.

Born in Scotland in 1847, Dowie came to the United States from Australia in 1888 and settled in Chicago in 1893 near the site of the WORLD'S COLUMBIAN EXPOSITION. In accord with reform efforts that swept through many American cities in the last part of the nineteenth century, Dowie desired that Zion City be free of crime and VICE. Dowie instituted the "Zion City Lease," which forbade GAMBLING, theaters, and circuses, as well as the manufacture and sale of alcohol and tobacco. In addition, the lease banned pork, dancing, swearing, spitting, politicians, doctors, oysters, and tan-colored shoes. Whistling on Sunday was punishable by jail time. Dowie especially opposed alcohol, having signed the temperance pledge at age six, and into the late twentieth century, Zion City remained "dry." The ban against medical doctors reflected Dowie's belief in "divine healing." Many of the original settlers in Zion City, primarily of DUTCH, GERMAN, and IRISH origin, had been attracted to the community because of Dowie's reputation as a "faith healer."

Initially, some 25 businesses and commercial interests jump-started Zion City's economy, providing work for the people who moved there from around the world. The Zion DEPARTMENT STORE and the factory of Zion Lace Industries together employed as many as 3,000 workers. But by 1905 Zion's local economy was in shambles. Despite new leadership after Dowie's death in 1907, industry never flourished in Zion City. Commonwealth Edison, which constructed two nuclear plants in Zion in 1973 and 1974, closed, both plants by 1998, after a history of safety and maintenance problems.

Despite the lack of industry and low level of employment in Zion City, the population increased steadily throughout the century. Zion City grew from 17,268 in 1970 to 22,866 in 2000. Although there had been only a small AFRICAN AMERICAN population in Zion City through much of the twentieth century, by the late 1990s blacks made up nearly 30 percent of Zion's population.

In 1987 the Illinois chapter of American Atheists filed suit against Zion City, citing that its city seal, which contained a cross, a dove, and the phrase "God Reigns," was unconstitutional. In 1992 the U.S. Supreme Court upheld a lower court decision that the city seal violated the principle of separation of church and state and that the Christian symbolism must be removed. Ironically, Zion City officials succeeded in incorporating the words "In God We Trust" on the new city seal, because the phrase was deemed acceptable religious language in the public arena.

Wallace Best

See also: Flags and Symbols; Prohibition and Temperance; Protestants; Religious Geography; Suburbs and Cities as Dual Metropolis; Sunday Closings

Further reading: Bateman, Newton, and Paul Selby, eds. *Historical Encyclopedia of Illinois and History of Lake County.* 1902. • Cook, Philip L. *Zion City, Illinois: Twentieth Century Utopia.* 1996. • Halsey, John J., ed. *A History of Lake County Illinois.* 1912.

Zionism. Chicago's Zionists claim the first organized Zionist group in the United States, the Chicago Zion Society (later the Knights of Zion), which first met in 1895. Although the Knights resisted affiliation with the Federation of American Zionists, they finally joined a national umbrella organization in 1918, when the Zionist Organization of America was created by Louis Brandeis and Judge Julian Mack of Chicago.

Bernard Horwich, the first president of the Knights of Zion and a leader long into the 1930s, was a proponent of this new organization, which was dedicated to the compatibility of Jewish nationalism and Americanism and also provided a unified fundraising framework. Other, more radical Zionists in Chicago chose to affiliate separately in organizations such as the *Poalei Tzion* (Workers of Zion). While numerically small, these organizations and their leaders continued to exert influence on Zionist policy in America and abroad. Golda Meir, a member of the regional *Poalei Tzion,* went on to become prime minister of Israel.

In the early period, Zionism faced opposition within Jewish Communities from both Orthodox and Reform leaders, including Rabbi Emil Hirsch of the Chicago Sinai Congregation. That opposition began to fade with the establishment of the state of Israel in 1948 and all but disappeared in the wake of the Six Day War in 1967.

Adam H. Stewart

See also: Fenianism; Israelis; Jews; Nation of Islam, The; Polish National Alliance

Further reading: Cutler, Irving. *The Jews of Chicago: From Shtetl to Suburb.* 1997. • Fishbein, J. I., ed. *The Sentinel's History of Chicago Jewry, 1911–1986.* 1986. • Siegel, Beverly. "Chicago's Zionist Romance." *JUF News,* 1997, 6–11.

Zoning. Controls on LAND USE in Chicago began during the mid-nineteenth century in response to concerns over PUBLIC HEALTH and safety. Although the city adopted the nation's first comprehensive BUILDING CODE after the FIRE OF 1871 and adopted nuisance laws to protect residents from some of the most onerous land-use problems, these measures did not provide adequate protection to residents. The city adopted an ordinance placing a height limit of 130 feet on downtown buildings in 1893 and gradually put into place a set of laws known as frontage consent ordinances. These ordinances, based on nuisance doctrines, required that the majority of residential owners on a block provide consent before certain land uses would be permitted. They were applicable only along blocks where two-thirds of the property was in residential use.

By the early 1910s, city officials were looking for more comprehensive ways to address concerns related to aesthetics and property values. After New York City adopted a citywide zoning ordinance in 1916, attention turned toward the possibility of a similar ordinance for Chicago. The city formed a Zoning Commission that year and in 1919 passed the Glackin Law, named after state senator Edward Glackin, which gave municipalities the authority to regulate land use if they had the approval of neighborhood property owners. If 40 percent approved the zoning plan, the municipality could formulate a zoning ordinance appropriate for the neighborhood. The state repealed the Glackin Law in 1921 and replaced it with a new state zoning-enabling act drafted by the zoning committee of the Chicago REAL ESTATE Board. The city adopted its first zoning ordinance in 1923.

The national zoning movement crossed an important legal milestone in 1926, when the Supreme Court issued its seminal ruling in *Village of Euclid (Ohio) v. Ambler Realty Company,* which affirmed a municipality's right to practice zoning. As it was first prescribed, zoning was envisioned as a tool primarily to protect the health and safety of residents of single-family homes. As time progressed, policymakers broadened the scope of zoning to protect other types of property and to manage issues related to property values, aesthetics, buildings and sites, and the environment.

The 1923 ordinance proved insufficient to handle the growing complexity of the city and was criticized for allowing nonconforming uses (land uses in violation of the ordinance) to continue. Although the ordinance was revised in 1942, dramatic changes, most notably the rise in automobile travel, necessitated a broad reassessment of the city's zoning policy. The product of this reassessment, the 1957 zoning ordinance, marked a critical moment in city PLANNING history and became nationally known for its emphasis on floor-area ratios, industrial performance standards, and other "scientific" measures to assess the desirability of developments.

The 1957 ordinance, created through the leadership of Harry F. Chaddick, the city's zoning director, played an enormous role in helping manage development in Chicago for more than 40 years. It included, for example, provisions for planned developments (or planned unit developments) that gave developers of larger projects substantially more flexibility than could be provided through conventional zoning. These provisions were gradually refined during the 1960s and proved instrumental to hundreds of development projects.

Over the next several decades, community involvement in zoning decisions gradually increased, and the city adopted several supplemental measures, including the Landmark Preservation Ordinance (1968), Lakefront Protection Ordinance (1973), a Townhouse Standards amendment (1998), and the Strip-Center Ordinance (1999). Although the city attempted to modernize the entire ordinance, these efforts were frustrated by the enormity of the task and the politically sensitive nature of this undertaking. Many felt the 1957 ordinance was too permissive with respect to high-density development.

In response to mounting concerns and a boom in residential construction, the city launched its long-anticipated initiative to overhaul its zoning ordinance on July 26, 2000. Mayor Richard M. Daley appointed a 21-member commission, the Zoning Reform Commission, to rewrite the ordinance. By 2004, the city council approved the text portion of the new ordinance, which included a variety of new regulations to enhance neighborhood aesthetics and encourage the development of pedestrian-oriented environments. That same year, the city began the difficult task of revising the zoning maps.

Zoning is also almost universally practiced in suburban communities. In more than 90 percent of municipalities in COOK, DUPAGE, and LAKE COUNTIES, zoning is established in accordance with a comprehensive plan, which outlines a municipality's goals and concerns for the quality of life. Although Chicago has many neighborhood and area plans to guide zoning decisions, it does not presently have a comprehensive plan.

Joseph P. Schwieterman
Dana Caspall

Suburban Zoning

Zoning practices in suburban areas of northern Illinois have shifted from agricultural county zoning to municipal incorporated zoning as development has spread outward from Chicago. Most northern Illinois municipalities use master plans as guides to their development and redevelopment.

For example, in NAPERVILLE the 1985 Master Land Use Plan (revised 1994) has guided development at the intersection of Route 59 and 95th Street. Although the Naperville and Aurora city limits were not far away, the four corners housed only a small church and remained essentially agricultural until the late 1990s. As outlined in the 1994 plan, the four corners of the intersection were slated for future commercial use, but they were actually zoned commercial only after the property was annexed to the city of Naperville. Two of the corners gained large shopping centers, each with a grocery store. The church soon relocated, giving way to a gas station, a tire store, and a fast-food outlet. The farm surrounding the church became town houses. The remaining corner was still planned for commercial use according to the 2002 revision to the Naperville Master Plan.

Judith Brodhead

See also: Building Codes; Built Environment of the Chicago Region; Planning Chicago

Further reading: Bosselman, Fred P. "The Commodification of 'Nature's Metropolis': The Historical Context of Illinois' Unique Zoning Standards." *Northern Illinois Law Review* 12 (Summer 1992): 545–546. • Caspall, Dana, and Joseph Schwieterman. *The Politics of Place: A History of Zoning in Chicago.* 2003. • King, Andrew J. *Law and Land Use in Chicago: A Prehistory of Modern Zoning.* 1976.

Zoroastrians. At the opening of the twenty-first century, approximately seven hundred Chicagoans were practicing the religion of Zoroastrianism, founded by the prophet Zoroaster (or Zarathustra) in ancient Persia, modern-day Iran. At least three-fourths were INDIAN and PAKISTANI immigrants and their children; most of the rest were IRANIAN.

Perhaps the first local Zoroastrian resident was a university student in the 1930s who stayed for employment. More students followed in the 1940s–1960s. In 1965, 30 local residents formed the Zoroastrian Association of America, conceiving it as a national organization, but it ceased functioning after a few years.

The number of Zoroastrian immigrants increased significantly after the liberalization of U.S. immigration laws in 1965. Another attempt at organizing the local community began with monthly meetings in 1974, first in homes, then at a Unitarian church in west suburban HINSDALE. This culminated in 1975 in the establishment of the Zoroastrian Association of Metropolitan Chicago. One of the association's first tasks was to purchase burial lots for the community in Elm Lawn CEMETERY in west suburban ELMHURST. Another important early task was to build a *darbe mehr* (worship center); the resulting facility opened in Hinsdale in 1983 with the distinction of being the first in North America constructed specifically as a *darbe mehr.*

The Zoroastrian Association of Metropolitan Chicago has played an important role in the institutional development of the North American Zoroastrian community, regularly hosting major conferences in Chicago. Representatives from Zoroastrian associations across North America met in Chicago in 1986 to form an umbrella organization, legally incorporated in the state of Illinois in 1987 as the Federation of Zoroastrian Associations of North America. The federation's first president was a leader of the Zoroastrian Association of Metropolitan Chicago.

Paul D. Numrich

See also: Religion, Chicago's Influence on; World's Parliament of Religions

Further reading: Lieblich, Julia. "1 of oldest religions, 1 of smallest." *Chicago Tribune,* July 8, 2002. • Williams, Raymond Brady. *Religions of Immigrants from India and Pakistan: New Threads in the American Tapestry.* 1988.

DICTIONARY OF LEADING CHICAGO BUSINESSES, 1820–2000

Mark R. Wilson was the principal compiler, with additional contributions from Steven R. Porter and Janice L. Reiff. Individual entries by other authors are credited at the end of the entry.

This dictionary provides brief summaries of the histories of leading private, for-profit business firms in the Chicago area from the 1820s through the end of the twentieth century.

WHICH COMPANIES APPEAR IN THIS DICTIONARY, AND WHY?

Only a small fraction of the business firms that have ever existed in the Chicago area are listed below. Tens of thousands of businesses—including restaurants, hair salons, real-estate firms, and many other important kinds of enterprises—do not appear here, simply because they were never large enough to rank among the area's largest or most distinctive businesses. Companies were included in the dictionary on the basis of several criteria. One of the primary measures used here has been local employment: those companies that employed more workers in the Chicago area, some not headquartered here, are more likely to appear. Longevity was also considered: those firms with a considerable presence in the area for many years were given special consideration. The composition of the dictionary also reflects companies' relative importance within their industries. That is, firms that ranked among the national or global leaders in their fields are more likely to appear, even if the story told in the dictionary emphasizes the Chicago part of the firm's history. Finally, the availability of information about a given company also influenced the shape of the dictionary.

UNDER WHICH NAME IS A GIVEN COMPANY LISTED, AND TO WHAT EXTENT ARE NAMES CROSS-REFERENCED?

This dictionary is organized alphabetically. Because companies tend to change their names frequently over time, it is not always possible to describe a given firm with a single title that was used throughout its history. Whenever possible, this dictionary adopts the policy of using the *name that lasted the longest* during the period that the firm was a leading Chicago company. If a given company ranked as one of the area's leading firms under more than one name, cross-references guide the reader to the complete entry, which appears under the longest-lasting name (as of the year 2003). For example, both the McCormick Harvesting Machine Co. and Navistar International Corp. were major Chicago companies in their own right, so they are both listed alphabetically in the dictionary; but both are followed by "see International Harvester Co." because International Harvester lasted for over 80 years, longer than either McCormick or Navistar. Whenever possible, a company's name changes over time are noted within its entry. Another potentially confusing problem occurs when companies use both the given names and family names of their founders. In this dictionary, such firms are listed alphabetically under *the last (family) name of the individual.* For example, Marshall Field & Co., founded by a real person named Marshall Field, appears as Field (Marshall) & Co. Any reader who fails to find a company in the alphabetical listings may consult the Encyclopedia's general index, which provides page references to names that appear anywhere in the volume, including the dictionary.

A

Abbott Laboratories

Chicago physician Wallace C. Abbott founded the Abbott Alkoloidal Co. in 1900. Abbott's experiments with the manufacture of alkaloid drugs and antiseptics proved successful, and the company's annual sales rose from about $200,000 in 1905 to $2 million by 1923. Renamed Abbott Laboratories in 1915, in 1920 the company moved to a new headquarters in North Chicago. In the mid-1930s, Abbott employed about 750 men and women in the Chicago area. Sales of anesthetics such as "Nembutal" and "Pentothal" drove annual sales up to $12 million by 1939. The company continued to grow during World War II, when it was one of the first mass-producers of penicillin. After the war, annual sales grew from about $100 million in the mid-1950s to $1 billion in the 1970s. The company built new headquarters in Abbott Park (in Lake County) during the 1960s. As Abbott continued to expand, the number of its Chicago-area employees grew from about 1,400 in the mid-1970s to roughly 10,000 by the late 1980s. During the 1980s and 1990s, the company pioneered blood tests for HIV, as well as drugs designed to combat AIDS; it also made a variety of other drugs and products, including infant formula. By 2002, Abbott's annual sales exceeded $16 billion and it employed roughly 17,000 Chicago-area residents, accounting for slightly less than a quarter of its global workforce.

Ace Hardware Corp.

Ace was created 1924 in Chicago by Richard Hesse and other Chicago hardware dealers who wanted to provide a centralized purchasing organization to supply their stores and others. The company was incorporated in 1928 as Ace Stores Inc. Its retail network expanded to hundreds of dealers by 1949, when annual sales reached about $10 million. After Hesse retired in 1973, Ace was sold to its retail dealers, and the headquarters moved to suburban Oak Brook. By 2002, the dealer-owned cooperative cleared about $3 billion in annual sales, supplied a network of over 5,000 retail stores in all 50 states and more than 60 countries, and employed about 1,000 Chicago-area residents.

Acme Steel Co.

The Acme Flexible Clasp Co. was founded in Chicago in 1884. In 1899, the company merged with the Quincy Hardware Manufacturing Co. of Quincy, Illinois, a manufacturer of barbed steel staples led by James E. MacMurray. The new company, based in Chicago, changed its name to the Acme Steel Goods Co. in 1907; in 1925, it became Acme Steel Co. By the mid-1930s (during the Great Depression), Acme employed about 1,400 Chicago-area residents. A new plant opened in Riverdale, Illinois, in 1918; by the end of the 1950s, when annual sales of well over $100 million placed Acme among the top 300 industrial corporations in the United States, the move from Chicago to Riverdale was complete. In 1964, Acme merged with the Interlake Iron Corp., a Cleveland-based company that owned plants in Chicago, to form the Interlake Steel Corp. In the mid-1970s, as its annual sales approached $700 million, Interlake had 3,500 workers in the Chicago area. A new Acme spun off from Interlake in 1986. The company had trouble staying afloat and employed only about 1,200 local residents by the end of the 1990s, a number that fell as a phased shutdown was begun in 2001. In 2002, the International Steel Group, organized by WL Ross & Co. LLC, bought the shuttered and bankrupt Acme Steel and reopened it as ISG Riverdale Inc., a sheet minimill employing about 200 workers.

Admiral Corp.

Admiral was a medium-sized manufacturer of consumer electronics goods and electric appliances during the late 1930s, when its annual sales were about $2 million. Led by Ross D. Siragusa, the company grew rapidly during the 1940s and 1950s, selling thousands of televisions manufactured at plants in Chicago. By the beginning of the 1960s, when annual sales approached $300 million, the company employed 8,500 people, many of them Chicago-area residents. Like many American electronics manufacturers, Admiral found it difficult to withstand foreign competition during the 1960s and 1970s. By the 1980s, the remnants of Admiral were owned by Maytag, an Iowa-based manufacturer of appliances.

Alberto-Culver Co.

In 1955, Leonard and Bernice Lavin bought Alberto-Culver Co. from Blaine Culver and moved it from Los Angeles to Chicago. Before the move, Alberto-Culver already had become a leading supplier of hair care products to the entertainment industry. The company built a new plant and headquarters in Melrose Park in 1960, and annual sales of products such as shampoos and deodorants rose from $25 million in 1961 to $100 million in 1964. In 1969, the company bought a 10-store retail chain called "Sally Beauty," which would grow over the next 30 years to a network of over 2,000 stores. By 2002, still based in Melrose Park, Alberto-Culver grossed about $2.6 billion in annual sales and employed about 1,400 people in the Chicago area and almost 17,000 worldwide.

Allstate Corp.

The Allstate Insurance Co. was created by Sears, Roebuck in 1931 after a friend suggested to Sears head Robert Wood that his company should sell auto insurance. Allstate soon became one of its parent company's fastest growing and most profitable divisions. In its first year, the company had a staff of about 20 people. Fifty years later, still a part of Sears, Allstate employed over 40,000 people around the world. The widely recognized slogan "You're in good hands with Allstate" first was used in 1950. The company began to offer life insurance during the 1950s, and the auto insurance business continued to boom. In 1967, Allstate's headquarters moved to suburban Northbrook. During the 1970s and 1980s, when many of Sears' operations faltered, Allstate remained profitable. In 1995, Allstate finally spun off from Sears. At the beginning of the twenty-first century, Allstate continued to be a U.S. insurance industry leader. With nearly $100 billion in assets, Allstate employed close to 10,000 people in the Chicago area and over 40,000 nationwide. *See also* SEARS, ROEBUCK & CO.

American Airlines Inc.

American Airlines has never been based in Chicago, but by the late twentieth century, it had become a leading employer in the region. In 1930 several small companies merged to form the American Airways Co., based in New York; it became American Airlines four years later. The company's headquarters moved to Dallas in 1979, and in 1982 its official name became AMR Corp. One of the world's leading passenger airlines, American employed about 3,500 Chicago-area residents by the early 1970s; during the late 1990s, when annual revenues stood at about $20 billion, it had as many as 12,000 workers in the area. Despite substantial layoffs in the aftermath of September 11, 2001, American employed approximately the same number of Chicago-area employees in 2002.

American Biscuit & Manufacturing Co.

See National Biscuit Co.

American Brake Shoe & Foundry Co.

See IC Industries Inc.

American Can Co.

This container industry giant was created in 1901 through the merger of dozens of plants around the country, including some in the Chicago area. Although it was not headquartered in Chicago, American Can became an important actor in the local economy during the early twentieth century. From the beginning of the century through the 1970s, the company employed thousands of men and women (the local workforce stood at about 2,700 in 1934 and 3,000 in 1974) at several plants around the city. During the final decades of the century, American Can diversified, became less important as a local employer, and eventually ceased to exist as an independent entity.

American Car & Foundry Co.

The firm of Wells, French & Co., which made railroad cars and bridges, was established in Chicago in 1866. By the early 1870s, with about 300 workers, the annual output of its plant on Blue Island Avenue surpassed $1 million. By 1880, Wells, French & Co. employed more than 400 men. In 1899, Wells, French & Co. was one of about a dozen American railway equipment producers that merged into the new American Car & Foundry Co., which had offices in Chicago but was headquartered in New York City. During the early 1900s, American Car employed about 1,500 people at its Chicago facilities, which specialized in the making of rail loaders, snowplows, and graders. American Car, like many firms in the railroad industry, suffered from the rise of the automobile and the airplane; the Chicago plant closed in 1950.

American Fur Co.

The American Fur Co., founded in New York in 1808 by John Jacob Astor, was the first big business enterprise to operate in Chicago. Between 1817, when the company first sent traders to Chicago, and 1832, American Fur was the most important economic institution in the tiny town. Several of the company's Chicago employees during the 1820s, including John Kinzie, John Crafts, Jean Beaubien,

Gurdon S. Hubbard, and Archibald Clybourn, became Chicago's most prominent citizens in the years that followed. Soon after Astor sold the company in 1834, its Chicago operations closed.

American Hospital Supply Corp.
American Hospital Supply Corp. descended from a hospital supply distribution company and was incorporated in 1922 in Illinois by Foster G. McGaw. It came to dominate its industry in the 1930s and '40s by changing the way hospital supplies were marketed. Eventually distributing both its own supplies and those of other companies to 19 of 20 hospitals in America, the company manufactured a range of products from intravenous solutions to uniforms. Its sales grew from $65 million in 1956 to nearly $200 million by 1965, at which time it was based in Evanston and had 6,200 employees nationwide. By the early 1970s, the company employed 2,500 workers locally. American Hospital Supply's sales revenue grew from $2 billion in 1979 to more than $3.4 billion in 1984. The next year, competitor Baxter Travenol Laboratories, a firm whose supplies American Hospital once distributed, acquired the company. In 1995, Baxter spun off its low-tech hospital supply division as an independent company, called Allegiance Corp. Allegiance was subsequently purchased by Cardinal Health Inc. of Ohio in 1998. *See also* BAXTER TRAVENOL LABORATORIES INC.

American Steel Foundries
This company was created in 1902 by the merger of eight separate foundries, including the American Steel Foundry Co. of Granite City, Illinois (near St. Louis), and the business of George M. Sargent, then based in the Chicago suburb of Englewood. The company's headquarters moved to Chicago in 1905. Over the next several decades, it operated large plants at East Chicago and Hammond, Indiana; the latter facility had about 2,600 workers during the 1930s. During World War II, the company produced about a quarter of the cast armor made in the United States. In 1962, when its name became Amsted Industries, the privately held company bested $100 million in annual sales and ranked as the leading manufacturer of steel castings in the United States. Amsted Industries continued to grow into the 1970s, when it employed about 2,500 Chicago-area residents. By 2002, Amsted reached about $1.4 billion in annual sales and employed fewer than 1,000 Chicago-area residents but over 9,000 people nationwide.

American Telephone & Telegraph Co.
See Western Electric Co.

Ameritech Corp.
See Illinois Bell Telephone Co.

Amoco Corp.
See Standard Oil Co. (Indiana)

AMR Corp.
See American Airlines Inc.

Amsted Industries Inc.
See American Steel Foundries

Andersen (Arthur) & Co.
This pioneering accounting services firm was founded in Chicago in 1913 by a young Northwestern University professor, Arthur Andersen, and a partner named Clarence DeLany. The firm started with two partners and six employees, who offered customers help with new federal income taxes and other accounting problems. During the 1920s, Andersen opened six new offices across the country, and annual billings rose to $2 million. The firm weathered the Great Depression and continued to expand after the founder's death in 1947. Between 1947 and 1973, Andersen's client base rose from 2,300 to 50,000, and the Chicago office increased from about 250 to more than 1,500 employees. Expansion continued during the late twentieth century, as the company became increasingly international and created a fast-growing management consulting division. In 1989, Arthur Andersen and Andersen Consulting became separate units, which were controlled by Arthur Andersen & Co., S.C.; this multibillion-dollar parent company soon became known as Andersen Worldwide. At the beginning of the twenty-first century, Andersen Consulting changed its name to Accenture Ltd.; and Arthur Andersen became simply Andersen. At that time, the consulting and accounting groups together employed nearly 8,500 Chicago-area residents. In the wake of the Enron scandal and the firm's indictment for obstruction of justice in 2002, Andersen ceased auditing clients in 2002 and began selling its overseas assets to other firms.

Andrew Corp.
In 1937, Victor J. Andrew founded a company near Midway Airport that made radio broadcasting equipment. During World War II, the company broadened its product line, manufacturing communications gear and cable for the military. After the war, Andrew made antennas, cables, and connectors. In 1953, six years after it was incorporated, Andrew moved its headquarters and some production to suburban Orland Park. The expansion of the telecommunications industry in the 1980s drove growth at Andrew, which saw annual sales rise to over $800 million by the end of the 1990s. By that time, Andrew had become an international corporation with about 2,000 employees in the Chicago area and over 4,500 worldwide.

Andrews (A. H.) & Co.
This furniture company was founded in 1865 by Alfred H. Andrews, a Connecticut native who moved to Chicago in 1857. By the end of the 1860s, Andrews employed about 70 men, who made about $150,000 worth of furniture each year. By the beginning of the 1880s, A. H. Andrews & Co. had become the largest firm in the city's robust furniture industry, employing about 500 people and manufacturing about $600,000 worth of school and office furniture each year. During the 1880s, the company opened branches in New York, Philadelphia, and Boston. Andrews & Co. started to produce metal furniture in the early 1890s, but it entered bankruptcy and went into decline soon thereafter.

Anglo-American Provision Co.
Founded by the Fowler brothers, Irish immigrants who had English investors, Anglo-American was one of the city's leading meatpacking firms in the years after the Civil War. By the mid-1870s, when it was still known as Fowler Bros., the company slaughtered more than 160,000 hogs each year, making it the third-largest packer in Chicago. By the end of the 1870s, using the name Anglo-American Provision Co., the Fowlers' company employed about 1,800 men at a seven-acre packing facility; annual sales at this time stood at about $8 million. Subsequently, it opened packing plants elsewhere in the United States as well. Anglo-American continued to stand among the more important second-tier Chicago packers until 1902, when it became part of the National Packing Co. established by Armour, Swift, and other large Chicago packers.

Anixter Bros. Inc.
Founded in 1957 by brothers Alan and William Anixter, this Skokie-based company grew into one of the country's leading wholesalers of wire. In 1986, when annual sales stood at about $600 million, Anixter was purchased for about $500 million by the Itel Corp., a large holding company controlled by Chicago financier Sam Zell. Itel soon sold many of its businesses, but retained Anixter. In 1995 Itel became Anixter International Inc., also based in Skokie. At the end of the 1990s, Anixter sold close to $3 billion annually and employed about 1,000 Chicago-area residents.

Aon Corp.
See Combined Insurance Co. of America

Armour & Co.
Philip D. Armour, a native of New York State, began to work in the pork-packing business in Milwaukee, where he made a substantial fortune in the immediate aftermath of the Civil War. In 1875, he moved to Chicago to take charge of Armour & Co. (a firm owned by Philip and his brothers), which had started its move to Chicago in 1867. During the late nineteenth century, when Chicago and its Union Stock Yard stood at the center of the meatpacking industry, Armour became a national operation and one of the country's largest businesses. By 1880, with an average of over 1,500 men on the

payroll at any given time and as many as 4,000 during the peak season to process $17.5 million worth of meat, Armour was Chicago's leading industrial enterprise and employer. By the late 1880s, Armour slaughtered more than 1.5 million animals each year and reached about $60 million in annual sales. Many of those sales derived from the processing of all the parts of the animal—"everything but the squeal"—making such products as glue, lard, gelatin, and fertilizer. When Philip died in 1901, the company employed about 7,000 Chicago residents and had a total workforce of 50,000 nationwide. In 1910, Armour had about 8,700 workers at its Union Stock Yard plants. In the early 1920s, the company had financial troubles and the Armour family ceded control of its operations. But Armour remained a leading Chicago employer. During the worst years of the Great Depression in the early 1930s, over 9,000 men and nearly 2,000 women worked for Armour at the Union Stock Yard, and another 1,400 men and 400 women worked for its Chicago-area auxiliaries, which produced soap, glue, and other goods made from packing-plant waste. Armour remained one of the nation's largest companies at the end of World War II, when annual sales stood at $1 billion, but its fortunes declined in the postwar period. In 1959, Armour stopped slaughtering in Chicago. In 1970, Armour was bought by the Greyhound Corp., which relocated the company to Arizona. *See also* GREYHOUND CORP.

Armour, Dole & Co.

Armour, Dole & Co. was founded in 1860 by George Armour, Charles Dole, and Wesley Munger. The company owned a grain elevator at the depot of the Chicago, Burlington & Quincy Railroad with a capacity of 850,000 bushels. After the Civil War, Armour, Dole & Co. remained among the city's leading grain warehousers; their elevators had a combined capacity of 2.1 million bushels in 1871. By the early 1880s, this figure had grown to 6.3 million bushels.

Arnold, Schwinn & Co.

In 1895, during the midst of a national bicycle craze, Ignaz Schwinn (who arrived in Chicago from Germany in 1891) and partner Adolph Arnold (a Chicago meat industry veteran) founded a bicycle manufacturing company. They joined a competitive industry: by 1900, when the Chicago region made more than half of all the bicycles and bicycle equipment produced in the United States, about 30 different bicycle makers were concentrated along Chicago's Lake Street. In 1901, Arnold, Schwinn & Co. moved its offices to North Kostner Avenue, where it stayed until 1986. By 1905, the company had become one of the leading firms in the industry. Many of its bicycles were sold by Sears, Roebuck & Co., the giant Chicago-based retailer. In 1908, Arnold sold his interest in the company, and a new factory was built on North Kildare Avenue in Chicago. Even during the Great Depression, the company still managed to build more than 100,000 bicycles each year; annual output rose to nearly 350,000 by 1941. After World War II, the company was led by Frank W. Schwinn, a son of Ignaz Schwinn, who died in 1948. By the 1950s, the company, still known as Arnold, Schwinn & Co., sold about one-quarter of all bicycles in the United States. Sales reached $20 million in 1961, when the company employed about 1,000 people in the Chicago area. From the 1950s through the 1970s, a third generation of Schwinn family members led the company and changed its name to Schwinn Bicycle. The "Phantom," "Sting Ray," and "Varsity" models were Schwinn's best sellers. The Schwinn factory on the city's West Side, which made one million bicycles in 1968, still employed as many as 1,800 people during the 1970s. But the company's share of the national bicycle market began to shrink. In 1980, there was a strike at the West Side factory; three years later, it closed for good. By this time, Edward Schwinn, Jr., a great-grandson of the founder, led the company. In 1992, when Schwinn's market share had declined to about 5 percent, it entered bankruptcy and was sold by the Schwinn family to a group of investors led by Chicago's Sam Zell. In 1993, Schwinn's general offices moved to Colorado.

AT&T

See Western Electric Co.; Illinois Bell Telephone Co.

Automatic Canteen Co. of America

The company that would become the leading firm in the American vending-machine industry was founded in 1929 by Nathaniel Leverone, who had arrived in Chicago as a 24-year-old in 1908. Leverone's company, the Automatic Canteen Co. of America, sold machines that dispensed candy bars, nuts, and chewing gum. By 1940, when the company's annual sales stood at about $10 million, about 230,000 of these vending machines were in use. After World War II, Automatic Canteen stocked the machines with cigarettes, among other items. Annual sales reached $200 million in the mid-1960s, when Automatic Canteen became the Canteen Corp. During the mid-1970s, the Canteen Corp. employed about 1,000 people in the Chicago area. At the end of the 1970s, the Trans World Corp. purchased the company, and management of its operations left Chicago.

Automatic Electric Co.

Like Western Electric, another industry-leading telephone equipment manufacturer located in the Chicago area, Automatic Electric spent most of its history as a subsidiary of another company. In 1889, a Kansas City resident named Almon B. Strowger invented an automatic telephone switch. In 1891, Joseph B. Harris of Chicago convinced Strowger to move to Chicago, and the Strowger Automatic Telephone Exchange was established. In 1901, the company changed its name to Automatic Electric and opened a six-story plant on Chicago's West Side. By 1910, this facility employed 850 workers to make automatic switches and other telephone equipment. Most of this equipment was sold to independent telephone companies around the country; some was also purchased by the Bell system of AT&T. In 1919, Automatic Electric was purchased by Theodore Gary & Co., a Kansas City–based enterprise that already owned several small telephone companies around the country. (In 1932, Gary & Co. would move its executive offices to Chicago.) During the 1920s, under Gary's leadership, a growing Automatic Electric established branches in Belgium, Italy, and Canada; meanwhile, it employed about 3,000 people at its West Side facilities. During this period, the company made roughly 80 percent of the world's dial-operated automatic telephone equipment. By the mid-1950s, Automatic Electric employed about 8,000 Chicago-area residents at a complex of 17 buildings on the West Side. In 1955, when Theodore Gary & Co. was acquired by the General Telephone Corp. (renamed the General Telephone & Electronics Corp., or GT&E, in 1959), Automatic Electric became a subsidiary of the nation's second-largest telephone company, which was headquartered in New York. In 1957, Automatic Electric moved from the West Side to a new 35-acre facility in suburban Northlake. At late as 1974, when it was still a division of GT&E, Automatic Electric employed about 10,000 Chicago area residents. The Northlake plant, however, found it increasingly difficult to develop new electronic and digital switching technologies that would allow GT&E to outpace its growing number of competitors. In 1983, just after the parent company changed its name to GTE Corp., the Automatic Electric name was scrapped, and the headquarters of GTE's new "Communication Systems" division, which included the Northlake operations, was moved to Phoenix, Arizona. This soon became part of AG Communications Systems Corp., a joint venture between GTE and its old rival AT&T. By the end of the twentieth century, the remnants of Automatic Electric (like those of Western Electric) had become part of Lucent Technologies, the manufacturing entity that separated from AT&T in 1996.

B

Baker & McKenzie

Soon after leaving the University of Chicago Law School in 1925, Russell Baker, a native of New Mexico, and friend Dana Simpson opened a small practice, Simpson & Baker. During the firm's early years, Baker frequently represented people from the city's growing Mexican American community. After Simpson retired in 1932, Baker formed a new firm, Freyberger, Baker & Rice; it soon represented major Chicago companies such as Abbott Laboratories. In 1949 Baker found a new partner in litigator John McKenzie; they started Baker & McKenzie, which began as a four-lawyer operation. This enterprise became the world's first multinational law firm when it began to open overseas offices in the late 1950s. By the late 1980s, the firm's franchises around the world had a total of about 1,000 lawyers, about 15 percent of whom were located in Chicago. By the end of the 1990s, the firm employed over 6,000 people in more than 60 offices around the world, and annual revenues were over $800 million.

Bally Manufacturing Corp.

Bally originated as the Lion Manufacturing Corp., a firm established in Chicago in 1931 by Raymond J. Moloney. Lion created the popular "Ballyhoo" pinball machine, produced by a subsidiary called the Bally Manufacturing Co. Lion began to make slot machines in the late 1930s; during World War II, it made detonator fuses and gun sights. In 1968, Lion became the Bally Manufacturing Corp., led by William O'Donnell. In the mid-1970s, annual sales reached $200 million, and the company employed about 2,300 people in the Chicago area. Although it suffered a setback in the late 1970s when O'Donnell was forced to resign because of alleged links to organized crime, Bally found success in the new video game industry. Bally's video arcades and electronic games, which included Space Invaders (introduced in 1979) and Pac Man (1980), soon accounted for half of its revenues. Meanwhile, the company bought health clubs, the Six Flags amusement park chain, and several casinos; by the late 1980s, annual revenues exceeded $2 billion, and Bally had about 33,000 workers nationwide. In 1996, two years after it changed its name to Bally Entertainment Corp., the company was acquired by Hilton Hotels Corp. of California. Its health club business, which had become an independent company a few years earlier, remained based in Chicago. At the end of the 1990s, Bally Total Fitness Holding Corp., the largest U.S. operator of health clubs, employed about 2,000 people in the Chicago area and had nearly $900 million in annual revenues from its 375 clubs nationwide.

Bankers Life & Casualty Co.

Bankers Life & Casualty Co. was small and nearly bankrupt when Chicago insurance salesman John D. MacArthur purchased it in 1935. The new owner used the company to sell insurance by mail, which proved to be a profitable business. By the 1950s, Bankers Life & Casualty was the nation's largest privately owned insurance company. By the mid-1970s, the company had nearly 5,000 Chicago-area employees. In 1978, after the death of MacArthur, his holdings in the company were transferred to the John D. and Catherine T. MacArthur Foundation, a large nonprofit organization based in Chicago. In 1992, Bankers Life was acquired by Conseco Inc. of Indiana.

Bank One Corp.

See First National Bank of Chicago

Baxter Travenol Laboratories Inc.

In 1931, physicians Donald Baxter of Los Angeles and Ralph Falk of Boise, Idaho, started the Don Baxter Intravenous Products Corp., which made supplies for IV systems in hospitals. In 1933, Baxter started a manufacturing plant in Glenview. A pioneer in blood preservation methods as well as IV supplies, Baxter grew steadily. In 1947, it moved its headquarters to Morton Grove; the company soon employed over 500 people in the Chicago area. Annual sales grew from about $10 million in the mid-1950s to more than $100 million by 1967, when the company was making dialysis equipment, heart-lung machines, and many other equipment items for hospitals. In 1975, when it employed about 2,200 in the Chicago area, the company moved its headquarters to suburban Glenview; the following year, its name changed to Baxter Travenol Laboratories. The company grew rapidly thereafter. In 1985, when annual sales stood at about $2 billion, Baxter bought the American Hospital Supply Corp., an even larger Chicago-area medical supply company. The new company, which in 1988 became Baxter International Inc., was an enormous entity that soon approached $10 billion in annual sales; about 10,000 of its 50,000 employees worldwide were in the Chicago area. During the 1990s, however, Baxter sold off several divisions, including many of the old American Hospital Supply Corp. operations. At the beginning of the twenty-first century, Baxter again began buying firms such as ESI Lederle. By 2002, Baxter's annual sales exceeded $8 billion; it had some 5,500 Chicago-area workers and 48,000 employees worldwide. *See also* American Hospital Supply Corp.

Beatrice Foods Co.

The Beatrice Creamery Co. was founded in Nebraska in the 1890s by partners George Everett Haskell and William W. Bosworth. By the time Beatrice moved its headquarters to Chicago in 1913 (settling in a large facility on South State Street in 1917), it was already a leading seller of dairy equipment and operator of dairies. By the early 1930s, its national network of 32 plants produced about 27 million gallons of milk and 9.5 million gallons of ice cream per year; its "Meadow Gold" brand of dairy products was particularly successful. In 1946, when the company became the Beatrice Foods Co., annual sales stood at about $170 million; sales doubled over the next decade. Starting in the 1960s, the company expanded rapidly by purchasing other food firms, and annual sales jumped to $12 billion by 1984. During the 1970s, Beatrice employed as many as 8,000 Chicago-area residents. After the company changed hands in 1986, however, it was dismantled with stunning speed. By 1990, the last of Beatrice was sold off, and the company that had once been one Chicago's largest was gone.

Bell & Howell Co.

Bell & Howell Co. was incorporated in 1907 by Albert Howell, a film projector inventor, and Donald Bell, a movie projectionist working in northern Illinois. From its headquarters in suburban Skokie, Bell & Howell made equipment used in the motion picture industry. It introduced an innovative all-metal camera in 1912 and a home movie camera in the 1920s, helped to make 35-millimeter film the industry standard, and served as a leading supplier to Hollywood. By 1925, when Bell & Howell had about 500 employees at its Larchmont Avenue plant, annual sales had reached $1 million. During World War II, a workforce of 2,000 made gun cameras and other optical equipment for the military. After the war, the company expanded into microfilm equipment and other products; annual sales passed $50 million in 1957. In 1966, Bell & Howell took over the DeVry Technical Institute (which it would sell in 1987), a for-profit school that offered electronics education. During the mid-1970s, when the company's annual sales approached $500 million, it employed about 4,000 people in the Chicago area. During the 1980s and 1990s, the company expanded its efforts in electronic imaging and information with the purchase of University Microfilms Incorporated and the creation of ProQuest Information service. In January 2000, the company, with sales nearing $1 billion, announced plans to create separate companies reflecting the firm's different interests. Eighteen months later, ProQuest Co., headquartered in Ann Arbor, Michigan, was launched as a separate company. In December 2002, Bell & Howell merged with Böwe Systec Inc. to form Böwe Bell & Howell, with two of its divisions now headquartered in Lincolnwood.

Ben Franklin Stores

See Butler Bros.; Household Finance Corp.

Bethlehem Steel Corp.

Bethlehem Steel came late to the Chicago area and never made its headquarters there, but it was a leading employer in the area during the last decades of the twentieth century. Founded in 1899 in Pennsylvania, Bethlehem Steel expanded rapidly during the 1920s and became the second-largest U.S. steelmaker by the eve of World War II. Unlike many other American steel companies, Bethlehem did not operate any large mills in the Chicago region during this period. It finally arrived in 1962, building a large new plant at Burns Harbor, Indiana. By the mid-1970s, about 7,000 people worked there; at the time, this amounted to only about 5 percent of Bethlehem's total workforce. But as the American steel industry declined and Bethlehem cut back, the Burns Harbor plant continued to operate. By the end of the 1990s, it accounted for half of the company's total revenues. In May 2003, its assets were acquired by the International Steel Group.

Booz Allen & Hamilton Inc.
One of the world's first management consulting firms originated in Chicago in 1914 under the leadership of Edwin G. Booz. In 1916, Booz formed the Business Research & Development Co., which became Business Surveys in 1924. Booz's company consisted of only three consultants as late as 1929, but it advised many Chicago companies. In 1936, Booz, Fry, Allen & Hamilton was established. The following year, the firm moved into offices in the Field Building. In 1943, when the firm's name became Booz Allen & Hamilton, it had about 400 clients. During the 1950s, Booz Allen & Hamilton became the world leader in the consulting field, and the firm employed over 500 people; at the end of the 1960s, when Booz Allen was still the largest American consulting firm, annual revenues were about $55 million. Starting in the 1970s, the firm fell behind its competitors and left the city in which it had grown up. After seven decades as a Chicago company, the firm moved to New York, where it remained during the 1980s; its headquarters later moved to the Washington DC area.

Borg-Warner Corp.
In 1918, after 14 years in Moline, Illinois, Charles W. Borg and Marshall Beck moved their automobile clutch manufacturing business to Chicago. In 1928, Borg & Beck merged with three other Midwestern auto parts makers—Warner Gear of Muncie, Indiana; Mechanics Universal Joint of Rockford, Illinois; and Marvel Carburetor of Flint, Michigan—to form Borg-Warner, headquartered on Michigan Avenue in Chicago. This new company expanded quickly. In 1929, the Ingersoll Steel Disc Co. of Galesburg, Illinois, joined Borg-Warner; in 1935, the company bought the re-rolling mill of the Calumet Steel Co. in Chicago Heights. Annual sales rose from about $50 million in 1929 to over $600 million by the late 1950s, when Borg-Warner became a leading manufacturer of automatic transmissions. Meanwhile, Borg-Warner entered the industrial plastics business and opened offices and plants overseas. In the early 1970s, the company employed more than 5,000 people in the Chicago area, along with tens of thousands around the world. In 1978, Borg-Warner began to build a large security services business; during the 1990s, this operation, known as Borg-Warner Security and later as Burns International Services, spun off and was soon bought by a Swedish corporation. Meanwhile, Borg-Warner sold its plastics and chemicals operations to General Electric. By the late 1990s, BorgWarner Inc. had again become an auto parts specialist, with about $2.5 billion in annual sales and about 1,300 employees in the Chicago area.

Bowman Dairy Co.
In 1874, J. R. Bowman of Clinton County, Illinois, headed west to St. Louis, where he established a dairy marketing business called J. R. Bowman & Co. In 1885, Bowman entered the Chicago market by purchasing the milk business of M. A. Devine. In 1891, Bowman and his brothers decided to sell their St. Louis operation and move to Chicago, where they formed the Bowman Dairy Co. This company soon became one of the leading suppliers of dairy products and eggs in the Chicago area. During the 1920s, it opened large bottling plants on the South Side. By the middle of the 1930s, Bowman employed over 3,000 Chicago-area residents. The company continued to carry on a large business until 1966, when it was purchased by a local rival, the Dean Foods Co. *See also* DEAN MILK CO.

Brach (E. J.) & Sons
In 1904, Emil J. Brach opened his "Palace of Sweets" at North Avenue and Towne Street in Chicago. The output of this candy factory grew quickly, producing more than 25 tons a week by 1911 and 1,000 tons a week by 1918. In 1922, the company built a large new plant on the city's West Side; this facility, the largest candy factory in the United States, soon employed hundreds of men and women. Brach's annual sales grew from about $8 million in 1925 to $22 million in 1945 and $62 million in 1961. Between 1966 and 1986, Brach was owned by the American Home Products Corp. of New York; it was then purchased by Jacobs Suchard, a Swiss company. By the end of the 1980s, Brach was still the clear leader in the bulk candy market, and the company's 3,500 workers made it the leading employer on the city's West Side. But Brach performed poorly under Suchard, which cut jobs and moved the executive offices to suburban Oakbrook Terrace. In 1994, Brach merged with the Brock Candy Co., creating a new company called Brach & Brock Confections Inc., based in Chattanooga, Tennessee.

Brunswick Corp.
By the beginning of the 1850s, Swiss-born John M. Brunswick and his half brothers David and Emanuel had begun to make billiard tables in Cincinnati, Chicago, and other cities. In 1873, when Brunswick Bros. became the J. M. Brunswick & Balke Co., the company operated a factory on Lake Street, where about 60 workers turned out two billiard tables a day. By the mid-1880s, when its name changed to the Brunswick-Balke-Collender Co., the company was the world's leading billiards equipment manufacturer. Its large Chicago production facility at Huron and Sedgwick Streets, which was housed in a building designed by Louis Sullivan, employed about 700 men by the beginning of the twentieth century. In 1908, Chicago became the official headquarters of the company, then led by Benjamin E. Beninger, a grandson of John Brunswick. In the 1910s, Brunswick manufactured phonographs and automobile tires; these businesses helped push annual sales up to about $30 million by the end of the 1920s. Revenues collapsed during the Great Depression, but the company began to recover during World War II; after the war, it enjoyed great success as a supplier of bowling equipment. During the bowling craze of the 1950s, Brunswick (along with rival AMF) sold thousands of automatic pinsetting machines and other bowling supplies. Annual sales skyrocketed from about $30 million in the early 1950s to about $400 million by 1960, when the company changed its name to Brunswick Corp. During the 1960s, when the company made many kinds of recreational equipment, the decline of the bowling craze meant losses for Brunswick; but it recovered somewhat in the 1970s, when annual sales reached $1 billion and it employed over 1,200 people in the Chicago area and about 25,000 worldwide. During the last decades of the twentieth century, Brunswick's main business was making boats and boat engines. In 1993, it moved its headquarters to suburban Lake Forest. As the century ended, Brunswick was doing over $4 billion in annual sales and employed about 1,000 Chicago-area residents.

Bunte Bros.
In 1876, Ferdinand Bunte, Gustav A. Bunte, and Charles A. Spoehr started a candy manufactory on State Street in Chicago. After a few years, Ferdinand's son Theodore W. Bunte took charge of the business. By the 1910s, when Bunte Bros. did annual sales of about $2.4 million, the company employed about 1,200 people. As late as the 1950s, it had over 1,000 workers in its Chicago plants. In 1954, Bunte Brothers Candy Co. was purchased by Chase Candy Co. of St. Joseph, Missouri, and a new firm, Bunte-Chase, was created. In 1961, the firm closed the Chicago plant, dropped the Bunte name, and returned to St. Joseph.

Burnham & Root
This famous partnership was formed in 1873 by Daniel H. Burnham and John W. Root, two young men who had been working for the Chicago architects Carter, Drake & Wight.

The new firm's first major commission came in 1874, when Root and Burnham designed a Prairie Avenue mansion for Chicago stockyards boss John B. Sherman. Over the next few decades, the firm designed dozens of large homes and commercial buildings in Chicago. Their 10-story Montauk Building, which went up in 1882, was the first of their contributions to the new field of skyscraper design. Among the partners' many contributions to the Chicago landscape were the Rookery; the original Art Institute; the Monadnock Building; the offices of the *Chicago Daily News*, then the city's leading newspaper; and the Masonic Temple, which became Chicago's first 20-story building when it was completed in 1892. After Root died in 1891, the name of the firm became D. H. Burnham & Co. Burnham and his associates continued to design many notable Chicago buildings, including the Reliance Building; the offices of the city's two leading banks (First National and Commercial & Continental); a department store for Marshall Field & Co.; and the Field Museum, completed in 1920. Outside Chicago, major works of the Burnham firm included the Flatiron Building in New York City and Union Station in Washington DC. At the time of Burnham's death in 1912, the firm had nearly 200 employees, making it one of the largest architectural businesses in the United States.

Burnett (Leo) Co.

After years working in the advertising business in cities around the Midwest, including a stint as a vice president at the Chicago ad firm of Erwin, Wasey & Co., the 44-year-old Leo Burnett started his own firm in Chicago in 1935. His venture soon became one of the world's leading advertising agencies. As Burnett took on more clients, billings rose from about $200,000 in 1935 to about $10 million by 1948 and $100 million by 1958. Among the most prominent of the company's ad campaigns were the Jolly Green Giant for Minnesota Valley Canning Co.; the Doughboy for Pillsbury; the Marlboro Man for Philip Morris; Charlie the Tuna for Star-Kist; Tony the Tiger for Kellogg's; and the lonely Maytag repairman. Burnett was known for the relatively conservative, Midwestern flavor of its ads. By the early 1970s, when billings stood at about $400 million and it employed about 1,200 people in the Chicago area, Burnett was the world's fifth-largest advertising firm. In 1989, when Burnett had dozens of offices around the world, the firm's headquarters moved into a new Chicago skyscraper, the Leo Burnett Building, located on Wacker Drive. The firm struggled against stiff competition in the 1990s, losing several major clients, including large Chicago-based companies United Airlines and McDonald's. At the end of the 1990s, when Burnett employed over 2,000 people in the Chicago area, it merged with a rival firm in New York and became part of the Bcom3 Group, a Chicago-based advertising giant that then ranked as the world's seventh-largest ad agency. In 2002, Bcom3 Group was bought out by the French Publicis Groupe S.A. As part of that firm, Leo Burnett USA continues its activities from offices in Chicago and New York.

Butler Bros.

George and Edward Butler founded a wholesale mail-order company in Boston in 1877. Butler Bros. opened a Chicago warehouse in 1879, and the city became home to the company's catalog department. (All of its operations were based in Chicago after 1930, when the purchasing department moved from New York.) By 1910, the Chicago offices employed about 1,000 people. Like Sears and Montgomery Ward, other Chicago companies that had large mail-order operations, Butler Bros. moved into brick-and-mortar retailing during the 1920s. By the beginning of the 1930s, it operated over 100 of its own "Scott" and "L. C. Burr" stores; at the same time, it had begun a franchising business that allowed independent retailers to become members of the "Ben Franklin" and "Federated" chains, which were supplied by Butler Bros. By 1936, there were about 2,600 Ben Franklin stores and 1,400 Federated stores around the country, mostly in small towns. During the 1940s and 1950s, Butler Bros. approached $120 million a year in wholesale and retail sales, ranking it among the leading wholesalers in the United States. In 1960, after it sold Ben Franklin and its other retail operations to the City Products Corp. of Ohio (which was bought in 1965 by the Household Finance Corp. of Chicago), Butler Bros. faded away.

C

Canteen Corp.

See Automatic Canteen Co. of America

Capsonic Group LLC

As a young engineer in the mid-1960s, Jim Liautaud conceived a process that binded plastic to metal to create parts for use in the electronics industry. In 1968 he started Capsonic Inc. and began applying his innovation to manufacture injection-molded parts in a small building in Elgin, Illinois. The company grew quickly, employing 40 workers in a new plant it occupied in 1970. By the mid-1990s, it had expanded beyond the electronics field and was supplying parts to the automotive, computer, appliance, and telecommunication industries, reaping over $40 million in sales a year. The company was called Capsonic Group LLC by the early 2000s and had spun off several related subsidiaries. Still owned by Liautaud and headquartered in Elgin, it had operations in Michigan and Mexico. With nearly 200 employees—most in the Chicago area—and revenues approaching $60 million, Capsonic Group ranked among Chicago's largest minority-owned firms.

Carson Pirie Scott & Co.

This leading Chicago department store originated with a business founded in Amboy, Illinois, in 1854 by Samuel Carson and John T. Pirie, two Scotch-Irish immigrants. By the end of the Civil War, Carson & Pirie was based on Lake Street in Chicago; during the late 1860s, annual sales (wholesale and retail) reached $800,000. In 1890, the entry of Robert Scott as a partner led the growing firm to change its name to Carson Pirie Scott & Co. By 1900, its two downtown Chicago stores on State and Washington and Franklin and Adams each employed about 1,000 men and women. In 1904, the company moved into a new Louis Sullivan–designed building at State and Madison. During the twentieth century, the retail operations of Carson's (as it came to be known) continued to grow; by the beginning of the 1960s, it operated 11 stores around the Chicago region, where it employed about 8,000 people and did about $150 million in annual sales. In 1989, Carson Pirie Scott was bought by P. A. Bergner & Co., a Milwaukee-based subsidiary of a Swiss company. After going through bankruptcy in 1991, this department store chain reemerged as Carson Pirie Scott & Co; but this entity was acquired in 1997 by Proffitt's Inc. of Knoxville Tennessee. At the end of the century, Carson's was still the name of several department stores around the Midwest, including the Sullivan-designed flagship store on State Street.

Castle (A. M.) & Co.

This distributor of steel products was founded in Chicago in 1890 by A. M. Castle. By the late 1920s, when the company had warehouses around the country, annual revenues were about $7 million. By the beginning of the 1960s, when sales reached about $35 million, Castle was based in suburban Franklin Park, Illinois. At the end of the twentieth century, the company employed about 500 people in the Chicago area and did about $700 million in annual sales.

CBI Industries

See Chicago Bridge & Iron Co.

CDW Computer Centers Inc.

This direct marketer of computers, originally named Computer Discount Warehouse, was established in Chicago in 1983 by Michael Krasny after he found it surprisingly easy to sell his own computer. Krasny soon started to buy and sell wholesale and publish a mail-order catalog; he opened a retail showroom in Chicago in 1989. The company became

CDW in 1993, when it started to sell stock to the public. At the beginning of the twenty-first century, CDW, based in suburban Vernon Hills, was exceeding $4.2 billion in annual sales and employing over 2,000 Chicago-area residents.

Ceco Corp.

The Concrete Engineering Co. was founded by C. Louis Meyer in Omaha, Nebraska, in 1912. The company manufactured reusable steel forms and reinforcing bars used by the commercial construction industry to create buildings out of concrete. By the end of the 1920s, when annual sales had climbed to $6 million, Meyer's company included a plant at Cicero, Illinois. In 1946, a decade after its name changed to the Ceco Steel Products Corp., the company moved its headquarters from Omaha to Cicero. By 1950, annual sales were about $40 million, and 1,500 of the company's 2,800 total employees worked in the Chicago area. In 1961, operating plants in suburban Lemont and Romeoville, as well as Cicero, the company name was shortened to Ceco Corp. In 1980, when annual sales stood at about $400 million, the headquarters moved from Cicero to Oak Brook Terrace. In 1990, Ceco merged with H. H. Robertson Inc. of Pittsburgh; the new entity, known as the Robertson-Ceco Corp., made its home in California.

CFS Continental Inc.

See Continental Coffee Co.

Chicago & North Western Railway Co.

The Chicago & North Western Railway, created during the late 1850s by the merger of several small railroads in Illinois and Wisconsin, was led during its early years by William B. Ogden, Chicago's first mayor. In 1864, the Chicago & North Western absorbed the Galena & Chicago Union, which in 1848 had been the city's first railroad. Between 1872 and 1910, under the leadership of Marvin Hughitt, the length of track in the road's rail network grew from about 1,400 miles to nearly 10,000 miles. The railroad served areas concentrated in Illinois, Wisconsin, Iowa, and Minnesota. Although the company went bankrupt during the Great Depression, it survived into the second half of the twentieth century. By 1961, the Chicago & North Western Railway had over $200 million in annual revenues and about 16,000 employees nationwide. In 1968, it absorbed the Chicago Great Western, a smaller competitor. That same year, the transportation company became part of a conglomerate, Northwest Industries; four years later, the railroad was spun off and sold to its employees, becoming the Chicago & North Western Transportation Co. In 1986, when the railroad's annual revenues were nearly $1 billion, it became known as CNW Corp. It finally ceased to exist as an independent railroad in 1995, when it was bought by another old railroad company, the Union Pacific Corp. *See also* NORTHWEST INDUSTRIES INC.

H. Roger Grant

Chicago American

See Hearst Newspapers

Chicago, Aurora & Elgin Railroad Co.

In 1906, the merger of several streetcar lines in Chicago's western suburbs created the Aurora, Elgin & Chicago Railroad. By 1909, the line had four routes between the western satellite cities and downtown Chicago. In 1922 its name became the Chicago, Aurora & Elgin Railroad Co. Owned briefly by Samuel Insull's Middle West Utilities Corp. during the late 1920s, the road entered bankruptcy in 1932. Despite financial difficulties, it continued to be an important commuter line. By 1940s, it carried about 30,000 riders a day over a network of 52 miles of track. The railroad eventually declined, ending passenger service in 1957 and freight service in 1959. The line was permanently abandoned in 1961.

Chicago Bridge & Iron Co.

Founded in 1889 by Horace Horton, Chicago Bridge & Iron Co. was created by the merger of several small firms that manufactured parts for iron bridges. Its two Chicago-area plants were located in Washington Heights, well south of downtown. By 1910, these facilities employed about 600 people. During World War II, when it had 12,000 workers making military vessels, Chicago Bridge temporarily became a large military contractor. For most of the second half of the twentieth century, it employed about 1,000 people in the Chicago area and more at other plants around the country. During the early 1960s, the company built new headquarters in suburban Oak Brook. In 1979, the company became known as CBI Industries; five years later, it acquired Liquid Carbonic, the nation's leading supplier of carbon dioxide. By 1995, when it was bought by rival Praxair of Connecticut, CBI was a leader in the field of industrial gases, with nearly $2 billion in annual sales and over 14,000 employees worldwide.

Chicago, Burlington & Quincy Railroad Co.

In 1855, the name of the Chicago & Aurora Railroad, which included several of the area's early rail lines, was changed to the Chicago, Burlington & Quincy. This road, which operated mainly in Illinois, Iowa, Missouri, and Nebraska, was a leading Chicago transportation line and local employer. In 1870, its car works in Aurora employed more than 1,200 men, making it the largest industrial employer in the Chicago region. As the company's rail network expanded, annual revenues rose to about $20 million by 1880. In 1901, the Chicago, Burlington & Quincy was purchased by James J. Hill, owner of the Northern Pacific and Great Northern railroads, based in St. Paul, Minnesota. By the early 1920s, the Burlington covered nearly 10,000 miles of road. Operating out of Union Station in Chicago, it became known as a technological pioneer in 1934, when it introduced the streamlined "Zephyr" high-speed diesel-electric passenger trains, and in 1950, when it ran air-conditioned, double-deck commuter cars out of Chicago. By the beginning of the 1960s, the road was collecting about $250 million in annual revenues and employed about 22,000 people nationwide. In 1970, the Burlington and the other lines in the old Hill empire finally merged, creating the Burlington Northern, which became the second-largest railroad system in the United States. In 1995, the Burlington Northern merged with the Atchison, Topeka & Santa Fe, forming the Burlington Northern Santa Fe, an even larger entity.

H. Roger Grant

Chicago Daily News Inc.

The *Chicago Daily News*, the city's first penny paper and the most widely read publication in Chicago during the late nineteenth century, was founded in 1875 by Melville H. Stone. When Victor F. Lawson bought the paper in 1876, he retained Stone as editor. The *Daily News* started with a one-cent afternoon edition; in 1881, it introduced a two-cent morning edition. By the late 1880s, when it lowered the price of the morning edition to a penny, it enjoyed a daily circulation of about 200,000, which made it one of the most widely read newspapers in the world. After Stone retired in 1888, Lawson took over complete control of the paper. It remained Chicago's most popular newspaper until 1918, when its circulation was surpassed by the *Chicago Tribune*. Even after Lawson died in 1925, however, the *Daily News* remained an important local publication. By the end of the 1920s, circulation was about 430,000, and the paper employed over 2,000 people at its headquarters on West Madison. At the end of World War II, when annual revenues approached $15 million, the paper ranked among the top 15 publishing companies in the United States. In 1959, with a circulation of around 600,000, the *Daily News* was purchased by Field Enterprises, owner of the *Chicago Sun-Times*. The *Daily News* ceased to exist in 1978, when it was absorbed by the *Sun-Times*.

Chicago Examiner

See Hearst Newspapers

Chicago Flexible Shaft Co.

Chicago Flexible Shaft Co., which would eventually be known as Sunbeam, was founded in Chicago in the early 1890s by John K. Stewart and Thomas J. Clark, who made mechanical horse clippers and sheep shearers. Between 1908 and 1936, Chicago Flexible Shaft operated as a subsidiary of Wm. Cooper & Nephews, an English company. During this time, the company began to manufacture a variety of electrical appliances, including irons, mixers, coffeemakers, and toasters; its plant on West Roosevelt Road employed about 500 people. In 1946, 10 years after Cooper sold the company, it became the Sunbeam Corp., with annual sales of about $15 million. After World War II, when it continued to introduce new appliances, Sunbeam employed over 1,000 people at the Roosevelt Road plant. Meanwhile, it continued to expand outside of Chicago; by the end of the 1970s, as the leading American manufacturer of small appliances, Sunbeam enjoyed about $1.3 billion in annual sales and employed nearly 30,000 people worldwide. In 1981, after Sunbeam was bought by Allegheny International Inc. of Pittsburgh, its Chicago-area factories were closed and the headquarters left the Chicago region.

Chicago Great Western Railway Co.

The Minnesota & Northwestern Railroad Co. began to run trains out of a station in suburban Forest Park in 1887; it soon became the Chicago, St. Paul & Kansas City. By the early 1890s, when its name changed to the Chicago Great Western Railway Co. and it ran over about 1,000 miles of track, this road had annual revenues of about $4 million. After the panic of 1907 helped push the road into bankruptcy, it was purchased by a group of investors that included New York banker J. P. Morgan. In 1920, the road had about 9,000 employees around the Midwest. The Chicago Great Western did not grow much over the next few decades. In 1967, federal regulators approved a merger with a longtime competitor, the Chicago & North Western.

Chicago Herald & Examiner

See Hearst Newspapers

Chicago, Milwaukee, St. Paul & Pacific Railway Co.

The Milwaukee & Waukesha Rail Road Co., founded in Wisconsin in 1847, soon became the Milwaukee & Mississippi; in the 1860s, it became part of the Milwaukee & St. Paul Railway Co. In 1874, one year after it completed a new line between Milwaukee and Chicago, the railroad became known as the Chicago, Milwaukee & St. Paul Railway Co. Between 1874 and 1887, the amount of track owned by this road—which operated mainly in Illinois, Wisconsin, Iowa, and Minnesota, but eventually reached Seattle—grew from 1,400 miles to nearly 5,700 miles. Over the same period, annual revenues rose from $3 million to $10 million. The company's general offices moved to Chicago at the turn of the twentieth century. By 1919, the Milwaukee Road's track exceeded 10,000 miles. The following decades were difficult ones for the company, which entered bankruptcy both in 1925 and again during the Great Depression. By 1965, the company still owned more than 10,000 miles of road, employed over 16,000 people nationwide, and had nearly $250 million in annual revenues. By the mid-1970s, the road still employed about 3,500 people in the Chicago area. The company entered bankruptcy again in 1977, reorganized, and divested itself of two-thirds of its track. In 1985, the Soo Line purchased the Milwaukee Road. Five years later, the Canadian Pacific acquired the Soo Line.

Chicago Motor Coach Co.

This enterprise was created between 1920 and 1922 through the merger of three motorbus carriers, Chicago Motor Bus Co., the Chicago Stage Co., and the Depot Motor Bus Lines. In 1922, when it was the second-largest urban bus company in the United States, Chicago Motor Coach was purchased by John D. Hertz, a Chicago auto dealer and owner of the Yellow Cab Co. In 1924, Hertz merged Chicago Motor Coach and the Fifth Avenue Motor Coach Corp. of New York City, creating the Omnibus Corp. In 1952, when it owned nearly 600 buses, Chicago Motor Coach's operations were taken over by the Chicago Transit Authority (CTA), the city's public mass-transit enterprise. With over 12,000 employees, the CTA at the beginning of the twenty-first century was one of the region's largest employers.

Chicago, North Shore & Milwaukee Railway Co.

This commuter rail line originated when a short street railway between North Chicago and Waukegan was finished in 1892. In 1908, the line extended to Milwaukee; 11 years later, when it was owned by local utilities titan Samuel Insull, it obtained access to downtown Chicago. The road's "Electroliner" train, introduced in 1941, was a popular innovation. By the latter part of the 1940s, annual revenues were about $10 million. By 1963, the road had ceased to operate.

Chicago Packing & Provision Co.

Benjamin P. Hutchinson, who would become one of the city's foremost grain traders, opened a meatpacking plant in Chicago in 1858. By the mid-1870s, when its several hundred employees handled 400,000 or more hogs per season, Hutchinson's Chicago Packing & Provision Co. was the leading meat processor in the United States. In 1880, the company employed as many as 1,600 people at once to produce over $8 million worth of meat during the year. By this time, the enterprise was being surpassed by other Chicago packers, such as Armour and Swift. Sold in 1890 to a group of English investors, Hutchinson's company was no longer an important packer by 1900.

Chicago Railways Co.

See Chicago Surface Lines

Chicago Rapid Transit Co.

This operator of elevated railways was the descendant of the Chicago Elevated Railways Collateral Trust, formed in 1913 as a voluntary association of the city's four elevated lines: the Chicago & South Side Rapid Transit Railroad (opened 1892); the Lake Street Elevated Railway Co. (1893); the Metropolitan West Side Elevated Railroad (1895); and the Northwestern Elevated Railroad (1899). These early elevated lines had been led by Chicago transit king Charles T. Yerkes (who died in 1905), among others. The Chicago Rapid Transit Co., which was led by Chicago utilities titan Samuel Insull, was created in 1924 after a formal merger among the lines associated in the Chicago Elevated Railways. During the 1920s, Chicago Rapid Transit employed about 5,000 men and 600 women and had annual revenues of roughly $20 million. In 1932, during the Great Depression, the company entered bankruptcy. In 1947 it was taken over by the new Chicago Transit Authority (CTA), a public entity that became the new owner of the city's famous "El."

Chicago, Rock Island & Pacific Railroad Co.

In 1854, this company completed a rail link between Chicago and Rock Island, Illinois; in 1856, it became the first railroad to bridge the Mississippi River. In 1866, the rail absorbed the Mississippi & Missouri Railroad Co. By the end of the nineteenth century, the railroad owned nearly 3,000 miles of track, most of it in the Midwest. In Chicago, the line's passenger service operated out of the LaSalle Street station. Too rapid expansion during the first decade of the twentieth century pushed the company into bankruptcy in 1914; it went bankrupt again in 1933. By the beginning of the 1960s, it operated over about 7,500 miles of track, had about $200 million in annual revenues, and employed nearly 16,000 people nationwide. The company failed again in 1975, leading to unsuccessful attempts to sell the railroad. Following a strike by its clerks in 1979, the Interstate Commerce Commission ordered the Kansas City Terminal Line to provide temporary "directed service." In early 1980, the bankruptcy court ordered the liquidation of the railroad. The few remaining assets when the company dissolved in 1984 were transferred to the Chicago Pacific Corp., a holding company since purchased by Maytag.

Chicago Ship Building Co.

The area's greatest shipyard, located in South Chicago, was founded in 1890 as a subsidiary of the Globe Iron Works of Cleveland. By 1900, just after it became part of the American Shipbuilding Co. (also based in Cleveland), the

Chicago Ship Building Co. employed 1,200 men and ranked as the leading builder of steel ships on the Great Lakes. The company, which remained part of American Shipbuilding, continued to operate on a relatively small scale through World War II; it never regained the leading position it had held in the 1890s.

Chicago, South Shore & South Bend Railroad Co.

This commuter line began in Northern Indiana in 1901; it started running in and out of Chicago in 1926, just after it was acquired by Samuel Insull's Middle West Utilities Corp. The road survived the Great Depression, and by 1945 annual revenues stood at about $6 million. After 1950, as more area residents used automobiles instead of trains, ridership declined. But the South Shore, unlike many other regional railroads, survived. In 1966, it was purchased by the Chesapeake & Ohio Railroad; in the 1970s, the state of Indiana prevented the line from closing. At the end of the twentieth century, it was known as the nation's last surviving interurban railroad.

Chicago Sun-Times

See Field Enterprises Inc.

Chicago Surface Lines

Chicago Surface Lines was created by city regulators in 1914 to consolidate operations of the city's two leading street railway companies, the Chicago Railways Co. and the Chicago City Railway Co. The Chicago Railways Co., which employed about 2,000 people around the city in 1910, was created in 1907 as a consolidation of several street railway lines that had been operating on the North and West Sides of the city since the 1860s. During the 1880s (when many lines made the transition from horse-powered to cable car systems), Charles T. Yerkes, the leading Chicago transit entrepreneur of his generation, purchased these lines. The main Yerkes lines were the North Chicago Street Railroad Co. and the West Chicago Street Railway Co., which each employed several hundred people during the late nineteenth century. In 1899, the lines consolidated into the new Chicago Union Traction Co., which in 1907 became Chicago Railways. The other half of Chicago Surface Lines was the Chicago City Railway Co., which was created in 1859 to offer horse-drawn car service between downtown and the South Side. By the end of the nineteenth century, Chicago City Railway owned nearly 2,000 cable cars, employed 3,000 people, and had $5 million in annual passenger revenues. When Chicago City Railway and Chicago Railways were associated in 1914 under the Chicago Surface Lines, this enterprise became the largest operator of streetcars in the United States. By the early 1920s, Chicago Surface Lines had over 16,000 workers, making it one of the leading employers in the Chicago area. The company suffered financial failures in the 1920s and during the Great Depression. Between 1945 and 1947, when it operated more than 3,500 streetcars and 400 motor buses, Chicago Surface Lines was absorbed by the Chicago Transit Authority (CTA), the city's public mass transit enterprise.

Chicago Telephone Co.

See Illinois Bell Telephone Co.

Chicago Times

This newspaper was founded in 1854 by editor James W. Sheahan with the backing of Stephen Douglas, the powerful U.S. Senator from Illinois and one of the leaders of the Democratic Party. In 1861, the *Times*—which was the leading rival of the pro-Republican *Chicago Tribune*—gained an energetic new Democratic editor when Wilbur F. Storey came to Chicago from Detroit. In 1863, Storey's hostility to the Lincoln administration inspired Union general Ambrose Burnside to suppress the paper; this ban was lifted immediately by Lincoln himself. By the end of the 1860s, the *Times* had a Sunday circulation of about 35,000, making it one of the leading papers in the Midwest. Before Storey died in 1884, the paper helped Carter H. Harrison, a Democrat, to begin a long term of service as Chicago's mayor. After 1895, when the *Times* merged with another Chicago daily, the *Herald*, it disappeared as an independent entity. (A new and distinct *Chicago Times*, founded in 1929 by Samuel E. Thomason as the city's first tabloid, became part of the *Chicago Sun-Times* in 1947.)

Chicago Tribune

See Tribune Co.

Chicago Yellow Cab Co.

See Yellow Cab Co. (of Chicago)

City Products Corp.

See Household Finance Corp.

CNA Financial Corp.

The Continental Assurance Co. of North America, founded in Detroit in 1897, soon changed its name to the Continental Casualty Co. In 1900, Continental Casualty merged with a Chicago insurer, the Metropolitan Accident Co., creating a new Chicago-based Continental Casualty that then ranked as the fifth-largest accident insurer in the United States. Six years later, it became an international firm when it began selling industrial health and accident policies in London. In 1911, when it began to offer automobile insurance, Continental Casualty created a new subsidiary, Continental Assurance, which sold life insurance. By the mid-1960s, Continental Casualty and Continental Assurance, which shared the same headquarters on Michigan Avenue, together collected roughly $850 million in annual premiums and employed nearly 8,000 people nationwide. In 1967, these two operations became part of a new parent company, the CNA Financial Corp. By the mid-1970s, when it was acquired by the Loews Corp., CNA employed about 5,000 Chicago-area residents. At the end of the 1990s, following a 1995 merger with the Continental Corp., CNA employed about 4,500 people in the Chicago area and another 20,000 around the world, and its annual revenues reached about $16 billion, making it one of the 10 largest insurance companies in the United States.

Combined Insurance Co. of America

Founded in Chicago by W. Clement Stone, this company would become the nation's largest door-to-door accident and health insurance company. Stone, who worked with his mother in the insurance business when he was still a teenager, opened his own small agency, the Combined Registry Co., in Chicago in 1922. Twenty-five years later, after his business had expanded considerably, Stone created the Combined Insurance Co. of America. By the beginning of the 1960s, Combined Insurance employed about 1,500 people and collected nearly $100 million in annual premiums. During the final decades of the twentieth century, Stone's company continued to expand, particularly after merging with the Ryan Insurance Group in 1982. By 1987, when Combined Insurance changed its name to Aon Corp., annual revenues stood at roughly $2.5 billion. The number of Chicago-area residents employed by the company rose from 1,500 in the mid-1970s to about 6,000 by the end of the 1990s. In 2002, Aon was a large international corporation with over 55,000 employees in 600 offices in 125 countries around the world.

Comdisco Inc.

In 1969, Kenneth Pontikes, a 29-year-old former salesman for IBM, borrowed $5,000 from his father to start a computer leasing business he named the Computer Discount Corp. In 1971, when Pontikes began to sell stock to the public, the name was changed to Comdisco. By the late 1970s, the company began to open offices overseas, and annual revenues topped $100 million. In the early 1990s, when revenues hit $2 billion, Comdisco ranked as the nation's leading computer equipment leasing company. By the end of the 1990s, the company, based in suburban Rosemont, was doing annual sales of $4 billion and employed nearly 1,500 people in the Chicago area. Comdisco expanded in the Internet boom, then collapsed, filing first for bankruptcy in July 2001 and then beginning liquidation in July 2002.

Commerce Clearing House Inc.

In 1892, William Kix Miller started Commerce Clearing House, a Chicago-based publisher of guides to commercial and tax regulations. The demand for legal information services provided by the company allowed it to prosper, and by 1960 its new Peterson Avenue facility on the city's far Northwest Side employed over 1,000 people. In 1986, the company moved its headquarters from Chicago to suburban Riverwoods. Annual revenues grew from about $30 million in the mid-1960s to $600 million by the mid-1990s. In 1995, Commerce Clearing House was purchased for nearly $2 billion by Wolters Kluwer, a Dutch company.

Commonwealth Edison Co.

The Western Edison Light Co. was founded in Chicago in 1882, three years after Thomas Edison developed a practical light bulb. In 1887, Western Edison became the Chicago Edison Co. Samuel L. Insull became president of Chicago Edison in 1892; in 1897 Insull incorporated another electric utility, the Commonwealth Electric Light & Power Co. In 1907, Insull's two companies formally merged to create the Commonwealth Edison Co. As more people became connected to the electric grid, Insull's company, which had an exclusive franchise from the city, grew steadily. By 1920, when it used more than two million tons of coal annually, the company's 6,000 employees served about 500,000 customers; annual revenues had reached nearly $40 million. During the 1920s, its largest generating stations included one on Fisk Street and West 22nd and one on Crawford Avenue and the Sanitary Canal. Although Insull went bankrupt and fled the country during the Great Depression, Commonwealth Edison survived; after World War II, it received a new 42-year franchise from the city. During the second half of the twentieth century, the company became a world leader in nuclear power. In 1959, it opened the Dresden nuclear generating plant near Morris, Illinois, southwest of Chicago. Over the next three decades, the company known as "ComEd" opened several plants around the region and became the largest operator of nuclear power facilities in the United States. Although the company received several warnings from federal regulators about safety problems at these plants, most of them continued to operate, and by the 1990s nuclear power accounted for well over half of the company's output. Meanwhile, the company employed a workforce of more than 15,000 men and women in the Chicago area. With its rates subject to approval by state regulators, the company saw its annual revenues rise to roughly $7 billion by the late 1990s, when it had about 3.4 million customers in the northern Illinois region. In 1994, ComEd became part of a parent company named Unicom; in 1999, after merging with the Philadelphia-based PECO Energy Co., the new parent company took the name of Exelon. In 2002, Exelon's revenues exceeded $12 billion. It employed over 12,000 persons in the Chicago area and, through ComEd, supplied electricity to over 3.4 million customers.

Consolidated Foods Corp.

The giant food company that was known by the end of the twentieth century as Sara Lee Corp. was the descendant of a Chicago grocery store called Sprague, Warner & Co. This enterprise, which started on State Street, was founded during the Civil War by Albert A. Sprague and Ezra J. Warner. By 1909, when it moved into a large new facility on Erie and Roberts Streets, Sprague, Warner & Co. was one of the leading wholesale grocery companies in the United States, famous for house brands such as "Richelieu" and "Batavia." In 1942, this company was acquired by Nathan Cummings, the Canadian-born owner of C. D. Kenny Co., a large grocery enterprise based in Baltimore. The new Chicago-based company, at first called Sprague Warner-Kenny Corp., ranked as the largest grocery wholesaler in the United States. Annual sales grew from about $20 million in 1942 to $120 million by 1946. After changing its name in 1945 to Consolidated Grocers, Cummings's company became the Consolidated Foods Corp. in 1953. In 1956, the company bought the Kitchens of Sara Lee, a five-year-old Chicago bakery named after the daughter of founder Charles Lubin; as a division of Consolidated, this became the world's leading producer of frozen pastries. In 1964, the company opened a large new automated bakery in suburban Deerfield. The company grew rapidly. Annual sales rose from $500 million in the early 1960s to nearly $5 billion by the late 1970s, when the company employed over 2,000 people in the Chicago area and about 75,000 more worldwide. By this time, Consolidated was selling not only food but also underwear and other products. In 1985, the company changed its name from Consolidated Foods to the Sara Lee Corp., with headquarters in Deerfield. By the early 2000s, Sara Lee, again headquartered in Chicago, was a huge international food and clothing company, amassing over $17 billion in annual sales, over one-third of which were made overseas. At the same time, its Deerfield bakery had closed, and only about 2,000 of the company's some 150,000 employees worldwide were Chicago-area residents.

Container Corp. of America

Walter P. Paepcke led the formation in 1926 of Container Corp. of America, which united several smaller manufacturers of paper boxes and containers and included 14 plants around the country. The enterprise had its national headquarters in Chicago, and by 1928, it operated four plants around the city, including those formerly owned by the Chicago Mill & Lumber Co., the Robert Gair Co., and the Sefton Manufacturing Co. By the mid-1930s, Container Corp. employed about 1,300 area residents. As the company grew, annual sales rose from about $20 million in 1936 to over $400 million by 1965, when Container Corp. employed over 20,000 people nationwide. In 1968, the company merged with Montgomery Ward Co., the giant Chicago-based retailer; the new parent company was called Marcor. In 1976, when Container Corp. had 150 plants around the world, Marcor was purchased by Mobil, the giant oil company. In 1986, Mobil sold Container Corp. to Jefferson Smurfit Corp., another box manufacturer. This company's 1998 merger with the Chicago-based Stone Container Corp., which created the Smurfit-Stone Container Corp., meant that the remnants of Container Corp. were again managed from Chicago. *See also* WARD (MONTGOMERY) & CO. and STONE CONTAINER CORP.

Continental Assurance Co.

See CNA Financial Corp.

Continental Can Co.

This company, the nation's second leading metal can maker (behind American Can) for much of the twentieth century, was founded in 1904 by Edwin Norton and T. G. Cranwell. Continental's main factories were in Chicago and Syracuse, New York, where it was headquartered. By the mid-1930s, with 38 plants nationwide, the company employed about 1,800 men and 1,200 women around the Chicago area. By the early 1970s, annual sales reached $2 billion and Continental Can ranked as the number one U.S. can manufacturer, with about 6,000 Chicago-area employees. In 1976, it became part of the Continental Group, a conglomerate with operations in many industries. By the end of the 1980s, the remnants of Continental Can became part of the U.S. Can Co., a new can-manufacturing company now headquartered in suburban Lombard.

Continental Casualty Co.

See CNA Financial Corp.

Continental Coffee Co.

This enterprise was founded in 1915 by Jacob Cohn, a 19-year-old Lithuanian immigrant. Cohn started by selling coffee to local restaurants and cafeterias. By 1920, he had 15 employees. By the 1940s, when the company marketed coffee through a national network of salesmen, annual sales approached $1 million. Starting in the 1950s, the company expanded rapidly by buying competitors. Annual sales rose from about $30 million in the early 1960s to over $1 billion by the early 1980s. By 1973, when the company changed its name to CFS Continental, coffee was only a small part of its food business. In 1988, when CFS ranked as the third-largest food distributor in the nation, it was purchased by a competitor, the Sysco Corp. of Houston, Texas.

Continental Illinois National Bank & Trust Co.

One of the city's two largest banks for most of the twentieth century, Continental was the product of a 1910 merger of two Chicago enterprises, the Commercial National Bank and the Continental National Bank. The older of the two was the Commercial National Bank, formed during the Civil War and led by Henry F. Eames. Commercial National Bank had become one of the city's leading banks by the early 1870s. The Continental National Bank, chartered in 1883, was led during its early years by John C. Black. By the turn of the century, both banks had grown by absorbing several competitors. In 1910, the merger of Commercial and Continental created a new entity, the Continental & Commercial National Bank of Chicago, which had $175 million in deposits, making it one of the largest banks in the United States. It continued to grow during the 1920s. In 1929 it merged with Illinois Merchants Trust Co.; three years later, the bank's name became Continental Illinois National Bank & Trust Co. During the Great Depression, the bank required a $50 million loan from Reconstruction Finance Corp. (a federal government agency) to stay afloat. After World War II, the bank grew: by the beginning of the 1960s, Continental had over $3 billion in deposits and employed 5,000 people. By the early 1970s, when it had 60 branches and affiliates around the world, the bank employed about 8,200 Chicago-area residents, many of whom worked at Continental's main offices on LaSalle Street in Chicago's loop. During the early 1980s, after many of its large loans to companies in the oil and gas industries went bad, the bank experienced a sudden and unexpected crisis. Continental's Great Depression–era experience was repeated as the Federal Deposit Insurance Corp. came to the rescue. In 1994, a diminished Continental was acquired by BankAmerica Corp. of San Francisco.

Corn Products Refining Co.

This company, created in 1902 by E. T. Bedford, had its executive offices in New York for most of the century, but its main manufacturing operation was located just outside Chicago. In 1910, Corn Products built a new $5 million plant at Summit, southwest of Chicago; the site of the plant was known as Argo, and the company sold cornstarch and other products under the "Argo" brand name. The company employed more than 1,000 Chicago-area residents at its Summit plant. In 1960, the Argo facility still ranked as the world's largest corn wet-milling plant. During the early 1970s, the plant employed as many as 4,000 people, but its workforce declined to about 1,000 by the 1990s. In the late 1990s, the general offices of the company finally came to the Chicago area when Corn Products International Inc. was spun off from Bestfoods Inc., a larger conglomerate. The new company, now based in suburban Westchester, achieved nearly $2 billion in annual sales at the end of the century and boasted nearly 30 plants in 20 countries.

Cotter & Co.

See True Value Hardware

Cracker Jack Co.

F. W. Rueckheim emigrated from Germany to Chicago in 1869. In 1872, Rueckheim and his brother Louis formed F. W. Rueckheim & Bro., a small candy and popcorn shop. Business grew steadily, and by the 1880s the brothers had relocated to a three-story plant on South Clinton Street. In 1896, the company began to sell its caramel-coated popcorn under the "Cracker Jack" brand name, a name that would be made famous by Jack Norworth's 1908 song, "Take Me Out to the Ball Game." In 1912, when the company employed about 450 women and girls and 250 men and boys at its large new factory on South Peoria and Harrison Streets, it began to insert small toys into the packages with the popcorn. This "prize in every box" marketing strategy proved successful. In 1922, the name of the company, which made marshmallows and candies as well as its signature popcorn product, became Cracker Jack Co. During the 1950s, the company employed over 1,000 Chicago-area residents. During the last decades of the twentieth century, Cracker Jack was purchased by a number of large international food companies. After being held for many years by Borden Foods Inc., the Cracker Jack brand was purchased in 1997 by the Frito Lay division of Pepsico, the food giant based in Purchase, New York.

Crain Communications Inc.

This business information company was founded by Gustavus D. Crain, Jr., who moved it in 1916 from Louisville to Chicago. He immediately started *Class* (now *BtoB*) and *Hospital Management*. In 1930, when the company's name became Advertising Publications Inc., it launched *Advertising Age*; by the late 1940s, this publication had a circulation of over 20,000. In 1969, the company changed its name to Crain Communications Inc., which continued to be operated by the Crain family. A new publication, *Crain's Chicago Business*, was launched in 1978; similar newspapers covering local business events were soon introduced in other cities, including Detroit, Cleveland, New York, and Mexico City. By the 1990s, when it was moving into electronic publishing, Crain's had close to $250 million in annual revenues, published 30 titles, and employed about 250 people in the Chicago area and another 750 people worldwide.

Crane Co.

Richard Teller Crane, a nephew of Chicago lumber dealer Martin Ryerson, moved to Chicago from New Jersey in 1855. Richard and his brother Charles soon formed R. T. Crane & Bro., which manufactured and sold brass goods and plumbing supplies. The new company soon won contracts to supply pipe and steam-heating equipment in large public buildings such as the Cook County courthouse and the state prison at Joliet. By 1865, when the name of the company was changed to the Northwestern Manufacturing Co., it ran a large pipe mill and manufactured engines and steam pumps; by 1870, when it employed about 160 people, it was making elevators as well. After the Chicago Fire of 1871, the company decided to expand its operations. Just after the firm became Crane Bros. Manufacturing Co. in 1872, it employed as many as 700 men and boys and manufactured over $1 million worth of products per year. In 1890, when it had sales branches in Omaha, Kansas City, Los Angeles, and Philadelphia, the company changed its name to Crane Co. By this time, Crane was supplying much of the pipe used for the large central heating systems in Chicago's new skyscrapers, and it was also selling the enameled cast-iron products that were soon found in bathrooms in residences across the country. In 1910, when Crane had begun to manufacture in a plant at Bridgeport, Connecticut, its Chicago plants employed more than 5,000 people. A large new Chicago plant on South Kedzie Avenue was built in the 1910s. During the 1920s, when Crane expanded overseas, the company was the world's leading manufacturer of valves and fittings. During the next few decades, Crane continued to employ thousands of Chicago-area residents at its Kedzie Avenue plant, and the company's annual sales rose to over $300 million by the mid-1950s. In 1959, however, the company was acquired by Thomas M. Evans, its first owner who was not a member of the Crane family. Evans proceeded to turn Crane into a global conglomerate that made aerospace equipment as well as plumbing supplies; the headquarters eventually moved from Chicago to Bridgeport. By the mid-1970s, Crane employed only about 1,000 people in the Chicago area. By the end of the century, Crane was doing annual sales of about $2 billion, but it was no longer a leading company in the city in which it was born.

Crate & Barrel

This house furnishings retail chain was created in 1962 by two young Chicago residents, Gordon and Carole Segal. The Segals began with a small store in the city's Old Town neighborhood; they began to issue catalogs in 1967. Between 1968 and 1975, they added new locations in Wilmette, Oak Brook, and downtown Chicago on Michigan Avenue. In 1983, soon after it started selling furniture, the company built a new warehouse and headquarters in suburban Northbrook. By the mid-1990s, when annual sales had climbed to roughly $300 million, the company already had 46 stores and was opening about 5 new stores each year. In 1998, Gordon Segal sold a controlling interest in the company to Otto Versand GmbH & Co., a German catalog company.

Cudahy Packing Co.
The Irish-born Cudahy brothers started working in the Milwaukee meat business in the early 1860s; there they met Philip Armour, whom they followed to Chicago during the 1870s. In the years that followed, the Cudahys operated small packing plants in Chicago. In 1887, with Armour's backing, Michael Cudahy and his brothers started an Armour-Cudahy packing plant in Omaha, Nebraska. The Cudahy Packing Co. was created in 1890, when Michael bought Armour's interest. Over the next 30 years, the company added branches across the country, including a cleaning products plant at East Chicago, Indiana, built in 1909. In 1911, the company's headquarters were transferred from Omaha to Chicago. By the mid-1920s, Cudahy was one of the nation's leading food companies, with over $200 million in annual sales and 13,000 employees around the country. Although it was hard hit by the Great Depression, the company still employed about 1,000 Chicago-area residents during the mid-1930s. Following World War II, the company moved its headquarters first to Omaha and, in 1965, to Phoenix, where it took the name Cudahy Co. During the 1970s, after it was purchased by General Host, Cudahy was dismantled.

Curtiss Candy Co.
Founded in Chicago in 1916 by Otto Schnering, Curtiss Candy did just under $100,000 in sales during its first year. The company grew quickly, and in 1919 it opened a new three-story factory on Briar Place that employed 400 men and women. Annual sales passed $1 million by 1921, when the company was turning out huge quantities of its "Baby Ruth" candy bars; among its other popular bars made were "Butterfinger" and "Polar Bar." In the mid-1930s, Curtiss employed over 300 men and nearly 1,900 women around the city. By the beginning of the 1960s, with $60 million in annual sales, the company ranked among the top 10 firms in the U.S. candy industry. Control of the company left the Chicago area in 1964, when Curtiss was purchased by Standard Brands, a large national food conglomerate. By the end of the century, the most popular of the old Curtiss brands were owned by Nestle, the Swiss food giant.

Dean Milk Co.
Sam Dean, an evaporated milk dealer who sold to Chicago-area customers, founded the Dean Evaporated Milk Co. in Pecatonica, Illinois (west of Rockford), in 1925. During the 1930s, Dean began to sell fresh dairy products, including fluid milk; it entered the ice cream business in 1947. During the 1950s and 1960s, Dean's business—now based in the Chicago suburb of Franklin Park and named the Dean Milk Co.—expanded by buying smaller dairy companies. By 1961, when it began to sell stock to the public, it employed about 1,300 people and did over $60 million in annual sales. Five years later, Dean doubled in size by purchasing the Bowman Dairy Co., another large Chicago-area food company. By 1985, when the company's annual sales hit $1 billion, it sold pickles and other foods, but dairy products still accounted for about two-thirds of its business. During the 1990s, with many dairy facilities around the Midwest, Dean became the largest milk processor in the United States, as well as diversifying to buy such brands as Birds Eye. By the end of the century, Dean had reached nearly $4 billion and annual sales, but only a few hundred of the company's some 14,000 employees worldwide were based in the Chicago area. In December 2001, Dean Foods was purchased by the Suiza Foods Corp., a rival company based in Dallas, Texas, which took the Dean name. *See also* BOWMAN DAIRY CO.

Deering Harvester Co.
See International Harvester Co.

Dick (A. B.) Co.
Albert B. Dick, who started a lumber business in Chicago in 1883, soon left that field to pioneer the manufacture of mimeograph machines, which were based on a design by Thomas Edison. The first of these primitive copiers were cranked by hand; eventually, Dick introduced larger and more automated models. In 1918, the company established the "Ditto" trademark. By the mid-1930s, Dick employed about 900 people in the Chicago area. In 1949, the company moved its headquarters to suburban Niles, where it opened a new plant. During the 1960s, Dick's mimeograph technology lost out to the new copy methods pioneered by Haloid/Xerox. By the mid-1970s, when Dick's annual sales approached $300 million, it had about 3,000 workers in the Chicago area. In 1979, the company was purchased by General Electric Co. of Great Britain. In the late 1990s, over a century after it was founded, A. B. Dick still called Chicago home; as a division of Nesco Inc. of Cleveland, it was a supplier of printing and graphics equipment, with about 1,000 employees.

Doggett, Bassett & Hills Co.
One of Chicago's first shoe dealers and manufacturers, this enterprise was founded as Ward & Doggett in 1846 by William E. Doggett and George L. Ward. In 1856, when the company was employing about 40 manufacturing workers and doing about $350,000 in annual wholesale sales, the name of the company became Doggett, Bassett & Hills. By the early 1870s, the company's factory on Lake Street had about 100 employees, who made $250,000 worth of shoes a year. By the 1880s, the firm's yearly sales had topped $1 million, but, soon after, the company declined and disappeared.

Dominick's Finer Foods Inc.
This retail grocery business was founded in Chicago by Dominick DiMatteo, who was eventually succeeded by his son Dominick Jr. In 1968, when it had grown to a chain of 18 stores, the company was purchased by Fisher Foods of Cleveland, Ohio. During the mid-1970s, the Dominick's chain employed about 6,000 Chicago-area residents. In 1981, when there were 71 stores in the chain, the DiMatteo family bought it back for $80 million. The chain proceeded to expand; its share of the retail grocery market in Chicago grew from about 13 percent in 1984 to about 25 percent by 1993. By the late 1980s, it had close to 18,000 workers in the Chicago area. In 1995, Oak Brook–based Dominick's was purchased by the Yucaipa Cos., a grocery company based in Los Angeles; three years later, it was acquired by a different California-based national chain, Safeway Inc. At the end of the century, the Safeway-owned Dominick's remained a leading grocery chain in the Chicago area and was still one of the area's top employers.

Donnelley (R. R.) & Sons Co.
In 1882, Richard R. Donnelley, a veteran of the printing and publishing business in Chicago, started his own printing company, R. R. Donnelley & Sons. Under the leadership of his son Thomas, the company grew quickly during the first decades of the twentieth century, when it printed the Montgomery Ward and Sears catalogs and launched efforts such as Lakeside Classics. It continued to expand by winning contracts to print major national magazines such as *Time* (introduced in 1927) and *Life* (1936). By the mid-1930s, Donnelley employed about 1,800 men and 700 women at its plant on East Cermak Avenue. By the beginning of the 1960s, as the number one company in the commercial printing industry, R. R. Donnelley grossed about $150 million in annual sales and employed nearly 10,000 people. A Los Angeles division was opened in 1978. In 1993, after Sears canceled its catalog, Donnelley closed its large plant on the city's South Side. By the end of the 1990s, when it was moving into electronic publishing and was printing paper manuals for computer industry companies such as Microsoft, annual sales stood at over $5 billion. Donnelley, which operated more than 50 plants in the United States, Mexico, South America, the United Kingdom, Central Europe, and Asia, ranked as the world's third-largest commercial printer. Of its some 34,000 employees, about 2,500 worked in the Chicago area.

Duchossois Industries Inc.

The Thrall Car Manufacturing Co. was founded in Chicago Heights in 1917. In 1946, Thrall was a small railroad equipment maker, with about 35 employees and $200,000 in annual sales. Richard L. Duchossois, a native of Chicago's South Side, joined the company after serving in World War II and marrying Beverly Thrall, daughter of the head of the firm. By the 1970s, the company was making as many as 90,000 railcars a year; but annual production dropped to about 10,000 cars during the 1980s, when annual sales were around $750 million. Meanwhile, Duchossois, who created a parent company named after himself that expanded into electronic consumer products, national defense supplies, and various capital goods, moved into the horse racing business by purchasing facilities in suburban Arlington Heights. By the mid-1990s, when railcar production reached 50,000 per year, annual revenues from horse racing approached $600 million. In 2001, Thrall was purchased by Trinity Industries of Dallas, Texas, a leading railcar manufacturer. At the beginning of the twenty-first century, the privately held company led by Craig Duchossois (Richard's son), still employed about 1,500 people in the Chicago area and grossed about $1 billion in annual sales.

E

Ekco Products Co.

In 1888, Austrian-born Edward Katzinger formed Edward Katzinger Co., which manufactured tin pans for bakeries. In 1923, the company built a large new factory on Chicago's Northwest Side. In 1945, led by Arthur Katzinger, a son of the founder, the company began to sell stock to the public and changed its name to the Ekco Products Co. The company continued to grow during the 1950s, when it was the nation's leading manufacturer of kitchen tools and cutlery. By the beginning of the 1960s, still based in Chicago, Ekco employed about 6,000 people and did about $90 million in annual sales. In 1965, American Home Products Corp. of New York purchased Ekco. By the 1980s, when it was purchased by Centronics Corp. of New Hampshire, Ekco was based in suburban Franklin Park, and it remained a leading manufacturer of bakeware.

Elgin National Watch Co.

This enterprise, which would quickly become one of the world's leading manufacturers of timepieces, was founded in Chicago during the Civil War by a group of investors that included Benjamin W. Raymond, a former mayor of the city, and John C. Adams, a Chicago watchmaker. Other founders of this new company, initially named the National Watch Co., included Ira G. Blake and P. S. Bartlett, both of whom had been involved with the famous Waltham Watch Co. in Massachusetts. By 1867, the company had begun to manufacture watches at a new plant in Elgin, west of Chicago. By 1870, the plant, which over the previous year had turned out 25,000 watches worth about $600,000, employed nearly 300 men and 200 women. In 1874, the name of the company was changed to the Elgin National Watch Co. Under the leadership of company president T. M. Avery, annual output rose from about 30,000 watches in the early 1870s to about 500,000 by the late 1880s, when the company employed nearly 2,500 people at its Elgin plant. By the early twentieth century, Elgin had surpassed its old rival Waltham and stood as the world's greatest mass producer of watches. The company built the Elgin Observatory in 1909; it opened the Elgin Watchmaker's College in 1920. By the late 1920s, Elgin National Watch was making about two million watches each year. But this production was followed by a steady decline. After World War II, the company struggled against competition from overseas. By the beginning of the 1960s, when the company was doing about $30 million in annual sales and still employed nearly 3,000 people, it had begun to fail. The Watchmaker's College closed in 1960. The large plant at Elgin was closed in 1965 and demolished the following year. Although remnants of the company continued to exist into the 1980s under the name Elgin National Industries, its days as a leading enterprise had ended.

Encyclopaedia Britannica Inc.

Founded in Scotland in 1768, the original *Encyclopaedia Britannica* consisted of three volumes, the last of which appeared in 1771. In 1901, the operation was purchased by American investors, who moved the general offices to New York City. Chicago's connection with the publication began in 1920, when Britannica was purchased by Julius Rosenwald, the Sears, Roebuck & Co. chief. Rosenwald's backing allowed the encyclopedia to publish its 14th edition in 1929. Three years later, Elkan H. "Buck" Powell, a University of Chicago graduate and Sears employee, took charge of Britannica, and the general offices moved to Chicago. In 1943, the operation was purchased by William Benton, who was backed by the University of Chicago. After World War II, Britannica salespeople solicited orders by telephone and by selling door-to-door. By the beginning of the 1960s, having purchased *Compton's Encyclopedia* and dictionary publisher G. & C. Merriam (later Merriam-Webster), and having published, in 1962, the *Great Books of the Western World* , the enterprise had nearly 4,000 employees nationwide and was doing about $75 million in annual sales. By the 1980s, when it was controlled by the William Benton Foundation, Britannica employed about 1,000 people in the Chicago area. During the 1990s, the company concentrated on producing electronic references, but competition in this field was heavy, and sales dropped. In 1995, Britannica was purchased by an investment group led by Jacob E. Safra of Switzerland.

Esmark Inc.

See Swift & Co.

Evans Food Products

Chicago attorney Lester W. Olin entered the pork rind business in 1947 when he purchased a large oil vat from a Mr. Evans, who had been renting a small office in the State Street building that Olin owned. Olin quickly patented his pork rind manufacturing process, and Evans Food Products was born. In the beginning, Olin sold his pork rinds, and soon corn chips, door-to-door to area homes and businesses. In 1955, Evans Food Products moved to a much larger manufacturing plant on South Halstead Street, about the same time that the company began selling to overseas markets. Evans continued to grow over the next several decades, employing several dozen people by the mid-1970s. Olin sold Evans Food Products to a subsidiary of Milwaukee-based Northwestern Mutual Life Insurance Co. in 1981. The next year, the company discontinued its corn chip line, focusing exclusively on pork rinds. Mexican pork rind manufacturers, Alejandro Silva, Carlos Silva, and Jose Garza purchased Evans in 1985. By the early 2000s, Evans Food Products was still headquartered at its plant on South Halsted, with manufacturing facilities in Texas, Ohio, and Mexico. Boasting annual revenues near $70 million, Evans was the world's top pork rind business, and one of Chicago's largest minority-owned firms. It employed about 100 people in Chicago and almost 150 more in its three other locations.

Evinrude Motor Co.

See Outboard Marine Corp.

Exelon Corp.

See Commonwealth Edison Co.

Fair, The

Founded in 1875 by Ernest J. Lehmann as a small Chicago retail shop, the Fair soon became a giant retail operation that is often regarded as the city's first department store. By the 1890s, when Ernest J. Lehmann, Jr., took charge of the business, a new store at State and Adams Streets contained 286,000 square feet of floor space. Promoting itself with the motto "everything for everybody under one roof," the Fair was now one of the largest retailers in the city. Offering a wide range of goods at low prices, the store offered services such as free wrapping, delivery, and an on-site nursery. In 1900, when annual sales were about $8 million, the store had nearly 3,800 workers; by the 1910s, floor space reached nearly 800,000 square feet. The Fair had 5,500 workers, making it one of the largest employers in the city. During the 1920s, the Fair was purchased by S. S. Kresge & Co., the Detroit-based dime store chain (which would eventually become known as Kmart). Under the new ownership, the Fair opened a branch in Oak Park in 1929; during the 1950s, it added locations in Evergreen Park and Skokie. In 1957, the Fair was purchased by Montgomery Ward, a larger Chicago-based competitor.

Fairbank (N. K.) & Co.

In 1864, Nathaniel K. Fairbank and John Peck established Fairbank, Peck & Co. as the successor to Smedley, Peck & Co., a Chicago lard processor and soap maker. Using materials generated by the city's large meatpacking industry, the company expanded. By 1870, its new plant at 19th and Blackwell Streets employed about 160 men, women, and children, and produced about $2 million worth of lard, soap, and cottonseed oil a year. In 1875, it was purchased by American Cotton Oil and was renamed N. K. Fairbank & Co. By 1880, it had 400 employees and $5 million in annual sales. A decade later, the company had sales branches in St. Louis, Omaha, and Montreal and had become famous for its distinctive advertising. The company employed over 1,000 people at the 19th Street plant in Chicago into the 1910s. In 1921, the plant was closed as American Cotton Oil moved its manufacturing to newer plants in the South.

Fairbank Canning Co.

See Morris (Nelson) & Co.

Fansteel Inc.

In 1907, Carl Pfanstiehl, a native of Highland Park, along with a friend, James M. Troxel, started the Pfanstiehl Electrical Laboratory, which made coils for x-ray equipment, automobiles, and other products. During the 1910s, the company pioneered the development of tungsten electrical contacts, as well as the industrial use of tantalum, a new metal. In 1918, the company's name was changed to Fansteel Products Co. Inc.; 17 years later, it would become the Fansteel Metallurgical Corp. During the 1920s, sales of radio battery chargers drove annual revenues past $5 million. In 1937, a sit-down strike by workers at the company's plant in North Chicago ended when police fired tear gas into the facility. During World War II, increased civilian and military demand for electrical contacts led to expansion at Fansteel: by the middle of the war, annual sales were up to $18 million, about seven times higher than they had been in 1940. After the war, the company expanded to other locations but still employed over 1,000 people in the Chicago area. It remained a medium-sized company that supplied specialty components for the aerospace industry and other users of exotic metallic goods. After the late 1960s, when annual sales were close to $100 million, Fansteel stopped growing. By the end of the 1990s, still based in North Chicago, the company sold about $150 million annually and employed fewer than 200 people in the Chicago area.

Farwell (John V.) & Co.

Now largely forgotten, this company was once one of the leading business enterprises in the United States. In 1838, when he was 13 years old, John V. Farwell moved with his family from New York to Illinois. In 1845, the young Farwell headed to Chicago, where he worked as a clerk for several merchant houses engaged in the sale of dry-goods such as textiles, clothing, and home furnishings. In 1857, Farwell became a partner in the largest of these Chicago dry-goods firms, which changed its name from Cooley, Wadsworth & Co. to Cooley, Farwell & Co. One of Farwell's associates in this company was the young Marshall Field, who would soon form his own dry goods company. By 1863, Cooley, Farwell had become Farwell, Field & Co.; in 1865, after Field departed, John V. Farwell & Co. was born. A wholesaler of dry goods who supplied smaller wholesalers and retailers all around the Midwest, Farwell & Co. operated on a very large scale. Annual sales reached nearly $10 million by 1870 and stood at about $20 million in 1883, when the company moved its 600 employees into a new eight-story, 400,000-square-foot building at Monroe and Market Streets. By the end of the 1880s, Farwell (along with Marshall Field, its great Chicago rival) ranked as one of the top three wholesalers in the country. Unlike Field, however, Farwell did not establish retail stores. During the first decades of the twentieth century, as more manufacturers sold directly to retailers (including large department stores, chain stores, and mail-order houses), traditional wholesalers such as Farwell & Co. suffered. During the 1910s, the company (now led by John V. Farwell, Jr.) still grossed around $20 million in annual sales and employed over 1,000 people at its Chicago headquarters, but it was no longer growing and profits were declining. In 1925, Farwell & Co. closed its wholesaling business, ending a 60-year reign as one of the city's foremost business enterprises.

Federal Sign & Signal Corp.

The Federal Electric Co., a manufacturer of electric signs, was incorporated in Illinois in 1901 by John Goehst and brothers John and James Gilchrist. In 1915, the company started making sirens. After spending a few years under the control of Chicago utilities titan Samuel Insull, the company became independent again in the 1930s, when it became the Federal Sign & Signal Corp. In 1958, Federal moved its main plant from 87th and State Streets on Chicago's South Side to Blue Island, the suburb a few miles to the southwest. By the middle of the 1960s, the company—a leader in the field of electric signs—was doing about $30 million in annual sales and had about 1,500 employees. After changing its name to the Federal Signal Corp. in 1975, the company's general offices were moved to suburban Oak Brook. By the end of the 1990s, when Federal Signal was a leading manufacturer of emergency vehicles and street sweepers as well as signs and sirens, the company approached $1 billion in annual sales and employed about 1,500 people in the Chicago area.

Felt & Tarrant Manufacturing Co.

See Victor Adding Machine Co.

Field (Marshall) & Co.

In 1856, the 21-year-old Marshall Field moved to Chicago from Massachusetts. He immediately began working at Cooley, Wadsworth & Co. By the Civil War, Field was a partner in the company, then led by John V. Farwell. Not satisfied as the junior partner in Farwell, Field & Co., Field left in 1865. That year, he joined Levi Leiter and Potter Palmer to create a new dry-goods house, Field, Palmer, Leiter & Co.; after Palmer sold out in 1867, this became Field, Leiter & Co. This new company operated on a very large scale, with about $9 million in wholesale and retail sales in 1867. Although two of its stores burned during the 1870s, the company continued to do an immense business. After Leiter retired in 1881, the name of the enterprise became Marshall Field & Co. By the late 1880s, when annual sales rose to over $30 million (about $5 million retail and $25 million wholesale), the company employed a total of nearly 3,000 people at its retail store on State and Washington Streets and its massive seven-story wholesale building at Quincy and Adams. The wholesale division, managed by John Shedd, made most of its purchases in New York City; meanwhile, by the 1890s, retail division chief Harry Selfridge was helping to create the modern department store by adding features such as a tearoom and large display windows. After Field died in 1906 (leaving $8 million for a natural history museum in Chicago that would bear his name), Shedd became president of a company that employed 12,000 people in Chicago (two-thirds of them in retail) and was doing about $25 million in yearly retail sales in addition to nearly $50 million wholesale. A new State Street store, completed in 1907, ranked as one of the largest retail establishments in the world. Under the leadership of Shedd and his successor James Simpson, Field & Co. expanded beyond Chicago during the 1920s. Shedd bought textile mills in North America and Asia; Simpson, who took over in 1923, concentrated on retail sales, opening branches in suburban Oak Park, Evanston, and Lake Forest, and acquiring a Seattle store at the end of the 1920s. Meanwhile, the company built the Merchandise Mart, a building in downtown Chicago that became the world's largest commercial structure when it was completed in 1931. Field & Co. would sell it in 1945. The expansion of the 1920s ended during the Great Depression, when the company closed its wholesale operations. At the end of World War II, Field & Co. ranked as one of the 20 largest retail enterprises in the United States. By the beginning of the 1960s, the company operated 10 stores, employed about 13,000 people, and did nearly $250 million in annual sales. In 1975, when it was adding stores across the country, Field opened a large new downtown Chicago store at Water Tower Place. In 1982, when it was purchased by BAT Industries of London, Field ceased to be an independent Chicago-based company. This continued to be the case after 1990, when Field (by then a 24-store chain) was purchased for about $1 billion by the Dayton Hudson Corp. of Minneapolis. By the end of the century, when Dayton Hudson became the Target Corp., it employed nearly 16,000 Chicago-area residents, who worked at Target discount stores as well as the department stores that retained the Marshall Field name.

Field Enterprises Inc.

In 1940, Marshall Field III, a wealthy grandson of the founder of the giant Chicago company, entered the publishing business by backing *PM*, a left-leaning newspaper published in New York City. In 1941, Field launched the *Chicago Sun*, which was conceived as a liberal alternative to the conservative *Tribune*. In 1947, Field bought the *Chicago Daily Times*, which had been founded in 1929 as the city's first tabloid, and merged it into the *Sun*. This created the *Chicago Sun-Times*, which during the second half of the twentieth century became the primary rival of the *Tribune*. By the 1950s, when it was led by Marshall Field IV, Field Enterprises was a major media company that owned not only the *Sun-Times* but also the *World Book Encyclopedia*, the book publisher Simon & Schuster, and several radio stations around the country. In 1959, Field Enterprises bought the *Chicago Daily News*, which had long been one of the city's leading newspapers. (In 1978, the *Daily News* was folded into the *Sun-Times*.) In the early 1980s, the Field family decided to get out of the media business, and Field Enterprises was dismantled. The *Sun-Times* was sold to international media titan Rupert Murdoch in 1984; 10 years later, it was acquired by Hollinger International Inc. of Vancouver, which soon opened offices in Chicago. By this time, Field Enterprises had ceased to exist as a media company.

First National Bank of Chicago

In 1863, a group of Chicago investors led by Edmund Aiken pooled $250,000 to establish a new bank under the guidelines established by new federal banking legislation. By 1876, First National ranked as the city's largest bank; it (and its descendants) would continue to be either Chicago's biggest or second biggest bank through the end of the twentieth century. By 1902, after it absorbed Union National Bank and Metropolitan National Bank, the $100 million in assets held by First National made it (temporarily) the nation's second-largest bank. In 1913, it became one of the original members of the Federal Reserve System. The bank managed to survive the Great Depression, and its assets passed $1 billion in 1938. By the beginning of the 1960s, when it opened an office in Tokyo, First National had over $3 billion in deposits and employed about 3,600 people. In 1969, when First National moved into a new skyscraper in Chicago's loop, it became part of the First Chicago Corp., a holding company for the bank. During the 1970s, when it employed more than 5,000 people in the Chicago area, the bank saw its assets rise from $8 billion to $30 billion. First Chicago continued to grow during the 1980s and early 1990s, when it was the city's largest bank. In comparison to many of the giant banking enterprises around the world, however, First Chicago was a relatively small, regional operation. This changed in 1995, when First Chicago merged with NBD of Detroit to create the First Chicago NBD Corp., which became the seventh-largest bank in the United States. Three years later, First Chicago NBD merged with the Banc One Corp. of Ohio to form Bank One, which had about $260 billion in assets, making it at that time the nation's fifth-largest bank. At the beginning of the century, the Chicago-based Bank One employed about 14,000 Chicago-area residents and more than 70,000 people worldwide.

Florsheim Shoe Co.

In 1892 Milton Florsheim, the son of a Chicago shoemaker, started a small shoe store. Florsheim soon moved into manufacturing, and by 1910 the company had 600 workers at its factory at Adams and Clinton Streets. By the end of the 1920s, when annual sales stood at $3 million, there were five Chicago-area factories, employing a total of 2,500 men and women. Business slowed during the Great Depression, but Florsheim emerged at the end of World War II as one of the top 10 firms in the industry, with nearly $18 million in annual sales. Control of the company left the Chicago area in 1953, when Florsheim was purchased by the International Shoe Co. (later Interco Inc.) of St. Louis. Florsheim became International Shoe's most profitable unit, leading the market for high-quality men's shoes. At the beginning of the 1970s, still a subsidiary, the Florsheim division consisted of 14 factories and 500 retail stores nationwide. During the 1980s, many of its manufacturing operations were moved overseas. In 1994, soon after Interco entered bankruptcy, Florsheim was spun off as an independent company with its headquarters in Chicago. By the end of the 1990s, Florsheim Shoe Group Inc. had about 10 percent of the market for men's dress shoes, making it the leading company in the trade. By that time, when it was doing close to $250 million in annual sales, only about 10 percent of its some 2,000 employees worldwide worked in the Chicago area.

Flying Food Group Inc.

In 1983, real-estate developer, bakery owner, and former Chinese restaurant worker Sue Ling Gin decided to start an airline catering business shortly after eating a particularly unsatisfying breakfast aboard a Midway Airlines flight. She founded Flying Food Group Inc. that same year, and made Midway Airlines her first client. The company's airline kitchen in Midway Airport was soon making 10,000 meals a day for air travelers. In subsequent years, Flying Food opened kitchens in several more airports around the country, including O'Hare, and began focusing on foreign-owned airlines flying internationally. By 2000 Flying Food produced meals for 80 airlines, employed over 2,000 people, and had $125 million in revenues. It had kitchens in nine U.S. airports, and a joint catering venture at Honggiao Airport in Shanghai. The September 11, 2001, terrorist attacks devastated the American air travel industry, and the air catering business along with it. While Flying Food's heavy reliance on non-American air carriers helped to insulate it partially from the industry downturn, it nevertheless laid off hundreds of its employees, and sales slumped. Gin quickly diversified Flying Food Group's operations, expanding into gourmet pre-packaged foods that the company sold to grocery stores. By mid-2003, the Chicago-based company had begun to grow back to its pre-9/11 levels, ranking a distant third among the world's largest airline caterers. With about 2,300 employees worldwide—including almost 1,000 in Chicago—and $120 million in revenues, Flying Food Group was one of Chicago's largest minority-owned firms.

FMC Corp.

This company traces its origins to the Food Machinery Corp., a California maker of agricultural and industrial pumps that was itself a successor to the John Bean Spray Pump Co., founded in 1904. During World War II, the California-based company made landing craft for the American military. Its name became FMC in 1961, when it had over $400 million in annual sales and employed nearly 19,000 people nationwide. In 1972, soon after it purchased the Link-Belt Corp. of Chicago, FMC moved its headquarters from San Jose to the Windy City. As the owner of Link-Belt's old operations, FMC became a major local employer, with about 10,000 workers in the Chicago area during the mid-1970s. By this time, the company was already operating in several fields, including machinery and chemicals; annual sales stood at about $2 billion. By the late 1980s, FMC, which was now a leading producer of agricultural chemicals, was one of the nation's leading exporters; its Defense Systems unit, which produced the Bradley Fighting Vehicle for the U.S. Army accounted for nearly one-third of sales. In the 1990s, FMC shed its military contracting division to concentrate on chemicals and products and services for the oil and gas industries. At the end of the century, with annual sales of over $4 billion, FMC still called Chicago home, but only a few hundred of its some 16,000 employees worldwide were based in the area.

Follett Corp.
In 1873, Charles Barnes started running a bookstore out of his home in Wheaton, Illinois. In 1917, after Barnes's son William moved to New York to create the company that became Barnes & Noble, the Illinois business changed hands. The new owners were John Wilcox and C. W. Follett, who had worked for many years as a salesman in the Barnes organization; the new enterprise was called the J. W. Wilcox & Follett Co. By 1923, Follett took charge; after his death in 1952, his son Dwight Follett became head of the company, then a leading wholesaler of textbooks. The company became the Follett Corp. in 1957, with headquarters in downtown Chicago. By the mid-1970s, Follett had about 800 employees in the Chicago area, and annual sales were around $50 million. Robert Follett, a son of Dwight, took over in 1977 and led a considerable expansion. The company bought dozens of college and university bookstores around the country, becoming a leading retailer of textbooks. By the end of the 1990s, Follett—based in River Grove, just west of Chicago—reached $1 billion in annual sales and employed about 2,000 people in the Chicago area.

Foote, Cone & Belding
This company was the descendant of one of the original American advertising firms, Lord & Thomas, which was founded in 1873 and became a national enterprise based in New York City. When Lord & Thomas chief Albert Lasker retired in 1942, several of the company's executives came together to create Foote, Cone & Belding, which was based in Chicago. By 1965, annual billings stood at nearly $230 million, and the firm had over 2,000 employees around the country. By this time, the firm was a leading producer of advertisements for television. Among the ad campaigns launched by the company were those that promoted Levi Strauss clothing, Coors beer, and the Kleenex and Kotex brands of Kimberly-Clark. Among Chicago-based ad agencies, Foote Cone trailed only Leo Burnett. During the 1990s, Foote Cone became part of True North Communications Inc., a new global ad firm headquartered in Chicago. At the end of the century, True North had nearly $1.5 billion in annual revenues and employed about 1,200 people in the Chicago area. In 2001, Interpublic purchased True North. By 2003, Foote, Cone & Belding, as a part of Interpublic, still ranked as Chicago's second-largest advertising agency, but it had only 425 local employees and its headquarters had moved to New York.

Fowler Bros.
See Anglo-American Provision Co.

Fraser & Chalmers
In 1872, Thomas Chalmers founded this Chicago manufacturer of mining machinery, boilers, and pumps. The company employed more than 170 workers in 1880, making engines, boilers, and other products worth $600,000. By 1890, when, under the leadership of William J. Chalmers, it had expanded its manufacturing to England and its sales worldwide, the company employed about 1,000 workers at its Chicago plant and had become one of the world's largest manufacturers of mining equipment. In 1901, Fraser & Chalmers (along with the Gates Iron Works of Chicago) merged with another leading machinery maker, Edward P. Allis & Co. of Milwaukee, to form Allis-Chalmers Co. This company, based in Milwaukee, soon became a leading manufacturer of farm equipment. The company's Chicago works were closed in the 1910s, but after World War II, Allis-Chalmers became a leading employer in the Chicago area. As late as the mid-1970s, it had over 4,000 workers around the Windy City. By the 1990s, Allis-Chalmers was part of AGCO Corp., a farm equipment maker based in Georgia.

Fuller (George A.) Co.
This construction company was founded in Chicago in 1882 as Clark & Fuller by C. E. Clark and George A. Fuller, a Boston architect and engineer. The company soon became the leading builder of the world's first skyscrapers going up around Chicago. By 1890, when Fuller's company became one of the first construction firms to be organized as a corporation (capitalized at $750,000), it had already built several skyscrapers, including the Tacoma Building designed by Holabird & Roche. Fuller was one of the first true general contractors: it completed large structures by coordinating the work of hundreds of men working under several subcontractors. The company opened a New York office during the 1890s and built several large structures in that city, including the New York Times Building and Daniel Burnham's Flatiron Building, which was known briefly as the Fuller Building because the company was headquartered there. By the time George Fuller died in 1900, his company—which between 1903 and 1922 was led by Paul Starrett—had started to serve as the general contractor for large commercial buildings around the country. Between 1900 and 1914 alone, Fuller Co. erected 600 buildings. In addition to the Tacoma Building, among the many structures the company built in Chicago were the Marquette, Pontiac, and Rand-McNally buildings; the Tribune Tower; and large department stores such as the Fair, Carson Pirie Scott, Marshall Field, and Montgomery Ward. Although headquartered in New York, the company still employed hundreds of people in the Chicago area through the 1960s. In the 1970s, the firm was sold and liquidated.

Gary (Theodore) & Co.
See Automatic Electric Co.

GATX Corp.
See General American Transportation Corp.

General American Transportation Corp.
In 1898, Max Epstein founded a Chicago-based railcar leasing firm called the Atlantic Seaboard Dispatch. One of the first companies to lease specialty cars to railroads, Epstein's operation started with only 28 used cars. In 1902, the name was changed to German-American Car Co. In 1907, when the company owned a fleet of 400 cars, it opened repair and maintenance shops in East Chicago, Indiana; it then began to manufacture new steel tank cars in addition to leasing used ones. By 1916, when the company began to sell stock to the public and changed its name to General American Tank Car Corp., it had a fleet of 2,300 cars and annual revenues of about $3 million. By the 1920s, General American had become a leading producer of tank cars, including specialty cars lined with glass or nickel for the transportation of milk, acids, and other liquids. By the early 1920s, the company's plants at East Chicago and Warren, Ohio, were turning out 10,000 new cars a year, worth about $20 million. In 1933, when it owned a fleet of nearly 50,000 cars, the company changed its name to the General American Transportation Corp. By the 1940s, when about 3,000 men worked at the East Chicago plant, General American was the nation's leading lessor of railcars. By the beginning of the 1960s, annual revenues

approached $250 million. Soon after changing its name to GATX Corp. in 1975, the company began to exit the car-manufacturing business. But GATX Corp. added to its traditional operations by leasing aircraft and setting up a large financial services division. By the end of the 1990s, GATX, still headquartered in Chicago, owned a fleet of nearly 90,000 railcars, employed about 6,000 people around the country, and had annual revenues of about $1.7 billion.

General Telephone & Electronics Corp.
See Automatic Electric Co.

Goldblatt Bros. Inc.
In 1905, Simon and Hannah Goldblatt moved with their children from Poland to Chicago. In 1914, two of their sons, Maurice and Nathan Goldblatt, opened a store at Chicago and Ashland Avenues, in a neighborhood that was then home to many Polish immigrants. Over the next 10 years, the firm's annual sales rose from about $15,000 to $1.4 million. As the operator of medium-size department stores that offered goods at low prices, Goldblatt Bros. prospered even during the Great Depression. By 1933, the company exceeded $20 million in annual sales, and owned five stores in Chicago, as well as stores in nearby Joliet, and Hammond, Indiana. Goldblatt's entered the city's high-rent retail district in 1936, when it opened a store on State Street. By the end of World War II, when younger brothers Louis and Joel Goldblatt began to lead the company, it had 15 stores and 2,500 employees. When the company's operations peaked in the 1970s, it had 47 stores, close to $250 million in annual sales, and about 8,000 employees in the Chicago area. Yet, the company was losing money quickly, having trouble competing with rival discount chains such as Kmart. After it entered bankruptcy, the chain was purchased in 1985 by JG Industries Inc. The flagship State Street store was purchased by DePaul University. By the 1990s, Goldblatt's was a chain of about 15 Chicago-area department stores, located mainly in the kind of low-income immigrant neighborhoods in which the company had started in the 1910s. In 2003, with only six stores remaining in Chicago, the company liquidated.

Grainger (W. W.) Inc.
William W. Grainger, an engineering graduate from the University of Illinois, started an electric motor wholesaling business on West Cermak Avenue in Chicago in 1927. Along with his sister Margaret, Grainger built a business based on mail-order catalog sales. By 1937, when annual sales hit $1 million, the company had sales offices around the country. In 1968, as sales passed $100 million and the company began to sell stock to the public, William Grainger retired and was succeeded as company chief by his son David. During the 1970s, the company bought electric motor factories and moved its headquarters to suburban Skokie; by this time, it employed about 700 people in the Chicago area. By the end of the 1990s, when its headquarters moved to suburban Lake Forest, Grainger's annual sales of motors and other industrial machines stood at $4.5 billion. At the turn of the twenty-first century, the company employed about 2,500 people in the Chicago area and another 14,000 in other parts of North America.

Greyhound Corp.
In 1926, several small bus companies founded in Minnesota during the 1910s merged to form the Motor Transit Corp., which had its main offices in Chicago. Led by E. C. Eckstrom and Eric Wickman, among others, the company used painted gray buses that were manufactured in Muskegon, Michigan. In 1930, the company changed its name to Greyhound Corp. Its fortunes were boosted by the 1933 World's Fair held in Chicago, during which it helped to move some 20 million attendees around the 428-acre fair site. By the beginning of the 1940s, Greyhound owned a fleet of 4,000 buses. In the 1960s, when it was the largest bus line in the United States, with 32,000 employees around the country and roughly $500 million in annual revenues, the company began to move into new lines of business. Its most significant venture came in 1970, when Greyhound began diversifying and acquired Armour-Dial, the old Chicago-based meatpacking giant. In 1971, when Greyhound moved its headquarters to Phoenix, about 1,000 jobs left the Chicago area. By the end of the century, after the company sold its Greyhound Lines to Laidlaw Inc. of Canada, Greyhound buses still ran in and out of Chicago, but the company had little presence in the city.

Hall (W. F.) Printing Co.
William Franklin Hall, an Indiana native who worked as a journeyman printer in Chicago during the 1880s, founded his own printing company in 1893. By 1910, Hall's company employed about 400 people at its plant on Superior Street. During the 1920s, with about 2,000 workers, Hall was one of the world's leading printers of magazines and catalogs. Hall continued to prosper during the next few decades. By the 1970s, it was still a leading U.S. printer, with about 5,000 employees in the Chicago area and over $100 million in annual revenues. In the 1980s, after it was purchased by the Krueger Co. of Arizona and Ringier AG, a Swiss firm, Hall closed its main catalog plant on West Diversey Avenue and moved many of its printing operations to Tennessee and Mississippi.

Hammond (George H.) Co.
George Henry Hammond, a pioneer in the use of refrigerated railcars for the transport of fresh meat, first used this method with his small packing company in Detroit, Michigan. In 1868, Hammond received a patent for a refrigerator car design. In the early 1870s, he built a new plant in Northern Indiana along the tracks of the Michigan Central Railroad. By 1873, the George H. Hammond Co. was selling $1 million worth of meat a year; by 1875, sales were nearly $2 million. The company's large packing house in Hammond, Indiana—the town had taken the name of its most powerful resident—rivaled those located at the Union Stock Yard in Chicago. By the middle of the 1880s, when it built a new plant in Omaha, Nebraska, Hammond was slaughtering over 100,000 cattle a year and owned a fleet of 800 refrigerator cars. After Hammond died in 1886, the company became less important and no longer challenged the giant Chicago packers, who acquired Hammond at the turn of the century and merged it into their National Packing Co.

Hammond Organ Co.
In 1928, Evanston resident Laurens Hammond founded the Hammond Clock Co. His enterprise had little success until 1934, when Hammond patented an electric organ and began to manufacture the instruments. In 1936 he sold more than 1,750 of the 275-pound organs, mainly to churches and households. During the 1950s, when the company employed over 1,000 people in the Chicago area, it changed its name from Hammond Musical Instrument Co. to Hammond Organ Co. By the early 1970s, with annual sales approaching $100 million, Hammond had four plants in the Chicago area and employed a total of 4,500 people nationwide. During the late 1970s, when organ sales declined, the company was purchased by the Marmon Group, a conglomerate owned by the Pritzker family of Chicago. By the 1990s, Hammond was owned by the Suzuki Group of Japan.

Hand (Peter) Brewing Co.
This company originated in a local brewery founded in 1891 on North Avenue by Peter Hand, a Prussian immigrant who had worked earlier for the Conrad Seipp Brewing Co. Before Hand died in 1899, his brewery already enjoyed considerable success with its "Meister Brau" brand. The enterprise survived Prohibition and employed nearly 600 people when it was purchased in 1965 by a group led by James Howard. Under the new management, the company was renamed Meister Brau Inc., and its operations expanded. By the end of the 1960s, annual production had reached one million barrels, and annual sales topped $50 million; this put Meister Brau among the top 30 beer companies in the United States. But the company was losing money, and in 1972 it sold

its brand names to the Milwaukee-based Miller Brewing Co. When the Peter Hand Brewery closed in 1978, there was not a single brewery left in the city of Chicago.

Harpo Productions Inc.

Talk-show host Oprah Winfrey, who worked in radio and television in Nashville and Baltimore during the 1970s and early 1980s, arrived in Chicago in 1984. Her *Oprah Winfrey Show*, which started in 1985, became one of the most popular talk shows on American television. In 1986, Winfrey founded Harpo Productions Inc., a production company that used her first name spelled backwards. In 1988, the company took full charge of Winfrey's show, which was produced in new facilities on the city's Near West Side. By the late 1990s, Winfrey's show had about 20 million regular viewers, and Harpo Productions had annual revenues of about $150 million with about 200 Chicago employees.

Harris Trust & Savings Bank

In 1883, 35-year-old Norman Wait Harris founded N. W. Harris & Co., a small Chicago-based investment banking firm. By 1890, when Harris opened an office in New York, the company had nearly $2 million in assets. Specializing in the marketing of municipal bonds, the firm grew. In 1907, when it was selling about $70 million worth of bonds a year, the company was incorporated as the Harris Trust & Savings Bank. By 1922, it employed about 440 people; by 1929, it had over $100 million in assets. After World War II, the company continued to grow and became one of Chicago's leading banks. During the 1970s, when assets passed $4 billion, Harris employed about 3,500 people in the Chicago area. In 1984, when Harris ranked as the third-largest bank in Chicago, it was purchased by the Bank of Montreal. By the early 2000s, Harris (still a division of its Canadian parent) remained one of Chicago's largest banks, boasting $1.3 billion in revenues and employing nearly 6,000 people in the Chicago area.

Hart, Schaffner & Marx

In 1872, Harry and Max Hart, German immigrants who arrived in Chicago as boys 14 years earlier, founded Harry Hart & Bro., a small men's clothing store on State Street. In 1879, along with brothers-in-law Levi Abt and Marcus Marx, the Harts formed Hart, Abt & Marx. By this time, the company not only sold clothing but also employed dozens of women around the city to manufacture close to $1 million worth of garments a year. In 1887, when Joseph Schaffner joined the firm, its name was changed to Hart, Schaffner & Marx. By the beginning of the twentieth century, it owned dozens of small garment factories—identified by many observers as "sweatshops"—around the city; about two-thirds of its several thousand employees were foreign-born men and women. In 1910, when its annual sales were roughly $15 million, the company became a target of one of the biggest strikes in Chicago. Hannah Shapiro, an 18-year-old Russian-born woman working at one of the Hart Schaffner shops, led a walkout in response to a wage cut. Within three weeks, about 40,000 Chicago garment workers went on strike. In 1911, Hart, Schaffner & Marx became one of the first companies to settle with the workers when it signed a collective bargaining agreement that was one of the most comprehensive ever to occur in the clothing industry; by 1915, the majority of the company's employees were members of the Amalgamated Clothing Workers of America, a new union that was an outgrowth of the Chicago strikes. During the years that followed, Hart, Schaffner & Marx continued to be a leading employer in the Chicago area, and it became the largest of all U.S. men's clothing companies. By the beginning of the 1970s, it had 38 factories and 250 retail stores around the country and over 5,000 workers in the Chicago area. During the 1970s, when the company was banned by U.S. Justice Department regulators from buying any more men's clothing stores, its sales grew slowly, from $360 million a year to $630 million a year. In 1983, after buying its old Chicago rival Kuppenheimer Manufacturing Co., a producer and retailer of inexpensive men's clothing, the company changed its name to Hartmarx Corp. At the beginning of the 1990s, the company endured its worst losses since the Great Depression; it responded by selling its retail businesses and manufacturing facilities. By the beginning of the century, Hartmarx was a leading men's clothing wholesaler, with over $600 million in annual sales to department stores, catalog companies, and other retailers; its headquarters remained in Chicago, where it employed about 1,000 people.

Hearst Newspapers

By the time he launched his first newspaper in Chicago, William Randolph Hearst was already famous as the influential publisher of the *Examiner* in San Francisco and the *New York Journal*. Hearst entered the Chicago market in 1900 by establishing the *Chicago American*, an evening paper; in 1902, he started a morning edition, the *Chicago Examiner*. In 1918, Hearst also bought the long-established *Chicago Herald* and merged it with his morning paper to form the *Herald-Examiner* . By the beginning of the 1920s, when Hearst owned 20 daily newspapers in 13 cities, his two Chicago papers each had a circulation of about 300,000, making them the third and fourth leading dailies in the city. Circulation peaked in 1929, when the *American* sold about 560,000 copies a day. By the mid-1930s, the Hearst papers employed about 2,500 people in Chicago. Declining sales during the Great Depression led to a merger of the morning and evening papers in 1939, creating the *Chicago Herald-American* (later reverting to the *Chicago American*). In 1956, the Hearst paper was purchased by the Tribune Co., which proceeded to publish it as an evening paper under the names *Chicago's American* and (starting in 1969) *Chicago Today*. In 1974, the remnants of the Hearst paper were absorbed by the *Chicago Tribune*.

Helene Curtis Industries Inc.

In 1927, Gerald Gidwitz and Louis Stein formed the National Mineral Co., which made the "Peach Bloom Facial Mask" and other beauty products. During the 1930s, the company had success selling shampoos, "Lanolin Creme," and "Suave" brands. After World War II, the company changed its name to Helene Curtis, which combined the names of Stein's wife and son. By the early 1960s, when it employed more than 1,000 people in Chicago, the company's annual sales of shampoo, hairspray, deodorant, and other products topped $50 million. During the 1970s and 1980s, when its "Suave" and "Finesse" brands were among the best-selling shampoos in the United States, Helene Curtis continued to grow. Annual sales reached $600 million during the 1980s, when the company's plant on North Avenue in Chicago employed nearly 1,000 people. In 1996, one year after Helene Curtis moved its headquarters to suburban Rolling Meadows, it was purchased by Unilever, the giant British-Dutch corporation. By the end of the century, Unilever announced that it would close the old North Avenue plant, leaving the company with little presence in the Chicago area.

Henderson (C. M.) & Co.

Charles M. Henderson moved from New England to Chicago in 1853, when he was 19, and joined the business of his uncle C. N. Henderson. In 1855, C. N. Henderson & Co. manufactured $12,000 worth of boots and sold another $250,000 worth of footwear made in Eastern factories. In 1859, the younger Henderson started his own business, C. M. Henderson & Co. By the early 1870s, when total sales reached about $2 million a year, this company's factory at the corner of Madison and Franklin Streets had about 150 employees, who made about $350,000 worth of boots and shoes per year. By this time, Henderson & Co. was one of the leading shoe companies in the Midwest. During the 1880s and early 1890s, annual wholesale sales had reached $3 million, and three Chicago-area factories employed nearly 1,000 people.

Hewitt Associates

In 1940, Ted Hewitt founded an insurance brokerage company in suburban Lake Forest providing financial planning for business executives and professionals. Hewitt Associates began offering compensation and benefit plan consulting services to area employers in the

1950s. With the opening of its Minneapolis branch office in 1959, Hewitt expanded nationally and, beginning with its Toronto office in the 1974, globally. After a half century of astonishing growth, Chicago's largest management consulting business went public in 2002. Globally, it boasted 86 offices in 37 countries, 15,000 employees, and revenues of nearly $2 billion. Its headquarters, located in the Chicago suburb of Lincolnshire, employed 3,400 full-time consultants.

Hibbard, Spencer, Bartlett & Co.

This leading hardware dealership was the descendant of a Chicago store called Tuttle, Hibbard & Co., which took that name in 1855 when William G. Hibbard became a partner. In 1865, Hibbard was joined by Franklin F. Spencer, and the enterprise was renamed Hibbard & Spencer. By 1867, the company's annual sales of hardware had reached $1 million. When longtime company employee A. C. Bartlett became a partner in 1882, the company's name became Hibbard, Spencer & Bartlett & Co. When Spencer died in 1890, the company was already among the leading wholesalers of hardware in the United States. In 1903, the year Hibbard died, the company opened a 10-story warehouse next to State Street Bridge in downtown Chicago. In 1932, the company introduced a new line of hand tools under the brand name "True Value." By 1948, Hibbard's annual sales reached nearly $30 million. Business slowed and profits were shrunk, however, as new hardware cooperatives began to bypass traditional wholesalers. In 1962, the company's owners, who wanted to move into the real-estate business, sold the hardware operations and the "True Value" brand to John Cotter for $2.5 million. *See also* TRUE VALUE HARDWARE.

Hilton Hotels Corp.

Conrad N. Hilton started in the hotel business in Texas during the late 1910s. In 1945, when it became the Hilton Hotels Corp., his company bought two large Chicago luxury properties: the Palmer House and the Stevens Hotel (which became the Conrad Hilton). Together, the two Chicago hotels had about 5,300 rooms and employed 4,500 men and women. Headquartered in Chicago, the new company started as a chain of nine large luxury hotels; by the early 1960s, it had about $230 million in annual revenues from 43 hotels around the world employing roughly 30,000 people. Hilton moved its general offices from Chicago during the 1970s, when the company became associated with TWA Airlines. At the end of the 1990s, Hilton, based in California, still owned luxury hotels in downtown Chicago.

Hines (Edward) Lumber Co.

After he moved with his family from Buffalo to Chicago in 1865, when he was still a boy, Edward Hines worked for some of the leading lumber companies in the city, including S. K. Martin. In 1892, Hines created his own lumber business, the E. Hines Lumber Co.; his enterprise sold more than 100 million feet of lumber in 1893. In 1896, Hines was able to buy the operations of S. K. Martin, his former employer. By the early part of the twentieth century, his company employed about 1,500 men in the Chicago area; it owned forests and mills in Wisconsin, Minnesota, and Mississippi. By the 1920s, the company's main wholesale lumberyard was a 45-acre facility on Chicago's South Side; it also had several smaller yards around the city. By the end of World War II, Hines grossed about $25 million in annual sales, making it one of the top 10 companies in the American lumber industry. By the mid-1970s, when the company employed about 500 people around Chicago, sales neared $300 million. Hines went out of business during the late 1980s.

Holabird & Root

In 1880, William Holabird and Ossian Simonds founded a Chicago architecture firm called Holabird & Simonds. In 1883, two years after the arrival of Martin Roche, the firm became Holabird & Roche. Soon after it was founded, the firm designed several of the city's first skyscrapers, including the Tacoma and Marquette buildings, in addition to homes and other structures. By the early 1890s, it employed as many as 40 draftsmen. By 1910, when Holabird & Roche had about 100 draftsmen, it stood as one of the largest architecture firms in the United States. In 1927, the company changed its name to Holabird & Root, as John Holabird (son of the founder) and John W. Root (the son of another Chicago architect) took over. By this time, the firm employed some 300 people. Holabird & Root continued to operate, with offices in Chicago and Rochester, Minnesota, through the end of the twentieth century, when it still employed several dozen architects and remained one of the city's 20 largest architectural firms.

Horner (Henry) & Co.

Henry Horner founded a grocery store in Chicago in 1842, two years after he emigrated from Bohemia. Horner's first store, at Randolph and Canal Streets, was one of Chicago's earliest retail groceries; Horner started a wholesaling operation in 1856. After Horner died in 1878, his wife Hannah and his four sons took charge of the business, which became one of the leading grocery wholesalers in the Midwest. In 1921, Horner & Co. merged with other companies to become Durand, McNeil, Horner Co.; it was no longer among the region's leading food distributors.

Household Finance Corp.

The Household Finance Corp., the descendant of a business founded in the late 1870s by Frank Mackey, moved from Minneapolis-St. Paul to Chicago in 1894. In 1905, Mackey's company added to its pioneering efforts in the field of consumer credit by introducing installment payment systems. By 1908, it had several dozen offices nationwide, with total loan accounts of $1.5 million. The Household Finance Corp. came into being in 1925 when Mackey merged 33 of his company's branch offices across the country into a single entity. At the end of the 1920s, Household Finance ranked as the largest personal finance company in the United States, with about $30 million in loans to tens of thousands of people. The company grew more slowly during the Great Depression and World War II, but during the postwar years Household Finance expanded quickly. By the early 1960s, when it employed about 7,000 people around the country, the company had about 1,200 offices with about $1.1 billion in outstanding loans. In 1965, Household Finance entered the retailing business on a large scale when it purchased the City Products Corp., owners of the "Ben Franklin" retail chain that had long been operated by Butler Bros. of Chicago. In 1981, Household Finance changed its name to Household International Inc. By 1985, just before it sold the Ben Franklin stores, Household had 28,000 employees worldwide and had about $3.4 billion in annual revenues. At the end of the 1990s, when it was based in suburban Prospect Heights, Household International employed about 4,700 people in the Chicago area. In 2003, Household International was bought out by British banking giant HSBC Holdings PLC.

Hoyt (William M.) & Co.

The descendant of a Chicago grocery store founded in the 1850s, William M. Hoyt & Co. was created during the Civil War. Hoyt became a leading grocery wholesaler, with annual sales of close to $1 million by the mid-1870s and nearly $5 million by the early 1890s, when it was among the region's leading food distributors. In 1920, Hoyt & Co. was sold to Austin Nichols & Co., based in Brooklyn, New York.

Hubbard (Gurdon S.) & Co.

One of Chicago's first business leaders, Gurdon S. Hubbard worked in the town during the 1820s, when it was little more than an outpost of the American Fur Co. In the 1830s, Hubbard became one of the town's first meatpackers. By the mid-1840s, his packing enterprise was slaughtering as many as 400 hogs a day during the winter months. Hubbard continued to be a leading Chicago packer during the 1850s, when he shipped barrels of salted beef and pork to customers in the East. Hubbard's company lasted through the Civil War, but by the 1870s it was no longer among the city's important packers.

Hyatt Hotels Corp.

In 1957, the Hyatt House hotel near the Los Angeles airport was purchased by Jay Pritzker, a member of the wealthy Chicago family descended from Nicholas Pritzker, who emigrated from Kiev to the Windy City in 1881. By 1961, Jay Pritzker had created a six-hotel chain. During the late 1960s, Hyatt spun off a separate entity, Hyatt International. By the end of the 1970s, Hyatt operated a 52-hotel chain with nearly $300 million in annual sales, placing it among the top 15 hotel chains in the United States. At the end of the century, still owned by the Pritzker family and still based in Chicago, Hyatt and Hyatt International together operated or licensed about 200 hotels and employed about 80,000 people around the world. In the Chicago area, the companies had about 3,500 workers.

I

IC Industries Inc.

Illinois Central Industries was created in 1962 as a holding company for the Illinois Central Railroad. In 1965, the company's annual revenues approached $300 million. William Johnson, who became president in 1966, transformed the company. In 1968, it purchased the Abex Corp. (formerly known as American Brake Shoe & Foundry), a manufacturer of automobile and railroad products that had been employing hundreds of workers in the Chicago area. During the early 1970s, the company bought Pepsi-Cola General Bottlers Inc. of Chicago, as well Midas International Corp., the Chicago-based chain of automobile maintenance shops. The company changed its name to IC Industries in 1975, and it employed about 8,000 people in the Chicago area. By that time, railroad transportation no longer constituted the larger part of its business. By the mid-1980s, when IC Industries sold food, aerospace equipment, and a variety of other goods and services, annual revenues were over $4 billion. At this point, the huge conglomerate stopped growing and began to sell off some of its operations. During the late 1980s, IC changed its name to Whitman Corp. and rid itself of the Illinois Central, the railroad that had once been the foundation of the company. By the end of the 1990s, Whitman was primarily a bottler of soft drinks, with about $2.6 billion in annual sales; it employed about 1,700 people in the Chicago area and another 10,000 around the country. In early 2001, the company substantially expanded its share of the soft drink bottling market by acquiring Minneapolis-based PepsiAmericas Inc. and adopting its onetime rival's name. The company moved its headquarters to Minneapolis but maintained most of its operations in Chicago. *See also* Illinois Central Railroad.

IGA Inc.

The Independent Grocers Alliance was created in 1926 by a group led by Chicago accountant J. Frank Grimes. It was designed as a network for independent grocers who sought to use the purchasing power of the association to compete with the rising chain-grocery companies. The enterprise was a success and lasted through the end of the century. By the 1980s, when it was known as IGA, the combined sales of its 3,000 affiliated stores made it the fourth-largest food retailer in the United States. At the end of the century, with annual sales of $18 billion, IGA was a wholesaling operation supplying the world's largest voluntary network of supermarkets.

Illinois Bell Telephone Co.

The Bell Telephone Co. of Illinois was chartered in 1878; three years later, it became part of the Chicago Telephone Co. By the beginning of the twentieth century, Chicago Telephone was associated with the Bell network of American Telephone & Telegraph Co. (AT&T), the largest phone company in the United States. The number of Chicago-area telephones served by this company grew from 34,000 in 1900 to roughly one million by 1930. By the early 1920s, Chicago Telephone employed about 16,000 people in the Chicago area; many of these employees were female operators. Illinois Bell continued to grow in the decades that followed, until it had roughly 36,000 Chicago-area employees by the early 1970s. After federal courts dismantled AT&T's Bell system in 1984, Illinois Bell became the largest division of Ameritech, the new, leading telecommunications company in the Midwest. At the end of the 1990s, when it employed about 20,000 people in the Chicago area and collected nearly $20 billion in annual revenues, Ameritech was purchased by SBC Communications Inc., another giant phone company and former "Baby Bell." At the turn of the new century, the executive offices of the corporation serving most of the phone customers in the Chicago area were now located in San Antonio, Texas.

Illinois Central Railroad

The first U.S. railroad promoted by a large (2.6 million acre) federal land grant, the Illinois Central cost about $25 million to build; as many as 10,000 workers at a time were engaged in building the railroad between 1851 and 1856. British and Dutch investors provided much of the capital required for construction. At its name suggested, the 700-mile road—the longest in the world at the time it was completed—ran down the length of the state, from Chicago and other northern towns all the way to the southern tip of Illinois, at the meeting of the Ohio and Mississippi Rivers. In Chicago, the principal terminus, the Illinois Central (which would become known as the IC) operated out of the Great Central Depot, located just south of the Chicago River near Lake Michigan. By the end of the 1850s, the road's annual revenues had reached $2 million a year. After the Civil War (when it transported troops and military supplies at a discount because of its land-grant status), under the leadership of William H. Osborn, the road expanded outside of Illinois. It reached Sioux City, Iowa, in 1867 and extended all the way to New Orleans by 1882. In 1887, when Stuyvesant Fish became president of the road, the Illinois Central owned 2,300 miles of track, had $12 million in annual revenues, and employed about 8,500 people. It continued to grow, and by the first years of the twentieth century it owned 5,000 miles of track in 13 states, as well as 800 locomotives, 700 passenger cars, and 33,000 freight cars. By this time, the IC employed more than 30,000 people nationwide, including about 5,000 men at its repair and maintenance shops at 95th and Cottage Grove on the South Side of Chicago. In the 1890s, the road opened a large new Chicago depot near Roosevelt Road called Central Station, which was torn down in the early 1970s. The IC's annual revenues stood at about $150 million by the 1920s, when it employed over 70,000 people around the country; but it was forced to cut back during the Great Depression. By the beginning of the 1960s, when it retired the last of its old steam locomotives, the IC had annual revenues of about $250 million; its national workforce had declined to about 20,000 people. In 1962, ownership of the company was transferred to a holding company called Illinois Central Industries, which proceeded to enter a variety of businesses; it became IC Industries in 1975. In 1971, the IC sold its passenger service to Amtrak; the following year, it merged with the Gulf, Mobile & Ohio Railroad to become the Illinois Central Gulf Railroad, which had nearly 10,000 miles of track. During the 1980s, it sold much of this track to concentrate the Chicago–New Orleans corridor, its primary route since the nineteenth century. In 1988, the IC sold its Chicago commuter lines to the Metropolitan Rail (Metra). One year later, the road left IC Industries and became an independent railway company, called Illinois Central Corp. In 1998, the road was purchased by the Canadian National Railway Co. for more than $2.4 billion. *See also* IC Industries Inc.

John P. Hankey

Illinois Steel Co.

See U.S. Steel Corp.

Illinois Tool Works Inc.

In 1912, Byron L. Smith, along with his sons and several veterans of the tool-and-die industry from Rockford, Illinois, started a small company at Huron and Franklin Streets in Chicago. After Byron Smith died, in 1914, his son Harold guided the firm, which specialized at first in the production of metal-cutting tools. During the 1920s, the company became a leading producer of metal fasteners. By the mid-1930s, Illinois Tool had about 500 workers in Chicago. After World War II, the company began to make plastic fasteners. Annual sales rose from about $30 million in 1960 to nearly $300 million by the mid-1970s, when the company had about 3,000 workers in the Chicago area. During the 1980s, under the leadership of John Nichols, Illinois Tool doubled in size by buying other companies, including Signode, another old Chicago-based fastener company. At the end of the 1990s, Illinois Tool bought Premark, a Chicago-area company that made kitchen appliances and plastics. By that time, Illinois Tool grossed over $9 billion in annual sales and employed nearly 5,000 people in the Chicago area, which the company still called home.

IMC Global

See International Minerals & Chemical Corp.

Independent Grocers' Alliance

See IGA Inc.

Inland Steel Co.

Chicago's leading homegrown steel company, Inland was founded in 1893 in Chicago Heights by Joseph Block and his son Philip. The Blocks' company started small after Philip had purchased the plant of the defunct Chicago Steel Works, a maker of farm equipment. In 1897, it had about 250 workers and only about $350,000 in sales. But in 1902, when it built a large new open-hearth steel mill at Indiana Harbor (in East Chicago, Indiana, 27 miles southeast of downtown Chicago), Inland Steel suddenly became a big business. By 1910, the Indiana Harbor facility had about 2,600 workers; by 1917, annual output passed one million tons. During the 1920s, when Inland made about 2 percent of all the steel produced in the United States, its workforce grew to about 7,000 people. In 1935, when annual output stood at two million tons, Inland purchased Joseph T. Ryerson & Son, an old Chicago wholesaler of steel products. Like all steel companies, Inland had all the business it could handle during World War II; annual output passed 3.5 million tons. During the 1950s, when Inland was among the 10 largest steel companies in the United States, annual sales grew to nearly $700 million. A new Chicago headquarters, the Inland Steel Building on Monroe Street, was built in 1957. During the 1960s and 1970s, about 25,000 people worked at the Indiana Harbor plant. Like most American steel companies, Inland declined and laid off thousands of workers during the 1980s. In 1998, it was purchased by Ispat International, a large corporation based in the Netherlands that specialized in acquiring underperforming companies to make them more profitable. Operating under a new name, Ispat Inland Inc., the company cut almost one-fifth of its workforce by 2002, to 7,800 employees. At that time, as the sixth-largest integrated steel producer in the United States, it produced about 5 percent of the country's steel.

Jonathan Keyes

Interlake Steel Corp.

See Acme Steel Co.

International Harvester Co.

Cyrus Hall McCormick, a Virginia inventor of plows and reapers, decided to move to Chicago in 1847, when he and his partner Charles M. Gray built a reaper factory on the north bank of the Chicago River. McCormick's mechanical reapers (which required horses to pull them) proved to be popular with farmers, and the enterprise expanded steadily. By the middle of the 1850s, the Chicago plant had 250 workers, who made more than 2,500 reapers a year, worth over $300,000. After the original plant burned in the 1871 fire, McCormick built a larger factory along the South Branch of the Chicago River. This facility soon employed about 800 men; annual sales well exceeded $1 million. After Cyrus died in 1884, his wife Nettie and his son Charles took over the business. Hostile toward labor unions and their demands for an eight-hour workday, the McCormicks faced strikes by their workers in 1885 and 1886; the second of these, often regarded as one of the more important events in American labor history, was associated with the explosion of a bomb at Haymarket Square in Chicago. Meanwhile, William Deering—a veteran dry-goods wholesaler who had been doing business in Maine and New York—had established a rival harvester factory at Plano, Illinois, southwest of the big city; in 1880, Deering moved his factory to Chicago. Weary of competition, the Deering and McCormick families began to talk about a merger of their companies during the late 1890s. By this time, McCormick had a plant at Blue Island and Western Avenues that employed over 5,000 people; the Deering Harvester works on Fullerton Avenue on the city's North Side employed about 7,000. In 1902, McCormick and Deering—along with the Plano Manufacturing Co. (which had about 1,400 workers at its West Pullman plant) and two smaller farm equipment makers—merged to form International Harvester. The new company was capitalized at $120 million and dominated the American market and, as its name suggested, played an important role in world markets as well. For most of the twentieth century, International Harvester (IH) was one of the leading industrial corporations in the United States; its operations were concentrated in Chicago and its suburbs. By 1910, when IH grossed about $100 million in annual sales, it had over 17,000 workers in the Chicago area, making it the leading employer in the region. By that time, IH had established its own steel mill on the city's far South Side, which it named Wisconsin Steel, as well as manufacturing plants in Sweden, Russia, and Germany. A manufacturer of trucks as well as tractors, during the first years of the twentieth century the company moved away from animal-powered equipment and toward motorized vehicles. By the 1930s, as the nation's leading manufacturer of trucks, IH had a sales network of about 11,000 dealers across the country. During the 1940s, when the company's national workforce grew to about 70,000 people, many IH workers joined one of two rival unions, the Farm Equipment Workers and United Auto Workers (UAW). During the 1950s, when annual sales passed $1 billion, John Deere surpassed IH as the nation's leading maker of agricultural equipment. By the 1970s, IH still employed about 20,000 people in the Chicago area and tens of thousands more around the world. But the company was beginning to struggle. Between 1977 and 1979, the company sold Wisconsin Steel to Envirodyne Inc.; IH then endured a five-month UAW strike from 1979 to 1980. By the early 1980s, the company was losing huge amounts of money, and it chose to sell its farm equipment business (as well as the International Harvester name) to Tenneco Inc., a competitor. By 1986, most of what had been International Harvester became Navistar International Corp. By the end of the 1990s, Navistar, headquartered in suburban Warrenville, had become the nation's leading manufacturer of large trucks. It employed about 2,500 people in the Chicago area, one-tenth of the number who once worked in and around the city for International Harvester. Its total revenues in 2002 stood at almost $7 billion.

International Minerals & Chemical Corp.

During the first decade of the twentieth century, Thomas C. Meadows, a Tennessee phosphate-mining entrepreneur, founded the International Agricultural Corp. International Agricultural, which had mines and plants in New Mexico and Tennessee, became a leading producer of phosphate rock and fertilizer. In 1941, the company changed its name to International Mineral & Chemical and moved its headquarters from Atlanta to Chicago. By the beginning of the 1960s, when its main offices were in Skokie, the company grossed about $130 million in annual sales and employed over 5,000 people around the country but only a few in the Chicago area. By the end of the 1990s, the company was called IMC Global; it had over $2 billion in annual revenues and employed about 250 people at its corporate headquarters in suburban Northbrook. In the early 2000s, the company's headquarters moved to nearby Lake Forest.

Itel Corp.

See Anixter Bros. Inc.

J

Jewel Cos.

The Jewel Tea Co. was founded in 1899 by Frank V. Skiff and Frank Ross, who sold coffee, tea, and other groceries to Chicagoans from their wagons. By 1915, the company had 850 routes and $8 million in annual sales. In 1930, when the company had traded in its old horse-drawn vehicles for motorized ones, it moved its headquarters from Chicago to suburban Barrington. Threatened by local ordinances that prohibited uninvited door-to-door sales, the company started to open retail stores around Chicago. By 1936, it owned 100 stores, which together grossed about $20 million in annual sales. By the end of World War II, Jewel was among the 10 largest retail grocery chains in the United States. At the beginning of the 1960s, when it purchased the 30-store Osco drug chain (founded in the late 1930s by L. L. Skaggs) and changed its own name to Jewel Cos. Inc., the company had over $500 million in annual sales and nearly 300 grocery stores. By the late 1960s, Jewel owned more 600 supermarkets in nine states and employed close to 20,000 people; it was the leading retail grocery chain in the Chicago area. In 1984, when its share of the Chicago-area grocery market was about 30 percent, Jewel was purchased by American Stores Inc. of Salt Lake City. By the end of the 1990s, when it was acquired by Albertson's Inc. (based in Boise, Idaho), Jewel had nearly 40,000 workers in the Chicago area, making it one of the leading employers in the region.

Johnson Motors

See Outboard Marine Corp.

Johnson Products Co.

George Johnson, a former door-to-door cosmetics salesman, formed this company in Chicago in 1954. At a plant on the city's South Side, Johnson manufactured hair care products for African Americans. The company's first product was a hair straightener called "Ultra Wave"; in 1957, it introduced its successful "Ultra Sheen" brand. Johnson responded to cultural shifts in the 1960s by creating a new line of products called "Afro Sheen." Meanwhile, Johnson Products was becoming one of the largest African American–owned manufacturing companies. Annual sales grew from about $4 million in 1967 to $40 million in 1976. By that time, Johnson had about 500 employees in Chicago, and it invested in a factory in Nigeria. But the company's profits declined in the late 1970s, as large cosmetics companies such as Revlon and Avon began to target African American consumers. In 1993, Johnson Products was purchased by the Ivax Corp. of Florida, a large drug and personal-care products company. At the end of the 1990s, Johnson became part of Carson Inc. of Georgia, a smaller company that specialized in cosmetics for African Americans. In 2000, Carson became part of L'Oreal USA. The Johnson Products division maintained its headquarters in Chicago but adopted the L'Oreal name.

Johnson Publishing Co.

John H. Johnson moved with his family from Arkansas City to Chicago in 1933, when he was a teenager. In 1942, after working for the Supreme Liberty Life Insurance Co., the 24-year-old Johnson began to publish *Negro Digest*, a weekly publication covering the nation's African American community. *Negro Digest* used a format similar to that of the mass-market weekly *Reader's Digest*. In 1945, Johnson introduced *Ebony* magazine, the large-format glossy magazine that became the company's flagship publication. By the 1950s, *Ebony*'s circulation had climbed to 500,000; it would reach one million during the 1970s. Another magazine intended for African American readers, *Jet*, was introduced in 1951. The company launched its annual Ebony Fashion Fair in 1958, a traveling fashion show that had raised $48 million for scholarships and charities by the early twenty-first century. By the 1970s, when it moved into the cosmetics business with Fashion Fair Cosmetics, Johnson Publishing ranked as the second-largest African American–owned company in the United States. Annual revenues passed $100 million in the early 1980s, when the company employed about 1,000 people in the Chicago area. By the end of the century, Johnson Publishing had added several more cosmetic lines, radio and television production, and a book division publishing African American authors to its family-owned business. John Johnson continued to lead the company, which posted over $400 million a year in revenues and employed 2,600 people nationwide.

Adam Green

Karpen (S.) & Bros.

In 1880 Solomon and Oscar Karpen, who emigrated from Germany to Chicago in 1872, started a furniture manufacturing enterprise. By the beginning of the twentieth century, when it ranked among the country's leading makers of upholstered furniture, S. Karpen & Bros. employed about 700 people at its large factory on West 22nd Street. In 1952, Karpen was acquired by the Schnadig Corp., led by Lawrence K. Schnadig of Chicago. By the end of the twentieth century, Schnadig was still based in the Chicago area (in suburban Des Plaines), but its plants were elsewhere.

Keebler Co.

See United Biscuit Co. of America

Keith Bros.

In 1858, Osborn R. Keith and Albert E. Faxon founded Keith & Faxon, a wholesale millinery business located on Lake Street. Sales during the first year reached nearly $75,000. In 1860, when Edson Keith became a partner, the firm became Keith, Faxon & Co. When Faxon retired in 1865, and Eldridge G. Keith joined, the company became Keith Bros. After the 1871 fire, the company moved to the southeast corner of Wabash Avenue and Monroe Street. In 1884, when annual sales stood at about $4.5 million, Keith Bros. became Edson Keith & Co. By this time, the company was a leading Midwestern dry-goods wholesaler, employing about 200 people at its Chicago headquarters, nearly 500 more at a factory in Milwaukee, and about 40 traveling salesmen. In 1896, the company's entire dry-goods stock was purchased by Ehrich Bros. of New York. The Edson Keith Mercantile Co. moved its headquarters to nearby Michigan Avenue in 1899, where it continued in business through the 1920s.

Kellogg (Charles P.) & Co.

A descendant of Chicago clothing companies founded in the 1850s, this large enterprise was founded in 1868 by C. P. Kellogg. By the 1870s, when the company was the leading manufacturer of clothing in the Midwest, it employed as many as 3,000 people and grossed about $2 million in annual sales. The founder and his son Charles P. Kellogg both died in 1883. The company faltered in the depression of 1893 and creditors assigned its assets.

Kellogg Switchboard & Supply Co.

In 1870, Milo G. Kellogg moved to Chicago from New York State and began working as a design engineer for telecommunications equipment maker Gray & Barton, which soon thereafter became Western Electric. In the late 1880s, he left Western Electric and began designing telecommunications devices on his own. By the time he had founded Kellogg Switchboard & Supply Co. in 1897, Kellogg had registered well over 100 patents, some of which would revolutionize the telecommunications industry. Kellogg Switchboard & Supply soon threatened the dominance of AT&T by selling its superior "divided-multiple" switchboards to the newly created independent telephone companies around the country. After Kellogg fell seriously ill in 1901, AT&T secretly purchased his stock in Kellogg Switchboard from Mr. Kellogg's temporary trustee. The Illinois Supreme Court canceled the surreptitious acquisition in 1909, and Milo Kellogg regained control of his company after eight years of phantom ownership by AT&T. After Mr. Kellogg's death that same year, Kellogg Switchboard continued to grow, eventually supplying equipment to AT&T's Western Electric. During the mid-1930s, Kellogg still employed about 400 Chicago-area residents. The company's entrance into the dial telephone business in 1939 buoyed sales, which hit $10 million by the mid-1940s. In 1952, Kellogg became a division of the International Telephone & Telegraph Co. (ITT). It was soon renamed ITT Kellogg, and many of ITT's telephone manufacturing operations were moved to the Kellogg plant on Cicero Avenue in 1959, where 1,000 people were employed. All of ITT Kellogg's Chicago operations were moved to Tennessee in 1962. ITT Kellogg changed its name to ITT Telecommunications in 1965 and was sold to a French company, Alcatel, in the late 1980s.

Kemper Corp.

In 1912, after the State of Illinois passed a workers' compensation law, James S. Kemper founded the Lumbermens Mutual Casualty Co., which sold accident insurance. Kemper's firm soon became one of the first to offer automobile insurance. By 1919, Lumbermens had offices around the country. The company continued to operate through World War II, and changed its name to James S. Kemper & Co. During the late 1960s, when annual revenues neared $150 million, the company moved its headquarters from Chicago to suburban Long Grove and became part of Kemperco Inc., a holding company. By the late 1970s, when the company was known as Kemper Corp., annual revenues had jumped to nearly $1 billion. Kemper expanded during the 1980s by moving into financial services. While Kemper would continue in the insurance business into the twenty-first century, its foray into the securities arena was short-lived. In 1995 Zurich Insurance of Switzerland acquired Kemper Corp. and promptly sold off the securities division to Kemper employees as a separate company named Everen Securities Inc. Kemper Insurance Companies, as it came to be called, dramatically downsized in the early 2000s, laying off thousands of employees in Chicago and nationwide and, in 2003, selling off its service organization.

Kent (A. E.) & Co.

Albert E. Kent and his brother Sydney Kent, who had been working in Chicago merchant houses, founded their own meatpacking company in 1860. The firm opened a New York office in 1862, which made it easier for the Kents to win contracts to supply salt pork to the Northern armies during the Civil War. During the winter of 1864–65, the company packed more than 62,000 hogs and 14,000 cattle at its Chicago facilities. Kent continued to rank among the city's leading packers into the early 1870s but faded in importance thereafter.

Kimball (W. W.) Co.

William W. Kimball, a native of Maine, moved from Iowa to Chicago in 1857, when he was 29 years old. Kimball made a living by renting pianos and selling sheet music. By the 1870s, his music store reported annual sales of nearly $1 million. At the beginning of the 1880s, Kimball opened his first factory, which made organs and pianos, at 26th and Rockwell Streets. By 1900, W. W. Kimball & Co. employed about 1,500 people at this facility. By the 1910s, the company was turning out more than 13,000 pianos each year, making it one of the top 10 manufacturers in the U.S. piano industry. During the 1950s, when it moved its main plant and general offices to suburban Melrose Park, the company continued to employ hundreds of Chicago-area residents. In 1959, Kimball was purchased by the Jasper Corp. of Jasper, Indiana, a maker of television cabinets; the piano plant moved to West Baden, Indiana. In 1974 the name of Jasper Corp. became Kimball International Inc.; at the end of the century, this company was still making Kimball pianos.

King (Henry W.) & Co.

In 1854, Henry W. King arrived in Chicago and helped to found Barrett, King & Co., a clothing company that grossed about $150,000 in sales in its first year. During the Civil War, the enterprise became known as King, Kellogg & Co. After the Kelloggs departed, Henry W. King & Co. was created in 1880 by King and his partners, most of whom lived in New York City. By the 1880s, King & Co. was a leading Midwestern clothing wholesaler and retailer, with about $5 million in annual sales. By the end of the nineteenth century, the company's main sales territories stretched from the Midwest to the Pacific. Most of the clothes sold by King, which reportedly employed about 5,000 people around the country, were made in Maine and New York by Browning, King & Co.

Kirk (James S.) & Co.

James S. Kirk, a native of Scotland who grew up in Montreal, moved his soap-manufacturing business from Utica, New York, to Chicago in 1859. In 1867, he set up a large new plant on North Water Street. In 1870, this facility employed about 30 men and 20 children and made nearly $600,000 worth of soap during the year. By 1880, the North Water Street plant was one of world's largest soap factories, with machinery driven by steam engines, a workforce of 250, and an annual output worth over $2 million. By the turn of the century, when there were close 600 workers at Kirk's factory, it made about 100 million pounds of soap per year. In 1929, the North Water Street plant was demolished, and the remnants of the company were sold to Proctor & Gamble of Cincinnati.

Kirkland & Ellis

This law firm was the descendant of a partnership formed in Chicago in 1908 by Stewart G. Shepard and Robert R. McCormick. (McCormick soon left to take charge of the *Chicago Tribune* newspaper, the family business.) In 1915, both Weymouth Kirkland and Howard Ellis started to work for the Shepard firm; their names eventually became those that identified the business. Among the firm's major clients were Chicago companies such as International Harvester, Inland Steel, Marshall Field, Motorola, and McCormick's own Tribune Co. The firm remained one of the city's largest into the twenty-first century, with revenues above $500 million and a workforce that included over 400 attorneys in Chicago and scores more at offices in New York and other cities around the world.

Kraft Inc.

James L. Kraft, born in Ontario, Canada, started a cheese-delivery business in Chicago in 1903. Within a few years, Kraft was producing cheese as well as distributing it, and the company grew. During the 1920s, it began operations in Australia and Europe. In 1928, a merger with Phenix Cheese created Kraft-Phenix, a large food company that supplied about 40 percent of all the cheese consumed in the United States. In 1930, Kraft-Phenix became a subsidiary of the National Dairy Products Corp., which was founded in 1923 by the Chicago pharmacist Thomas H. McInnerney. By the early 1930s, when National Dairy's annual sales of nearly $400 million made it one of the largest companies in the United States, Kraft-Phenix employed about 700 people in the Chicago area. In 1969, Kraft and National Dairy became known as Kraftco; in 1976, when annual sales stood at about $5 billion, the name changed to Kraft Inc. By this time, the company employed nearly 50,000 people around the world, including about 3,000 in the Chicago area. Kraft merged with Dart Industries in 1980, creating Dart & Kraft Inc.; the two companies split in 1986. In 1988, when it was based in suburban Glenview, Kraft was purchased by Philip Morris, the tobacco and food giant. The following year, it was merged with General Foods, another Philip Morris acquisition, and renamed Kraft General Foods. The new company had a much larger product offering, which it expanded in the 1990s, when the company again took the name Kraft Foods, through the purchase of international corporations. In 2001 Philip Morris (renamed the Altria Group in 2003) sold a large portion of Kraft stock to the public but maintained a controlling interest in the company, now based in suburban Northfield.

Kroehler Manufacturing Co.

In 1902, Peter E. Kroehler bought the Naperville Lounge Co., a maker of wooden lounge chairs and upholstered furniture. Kroehler built a new factory in Naperville in 1913 after the original facility was destroyed by a tornado. Soon thereafter, he renamed the company Kroehler Manufacturing Co. This enterprise soon operated across the country and employed several hundred men and women in the Chicago area. By the middle of the 1940s, with over $20 million in annual sales, Kroehler was the second-largest furniture maker in the United States. During the 1960s, when the company employed close to 8,000 people around the country, annual revenues passed $100 million. The company struggled during the 1970s, closing its historic Naperville factory in 1978 and ending its operations in the area. In 1981 Kroehler was acquired by the ATR Group of Northbrook, which put the company up for sale. By the early 2000s, furniture was still manufactured under the Kroehler name by two unrelated companies, one in North Carolina and the other in Ontario, Canada.

Kuppenheimer (B.) & Co.

Bernard Kuppenheimer emigrated from Germany to the United States in 1850 when he was 21 years old. In 1865, he became a partner in the Chicago clothing firm of Kohn, Claybugh & Einstein, which had been established two years earlier. In 1876, the old firm dissolved, and B. Kuppenheimer and his son Jonas started their own men's clothing company. By the 1880s, when they employed as many as 1,000 people to manufacture garments, annual sales reached $1 million. By 1910, the company employed close to 2,000 men and women at shops around the city. Kuppenheimer continued to operate independently as a leading manufacturer of men's clothing until 1982, when it was purchased by another old Chicago clothing company, Hart, Schaffner & Marx (later Hartmarx). By the mid-1990s, when the company was headquartered in Atlanta, sales were lagging, many of its stores were closing, and it entered into bankruptcy. After Hartmarx sold the troubled company to an intermediate investment group, Kuppenheimer was purchased in 1997 by the Men's Warehouse suit retailer, who closed many more Kuppenheimer stores and eventually folded the Kuppenheimer business into its own. *See also* Hart, Schaffner & Marx.

L

LaSalle National Bank

National Builders' Bank was chartered in downtown Chicago in 1927 and managed to weather the Great Depression that followed shortly thereafter. It moved to the recently constructed Art Deco building on the northeast corner of Adams and LaSalle in 1940, changing its name to LaSalle National Bank and maintaining its headquarters there through the early twenty-first century. LaSalle soon grew to become one of Chicago's largest banks, boasting over $100 million in deposits by the early 1950s. By 1965, deposits exceeded $300 million and the bank employed over 500 people. In 1979, LaSalle became a division of Algemene Bank Nederland (ABN), a giant Dutch bank. LaSalle continued to grow after this acquisition, purchasing numerous banks on its own throughout the Midwest over the next two decades. In the early years of the new century, LaSalle was Chicago's second-largest bank, with more than one hundred branches in the Midwest, over $50 billion in assets, and 10,000 employees in the Chicago area.

Lettuce Entertain You Enterprises Inc.

In 1971, Richard Melman opened a restaurant in the Lincoln Park neighborhood of Chicago that he called R. J. Grunts. Over the next five years, Melman opened four more restaurants in the Chicago area. By the mid-1980s, his network of restaurants employed about 2,000 people in the Chicago area and annual revenues stood at about $40 million. Among the restaurants in the Lettuce empire were Ed Debevic's, Maggiano's, and Big Bowl. By the end of the 1990s, the company had over $200 million in annual revenues and owned a total of 75 restaurants worldwide. Most of these were in the Chicago area, where Lettuce employed about 4,000 people.

Levy (Chas.) Circulating Co.

In 1893, the 15-year-old Charles Levy won a horse and wagon in a raffle and began to haul newspapers around Chicago's West Side. By the 1920s, his company was distributing newspapers to the suburbs as well. In 1949, when the company was distributing not only newspapers but also magazines and paperback books, the center of operations moved to Goose Island, in the middle of the Chicago River. By the early 1950s, the company owned a fleet of over 60 trucks and amassed annual sales of about $5 million. Over time, the company began to increase its business outside the Chicago region. By the end of the 1980s, when Barbara Levy Kipper headed the company, over half of its some $360 million in annual sales occurred outside the Chicago area, where it still employed as many as 1,600 people. By the end of the 1990s, the Chas. Levy Co. was the largest distributor of periodicals in the Midwest and one of the largest in the nation; it continued to call Chicago home and employed several hundred people in the area.

Libby, McNeill & Libby

One of the world's leading producers of canned foods, this company was created in 1868 by Archibald McNeill and the brothers Arthur and Charles Libby, who sold beef packed in brine. In 1875, the company began to can its meat in pyramid-shaped metal containers. This product proved popular, and by the 1880s, when it employed 1,500 people, the company was slaughtering as many as 200,000 cattle and selling several millions of dollars' worth of canned meat each year. Like other large Chicago meat companies, Libby slaughtered at the Union Stock Yard. Many of its cans of meat were sold in Europe, where they were consumed by both civilians and soldiers. Between 1888 and 1920, Libby was controlled by Swift & Co., the giant Chicago-based meatpacker. During the first years of the twentieth century, Libby began to can vegetables and fruits. By the middle of the 1930s, it employed some 9,000 people in the Chicago area. Annual sales passed $100 million during the 1940s. During the 1970s, when Libby was purchased by Nestlé of Switzerland, the company had annual sales of close to $500 million and about 1,300 workers in the Chicago area.

Link-Belt Co.

A few years after the end of the Civil War, an Iowa farm-equipment dealer named William D. Ewart invented a new kind of detachable-link drive train. In 1875, with the aid of John C. Coonley of the Chicago Malleable Iron Co. and other investors, Ewart established the William D. Ewart Manufacturing Co. In 1880, he founded a sister enterprise, the Link-Belt Machinery Co., based in Chicago. The company manufactured conveyors and other machines for use in agriculture and industry. In 1906, Ewart Manufacturing merged with Link-Belt, bringing a family of companies under a single Chicago-based head. By the 1920s, the company operated plants in Chicago, Indianapolis, Philadelphia, and San Francisco. Over the next several decades, Link-Belt employed over 1,000 people in the Chicago area. In 1967, Link-Belt, with annual sales topping $200 million and about 10,000 workers nationwide, was purchased by California-based FMC Corp., which moved its own headquarters from California to Chicago in 1972. *See also* FMC Corp.

LTV Steel Co.

See Youngstown Sheet & Tube Co.; Republic Steel Corp.

Lumbermens Mutual Casualty Co.

See Kemper Corp.

Mandel Bros.

This retail enterprise, which would become one of Chicago's leading department stores, was founded in 1855 by Bavarian immigrants

Solomon Mandel and his uncle Simon Klein. Their first store was located on Clark Street. In 1865, after Solomon's brothers Leon and Emanuel joined the firm, its name became Mandel Bros. Purchasing in New York and Paris and selling in Chicago, the enterprise grew. By the 1880s, its new store on the corner of State and Madison Streets employed about 800 people. By the beginning of the twentieth century, the workforce had grown to over 3,000 people. Rebuilt in 1912 and renovated in 1948, the State Street store continued to operate into the 1970s, when the company folded amid State Street's demise as a major retail center.

MarchFirst Inc.

See Whittman-Hart Inc.

Marcor Inc.

See Ward (Montgomery) & Co.

Marmon Group Inc.

This large conglomerate, a creation of Chicago's Pritzker family, was the descendant of Pritzker & Pritzker, a law firm founded at the beginning of the twentieth century. By 1940, the firm had evolved into an investment company. In 1963, Jay and Robert Pritzker bought a large part of the Marmon-Herrington Co., a descendant of an automobile manufacturer. During the 1970s, the Pritzkers acquired the Cerro Corp., which had mining, trucking, and real-estate operations; their company was known for a time as the Cerro-Marmon Corp. The Marmon Group continued to grow during the 1980s, when annual revenues passed $3 billion. Among its holdings were the Trans Union Corp., a lessor of railroad cars; Braniff Airlines; and the Ticketmaster chain. By the early 2000s, Marmon owned about 150 companies—mostly in the service and manufacturing industries—had nearly $7 billion in assets, and employed 30,000 people worldwide, with over 2,500 in the Chicago area. In 2002, Robert Pritzker retired from Marmon after spending 48 years at the company's helm in its Chicago headquarters. Soon thereafter, efforts were launched to liquidate large portions of the immense assets of what was still Chicago's largest privately held company.

Material Service Corp.

The Material Service Corp. (MSC) was formed with $10,000 by brothers Henry, Irving, and Sol Crown in 1919. Henry Crown became president after Sol died in 1921. Originally a brokerage that bought and resold sand and gravel, MSC expanded rapidly by purchasing pits, mines, quarries, and factories to produce lime, pipe, stone, coal, and cement. Starting in 1938, the company operated the Thornton Quarry, one of the world's largest limestone quarries, in Thornton, just south of Chicago. The company soon benefited from large war-related contracts, enabling it to acquire coal mines and more limestone quarries, and to become one of the city's most prominent builders of commercial property. Among the major Chicago structures that MSC helped to build were the Merchandise Mart, the Loop Railway, and the Civic Opera House. Friendly ties to Chicago mayors Anton Cermak and Richard J. Daley allegedly boosted the firm's fortunes. In a stock-for-stock merger in 1959, MSC became part of the General Dynamics Corp. (GD), a leading military contractor. The Crown family obtained a major interest in GD through the deal, a move that would quickly come to haunt them, as GD's bad financial health forced the Crowns in 1961 to sell one of their prized possessions, the Empire State Building in New York City. The Crown family was forced to sell their interest in GD, and thus MSC, in 1965. Within five years, however, the Crowns had re-accumulated enough General Dynamics stock to gain control of the company, including the Material Service division. Around this time, the Crowns created Henry Crown & Co., a holding company that would eventually form the massive core of Crown family investments nationwide, including its stake in GD, major real estate and resort properties, Maytag Corp., and a 10 percent share of the New York Yankees. By the early 1980s, Material Service had become the leading distributor and producer of building materials in the Midwest; it employed more than 3,000 people.

Andrew W. Cohen

Mayer (Oscar) & Co.

In 1883, German immigrants Oscar F. Mayer and Gottfried Mayer started a small sausage-making operation on Chicago's North Side. They opened a meatpacking plant in 1888; by 1909, the plant employed about 70 people. Starting in the 1910s, the company expanded more quickly. Annual sales rose from about $3 million in 1913 to $11 million by 1918. By the early 1930s, when a son of the founder named Oscar G. Mayer was running the company, it employed over 400 people in the Chicago area. Annual sales rose to about $275 million by the early 1960s, when the company had about 8,000 workers nationwide, including many in Madison, Wisconsin, as well as Chicago. By the 1970s, the company had moved its headquarters to Madison, and annual sales reached $1 billion. In the 1980s, Oscar Mayer became part of Philip Morris (Altria Group since 2003) and its Kraft Foods division.

Mayer, Brown & Platt

Descended from a law partnership founded in Chicago in 1881, this firm was known by the mid-twentieth century as Mayer, Meyer, Austrian & Platt. Major clients included large Chicago companies such as Continental Bank and Sears. Starting in the 1970s, the firm expanded by adding offices in New York City and around the world. In early 2003, the firm grew even larger after merging with area competitor Rowe & Maw to become Mayer, Brown, Rowe & Maw. The new firm employed approximately 550 attorneys and 2,000 staff members in its Chicago office alone, and boasted 18 additional offices nationwide.

McCormick Harvesting Machine Co.

See International Harvester Co.

McDonald's Corp.

McDonald's was founded in 1955 by Oak Park native Ray Kroc, who worked as a salesman of milk shake machines. In 1954, Kroc encountered the hamburger stand of the McDonald brothers in San Bernardino, California, which used Kroc's mixers. After convincing the McDonalds to name him their exclusive franchising agent, Kroc opened a restaurant in Des Plaines; it was the first McDonald's in the Chicago area. The chain grew at an extraordinary rate: there were 14 restaurants in 1957 and 100 by 1959. In 1961, when there were 250 restaurants in the chain, Kroc purchased the interest of the McDonald brothers for $2.7 million. By 1968, three years after it started to advertise on television, Kroc's company oversaw 1,000 McDonald's franchises. The remarkable growth continued during the 1970s, when McDonald's—now based in Oak Brook—added 500 new restaurants each year in locations around the world. With this rapid expansion, annual revenues passed $1 billion. The company had become one of the world's largest users of beef, potatoes, ketchup, and other foods; its distinctive golden arches had become a familiar part of the landscape. By the beginning of the century, there were about 25,000 McDonald's restaurants around the world, annual revenues stood at about $15 billion, and over 400,000 employees worked for the company, which had become a symbol of America around the world. In the Chicago area, the company employed about 6,000 people.

McGraw-Edison Co.

Max McGraw started an electrical-contracting business around 1900, when he was still a teenager in Iowa. In 1926, McGraw moved to Chicago, purchased a toaster company, and set up an electrical appliance business, the McGraw Electric Co. By the mid-1950s, the company had over 1,000 workers in the Chicago area. In 1957, McGraw bought Thomas A. Edison Inc. and formed McGraw-Edison Co., a maker of appliances, tools, and electrical equipment. By the mid-1960s, annual sales topped $450 million, and the company had about 20,000 workers at plants around the country. In the mid-1970s, sales passed $1 billion, and the company had about 2,200 employees in the Chicago area. In 1985, McGraw-Edison was purchased by Cooper Industries of Houston, Texas.

Mears, Bates & Co.
Charles Mears, a Massachusetts native, went into the lumber business in Michigan as a young man and was trading lumber in Chicago as early as 1838. By 1850, when his brother Nathan Mears became part of C. Mears & Co., the business was based in Chicago. In 1859, Charles Mears departed to concentrate on his lumber interests in Michigan; the old company became Mears & Bates, which was led by Nathan Mears and Eli Bates. Charles H. Mears, a son of Nathan, joined Mears, Bates & Co. in 1881. By the early 1890s, when the name of the enterprise had become Charles H. Mears & Co., it handled up to 60 million feet of lumber per year.

Meister Brau Inc.
See Hand (Peter) Brewing Co.

Midas International Corp.
See IC Industries Inc.

Midway Airlines Inc.
Founded in 1976 by Irving T. Tague, Midway started flying in 1979, when it had about 200 employees at its main hub at Midway Airport in Chicago. One of the first new airline companies to begin operating after the federal Airline Deregulation Act of 1978, Midway Airlines started with three DC9-15 airplanes, which it used to ferry passengers between Chicago and Cleveland, Detroit, and Kansas City. By the end of 1982, Midway served 15 cities with a fleet of 16 airplanes. After the company bought the assets of the bankrupt Air Florida in 1984, it had over 2,000 employees. By the late 1980s, Midway owned more than 70 planes, flew to 50 airports, employed 6,000 people, and had annual revenues of over $400 million. The expansion continued in 1989, when Midway purchased the Philadelphia operations of Eastern Airlines; but this venture ended up driving the company into bankruptcy. Before going out of business in 1991, Midway employed about 4,000 people in the Chicago area. A North Carolina–based airline with the Midway name and owned by Sam Zell of Chicago appeared in 1994, filed for bankruptcy in September 2001, and suspended operations in 2002.

Molex Inc.
In 1938, Frederick Krehbiel founded a company in Brookfield that made plastic goods. In the 1940s, led by John Krehbiel, the company moved into electric and electronics products at its Brookfield factory. Annual sales passed $1 million in 1962. Molex became a leading manufacturer of electrical switches and connectors. At the beginning of the twenty-first century, Molex, based in Lisle, grossed about $1.7 billion in annual sales and ranked as the world's second leading maker of connectors, with factories and sales offices throughout the world. At the beginning of the century, approximately 1,600 of its 16,000 employees worldwide worked in the Chicago area.

Morris (Nelson) & Co.
German-born Nelson Morris arrived in Chicago in 1854 and found work with meatpacker John B. Sherman. Morris started packing under his own name in 1859. During the Civil War, he sold cattle to the Union armies. Morris's company was one of the original meatpacking companies at the city's Union Stock Yard, which opened in 1865. By 1873, the company's annual sales were about $11 million. Like other leading Chicago packers such as Swift and Armour, Morris's operations extended across the nation during the last decades of the nineteenth century. The company owned packing plants in East St. Louis and Kansas City, as well as cattle ranches in Texas and the Dakotas. The Morris-owned Fairbank Canning Co. slaughtered more than 500,000 cattle a year by the beginning of the 1890s. At the turn of the century, Nelson Morris & Co. had nearly 100 branches across the United States and employed over 3,700 people at the Union Stock Yard. By the time the founder died, in 1907, annual sales had reached about $100 million. Still a leading American food company at the end of the 1910s, it was merged into Armour & Co. in 1923.

Morrison, Plummer & Co.
In 1876, Robert Morrison and Jonathan W. Plummer moved their three-year-old drug wholesaling business from Richmond, Indiana, to Chicago. At the turn of the century, Morrison's son James became the company's president. In 1915, when the company employed about 300 people, an association with the business of Charles Fuller created the Fuller-Morrison Co., one of the leading drug wholesalers in the United States. Like many other wholesale drug distributors, Fuller-Morrison eventually joined with the McKesson & Robbins; in the 1930s, the Chicago-based firm was known as McKesson-Fuller-Morrison.

Morton Salt Co.
In 1880, a 25-year-old Nebraskan named Joy Morton arrived in Chicago to become a new partner in E. I. Wheeler & Co., a salt-marketing firm. Wheeler & Co. originated as a Chicago firm called Richmond & Co., which in 1848 had become a sales agent of the New York State Salt Manufacturing Co. After Wheeler died in 1895, the firm became Joy Morton & Co. Morton soon began to invest in salt evaporation plants in Michigan, and the company grew. The Morton Salt Co. was incorporated in 1910, and the company's "Umbrella Girl" logo and its "when it rains it pours" slogan soon became familiar to consumers across the United States. During the mid-1930s, the company had about 250 employees in the Chicago area. After World War II, Morton expanded into new regions and new products, including chemicals, drugs, and adhesives. Between 1961 and 1967, annual sales grew from $50 million to $250 million. A merger with a drug company in 1969 led the company to adopt the name Morton-Norwich. By the end of the 1970s, this company grossed $700 million in annual sales and had more than 10,000 workers around the world. In 1982, the company sold its drug business and purchased Thiokol Inc., a maker of cleaners, chemicals, and rockets; the new entity was named Morton Thiokol Inc. In 1989, soon after the company's work was connected to the 1986 explosion of the U.S. Space Shuttle *Challenger*, Morton separated from Thiokol to focus on making chemicals. At the same time, it moved quickly into the production of safety airbags for automobiles and soon became a leader in the airbag business. By the 1990s, Morton International was still based in Chicago, where it employed about 1,500 people. Morton continued to earn profits from its market-leading salt brand, but most of its $3 billion in annual revenues came from sales of airbags and specialty chemicals. Two years after selling its airbag division in 1997, Morton was purchased by Rohm & Haas, a Philadelphia company, largely ending Morton's century-long relationship with Chicago. It still maintained a riverside distribution facility on North Elston Avenue in 2003, receiving regular shipments of Louisiana salt by barges.

Motorola Inc.
In 1928, brothers Paul V. Galvin and Joseph E. Galvin purchased a battery eliminator business from the bankrupt Stewart Storage Battery Co. of Chicago. The brothers' new company, located on the West Side of Chicago, was called the Galvin Manufacturing Corp.; it began with five employees. The company began to make car radios in 1930 and manufactured larger radio sets for homes starting in 1937. During World War II, Galvin made hand-held, two-way FM portable radios—which became known as "walkie-talkies"—for the use of the U.S. military. Although the company experienced a severe decline immediately after the end of the war, as the end of large military contracts pushed its annual sales down from $68 million in 1945 to $23 million in 1946, it soon recovered in spectacular fashion. In 1947, the company changed its name to Motorola Inc. Six years later, it opened a large television assembly plant in the Chicago suburb of Franklin Park, where Motorola made the first television sets to sell for under $200. Motorola introduced new electronics products year after year. An all-transistor car radio appeared 1959; later, the company pioneered eight-track tape players for automobiles and began to sell an all-transistor television set, the "Quasar." In 1958, two years after Robert W. Galvin succeeded his father Paul as company president, Motorola started a semiconductors

division, based in Phoenix, Arizona. By the middle of the 1960s, the company grossed $500 million in annual sales and employed some 30,000 people nationwide. One of Motorola's customers was NASA, which bought communications for its space missions. In 1974, the year it stopped making televisions, Motorola introduced its first microprocessor. By 1976, when the company moved its headquarters to a 325-acre campus in the Chicago suburb of Schaumburg, it employed over 7,500 people around the Chicago area. Expansion continued during the 1980s, when Motorola began to sell pagers and cellular telephones, boosting annual sales past $10 billion and the total number of employees (worldwide) beyond 100,000. Meanwhile, the company had become the nation's fourth-largest manufacturer of semiconductors for the booming computer industry. In 1993, Robert Galvin's son Christopher was named company president. By the end of the 1990s, annual sales had passed $30 billion, and there were over 20,000 Motorola employees working in the Chicago area. Strong telecommunications competition with new rivals such as Nokia (a giant cellular phone manufacturer based in Finland) and slumping semiconductor markets in the early 2000s hit Motorola hard. Three-quarters of a century of rapid growth came to an end, as Motorola slashed tens of thousands of jobs in Chicago and worldwide. Christopher Galvin was replaced by the first non-Galvin to head Motorola in its storied history, a former executive at General Electric with a reputation for instituting relentless cost-cutting measures. By 2002, however, Motorola remained one of Chicago's largest corporations, with net revenues of almost $27 billion and 97,000 employees worldwide.

Timothy J. Gilfoyle

Munger, Wheeler & Co.

In 1854, Wesley Munger and George Armour started a Chicago grain-warehousing company called Munger & Armour. In 1863, Hiram Wheeler entered the firm, which became Munger, Wheeler & Co. The company owned large grain elevators next to the depot of the Chicago & North Western Railroad. When Wesley Munger died in 1868, his son Albert entered the firm. All three of the company's elevators, with a total capacity of 1.5 million barrels, were destroyed in the Chicago Fire of 1871, but the firm rebounded. In 1880, Munger, Wheeler & Co. owned 8 of the city's 23 large-scale grain warehouses; these eight elevators had a capacity of 6.4 million bushels. In 1889, the company was purchased by the City of Chicago Grain Elevators Co., Ltd., a corporation owned by English investors.

Munn & Scott

This grain-warehousing company traced its origins to a company founded in 1844 in Spring Bay, Illinois, north of Peoria. By 1856, Ira Y. Munn and his partners owned a large Chicago grain elevator with a capacity of 200,000 bushels. Two years later, George L. Scott joined the enterprise, which changed its name from Munn, Gill & Co. to Munn & Scott. By the end of the Civil War, the company owned four Chicago grain elevators with a total capacity of 2.3 million bushels, nearly a third of the total capacity of all of the city's large elevators. By this time, Munn had already served as president of the Chicago Board of Trade. Annual revenues reached about $4 million in 1867; by 1870, the company still ranked as the city's leading warehouser of grain. Munn rapidly declined during the early 1870s. In 1872, speculative transactions in the grain market had bankrupted the company, which sold many of its assets to George Armour, another leading elevator operator. In the same year, Munn & Scott was charged with violating new Illinois regulations that enabled the state to inspect and regulate the elevators. Munn and his company achieved their most lasting fame in 1876–77, when the U.S. Supreme Court rejected Munn's argument that the state had no right to regulate privately owned enterprises such as grain elevators.

N

Nalco Chemical Co.

In 1920, Herbert A. Kern founded the Chicago Chemical Co., which sold water-treatment chemicals such as sodium aluminate. Two years later, P. Wilson Evans started the Aluminate Sales Corp. In 1928, a merger between these two companies created the National Aluminate Corp., based in Chicago. Annual sales neared $4 million by the end of the 1930s, and the company continued to grow thereafter. By 1959, when the company's name changed to Nalco Chemical, annual sales approached $50 million. Sales rose to $400 million by the mid-1970s, when Nalco—now a Fortune 500 company operating on a global scale—had about 1,700 workers in the Chicago area. In the 1980s, still specializing in the production of water-treatment chemicals, the company built a large new technical center in the Chicago suburb of Naperville. At the end of the 1990s, Nalco was purchased by Suez Lyonnaise des Eaux, a French company. Shortly thereafter, the company's name was changed to Ondeo Nalco, reflecting the name for its parent company's water-treatment divisions. As of the early 2000s, Nalco maintained its Naperville headquarters and continued to be a world leader in its field.

National Biscuit Co.

In 1890, Chicago lawyer Adolphus W. Green helped to found the American Biscuit Co., a large food company that took control of 40 bakeries around the Midwest. American Biscuit set up its headquarters in Chicago, where it owned three large bakeries on the city's West Side. In 1898, American Biscuit became part of the new National Biscuit Co., a 114-bakery cracker-making giant that also included the old operations of the New York Biscuit Co. National Biscuit dominated the American market for mass-produced cookies and crackers. During the first eight years of its existence, when annual sales were about $40 million, the company was based in Chicago; in 1906, the corporate headquarters was moved to New York. By 1910, National Biscuit employed nearly 1,300 men and women at its bakeries in Chicago, one of which was built especially to produce the company's popular "Uneeda" brand. By the late 1950s, when annual sales passed $400 million, National Biscuit (also known as Nabisco) still had over 1,000 workers in the Chicago area. In 1985, Nabisco was purchased by tobacco giant R. J. Reynolds but continued to operate out of the Chicago area. After 15 years of solid growth, Nabisco was purchased by another major American tobacco company, Phillip Morris (renamed Altria Group Inc. in 2003), for $19 billion. The Nabisco product line would soon fall under the operations of another Phillip Morris subsidiary, Kraft Foods of suburban Northfield. *See* KRAFT INC.

National Dairy Products Corp.

See Kraft Inc.

National Malleable & Steel Castings Co.

The Chicago Malleable Iron Co. was founded 1873 by Alfred A. Pope and John C. Coonley, who operated similar companies in Ohio and Indiana. By the late 1880s, the company employed nearly 1,000 men at its 26th and Western Chicago works, which made metal products for the railroad, farm wagon, and horse-drawn carriage industries. In 1891, Chicago Malleable became part of the new National Malleable Castings Co., a Cleveland-based company with plants across the Midwest. At the turn of the century, the Chicago plant had about 2,000 workers. National Malleable purchased the Latrobe Steel & Coupler Co.'s plant in Melrose Park, Illinois in 1909. In 1923, when it had begun to supply the automobile industry, the company changed its name to National Malleable & Steel Castings Co. Its stock was listed on the New York Stock Exchange beginning in 1936, but company employees continued to own a large portion of National Malleable. By the early 1950s, when it still had plants in Cicero and Melrose Park, the company employed nearly 6,000 workers across the nation and had annual sales of over $50 million. In 1961, the company changed its name to National Castings and, in 1965, was absorbed by Midland-Ross. In 1985, Midland-Ross divested itself of the former company, which returned to Chicago as National Castings Inc. and continued to operate the plants in Cicero and Melrose Park.

National Packing Co.

In 1902, the leading Chicago-based packing companies (including Armour, Swift, and Morris) agreed to merge into a giant corporation called the National Packing Co. Conceived primarily as a holding company, National Packing soon began buying up smaller meat companies, such as G. H. Hammond and Fowler. Between 1904 and 1910, National Packing acquired 23 stockyards and slaughtering plants nationwide, which gave it control over about one-tenth of U.S. meat production. The company owned branches in over 150 cities around the world, along with a fleet of 2,600 refrigerated railcars. Pressure from U.S. government regulators forced the dissolution of the company in 1912, leaving the structure of the American meat industry about the same as it had been before 1902.

National Tea Co.

Beginning with one store on North Avenue in 1899, National Tea became the region's largest retail grocery chain. By 1920, when there were about 160 stores in the chain, annual sales approached $13 million. By the end of the 1920s, National Tea had over 600 locations in the Chicago area and another 1,000 stores nationwide; sales had grown to about $90 million a year. Many of these stores were closed or sold during the Great Depression, but National Tea remained among the 10 largest grocery chains in the United States for most of the twentieth century. During the 1950s, it acquired about 500 new stores by buying up smaller chains. In 1956, when annual sales topped $600 million and the company had nearly 20,000 employees nationwide, National Tea was purchased by George Weston Ltd., a Canadian company. There was little growth during the 1960s, when the company operated about 240 stores in the Chicago area (where it had fallen behind Jewel as the number one chain). During the mid-1970s, when it still employed about 9,000 people around the region, National Tea/George Weston suddenly abandoned the Chicago grocery market. By the end of the century, there was little trace remaining of what had once stood as one of the area's leading enterprises and the source of groceries for a large fraction of Chicago's population.

Navistar International Corp.

See International Harvester Co.

Nicor Inc.

This company traces its origins to some of the gas companies founded in northern Illinois during the 1850s, such as the Ottawa Gas Light & Coke Co. The first steps toward the formation of the large company that eventually became Nicor occurred during the early 1910s. In 1911, a group of investors including Chicago utilities titan Samuel Insull created the Public Service Co. of Northern Illinois; one year later, a different merger of small gas companies in the region created the Illinois Northern Utilities Co. These two entities were united in 1954 as Northern Illinois Gas, which had about $60 million in sales during its first year. By the early 1960s, the company employed about 3,600 people around the region. In 1976, Northern Illinois Gas became a subsidiary of Nicor Inc., a holding company. By the early 2000s, Naperville-based Nicor had revenues approaching $2 billion and still employed some 3,500 people.

Nielsen (A. C.) Co.

In 1923, Arthur C. Nielsen opened a statistical consulting firm in Chicago. During the 1930s, he added a service that provided radio ratings, which allowed advertisers to estimate the size of the audiences of particular stations and programs. The company soon introduced machines that recorded consumers' selection of radio and television programs; for many years, Nielsen dominated the market for television ratings information, much of which came from some 1,200 of these machines placed in homes around the country. By the middle of the 1960s, the company's annual revenues were about $60 million, and it employed nearly 7,000 people around the country. At the end of the 1970s, when Nielsen had begun to use computers to analyze large quantities of retail-sales data, the company had become the nation's leading market-research firm, with $400 million in annual sales and 17,000 employees nationwide. Between 1984 and 1996, the company was a division of the Dun & Bradstreet Corp. of New York City. At the turn of the century, the descendant of Arthur Nielsen's small Chicago firm was a worldwide marketing information company with 21,000 employees in 100 countries. ACNielsen Corp.'s American headquarters were still located in the Chicago area, in Schaumburg.

Nipsco Industries Inc.

See Northern Indiana Public Service Co.

North Chicago Rolling Mill Co.

The first large iron and steel plant in the Chicago area, the North Chicago Rolling Mill, was founded in 1857 by Eber B. Ward, an owner of iron mines in the Lake Superior region who had made his fortune in shipping around the Great Lakes. Along with partners Stephen and Orrin Potter, Ward built a large facility along the North Branch of the Chicago River, about two and a half miles northwest of the city's center. By 1860, when it employed about 200 men and manufactured nearly $700,000 worth of iron railroad rails, the plant was one of the largest manufacturing enterprises in the Chicago region. In 1865, the mill rolled a few experimental steel rails, which may have been the first ever produced in the United States. In the early 1870s, when it employed about 1,500 men, the company added a Bessemer furnace, which allowed it to produce steel rails in huge quantities. At the beginning of the 1880s, the company opened a large new plant at South Chicago that also made steel rails. By the mid-1880s, the two mills together employed about 6,000 people; annual output exceeded 600,000 tons. In 1889, the two plants of the North Chicago Rolling Mill Co. became the heart of the new Illinois Steel Co., an entity that merged several of the largest Chicago-area mills into what was then the largest steel company in the world. At the beginning of the twentieth century, Illinois Steel became part of U.S. Steel, a much larger entity. Until it was closed permanently in 1992, the South Works of the old North Chicago Rolling Mill Co. served as one of U.S. Steel's main plants. *See also* U.S. STEEL CORP.

Northern Illinois Gas Co.

See Nicor Inc.

Northern Indiana Public Service Co.

This regional utility was the descendant of several small enterprises founded during the nineteenth century, including the South Bend Gas Light Co., established in 1868 by the Studebaker brothers, of the famous wagon-making firm. During the first decade of the twentieth century, a series of mergers caused the Hammond Illuminating Co. (founded in 1901) to become the South Shore Gas & Electric Co., which by 1909 would become the Northern Indiana Gas & Electric Co. In 1923, Northern Indiana was purchased by Samuel Insull, who owned utilities all around the Chicago area. In 1926, Insull combined Northern Indiana Gas & Electric with his Calumet Electric Co., forming the Northern Indiana Public Service Co. By the middle of the 1960s, this Hammond-based company grossed nearly $200 million in annual sales and employed over 4,000 people. In 1988, the name of the company was changed to Nipsco Industries Inc. By the 1990s, Nipsco was providing electricity to 400,000 customers in Northern Indiana; it also had about 700,000 gas customers. After several more mergers and acquisitions at the end of the twentieth century, the company operated out of Merrillville, Indiana, and became known as NiSource Inc., with more than $6 billion in annual revenues and 7,500 employees.

Northern Trust Co.

In 1889, Byron L. Smith collected about $1 million from leading Chicago businessmen, including Marshall Field and Philip D. Armour, to start a banking enterprise. Buoyed by the exposure it gained from opening a branch at the 1893 World's Columbian Exposition, the company's deposits grew to $10 million by the mid-1890s. From 1914 to 1963, the bank—which made its home on LaSalle Street in the Loop—was led by Solomon A. Smith, a son of the founder. Unlike many banks, Northern Trust grew during the Great Depression: deposits increased from about $50 million in 1929 to $300 million in 1935. By the beginning of the 1960s, when deposits totaled nearly $1 billion, Northern Trust was Chicago's fourth-largest bank. In 1974, when, after opening a branch in London and expanding to a new building at Wacker and Adams, the bank employed about 3,000 people in the Chicago area, its fortunes were boosted by a new federal law requiring that the assets in corporate benefit and pension funds be overseen by independent custodians. In 1982, it added banking operations in Florida. Despite the bear stock market of the early 2000s, Northern had become Chicago's third-largest bank, with over $1.3 trillion in assets under custody and over 9,300 employees worldwide and almost 6,000 in the Chicago area.

Northwest Industries Inc.

After Frank Lyon bought the Chicago & North Western Railway in 1956, he installed a young lawyer named Ben Heineman as president. After returning the railroad to profitability, Heineman created a holding company called Northwest Industries in 1968. Four years later, when Northwest Industries had become a conglomerate with interests in a variety of businesses around the country, Heineman sold the railroad. Unlike IC Industries, another conglomerate born out of a Chicago-based railroad, Northwest Industries employed only a small number of people in the Chicago area by the mid-1970s, when annual revenues were approaching $2 billion. By this time, the company owned plants around the world and made boots, batteries, underwear (including the "Fruit of the Loom" brand), and a variety of other goods. In 1985, Northwest Industries was purchased by William F. Farley, who changed its name to Farley Industries Inc. but kept the headquarters in Chicago. This company had about 50,000 employees worldwide and nearly $4 billion in annual sales by the late 1980s, but in 1991 it went bankrupt and was dismantled. *See also* CHICAGO & NORTH WESTERN RAILROAD CO.

Northwestern Terra Cotta Co.

Founded in Chicago in 1878 by a group of investors including John R. True, this company became a major producer of terra cotta trimmings used by the construction industry. By the early 1890s, when Northwestern Terra Cotta employed approximately 500 men, annual sales approached $600,000. By 1910, its large plant at Clybourn and Wrightwood Avenues had about 1,000 workers. The popularity of placing terra cotta moldings on building facades peaked in the 1920s, and Northwestern Terra Cotta led the way, in Chicago and around the country. Around this time, the company opened plants in St. Louis and Denver. Beginning with Louis Sullivan earlier in the century, prominent Chicago architects like Frank Lloyd Wright had extensive contracts with the company. Included among the many landmark Chicago buildings for which Northwestern supplied extensive decorative moldings were the Civic Opera House, the Chicago Theater, the Wrigley Building, and the Randolph Tower. Northwestern's operations in Chicago declined alongside the construction industry during Great Depression and never returned to their 1920s levels. In 1965, Northwestern Terra Cotta Co.'s only remaining plant, in Denver, closed.

Nuveen (John) Co.

John Nuveen emigrated from Germany to Chicago with his family in 1866, when he was two years old. After working for several of the city's merchant houses and real-estate companies as a young man, Nuveen founded his own investment banking firm in Chicago in 1898. The company specialized in the marketing of municipal bonds issued by towns around the Midwest, as well as in Puerto Rico. In 1917, the annual revenues of this small firm passed $300,000. Nuveen expanded during the Great Depression by handling financial instruments issued by new public utilities, and it continued to grow after World War II. By the 1950s, with more than 100 employees, Nuveen had become a national leader in the municipal bond and public finance business. A downturn in the bond market in 1969 caused the company to suffer huge losses, and Nuveen was purchased by Investor's Diversified Services (IDS) of Minneapolis. In 1974, it was acquired by another Minnesota business, an insurance group known as the St. Paul Companies of Minnesota. During the 1990s, as a Chicago-based division of St. Paul, Nuveen began to specialize in the management of assets. At the end of the century, it employed over 400 people in the Chicago area and had annual revenues close to $350 million.

Osco Drug Inc.

See Jewel Cos.

Outboard Marine Corp.

In 1882, when he was five years old, Ole Evinrude emigrated with his family from Norway to Wisconsin. In 1907, he founded the Evinrude Motor Co. in Milwaukee. By 1911, the company was selling 2,000 boat motors a year. In 1929 Evinrude and Stephen Briggs of the gasoline engine company Briggs & Stratton created the Outboard Motors Corp., which became the world leader in this field. In 1935, just after Ole Evinrude passed away and was succeeded by his son Ralph, Outboard Motors purchased the assets of the bankrupt Johnson Bros. Motor Co., an Indiana company that had built a new marine plant in Waukegan just before the Great Depression. For the rest of the century, the company would manufacture such well-known marine products as Evinrude & Johnson marine motors as well as Chris-Craft boats. In 1936, when it employed a total of about 1,000 people, Evinrude's company changed its name to Outboard Marine & Manufacturing Co.; 20 years later, it became Outboard Marine Corp. (OMC). After serving as a military contractor during World War II, the company turned back toward civilian markets. During the 1950s, when the Waukegan facility became its main plant, Outboard Marine manufactured the popular "Lawn-Boy" power mowers, as well as boat motors. By the beginning of the 1960s, annual sales had reached $130 million. In the mid-1970s, the company had about 7,000 workers in the Chicago region, most of them in Waukegan. By the beginning of the 1990s, when Outboard Marine was the nation's second leading manufacturer of boats (the Chicago-based Brunswick Corp. was the leader), the company was losing money and cutting jobs. A highly leveraged acquisition of OMC by a New York–based partnership led by billionaire investor George Soros accelerated the company's decline. Burdened by heavy debt, Outboard Marine declared bankruptcy in late 2000. A Montreal sporting goods retailer purchased the Evinrude & Johnson motors division, but the Waukegan plant relocated to Wisconsin. As the remainder of OMC's assets were sold off to various buyers, plants around the country either closed or downsized, throwing thousands out of work.

Palmer, Fuller & Co.

This company, a major producer of wooden building materials during the late nineteenth century, was founded in Chicago in 1866 by A. R. Palmer and W. A. Fuller. In 1869 the partners built a large lumber mill at 22nd and Union Streets. By 1873 that facility employed about 400 men and produced about $800,000 a year worth of sash, doors, and other goods. In 1880, the plant employed more than 500 workers.

People's Gas Light & Coke Co.

Chicago's first gas company, the Chicago Gas Light & Coke Co., was organized in 1849 and began to sell gas (used for lighting) in 1850. People's Gas Light & Coke Co. was chartered in 1855 and started delivering gas to Chicago customers in 1862. In 1897, after the Illinois legislature authorized gas company mergers, People's Gas merged with seven other firms. By this time, the company was a leading seller of gas stoves: it sold over 20,000 stoves to Chicago customers in 1898 alone. By 1907, People's Gas had a local monopoly, and it struggled with the city to establish fair rates. In 1913, Illinois created a Public Utilities Commission (which became the Illinois Commerce Commission in 1921) to regulate gas companies. By the beginning of the 1920s, People's Gas was delivering about 22 billion cubic feet of gas a year to Chicago customers via 3,100 miles of street mains. At this time, the company still manufactured gas out of coal and oil; in 1921, it used over 700,000 tons of coal and coke and 77 million gallons of oil. A critical shift in the company's operations occurred at the end of the 1920s, when it invested in long pipelines that connected Chicago to natural gas fields in Texas. By 1950, People's Gas had annual sales of over $80 million and employed over 4,500 people. The company changed its name to People's Gas Co. in 1968; 12 years later, it became part of People's Energy Corp. This entity controlled both People's Gas and the North Shore Gas Co., which operated in northeastern Illinois. By the early 2000s, People's Energy grossed more than $2 billion and had employed over 3,000 workers in the Chicago area.

Pepper Construction Co.

During the first years of the twentieth century, Frederick Pepper headed the carpentry shop at Marshall Field & Co., the leading Chicago retailer. His son, Stanley Pepper, started his own construction company in Chicago in 1927. For the next 75 years, Pepper Construction would be led by successive generations of Frederick Pepper's sons and grandsons. Richard S. Pepper took over the business from his father in 1957 and continued to establish Pepper Construction as one of the region's leading general contractors for the next three and a half decades. Richard's son, J. Stanley Pepper, claimed the company reigns in the early 1990s. Over the next decade, he expanded Pepper Construction to Texas, California, and Indiana, eventually placing all business operations under a newly formed holding company in Chicago, Pepper Construction Group LLC. Pepper Construction Co. continued to operate out of Chicago in the early 2000s, claiming about 1,000 employees and $900 million in revenues.

Perkins & Will

This architecture firm was founded in 1935 by Lawrence B. Perkins and Philip Will, Jr., who began his career designing houses. By 1950, the firm had a staff of 50, and it specialized in designing schools and colleges. A New York office opened in 1952. By 1970, the firm was nationally prominent, designing large office buildings and a variety of other structures. By the 1980s, when it employed about 250 people around the country, Perkins & Will ranked as Chicago's leading architecture firm in terms of local construction volume. At the beginning of the century, it employed about 100 architects in Chicago, working on such projects as the Chicago Park District Headquarters and the Halsted Street Sky Bridge downtown.

Pettibone Mulliken Corp.

Organized in 1880, this company was a leading manufacturer of railroad track equipment such as such as frogs, crossings, and switches. The company's main railroad equipment plant was on Chicago's West Side. In 1945, when most of the company's business was still related to railroad supply, the West Side plant, which then had about 1,700 workers, was Pettibone's only manufacturing facility. During the postwar era, however, the company added new plants around the country and began to focus on making construction and foundry equipment such as graders, lifts, and loaders. Annual sales passed $100 million during the late 1960s. Sales rose from $42 million in 1957 to $94 million in 1965, when there were about 3,000 employees nationwide. In 1961, Pettibone Mulliken grossed $38 million in sales and employed 2,000 nationwide. During the 1970s, when the company was still based in Chicago but had few local workers, it became known as Pettibone Corp. After a series of ownership and name changes (including Nucorp Inc. and Hako Minuteman Inc.) in the early 1990s, the company was purchased by a privately owned holding company called Heico Corp. in 1994; its name became Pettibone Corp. once again. By 2000, Pettibone was based out of Des Plaines, Illinois, and manufactured construction, forestry, foundry, railroad, and scrap-processing equipment. It claimed revenues of nearly $130 million but did not employ a large workforce in the Chicago area.

Phelps, Dodge & Palmer

This shoe company had its start in 1864, when Erskine M. Phelps and George E. P. Dodge moved from Boston to Chicago and founded Phelps & Dodge, a shoe wholesaling business. N. B. Palmer became a partner the following year, and in 1867 the company's name became Phelps, Dodge & Palmer. By the early 1870s, when annual sales hit $1 million, the company owned its own factory on Wabash Avenue, where about 90 employees produced about one-quarter of the shoes the company sold. Manufacturing operations expanded during the 1880s, when annual sales rose to $3 million and the company employed some 900 workers in its factories, which produced about 2,000 pairs of shoes a day. By this time, Phelps, Dodge & Palmer had become one of the leading shoe companies in the Midwest.

Pinkerton National Detective Agency

Allan Pinkerton emigrated from Scotland to the United States in 1842, when he was 23 years old; he soon settled in the town of Dundee, northwest of Chicago. By the beginning of the 1850s, Pinkerton and a partner had established the North-Western Police Agency, which had its offices at Washington and Dearborn Streets in Chicago. One of the first private detective agencies in the United States, this company worked for the Illinois Central and other railroads. By late 1850s, Pinkerton employed 15 operatives. During the Civil War, the company provided intelligence to the Northern armies that was not particularly accurate. After the war, promoting itself with the slogan "we never sleep," the company opened offices in New York City and Philadelphia. Much of its business came from banks and express companies, who wanted to deter robberies. Starting in the 1870s, Pinkerton detectives also began to work for industrial companies as spies and strikebreakers, and they quickly became despised by American labor. The company's most infamous strike-busting operation came in 1892, when 300 Pinkerton employees fought with workers at the Homestead, Pennsylvania, steel plant owned by Andrew Carnegie. When the two sides exchanged gunfire, nine strikers and seven Pinkerton agents were killed. By the time Allan Pinkerton died in 1884, his sons William and Robert Pinkerton were leading the company, which had about 2,000 full-time employees and several thousand "reservists." During the 1920s, annual revenues approached $2 million. In 1937, Robert Pinkerton II, a great-grandson of the founder, ended the firm's antiunion operations. By the late 1960s, just after the name of the enterprise became Pinkerton's Inc. and the corporate headquarters moved to California, it had 70 branch offices (including central offices in Chicago and New York), about $75 million in annual revenues, and some 13,000 full-time employees worldwide. In the mid-1970s, the company had about 800 employees in the Chicago area. By the end of the century, the enterprise founded a century and a half earlier had become a subsidiary of a large Swedish corporation called Securitas.

Plano Manufacturing Co.

See International Harvester Co.

Platinum Technology Inc.

Founded in 1987 by Andrew Filipowski, this computer software company was one of the fastest-growing firms in the Chicago area during the 1990s. The company began by specializing in database software and then moved into other software products. In 1989, Platinum grossed $6 million in sales and employed about 40 people. Nine years later, the company's annual sales reached about $1 billion, and it employed 5,000 people around the country, including 1,500 in the Chicago area. In 1999, Platinum was purchased for $3.5 billion by Computer Associates, a larger competitor based in New York that assumed both its operations and its name. Filipowski soon used some of his proceeds to begin an Internet "incubator" company called Divine InterVentures Inc., which, after being billed as the harbinger of a burgeoning Internet industry in Chicago, quickly sank along with the rest of the high-tech industry of the early 2000s.

Playboy Enterprises Inc.

Twenty-seven-year-old Hugh Hefner, a former sociology student at Northwestern University, started *Playboy* magazine in Chicago in 1953. The first printing of 50,000 copies, which featured Marilyn Monroe on the cover, sold out quickly. By publishing photographs of nude women and promoting the concept of sex as recreation, the magazine became a much-discussed phenomenon of American popular culture. Annual sales of *Playboy* grew from $4 million in 1960 to about $175 million at the end of the 1970s, when it had a circulation of about six million and ranked among the top 10 magazines (in terms of circulation as well as sales) in the United States. Meanwhile, from 1960 to 1986, Hefner's company operated the "Playboy Club" chain of nightclubs. By the late 1970s, Playboy employed about 4,000 people around the country. In 1982, Christie Hefner, the 29-year-old daughter of the founder, took charge of the company, which was moving into television and video products. By the end of the century, annual revenues stood at about $350 million, and Playboy employed about 500 people in the Chicago area. Playboy's revenues and circulation fell in the early 2000s as it faced tough competition from a series of new so-called lad mags, such as *Maxim* and *FHM*. It soon began to offset these losses, however, by emulating the graphics and photograph-heavy pages of its new competitors and expanding into the Internet market with Playboy .com.

Max Grinnell

Playskool Inc.

The Playskool Institute was founded in 1928 by Lucille King and another teacher from Wisconsin. During the early 1930s, the enterprise was purchased by a Chicago company, which changed its name to Playskool Inc. In 1938, Playskool was purchased by the Joseph Lumber Co., another Chicago company. During this period, Playskool's toy factory was running on the city's Northwest Side. In 1943, Playskool acquired the J. L. Wright Co., known for its founder's famous father, Frank Lloyd Wright, and the "Lincoln Logs" it produced. The company's annual sales grew from $6 million in 1957 to $23 million in 1965. In 1968, Playskool was purchased by the Milton Bradley Co. of Massachusetts. In 1973, Playskool, a division of Milton Bradley, renovated its plant on Chicago's Northwest Side, where it employed over 1,200 people. In 1984, Milton Bradley was acquired by Hasbro Inc. of Rhode Island. Much to the dismay of Chicago residents, who had recently helped to finance the Playskool plant renovations, Hasbro shut down the factory.

Premark International Inc.

See Kraft Inc.; Illinois Tool Works Inc.

Pressed Steel Car Co.

See General American Transportation Corp.

Pullman Inc.

Toward the end of the 1850s, George M. Pullman of Chicago began to remodel passenger coach railroad cars. The Pullman's Palace Car Co. was incorporated in Illinois in 1867; its first manufacturing shops were located in Detroit and Elmira, New York. By 1877, it operated about 460 luxury passenger cars, service on which was supervised by white conductors and African American porters. In 1880, Pullman decided to build a new manufacturing plant and a company town on a site about 14 miles south of downtown Chicago. By 1885, the population of the town had risen to nearly 9,000 men, women, and children. In the early 1890s, nearly 6,000 of the company's 14,000 employees nationwide worked in Pullman, where annual output stood at about 12,000 freight cars and 1,000 passenger cars. After an economic downturn in 1893, the company laid off thousands of workers; Pullman employees responded in 1894 by going on strike. This strike soon had national effects, because tens of thousands of American Railway Union members showed their support for Pullman workers by launching a boycott of trains pulling Pullman cars. In 1898, the Illinois courts ordered the company to sell its non-factory lands in the town. The company, however, continued to grow. By 1900, when the company changed its name to Pullman Co. after acquiring the assets of its only real competitor, the main plant had nearly 6,000 employees and produced about $14 million worth of railroad cars per year. Ten years later, when the company completed its transition from wooden cars to steel cars, there were about 10,000 workers at the Pullman plant. Meanwhile, the company operated about 7,500 passenger cars, which it leased—complete with porters and other workers—to railroad companies around the world. During the 1920s, when the workforce at Pullman reached a peak of about 20,000 people, the company was reorganized. In 1927, a holding company called Pullman Inc. was established to oversee two separate divisions: the Pullman Car & Manufacturing Corp., the company's manufacturing division, and the Pullman Co., which operated the world-famous passenger cars. The latter company's labor policies gave birth to the Brotherhood of Sleeping Car Porters. In 1929, Pullman Car merged with the Standard Steel Car Co. (another leading railroad car maker), creating the Pullman-Standard Car Manufacturing Co., which had plants in Hammond and Michigan City, Indiana, as well as other U.S. locations. During the 1930s, Pullman-Standard was the nation's largest manufacturer of freight cars and passenger cars. After World War II, the U.S. Department of Justice forced Pullman Inc. to sell one of its two divisions. The operating company, which kept the Pullman Co. name, was purchased by a group of railroad companies. Pullman Inc. kept Pullman-Standard, which declined steadily through the 1970s, by which time it was no longer an important manufacturer of railcars. In 1977, Pullman Inc., still based in Chicago, had annual revenues of $2 billion and employed 32,000 people nationwide. In 1980, Pullman Inc. was purchased by Wheelabrator-Frye Inc., a New Hampshire–based conglomerate. Two years later, the Pullman Car Works closed. Most of its rail-car manufacturing assets and its remaining freight car plants were subsequently sold to Dallas-based Trinity Industries.

Martha T. Briggs and Cynthia H. Peters

Pure Oil Co.

In 1914 in Columbus, Ohio, Fletcher Heath and Beman Dawes started the Ohio Cities Gas Co., which built its first oil refinery in West Virginia. In 1926, six years after the name of the company was changed to Pure Oil, its headquarters were moved to Chicago. From their offices in the Pure Oil building, company executives oversaw oil wells and refineries located in Ohio, West Virginia, Oklahoma, and Texas. A new research laboratory opened in 1950 in suburban Crystal Lake; eventually, Pure Oil operated a refinery at Lemont, Illinois. The company's annual sales grew from about $80 million in the late 1920s to over $700 million by the early 1960s, when it ranked among the 100 largest industrial corporations in the United States and employed more than 1,000 people in the Chicago area. In 1965, Pure Oil was purchased by the Union Oil Co. of California. As late as the mid-1970s, about 2,200 Chicago-area residents were employed by Union Oil.

Quaker Oats Co.

In 1879, the Imperial Mill was built at 16th and Dearborn Streets in Chicago by a group of investors that included John and Robert Stuart. At the end of the 1880s, this oat mill and several other leading mills around the Midwest became part of the American Cereal Co., a grain-milling giant that had its headquarters in Chicago. In 1901, American Cereal became the Quaker Oats Co. (The "Quaker" brand name came from an Ohio mill owned by Henry P. Crowell.) By 1907, Quaker's annual sales of oatmeal, flour, and feed amounted to $20 million. In 1909, the company used new machines to produce its "Puffed Rice" and "Puffed Wheat" ready-to-eat cereals, which proved popular. Annual sales in 1918 exceeded $120 million. In 1925, the company bought the "Aunt Jemima" mills of St. Joseph, Missouri. By that time, Quaker had begun to use oat hulls to produce the chemical furfural, which was soon used by industry to manufacture nylon and synthetic rubber. The company also became a leading maker of pet foods. In 1942, Quaker purchased Ken-L-Ration Dog Foods of Rockford, Illinois. By the middle of the 1960s, annual sales approached $500 million, and the company employed about 12,000 people nationwide (only a few hundred of these worked in the Chicago area). The company proceeded to introduce new lines of ready-to-eat breakfast cereals, including its popular "Life" and "Cap'n Crunch" brands, as well as Quaker instant oatmeal. By the middle of the 1970s, when the company employed about 1,800 people in the Chicago area, annual sales were about $1.5 billion. Over the last decades of the century, Quaker continued to make cereals, but its greatest success and greatest failure came with beverages. Its "Gatorade" sports drink brand became an immensely popular and profitable product and helped push Quaker's global workforce up to 32,000 by 1989. The company suffered in 1994, however, after paying $1.7 billion to acquire the "Snapple" drink brand, which it dumped in 1997 at a huge loss. At the beginning of the twenty-first century, when Quaker grossed nearly $5 billion in annual sales and had about 1,200 workers in the Chicago area and another 10,000 worldwide, the company was acquired by PepsiCo Inc. of New York.

Quill Corp.

This office supply business was founded in 1956 on Chicago's North Side by Jack Miller, who was joined in the business by his brothers Harvey and Arnold. The Millers' office supply business moved to the Irving Park neighborhood in western Chicago in 1960; during the 1970s it would relocate again, first to Northbrook and then to Lincolnshire. A successful catalog business pushed the company's annual sales up from $3.5 million in 1973 to over $400 million by the mid-1990s, when Quill was the largest independent mail-order office supply company in the country. Before the Millers sold the company in 1998 for $685 million to Massachusetts-based Staples Inc., Quill employed about 1,200 people in the Chicago area. Under new ownership, Quill kept its name and continued operations in Chicago without other major changes.

R

Rand McNally & Co.

In 1856, William H. Rand arrived in Chicago from Boston and set up a printing shop. Rand soon hired Andrew McNally, an Irish immigrant and a trained printer. In 1859, the two men started managing the printing shop of the *Chicago Tribune* newspaper. Rand, McNally & Co. was created in 1868, when it began to publish business directories and railroad guides. After publishing its first map in an 1872 railroad guide, the company became a pioneer in the field of mapmaking. Applying a wax engraving method, which made it possible to mass-produce maps at low cost, Rand McNally became the largest maker of maps in the United States. In 1880, when the company employed about 200 men and 50 women at its shops, its annual sales were about $500,000. The company soon moved into atlas and textbook publishing. Rand sold his interest in the company to McNally in 1899; both of the founders died in 1904–5. For most of the twentieth century, McNally's descendants ran the company. Annual sales reached $2 million in 1913, soon after the company began to make road maps to serve the growing numbers of automobile users. Rand McNally published its first road atlas, the "Auto Chum," in 1924. In 1952, when it employed over 1,000 people in the Chicago area, the company moved its headquarters from downtown Chicago to nearby Skokie. Annual sales passed $100 million in the 1970s, when there were about 750 employees in the Chicago area. In 1989, Rand McNally started to open retail stores; 10 years later, it owned about 30 stores around the country. Meanwhile, it moved quickly into electronic map products, including its "Streetfinder" brand. In 1998, the McNally family sold the company to a private investment group, AEA Investors Inc. of New York, for $500 million. The 30-year-old AEA, whose founders included the Mellon and Rockefeller families, had hoped to transform Rand into a high-tech multimedia company. A series of financial and strategic missteps, however, put the once venerable Chicago company on thin ice. It filed for Chapter 11 bankruptcy protection in 2003, emerging later that year with a new majority owner, Los Angeles–based acquisitions company Leonard Green & Partners LP.

Republic Steel Corp.

This large American steel company was formed in 1899 as the Republic Iron & Steel Co. through the merger of 30 small mills in Alabama; Youngstown, Ohio; and the Chicago area. In 1910, it employed about 900 men at its plant in East Chicago, Indiana. In 1930, following more mergers, the company changed its name to the Republic Steel Corp. The company operated a large mill in South Chicago that employed about 1,300 men during the mid-1930s. At that time its production capacity stood at 400,000 tons, less than 10 percent of the total capacity of Republic's plants across the country. By the late 1940s, the capacity of the South Chicago plant was over one million tons, representing about one-seventh of Republic's total capacity. As late as the 1970s, Republic still employed about 5,000 people in the Chicago area. Republic was purchased by Texas-based steel conglomerate LTV Corp. in 1984. The proliferation of inexpensive imported steel around that time, however, hurt the entire American steel industry, and LTV declared reorganization bankruptcy in 1986, one of several bankruptcies it endured through the 1980s and 1990s. While some of Republic's operations continued in southeastern Chicago for a time, a successive wave of additional LTV bankruptcies over the next 15 years prompted the closing of all of its mills and refineries by the early 2000s.

Ritchie (W. C.) & Co.

This manufacturer of paper boxes, founded by the Canadian-born William C. Ritchie, began to operate in Chicago in 1866 as Ritchie & Duck. Its name became W. C. Ritchie & Co. in 1881. By 1910, the company employed 1,100 workers at two Chicago box plants; it also owned a factory in nearby Aurora. In 1955, W. C. Ritchie was purchased by the Stone Container Corp., another Chicago-based paper box manufacturer. *See also* STONE CONTAINER CORP.

Ryerson (Joseph T.) & Son

Soon after he arrived in Chicago in 1842 as an agent for a Pittsburgh iron manufacturer, Joseph T. Ryerson opened his own store, which sold boilers and other iron products. Over the next few decades, Ryerson's company became one of the leading American processors and wholesalers of steel products. In 1926, the company became one of the first to offer stainless steel goods. By 1929, when the founder's grandson Edward L. Ryerson, Jr., became president of the company, it operated 10 distribution centers across the United States. In 1935, Ryerson was acquired by Inland Steel, the Chicago steel producer, which used Ryerson as its processing and distribution arm. By the late 1960s, the Ryerson division remained a major distributor of steel products; it was also the nation's leading aluminum distributor and a major dealer of plastics. In 1986, Inland Steel acquired another distributor, the Atlanta-based J. M. Tull. During the early 1990s, Inland spun off its distribution wing, creating an independent company called Ryerson Tull Inc. By the end of the twentieth century, this company had become the leading processor and distributor of metals in North

America, with close to $3 billion in annual sales and about 1,600 employees in the Chicago area. Despite weakened market conditions, as of 2003 the steel supplier had managed to avoid major layoffs in the Chicago area, but it had become the object of considerable acquisition speculation. *See also* INLAND STEEL CO.

S

S&C Electric Co.

This manufacturer of electrical fuses and switches, first called Schweitzer & Conrad, was founded in 1911 by Nicholas J. Conrad and Edmund O. Schweitzer, who were then employees of Commonwealth Edison, Chicago's electric utility. The company served as a military contractor during World War II and grew during the 1950s. In 1961, it opened a large Chicago facility called the Conrad Laboratory. By the mid-1970s, S&C employed about 1,400 people in the Chicago area. By the early 2000s, S&C was still a leading manufacturer of electric switches, grossing more than $100 million in annual sales and employing 1,700 workers at its Chicago headquarters. At that time, the company had a handful of manufacturing, engineering, and research and development operations in the United States, Canada, Brazil, China, and Mexico.

Safety-Kleen Corp.

Safety-Kleen, founded in Milwaukee in 1963 by Ben Palmer, pioneered the practice of recycling the solvents used to clean auto parts. In 1968, Palmer's company was purchased by the Elgin-Based Chicago Rawhide Manufacturing Co., then led by Donald W. Brinckman. Safety-Kleen's annual revenues increased from $1 million in 1969 to $28 million by 1974, when it was spun off as an independent company. From 1979, when it went public, to the late 1990s, Safety-Kleen enjoyed an astonishing streak of annual growth rates of 20 percent or more. Whenever significant competition cropped up, Safety-Kleen acquired it. By the end of the 1980s, it had 160 branches around the country and owned 2,500 trucks and 350,000 cleaning machines, which handled dirty automobile parts, dry-cleaning solvents, flammable liquids, and other items requiring cleaning, recycling, or disposal. By the early 1990s, Safety-Kleen employed nearly 7,000 people around the country and grossed nearly $800 million in annual sales. In 1991, the company opened a large oil-recycling plant in East Chicago, Indiana. The company's profits and rate of growth slowed sharply during the 1990s, partly because of environmental violations at one of its solvent-disposal plants in Puerto Rico. In 1998, it was acquired by South Carolina–based Laidlaw Environmental Services Inc., a company with origins in and continuing ties to Laidlaw Inc. Laidlaw moved Safety-Kleen's headquarters to Columbia, South Carolina, and adopted the company's famous name. Among the 650 people laid off at the Elgin headquarters were a handful of executives who began two environmental services companies in Elgin, Heritage-Crystal Clean LLC and Water Works Cleaning Systems LLC, designed to rival the troubled but still dominant Safety-Kleen in the early 2000s.

Sara Lee Corp.

See Consolidated Foods Corp.

Sayers Group LLC

In 1984, former Chicago Bears Hall of Fame running back Gale Sayers and his wife, Ardythe Sayers, founded the Sayers Group LLC in the Chicago suburb of Mount Prospect. In the beginning, the small company sold computer-related supplies such as printer cartridges and fax machines. By the mid-1990s, the Sayers Group had expanded to establish itself as a national leader in selling used and refurbished computers to households and businesses. The Sayers Group took advantage of the technology sector bust of the early 2000s by acquiring devalued computer and Internet-related companies. By 2003, the company was still involved in its earlier operations but had diversified into the fields of Internet consultancy and asset management, with offices in several states. At that time, the Sayers Group employed about 100 people nationwide; 60 of those worked at its Mount Prospect headquarters. With annual revenues around $300 million, the Sayers Group was one of the Chicago's largest minority-owned firms.

Schlesinger & Mayer

This dry-goods merchant house was founded in Chicago in 1872 by Leopold Schlesinger and David Mayer, both immigrants from Germany. The company soon opened branches in New York and Europe. In 1899, the company commissioned architect Louis Sullivan to dramatically redesign its large downtown Chicago department store at State and Madison Streets, where it employed nearly 2,500 people. When the refurbished structure was completed in 1904, Schlesinger & Mayer was no longer financially able to operate there. Rival Carson Pirie Scott moved in immediately, attaching its name to the ornate building that would become an architectural landmark for decades to come.

Schoenhofen (Peter) Brewing Co.

Peter Schoenhofen, a Prussian immigrant, was in Chicago working in the brewing trade by the 1850s. In 1861, he started a partnership with Matheus Gottfried; they were soon operating a brewery at Canalport Avenue and 18th Street where, during the early 1860s, they made about 600 barrels of lager beer a year. In 1867, Schoenhofen bought out his partner, and the company became the Peter Schoenhofen Brewing Co. By 1868, annual output had increased to about 10,000 barrels. During the 1890s, when the business was owned by the City Contract Co. of London, England, annual output reached 180,000 barrels. Around 1900, the Schoenhofen family regained control of the company, which employed about 500 people at its brewery on West 12th Street by 1910. During this time, the company was also known as the National Brewing Co. The company's "Edelweiss" brand of beer was a big seller. Operations shut down during Prohibition, but by 1933, after the national ban on alcohol production was lifted, the company was back in business as the Schoenhofen-Edelweiss Co. After being purchased by the Atlas Brewing Co. in the late 1940s, Schoenhofen became part of Dewery's Ltd. of South Bend, Indiana, in 1951, and thereafter assumed the Dewery's name. By the beginning of the 1970s, there was nothing left of its Chicago operations, although Dewery's reintroduced the famous Edelweiss brand in 1972 after nearly a decade-long hiatus.

Scholl Inc.

William Mathias Scholl graduated from Illinois Medical College (now Loyola University) in 1904 and founded a business that designed, manufactured, and sold orthopedic foot products. While most of its operations were based in Chicago, the company was incorporated in New York in 1913. Many of its products were sold under the "Dr. Scholl's" brand name. By the mid-1930s, Scholl employed nearly 400 people at its facilities on West Schiller Street in Chicago. Annual sales reached $65 million in 1967 and passed $200 million during the 1970s. By this time, the company was operating hundreds of "Foot Comfort Shops," and it employed about 7,000 people across the country, including about 750 in the Chicago area. At the end of the 1970s, Scholl was acquired by Schering-Plough, a drug company based in New Jersey. By the early 2000s, the Brown Shoe Co. owned the famous Dr. Scholl's brand name.

Schuttler (Peter) Co.

This important manufacturer of wagons was founded by Peter Schuttler, who emigrated from Germany to the United States in 1834 when he was 22 years old. After working as a wagon maker in Sandusky, Ohio, Schuttler moved to Chicago in 1843. He soon set up a new wagon shop and took advantage of the growing demand for heavy vehicles with the rise in westward migration to California after the 1849 Gold Rush. By the middle of the 1850s, Schuttler employed about 100 men at his wagon-making facility, which turned out about 1,800 wagons (worth about $75 each) per year. By this time, Schuttler was one of the leading wagon makers in the United States.

Although his company did not serve as a major military contractor during the Civil War, civilian demand allowed Schuttler's business to prosper. In 1863, he was one of only three Chicago residents (Potter Palmer and John V. Farwell were the others) to pay taxes on an income of over $100,000 . After the founder died in 1865, his son Peter took charge of the business, which continued to produce large numbers of wagons. By 1880, about 300 workers produced over $400,000 worth of wagons per year. As late as 1910, when Peter Schuttler III led the company, it still employed about 300 people at its factory on 22nd Street. But the dawn of the automobile age meant the end of the line for the Schuttler wagon works, which closed by the mid-1920s.

Schwartzchild & Sulzberger

See Wilson & Co.

Schwinn Bicycle Co.

See Arnold, Schwinn & Co.

Searle (G. D.) & Co.

This company was founded by Gideon D. Searle, a Civil War veteran, and Indiana drug store owner Frank Hereth, who had formerly worked as chief chemist of Eli Lilly & Co., the Indiana pharmaceutical company. At the beginning of the 1890s, Searle and Hereth moved their operation from Omaha, Nebraska, to Chicago's North Side. After Searle died in 1917, the company was led by his son C. Howard Searle; family members continued to manage the company for several decades. Searle, which bought an old Abbott Laboratories plant in Chicago's Ravenswood neighborhood in 1925, moved its operations to nearby Skokie in 1942. By 1950, the company's annual sales were nearly $20 million; among its best-selling products was Dramamine, a drug used to counter motion sickness. In 1960, Searle became the first American company to sell an oral contraceptive, which it marketed under the "Enovid" brand name. Searle grew rapidly during the 1960s. By the middle of the 1970s, annual sales had risen to $700 million, and the company employed about 4,500 people in the Chicago area. In 1981, after an extended controversy between Searle and the Food and Drug Administration, the U.S. government approved the sale of a new artificial sweetener, aspartame, which Searle sold under the "NutraSweet" brand name. In 1985, the company was acquired by the Monsanto Co., a chemical producer based in St. Louis. Searle, which retained considerable autonomy, continued to reside in Skokie. Searle's longtime Chicago history began to fade in 2000 when Monsanto was acquired by New Jersey–based Pharmacia & Upjohn Inc. Upjohn maintained Searle's research, development, and manufacturing plant in Skokie but closed the headquarters. New York pharmaceutical giant Pfizer purchased Pharmacia in 2003 and announced it would close Searle's Skokie plant, thereby laying off its 1,500 employees.

Sears, Roebuck & Co.

The business that would become Chicago's leading company and America's leading retailer for much of the twentieth century was founded in 1893 by Richard W. Sears. In 1887, Sears moved his watch-selling business from Minneapolis to Chicago and hired watchmaker Alvah C. Roebuck to assist him. While Roebuck's name would remain with the company for decades, ill health forced his retirement around the turn of the century. Sears soon sold the watch business and returned to Minneapolis for a time, but by 1895 Sears returned to Chicago to head a general mail-order firm. This enterprise expanded at an extraordinary pace and soon surpassed Montgomery Ward, the Chicago firm that had pioneered large-scale mail-order retailing. Like Ward, Sears issued thick catalogs and sold all sorts of goods, including clothing, appliances, and furniture. By 1906, when it first issued stock to the public, the company was capitalized at $40 million, had about 9,000 employees, and was approaching $50 million in annual sales. Mail-order branch houses soon opened in Dallas and Seattle. In 1908, Sears retired, and Julius Rosenwald, a partner since 1895, took charge of the company. Although the company was successful with its "No Money Down" policy of generous consumer credit, which helped to push annual sales to $235 million by 1920, the tremendous growth of the mail-order industry was slowing. In 1924, the company made a significant change in its operations by opening its first retail store. By 1929, there were over 300 Sears stores across the country. The move into retail stores was engineered by Robert E. Wood, a former U.S. Army supply officer who joined Sears after World War I. In 1928, Wood took over leadership of the company from Rosenwald; during the Great Depression, Wood managed to keep the firm growing. The company's "Allstate" automobile insurance business, established in 1931 after Wood's neighbor and fellow commuter suggested that Sears sell auto insurance, was a major success. In 1932, the company moved into its famous flagship store on State and Van Buren Streets in Chicago's Loop, where it would remain until 1986. By 1941, Sears' annual sales neared $1 billion. Meanwhile, Wood, a staunch political conservative, served as a leader of the isolationist America First movement, and he opposed efforts among Sears workers during the New Deal and World War II to join unions. In the seven years after the end of the war, the company opened nearly 100 new stores, including one in Mexico City, and expanded several others. By the time Wood retired in 1954, the company's annual sales had surpassed $3 billion, and Sears had become America's leading retailer. But by the beginning of the 1970s, although annual sales had risen to $10 billion, and although it was about to move its headquarters into the world's tallest building (the Sears Tower), the company's fortunes were declining. Other discount retail chains such as Kmart were competing successfully against Sears, which by 1975 had over 850 stores and close to 400,000 employees (about 30,000 of them in the Chicago area). Between 1979 and 1986, the company spent about $100 million to defend itself against a lawsuit (in which Sears eventually prevailed) by the U.S. government for alleged discrimination against female and minority employees. By the early 1990s, the company's payrolls had shrunk by tens of thousands of workers. At the end of the 1990s, when the company's annual sales stood at about $40 billion, Sears, headquartered in suburban Hoffman Estates, employed about 8,000 men and women in the Chicago area. The year 2001 was a milestone for Sears in Chicago, as it opened a large store on downtown State Street after having been gone from the historic location for 15 years. In 2002, the company purchased Lands' End, a mail-order company that had its beginnings in 1963 on North Elston Avenue. In 2003, Sears divested itself of its credit division, a division that had helped spur its growth 90 years earlier. *See also* ALLSTATE CORP.

Seipp (Conrad) Brewing Co.

Conrad Seipp, an immigrant from Germany, started making beer in Chicago in 1854, after buying a small brewery from Mathias Best. By 1856, Seipp had six employees, who helped him produce about 1,100 barrels of beer each year. In 1858, Frederick Lehman joined the company, which became Seipp & Lehman. By the end of the 1860s, when Seipp & Lehman was one of Chicago's leading brewers, about 50 employees made more than 50,000 barrels of beer (worth close to $500,000) per year. After Lehman died in 1872, Seipp organized the Conrad Seipp Brewing Co. Dominating the Chicago beer market by the late 1870s, Seipp was among the largest breweries in the United States, producing over 100,000 barrels a year. After Conrad Seipp died in 1890, the company merged with several smaller Chicago breweries to form the City of Chicago Consolidated Brewing & Malting Co., which was controlled by British investors, although Seipp was allowed to operate with considerable autonomy and under the Seipp name. At the turn of the century, the Seipp brewery was still active; annual output had reached about 250,000 barrels. The widespread establishment of neighborhood liquor stores around 1910 siphoned off sales from Seipp and other city breweries, but Seipp managed to stay afloat by introducing home beer deliveries. Grain and coal shortages during World War I stifled Seipp's production before the enactment of Prohibition in 1919 dealt a devastating blow to the beer industry as a whole. The company limped along through the Prohibition years by producing low-alcohol "near bear" and distributing soda pop. Many speculated that Seipp also produced bootleg beer for the Torrio-Capone crime organization. Ironically, Seipp operations ceased in 1933, just before Prohibition was lifted. The brewery was destroyed that year to make room for a new hospital.

Selz, Schwab & Co.

Morris Selz, a native of Württemberg, Germany, arrived in Chicago in 1854 after working in sales for companies in Connecticut and Georgia. Selz started in the clothing business in Chicago with Selz & Cohn, but in 1871 he entered the wholesale shoe trade, founding M. Selz & Co. By the following year, the East Madison Street factory of the firm had about 350 employees, who made about $1 million worth of hand-pegged boots and shoes each year. Selz's company now ranked among the leading shoe manufacturers in the Midwest. The enterprise became Selz, Schwab & Co. in 1878, when Charles H. Schwab—another German immigrant who had arrived in Chicago in 1854—joined the firm. By the beginning of the twentieth century, the company employed about 1,500 workers at its factories around northern Illinois, which were located in Chicago, Joliet, Genoa, and Elgin. By this time, Selz, Schwab & Co. manufactured about 12,000 pairs of boots and shoes per day, which placed the company among the leading makers of footwear in the United States. Selz remained a major footwear company throughout the 1920s, before the Great Depression crippled its sales and forced its factories to close.

ServiceMaster Industries Inc.

Marion Wade owned a carpet-cleaning business as early as 1929. In 1947, Wade started a new cleaning company with Kenneth Hansen, a graduate of Wheaton College. In 1958, the company became known as ServiceMaster—a name that referred not only to the firm's business, but also to the founders' commitment to Christian ethics. In 1962, as ServiceMaster began to sell stock to the public, it also started to serve as a cleaning contractor for hospitals. Over the next decade, the company enjoyed remarkable growth. Annual sales rose from about $20 million in 1967 to over $200 million by the mid-1970s, when ServiceMaster had about 600 employees in the Chicago area. The company diversified in the 1980s and 1990s by purchasing a wide range of companies involved in home services, including pest control, lawn treatment, and even day care. ServiceMaster's fortunes turned downward in the late 1990s, however, after the company made two particularly unprofitable acquisitions. After selling some of its less profitable companies overseas and working to integrate its diverse remaining divisions, ServiceMaster began returning to solid profitability in the early 2000s. Still headquartered in Downers Grove, the company had annual revenues of $3.6 billion and employed about 2,500 workers in the Chicago area.

Sidley & Austin

This law firm traced its roots to Williams & Thompson, a Chicago firm founded in 1866 by Norman Williams and John L. Thompson. The name Sidley—from William Pratt Sidley, who started working for the firm as a young lawyer in 1892—entered the firm's title in 1900, when it became Holt, Wheeler & Sidley. Edwin C. Austin joined the firm in 1914. By this time, the firm's list of clients included many of Chicago's largest businesses, including Pullman, Western Electric, and Illinois Steel. In 1916, the firm consisted of nine lawyers and their office staff. In 1920, the firm's offices moved from the Tacoma Building to the Roanoke Building, a newer skyscraper. By 1941, when the firm was known as Sidley, McPherson, Austin & Burgess, it employed 32 lawyers. From 1950 to 1967, the firm was called Sidley, Austin, Burgess & Smith. In 1967, when it changed its name to Sidley & Austin, it consisted of 80 lawyers, half of whom were partners; two years later, the firm moved into new offices at One First National Plaza, a new skyscraper in Chicago's Loop. A 1972 merger with Liebman, Williams, Bennett, Baird & Minow, another large Chicago law firm, created a firm of 150 lawyers. Over the next 25 years Sidley & Austin grew to rank consistently as one of Chicago's largest law firms and opened offices in other cities around the country. In 1999, it merged with competitor Brown & Wood to become Sidley, Austin, Brown & Wood LLP. Under its new name, the firm claimed 400 attorneys and 1,400 staff in its Chicago headquarters alone, with fourteen additional offices nationwide.

Siegel, Cooper & Co.

This discount department store, located on State Street in Chicago's Loop, was established in 1887 by Henry Siegel, Frank H. Cooper, and Isaac Keim. In 1891, the company moved into the Siegel, Cooper & Co. Building on State and Van Buren Streets. The eight-story building, designed by William Le Baron Jenney and internationally recognized as one of the early "Chicago School" skyscrapers, was however not nearly as opulent as the company's New York store, designed by DeLemos & Cordes and located on Sixth Avenue on what was known as the "Ladies' Mile." By 1900, the "Big Store," as Siegel was popularly known, employed about 2,000 people. In 1913–14 Siegel's stores, along with those of other merchants, were reorganized into the Associated Dry Goods Corp. with the help of J. P. Morgan. The Chicago store closed around 1930, its building soon occupied by Sears & Roebuck's flagship store.

Signode Steel Strapping Co.

In 1913, Ellsworth Flora and J. Fremont Murphy formed the Seal & Fastener Co. in Chicago. The company made steel strapping systems, which could be used to seal and reinforce large containers. In 1916, the company's name became Signode System. In 1928, when annual sales surpassed $3 million, the name changed to Signode Steel Strapping Co. During World War II, with about 400 employees, the company made radar equipment and other military supplies; sales in 1945 approached $16 million. During the postwar era, Signode expanded nationwide and overseas. Starting in 1955, many of its operations were transferred to Glenview, northwest of Chicago. By the early 1960s, when annual sales reached $60 million, the company employed more than 1,000 people in the Chicago area. In 1964, when the company was renamed Signode Corp., it opened a new plant in Bridgeview, southwest of Chicago. By this time, Signode had begun to sell nylon and plastic strapping, and annual sales had reached $100 million. In the mid-1980s, when the company became known as Signode Industries Inc., it employed nearly 2,000 people in the Chicago area, and annual sales reached about $750 million. In 1986, Signode was purchased by another Chicago-area company, Illinois Tool Works. By the early 2000s, Signode was still a steel strapping division of Illinois Tool Works, operating out of suburban Glenview. *See also* ILLINOIS TOOL WORKS INC.

Skidmore, Owings & Merrill

This architecture firm was founded in 1936 in Chicago as Skidmore & Owings by Louis Skidmore and his brother-in-law, Nathaniel Owings. Before creating this firm, Skidmore had served as the chief architect (Owings assisted him) for the 1933 Century of Progress Exposition in Chicago. The partners opened a New York office in 1937. After John Merrill joined the firm in 1939, the name changed to Skidmore, Owings & Merrill. By 1952, the firm was one of the few American architecture enterprises to employ more than 1,000 people around the country. During the 1960s and 1970s, it designed many large buildings in Chicago, including the Brunswick Building, the John Hancock Center, the Sears Tower, the main libraries for the University of Chicago and Northwestern University, and much of the University of Illinois at Chicago. In the late 1980s, when it employed about 700 people in Chicago, Skidmore, Owings & Merrill was the city's largest architecture firm. At the end of the 1990s, Chicago-area projects accounted for about one-third of the firm's $90 million in annual billings across the country. Although a decline in new commercial construction in the early 2000s led to cutbacks in the firm's local workforce, it maintained offices in Chicago, New York, San Francisco, Washington DC, Los Angeles, London, Hong Kong, and São Paulo and had annual billings near $176 million in the United States.

Smurfit-Stone Container Corp.
See Stone Container Corp.

Southwest Airlines Inc.
Founded in 1966 in Dallas, Texas, by Herbert D. Kelleher and other investors, Southwest started flying in 1971. In 1985, the discount airline began to serve Chicago's Midway Airport. Although it continued to call Texas home, Southwest became an important Chicago airline in the early 1990s, when it purchased many of the Midway Airport gates of the bankrupt Midway Airlines. By 1994, it employed about 1,200 people in the Chicago area. As the rest of the airline industry floundered in the early 2000s, Southwest remained profitable, substantially increasing its Chicago presence after Midway Airport added a new terminal.

Spalding (A. G.) Co.
Albert G. Spalding, a native of Illinois, played baseball professionally with the Boston Red Stockings and the Chicago White Stockings during the 1870s. In 1876, Spalding started a sporting goods business in Chicago, helped found baseball's National League, and served as both player and manager of the new Chicago Club baseball team. By the 1880s, the company had branches around the country. The Spalding Co. developed the ball for the first-ever organized basketball game in 1891. In 1938, when Spalding was purchased by BTR of England, it employed about 250 people at a plant on Chicago's South Side. Sold by BTR during the 1960s, Spalding was purchased by a New York investment company in the 1990s. By the early 2000s, Spalding was based in Massachusetts, and still a sporting goods powerhouse.

Spiegel Inc.
Joseph Spiegel emigrated with his family from Germany to the United States in 1848, when he was eight years old. In 1865, Spiegel started a home furnishings store in Chicago. A 1903 merger with another furniture company created Spiegel, May, Stern & Co. In 1905, Joseph and his son Arthur Spiegel started a large-scale mail-order business; mail-order sales for 1906 totaled about $1 million. By 1910, the company employed about 300 people at its offices on West 35th Street. In 1912, the company began to sell women's clothing. Thanks to its mail-order operations, Spiegel grew rapidly during the 1920s, as annual sales rose from $4 million to $24 million. Sales dropped during the first part of the Great Depression, but Spiegel grew between 1933 and 1937 (when its name became Spiegel Inc.) by offering installment buying plans and pursuing a strategy of high-volume discount sales. Business slowed during World War II, when the company experimented unsuccessfully with operating retail stores. After shedding these stores in 1953, Spiegel reached $200 million in annual mail-order sales by the end of the 1950s. In 1965, Spiegel was acquired by the Beneficial Finance Co., another mail-order company, which moved Spiegel into the field of high-priced designer clothing. By the early 1970s, when annual sales reached about $400 million, Spiegel employed about 5,000 people in the Chicago area. In 1982, Spiegel was acquired by Otto-Versand, a German catalog company. Under the new ownership, Spiegel expanded. In 1988, when orders placed by telephone accounted for the bulk of its business, Spiegel purchased the "Eddie Bauer" clothing chain and brand from General Mills Inc. At the beginning of the 1990s, Spiegel, based in suburban Downers Grove, still employed about 2,200 people at its catalog warehouse on Chicago's South Side, but this facility would soon close. During the 1990s, when Spiegel mailed as many as 340 million catalogs a year and operated about 350 Eddie Bauer stores worldwide, annual sales rose to $3 billion. At the turn of the new century, when the Otto family of Germany still controlled Spiegel, the company employed about 1,600 people in the Chicago area. The economic recession of the early 2000s hit the company's catalog and credit card divisions hard. Spiegel entered Chapter 11 reorganization bankruptcy in early 2003 and planned to close at least 60 of its 540 Eddie Bauer stores nationally, including several in the Chicago area.

Sprague, Warner & Co.
See Consolidated Foods Corp.

Standard Oil Co. (Indiana)
In 1889, John D. Rockefeller's Standard Oil Co. established an Indiana-based subsidiary. The next year, the company began to process oil at an enormous new refinery at Whiting, Indiana, southeast of Chicago. By the mid-1890s, the Whiting plant had become the largest refinery the United States, handling 36,000 barrels of oil per day and accounting for nearly 20 percent of the total U.S. refining capacity. During these years, the company's main product was kerosene, which was used in lamps. By 1910, when it was connected by pipeline to oil fields in Kansas and Oklahoma, as well as Ohio and Indiana, the Whiting facility had about 2,400 workers. In 1911, when the U.S. government forced Rockefeller to break up his oil giant, Standard of Indiana—which had its main offices in downtown Chicago—emerged as an independent company; it soon began to purchase oil wells of its own. During the 1910s, the company pioneered a new thermal "cracking" process, in which crude oil was processed under pressure in order to produce higher yields of gasoline. By this time, the beginning of the automobile age, gasoline had become the leading product of oil refineries. In 1920, Standard Indiana ranked as the third-largest oil refiner in the United States, behind Standard New Jersey and Standard California. In 1925, when it already had more than 25,000 employees around the country, Standard Indiana merged with the American Oil Co. (Amoco). During the mid-1930s, the company employed about 7,000 people at its Whiting plant and Chicago offices. Standard Indiana ranked as the second-largest American oil company at the beginning of the 1950s, when annual sales grossed $1.5 billion. In the early 1970s, when the company moved into new offices on East Randolph Drive near Chicago's lakefront, Standard Indiana still employed about 8,000 people in the area. In 1985, as annual sales neared $30 billion, the company changed its name to Amoco, which then ranked as the nation's sixth-largest oil company. By that time, Amoco and other leading oil companies were huge global corporations that not only refined oil but also explored and drilled for it; Amoco also had a large chemicals division. At the end of the 1990s, when Amoco employed about 4,000 people in the Chicago area, it merged with British Petroleum (BP). While most of the company's jobs still remained in Chicago by the early 2000s, Amoco's old operations had become known by the BP name, and management of the company was directed from London.

Stewart-Warner Corp.
In 1905, John K. Stewart and Thomas J. Clark—the same men who in 1897 had created the Chicago Flexible Shaft Co. (which became Sunbeam)—founded Stewart & Clark, which manufactured speedometers for automobiles. Between 1906 and 1908, annual sales rose from about $35,000 to $350,000. Although Clark died in a 1907 accident while demonstrating the product, the company continued to expand. By 1910, it had about 375 workers at its factory on Chicago's Diversey Avenue. In 1912, after buying the Warner Instrument Co. of Beloit, Wisconsin, another speedometer maker, the company became the Stewart-Warner Corp. In 1924, Stewart-Warner bought Bassick-Alemite, a maker of high-pressure auto lubrication equipment formed out of companies based in Chicago, Connecticut, and Cleveland. By the end of the 1920s, annual sales had reached about $40 million. Although business lagged during the Great Depression, Stewart-Warner employed about 2,500 people in the Chicago area in the mid-1930s, when the company made refrigerators and radios as well as auto parts. During World War II, the company manufactured bombs and shells, fuses, and engine parts, becoming one of the nation's top 100 military contractors in terms

of volume of sales to the U.S. government (which came to about $330 million over the course of the war). The company did not grow much during the postwar years, but by the early 1970s, when annual sales stood at about $260 million, it still employed about 5,000 people in the Chicago area, many of them at plants on the city's West Side. In 1987, most of Stewart-Warner's operations were purchased by BTR, a British conglomerate. Over the next decade, the company's remaining divisions either downsized area operations or were acquired by larger companies. By the late 1990s, Stewart-Warner's Chicago presence had dwindled to the 20 employees at navigational equipment maker Stewart-Warner Electronics Corp. in Schiller Park.

Stone Container Corp.

After emigrating from Russia to the United States around 1888, Joseph H. Stone made his way to Chicago, where he worked as a cigar maker. By the late 1910s, Stone was a wholesaler of paper products. In 1926, Stone and his sons Norman and Marvin formed J. H. Stone & Sons, a small enterprise that sold paper and twine. The Stones' sales in 1927 amounted to about $70,000. During the late 1930s, the company built a large corrugated cardboard box factory at 42nd Place and Keeler Avenue in Chicago. In 1945, by which time the company owned another plant in Philadelphia, its name changed to Stone Container Corp. By the early 1960s, annual sales reached $50 million, and Stone Container had over 1,000 employees in the Chicago area and hundreds more nationwide. In the late 1970s, Roger W. Stone, a son of Marvin, took charge of the company, leading it through a period of great expansion. The new chief made Stone bigger by buying other paper companies, including Consolidated-Bathhurst of Canada, a newsprint maker acquired in 1989. Stone's annual sales rose from nearly $300 million in 1979 to about $6 billion in the mid-1990s, when it employed about 30,000 people around the world and ranked as the world's leading manufacturer of paper packaging. In 1998, Stone merged with the Jefferson Smurfit Corp., a smaller paper company based in St. Louis. The resulting entity was named Smurfit-Stone Container Corp., which at the end of the twentieth century grossed more than $7 billion in annual sales and employed about 1,200 people in the Chicago area, where it made its headquarters.

Sturges, Buckingham & Co.

This grain elevator company was founded in 1855 by Solomon Sturges and his brothers-in-law C. P. Buckingham and Alvah Buckingham. By 1857, they owned 120-foot elevators at the Illinois Central Railroad depot. During the Civil War, their two elevators had a capacity of 700,000 bushels each, which made Sturges, Buckingham & Co. the city's leading grain warehousing firm. In 1865, John Buckingham and Ebenezer Buckingham took over management of the elevators. By 1873, the Buckinghams' elevators had a capacity of nearly 2.9 million bushels of grain. The partnership ended with death of John Buckingham in 1881.

Sunbeam Co.

See Chicago Flexible Shaft Co.

Swift & Co.

During the 1850s, when he was still a teenager, Gustavus F. Swift started to work in the beef business in Massachusetts. In 1875, Swift began buying cattle in Chicago to send to his family's butcher operations back East. He quickly revolutionized the meat industry by using newly developed refrigerated railcars to ship fresh meat from Chicago to Eastern markets. The company soon set up a national network of branch offices, which allowed it to control the distribution of its meat across the country. By 1886, when the company slaughtered more than 400,000 cattle a year, Swift employed about 1,600 people. Between 1887 and 1892, new packing plants were opened in Kansas City, Omaha, and St. Louis. By the time the founder died in 1903, his company grossed $200 million in annual sales and employed about 23,000 people across the country, including over 5,000 workers at its slaughtering plant in Chicago's Union Stock Yard. In 1908, Swift plants across the country slaughtered a total of about eight million animals. By this time, Swift owned a fleet of nearly 5,000 refrigerated railcars. Annual sales reached $700 million by the late 1920s, when the total workforce of the company—which ranked as one of the largest industrial corporations in the United States—consisted of about 55,000 people. Swift stopped slaughtering in Chicago in 1953, but its corporate headquarters remained in the city. In 1973, by which time meat had become only one of its businesses, Swift became part of Esmark Inc., a holding company. During the 1980s, Esmark's meat division was spun off and moved to Texas. Swift, once one of Chicago's leading employers and largest companies, no longer has a presence in the city. From the early 1990s through the early 2000s, food conglomerate Conagra owned Swift's operations. Swift & Co.'s divisional headquarters were located in Greeley, Colorado.

T

Target Corp.

See Field (Marshall) & Co.

Telephone & Data Systems Inc.

This company, which grew by buying small independent telephone companies, was founded in 1968 by LeRoy T. Carlson, a Chicago native. In 1983, when Telephone & Data Systems (TDS) had its headquarters in Chicago, it created a subsidiary called United States Cellular Corp., which grew into one of the 10 largest wireless telecommunications companies in the country. After purchasing numerous smaller companies around the country, TDS claimed over five million customers in 35 states by the early 2000s. Led by one of LeRoy Carlson's sons at the LaSalle Street headquarters, the company grossed about $3 billion dollars in revenues and employed over 8,000 people in the Chicago area at that time.

Teletype Corp.

See Western Electric Co.

Tellabs Inc.

This manufacturer of telecommunications equipment was established in 1975 by Michael Birk and others in Lisle, just west of Chicago. The company started with 20 employees and grossed about $300,000 in sales during its first year. The federally mandated breakup of AT&T in the early 1980s helped Tellabs by increasing the number of potential customers. Annual sales surpassed $100 million in 1985. The strong telecommunications market of the middle to late 1990s provided fertile ground for Tellabs' exponential growth during that decade. The company was headquartered in suburban Naperville by 2000, boasting $4 billion in revenues and 8,000 employees around the world, almost half of those in Chicago. Tellabs followed its industry downward in the early 2000s, dropping two-thirds of its sales and cutting its workforce to about 4,000, one-third of whom worked outside the United States.

Tootsie Roll Industries Inc.

The first "Tootsie Roll" candies were made in New York City during the early 1890s by Austrian immigrant Leo Hirschfeld. In 1922, Hirschfeld's company was renamed Sweets Co. of America. When William Rubin bought the company in 1935, it operated a large candy factory in New Jersey. In 1966, Tootsie Roll opened a large factory in the Ford City industrial park in southwest Chicago. Soon, all of the company's operations were centralized in Chicago, where it employed about 900 people by the mid-1970s. By that time, the company was led by Rubin's daughter Ellen Gordon and her husband Melvin Gordon. In 1988, Tootsie Roll bought Charms Co., a maker of lollipops. By 1990, when annual sales were close to $200 million, Tootsie Roll was the nation's leading producer of lollipops. The company continued a pattern of solid growth through the 1990s, with annual sales of $400 million and about 1,700 employees in the Chicago area by the end of the decade, when sales began to flatten. In the early 2000s, the company was still headed by William Rubin's daughter and son-in-law.

Trans Union Corp.

See Union Tank Car Co.

Tribune Co.

The *Chicago Daily Tribune* newspaper was founded in 1847. In 1861, six years after Joseph Medill became associated with the paper, the name changed to *Chicago Tribune*. After a few years in other pursuits, Medill regained control of the paper in 1874 and directed it until 1899. In 1880, Medill's company had about 200 production workers in Chicago. During the 1910s, Medill's grandsons Robert R. McCormick and Joseph Medill Patterson took over the management of the company that owned the *Tribune*, which became more than just a publisher of a leading Chicago newspaper. In 1919, the Tribune Co. established a new paper in the country's largest city called the New York *News* (later the *Daily News*), led by Patterson, who had moved to New York. Back in Chicago, McCormick had made the *Tribune* the most widely read of the city's several daily newspapers, even as he built the Tribune Co. into a diversified media company. Daily circulation of the paper rose from about 230,000 in 1912 to 660,000 by 1925. The WGN radio station was launched in 1924, just before the company and its flagship newspaper moved into the new Tribune Tower on North Michigan Avenue in downtown Chicago. The Tribune Tower provided space for some 2,000 employees. The company's WGN television station was established in 1948, becoming Chicago's only "superstation" 30 years later, with broadcast outlets around the country. After McCormick died in 1955, the Tribune Co. continued to grow. During the 1960s, it purchased newspapers in Florida. In 1981, when it created a subsidiary called the Tribune Broadcasting Co., the company bought the Chicago Cubs baseball team from the Wrigley family. In 1983, as annual revenues approached $2 billion, the Tribune Co. began to sell stock to the public. The New York *Daily News* was sold off in 1991, and the Tribune Co.'s total workforce across the country dropped from nearly 19,000 in 1985 to about 10,000 in 1994. During the 1990s, the company launched an electronic version of the *Tribune* newspaper. At the end of the century, with over $3 billion in annual sales, the company expanded by purchasing the Times Mirror Co., publisher of the *Los Angeles Times* and other newspapers around the country. This acquisition turned the Tribune Co.—which now owned 10 major papers—into the nation's third-largest newspaper company in terms of total circulation. It also owned some 20 television stations nationwide. By 1999, the company employed nearly 6,000 people in the Chicago area. It continued to grow vigorously through the early 2000s, with annual revenues reaching over $5 billion.

True Value Hardware

In 1948, John Cotter, a veteran hardware salesman from St. Paul, Minnesota, created Cotter & Co., a wholesaler that supplied a cooperative of 25 hardware retailers in Illinois and other Midwestern states. This company, which sold through catalogs, had about 200 employees and $20 million in annual sales by the beginning of the 1960s, when the retail network had expanded to about 500 stores. In 1963, Cotter spent $2.5 million to acquire the hardware operations and "True Value" trademark of the venerable Chicago hardware company Hibbard, Spencer & Bartlett. This brought 400 new retailers into the Cotter cooperative and doubled the size of the business. Annual sales proceeded to grow from $100 million in 1966 to about $2 billion by the end of the 1980s, when the company employed about 1,000 people in the Chicago area. In 1997, after Cotter & Co. merged with Pittsburgh-based competitor ServiStar Coast to Coast Corp., the company became known as the TruServ Corp. Based in Chicago, TruServ was a member-owned cooperative supplying over 10,000 independent hardware retailers worldwide and with annual sales of over $4 billion and nearly 2,000 employees in the Chicago area. *See also* HIBBARD, SPENCER, BARTLETT & CO.

U

Unicom Corp.

See Commonwealth Edison Co.

Union Stock Yard & Transit Co.

This company, which ran the huge stockyards that made Chicago the center of the American meat industry for decades, was organized during the Civil War by a group of Chicago meatpackers and railroad executives that included Rosell Hough and John Hancock. On Christmas Day, 1865, the Union Stock Yard—a 320-acre facility on Chicago's South Side—was opened. For many years, Union Stock Yard & Transit was managed by John B. Sherman, a veteran of the livestock industry. By the beginning of the 1890s, when the Union Stock Yard could hold more than 400,000 live animals at a time, the company employed about 1,000 people to help run the facility, which housed the plants of leading Chicago-based meat companies such as Swift and Armour. Between 1865 and 1900, about 400 million animals were killed within the confines of the yards. The company's workforce grew to 2,000 by the beginning of the 1920s. Just as America's railroad system had helped to centralize the meatpacking industry after the Civil War, the post–World War II highway system and trucking industry worked to disperse operations as the twentieth century progressed. Faster, more modern transportation methods made it cheaper to slaughter animals where they were raised—in western states, such as Nebraska, Kansas, Iowa, Colorado, and Montana—before shipping them for sale. The major meat companies joined together to resist the change for a time. Eventually, Swift and Armour acquiesced and left the Union Stock Yard in the late 1950s, effectively relegating the historical yards to a minor position in the meat industry. The Union Stock Yard completely stopped operations in 1971.

Union Tank Car Co.

Founded in 1866 by one of Standard Oil Co.'s early competitors, J. J. Vandergrift, the Star Tank Line shipped oil from the fields of Pennsylvania to Chicago. The company was purchased by Standard Oil in 1873 and its headquarters moved to Ohio. Five years later, its name was changed to Union Tank Car Co. As part of John D. Rockefeller's innovative scheme to avoid state antitrust measures, Union Tank Car was incorporated in New Jersey in 1891 as a subsidiary of the newly incorporated Standard Oil Trust. By 1904, Union Tank Car owned a fleet of 10,000 cars, far more than any other private car operator. It shipped products solely for its parent company until 1911, when the Standard Oil Trust was dissolved by the federal government. During the 1920s, when its fleet consisted of about 30,000 cars, the company changed its name to UTCC and its headquarters were moved to Chicago. In 1931, it began shipping chemicals and producing tank cars. Over the next several decades, UTCC acquired other companies and became one of the world's largest tank carrier companies. By the early 1960s, when the company moved into the new Union Tank Car Building in Chicago's Loop, annual sales exceeded $100 million. A decade later, UTCC and its newly created holding company, Trans Union Corp., employed about 1,500 people in the Chicago area. Trans Union Corp. and its subsidiaries (UTCC included) were purchased by the Chicago-based Marmon Group investment company in 1981. *See also* MARMON GROUP INC.

United Air Lines

United Air Lines and the modern American commercial airline industry were born out of small private companies that contracted in the 1920s with the U.S. postal service to deliver mail to the Pacific coast. One of these early airlines, the Boeing Air Transport Co., was founded by William Boeing in 1927; it flew between Chicago and San Francisco. By 1931, Boeing Air Transport—along with National Air Transport, another airline that flew out of Chicago—was part of the United Aircraft & Transport Co., which included Boeing's airplane manufacturing operations. In 1934, a new federal law forced this company to split into separate, independent airline and aircraft manufacturing companies. The airline became

United Air Lines Transport Corp., which was led by William Patterson. In 1939, the company built its headquarters next to Midway (then Chicago Municipal) Airport. During the middle of World War II, when it sold aircraft to the U.S. military, the company's name was shortened to United Air Lines. During the postwar era, United and the whole commercial airline industry grew rapidly. Annual revenues, which came primarily from passenger tickets, rose from about $16 million in 1940 to $130 million in 1951. By this time, the company employed about 600 female flight attendants. In 1959, United started to fly its first jets, which were DC-8 models. At the beginning of the 1960s, when the company's home moved from Chicago Midway to Chicago O'Hare, United owned a fleet of more than 200 airplanes and employed over 28,000 people worldwide. Soon, United was grossing $500 million in annual sales and ranked as the world's largest passenger airline, ahead of competitors such as American and Eastern. In 1969, United Air Lines became part of a holding company named UAL Inc., which had its headquarters in Elk Grove Village, a suburb just west of O'Hare Airport. By the early 1970s, UAL employed about 10,000 Chicago-area residents, making it one of the region's leading employers. Despite financial difficulties and strikes by its workers, UAL continued to expand. By the end of the 1970s, annual revenues approached $4 billion, and the company employed over 70,000 people around the world. When the U.S. government deregulated the airline industry in 1978, United was the number one passenger carrier. By 1985, when United pilots engaged in a one-month strike, the company owned a fleet of over 300 planes. For a brief period during the late 1980s, United's name was changed to the Allegis Corp. In 1994, the company's employees became its new owners, as they received a majority of stock in exchange for wage concessions. By the end of the 1990s, when the company was once again the world's largest passenger airline, annual revenues had grown to about $18 billion. At this point, UAL employed about 100,000 people around the world, including about 21,000 Chicago-area residents. United's fortunes turned dramatically in the twenty-first century. Corporate policies combined with the September 11, 2001, attacks that involved two United flights to weaken the company, which filed for bankruptcy protection in 2002. Nonetheless, UAL, at the end of that year, continued to employ some 18,000 persons in Chicago and 72,000 worldwide and had revenues in excess of $14 billion.

United Biscuit Co. of America

In 1927, United Biscuit was created by the merger of several cracker bakeries around the Midwest, including the Sawyer Biscuit Co. of Chicago. United Biscuit made its headquarters in Chicago, which was also the location of its packaging materials division, the Chicago Carton Co. During the mid-1930s, the Sawyer bakery on the city's Near West Side employed about 350 people. Annual sales passed $100 million during the 1950s, when the company employed over 1,000 people in the Chicago area. In 1953, United Biscuit built a new bakery—one of some 20 plants around the country—in Melrose Park, just west of Chicago. The company also moved its general offices from Chicago to Melrose Park. In 1966, United Biscuit changed its name to Keebler Co., and the headquarters moved to Elmhurst, just a few miles west of Melrose Park. By this time, the company employed nearly 7,000 people around the country. Over the next few years, Keebler grew. During the 1980s, when Keebler had become the second-largest American manufacturer of cookies (behind Nabisco), annual revenues passed $1 billion. In 2001, the company was purchased by the Kellogg Co., based in Battle Creek, Michigan. Keebler and its nearly 2,000 employees continued to operate from Elmhurst under the Keebler name.

United States Gypsum Co.

This leading maker of common construction materials such as wallboard and "Sheetrock" was established in Chicago in 1901. Created from a merger of several smaller operations, U.S. Gypsum started with $7.5 million in capital. Its operations around the country, which included a plant in East Chicago, Indiana, mined gypsum (hydrous calcium sulfate) and turned it into building products. By the mid-1930s, the East Chicago plant employed about 300 people. The company's annual sales rose from about $8 million in 1919 to $175 million in 1950. By the beginning of the 1960s, United States Gypsum had about 13,000 employees around the country, including over 1,000 in the Chicago area. In 1985, the company changed its name to USG Corp. By the end of the century, USG grossed about $3.6 billion in annual sales and employed some 1,200 Chicago-area residents. Facing almost 200,000 asbestos-related lawsuits, the company filed for Chapter 11 bankruptcy protection in 2001, but its sales continued to climb.

United Stationers Supply Co.

In 1921, Morris Wolf, Harry Hecktman, and Israel Kriloff bought the Utility Supply Co. and started selling office products in Chicago. By the 1930s, they had retail stores as well as wholesale and retail catalog operations. The company's annual sales rose from about $120,000 during its first year to $2 million by 1948, when mail-order sales accounted for about 40 percent of the business. In 1960, when it was still based in Chicago, the company changed its name to United Stationers Supply Co. When Howard Wolf, a son of the founder, became United Stationers president in 1967, annual sales hit $10 million. By the early 1980s, when it had exited the retail business, United Stationers ranked as the nation's leading wholesaler of office supplies. Annual sales reached about $180 million by 1986. In 1995, an investment company called Wingate Partners bought a large piece of United Stationers and merged it with Associated Stationers, creating United Stationers Inc. By the end of the 1990s, the company grossed about $3.4 billion in annual sales; about one-sixth of its 6,000 employees nationwide worked in the Chicago area.

U.S. Cellular Corp.

See Telephone & Data Systems Inc.

U.S. Gypsum Co./USG Corp.

See United States Gypsum Co.

U.S. Robotics Inc.

This enterprise was founded in 1976 by Casey Cowell, Stephen Muka, and three other alumni of the University of Chicago. From its first headquarters on Lincoln Avenue in Chicago, the company introduced the first commercial computer modem, which communicated at a speed of 0.3 kilobits per second. When the company arranged a public stock offering in 1991, annual sales were up to about $80 million. In 1995, when annual revenues approached $900 million, the company employed about 3,500 people at its Chicago-area plants in the suburbs of Skokie, Morton Grove, and Mount Prospect; it also had another 1,600 workers elsewhere in the country. By this time, U.S. Robotics had become the world's leading manufacturer of modems; it was the first to market modems that handled 14.4 and 28.8 kilobits per second. In 1997, the company was introducing the first 56 kilobit per second modems and also sold the "Palm" brand of handheld computers. U.S. Robotics, with $2 billion in annual sales by 1997, was purchased by 3Com Corp. of Santa Clara, California, a maker of computer networking gear. Over the next few months, hundreds of U.S. Robotics workers lost their jobs. At the beginning of the twenty-first century, the remnants of U.S. Robotics were owned by NatSteel Electronics Ltd. of Singapore and Accton Technology of Taiwan.

U.S. Steel Corp.

This giant Pittsburgh-based company never had its headquarters in Chicago, but it was a leading local employer throughout the twentieth century, and Chicago-area plants produced a large fraction of all of the steel made by its plants across the country. When U.S. Steel was created by New York banker J. P. Morgan and others in 1901, it was the world's largest business enterprise, controlling about two-thirds of the steel-making capacity in the United States. Among the companies that merged into U.S. Steel in 1901 was Illinois Steel (established in 1889), which operated most of the large steel mills in the Chicago region, including the original plant and South Works of the North Chicago Rolling Mill, as well as mills in Joliet and Milwaukee. The U.S. Steel plant in Southeast Chicago, which had about 6,500 workers at the beginning of the twentieth century, became one of the company's leading production facilities. In 1906, U.S. Steel built a giant new plant in Gary, Indiana, southeast of Chicago. By the 1910s, the company's South Chicago and Gary plants employed a total of about 17,000 Chicago-area residents. These two plants ranked as U.S. Steel's most productive facilities for much of the twentieth century. As late as the mid-1970s, U.S. Steel still employed about 40,000 people in the Chicago area, more than any other company. The sudden decline of the American steel industry in the late 1970s adversely affected U.S. Steel's Chicago-area plants. In 1983, the company (which would soon be known as USX) announced that it would close the South Works, which still employed 3,900 people. At the end of the century, USX was still based in Pittsburgh and was still the nation's leading steel producer; over half of the of steel it produced (then about $5 billion worth per year) was made at the plant in Gary. In the early 2000s, USX began selling large portions of the former South Works plant, closed permanently in 1992, to industrial developers.

V

Veluchamy Enterprises

In 1974 Indian native Pethinaidu Veluchamy began selling magazine subscriptions door-to-door while taking graduate courses at the University of Illinois, Chicago. As the enterprise became increasingly profitable, Veluchamy left his program, hired sales associates, and rented an office space in suburban Downers Grove where his company could solicit magazine subscriptions by mail. By the late 1970s, Veluchamy began to acquire other Chicago-area direct mailing companies as well as commercial and industrial real estate. By the late 1980s, Veluchamy Enterprises, as it became known, had developed a vertically integrated direct marketing operation that included nine individual companies specializing in printing, data entry, automated mailing services, embossing, gift cards, and the encoding of credit and ATM cards. At that time it employed nearly 1,000 people around Chicago and had sales of about $60 million. In 1995, the company purchased the single branch of Security Bank. By the early 2000s, Veluchamy Enterprises owned and leased over two million square feet of retail and industrial real-estate space, including the building that housed the former Michael Jordan's Restaurant downtown. It owned two banks with eight branches by that time. Still headquartered in Downers Grove, it owned nearly a dozen direct marketing businesses in the Chicago area, and one each in New Jersey and India. With 1,500 Chicago-area employees, 1,500 more worldwide, and over $200 million in annual revenues, this family-owned and -operated company was one of Chicago's largest minority-owned firms.

Victor Adding Machine Co.

This manufacturer of office machines was founded in 1918 by Carl Buehler, a Chicago merchant who already owned a chain of retail stores called Buehler Bros. Victor Adding Machine made the first portable desk calculators. Between 1921 and 1925, Victor's annual sales jumped from less than $300,000 to nearly $2 million. From the 1920s through the 1960s, the adding machines were manufactured at its main plant at on North Rockwell Street in Chicago. Albert C. Buehler, a son of the founder, led Victor for many years. During World War II, when the company served as a military contractor, the number of workers at the North Rockwell plant increased from about 350 to 1,400. After the war, the company continued to grow. Annual sales rose from about $5 million in 1946 to $28 million in 1956, when Victor was selling printing calculators and enjoyed a one-quarter share of national market for adding machines. Between 1918 and 1958, the company manufactured 1.5 million calculators. In 1961, the Victor Adding Machine Co. merged with the Comptometer Corp. of Chicago, a smaller but older company. Comptometer was a new name taken in 1957 by the Felt & Tarrant Manufacturing Co., which had been founded in Chicago in 1887 by Dorr E. Felt and Robert Tarrant. This pioneering adding machine maker had been an industry leader in the 1930s, when it employed about 200 men and 200 women at its North Paulina Street plant in Chicago, but by 1960 Comptometer was only half the size of Victor. By 1968, Victor Comptometer owned 18 plants in the United States and Canada and employed about 8,000 people worldwide. In 1969, when Victor sold its electronics division to Nixdorf, a German company, it effectively abandoned the adding machine market. In 1975, when annual sales exceeded $200 million, the company still employed about 1,300 people in the Chicago area. At the end of the 1970s, Victor Comptometer was purchased by Kidde Inc. of New Jersey.

Walgreen Co.

In 1901, Charles R. Walgreen, a son of Swedish immigrants, started a small pharmacy at Cottage Grove and Bowen Avenues on Chicago's South Side. A second Walgreen store opened in 1909; over the next few years, the chain grew rapidly, until there were nearly 400 Walgreen pharmacies nationwide by 1929. The chain's annual sales rose from about $1.5 million in 1920 to nearly $50 million by 1929. By the mid-1930s, the company employed about 1,300 men and 1,400 women at its large manufacturing laboratory and warehouse on the South Side. After the founder died in 1939, his son Charles R. Walgreen, Jr., led the firm. The company's first self-service store (a retailing design that would become the rule throughout the industry) opened on the South Side in 1952. Annual sales for the entire chain passed $200 million during the 1950s and $1 billion in the 1970s, when Charles R. Walgreen III led the company. By that time, Walgreen employed about 10,000 people in the Chicago area, and it was the nation's leading drug retailer, with 650 stores nationwide (most of them in the Midwest). The corporate headquarters moved to Deerfield in 1975. The company grew quickly during the last years of the twentieth century. By the early 2000s, Walgreens could boast nearly $25 billion in annual sales from over 3,000 stores nationwide. It employed over 14,000 people in the greater Chicago area.

Ward (Montgomery) & Co.

The world's first great mail-order retail company was founded in Chicago in 1872 by Aaron Montgomery Ward. Ward, a New Jersey native, arrived in Chicago in 1866 and found a job with Field, Palmer & Leiter, the large dry-goods business that would become Marshall Field & Co. After selling Field's products in hard-to-reach rural areas for several years, Ward decided to create an easier means to market merchandise. In 1892, Ward and brother-in-law George R. Thorne invested $2,400 in a new mail-order business. Boosted by orders from members of the Patrons of Husbandry (or "Grange"), the Midwestern farmers' association for which it served as an official supply house, the business grew rapidly. In 1874, the catalog was 32 pages long; by 1876, a 152-page Ward catalog listed 3,000 items. The slogan adopted in 1875, "satisfaction guaranteed or your money back," proved to be appealing to consumers, who used Ward's catalogs to order all sorts of goods, including clothing, barbed wire, saddles, windmills, and even steam engines. By 1897, annual sales had reached $7 million and the catalog was nearly 1,000 pages long. In 1900, there were about 1,400 workers at the company's Michigan Avenue headquarters; 10 years later, when annual sales stood at nearly $19 million, Ward employed more than 7,000 Chicago-area residents at its huge new facility along the North Branch of the Chicago River. As branches were added around the country, annual sales grew to over $100 million by 1920. The company entered a new era in 1926, when it decided to follow the lead of Sears, Roebuck & Co., its main rival, by opening retail stores. By 1931, there were more than 530 Montgomery Ward stores across the country. Led by Sewell Avery, the company continued to grow during the Great Depression: between 1928 and 1941, annual sales grew from $200 million to $600 million. By the early 1940s, Ward employed over 70,000 people nationwide. During World War II, when Avery refused to recognize an employees' union that was backed by the government's War Labor Board, the Army seized much of the company's property. Although annual sales passed $1 billion in 1956, Ward grew much more slowly during the second half of the twentieth century than it had previously. In 1968, Ward merged with the Container Corp. of America, another Chicago-based company. In 1974, with about 450 stores across the country and nearly $900 million in annual sales, Ward was purchased by the Mobil Oil Corp. After Mobil sold Ward in 1985, the retailer became a private company. But profits proved elusive. At the beginning of the twenty-first century, when it grossed $7 billion in annual sales and still employed close to 7,000 people in the Chicago area, Ward announced that it would shut down permanently. After nearly 130 years in business as a major Chicago company and leading American retailer, the company founded by Aaron Montgomery Ward was gone.

Waste Management Inc.

Dean Waste Management had its origins in the Dutch-dominated Chicago garbage business. In 1965, the U.S. Congress passed new laws that set stricter requirements for waste disposal, opening the field for new, larger companies in the industry. One of these companies was Waste Management, a Chicago-based enterprise founded in 1968 by Dean Buntrock and Wayne Huizenga through a merger of several garbage companies in Illinois, Wisconsin, and Florida. The annual revenues of this enterprise rose from about $5 million in 1968 to $17 million in 1971, when the company began to sell stock to the public under the name Waste Management Inc. During the next few years, the company grew at an extraordinary rate. At the beginning of the 1980s, when annual revenues neared $800 million, Waste Management owned about 4,500 vehicles and had about 12,000 workers worldwide. Waste Management had become the leading garbage disposal company in the United States. One of the company's divisions, Chemical Waste Management—which had a large laboratory in Riverdale, outside of Chicago—was spun off as an independent entity in 1986. By 1993, when the company changed its name to WMX Technologies, it was a giant international corporation claiming about $10 billion in annual revenues and some 75,000 employees around the world. In 1998, WMX was purchased by USA Waste Services Inc. of Texas for nearly $19 billion; the new owner returned the company's name to Waste Management Inc., and the headquarters of the operation were based in Houston, Texas.

Wells, French & Co.

See American Car & Foundry Co.

Western Electric Co.

Gray & Barton, a telegraph industry supply company founded in 1869 by Elisha Gray and Enos Barton, moved from Cleveland to Chicago immediately after it was established. In 1872, the company changed its name to the Western Electric Manufacturing Co., which was located at Kinzie and State Streets. Led by Barton and company president Anson Stager, Western Electric expanded during the 1870s from 20 people in 1870 to a workforce of 105 men and 25 women by 1880. In 1881, when annual sales had already grown to nearly $1 million, the firm was purchased by the American Bell Telephone Co. (the company that would become AT&T); it was renamed the Western Electric Co. and became Bell's manufacturing arm. When Barton succeeded Stager as president in 1886, Western Electric was prospering at its new plant at Clinton and Van Buren Streets. By the turn of the century, this facility employed about 5,300 workers. In 1904, when annual sales neared $32 million, the company relocated to suburban Cicero, where it had built a large new manufacturing complex known as the Hawthorne Works. By 1917, this facility employed 25,000 people, many of them Cicero residents of Czech or Polish descent, making it one of the largest manufacturing plants in the world. In 1915, Western Electric was associated with one of the worst accidents in Chicago history, when the *Eastland*, a vessel filled with employees and their family members attending the company's annual outing, capsized at its dock in the Chicago River, killing more than 800 people. By the 1920s, when annual sales reached $300 million and the company opened a new plant in New Jersey, Western Electric supplied roughly 90 percent of all the telephone equipment used in the United States. At the same time, its Hawthorne Works became famous as a leader in the "scientific management" of employees and the production process. During the 1910s, researchers at the Hawthorne Works pioneered new technologies such as the high-vacuum tube, the condenser microphone, and radio systems for airplanes. During the Great Depression, the company laid off thousands of workers, but business recovered during World War II, when Western Electric became a leading producer of radar equipment. During the war years, when it was subject to federal rules for government contractors, the company began to employ African Americans for the first time. During the 1950s and 1960s, when its Hawthorne plant was one of several around the country, Western Electric continued to grow, as annual sales rose from about $1 billion to $5 billion. After 1970, when there were still 25,000 employees at the Hawthorne Works and another 190,000 workers worldwide, Western Electric slipped. As part of the Federal Communications Commission's ordered break-up of AT&T, Western Electric was subsumed under a new entity, AT&T Technologies, in 1984. The Hawthorne Works plant was closed for good, and Western Electric effectively ceased operations under its old name. In the middle 1990s, AT&T Technologies and its divisional branches joined Bell Labs to become New Jersey-based Lucent Technologies. By early 2001, Lucent employed about 11,000 people in Illinois, most of them in suburban Naperville and Lisle, but companywide layoffs had cut that number in half within only two years.

Whitman Corp.

See IC Industries Inc.

Whittman-Hart Inc.

Robert F. Bernard, a son of an electrician who worked for Chicago's Inland Steel Co., founded this computer software and consulting firm in 1984 when he was 22 years old. In 1990 his partner William Merchantz departed with the software side of the company, leaving Bernard in charge of the consulting business, which then had revenues of $9 million a year. In 1996, the company began to sell stock to the public. In 1999, Whittman-Hart acquired the USWeb Corp. of San Francisco, a Web design and strategy firm, for nearly $6 billion. The new company, which changed its name to MarchFirst Inc., had 9,000 employees around the world, including about 1,500 in the Chicago area. At the time, MarchFirst ranked as the world's largest Internet services company, with annual sales of about $500 million. At the beginning of the new century, MarchFirst's fortunes began dropping quickly along with the high-tech Internet sector. Its assets were liquidated in the middle of 2001, its remaining corporate shell mired in bankruptcy proceedings for the next two years. In mid-2003, Robert Bernard reacquired some of his old company's liquidated units and launched a slimmed-down Internet technology consulting company. The new firm, operating in five Midwestern cities including Chicago, reincarnated the well-known WhittmanHart name (minus the hyphen).

Wieboldt Stores Inc.

This retailing enterprise, which became a Chicago-area chain of department stores, was founded in 1883 by William A. Wieboldt. By the beginning of the 1910s, the Wieboldt store on Milwaukee Avenue in Chicago employed about 700 people and grossed $3 million in annual sales. The company added new locations over the next few years. By 1930, Wieboldt had five stores with a combined $21 million in sales. The company enjoyed another growth spurt after World War II, and by 1960 there were 10 Wieboldt stores grossing a combined total of over $80 million in annual sales. During the mid-1970s, the company still employed about 6,000 people in the Chicago area, but Wieboldt had trouble remaining profitable. In 1986, it was forced into bankruptcy, from which it never recovered.

Wilson & Co.

The giant Chicago-based meatpacker Wilson & Co. began as a New York slaughterhouse in the 1850s called Schwartzchild & Sulzberger, which expanded to Kansas City in 1893. After the company hastily opened slaughterhouses in the early twentieth century in places like Chicago, Oklahoma City, and Cedar Rapids, Iowa, it quickly fell into financial trouble. In 1916, control of the company went to Thomas E. Wilson, a former president of Chicago-based Morris & Co. packinghouse, and the firm's health was soon revived. The company's name changed to Wilson & Co., its headquarters moved to Chicago's Union Stock Yard, and it joined Armour and Swift at the top of the American meat industry. In 1917, when it had already established a sporting goods subsidiary, Wilson ranked as one of the 50 largest industrial corporations in the country. By the mid-1930s, the company employed about 3,900 men and 1,000 women at its plant on Chicago's South Side. At the end of World War II, Wilson's annual sales neared $440 million. Like other leading packers, Wilson stopped slaughtering in Chicago during the 1950s, but kept its headquarters in the city for several years afterwards. By the middle of the 1960s, the company grossed over $800 million in annual sales and employed about 17,000 people in the United States. In 1967, Wilson was purchased by Jim Ling of the Ling-Temco-Vought (LTV) conglomerate, and its executive offices were transferred from Chicago to Dallas, Texas. Over the next few years, parts of the old Wilson were gradually sold off, until it was no longer a coherent entity. *See also* Wilson Sporting Goods Co.

Wilson Sporting Goods Co.

This Chicago-based manufacturer of athletic gear began in 1913 as Ashland Manufacturing, which was as a subsidiary of the Wilson & Co. meat company. At one point, the enterprise became known as the Thomas E. Wilson Co., taking the name of an early chief executive. In 1931, the name was changed to Wilson Sporting Goods Co. During the mid-1930s, the company's plant on Powell Avenue in Chicago employed about 800 people. By the middle of the century, Wilson had become the leading sporting goods manufacturer in the United States. The company's headquarters moved from Chicago to the suburb of River Grove in 1957. After LTV purchased Wilson & Co. in 1967, Wilson Sporting Goods was spun off as a separate company and grossed about $100 million in annual sales. In 1970, Wilson Sporting Goods was acquired by Pepsico, the New York–based beverage giant. In 1985 the company reemerged as an independent entity, Wilson Sporting Goods Inc., which had its headquarters in River Grove and employed about 400 Chicago-area residents among its 4,200 workers nationwide. At the end of the 1980s, when Wilson Sporting Goods was purchased by the Amer Group of Finland, annual sales had exceeded $400 million. In the early 1990s, the executive offices were moved back to Chicago from River Grove. By the early 2000s, Wilson was still headquartered in Chicago and had annual sales over $600 million. *See also* Wilson & Co.

John H. Long

Wirtz Corp.

This large family business was created in 1922 by Arthur M. Wirtz, who made money in real estate and liquor distribution in Chicago. After struggling through Prohibition and the Great Depression, Wirtz bought the large Judge & Dolph liquor wholesaler from the Walgreen Drug Co. in 1945. The Wirtz Corp., headquartered in Chicago with branches around the city, continued acquiring liquor companies and real estate through the ensuing decades, serving as a holding company. When the founder died in 1983, his son William Wirtz, in charge of Judge & Dolph since 1950, took the reigns of Wirtz Corp. By the end of the century, the Wirtz Corp. also owned Edison Liquor Co., distributed about half the liquor sold in Illinois, and ranked among the 10 largest liquor distributors in the United States. Wirtz had annual revenues of $700 and employed about 1,600 people in the Chicago area. The real-estate arm of the corporation owned property in Illinois, Wisconsin, Mississippi, Texas, Nevada, and Florida at the beginning of the next century. Wirtz Corp. also owned the Chicago Blackhawks hockey team and co-owned the United Center arena—where the Blackhawks and the Chicago Bulls basketball team played—with Bulls majority owner Jerry Reinsdorf.

Wisconsin Steel Co.

See International Harvester Co.

Wolff (L.) Manufacturing Co.

Ludwig Wolff emigrated with his family from Germany to Chicago in 1854, when he was 18 years old. The following year, he started a small plumbing business with Torrence McGuire that specialized in making copper and brass plumbing devices for candy and alcohol manufacturers, even making its own alcohol for a time. By 1876, Wolff had a large plumbing supply factory, and his company took the name L. Wolff Manufacturing Co. Wolff built a large new Chicago plant at Carroll and Fulton Streets in 1887; this facility soon employed about 1,000 men and produced $1.5 million worth of goods a year. As indoor plumbing became more common by the late nineteenth century, Wolff began producing a wider array of plumbing items for homes, hospitals, businesses, and schools. By 1910, the company had about 3,500 workers at two Chicago-area plants and sales and service operations in about 10 other cities. Wolff's operations shrank during the Great Depression, when it employed only about 450 people at its Fullerton Avenue site. The company stopped operating shortly after World War II.

Wrigley (Wm. Jr.) Co.

After working as a soap salesman for his father in Philadelphia, the 29-year-old William Wrigley, Jr., moved to Chicago in 1891. He continued to sell soap, but soon offered other products, including baking soda. Wrigley's best-selling item proved to be chewing gum, which he started buying in 1892 from the Zeno Manufacturing Co. of Chicago. Among the early brands of gum made for Wrigley by Zeno were "Lotta," "Vassar," "Juicy Fruit," and "Spearmint." By 1897, Wrigley's annual gum sales passed $1 million, and Wrigley and Zeno together employed about 500 people. In 1910, Wrigley and Zeno formally combined their businesses, creating the William Wrigley Jr. Co. National advertising helped the company's annual sales rise to nearly $4.5 million in 1910, when "Spearmint" was the industry's leading brand. A new brand, "Double Mint," was introduced in 1914. As the company's operations expanded nationally and overseas, annual sales grew to $27 million by 1919. Some of Wrigley's profits went toward the construction of the Wrigley Building, the Michigan Avenue tower that was Chicago's tallest structure when it was completed in 1921. Meanwhile, William Wrigley, Jr., had become the primary owner of the Chicago Cubs baseball team, which now played in a stadium called Wrigley Field. The Wrigley family also purchased and developed Catalina Island, near Los Angeles. In 1932, after the founder died, his son Philip K. Wrigley took charge of the company, which would continue to be headed by family members through the end of the twentieth century. During World War II, government-ordered rationing forced Wrigley to stop much of its normal production; the company temporarily introduced "Orbit," an inferior product. Business recovered after the war, as annual sales grew from about $38 million in 1946 to over $100 million by 1961; the company employed over 1,000 people in the Chicago area during this period. Sales topped $500 million by the end of the 1970s, when new brands such as "Freedent," "Big Red," and "Hubba Bubba" helped Wrigley to maintain a hold over about one-third of the domestic market for gum. In the early twenty-first century, William Wrigley's great-grandson oversaw the company's now global empire from its Chicago headquarters. With 60 percent of its business occurring overseas, Wrigley had nearly $3 billion in annual sales and almost 10,000 employees worldwide.

Yellow Cab Co. (of Chicago)

Chicago automobile salesman John Hertz entered the taxicab business with Walden W. Shaw in 1907 by transforming used trade-in cars into taxicabs. Hertz began painting the taxis yellow to attract the attention of would-be riders. Hertz, an Austrian native who grew up in Chicago, incorporated the Yellow Cab Co. in 1915 with a fleet of 40 taxis. By 1925, when publicly owned Yellow Cab was the largest taxi company in the world, the fleet had grown to 2,700 vehicles, most built by the Yellow Cab Manufacturing Co. During that time, the company, still controlled by Hertz, helped launch several important innovations: automatic windshield wipers, smooth-riding Firestone balloon tires, and telephone dispatching of taxis. In 1929, Hertz sold his share of Yellow Cab in order to focus on the rental car business he had purchased from fellow Chicagoan Walter L. Jacobs in 1923. The new majority owners of Yellow Cab, a partnership led by Russian-born Morris Markin, also owned Checker Taxi; its parent company, Checker Cab Manufacturing Co. of Kalamazoo, Michigan; and numerous smaller taxi companies in New York City, Minneapolis, and Pittsburgh. By 1935, the Markin partnership had turned Yellow Cab back into a privately held company and would maintain control of the company for the next seven decades. At the beginning of the 1960s, when it had about 3,000 employees and $16 million in annual revenues, Chicago Yellow Cab was formally merged into the Checker Motors Corp. During the middle and late 1990s, Yellow Cab changed hands several times and effectively ended its legal relationship with Checker. Yellow Cab eventually split into multiple companies across the nation bearing the Yellow Cab name. In Chicago, the Yellow Cab Management Co. operated a fleet of 2,000 taxis—the most in Chicago—leasing the cabs to drivers belonging to the Yellow Cab Association for about $150 a week. At the end of the century, Yellow Cab Management Co. founded the Wolley Cab Association ("yellow" spelled backwards), a bright orange fleet of 120 taxis in Chicago.

Youngstown Sheet & Tube Co.

Although never based in Chicago, this steel company was a leading local employer for much of the twentieth century. Youngstown Sheet & Tube was established in Youngstown, Ohio, in 1900. In 1923, the company acquired plants in South Chicago and East Chicago, Indiana. During the mid-1930s, Youngstown employed about 6,300 Chicago-area residents. By the 1940s, the company's Chicago-area plants made about $400 million worth of steel products a year and represented about one-third of Youngstown's total national production capacity. By the mid-1970s, when Youngstown Sheet & Tube had become a subsidiary of Lykes Industries, it still had about 10,000 employees in the Chicago area. At the end of the 1970s, just as the American steel industry entered a severe slump, Lykes was purchased by LTV, a large Texas-based conglomerate led by James J. Ling. As part of LTV Steel, which spent much of the 1980s and 1990s in bankruptcy, the old Youngstown steel plants in the Chicago area laid off thousands of workers. By the end of the 1990s, LTV, which also owned the old Chicago plants of Republic Steel, employed approximately 4,000 people in the Chicago area.

Z

Zenith Radio Corp.

Karl Hassel and Ralph H. G. Mathews founded Chicago Radio Laboratory in 1919 as a small manufacturer of radio equipment. The brand name "Z-Nith" came from the call letters of their small Chicago radio station, 9ZN. In 1923, Hassel, Mathews, and investor Eugene F. McDonald, Jr., formed the Zenith Radio Corp., which soon moved into a large factory on the 3600 block of South Iron Street. The company pioneered the manufacture of portable radios in 1924, and in 1926 it introduced the first home radio receivers to operate on AC power instead of batteries. Annual sales grew from about $5 million in 1928 to $11 million in 1930. By the mid-1930s, about 450 people worked at Zenith's Iron Street plant. During World War II, the company expanded as it filled military orders for bomb fuses and other devices. In the late 1940s, Zenith began to manufacture televisions; during the 1950s and 1960s, it was the number one maker of black-and-white sets. Annual sales reached $100 million in 1950 and approached $500 million by the mid-1960s, when Zenith had more than 15,000 employees, most of whom worked at factories around the Chicago area. Zenith's headquarters remained in Chicago at this time. The company still employed about 12,000 Chicago-area residents in the early 1970s, but international competition was beginning to take its toll. By 1984, when it was renamed Zenith Electronics, the company had laid off thousands of employees and moved some operations overseas. Thanks in part to a move into computer manufacturing, Zenith still employed about 5,000 Chicago-area workers by 1990. Losses mounted, however, and in the mid-1990s a declining Zenith was acquired by LG Electronics Inc., a company based in South Korea. Zenith declared Chapter 11 reorganization bankruptcy in the late 1990s, as company layoffs in Chicago and around the country mounted. At the beginning of the next century, its sales continued to decline, from $740 million in 2000 to $560 million just one year later. Its once substantial Glenview headquarters moved to smaller facilities in suburban Lincolnshire.

Select Bibliography

The above dictionary is based on information located in hundreds of sources, not all of which can be listed here. Those sources listed below all contain information on multiple firms.

Achilles, Rolf. *Made in Illinois: A Story of Illinois Manufacturing.* 1993.

A. G. Becker Guide to Publicly Held Corporations in the Chicago Area. 1966–1984.

Andreas, A. T. *History of Chicago.* 3 Vols. 1884–1886.

Cahan, Richard. *Chicago: Rising from the Prairie.* 2000.

Chicago Enterprise. 1986–1993.

Chicago Association of Commerce. *Manufacturers in the Chicago and Metropolitan Area Employing 50 or More Persons.* 1934.

Chicago Commerce. 1908–1990.

Chicago Tribune. Historical Archive, 1849–1977.

Chicago Tribune Online. 1985–2003.

Clipping Files, Chicago Historical Society.

Crain's Chicago Business. 1978–2003.

Currey, J. Seymour. *Manufacturing and Wholesale Industries of Chicago.* 3 Vols. 1918.

Darling, Sharon. *Chicago Furniture: Art, Craft, and Industry, 1833–1983.* 1984.

Downard, William L. *Dictionary of the History of the American Brewing and Distilling Industries.* 1970.

First Chicago Guide: Major Publicly Held Corporations and Financial Institutions Headquartered in Northern Illinois. 1985–86 to 1995–96.

German Press Club of Chicago. *Prominent Citizens and Industries of Chicago.* 1901.

Half-Century's Progress of the City of Chicago: The City's Leading Manufacturers and Merchants. 1887.

Heise, Kenan and Michael Edgerton. *Chicago: Center for Enterprise.* 2 Vols. 1982.

Hoover's Guide to the Top Chicago Companies. 1996.

Hoover's Handbook of American Business, 2001. 2000.

Illinois, Factory Inspector. *Eighth Annual Report . . . for the Year Ending December 15, 1900.* 1901.

Illinois, Factory Inspector, *Eighteenth Annual Report . . . 1910.* 1911.

Indiana, State Bureau of Inspection. *First Annual Report . . . 1912.* 1913.

Industrial Chicago. Vols. 2–4. 1891, 1894.

International Directory of Company Histories. Multivolume ongoing series. 1988–.

LaSalle Bank Guide . . . Major Publicly Held Corporations and Financial Institutions Headquartered in Illinois. 1997–98 to 2000–1 editions.

Moskowitz, Milton, Michael Katz, and Robert Levering, eds. *Everybody's Business, an Almanac: The Irreverent Guide to Corporate America.* 1980.

———. *Everybody's Business: A Field Guide to the 400 Leading Companies in America.* 1990.

News Front. *12,000 Leading U.S. Corporations.* 1962.

New York Times (historical backfile). 1851–1999.

New York Times. 1999–2003.

Press Club of Chicago. *Official Reference Book.* 1922.

Robinson, Richard. *United States Business History, 1602–1988: A Chronology.* 1990.

Schoff, S. S. *The Industrial Interests of Chicago.* 1873.

Schroeder, Gertrude G. *The Growth of Major Steel Companies, 1900–1950.* 1953.

Skilnik, Bob. *The History of Beer and Brewing in Chicago, 1833–1978.* 1999.

Taylor, Charles H. *History of the Board of Trade of the City of Chicago.* 3 Vols. 1917.

U.S. Census, Industry. Manuscript returns, 1860, 1870, and 1880 (microfilm).

U.S. Federal Trade Commission. *Report of the Federal Trade Commission on Interlocking Directorates.* 1951.

Wall Street Journal (historical backfile). 1889–1985.

Wall Street Journal. 1984–2003.

Young, David M. *Chicago Transit: An Illustrated History.* 1998.

BIOGRAPHICAL DICTIONARY

Compiled by Christina A. Reynen

his dictionary provides brief reference information for more than 2,000 deceased Chicagoans who are mentioned in the main body of the *Encyclopedia of Chicago.* Individuals mentioned in *Encyclopedia* entries but whose lives were not primarily connected with metropolitan Chicago, such as international heads of state or national figures, have not been included; nor have persons who were living at the time this list was compiled. Inclusion or exclusion from the dictionary is not in itself intended as an evaluation of significance.

We have attempted to include birth and death dates, places of birth and death, and brief descriptions for each person in the dictionary. Newberry Library staff have consulted hundreds of sources and have to the extent possible resolved the many discrepancies in those sources.

The dictionary includes incomplete and uncertain information where it might be of use as a starting point for further research. Where we were unable to determine exact dates, we have indicated months, years, decades, or broader time categories with as much specificity as the sources warrant. Dates and places that we were unable to confirm in reliable sources have been indicated with question marks. Where sources have disagreed on dates and we have been unable to determine which is correct, we have provided both alternatives. If the dictionary does not include any information on an individual's birth or death, readers may infer that our research turned up nothing.

A

Abbott, Edith b Sept. 26, 1876, Grand Island, NE; d July 28, 1957, Grand Island, NE. Social reformer; dean of School of Social Service Administration, Univ. of Chicago.

Abbott, Grace b Nov. 17, 1878, Grand Island, NE; d June 19, 1939, Chicago. Social worker; worked at Hull House; director of U.S. Children's Bureau.

Abbott, Merriel b Apr. 27, 1893, Chicago; d Nov. 6, 1977, Chicago. Dance teacher; troupe performed at Palmer House for 24 years.

Abbott, Robert Sengstacke b Nov. 28, 1868, St. Simons Island, GA; d Feb. 29, 1940, Chicago. Newspaper publisher; founded *Chicago Defender.*

Abbott, Wallace Calvin b Oct. 12, 1857, Bridgewater, VT; d July 4, 1921, Chicago, IL. Physician; drug manufacturer; founded Abbott Laboratories.

Abercrombie, Gertrude b Feb. 17, 1909, Austin, TX; d July 1977, Chicago. Painter; associated with Chicago's surrealist school.

Abner, Ewart, Jr. b May 11, 1923, Chicago; d Dec. 27, 1997, Los Angeles, CA. Record executive; president of Vee-Jay Records and Motown Records.

Accardo, Anthony "Tony" J. b Apr. 28, 1906, Chicago; d May 27, 1992, Chicago. Organized crime boss; heir to Al Capone.

Acheson, Henry active 1850s. Lithographer; map engraver.

Acklin, Barbara b Feb. 28, 1944, Chicago; d Nov. 27, 1998, Omaha, NE. Soul performer; singer-songwriter.

Adamowski, Benjamin b Nov. 20, 1906, Chicago; d Mar. 1, 1982, Chicago. Attorney; state legislator (1931–1941); Cook County state's attorney; lost mayoral race against Richard J. Daley (1963).

Adams, John McGregor b Mar. 11, 1834, Londonderry, NH; d Sept. 17, 1904, Highland Park, IL. Manufacturer; railroad supply industry executive.

Adams, John Quincy b 1824, Hopkinton, MA; d Feb. 8, 1899, Wheaton, IL. Grain merchant; financier; endowed first library in Wheaton.

Adams, Milward b Jan. 6, 1857, Lexington, KY; d June 18, 1923, Chicago. Theatrical manager; impresario; managed Chicago Auditorium Theater.

Addams, Jane b Sept. 6, 1860, Cedarville, IL; d May 21, 1935, Chicago. Social reformer; founded Hull House; won Nobel Peace Prize (1931).

Ade, George b Feb. 9, 1866, Kentland, IN; d May 16, 1944, Brook, IN. Humorist; journalist at the *Chicago Morning Record*; playwright.

Adler, Dankmar b July 3, 1844, Stadt Lengsfeld, Germany; d Apr. 16, 1900, Chicago.

Architect; engineer; partner of Louis Sullivan.

Adler, Max b 1866, Elgin, IL; d Nov. 4, 1952, Beverly Hills, CA. Philanthropist; founded Adler Planetarium; vice president of Sears, Roebuck & Co.

Ahner, Henry active 1850s. Trumpeter; associated with Germania Orchestra.

Aitken, William b ca. 1878; d Sept. 10, 1952, Chadron, NE. Developer, builder, and real-estate operator; founded Bannockburn.

Albertieri, Luigi b 1860 or 1869, Rome, Italy; d Aug. 25, 1930, New York, NY. Dancer; ballet teacher; ballet master for the Chicago Lyric Opera.

Albright, Ivan b Feb. 20, 1897, North Harvey, IL; d Nov. 18, 1983, Woodstock, VT. Artist; painter; identified with "magic realism."

Aldis, Arthur T. b July 7, 1861, St. Albans, VT; d Nov. 23, 1933, Winter Park, FL. Real-estate investor; art patron; helped bring Armory Show to Chicago.

Aldis, Mary [Mary Reynolds] b June 8, 1872, Chicago; d June 20, 1949. Poet; playwright; founded Aldis Playhouse.

Alexander, Franz Gabriel b Jan. 22, 1891, Budapest, Hungary; d Mar. 8, 1964, Palm Springs, CA. Psychiatrist; first director of Chicago Institute for Psychoanalysis.

Alexandroff, Mirron "Mike" b Mar. 3, 1923, Chicago; d Apr. 20, 2001, Chicago. President of Columbia College (1964–1992).

Algren, Nelson b Mar. 28, 1909, Detroit, MI; d May 9, 1981, Sag Harbor, NY. Writer; won first National Book Award for *The Man with the Golden Arm* (1949).

Ali, Noble Drew [Timothy Drew] b Jan. 8, 1886, NC; d July 20, 1929, Chicago. Founded Moorish Science Temple.

Alinsky, Saul David b Jan. 30, 1909, Chicago; d June 12, 1972, Carmel, CA. Sociologist; community organizer; author of *Reveille for Radicals* (1946).

Allee, Warder Clyde b June 5, 1885, Bloomington, IN; d Mar. 18, 1955, Gainesville, FL. Biologist; Univ. of Chicago professor; ecological research pioneer.

Allen, Alfred P. active 1950s. Architect; designed terminal for Sky Harbor Airport (ca. 1929).

Allison, Fran [Frances Levington] b Nov. 20, 1907, La Porte City, IA; d June 13, 1989, Sherman Oaks, CA. Chicago radio performer (1937–1967); part of *Kukla, Fran and Ollie*.

Allouez, Claude b June 6, 1622, Saint-Didier, Haute Loire, France; d 1689, near present Niles, IL. Jesuit missionary.

Allport, Walter Webb b June 10, 1824, Lorain, NY; d Mar. 21, 1893, Chicago. Dentist; educator; researcher; first chairman of American Dental Association.

Aloma, Luis b July 23, 1923, Havana, Cuba; d Apr. 7, 1997, Park Ridge, IL. Baseball player; White Sox pitcher.

Alschuler, Alfred Samuel b Nov. 2, 1876, Chicago; d Nov. 6, 1940, Chicago. Architect; pioneer in reinforced concrete; designed Wrigley Building, KAM Temple.

Alsdorf, James William b Aug. 16, 1913, Chicago; d Apr. 21, 1990, Chicago. Businessman; patron of the arts.

Alsip, Charles H. b Jan. 28, 1877, Chicago; d June 15, 1946, Chicago. Brick manufacturer; president of Alsip manufacturing company.

Alsip, Frank b Nov. 7, 1827, Pittsburgh, PA; d Dec. 20, 1907, Chicago. Brick manufacturer; founded Alsip Brick Co. in Blue Island.

Altgeld, John Peter b Dec. 30, 1847, Nieder Selters, Germany; d Mar. 12, 1902, Joliet, IL. Illinois governor; pardoned Haymarket anarchists; chief justice of Cook County Superior Court.

Amberg, Agnes Ward [Sarah Agnes Ward] b Nov. 4, 1847, Chicago; d Nov. 14, 1919, Chicago. Cofounded Madonna Center.

Amberg, Mary Agnes b Aug. 6, 1874, Chicago; d Aug. 28, 1962, Chicago. Resident director of Madonna Center (1913–1962).

Amberg, William A. b July 6, 1847, Albstadt, Bavaria, Germany; d Sept. 5, 1918, Mackinac Island, MI. Inventor; manufacturer; printer.

Ameche, Don [Dominic Felix Ameche] b May 31, 1908, Kenosha, WI; d Dec. 6, 1993, Scottsdale, AZ. Actor in Broadway, film, television, and radio.

Ammons, Albert C. b Sept. 23, 1907, Chicago; d Dec. 3, 1949, Chicago. Jazz pianist; boogie-woogie pioneer.

Ammons, Gene [Eugene Ammons] b Apr. 14, 1925, Chicago; d Aug. 6, 1974, Chicago. Jazz tenor saxophonist.

Andersen, Arthur Edward b May 30, 1885, Plano, IL; d Jan. 10, 1947, Chicago. Certified public accountant; founded Arthur Andersen Co.

Anderson, A. Harold b Mar. 29, 1911; d Aug. 6, 1997, Northbrook, IL. Developer; project engineer for O'Hare International Airport.

Anderson, Gilbert Maxwell [Max Aronson; "Broncho Billy"] b Mar. 21, 1882, Little Rock, AR; d Jan. 20, 1971, South Pasadena, CA. First western film hero; established Essanay Studios.

Anderson, Heartley "Hunk" b Sept. 22, 1898, Tamarack, MI; d Apr. 24, 1978, West Palm Beach, FL. Football player and coach for Chicago Bears.

Anderson, Margaret Carolyn b Nov. 24, 1886, Indianapolis, IN; d Oct. 19, 1973, Cannes, France. Founded *Little Review* (1914); feminist; lesbian editor and author.

Anderson, Mary b ca. 1873, Lidkoping, Sweden; d Jan. 29, 1964, Washington, DC. Trade union leader; first director of U.S. Women's Bureau.

Anderson, Sherwood B. b Sept. 13, 1876, Camden, OH; d Mar. 8, 1941, Colon, Panama Canal Zone. Writer (*Winesburg, Ohio*).

Andreas, Alfred T. b May 29, 1839, Amity, NY; d Feb. 1, 1900, New Rochelle, NY. Atlas publisher; author of early three-volume history of Chicago.

Andrews, Wilbur J. b Mar. 24, 1859, Rockford, IL; d Dec. 25, 1931, Berwyn, IL. Early Berwyn settler; partner in real-estate firm of Andrews & Piper.

Andrus, Thomas b Jan. 26, 1801, Cass County, VT; d May 31, 1888, Darien, IL. Settled in Darien area in 1832.

Angle, Paul b Dec. 25, 1900, Mansfield, OH; d May 11, 1975, Chicago. Director of Chicago Historical Society.

Angsman, Elmer J. b Dec. 11, 1925, Chicago; d Apr. 11, 2002, West Palm Beach, FL. Football player for Chicago Cardinals.

Anson, Adrian "Cap" b Apr. 17, 1852, Marshalltown, IA; d Apr. 14, 1922, Chicago. Baseball player; manager; associated with Chicago White Stockings for 22 years.

Ap-ta-ke-sic b ca. 1780s. Indian leader; Chief Half Day of the Potawatomis.

Appling, Luke (Lucius) Benjamin b Apr. 2, 1907; d Jan. 3, 1991. Baseball player (shortstop), Chicago White Sox; Hall of Fame.

Archer, William Beatty b Jan. 30, 1792; d Aug. 9, 1870, Clark County, IL. I&M Canal commissioner; civil engineer, land speculator; state legislator.

Armin, Emil b Apr. 1, 1883, Raudautz, Romania; d July 2, 1971, Chicago. Artist; painter; sculptor.

Armondo, Joseph b May 12, 1909; d June 11, 1988. Village president of Fox Lake, IL; owner of Joseph Armondo Distributing Co.

Armour, Philip Danforth, III b 1893; d Jan. 19, 1958, Palm Beach, FL. Third generation of Armour meatpacking family.

Armour, George b Apr. 24, 1812, Campbelltown, Argyleshire, Scotland; d June 13, 1881, Brighton, England. Businessman; founded Armour, Dole & Co.; president of Chicago Board of Trade.

Armour, J[onathan] Ogden b Nov. 11, 1863, Milwaukee, WI; d Aug. 16, 1927, London, England. Meatpacker; philanthropist; president of Armour & Co.

Armour, Malvina Belle Ogden b May 7, 1842, Cincinnati, OH; d July 25, 1927, Chicago. Founded Woman's Athletic Club of Chicago.

Armour, Philip Danforth b May 16, 1832, Stockbridge, NY; d Jan. 6, 1901, Chicago. Meatpacker; philanthropist; built Armour & Co., Chicago's largest meatpacking company.

Armstrong, Alberta active 1940s. Community leader; helped raise funds for fire truck in East Chicago Heights (Ford Heights).

Armstrong, George Buchanan b Oct. 27, 1822, Armagh, Ireland; d May 5, 1871, Chicago. Chicago postal administrator; credited with establishment of Railway Mail Service.

Armstrong, Lil Hardin b Feb. 3, 1902, Memphis, TN; d Aug. 27, 1971, Chicago. Jazz musician; singer; pianist; composer; played in King Oliver's Band.

Armstrong, Louis b Aug. 4, 1901, New Orleans, LA; d July 6, 1971, Queens, NY. Jazz trumpet musician; bandleader; composer; singer.

Arnold, Adolph b 1849; d Aug. 6, 1912, Chicago. Meatpacker; partner of Schwinn in bicycle company.

Arnold, Rus b May 29, 1909, Russia; d Nov. 27, 1973, Honolulu, HI. Photographer; writer; lighting expert.

Aronson, Max *See* **Anderson, Gilbert Maxwell**

Arvey, Jacob M. b Nov. 3, 1896, Chicago; d Aug. 25, 1977, Chicago. Attorney; Chicago Democratic Party chairman.

Asbjornsen, Sigvald b Oct. 11, 1867, Christiania, Norway; d Sept. 8, 1954, Skokie, IL. Sculptor; created statue of Leif Ericson (Humboldt Park) and Louis Jolliet (Joliet).

Assman, Henry E. b Mar. 28, 1843, Hanover, Germany; d Apr. 6, 1929, Lombard, IL. Brick mason contractor; cofounded Elmhurst-Chicago Stone Co. (1883).

Atkins, Jearum b ca. 1816, VT. Machinist; developed self-rake reaper.

Atlass, H. Leslie b Nov. 29, 1894, Lincoln, IL; d Nov. 18, 1960. Radio executive; president and cofounder of WBBM.

Atlass, Ralph Leigh b Mar. 31, 1903, Lincoln, IL; d June 1979. Radio executive; cofounded WBBM.

Attaway, William Alexander b Nov. 19, 1911, Greenville, MS; d June 17, 1986, Los Angeles, CA. Novelist; composer; scriptwriter; involved with Illinois Federal Writers' Project.

Atwood, Charles Bowler b May 18, 1849, Charlestown, MA; d Dec. 19, 1895, Chicago. Architect; designer-in-chief of World's Columbian Exposition; early skyscraper designer.

Austin, Henry W. b Aug. 1, 1828, Skaneateles, NY; d Dec. 24, 1889, Oak Park, IL. Founded Austin; state legislator; wrote Illinois Temperance Law (1872).

Austin, Richard Bevan b Jan. 23, 1901, Chicago; d Feb. 7, 1977, Chicago. Federal district court judge; chief justice of Criminal Court of Cook County.

Avdich, Kamil b Apr. 10, 1913, Bileca, Yugoslavia; d Dec. 2, 1979. Librarian; leader of Islamic Cultural Center of Greater Chicago.

Avery, Sewell b Nov. 4, 1873, Saginaw, MI; d Oct. 31, 1960, Chicago. Business executive; chairman of Montgomery Ward.

Ayer, Elbridge Gerry b July 25, 1813, Haverhill, MA; d Apr. 13, 1887, Harvard, IL. Platted Harvard, IL.

Ayres, Anson b Feb. 17, 1819, Romulus, NY; d 1894, Hinsdale, IL. Farmer; arrived in Naperville in 1867.

B

Babcock, Morgan b 1806, De Ruyter, NY. Farmer; settled along DuPage River in 1833 in area that became Babcock's Grove.

Babcock, Ralph b Dec. 1, 1810, Tully, Onondaga, NY; d Sept. 19, 1897, Elroy, WI. Farmer; settled along DuPage River in 1833 in area that became Babcock's Grove.

Bachrach, William A. b May 15, 1879, Elgin, IL; d July 15, 1959, Chicago. Swimming instructor; coach of Illinois Athletic Club and U.S. Olympic team.

Bailen, Maurice b Apr. 10, 1902, Chicago; d Oct. 15, 1980, Maywood, IL. Filmmaker (*The Great Depression*); organized Chicago Film and Photo League.

Bailly, Joseph [Honore Gratien Joseph Bailly de Messein] b Apr. 7, 1774, Varennes, Quebec; d Dec. 21, 1835, Porter County, IN. Fur trader in northern Indiana.

Bailly, Marie b ca. 1783; d 1866. Trader; ran trading post with husband Joseph; namesake of village of Monee.

Baker, Ray Stannard b Apr. 17, 1870, Lansing, MI; d July 12, 1946, Amherst, MA. Muckraking writer; reformer; journalist for *Chicago News-Record;* won 1940 Pulitzer Prize.

Balaban, Abraham Joseph b Apr. 20, 1889, Chicago; d Nov. 1, 1962, New York, NY. Motion picture executive; cofounded Balaban & Katz.

Balaban, Barney b June 8, 1887, Chicago; d Mar. 7, 1917, Byram, CT. Motion picture executive; cofounded Balaban & Katz; chairman of Paramount Corp.

Balatka, Hans b Mar. 5, 1826, Hoffnungsthal, Moravia, Austria; d Apr. 17, 1899, Chicago. Musician; composer; led Philharmonic Society of Chicago; founded Balatka Academy of Musical Art.

Balbo, Italo b June 5, 1896, Ferrara, Italy; d June 28, 1940, Tobruk, Libya. Aviator; Italian air minister; led goodwill air convoy to Chicago.

Balch, O. H. active 1830s. Editor of *Juliet Courier,* 1839.

Baldwin, Thomas F. active 1850s; d Sept. 21, 1876. Early settler; riverboat captain; purchased land in Berwyn around 1856.

Ball, Charles B. b Aug. 3, 1854, New Haven, CT; d Oct. 18, 1928, Chicago. Chief sanitary inspector for Chicago Dept. of Health.

Ballard, J. P. active 1830s. Built first house in Portersville (later Valparaiso) in 1834.

Banga, Henry b Feb. 14, 1848, Liestal, Switzerland; d Dec. 24, 1913, Chicago. Physician; surgeon; pioneer of antiseptic surgery at Michael Reese Hospital.

Bangs, George S. b Feb. 20, 1823, Akron, OH; d Nov. 17, 1877, Washington, DC. General Superintendent of Railway Service; instituted "fast mail" train in 1875 to New York.

Bangs, Justus b Mar. 16, 1806, Montague, MA; d Dec. 13, 1895, Wauconda Lake, IL. Founded Wauconda.

Banks, Paul N. b Apr. 15, 1934, Montebello, CA; d May 10, 2000, New York, NY. Book conservator at Newberry Library.

Barber, John b ca. 1796; d Dec. 19, 1876, Bolingbrook, IL. Early Bolingbrook resident.

Barbour, J. Berni b Danville, KY; active early twentieth century. Music publisher; established first black-owned music publishing company.

Barnett, Claude Albert b Sept. 16, 1889, Sanford FL; d Aug. 2, 1967, Chicago. Entrepreneur; newspaper executive; founded Associated Negro Press.

Barnett, Ferdinand Lee b ca. 1859, Nashville, TN; d Mar. 11, 1936, Chicago. Attorney; journalist; founded *Chicago Conservator* newspaper.

Barnett, Ida B. Wells *See* **Wells, Ida Bell**

Barrett, Nathan Franklin b 1845, Staten Island, NY; d Oct. 1919. Landscape architect; designed Pullman community.

Barrows, John Henry b July 11, 1847, Medina, MI; d June 3, 1902, Oberlin, OH. Minister; planned and chaired World's Parliament of Religions (1893).

Bartlett, Edwin b Oct. 6, 1812, Conway, MA. Farmer; established Ontarioville; first postmaster of Ontarioville.

Bartlett, Frederic C. b June 1, 1873, Chicago; d June 25, 1953, Beverly, MA. Painter; muralist.

Bartlett, Frederick H. b Feb. 6, 1875, Binghamton, NY; d July 27, 1948, Pasadena, CA. Real-estate developer; developed Beverly Shores (1933).

Bartlett, Luther b July 21, 1817, Conway, MA; d June 25, 1882, Bartlett, IL. Founder and first postmaster of Bartlett.

Bartlett, Lyman b Nov. 21, 1807, Conway, MA; d June 6, 1865. Purchased farm in Wayne Township in 1844.

Bartlett, Robert b Aug. 22, 1884; d May 2, 1967, Chicago. Real-estate developer; developed Lake Barrington.

Barzynski, John b 1848 or 1849; d 1886, Chicago. Editor and publisher; founded *Gazeta Katolicka* (Polish Catholic Gazette).

Barzynski, Vincent b Sept. 20, 1838, Sulislawice, Poland; d May 2, 1899, Chicago. Roman Catholic priest; established first Polish Catholic parish in the United States in Chicago.

Basker, Robert S. b Sept. 29, 1918, East Harlem, NY; d Apr. 6, 2001, San Francisco, CA. Activist; leader of reconstituted Mattachine Midwest (1964).

Bates, Gerry b Aug. 24, 1800, Chesterfield, MA; d July 29, 1878, Elmhurst, IL. Innkeeper; postmaster; founded Cottage Hill (Elmhurst).

Bates, William Wallace b 1826, Nova Scotia; d Nov. 26, 1911, Denver, CO. Shipbuilder; U.S. commissioner of navigation.

Bauer, Sybil b Sept. 18, 1903, Chicago; d Jan. 31, 1927, Chicago. Swimmer; Olympic backstroke champion (1924).

Bauler, Mathias "Paddy" b Jan. 27, 1890, Chicago; d Aug. 20, 1977, Melrose Park, IL. Saloon owner; alderman; Democratic boss of Forty-third Ward (1933–1967).

Baum, L. Frank b May 15, 1856, Chittenango, NY; d May 6, 1919, Hollywood, CA. Children's author (*The Wonderful Wizard of Oz*); journalist; playwright.

Baumann, Frederick H. b Jan. 6, 1826, Augernmunder, Germany; d Mar. 18, 1921, Chicago. Architect; engineer; designed Chicago's first skyscraper.

Baxter, Donald E. b 1882, Southington, OH; d July 20, 1935, on a plane en route to Los Angeles, CA. Founded Baxter International; developed intravenous medical device.

Bayer, Herbert b Apr. 5, 1900, Haag (Salzburg), Austria; d Sept. 30, 1985, Montecito, CA. Artist; industrial designer; taught at Institute of Design.

Beardsley, Ziba b Aug. 3, 1800; d July 14, 1878, Crystal Lake, IL. McHenry County clerk (1839–1843).

Beatty, Talley b Dec. 22, 1918, Cedar Grove, LA; d Apr. 29, 1995, New York, NY. Dancer; choreographer.

Beaubien, Jean-Baptiste b Sept. 5, 1787, Detroit, MI; d Jan. 5, 1863, Naperville, IL. Fur trader; owned Fort Dearborn site.

Beaubien, Madore B. b 1809; d 1883. Fur trader.

Beaubien, Mark b Apr. 25, 1800, Detroit or Monroe, MI; d Apr. 11, 1881, Kankakee, IL. Innkeeper; fiddler; built and owned Sauganash Tavern.

Beck, Dave Daniel b June 16, 1894, Stockton CA; d Dec. 26, 1993, Seattle, WA. President of International Brotherhood of Teamsters.

Beck, L. W. active 1860s. Real-estate developer; donated land for Cook County Normal School.

Beebe, George W. active 1840s; d 1864, Willow Springs, IL. Contractor; did extensive work on the I&M Canal.

Beecher, William John b May 23, 1915, Chicago; d July 27, 2002, Wood Dale, IL. Ornithologist; biologist; director of Chicago Academy of Sciences.

Begley, William active 1860s. Brewer; owned Waukegan Brewing Co. in 1860s.

Beifeld, Joseph [Joseph Byfield] b Aug. 22, 1853, Budapest, Hungary; d Sept. 17, 1926, Chicago. Wholesale manufacturer of cloaks; bought Sherman Hotel in 1902.

Bell, Robert b Jan. 18, 1922, Flint, MI; d Dec. 8, 1997, Lake San Marcos, CA. Actor; portrayed Bozo the Clown for 25 years on WGN-TV.

Belushi, John b Jan. 24, 1949, Chicago; d Mar. 5, 1982, Hollywood, CA. Actor; comedian (Second City, *Saturday Night Live*, *The Blues Brothers*).

Beman, Solon Spencer b Oct. 1, 1853, Brooklyn, NY; d Apr. 23, 1914, Chicago. Architect; designed city of Pullman and Fine Arts Building.

Bengson, Emil H. b Feb. 15, 1881, Holstein, Germany; d Jan. 11, 1943, Chicago. Businessman in Portage Park; president of storage warehouse and coal companies.

Bennett, Edward H. b May 12, 1874, Cheltenham, England; d Oct. 14, 1954, Tryon, NC. Architect; city planner; coauthored *Plan of Chicago* (1909); designed Century of Progress Exposition.

Bennett, Helen Marie b ca. 1879, Washington, IA; d Apr. 21, 1962, East Providence, RI. Feminist; reporter for *Chicago Record-Herald*; initiated Women's World's Fair.

Bennett, Richard M. b Feb. 4, 1907, Braddock, PA; d May 2, 1996. Architect; designed Park Forest Plaza.

Benny, Jack [Benjamin Kubelsky] b Feb. 14, 1894, Chicago; d Dec. 26, 1974, Beverly Hills, CA. Comedian for radio, films, and television.

Benson, Al [Arthur B. Leaner] b June 30, 1908, Jackson, MS; d Sept. 6, 1978, Berrien, MI. Disc jockey at WGES (WVON).

Bergman, Edwin A. b July 18, 1917, Chicago; d Feb. 17, 1986, Chicago. Businessman; art collector; philanthropist.

Bernard, L. Cosby b July 14, 1890, Junction City, KY; d Aug. 1963, Sylva, NC. Residential architect in Hammond.

Bernardin, Joseph b Apr. 2, 1928, Columbia, SC; d Nov. 14, 1996, Chicago. Archbishop of Chicago Diocese (1982–1996); cardinal.

Berry, Addison b ca. 1866, Hackensack, NJ; d Feb. 13, 1940, Hammond, IN. Hammond architect; active in 1920s.

Berry, Edwin Carlos "Bill" b Nov. 11, 1910, Oberlin, OH; d May 13, 1987, Chicago. Civil rights leader; executive director Chicago Urban League.

Berry, Parker N. b Sept. 2, 1888, Hastings, NE; d Dec. 16, 1918, Princeton, IL. Architect; chief designer for Louis H. Sullivan.

Besinger, Leonard W. b June 26, 1907; d Aug. 9, 1982, Elgin, IL. Northwest suburban builder and developer.

Bickerdike, George N. b 1806, Yorkshire, England; d Nov. 4, 1880, Yorkshire, England. Resident at Fort Dearborn; owned land near Oak Park.

Biegler, Martha A. b Dec. 1, 1864, IN; d Apr. 29, 1947, Kankakee, IL. Feminist; journalist (*Chicago Daily Socialist*).

Bielfeldt, John S. b Jan. 26, 1834, Holstein, Germany; d Dec. 31, 1899, buried in Thornton, IL. Established brewery in Thornton, 1852.

Biesel, Fred b 1863; d 1964. Painter; head of Illinois Art Project (1941–1943).

Bilandic, Michael A. b Feb. 13, 1923, Bridgeport, IL; d Jan. 15, 2002, Chicago. Mayor of Chicago (1976–1979); chief justice of Illinois Supreme Court.

Binder, Joseph b Mar. 3, 1898, Vienna, Austria; d June 26, 1972, Vienna, Austria. Graphic designer; illustrator; lecturer.

Binga, Eudora Johnson b Feb. 22, 1869, Chicago; d Mar. 26, 1933, Chicago. Socialite; philanthropist.

Binga, Jesse b Apr. 10, 1865, Detroit, MI; d June 13, 1950, Chicago. Banker; real-estate investor.

Bistor, James E. b July 30, 1890, Macomb, IL; d Mar. 3, 1945, Chicago. Real-estate broker; leader in Association of Real Estate Taxpayers (ARET).

Black Hawk [Makataimeshekiakiak] b 1767, Sauk Village (Rock River, IL); d Oct. 3, 1838, near Des Moines River, IA. Sauk leader; launched Black Hawk War (1832).

Black Partridge active 1800s. Potawatomi chief.

Black, Greene Vardiman b Aug. 3, 1836, Scott County, IL; d Aug. 31, 1915. Dentist; dean of dentistry at Northwestern Univ.

Black, Neville b Jamaica; d Apr. 2000. Dancer; choreographer; founding director Chicago Contemporary Dance Co.

Blackbird [Chief J. B. Assikinock] b 1768, L'Arbor Croche, MI; d Nov. 3, 1866, Wekwemiking, Manitoulin Island, MI. Ottawa chief; led Aug. 1812 attack on Fort Dearborn.

Blackshear, Kathleen b June 6, 1897, Navasota, TX; d Oct. 14, 1988, Navasota, TX. Painter; lecturer at Art Institute of Chicago.

Blackstone, John active 1830s. Established sawmill on Thorn Creek with John Kinzie and Gurdon Hubbard.

Blair, Lucy McCormick Linn b Feb. 4, 1886; d Nov. 16, 1978, Lake Forest, IL. Founder and first president of Junior League Chicago.

Blanchard, Charles A. b Nov. 8, 1848, Galesburg, IL; d Dec. 20, 1925, Wheaton, IL. Educator; president of Wheaton College.

Blanchard, Jonathan b Jan. 19, 1811, Rockingham, VT; d May 14, 1892, Wheaton, IL. Educator; social reformer; first president of Wheaton College.

Blanchard, Joseph active 1830s. Constructed first city market in 1834.

Blanchard, Rufus b Mar. 7, 1821, Lyndeboro, NH; d Jan. 3, 1904, Wheaton, IL. Mapmaker; publisher; historian.

Blanchard, Walter b Mar. 31, 1807, Newhampton, NH; d Dec. 4, 1863, Ringgold Gap, Taylor's Ridge, GA. Farmer, Downers Grove area; judge; infantry captain in Civil War.

Blaney, James Van Zandt b May 1, 1820, Newcastle, DE; d Dec. 11, 1874, Chicago. Chemical manufacturer; cofounded Rush Medical College.

Blatchford, Eliphalet Wickes b May 31, 1826, Stillwater, NY; d Jan. 25, 1914, Chicago. Lead manufacturer; trustee for Newberry and Crerar Libraries; helped found Chicago Academy of Sciences.

Bliss, Philip b July 9, 1838, Clearfield County, PA; d Dec. 29, 1876, Ashtabula, OH.

Christian composer; hymnodist; musical evangelist.

Block, Leigh B. b Apr. 7, 1905, Chicago; d Dec. 9, 1987, Santa Barbara, CA. Steel executive; chairman of Art Institute of Chicago (1970–1975).

Block, Mary Lasker b Sept. 16, 1904, Chicago; d Feb. 17, 1981, Chicago. Business executive; trustee of Art Institute; founded Block Museum at Northwestern Univ.

Blodgett, Henry W. b July 21, 1821, Amherst, MA; d Feb. 9, 1905, Waukegan, IL. Railroad builder; federal judge; Illinois state representative and senator.

Blodgett, Israel b 1779, Amherst, MA; d 1861. Early resident of Downers Grove.

Blood, Mary A. b June 20, 1851, Hollis, NH; d July 25, 1927, Chicago. Educator at Columbia College.

Blum, Jerome S. b 1884, Chicago; d July 23, 1956, New York, NY. Painter; assisted Frank Lloyd Wright in planning color scheme for Midway Gardens.

Bodenheim, Maxwell b May 26, 1892, Hermanville, MS; d Feb. 7, 1954, New York, NY. Poet; critic; novelist; associated with Chicago Renaissance.

Bogan, William Joseph b Oct. 26, 1870, Mackinac Island, MI; d Mar. 24, 1936, Chicago. Educator; superintendent of Chicago Public Schools.

Bohac, Ben F. b Jan. 4, 1893, Chicago; d Mar. 19, 1975, Chicago. President and founder of Talman Federal Savings & Loan Association.

Boldt, Melvin H. b 1917; d 1981. Industrial designer; designed household appliances, jukeboxes, and powerboats.

Bolm, Adolph R. b Sept. 25, 1884, St. Petersburg, Russia; d Apr. 16, 1951, Hollywood, CA. Ballet dancer; teacher; choreographer for Chicago Opera Company.

Bonfield, John b Apr. 12, 1836, Bathurst, New Brunswick, Canada; d Oct. 19, 1898, Chicago. Police inspector; headed platoon at Haymarket Square riot.

Bontemps, Arna Wendell b Oct. 13, 1902, Alexandria, LA; d June 4, 1973, Nashville, TN. Writer; worked for the WPA Illinois Writers' Project; taught at Univ. of Illinois.

Boone, Levi D. b Dec. 6 or 8, 1808, Lexington, KY; d Jan. 24, 1882, Chicago. Doctor; captain in Black Hawk War; mayor of Chicago (1855–1856).

Booz, Edwin G. b Sept. 2, 1887, Reading, PA; d Oct. 14, 1951, Evanston, IL. Management consultant; founded Booz, Allen & Hamilton.

Borden, Gail b Nov. 9, 1801, Norwich, NY; d Jan. 11, 1874, Borden, TX. Surveyor; invented condensed milk; opened milk factory in Elgin.

Borowski, Felix b Mar. 10, 1872, Burton, Westmoreland, England; d Sept. 6, 1956, Chicago. Composer; musical critic; president of Chicago Musical College.

Boudreau, Lou b July 17, 1917, Harvey, IL; d Aug. 10, 2001, Olympia Fields, IL. Baseball player; Hall of Fame shortstop; Chicago Cubs broadcaster.

Boulden, Jesse Freeman b Oct. 8, 1820, DE. Editor; minister; pastor of Olivet Baptist Church in 1860s.

Bourassa, Leon b 1798 or 1799. French-Indian trader; settled on land which is now Forest Home Cemetery.

Bouscaren, Louis G. b Mar. 13, 1882; d Aug. 4, 1966, Evanston, IL. Businessman; platted South Riverwoods area.

Bowen, James H. b Mar. 7, 1822, Mannheim, NY; d May 1, 1881, Chicago. President of Calumet & Chicago Canal & Dock Co.

Bowen, Louise de Koven b Feb. 26, 1859, Chicago; d Nov. 9, 1953, Chicago. Social reformer; benefactor and president of Hull House; president of Juvenile Protective Association.

Bowles, Lillian b 1884? d 1949? Owner of music publishing house specializing in gospel music.

Boyce, William D. b June 16, 1858 or 1860, Plum Township, PA; d June 11, 1929, Chicago. Publisher; founded Boy Scouts of America.

Boyington, William W. b July 22, 1818, Southwick, MA; d Oct. 16, 1898, Highland Park, IL. Architect; designed Chicago Water Tower and Pumping Station.

Boykin, Randson b Sept. 4, 1949; d Nov. 15, 1995. Poet; performance artist; founder and executive director of Katherine Dunham Foundation.

Boyton, Paul b June 29, 1848, Dublin, Ireland; d Apr. 18, 1924, Brooklyn, NY. Aquatic showman; invented "Shoot the Chute."

Brach, Emil J. b May 21, 1859, Schoenwald, Germany; d Oct. 29, 1947, Chicago. President and founder of E. J. Brach Candy Manufacturers.

Bracken, Jimmy b May 23, 1908; d Feb. 20 or 22, 1972, Chicago. Record producer; cofounded Vee-Jay Records.

Bradley, Cyrus P. b Nov. 14, 1819, Concord, NH; d Mar. 6, 1865, Chicago. First chief of police in Chicago; sheriff of Cook County.

Bradley, Preston b Aug. 18, 1888, Linden, MI; d June 1, 1983, Morrisville, VT. Christian Unitarian minister; civic leader; founder and pastor of Peoples Church.

Bradley, Will H. b July 10, 1868, Boston, MA; d Jan. 25, 1962, La Mesa, CA. Illustrator; graphic designer; painter.

Bradley, William Henry b Nov. 29, 1816, Ridgefield, CT; d Mar. 1, 1892, Chicago. Circuit court clerk; Newberry Library trustee.

Bradwell, Myra Colby b Feb. 12, 1831, Manchester, VT; d Feb. 14, 1894, Chicago. Attorney; publisher; established *Chicago Legal News;* first woman member of Illinois State Bar Association.

Braidwood, James b Mar. 1, 1831, Johnstone, Renfrewshire, Scotland; d Feb. 1, 1879, Braidwood, IL. Sunk first coal shaft in Will County; founded city of Braidwood.

Brand, Edwin b Oct. 16, 1835, Edmeston, NY; d Dec. 25, 1900, Chicago. Photographer.

Brand, Michael b Mar. 23, 1826 or 1828, Odenheim, Rheinhessen, Germany; d Oct. 26, 1897, Chicago. Brewer; alderman; Illinois state legislator; founded Michael Brand Brewing Co.

Brass, Allen H. b June 2, 1818, NY; d Jan. 23, 1892, Crown Point, IN. Innkeeper in Munster in 1840s.

Breasted, James Henry b Aug. 27, 1865, Rockford, IL; d Dec. 2, 1935, New York, NY. Egyptologist; archeologist; historian; founded Oriental Institute at Univ. of Chicago.

Breckenridge, James D. b Aug. 8, 1926, Brooklyn, NY; d Dec. 18, 1982, Evanston, IL. Art history professor, Northwestern Univ.; wrote for *Herald-American.*

Breckinridge, Sophonisba Preston b Apr. 1, 1866, Lexington, KY; d July 30, 1948, Chicago. Social scientist; reformer; Univ. of Chicago faculty, School of Social Service Administration.

Brennan, Edward P. b June 30, 1866, Chicago; d Jan. 10, 1942, Chicago. Building superintendent; introduced street numbering system.

Brennan, George E. b May 20, 1865, Port Byron, NY; d Aug. 8, 1928, Chicago. Democratic Party leader; Illinois National Committeeman.

Brentano, Lorenz b Nov. 4, 1813, Mannheim, Germany; d Sept. 17, 1891, Chicago. Journalist; attorney; school board chairman; co-owner *Illinois Staats-Zeitung*; U.S. congressman.

Brickman, Joseph M. b Dec. 11, 1901; d Dec. 14, 1977, Evanston, IL. Founded home building firm; helped found Highland Park Country Club.

Brinkman, William J. b 1874; d Feb. 24, 1911, Chicago. Architect; designed St. Josephat Church; designed exhibits at World's Columbian Exposition.

Britten, Frederick Albert b Nov. 18, 1871, Chicago; d May 4, 1946, Bethesda, MD. U.S. congressman.

Britton, Edgar b Apr. 15, 1901, Kearney, NE; d Apr. 1982, Denver, CO. Artist; muralist; painter; sculptor.

Brodman, Howard Charles b Mar. 15, 1885, Peoria, IL; d Feb. 25, 1861, Chicago. Superintendent of Department of Maps and Plats; involved in street naming.

Brooks, C. Wayland b Mar. 8, 1897, West Bureau, IL; d Jan. 14, 1957, Chicago. Attorney; U.S. senator.

Brooks, Gwendolyn [Gwendolyn Brooks Blakely] b June 7, 1917, Topeka, KS; d Dec. 3, 2000, Chicago. Poet; first African American Pulitzer Prize winner (*Annie Allen*); poet laureate of Illinois.

Brooks, James active 1830s. Landowner; owned property around the I&M Canal in 1838.

Broonzy, William Lee "Big Bill" [William Lee Conley] b June 26, 1893, Scott, MS; d Aug. 14, 1958, Chicago. Blues singer; guitarist; recording artist.

Brophy, Truman William b Apr. 12, 1848, Goodings Grove, IL; d Feb. 4, 1928, Chicago. Oral surgeon; pioneer in cleft palate surgery; an organizer of Chicago College of Dental Surgery.

Bross, William b Nov. 4, 1813, Montague, NJ; d Jan. 27, 1890, Chicago. Journalist; newspaper editor and publisher; Lieutenant Governor; founded *Democratic Press.*

Brown, Adam b 1805? Guilford, NC; d Mar. 8, 1895. Arrived in South Chicago Heights area ("Brown's Corners") in 1833.

Brown, Arthur, Jr. b May 21, 1874, Oakland, CA; d July 7, 1957, Burlingame, CA. Architect; member of Architectural Commission, Century of Progress.

Brown, Christopher b 1832, OH. Son of Adam and Phoebe Brown, who arrived in South Chicago Heights area in 1833.

Brown, Corinne Stubbs b ca. Dec. 14, 1849, Chicago; d Mar. 15, 1914, New York, NY. Suffrage leader; labor reformer; socialist; president of Illinois Women's Alliance.

Brown, H. D. "Curly" d May 1930. Millionaire; founded Arlington Heights racetrack.

Brown, James Stanley b Sept. 1863, Cumberland, OH; d Sept. 6, 1939, Frankfurt, MI. Educator; superintendent and principal of Joliet Township High School and Junior College (1893–1899).

Brown, John G. active early twentieth century. Village president of Fox Lake after incorporation in 1907.

Brown, Joseph H. active early 1900s. Steel industry executive.

Brown, Nathaniel J. b Jan. 27, 1812, Windsor, VT; d Aug. 2, 1900, buried in Lemont, IL. I&M Canal builder; large Lemont property owner.

Brown, Ned active twentieth century; d 1959. Member Potawatomi tribe; advisor to Cook County Forest Preserve commission.

Brown, Phoebe b ca. 1810, TN; d 1892. Arrived in South Chicago Heights area ("Brown's Corners") in 1833.

Brown, Roger [James Roger Brown] b Dec. 10, 1941, Hamilton, AL; d Nov. 22, 1997, Opelika, AL. Artist; Chicago Imagist.

Brown, Roy Thomas b July 8, 1932, Tucson, AZ; d Jan. 22, 2001, Chicago. Puppeteer; "Cooky the Cook" on *Bozo's Circus*; *Garfield Goose* puppeteer.

Browne, Francis Fisher b Dec. 1, 1843, S. Halifax, VA; d May 11, 1913, Chicago. Editor; founded the *Dial.*

Browne, Maurice b Feb. 12, 1881, Reading, England; d Jan. 21, 1955, London, England. Actor; theatrical director; founded Chicago Little Theatre (1912).

Browning, Charles Patrick b Apr. 9, 1915, Louisville, KY; d Jan. 20, 1954, Little Rock, AR. Vice president *Chicago Defender*; active in South Side Community Art Center.

Brownlow, Louis H. b Aug. 29, 1879, Buffalo, MO; d Sept. 1963, Arlington, VA. Journalist; director of Public Administration Clearing House.

Broyles, Paul W. b Feb. 3, 1896, McLeansboro, IL; d Feb. 25, 1974, St. Louis, MO. Republican state senator; chaired anti-Communist commission.

Brundage, Myron "Slim" b Nov. 29, 1903, Blackfoot, Idaho; d Oct. 18, 1990, El Centro, CA. Tavern owner (College of Complexes); organizer for the Industrial Workers of the World.

Bryan, Thomas Barbour b Dec. 22, 1828, Alexandria, VA; d Jan. 25, 1906, Washington, DC. Attorney; early businessman; founded Graceland Cemetery; real-estate developer.

Bubacz, Stephen S. b Aug. 17, 1909, Chicago; d Dec. 15, 1968, Chicago. Neighborhood organizer; led Russell Square Community Committee (1938–1968).

Buck, Dudley b Mar. 10, 1839, Hartford, CT; d Oct. 6, 1909, West Orange, NJ. Organist; composer.

Buell, Dorothy R. b 1886 or 1887, Menasha, WI; d May 17, 1977, San Jose, CA. Conservationist; organized Save the Dunes Council.

Bulliet, Clarence Joseph b Mar. 16, 1883, Corydon, IN; d Oct. 20, 1952, Chicago. Art, drama, and music critic for *Chicago Evening Post* and *Chicago Daily News.*

Bullock, Carrie E. b June 16, 1887, Laurens, SC; d Dec. 31, 1962, Chicago. Nurse; associated with Visiting Nurse Association for 47 years.

Bundesen, Herman N. b Apr. 27, 1882, Berlin, Germany; d Aug. 25, 1960, Chicago. Physician; author; politician; president of Chicago Board of Health; Cook County coroner.

Burdell, Nicholas active 1840s. Band leader in 1840.

Burgess, Ernest Watson b May 16, 1886, Tilbury, Ontario, Canada; d Dec. 27, 1966, Chicago. Sociologist at Univ. of Chicago; involved with Chicago Area Project; developed "concentric zone theory."

Burke, Jack active 1880s. Boxer; fought in first prizefight in Chicago in 1885.

Burke, Ralph H. b ca. 1884, Chicago; d Aug. 23, 1956, Chicago. Engineer; city airport consultant; involved in development of O'Hare Airport; chief engineer of Chicago Park District.

Burmeister, Charles G. b ca. 1876; d Oct. 12, 1950, Chicago. Undertaker.

Burnett, Leo b Oct. 21, 1891, St. Johns, MI; d June 7, 1971, Lake Zurich, IL. Founded Leo Burnett advertising agency.

Burnham, Daniel Hudson, Jr. b Feb. 22, 1886, Chicago; d Nov. 3, 1961, Chicago. Architect; director of works at Century of Progress Exposition.

Burnham, Daniel Hudson b Sept. 4, 1846, Henderson, NY; d June 1, 1912, Heidelberg, Germany. City planner; architect; created 1909 *Plan of Chicago*; developed early skyscraper.

Burnham, Hubert b Sept. 7, 1882, Chicago; d Dec. 31, 1968, La Jolla, CA. Architect (son of Daniel H. Burnham); designed Union Carbide Building; architect for Century of Progress Exposition.

Burnham, Telford b Oct. 23, 1843, Cincinnati, OH; d Apr. 29, 1923, Kankakee, IL. Attorney; developed plan for area that became Burnham.

Burroughs, Charles b Feb. 28, 1919; d Feb. 26, 1994. Cofounded DuSable Museum of African American History.

Burroughs, Edgar Rice b Sept. 1, 1875, Chicago; d Mar. 19, 1950, Encino, CA. Novelist; creator of the character Tarzan.

Burton, Charles W. b Apr. 19, 1884, Meridian, MS; d Sept. 23, 1957, Chicago. Clergyman; lawyer; head of National Negro Congress until 1940.

Burton, William Merriam b Nov. 17, 1865, Cleveland, OH; d Dec. 29, 1954, Miami, FL. Chemist; president of Standard Oil (Indiana); pioneer in oil refining technology.

Busby, Denver A. b Oct. 8, 1896, Trenton, MO; d Apr. 22, 1981, San Diego, CA. Farmer; his dairy farm was later developed into Burr Ridge.

Busse, Fred A. b Mar. 3, 1866, Chicago; d July 9, 1914, Chicago. Mayor of Chicago (1907–1911); state treasurer; postmaster; president of Busse Coal Co.

Busse, William b Jan. 27, 1864, Elk Grove, IL; d July 17, 1955, Elgin, IL. Farmer; Cook County commissioner; Republican leader.

Buswell, James Oliver b Jan. 16, 1895, Burlington, WI; d Feb. 3, 1977. Clergyman; president of Wheaton College (1925–1940).

Butler, Burridge D. b Feb. 5, 1868, Louisville, KY; d Mar. 30, 1948, Phoenix, AZ. Publisher; owned *Prairie Farmer* and radio station WLS.

Butler, Frank Osgood b Apr. 22, 1861, Chicago; d Mar. 18, 1955, West Palm Beach, FL. Paper manufacturer; president of Natoma Farm, Hinsdale.

Butler, Paul b June 25, 1892, Chicago; d June 24, 1981, Oak Brook, IL. Business executive; real-estate developer; founded Oak Brook; founded Butler Aviation.

Butterfield, Justin b 1790, Keene, NH; d Oct. 23, 1855, Chicago. Lawyer; Whig Party organizer; commissioner of Land Office under President Taylor.

Buttrick, Hiram b Dec. 17, 1811, Middletown, Concord, MA; d Dec. 1, 1886, Waukegan, IL. Built sawmill in Antioch in 1839.

Butts, Magnolia Lewis b ca. 1894–1896, Tipton, MA; d Dec. 10, 1949, Chicago. Gospel choir organizer; soloist; assistant to director of the Metropolitan Choir; director of W. G. Cook Gospel Choir.

Byfield, Joseph *See* **Beifeld, Joseph**

Byford, William Heath b Mar. 20, 1817, Eaton, OH; d May 21, 1870, Chicago. Physician; author; cofounded Chicago Medical

College and Woman's Hospital Medical College.

Byrne, Francis Barry b Dec. 19, 1883, Chicago; d Dec. 17, 1967, Evanston, IL. Architect; apprentice to Frank Lloyd Wright; designed churches and schools for Chicago Archdiocese.

C

Cabrini, Frances Xavier b July 15, 1850, Saint Angelo Lodigiano, Italy; d Dec. 22, 1917, Chicago. Educator; social worker; founded schools and orphanages; canonized in 1946.

Cadwell, Jacob b 1770 or 1771, Addison County, VT; d July 27, 1848. First Euro-American settler in Deerfield in 1835.

Cady, Ezekiel b Apr. 29, 1791, Oneida, NY? d Oct. 1, 1873, buried Cady Cemetery. Landowner in Deer Grove in 1850s.

Caldwell, Alfred b May 26, 1903, St. Louis, MO; d July 3, 1998, Bristol, WI. Landscape architect; engineer; educator; designed Lily Pond in Lincoln Park.

Caldwell, Billy [Sauganash] b Mar. 17, 1780, Niagara Frontier (NY); d Sept. 27, 1841, Council Bluffs, IA. Fur trader; justice of the peace; Potawatomi chief; officer in British Indian Dept.; business chief of the Prairie Bands.

Calhoun, John b Apr. 14, 1808, Watertown, NY; d Feb. 20, 1859, Chicago. Editor; founded *Chicago Weekly Democrat*.

Callahan, Harry b Oct. 22, 1912, Detroit, MI; d Mar. 15, 1999, Atlanta, GA. Photographer; taught at the Institute of Design.

Cameron, Daniel R. b Aug. 16, 1836, Summerstown, Ontario, Canada; d June 26, 1918, Altadena, CA. Stationery manufacturer; printer; president of Chicago Board of Education.

Campanini, Cleofante b Sept. 1, 1860, Parma, Italy; d Dec. 19, 1919, Chicago. Opera director for Chicago-Philadelphia Grand Opera.

Campbell, James B. active 1830s. I&M Canal commissioner; laid out village of Joliet in 1834.

Campbell, Lucie E. [Lucie Campbell Williams] b Apr. 30, 1885, Duck Hill, MS; d Jan. 3, 1963, Nashville, TN. Gospel composer; teacher; pioneer in twentieth-century gospel music.

Campbell, Robert C. active 1850s. Railroad engineer; worked for Fond du Lac railroad.

Campbell, Robert W. b July 30, 1874, Frankfort, IN; d Feb. 16, 1947. Lawyer; first president of National Council for Industrial Safety (1913); chief attorney for Illinois Steel.

Campbell, Thomas A. E. b July 1810, Montgomery County, NY; d May 14, 1878? Valparaiso, IN. Early postmaster of Valparaiso Township.

Camras, Marvin b Jan. 1, 1916, Chicago; d June 23, 1995, Evanston, IL. Educator; inventor; pioneered magnetic tape recording.

Camryn, Walter [Walter Cameron] b July 31, 1903, Helena, MT; d Feb. 29, 1984, Chicago. Choreographer; principal dancer Chicago Opera Ballet; established Stone-Camryn School of Dance.

Canfield, Florence C. b ca. 1847, NY; d Nov. 5, 1926? Bremen Township, IL. Farm owner; sold land in 1900 to Chicago, Aurora & Elgin Railway.

Cantwell, Daniel M. b June 29, 1914, Chicago; d Jan. 2, 1996, Chicago. Roman Catholic priest; founder and chaplain of Catholic Interracial Council; pastor of St. Clotilde parish.

Capone, Alphonse b Jan. 17, 1899, Brooklyn, NY; d Jan. 25, 1947, Miami, FL. Chicago gangster, bootlegger, and racketeer.

Capone, Ralph b Jan. 12, 1894, Naples, Italy; d Nov. 20, 1974, Hurley, WI. Prohibition-era gangster (brother of Al Capone).

Capone, Theresa Angelina b ca. 1867, Italy; d Nov. 29, 1952, Chicago. Mother of Al Capone.

Caray, Harry [Harry Christopher Carabina] b Mar. 1, 1914, St. Louis, MO; d Feb. 18, 1998, Rancho Mirage, CA. Baseball broadcaster for White Sox and Cubs.

Carbutt, John b Dec. 2, 1832, Sheffield, England; d July 26, 1905, Philadelphia, PA. Photographer; chemist; invented new photographic methods.

Carey, Archibald James (Sr.) b Aug. 1867 or 1868, Atlanta, GA; d Mar. 23, 1931, Chicago. African Methodist Episcopal minister; political activist.

Carey, Thomas b 1860, West Brookfield, MA; d Sept. 1, 1925, Los Angeles, CA. Alderman; owned Hawthorne Race Track.

Carkeek, Jack b Jan. 22, 1861, Rockland, MI; d Mar. 12, 1924, Havana, Cuba. Wrestler; competitor in first professional heavyweight championship in Chicago.

Carnevali, Emanuel b Dec. 4, 1897, Firenze (Toscana), Italy; d Nov. 1, 1942, Bologna, Italy. Poet; associate editor of *Poetry* magazine; author, *A Hurried Man* (1925).

Carpenter, Angelo b Aug. 19, 1827, Uxbridge, MA; d Mar. 30, 1880, Dundee, IL. Platted Carpentersville in 1851; state legislator.

Carpenter, Charles V. b Oct. 31, 1806, Uxbridge, MA; d Feb. 10, 1878, Dundee, IL. Farmer; arrived with his brother in 1837 in Carpentersville.

Carpenter, Daniel b Apr. 27, 1801, Uxbridge, MA; d Jan. 6, 1874, Dundee, IL. Farmer; arrived with his brother in 1837 in Carpentersville.

Carpenter, Henry b Feb. 22, 1810, Washington County, NY; d June 7, 1891, Downers Grove, IL. First store owner in Downers Grove; postmaster; justice of the peace.

Carpenter, Jacob b Dec. 17, 1811, OH; d Sept. 20, 1836, Aurora, IL. Staked out a land claim in what is now Montgomery, ca. 1834.

Carpenter, John Alden b Feb. 28, 1876, Park Ridge, IL; d Apr. 26, 1951, Chicago. Composer (*The Birthday of the Infanta*); early works premiered in Chicago.

Carpenter, Philo b Feb. 27, 1805, Savoy, MA; d Aug. 7, 1886, Chicago. Pharmacist; cofounded First Presbyterian Church; temperance advocate; participant in Underground Railroad.

Carroll, Cora b Aug. 16, 1924, Indianola, MS; d July 2000, Chicago. Winner of *Chicago Defender*'s "Mayor of Bronzeville" contests (1958–1962).

Carroll, Paul D. b July 15, 1927, Chicago; d Aug. 31, 1996, Vilas, NC. Educator; Beat-generation editor; poet; Univ. of Illinois at Chicago faculty member.

Carse, Matilda b Nov. 19, 1835, Belfast, Ireland; d June 3, 1917, Park Hill-on-Hudson, NY. Temperance activist; suffragist; editor; entrepreneur; president Chicago Central Woman's Christian Temperance Union.

Cary, William D. b Sept. 7, 1807, Sandy Creek Onondaga, NY; d Feb. 3, 1861, buried in Cary Cemetery, Cary, IL. Farmer; platted Cary in 1856.

Cassidy, Claudia b Nov. 18, 1899, Shawneetown, IL; d July 21, 1996, Chicago. Theatre, dance, and music critic for Chicago newspapers.

Castle, George b ca. 1850, Syracuse, NY; d Dec. 29, 1917, Miami, FL. Owner of Majestic and Olympic Theatres; vaudeville manager.

Cather, Willa b Dec. 7, 1873, Back Creek Valley (now Gore), VA; d Apr. 24, 1947, New York, NY. Novelist (*The Song of the Lark*); short story writer.

Caton, Edward b Apr. 3, 1900, St. Petersburg, Russia; d Oct. 22, 1981, New York, NY. Dancer; teacher; choreographer; danced with Chicago Opera Ballet.

Caverly, John R. b Dec. 6, 1861, London, England; d Aug. 4, 1939, at sea en route to Bermuda. Lawyer; chief justice of Criminal Court; sentenced Leopold and Loeb.

Cayton, Horace Roscoe b Apr. 12, 1903, Seattle, WA; d Jan. 22, 1970, Paris, France. Sociologist; social reformer; coauthor *Black Metropolis* (1945).

Cermak, Anton b May 9, 1873, Kladno, Czechoslovakia; d Mar. 6, 1933, Miami, FL. Mayor of Chicago (1931–1933).

Cernocky, Louis, Jr. b Nov. 1, 1909, Chicago; d June 27, 1991, Fox River Grove, IL. Purchased Fox River Picnic Grove in 1942 (with wife Clara Opatrny).

Cernocky, Louis, Sr. b June 11, 1885, Austria; d Sept. 20, 1934, Fox River Grove, IL. Harness maker.

Chaddick, Harry F. b Aug. 27, 1901, Chicago; d May 31, 1994, Chicago. Real-estate developer; businessman; city zoning director.

Chakonas, Christ b 1848, Zoupena, Greece; d 1930s? Early leader of Greek community.

Chamberlin, Henry Barrett b Mar. 10, 1867, Washington, DC; d Aug. 7, 1941, Chicago. Lawyer; journalist; editor; director Chicago Crime Commission.

Chance, Frank Leroy b Sept. 9, 1877, Fresno, CA; d Sept. 15, 1924, Los Angeles, CA. Baseball player; Cubs first baseman and manager; Hall of Fame.

Chapin, John P. b Apr. 21, 1810, Rutland or Bradford, VT; d June 27, 1864, Chicago. Boat builder; mayor of Chicago (1846–1847); vice president of Chicago Board of Trade.

Chaplin, Ralph Hosea b Aug. 30, 1887; d Mar. 23, 1961, Tacoma, WA. Radical labor activist; journalist; songwriter; poet; wrote "Solidarity Forever."

Chatfield-Taylor, Hobart b Mar. 24, 1865, Chicago; d Jan. 16, 1945. Writer; established political review *America*; foreign correspondent, *Daily News*.

Chatfield, Alonzo B. b Nov. 26, 1810, Armenia, NY; d May 31, 1893. Early settler, Lisle area.

Che Che Pin Qua *See* **Robinson, Alexander**

Cheney, Flora b Mar. 11, 1872, Fond du Lac, WI; d Apr. 8, 1929, Chicago. Women's suffrage and good government activist; first president of Illinois League of Women Voters; state legislator (1928).

Chermayeff, Serge Ivan b Oct. 8, 1900, Grozny, Caucasus; d May 8, 1996, Wellfleet, MA. Architect; Illinois Institute of Technology faculty; president of Chicago Institute of Design.

Chesbrough, Ellis Sylvester b July 6, 1813, Baltimore, MD; d Aug. 18 or 19, 1886, Chicago. Civil engineer; Public Works commissioner; planned Chicago sewerage system.

Chess, Leonard S. b Mar. 12, 1907, Motele, Poland; d Oct. 16, 1969, Chicago. Founded Chess Records; owned radio station and nightclub.

Chester, Art b Dec. 10, 1899, Downers Grove, IL; d 1949, San Diego, CA. Air racing champion; aircraft designer.

Chevalier, Marie Réaume L'Archeveque active eighteenth century. Illini woman living at Fort St. Joseph; fur trader.

Chicago active early eighteenth century. Illinois tribal leader; Michigamea chief; visited Paris in 1725; (note: not namesake for city).

Childs, Charles R. b Mar. 28, 1875, Elmwood, IL; d Jan. 14, 1960, Chicago. Postcard photographer.

Chmielinska, Stefania b Mar. 16, 1866, Warsaw, Poland; d Feb. 24, 1939, Chicago. Seamstress; women's rights activist; organized Polish Women's Alliance of America.

Chorpenning, Charlotte b Jan. 3 or 5, 1872; d Jan. 7, 1955, Warwick, NY. Playwright; teacher; developed children's theater at Goodman Theatre.

Christman, Paul J. b Mar. 5, 1918, St. Louis, MO; d Mar. 2, 1970, Lake Forest, IL. Football player, Chicago Cardinals; television commentator.

Churchill, Deacon Winslow b Dec. 30, 1770, Plympton, MA; d Sept. 18, 1847. Early settler of the present Glen Ellyn Township.

Chute, Walter H. b Apr. 12, 1891; d Apr. 28, 1981, Tucson, AZ. Director of Shedd Aquarium.

Cicotte, Eddie b June 19, 1884, Detroit, MI; d May 5, 1969, Detroit, MI. Baseball player; Chicago White Sox pitcher; involved in "Black Sox Scandal."

Cincotta, Gale A. [Gail Angeles] b Dec. 28, 1929, Chicago; d Aug. 15, 2001, Maywood, IL. Neighborhood activist; president of Organization for a Better Austin.

Clark, Dee b Nov. 7, 1938, Blythesville, AR; d Dec. 7, 1990, Smyrna, GA. R&B vocalist; member, Kool Gents; recorded for Vee-Jay Records.

Clark, Frank active late nineteenth century. Community leader; president of incorporated Lake Zurich in 1896.

Clark, John Kinzie b ca. 1784, near Fort Wayne, IN? d 1865, Chicago. Fur trader; known as "Indian Clark."

Clark, Mark b June 28, 1947, Peoria, IL; d Dec. 4, 1969, Chicago. Black Panther chairman in Peoria; killed in 1969 police raid.

Clarke, Caroline Palmer b Dec. 31, 1806, Sangerfield, NY; d Jan. 9, 1860, Buffalo, NY. Resident of Clarke House (one of Chicago's oldest surviving structures).

Clarke, George "Colonel" R. b Feb. 22, 1827, Otsego County, NY; d June 22, 1892. Cofounder of Pacific Garden Mission; lawyer.

Clarke, George W. b Feb. 8, 1810, Brownsville, PA; d Aug. 15, 1866, Chicago. Civil. engineer; owned large portion of Indiana Territory.

Clarke, Sarah D. b Nov. 3, 1835, Cayuga County, NY; d Jan. 29, 1918, Hinsdale, IL. Founded Pacific Garden Mission.

Clarkson, Ralph b Aug. 3, 1861, Amesbury, MA; d Apr. 5, 1942, Orlando, FL. Portrait painter; promoted art in Chicago; president of Chicago Society of Artists.

Clavey, Gordon E. b June 1, 1917, Highland Park, IL; d July 14, 1998, FL. Nurseryman; owned land that became Vernon Hills.

Cleaver, Charles b July 21, 1814, London, England; d Oct. 27, 1893, Chicago. Real-estate developer; founded Cleaverville.

Cleveland, Horace William Shaler b Dec. 16, 1814, Lancaster, MA; d Dec. 5, 1900, Hinsdale, IL. Landscape architect; planned Drexel Boulevard, Washington Park, and Downers Grove.

Cloes, Catherine b Germany; d 1872. Resident of Lake Bluff, 1830s; established Cloes brickyard in 1860.

Cloes, John b 1797, Germany; d declared legally dead in Jan. 1851. First Euro-American Lake Bluff resident; blacksmith; joined Gold Rush in 1840s.

Close, Del b Mar. 9, 1934, Manhattan, KS; d Mar. 4, 1999, Chicago. Actor; improvisational comic; performer and director of Second City.

Clybourne, Archibald b Aug. 28, 1802, Pearisburgh, VA; d Aug. 23, 1872, Chicago. Butcher; built the city's first slaughterhouse; first Justice of the Peace (1831).

Cobb, Henry Ives b Aug. 19, 1859, Brookline, MA; d Mar. 27, 1931, New York, NY. Architect; designed Chicago Opera House, Newberry Library, buildings at Univ. of Chicago.

Cochran, John Lewis b Mar. 23, 1857, Sacramento, CA; d Sept. 25, 1923, Chicago. Real-estate developer; founded Edgewater; promoter and first president, Northwestern Elevated Railroad.

Cody, John Patrick b Dec. 24, 1907, St. Louis, MO; d Apr. 25, 1982, Chicago. Roman Catholic archbishop of Chicago (1965–1982); cardinal (1967–1982).

Coey, Charles A. b 1870, Redfield, NY; d July 2, 1952, Chicago. Automobile livery owner; opened first public garage in Chicago.

Coffey, Cornelius b Sept. 6, 1902; d Mar. 2, 1994, Chicago. Aviator; trained many of Tuskegee Airmen.

Cogley, John b Mar. 16, 1916, Chicago; d Mar. 29, 1976, Santa Barbara, CA. Journalist; editor of *Catholic Worker*; operated a house for homeless men in Chicago.

Cohen, George b Aug. 4, 1919; d Apr. 18, 1999, Evanston, IL. Artist; figure painter; Northwestern Univ. faculty.

Cole, George E. b Mar. 2, 1845, Jackson, MI; d Aug. 18, 1930, Winnetka, IL. Stationer; printer; organized 1896 Municipal Voters League.

Cole, Nat "King" b Mar. 17, 1919, Montgomery, AL; d Feb. 15, 1965, Santa Monica, CA. Jazz pianist; singer; first African American to host TV show on NBC.

Cole, Robert Alexander b Oct. 8, 1882, Mount Carmel, TN; d July 27, 1956, Chicago. Founded Metropolitan Funeral System; chairman, Metropolitan Mutual Assurance Co.

Coleman, Bessie b Jan. 26, 1892, Atlanta, TX; d Apr. 30, 1926, Jacksonville, FL. Aviator; first black woman pilot.

Collins, Edward Trowbridge b May 2, 1887, Millerton, NY; d Mar. 25, 1951, Boston, MA. Baseball player in Hall of Fame; manager of White Sox.

Colosimo, James b 1877, Cosenza, Calabria, Italy; d May 11, 1920, Chicago. Restaurant owner; Chicago mob boss before Capone.

Colvin, Harvey Doolittle b Dec. 18, 1815, Herkimer County, NY; d Apr. 16, 1892, Jacksonville, FL. Mayor of Chicago (1873–1875).

Comiskey, Charles A. b Aug. 15, 1859, Chicago; d Oct. 26, 1931, Eagle River, WI. Baseball player; owned and managed Chicago White Sox.

Comiskey, John "Honest John" sb ca. 1830, Crosserlough, Ireland; d Jan. 8, 1900, Chicago. Alderman; father of Charles A. Comiskey.

Compton, Arthur Holly b Sept. 10, 1892, Wooster, OH; d Mar. 15, 1962, Berkeley, CA. Physicist; directed Manhattan Project at Univ. of Chicago; shared 1927 Nobel Prize for Physics.

Compton, Frank E. b 1874 or 1875, Wisconsin Rapids, WI; d May 13, 1950, La Jolla, CA. Chairman of F. E. Compton & Co.; publisher of *Compton's Encyclopedia*.

Condon, Eddie [Albert Edwin Condon] b Nov. 16, 1905, Goodland, IN; d Aug. 4, 1973, New York, NY. Jazz banjo player; club owner; bandleader; recorded with "The Chicagoans."

Condon, John b ca. 1855; d Aug. 9, 1915, Chicago. Racetrack owner; gambler; opened Harlem Race Track (1894).

Cone, Fairfax M. b Feb. 21, 1903, San Francisco, CA; d June 20, 1977, Carmel, CA. Founder and chairman of Foote, Cone & Belding advertising company.

Connolly, James b June 5, 1868, Edinburgh, Scotland; d May 12, 1916, Dublin, Ireland. Socialist; trade union organizer.

Conroy, Jack [John Wesley Conroy] b Dec. 5, 1898, Moberly, MO; d Feb. 28, 1990, Moberly, MO. Author (*Anyplace but Here*, with Arna Bontemps); folklorist; editor; worked on Illinois Writers' Project (1938–1941).

Conti, Elmer W. b Apr. 9, 1921; d Jan. 4, 1988, Elmwood Park, IL. Bank president; village president of Elmwood (1953–1985); state representative.

Conzelman, James [James Gleason Dunn] b Mar. 6, 1898, St. Louis, MO; d July 31, 1970, St. Louis, MO. Football player; coached Chicago Cardinals to NFL championship in 1947.

Cook, Andrew b Nov. 5, 1801, Stamford, VT; d Dec. 31, 1884. Platted Wauconda, originally called Bangs Lake.

Cook, Ansel Brainerd b Aug. 18, 1823, Haddom, CT; d June 10, 1898, Libertyville, IL. Sidewalk contractor; president of Chicago City Council (late 1860s).

Cook, Daniel Pope b 1794 or 1795, Scott County, KY; d Oct. 16, 1827, Scott County, KY. Lawyer; first attorney general of Illinois; U.S. congressman (1819–1827); namesake of Cook County.

Cook, Ezra A. b Nov. 5, 1841, Windsor, CT; d Sept. 15, 1911, Wheaton, IL. Publisher; temperance leader.

Cooke, David Brainerd b Feb. 10, 1826, OH or Northampton, MA; d Oct. 21, 1884, Chicago. Early Chicago bookseller; publisher of "Blackwell's Reports"; partner of S. C. Griggs.

Cooke, Flora J. b Dec. 25, 1864, Bainbridge, OH; d Feb. 21, 1953, Chicago. Progressive educator; founding principal, Francis W. Parker School; aided in establishing North Shore Country Day School and Roosevelt Univ.

Cooke, Sam b Jan. 22, 1931, Clarksdale, MS; d Dec. 11, 1964, Hollywood, CA. Musician; singer; songwriter; known for "Twisting the Night Away."

Cooley, Edwin G. b Mar. 12, 1854, Strawberry Point, IA; d Sept. 28, 1923, New Trier, IL. Educator; principal of Chicago Normal College; Superintendent of Chicago schools.

Coon, W. D. active 1850s. Established farm in Vernon Hills in 1851.

Cooper, Jack L. b Sept. 18, 1888, Memphis, TN; d Jan. 12, 1970, Chicago. Radio personality; first African American disc jockey in Chicago; began radio career in 1926.

Cooper, Oswald Bruce b Apr. 13, 1879, Mount Gilead, OH; d Dec. 17, 1940, Chicago. Calligrapher; typographic designer.

Coopersmith, Harry b Dec. 5, 1902, Russia; d Dec. 1975. Composer; musical director; founded Halevi Choral Society in 1926.

Copley, Ira C. b Oct. 25, 1864, Copley Township, IL; d Nov. 2, 1947, Aurora, IL. Newspaper chain founder; publisher of newspapers in Illinois and California.

Corbett, Harvey Wiley b Jan. 8, 1873, San Francisco, CA; d Apr. 21, 1954, NY. Architect; chairman of Architectural Commission for Century of Progress.

Cornell, Paul b Aug. 5, 1822, White Creek, NY; d Mar. 3, 1904, Chicago. Lawyer; real-estate developer; founded Hyde Park; South Park commissioner.

Cornish, Andrew b June 27, 1782, New Ashford, Berkshire, MA; d Jan. 2, 1846, Algonquin, IL. Physician; Cornish's Ferry was renamed Algonquin around 1836.

Correll, Charles J. b Feb. 2, 1890, Peoria, IL; d Sept. 26, 1972, Chicago. Radio comedian; cocreator of "Amos 'n' Andy."

Corrigan, Edward b ca. 1842, Ireland; d July 4, 1924, Kansas City, MO. Racetrack owner; controlled Hawthorne Race Track.

Cortelyou, John R. b July 21, 1914, Chicago; d Nov. 9, 1996, Chicago. Natural scientist; priest; president of DePaul Univ. (1964–1981).

Cosimi, Serfino active late nineteenth century. Priest; established St. Stanislaus Bishop and Martyr Catholic Church in 1893.

Cossitt, Franklin Dwight b Sept. 19, 1821, Granby, CT; d July 9, 1900, La Grange, IL. Real-estate owner; founded village of La Grange.

Couch, Ira b Nov. 22, 1806, Saratoga County, NY; d Feb. 28, 1857, Havana, Cuba. Real-estate developer; built Tremont House hotel.

Coughlin, "Bathhouse" John b Aug. 15, 1860, Connelly's Patch, Chicago; d Nov. 11, 1938, Chicago. First Ward alderman (1892–1938).

Coulon, Johnny b Feb. 12, 1889, Toronto, Canada; d Oct. 29, 1973, Chicago. Boxer; world bantamweight champion (1910–1914); founded Coulon's Gym (1925).

Covell, Marion Francis b Jan. 10, 1831, Plainfield, IL; d Jan. 20, 1917, Hillside, IL. Farmer; owned Covell quarries; held public offices in Proviso Township.

Cowles, Henry C. b Feb. 27, 1869, Kensington, CT; d Sept. 12, 1939, Chicago. Botanist; worked to establish Cook County Forest Preserve; professor at Univ. of Chicago.

Cowling, Sam b Jan. 8, 1914, Jeffersonville, IN; d Feb. 14, 1983, Fresno, CA. Comic; radio-TV writer on Don McNeill's *Breakfast Club*.

Crain, Gustavus Dedman, Jr. b Nov. 19, 1885, Lawrenceburg, KY; d Dec. 15, 1973, Evanston, IL. Publisher; founded Crain Communications; published *Advertising Age*.

Cram, George F. b May 20, 1842, Lowell, MA; d Mar. 24, 1928. Engraver; published maps and atlases.

Crandall, Beman b Oct. 12, 1794, Cicero, NY; d Oct. 25, 1884, Brownsville, MO. Arrived in IL ca. 1832; platted east shore village in Crystal Lake in 1840.

Crane, Richard T. b May 15, 1832, Paterson, NJ; d Jan. 8, 1912, Chicago. Inventor; manufacturer; founded plumbing company in 1855.

Crawford, Peter b 1795 or 1796, Argyleshire, Scotland; d Dec. 7, 1876, Chicago. Real-estate speculator; lumber dealer; early carpenter and home builder.

Crawford, Ruth [Ruth Porter Crawford Seeger] b July 3, 1901, East Liverpool, OH; d Nov. 18, 1953, Chevy Chase, MD. Composer; teacher; scholar of American folk music.

Crerar, John b Mar. 8, 1827, New York, NY; d Oct. 19, 1889, Chicago. Merchant; banker; philanthropist; endowed John Crerar Library.

Cret, Paul Philippe b Oct. 23, 1876, Lyon, France; d Sept. 8, 1945, Philadelphia, PA. Architect; educator; member of architectural commission for Century of Progress Exposition.

Crilly, Daniel Francis b Oct. 14, 1838, Mercersburg, PA; d June 19, 1921, Chicago. Early builder; real-estate developer; designed Crilly Court and built much of what is now Old Town.

Cromie, Robert A. b Feb. 28, 1909, Detroit, MI; d May 22, 1999, Grayslake, IL. War correspondent; sports writer; columnist; radio and television host.

Crooks, Ramsay b Jan. 2, 1787, Greenock, Scotland; d June 6, 1859, New York, NY. Fur trader; agent and president of American Fur Trade Co.

Crosby, Uranus (Uriah) H. b Aug. 17, 1831, Brewster, MA; d Mar. 25, 1903, Brewster, MA. Distiller; founded Crosby Opera House in 1865.

Crowen, Samuel N. b July 17, 1873, Bresla, Germany; d Jan. 16, 1935, Lake Forest, IL. Architect specializing in apartment houses; designed Willoughby Tower in Chicago.

Crowley, Ruth b ca. 1907; d July 19, 1955, Lake Forest, IL. Television personality; feature writer for *Chicago Sun-Times*.

Crown, Henry b June 13, 1896, Chicago; d Aug. 14, 1990, Chicago. Entrepreneur; philanthropist; cofounded Material Service Corp.

Crown, Irving b Dec. 9, 1894, Chicago; d Mar. 1, 1987, Chicago. Philanthropist; cofounded Material Services Corp.

Crunelle, Leonard b July 8, 1872, Pas-de-Calais, France; d Sept. 10, 1944, Chicago. Sculptor; designed Victory Monument honoring World War I Africans.

Cullerton, "Foxy Ed" Edward F. b Oct. 12, 1841, Chicago; d Feb. 1, 1920, Chicago. Alderman (1871–1892, 1892–1920); state legislator.

Cuneo, John F. b Dec. 24, 1884, Chicago; d Apr. 30, 1977, Chicago. Real-estate developer; philanthropist; founded Cuneo Press.

Currey, Margery b ca. 1876, NY; d Aug. 15, 1959, New York, NY. Society editor for *Chicago Tribune* in the 1920s.

Curtiss, Glenn Hammond b May 21, 1878, Hammondsport, NY; d July 23, 1930, Buffalo, NY. Aviator; airplane designer and builder; built Curtiss-Reynolds Field in Glenview.

Curtiss, Samuel b 1789, CT; d Feb. 25, 1867, Downers Grove, IL. Farmer; established subdivision in Downers Grove.

Cutler, Charlie active 1910s. Wrestler; national champion (1914–1915).

D

Daley, Richard J. b May 15, 1902, Chicago; d Dec. 20, 1976, Chicago. Mayor of Chicago (1955–1976); state legislator (1936–1946); chairman, Cook County Democratic Party (1953–1976).

Damen, Arnold b Mar. 20, 1815, Leur, North Brabant, Holland; d Jan. 1, 1890, Omaha, NE. Founded St. Ignatius College (now Loyola Univ.).

Damski, Jon-Henri b Mar. 31, 1937, Seattle. WA; d Nov. 1, 1997, Chicago. Columnist; poet; contributor to gay publications in Chicago.

Darden, Severn T. b Nov. 9, 1929, New Orleans, LA; d May 26, 1995, Santa Fe, NM. Actor; founding cast member of the Second City Theatre (1959).

Darger, Henry Joseph b Apr. 12, 1892, Chicago; d Apr. 13, 1973, Chicago. Painter; writer (*In the Realms of the Unreal*); folk artist.

Darrow, Clarence Seward b Apr. 18, 1857, Kinsman, OH; d Mar. 13, 1938, Chicago. Lawyer; orator; defense attorney in Scopes and Leopold and Loeb trials.

Dart, Edward D. b May 28, 1922, New Orleans, LA; d July 9, 1975, Elgin, IL. Architect; designed Water Tower Plaza and Chicago churches.

Davenport, Charles "Cow Cow" b Apr. 26, 1895, Anniston, AL; d Dec. 2, 1955, Cleveland, OH. Boogie-woogie pianist; blues composer and artist.

Davis, Dantrell b 1985; d Oct. 13, 1992, Chicago. Murder victim; shot at age 7 in Cabrini-Green.

Davis, Frank Marshall b Dec. 31, 1905, Arkansas City, KS; d July 15 or 26, 1987, Honolulu, HI. Journalist; poet; wrote *47th Street*; editor at Associated Negro Press.

Davis, George Royal b Jan. 3, 1840, Three Rivers, MA; d Nov. 25, 1899, Chicago. Lawyer; U.S. Republican congressman (1879–1885); director general of 1893 World's Columbian Exposition.

Davis, Maxwell Street Jimmy [Charles W. Thompson] b Mar. 2, 1925; d Dec. 28, 1995, Chicago. Blues singer; guitarist; performed on Maxwell Street.

Davis, Nathan Smith b Jan. 9, 1817, Greene, NY; d June 16, 1904, Chicago. Physician; founded Mercy Hospital; cofounded Northwestern Univ. Medical School and Chicago Academy of Science.

Davis, Zachary Taylor b May 26, 1872, Aurora, IL; d Dec. 16, 1946, Chicago. Architect for Comiskey Park, Wrigley Field, and Board of Education.

Dawes, Charles Gates b Aug. 27, 1865, Marietta, OH; d Apr. 23, 1951, Evanston, IL. Chicago banker; U.S. vice president under Coolidge; won Nobel Peace Prize (1925); originated Dawes Plan.

Dawes, Rufus Cutler b July 30, 1867, Marietta, OH; d Jan. 8, 1940, Evanston, IL. Public utility executive; chairman of 1933 Century of Progress Exhibition; president of Museum of Science and Industry.

Dawson, Charles Clarence b June 12, 1889, Brunswick, GA; d 1940. Painter; designer; illustrator.

Dawson, Manierre b Dec. 22, 1887; d Aug. 1969. Cubist-style painter.

Dawson, William Levi b Apr. 26, 1886, Albany, GA; d Nov. 9, 1970, Chicago. Lawyer; Second Ward alderman (1933–1939); U.S. representative (1943–1970).

Dawson, William R. b Oct. 20, 1901, Huntsville, AL; d July 1, 1990, Chicago. Folk artist; wood sculptor; painter.

De Baptiste, Richard b Nov. 11, 1831, Fredericksburg, Spotsylvania, VA; d Apr. 21, 1901. Minister; pastor of Olivet Baptist Church (1863–1882).

De Vry, Cyrus B. b c. 1859, Harrisburg, PA; d Oct. 3, 1934, Los Angeles, CA. Animal trainer; director of Lincoln Park Zoo (1881–1912).

Dean, Charles E., Sr. b Feb. 13, 1867, Palatine, IL; d May 31, 1922, Chicago. Racehorse trainer; operated racetrack in Palatine Township.

Dean, Samuel Edward b Sept. 16, 1875, Sherman, MI; d Nov. 15, 1946, Hinsdale, IL. Founded Dean Milk Co.; pioneered introduction of paper milk carton.

Dean, Silas T. b 1818, Lowell, MA; d Jan. 12? 1889, Chicago. Musician; organized band.

Dearborn, Henry b Feb. 23, 1751, Hampton, NH; d June 6, 1829, Roxbury, MA. Soldier; U.S. secretary of war under Jefferson; namesake of Fort Dearborn.

Debs, Eugene Victor b Nov. 5, 1855, Terre Haute, IN; d Oct. 20, 1926, Chicago. Labor organizer; union leader; jailed during Pullman strike; socialist candidate for U.S. president.

Deering, William b Apr. 25, 1826, South Paris, ME; d Dec. 9, 1913, Coconut Grove, FL. Manufacturer; founded Deering reaper company.

Defauw, Désiré b Sept. 5, 1885, Ghent, Belgium; d July 25, 1960, Gary, IN. Conductor; music director of Chicago Symphony Orchestra (1943–1947) and Youth Symphony Orchestra (1954–1958).

DeGolyer, Robert b June 9, 1876, Chicago; d Oct. 11, 1952, Evanston, IL. Architect; designer of apartment buildings on the North Side.

Delano, Frederic A. b Sept. 10, 1863, Hong Kong, China; d Mar. 28, 1953, Washington, DC. Railroad executive; active in Commercial Club.

De Lee, Joseph Bolivar b Oct. 28, 1869, Cold Spring, NY; d Apr. 2, 1942, Chicago. Obstetrician; founded Chicago Lying-In Hospital and Dispensary (1895); faculty of Northwestern Univ. and Univ. of Chicago.

Dell, Floyd b June 28, 1887, Barry, IL; d July 23, 1969, Bethesda, MD. Novelist; editor; playwright; social critic; Chicago Literary Renaissance personality.

Dempsey, Jack [William Harrison Dempsey] b June 24, 1895, Manassa, CO; d May 31, 1983, New York, NY. World heavyweight boxing champion; lost to Gene Tunney in 1927 bout at Soldier Field.

Denny, Allen b ca. 1791. Founded village of Mokena; platted area of Rock Island in 1852.

Denny, Charles b Dec. 25, 1759, Dutchess County, NY; d Aug. 6, 1839, Will County, IL. Revolutionary war veteran buried in Will County.

DePriest, Oscar Stanton b Mar. 9, 1871, Florence, AL; d May 12, 1951, Chicago. Real-estate agent; alderman (1915–1917, 1943–1947); U.S. representative (1929–1935).

Derx, Jacob b June 26, 1869, Cincinnati, OH; d Dec. 1, 1937, Chicago. Printer; published the *Weekly Bulletin*.

Deschamps, Antoine active 1800s. Fur trader; agent of American Fur Co., early nineteenth century.

Dever, William Emmett b Mar. 13, 1862, Woburn, MA; d Sept. 3, 1929, Chicago. Lawyer; judge; alderman; mayor of Chicago (1923–1927).

DeVry, Herman A. b 1877, Mecklenburg, Germany; d 1941. Inventor; manufacturer of motion picture equipment; founded DeVry Institutes.

Deweese, Thomas b Nov. 29, 1798, Knox Co. KY; d Mar. 28, 1864. Platted land east of Fox River in 1837.

Dewes, John active 1830s. Owned farmlands in Golf beginning in 1832.

Dewey, Alice C. [Alice Chipman] b Sept. 7, 1858, Fenton, MI; d July 14, 1927, New York, NY. Educator; feminist; cofounded Univ. of Chicago Laboratory School.

Dewey, John b Oct. 20, 1859, Burlington, VT; d June 1, 1952, New York, NY. Philosopher; education reformer; professor at Univ. of Chicago.

DeWolf, Calvin b Feb. 18, 1815, Braintrim, PA; d Nov. 28, 1899, Chicago. Lawyer; abolitionist; Justice of the Peace; participant in Underground Railroad.

Dickerson, Carroll b 1895; d Oct. 1957, Chicago. Bandleader for Chicago jazz bands during 1920s.

Dickerson, Earl B. b June 22, 1891, Canton, MS; d Sept. 1, 1986, Chicago. Lawyer; alderman; activist for racial equality; argued restrictive covenants before U.S. Supreme Court.

Dickinson, Chester b ca. 1820, MA. Farmer; innkeeper; postmaster in Portage Park.

Dietrich, Henry S. b 1844; d July 1, 1909, Chicago. Real-estate developer; Civil War veteran; developed Mt. Forest subdivision near Willow Springs.

Dilg, Will H. b ca. 1869; d Mar. 27, 1927, Washington, DC. Advertising man; conservation activist; founder and president of Izaak Walton League.

Dillinger, John b June 22, 1903, Indianapolis, IN; d July 22, 1934, Chicago. Bank robber; prison escapee; shot to death by FBI at Biograph Theater.

Dillon, George Hill b Nov. 12, 1906, Jacksonville, FL; d May 9, 1968, Charleston, SC. Poet; editor of *Poetry* magazine (1937–1949); won Pulitzer Prize (1932).

Dingan, Patrick active 1880s. Undertaker.

Dinkins, Fitzhugh b Apr. 25, 1919, Houston, TX; d Mar. 12, 1993, Chicago. Graphic design artist; involved with South Side Community Art Center.

Dirksen, Everett McKinley b Jan. 4, 1896, Pekin, IL; d Sept. 7, 1969, Washington, DC. U.S. representative and senator from central Illinois.

Disney, Elias b Feb. 6, 1859, Ontario, Canada; d Sept. 13, 1941, North Hollywood, CA. Father of Walt Disney; manual laborer at 1893 World's Columbian Exposition.

Disney, Walter Elias b Dec. 5, 1901, Chicago; d Dec. 15, 1966, Burbank, CA. Animator; motion picture producer; founded Disneyland; studied at Art Institute of Chicago.

Diversey, Michael b Dec. 10, 1810, Germany; d Dec. 12, 1869, Chicago. Brewer; philanthropist; alderman (1844–45; 1856–1868); partner in Lill & Diversey; donated land for St. Michael's Church.

Dixon, Arthur b Mar. 27, 1837, Fermanagh, Ireland; d Oct. 26, 1917, Chicago. Businessman; alderman (1867–1875; 1879–1891).

Dixon, Willie b July 1, 1915, Vicksburg, MS; d Jan. 19, 1992, Burbank, CA. Blues musician and composer; recording artist for Chess Records; six-time Grammy nominee (won 1989).

Dobbins, T. R. active 1870s. Landowner; purchased land in Bensenville around 1870s.

Doblin, Jay b Dec. 10, 1920, New York, NY; d May 11, 1989, Chicago. Industrial designer; educator; director of Institute of Design; cofounded Unimark International Design Co.

Dodds, John M. b Apr. 12, 1892, New Orleans, LA; d Aug. 8, 1940, Chicago. Jazz clarinetist; alto saxophonist; member of King Oliver's Creole Jazz Band.

Dodds, Warren "Baby" b Dec. 24, 1898, New Orleans, LA; d Feb. 14, 1959, Chicago. Jazz drummer; performed with King Oliver's Creole Jazz Band.

Doggett, Kate Newell b Nov. 5, 1828, Castleton, VT; d Mar. 13, 1884, Cuba. Reformer; suffragist; founded the Fortnightly and Sorosis Clubs.

Dole, Charles S. b Nov. 2, 1818 or 1819, Bloomfield, MI; d Sept. 2, 1904, Kansas City, MO. Operated grain warehousing and elevator business.

Dole, George W. b Feb. 29, 1800, Troy, NY; d Apr. 13, 1860, Chicago. Postmaster; water commissioner; meatpacker; grocer.

Dolton, George b June 11, 1797, Baltimore, MD; d 1861. Operated a ferry in mid-1830s (with J. C. Matthews).

Donnelley, Richard Robert b Nov. 15, 1836 or 1837 or 1838, Hamilton, Ontario, Canada; d Apr. 8, 1899, Chicago. Printer; owned Lakeside Press and R. R. Donnelley & Sons; published *Chicago Directory* and *Chicago Blue Book*.

Donnelly, Michael active 1898–1916 (disappeared). Labor organizer; butcher; first president of Amalgamated Meat Cutters and Butcher Workmen.

Donoghue, John Talbott b 1853, Chicago; d July 1, 1903, Lake Whitney, CT. Artist; sculptor.

Dore, John C. b Mar. 22, 1822, Ossipee, NH; d Dec. 14, 1900, Boston, MA. First superintendent of Chicago Public Schools in 1854; president of Chicago Board of Education.

Dorsey, Thomas Andrew b July 1, 1899, Villa Rica, GA; d Jan. 23, 1993, Chicago. Gospel and blues writer; composer; coorganized first gospel choir in Chicago at Ebenezer Baptist Church.

Douglas, Elizabeth *See* **Memphis Minnie**

Douglas, Paul Howard b Mar. 26, 1892, Salem, MA; d Sept. 24, 1976, Washington, DC. Economist at Univ. of Chicago; alderman (1939–1942); U.S. senator (1949–1967).

Douglas, Stephen Arnold b Apr. 23, 1813, Brandon, VT; d June 3, 1861, Chicago. Lawyer; U.S. congressman (1843–1847); U.S. senator (1847–1861); presidential candidate; real-estate developer.

Dowie, John Alexander b May 25, 1847, Edinburgh, Scotland; d Mar. 9, 1907, Zion City, IL. Evangelist; organized Christian Catholic Apostolic Church; founded Zion.

Downer, Pierce b July 25, 1782, Plainfield, VT; d Mar. 26, 1863, Downers Grove, IL. Namesake of Downers Grove community.

Downer, Stephen Ellis b Sept. 28, 1809, Rutland, NY; d June 30, 1884, Harrisonville, MD. Brick mason; helped build Chicago's first lighthouse.

Downs, James C. b Oct. 18, 1905, Des Moines, IA; d Oct. 26, 1981, Naples, FL. Founded Real Estate Research Corp.; Chicago housing coordinator (1952–1956).

Dowst, Charles O. b July 23, 1853, Waukegan, IL; d May 22, 1919, Evanston, IL. Editor; publisher; founded Tootsietoys.

Drake, St. Clair, Jr. sb Jan. 2, 1911, Suffolk, VA; d June 15, 1990, Palo Alto, CA. Anthropologist; coauthor of *Black Metropolis* (1945); faculty at Roosevelt Univ.

Dreier, Emil b 1832, Viborg, Denmark; d 1892, Viborg. Danish consul; druggist.

Dreiser, Theodore Herman b Aug. 27, 1871, Terre Haute, IN; d Dec. 8, 1945, Hollywood, CA. Writer (*Sister Carrie*, 1900; *The Song of the Lark*, 1915).

Driscoll, John "Paddy" b Jan. 11, 1895, Evanston, IL; d June 29, 1968, Chicago. Bears football player (1920s); coach (1956–1957).

Druggan, George b ca. 1902; d Nov. 10, 1943, Oak Park, IL. Beer baron; brother of mobster Terry Druggan.

Druggan, Terry b ca. 1903, Chicago; d Mar. 4, 1954, Chicago. Prohibition-era gangster and beer baron.

Drummond, Thomas J. b Oct. 16, 1809, Bristol Mills, ME; d May 15, 1890, Wheaton, IL. Federal district and appeals court judge; state legislator; decided 1860 fugitive slave law case.

Drummond, William E. b Mar. 28, 1876, Newark, NJ; d Sept. 13, 1948, Chicago. Architect; associated with Prairie School.

Dryer, Emma b Jan. 28, 1835, West Stockbridge, MA; d Apr. 16, 1925, Wheaton, IL. Religious educator; helped establish Moody Bible Institute.

Dubuis, Oscar F. b June 1848 or 1849, Givrins, Vaud, Switzerland; d Apr. 1906. Landscape architect; civil engineer; superintendent of West Chicago Park System.

Ducat, Arthur C. b Feb. 24, 1830, Dublin, Ireland; d Jan. 29, 1896, Downers Grove, IL. Civil engineer; U.S. Army inspector general during Civil War; reorganized Illinois state militia.

Ducoigne, Jean Baptiste active late eighteenth, early nineteenth century. Chief of Kaskaskia Indians.

Dudley, Frank Virgil b Nov. 14, 1868, Delavan, WI; d Mar. 5, 1957, Chicago. Painter, especially of landscapes.

Dudley, Oscar L. b Aug. 2, 1844, North Troy, VT; d May 3, 1918, Bangor, MI. Educator; active in Illinois Humane Society; founded Glenwood School.

Dudzik, Josephine (Sister Theresa) [Sister Theresa Dudzik] b Aug. 30, 1860, Plocicz, Poland; d Sept. 20, 1918, Chicago. Founded religious order of Franciscan Sisters of Blessed Kunegunda in Chicago (1894).

Duggan, James b May 22, 1825, Maynooth, Ireland; d Mar. 27, 1899, St. Louis, MO. Roman Catholic Bishop of Chicago (1859–1870).

Dukes, James b 1924 or 1925; d Aug. 24, 1962, Chicago. Convicted murderer; last man executed in Cook County jail.

Duncan, Hugh Dalziel b Oct. 6, 1909, Bo'ness, Scotland; d Aug. 8, 1970, Harvey, IL. Writer; sociologist.

Dunham, Mark Wentworth b June 22, 1842, St. Charles Township, IL; d Feb. 11, 1899, Chicago. Importer and breeder of Percheron horses; built "Dunham Castle."

Dunham, Solomon b 1791 or 1794, Saratoga County, NY; d Apr. 2, 1865. County commissioner and assessor in Kane County.

Dunklee, Hezekiah b Feb. 14, 1793, Hillsboro, NH; d July 25, 1852. Arrived in Chicago in 1833; made a claim (with George Mason) on land called Dunklee's Grove.

Dunne, Charlotte b Oct. 15, 1872, Chicago; d Oct. 23, 1962, Chicago. Youngest sister of Finley Peter Dunne.

Dunne, Dennis b Feb. 24, 1824, Queen's County, Ireland; d Dec. 23, 1868, Chicago. Pastor at St. Patrick's Church; brought Society of St. Vincent de Paul to Chicago; vicar general of Chicago Archdiocese.

Dunne, Edward Fitzsimmons b Oct. 12, 1853, Waterville, CT; d May 24, 1937, Chicago. Lawyer; circuit court judge; mayor of Chicago (1905–1907); Illinois governor.

Dunne, Finley Peter b July 10, 1867, Chicago; d Apr. 24, 1936, New York, NY. Journalist; created "Mr. Dooley" character.

Dunne, Katherine b Oct. 8, 1859, Chicago; d May 16, 1928, Chicago. Teacher; sister of Finley Peter Dunne.

Dunne, Mary b Aug. 28, 1863, Chicago; d Jan. 2, 1929, Chicago. Teacher; sister of Finley Peter Dunne.

Dunning, Andrew b Aug. 23, 1839, Chicago. Farmer; engaged in real-estate and nursery business; laid out the village of Dunning.

Dunning, Daniel S. active 1830s. Bought and sold land in Wood Dale around 1836.

Dunton, Asa b Oct. 29, 1788, Dorset, VT; d Feb. 1, 1870, Arlington Heights, IL. Stonecutter; founded Dunton, predecessor of Arlington Heights.

Durocher, Leo Ernest b July 27, 1905, West Springfield, MA; d Oct. 7, 1991, Palm Springs, CA. Baseball player; manager; managed Chicago Cubs (1966–1972).

DuSable, Catherine active late eighteenth century. Interpreter (Illiniwek); wife of Jean Baptiste Point DuSable.

DuSable, Jean Baptiste Point b ca. 1745, San Marc, Haiti; d Aug. 28, 1818, St. Charles, MO. Merchant; trader; farmer; considered Chicago's first permanent settler.

Dyer, Charles Volney b June 12, 1808, Clarendon, VT; d Apr. 24, 1878, Lake View, IL. Physician; abolitionist; Underground Railroad activist.

Dyett, Walter Henri b Jan. 11, 1901, St. Joseph, MO; d Nov. 17, 1969, Chicago. Music teacher; arranger; conductor.

Dyhrenfurth, Julius b Apr. 9, 1814, Breslau, Silesia, Prussia. Musician; conductor; conducted Philharmonic Society.

E

Earle, Frederick Hobart b Aug. 22, 1820, Falmouth, Cornwall, England; d 1894, Falmouth, Cornwall, England. Namesake of Hobart, IN.

Earle, George b Feb. 5, 1807, Falmouth, Cornwall, England; d Jan. 22, 1876, Philadelphia, PA. Founded Hobart; landowner in Lake County, IN.

Earle, Lawrence C. b Nov. 11, 1845, New York, NY; d Nov. 20, 1921, Grand Rapids, MI. Artist; muralist; painter.

Earling, Albert J. b Jan. 19, 1848, Richfield, WI; d Nov. 10, 1925, Milwaukee, WI. President of Chicago, Milwaukee & St. Paul Railway.

Easley, Ralph Montgomery b Feb. 25, 1856, Browning, IL; d Sept. 7, 1939, Rye, NY. Journalist; cofounded Civic Federation of Chicago; founded National Civic Federation.

Easterly, George active mid-nineteenth century. Manufacturer; produced agricultural machinery.

Eckerstrom, Ralph E. b Dec. 5, 1921; d Sept. 15, 1996, La Grange, IL. Graphic designer; cofounder and president of Unimark International.

Eckstein, Louis b Feb. 10, 1865, Milwaukee, WI; d Nov. 21, 1935, Chicago. Businessman; sponsored Ravinia opera for over 20 years.

Eddy, Arthur Jerome b Nov. 5, 1859, Flint, MI; d July 21, 1920, New York, NY. Lawyer; art patron.

Eddy, Clarence b June 23, 1851, Greenfield, MA; d Jan. 10, 1937, Winnetka, IL. Organist (at dedication of Auditorium Theater); author.

Edgar, William H. active late nineteenth century. Chemist; founded Dearborn Chemical Co. 1888.

Egan, James J. b 1839 or 1841, Cork, Ireland; d Dec. 2, 1914, Chicago. Architect; designed many public buildings and churches after the fire of 1871.

Egan, John J. b Oct. 9, 1916; d May 19, 2001, Chicago. Monsignor; civil rights activist; namesake of Egan Center at DePaul Univ.

Egan, William B. b Sept. 28, 1808, Killarney, Ireland; d Oct. 27, 1860, Chicago. Physician; real-estate developer; state legislator (1841–1842); recorder of city and county.

Eggleston, Edward b Dec. 10, 1837, Vevay, IN; d Sept. 3, 1902, Lake George, NY. Historian; editor; novelist *(The Hoosier School-Master)*.

Eggleston, Ezra Carpenter b NY; active 1870s. Real-estate agent; built four-block residential subdivision in Mount Prospect in 1871.

Ela, George b 1805, Lebanon, NH; d 1882, Barrington, IL. Postmaster; state legislator; namesake of Ela Township.

Elfrink, Barney b 1807; d 1879. Landowner in Deer Grove in 1850s.

Ellington, Duke b Apr. 29, 1889, Washington, DC; d May 24, 1974, New York, NY. Jazz pianist; composer; bandleader; played at the Oriental Theatre and Blue Note.

Elliott, John H. b July 17, 1810 or 1816, Sussex, England; d Apr. 25, 1881, buried Hillside Cemetery, Antioch, IL. Built steam gristmill in Antioch in 1856.

Elliott, William T. b June 10 or 11, 1811, Killingworth, CT; d May 1894? Blacksmith; moved to Montgomery ca. 1834.

Ellis, Hilliard b Jan. 6 or 27, 1915, St. Matthews, GA; d July 22, 1989, Savannah, GA. Labor official; United Automobile Workers official in 1940s.

Ellis, Samuel active 1850s. Early landowner; sold land to industrialist Charles Cleaver.

Ellsworth, James W. b Oct. 13, 1849, Hudson, OH; d June 3, 1925, Florence, Italy. Book and art collector; an organizer of World's Columbian Exposition.

Elmslie, George Grant b Feb. 20, 1871, Aberdeenshire, Scotland; d Apr. 23, 1952, Chicago. Architect; associated with Prairie School; apprenticed with Louis Sullivan.

Elston, Daniel active mid-nineteenth century. Merchant; brickyard owner; school inspector.

Elston, Isaac C. b Oct. 4, 1794, Elizabethtown, NJ; d Oct. 24, 1867, Crawfordville, IN. Real-estate speculator; bought land in Michigan City in 1831.

Ely, Richard Theodore b Apr. 13, 1854, Ripley, NY; d Oct. 4, 1943, Old Lyme, CT. Economist; reformer; faculty at Northwestern Univ.

Embree, Edwin R. b July 31, 1883, Osceola, NE; d Feb. 21, 1950, New York, NY. Sociologist; chairman of the Mayor's Commission on Race Relations; president of Julius Rosenwald Fund.

Emery, Henry active mid-nineteenth century. Publisher; merged *Prairie Farmer* with his *Emery's Journal of Agriculture*.

Engel, George b Apr. 15, 1836, Cassel, Germany; d Nov. 11, 1887, Chicago. Anarchist; convicted in Haymarket Square riot; executed.

Epstein, Abraham b Dec. 24, 1887, Kiev, Russia; d Dec. 7, 1958, Chicago. Engineer; architect; designed International Amphitheatre.

Epstein, Max b Feb. 6, 1875, Eisenach, Germany; d Aug. 21 or 22, 1954, Winnetka, IL. Business executive; art patron; manufactured and rented railroad tank cars.

Epton, Bernard Edward b Aug. 25, 1921, Chicago; d Dec. 13, 1987, Ann Arbor, MI. State legislator; Republican opponent of Harold Washington in 1983 mayoral race.

Erbstein, Charles b Nov. 18, 1876, Cleveland, OH; d May 27, 1927, Chicago. Lawyer; radio broadcaster; real-estate developer; owned Villa Olivia in Bartlett.

Evans, Charles "Chick," Jr. b July 18, 1890, Indianapolis, IN; d Nov. 6, 1979, Chicago. Amateur golf champion; won both U.S. Open and Amateur in 1916.

Evans, Hannah Simpson b 1861, England; d 1931. Salvation Army captain; helped found Salvation Army in Chicago, 1885.

Evans, John b Mar. 9, 1814, Waynesville, OH; d July 3, 1897, Denver, CO. Physician; businessman; alderman (1852); cofounded Chicago's first hospital; founded Northwestern Univ.

Evans, Samuel J. "Sam" b May 25, 1911; d Feb. 14, 1971, Chicago. Radio personality; hosted rhythm and blues show on WVON radio.

Evans, William b Sept. 21, 1859, Penarth, Wales. Salvation Army Captain; started Salvation Army's first Chicago station.

Everett, David active 1830s. Landowner in River Grove in early 1830s; purchased portion of LaFramboise reserve.

Evers, John Joseph "Johnny" b July 21, 1881, Troy, NY; d Mar. 28, 1947, Albany, NY. Baseball player in Hall of Fame; played second base for Cubs and White Sox.

F

Fabyan, George b Mar. 15, 1867, Boston, MA; d May 17, 1936, Geneva, IL. Dry-goods merchant; scientist; established Geneva's first research and development facility.

Fabyan, Nelle Wright b Nov. 19, 1872, Marinette, WI; d July 22, 1939, Chicago. Geneva estate later housed the Riverbank Laboratories.

Falk, Harry active 1930s. Businessman; involved with startup of Baxter International.

Falk, Ralph b Aug. 6, 1884, Boise, ID; d Nov. 2, 1960, Chicago. Surgeon; board chairman of Baxter Laboratories.

Farley, Chris b Feb. 15, 1964, Madison, WI; d Dec. 18, 1997, Chicago. Improv comedian; actor; performed with Second City and Saturday Night Live.

Farmer, James b Jan. 12, 1920, Marshall, TX; d July 9, 1999, Fredericksburg, VA. Civil rights leader; founded Congress of Racial Equality (1942); received Presidential Medal of Freedom (1998).

Farnam, Henry b Nov. 9, 1803, Scipio, NY; d Oct. 4, 1883, New Haven, CT. Railroad builder; philanthropist; built Chicago & Rock Island Railroad.

Farr, Newton C. b Dec. 25, 1887, Chicago; d Nov. 8, 1967, Chicago. Real-estate executive; pioneer in concept of urban renewal; oversaw Hyde Park urban renewal.

Farrell, James Thomas b Feb. 27, 1904, Chicago; d Aug. 22, 1979, New York, NY. Writer; novelist (*Studs Lonigan*).

Farwell, Charles Benjamin b July 1, 1823, Painted Post, NY; d Sept. 23, 1903, Lake Forest, IL. Early merchant; clerk of Cook County and Cook County Board of Supervisors; U.S. representative and senator.

Fassett, Samuel Montague b 1825, Chicago; d Aug. 2, 1910, Washington, DC. Cabinet card photographer (1855–1860).

Fauntz, Jane [Jane Fauntz Manske] b Dec. 19, 1910, New Orleans, LA; d May 30, 1989. Olympic swimmer; won 1928 Olympic bronze medal.

Fay, C. Norman b Aug. 13, 1848, Burlington, VT; d Apr. 7, 1944, Cambridge, MA. Utilities executive; author; classical music patron.

Feehan, Patrick Augustine b Aug. 29, 1829, Killenaule, Ireland; d July 12, 1902, Chicago. Roman Catholic archbishop of Chicago (1880–1902).

Feldman, Eugene Pieter b Sept. 14, 1915, Sheboygan, WI; d Nov. 28, 1987, Montgomery, AL. Museum administrator; helped establish DuSable Museum.

Felsenthal, Bernhard b Jan. 2, 1822, Munchweiler, Bavaria; d Jan. 12, 1908, Chicago. Jewish theologian; rabbi; writer; founded Zion congregation on Chicago's West Side.

Fenger, Christian b Nov. 3, 1840, Copenhagen, Denmark; d Mar. 7, 1902, Chicago. Surgeon; medical educator.

Ferber, Edna Jessica b Aug. 15, 1885, Kalamazoo, MI; d Apr. 16, 1968, New York, NY. Novelist; playwright; short story writer; Pulitzer Prize (1924) for *So Big*.

Fergus, Robert b Aug. 14, 1815, Glasgow, Scotland; d June 23, 1897, Evanston, IL. Early printer in Chicago; local historian; published Fergus Historical Series.

Ferguson, Benjamin Franklin b 1837 or 1839, Columbus, PA; d Apr. 11, 1905, Chicago. Early lumber dealer; endowed Ferguson Fund to construct statues and fountains in parks.

Fermi, Enrico b Sept. 29, 1901, Rome, Italy; d Nov. 28, 1954, Chicago. Physicist; coarchitect of the Manhattan Project at Univ. of Chicago; won Nobel Prize in Physics (1938).

Ferris, George Washington Gale b Feb. 14, 1859, Galesburg, IL; d Nov. 22, 1896, Pittsburgh, PA. Civil engineer; invented the Ferris Wheel for 1893 World's Columbian Exposition.

Ferris, William b Feb. 26, 1937, Chicago; d May 16, 2000, Chicago. Composer; conductor; founder and director of William Ferris Chorale.

Field, Marshall, III b Sept. 28, 1893, Chicago; d Nov. 8, 1956, New York, NY. Investor; newspaper publisher; philanthropist.

Field, Eugene b Sept. 2, 1850, St. Louis, MO; d Nov. 4, 1895, Chicago. Journalist; poet; humorist; *Chicago Daily News* columnist.

Field, Marshall b Aug. 18, 1834, Conway, MA; d Jan. 16, 1906, New York, NY. Merchant; founded Marshall Field's department store.

Fielden, Samuel b Feb. 25, 1847, Todmorden, Lancashire, England; d Feb. 7, 1922, La Veta, CO. Anarchist; convicted in Haymarket Square riot; pardoned by Governor John P. Altgeld.

Filkins, Joseph b July 4, 1806, Berne, NY; d Nov. 12, 1857, Chicago. Hardware dealers; Wheeling Township supervisor; operated stagecoach stop and hotel.

Finerty, John Frederick b Sept. 10, 1846, Galway, Ireland; d June 10, 1908, Chicago. Journalist; U.S. congressman (1883–1885); established the Irish newspaper *Chicago Citizen* (1882).

Finkelman, Max Y. b Apr. 4, 1900; d Jan. 4, 1983, Chicago. Diamond merchant; founded wholesale jewelry firm in Jeweler's Row.

Fischer, Adolph b ca. 1857, Bremen, Germany; d Nov. 11, 1887, Chicago. Anarchist; convicted in Haymarket Square riot; executed.

Fish, Elisha b ca. 1785; d ca. 1852. Arrived in Elmhurst in 1834.

Fishbein, Morris b July 22, 1889, St. Louis, MO; d Sept. 27, 1976, Chicago. Physician; writer; editor of *Journal of the American Medical Association*.

Fisher, Elijah John b Aug. 2, 1858, LaGrange, GA; d July 31, 1915, Chicago. Minister at Olivet Baptist Church (1902–1915).

Fitzpatrick, John b Apr. 21, 1870, Athlone, Ireland; d Sept. 27, 1946, Chicago. Labor leader; president of Chicago Federation of Labor; organized Stockyards Labor Council.

Florsheim, Harold Milton b June 20, 1899, Chicago; d Jan. 30, 1987, Palm Springs, CA. Shoe manufacturer; established Harham Farms in Mettawa in early 1930s.

Flower, Lucy Louisa Coues b May 10, 1837, Boston, MA; d Apr. 27, 1921, CA. Social reformer; president of Chicago Woman's Club (1890); worked to establish Cook County Juvenile Court.

Flower, Walter L. active 1860s. Created first landownership map of Cook County in 1861.

Flynn, Elizabeth Gurley b Aug. 7, 1890, Concord, NH; d Sept. 5, 1964, Soviet Union. Labor organizer; radical.

Foley, Edna L. b Dec. 17, 1878, Hartford, CT; d Aug. 4, 1973, New York, NY. Head of Chicago Visiting Nurse Association.

Foley, Thomas b Mar. 6, 1822, Baltimore, MD; d Feb. 19, 1879, Chicago. Roman Catholic coadjutor bishop and administrator of Chicago (1870–1879).

Forbes, John Murray b Feb. 23, 1813, Bordeaux, France; d Oct. 12, 1898, Milton, MA. Merchant; financier; railroad developer; organized Chicago, Burlington & Quincy Railroad.

Ford, Orrin b ca. 1802; d July 3, 1869. Arrived in Rolling Meadows ca. 1836.

Foresman, Hugh Austin b July 8, 1867, Easton, PA; d Jan. 13, 1960, Winnetka, IL. Publisher; chairman of Scott, Foresman & Co. textbook publishing company.

Forgan, James B. b Apr. 11, 1852, St. Andrews, Scotland; d Oct. 28, 1924, Chicago. Banker; president of First National Bank; helped form Federal Reserve.

Forrest, Leon Richard b Jan. 8, 1937, Chicago; d Nov. 6, 1997, Chicago. Writer; novelist; editor; chair of African American Studies at Northwestern Univ.

Forsyth(e), Jessie P. b Feb. 12, 1859; d Apr. 1, 1909, Chicago. Founded Jessie P. Forsythe rest home (renamed Chicago-Winfield Tuberculosis Sanatorium).

Fortmann, Danny b Apr. 11, 1916, Pearl River, NY; d May 23, 1995, Los Angeles, CA. Football player; guard for Chicago Bears (1936–1943); team physician for Los Angeles Rams.

Fosse, Bob (Robert Louis) b June 23, 1927, Chicago; d Sept. 23, 1987, Washington, DC. Choreographer; musical director; filmmaker.

Foster, Andrew "Rube" b Sept. 17, 1879, Calvert, TX; d Dec. 9, 1930, Kankakee, IL. Baseball pitcher; owned and managed Chicago American Giants; established Negro National League.

Foster, William D. b 1884; d ca. 1962, Los Angeles, CA. Early film producer; started Foster Photoplay Co.

Foster, William Z. b Feb. 25, 1881, Taunton, MA; d Sept. 1, 1961, Moscow, Soviet Union. Labor organizer; cofounder and secretary of Stockyards Labor Council; led 1919 steel strike; national chairman, Communist Party.

Fox, Carol b June 15, 1926, Chicago; d July 21, 1981, Chicago. Cofounded Lyric Opera; general manager for 26 years.

Fox, Nellie [Jacob Nelson Fox] b Dec. 25, 1927, St. Thomas, PA; d Dec. 1, 1975, Baltimore, MD. Baseball player for White Sox; Hall of Fame.

Fox, Philip b Mar. 7, 1878, Manhattan, KS; d July 21, 1944, Boston, MA. Astronomer; Univ. of Chicago and Northwestern Univ. faculty; first director of Adler Planetarium (1929–1937).

Franck, James b Aug. 26, 1882, Hamburg, Germany; d May 21, 1964, Gottingen, Germany. Physicist; Univ. of Chicago faculty; directed Manhattan Project; won 1925 Nobel Prize in Physics.

Franklin, Lesser b ca. 1852, Germany; d Apr. 19, 1910, Chicago. Real-estate developer; founded Franklin Park and other suburbs.

Franks, Robert (Bobby) E. b Sept. 19, 1909, Chicago; d May 21, 1924, Chicago. Murder victim; murdered by Leopold and Loeb.

Frazier, Edward Franklin b Sept. 24, 1894, Baltimore, MD; d May 17, 1962, Washington, DC. Sociologist; wrote *The Negro Family in Chicago* (1932); and *Black Bourgeoisie* (1957).

Frederick, John T. b Feb. 1, 1893, Corning, IA; d Jan. 1975. Writer; editor; journalism professor at Northwestern Univ.; founded and edited the *Midland*.

Freeman, Allen B. active 1830s. Clergyman; sent to Chicago by American Baptist Home Mission Society in 1833.

Freeman, Lawrence "Bud" b Apr. 13, 1906, Chicago; d Mar. 15, 1991, Chicago. Jazz tenor saxophonist; played a mix of Dixieland jazz and swing that became known as Chicago jazz.

Freer, Lemuel Covell Paine b Sept. 18, 1813, North East, NY; d Apr. 14, 1892, Chicago. Attorney; abolitionist; Underground Railroad activist.

French, Daniel Chester b Apr. 20, 1850, Exeter, NH; d Oct. 7, 1931, Stockbridge, MA. Sculptor; designed statue *The Republic* for 1893 World's Columbian Exposition.

French, William M. R. b Oct. 1, 1843, Exeter, NH; d June 3, 1914, Chicago. Civil engineer; landscape architect; director of the Art Institute of Chicago for 35 years.

Friberg, Conrad [Conrad O. Nelson] b May 9, 1896, IL; d Sept. 2, 1989, Alameda County, CA. Filmmaker; made documentary labor films in the 1930s.

Friedman, Esther *See* **Landers, Ann**

Fritz, Art b Oct. 18, 1898; d Mar. 16, 1967. Founded Kiddieland in Melrose Park in 1929.

Fromm, Paul b Sept. 28, 1906, Kitzingen, Germany; d July 4, 1987, Chicago. Wine merchant; music philanthropist.

Frost, Albert Carl b Mar. 20, 1865, Berend, Germany; d July 25, 1941, AK. Banker; railroad official; founded Ravinia Music Festival (1904).

Frost, Charles Sumner b May 31, 1956, Lewiston, ME; d Dec. 11, 1931, Lake Forest, IL. Architect; erected railway stations; designed Navy Pier and Potter Palmer residence on Lake Shore Drive.

Fry, George Arthur b Oct. 20, 1901, Swayzee, IN; d Sept. 29, 1973, Wilmette, IL. Management consultant; founder and chairman of George A. Fry.

Frye, Theodore Roosevelt b Sept. 10, 1899; d Aug. 26, 1963, Chicago. Gospel pianist; composer; co-organized with Thomas A. Dorsey the first gospel choir in Chicago at Ebenezer Baptist Church.

Fuller, Benjamin b 1812, Broome County, NY; d 1868. Platted the town of Fullersburg, which became part of Hinsdale.

Fuller, George A. b Oct. 21, 1851, Templeton, Worcester, MA; d Dec. 14, 1900, Mamaroneck-on-Sound, NY. Pioneer of modern steel skeleton building; president, George A. Fuller Co.

Fuller, Henry Blake b Jan. 9, 1857, Chicago; d July 28, 1929, Chicago. Novelist; newspaper editorial writer; wrote *Cliff Dwellers* (1893).

Fuller, Hoyt William b 1923 or 1927, Atlanta, GA; d May 11, 1981, Fulton County, GA. Writer; literary critic; managing editor of *Negro Digest*; founding member of Organization of Black American Culture.

Fuller, Margaret b May 23, 1810, Cambridgeport, MA; d July 19, 1850, off Fire Island, NY. Author; feminist; wrote *Summer on the Lakes*.

Fuller, Melville Weston b Feb. 11, 1833, Augusta, ME; d July 4, 1910, Sorrento, ME. Lawyer; state legislator (1863–1865); chief justice of U.S. Supreme Court (1888–1910); namesake of Fuller Park.

Fuller, R. Buckminster b July 12, 1895, Milton, MA; d July 1, 1983, Los Angeles, CA. Architect; designed geodesic dome; faculty member, Institute of Design.

Fuller, Samuel B. b June 4, 1905, Ouachita, LA; d Oct. 24, 1988, Blue Island, IL. Entrepreneur; founder and president of Fuller Products Co.

Fullerton, Hugh S. b Sept. 10, 1873, Hillsboro, OH; d Dec. 27, 1945, Dunedin, FL. Baseball journalist for several Chicago newspapers; broke "Black Sox" scandal of 1919.

Fulmer, Harriet b ca. 1877, Fulmerville, PA; d Nov. 27, 1952, Chicago. Nurse; leader in public health programs.

Fulton, John b 1813, Belfast, Ireland; d Mar. 7, 1883, Bremen Township, IL. Early landowner in Bremen Township.

G

Gage, Darius Benjamin b July 29, 1801, Onondaga County, NY; d Mar. 8, 1875 or 1877, IL. Filed early land claims along Sequoit Creek in Antioch.

Gage, David A. active 1830s. Landowner along Des Plaines River; treasurer of city of Chicago.

Gage, George W. active late nineteenth century. Landowner; namesake of Gage Park.

Gage, Lyman Judson b June 28, 1836, De Ruyter, NY; d Jan. 26, 1927, Point Loma, CA. Banker; financier; U.S. secretary of the treasury (1897–1902); president of First National Bank of Chicago.

Gage, Matilda Joslyn b Mar. 24, 1826, Cicero, NY; d Mar. 18, 1898, Chicago. Suffragist; writer; editor; founding member of National Woman Suffrage Association.

Gage, Thomas Q. b 1809, Ontongon, MI; d May 18, 1881. Arrived in Antioch in 1837.

Galvin, Paul V. b June 29, 1895, Harvard, IL; d Nov. 5, 1959, Evanston, IL. Founded Galvin Manufacturing Co. (now Motorola); pioneered the car radio.

Gandil, "Chick" b Jan. 19, 1888; d Dec. 13, 1970, Calistoga, CA. Baseball player; 3rd baseman, Chicago White Sox; involved in "Black Sox" scandal; banned from baseball for life.

Ganz, Rudolph b Feb. 24, 1877, Zurich, Switzerland; d Aug. 2, 1972, Chicago. Pianist; conductor; president of Chicago Musical College (1933–1954).

García-Camilo, Ramón b Aug. 9, 1918, La Vega, Dominican Republic; d Feb. 18, 1997, Park Ridge, IL. Physician; founded Camilo Medical Center and Washington National Bank; Dominican Republic's consul general in Chicago.

Garden, Hugh M. G. b July 9, 1873, Toronto, Canada; d Oct. 6, 1961, Chicago. Architect; designed Montgomery Ward warehouse; senior partner in Schmidt, Garden & Erikson.

Garden, Mary b Feb. 20, 1874, Aberdeen, Scotland; d Jan. 3, 1967, Aberdeen, Scotland. Operatic soprano; Chicago Grand Opera (1910–1930).

Gardiner, Alexander b Jan. 31, 1812, Dundee, Scotland; d June 5, 1875, Woodstock, IL. Named town of Dundee for his Scottish hometown.

Gardner, Helen b Mar. 17, 1878, Manchester, NH; d June 4, 1946, Chicago. Art historian; author; faculty of Art Institute of Chicago and Univ. of Chicago.

Gardner, Joseph C. b June 10, 1821, Chautauqua, NY; d Oct. 29, 1906. Banker; established Valparaiso Savings Bank and Chesterton Bank.

Garland, (Hannibal) Hamlin b Sept. 14, 1860, West Salem, WI; d Mar. 4, 1940, Los Angeles, CA. Writer; novelist; essayist; won Pulitzer Prize (1922) for *A Daughter of the Middle Border*.

Garrett, Augustus b 1801, New York, NY; d Nov. 30, 1848, Chicago. Early landowner; alderman (1840–1843); mayor of Chicago (1843–1846).

Garroway, David Cunningham b July 13, 1913, Schenectady, NY; d July 21, 1982, Swarthmore, PA. Radio personality; television broadcaster; telecast "Garroway at Large" from NBC Chicago (1940s–early 1950s).

Gary, Charles Wesley b Nov. 1, 1801, Pomfret or Putnam, CT; d Aug. 31, 1871, Gary's Mill, IL. DuPage County justice; founded Warrenville Methodist Church; family founded Gary's Mill.

Gary, Elbert Henry b Oct. 8, 1846, Wheaton, IL; d Aug. 15, 1927, New York, NY. Lawyer; first mayor of Wheaton; founded U.S. Steel Corp. and Gary, IN.

Gary, Erastus b Apr. 5, 1806, Pomfret, CT; d May 7, 1888, Wheaton, IL. Staked first land claim in Winfield Township, 1831; cofounded Gary's Mill; helped establish Wheaton College.

Gary, Joseph Easton b July 9, 1821, Potsdam, NY; d 1906. Judge, Superior Court of Cook County; presided over in Haymarket anarchists' trial.

Gary, Jude Perrin b Feb. 3, 1811, Pomfret, CT; d May 11, 1881, Warrenville, IL. Early settler of Winfield Township and DuPage County.

Gates, Simon S. b Oct. 1, 1799, Stockbridge, VT; d June 24, 1878 or 1879, Crystal Lake, IL. Landowner; platted village of Nunda (later North Central Lake).

Gaudette, Thomas (Tom) A. b Mar. 22, 1923; d Sept. 19, 1998, Chicago. Community organizer; trained by Saul Alinsky; founded mid-American Center and Northwest Community Organization.

Gautreaux, Dorothy b 1927; d 1968. Civil rights activist; plaintiff in Chicago Housing Authority segregation suit.

Gay, Edwin b ca. 1861, England. Brigadier in Salvation Army; helped found Salvation Army in Chicago (1885).

Gelert, Johannes Sophus b Dec. 10, 1852, Nybel, Denmark; d Nov. 4, 1923. Sculptor; designed Haymarket monument (Chicago) and statue of General Grant (Galena, IL).

Gerber, Henry [Joseph Henry Dittmar] b June 29, 1892, Bavaria, Germany; d Dec. 31, 1972, Washington, DC. Gay rights activist; founded Society for Human Rights.

Gerhardt, Paul, Jr. b Jan. 23, 1899, Chicago; d Oct. 11, 1966, Chicago. City architect (1928–1966); designed Chicago Free Academy and South District Filtration Plant.

Germano, Joseph S. b Feb. 12, 1904, Chicago; d Jan. 2, 1992, Honolulu, HI. Labor organizer; district director, United Steel Workers of America (1940–1973).

Gerstenberg, Alice b Aug. 2, 1885, Chicago; d July 28, 1972, Minneapolis, MN. Playwright; novelist; associated with Chicago Literary Renaissance.

Gherkin, Henry b Prussia; active 1830s. Gravedigger; one of the first gravediggers in Chicago.

Giancana, Sam b May 24, 1908, Chicago; d June 19, 1975, Oak Park, IL. Crime syndicate boss; ruled Chicago Mafia in 1950s and 1960s.

Gillespie, Frank L. b Nov. 8, 1876, Osceola, AR; d May 1, 1925, Chicago. Founded Supreme Liberty Life Insurance Co.

Gilmore, Patrick b Dec. 25, 1829, Ballygar, Ireland; d Sept. 24, 1882, St. Louis, MO. Band leader; 1873 Chicago Jubilee.

Gingrich, Arnold b Dec. 5, 1903, Grand Rapids, MI; d July 9, 1976, Ridgewood, NJ. Editor; cofounded *Esquire* magazine.

Givins, Robert C. b 1845, Yorkville, Canada; d Apr. 14, 1915, San Francisco, CA. Real-estate developer; novelist; charter member and vice president of Chicago Real Estate Board.

Glackin, Edward J. b May 9, 1867, Montreal, Canada; d June 15, 1939, Chicago. State senator (1904–1926); sponsored early zoning law (1919).

Gleason, Frederick Grant b Dec. 18, 1848, Middletown, CT; d Dec. 6, 1903, Chicago. Musician; composer; music editor of *Chicago Tribune*.

Glessner, John J. b Jan. 26, 1843, Zanesville, OH; d Jan. 20, 1936, Chicago. Industrialist; cofounded International Harvester Co.

Gnesin, Maurice b Nov. 16, 1896, Odessa, Russia; d Feb. 26, 1957. Play producer; theater director; head of Goodman School of Drama.

Godie, Lee b 1908; d Mar. 2, 1994, Chicago. Folk artist; painter; homeless collage artist.

Goggin, Catharine b 1855, Adirondack, NY; d Jan. 4, 1916, Chicago. Teacher; labor leader; cofounded Chicago Teachers Federation.

Goins, Irene [Irene V. Sappington] b Dec. 18, 1876, Moberly, MO Or Quincy, IL; d Mar. 12, 1929, Chicago. Clubwoman; suffragist; labor activist; president of Federation of Colored Women's Clubs.

Goldberg, Arthur Joseph b Aug. 8, 1908, Chicago; d Jan. 19, 1990, Washington, DC. Lawyer; diplomat; U.S. secretary of labor; U.S. Supreme Court justice.

Goldberg, Bertrand b July 17, 1913, Chicago; d Oct. 8, 1997, Chicago. Architect; student of Ludwig Mies van der Rohe; designed Marina City.

Goldman, Emma b June 27, 1869, Kovno, Lithuania; d May 14, 1940, Toronto, Canada. Anarchist; editor; lecturer; free-speech advocate; buried next to Haymarket Martyrs in Waldheim Cemetery.

Goldman, Solomon b Aug. 19, 1893, Volhynia, Russia; d May 14, 1953, Chicago. Conservative rabbi; led Anshe Emet Congregation (1929 to 1953).

Goldsholl, Morton b Dec. 21, 1911; d Feb. 27, 1995. Graphic designer; created packaging and corporate symbols.

Goldsmith, Charles W. active late nineteenth century. Agent of American Lithographics Co. of NY in Chicago; produced picture postcards for 1893 World's Columbian Exposition.

Goldsmith, Myron b Sept. 15, 1918, Chicago; d July 15, 1996, Wilmette, IL. Architect; engineer; student of Ludwig Mies van der Rohe; professor of architecture at Illinois Institute of Technology; designed Hancock Center.

Goode, George Brown b Feb. 13, 1851, Albany, IN; d Sept. 6, 1896, Washington, DC. Taxonomist; classified and designed exhibits at 1893 World's Columbian Exposition; director of Smithsonian Museum of Natural History.

Gooding, William b 1803, Bristol, NY; d 1878, Lockport, IL. Civil engineer; worked on I&M Canal.

Goodman, Benjamin David b May 30, 1909, Chicago; d June 13, 1986, New York,

NY. Jazz clarinetist; composer; band leader; "King of Swing."

Goodman, Kenneth Sawyer b Sept. 19, 1883, Chicago; d Nov. 29, 1918, Chicago. Playwright; energized Chicago's Little Theatre movement; Goodman Theatre funded by parents in his honor.

Goodrich, Grant b Aug. 11, 1812, Milton, NY; d Mar. 15, 1889, Chicago. Lawyer, temperance activist; circuit court judge; Illinois Supreme Court justice; cofounded Northwestern Univ.

Goodrich, Pomeroy b Dec. 13, 1776 or 1797, Benson Township, Rutland, VT. Farmer in Woodbridge area.

Gosden, Freeman Fisher b May 5, 1899, Richmond, VA; d Dec. 10, 1982, Beverly Hills, CA. Producer; writer; radio performer; cocreator of "Amos 'n' Andy."

Gosnell, Harold Foote b Dec. 24, 1896, Lockport, NY; d Jan. 8, 1997, Bethesda, MD. Political scientist; Univ. of Chicago faculty; studied politics and African American politicians.

Goss, Bernard b 1913, Sedalia, MO; d June 20, 1966, Chicago. Painter; muralist; printmaker.

Goudy, Frederic William b Mar. 18, 1865, Bloomington, IL; d May 11, 1947, Marlboro, NY. Typographer; taught at Frank Holme School of Illustration; designed 116 typefaces.

Gould, Chester b Nov. 20, 1900, Pawnee, OK; d May 11, 1985, Woodstock, IL. Cartoonist; created comic strip *Dick Tracy*.

Govier, Sheldon W. b Jan. 11, 1883, Glasgow, Scotland; d July 24, 1948, Chicago. Soccer player; alderman (1918–1932).

Graff, Grace Cornell b June 28 or 29, 1906, Chicago; d Oct. 31, 1992, Stockbridge, MA. Dancer; cofounded Graff Ballet.

Graff, Kurt b Jan. 12, 1910, Bonn, Germany; d Nov. 8, 1993, Great Barrington, MA. Dancer; cofounded Graff Ballet.

Grange, Harold Edward "Red" b June 13, 1903, Forksville, PA; d Jan. 28, 1991, Lake Wales, FL. Football player; Chicago Bears running back; radio and TV announcer for NBC (1947–1961).

Graue, Frederick b Jan. 25, 1819, Landesbergen, Germany; d Jan. 13, 1892. Miller; abolitionist; built Graue Mill in Oak Brook (1852); participated in Underground Railroad.

Gravier, Jacques b May 17, 1651, Moulins, France; d 1708, Mobile, AL. Priest; French Jesuit missionary to Kaskaskias and Peorias.

Gray, Alice Mabel b Nov. 25, 1881, Chicago; d Feb. 8, 1925, Indiana Dunes, IN. Lived as recluse in Lake Michigan Dunes; known as "Diana of the Dunes."

Gray, Charles McNeill b June 13, 1807, Sherburne, NY; d Oct. 17, 1883, Chicago. Businessman; early partner of Cyrus McCormick; mayor of Chicago (1853–1854).

Gray, Daniel b Jan. 23, 1795, Montgomery County, NY; d 1854 or 1855, Montgomery, IL. Businessman; store and tavern owner in Montgomery.

Gray, Nicholas J. b Apr. 8, 1783, German Flats, Herkimer, NY; d May 15, 1875, Aurora, IL. Early resident of Montgomery.

Gray, William Augustus b Aug. 16, 1814, MA; d Dec. 4, 1880, Appleton, WI. Purchased land in western Lake County in 1840.

Green, Adolphus Williamson b Jan. 14, 1843, Boston, MA; d Mar. 8, 1917, New York, NY. Lawyer; businessman; cofounder and president of National Biscuit Co. (Nabisco).

Green, Arthur active 1970s. Clergyman; founded Metropolitan Community Church in 1970.

Green, Henry Delorval b Nov. 24, 1896, Linwood, NE; d Mar. 26, 1984, Chicago. Photographer; documented everyday life on the North Side in 1940s and 1950s.

Green, Lillian "Lil" b Dec. 22, 1919, Clarksdale, MS; d Apr. 14, 1954, Chicago. Blues singer; performed in Chicago clubs with Bill Broonzy in mid-1930s.

Greene, William B. b Oct. 20, 1818, Madison County, NY. Established farm in Woodbridge, IL, in 1841.

Greening, Dawn L. b May 4, 1922; d Mar. 20, 1993, Ft. Collins, CO. Cofounded Old Town School of Music.

Greenwald, Herbert S. b 1916, St. Louis, MO; d 1959, Flushing Bay, NY. Builder; real-estate developer; built skyscraper apartments on Chicago lakefront; collaborated with Ludwig Mies van der Rohe on 860–880 North Lake Shore Drive.

Greenwood, Isabella b ca. 1838, Atlanta, GA; d Jan. 5, 1942, Bloom Township, IL. Early resident of East Chicago Heights (now Ford Heights).

Gregg, William L. b Jan. 11, 1831? Carlisle, PA? d 1887. Manufacturer; lumber trader; founded Excelsior Brick Co. (1872).

Gregory, Clifford V. b Oct. 20, 1883, Mason City, IA; d Nov. 18, 1941, Des Moines, IA. Edited *Prairie Farmer* (1911–1937).

Gridley, John active 1840s. Settled near Long Grove ca. 1840.

Griffin, Marion Lucy Mahony b Feb. 14, 1871, Chicago; d Aug. 10, 1961, Chicago. Architect; worked with Dwight Perkins and Frank Lloyd Wright.

Griffin, Walter Burley b Nov. 24, 1876, Maywood, IL; d Feb. 11, 1937, Lucknow, India. Architect; city planner; landscape designer; associated with Prairie School of architecture.

Griggs, S(amuel) C. b 1819, Tolland County, CT; d Apr. 5, 1897. Early bookseller; established book publishing firm of S. C. Griggs & Co.

Gross, Oskar Carl b Nov. 29, 1871, Vienna, Austria; d Aug. 19, 1963, Chicago. Muralist; painted murals for Louis Sullivan and Daniel Burnham.

Gross, Samuel Eberly b Nov. 11, 1843, Dauphin, PA; d Oct. 24, 1913, Battle Creek, MI. Suburban real-estate developer; built 21 subdivisions and 10,000 houses in Chicago metropolitan area.

Groves, Leslie Richard, Jr. b Aug. 17, 1896, Albany, NY; d July 13, 1970, Washington, DC. Army officer; engineer; military leader of Manhattan Project at Univ. of Chicago.

Grudzinski, Louis b Aug. 2, 1878, Posen, Poland; d Sept. 23, 1948, Chicago. Pastor of St. John of God; founded Guardian Angel Day Nursery.

Gruelle, John Barton b Dec. 24, 1880, Arcalo, IL; d 1938, Miami, FL. Author; cartoonist; created Raggedy Ann and Andy series.

Guerin, Jules Vallee b Nov. 18, 1866, St. Louis, MO; d 1946, Avon, NJ. Painter; illustrator of Burnham's *Plan of Chicago*; decorated Chicago Civic Opera and Merchandise Mart.

Gunderson, Seward Miles b Feb. 23, 1866, Chicago; d July 6, 1950, Chicago. Early real-estate developer in Oak Park.

Gunsaulus, Frank Wakely b Jan. 1, 1856, Chesterville, OH; d Mar. 17, 1921, Chicago. Methodist minister; educator; member of Chicago Vice Commission; president of Armour Institute of Technology.

Gunther, Charles Frederick b Mar. 6, 1837, Wildberg, Germany; d Feb. 10, 1920, Chicago. Candy manufacturer; alderman (1896–1900); collector.

Gurnee, Walter S. b Mar. 9, 1813, Haverstraw, NY; d Apr. 18, 1903, New York, NY. Early land speculator in Chicago's North Shore; owned saddlery and harness business; president of Chicago & Milwaukee Railroad; mayor of Chicago (1851–1853).

Gustafson, Vic b Mar. 2, 1905, Chicago; d Oct. 9, 1964, Geneva, IL. Football player; played for Wheaton High School in 1920s; coached at Wheaton College.

Guzik, Jack (or Jake) b 1880s, Russia; d Feb. 21, 1956, Chicago. Bootlegger; gambling entrepreneur; close associate of Al Capone.

H

Haas, William active 1830s. Brewer; opened brewery in 1833 on the West Side.

Haase, Ferdinand b Apr. 27, 1826, Maedlich, Germany; d Jan. 6, 1911, Chicago. President of the Forest Home Cemetery Co.

Hack, John b Nov. 18, 1787; d Nov. 21, 1856, St. John, IN. Farmer; first postmaster of St. John, IN.

Hackett, Francis b Jan. 21, 1883, Kilkenny, Ireland; d Apr. 25, 1962, Virum, Denmark. Literary critic; novelist; editorial writer for *Chicago Evening Post* (1906–1909); founded *Post's Friday Literary Review*.

Hackney, William active early twentieth century. Promoter of big concerts; involved with "All-Colored Composers' Concerts."

Hadley, Marian M. b 1898? Nashville, TN; d 1974? Chicago. Librarian; active in early development of DuSable Museum.

Haeger, David H. b Aug. 7, 1837, Mecklenburg, Germany; d June 9, 1900, Dundee, IL. Founded brickyard; manufacturer of pottery and ceramics.

Haentze, Albert b July 20, 1869, Fond du Lac, WI; d July 16, 1947, CA. Businessman; real-estate developer.

Haines, Elijah Middlebrook b Apr. 21, 1822, Oneida County, NY; d Apr. 25, 1889, Waukegan, IL. Lawyer; farmer; state legislator; platted Hainesville; editor of the *MISK-WI-NEN-NE*.

Halas, George Stanley b Feb. 2, 1895, Chicago; d Oct. 31, 1983, Chicago. Football player and coach; founded Chicago Bears; coach (1920–1929, 1933–1942, 1946–1955, 1958–1967); charter member of football Hall of Fame.

Hale, Raleigh P. b Oct. 2, 1889, Selvind, IN; d Dec. 1, 1931, East Chicago, IN. Dentist; mayor of East Chicago (1926–1930).

Haley, Margaret Angela b Nov. 15, 1861, Joliet, IL; d Jan. 5, 1939, Chicago. Teacher; led Chicago Teachers Federation.

Hall, Benjamin active 1830s. First proprietor of tavern on Dutchman's Point in Niles.

Hall, Benjamin Franklin b Nov. 17, 1812, West Bloomfield, NY; d Sept. 8, 1860, on a steamer in Lake Michigan, IL. Banker; first mayor of Aurora; cofounded *Aurora Beacon* (1846).

Hall, Myron Volney b early 1810s; d June 21, 1881, Chicago. Printer; banker; cofounded *Aurora Beacon* in 1846.

Hammerschmidt, Adolph b Jan. 30, 1827; d July 25, 1914. Cofounded Elmhurst Chicago Stone Co. in 1883.

Hammond, Alexander b Sept. 28, 1818, Homer, NY; d May 20, 1905, Milwaukee, WI. Physician; developer; formed residential community at Glencoe.

Hammond, George b May 5, 1838, Fitchburg, MA; d Dec. 29, 1886, Detroit, MI. Meatpacking executive; pioneered use of refrigerated railcars.

Hampton, Fred b Aug. 30, 1948; d Dec. 4, 1969, Chicago. Civil rights activist; leader of Chicago Black Panther Party; killed in 1969 police raid.

Hancock, George active 1880s. Inventor of softball.

Hand, John "Johnny" A. b Oct. 26, 1828, Wadern, Prussia; d Oct. 18, 1916, Chicago. Bandleader; known as Chicago's "music master."

Handy, Henry Jamison b Mar. 6, 1886; d Nov. 13, 1983. Swimmer; won Olympic medals 20 years apart (1904, 1924); founded company that made industrial training films.

Hankins, George V. b ca. 1845; d Aug. 18, 1912, Chicago. Gambler; opened Harlem Race Track (1894).

Hansberry, Carl Augustus b ca. 1895, Gloster, MS; d Mar. 7, 1946, Mexico. Real-estate broker; landlord; U.S. deputy marshal; active in Urban League and NAACP; challenged restrictive covenants in *Hansberry v. Lee* (1940).

Hansberry, Lorraine b May 19, 1930, Chicago; d Jan. 12, 1965, New York, NY. Playwright; wrote *A Raisin in the Sun*.

Happ, John b Oct. 13, 1794? Trier, Germany. Blacksmith; justice of the peace in 1849.

Harbert, Elizabeth Boynton b Apr. 15, 1843, Crawfordsville, IN; d Jan. 19, 1925, Pasadena, CA. Journalist; social reformer; *Chicago Inter-Ocean* columnist; organized Evanston Woman's Club; president of Illinois Equal Suffrage Association.

Hard, William b Sept. 15, 1878, Painted Post, NY; d Jan. 30, 1962, New Canaan, CT. Journalist; editorial writer of *Chicago Tribune*; pioneer radio news commentator in 1920s.

Harder, Pat b May 6, 1922, Milwaukee, WI; d Sept. 6, 1992, Waukesha, WI. Football player, Chicago Cardinals; three-time NFL All-Pro.

Hardy, Thomas b ca. 1813, Ireland. Came to Orland Park in 1836.

Harmon, Patrick T. "Paddy" b May 25, 1876, Chicago; d July 22, 1930, Des Plaines, IL. Sports promoter; built Chicago Stadium.

Harper, Lucius C. b Nov. 11, 1895, Augusta, GA; d Feb. 10, 1952, Chicago. Managing editor of *Chicago Defender*; cofounded Bud Billiken Club.

Harper, William Rainey b July 24, 1856, New Concord, OH; d Jan. 10, 1906, Chicago. First president of Univ. of Chicago; biblical scholar.

Harris, Albert Wadsworth b Nov. 4, 1867, Cincinnati, OH; d Nov. 9, 1958, Chicago. Banker; endowed Chicago Community Trust; bred Arabian horses.

Harris, Paul Percy b Apr. 19, 1868, Racine, WI; d Jan. 27, 1947, Chicago. Lawyer; founder and president of Rotary International (1919).

Harrison, Carter H., II b Apr. 23, 1860, Chicago; d Dec. 25, 1953, Chicago. Lawyer; publisher of *Chicago Times*; mayor of Chicago (1897–1905, 1911–1915).

Harrison, Carter H. b Feb. 15, 1825, Fayette County, KY; d Oct. 28, 1893, Chicago. Congressman; mayor of Chicago (1879–1887, 1893).

Harrison, Elizabeth b Sept. 1, 1849, Athens, KY; d Oct. 31, 1927, San Antonio, TX. Educator; founded Chicago Kindergarten Training School, first institution in the United States to provide professional training for kindergarten teachers.

Harrison, Robert active late nineteenth century. Businessman; first president of incorporated Wauconda in 1877.

Hart, Aaron Norton b Apr. 16, 1816, Akron, OH; d Jan. 12, 1883, Plum Creek, IN. Early farmer in Dyer; developed local drainage system; Philadelphia publisher.

Hart, Harry b Feb. 17, 1850, Eppelsheim, Germany; d Nov. 20, 1929, Chicago. Clothing manufacturer; founder and president of Hart, Schaffner & Marx.

Hart, Henry active 1850s. Mapmaker; published "City of Chicago" map in 1853.

Hart, Pearl M. [Pearl M. Harchovsky] b Apr. 7, 1890, Traverse City, MI; d Mar. 22, 1975, Chicago. Lawyer; civil rights activist; professor at John Marshall Law School; cofounded Mattachine Midwest.

Hartnett, Gabby [Charles Leo Hartnett] b Dec. 20, 1900, Woonsocket, RI; d Dec. 20, 1972, Park Ridge, IL. Baseball player and manager with the Chicago Cubs (1922–1940); Hall of Fame.

Harvey, Alonzo active 1840s. Built first house within present limits of West Chicago.

Harvey, Turlington Walker b Mar. 10, 1835, Siloam, NY; d Sept. 12, 1909, Littleton, NH. Lumber merchant; philanthropist; founded Harvey, IL.

Harvey, William "Coin" b Aug. 16, 1851, Buffalo, WV; d Feb. 11, 1936, Monte Ne, AR. Lawyer; economic reformer; "free silver" activist; author of *Coin's Financial School* (1894), an influential populist tract.

Hathaway, Joshua b 1810; d 1863. Mapmaker.

Hatzfeld, Clarence b ca. 1873; d Aug. 25, 1943, Washington, DC. Architect; designed park district fieldhouses (ca. 1920s).

Hauser, Jon William b June 8, 1916, Sault Ste. Marie, MI; d Mar. 20, 1999, Geneva, IL. Industrial designer; Sears' director of design (1943–1945).

Havighurst, Robert J. b June 5, 1900, De Pere, WI; d Jan. 31, 1991. Education scholar; Univ. of Chicago faculty; prepared 1964 Chicago Public Schools evaluation.

Hayden, Sophia Gregoria b Oct. 17, 1868, Santiago, Chile; d Feb. 3, 1953, Winthrop, MA. Architect; designed Woman's Building for 1893 World's Columbian Exposition.

Haydon, Harold E. b Apr. 22, 1909, Fort William, Canada; d Jan. 18, 1994, Chicago. Artist; art teacher; art critic for the *Chicago Sun-Times*.

Haynes, Charles active nineteenth century. Musician; wrote "eight-hour songs" around 1865.

Haywood, William D. b Feb. 4, 1869, Salt Lake City, UT; d May 18, 1928, Moscow, Russia. Labor activist; played leading role at IWW convention in Chicago (1905).

Hazelton, Charles active 1880s. Founded first church in Forest Glen area.

Heacock, Russell E. b 1779, Litchfield, CT; d end June 1849, Summit, IL. Carpenter; lawyer; came to Chicago in 1827; farmer and innkeeper in Summit; promoted I&M Canal.

Head, Cloyd b Sept. 24, 1886; d Feb. 7, 1969, Chicago. Playwright; active with Little Theatre in 1910s; business manager Goodman Theatre 1920s.

Heald, Nathan b Sept. 24, 1775, New Ipswich, NH; d Apr. 27, 1832, St. Charles, MO. Commander at Fort Dearborn; taken prisoner with his wife during Fort Dearborn attack of 1812.

Heald, Rebekah Wells b between 1785 and 1790, Louisville, KY; d 1857, St. Charles, MO. Taken prisoner with her husband Nathan Heald after Fort Dearborn attack of 1812.

Healy, George Peter Alexander b July 15, 1813, Boston, MA; d June 24, 1894, Chicago. Artist; portrait painter.

Healy, William b 1869, Beaconsfield, England; d Mar. 15, 1963, Clearwater, FL. Psychiatrist; founder and director of Chicago Juvenile Psychopathic Institute (later the Institute for Juvenile Research).

Heap, Jane b Nov. 1, 1883, Topeka, KS; d June 16, 1964, London, England. Editor of *Little Review*; artist.

Hebner, Harry b June 15, 1891; d Oct. 1968. Water polo player; Olympic swimming champion (1912).

Hecht, Ben b Feb. 28, 1894, New York, NY; d Apr. 18, 1964, New York, NY. Journalist; writer; playwright (*The Front Page*); Academy Award–winning screenwriter.

Hegewisch, Adolph active 1880s. President of U.S. Rolling Stock Co.; founded Hegewisch as workers' community.

Heinrich, John C. b June 23, 1927; d Jan. 16, 1993, Valparaiso, IN. Architect; codesigned Lake Point Tower; student of Ludwig Mies van der Rohe.

Helgason, Arni b Mar. 16, 1891, Iceland; d Dec. 1968. Engineer; director of Chicago Transformer Corp.

Helm, Margaret active early nineteenth century. Stepdaughter of John Kinzie; wife of American officer at Fort Dearborn.

Helm, Nathan B. b Feb. 9, 1825, Cayuga County, NY; d Apr. 26 or 27, 1904, Harvard, IL. Hardware merchant; first mayor of Harvard around 1891.

Hemingway, Ernest Miller b July 21, 1899, Oak Park, IL; d July 2, 1961, Ketchum, ID. Writer; spent childhood and adolescence in Oak Park; won Nobel Prize in Literature (1954).

Henderson, Charles Richmond b Dec. 17, 1848, Covington, IN; d Mar. 29, 1915, Charleston, SC. Sociologist; minister; chair of Sociology Department, Univ. of Chicago.

Henderson, David b Apr. 26, 1853, Edinburgh, Scotland; d May 27, 1908, Chicago. Journalist; theatrical manager; producer; built Chicago Opera House.

Henderson, William Penhallow b June 4, 1877, Medford, MA; d Oct. 15, 1943, Santa Fe, NM. Artist; muralist.

Henius, Max b June 16, 1859, Aalborg, Denmark; d Nov. 15, 1935, Aalborg. Chemist; founded American Academy of Brewing; president of Chicago Public Library.

Henneberry, William active 1860s. Discovered coal deposits in Will County in 1864.

Hennepin, Louis b Apr. 7, 1640, Ath, Belgium; d between 1701 and 1705. Clergyman; explorer; writer; accompanied La Salle on expedition to central Illinois.

Henrotin, Ellen Martin b July 6, 1847, Portland, ME; d June 29, 1922, Cherryplain, NY. Women's club leader; social reformer; member of Chicago Vice Commission.

Henrotin, Fernand b Sept. 28, 1847, Brussels, Belgium; d Dec. 9, 1906, Chicago. Surgeon; Cook County physician; physician of police and fire dept.; president of Chicago Medical Society (1896).

Henrotin, Joseph F. b Aug. 2, 1813? Tellin, Belgium; d Mar. 17, 1876, Chicago. Physician; Belgian consul in Chicago.

Herbert, Fred B. b ca. 1888, Canada; d June 1955, London, England. Kentucky Derby winner in 1910; Chicago Ridge resident.

Herrick, Robert b Apr. 26, 1868, Cambridge, MA; d Dec. 23, 1938, Charlotte Amalie, Virgin Islands. Writer; English professor at Univ. of Chicago (1893–1923).

Herrington, James, Jr. b June 6, 1824, Mercer, PA; d July 7, 1890, Geneva, IL. Farmer; journalist; first mayor of Geneva, IL.

Herrington, Augustus M. b July 27, 1820, Mercer, PA; d Aug. 14, 1883, Geneva, IL. Lawyer; U.S. district attorney.

Herrington, Charity b Sept. 6, 1799, Cumberland County, PA; d Sept. 22, 1879, Geneva, IL. Cofounded Geneva, IL.

Herrington, James Clayton b May 8, 1798, York County, PA; d Mar. 25, 1839, Geneva, IL. Land speculator; sheriff; cofounded Geneva, IL.

Herskovits, Melville Jean b Sept. 10, 1895, Bellefontaine, OH; d Feb. 25, 1963, Evanston, IL. Anthropologist; created Department of Anthropology and Program of African Studies at Northwestern Univ.; member of Mayor's Commission on Race Relations.

Hertz, John Daniel b Apr. 10, 1879, Ruttka (now Slovakia); d Oct. 8, 1961, Los Angeles, CA. Transportation entrepreneur; founded Yellow Cab Co. (1915).

Hesing, Anton Casper b Jan. 6, 1823, Vechta, Germany; d Mar. 31, 1895, Chicago. Owner and editor of *Illinois-Staatszeitung*; Cook County sheriff.

Hesler, Alexander b July 1823, Montreal, Canada; d July 5, 1895, Evanston, IL. Photographer; known for landscapes and portraits of Lincoln.

Hess, Julius H. b 1876, Ottawa, IL; d Nov. 2, 1955, Los Angeles, CA. Pediatrician; established premature infant clinic at Michael Reese Hospital; invented infant incubator.

Hesse, Richard C. b Oct. 4, 1895, Chicago; d Oct. 20, 1975, Chicago. Hardware executive; founded Ace Hardware, 1924.

Hetherington, John Todd b Aug. 15, 1859, Uxbridge, Canada; d Dec. 26, 1936, Chicago. Architect; designed fieldhouse for Ridge Park in Beverly (1912).

Hibbard, William G. b ca. 1825, Dryden, NY; d Oct. 11, 1903, Chicago. Founded hardware wholesaling firm; president of Hibbard, Spencer, Bartlett & Co.

Hicks, Bob b Oct. 9, 1899; d May 19, 1987, Ojai, CA. Wrestling coach, Tilden Tech; won city titles and two state championships.

Higgins, Hiram M. b Oct. 13, 1820, Chautauqua County, NY; d July 13, 1897, San Diego, CA. Music composer; publisher; opened first music publishing house in Chicago.

Higinbotham, Harlow Niles b Oct. 10, 1838, Joliet, IL; d Apr. 18, 1919, New York, NY. Merchant; president of 1893 World's Columbian Exposition; partner at Marshall Field & Co.; philanthropist.

Hildebrandt, August b Nov. 8, 1801, Prussia; d Mar. 16, 1891, Lansing, IL. Arrived in 1843 in Lansing.

Hill, Ellen Marie b Apr. 19, 1839, MA; d Jan. 4, 1916, Glen Ellyn, IL. Namesake of Lake Glen Ellyn.

Hill, George b Mar. 21, 1870, Stratfordshire, England; d July 29, 1963, Chicago. Businessman; established first business, a hardware store, in Clearing, in 1909.

Hill, James Jerome b Sept. 16, 1838, Rockwood, Canada; d May 29, 1916, St. Paul, MN. Railroad developer; headed Chicago, Burlington & Quincy Railroad.

Hill, Joe [Joel Hagglund; Joseph Hillstrom] b Oct. 7, 1879, Gavle, Sweden; d Nov. 19, 1915, Salt Lake City, UT. Labor songwriter; member of the IWW; massive funeral in Chicago after execution in Utah.

Hill, Kimball b Oct. 10, 1910, Chicago; d Nov. 9, 1993, Evanston, IL. Builder; lawyer; pioneer in building prefabricated homes; created Rolling Meadows.

Hill, Thomas Arnold b Aug. 23, 1888, Richmond, VA; d Aug. 1, 1947, Cleveland, OH. Led Chicago Urban League during World War I.

Hill, Thomas Clarkson b Mar. 11, 1831, Guilford County, NC; d 1896, Western Springs, IL. Land promoter in 1870; first president of incorporated Western Springs in 1886.

Hill, Thomas E. b Feb. 29, 1832, Sandgate, VT; d 1915. Publishing executive; village president and developer of Glen Ellyn.

Hill, William "Big Bill" b Apr. 6, 1914; d Apr. 16, 1983, Chicago. Radio minister; rhythm and blues disc jockey (1950s).

Hill, William b Aberdeen, Scotland; d Oct. 15, 1875, West Dundee, IL. Nurseryman; founded D. Hill Nursery in 1855.

Hillenbrand, Reynold b July 19, 1904 or 1905, Chicago; d May 22, 1979, Chicago.

Monsignor; social activist; pastor of Sacred Heart Church in Winnetka.

Hilliard, Laurin P. b Oct. 11, 1814, Unadilla, NY; d Nov. 2, 1895, Chicago. Real-estate agent; Cook County clerk; cofounded Washington Heights, Longwood, and Beverly Hills.

Hilliard, Raymond Marcellus b Aug. 8, 1907; d July 4, 1966, Chicago. Lawyer; director of Cook County Department of Welfare.

Hillis, Margaret b Oct. 1, 1921, Kokomo, IN; d Feb. 4, 1998, Evanston, IL. Founder and director of Chicago Symphony Chorus (1957).

Hillman, Sidney b Mar. 23, 1887, Zagare, Lithuania; d July 10, 1946, Point Lookout, NY. Labor leader; first president of Amalgamated Clothing Workers of America; cofounded Congress of Industrial Organizations (CIO).

Hines, Earl Kenneth b Dec. 28, 1905, Duquesne, PA; d Apr. 22, 1983, Oakland, CA. Jazz pianist; band leader; performed regularly at Grand Terrace Club.

Hines, Edward b July 31, 1863, Buffalo, NY; d Dec. 1, 1931, Evanston, IL. Lumber merchant; philanthropist; founded Edward Hines Lumber Co.

Hinman, Mary Wood b Feb. 14, 1878, OH; d July 4, 1952, Los Angeles, CA. Teacher of folk and social dance; choreographer; taught dance at Hull House and Francis W. Parker School (1906–1919).

Hirsch, Emil Gustav b May 22, 1851, Luxembourg; d Jan. 7, 1923, Chicago. Rabbi; led Sinai Congregation for 43 years; founding editor of *Reform Advocate*.

Hitchcock, Annie McClure b 1839 or 1840; d June 29, 1922, Berea, KY. Cofounded Chicago's Woman's Club.

Hitt, Willis M. b ca. 1826, MD. Early developer; subdivided land around 1866.

Hobson, Bailey b Apr. 30, 1798, Jefferson County, TN; d Mar. 25, 1850, Naperville, IL. Built first water powered flour mill in DuPage County; served in first county government.

Hobson, Clarissa Stewart b Dec. 13, 1804, GA; d Mar. 27, 1884. Early resident of DuPage County; arrived in 1832.

Hodes, Art b Nov. 14, 1904, Nikolaev, Russia; d Mar. 4, 1993, Harvey, IL. Jazz-blues pianist; writer.

Hodge, Emma B. b Apr. 16, 1862, Milwaukee, WI; d July 1, 1928, Chicago. Book collector; authority on ceramics, textiles, and needlework.

Hodgkins, Jefferson b Oct. 27, 1843 or 1844, ME; d Jan. 2, 1921? FL. Quarryman; crushed stone contractor; president Kimball & Cobb Stone Co.

Hoellen, John b Sept. 24, 1914, Chicago; d Jan. 30, 1999. Lawyer; alderman (1947–1975); lost mayoral race to Richard J. Daley in 1975.

Hoffman, George, Jr. b May 8, 1855, Chicago; d Mar. 18, 1942, Lyons, IL. Brewer; built a dam on Des Plaines River; erected Hoffman Tower.

Hoffman, Abbott Howard "Abbie" b Nov. 30, 1936, Worcester, MA; d Apr. 12, 1989, Solebury Township, PA. Antiwar activist; cofounded Youth International Party ("Yippies"); one of the "Chicago Seven" arrested at 1968 Democratic Convention in Chicago.

Hoffman, Julius Jennings b July 7, 1895, Chicago; d July 1, 1983, Chicago. Lawyer; federal judge; presided over Chicago Seven conspiracy trial.

Hoffman, Sam b July 20, 1900, Russia; d Oct. 13, 1959, Phoenix, AZ. Developer of Hoffman Estates.

Hogan, Quintin "Quinn" b Mar. 26, 1922, Chicago; d Dec. 7, 1993, Seminole, FL. Land developer; developed Vernon Hills.

Hoge, Jane C. b July 31, 1811, Philadelphia, PA; d Aug. 26, 1890, Chicago. Welfare worker; fundraiser; cochaired Chicago branch of Sanitary Commission.

Hohman, Caroline Sibley [Caroline Sibley] b 1828 or 1830, Wales, England; d Oct. 1900. Arrived in Chicago in 1849; created Hohman Opera House.

Hohman, Ernest b Sept. 5, 1817, Koenigsburg, Prussia; d buried Dec. 18, 1872, Hammond, IN. Large landowner in North, IN; Justice of the Peace in North Township.

Holabird, John A. b May 4, 1886, Evanston, IL; d May 4, 1945, Chicago. Architect; designed Art Institute and Soldier Field.

Holabird, William b Sept. 11, 1854, Amenia Union, NY; d July 19, 1923, Evanston, IL. Architect; partner at Holabird & Roche; pioneer in engineering skeleton steel skyscrapers.

Holcomb, John b Apr. 21, 1816 or 1819, Jefferson County, NY; d Jan. 25, 1889. Namesake of Holcomb, which became Mundelein in 1924; donated land for station and village plat in 1880.

Holdom, Jesse b Aug. 23, 1851, London, England; d July 14, 1930, Chicago. Lawyer; judge of the Superior Court of Cook County.

Holland, Bud C. b Dec. 27, 1922, Chicago; d Dec. 29, 1994, Chicago. Art dealer; gallery owner.

Holloway, Milton J. b Jan. 24, 1896, Chicago; d Mar. 15, 1972, Portola Valley, CA. Candy manufacturer; founder and president of M. J. Holloway Candy Co.

Holme, Frank b 1868, Corinth, WV; d July 27, 1904, Denver, CO. Graphic designer; newspaper artist; founded Chicago School of Illustration.

Holmes, Berenice b Feb. 4, 1905, Chicago; d Apr. 2, 1982, Chicago. Ballet dancer; dance teacher; choreographer.

Holmes, Edward Lorenzo b Jan. 28, 1828, Dedham, MA; d Feb. 12, 1900, Chicago. Early ophthalmologist; director of Illinois Charitable Eye and Ear Infirmary; president of Rush Medical College.

Holmes, Joseph b 1948, Chicago; d Apr. 11, 1986, Chicago. Dancer; founder and artistic director of Joseph Holmes Dance Theatre.

Holt, Nora Douglas b 1885, Kansas City, KS; d 1974. Composer; cofounded National Association of Negro Musicians.

Holton, Frank b Mar. 10, 1858, Allegan, MI; d Apr. 17, 1942, Elkhorn, WI. Musician; trombonist with John Philip Sousa Band; founded Frank Holton Band Instrument Manufacturing Co.

Hood, Raymond Mathewson b Mar. 29, 1881, Pawtucket, RI; d Aug. 14, 1934, Stamford, CT. Architect; collaborated on winning design for 1922 Tribune Tower competition; designed Electrical Building at Century of Progress Exposition.

Hooker, John Lee b Aug. 22? 1917, Clarksdale, MS; d June 21, 2001, San Francisco, CA. Blues musician; influenced postwar blues and rock 'n' roll.

Hookway, Amelia Marcella Dunne b Apr. 24, 1858, Chicago; d Nov. 14, 1914, Chicago. Educator; principal, Howland School; sister of Finley Peter Dunne.

Hopkins, Claude C. b 1866, Spring Lake, MI; d Sept. 21, 1932, Grand Haven, MI. Advertising copywriter; developed advertising slogans for well-known products.

Hopkins, Emma Curtis b Sept. 2, 1849, Killingly, CT; d Apr. 8, 1925, Killingly. Feminist; theologian; teacher; writer; founded New Thought ministry in Chicago.

Hopkins, Howard D. "Doc" b Jan. 26, 1900, Wallins Creek, KY; d Jan. 3, 1988, Evanston, IL. Folk and country music singer; regular on WLS *National Barn Dance* music program.

Hopkins, John Patrick b Oct. 29, 1858, Buffalo, NY; d Oct. 13, 1918, Chicago. Businessman; first Irish Catholic mayor of Chicago (1893–1895).

Horn, Milton b Sept. 1, 1905, Kiev, Ukraine; d Mar. 29, 1995, Chicago. Artist; sculptor; worked with wood, metal, and stone.

Horner, Henry b Dec. 29, 1818, Bohemia; d Feb. 11, 1878, Chicago. Grocer; founded Henry Horner & Co.; charter member of Chicago Board of Trade.

Horner, Henry b Nov. 30, 1878, Chicago; d Oct. 6, 1940, Winnetka, IL. Governor of Illinois (1933–1936); judge of Cook County Probate Court.

Horwich, Bernard b ca. 1861; d Apr. 23, 1949, Chicago. Manufacturer; banker; active in Chicago Zion Society.

Horwich, Frances R. b July 16, 1907, Ottawa, OH; d July 22, 2001, Scottsdale, AZ. Educator; host of *Ding Dong School* TV program.

Hossack, John b Dec. 6, 1806, Elgin, Scotland; d Nov. 8, 1891, Ottawa, IL. Grain and lumber dealer; convicted in 1860 of breaking fugitive slave law.

Hostetler, Lana b ca. 1942, IL; d Feb. 4, 1999, Springfield, IL. Activist; lobbied for children's issues and gay rights; founding member of Illinois Federation for Human Rights.

Hotchkiss, Almerin b June 6, 1816, CT; d Jan. 17, 1903, St. Louis, MO. Landscape architect; designed layout of Lake Forest; designed cemeteries.

Hough, Electa b 1791, CT; d Jan. 16, 1864, Bloomingdale, IL. Came to Roselle in 1836.

Hough, Elijah b Sept. 20, 1785, Hampshire County, MA; d June 5, 1851, Bloomingdale, IL. Came to Roselle in 1836.

Hough, Roselle M. b 1820, NY; d Mar. 9, 1892, Chicago. Businessman; early landowner in Bloomingdale Township; first president of Chicago Chamber of Commerce.

Howe, Frank b 1849, Arlington, MA; d Jan. 4, 1909, Kansas City, MO. Architect; designed Electricity Building at the 1893 World's Columbian Exposition.

Howlin' Wolf [Chester Arthur Bennett] b June 10, 1910 or 1911, West Point, MS; d Jan. 10, 1976, Hines, IL. Blues musician; recorded for Chess Records.

Hoyne, Thomas b Feb. 11, 1817, New York, NY; d July 27, 1883, Carlton Station, NY. Justice of the peace; mayor of Chicago (1876).

Hoyt, Homer b June 14, 1896, St. Joseph, MO; d Nov. 29, 1984, Silver Springs, MD. Real-estate economist; director of research for Chicago Plan Commission; chief housing economist for Federal Housing Authority.

Hubbard, Gurdon Saltonstall b Aug. 22, 1802, Windsor, VT; d Sept. 14, 1886, Chicago. Businessman; partner at American Fur Co.

Hubble, Edwin Powell b Nov. 20, 1889, Marshfield, MO; d Sept. 28, 1953, San Marino, CA. Astronomer.

Hubschman, Jorgen b Aug. 4, 1897; d Feb. 21, 1983, Juno Beach, FL. Cofounded Lake Barrington; founder and president of Hubschman Construction Co.; mayor of Lake Barrington (1960–1977).

Huck, John A. b May 15, 1819, Uttenhofen, Baden; d Jan. 26 or 27, 1878, Chicago. Brewer; owned lager beer brewery in Chicago.

Hudlun, Anna Elizabeth Lewis b Feb. 6, 1840, Uniontown, PA; d Nov. 21, 1914, probably Chicago. Underground Railroad activist.

Hudlun, Joseph Henry b Oct. 4, 1839, Culpepper Courthouse, VA. Early black homeowner; born a slave; worked at Chicago Board of Trade.

Huebert, Diana [Diana Faidy] b Feb. 22, 1899, Chicago; d Dec. 1983. Chicago dancer; choreographer; dance teacher.

Hughes, Everett C. b Nov. 30, 1897, Beaver, OH; d Jan. 5, 1983, Cambridge, MA. Sociologist; professor at Univ. of Chicago; associated with Chicago School of Sociology.

Hughes, Langston b Feb. 1, 1902, Joplin, MO; d May 22, 1967, New York, NY. Writer; associated with Harlem Renaissance but spent time in Chicago; set *Not Without Laughter* in Chicago.

Hulbert, Thomas H. b Sept. 20, 1848, Lee, MA; d Mar. 23, 1932, Chicago. Early real-estate developer; built homes in south Oak Park.

Hull, Denison B. b Mar. 25, 1897, Chicago; d Jan. 31, 1988, Scottsdale, AZ. Architect; designed First Congregational Church; Greek scholar.

Hummert, Anne Ashenhurst [Anne Schumacher] b Jan. 19, 1905, Baltimore, MD; d July 5, 1996, New York, NY. Soap opera writer; created radio soap opera *Just Plain Bill*.

Hummert, Frank b 1882 or 1887, St. Louis, MO; d Mar. 12, 1966, Manhattan, NY. Writer; creator of radio soap opera.

Humphrey, Doris b Oct. 17, 1895, Oak Park, IL; d Dec. 29, 1958, New York, NY. Choreographer; dance teacher; founded ballet school in Oak Park (1913).

Humphrey, John b June 20, 1838, Walpole, England; d Oct. 3, 1914, Chicago. Lawyer; state legislator (1871–1872; 1885–1910); supervisor of Orland Park for 35 years.

Humphreys, Llewel(l)yn Morris b ca. Apr. 20, 1899, Chicago; d Nov. 23, 1965, Chicago. Crime syndicate leader; protégé of Al Capone.

Hundley, Elisha active 1850s. Built Lakeview House in 1854.

Hunt, Herold Christian b Feb. 9, 1902, Northville, MI; d Oct. 17, 1996, Lexington, MA. Educator; superintendent of Chicago Public Schools (1947–1953); undersecretary of Dept. of Health, Education, and Welfare.

Hunt, Myron b Feb. 17, 1868, Sunderland, MA; d May 26, 1952, Pasadena, CA. Architect; associated with Prairie School.

Hunt, Richard Morris b Oct. 31, 1827, Brattleboro, VT; d July 31, 1895, Newport, RI. Architect; built Administration Building at 1893 World's Fair; built Marshall Field mansion.

Hunter, Alberta b Apr. 1, 1895, Memphis, TN; d Oct. 17, 1984, Roosevelt Island, NY. Blues musician; singer; performed extensively in small cabaret clubs in Chicago.

Hunter, Norman L. b Aug. 28, 1832, Forkland, AL; d Dec. 10, 1992, Chicago. Graphic designer; photographer; art director for African American magazines.

Hunter, Robert b Apr. 10, 1874, Terre Haute, IN; d May 15, 1942, Montecito, CA. Social worker and reformer; authored *Tenement Conditions in Chicago* (1901).

Huntley, Thomas Stilwell b Mar. 27, 1807, Cicinnatus, NY; d May 21, 1894. Businessman; platted the town of Huntley.

Hurley, Timothy David b Aug. 31, 1863, Maysville, KY; d July 22, 1926, Evanston, IL. Lawyer; president of Visitation and Aid Society; president of Illinois State Council of the Catholic Benevolent Legion.

Hutchins, Robert Maynard b Jan. 17, 1899, Brooklyn, NY; d May 14, 1977, Santa Barbara, CA. Educator; president of Univ. of Chicago (1929–1951); developed "Chicago Plan" for undergraduate education.

Hutchinson, Charles Lawrence b Mar. 7, 1854, Lynn, MA; d Oct. 7, 1924, Chicago. Merchant; banker; founder and president of Art Institute.

I

Iannelli, Alfonso b 1888, Andretta, Italy; d Mar. 23, 1965, Chicago. Sculptor; designer; painter; worked on Midway Gardens, Pickwick Theatre, Adler Planetarium.

Ickes, Anna Wilmarth Thompson b Jan. 27, 1873, Chicago; d Aug. 31, 1935, Velarde, NM. Social reformer; suffragist; state legislator (1929–1934); president of Chicago Woman's Club.

Ilg, Robert b Jan. 21, 1879, Paris, France; d Dec. 25, 1964. Electric ventilating company executive; donated Leaning Tower replica to the town of Niles.

Ingalls, Frederick b Dec. 22, 1855, Waukegan, IL; d Dec. 12, 1938, Pebble Beach, CA. Manufacturer; lawyer; endowed hospital in Harvey.

Insull, Samuel b Nov. 11, 1859, London, England; d July 16, 1938, Paris, France. Electric utilities executive; president of Chicago Edison (later Commonwealth Edison).

Ireland, George b June 15, 1913, Madison, WI; d Sept. 14, 2001, Chicago. College basketball coach; guided Loyola Univ. to 1963 NCAA National Championship.

Isherwood, Harry active 1830s. Theatre manager; scene painter; comanager of early Chicago theater company.

Itkin, David b July 29, 1890; d May 18, 1971, Palm Springs, CA. Theater director; professor of drama at Goodman Theatre; head drama department at DePaul Univ.

Ivan, Thomas Nathaniel b Jan. 31, 1911, Toronto, Canada; d June 24, 1999, Lake Forest, IL. Hockey executive; general manager of Blackhawks in 1950s.

J

Jablonski, Francis Jerome Roman b Aug. 9, 1863, Inowroclaw, Poland; d Feb. 23, 1908, Chicago. Writer; editor of Polish newspaper *Dziennik Zwizkowy*.

Jackson, Daniel McKee b Sept. 9, 1870, Pittsburgh, PA; d May 17, 1929, Chicago. Undertaker; president of Emanuel Jackson Undertaking Co.; gambling king.

Jackson, Joseph "Shoeless Joe" Jefferson b July 6, 1887, Dickens County, SC; d Dec. 5,

1951, Greenville, SC. Baseball player; Chicago White Sox outfielder; acquitted of participating in 1919 "Black Sox" scandal but banned from Major League Baseball for life.

Jackson, Joseph Harrison b Sept. 11, 1900, Rudyard, MS; d Aug. 18, 1990, Chicago. Minister, Olivet Baptist Church; president of National Baptist Convention (1953–1982).

Jackson, Mahalia b Oct. 26, 1911, New Orleans, LA; d Jan. 27, 1972, Evergreen Park, IL. Gospel singer; collaborated with Thomas Dorsey; held annual concerts at Carnegie Hall, 1937–1946.

Jackson, Robert R. b Sept. 1, 1870, Malta, IL; d June 12, 1942, Chicago. State senator (1912–1916); alderman (1918–1942).

Jackson, Tony b June 5, 1876, New Orleans, LA; d Apr. 20, 1921, Chicago. Pianist; composer; ragtime vaudeville artist; wrote "Pretty Baby."

Jackson, Walter b Mar. 19, 1938, Pensacola, FL; d June 20, 1983, Chicago. Soul singer; known for long ballads.

Jacob, W. V. active late nineteenth century. Developer of Burnside area in 1890s.

Jacobs, Arnold M. b June 11, 1915, Philadelphia, PA; d Oct. 7, 1998, Chicago. Tuba player; member of Chicago Symphony Orchestra; brass instrument teacher.

Jacobson, Egbert b Sept. 27, 1890, New York, NY; d Jan. 1966, Clearwater, FL. Graphic designer; first director of Container Corp. of America (CCA) Department of Design.

James, Elmore b Jan. 27, 1918, Holmes County, MS; d May 24, 1963, Chicago. Blues singer and slide guitarist; recorded for Meteor label and Chess Records.

James, John b 1829, Nitshill, Renfrewshire, Scotland; d 1902, Santa Monica, CA. Coal miner; union leader.

Janowitz, Morris b Oct. 22, 1919, Paterson, NJ; d Nov. 7, 1988, Chicago. Sociologist; chairman of Univ. of Chicago sociology department; wrote *The Community Press in an Urban Setting*.

Janowski, Max b Jan. 29, 1912, Berlin, Germany; d Apr. 8, 1991, Chicago. Music director; composer of Jewish liturgical music; voice teacher.

Jefferson, "Blind Lemon" b July 11, 1897? Couch, TX; d Dec. 1929, Chicago. Blues singer and guitarist; performed and recorded in 1920s; member of Blues Hall of Fame.

Jefferson, Cornelia Frances b Oct. 1, 1796, NY; d Nov. 1849, Philadelphia, PA. Actress; performed in opening production of Chicago Theatre.

Jefferson, Joseph, II b 1804, Philadelphia, PA; d Nov. 24, 1842, Mobile, AL. Actor; scene painter; partner of Alexander McKinzie in theater company.

Jefferson, Joseph, III b Feb. 20, 1829, Philadelphia, PA; d Apr. 23, 1905, Palm Beach, FL. Actor; identified with role of "Rip van Winkle"; member of Illinois Theatrical Company; namesake of "Jeff" awards in Chicago theater.

Jeffery, Thomas B. b Feb. 5, 1845, Stoke, England; d Apr. 2, 1910, Pompeii, Italy. Bicycle manufacturer; mass producer of motor cars; developed Rambler auto.

Jeffries, Zay b Apr. 22, 1888, Willow Lake, Dakota Territory; d May 21, 1965, Pittsfield, MA. Metallurgist; scientist; participated in Manhattan Project.

Jemsek, Joe b Dec. 24, 1912 or 1913, IL; d Apr. 2, 2002, Chicago. Pro golfer; golf course owner; early developer of public golf courses.

Jenkins, Thomas active 1830s. Built structure on northern bank of Lake Michigan in 1835.

Jenney, William Le Baron b Sept. 25, 1832, Fairhaven, MA; d June 15, 1907, Los Angeles, CA. Engineer; architect; built Home Insurance Building.

Jensen, Jens b Sept. 13 or Sept. 30, 1860, Dybbol, Denmark; d Oct. 1, 1951, Ellison Bay, WI. Landscape architect; designed Humboldt Park, Columbus Park, and Garfield Park Conservatory.

Jepson, Ivar Per b Nov. 2, 1903, Onnestad, Sweden; d Nov. 1968. Industrial designer; engineer; chief designer at Sunbeam.

Jewett, Eleanor [Eleanor Jewett Lundberg] b Feb. 9, 1892, Chicago; d June 1968. Newspaper writer; art critic for *Tribune* beginning in 1917.

Job, Samuel b Nov. 19, 1842, Beaufort, South Wales, England. Businessman; active in Welsh exhibition at World's Columbian Exposition in 1893.

Joffrey, Robert [Abdullah Jaffa Anver Bey Khan] b Dec. 24, 1930, Seattle, WA; d Mar. 25, 1988, New York, NY. Founder and artistic director of Joffrey Ballet.

Johnson, Charles Nelson b Mar. 16, 1860, Brock Township, Ontario, Canada; d July 17, 1938, Chicago. Dentist; professor at Chicago College of Dental Surgery; editor of *Dental Review*.

Johnson, Charles Spurgeon b July 24, 1893, Bristol, VA; d Oct. 27, 1956, Louisville, KY. Sociologist; president of Fisk Univ.; research director for Chicago Urban League; coauthor of Chicago's Commission on Race Relations report, *The Negro in Chicago* (1922).

Johnson, David active 1830s. Norwegian sailor; arrived in 1834.

Johnson, John "Mushmouth" V. b ca. 1857, St. Louis, MO; d Sept. 12, 1907, Brooklyn, NY. Gambling-house proprietor.

Johnson, Robert Leroy b May 8, 1911, Hazelhurst, MS; d Aug. 16, 1938, Greenwood, MS. Blues guitarist; harmonica player; exemplified Mississippi Delta blues tradition.

Johnson, William H. b Sept. 20, 1895, Chicago; d May 1, 1981, Fort Lauderdale, FL. Educator; superintendent of Chicago Public Schools (1936–1946).

Johnsos, Luke b Dec. 9, 1905, Chicago; d Dec. 10, 1984, Evanston, IL. Professional football player; coach; spent nearly 40 years with Chicago Bears.

Joliet, Louis b Sept. 21, 1645, Quebec City, Canada; d May 1700, Canada. Explorer; cartographer; one of the first Europeans to visit Chicago (1673).

Jones, J. Wesley b Sept. 8, 1884, Nashville, TN; d Feb. 11, 1961, Chicago. Choral leader; musician.

Jones, Jenkin Lloyd b Nov. 14, 1843, Llandysul, Wales; d Sept. 12, 1918, Tower Hill, WI. Clergyman; established All Souls' Church; secretary of World Parliament of Religions (1893).

Jones, John b Nov. 3, 1816, Greene County, NC; d May 21, 1879, Chicago. Tailor; businessman; philanthropist; Underground Railroad activist; abolitionist; civil rights activist; county commissioner; first African American to hold elective office in Illinois (1871).

Jones, John A. "Jack" b Oct. 12, 1876, Kingston, Ontario, Canada; d Dec. 12, 1940, Chicago. Owner and proprietor of Dill Pickle Club; labor activist; participant in IWW founding convention in Chicago (1905).

Jones, Mary Jane Richardson b Oct. 28, 1819, TN; d Jan. 2, 1910. Abolitionist; Underground Railroad activist; clubwoman; philanthropist.

Jones, Mary Harris "Mother" [Mary Harris] b baptized Aug. 1, 1837, Cork, Ireland; d Nov. 30, 1930, Silver Springs, MD. Dressmaker; union organizer for United Mine Workers, Knights of Labor, and others; participant in IWW founding convention in Chicago (1905).

Jones, Ralph R. b ca. 1880, IN; d July 25, 1951, Boulder, CO. Football coach for Chicago Bears (1931–1932); refined T formation.

Jones, Robert Edmond b Dec. 12, 1887, Milton, NH; d Nov. 26, 1954, Milton, NH. Theater director; set designer; painter.

Jones, Wilbur Cox b 1923, Nashville, TN; d 1978, Chicago. Active in early development of DuSable Museum.

Jordan, James Edward b Nov. 16, 1896, Peoria, IL; d Apr. 1 or 2, 1988, Los Angeles, CA. Radio entertainer; broadcast *Fibber McGee & Molly* show from Chicago.

Jordan, Marian Driscoll [Marian Driscoll] b Apr. 16, 1898, Peoria, IL; d Apr. 7, 1961, Encino, CA. Radio entertainer; broadcast "Fibber McGee & Molly" show from Chicago.

Judd, Charles Hubbard b Feb. 23, 1873, Bareilly, India; d July 18 or 19, 1946, Santa Barbara, CA. Psychologist; educator; chaired Univ. of Chicago Department of Education.

Judd, Norman Buel b Jan. 10, 1815, Rome, NY; d Nov. 11, 1878, Chicago. Lawyer; diplomat; U.S. congressman; Lincoln's ambassador to Prussia.

Judson, Harry Pratt b Dec. 20, 1849, Jamestown, NY; d Mar. 4, 1927, Chicago.

Educator; president of Univ. of Chicago (1907–1923).

Judson, Philo b Mar. 1, 1807, Otsego County, NY; d Mar. 23, 1876, Evanston, IL. Methodist minister; first business agent of Northwestern Univ.; platted village of Evanston.

K

Kane, Elias Kent b June 7, 1894, New York, NY; d Dec. 12, 1835, Washington, DC. Lawyer; state legislator (1818–1822); U.S. senator (1824–1835); namesake of Kane County.

Kapp, Jack b June 15, 1901, Chicago; d Mar. 25, 1949, New York, NY. Record producer; worked for Columbia Records in Chicago; brought Decca Records to the United States.

Katz, Sam b ca. 1892, Chicago; d Jan. 11, 1961, Beverly Hills, CA. Founded Balaban & Katz; head of production at MGM.

Kearney, Andrew Thomas b July 5, 1892, Brockway, PA; d Jan. 11, 1962, Chicago. Management consultant.

Keck, George Fred b May 17, 1895, Watertown, WI; d Nov. 21, 1980, Chicago. Architect; designed 12-sided glass House of Tomorrow for Century of Progress Exposition.

Keeley, James b Oct. 14, 1867, London, England; d June 7, 1934, Lake Forest, IL. Managing editor of *Chicago Tribune*; owner of *Chicago Herald*.

Kehl, Frederick W. b Aug. 19, 1862, Eiterfeld, Germany; d Aug. 11, 1938, Chicago. Ballroom dancer; dance teacher; founded Chicago Association of Dancing Masters.

Kelley, Daniel b May 3, 1818, Rutland County, VT; d 1900. Wool grower; donated land for railroad station near what became Carol Stream.

Kelley, Florence b Sept. 12, 1859, Philadelphia, PA; d Feb. 17, 1932, Germantown, PA. Lawyer; social reformer; Hull House resident; first woman chief inspector of factories for Illinois; secretary of National Consumers' League; cofounded U.S. Children's Bureau.

Kellogg, Alice D. [Alice Kellogg Tyler] b Dec. 27, 1862, Chicago; d Feb. 14, 1900, Chicago. Painter; teacher; one of the first pupils at Art Institute of Chicago.

Kelly, Edward Joseph b May 1, 1876, Chicago; d Oct. 20, 1950, Chicago. Mayor of Chicago (1933–1947).

Kelly, Lawrence V. b May 30, 1928, Chicago; d Sept. 16, 1974, Kansas City, MO. Dancer; cofounded Lyric Theatre of Chicago and Dallas Civic Opera.

Kemper, James Scott b Nov. 18, 1886, Van Wert, OH; d Sept. 17, 1981, Chicago. Insurance executive; ambassador; philanthropist; organized Kemper Insurance group and James S. Kemper & Co.

Kempf, Tud b Oct. 22, 1886, Jasper, IN. Artist; sculptor; woodcarver; active in WPA projects.

Kendall, Curtis P. b July 25, 1898, Louisville, KY; d July 4, 1949, Kenilworth, IL. Businessman; Washington National Insurance Co.; benefactor of Kendall College.

Kenna, "Hinky Dink" Mike b Aug. 20, 1857, Chicago; d Oct. 9, 1946, Chicago. Alderman; bossed First Ward with "Bathhouse" John Coughlin.

Kennedy, Joseph Patrick b Sept. 6, 1888, Boston, MA; d Nov. 18, 1969, Hyannis, MA. Entrepreneur; ambassador to England; first chairman of Securities and Exchange Commission; bought Merchandise Mart (1945).

Kennelly, Martin H. b Aug. 11, 1887, Chicago; d Nov. 29, 1961, Chicago. Warehouse and trucking executive; mayor of Chicago (1947–1955).

Kennicott, John A. b Jan. 5, 1802, NY; d June 4, 1863, Glenview, IL. Doctor; early nursery man; horticultural editor of *Prairie Farmer*; promoted Morrill Act establishing land grant colleges.

Kennicott, Robert b Nov. 13, 1835, New Orleans, LA; d May 13, 1866, Ft. Nulato, AL. Naturalist; cofounded Chicago Academy of Sciences.

Kent, Trumbull b ca. 1827, Oswego County, NY. Farmer in Palatine; arrived in 1835.

Kenyon, William Asbury b Aug. 22, 1817, Hingham, MA; d Jan. 25, 1862, Hingham, MA. Early Chicago Poet.

Keppard, Freddie b Feb. 27, 1890, New Orleans, LA; d July 15, 1933, Chicago. Musician; cornetist; played in Chicago clubs.

Kern, Herbert Arthur b Aug. 31, 1890, Lake Elmo, MN; d Feb. 28, 1963, La Grange, IL. Chemical firm executive; founded Chicago Chemical Co. (1920), later Nalco Chemical Co.

Kern, Peter active 1850s. Landowner; assessor; bought land in what would become Summit.

Kerner, Otto b Aug. 15, 1908, Chicago; d May 9, 1976, Chicago. Federal judge; governor of Illinois; chaired National Advisor Commission on Civil Disorders (1967); convicted in racetrack scandal.

Kerr, Charles Hope b Apr. 23, 1860, La-Grange, GA; d June 1, 1944, Los Angeles, CA. Socialist publisher; cofounded Charles H. Kerr publishing house; published *International Socialist Review*.

Kettlestrings, Joseph b Nov. 7, 1808, Newton, England; d Nov. 17, 1883, probably Chicago. Early landowner in Oak Park; member of Bickerdike & Noble firm.

Khan, Fazlur Rahman b Apr. 3, 1929, Dacca, Bangladesh; d Mar. 27, 1982, Jeddah, Saudi Arabia. Structural engineer; innovator in skyscraper design; designed Sears Tower and John Hancock Center.

Kikulski, John b Aug. 29, 1876, Poland; d May 21, 1920, Chicago. Union organizer of Stockyards Labor Council.

Kimball, Ingalls b Apr. 2, 1874, West Newton, MA; d Oct. 16, 1933, Mt. McGregor, NY. Publisher; insurance executive; founded publishing house Stone & Kimball.

Kimbell, Martin Nelson b Jan. 24, 1812, Stillwater, NY; d Feb. 13, 1895, Chicago. Early farmer; claimed land in Jefferson Township (now Logan Square).

Kimberly, Edmund S. b 1803; d 1874, Libertyville, IL. Physician; Chicago's first village clerk; elected to first Board of Trustees.

Kimmelman, Susan b July 15, 1948, Brooklyn, NY; d Aug. 26, 2001, Chicago. Choreographer; lawyer; cofounded MoMing Dance and Arts Center.

Kincaid, Bradley b July 13, 1895, Garrard County, KY; d Sept. 23, 1989, Springfield, OH. Country singer; composer; known for his arrangement of "Barbara Allen."

Kincheloe, Samuel C. b Nov. 20, 1890, Georgetown, OH; d July 15, 1981. Sociologist; professor; applied scientific methods to study of religious institutions; wrote *The American City and Its Church* (1938).

King, Martin Luther, Jr. b Jan. 15, 1929, Atlanta, GA; d Apr. 4, 1968, Memphis, TN. Baptist minister; civil rights leader; received 1964 Nobel Peace Prize; played prominent role in Chicago open-housing movement.

Kingery, Robert b Sept. 26, 1890, Emporia, KS; d Nov. 13, 1951, Evanston, IL. Engineer; general manager of Chicago Regional Planning Association; chairman of Chicago Port Authority.

Kinzie, Eleanor Lyttle b ca. 1769–1771; d early 1834, NY. Early settler in Chicago.

Kinzie, John b Dec. 3, 1763, Quebec, Canada; d Jan. 6, 1828, Chicago. Fur trader; agent of the American Fur Co. (1827).

Kinzie, John H. b July 7, 1803, Sandwich, Ontario; d June 21, 1865, on the Pittsburgh, Fort Wayne & Chicago Railroad. Fur trader, first president of Chicago Historical Society.

Kinzie, Juliette Augusta Magill b Sept. 11, 1806, Middletown, CT; d Sept. 14, 1870, Amagansett, Long Island. Early Chicago settler; wrote *Wau-Bun, the "Early Day" in the North-West* (1856).

Kiolbassa, Peter b Oct. 13, 1838, Swibiu, Poland; d June 23, 1905, Chicago. Businessman; building commissioner; city treasurer; state legislator (1877–1879); alderman; leading role in establishment of St. Stanislaus Kostka parish.

Kirkland, Joseph b Jan. 7, 1830, Geneva, NY; d Apr. 29, 1894, Chicago. Writer; soldier; lawyer; wrote local histories of Chicago and novel *Zury*.

Kissel, Ben D. b Feb. 17, 1897; d Jan. 4, 1967, Chicago. Parking entrepreneur; converted old buildings to parking garages.

Kitchell, Iva b Mar. 31, 1912, Junction City, KS; d Nov. 9, 1983, Ormond Beach, FL. Concert dancer; dance satirist; performed with Chicago Grand Opera Ballet Company.

Kittredge, William A. b May 28, 1891, Lowell, MA; d July 26, 1945, Evanston, IL. Typographer; author; printer; director of design at Lakeside Press.

Klehm, John Adam b July 14, 1834, Hesse-Darmstadt, Germany; d Mar. 16, 1916, Arlington Heights, IL. Bricklayer; farmer; established nursery business in Arlington Heights.

Klootwyck, Peter b 1847, Holland; d 1914, Munster, IN. Operated small store in Munster in nineteenth century.

Kluczynski, John Carl b Feb. 15, 1896, Chicago; d Jan. 26, 1975, Chicago. State representative (1933–1948); U.S. representative (1951–1975).

Klutznick, Philip M. b July 9, 1907, Kansas City, MO; d Aug. 14, 1999, Chicago. Lawyer; real-estate developer; philanthropist; developed Park Forest.

Knapp, Albert A. b Jan. 20, 1852, IL; d Dec. 20, 1932, Oak Park, IL. Businessman; built a combination creamery and cheese factory in 1873.

Kner, Albert b Feb. 19, 1899, Gyoma, Hungary; d Aug. 1976. Entrepreneur; pioneer in development of package design and market research; worked for Container Corp. of America.

Kner, Elizabeth b Oct. 7, 1897, Gyoma, Hungary; d Feb. 26, 1998, Chicago. Printer; bookbinder at Newberry Library.

Knight, Frank Hyneman b Nov. 7, 1885, White Oak, IL; d Apr. 15, 1972, Chicago. Economist; part of Chicago School of Economics; Univ. of Chicago faculty.

Knox, William Franklin b Jan. 1, 1874, Boston, MA; d Apr. 28, 1944, Washington, DC. Newspaper editor and publisher; U.S. secretary of the navy; owned controlling interest in *Chicago Daily News*.

Kochs, August b Aug. 13, 1871, Lichtenau, Germany; d Nov. 21, 1960, Chicago. Chemical manufacturer; founded Victor Chemical Works (1902).

Kogan, Herman S. b Nov. 6, 1914, Chicago; d Mar. 8, 1989, New Buffalo, MI. Journalist; popular historian.

Kohl, Charles E. b Mar. 28, 1855, Brooklyn, NY; d Nov. 12, 1910, Oconomowoc, WI. Vaudeville manager; operated Kohl & Castle dime museum.

Kohlsaat, Herman H. b Mar. 22, 1853, Edwards County, IL; d Oct. 17, 1924, Washington, DC. Merchant; newspaper publisher; owned chain of bakeries and restaurants.

Kolze, Henry J. b June 23, 1859, Leyden, IL; d June 11, 1926, Chicago. Early restaurant owner; built Kolze's hotel in Dunning; county commissioner.

Kolze, Julia M. b Aug. 28, 1880, Chicago; d Nov. 12, 1938, Schiller Park, IL. Mayor of Schiller Park; first woman mayor in Illinois (1932).

Kolze, William b June 9, 1836, Germany; d June 23, 1896, Chicago. Early landowner near Des Plaines River; honorary mayor of unincorporated Kolze.

Korhumel, Newton F. b Aug. 21, 1905; d Feb. 5, 2001, Chicago. Steel manufacturer; developer in Mettawa.

Kotas, Helen [Helen Kotas Hirsch] b June 7, 1916, Chicago; d Dec. 15, 2000, Chicago. French horn player; member of Chicago Symphony Orchestra.

Kovler, Marjorie b May 10, 1921, Chicago; d Dec. 20, 1970, Chicago. Owner of Kovler Art Gallery; namesake of Center for the Treatment of Survivors of Torture.

Kraft, James Lewis b Nov. 11, 1874, Fort Erie, Canada; d Feb. 16, 1953, Chicago. Inventor; cheese manufacturer; founded Kraft Foods.

Krainik, Ardis Joan b Mar. 8, 1929, Manitowoc, WI; d Jan. 18, 1997, Chicago. Director of Lyric Opera of Chicago (1981–1997).

Kramer, Ferdinand "Ferd" b Aug. 10, 1901, Chicago; d July 16, 2002, Chicago. Businessman; head of real-estate firm Draper & Kramer; president of Metropolitan Housing and Planning Council; managed Lake Meadows; developed Prairie Shores.

Kraus, Adolf b Feb. 26, 1850, Blowitz, Bohemia; d Oct. 22, 1928, Chicago. Lawyer; president of the Chicago Board of Education; head of City Law Department.

Kroc, Raymond Albert b Oct. 5, 1902, Oak Park, IL; d Jan. 14, 1984, La Jolla, CA. Founded McDonald's Corp. and Ronald McDonald House; pioneer in fast-food chain stores; opened first McDonald's franchise restaurant in Des Plaines.

Kruger, John active late nineteenth century. Restaurateur; began a small chain of cafeterias in 1890s.

Krumske, Paul A. b July 25, 1912; d July 23, 1979, Boca Raton, FL. Hall of Fame bowler; television bowling host on WBKB-TV.

Krupa, Gene b Jan. 15, 1909, Chicago; d Oct. 16, 1973, Yonkers, NY. Jazz drummer; played with Benny Goodman in the 1930s and 1940s.

Kryl, Bohumir b May 2, 1875, Horice, Czechoslovakia; d Aug. 7, 1961, Wilmington, NY. Conductor; cornetist; joined John Philip Sousa's band in 1898; led "Chicago Band" (ca. 1910s).

Kubelik, Rafael b June 29, 1914, Bychory, Czechoslovakia; d Aug. 11, 1996, Lucerne, Switzerland. Conductor; composer; directed Chicago Symphony Orchestra (1950–1953).

Kuh, Katherine W. [Katherine Woolf] b July 15, 1904, St. Louis, MO; d Jan. 10, 1994, New York, NY. Art critic; art consultant; first curator of modern art at Art Institute Chicago (1942–1959).

Kuné, Julian b 1831; d Aug. 29, 1914, Chicago. Newspaper music critic; member of Chicago Board of Trade; organized 24th Illinois Infantry in Civil War.

Kuppenheimer, Bernard b 1829, Baden, Germany; d Oct. 27, 1903, Chicago. Founded B. Kuppenheimer & Co., wholesale clothier.

L

La Salle, Robert Cavelier de b 1643, Rouen, France; d 1687, East Texas. Explorer; came through Chicago portage to reach the Mississippi Valley.

Laemmle, Carl b Jan. 17, 1867, Laupheim, Germany; d Sept. 24, 1939, Beverly Hills, CA. Pioneer motion picture producer; owned. first nickelodeon movie theaters in Chicago.

Laflin, Matthew b Dec. 16, 1803, Southwick, MA; d May 20, 1897, Chicago. Pioneer powder manufacturer; helped build Academy of Sciences in Lincoln Park.

LaFramboise, Claude b Nov. 16, 1771, Trois Rivieres, Quebec. Landowner; his land received in 1829 treaty became River Grove.

LaFromboise, Madelaine b c. 1780; d 1846. Ottawa woman; operated trading company.

Lalime, Jean B. active early nineteenth century; d spring 1812, Chicago. Indian interpreter; occupied former DuSable residence.

Lance, Major b ca. 1939; d Sept. 3, 1994, Decatur, GA. Bandleader; shaped Chicago's soul sound in 1960s.

Landers, Ann [Eppie Lederer; Esther Pauline Friedman] b July 4, 1918, Sioux City, IA; d June 22, 2002, Chicago. Syndicated newspaper advice columnist (1955–2002).

Landis, Kenesaw Mountain b Nov. 20, 1866, Millville, OH; d Nov. 25, 1944, Chicago. Lawyer; federal judge; first baseball commissioner; banned "Black Sox" players from Major League Baseball; presided over conviction of IWW leaders in 1918.

Landon, Margaret Mortenson b Sept. 3, 1903; d Dec. 4, 1993. Writer; wrote *Anna and the King of Siam.*

Lane, Albert G. b May 15, 1841; d Aug. 22, 1906, Chicago. Educator; superintendent of Chicago Public Schools (1891–1898).

Lane, Frank "Trader" b Feb. 1, 1895 or 1896, Cincinnati, OH; d Mar. 19, 1981, Richardson, TX. Baseball executive; White Sox general manager (1950s).

Lane, Hannah b July 15, 1780, Kingsbury, NY; d Sept. 16, 1853, Worth Township, Cook County, IL. Arrived in Alsip in 1834.

Lane, Joseph b Aug. 10, 1773, Champlain, Clinton, NY; d June 10, 1877, Worth Township, Cook County, IL. Arrived in Alsip in 1834.

Lanigan, James (Jim) W. b Jan. 30, 1902, Chicago; d Apr. 9, 1983, Elburn, IL. Classical and jazz musician; violinist with Chicago Symphony Orchestra; string bass/tuba player with original Austin High School jazz band.

Lansett, Peter b Canada. Credited with 1820 discovery of coal near Coal City.

Lansing, George b NY. Arrived in Lansing area in 1846.

Lansing, Henry b Chenango County, NY; active 1840s–1860s. Early Lansing postmaster; operated general store.

Lansing, John b NY. Platted village of Lansing in 1865.

Lardner, Ring b Mar. 6, 1885, Niles, MI; d Sept. 25, 1933, Long Island, NY. Sports journalist; playwright; lyricist.

Lasker, Albert Davis b May 1, 1880, Freiburg, Germany; d May 30, 1952, New York, NY. Advertising executive; philanthropist; pioneered modern advertising methods.

Lasker, Mary *See* **Block, Mary Lasker**

Lathrop, Jedediah H. b July 5, 1806, Lebanon, NH; d Nov. 23, 1889. Early settler of Elmhurst; planted elm trees along Cottage Grove.

Lathrop, Julia b June 29, 1858, Rockford, IL; d Apr. 15, 1932, Rockford, IL. Social reformer; Hull House resident; first head of U.S. Children's Bureau.

Laughlin, Clara Elizabeth b Aug. 3, 1873, New York, NY; d Mar. 3, 1941, Chicago. Travel writer; founder and editor of *So You're Going* travel monthly.

Laughton, Bernardus H. active 1820s–1830s. Indian trader; established trading post in Lyons with brother David.

Laughton, David active 1820s–1830s. Early settler; established trading post in Lyons with brother Bernardus.

Lawrence, George R. b Feb. 24, 1867, Ottawa, IL; d Dec. 15, 1938, Chicago. Photographer; pioneer in aerial and panoramic photography; banquet photographer.

Lawson, Victor Fremont b Sept. 9, 1850, Chicago; d Aug. 19, 1925, Chicago. Owner and editor of *Chicago Daily News* (1876–1925); philanthropist.

Le Beau, Emily Beaubien b July 8 or 28, 1825, River Raisin, Washtenaw, MI; d Nov. 4, 1919, Aurora, IL. Daughter of Mark Beaubien.

Le Grand Saulteur [Mineweweh; Ninkaton; Minavavana] b c. 1710; d Autumn 1770. Ojibwa chief; prominent leader from Sault Ste. Marie District.

Leahy, Mary Clemenza active 1910s. Nun; one of the first women to earn a bachelor's degree at DePaul, 1912.

Leaner, Arthur *See* **Benson, Al**

Leaner, George b June 1, 1917, MS; d Sept. 18, 1983, Chicago. Record producer; founded "One-derful" record label in 1962.

Leavensworth, Jessie active 1840s. Resident near Riverwoods and Deerfield Road in 1841.

Lederer, Eppie *See* **Landers, Ann**

Lee, Charles active 1800s. Farmer before 1812.

Lee, William A. b Apr. 11, 1895, Chicago; d June 16, 1984, Chicago. Labor leader; head of Bakery Truck Drivers Union (1916–1960); president of Chicago Federation of Labor (1946–1984).

Legge, Katherine [Katherine McMahan] b 1870, Butler County, PA; d Aug. 22, 1924, Pasadena, CA. Wife of president of International Harvester; husband donated land for memorial park in her honor.

Legler, Henry Eduard b Feb. 22, 1861, Palermo, Italy; d Sept. 13, 1917, Chicago. Librarian of Chicago Public Library (1909–1917); proposed network of neighborhood libraries.

Lehmann, Ernst E. b Oct. 28, 1886, Chicago; d Jan. 18, 1930, Chicago. Cattle breeder; son of founder of Lake Villa.

Lehmann, Ernst J. b Jan. 27, 1849, Tetrow, Germany; d Jan. 4, 1900, White Plains, NY. Originator of the department store concept in Chicago; owned "The Fair Store"; founded Lake Villa and Lindenhurst.

Leigh, Edward Baker b Apr. 23, 1853, Townsend, MA; d May 17, 1932, Kerr County, TX. President of Chicago Railway Equipment Co.

Leiter, Levi Z. b Nov. 2, 1834, Leitersburg, MD; d June 9, 1904, Bar Harbor, ME. Merchant; partner in Field, Leiter & Co. (later Marshall Field & Co.); president of Commercial Club and Art Institute of Chicago.

Leopold, Nathan, Jr. b Nov. 19, 1904, Chicago; d Aug. 30, 1971, San Juan, Puerto Rico. Thrill murderer; coperpetrator in 1924 kidnapping and murder of Bobby Franks.

Lester, Frederick E. b July 3, 1828, Clinton, NY; d Jan. 21, 1891. Merchant; postmaster; founded Wood Dale.

Levy, Felix Alexander b Oct. 20, 1884, New York, NY; d June 16, 1963, New York, NY. Rabbi of Congregation Emanuel (1907–1956); president of Central Conference of American Rabbis.

Lew, Gerard b May 7, 1888, MA; d Mar. 11, 1965, Chicago. First president of DuSable Museum Board; poet.

Lewis, Allen C. b 1821, Sterling, CT; d Oct. 27, 1877, Chicago. Businessman; established Polytechnic School (forerunner of Illinois Institute of Technology).

Lewis, Arthur Morrow b ca. 1873, England; d Aug. 22, 1922, Chicago. Lecturer; socialist; speaker at Dill Pickle Club.

Lewis, Benjamin Franklin b Nov. 23, 1842, Union County, IN; d Feb. 2, 1928, Pasadena, CA. Publisher of county histories.

Lewis, Evan "Strangler" active late nineteenth century. Wrestler; fought in first recognized professional heavyweight championship.

Lewis, Frank J. b Apr. 9, 1867, Chicago; d Dec. 21, 1960, Chicago. Businessman; philanthropist; founded Lewis Univ.

Lewis, Henry B. b 1825, Madison County, NY; d June 6, 1901, Chicago. Early real-estate dealer in Englewood; member of Chicago Board of Trade.

Lewis, Lloyd Downs b May 2, 1891, Pendleton, IN; d Apr. 21, 1949, Libertyville, IN. Journalist and managing editor at *Chicago Daily News*; biographer.

Lewis, Meade Lux b Sept. 4, 1905, Chicago; d June 7, 1964, Minneapolis, MN. Boogie-woogie pianist; discovered in Chicago clubs.

Lewis, Samuel active 1830s. Music teacher; opened school of music around 1835.

Leyendecker, Joseph Christian b Mar. 23, 1874, Montabaur, Germany; d July 25, 1951, New Rochelle, NY. Artist; illustrator; known for magazine cover illustrations; did first Arrow collar advertisements.

Lieb, Hermann b May 24, 1826, Turgau, Switzerland; d Mar. 4, 1908, Chicago. Lawyer; county clerk; cofounded *Abend Zeitung*; owner and editor of *Chicago Democrat*.

Liesegang, Adolph active late nineteenth century. Bandleader; organized band after the fire of 1871.

Lincoln, Abraham b Feb. 12, 1809, Hodgenville, KY; d Apr. 14, 1865, Washington, DC. U.S. president; nominated at 1860 Republican Convention in Chicago; cofounded Republican Party in Illinois; congressman (1847–1849).

Lincoln, Benjamin B. b 1806, VT; d 1855, Palatine, IL. Arrived in Palatine around 1835; first justice of the peace in Palatine.

Lincoln, Mary Todd b Dec. 13, 1818, Lexington, Kentucky; d July 16, 1882, Springfield, IL. U.S. First Lady; hospitalized at Bellevue Place sanatorium in Batavia.

Lincoln, Robert Todd b Aug. 1, 1843, Springfield, IL; d July 26, 1926, Manchester, VT. Lawyer; railroad executive; founded Glenwood School; U.S. secretary of war; diplomat.

Lindheimer, Benjamin Franklin b Oct. 1, 1889, Chicago; d June 5, 1960, Beverly Hills, CA. Real-estate dealer; racetrack owner.

Lindsay, Vachel b Nov. 10, 1879, Springfield, IL; d Dec. 5, 1931, Springfield, IL. Poet; associated with Chicago Renaissance; wrote *The Congo and Other Poems*.

Lingg, Louis b Sept. 9, 1864, Mannheim, Germany; d Nov. 10, 1887, Chicago. Anarchist; convicted in Haymarket Square riot; committed suicide before his execution.

Lingle, Alfred Philip "Jake" b July 2, 1891, Chicago; d June 9, 1930, Cicero, IL. Crime reporter for *Chicago Tribune*.

Little Turtle b ca. 1752, Ft. Wayne, IN; d July 14, 1812, Fort Wayne, IN. Chief and military leader of the Miami Indians.

Livermore, Mary Ashton Rice b Dec. 19, 1820, Boston, MA; d May 23, 1905, Melrose, MA. Writer; abolitionist; suffragist; founded Illinois Woman Suffrage Association.

Llapitan, Carmelito b Dec. 14, 1910; d Apr. 2, 1988. Founded Filipino American Council of Chicago; served as council president 1961–1965 and 1970–1978.

Lloyd, Henry Demarest b May 1, 1847, New York, NY; d Sept. 28, 1903, Chicago. Social reformer; economist; *Chicago Tribune* journalist; wrote *Wealth vs. Commonwealth* (1894).

Locke, Ned b Dec. 25, 1919, Redwing, MN; d Feb. 4, 1992, Kimberling, MO. Ringmaster on *Bozo's Circus* television show.

Loeb, Jacob M. b Sept. 17, 1875, Chicago; d Feb. 17, 1944, Chicago. Insurance executive; president of Chicago Board of Education (1910s).

Loeb, Richard b June 11, 1905, Chicago; d Jan. 28, 1936, Lockport, IL. Thrill murderer; coperpetrator of 1924 kidnapping and murder of Bobby Franks; killed in prison.

Loewy, Raymond b Nov. 5, 1893, Paris, France; d July 14, 1986, Monte Carlo, Monaco. Industrial designer; designed Studebaker car and Coca-Cola bottle.

Logan, John Alexander b Feb. 9, 1826, Murphysnoro, IL; d Dec. 26, 1886, Washington, DC. Lawyer; U.S. Army general; state legislator (1853–1854; 1857–1858); U.S. representative (1859–1862; 1867–1870), U.S. senator (1871–1876; 1879–1886).

Logan, Josephine Hancock b May 1, 1862, Chicago; d Nov. 1, 1943, Chicago. Arts patron; writer; established "Sanity in Art" committee (1936).

Lohr, Lenox R. b Aug. 15, 1891, Washington, DC; d 1968. General manager of Century of Progress World's Fair, 1933.

Long, Birch Burdette b ca. 1878, Columbus, OH; d Mar. 1, 1927, New York, NY. Artist; painter; illustrator.

Loomis, Frank D. b Dec. 14, 1880, Bowling Green, OH; d Nov. 1969, Hopedale, IL. Executive director of Chicago Community Trust; founded Crusade of Mercy in 1934.

Lorimer, William b Apr. 27, 1861, Manchester, England; d Sept. 13, 1934, Chicago. U.S. congressman and U.S. senator; led Republican political machine in Chicago.

Lott, George b Oct. 16, 1906, Springfield, IL; d Dec. 3, 1991, Chicago. Tennis player; outstanding doubles player in the 1930s; tennis coach at DePaul Univ.

Loughman, John Patrick b May 12, 1894, Chicago; d Dec. 5, 1946, Chicago. Labor speaker; known as King of the Soapboxers; captain of Hobo College.

Louis, Joseph b May 13, 1914, Lafayette, AL; d Apr. 12, 1981, Las Vegas, NV. Heavyweight boxing champion; became a professional boxer in Chicago.

Lovett, Harriett [Harriett Lovett Sayre] b ca. 1820; d Nov. 16, 1913, Chicago. Arrived in Chicago in 1835; farmed in Montclare area.

Lovett, Robert Morss b Dec. 25, 1870, Boston, MA; d Feb. 8, 1952, Chicago. Reformer; educator; editor; English professor at Univ. of Chicago; Hull House resident.

Lowden, Frank Orren b Jan. 26, 1861, Sunrise City, MN; d Mar. 30, 1943, Tucson, AZ. Lawyer; businessman; governor of Illinois (1917–1921); agriculturist.

Lowe, Julia R. active late nineteenth century. Physician; led campaign for public baths.

Lozano, Rudy b July 17, 1951, Harlingen, TX; d June 8, 1983, Chicago. Labor organizer; community activist; Midwest director of International Ladies Garment Workers Union.

Lubin, Charles W. b Nov. 16, 1903, Chicago; d July 15, 1988, Chicago. Businessman; founded Kitchens of Sara Lee.

Luckman, Sidney b Nov. 21, 1916, Brooklyn, NY; d July 5, 1998, Aventura, FL. Professional football player; Bears quarterback (1940s).

Ludby, Peter active 1830s. Arrived in Dunning in 1839.

Ludmila, Anna [Jean Cahley; Jean Marie Gee] b Jan. 12, 1903, Chicago; d Apr. 18, 1990, Houston, TX. Ballet dancer; principal dancer of Chicago Opera Ballet in the 1920s.

Lumbard, Frank active 1840s. Educator; appointed vocal teacher in public schools, 1847.

Lundgren, Harriet b Nov. 20, 1907, Chicago; d Jan. 9, 1996, Chicago. Ballet dancer; principal dancer with Chicago Grand Opera Ballet; conducted ballet school in Chicago.

Lundin, Frederick b May 18, 1868, West Tollstad, Sweden; d Aug. 29, 1947, Beverly Hills, CA. Manufacturer; state senator (1894–1898); U.S. congressman (1909–1911); president of Lundin & Co.

Lunt, Orrington b Dec. 24, 1815, Bowdoinham, ME; d Apr. 5, 1897, Evanston, IL. Grain merchant; philanthropist; cofounded Northwestern Univ.

Lush, Marion b Aug. 10, 1931, Chicago; d May 4, 1993, Hollywood, FL. Singer; polka bandleader and musician.

Lux, John Andrew b Sept. 3, 1849, Buffalo, NY; d Mar. 27, 1926, Waukegan, IL. Farmer; platted a village site named Wadsworth in 1874.

Lydy, Richard Grant b Dec. 27, 1895, Springfield, MO; d Apr. 22, 1976, Chicago. Business executive; opened first parking garage for automobiles in the Loop.

Lynch, John J. active twentieth century. Community leader; temporary president of Round Lake Beach immediately after incorporation (1937).

Lyon, Paulina Harriette active late nineteenth century, early twentieth century. Clubwoman; founded Woman's Athletic Club (1898).

Lyser, Gustav b 1840 or 1841; d Oct. 7, 1909, Milwaukee, WI. Socialist journalist; editor of the *Verbote* and *Chicagoer Arbeiter-Zeitung*.

M

Mabon, Willie b Oct. 24, 1925, Hollywood, TN; d Apr. 19, 1985, Paris, France. Blues pianist; harmonica player; recorded for Chess Records.

MacArthur, Catherine T. [Catherine T. Hyland] b Nov. 23, 1908, Chicago; d Dec. 15, 1981, Palm Beach Shores, FL. Philanthropist; cofounded John D. and Catherine T. MacArthur Foundation.

MacArthur, Charles b Nov. 5, 1895, Scranton, PA; d Apr. 21, 1956, New York, NY. Playwright; screenwriter; journalist; worked with Ben Hecht on *The Front Page*.

MacArthur, John Donald b Mar. 6, 1897, Pittston, PA; d Jan. 6, 1978, West Palm Beach, FL. Insurance and real-estate executive; philanthropist; established the John D. and Catherine T. MacArthur Foundation.

MacChesney, Nathan William b June 2, 1878, Chicago; d Sept. 25, 1954. Lawyer; diplomat; member of Chicago Plan Commission; drafted standard restrictive covenant.

Macdonald, Charles Blair b Nov. 14, 1855, Niagara Falls, Canada; d Apr. 21, 1939, Southampton, NY. Stock broker; amateur golf champion; golf course designer.

MacDonald, Jessica N. *See* **North, Jessica Nelson**

Mack, Julian (Judge) b July 19, 1866, San Francisco, CA; d Sept. 5, 1943, New York, NY. Lawyer; Cook County and federal judge; Zionist leader; cofounded *Harvard Law Review*.

Mackey, Frank b Mar. 20, 1852, Bilbao, NY; d Feb. 24, 1927, Minneapolis, MN. Businessman; founded Household Finance Corp. (now Household International) around 1885.

MacLagan, James b Nov. 14, 1858, Ayreshire, Scotland; d Mar. 29, 1929, Chicago. Pastor of First Scotch Presbyterian Church.

MacLean, Annie b 1870? St. Peters Bay, Prince Edward Island, Canada; d May 1, 1934, Pasadena, CA. Sociologist; studied retail workers in late 1890s.

Maclean, Norman b Dec. 23, 1902, Clarinda, IA; d Aug. 2, 1990, Chicago. Writer; English professor at Univ. of Chicago; wrote *A River Runs Through It*.

Mad Sturgeon [Bad Sturgeon; Nuscotomeg] active early nineteenth century. Led Potawatomi in attacking Fort Dearborn in 1812.

Madden, Martin B. "Skinny" b Mar. 20, 1855, Darlington, England; d Apr. 27, 1928, Washington, DC. Chicago city council member (1889–1897); U.S. congressman (1905–1928).

Maggio, Michael J. b July 3, 1951, Chicago; d Aug. 19, 2000, Chicago. Stage director; Dean at DePaul Univ.; directed Theatre School at Goodman Theatre.

Magic Sam [Samuel Maghett] b Feb. 14, 1937, Grenada, MS; d Dec. 1, 1969, Chicago. Guitarist; helped to develop the West Side generation of great Chicago bluesmen; performed with Willie Dixon.

Maher, George W. b Dec. 25, 1864, Mill Creek, WV; d Sept. 12, 1916, Douglas, MI. Architect in Prairie Style; designed numerous residences.

Main Poc b c. 1765, probably southern MI; d 1816, near Manistee, Michigan Territory. Potawatomi war leader and shaman.

Majdak, Ivan active 1930s. President of Croatian-American Radio Club in Berwyn in 1935.

Malnati, Luciano "Lou" Ernesto Giuseppe b June 27, 1929, Varese, Italy; d Feb. 28, 1978, Chicago. Businessman; manager of Pizzeria Uno, 1940s; founded Lou Malnati's restaurant.

Maloney, Elizabeth b Nov. 19, 1880, Joliet, IL; d Oct. 26, 1921, Chicago. Waitress; union organizer; suffragist.

Manilow, Nathan b Apr. 10, 1898, Baltimore, MD; d Oct. 28, 1971, Miami Beach, FL. Chicago area home builder; developed Park Forest and Park Forest South.

Mann, Fred b Oct. 9, 1873, Germany; d Oct. 8, 1930, Chicago. Restaurateur; owner of Rainbo Gardens.

Mann, James R. b Oct. 20, 1856, Bloomington, IL; d Nov. 30, 1922, Washington, DC. Lawyer; U.S. congressman; sponsored White Slave Traffic Act of 1910 (Mann Act).

Mansfield, Portia b Nov. 19, 1887, Chicago; d Jan. 29, 1979, Carmel, CA. Dancer; choreographer; camp director; taught social dance.

March, Herbert b Nov. 8, 1912, Brooklyn, NY; d Feb. 10, 2002. Trade union organizer; led United Packinghouse Workers (1930s–1940s).

Marcy, Mary Edna Tobias b May 8, 1877, Belleville, IL; d Dec. 8, 1922, Chicago. Editor; radical writer; editor of *International Socialist Review* in early 1900s.

Maremont, Arnold Harold b Aug. 24, 1904, Chicago; d Nov. 1, 1978, New York, NY. Industrialist; philanthropist; advocated birth control; housing reformer.

Markham, Charles H. b May 22, 1861, Clarksdale, TN; d Nov. 24, 1930. Railroad executive; president and chairman of Illinois Central Railroad.

Markin, Morris b July 15, 1892, Russia; d July 7, 1970, Kalamazoo, MI. Businessman; founder and president of Checker Cab.

Marquette, Jacques b June 1, 1637, Laon, France; d May 18, 1675, Ludington, MI. Missionary and explorer; with Joliet the first Europeans to visit Chicago (1673).

Marquis, A. Nelson b Jan. 10, 1855, Brown County, OH; d Dec. 21, 1943, Evanston, IL. Founder and publisher of *Who's Who in America*; published first Chicago business directory.

Marsh, Sylvester b Sept. 30, 1803, Compton, NH; d Dec. 30, 1884, Concord, NH. Grain dealer; invented more efficient grain dryers.

Marshall, Benjamin Howard b May 5, 1874, Chicago; d June 19, 1944, Chicago. Architect; designed Blackstone Theatre, Drake Hotel, and Edgewater Beach Apartments.

Marshall, Charles [Carlo Marziali] b Sept. 15, 1886, Auburn, ME; d May 8, 1951, Assembly Point, Lake George, NY. Operatic tenor; American debut as Otello with Chicago Civic Opera in 1920.

Marshall, John active 1830s. Early settler; builder of tavern at Dutchman's Point in 1830s.

Martin, Halloween b Apr. 14, 1902. Chicago's first disc jockey; had a show "Musical Clock" (1929–1946).

Martin, Horace Hawes b Sept. 22, 1855, Olean, NY; d Oct. 19, 1925, Lake Forest, IL. Book collector; lawyer; trustee of Newberry Library.

Martin, Roberta [Roberta Evelyn Winston] b Feb. 12, 1907, Helena, AR; d Jan. 18, 1969, Chicago. Gospel singer; pianist; composer/arranger; music publisher.

Martin, Sallie b Nov. 20, 1895, Pittfield, GA; d June 18, 1988, Chicago. Gospel singer; composer.

Martinon, Jean b Jan. 10, 1910, Lyon, France; d Mar. 1, 1976, Paris, France. Composer; conductor of Chicago Symphony Orchestra (1963–1968).

Marwood, Fryer b June 2, 1830, Kirby, Ravensworth, Yorkshire, England; d Jan. 16, 1910, Ellsworth, IL. Landowner; bought property in 1865 on what is now Harlem Avenue.

Marwood, Merritt B. b Sept. 4, 1867, Orison, IL; d CA. First mayor of incorporated Elmwood Park.

Marx, Julius "Groucho" Henry [Julius Henry Marx] b Oct. 2, 1890, New York, NY; d Aug. 19, 1977, Los Angeles, CA. Comedian; member of Marx Brothers comedy team.

Mason, Charles Max b Oct. 26, 1877, Madison, WI; d Mar. 23, 1961, Claremont, CA. Mathematical physicist; president of Univ. of Chicago (1925–1928).

Mason, Roswell B. b Sept. 19, 1805, New Hartford, NY; d Jan. 1, 1892, Chicago. Civil engineer; mayor of Chicago (1869–1871).

Masters, Edgar Lee b Aug. 23, 1869, Garnett, Kansas; d Mar. 5, 1950, Philadelphia, PA. Lawyer; novelist; poet; wrote *Spoon River Anthology*.

Mather, Stephen T. b July 4, 1867, San Francisco, CA; d Jan. 22, 1930, Brookline, MA. Reformer; organizer and first director of National Park Service; advocated a dunes park.

Matsuoka Roshi, Soyu active mid-twentieth century. Abbot; led Zen Buddhist Temple of Chicago early 1960s.

Matteson, Joel Aldrich b Aug. 2, 1808, Watertown, NY; d Jan. 31, 1873, Chicago. Railroad executive; governor of Illinois (1853–1857); contractor in building I&M Canal.

Matthews, J. C. active 1830s–1840s. Operated ferry in mid-1830s (with George Dolton).

Matthews, Vincent active 1830s–1840s. Operated ferry ca. 1836–1842.

Mau-Me-Nass active early nineteenth century. Potawatomi woman; owned land at site that became Chesterton, IN.

May, George S. b June 5, 1890, Windsor, IL; d Mar. 12, 1962, Niles, IL. Management consultant; established and directed golf tournaments.

Mayer, Harold Melvin b Mar. 27, 1916, New York, NY; d July 23, 1994, Milwaukee, WI. Urban planner; geographer; Univ. of Chicago faculty member; research director of Chicago Plan Commission; coauthor of *Chicago: Growth of a Metropolis*.

Mayer, Oscar Ferdinand b Mar. 29, 1859, Kissingen, Germany; d Mar. 11, 1955, Chicago. Meatpacker; founded Oscar Mayer & Co.

Mayfield, Curtis b June 3, 1942, Chicago; d Dec. 26, 1999, Roswell, GA. Singer; songwriter; guitarist.

McAlpine, William J. b Apr. 30, 1812, New York, NY; d Feb. 16, 1890. Civil engineer; designed Chicago municipal water supply, 1850s.

McAndrew, William b Aug. 20, 1863, Ypsilanti, MI; d June 28, 1937, Mamaroneck, NY. Educator; editor of *Educational Review*; superintendent of Chicago Public Schools.

McCarthy, Joseph Vincent b Apr. 21, 1887, Philadelphia, PA; d Jan. 13, 1978, Buffalo, NY. Baseball player; manager; took over Chicago Cubs in 1925.

McCarty, Joseph b 1808, Morrison, NJ; d May 8 or 10, 1839, Tombigbee River, AL. Early settler in Aurora.

McCarty, Samuel b Mar. 9, 1810, Morrison, NJ; d Mar. 30, 1889, Aurora, IL. Founded Aurora.

McClellan, George B. b Dec. 3, 1826, Philadelphia, PA; d Oct. 29, 1885, Orange, NJ. Engineer and vice president of Illinois Central Railroad; commander of Army of the Potomac during Civil War.

McClintock, Carrie E. b ca. 1866, OH; d May 13, 1941, Harvey, IL. Cofounded South Harvey (later Hazel Crest); wife of William McClintock.

McClintock, William C. b ca. 1847; d July 22, 1903. Real-estate owner; cofounded South Harvey (later Hazel Crest).

McClurg, Alexander Caldwell b 1832 or 1833, Philadelphia, PA; d Apr. 15, 1901, St. Augustine, FL. Bookseller; publisher; president of McClurg Publishing Co.

McConnell, Joseph b ca. 1810, NY; d 1877. Founded Turner (now West Chicago).

McConnell, Mary Thompson b ca. 1810; d 1890. Platted Town of Turner (now West Chicago).

McCook, John James b May 26, 1845, Carrollton, OH; d Sept. 17, 1911. Civil war veteran; Santa Fe Railroad director.

McCormick, Cyrus Hall, Jr. b May 16, 1859, Washington, DC; d June 2, 1936, Lake Forest, IL. Manufacturer; managed and chaired International Harvester.

McCormick, Chauncey b Dec. 7, 1884, Chicago; d Sept. 8, 1954, Bar Harbor, ME. Business executive; philanthropist; president of Art Institute.

McCormick, Cyrus Hall b Feb. 15, 1809, Rockbridge County, VA; d May 13, 1884,

Chicago. Businessman; philanthropist; invented the reaper.

McCormick, Edith Rockefeller b Aug. 31, 1872, Cleveland, OH; d Aug. 25, 1932, Chicago. Philanthropist; promoted Chicago Civic Opera; financially supported Chicago Juvenile Court.

McCormick, Harold Fowler b May 2, 1872, Chicago; d Oct. 16, 1941, Beverly Hills, CA. Manufacturer; International Harvester Co. executive; founded Chicago Grand Opera (1910).

McCormick, Joseph Medill b May 16, 1877, Chicago; d Feb. 25, 1925, Washington, DC. Publisher; U.S. congressman and senator; owned *Chicago Daily Tribune.*

McCormick, Nettie Fowler b Feb. 8, 1835, Brownsville, NY; d July 5, 1923, Lake Forest, IL. Businesswoman; philanthropist.

McCormick, Robert Rutherford b July 30, 1880, Chicago; d Apr. 1, 1955, Wheaton, IL. Newspaper editor; publisher of *Chicago Tribune*; alderman; founded WGN radio station; president of Sanitary District.

McCormick, Ruth Hanna b Mar. 27, 1880, Cleveland, OH; d Dec. 31, 1944, Chicago. U.S. representative; woman suffrage activist; organizer and leader of Republican Women's Clubs in Chicago.

McCormick, Stanley b Nov. 2, 1874, Chicago; d Jan. 19, 1947, Santa Barbara, CA. Businessman with McCormick Harvesting Machine Co.

McCoy, John b Nov. 16, 1793, NH; d July 24, 1854. Farmer; established farm in 1830s; home was Underground Railroad stop.

McCoy, Sabra b July 21, 1799, Wells, Rutland, VT; d July 26, 1884. Farmer; established farm in 1830s; home was Underground Railroad stop.

McCulloch, Catharine Waugh b June 4, 1862, Ransomville, NY; d Apr. 20, 1945, Evanston, IL. Lawyer; suffragist; active in Chicago Political Equality League; first woman Justice of the Peace in Illinois.

McCutcheon, John T. b May 6, 1870, South Raub, IN; d June 10, 1949, Lake Forest, IL. Editorial cartoonist for *Chicago Tribune*; writer; war correspondent; won 1932 Pulitzer Prize.

McDermott, John Andrew b June 12, 1926, Philadelphia, PA; d Aug. 17, 1996, Chicago. Civil rights activist; founded *Chicago Reporter.*

McDermott, John J. b Aug. 10 or 12, 1891, Philadelphia, PA; d Aug. 2, 1917, Yeadon, PA. Professional golfer; first American-born winner of U.S. Open (1911).

McDonald, Eugene F. b Mar. 11, 1890, Syracuse, NY; d May 15, 1958. President of Zenith Radio Corp.

McDonald, Michael Cassius b 1839; d Aug. 9, 1907, Chicago. Gambling-house owner; Democratic Party leader in Chicago.

McDowell, Mary b Nov. 30, 1854, Cincinnati, OH; d Oct. 14, 1936, Chicago. Social worker; reformer; kindergarten teacher at Hull House; directed Univ. of Chicago Settlement House; president of Woman's City Club; Chicago commissioner of social welfare; cofounded Women's Trade Union League.

McFetridge, William Lane b Nov. 28, 1893, Chicago; d Mar. 15, 1969, Chicago. Labor leader; president of Building Service Employees International Union.

McGaw, Foster G. b Mar. 7, 1897, Hot Springs, NC; d Apr. 16, 1986, Lake Forest, IL. Founder and chairman of American Hospital Supply Corp.; philanthropist.

McGee, Henry Wadworth b Feb. 7, 1910, Hillsboro, TX; d Mar. 18, 2000, Evanston, IL. First black postmaster in Chicago (1966); president of Chicago chapter of NAACP.

McGillivray, Perry b Aug. 5, 1893, Oak Park, IL; d July 27, 1944, Chicago. Olympic water polo player.

McGinley, William Joseph b July 14, 1923, Hinsdale, IL; d Jan. 21 or 22, 2001, Key Largo, FL. Founded Methode Electronics, Inc.; owned Horizon Farms and bred thoroughbred horses.

McIntosh, Arthur T. b Mar. 28, 1877, Clear Lake, IA; d Nov. 7, 1955, Chicago. Real-estate developer; built communities in Glenview, Inverness, and Barrington.

McKay, Henry Donald b Dec. 6, 1899, Orient, SD; d Apr. 1980? Sociologist; Institute for Juvenile Research; collaborator of Clifford R. Shaw.

McKenzie, Roderick D. b Feb. 3, 1885, Carman, Manitoba; d May 6, 1940, Ann Arbor, MI. Sociologist; associated with Chicago School of Sociology.

McKibbin, George Baldwin b Apr. 26, 1888, Keosauqua, IA; d Sept. 14, 1960, Chicago. Lawyer; chairman of Illinois Public Aid Commission; unsuccessful candidate for mayor of Chicago (1943).

McKim, Charles b Aug. 24, 1847, Isabella Furnace, PA; d Sept. 14, 1909, St. James, NY. Architect; firm designed Agriculture Building at World's Columbian Exposition.

McKinsey, James Oscar b June 4, 1889, Gamma, MO; d Nov. 30, 1937, Chicago. Management consultant; founded McKinsey & Co.

McKinzie, Alexander active mid-nineteenth century. Actor; manager of Isherwood and McKinzie, first dramatic organization in Chicago.

McLaughlin, Daniel b Aug. 9, 1831, Lanarkshire, Scotland; d May 1, 1901, Chicago. Coal miner, union leader; mayor of Braidwood.

McLaughlin, Frederick b June 27, 1877, Chicago; d Dec. 17, 1944, Lake Forest, IL. Coffee executive; purchased Blackhawks hockey team in 1920s.

McMurtrie, Douglas C. b July 20, 1888, Belmar, NJ; d Sept. 19, 1944, Evanston, IL. Type designer; director of typography at Ludlow Co. and Cuneo Press.

McNear, Everett b Sept. 30, 1904; d Oct. 1984. Artist; designer; donated a collection of Persian miniatures to Art Institute of Chicago.

McNeill, Don b Dec. 23, 1907, Galena, IL; d May 7, 1996, Evanston, IL. Radio broadcaster; host of Don McNeill's *Breakfast Club* (1933–1968).

McParlan, James b 1844, Ulster, Ireland; d May 19, 1919, Denver, CO. Liquor store and saloon owner; detective; joined Pinkerton agency in early 1870s; noted for work in Molly Maguire case in Pennsylvania.

McPartland, James "Jimmy" Dougald b Mar. 15, 1907, Chicago; d Mar. 13, 1991, Port Washington, NY. Jazz cornetist; member of Austin High Gang.

McPartland, Richard "Dick" G. b May 18, 1905, Chicago; d Nov. 30, 1957, Elmhurst, IL. Guitarist; banjo player; member of Austin High Gang; performed in Chicago for over 30 years.

McPherson, Scott William b Oct. 13, 1959, OH; d Nov. 7, 1992, Chicago. Playwright; wrote *Marvin's Room*, which premiered at Goodman Theatre.

McRae, Edna b June 15, 1901, Chicago; d June 7, 1990, Evanston, IL. Contemporary dancer; dance teacher; owned dance school.

McSwiggin, William H. b Feb. 8, 1900, Chicago; d Apr. 27, 1926, Cicero, IL. Assistant state's attorney; posthumously exposed as associated with Al Capone.

McVickar, Brockholst H. b May 1810, New York, NY; d Oct. 14, 1883, Buffalo, NY. First city physician; surgeon at Marine Hospital; health commissioner.

McVicker, James H. b Feb. 14, 1822, New York, NY; d Mar. 7, 1896, Chicago. Theater manager; built McVicker's Theatre in Chicago (1857).

Meacham, Benjamin Franklin b 1813, Oswego County, NY; d 1879. Large landholder; promoted development near Bloomingdale.

Meacham, Harvey b Aug. 9, 1800, Pawlet, VT; d Nov. 11, 1878, Belgrade, OH. Early land purchaser in DuPage County.

Meacham, Lyman b ca. 1796, Pawlet, VT; d ca. 1892. Justice of the peace in Bloomingdale in 1834.

Meacham, Silas b July 2, 1789, Pawlet, VT; d July 21, 1852, Maine, IL. Early land purchaser in DuPage County; postmaster of Des Plaines (1840s).

Mead, Edward b Mar. 21, 1819, Leeds, England; d 1883, coast of Pico near Azores. Physician; founded Chicago Retreat for the Insane in 1847.

Mead, George Herbert b Feb. 27, 1863, South Hadley, MA; d Apr. 26, 1931, Chicago. Philosopher; social theorist; helped establish philosophy department at Univ. of Chicago.

Mead, William Rutherford b Aug. 20, 1946, Brattleboro, VT; d June 20, 1928, Paris,

France. Architect; firm designed Agriculture Building for World's Columbian Exposition.

Mears, Charles H. b Dec. 27, 1851, Chicago; d June 20, 1916, Pasadena, CA. Lumber dealer; identified with Mears-Slayton lumber company.

Medill, James C. b May 1, 1828; d Nov. 3, 1864. Printer; engaged with brother William in publication of *Prairie Farmer* in late 1850s.

Medill, Joseph E. b Apr. 6, 1823, St. John, New Brunswick; d Mar. 16, 1899, San Antonio, TX. Journalist; publisher of *Chicago Tribune*; mayor of Chicago (1871–1873).

Medill, William H. b Nov. 5, 1835, Massillon, OH; d July 16, 1863, Frederick City, MD. Printer; engaged with his brother James in publication of *Prairie Farmer* in late 1850s.

Mee, D. D. b June 9, 1850, Cedar Creek, IN; d June 14, 1919, Chicago. Owned D. D. Mee grocery, an early store in Irving Park area.

Meegan, Joseph B. b Aug. 5, 1911, Chicago; d July 8, 1994, Hinsdale, IL. Sociologist; cofounder and executive director of Back of the Yards Neighborhood Council for almost 50 years.

Meigs, Merrill C. b Nov. 25, 1883, Malcom, IA; d Jan. 25, 1968, Palm Beach, FL. Newspaper publisher; executive at Hearst Corp.; head of Chicago Aeronautics Commission.

Meinken, Johnny b Nov. 4, 1866, Bremen, Germany; d Aug. 29, 1924, Norwood Park, IL. Musician.

Meir, Golda [Golda Mabovitch Meyerson] b May 3, 1898, Kiev; d Dec. 8, 1978, Jerusalem, Israel. Member of Chicago "Poalei Tzion" (Workers of Zion); worked at Chicago Public Library; prime minister of Israel (1969–1974).

Memphis Minnie [Lizzie Douglas] b June 3, 1897, Algiers, LA; d Aug. 6, 1973, Memphis, TN. Early blues singer; guitarist; banjo player; popular Chicago club performer.

Memphis Slim [John Len Chatman] b Sept. 3, 1915, Memphis, TN; d Feb. 24, 1988, Paris, France. Blues singer; pianist; performed with Big Bill Broonzy.

Mendel, Edward b June 24, 1827; d Apr. 4, 1884. Early Chicago lithographer.

Mentch, Luna Elburn b June 3, 1860, Omro, WI; d Oct. 6, 1937, Cary, IL. Entrepreneur; opened first bank and real-estate agency in Cary; first president of incorporated Cary in 1893.

Merriam, Charles Edward b Nov. 15, 1874, Hopkinton, IA; d Jan. 8, 1953, Rockville, MD. Political scientist; alderman (1909–1911, 1913–1917); Univ. of Chicago faculty; Social Science Research Council founder.

Merriam, Robert Edward b Oct. 2, 1918, Chicago; d Aug. 25, 1988, Chicago. Business executive; alderman; unsuccessful 1955 GOP Chicago mayoral candidate; presidential adviser.

Merrill, Dudley b Sept. 15, 1814, VT; d July 8, 1890, Merrillville, IN. Arrived in 1837; namesake of Merrillville.

Merrill, George active 1830s. Saloonkeeper at Whiskey Point in Belmont Cragin.

Merrill, William b Apr. 16, 1808, VT; d Jan. 1, 1860, Merrillville, IN. Early settler; namesake of Merrillville.

Merrion, Joseph E. b Oct. 19, 1898, Chicago; d Nov. 28, 1971, Long Beach, IN. Real-estate developer of Hometown, Merrionette Park, and Country Club Hills; president of J. E. Merrion & Co.

Mestrovic, Ivan b Aug. 15, 1883, Vrpolje, Croatia; d Jan. 16, 1962, South Bend, IN. Sculptor; architect.

Metcalfe, Ralph Harold b May 30, 1910, Atlanta, GA; d Oct. 10, 1978, Chicago. Track and field athlete; alderman (1955–1970); U.S. representative (1971–1978); Olympic medal winner (1932, 1936).

Meyer, Albert Gregory b Mar. 9, 1903, Milwaukee, WI; d Apr. 9, 1965, Chicago. Roman Catholic archbishop of Chicago (1958–1965); cardinal (1959–1965); a leader at Vatican Council II.

Meyer, Fred J. b May 17, 1900; d Mar. 1983. Wrestler; 1920 Olympic wrestling medalist; trained at Chicago Hebrew Institute.

Meyer, Louis J. b Nov. 8, 1851, Elmhurst, IL; d Dec. 8, 1929, Addison Township, IL. Farmer; sold land to Chicago, Aurora & Elgin Railway.

Meyer, Lucy Rider b Sept. 9, 1849, New Haven, VT; d Mar. 16, 1922, Chicago. Educator; founded Chicago Training School for City, Home, and Foreign Missions.

Mezzrow, Milton "Mezz" [Milton Mesirow] b Nov. 9, 1899, Chicago; d Aug. 5, 1972, Paris, France. Jazz clarinetist; saxophone player; promoter.

Michaels, Kelly b Mar. 12, 1957, Morton Grove, IL; d Mar. 18, 1995, Chicago. Dancer; cofounded Chicago Human Rhythm Project (1990).

Michelson, Albert Abraham b Dec. 19, 1852, Strelno, Prussia (later Strzelno, Poland); d May 9, 1931, Pasadena, CA. Physicist; first chair of physics department at Univ. of Chicago; won Nobel Prize in Physics (1907).

Middaugh, Henry C. b Feb. 19, 1833, Scio, NY; d Oct. 28, 1916, Clarendon Hills, IL. Early landowner in Clarendon Hills.

Middeldorf, Ulrich Alexander b June 23, 1901; d Feb. 19, 1983. Art historian; faculty at School of the Art Institute of Chicago and Univ. of Chicago; active in Hyde Park Art Center.

Middleton, George b 1842; d Feb. 15, 1926, Pasadena, CA. Museum owner; opened first vaudeville entertainment in Chicago.

Middleton, Robert Hunter b May 6, 1898, Glasgow, Scotland; d Aug. 3, 1985, Chicago. Type designer; printer; worked at Ludlow Typographic Co. for 50 years.

Midney, Frank b 1876, Brooklyn, NY; d Dec. 12, 1939, Kankakee, IL. Socialist lecturer; Bughouse Square speaker.

Mies van der Rohe, Ludwig b Mar. 27, 1886, Aachen, Germany; d Aug. 17, 1969, Chicago. Architect; created International Style of steel and glass skyscrapers.

Mihalótzy, Géza b Apr. 21, 1825, Hungary; d Mar. 11, 1864, Chattanooga, TN. Soldier; organized Slovak military unit in Civil War (part of 24th Illinois Infantry).

Milleman, Jacob d 1849 or 1850. Cholera victim; estate was added to city cemetery.

Millen, John b 1796; d Aug. 11, 1853. Arrived in Chicago in 1838; resident in Deerfield; suggested name for Deerfield.

Miller, Howard b Dec. 17, 1912, Chicago; d Nov. 8, 1994, Naples, FL. Disc jockey; radio personality (1940s–1970s); program director at WIND.

Miller, Jacob b Nov. 4 or 5, 1804, Alsace, France; d May 19, 1874. Built saw- and gristmill along a tributary of Des Plaines River, naming it Mill Creek.

Miller, James Roscoe b Oct. 26, 1905, Murray, UT; d Oct. 16, 1977, Evanston, IL. Educator; dean of Northwestern Medical School (1941–1949); president of Northwestern Univ. (1949–1974).

Miller, Jesse active 1830s. Arrived in Barrington Hills in 1834.

Miller, Loren R. b July 1, 1877; d Mar. 19, 1967, Chicago. Merchant; Loren Miller's department store became Goldblatt's in Uptown area.

Miller, Merton H. b May 16, 1923, Boston, MA; d June 3, 2000, Chicago. Economist; Univ. of Chicago faculty specializing in finance; won Nobel Prize (1990).

Miller, Samuel active 1820s; d Michigan City, IN. Businessman; proprietor of Miller House, an early tavern; Cook County Commissioner.

Miller, Timothy Lathrop b Apr. 7, 1817, Middletown, CT; d Mar. 15, 1900, De Funiak Springs, FL. Breeder of Hereford cattle in area near Beecher (1870s).

Millis, Harry b May 14, 1873, Paoli, IN; d June 25, 1948, Chicago. Educator; Univ. of Chicago economist; chairman of National Labor Relations Board in 1940.

Mills, John b Apr. 17, 1854, Kingston, Ontario, Canada; d Dec. 7, 1841, Wilmette, IL. Developer; laid out Westwood subdivision.

Mills, Make b ca. 1871, Kuibyshev, Russia; d Sept. 26, 1956, Chicago. Police lieutenant; led Chicago's Red Squad in 1920s.

Mills, Theodore Sedgwick b July 1823 or 1824, Williamstown, MA. Started farm in Vernon Hills in 1851.

Miltimore, Ira b Sept. 28, 1813, Andover, VT; d June 8, 1879, Janesville, WI. Abolitionist; alderman; chairman of school committee.

Minton, Sherman b Oct. 20, 1890, Georgetown, IN; d Apr. 9, 1965, New Albany, IN.

U.S. senator; U.S. Supreme Court justice; U.S. Court of Appeals judge.

Mitchell, McKinley b ca. 1935, Jackson, MS; d Jan. 18, 1986, Chicago. Blues singer.

Moczygemba, Leopold b Oct. 18, 1824, Pluznica, Poland; d Feb. 23, 1891, Dearborn, MI. First Polish priest in Chicago; pastor at St. Alphonsus Church in Lemont, IL (1882–1887).

Moholy-Nagy, László b July 20, 1945, Bacsborsod, Hungary; d Nov. 24, 1946, Chicago. Painter; author; photographer; first director of New Bauhaus, Chicago (1937); president of Institute of Design.

Monroe, Day b Oct. 10 or 19, 1888, Wakeeney, KS; d June 1982. Sociologist.

Monroe, Harriet b Dec. 23, 1860, Chicago; d Sept. 26, 1936, Arequipa, Peru. Editor; poet; wrote official poem of World's Columbian Exposition; founding editor of *Poetry*.

Monroe, Lucy [Lucy Calhoun] b Mar. 1865, Chicago; d Sept. 5, 1950, Chicago. Writer; helped found Little Theatre; art critic for *Chicago Herald*.

Monroe, William "Bill" Smith b Sept. 13, 1911, Rosine, KY; d Sept. 9, 1996, Nashville, TN. Bluegrass musician; known as "Father of Bluegrass Music"; WLS *National Barn Dance* dancer.

Moody, Dwight Lyman b Feb. 5, 1837, Northfield, MA; d Dec. 22, 1899, Northfield, MA. Evangelist; revivalist; first president of Chicago YMCA (1866); founded Chicago (now Moody) Bible Institute (1886).

Moody, Walter Dwight b Jan. 16, 1874, Detroit, MI; d Nov. 21, 1920, Chicago. Business executive; promoted Burnham's *Plan of Chicago*; managing director of Chicago Plan Commission.

Moore, Christopher b ca. 1930; d June 26, 1987, Little Rock, AR. Minister; founded Chicago Children's Choir (1956).

Moore, J. Howard b Dec. 4, 1862, Linden, MO; d June 17, 1916, Chicago. Educator; writer; animal rights activist.

Moore, William Henry b Oct. 25, 1848, Utica, NY; d Jan. 11, 1923, NY. Lawyer; reorganized industrial companies (Rock Island Railroad, National Biscuit Co.).

Moran, George "Bugs" b 1893; d Feb. 25, 1957, Leavenworth, KS. Prohibition-era gangster; led North Side gang after the deaths of Dion O'Banion and Hymie Weiss.

Moran, Michael b Dec. 15, 1844, Longford, Ireland. Postmaster; opened Whiskey Point Hotel in Belmont-Cragin area.

Morgan, Anna b Feb. 24, 1851, Fleming, NY; d Aug. 27, 1936, Chicago. Speech and drama teacher; cofounded the Little Room literary salon.

Morgan, George C. b Sept. 11, 1830; d Mar. 21, 1895. Founded Chesterton State Bank.

Morgan, Jesse b May 12, 1787, Monongalia County, VA; d Feb. 3, 1853, Chesterton, IN. Early resident of Chesterton; first postmaster in Porter County.

Morgan, John "Jack" R. b July 14, 1903, Guatemala City, Guatemala; d Feb. 10, 1986, WI. Industrial designer; head of design at Sears (1934–1944).

Morgan, Thomas b Mar. 9, 1783, Surrey, England; d Mar. 19, 1857. Early English immigrant to Chicago.

Morris, Buckner Stith b Aug. 19, 1800, Augusta, KY; d Dec. 16, 1879, Chicago. Lawyer; alderman; circuit court judge; mayor of Chicago (1838–1839).

Morris, Kenneth b Aug. 28, 1917, New York, NY; d Feb. 1, 1989, Chicago. Pianist; music publisher; composed hundreds of gospel songs; cofounded Martin & Morris Music Co.

Morris, Nelson b Jan. 21, 1838, Hechingen, Germany; d Aug. 27, 1907, Chicago. Early cattle trader; meatpacker; central figure at Union Stock Yard for 50 years; founded Morris & Co.

Morrison, Charles Clayton b Dec. 4, 1874, Harrison, OH; d Mar. 2, 1966, Chicago. Minister; editor of the *Christian Century* magazine for 39 years; taught at Chicago Theological Seminary.

Morrison, Robert b Dec. 27, 1842, Richmond, IN; d 1888? Druggist; founded Fuller-Morrison drug company.

Morrissette, Bruce Archer b Apr. 26, 1911, Richmond, VA; d Feb. 6, 2000, Chicago. Univ. of Chicago professor of Romance Languages; film and novel scholar.

Morse, T. Vernette b 1852? Cortland, NY; d Feb. 19, 1925, Chicago. Artist; writer; philanthropist; art writer during World's Columbian Exposition.

Morton, Ferdinand "Jelly Roll" b Oct. 20, 1890, New Orleans, LA; d July 10, 1941, Los Angeles, CA. Jazz composer; ragtime, blues pianist; jazz bandleader; regarded as first jazz composer.

Morton, Joy b Sept. 27, 1855, Detroit, MI; d May 9, 1934, Lisle, IL. Salt merchant; president of Morton Salt Co.; founded Morton Arboretum.

Moser, Harold b c. 1914, IN; d Dec. 17, 2001, Naperville, IL. Real-estate developer, especially in Naperville; philanthropist.

Mosher, Charles Delevan b Feb. 10, 1829, NY; d June 7, 1897, Chicago. Photographer specializing in "cartes de visite."

Motley, Archibald John, Jr. b Oct. 7, 1891, New Orleans, LA; d Jan. 19, 1981, Chicago. Painter; active in South Side Community Art Center.

Motley, Willard Francis b July 14, 1909, Chicago; d Mar. 4, 1965, Mexico City, Mexico. Novelist; WPA writer; wrote *Knock on Any Door*, set in Chicago.

Motts, Robert T. b 1861, Washington, IA; d July 10, 1911, Chicago. Music hall proprietor; owned Pekin Theater.

Mould, Brooks K. active 1840s–1850s. Music publisher; prominent in Chicago music trade 1847–1859; operated his own music store.

Muddy Waters [McKinley Morganfield] b Apr. 4, 1915, Rolling Forks, MS; d Apr. 30, 1983, Chicago. Blues singer; guitarist; recorded for 30 years with Chess Records; transformed Delta Blues into Chicago Blues.

Mudgett, Herman Webster [H. H. Holmes] b 1861, Gilmanton, NH; d May 7, 1896, Philadelphia, PA. Serial killer; confessed to 27 murders.

Mueller, Vinzenz b Jan. 21, 1865, Liptingen, Germany; d June 6, 1942, Oak Park, IL. Founded a surgical instruments company.

Muhammad, Clara Evans b Nov. 2, 1898, GA; d Aug. 12, 1972, Chicago. Instrumental in creating the Clara Muhammad Elementary Schools.

Muhammad, Elijah [Robert Poole] b Oct. 1897, Sandersville, GA; d Feb. 25, 1975, Chicago. Leader of the Nation of Islam (1934–1975).

Mundelein, George William b July 2, 1872, New York, NY; d Oct. 2, 1939, Chicago. Roman Catholic archbishop of Chicago (1915–1939); cardinal (1924–1939).

Mundie, William Bryce b Apr. 30, 1863, Hamilton, Ontario, Canada; d Mar. 27, 1939, Evanston, IL. Architect; partner of William LeBaron Jenney; designed Horticultural Building for World's Columbian Exposition.

Mundy, James A. b July 9, 1886, Maysville, KY; d Dec. 25, 1978, Chicago. Choral director; trained thousands of black singers; known for "Battles of the Choirs."

Muni, Paul [Muni Weisenfreund] b Sept. 22, 1895, Lemberg, Austria (now Lviv, Ukraine); d Aug. 25, 1967, Santa Barbara, CA. Broadway and Hollywood actor; began acting career in Maxwell Street Yiddish theater; won Academy Award for *The Story of Louis Pasteur* (1936).

Munn, Ira Y. b ca. 1818, NJ; d 1882, Ouray, CO. President, Board of Trade; plaintiff in Supreme Court case *Munn v. Illinois* (1877).

Munster, Jacob [Monster] b ca. 1846, Holland; d 1924, Munster, IN. Early postmaster of Munster.

Murphy, John Benjamin b Dec. 21, 1857, Appleton, WI; d Aug. 11, 1916, Mackinac Island, MI. Surgeon; chair of Rush Medical College; performed first successful appendectomy in the United States in Chicago.

Musso, George b Apr. 8, 1910, Collinsville, IL; d Sept. 5, 2000, Edwardsville, IL. Professional football player; Bears player and team captain (1940s).

N

Nagurski, Bronislau "Bronko" b Nov. 3 or 4, 1908, Rainy River, Ontario, Canada; d Jan. 7, 1990, International Falls, MN. College and professional football player; Bears fullback (1940s).

Naper, Joseph b ca. 1798, VT; d Aug. 17, 1862, Naperville, IL. Platted Naperville; state legislator (1836–1840); first village president of Naperville (1857).

Napieralska, Stella active 1910s. Physician; supervised Guardian Angel Day Nursery Dispensary.

Napieralski, John b Poland; active 1830s. Captain in the Polish army; first Pole to arrive in Chicago.

Nash, Joseph b Apr. 6, 1828, England; d Apr. 12, 1903, Hobart, IN. Brickmaker and journeyman; established first large brickyard in Hobart, IN (1863).

Nash, Patrick A. b Mar. 2, 1863, Chicago; d Oct. 6, 1943, Chicago. Politician; chairman of Cook County Democratic Party; built "Kelly-Nash" machine.

Nathan, Marks b 1845, Lidvinowa, Russia; d Nov. 6, 1903. Businessman; endowed Marks Nathan Jewish Orphan Home.

Neal, George Edward b Nov. 10, 1907, Memphis, TN; d Aug. 22, 1938, Chicago. Painter, art teacher; worked for South Side Community Art Center.

Neebe, Oscar W. b July 12, 1850, New York, NY; d Apr. 22, 1916, Chicago. Anarchist; convicted in Haymarket Square riot; pardoned by Governor John P. Altgeld.

Nelson, Swain b Jan. 30, 1828, Fjelkestad, Sweden; d Jan. 18, 1917, Glenview, IL. Landscape designer; designed Lincoln and Union Parks.

Ness, Eliot b Apr. 19, 1903, Chicago; d May 16, 1957, Coudersport, PA. Federal law enforcement agent; headed the Untouchables; helped send Capone to prison.

Nestor, Agnes b June 24, 1880, Grand Rapids, MI; d Dec. 28, 1948, Chicago. Union organizer; president of International Glove Workers Union; president of Chicago Women's Trade Union League.

Nevans, Billy b July 17, 1833, Brooklyn, NY; d Mar. 27, 1894, Chicago. Bandleader; an organizer of Nevans & Dean's band.

Newberry, Julia Butler b May 12, 1818, Oxford, NY; d Dec. 9, 1885, Paris, France. Arrived in Chicago in 1843; wife of founder of Newberry Library.

Newberry, Walter Cass b Dec. 23, 1835, Sangerfield, NY; d July 20, 1912, Chicago. Businessman; U.S. representative; postmaster of Chicago; Civil War soldier.

Newberry, Walter Loomis b Sept. 18, 1804, Windsor, CT; d Nov. 6, 1868, Died at sea; buried in Chicago. Merchant banker; real-estate investor; bequeathed funds to establish Newberry Library.

Newhouse, Henry L. b Apr. 11, 1874, Chicago; d Oct. 26, 1929, Chicago. Architect; designer of Queen Anne homes in Fuller Park in mid-1880s.

Newton, Lewey Q. b ca. 1798, VT; d Apr. 11, 1868. First physician in Glen Ellyn; built a railroad station.

Nichols, May b after 1856? d Oct. 11, 1865, VT? Village of Maywood named for her by her father, William T. Nichols.

Nichols, Thomas F. active 1870s. Laid out Morgan Park in 1870s.

Nichols, William T. b Mar. 24, 1829, Clarendon, VT; d Apr. 10, 1882, Maywood, IL. Businessman; president of Maywood Co.; founded Maywood.

Nielubowski, Alex M. b Feb. 15, 1885, Chicago; d Nov. 1968. Packinghouse union leader.

Nims, John Frederick b Nov. 20, 1913, Muskegon, MI; d Jan. 19, 1999, Chicago. Educator; poet; editor of *Poetry Magazine*.

Noble, Mark, Jr. b Nov. 20, 1810, Yorkshire, England. Farmer; partner of George Bickerdike; constructed sawmill on Aux Plaines (now Des Plaines) River.

Noble, Mark, Sr. b c. 1765, England; d Nov. 25, 1839, Chicago. Farmer; butcher; arrived in Chicago in 1831; lived in Kinzie's cabin.

Noone, Jimmie b Apr. 23, 1895, Cut Off, LA; d Apr. 19, 1944, Los Angeles, CA. Jazz clarinetist; bandleader (1920s); jazz pioneer in transition from New Orleans style to Chicago style.

Nordfeldt, Bror Julius Olsson b Apr. 13, 1878, Tullstrop, Skane, Sweden; d Apr. 21, 1955, Henderson, TX. Artist; trained and exhibited at Chicago Art Institute.

Norris, Benjamin "Frank" Franklin b Mar. 5, 1870, Chicago; d Oct. 25, 1902, San Francisco, CA. Novelist; author of *The Pit*.

Norris, James D. b Nov. 6, 1906, Chicago; d Feb. 25, 1966, Chicago. Boxing promoter; formed International Boxing Club (1949); co-owned Chicago Blackhawks.

North, Dave active 1920s. Musician; played in Austin High Gang band.

North, Jessica Nelson [Jessica N. MacDonald] b Sept. 7, 1891, Madison, WI; d June 3, 1988. Poet; novelist; wrote *Arden Acres* (1935).

Norton, Hiram b Feb. 26, 1799, Skaneateles, NY; d Apr. 1, 1875, Lockport, IL. Contractor for I&M Canal; established firm of Norton & Co.; state legislator.

Nosek, Joseph active 1920s. Attorney; suggested incorporating Forest View in 1924.

Novikoff, Laurent b Aug. 3, 1888, Moscow, Russia; d June 18, 1956, New Buffalo, MI. Dancer; ballet master of Chicago Civic Opera Ballet.

O

O'Banion, Dion b July 8, 1892, Aurora, IL; d Nov. 10, 1924, Chicago. Flower shop owner; led North Side gang; adversary of Al Capone.

O'Brien, Agatha active mid-nineteenth century. Roman Catholic nun; led group of Sisters of Mercy to Chicago in 1846; helped establish orphanage, Mercy Hospital, other social services.

O'Brien, Christopher b ca. 1881, Meath, Ireland; d June 3, 1951, Chicago. Football executive and scout; cofounder and owner of Cardinals football team.

O'Connor, Leonard "Len" John b June 28, 1912; d July 5, 1991, Tubac, AZ. Radio and TV journalist; writer and commentator for nearly 40 years.

O'Connor, Timothy J. b Jan. 27, 1902; d Dec. 31, 1967, Chicago. Police commissioner (1950–1960); resigned after "burglar in blue" scandal.

O'Hare, Edward H. "Butch" b Mar. 13, 1914, St. Louis, MO; d Nov. 26, 1943, Gilbert Islands, Pacific. World War II fighter pilot; awarded Congressional Medal of Honor (1942); shot down during volunteer mission in the Pacific; namesake of O'Hare Airport.

O'Kennard, James b May 22, 1926, Chicago; d July 1971, Chicago. Active in early development of DuSable Museum.

O'Leary, Catherine b ca. 1827, Ireland; d July 3, 1895, Chicago. Owner of barn where 1871 fire allegedly originated.

O'Leary, Patrick b ca. 1819, Ireland; d Sept. 15, 1894. Husband of Catherine O'Leary; owned barn in which 1871 fire began.

O'Neill, Francis b Aug. 25, 1849, Cork, Ireland; d Jan. 28, 1936, Chicago. Chief of Chicago Police (1901–1905); authority on Irish folk tunes.

O'Neill, Lottie Holman b Nov. 7, 1878, Barry, IL; d Feb. 17, 1967, Downers Grove, IL. State legislator (1923–1931; 1933–1963).

O'Shaughnessy, Thomas A. b Apr. 14, 1870, Chariton, MO; d Feb. 11, 1956, Chicago. Mural artist; created stained-glass windows in Old St. Patrick's Church.

O'Toole, Donald b Apr. 4, 1909, Chicago; d Sept. 21? 1996, Frankfort, IL. Banker; involved with Princeton Park Homes development on Chicago's South Side.

Oakes, Grant Wilson b Apr. 1905, Westfield, NY; d July 1967? Labor union official; leader of Farm Equipment Workers.

Oatman, Elder John b July 14, 1787, Jefferson, KY; d 1875, Llano, TX. Early store and tavern owner in West Dundee; minister; helped establish Eureka College.

Oatman, Nancy b Mar. 22, 1876, Pennsylvania, VA; d 1864, Llano, TX. Established store and tavern in 1835.

Ochsner, Albert J. b Apr. 3, 1858, Baraboo, WI; d July 25, 1925, Chicago. Chief surgeon at Augustana Hospital.

Ogden, William Butler b June 15, 1805, Walton, NY; d Aug. 3, 1877, Fordham Heights, NY. Businessman; first mayor of Chicago (1837–1838).

Ogle, George Alden b July 5, 1863, Zanesville, OH; d May 27, 1930, Santa Monica,

CA. Publisher; head of map publishing company specializing in county atlases.

Oliver, Joe "King" b May 11, 1885, near New Orleans. LA; d Apr. 8, 1938, Savannah, GA. Jazz cornetist and bandleader; created King Oliver's Creole Jazz Band; gave Louis Armstrong his start.

Olmsted, Frederick Law b Apr. 26, 1822, Hartford, CT; d Aug. 23, 1903, Waverly, MA. Landscape architect; travel writer; designed World's Columbian Exposition, Washington and Jackson Parks.

Olson, Arthur H. b May 17, 1927, Gary, IN; d Oct. 3, 1981, Portage, IN. First mayor of Portage (1968–1971).

Onahan, William J. b Nov. 24, 1836, Carlow, Ireland; d Jan. 12, 1919, Chicago. Businessman; city clerk; city collector and city comptroller; president of Chicago Public Library.

Opatrny, Clara [Clara Cernocky] b Oct. 28, 1910, Fox River Grove, IL; d Jan. 27, 1993, Barrington, IL. Purchased Fox River Picnic Grove in 1942 with husband Louis Cernocky, Jr.

Opatrny, Eman b Jan. 8, 1877, IL; d Aug. 19, 1916, Algonquin, IL. Farmer; first developer of Fox River Grove and builder of Castle Pavilion.

Opatrny, Frank b 1830 or 1832, Bohemia, Austria; d Mar. 2, 1908, Fox River Grove, IL. Landowner; purchased 80 acres along the Fox River in 1869.

Oremus, John A. b Dec. 29, 1913, Chicago; d Apr. 4, 2002, Bridgeview, IL. Businessman; mayor of Bridgeview for 42 years.

Orvis, Justin K. b Nov. 6, 1870, Camp Lake, WI; d Aug. 7, 1939, Chicago. Lawyer; supported construction of a rail line linking Lake Zurich to Chicago.

Ouilmette, Antoine b 1760, Montreal, Canada; d 1841, Council Bluffs, IA. Fur trader; among the earliest European settlers in Chicago area.

Ouilmette, Archange b 1764, Sugar Creek, MI; d Nov. 25, 1840, Council Bluffs, IA. Potawatomi wife of Antoine Ouilmette; granted land in 1829 Indian treaty.

Oukrainsky, Serge [Leonide Orlay de Carva] b Dec. 2, 1885, Odessa, Russia; d Nov. 1, 1972, Los Angeles, CA. Ballet and opera dancer; choreographer and director of Chicago Grand Opera Ballet; created Pavley-Oukrainsky ballet company.

Overton, Anthony b Mar. 21, 1865, Monroe, LA; d July 2, 1946, Chicago. Lawyer; business executive; published *Chicago Bee*; organized Douglass National Bank; founded Overton Hygienic Manufacturing Co.

Owen, William B. b June 5, 1834, Crown Point, NY; d 1901. Manufacturer of brick and terra cotta; founded Owen works.

Owings, Nathaniel Alexander b Feb. 5, 1903, Indianapolis, IN; d June 13, 1984, Santa Fe, NM. Architect; environmentalist; partner at Skidmore, Owings & Merrill.

P

Paddock, Charles S. b Sept. 10, 1883, Chicago; d May 23, 1967, Arlington Heights, IL. Newspaper publisher; published *Daily Herald*.

Paddock, Hosea C. b Aug. 5, 1852, Western NY; d Nov. 15, 1935, Arlington Heights, IL. Newspaper publisher; founded Paddock Publications, owner of *Daily Herald*.

Paddock, Stuart Ransom b Aug. 10, 1881, Plainfield, IL; d May 4, 1968, Dunedin, FL. Newspaper publisher; published *Daily Herald*.

Paepcke, Walter b June 29, 1896, Chicago; d Apr. 13, 1960, Chicago. Founder and president of Container Corp. of America.

Page, Geraldine b Nov. 22, 1924, Kirksville, MO; d June 13, 1987, New York, NY. Actor; trained at Goodman Theatre Dramatic School in Chicago.

Page, H. R. active 1870s. Mapmaker; compiled real-estate atlas in 1879.

Page, Harlan (Pat) O. b Mar. 20, 1887, Watervliet, MI; d Nov. 23, 1965, St. Joseph, MI. Athlete; Univ. of Chicago football player; basketball player and coach; in Basketball Hall of Fame.

Page, Ruth [Ruth Fischer] b Mar. 22, 1899, Indianapolis, IN; d Apr. 7, 1991, Chicago. Ballet dancer; director of Chicago Opera Ballet; founded Ruth Page Ballet.

Page, William R. active 1870s. Lawyer; land promoter in Western Springs around 1870.

Pahlman, Hermann H. b Apr. 25, 1812, Latbergan, Hanover, Prussia; d Feb. 21, 1900. Built cabin near Long Grove Road in Kildeer around 1837.

Paine, Seth b ca. 1815, New England; d 1871? Merchant; purchased lakeshore tract and developed it as Lake Zurich.

Pajeau, Charles H. b Aug. 18, 1875, New Ipswich, NH; d Dec. 17, 1952, Evanston, IL. Toy manufacturer; invented Tinker Toys.

Palandech, John R. b Sept. 23, 1873, Sulina, Roumania; d Sept. 14, 1959, Chicago. Editor and publisher of the *United Serbian*; founded Palandech Press.

Paley, William S b Sept. 27 or 28, 1901, Chicago; d Oct. 26, 1990, New York, NY. Broadcasting executive; president of CBS.

Palmer, Bertha Honoré b May 22, 1849, Louisville, KY; d May 5, 1918, Osprey, FL. Philanthropist; art collector.

Palmer, Potter b May 20, 1826, Potter's Hollow, NY; d May 4, 1902, Chicago. Merchant and innovator of retail practices; early developer of State Street; built the Palmer House.

Pargellis, Stanley b June 25, 1898, Toledo, OH; d Jan. 6, 1968, Chicago. Librarian of Newberry Library (1942–1962).

Park, Robert Ezra b Feb. 14, 1864, Luzerne County, PA; d Feb. 7, 1944, Nashville, TN. Sociologist; Univ. of Chicago professor; associated with Chicago School of Sociology; first president of Chicago Urban League.

Parker, Francis Wayland b Oct. 9, 1837, Bedford, NH; d Mar. 2, 1902, Pass Christian, MS. Educational reformer; principal of Cook County Normal School; founded Francis W. Parker School.

Parmelee, Frank b Aug. 11, 1816, Byron, NJ; d Oct. 1, 1904, Chicago. Transportation executive; founded Chicago Omnibus Line, the first in the city.

Parsons, Albert R. b June 24, 1848, Montgomery, AL; d Nov. 11, 1887, Chicago. Anarchist; convicted in Haymarket Square riot; executed.

Parsons, Lucy Eldine b Mar. 1853, Waco, TX; d Mar. 7, 1942, Chicago. Free-speech advocate; labor activist; active in anarchist, socialist and Communist movements in Chicago.

Passavant, William b Oct. 9, 1821, Zelienople, PA; d June 3, 1894, Pittsburgh, PA. Lutheran clergyman; founded hospitals and orphanages; principal founder of Chicago Lutheran Seminary (1891).

Patrick, Hiram Blanchard b 1819, Courtland County, NY; d 1906. Farmer; arrived in DuPage County in 1843.

Patterson, Erastus b Woodstock, VT; d 1837. Established Patterson Tavern along Green Bay Trail in 1836 (with Zeruah Patterson).

Patterson, George A. b Oct. 27, 1907, Scotland; d Oct. 3, 1988, Chicago. Union organizer; founding president of Local 65 of United Steelworkers of America; picket captain at Memorial Day Massacre in 1937.

Patterson, Joseph Medill b Jan. 6, 1879, Chicago; d May 25, 1946, New York, NY. Newspaper publisher; editor of *Chicago Tribune*; state legislator (1903–1904); Pulitzer Prize (1940).

Patterson, Richard J. b Nov. 14, 1817, Berkshire County, MA; d Apr. 27, 1893, Batavia, IL. Physician specializing in mental illness; founded Bellevue Place; physician in charge during Mary Todd Lincoln's stay.

Patterson, Robert Wilson b Nov. 30, 1850, Chicago; d Apr. 1, 1910, Philadelphia, PA. Journalist; editor-in-chief of *Chicago Tribune*.

Patterson, Zeruah (or Zernah) b ca. 1794, Woodstock, VT. Established Patterson Tavern in 1836 along Green Bay Trail (with Erastus Patterson).

Patti, Adelina Juana b Feb. 19, 1843, Madrid, Spain; d Sept. 27, 1919, Craig-y-Nos, Wales, England. Soprano; performed in Chicago during 1850s as a child prodigy.

Patton, Francis Landry b Jan. 22, 1843, Warwick, Bermuda; d Nov. 25, 1932. Presbyterian preacher; taught at McCormick Seminary; accused David Swing of heresy.

Patton, John b ca. 1883; d Dec. 23, 1956, Earl Park, IN. Capone vice overlord; had 42-year career as "boy mayor of Burnham" (1908–1949).

Paul, René active 1820s. Surveyor; made first survey of possible I&M Canal routes (with Justus Post).

Pavley, Andreas [Andreas van Dorp de Weyer] b Nov. 1, 1892, Batavia, Java (now Indonesia); d June 26, 1931, Chicago. Dancer; ballet master of Chicago Civic Opera; founded Pavley-Oukrainsky ballet.

Payne, Jimmy b Aug. 21, 1905; d Nov. 13, 2000, Chicago. Artist; tap dancer and teacher in Chicago in the 1940s.

Payne, William Morton b Feb. 14, 1858, Newburyport, MA; d July 11, 1919, Chicago. Educator; writer; associate editor of the *Dial*; literary editor of *Chicago Morning News* and *Chicago Evening Journal*.

Payton, Walter Jerry b July 25, 1954, Columbia, MS; d Nov. 1, 1999, Barrington, IL. Hall of Fame football player; Chicago Bears running back (1975–1987); businessman.

Peabody, Robert Swain b Feb. 22, 1845, New Bedford, MA; d Sept. 23, 1917, Marblehead, MA. Architect; designed Machinery Hall on the Court of Honor and Massachusetts Building for World's Columbian Exposition.

Peattie, Donald Culross b June 21, 1898, Chicago; d Nov. 16, 1964, Santa Barbara, CA. Naturalist; writer; author of *Flora of the Indiana Dunes*.

Peattie, Elia Wilkinson b Jan. 15, 1862, Kalamazoo, MI; d July 12, 1935, Wellingford, VT. Writer; literary critic; journalist for *Chicago Tribune* and the *Daily News*.

Peck, Charles Edwin b Sept. 2, 1816, Washington, VT; d Aug. 12, 1904. Cofounded village of Winnetka; postmaster of Winnetka; Chicago fire chief.

Peck, Ferdinand Wythe b July 15, 1848, Chicago; d Nov. 4, 1924, Chicago. Lawyer; president of opera festival; promoted building of the Auditorium Theatre.

Peck, Phillip F. W. b Jan. 16, 1809, Providence, RI; d Oct. 23, 1871, Chicago. Early Chicago merchant; real-estate developer.

Peel, Peter J. b May 14, 1874, Dublin, Ireland; d May 4, 1969, Chicago. Soccer player; considered the "father of American soccer"; led first U.S. Olympic soccer team (1924).

Penny, George W. b ca. 1820s, Bangor, ME; d Sept. 11, 1868. Brickyard owner in Park Ridge; built Park Ridge residence in 1857.

Perez, Manuel b Dec. 28, 1871, New Orleans, LA; d 1946, New Orleans, LA. Bandleader; cornetist; played ragtime and jazz; performed with Charles Elgar's Creole Orchestra in Chicago.

Periolat, Napoleon active mid-nineteenth century. Businessman; built brewery in Wheeling in 1850.

Perkins, Charles Elliott b Nov. 24, 1840, Cincinnati, OH; d Nov. 8, 1907, Westwood, MA. Railroad executive; president of Chicago, Burlington & Quincy Railroad (1875–1907).

Perkins, Dwight Heald b Mar. 26, 1867, Memphis, TN; d Nov. 2, 1941, Lordsburg, NM. Architect; specialist in school architecture; designed over 200 Chicago public buildings; campaigned for creation of forest preserves.

Perkins, Lawrence Bradford b Feb. 12, 1907, Evanston, IL; d Dec. 3, 1997, Evanston, IL. Architect; designed Crow Island Elementary School in Winnetka, IL, and First National Bank of Chicago.

Perkins, Marion M. b 1908, Marche, AR; d Dec. 17, 1961, Chicago. Artist; sculptor.

Perkins, Marlin b Mar. 28, 1905, Carthage, MO; d June 14, 1986, St. Louis, MO. Naturalist; television personality; Lincoln Park Zoo director for 18 years.

Perren, Julius b Germany; d ca. 1878, Niles, IL. Farmer; settled in Niles in early 1830s.

Petersdorf, Frederick active 1850s. Landowner; purchased land from Peter Kern around 1850s.

Petersen, Louis P. b ca. 1884, Detroit, MI; d June 13, 1958, Chicago. Bowling alley owner; organized Petersen Bowling Classic; founded Chicago Bowling Proprietors Association.

Peterson, Gunnar A. b Jan. 3, 1915, Pittsfield, MA; d June 7, 1976, Halifax, Nova Scotia. Preservation activist; founding executive director of Openlands Project (1963–1975).

Peterson, Per S. b June 15, 1830, Vä, Skåne, Sweden; d Jan. 19, 1903, Chicago. First professional nurseryman in Middle West; started Rose Hill Nursery.

Peterson, Virgil W. b Nov. 16, 1904, Olds, IA; d Feb. 20, 1989, Berwyn, IL. Lawyer; FBI agent; directed Chicago Crime Commission for 27 years.

Petrillo, James Caesar b Mar. 16, 1892, Chicago; d Oct. 23, 1984, Chicago. Labor leader; musician; president of American Federation of Musicians.

Pettibone, Holman b Feb. 27, 1889, Albion, NE; d July 24, 1962, Lac du Flambeau, WI. Banker; chairman of the board of Chicago Title & Trust Co.

Phillips, Irna b July 1, 1903, Chicago; d Dec. 23, 1973, Chicago. Radio and television writer; created radio and television daytime serials including *The Guiding Light* and *As the World Turns*.

Phillips, James F. ["The Fox"] b Nov. 20, 1930, Aurora, IL; d Oct. 3, 2001, Aurora. Environmental activist.

Piacenza, Aldo b Aug. 13, 1888, Italy; d Feb. 1976. Self-taught artist; made elaborate painted birdhouses.

Piatkiewicz, Karol b Oct. 29, 1891; d Apr. 23, 1971, Hot Springs, AR. Chief editor of Polish National Alliance newspaper (*Dziennik Zwizkowy*) for 36 years.

Pierce, Bessie Louise b Apr. 20, 1888, Caro, MI; d Oct. 3, 1974, Iowa City, IA. Historian; Univ. of Chicago faculty; wrote three-volume history of Chicago.

Pierce, Elijah active 1820s. Opened tavern near Montgomery in mid-1830s.

Pihlfeldt, Thomas G. b Oct. 11, 1858, Vadso, Norway; d Jan. 23, 1941, Chicago. Engineer; city engineer of bridges.

Pinet, Pierre b ca. 1660; d July 16, 1704, Cahokia, IL. Roman Catholic priest; established Mission of the Guardian Angel in 1696.

Pingree, Andrew b July 16, 1803, Weare, NH; d Aug. 18, 1879, Pingree Grove, IL. Minister; farmer; surveyor of Burlington; established Pingree Grove.

Pinkerton, Allan b Aug. 25, 1819, Gorbals, Glasgow, Scotland; d July 1, 1894, Chicago. Private detective; founded Pinkerton National Detective Agency in Chicago (1850).

Pinkerton, Robert Allen b Dec. 2, 1848, Dundee, IL; d Aug. 12 or 13, 1907, aboard ship to Europe. Private detective; head of Pinkerton Detective agency's eastern division.

Pinkerton, William Allen b Apr. 7, 1846, Dundee, IL; d Dec. 11, 1923, Los Angeles, CA. Private detective; chief of Pinkerton Detective Agency during Haymarket Affair; secret service agent during Civil War.

Piper, Alexander Ross b Mar. 1, 1865, Fort Wadsworth, Staten Island, NY; d Nov. 1, 1952, South Salem, NY. Police captain; led internal investigation of Chicago Police Department in 1904.

Piper, Charles E. b June 12, 1858, Chicago; d Jan. 28, 1923, Black Mountain, NC. Lawyer; real-estate investor in Berwyn.

Piven, Byrne b Sept. 24, 1929, Scranton, PA; d Feb. 18, 2002, Evanston, IL. Actor; director; teacher; founded Piven Theatre Workshop.

Plagge, Christoph active 1850s. Music writer; wrote "The Garden City Polka" in 1854.

Plamondon, Marie b Sept. 27, 1880; d May 14, 1967, Chicago. Social worker; codirector of Madonna Center (1932–1967).

Plawinski, Edward E. b Oct. 18, 1903, Chicago; d Feb. 16, 1986, Ft. Lauderdale, FL. Pastor at St. Simeon (Bellwood) for 26 years; president of Back of the Yards Neighborhood Council (1940–1945).

Plummer, Jonathan W. b Mar. 25, 1835, Richmond, IN; d Feb. 2, 1918, Dixon, IL. Wholesale druggist; founded wholesale drug firm of Morrison, Plummer & Co. (later Fuller-Morrison).

Polacheck, Hilda Satt [Hinda] b Oct. 12, 1882, Wloclawek, Poland; d May 18, 1967, Chicago. Writer; involved in labor, peace, and woman suffrage movements; active participant in Hull House.

Poncelet, Adolphe b May 15, 1819, Neufchateau, Belgium; d May 11, 1857, Blue Island, IL. Belgian consul in Chicago (1850s).

Pond, Allen B. b Nov. 21, 1858, Ann Arbor, MI; d Mar. 17, 1929, Chicago. Architect; codesigned Hull House buildings.

Pond, Irving Kane b May 1, 1857, Ann Arbor, MI; d Sept. 29, 1939, Washington, DC. Architect; structural engineer; codesigned Hull House buildings.

Pontiac b ca. 1714, Ottawa village on the Detroit River; d Apr. 20, 1769, Cahokia, IL. Ottawa chief; led Indian mobilization, 1763–1764.

Poole, George A. b Apr. 8, 1907, Chicago; d Mar. 21, 1990. Printer; philanthropist; rare book collector.

Poole, William Frederick b Dec. 24, 1821, Salem/Peabody, MA; d Mar. 1, 1894, Evanston, IL. Librarian; bibliographer; president of American Library Association; librarian of Chicago Public Library (1873–1887); librarian of Newberry Library (1887–1894).

Pooley, Georgia Bitzis b Jan. 20, 1857, Corfu, Greece; d June 1, 1945, Chicago. First known Greek woman in Chicago (1885).

Pooley, Peter b 1844, Corfu, Greece; d 1914, Chicago. Sea captain.

Poorman, John G. b Jan. 27, 1882, Cincinnati, OH; d Sept. 22, 1955, Beaumont, CA. Inventor; poultry farmer; invented a chicken brooder.

Porter, Benjamin M. b July 3, 1816, Pawlet, VT; d Jan. 6, 1897, Palatine, IL. Arrived in Chicago area around 1835.

Porter, Eliza Emily Chappell b Nov. 5, 1807, Geneseo, NY; d Jan. 1, 1888, Santa Barbara, CA. Educator; relief worker; missionary; Underground Railroad activist.

Porter, Jeremiah b Dec. 27, 1804, Hadley, MA; d July 25, 1893, Beloit, WI. Early clergyman; organized First Presbyterian Church in Chicago (1833).

Porter, Julia Foster b Aug. 22, 1846, Chicago; d Aug. 23, 1936, Chicago. Administrator; philanthropist; founded Children's Hospital.

Porthier, Victoire Mirandeau b 1800 or 1801; d after 1883. Métis member of Ouilmette and Kinzie households; eyewitness to Lalime homicide.

Post, George Browne b Dec. 15, 1837, New York, NY; d Nov. 28, 1913, Bernardsville, NJ. Architect; designed Manufacturers and Liberal Arts Buildings at World's Columbian Exposition.

Post, Justus b ca. 1781, NJ; d Mar. 14, 1846, Caledonia, IL. Engineer; made the first survey of possible I&M Canal routes (with René Paul).

Post, Louis Freeland b Nov. 15, 1849, Warren County, NJ; d Jan. 10, 1928, Washington, DC. Writer; reformer; member of Chicago Board of Education; assistant U.S. secretary of labor.

Powers, Johnny b Feb. 15, 1852, Brannon, Kilkenny, Ireland; d May 19, 1930, Chicago. Alderman (1888–1927); businessman; Democratic Party power broker.

Pratt, John Morgan b Mar. 23, 1886, Sharpsville, IN; d June 14, 1954, Chicago. Lawyer; newspaper executive; active in Association of Real Estate Taxpayers (ARET); leader in 1930s tax strikes.

Prendergast, Patrick Eugene b ca. 1868, Ireland; d July 13, 1894, Chicago. Assassinated mayor Carter Harrison (1893); executed for the murder.

Price, Florence Beatrice b Apr. 9, 1888, Little Rock, AR; d June 3, 1953, Chicago. Composer; organist; pianist.

Priebe, Karl b July 1, 1914, Milwaukee, WI; d July 6, 1976, Milwaukee, WI. Artist; painter; teacher.

Prince, Earl H. b Oct. 10, 1861, Roxbury, VT; d Feb. 8, 1940, Dixon, IL. Real-estate developer; platted a subdivision of Downers Grove.

Prince, Frederick Henry b Nov. 24, 1859, Winchester, MA; d Feb. 2, 1953, Biarritz, France. Financier; incorporated Chicago Stock Yards Co.; founded Central Manufacturing District (1905).

Prince, Richard b Sept. 18, 1922, Chicago; d July 6, 1996, Holland, MI. Helped found Trinity Christian College; served as dean.

Proudfoot, Malcolm b July 18, 1907, Chicago; d Nov. 21, 1955, Oxford, England. Geographer; professor at Northwestern Univ.

Pucinski, Roman C. b May 13, 1919, Buffalo, NY; d Sept. 25, 2002, Park Ridge, IL. U.S. congressman (1959–1973); alderman; reporter for *Sun-Times.*

Puffer, Henry b Feb. 15, 1790, Berlin, MA; d Mar. 12, 1851 or 1857, Downers Grove, IL. Early resident of Downers Grove area.

Pullman, George Mortimer b Mar. 3, 1831, Brocton, NY; d Oct. 19, 1897, Chicago. Manufacturing innovator and entrepreneur, founded town of Pullman, Pullman Palace Car Co.

Purcell, William b 1880, Wilmette, IL; d Apr. 11, 1965. Architect.

Purington, Dillwyn V. b Jan. 22, 1841, Sidney, ME; d Apr. 2, 1914, Ocean Springs, MS. Manufacturer; founded brick companies.

Purvin, Jennie Franklin b Aug. 23, 1873, Chicago; d Nov. 1, 1958, Chicago. Civic reformer; active in Chicago's women's clubs; campaigned for public bathing along Lake Michigan.

Putnam, Alice Harvey Whiting b Jan. 18, 1841, Chicago; d Jan. 19, 1919, Chicago. Leader in kindergarten movement; president of Chicago Kindergarten Club.

Putnam, Frederic Ward b Apr. 16, 1839, Salem, MA; d Aug. 14, 1915, Cambridge, MA. Anthropologist; curator of Harvard's Peabody Museum; director of anthropological section World's Columbian Exposition.

Pyle, Charles C. b Mar. 25, 1882, Van Wert, OH; d Feb. 3, 1939, Los Angeles, CA. Sports promoter; agent for football star Red Grange.

Q

Quaife, Milo M. b Oct. 6, 1880, Nashua, IA; d Sept. 1, 1959, Detroit, MI. Historian of the Midwest; superintendent of Wisconsin Historical Society.

Quarter, William James b Jan. 21, 1806, King's County, Ireland; d Apr. 10, 1848, Chicago. First bishop of Roman Catholic Diocese of Chicago (1844–1848).

Quesse, William F. b Apr. 4, 1878, Chebanse, IL; d Feb. 16, 1927, Chicago. Labor leader; organizer and first international president of Chicago Flat Janitor's Union (1912).

Quick, Henry b Harlem, NY. Arrived in Noyesville in 1850s; prominent landowner; owned farm on what is now River Forest.

Quick, John Henry b Jan. 13, 1837, Newark, NJ; d Mar. 2, 1921. Lawyer; landowner in Forest Park in 1850s.

Quigley, James Edwar b Oct. 15, 1854, Oshawa, Ontario, Canada d July 10, 1915, Rochester, NY. Roman Catholic archbishop of Chicago (1903–1915).

Quinn, Don b Nov. 18, 1900, Grand Rapids, MI; d Dec. 30, 1967, Los Angeles, CA. Comedy writer; creator and head writer of *Fibber McGee and Molly* show.

Quinn, Robert J. b May 12, 1905, Chicago; d Jan. 19, 1979, Naples, FL. Chicago fire commissioner (1957–1978).

R

Rabinowitch, Eugene b 1901, St. Petersburg, Russia; d May 15, 1973, Washington, DC. Chemist; member of Manhattan Project; leader in international movement for nuclear arms control.

Raby, Al(bert) A. b Feb. 19, 1933, Chicago; d Nov. 23, 1988, Chicago. Civil rights activist; aide to Rev. Martin Luther King Jr.; campaign manager for Harold Washington mayoral run.

Race, Charles T. b Nov. 1810, Greene, NY; d Apr. 20, 1888, Chicago. Farmer; real-estate developer; organized Irving Park Land Co.

Raday, Harry b Nov. 10, 1927, Chicago; d Oct. 1989. General contractor; mayor of Midlothian (1961–1985).

Rader, Paul b Aug. 24, 1879, Denver, CO; d June 19, 1938, Hollywood, CA. Evangelist; pastor at Moody Church; founded Chicago Gospel Tabernacle; early radio evangelist.

Ragen, Frank M. b Mar. 23, 1871, Chicago; d July 1, 1945, Chicago. County commissioner; Democratic ward committeeman; founded Ragen's Colts, an athletic club active in 1919 riot.

Rainey, Ma [Gertrude Pridgett] b Apr. 26, 1886, Columbus, GA; d Dec. 22, 1939, Columbus, GA. Blues singer; songwriter; known as "Mother of the Blues"; recorded for Paramount Records in Chicago (1920s).

Raisa, Rosa [Raisa Burchstein] b May 30, 1893, Bialystok, Poland; d Sept. 28, 1963, Pacific Palisades, CA. Soprano; voice teacher; joined Chicago Opera Company.

Rakove, Milton Leon b Oct. 30, 1918, Buhl, MN; d Nov. 5, 1983, Chicago. Political scientist; professor at Univ. of Illinois of Chicago;

author of *Don't Make No Waves, Don't Back No Losers*; expert on Richard M. Daley's city politics.

Ramanujan, A. K. b Mar. 16, 1929, Mysore, India; d July 13, 1993, Chicago. Poet; writer; Univ. of Chicago professor specializing in Indian literature.

Ramberg, Christina b Aug. 21, 1946, Fort Campbell, KY; d Dec. 10, 1995, Naperville, IL. Artist; professor at the School of the Art Institute; associated with Imagist movement.

Rand, Sally [Helen Gould Beck] b Jan. 2, 1904, Elkton, MO; d Aug. 31, 1979, Glendora, CA. Fan dancer; sensation at Century of Progress World's Fair.

Rand, Socrates b ca. 1804, Franklin County, MA; d ca. 1890, Des Plaines, IL. Early farmer; justice of the peace in Des Plaines.

Rand, William H. b May 2, 1828, Quincy, MA; d June 20, 1915, New Canaan, CT. Publisher; cofounded Rand, McNally & Co. in 1856.

Randall, Dudley b Feb. 17, 1832, Stonington, CT. Editor; worked for *Aurora Beacon* and various other Illinois newspapers.

Randolph, A. Philip b Apr. 15, 1889, Crescent City, FL; d May 16, 1979, Manhattan, NY. Founded Brotherhood of Sleeping Car Porters; editor of the *Messenger* (NY).

Randolph, Paul Johnston b Sept. 5, 1905, Beason, IL; d Nov. 19 or 20, 1990, on a cruise ship in Florida. State representative; influential in creating Chicago's Transportation Authority.

Ransom, Anning S. b 1795, NY; d 1883, Wheaton, IL. Early farmer in Carol Stream area (1830s); soldier in War of 1812.

Ransom, Reverdy Cassius b Jan. 4, 1861, Flushing, OH; d Apr. 22, 1959, Wilberforce, OH. Bishop; civil rights leader; organized African Methodist Episcopal Institutional Church and Social Settlement.

Ransom, Will b 1878, Saint Louis, MI; d May 24, 1955, Norman, OK. Typographer; book artist; writer on the printing arts.

Rascher, Charles b ca. 1844, Germany; d Nov. 8, 1900, Chicago. Surveyor; mapmaker and map publisher, 1880–1892.

Rascoe, Burton b Oct. 22, 1892, Fulton, KY; d Mar. 19, 1957, New York, NY. Writer; editor; drama critic; worked for *Chicago Tribune* (1912–1920).

Rauch, John H. b Sept. 4, 1828, Lebanon, PA; d Mar. 24, 1894, Lebanon, PA. Physician; president of Illinois State Board of Health; park district advocate.

Rauhoff, John M. b May 15, 1868, Russellville, AL; d Oct. 18, 1927, Tinley Park, IL. Engineer; created "Ironite," an additive for waterproofing cement used in the Hoover Dam.

Raupp, Melchior b Mar. 11, 1814, Baden, Bavaria, Germany; d Jan. 8, 1891, Buffalo Grove, IL. Moved to Buffalo Grove around 1840s.

Raycroft, Joseph Edward b Nov. 15, 1867, Williamstown, VT; d Sept. 30, 1955, Trenton, NJ. College basketball coach; coached Univ. of Chicago to four straight Big Ten championships.

Raymond, Benjamin Wright b June 15, 1801, Rome, NY; d Apr. 6, 1883, Chicago. Merchant; watch manufacturer in Elgin; mayor of Chicago (1839–40; 1842–43).

Read, Opie b Dec. 22, 1852, Nashville, TN; d Nov. 2, 1939, Chicago. Novelist; newspaper journalist; member of the Chicago Press Club.

Rebori, Andrew Nicholas b Feb. 21, 1886, New York, NY; d May 31, 1966, Chicago. Chicago architect; designed Madonna della Strada Chapel (1938–1939).

Redenbacher, Orville Clarence b July 16, 1907, Brazil, IN; d Sept. 19, 1995, Coronado, CA. Food manufacturer; introduced gourmet popcorn.

Redmond, James F. b Sept. 13, 1915, Kansas City, MO; d Mar. 21, 1993, La Grange, IL. Superintendent of Chicago Public Schools (1966–1975).

Reed, Charles b Apr. 16, 1784, VA; d Aug. 26, 1863, Rockton, IL. Founded Joliet.

Reed, Guy Euclid b July 11, 1890, Holdrege, NE; d Jan. 2, 1959, Northbrook, IL. Banker; president of Chicago Crime Commission; president of village of Long Grove.

Reed, Mathis James "Jimmy" b Sept. 6, 1925, Dunleith, MS; d Aug. 29, 1976. Blues musician; singer; songwriter; recorded for Vee-Jay Records.

Reeder, John active 1840s. Arrived in area known as Reeder Station (later Schererville, IN) around 1840.

Rees, James H. b Apr. 24, 1813, PA; d Sept. 21, 1880, Chicago. Built hotel in 1854 in Lake View (Lakeview House).

Reese, Michael b Aug. 15, 1817, Hainsfurth, Bavaria, Germany; d Aug. 1, 1878, Wallenstein, Bavaria, Germany. Financier; his heirs donated part of his fortune to build Michael Reese Hospital.

Regensteiner, Theodore b May 17, 1868, Munich, Germany; d July 15, 1952, Chicago. Founder and president of Regensteiner Corp.; pioneer in field of color printing.

Regnery, Henry b Jan. 5, 1912, Hinsdale, IL; d June 18, 1996, Chicago. Publisher; established trade publishing firm in Chicago; nurtured conservative authors.

Reich, John b Sept. 30, 1906, Vienna, Austria; d Feb. 9, 1988. Theater producer and director; led the Goodman Theatre (1957–1972).

Reinecke, Jean Otis b July 9, 1909, Ft. Scott, KS; d Dec. 18, 1987. Industrial designer; designed 1947 Toastmaster; established Barnes & Reinecke.

Reiner, Fritz b Dec. 19, 1888, Budapest, Hungary; d Nov. 15, 1963, New York, NY. Conductor; music director of Chicago Symphony Orchestra (1953–1962); conductor of several orchestras in the Eastern United States.

Reitman, Benjamin L. b Jan. 1, 1879, St. Paul, MN; d Nov. 16, 1942, Chicago. Physician; activist on behalf of hobo community; founded Hobo College.

Reitzel, Robert b Jan. 27, 1849, Weitenau amt Schopfheim, Baden Germany; d Mar. 31, 1898, Detroit, MI. German American poet; publisher; founded anarchist newspaper *Der Arme Teufel*; defended and eulogized Haymarket anarchists.

Revell, Fleming Hewitt b Dec. 11, 1849, Chicago; d Oct. 11, 1931, Yonkers, NY. Publisher of religious books; founded Fleming H. Revell Co.

Rexroth, Kenneth b Dec. 22, 1905, South Bend, IN; d June 6, 1982, Santa Barbara, CA. Poet; critic; translator; active in Dill Pickle Club; prominent during Beat movement.

Reynolds, George M. b 1864 or 1865, Panora, IA; d Feb. 26, 1940, Pasadena, CA. Banker; owned Continental & Commercial National Bank of Chicago.

Reznick, Hyman b Jan. 15, 1904, Chicago; d June 6, 1973, Portland, OR. Music director; founded Halevi Choral Society.

Rhea, Delbert "Dell" F. b Apr. 27, 1907, Springfield, MO; d Oct. 16, 1992, Chicago. Restaurateur; owned Dell Rhea's Chicken Basket restaurant in Willowbrook.

Rhode, Paul P. b Sept. 16, 1870 or 1871, Wejherowo, Poland; d Mar. 3, 1945, Green Bay, WI. Pastor of St. Michael's Catholic Church; first Polish bishop in Chicago and the United States (1908).

Rhodes, B. b England; active 1840s. Early landowner in Elmwood Park.

Rhodes, Richard S. b Nov. 5, 1843, Providence, RI; d May 13, 1902, River Grove, IL. Book publisher; president of Rhodes & McClure Publishing Co.

Rhodus, Charlotte C. active 1910s. President of Woman Suffrage Party of Cook County (1912).

Rhymer, Paul b c. 1905, Fulton, IL; d Oct. 26, 1964, Chicago. Comedy writer; wrote *Vic and Sade* radio serial.

Riccardo, Ric b ca. 1903, Italy; d Oct. 11, 1954, Chicago. Artist; restaurateur; owner Riccardo Studio restaurant.

Rice, John Blake b May 28, 1809, Easton, MD; d Dec. 17, 1874, Norfolk, VA. Actor; theater manager; state and national legislator; mayor of Chicago (1865–1869).

Rice, Joseph Mayer b May 20, 1857, Philadelphia, PA; d June 24, 1934, Philadelphia. Physician; education critic.

Richardson, Henry Hobson b Sept. 29, 1838, St. James Parish, LA; d Apr. 27, 1886, Brookline, MA. Architect; designed Marshall Field wholesale store and J. J. Glessner House.

Ricketts, Coella Lindsay b May 24, 1859, Shepardstown, OH; d Feb. 19, 1941, Wilmette, IL. Electric company executive; calligrapher; illustrator.

Rieck, Emilie b May 1850, Hamburg, Germany; d Jan. 1, 1929? Chicago? Brothel owner; operated Arena Hotel in Glen Ellyn.

Riley, Ida M. d Mar. 7, 1901, Chicago. Teacher; cofounded Columbia School of Oratory.

Riley, Jack H. b June 13, 1909; d Mar. 22, 1993. Wrestler; won Olympic silver medal (1932); All-American in football and wrestling at Northwestern Univ.

Riley, John D. b Dec. 29, 1870, Blackburn, England; d Mar. 14, 1933, Chicago. Superintendent, Chicago Bureau of Maps.

Risberg, Charles "Swede" b Oct. 13, 1894, San Francisco, CA; d Oct. 16, 1975, Red Bluff, CA. Professional baseball player for Chicago White Sox; involved in "Black Sox Scandal"; banned from baseball for life.

Robbins, Eugene S. b Oct. 12, 1862, Jordan, NY; d Apr. 25, 1944, Chicago. Real-estate agent.

Robbins, Henry b Nov. 27, 1836, Brooklyn, MA; d Apr. 20, 1950, Chicago. Real-estate agent.

Robbins, Samuel P. active 1830s. Farmer; arrived in Portage around 1838.

Robbins, William b July 20, 1824, Oswego County, NY; d June 1889, Hinsdale, IL. Early landowner in what is now Hinsdale.

Roberts, Eben Ezra b 1865 or 1866, Boston, MA; d Aug. 4, 1943, Muskegon, MI. Architect; designed homes in Oak Park; associated with Prairie style.

Robie, Frederick Carleton b Aug. 14, 1876, Chicago; d Dec. 17, 1962, OH. Merchant; inventor; home in Hyde Park notable for Frank Lloyd Wright design.

Robins, Margaret Dreier b Sept. 6, 1868, Brooklyn, NY; d Feb. 21, 1945, Hernando County, FL. Social reformer; labor leader; president of National Women's Trade Union League.

Robins, Raymond b Sept. 17, 1873, Staten Island, NY; d Sept. 26, 1954, Brooksville, FL. Progressive reformer; headed Northwestern Univ. Settlement; member of Chicago Charter Convention (1906–1909).

Robinson, Alexander [Che Che Pin Qua] b ca. 1772, Mackinac, MI; d Apr. 22, 1872, Leyden, IL. Potawatomi chief; government interpreter.

Robinson, Elisha active 1880s. Mapmaker; published real-estate atlas in 1886.

Robinson, Increase [Josephine Dorothea Reichmann] b 1890, Chicago; d 1981. Painter; gallery owner; state director of Federal Art Project (1935–1938).

Robinson, John (Johnny) C. b Nov. 26, 1903, Carabelle, FL; d Mar. 27, 1954, Addis Ababa, Ethiopia. Aviator; cofounded Robbins Airport; pilot of Ethiopian emperor Haile Selassie.

Robinson, John b England. Swimming instructor at Chicago Athletic Association; introduced water polo to Chicago in 1893.

Roche, Martin b Aug. 15, 1855, Cleveland, OH; d June 4, 1927, Chicago. Architect; partner at Holabird & Roche; an originator of the skeleton skyscraper office building; designed Soldier Field, Palmer House, Board of Trade.

Rockefeller, John D. b July 8, 1839, Richford, NY; d May 23, 1937, Ormond Beach, FL. Oil magnate; philanthropist; owned Standard Oil Co.; endowed Univ. of Chicago.

Rockne, Knute Kenneth b Mar. 4, 1888, Voss, Norway; d Mar. 31, 1931, airplane crash near Bazaar, KS. Head football coach at Notre Dame (1918–1931).

Rodchenko, Alexander Mikhailovich b Nov. 23, 1891, St. Petersburg, Russia; d Dec. 3, 1956, Moscow, Russia. Artist; faculty member at Institute of Design.

Rodeheaver, Homer Alvan b Oct. 4, 1880, Union Furnace, OH; d Dec. 18, 1955, Winona Lake, IN. Evangelist, musician, musical director for Billy Sunday.

Roden, Carl B. b June 7, 1870, Kansas City, MO; d Oct. 25, 1956, Palatine, IL. Librarian; head librarian at Chicago Public Library (1918–1950).

Rodzinski, Artur b Jan. 1, 1892, Spalato (now Split, Croatia); d Nov. 27, 1958, Boston, MA. Conductor; music director, Chicago Symphony Orchestra (1947–1948).

Roe, Clifford Griffith b June 26, 1875, Rowling Prairie, IN; d June 28, 1934, Chicago. Lawyer; assistant state's attorney of Cook County; prosecuted "white slaves trade."

Roe, Hiram active 1850s. Proprietor of tavern at Roe's Hill (later Rosehill Cemetery) around 1859.

Roebuck, Alvah Curtis b ca. 1864, Lafayette, IN; d June 18, 1948, Evanston, IL. Retail executive; cofounded Sears, Roebuck & Co.

Roeh, Hans active twentieth century. Community leader; elected president of Round Lake Beach in 1937.

Rogers, Henry Wade b Oct. 10, 1853, Holland Patent, NY; d Aug. 16, 1926, Pennington, NJ. Lawyer; educator; president of Northwestern Univ. (1890–1900); federal judge.

Rogers, James Gamble b Mar. 3, 1867, Bryant's Station, KY; d Oct. 1, 1947, New York, NY. Architect; designed downtown Chicago campus of Northwestern Univ.

Rogers, Jimmy [James A. Lane] b June 13, 1924, Ruleville, MS; d Dec. 19, 1997, Chicago. Blues guitarist; pioneer of Chicago electric blues; played with Muddy Waters.

Rogers, Phillip M. b Aug. 15, 1812, Dublin, Ireland; d Dec. 13, 1856, Rogers Park, IL. Evanston assessor; early landowner in Lakeview Township; purchased 1,600 acres of government land.

Rohl-Smith, Carl b 1848; d Aug. 22, 1900, Copenhagen, Denmark. Sculptor (Benjamin Franklin at World's Columbian Exposition; *The Indian Massacre*; General Sherman).

Rohn, Ferdinand b ca. 1826. Austrian truck farmer around South Shore; butcher.

Rokosz, Stanley d Apr. 20, 1921, Chicago. Labor leader; business agent for Butchers' Union; president of Polish National Alliance.

Rold, June D. b Nov. 28, 1905; d Oct. 11, 1993. Dance teacher; owner and operator of June Rold School of Dance for 50 years.

Root, George Frederick b Aug. 30, 1820, Sheffield, MA; d Aug. 6, 1895, Bailey's Island, ME. Composer; music educator; partner in music firm Root & Cady; wrote "Battle Cry of Freedom."

Root, John Wellborn b Jan. 10, 1850, Lumpkin, GA; d Jan. 15, 1891, Chicago. Architect; collaborated with Daniel H. Burnham; best known for Montauk and Monadnock Buildings; consulted for World's Columbian Exposition.

Rosenthal, Benjamin J. b Nov. 5, 1867, Chicago; d May 14, 1936, Chicago. Businessman; founded Chicago mail-order company; built subsidized housing.

Rosenwald, Julius b Aug. 12, 1862, Springfield, IL; d Jan. 6, 1932, Chicago. Merchandiser; philanthropist; early partner of Sears & Roebuck; established Museum of Science and Industry; major donor to African American schools in rural South and to African American YMCAs.

Ross, Barney [Barnet David Rosofsky] b Dec. 23, 1909, New York, NY; d Jan. 18, 1967, Chicago. Lightweight and welterweight boxing champion; learned boxing on Chicago's West Side.

Ross, Norman DeMille b Mar. 16, 1896, Portland, OR; d June 19, 1953, Evanston, IL. Radio announcer; classical music disk jockey; won Olympic gold medal in swimming (1920).

Ross, Sam b Mar. 10, 1911, Kiev, Ukraine; d Mar. 30, 1998. Writer; member of Illinois Writers' Project.

Rossiter, Will b Mar. 15, 1867, Wells, Somerset, England; d June 10, 1954, Oak Park, IL. Music publisher; composer; wrote "I'd Love to Live in Loveland."

Rouensa b ca. 1650, Kaskaskia, IL. Illinois tribal leader; chief of Kaskaskia tribe.

Rowe, Louise Osborn b ca. 1889, Jacksonville, IL; d Mar. 26, 1962, Elgin, IL. First Commissioner of Public Welfare (1915).

Royko, Michael Melvin b Sept. 19, 1932, Chicago; d Apr. 29, 1997, Evanston, IL. Newspaper columnist; wrote for *Chicago Daily News*, *Sun-Times*, and *Chicago Tribune*; won Pulitzer Prize in 1972.

Rubloff, Arthur b June 25, 1902, Duluth, MN; d May 24, 1986. Real-estate developer; philanthropist; president of Arthur Rubloff & Co.

Ruby, Jack [Jacob Rubenstein] b ca. 1911, Chicago; d Jan. 3, 1967, Dallas, TX. Assassinated Lee Harvey Oswald; grew up around Maxwell Street.

Rucker, Edward A. b Jan. 24, 1822, Cook County, IL; d June 19, 1872, Chicago.

Pioneered title indexing; firm was forerunner of Chicago Title & Trust.

Rudowitz, Christian A. b ca. 1873, Courland Province, Russia. Latvian revolutionary; his U.S. extradition case set legal precedent.

Rueckheim, Frederick William b Apr. 18, 1846, Japenzin, Germany; d Jan. 12, 1934, Chicago. Popcorn manufacturer; created "Cracker Jack" snacks.

Ruml, Beardsley b Nov. 5, 1894, Cedar Rapids, IA; d Apr. 18, 1960, Danbury, CT. Economist; Social Science Division dean at Univ. of Chicago; originated pay-as-you-go income tax collection.

Rumsey, Julian S. b Apr. 3, 1823, Batavia, NY; d Apr. 20, 1886, Chicago. Grain merchant; county treasurer; president of Board of Trade; mayor of Chicago (1861–1862).

Russ, Alamondo B. b ca. 1829, VT. Undertaker; furniture dealer.

Russell, Charles Edward b Sept. 25, 1860, Davenport, IA; d Apr. 23, 1941, Washington, DC. Journalist; reformer; published *Chicago American*; wrote exposé of meatpacking industry; attended founding meeting of NAACP.

Russo, William Joseph b June 25, 1928, Chicago; d Jan. 11, 2003, Chicago. Jazz composer; founded Chicago Jazz Ensemble; initiated music department at Columbia College.

Ruud, Helga M. b Dec. 28, 1860, Kongsberg, Norway; d Jan. 29, 1956, Chicago. Doctor; taught at women's medical college of Northwestern Univ.

Ryerson, Edward L. b Dec. 3, 1886, Chicago; d Aug. 2, 1971, Chicago. Steel manufacturer; president of Inland Steel Co.

Ryerson, Joseph T. b Mar. 25, 1813, Chester, PA; d Mar. 10, 1883, Chicago. Iron merchant; founded Ryerson-Tull (later Inland Steel).

Ryerson, Martin Antoine b Oct. 26, 1856, Grand Rapids, MI; d Aug. 11, 1932, Lake Geneva, WI. Lumber executive; Art Institute trustee and patron.

S

Sachs, Leonard (Lennie) David b Aug. 7, 1897, Chicago; d Oct. 27, 1942, Chicago. Football player; basketball coach at Loyola Univ.

Sachs, Theodore B. b May 2, 1868, Dinaberg, Russia; d Apr. 2, 1916, Naperville, IL. Physician; founded Chicago Municipal Tuberculosis Sanatorium; led antituberculosis movement.

Sadauskas, Ildefonsas b June 1, 1902, Lithuania; d Feb. 1981, Chicago. Brewer; operated White Bear Brewery in Thornton 1930s and 1940s.

Saint-Gaudens, Augustus b Mar. 1, 1848, Dublin, Ireland; d Aug. 3, 1907, Cornish, NH. Sculptor; educator; created *The Standing Lincoln* (Lincoln Park, 1887); *Logan Monument* (Michigan Avenue, 1897).

Salathe, Frederick active 1920s. Founded Chicago Chemical Co.

Sandburg, Carl b Jan. 6, 1878, Galesburg, IL; d July 22, 1967, Flat Rock, NC. Writer; poet; biographer; folk musician; won Pulitzer Prize.

Sandegren, Andrew b June 25, 1867, Halmsted, Sweden; d Jan. 23, 1924, Chicago. Architect; designed apartment buildings, offices, and Swedish Old People's Home.

Sanders, Alvin H. b Sept. 8, 1860, Talleyrand, IA; d July 18, 1948, Wayne, PA. Writer; managing editor and part owner of *Breeders' Gazette.*

Sanders, James Harvey b Oct. 9, 1832, Union County, OH; d Dec. 22, 1899, Memphis, TN. Agricultural journalist; founded *Breeders' Gazette* (ca. 1881).

Sankey, Ira David b Aug. 28, 1840, Edinburgh, PA; d Aug. 13, 1908, Brooklyn, NY. Singing evangelist; gospel songwriter; musical director for evangelist Dwight L. Moody.

Saperstein, Abraham Michael b July 4, 1902, London, England; d Mar. 15, 1966, Chicago. Basketball promoter; founded Harlem Globetrotters in Chicago (1926).

Saperstein, Esther Richman b Oct. 22, 1901, Chicago; d May 17, 1988, Chicago. Alderman (1975–1979); state representative (1957–1967); first female state senator (1967–1975); head of Illinois Commission on the Status of Women.

Sauganash *See* **Caldwell, Billy**

Sayre, William active 1830s. Farmer; landowner in Montclare area in 1836.

Scammon, J. Young b July 27, 1812, Whitefield, ME; d Mar. 17, 1890, Chicago. Lawyer; financier; established Marine Bank (1851); president of Chicago Board of Education.

Scanlon, John active 1860s. Journalist; Chicago Irish American leader in Civil War era.

Scanlon, William active 1860s. Journalist; Chicago Irish American leader in Civil War era.

Schaack, Michael John b Aug. 23, 1843, Grand Duchy of Luxembourg; d May 18, 1898, Chicago. Police inspector and captain; investigated Haymarket anarchists, Cronin murder case and Luetgert murder case.

Schadiger, John b Germany. Farmer; settled in Niles in early 1830s.

Schaffner, Joseph b Mar. 23, 1848, Reedsburg, OH; d Apr. 19, 1918, Chicago. Clothing manufacturer; cofounder and co-owner of Hart Schaffner & Marx clothing business.

Scherer, Mathias b June 16, 1818, Germany. Opened saloon/hotel in St. John, IN, in 1849.

Scherer, Nicholas b June 29, 1830, Prussia, Germany; d Apr. 24, 1907, Schererville, IN. Founded Schererville, IN.

Schlacks, Henry J. b 1868, Chicago; d Jan. 6, 1938, Chicago. Architect; designed St. Adalbert's, St. Paul's, and other Catholic churches.

Schmidt, George A. b ca. 1885; d July 3, 1957, Palm Springs, CA. Businessman; opened Riverview Park amusement park in 1904.

Schmidt, Otto L. b Mar. 21, 1863, Chicago; d Aug. 20, 1935, Chicago. Physician; historian; president of German American Historical Society of Illinois; president of Chicago Historical Society.

Schneider, John Peter b Apr. 1801, Frankfort-on-the-Rhine, Germany; d June 26, 1883, Aurora, IL. Settled in Schneider's Mills (now North Aurora) ca. 1834.

Schock, Frederick R. b Apr. 7, 1854, Chicago; d Sept. 28, 1934, Chicago. Architect; designed Queen Anne–style homes in central Austin.

Schoenhofen, Peter b Feb. 2, 1827, Derbach, Kreiswitt, Germany; d Jan. 2, 1893, Chicago. Brewer; founded Schoenhofen Brewing Co.

Schommer, John Joseph b Jan. 29, 1884, Chicago; d Jan. 11, 1960. Basketball player; played on Univ. of Chicago 1910 Big Ten Championship team.

Schorling, John M. b Dec. 16, 1865, Michigan City, IN; d Mar. 23, 1940, Chicago. Tavern owner; sports promoter; co-owned Leland Giants baseball team; owned Schorling Park baseball field.

Schrage, Henry b Jan. 21, 1844, Auchen, Germany. Grocer; banker; owner Whiting Bank and East Chicago Bank; Whiting postmaster.

Schultz, Theodore William b Apr. 30, 1902, Arlington, SD; d Feb. 26, 1998, Evanston, IL. Economist; identified with Chicago School of Economics; won Nobel Prize for Economics (1979).

Schutze, Eva (Eve) Watson b 1867; d May 20, 1935, Chicago. Photographer; Director of Renaissance Society at the Univ. of Chicago.

Schwab, Michael b Aug. 9, 1853, Kitringen, Germany; d June 29, 1898. Anarchist; convicted in Haymarket Square riot; pardoned by Governor John P. Altgeld.

Schwinn, Ignaz b Apr. 1, 1860, Hardheim, Germany; d Aug. 31, 1948, Chicago. Bicycle manufacturer; cofounded Arnold Schwinn & Co.

Scott, Walter Dill b May 1, 1869, Cooksville, IL; d Sept. 13, 1955, Evanston, IL. Psychologist; president of Northwestern Univ. (1920–1939).

Scoville, James Wilmarth b Oct. 14, 1825, Pompey, NY; d Nov. 2, 1893, Pasadena, CA. Early Oak Park landowner.

Scripps, John Locke b Feb. 27, 1818, Jackson County, MO; d Sept. 21, 1866, Minneapolis, MN. Journalist; Chicago postmaster during Civil War; founded *Chicago Tribune.*

Searle, Gideon Daniel b Feb. 13, 1846, Deerfield, IN; d Jan. 25, 1917, Chicago. Chemist; pharmacist; founded G. D. Searle & Co.; Civil War veteran.

Sears, Paul Bigelow b Dec. 17, 1891, Bucyrus, OH; d Apr. 30, 1990, Taos, NM. Botanist; ecologist; conservationist; researched Indiana dunes.

Sears, Richard Warren b Dec. 7, 1863, Stewartville, MN; d Sept. 28, 1914, Waukesha, WI. Retail merchant; founded Sears, Roebuck & Co.

Seipp, Conrad b 1825; d Jan. 18, 1890, Chicago. Early brewer in Chicago.

Selig, William Nicholas b Mar. 14, 1864, Chicago; d July 15, 1948, Los Angeles, CA. Motion picture producer; invented Selig Polyscope.

Seman, Philip L. b Nov. 11, 1881, Warsaw, Poland; d Sept. 25, 1957, Los Angeles, CA. Social worker; director of Chicago Hebrew Institute (1913–1945).

Sengstacke, John H. b Nov. 25, 1912, Savannah, GA; d May 28, 1997, Chicago. Publisher of *Chicago Defender.*

Senn, Nicholas b Oct. 31, 1844, Buchs, Switzerland; d Jan. 2, 1908, Chicago. Surgeon; writer; Rush Medical College faculty; philanthropist; book collector; pioneered surgical pathology; founded Association of Military Surgeons of the United States.

Sergel, Annie M. [Annie Meyers] b Aug. 18, 1857, Philadelphia, PA; d Dec. 23, 1927, Chicago. President of Illinois Woman's Press Club; organized Anti-Smoke League.

Sewell, Florence Lenore Davis b May 24, 1903, Holton, KS; d Apr. 9, 2000, Chicago. Philanthropist; silent partner in Pizzerias Uno and Due.

Sewell, Ike b Sept. 9, 1903, Wills Point, TX; d Aug. 20, 1990, Chicago. Liquor executive; owner of Pizzeria Uno and Su Casa restaurants; invented "Chicago-style" deep-dish pizza.

Seymour, Henry active 1830s. Farmer; subdivided land on Pershing Road in 1835.

Seymour, Ralph Fletcher b Mar. 18, 1876, Milan, Italy; d Jan. 1, 1966, Elburn, IL. Artist; illustrator; publisher; hand-lettered Baum's *Father Goose: His Book* (1899).

Shabbona [Shabonna; Shaubena] b ca. 1775, Maumee River, OH, or Kankakee River, IL; d July 17, 1859, Morris, IL. Potawatomi-Ottawa chief; ally of Tecumseh in War of 1812.

Shapey, Ralph b Mar. 21, 1921, Philadelphia, PA; d June 13, 2002, Chicago. Classical composer; violin prodigy; influential teacher.

Shapiro, Jory b ca. 1911; d Apr. 1993. Art collector; supporter of Museum of Contemporary Art.

Shapiro, Joseph Randall b Dec. 22, 1904, Russia; d June 16, 1996, Oak Park, IL. Art collector; helped found Museum of Contemporary Art.

Shapiro, Karl J. b Nov. 10, 1913, Baltimore, MD; d May 14, 2000, New York, NY. Poet; editor of *Poetry* magazine; literature professor at Univ. of Illinois at Chicago; won Pulitzer Prize (1944).

Shaughnessy, Clark Daniel b Mar. 6, 1892, St. Cloud, MN; d May 15, 1970, Santa Monica, CA. Football coach; coached Chicago Bears; refined T formation.

Shaw, Clifford R. b 1895 or 1896, Luray, IN; d Aug. 1, 1957, St. Charles, IL. Sociologist; founded Chicago Area Project; worked for Institute for Juvenile Research.

Shaw, Howard Van Doren b May 7, 1869, Chicago; d May 6, 1926, Baltimore, MD. Architect; designed Goodman Theatre, Market Square in Lake Forest, and the model steel town of Indiana Harbor.

Shedd, John Graves b July 20, 1850, Alstead, NH; d Oct. 22, 1926, Chicago. Retail merchant; president of Marshall Field & Co.; funded Shedd Aquarium.

Shefferman, Nathan W. b July 19, 1887, Baltimore, MD; d Feb. 3, 1968, Chicago. Labor relations consultant; antiunion consultant to Sears, Roebuck.

Sheil, Bernard James b Feb. 18, 1886, Chicago; d Sept. 13, 1969, Tucson, AZ. Roman Catholic bishop; founded Catholic Youth Organization (1930).

Sheldon, Arthur Frederick b May 1, 1868, Vernon, MI; d Dec. 21, 1935, Mission, TX. Educator; writer; founded Sheldon School for the teaching of business science.

Shelford, Victor Ernest b Sept. 22, 1877, Chemung County, NY; d Dec. 1968, Urbana, IL. Ecologist; zoologist at Univ. of Chicago; wrote *Animal Communities in Temperate America as Illustrated in the Chicago Region.*

Shepard, Otis Franklin b May 16, 1893 or 1894, Linden, KS; d Feb. 9, 1969, Ross, CA. Graphic designer; art director for Wrigley Co.; designed Chicago Cubs uniforms.

Sheridan, Jack b Jan. 11, 1905; d Feb. 1967, Chicago. Bughouse Square speaker.

Sheridan, James "Jimmie" b Jan. 11, 1905; d Feb. 6, 1972, Oak Park, IL. Bughouse Square speaker; hobo activist; twin of Jack Sheridan.

Sherman, Alson Smith b Apr. 21, 1811, Barre, VT; d Sept. 22, 1903, Waukegan, IL. Builder; fire chief; alderman (1842, 1846), trustee of Northwestern Univ.; mayor of Chicago (1844–1845).

Sherman, Francis Cornwall b Sept. 18, 1805, Newton, CT; d Nov. 6, 1870, Chicago. Builder; mayor of Chicago (1841–1842; 1862–1865).

Sherman, Silas W. active 1840s. First sheriff of Cook County; filed claim for 160 acres in Northbrook area in 1843.

Shimer, Frances Wood b Aug. 31, 1826, Milton, NY? d 1901. College president; founder and president of Mount Carroll Seminary and Conservatory of Music of Mount Carroll.

Shober, Charles active 1850s. Lithographer; engraver.

Siedenburg, Frederic b Jan. 28, 1872, Cincinnati, OH; d Feb. 20, 1939, Detroit, MI. Educator; sociologist; helped establish School of Social Work at Loyola Univ.

Silber, Saul b ca. 1882, Dvinsk, Latvia; d Sept. 1, 1946, Chicago. Rabbi of Anshe Sholom Congregation; president of Hebrew Theological College.

Silsbee, Joseph Lyman b ca. 1849, Salem, MA; d Jan. 31, 1913, Chicago. Architect; designed Lincoln Park Conservatory.

Simonds, Ossian Cole b Nov. 11, 1855, Grand Rapids, MI; d Nov. 20, 1931, Chicago. Landscape architect; redesigned Graceland Cemetery; designed Lincoln Park extension.

Simons, Algie Martin b Oct. 9, 1870, North Freedom, WI; d Mar. 11, 1950, New Martinsville, WV. Socialist theorist; journalist; social activist; edited *International Socialist Review* (1900–1918).

Simpson, Herbert D. b May 21, 1876, Carnegie, PA; d June 4, 1952, Evanston, IL. Economist; public finance professor at Northwestern Univ.; expert on city and federal taxes.

Simpson, John A. b Nov. 3, 1916, Portland, OR; d Aug. 31, 2000, Chicago. Nuclear physicist; founded Atomic Scientists of Chicago, Inc.

Sinclair, Upton Beall b Sept. 20, 1878, Baltimore, MD; d Nov. 25, 1968, Bound Brook, NJ. Writer; reformer; socialist; wrote *The Jungle* (1906).

Singer, Horace b Oct. 1, 1823, Schenectady, NY; d Dec. 28, 1896, Pasadena, CA. Businessman; moved to Lockport in 1836; state legislator; Cook County commissioner.

Singleton, Arthur "Zutty" James b May 14, 1898, Bunkie, LA; d July 14, 1975, New York, NY. Jazz drummer; played in various Chicago jazz bands.

Siporin, Mitchell b May 5, 1910, New York, NY; d June 11, 1976, Newton, MA. Educator; artist.

Siskel, Eugene Kal b Jan. 20, 1946, Chicago; d Feb. 20, 1999, Evanston, IL. Film critic; critic for *Chicago Tribune* and on television with Roger Ebert.

Siskind, Aaron b Dec. 4, 1903, New York, NY; d Feb. 8, 1991, Providence, RI. Photographer; taught at Institute of Design (1951–1970).

Skidmore, Louis b Apr. 8, 1897, Lawrenceburg, IN; d Sept. 27, 1962, Winter Haven, FL. Architect; founding partner of Skidmore, Owings & Merrill; chief designer of Century of Progress Exposition.

Skinner, Mark b Sept. 13, 1813, Manchester, VT; d Sept. 16, 1887. Cook County Judge; city attorney; prominent Democrat during Civil War.

Slater, Frederick W. b Dec. 19, 1898, Normal, IL; d Aug. 14, 1966, Chicago. First African American circuit court judge in Illinois.

Sleight, Morris b 1795, Hyde Park, NY; d 1863. Real-estate trader; entrepreneur in Naperville.

Small, Albion Woodbury b May 11, 1854, Buckfield, ME; d Mar. 24, 1926, Chicago. Sociologist; founded department of sociology at Univ. of Chicago; founded *American Journal of Sociology.*

Smart, Alfred b June 17, 1894, Omaha, NE; d Feb. 3, 1951, Chicago. Publisher; cofounded *Esquire* magazine.

Smart, David Archibald b Oct. 4, 1892, Omaha, NE; d Oct. 15 or 16, 1952, Chicago. Publisher; cofounded *Esquire* magazine; founded Smart Museum.

Smarzewski-Schermann, Anthony b May 24, 1818, Kcynia, Poznan Duchy, Poland; d Sept. 22, 1900, Chicago. Arrived in Chicago in 1851; early Polish resident of Chicago; helped organized St. Stanislaus Kostka parish.

Smith, Amanda Berry b Jan. 23, 1837, Long Green, MD; d Feb. 24, 1915, Sebring, FL. Evangelist; reformer; founded a home for African American orphans in Harvey, IL.

Smith, Clarence "Pine Top" b June 11, 1904, Troy, AL; d Mar. 15, 1929, Chicago. Boogie-woogie pianist; played and recorded in Chicago.

Smith, David Sheppard b Apr. 28, 1816, Camden, NJ; d Apr. 29, 1891, Chicago. Doctor; introduced homeopathy in Chicago; president of Hahnemann College.

Smith, Dolly active 1860s. Named town of Minooka.

Smith, Elijah J. b May 8, 1815, Morristown, NJ; d 1888. Dairy farmer; physician; founded Itasca (ca. 1840s).

Smith, George b Feb. 10, 1808, Aberdeenshire, Scotland; d Oct. 7, 1899, London, England. Financier; early Chicago banker; founded Wisconsin Marine & Fire Insurance Co.

Smith, Henry Justin b June 19, 1875, Chicago; d Feb. 9, 1936, Evanston, IL. Editor and journalist at *Chicago Daily News*.

Smith, Mason b ca. 1807, Potsdam, NY. Farmer; filed claim (with George Mason) on land called Dunklee's Grove in Bensenville area.

Smith, Milton b 1810, NY; d 1874. Farmer; abolitionist; founded Wesleyan Methodist Church in Wheaton.

Smith, Nathaniel Clark b July 31, 1877, Fort Leavenworth, KS; d Oct. 8, 1935, Kansas City, MO. Band director; composer; established first black-owned music publishing company.

Smith, Perry Dunlap b Dec. 16, 1888, Chicago; d Feb. 4, 1967, Winnetka, IL. Educator; founded North Shore Country Day School; cofounded Winnetka Teachers College.

Smith, Tempel J. b Aug. 10, 1909; d Dec. 19, 1980, Chicago. Founder and president of Tempel Steel Co.; bred Lipizzan show horses.

Smith, Thomas Vernor b Apr. 26, 1890, Blanket, TX; d May 24, 1964, Hyattsville, MD. Philosophy professor at Univ. of Chicago; state senator; congressman-at-large from Illinois.

Smulski, John F. b Feb. 4, 1867, Posen, Poland; d Mar. 18, 1928, Chicago. Lawyer; banker; alderman (1898–1903); city attorney; founded Northwestern Trust & Savings Bank (1906).

Snow, George Washington b Sept. 16, 1797, Keene, NH; d July 29, 1870, Altoona, PA. City surveyor; lumber dealer; innovator in balloon frame construction.

Solomon, Hannah Greenbaum b Jan. 14, 1858, Chicago; d Dec. 7, 1942, Chicago. Social reformer; one of the first Jewish women admitted in Chicago Woman's Club; founded National Council of Jewish Women.

Solti, Sir Georg b Oct. 21, 1912, Budapest, Hungary; d Sept. 5, 1971, Antibes, France. Conductor; music director of the Chicago Symphony Orchestra (1969–1991); made over 50 recordings with CSO; won 32 Grammy awards.

Soltker, Gertrude b July 22, 1912; d Oct. 1981? Cofounded Old Town School of Folk Music.

Sowerby, Leo b May 1, 1865, Grand Rapids, MI; d July 7, 1968, Fort Clinton, OH. Composer; organist at St. James Church; won Pulitzer Prize for *Canticle of the Sun* (1946).

Spacek, Leonard Paul b Sept. 12, 1907, Cedar Rapids, IA; d Mar. 19, 2000, Chicago. Accountant; managing partner at Arthur Andersen in 1950s.

Spalding, Albert G. b Sept. 2, 1850, Byron, IL; d Sept. 9, 1915, Point Loma, CA. Baseball player and executive; sporting goods manufacturer.

Spanier, Francis Joseph "Muggsy" b Nov. 9, 1901, Chicago; d Feb. 12, 1967, Sausalito, CA. Jazz cornetist; bandleader; performed in numerous Chicago clubs; recorded with his ragtime band.

Spann, Otis b Mar. 21, 1930, Jackson, MS; d Apr. 24, 1970, Chicago. Blues pianist and singer; played with Muddy Waters band; recorded on Chess and Checker labels.

Spaulding, Henry A. b Nov. 11, 1837, New York, NY. Jewel merchant; established jewelry firm in Chicago in 1888.

Spears, Ethel b Oct. 5, 1903, Chicago; d Aug. 2, 1974, Navasota, TX. Artist; painter; illustrator.

Spencer, Robert Clossen, Jr. b Apr. 13, 1864, Milwaukee, WI; d Sept. 9, 1953, Tucson, AZ. Architect; writer; designed interior of Chicago Public Library and the Art Institute.

Spiegel, Arthur H. b ca. 1885; d Apr. 7, 1916, New York, NY. Founded Spiegel company, 1904.

Spiegel, Joseph b Sept. 23, 1840, Hesse-Darmstadt, Germany; d Sept. 13, 1918, Chicago. Merchant; founder and president of Spiegel House Furnishing Co., 1904.

Spies, August Vincent Theodore b Dec. 10, 1855, Landeck, Germany; d Nov. 11, 1887, Chicago. Anarchist; convicted in Haymarket Square riot; executed.

Spolin, Viola b Nov. 7, 1906, Chicago; d Nov. 22, 1994, Los Angeles, CA. Theatre educator; developed "Theater Games" improvisation method to train actors.

Spoor, George K. b Dec. 18, 1871, Highland Park, IL; d Nov. 24, 1953, Chicago. Cofounded Essanay Film Co.; pioneered moving picture industry in Chicago; invented movie equipment.

Spoor, John A. b Sept. 30, 1851, Freehold, NY; d Oct. 15, 1926, Chicago. Rare book collector; president of Union Stock Yard.

Squire, Belle b Jan. 28, 1870; d Apr. 17, 1939, Chicago. Teacher; suffragist; coestablished Alpha Suffrage Club (1913).

Stacy, Philo W. b Jan. 13, 1833, Ashford, NY; d Mar. 2, 1917, Glen Ellyn, IL. Early settler of Milton Township; donated Stacy Park to Glen Ellyn.

Stagg, Amos Alonzo b Aug. 16, 1862, West Orange, NJ; d Mar. 17, 1965, Stockton, CA. Football coach for 40 years at Univ. of Chicago; brought collegiate basketball to Chicago.

Stallbohm, Johann Friedrich Willhelm b 1823, Germany; d 1899, Munster, IN. Innkeeper; ran Stallbohm's Inn, also called the Green House, in Munster.

Stanley, Dexter b Oct. 1780, Taunton, MA; d Feb. 12, 1849. Downers Grove resident in 1840s.

Stark, Inez Cunningham [Inez Stark Boulton] d Aug. 16, 1958, Washington, DC. Poet; teacher; active in Renaissance Society at Univ. of Chicago.

Starks, Edward Albert b Mar. 26, 1928, Robbins, IL; d Apr. 3, 1987, Robbins, IL. Real-estate developer in 1960s; opened Golden Acres subdivision in Robbins, IL.

Starr, Ellen Gates b Mar. 19, 1859, Laona, IL; d Feb. 10, 1940, Suffern, NY. Settlement worker; labor activist; bookbinder; cofounded Hull House (1898).

Stead, William T. b July 5, 1849, Embleton, Northumberland, England; d Apr. 15, 1912, on the *Titanic*. Journalist; wrote *If Christ Came to Chicago* (1894).

Stearns, John Goddard b 1843, New York, NY; d Sept. 16, 1917. Architect; designed Machinery Hall at the World's Columbian Exposition.

Steele, Ashbel b 1794, Derby, England; d Sept. 26, 1861, River Forest, IL. Coroner and sheriff of Cook County; arrived in Chicago in 1833; settled in River Forest.

Steger, John Valentine b Mar. 24, 1854, Ulm, Württemberg, Germany; d June 11, 1916, Steger, IL. Piano manufacturer; founded village of Steger.

Steghagen, Emma b Mar. 5, 1856, Germany; d Oct. 31, 1948? Hartford, MI. Labor organizer; organized the Wage Earners' Suffrage League; secretary of Chicago Women's Trade Union League.

Stein, Jules b Apr. 26, 1896, South Bend, IN; d Apr. 29, 1981, Los Angeles, CA. Entertainment executive; ophthalmologist; philanthropist; founded Music Corp. of America (MCA).

Stein, Louis P. b Sept. 18, 1893, Warsaw, Poland; d June 24, 1952, Chicago. Beauty supply manufacturer; organized Helene Curtis Industries.

Steinfeldt, Harry M. b Sept. 29, 1877, St. Louis, MO; d Aug. 17, 1914, Bellevue, KY. Baseball player; Cubs third baseman.

Sternaman, Edward C. "Dutch" b Feb. 9, 1895; d Feb. 2, 1973, Chicago. Football and hockey coach; cofounder and coach of Decatur Staleys and Chicago Bears; first coach of Chicago Blackhawks.

Stevens, Alzina Parsons b May 27, 1849, Parsonsfield, ME; d June 3, 1900, Chicago. Printer; labor organizer; journalist; settlement worker; Chicago's first probation officer (1899).

Stevens, Thomas Wood b Jan. 26, 1880, Daysville, IL; d Jan. 29, 1942, Tucson, AZ. Writer; cofounded Goodman Theatre; founded Blue Sky Press.

Stevenson, Adlai Ewing, II b Feb. 5, 1900, Los Angeles, CA; d July 14, 1965, London, England. Lawyer; Illinois governor; diplomat; two-time candidate for U.S. president.

Stevenson, Adlai Ewing b Oct. 23, 1835, Christian County, KY; d June 14, 1914, Chicago. Lawyer; U.S. representative; vice president of the United States (1893–1896).

Stevenson, Sarah Hackett b Feb. 2, 1841, Buffalo Grove (now Polo), IL; d Aug. 14, 1909, Chicago. Doctor; settlement worker; founded Illinois Training School for Nurses.

Stewart, Bill (William) b 1894, Fitchburg, MA; d Feb. 18, 1964, Boston, MA. Hockey coach; coached Chicago Blackhawks (1937–1939); led team to Stanley Cup win (1938).

Stewart, William Larry b Mar. 24, 1937, Washington, DC; d Jan. 17, 1970, Neuse River, NC. Vocalist; soul performer in the 1960s.

Stickney, Alpheus Beede b June 27, 1840, Wilton, ME; d Aug. 9, 1916, St. Paul, MN. Lawyer; railway executive; president of Chicago Great Western Railway.

Stigler, George J. b Jan. 17, 1911, Renton, WA; d Dec. 1, 1991, Chicago. Economist; associated with Chicago School of Economics; won Nobel Prize.

Stillman, Alexander b Sept. 29, 1911, New York, NY; d Jan. 10, 1984, Barrington, IL. Philanthropist; donated land to Audubon Society of Chicago in 1976.

Stimpson, William b Feb. 14, 1832, Roxbury, MA; d May 26, 1872, Ilchester, MD. Marine zoologist; museum administrator; director of Chicago Academy of Sciences.

Stinson, Katherine b Feb. 14, 1891, Fort Payne, AL; d July 8, 1977, Santa Fe, NM. Early airmail pilot; first woman pilot to carry the U.S. mail.

Stoch, Karol C. b Nov. 1, 1889, Zubsuche, Poland; d Aug. 25, 1947, Chicago. Tavernkeeper; Polish mountain fiddler.

Stock, Frederick August b Nov. 11, 1872, Julich near Cologne, Germany; d Oct. 20, 1942, Chicago. Orchestra conductor; head of Chicago Symphony Orchestra (1905–1942); first director of Civic Orchestra.

Stockham, Alice Bunker b Nov. 8, 1833, Cardington, OH; d Dec. 2, 1912, Alhambra, CA. Physician; publisher; suffragist; social reformer.

Stone, Bentley b Aug. 31, 1907, Plankinton, SD; d Feb. 10, 1984, Chicago. Ballet dancer; teacher; choreographer; performed with Ruth Page.

Stone, Herbert Stuart b 1870 or 1871, Chicago; d May 7, 1915, died at sea during sinking of Lusitania. Journalist; publisher; editor and owner of the *Chap-Book*; founded Stone & Kimball publishers.

Stone, Melville Elijah b Aug. 22, 1848, Hudson, IL; d Feb. 15, 1929, New York, NY. Journalist; founded *Chicago Daily News*; general manager of Associated Press.

Stone, W. Clement b May 4, 1902, Chicago; d Sept. 3, 2002, Evanston, IL. Insurance executive; founded Combined Insurance Co. of America.

Storey, Wilbur Fiske b Dec. 19, 1819, Salisbury, VT; d Oct. 27, 1884, Chicago. Journalist; editor and publisher of *Chicago Times*.

Storrs, John Henry Bradley b June 28, 1885, Chicago; d Apr. 23, 1956, Mer, France. Sculptor; designed Ceres statue atop Board of Trade building.

Stracke, Winfred "Win" J. b Feb. 20, 1908; d June 29, 1991, Chicago. Folk singer; songwriter; pioneer of early Chicago television; cofounded Old Town School of Folk Music.

Strasser, Adolph b Jan. 23, 1846? Austria-Hungary; d Jan. 1, 1939, Lakeland, FL. Labor leader; cofounded American Federation of Labor.

Stratton, William Grant b Feb. 26, 1914, Ingleside, IL; d Mar. 2, 2001, Chicago. Republican governor of Illinois (1953–1961).

Strauss, C. T. active late nineteenth century. Businessman; converted to Buddhism at 1893 World's Parliament of Religions.

Streeter, George Wellington b 1837; d Jan. 22, 1921, East Indiana Harbor Canal, near Forsythe, IN. Sea captain; claimed the Gold Coast area by right of original discovery; namesake of "Streeterville."

Stritch, Samuel Alphonsus b Aug. 17, 1887, Nashville, TN; d May 27, 1958, Rome, Italy. Roman Catholic archbishop of Chicago (1940–1958); created cardinal (1946).

Strode, James M. active 1840s. Attorney; state senator (1832–1836).

Struckmann, Dietrich b Nov. 29, 1818, Landesbergen, Germany; d May 4, 1879, Elmhurst, IL. Landowner; purchased land around Bensenville in early 1870s.

Stydahar, Joseph Lee b Mar. 17, 1912, Kaylor, PA; d Mar. 23, 1977, Beckley, WV. Football player and coach for Chicago Bears; Bears' first draft pick, 1936.

Sullivan, Joseph Michael b Nov. 4, 1906, Chicago; d Oct. 13, 1971, San Francisco, IL. Jazz pianist; composer; performed with several Chicago bands; recorded with Lionel Hampton and Billie Holiday.

Sullivan, Louis Henri b Sept. 3, 1856, Boston, MA; d Apr. 14, 1924, Chicago. Architect; designed early skyscrapers, Auditorium Building, Carson Pirie Scott store, and numerous other notable buildings.

Sullivan, Margaret Frances Buchanan b 1847, Ireland; d Dec. 28, 1903. Journalist; editorial writer for Chicago newspapers.

Sullivan, Roger C. b Feb. 2, 1861, Belvidere, IL; d Apr. 14, 1920, Chicago. President of Ogden Gas Co.; leader of Democratic Party in Illinois.

Sulzer, Andrew active 1830s. Established brewery in 1833.

Sulzer, Conrad b May 3, 1807, Bussnang, Thurgau, Switzerland; d Dec. 24, 1873, Chicago. Settled in Lakeview area in 1837.

Sun Ra [Herman Lee; Herman Blount] b May 22, 1914, Birmingham, AL; d May 30, 1993, Birmingham, AL. Jazz pianist; electric keyboardist; bandleader; composer; founded avant-garde jazz band, Solar Arkestra.

Sunday, Billy b Nov. 19, 1862, Story County, IA; d Nov. 6, 1935, Chicago. Major League baseball player; conservative Protestant evangelist.

Sundstrom, Ebba [Ebba Sundstrom Nylander] b Feb. 26, 1896, Lindsborg, KS; d Jan. 4 or 5, 1963, Evanston, IL. Conductor; violist; teacher; formed Women's Symphony Orchestra of Chicago.

Sutherland, E. B. active 1840s. Established tavern in 1841; first postmaster in Portage Park.

Swainson, Anne b c. 1900, Sweden; d May 19, 1955, Chicago. Industrial designer; formed Bureau of Design at Montgomery Ward, 1931.

Swanson, Gloria [Gloria May Josephine Svennson] b Mar. 27, 1899, Chicago; d Apr. 4, 1983, New York, NY. Film actress; career began at Chicago's Essanay film studio; known as one of the first glamour queens.

Sweet, Carroll F. b June 24, 1877, Grand Rapids, MI; d Sept. 26, 1955, Dolton, IL. Real-estate developer; construction executive; codeveloped Park Forest.

Swenie, Denis J. b July 29, 1834, Glasgow, Scotland; d Feb. 16, 1903, Chicago. Fireman; chief of Chicago's volunteer fire department (1858–1901).

Swift, Gustavus Franklin b June 24, 1839, Sandwich, Cape Cod, MA; d Mar. 29, 1903, Lake Forest, IL. Meatpacker; philanthropist; founder and president of Swift & Co.; pioneer in use of refrigerated railcars for shipping meat.

Swift, Louis F. b Sept. 27, 1861, Sagamore, MA; d May 12, 1937, Chicago. Meatpacker; president of Swift & Co. (1903–1931).

Swing, David b Aug. 23, 1830, Cincinnati, OH; d Oct. 3, 1884, Chicago. Minister at Fourth Presbyterian Church; accused of heresy;

formed nondenominational congregation of Central Church (1875).

Szukalski, Stanislaus b Dec. 13, 1893, Warta, Poland; d May 19, 1987, Burbank, CA. Sculptor; painter.

T

Taft, Lorado Zadok b Apr. 29, 1860, Elmwood, IL; d Oct. 30, 1936, Chicago. Sculptor; designed sculpture for World's Columbian Exposition, *Eternal Silence* grave monument in Graceland, *Fountain of Time* on Midway, and *Fountain of the Great Lakes* at Art Institute.

Talcott, Mancel b Oct. 12, 1817, Rome, NY; d June 5, 1878, Chicago. Alderman; partner at Singer & Talcott Stone Co.; founded First National Bank of Chicago.

Tallmadge, Emily b Feb. 14, 1840? Dutchess, NY. Printer; labor songwriter.

Tallmadge, James D. b Feb. 4, 1822? Tioga, NY. Printer; labor songwriter.

Tallmadge, Thomas Eddy b Apr. 24, 1876, Washington, DC; d Jan. 1, 1940, Arcola, IL. Architect; teacher; writer.

Tampa Red [Hudson Whittaker; Hudson Woodbridge] b Jan. 8, 1903, Smithville, GA; d Mar. 19, 1981, Chicago. Blues singer; slide guitarist; popular performer on Chicago club circuit.

Taylor, Anson H. b ca. 1805, Hartford, CT? d 1878. Storekeeper; builder; operated inn near Glencoe site in 1835.

Taylor, Augustine Deodat b Apr. 28, 1796, Hartford, CT; d Mar. 31, 1891, Chicago. Carpenter; builder; worked on St. James' (Episcopal) Church and St. Patrick's Church.

Taylor, Benjamin Franklin b July 19, 1819 or 1822, Lowville, NY; d Feb. 24, 1887, Cleveland, OH. Journalist; poet; Civil War correspondent; editor for *Chicago Evening Journal* and *Chicago Journal*.

Taylor, Bert Leston b Nov. 13, 1866, Goshen, MA; d Mar. 19, 1921, Glencoe, IL. Writer; newspaper columnist.

Taylor, Graham b May 2, 1851, Schenectady, NY; d Sept. 26, 1938, Ravinia, IL. Clergyman; social reformer; educator; founded Chicago Commons settlement; president of Chicago School of Civics and Philanthropy.

Taylor, Henry active 1830s. Came to Orland Park in 1834.

Taylor, John W. b 1846; d early 1920s? Photographer; architectural and view photography; landscapes; view albums.

Taylor, Lea Demarest b June 24, 1883, Hartford, CT; d Dec. 3, 1975, Highstown, NJ. Social reformer; director of Chicago Commons settlement house (1922–1954).

Taylor, Lisa active 1830s. Operated inn with husband Anson H. Taylor beginning 1835.

Taylor, Marshall W. "Major" b Nov. 26, 1878, Indianapolis, IN; d June 21, 1932, Chicago. Cyclist; champion racer in 1890s.

Taylor, Robert Rochon b ca. 1899 or 1900; d Mar. 1, 1957, Chicago. Housing developer; manager of Michigan Boulevard Garden Apartments; chairman of Chicago Housing Authority.

Taylor, Theodore Roosevelt "Hound Dog" b Apr. 12, 1917, Natchez, MS; d Dec. 17, 1975, Chicago. Blues singer; guitarist; played Maxwell Street market district; part of the 1970s blues revival on Alligator records.

Teale, Edwin Way b June 2, 1899, Joliet, IL; d Oct. 18, 1980, Norwich, CT. Naturalist; writer; photographer; worked to save the Indiana Dunes from development.

Tecumseh b c. 1768, probably along Scioto River, OH; d Oct. 5, 1813. Shawnee chief; led movement to unite tribes against U.S. military; killed in War of 1812.

Teich, Curt Otto b Mar. 23, 1877, Lobenstein, Germany; d Jan. 12, 1974, Clearwater, FL. Postcard printer; founded Curt Teich Co.

Tennes, Mont Jacob b Jan. 16, 1874, Chicago; d Aug. 6, 1941, Chicago. Gambler; inherited Mike McDonald's gambling empire; dominant force in racetrack gambling.

Tenskwatawa [Shawnee Prophet] b 1775, Old Piqua, OH; d Nov. 1836, Kansas City, KS. American Indian; active around Fort Dearborn in 1803 in Pan-Indian Movement.

Teresita, Mary active 1910s. Nun; one of the first women to earn bachelor's degree at DePaul, 1912.

Terra, Daniel J. b June 8, 1911, Philadelphia, PA; d June 28, 1996, Washington, DC. Businessman; art collector; founded Terra Museum of American Art.

Teschemacher, Frank M. b Mar. 13, 1906, Kansas City, MO; d Mar. 1, 1932, Chicago. Jazz musician; clarinetist; alto saxophonist; member of Austin High Gang.

Thatcher, David C. b 1810, Cooperstown, NY; d Apr. 1869, River Forest, IL. Merchant; moved to River Forest in 1858; owned arms and ammunition store.

Thomas, Danny [Muzyad Yakhoob; Amos Jacobs] b Jan. 6, 1912, Deerfield, MI; d Feb. 6, 1991, Los Angeles, CA. Radio and television actor, comedian; philanthropist; star of *Make Room for Daddy*; career began in Chicago clubs and radio.

Thomas, Frazier b June 13, 1918, Rushville, IN; d Apr. 3, 1985, Chicago. Television entertainer; hosted children's programs on WGN-TV for 30 years; created character Garfield Goose.

Thomas, Frederick active 1830s. Barber-surgeon; ran retail drug business in 1830s.

Thomas, Henry b 1874, Big Sandy, TX; d 1950s? Ragtime folk musician; recorded in Chicago in 1920s.

Thomas, Hiram Washington b Apr. 29, 1832, Hampshire County, VA; d Aug. 12, 1909, De Funiak Springs, FL. Preacher; Methodist; founded People's Church of Chicago.

Thomas, John W. E. b May 1, 1847, Montgomery, AL; d Dec. 18, 1899, Chicago. Lawyer; ex-slave and civil rights leader; first African American state legislator (1878).

Thomas, Theodore b Oct. 11, 1835, Esens, Germany; d Jan. 4, 1905, Chicago. Founder and first conductor of Chicago Symphony Orchestra (1891).

Thomas, William b 1777; d Sept. 27, 1838. Early landowner; owned cabin, sawmill and general store near Coffee Creek in Chesterton, IN.

Thomas, William Isaac b Aug. 13, 1863, Russell County, VA; d Dec. 5, 1947, Berkeley, CA. Sociologist; professor at Univ. of Chicago; coauthor of *The Polish Peasant in Europe and America* (1918).

Thompson, Daniel M. active 1870s. Businessman; owner of grain elevators; built first large home on Prairie Avenue in 1870.

Thompson, James b Jan. 2, 1789, Abbeville, SC; d Oct. 6, 1872, Preston, IL. Farmer; judge; first surveyor of Chicago.

Thompson, Mary Harris b Apr. 15, 1829, Fort Ann, NY; d Mar. 21, 1895, Chicago. Surgeon; established Chicago Hospital for Women and Children and Woman's Hospital Medical College.

Thompson, William Hale b May 14, 1867, Boston, MA; d Mar. 19, 1944, Chicago. Mayor of Chicago (1915–1923, 1927–1931).

Thomson, George b Oct. 3, 1864 or 1865, Fort Hill, IL; d June 17, 1912, Grayslake, IL. Merchant; first president of Grayslake in 1895.

Thordarson, Chester Hjortur b May 12, 1867, Stadur, Hrutafjordur, Iceland; d Feb. 6, 1945, Chicago. Electrical inventor; businessman; specialized in the field of electrical transformers.

Thorne, George R. b Sept. 29, 1837, Vergennes, VT; d Sept. 24, 1918, Lake Forest, IL. Cofounded Montgomery Ward; founded country club in Midlothian.

Thornton, William F. b ca. 1789, VA; d Oct. 21, 1873, Shelbyville, IL. State representative; I&M Canal commissioner and president of its board.

Thorp, George G. b 1904; d 1972. Artist; head of Illinois Art Project (1938–1941).

Thurber, W. Scott b July 24, 1848, St. Lawrence County, NY; d Sept. 24, 1913, Chicago. Art dealer; gallery owner; displayed radical modern art in 1912.

Tiffany, Joel b Sept. 6, 1811, Brakhamsted, CT; d 1893. Judge; first village president of Hinsdale.

Tillstrom, Burr b Oct. 13, 1917, Chicago; d Dec. 6, 1985, Palm Springs, CA. Puppeteer; created *Kukla, Fran and Ollie* children's television show.

Tilton, George W. b Jan. 12, 1830, Manchester, NH; d Aug. 17, 1890, Chicago. Superintendent for Northwestern Railroad for 25 years.

Tinker, Joseph Bert b July 27, 1880, Muscotah, KS; d July 27, 1948, Orlando, FL. Baseball player; Chicago Cubs shortstop; in Hall of Fame.

Tinley, Samuel, Sr. b Sept. 2, 1808, Nottinghamshire, England; d July 31, 1882, Tinley Park, IL. Longtime Rock Island stationmaster; came to Chicago in 1848.

Tomlins, William Lawrence b Feb. 8, 1844, London, England; d Sept. 26, 1930, Delafield, WI. Music teacher; directed Apollo Chorus.

Tonti, Henri de [Tonty] b 1649 or 1650, France; d Sept. 1704, Mobile, AL. Fur trader; explorer; French "Governor of the Illinois" (late 1680s).

Toomer, Jean [Nathan Pinchback Toomer; Eugene Pinchback] b Dec. 26, 1894, Washington, DC; d Mar. 3, 1967, Doylestown, PA. Writer; philosopher; poet; wrote *Cane*; taught Gurdjieff gospel of higher consciousness while living in Chicago.

Torres, Rubin J. b Feb. 25, 1918; d July 4, 1998. Published Pilsen neighborhood newsletter for over 60 years.

Torrio, John b Feb. 1882, Orsara, Italy; d Apr. 16, 1957, Brooklyn, NY. Saloon and brothel keeper; gangster; Prohibition-era bootlegger; established West Side syndicate; mentor of Al Capone.

Tough, David Jaffray b Apr. 26, 1907, Oak Park, IL; d Dec. 9, 1948, Newark, NJ. Jazz drummer; performed with Austin High Gang, Tommy Dorsey, and Benny Goodman.

Touhy, Patrick L. b 1839 or 1842, Feakle, Ireland; d Oct. 16 or 17, 1911, Chicago. Real-estate developer; founded Rogers Park.

Towle, Marcus b ca. 1841 or 1843; d 1910. First mayor of Hammond.

Towner, Lawrence William b Sept. 10, 1921, St. Paul, MN; d June 12, 1992, Chicago. Historian; directed Newberry Library for 24 years.

Traynor, William B. b Jan. 10, 1886, New York, NY; d Jan. 7, 1968, Chicago. Businessman; president of Chicago Board of Education (1949–1955).

Tree, Anna Magie b ca. 1832, NJ; d Oct. 8, 1908, at sea near New York. Artist; cofounded Tree Studios to attract artists.

Tree, Lambert b Nov. 29, 1832, Washington, DC; d Oct. 9, 1910, New York, NY. Lawyer; Circuit Court judge (elected 1864); state legislator; diplomat; cofounded Tree Studios.

Tripp, Sylvester L. b Oct. 22, 1865, Half Day, IL; d 1939. President of incorporated Mundelein in 1909.

Trowbridge, Raymond W. b July 1886, Seneca, IL; d Dec. 16, 1936, Chicago. Architect; photographer.

Truax, Charles Henry b Sept. 24, 1852, Milton, WI; d Feb. 5, 1918, Chicago. Surgical supply wholesaler; president and founder of Truax & Co.

Trumbull, Lyman b Oct. 12, 1813, Colchester, CT; d June 25, 1896, Chicago. Lawyer; U.S. senator.

Tucker, Preston Thomas b Sept. 21, 1903, Capac, MI; d Dec. 26, 1956, Ypsilanti, MI. Automobile manufacturer; built Tucker sedans, rear-engine six-cylinder cars.

Tucker, Sophie Abuza b Jan. 13, 1889, Russia; d Feb. 9, 1966, New York, NY. Singer; vaudeville star; performed in Chicago vaudeville and nightclubs.

Tufts, James Hayden b July 9, 1862, Monson, MA; d Aug. 5, 1942, Berkeley, CA. Philosopher; professor and department head at Univ. of Chicago.

Tuley, Murray F. b Mar. 4, 1827, Louisville, KY; d Dec. 25, 1905, Kenosha, WI. Circuit court judge; alderman (1879–1883); attorney general of New Mexico.

Tumbelston, Peter G. b Mar. 15, 1957, Philadelphia, PA; d Jan. 27, 1992, Chicago. Independent dance producer; dance consultant; executive director of MoMing Dance and Arts Center.

Tunney, James Joseph "Gene" b May 25, 1897, New York, NY; d Nov. 7, 1978, Greenwich, CT. World heavyweight boxing champion; defeated Jack Dempsey in 1927 bout at Soldier Field.

Tupper, Chester b Sept. 1797, NY; d Feb. 3, 1861, CA. House mover; ca. 1840s–1850s.

Turbyfill, Mark b June 29, 1896, Wynnewood, OK; d June 6, 1990, Chicago. Dancer; poet; painter; choreographer; principal dancer of Chicago Allied Art; danced with Ruth Page.

Turner, Clyde "Bulldog" b Mar. 10, 1919, TX; d Oct. 30, 1998, Gatesville, TX. Football player; played for the Chicago Bears for 13 seasons.

Turner, George Kibbe b Mar. 23, 1869, Quincy, IL; d Feb. 15, 1952, Miami, FL. Magazine journalist; editor; wrote "The City of Chicago: A Study of the Great Immoralities" for *McClure's* (1907).

Turner, John active 1870s. Landowner in North Center.

Turner, John Bice b Jan. 14, 1799, Colchester, NY; d Feb. 26, 1871, Chicago. Founded Galena & Chicago Union Railroad (later the Chicago & North Western Railway).

Turner, Ralph G. b 1898; d Sept. 2, 1980, Chicago. Railroad worker; civil rights leader; founding member of DuSable Museum.

Tyler, Alice Kellogg *See* **Kellogg, Alice D.**

U

Upton, George Putnam b Oct. 25, 1834, Boston, MA; d May 19, 1919, Chicago. Writer; music critic for *Chicago Journal* and *Chicago Tribune*; founded Apollo Club.

Urban, Joseph Karl Maria Georg b May 26, 1872, Vienna, Austria; d July 10, 1933, New York, NY. Architect; artist; scenic designer; determined color scheme at Century of Progress Exposition.

Utley, Clifton Maxwell b May 31, 1904, Chicago; d Jan. 20, 1978, Kahului, Maui, HI. Newspaper columnist; radio and television commentator; specialized in foreign affairs.

V

Van Brunt, Henry b Sept. 5, 1832, Boston, MA; d Apr. 8, 1903, Boston, MA. Architect; designed Electricity Building at World's Columbian Exposition.

Van de Velde, James Oliver b Apr. 3, 1795, Lebbeke, Belgium; d Nov. 13, 1855, Natchez, MS. Roman Catholic bishop; second bishop of Archdiocese of Chicago.

Van Depoele, Charles J. b Apr. 27, 1846, Lichtervelde, Belgium; d Mar. 18, 1892, Lynn, MA. Scientist; inventor; demonstrated electric streetcar system at Chicago Exposition of Railway Appliances (1883).

Van Orsdal, William active 1830s. Arrived in Barrington Hills in 1834.

Van Osdel, John M. b July 31, 1811, Baltimore, MD; d Dec. 21, 1891, Chicago. Architect; designed Palmer House and Tremont House; secured passage of city's first building code.

Van Vlissingen, James Henry b Feb. 16, 1857, Spijkenisse, Province of Zuid-Holland, Netherlands. Developer; first village president of Winthrop Harbor.

Van Volkenburg, Ellen b 1880. Artist; cofounded Little Theatre with husband, Maurice Browne.

Vandercook, Robert Oatman b Aug. 26, 1866, Bennington, VT; d June 8, 1951, Evanston, IL. Inventor; printing press manufacturer; founded Evanston Press.

Vardin, George active 1830s. Arrived in Libertyville (originally Vardin's Grove) around 1830.

Vaux, Calvert b Dec. 20, 1824, London, England; d Nov. 19? 1895, disappeared in Bensonhurst, Long Island, NY. Architect; landscape architect; codesigned Jackson and Washington Parks and Riverside planned community.

Veeck, William Louis b Feb. 9, 1914, Chicago; d Jan. 2, 1986, Chicago. Baseball entrepreneur; owned Cleveland Indians, St. Louis Browns, and Chicago White Sox; elected to Hall of Fame (1991).

Vial, Joseph b Aug. 23, 1791; d Nov. 18, 1853, La Grange, IL. Early settler of Lyons Township; built general store and hotel in Western Springs in 1834.

Vitzthum, Karl b Jan. 2, 1880, Munich, Germany; d Oct. 30, 1967, Chicago. Architect; designer of St. Peter's Catholic Church and Cook County Hospital.

Vogt, Carl F. b Sept. 27, 1839, Rockensuess, Hessen, Germany; d Mar. 7, 1888, Bremen, IL. Early settler in village of Bremen.

Volk, Leonard Wells b Nov. 7, 1828, Wellstown (now Wells), NY; d Aug. 19, 1895,

Osceola, WI. Sculptor; organized first art exhibition in Chicago in 1859.

Volland, Paul Frederick b Oct. 24, 1875, Germany; d May 5, 1919, Chicago. Engraver; publisher of juvenile and gift books; founded P. F. Volland & Co.

W

Wachter, Josephina b ca. 1820, Bavaria, Germany. Arrived in Hickory Hills in 1858.

Wachter, Mathias b ca. 1808, Bavaria, Germany. Farmer; arrived in Hickory Hills in 1858.

Wacker, Charles Henry b Aug. 29, 1856, Chicago; d Oct. 31, 1929, Lake Geneva, WI. Business executive; philanthropist; chairman of Chicago Plan Commission (1909–1926); namesake of Wacker Drive.

Wadsworth, Elisha b May 10, 1813, New Hartford, CT; d Nov. 25, 1890, Clifton Springs, NY. Dry-goods merchant; cofounded Wadsworth, Dyer & Chapin.

Wagoner, Henry O. b Feb. 27, 1816, Hagerstown, MD; d Jan. 27, 1901, Denver, CO. Businessman; abolitionist; participant in Underground Railroad.

Waite, George active late 1870s. Landowner; his land became Mount Greenwood Cemetery.

Walgreen, Charles Rudolph b Oct. 9, 1873, Knox County, IL; d Aug. 20, 1971, Chicago. Pharmacist; chain store executive; started first Walgreen drugstore in Chicago in 1901.

Walker, George Clarke b Nov. 5, 1835, Burlington Flats, NY; d Apr. 12, 1905, Chicago. President of Blue Island Land & Building Co.; donated library to Esmond Public School.

Walker, Jesse b June 9, 1766, Buckingham County, VA; d Oct. 4, 1835, Leyden Township, IL. Missionary; preacher; founded Methodist Episcopal Church in Illinois; held first Methodist services in Chicago.

Walker, M. O. b June 9, 1809, Hubbardton, VT; d May 28, 1874, Chicago. Brick manufacturer; omnibus entrepreneur.

Walker, Margaret [Margaret Walker Alexander] b July 7, 1915, Birmingham AL; d Nov. 30, 1998, Chicago. Writer; participant in Federal Writers' Project in Chicago; member of South Side Writers Group.

Walker, Ralph T. b Nov. 27 or 28, 1889, Waterbury, CT; d Jan. 17, 1973, Chappaqua, NY. Architect; member of Board of Design for Century of Progress Exposition.

Walker, Samuel J. b Jan. 9, 1827, Dayton, KY; d Apr. 15, 1884, Chicago. Real-estate developer on the Near West Side; renamed Ashland Avenue.

Walker, William Ernest b Nov. 19, 1869, Covington, KY; d Dec. 26, 1918, Chicago. Architect; built apartment buildings.

Walkup, Christopher b 1785, Rockbridge County, VA; d 1869, Crystal Lake, IL. Platted east shore village of Crystal Lake in 1840.

Waller, Edward Carson b Nov. 21, 1845, Maysville, KY; d Jan. 13, 1931, River Forest, IL. Real-estate developer; built Francisco Terrace, Chicago's first subsidized housing project.

Waller, Judith Cary b Feb. 19, 1889, Oak Park, IL; d Oct. 28, 1973, Evanston, IL. Radio broadcaster; first general manager of WMAQ radio station; produced *Amos 'n' Andy Show.*

Walley, John E. b Feb. 2, 1910, Sheridan, WY; d June 9, 1974. Mural painter; 1930s art at Lane Tech High School.

Walrath, Florence Dahl b Aug. 18, 1877, Chicago; d Nov. 7, 1958, Evanston, IL. Founder and director of Cradle Society adoption agency.

Walter, Charles active 1850s. Businessman; cofounded Chicago & North Western Railway system.

Walter, Little [Marion Walter Jacobs] b May 1, 1923, Marksville, LA; d Feb. 15, 1968, Chicago. Blues guitarist; harmonica player; played with Muddy Waters; recorded for Chess Records.

Walton, Seymour b Feb. 15, 1846, New Orleans, LA; d June 26, 1920, Chicago. Accountant; Northwestern Univ. faculty.

Wanamaker, Sam b June 14, 1919, Chicago; d Dec. 18, 1993, London, England. Actor; trained at Goodman School.

Waner, John L. b Aug. 3, 1914; d June 21, 1994, Naperville, IL. Regional director of HUD in Chicago; mayoral candidate (1967).

Ward, Aaron Montgomery b Feb. 17, 1843 or 1844, Chatham, NJ; d Dec. 7, 1913, Highland Park, IL. Merchant; founded A. Montgomery Ward mail-order business; lakefront preservation activist.

Ward, Archibald "Arch" Burdette b Dec. 27, 1896, Irwin, IL; d July 9, 1955, Chicago. *Chicago Tribune* sports writer; founded baseball All-Star Game, Chicago College All-Star Football Game, and the All-America Football Conference.

Warder, John Aston b Jan. 19, 1812, Philadelphia, PA; d July 14, 1883, North Bend, OH. Physician; early horticulturist.

Waring, Mary Fitzbutler b Nov. 1, 1869, Louisville, KY; d Dec. 3, 1958, Chicago. Physician; educator; headed National Association of Colored Women's Clubs.

Warren, Clinton J. b 1858 or 1860; d 1938. Architect; built elevator apartments around 1900.

Warren, Julius M. b June 13, 1811, Fredonia, NY; d May 1, 1893, Warrenville, IL. Platted town of Warrenville, IL; state legislator (1840–1843).

Washburne, Carleton b Dec. 2, 1889, Chicago; d Nov. 26, 1968, Lansing, MI. Educator; superintendent of Winnetka schools; progressive education leader.

Washburne, Hempstead b Nov. 11, 1851, Galena, IL; d Apr. 13, 1918, Chicago. Mayor of Chicago (1891–1893).

Washington, Dinah [Ruth Lee Jones] b Aug. 29, 1924, Tuscaloosa, AL; d Dec. 14, 1963, Detroit, MI. Blues and gospel singer; pianist.

Washington, Harold L. b Apr. 15, 1922, Chicago; d Nov. 25, 1987, Chicago. Mayor of Chicago (1983–1987), state legislator, congressman.

Watts, May Theilgaard b May 1, 1893, Chicago; d Aug. 20, 1975, Naperville, IL. Naturalist; teacher; associated with Morton Arboretum.

Way, W. Irving b Feb. 24, 1853, Trenton, Ontario; d Oct. 19, 1931, Los Angeles, CA. Book publisher and bookseller.

Weaver, George "Buck" b Aug. 18, 1890, Pottstown, PA; d Jan. 31, 1956, Chicago. White Sox baseball player; involved in "Black Sox" scandal; banned from baseball for life.

Webster, Maurice b Sept. 20, 1892; d May 17, 1982, Evanston, IL. Architect; designed terminal for Sky Harbor Airport (ca. 1929).

Webster, Milton Price b ca. 1887 or 1888, Clarksville, TN; d Feb. 24, 1965, Bal Harbour, FL. Porter; labor organizer; first international vice president of Brotherhood of Sleeping Car Porters.

Webster, Roderick Sheldon b Sept. 14, 1915; d July 31, 1997, Evanston, IL. Curator at Adler Planetarium.

Weeghman, Charles H. b Mar. 8, 1874, Richmond, IN; d Nov. 2, 1938, Chicago. Restaurant owner; owned Chicago Cubs; built a chain of lunchrooms.

Weese, Harry Mohr b June 30, 1915, Evanston, IL; d Oct. 29, 1998, Manteno, IL. Architect; renovated Adler & Sullivan Auditorium, Field Museum, and Orchestra Hall.

Weidner, John B. b Feb. 12, 1860, Buffalo Grove, IL; d Nov. 19, 1922, Buffalo Grove, IL. Builder of cheese factory in Buffalo Grove around 1900.

Weimhoff, Henry active 1970s. Activist; organized Univ. of Chicago Gay Liberation Front in 1970s.

Weinstein, Jacob Joseph b June 6, 1902, Stephin, Poland; d Nov. 2, 1974, San Francisco, CA. Rabbi at Kehilath Anshe Mayriv Congregation (1939–1967); social reformer.

Weisenborn, Rudolph b Oct. 31, 1881, Chicago; d Mar. 1974, Chicago. Artist; abstract painter.

Weiss, Hymie [Earl Wojciechowski] b ca. 1898, Chicago; d Oct. 11, 1926, Chicago. Crime boss of O'Banion gang.

Weissmuller, Janos "Johnny" b June 2, 1904, Freidorf, Romania; d Jan. 20, 1984, Acapulco, Mexico. Olympic swimming champion; star of Tarzan movies; trained at the Illinois Athletic Club.

Weldon, Aldred F. b June 14, 1862, Hartford, CT; d May 5, 1914, Chicago. Composer; bandleader; conductor of Second Regiment Band in 1890s.

Wellington, Gertrude Gail active late nineteenth century. Physician; led campaign for public baths; president of the Free Bath and Sanitary League.

Wells, Absalom active 1830s. Built cabin in Chicago Heights around 1830s.

Wells, Ida Bell [Ida B. Wells-Barnett] b July 16, 1862, Holly Springs, MS; d Mar. 25, 1931, Chicago. Journalist; social reformer; suffrage and civil rights activist; headed NAACP founding meeting; established Alpha Suffrage Club.

Wells, William b 1770, Jacob's Creek, PA; d Aug. 15, 1812, Fort Dearborn, Chicago. Army scout; adopted by Miami Indians; mediated Indian-white relations.

Wells, William Harvey b Feb. 27, 1812, Tolland, CT; d Jan. 21, 1885, Chicago. Educator; superintendent of Chicago Public Schools (1956–1964).

Wentworth, "Long John" b Mar. 5, 1815, Sandwich, NH; d Oct. 16, 1888, Chicago. Mayor of Chicago (1857–1858; 1860–1861).

Westermann, Horace Clifford b Dec. 11, 1922, Los Angeles, CA; d Nov. 3, 1981, Danbury, CT. Artist; sculptor; worked in wood and metal.

Wetmore, Frances K. b ca. 1873; d Jan. 25, 1949, Chicago. Founded Americanization and adult education program in Chicago Public Schools.

Weydemeyer, Joseph b ca. 1818, Westphalia, Rhenish Prussia; d Aug. 1866, St. Louis, MO. Journalist; Civil War veteran; published *Die Stimme des Volkes* in Chicago.

Wheaton, Jesse C. b May 27, 1813, Pomfret, CT; d 1895. Farmer; cofounded Wheaton College.

Wheaton, Warren L. b Mar. 6, 1812, Pomfret, CT; d 1903. Cofounded Wheaton; first village president of Wheaton.

Wheeler, Charles Martin b Sept. 24, 1854, Ferrisburg, VT. In real-estate business with Albert Haentze.

Wheeler, Harry A. b May 26, 1866, Brooklyn, NY; d Jan. 23, 1960, Altadena, CA. Banker; civic leader; first president United States Chamber of Commerce (1912).

Whistler, John b ca. 1756, Ulster, Ireland; d Sept. 3, 1829, Jefferson Barracks, MO. Soldier; builder and first commander of Fort Dearborn.

White, Amarias M. b Sept. 19, 1849, Avon Township, IL; d Feb. 9, 1928, Round Lake, IL. Real-estate developer; landowner near Hainesville.

White, Charles b Apr. 2, 1918, Chicago; d Oct. 3, 1979, Los Angeles, CA. Painter; printmaker; muralist; taught at South Side Community Art Center.

White, Charles A. active 1910s. Illinois assemblyman; admitted being bribed for Lorimer Senate vote.

White, Horace b Aug. 10, 1834, Colebrook, NH; d Sept. 16, 1916, New York, NY. Journalist; editor-in-chief of *Chicago Tribune*.

White, Stanford b Nov. 9, 1853, New York, NY; d June 25, 1906, New York, NY. Architect; partner at McKim, Mead & White.

Whitehead, Richard F. b Jan. 1, 1884, Fall River, MA; d Mar. 11, 1993, Chicago. Naval officer; corporate executive; converted two merchant ships into aircraft carriers.

Whitlock, Brand b Mar. 4, 1869, Urbana, OH; d May 24, 1934, Cannes, France. Novelist; journalist at *Chicago Herald*; ambassador to Belgium during WWI.

Whyte, William H. b Oct. 1, 1917, West Chester, PA; d Jan. 12, 1999, Manhattan, NY. Journalist; wrote *The Organization Man* (1956; based on suburb of Park Forest).

Wieboldt, William A. b Mar. 8, 1857, Altenbruch, Hanover, Germany; d Dec. 9, 1954, Evanston, IL. Merchant; philanthropist; founded Wieboldt Stores.

Wiggins, Jeremiah active 1830s. Early settler; purchased land claim in 1835 and named it Wiggins Point (later Merrillville).

Wight, Peter Bonnett b Aug. 1, 1838, New York, NY; d Sept. 8, 1925, Pasadena, CA. Architect; prominent in rebuilding of Chicago after 1871 fire; employed Daniel Burnham.

Wilkerson, James Herbert b Dec. 11, 1869, Savannah, MO; d Sept. 30, 1948, Evanston, IL. Lawyer; federal judge; presiding judge at Al Capone trial.

Wilkie, Franc Bangs b July 2, 1832, West Charlton, NY; d Apr. 12, 1892, Norwood, IL. Journalist; wrote for *Chicago Times* for 25 years.

Will, Conrad b June 1778 or 1779, Philadelphia, PA; d June 11, 1835, Brownsville, IL. Physician; founded Brownsville, IL; Will County named for him.

Willard, Frances Elizabeth Caroline b Sept. 28, 1839, Churchville, NY; d Feb. 17, 1898, NY. Educator; lecturer; local, national, and international president of Woman's Christian Temperance Union.

Williams, Benezette b Nov. 9, 1844, West Liberty, OH; d June 22, 1914, Western Springs, IL. Engineer; first engineer of Chicago drainage canal.

Williams, Daniel Hale b Jan. 18, 1856, Hollidaysburg, PA; d Aug. 4, 1931, Idlewild, MI. Surgeon; hospital administrator; founded Provident Hospital (1891).

Williams, Edgar b July 29, 1851, Sheboygan, WI; d Dec. 8, 1945, Western Springs, IL. Engineer; built Western Springs waterworks system in 1890.

Williams, J. Mayo "Ink" b July 25, 1894, Monmouth, IL; d Jan. 2, 1980, Chicago. Jazz and blues record producer; manager of "Race Artist Series" for Paramount Records.

Williams, Lacey Kirk b July 11, 1871, Eufaula, AL; d Oct. 29, 1940, Olivet, MI. Clergyman; pastor of Olivet Baptist Church.

Williams, Sidney R. b Mar. 7, 1909, Elloree, SC; d Mar. 21, 1992, Chicago. Civil rights activist; executive director of Chicago Urban League (1947–1955).

Williamson, John Lee Curtis b Mar. 30, 1914, Jackson, TN; d June 1, 1948, Chicago. Blues harmonica player; songwriter; played in Chicago blues clubs; regular performer in Maxwell Street open-air market.

Williamson, Sonny Boy [Aleck Miller] b Dec. 5, 1899? Glendora, MS; d May 25, 1965, Helena, AR. Blues artist; recorded for Chess Records.

Willis, Benjamin C. b Dec. 23, 1901, Baltimore, MD; d Aug. 27, 1988, Plantation, FL. Superintendent of Chicago Public Schools; namesake of "Willis Wagons."

Willmarth, Homer b Mar. 5, 1807, North Adams, MA; d Mar. 29, 1882, Barrington, IL. Farmer; Cook County Commissioner; justice of the peace.

Wilmarth, Mary H. b May 21, 1837, New Bedford, MA; d Aug. 28, 1919, Lake Geneva, WI. Social reformer; suffragist; member of first board of trustees at Hull House; president of the Fortnightly Club.

Wilson, Isaac G. b June 25, 1780, Danby, VT; d Oct. 25, 1848, Batavia, IL. Lawyer; circuit and appellate court judge; founded Batavia and named it after his hometown in New York.

Wilson, Jack "Jackie" Leroy b June 9, 1934, Detroit, MI; d Jan. 21, 1984, Mount Holly, NJ. Soul singer; musician.

Wilson, Lewis Robert "Hack" b Apr. 26, 1900, Elwood City, PA; d Nov. 23, 1948, Baltimore, MD. Baseball player, Chicago Cubs (1926–1931).

Wilson, Orlando W. b May 15, 1900, Veblen, SD; d Oct. 18, 1972, Poway, CA. Criminologist; police superintendent (1960–1967).

Wilson, Robert Rathbun b Mar. 4, 1914, Frontier, WY; d Jan. 16, 2000, Ithaca, NY. Physicist; designed Fermi National Accelerator Laboratory; worked on Manhattan Project.

Wilson, Thomas E. b July 22, 1868, London, Ontario, Canada; d Aug. 4, 1958, Lake Forest, IL. Meatpacking executive; chairman of Wilson & Co.

Winslow, Eugene b Nov. 17, 1919, Dayton, OH; d July 7, 2001, Chicago. Graphic designer; advertising executive; Tuskegee Airman.

Winslow, William Herman b May 2, 1857, Brooklyn, NY; d Dec. 24, 1934, North Haven, MI. Manufacturer; inventor; owned firm making ornamental bronze and iron work.

Wirt, William Albert b Jan. 21, 1874, Markle, IN; d Mar. 11, 1938, Gary, IN. Educator; superintendent of Gary, IN, schools; initiated "Gary System" in schools.

Wirth, Louis b Aug. 28, 1897, Gemunden, Germany; d May 3, 1952, Buffalo, NY. Sociologist; associated with Chicago School of Sociology; director of planning for Illinois Post War Planning Commission.

Wirtz, Arthur Michael b Jan. 23, 1901, Chicago; d July 21, 1983, Chicago. Sports and real-estate executive; owned Chicago Stadium; formed International Boxing Club in 1949.

Witkowsky, Flora Mayer b Nov. 2, 1869, Chicago; d Nov. 8, 1944, Chicago. Leader of Jewish Chicago Woman's Aid; president of Illinois Federation of Women's Clubs.

Wolf, Jacob b Aug. 13, 1784, Westmoreland County, PA; d Apr. 15, 1851, Porter, IN. Farmer in Portage, IN, in late 1830s.

Wolff, Ludwig b Mar. 11, 1836, Mecklenburg-Schwerin, Germany; d Apr. 14, 1911, Chicago. Manufacturer; plumbing and coppersmith business.

Womer, Mary Louise b Dec. 9, 1909, Springfield, MO; d Nov. 4, 1997, Valparaiso, IN. Gallery owner; founded 57th Street Art Fair in Hyde Park.

Wood, Diantha S. Boardman b Sept. 10, 1811, Morristown, VT; d Sept. 24, 1865, Crete, IL. Cofounded Crete.

Wood, Elizabeth b Mar. 4, 1899; d Jan. 16, 1993. Executive director of Chicago Housing Authority (1937–1954).

Wood, Robert Elkington b June 13, 1879, Kansas City, MO; d Nov. 6, 1969, Lake Forest, IL. Army officer; businessman; president of Sears, Roebuck & Co. for 26 years.

Wood, Willard b Aug. 28, 1808, Randolph, VT; d Nov. 27, 1899, Crete, IL. Lawyer; cofounded Crete; justice of the peace.

Woodbridge, William active 1830s. Arrived in Thornton area in 1834.

Woodman, William E. b Oct. 1, 1932, New York, NY; d Dec. 19, 1995, New York, NY. Artistic director of Goodman Theatre (1973–1978).

Woodworth, James H. b Dec. 4, 1804, Greenwich, NY; d Mar. 26, 1869, Highland Park, IL. Mayor of Chicago (1848–1850).

Wooldridge, Clifton Rodman b ca. 1854; d Aug. 14, 1933, Chicago. Police detective; writer; investigated fake fire insurance companies.

Wooley, Jedediah, Jr. b 1781, Monmouth, NJ. Mill owner on DuPage River in 1830s; county surveyor.

Woolley, Celia Parker b June 14, 1848, Toledo, OH; d Mar. 9, 1918, Chicago. Unitarian minister; writer; clubwoman; attended founding meeting of NAACP; president of Chicago Woman's Club; cofounded Chicago Political Equality League.

Work, Henry Clay b Oct. 1, 1832, Middletown, CT; d June 8, 1884, Hartford, CT. Composer; songwriter.

Worth, William Jenkins b Mar. 1, 1794, Hudson, NY; d 1849, San Antonio, TX. Army officer; fought in War of 1812; Mexican War general; namesake of Worth, IL.

Wrenn, John H. b Sept. 11, 1841, Middletown, OH; d May 13, 1911, Los Angeles, CA. Early Chicago Board of Trade operator; book collector.

Wright, Edward H. b ca. 1867, NY; d Aug. 6, 1930, Rochester, MN. Lawyer; politician; first president of Cook County Bar Association (1914).

Wright, Frank Lloyd b June 8, 1867, Richland Center, WI; d Apr. 9, 1959, Phoenix, AZ. Architect, student of Louis Sullivan; designed Robie House.

Wright, John Lloyd b Dec. 12, 1892, Oak Park, IL; d Dec. 20, 1972, La Jolla, CA. Architect; toy designer in Chicago; created Lincoln Logs toys.

Wright, John Stephen b July 16, 1815, Sheffield, MA; d Sept. 26, 1874, Philadelphia, PA. City promoter; editor of the *Prairie Farmer*.

Wright, Richard Nathaniel b Sept. 4, 1908, Natchez, MS; d Nov. 28, 1960, Paris, France. Writer; wrote *Native Son* (1940), *Black Boy*; worked for Federal Writers Project.

Wrigley, Philip Knight b Dec. 5, 1904, Chicago; d Apr. 12, 1977, Elkhorn, WI. Chewing gum manufacturer; owned Chicago Cubs baseball team.

Wrigley, William, Jr. b Sept. 30, 1861, Philadelphia, PA; d Jan. 26, 1932, Phoenix, AZ. Chewing gum manufacturer; founded Wrigley Chewing Gum Co.

Wyatt, Edith Franklin b Sept. 14, 1873, Tomah, WI; d Oct. 1958. Writer; wrote *True Love*.

Wynkoop, Archimedes b ca. 1812, NY? Farmer; town court recorder; renamed settlement as Libertyville.

Wynn, Robert David b Dec. 18, 1865, Shields Township, Lake County, IL; d Apr. 12, 1940, Jacksonville, FL. Railroad entrepreneur; promoted building traction rail line in 1910.

Wynne, Madeline Y. b Sept. 25, 1847, Newport, NY; d Jan. 4, 1918, Asheville, NC. Writer; wrote *The Little Room*.

Y

Yackley, Joseph b Dec. 24, 1829, Alsace, France; d May 16, 1921, Naperville, IL. Longtime resident of Naperville beginning in the 1840s.

Yarros, Rachelle Slobodinsky b May 18, 1869, Berdechev, near Kiev in Ukraine; d Mar. 17, 1946, San Diego, CA. Physician; Chicago obstetrician; pioneer in social hygiene; birth control advocate.

Yerby, Frank Garvin b Sept. 5, 1916, Augusta, GA; d Nov. 29, 1991, Madrid, Spain. Writer; worked for Federal Writers Project; wrote *Foxes of Harrow* and other historical novels.

Yerkes, Charles Tyson, Jr. b June 25, 1837, Philadelphia, PA; d Dec. 29, 1905, New York, NY. Transportation business executive; built Chicago elevated railway in the Loop.

Yoakum, Joseph b Feb. 20, 1890, Window Rock, AZ; d Dec. 1972, Chicago. Painter; folk artist; known for his landscape drawings.

Young, Albert active early twentieth century. Labor official; president of Chicago Teamsters' Union; toppled by graft charges 1904–1905.

Young, Edward active late nineteenth century. Civil War general; built home around Pleasant Avenue in 1890s.

Young, Ella Flagg b Jan. 15, 1845, Buffalo, NY; d Oct. 26, 1918, Washington, DC. Educator; superintendent of Chicago Public Schools (1909–1913).

Z

Zeckendorf, William b June 20, 1905, Paris, IL; d Sept. 30, 1976, New York, NY. Real-estate developer; partner of Arthur Rubloff in the development of the Magnificent Mile.

Zelzer, Harry b Apr. 15, 1897, Warsaw, Poland; d June 14, 1979, Chicago. Banker; major presenter of classical music and dance attractions.

Zelzer, Sarah Schectman b Jan. 23, 1909, Philadelphia, PA; d Mar. 29, 1998, Chicago. Cofounded Allied Arts organization; influential in Chicago's musical scene.

Ziegfeld, Florenz b June 10, 1841, Jever, Oldenburg, Germany; d May 20, 1923, Chicago. Founder and president of Chicago Musical College.

Zima, Edwin "Eddie" b Feb. 20, 1923, Chicago; d July 1966. Polka musician; shaped Chicago-style polka.

Znaniecki, Florian Witold b Jan. 15, 1882, Swiatniki, Poland; d Mar. 23, 1958, Urbana, IL. Sociologist; coauthored *The Polish Peasant in Europe and America*.

Zorbaugh, Harvey Warren b Sept. 20, 1896, East Cleveland, OH; d Jan. 1965. Sociologist; wrote *The Gold Coast and the Slum*.

Zueblin, Charles b May 4, 1866, Pendleton, IN; d Sept. 15, 1924, Corsier-Port, Switzerland. Educator; founded Northwestern Univ. Settlement; sociology chair at Univ. of Chicago.

APPENDIXES

CHICAGO MAYORS

Years in office	Name	Birth and death	Birthplace	Vote	Candidate and party
1837–1838	William Butler Ogden	(June 15, 1805–Aug. 3, 1877)	Walton, NY	489 217	William Butler Ogden (Dem.) John H. Kinzie (Whig)
1838–1839	Buckner Stith Morris	(Aug. 19, 1800–Dec. 16, 1879)	Augusta, KY	377 318	Buckner Stith Morris (Whig) William Jones (Dem.)
1839–1840	Benjamin Wright Raymond	(June 15, 1801–Apr. 6, 1883)	Rome, NY	353 212	Benjamin Wright Raymond (Whig) James Curtiss (Dem.)
1840–1841	Alexander Loyd	(Aug. 19, 1805–May 7, 1872)	Orange County, NY	582 423	Alexander Loyd (Dem.) Benjamin Raymond (Whig)
1841–1842	Francis Cornwall Sherman	(Sept. 18, 1805–Nov. 7, 1870)	Newton, CT	460 419	Francis Cornwall Sherman (Dem.) Isaac R. Gavin (Whig)
1842–1843	Benjamin Wright Raymond			490 432 53	Benjamin Wright Raymond (Whig) Augustus Garrett (Dem.) Henry Smith (Liberty)
1843–1844	Augustus Garrett	(1801–Nov. 30, 1848)	New York, NY	671 381 45	Augustus Garrett (Dem.) Thomas Church (Whig) Henry Smith (Liberty)
1844–1845	Alson Smith Sherman	(Apr. 21, 1811–Sept. 22, 1903)	Barre, VT	837 694 126	Alson Smith Sherman (Ind. Dem.) Augustus Garrett (Dem.) Henry Smith (Liberty)
1845–1846	Augustus Garrett			1,072 913 131	Augustus Garrett (Dem.) John H. Kinzie (Whig) Henry Smith (Liberty)
1846–1847	John P. Chapin	(Apr. 21, 1810–June 27, 1864)	Rutland, VT	1,104 667 229	John P. Chapin (Whig) Charles Follansbee (Dem.) Philo Carpenter (Liberty)
1847–1848	James Curtiss	(Apr. 7, 1803–Nov. 2, 1859)	Weathersford, VT	1,281 1,220 238	James Curtiss (Dem.) Philo Carpenter (Liberty) John H. Kinzie (Whig)
1848–1849	James H. Woodworth	(Dec. 4, 1804–Mar. 26, 1869)	Greenwich, NY	1,971 1,361	James H. Woodworth (Ind. Dem.) James Curtiss (Dem.)
1849–1850	James H. Woodworth			2,668 399 245 22	James H. Woodworth Timothy Wait Lewis C. Kerchival S. D. Childs
1850–1851	James Curtiss			1,697 1,227 805	James Curtiss Levi D. Boone Lewis C. Kerchival
1851–1852	Walter S. Gurnee	(Mar. 9, 1813–Apr. 18, 1903)	Haverstraw, NY	2,032 1,092 1,001 226	Walter S. Gurnee Eli B. Williams James Curtiss Edward K. Rogers

Years in office	Name	Birth and death	Birthplace	Vote	Candidate and party
1852–1853	Walter S. Gurnee			1,749 1,294 1,142 269	Walter S. Gurnee James Curtiss Amos G. Throop (Temperance) Peter Page
1853–1854	Charles McNeill Gray	(Mar. 7, 1807–Oct. 17, 1885)	Chenango County, NY	3,270 971	Charles McNeill Gray Josiah L. James
1854–1855	Isaac Lawrence Milliken	(Aug. 29, 1815–Dec. 2, 1889)	Saco, ME	3,800 2,556	Isaac Lawrence Milliken (Dem.) Amos G. Throop (Temperance)
1855–1856	Levi D. Boone	(Dec. 8, 1808–Jan. 24, 1882)	Lexington, KY	3,186 2,841	Levi D. Boone (Know-Nothing) Isaac Lawrence Milliken (Dem.)
1856–1857	Thomas Dyer	(Jan. 13, 1805–June 6, 1862)	Canton, CT	4,712 4,123	Thomas Dyer (Dem. [Pro-Nebraska]) Francis Cornwall Sherman (Dem. [Anti-Nebraska])
1857–1858	John Wentworth	(Mar. 5, 1815–Oct. 16, 1888)	Sandwich, NH	5,933 4,842	John Wentworth (Rep.-Fusion) Benjamin F. Carver (Dem.)
1858–1859	John C. Haines	(May 26, 1818–July 4, 1896)	Deerfield, NY	8,642 7,481	John C. Haines (Rep.) Daniel Brainard (Dem.)
1859–1860	John C. Haines			8,587 7,728	John C. Haines (Rep.) Marcus G. Gilman (Dem.)
1860–1861	John Wentworth			9,998 8,739	John Wentworth (Rep.-Fusion) Walter S. Gurnee (Dem.)
1861–1862	Julian S. Rumsey	(Apr. 3, 1823–Apr. 20, 1886)	Batavia, NY	8,274 6,601	Julian S. Rumsey (Rep.) Thomas B. Bryan (Union)
1862–1865	Francis Cornwall Sherman			7,437 6,254	Francis Cornwall Sherman (Dem.) Charles Holden (Rep.)
1865–1867	John B. Rice	(May 28, 1809–Dec. 17, 1874)	Easton, MD	11,078 5,600	John B. Rice (Rep.) Francis Cornwall Sherman (Dem.)
1867–1869	John B. Rice			11,904 7,971	John B. Rice (Rep.) Francis Cornwall Sherman (Dem.)
1869–1871	Roswell B. Mason	(Sept. 19, 1805–Jan. 11, 1892)	New Hartford, NY	19,826 11,410	Roswell B. Mason (Citizens') George W. Gage (Rep.)
1871–1873	Joseph E. Medill	(Apr. 6, 1823–Mar. 16, 1899)	Nova Scotia	16,125 5,988	Joseph E. Medill (Union-Fireproof) C. C. P. Holden (Dem.)
1873	Lester Legrant Bond *Acting mayor following Medill's resignation*	(Oct. 27, 1829–Apr. 15, 1903)	Ravenna, OH		
1873–1876	Harvey Doolittle Colvin	(Dec. 18, 1815–Apr. 16, 1892)	Herkimer County, NY	28,791 18,540	Harvey Doolittle Colvin (Dem./People's) Lester Legrant Bond (Union)
1876–1877	Monroe Heath	(Mar. 27, 1828–Oct. 21, 1894)	Grafton, NH	19,248 7,509 3,363	Monroe Heath (Rep.) Mark Kimball (Dem.) J. J. McGrath (Ind.)
1877–1879	Monroe Heath			30,881 19,449	Monroe Heath (Rep.) Perry H. Smith (Dem.)
1879–1881	Carter Henry Harrison	(Feb. 25, 1825–Oct. 28, 1893)	Lexington, KY	25,685 20,496 11,829	Carter Henry Harrison (Dem.) Abner Wright (Rep.) Ernest Schmidt (Socialist Labor)
1881–1883	Carter Henry Harrison			35,668 27,925 764 240	Carter Henry Harrison (Dem.) John Clark (Rep.) Timothy O'Mara (Ind.) George Schilling (Socialist Labor)
1883–1885	Carter Henry Harrison			41,226 30,963	Carter Henry Harrison (Dem.) Eugene Cary (Rep.)
1885–1887	Carter Henry Harrison			43,352 42,977 221	Carter Henry Harrison (Dem.) Sidney Smith (Rep.) William Bush (Prohibition)
1887–1889	John A. Roche	(Aug. 12, 1844–Feb. 10, 1904)	Utica, NY	51,249 23,490 376	John A. Roche (Rep.) Robert S. Nelson (Labor) Joseph L. Whitlock (Prohibition)
1889–1891	DeWitt Clinton Cregier	(June 1, 1829–Nov. 9, 1898)	New York, NY	57,340 45,328 411 304	Dewitt C. Cregier (Dem.) John A. Roche (Rep.) Ira J. Mason (Prohibition) Charles Orchardson (Socialist)
1891–1893	Hempstead Washburne	(Nov. 11, 1852–Apr. 13, 1918)	Galena, IL	46,957 46,558 42,931 24,027 2,376	Hempstead Washburne (Reform) Dewitt C. Cregier (Dem.) Carter Harrison (Ind. Dem.) Elmer Washburn (Citizens) Thomas J. Morgan (Socialist)
1893	Carter Henry Harrison *Died in office*			114,237 93,148 3,033 1,000	Carter Henry Harrison (Dem.) Samuel W. Allerton (Rep.) Dewitt C. Cregier (Union Citizens) Henry Ehrenpreis (Socialist Labor)
1893	George Bell Swift *Mayor pro tem after Harrison's death until election*	(Dec. 14, 1845–July 2, 1912)	Cincinnati, OH		

Years in office	Name	Birth and death	Birthplace	Vote	Candidate and party
1893–1895	John Patrick Hopkins	(Oct. 29, 1858–Oct. 13, 1918)	Buffalo, NY	112,959 111,660 2,599	John Patrick Hopkins (Dem.) George Bell Swift (Rep.) Socialist and People's candidates combined
1895–1897	George Bell Swift			143,884 103,125 12,882	George Bell Swift (Rep.) Frank Wenter (Dem.) Bayard Holmes (People's)
1897–1899	Carter Henry Harrison II	(Apr. 23, 1860–Dec. 25, 1953)	Chicago, IL	148,880 69,730 59,542 18,238	Carter Henry Harrison, II (Dem.) John M. Harlan (Ind. Rep.) Nathaniel C. Sears (Rep.) six others combined
1899–1901	Carter Henry Harrison II			148,496 107,437 47,169 2,565	Carter Henry Harrison, II (Dem.) Zina R. Carter (Rep.) John P. Altgeld (Municipal Ownership) three others combined
1901–1903	Carter Henry Harrison II			156,756 128,413 7,078 5,384	Carter Henry Harrison, II (Dem.) Elbridge Hanecy (Rep.) four others combined John Collins (Socialist)
1903–1905	Carter Henry Harrison II			146,208 138,548 13,635 11,124	Carter Henry Harrison, II (Dem.) Graeme Stewart (Rep.) three others combined Charles L. Breckon (Socialist)
1905–1907	Edward Fitzsimmons Dunne	(Oct. 12, 1853–May 24, 1937)	Waterville, CT	163,189 138,548 23,034 3,294	Edward Fitzsimmons Dunne (Dem.) John M. Harlan (Rep.) John Collins (Socialist) Oliver W. Stewart (Prohibition)
1907–1911	Fred A. Busse	(Mar. 3, 1866–July 9, 1914)	Chicago, IL	164,702 151,779 13,429 6,020	Fred A. Busse (Rep.) Edward Fitzsimmons Dunne (Dem.) George Koop (Socialist) W. A. Brubaker (Prohibition)
1911–1915	Carter Henry Harrison II			177,997 160,672 24,825 3,297	Carter Henry Harrison, II (Dem.) Charles E. Merriam (Rep.) William E. Rodriguez (Socialist) two others combined
1915–1919	William Hale Thompson	(May 14, 1867–Mar. 18, 1944)	Boston, MA	398,538 251,061 24,452 3,974	William Hale Thompson (Rep.) Robert M. Sweitzer (Dem.) Seymour Stedman (Socialist) John H. Hill (Prohibition)
1919–1923	William Hale Thompson			259,828 238,206 110,851 55,990 24,079 1,848	William Hale Thompson (Rep.) Robert M. Sweitzer (Dem.) Maclay Hoyne (Ind.) John Fitzpatrick (Labor) John Collins (Socialist) Adolph S. Carm (Socialist Labor)
1923–1927	William Emmett Dever	(Mar. 13, 1862–Sept. 3, 1929)	Woburn, MA	390,413 285,094 41,186	William Emmett Dever (Dem.) Arthur C. Leuder (Rep.) William A. Cunnea (Socialist)
1927–1931	William Hale Thompson			515,716 432,678 51,347	William Hale Thompson (Rep.) William Emmett Dever (Dem.) J. D. Robertson (People's Ownership Smash Crime Rings)
1931–1933	Anton J. Cermak *Died in office*	(May 9, 1873–Mar. 6, 1933)	Kladno, Bohemia	671,189 476,922	Anton J. Cermak (Dem.) William Hale Thompson (Rep.)
1933	Frank J. Corr *Acting mayor pending election*	(Jan. 12, 1877–June 3, 1934)	Brooklyn, NY		
1933–1935	Edward J. Kelly *Elected by city council*	(May 1, 1876–Oct. 20, 1950)	Chicago, IL		
1935–1939	Edward J. Kelly			798,150 166,571 87,726	Edward J. Kelly (Dem.) Emil C. Welten (Rep.) Newton Jenkins (Third Party)
1939–1943	Edward J. Kelly			822,469 638,068 4,921	Edward J. Kelly (Dem.) Dwight H. Green (Rep.) Arthur P. Reilly (Third Party)
1943–1947	Edward J. Kelly			685,567 571,547	Edward J. Kelly (Dem.) George B. McKibbin (Rep.)
1947–1951	Martin H. Kennelly	(Aug. 11, 1887–Nov. 29, 1961)	Chicago, IL	919,593 646,239	Martin H. Kennelly (Dem.) Russell W. Root (Rep.)
1951–1955	Martin H. Kennelly			697,871 545,326	Martin H. Kennelly (Dem.) Robert L. Hunter (Rep.)
1955–1959	Richard J. Daley	(May 15, 1902–Dec. 20, 1976)	Chicago, IL	708,660 581,461	Richard J. Daley (Dem.) Robert E. Merriam (Rep.)
1959–1963	Richard J. Daley			778,612 311,940	Richard J. Daley (Dem.) Timothy Sheehan (Rep.)
1963–1967	Richard J. Daley			679,497 540,705	Richard J. Daley (Dem.) Benjamin Adamowski (Rep.)

Years in office	Name	Birth and death	Birthplace	Vote	Candidate and party
1967–1971	Richard J. Daley			792,238 272,542	Richard J. Daley (Dem.) John Waner (Rep.)
1971–1975	Richard J. Daley			740,137 315,969	Richard J. Daley (Dem.) Richard Friedman (Rep.)
1975–1976	Richard J. Daley *Died in office*			542,817 139,335 16,693	Richard J. Daley (Dem.) John Hoellen (Rep.) Willie Mae Reid (Socialist Workers)
1977–1979	Michael A. Bilandic *Acting mayor, then won special election*	(Feb. 13, 1923–)	Chicago, IL	490,688 5,546 2,497	Michael A. Bilandic (Dem.) Dennis Brasky (Socialist Workers) Gerald Rose (U.S. Labor)
1979–1983	Jane M. Byrne	(May 24, 1934–)	Chicago, IL	700,874 137,664 15,625	Jane M. Byrne (Dem.) Wallace Johnson (Rep.) Andrew Pulley (Socialist Workers)
1983–1987	Harold Washington	(Apr. 15, 1922–Nov. 25, 1987)	Chicago, IL	668,176 619,926 3,756	Harold L. Washington (Dem.) Bernard E. Epton (Rep.) Ed Warren (Socialist Workers)
1987	Harold Washington *Died in office*			600,290 468,493 47,652	Harold L. Washington (Dem.) Edward R. Vroldyak (IL Solidarity) Donald H. Haider (Rep.)
1987–1989	Eugene Sawyer *Appointed by city council after Washington's death*	(Sept. 3, 1934–)	Greensboro, AL		
1989–1991	Richard M. Daley	(Apr. 24, 1942–)	Chicago, IL	577,141 428,105 35,998	Richard M. Daley (Dem.) Timothy C. Evans (Harold Washington Party) Edward R. Vrdolyak (Rep.)
1991–1995	Richard M. Daley			450,581 160,302 23,421 3,581	Richard M. Daley (Dem.) R. Eugene Pincham (Harold Washington Party) George S. Gottlieb (Rep.) James Warren (Socialist Workers)
1995–1999	Richard M. Daley			360,372 217,315 16,592 5,165	Richard M. Daley (Dem.) Roland Burris (Ind.) Ray Wardlingley (Rep.) Lawrence Redmond (Harold Washington Party)
1999–2003	Richard M. Daley			429,746 167,845	Richard M. Daley (Nonpartisan) Bobby L. Rush (Nonpartisan)
2003–	Richard M. Daley			363,553 64,941 27,350 7,488	Richard M. Daley (Nonpartisan) Paul L. Jakes, Jr. (Nonpartisan) Patricia McAllister (Nonpartisan) Joseph McAfee (Nonpartisan)

CHICAGO METROPOLITAN POPULATION

The table below provides census data for counties, municipalities, and Chicago community areas at 30-year intervals from 1840 through 1990, with additional data from the 2000 census. Census questions and categories have changed over time, including racial categories. The "Hispanic" category (*) in the 1990 and 2000 censuses was independent of racial categories.

Counties

Cook County, IL

Year	Total (and by category)	Category	Foreign born	Native with foreign parentage	Males per 100 females
1840	10,201		—	—	142
	10,146	Free white (99.5%)			
	55	Free colored (0.5%)			
1870	349,966		47.7%	79.8%	106
	346,102	White (98.9%)			
	3,858	Colored (1.1%)			
	6	Indian (0.0%)			
1900	1,838,735		34.0%	42.6%	103
	1,805,561	White (98.2%)			
	31,838	Negro (1.7%)			
	1,253	Chinese (0.1%)			
	74	Japanese (0.0%)			
	9	Indian (0.0%)			
1930	3,982,123		24.0%	39.0%	102
	3,708,281	White (93.1%)			
	246,992	Negro (6.2%)			
	275	Indian (0.0%)			
	2,875	Chinese (0.1%)			
	517	Japanese (0.0%)			
	21,087	Mexican (0.5%)			
	2,096	Other (0.1%)			
1960	5,129,725		10.6%	23.6%	95
	4,240,873	White (82.7%)			
	861,146	Negro (16.8%)			
	227,706	Other races (4.4%)			
1990	5,105,067		14.1%	—	93
	3,208,115	White (62.8%)			
	1,314,859	Black (25.8%)			
	10,387	American Indian (0.2%)			
	188,447	Asian/Pacific Islander (3.7%)			
	383,259	Other race (7.5%)			
	677,949	Hispanic Origin* (13.3%)			
2000	5,376,741		19.8%	—	94
	3,025,760	White alone (56.3%)			
	1,405,361	Black or African American alone (26.1%)			
	15,496	American Indian and Alaska Native alone (0.3%)			
	260,170	Asian alone (4.8%)			
	2,561	Native Hawaiian and Other Pacific Islander alone (0.0%)			
	531,170	Some other race alone (9.9%)			
	136,223	Two or more races (2.5%)			
	1,071,740	Hispanic or Latino* (19.9%)			

DuPage County, IL

Year	Total (and by category)	Category	Foreign born	Native with foreign parentage	Males per 100 females
1840	3,535		—	—	123
	3,531	Free white (99.9%)			
	4	Free colored (0.1%)			
1870	16,685		31.2%	50.4%	111
	16,652	White (99.8%)			
	33	Colored (0.2%)			
1900	28,196		23.3%	40.3%	105
	28,021	White (99.4%)			
	165	Negro (0.6%)			
	10	Chinese (0.0%)			
1930	91,998		12.8%	31.7%	101
	91,410	White (99.4%)			
	319	Negro (0.3%)			
	3	Indian (0.0%)			
	14	Chinese (0.0%)			
	8	Japanese (0.0%)			
	230	Mexican (0.3%)			
	14	Other (0.0%)			
1960	313,459		5.0%	20.1%	99
	312,200	White (99.6%)			
	677	Negro (0.2%)			
	582	Other races (0.2%)			
1990	781,666		9.1%	—	97
	715,304	White (91.5%)			
	15,354	Black (2.0%)			
	1,015	American Indian (0.1%)			
	39,841	Asian/Pacific Islander (5.1%)			
	10,152	Other race (1.3%)			
	32,795	Hispanic Origin* (4.2%)			
2000	904,161		15.3%	—	97
	759,924	White alone (84.0%)			
	27,600	Black or African American alone (3.1%)			
	1,520	American Indian and Alaska Native alone (0.2%)			
	71,252	Asian alone (7.9%)			
	217	Native Hawaiian and Other Pacific Islander alone (0.0%)			
	28,166	Some other race alone (3.1%)			
	15,482	Two or more races (1.7%)			
	81,366	Hispanic or Latino* (9.0%)			

Kane County, IL

Year	Total (and by category)	Category	Foreign born	Native with foreign parentage	Males per 100 females
1840	6,501		—	—	119
	6,497	Free white (99.9%)			
	4	Free colored (0.1%)			
1870	39,091		26.4%	50.1%	103
	38,724	White (99.1%)			
	367	Colored (0.9%)			
1900	78,792		24.4%	34.3%	99
	78,165	White (99.2%)			
	612	Negro (0.8%)			
	15	Chinese (0.0%)			
1930	125,327		14.4%	32.9%	100
	122,897	White (98.1%)			
	1,787	Negro (1.4%)			
	4	Indian (0.0%)			
	21	Chinese (0.0%)			
	6	Japanese (0.0%)			
	610	Mexican (0.5%)			
	2	Other (0.0%)			
1960	208,246		4.6%	16.9%	97
	203,321	White (97.6%)			
	4,675	Negro (2.2%)			
	250	Other races (0.1%)			
1990	317,471		8.2%	—	99
	270,301	White (85.1%)			
	18,981	Black (6.0%)			
	612	American Indian (0.2%)			
	4,320	Asian/Pacific Islander (1.4%)			
	23,257	Other race (7.3%)			
	42,234	Hispanic Origin* (13.3%)			
2000	404,119		15.7%	—	101
	320,340	White alone (79.3%)			
	23,279	Black or African American alone (5.8%)			
	1,255	American Indian and Alaska Native alone (0.3%)			
	7,296	Asian alone (1.8%)			
	144	Native Hawaiian and Other Pacific Islander alone (0.0%)			
	42,870	Some other race alone (10.6%)			
	8,935	Two or more races (2.2%)			
	95,924	Hispanic or Latino* (23.7%)			

Lake County, IL

Year	Total (and by category)	Category	Foreign born	Native with foreign parentage	Males per 100 females
1840	2,634		—	—	117
	2,628	Free white (99.8%)			
	6	Free colored (0.2%)			
1870	21,014		27.2%	59.2%	104
	20,948	White (99.7%)			
	62	Colored (0.3%)			
	4	Indian (0.0%)			
1900	34,504		23.8%	37.1%	111
	34,316	White (99.5%)			
	185	Negro (0.5%)			
	3	Chinese (0.0%)			

Counties *(continued)*

	Total (and by category)	Foreign born	Native with foreign parentage	Males per 100 females
1930	104,387	18.8%	32.7%	112
	101,430 White (97.2%)			
	2,356 Negro (2.3%)			
	12 Indian (0.0%)			
	19 Chinese (0.0%)			
	5 Japanese (0.0%)			
	822 Mexican (0.8%)			
	43 Other (0.0%)			
1960	293,656	6.1%	18.4%	111
	280,961 White (95.7%)			
	11,719 Negro (4.0%)			
	976 Other races (0.3%)			
1990	516,418	8.1%	—	102
	451,157 White (87.4%)			
	34,698 Black (6.7%)			
	1,405 American Indian (0.3%)			
	12,488 Asian/Pacific Islander (2.4%)			
	16,670 Other race (3.2%)			
	36,735 Hispanic Origin* (7.1%)			
2000	644,356	14.8%	—	101
	516,189 White alone (80.1%)			
	44,741 Black or African American alone (6.9%)			
	1,801 American Indian and Alaska Native alone (0.3%)			
	25,105 Asian alone (3.9%)			
	308 Native Hawaiian and Other Pacific Islander alone (0.0%)			
	43,283 Some other race alone (6.7%)			
	12,929 Two or more races (2.0%)			
	92,716 Hispanic or Latino* (14.4%)			

Lake County, IN

	Total (and by category)	Foreign born	Native with foreign parentage	Males per 100 females
1840	1,468	—	—	130
	1,466 Free white (99.9%)			
	2 Free colored (0.1%)			
1870	12,339	29.2%	60.9%	109
	12,336 White (100.0%)			
	3 Colored (0.0%)			
1900	37,892	24.9%	38.9%	115
	37,838 White (99.9%)			
	41 Negro (0.1%)			
	12 Chinese (0.0%)			
	1 Indian (0.0%)			
1930	261,310	18.7%	29.7%	117
	228,473 White (87.4%)			
	23,748 Negro (9.1%)			
	9 Indian (0.0%)			
	47 Chinese (0.0%)			
	11 Japanese (0.0%)			
	9,007 Mexican (3.4%)			
	15 Other (0.0%)			
1960	513,269	7.1%	16.8%	101
	425,641 White (82.9%)			
	87,109 Negro (17.0%)			
	519 Other races (0.1%)			
1990	475,594	4.1%	—	92
	334,459 White (70.3%)			
	116,572 Black (24.5%)			
	1,097 American Indian (0.2%)			
	2,345 Asian/Pacific Islander (0.5%)			
	21,121 Other race (4.4%)			
	43,446 Hispanic Origin* (9.1%)			
2000	484,564	5.3%	—	93
	323,290 White alone (66.7%)			
	122,723 Black or African American alone (25.3%)			
	1,343 American Indian and Alaska Native alone (0.3%)			
	3,983 Asian alone (0.8%)			
	195 Native Hawaiian and Other Pacific Islander alone (0.0%)			
	24,051 Some other race alone (5.0%)			
	8,979 Two or more races (1.9%)			
	59,128 Hispanic or Latino* (12.2%)			

McHenry County, IL

	Total (and by category)	Foreign born	Native with foreign parentage	Males per 100 females
1840	2,578	—	—	120
	2,578 Free white (100.0%)			
1870	23,762	19.5%	43.9%	105
	23,698 White (99.7%)			
	64 Colored (0.3%)			
1900	29,759	19.4%	36.0%	111
	29,735 White (99.9%)			
	24 Negro (0.1%)			
1930	35,079	11.9%	32.5%	110
	35,006 White (99.8%)			
	35 Negro (0.1%)			
	1 Japanese (0.0%)			
	37 Mexican (0.1%)			
1960	84,210	5.2%	18.0%	99
	84,094 White (99.9%)			
	22 Negro (0.0%)			
	94 Other races (0.1%)			
1990	183,241	4.3%	—	100
	178,873 White (97.6%)			
	423 Black (0.2%)			
	353 American Indian (0.2%)			
	1,187 Asian/Pacific Islander (0.6%)			
	2,405 Other race (1.3%)			
	5,900 Hispanic Origin* (3.2%)			
2000	260,077	7.2%	—	101
	244,240 White alone (93.9%)			
	1,523 Black or African American alone (0.6%)			
	445 American Indian and Alaska Native alone (0.2%)			
	3,782 Asian alone (1.5%)			
	55 Native Hawaiian and Other Pacific Islander alone (0.0%)			
	7,211 Some other race alone (2.8%)			
	2,821 Two or more races (1.1%)			
	19,602 Hispanic or Latino* (7.5%)			

Porter County, IN

	Total (and by category)	Foreign born	Native with foreign parentage	Males per 100 females
1840	2,162	—	—	119
	2,155 Free white (99.7%)			
	7 Free colored (0.3%)			
1870	13,942	20.4%	39.2%	107
	13,903 White (99.7%)			
	39 Colored (0.3%)			
1900	19,175	15.0%	30.2%	109
	19,161 White (99.9%)			
	11 Negro (0.1%)			
	1 Chinese (0.0%)			
	2 Indian (0.0%)			
1930	22,821	8.7%	24.0%	107
	22,776 White (99.8%)			
	17 Negro (0.1%)			
	2 Chinese (0.0%)			
	1 Japanese (0.0%)			
	25 Mexican (0.1%)			
1960	60,279	2.8%	12.0%	102
	60,183 White (99.8%)			
	69 Negro (0.1%)			
	27 Other races (0.0%)			
1990	128,932	2.3%	—	96
	126,474 White (98.1%)			
	431 Black (0.3%)			
	280 American Indian (0.2%)			
	1,021 Asian/Pacific Islander (0.8%)			
	726 Other race (0.6%)			
	3,670 Hispanic Origin* (2.8%)			
2000	146,798	3.0%	—	96
	139,946 White alone (95.3%)			
	1,344 Black or African American alone (0.9%)			
	326 American Indian and Alaska Native alone (0.2%)			
	1,341 Asian alone (0.9%)			
	42 Native Hawaiian and Other Pacific Islander alone (0.0%)			
	1,855 Some other race alone (1.3%)			
	1,944 Two or more races (1.3%)			
	7,079 Hispanic or Latino* (4.8%)			

Will County, IL

	Total (and by category)	Foreign born	Native with foreign parentage	Males per 100 females
1840	10,167	—	—	184
	10,157 Free white (99.9%)			
	10 Free colored (0.1%)			
1870	43,013	33.9%	65.2%	117
	42,771 White (99.4%)			
	242 Colored (0.6%)			
1900	74,764	26.4%	42.0%	113
	73,504 White (98.3%)			
	1,244 Negro (1.7%)			
	16 Chinese (0.0%)			
1930	110,732	14.9%	37.4%	113
	106,235 White (95.9%)			
	3,131 Negro (2.8%)			
	16 Indian (0.0%)			
	41 Chinese (0.0%)			
	1,308 Mexican (1.2%)			
	1 Other (0.0%)			
1960	191,617	4.3%	18.1%	103
	179,463 White (93.7%)			
	11,915 Negro (6.2%)			
	239 Other races (0.1%)			
1990	357,313	4.4%	—	100
	303,506 White (84.9%)			
	37,808 Black (10.6%)			
	797 American Indian (0.2%)			
	4,972 Asian/Pacific Islander (1.4%)			
	10,230 Other race (2.9%)			
	19,524 Hispanic Origin* (5.5%)			
2000	502,266	7.1%	—	100
	411,027 White alone (81.8%)			
	52,509 Black or African American alone (10.5%)			
	1,038 American Indian and Alaska Native alone (0.2%)			
	11,125 Asian alone (2.2%)			
	162 Native Hawaiian and Other Pacific Islander alone (0.0%)			
	18,219 Some other race alone (3.6%)			
	8,186 Two or more races (1.6%)			
	43,768 Hispanic or Latino* (8.7%)			

Municipalities

Addison, IL (inc. 1884)

	Total (and by category)	Foreign born	Native with foreign parentage	Males per 100 females
1900	591	—	—	—
1930	916	—	—	—
1960	6,741	4.5%	21.3%	102
	6,727 white (99.8%)			
	1 Negro (0.0%)			
	13 Other races (0.2%)			
1990	32,058	19.5%	—	100
	28,285 White (88.2%)			
	492 Black (1.5%)			
	14 American Indian (0.0%)			
	1,907 Asian/Pacific Islander (5.9%)			
	1,360 Other race (4.2%)			
	4,131 Hispanic Origin* (12.9%)			
2000	35,914	34.1%	—	103
	27,076 White alone (75.4%)			
	902 Black or African American alone (2.5%)			
	127 American Indian and Alaska Native alone (0.4%)			
	2,850 Asian alone (7.9%)			
	5 Native Hawaiian and Other Pacific Islander alone (0.0%)			
	4,091 Some other race alone (11.4%)			
	863 Two or more races (2.4%)			
	10,198 Hispanic or Latino* (28.4%)			

Algonquin, IL (inc. 1890)

	Total (and by category)	Foreign born	Native with foreign parentage	Males per 100 females
1900	550	—	—	
1930	866	—	—	
1960	2,014	—	—	94
	2,013 White (100.0%)			
	1 Negro (0.0%)			
1990	11,663	4.5%	—	101
	11,478 White (98.4%)			
	12 Black (0.1%)			
	56 American Indian (0.5%)			
	137 Asian/Pacific Islander (1.2%)			
	22 Other race (0.2%)			
	188 Hispanic Origin* (1.6%)			

2000	23,276	6.4%	—	99
	21,939	White alone (94.3%)		
	214	Black or African American alone (0.9%)		
	24	American Indian and Alaska Native alone (0.1%)		
	546	Asian alone (2.3%)		
	3	Native Hawaiian and Other Pacific Islander alone (0.0%)		
	280	Some other race alone (1.2%)		
	270	Two or more races (1.2%)		
	948	Hispanic or Latino* (4.1%)		

Alsip, IL (inc. 1927)

1930	327	—	—	
1960	3,770	5.5%	22.0%	102
	3,728	White (98.9%)		
	31	Negro (0.8%)		
	11	Other races (0.3%)		
1990	18,227	5.6%	—	96
	16,761	White (92.0%)		
	894	Black (4.9%)		
	79	American Indian (0.4%)		
	414	Asian/Pacific Islander (2.3%)		
	79	Other race (0.4%)		
	753	Hispanic Origin* (4.1%)		
2000	19,725	8.9%	—	93
	16,104	White alone (81.6%)		
	1,991	Black or African American alone (10.1%)		
	29	American Indian and Alaska Native alone (0.1%)		
	415	Asian alone (2.1%)		
	6	Native Hawaiian and Other Pacific Islander alone (0.0%)		
	635	Some other race alone (3.2%)		
	545	Two or more races (2.8%)		
	1,727	Hispanic or Latino* (8.8%)		

Antioch, IL (inc. 1857)

1900	522	—	—	
1930	1,101	12.3%	32.0%	106
	1,101	White (100.0%)		
1960	2,268	—	—	96
	2,268	White (100.0%)		
1990	6,105	2.7%	—	93
	6,017	White (98.6%)		
	7	Black (0.1%)		
	11	American Indian (0.2%)		
	15	Asian/Pacific Islander (0.2%)		
	55	Other race (0.9%)		
	120	Hispanic Origin* (2.0%)		
2000	8,788	3.4%	—	96
	8,365	White alone (95.2%)		
	94	Black or African American alone (1.1%)		
	31	American Indian and Alaska Native alone (0.4%)		
	102	Asian alone (1.2%)		
	1	Native Hawaiian and Other Pacific Islander alone (0.0%)		
	95	Some other race alone (1.1%)		
	100	Two or more races (1.1%)		
	388	Hispanic or Latino* (4.4%)		

Arlington Heights, IL (inc. 1887)

1900	1,380	—	—	—
1930	4,997	17.5%	37.0%	105
	4,994	White (99.9%)		
	3	Negro (0.1%)		
1960	27,878	3.3%	17.6%	96
	27,849	White (99.9%)		
	4	Negro (0.0%)		
	25	Other races (0.1%)		
1990	75,460	9.3%	—	93
	71,493	White (94.7%)		
	500	Black (0.7%)		
	49	American Indian (0.1%)		
	2,813	Asian/Pacific Islander (3.7%)		
	605	Other race (0.8%)		
	1,989	Hispanic Origin* (2.6%)		

2000	76,031	13.9%	—	93
	68,854	White alone (90.6%)		
	728	Black or African American alone (1.0%)		
	58	American Indian and Alaska Native alone (0.1%)		
	4,548	Asian alone (6.0%)		
	30	Native Hawaiian and Other Pacific Islander alone (0.0%)		
	907	Some other race alone (1.2%)		
	906	Two or more races (1.2%)		
	3,393	Hispanic or Latino* (4.5%)		

Aurora, IL (inc. 1853)

1870	11,162	27.5%	—	96
	11,013	White (98.7%)		
	149	Colored (1.3%)		
1900	24,147	21.0%	38.1%	94
	23,929	White (99.1%)		
	211	Negro (0.9%)		
	7	Chinese (0.0%)		
1930	46,589	12.9%	32.3%	97
	45,348	White (97.3%)		
	936	Negro (2.0%)		
	6	Chinese (0.0%)		
	299	Mexican (0.6%)		
1960	63,715	5.5%	16.5%	94
	61,417	White (96.4%)		
	2,227	Negro (3.5%)		
	71	Other races (0.1%)		
1990	99,581	12.0%	—	98
	74,019	White (74.3%)		
	11,806	Black (11.9%)		
	191	American Indian (0.2%)		
	1,245	Asian/Pacific Islander (1.3%)		
	12,320	Other race (12.4%)		
	22,534	Hispanic Origin* (22.6%)		
2000	142,990	21.6%	—	101
	97,340	White alone (68.1%)		
	15,817	Black or African American alone (11.1%)		
	511	American Indian and Alaska Native alone (0.4%)		
	4,370	Asian alone (3.1%)		
	47	Native Hawaiian and Other Pacific Islander alone (0.0%)		
	20,762	Some other race alone (14.5%)		
	4,143	Two or more races (2.9%)		
	46,557	Hispanic or Latino* (32.6%)		

Bannockburn, IL (inc. 1929)

1930	186	—	—	—
1960	466	—	—	—
1990	1,388	17.4%	—	98
	1,130	White (81.4%)		
	99	Black (7.1%)		
	156	Asian/Pacific Islander (11.2%)		
	3	Other race (0.2%)		
	9	Hispanic Origin* (0.6%)		
2000	1,429	12.9%	—	103
	1,251	White alone (87.5%)		
	48	Black or African American alone (3.4%)		
	1	American Indian and Alaska Native alone (0.1%)		
	73	Asian alone (5.1%)		
	1	Native Hawaiian and Other Pacific Islander alone (0.1%)		
	24	Some other race alone (1.7%)		
	31	Two or more races (2.2%)		
	50	Hispanic or Latino* (3.5%)		

Barrington Hills, IL (inc. 1957)

1960	1,726	—	—	99
	1,689	White (97.9%)		
	32	Negro (1.9%)		
	5	Other races (0.3%)		
1990	4,202	8.2%	—	100
	3,830	White (91.1%)		
	250	Asian/Pacific Islander (5.9%)		
	24	Hispanic Origin* (0.6%)		

2000	3,915	5.5%	—	98
	3,692	White alone (94.3%)		
	18	Black or African American alone (0.5%)		
	153	Asian alone (3.9%)		
	29	Some other race alone (0.7%)		
	23	Two or more races (0.6%)		
	75	Hispanic or Latino* (1.9%)		

Barrington, IL (inc. 1865)

1900	1,162	—	—	—
1930	3,213	9.7%	33.4%	104
	3,191	White (99.3%)		
	2	Negro (0.1%)		
	22	Other (0.7%)		
1960	5,434	4.7%	19.7%	90
	5,422	White (99.8%)		
	4	Negro (0.1%)		
	8	Other races (0.1%)		
1990	9,504	5.7%	—	90
	9,354	White (98.4%)		
	16	Black (0.2%)		
	8	American Indian (0.1%)		
	99	Asian/Pacific Islander (1.0%)		
	25	Other race (0.3%)		
	210	Hispanic Origin* (2.2%)		
2000	10,168	6.5%	—	90
	9,778	White alone (96.2%)		
	63	Black or African American alone (0.6%)		
	13	American Indian and Alaska Native alone (0.1%)		
	203	Asian alone (2.0%)		
	1	Native Hawaiian and Other Pacific Islander alone (0.0%)		
	32	Some other race alone (0.3%)		
	78	Two or more races (0.8%)		
	237	Hispanic or Latino* (2.3%)		

Bartlett, IL (inc. 1891)

1900	360	—	—	—
1930	504	—	—	—
1960	1,540	—	—	93
	1,514	White (98.3%)		
	26	Negro (1.7%)		
1990	19,373	5.4%	—	98
	18,037	White (93.1%)		
	439	Black (2.3%)		
	67	American Indian (0.3%)		
	708	Asian/Pacific Islander (3.7%)		
	111	Other race (0.6%)		
	440	Hispanic Origin* (2.3%)		
2000	36,706	11.0%	—	97
	32,020	White alone (87.2%)		
	725	Black or African American alone (2.0%)		
	52	American Indian and Alaska Native alone (0.1%)		
	2,871	Asian alone (7.8%)		
	8	Native Hawaiian and Other Pacific Islander alone (0.0%)		
	497	Some other race alone (1.4%)		
	533	Two or more races (1.5%)		
	2,024	Hispanic or Latino* (5.5%)		

Batavia, IL (inc. 1872)

1900	3,871	28.6%	35.3%	98
	3,809	White (98.4%)		
	62	Negro (1.6%)		
1930	5,045	19.3%	21.2%	98
	4,935	White (97.8%)		
	108	Negro (2.1%)		
	2	Other (0.0%)		
1960	7,496	5.2%	21.3%	96
	7,248	White (96.7%)		
	245	Negro (3.3%)		
	3	Other races (0.0%)		
1990	17,076	3.3%	—	93
	16,204	White (94.9%)		
	485	Black (2.8%)		
	13	American Indian (0.1%)		
	168	Asian/Pacific Islander (1.0%)		
	206	Other race (1.2%)		
	524	Hispanic Origin* (3.1%)		

Municipalities *(continued)*

	Total (and by category)	Foreign born	Native with foreign parentage	Males per 100 females
2000	23,866	5.2%	—	95
	22,245	White alone (93.2%)		
	577	Black or African American alone (2.4%)		
	26	American Indian and Alaska Native alone (0.1%)		
	321	Asian alone (1.3%)		
	1	Native Hawaiian and Other Pacific Islander alone (0.0%)		
	364	Some other race alone (1.5%)		
	332	Two or more races (1.4%)		
	1,257	Hispanic or Latino* (5.3%)		

Beach Park, IL (inc. 1988)

	Total (and by category)	Foreign born	Native with foreign parentage	Males per 100 females
1990	9,513	3.5%	—	101
	8,824	White (92.8%)		
	293	Black (3.1%)		
	48	American Indian (0.5%)		
	118	Asian/Pacific Islander (1.2%)		
	230	Other race (2.4%)		
	543	Hispanic Origin* (5.7%)		
2000	10,072	7.2%	—	99
	8,592	White alone (85.3%)		
	457	Black or African American alone (4.5%)		
	28	American Indian and Alaska Native alone (0.3%)		
	150	Asian alone (1.5%)		
	3	Native Hawaiian and Other Pacific Islander alone (0.0%)		
	616	Some other race alone (6.1%)		
	226	Two or more races (2.2%)		
	1,368	Hispanic or Latino* (13.6%)		

Bedford Park, IL (inc. 1940)

	Total (and by category)	Foreign born	Native with foreign parentage	Males per 100 females
1960	737	—	—	—
1990	566	1.9%	—	86
	565	White (99.8%)		
	8	American Indian (1.4%)		
	4	Other race (0.7%)		
	28	Hispanic Origin* (4.9%)		
2000	574	4.5%	—	87
	556	White alone (96.9%)		
	6	Black or African American alone (1.0%)		
	3	American Indian and Alaska Native alone (0.5%)		
	1	Asian alone (0.2%)		
	1	Some other race alone (0.2%)		
	7	Two or more races (1.2%)		
	38	Hispanic or Latino* (6.6%)		

Beecher, IL (inc. 1883)

	Total (and by category)	Foreign born	Native with foreign parentage	Males per 100 females
1900	410	—	—	—
1930	772	—	—	—
1960	1,367	—	—	88
	1,367	White (100.0%)		
1990	2,032	1.3%	—	98
	2,022	White (99.5%)		
	2	American Indian (0.1%)		
	8	Asian/Pacific Islander (0.4%)		
	9	Hispanic Origin* (0.4%)		
2000	2,033	2.5%	—	91
	1,993	White alone (98.0%)		
	3	American Indian and Alaska Native alone (0.1%)		
	9	Asian alone (0.4%)		
	7	Some other race alone (0.3%)		
	21	Two or more races (1.0%)		
	36	Hispanic or Latino* (1.8%)		

Bellwood, IL (inc. 1900)

	Total (and by category)	Foreign born	Native with foreign parentage	Males per 100 females
1930	4,991	21.1%	40.3%	110
	4,986	White (99.9%)		
	5	Other (0.1%)		
1960	20,729	7.9%	26.4%	96
	20,709	White (99.9%)		
	1	Negro (0.0%)		
	19	Other races (0.1%)		
1990	20,241	5.3%	—	94
	4,825	White (23.8%)		
	14,491	Black (71.6%)		
	267	Asian/Pacific Islander (1.3%)		
	658	Other race (3.3%)		
	1,006	Hispanic Origin* (5.0%)		
2000	20,535	6.1%	—	88
	2,412	White alone (11.7%)		
	16,783	Black or African American alone (81.7%)		
	49	American Indian and Alaska Native alone (0.2%)		
	197	Asian alone (1.0%)		
	4	Native Hawaiian and Other Pacific Islander alone (0.0%)		
	779	Some other race alone (3.8%)		
	311	Two or more races (1.5%)		
	1,631	Hispanic or Latino* (7.9%)		

Bensenville, IL (inc. 1894)

	Total (and by category)	Foreign born	Native with foreign parentage	Males per 100 females
1900	374	—	—	—
1930	1,680	13.9%	33.2%	108
	1,628	White (96.9%)		
	1	Negro (0.1%)		
	51	Other (3.0%)		
1960	9,141	6.5%	23.0%	101
	9,135	White (99.9%)		
	2	Negro (0.0%)		
	4	Other races (0.0%)		
1990	17,767	19.2%	—	103
	15,374	White (86.5%)		
	146	Black (0.8%)		
	43	American Indian (0.2%)		
	1,141	Asian/Pacific Islander (6.4%)		
	1,063	Other race (6.0%)		
	3,372	Hispanic Origin* (19.0%)		
2000	20,703	31.2%	—	106
	14,615	White alone (70.6%)		
	579	Black or African American alone (2.8%)		
	94	American Indian and Alaska Native alone (0.5%)		
	1,318	Asian alone (6.4%)		
	5	Native Hawaiian and Other Pacific Islander alone (0.0%)		
	3,438	Some other race alone (16.6%)		
	654	Two or more races (3.2%)		
	7,690	Hispanic or Latino* (37.1%)		

Berkeley, IL (inc. 1924)

	Total (and by category)	Foreign born	Native with foreign parentage	Males per 100 females
1930	779	—	—	—
1960	5,792	5.4%	25.4%	99
	5,788	White (99.9%)		
	4	Other races (0.1%)		
1990	5,137	8.8%	—	96
	4,576	White (89.1%)		
	231	Black (4.5%)		
	221	Asian/Pacific Islander (4.3%)		
	109	Other race (2.1%)		
	279	Hispanic Origin* (5.4%)		
2000	5,245	13.4%	—	97
	3,114	White alone (59.4%)		
	1,455	Black or African American alone (27.7%)		
	6	American Indian and Alaska Native alone (0.1%)		
	202	Asian alone (3.9%)		
	1	Native Hawaiian and Other Pacific Islander alone (0.0%)		
	354	Some other race alone (6.7%)		
	113	Two or more races (2.2%)		
	814	Hispanic or Latino* (15.5%)		

Berwyn, IL (inc. 1901)

	Total (and by category)	Foreign born	Native with foreign parentage	Males per 100 females
1930	47,027	21.9%	46.1%	102
	45,005	White (95.7%)		
	8	Negro (0.0%)		
	5	Indian (0.0%)		
	5	Chinese (0.0%)		
	4	Other (0.0%)		
1960	54,224	12.4%	37.4%	91
	54,171	White (99.9%)		
	6	Negro (0.0%)		
	47	Other races (0.1%)		
1990	45,426	12.0%	—	87
	43,125	White (94.9%)		
	41	Black (0.1%)		
	50	American Indian (0.1%)		
	886	Asian/Pacific Islander (2.0%)		
	1,324	Other race (2.9%)		
	3,527	Hispanic Origin* (7.8%)		
2000	54,016	25.1%	—	95
	39,667	White alone (73.4%)		
	702	Black or African American alone (1.3%)		
	239	American Indian and Alaska Native alone (0.4%)		
	1,400	Asian alone (2.6%)		
	14	Native Hawaiian and Other Pacific Islander alone (0.0%)		
	10,040	Some other race alone (18.6%)		
	1,954	Two or more races (3.6%)		
	20,543	Hispanic or Latino* (38.0%)		

Beverly Shores, IN (inc. 1947)

	Total (and by category)	Foreign born	Native with foreign parentage	Males per 100 females
1960	773	—	—	—
1990	622	23.6%	—	101
	628	White (101.0%)		
	3	Black (0.5%)		
	7	American Indian (1.1%)		
2000	708	9.0%	—	110
	691	White alone (97.6%)		
	5	Black or African American alone (0.7%)		
	3	Asian alone (0.4%)		
	1	Some other race alone (0.1%)		
	8	Two or more races (1.1%)		
	2	Hispanic or Latino* (0.3%)		

Bloomingdale, IL (inc. 1923)

	Total (and by category)	Foreign born	Native with foreign parentage	Males per 100 females
1900	235	—	—	—
1930	337	—	—	—
1960	1,262	—	—	104
	1,257	White (99.6%)		
	5	Negro (0.4%)		
1990	16,614	9.1%	—	93
	15,429	White (92.9%)		
	242	Black (1.5%)		
	14	American Indian (0.1%)		
	830	Asian/Pacific Islander (5.0%)		
	99	Other race (0.6%)		
	383	Hispanic Origin* (2.3%)		
2000	21,675	13.2%	—	93
	18,505	White alone (85.4%)		
	557	Black or African American alone (2.6%)		
	26	American Indian and Alaska Native alone (0.1%)		
	1,916	Asian alone (8.8%)		
	3	Native Hawaiian and Other Pacific Islander alone (0.0%)		
	325	Some other race alone (1.5%)		
	343	Two or more races (1.6%)		
	1,074	Hispanic or Latino* (5.0%)		

Blue Island, IL (inc. 1843)

	Total (and by category)	Foreign born	Native with foreign parentage	Males per 100 females
1900	6,114	24.8%	46.4%	101
	6,110	White (99.9%)		
	1	Negro (0.0%)		
	3	Chinese (0.0%)		
1930	16,534	15.7%	39.2%	103
	16,216	White (98.1%)		
	9	Negro (0.1%)		
	309	Other (1.9%)		
1960	19,618	8.3%	25.8%	96
	19,295	White (98.4%)		
	319	Negro (1.6%)		
	4	Other races (0.0%)		
1990	21,203	14.5%	—	97
	16,029	White (75.6%)		
	2,974	Black (14.0%)		
	24	American Indian (0.1%)		
	78	Asian/Pacific Islander (0.4%)		
	2,098	Other race (9.9%)		
	5,196	Hispanic Origin* (24.5%)		

2000	23,463	22.0%	—	96
	12,596	White alone (53.7%)		
	5,655	Black or African American alone (24.1%)		
	135	American Indian and Alaska Native alone (0.6%)		
	87	Asian alone (0.4%)		
	8	Native Hawaiian and Other Pacific Islander alone (0.0%)		
	4,149	Some other race alone (17.7%)		
	833	Two or more races (3.6%)		
	8,899	Hispanic or Latino* (37.9%)		

Bolingbrook, IL (inc. 1965)

1990	40,843	7.9%	—	99
	31,219	White (76.4%)		
	6,343	Black (15.5%)		
	108	American Indian (0.3%)		
	2,015	Asian/Pacific Islander (4.9%)		
	1,072	Other race (2.6%)		
	2,548	Hispanic Origin* (6.2%)		
2000	56,321	14.4%	—	100
	36,330	White alone (64.5%)		
	11,494	Black or African American alone (20.4%)		
	130	American Indian and Alaska Native alone (0.2%)		
	3,591	Asian alone (6.4%)		
	36	Native Hawaiian and Other Pacific Islander alone (0.1%)		
	3,182	Some other race alone (5.6%)		
	1,558	Two or more races (2.8%)		
	7,371	Hispanic or Latino* (13.1%)		

Braidwood, IL (inc. 1873)

1900	3,279	32.6%	54.9%	109
	3,146	White (95.9%)		
	133	Negro (4.1%)		
1930	1,161	24.1%	38.8%	98
	1,105	White (95.2%)		
	56	Negro (4.8%)		
1960	1,944	—	—	100
	1,899	White (97.7%)		
	45	Negro (2.3%)		
1990	3,584	1.2%	—	97
	3,488	White (97.3%)		
	68	American Indian (1.9%)		
	18	Asian/Pacific Islander (0.5%)		
	17	Other race (0.5%)		
	39	Hispanic Origin* (1.1%)		
2000	5,203	1.5%	—	101
	5,072	White alone (97.5%)		
	14	Black or African American alone (0.3%)		
	5	American Indian and Alaska Native alone (0.1%)		
	17	Asian alone (0.3%)		
	41	Some other race alone (0.8%)		
	54	Two or more races (1.0%)		
	147	Hispanic or Latino* (2.8%)		

Bridgeview, IL (inc. 1947)

1960	7,334	4.3%	17.1%	103
	7,330	White (99.9%)		
	1	Negro (0.0%)		
	3	Other races (0.0%)		
1990	14,402	9.0%	—	93
	13,977	White (97.0%)		
	13	American Indian (0.1%)		
	218	Asian/Pacific Islander (1.5%)		
	183	Other race (1.3%)		
	632	Hispanic Origin* (4.4%)		
2000	15,335	18.9%	—	98
	13,406	White alone (87.4%)		
	126	Black or African American alone (0.8%)		
	46	American Indian and Alaska Native alone (0.3%)		
	341	Asian alone (2.2%)		
	609	Some other race alone (4.0%)		
	807	Two or more races (5.3%)		
	1,445	Hispanic or Latino* (9.4%)		

Broadview, IL (inc. 1913)

1930	2,334	26.3%	12.0%	305
	2,151	White (92.2%)		
	111	Negro (4.8%)		
	72	Other (3.1%)		
1960	8,588	5.5%	27.4%	98
	8,526	White (99.3%)		
	14	Negro (0.2%)		
	18	Other races (0.2%)		
1990	8,713	3.9%	—	94
	3,799	White (43.6%)		
	4,667	Black (53.6%)		
	88	Asian/Pacific Islander (1.0%)		
	159	Other race (1.8%)		
	205	Hispanic Origin* (2.4%)		
2000	8,264	3.9%	—	86
	1,815	White alone (22.0%)		
	6,043	Black or African American alone (73.1%)		
	13	American Indian and Alaska Native alone (0.2%)		
	110	Asian alone (1.3%)		
	126	Some other race alone (1.5%)		
	157	Two or more races (1.9%)		
	325	Hispanic or Latino* (3.9%)		

Brookfield, IL (inc. 1893)

1900	1,111	—	—	—
1930	10,035	18.2%	38.1%	102
	18,016	White (179.5%)		
	4	Negro (0.0%)		
	15	Other (0.1%)		
1960	20,429	8.0%	28.9%	96
	20,399	White (99.9%)		
	4	Negro (0.0%)		
	26	Other races (0.1%)		
1990	18,876	6.4%	—	92
	18,492	White (98.0%)		
	31	American Indian (0.2%)		
	201	Asian/Pacific Islander (1.1%)		
	152	Other race (0.8%)		
	513	Hispanic Origin* (2.7%)		
2000	19,085	9.2%	—	91
	17,850	White alone (93.5%)		
	169	Black or African American alone (0.9%)		
	27	American Indian and Alaska Native alone (0.1%)		
	237	Asian alone (1.2%)		
	2	Native Hawaiian and Other Pacific Islander alone (0.0%)		
	550	Some other race alone (2.9%)		
	250	Two or more races (1.3%)		
	1,537	Hispanic or Latino* (8.1%)		

Buffalo Grove, IL (inc. 1958)

1960	1,492	—	—	102
	1,490	White (99.9%)		
	2	Other races (0.1%)		
1990	36,427	7.9%	—	96
	34,383	White (94.4%)		
	407	Black (1.1%)		
	1,568	Asian/Pacific Islander (4.3%)		
	69	Other race (0.2%)		
	545	Hispanic Origin* (1.5%)		
2000	42,909	20.3%	—	94
	38,059	White alone (88.7%)		
	325	Black or African American alone (0.8%)		
	24	American Indian and Alaska Native alone (0.1%)		
	3,618	Asian alone (8.4%)		
	6	Native Hawaiian and Other Pacific Islander alone (0.0%)		
	389	Some other race alone (0.9%)		
	488	Two or more races (1.1%)		
	1,425	Hispanic or Latino* (3.3%)		

Bull Valley, IL (inc. 1977)

1990	574	5.7%	—	89
	554	White (96.5%)		
	20	Black (3.5%)		
	10	Asian/Pacific Islander (1.7%)		
	6	Hispanic Origin* (1.0%)		
2000	726	4.0%	—	86
	702	White alone (96.7%)		
	4	Black or African American alone (0.6%)		
	8	Asian alone (1.1%)		
	1	Native Hawaiian and Other Pacific Islander alone (0.1%)		
	5	Some other race alone (0.7%)		
	6	Two or more races (0.8%)		
	16	Hispanic or Latino* (2.2%)		

Burbank, IL (inc. 1970)

1990	27,600	10.2%	—	95
	26,903	White (97.5%)		
	10	Black (0.0%)		
	72	American Indian (0.3%)		
	294	Asian/Pacific Islander (1.1%)		
	321	Other race (1.2%)		
	1,211	Hispanic Origin* (4.4%)		
2000	27,902	21.8%	—	96
	25,299	White alone (90.7%)		
	73	Black or African American alone (0.3%)		
	47	American Indian and Alaska Native alone (0.2%)		
	490	Asian alone (1.8%)		
	6	Native Hawaiian and Other Pacific Islander alone (0.0%)		
	1,102	Some other race alone (3.9%)		
	885	Two or more races (3.2%)		
	3,095	Hispanic or Latino* (11.1%)		

Burlington, IL (inc. 1906)

1930	224	—	—	—
1960	360	—	—	—
1990	400	1.0%	—	92
	385	White (96.3%)		
2000	452	6.2%	—	84
	438	White alone (96.9%)		
	6	Asian alone (1.3%)		
	1	Some other race alone (0.2%)		
	7	Two or more races (1.5%)		
	3	Hispanic or Latino* (0.7%)		

Burnham, IL (inc. 1907)

1930	994	—	—	—
1960	2,478	—	—	107
	2,478	White (100.0%)		
1990	3,916	6.0%	—	94
	3,166	White (80.8%)		
	576	Black (14.7%)		
	22	Asian/Pacific Islander (0.6%)		
	152	Other race (3.9%)		
	490	Hispanic Origin* (12.5%)		
2000	4,170	6.8%	—	93
	1,451	White alone (34.8%)		
	2,259	Black or African American alone (54.2%)		
	9	American Indian and Alaska Native alone (0.2%)		
	42	Asian alone (1.0%)		
	1	Native Hawaiian and Other Pacific Islander alone (0.0%)		
	316	Some other race alone (7.6%)		
	92	Two or more races (2.2%)		
	635	Hispanic or Latino* (15.2%)		

Burns Harbor, IN (inc. 1967)

1990	788	0.9%	—	107
	778	White (98.7%)		
	3	Black (0.4%)		
	3	American Indian (0.4%)		
	2	Asian/Pacific Islander (0.3%)		
	7	Hispanic Origin* (0.9%)		
2000	766	2.2%	—	104
	722	White alone (94.3%)		
	2	Black or African American alone (0.3%)		
	9	American Indian and Alaska Native alone (1.2%)		
	8	Asian alone (1.0%)		
	3	Some other race alone (0.4%)		
	22	Two or more races (2.9%)		
	33	Hispanic or Latino* (4.3%)		

Municipalities *(continued)*

Burr Ridge, IL (inc. 1956)

Year	Total (and by category)	Foreign born	Native with foreign parentage	Males per 100 females
1960	299	—	—	—
1990	7,669	9.5%	—	97
	6,974 White (90.9%)			
	35 Black (0.5%)			
	619 Asian/Pacific Islander (8.1%)			
	40 Other race (0.5%)			
	186 Hispanic Origin* (2.4%)			
2000	10,408	13.1%	—	96
	8,919 White alone (85.7%)			
	102 Black or African American alone (1.0%)			
	3 American Indian and Alaska Native alone (0.0%)			
	1,138 Asian alone (10.9%)			
	3 Native Hawaiian and Other Pacific Islander alone (0.0%)			
	78 Some other race alone (0.7%)			
	165 Two or more races (1.6%)			
	304 Hispanic or Latino* (2.9%)			

Calumet City, IL (inc. 1911)

Year	Total (and by category)	Foreign born	Native with foreign parentage	Males per 100 females
1900	2,935	43.6%	50.1%	109
	2,935 White (100.0%)			
1930	12,298	17.9%	42.7%	106
	12,973 White (105.5%)			
	24 Negro (0.2%)			
	1 Other (0.0%)			
1960	25,000	6.2%	24.7%	99
	24,966 White (99.9%)			
	23 Negro (0.1%)			
	11 Other races (0.0%)			
1990	37,840	5.1%	—	90
	27,724 White (73.3%)			
	8,945 Black (23.6%)			
	47 American Indian (0.1%)			
	226 Asian/Pacific Islander (0.6%)			
	898 Other race (2.4%)			
	2,380 Hispanic Origin* (6.3%)			
2000	39,071	7.3%	—	87
	15,137 White alone (38.7%)			
	20,673 Black or African American alone (52.9%)			
	97 American Indian and Alaska Native alone (0.2%)			
	207 Asian alone (0.5%)			
	21 Native Hawaiian and Other Pacific Islander alone (0.1%)			
	2,097 Some other race alone (5.4%)			
	839 Two or more races (2.1%)			
	4,242 Hispanic or Latino* (10.9%)			

Calumet Park, IL (inc. 1912)

Year	Total (and by category)	Foreign born	Native with foreign parentage	Males per 100 females
1930	1,429	31.1%	53.3%	114
	1,335 White (93.4%)			
	14 Negro (1.0%)			
1960	8,448	6.0%	26.6%	101
	8,410 White (99.6%)			
	32 Negro (0.4%)			
	6 Other races (0.1%)			
1990	8,418	6.2%	—	91
	1,954 White (23.2%)			
	6,047 Black (71.8%)			
	55 American Indian (0.7%)			
	362 Other race (4.3%)			
	713 Hispanic Origin* (8.5%)			
2000	8,516	4.0%	—	88
	1,034 White alone (12.1%)			
	7,058 Black or African American alone (82.9%)			
	26 American Indian and Alaska Native alone (0.3%)			
	6 Asian alone (0.1%)			
	1 Native Hawaiian and Other Pacific Islander alone (0.0%)			
	262 Some other race alone (3.1%)			
	129 Two or more races (1.5%)			
	659 Hispanic or Latino* (7.7%)			

Carol Stream, IL (inc. 1959)

Year	Total (and by category)	Foreign born	Native with foreign parentage	Males per 100 females
1960	836	—	—	—
1990	31,716	9.8%	—	98
	28,046 White (88.4%)			
	1,125 Black (3.5%)			
	44 American Indian (0.1%)			
	1,862 Asian/Pacific Islander (5.9%)			
	639 Other race (2.0%)			
	1,721 Hispanic Origin* (5.4%)			
2000	40,438	16.5%	—	97
	31,749 White alone (78.5%)			
	1,716 Black or African American alone (4.2%)			
	71 American Indian and Alaska Native alone (0.2%)			
	4,531 Asian alone (11.2%)			
	4 Native Hawaiian and Other Pacific Islander alone (0.0%)			
	1,534 Some other race alone (3.8%)			
	833 Two or more races (2.1%)			
	4,055 Hispanic or Latino* (10.0%)			

Carpentersville, IL (inc. 1887)

Year	Total (and by category)	Foreign born	Native with foreign parentage	Males per 100 females
1900	1,002	—	—	—
1930	1,461	20.0%	39.1%	121
	1,461 White (100.0%)			
1960	17,424	2.1%	15.0%	102
	17,400 White (99.9%)			
	1 Negro (0.0%)			
	23 Other races (0.1%)			
1990	23,049	9.9%	—	100
	19,606 White (85.1%)			
	1,033 Black (4.5%)			
	92 American Indian (0.4%)			
	347 Asian/Pacific Islander (1.5%)			
	1,971 Other race (8.6%)			
	3,748 Hispanic Origin* (16.3%)			
2000	30,586	26.2%	—	107
	21,031 White alone (68.8%)			
	1,279 Black or African American alone (4.2%)			
	197 American Indian and Alaska Native alone (0.6%)			
	606 Asian alone (2.0%)			
	30 Native Hawaiian and Other Pacific Islander alone (0.1%)			
	6,372 Some other race alone (20.8%)			
	1,071 Two or more races (3.5%)			
	12,410 Hispanic or Latino* (40.6%)			

Cary, IL (inc. 1893)

Year	Total (and by category)	Foreign born	Native with foreign parentage	Males per 100 females
1900	398	—	—	—
1930	731	—	—	—
1960	2,530	3.3%	20.9%	101
	2,528 White (99.9%)			
	1 Negro (0.0%)			
	1 Other races (0.0%)			
1990	10,043	3.7%	—	98
	9,801 White (97.6%)			
	52 Black (0.5%)			
	22 American Indian (0.2%)			
	65 Asian/Pacific Islander (0.6%)			
	103 Other race (1.0%)			
	252 Hispanic Origin* (2.5%)			
2000	15,531	4.3%	—	98
	14,837 White alone (95.5%)			
	61 Black or African American alone (0.4%)			
	24 American Indian and Alaska Native alone (0.2%)			
	210 Asian alone (1.4%)			
	4 Native Hawaiian and Other Pacific Islander alone (0.0%)			
	285 Some other race alone (1.8%)			
	110 Two or more races (0.7%)			
	843 Hispanic or Latino* (5.4%)			

Cedar Lake, IN (inc. 1966)

Year	Total (and by category)	Foreign born	Native with foreign parentage	Males per 100 females
1960	5,766	4.0%	11.4%	107
	5,763 White (99.9%)			
	1 Negro (0.0%)			
	2 Other races (0.0%)			
1990	8,885	1.0%	—	98
	8,733 White (98.3%)			
	75 American Indian (0.8%)			
	30 Asian/Pacific Islander (0.3%)			
	47 Other race (0.5%)			
	147 Hispanic Origin* (1.7%)			
2000	9,279	1.2%	—	104
	9,038 White alone (97.4%)			
	8 Black or African American alone (0.1%)			
	22 American Indian and Alaska Native alone (0.2%)			
	19 Asian alone (0.2%)			
	82 Some other race alone (0.9%)			
	110 Two or more races (1.2%)			
	325 Hispanic or Latino* (3.5%)			

Channahon, IL (inc. 1961)

Year	Total (and by category)	Foreign born	Native with foreign parentage	Males per 100 females
1990	4,266	1.3%	—	102
	4,190 White (98.2%)			
	36 Black (0.8%)			
	5 American Indian (0.1%)			
	15 Asian/Pacific Islander (0.4%)			
	18 Other race (0.4%)			
	117 Hispanic Origin* (2.7%)			
2000	7,344	1.3%	—	106
	7,140 White alone (97.2%)			
	31 Black or African American alone (0.4%)			
	8 American Indian and Alaska Native alone (0.1%)			
	20 Asian alone (0.3%)			
	70 Some other race alone (1.0%)			
	75 Two or more races (1.0%)			
	267 Hispanic or Latino* (3.6%)			

Chesterton, IN (inc. 1899)

Year	Total (and by category)	Foreign born	Native with foreign parentage	Males per 100 females
1900	788	—	—	—
1930	2,231	—	—	—
1960	4,335	2.5%	15.8%	97
	4,334 White (100.0%)			
	1 Negro (0.0%)			
1990	9,124	1.3%	—	92
	8,990 White (98.5%)			
	44 American Indian (0.5%)			
	90 Asian/Pacific Islander (1.0%)			
	90 Hispanic Origin* (1.0%)			
2000	10,488	2.2%	—	96
	10,099 White alone (96.3%)			
	46 Black or African American alone (0.4%)			
	22 American Indian and Alaska Native alone (0.2%)			
	144 Asian alone (1.4%)			
	2 Native Hawaiian and Other Pacific Islander alone (0.0%)			
	53 Some other race alone (0.5%)			
	122 Two or more races (1.2%)			
	347 Hispanic or Latino* (3.3%)			

Chicago Heights, IL (inc. 1892)

Year	Total (and by category)	Foreign born	Native with foreign parentage	Males per 100 females
1900	5,100	30.0%	36.9%	145
	5,048 White (99.0%)			
	47 Negro (0.9%)			
	5 Chinese (0.1%)			
1930	22,321	21.6%	39.5%	108
	19,987 White (89.5%)			
	2,198 Negro (9.8%)			
	136 Other (0.6%)			
1960	34,331	7.7%	20.4%	97
	27,767 White (80.9%)			
	6,529 Negro (19.0%)			
	35 Other races (0.1%)			
1990	33,072	6.4%	—	90
	18,141 White (54.9%)			
	11,611 Black (35.1%)			
	33 American Indian (0.1%)			
	121 Asian/Pacific Islander (0.4%)			
	3,166 Other race (9.6%)			
	4,818 Hispanic Origin* (14.6%)			

2000	32,776	11.3%	—	95
	14,756	White alone (45.0%)		
	12,421	Black or African American alone (37.9%)		
	146	American Indian and Alaska Native alone (0.4%)		
	144	Asian alone (0.4%)		
	12	Native Hawaiian and Other Pacific Islander alone (0.0%)		
	4,411	Some other race alone (13.5%)		
	886	Two or more races (2.7%)		
	7,790	Hispanic or Latino* (23.8%)		

Chicago Ridge, IL (inc. 1914)

1930	269	—	—	—
1960	5,748	2.9%	16.1%	105
	5,729	White (99.7%)		
	19	Other races (0.3%)		
1990	13,643	7.9%	—	94
	13,400	White (98.2%)		
	40	Black (0.3%)		
	24	American Indian (0.2%)		
	96	Asian/Pacific Islander (0.7%)		
	83	Other race (0.6%)		
	519	Hispanic Origin* (3.8%)		
2000	14,127	13.5%	—	94
	12,592	White alone (89.1%)		
	345	Black or African American alone (2.4%)		
	32	American Indian and Alaska Native alone (0.2%)		
	207	Asian alone (1.5%)		
	277	Some other race alone (2.0%)		
	674	Two or more races (4.8%)		
	883	Hispanic or Latino* (6.3%)		

Chicago, IL (inc. 1837)

1840	4,470	—	—	119
	4,417	Free white (98.8%)		
	53	Free colored (1.2%)		
1870	298,977	48.4%	—	105
	295,281	White (98.8%)		
	3,691	Colored (1.2%)		
	5	Indian (0.0%)		
1900	1,698,575	34.6%	42.8%	103
	1,667,140	White (98.1%)		
	30,150	Negro (1.8%)		
	1,209	Chinese (0.1%)		
	68	Japanese (0.0%)		
	8	Indian (0.0%)		
1930	3,376,438	24.9%	39.5%	103
	3,117,731	White (92.3%)		
	233,903	Negro (6.9%)		
	246	Indian (0.0%)		
	2,757	Chinese (0.1%)		
	486	Japanese (0.0%)		
	19,362	Mexican (0.6%)		
1960	3,550,404	12.3%	23.7%	95
	2,712,748	White (76.4%)		
	812,637	Negro (22.9%)		
	25,019	Other races (0.7%)		
1990	2,783,726	16.9%	—	92
	1,265,953	White (45.5%)		
	1,086,389	Black (39.0%)		
	6,761	American Indian (0.2%)		
	104,141	Asian/Pacific Islander (3.7%)		
	320,482	Other race (11.5%)		
	535,315	Hispanic Origin* (19.2%)		
2000	2,896,016	21.7%	—	94
	1,215,315	White alone (42.0%)		
	1,065,009	Black or African American alone (36.8%)		
	10,290	American Indian and Alaska Native alone (0.4%)		
	125,974	Asian alone (4.3%)		
	1,788	Native Hawaiian and Other Pacific Islander alone (0.1%)		
	393,203	Some other race alone (13.6%)		
	84,437	Two or more races (2.9%)		
	753,644	Hispanic or Latino* (26.0%)		

Cicero, IL (inc. 1867)

1870	1,545	34.6%	—	—
	1,541	White (99.7%)		
	4	Colored (0.3%)		
1900	16,310	—	—	—
1930	66,602	29.3%	—	106
	66,436	White (99.8%)		
	5	Negro (0.0%)		
	9	Chinese (0.0%)		
	1	Japanese (0.0%)		
	151	Mexican (0.2%)		
1960	69,130	14.9%	34.7%	96
	69,093	White (99.9%)		
	4	Negro (0.0%)		
	33	Other races (0.0%)		
1990	67,436	23.9%	—	99
	50,717	White (75.2%)		
	173	Black (0.3%)		
	249	American Indian (0.4%)		
	1,157	Asian/Pacific Islander (1.7%)		
	15,140	Other race (22.5%)		
	24,148	Hispanic Origin* (35.8%)		
2000	85,616	43.6%	—	106
	41,327	White alone (48.3%)		
	956	Black or African American alone (1.1%)		
	759	American Indian and Alaska Native alone (0.9%)		
	828	Asian alone (1.0%)		
	38	Native Hawaiian and Other Pacific Islander alone (0.0%)		
	38,277	Some other race alone (44.7%)		
	3,431	Two or more races (4.0%)		
	66,299	Hispanic or Latino* (77.4%)		

Clarendon Hills, IL (inc. 1924)

1930	933	—	—	—
1960	5,885	4.0%	18.9%	94
	5,874	White (99.8%)		
	2	Negro (0.0%)		
	9	Other races (0.2%)		
1990	6,994	6.1%	—	92
	6,798	White (97.2%)		
	26	Black (0.4%)		
	5	American Indian (0.1%)		
	154	Asian/Pacific Islander (2.2%)		
	11	Other race (0.2%)		
	177	Hispanic Origin* (2.5%)		
2000	7,610	8.3%	—	92
	7,159	White alone (94.1%)		
	64	Black or African American alone (0.8%)		
	1	American Indian and Alaska Native alone (0.0%)		
	268	Asian alone (3.5%)		
	32	Some other race alone (0.4%)		
	86	Two or more races (1.1%)		
	180	Hispanic or Latino* (2.4%)		

Coal City, IL (inc. 1881)

1900	2,607	40.3%	48.7%	115
	2,607	White (100.0%)		
1930	1,637	20.9%	45.8%	102
	1,637	White (100.0%)		
1960	2,852	5.4%	27.1%	94
	2,852	White (100.0%)		
1990	3,907	1.6%	—	94
	3,857	White (98.7%)		
	6	American Indian (0.2%)		
	6	Asian/Pacific Islander (0.2%)		
	22	Other race (0.6%)		
	98	Hispanic Origin* (2.5%)		
2000	4,797	1.1%	—	96
	4,723	White alone (98.5%)		
	6	Black or African American alone (0.1%)		
	12	American Indian and Alaska Native alone (0.3%)		
	1	Asian alone (0.0%)		
	1	Native Hawaiian and Other Pacific Islander alone (0.0%)		
	26	Some other race alone (0.5%)		
	28	Two or more races (0.6%)		
	91	Hispanic or Latino* (1.9%)		

Country Club Hills, IL (inc. 1958)

1960	3,421	1.4%	14.0%	106
	3,420	White (100.0%)		
	1	Other races (0.0%)		
1990	15,431	3.9%	—	92
	6,066	White (39.3%)		
	8,938	Black (57.9%)		
	17	American Indian (0.1%)		
	335	Asian/Pacific Islander (2.2%)		
	75	Other race (0.5%)		
	338	Hispanic Origin* (2.2%)		
2000	16,169	2.4%	—	85
	2,346	White alone (14.5%)		
	13,243	Black or African American alone (81.9%)		
	24	American Indian and Alaska Native alone (0.1%)		
	164	Asian alone (1.0%)		
	88	Some other race alone (0.5%)		
	304	Two or more races (1.9%)		
	280	Hispanic or Latino* (1.7%)		

Countryside, IL (inc. 1960)

1990	5,716	6.4%	—	95
	5,632	White (98.5%)		
	59	Black (1.0%)		
	6	American Indian (0.1%)		
	6	Asian/Pacific Islander (0.1%)		
	13	Other race (0.2%)		
	195	Hispanic Origin* (3.4%)		
2000	5,991	16.1%	—	90
	5,529	White alone (92.3%)		
	129	Black or African American alone (2.2%)		
	6	American Indian and Alaska Native alone (0.1%)		
	93	Asian alone (1.6%)		
	131	Some other race alone (2.2%)		
	103	Two or more races (1.7%)		
	410	Hispanic or Latino* (6.8%)		

Crest Hill, IL (inc. 1960)

1960	5,887	3.8%	23.1%	102
	5,873	White (99.8%)		
	14	Other races (0.2%)		
1990	10,643	3.1%	—	149
	8,284	White (77.8%)		
	1,979	Black (18.6%)		
	84	American Indian (0.8%)		
	89	Asian/Pacific Islander (0.8%)		
	207	Other race (1.9%)		
	635	Hispanic Origin* (6.0%)		
2000	13,329	4.3%	—	148
	9,912	White alone (74.4%)		
	2,606	Black or African American alone (19.6%)		
	26	American Indian and Alaska Native alone (0.2%)		
	150	Asian alone (1.1%)		
	17	Native Hawaiian and Other Pacific Islander alone (0.1%)		
	425	Some other race alone (3.2%)		
	193	Two or more races (1.4%)		
	1,174	Hispanic or Latino* (8.8%)		

Crestwood, IL (inc. 1928)

1960	1,213	—	—	98
	1,012	White (83.4%)		
	193	Negro (15.9%)		
	8	Other races (0.7%)		
1990	10,823	3.4%	—	87
	10,171	White (94.0%)		
	443	Black (4.1%)		
	37	American Indian (0.3%)		
	58	Asian/Pacific Islander (0.5%)		
	114	Other race (1.1%)		
	309	Hispanic Origin* (2.9%)		
2000	11,251	3.4%	—	85
	10,403	White alone (92.5%)		
	508	Black or African American alone (4.5%)		
	14	American Indian and Alaska Native alone (0.1%)		
	82	Asian alone (0.7%)		
	117	Some other race alone (1.0%)		
	127	Two or more races (1.1%)		
	414	Hispanic or Latino* (3.7%)		

Municipalities *(continued)*

Crete, IL (inc. 1880)

Year	Total (and by category)	Foreign born	Native with foreign parentage	Males per 100 females
1900	760	—	—	—
1930	1,429	5.9%	31.1%	104
	1,428 White (99.9%)			
	1 Negro (0.1%)			
1960	3,463	2.2%	15.0%	94
	3,463 White (100.0%)			
1990	6,773	2.0%	—	96
	6,395 White (94.4%)			
	303 Black (4.5%)			
	41 Asian/Pacific Islander (0.6%)			
	34 Other race (0.5%)			
	151 Hispanic Origin* (2.2%)			
2000	7,346	1.6%	—	96
	6,351 White alone (86.5%)			
	769 Black or African American alone (10.5%)			
	5 American Indian and Alaska Native alone (0.1%)			
	55 Asian alone (0.7%)			
	1 Native Hawaiian and Other Pacific Islander alone (0.0%)			
	68 Some other race alone (0.9%)			
	97 Two or more races (1.3%)			
	267 Hispanic or Latino* (3.6%)			

Crown Point, IN (inc. 1868)

Year	Total (and by category)	Foreign born	Native with foreign parentage	Males per 100 females
1900	2,336	—	—	—
1930	4,046	8.8%	25.9%	106
	3,918 White (96.8%)			
	87 Negro (2.2%)			
	41 Other (1.0%)			
1960	8,443	3.6%	12.0%	94
	8,421 White (99.7%)			
	20 Negro (0.2%)			
	2 Other races (0.0%)			
1990	17,728	5.8%	—	92
	17,236 White (97.2%)			
	264 Black (1.5%)			
	134 Asian/Pacific Islander (0.8%)			
	94 Other race (0.5%)			
	390 Hispanic Origin* (2.2%)			
2000	19,806	6.3%	—	90
	18,879 White alone (95.3%)			
	280 Black or African American alone (1.4%)			
	36 American Indian and Alaska Native alone (0.2%)			
	195 Asian alone (1.0%)			
	8 Native Hawaiian and Other Pacific Islander alone (0.0%)			
	202 Some other race alone (1.0%)			
	206 Two or more races (1.0%)			
	793 Hispanic or Latino* (4.0%)			

Crystal Lake, IL (inc. 1914)

Year	Total (and by category)	Foreign born	Native with foreign parentage	Males per 100 females
1900	950	—	—	—
1930	3,732	15.0%	33.9%	100
	3,713 White (99.5%)			
	4 Negro (0.1%)			
	15 Other (0.4%)			
1960	8,314	6.0%	20.6%	95
	8,303 White (99.9%)			
	2 Negro (0.0%)			
	9 Other races (0.1%)			
1990	24,512	4.2%	—	96
	24,137 White (98.5%)			
	45 Black (0.2%)			
	217 Asian/Pacific Islander (0.9%)			
	113 Other race (0.5%)			
	635 Hispanic Origin* (2.6%)			
2000	38,000	7.3%	—	98
	35,746 White alone (94.1%)			
	212 Black or African American alone (0.6%)			
	62 American Indian and Alaska Native alone (0.2%)			
	747 Asian alone (2.0%)			
	8 Native Hawaiian and Other Pacific Islander alone (0.0%)			
	826 Some other race alone (2.2%)			
	399 Two or more races (1.1%)			
	2,662 Hispanic or Latino* (7.0%)			

Darien, IL (inc. 1969)

Year	Total (and by category)	Foreign born	Native with foreign parentage	Males per 100 females
1990	18,341	9.4%	—	94
	16,327 White (89.0%)			
	213 Black (1.2%)			
	1,662 Asian/Pacific Islander (9.1%)			
	139 Other race (0.8%)			
	336 Hispanic Origin* (1.8%)			
2000	22,860	15.2%	—	96
	19,225 White alone (84.1%)			
	451 Black or African American alone (2.0%)			
	26 American Indian and Alaska Native alone (0.1%)			
	2,635 Asian alone (11.5%)			
	6 Native Hawaiian and Other Pacific Islander alone (0.0%)			
	222 Some other race alone (1.0%)			
	295 Two or more races (1.3%)			
	831 Hispanic or Latino* (3.6%)			

Deer Park, IL (inc. 1957)

Year	Total (and by category)	Foreign born	Native with foreign parentage	Males per 100 females
1960	476	—	—	—
1990	2,887	5.9%	—	103
	2,806 White (97.2%)			
	18 Black (0.6%)			
	63 Asian/Pacific Islander (2.2%)			
	13 Hispanic Origin* (0.5%)			
2000	3,102	8.7%	—	101
	2,977 White alone (96.0%)			
	18 Black or African American alone (0.6%)			
	2 American Indian and Alaska Native alone (0.1%)			
	75 Asian alone (2.4%)			
	1 Native Hawaiian and Other Pacific Islander alone (0.0%)			
	8 Some other race alone (0.3%)			
	21 Two or more races (0.7%)			
	47 Hispanic or Latino* (1.5%)			

Deerfield, IL (inc. 1903)

Year	Total (and by category)	Foreign born	Native with foreign parentage	Males per 100 females
1930	1,852	10.6%	29.9%	104
	1,849 White (99.8%)			
	3 Negro (0.2%)			
1960	11,786	4.1%	19.3%	100
	11,771 White (99.9%)			
	12 Negro (0.1%)			
	3 Other races (0.0%)			
1990	17,327	7.4%	—	95
	16,884 White (97.4%)			
	55 Black (0.3%)			
	7 American Indian (0.0%)			
	336 Asian/Pacific Islander (1.9%)			
	45 Other race (0.3%)			
	242 Hispanic Origin* (1.4%)			
2000	18,420	8.8%	—	93
	17,662 White alone (95.9%)			
	61 Black or African American alone (0.3%)			
	7 American Indian and Alaska Native alone (0.0%)			
	465 Asian alone (2.5%)			
	4 Native Hawaiian and Other Pacific Islander alone (0.0%)			
	79 Some other race alone (0.4%)			
	142 Two or more races (0.8%)			
	312 Hispanic or Latino* (1.7%)			

Des Plaines, IL (inc. 1869)

Year	Total (and by category)	Foreign born	Native with foreign parentage	Males per 100 females
1900	1,666	—	—	—
1930	8,798	13.9%	36.2%	106
	8,788 White (99.9%)			
	10 Other (0.1%)			
1960	34,886	1.1%	21.7%	98
	34,838 White (99.9%)			
	5 Negro (0.0%)			
	43 Other races (0.1%)			
1990	53,223	13.5%	—	93
	49,244 White (92.5%)			
	248 Black (0.5%)			
	28 American Indian (0.1%)			
	2,680 Asian/Pacific Islander (5.0%)			
	1,023 Other race (1.9%)			
	3,265 Hispanic Origin* (6.1%)			
2000	58,720	23.9%	—	94
	49,586 White alone (84.4%)			
	594 Black or African American alone (1.0%)			
	151 American Indian and Alaska Native alone (0.3%)			
	4,492 Asian alone (7.6%)			
	13 Native Hawaiian and Other Pacific Islander alone (0.0%)			
	2,726 Some other race alone (4.6%)			
	1,158 Two or more races (2.0%)			
	8,229 Hispanic or Latino* (14.0%)			

Diamond, IL (inc. 1895)

Year	Total (and by category)	Foreign born	Native with foreign parentage	Males per 100 females
1900	672	—	—	—
1930	92	—	—	—
1960	250	—	—	—
1990	1,077	1.0%	—	97
	1,090 White (101.2%)			
	8 Other race (0.7%)			
	25 Hispanic Origin* (2.3%)			
2000	1,393	0.4%	—	95
	1,353 White alone (97.1%)			
	9 American Indian and Alaska Native alone (0.6%)			
	1 Asian alone (0.1%)			
	12 Some other race alone (0.9%)			
	18 Two or more races (1.3%)			
	49 Hispanic or Latino* (3.5%)			

Dixmoor, IL (inc. 1922)

Year	Total (and by category)	Foreign born	Native with foreign parentage	Males per 100 females
1930	944	—	—	—
1960	3,076	4.0%	9.6%	102
	1,221 White (39.7%)			
	1,855 Negro (60.3%)			
1990	3,647	4.5%	—	94
	1,242 White (34.1%)			
	2,216 Black (60.8%)			
	16 American Indian (0.4%)			
	207 Other race (5.7%)			
	255 Hispanic Origin* (7.0%)			
2000	3,934	9.6%	—	92
	1,212 White alone (30.8%)			
	2,247 Black or African American alone (57.1%)			
	10 American Indian and Alaska Native alone (0.3%)			
	6 Asian alone (0.2%)			
	373 Some other race alone (9.5%)			
	86 Two or more races (2.2%)			
	716 Hispanic or Latino* (18.2%)			

Dolton, IL (inc. 1892)

Year	Total (and by category)	Foreign born	Native with foreign parentage	Males per 100 females
1900	1,229	—	—	—
1930	2,923	15.9%	38.3%	110
	2,886 White (98.7%)			
	37 Negro (1.3%)			
1960	18,746	3.3%	20.2%	99
	18,730 White (99.9%)			
	16 Other races (0.1%)			
1990	23,930	4.3%	—	91
	13,901 White (58.1%)			
	9,097 Black (38.0%)			
	59 American Indian (0.2%)			
	356 Asian/Pacific Islander (1.5%)			
	517 Other race (2.2%)			
	1,061 Hispanic Origin* (4.4%)			

2000	25,614	3.7%	—	87
	3,671	White alone (14.3%)		
	21,098	Black or African American alone (82.4%)		
	44	American Indian and Alaska Native alone (0.2%)		
	144	Asian alone (0.6%)		
	4	Native Hawaiian and Other Pacific Islander alone (0.0%)		
	365	Some other race alone (1.4%)		
	288	Two or more races (1.1%)		
	791	Hispanic or Latino* (3.1%)		

Downers Grove, IL (inc. 1873)

1900	2,103	—	—	—
1930	8,977	11.1%	30.4%	98
	8,951	White (99.7%)		
	17	Negro (0.2%)		
	9	Other (0.1%)		
1960	21,154	5.0%	20.1%	95
	21,098	White (99.7%)		
	25	Negro (0.1%)		
	31	Other races (0.1%)		
1990	46,858	6.9%	—	94
	43,681	White (93.2%)		
	767	Black (1.6%)		
	78	American Indian (0.2%)		
	1,947	Asian/Pacific Islander (4.2%)		
	385	Other race (0.8%)		
	934	Hispanic Origin* (2.0%)		
2000	48,724	9.8%	—	92
	43,924	White alone (90.1%)		
	936	Black or African American alone (1.9%)		
	55	American Indian and Alaska Native alone (0.1%)		
	2,782	Asian alone (5.7%)		
	6	Native Hawaiian and Other Pacific Islander alone (0.0%)		
	488	Some other race alone (1.0%)		
	533	Two or more races (1.1%)		
	1,747	Hispanic or Latino* (3.6%)		

Dune Acres, IN (inc. 1923)

1930	12	—	—	—
1960	238	—	—	—
1990	263	7.6%	—	95
	256	White (97.3%)		
	9	Asian/Pacific Islander (3.4%)		
2000	213	7.5%	—	105
	211	White alone (99.1%)		
	2	Two or more races (0.9%)		
	3	Hispanic or Latino* (1.4%)		

Dyer, IN (inc. 1910)

1930	672	—	—	—
1960	3,993	1.5%	11.6%	96
	3,990	White (99.9%)		
	3	Negro (0.1%)		
1990	10,923	4.3%	—	95
	10,658	White (97.6%)		
	63	Black (0.6%)		
	10	American Indian (0.1%)		
	93	Asian/Pacific Islander (0.9%)		
	99	Other race (0.9%)		
	431	Hispanic Origin* (3.9%)		
2000	13,895	4.9%	—	95
	13,258	White alone (95.4%)		
	91	Black or African American alone (0.7%)		
	19	American Indian and Alaska Native alone (0.1%)		
	222	Asian alone (1.6%)		
	5	Native Hawaiian and Other Pacific Islander alone (0.0%)		
	175	Some other race alone (1.3%)		
	125	Two or more races (0.9%)		
	696	Hispanic or Latino* (5.0%)		

East Chicago, IN (inc. 1889)

1900	3,411	39.0%	42.1%	130
	3,408	White (99.9%)		
	1	Negro (0.0%)		
	2	Chinese (0.1%)		
1930	54,784	25.2%	34.7%	127
	44,308	White (80.9%)		
	5,088	Negro (9.3%)		
	7	Indian (0.0%)		
	30	Chinese (0.1%)		
	5,343	Mexican (9.8%)		
	8	Other (0.0%)		
1960	57,669	15.4%	22.6%	107
	43,831	White (76.0%)		
	13,766	Negro (23.9%)		
	72	Other races (0.1%)		
1990	33,892	11.6%	—	91
	12,936	White (38.2%)		
	11,395	Black (33.6%)		
	102	American Indian (0.3%)		
	33	Asian/Pacific Islander (0.1%)		
	9,426	Other race (27.8%)		
	15,889	Hispanic Origin* (46.9%)		
2000	32,414	14.7%	—	92
	11,843	White alone (36.5%)		
	11,695	Black or African American alone (36.1%)		
	166	American Indian and Alaska Native alone (0.5%)		
	66	Asian alone (0.2%)		
	26	Native Hawaiian and Other Pacific Islander alone (0.1%)		
	7,774	Some other race alone (24.0%)		
	844	Two or more races (2.6%)		
	16,728	Hispanic or Latino* (51.6%)		

East Dundee, IL (inc. 1887)

1900	1,417	—	—	—
1930	1,341	16.4%	43.3%	105
	1,340	White (99.9%)		
	1	Other (0.1%)		
1960	2,221	—	—	102
	2,210	White (99.5%)		
	1	Negro (0.0%)		
	10	Other races (0.5%)		
1990	2,721	3.0%	—	100
	2,663	White (97.9%)		
	23	Asian/Pacific Islander (0.8%)		
	32	Other race (1.2%)		
	109	Hispanic Origin* (4.0%)		
2000	2,955	6.7%	—	96
	2,782	White alone (94.1%)		
	29	Black or African American alone (1.0%)		
	3	American Indian and Alaska Native alone (0.1%)		
	51	Asian alone (1.7%)		
	51	Some other race alone (1.7%)		
	39	Two or more races (1.3%)		
	116	Hispanic or Latino* (3.9%)		

East Hazel Crest, IL (inc. 1918)

1930	686	—	—	—
1960	1,457	—	—	103
	1,364	White (93.6%)		
	93	Negro (6.4%)		
1990	1,570	4.8%	—	101
	1,141	White (72.7%)		
	381	Black (24.3%)		
	2	American Indian (0.1%)		
	6	Asian/Pacific Islander (0.4%)		
	40	Other race (2.5%)		
	114	Hispanic Origin* (7.3%)		
2000	1,607	4.9%	—	89
	904	White alone (56.3%)		
	600	Black or African American alone (37.3%)		
	10	Asian alone (0.6%)		
	45	Some other race alone (2.8%)		
	48	Two or more races (3.0%)		
	116	Hispanic or Latino* (7.2%)		

Elburn, IL (inc. 1886)

1900	606	—	—	—
1930	548	—	—	—
1960	960	—	—	—
1990	1,275	0.9%	—	101
	1,255	White (98.4%)		
	16	American Indian (1.3%)		
	4	Other race (0.3%)		
	10	Hispanic Origin* (0.8%)		
2000	2,756	3.4%	—	92
	2,703	White alone (98.1%)		
	3	Black or African American alone (0.1%)		
	4	American Indian and Alaska Native alone (0.1%)		
	9	Asian alone (0.3%)		
	13	Some other race alone (0.5%)		
	24	Two or more races (0.9%)		
	59	Hispanic or Latino* (2.1%)		

Elgin, IL (inc. 1854)

1870	5,441	26.7%	—	98
	5,360	White (98.5%)		
	81	Colored (1.5%)		
1900	22,433	24.2%	36.8%	89
	22,238	White (99.1%)		
	187	Negro (0.8%)		
	8	Chinese (0.0%)		
1930	35,929	15.3%	32.5%	94
	35,539	White (98.9%)		
	310	Negro (0.9%)		
	12	Chinese (0.0%)		
	1	Japanese (0.0%)		
	67	Mexican (0.2%)		
1960	49,447	4.6%	18.1%	91
	47,795	White (96.7%)		
	595	Negro (1.2%)		
	57	Other races (0.1%)		
1990	77,010	12.9%	—	98
	60,040	White (78.0%)		
	5,588	Black (7.3%)		
	122	American Indian (0.2%)		
	2,663	Asian/Pacific Islander (3.5%)		
	8,597	Other race (11.2%)		
	14,201	Hispanic Origin* (18.4%)		
2000	94,487	23.6%	—	100
	66,600	White alone (70.5%)		
	6,427	Black or African American alone (6.8%)		
	382	American Indian and Alaska Native alone (0.4%)		
	3,668	Asian alone (3.9%)		
	58	Native Hawaiian and Other Pacific Islander alone (0.1%)		
	14,537	Some other race alone (15.4%)		
	2,815	Two or more races (3.0%)		
	32,430	Hispanic or Latino* (34.3%)		

Elk Grove Village, IL (inc. 1956)

1960	6,608	2.3%	16.9%	98
	6,606	White (100.0%)		
	2	Other races (0.0%)		
1990	33,429	9.4%	—	97
	30,644	White (91.7%)		
	197	Black (0.6%)		
	27	American Indian (0.1%)		
	2,292	Asian/Pacific Islander (6.9%)		
	269	Other race (0.8%)		
	1,194	Hispanic Origin* (3.6%)		
2000	34,727	14.3%	—	95
	29,874	White alone (86.0%)		
	490	Black or African American alone (1.4%)		
	33	American Indian and Alaska Native alone (0.1%)		
	3,051	Asian alone (8.8%)		
	15	Native Hawaiian and Other Pacific Islander alone (0.0%)		
	797	Some other race alone (2.3%)		
	467	Two or more races (1.3%)		
	2,165	Hispanic or Latino* (6.2%)		

Elmhurst, IL (inc. 1882)

1870	329	50.2%	—	—
	323	White (98.2%)		
	6	Colored (1.8%)		
1900	1,728	—	—	—

Municipalities *(continued)*

	Total (and by category)	Foreign born	Native with foreign parentage	Males per 100 females
1930	14,055	13.5%	34.1%	100
	14,023 White (99.8%)			
	13 Negro (0.1%)			
	19 Other (0.1%)			
1960	36,991	5.2%	22.3%	95
	36,928 White (99.8%)			
	18 Negro (0.0%)			
	45 Other races (0.1%)			
1990	42,029	6.8%	—	94
	40,353 White (96.0%)			
	169 Black (0.4%)			
	37 American Indian (0.1%)			
	1,317 Asian/Pacific Islander (3.1%)			
	153 Other race (0.4%)			
	720 Hispanic Origin* (1.7%)			
2000	42,762	8.0%	—	93
	39,940 White alone (93.4%)			
	400 Black or African American alone (0.9%)			
	24 American Indian and Alaska Native alone (0.1%)			
	1,568 Asian alone (3.7%)			
	8 Native Hawaiian and Other Pacific Islander alone (0.0%)			
	416 Some other race alone (1.0%)			
	406 Two or more races (0.9%)			
	1,717 Hispanic or Latino* (4.0%)			

Elmwood Park, IL (inc. 1914)

	Total (and by category)	Foreign born	Native with foreign parentage	Males per 100 females
1930	11,270	21.9%	40.8%	103
	11,269 White (100.0%)			
	1 Other (0.0%)			
1960	23,866	13.2%	32.8%	95
	23,851 White (99.9%)			
	9 Negro (0.0%)			
	6 Other races (0.0%)			
1990	23,206	13.3%	—	84
	22,762 White (98.1%)			
	28 Black (0.1%)			
	20 American Indian (0.1%)			
	176 Asian/Pacific Islander (0.8%)			
	220 Other race (0.9%)			
	1,032 Hispanic Origin* (4.4%)			
2000	25,405	24.3%	—	91
	23,255 White alone (91.5%)			
	132 Black or African American alone (0.5%)			
	45 American Indian and Alaska Native alone (0.2%)			
	530 Asian alone (2.1%)			
	7 Native Hawaiian and Other Pacific Islander alone (0.0%)			
	842 Some other race alone (3.3%)			
	594 Two or more races (2.3%)			
	2,798 Hispanic or Latino* (11.0%)			

Elwood, IL (inc. 1873)

	Total (and by category)	Foreign born	Native with foreign parentage	Males per 100 females
1900	244	—	—	—
1930	257	—	—	—
1960	746	—	—	—
1990	951	0.2%	—	104
	948 White (99.7%)			
	11 Hispanic Origin* (1.2%)			
2000	1,620	2.0%	—	93
	1,581 White alone (97.6%)			
	9 American Indian and Alaska Native alone (0.6%)			
	5 Asian alone (0.3%)			
	1 Native Hawaiian and Other Pacific Islander alone (0.1%)			
	5 Some other race alone (0.3%)			
	19 Two or more races (1.2%)			
	65 Hispanic or Latino* (4.0%)			

Evanston, IL (inc. 1872)

	Total (and by category)	Foreign born	Native with foreign parentage	Males per 100 females
1900	19,259	23.1%	32.0%	82
	18,513 White (96.1%)			
	737 Negro (3.8%)			
	3 Chinese (0.0%)			
	6 Japanese (0.0%)			
1930	63,338	15.2%	26.4%	88
	58,338 White (92.1%)			
	4,938 Negro (7.8%)			
	4 Indian (0.0%)			
	20 Chinese (0.0%)			
	5 Japanese (0.0%)			
	3 Mexican (0.0%)			
	30 Other (0.0%)			
1960	79,283	8.8%	19.4%	85
	69,739 White (88.0%)			
	9,126 Negro (11.5%)			
	418 Other races (0.5%)			
1990	73,233	11.5%	—	88
	51,752 White (70.7%)			
	16,604 Black (22.7%)			
	219 American Indian (0.3%)			
	3,570 Asian/Pacific Islander (4.9%)			
	1,088 Other race (1.5%)			
	2,379 Hispanic Origin* (3.2%)			
2000	74,239	15.4%	—	89
	48,429 White alone (65.2%)			
	16,704 Black or African American alone (22.5%)			
	140 American Indian and Alaska Native alone (0.2%)			
	4,524 Asian alone (6.1%)			
	64 Native Hawaiian and Other Pacific Islander alone (0.1%)			
	2,116 Some other race alone (2.9%)			
	2,262 Two or more races (3.0%)			
	4,539 Hispanic or Latino* (6.1%)			

Evergreen Park, IL (inc. 1893)

	Total (and by category)	Foreign born	Native with foreign parentage	Males per 100 females
1900	445	—	—	—
1930	1,594	20.9%	45.7%	113
	1,589 White (99.7%)			
	3 Negro (0.2%)			
	2 Other (0.1%)			
1960	24,178	7.5%	28.5%	94
	24,154 White (99.9%)			
	5 Negro (0.0%)			
	19 Other races (0.1%)			
1990	20,874	5.5%	—	88
	20,499 White (98.2%)			
	74 Black (0.4%)			
	6 American Indian (0.0%)			
	225 Asian/Pacific Islander (1.1%)			
	70 Other race (0.3%)			
	434 Hispanic Origin* (2.1%)			
2000	20,821	4.2%	—	90
	18,388 White alone (88.3%)			
	1,644 Black or African American alone (7.9%)			
	29 American Indian and Alaska Native alone (0.1%)			
	257 Asian alone (1.2%)			
	3 Native Hawaiian and Other Pacific Islander alone (0.0%)			
	258 Some other race alone (1.2%)			
	242 Two or more races (1.2%)			
	831 Hispanic or Latino* (4.0%)			

Flossmoor, IL (inc. 1924)

	Total (and by category)	Foreign born	Native with foreign parentage	Males per 100 females
1930	808	—	—	—
1960	4,624	3.1%	20.2%	97
	4,594 White (99.4%)			
	30 Negro (0.6%)			
1990	8,651	6.0%	—	95
	7,295 White (84.3%)			
	910 Black (10.5%)			
	446 Asian/Pacific Islander (5.2%)			
	9 Hispanic Origin* (0.1%)			
2000	9,301	10.0%	—	92
	6,167 White alone (66.3%)			
	2,522 Black or African American alone (27.1%)			
	8 American Indian and Alaska Native alone (0.1%)			
	393 Asian alone (4.2%)			
	51 Some other race alone (0.5%)			
	160 Two or more races (1.7%)			
	223 Hispanic or Latino* (2.4%)			

Ford Heights, IL (inc. 1949)

	Total (and by category)	Foreign born	Native with foreign parentage	Males per 100 females
1960	3,270	2.4%	6.1%	96
	460 White (14.1%)			
	16 Negro (0.5%)			
	2,794 Other races (85.4%)			
1990	4,259	0.0%	—	85
	24 White (0.6%)			
	4,226 Black (99.2%)			
	9 American Indian (0.2%)			
	23 Hispanic Origin* (0.5%)			
2000	3,456	0.6%	—	87
	61 White alone (1.8%)			
	3,314 Black or African American alone (95.9%)			
	2 American Indian and Alaska Native alone (0.1%)			
	4 Asian alone (0.1%)			
	40 Some other race alone (1.2%)			
	35 Two or more races (1.0%)			
	87 Hispanic or Latino* (2.5%)			

Forest Park, IL (inc. 1907)

	Total (and by category)	Foreign born	Native with foreign parentage	Males per 100 females
1900	4,085	38.0%	13.6%	121
	3,975 White (97.3%)			
	106 Negro (2.6%)			
	4 Chinese (0.1%)			
1930	14,555	23.2%	42.0%	101
	14,536 White (99.9%)			
	1 Negro (0.0%)			
	18 Other (0.1%)			
1960	14,452	11.8%	28.9%	92
	14,419 White (99.8%)			
	6 Negro (0.0%)			
	27 Other races (0.2%)			
1990	14,918	14.4%	—	89
	11,467 White (76.9%)			
	1,953 Black (13.1%)			
	1,260 Asian/Pacific Islander (8.4%)			
	238 Other race (1.6%)			
	698 Hispanic Origin* (4.7%)			
2000	15,688	14.8%	—	90
	8,808 White alone (56.1%)			
	4,892 Black or African American alone (31.2%)			
	23 American Indian and Alaska Native alone (0.1%)			
	1,071 Asian alone (6.8%)			
	11 Native Hawaiian and Other Pacific Islander alone (0.1%)			
	440 Some other race alone (2.8%)			
	443 Two or more races (2.8%)			
	1,230 Hispanic or Latino* (7.8%)			

Forest View, IL (inc. 1924)

	Total (and by category)	Foreign born	Native with foreign parentage	Males per 100 females
1930	125	—	—	—
1960	1,042	—	—	101
	1,042 White (100.0%)			
1990	743	3.6%	—	88
	724 White (97.4%)			
	2 Asian/Pacific Islander (0.3%)			
	10 Other race (1.3%)			
	33 Hispanic Origin* (4.4%)			
2000	778	5.1%	—	100
	723 White alone (92.9%)			
	3 Black or African American alone (0.4%)			
	37 Some other race alone (4.8%)			
	15 Two or more races (1.9%)			
	81 Hispanic or Latino* (10.4%)			

Fox Lake, IL (inc. 1906)

	Total (and by category)	Foreign born	Native with foreign parentage	Males per 100 females
1930	880	—	—	—
1960	3,700	9.7%	24.8%	102
	3,693 White (99.8%)			
	7 Other races (0.2%)			
1990	7,478	3.4%	—	96
	7,256 White (97.0%)			
	18 American Indian (0.2%)			
	59 Asian/Pacific Islander (0.8%)			
	97 Other race (1.3%)			
	160 Hispanic Origin* (2.1%)			

Year	Population	Race/Origin			
2000	9,178		6.7%	—	101
	8,764	White alone (95.5%)			
	70	Black or African American alone (0.8%)			
	22	American Indian and Alaska Native alone (0.2%)			
	60	Asian alone (0.7%)			
	5	Native Hawaiian and Other Pacific Islander alone (0.1%)			
	141	Some other race alone (1.5%)			
	116	Two or more races (1.3%)			
	533	Hispanic or Latino* (5.8%)			

Fox River Grove, IL (inc. 1919)

Year	Population	Race/Origin			
1930	641		—	—	—
1960	1,866		—	—	91
	1,865	White (99.9%)			
	1	Negro (0.1%)			
1990	3,551		5.5%	—	100
	3,645	White (102.6%)			
	4	Black (0.1%)			
	28	Other race (0.8%)			
	102	Hispanic Origin* (2.9%)			
2000	4,862		4.4%	—	105
	4,663	White alone (95.9%)			
	33	Black or African American alone (0.7%)			
	6	American Indian and Alaska Native alone (0.1%)			
	62	Asian alone (1.3%)			
	55	Some other race alone (1.1%)			
	43	Two or more races (0.9%)			
	186	Hispanic or Latino* (3.8%)			

Fox River Valley Gardens, IL (inc. 1969)

Year	Population	Race/Origin			
1990	665		1.7%	—	94
	652	White (98.0%)			
	11	Other race (1.7%)			
	19	Hispanic Origin* (2.9%)			
2000	788		9.1%	—	97
	769	White alone (97.6%)			
	4	Black or African American alone (0.5%)			
	8	Asian alone (1.0%)			
	1	Native Hawaiian and Other Pacific Islander alone (0.1%)			
	2	Some other race alone (0.3%)			
	4	Two or more races (0.5%)			
	22	Hispanic or Latino* (2.8%)			

Frankfort, IL (inc. 1879)

Year	Population	Race/Origin			
1900	250		—	—	—
1930	590		—	—	—
1960	1,135		—	—	97
	1,135	White (100.0%)			
1990	7,180		4.1%	—	97
	7,081	White (98.6%)			
	5	Black (0.1%)			
	12	American Indian (0.2%)			
	65	Asian/Pacific Islander (0.9%)			
	17	Other race (0.2%)			
	93	Hispanic Origin* (1.3%)			
2000	10,391		4.2%	—	94
	9,753	White alone (93.9%)			
	258	Black or African American alone (2.5%)			
	18	American Indian and Alaska Native alone (0.2%)			
	221	Asian alone (2.1%)			
	64	Some other race alone (0.6%)			
	77	Two or more races (0.7%)			
	240	Hispanic or Latino* (2.3%)			

Franklin Park, IL (inc. 1892)

Year	Population	Race/Origin			
1900	483		—	—	—
1930	2,425		15.8%	33.9%	118
	2,378	White (98.1%)			
	47	Other (1.9%)			
1960	18,322		7.6%	27.5%	102
	18,299	White (99.9%)			
	1	Negro (0.0%)			
	22	Other races (0.1%)			
1990	18,485		20.5%	—	97
	16,023	White (86.7%)			
	38	Black (0.2%)			
	14	American Indian (0.1%)			
	202	Asian/Pacific Islander (1.1%)			
	2,208	Other race (11.9%)			
	3,813	Hispanic Origin* (20.6%)			
2000	19,434		32.8%	—	100
	15,401	White alone (79.2%)			
	147	Black or African American alone (0.8%)			
	57	American Indian and Alaska Native alone (0.3%)			
	481	Asian alone (2.5%)			
	9	Native Hawaiian and Other Pacific Islander alone (0.0%)			
	2,840	Some other race alone (14.6%)			
	499	Two or more races (2.6%)			
	7,399	Hispanic or Latino* (38.1%)			

Gary, IN (inc. 1906)

Year	Population	Race/Origin			
1930	100,426		19.3%	25.9%	119
	78,992	White (78.7%)			
	17,922	Negro (17.8%)			
	2	Indian (0.0%)			
	13	Chinese (0.0%)			
	7	Japanese (0.0%)			
	3,486	Mexican (3.5%)			
	4	Other (0.0%)			
1960	178,415		7.7%	14.7%	99
	108,980	White (61.1%)			
	69,123	Negro (38.7%)			
	217	Other races (0.1%)			
1990	116,646		1.4%	—	85
	18,995	White (16.3%)			
	94,013	Black (80.6%)			
	207	American Indian (0.2%)			
	145	Asian/Pacific Islander (0.1%)			
	3,286	Other race (2.8%)			
	6,282	Hispanic Origin* (5.4%)			
2000	102,746		1.6%	—	85
	12,245	White alone (11.9%)			
	86,340	Black or African American alone (84.0%)			
	213	American Indian and Alaska Native alone (0.2%)			
	140	Asian alone (0.1%)			
	24	Native Hawaiian and Other Pacific Islander alone (0.0%)			
	2,023	Some other race alone (2.0%)			
	1,761	Two or more races (1.7%)			
	5,065	Hispanic or Latino* (4.9%)			

Geneva, IL (inc. 1867)

Year	Population	Race/Origin			
1900	2,446		—	—	—
1930	4,607		18.2%	32.8%	76
	4,415	White (95.8%)			
	169	Negro (3.7%)			
	23	Other (0.5%)			
1960	7,646		6.2%	21.5%	87
	7,420	White (97.0%)			
	208	Negro (2.7%)			
	13	Other races (0.2%)			
1990	12,617		2.8%	—	97
	12,340	White (97.8%)			
	31	Black (0.2%)			
	55	American Indian (0.4%)			
	191	Asian/Pacific Islander (1.5%)			
	79	Hispanic Origin* (0.6%)			
2000	19,515		4.5%	—	100
	18,832	White alone (96.5%)			
	199	Black or African American alone (1.0%)			
	11	American Indian and Alaska Native alone (0.1%)			
	244	Asian alone (1.3%)			
	5	Native Hawaiian and Other Pacific Islander alone (0.0%)			
	114	Some other race alone (0.6%)			
	110	Two or more races (0.6%)			
	541	Hispanic or Latino* (2.8%)			

Gilberts, IL (inc. 1890)

Year	Population	Race/Origin			
1900	222		—	—	—
1930	130		—	—	—
1960	238		—	—	—
1990	987		3.6%	—	94
	963	White (97.6%)			
	2	Asian/Pacific Islander (0.2%)			
	2	Other race (0.2%)			
	15	Hispanic Origin* (1.5%)			
2000	1,279		2.3%	—	98
	1,226	White alone (95.9%)			
	2	Black or African American alone (0.2%)			
	4	American Indian and Alaska Native alone (0.3%)			
	21	Asian alone (1.6%)			
	20	Some other race alone (1.6%)			
	6	Two or more races (0.5%)			
	43	Hispanic or Latino* (3.4%)			

Glen Ellyn, IL (inc. 1892)

Year	Population	Race/Origin			
1900	793		—	—	—
1930	7,680		10.0%	27.8%	97
	7,637	White (99.4%)			
	36	Negro (0.5%)			
	7	Other (0.1%)			
1960	15,972		3.9%	17.2%	95
	15,890	White (99.5%)			
	61	Negro (0.4%)			
	21	Other races (0.1%)			
1990	24,944		6.5%	—	97
	23,530	White (94.3%)			
	345	Black (1.4%)			
	25	American Indian (0.1%)			
	762	Asian/Pacific Islander (3.1%)			
	282	Other race (1.1%)			
	704	Hispanic Origin* (2.8%)			
2000	26,999		10.8%	—	95
	24,163	White alone (89.5%)			
	575	Black or African American alone (2.1%)			
	39	American Indian and Alaska Native alone (0.1%)			
	1,280	Asian alone (4.7%)			
	2	Native Hawaiian and Other Pacific Islander alone (0.0%)			
	493	Some other race alone (1.8%)			
	447	Two or more races (1.7%)			
	1,275	Hispanic or Latino* (4.7%)			

Glencoe, IL (inc. 1869)

Year	Population	Race/Origin			
1900	1,020		—	—	—
1930	6,295		16.9%	27.0%	82
	5,975	White (94.9%)			
	313	Negro (5.0%)			
	7	Other (0.1%)			
1960	10,472		6.8%	28.2%	88
	9,794	White (93.5%)			
	655	Negro (6.3%)			
	23	Other races (0.2%)			
1990	8,499		7.1%	—	92
	8,000	White (94.1%)			
	279	Black (3.3%)			
	202	Asian/Pacific Islander (2.4%)			
	18	Other race (0.2%)			
	77	Hispanic Origin* (0.9%)			
2000	8,762		6.5%	—	95
	8,330	White alone (95.1%)			
	176	Black or African American alone (2.0%)			
	4	American Indian and Alaska Native alone (0.0%)			
	147	Asian alone (1.7%)			
	23	Some other race alone (0.3%)			
	82	Two or more races (0.9%)			
	108	Hispanic or Latino* (1.2%)			

Glendale Heights, IL (inc. 1959)

Year	Population	Race/Origin			
1990	27,973		15.3%	—	102
	22,856	White (81.7%)			
	754	Black (2.7%)			
	40	American Indian (0.1%)			
	3,718	Asian/Pacific Islander (13.3%)			
	605	Other race (2.2%)			
	1,737	Hispanic Origin* (6.2%)			

Municipalities *(continued)*

	Total (and by category)	Foreign born	Native with foreign parentage	Males per 100 females
2000	31,765	30.2%	—	104
	20,263	White alone (63.8%)		
	1,537	Black or African American alone (4.8%)		
	95	American Indian and Alaska Native alone (0.3%)		
	6,345	Asian alone (20.0%)		
	25	Native Hawaiian and Other Pacific Islander alone (0.1%)		
	2,576	Some other race alone (8.1%)		
	924	Two or more races (2.9%)		
	5,842	Hispanic or Latino* (18.4%)		

Glenview, IL (inc. 1899)

	Total (and by category)	Foreign born	Native with foreign parentage	Males per 100 females
1930	1,886	17.0%	35.7%	109
	1,886	White (100.0%)		
1960	18,132	4.4%	20.2%	97
	18,116	White (99.9%)		
	14	Negro (0.1%)		
	2	Other races (0.0%)		
1990	37,093	11.3%	—	95
	33,847	White (91.2%)		
	233	Black (0.6%)		
	38	American Indian (0.1%)		
	2,641	Asian/Pacific Islander (7.1%)		
	334	Other race (0.9%)		
	912	Hispanic Origin* (2.5%)		
2000	41,847	19.4%	—	92
	35,817	White alone (85.6%)		
	665	Black or African American alone (1.6%)		
	41	American Indian and Alaska Native alone (0.1%)		
	4,207	Asian alone (10.1%)		
	7	Native Hawaiian and Other Pacific Islander alone (0.0%)		
	532	Some other race alone (1.3%)		
	578	Two or more races (1.4%)		
	1,702	Hispanic or Latino* (4.1%)		

Glenwood, IL (inc. 1903)

	Total (and by category)	Foreign born	Native with foreign parentage	Males per 100 females
1930	603	—	—	—
1960	882	—	—	—
1990	9,289	3.4%	—	91
	6,763	White (72.8%)		
	2,356	Black (25.4%)		
	11	American Indian (0.1%)		
	83	Asian/Pacific Islander (0.9%)		
	76	Other race (0.8%)		
	197	Hispanic Origin* (2.1%)		
2000	9,000	3.5%	—	87
	4,615	White alone (51.3%)		
	4,008	Black or African American alone (44.5%)		
	9	American Indian and Alaska Native alone (0.1%)		
	56	Asian alone (0.6%)		
	9	Native Hawaiian and Other Pacific Islander alone (0.1%)		
	203	Some other race alone (2.3%)		
	100	Two or more races (1.1%)		
	452	Hispanic or Latino* (5.0%)		

Godley, IL (inc. 1888)

	Total (and by category)	Foreign born	Native with foreign parentage	Males per 100 females
1900	329	—	—	—
1930	60	—	—	—
1960	97	—	—	—
1990	322	0.3%	—	94
	323	White (100.3%)		
	15	Hispanic Origin* (4.7%)		
2000	594	1.9%	—	98
	573	White alone (96.5%)		
	1	Black or African American alone (0.2%)		
	18	Some other race alone (3.0%)		
	2	Two or more races (0.3%)		
	36	Hispanic or Latino* (6.1%)		

Golf, IL (inc. 1928)

	Total (and by category)	Foreign born	Native with foreign parentage	Males per 100 females
1930	112	—	—	—
1960	409	—	—	—
1990	454	6.6%	—	102
	447	White (98.5%)		
	10	Asian/Pacific Islander (2.2%)		
	8	Hispanic Origin* (1.8%)		
2000	451	3.8%	—	95
	446	White alone (98.9%)		
	4	Asian alone (0.9%)		
	1	Some other race alone (0.2%)		
	3	Hispanic or Latino* (0.7%)		

Grayslake, IL (inc. 1895)

	Total (and by category)	Foreign born	Native with foreign parentage	Males per 100 females
1900	416	—	—	—
1930	1,120	10.8%	27.9%	100
	1,120	White (100.0%)		
1960	3,762	3.4%	15.2%	100
	3,672	White (97.6%)		
1990	7,388	2.8%	—	95
	7,281	White (98.6%)		
	7	American Indian (0.1%)		
	76	Asian/Pacific Islander (1.0%)		
	24	Other race (0.3%)		
	199	Hispanic Origin* (2.7%)		
2000	18,506	8.4%	—	96
	16,840	White alone (91.0%)		
	293	Black or African American alone (1.6%)		
	35	American Indian and Alaska Native alone (0.2%)		
	783	Asian alone (4.2%)		
	6	Native Hawaiian and Other Pacific Islander alone (0.0%)		
	314	Some other race alone (1.7%)		
	235	Two or more races (1.3%)		
	920	Hispanic or Latino* (5.0%)		

Green Oaks, IL (inc. 1960)

	Total (and by category)	Foreign born	Native with foreign parentage	Males per 100 females
1990	2,101	9.5%	—	104
	1,989	White (94.7%)		
	7	Black (0.3%)		
	101	Asian/Pacific Islander (4.8%)		
	4	Other race (0.2%)		
	13	Hispanic Origin* (0.6%)		
2000	3,572	9.8%	—	101
	3,245	White alone (90.8%)		
	62	Black or African American alone (1.7%)		
	5	American Indian and Alaska Native alone (0.1%)		
	195	Asian alone (5.5%)		
	15	Some other race alone (0.4%)		
	50	Two or more races (1.4%)		
	94	Hispanic or Latino* (2.6%)		

Greenwood, IL (inc. 1995)

	Total (and by category)	Foreign born	Native with foreign parentage	Males per 100 females
1990	203	—	—	—
2000	244	0.0%	—	102
	227	White alone (93.0%)		
	6	Asian alone (2.5%)		
	2	Some other race alone (0.8%)		
	9	Two or more races (3.7%)		
	16	Hispanic or Latino* (6.6%)		

Griffith, IN (inc. 1904)

	Total (and by category)	Foreign born	Native with foreign parentage	Males per 100 females
1930	1,176	9.0%	23.3%	101
	1,170	White (99.5%)		
	6	Negro (0.5%)		
1960	9,483	2.9%	14.8%	102
	9,468	White (99.8%)		
	13	Negro (0.1%)		
	2	Other races (0.0%)		
1990	17,916	3.4%	—	98
	17,033	White (95.1%)		
	450	Black (2.5%)		
	15	American Indian (0.1%)		
	144	Asian/Pacific Islander (0.8%)		
	274	Other race (1.5%)		
	949	Hispanic Origin* (5.3%)		
2000	17,334	3.1%	—	94
	14,562	White alone (84.0%)		
	1,753	Black or African American alone (10.1%)		
	60	American Indian and Alaska Native alone (0.3%)		
	140	Asian alone (0.8%)		
	7	Native Hawaiian and Other Pacific Islander alone (0.0%)		
	495	Some other race alone (2.9%)		
	317	Two or more races (1.8%)		
	1,461	Hispanic or Latino* (8.4%)		

Gurnee, IL (inc. 1928)

	Total (and by category)	Foreign born	Native with foreign parentage	Males per 100 females
1930	503	—	—	—
1960	1,831	—	—	99
	1,827	White (99.8%)		
	4	Other races (0.2%)		
1990	13,701	5.9%	—	96
	12,558	White (91.7%)		
	457	Black (3.3%)		
	69	American Indian (0.5%)		
	529	Asian/Pacific Islander (3.9%)		
	88	Other race (0.6%)		
	366	Hispanic Origin* (2.7%)		
2000	28,834	11.7%	—	94
	23,679	White alone (82.1%)		
	1,459	Black or African American alone (5.1%)		
	52	American Indian and Alaska Native alone (0.2%)		
	2,364	Asian alone (8.2%)		
	15	Native Hawaiian and Other Pacific Islander alone (0.1%)		
	621	Some other race alone (2.2%)		
	644	Two or more races (2.2%)		
	1,738	Hispanic or Latino* (6.0%)		

Hainesville, IL (inc. 1847)

	Total (and by category)	Foreign born	Native with foreign parentage	Males per 100 females
1930	81	—	—	—
1960	132	—	—	—
1990	134	3.7%	—	79
	134	White (100.0%)		
	1	Other race (0.7%)		
	13	Hispanic Origin* (9.7%)		
2000	2,129	14.7%	—	102
	1,833	White alone (86.1%)		
	37	Black or African American alone (1.7%)		
	2	American Indian and Alaska Native alone (0.1%)		
	120	Asian alone (5.6%)		
	1	Native Hawaiian and Other Pacific Islander alone (0.0%)		
	98	Some other race alone (4.6%)		
	38	Two or more races (1.8%)		
	198	Hispanic or Latino* (9.3%)		

Hammond, IN (inc. 1883)

	Total (and by category)	Foreign born	Native with foreign parentage	Males per 100 females
1900	12,376	25.5%	39.1%	111
	12,356	White (99.8%)		
	17	Negro (0.1%)		
	2	Chinese (0.0%)		
	1	Indian (0.0%)		
1930	64,560	15.0%	30.3%	109
	63,845	White (98.9%)		
	623	Negro (1.0%)		
	4	Chinese (0.0%)		
	86	Mexican (0.1%)		
	2	Other (0.0%)		
1960	111,698	6.1%	19.5%	100
	109,112	White (97.7%)		
	2,434	Negro (2.2%)		
	152	Other races (0.1%)		
1990	84,236	4.4%	—	94
	71,553	White (84.9%)		
	7,611	Black (9.0%)		
	350	American Indian (0.4%)		
	268	Asian/Pacific Islander (0.3%)		
	4,454	Other race (5.3%)		
	9,851	Hispanic Origin* (11.7%)		

2000	83,048	7.3%	—	95
	60,089	White alone (72.4%)		
	12,102	Black or African American alone (14.6%)		
	339	American Indian and Alaska Native alone (0.4%)		
	383	Asian alone (0.5%)		
	64	Native Hawaiian and Other Pacific Islander alone (0.1%)		
	7,741	Some other race alone (9.3%)		
	2,330	Two or more races (2.8%)		
	17,473	Hispanic or Latino* (21.0%)		

Hampshire, IL (inc. 1876)

1900	760	—	—	—
1930	656	—	—	—
1960	1,309	—	—	96
	1,308	White (99.9%)		
	1	Other races (0.1%)		
1990	1,843	1.7%	—	96
	1,835	White (99.6%)		
	2	Black (0.1%)		
	9	American Indian (0.5%)		
	3	Asian/Pacific Islander (0.2%)		
	9	Other race (0.5%)		
	39	Hispanic Origin* (2.1%)		
2000	2,900	2.0%	—	93
	2,848	White alone (98.2%)		
	3	Black or African American alone (0.1%)		
	11	American Indian and Alaska Native alone (0.4%)		
	4	Asian alone (0.1%)		
	18	Some other race alone (0.6%)		
	16	Two or more races (0.6%)		
	70	Hispanic or Latino* (2.4%)		

Hanover Park, IL (inc. 1958)

1960	451	—	—	—
1990	32,895	13.7%	—	106
	28,048	White (85.3%)		
	1,258	Black (3.8%)		
	173	American Indian (0.5%)		
	2,432	Asian/Pacific Islander (7.4%)		
	970	Other race (2.9%)		
	3,462	Hispanic Origin* (10.5%)		
2000	38,278	28.5%	—	106
	26,077	White alone (68.1%)		
	2,348	Black or African American alone (6.1%)		
	109	American Indian and Alaska Native alone (0.3%)		
	4,574	Asian alone (11.9%)		
	6	Native Hawaiian and Other Pacific Islander alone (0.0%)		
	3,967	Some other race alone (10.4%)		
	1,197	Two or more races (3.1%)		
	10,233	Hispanic or Latino* (26.7%)		

Harvard, IL (inc. 1867)

1870	1,120	17.9%	—	—
	1,102	White (98.4%)		
	18	Colored (1.6%)		
1900	2,602	16.0%	30.0%	103
	2,601	White (100.0%)		
	1	Negro (0.0%)		
1930	2,988	9.5%	30.7%	97
	2,975	White (99.6%)		
	2	Negro (0.1%)		
	11	Other (0.4%)		
1960	4,248	3.6%	17.4%	93
	4,246	White (100.0%)		
	1	Negro (0.0%)		
	1	Other races (0.0%)		
1990	5,975	9.3%	—	100
	5,357	White (89.7%)		
	10	American Indian (0.2%)		
	18	Asian/Pacific Islander (0.3%)		
	590	Other race (9.9%)		
	652	Hispanic Origin* (10.9%)		

2000	7,996	27.3%	—	108
	6,097	White alone (76.3%)		
	68	Black or African American alone (0.9%)		
	30	American Indian and Alaska Native alone (0.4%)		
	114	Asian alone (1.4%)		
	1	Native Hawaiian and Other Pacific Islander alone (0.0%)		
	1,500	Some other race alone (18.8%)		
	186	Two or more races (2.3%)		
	3,023	Hispanic or Latino* (37.8%)		

Harvey, IL (inc. 1891)

1900	5,395	18.2%	29.2%	111
	5,312	White (98.5%)		
	83	Negro (1.5%)		
1930	16,374	16.4%	29.8%	107
	15,957	White (97.5%)		
	405	Negro (2.5%)		
	12	Other (0.1%)		
1960	29,071	5.3%	17.3%	100
	27,065	White (93.1%)		
	1,986	Negro (6.8%)		
	20	Other races (0.1%)		
1990	29,771	4.4%	—	92
	4,459	White (15.0%)		
	23,962	Black (80.5%)		
	39	American Indian (0.1%)		
	19	Asian/Pacific Islander (0.1%)		
	1,288	Other race (4.3%)		
	1,762	Hispanic Origin* (5.9%)		
2000	30,000	8.3%	—	92
	3,005	White alone (10.0%)		
	23,871	Black or African American alone (79.6%)		
	79	American Indian and Alaska Native alone (0.3%)		
	114	Asian alone (0.4%)		
	16	Native Hawaiian and Other Pacific Islander alone (0.1%)		
	2,382	Some other race alone (7.9%)		
	533	Two or more races (1.8%)		
	3,834	Hispanic or Latino* (12.8%)		

Harwood Heights, IL (inc. 1947)

1960	5,688	9.3%	30.3%	101
	5,682	White (99.9%)		
	6	Other races (0.1%)		
1990	7,680	23.9%	—	86
	7,393	White (96.3%)		
	209	Asian/Pacific Islander (2.7%)		
	78	Other race (1.0%)		
	256	Hispanic Origin* (3.3%)		
2000	8,297	33.8%	—	88
	7,644	White alone (92.1%)		
	26	Black or African American alone (0.3%)		
	20	American Indian and Alaska Native alone (0.2%)		
	367	Asian alone (4.4%)		
	2	Native Hawaiian and Other Pacific Islander alone (0.0%)		
	128	Some other race alone (1.5%)		
	110	Two or more races (1.3%)		
	484	Hispanic or Latino* (5.8%)		

Hawthorn Woods, IL (inc. 1958)

1960	239	—	—	—
1990	4,423	5.5%	—	106
	4,280	White (96.8%)		
	43	Black (1.0%)		
	107	Asian/Pacific Islander (2.4%)		
	32	Hispanic Origin* (0.7%)		
2000	6,002	7.6%	—	101
	5,675	White alone (94.6%)		
	42	Black or African American alone (0.7%)		
	1	American Indian and Alaska Native alone (0.0%)		
	186	Asian alone (3.1%)		
	4	Native Hawaiian and Other Pacific Islander alone (0.1%)		
	34	Some other race alone (0.6%)		
	60	Two or more races (1.0%)		
	124	Hispanic or Latino* (2.1%)		

Hazel Crest, IL (inc. 1911)

1930	1,162	13.9%	29.3%	106
	1,162	White (100.0%)		
1960	6,205	2.8%	17.1%	98
	6,202	White (100.0%)		
	1	Negro (0.0%)		
	2	Other races (0.0%)		
1990	13,334	3.0%	—	89
	6,179	White (46.3%)		
	6,889	Black (51.7%)		
	30	American Indian (0.2%)		
	154	Asian/Pacific Islander (1.2%)		
	82	Other race (0.6%)		
	471	Hispanic Origin* (3.5%)		
2000	14,816	3.4%	—	84
	2,885	White alone (19.5%)		
	11,308	Black or African American alone (76.3%)		
	18	American Indian and Alaska Native alone (0.1%)		
	138	Asian alone (0.9%)		
	3	Native Hawaiian and Other Pacific Islander alone (0.0%)		
	220	Some other race alone (1.5%)		
	244	Two or more races (1.6%)		
	494	Hispanic or Latino* (3.3%)		

Hebron, IL (inc. 1895)

1900	611	—	—	—
1930	608	—	—	—
1960	701	—	—	—
1990	809	1.0%	—	99
	780	White (96.4%)		
	4	Black (0.5%)		
	3	Other race (0.4%)		
	3	Hispanic Origin* (0.4%)		
2000	1,038	1.3%	—	100
	1,015	White alone (97.8%)		
	4	Black or African American alone (0.4%)		
	1	Asian alone (0.1%)		
	12	Some other race alone (1.2%)		
	6	Two or more races (0.6%)		
	55	Hispanic or Latino* (5.3%)		

Hebron, IN (inc. 1886)

1900	794	—	—	—
1930	693	—	—	—
1960	1,401	—	—	100
	1,401	White (100.0%)		
1990	3,183	1.0%	—	90
	3,169	White (99.6%)		
	7	American Indian (0.2%)		
	7	Asian/Pacific Islander (0.2%)		
	47	Hispanic Origin* (1.5%)		
2000	3,596	1.8%	—	92
	3,466	White alone (96.4%)		
	10	Black or African American alone (0.3%)		
	4	American Indian and Alaska Native alone (0.1%)		
	10	Asian alone (0.3%)		
	46	Some other race alone (1.3%)		
	60	Two or more races (1.7%)		
	148	Hispanic or Latino* (4.1%)		

Hickory Hills, IL (inc. 1951)

1960	2,707	4.4%	25.5%	101
	2,704	White (99.9%)		
	3	Other races (0.1%)		
1990	13,021	7.8%	—	98
	12,681	White (97.4%)		
	63	Black (0.5%)		
	8	American Indian (0.1%)		
	112	Asian/Pacific Islander (0.9%)		
	157	Other race (1.2%)		
	506	Hispanic Origin* (3.9%)		

Municipalities *(continued)*

Year	Total (and by category)		Foreign born	Native with foreign parentage	Males per 100 females
2000	13,926		16.8%	—	98
	12,657	White alone (90.9%)			
	172	Black or African American alone (1.2%)			
	32	American Indian and Alaska Native alone (0.2%)			
	290	Asian alone (2.1%)			
	1	Native Hawaiian and Other Pacific Islander alone (0.0%)			
	331	Some other race alone (2.4%)			
	443	Two or more races (3.2%)			
	1,129	Hispanic or Latino* (8.1%)			

Highland Park, IL (inc. 1869)

Year	Total (and by category)		Foreign born	Native with foreign parentage	Males per 100 females
1900	2,806		23.3%	38.5%	100
	2,793	White (99.5%)			
	12	Negro (0.4%)			
	1	Chinese (0.0%)			
1930	12,203		18.5%	—	90
	12,004	White (98.4%)			
	177	Negro (1.5%)			
	22	Other (0.2%)			
1960	25,532		26.5%	34.9%	91
	24,979	White (97.8%)			
	504	Negro (2.0%)			
	49	Other races (0.2%)			
1990	30,575		10.9%	—	96
	28,756	White (94.1%)			
	684	Black (2.2%)			
	8	American Indian (0.0%)			
	775	Asian/Pacific Islander (2.5%)			
	352	Other race (1.2%)			
	1,274	Hispanic Origin* (4.2%)			
2000	31,365		15.3%	—	96
	28,606	White alone (91.2%)			
	559	Black or African American alone (1.8%)			
	24	American Indian and Alaska Native alone (0.1%)			
	716	Asian alone (2.3%)			
	4	Native Hawaiian and Other Pacific Islander alone (0.0%)			
	1,086	Some other race alone (3.5%)			
	370	Two or more races (1.2%)			
	2,792	Hispanic or Latino* (8.9%)			

Highland, IN (inc. 1910)

Year	Total (and by category)		Foreign born	Native with foreign parentage	Males per 100 females
1930	1,553		15.9%	38.4%	109
	1,551	White (99.9%)			
	2	Negro (0.1%)			
1960	16,284		4.2%	19.0%	103
	16,280	White (100.0%)			
	4	Other races (0.0%)			
1990	23,696		4.5%	—	93
	23,172	White (97.8%)			
	66	Black (0.3%)			
	156	Asian/Pacific Islander (0.7%)			
	302	Other race (1.3%)			
	966	Hispanic Origin* (4.1%)			
2000	23,546		4.5%	—	92
	22,240	White alone (94.5%)			
	296	Black or African American alone (1.3%)			
	36	American Indian and Alaska Native alone (0.2%)			
	260	Asian alone (1.1%)			
	5	Native Hawaiian and Other Pacific Islander alone (0.0%)			
	425	Some other race alone (1.8%)			
	284	Two or more races (1.2%)			
	1,557	Hispanic or Latino* (6.6%)			

Highwood, IL (inc. 1886)

Year	Total (and by category)		Foreign born	Native with foreign parentage	Males per 100 females
1900	1,575		—	—	—
1930	3,590		36.8%	40.2%	128
	3,589	White (100.0%)			
	1	Other (0.0%)			
1960	4,499		27.9%	25.4%	103
	4,350	White (96.7%)			
	102	Negro (2.3%)			
	47	Other races (1.0%)			
1990	5,331		29.0%	—	108
	4,554	White (85.4%)			
	239	Black (4.5%)			
	13	American Indian (0.2%)			
	85	Asian/Pacific Islander (1.6%)			
	440	Other race (8.3%)			
	1,261	Hispanic Origin* (23.7%)			
2000	4,143		38.0%	—	99
	3,030	White alone (73.1%)			
	89	Black or African American alone (2.1%)			
	24	American Indian and Alaska Native alone (0.6%)			
	88	Asian alone (2.1%)			
	2	Native Hawaiian and Other Pacific Islander alone (0.0%)			
	712	Some other race alone (17.2%)			
	198	Two or more races (4.8%)			
	1,584	Hispanic or Latino* (38.2%)			

Hillside, IL (inc. 1905)

Year	Total (and by category)		Foreign born	Native with foreign parentage	Males per 100 females
1930	1,004		18.7%	43.4%	126
	1,004	White (100.0%)			
1960	7,794		4.6%	23.7%	99
	7,778	White (99.8%)			
	3	Negro (0.0%)			
	13	Other races (0.2%)			
1990	7,672		9.3%	—	94
	6,620	White (86.3%)			
	482	Black (6.3%)			
	7	American Indian (0.1%)			
	374	Asian/Pacific Islander (4.9%)			
	189	Other race (2.5%)			
	287	Hispanic Origin* (3.7%)			
2000	8,155		13.7%	—	93
	4,020	White alone (49.3%)			
	3,008	Black or African American alone (36.9%)			
	14	American Indian and Alaska Native alone (0.2%)			
	418	Asian alone (5.1%)			
	5	Native Hawaiian and Other Pacific Islander alone (0.1%)			
	472	Some other race alone (5.8%)			
	218	Two or more races (2.7%)			
	1,068	Hispanic or Latino* (13.1%)			

Hinsdale, IL (inc. 1873)

Year	Total (and by category)		Foreign born	Native with foreign parentage	Males per 100 females
1900	2,578		22.7%	30.7%	91
	2,517	White (97.6%)			
	37	Negro (1.4%)			
1930	6,923		14.0%	30.6%	87
	5,788	White (83.6%)			
	86	Negro (1.2%)			
	4	Other (0.1%)			
1960	12,859		4.4%	17.5%	93
	12,763	White (99.3%)			
	68	Negro (0.5%)			
	28	Other races (0.2%)			
1990	16,029		6.1%	—	93
	15,181	White (94.7%)			
	124	Black (0.8%)			
	10	American Indian (0.1%)			
	699	Asian/Pacific Islander (4.4%)			
	26	Other race (0.2%)			
	146	Hispanic Origin* (0.9%)			
2000	17,349		9.1%	—	92
	16,187	White alone (93.3%)			
	136	Black or African American alone (0.8%)			
	12	American Indian and Alaska Native alone (0.1%)			
	777	Asian alone (4.5%)			
	4	Native Hawaiian and Other Pacific Islander alone (0.0%)			
	86	Some other race alone (0.5%)			
	147	Two or more races (0.8%)			
	414	Hispanic or Latino* (2.4%)			

Hobart, IN (inc. 1889)

Year	Total (and by category)		Foreign born	Native with foreign parentage	Males per 100 females
1870	1,037		39.9%	—	—
	1,037	White (100.0%)			
1900	1,390		—	—	—
1930	5,787		11.5%	29.3%	100
	5,779	White (99.9%)			
	4	Negro (0.1%)			
	4	Other (0.1%)			
1960	18,680		3.7%	14.4%	98
	18,673	White (100.0%)			
	7	Negro (0.0%)			
	10	Other races (0.1%)			
1990	21,822		2.9%	—	94
	21,370	White (97.9%)			
	46	Black (0.2%)			
	45	American Indian (0.2%)			
	109	Asian/Pacific Islander (0.5%)			
	252	Other race (1.2%)			
	1,045	Hispanic Origin* (4.8%)			
2000	25,363		2.9%	—	94
	23,773	White alone (93.7%)			
	353	Black or African American alone (1.4%)			
	53	American Indian and Alaska Native alone (0.2%)			
	136	Asian alone (0.5%)			
	4	Native Hawaiian and Other Pacific Islander alone (0.0%)			
	660	Some other race alone (2.6%)			
	384	Two or more races (1.5%)			
	2,042	Hispanic or Latino* (8.1%)			

Hodgkins, IL (inc. 1896)

Year	Total (and by category)		Foreign born	Native with foreign parentage	Males per 100 females
1900	195		—	—	—
1930	302		—	—	—
1960	1,126		—	—	103
	1,126	White (100.0%)			
1990	1,963		22.9%	—	121
	1,473	White (75.0%)			
	2	Black (0.1%)			
	8	American Indian (0.4%)			
	52	Asian/Pacific Islander (2.6%)			
	409	Other race (20.8%)			
	589	Hispanic Origin* (30.0%)			
2000	2,134		33.3%	—	123
	1,746	White alone (81.8%)			
	3	Black or African American alone (0.1%)			
	10	American Indian and Alaska Native alone (0.5%)			
	1	Asian alone (0.0%)			
	347	Some other race alone (16.3%)			
	27	Two or more races (1.3%)			
	933	Hispanic or Latino* (43.7%)			

Hoffman Estates, IL (inc. 1959)

Year	Total (and by category)		Foreign born	Native with foreign parentage	Males per 100 females
1960	8,296		1.3%	13.6%	104
	8,203	White (98.9%)			
	13	Other races (0.2%)			
1990	46,561		12.4%	—	101
	40,585	White (87.2%)			
	1,312	Black (2.8%)			
	78	American Indian (0.2%)			
	3,715	Asian/Pacific Islander (8.0%)			
	871	Other race (1.9%)			
	2,450	Hispanic Origin* (5.3%)			
2000	49,495		23.5%	—	99
	36,837	White alone (74.4%)			
	2,166	Black or African American alone (4.4%)			
	86	American Indian and Alaska Native alone (0.2%)			
	7,461	Asian alone (15.1%)			
	12	Native Hawaiian and Other Pacific Islander alone (0.0%)			
	1,857	Some other race alone (3.8%)			
	1,076	Two or more races (2.2%)			
	5,198	Hispanic or Latino* (10.5%)			

Holiday Hills, IL (inc. 1976)

Year	Total (and by category)		Foreign born	Native with foreign parentage	Males per 100 females
1990	807		2.6%	—	110
	822	White (101.9%)			
	3	Black (0.4%)			
	4	Asian/Pacific Islander (0.5%)			
	10	Other race (1.2%)			
	26	Hispanic Origin* (3.2%)			

2000 831 3.4% — 103
785 White alone (94.5%)
10 Black or African American alone (1.2%)
3 American Indian and Alaska Native alone (0.4%)
3 Asian alone (0.4%)
1 Native Hawaiian and Other Pacific Islander alone (0.1%)
25 Some other race alone (3.0%)
4 Two or more races (0.5%)
43 Hispanic or Latino* (5.2%)

Hometown, IL (inc. 1953)

1960 7,479 3.4% 18.2% 96
7,479 White (100.0%)
1990 4,769 2.4% — 83
4,726 White (99.1%)
34 American Indian (0.7%)
9 Asian/Pacific Islander (0.2%)
31 Hispanic Origin* (0.7%)
2000 4,467 2.9% — 83

Homewood, IL (inc. 1893)

1900 352 — —
1930 3,227 14.8% 33.5% 102
3,225 White (99.9%)
2 Negro (0.1%)
1960 13,371 4.7% 20.6% 98
13,361 White (99.9%)
8 Negro (0.1%)
2 Other races (0.0%)
1990 19,278 3.9% — 89
17,674 White (91.7%)
1,216 Black (6.3%)
13 American Indian (0.1%)
298 Asian/Pacific Islander (1.5%)
77 Other race (0.4%)
310 Hispanic Origin* (1.6%)
2000 19,543 4.4% — 85
15,270 White alone (78.1%)
3,422 Black or African American alone (17.5%)
20 American Indian and Alaska Native alone (0.1%)
307 Asian alone (1.6%)
13 Native Hawaiian and Other Pacific Islander alone (0.1%)
207 Some other race alone (1.1%)
304 Two or more races (1.6%)
597 Hispanic or Latino* (3.1%)

Huntley, IL (inc. 1872)

1900 606 — — —
1930 670 — — —
1960 1,143 — — 95
1,137 White (99.5%)
6 Other races (0.5%)
1990 2,453 3.2% — 100
2,425 White (98.9%)
9 American Indian (0.4%)
13 Asian/Pacific Islander (0.5%)
6 Other race (0.2%)
45 Hispanic Origin* (1.8%)
2000 5,730 5.5% — 95
5,440 White alone (94.9%)
25 Black or African American alone (0.4%)
10 American Indian and Alaska Native alone (0.2%)
122 Asian alone (2.1%)
72 Some other race alone (1.3%)
61 Two or more races (1.1%)
245 Hispanic or Latino* (4.3%)

Indian Creek, IL (inc. 1958)

1960 239 — — —
1990 247 4.0% — 109
208 White (84.2%)
7 Asian/Pacific Islander (2.8%)

2000 194 2.6% — 106
188 White alone (96.9%)
1 Asian alone (0.5%)
4 Some other race alone (2.1%)
1 Two or more races (0.5%)
8 Hispanic or Latino* (4.1%)

Indian Head Park, IL (inc. 1959)

1960 385 — — —
1990 3,503 6.0% — 80
3,460 White (98.8%)
32 Asian/Pacific Islander (0.9%)
38 Hispanic Origin* (1.1%)
2000 3,685 6.8% — 79
3,535 White alone (95.9%)
32 Black or African American alone (0.9%)
2 American Indian and Alaska Native alone (0.1%)
73 Asian alone (2.0%)
1 Native Hawaiian and Other Pacific Islander alone (0.0%)
19 Some other race alone (0.5%)
23 Two or more races (0.6%)
72 Hispanic or Latino* (2.0%)

Inverness, IL (inc. 1962)

1990 6,503 7.8% — 101
6,151 White (94.6%)
66 Black (1.0%)
270 Asian/Pacific Islander (4.2%)
16 Other race (0.2%)
59 Hispanic Origin* (0.9%)
2000 6,749 10.5% — 99
6,207 White alone (92.0%)
45 Black or African American alone (0.7%)
6 American Indian and Alaska Native alone (0.1%)
421 Asian alone (6.2%)
6 Native Hawaiian and Other Pacific Islander alone (0.1%)
28 Some other race alone (0.4%)
36 Two or more races (0.5%)
128 Hispanic or Latino* (1.9%)

Island Lake, IL (inc. 1950)

1960 1,639 — — 97
1,633 White (99.6%)
3 Negro (0.2%)
3 Other races (0.2%)
1990 4,449 2.4% — 100
4,345 White (97.7%)
23 Black (0.5%)
56 Asian/Pacific Islander (1.3%)
46 Other race (1.0%)
194 Hispanic Origin* (4.4%)
2000 8,153 5.6% — 99
7,647 White alone (93.8%)
40 Black or African American alone (0.5%)
13 American Indian and Alaska Native alone (0.2%)
132 Asian alone (1.6%)
1 Native Hawaiian and Other Pacific Islander alone (0.0%)
222 Some other race alone (2.7%)
98 Two or more races (1.2%)
679 Hispanic or Latino* (8.3%)

Itasca, IL (inc. 1890)

1900 256 — — —
1930 594 — — —
1960 3,564 4.0% 23.6% 99
3,563 White (100.0%)
1 Other races (0.0%)
1990 6,947 10.0% — 99
6,552 White (94.3%)
110 Black (1.6%)
8 American Indian (0.1%)
227 Asian/Pacific Islander (3.3%)
50 Other race (0.7%)
324 Hispanic Origin* (4.7%)

2000 8,302 18.7% — 94
7,309 White alone (88.0%)
140 Black or African American alone (1.7%)
22 American Indian and Alaska Native alone (0.3%)
484 Asian alone (5.8%)
2 Native Hawaiian and Other Pacific Islander alone (0.0%)
143 Some other race alone (1.7%)
202 Two or more races (2.4%)
581 Hispanic or Latino* (7.0%)

Johnsburg, IL (inc. 1956)

1990 1,529 1.4% — 107
1,525 White (99.7%)
1 American Indian (0.1%)
3 Asian/Pacific Islander (0.2%)
13 Hispanic Origin* (0.9%)
2000 5,391 0.8% — 102
5,328 White alone (98.8%)
7 Black or African American alone (0.1%)
3 American Indian and Alaska Native alone (0.1%)
10 Asian alone (0.2%)
9 Some other race alone (0.2%)
34 Two or more races (0.6%)
82 Hispanic or Latino* (1.5%)

Joliet, IL (inc. 1845)

1840 2,558 — — —
2,552 Free white (99.8%)
6 Free colored (0.2%)
1870 7,263 31.7% — 100
7,228 White (99.5%)
35 Colored (0.5%)
1900 29,353 29.1% 32.3% 109
28,688 White (97.7%)
175 Negro (0.6%)
15 Chinese (0.1%)
1930 42,993 16.4% 38.4% 102
40,797 White (94.9%)
1,309 Negro (3.0%)
30 Indian (0.1%)
14 Chinese (0.0%)
845 Mexican (2.0%)
1 Other (0.0%)
1960 66,780 6.1% 22.2% 98
62,077 White (93.0%)
4,638 Negro (6.9%)
65 Other races (0.1%)
1990 76,836 7.3% — 94
53,308 White (69.4%)
16,544 Black (21.5%)
128 American Indian (0.2%)
729 Asian/Pacific Islander (0.9%)
6,127 Other race (8.0%)
9,483 Hispanic Origin* (12.3%)
2000 106,221 10.9% — 98
73,633 White alone (69.3%)
19,294 Black or African American alone (18.2%)
301 American Indian and Alaska Native alone (0.3%)
1,215 Asian alone (1.1%)
22 Native Hawaiian and Other Pacific Islander alone (0.0%)
9,532 Some other race alone (9.0%)
2,224 Two or more races (2.1%)
19,552 Hispanic or Latino* (18.4%)

Justice, IL (inc. 1911)

1930 377 — — —
1960 2,803 5.2% 20.4% 103
2,803 White (100.0%)
1990 11,137 7.7% — 101
9,161 White (82.3%)
1,605 Black (14.4%)
185 Asian/Pacific Islander (1.7%)
186 Other race (1.7%)
515 Hispanic Origin* (4.6%)

Municipalities *(continued)*

Year	Total (and by category)	Foreign born	Native with foreign parentage	Males per 100 females
2000	12,193	19.1%	—	97
	8,639 White alone (70.9%)			
	2,456 Black or African American alone (20.1%)			
	23 American Indian and Alaska Native alone (0.2%)			
	213 Asian alone (1.7%)			
	3 Native Hawaiian and Other Pacific Islander alone (0.0%)			
	336 Some other race alone (2.8%)			
	523 Two or more races (4.3%)			
	928 Hispanic or Latino* (7.6%)			

Kenilworth, IL (inc. 1896)

Year	Total (and by category)	Foreign born	Native with foreign parentage	Males per 100 females
1900	336	—	—	—
1930	2,501	12.3%	21.6%	76
	2,390 White (95.6%)			
	107 Negro (4.3%)			
	4 Other (0.2%)			
1960	2,959	4.8%	14.8%	86
	2,920 White (98.7%)			
	39 Negro (1.3%)			
1990	2,402	9.8%	—	89
	2,480 White (103.2%)			
	15 Black (0.6%)			
	67 Asian/Pacific Islander (2.8%)			
	14 Hispanic Origin* (0.6%)			
2000	2,494	8.5%	—	90
	2,426 White alone (97.3%)			
	4 Black or African American alone (0.2%)			
	1 American Indian and Alaska Native alone (0.0%)			
	56 Asian alone (2.2%)			
	7 Two or more races (0.3%)			
	34 Hispanic or Latino* (1.4%)			

Kildeer, IL (inc. 1958)

Year	Total (and by category)	Foreign born	Native with foreign parentage	Males per 100 females
1960	173	—	—	—
1990	2,257	5.8%	—	103
	2,208 White (97.8%)			
	3 American Indian (0.1%)			
	44 Asian/Pacific Islander (1.9%)			
	2 Other race (0.1%)			
	25 Hispanic Origin* (1.1%)			
2000	3,460	8.5%	—	98
	3,246 White alone (93.8%)			
	32 Black or African American alone (0.9%)			
	148 Asian alone (4.3%)			
	13 Some other race alone (0.4%)			
	21 Two or more races (0.6%)			
	80 Hispanic or Latino* (2.3%)			

Kouts, IN (inc. 1921)

Year	Total (and by category)	Foreign born	Native with foreign parentage	Males per 100 females
1930	583	—	—	—
1960	1,007	—	—	—
1990	1,603	1.1%	—	96
	1,580 White (98.6%)			
	10 Black (0.6%)			
	2 American Indian (0.1%)			
	11 Asian/Pacific Islander (0.7%)			
	7 Hispanic Origin* (0.4%)			
2000	1,698	0.7%	—	97
	1,681 White alone (99.0%)			
	2 Asian alone (0.1%)			
	11 Some other race alone (0.6%)			
	4 Two or more races (0.2%)			
	21 Hispanic or Latino* (1.2%)			

La Grange Park, IL (inc. 1892)

Year	Total (and by category)	Foreign born	Native with foreign parentage	Males per 100 females
1900	730	—	—	—
1930	2,939	11.9%	29.9%	92
	2,933 White (99.8%)			
	6 Negro (0.2%)			
1960	13,793	5.7%	26.3%	89
	13,786 White (99.9%)			
	2 Negro (0.0%)			
	5 Other races (0.0%)			
1990	12,861	7.5%	—	82
	12,545 White (97.5%)			
	40 Black (0.3%)			
	14 American Indian (0.1%)			
	227 Asian/Pacific Islander (1.8%)			
	35 Other race (0.3%)			
	107 Hispanic Origin* (0.8%)			
2000	13,295	6.6%	—	84
	12,394 White alone (93.2%)			
	409 Black or African American alone (3.1%)			
	14 American Indian and Alaska Native alone (0.1%)			
	218 Asian alone (1.6%)			
	5 Native Hawaiian and Other Pacific Islander alone (0.0%)			
	121 Some other race alone (0.9%)			
	134 Two or more races (1.0%)			
	472 Hispanic or Latino* (3.6%)			

La Grange, IL (inc. 1879)

Year	Total (and by category)	Foreign born	Native with foreign parentage	Males per 100 females
1900	3,969	19.9%	28.7%	90
	3,919 White (98.7%)			
	47 Negro (1.2%)			
	3 Chinese (0.1%)			
1930	10,103	10.9%	25.9%	88
	9,749 White (96.5%)			
	350 Negro (3.5%)			
	4 Other (0.0%)			
1960	15,285	4.2%	17.7%	93
	14,170 White (92.7%)			
	1,084 Negro (7.1%)			
	31 Other races (0.2%)			
1990	15,362	3.8%	—	93
	14,173 White (92.3%)			
	987 Black (6.4%)			
	20 American Indian (0.1%)			
	96 Asian/Pacific Islander (0.6%)			
	86 Other race (0.6%)			
	303 Hispanic Origin* (2.0%)			
2000	15,608	5.6%	—	94
	14,206 White alone (91.0%)			
	939 Black or African American alone (6.0%)			
	14 American Indian and Alaska Native alone (0.1%)			
	156 Asian alone (1.0%)			
	3 Native Hawaiian and Other Pacific Islander alone (0.0%)			
	155 Some other race alone (1.0%)			
	135 Two or more races (0.9%)			
	572 Hispanic or Latino* (3.7%)			

Lake Barrington, IL (inc. 1959)

Year	Total (and by category)	Foreign born	Native with foreign parentage	Males per 100 females
1960	172	—	—	—
1990	3,855	5.1%	—	95
	3,798 White (98.5%)			
	4 Black (0.1%)			
	7 American Indian (0.2%)			
	46 Asian/Pacific Islander (1.2%)			
	28 Hispanic Origin* (0.7%)			
2000	4,757	5.1%	—	94
	4,634 White alone (97.4%)			
	20 Black or African American alone (0.4%)			
	9 American Indian and Alaska Native alone (0.2%)			
	51 Asian alone (1.1%)			
	3 Native Hawaiian and Other Pacific Islander alone (0.1%)			
	7 Some other race alone (0.1%)			
	33 Two or more races (0.7%)			
	47 Hispanic or Latino* (1.0%)			

Lake Bluff, IL (inc. 1895)

Year	Total (and by category)	Foreign born	Native with foreign parentage	Males per 100 females
1900	490	—	—	—
1930	1,452	10.7%	28.9%	89
	1,429 White (98.4%)			
	14 Negro (1.0%)			
	9 Other (0.6%)			
1960	3,494	4.5%	15.6%	98
	3,476 White (99.5%)			
	12 Negro (0.3%)			
	6 Other races (0.2%)			
1990	5,513	5.0%	—	98
	5,382 White (97.6%)			
	42 Black (0.8%)			
	5 American Indian (0.1%)			
	84 Asian/Pacific Islander (1.5%)			
	24 Hispanic Origin* (0.4%)			
2000	6,056	7.4%	—	93
	5,771 White alone (95.3%)			
	31 Black or African American alone (0.5%)			
	2 American Indian and Alaska Native alone (0.0%)			
	200 Asian alone (3.3%)			
	2 Native Hawaiian and Other Pacific Islander alone (0.0%)			
	14 Some other race alone (0.2%)			
	36 Two or more races (0.6%)			
	72 Hispanic or Latino* (1.2%)			

Lake Forest, IL (inc. 1861)

Year	Total (and by category)	Foreign born	Native with foreign parentage	Males per 100 females
1900	2,215	—	—	—
1930	6,554	30.1%	28.3%	84
	6,318 White (96.4%)			
	228 Negro (3.5%)			
	8 Other (0.1%)			
1960	10,687	8.6%	17.2%	82
	10,427 White (97.6%)			
	224 Negro (2.1%)			
	36 Other races (0.3%)			
1990	17,836	6.8%	—	93
	17,081 White (95.8%)			
	136 Black (0.8%)			
	19 American Indian (0.1%)			
	438 Asian/Pacific Islander (2.5%)			
	162 Other race (0.9%)			
	269 Hispanic Origin* (1.5%)			
2000	20,059	6.5%	—	91
	18,815 White alone (93.8%)			
	271 Black or African American alone (1.4%)			
	12 American Indian and Alaska Native alone (0.1%)			
	692 Asian alone (3.4%)			
	26 Native Hawaiian and Other Pacific Islander alone (0.1%)			
	89 Some other race alone (0.4%)			
	154 Two or more races (0.8%)			
	376 Hispanic or Latino* (1.9%)			

Lake in the Hills, IL (inc. 1952)

Year	Total (and by category)	Foreign born	Native with foreign parentage	Males per 100 females
1960	2,046	—	—	101
	2,046 White (100.0%)			
1990	5,866	1.9%	—	106
	5,857 White (99.8%)			
	9 American Indian (0.2%)			
	70 Hispanic Origin* (1.2%)			
2000	23,152	8.6%	—	101
	21,206 White alone (91.6%)			
	347 Black or African American alone (1.5%)			
	33 American Indian and Alaska Native alone (0.1%)			
	770 Asian alone (3.3%)			
	4 Native Hawaiian and Other Pacific Islander alone (0.0%)			
	430 Some other race alone (1.9%)			
	362 Two or more races (1.6%)			
	1,462 Hispanic or Latino* (6.3%)			

Lake Station, IN (inc. 1908)

Year	Total (and by category)	Foreign born	Native with foreign parentage	Males per 100 females
1930	2,409	—	—	—
1960	9,858	—	—	—
1990	13,899	2.7%	—	98
	12,878 White (92.7%)			
	66 Black (0.5%)			
	19 American Indian (0.1%)			
	7 Asian/Pacific Islander (0.1%)			
	836 Other race (6.0%)			
	1,832 Hispanic Origin* (13.2%)			

2000	13,948	4.3%	—	100
	12,027	White alone (86.2%)		
	107	Black or African American alone (0.8%)		
	70	American Indian and Alaska Native alone (0.5%)		
	42	Asian alone (0.3%)		
	7	Native Hawaiian and Other Pacific Islander alone (0.1%)		
	1,298	Some other race alone (9.3%)		
	397	Two or more races (2.8%)		
	2,875	Hispanic or Latino* (20.6%)		

Lake Villa, IL (inc. 1901)

1930	487	—	—	—
1960	903	—	—	—
1990	2,857	3.5%	—	100
	2,823	White (98.8%)		
	13	Black (0.5%)		
	12	American Indian (0.4%)		
	7	Asian/Pacific Islander (0.2%)		
	31	Hispanic Origin* (1.1%)		
2000	5,864	4.8%	—	99
	5,450	White alone (92.9%)		
	145	Black or African American alone (2.5%)		
	7	American Indian and Alaska Native alone (0.1%)		
	96	Asian alone (1.6%)		
	5	Native Hawaiian and Other Pacific Islander alone (0.1%)		
	52	Some other race alone (0.9%)		
	109	Two or more races (1.9%)		
	181	Hispanic or Latino* (3.1%)		

Lake Zurich, IL (inc. 1896)

1900	215	—	—	—
1930	368	—	—	—
1960	3,458	4.5%	19.4%	100
	3,451	White (99.8%)		
	7	Other races (0.2%)		
1990	14,947	5.4%	—	100
	14,414	White (96.4%)		
	130	Black (0.9%)		
	7	American Indian (0.0%)		
	300	Asian/Pacific Islander (2.0%)		
	96	Other race (0.6%)		
	513	Hispanic Origin* (3.4%)		
2000	18,104	8.8%	—	101
	16,711	White alone (92.3%)		
	146	Black or African American alone (0.8%)		
	30	American Indian and Alaska Native alone (0.2%)		
	691	Asian alone (3.8%)		
	2	Native Hawaiian and Other Pacific Islander alone (0.0%)		
	357	Some other race alone (2.0%)		
	167	Two or more races (0.9%)		
	1,005	Hispanic or Latino* (5.6%)		

Lakemoor, IL (inc. 1951)

1960	736	—	—	—
1990	1,322	3.8%	—	101
	1,313	White (99.3%)		
	3	American Indian (0.2%)		
	18	Other race (1.4%)		
	55	Hispanic Origin* (4.2%)		
2000	2,788	4.0%	—	108
	2,585	White alone (92.7%)		
	18	Black or African American alone (0.6%)		
	4	American Indian and Alaska Native alone (0.1%)		
	51	Asian alone (1.8%)		
	5	Native Hawaiian and Other Pacific Islander alone (0.2%)		
	80	Some other race alone (2.9%)		
	45	Two or more races (1.6%)		
	196	Hispanic or Latino* (7.0%)		

Lakewood, IL (inc. 1933)

1960	635	—	—	—
1990	1,609	3.7%	—	103
	1,587	White (98.6%)		
	3	Black (0.2%)		
	3	American Indian (0.2%)		
	10	Asian/Pacific Islander (0.6%)		
	32	Hispanic Origin* (2.0%)		
2000	2,337	5.0%	—	96
	2,246	White alone (96.1%)		
	18	Black or African American alone (0.8%)		
	4	American Indian and Alaska Native alone (0.2%)		
	36	Asian alone (1.5%)		
	16	Some other race alone (0.7%)		
	17	Two or more races (0.7%)		
	55	Hispanic or Latino* (2.4%)		

Lansing, IL (inc. 1893)

1900	830	—	—	—
1930	3,378	15.4%	38.0%	109
	3,365	White (99.6%)		
	13	Other (0.4%)		
1960	18,098	4.5%	22.0%	98
	18,091	White (100.0%)		
	7	Other races (0.0%)		
1990	28,086	3.5%	—	91
	26,821	White (95.5%)		
	843	Black (3.0%)		
	9	American Indian (0.0%)		
	104	Asian/Pacific Islander (0.4%)		
	309	Other race (1.1%)		
	787	Hispanic Origin* (2.8%)		
2000	28,332	5.5%	—	90
	24,295	White alone (85.8%)		
	3,029	Black or African American alone (10.7%)		
	36	American Indian and Alaska Native alone (0.1%)		
	203	Asian alone (0.7%)		
	13	Native Hawaiian and Other Pacific Islander alone (0.0%)		
	437	Some other race alone (1.5%)		
	319	Two or more races (1.1%)		
	1,624	Hispanic or Latino* (5.7%)		

Lemont, IL (inc. 1873)

1900	2,449	—	—	—
1930	2,582	13.8%	45.3%	104
	2,582	White (100.0%)		
1960	3,397	2.9%	23.7%	96
	3,393	White (99.9%)		
	4	Other races (0.1%)		
1990	7,348	4.7%	—	98
	7,248	White (98.6%)		
	14	Black (0.2%)		
	10	American Indian (0.1%)		
	33	Asian/Pacific Islander (0.4%)		
	43	Other race (0.6%)		
	250	Hispanic Origin* (3.4%)		
2000	13,098	9.7%	—	90
	12,757	White alone (97.4%)		
	40	Black or African American alone (0.3%)		
	19	American Indian and Alaska Native alone (0.1%)		
	107	Asian alone (0.8%)		
	4	Native Hawaiian and Other Pacific Islander alone (0.0%)		
	87	Some other race alone (0.7%)		
	84	Two or more races (0.6%)		
	393	Hispanic or Latino* (3.0%)		

Libertyville, IL (inc. 1882)

1900	864	—	—	—
1930	3,791	10.9%	29.1%	106
	3,723	White (98.2%)		
	2	Negro (0.1%)		
	66	Other (1.7%)		
1960	8,560	5.4%	17.9%	98
	8,553	White (99.9%)		
	3	Negro (0.0%)		
	4	Other races (0.0%)		

1990	19,174	6.7%	—	94
	18,314	White (95.5%)		
	72	Black (0.4%)		
	28	American Indian (0.1%)		
	712	Asian/Pacific Islander (3.7%)		
	69	Other race (0.4%)		
	420	Hispanic Origin* (2.2%)		
2000	20,742	10.2%	—	93
	19,121	White alone (92.2%)		
	211	Black or African American alone (1.0%)		
	18	American Indian and Alaska Native alone (0.1%)		
	949	Asian alone (4.6%)		
	6	Native Hawaiian and Other Pacific Islander alone (0.0%)		
	231	Some other race alone (1.1%)		
	206	Two or more races (1.0%)		
	566	Hispanic or Latino* (2.7%)		

Lily Lake, IL (inc. 1990)

1990	542	—	—	—
2000	825	3.5%	—	115
	811	White alone (98.3%)		
	7	Black or African American alone (0.8%)		
	2	Asian alone (0.2%)		
	5	Two or more races (0.6%)		
	17	Hispanic or Latino* (2.1%)		

Lincolnshire, IL (inc. 1957)

1960	555	—	—	—
1990	4,931	7.1%	—	100
	4,748	White (96.3%)		
	37	Black (0.8%)		
	2	American Indian (0.0%)		
	139	Asian/Pacific Islander (2.8%)		
	5	Other race (0.1%)		
	83	Hispanic Origin* (1.7%)		
2000	6,108	10.8%	—	95
	5,748	White alone (94.1%)		
	31	Black or African American alone (0.5%)		
	2	American Indian and Alaska Native alone (0.0%)		
	227	Asian alone (3.7%)		
	4	Native Hawaiian and Other Pacific Islander alone (0.1%)		
	30	Some other race alone (0.5%)		
	66	Two or more races (1.1%)		
	153	Hispanic or Latino* (2.5%)		

Lincolnwood, IL (inc. 1911)

1930	473	—	—	—
1960	11,744	10.6%	38.7%	95
	11,683	White (99.5%)		
	44	Negro (0.4%)		
	17	Other races (0.1%)		
1990	11,365	27.6%	—	90
	9,396	White (82.7%)		
	46	Black (0.4%)		
	1,773	Asian/Pacific Islander (15.6%)		
	150	Other race (1.3%)		
	379	Hispanic Origin* (3.3%)		
2000	12,359	34.1%	—	89
	9,211	White alone (74.5%)		
	47	Black or African American alone (0.4%)		
	4	American Indian and Alaska Native alone (0.0%)		
	2,605	Asian alone (21.1%)		
	3	Native Hawaiian and Other Pacific Islander alone (0.0%)		
	152	Some other race alone (1.2%)		
	337	Two or more races (2.7%)		
	517	Hispanic or Latino* (4.2%)		

Lindenhurst, IL (inc. 1956)

1960	1,259	—	—	99
	1,258	White (99.9%)		
	1	Other races (0.1%)		

Municipalities *(continued)*

	Total (and by category)	Foreign born	Native with foreign parentage	Males per 100 females
1990	8,038	3.2%	—	103
	7,845 White (97.6%)			
	63 Black (0.8%)			
	35 American Indian (0.4%)			
	79 Asian/Pacific Islander (1.0%)			
	16 Other race (0.2%)			
	169 Hispanic Origin* (2.1%)			
2000	12,539	5.4%	—	97
	11,640 White alone (92.8%)			
	184 Black or African American alone (1.5%)			
	19 American Indian and Alaska Native alone (0.2%)			
	377 Asian alone (3.0%)			
	1 Native Hawaiian and Other Pacific Islander alone (0.0%)			
	165 Some other race alone (1.3%)			
	153 Two or more races (1.2%)			
	508 Hispanic or Latino* (4.1%)			

Lisle, IL (inc. 1956)

	Total (and by category)	Foreign born	Native with foreign parentage	Males per 100 females
1960	4,219	4.1%	21.9%	104
	4,218 White (100.0%)			
	1 Negro (0.0%)			
1990	19,512	7.4%	—	101
	17,679 White (90.6%)			
	538 Black (2.8%)			
	42 American Indian (0.2%)			
	1,104 Asian/Pacific Islander (5.7%)			
	149 Other race (0.8%)			
	555 Hispanic Origin* (2.8%)			
2000	21,182	13.0%	—	101
	17,661 White alone (83.4%)			
	736 Black or African American alone (3.5%)			
	40 American Indian and Alaska Native alone (0.2%)			
	2,073 Asian alone (9.8%)			
	6 Native Hawaiian and Other Pacific Islander alone (0.0%)			
	355 Some other race alone (1.7%)			
	311 Two or more races (1.5%)			
	1,163 Hispanic or Latino* (5.5%)			

Lockport, IL (inc. 1853)

	Total (and by category)	Foreign born	Native with foreign parentage	Males per 100 females
1870	1,772	33.4%	—	107
	1,766 White (99.7%)			
	6 Colored (0.3%)			
1900	2,659	20.8%	38.6%	99
	2,529 White (95.1%)			
	130 Negro (4.9%)			
1930	3,383	12.5%	34.4%	103
	3,306 White (97.7%)			
	32 Negro (0.9%)			
	45 Other (1.3%)			
1960	7,560	4.2%	20.3%	95
	7,440 White (98.4%)			
	119 Negro (1.6%)			
	1 Other races (0.0%)			
1990	9,401	1.8%	—	94
	9,272 White (98.6%)			
	25 Black (0.3%)			
	16 American Indian (0.2%)			
	96 Other race (1.0%)			
	242 Hispanic Origin* (2.6%)			
2000	15,191	3.9%	—	97
	14,556 White alone (95.8%)			
	168 Black or African American alone (1.1%)			
	34 American Indian and Alaska Native alone (0.2%)			
	114 Asian alone (0.8%)			
	1 Native Hawaiian and Other Pacific Islander alone (0.0%)			
	143 Some other race alone (0.9%)			
	175 Two or more races (1.2%)			
	660 Hispanic or Latino* (4.3%)			

Lombard, IL (inc. 1869)

	Total (and by category)	Foreign born	Native with foreign parentage	Males per 100 females
1900	590	—	—	—
1930	6,197	13.0%	33.2%	101
	6,194 White (100.0%)			
	1 Negro (0.0%)			
	2 Mexican (0.0%)			
1960	22,561	4.6%	20.9%	97
	22,537 White (99.9%)			
	1 Negro (0.0%)			
	23 Other races (0.1%)			
1990	39,408	6.8%	—	94
	36,939 White (93.7%)			
	526 Black (1.3%)			
	40 American Indian (0.1%)			
	1,656 Asian/Pacific Islander (4.2%)			
	247 Other race (0.6%)			
	957 Hispanic Origin* (2.4%)			
2000	42,322	11.5%	—	94
	36,829 White alone (87.0%)			
	1,141 Black or African American alone (2.7%)			
	62 American Indian and Alaska Native alone (0.1%)			
	2,982 Asian alone (7.0%)			
	7 Native Hawaiian and Other Pacific Islander alone (0.0%)			
	606 Some other race alone (1.4%)			
	695 Two or more races (1.6%)			
	2,012 Hispanic or Latino* (4.8%)			

Long Grove, IL (inc. 1956)

	Total (and by category)	Foreign born	Native with foreign parentage	Males per 100 females
1960	640	—	—	—
1990	4,740	9.5%	—	99
	4,547 White (95.9%)			
	66 Black (1.4%)			
	119 Asian/Pacific Islander (2.5%)			
	8 Other race (0.2%)			
	66 Hispanic Origin* (1.4%)			
2000	6,735	8.2%	—	99
	6,116 White alone (90.8%)			
	63 Black or African American alone (0.9%)			
	1 American Indian and Alaska Native alone (0.0%)			
	456 Asian alone (6.8%)			
	36 Some other race alone (0.5%)			
	63 Two or more races (0.9%)			
	202 Hispanic or Latino* (3.0%)			

Lowell, IN (inc. 1868)

	Total (and by category)	Foreign born	Native with foreign parentage	Males per 100 females
1900	1,275	—	—	—
1930	1,274	—	—	—
1960	2,270	—	—	—
1990	6,430	0.9%	—	98
	6,386 White (99.3%)			
	6 American Indian (0.1%)			
	14 Asian/Pacific Islander (0.2%)			
	24 Other race (0.4%)			
	135 Hispanic Origin* (2.1%)			
2000	7,505	1.4%	—	96

Lynwood, IL (inc. 1959)

	Total (and by category)	Foreign born	Native with foreign parentage	Males per 100 females
1960	255	—	—	
1990	6,535	3.7%	—	93
	5,380 White (82.3%)			
	1,024 Black (15.7%)			
	23 American Indian (0.4%)			
	61 Asian/Pacific Islander (0.9%)			
	47 Other race (0.7%)			
	230 Hispanic Origin* (3.5%)			
2000	7,377	5.0%	—	91
	3,699 White alone (50.1%)			
	3,349 Black or African American alone (45.4%)			
	17 American Indian and Alaska Native alone (0.2%)			
	72 Asian alone (1.0%)			
	114 Some other race alone (1.5%)			
	126 Two or more races (1.7%)			
	337 Hispanic or Latino* (4.6%)			

Lyons, IL (inc. 1888)

	Total (and by category)	Foreign born	Native with foreign parentage	Males per 100 females
1900	951	—	—	—
1930	4,787	27.6%	49.2%	107
	4,786 White (100.0%)			
	1 Other (0.0%)			
1960	9,936	10.0%	29.2%	101
	9,914 White (99.8%)			
	1 Negro (0.0%)			
	21 Other races (0.2%)			
1990	9,828	10.3%	—	97
	9,565 White (97.3%)			
	7 Black (0.1%)			
	74 American Indian (0.8%)			
	90 Asian/Pacific Islander (0.9%)			
	92 Other race (0.9%)			
	548 Hispanic Origin* (5.6%)			
2000	10,255	17.5%	—	99
	8,911 White alone (86.9%)			
	103 Black or African American alone (1.0%)			
	25 American Indian and Alaska Native alone (0.2%)			
	143 Asian alone (1.4%)			
	4 Native Hawaiian and Other Pacific Islander alone (0.0%)			
	703 Some other race alone (6.9%)			
	366 Two or more races (3.6%)			
	1,668 Hispanic or Latino* (16.3%)			

Manhattan, IL (inc. 1886)

	Total (and by category)	Foreign born	Native with foreign parentage	Males per 100 females
1900	393	—	—	—
1930	628	—	—	—
1960	1,117	—		94
	1,117 White (100.0%)			
1990	2,059	0.6%	—	96
	2,026 White (98.4%)			
	17 American Indian (0.8%)			
	5 Asian/Pacific Islander (0.2%)			
	11 Other race (0.5%)			
	31 Hispanic Origin* (1.5%)			
2000	3,330	2.5%	—	104
	3,237 White alone (97.2%)			
	7 Black or African American alone (0.2%)			
	4 American Indian and Alaska Native alone (0.1%)			
	7 Asian alone (0.2%)			
	39 Some other race alone (1.2%)			
	36 Two or more races (1.1%)			
	101 Hispanic or Latino* (3.0%)			

Maple Park, IL (inc. 1872)

	Total (and by category)	Foreign born	Native with foreign parentage	Males per 100 females
1900	391	—	—	—
1930	389	—	—	—
1960	592	—	—	—
1990	641	0.3%	—	102
	648 White (101.1%)			
	6 Hispanic Origin* (0.9%)			
2000	765	0.4%	—	106
	746 White alone (97.5%)			
	3 American Indian and Alaska Native alone (0.4%)			
	1 Asian alone (0.1%)			
	7 Some other race alone (0.9%)			
	8 Two or more races (1.0%)			
	19 Hispanic or Latino* (2.5%)			

Marengo, IL (inc. 1857)

	Total (and by category)	Foreign born	Native with foreign parentage	Males per 100 females
1870	1,327	8.9%	—	—
1900	2,005	—	—	—
1930	1,948	10.6%	27.4%	99
	1,947 White (99.9%)			
	1 Negro (0.1%)			
	2 Indian (0.1%)			
1960	3,568	4.1%	14.9%	98
	3,558 White (99.7%)			
	10 Other races (0.3%)			
1990	4,768	3.2%	—	101
	4,581 White (96.1%)			
	89 Black (1.9%)			
	19 American Indian (0.4%)			
	79 Other race (1.7%)			
	280 Hispanic Origin* (5.9%)			

2000	6,355	7.0%	—	96
	5,851	White alone (92.1%)		
	19	Black or African American alone (0.3%)		
	17	American Indian and Alaska Native alone (0.3%)		
	18	Asian alone (0.3%)		
	1	Native Hawaiian and Other Pacific Islander alone (0.0%)		
	352	Some other race alone (5.5%)		
	97	Two or more races (1.5%)		
	826	Hispanic or Latino* (13.0%)		

Markham, IL (inc. 1925)

1930	349	—	—	—
1960	11,704	2.1%	12.6%	101
	9,180	White (78.4%)		
	2,505	Negro (21.4%)		
	19	Other races (0.2%)		
1990	13,136	1.2%	—	91
	2,936	White (22.4%)		
	10,048	Black (76.5%)		
	41	American Indian (0.3%)		
	111	Other race (0.8%)		
	181	Hispanic Origin* (1.4%)		
2000	12,620	2.8%	—	87
	2,183	White alone (17.3%)		
	9,952	Black or African American alone (78.9%)		
	20	American Indian and Alaska Native alone (0.2%)		
	75	Asian alone (0.6%)		
	3	Native Hawaiian and Other Pacific Islander alone (0.0%)		
	203	Some other race alone (1.6%)		
	184	Two or more races (1.5%)		
	396	Hispanic or Latino* (3.1%)		

Matteson, IL (inc. 1889)

1900	449	—	—	—
1930	736	—	—	—
1960	3,225	3.8%	16.4%	100
	3,225	White (100.0%)		
1990	11,378	3.8%	—	94
	5,871	White (51.6%)		
	5,070	Black (44.6%)		
	4	American Indian (0.0%)		
	219	Asian/Pacific Islander (1.9%)		
	214	Other race (1.9%)		
	420	Hispanic Origin* (3.7%)		
2000	12,928	3.9%	—	86
	4,230	White alone (32.7%)		
	8,098	Black or African American alone (62.6%)		
	16	American Indian and Alaska Native alone (0.1%)		
	201	Asian alone (1.6%)		
	144	Some other race alone (1.1%)		
	239	Two or more races (1.8%)		
	436	Hispanic or Latino* (3.4%)		

Maywood, IL (inc. 1881)

1900	4,532	25.1%	38.5%	101
	4,508	White (99.5%)		
	19	Negro (0.4%)		
	5	Chinese (0.1%)		
1930	25,829	15.5%	33.6%	102
	25,087	White (97.1%)		
	722	Negro (2.8%)		
	3	Indian (0.0%)		
	5	Chinese (0.0%)		
	6	Japanese (0.0%)		
	1	Mexican (0.0%)		
	5	Other (0.0%)		
1960	27,330	7.2%	19.6%	93
	22,010	White (80.5%)		
	5,229	Negro (19.1%)		
	91	Other races (0.3%)		
1990	27,139	5.1%	—	89
	3,348	White (12.3%)		
	22,696	Black (83.6%)		
	19	American Indian (0.1%)		
	165	Asian/Pacific Islander (0.6%)		
	911	Other race (3.4%)		
	1,623	Hispanic Origin* (6.0%)		

2000	26,987	7.2%	—	88
	2,625	White alone (9.7%)		
	22,308	Black or African American alone (82.7%)		
	34	American Indian and Alaska Native alone (0.1%)		
	80	Asian alone (0.3%)		
	1	Native Hawaiian and Other Pacific Islander alone (0.0%)		
	1,500	Some other race alone (5.6%)		
	439	Two or more races (1.6%)		
	2,843	Hispanic or Latino* (10.5%)		

McCook, IL (inc. 1926)

1930	367	—	—	—
1960	441	—	—	—
1990	235	3.0%	—	88
	255	White (108.5%)		
	3	Hispanic Origin* (1.3%)		
2000	254	0.0%	—	91
	242	White alone (95.3%)		
	12	Some other race alone (4.7%)		
	20	Hispanic or Latino* (7.9%)		

McCullom Lake, IL (inc. 1955)

1960	759	—	—	—
1990	1,033	4.3%	—	103
	1,003	White (97.1%)		
	2	Asian/Pacific Islander (0.2%)		
	28	Other race (2.7%)		
	48	Hispanic Origin* (4.6%)		
2000	1,038	2.6%	—	100
	1,001	White alone (96.4%)		
	9	Black or African American alone (0.9%)		
	5	American Indian and Alaska Native alone (0.5%)		
	3	Asian alone (0.3%)		
	1	Native Hawaiian and Other Pacific Islander alone (0.1%)		
	13	Some other race alone (1.3%)		
	6	Two or more races (0.6%)		
	44	Hispanic or Latino* (4.2%)		

McHenry, IL (inc. 1855)

1900	1,013	—	—	—
1930	1,354	7.5%	34.0%	95
	1,354	White (100.0%)		
1960	3,336	3.2%	15.3%	92
	3,336	White (100.0%)		
1990	16,177	3.1%	—	91
	15,970	White (98.7%)		
	23	Black (0.1%)		
	38	American Indian (0.2%)		
	69	Asian/Pacific Islander (0.4%)		
	77	Other race (0.5%)		
	368	Hispanic Origin* (2.3%)		
2000	21,501	6.2%	—	95
	20,250	White alone (94.2%)		
	75	Black or African American alone (0.3%)		
	45	American Indian and Alaska Native alone (0.2%)		
	192	Asian alone (0.9%)		
	8	Native Hawaiian and Other Pacific Islander alone (0.0%)		
	711	Some other race alone (3.3%)		
	220	Two or more races (1.0%)		
	1,527	Hispanic or Latino* (7.1%)		

Melrose Park, IL (inc. 1893)

1900	2,592	38.4%	44.9%	113
	2,583	White (99.7%)		
	7	Negro (0.3%)		
	2	Chinese (0.1%)		
1930	10,741	27.5%	45.7%	113
	10,428	White (97.1%)		
	121	Negro (1.1%)		
	192	Other (1.8%)		
1960	22,291	11.2%	28.9%	102
	22,172	White (99.5%)		
	57	Negro (0.3%)		
	62	Other races (0.3%)		

1990	20,859	23.8%	—	98
	17,561	White (84.2%)		
	159	Black (0.8%)		
	24	American Indian (0.1%)		
	532	Asian/Pacific Islander (2.6%)		
	2,583	Other race (12.4%)		
	6,188	Hispanic Origin* (29.7%)		
2000	23,171	35.4%	—	101
	16,575	White alone (71.5%)		
	676	Black or African American alone (2.9%)		
	114	American Indian and Alaska Native alone (0.5%)		
	461	Asian alone (2.0%)		
	3	Native Hawaiian and Other Pacific Islander alone (0.0%)		
	4,653	Some other race alone (20.1%)		
	689	Two or more races (3.0%)		
	12,485	Hispanic or Latino* (53.9%)		

Merrillville, IN (inc. 1971)

1990	27,257	7.0%	—	92
	25,067	White (92.0%)		
	1,367	Black (5.0%)		
	71	American Indian (0.3%)		
	134	Asian/Pacific Islander (0.5%)		
	618	Other race (2.3%)		
	1,867	Hispanic Origin* (6.8%)		
2000	30,560	7.1%	—	91
	21,286	White alone (69.7%)		
	6,987	Black or African American alone (22.9%)		
	100	American Indian and Alaska Native alone (0.3%)		
	460	Asian alone (1.5%)		
	6	Native Hawaiian and Other Pacific Islander alone (0.0%)		
	1,035	Some other race alone (3.4%)		
	686	Two or more races (2.2%)		
	2,950	Hispanic or Latino* (9.7%)		

Merrionette Park, IL (inc. 1947)

1960	2,354	—	—	99
	2,352	White (99.9%)		
	1	Negro (0.0%)		
	1	Other races (0.0%)		
1990	2,065	3.1%	—	87
	2,024	White (98.0%)		
	26	Black (1.3%)		
	3	American Indian (0.1%)		
	7	Asian/Pacific Islander (0.3%)		
	5	Other race (0.2%)		
	15	Hispanic Origin* (0.7%)		
2000	1,999	2.6%	—	91
	1,805	White alone (90.3%)		
	132	Black or African American alone (6.6%)		
	1	American Indian and Alaska Native alone (0.1%)		
	10	Asian alone (0.5%)		
	23	Some other race alone (1.2%)		
	28	Two or more races (1.4%)		
	83	Hispanic or Latino* (4.2%)		

Mettawa, IL (inc. 1960)

1960	126	—	—	—
1990	348	4.0%	—	107
	305	White (87.6%)		
	3	American Indian (0.9%)		
	12	Asian/Pacific Islander (3.4%)		
	7	Other race (2.0%)		
	3	Hispanic Origin* (0.9%)		
2000	367	18.3%	—	104
	351	White alone (95.6%)		
	9	Asian alone (2.5%)		
	4	Some other race alone (1.1%)		
	3	Two or more races (0.8%)		
	15	Hispanic or Latino* (4.1%)		

Michigan City, IN (inc. 1836)

1870	3,985	39.8%	—	100
	3,940	White (98.9%)		
	45	Colored (1.1%)		
1900	14,850	24.7%	42.7%	120
	14,653	White (98.7%)		
	197	Negro (1.3%)		

Municipalities *(continued)*

Year	Total (and by category)		Foreign born	Native with foreign parentage	Males per 100 females
1930	26,735		12.3%	31.6%	124
	25,533	White (95.5%)			
	1,071	Negro (4.0%)			
	131	Other (0.5%)			
1960	36,653		3.8%	14.9%	109
	36,624	White (99.9%)			
	12	Negro (0.0%)			
	17	Other races (0.0%)			
1990	33,822		2.0%	—	99
	25,570	White (75.6%)			
	7,699	Black (22.8%)			
	144	American Indian (0.4%)			
	193	Asian/Pacific Islander (0.6%)			
	225	Other race (0.7%)			
	488	Hispanic Origin* (1.4%)			
2000	32,900		2.0%	—	102
	22,848	White alone (69.4%)			
	8,657	Black or African American alone (26.3%)			
	86	American Indian and Alaska Native alone (0.3%)			
	167	Asian alone (0.5%)			
	6	Native Hawaiian and Other Pacific Islander alone (0.0%)			
	361	Some other race alone (1.1%)			
	775	Two or more races (2.4%)			
	1,035	Hispanic or Latino* (3.1%)			

Midlothian, IL (inc. 1927)

Year	Total (and by category)		Foreign born	Native with foreign parentage	Males per 100 females
1930	1,775		12.5%	30.0%	109
	1,775	White (100.0%)			
1960	6,605		4.7%	21.6%	100
	6,600	White (99.9%)			
	5	Other races (0.1%)			
1990	14,372		2.2%	—	96
	13,691	White (95.3%)			
	352	Black (2.4%)			
	38	American Indian (0.3%)			
	126	Asian/Pacific Islander (0.9%)			
	165	Other race (1.1%)			
	490	Hispanic Origin* (3.4%)			
2000	14,315		3.8%	—	95
	12,636	White alone (88.3%)			
	877	Black or African American alone (6.1%)			
	22	American Indian and Alaska Native alone (0.2%)			
	236	Asian alone (1.6%)			
	3	Native Hawaiian and Other Pacific Islander alone (0.0%)			
	322	Some other race alone (2.2%)			
	219	Two or more races (1.5%)			
	976	Hispanic or Latino* (6.8%)			

Minooka, IL (inc. 1869)

Year	Total (and by category)		Foreign born	Native with foreign parentage	Males per 100 females
1900	424		—	—	—
1930	346		—	—	—
1960	539		—	—	—
1990	2,561		1.4%	—	106
	2,529	White (98.8%)			
	12	American Indian (0.5%)			
	22	Other race (0.9%)			
	34	Hispanic Origin* (1.3%)			
2000	3,971		1.9%	—	99
	3,893	White alone (98.0%)			
	10	Black or African American alone (0.3%)			
	8	American Indian and Alaska Native alone (0.2%)			
	12	Asian alone (0.3%)			
	21	Some other race alone (0.5%)			
	27	Two or more races (0.7%)			
	113	Hispanic or Latino* (2.8%)			

Mokena, IL (inc. 1880)

Year	Total (and by category)		Foreign born	Native with foreign parentage	Males per 100 females
1900	281		—	—	—
1930	562		—	—	—
1960	1,332		—	—	89
	1,332	White (100.0%)			
1990	6,128		1.4%	—	99
	6,097	White (99.5%)			
	31	Other race (0.5%)			
	78	Hispanic Origin* (1.3%)			
2000	14,583		4.1%	—	102
	14,126	White alone (96.9%)			
	72	Black or African American alone (0.5%)			
	10	American Indian and Alaska Native alone (0.1%)			
	183	Asian alone (1.3%)			
	8	Native Hawaiian and Other Pacific Islander alone (0.1%)			
	92	Some other race alone (0.6%)			
	92	Two or more races (0.6%)			
	421	Hispanic or Latino* (2.9%)			

Monee, IL (inc. 1874)

Year	Total (and by category)		Foreign born	Native with foreign parentage	Males per 100 females
1870	598		44.5%	—	—
1900	462		—	—	—
1930	383		—	—	—
1960	646		—	—	—
1990	1,044		3.4%	—	110
	1,042	White (99.8%)			
	2	Other race (0.2%)			
	27	Hispanic Origin* (2.6%)			
2000	2,924		1.7%	—	101
	2,745	White alone (93.9%)			
	62	Black or African American alone (2.1%)			
	2	American Indian and Alaska Native alone (0.1%)			
	13	Asian alone (0.4%)			
	55	Some other race alone (1.9%)			
	47	Two or more races (1.6%)			
	118	Hispanic or Latino* (4.0%)			

Montgomery, IL (inc. 1858)

Year	Total (and by category)		Foreign born	Native with foreign parentage	Males per 100 females
1900	350		—	—	—
1930	546		—	—	—
1960	2,122		—	—	103
	2,118	White (99.8%)			
	1	Negro (0.0%)			
	3	Other races (0.1%)			
1990	4,267		4.7%	—	101
	4,107	White (96.3%)			
	95	Black (2.2%)			
	56	Asian/Pacific Islander (1.3%)			
	117	Other race (2.7%)			
	150	Hispanic Origin* (3.5%)			
2000	5,471		5.3%	—	94
	4,887	White alone (89.3%)			
	165	Black or African American alone (3.0%)			
	23	American Indian and Alaska Native alone (0.4%)			
	44	Asian alone (0.8%)			
	2	Native Hawaiian and Other Pacific Islander alone (0.0%)			
	267	Some other race alone (4.9%)			
	83	Two or more races (1.5%)			
	741	Hispanic or Latino* (13.5%)			

Morris, IL (inc. 1853)

Year	Total (and by category)		Foreign born	Native with foreign parentage	Males per 100 females
1870	3,138		26.3%	—	94
	3,119	White (99.4%)			
	19	Colored (0.6%)			
1900	4,273		22.1%	37.9%	97
	4,251	White (99.5%)			
	20	Negro (0.5%)			
	2	Chinese (0.0%)			
1930	5,568		11.0%	33.1%	99
	5,523	White (99.2%)			
	9	Negro (0.2%)			
	36	Other (0.6%)			
1960	7,935		3.0%	17.3%	94
	7,915	White (99.7%)			
	8	Negro (0.1%)			
	12	Other races (0.2%)			
1990	10,270		2.6%	—	92
	10,047	White (97.8%)			
	9	Black (0.1%)			
	33	American Indian (0.3%)			
	44	Asian/Pacific Islander (0.4%)			
	137	Other race (1.3%)			
	363	Hispanic Origin* (3.5%)			
2000	11,928		3.9%	—	95
	11,373	White alone (95.3%)			
	41	Black or African American alone (0.3%)			
	27	American Indian and Alaska Native alone (0.2%)			
	61	Asian alone (0.5%)			
	3	Native Hawaiian and Other Pacific Islander alone (0.0%)			
	292	Some other race alone (2.4%)			
	131	Two or more races (1.1%)			
	828	Hispanic or Latino* (6.9%)			

Morton Grove, IL (inc. 1895)

Year	Total (and by category)		Foreign born	Native with foreign parentage	Males per 100 females
1900	564		—	—	—
1930	1,974		26.2%	38.1%	130
	1,961	White (99.3%)			
	13	Negro (0.7%)			
1960	20,533		6.1%	27.0%	99
	20,394	White (99.3%)			
	22	Negro (0.1%)			
	117	Other races (0.6%)			
1990	22,408		22.7%	—	93
	18,862	White (84.2%)			
	47	American Indian (0.2%)			
	3,289	Asian/Pacific Islander (14.7%)			
	207	Other race (0.9%)			
	637	Hispanic Origin* (2.8%)			
2000	22,451		33.6%	—	91
	16,606	White alone (74.0%)			
	142	Black or African American alone (0.6%)			
	27	American Indian and Alaska Native alone (0.1%)			
	4,980	Asian alone (22.2%)			
	1	Native Hawaiian and Other Pacific Islander alone (0.0%)			
	261	Some other race alone (1.2%)			
	434	Two or more races (1.9%)			
	988	Hispanic or Latino* (4.4%)			

Mount Prospect, IL (inc. 1917)

Year	Total (and by category)		Foreign born	Native with foreign parentage	Males per 100 females
1930	1,225		11.3%	33.7%	108
	1,218	White (99.4%)			
1960	18,906		2.9%	19.8%	99
	18,876	White (99.8%)			
	3	Negro (0.0%)			
	27	Other races (0.1%)			
1990	53,170		16.2%	—	99
	47,943	White (90.2%)			
	549	Black (1.0%)			
	185	American Indian (0.3%)			
	3,421	Asian/Pacific Islander (6.4%)			
	1,072	Other race (2.0%)			
	3,224	Hispanic Origin* (6.1%)			
2000	56,265		26.9%	—	99
	45,338	White alone (80.6%)			
	1,026	Black or African American alone (1.8%)			
	110	American Indian and Alaska Native alone (0.2%)			
	6,292	Asian alone (11.2%)			
	28	Native Hawaiian and Other Pacific Islander alone (0.0%)			
	2,332	Some other race alone (4.1%)			
	1,139	Two or more races (2.0%)			
	6,620	Hispanic or Latino* (11.8%)			

Mundelein, IL (inc. 1909)

Year	Total (and by category)		Foreign born	Native with foreign parentage	Males per 100 females
1930	1,011		12.9%	30.9%	110
	1,011	White (100.0%)			
1960	10,526		2.9%	16.7%	101
	10,500	White (99.8%)			
	1	Negro (0.0%)			
	25	Other races (0.2%)			
1990	21,215		12.2%	—	102
	18,918	White (89.2%)			
	272	Black (1.3%)			
	17	American Indian (0.1%)			
	642	Asian/Pacific Islander (3.0%)			
	1,366	Other race (6.4%)			
	2,822	Hispanic Origin* (13.3%)			

2000 30,935 23.6% — 105
- 24,340 White alone (78.7%)
- 494 Black or African American alone (1.6%)
- 87 American Indian and Alaska Native alone (0.3%)
- 2,041 Asian alone (6.6%)
- 23 Native Hawaiian and Other Pacific Islander alone (0.1%)
- 3,298 Some other race alone (10.7%)
- 652 Two or more races (2.1%)
- 7,487 Hispanic or Latino* (24.2%)

Munster, IN (inc. 1907)

1930 975 — — —

1960 10,313 4.6% 20.6% 97
- 10,303 White (99.9%)
- 9 Negro (0.1%)
- 1 Other races (0.0%)

1990 19,949 6.3% — 92
- 19,087 White (95.7%)
- 77 Black (0.4%)
- 662 Asian/Pacific Islander (3.3%)
- 123 Other race (0.6%)
- 534 Hispanic Origin* (2.7%)

2000 21,511 7.9% — 92
- 19,851 White alone (92.3%)
- 222 Black or African American alone (1.0%)
- 13 American Indian and Alaska Native alone (0.1%)
- 965 Asian alone (4.5%)
- 4 Native Hawaiian and Other Pacific Islander alone (0.0%)
- 237 Some other race alone (1.1%)
- 219 Two or more races (1.0%)
- 1,050 Hispanic or Latino* (4.9%)

Naperville, IL (inc. 1857)

1870 1,713 23.3% —
- 1,713 White (100.0%)

1900 2,629 20.0% 33.2% 99
- 2,626 White (99.9%)
- 1 Negro (0.0%)
- 2 Chinese (0.1%)

1930 5,118 10.7% 30.3% 96
- 5,098 White (99.6%)
- 20 Other (0.4%)

1960 12,933 3.3% 15.4% 97
- 12,904 White (99.8%)
- 12 Negro (0.1%)
- 17 Other races (0.1%)

1990 85,351 6.3% — 97
- 79,256 White (92.9%)
- 1,622 Black (1.9%)
- 75 American Indian (0.1%)
- 4,121 Asian/Pacific Islander (4.8%)
- 277 Other race (0.3%)
- 1,524 Hispanic Origin* (1.8%)

2000 128,358 11.7% — 96
- 109,346 White alone (85.2%)
- 3,887 Black or African American alone (3.0%)
- 154 American Indian and Alaska Native alone (0.1%)
- 12,380 Asian alone (9.6%)
- 24 Native Hawaiian and Other Pacific Islander alone (0.0%)
- 967 Some other race alone (0.8%)
- 1,600 Two or more races (1.2%)
- 4,160 Hispanic or Latino* (3.2%)

New Chicago, IN (inc. 1908)

1930 481 — — —

1960 2,312 — — —

1990 2,066 4.3% — 97
- 1,968 White (95.3%)
- 5 Black (0.2%)
- 11 American Indian (0.5%)
- 1 Asian/Pacific Islander (0.0%)
- 81 Other race (3.9%)
- 197 Hispanic Origin* (9.5%)

2000 2,063 4.9% — 95

New Lenox, IL (inc. 1946)

1960 1,750 — — 100
- 1,748 White (99.9%)
- 2 Other races (0.1%)

1990 9,627 1.2% — 95
- 9,550 White (99.2%)
- 6 Black (0.1%)
- 17 American Indian (0.2%)
- 21 Asian/Pacific Islander (0.2%)
- 33 Other race (0.3%)
- 181 Hispanic Origin* (1.9%)

2000 17,771 1.3% — 95
- 17,354 White alone (97.7%)
- 54 Black or African American alone (0.3%)
- 11 American Indian and Alaska Native alone (0.1%)
- 65 Asian alone (0.4%)
- 2 Native Hawaiian and Other Pacific Islander alone (0.0%)
- 150 Some other race alone (0.8%)
- 135 Two or more races (0.8%)
- 563 Hispanic or Latino* (3.2%)

Niles, IL (inc. 1899)

1900 514 — — —

1930 2,135 16.0% 58.8% 116
- 2,134 White (100.0%)
- 2 Negro (0.1%)

1960 20,393 7.4% 29.5% 98
- 20,374 White (99.9%)
- 3 Negro (0.0%)
- 16 Other races (0.1%)

1990 28,284 21.8% — 88
- 25,928 White (91.7%)
- 61 Black (0.2%)
- 32 American Indian (0.1%)
- 1,966 Asian/Pacific Islander (7.0%)
- 297 Other race (1.1%)
- 871 Hispanic Origin* (3.1%)

2000 30,068 33.7% — 87
- 25,022 White alone (83.2%)
- 139 Black or African American alone (0.5%)
- 27 American Indian and Alaska Native alone (0.1%)
- 3,812 Asian alone (12.7%)
- 4 Native Hawaiian and Other Pacific Islander alone (0.0%)
- 502 Some other race alone (1.7%)
- 562 Two or more races (1.9%)
- 1,512 Hispanic or Latino* (5.0%)

Norridge, IL (inc. 1948)

1960 14,087 8.0% 30.5% 96
- 14,059 White (99.8%)
- 1 Negro (0.0%)
- 27 Other races (0.2%)

1990 14,459 20.1% — 88
- 14,297 White (98.9%)
- 10 American Indian (0.1%)
- 128 Asian/Pacific Islander (0.9%)
- 24 Other race (0.2%)
- 312 Hispanic Origin* (2.2%)

2000 14,582 32.7% — 87
- 13,829 White alone (94.8%)
- 15 Black or African American alone (0.1%)
- 11 American Indian and Alaska Native alone (0.1%)
- 399 Asian alone (2.7%)
- 1 Native Hawaiian and Other Pacific Islander alone (0.0%)
- 180 Some other race alone (1.2%)
- 147 Two or more races (1.0%)
- 553 Hispanic or Latino* (3.8%)

North Aurora, IL (inc. 1905)

1930 682 — — —

1960 2,088 — — 98
- 2,085 White (99.9%)
- 1 Negro (0.0%)
- 2 Other races (0.1%)

1990 5,940 6.0% — 98
- 5,496 White (92.5%)
- 184 Black (3.1%)
- 12 American Indian (0.2%)
- 183 Asian/Pacific Islander (3.1%)
- 65 Other race (1.1%)
- 270 Hispanic Origin* (4.5%)

2000 10,585 8.0% — 98
- 9,284 White alone (87.7%)
- 474 Black or African American alone (4.5%)
- 22 American Indian and Alaska Native alone (0.2%)
- 269 Asian alone (2.5%)
- 3 Native Hawaiian and Other Pacific Islander alone (0.0%)
- 352 Some other race alone (3.3%)
- 181 Two or more races (1.7%)
- 1,025 Hispanic or Latino* (9.7%)

North Barrington, IL (inc. 1959)

1960 282 — —

1990 1,787 5.0% — 102
- 1,771 White (99.1%)
- 7 Black (0.4%)
- 7 Asian/Pacific Islander (0.4%)
- 2 Other race (0.1%)
- 34 Hispanic Origin* (1.9%)

2000 2,918 6.8% — 99
- 2,816 White alone (96.5%)
- 14 Black or African American alone (0.5%)
- 47 Asian alone (1.6%)
- 1 Native Hawaiian and Other Pacific Islander alone (0.0%)
- 10 Some other race alone (0.3%)
- 30 Two or more races (1.0%)
- 71 Hispanic or Latino* (2.4%)

North Chicago, IL (inc. 1895)

1900 1,150 — — —

1930 8,466 26.1% 47.7% 108
- 7,903 White (93.3%)
- 521 Negro (6.2%)
- 42 Other (0.5%)

1960 22,938 5.2% 14.8% 100
- 15,715 White (68.5%)
- 4,577 Negro (20.0%)
- 225 Other races (1.0%)

1990 34,978 6.2% — 187
- 19,813 White (56.6%)
- 11,977 Black (34.2%)
- 177 American Indian (0.5%)
- 1,357 Asian/Pacific Islander (3.9%)
- 1,654 Other race (4.7%)
- 3,277 Hispanic Origin* (9.4%)

2000 35,918 12.9% — 156
- 17,140 White alone (47.7%)
- 13,024 Black or African American alone (36.3%)
- 301 American Indian and Alaska Native alone (0.8%)
- 1,289 Asian alone (3.6%)
- 53 Native Hawaiian and Other Pacific Islander alone (0.1%)
- 2,750 Some other race alone (7.7%)
- 1,361 Two or more races (3.8%)
- 6,552 Hispanic or Latino* (18.2%)

North Riverside, IL (inc. 1923)

1930 969 — —

1960 7,989 9.6% 35.0% 103
- 7,879 White (98.6%)
- 89 Negro (1.1%)
- 22 Other races (0.3%)

1990 6,005 7.1% — 85
- 5,834 White (97.2%)
- 86 Asian/Pacific Islander (1.4%)
- 85 Other race (1.4%)
- 173 Hispanic Origin* (2.9%)

Municipalities *(continued)*

	Total (and by category)	Foreign born	Native with foreign parentage	Males per 100 females
2000	6,688	14.5%	—	89
	6,066	White alone (90.7%)		
	198	Black or African American alone (3.0%)		
	9	American Indian and Alaska Native alone (0.1%)		
	175	Asian alone (2.6%)		
	1	Native Hawaiian and Other Pacific Islander alone (0.0%)		
	164	Some other race alone (2.5%)		
	75	Two or more races (1.1%)		
	544	Hispanic or Latino* (8.1%)		

Northbrook, IL (inc. 1923)

1930	1,193	17.9%	38.6%	105
	1,193	White (100.0%)		
1960	11,635	4.0%	18.6%	100
	11,599	White (99.7%)		
	20	Negro (0.2%)		
	16	Other races (0.1%)		
1990	32,308	10.1%	—	95
	30,122	White (93.2%)		
	32	Black (0.1%)		
	7	American Indian (0.0%)		
	2,083	Asian/Pacific Islander (6.4%)		
	64	Other race (0.2%)		
	424	Hispanic Origin* (1.3%)		
2000	33,435	15.2%	—	93
	29,830	White alone (89.2%)		
	190	Black or African American alone (0.6%)		
	13	American Indian and Alaska Native alone (0.0%)		
	2,958	Asian alone (8.8%)		
	3	Native Hawaiian and Other Pacific Islander alone (0.0%)		
	119	Some other race alone (0.4%)		
	322	Two or more races (1.0%)		
	616	Hispanic or Latino* (1.8%)		

Northfield, IL (inc. 1926)

1930	311	—	—	—
1960	4,005	5.7%	16.3%	97
	3,977	White (99.3%)		
	28	Negro (0.7%)		
1990	4,635	9.8%	—	92
	4,429	White (95.6%)		
	200	Asian/Pacific Islander (4.3%)		
	6	Other race (0.1%)		
	44	Hispanic Origin* (0.9%)		
2000	5,389	12.4%	—	91
	4,984	White alone (92.5%)		
	28	Black or African American alone (0.5%)		
	2	American Indian and Alaska Native alone (0.0%)		
	300	Asian alone (5.6%)		
	23	Some other race alone (0.4%)		
	52	Two or more races (1.0%)		
	90	Hispanic or Latino* (1.7%)		

Northlake, IL (inc. 1949)

1960	12,318	6.5%	23.5%	102
	12,292	White (99.8%)		
	26	Other races (0.2%)		
1990	12,505	16.9%	—	94
	10,827	White (86.6%)		
	178	Black (1.4%)		
	7	American Indian (0.1%)		
	436	Asian/Pacific Islander (3.5%)		
	1,057	Other race (8.5%)		
	1,972	Hispanic Origin* (15.8%)		
2000	11,878	24.4%	—	96
	8,964	White alone (75.5%)		
	285	Black or African American alone (2.4%)		
	59	American Indian and Alaska Native alone (0.5%)		
	436	Asian alone (3.7%)		
	6	Native Hawaiian and Other Pacific Islander alone (0.1%)		
	1,825	Some other race alone (15.4%)		
	303	Two or more races (2.6%)		
	4,133	Hispanic or Latino* (34.8%)		

Oak Brook, IL (inc. 1958)

1960	324	—	—	—
1990	9,178	18.6%	—	99
	7,457	White (81.2%)		
	121	Black (1.3%)		
	1,576	Asian/Pacific Islander (17.2%)		
	24	Other race (0.3%)		
	157	Hispanic Origin* (1.7%)		
2000	8,702	21.5%	—	91
	6,666	White alone (76.6%)		
	119	Black or African American alone (1.4%)		
	1,750	Asian alone (20.1%)		
	1	Native Hawaiian and Other Pacific Islander alone (0.0%)		
	19	Some other race alone (0.2%)		
	147	Two or more races (1.7%)		
	208	Hispanic or Latino* (2.4%)		

Oak Forest, IL (inc. 1947)

1960	3,724	6.6%	17.4%	99
	3,724	White (100.0%)		
1990	26,203	3.7%	—	97
	25,480	White (97.2%)		
	99	Black (0.4%)		
	62	American Indian (0.2%)		
	417	Asian/Pacific Islander (1.6%)		
	145	Other race (0.6%)		
	720	Hispanic Origin* (2.7%)		
2000	28,051	5.8%	—	99
	25,353	White alone (90.4%)		
	1,021	Black or African American alone (3.6%)		
	42	American Indian and Alaska Native alone (0.1%)		
	744	Asian alone (2.7%)		
	4	Native Hawaiian and Other Pacific Islander alone (0.0%)		
	468	Some other race alone (1.7%)		
	419	Two or more races (1.5%)		
	1,645	Hispanic or Latino* (5.9%)		

Oak Lawn, IL (inc. 1909)

1930	2,045	15.6%	36.5%	106
	2,043	White (99.9%)		
	2	Negro (0.1%)		
1960	27,471	3.9%	23.7%	99
	27,445	White (99.9%)		
	5	Negro (0.0%)		
	21	Other races (0.1%)		
1990	56,182	7.5%	—	87
	55,127	White (98.1%)		
	50	Black (0.1%)		
	43	American Indian (0.1%)		
	680	Asian/Pacific Islander (1.2%)		
	282	Other race (0.5%)		
	1,240	Hispanic Origin* (2.2%)		
2000	55,245	11.5%	—	88
	51,570	White alone (93.3%)		
	673	Black or African American alone (1.2%)		
	92	American Indian and Alaska Native alone (0.2%)		
	953	Asian alone (1.7%)		
	5	Native Hawaiian and Other Pacific Islander alone (0.0%)		
	905	Some other race alone (1.6%)		
	1,047	Two or more races (1.9%)		
	2,942	Hispanic or Latino* (5.3%)		

Oak Park, IL (inc. 1901)

1930	63,982	13.1%	33.4%	89
1960	61,093	8.3%	26.0%	82
	60,876	White (99.6%)		
	57	Negro (0.1%)		
	160	Other races (0.3%)		
1990	53,648	6.6%	—	87
	41,244	White (76.9%)		
	9,944	Black (18.5%)		
	84	American Indian (0.2%)		
	1,806	Asian/Pacific Islander (3.4%)		
	570	Other race (1.1%)		
	1,626	Hispanic Origin* (3.0%)		
2000	52,524	9.8%	—	87
	36,124	White alone (68.8%)		
	11,788	Black or African American alone (22.4%)		
	81	American Indian and Alaska Native alone (0.2%)		
	2,178	Asian alone (4.1%)		
	16	Native Hawaiian and Other Pacific Islander alone (0.0%)		
	857	Some other race alone (1.6%)		
	1,480	Two or more races (2.8%)		
	2,374	Hispanic or Latino* (4.5%)		

Oakbrook Terrace, IL (inc. 1958)

1960	1,121	—	—	105
	1,121	White (100.0%)		
1990	1,907	9.7%	—	87
	1,784	White (93.6%)		
	8	Black (0.4%)		
	108	Asian/Pacific Islander (5.7%)		
	7	Other race (0.4%)		
	39	Hispanic Origin* (2.0%)		
2000	2,300	15.5%	—	90
	1,852	White alone (80.5%)		
	95	Black or African American alone (4.1%)		
	281	Asian alone (12.2%)		
	1	Native Hawaiian and Other Pacific Islander alone (0.0%)		
	20	Some other race alone (0.9%)		
	51	Two or more races (2.2%)		
	95	Hispanic or Latino* (4.1%)		

Oakwood Hills, IL (inc. 1958)

1960	213	—	—	—
1990	1,498	2.1%	—	107
	1,486	White (99.2%)		
	2	Black (0.1%)		
	2	American Indian (0.1%)		
	6	Other race (0.4%)		
	42	Hispanic Origin* (2.8%)		
2000	2,194	5.4%	—	102
	2,151	White alone (98.0%)		
	8	Black or African American alone (0.4%)		
	5	American Indian and Alaska Native alone (0.2%)		
	7	Asian alone (0.3%)		
	4	Some other race alone (0.2%)		
	19	Two or more races (0.9%)		
	74	Hispanic or Latino* (3.4%)		

Ogden Dunes, IN (inc. 1925)

1930	50	—	—	—
1960	947	—	—	—
1990	1,499	2.5%	—	97
	1,483	White (98.9%)		
	10	Asian/Pacific Islander (0.7%)		
	6	Other race (0.4%)		
	46	Hispanic Origin* (3.1%)		
2000	1,313	3.4%	—	99
	1,294	White alone (98.6%)		
	3	Black or African American alone (0.2%)		
	2	American Indian and Alaska Native alone (0.2%)		
	1	Asian alone (0.1%)		
	3	Some other race alone (0.2%)		
	10	Two or more races (0.8%)		
	31	Hispanic or Latino* (2.4%)		

Old Mill Creek, IL (inc. 1958)

1960	149	—	—	—
1990	73	0.0%	—	115
	83	White (113.7%)		
2000	251	14.7%	—	96
	219	White alone (87.3%)		
	6	Black or African American alone (2.4%)		
	16	Asian alone (6.4%)		
	3	Some other race alone (1.2%)		
	7	Two or more races (2.8%)		
	6	Hispanic or Latino* (2.4%)		

Olympia Fields, IL (inc. 1927)

1930	143	—	—	—
1960	1,503	—	—	103
	1,497	White (99.6%)		
	6	Negro (0.4%)		
1990	4,248	8.0%	—	98
	3,256	White (76.6%)		
	685	Black (16.1%)		
	252	Asian/Pacific Islander (5.9%)		
	55	Other race (1.3%)		
	84	Hispanic Origin* (2.0%)		
2000	4,732	8.3%	—	91
	2,018	White alone (42.6%)		
	2,466	Black or African American alone (52.1%)		
	2	American Indian and Alaska Native alone (0.0%)		
	160	Asian alone (3.4%)		
	1	Native Hawaiian and Other Pacific Islander alone (0.0%)		
	27	Some other race alone (0.6%)		
	58	Two or more races (1.2%)		
	86	Hispanic or Latino* (1.8%)		

Orland Hills, IL (inc. 1961)

1990	5,510	4.3%	—	96
	5,027	White (91.2%)		
	216	Black (3.9%)		
	7	American Indian (0.1%)		
	100	Asian/Pacific Islander (1.8%)		
	160	Other race (2.9%)		
	239	Hispanic Origin* (4.3%)		
2000	6,779	8.8%	—	97
	5,878	White alone (86.7%)		
	346	Black or African American alone (5.1%)		
	17	American Indian and Alaska Native alone (0.3%)		
	225	Asian alone (3.3%)		
	117	Some other race alone (1.7%)		
	196	Two or more races (2.9%)		
	409	Hispanic or Latino* (6.0%)		

Orland Park, IL (inc. 1892)

1900	366	—	—	—
1930	571	—	—	—
1960	2,592	1.1%	13.0%	103
	2,585	White (99.7%)		
	7	Other races (0.3%)		
1990	35,720	7.4%	—	96
	34,052	White (95.3%)		
	92	Black (0.3%)		
	20	American Indian (0.1%)		
	1,309	Asian/Pacific Islander (3.7%)		
	247	Other race (0.7%)		
	867	Hispanic Origin* (2.4%)		
2000	51,077	9.4%	—	92
	47,772	White alone (93.5%)		
	374	Black or African American alone (0.7%)		
	34	American Indian and Alaska Native alone (0.1%)		
	1,770	Asian alone (3.5%)		
	18	Native Hawaiian and Other Pacific Islander alone (0.0%)		
	530	Some other race alone (1.0%)		
	579	Two or more races (1.1%)		
	1,874	Hispanic or Latino* (3.7%)		

Oswego, IL (inc. 1857)

1900	618	—	—	—
1930	932	—	—	—
1960	1,510	—	—	99
	1,509	White (99.9%)		
	1	Other races (0.1%)		
1990	3,876	1.4%	—	95
	3,848	White (99.3%)		
	11	Asian/Pacific Islander (0.3%)		
	17	Other race (0.4%)		
	45	Hispanic Origin* (1.2%)		
2000	13,326	4.7%	—	96
	12,459	White alone (93.5%)		
	239	Black or African American alone (1.8%)		
	24	American Indian and Alaska Native alone (0.2%)		
	183	Asian alone (1.4%)		
	4	Native Hawaiian and Other Pacific Islander alone (0.0%)		
	238	Some other race alone (1.8%)		
	179	Two or more races (1.3%)		
	665	Hispanic or Latino* (5.0%)		

Palatine, IL (inc. 1869)

1900	1,020	—	—	—
1930	2,118	11.2%	39.1%	100
	2,118	White (100.0%)		
1960	11,504	3.1%	19.1%	94
	11,482	White (99.8%)		
	1	Negro (0.0%)		
	21	Other races (0.2%)		
1990	39,253	8.3%	—	95
	36,824	White (93.8%)		
	334	Black (0.9%)		
	55	American Indian (0.1%)		
	1,316	Asian/Pacific Islander (3.4%)		
	724	Other race (1.8%)		
	1,443	Hispanic Origin* (3.7%)		
2000	65,479	21.8%	—	99
	54,381	White alone (83.1%)		
	1,407	Black or African American alone (2.1%)		
	147	American Indian and Alaska Native alone (0.2%)		
	4,953	Asian alone (7.6%)		
	27	Native Hawaiian and Other Pacific Islander alone (0.0%)		
	3,327	Some other race alone (5.1%)		
	1,237	Two or more races (1.9%)		
	9,247	Hispanic or Latino* (14.1%)		

Palos Heights, IL (inc. 1959)

1960	3,775	4.9%	23.2%	102
	3,775	White (100.0%)		
1990	11,478	5.2%	—	91
	11,097	White (96.7%)		
	51	Black (0.4%)		
	7	American Indian (0.1%)		
	316	Asian/Pacific Islander (2.8%)		
	7	Other race (0.1%)		
	102	Hispanic Origin* (0.9%)		
2000	11,260	6.4%	—	86
	10,853	White alone (96.4%)		
	49	Black or African American alone (0.4%)		
	10	American Indian and Alaska Native alone (0.1%)		
	232	Asian alone (2.1%)		
	28	Some other race alone (0.2%)		
	88	Two or more races (0.8%)		
	161	Hispanic or Latino* (1.4%)		

Palos Hills, IL (inc. 1959)

1960	3,766	5.2%	21.1%	101
	3,762	White (99.9%)		
	4	Other races (0.1%)		
1990	17,803	10.7%	—	92
	17,061	White (95.8%)		
	385	Black (2.2%)		
	16	American Indian (0.1%)		
	227	Asian/Pacific Islander (1.3%)		
	114	Other race (0.6%)		
	513	Hispanic Origin* (2.9%)		
2000	17,665	16.5%	—	88
	15,401	White alone (87.2%)		
	968	Black or African American alone (5.5%)		
	19	American Indian and Alaska Native alone (0.1%)		
	472	Asian alone (2.7%)		
	2	Native Hawaiian and Other Pacific Islander alone (0.0%)		
	277	Some other race alone (1.6%)		
	526	Two or more races (3.0%)		
	854	Hispanic or Latino* (4.8%)		

Palos Park, IL (inc. 1914)

1930	456	—	—	—
1960	2,169	—	—	101
	2,169	White (100.0%)		
1990	4,199	10.7%	—	101
	3,973	White (94.6%)		
	216	Asian/Pacific Islander (5.1%)		
	10	Other race (0.2%)		
	88	Hispanic Origin* (2.1%)		
2000	4,689	8.3%	—	94
	4,556	White alone (97.2%)		
	13	Black or African American alone (0.3%)		
	2	American Indian and Alaska Native alone (0.0%)		
	81	Asian alone (1.7%)		
	9	Some other race alone (0.2%)		
	28	Two or more races (0.6%)		
	99	Hispanic or Latino* (2.1%)		

Park City, IL (inc. 1958)

1960	1,408	—	—	107
	1,404	White (99.7%)		
	1	Negro (0.1%)		
	3	Other races (0.2%)		
1990	4,677	12.8%	—	99
	3,868	White (82.7%)		
	220	Black (4.7%)		
	25	American Indian (0.5%)		
	215	Asian/Pacific Islander (4.6%)		
	349	Other race (7.5%)		
	707	Hispanic Origin* (15.1%)		
2000	6,637	32.1%	—	103
	4,008	White alone (60.4%)		
	500	Black or African American alone (7.5%)		
	15	American Indian and Alaska Native alone (0.2%)		
	586	Asian alone (8.8%)		
	10	Native Hawaiian and Other Pacific Islander alone (0.2%)		
	1,149	Some other race alone (17.3%)		
	369	Two or more races (5.6%)		
	2,506	Hispanic or Latino* (37.8%)		

Park Forest, IL (inc. 1949)

1960	29,993	3.7%	14.7%	99
	29,801	White (99.4%)		
	8	Negro (0.0%)		
	184	Other races (0.6%)		
1990	24,656	3.4%	—	91
	17,892	White (72.6%)		
	5,978	Black (24.2%)		
	39	American Indian (0.2%)		
	284	Asian/Pacific Islander (1.2%)		
	463	Other race (1.9%)		
	889	Hispanic Origin* (3.6%)		
2000	23,462	3.1%	—	87
	13,003	White alone (55.4%)		
	9,247	Black or African American alone (39.4%)		
	53	American Indian and Alaska Native alone (0.2%)		
	193	Asian alone (0.8%)		
	17	Native Hawaiian and Other Pacific Islander alone (0.1%)		
	362	Some other race alone (1.5%)		
	587	Two or more races (2.5%)		
	1,169	Hispanic or Latino* (5.0%)		

Municipalities *(continued)*

Park Ridge, IL (inc. 1873)

Year	Total (and by category)	Foreign born	Native with foreign parentage	Males per 100 females
1900	1,340	—	—	—
1930	10,417	11.6%	34.3%	94
	10,403 White (99.9%)			
	14 Negro (0.1%)			
1960	32,659	4.9%	25.0%	94
	32,623 White (99.9%)			
	5 Negro (0.0%)			
	31 Other races (0.1%)			
1990	36,175	10.5%	—	88
	35,225 White (97.4%)			
	8 Black (0.0%)			
	5 American Indian (0.0%)			
	835 Asian/Pacific Islander (2.3%)			
	102 Other race (0.3%)			
	467 Hispanic Origin* (1.3%)			
2000	37,775	12.7%	—	90
	36,031 White alone (95.4%)			
	90 Black or African American alone (0.2%)			
	24 American Indian and Alaska Native alone (0.1%)			
	1,004 Asian alone (2.7%)			
	18 Native Hawaiian and Other Pacific Islander alone (0.0%)			
	329 Some other race alone (0.9%)			
	279 Two or more races (0.7%)			
	1,113 Hispanic or Latino* (2.9%)			

Peotone, IL (inc. 1869)

Year	Total (and by category)	Foreign born	Native with foreign parentage	Males per 100 females
1900	1,003	—	—	—
1930	1,154	13.7%	37.4%	90
	1,142 White (99.0%)			
	12 Negro (1.0%)			
1960	1,788	—	—	94
	1,777 White (99.4%)			
	9 Negro (0.5%)			
	2 Other races (0.1%)			
1990	2,947	1.1%	—	98
	2,890 White (98.1%)			
	5 Asian/Pacific Islander (0.2%)			
2000	3,385	1.0%	—	93
	3,315 White alone (97.9%)			
	9 Black or African American alone (0.3%)			
	2 American Indian and Alaska Native alone (0.1%)			
	16 Asian alone (0.5%)			
	10 Some other race alone (0.3%)			
	33 Two or more races (1.0%)			
	46 Hispanic or Latino* (1.4%)			

Phoenix, IL (inc. 1900)

Year	Total (and by category)	Foreign born	Native with foreign parentage	Males per 100 females
1930	3,033	24.9%	46.5%	115
	2,554 White (84.2%)			
	457 Negro (15.1%)			
	22 Other (0.7%)			
1960	4,203	3.5%	9.5%	101
	1,459 White (34.7%)			
	2,744 Negro (65.3%)			
1990	2,217	3.2%	—	86
	111 White (5.0%)			
	2,029 Black (91.5%)			
	9 American Indian (0.4%)			
	72 Other race (3.2%)			
	165 Hispanic Origin* (7.4%)			
2000	2,157	2.7%	—	87
	63 White alone (2.9%)			
	2,024 Black or African American alone (93.8%)			
	8 American Indian and Alaska Native alone (0.4%)			
	1 Asian alone (0.0%)			
	33 Some other race alone (1.5%)			
	28 Two or more races (1.3%)			
	87 Hispanic or Latino* (4.0%)			

Pingree Grove, IL (inc. 1907)

Year	Total (and by category)	Foreign born	Native with foreign parentage	Males per 100 females
1930	125	—	—	—
1960	173	—	—	—
1990	138	4.3%	—	109
	150 White (108.7%)			
	4 Hispanic Origin* (2.9%)			
2000	124	0.0%	—	91
	123 White alone (99.2%)			
	1 Some other race alone (0.8%)			
	5 Hispanic or Latino* (4.0%)			

Plainfield, IL (inc. 1869)

Year	Total (and by category)	Foreign born	Native with foreign parentage	Males per 100 females
1870	723	7.7%	—	—
	723 White (100.0%)			
1900	920	—	—	—
1930	1,428	4.3%	24.2%	96
	1,418 White (99.3%)			
1960	2,183	—	—	96
	2,183 White (100.0%)			
1990	4,557	1.3%	—	97
	4,507 White (98.9%)			
	10 American Indian (0.2%)			
	23 Asian/Pacific Islander (0.5%)			
	17 Other race (0.4%)			
	59 Hispanic Origin* (1.3%)			
2000	13,038	3.9%	—	101
	12,497 White alone (95.9%)			
	110 Black or African American alone (0.8%)			
	10 American Indian and Alaska Native alone (0.1%)			
	163 Asian alone (1.3%)			
	1 Native Hawaiian and Other Pacific Islander alone (0.0%)			
	132 Some other race alone (1.0%)			
	125 Two or more races (1.0%)			
	504 Hispanic or Latino* (3.9%)			

Portage, IN (inc. 1959)

Year	Total (and by category)	Foreign born	Native with foreign parentage	Males per 100 females
1870	728	37.5%	—	—
	723 White (99.3%)			
	5 Colored (0.7%)			
1960	11,822	2.7%	9.9%	103
	11,807 White (99.9%)			
	13 Negro (0.1%)			
	2 Other races (0.0%)			
1990	29,060	2.4%	—	95
	28,270 White (97.3%)			
	83 Black (0.3%)			
	57 American Indian (0.2%)			
	144 Asian/Pacific Islander (0.5%)			
	506 Other race (1.7%)			
	1,833 Hispanic Origin* (6.3%)			
2000	33,496	3.1%	—	94
	30,992 White alone (92.5%)			
	485 Black or African American alone (1.4%)			
	90 American Indian and Alaska Native alone (0.3%)			
	215 Asian alone (0.6%)			
	19 Native Hawaiian and Other Pacific Islander alone (0.1%)			
	1,072 Some other race alone (3.2%)			
	623 Two or more races (1.9%)			
	3,330 Hispanic or Latino* (9.9%)			

Porter, IN (inc. 1908)

Year	Total (and by category)	Foreign born	Native with foreign parentage	Males per 100 females
1870	1,006	21.9%	—	—
	1,086 White (108.0%)			
1930	805	—	—	—
1960	2,189	—	—	101
	2,189 White (100.0%)			
1990	3,118	2.4%	—	100
	3,055 White (98.0%)			
	51 Asian/Pacific Islander (1.6%)			
	12 Other race (0.4%)			
	78 Hispanic Origin* (2.5%)			
2000	4,972	2.4%	—	95
	4,780 White alone (96.1%)			
	41 Black or African American alone (0.8%)			
	11 American Indian and Alaska Native alone (0.2%)			
	29 Asian alone (0.6%)			
	31 Some other race alone (0.6%)			
	80 Two or more races (1.6%)			
	233 Hispanic or Latino* (4.7%)			

Posen, IL (inc. 1900)

Year	Total (and by category)	Foreign born	Native with foreign parentage	Males per 100 females
1930	1,329	28.2%	58.3%	112
	1,329 White (100.0%)			
1960	4,517	6.1%	21.8%	97
	4,513 White (99.9%)			
	4 Other races (0.1%)			
1990	4,226	4.9%	—	98
	3,995 White (94.5%)			
	60 Black (1.4%)			
	29 Asian/Pacific Islander (0.7%)			
	142 Other race (3.4%)			
	310 Hispanic Origin* (7.3%)			
2000	4,730	10.5%	—	101
	3,703 White alone (78.3%)			
	413 Black or African American alone (8.7%)			
	16 American Indian and Alaska Native alone (0.3%)			
	11 Asian alone (0.2%)			
	3 Native Hawaiian and Other Pacific Islander alone (0.1%)			
	462 Some other race alone (9.8%)			
	122 Two or more races (2.6%)			
	1,087 Hispanic or Latino* (23.0%)			

Prairie Grove, IL (inc. 1973)

Year	Total (and by category)	Foreign born	Native with foreign parentage	Males per 100 females
1990	654	4.9%	—	102
	647 White (98.9%)			
	3 Black (0.5%)			
	6 Asian/Pacific Islander (0.9%)			
	10 Hispanic Origin* (1.5%)			
2000	960	4.1%	—	97
	931 White alone (97.0%)			
	6 Black or African American alone (0.6%)			
	2 American Indian and Alaska Native alone (0.2%)			
	10 Asian alone (1.0%)			
	4 Some other race alone (0.4%)			
	7 Two or more races (0.7%)			
	12 Hispanic or Latino* (1.3%)			

Prospect Heights, IL (inc. 1976)

Year	Total (and by category)	Foreign born	Native with foreign parentage	Males per 100 females
1990	15,239	20.0%	—	104
	13,248 White (86.9%)			
	273 Black (1.8%)			
	25 American Indian (0.2%)			
	706 Asian/Pacific Islander (4.6%)			
	987 Other race (6.5%)			
	2,126 Hispanic Origin* (14.0%)			
2000	17,081	37.5%	—	104
	13,223 White alone (77.4%)			
	300 Black or African American alone (1.8%)			
	42 American Indian and Alaska Native alone (0.2%)			
	746 Asian alone (4.4%)			
	8 Native Hawaiian and Other Pacific Islander alone (0.0%)			
	2,361 Some other race alone (13.8%)			
	401 Two or more races (2.3%)			
	4,711 Hispanic or Latino* (27.6%)			

Richmond, IL (inc. 1865)

Year	Total (and by category)	Foreign born	Native with foreign parentage	Males per 100 females
1900	576	—	—	—
1930	514	—	—	—
1960	855	—	—	—
1990	1,016	3.4%	—	93
	1,011 White (99.5%)			
	5 Black (0.5%)			
	8 Hispanic Origin* (0.8%)			

2000	1,091	3.4%	—	99
	1,068	White alone (97.9%)		
	3	Black or African American alone (0.3%)		
	2	American Indian and Alaska Native alone (0.2%)		
	7	Asian alone (0.6%)		
	10	Some other race alone (0.9%)		
	1	Two or more races (0.1%)		
	44	Hispanic or Latino* (4.0%)		

Richton Park, IL (inc. 1926)

1930	137	—	—	—
1960	933	—	—	—
1990	10,523	4.6%	—	87
	7,839	White (74.5%)		
	2,335	Black (22.2%)		
	25	American Indian (0.2%)		
	185	Asian/Pacific Islander (1.8%)		
	139	Other race (1.3%)		
	312	Hispanic Origin* (3.0%)		
2000	12,533	4.6%	—	85
	4,474	White alone (35.7%)		
	7,407	Black or African American alone (59.1%)		
	30	American Indian and Alaska Native alone (0.2%)		
	192	Asian alone (1.5%)		
	5	Native Hawaiian and Other Pacific Islander alone (0.0%)		
	167	Some other race alone (1.3%)		
	258	Two or more races (2.1%)		
	484	Hispanic or Latino* (3.9%)		

Ringwood, IL (inc. 1994)

1990	520	—	—	—
2000	471	6.6%	—	104
	465	White alone (98.7%)		
	1	Black or African American alone (0.2%)		
	3	Asian alone (0.6%)		
	1	Some other race alone (0.2%)		
	1	Two or more races (0.2%)		
	2	Hispanic or Latino* (0.4%)		

River Forest, IL (inc. 1880)

1900	1,539	—	—	—
1930	8,829	12.3%	32.0%	87
	8,713	White (98.7%)		
	101	Negro (1.1%)		
	15	Other (0.2%)		
1960	12,695	5.3%	23.2%	82
	12,652	White (99.7%)		
	35	Negro (0.3%)		
	8	Other races (0.1%)		
1990	11,669	7.9%	—	83
	11,045	White (94.7%)		
	182	Black (1.6%)		
	7	American Indian (0.1%)		
	355	Asian/Pacific Islander (3.0%)		
	80	Other race (0.7%)		
	280	Hispanic Origin* (2.4%)		
2000	11,635	7.6%	—	85
	10,396	White alone (89.4%)		
	560	Black or African American alone (4.8%)		
	11	American Indian and Alaska Native alone (0.1%)		
	364	Asian alone (3.1%)		
	5	Native Hawaiian and Other Pacific Islander alone (0.0%)		
	114	Some other race alone (1.0%)		
	185	Two or more races (1.6%)		
	466	Hispanic or Latino* (4.0%)		

River Grove, IL (inc. 1888)

1900	333	—	—	—
1930	2,741	17.4%	39.4%	104
	2,740	White (100.0%)		
	1	Negro (0.0%)		
1960	8,464	6.8%	28.5%	100
	8,456	White (99.9%)		
	3	Negro (0.0%)		
	5	Other races (0.1%)		
1990	9,961	16.6%	—	88
	9,713	White (97.5%)		
	11	American Indian (0.1%)		
	132	Asian/Pacific Islander (1.3%)		
	105	Other race (1.1%)		
	403	Hispanic Origin* (4.0%)		
2000	10,668	25.0%	—	93
	9,841	White alone (92.2%)		
	38	Black or African American alone (0.4%)		
	31	American Indian and Alaska Native alone (0.3%)		
	217	Asian alone (2.0%)		
	6	Native Hawaiian and Other Pacific Islander alone (0.1%)		
	389	Some other race alone (3.6%)		
	146	Two or more races (1.4%)		
	1,043	Hispanic or Latino* (9.8%)		

Riverdale, IL (inc. 1892)

1900	558	—	—	—
1930	2,504	15.3%	32.6%	110
	2,373	White (94.8%)		
	131	Other (5.2%)		
1960	12,008	6.1%	24.9%	98
	12,000	White (99.9%)		
	3	Negro (0.0%)		
	5	Other races (0.0%)		
1990	13,671	3.5%	—	85
	8,016	White (58.6%)		
	5,463	Black (40.0%)		
	24	American Indian (0.2%)		
	9	Asian/Pacific Islander (0.1%)		
	125	Other race (0.9%)		
	334	Hispanic Origin* (2.4%)		
2000	15,055	3.3%	—	84
	1,667	White alone (11.1%)		
	13,004	Black or African American alone (86.4%)		
	24	American Indian and Alaska Native alone (0.2%)		
	29	Asian alone (0.2%)		
	7	Native Hawaiian and Other Pacific Islander alone (0.0%)		
	157	Some other race alone (1.0%)		
	167	Two or more races (1.1%)		
	366	Hispanic or Latino* (2.4%)		

Riverside, IL (inc. 1875)

1900	1,551	—	—	—
1930	6,770	13.9%	35.5%	93
	6,752	White (99.7%)		
	16	Negro (0.2%)		
	2	Other (0.0%)		
1960	9,750	7.1%	31.0%	89
	9,742	White (99.9%)		
	6	Negro (0.1%)		
	2	Other races (0.0%)		
1990	8,774	8.2%	—	90
	8,679	White (98.9%)		
	8	American Indian (0.1%)		
	68	Asian/Pacific Islander (0.8%)		
	19	Other race (0.2%)		
	186	Hispanic Origin* (2.1%)		
2000	8,895	9.2%	—	93
	8,484	White alone (95.4%)		
	23	Black or African American alone (0.3%)		
	7	American Indian and Alaska Native alone (0.1%)		
	142	Asian alone (1.6%)		
	1	Native Hawaiian and Other Pacific Islander alone (0.0%)		
	140	Some other race alone (1.6%)		
	98	Two or more races (1.1%)		
	489	Hispanic or Latino* (5.5%)		

Riverwoods, IL (inc. 1959)

1960	96	—	—	—
1990	2,868	7.4%	—	96
	2,797	White (97.5%)		
	4	American Indian (0.1%)		
	67	Asian/Pacific Islander (2.3%)		
	8	Hispanic Origin* (0.3%)		
2000	3,843	13.5%	—	94
	3,617	White alone (94.1%)		
	14	Black or African American alone (0.4%)		
	173	Asian alone (4.5%)		
	1	Native Hawaiian and Other Pacific Islander alone (0.0%)		
	7	Some other race alone (0.2%)		
	31	Two or more races (0.8%)		
	76	Hispanic or Latino* (2.0%)		

Robbins, IL (inc. 1917)

1930	753	—	—	—
1960	7,511	0.4%	0.3%	96
	66	White (0.9%)		
	7,410	Negro (98.7%)		
	35	Other races (0.5%)		
1990	7,498	0.1%	—	90
	71	White (0.9%)		
	7,391	Black (98.6%)		
	30	American Indian (0.4%)		
	6	Other race (0.1%)		
	27	Hispanic Origin* (0.4%)		
2000	6,635	0.6%	—	89
	187	White alone (2.8%)		
	6,320	Black or African American alone (95.3%)		
	8	American Indian and Alaska Native alone (0.1%)		
	5	Asian alone (0.1%)		
	62	Some other race alone (0.9%)		
	53	Two or more races (0.8%)		
	129	Hispanic or Latino* (1.9%)		

Rockdale, IL (inc. 1903)

1930	1,701	28.7%	50.3%	115
	1,591	White (93.5%)		
1960	1,272	—	—	104
	1,272	White (100.0%)		
1990	1,709	5.3%	—	95
	1,550	White (90.7%)		
	4	Black (0.2%)		
	4	American Indian (0.2%)		
	5	Asian/Pacific Islander (0.3%)		
	146	Other race (8.5%)		
	252	Hispanic Origin* (14.7%)		
2000	1,888	9.2%	—	101
	1,565	White alone (82.9%)		
	16	Black or African American alone (0.8%)		
	9	American Indian and Alaska Native alone (0.5%)		
	7	Asian alone (0.4%)		
	205	Some other race alone (10.9%)		
	86	Two or more races (4.6%)		
	415	Hispanic or Latino* (22.0%)		

Rolling Meadows, IL (inc. 1955)

1960	10,879	1.7%	15.4%	104
	10,865	White (99.9%)		
	14	Other races (0.1%)		
1990	22,591	13.2%	—	103
	20,944	White (92.7%)		
	343	Black (1.5%)		
	30	American Indian (0.1%)		
	800	Asian/Pacific Islander (3.5%)		
	474	Other race (2.1%)		
	2,519	Hispanic Origin* (11.2%)		
2000	24,604	21.3%	—	102
	20,256	White alone (82.3%)		
	696	Black or African American alone (2.8%)		
	67	American Indian and Alaska Native alone (0.3%)		
	1,627	Asian alone (6.6%)		
	7	Native Hawaiian and Other Pacific Islander alone (0.0%)		
	1,463	Some other race alone (5.9%)		
	488	Two or more races (2.0%)		
	4,725	Hispanic or Latino* (19.2%)		

Romeoville, IL (inc. 1895)

1900	113	—	—	—
1930	133	—	—	—

Municipalities *(continued)*

	Total (and by category)	Foreign born	Native with foreign parentage	Males per 100 females
1960	3,574	0.9%	8.9%	102
	3,547 White (99.2%)			
	27 Other races (0.8%)			
1990	14,074	4.4%	—	108
	12,807 White (91.0%)			
	304 Black (2.2%)			
	31 American Indian (0.2%)			
	213 Asian/Pacific Islander (1.5%)			
	724 Other race (5.1%)			
	1,442 Hispanic Origin* (10.2%)			
2000	21,153	9.4%	—	102
	17,872 White alone (84.5%)			
	1,137 Black or African American alone (5.4%)			
	82 American Indian and Alaska Native alone (0.4%)			
	518 Asian alone (2.4%)			
	5 Native Hawaiian and Other Pacific Islander alone (0.0%)			
	1,039 Some other race alone (4.9%)			
	500 Two or more races (2.4%)			
	2,781 Hispanic or Latino* (13.1%)			

Roselle, IL (inc. 1922)

	Total (and by category)	Foreign born	Native with foreign parentage	Males per 100 females
1930	807	—	—	—
1960	3,581	3.2%	20.3%	95
	3,581 White (100.0%)			
1990	20,819	8.9%	—	96
	19,149 White (92.0%)			
	358 Black (1.7%)			
	19 American Indian (0.1%)			
	1,064 Asian/Pacific Islander (5.1%)			
	193 Other race (0.9%)			
	540 Hispanic Origin* (2.6%)			
2000	23,115	15.2%	—	96
	20,315 White alone (87.9%)			
	383 Black or African American alone (1.7%)			
	48 American Indian and Alaska Native alone (0.2%)			
	1,685 Asian alone (7.3%)			
	11 Native Hawaiian and Other Pacific Islander alone (0.0%)			
	333 Some other race alone (1.4%)			
	340 Two or more races (1.5%)			
	1,197 Hispanic or Latino* (5.2%)			

Rosemont, IL (inc. 1956)

	Total (and by category)	Foreign born	Native with foreign parentage	Males per 100 females
1960	978	—	—	—
1990	3,995	21.1%	—	106
	3,245 White (81.2%)			
	30 Black (0.8%)			
	11 American Indian (0.3%)			
	180 Asian/Pacific Islander (4.5%)			
	529 Other race (13.2%)			
	773 Hispanic Origin* (19.3%)			
2000	4,224	36.8%	—	111
	3,347 White alone (79.2%)			
	57 Black or African American alone (1.3%)			
	37 American Indian and Alaska Native alone (0.9%)			
	186 Asian alone (4.4%)			
	1 Native Hawaiian and Other Pacific Islander alone (0.0%)			
	488 Some other race alone (11.6%)			
	108 Two or more races (2.6%)			
	1,493 Hispanic or Latino* (35.3%)			

Round Lake Beach, IL (inc. 1937)

	Total (and by category)	Foreign born	Native with foreign parentage	Males per 100 females
1960	5,011	5.2%	21.2%	101
1990	16,434	8.4%	—	98
	15,034 White (91.5%)			
	169 Black (1.0%)			
	60 American Indian (0.4%)			
	261 Asian/Pacific Islander (1.6%)			
	910 Other race (5.5%)			
	2,316 Hispanic Origin* (14.1%)			
2000	25,859	21.3%	—	102
	19,227 White alone (74.4%)			
	792 Black or African American alone (3.1%)			
	161 American Indian and Alaska Native alone (0.6%)			
	534 Asian alone (2.1%)			
	11 Native Hawaiian and Other Pacific Islander alone (0.0%)			
	4,387 Some other race alone (17.0%)			
	747 Two or more races (2.9%)			
	8,084 Hispanic or Latino* (31.3%)			

Round Lake Heights, IL (inc. 1960)

	Total (and by category)	Foreign born	Native with foreign parentage	Males per 100 females
1990	1,251	6.6%	—	105
	1,180 White (94.3%)			
	3 Black (0.2%)			
	7 American Indian (0.6%)			
	9 Asian/Pacific Islander (0.7%)			
	52 Other race (4.2%)			
	164 Hispanic Origin* (13.1%)			
2000	1,347	12.2%	—	101
	1,109 White alone (82.3%)			
	28 Black or African American alone (2.1%)			
	2 American Indian and Alaska Native alone (0.1%)			
	15 Asian alone (1.1%)			
	1 Native Hawaiian and Other Pacific Islander alone (0.1%)			
	142 Some other race alone (10.5%)			
	50 Two or more races (3.7%)			
	288 Hispanic or Latino* (21.4%)			

Round Lake Park, IL (inc. 1947)

	Total (and by category)	Foreign born	Native with foreign parentage	Males per 100 females
1960	2,565	5.5%	17.8%	101
	2,546 White (99.3%)			
	19 Other races (0.7%)			
1990	4,045	6.3%	—	103
	3,825 White (94.6%)			
	24 American Indian (0.6%)			
	5 Asian/Pacific Islander (0.1%)			
	191 Other race (4.7%)			
	518 Hispanic Origin* (12.8%)			
2000	6,038	15.3%	—	101
	4,905 White alone (81.2%)			
	104 Black or African American alone (1.7%)			
	22 American Indian and Alaska Native alone (0.4%)			
	33 Asian alone (0.5%)			
	1 Native Hawaiian and Other Pacific Islander alone (0.0%)			
	817 Some other race alone (13.5%)			
	156 Two or more races (2.6%)			
	1,584 Hispanic or Latino* (26.2%)			

Round Lake, IL (inc. 1908)

	Total (and by category)	Foreign born	Native with foreign parentage	Males per 100 females
1930	338	—	—	—
1960	997	—	—	—
1990	3,550	8.5%	—	97
	3,301 White (93.0%)			
	15 Black (0.4%)			
	12 American Indian (0.3%)			
	78 Asian/Pacific Islander (2.2%)			
	143 Other race (4.0%)			
	419 Hispanic Origin* (11.8%)			
2000	5,842	20.6%	—	102
	4,782 White alone (81.9%)			
	116 Black or African American alone (2.0%)			
	23 American Indian and Alaska Native alone (0.4%)			
	112 Asian alone (1.9%)			
	2 Native Hawaiian and Other Pacific Islander alone (0.0%)			
	630 Some other race alone (10.8%)			
	177 Two or more races (3.0%)			
	1,292 Hispanic or Latino* (22.1%)			

Sauk Village, IL (inc. 1957)

	Total (and by category)	Foreign born	Native with foreign parentage	Males per 100 females
1960	4,687	1.9%	10.8%	106
	4,672 White (99.7%)			
	15 Other races (0.3%)			
1990	9,926	2.1%	—	99
	7,452 White (75.1%)			
	1,790 Black (18.0%)			
	31 American Indian (0.3%)			
	110 Asian/Pacific Islander (1.1%)			
	543 Other race (5.5%)			
	934 Hispanic Origin* (9.4%)			
2000	10,411	4.0%	—	98
	6,221 White alone (59.8%)			
	3,382 Black or African American alone (32.5%)			
	26 American Indian and Alaska Native alone (0.2%)			
	69 Asian alone (0.7%)			
	4 Native Hawaiian and Other Pacific Islander alone (0.0%)			
	348 Some other race alone (3.3%)			
	361 Two or more races (3.5%)			
	1,224 Hispanic or Latino* (11.8%)			

Schaumburg, IL (inc. 1956)

	Total (and by category)	Foreign born	Native with foreign parentage	Males per 100 females
1960	986	—	—	—
1990	68,586	9.6%	—	95
	62,156 White (90.6%)			
	1,487 Black (2.2%)			
	38 American Indian (0.1%)			
	4,414 Asian/Pacific Islander (6.4%)			
	491 Other race (0.7%)			
	1,649 Hispanic Origin* (2.4%)			
2000	75,386	18.9%	—	95
	59,391 White alone (78.8%)			
	2,526 Black or African American alone (3.4%)			
	77 American Indian and Alaska Native alone (0.1%)			
	10,697 Asian alone (14.2%)			
	43 Native Hawaiian and Other Pacific Islander alone (0.1%)			
	1,307 Some other race alone (1.7%)			
	1,345 Two or more races (1.8%)			
	3,988 Hispanic or Latino* (5.3%)			

Schererville, IN (inc. 1911)

	Total (and by category)	Foreign born	Native with foreign parentage	Males per 100 females
1930	580	—	—	—
1960	2,875	3.8%	14.5%	103
	2,873 White (99.9%)			
	2 Other races (0.1%)			
1990	19,926	5.5%	—	100
	19,303 White (96.9%)			
	114 Black (0.6%)			
	36 American Indian (0.2%)			
	223 Asian/Pacific Islander (1.1%)			
	250 Other race (1.3%)			
	743 Hispanic Origin* (3.7%)			
2000	24,851	8.3%	—	97
	22,726 White alone (91.4%)			
	533 Black or African American alone (2.1%)			
	28 American Indian and Alaska Native alone (0.1%)			
	636 Asian alone (2.6%)			
	11 Native Hawaiian and Other Pacific Islander alone (0.0%)			
	504 Some other race alone (2.0%)			
	413 Two or more races (1.7%)			
	1,576 Hispanic or Latino* (6.3%)			

Schiller Park, IL (inc. 1914)

	Total (and by category)	Foreign born	Native with foreign parentage	Males per 100 females
1930	709	—	—	—
1960	5,687	5.9%	24.9%	104
	5,684 White (99.9%)			
	1 Negro (0.0%)			
	2 Other races (0.0%)			
1990	11,189	18.8%	—	106
	10,001 White (89.4%)			
	106 Black (0.9%)			
	51 American Indian (0.5%)			
	439 Asian/Pacific Islander (3.9%)			
	592 Other race (5.3%)			
	1,394 Hispanic Origin* (12.5%)			

2000	11,850	38.9%	—	104
	9,596	White alone (81.0%)		
	235	Black or African American alone (2.0%)		
	33	American Indian and Alaska Native alone (0.3%)		
	609	Asian alone (5.1%)		
	2	Native Hawaiian and Other Pacific Islander alone (0.0%)		
	961	Some other race alone (8.1%)		
	414	Two or more races (3.5%)		
	2,598	Hispanic or Latino* (21.9%)		

Schneider, IN (inc. 1915)

1930	264	—	—	—
1960	405	—	—	—
1990	310	0.6%	—	88
	303	White (97.7%)		
	6	American Indian (1.9%)		
	1	Other race (0.3%)		
	4	Hispanic Origin* (1.3%)		
2000	317	1.3%	—	105

Shorewood, IL (inc. 1957)

1960	358	—	—	—
1990	6,264	2.4%	—	99
	6,009	White (95.9%)		
	93	Black (1.5%)		
	5	American Indian (0.1%)		
	107	Asian/Pacific Islander (1.7%)		
	50	Other race (0.8%)		
	110	Hispanic Origin* (1.8%)		
2000	7,686	4.3%	—	100
	7,126	White alone (92.7%)		
	184	Black or African American alone (2.4%)		
	21	American Indian and Alaska Native alone (0.3%)		
	102	Asian alone (1.3%)		
	1	Native Hawaiian and Other Pacific Islander alone (0.0%)		
	152	Some other race alone (2.0%)		
	100	Two or more races (1.3%)		
	341	Hispanic or Latino* (4.4%)		

Skokie, IL (inc. 1888)

1900	529	—	—	—
1930	5,007	14.9%	35.1%	101
	4,994	White (99.7%)		
	2	Negro (0.0%)		
	11	Other (0.2%)		
1960	59,364	8.8%	33.9%	96
	59,093	White (99.5%)		
	147	Negro (0.2%)		
	124	Other races (0.2%)		
1990	59,432	27.9%	—	88
	48,361	White (81.4%)		
	1,276	Black (2.1%)		
	83	American Indian (0.1%)		
	9,218	Asian/Pacific Islander (15.5%)		
	494	Other race (0.8%)		
	2,477	Hispanic Origin* (4.2%)		
2000	63,348	37.0%	—	90
	43,661	White alone (68.9%)		
	2,854	Black or African American alone (4.5%)		
	109	American Indian and Alaska Native alone (0.2%)		
	13,483	Asian alone (21.3%)		
	16	Native Hawaiian and Other Pacific Islander alone (0.0%)		
	1,178	Some other race alone (1.9%)		
	2,047	Two or more races (3.2%)		
	3,620	Hispanic or Latino* (5.7%)		

Sleepy Hollow, IL (inc. 1958)

1960	311	—	—	—
1990	3,241	4.6%	—	99
	3,158	White (97.4%)		
	6	Black (0.2%)		
	22	American Indian (0.7%)		
	55	Asian/Pacific Islander (1.7%)		
	64	Hispanic Origin* (2.0%)		

2000	3,553	9.0%	—	103
	3,316	White alone (93.3%)		
	23	Black or African American alone (0.6%)		
	2	American Indian and Alaska Native alone (0.1%)		
	77	Asian alone (2.2%)		
	1	Native Hawaiian and Other Pacific Islander alone (0.0%)		
	63	Some other race alone (1.8%)		
	71	Two or more races (2.0%)		
	134	Hispanic or Latino* (3.8%)		

South Barrington, IL (inc. 1959)

1960	473	—	—	—
1990	2,937	10.0%	—	98
	2,741	White (93.3%)		
	34	Black (1.2%)		
	2	American Indian (0.1%)		
	158	Asian/Pacific Islander (5.4%)		
	21	Hispanic Origin* (0.7%)		
2000	3,760	19.3%	—	98
	3,096	White alone (82.3%)		
	33	Black or African American alone (0.9%)		
	2	American Indian and Alaska Native alone (0.1%)		
	541	Asian alone (14.4%)		
	1	Native Hawaiian and Other Pacific Islander alone (0.0%)		
	20	Some other race alone (0.5%)		
	67	Two or more races (1.8%)		
	69	Hispanic or Latino* (1.8%)		

South Chicago Heights, IL (inc. 1907)

1930	1,691	15.1%	33.5%	114
	1,678	White (99.2%)		
	13	Negro (0.8%)		
1960	4,043	8.7%	24.0%	103
	4,032	White (99.7%)		
	9	Negro (0.2%)		
	2	Other races (0.0%)		
1990	3,597	6.1%	—	100
	3,341	White (92.9%)		
	38	Black (1.1%)		
	218	Other race (6.1%)		
	489	Hispanic Origin* (13.6%)		
2000	3,970	7.9%	—	96
	3,142	White alone (79.1%)		
	288	Black or African American alone (7.3%)		
	20	American Indian and Alaska Native alone (0.5%)		
	42	Asian alone (1.1%)		
	2	Native Hawaiian and Other Pacific Islander alone (0.1%)		
	356	Some other race alone (9.0%)		
	120	Two or more races (3.0%)		
	718	Hispanic or Latino* (18.1%)		

South Elgin, IL (inc. 1897)

1900	515	—	—	—
1930	745	—	—	—
1960	2,624	4.2%	14.7%	100
	2,590	White (98.7%)		
	33	Negro (1.3%)		
	1	Other races (0.0%)		
1990	7,474	5.4%	—	95
	6,949	White (93.0%)		
	176	Black (2.4%)		
	12	American Indian (0.2%)		
	204	Asian/Pacific Islander (2.7%)		
	144	Other race (1.9%)		
	403	Hispanic Origin* (5.4%)		
2000	16,100	8.8%	—	100
	13,850	White alone (86.0%)		
	415	Black or African American alone (2.6%)		
	27	American Indian and Alaska Native alone (0.2%)		
	881	Asian alone (5.5%)		
	2	Native Hawaiian and Other Pacific Islander alone (0.0%)		
	625	Some other race alone (3.9%)		
	300	Two or more races (1.9%)		
	1,664	Hispanic or Latino* (10.3%)		

South Holland, IL (inc. 1894)

1900	766	—	—	—
1930	1,873	12.7%	37.0%	100
	1,873	White (100.0%)		
1960	10,412	4.7%	22.3%	95
	10,396	White (99.8%)		
	16	Other races (0.2%)		
1990	22,105	4.1%	—	94
	18,993	White (85.9%)		
	2,563	Black (11.6%)		
	14	American Indian (0.1%)		
	371	Asian/Pacific Islander (1.7%)		
	164	Other race (0.7%)		
	509	Hispanic Origin* (2.3%)		
2000	22,147	5.2%	—	89
	9,975	White alone (45.0%)		
	11,253	Black or African American alone (50.8%)		
	37	American Indian and Alaska Native alone (0.2%)		
	190	Asian alone (0.9%)		
	2	Native Hawaiian and Other Pacific Islander alone (0.0%)		
	428	Some other race alone (1.9%)		
	262	Two or more races (1.2%)		
	836	Hispanic or Latino* (3.8%)		

Spring Grove, IL (inc. 1902)

1930	184	—	—	—
1960	301	—	—	—
1990	1,066	1.7%	—	108
	1,077	White (101.0%)		
	4	American Indian (0.4%)		
	2	Asian/Pacific Islander (0.2%)		
	5	Other race (0.5%)		
	14	Hispanic Origin* (1.3%)		
2000	3,880	2.1%	—	101
	3,778	White alone (97.4%)		
	5	Black or African American alone (0.1%)		
	6	American Indian and Alaska Native alone (0.2%)		
	35	Asian alone (0.9%)		
	4	Native Hawaiian and Other Pacific Islander alone (0.1%)		
	14	Some other race alone (0.4%)		
	38	Two or more races (1.0%)		
	69	Hispanic or Latino* (1.8%)		

St. Charles, IL (inc. 1839)

1900	2,675	28.2%	35.6%	105
	2,640	White (98.7%)		
	35	Negro (1.3%)		
1930	5,377	25.6%	36.8%	106
	5,330	White (99.1%)		
	43	Negro (0.8%)		
	4	Other (0.1%)		
1960	9,269	7.9%	22.9%	95
	9,227	White (99.5%)		
	28	Negro (0.3%)		
	14	Other races (0.2%)		
1990	22,501	3.2%	—	96
	22,081	White (98.1%)		
	82	Black (0.4%)		
	25	American Indian (0.1%)		
	163	Asian/Pacific Islander (0.7%)		
	161	Other race (0.7%)		
	585	Hispanic Origin* (2.6%)		
2000	27,896	6.6%	—	99
	26,169	White alone (93.8%)		
	462	Black or African American alone (1.7%)		
	39	American Indian and Alaska Native alone (0.1%)		
	499	Asian alone (1.8%)		
	1	Native Hawaiian and Other Pacific Islander alone (0.0%)		
	463	Some other race alone (1.7%)		
	263	Two or more races (0.9%)		
	1,535	Hispanic or Latino* (5.5%)		

Municipalities *(continued)*

St. John, IN (inc. 1911)

Year	Total (and by category)	Category	Foreign born	Native with foreign parentage	Males per 100 females
1870	1,442		38.3%	—	—
1930	332		—	—	—
1960	1,128		—	—	104
	1,128	White (100.0%)			
1990	4,921		1.8%	—	100
	4,904	White (99.7%)			
	17	American Indian (0.3%)			
	112	Hispanic Origin* (2.3%)			
2000	8,382		3.3%	—	101
	8,177	White alone (97.6%)			
	11	Black or African American alone (0.1%)			
	14	American Indian and Alaska Native alone (0.2%)			
	39	Asian alone (0.5%)			
	63	Some other race alone (0.8%)			
	78	Two or more races (0.9%)			
	352	Hispanic or Latino* (4.2%)			

Steger, IL (inc. 1896)

Year	Total (and by category)	Category	Foreign born	Native with foreign parentage	Males per 100 females
1900	712		—	—	—
1930	2,985		16.2%	35.0%	112
	2,977	White (99.7%)			
	8	Negro (0.3%)			
1960	6,432		6.0%	19.2%	99
	6,394	White (99.4%)			
	36	Negro (0.6%)			
	2	Other races (0.0%)			
1990	8,584		3.0%	—	100
	8,026	White (93.5%)			
	230	Black (2.7%)			
	14	American Indian (0.2%)			
	45	Asian/Pacific Islander (0.5%)			
	269	Other race (3.1%)			
	620	Hispanic Origin* (7.2%)			
2000	9,682		4.6%	—	100
	8,482	White alone (87.6%)			
	610	Black or African American alone (6.3%)			
	33	American Indian and Alaska Native alone (0.3%)			
	47	Asian alone (0.5%)			
	9	Native Hawaiian and Other Pacific Islander alone (0.1%)			
	298	Some other race alone (3.1%)			
	203	Two or more races (2.1%)			
	781	Hispanic or Latino* (8.1%)			

Stickney, IL (inc. 1913)

Year	Total (and by category)	Category	Foreign born	Native with foreign parentage	Males per 100 females
1930	2,005		28.0%	45.5%	106
	2,005	White (100.0%)			
1960	6,239		8.2%	34.5%	96
	6,239	White (100.0%)			
1990	5,678		8.0%	—	97
	5,379	White (94.7%)			
	90	Asian/Pacific Islander (1.6%)			
	209	Other race (3.7%)			
	363	Hispanic Origin* (6.4%)			
2000	6,148		16.2%	—	99
	5,581	White alone (90.8%)			
	26	Black or African American alone (0.4%)			
	14	American Indian and Alaska Native alone (0.2%)			
	67	Asian alone (1.1%)			
	388	Some other race alone (6.3%)			
	72	Two or more races (1.2%)			
	1,323	Hispanic or Latino* (21.5%)			

Stone Park, IL (inc. 1939)

Year	Total (and by category)	Category	Foreign born	Native with foreign parentage	Males per 100 females
1960	3,038		5.7%	18.1%	103
	3,033	White (99.8%)			
	5	Other races (0.2%)			
1990	4,383		36.9%	—	107
	2,689	White (61.4%)			
	11	American Indian (0.3%)			
	153	Asian/Pacific Islander (3.5%)			
	1,530	Other race (34.9%)			
	2,537	Hispanic Origin* (57.9%)			
2000	5,127		50.1%	—	116
	2,768	White alone (54.0%)			
	93	Black or African American alone (1.8%)			
	24	American Indian and Alaska Native alone (0.5%)			
	104	Asian alone (2.0%)			
	1	Native Hawaiian and Other Pacific Islander alone (0.0%)			
	1,992	Some other race alone (38.9%)			
	145	Two or more races (2.8%)			
	4,057	Hispanic or Latino* (79.1%)			

Streamwood, IL (inc. 1957)

Year	Total (and by category)	Category	Foreign born	Native with foreign parentage	Males per 100 females
1960	4,821		1.6%	12.8%	104
	4,812	White (99.8%)			
	9	Other races (0.2%)			
1990	30,987		9.2%	—	100
	28,338	White (91.5%)			
	540	Black (1.7%)			
	9	American Indian (0.0%)			
	1,324	Asian/Pacific Islander (4.3%)			
	776	Other race (2.5%)			
	2,295	Hispanic Origin* (7.4%)			
2000	36,407		20.1%	—	100
	28,225	White alone (77.5%)			
	1,398	Black or African American alone (3.8%)			
	106	American Indian and Alaska Native alone (0.3%)			
	3,145	Asian alone (8.6%)			
	12	Native Hawaiian and Other Pacific Islander alone (0.0%)			
	2,570	Some other race alone (7.1%)			
	951	Two or more races (2.6%)			
	6,108	Hispanic or Latino* (16.8%)			

Sugar Grove, IL (inc. 1957)

Year	Total (and by category)	Category	Foreign born	Native with foreign parentage	Males per 100 females
1960	326		—	—	—
1990	2,005		2.6%	—	95
	1,973	White (98.4%)			
	5	Black (0.2%)			
	6	American Indian (0.3%)			
	21	Other race (1.0%)			
	44	Hispanic Origin* (2.2%)			
2000	3,909		1.8%	—	103
	3,747	White alone (95.9%)			
	54	Black or African American alone (1.4%)			
	1	American Indian and Alaska Native alone (0.0%)			
	20	Asian alone (0.5%)			
	50	Some other race alone (1.3%)			
	37	Two or more races (0.9%)			
	173	Hispanic or Latino* (4.4%)			

Summit, IL (inc. 1890)

Year	Total (and by category)	Category	Foreign born	Native with foreign parentage	Males per 100 females
1900	547		—	—	—
1930	6,548		23.3%	40.6%	114
	5,986	White (91.4%)			
	493	Negro (7.5%)			
	69	Other (1.1%)			
1960	10,374		11.5%	22.6%	104
	8,484	White (81.8%)			
	1,870	Negro (18.0%)			
	20	Other races (0.2%)			
1990	9,971		25.3%	—	103
	6,702	White (67.2%)			
	1,339	Black (13.4%)			
	39	American Indian (0.4%)			
	208	Asian/Pacific Islander (2.1%)			
	1,683	Other race (16.9%)			
	3,095	Hispanic Origin* (31.0%)			
2000	10,637		34.1%	—	106
	6,734	White alone (63.3%)			
	1,282	Black or African American alone (12.1%)			
	32	American Indian and Alaska Native alone (0.3%)			
	150	Asian alone (1.4%)			
	2	Native Hawaiian and Other Pacific Islander alone (0.0%)			
	2,089	Some other race alone (19.6%)			
	348	Two or more races (3.3%)			
	5,156	Hispanic or Latino* (48.5%)			

Symerton, IL (inc. 1904)

Year	Total (and by category)	Category	Foreign born	Native with foreign parentage	Males per 100 females
1930	77		—	—	—
1960	123		—	—	—
1990	110		0.0%	—	86
	113	White (102.7%)			
2000	106		0.0%	—	100
	105	White alone (99.1%)			
	1	Black or African American alone (0.9%)			

Third Lake, IL (inc. 1959)

Year	Total (and by category)	Category	Foreign born	Native with foreign parentage	Males per 100 females
1990	1,248		3.0%	—	106
	1,228	White (98.4%)			
	7	Black (0.6%)			
	13	Asian/Pacific Islander (1.0%)			
	4	Hispanic Origin* (0.3%)			
2000	1,355		5.2%	—	106
	1,294	White alone (95.5%)			
	7	Black or African American alone (0.5%)			
	26	Asian alone (1.9%)			
	8	Some other race alone (0.6%)			
	20	Two or more races (1.5%)			
	45	Hispanic or Latino* (3.3%)			

Thornton, IL (inc. 1900)

Year	Total (and by category)	Category	Foreign born	Native with foreign parentage	Males per 100 females
1930	1,012		18.9%	41.0%	123
	1,012	White (100.0%)			
1960	2,895		6.5%	21.3%	102
	2,892	White (99.9%)			
	3	Other races (0.1%)			
1990	2,778		3.3%	—	94
	2,773	White (99.8%)			
	5	Black (0.2%)			
	60	Hispanic Origin* (2.2%)			
2000	2,582		1.4%	—	88
	2,496	White alone (96.7%)			
	21	Black or African American alone (0.8%)			
	3	American Indian and Alaska Native alone (0.1%)			
	6	Asian alone (0.2%)			
	22	Some other race alone (0.9%)			
	34	Two or more races (1.3%)			
	107	Hispanic or Latino* (4.1%)			

Tinley Park, IL (inc. 1892)

Year	Total (and by category)	Category	Foreign born	Native with foreign parentage	Males per 100 females
1900	300		—	—	—
1930	823		—	—	—
1960	6,392		3.4%	16.8%	101
	6,388	White (99.9%)			
	1	Negro (0.0%)			
	3	Other races (0.0%)			
1990	37,121		3.4%	—	95
	35,689	White (96.1%)			
	565	Black (1.5%)			
	7	American Indian (0.0%)			
	521	Asian/Pacific Islander (1.4%)			
	368	Other race (1.0%)			
	795	Hispanic Origin* (2.1%)			
2000	48,401		5.8%	—	94
	45,092	White alone (93.2%)			
	931	Black or African American alone (1.9%)			
	63	American Indian and Alaska Native alone (0.1%)			
	1,153	Asian alone (2.4%)			
	9	Native Hawaiian and Other Pacific Islander alone (0.0%)			
	539	Some other race alone (1.1%)			
	614	Two or more races (1.3%)			
	1,998	Hispanic or Latino* (4.1%)			

Tower Lakes, IL (inc. 1966)

1990	1,333	4.1%	—	100
	1,312	White (98.4%)		
	2	Black (0.2%)		
	15	Asian/Pacific Islander (1.1%)		
	4	Other race (0.3%)		
	19	Hispanic Origin* (1.4%)		
2000	1,310	7.5%	—	95
	1,278	White alone (97.6%)		
	4	Black or African American alone (0.3%)		
	1	American Indian and Alaska Native alone (0.1%)		
	10	Asian alone (0.8%)		
	4	Some other race alone (0.3%)		
	13	Two or more races (1.0%)		
	18	Hispanic or Latino* (1.4%)		

Town of Pines, IN (inc. 1954)

1960	939	—	—	—
1990	789	2.3%	—	102
	768	White (97.3%)		
	7	Black (0.9%)		
	1	American Indian (0.1%)		
	9	Asian/Pacific Islander (1.1%)		
	4	Other race (0.5%)		
	9	Hispanic Origin* (1.1%)		
2000	798	2.1%	—	109

Trout Valley, IL (inc. 1996)

1990	612	—	—	—
2000	599	4.2%	—	102
	567	White alone (94.7%)		
	4	Black or African American alone (0.7%)		
	6	Asian alone (1.0%)		
	7	Some other race alone (1.2%)		
	15	Two or more races (2.5%)		
	25	Hispanic or Latino* (4.2%)		

Union, IL (inc. 1897)

1900	322	—	—	—
1930	367	—	—	—
1960	480	—	—	—
1990	542	1.8%	—	98
	545	White (100.6%)		
	3	American Indian (0.6%)		
	10	Hispanic Origin* (1.8%)		
2000	576	2.1%	—	93
	565	White alone (98.1%)		
	2	American Indian and Alaska Native alone (0.3%)		
	5	Some other race alone (0.9%)		
	4	Two or more races (0.7%)		
	23	Hispanic or Latino* (4.0%)		

University Park, IL (inc. 1967)

1990	6,204	1.8%	—	84
	1,190	White (19.2%)		
	4,915	Black (79.2%)		
	18	American Indian (0.3%)		
	25	Asian/Pacific Islander (0.4%)		
	56	Other race (0.9%)		
	149	Hispanic Origin* (2.4%)		
2000	6,662	3.6%	—	85
	801	White alone (12.0%)		
	5,591	Black or African American alone (83.9%)		
	5	American Indian and Alaska Native alone (0.1%)		
	22	Asian alone (0.3%)		
	1	Native Hawaiian and Other Pacific Islander alone (0.0%)		
	41	Some other race alone (0.6%)		
	201	Two or more races (3.0%)		
	120	Hispanic or Latino* (1.8%)		

Valparaiso, IN (inc. 1850)

1870	2,765	20.3%	—	—
	2,760	White (99.8%)		
	5	Colored (0.2%)		
1900	6,280	10.5%	63.8%	102
	6,273	White (99.9%)		
	5	Negro (0.1%)		
	2	Indian (0.0%)		
1930	8,079	6.9%	20.3%	96
	8,066	White (99.8%)		
	3	Negro (0.0%)		
	10	Other (0.1%)		
1960	15,227	2.3%	11.9%	99
	15,201	White (99.8%)		
	10	Negro (0.1%)		
	16	Other races (0.1%)		
1990	24,414	3.0%	—	89
	23,916	White (98.0%)		
	183	Black (0.7%)		
	68	American Indian (0.3%)		
	218	Asian/Pacific Islander (0.9%)		
	29	Other race (0.1%)		
	274	Hispanic Origin* (1.1%)		
2000	27,428	4.1%	—	92
	25,879	White alone (94.4%)		
	440	Black or African American alone (1.6%)		
	62	American Indian and Alaska Native alone (0.2%)		
	410	Asian alone (1.5%)		
	5	Native Hawaiian and Other Pacific Islander alone (0.0%)		
	216	Some other race alone (0.8%)		
	416	Two or more races (1.5%)		
	917	Hispanic or Latino* (3.3%)		

Vernon Hills, IL (inc. 1958)

1960	123	—	—	—
1990	15,319	10.1%	—	92
	13,943	White (91.0%)		
	249	Black (1.6%)		
	42	American Indian (0.3%)		
	951	Asian/Pacific Islander (6.2%)		
	166	Other race (1.1%)		
	577	Hispanic Origin* (3.8%)		
2000	20,120	21.7%	—	94
	16,470	White alone (81.9%)		
	340	Black or African American alone (1.7%)		
	21	American Indian and Alaska Native alone (0.1%)		
	2,348	Asian alone (11.7%)		
	6	Native Hawaiian and Other Pacific Islander alone (0.0%)		
	588	Some other race alone (2.9%)		
	347	Two or more races (1.7%)		
	1,446	Hispanic or Latino* (7.2%)		

Villa Park, IL (inc. 1914)

1930	6,220	13.3%	32.2%	101
	6,214	White (99.9%)		
	6	Other (0.1%)		
1960	20,391	5.6%	20.7%	100
	20,360	White (99.8%)		
	31	Other races (0.2%)		
1990	22,253	8.1%	—	99
	20,920	White (94.0%)		
	266	Black (1.2%)		
	45	American Indian (0.2%)		
	740	Asian/Pacific Islander (3.3%)		
	282	Other race (1.3%)		
	1,204	Hispanic Origin* (5.4%)		
2000	22,075	14.5%	—	101
	19,679	White alone (89.1%)		
	369	Black or African American alone (1.7%)		
	39	American Indian and Alaska Native alone (0.2%)		
	805	Asian alone (3.6%)		
	7	Native Hawaiian and Other Pacific Islander alone (0.0%)		
	806	Some other race alone (3.7%)		
	370	Two or more races (1.7%)		
	2,770	Hispanic or Latino* (12.5%)		

Virgil, IL (inc. 1990)

1990	319	—	—	—
2000	266	0.0%	—	99
	259	White alone (97.4%)		
	3	Black or African American alone (1.1%)		
	1	Asian alone (0.4%)		
	1	Some other race alone (0.4%)		
	2	Two or more races (0.8%)		
	5	Hispanic or Latino* (1.9%)		

Volo, IL (inc. 1993)

1990	193	—	—	—
2000	180	34.4%	—	128
	167	White alone (92.8%)		
	2	Asian alone (1.1%)		
	1	Some other race alone (0.6%)		
	10	Two or more races (5.6%)		
	42	Hispanic or Latino* (23.3%)		

Wadsworth, IL (inc. 1962)

1990	1,826	3.3%	—	102
	1,801	White (98.6%)		
	3	American Indian (0.2%)		
	22	Asian/Pacific Islander (1.2%)		
	30	Hispanic Origin* (1.6%)		
2000	3,083	5.0%	—	102
	2,902	White alone (94.1%)		
	53	Black or African American alone (1.7%)		
	4	American Indian and Alaska Native alone (0.1%)		
	32	Asian alone (1.0%)		
	32	Some other race alone (1.0%)		
	60	Two or more races (1.9%)		
	109	Hispanic or Latino* (3.5%)		

Warrenville, IL (inc. 1967)

1960	3,134	3.7%	17.9%	97
	3,114	White (99.4%)		
	2	Negro (0.1%)		
	18	Other races (0.6%)		
1990	11,333	5.1%	—	99
	10,811	White (95.4%)		
	87	Black (0.8%)		
	13	American Indian (0.1%)		
	369	Asian/Pacific Islander (3.3%)		
	53	Other race (0.5%)		
	328	Hispanic Origin* (2.9%)		
2000	13,363	9.3%	—	98
	11,910	White alone (89.1%)		
	319	Black or African American alone (2.4%)		
	39	American Indian and Alaska Native alone (0.3%)		
	459	Asian alone (3.4%)		
	5	Native Hawaiian and Other Pacific Islander alone (0.0%)		
	463	Some other race alone (3.5%)		
	168	Two or more races (1.3%)		
	1,349	Hispanic or Latino* (10.1%)		

Wauconda, IL (inc. 1877)

1900	397	—	—	—
1930	554	—	—	—
1960	3,227	4.5%	15.6%	97
	3,226	White (100.0%)		
	1	Other races (0.0%)		
1990	6,294	3.7%	—	100
	6,140	White (97.6%)		
	22	American Indian (0.3%)		
	29	Asian/Pacific Islander (0.5%)		
	103	Other race (1.6%)		
	250	Hispanic Origin* (4.0%)		
2000	9,448	11.8%	—	102
	8,526	White alone (90.2%)		
	39	Black or African American alone (0.4%)		
	25	American Indian and Alaska Native alone (0.3%)		
	169	Asian alone (1.8%)		
	4	Native Hawaiian and Other Pacific Islander alone (0.0%)		
	600	Some other race alone (6.4%)		
	85	Two or more races (0.9%)		
	1,125	Hispanic or Latino* (11.9%)		

Municipalities *(continued)*

Waukegan, IL (inc. 1852)

Year	Total (and by category)	Category	Foreign born	Native with foreign parentage	Males per 100 females
1870	4,507		26.3%	—	90
	4,494	White (99.7%)			
	13	Colored (0.3%)			
1900	9,426		26.6%	35.0%	105
	9,380	White (99.5%)			
	44	Negro (0.5%)			
	2	Chinese (0.0%)			
1930	33,499		19.3%	33.3%	111
	31,925	White (95.3%)			
	1,017	Negro (3.0%)			
	5	Indian (0.0%)			
	4	Chinese (0.0%)			
	537	Mexican (1.6%)			
	10	Other (0.0%)			
1960	55,719		7.0%	19.5%	96
	51,036	White (91.6%)			
	4,485	Negro (8.0%)			
	198	Other races (0.4%)			
1990	69,392		15.5%	—	97
	44,537	White (64.2%)			
	13,974	Black (20.1%)			
	382	American Indian (0.6%)			
	1,974	Asian/Pacific Islander (2.8%)			
	8,525	Other race (12.3%)			
	15,755	Hispanic Origin* (22.7%)			
2000	87,901		30.2%	—	103
	44,073	White alone (50.1%)			
	16,890	Black or African American alone (19.2%)			
	471	American Indian and Alaska Native alone (0.5%)			
	3,146	Asian alone (3.6%)			
	57	Native Hawaiian and Other Pacific Islander alone (0.1%)			
	20,185	Some other race alone (23.0%)			
	3,079	Two or more races (3.5%)			
	39,396	Hispanic or Latino* (44.8%)			

Wayne, IL (inc. 1958)

Year	Total (and by category)	Category	Foreign born	Native with foreign parentage	Males per 100 females
1960	373		—	—	—
1990	1,541		4.2%	—	96
	1,580	White (102.5%)			
	28	Asian/Pacific Islander (1.8%)			
	2	Other race (0.1%)			
	2	Hispanic Origin* (0.1%)			
2000	2,137		4.9%	—	93
	2,026	White alone (94.8%)			
	8	Black or African American alone (0.4%)			
	1	American Indian and Alaska Native alone (0.0%)			
	60	Asian alone (2.8%)			
	16	Some other race alone (0.7%)			
	26	Two or more races (1.2%)			
	80	Hispanic or Latino* (3.7%)			

West Chicago, IL (inc. 1873)

Year	Total (and by category)	Category	Foreign born	Native with foreign parentage	Males per 100 females
1900	1,877		—	—	—
1930	3,477		9.6%	32.8%	97
	3,428	White (98.6%)			
	49	Other (1.4%)			
1960	6,854		4.6%	17.7%	96
	6,842	White (99.8%)			
	12	Other races (0.2%)			
1990	14,796		21.0%	—	108
	12,245	White (82.8%)			
	270	Black (1.8%)			
	29	American Indian (0.2%)			
	190	Asian/Pacific Islander (1.3%)			
	2,062	Other race (13.9%)			
	4,416	Hispanic Origin* (29.8%)			
2000	23,469		34.7%	—	114
	18,271	White alone (77.9%)			
	395	Black or African American alone (1.7%)			
	85	American Indian and Alaska Native alone (0.4%)			
	457	Asian alone (1.9%)			
	7	Native Hawaiian and Other Pacific Islander alone (0.0%)			
	3,547	Some other race alone (15.1%)			
	707	Two or more races (3.0%)			
	11,405	Hispanic or Latino* (48.6%)			

West Dundee, IL (inc. 1887)

Year	Total (and by category)	Category	Foreign born	Native with foreign parentage	Males per 100 females
1900	1,348		—	—	—
1930	1,697		12.2%	35.9%	94
	1,697	White (100.0%)			
1960	2,530		4.5%	18.6%	96
	2,525	White (99.8%)			
	2	Negro (0.1%)			
	3	Other races (0.1%)			
1990	3,728		3.4%	—	94
	3,700	White (99.2%)			
	7	Black (0.2%)			
	21	Asian/Pacific Islander (0.6%)			
	26	Hispanic Origin* (0.7%)			
2000	5,428		6.8%	—	94
	5,098	White alone (93.9%)			
	33	Black or African American alone (0.6%)			
	21	American Indian and Alaska Native alone (0.4%)			
	120	Asian alone (2.2%)			
	76	Some other race alone (1.4%)			
	80	Two or more races (1.5%)			
	231	Hispanic or Latino* (4.3%)			

Westchester, IL (inc. 1925)

Year	Total (and by category)	Category	Foreign born	Native with foreign parentage	Males per 100 females
1930	358		—	—	—
1960	18,092		6.1%	28.7%	96
	18,084	White (100.0%)			
	3	Negro (0.0%)			
	5	Other races (0.0%)			
1990	17,301		7.8%	—	90
	16,709	White (96.6%)			
	55	Black (0.3%)			
	20	American Indian (0.1%)			
	450	Asian/Pacific Islander (2.6%)			
	67	Other race (0.4%)			
	270	Hispanic Origin* (1.6%)			
2000	16,824		9.4%	—	87
	14,494	White alone (86.2%)			
	1,212	Black or African American alone (7.2%)			
	11	American Indian and Alaska Native alone (0.1%)			
	579	Asian alone (3.4%)			
	1	Native Hawaiian and Other Pacific Islander alone (0.0%)			
	334	Some other race alone (2.0%)			
	193	Two or more races (1.1%)			
	956	Hispanic or Latino* (5.7%)			

Western Springs, IL (inc. 1886)

Year	Total (and by category)	Category	Foreign born	Native with foreign parentage	Males per 100 females
1900	662		—	—	—
1930	3,894		9.7%	28.4%	95
	3,875	White (99.5%)			
	17	Negro (0.4%)			
	2	Other (0.1%)			
1960	10,838		3.9%	20.2%	95
	10,828	White (99.9%)			
	6	Negro (0.1%)			
	4	Other races (0.0%)			
1990	11,984		4.5%	—	93
	11,716	White (97.8%)			
	29	Black (0.2%)			
	30	American Indian (0.3%)			
	209	Asian/Pacific Islander (1.7%)			
	98	Hispanic Origin* (0.8%)			
2000	12,493		3.8%	—	93
	12,283	White alone (98.3%)			
	23	Black or African American alone (0.2%)			
	5	American Indian and Alaska Native alone (0.0%)			
	90	Asian alone (0.7%)			
	26	Some other race alone (0.2%)			
	66	Two or more races (0.5%)			
	212	Hispanic or Latino* (1.7%)			

Westmont, IL (inc. 1921)

Year	Total (and by category)	Category	Foreign born	Native with foreign parentage	Males per 100 females
1930	2,733		17.8%	35.3%	107
	2,724	White (99.7%)			
	4	Other (0.1%)			
1960	5,997		7.2%	24.3%	94
	5,993	White (99.9%)			
	4	Other races (0.1%)			
1990	21,228		10.8%	—	89
	18,490	White (87.1%)			
	736	Black (3.5%)			
	38	American Indian (0.2%)			
	1,811	Asian/Pacific Islander (8.5%)			
	153	Other race (0.7%)			
	741	Hispanic Origin* (3.5%)			
2000	24,554		19.5%	—	87
	19,156	White alone (78.0%)			
	1,321	Black or African American alone (5.4%)			
	33	American Indian and Alaska Native alone (0.1%)			
	2,935	Asian alone (12.0%)			
	591	Some other race alone (2.4%)			
	518	Two or more races (2.1%)			
	1,714	Hispanic or Latino* (7.0%)			

Wheaton, IL (inc. 1859)

Year	Total (and by category)	Category	Foreign born	Native with foreign parentage	Males per 100 females
1870	998		14.6%	—	—
	985	White (98.7%)			
	13	Colored (1.3%)			
1900	2,345		—	—	—
1930	7,258		10.0%	63.2%	95
	7,118	White (98.1%)			
	129	Negro (1.8%)			
	11	Other (0.2%)			
1960	24,312		4.2%	17.5%	94
	23,919	White (98.4%)			
	347	Negro (1.4%)			
	46	Other races (0.2%)			
1990	51,464		6.5%	—	94
	47,833	White (92.9%)			
	1,373	Black (2.7%)			
	35	American Indian (0.1%)			
	1,945	Asian/Pacific Islander (3.8%)			
	278	Other race (0.5%)			
	1,035	Hispanic Origin* (2.0%)			
2000	55,416		9.5%	—	95
	49,791	White alone (89.8%)			
	1,565	Black or African American alone (2.8%)			
	63	American Indian and Alaska Native alone (0.1%)			
	2,687	Asian alone (4.8%)			
	11	Native Hawaiian and Other Pacific Islander alone (0.0%)			
	571	Some other race alone (1.0%)			
	728	Two or more races (1.3%)			
	2,023	Hispanic or Latino* (3.7%)			

Wheeling, IL (inc. 1894)

Year	Total (and by category)	Category	Foreign born	Native with foreign parentage	Males per 100 females
1900	331		—	—	—
1930	467		—	—	—
1960	7,169		3.4%	14.7%	101
	7,154	White (99.8%)			
	4	Negro (0.1%)			
	11	Other races (0.2%)			
1990	29,911		12.7%	—	95
	27,073	White (90.5%)			
	406	Black (1.4%)			
	29	American Indian (0.1%)			
	1,410	Asian/Pacific Islander (4.7%)			
	993	Other race (3.3%)			
	2,469	Hispanic Origin* (8.3%)			

2000	34,496	31.4%	—	97
	26,452	White alone (76.7%)		
	843	Black or African American alone (2.4%)		
	80	American Indian and Alaska Native alone (0.2%)		
	3,193	Asian alone (9.3%)		
	25	Native Hawaiian and Other Pacific Islander alone (0.1%)		
	3,168	Some other race alone (9.2%)		
	735	Two or more races (2.1%)		
	7,135	Hispanic or Latino* (20.7%)		

Whiting, IN (inc. 1895)

1900	3,983	40.1%	6.2%	148
	3,978	White (99.9%)		
	2	Negro (0.1%)		
	3	Chinese (0.1%)		
1930	10,880	25.2%	42.5%	123
	10,865	White (99.9%)		
	15	Other (0.1%)		
1960	8,137	10.3%	27.6%	105
	8,134	White (100.0%)		
	2	Negro (0.0%)		
	1	Other races (0.0%)		
1990	5,155	6.3%	—	95
	4,720	White (91.6%)		
	17	Asian/Pacific Islander (0.3%)		
	418	Other race (8.1%)		
	730	Hispanic Origin* (14.2%)		
2000	5,137	10.8%	—	92
	4,488	White alone (87.4%)		
	29	Black or African American alone (0.6%)		
	15	American Indian and Alaska Native alone (0.3%)		
	47	Asian alone (0.9%)		
	4	Native Hawaiian and Other Pacific Islander alone (0.1%)		
	467	Some other race alone (9.1%)		
	87	Two or more races (1.7%)		
	1,313	Hispanic or Latino* (25.6%)		

Willow Springs, IL (inc. 1892)

1900	378	—	—	—
1930	733	—	—	—
1960	2,348	—	—	103
	2,347	White (100.0%)		
	1	Other races (0.0%)		
1990	4,509	6.5%	—	102
	4,370	White (96.9%)		
	97	Asian/Pacific Islander (2.2%)		
	42	Other race (0.9%)		
	39	Hispanic Origin* (0.9%)		
2000	5,027	13.1%	—	101
	4,721	White alone (93.9%)		
	36	Black or African American alone (0.7%)		
	6	American Indian and Alaska Native alone (0.1%)		
	93	Asian alone (1.9%)		
	1	Native Hawaiian and Other Pacific Islander alone (0.0%)		
	54	Some other race alone (1.1%)		
	116	Two or more races (2.3%)		
	254	Hispanic or Latino* (5.1%)		

Willowbrook, IL (inc. 1960)

1960	157	—	—	—
1990	8,598	11.7%	—	91
	7,618	White (88.6%)		
	125	Black (1.5%)		
	13	American Indian (0.2%)		
	783	Asian/Pacific Islander (9.1%)		
	59	Other race (0.7%)		
	178	Hispanic Origin* (2.1%)		
2000	8,967	16.9%	—	85
	7,589	White alone (84.6%)		
	217	Black or African American alone (2.4%)		
	4	American Indian and Alaska Native alone (0.0%)		
	898	Asian alone (10.0%)		
	4	Native Hawaiian and Other Pacific Islander alone (0.0%)		
	104	Some other race alone (1.2%)		
	151	Two or more races (1.7%)		
	382	Hispanic or Latino* (4.3%)		

Wilmette, IL (inc. 1872)

1900	2,300	—	—	—
1930	15,233	13.0%	29.2%	90
	15,027	White (98.6%)		
	192	Negro (1.3%)		
	14	Other (0.1%)		
1960	28,268	5.5%	21.0%	92
	28,042	White (99.2%)		
	156	Negro (0.6%)		
	70	Other races (0.2%)		
1990	26,690	13.1%	—	90
	24,481	White (91.7%)		
	84	Black (0.3%)		
	24	American Indian (0.1%)		
	1,848	Asian/Pacific Islander (6.9%)		
	93	Other race (0.3%)		
	403	Hispanic Origin* (1.5%)		
2000	27,651	13.2%	—	92
	24,791	White alone (89.7%)		
	156	Black or African American alone (0.6%)		
	10	American Indian and Alaska Native alone (0.0%)		
	2,255	Asian alone (8.2%)		
	4	Native Hawaiian and Other Pacific Islander alone (0.0%)		
	117	Some other race alone (0.4%)		
	318	Two or more races (1.2%)		
	574	Hispanic or Latino* (2.1%)		

Wilmington, IL (inc. 1837)

1870	1,118	28.1%	—	—
	1,819	White (162.7%)		
	9	Colored (0.8%)		
1900	1,420	—	—	—
1930	1,741	7.2%	25.0%	86
	1,739	White (99.9%)		
	2	Negro (0.1%)		
1960	4,210	1.2%	9.9%	95
	4,207	White (99.9%)		
	3	Other races (0.1%)		
1990	4,743	1.6%	—	96
	4,684	White (98.8%)		
	21	Black (0.4%)		
	33	Asian/Pacific Islander (0.7%)		
	5	Other race (0.1%)		
	12	Hispanic Origin* (0.3%)		
2000	5,134	1.4%	—	93
	4,987	White alone (97.1%)		
	38	Black or African American alone (0.7%)		
	18	American Indian and Alaska Native alone (0.4%)		
	15	Asian alone (0.3%)		
	1	Native Hawaiian and Other Pacific Islander alone (0.0%)		
	31	Some other race alone (0.6%)		
	44	Two or more races (0.9%)		
	100	Hispanic or Latino* (1.9%)		

Winfield, IL (inc. 1921)

1930	445	—	—	—
1960	1,575	—	—	104
	1,558	White (98.9%)		
	17	Other races (1.1%)		
1990	7,096	6.7%	—	96
	6,875	White (96.9%)		
	18	Black (0.3%)		
	5	American Indian (0.1%)		
	184	Asian/Pacific Islander (2.6%)		
	14	Other race (0.2%)		
	180	Hispanic Origin* (2.5%)		
2000	8,718	6.5%	—	95
	8,160	White alone (93.6%)		
	108	Black or African American alone (1.2%)		
	9	American Indian and Alaska Native alone (0.1%)		
	258	Asian alone (3.0%)		
	2	Native Hawaiian and Other Pacific Islander alone (0.0%)		
	79	Some other race alone (0.9%)		
	102	Two or more races (1.2%)		
	233	Hispanic or Latino* (2.7%)		

Winfield, IN (inc. 1993)

2000	2,298	8.9%	—	93

Winnetka, IL (inc. 1869)

1900	1,833	—	—	—
1930	12,166	16.5%	23.2%	79
	11,897	White (97.8%)		
	256	Negro (2.1%)		
	13	Other (0.1%)		
1960	13,368	7.0%	16.2%	87
	13,095	White (98.0%)		
	252	Negro (1.9%)		
	21	Other races (0.2%)		
1990	12,174	5.8%	—	96
	11,888	White (97.7%)		
	12	Black (0.1%)		
	269	Asian/Pacific Islander (2.2%)		
	5	Other race (0.0%)		
	92	Hispanic Origin* (0.8%)		
2000	12,419	5.0%	—	94
	11,958	White alone (96.3%)		
	31	Black or African American alone (0.2%)		
	2	American Indian and Alaska Native alone (0.0%)		
	302	Asian alone (2.4%)		
	37	Some other race alone (0.3%)		
	89	Two or more races (0.7%)		
	156	Hispanic or Latino* (1.3%)		

Winthrop Harbor, IL (inc. 1901)

1930	661	—	—	—
1960	3,848	3.5%	14.7%	102
	3,841	White (99.8%)		
	7	Other races (0.2%)		
1990	6,240	4.2%	—	100
	6,050	White (97.0%)		
	18	American Indian (0.3%)		
	160	Asian/Pacific Islander (2.6%)		
	12	Other race (0.2%)		
	118	Hispanic Origin* (1.9%)		
2000	6,670	3.0%	—	100
	6,256	White alone (93.8%)		
	38	Black or African American alone (0.6%)		
	33	American Indian and Alaska Native alone (0.5%)		
	127	Asian alone (1.9%)		
	1	Native Hawaiian and Other Pacific Islander alone (0.0%)		
	101	Some other race alone (1.5%)		
	114	Two or more races (1.7%)		
	303	Hispanic or Latino* (4.5%)		

Wonder Lake, IL (inc. 1974)

1960	3,543	5.4%	21.2%	99
	3,537	White (99.8%)		
	1	Negro (0.0%)		
	5	Other races (0.1%)		
1990	1,024	2.8%	—	102
	1,018	White (99.4%)		
	5	Asian/Pacific Islander (0.5%)		
	1	Other race (0.1%)		
	14	Hispanic Origin* (1.4%)		
2000	1,345	2.2%	—	106
	1,307	White alone (97.2%)		
	5	Black or African American alone (0.4%)		
	1	American Indian and Alaska Native alone (0.1%)		
	4	Asian alone (0.3%)		
	15	Some other race alone (1.1%)		
	13	Two or more races (1.0%)		
	60	Hispanic or Latino* (4.5%)		

Wood Dale, IL (inc. 1928)

1930	230	—	—	—
1960	3,071	8.8%	19.4%	98
	3,061	White (99.7%)		
	10	Other races (0.3%)		

Municipalities *(continued)*

	Total (and by category)	Foreign born	Native with foreign parentage	Males per 100 females
1990	12,425	13.1%	—	94
	11,905	White (95.8%)		
	25	American Indian (0.2%)		
	333	Asian/Pacific Islander (2.7%)		
	162	Other race (1.3%)		
	842	Hispanic Origin* (6.8%)		
2000	13,535	21.9%	—	98
	12,076	White alone (89.2%)		
	78	Black or African American alone (0.6%)		
	20	American Indian and Alaska Native alone (0.1%)		
	439	Asian alone (3.2%)		
	10	Native Hawaiian and Other Pacific Islander alone (0.1%)		
	650	Some other race alone (4.8%)		
	262	Two or more races (1.9%)		
	1,768	Hispanic or Latino* (13.1%)		

Woodridge, IL (inc. 1959)

	Total	Foreign born	Native with foreign parentage	Males per 100 females
1960	542	—	—	—
1990	26,256	9.1%	—	99
	22,655	White (86.3%)		
	1,614	Black (6.1%)		
	93	American Indian (0.4%)		
	1,648	Asian/Pacific Islander (6.3%)		
	327	Other race (1.2%)		
	901	Hispanic Origin* (3.4%)		
2000	30,934	17.4%	—	99
	23,289	White alone (75.3%)		
	2,482	Black or African American alone (8.0%)		
	49	American Indian and Alaska Native alone (0.2%)		
	3,485	Asian alone (11.3%)		
	6	Native Hawaiian and Other Pacific Islander alone (0.0%)		
	962	Some other race alone (3.1%)		
	661	Two or more races (2.1%)		
	2,839	Hispanic or Latino* (9.2%)		

Woodstock, IL (inc. 1852)

	Total	Foreign born	Native with foreign parentage	Males per 100 females
1870	1,574	20.3%	—	—
	1,563	White (99.3%)		
	11	Colored (0.7%)		
1900	2,502	16.2%	29.3%	106
	2,496	White (99.8%)		
	6	Negro (0.2%)		
1930	5,471	11.0%	30.7%	100
	5,451	White (99.6%)		
	20	Negro (0.4%)		
1960	8,897	3.7%	16.3%	92
	8,881	White (99.8%)		
	7	Negro (0.1%)		
	9	Other races (0.1%)		
1990	14,353	6.9%	—	94
	13,539	White (94.3%)		
	81	Black (0.6%)		
	6	American Indian (0.0%)		
	201	Asian/Pacific Islander (1.4%)		
	526	Other race (3.7%)		
	1,067	Hispanic Origin* (7.4%)		
2000	20,151	16.9%	—	101
	17,628	White alone (87.5%)		
	214	Black or African American alone (1.1%)		
	47	American Indian and Alaska Native alone (0.2%)		
	406	Asian alone (2.0%)		
	1,550	Some other race alone (7.7%)		
	306	Two or more races (1.5%)		
	3,830	Hispanic or Latino* (19.0%)		

Worth, IL (inc. 1914)

	Total	Foreign born	Native with foreign parentage	Males per 100 females
1930	411	—	—	—
1960	8,196	3.2%	20.3%	101
	8,190	White (99.9%)		
	6	Other races (0.1%)		
1990	11,208	4.1%	—	95
	11,063	White (98.7%)		
	32	Black (0.3%)		
	19	American Indian (0.2%)		
	94	Other race (0.8%)		
	298	Hispanic Origin* (2.7%)		
2000	11,047	9.2%	—	97
	10,211	White alone (92.4%)		
	176	Black or African American alone (1.6%)		
	20	American Indian and Alaska Native alone (0.2%)		
	135	Asian alone (1.2%)		
	2	Native Hawaiian and Other Pacific Islander alone (0.0%)		
	241	Some other race alone (2.2%)		
	262	Two or more races (2.4%)		
	669	Hispanic or Latino* (6.1%)		

Yorkville, IL (inc. 1873)

	Total	Foreign born	Native with foreign parentage	Males per 100 females
1900	413	—	—	—
1930	492	—	—	—
1960	1,568	25.1%	75.6%	93
	1,568	White (100.0%)		
1990	3,925	2.3%	—	97
	3,824	White (97.4%)		
	13	Asian/Pacific Islander (0.3%)		
	88	Other race (2.2%)		
	93	Hispanic Origin* (2.4%)		
2000	6,189	3.7%	—	97
	6,003	White alone (97.0%)		
	26	Black or African American alone (0.4%)		
	12	American Indian and Alaska Native alone (0.2%)		
	24	Asian alone (0.4%)		
	3	Native Hawaiian and Other Pacific Islander alone (0.0%)		
	45	Some other race alone (0.7%)		
	76	Two or more races (1.2%)		
	182	Hispanic or Latino* (2.9%)		

Zion, IL (inc. 1902)

	Total	Foreign born	Native with foreign parentage	Males per 100 females
1930	5,991	16.8%	27.2%	89
	5,916	White (98.7%)		
	70	Negro (1.2%)		
	5	Other (0.1%)		
1960	11,941	3.3%	9.9%	97
	11,366	White (95.2%)		
	564	Negro (4.7%)		
	11	Other races (0.1%)		
1990	19,775	3.5%	—	94
	14,542	White (73.5%)		
	4,396	Black (22.2%)		
	61	American Indian (0.3%)		
	253	Asian/Pacific Islander (1.3%)		
	523	Other race (2.6%)		
	1,144	Hispanic Origin* (5.8%)		
2000	22,866	8.9%	—	94
	13,435	White alone (58.8%)		
	6,196	Black or African American alone (27.1%)		
	88	American Indian and Alaska Native alone (0.4%)		
	428	Asian alone (1.9%)		
	16	Native Hawaiian and Other Pacific Islander alone (0.1%)		
	1,783	Some other race alone (7.8%)		
	920	Two or more races (4.0%)		
	3,487	Hispanic or Latino* (15.2%)		

Community Areas (1930–2000)

Albany Park (CA 14)

	Total (and by category)	Foreign born	Native with foreign parentage	Males per 100 females
1930	55,577	32.2%	45.7%	96
	55,495	White (99.9%)		
	46	Negro (0.1%)		
	36	Other (0.1%)		
1960	49,450	27.3%	35.8%	93
	49,250	White (99.6%)		
	19	Negro (0.0%)		
	181	Other races (0.4%)		
1990	49,501	46.6%	—	103
	28,737	White (58.1%)		
	1,697	Black (3.4%)		
	152	American Indian (0.3%)		
	11,966	Asian/Pacific Islander (24.2%)		
	6,949	Other race (14.0%)		
	15,738	Hispanic Origin* (31.8%)		
2000	57,655	52.2%	—	109
	28,568	White alone (49.5%)		
	2,207	Black or African American alone (3.8%)		
	260	American Indian and Alaska Native alone (0.5%)		
	10,233	Asian alone (17.7%)		
	36	Native Hawaiian and Other Pacific Islander alone (0.1%)		
	12,491	Some other race alone (21.7%)		
	3,860	Two or more races (6.7%)		
	26,741	Hispanic or Latino* (46.4%)		

Archer Heights (CA 57)

	Total	Foreign born	Native with foreign parentage	Males per 100 females
1930	8,120	32.0%	56.6%	110
	8,075	White (99.4%)		
	6	Negro (0.1%)		
	39	Other (0.5%)		
1960	10,584	16.5%	39.0%	96
	10,583	White (100.0%)		
	1	Negro (0.0%)		
1990	9,227	26.7%	—	91
	8,834	White (95.7%)		
	21	Black (0.2%)		
	61	Asian/Pacific Islander (0.7%)		
	311	Other race (3.4%)		
	779	Hispanic Origin* (8.4%)		
2000	12,644	43.8%	—	99
	9,109	White alone (72.0%)		
	82	Black or African American alone (0.6%)		
	43	American Indian and Alaska Native alone (0.3%)		
	55	Asian alone (0.4%)		
	10	Native Hawaiian and Other Pacific Islander alone (0.1%)		
	2,896	Some other race alone (22.9%)		
	449	Two or more races (3.6%)		
	5,485	Hispanic or Latino* (43.4%)		

Armour Square (CA 34)

	Total	Foreign born	Native with foreign parentage	Males per 100 females
1930	21,450	25.0%	37.1%	122
	15,207	White (70.9%)		
	4,058	Negro (18.9%)		
	2,185	Other (10.2%)		
1960	15,783	14.1%	22.1%	103
	9,096	White (57.6%)		
	4,960	Negro (31.4%)		
	1,727	Other races (10.9%)		
1990	10,801	44.6%	—	90
	2,505	White (23.2%)		
	2,408	Black (22.3%)		
	5,616	Asian/Pacific Islander (52.0%)		
	272	Other race (2.5%)		
	471	Hispanic Origin* (4.4%)		

2000	12,032	52.0%	—	90
	2,287	White alone (19.0%)		
	2,053	Black or African American alone (17.1%)		
	31	American Indian and Alaska Native alone (0.3%)		
	7,324	Asian alone (60.9%)		
	2	Native Hawaiian and Other Pacific Islander alone (0.0%)		
	142	Some other race alone (1.2%)		
	193	Two or more races (1.6%)		
	448	Hispanic or Latino* (3.7%)		

Ashburn (CA 70)

1930	733	14.3%	33.0%	136
	677	White (92.4%)		
	56	Other (7.6%)		
1960	38,638	6.2%	27.9%	99
	38,604	White (99.9%)		
	1	Negro (0.0%)		
	33	Other races (0.1%)		
1990	37,092	8.2%	—	91
	32,084	White (86.5%)		
	3,786	Black (10.2%)		
	18	American Indian (0.0%)		
	304	Asian/Pacific Islander (0.8%)		
	900	Other race (2.4%)		
	2,331	Hispanic Origin* (6.3%)		
2000	39,584	11.4%	—	91
	17,099	White alone (43.2%)		
	17,171	Black or African American alone (43.4%)		
	122	American Indian and Alaska Native alone (0.3%)		
	423	Asian alone (1.1%)		
	15	Native Hawaiian and Other Pacific Islander alone (0.0%)		
	3,585	Some other race alone (9.1%)		
	1,169	Two or more races (3.0%)		
	6,674	Hispanic or Latino* (16.9%)		

Auburn Gresham (CA 71)

1930	57,381	17.5%	42.1%	98
	57,343	White (99.9%)		
	17	Negro (0.0%)		
	21	Other (0.0%)		
1960	59,484	12.6%	32.1%	88
	59,346	White (99.8%)		
	91	Negro (0.2%)		
	47	Other races (0.1%)		
1990	59,808	0.8%	—	84
	632	White (1.1%)		
	59,059	Black (98.7%)		
	30	American Indian (0.1%)		
	52	Asian/Pacific Islander (0.1%)		
	35	Other race (0.1%)		
	204	Hispanic Origin* (0.3%)		
2000	55,928	1.2%	—	81
	266	White alone (0.5%)		
	55,050	Black or African American alone (98.4%)		
	80	American Indian and Alaska Native alone (0.1%)		
	48	Asian alone (0.1%)		
	4	Native Hawaiian and Other Pacific Islander alone (0.0%)		
	81	Some other race alone (0.1%)		
	399	Two or more races (0.7%)		
	347	Hispanic or Latino* (0.6%)		

Austin (CA 25)

1930	131,114	19.6%	40.5%	95
	130,932	White (99.9%)		
	132	Negro (0.1%)		
	50	Other (0.0%)		
1960	125,133	14.4%	32.9%	89
	124,916	White (99.8%)		
	31	Negro (0.0%)		
	186	Other races (0.1%)		
1990	114,079	3.0%	—	87
	12,211	White (10.7%)		
	99,046	Black (86.8%)		
	177	American Indian (0.2%)		
	1,016	Asian/Pacific Islander (0.9%)		
	1,629	Other race (1.4%)		
	4,154	Hispanic Origin* (3.6%)		
2000	117,527	3.0%	—	85
	7,234	White alone (6.2%)		
	106,029	Black or African American alone (90.2%)		
	147	American Indian and Alaska Native alone (0.1%)		
	665	Asian alone (0.6%)		
	31	Native Hawaiian and Other Pacific Islander alone (0.0%)		
	2,200	Some other race alone (1.9%)		
	1,221	Two or more races (1.0%)		
	4,841	Hispanic or Latino* (4.1%)		

Avalon Park (CA 45)

1930	10,023	16.4%	35.6%	101
	10,019	White (100.0%)		
	4	Negro (0.0%)		
1960	12,710	10.3%	4.0%	94
	12,660	White (99.6%)		
	6	Negro (0.0%)		
	44	Other races (0.3%)		
1990	11,711	0.6%	—	82
	88	White (0.8%)		
	11,587	Black (98.9%)		
	36	American Indian (0.3%)		
	81	Hispanic Origin* (0.7%)		
2000	11,147	2.7%	—	79
	109	White alone (1.0%)		
	10,851	Black or African American alone (97.3%)		
	17	American Indian and Alaska Native alone (0.2%)		
	20	Asian alone (0.2%)		
	1	Native Hawaiian and Other Pacific Islander alone (0.0%)		
	32	Some other race alone (0.3%)		
	117	Two or more races (1.0%)		
	85	Hispanic or Latino* (0.8%)		

Avondale (CA 21)

1930	48,433	25.4%	48.3%	99
	48,422	White (100.0%)		
	4	Negro (0.0%)		
	7	Other (0.0%)		
1960	39,748	14.6%	32.6%	94
	39,613	White (99.7%)		
	3	Negro (0.0%)		
	132	Other races (0.3%)		
1990	35,579	39.4%	—	98
	26,228	White (73.7%)		
	335	Black (0.9%)		
	137	American Indian (0.4%)		
	1,245	Asian/Pacific Islander (3.5%)		
	7,634	Other race (21.5%)		
	13,359	Hispanic Origin* (37.5%)		
2000	43,083	44.0%	—	104
	22,437	White alone (52.1%)		
	930	Black or African American alone (2.2%)		
	230	American Indian and Alaska Native alone (0.5%)		
	987	Asian alone (2.3%)		
	35	Native Hawaiian and Other Pacific Islander alone (0.1%)		
	15,096	Some other race alone (35.0%)		
	3,368	Two or more races (7.8%)		
	26,700	Hispanic or Latino* (62.0%)		

Belmont Cragin (CA 19)

1930	60,221	26.9%	48.6%	104
	60,182	White (99.9%)		
	4	Negro (0.0%)		
	40	Other (0.1%)		
1960	60,883	16.9%	37.4%	94
	60,838	White (99.9%)		
	3	Negro (0.0%)		
	42	Other races (0.1%)		
1990	56,787	32.0%	—	96
	46,791	White (82.4%)		
	647	Black (1.1%)		
	32	American Indian (0.1%)		
	2,058	Asian/Pacific Islander (3.6%)		
	7,259	Other race (12.8%)		
	17,066	Hispanic Origin* (30.1%)		
2000	78,144	42.2%	—	100
	45,509	White alone (58.2%)		
	2,369	Black or African American alone (3.0%)		
	479	American Indian and Alaska Native alone (0.6%)		
	2,025	Asian alone (2.6%)		
	50	Native Hawaiian and Other Pacific Islander alone (0.1%)		
	23,992	Some other race alone (30.7%)		
	3,720	Two or more races (4.8%)		
	50,881	Hispanic or Latino* (65.1%)		

Beverly (CA 72)

1930	13,793	11.2%	31.1%	89
	13,740	White (99.6%)		
	50	Negro (0.4%)		
	3	Other (0.0%)		
1960	24,814	5.6%	25.5%	88
	24,791	White (99.9%)		
	14	Negro (0.1%)		
	9	Other races (0.0%)		
1990	22,385	2.5%	—	89
	16,759	White (74.9%)		
	5,428	Black (24.2%)		
	45	American Indian (0.2%)		
	95	Asian/Pacific Islander (0.4%)		
	58	Other race (0.3%)		
	393	Hispanic Origin* (1.8%)		
2000	21,992	2.6%	—	89
	14,221	White alone (64.7%)		
	7,036	Black or African American alone (32.0%)		
	41	American Indian and Alaska Native alone (0.2%)		
	121	Asian alone (0.6%)		
	4	Native Hawaiian and Other Pacific Islander alone (0.0%)		
	156	Some other race alone (0.7%)		
	413	Two or more races (1.9%)		
	643	Hispanic or Latino* (2.9%)		

Bridgeport (CA 60)

1930	53,553	28.7%	49.7%	108
	53,051	White (99.1%)		
	1	Negro (0.0%)		
	501	Other (0.9%)		
1960	41,560	12.9%	29.8%	99
	41,436	White (99.7%)		
	65	Negro (0.2%)		
	59	Other races (0.1%)		
1990	29,877	23.8%	—	96
	20,189	White (67.6%)		
	26	Black (0.1%)		
	37	American Indian (0.1%)		
	5,072	Asian/Pacific Islander (17.0%)		
	4,553	Other race (15.2%)		
	7,796	Hispanic Origin* (26.1%)		
2000	33,694	32.2%	—	99
	18,067	White alone (53.6%)		
	397	Black or African American alone (1.2%)		
	226	American Indian and Alaska Native alone (0.7%)		
	8,851	Asian alone (26.3%)		
	14	Native Hawaiian and Other Pacific Islander alone (0.0%)		
	5,203	Some other race alone (15.4%)		
	936	Two or more races (2.8%)		
	10,165	Hispanic or Latino* (30.2%)		

Brighton Park (CA 58)

1930	46,552	30.3%	51.4%	108
	46,065	White (99.0%)		
	41	Negro (0.1%)		
	446	Other (1.0%)		
1960	38,019	20.4%	33.7%	99
	37,948	White (99.8%)		
	36	Negro (0.1%)		
	35	Other races (0.1%)		
1990	32,207	29.3%	—	95
	23,861	White (74.1%)		
	19	Black (0.1%)		
	60	American Indian (0.2%)		
	698	Asian/Pacific Islander (2.2%)		
	7,569	Other race (23.5%)		
	12,044	Hispanic Origin* (37.4%)		

Community Areas (1930–2000) *(continued)*

Year	Total (and by category)		Foreign born	Native with foreign parentage	Males per 100 females
2000	44,912		46.3%	—	106
	22,861	White alone (50.9%)			
	330	Black or African American alone (0.7%)			
	415	American Indian and Alaska Native alone (0.9%)			
	1,326	Asian alone (3.0%)			
	29	Native Hawaiian and Other Pacific Islander alone (0.1%)			
	18,054	Some other race alone (40.2%)			
	1,897	Two or more races (4.2%)			
	34,409	Hispanic or Latino* (76.6%)			

Burnside (CA 47)

Year	Total (and by category)		Foreign born	Native with foreign parentage	Males per 100 females
1930	3,483		37.1%	53.7%	109
	3,478	White (99.9%)			
	5	Other (0.1%)			
1960	3,463		21.9%	1.2%	106
	3,454	White (99.7%)			
	9	Other races (0.3%)			
1990	3,445		2.1%	—	88
	57	White (1.7%)			
	3,388	Black (98.3%)			
	16	Hispanic Origin* (0.5%)			
2000	3,294		2.7%	—	86
	47	White alone (1.4%)			
	3,198	Black or African American alone (97.1%)			
	1	American Indian and Alaska Native alone (0.0%)			
	7	Asian alone (0.2%)			
	4	Some other race alone (0.1%)			
	37	Two or more races (1.1%)			
	34	Hispanic or Latino* (1.0%)			

Calumet Heights (CA 48)

Year	Total (and by category)		Foreign born	Native with foreign parentage	Males per 100 females
1930	7,343		22.2%	42.6%	111
	7,167	White (97.6%)			
	19	Negro (0.3%)			
	157	Other (2.1%)			
1960	19,352		12.8%	2.4%	98
	19,313	White (99.8%)			
	8	Negro (0.0%)			
	31	Other races (0.2%)			
1990	17,453		3.9%	—	85
	687	White (3.9%)			
	16,179	Black (92.7%)			
	11	American Indian (0.1%)			
	576	Other race (3.3%)			
	920	Hispanic Origin* (5.3%)			
2000	15,974		4.1%	—	80
	472	White alone (3.0%)			
	14,889	Black or African American alone (93.2%)			
	32	American Indian and Alaska Native alone (0.2%)			
	36	Asian alone (0.2%)			
	5	Native Hawaiian and Other Pacific Islander alone (0.0%)			
	330	Some other race alone (2.1%)			
	210	Two or more races (1.3%)			
	747	Hispanic or Latino* (4.7%)			

Chatham (CA 44)

Year	Total (and by category)		Foreign born	Native with foreign parentage	Males per 100 females
1930	36,228		19.3%	38.5%	98
	36,137	White (99.7%)			
	10	Negro (0.0%)			
	81	Other (0.2%)			
1960	41,962		5.6%	1.2%	90
	15,090	White (36.0%)			
	26,756	Negro (63.8%)			
	116	Other races (0.3%)			
1990	36,779		1.1%	—	79
	363	White (1.0%)			
	36,307	Black (98.7%)			
	23	American Indian (0.1%)			
	29	Asian/Pacific Islander (0.1%)			
	57	Other race (0.2%)			
	198	Hispanic Origin* (0.5%)			
2000	37,275		1.3%	—	77
	157	White alone (0.4%)			
	36,648	Black or African American alone (98.3%)			
	34	American Indian and Alaska Native alone (0.1%)			
	26	Asian alone (0.1%)			
	21	Native Hawaiian and Other Pacific Islander alone (0.1%)			
	64	Some other race alone (0.2%)			
	325	Two or more races (0.9%)			
	220	Hispanic or Latino* (0.6%)			

Chicago Lawn (CA 66)

Year	Total (and by category)		Foreign born	Native with foreign parentage	Males per 100 females
1930	47,462		21.4%	43.1%	101
	47,441	White (100.0%)			
	6	Negro (0.0%)			
	15	Other (0.0%)			
1960	51,347		19.7%	34.0%	92
	51,294	White (99.9%)			
	3	Negro (0.0%)			
	50	Other races (0.1%)			
1990	51,243		22.0%	—	93
	26,837	White (52.4%)			
	13,655	Black (26.6%)			
	208	American Indian (0.4%)			
	967	Asian/Pacific Islander (1.9%)			
	9,576	Other race (18.7%)			
	14,549	Hispanic Origin* (28.4%)			
2000	61,412		21.0%	—	92
	14,518	White alone (23.6%)			
	32,541	Black or African American alone (53.0%)			
	319	American Indian and Alaska Native alone (0.5%)			
	421	Asian alone (0.7%)			
	22	Native Hawaiian and Other Pacific Islander alone (0.0%)			
	11,726	Some other race alone (19.1%)			
	1,865	Two or more races (3.0%)			
	21,534	Hispanic or Latino* (35.1%)			

Clearing (CA 64)

Year	Total (and by category)		Foreign born	Native with foreign parentage	Males per 100 females
1930	5,434		22.9%	40.1%	123
	5,417	White (99.7%)			
	17	Other (0.3%)			
1960	18,797		8.1%	28.3%	103
	18,777	White (99.9%)			
	2	Negro (0.0%)			
	18	Other races (0.1%)			
1990	21,490		9.5%	—	93
	20,722	White (96.4%)			
	100	American Indian (0.5%)			
	203	Asian/Pacific Islander (0.9%)			
	635	Other race (3.0%)			
	1,615	Hispanic Origin* (7.5%)			
2000	22,331		17.0%	—	96
	19,201	White alone (86.0%)			
	155	Black or African American alone (0.7%)			
	36	American Indian and Alaska Native alone (0.2%)			
	165	Asian alone (0.7%)			
	8	Native Hawaiian and Other Pacific Islander alone (0.0%)			
	2,260	Some other race alone (10.1%)			
	506	Two or more races (2.3%)			
	4,688	Hispanic or Latino* (21.0%)			

Douglas (CA 35)

Year	Total (and by category)		Foreign born	Native with foreign parentage	Males per 100 females
1930	50,285		2.9%	3.5%	103
	5,517	White (11.0%)			
	44,644	Negro (88.8%)			
	124	Other (0.2%)			
1960	52,325		1.6%	1.8%	91
	3,880	White (7.4%)			
	48,031	Negro (91.8%)			
	414	Other races (0.8%)			
1990	30,652		3.7%	—	71
	1,683	White (5.5%)			
	27,976	Black (91.3%)			
	123	American Indian (0.4%)			
	806	Asian/Pacific Islander (2.6%)			
	64	Other race (0.2%)			
	253	Hispanic Origin* (0.8%)			
	26,470		5.5%	—	81
	1,841	White alone (7.0%)			
	22,719	Black or African American alone (85.8%)			
	67	American Indian and Alaska Native alone (0.3%)			
	1,393	Asian alone (5.3%)			
	9	Native Hawaiian and Other Pacific Islander alone (0.0%)			
	111	Some other race alone (0.4%)			
	330	Two or more races (1.2%)			
	295	Hispanic or Latino* (1.1%)			

Dunning (CA 17)

Year	Total (and by category)		Foreign born	Native with foreign parentage	Males per 100 females
1930	19,659		23.3%	42.3%	107
	19,648	White (99.9%)			
	3	Negro (0.0%)			
	8	Other (0.0%)			
1960	41,626		14.5%	33.8%	96
	41,560	White (99.8%)			
	2	Negro (0.0%)			
	64	Other races (0.2%)			
1990	36,957		19.6%	—	92
	35,360	White (95.7%)			
	157	Black (0.4%)			
	98	American Indian (0.3%)			
	861	Asian/Pacific Islander (2.3%)			
	481	Other race (1.3%)			
	1,882	Hispanic Origin* (5.1%)			
2000	42,164		34.5%	—	93
	37,439	White alone (88.8%)			
	265	Black or African American alone (0.6%)			
	69	American Indian and Alaska Native alone (0.2%)			
	1,361	Asian alone (3.2%)			
	19	Native Hawaiian and Other Pacific Islander alone (0.0%)			
	2,019	Some other race alone (4.8%)			
	992	Two or more races (2.4%)			
	5,441	Hispanic or Latino* (12.9%)			

East Garfield Park (CA 27)

Year	Total (and by category)		Foreign born	Native with foreign parentage	Males per 100 females
1930	63,353		23.9%	37.5%	105
	61,339	White (96.8%)			
	1,848	Negro (2.9%)			
	166	Other (0.3%)			
1960	66,871		5.4%	7.1%	98
	25,409	White (38.0%)			
	41,097	Negro (61.5%)			
	365	Other races (0.5%)			
1990	24,030		0.4%	—	90
	213	White (0.9%)			
	23,644	Black (98.4%)			
	42	American Indian (0.2%)			
	33	Asian/Pacific Islander (0.1%)			
	98	Other race (0.4%)			
	151	Hispanic Origin* (0.6%)			
2000	20,881		0.7%	—	88
	270	White alone (1.3%)			
	20,378	Black or African American alone (97.6%)			
	16	American Indian and Alaska Native alone (0.1%)			
	25	Asian alone (0.1%)			
	5	Native Hawaiian and Other Pacific Islander alone (0.0%)			
	67	Some other race alone (0.3%)			
	120	Two or more races (0.6%)			
	207	Hispanic or Latino* (1.0%)			

East Side (CA 52)

Year	Total (and by category)		Foreign born	Native with foreign parentage	Males per 100 females
1930	16,839		26.1%	46.5%	112
	16,795	White (99.7%)			
	44	Other (0.3%)			
1960	23,214		11.5%	31.1%	103
	23,191	White (99.9%)			
	4	Negro (0.0%)			
	19	Other races (0.1%)			

1990 20,450 18.0% — 94
15,896 White (77.7%)
2 Black (0.0%)
73 American Indian (0.4%)
53 Asian/Pacific Islander (0.3%)
4,426 Other race (21.6%)
8,177 Hispanic Origin* (40.0%)
2000 23,653 28.6% — 98
13,239 White alone (56.0%)
318 Black or African American alone (1.3%)
188 American Indian and Alaska Native alone (0.8%)
69 Asian alone (0.3%)
6 Native Hawaiian and Other Pacific Islander alone (0.0%)
9,039 Some other race alone (38.2%)
794 Two or more races (3.4%)
16,113 Hispanic or Latino* (68.1%)

Edgewater (CA 77)

1930 53,938 — — —
1990 60,703 29.6% — 98
35,274 White (58.1%)
12,009 Black (19.8%)
384 American Indian (0.6%)
7,272 Asian/Pacific Islander (12.0%)
5,764 Other race (9.5%)
3,331 Hispanic Origin* (5.5%)
2000 62,198 36.1% — 102
35,404 White alone (56.9%)
10,813 Black or African American alone (17.4%)
283 American Indian and Alaska Native alone (0.5%)
7,210 Asian alone (11.6%)
98 Native Hawaiian and Other Pacific Islander alone (0.2%)
5,492 Some other race alone (8.8%)
2,898 Two or more races (4.7%)
12,176 Hispanic or Latino* (19.6%)

Edison Park (CA 9)

1930 5,370 12.2% 36.6% 95
5,366 White (99.9%)
4 Negro (0.1%)
1960 12,568 8.0% 30.4% 92
12,565 White (100.0%)
3 Other races (0.0%)
1990 11,426 9.3% — 85
11,316 White (99.0%)
100 Asian/Pacific Islander (0.9%)
10 Other race (0.1%)
217 Hispanic Origin* (1.9%)
2000 11,259 11.4% — 88
10,839 White alone (96.3%)
21 Black or African American alone (0.2%)
14 American Indian and Alaska Native alone (0.1%)
201 Asian alone (1.8%)
67 Some other race alone (0.6%)
117 Two or more races (1.0%)
463 Hispanic or Latino* (4.1%)

Englewood (CA 68)

1930 89,063 21.8% 36.4% 101
87,873 White (98.7%)
1,126 Negro (1.3%)
64 Other (0.1%)
1960 97,595 4.3% 8.1% 94
30,107 White (30.8%)
67,216 Negro (68.9%)
272 Other races (0.3%)
1990 48,434 0.9% — 83
209 White (0.4%)
47,963 Black (99.0%)
51 American Indian (0.1%)
105 Asian/Pacific Islander (0.2%)
106 Other race (0.2%)
231 Hispanic Origin* (0.5%)

2000 40,222 1.0% — 83
242 White alone (0.6%)
39,501 Black or African American alone (98.2%)
44 American Indian and Alaska Native alone (0.1%)
28 Asian alone (0.1%)
7 Native Hawaiian and Other Pacific Islander alone (0.0%)
122 Some other race alone (0.3%)
278 Two or more races (0.7%)
347 Hispanic or Latino* (0.9%)

Forest Glen (CA 12)

1930 4,065 22.5% 42.9% 103
4,058 White (99.8%)
2 Negro (0.0%)
5 Other (0.1%)
1960 19,228 10.8% 34.9% 91
19,203 White (99.9%)
6 Negro (0.0%)
19 Other races (0.1%)
1990 17,655 14.7% — 93
16,521 White (93.6%)
35 American Indian (0.2%)
1,016 Asian/Pacific Islander (5.8%)
83 Other race (0.5%)
583 Hispanic Origin* (3.3%)
2000 18,165 19.8% — 93
15,746 White alone (86.7%)
80 Black or African American alone (0.4%)
37 American Indian and Alaska Native alone (0.2%)
1,594 Asian alone (8.8%)
4 Native Hawaiian and Other Pacific Islander alone (0.0%)
309 Some other race alone (1.7%)
395 Two or more races (2.2%)
1,389 Hispanic or Latino* (7.6%)

Fuller Park (CA 37)

1930 14,437 28.1% 39.5% 108
12,857 White (89.1%)
1,093 Negro (7.6%)
487 Other (3.4%)
1960 12,181 1.0% 1.5% 94
476 White (3.9%)
11,692 Negro (96.0%)
13 Other races (0.1%)
1990 4,364 0.2% — 85
22 White (0.5%)
4,342 Black (99.5%)
41 Hispanic Origin* (0.9%)
2000 3,420 2.3% — 88
46 White alone (1.3%)
3,239 Black or African American alone (94.7%)
11 American Indian and Alaska Native alone (0.3%)
6 Asian alone (0.2%)
3 Native Hawaiian and Other Pacific Islander alone (0.1%)
78 Some other race alone (2.3%)
37 Two or more races (1.1%)
116 Hispanic or Latino* (3.4%)

Gage Park (CA 63)

1930 31,535 25.6% 49.2% 105
31,529 White (100.0%)
6 Other (0.0%)
1960 28,244 15.8% 36.3% 93
28,222 White (99.9%)
2 Negro (0.0%)
20 Other races (0.1%)
1990 26,957 22.9% — 98
18,859 White (70.0%)
1,366 Black (5.1%)
46 American Indian (0.2%)
94 Asian/Pacific Islander (0.3%)
6,592 Other race (24.5%)
10,574 Hispanic Origin* (39.2%)

2000 39,193 45.2% — 103
18,596 White alone (47.4%)
2,862 Black or African American alone (7.3%)
285 American Indian and Alaska Native alone (0.7%)
202 Asian alone (0.5%)
23 Native Hawaiian and Other Pacific Islander alone (0.1%)
15,656 Some other race alone (39.9%)
1,569 Two or more races (4.0%)
31,079 Hispanic or Latino* (79.3%)

Garfield Ridge (CA 56)

1930 6,050 29.5% 55.1% 110
6,018 White (99.5%)
32 Other (0.5%)
1960 40,449 8.6% 32.2% 98
37,675 White (93.1%)
2,686 Negro (6.6%)
88 Other races (0.2%)
1990 33,948 11.2% — 89
28,308 White (83.4%)
4,302 Black (12.7%)
24 American Indian (0.1%)
421 Asian/Pacific Islander (1.2%)
893 Other race (2.6%)
2,509 Hispanic Origin* (7.4%)
2000 36,101 19.4% — 90
27,897 White alone (77.3%)
4,437 Black or African American alone (12.3%)
57 American Indian and Alaska Native alone (0.2%)
347 Asian alone (1.0%)
22 Native Hawaiian and Other Pacific Islander alone (0.1%)
2,567 Some other race alone (7.1%)
774 Two or more races (2.1%)
5,948 Hispanic or Latino* (16.5%)

Grand Boulevard (CA 38)

1930 87,005 1.4% 1.9% 96
4,550 White (5.2%)
82,329 Negro (94.6%)
126 Other (0.1%)
1960 80,036 0.3% 0.0% 91
398 White (0.5%)
79,537 Negro (99.4%)
101 Other races (0.1%)
1990 35,897 0.3% — 79
47 White (0.1%)
35,715 Black (99.5%)
12 American Indian (0.0%)
51 Asian/Pacific Islander (0.1%)
72 Other race (0.2%)
146 Hispanic Origin* (0.4%)
2000 28,006 0.7% — 79
182 White alone (0.6%)
27,502 Black or African American alone (98.2%)
36 American Indian and Alaska Native alone (0.1%)
22 Asian alone (0.1%)
3 Native Hawaiian and Other Pacific Islander alone (0.0%)
88 Some other race alone (0.3%)
173 Two or more races (0.6%)
236 Hispanic or Latino* (0.8%)

Greater Grand Crossing (CA 69)

1930 60,007 21.4% 37.6% 101
59,667 White (99.4%)
254 Negro (0.4%)
86 Other (0.1%)
1960 63,169 2.5% 4.5% 91
8,687 White (13.8%)
54,257 Negro (85.9%)
225 Other races (0.4%)
1990 38,644 0.7% — 79
228 White (0.6%)
38,298 Black (99.1%)
24 American Indian (0.1%)
11 Asian/Pacific Islander (0.0%)
83 Other race (0.2%)
189 Hispanic Origin* (0.5%)

Community Areas (1930–2000) *(continued)*

	Total (and by category)		Foreign born	Native with foreign parentage	Males per 100 females
2000	38,619		1.1%	—	81
	169	White alone (0.4%)			
	37,952	Black or African American alone (98.3%)			
	54	American Indian and Alaska Native alone (0.1%)			
	28	Asian alone (0.1%)			
	6	Native Hawaiian and Other Pacific Islander alone (0.0%)			
	85	Some other race alone (0.2%)			
	325	Two or more races (0.8%)			
	276	Hispanic or Latino* (0.7%)			

Hegewisch (CA 55)

1930	7,890		32.3%	50.1%	122
	7,798	White (98.8%)			
	92	Other (1.2%)			
1960	8,936		12.7%	32.0%	106
	8,900	White (99.6%)			
	32	Negro (0.4%)			
	4	Other races (0.0%)			
1990	10,136		9.1%	—	99
	9,550	White (94.2%)			
	76	Black (0.7%)			
	19	American Indian (0.2%)			
	57	Asian/Pacific Islander (0.6%)			
	434	Other race (4.3%)			
	1,290	Hispanic Origin* (12.7%)			
2000	9,781		13.5%	—	95
	7,835	White alone (80.1%)			
	131	Black or African American alone (1.3%)			
	67	American Indian and Alaska Native alone (0.7%)			
	39	Asian alone (0.4%)			
	3	Native Hawaiian and Other Pacific Islander alone (0.0%)			
	1,294	Some other race alone (13.2%)			
	412	Two or more races (4.2%)			
	2,820	Hispanic or Latino* (28.8%)			

Hermosa (CA 20)

1930	23,518		26.5%	43.7%	102
	23,506	White (99.9%)			
	7	Negro (0.0%)			
	5	Other (0.0%)			
1960	21,429		15.6%	33.3%	92
	21,401	White (99.9%)			
	28	Other races (0.1%)			
1990	23,131		23.7%	—	99
	13,337	White (57.7%)			
	362	Black (1.6%)			
	57	American Indian (0.2%)			
	689	Asian/Pacific Islander (3.0%)			
	8,686	Other race (37.6%)			
	15,923	Hispanic Origin* (68.8%)			
2000	26,908		32.3%	—	100
	11,094	White alone (41.2%)			
	900	Black or African American alone (3.3%)			
	184	American Indian and Alaska Native alone (0.7%)			
	348	Asian alone (1.3%)			
	32	Native Hawaiian and Other Pacific Islander alone (0.1%)			
	13,203	Some other race alone (49.1%)			
	1,147	Two or more races (4.3%)			
	22,574	Hispanic or Latino* (83.9%)			

Humboldt Park (CA 23)

1930	80,835		31.4%	45.0%	104
	80,679	White (99.8%)			
	43	Negro (0.1%)			
	113	Other (0.1%)			
1960	71,609		20.5%	31.4%	97
	70,972	White (99.1%)			
	425	Negro (0.6%)			
	212	Other races (0.3%)			
1990	67,573		13.0%	—	95
	15,279	White (22.6%)			
	34,199	Black (50.6%)			
	275	American Indian (0.4%)			
	707	Asian/Pacific Islander (1.0%)			
	17,193	Other race (25.4%)			
	29,735	Hispanic Origin* (44.0%)			
2000	65,836		18.8%	—	94
	12,781	White alone (19.4%)			
	31,960	Black or African American alone (48.5%)			
	295	American Indian and Alaska Native alone (0.4%)			
	294	Asian alone (0.4%)			
	96	Native Hawaiian and Other Pacific Islander alone (0.1%)			
	18,800	Some other race alone (28.6%)			
	1,610	Two or more races (2.4%)			
	31,607	Hispanic or Latino* (48.0%)			

Hyde Park (CA 41)

1930	48,017		20.1%	32.8%	85
	47,198	White (98.3%)			
	521	Negro (1.1%)			
	298	Other (0.6%)			
1960	45,577		11.0%	1.8%	93
	27,214	White (59.7%)			
	17,163	Negro (37.7%)			
	1,200	Other races (2.6%)			
1990	28,630		14.5%	—	99
	14,881	White (52.0%)			
	10,957	Black (38.3%)			
	61	American Indian (0.2%)			
	2,506	Asian/Pacific Islander (8.8%)			
	257	Other race (0.9%)			
	895	Hispanic Origin* (3.1%)			
2000	29,920		16.3%	—	94
	13,689	White alone (45.8%)			
	11,413	Black or African American alone (38.1%)			
	40	American Indian and Alaska Native alone (0.1%)			
	3,372	Asian alone (11.3%)			
	21	Native Hawaiian and Other Pacific Islander alone (0.1%)			
	448	Some other race alone (1.5%)			
	937	Two or more races (3.1%)			
	1,230	Hispanic or Latino* (4.1%)			

Irving Park (CA 16)

1930	66,783		23.9%	43.1%	98
	66,708	White (99.9%)			
	37	Negro (0.1%)			
	38	Other (0.1%)			
1960	58,298		14.7%	32.3%	91
	58,125	White (99.7%)			
	20	Negro (0.0%)			
	153	Other races (0.3%)			
1990	50,159		26.1%	—	95
	39,801	White (79.3%)			
	497	Black (1.0%)			
	208	American Indian (0.4%)			
	4,237	Asian/Pacific Islander (8.4%)			
	5,416	Other race (10.8%)			
	12,222	Hispanic Origin* (24.4%)			
2000	58,643		35.8%	—	100
	37,216	White alone (63.5%)			
	1,342	Black or African American alone (2.3%)			
	307	American Indian and Alaska Native alone (0.5%)			
	4,417	Asian alone (7.5%)			
	39	Native Hawaiian and Other Pacific Islander alone (0.1%)			
	12,092	Some other race alone (20.6%)			
	3,230	Two or more races (5.5%)			
	25,401	Hispanic or Latino* (43.3%)			

Jefferson Park (CA 11)

1930	20,532		23.4%	45.8%	102
	20,522	White (100.0%)			
	2	Negro (0.0%)			
	8	Other (0.0%)			
1960	27,494		13.3%	35.2%	94
	27,475	White (99.9%)			
	19	Other races (0.1%)			
1990	23,649		16.9%	—	88
	22,337	White (94.5%)			
	15	Black (0.1%)			
	250	American Indian (1.1%)			
	761	Asian/Pacific Islander (3.2%)			
	286	Other race (1.2%)			
	1,041	Hispanic Origin* (4.4%)			
2000	25,859		27.4%	—	90
	22,767	White alone (88.0%)			
	91	Black or African American alone (0.4%)			
	61	American Indian and Alaska Native alone (0.2%)			
	1,263	Asian alone (4.9%)			
	13	Native Hawaiian and Other Pacific Islander alone (0.1%)			
	1,011	Some other race alone (3.9%)			
	653	Two or more races (2.5%)			
	2,881	Hispanic or Latino* (11.1%)			

Kenwood (CA 39)

1930	26,942		18.4%	30.2%	83
	26,713	White (99.2%)			
	185	Negro (0.7%)			
	44	Other (0.2%)			
1960	41,533		2.9%	0.3%	92
	6,282	White (15.1%)			
	34,838	Negro (83.9%)			
	413	Other races (1.0%)			
1990	18,178		5.1%	—	79
	3,645	White (20.1%)			
	13,954	Black (76.8%)			
	40	American Indian (0.2%)			
	442	Asian/Pacific Islander (2.4%)			
	97	Other race (0.5%)			
	241	Hispanic Origin* (1.3%)			
2000	18,363		8.7%	—	78
	3,012	White alone (16.4%)			
	13,968	Black or African American alone (76.1%)			
	37	American Indian and Alaska Native alone (0.2%)			
	790	Asian alone (4.3%)			
	11	Native Hawaiian and Other Pacific Islander alone (0.1%)			
	133	Some other race alone (0.7%)			
	412	Two or more races (2.2%)			
	301	Hispanic or Latino* (1.6%)			

Lake View (CA 6)

1930	114,872		28.8%	35.6%	96
	114,435	White (99.6%)			
	198	Negro (0.2%)			
	239	Other (0.2%)			
1960	118,764		20.1%	27.8%	89
	115,018	White (96.8%)			
	168	Negro (0.1%)			
	3,578	Other races (3.0%)			
1990	91,031		15.0%	—	98
	74,864	White (82.2%)			
	5,932	Black (6.5%)			
	337	American Indian (0.4%)			
	3,983	Asian/Pacific Islander (4.4%)			
	5,915	Other race (6.5%)			
	12,932	Hispanic Origin* (14.2%)			
2000	94,817		13.8%	—	100
	79,814	White alone (84.2%)			
	4,305	Black or African American alone (4.5%)			
	234	American Indian and Alaska Native alone (0.2%)			
	5,165	Asian alone (5.4%)			
	67	Native Hawaiian and Other Pacific Islander alone (0.1%)			
	3,187	Some other race alone (3.4%)			
	2,045	Two or more races (2.2%)			
	8,268	Hispanic or Latino* (8.7%)			

Lincoln Park (CA 7)

1930	97,873		33.8%	36.8%	106
	97,393	White (99.5%)			
	143	Negro (0.1%)			
	337	Other (0.3%)			
1960	88,836		17.3%	21.7%	97
	84,604	White (95.2%)			
	1,358	Negro (1.5%)			
	2,874	Other races (3.2%)			

1990 61,092 7.6% — 92
53,900 White (88.2%)
3,717 Black (6.1%)
79 American Indian (0.1%)
1,504 Asian/Pacific Islander (2.5%)
1,892 Other race (3.1%)
3,981 Hispanic Origin* (6.5%)
2000 64,320 8.1% — 96
56,140 White alone (87.3%)
3,394 Black or African American alone (5.3%)
129 American Indian and Alaska Native alone (0.2%)
2,337 Asian alone (3.6%)
27 Native Hawaiian and Other Pacific Islander alone (0.0%)
1,245 Some other race alone (1.9%)
1,048 Two or more races (1.6%)
3,254 Hispanic or Latino* (5.1%)

Lincoln Square (CA 4)

1930 46,419 22.5% 40.4% 94
46,384 White (99.9%)
11 Negro (0.0%)
24 Other (0.1%)
1960 49,850 19.4% 32.6% 87
49,544 White (99.4%)
30 Negro (0.1%)
276 Other races (0.6%)
1990 44,891 37.7% — 92
32,524 White (72.5%)
1,174 Black (2.6%)
250 American Indian (0.6%)
6,237 Asian/Pacific Islander (13.9%)
4,706 Other race (10.5%)
10,353 Hispanic Origin* (23.1%)
2000 44,574 38.6% — 96
29,801 White alone (66.9%)
1,455 Black or African American alone (3.3%)
220 American Indian and Alaska Native alone (0.5%)
6,004 Asian alone (13.5%)
39 Native Hawaiian and Other Pacific Islander alone (0.1%)
4,820 Some other race alone (10.8%)
2,235 Two or more races (5.0%)
11,831 Hispanic or Latino* (26.5%)

Logan Square (CA 22)

1930 114,174 29.7% 47.3% 101
114,086 White (99.9%)
19 Negro (0.0%)
69 Other (0.1%)
1960 94,799 17.4% 30.6% 97
94,076 White (99.2%)
371 Negro (0.4%)
352 Other races (0.4%)
1990 82,605 25.6% — 101
39,522 White (47.8%)
5,418 Black (6.6%)
196 American Indian (0.2%)
1,356 Asian/Pacific Islander (1.6%)
36,113 Other race (43.7%)
54,740 Hispanic Origin* (66.3%)
2000 82,715 28.2% — 104
40,073 White alone (48.4%)
4,999 Black or African American alone (6.0%)
463 American Indian and Alaska Native alone (0.6%)
1,155 Asian alone (1.4%)
64 Native Hawaiian and Other Pacific Islander alone (0.1%)
31,502 Some other race alone (38.1%)
4,459 Two or more races (5.4%)
53,833 Hispanic or Latino* (65.1%)

Loop (CA 32)

1930 7,851 28.2% 30.3% 394
7,639 White (97.3%)
98 Negro (1.2%)
114 Other (1.5%)
1960 4,337 7.1% 13.8% 502
3,841 White (88.6%)
449 Negro (10.4%)
47 Other races (1.1%)

1990 11,954 9.0% — 112
8,924 White (74.7%)
2,451 Black (20.5%)
44 American Indian (0.4%)
448 Asian/Pacific Islander (3.7%)
78 Other race (0.7%)
679 Hispanic Origin* (5.7%)
2000 16,388 15.1% — 105
10,744 White alone (65.6%)
3,249 Black or African American alone (19.8%)
46 American Indian and Alaska Native alone (0.3%)
1,631 Asian alone (10.0%)
16 Native Hawaiian and Other Pacific Islander alone (0.1%)
293 Some other race alone (1.8%)
409 Two or more races (2.5%)
975 Hispanic or Latino* (5.9%)

Lower West Side (CA 31)

1930 66,198 36.6% 51.6% 112
65,714 White (99.3%)
5 Negro (0.0%)
479 Other (0.7%)
1960 48,448 19.9% 32.0% 104
47,795 White (98.7%)
530 Negro (1.1%)
123 Other races (0.3%)
1990 45,654 49.1% — 112
14,039 White (30.8%)
415 Black (0.9%)
109 American Indian (0.2%)
112 Asian/Pacific Islander (0.2%)
30,979 Other race (67.9%)
40,227 Hispanic Origin* (88.1%)
2000 44,031 49.1% — 113
17,273 White alone (39.2%)
979 Black or African American alone (2.2%)
430 American Indian and Alaska Native alone (1.0%)
174 Asian alone (0.4%)
26 Native Hawaiian and Other Pacific Islander alone (0.1%)
23,743 Some other race alone (53.9%)
1,406 Two or more races (3.2%)
39,144 Hispanic or Latino* (88.9%)

McKinley Park (CA 59)

1930 22,032 23.0% 50.4% 107
22,020 White (99.9%)
3 Negro (0.0%)
9 Other (0.0%)
1960 16,908 10.0% 32.2% 98
16,885 White (99.9%)
23 Other races (0.1%)
1990 13,297 18.9% — 96
9,930 White (74.7%)
10 Black (0.1%)
53 American Indian (0.4%)
342 Asian/Pacific Islander (2.6%)
2,962 Other race (22.3%)
5,255 Hispanic Origin* (39.5%)
2000 15,962 37.9% — 100
8,643 White alone (54.1%)
172 Black or African American alone (1.1%)
109 American Indian and Alaska Native alone (0.7%)
1,228 Asian alone (7.7%)
2 Native Hawaiian and Other Pacific Islander alone (0.0%)
5,203 Some other race alone (32.6%)
605 Two or more races (3.8%)
9,819 Hispanic or Latino* (61.5%)

Montclare (CA 18)

1930 8,500 26.6% 44.0% 103
8,493 White (99.9%)
5 Negro (0.1%)
2 Other (0.0%)
1960 11,802 18.8% 36.1% 94
11,785 White (99.9%)
1 Negro (0.0%)
16 Other races (0.1%)

1990 10,573 21.0% — 88
9,885 White (93.5%)
41 Black (0.4%)
6 American Indian (0.1%)
178 Asian/Pacific Islander (1.7%)
463 Other race (4.4%)
1,199 Hispanic Origin* (11.3%)
2000 12,646 33.6% — 96
8,964 White alone (70.9%)
297 Black or African American alone (2.3%)
34 American Indian and Alaska Native alone (0.3%)
345 Asian alone (2.7%)
8 Native Hawaiian and Other Pacific Islander alone (0.1%)
2,445 Some other race alone (19.3%)
553 Two or more races (4.4%)
4,865 Hispanic or Latino* (38.5%)

Morgan Park (CA 75)

1930 12,747 9.0% 20.0% 95
8,267 White (64.9%)
4,466 Negro (35.0%)
14 Other (0.1%)
1960 27,912 4.7% 17.3% 91
18,082 White (64.8%)
9,797 Negro (35.1%)
33 Other races (0.1%)
1990 26,740 1.8% — 87
9,183 White (34.3%)
17,365 Black (64.9%)
55 American Indian (0.2%)
72 Asian/Pacific Islander (0.3%)
65 Other race (0.2%)
340 Hispanic Origin* (1.3%)
2000 25,226 2.4% — 84
7,794 White alone (30.9%)
16,904 Black or African American alone (67.0%)
16 American Indian and Alaska Native alone (0.1%)
84 Asian alone (0.3%)
4 Native Hawaiian and Other Pacific Islander alone (0.0%)
139 Some other race alone (0.6%)
285 Two or more races (1.1%)
533 Hispanic or Latino* (2.1%)

Mount Greenwood (CA 74)

1930 3,310 24.4% 42.3% 107
3,310 White (100.0%)
1960 21,941 6.8% 27.1% 95
21,918 White (99.9%)
4 Negro (0.0%)
19 Other races (0.1%)
1990 19,179 3.6% — 95
18,781 White (97.9%)
233 Black (1.2%)
27 American Indian (0.1%)
48 Asian/Pacific Islander (0.3%)
90 Other race (0.5%)
362 Hispanic Origin* (1.9%)
2000 18,820 3.8% — 97
17,612 White alone (93.6%)
676 Black or African American alone (3.6%)
20 American Indian and Alaska Native alone (0.1%)
61 Asian alone (0.3%)
8 Native Hawaiian and Other Pacific Islander alone (0.0%)
159 Some other race alone (0.8%)
284 Two or more races (1.5%)
723 Hispanic or Latino* (3.8%)

Near North Side (CA 8)

1930 79,554 26.4% 31.5% 114
74,410 White (93.5%)
4,321 Negro (5.4%)
823 Other (1.0%)
1960 75,509 7.7% 12.6% 101
50,569 White (67.0%)
23,114 Negro (30.6%)
1,826 Other races (2.4%)

Community Areas (1930–2000) *(continued)*

	Total (and by category)	Foreign born	Native with foreign parentage	Males per 100 females
1990	62,842	8.9%	—	86
	45,972 White (73.2%)			
	14,530 Black (23.1%)			
	52 American Indian (0.1%)			
	1,765 Asian/Pacific Islander (2.8%)			
	523 Other race (0.8%)			
	1,856 Hispanic Origin* (3.0%)			
2000	72,811	13.4%	—	87
	52,186 White alone (71.7%)			
	14,023 Black or African American alone (19.3%)			
	92 American Indian and Alaska Native alone (0.1%)			
	4,457 Asian alone (6.1%)			
	47 Native Hawaiian and Other Pacific Islander alone (0.1%)			
	773 Some other race alone (1.1%)			
	1,233 Two or more races (1.7%)			
	2,805 Hispanic or Latino* (3.9%)			

Near South Side (CA 33)

	Total	Foreign born	Native with foreign parentage	Males per 100 females
1930	10,416	18.5%	21.7%	138
	7,745 White (74.4%)			
	2,474 Negro (23.8%)			
	197 Other (1.9%)			
1960	10,350	3.1%	3.1%	103
	54 White (0.5%)			
	7,942 Negro (76.7%)			
	2,354 Other races (22.7%)			
1990	6,828	1.7%	—	69
	374 White (5.5%)			
	6,424 Black (94.1%)			
	30 Asian/Pacific Islander (0.4%)			
	108 Hispanic Origin* (1.6%)			
2000	9,509	5.9%	—	82
	2,502 White alone (26.3%)			
	6,103 Black or African American alone (64.2%)			
	16 American Indian and Alaska Native alone (0.2%)			
	517 Asian alone (5.4%)			
	5 Native Hawaiian and Other Pacific Islander alone (0.1%)			
	208 Some other race alone (2.2%)			
	158 Two or more races (1.7%)			
	377 Hispanic or Latino* (4.0%)			

Near West Side (CA 28)

	Total	Foreign born	Native with foreign parentage	Males per 100 females
1930	152,457	25.1%	33.4%	127
	119,696 White (78.5%)			
	25,239 Negro (16.6%)			
	7,522 Other (4.9%)			
1960	126,610	7.5%	10.5%	113
	788 White (0.6%)			
	68,146 Negro (53.8%)			
	57,676 Other races (45.6%)			
1990	46,197	9.8%	—	88
	10,332 White (22.4%)			
	31,052 Black (67.2%)			
	109 American Indian (0.2%)			
	2,374 Asian/Pacific Islander (5.1%)			
	2,321 Other race (5.0%)			
	4,416 Hispanic Origin* (9.6%)			
2000	46,419	12.6%	—	95
	13,486 White alone (29.1%)			
	24,706 Black or African American alone (53.2%)			
	88 American Indian and Alaska Native alone (0.2%)			
	4,926 Asian alone (10.6%)			
	95 Native Hawaiian and Other Pacific Islander alone (0.2%)			
	2,212 Some other race alone (4.8%)			
	906 Two or more races (2.0%)			
	4,415 Hispanic or Latino* (9.5%)			

New City (CA 61)

	Total	Foreign born	Native with foreign parentage	Males per 100 females
1930	87,103	29.3%	49.8%	110
	84,866 White (97.4%)			
	79 Negro (0.1%)			
	2,158 Other (2.5%)			
1960	67,428	14.0%	31.5%	99
	67,172 White (99.6%)			
	166 Negro (0.2%)			
	90 Other races (0.1%)			
1990	53,226	20.7%	—	100
	16,937 White (31.8%)			
	22,245 Black (41.8%)			
	114 American Indian (0.2%)			
	186 Asian/Pacific Islander (0.3%)			
	13,744 Other race (25.8%)			
	20,906 Hispanic Origin* (39.3%)			
2000	51,721	29.5%	—	102
	17,877 White alone (34.6%)			
	18,489 Black or African American alone (35.7%)			
	276 American Indian and Alaska Native alone (0.5%)			
	175 Asian alone (0.3%)			
	42 Native Hawaiian and Other Pacific Islander alone (0.1%)			
	13,497 Some other race alone (26.1%)			
	1,365 Two or more races (2.6%)			
	25,948 Hispanic or Latino* (50.2%)			

North Center (CA 5)

	Total	Foreign born	Native with foreign parentage	Males per 100 females
1930	47,651	27.3%	40.0%	101
	47,615 White (99.9%)			
	19 Negro (0.0%)			
	17 Other (0.0%)			
1960	43,877	18.1%	29.4%	90
	43,622 White (99.4%)			
	48 Negro (0.1%)			
	207 Other races (0.5%)			
1990	33,010	19.7%	—	93
	25,667 White (77.8%)			
	1,008 Black (3.1%)			
	207 American Indian (0.6%)			
	1,731 Asian/Pacific Islander (5.2%)			
	4,397 Other race (13.3%)			
	9,048 Hispanic Origin* (27.4%)			
2000	31,895	14.5%	—	98
	24,940 White alone (78.2%)			
	1,422 Black or African American alone (4.5%)			
	186 American Indian and Alaska Native alone (0.6%)			
	1,356 Asian alone (4.3%)			
	27 Native Hawaiian and Other Pacific Islander alone (0.1%)			
	2,944 Some other race alone (9.2%)			
	1,020 Two or more races (3.2%)			
	6,496 Hispanic or Latino* (20.4%)			

North Lawndale (CA 29)

	Total	Foreign born	Native with foreign parentage	Males per 100 females
1930	112,261	45.0%	45.7%	104
	111,821 White (99.6%)			
	374 Negro (0.3%)			
	66 Other (0.1%)			
1960	124,937	1.8%	2.6%	93
	10,792 White (8.6%)			
	113,827 Negro (91.1%)			
	318 Other races (0.3%)			
1990	47,296	1.2%	—	85
	796 White (1.7%)			
	45,527 Black (96.3%)			
	56 American Indian (0.1%)			
	31 Asian/Pacific Islander (0.1%)			
	886 Other race (1.9%)			
	1,471 Hispanic Origin* (3.1%)			
2000	41,768	2.3%	—	80
	1,060 White alone (2.5%)			
	39,363 Black or African American alone (94.2%)			
	64 American Indian and Alaska Native alone (0.2%)			
	68 Asian alone (0.2%)			
	6 Native Hawaiian and Other Pacific Islander alone (0.0%)			
	900 Some other race alone (2.2%)			
	307 Two or more races (0.7%)			
	1,896 Hispanic or Latino* (4.5%)			

North Park (CA 13)

	Total	Foreign born	Native with foreign parentage	Males per 100 females
1930	11,052	27.2%	43.8%	94
	10,951 White (99.1%)			
	66 Negro (0.6%)			
	35 Other (0.3%)			
1960	17,866	22.3%	40.1%	93
	17,820 White (99.7%)			
	517 Negro (2.9%)			
	69 Other races (0.4%)			
1990	16,236	33.8%	—	85
	12,139 White (74.8%)			
	130 Black (0.8%)			
	21 American Indian (0.1%)			
	3,373 Asian/Pacific Islander (20.8%)			
	573 Other race (3.5%)			
	1,481 Hispanic Origin* (9.1%)			
2000	18,514	38.4%	—	91
	11,828 White alone (63.9%)			
	469 Black or African American alone (2.5%)			
	60 American Indian and Alaska Native alone (0.3%)			
	4,447 Asian alone (24.0%)			
	17 Native Hawaiian and Other Pacific Islander alone (0.1%)			
	888 Some other race alone (4.8%)			
	805 Two or more races (4.3%)			
	2,652 Hispanic or Latino* (14.3%)			

Norwood Park (CA 10)

	Total	Foreign born	Native with foreign parentage	Males per 100 females
1930	14,408	18.0%	41.6%	98
	14,402 White (100.0%)			
	4 Negro (0.0%)			
	2 Other (0.0%)			
1960	40,953	10.2%	33.7%	94
	40,915 White (99.9%)			
	12 Negro (0.0%)			
	26 Other races (0.1%)			
1990	37,530	16.6%	—	86
	36,166 White (96.4%)			
	17 Black (0.0%)			
	13 American Indian (0.0%)			
	1,035 Asian/Pacific Islander (2.8%)			
	299 Other race (0.8%)			
	1,005 Hispanic Origin* (2.7%)			
2000	37,669	18.7%	—	88
	34,933 White alone (92.7%)			
	336 Black or African American alone (0.9%)			
	48 American Indian and Alaska Native alone (0.1%)			
	1,232 Asian alone (3.3%)			
	20 Native Hawaiian and Other Pacific Islander alone (0.1%)			
	592 Some other race alone (1.6%)			
	508 Two or more races (1.3%)			
	2,409 Hispanic or Latino* (6.4%)			

O'Hare (CA 76)

	Total	Foreign born	Native with foreign parentage	Males per 100 females
1960	763	—	—	
1990	11,381	21.3%	—	95
	10,552 White (92.7%)			
	319 Black (2.8%)			
	315 Asian/Pacific Islander (2.8%)			
	195 Other race (1.7%)			
	525 Hispanic Origin* (4.6%)			
2000	11,956	39.7%	—	97
	10,244 White alone (85.7%)			
	269 Black or African American alone (2.2%)			
	18 American Indian and Alaska Native alone (0.2%)			
	891 Asian alone (7.5%)			
	7 Native Hawaiian and Other Pacific Islander alone (0.1%)			
	202 Some other race alone (1.7%)			
	325 Two or more races (2.7%)			
	773 Hispanic or Latino* (6.5%)			

Oakland (CA 36)

	Total	Foreign born	Native with foreign parentage	Males per 100 females
1930	14,962	13.9%	19.2%	105
	10,452 White (69.9%)			
	4,317 Negro (28.9%)			
	193 Other (1.3%)			

1960	24,378	0.4%	0.4%	88
	311	White (1.3%)		
	23,955	Negro (98.3%)		
	112	Other races (0.5%)		
1990	8,197	0.8%	—	72
	29	White (0.4%)		
	8,153	Black (99.5%)		
	7	American Indian (0.1%)		
	8	Asian/Pacific Islander (0.1%)		
	34	Hispanic Origin* (0.4%)		
2000	6,110	2.7%	—	78
	52	White alone (0.9%)		
	5,989	Black or African American alone (98.0%)		
	2	American Indian and Alaska Native alone (0.0%)		
	8	Asian alone (0.1%)		
	1	Native Hawaiian and Other Pacific Islander alone (0.0%)		
	13	Some other race alone (0.2%)		
	45	Two or more races (0.7%)		
	58	Hispanic or Latino* (0.9%)		

Portage Park (CA 15)

1930	64,203	23.7%	46.1%	101
	64,181	White (100.0%)		
	9	Negro (0.0%)		
	13	Other (0.0%)		
1960	65,925	14.0%	35.4%	91
	65,841	White (99.9%)		
	17	Negro (0.0%)		
	67	Other races (0.1%)		
1990	56,513	23.1%	—	90
	53,278	White (94.3%)		
	143	Black (0.3%)		
	82	American Indian (0.1%)		
	1,877	Asian/Pacific Islander (3.3%)		
	1,133	Other race (2.0%)		
	4,419	Hispanic Origin* (7.8%)		
2000	65,340	37.3%	—	95
	52,623	White alone (80.5%)		
	461	Black or African American alone (0.7%)		
	218	American Indian and Alaska Native alone (0.3%)		
	2,495	Asian alone (3.8%)		
	38	Native Hawaiian and Other Pacific Islander alone (0.1%)		
	6,670	Some other race alone (10.2%)		
	2,835	Two or more races (4.3%)		
	15,022	Hispanic or Latino* (23.0%)		

Pullman (CA 50)

1930	6,705	41.3%	43.3%	123
	6,634	White (98.9%)		
	71	Other (1.1%)		
1960	8,412	16.2%	1.8%	101
	8,400	White (99.9%)		
	12	Other races (0.1%)		
1990	9,344	6.5%	—	82
	1,419	White (15.2%)		
	7,367	Black (78.8%)		
	9	American Indian (0.1%)		
	31	Asian/Pacific Islander (0.3%)		
	518	Other race (5.5%)		
	780	Hispanic Origin* (8.3%)		
2000	8,921	5.3%	—	82
	1,070	White alone (12.0%)		
	7,285	Black or African American alone (81.7%)		
	15	American Indian and Alaska Native alone (0.2%)		
	21	Asian alone (0.2%)		
	417	Some other race alone (4.7%)		
	113	Two or more races (1.3%)		
	795	Hispanic or Latino* (8.9%)		

Riverdale (CA 54)

1930	1,486	29.6%	47.4%	110
	1,486	White (100.0%)		
1960	11,448	1.1%	2.6%	88
	1,127	White (9.8%)		
	10,306	Negro (90.0%)		
	15	Other races (0.1%)		
1990	10,821	0.7%	—	76
	113	White (1.0%)		
	10,583	Black (97.8%)		
	28	American Indian (0.3%)		
	97	Other race (0.9%)		
	150	Hispanic Origin* (1.4%)		
2000	9,809	2.3%	—	77
	93	White alone (0.9%)		
	9,494	Black or African American alone (96.8%)		
	22	American Indian and Alaska Native alone (0.2%)		
	8	Asian alone (0.1%)		
	3	Native Hawaiian and Other Pacific Islander alone (0.0%)		
	117	Some other race alone (1.2%)		
	72	Two or more races (0.7%)		
	160	Hispanic or Latino* (1.6%)		

Rogers Park (CA 1)

1930	57,094	15.8%	34.3%	87
	56,895	White (99.7%)		
	128	Negro (0.2%)		
	71	Other (0.1%)		
1960	56,888	17.7%	30.7%	83
	56,503	White (99.3%)		
	57	Negro (0.1%)		
	328	Other races (0.6%)		
1990	60,378	29.1%	—	99
	33,036	White (54.7%)		
	16,593	Black (27.5%)		
	230	American Indian (0.4%)		
	5,305	Asian/Pacific Islander (8.8%)		
	5,214	Other race (8.6%)		
	12,005	Hispanic Origin* (19.9%)		
2000	63,484	33.8%	—	104
	29,457	White alone (46.4%)		
	19,160	Black or African American alone (30.2%)		
	365	American Indian and Alaska Native alone (0.6%)		
	4,111	Asian alone (6.5%)		
	65	Native Hawaiian and Other Pacific Islander alone (0.1%)		
	6,865	Some other race alone (10.8%)		
	3,461	Two or more races (5.5%)		
	17,639	Hispanic or Latino* (27.8%)		

Roseland (CA 49)

1930	43,206	28.9%	42.8%	106
	41,917	White (97.0%)		
	1,256	Negro (2.9%)		
	33	Other (0.1%)		
1960	58,750	5.6%	2.3%	94
	45,392	White (77.3%)		
	13,255	Negro (22.6%)		
	103	Other races (0.2%)		
1990	56,493	0.5%	—	86
	493	White (0.9%)		
	55,861	Black (98.9%)		
	32	American Indian (0.1%)		
	40	Asian/Pacific Islander (0.1%)		
	67	Other race (0.1%)		
	283	Hispanic Origin* (0.5%)		
2000	52,723	0.8%	—	82
	330	White alone (0.6%)		
	51,741	Black or African American alone (98.1%)		
	65	American Indian and Alaska Native alone (0.1%)		
	32	Asian alone (0.1%)		
	5	Native Hawaiian and Other Pacific Islander alone (0.0%)		
	106	Some other race alone (0.2%)		
	444	Two or more races (0.8%)		
	363	Hispanic or Latino* (0.7%)		

South Chicago (CA 46)

1930	56,683	23.6%	23.6%	114
	51,659	White (91.1%)		
	738	Negro (1.3%)		
	4,286	Other (7.6%)		
1960	49,913	13.9%	1.3%	98
	47,338	White (94.8%)		
	2,448	Negro (4.9%)		
	127	Other races (0.3%)		
1990	40,645	15.4%	—	89
	6,835	White (16.8%)		
	25,016	Black (61.5%)		
	78	American Indian (0.2%)		
	184	Asian/Pacific Islander (0.5%)		
	8,532	Other race (21.0%)		
	13,644	Hispanic Origin* (33.6%)		
2000	38,596	13.2%	—	86
	5,008	White alone (13.0%)		
	26,647	Black or African American alone (69.0%)		
	161	American Indian and Alaska Native alone (0.4%)		
	55	Asian alone (0.1%)		
	27	Native Hawaiian and Other Pacific Islander alone (0.1%)		
	5,775	Some other race alone (15.0%)		
	923	Two or more races (2.4%)		
	10,565	Hispanic or Latino* (27.4%)		

South Deering (CA 51)

1930	7,898	28.7%	45.7%	125
	6,901	White (87.4%)		
	997	Other (12.6%)		
1960	18,794	13.1%	33.9%	101
	18,637	White (99.2%)		
	125	Negro (0.7%)		
	32	Other races (0.2%)		
1990	17,755	10.8%	—	86
	4,145	White (23.3%)		
	10,467	Black (59.0%)		
	53	American Indian (0.3%)		
	3,090	Other race (17.4%)		
	5,038	Hispanic Origin* (28.4%)		
2000	16,990	12.9%	—	85
	3,522	White alone (20.7%)		
	10,397	Black or African American alone (61.2%)		
	52	American Indian and Alaska Native alone (0.3%)		
	20	Asian alone (0.1%)		
	5	Native Hawaiian and Other Pacific Islander alone (0.0%)		
	2,644	Some other race alone (15.6%)		
	350	Two or more races (2.1%)		
	5,176	Hispanic or Latino* (30.5%)		

South Lawndale (CA 30)

1930	76,749	31.5%	52.1%	107
	75,950	White (99.0%)		
	679	Negro (0.9%)		
	120	Other (0.2%)		
1960	60,940	17.8%	32.0%	102
	57,278	White (94.0%)		
	3,568	Negro (5.9%)		
	94	Other races (0.2%)		
1990	81,155	46.9%	—	122
	22,144	White (27.3%)		
	7,159	Black (8.8%)		
	126	American Indian (0.2%)		
	120	Asian/Pacific Islander (0.1%)		
	51,583	Other race (63.6%)		
	69,131	Hispanic Origin* (85.2%)		
2000	91,071	48.3%	—	136
	26,905	White alone (29.5%)		
	12,097	Black or African American alone (13.3%)		
	610	American Indian and Alaska Native alone (0.7%)		
	173	Asian alone (0.2%)		
	68	Native Hawaiian and Other Pacific Islander alone (0.1%)		
	48,137	Some other race alone (52.9%)		
	3,081	Two or more races (3.4%)		
	75,613	Hispanic or Latino* (83.0%)		

South Shore (CA 43)

1930	78,755	16.6%	35.6%	87
	78,538	White (99.7%)		
	171	Negro (0.2%)		
	46	Other (0.1%)		
1960	73,086	13.3%	3.4%	83
	65,507	White (89.6%)		
	7,018	Negro (9.6%)		
	561	Other races (0.8%)		

Community Areas (1930–2000) *(continued)*

Year	Total (and by category)		Foreign born	Native with foreign parentage	Males per 100 females
1990	61,517		1.6%	—	80
	1,295	White (2.1%)			
	59,933	Black (97.4%)			
	90	American Indian (0.1%)			
	80	Asian/Pacific Islander (0.1%)			
	119	Other race (0.2%)			
	497	Hispanic Origin* (0.8%)			
2000	61,556		2.6%	—	78
	778	White alone (1.3%)			
	59,732	Black or African American alone (97.0%)			
	75	American Indian and Alaska Native alone (0.1%)			
	88	Asian alone (0.1%)			
	20	Native Hawaiian and Other Pacific Islander alone (0.0%)			
	224	Some other race alone (0.4%)			
	639	Two or more races (1.0%)			
	636	Hispanic or Latino* (1.0%)			

Uptown (CA 3)

Year	Total (and by category)		Foreign born	Native with foreign parentage	Males per 100 females
1930	67,699		—	—	—
	120,704	White (178.3%)			
	531	Negro (0.8%)			
	402	Other (0.6%)			
1960	76,103		—	—	—
	122,595	White (161.1%)			
	423	Negro (0.6%)			
	4,664	Other races (6.1%)			
1990	63,839		32.6%	—	104
	30,113	White (47.2%)			
	15,842	Black (24.8%)			
	429	American Indian (0.7%)			
	9,263	Asian/Pacific Islander (14.5%)			
	8,192	Other race (12.8%)			
	24,965	Hispanic Origin* (39.1%)			
2000	63,551		33.0%	—	110
	32,750	White alone (51.5%)			
	13,680	Black or African American alone (21.5%)			
	383	American Indian and Alaska Native alone (0.6%)			
	8,238	Asian alone (13.0%)			
	102	Native Hawaiian and Other Pacific Islander alone (0.2%)			
	5,567	Some other race alone (8.8%)			
	2,831	Two or more races (4.5%)			
	12,674	Hispanic or Latino* (19.9%)			

Washington Heights (CA 73)

Year	Total (and by category)		Foreign born	Native with foreign parentage	Males per 100 females
1930	17,865		16.0%	39.4%	100
	17,790	White (99.6%)			
	33	Negro (0.2%)			
	42	Other (0.2%)			
1960	29,793		8.1%	26.5%	92
	26,017	White (87.3%)			
	3,711	Negro (12.5%)			
	65	Other races (0.2%)			
1990	32,114		0.9%	—	86
	317	White (1.0%)			
	31,705	Black (98.7%)			
	38	American Indian (0.1%)			
	20	Asian/Pacific Islander (0.1%)			
	34	Other race (0.1%)			
	140	Hispanic Origin* (0.4%)			
2000	29,843		1.3%	—	82
	233	White alone (0.8%)			
	29,210	Black or African American alone (97.9%)			
	37	American Indian and Alaska Native alone (0.1%)			
	10	Asian alone (0.0%)			
	10	Native Hawaiian and Other Pacific Islander alone (0.0%)			
	69	Some other race alone (0.2%)			
	274	Two or more races (0.9%)			
	231	Hispanic or Latino* (0.8%)			

Washington Park (CA 40)

Year	Total (and by category)		Foreign born	Native with foreign parentage	Males per 100 females
1930	44,016		2.0%	2.8%	96
	3,448	White (7.8%)			
	40,460	Negro (91.9%)			
	108	Other (0.2%)			
1960	43,690		0.5%	0.1%	92
	332	White (0.8%)			
	43,310	Negro (99.1%)			
	48	Other races (0.1%)			
1990	19,425		0.3%	—	84
	92	White (0.5%)			
	19,249	Black (99.1%)			
	49	American Indian (0.3%)			
	35	Asian/Pacific Islander (0.2%)			
	48	Hispanic Origin* (0.2%)			
2000	14,146		1.1%	—	81
	95	White alone (0.7%)			
	13,875	Black or African American alone (98.1%)			
	22	American Indian and Alaska Native alone (0.2%)			
	5	Asian alone (0.0%)			
	5	Native Hawaiian and Other Pacific Islander alone (0.0%)			
	26	Some other race alone (0.2%)			
	118	Two or more races (0.8%)			
	134	Hispanic or Latino* (0.9%)			

West Elsdon (CA 62)

Year	Total (and by category)		Foreign born	Native with foreign parentage	Males per 100 females
1930	2,861		31.5%	542.6%	114
	2,807	White (98.1%)			
	54	Other (1.9%)			
1960	14,215		12.7%	38.3%	95
	14,210	White (100.0%)			
	5	Other races (0.0%)			
1990	12,266		20.6%	—	89
	11,683	White (95.2%)			
	28	American Indian (0.2%)			
	97	Asian/Pacific Islander (0.8%)			
	458	Other race (3.7%)			
	1,135	Hispanic Origin* (9.3%)			
2000	15,921		37.5%	—	95
	10,597	White alone (66.6%)			
	94	Black or African American alone (0.6%)			
	60	American Indian and Alaska Native alone (0.4%)			
	138	Asian alone (0.9%)			
	16	Native Hawaiian and Other Pacific Islander alone (0.1%)			
	4,330	Some other race alone (27.2%)			
	686	Two or more races (4.3%)			
	7,875	Hispanic or Latino* (49.5%)			

West Englewood (CA 67)

Year	Total (and by category)		Foreign born	Native with foreign parentage	Males per 100 females
1930	63,845		22.9%	43.0%	102
	61,854	White (96.9%)			
	1,967	Negro (3.1%)			
	24	Other (0.0%)			
1960	58,516		11.6%	26.4%	94
	51,583	White (88.2%)			
	6,842	Negro (11.7%)			
	91	Other races (0.2%)			
1990	52,772		0.8%	—	88
	706	White (1.3%)			
	51,762	Black (98.1%)			
	100	American Indian (0.2%)			
	37	Asian/Pacific Islander (0.1%)			
	167	Other race (0.3%)			
	331	Hispanic Origin* (0.6%)			
2000	45,282		1.0%	—	86
	278	White alone (0.6%)			
	44,429	Black or African American alone (98.1%)			
	48	American Indian and Alaska Native alone (0.1%)			
	30	Asian alone (0.1%)			
	3	Native Hawaiian and Other Pacific Islander alone (0.0%)			
	156	Some other race alone (0.3%)			
	338	Two or more races (0.7%)			
	459	Hispanic or Latino* (1.0%)			

West Garfield Park (CA 26)

Year	Total (and by category)		Foreign born	Native with foreign parentage	Males per 100 females
1930	50,014		25.9%	42.7%	99
	49,910	White (99.8%)			
	46	Negro (0.1%)			
	58	Other (0.1%)			
1960	45,611		12.4%	18.6%	98
	38,152	White (83.6%)			
	7,204	Negro (15.8%)			
	255	Other races (0.6%)			
1990	24,095		0.2%	—	86
	32	White (0.1%)			
	23,923	Black (99.3%)			
	42	American Indian (0.2%)			
	20	Asian/Pacific Islander (0.1%)			
	78	Other race (0.3%)			
	133	Hispanic Origin* (0.6%)			
2000	23,019		1.5%	—	85
	160	White alone (0.7%)			
	22,651	Black or African American alone (98.4%)			
	20	American Indian and Alaska Native alone (0.1%)			
	20	Asian alone (0.1%)			
	1	Native Hawaiian and Other Pacific Islander alone (0.0%)			
	83	Some other race alone (0.4%)			
	84	Two or more races (0.4%)			
	201	Hispanic or Latino* (0.9%)			

West Lawn (CA 65)

Year	Total (and by category)		Foreign born	Native with foreign parentage	Males per 100 females
1930	8,919		20.0%	43.6%	105
	8,916	White (100.0%)			
	3	Negro (0.0%)			
1960	26,910		10.9%	35.5%	97
	26,893	White (99.9%)			
	5	Negro (0.0%)			
	12	Other races (0.0%)			
1990	23,402		11.9%	—	91
	22,006	White (94.0%)			
	109	Black (0.5%)			
	67	American Indian (0.3%)			
	253	Asian/Pacific Islander (1.1%)			
	967	Other race (4.1%)			
	2,519	Hispanic Origin* (10.8%)			
2000	29,235		30.7%	—	96
	18,375	White alone (62.9%)			
	810	Black or African American alone (2.8%)			
	99	American Indian and Alaska Native alone (0.3%)			
	286	Asian alone (1.0%)			
	10	Native Hawaiian and Other Pacific Islander alone (0.0%)			
	8,412	Some other race alone (28.8%)			
	1,243	Two or more races (4.3%)			
	15,179	Hispanic or Latino* (51.9%)			

West Pullman (CA 53)

Year	Total (and by category)		Foreign born	Native with foreign parentage	Males per 100 females
1930	28,474		31.2%	48.6%	111
	28,014	White (98.4%)			
	170	Negro (0.6%)			
	290	Other (1.0%)			
1960	35,397		12.7%	33.2%	97
	35,328	White (99.8%)			
	62	Negro (0.2%)			
	7	Other races (0.0%)			
1990	39,846		3.2%	—	89
	1,328	White (3.3%)			
	37,447	Black (94.0%)			
	41	American Indian (0.1%)			
	37	Asian/Pacific Islander (0.1%)			
	993	Other race (2.5%)			
	1,771	Hispanic Origin* (4.4%)			
2000	36,649		3.4%	—	86
	945	White alone (2.6%)			
	34,399	Black or African American alone (93.9%)			
	78	American Indian and Alaska Native alone (0.2%)			
	20	Asian alone (0.1%)			
	4	Native Hawaiian and Other Pacific Islander alone (0.0%)			
	801	Some other race alone (2.2%)			
	402	Two or more races (1.1%)			
	1,699	Hispanic or Latino* (4.6%)			

West Ridge (CA 2)

1930	39,759	17.5%	39.4%	94
	39,701	White (99.9%)		
	46	Negro (0.1%)		
	12	Other (0.0%)		
1960	63,884	18.2%	40.9%	91
	63,696	White (99.7%)		
	81	Negro (0.1%)		
	107	Other races (0.2%)		
1990	65,374	38.9%	—	89
	50,264	White (76.9%)		
	2,132	Black (3.3%)		
	127	American Indian (0.2%)		
	10,846	Asian/Pacific Islander (16.6%)		
	2,005	Other race (3.1%)		
	5,398	Hispanic Origin* (8.3%)		
2000	73,199	45.6%	—	97
	41,947	White alone (57.3%)		
	5,119	Black or African American alone (7.0%)		
	256	American Indian and Alaska Native alone (0.3%)		
	16,437	Asian alone (22.5%)		
	59	Native Hawaiian and Other Pacific Islander alone (0.1%)		
	5,095	Some other race alone (7.0%)		
	4,286	Two or more races (5.9%)		
	11,353	Hispanic or Latino* (15.5%)		

West Town (CA 24)

1930	187,292	38.6%	50.3%	108
	186,271	White (99.5%)		
	841	Negro (0.4%)		
	180	Other (0.1%)		
1960	139,657	24.9%	25.8%	104
	136,479	White (97.7%)		
	2,366	Negro (1.7%)		
	812	Other races (0.6%)		
1990	87,703	28.4%	—	103
	44,514	White (50.8%)		
	9,207	Black (10.5%)		
	482	American Indian (0.5%)		
	1,157	Asian/Pacific Islander (1.3%)		
	31,949	Other race (36.4%)		
	54,361	Hispanic Origin* (62.0%)		
2000	87,435	22.8%	—	108
	50,896	White alone (58.2%)		
	8,674	Black or African American alone (9.9%)		
	446	American Indian and Alaska Native alone (0.5%)		
	1,575	Asian alone (1.8%)		
	105	Native Hawaiian and Other Pacific Islander alone (0.1%)		
	21,676	Some other race alone (24.8%)		
	4,063	Two or more races (4.6%)		
	40,966	Hispanic or Latino* (46.9%)		

Woodlawn (CA 42)

1930	66,052	15.0%	26.7%	97
	57,182	White (86.6%)		
	8,578	Negro (13.0%)		
	292	Other (0.4%)		
1960	81,279	1.8%	0.3%	94
	8,450	White (10.4%)		
	72,397	Negro (89.1%)		
	432	Other races (0.5%)		
1990	27,473	1.7%	—	80
	879	White (3.2%)		
	26,388	Black (96.1%)		
	7	American Indian (0.0%)		
	168	Asian/Pacific Islander (0.6%)		
	31	Other race (0.1%)		
	178	Hispanic Origin* (0.6%)		
2000	27,086	2.0%	—	81
	821	White alone (3.0%)		
	25,627	Black or African American alone (94.6%)		
	42	American Indian and Alaska Native alone (0.2%)		
	209	Asian alone (0.8%)		
	7	Native Hawaiian and Other Pacific Islander alone (0.0%)		
	75	Some other race alone (0.3%)		
	305	Two or more races (1.1%)		
	288	Hispanic or Latino* (1.1%)		

*Independent of racial categories in 1990 and 2000 censuses

CREDITS

Abbreviations

CHS = Chicago Historical Society
CPL = Chicago Public Library
LOC = Library of Congress
NL = Newberry Library
UIC = University of Illinois at Chicago

ILLUSTRATION CREDITS

ii (frontispiece) Dearborn and Randolph. CHS, ICHi-04192.

A **2** Actors. CHS, ICHi-14718. © Irene Siegel. **4** Ad agency office. NL, *Land Owner* 6 (April 1874): 61. **5** McLaughlin's card. NL, John M. Wing Collection. **8** *Breeder's Gazette*. CHS, *Breeder's Gazette*, Dec. 18, 1881. **10** Holstein farm. NL, *Combination Atlas Map of DuPage County,* 1874. **12** United flight crew. CHS, ICHi-26512. © United Airlines. **16** Kids under tracks. LOC, Prints & Photographs Division, FSA/OWI Collection, LC-USF34-038601-D. **16** DuPage Co. Almshouse. DuPage County Historical Museum, 84.29.4.45. **19** Pageant. CHS, ICHi-18430. © CHS. **20** Amos n' Andy. CHS, Chicago Daily News Collection, DN-0094569. © CHS. **21** Riverview Park. CHS, ICHi-23578. **24** Traffic jam. Lakes Region Historical Society. **26** Addams and McDowell. CHS, ICHi-09371. **28** 1935 skyline panorama. CPL, CCW 1.8. **29** Rookery. CHS, ICHi-26160. **30** Carson Pirie Scott ironwork. CHS, HB-19321-C. © CHS. **31** Grand Basin. CHS, ICHi-02524. **32** Wacker Dr. CHS. **32** *Plan of Chicago*. CHS, Charles Moore, *Daniel H. Burnham: Architect, Planner of Cities,* 1921. **33** Midway Gardens. CHS. **34** Crown Hall. CHS, HB-18506-S2. © CHS. **35** Hancock Tower. CPL, CCW 14.1. **36** Marina City. CHS, HB-23215-C5. © CHS. **36** Post Office demolition. CHS, ICHi-26381. **37** Argonne. CHS, HB-19294-C. © CHS. **39** First Regiment Armory. CHS, ICHi-19108. **42** Daley Plaza Picasso. CHS, HB-25252-G7. © CHS. **46** *Fountain of the Great Lakes.* CHS, Chicago Daily News Collection, DN-0087290. © CHS. **49** Frontispiece. CHS, Oscar Lovell Triggs, *Chapters in the History of the Arts and Crafts Movement,* 1902. **52** Auditorium interior. CHS, ICHi-21989.

B **58** Stockyards. CHS, ICHi-14486. **59** Dancers. NL, Barzel Collection. **59** Baha'i Temple. CHS, G1988.67, box 1, folder 19. © CHS. **61** Band. CHS, ICHi-27382. **62** I&M Canal scrip. CHS, ICHi-14151. **63** Bank failure. CHS, Chicago Daily News Collection, DN-0003927. **67** Baseball game. CPL, Harold Washington Library, Municipal Reference Collection, Special Park Commission, *Annual Report* 1907 (published 1908), 26. **68** Foster. CHS, Chicago Daily News Collection, SDN-055355. **70** Public bath. CHS, ICHi-21723. © CHS. **71** Halas and team. CHS, Chicago Daily News Collection, DN-76921. © CHS. **80** Babies. LOC, Prints & Photographs Division, FSA/OWI Collection, LC-USW3-000578-D. **84** Musicians. CHS, Jerome Joseph Collection. © Jerome Joseph. **87** Village Press. NL, John M. Wing Collection. **89** Bowling event. CHS, ICHi-14859. **90** Golden Gloves. CHS. © Chicago Tribune Charities. **93** Bridges. CHS, Chicago Daily News Collection, DN-0086258. © CHS. **95** Program cover. CHS, ML42 J8. **98** Zoo poster. LOC, Prints & Photographs Division, WPA Poster Collection, LC-USZ62-117505. **100** Inspectors. CHS, Chicago Daily News Collection, DN-6053. © CHS. **110** CTA bus. CHS, ICHi-23701. © CHS. **113** Pullman Co. map. CHS. **114** Warehouse. CHS, WS 1.263. **114** Trains. CHS. © CHS.

C **116** Cabrini Homes. UIC, Italian American Collection, IAC neg. 91.152. **118** Calumet River. LOC, Prints & Photographs Division, Detroit Publishing Company Collection, LC-D418-8786. **125** Travel pavilion. CHS, ICHi-23087. **125** Greyhound bus. CHS, ICHi-23853. **131** Neighborhood leaders. CHS, 1x6 1986.278. © Chicago Area Project. **136** Wells Homes poster. LOC, Prints & Photographs Division, WPA Poster Collection, LC-USZC2-5196. **152** Teachers meeting. CPL, CCW 1.45. **153** Sailboat race. CHS, Chicago Daily News Collection, DN-4707. **156** Baby. UIC, Jane Addams Memorial Collection, JAMC neg. 107. **156** Milk. CHS, ICHi-20210. **158** Parade. CHS, Chicago Daily News Collection, DN-0086651. © CHS. **159** Registering for draft. CHS, Chicago Daily News Collection, DN-0068166. **160** Apollo Chorus. CHS. **162** Chicago Temple. CHS, ICHi-25406. **162** Holy Name Cathedral. CHS, G1989.347.6. **162** St. Mary's. CHS. **162** Second Presbyterian. CPL, CCW 5.72. **163** St. Stanislaus. NL, case folio oF 548.7 .S56, v. 1. **163** St. Ignatius. NL, case folio oF 548.7 .S56, v. 1. **163** St. Stanislaus Kostka. CHS, ICHi-14073. © CHS. **163** Holy Trinity Russian Orthodox. CHS, Chicago Daily News Collection, DN-Alpha-9336. © CHS. **164** Pilgrim Baptist. LOC, Prints & Photographs Division, FSA/OWI Collection, LC-USF33-013000-M3. **164** Unity Temple interior. CHS, HB-19311-E. © CHS. **164** Unity Temple exterior. NL, case folio oF 548.7 .S56, v. II. **165** St. Nicholas. CHS, G81:097, #3. © St. Nicholas Ukrainian Church. **165** Rockefeller Chapel. CHS. **165** Madonna della Strada. CHS, ICHi-25872. **165** Church of Christ, Scientist. CHS, HB-32111. © CHS. **168** Protestors. CHS, ICHi-17209. **171** Chicago Symphony Orchestra. CHS, ICHi-22677. **172** Women's Symphony Orchestra. CHS, ICHi-24032. **174** Civil service exam. CHS, Chicago Daily News Collection, DN-0007016. **175** Sanitarium. LOC, Prints & Photographs Division, FSA/OWI Collection, LC-USF33-005134-M2. **177** Margaret Dreier Robbins. CHS, Chicago Daily News Collection, DN-0065049. **177** Tailor shop. UIC, Italian American Collection, IAC neg. 135.38. **179** Drum corps. CHS, Chicago Daily News Collection, DN-0003818. **180** American Legion. CHS. **181** Women's Federated Club. CPL, Bethel New Life Collection, photograph 15.6. **182** Chicago

Hebrew Institute. CHS, ICHi-17310. **183** Coffee shop. LOC, Prints & Photographs Division, FSA/OWI Collection, LC-USF33-016075-M5. **186** Comiskey Park. CHS, ICHi-19088. **188** Board of Trade. CHS, ICHi-18146. **189** Chalkboard. CHS. © CHS. **194** Commuters. LOC, Prints & Photographs Division, FSA/OWI Collection, LC-USF33-016119-M3. **197** American Furniture Mart. CHS, HB-SN891C. © CHS. **199** Lincoln Park Conservatory. CHS, Chicago Daily News Collection, DN-0004421. **200** Washington Park Conservatory. CHS, ICHi-03498. **201** High-rise construction. NL, *Inland Architect* 5.18, no. 4 (November 1891). **202** Loan store. CHS, ICHi-27835. **203** Furniture ad. CHS, *Woman's Magazine* (1905). **203** Color line cartoon. *Chicago Tribune,* July 28, 1919. **204** Illinois-Wisconsin boundary. NL, Charles O. Paullin, *Atlas of the Historical Geography of the U.S.*, 1932, plate 99C. © Carnegie Institution of Washington. **206** Combine harvester. *Chicago Tribune,* Oct. 13, 2000. © Chicago Tribune. **208** Hospital ward. CHS, ICHi-22455. **212** Fairgoers. CHS, Chicago Daily News Collection, DN-0066676. **213** Court. CHS, Chicago Daily News Collection, DN-0008505. **216** Soccer team. CHS, Chicago Daily News Collection, SDN-064029. **216** Fitzsimmons. CHS. **219** "What Dante Missed." CHS, Robert O. Harland, *The Vice Bondage of a Great City,* 1912, 14.

D **225** Page. NL, Midwest Dance Collection. © Sheila Malkind. **226** Pavley, Ludmila, and Oukrainsky. NL, Barzel Collection. **227** *Nutcracker* auditions. NL, Midwest Dance Collection. © Sheila Malkind. **228** Dance hall. CHS, Chicago Daily News Collection, DN-0057995. **232** 1932 Democratic Convention. CPL, WS 1.27a. **235** Causes of death chart from *Chicago–Cook County Health Survey,* by the U.S. Public Health Service. NL. © Columbia University Press, 1949. Reprinted with the permission of the publisher. **235** Mortality. NL, Frederick L. Hoffman, "American Mortality Progress during the Last Half Century," in Mazÿck Porcher Ravenel, ed., *A Half Century of Public Health,* 1921, 111. **238** Marshall Field's cartoon. NL, Modern Manuscripts, John T. McCutcheon Papers. **247** Dunes. CHS, Henry Chandler Cowles, *The Ecological Relations of the Vegetation on the Sand Dunes of Lake Michigan,* 1899, 39. **248** Elm Tree Grove. Lake County (IL) Discovery Museum, Curt Teich Postcard Archives, 7280. **249** Highways. DuPage County Historical Museum, 86.87.5.5. **250** Dancers. CPL, CRCC 1.134.

E **255** Union Stock Yard. NL, J. W. Sheahan, *Chicago Illustrated, 1830–1860,* 1866. **255** Grain elevators and ships. CHS, ICHi-17111. **257** Midwest Stock Exchange. CHS, ICHi-29229. **260** "Chicago's Place." CHS, Chicago Plan Commission, *Chicago Industrial Study* Summary Report, 1952, fig. 1. © Chicago Plan Commission. **264** Edgewater ad. CHS. **267** Holiday Inn. Lake County (IL) Discovery Museum, Curt Teich Postcard Archives, 8DK705. **267** "Old Main." Lake County (IL) Discovery Museum, Curt Teich Postcard Archives, 3BH1613. **268** Swenson's Greenhouse. DuPage County Historical Museum, 85.16.2.1. **270** Sauganash Hotel. CHS, ICHi-00755. **271** Aragon Ballroom. CHS, ICHi-27263. © CHS. **272** Plantation Café. CHS, ICHi-14428. **273** Benny Goodman. CHS, ICHi-18516. © Conn-Selmer Company/Estate of Benny Goodman. **279** Municipal Tuberculosis Sanitarium. CHS, Chicago Daily News Collection, DN-0075840. © CHS. **282** Dance and Rhythm Festival. UIC, Jane Addams Memorial Collection photos, JAMC neg. 2512. **284** Polish Mountaineers. CHS. **286** Congress Parkway. CHS.

F **292** Field Museum. CHS. **294** Selig Polyscope. CHS, Chicago Daily News Collection, DN-0062406. **294** Essanay Studios. CHS, ICHi-16886. **296** Monroe and LaSalle. NL, Oliver Barrett–Carl Sandburg Papers. **297** Fire aftermath. CPL, ECC 1.1966. **298** Elmhurst Fire Department. DuPage County Historical Museum, 80.50.1.10. **299** Fighting a fire. CHS, RD-Fires-1940-59. **299** Connell and Halverson. CHS, Chicago Daily News Collection, SDN-069501. © CHS. **300** Plzensky Sokol. Paul Nemecek. © Paul Nemecek. **302** Dancing children. UIC, Jane Addams Memorial Collection, JAMC neg. 581. **305** Dairy cart. UIC, Italian American Collection, IAC neg. 144.4. **306** Grain elevator. CHS, ICHi-24684. © Joan M. Colby. **307** Sara Lee billboard. CHS, HB-17280. © CHS. **308** Church and diner. LOC, Prints & Photographs Division, FSA/OWI Collection, LC-USF33-005184-M4. **309** Donut tower. Janice L. Reiff. © Janice L. Reiff. **310** Stagg Field. CHS. **313** Fort Dearborn. CHS. **315** Fox River dam. CHS, CHS 000152. © CHS. **317** Marquette map. NL. **320** Furniture factory. CHS. **321** Tonk Mfg. Co. CHS.

G **326** Garfield Park. CHS. **329** Electrical substation. CHS. **329** Com Ed ad. CHS, ICHi-20010. **330** Gas station. Lakes Region Historical Society. **334** Turnverein. CHS, ICHi-14858. **335** Schwäbischer Sängerbund. CHS, ICHi-21436. **339** Milk depot. DuPage County Historical Museum, 86.61.1. **344** Zephyr ticket counter. LOC, Prints & Photographs Division, FSA/OWI Collection, LC-USW3-015943-D. **345** Gold Coast. NL, *Stanolind Record* 10.11 (September 1929): 2. **346** Golfers. CHS, Chicago Daily News Collection, SDN-053326. **347** Mass meeting ad. CHS, ICHi-20741. **348** Spells Brothers. CHS, Scotty Piper Collection. **349** Cook Co. government. NL, League of Women Voters, *This Is Cook County,* 1958. © League of Women Voters of Chicago. **354** Act of incorporation. CHS, *An Act to Incorporate the City of Chicago,* 1837. **355** Dolton Building. CHS, ICHi-17219. © CHS. **357** 49th and Champlain. CHS, from John Taitt, comp., *The Souvenir of Negro Progress: Chicago 1779–1925,* 1925[?]. **358** Grant Park. NL. **358** Interstate Exposition Building. CHS, ICHi-05719. **359** Society of Typographic Arts. NL, John M. Wing Collection. **361** Men with cabbage. CHS, ICHi-20837. **361** WPA workers. CHS, ICHi-05955. **365** Dancers. UIC, Jane Addams Memorial Collection, JAMC neg. 484. **368** Grocery. CHS. **371** Gypsies. LOC, Prints & Photographs Division, FSA/OWI Collection, LC-USF33-012985-M2.

H **377** May Day poster. Janice L. Reiff. © Janice L. Reiff. **382** Hinsdale ad. NL, *Land Owner* (July 1873): 112. **383** Preservation picketing. CHS, Arthur Siegel Collection. © Irene Siegel. **383** Clarke House. CHS, Chicago Daily News Collection, DN-A-4601. © CHS. **390** Derby Day. CHS, Chicago Daily News Collection, DN-0000597. **392** Hospital room. CHS, ICHi-24758. **393** Technicians. CHS, ICHi-18890. **394** Grand Pacific Hotel. NL, *Land Owner* (May 1872). **394** Edgewater Beach hotel. Lake County (IL) Discovery Museum, Curt Teich Postcard Archives, 2586-30. **396** Cookware ad. Lake County (IL) Discovery Museum, Curt Teich Postcard Archives, A36096. **398** Storefront apartments. UIC, Metropolitan Planning Council Collection, MPC neg. 134. **399** Inspection report. CHS, Chicago Daily News Collection, DN-P-6059. © CHS. **400** Frame two-flats. UIC, Metropolitan Planning Council Collection, MPC neg. 118. **400** 44th and Wood. CHS, ICHi-01871. © CHS. **401** Ontario Flat Building. CHS, Chicago Daily News Collection, DN-0000650. **401** Bungalow. CHS, ICHi-17915.

I **407** Trains. CHS, ICHi-31457. **410** Patel Brothers grocery. CHS, ICHi-26012. © CHS. **412** *I.W.W. Songs.* CHS. **413** Pullman water tower. LOC, Prints & Photographs Division, Detroit Publishing Company Collection, LC-D4-12560. **416** Grading grain. CHS. © CHS. **418** Insurance office. LOC, Prints & Photographs Division, FSA/OWI Collection, LC-USF33-005139-M1 DLC. **426** Illinois Steel Works. LOC, Prints & Photographs Division, FSA/OWI Collection, Detroit Publishing Company Collection, LC-D4-5935. **427** Blast furnace. CHS. **429** Tosi funeral. UIC, Italian American Collection, IAC neg. 60.5.

J **432** Bridewell Prison. CHS, Chicago Daily News Collection, DN-0000314. **436** Physical education class. CHS. **437** Band. CHS, ICHi-17321. **440** Copy desk. CHS, ICHi-26644. © *Chicago Tribune.* **441** Religious services. CHS, CHS 9328.

K **447** Parsons ad. NL, Modern Manuscripts, Charles H. Kerr Company Collection.

L **449** "L." CHS, *Chicago,* 1893. **451** Mud Lake. CHS, Chicago Daily News Collection, DN-0053290. **454** Loading ice. Lakes Region Historical Society. **457** Lake View town hall. CHS. **459** Freight yards. CHS, CHS 14648. **460** Cary Station Hills. Lake County (IL) Discovery Museum, Curt Teich Postcard Archives, C56249. **461** Union Park. NL, *Land Owner* (1870). **465** Suitcase factory. CHS, ICHi-21789. **468** Col. Wood's Museum. CHS. **469** Chicago and North-Western ad. CHS, ICHi-14973. **469** Lake View Cycling Club. CHS,

ICHi-22247. **469** Bathers. UIC, Italian American Collection, IAC neg. 82.3. **471** Buffalo Bill. CHS, Chicago Daily News Collection, DN-0066931. **471** Sans Souci. CHS, Chicago Daily News Collection, DN-0006357. **474** Hawthorne Race Track. CHS, Chicago Daily News Collection, SDN-064900. © CHS. **478** Playground race. CPL, Municipal Reference Collection, Special Park Commission, *Annual Report,* 1907, 34. **481** Schlitz cart. UIC, Italian American Collection, IAC neg. 55.17. **482** *Artie.* NL. **483** *Cavalcade of the American Negro.* LOC, Prints & Photographs Division, WPA Poster Collection, LC-USZ62-97018. **485** Dill Pickle Club. NL, Midwest Manuscripts, Dill Pickle Club Collection. **485** *The Chap-Book.* NL. **487** Book cover of 1968 hardcover edition of *In the Mecca* by Gwendolyn Brooks. CHS. © HarperCollins. Reprinted by permission of HarperCollins Publishers Inc. **493** Clark and Jackson. NL, *Stanolind Record* 10:11 (September 1929): 12. **494** Arcades and theaters. CHS. **496** Lumber district. CHS.

M **499** Politicians. CHS, ICHi-09764. **500** "Bathhouse John's Ball." *Chicago Tribune,* December 14, 1908. **502** Wrigley and Tribune buildings. CHS, ICHi-23790. **503** Mail streetcar. CHS, ICHi-21189. **504** Sears catalog. CHS. **510** Harlan ad. CHS, ICHi-14896 V. **511** William Hale Thompson. CHS, Chicago Daily News Collection, DN-0064356. **512** Daley tribute. CHS, ICHi-22462. **516** Cattle pens. CHS, ICHi-20649. **516** Canning room. CHS, ICHi-21839. **517** Surgical clinic. CHS. **518** School for Nurses. NL, Hahnemann Hospital *Annual Report,* 1909. **519** Lab workers. LOC, Prints & Photographs Division, FSA/OWI Collection, LC-USE6-D-008615. **527** Chicago, bird's-eye view. NL, *Land Owner* 6.2 (February 1874): cover. **530** Graue Mill. Lake County (IL) Discovery Museum, Curt Teich Postcard Archives, 4DK1934. **533** Farm workers. CHS, Chicago Daily News Collection, DN-0068516. **534** Parade. CHS, ICHi-31808. © CHS. **536** Municipal Airport. CHS, ICHi-25924. © Chicago Aerial Survey Co. **544** Cabins. Lake County (IL) Discovery Museum, Curt Teich Postcard Archives, 8B383. **546** Nortown Theater. CHS, ICHi-25888. **547** Regal Theater. LOC, Prints & Photographs Division, FSA/OWI Collection, LC-USF34-038808-D. **548** Moving day. CHS, Chicago Daily News Collection, DN-0051354. **552** Maxwell St. LOC, Prints & Photographs Division, FSA/OWI Collection, LC-USF33-012984-M1. **556** *Music of Ireland.* NL, O'Neill's *Music of Ireland,* 1903.

N **561** IC depot. CHS, ICHi-05211. **561** Navy Pier. CHS, ICHi-14115. **563** South Side Levee. CHS, F38KG A18. **571** Newsboy. LOC, Prints & Photographs Division, FSA/OWI Collection, LC-USW3-000698-D. **581** Visiting nurse. CHS, ICHi-03929.

O **587** John F. Kennedy. CHS, ICHi-32484. **590** Blue Island Opera House. Lake County (IL) Discovery Museum, Curt Teich Postcard Archives, 9388. **590** Opera program. NL, WSB Matthews Music Scrapbooks. **591** Puppet theater. CHS. **594** Ravinia. CHS, ICHi-07490.

P **595** Packinghouse. CHS, ICHi-04076. **598** Reactor monument. CHS. © Robert C. Long. **601** Park districts. CHS, Map #2794-A. **605** Cotillion. CHS. **607** Hedrich Blessing. CHS, HB-03300-I. © CHS. **609** Saloon Building. CHS, A. T. Andreas, *History of Chicago,* vol. 1, 1884, 180. **610** Wigwam. CHS. **610** Old Farwell Hall. CHS, ICHi-25624. **611** Coliseum. CHS. **611** Dexter Park. CHS, Chicago Daily News Collection, DN-0006021. **613** Subdivision map. NL, *Land Owner* 1 (1869): after 28. **617** Planned civic center. NL, *Plan of Chicago,* 1909, 129. **618** Union Station. CHS, ICHi-31909. © Chicago Architectural Photographing Co. **619** Lotus beds. CHS, ICHi-24053. **620** Buroak. NL. **623** *Poetry.* NL. **625** Kosciusko Guards. CHS, ICHi-03021. **627** Sergeants exam. CHS, Chicago Daily News Collection, DN-0000739. **628** Mounted police. LOC, Prints & Photographs Division, FSA/OWI Collection, LC-USF33-016163-M2. **629** Exhibition poster. LOC, Prints & Photographs Division, WPA Poster Collection, LC-USZC2-5226. **630** "America Needs Stevenson," July 24, 1952. CHS, ICHi-26175. © *Chicago Sun-Times.* Reprinted with special permission from the Chicago Sun-Times, Inc. **631** Coliseum. CHS. **632** Dever flyer. CHS, ICHi-06410. **633** Harrison flyer. CHS, ICHi-21392. **635** Dickerson ad. CHS. **636** Drake tea party. CHS, Chicago Daily News Collection, DN-0062308. **638** "Smash Tammany!" CHS, ICHi-22475. **647** Printing press. NL, Rand McNally Archives. **649** Classroom. CHS, HB-6184. © CHS. **650** Temperance parade. CHS. **650** Harrison ad. CHS, ICHi-14843. **653** Picnic. CPL, WGP 1.47. **654** Storefront church. LOC, Prints & Photographs Division, FSA/OWI Collection, LC-USF34-038830-D. **656** Demolition. CHS. **657** Federal Building. CHS. © CHS. **659** Smallpox poster. LOC, Prints & Photographs Division, WPA Poster Collection, LC-USZC2-5173. **659** Syphilis poster. LOC, Prints & Photographs Division, WPA Poster Collection, LC-USZC2-1655. **660** Horse-drawn bus. CHS. **660** Cable car. CHS. **661** Trolley bus. CPL, ACC 2.169. **661** Streetcar. UIC, Marcy Newberry Center Records, MN neg. 165. **663** DuBois contract. NL, Modern Manuscripts, A. C. McClurg & Co. Collection. **664** Printing form. CHS.

R **668** Irishmen poster. CHS, ICHi-14837. **671** IC Railroad station. CHS, ICHi-23805. **671** Lake Shore & Michigan Southern Railroad station. NL, *Land Owner* (November 1872): 184–185. **672** Union Station steps. LOC, Prints & Photographs Division, FSA/OWI Collection, LC-USW3-015561-E. **673** Pullman car. NL, Pullman Archives, 13/01/03. **675** Labor Day parade. CPL, HPC 1.62. **676** Rail yards. UIC, Jane Addams Memorial Collection, JAMC neg. 857. **680** Calumet Harbor. NL, *Land Owner* (May 1873): 81. **682** Alley. UIC, Metropolitan Planning Council Collection, MPC neg. 117. **686** State Board of Charities. CHS, Chicago Daily News Collection, DN-0005711. **686** Bread line. CHS, Chicago Daily News Collection, DN-98013. © CHS. **689** Billy Sunday. CHS, Chicago Daily News Collection, DN-0065330. **700** Lincoln funeral. CHS, ICHi-22122. **701** 1895 restaurant. CHS, ICHi-30447. **702** Terrace Garden. CHS, ICHi-22994. **703** S. Michigan Ave. Lake County (IL) Discovery Museum, Curt Teich Postcard Archives, A54790. **705** Dime store. Grayslake Historical Society. **708** Store. NL, *Land Owner* (March 1873). **711** Ravine. Lake County (IL) Discovery Museum, Curt Teich Postcard Archives. **716** High Mass. CHS. **717** Good Friday parade. CHS, ICHi-26666. © CHS. **718** Church float. UIC, Italian American Collection, IAC neg. 91.1c. **719** St. Anthony's. UIC, Italian American Collection, IAC neg. 55.23.2. **720** Choir loft. LOC, Prints & Photographs Division, FSA/OWI Collection, LC-USW3-000147-D.

S **727** Choir boys. CHS, Chicago Daily News Collection, DN-0007607. **727** Hymn book. CHS. **729** Steinmetz Saloon. CHS. **731** Canal construction. CHS, ICHi-05859. **734** Lane Tech. CHS. **736** Chicago Hebrew Institute class. CHS, ICHi-21693. **738** St. Joseph's Bohemian Orphanage class. Lake County (IL) Discovery Museum, Curt Teich Postcard Archives, R88925. **738** Siebel's brewing academy. CHS, ICHi-17537. **739** Dearborn School. NL, Modern Manuscripts, Rand McNally VIII Photographs, box 1. **743** Juarez High yearbook, 1981. CHS. © Chicago Public Schools. **744** Boy Scouts. CHS, Chicago Daily News Collection, DN-0064654. **748** Maypole dancing. CHS. **750** Ship construction. CHS. © CHS. **751** St. Charles. CHS, Chicago Daily News Collection, DN-0088210. © CHS. **752** Pullman arcade building. NL, *Harpers* 70:17 (February 1885): 456. **754** Starr Hotel. CHS, ICHi-20654. **755** *State Street Bridge.* NL, Midwest Manuscripts, McIlvaine Clippings; Sunday *Tribune,* November 30, 1930. © *Chicago Tribune.* **756** Tall buildings compared. CHS, ICHi-30460. **757** Home Insurance Building. CHS, ICHi-19291. **760** Sparta A.B.A. CHS. **762** Cook County Poor House. CHS, ICHi-23498. **763** *The Care of the Immigrant.* CHS, ICHi-14353-D. **769** *South Holland.* NL, Richard A. Cook, *South Holland, Illinois: A History, 1846–1966,* 1966. © South Holland Trust and Savings Bank. **769** Paarlberg house and migrant worker's home. NL, Richard A. Cook, *South Holland, Illinois: A History, 1846–1966,* 1966, 27. © South Holland Trust and Savings Bank. **771** South Shore Country Club. CHS, Chicago Daily News Collection, DN-0052788. **775** Navy Pier. CHS, ICHi-25730. © Jim Parker/Copelin Commercial Photographers. **776** Sporting goods factory. CHS. © Wilson Sporting Goods Co. **778** DuSable High basketball team. CHS. © CHS. **778** Armour football team. CHS. **780** St. Charles bridge. CHS. **781** St. Valentine's Day Massacre. CHS, ICHi-14406. **786** Street raising. NL, Modern Manuscripts, Rand McNally Collection. **787** St. Patrick's Day parade. CPL, EGP 1.25. **787**

Wrecked buggy. DuPage County Historical Museum, 84.29.4.84. **788** Dearborn and Randolph. CHS, ICHi-04192. **790** Musician. CHS, ICHi-12834. © CHS. **792** Huckster. CHS, ICHi-22802. © CHS. **795** Messenger boys. CHS, Chicago Daily News Collection, DN-0000022. **796** Subdivision plan. NL, Chicago Plan Commission, *Building New Neighborhoods,* 1943, 17. © Chicago Plan Commission. **797** Michigan Boulevard Garden Apartments. CHS, ICHi-09273. © CHS. **797** Stateway Gardens. CHS, ICHi-23483. © CHS. **798** Cabrini Extension. CHS, ICHi-23200. © CHS. **801** Buffalo Grove. CHS, HB-31832-PPN. © CHS. **801** Woodfield Mall. CHS. © CHS. **803** Ballot. CHS, ICHi-14325. **806** Swedish Old People's Home. CHS, Chicago Daily News Collection, DN-0078707. © CHS. **807** Beach. LOC, Prints & Photographs Division, FSA/OWI Collection, LC-USF33-016072-M4.

T **811** Western Electric plant. Lake County (IL) Discovery Museum, Curt Teich Postcard Archives, 1CH179. **813** Alley. UIC, Jane Addams Memorial Collection, JAMC neg. 1054. **815** Tooker Alley poster. NL, Midwest Manuscripts, Dill Pickle Club Collection. **816** Rehearsal. LOC, Prints & Photographs Division, FSA/OWI Collection, LC-USW3-000678-D. **817** McVicker's Theatre. CHS. **818** Great Northern Theatre poster. LOC, Prints & Photographs Division, WPA Poster Collection, LC-USZC2-5468. **821** Toll plaza. CHS. © CHS. **823** Attractions. NL, Modern Manuscripts, John T. McCutcheon Papers. © *Chicago Tribune.* **824** *Pictorial Guide.* CHS. **828** Canal reopening. CHS, ICHi-05836. **828** Locomotive. CHS, ICHi-23545. **828** Railway ad. CHS. **831** Swimming race. CHS, Chicago Daily News Collection, SDN-054202. **832** State and Madison. CHS. **832** Horsecar. CHS. **836** Turnverein. Lake County (IL) Discovery Museum, Curt Teich Postcard Archives, RD10872.

U **838** Free lunch. CHS, Chicago Daily News Collection, DN-93843. © CHS. **838** Smashing slot machine. CHS, Chicago Daily News Collection, DN-0004942. **840** Demonstration. CHS, ICHi-23242. **842** Strikers. CHS, Chicago Daily News Collection, DN-0056264. **848** Schloesser & Co. CHS, ICHi-24371. **849** Urban League pamphlet. CHS. **850** Polk St. UIC, Italian American Collection, IAC neg. 140.4. **850** Vacant property. CHS, ICHi-14396. © CHS.

V **855** Vice district. LOC, Prints & Photographs Division, FSA/OWI Collection, LC-USF33-016121-M4.

W **861** Alley. CHS, ICHi-00798. **862** "Great Chicago Sewer." NL, *Land Owner* (August 1871): after 248. **863** Skokie Marsh. CHS, ICHi-20511. **864** Water system. NL, *Land Owner* (November 1873): 204–205. **865** Pier construction. CHS, Chicago Daily News Collection, DN-0063456. **865** Beach. CPL, Municipal Reference Collection, Special Park Commission, *Annual Report,* 1916, 2. **878** S. Water St. CHS, *Chicago,* 1892. **882** Windy City. Ohio Historical Society. **884** Woman's City Club. CHS, ICHi-7386. **888** Beef-dressing floor. CHS, ICHi-14233. **889** Construction workers. CHS, Chicago Daily News Collection, DN-0085101. © CHS. **890** Egg-breaking plant. LOC, Prints & Photographs Division, FSA/OWI Collection, LC-USF34-063119-D. **892** Manufacturing employment map. CHS, Chicago Plan Commission, *Chicago Industrial Study,* Summary Report, 1952, 20. © Chicago Plan Commission. **894** Saloons. NL, Modern Manuscripts, Graham Taylor Papers. **895** Labor Day parade. DuPage County Historical Museum, 86.64.1. **896** Anti-German sign. CHS, Chicago Daily News Collection, DN-0069264. **897** Charles W. Folds. CHS, Chicago Daily News Collection, DN-0070050. **898** Exposition map. CHS. **899** Produce exhibit. NL, *World's Columbian Exposition Illustrated* 3.9 (November 1893): 231. **899** Court of Honor. CHS, ICHi-18013. **900** Street in Cairo. CHS. **901** Ferris wheel. NL, Hubert Howe Bancroft, *The Book of the Fair,* 1895. **901** Woman's Building. CHS, ICHi-23353. **903** Wrigley Field. CHS, ICHi-17617.

"The City as Artifact"

A1 *Michigan Avenue with View of the Art Institute* by Richard Estes, American, b. 1937. Oil on canvas, 91.4 x 121.9 cm. Gift of the Capital Campaign Fund, 1984.177. The Art Institute of Chicago. © Richard Estes, courtesy, Marlborough Gallery, New York. **A2** *The Running Horse—Dan Ryan Expressway.* Jay Wolke. © Jay Wolke. **A3** *Homage to the Chicago School.* Thomas Schlereth. © Thomas Schlereth. Mural © Richard Haas. **A4** *History of the Packinghouse Worker.* NL. © NL. Mural © William Walker/Chicago Public Art Group. **A4** *I Welcome Myself to a New Place.* NL. © NL. Mural © Olivia Gude, Jon Pounds, and Marcus Jefferson/Chicago Public Art Group. **A5** *Casa Aztlan.* Thomas Schlereth. © Thomas Schlereth. Mural © Marcos Raya. **A6** *Fragments of Chicago's Past,* permanent installation, gallery 200 (Architecture), view of north wall. The Art Institute of Chicago. © The Art Institute of Chicago. **A6** *Land of Lincoln.* The School of the Art Institute of Chicago. © The School of the Art Institute of Chicago and the Brown family. **A7** *Big Bil-Bored.* Thomas Schlereth. © Thomas Schlereth. Sculpture © Nancy Rubins. **A8** *Haymarket Riot Monument.* CHS, ICHi-14452. **A8** *Haymarket Martyrs' Monument.* CHS, ICHi-16157.

Timeline and Year Pages

B22 Map of the Northwest Territory. Cartographer: Thomas Valentine. CHS, ICHi-14169. **B22** Treaty of Greenville. CHS. **B22** Painting of treaty negotiations. Artist: Unknown. CHS. **B23** Depiction of DuSable's house. Artist: Unknown. NL, A. T. Andreas, *History of Chicago,* vol. 1, 1884, detail of frontispiece. **B23** Silver brooch. CHS. © CHS. **B23** Brass holy water font. CHS. © CHS. **B24** "Chicago in 1812." Cartographer: Unknown. NL, *Chicago Magazine* 1 (1857): 104. **B24** Rebekah Wells Heald. Photographer: Unknown. CHS, ICHi-13957. **B24** Tortoise-shell comb. CHS. © CHS. **B25** Silver cross. CHS. © CHS. **B25** Victoire Mirandeau Porthier. Photographer: Unknown. CHS, ICHi-15043. **B25** Depiction of Kinzie house. Artist: Unknown. NL, A. T. Andreas, *History of Chicago,* vol. 1, 1884, 75. **B25** Black Hawk. Artist: Unknown. NL, Thomas Loraine McKenney, *History of the Indian Tribes of North America,* 1848, plate opposite 213. **B26** Public square. Artist: Unknown. NL, *Chicago Daily Journal,* April 25, 1848. **B26** 1850 census. NL, manuscript census for Chicago, 930. **B27** Telegram. Illinois State Archives, RG 491.114. **B27** Railroad depot. Photographer: Unknown. CHS, ICHi-05266. **B28** *City of Chicago.* Artist: William Flint. LOC, g4104c pm001493. **B28** People fleeing. Artists: Currier & Ives. CHS. **B29** State and Madison. Photographer: Unknown. CHS, ICHi-02811. **B29** O'Leary house. Photographer: Unknown. CHS, ICHi-02737. **B29** "Homeless Citizens." Artist: Unknown. CHS, ICHi-02889. **B30** Vice map. Creator: William T. Stead. NL, William T. Stead, *If Christ Came to Chicago,* 1894, opposite title page. **B30** Unrest at Blue Island. Artist: Unknown. NL, Case Pullman 12/00/03, Pullman Strike Scrapbook, clipping from *Chicago Tribune,* July 2, 1894. **B31** Troops on the lakefront. Artist: T. Dacy Walker. NL, *Harper's Weekly,* July 21, 1884, 668. **B31** Fairground buildings in ruins. Photographer: Unknown. CHS, ICHi-02551. **B31** Chicago Commons. Photographer: Unknown. CHS, ICHi-03795. **B32** Gary steel strike. Photographer: *Chicago Daily News* staff. CHS, Chicago Daily News Collection, DN- 0071498. **B32** Jackson subpoena. Circuit Court of Cook County. **B32** Thompson voting. Photographer: *Chicago Daily News* staff. CHS, Chicago Daily News Collection, DN-0065980. **B33** Red Cross volunteers. Photographer: *Chicago Daily News* staff. CHS, Chicago Daily News Collection, DN-0070539. **B33** National Guardsmen. Photographer: Jun Fujita. CHS, ICHi-25571. **B34** Police confrontation. Photographer: *Chicago Daily News* staff. CHS, Chicago Daily News Collection, DN C-8769. © CHS. **B34** Brotherhood Week. NL, Pullman Company Archive, 06/01/04; box 17, folder 492. **B34** Braddock vs. Louis ticket. Jim Themelis. **B35** Outer Drive Bridge. Photographer: Unknown. CHS. **B35** Lathrop Homes. Photographer: Unknown. NL, *Survey Graphic* (December 1937). **B36** Line of police. Photographer: Unknown. CHS, ICHi-20689. **B36** "Hello Democrats!" CHS. **B36** Protesters in Grant Park. Photographer: Unknown. CHS, ICHi-14788. **B37** *Chicago Seed* cover. Artist: Unknown. University of Connecticut. **B37** Police on West Madison. Photographer: AP/Wide World Photos. CHS, ICHi-19851. © AP/Wide World Photos. **B37** "We Support Mayor Daley." CHS, ICHi-26272. **B38** Epton campaign headquarters. Photographer: Thomas Favelli. CHS. **B38** Washington button. CPL. **B38** Washington taking oath. Photographer: Ernie Cox, Jr. *Chicago Tribune.* © Chicago Tribune. **B39** Poverty map. Cartographer: Janice L. Reiff. Based on a map in Tom Brune and Eduardo Camacho, *A Special Report: Race and Poverty in Chicago,* 1983, 15. **B39** Peace march. Photographer: Anne Cusack. *Chicago Tribune.* © Chicago Tribune.

TEXT CREDITS

35 Excerpts from interview with Bruce Graham. Reprinted with permission of the CHS. **69** Excerpts from Roger Ebert, "Hoop Dreams." Taken from the Roger Ebert column by Roger Ebert, © 1994. Distributed by Universal Press Syndicate. Reprinted with permission. All rights reserved. **104** Excerpt from Philip M. Klutznick and Sidney Hyman, *Angles of Vision*. Reprinted with permission of Ivan R. Dee, Publisher. **115** Excerpt from interview with Patrick Ryan. Reprinted with permission of the CHS. **122** Excerpts from interview with Robert Galvin. Reprinted with permission of the CHS. **177** Excerpts from "The Fate of Women Workers." © 1988 by the Board of Trustees of the University of Illinois. Reprinted with permission of the University of Illinois Press. **178** Excerpt from Mike Royko, "What Clout Is and Isn't." © by Mike Royko. Reprinted with permission of Sterling Lord Literistic, Inc. **199** Excerpt from Howell Raines, "Prelude," in *My Soul Is Rested*. © 1977 by Howell Raines. Reprinted with permission of G. P. Putnam's Sons, a division of Penguin Group (USA) Inc. **290** Excerpt from Leon Lederman and Dick Teresi, *The God Particle*. © 1993 by Leon Lederman and Dick Teresi. Reprinted with permission of Houghton Mifflin Company. All rights reserved. **447** Gwendolyn Brooks, "kitchenette building." Reprinted with permission of Brooks Permissions. **467** Excerpts from "The Desplaines Hall Workers Club Picnics in Ogden's Grove." © 1988 by the Board of Trustees of the University of Illinois. Reprinted with permission of the University of Illinois Press. **483** Excerpts from interview with Studs Terkel. Reprinted with permission of the CHS. **486** Excerpt from Saul Bellow, *The Adventures of Augie March*. © 1949, 1951, 1952, 1953 by Saul Bellow. Reprinted with permission of Viking Penguin, a division of Penguin Group (USA) Inc., and the Wylie Agency, Inc. **486** Excerpt from Saul Bellow, *Humboldt's Gift*. © 1973, 1974, 1975 by Saul Bellow. Reprinted with permission of Viking Penguin, a division of Penguin Group (USA) Inc., and the Wylie Agency, Inc. **487** Excerpt from Gwendolyn Brooks, "Of De Witt Williams on His Way to Lincoln Cemetery." Reprinted with permission of Brooks Permissions. **669** Excerpts from Langston Hughes, *The Collected Poems of Langston Hughes*. © 1994 by The Estate of Langston Hughes. Reprinted with permission of Alfred A. Knopf, a division of Random House, Inc., and Harold Ober Associates Incorporated. **689** Excerpts from Dwight L. Moody, "Heaven and Who Are There." Reprinted with permission of the Moody Press. **742** Excerpt from George S. Counts, *School and Society in Chicago*. © 1928 by Harcourt, Inc., renewed 1984 by George S. Counts. Reprinted with permission of the publisher. **851** Excerpts from Hilda Satt Polachek, *I Came a Stranger*. © 1989 by the Board of Trustees of the University of Illinois. Reprinted with permission of the University of Illinois Press. **900** Excerpt from Alfreda M. Duster, ed., *Crusade for Justice: The Autobiography of Ida B. Wells*. © 1970 by the University of Chicago. Reprinted with permission of the University of Chicago Press. **B22** Excerpt from Helen Hornbeck Tanner, *Atlas of Great Lakes Indian History*. Reprinted with permission of the author.

MAP SOURCES

xxx **Metropolitan Chicago Reference Map**

Sources: Generalized from U.S. Geological Survey 1:100,000 scale topographic maps.

22 **Annexations and Additions to the City of Chicago (Ann Durkin Keating)**

Research assistance: Dennis McClendon

Sources: Chicago Department of Public Works, Bureau of Maps & Plats, "Map of Chicago Showing Growth of the City by Annexations and Accretions," November 1974 (revised 1985); Cook Co. Dept of Highways, *Cook County Township Maps Including the City of Chicago* (Chicago, 1999); Barbara Mercedes Posadas, "Community Structures of Chicago's Northwest Side: The Transition from Rural to Urban, 1830–1889" (Ph.D. dissertation, Northwestern University, 1976); *Industrial Chicago*, vol. 2, *Building Interests* (Chicago: Goodspeed Publishing Co., 1891), 42.

85 **Blues Clubs in Chicago (Michael P. Conzen and Max Grinnell)**

Research assistance: Christopher P. Thale

Sources: Based primarily on newspaper ads and listings; Karl M. Grinnell, "The Blues Fell Down This Morning: Blues and Chicago's Black Belt in the Post–World War II Era" (Bachelor's thesis, Committee on Geographical Studies, University of Chicago, 1998). Areas of black population based on census tract statistics for 1950, 1970, and 2000.

117 **The Calumet Region (Dennis McClendon)**

Sources: Generalized from U.S. Geological Survey 1:100,000 scale topographic maps; F. M. Fryxell, *The Physiography of the Region of Chicago* (Chicago: University of Chicago Press, 1927), fig. 11.

134 **Southern Distribution of the *Chicago Defender* (James R. Grossman)**

Source: James R. Grossman, *Land of Hope: Chicago, Black Southerners, and the Great Migration* (Chicago: University of Chicago Press, 1989), 76–77.

137 **Chicago Housing Authority Family Projects, 1985 (Dennis McClendon)**

Sources: Chicago Housing Authority 1984/85 Statistical Report, 7–13; "Areas of Negro Residence in Chicago," prepared by Research Department, Chicago Urban League, 1965.

138 **Ancient Indian Earthworks in the Chicago Region (Michael P. Conzen and James A. Marshall)**

Sources: James A. Marshall, "Astronomical Alignments Claimed to Exist on the Eastern North American Prehistoric Earthworks and the Evidence and Arguments against Them," *Ohio Archaeologist* 45.1 (Spring 1995): 4–16; James A. Marshall, "Architecture of Prehistoric Chicagoland," paper given to the Midwest Archaeological Conference, Grand Rapids, Michigan, October 16–18, 1992.

139 **Chicago's Place in the Water Routes of the Indian World, 1600–1830 (Helen Hornbeck Tanner and Michael P. Conzen)**

Source: Helen H. Tanner, ed., *Atlas of Great Lakes Indian History* (Norman: University of Oklahoma Press, 1987), map 2.

140 **Indian Settlement Pattern in the Chicago Region, circa 1830 (Helen Hornbeck Tanner and Michael P. Conzen)**

Source: Helen H. Tanner, ed., *Atlas of Great Lakes Indian History* (Norman: University of Oklahoma Press, 1987), maps 25–27.

176 **Women's Garment Factories in Chicago in 1925**

Source: City of Chicago, *Mid-Chicago Economic Development Study* (Chicago: Mayor's Committee for Economic and Cultural Development of Chicago, 1966), plate 17.

190 **Chicago's Community Areas**

Sources: The original version of this map appeared in Robert E. Park, Ernest W. Burgess, and Roderick D. McKenzie, *The City* (Chicago: University of Chicago Press, 1925 [1984]; updated a number of times since, reproduced in the various editions of the Chicago Community Fact Books).

193 **Chicago: Commuting in the Walking City in 1854 (Michael P. Conzen)**

Sources: Hall & Co.'s Chicago City Directory and Business Advertiser for 1854–'55.

194 **Railroad Commuting to Chicago in 1934**

Research assistance: Dennis McClendon

Sources: Chicago Regional Planning Association, "Railway Commutation Time in the Region of Chicago, March 1934."

195 **Commuting to Chicago in 1970**

Sources: Brian J. L. Berry et al., *Chicago: Transformations of an Urban System* (Cambridge, MA: Ballinger Pub. Co., for the Comparative Metropolitan Analysis Project of the Association of American Geographers, 1976), 14, 22, and 31.

196 **The Journey to Work in Chicago in 1980 (Michael P. Conzen)**

Research assistance: Dennis McClendon

Source: U.S. Census Bureau, *1980 Census of Population and Housing: Summary Characteristics for Governmental Units and Standard Metropolitan Statistical Areas, Illinois* (U.S. Department of Commerce, 1982), 69–103.

205 **Racial Restrictive Covenants on Chicago's South Side in 1947**

Source: Map submitted as defendant's exhibit 2, in *Tovey v. Levy*, 401 Ill. 393 (1948).

220 **Organized Crime in 1920s Chicago**

Source: Herbert Asbury, *Gem of the Prairie: An Informal History of the Chicago Underworld* (New York: Knopf, 1940), 329 (credited to the *Chicago Tribune*).

231 **Chicago's Deep Tunnel System in 2003 (Dennis McClendon)**

Sources: Maps and plans provided by the Metropolitan Water Reclamation District of Greater Chicago, September 2003.

236 **Changing Origins of Metropolitan Chicago's Foreign-Born Population (Michael P. Conzen)**

Research assistance: Christopher P. Thale

Sources: U.S. Censuses for 1910, 1990, for Cook, DuPage, Kane, Lake, McHenry, and Will Counties, Illinois, and Lake and Porter Counties, Indiana.

258 **Chicago's Evolving Economic Geography (Michael P. Conzen and Mark Donovan)**

Research assistance: Dennis McClendon

Sources: Hall & Co.'s Chicago City Directory and Business Advertiser for 1854–'55 (Chicago, 1854); Chicago Local Community Research Committee and the Chicago Commonwealth Club, *Present Use of Land and Its Probable Future Use in the Region of Chicago* (Chicago: Chicago Regional Planning Association, 1926); industrial areas generalized from Chicago Zoning Commission, *Tentative Report and a Proposed Zoning Ordinance for the City of Chicago, 1954* (Chicago, 1923), 6; and from U.S. Geological Survey 7.5 Minute Series topographic maps; 1990 office locations from a dissertation in preparation by Mark P. Donovan (University of Chicago) using real estate data provided by CoStar Inc.

262 **The Chicago Area before Human Transformation (Michael P. Conzen)**

Sources: F. M. Fryxell, *The Physiography of the Region of Chicago* (Chicago: University of Chicago Press, 1927), fig. 2; Louis R. Iverson and Mark Joselyn, "Forest Cover in Illinois, 1820–1980; with maps on Forest Composition, Volume, Diversity, and Cover," Illinois Natural History Survey, Illinois Department of Energy and Natural Resources, 1980; Alfred H. Meyer, "Fundament Vegetation of the Calumet Region, Northwest Indiana–Northeast Illinois," *Papers of the Michigan Academy of Sciences, Arts, and Letters, 1950*, vol. 34 (1952), fig. 1; Philip C. Hanson, "The Presettlement Vegetation of the Plain of Glacial Lake Chicago in Cook County, Illinois," *Biological Notes*, Ohio Biological Survey 15 (1981): 159–164.

287 **Chicago-Area Expressways in 2003 (Dennis McClendon)**

Sources: Ed J. Christopher and Maryanne A. C. Custodio, "A History of the Northeastern Illinois Expressway System" (Chicago Area Transportation Study Working Paper 97–04, 1997).

342 **Chicago's World—Within a Day's Travel (Michael P. Conzen and Dennis McClendon)**

Research assistance: J. Ryan Lowry

Sources: *Appleton's Railway, Canal, and Steamship Guide*, 1850; *Official Railway Guide to the United States, Canada, and Mexico* (New York: National Railway Publication Co., 1900); *Official Railway Guide to the United States, Puerto Rico, Canada, Mexico, and Cuba* (New York: National Railway Publication Co., 1950); *OAG Flight Guide Worldwide* 2.1 (July 2000).

351 **County Boundaries in the Chicago Area (John H. Long and Robert Will)**

Sources: Gordon DenBoer, *Atlas of Historical County Boundaries: Illinois,* ed. John H. Long (New York: Charles Scribner's Sons, 1997); Peggy Tuck Sinko, *Atlas of Historical County Boundaries: Indiana,* ed. John H. Long (New York: Simon & Schuster, 1996).

362 **The Great Lakes**

Sources: Environment Canada, "The Great Lakes Basin: Eco-regions, Drainage, and Urban Areas" (Ottawa, ON: Environment Canada, 1977); U.S. Coast Survey, "Great Lakes: Lake Champlain to Lake of the Woods," Nautical Chart 14500 (Washington, DC: Coast Survey, 2002).

363 **Illinois Central Railroad Links to Chicago (James R. Grossman)**

Source: James R. Grossman, *Land of Hope: Chicago, Black Southerners, and the Great Migration* (Chicago: University of Chicago Press, 1989), 100–101.

376 **Labor Unrest in Chicago, April 25–May 4, 1886 (Michael P. Conzen and Christopher P. Thale)**

Sources: *Chicago Times*, *Chicago Tribune*, April 25–May 5, 1886. Base map: U.S. Geological Survey Topographic Map, 15 Minute Series, Chicago Quadrangle, Washington, DC, 1891.

420 **Interurbans in the Chicago Region (Dennis McClendon)**

Research assistance: Roy J. Benedict

Sources: George W. Hilton & John F. Due, *The Electric Interurban Railways in America* (Stanford, CA: Stanford University Press, 1960 [2000]); John Szwajkart, *The Train Watcher's Guide to Chicago* (Brookfield, IL: John Szwajkart, 1976); Rand, McNally & Co., *Commercial Atlas of America* (Chicago: Rand, McNally & Co., 1918).

424 **The Chicago Area's Iron and Steel Industry (Michael P. Conzen and Christopher P. Thale)**

Sources: American Iron and Steel Works Directories, for 1888, 1920, 1935, 1951, 1967, and 1984; Association of Iron and Steel Engineers, Works Directory, 2000; *The Iron and Steel Interests of Chicago* (1890); various telephone books, city directories, Sanborn fire insurance maps, community maps, company Web sites, and Dun and Bradstreet industrial guides; William T. Hogan, *Economic History of the Iron and Steel Industry of the United States*, 5 vols. (Lexington, MA: Heath, 1971); A. T. Andreas, *History of Chicago*, 3 vols. (Chicago: A. T. Andreas, 1884–1886); A. T. Andreas, *History of Cook County, Illinois* (Chicago: A. T. Andreas, 1886); John B. Appleton, *The Iron and Steel Industry of the Calumet District,* University of Illinois, Studies in the Social Sciences, vol. 13 (Urbana: University of Illinois, 1927).

470 **Recreation Facilities in Chicago's Loop (Michael P. Conzen and Katharine W. Hannaford)**

Sources: Chicago city directory, 1885; Arthur J. Todd et al., *The Chicago Recreation Survey 1937,* vol. 2, *Commercial Recreation* (Chicago, 1938).

472 **Movie Theaters in Chicago, 1926, 1937, and 2002 (Michael P. Conzen and Christopher P. Thale)**

Sources: Arthur J. Todd et al., *The Chicago Recreation Survey 1937,* vol. 2, *Commercial Recreation* (Chicago, 1938); 2002 newspaper ads and listings.

526 **Economic Origins of Metropolitan Chicago's Communities (Ann Durkin Keating and Michael P. Conzen)**

Sources: Based primarily on entries in this Encyclopedia for individual communities outside Chicago; also Ann Durkin Keating, *Building Chicago: Suburban Developers and the Creation of a Divided Metropolis* (Columbus: Ohio State University Press, 1988), tables 1, 4, 6, 8, 10, and 18, and maps 1, 2, 3, 4, and 8.

528 **Land Subdivision and Urbanization on Chicago's Northwest Side (Michael P. Conzen and Ann Durkin Keating)**

Sources: James H. Rees, "Map of Cook and DuPage Counties, Illinois, 1851," Land Ownership Maps of the United States, Library of Congress fiche series, no. 583; Public Domain Alienation Records, Geographical Series, State of Illinois; William L. Flower, "Map of Cook and DuPage Counties, Illinois, 1861," Land Ownership Maps of the United States, Library of Congress fiche series, no. 584; William L. Flower, "Map of Cook and DuPage Counties, Illinois, 1870," Land Ownership Maps of the United States, Library of Congress fiche series, no. 586; U.S. Geological Survey Topographic Map, 15 Minute Series, Riverside Quadrangle, Washington, DC, 1901; U.S. Geological Survey Topographic Map, 7.5 Minute Series, River Forest Quadrangle, Washington, DC, 1928; U.S. Geological Survey Topographic Map, 7.5 Minute Series, River Forest Quadrangle, Washington, DC, 1963; Cook County (IL) Office of Assessor, Unit Value Land Maps of the 1931 Quadrennial Real Estate Assessment, Cook County, Illinois.

660 **Chicago's Street Railways in 1890 (Dennis McClendon)**

Research assistance: James J. Buckley, Robert D. Heinlein, Andris J. Kristopans, Richard B. Kunz, Charles L. Tauscher

Sources: George W. Hilton, *Cable Railways of Chicago* (Chicago: Electric Railway Historical Society, 1954). Base map: U.S. Geological Survey Topographic Map, 15 Minute Series, Chicago and Calumet Quadrangles, Washington, DC, 1891.

678 **Chicago's Rapid Transit Lines (Dennis McClendon)**

Research assistance: Roy J. Benedict, Bruce G. Moffat, Graham Garfield

Sources: Bruce G. Moffat, *The "L": The Development of Chicago's Rapid Transit System, 1888–1932,* Bulletin 131 of the Central Electric Railfans' Association (Chicago: Central Electric Railfans' Association, 1995); Chicago Transit Authority, "Chicago's Rapid Transit System: History of Service Changes," photocopy, 1997; Chicago Rapid Transit Co., "1940 Transportation Map of Chicago"; Walter R. Keevil and Norman Carlson, eds., *Chicago's Rapid Transit*, vol. 2, *Rolling Stock/1947–1976,* Bulletin 115 of the Central

Electric Railfans' Association (Chicago: Central Electric Railfans' Association, 1976), 226–256.

691 Jewish Congregations on the Move in Chicago, 1849–2002 (Michael P. Conzen)

Sources: Hyman L. Meites, *History of the Jews of Chicago* (Chicago: Chicago Jewish Historical Society and Wellington Publishing, 1990); Morris A. Gutstein, *A Priceless Heritage: The Epic Growth of Nineteenth Century Chicago Jewry* (New York: Bloch, 1953), 57–92; Morris A. Gutstein, "Historical Listing of Synagogues in Illinois," in *Faith and Form: An Exhibition Organized by the Maurice Spertus Museum of Judaica*, catalog, 1976, 91–98; Irving Cutler, Norman D. Schwartz, and Sidney Sorkin, eds., *Synagogues of Chicago*, part 1, *Compiled from Chicago City Directories;* part 2, *Compiled from Chicago Classified Telephone Directories* (Chicago: Chicago Jewish Historical Society, 1991); Sara Ann Rubin, "The Wandering Jew: Jewish Movement into Hyde Park, 1909–1928" (Bachelor's thesis, Department of Geography, University of Chicago, 1978); Irving Cutler, *The Jews of Chicago: From Shtetl to Suburb* (Urbana: University of Illinois Press, 1996).

692 Churches of the Presbyterian Church (USA) in the Chicago Area (Michael P. Conzen)

Research assistance: Lowell Livezey, Mark Bouman

Sources: Minutes of the Synod of Illinois of the Presbyterian Church in the United States of America, Centralia, Illinois, October 19–21, 1920; Chicago church locations from 1923 city directory; online directory of Presbyterian Church (USA) congregations at www.pcusa.org. Municipal boundaries generalized from Regional Planning Association map "Region of Chicago" (Chicago, 1926) and from Illinois official highway map 2001–2002.

693 Locational Stability: Saint Aloysius Parish, Chicago, in 1951 (Michael P. Conzen)

Research assistance: Ray Gadke

Sources: Harry C. Koenig, ed., *A History of the Parishes of the Archdiocese of Chicago* (Chicago: The Archdiocese, 1980), 2 vols.; Sanborn Map Co., *Sanborn Fire Insurance Map of Chicago*, 1951.

694 Religious Diversity on Chicago's Southwest Side, 2002 (Michael P. Conzen)

Research assistance: Lowell Livezey, Mark Bouman

Sources: Lowell W. Livezey, ed., *Public Religion and Urban Transformation: Faith in the City* (New York: New York University Press, 2000), 106; telephone books, 2002; fieldwork by Michael P. Conzen, March 2002; City of Chicago Community Policing information on church locations. Areas of Hispanic population based on 2000 census block group statistics.

695 Chicago's Non-Judeo-Christian Congregations in 2002 (Michael P. Conzen)

Research assistance: Douglas Knox, Lowell Livezey

Source: *Directory of Religious Centers* (electronic database), Pluralism Project, Committee on the Study of Religion, Harvard University, http://www.pluralism.org/directory/.

704 Chicago's Retail Centers in 1948 (Michael P. Conzen and Dennis McClendon)

Sources: Northeastern Illinois Planning Commission, *The Chicago Urbanized Area* (Chicago: Northeastern Illinois Metropolitan Area Planning Commission, 1960); sales data Albert J. Reiss, Jr., and Leonard Z. Breen, eds., *Geographic Distribution of Retail Trade in the Chicago Metropolitan Area, 1948* (Chicago: Chicago Community Inventory, 1952).

706 Chicago's Retail Centers in 2000 (Michael P. Conzen and Ann T. Natunewicz)

Source: Data from the National Research Bureau, Chicago, 2000.

772 Chicago's Prairie Avenue Elite in 1886 (Michael P. Conzen and Douglas Knox)

Sources: Chicago City Directory, 1886; *Land Owner* (May 1874); *Ladies' Exclusive Directory and Calling List,* 1895; *Elite of Chicago,* reversed directory, ca. 1881; *Bon-Ton Directory,* 1879–1880; 1900 U.S. census, manuscript population schedules, Chicago; *Prairie Avenue Historic District Interpretive Plan,* July 1977.

826 The Historic Illinois & Michigan Canal Corridor in 1851 (Michael P. Conzen)

Research assistance: John T. Monckton

Sources: Michael P. Conzen, "The Historical and Geographical Development of the Illinois & Michigan Canal National Heritage Corridor," chapter 1 in *The Illinois & Michigan Canal National Heritage Corridor A Guide to Its History and Sources,* edited by Michael P. Conzen and Kay J. Carr (DeKalb: Northern Illinois University Press, 1988), 325; Milo F. Quaife, *Chicago's Highways, Old and New, From Indian Trail to Motor Road* (Chicago: D. F. Keller & Co., 1923).

829 Chicago's Railroad Pattern in 1950 (Michael P. Conzen)

Research assistance: John Hankey, Andris J. Kristopans, Dennis McClendon

Sources: Pei-Lin Tan, "The Belt and Switching Railroads of Chicago Terminal Area" (Ph.D. diss., University of Chicago, 1931); John Szwajkart, *The Train Watcher's Guide to Chicago* (Brookfield, IL: John Szwajkart, 1976).

834 Chicago's Freight Tunnels, circa 1930 (Dennis McClendon)

Sources: Bruce G. Moffat, *The Chicago Tunnel Story: Exploring the Railroad "Forty Feet Below,"* Bulletin 135 of the Central Electric Railfans' Association (Chicago: Central Electric Railfans' Association, 2002); Chicago Tunnel Co., *What the Freight Tunnels Mean to Chicago* (Chicago, 1928); City of Chicago Committee on Railway Terminals, *The Railway Passenger Terminal Problem at Chicago* (Chicago: 1933), 20.

866 Chicago's Lakefront Landfill (Dennis McClendon)

Sources: Manuscript maps compiled by the U.S. Surveyor General, accessible as "Federal Township Plats of Illinois (1804–1891)" on the Illinois State Archives website; U.S. Geological Survey topographic maps; U.S. Lake Survey charts;*Greeley, Carlson & Co.'s Atlas of the City of Chicago* (Chicago: Greeley, Carlson & Co., 1884).

B40 Growth of the Chicago Metropolitan Area (Michael P. Conzen)

Research assistance: Dennis McClendon

Source: Michael P. Conzen, "The Changing Character of Metropolitan Chicago," *Journal of Geography* 85.5 (September 1986): 224–236; 1990s areas generalized from U.S. Geological Survey 7.5 Minute Series topographic maps.

C1 Initial Land Sales in Northeastern Illinois (Erich K. Schroeder)

Source: Erich K. Schroeder, "Public Domain Lands in Illinois, 1813–1870," color map, Illinois State Museum, http://museum.state.il.us/research/GISlab/posters/schroeder1994.html; also discussed in Erich K. Schroeder, "Integrating 19th-Century Land Office Records and a Geographic Information System," *Illinois GIS & Mapnotes* 13 (Fall 1995): 12–17.

C2 Progress of the Chicago Fire of 1871 (Michael P. Conzen)

Research assistance: Christopher P. Thale

Source: H. A. Musham, "The Great Chicago Fire, October 8–10, 1871," *Papers in Illinois History and Transactions for the Year 1940* (Springfield, IL: Illinois State Historical Society, 1941), 69–189. Jonathan J. Keyes, "The Forgotten Fire," *Chicago History* 26:3 (Fall 1997): 52.

C2 Fire Limits in Chicago in the 1870s (Michael P. Conzen)

Sources: Chicago City Council Proceedings, February 12, 1872; Homer Hoyt, *One Hundred Years of Land Values in Chicago: The Relationship of the Growth of Chicago to the Rise in Its Land Values, 1830–1933* (Chicago: University of Chicago Press, 1933), fig. 17; Christine Rosen, *The Limits to Power: Great Fires and the Process of City Growth in America* (Cambridge: Cambridge University Press, 1986), fig. 6.2; H. A. Musham, "The Great Chicago Fire, October 8–10, 1871," *Papers in Illinois History and Transactions for the Year 1940* (Springfield, IL: Illinois State Historical Society, 1941), 69–189.

C3 Railroads and Chicago's Loop, circa 1930 (Michael P. Conzen)

Sources: U.S. Geological Survey Topographic Map, 7.5 Minute Series, Chicago Loop Quadrangle, Washington, DC, 1929; Chicago Switching Committee, Illinois Freight Association, Official Map of the Chicago Terminal District, 1934.

C4 Neighborhood Change: Prairie Avenue, 1853–2003 (Michael P. Conzen, Douglas Knox, and Dennis McClendon)

Sources: Henry Hart, *City of Chicago, Cook Co., Illinois, 1853* (New York: Sarony & Co., n.d.); *Rascher's Fire Insurance Map of Chicago,* 1877, Library of Congress, DLC-1-0740; Elisha Robinson, *Robinson's Atlas of the City of Chicago* (New York: Robinson, 1886), vol. 1, plates 10 and 11; Sanborn Map Co., *Sanborn Fire Insurance Map of Chicago*, 1911, vol. 3; Sanborn Map Co., *Sanborn*

Fire Insurance Map of Chicago, 1911, updated through 1950, vol. 3; The Sidwell Co., *Atlas of Cook County, Illinois,* vol. 9, 2000; field checking in February 2003 by Dennis McClendon.

C6 Chicago's Ethnic Mosaic in 1980 (Michael P. Conzen)

Research assistance: J. Ryan Lowry

Source: U.S. Census, 2000, files for Cook, DuPage, and Will counties, Illinois, giving race, Hispanic, first-ancestry, and country-of-birth data by census tract.

C7 Chicago's Ethnic Mosaic in 2000 (Michael P. Conzen)

Research assistance: J. Ryan Lowry

Source: U.S. Census, 2000, files for Cook, DuPage, and Will counties, Illinois, giving race, Hispanic, first-ancestry, and country-of-birth data by census tract.

C8 Chicago's Residential Patterns According to Census Racial Categories in 2000 (Dennis McClendon)

Research assistance: Christopher Winters

Sources: U.S. Census of Population 2000, Chicago digital files.

INDEX

Note: Bold page numbers indicate the main site of information on that topic; italic page numbers indicate maps, tables, and illustrations.